2022
Harris
Florida
Manufacturers Directory

MERGENT
Exclusive Provider of
Dun & Bradstreet Library Solutions

dun & bradstreet

HOOVERS™   ᵞ First Research    HARRIS INFOSOURCE™

Published December 2022 next update December 2023

Publisher

Mergent Inc.
444 Madison Ave
New York, NY 10022

©Mergent Inc All Rights Reserved
2022 Mergent Business Press
ISSN 1080-2614
ISBN 978-1-164972-578-3

MERGENT
BUSINESS PRESS
by FTSE Russell

TABLE OF CONTENTS

SUMMARY OF CONTENTS

Number of Companies 18,641

Number of Decision Makers 38,459

Minimum Number of Employees.. 4

EXPLANATORY NOTES

How to Cross-Reference in This Directory

Sequential Entry Numbers. Each establishment in the Geographic Section is numbered sequentially (G-0000). The number assigned to each establishment is referred to as its "entry number." To make cross-referencing easier, each listing in the Geographic, SIC, Alphabetic and Product Sections includes the establishment's entry number. To facilitate locating an entry in the Geographic Section, the entry numbers for the first listing on the left page and the last listing on the right page are printed at the top of the page next to the city name.

Source Suggestions Welcome

Although all known sources were used to compile this directory, it is possible that companies were inadvertently omitted. Your assistance in calling attention to such omissions would be greatly appreciated. A special form on the facing page will help you in the reporting process.

Analysis

Every effort has been made to contact all firms to verify their information. The one exception to this rule is the annual sales figure, which is considered by many companies to be confidential information. Therefore, estimated sales have been calculated by multiplying the nationwide average sales per employee for the firm's major SIC/NAICS code by the firm's number of employees. Nationwide averages for sales per employee by SIC/NAICS codes are provided by the U.S. Department of Commerce and are updated annually. All sales—sales (est)—have been estimated by this method. The exceptions are parent companies (PA), division headquarters (DH) and headquarter locations (HQ) which may include an actual corporate sales figure—sales (corporate-wide) if available.

Types of Companies

Descriptive and statistical data are included for companies in the entire state. These comprise manufacturers, machine shops, fabricators, assemblers and printers. Also identified are corporate offices in the state.

Employment Data

The employment figure shown in the Geographic Section includes male and female employees and embraces all levels of the company: administrative, clerical, sales and maintenance. This figure is for the facility listed and does not include other plants or offices. It should be recognized that these figures represent an approximate year-round average. These employment figures are broken into codes A through G and used in the Product and SIC Sections to further help you in qualifying a company. Be sure to check the footnotes on the bottom of pages for the code breakdowns.

Standard Industrial Classification (SIC)

The Standard Industrial Classification (SIC) system used in this directory was developed by the federal government for use in classifying establishments by the type of activity they are engaged in. The SIC classifications used in this directory are from the 1987 edition published by the U.S. Government's Office of Management and Budget. The SIC system separates all activities into broad industrial divisions (e.g., manufacturing, mining, retail trade). It further subdivides each division. The range of manufacturing industry classes extends from two-digit codes (major industry group) to four-digit codes (product).

For example:

Industry Breakdown	Code	Industry, Product, etc.
*Major industry group	20	Food and kindred products
Industry group	203	Canned and frozen foods
*Industry	2033	Fruits and vegetables, etc.

*Classifications used in this directory

Only two-digit and four-digit codes are used in this directory.

Arrangement

1. The **Geographic Section** contains complete in-depth corporate data. This section is sorted by cities listed in alphabetical order and companies listed alphabetically within each city. A County/City Index for referencing cities within counties precedes this section.

IMPORTANT NOTICE: It is a violation of both federal and state law to transmit an unsolicited advertisement to a facsimile machine. Any user of this product that violates such laws may be subject to civil and criminal penalties, which may exceed $500 for each transmission of an unsolicited facsimile. Mergent Inc. provides fax numbers for lawful purposes only and expressly forbids the use of these numbers in any unlawful manner.

2. The **Standard Industrial Classification (SIC) Section** lists companies under approximately 500 four-digit SIC codes. An alphabetical and a numerical index precedes this section. A company can be listed under several codes. The codes are in numerical order with companies listed alphabetically under each code.

3. The **Alphabetic Section** lists all companies with their full physical or mailing addresses and telephone number.

4. The **Product Section** lists companies under unique Harris categories. An index preceding this section lists all product categories in alphabetical order. Companies can be listed under several categories.

USER'S GUIDE TO LISTINGS

GEOGRAPHIC SECTION

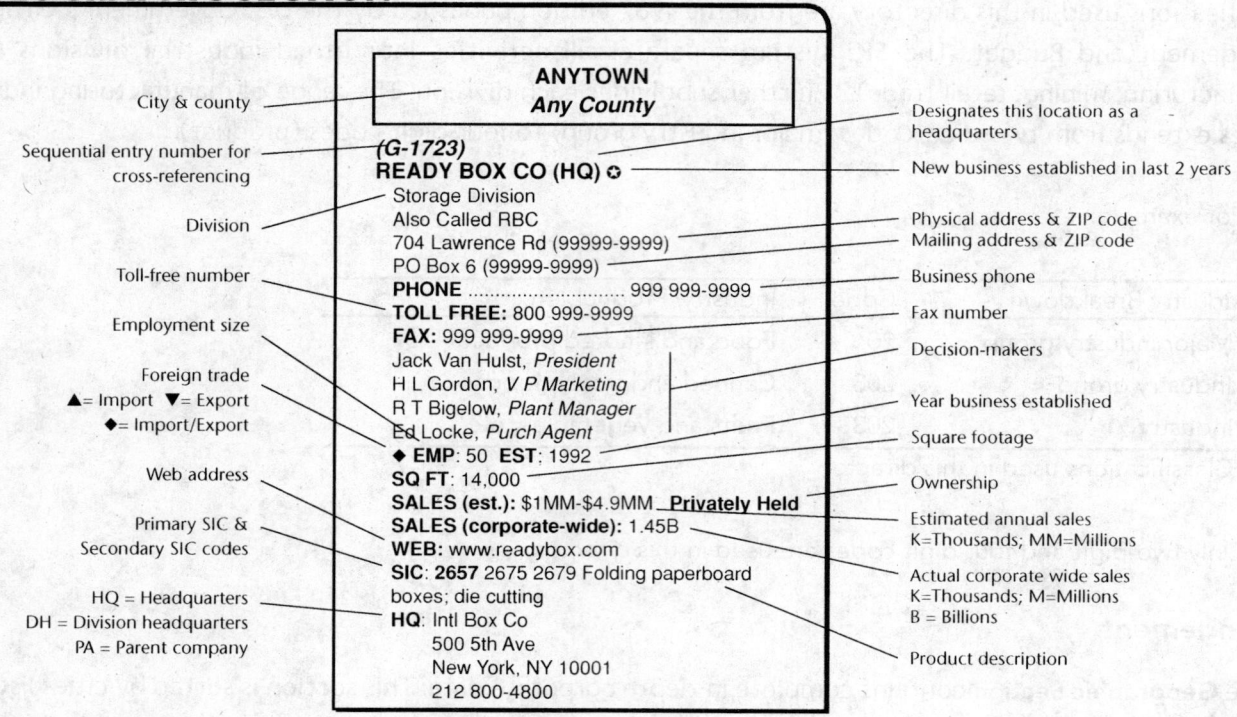

City & county

Sequential entry number for cross-referencing

Division

Toll-free number

Employment size

Foreign trade
▲= Import ▼= Export
◆= Import/Export

Web address

Primary SIC & Secondary SIC codes

HQ = Headquarters
DH = Division headquarters
PA = Parent company

ANYTOWN
Any County

(G-1723)
READY BOX CO (HQ) ✿
Storage Division
Also Called RBC
704 Lawrence Rd (99999-9999)
PO Box 6 (99999-9999)
PHONE 999 999-9999
TOLL FREE: 800 999-9999
FAX: 999 999-9999
Jack Van Hulst, *President*
H L Gordon, *V P Marketing*
R T Bigelow, *Plant Manager*
Ed Locke, *Purch Agent*
◆ **EMP**: 50 **EST**: 1992
SQ FT: 14,000
SALES (est.): $1MM-$4.9MM Privately Held
SALES (corporate-wide): 1.45B
WEB: www.readybox.com
SIC: 2657 2675 2679 Folding paperboard
boxes; die cutting
HQ: Intl Box Co
500 5th Ave
New York, NY 10001
212 800-4800

Designates this location as a headquarters

New business established in last 2 years

Physical address & ZIP code
Mailing address & ZIP code

Business phone

Fax number

Decision-makers

Year business established

Square footage

Ownership

Estimated annual sales K=Thousands; MM=Millions

Actual corporate wide sales K=Thousands; M=Millions B = Billions

Product description

SIC SECTION

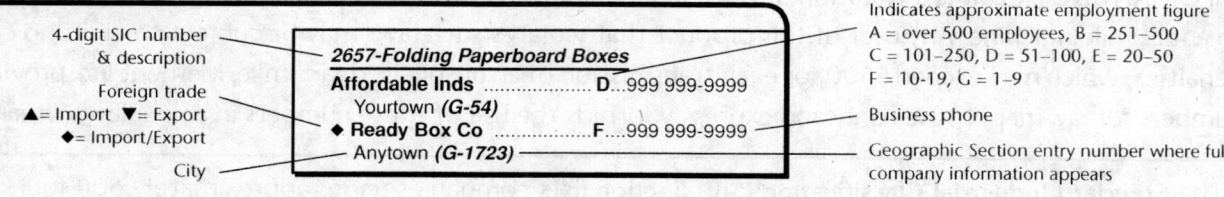

4-digit SIC number & description

Foreign trade
▲= Import ▼= Export
◆= Import/Export

City

2657-Folding Paperboard Boxes
Affordable Inds .... D...999 999-9999
Yourtown *(G-54)*
◆ **Ready Box Co** .... F....999 999-9999
Anytown *(G-1723)*

Indicates approximate employment figure
A = over 500 employees, B = 251-500
C = 101-250, D = 51-100, E = 20-50
F = 10-19, G = 1-9

Business phone

Geographic Section entry number where full company information appears

ALPHABETIC SECTION

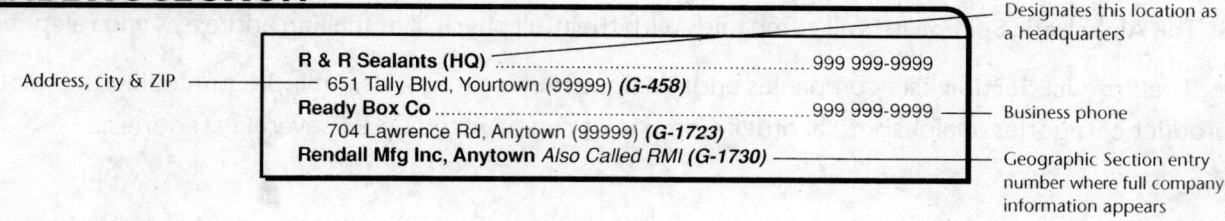

Address, city & ZIP

R & R Sealants (HQ) 999 999-9999
651 Tally Blvd, Yourtown (99999) *(G-458)*
Ready Box Co 999 999-9999
704 Lawrence Rd, Anytown (99999) *(G-1723)*
Rendall Mfg Inc, Anytown *Also Called RMI (G-1730)*

Designates this location as a headquarters

Business phone

Geographic Section entry number where full company information appears

PRODUCT SECTION

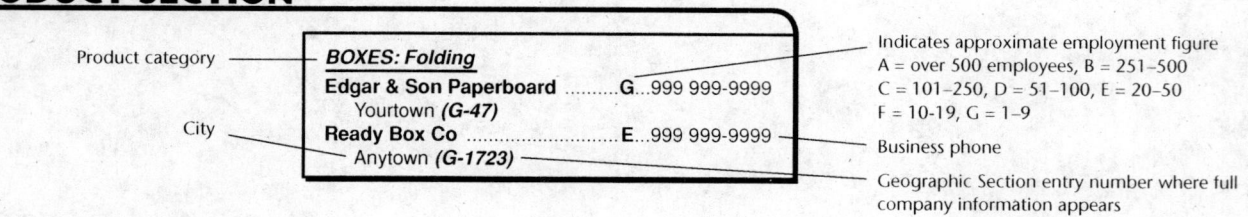

Product category

City

BOXES: Folding
Edgar & Son Paperboard ....G...999 999-9999
Yourtown *(G-47)*
Ready Box Co ....E...999 999-9999
Anytown *(G-1723)*

Indicates approximate employment figure
A = over 500 employees, B = 251-500
C = 101-250, D = 51-100, E = 20-50
F = 10-19, G = 1-9

Business phone

Geographic Section entry number where full company information appears

GEOGRAPHIC SECTION

Companies sorted by city in alphabetical order

In-depth company data listed

STANDARD INDUSTRIAL CLASSIFICATIONS

Alphabetical index of classifcation descriptions

Numerical index of classifcation descriptions

Companies sorted by SIC product groupings

ALPHABETIC SECTION

Company listings in alphabetical order

PRODUCT INDEX

Product categories listed in alphabetical order

PRODUCT SECTION

Companies sorted by product and manufacturing service classifications

GEOGRAPHIC

SIC

ALPHABETIC

PRDT INDEX

PRODUCT

Florida
County Map

Escambia
Santa Rosa
Okaloosa
Walton
Holmes
Washington
Jackson
Calhoun
Bay
Liberty
Gadsden
Leon
Wakulla
Jefferson
Madison
Taylor
Hamilton
Suwannee
Lafayette
Columbia
Gilchrist
Dixie
Union
Alachua
Levy
Nassau
Duval
Baker
Bradford
Clay
St. John's
Putnam
Flagler
Marion
Volusia
Citrus
Sumter
Lake
Seminole
Hernando
Orange
Pasco
Osceola
Pinellas
Hillsborough
Polk
Brevard
Indian River
Manatee
Hardee
Okeechobee
St. Lucie
Highlands
Sarasota
De Soto
Martin
Charlotte
Glades
Palm Beach
Lee
Hendry
Collier
Broward
Monroe
Miami Dade
Gulf
Franklin

Key West
(Monroe County)

COUNTY/CITY CROSS-REFERENCE INDEX

	ENTRY #		ENTRY #		ENTRY #		ENTRY #		ENTRY #
Key Biscayne	(G-6833)	Belle Isle	(G-348)	Hudson	(G-5761)	East Palatka	(G-3471)	Lake Panasoffkee	(G-7119)
Medley	(G-8191)	Christmas	(G-1462)	Land O Lakes	(G-7488)	Florahome	(G-3610)	Oxford	(G-12853)
Miami	(G-8605)	Gotha	(G-4806)	New Port Richey	(G-10961)	Grandin	(G-4810)	Sumterville	(G-16262)
Miami Beach	(G-10159)	Lake Buena Vista	(G-6998)	Port Richey	(G-14355)	Hollister	(G-5508)	The Villages	(G-17553)
Miami Gardens	(G-10248)	Maitland	(G-8048)	San Antonio	(G-15246)	Interlachen	(G-5820)	Webster	(G-17832)
Miami Lakes	(G-10279)	Oakland	(G-11226)	Spring Hill	(G-16084)	Melrose	(G-8571)	Wildwood	(G-18308)
Miami Shores	(G-10382)	Ocoee	(G-11520)	Trinity	(G-17632)	Palatka	(G-12861)	**Suwannee**	
Miami Springs	(G-10385)	Orlando	(G-11848)	Wesley Chapel	(G-17870)	Welaka	(G-17840)	Branford	(G-1111)
North Bay Village	(G-11057)	Windermere	(G-18347)	Zephyrhills	(G-18601)	**Santa Rosa**		Live Oak	(G-7841)
North Miami	(G-11087)	Winter Garden	(G-18372)	**Pinellas**		Gulf Breeze	(G-4874)	Mc Alpin	(G-8187)
North Miami Beach	(G-11130)	Winter Park	(G-18480)	Belleair	(G-352)	Jay	(G-6647)	O Brien	(G-11223)
Opa Locka	(G-11710)	Zellwood	(G-18595)	Belleair Beach	(G-354)	Milton	(G-10415)	**Taylor**	
Palmetto Bay	(G-13207)	**Osceola**		Belleair Bluffs	(G-355)	Navarre	(G-10947)	Perry	(G-13629)
Pinecrest	(G-13661)	Celebration	(G-1438)	Clearwater	(G-1469)	Pace	(G-12857)	Steinhatchee	(G-16106)
Princeton	(G-14486)	Harmony	(G-4987)	Clearwater Beach	(G-1860)	**Sarasota**		**Union**	
South Miami	(G-16031)	Kissimmee	(G-6890)	Dunedin	(G-3439)	Englewood	(G-3526)	Lake Butler	(G-7000)
Sunny Isles Beach	(G-16268)	Reunion	(G-14555)	Gulfport	(G-4897)	Lakewood Ranch	(G-7481)	**Volusia**	
Surfside	(G-16395)	Saint Cloud	(G-14918)	Indian Rocks Beach	(G-5809)	Nokomis	(G-11041)	Daytona Beach	(G-2504)
Sweetwater	(G-16401)	**Palm Beach**		Indian Shores	(G-5810)	North Port	(G-11186)	De Land	(G-2620)
Virginia Gardens	(G-17820)	Belle Glade	(G-338)	Kenneth City	(G-6832)	North Venice	(G-11207)	De Leon Springs	(G-2621)
West Miami	(G-17904)	Boca Raton	(G-382)	Largo	(G-7518)	Osprey	(G-12801)	Debary	(G-2630)
Monroe		Boynton Beach	(G-834)	Madeira Beach	(G-8039)	Sarasota	(G-15581)	Deland	(G-2846)
Big Pine Key	(G-371)	Canal Point	(G-1260)	Oldsmar	(G-11624)	Venice	(G-17671)	Deltona	(G-3039)
Islamorada	(G-5836)	Delray Beach	(G-2922)	Ozona	(G-12856)	**Seminole**		Edgewater	(G-3479)
Key Largo	(G-6842)	Greenacres	(G-4844)	Palm Harbor	(G-13095)	Altamonte Springs	(G-26)	Holly Hill	(G-5509)
Key West	(G-6853)	Haverhill	(G-5004)	Pinellas Park	(G-13671)	Casselberry	(G-1411)	Lake Helen	(G-7055)
Marathon	(G-8105)	Highland Beach	(G-5459)	Redington Shores	(G-14554)	Chuluota	(G-1463)	New Smyrna	(G-10992)
Summerland Key	(G-16261)	Hypoluxo	(G-5794)	Safety Harbor	(G-14782)	Fern Park	(G-3578)	New Smyrna Beach	(G-10993)
Tavernier	(G-17531)	Juno Beach	(G-6660)	Saint Petersburg	(G-14948)	Geneva	(G-4786)	Orange City	(G-11804)
Nassau		Jupiter	(G-6673)	Seminole	(G-15967)	Lake Mary	(G-7056)	Ormond Beach	(G-12738)
Amelia Island	(G-85)	Lake Harbor	(G-7054)	South Pasadena	(G-16050)	Longwood	(G-7861)	Ponce Inlet	(G-14252)
Bryceville	(G-1225)	Lake Park	(G-7121)	St Pete Beach	(G-16089)	Oviedo	(G-12803)	Port Orange	(G-14326)
Callahan	(G-1250)	Lake Worth	(G-7180)	Tarpon Springs	(G-17456)	Sanford	(G-15256)	South Daytona	(G-16018)
Fernandina Beach	(G-3580)	Lake Worth Beach	(G-7246)	Treasure Island	(G-17628)	Winter Springs	(G-18557)	**Wakulla**	
Hilliard	(G-5463)	Lantana	(G-7508)	**Polk**		**St. Johns**		Crawfordville	(G-2231)
Yulee	(G-18584)	Loxahatchee	(G-7964)	Auburndale	(G-218)	Elkton	(G-3507)	Panacea	(G-13224)
Okaloosa		Mangonia Park	(G-8087)	Bartow	(G-297)	Hastings	(G-4988)	Sopchoppy	(G-16009)
Baker	(G-290)	North Palm Beach	(G-11173)	Davenport	(G-2362)	Jacksonville	(G-6624)	**Walton**	
Crestview	(G-2240)	Ocean Ridge	(G-11517)	Dundee	(G-3434)	Ponte Vedra	(G-14253)	Defuniak Springs	(G-2837)
Destin	(G-3058)	Pahokee	(G-12860)	Eloise	(G-3514)	Ponte Vedra Beach	(G-14260)	Destin	(G-3083)
Eglin Afb	(G-3504)	Palm Beach	(G-12928)	Fort Meade	(G-4150)	Saint Augustine	(G-14803)	Freeport	(G-4621)
Fort Walton Beach	(G-4558)	Palm Beach Gardens		Frostproof	(G-4633)	Saint Johns	(G-14944)	Inlet Beach	(G-5819)
Holt	(G-5693)	(G-12944)		Haines City	(G-4901)	**St. Lucie**		Miramar Beach	(G-10568)
Hurlburt Field	(G-5792)	Palm Springs	(G-13141)	Kissimmee	(G-6975)	Fort Pierce	(G-4457)	Mossy Head	(G-10595)
Mary Esther	(G-8177)	Riviera Beach	(G-14584)	Lake Alfred	(G-6995)	Hutchinson Island	(G-5793)	Panama City	(G-13323)
Niceville	(G-11028)	Royal Palm Beach	(G-14759)	Lake Hamilton	(G-7050)	Port Saint Lucie	(G-14393)	Ponce De Leon	(G-14248)
Shalimar	(G-16001)	South Bay	(G-16015)	Lake Wales	(G-7151)	Port St Lucie	(G-14469)	Santa Rosa Beach	(G-15420)
Valparaiso	(G-17654)	Tequesta	(G-17550)	Lakeland	(G-7265)	**Sumter**		**Washington**	
Okeechobee		Wellington	(G-17841)	Mulberry	(G-10618)	Bushnell	(G-1240)	Chipley	(G-1452)
Okeechobee	(G-11598)	West Palm Beach	(G-17905)	Polk City	(G-13903)	Center Hill	(G-1440)	Wausau	(G-17831)
Orange		**Pasco**		Winter Haven	(G-18410)	Lady Lake	(G-6994)		
Apopka	(G-98)	Dade City	(G-2313)	**Putnam**					
		Holiday	(G-5487)	Crescent City	(G-2234)				

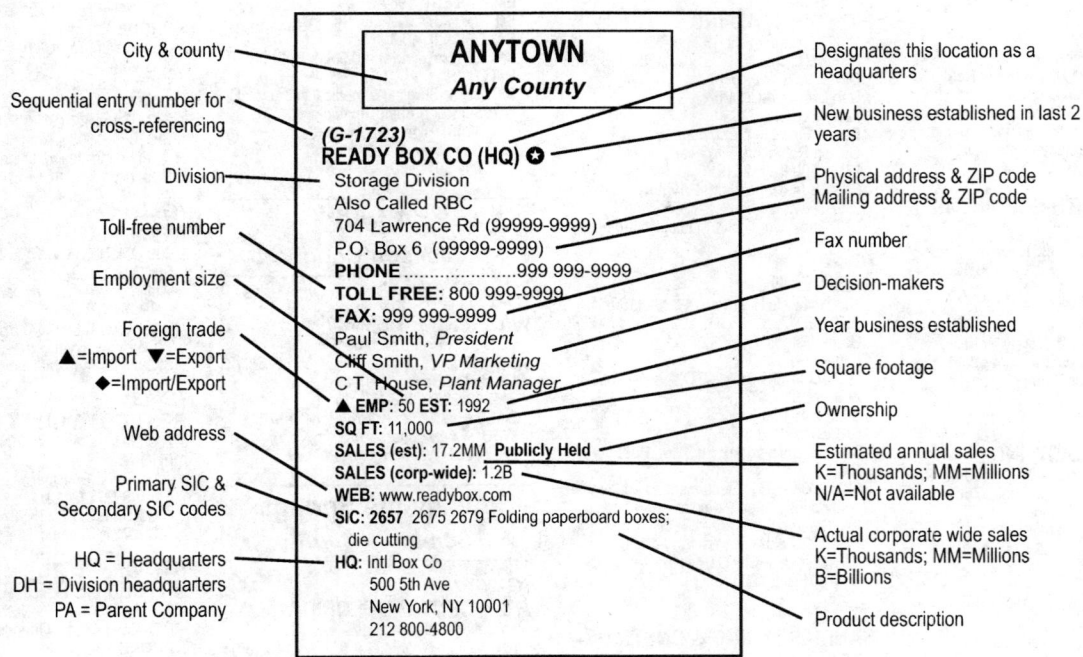

On the left side of the diagram (labels):
- City & county
- Sequential entry number for cross-referencing
- Division
- Toll-free number
- Employment size
- Foreign trade ▲=Import ▼=Export ◆=Import/Export
- Web address
- Primary SIC & Secondary SIC codes
- HQ = Headquarters
- DH = Division headquarters
- PA = Parent Company

Center box:

ANYTOWN
Any County

(G-1723)
READY BOX CO (HQ) ✪
Storage Division
Also Called RBC
704 Lawrence Rd (99999-9999)
P.O. Box 6 (99999-9999)
PHONE.....................999 999-9999
TOLL FREE: 800 999-9999
FAX: 999 999-9999
Paul Smith, *President*
Cliff Smith, *VP Marketing*
C T House, *Plant Manager*
▲ EMP: 50 EST: 1992
SQ FT: 11,000
SALES (est): 17.2MM **Publicly Held**
SALES (corp-wide): 1.2B
WEB: www.readybox.com
SIC: 2657 2675 2679 Folding paperboard boxes; die cutting
HQ: Intl Box Co
500 5th Ave
New York, NY 10001
212 800-4800

On the right side of the diagram (labels):
- Designates this location as a headquarters
- New business established in last 2 years
- Physical address & ZIP code
- Mailing address & ZIP code
- Fax number
- Decision-makers
- Year business established
- Square footage
- Ownership
- Estimated annual sales K=Thousands; MM=Millions N/A=Not available
- Actual corporate wide sales K=Thousands; MM=Millions B=Billions
- Product description

See footnotes for symbols and codes identification.
- This section is in alphabetical order by city.
- Companies are sorted alphabetically under their respective cities.
- To locate cities within a county refer to the County/City Cross Reference Index.

IMPORTANT NOTICE: It is a violation of both federal and state law to transmit an unsolicited advertisement to a facsimile machine. Any user of this product that violates such laws may be subject to civil and criminal penalties which may exceed $500 for each transmission of an unsolicited facsimile. Harris InfoSource provides fax numbers for lawful purposes only and expressly forbids the use of these numbers in any unlawful manner.

Alachua
Alachua County

(G-1)
ALACHUA TODAY INC
14804 Main St (32615-8590)
P.O. Box 2135 (32616-2135)
PHONE.....................386 462-3355
Gail Luparello, *President*
EMP: 6 EST: 2000
SQ FT: 1,472
SALES (est): 660.3K **Privately Held**
WEB: www.alachuacountytoday.com
SIC: 2711 Newspapers, publishing & printing

(G-2)
AMEND SURGICAL INC
14000 Nw 126th Ter (32615-4884)
PHONE.....................844 281-3169
Robby Lane, *CEO*
EMP: 10 EST: 2015
SALES (est): 1.1MM **Privately Held**
WEB: www.amendsurgical.com
SIC: 3841 Surgical & medical instruments

(G-3)
AP LIFESCIENCES LLC
12085 Research Dr Ste 155 (32615-6837)
PHONE.....................954 300-7469
Ammon Peck, *COO*
Benjamin Canales, *Senior VP*
Nigel Richards, *Senior VP*
Cuong Nguyen,
EMP: 10 EST: 2015
SALES (est): 556.7K **Privately Held**
SIC: 2835 In vitro diagnostics

(G-4)
APPAREL PRINTERS
13201 Rachael Blvd (32615-6688)
P.O. Box 1649 (32616-1649)
PHONE.....................352 463-8850
Harold M Hofstetter, *Owner*
EMP: 7 EST: 1988
SQ FT: 6,000
SALES (est): 300K **Privately Held**
WEB: www.apparel-printers.com
SIC: 2262 7389 5199 2759 Screen printing: manmade fiber & silk broadwoven fabrics; sign painting & lettering shop; advertising specialties; screen printing; embroidery products, except schiffli machine

(G-5)
APPLIED GENETIC TECH CORP
14193 Nw 119th Ter Ste 10 (32615-9410)
PHONE.....................386 462-2204
Scott Koenig, *Ch of Bd*
Susan B Washer, *President*
William A Sullivan, *CFO*
Matthew Feinsod, *Chief Mktg Ofcr*
Brian Krex, *General Counsel*
EMP: 78 EST: 1999
SQ FT: 21,000
SALES (est): 325K **Privately Held**
WEB: www.agtc.com
SIC: 2836 8731 Biological products, except diagnostic; biological research

(G-6)
AXOGEN INC (PA)
13631 Progress Blvd # 400 (32615-9409)
PHONE.....................386 462-6800
Karen Zaderej, *Ch of Bd*
Alicia Carney, *Partner*
Brad Alexander, *Area Mgr*
Phillip Edmondson, *Area Mgr*
Chad McDermott, *Area Mgr*
▲ EMP: 97 EST: 1977
SQ FT: 11,761
SALES (est): 127.3MM **Publicly Held**
WEB: www.axogeninc.com
SIC: 3845 Electrotherapeutic apparatus

(G-7)
AXOGEN CORPORATION
13631 Progress Blvd # 400 (32615-9409)
P.O. Box 357787, Gainesville (32635-7787)
PHONE.....................386 462-6800
Karen Zaderej, *CEO*
Stacy Arnold, *Vice Pres*
John Engels, *Vice Pres*
Mark Friedman, *Vice Pres*
Brad Hedger, *Vice Pres*
EMP: 32 EST: 2002
SALES (est): 13MM
SALES (corp-wide): 127.3MM **Publicly Held**
WEB: www.axogeninc.com
SIC: 3842 Implants, surgical
PA: Axogen, Inc.
13631 Progress Blvd # 400
Alachua FL 32615
386 462-6800

(G-8)
BACK TO GODHEAD INC
Also Called: B T G
13921 Nw 146th Ave (32615-6193)
P.O. Box 430 (32616-0430)
PHONE.....................386 462-0481
Norman Comtois, *President*
▲ EMP: 13 EST: 1944
SALES (est): 715.7K **Privately Held**
WEB: www.back2godhead.com
SIC: 2721 Magazines: publishing only, not printed on site

(G-9)
BIOENERGETICS PRESS
19802 Old Bellamy Rd (32615-3867)
PHONE.....................386 462-5155
EMP: 10
SALES (est): 557.5K **Privately Held**
SIC: 2741 Misc Publishing

(G-10)
BRAMMER BIO LLC
13859 Progress Blvd (32615-9403)
PHONE.....................386 418-8199
Shaun Eckerle, *General Mgr*
EMP: 309
SALES (corp-wide): 39.2B **Publicly Held**
SIC: 2834 Pharmaceutical preparations
HQ: Brammer Bio, Llc
13702 Innovation Dr
Alachua FL 32615
386 418-1482

(G-11)
ENCELL TECHNOLOGY INC
12887 Nw Us Highway 441 (32615-8503)
PHONE.....................386 462-2643
Mohan Krishnan, *CEO*
Robert Guyton, *Chairman*
Alan Seidel, *Engineer*
Chris Maier, *CFO*
Christopher Maier, *CFO*
▲ EMP: 28 EST: 2006
SQ FT: 30,000
SALES (est): 5.2MM **Privately Held**
WEB: www.encell.com
SIC: 3691 Storage batteries

(G-12)
INTERMED GROUP INC (PA)
13301 Nw Us Highway 441 (32615-8512)
PHONE.....................561 586-3667

Rick Staab, *CEO*
Mica Hendricks, *Regional Mgr*
Kyle Cole, *Area Mgr*
Larry Hertzler, *COO*
Scott Nudelman, *COO*
EMP: 43 **EST:** 1984
SQ FT: 4,000
SALES (est): 29.8MM **Privately Held**
WEB: www.intermed1.com
SIC: 3841 3842 5047 Surgical & medical instruments; surgical appliances & supplies; medical equipment & supplies

(G-13)
LIBERTY HEALTH SCIENCES INC
14810 Nw 94th Ave (32615-6702)
PHONE..................386 462-0141
Darrin Potter, *Vice Pres*
Luis Marcano, *Store Mgr*
EMP: 9 **EST:** 2018
SALES (est): 1MM **Privately Held**
WEB: www.libertyhealthsciences.com
SIC: 2833 Alkaloids & other botanical based products

(G-14)
LINDSAY PRECAST INC
13365 Southern Precast Dr (32615-8548)
PHONE..................800 669-2278
Roland C Lindsay, *President*
Randy Trimm, *Project Mgr*
Mark Severance, *Purchasing*
Nikki Rose, *Admin Asst*
EMP: 50
SALES (corp-wide): 55.8MM **Privately Held**
WEB: www.lindsayprecast.com
SIC: 3272 Concrete products
PA: Lindsay Precast, Llc
6845 Erie Ave Nw
Canal Fulton OH 44614
800 837-7788

(G-15)
NEUROTRONICS INC
13800 Tech City Cir 400 (32615-6094)
PHONE..................352 372-9955
Kazuteru Yanagihara, *President*
Randy Widell, *Vice Pres*
James Schubert, *VP Engrg*
David Pezet, *QC Mgr*
Brad Dotson, *Sales Staff*
EMP: 7 **EST:** 1997
SALES (est): 1.2MM **Privately Held**
WEB: www.neurotronics.com
SIC: 3841 Surgical & medical instruments
PA: Nihon Kohden Corporation
1-31-4, Nishiochiai
Shinjuku-Ku TKY 161-0

(G-16)
OPTIMAL VENDING SYSTEMS LLC
Also Called: Optimal Station
22806 Nw County Road 241 (32615-3929)
PHONE..................301 633-2353
Michele Sparks, *CEO*
Alex Garnier, *Project Mgr*
Pamela Patterson, *Director*
EMP: 8 **EST:** 2017
SALES (est): 708.9K **Privately Held**
WEB: www.optimalstation.com
SIC: 3581 Automatic vending machines

(G-17)
PIONEER SURGICAL TECHNOLOGY
11621 Research Cir (32615-6825)
PHONE..................906 225-5629
EMP: 10 **EST:** 2018
SALES (est): 184.9K **Privately Held**
SIC: 3841 Surgical & medical instruments

(G-18)
REGENERATION TECHNOLOGIES INC
11621 Research Cir (32615-6825)
PHONE..................386 418-8888
Caroline Hartill, *Exec VP*
Keith Koford, *VP Legal*
Eric Baldwin, *Vice Pres*
Johannes Louw, *Vice Pres*
William Cassarly, *Opers Mgr*
EMP: 22 **EST:** 2019

SALES (est): 1.5MM **Privately Held**
SIC: 3841 Surgical & medical instruments

(G-19)
RTI SURGICAL INC
11621 Research Cir (32615-6825)
PHONE..................386 418-8888
Olivier Visa, *President*
Dan Crowder, *QC Mgr*
Kerry Pearson, *QC Mgr*
Darian Flewellen, *Engineer*
Garrett Robinson, *Engineer*
EMP: 200 **EST:** 2019
SALES (est): 33.3MM **Privately Held**
WEB: www.rtix.com
SIC: 3841 Surgical & medical instruments

(G-20)
SABINE INC
13301 Nw Us Highway 441 (32615-8512)
PHONE..................386 418-2000
Doran Oster, *CEO*
Kim Kelley, *CFO*
Michael Mychalczuk, *CTO*
◆ **EMP:** 81 **EST:** 1971
SQ FT: 45,000
SALES (est): 1.1MM
SALES (corp-wide): 28.9MM **Publicly Held**
SIC: 3699 3931 Electric sound equipment; string instruments & parts
PA: Clearone, Inc.
5225 W Wiley Post Way # 500
Salt Lake City UT 84116
801 975-7200

(G-21)
SANDVIK MINING & CNSTR USA LLC (DH)
13500 Nw County Road 235 (32615-6150)
PHONE..................386 462-4100
Olof Faxander, *CEO*
David Levy, *Vice Pres*
Petri Liljaranta, *Vice Pres*
Tim Clayton, *Engineer*
Mats Backman, *CFO*
◆ **EMP:** 150 **EST:** 1998
SQ FT: 70,000
SALES (est): 62.6MM
SALES (corp-wide): 10.8B **Privately Held**
SIC: 3532 Drills, core; oil field machinery & equipment; water well drilling equipment

(G-22)
THE CALDWELL MANUFACTURING CO
11600 Nw 173rd St Ste 110 (32615-6059)
PHONE..................386 418-3525
Wayne Sutton, *Manager*
EMP: 52
SALES (corp-wide): 10.3B **Privately Held**
WEB: www.caldwellmfgco.com
SIC: 3999 Barber & beauty shop equipment
HQ: The Caldwell Manufacturing Company
2605 Manitou Rd Ste 100
Rochester NY 14624
585 352-3790

(G-23)
TUCKER-DAVIS TECHNOLOGIES INC
11930 Research Cir (32615-6826)
PHONE..................386 462-9622
Timothy J Tucker, *President*
Myles Billard, *Engineer*
Kurtys Randolph, *Engineer*
Jennifer Sanders, *Controller*
April Hatfield, *Sales Staff*
EMP: 29 **EST:** 1980
SQ FT: 15,000
SALES (est): 5.3MM **Privately Held**
WEB: www.tdt.com
SIC: 3829 3825 Measuring & controlling devices; digital test equipment, electronic & electrical circuits

(G-24)
TUTOGEN MEDICAL INC (DH)
11621 Research Cir (32615-6825)
P.O. Box 2650 (32616-2650)
PHONE..................386 418-8888
Roy D Crowninshield, *Ch of Bd*
Guy L Mayer, *President*

David C Greenspan, *Vice Pres*
Claude O Pering, *Vice Pres*
Clifton Seliga, *Vice Pres*
EMP: 49 **EST:** 1985
SQ FT: 34,384
SALES (est): 48.3MM
SALES (corp-wide): 90.5MM **Publicly Held**
SIC: 3841 Surgical & medical instruments
HQ: Surgalign Spine Technologies, Inc.
12481 High Bluff Dr Ste 3
San Diego CA 92130
844 894-7752

Alford
Jackson County

(G-25)
WASHERS-R-US INC
2205 Park Rd (32420-6819)
PHONE..................850 573-0221
Michael W Baxley, *Partner*
EMP: 9 **EST:** 2008
SALES (est): 62.6K **Privately Held**
WEB: www.washers-r-us.com
SIC: 3452 Washers

Altamonte Springs
Seminole County

(G-26)
A & A CENTRAL FLORIDA
Also Called: Elite Awnings
540 N State Road 434 # 53 (32714-2166)
PHONE..................407 648-5666
Steve Alvin, *Owner*
EMP: 12 **EST:** 1991
SQ FT: 2,200
SALES (est): 273.2K **Privately Held**
SIC: 2394 1799 5999 5211 Awnings, fabric: made from purchased materials; awning installation; awnings; energy conservation products

(G-27)
AEROSPC/DFENSE COATINGS GA INC
378 Centerpointe Cir # 1272 (32701-3438)
PHONE..................407 843-1140
Tom Scott, *Owner*
EMP: 9 **EST:** 2008
SALES (est): 161.1K **Privately Held**
SIC: 3479 Metal coating & allied service

(G-28)
AFFORDABLE GRANITE CONCEPTS
1025 Miller Dr Ste 139 (32701-2082)
PHONE..................407 332-0057
Walter S Pianta, *President*
EMP: 13 **EST:** 2009
SQ FT: 14,000
SALES (est): 4.5MM **Privately Held**
WEB: www.affordablegraniteconcepts.com
SIC: 3281 Cut stone & stone products

(G-29)
AGM ORLANDO INC
223 Altamonte Commerce Bl (32714-2550)
PHONE..................407 865-9522
Carmine Parente, *President*
Bill Shoewalter, *Vice Pres*
▲ **EMP:** 5 **EST:** 1998
SQ FT: 4,000
SALES (est): 1MM **Privately Held**
SIC: 3088 Shower stalls, fiberglass & plastic

(G-30)
AM CABINETS LLC
628 Alpine St (32701-2634)
PHONE..................321 663-4319
Yennisey Fenandez, *Manager*
EMP: 6 **EST:** 2017
SALES (est): 993.4K **Privately Held**
WEB: www.amcabinetsllc.com
SIC: 2434 Wood kitchen cabinets

(G-31)
AMRAV INC
Also Called: Frame Tech of Orlando
1026 Miller Dr (32701-2032)
PHONE..................407 831-1550
Drew Vargo, *President*
Rita Vargo, *Vice Pres*
EMP: 7 **EST:** 1992
SQ FT: 5,000
SALES (est): 579.1K **Privately Held**
SIC: 3555 5084 Printing trades machinery; printing trades machinery, equipment & supplies

(G-32)
AVYM LLC
639 Oak Hollow Way (32714-1811)
PHONE..................407 970-7746
Vitalie C Avram, *Principal*
EMP: 7 **EST:** 2009
SALES (est): 180.6K **Privately Held**
WEB: www.avym.com
SIC: 2819 Industrial inorganic chemicals

(G-33)
BEST COMMUNITY MAGAZINE
260 Maitland Ave Ste 2000 (32701-5510)
PHONE..................407 571-2980
John Foret, *Principal*
EMP: 9 **EST:** 2010
SALES (est): 325.7K **Privately Held**
SIC: 2721 Periodicals

(G-34)
BRYCE FOSTER INC
215 Rollingwood Trl (32714-3412)
P.O. Box 547841, Orlando (32854-7841)
PHONE..................800 371-0395
Alec E String, *President*
▲ **EMP:** 9 **EST:** 1995
SALES (est): 690.3K **Privately Held**
WEB: www.brycefoster.com
SIC: 2674 Shipping & shopping bags or sacks

(G-35)
BUBBA ROPE LLC
998 Explorer Cv Ste 130 (32701-7500)
PHONE..................877 499-8494
Kristopher Balser, *Prdtn Mgr*
Douglas J Worswick, *Administration*
EMP: 10 **EST:** 2015
SALES (est): 886.2K **Privately Held**
WEB: www.bubbarope.com
SIC: 2298 Ropes & fiber cables; rope, except asbestos & wire

(G-36)
BUILDERS PUBLISHING GROUP LLC
Also Called: Bpg
815 Orienta Ave Ste 1050 (32701-5624)
PHONE..................407 539-2938
David A Konkol, *Mng Member*
EMP: 7 **EST:** 2010
SALES (est): 363.9K **Privately Held**
WEB: www.builderspublishinggroup.com
SIC: 2741 2731 Miscellaneous publishing; book publishing

(G-37)
CENTURY GRAPHICS & METALS INC
350 Northlake Blvd # 100 (32701-5223)
PHONE..................407 262-8290
Ken Levitt, *President*
Jacqueline Levitt, *Vice Pres*
EMP: 20 **EST:** 1973
SQ FT: 15,000
SALES (est): 2MM **Privately Held**
WEB: www.centurygraphics.com
SIC: 3993 2759 Signs & advertising specialties; commercial printing

(G-38)
CLEAR CHOICE INC
1045 Miller Dr (32701-2067)
PHONE..................407 830-6968
Brian Smith, *President*
Adam Salinas, *Sales Staff*
Michelle Salinas, *Office Mgr*
EMP: 5 **EST:** 2000
SALES (est): 1.1MM **Privately Held**
WEB: www.clearchoicelaminating.com
SIC: 2759 Promotional printing

▲ = Import ▼=Export
◆ =Import/Export

(G-39)
COMPRHNSIVE SLEEP DISORDER CTR
851 Douglas Ave Ste 148 (32714-2085)
PHONE....................................407 834-1023
T Benjamin Thomas, *President*
Mike Kalor, *Vice Pres*
EMP: 11 EST: 1999
SALES (est): 138.9K Privately Held
SIC: 3821 Laboratory apparatus & furniture

(G-40)
CONNECTED LIFE SOLUTIONS LLC
Also Called: Consulting
153 Dahlia Dr (32714-2124)
PHONE....................................214 507-9331
Mario J Pino, *Mng Member*
Mario Pino, *Mng Member*
Marc Eskenas, *Manager*
Mario J Pino, *Manager*
Ramiro Ruiz, *Manager*
EMP: 10 EST: 2014
SALES (est): 627.8K Privately Held
WEB: www.connectedls.com
SIC: 7372 8748 7379 8742 Prepackaged
software; communications consulting; ;
marketing consulting services;

(G-41)
CREATIVE CANVAS CENTL FLA INC
436 Wekiva Rapids Dr (32714-7546)
PHONE....................................407 661-1211
Beverly Costello, *Principal*
Theresa Castle, *Vice Pres*
Daniel Jarrous, *Project Mgr*
Edward Ortiz, *Opers Staff*
Carlos Vargas, *Production*
EMP: 8 EST: 2014
SALES (est): 218K Privately Held
SIC: 2211 Canvas

(G-42)
DIGITAL LIVING
4303 Vineland Rd (32714)
PHONE....................................407 332-9998
EMP: 8
SALES (est): 780K Privately Held
SIC: 3823 Mfg Process Control Instruments

(G-43)
DJ LIVE PRODUCTIONS LLC
999 Douglas Ave (32714-2064)
PHONE....................................407 383-1740
Austin Beeghly, *Principal*
EMP: 7 EST: 2015
SALES (est): 269.8K Privately Held
WEB: www.djliveproductions.com
SIC: 3651 5999 3648 Amplifiers: radio,
public address or musical instrument;
audio-visual equipment & supplies; stage
lighting equipment

(G-44)
EIZO RUGGED SOLUTIONS INC
442 Northlake Blvd # 1008 (32701-5244)
PHONE....................................407 262-7100
Selwyn L Henriques, *President*
Colin Woodley, *Managing Dir*
David Hindon, *Business Mgr*
Mike Kreischer, *Business Mgr*
Kyana Brooks, *Opers Mgr*
EMP: 27 EST: 1984
SQ FT: 13,000
SALES (est): 10.5MM Privately Held
WEB: www.eizorugged.com
SIC: 3577 7371 Graphic displays, except
graphic terminals; custom computer pro-
gramming services
HQ: Eizo Inc.
5710 Warland Dr
Cypress CA 90630
562 431-5011

(G-45)
ETERNAL ELEMENTS LLC
1045 Miller Dr (32701-2067)
PHONE....................................407 830-6968
Michelle Salinas, *Principal*
EMP: 8 EST: 2010
SALES (est): 542.5K Privately Held
SIC: 2819 Industrial inorganic chemicals

(G-46)
EUROPRINT INC
620 Douglas Ave Ste 1308 (32714-2546)
PHONE....................................407 869-9955
Scott Johnson, *President*
EMP: 10 EST: 1994
SQ FT: 5,000
SALES (est): 746K Privately Held
SIC: 2711 Newspapers

(G-47)
FLORIDA MEDIA INC
Also Called: Florida Monthly
1268 Bent Oak Trl (32714-1102)
PHONE....................................407 816-9596
Doug Cifers, *President*
Kristen Cifers, *Vice Pres*
EMP: 10 EST: 1997
SALES (est): 725.3K Privately Held
WEB: www.floridamagazine.com
SIC: 2721 Magazines: publishing only, not
printed on site

(G-48)
FLORIDAS BEST INC
839 Sunshine Ln (32714-3901)
PHONE....................................407 682-9570
James L Toler, *President*
EMP: 6 EST: 2011
SALES (est): 601.4K Privately Held
WEB: www.floridasbest.com
SIC: 2834 Lip balms

(G-49)
GALAXY SCREENPRINTING INC
925 Sunshine Ln (32714-3825)
PHONE....................................407 862-2224
Ryan T Panacek, *Principal*
EMP: 7 EST: 2001
SALES (est): 73.2K Privately Held
SIC: 2759 Screen printing

(G-50)
GALLEON INDUSTRIES INC
Also Called: Galleon Decals & Die Cuts
279 Douglas Ave Ste 1112 (32714-3324)
PHONE....................................708 478-5444
Paul Turay, *President*
Craig Turay, *Vice Pres*
Jeff Turay, *Vice Pres*
EMP: 5 EST: 1993
SALES (est): 738.6K Privately Held
WEB: www.galleonindustries.com
SIC: 2759 7389 Screen printing; printing
broker

(G-51)
GF WOODWORKS
1306 Pressview Ave (32701-7742)
P.O. Box 181735, Casselberry (32718-
1735)
PHONE....................................407 716-3712
Gary Fliess, *Manager*
EMP: 8 EST: 2006
SALES (est): 74.9K Privately Held
SIC: 2431 Millwork

(G-52)
HEMCO CORPORATION
260 E Altamonte Dr (32701-4328)
PHONE....................................904 993-0380
Robert Marsh Jr, *Principal*
EMP: 7 EST: 2011
SALES (est): 110.3K Privately Held
SIC: 3821 Laboratory apparatus & furniture

(G-53)
INNOVATIVE SUPPORT SYSTEMS INC
1030 Sunshine Ln Ste 1000 (32714-3882)
PHONE....................................407 682-7570
Wood Breazeale, *President*
W Breazeale, *Owner*
Patrick Saldana, *Sales Staff*
Ileane Elliotte, *Manager*
Randy Carroll, *Associate*
EMP: 8 EST: 2001
SALES (est): 1.4MM Privately Held
WEB: www.issifl.com
SIC: 3585 5075 Air conditioning units,
complete: domestic or industrial; warm air
heating equipment & supplies

(G-54)
KROHN LIGHTING LLC
191 Varsity Cir (32714-2836)
PHONE....................................407 949-7231
Ann K Krohn, *Principal*
EMP: 7 EST: 2010
SALES (est): 183.9K Privately Held
SIC: 3648 Lighting equipment

(G-55)
LORENZE & ASSOCIATES INC
1030 Sunshine Ln Ste 1000 (32714-3830)
PHONE....................................407 682-7570
Dewayne Lorenze, *President*
Sharon Lorenze, *Admin Sec*
EMP: 9 EST: 1979
SQ FT: 1,800
SALES (est): 704.9K Privately Held
SIC: 3585 Heating & air conditioning com-
bination units

(G-56)
M12 LENSES INC
350 Pinestraw Cir (32714-5415)
PHONE....................................407 973-4403
Priyangika Goonetilleke, *Principal*
EMP: 7 EST: 2010
SALES (est): 246.8K Privately Held
WEB: www.m12lenses.com
SIC: 3851 Ophthalmic goods

(G-57)
MAGGARD FNDTION FOR BLIND PHYS
1270 Marty Blvd Ste 101 (32714-2725)
PHONE....................................407 637-5302
Diane M Maggard, *Principal*
EMP: 7 EST: 2020
SALES (est): 86.9K Privately Held
SIC: 2591 Window blinds

(G-58)
MANNS DIVERSIFIED INDS INC
380 S State Road 434 # 10 (32714-3810)
PHONE....................................407 310-5938
Roy Harold Mann Jr, *Principal*
EMP: 7 EST: 2012
SALES (est): 270.2K Privately Held
SIC: 3999 Manufacturing industries

(G-59)
NORTH AMRCN PRTECTION CTRL LLC
190 N Westmonte Dr (32714-3342)
P.O. Box 161060 (32716-1060)
PHONE....................................407 788-3717
EMP: 7
SALES (est): 659.3K Privately Held
SIC: 3462 3568 Iron And Steel Forgings,
Nsk

(G-60)
OAKTREE SOFTWARE INC
Also Called: Accordance Bible Software
222 S Westmonte Dr # 251 (32714-4269)
PHONE....................................407 339-5855
Roy B Brown, *President*
Helen Brown, *Vice Pres*
Kristen Linduff, *CFO*
Darin Allen, *Marketing Staff*
Jackie Bolton, *Marketing Staff*
EMP: 10 EST: 1989
SALES (est): 2MM Privately Held
WEB: www.accordancebible.com
SIC: 7372 Prepackaged software

(G-61)
PARADISE BUILDING MTLS LLC
665 Youngstown Pkwy # 268 (32714-4550)
PHONE....................................407 267-3378
Kevin Fagan,
EMP: 7 EST: 2017
SALES (est): 228.2K Privately Held
SIC: 3999 Manufacturing industries

(G-62)
PATHFINDER SHIRTS
865 Sunshine Ln (32714-3952)
PHONE....................................407 865-6530
Karen Lillard, *Principal*
EMP: 7 EST: 2014
SALES (est): 427.5K Privately Held
WEB: www.pathfindershirts.com
SIC: 2759 Screen printing

(G-63)
PAVER WAY LLC
160 N Spring Trl (32714-3461)
PHONE....................................321 303-0968
John Gilmore, *Principal*
EMP: 10 EST: 2010
SALES (est): 2.6MM Privately Held
SIC: 3531 Pavers

(G-64)
PHARMA RESOURCES INC
380 S State Road 434 (32714-3810)
PHONE....................................973 780-5241
Gregory A Longo, *President*
EMP: 11 EST: 2003
SALES (est): 355.3K Privately Held
SIC: 2834 Pharmaceutical preparations

(G-65)
PRISTINE LASER CENTER
1180 Spring Cntre S Blvd (32714)
PHONE....................................407 389-1200
Mohammad Eskandari, *Manager*
EMP: 8 EST: 2011
SALES (est): 765K Privately Held
WEB: www.removery.com
SIC: 3845 Laser systems & equipment,
medical

(G-66)
PRODIGY CUSTOMS
527 Little Wekiva Rd (32714-7403)
PHONE....................................407 832-1752
Frank Serafine, *Principal*
EMP: 7 EST: 2005
SALES (est): 81K Privately Held
SIC: 2395 Embroidery & art needlework

(G-67)
PROTECTIVE ENCLOSURES CO LLC
Also Called: TV Shield, The
277 Douglas Ave Ste 1012 (32714-3300)
PHONE....................................321 441-9689
Mary Martinez, *Business Mgr*
Justin King, *Mng Member*
King Justin, *Mng Member*
John Lupo, *Director*
Jarad King,
▲ **EMP: 6 EST: 2011**
SALES (est): 1MM Privately Held
WEB: www.protectiveenclosures.com
SIC: 3089 Plastic hardware & building
products

(G-68)
RAIL TECH
674 Maitland Ave (32701-6862)
PHONE....................................407 834-6966
John Heath, *Principal*
EMP: 7 EST: 1998
SALES (est): 80K Privately Held
SIC: 3999 Manufacturing industries

(G-69)
RAPID RESPONSE
250 Altmnte Commerce 10 (32714-2535)
PHONE....................................407 774-9877
Donald Dass, *Manager*
EMP: 8 EST: 2010
SALES (est): 456.8K Privately Held
WEB: www.rapiddeploy.com
SIC: 1389 Construction, repair & disman-
tling services

(G-70)
SAFARI SUN LLC
928 Josiane Ct Ste 1007 (32701-3617)
PHONE....................................407 339-7291
Tara Montano, *Accounts Mgr*
Melissa Battista, *Cust Mgr*
Allan Gehr, *Sales Staff*
Marlene McQuaig, *Sales Staff*
Heather Eshack, *Marketing Mgr*
EMP: 30 EST: 1980
SQ FT: 6,000
SALES (est): 5.1MM Privately Held
WEB: www.safarisun.com
SIC: 2759 Directories, telephone: printing

GEOGRAPHIC

(G-71)
SPECIAL EDITIONSPUBLISHING
Also Called: Special Editions Publishing
999 Douglas Ave Ste 3317 (32714-2063)
P.O. Box 953813, Lake Mary (32795-3813)
PHONE..............................407 862-7737
Albert Sciuto, *President*
Mark Heagy, *Advt Staff*
Rosalyn Porter, *Manager*
Lydia Enriquez, *Bd of Directors*
EMP: 5 **EST:** 1976
SQ FT: 3,000
SALES (est): 790.6K **Privately Held**
SIC: 2721 Magazines: publishing only, not printed on site

(G-72)
SUNSHINE METAL PRODUCTS INC
195 Magnolia St (32701-7512)
PHONE..............................407 331-1300
Benjamin J Coble, *President*
EMP: 5 **EST:** 2003
SQ FT: 4,794
SALES (est): 476K **Privately Held**
WEB: www.sunshinemetalproducts.com
SIC: 3444 Sheet metalwork

(G-73)
SUPERLITE ALUMINUM PDTS INC
Also Called: Racestar Manufacturing
1090 Rainer Dr (32714-3846)
P.O. Box 162245 (32716-2245)
PHONE..............................407 682-2121
Todd A Vallancourt, *President*
Ellen Vallancourt, *Vice Pres*
EMP: 6 **EST:** 2001
SALES (est): 814.2K **Privately Held**
SIC: 3354 Aluminum extruded products

(G-74)
TWO GUYS PLUMBING SUPPLY LLC
1030 Sunshine Ln Ste 1020 (32714-3882)
PHONE..............................321 263-0021
Frank J Altilio, *Vice Pres*
EMP: 9 **EST:** 2010
SALES (est): 420.1K **Privately Held**
SIC: 3088 Plastics plumbing fixtures

(G-75)
ULTIMATE SWIMWEAR INC
247 N Westmonte Dr (32714-3345)
PHONE..............................386 668-8900
Gwyn R Picerne, *President*
EMP: 12 **EST:** 1993
SQ FT: 12,000
SALES (est): 307.2K **Privately Held**
WEB: www.ultimateswimwear.com
SIC: 2339 2329 5699 Bathing suits: women's, misses' & juniors'; bathing suits & swimwear: men's & boys'; bathing suits

(G-76)
VEDIC ORIGINS INC
478 E Altamonte Dr # 108 (32701-4628)
PHONE..............................407 712-5614
Chirag Patel, *Principal*
EMP: 9 **EST:** 2010
SALES (est): 328.2K **Privately Held**
SIC: 2833 Vitamins, natural or synthetic: bulk, uncompounded

(G-77)
VINTAGE IRONWORKS LLC
671 Newburyport Ave (32701-2740)
PHONE..............................407 339-2555
William J Walters, *Mng Member*
EMP: 10 **EST:** 2005
SALES (est): 965.4K **Privately Held**
WEB: www.vintageirondoors.com
SIC: 3446 Architectural metalwork

Altha
Calhoun County

(G-78)
TRI-COUNTY CABINETRY WDWRK LLC
16050 Nw Ashley Shiver Rd (32421-4820)
PHONE..............................850 238-6226

Xavier Pena-Cintron, *Principal*
EMP: 7 **EST:** 2016
SALES (est): 169.5K **Privately Held**
SIC: 2431 Millwork

(G-79)
WALDEN TIMBER HARVESTING INC
13851 Nw Sand Cut Trl (32421-4940)
PHONE..............................850 674-4884
Troy Walden, *President*
Garnet Walden, *Vice Pres*
EMP: 10 **EST:** 1983
SALES (est): 843.9K **Privately Held**
SIC: 2411 Logging camps & contractors

Alva
Lee County

(G-80)
EZ TRUCK SERVICES INC
19595 N River Rd (33920-3247)
PHONE..............................239 728-3022
Edward P Zengel Sr, *President*
Marie Zengel, *Corp Secy*
Edward A Zengel Jr, *Vice Pres*
EMP: 17 **EST:** 1988
SALES (est): 428.8K **Privately Held**
SIC: 3715 Truck trailers

(G-81)
JNJ & COMPANY INC
17650 Oak Creek Rd (33920-3517)
PHONE..............................239 489-0053
John Barr, *Principal*
EMP: 13 **EST:** 2008
SALES (est): 892.4K **Privately Held**
WEB: www.jnj.com
SIC: 2834 Pharmaceutical preparations

(G-82)
NPC&UG INC
22021 Luckey Lee Ln (33920-4013)
PHONE..............................239 694-7255
Mitchell Nobles, *Principal*
EMP: 8 **EST:** 2007
SALES (est): 1.2MM **Privately Held**
SIC: 2911 Gases & liquefied petroleum gases

(G-83)
RABER INDUSTRIES INC
2190 Sebastian Ct (33920-3824)
PHONE..............................239 728-5527
Thomas E Raber Jr, *President*
Bill Bolek, *Manager*
Dan Subbert, *Admin Sec*
EMP: 9 **EST:** 2000
SALES (est): 1.8MM **Privately Held**
WEB: www.raberindustries.com
SIC: 3441 Fabricated structural metal

(G-84)
SIMPLY CLOSETS & CABINETS
10105 Amberwood Rd Ste 6 (33920)
PHONE..............................239 994-4264
Barbara Roessner, *Owner*
EMP: 7 **EST:** 2013
SALES (est): 304.3K **Privately Held**
WEB: www.simplyclosetsandcabinets.com
SIC: 2434 Wood kitchen cabinets

Amelia Island
Nassau County

(G-85)
AMERICAN MAGLEV TECH FLA INC
8030 Frst Cast Hwy Apt 10 (32034)
PHONE..............................404 386-4036
Tony Morris, *CEO*
Jordan Morris, *CFO*
EMP: 10 **EST:** 1994
SALES (est): 940.1K **Privately Held**
WEB: www.american-maglev.com
SIC: 3764 Propulsion units for guided missiles & space vehicles

Anthony
Marion County

(G-86)
AUSTIN POWDER COMPANY
5299 Ne 97th Street Rd (32617-3952)
P.O. Box 58 (32617-0058)
PHONE..............................352 690-7060
Mike Kaufman, *Manager*
EMP: 8
SALES (corp-wide): 734.5MM **Privately Held**
WEB: www.austinpowder.com
SIC: 2892 Explosives
HQ: Austin Powder Company
25800 Science Park Dr # 300
Cleveland OH 44122
216 464-2400

(G-87)
KEEPIT NEAT
11630 Ne Jacksonville Rd (32617-2601)
P.O. Box 84 (32617-0084)
PHONE..............................352 867-0541
Brent R Long, *Principal*
EMP: 7 **EST:** 2008
SALES (est): 73.8K **Privately Held**
SIC: 2631 Container, packaging & boxboard

Apalachicola
Franklin County

(G-88)
BUDDY WARD & SONS SEAFOOD
Also Called: Buddy Ward Sons Seafood Trckg
3022 C 30 13 Mile Rd (32320)
P.O. Box 698 (32329-0698)
PHONE..............................850 653-8522
Thomas Ward, *Manager*
EMP: 7 **Privately Held**
SIC: 2092 4212 Seafoods, fresh: prepared; local trucking, without storage
PA: Buddy Ward & Sons Seafood
233 Water St
Apalachicola FL 32320

(G-89)
MIRACLE SEAFOOD MANUFACTURERS
Also Called: S & W Nash Seafood
610 Us Highway 98 (32320-1243)
P.O. Box 494 (32329-0494)
PHONE..............................850 653-2114
Stephen Nash, *Partner*
Wayne Nash, *Partner*
EMP: 8 **EST:** 1972
SQ FT: 2,600
SALES (est): 218K **Privately Held**
SIC: 2091 2092 Oysters: packaged in cans, jars, etc.; fresh or frozen packaged fish

Apollo Beach
Hillsborough County

(G-90)
ALTERNATIVE MEDICAL ENTPS LLC
Also Called: Altmed Enterprises
6944 N Us Highway 41 (33572-1500)
PHONE..............................941 702-9955
Todd Beckwith, *Marketing Staff*
Judy Firek, *Marketing Staff*
Tyler Hayden, *Manager*
Ron Watson, *Director*
Gary Merlino,
EMP: 17 **EST:** 2014
SALES (est): 579.2K **Privately Held**
WEB: www.altmed.co
SIC: 2834 Pharmaceutical preparations

(G-91)
ELSTONS INC
Also Called: Elstons Lmnted Toil Partitions
703 Islebay Dr (33572-3338)
PHONE..............................727 527-7929
EMP: 6

SQ FT: 3,200
SALES (est): 1MM **Privately Held**
SIC: 3088 Mfg Toilet Partitions

(G-92)
FOUR SEAS DISTILLING CO LLC
Also Called: Copper Bottom Craft Distillery
915 Bunker View Dr (33572-2813)
PHONE..............................813 645-0057
Joanne Craig, *Principal*
EMP: 8 **EST:** 2015
SALES (est): 462.7K **Privately Held**
WEB: www.copperbottomspirits.com
SIC: 2085 Distilled & blended liquors

(G-93)
JORDAN LOGISTICS CO LLC
216 Apollo Beach Blvd (33572-2200)
PHONE..............................813 787-7791
Melvin, *Principal*
EMP: 15
SALES (est): 591.4K **Privately Held**
SIC: 3537 Trucks: freight, baggage, etc.: industrial, except mining

(G-94)
LIFESAVING SYSTEMS CORPORATION
220 Elsberry Rd (33572-2291)
PHONE..............................813 645-2748
Samuel G Maness, *CEO*
Jason A Glazer, *President*
Barbara A Maness, *Vice Pres*
Taran Fleming, *Opers Staff*
Amy O'Hara, *Sales Mgr*
◆ **EMP:** 36 **EST:** 1981
SQ FT: 20,000
SALES (est): 5.9MM **Privately Held**
WEB: www.lifesavingsystems.com
SIC: 3842 5099 5999 Personal safety equipment; safety equipment & supplies; safety supplies & equipment

(G-95)
MATERIAL CONVEYING MAINT INC
6535 Carrington Sky Dr (33572-1732)
PHONE..............................813 677-3740
Nelson G Castellano, *Branch Mgr*
EMP: 41
SALES (corp-wide): 2.4MM **Privately Held**
WEB: www.gomcmi.com
SIC: 3535 Conveyors & conveying equipment
PA: Material Conveying Maintenance, Inc.
4901 30th Ave S
Tampa FL 33619
813 740-1111

(G-96)
TAMPA BAY CABINETS INC
6509 Santiago Ct (33572-2111)
PHONE..............................813 781-9468
Jeffrey A Smith, *Principal*
EMP: 7 **EST:** 2016
SALES (est): 137K **Privately Held**
WEB: www.tampabaycabinets.net
SIC: 2434 Wood kitchen cabinets

(G-97)
TROPIC GUARD INDUSTRIES LLC
6727 Clair Shore Dr (33572-3359)
PHONE..............................813 447-3938
John G Hough, *Principal*
EMP: 7 **EST:** 2016
SALES (est): 245.5K **Privately Held**
WEB: www.tropicguardfl.com
SIC: 3999 Manufacturing industries

Apopka
Orange County

(G-98)
ACCURATE REPRODUCTIONS INC
2060 Apopka Blvd (32703-7735)
PHONE..............................407 814-1622
Barry West, *President*
EMP: 9 **EST:** 1988
SQ FT: 10,000

▲ = Import ▼=Export
◆ =Import/Export

SALES (est): 457K **Privately Held**
SIC: 2221 Fiberglass fabrics

(G-99)
ADVANCED HERMETICS INC
2052 Platinum Rd (32703-7738)
PHONE...................................407 464-0539
John Wilson, *President*
Patricia Wilson, *Vice Pres*
▲ EMP: 5 EST: 1988
SQ FT: 5,100
SALES (est): 608.4K **Privately Held**
WEB: www.advancedhermetics.com
SIC: 3585 Compressors for refrigeration &
air conditioning equipment

(G-100)
ALL AMRCAN BLDG STRCTRES CNTR
401 E Cleveland St (32703-7224)
PHONE...................................407 466-4959
Lamar Hughley, *Principal*
EMP: 9 EST: 2010
SALES (est): 131.2K **Privately Held**
SIC: 3448 Prefabricated metal buildings

(G-101)
ALL BECAUSE LLC
Also Called: Printers, The
2098 Sprint Blvd (32703-7761)
PHONE...................................407 884-6700
Marcia Van Vliet, *Office Mgr*
John Sciandra, *Mng Member*
John Cravey, *Mng Member*
Terry Cravey, *Admin Sec*
EMP: 7 EST: 2009
SALES (est): 1MM **Privately Held**
WEB: www.the-printers.net
SIC: 2752 Commercial printing, offset

(G-102)
ANDERSONS CAN LINE FBRCTION EQ
2208 Stillwater Ave (32703-9003)
P.O. Box 116, Ocoee (34761-0116)
PHONE...................................407 889-4665
Frank L Anderson Jr, *President*
EMP: 10 EST: 1976
SQ FT: 40,000
SALES (est): 4.5MM **Privately Held**
SIC: 3411 3535 3494 Aluminum cans;
conveyors & conveying equipment; valves
& pipe fittings

(G-103)
ARTISAN ARMS INC
2516 Jmt Industrial Dr # 105 (32703-2135)
PHONE...................................321 299-4053
Philip Picardat, *President*
James Krosky, *Principal*
Robert Soong, *Principal*
Lisa Wise-Picardat, *CFO*
EMP: 6 EST: 2009
SALES (est): 517.1K **Privately Held**
SIC: 3484 Guns (firearms) or gun parts, 30
mm. & below

(G-104)
BAVARIA CORPORATION
Also Called: Bavaria Corp International
515 Cooper Commerce Dr # 10
(32703-5135)
PHONE...................................407 880-0322
Peter F Schaeflein, *President*
Bruce Hopkins, *General Mgr*
Faye Reed, *Vice Pres*
Victor Moreno, *Marketing Mgr*
Dennis Koo, *Manager*
◆ EMP: 15 EST: 1986
SQ FT: 15,000
SALES (est): 3.2MM **Privately Held**
WEB: www.bavariacorp.com
SIC: 2099 5149 Seasonings & spices;
seasonings, sauces & extracts

(G-105)
BDJL ENTERPRISES LLC
Also Called: Blue Water Spa Covers
2591 Clark St Ste 208 (32703-2108)
PHONE...................................407 678-9960
Brian Keihner, *Mng Member*
Seth Keihner, *Manager*
EMP: 18 EST: 2015
SQ FT: 12,000
SALES (est): 2MM **Privately Held**
SIC: 3999 Hot tub & spa covers

(G-106)
BEST OF ORLANDO PNTG & STUCCO
3000 Clarcona Rd Lot 763 (32703-8723)
PHONE...................................407 947-4174
Gary Baugh, *Principal*
EMP: 9 EST: 2009
SALES (est): 415.9K **Privately Held**
WEB: best-of-orlando-painting-stucco-
inc.business.site
SIC: 3299 Stucco

(G-107)
BLAQ LUXURY COLLECTION LLC
Also Called: Blaq Luxury Realty
2164 Platinum Rd Ste D (32703-7764)
PHONE...................................407 496-7517
Cherice Williams, *CEO*
EMP: 5 EST: 2019
SALES (est): 2.8MM **Privately Held**
SIC: 2844 Hair preparations, including
shampoos

(G-108)
BLOEM LLC
3000 Orange Ave (32703-3347)
PHONE...................................407 889-5533
Kevin McCarron, *Engineer*
EMP: 16
SALES (corp-wide): 11.4MM **Privately Held**
WEB: www.bloemliving.com
SIC: 3089 Planters, plastic
PA: Bloem, Llc
3301 Hudson Trail Dr
Hudsonville MI 49426
616 622-6344

(G-109)
CELLEC GAMES INC
Also Called: Cg Solutionsgroup
2736 Candlewood Ct (32703-4995)
PHONE...................................407 476-3590
Gerard Merritt, *CEO*
Prashanth Yaramosu, *Prgrmr*
EMP: 5 EST: 2011
SALES (est): 782.6K **Privately Held**
WEB: www.cellecgames.com
SIC: 7372 7389 7371 Educational com-
puter software; ; custom computer pro-
gramming services

(G-110)
CHIP SUPPLY INC (HQ)
Also Called: Micross Components
1810 S Orange Blossom Trl (32703-9419)
PHONE...................................407 298-7100
Vince Buffa, *CEO*
Brad Buser, *Vice Pres*
Cyndy Hernandez, *Vice Pres*
Dale Pullis, *Vice Pres*
Farokh Sooudi, *Engineer*
▲ EMP: 38 EST: 1979
SQ FT: 5,000
SALES (est): 52.2MM
SALES (corp-wide): 332.8MM **Privately Held**
WEB: www.micross.com
SIC: 3674 Microcircuits, integrated (semi-
conductor); wafers (semiconductor de-
vices)
PA: Micross Inc.
1810 S Orange Blossom Trl
Apopka FL 32703
407 298-7100

(G-111)
COCA-COLA COMPANY
2659 Orange Ave (32703-3346)
PHONE...................................407 886-1568
Katherine Larid, *Manager*
Anthony Rapaglia,
EMP: 27
SALES (corp-wide): 33B **Publicly Held**
WEB: www.coca-colacompany.com
SIC: 2086 2087 Bottled & canned soft
drinks; fruit juices: concentrated for foun-
tain use; syrups, drink
PA: The Coca-Cola Company
1 Coca Cola Plz Nw
Atlanta GA 30313
404 676-2121

(G-112)
COCA-COLA COMPANY
2651 Orange Ave (32703-3346)
PHONE...................................404 676-2121
◆ EMP: 20
SALES (est): 3.2MM **Privately Held**
SIC: 2086 Carb Sft Drnkbtlcn

(G-113)
COCA-COLA COMPANY
2651 Orange Ave (32703-3346)
PHONE...................................407 565-2465
EMP: 7
SALES (corp-wide): 33B **Publicly Held**
WEB: www.coca-cola.com
SIC: 2087 2086 2033 2037 Concen-
trates, drink; soft drinks: packaged in
cans, bottles, etc.; fruit juices: fresh; fruit
juice concentrates, frozen
PA: The Coca-Cola Company
1 Coca Cola Plz Nw
Atlanta GA 30313
404 676-2121

(G-114)
COCA-COLA COMPANY
2501 Orange Ave (32703-3346)
PHONE...................................407 358-6758
Oneal Michael, *Opers Staff*
Eric Bennett, *Branch Mgr*
EMP: 90
SALES (corp-wide): 33B **Publicly Held**
WEB: www.coca-colacompany.com
SIC: 2095 2087 Freeze-dried coffee; fruit
juices: concentrated for fountain use
PA: The Coca-Cola Company
1 Coca Cola Plz Nw
Atlanta GA 30313
404 676-2121

(G-115)
COCA-COLA COMPANY DISTRIBUTION
1451 Ocoee Apopka Rd (32703-9209)
PHONE...................................407 814-1327
EMP: 7 EST: 2017
SALES (est): 383.2K **Privately Held**
WEB: www.coca-cola.com
SIC: 2086 Bottled & canned soft drinks

(G-116)
COLLINS MFG INC
672 Johns Rd (32703-6203)
PHONE...................................407 889-9669
Jim Whittaker, *President*
Bill Poole, *Opers Mgr*
Ryan Tobyansen, *Production*
Susana Olbrych, *Human Res Mgr*
Wendy Ritchey, *Human Res Mgr*
EMP: 100 EST: 1995
SQ FT: 37,000
SALES (est): 16.3MM **Privately Held**
WEB: www.collinsmanufacturing.com
SIC: 3369 Castings, except die-castings,
precision

(G-117)
CREATIVE METAL STUDIO INC (PA)
849 Monroe Ave (32703-4472)
PHONE...................................321 206-6112
Bilyana P Vladimirova, *President*
EMP: 5 EST: 2007
SALES (est): 546.2K **Privately Held**
WEB: www.creativemetalstudioinc.com
SIC: 3446 Architectural metalwork

(G-118)
CREATIVE SIGNS INC
2301 N Hiawassee Rd (32703-2604)
P.O. Box 608070, Orlando (32860-8070)
PHONE...................................407 293-9393
Antonio Di Salvatore, *President*
Carol Tredway, *Production*
Cheryl Disalvatore, *Treasurer*
EMP: 31 EST: 1982
SALES (est): 5.6MM **Privately Held**
WEB: www.creativesignsinc.com
SIC: 3993 Signs & advertising specialties

(G-119)
CUSTOM MEDICAL PRODUCTS INC
3909 E Semrn Blvd Ste 599 (32703-6103)
PHONE...................................407 865-7211

Carl Shumate, *President*
EMP: 9 EST: 2004
SALES (est): 257.9K **Privately Held**
SIC: 3841 Surgical & medical instruments

(G-120)
DESIGN & PRINT SOLUTIONS INC
Also Called: Romine Reprographics Svcs
553 Sheeler Ave (32703-5555)
PHONE...................................407 703-7861
Chet Carter, *Principal*
EMP: 7 EST: 2016
SALES (est): 156.7K **Privately Held**
SIC: 2752 Commercial printing, litho-
graphic

(G-121)
DGW TECHNOLOGIES LLC
Also Called: Everest Ice and Water Systems
1000 Ocoee Apopka Rd # 4 (32703-9238)
PHONE...................................407 930-4437
Daniel Doromal, *Mng Member*
Robert Gaskill,
EMP: 11 EST: 2015
SALES (est): 1.2MM **Privately Held**
SIC: 3581 Automatic vending machines

(G-122)
DJ PLASTICS INC
946 Century Ln (32703-3709)
PHONE...................................407 656-6677
Dominick P Dichiria, *President*
Page Bowlen, *President*
EMP: 5 EST: 1998
SQ FT: 18,500
SALES (est): 646.5K **Privately Held**
WEB: www.seelyeinc-orl.com
SIC: 2821 3089 Thermoplastic materials;
thermoformed finished plastic products

(G-123)
DRISCOLL INDUSTRIES LLC
522 S Hunt Club Blvd # 570 (32703-4960)
PHONE...................................407 848-7127
Ernest D Nash Jr, *Manager*
EMP: 6 EST: 2017
SALES (est): 334.5K **Privately Held**
SIC: 3999 Barber & beauty shop equip-
ment

(G-124)
EARTHMOVER CNSTR EQP LLC
2325 Clark St (32703-2110)
P.O. Box 1649, Windermere (34786-1649)
PHONE...................................407 401-8956
Howard W Abell, *President*
Brian Darville, *Sales Staff*
EMP: 16 EST: 2013
SALES (est): 2.6MM **Privately Held**
SIC: 3537 Industrial trucks & tractors

(G-125)
ELRO MANUFACTURING LLC
516 Cooper Commerce Dr (32703-6223)
PHONE...................................407 410-6006
Robert Asta, *CEO*
Paul Wolmarans, *Ch of Bd*
Philip Klote, *Vice Pres*
EMP: 10 EST: 2014
SALES (est): 1.1MM **Privately Held**
WEB: www.elro-mfg.com
SIC: 3441 Fabricated structural metal

(G-126)
ENERGY TASK FORCE LLC (HQ)
2501 Clark St Ste 101 (32703-2132)
PHONE...................................407 523-3770
Jay Newell, *Mng Member*
EMP: 15 EST: 2000
SQ FT: 38,000
SALES (est): 9.8MM
SALES (corp-wide): 93.4MM **Privately Held**
WEB: www.energytaskforce.com
SIC: 3498 Fabricated pipe & fittings
PA: Venture Management Group, Inc.
110 East Dr Ste 1
Melbourne FL 32904
321 726-8543

(G-127)
ENVIROWORKS INC
Also Called: Solartex
3000 Orange Ave (32703-3347)
PHONE...................................407 889-5533

Dave Smith, *President*
EMP: 33 **EST:** 1982
SQ FT: 420,000
SALES (est): 3.3MM
SALES (corp-wide): 1.4B **Privately Held**
WEB: www.enviroworks.co.uk
SIC: 2295 3089 0782 Chemically coated & treated fabrics; flower pots, plastic; plastic hardware & building products; lawn services
HQ: Fiskars Brands, Inc.
7800 Discovery Dr
Middleton WI 53562
866 348-5661

(G-128)
ER PRECISION OPTICAL CORP
1676 E Semoran Blvd (32703-5673)
PHONE............................407 292-5395
Mark Hess, *President*
Jason Hess, *Vice Pres*
◆ **EMP:** 18 **EST:** 1991
SQ FT: 25,000
SALES (est): 4.6MM **Privately Held**
WEB: www.eroptics.com
SIC: 3827 Optical instruments & apparatus

(G-129)
ETF WEST LLC
2501 Clark St (32703-2132)
PHONE............................407 523-3770
EMP: 10 **EST:** 2007
SALES (est): 500.1K **Privately Held**
SIC: 3498 Fabricated pipe & fittings

(G-130)
FINFROCK DESIGN INC
2400 Apopka Blvd (32703-7743)
PHONE............................407 293-4000
Robert D Finfrock, *President*
William Finfrock, *Exec VP*
Jorge Arboleda, *Vice Pres*
Allen R Finfrock, *Vice Pres*
William A Finfrock, *Vice Pres*
EMP: 44 **EST:** 2000
SALES (est): 4MM **Privately Held**
WEB: www.finfrock.com
SIC: 3272 Concrete products

(G-131)
FINFROCK INDUSTRIES INC
2400 Apopka Blvd (32703-7743)
P.O. Box 607754, Orlando (32860-7754)
PHONE............................407 293-4000
Robert D Finfrock, *Ch of Bd*
Jeff Harrison, *Superintendent*
Jonn Hoffman, *Superintendent*
Daniel J Finfrock, *Vice Pres*
William A Finfrock, *Vice Pres*
EMP: 200 **EST:** 1945
SQ FT: 30,000
SALES (est): 44.7MM **Privately Held**
WEB: www.finfrock.com
SIC: 3272 Prestressed concrete products

(G-132)
FISKARS BRANDS INC
Fiskars Home Leisure Division
3000 Orange Ave (32703-3347)
PHONE............................407 889-5533
William Denton, *President*
Rob Carroll, *Vice Pres*
Melissa Dunn, *Vice Pres*
Joelle Onorato, *Vice Pres*
Ashley Brantner, *Project Mgr*
EMP: 88
SALES (corp-wide): 1.4B **Privately Held**
WEB: www.gilmour.com
SIC: 2295 3089 Chemically coated & treated fabrics; flower pots, plastic; plastic hardware & building products
HQ: Fiskars Brands, Inc.
7800 Discovery Dr
Middleton WI 53562
866 348-5661

(G-133)
FLORIDA FABRICATION INC
800 Johns Rd (32703-6207)
PHONE............................407 212-0105
Katherine Starkey, *Principal*
EMP: 10 **EST:** 2013
SALES (est): 2.4MM **Privately Held**
WEB: www.floridafabrication.net
SIC: 3441 Fabricated structural metal

(G-134)
FOLIAGE ENTERPRISES INC
Also Called: Apopka Chief, The
400 N Park Ave (32712-4152)
P.O. Box 880 (32704-0880)
PHONE............................407 886-2777
John E Ricketson, *President*
Eileen Ricketson, *Vice Pres*
EMP: 22 **EST:** 1923
SQ FT: 8,000
SALES (est): 2MM **Privately Held**
WEB: www.theapopkachief.com
SIC: 2711 Newspapers, publishing & printing

(G-135)
FOSTER & FOSTER WORLDWIDE LLC
635 Lexington Pkwy (32712-4420)
PHONE............................352 362-9102
Steven Foster, *President*
EMP: 10 **EST:** 2019
SALES (est): 267.5K **Privately Held**
SIC: 1389 Oil consultants

(G-136)
GREATHOUSE SIGNS LLC
156 Holly St (32712-5705)
P.O. Box 1016 (32704-1016)
PHONE............................407 247-2668
Bob Greathouse, *Principal*
EMP: 7 **EST:** 2010
SALES (est): 289.1K **Privately Held**
WEB: www.greathousesigns.com
SIC: 3993 Signs & advertising specialties

(G-137)
GREEN RHINO ENRGY SLUTIONS LLC (PA)
1451 Ocoee Apopka Rd (32703-9209)
PHONE............................407 925-5868
Victor Diaz Estrada, *Project Mgr*
Bishoy Rezk, *Electrical Engi*
Nick Bussanich, *VP Bus Dvlpt*
Tom Mangone, *VP Bus Dvlpt*
Mario Wilhelm, *VP Bus Dvlpt*
EMP: 29 **EST:** 2016
SALES (est): 4.7MM **Privately Held**
WEB: www.greenrhino-energy.com
SIC: 3621 Power generators

(G-138)
GUY WINGO SIGNS
Also Called: Capital Signs
2682 Pemberton Dr (32703-9402)
PHONE............................407 578-1132
Guy Wingo, *Principal*
EMP: 5 **EST:** 2008
SALES (est): 725.3K **Privately Held**
SIC: 3993 Electric signs

(G-139)
HEIRLOOM DESIGN GROUP LLC
2770 Apopka Blvd (32703-9345)
PHONE............................407 735-2224
Brian Dreyer, *Mng Member*
EMP: 9 **EST:** 2008
SALES (est): 1.2MM **Privately Held**
WEB: www.heirloomdesigngroup.com
SIC: 2434 Wood kitchen cabinets

(G-140)
ITT WATER & WASTEWATER USA INC
2152 Sprint Blvd (32703-7761)
PHONE............................407 880-2900
Frank Jones, *Regional Mgr*
EMP: 8
SALES (corp-wide): 2.7B **Publicly Held**
SIC: 3561 Pumps & pumping equipment
HQ: Itt Water & Wastewater U.S.A., Inc.
1 Greenwich Pl Ste 2
Shelton CT 06484
262 548-8181

(G-141)
JK2 SCENIC LLC
541 Live Pine Cir (32703-3330)
PHONE............................407 703-2977
Julie Holmes, *General Mgr*
Tim Bartell,
Paul Holmes,
EMP: 26 **EST:** 2017

SALES (est): 2.5MM **Privately Held**
WEB: www.jk2.com
SIC: 2431 Millwork

(G-142)
JOHN ANDERSEN
923 Ridgeside Ct (32712-4006)
PHONE............................407 702-4891
John Andersen, *Principal*
EMP: 8 **EST:** 2011
SALES (est): 445.6K **Privately Held**
SIC: 2491 Structural lumber & timber, treated wood

(G-143)
K & T MANUFACTURING INC
557 Cooper Indus Pkwy (32703-6232)
PHONE............................407 814-7700
Nick Geisel, *CEO*
Rick Liesner, *Vice Pres*
EMP: 5 **EST:** 2001
SALES (est): 759.5K **Privately Held**
WEB: www.kandtmanufacturing.com
SIC: 3441 Fabricated structural metal

(G-144)
KEYS INTERNATIONAL GROUP LLC
2674 Grassmoor Loop (32712-5004)
PHONE............................855 213-0399
Maniram M Jagmohan,
Stephanie A Jagmohan,
EMP: 7 **EST:** 2015
SALES (est): 246.7K **Privately Held**
WEB: www.keysintgroup.com
SIC: 3714 Motor vehicle parts & accessories; motor vehicle engines & parts

(G-145)
KHALED W AKKAWI
1349 S Orange Blossom Trl (32703-7605)
PHONE............................321 396-3108
Khalid Akkawi, *Principal*
EMP: 7 **EST:** 2006
SALES (est): 134.3K **Privately Held**
SIC: 3484 Guns (firearms) or gun parts, 30 mm. & below

(G-146)
LASER CREATIONS INCORPORATED
Also Called: Laser Magic
946 Century Ln (32703-3709)
PHONE............................800 771-7151
Phillip Kimmell, *President*
Philip Kimmel, *Cust Mgr*
Tish Figueroa, *Director*
▲ **EMP:** 26 **EST:** 1990
SQ FT: 6,000
SALES (est): 1.5MM **Privately Held**
WEB: www.lasercreations.com
SIC: 3993 3089 5199 Advertising novelties; plastic processing; advertising specialties

(G-147)
LINDLEY FOODS LLC
Also Called: Selma's Cookies
2023 Apex Ct (32703-7720)
PHONE............................407 884-9433
Stephanie Lindley, *Principal*
EMP: 6 **EST:** 2020
SALES (est): 405.2K **Privately Held**
SIC: 2052 Cookies

(G-148)
MARNIS DOLCE
2928 Rapollo Ln (32712-2431)
PHONE............................407 915-7607
Annie Resnick, *President*
EMP: 8 **EST:** 2017
SALES (est): 478.5K **Privately Held**
WEB: www.ozlan.us
SIC: 2051 Bread, cake & related products

(G-149)
MATTHEWS INTERNATIONAL CORP
Matthews Envmtl Solutions
2045 Sprint Blvd (32703-7762)
PHONE............................407 886-5533
Paul Rayhill, *Division Pres*
Rich Bobrzynski, *Opers Spvr*
Michael Tricoche, *Engineer*
Louis Serventi, *Controller*

Robert Martinac, *Credit Staff*
EMP: 170
SALES (corp-wide): 1.6B **Publicly Held**
WEB: www.matw.com
SIC: 3569 7699 5085 3567 Cremating ovens; industrial machinery & equipment repair; industrial supplies; industrial furnaces & ovens; nonclay refractories
PA: Matthews International Corporation
2 N Shore Ctr Ste 200
Pittsburgh PA 15212
412 442-8200

(G-150)
METAL ROCK INC
174a Semoran Commerce Pl # 103 (32703-4670)
PHONE............................407 886-6440
▲ **EMP:** 10
SALES (est): 1.1MM **Privately Held**
SIC: 3911 3914 Mfg Custom Jewelry & Pewter Ware

(G-151)
MICRO ENGINEERING INC
1428 E Semrn Blvd Ste 120 (32703-5672)
PHONE............................407 886-4849
Larry A Laforest, *President*
Joseph Nguyen, *Vice Pres*
William Noble, *Vice Pres*
Samuel Pereira, *Design Engr*
Sharkey Raymond, *Director*
EMP: 36 **EST:** 1981
SALES (est): 5.2MM **Privately Held**
WEB: www.microeng.com
SIC: 3674 3672 Hybrid integrated circuits; printed circuit boards

(G-152)
MICROSS INC (PA)
1810 S Orange Blossom Trl (32703-9419)
PHONE............................407 298-7100
Vincent Buffa, *CEO*
Stephen Bahmueller, *General Mgr*
John Lannon, *General Mgr*
John Riordan, *Business Mgr*
Erik Everett, *Vice Pres*
EMP: 66 **EST:** 2009
SALES (est): 332.8MM **Privately Held**
WEB: www.micross.com
SIC: 3674 Semiconductors & related devices

(G-153)
MICROSS MINCO LLC
1810 S Orange Blossom Trl (32703-9419)
PHONE............................512 339-3422
Richard Kingeon, *President*
David Harrison, *Engineer*
Mellisa Martin, *Finance*
Jeff Weiss, *Sales Staff*
EMP: 55 **EST:** 2010
SQ FT: 3,200
SALES (est): 160MM
SALES (corp-wide): 332.8MM **Privately Held**
WEB: www.micross.com
SIC: 3674 Microcircuits, integrated (semiconductor)
PA: Micross Inc.
1810 S Orange Blossom Trl
Apopka FL 32703
407 298-7100

(G-154)
MJR WOODWORKS LLC
552 Cooper Indus Pkwy (32703-6202)
PHONE............................407 403-5430
Jason E Ryan, *President*
Matthew Ryan, *Vice Pres*
Matthew Panessidi, *Project Mgr*
EMP: 15 **EST:** 2010
SALES (est): 2.8MM **Privately Held**
WEB: www.mjrwoodworks.com
SIC: 2431 Millwork

(G-155)
MOTOR PROTECTION ELECTRONICS
Also Called: M P E
2464 Vulcan Rd (32703-2015)
PHONE............................407 299-3825
James E Gallagher, *CEO*
John Evans, *President*
EMP: 10 **EST:** 1983
SQ FT: 6,000

▲ = Import ▼=Export
◆ =Import/Export

SALES (est): 1.7MM **Privately Held**
WEB: www.mpelectronics.com
SIC: 3625 3613 Motor controls & accessories; switchgear & switchboard apparatus

(G-156)
NEED A DUMPSTER LLC
1733 Benbow Ct Ste 5 (32703-7798)
PHONE..................................888 407-3867
Chiara Carrier, *Mng Member*
EMP: 7 EST: 2018
SALES (est): 755.1K **Privately Held**
WEB: www.needadumpsterrent.com
SIC: 3443 Dumpsters, garbage

(G-157)
NEON COWBOYS LLC
2312 Clark St Ste 5 (32703-2117)
PHONE..................................949 514-5557
Asia Hall, *President*
EMP: 5 EST: 2015
SALES (est): 584.3K **Privately Held**
WEB: www.neoncowboys.com
SIC: 2813 Neon

(G-158)
NORTHROP GRUMMAN SYSTEMS CORP
2787 S Orange Blossom Trl (32703-4397)
P.O. Box 609555, Orlando (32860-9555)
PHONE..................................407 295-4010
Loshuertos Bill, *Opers Mgr*
Gavin Clark, *Engineer*
Fred Dant, *Engineer*
Sam Ervolino, *Engineer*
Virgil Blanton, *Design Engr*
EMP: 400 **Publicly Held**
WEB: www.northropgrumman.com
SIC: 3674 3812 Infrared sensors, solid state; search & navigation equipment
HQ: Northrop Grumman Systems Corporation
2980 Fairview Park Dr
Falls Church VA 22042
703 280-2900

(G-159)
ORANGE COUNTY COUNTERTOPS
2600 Pemberton Dr (32703-9402)
PHONE..................................407 294-8677
Mihaela Debille, *President*
EMP: 19 EST: 2013
SALES (est): 1.6MM **Privately Held**
WEB: www.occtopshop.com
SIC: 2541 Counter & sink tops; table or counter tops, plastic laminated

(G-160)
OUM LLC
Also Called: Best Global Source
531 Cooper Indus Pkwy (32703-6232)
PHONE..................................407 886-1511
Prafulchanbra Bhakta, *Vice Pres*
Janak Bhakta,
Kunal Bhakta,
EMP: 18 EST: 2013
SALES (est): 2.8MM **Privately Held**
SIC: 3672 Printed circuit boards

(G-161)
PIONEER WELDING & FABRICATION
532 Hillend Ct (32712-4732)
PHONE..................................407 880-4997
Paula Marn, *President*
Casey Stroup, *General Mgr*
EMP: 5 EST: 1991
SALES (est): 1.5MM **Privately Held**
WEB: www.pioneerwelding.com
SIC: 3446 5051 Stairs, fire escapes, balconies, railings & ladders; iron & steel (ferrous) products

(G-162)
PLUMB RITE OF CENTRAL FLORIDA
2850 Overland Rd (32703-9446)
PHONE..................................407 292-0750
Harold H Harris, *Director*
EMP: 5 EST: 2001
SALES (est): 465.9K **Privately Held**
SIC: 3432 Plumbing fixture fittings & trim

(G-163)
PRO STREET CHOPPERS INC
917 Suwannee Dr (32703-5935)
PHONE..................................407 389-2047
Robert Alford, *President*
EMP: 8 EST: 2004
SALES (est): 122.8K **Privately Held**
SIC: 3751 Motorcycles & related parts

(G-164)
QORVO INC
1818 S Orange Blossom Trl (32703-9419)
PHONE..................................407 886-8860
Stephanie Stout, *Mfg Spvr*
Armando Hernandez, *Buyer*
Kalyan Karnati, *Research*
Marcela Aguirre, *Design Engr Mgr*
Timothy Kraus, *Design Engr Mgr*
EMP: 470
SALES (corp-wide): 4.6B **Publicly Held**
WEB: www.qorvo.com
SIC: 3674 Semiconductors & related devices
PA: Qorvo, Inc.
7628 Thorndike Rd
Greensboro NC 27409
336 664-1233

(G-165)
QORVO US INC
1818 S Orange Blossom Trl (32703-9419)
PHONE..................................407 886-8860
EMP: 447
SALES (corp-wide): 4.6B **Publicly Held**
WEB: www.qorvo.com
SIC: 3674 Semiconductors & related devices
HQ: Qorvo Us, Inc.
2300 Ne Brookwood Pkwy
Hillsboro OR 97124
336 664-1233

(G-166)
QUICK ADVERTISING INC
Also Called: Fastsigns
3030 E Semrn Blvd Ste 236 (32703-5953)
PHONE..................................407 774-0003
Roderick A Quick, *President*
EMP: 10 EST: 2001
SQ FT: 2,600
SALES (est): 1.6MM **Privately Held**
SIC: 3993 Signs & advertising specialties

(G-167)
R & D SLEEVES LLC (PA)
520 W Orange Blossom Trl (32712-3454)
P.O. Box 460, Plymouth (32768-0460)
PHONE..................................407 886-9010
Steven McCoy,
EMP: 24 EST: 1981
SALES (est): 2.1MM **Privately Held**
WEB: www.randdsleeves.com
SIC: 2679 2673 Paper products, converted; bags: plastic, laminated & coated

(G-168)
RELIANCE MEDIA INC
515 Cooper Commerce Dr # 140 (32703-6222)
PHONE..................................505 243-1821
Patrick McGuffin, *President*
EMP: 12 EST: 1990
SQ FT: 120,000
SALES (est): 893.1K **Privately Held**
WEB: www.new-book-publishing.com
SIC: 2732 2731 7336 Book printing; books: publishing only; commercial art & graphic design

(G-169)
RIGID COATINGS & CASTINGS INC
2585 Clark St (32703-2112)
PHONE..................................352 396-8738
Billy Barham, *Principal*
EMP: 7 EST: 2018
SALES (est): 138.5K **Privately Held**
SIC: 3479 Metal coating & allied service

(G-170)
RIGID MACHINE SERVICES INC
3290 Overland Rd (32703-9473)
PHONE..................................352 396-8738
Parke Daniel, *Principal*
EMP: 8 EST: 2015

SALES (est): 109.2K **Privately Held**
SIC: 3479 Metal coating & allied service

(G-171)
ROCKPACK INC
Also Called: Weigle's Equipment Repair
2549 Clark St (32703-2112)
PHONE..................................407 757-0798
Sheetal Sood, *Principal*
EMP: 26 EST: 2015
SALES (est): 3.5MM **Privately Held**
WEB: www.rockpack.net
SIC: 1442 Construction sand & gravel

(G-172)
ROOMY DESIGN ORGANIZERS LLC
330 Cooper Palms Pkwy A (32703-0011)
PHONE..................................407 703-9550
Raul Segarra, *Mng Member*
Armando Pacheco, *Administration*
EMP: 13 EST: 2005
SALES (est): 1.9MM **Privately Held**
WEB: roomy-design-organizers.business.site
SIC: 2541 1751 Bar fixtures, wood; cabinet building & installation

(G-173)
ROWELL LABORATORIES INC
Also Called: Rowell Labs
174 Semoran Commerce Pl # 110 (32703-1407)
PHONE..................................407 929-9445
Bill Rowell, *President*
EMP: 10 EST: 2008
SALES (est): 1.6MM
SALES (corp-wide): 56.2B **Publicly Held**
WEB: www.rowelllaboratories.com
SIC: 2834 5122 Pharmaceutical preparations; pharmaceuticals
PA: Abbvie Inc.
1 N Waukegan Rd
North Chicago IL 60064
847 932-7900

(G-174)
SEELYE ACQUISITIONS INC
946 Century Ln (32703-3709)
PHONE..................................407 656-6677
Dominick P Dichiria, *CEO*
Paige Bowen, *President*
▲ EMP: 7 EST: 1978
SQ FT: 18,500
SALES (est): 663K **Privately Held**
WEB: www.seelyeinc-orl.com
SIC: 3548 5084 5162 3087 Welding & cutting apparatus & accessories; welding machinery & equipment; plastics materials; custom compound purchased resins

(G-175)
SELMAS COOKIES INC (PA)
2023 Apex Ct (32703-7720)
P.O. Box 160756, Altamonte Springs (32716-0756)
PHONE..................................407 884-9433
Selma Sayin, *President*
Dawn Fowler, *CFO*
Karen Brandenburg, *Mktg Dir*
EMP: 23 EST: 1990
SQ FT: 20,000
SALES (est): 5MM **Privately Held**
WEB: www.selmas.com
SIC: 2052 5461 Cookies; cookies

(G-176)
SHADES TO YOU LLC
1676 E Semoran Blvd (32703-5673)
PHONE..................................407 889-0049
Nicholas Czesnakowicz, *President*
Carlene Garst, *Sales Staff*
Marcia Rosen, *Consultant*
Robert Czesnakowicz,
▲ EMP: 9 EST: 1987
SALES (est): 1.4MM **Privately Held**
WEB: shadestoyou.windowblindsorlando.com
SIC: 2431 2591 Blinds (shutters), wood; blinds vertical

(G-177)
STA-CON INCORPORATED (PA)
2525 S Orange Blossom Trl (32703-2002)
PHONE..................................407 298-5940
James E Gallagher, *CEO*

Mark S McCartney, *President*
Donna Bender, *General Mgr*
Philip Gallagher, *Vice Pres*
Tommy Wandzilak, *Prdtn Mgr*
EMP: 50 EST: 1973
SQ FT: 17,000
SALES (est): 10.3MM **Privately Held**
WEB: www.stacon.com
SIC: 3625 Control equipment, electric

(G-178)
STEVE BAIE ENTERPRISES INC
2456 Clark St (32703-2109)
PHONE..................................407 822-3997
Steve Baie, *President*
EMP: 5 EST: 1998
SALES (est): 431.7K **Privately Held**
SIC: 3661 Telephones & telephone apparatus

(G-179)
SUNBELT METALS & MFG INC
920 S Bradshaw Rd (32703-5168)
PHONE..................................407 889-8960
Kevin P Harbin, *President*
Bill Harbin, *General Mgr*
Billy R Harbin, *Corp Secy*
Christopher A Harbin, *Vice Pres*
Robert Hernandez, *Foreman/Supr*
EMP: 48 EST: 1992
SQ FT: 24,000
SALES (est): 12.9MM **Privately Held**
WEB: www.sunbeltmetals.com
SIC: 3441 3443 3444 3446 Building components, structural steel; fabricated plate work (boiler shop); sheet metalwork; architectural metalwork

(G-180)
SUPERIOR TRIM & DOOR INC (PA)
615 Sprior Cmmrce Blvd St (32703-3399)
PHONE..................................407 408-7624
Keith Lemieux, *President*
David Buzzella, *Vice Pres*
▲ EMP: 41 EST: 1983
SQ FT: 67,500
SALES (est): 2.7MM **Privately Held**
WEB: www.superiortrim.com
SIC: 2431 3442 Doors, wood; trim, wood; metal doors; moldings & trim, except automobile: metal

(G-181)
TRI-COUNTY CHEMICAL CO
2578 Park St Unit 5 (32712)
P.O. Box 917177, Longwood (32791-7177)
PHONE..................................407 682-3550
Terry Schultz, *President*
Pat Schultz, *Admin Sec*
EMP: 7 EST: 1986
SALES (est): 476.4K **Privately Held**
SIC: 3949 5999 Swimming pools, except plastic; swimming pool chemicals, equipment & supplies

(G-182)
UNITRON PRCISION MACHINING INC
2482 Clark St (32703-2111)
PHONE..................................407 299-4180
George De Vlugt, *President*
EMP: 10 EST: 1977
SQ FT: 1,800
SALES (est): 1.1MM **Privately Held**
WEB: www.unitronmachining.com
SIC: 3599 Machine shop, jobbing & repair

(G-183)
VERTPAC LLC
520 W Orange Blossom Trl (32712-3454)
PHONE..................................407 886-9010
Stefanos Stamos, *Partner*
Annie Sauceda, *Manager*
EMP: 40 EST: 2016
SQ FT: 18,500
SALES (est): 5MM **Privately Held**
WEB: www.vertpac.com
SIC: 2621 5261 Kraft paper; nursery stock, seeds & bulbs

(G-184)
VISION SOURCE INC
9262 Bent Arrow Cv (32703-1965)
PHONE..................................407 435-9958
Letiza Christensen, *Manager*

EMP: 7 EST: 2017
SALES (est): 104.7K **Privately Held**
WEB: www.visionsource.com
SIC: 3851 Magnifiers (readers & simple
magnifiers)

(G-185)
WHOLE 9 GOLF & CIGARS
1710 Stefan Cole Ln (32703-4695)
PHONE......................................407 814-9994
Jonathan Wilson, *Principal*
EMP: 7 EST: 2001
SALES (est): 110K **Privately Held**
WEB: www.whole9golf.com
SIC: 3949 5091 Golf equipment; golf
equipment

(G-186)
**XYLEM WATER SOLUTIONS FLA
LLC**
Also Called: ITT Flygt LLC
2152 Sprint Blvd (32703-7761)
PHONE......................................561 848-1200
Joseph Johnston, *President*
EMP: 35 EST: 2010
SALES (est): 5.9MM **Publicly Held**
SIC: 3561 Pumps & pumping equipment
PA: Xylem Inc.
1 International Dr
Rye Brook NY 10573

Arcadia
Desoto County

(G-187)
ADAMS BROS CABINETRY INC
9300 Sw Ft Winder St (34269-7003)
PHONE......................................863 993-0501
Ethan M Adams, *Principal*
EMP: 7 EST: 2010
SALES (est): 61.1K **Privately Held**
SIC: 2434 Wood kitchen cabinets

(G-188)
ARCADIA THRIFT LLC
129 S Mills Ave (34266-4619)
PHONE......................................863 993-2004
Michael Owens,
EMP: 8 EST: 2016
SALES (est): 343.5K **Privately Held**
SIC: 2519 Fiberglass & plastic furniture;
fiberglass furniture, household: padded or
plain; furniture, household: glass, fiber-
glass & plastic; household furniture, ex-
cept wood or metal: upholstered

(G-189)
CCF HOLDCO LLC
Also Called: Columbia Care Florida
1528 Sw Highway 17 (34266-6436)
PHONE......................................800 714-9215
Nicholas Vita, *Manager*
Michael Abbott, *Manager*
David Hart, *Manager*
EMP: 10 EST: 2018
SALES (est): 567.3K **Privately Held**
SIC: 2833 Drugs & herbs: grading, grinding
& milling

(G-190)
**COOPER TIMBER HARVESTING
INC**
2056 Ne Newberry Dr (34266-5695)
PHONE......................................863 494-0240
Wayne R Cooper, *President*
Essie E Cooper, *Corp Secy*
EMP: 11 EST: 1979
SALES (est): 1.6MM **Privately Held**
WEB: www.coopertimberfl.com
SIC: 2411 Logging camps & contractors

(G-191)
**CROWN BUILDING PDTS FLA
LLC**
Also Called: Crown Roof Tiles
6018 Sw Highway 72 (34266-6539)
PHONE......................................863 993-4004
Gus Lavin, *Vice Pres*
Jerry Vandewater, *Vice Pres*
Darby Gippert, *Sales Staff*
George McMahon, *Sales Staff*
Edson Rodriguez, *Sales Staff*
▲ EMP: 76 EST: 2013

SALES (est): 8.3MM **Privately Held**
WEB: www.crownrooftiles.com
SIC: 3259 Clay sewer & drainage pipe &
tile

(G-192)
DYCO VENTURES LLC
2692 Ne Nat Ave (34266-5737)
PHONE......................................863 491-7211
Peter Dyck, *CEO*
EMP: 9 EST: 2006
SALES (est): 299.1K **Privately Held**
WEB: www.dycoventures.com
SIC: 2542 Cabinets: show, display or stor-
age: except wood

(G-193)
**FINE LINE CUSTOM MILLWORK
LLC**
1683 Ne Bishop St (34266-5831)
PHONE......................................941 628-9611
Nicole Adams, *Principal*
EMP: 23 EST: 2015
SALES (est): 1MM **Privately Held**
SIC: 2499 Laundry products, wood

(G-194)
SOUTH COUNTRY SHEDS LLC
1460 Sw Price Child St (34266-3851)
PHONE......................................863 491-8700
Orlando Penner,
Mary K Penner,
EMP: 10 EST: 2014
SALES (est): 1.2MM **Privately Held**
WEB: www.southcountrysheds.com
SIC: 2452 Prefabricated wood buildings

(G-195)
TREMRON LLC
Also Called: Tremron Group
3144 Ne Highway 17 (34266-5781)
PHONE......................................863 491-0990
EMP: 59
SALES (corp-wide): 36.1MM **Privately
Held**
WEB: www.tremron.com
SIC: 3271 3272 2951 Blocks, concrete:
drystack interlocking; concrete products;
asphalt paving mixtures & blocks
PA: Tremron, Llc
2885 Saint Clair St
Jacksonville FL 32254
904 359-5900

Archer
Alachua County

(G-196)
**CARSONS CABINETRY &
DESIGN INC**
13411 Sw County Road 346 (32618-4221)
PHONE......................................352 373-8292
Stephen Carson, *President*
EMP: 5 EST: 1980
SALES (est): 359.1K **Privately Held**
WEB: www.carsonscabinetry.com
SIC: 2511 5712 Wood household furniture;
customized furniture & cabinets

(G-197)
**FLORIDA CONCRETE
RECYCLING INC**
18515 Sw Archer Rd (32618-4645)
PHONE......................................352 495-2044
Timothy Renfroe, *President*
EMP: 17 EST: 1992
SALES (est): 4.7MM **Privately Held**
WEB: www.flcrinc.net
SIC: 3273 Ready-mixed concrete

(G-198)
**MADDOX FOUNDRY & MCH
WORKS LLC**
13370 Sw 170th St (32618-3858)
P.O. Box 7 (32618-0007)
PHONE......................................352 495-2121
Chase A Hope, *COO*
Fletcher J Hope, *Officer*
Mary M Hope,
EMP: 30 EST: 1905
SQ FT: 100,000

SALES (est): 2MM **Privately Held**
WEB: www.maddoxfoundry.com
SIC: 3321 3325 Gray & ductile iron
foundries; steel foundries

Astatula
Lake County

(G-199)
**FLORIDA CONCRETE PIPE
CORP**
25750 C R 561 (34705)
PHONE......................................352 742-2232
Carolyn Sonnentag, *President*
Teresa Whybrew, *Vice Pres*
▲ EMP: 20 EST: 1987
SQ FT: 800
SALES (est): 1.1MM **Privately Held**
WEB: florida.concretepipe.org
SIC: 3272 Pipe, concrete or lined with con-
crete

(G-200)
**MACK CONCRETE INDUSTRIES
INC**
23902 County Road 561 (34705-9420)
P.O. Box 157 (34705-0157)
PHONE......................................352 742-2333
Betsy Mack Nespeca, *President*
Barbara Mack, *Corp Secy*
EMP: 125 EST: 1986
SALES (est): 19.2MM
SALES (corp-wide): 134.5MM **Privately
Held**
WEB: www.mackconcrete.com
SIC: 3272 Concrete products, precast
PA: Mack Industries, Inc.
1321 Industrial Pkwy N # 500
Brunswick OH 44212
330 460-7005

(G-201)
MACK INDUSTRIES INC
Also Called: Mack Concrete
23902 County Road 561 (34705-9420)
P.O. Box 157 (34705-0157)
PHONE......................................352 742-2333
Samir Soliman, *Engineer*
Greg Liskey, *Manager*
Ricardo Acevedo, *Technician*
EMP: 24
SALES (corp-wide): 134.5MM **Privately
Held**
WEB: www.mackconcrete.com
SIC: 3272 1771 Burial vaults, concrete or
precast terrazzo; concrete work
PA: Mack Industries, Inc.
1321 Industrial Pkwy N # 500
Brunswick OH 44212
330 460-7005

Astor
Lake County

(G-202)
BOARD SHARK PCB INC
53717 Rivertrace Rd (32102-3514)
PHONE......................................352 759-2100
Cheri Surface, *Principal*
EMP: 7 EST: 2016
SALES (est): 249.4K **Privately Held**
WEB: www.boardsharkpcb.com
SIC: 3672 Printed circuit boards

Atlantic Beach
Duval County

(G-203)
AMEE BAY LLC
1701 Mayport Rd (32233-1930)
PHONE......................................904 553-9873
EMP: 30
SALES (corp-wide): 89.1MM **Privately
Held**
WEB: www.ameebay.com
SIC: 3731 Shipbuilding & repairing
HQ: Amee Bay, Llc
2702 Denali St Ste 104
Anchorage AK 99503

(G-204)
ART IN SPOTLIGHT
1578 Linkside Dr (32233-7307)
PHONE......................................904 853-6661
Joann Germea Wallace, *Principal*
EMP: 8 EST: 2011
SALES (est): 110K **Privately Held**
SIC: 3648 Spotlights

(G-205)
BEACHES WOODCRAFT INC
14 Dutton Island Rd E (32233-6951)
PHONE......................................904 249-0785
Jerry Hoey, *President*
Jason Hay, *Vice Pres*
Dan Hoey, *Vice Pres*
Jason Hoey, *Vice Pres*
Luke Hoey, *Engineer*
EMP: 15 EST: 1978
SQ FT: 7,500
SALES (est): 1.8MM **Privately Held**
WEB: www.beacheswoodcrafts.com
SIC: 2434 2511 Wood kitchen cabinets;
wood household furniture

(G-206)
COLONNA SHIPYARD
1701 Mayport Rd (32233-1930)
PHONE......................................904 246-1183
EMP: 7 EST: 2015
SALES (est): 108.7K **Privately Held**
WEB: www.colonnaship.com
SIC: 3731 Shipbuilding & repairing

(G-207)
DIRTBAG CHOPPERS INC
27 W 11th St (32233-3460)
PHONE......................................904 725-7600
Jeff Gordon, *CEO*
EMP: 14 EST: 2014
SALES (est): 603.8K **Privately Held**
SIC: 3751 7389 Motorcycles & related
parts;

(G-208)
**FLORIDA MINING ENTERPRISES
LLC**
2207 Alicia Ln (32233-5975)
PHONE......................................904 270-2646
David Johnston, *Principal*
EMP: 12 EST: 2007
SALES (est): 528.2K **Privately Held**
SIC: 3273 Ready-mixed concrete

(G-209)
**GENERAL SIGNS AND SERVICE
INC**
Also Called: Beach Neon & Sign Co
20 Donner Rd (32233-4209)
PHONE......................................904 372-4238
Randall Ginseg, *President*
Sybil Vinson, *Manager*
EMP: 6 EST: 1988
SALES (est): 539.6K **Privately Held**
SIC: 3993 1799 Electric signs; neon signs;
sign installation & maintenance

(G-210)
GREYMATTER DISTILLERY
1221 Mayport Rd (32233-3435)
PHONE......................................904 723-1114
Paul Grey, *Marketing Staff*
EMP: 7 EST: 2019
SALES (est): 278K **Privately Held**
WEB: www.greymatterdistillery.com
SIC: 2085 Distilled & blended liquors

(G-211)
H2C BRANDS LLC
5831 Fleet Landing Blvd (32233-7527)
PHONE......................................360 338-0449
Paul M Eakin, *Administration*
EMP: 20
SALES (corp-wide): 321.6K **Privately
Held**
WEB: www.voltheat.com
SIC: 2253 Warm weather knit outerwear,
including beachwear
PA: H2c Brands, Llc
110 Cumberland Park Dr # 205
Saint Augustine FL 32095
904 342-7485

(G-212)
NPHASE INC
1015 Atl Blvd Pmb 328 328 Pmb (32233)
PHONE.....................805 750-8580
Scott A Climes, *CEO*
EMP: 95 **EST:** 2014
SALES (est): 3.9MM **Privately Held**
SIC: 7372 Business oriented computer
software

(G-213)
OCEAN WOODWORKS INC
1701 Mayport Rd Ste 1 (32233-1930)
PHONE.....................904 246-7178
Bill Henry, *President*
EMP: 8 **EST:** 1986
SQ FT: 3,200
SALES (est): 660.5K **Privately Held**
WEB: www.oceanwoodworksinc.com
SIC: 2431 Millwork

(G-214)
PINK CUPCAKE INC
1013 Atlantic Blvd (32233-3313)
PHONE.....................904 434-9599
Hugh J Pickens Sr, *Vice Pres*
EMP: 7 **EST:** 2013
SALES (est): 104.4K **Privately Held**
WEB: cupcakefriday.webs.com
SIC: 2051 Bread, cake & related products

(G-215)
SANDAR INDUSTRIES INC
1545 Main St (32233-1938)
P.O. Box 330106 (32233-0106)
PHONE.....................904 246-4309
Jason Rodriguez, *Principal*
Peter Rodriguez, *Chairman*
Delia M Rodriguez, *Vice Pres*
Erika Chaves, *Cust Mgr*
◆ **EMP:** 22 **EST:** 1975
SQ FT: 10,800
SALES (est): 4.6MM **Privately Held**
WEB: www.sandar.com
SIC: 3545 5084 Precision tools, machin-
ists'; paper manufacturing machinery

(G-216)
TECNICO CORPORATION
490 Levy Rd (32233-2618)
PHONE.....................904 853-6118
Jeff Barrett, *Program Mgr*
Jim Pickney, *Manager*
EMP: 14 **Privately Held**
WEB: www.tecnicocorp.com
SIC: 3731 Shipbuilding & repairing
PA: Tecnico Corporation
831 Industrial Ave
Chesapeake VA 23324

(G-217)
WATTS JUICERY
1013 Atlantic Blvd (32233-3313)
PHONE.....................904 372-0693
Annie Tuttle, *Owner*
Taylor Willneth, *General Mgr*
EMP: 10 **EST:** 2015
SALES (est): 583.1K **Privately Held**
WEB: www.wattsjuicery.com
SIC: 2033 5499 Fruit juices: fresh; juices,
fruit or vegetable

Auburndale
Polk County

(G-218)
**AGRIFLEET LEASING
CORPORATION**
100 Thornhill Rd (33823-3938)
PHONE.....................239 293-3976
Robert Swander, *President*
Darren Swander, *Vice Pres*
Mike Bailey, *Parts Mgr*
EMP: 20 **EST:** 1997
SQ FT: 3,000
SALES (est): 4.4MM **Privately Held**
WEB: www.agrifleet.com
SIC: 3523 7519 7359 Fertilizing machin-
ery, farm; utility trailer rental; equipment
rental & leasing

(G-219)
BANKS LUMBER CO INC
105 Progress Rd (33823-2728)
P.O. Box 217 (33823-0217)
PHONE.....................863 687-6068
Chris Aloia, *Principal*
EMP: 7 **EST:** 2011
SALES (est): 101.1K **Privately Held**
SIC: 2439 Trusses, wooden roof

(G-220)
BRANDON ALAN CHAPMAN
Also Called: Custom Exotic Welding
114 Deen Blvd (33823-2537)
PHONE.....................863 651-9189
Brandon Chapman, *Principal*
EMP: 7 **EST:** 2018
SALES (est): 77.4K **Privately Held**
SIC: 7692 Welding repair

(G-221)
CANTEX INC
101 Gandy Rd (33823-2733)
P.O. Box 365 (33823-0365)
PHONE.....................863 967-4161
John Davies, *Branch Mgr*
EMP: 98
SQ FT: 4,000 **Privately Held**
WEB: www.cantexinc.com
SIC: 3644 3498 3084 Electric conduits &
fittings; fabricated pipe & fittings; plastics
pipe
HQ: Cantex Inc.
301 Commerce St Ste 2700
Fort Worth TX 76102

(G-222)
CENTER SEAL INC
2714 K Ville Ave (33823-4963)
PHONE.....................863 965-7124
Greg Arnold, *President*
Jamie Arnold, *Corp Secy*
EMP: 8 **EST:** 1995
SQ FT: 7,000
SALES (est): 681.3K **Privately Held**
WEB: www.centerseal.com
SIC: 2451 Mobile homes

(G-223)
**CENTRAL FLORIDA SALES &
SVC**
307 Mckean St (33823-3226)
P.O. Box 402 (33823-0402)
PHONE.....................863 967-6678
Marvin Brown, *President*
Danny Kniskern, *Purch Agent*
Bruce Barber, *Admin Sec*
EMP: 25 **EST:** 1968
SALES (est): 1.7MM **Privately Held**
SIC: 3599 3565 Machine shop, jobbing &
repair; packaging machinery

(G-224)
CHEMCLAD LLC
1701 Hobbs Rd (33823-4692)
P.O. Box 1804 (33823-1804)
PHONE.....................863 967-1156
Stephanie S Whiddon, *President*
Conley Whiddon, *Vice Pres*
Shain Brown, *Prdtn Mgr*
Harry W Hazelwood, *Treasurer*
Harry Hazelwood, *Manager*
▲ **EMP:** 15 **EST:** 1981
SQ FT: 20,000
SALES (est): 3.7MM **Privately Held**
WEB: www.chemclad.com
SIC: 3083 Laminated plastics plate & sheet

(G-225)
**COCA-COLA REFRESHMENTS
USA INC**
705 Main St (33823-4425)
PHONE.....................863 551-3700
Nicole Langone, *Production*
EMP: 57
SALES (corp-wide): 33B **Publicly Held**
WEB: www.coca-cola.com
SIC: 2086 Bottled & canned soft drinks
HQ: Coca-Cola Refreshments Usa, Inc.
2500 Windy Ridge Pkwy Se
Atlanta GA 30339
770 989-3000

(G-226)
**CRUMPTON WELDING SUP &
EQP INC**
601 Charlotte Rd (33823-4539)
PHONE.....................863 965-8423
EMP: 7
SALES (corp-wide): 12.8MM **Privately
Held**
WEB: www.crumptonws.info
SIC: 7692 Welding repair
PA: Crumpton Welding Supply And Equip-
ment, Inc.
1602 N 34th St
Tampa FL 33605
813 248-8150

(G-227)
**CUSTOM WLDG & FABRICATION
INC**
364 Recker Hwy (33823-4075)
P.O. Box 3538, Plant City (33563-0010)
PHONE.....................863 967-1000
Yvonne M Hampton, *President*
Michael E Hampton, *Vice Pres*
EMP: 71 **EST:** 1991
SQ FT: 2,480
SALES (est): 3MM **Privately Held**
WEB: www.customwelding.com
SIC: 3441 1799 Fabricated structural
metal; welding on site

(G-228)
CUTRALE FARMS INC
Also Called: Cutrale Citrus Juices
602 Mckean St (33823-4070)
PHONE.....................863 965-5000
Joe A Birge, *President*
Daniel Marques, *Corp Secy*
Andrew Sharrock, *Project Mgr*
Dan Marques, *Opers Mgr*
Antonio Violante, *Purchasing*
▲ **EMP:** 66 **EST:** 1998
SALES (est): 11.9MM **Privately Held**
SIC: 2033 Fruit juices: fresh

(G-229)
DI JAM HOLDINGS INC
Also Called: Custom Trade Printing.com
123 Main St (33823-3401)
PHONE.....................863 967-6949
James Murray, *President*
EMP: 13 **EST:** 2011
SALES (est): 351.5K **Privately Held**
WEB: www.customtradeprinting.net
SIC: 2752 Commercial printing, litho-
graphic

(G-230)
FI-FOIL COMPANY INC
Also Called: Fl Foil Co
612 W Bridgers Ave (33823-3154)
P.O. Box 800 (33823-0800)
PHONE.....................863 965-1846
William A Lippy, *President*
Matt Belman, *Division Mgr*
James Hayes, *Vice Pres*
Douglas F Kinninger, *Vice Pres*
James T Sheridan, *CFO*
◆ **EMP:** 33 **EST:** 2000
SQ FT: 50,000
SALES (est): 8.5MM **Privately Held**
WEB: www.fifoil.com
SIC: 3999 Curling feathers

(G-231)
**FLORIDA ALUMINUM AND
STEEL INC**
100 Thornhill Rd (33823-3938)
PHONE.....................863 967-4191
Darren Swander, *Branch Mgr*
EMP: 10
SALES (corp-wide): 8.9MM **Privately
Held**
WEB: www.flasf.com
SIC: 3312 1799 3444 3441 Structural
shapes & pilings, steel; ornamental metal
work; sheet metalwork; fabricated struc-
tural metal
PA: Florida Aluminum And Steel, Inc.
1 Tom Rab Ln
Fort Myers FL
239 936-8153

(G-232)
FLORIDA BREWERY INC
202 Gandy Rd (33823-2726)
P.O. Box 6 (33823-0006)
PHONE.....................863 965-1825
Julie Williams, *President*
Phil Keck, *Maint Spvr*
Steven Carter, *Engineer*
Frank Nunez, *Engineer*
Stacey Oakley, *CFO*
◆ **EMP:** 27 **EST:** 1971
SQ FT: 57,863
SALES (est): 6.1MM **Privately Held**
WEB: www.floridabrewery.com
SIC: 2083 2082 Malt; malt beverages;
beer (alcoholic beverage)

(G-233)
FLORIDA DISTILLERS CO
Also Called: Florida Caribbean Distillers
425 Recker Hwy (33823-4035)
PHONE.....................863 967-4481
Mike Ryan, *Vice Pres*
Felicie Iris, *Vice Pres*
Joseph Pickett, *Production*
Jose Dones, *Engineer*
Lilly Torres, *Human Res Mgr*
EMP: 19 **EST:** 2015
SALES (est): 11.8MM
SALES (corp-wide): 27.9MM **Privately
Held**
WEB: www.floridadistillers.com
SIC: 2085 Distillers' dried grains & solubles
& alcohol
HQ: Imperial Brands, Inc.
100 W Cypress Creek Rd # 1050
Fort Lauderdale FL 33309

(G-234)
GLASRITE INC
627 W Bridgers Ave (33823-3103)
PHONE.....................863 967-8151
Barlow Brannon, *Manager*
◆ **EMP:** 10 **EST:** 2004
SALES (est): 635.3K **Privately Held**
SIC: 2221 Fiberglass fabrics

(G-235)
GREIF INC
211 Sandra Jackson Rd (33823-4689)
PHONE.....................863 967-2419
Jeff Brozio, *Branch Mgr*
EMP: 18
SALES (corp-wide): 5.5B **Publicly Held**
WEB: www.greif.com
SIC: 2655 Fiber cans, drums & similar
products
PA: Greif, Inc.
425 Winter Rd
Delaware OH 43015
740 549-6000

(G-236)
GTI SYSTEMS INC (PA)
1250 Hobbs Rd (33823-4638)
PHONE.....................863 965-2002
Peter Shin, *President*
Danielle Lynch, *Manager*
EMP: 20 **EST:** 2002
SQ FT: 20,000
SALES (est): 7.2MM **Privately Held**
SIC: 3482 3471 3483 3451 Small arms
ammunition; anodizing (plating) of metals
or formed products; ammunition, except
for small arms; screw machine products

(G-237)
**J & J WLDG STL FBRCTION FLA
IN**
364 Recker Hwy (33823-4075)
PHONE.....................813 754-0771
James Davis, *Principal*
EMP: 18 **EST:** 2012
SALES (est): 2.2MM **Privately Held**
WEB: www.jnjwelding.com
SIC: 3441 5051 Fabricated structural
metal; structural shapes, iron or steel

(G-238)
**JENNINGS MOBILE HM SET UP
LLC**
1048 Us Highway 92 W (33823-9514)
P.O. Box 1428 (33823-1428)
PHONE.....................863 965-0883
Thomas Jennings,

GEOGRAPHIC

EMP: 13 EST: 2002
SALES (est): 1.7MM Privately Held
SIC: 2452 Modular homes, prefabricated, wood

(G-239)
MAGNOLIA MACHINE COMPANY
1088 Us Highway 92 W (33823-9622)
P.O. Box 657 (33823-0657)
PHONE..................................863 965-8201
EMP: 23
SALES (est): 3.1MM Privately Held
SIC: 3599 Mfg Industrial Machinery

(G-240)
MASTER-KRAFT CABINETRY
305 Keystone Rd (33823-2343)
PHONE..................................863 661-2083
Jonathan C Ammerman, President
▼ EMP: 7 EST: 2004
SALES (est): 137.2K Privately Held
SIC: 2434 Wood kitchen cabinets

(G-241)
MEDLINE INDUSTRIES LP
1062 Old Dixie Hwy (33823-9651)
PHONE..................................863 337-4797
EMP: 14
SALES (corp-wide): 7.7B Privately Held
WEB: www.medline.com
SIC: 3841 Surgical & medical instruments
PA: Medline Industries, Lp
　　3 Lakes Dr
　　Northfield IL 60093
　　847 949-5500

(G-242)
PRECISE PAVERS INC
2581 Nelson St (33823-4816)
PHONE..................................863 528-8000
Jose C Gomez, Principal
EMP: 9 EST: 2012
SALES (est): 326.3K Privately Held
SIC: 3531 Pavers

(G-243)
RAT-TRAP BAIT COMPANY INC
106 Adams St (33823-3612)
P.O. Box 845 (33823-0845)
PHONE..................................863 967-2148
Ralph Robinson, President
Yolanda Dyer, President
Charles Davis Jr, Corp Secy
Ralph Robbins, Vice Pres
Darcy Hurley, Office Mgr
EMP: 9 EST: 1940
SQ FT: 10,000
SALES (est): 493.7K Privately Held
SIC: 3949 3496 2869 2298 Fishing tackle, general; miscellaneous fabricated wire products; industrial organic chemicals; cordage & twine

(G-244)
SEWELL PRODUCTS FLORIDA LLC
Also Called: Kik Custom Products
909 Magnolia Ave (33823-4007)
PHONE..................................863 967-4463
David G Cynamon, President
Paul C Anderson, Senior VP
Bob Clarke, Manager
Leah Smith, Manager
Richard L Pfab, Admin Sec
EMP: 72 EST: 1996
SQ FT: 200,000
SALES (est): 28.5MM
SALES (corp-wide): 111.1MM Privately Held
SIC: 2842 Bleaches, household: dry or liquid
HQ: Sewell Products, Inc.
　　27 Mill Ln
　　Salem VA 24153
　　540 389-5401

(G-245)
SMITHBILT INDUSTRIES INC (PA)
1061 Us Highway 92 W (33823-4077)
PHONE..................................321 690-0902
Donald E Smith, President
Jeanette K Smith, Corp Secy
EMP: 75 EST: 1982
SQ FT: 40,000

SALES (est): 10.1MM Privately Held
WEB: www.smithbilt.com
SIC: 3448 Buildings, portable: prefabricated metal

(G-246)
TAYLOR BUILDING ELEMENTS LLC
116 Van Fleet Ct (33823-2059)
PHONE..................................863 287-2228
Alison A Taylor, Principal
EMP: 7 EST: 2012
SALES (est): 1.9MM Privately Held
SIC: 2819 Industrial inorganic chemicals

(G-247)
WINANS ELECTRIC MOTORS LLC
1150 Us Highway 92 W (33823-4046)
PHONE..................................863 875-5710
Michael Wenners, Mng Member
Janet Gangraw,
EMP: 5 EST: 1989
SALES (est): 476.1K Privately Held
SIC: 3621 Motors & generators

Ave Maria
Collier County

(G-248)
HOUSE DOCTAIR INC
5438 Ferrari Ave (34142-9554)
PHONE..................................239 349-7497
Matthew Foster, President
EMP: 10 EST: 2020
SALES (est): 293.1K Privately Held
WEB: www.housedoctors.com
SIC: 1389 Construction, repair & dismantling services

(G-249)
P & M SHEET METAL CORP
4963 Frattina St (34142-5123)
PHONE..................................954 618-8513
Ro Y Perez, Principal
EMP: 9 EST: 2018
SALES (est): 529.9K Privately Held
SIC: 3444 Sheet metalwork

Aventura
Miami-Dade County

(G-250)
ACTION CONTROLS INC
Also Called: Aci
3701 N Country Club Dr # 201 (33180-1717)
PHONE..................................253 243-7703
James Waite, President
Kristi Waite, Vice Pres
EMP: 7 EST: 1991
SQ FT: 5,400
SALES (est): 992.6K Privately Held
WEB: www.actioncontrols.com
SIC: 3625 Relays & industrial controls

(G-251)
AMERICAN FOODS INTL LLC
2875 Ne 191st St Ph 1 (33180-2841)
PHONE..................................877 894-7675
Mike Sanchez, Purchasing
Daniel Azevedo,
EMP: 45 EST: 2019
SALES (est): 30MM Privately Held
WEB: www.americanfoodsllc.com
SIC: 2015 2011 5143 Ham, poultry; pork products from pork slaughtered on site; cheese

(G-252)
AMERICAN WIRE GROUP LLC (PA)
2980 Ne 207th St Ste 901 (33180-1467)
PHONE..................................954 455-3050
Joshua Dorfman, Vice Pres
Qortez McGaughey, Warehouse Mgr
Bill Brewer, Sales Engr
Robert Dorfman,
Mary Brewer, Administration
◆ EMP: 12 EST: 2001
SQ FT: 3,000

SALES (est): 200MM Privately Held
WEB: www.buyawg.com
SIC: 3351 3355 5063 2298 Wire, copper & copper alloy; aluminum wire & cable; wire & cable; power wire & cable; cable, fiber

(G-253)
APPO GROUP INC
7000 Island Blvd Apt 2309 (33160-2474)
PHONE..................................410 992-5500
Stephen Wigler, President
Cindy Jones, Senior VP
Tom Wuhas, Senior VP
EMP: 7 EST: 2013
SALES (est): 467.2K Privately Held
WEB: www.appogroup.com
SIC: 7372 Prepackaged software

(G-254)
AYAM BEAUTYCARE LLC
19495 Biscayne Blvd # 608 (33180-2318)
PHONE..................................305 318-2598
Moises Alex Guenoun,
EMP: 7 EST: 2019
SALES (est): 258.9K Privately Held
WEB: www.ayambeautycare.com
SIC: 2844 Shampoos, rinses, conditioners: hair.

(G-255)
BASHERT DIAMONDS INC
3201 Ne 183rd St Apt 408 (33160-2488)
PHONE..................................305 466-1881
Kyla Fajerstein, President
EMP: 5 EST: 2012
SQ FT: 1,000
SALES (est): 447.3K Privately Held
WEB: www.bashertdiamonds.com
SIC: 3911 3915 Jewelry, precious metal; diamond cutting & polishing

(G-256)
BERG LLC
3201 Ne 183rd St Apt 704 (33160-2493)
PHONE..................................786 201-2625
Paul L Berg, Principal
EMP: 12 EST: 2010
SALES (est): 141.8K Privately Held
WEB: www.bergpipe.com
SIC: 3312 Blast furnaces & steel mills

(G-257)
BOSSY PRINCESS LLC
18117 Biscayne Blvd # 1194 (33160-2535)
PHONE..................................786 285-4435
Christopher Mesa, CEO
Akyng Mesa, COO
Nia Mesa, COO
Dominique Lewis, CFO
EMP: 8 EST: 2020
SALES (est): 534.9K Privately Held
WEB: www.bossy-princess.com
SIC: 2361 5641 Girls' & children's blouses & shirts; children's & infants' wear stores

(G-258)
EGD EURO GOURMET DELI INC
18650 Ne 28th Ct (33180-2931)
PHONE..................................305 937-1515
Monique Seelinger, President
Harold Aumenta, Vice Pres
Hans Christian Seelinger, Vice Pres
EMP: 8 EST: 2013
SALES (est): 170.4K Privately Held
SIC: 3411 5149 Food & beverage containers; beverage concentrates

(G-259)
EILEEN KRAMER INC
19955 Ne 38th Ct Apt 504 (33180-3428)
PHONE..................................315 395-3831
Eileen Favor Kramer, Principal
EMP: 8 EST: 2011
SALES (est): 243.8K Privately Held
WEB: www.lilbbonnet.com
SIC: 3199 Leather goods

(G-260)
GAIN SOLAR LLC
18205 Biscayne Blvd (33160-2106)
P.O. Box 2604, Windermere (34786-2604)
PHONE..................................305 933-1060
Daniel Halberstin,
EMP: 7 EST: 2010

SALES (est): 712.8K Privately Held
SIC: 3433 Solar heaters & collectors

(G-261)
GLOBAL PRIME WOOD LLC
2875 Ne 191st St Ste 500 (33180-2832)
PHONE..................................770 292-9200
Cesar Alberto Cemin, Mng Member
Leonardo Souza De Zorzi, Mng Member
Joao Carlos Nesello, Mng Member
▲ EMP: 9 EST: 2012
SALES (est): 518.7K Privately Held
SIC: 2421 1752 Outdoor wood structural products; wood floor installation & refinishing

(G-262)
GOURMET FOOD SOLUTIONS LLC
19950 W Country Club Dr # 101 (33180-4602)
PHONE..................................413 687-3285
Irvin Rhodes, CEO
EMP: 30 EST: 2014
SALES (est): 2.2MM Privately Held
SIC: 2099 Sauces: gravy, dressing & dip mixes

(G-263)
HERBKO INC
3000 Island Blvd Ph 5 (33160-4927)
PHONE..................................305 932-3572
Herbert Sternberg, President
Tracey Sternberg, Vice Pres
Marlene Sternberg, CFO
EMP: 8 EST: 1978
SQ FT: 5,000
SALES (est): 415.7K Privately Held
SIC: 3944 Games, toys & children's vehicles

(G-264)
JMS CORPORATE GROUP LLC
21205 Ne 37th Ave (33180-4051)
PHONE..................................786 219-6114
Juan M Santos, Mng Member
EMP: 7 EST: 2017
SALES (est): 500K Privately Held
SIC: 3714 Motor vehicle parts & accessories

(G-265)
LEVARIO COATINGS INTL USA
4000 Island Blvd Apt 70 (33160-5203)
PHONE..................................954 871-6461
Saverio Marotta, Principal
EMP: 7 EST: 2016
SALES (est): 78.4K Privately Held
SIC: 3479 Coating of metals & formed products

(G-266)
M PET GROUP CORP
2980 Ne 207th St Ste 701 (33180-1465)
PHONE..................................954 455-5003
Isaac Mendal, President
EMP: 11 EST: 2018
SALES (est): 498.7K Privately Held
SIC: 3999 Pet supplies

(G-267)
NEXTPLAT CORP (PA)
Also Called: ORBSAT
18851 Ne 29th Ave Ste 700 (33180-2845)
PHONE..................................305 560-5355
Charles M Fernandez, Ch of Bd
David Phipps, President
Andrew Cohen, Senior VP
Thomas Seifert, CFO
Paul R Thomson, CFO
EMP: 7 EST: 1984
SALES (est): 7.7MM Publicly Held
WEB: www.nextplat.com
SIC: 3663 Satellites, communications

(G-268)
ONE BIO CORP
19950 W Country Club Dr (33180-4601)
PHONE..................................305 328-8662
Marius Silvasan, President
Cris Neely, Officer
EMP: 358 EST: 2000

SALES (est): 34.5MM **Privately Held**
SIC: 2833 Organic medicinal chemicals: bulk, uncompounded; drugs & herbs: grading, grinding & milling; medicinal chemicals

(G-269)
ORIGINATES INC
20900 Ne 30th Ave Ste 707 (33180-2164)
PHONE.....................................954 233-2500
Meyer Minski, *President*
Jose Minski, *Vice Pres*
Julia Restrepo, *Purch Agent*
Daniel Minski, *Sales Mgr*
◆ **EMP:** 14 **EST:** 1976
SQ FT: 1,500
SALES (est): 24.4MM **Privately Held**
WEB: www.originates.com
SIC: 2869 Fatty acid esters, aminos, etc.

(G-270)
PHIDAL INC
2875 Ne 191st St Ste 704 (33180-2834)
PHONE.....................................786 288-0339
David Soussan, *President*
EMP: 8 **EST:** 2014
SQ FT: 2,400
SALES (est): 12.1MM
SALES (corp-wide): 6.7MM **Privately Held**
WEB: www.phidal.com
SIC: 2731 Book publishing
PA: Phidal Publishing Inc
5740 Rue Ferrier
Mont-Royal QC H4P 1
514 738-0202

(G-271)
PIKANTITOS LLC
19500 W Dixie Hwy # 101 (33180-2216)
PHONE.....................................305 937-4827
Emilio Suaya, *Manager*
EMP: 16
SALES (corp-wide): 86.1K **Privately Held**
SIC: 2099 Food preparations
PA: Pikantitos, Llc
19500 Turnberry Way
Aventura FL

(G-272)
PRINT & POST INC
18117 Biscayne Blvd (33160-2535)
PHONE.....................................786 603-9279
Michael R Kroth, *Principal*
EMP: 7 **EST:** 2019
SALES (est): 254.1K **Privately Held**
WEB: www.printandpost.us
SIC: 2752 Commercial printing, offset

(G-273)
REMETALL USA INC ☼
3000 Ne 190th St Apt 202 (33180-3182)
PHONE.....................................888 212-3812
Dorel Mitrut, *CEO*
EMP: 10 **EST:** 2021
SALES (est): 1MM **Privately Held**
SIC: 3714 5015 Exhaust systems & parts, motor vehicle; automotive parts & supplies, used

(G-274)
RGRAUTO INC
20801 Biscayne Blvd (33180-1430)
PHONE.....................................305 952-5522
Roman Ferster, *CEO*
EMP: 20 **EST:** 2020
SALES (est): 1.1MM **Privately Held**
SIC: 3663

(G-275)
SERVICES NS 18 LLC
Also Called: Renue Systems South East Fla
19900 E Country Club Dr (33180-3327)
PHONE.....................................786 546-3295
Enrique Nessim, *Mng Member*
EMP: 5 **EST:** 2011
SALES (est): 469.3K **Privately Held**
SIC: 2842 Specialty cleaning preparations

(G-276)
VMOVILES INC
Also Called: Vmoviles Power Solar Energy
17111 Biscayne Blvd (33160-5097)
PHONE.....................................954 609-2510
Francisco Pages, *President*
EMP: 7 **EST:** 2009

SALES (est): 1.9MM **Privately Held**
WEB: www.vmoviles.com
SIC: 3663 Radio & TV communications equipment
PA: Fertiven Operaciones Ca
Urbanizacion El Vinedo
Valencia

(G-277)
YIELDX INC
2980 Ne 207th St Ste 504 (33180-1463)
PHONE.....................................646 328-9803
Adam Green, *President*
EMP: 13 **EST:** 2019
SALES (est): 260.1K **Privately Held**
WEB: www.yieldx.app
SIC: 7372 Application computer software

Avon Park
Highlands County

(G-278)
AGRA CHEM SALES CO INC
959 S Angelo Lake Rd (33825-6501)
P.O. Box 1356 (33826-1356)
PHONE.....................................863 453-6450
Rick Brant, *President*
Bill Engel, *Vice Pres*
◆ **EMP:** 8 **EST:** 1962
SQ FT: 40,000
SALES (est): 636K **Privately Held**
SIC: 2879 Trace elements (agricultural chemicals)

(G-279)
DESIGNERS TOP SHOP INC
12 N Anoka Ave (33825-3309)
P.O. Box 1952 (33826-1952)
PHONE.....................................863 453-3855
Justine Jackson, *President*
Christine Jackson, *Vice Pres*
EMP: 8 **EST:** 1983
SQ FT: 3,500
SALES (est): 494.5K **Privately Held**
WEB: www.designertopshop.com
SIC: 2759 2395 Screen printing; embroidery & art needlework

(G-280)
DS COATINGS INC
18 S Butler Ave (33825-3804)
PHONE.....................................321 848-4719
Daniel Sauls, *Principal*
EMP: 9 **EST:** 2015
SALES (est): 320.1K **Privately Held**
SIC: 3479 Metal coating & allied service

(G-281)
FLOWERS BKG CO BRADENTON LLC
Also Called: Flowers Baking Company
1202 State Road 64 W (33825-3302)
PHONE.....................................941 758-5656
Chris Peer, *Manager*
EMP: 15
SALES (corp-wide): 4.3B **Publicly Held**
WEB: www.flobradconf.com
SIC: 2051 Bread, cake & related products
HQ: Flowers Baking Co. Of Bradenton, Llc
6490 Parkland Dr
Sarasota FL 34243

(G-282)
JAHNA CONCRETE INC (PA)
103 County Road 17a W (33825-2239)
PHONE.....................................863 453-4353
Frederick W Jahna Jr, *President*
Candis Davis, *Corp Secy*
David Jahna, *Vice Pres*
Dawn Robinson, *Bookkeeper*
Fedeila Jahna, *Shareholder*
EMP: 12 **EST:** 1925
SALES (est): 12.8MM **Privately Held**
WEB: www.jahnaconcrete.com
SIC: 3271 5032 3273 3272 Blocks, concrete or cinder: standard; concrete mixtures; ready-mixed concrete; concrete products

(G-283)
JAHNA CONCRETE INC
104 S Railroad Ave (33825-3181)
PHONE.....................................863 453-4353
Fredy Yahna, *President*

EMP: 20
SALES (corp-wide): 12.8MM **Privately Held**
WEB: www.jahnaconcrete.com
SIC: 3273 Ready-mixed concrete
PA: Jahna Concrete, Inc.
103 County Road 17a W
Avon Park FL 33825
863 453-4353

(G-284)
PEPSI BOTTLING GROUP
Also Called: Pepsico
1006 W Cornell St (33825-3510)
PHONE.....................................863 452-9920
EMP: 7 **EST:** 2010
SALES (est): 98.1K **Privately Held**
WEB: www.pepsico.com
SIC: 2086 Carbonated soft drinks, bottled & canned

(G-285)
PLASTIREX LLC
1552 Sun Pure Rd (33825-8713)
PHONE.....................................305 471-1111
Janice Roller, *Office Mgr*
Roberto Panzarasa,
Raffaele Chierchia,
Gianpaolo Girardello,
EMP: 18 **EST:** 2018
SALES (est): 5MM **Privately Held**
WEB: www.florida-corp.com
SIC: 2821 Carbohydrate plastics

(G-286)
PRO-WELD INC
222 S Forest Ave Unit 1 (33825-3815)
PHONE.....................................863 453-9353
Richard Tindell, *President*
EMP: 5 **EST:** 1990
SQ FT: 10,000
SALES (est): 893.1K **Privately Held**
WEB: www.proweldincfl.com
SIC: 7692 Welding repair

(G-287)
SIMCO MACHINE AND TOOL INC
2029 State Road 64 W (33825-8417)
P.O. Box 997 (33826-0997)
PHONE.....................................863 452-1151
Drema Zimmerman, *CEO*
EMP: 10 **EST:** 1998
SALES (est): 849K **Privately Held**
WEB: www.simcobox.com
SIC: 3089 Injection molding of plastics

(G-288)
SIMPSON CONSTRUCTION AND ROOFG
418 E Elm St (33825-3206)
PHONE.....................................863 443-0710
Thomas Simpson, *President*
EMP: 15 **EST:** 2010
SALES (est): 558.8K **Privately Held**
WEB: www.simpsonconstructionandroofing.com
SIC: 3842 Clothing, fire resistant & protective

(G-289)
STANDARD INJECTION MOLDING INC
Also Called: Simco
2027 State Road 64 W (33825-8417)
P.O. Box 997 (33826-0997)
PHONE.....................................863 452-9090
Drema Zimmerman, *President*
Susan R Crull, *Vice Pres*
EMP: 10 **EST:** 1982
SQ FT: 30,000
SALES (est): 988.1K **Privately Held**
WEB: www.simcobox.com
SIC: 3089 Injection molding of plastics

Baker
Okaloosa County

(G-290)
4F MOBILE WELDING LLC
Also Called: 4f Contracting
6289 Holloway Rd (32531-8131)
PHONE.....................................850 537-2290
Aaron Fortner, *Principal*

EMP: 6 **EST:** 2016
SALES (est): 398.4K **Privately Held**
SIC: 7692 Welding repair

(G-291)
BAKER METAL WORKS & SUPPLY LLC (PA)
5846 Highway 189 N (32531-2506)
PHONE.....................................850 537-2010
Carrie N Norton,
Jason C Norton,
EMP: 6 **EST:** 2007
SALES (est): 7.2MM **Privately Held**
WEB: www.bakermetalworks.com
SIC: 3444 Metal roofing & roof drainage equipment

(G-292)
BAKER METALWORKS AND SUP INC
5846 Highway 189 N (32531-2506)
PHONE.....................................850 537-2010
Carrie N Norton, *President*
EMP: 18 **EST:** 2001
SALES (est): 409.6K **Privately Held**
WEB: www.bakermetalworks.com
SIC: 3441 Fabricated structural metal

Bal Harbour
Miami-Dade County

(G-293)
BROADBAND FIBERS & SUPPLIES
10225 Collins Ave (33154-1443)
PHONE.....................................786 258-5746
Carlos M Terzian, *President*
Nestor R Terzian, *Vice Pres*
EMP: 9 **EST:** 2018
SALES (est): 360K **Privately Held**
SIC: 3315 Wire & fabricated wire products

(G-294)
GOYARD MIAMI LLC
Also Called: Maison Goyard
9700 Collins Ave Ste 118 (33154-2200)
PHONE.....................................305 894-9235
Deborah Ruiz, *Branch Mgr*
EMP: 92
SALES (corp-wide): 55.2MM **Privately Held**
SIC: 3161 Wardrobe bags (luggage)
HQ: Goyard Miami, Llc
20 E 63rd St
New York NY 10065
212 813-0005

(G-295)
MOBA CORP
10155 Collins Ave # 1807 (33154-1655)
PHONE.....................................305 868-3700
EMP: 16 **EST:** 1946
SALES (est): 1.2MM **Privately Held**
SIC: 3911 Manufactures Precious Jewelry & Works Of Art With Precious Metals & Stones

(G-296)
SMART SNACKS LLC
10205 Collins Ave Apt 206 (33154-1426)
PHONE.....................................954 860-8833
Tammy Cohen, *Managing Dir*
EMP: 6 **EST:** 2012
SALES (est): 483.5K **Privately Held**
SIC: 2052 Cookies

Bartow
Polk County

(G-297)
ALL WOOD CABINETRY LLC
Also Called: Ideal Cabinetry
210 Century Blvd (33830-7704)
PHONE.....................................866 367-2516
Richard Heley,
Kristi R Dunbar,
◆ **EMP:** 45 **EST:** 2006
SALES (est): 16.2MM **Privately Held**
WEB: www.idealcabinetry.com
SIC: 2434 Wood kitchen cabinets

GEOGRAPHIC

(G-298)
AMERICAN CMMERCE SOLUTIONS INC (PA)
1400 Chamber Dr (33830-8428)
P.O. Box 269 (33831-0269)
PHONE................................863 533-0326
Robert E Maxwell, *Ch of Bd*
Daniel L Hefner, *President*
Frank D Puissegur, *CFO*
EMP: 2 **EST:** 1991
SQ FT: 38,000
SALES (est): 3.4MM **Privately Held**
WEB: www.aacssymbol.com
SIC: 3549 Metalworking machinery

(G-299)
B & R PROFILES LLC (PA)
216 Homeland Cemetery Rd (33830-8555)
PHONE................................305 479-8308
Harold Brandan, *Mng Member*
EMP: 25 **EST:** 2015
SALES (est): 8MM **Privately Held**
SIC: 3674 Light sensitive devices

(G-300)
BARTOW ETHANOL FLORIDA LC
1705 E Mann Rd (33830-7542)
PHONE................................863 533-2498
Charles R Ritley, *CEO*
Anthony Senagore, *President*
Jim Munzt, *COO*
James Muntz, *Vice Pres*
Matt Dunbar, *Controller*
◆ **EMP:** 15 **EST:** 2004
SQ FT: 10,000
SALES (est): 6.3MM **Privately Held**
WEB: www.bartowethanol.com
SIC: 2869 Industrial organic chemicals

(G-301)
BARTOW MACHINE WORKS INC
441 W Vine St (33830-5440)
PHONE................................863 533-6361
Patrick Frankenburger, *President*
Beverly Heath, *Office Mgr*
Gail Frankenburger, *Admin Sec*
EMP: 7 **EST:** 1941
SQ FT: 10,000
SALES (est): 491.1K **Privately Held**
SIC: 3599 7692 Machine shop, jobbing & repair; welding repair

(G-302)
BEARS METAL WORKS INC
320 S 1st Ave (33830-4900)
PHONE................................863 537-5644
David Fox, *President*
Phyllis Fox, *Corp Secy*
Kevin Fox, *Vice Pres*
Tim Fox, *Vice Pres*
EMP: 10 **EST:** 1979
SQ FT: 6,000
SALES (est): 1.1MM **Privately Held**
SIC: 3599 Machine shop, jobbing & repair

(G-303)
BEST FABRICATIONS INC
2145 Bravo Ave (33830-6642)
PHONE................................863 519-6611
Nicholas G Ruys, *CEO*
Anthony Easton, *President*
Pamela Byrd, *Treasurer*
Barry Boucher, *Sales Mgr*
Carolyn Rodriguezthomas, *Office Mgr*
▼ **EMP:** 15 **EST:** 1992
SQ FT: 18,000
SALES (est): 2.7MM **Privately Held**
WEB: www.bestfab.com
SIC: 3441 Fabricated structural metal

(G-304)
CENTRAL FLORIDA TRUSS INC (PA)
1500 Us Highway 17 N (33830-7602)
P.O. Box 455 (33831-0455)
PHONE................................863 533-0821
Gary N Newell, *President*
Steven Newell, *Vice Pres*
Larry Braswell, *Manager*
Alec Monies, *Manager*
▼ **EMP:** 20 **EST:** 1977
SQ FT: 2,000

SALES (est): 10.9MM **Privately Held**
WEB: www.cftruss.com
SIC: 2439 Trusses, wooden roof

(G-305)
CF INDUSTRIES INC
Also Called: CF Terminal
2501 Bonnie Mine Rd (33830-8461)
P.O. Box 1480 (33831-1480)
PHONE................................813 782-1591
A L Holmes, *Branch Mgr*
EMP: 27 **Publicly Held**
WEB: www.cfindustries.com
SIC: 2873 4225 Anhydrous ammonia; general warehousing & storage
HQ: Cf Industries, Inc.
     4 Parkway North Blvd # 400
     Deerfield IL 60015
     847 405-2400

(G-306)
CORSICANA BEDDING LLC
Also Called: Corsicana Mattress Company
450 Polk St (33830-3749)
PHONE................................863 534-3450
Carroll Moran, *Branch Mgr*
EMP: 64
SALES (corp-wide): 636.6MM **Privately Held**
WEB: www.corsicanamattress.com
SIC: 2515 Mattresses, innerspring or box spring
PA: Corsicana Bedding, Llc
     1420 W Mockingbird Ln
     Dallas TX 75247
     800 323-4349

(G-307)
EPIC METALS CORPORATION
1930 State Road 60 W (33830-9321)
PHONE................................863 533-7404
Daryl Paw, *Manager*
EMP: 9
SALES (corp-wide): 20.1MM **Privately Held**
WEB: www.epicmetals.com
SIC: 3444 Roof deck, sheet metal
PA: Epic Metals Corporation
     11 Talbot Ave
     Rankin PA 15104
     412 351-3913

(G-308)
ERIE MANUFACTURING INC
1520 Centennial Blvd (33830-7707)
PHONE................................863 534-3743
Phil Dosso, *President*
EMP: 10 **EST:** 1962
SQ FT: 40,000
SALES (est): 1.9MM **Privately Held**
WEB: www.eriemanufacturinginc.com
SIC: 3535 Conveyors & conveying equipment

(G-309)
HARLEY BOAT CORPORATION
Also Called: Harley Boats
300 S 1st Ave (33830-4935)
PHONE................................863 533-2800
Howard Harley, *President*
Dorothy E Harley, *Corp Secy*
Richard C Harley, *Vice Pres*
EMP: 5 **EST:** 2007
SQ FT: 26,000
SALES (est): 451.1K **Privately Held**
WEB: www.harleyboats.com
SIC: 3732 Boats, fiberglass: building & repairing

(G-310)
HARLEY SHIPBUILDING CORP
Also Called: Harley Boat
300 S 1st Ave (33830-4935)
PHONE................................863 533-2800
Howard Harley, *President*
EMP: 9 **EST:** 1997
SALES (est): 756.3K **Privately Held**
WEB: www.harleyshipbuilding.net
SIC: 3732 Boat kits, not models

(G-311)
HCO HOLDING I CORPORATION
2701 State Road 60 W (33830-8750)
PHONE................................863 533-0522
Jimmy Sellers, *Plant Mgr*
P James Grauer, *Sales & Mktg St*

James Sellers, *Manager*
EMP: 10
SALES (corp-wide): 254.1MM **Privately Held**
SIC: 3531 3241 2952 2851 Asphalt plant, including gravel-mix type; cement, hydraulic; asphalt felts & coatings; paints & allied products; roofing, asphalt & sheet metal
HQ: Hco Holding I Corporation
     999 N Pacific Coast Hwy # 80
     El Segundo CA 90245
     323 583-5000

(G-312)
HINES ENERGY COMPLEX
7700 County Road 555 S (33830-8454)
PHONE................................863 519-6106
Robert Miller, *President*
EMP: 10 **EST:** 2003
SALES (est): 383K **Privately Held**
SIC: 3462 Turbine engine forgings, ferrous

(G-313)
INNOVATED INDUSTRIAL SVCS INC
1416 Chamber Dr (33830-8428)
PHONE................................863 701-2711
Thomas N Taphorn, *President*
Steven J Hasley, *Vice Pres*
EMP: 12 **EST:** 2000
SQ FT: 2,400
SALES (est): 3.8MM **Privately Held**
WEB: www.innovatedindustrial.com
SIC: 3569 Assembly machines, non-metalworking

(G-314)
KMR CONCRETE INC
2835 State Road 60 E (33830-8917)
P.O. Box 428 (33831-0428)
PHONE................................863 519-9077
Kennedy M Heidel, *President*
Gary Thomas, *General Mgr*
Ashley Bass, *Manager*
Kerry L Hammock, *Director*
EMP: 17 **EST:** 2005
SQ FT: 400
SALES (est): 2.2MM **Privately Held**
WEB: www.kmrconcrete.com
SIC: 3273 Ready-mixed concrete

(G-315)
L & M PALLET SERVICES INC
1190 Us Highway 17 S (33830-6028)
P.O. Box 1846 (33831-1846)
PHONE................................863 519-3502
Tim Long, *President*
Eddie Martin, *Vice Pres*
EMP: 15 **EST:** 1999
SALES (est): 1.8MM **Privately Held**
WEB: www.lmpallets.com
SIC: 2448 2441 Pallets, wood; nailed wood boxes & shook

(G-316)
MAINTNNCE RELIABILITY TECH INC
Also Called: M & R Technologies
1421 Chamber Dr (33830-8429)
P.O. Box 2286 (33831-2286)
PHONE................................863 533-0300
Robert Radford, *President*
James Radford, *Vice Pres*
Marty Thurman, *Vice Pres*
Mike Kautz, *Manager*
Dean Newman, *Manager*
EMP: 35 **EST:** 2004
SQ FT: 9,024
SALES (est): 6.2MM **Privately Held**
WEB: www.mrtechnologies.net
SIC: 3822 Building services monitoring controls, automatic

(G-317)
METAL MART SYSTEMS INC
255 Century Blvd (33830-7705)
PHONE................................863 533-4040
Henry T Boggs, *President*
Debbie Beckelheimer, *Controller*
▼ **EMP:** 50 **EST:** 1988
SQ FT: 85,000
SALES (est): 8.1MM **Privately Held**
WEB: www.metalmartsystems.com
SIC: 3444 Ducts, sheet metal

(G-318)
MID-FLRIDA LBR ACQISITIONS INC
4281 Echo Ave (33830-6662)
PHONE................................863 533-0155
Tim Delph, *President*
Vj Creech, *Sales Staff*
EMP: 50 **EST:** 1991
SQ FT: 9,600
SALES (est): 6.5MM **Privately Held**
WEB: www.midflorida.com
SIC: 2439 4226 Trusses, wooden roof; lumber terminal (storage for hire)

(G-319)
PALLET ONE OF MOBILE LLC
6001 Foxtrot Ave (33830-6665)
PHONE................................251 960-1107
EMP: 13 **EST:** 2019
SALES (est): 241.8K **Privately Held**
WEB: www.palletone.com
SIC: 2448 Pallets, wood

(G-320)
PALLETONE INC (HQ)
6001 Foxtrot Ave (33830-6665)
P.O. Box 819 (33831-0819)
PHONE................................800 771-1147
Howe Wallace, *President*
Bridget Kennedy Hull, *Vice Pres*
Donnie Isaacson, *Vice Pres*
Bo Reese, *Vice Pres*
Gary Creamer, *Safety Mgr*
◆ **EMP:** 30 **EST:** 2001
SQ FT: 5,000
SALES (est): 50.4MM
SALES (corp-wide): 8.6B **Publicly Held**
WEB: www.palletone.com
SIC: 2448 Pallets, wood
PA: Ufp Industries, Inc.
     2801 E Beltline Ave Ne
     Grand Rapids MI 49525
     616 364-6161

(G-321)
PALLETONE OF TEXAS LP (HQ)
1470 Us Highway 17 S (33830-6627)
P.O. Box 97, New Boston TX (75570-0097)
PHONE................................903 628-5695
Howe Wallace, *Partner*
▲ **EMP:** 51 **EST:** 1994
SQ FT: 60,000
SALES (est): 31.4MM
SALES (corp-wide): 8.6B **Publicly Held**
SIC: 2448 Pallets, wood
PA: Ufp Industries, Inc.
     2801 E Beltline Ave Ne
     Grand Rapids MI 49525
     616 364-6161

(G-322)
PHANTOM SALES GROUP INC
1550 Centennial Blvd (33830-7707)
PHONE................................888 614-1232
Diane Sehleicher, *CEO*
Diane Arroyo, *President*
Melvin Smith, *Vice Pres*
▲ **EMP:** 7 **EST:** 2009
SALES (est): 685.7K **Privately Held**
WEB: www.phantompumps.com
SIC: 3569 8711 Lubrication equipment, industrial; industrial engineers

(G-323)
ROCKYMOUNTAIN LIFENET
5581 Airport Blvd (33830-6635)
PHONE................................863 533-5168
Tracy Sanderson, *Manager*
EMP: 7 **EST:** 2002
SALES (est): 83.9K **Privately Held**
SIC: 3721 Helicopters

(G-324)
RSR INDUSTRIAL COATINGS INC
Also Called: Painting & Specialty Coatings
1577 Centennial Blvd (33830-7708)
P.O. Box 1035, Lithia (33547-1035)
PHONE................................863 537-1110
Sonya Toney, *President*
EMP: 12 **EST:** 2006

SALES (est): 1.7MM **Privately Held**
WEB: www.rsrcoatings.com
SIC: 3479 1799 2295 Coating of metals &
formed products; painting of metal products; sandblasting of building exteriors;
sealing or insulating tape for pipe: coated
fiberglass

(G-325)
S & S WELDING INC
2850 Us Highway 17 S (33830-7561)
PHONE..................863 533-2888
Dale J Piechowiak, *President*
Roy Hernandez, *Vice Pres*
Sharon L Piechowiak, *Vice Pres*
Sharon Piechowiak, *Vice Pres*
Hannah Ramer, *Manager*
EMP: 12 EST: 1983
SQ FT: 46,000
SALES (est): 5.9MM **Privately Held**
WEB: www.s-swelding.com
SIC: 3444 3449 3446 7692 Sheet metal-
work; bars, concrete reinforcing: fabri-
cated steel; architectural metalwork;
welding repair

(G-326)
SUNBELT FOREST VENTURES
LLC
6001 Foxtrot Ave (33830-6665)
P.O. Box 819 (33831-0819)
PHONE..................863 496-3054
Casey Fletcher,
EMP: 1 EST: 2018
SALES (est): 4.4MM
SALES (corp-wide): 8.6B **Publicly Held**
SIC: 2448 Pallets, wood
HQ: Palletone, Inc.
6001 Foxtrot Ave
Bartow FL 33830
800 771-1147

(G-327)
SUPERHEAT FGH SERVICES
INC
895 E Lemon St (33830-4926)
PHONE..................519 396-1324
Jason Aulwurm, *Area Mgr*
Nigel Ford, *Area Mgr*
Gregory Teofilo, *Area Mgr*
Scotty Weatherman, *Business Mgr*
David Ziada, *Business Mgr*
EMP: 7
SALES (corp-wide): 49.6MM **Privately**
Held
SIC: 3398 Metal heat treating
PA: Superheat Fgh Services, Inc.
313 Garnet Dr
New Lenox IL 60451
708 478-0205

(G-328)
VALMONT NEWMARK INC
Also Called: Newmark International
4131 Us Highway 17 S (33830-7567)
PHONE..................863 533-6465
Chris Aycock, *Foreman/Supr*
Tony Gabel, *Engineer*
Ronald Barnett, *Manager*
EMP: 50
SALES (corp-wide): 3.5B **Publicly Held**
SIC: 3272 Pipe, concrete or lined with con-
crete; panels & sections, prefabricated
concrete
HQ: Valmont Newmark, Inc.
2 Perimeter Park S 475w
Birmingham AL 35243
205 968-7200

Bascom
Jackson County

(G-329)
HAY TECH
6468 Wolf Pond Rd (32423-9374)
P.O. Box 65, Donalsonville GA (39845-
0065)
PHONE..................850 592-2424
Steve Crutchfield, *Principal*
EMP: 5 EST: 2002
SALES (est): 307.1K **Privately Held**
WEB: www.hay-tech.co.uk
SIC: 2048 7692 Hay, cubed; welding re-
pair

Bay Harbor Islands
Miami-Dade County

(G-330)
ALLIANCE METALS LLC
1111 Kane Concourse # 518 (33154-2029)
PHONE..................305 343-9536
Larry Gitman, *CEO*
EMP: 6 EST: 2017
SALES (est): 1.4MM **Privately Held**
WEB: www.alliancemetalsusa.com
SIC: 3341 Aluminum smelting & refining
(secondary)

(G-331)
AMERICAN METAL GATE CORP
9901 E Bay Harbor Dr (33154-1878)
PHONE..................516 659-7952
Kia-Lynn Bazon, *President*
EMP: 10
SALES (est): 622.1K **Privately Held**
WEB: www.americanmetalgate.com
SIC: 3446 7389 Gates, ornamental metal;

(G-332)
DEERS HOLDINGS INC
1108 Kane Cncurse Ste 206 (33154)
PHONE..................805 323-6899
Bentzion Shemtov, *President*
EMP: 3 EST: 2016
SALES (est): 5MM **Privately Held**
SIC: 3639 3949 Major kitchen appliances,
except refrigerators & stoves; sporting &
athletic goods

(G-333)
SAL PRASCHNIK INC
1090 Kane Cncurse Ste 101 (33154)
PHONE..................305 866-4323
Sal Praschnik, *President*
David Praschnik, *Vice Pres*
EMP: 10 EST: 1968
SQ FT: 5,100
SALES (est): 683.4K **Privately Held**
WEB: www.salpraschnik.com
SIC: 3911 6531 Jewelry, precious metal;
real estate agents & managers

Bell
Gilchrist County

(G-334)
ABT TRUSSES INC
1310 Sw 32nd Pl (32619-1500)
PHONE..................352 221-4867
Jeffery D Jordan, *Principal*
EMP: 10 EST: 2018
SALES (est): 291.5K **Privately Held**
WEB: www.abttrusses.com
SIC: 2439 Trusses, wooden roof

(G-335)
BELL CONCRETE PRODUCTS
INC (PA)
2480 N Us Highway 129 (32619-3160)
P.O. Box 7 (32619-0007)
PHONE..................352 463-6103
Chad A Smith, *President*
Mark Smith, *Vice Pres*
Marilyn Smith, *Treasurer*
▲ EMP: 25 EST: 1972
SQ FT: 2,000
SALES (est): 4.9MM **Privately Held**
WEB: www.bellconcreteproducts.com
SIC: 3273 3271 Ready-mixed concrete;
concrete block & brick

(G-336)
RIDGEWAY TIMBER INC
3949 Nw County Road 341 (32619-3587)
PHONE..................352 463-6013
Duane J Ridgeway, *President*
Celeste Ridgeway, *Vice Pres*
EMP: 9 EST: 2003
SALES (est): 290K **Privately Held**
SIC: 2411 Logging camps & contractors

(G-337)
SANTA FE TRUSS COMPANY
INC
5079 Sw 80th Ave (32619-1940)
P.O. Box 1298, High Springs (32655-1298)
PHONE..................386 454-7711
Laurie T Wootton Jr, *President*
EMP: 11 EST: 1993
SQ FT: 10,000
SALES (est): 421.3K **Privately Held**
WEB: www.sftruss.com
SIC: 2439 Trusses, wooden roof

Belle Glade
Palm Beach County

(G-338)
ATLANTIC SUGAR
ASSOCIATION
26400 County Rd 880 (33430-3127)
P.O. Box 1570 (33430-6570)
PHONE..................561 996-6541
Val Galan, *Controller*
Eduardo Recio, *Director*
Donald Carson, *Director*
Christopher Hopper, *Director*
Jose F Valdivia Jr, *Director*
EMP: 16 EST: 1963
SQ FT: 10,000
SALES (est): 915.8K **Privately Held**
SIC: 2061 2062 Raw cane sugar; cane
sugar refining

(G-339)
BELLE GLADE ELECTRIC
MOTOR SVC
900 Nw 13th St (33430-1710)
PHONE..................561 996-3333
Bret E Mc Cormick, *President*
Betty Mc Cormick, *Controller*
EMP: 9 EST: 1964
SQ FT: 4,800
SALES (est): 610K **Privately Held**
SIC: 7694 3825 Electric motor repair;
electrical power measuring equipment

(G-340)
CEMEX CNSTR MTLS FLA LLC
Also Called: Belle Glade FL Block
State Rd 80 & Fec Rr (33430)
P.O. Box 1986 (33430-6986)
PHONE..................561 996-5249
Toll Free:..................888 -
Norval Krast, *Branch Mgr*
EMP: 8 **Privately Held**
SIC: 3273 Ready-mixed concrete
HQ: Cemex Construction Materials Florida,
Llc
1501 Belvedere Rd
West Palm Beach FL 33406

(G-341)
GLADES FORMULATING
CORPORATION
Also Called: G F C
909 Nw 13th St (33430-1709)
P.O. Box 1690 (33430-6690)
PHONE..................561 996-4200
Juan Montalvo Jr, *President*
▲ EMP: 10 EST: 1987
SQ FT: 35,000
SALES (est): 2.5MM **Privately Held**
WEB: www.gladesformulating.com
SIC: 2879 5191 Pesticides, agricultural or
household; pesticides

(G-342)
OKEE-B INC
1125 Ne 18th St (33430-2209)
PHONE..................561 996-3040
EMP: 58 EST: 1995
SALES (est): 6.7MM **Privately Held**
SIC: 3523 7389 Mfg Farm
Machinery/Equipment Business Services
At Non-Commercial Site

(G-343)
SUGAR CANE GROWERS COOP
FLA (PA)
Also Called: Glades Sugar House
1500 George Wedgworth Way
(33430-5400)
PHONE..................561 996-5556
Matthew B Hoffman, *CEO*
Robert J Underbrink, *Ch of Bd*
Antonio L Contreras, *President*
C David Goodlett, *Senior VP*
Jose F Alvarez, *Vice Pres*
▲ EMP: 469 EST: 1960
SALES (est): 106.8MM **Privately Held**
WEB: www.scgc.org
SIC: 2061 Raw cane sugar

(G-344)
TELLUS PRODUCTS LLC (HQ)
1500 George Wedgworth Way
(33430-5400)
P.O. Box 666 (33430-0666)
PHONE..................561 996-5556
Matthew F Hoffman,
Jose F Alvarez,
Erik J Blomqvist,
Gustavo R Cepero,
Antonio L Contreras,
EMP: 13 EST: 2014
SQ FT: 120,000
SALES (est): 21MM
SALES (corp-wide): 25.7MM **Privately**
Held
SIC: 2656 Sanitary food containers
PA: Tellus Holdings, Llc
1500 W Sugarhouse Rd
Belle Glade FL 33430
561 829-2600

(G-345)
TRIPP ELECTRIC MOTORS INC
1233 Nw Avenue L (33430-1719)
P.O. Box 1059 (33430-1059)
PHONE..................561 996-3333
Jimmy Tripp, *President*
Ashley Tripp, *Vice Pres*
▼ EMP: 9 EST: 1992
SQ FT: 15,000
SALES (est): 2.4MM **Privately Held**
WEB: www.trippmotors.com
SIC: 7694 Electric motor repair

(G-346)
TRU-FLO CORP
924 Nw 13th St (33430-1799)
P.O. Box 248 (33430-0248)
PHONE..................561 996-5850
Julio Sanchez, *President*
Harold Peacock, *Vice Pres*
EMP: 15 EST: 1961
SQ FT: 6,000
SALES (est): 1.8MM **Privately Held**
WEB: www.truflopumps.com
SIC: 3561 3523 Industrial pumps & parts;
farm machinery & equipment

(G-347)
WEDGWORTHS INC (PA)
651 Nw 9th St (33430-1747)
P.O. Box 2076 (33430-7076)
PHONE..................561 996-2076
Dennis Wedgworth, *President*
Brittany Meeks, *Principal*
Barbara Oetzman, *Principal*
Wayne Boynton, *Vice Pres*
James Matthews, *Vice Pres*
▼ EMP: 1 EST: 1921
SQ FT: 6,000
SALES (est): 12MM **Privately Held**
WEB: www.wedgworth.com
SIC: 2875 Fertilizers, mixing only

Belle Isle
Orange County

(G-348)
BELLE ISLE FURNITURE LLC
(PA)
7210 Seminole Dr Apt 1 (32812-3749)
PHONE..................407 408-1266
Troy Buswell,
Matt Brannon,
Chris Wyman,

EMP: 2 EST: 2018
SALES (est): 5MM **Privately Held**
SIC: 2511 Wood household furniture

(G-349)
EEP
3307 Trentwood Blvd (32812-4848)
PHONE.............................407 380-2828
Stephen Edwards, *Principal*
EMP: 12 EST: 2010
SALES (est): 504.8K **Privately Held**
WEB:
www.edwardselectronicprocessing.com
SIC: 3578 Automatic teller machines (ATM)

(G-350)
RESORT POOLSIDE SHOPS INC
2912 Nela Ave (32809-6177)
PHONE.............................407 256-5853
Paul Mullican, *President*
▲ EMP: 8 EST: 1999
SALES (est): 730.2K **Privately Held**
SIC: 2369 5611 Beachwear: girls', children's & infants'; clothing, sportswear, men's & boys'

(G-351)
SUNCOAST ASSEMBLERS LLC
2114 Belle Isle Ave (32809-3304)
PHONE.............................407 947-8835
Manuel Antonio Umpierre, *Principal*
EMP: 5 EST: 2008
SALES (est): 309.9K **Privately Held**
WEB: www.suncoastassemblers.com
SIC: 3999 Manufacturing industries

Belleair
Pinellas County

(G-352)
MORCENT IMPORT EXPORT INC
Also Called: True Back
1702 Indian Rocks Rd (33756-1656)
PHONE.............................727 442-9735
Rodney D Vincent, *President*
Rodney Vincent, *President*
EMP: 5 EST: 1995
SQ FT: 2,500
SALES (est): 562.6K **Privately Held**
WEB: www.trueback.com
SIC: 3841 Ophthalmic instruments & apparatus

(G-353)
TRX INTEGRATION INC
401 Corbett St Ste 470 (33756-7311)
PHONE.............................727 797-4707
EMP: 10
SQ FT: 1,600
SALES (est): 1.6MM **Privately Held**
SIC: 7372 7373 8742 Prepackaged Software

Belleair Beach
Pinellas County

(G-354)
TALON INDUSTRIES INC
111 8th St (33786-3220)
PHONE.............................727 517-0052
Michael Mone, *President*
EMP: 7 EST: 2018
SALES (est): 39.6K **Privately Held**
WEB: www.talon-industries.com
SIC: 3999 Manufacturing industries

Belleair Bluffs
Pinellas County

(G-355)
MARLIN DARLIN AIR LLC
2819 West Bay Dr (33770-2619)
P.O. Box 368, Safety Harbor (34695-0368)
PHONE.............................727 726-1136
William Jacobsen, *Administration*
EMP: 8 EST: 2005
SALES (est): 174.7K **Privately Held**
SIC: 2451 Mobile homes

(G-356)
SCS SOFTWARE INC
2840 West Bay Dr Ste 125 (33770-2620)
PHONE.............................727 871-8366
Josh Lasov, *VP Opers*
Michael Manter, *Sales Engr*
Jessica Elias, *Manager*
Gabriel Bara, *Consultant*
Henry Abbott, *Technical Staff*
EMP: 17 EST: 2015
SALES (est): 2.6MM **Privately Held**
WEB: www.scscloud.com
SIC: 7372 Prepackaged software

Belleview
Marion County

(G-357)
ACTION PLASTICS INC
11665 Se Us Highway 301 (34420-4427)
PHONE.............................352 342-4122
Harry Severt, *President*
EMP: 5 EST: 2006
SALES (est): 512.2K **Privately Held**
WEB: www.acticnplasticsinc.com
SIC: 3089 5162 Plastic containers, except foam; plastics products

(G-358)
AL & SONS MILLWORK INC
6323 Se 113th St (34420-4122)
PHONE.............................352 245-9191
Michael Madore, *President*
Susan Graves, *Office Mgr*
EMP: 36 EST: 1978
SQ FT: 27,500
SALES (est): 11MM **Privately Held**
WEB: www.alandsonsmw.com
SIC: 2431 3442 Door frames, wood; metal doors

(G-359)
ASECURE AMERICA INC
10080 Se 67th Ter (34420-9350)
PHONE.............................352 347-7951
Charles Butler, *President*
Tamra Butler, *Manager*
EMP: 8 EST: 2003
SALES (est): 82.6K **Privately Held**
SIC: 3699 Security devices

(G-360)
DOLMAR FOODS INC
5920 Se Hames Rd (34420-7312)
P.O. Box 771, Herndon VA (20172-0771)
PHONE.............................262 303-6026
EMP: 15 EST: 2012
SALES (est): 585.3K **Privately Held**
SIC: 2099 Food preparations

(G-361)
GATOR FABRICATIONS LLC
3450 Se 132nd Ln (34420-5650)
PHONE.............................352 245-7227
Anthony Hamblen, *Principal*
EMP: 8 EST: 2015
SALES (est): 240K **Privately Held**
SIC: 3999 Manufacturing industries

(G-362)
HEAT TREATING INCORPORATED
Also Called: H T I
6740 Se 110th St Unit 508 (34420-8433)
PHONE.............................352 245-8811
Steve Knapke, *President*
Rodney E Ingram, *Vice Pres*
Doug Knapke, *Vice Pres*
Chad Tester, *Vice Pres*
Ali Alobaidi, *QC Mgr*
EMP: 68 EST: 1995
SQ FT: 3,400
SALES (est): 9.4MM **Privately Held**
WEB: www.heattreatinginc.com
SIC: 3398 Metal heat treating

(G-363)
HYDROGEN ONE INC
6880 Se 104th St (34420-9326)
PHONE.............................352 361-6974
Tim Burrall, *Principal*
EMP: 9 EST: 2008

SALES (est): 153.6K **Privately Held**
SIC: 2813 Hydrogen

(G-364)
NOBILITY HOMES INC
Also Called: Nobility Plant 8
6432 Se 115th Ln (34420-4452)
PHONE.............................352 245-5126
Mick Jones, *Manager*
EMP: 50
SQ FT: 31,180
SALES (corp-wide): 45MM **Publicly Held**
WEB: www.nobilityhomes.com
SIC: 2451 Mobile homes, except recreational
PA: Nobility Homes, Inc.
3741 Sw 7th St
Ocala FL 34474
352 732-5157

(G-365)
PETROLEUM GROUP LLC
Also Called: Petroimage
6432 Se 115th Ln (34420-4452)
PHONE.............................352 304-5500
Colleen Collins, *Project Mgr*
Dennis Soucey,
Sadiq S Fazal,
EMP: 10 EST: 2014
SALES (est): 3.1MM **Privately Held**
WEB: www.petroleum.group
SIC: 2911 Petroleum refining

(G-366)
RAIMONDA INVESTMENT GROUP INC
Also Called: Sign Source The
5911 Se Hames Rd (34420-3321)
P.O. Box 3688 (34421-3688)
PHONE.............................352 347-8899
Ron Raimonda, *President*
EMP: 5 EST: 1995
SALES (est): 496.2K **Privately Held**
SIC: 3993 Signs & advertising specialties

(G-367)
VOICE OF SOUTH MARION
5513 Se 113th St (34420-4039)
P.O. Box 700 (34421-0700)
PHONE.............................352 245-3161
Sandra Walron, *Owner*
EMP: 6 EST: 1969
SALES (est): 478K **Privately Held**
WEB: www.thevosm.net
SIC: 2711 Newspapers: publishing only, not printed on site

Beverly Hills
Citrus County

(G-368)
NEW ERA TECHNOLOGY CORP
620 W Sunset Strip Dr (34465-8744)
PHONE.............................352 746-3569
Joan Ward, *President*
Jesse Ward, *Vice Pres*
Joanne Jean, *Admin Sec*
EMP: 10 EST: 1986
SQ FT: 10,000
SALES (est): 969.9K **Privately Held**
SIC: 3679 Electronic circuits

(G-369)
PET SERVICES OF FLORIDA LLC
3404 N Lecanto Hwy (34465-3569)
PHONE.............................352 746-6888
Joseph Campbell, *Owner*
EMP: 5 EST: 2005
SALES (est): 668.7K **Privately Held**
WEB: www.petctfla.com
SIC: 3829 Medical diagnostic systems, nuclear

(G-370)
VENKATA SAI CORPORATION
3502 N Lecanto Hwy (34465-3512)
PHONE.............................352 746-7076
Kanaka V Yegalapati, *Principal*
EMP: 10 EST: 2009
SALES (est): 2.6MM **Privately Held**
SIC: 1311 Crude petroleum production

Big Pine Key
Monroe County

(G-371)
BLUE NATIVE OF FLA KEYS INC
197 Industrial Rd (33043-3408)
PHONE.............................305 345-5305
Louis Perez Jr, *President*
Andrew Fenaughty, *Business Mgr*
EMP: 6 EST: 2017
SALES (est): 566.3K **Privately Held**
WEB: www.bluenativekeys.com
SIC: 3271 Blocks, concrete: landscape or retaining wall

(G-372)
COCA-COLA BEVERAGES FLA LLC
30801 Avenue A (33043-4824)
PHONE.............................305 872-9715
Carl Skapepis, *Branch Mgr*
EMP: 8
SALES (corp-wide): 366.5MM **Privately Held**
WEB: www.cocacolaflorida.com
SIC: 2086 Bottled & canned soft drinks
PA: Coca-Cola Beverages Florida, Llc
10117 Princess Palm Ave
Tampa FL 33610
800 438-2653

(G-373)
STOCKING FACTORY
30554 5th Ave (33043-3401)
PHONE.............................305 745-2681
Eugenie Livingstone, *Partner*
▲ EMP: 5 EST: 1989
SALES (est): 585.6K **Privately Held**
WEB: www.stockingfactory.com
SIC: 3999 Christmas tree ornaments, except electrical & glass

Biscayne Park
Miami-Dade County

(G-374)
AUDIO VIDEO IMAGINEERING INC
11853 Griffing Blvd (33161-6242)
PHONE.............................305 947-6991
David Rubinstein, *President*
EMP: 6 EST: 1995
SALES (est): 360.7K **Privately Held**
WEB: www.wow305.com
SIC: 3651 Audio electronic systems

Blountstown
Calhoun County

(G-375)
BAILEY TIMBER CO INC
19872 State Road 20 W # 2 (32424-4021)
P.O. Box 880 (32424-0880)
PHONE.............................850 674-2080
Aurther Bailey Sr, *President*
Arthur Bailey Jr, *Vice Pres*
EMP: 11 EST: 1993
SALES (est): 342.6K **Privately Held**
SIC: 2411 2421 Timber, cut at logging camp; sawmills & planing mills, general

(G-376)
MIKE BLACKBURN WELDING LLC
19983 Ne Hentz Ave (32424-1080)
PHONE.............................850 643-8464
Sheila A Blackburn, *Principal*
EMP: 8 EST: 2009
SALES (est): 300.9K **Privately Held**
SIC: 7692 Welding repair

(G-377)
SOUTHERN CONTRACTING N FL INC
19073 Ne State Road 69 (32424-4742)
P.O. Box 297 (32424-0297)
PHONE.............................850 674-3570
James Clemons Jr, *President*

▲ = Import ▼=Export
◆ =Import/Export

EMP: 8 EST: 2003
SALES (est): 80.3K **Privately Held**
SIC: **1411** Limestone & marble dimension stone

(G-378)
SOUTHLAND MILLING CO
21474 Se Coastal St (32424-2702)
P.O. Box 351 (32424-0351)
PHONE..........................850 674-8448
John H Schmarje, *President*
EMP: 6 EST: 1987
SQ FT: 1,000
SALES (est): 528.5K **Privately Held**
SIC: **2041** 5153 Grain mills (except rice); grains

(G-379)
VERTICAL ASSESMENT ASSOC LLC
17752 Ne Charlie Johns St (32424-1056)
PHONE..........................850 210-0401
Lee Rigby, *President*
Bill Strawn, *Vice Pres*
William Boedicker, *Project Mgr*
Kirsten Dobbs, *Project Mgr*
Dan Tyler, *Consultant*
EMP: 20 EST: 2001
SALES (est): 2.9MM **Privately Held**
SIC: **2591** Blinds vertical

Boca Grande
Lee County

(G-380)
AUTOMATED SONIX CORPORATION
5800 Gasparilla Rd (33921-1117)
P.O. Box 1888 (33921-1888)
PHONE..........................941 964-1361
I J Cagan, *President*
EMP: 7 EST: 1987
SQ FT: 2,200
SALES (est): 1.2MM **Privately Held**
WEB: www.automatedsonix.com
SIC: **3823** Industrial instrmnts msrmnt display/control process variable

(G-381)
HOPKINS & DAUGHTER INC
Also Called: Boca Beacon Co
431 Park Ave (33921-1000)
P.O. Box 313 (33921-0313)
PHONE..........................941 964-2995
Philip Hopkins, *President*
Marcy Shortuse, *Editor*
Julianne Greenberg, *Advt Staff*
Daniel Godwin, *Art Dir*
EMP: 9 EST: 1988
SALES (est): 1.3MM **Privately Held**
SIC: **2711** Newspapers: publishing only, not printed on site

Boca Raton
Palm Beach County

(G-382)
5D BIO GOLD LLC
1725 Avenida Del Sol (33432-1742)
PHONE..........................561 756-8291
Kenneth B Morrow, *Administration*
EMP: 7 EST: 2013
SALES (est): 194.3K **Privately Held**
SIC: **2834** Pharmaceutical preparations

(G-383)
A & A PUBLISHING CORP
Also Called: Boca Raton Observer Magazine
950 Peninsula Corporate C (33487-1378)
PHONE..........................561 982-8960
Linda Behmoiras, *President*
Chelsea Greenwood Lassm, *Editor*
Ralph Behmoiras, *Vice Pres*
EMP: 19 EST: 2004
SQ FT: 2,000
SALES (est): 2.6MM **Privately Held**
WEB: www.bocaratonobserver.com
SIC: **2721** Magazines: publishing only, not printed on site

(G-384)
A PERFECT VIEW WINDOW TINT
1031 Cornwall B (33434-2946)
PHONE..........................954 937-0400
Gina Nelson, *Principal*
EMP: 7 EST: 2011
SALES (est): 123K **Privately Held**
SIC: **3356** Tin

(G-385)
A&D WOODWORK FLORIDA LLC
7595 San Mateo Dr E (33433-4128)
PHONE..........................561 465-2863
EMP: 27
SALES (corp-wide): 104K **Privately Held**
SIC: **2431** Millwork
PA: A&D Woodwork Florida Llc
651 Ne 23rd Pl
Pompano Beach FL

(G-386)
ADCON TELEMETRY INC (PA)
1001 Nw 51st St Ste 305 (33431-4403)
PHONE..........................561 989-5309
EMP: 8
SALES (est): 1.7MM **Privately Held**
SIC: **3661** Telephone And Telegraph Apparatus

(G-387)
ADMA
5800 Pk Of Commerce Blvd (33487-8222)
PHONE..........................561 989-5800
Michael Space, *Vice Pres*
Maureen Garrity, *Human Resources*
Marc Gelberg, *Director*
EMP: 31 EST: 2018
SALES (est): 1.4MM **Privately Held**
WEB: www.admabiologics.com
SIC: **3999** Manufacturing industries

(G-388)
ADMA BIOLOGICS INC
5800 Pk Of Cmmrce Blvd Nw (33487-8222)
PHONE..........................561 989-5800
Drew Pantello, *Vice Pres*
Adam Pinkert, *Vice Pres*
EMP: 67 **Publicly Held**
WEB: www.admabiologics.com
SIC: **2834** Pharmaceutical preparations
PA: Adma Biologics, Inc.
465 State Rt 17
Ramsey NJ 07446

(G-389)
ADMA BIOMANUFACTURING LLC
5800 Pk Of Commerce Blvd (33487-8222)
PHONE..........................201 478-5552
Adam Grossman, *Mng Member*
Brian Lenz, *Mng Member*
James Mond, *Mng Member*
EMP: 254 EST: 2017
SALES (est): 22.4MM **Publicly Held**
WEB: www.admabiologics.com
SIC: **2836** Biological products, except diagnostic
PA: Adma Biologics, Inc.
465 State Rt 17
Ramsey NJ 07446

(G-390)
ADVANCED CMMNICATIONS TECH INC
108 Nw 20th St (33431-7948)
PHONE..........................954 444-4119
Dennis Goodman, *President*
◆ EMP: 12 EST: 1997
SQ FT: 6,000
SALES (est): 1.1MM **Privately Held**
SIC: **3651** Loudspeakers, electrodynamic or magnetic; microphones

(G-391)
ADVANTAGE AIRLINE PARTS INC (PA)
17735 Boniello Rd (33496-1505)
PHONE..........................770 521-1107
Friedrich Lachner, *CEO*
▲ EMP: 5 EST: 2010
SALES (est): 1.6MM **Privately Held**
WEB: www.airlinegse.com
SIC: **3724** Aircraft engines & engine parts

(G-392)
AEROSPACE TECH GROUP INC
Also Called: Atg
620 Nw 35th St (33431-6404)
PHONE..........................561 244-7400
Simon R Kay, *CEO*
Raymond P Caldiero, *Ch of Bd*
Jeffrey L Booher, *Vice Pres*
Christopher Bellido, *Engineer*
Viet Le, *Engineer*
▲ EMP: 75 EST: 1998
SQ FT: 64,000
SALES (est): 24.9MM **Privately Held**
WEB: www.atgshades.com
SIC: **2591** Window shades

(G-393)
AG SIGNS PLUS INC (PA)
9139 Sw 20th St Apt F (33428-7603)
PHONE..........................954 709-8422
Edwin A Granda, *Principal*
EMP: 7 EST: 2010
SALES (est): 124K **Privately Held**
WEB: www.agsignsplus.com
SIC: **3993** Signs & advertising specialties

(G-394)
AIR TURBINE TECHNOLOGY INC
1225 Broken Sound Pkwy Nw D (33487-3500)
PHONE..........................561 994-0500
Bill Doyle, *Principal*
Simon Shane, *Chairman*
Terrence Collins, *Senior VP*
Kemma Dodds, *Engineer*
Terry Collins, *Manager*
▲ EMP: 10 EST: 1978
SQ FT: 8,000
SALES (est): 1.9MM **Privately Held**
WEB: www.airturbinetools.com
SIC: **3546** Power-driven handtools

(G-395)
AIRGROUP INC
9858 Glades Rd (33434-3983)
PHONE..........................561 279-0680
Robert Ejr Peach, *President*
EMP: 12 EST: 2008
SALES (est): 175.3K **Privately Held**
WEB: www.airgroup.com
SIC: **3569** Lubrication equipment, industrial

(G-396)
AIRSPAN NETWORKS INC (PA)
777 W Yamato Rd Ste 310 (33431-4406)
PHONE..........................561 893-8670
Eric D Stonestrom, *President*
Pilar Diaz, *General Mgr*
Uzi Shalev, *COO*
Paul Senior, *Senior VP*
David M Brant, *Vice Pres*
▲ EMP: 30 EST: 1992
SQ FT: 5,400
SALES (est): 63.3MM **Privately Held**
WEB: www.airspan.com
SIC: **3663** Radio & TV communications equipment

(G-397)
ALEVO AUTOMOTIVE INC
301 Ne 51st St Ste 1240 (33431-4931)
PHONE..........................954 593-4215
Stein Christiansen, *Exec VP*
EMP: 7 EST: 2009
SALES (est): 501.5K **Privately Held**
SIC: **3711** Automobile assembly, including specialty automobiles

(G-398)
ALL-TAG CORPORATION (PA)
Also Called: All-Tag Security Americas
1155 Broken Sound Pkwy Nw E (33487-3538)
PHONE..........................561 998-9983
Stuart Seidel, *President*
Cynthia Dale, *Accounting Mgr*
Jeanne Simenc, *Accounts Exec*
▲ EMP: 22 EST: 2000
SQ FT: 21,000
SALES (est): 5.5MM **Privately Held**
WEB: www.all-tag.com
SIC: **3825** 5131 Oscillators, audio & radio frequency (instrument types); labels

(G-399)
ALMACO GROUP INC
7900 Glades Rd Ste 630 (33434-4105)
PHONE..........................561 558-1600
Vilhelm Roberts, *President*
Guillaume Faysse, *Vice Pres*
Mikael Hedberg, *Vice Pres*
Leena Ades, *Admin Asst*
◆ EMP: 16 EST: 1998
SQ FT: 6,960
SALES (est): 8.3MM **Privately Held**
WEB: www.almaco.cc
SIC: **3731** Shipbuilding & repairing
PA: Almaco Group Oy
Uudenmaantie 100
Piispanristi 20760

(G-400)
ALTELIX LLC
1201 Clint Moore Rd (33487-2718)
PHONE..........................561 660-9434
Peter Roth, *President*
EMP: 10 EST: 2016
SQ FT: 30,000
SALES (est): 1MM **Privately Held**
WEB: www.altelix.com
SIC: **3663** 3678 Antennas, transmitting & communications; electronic connectors

(G-401)
ALUDISC LLC
2127 Nw 53rd St (33496-3451)
PHONE..........................910 299-0911
▲ EMP: 40
SALES (est): 9.1MM **Privately Held**
SIC: **3354** 3355 Mfg Aluminum Extruded Products Aluminum Rolling/Drawing

(G-402)
AM PAVERS INC
19722 Black Olive Ln (33498-4854)
PHONE..........................954 275-1590
Angela Vicente, *President*
EMP: 7 EST: 2005
SALES (est): 124.9K **Privately Held**
SIC: **3531** Pavers

(G-403)
AMARANTH LF SCIENCES PHRM INC
1731 Avenida Del Sol (33432-1742)
PHONE..........................561 756-8291
Walter M Wolf, *CEO*
EMP: 10 EST: 2016
SALES (est): 409K **Privately Held**
SIC: **2099** Food preparations

(G-404)
AMERICAN AGGREGATES LLC
9040 Kimberly Blvd Ste 61 (33434-2836)
PHONE..........................813 352-2124
Roberto Servija, *CFO*
EMP: 11 EST: 2017
SALES (est): 924K **Privately Held**
SIC: **1081** Metal mining services

(G-405)
AMERICAN BHVIORAL RES INST LLC
Also Called: Relaxium
1515 N Federal Hwy # 300 (33432-1911)
PHONE..........................888 353-1205
Timea Ciliberti, *CEO*
Eric Ciliberti, *Research*
Eric C D, *Mng Member*
EMP: 85 EST: 2009
SALES: 10.6MM **Privately Held**
WEB: www.tryrelaxium.com
SIC: **2834** Pills, pharmaceutical

(G-406)
AMERICAN DIAMOND BLADES CORP
433 Plaza Real Ste 275 (33432-3999)
PHONE..........................561 571-2166
Eduardo Velez, *President*
EMP: 18 EST: 2018
SALES (est): 1.3MM **Privately Held**
WEB: www.americandiamondblades.com
SIC: **3425** 5072 3291 1795 Saw blades & handsaws; saw blades for hand or power saws; saw blades; abrasive wheels & grindstones, not artificial; concrete breaking for streets & highways

(G-407)
AMERICAN HOUSEHOLD INC (DH)
Also Called: Sunbeam Outdoor Products
2381 Nw Executive Ctr Dr (33431-8560)
PHONE..................................561 912-4100
Jerry Levin, *Ch of Bd*
▲ EMP: 60 EST: 1900
SQ FT: 27,003
SALES (est): 314.4MM
SALES (corp-wide): 10.5B **Publicly Held**
SIC: 3631 2514 3421 3634 Barbecues, grills & braziers (outdoor cooking); metal lawn & garden furniture; lawn furniture: metal; scissors, shears, clippers, snips & similar tools; shears, hand; clippers, fingernail & toenail; electric housewares & fans; hair dryers, electric; blenders, electric; food mixers, electric; household; thermometers & temperature sensors; temperature sensors, except industrial process & aircraft; thermometers, liquid-in-glass & bimetal type; geophysical & meteorological testing equipment; blood pressure apparatus

(G-408)
AMI CELEBRITY PUBLICATIONS LLC
1000 American Media Way (33464-1000)
PHONE..................................561 997-7733
David J Pecker, *CEO*
EMP: 203 EST: 2011
SALES (est): 2.5MM
SALES (corp-wide): 1.2B **Privately Held**
SIC: 2741 Miscellaneous publishing
PA: Worldwide Media Services Group Inc.
4 New York Plz Fl 2
New York NY 10004
800 929-8274

(G-409)
AMI DIGITAL INC
1000 American Media Way (33464-1000)
PHONE..................................561 997-7733
EMP: 360 EST: 2014
SALES (est): 2.6MM
SALES (corp-wide): 1.2B **Privately Held**
SIC: 2741 Miscellaneous publishing
PA: Worldwide Media Services Group Inc.
4 New York Plz Fl 2
New York NY 10004
800 929-8274

(G-410)
AMJ DOT LLC
Also Called: City Fashion, The
22304 Calibre Ct Apt 1304 (33433-5507)
PHONE..................................646 249-0273
Assaf Joseth, *CEO*
Assaf Joseph, *CEO*
Ruth Elmann, *COO*
David Yakobov, *CFO*
▲ EMP: 7 EST: 2013
SALES (est): 470.1K **Privately Held**
SIC: 2335 5621 Women's, juniors' & misses' dresses; women's clothing stores

(G-411)
AONEA
5400 N Dixie Hwy (33487-4902)
PHONE..................................561 989-0067
Phyllis Cullen, *Principal*
EMP: 7 EST: 2010
SALES (est): 94.3K **Privately Held**
SIC: 3993 Signs & advertising specialties

(G-412)
APEX FLOOD FIRE MOLD CLNUP INC
1340 Sw 19th Ave (33486-8514)
PHONE..................................305 975-1710
Sagi Dayan, *Principal*
EMP: 9 EST: 2008
SALES (est): 103.3K **Privately Held**
SIC: 3544 Industrial molds

(G-413)
APPERALS CUSTOM FINISH WDWRK
22446 Sw 66th Ave (33428-5936)
PHONE..................................754 264-2296
Ricardo Espineira, *Principal*
EMP: 8 EST: 2008

SALES (est): 144.6K **Privately Held**
SIC: 2431 Millwork

(G-414)
AQUATEC SOLUTIONS LLC
140 Nw 11th St (33432-2605)
PHONE..................................561 717-6933
Philip Root, *President*
Sondra Bennett, *Vice Pres*
EMP: 12 EST: 2017
SALES (est): 341.1K **Privately Held**
WEB: www.aquatec.com
SIC: 3589 Water treatment equipment, industrial

(G-415)
ARTISTIC ELEMENTS INC
400 E Palmetto Park Rd (33432-5018)
PHONE..................................561 750-1554
Leigh A Auger, *President*
EMP: 9 EST: 2017
SALES (est): 835.8K **Privately Held**
WEB: www.theartisticelements.com
SIC: 2819 Industrial inorganic chemicals

(G-416)
ARTY-SUN LLC
9045 La Fontana Blvd (33434-5636)
PHONE..................................561 705-2222
EMP: 8
SALES (est): 400K **Privately Held**
SIC: 3911 Mfg Precious Metal Jewelry

(G-417)
ASTOR EXPLORATIONS CORP
5030 Champion Blvd G6162 (33496-2473)
PHONE..................................561 241-3621
Philip Langerman, *Principal*
EMP: 7 EST: 2010
SALES (est): 122K **Privately Held**
WEB: www.astorexplorations.com
SIC: 1041 Gold ores

(G-418)
ATI AGENCY INC
123 Nw 13th St Ste 305b (33432-1645)
PHONE..................................954 895-7909
EMP: 16 EST: 2018
SALES (est): 441.6K **Privately Held**
WEB: www.atiagencyinc.com
SIC: 3312 Stainless steel

(G-419)
ATKORE INTERNATIONAL INC
1 Town Center Rd (33486-1039)
PHONE..................................800 882-5543
EMP: 19 **Publicly Held**
WEB: www.atkore.com
SIC: 3317 Steel pipe & tubes
HQ: Atkore International, Inc.
16100 Lathrop Ave
Harvey IL 60426

(G-420)
ATM VAULT CORP
2151 Nw Boca Raton Blvd (33431-7456)
PHONE..................................561 441-9294
John Schuttler, *Principal*
EMP: 10 EST: 2012
SALES (est): 292K **Privately Held**
SIC: 3272 Burial vaults, concrete or precast terrazzo

(G-421)
AVON ASSOC
4101 N Ocean Blvd (33431-5341)
PHONE..................................561 391-7188
Marilyn Schrager, *Principal*
EMP: 5 EST: 2005
SALES (est): 630.5K **Privately Held**
SIC: 2821 Plastics materials & resins

(G-422)
B C CABINETRY
10625 Mendocino Ln (33428-1229)
PHONE..................................561 393-8937
Bruce Carlson, *Owner*
EMP: 6 EST: 1985
SALES (est): 377.6K **Privately Held**
SIC: 2511 Wood household furniture

(G-423)
B F INDUSTRIES INC
4201 Oak Cir Ste 29 (33431-4237)
PHONE..................................561 368-6662
Sidney Z Bors, *President*

Bob McDonald, *Plant Mgr*
EMP: 10 EST: 1972
SQ FT: 10,000
SALES (est): 927.5K **Privately Held**
WEB: www.bfindustries.com
SIC: 3841 Surgical & medical instruments

(G-424)
B J AND ME INC
Also Called: Insty-Prints
2284 N Dixie Hwy Fl 1 (33431-8025)
PHONE..................................561 368-5470
Howard Rothberg, *President*
Barbara Rothberg, *Vice Pres*
EMP: 5 EST: 1984
SQ FT: 1,000
SALES (est): 450K **Privately Held**
WEB: www.instyprints.com
SIC: 2752 7334 2791 2789 Commercial printing, offset; photocopying & duplicating services; typesetting; bookbinding & related work

(G-425)
BA PRECISION PRODUCTS CORP
2920 Nw 2nd Ave Ste 3 (33431-6687)
PHONE..................................561 859-3400
Gary Becher, *President*
Lynn Ossian, *Engineer*
EMP: 6 EST: 1991
SALES (est): 918.4K **Privately Held**
WEB: www.baprecision.com
SIC: 3599 Machine shop, jobbing & repair

(G-426)
BABBALA LLC
Also Called: Teething Egg, The
2901 Clint Moore Rd (33496-2041)
PHONE..................................844 869-5747
Jessica Luntz, *President*
Dean Luntz, *Vice Pres*
EMP: 5 EST: 2015
SALES (est): 589.6K **Privately Held**
SIC: 3069 Teething rings, rubber

(G-427)
BASIC FUN INC (PA)
301 E Yamato Rd Ste 4200 (33431-4933)
PHONE..................................561 997-8901
Jay Foreman, *CEO*
Craig Leaf, *President*
Jeff Lebron, *General Mgr*
Steve Littman, *COO*
Steve Beilman, *Vice Pres*
▲ EMP: 28 EST: 2009
SALES (est): 26.3MM **Privately Held**
SIC: 3944 3942 Games, toys & children's vehicles; electronic games & toys; dolls & stuffed toys

(G-428)
BEDDING ACQUISITION LLC (PA)
Also Called: Hollander Sleep & Decor
901 W Yamato Rd Ste 250 (33431-4415)
PHONE..................................561 997-6900
Mark Eichhorn, *Mng Member*
Beth Mack
EMP: 8 EST: 2019
SALES (est): 12.7MM **Privately Held**
SIC: 2392 2221 Cushions & pillows; bedding, manmade or silk fabric

(G-429)
BEDESCHI AMERICA INC (HQ)
2600 N Military Trl # 245 (33431-6330)
PHONE..................................954 602-2175
Rino Bedeschi, *President*
Vladimir Grubacic, *General Mgr*
Thomas C Turano, *Vice Pres*
Marco Bertorelle, *Sales Staff*
Fabio Iurzolla, *Sales Staff*
▲ EMP: 6 EST: 2004
SALES (est): 18.8MM
SALES (corp-wide): 173.5MM **Privately Held**
WEB: www.bedeschi.com
SIC: 3542 Extruding machines (machine tools); metal
PA: Bedeschi Spa
Via Praimbole 38
Limena PD 35010
049 766-3100

(G-430)
BF AMERICAN BUSINESS LLC
22285 Sw 66th Ave Apt 200 (33428-5929)
PHONE..................................561 856-7094
Alberto Bracho, *Manager*
EMP: 7 EST: 2015
SALES (est): 230.6K **Privately Held**
SIC: 3011 Tires & inner tubes

(G-431)
BIG L BRANDS INC (PA)
Also Called: Beer Bread Company
7750 Ne Spanish Trail Ct (33487-1718)
PHONE..................................888 552-9768
Molly Wilson Kohler, *President*
Andrew Yochum, *President*
EMP: 7 EST: 2003
SALES (est): 2MM **Privately Held**
WEB: www.linktr.ee
SIC: 2045 5149 Prepared flour mixes & doughs; groceries & related products

(G-432)
BLACK ICE SOFTWARE LLC (PA)
950 Peninsula Corporate C (33487-1389)
PHONE..................................561 757-4107
Jozsef Nemeth, *CEO*
Ilona Colaire, *Manager*
Zsolt Jancsik, *Web Dvlpr*
EMP: 6 EST: 1987
SQ FT: 1,600
SALES (est): 1.5MM **Privately Held**
WEB: www.blackice.com
SIC: 7372 Prepackaged software

(G-433)
BLUM & FINK INC
Also Called: Fleurette
1200 N Federal Hwy # 200 (33432-2813)
PHONE..................................212 695-2606
Stanley Blum, *President*
▲ EMP: 12 EST: 1961
SALES (est): 1.7MM **Privately Held**
SIC: 2371 5137 Fur coats & other fur apparel; fur clothing, women's & children's

(G-434)
BOCA COATINGS INC
6135 Belleza Ln (33433-1792)
PHONE..................................561 400-8183
Robert Cox, *Principal*
EMP: 7 EST: 2013
SALES (est): 71.7K **Privately Held**
SIC: 3479 Metal coating & allied service

(G-435)
BOCA COLOR GRAPHICS INC
139 Nw 3rd St (33432-3824)
PHONE..................................561 391-2229
Joseph W Massarella, *Ch of Bd*
Michael Massarella, *President*
Gerard Massarella, *Vice Pres*
Mike Massarella, *Officer*
Amy Mollica, *Admin Sec*
EMP: 11 EST: 1967
SQ FT: 12,000
SALES (est): 1.8MM **Privately Held**
WEB: www.bocacolorgraphics.com
SIC: 2752 2796 2791 2789 Commercial printing, offset; platemaking services; typesetting; bookbinding & related work

(G-436)
BOCA DENTAL SUPPLY LLC
3401 N Federal Hwy # 211 (33431-6007)
PHONE..................................800 768-5691
Alvaro Betancur, *President*
EMP: 7 EST: 2015
SALES (est): 216.5K **Privately Held**
WEB: www.bocadentalregenerative.com
SIC: 3843 Dental equipment & supplies

(G-437)
BOCA RATON PRINTING CO
1000 Clint Moore Rd # 205 (33487-2807)
PHONE..................................561 395-8404
Dan Garber, *President*
Edward Harper Jr, *Principal*
EMP: 8 EST: 1961
SALES (est): 574.6K **Privately Held**
WEB: www.bocaprinting.com
SIC: 2752 2796 2791 Commercial printing, offset; platemaking services; typesetting

(G-438)
BOCA SEMICONDUCTOR CORPORATION
4260 Nw 1st Ave Ste 50 (33431-4264)
PHONE.................................561 226-8500
Richard Rosenstein, CEO
L Scott Rosenstein, President
EMP: 20 **EST:** 2000
SQ FT: 3,000
SALES (est): 837.3K **Privately Held**
WEB: www.bocasemi.com
SIC: 3674 5065 Transistors; semiconductor devices

(G-439)
BOCA SIGNWORKS
174 Glades Rd (33432-1605)
PHONE.................................561 393-6010
Jason Goulet, Principal
EMP: 5 **EST:** 2008
SALES (est): 472.3K **Privately Held**
SIC: 3993 Signs, not made in custom sign painting shops

(G-440)
BOCA STONE DESIGN INC
3601 N Dixie Hwy Ste 5 (33431-5901)
PHONE.................................561 362-2085
Rosana Marchelli, Principal
EMP: 9 **EST:** 2016
SALES (est): 1.2MM **Privately Held**
WEB: www.bocastonedesign.com
SIC: 3469 Appliance parts, porcelain enameled

(G-441)
BOCA SYSTEMS INC
1065 S Rogers Cir (33487-2816)
PHONE.................................561 998-9600
Larry Gross, CEO
Joseph Gross, Ch of Bd
Rob Kohn, Vice Pres
Robert Kohn, Vice Pres
Louis Rosner, Sales Staff
▼ **EMP:** 135 **EST:** 1990
SQ FT: 80,000
SALES (est): 27.8MM **Privately Held**
WEB: www.bocasystems.com
SIC: 3577 Computer peripheral equipment

(G-442)
BODYLASTICS INTERNATIONAL INC (PA)
23026 Clear Echo Dr (33433-6452)
PHONE.................................561 254-0475
Blake Kassel, President
◆ **EMP:** 6 **EST:** 1998
SALES (est): 1.2MM **Privately Held**
WEB: www.bodylastics.com
SIC: 3949 Exercise equipment

(G-443)
BODYLASTICS INTERNATIONAL INC
3500 Nw 2nd Ave Ste 606 (33431-5868)
PHONE.................................561 562-4745
Blake A Kassel, Branch Mgr
EMP: 17
SALES (corp-wide): 1.2MM **Privately Held**
WEB: www.bodylastics.com
SIC: 3949 Exercise equipment
PA: Bodylastics International Inc.
   23026 Clear Echo Dr
   Boca Raton FL 33433
   561 254-0475

(G-444)
BODYLOGICMD FRANCHISE CORP
5000 T Rex Ave (33431-4491)
PHONE.................................561 972-9580
Patrick Savage, President
EMP: 86 **EST:** 2009
SALES (est): 9.1MM **Privately Held**
SIC: 2833 Hormones or derivatives

(G-445)
BPC PLASMA INC
901 W Yamato Rd Ste 101 (33431-4409)
PHONE.................................561 989-5800
EMP: 14

SALES (corp-wide): 480.7MM **Privately Held**
WEB: www.biotestplasma.com
SIC: 2834 8731 Pharmaceutical preparations; biological research
HQ: Bpc Plasma, Inc.
   901 W Yamato Rd Ste 101
   Boca Raton FL 33431

(G-446)
BPC PLASMA INC (DH)
Also Called: Biotest Plasma Center
901 W Yamato Rd Ste 101 (33431-4409)
PHONE.................................561 569-3100
Ilana Carlisle, CEO
Johann Vaz, Vice Pres
Stephanie Williams, Production
Joan Hoggatt, Buyer
Zach Mozingo, QC Mgr
EMP: 50 **EST:** 2007
SALES (est): 106.9MM
SALES (corp-wide): 480.7MM **Privately Held**
WEB: www.biotestplasma.com
SIC: 2834 8731 Pharmaceutical preparations; biological research; medical research, commercial
HQ: Grifols Shared Services North America, Inc.
   2410 Lillyvale Ave
   Los Angeles CA 90032
   323 225-2221

(G-447)
BRIAN SLATER & ASSOCIATES LLC
Also Called: Slater Lighting Solutions
5301 N Federal Hwy # 195 (33487-4917)
PHONE.................................561 886-7705
Ginamaria Rivara, Project Mgr
Chad Sample, Sales Staff
Brian Slater,
Meta Jamison,
EMP: 7 **EST:** 2011
SALES (est): 200.5K **Privately Held**
WEB: www.slaterlighting.com
SIC: 3645 Residential lighting fixtures

(G-448)
BRIANAS SALAD LLC
5400 N Dixie Hwy Ste 7 (33487-4902)
PHONE.................................954 608-0953
Maryann Murphy, Principal
EMP: 7 **EST:** 2013
SALES (est): 212.1K **Privately Held**
SIC: 2099 Salads, fresh or refrigerated

(G-449)
BRIJOT IMAGING SYSTEMS INC
951 W Yamato Rd Ste 205 (33431-4440)
PHONE.................................407 641-4370
Mitchel J Laskey, President
Robert Daly, Senior VP
Leon Chlimper, Vice Pres
Gregory Chouljian, Vice Pres
Troy Techau, Vice Pres
▼ **EMP:** 21 **EST:** 2004
SQ FT: 24,000
SALES (est): 1.8MM **Privately Held**
SIC: 3699 Security devices

(G-450)
BROKERAGE MGT SOLUTIONS INC
1095 Broken Sound Pkwy Nw # 200 (33487-3503)
PHONE.................................561 766-0409
Michael Mosseri, CEO
EMP: 15 **EST:** 2015
SALES (est): 555K **Privately Held**
WEB: www.totalbrokerage.com
SIC: 7372 Prepackaged software

(G-451)
BROWNBAG POPCORN COMPANY LLC
Also Called: Bbpco
900 Ne 4th St Apt A (33432-4200)
PHONE.................................561 212-5664
Karen Barnes, Director
Lynne E Szymanski,
Jill G Fine,
EMP: 7 **EST:** 2014

SALES (est): 585.2K **Privately Held**
WEB: www.brownbagpopcornco.com
SIC: 2064 5145 Popcorn balls or other treated popcorn products; popcorn & supplies

(G-452)
BTB REFINING LLC
925 S Federal Hwy Ste 375 (33432-6144)
PHONE.................................561 999-9916
Kevin G Kirkeide, Manager
EMP: 10 **EST:** 2014
SALES (est): 297.9K **Privately Held**
SIC: 2951 Asphalt paving mixtures & blocks

(G-453)
CAPITOL FURNITURE MFG LLC
850 Broken Sound Pkwy Nw (33487-3624)
PHONE.................................954 485-5000
Joan Steele, Exec VP
Robert Steinman, Mng Member
Kenneth Croll, Mng Member
Sheardon Thomas, IT/INT Sup
EMP: 8 **EST:** 2014
SQ FT: 2,500
SALES (est): 447.7K **Privately Held**
WEB: www.capitolfurniture.com
SIC: 2512 2511 Upholstered household furniture; wood bedroom furniture

(G-454)
CASEBRIEFS LLC
2234 N Federal Hwy 413 (33431-7710)
PHONE.................................646 240-4401
David E Gray, Principal
EMP: 8 **EST:** 2013
SALES (est): 277.2K **Privately Held**
WEB: www.casebriefs.com
SIC: 2731 Book publishing

(G-455)
CAVASTONE LLC
Also Called: Cavastone By Connie Davalos
506 Nw 77th St (33487-1323)
PHONE.................................561 994-9100
Norma Davalos, Mng Member
Juan C Reyes, Mng Member
▲ **EMP:** 7 **EST:** 2006
SALES (est): 3.2MM **Privately Held**
WEB: www.cavastone.com
SIC: 1411 Dimension stone

(G-456)
CEAUTAMED WORLDWIDE LLC
Also Called: Greens First
1289 Clint Moore Rd (33487-2718)
PHONE.................................866 409-6262
Ryan Benson, CEO
▲ **EMP:** 6 **EST:** 2009
SALES (est): 1.1MM **Privately Held**
WEB: www.greensfirst.com
SIC: 2834 5122 Vitamin preparations; pharmaceuticals

(G-457)
CEBEV LLC
2424 N Federal Hwy # 101 (33431-7735)
PHONE.................................918 830-4417
Bill Towler, General Mgr
EMP: 5 **EST:** 2016
SQ FT: 1,500
SALES (est): 528.3K **Privately Held**
SIC: 2037 Fruit juices

(G-458)
CELSIUS INC
2424 N Federal Hwy # 208 (33431-7780)
PHONE.................................561 276-2239
John Fieldly, CEO
Tony Lau, Chairman
William Milmoe, Chairman
Rona Miles, Production
Bryan Alesiano, Sales Staff
▼ **EMP:** 18 **EST:** 2004
SQ FT: 3,000
SALES (est): 12.6MM **Publicly Held**
WEB: www.celsius.com
SIC: 2087 Beverage bases
PA: Celsius Holdings, Inc.
   2424 N Federal Hwy # 208
   Boca Raton FL 33431

(G-459)
CELSIUS HOLDINGS INC (PA)
2424 N Federal Hwy # 208 (33431-7780)
PHONE.................................561 276-2239
John Fieldly, President
Ronnie Char, Managing Dir
Thorsten Brandt, Senior VP
Lex Shankle, Senior VP
Jason Burke, Vice Pres
EMP: 31 **EST:** 2004
SQ FT: 2,140
SALES (est): 314.2MM **Publicly Held**
WEB: www.celsius.com
SIC: 2086 Iced tea & fruit drinks, bottled & canned

(G-460)
CIAO GROUP INC (PA)
951 W Yamato Rd Ste 101 (33431-4437)
PHONE.................................347 560-5040
EMP: 20
SALES (est): 1.4MM **Privately Held**
SIC: 3661 4813 6794 Mfg Telecommunications Products & Solutions Franchising Stores

(G-461)
CIRCLE PRESS
5749 Camino Del Sol (33433-6564)
PHONE.................................561 213-5831
EMP: 7 **EST:** 2008
SALES (est): 98.9K **Privately Held**
SIC: 2741 Miscellaneous publishing

(G-462)
CITY NEWS PUBLISHING LLC
12364 Clearfalls Dr (33428-4845)
PHONE.................................305 332-9101
Gerald S Spielman, Principal
EMP: 7 **EST:** 2019
SALES (est): 383.8K **Privately Held**
SIC: 2741 Miscellaneous publishing

(G-463)
CLASSIC METAL FABRICATION INC
121 Nw 11th St (33432-2639)
PHONE.................................561 305-9532
Siegfried James Mahar, President
EMP: 6 **EST:** 2013
SQ FT: 3,500
SALES (est): 728.6K **Privately Held**
WEB: www.classicmetalfab.com
SIC: 3441 Fabricated structural metal

(G-464)
CLASSIQUE STYLE INC
6590 W Rogers Cir Ste 8 (33487-2739)
PHONE.................................561 995-7557
Dominic Graci, President
Stephanie Graci, Vice Pres
EMP: 9 **EST:** 1998
SQ FT: 3,000
SALES (est): 433.8K **Privately Held**
SIC: 3911 Jewelry, precious metal

(G-465)
CLEARLY DERM LLC (PA)
7050 W Palmetto Park Rd # 30 (33433-3426)
PHONE.................................561 353-3376
Brooke Boland, Med Doctor
Andrea Colton, Med Doctor
Nicole Conrad, Med Doctor
Meredith Hancock, Med Doctor
Erika Luceri, Med Doctor
EMP: 14 **EST:** 2010
SALES (est): 12.7MM **Privately Held**
WEB: www.clearlyderm.com
SIC: 2834 Dermatologicals

(G-466)
CLEVA TECHNOLOGIES LLC
Also Called: Cleva Power
1951 Nw 19th St Ste 101 (33431-7344)
PHONE.................................561 654-5279
Mitchel Robbins, CEO
Larry K Canipe, President
EMP: 15 **EST:** 2006
SALES (est): 3.8MM **Privately Held**
WEB: www.clevatec.com
SIC: 3691 3694 Alkaline cell storage batteries; battery charging alternators & generators

GEOGRAPHIC

(G-467)
COASTAL COMMUNICATIONS CORP
Also Called: Corporate & Incentive Travel
2500 N Military Trl # 283 (33431-6322)
PHONE......................................561 989-0600
Harvey Grotsky, *President*
David Middlebrook, *Vice Pres*
Henry Fitzgerald, *Manager*
EMP: 15 EST: 1977
SALES (est): 1.4MM **Privately Held**
WEB: www.themeetingmagazines.com
SIC: 2721 8742 Magazines: publishing only, not printed on site; management consulting services

(G-468)
COLLFIX INC
365 Sw 16th St (33432-7213)
PHONE......................................754 264-0959
Tadeusz Torkowski, *Principal*
EMP: 7 EST: 2014
SALES (est): 158.8K **Privately Held**
WEB: www.babawenda.com
SIC: 2834 Pharmaceutical preparations

(G-469)
COMPACT CONTAINER SYSTEMS LLC
2500 N Military Trl # 400 (33431-6344)
PHONE......................................561 392-6910
Charlie Santos Busch, *Mng Member*
EMP: 10 EST: 2014
SALES (est): 547.2K **Privately Held**
WEB: www.compactcontainers.com
SIC: 2448 Cargo containers, wood & metal combination

(G-470)
COOPER BUSSMANN LLC
Also Called: Cooper Bussmann-Automotive
1225 Broken Sound Pkwy Nw S (33487-3533)
PHONE......................................561 998-4100
Norman Campbell, *Design Engr*
Renford Hanley, *Design Engr*
Johnathan Janis, *Sales Mgr*
Helio Sakaya, *Branch Mgr*
EMP: 111 **Privately Held**
SIC: 3677 Electronic transformers
HQ: Cooper Bussmann, Llc
    114 Old State Rd
    Ellisville MO 63021
    636 527-1324

(G-471)
COPPERCOM INC
Also Called: Coppercom, A Heico
3600 Fau Blvd Ste 100 (33431-6474)
PHONE......................................561 322-4000
Julian Thomson, *President*
Manuel Vexler, *CTO*
EMP: 62 EST: 1997
SQ FT: 15,000
SALES (est): 5.2MM **Privately Held**
SIC: 3661 Telephone & telegraph apparatus
PA: The Heico Companies L L C
    70 W Madison St Ste 5600
    Chicago IL 60602

(G-472)
COSMETIC SOLUTIONS LLC (PA)
6101 Pk Of Commerce Blvd (33487-8208)
PHONE......................................561 226-8600
Mervyn Becker, *President*
Warren Becker, *COO*
Jose Rodriguez, *Prdtn Mgr*
Elana Durbin, *Production*
Les Herz, *CFO*
◆ EMP: 30 EST: 1992
SQ FT: 40,000
SALES (est): 32.2MM **Privately Held**
WEB: www.naturalskincare.com
SIC: 2844 5122 Cosmetic preparations; cosmetics, perfumes & hair products

(G-473)
CRC PRESS LLC (DH)
Also Called: Critical Review Journals, Crj
6000 Broken Sound Pkwy Nw # 300 (33487-5704)
PHONE......................................561 994-0555
Polly Dodson, *Publisher*

Natalie Foster, *Publisher*
Nicola Parkin, *Publisher*
Louisa Semlyen, *Publisher*
Lian Sun, *Publisher*
EMP: 30 EST: 1913
SQ FT: 40,354
SALES (est): 31.1MM
SALES (corp-wide): 2.4B **Privately Held**
WEB: www.routledge.com
SIC: 2731 Books: publishing only
HQ: Taylor & Francis Limited
    Oakfield Road Adams Corner
    Aylesbury BUCKS
    129 674-7270

(G-474)
CRC PRESS LLC
3848 Fau Blvd Ste 310 (33431-6437)
PHONE......................................561 361-6000
Fenton Markevich, *CEO*
EMP: 55
SALES (corp-wide): 2.4B **Privately Held**
WEB: www.routledge.com
SIC: 2731 Books: publishing only
HQ: Crc Press Llc
    6000 Broken Sound Pkwy Nw # 300
    Boca Raton FL 33487
    561 994-0555

(G-475)
CROWN LEAO INDUSTRIES INC
150 E Palmetto Park Rd # 80 (33432-4827)
PHONE......................................561 866-1218
Achilles A Utsch De Leao, *Principal*
EMP: 9 EST: 2015
SALES (est): 463.6K **Privately Held**
SIC: 3999 Manufacturing industries

(G-476)
CUSTOM INSTALL SOLUTIONS INC
3632 Nw 5th Ter (33431-5746)
PHONE......................................916 601-1190
Peter Gokun, *President*
Mikhail Kosachevich, *Vice Pres*
EMP: 10 EST: 2017
SALES (est): 918K **Privately Held**
SIC: 2431 7389 Millwork;

(G-477)
DALIAN PLATINUM CHEM LTD CORP
263 Fan Palm Rd (33432-7501)
PHONE......................................954 501-0564
Klaus J Grau Sr, *President*
Catalina M Grau Atuesta, *Treasurer*
EMP: 8 EST: 2017
SALES (est): 315.9K **Privately Held**
SIC: 2048 Prepared feeds

(G-478)
DAZMED INC
Also Called: Dazmed Pharmaceuticals
508 Nw 77th St (33487-1323)
PHONE......................................561 571-2020
Amio Das, *President*
EMP: 8 EST: 2011
SALES (est): 991.6K **Privately Held**
WEB: www.dazmed.com
SIC: 2834 Pharmaceutical preparations

(G-479)
DECO LAV INC (PA)
4920 Bocaire Blvd (33487-1162)
PHONE......................................561 274-2110
Robert Mayer, *President*
Johnny Kong, *Managing Dir*
Elyshia Schemmel, *Exec VP*
Courtney Casperson, *Vice Pres*
Linda M Persaud, *Vice Pres*
▲ EMP: 12 EST: 2001
SALES (est): 25.2MM **Privately Held**
WEB: partners.decolav.com
SIC: 3431 Bathroom fixtures, including sinks

(G-480)
DEFENSTECH INTERNATIONAL INC
Also Called: Defend-X
2790 N Federal Hwy # 400 (33431-7784)
PHONE......................................202 688-1988
Alan R Sporn, *President*
▼ EMP: 10 EST: 2005

SALES (est): 2.1MM **Privately Held**
WEB: www.defenstech.com
SIC: 3812 Defense systems & equipment

(G-481)
DESIGN & PRINT
199 W Palmetto Park Rd (33432-3809)
PHONE......................................561 361-8299
Carol Inman, *President*
EMP: 5 EST: 1991
SALES (est): 339.2K **Privately Held**
SIC: 2752 7336 Commercial printing, lithographic; graphic arts & related design

(G-482)
DEVCON INTERNATIONAL CORP (HQ)
595 S Federal Hwy Ste 500 (33432-5542)
PHONE......................................954 926-5200
Mr Steve Hafen, *CEO*
Mr Donald L Smith, *Principal*
Ms Ann Macdonald, *Senior VP*
Mr Mark M McIntosh, *Senior VP*
Mr Sean Forrest, *CFO*
◆ EMP: 11 EST: 1951
SALES (est): 4.9MM
SALES (corp-wide): 1.6B **Privately Held**
SIC: 3699 3273 3281 3271 Security devices; ready-mixed concrete; stone, quarrying & processing of own stone products; concrete block & brick; asphalt paving mixtures & blocks; cement
PA: Golden Gate Private Equity Incorporated
    1 Embarcadero Ctr Fl 39
    San Francisco CA 94111
    415 983-2706

(G-483)
DIAGNOSTIC TEST GROUP LLC
Also Called: Clarity Diagnostics
1060 Holland Dr Ste A (33487-2758)
PHONE......................................561 347-5760
Rick Simpson, *CEO*
Dave Wilbert, *President*
Jason Lustig, *CFO*
EMP: 12 EST: 2003
SALES (est): 1.5MM **Privately Held**
WEB: www.claritydiagnostics.com
SIC: 3841 Diagnostic apparatus, medical

(G-484)
DILIGENT WLDG FABRICATION LLC (HQ)
Also Called: Phillips Metal Products
3500 Nw Boca Raton Blvd (33431-5851)
PHONE......................................561 620-4900
Ivana Montague,
EMP: 7 EST: 2019
SALES (est): 299.2K
SALES (corp-wide): 10.7MM **Privately Held**
SIC: 7692 Welding repair
PA: Diligent Holdings, Llc
    2730 Nw 1st Ave
    Boca Raton FL 33431
    561 699-9000

(G-485)
DIOXIDE MATERIALS INC
1100 Holland Dr (33487-2701)
PHONE......................................217 239-1400
Rich Masel, *CEO*
Jerry Kaczur, *Senior Engr*
Sharon Collinsmasel, *Human Resources*
EMP: 12 EST: 2009
SALES (est): 2.6MM **Privately Held**
WEB: www.dioxidematerials.com
SIC: 2821 8731 3629 Polystyrene resins; commercial research laboratory; electro-chemical generators (fuel cells)

(G-486)
DIRECT MAIL VELOCITY LLC ✪
1200 S Rogers Cir Ste 8 (33487-5703)
PHONE......................................561 393-4722
David P Adams, *CEO*
Greg Nelson, *President*
Owen McCullough, *Manager*
EMP: 7 EST: 2022
SALES (est): 125.5K **Privately Held**
WEB: www.maildmi.com
SIC: 2752 Commercial printing, lithographic

(G-487)
DIRECT RESPONSE PUBLICATION
Also Called: D R P
315 Se Mizner Blvd # 208 (33432-6086)
PHONE......................................561 620-3010
Richard Giarratana, *President*
Kyle Franch, *General Mgr*
▲ EMP: 19 EST: 1985
SQ FT: 1,000
SALES (est): 1.1MM **Privately Held**
WEB: www.designtrade.net
SIC: 2721 2731 Magazines: publishing only, not printed on site; books: publishing only

(G-488)
DIVINE DOVETAIL
1050 Nw 1st Ave Ste 7 (33432-2603)
PHONE......................................561 245-7601
Chris G Goddard, *Principal*
EMP: 9 EST: 2007
SALES (est): 244.9K **Privately Held**
SIC: 3429 Cabinet hardware

(G-489)
DOCTOR PICKLE LLC
1279 W Palmetto Park Rd (33427-0801)
PHONE......................................772 985-5919
Harold Pitts, *Mng Member*
EMP: 17
SALES (est): 1MM **Privately Held**
WEB: www.doctorpickle.com
SIC: 2035 Pickles, sauces & salad dressings

(G-490)
DOLPHINE JEWELRY CONTRACTING
Also Called: Stal Creations
9064 Villa Portofino Cir (33496-1752)
PHONE......................................561 488-0355
Emanuel Friedman, *President*
EMP: 7 EST: 1971
SQ FT: 1,600
SALES (est): 89.1K **Privately Held**
SIC: 3911 Jewelry, precious metal

(G-491)
DONNA M WALKER PA
11137 Harbour Springs Cir (33428-1246)
PHONE......................................561 289-0437
Donna Walker, *Principal*
EMP: 7 EST: 2008
SALES (est): 235.7K **Privately Held**
SIC: 3842 Walkers

(G-492)
DOUG SPECIALTIES LLC
5223 Sapphire Vly (33486-1409)
PHONE......................................954 675-6866
Jason R Lurie,
EMP: 24
SALES (corp-wide): 640.5K **Privately Held**
SIC: 2542 Postal lock boxes, mail racks & related products
PA: Doug Specialties Llc
    1259 W Atl Blvrd Ste 122a
    Pompano Beach FL 33069
    954 675-6866

(G-493)
DOVO INC
Also Called: Chemical Manufacturers
11898 Cove Pl (33428-5678)
PHONE......................................754 244-5120
Tammy Dovo, *CEO*
EMP: 10 EST: 2014
SALES (est): 625.8K **Privately Held**
WEB: www.dovo.com
SIC: 2899 Chemical preparations

(G-494)
DR LIPS LLC
11 Plaza Real S Apt 304 (33432-4892)
PHONE......................................352 203-3182
Robert W Gordon, *Principal*
EMP: 7 EST: 2011
SALES (est): 98.6K **Privately Held**
SIC: 2834 Pharmaceutical preparations

(G-495)
DR PEPPER/SEVEN UP INC
Also Called: Dr. Pepper Snapple
7251 W Plmtt Prk Rd Ste 3 (33433-3487)
PHONE...................................561 995-6260
Kathy Gray, *Branch Mgr*
EMP: 12 **Publicly Held**
WEB: www.drpepper.com
SIC: 2086 Soft drinks: packaged in cans, bottles, etc.
HQ: Dr Pepper/Seven Up, Inc.
   6425 Hall Of Fame Ln
   Frisco TX 75034
   972 673-7000

(G-496)
DRAGONS MIRACLE LLC
160 W Camino Real Ste 154 (33432-5942)
PHONE...................................561 670-5546
Angelo Cairo, *Administration*
EMP: 7 EST: 2015
SALES (est): 375.1K **Privately Held**
WEB: www.dragonsmiracle.com
SIC: 2833 Organic medicinal chemicals: bulk, uncompounded

(G-497)
DRIVERS WORLD CORP
20606 Carousel Cir W (33434-3934)
PHONE...................................561 852-5545
Joseph Gimenez, *Principal*
EMP: 9 EST: 2005
SALES (est): 173.7K **Privately Held**
SIC: 3651 5064 Household audio & video equipment; radios, motor vehicle

(G-498)
EAGLE ARTISTIC PRINTING INC
10277 Shireoaks Ln (33498-6402)
PHONE...................................973 476-6301
Julia Leung, *Principal*
EMP: 8 EST: 2010
SALES (est): 19.4K **Privately Held**
SIC: 2752 Commercial printing, offset

(G-499)
ECOSOULIFE USA DIST LLC
3651 Fau Blvd Ste 400 (33431-6489)
PHONE...................................754 212-5456
Romualdo Munoz Jr, *Mng Member*
Brita McGrath,
Yamit Sadok,
EMP: 12 EST: 2015
SQ FT: 7,000
SALES (est): 970K **Privately Held**
SIC: 3229 Tableware, glass or glass ceramic

(G-500)
EDGEONE LLC
Also Called: Edgetech
1141 Holland Dr Ste 1 (33487-2737)
PHONE...................................561 995-7767
David Deveau, *Engineer*
John Spruance, *Manager*
EMP: 22
SALES (corp-wide): 20.3MM **Privately Held**
WEB: www.edgetech.com
SIC: 3826 3812 Analytical instruments; search & navigation equipment
PA: Edgeone Llc
   4 Little Brook Rd
   West Wareham MA 02576
   508 291-0057

(G-501)
EI GLOBAL GROUP LLC
1515 N Federal Hwy # 200 (33432-1911)
PHONE...................................561 999-8989
Steven Megur, *CEO*
Michael Schwartz, *Administration*
Scott Everett,
▲ EMP: 8 EST: 2006
SALES (est): 1.2MM **Privately Held**
WEB: www.eigpersonalcare.com
SIC: 3089 2844 Novelties, plastic; shampoos, rinses, conditioners: hair; face creams or lotions

(G-502)
ELEMENT AIRCRAFT SALES LLC
1001 Sw 20th St (33486-6833)
PHONE...................................954 494-2242

Christopher A Blanchard, *Manager*
EMP: 7 EST: 2017
SALES (est): 494.1K **Privately Held**
WEB: www.element-aviation.com
SIC: 2819 Industrial inorganic chemicals

(G-503)
ELMRIDGE PROTECTION PDTS LLC
1200 Clint Moore Rd Ste 1 (33487-2731)
PHONE...................................561 244-8337
Jonathan Tyfield, *Opers Mgr*
Ira J Gurvitch,
▲ EMP: 8 EST: 2006
SALES (est): 986K **Privately Held**
WEB: www.elmridgeprotection.com
SIC: 3842 Surgical appliances & supplies

(G-504)
ENGLERT ARTS INC
1021 S Rogers Cir Ste 18 (33487-2857)
PHONE...................................561 241-9924
Frank Englert, *President*
Patricia Englert, *Vice Pres*
▼ EMP: 9 EST: 1979
SQ FT: 3,500
SALES (est): 954.6K **Privately Held**
WEB: www.englertarts.com
SIC: 2273 3931 3281 Floor coverings, textile fiber; musical instruments; cut stone & stone products

(G-505)
EPIC PROMOS LLC
6451 E Rogers Cir Ste 3 (33487-2601)
PHONE...................................561 479-8055
Herman Craig, *Principal*
EMP: 8 EST: 2016
SALES (est): 470.8K **Privately Held**
WEB: www.epicpromosfla.com
SIC: 2759 Screen printing

(G-506)
ERAN GROUP INC
3500 Nw 2nd Ave (33431-5866)
PHONE...................................561 289-5021
Ron Ahayon, *Principal*
EMP: 11 EST: 2009
SALES (est): 1.1MM **Privately Held**
WEB: www.eranindustrial.com
SIC: 3646 Commercial indusl & institutional electric lighting fixtures

(G-507)
ESSENTIAL PUBLISHING GROUP LLC (PA)
1140 Holland Dr Ste 21 (33487-2751)
PHONE...................................410 440-5777
EMP: 6 EST: 2017
SALES (est): 456.5K **Privately Held**
WEB: www.essentialpublishinggroup.com
SIC: 2741 Miscellaneous publishing

(G-508)
EUROCRAFT CABINETS INC
1217 Clint Moore Rd (33487-2718)
PHONE...................................561 948-3034
Jeff Canter, *Principal*
▼ EMP: 8 EST: 2003
SALES (est): 756.8K **Privately Held**
WEB: www.eurocraftcabinets.com
SIC: 2434 Wood kitchen cabinets

(G-509)
EXELAN PHARMACEUTICALS INC
370 W Cmino Grdns Blvd St (33432)
PHONE...................................561 287-6631
Brian Christensen, *President*
Terri Arndt, *General Mgr*
Deepak Argawal, *CFO*
Sudip Jadhav, *Associate Dir*
EMP: 3 EST: 2011
SQ FT: 3,500
SALES: 101.5MM **Privately Held**
WEB: www.exelanpharma.com
SIC: 2834 Pharmaceutical preparations
HQ: Cipla Usa Inc.
   10 Independence Blvd # 300
   Warren NJ 07059
   908 356-8900

(G-510)
EXTREME CRAFTS LLC
999 Nw 51st Ste 100 (33431-4478)
PHONE...................................561 989-7400
Frederick M Middleton, *Mng Member*
EMP: 10 EST: 2003
SALES (est): 252.3K **Privately Held**
SIC: 3721 Autogiros

(G-511)
FAF DISTRIBUTION LLC
2200 Nw Corp Blvd Ste 407 (33431-7369)
PHONE...................................561 717-3353
Fatima A Fernandez, *Mng Member*
EMP: 6 EST: 2019
SALES (est): 600.7K **Privately Held**
WEB: www.fafdistribution.com
SIC: 3861 Photographic equipment & supplies

(G-512)
FASTSIGNS2043
2401 N Federal Hwy (33431-7756)
PHONE...................................305 988-5264
Chris Kirby, *CEO*
Ron Herbert, *CFO*
EMP: 14 EST: 2016
SALES (est): 1MM **Privately Held**
WEB: www.fastsigns.com
SIC: 3993 Signs & advertising specialties

(G-513)
FBS FORTIFIED & BALLISTIC SEC
3350 Nw Boca Raton Blvd (33431-6657)
PHONE...................................561 409-6300
David Vranicar, *Mng Member*
EMP: 6 EST: 2011
SALES (est): 343.1K **Privately Held**
WEB: www.customsecuritydoors.com
SIC: 3499 Doors, safe & vault: metal

(G-514)
FIIK SKATEBOARDS LLC (PA)
7050 W Palmetto Park Rd (33433-3426)
PHONE...................................561 316-8234
EMP: 5 EST: 2012
SALES (est): 301.3K **Privately Held**
WEB: www.fiik.com
SIC: 3949 Skateboards

(G-515)
FIRST WAVE BIOPHARMA INC
Also Called: Azurrx
777 W Yamato Rd Ste 502 (33431-4475)
PHONE...................................561 589-7020
James Sapirstein, *Ch of Bd*
Sarah Romano, *CFO*
James E Pennington, *Chief Mktg Ofcr*
Edward J Borkowski, *Director*
EMP: 17 EST: 2014 **Privately Held**
WEB: www.firstwavebio.com
SIC: 2834 Pharmaceutical preparations

(G-516)
FLEXSHOPPER LLC
2700 N Military Trl # 200 (33431-6394)
PHONE...................................561 922-6609
Brad Bernstein, *President*
John Brann, *Partner*
Justin Metzl, *Vice Pres*
Mario Carballosa, *Engineer*
Alisia Onderlinde, *Bookkeeper*
EMP: 30 EST: 2013
SQ FT: 6,400
SALES (est): 17.3MM **Publicly Held**
WEB: www.flexshopper.com
SIC: 3639 2519 3931 Floor waxers & polishers, electric: household; household furniture, except wood or metal: upholstered; musical instruments
PA: Flexshopper, Inc.
   901 W Yamato Rd Ste 260
   Boca Raton FL 33431

(G-517)
FLORIDA DESIGN INC
621 Nw 53rd St Ste 370 (33487-8241)
PHONE...................................561 997-1660
Jeff Lichtenstein, *President*
Ken Baxley, *Publisher*
Linda Donnelly, *Publisher*
Paul Lichtenstein, *Vice Pres*
Jenny Ortegon, *Human Resources*
EMP: 37 EST: 1990

SQ FT: 5,500
SALES (est): 4.8MM **Privately Held**
WEB: www.floridadesign.com
SIC: 2721 Magazines: publishing only, not printed on site

(G-518)
FLORIDA NBTY MANUFACTURING
901 Broken Sound Pkwy Nw (33487-3528)
PHONE...................................561 922-4800
Lynn Boland, *Principal*
Oscar Giraldo, *Technical Mgr*
Jan Przenioslo, *Research*
EMP: 11 EST: 2008
SALES (est): 1.6MM **Privately Held**
SIC: 3999 Manufacturing industries

(G-519)
FLORIDA STUCCO CORP
21195 Boca Rio Rd (33433-2201)
P.O. Box 880023 (33488-0023)
PHONE...................................561 487-1301
Rick Howell, *President*
Tom Skehan, *Sales Staff*
▼ EMP: 21 EST: 1980
SQ FT: 13,000
SALES (est): 4MM **Privately Held**
WEB: www.floridastucco.com
SIC: 3299 3949 Stucco; sporting & athletic goods

(G-520)
FLOSPINE LLC
3651 Fau Blvd Ste 400 (33431-6489)
PHONE...................................561 705-3080
Peter Harris, *President*
James Szalas, *Engineer*
Madison Malloch, *Sales Staff*
EMP: 5 EST: 2011
SQ FT: 800
SALES (est): 540K **Privately Held**
WEB: www.flospine.com
SIC: 3841 Surgical & medical instruments

(G-521)
FOAM FACTORY INC
10137 Spyglass Way (33498-6448)
PHONE...................................954 485-6700
Stan Regent, *President*
Lori Weiss, *Vice Pres*
Loriann Kaczynski, *Sales Staff*
◆ EMP: 40 EST: 1976
SQ FT: 30,000
SALES (est): 2.5MM **Privately Held**
WEB: www.foamfactory.com
SIC: 3086 Packaging & shipping materials, foamed plastic

(G-522)
FOREVER CURRENT STUDIOS LLC
1161 Holland Dr (33487-2702)
PHONE...................................561 544-7303
Gabriel Galinsky, *Director*
EMP: 5 EST: 2018
SALES (est): 343.9K **Privately Held**
WEB: www.forevercurrent.com
SIC: 2741 Miscellaneous publishing

(G-523)
FOREWARN LLC
2650 N Military Trl # 300 (33431-6350)
PHONE...................................561 757-4550
James Reilly, *President*
Aaron Solomon, *Senior VP*
EMP: 5 EST: 2017
SALES (est): 1.3MM **Publicly Held**
WEB: www.forewarn.com
SIC: 7372 Prepackaged software
PA: Fluent, Inc.
   1 N End Ave Fl 9
   New York NY 10282

(G-524)
FRESH START BEVERAGE COMPANY (PA)
Also Called: Fsbc
4001 N Ocean Blvd Apt B30 (33431-5363)
PHONE...................................561 757-6541
Steven Gelerman, *CEO*
Claudette Patron, *President*
Sonia Jackson-Myles, *Principal*
Jack Knott, *Principal*
He Neter Kush Ben Alkebulan, *COO*

EMP: 7 EST: 2013
SQ FT: 1,300
SALES (est): 2.4MM **Privately Held**
WEB: www.bananawave.com
SIC: 2087 5149 2086 2023 Beverage bases; groceries & related products; beverage concentrates; beverages, except coffee & tea; iced tea & fruit drinks, bottled & canned; carbonated beverages, nonalcoholic; bottled & canned; dietary supplements, dairy & non-dairy based

(G-525)
FUEL U FAST INC
5660 Wind Drift Ln (33433-5446)
PHONE.....................................561 654-0212
Derren Garber, *President*
EMP: 6 EST: 2012
SALES (est): 443.6K **Privately Held**
WEB: www.fuelufast.com
SIC: 2869 Fuels

(G-526)
GEOCOMMAND INC
3700 Airport Rd Ste 410 (33431-6423)
PHONE.....................................561 347-9215
EMP: 6
SQ FT: 700
SALES (est): 672.5K **Privately Held**
SIC: 7372 Prepackaged Software Services

(G-527)
GLM PUBLISHING LLC
2165 Nw 30th Rd (33431-6367)
PHONE.....................................561 409-7696
Guy Mancini, *Principal*
EMP: 7 EST: 2013
SALES (est): 251.4K **Privately Held**
WEB: www.seakidstv.com
SIC: 2741 Miscellaneous publishing

(G-528)
GNS TECHNOLOGIES LLC
5612 Pacific Blvd Apt 704 (33433-6793)
PHONE.....................................561 367-3774
Edith Adessa, *Principal*
EMP: 10 EST: 2008
SALES (est): 1.4MM
SALES (corp-wide): 54.9B **Publicly Held**
SIC: 2819 Industrial inorganic chemicals
HQ: The Dow Chemical Company
2211 H H Dow Way
Midland MI 48642
989 636-1000

(G-529)
GOLDEN GLOBAL CORP
21573 San Germain Ave (33433-1004)
PHONE.....................................954 695-7025
Erik Blum, *President*
EMP: 7 EST: 2016
SALES (est): 116.8K **Privately Held**
SIC: 1081 Metal mining services

(G-530)
GOOD JAMS LLC
6450 N Federal Hwy (33487-3155)
PHONE.....................................702 379-5551
EMP: 10 EST: 2017
SALES (est): 802.1K **Privately Held**
SIC: 2033 Jams, jellies & preserves: packaged in cans, jars, etc.

(G-531)
GOT IT INC
Also Called: Kitchens, Baths & Closets
107 E Palmetto Park Rd (33432-4818)
PHONE.....................................954 899-0001
Paul Remolina, *President*
Holly Sauer, *Vice Pres*
EMP: 8 EST: 2015
SALES (est): 411.6K **Privately Held**
SIC: 2514 2394 Metal lawn & garden furniture; canvas awnings & canopies

(G-532)
GRAPHIC PRINTING CORP
751 Park Of Commerce Dr (33487-3626)
PHONE.....................................561 994-3586
Matthew Stern, *President*
Sam Ghanem, *Exec VP*
Mindy Stern, *CFO*
EMP: 27 EST: 1983
SQ FT: 6,000

SALES (est): 5MM **Privately Held**
WEB: www.gpclabels.com
SIC: 2759 Flexographic printing; screen printing

(G-533)
GRINNELL LLC (DH)
Also Called: Grinnell Fire Prtction Systems
1501 Nw 51st St (33431-4438)
PHONE.....................................561 988-3658
John F Fort, *CEO*
Jerry Boggess, *Exec VP*
Robert Mead, *Exec VP*
Stephanie Trammell, *Opers Staff*
Brandon Mann, *Technical Staff*
▲ EMP: 500 EST: 1895
SALES (est): 245.4MM **Privately Held**
SIC: 3569 3491 Sprinkler systems, fire: automatic; automatic regulating & control valves; fire hydrant valves; water works valves; gas valves & parts, industrial
HQ: Johnson Controls Fire Protection Lp
6600 Congress Ave
Boca Raton FL 33487
561 988-7200

(G-534)
GROM SOCIAL ENTERPRISES INC (PA)
2060 Nw Boca Raton Blvd (33431-7414)
PHONE.....................................561 287-5776
Darren Marks, *Ch of Bd*
Ismael Llera, *Vice Pres*
Melvin Leiner, *CFO*
EMP: 34 EST: 2014
SQ FT: 2,100
SALES (est): 6.3MM **Publicly Held**
WEB: www.gromsocial.com
SIC: 7372 Prepackaged software

(G-535)
GULFSTREAM GOODWILL INDS INC
1662 N Federal Hwy (33432-1930)
PHONE.....................................561 362-8662
EMP: 42
SALES (corp-wide): 48.6MM **Privately Held**
WEB: www.goggi.org
SIC: 3999 Atomizers, toiletry
PA: Gulfstream Goodwill Industries, Inc.
1715 E Tiffany Dr
Mangonia Park FL 33407
561 848-7200

(G-536)
HAND CARVED CREATIONS
5331 N Dixie Hwy Ste 3 (33487-4920)
PHONE.....................................561 893-0292
Errol Palmer, *President*
EMP: 5 EST: 2003
SALES (est): 402K **Privately Held**
WEB: www.handcarvedcreation.com
SIC: 2434 Wood kitchen cabinets

(G-537)
HANDCRAFT WOODWORKING INC
7608 Nw 6th Ave (33487-1319)
PHONE.....................................561 241-9911
EMP: 7 EST: 2011
SALES (est): 353.7K **Privately Held**
SIC: 2431 Millwork

(G-538)
HARDWARE PARTS CORPORATION
5030 Champion Blvd 6250 (33496-2473)
PHONE.....................................561 994-2121
Bernice Cornfield, *President*
▲ EMP: 5 EST: 1988
SALES (est): 426.1K **Privately Held**
SIC: 3325 Steel foundries

(G-539)
HOOT/WISDOM MUSIC PUBG LLC
777 Glades Rd (33431-6424)
PHONE.....................................561 297-3205
Sid M Breman, *Principal*
EMP: 7 EST: 2010
SALES (est): 67.4K **Privately Held**
WEB: www.hootwisdom.com
SIC: 2741 Miscellaneous publishing

(G-540)
HUT GLOBAL INC
Also Called: Volume Cases
131 S Federal Hwy Apt 721 (33432-4961)
P.O. Box 654 (33429-0654)
PHONE.....................................561 571-2523
Michael Bordack, *Vice Pres*
EMP: 5 EST: 2014
SALES (est): 593.6K **Privately Held**
SIC: 3161 5045 Cases, carrying; printers, computer

(G-541)
IMAGE 360
6560 E Rogers Cir (33487-2655)
PHONE.....................................561 395-0745
Mary Sol Gonzalez, *Principal*
Les Lipman, *Consultant*
EMP: 7 EST: 2013
SALES (est): 165.9K **Privately Held**
SIC: 3993 Signs & advertising specialties

(G-542)
IMPERX INC (PA)
6421 Congress Ave Ste 204 (33487-2859)
PHONE.....................................561 989-0006
Petko Dinev, *President*
Melissa Pangburn, *Opers Staff*
Gregory A Pangburn, *CFO*
Gregory Pangburn, *CFO*
EMP: 25 EST: 2001
SQ FT: 10,833
SALES (est): 11.5MM **Privately Held**
WEB: www.imperx.com
SIC: 3861 Cameras & related equipment

(G-543)
IMPRESSIONS DRY CLEANERS INC
6201 N Federal Hwy Ste 1 (33487-3200)
PHONE.....................................561 988-3030
Pete Averill,
EMP: 10 EST: 2001
SALES (est): 507K **Privately Held**
WEB: www.mydrycleantogo.com
SIC: 2842 Specialty cleaning preparations

(G-544)
INFOR (US) LLC
5464 Fox Hollwo Dr (33486)
PHONE.....................................407 916-9100
Toshia Kaar, *Project Mgr*
Elaine Schroeder, *VP Sales*
Bill Von Goetz, *Accounts Mgr*
Tyler Johnson, *Business Anlyst*
Bryon Young, *Branch Mgr*
EMP: 22
SALES (corp-wide): 36.9B **Privately Held**
WEB: www.infor.com
SIC: 7372 Prepackaged software
HQ: Infor (Us), Llc
641 Ave Of The Americas
New York NY 10011
866 244-5479

(G-545)
INSTAZORB INTERNATIONAL INC
500 Ne Spanish River Blvd (33431-4515)
P.O. Box 58, Hallandale (33008-0058)
PHONE.....................................561 416-7302
Tom Payne, *CEO*
Siren Corn, *Admin Sec*
EMP: 5 EST: 1997
SALES (est): 883.2K **Privately Held**
WEB: www.instazorb.com
SIC: 3559 Degreasing machines, automotive & industrial

(G-546)
INTEGRAL WD CSTM CABINETRY LLC
Also Called: C.A.c Custom Artisan Cabinetry
176 Glades Rd Ste A (33432-1649)
PHONE.....................................561 361-5111
Enzo Barni, *Mng Member*
Elvio Barni,
Jose Barni,
EMP: 12 EST: 2015
SQ FT: 11,600
SALES (est): 2.7MM **Privately Held**
SIC: 2434 Wood kitchen cabinets

(G-547)
INTERACTIVE MEDIA TECH INC (PA)
Also Called: Globaltel
7999 N Federal Hwy # 400 (33487-1673)
PHONE.....................................561 999-9116
Steven Williams, *President*
Lee Parmeter, *Engineer*
Melissa Allison, *Controller*
Steve Wlliams, *Technology*
EMP: 12 EST: 1991
SQ FT: 6,000
SALES (est): 7.3MM **Privately Held**
WEB: www.globaltel.com
SIC: 2833 7389 Vitamins, natural or synthetic: bulk, uncompounded; telephone services

(G-548)
INTERIOR DESIGN
3651 Fau Blvd Ste 200 (33431-6489)
PHONE.....................................646 805-0200
Nora Fried, *Business Mgr*
Julie Arkin, *Director*
Mark McMenamin, *Senior Editor*
EMP: 15 EST: 2018
SALES (est): 3.1MM **Privately Held**
WEB: www.interiordesign.net
SIC: 2721 Magazines: publishing only, not printed on site

(G-549)
INTERIOR DSIGN MEDIA GROUP LLC
3731 Fau Blvd Ste 1 (33431-6412)
PHONE.....................................561 750-0151
Katie Brockman, *Publisher*
Stacey Callahan, *Publisher*
Debby Steiner, *Publisher*
Amy Tambini, *Publisher*
Jim Wilson, *Publisher*
EMP: 77 EST: 2010
SALES (est): 3.5MM
SALES (corp-wide): 78.7MM **Privately Held**
SIC: 2721 Magazines: publishing only, not printed on site
PA: Sandow Media, Llc
3651 Nw 8th Ave Ste 200
Boca Raton FL 33431
561 961-7749

(G-550)
INTERNATIONAL FINISHES INC
7777 Glades Rd (33434-4194)
PHONE.....................................561 948-1066
George M Deacon, *Director*
Vicky A Deacon, *Director*
EMP: 13 EST: 1995
SALES (est): 899.9K **Privately Held**
SIC: 2843 Finishing agents

(G-551)
INTERTECH WORLDWIDE CORP (PA)
4400 N Federal Hwy # 125 (33431-5187)
PHONE.....................................561 395-5441
David A Igdaloff, *President*
Nilma M Igdaloff, *Vice Pres*
▲ EMP: 5 EST: 1978
SALES (est): 2.7MM **Privately Held**
SIC: 3433 Gas-oil burners, combination

(G-552)
INTRALOCK INTERNATIONAL INC
6560 W Rogers Cir Ste 24 (33487-2746)
PHONE.....................................561 447-8282
Thierry Girono, *CEO*
Angie Fratichelli, *Office Mgr*
Mary Jean, *Manager*
Rob Rhees, *Education*
EMP: 9 EST: 2019
SALES (est): 539.7K **Privately Held**
WEB: www.intra-lock.com
SIC: 3843 Dental equipment & supplies

(G-553)
ISLAND NATURAL ORIGINALS LLC
150 Nw 16th St (33432-1607)
PHONE.....................................561 287-0095
Melody Legore, *Principal*
EMP: 9 EST: 2016

SALES (est): 247.5K **Privately Held**
SIC: 2911 Mineral oils, natural

(G-554)
ISOCIALMEDIA DIGITAL MARKETING
433 Plaza Real Ste 275 (33432-3999)
PHONE..............................561 510-1124
Celeste Velez, *President*
EMP: 9 EST: 2019
SALES (est): 342K **Privately Held**
WEB: isocialmedia.business.site
SIC: 2741

(G-555)
ITILES LLC
2255 Glades Rd Ste 324a (33431-8571)
PHONE..............................954 609-0984
Nicola Borelli,
EMP: 6 EST: 2011
SQ FT: 3,000
SALES (est): 1.2MM **Privately Held**
SIC: 3272 Floor slabs & tiles, precast concrete

(G-556)
JAMERICA INC
11188 Jasmine Hill Cir (33498-1923)
PHONE..............................561 488-6247
John Maslauskas, *Principal*
EMP: 8 EST: 2010
SALES (est): 201.9K **Privately Held**
SIC: 2329 Men's & boys' clothing

(G-557)
JARDEN PLASTIC SOLUTIONS
2381 Nw Executive Ctr Dr (33431-8560)
PHONE..............................864 879-8100
Martin E Franklin, *Principal*
EMP: 7 EST: 2010
SALES (est): 476.6K **Privately Held**
SIC: 3089 8748 Injection molding of plastics; systems analysis & engineering consulting services

(G-558)
JAZZIZ MAGAZINE INC
2650 N Military Trl # 140 (33431-6350)
P.O. Box 880189 (33488-0189)
PHONE..............................561 893-6868
Michael Fagien, *President*
Lori Fagien, *Owner*
Brian Zimmerman, *Editor*
Karen Rosenfeld, *CPA*
Geoffrey Fagien, *Adv Dir*
EMP: 36 EST: 1983
SQ FT: 2,500
SALES (est): 2.4MM **Privately Held**
WEB: www.jazziz.com
SIC: 2721 3652 Magazines: publishing only, not printed on site; pre-recorded records & tapes

(G-559)
JC VOYAGE LLC (PA)
2403 Nw 30th Rd (33431-6214)
PHONE..............................603 686-0065
Jessica Huber, *Mng Member*
Colette Shoemaker, *Mng Member*
EMP: 6 EST: 2019
SALES (est): 463.6K **Privately Held**
SIC: 2341 Women's & children's undergarments

(G-560)
JES PUBLISHING CORP
Also Called: Boca Raton Magazine
1000 Clint Moore Rd # 103 (33487-2806)
P.O. Box 820 (33429-0820)
PHONE..............................561 997-8683
Margaret Shuff, *President*
Maureen Hahn, *Research*
John Shuff, *Treasurer*
Gary Kot, *Manager*
Thomas Graziano, *Director*
EMP: 24 EST: 1981
SQ FT: 3,208
SALES (est): 3.8MM **Privately Held**
WEB: www.bocamag.com
SIC: 2721 Magazines: publishing only, not printed on site

(G-561)
JIBE LTG N AMER LTD LBLTY CO
9825 Marina Blvd (33428-6628)
PHONE..............................954 899-4040
Todd Darling, *Mng Member*
EMP: 11 EST: 2019
SALES (est): 32MM **Privately Held**
SIC: 3648 Lighting fixtures, except electric: residential

(G-562)
JKG GROUP
160 Nw 51st St (33431-4226)
PHONE..............................561 866-2850
Josh Aragon, *Director*
EMP: 8 EST: 2014
SALES (est): 201.9K **Privately Held**
SIC: 2752 Commercial printing, offset

(G-563)
JO MO ENTERPRISES INC
Also Called: Vince & Sons Pasta Co
20966 Estada Ln (33433-1756)
PHONE..............................708 599-8098
Robert Okon, *President*
Michael Okon, *Vice Pres*
EMP: 8 EST: 2013
SQ FT: 10,000
SALES (est): 237.6K **Privately Held**
SIC: 2099 2038 2098 5142 Packaged combination products: pasta, rice & potato; spaghetti & meatballs, frozen; macaroni & spaghetti; dinners, frozen

(G-564)
JODAR INC
354 Ne 5th St (33432-4051)
PHONE..............................561 375-6277
Darin Matera, *Principal*
EMP: 15 EST: 2005
SALES (est): 374.5K **Privately Held**
SIC: 3714 Motor vehicle parts & accessories

(G-565)
KAY DIAMOND PRODUCTS LLC
1080 Holland Dr Ste 2 (33487-2782)
PHONE..............................561 994-5400
George Clesi, *QC Mgr*
John Kay, *Mng Member*
EMP: 12 EST: 2002
SALES (est): 996K **Privately Held**
WEB: www.kaydp.com
SIC: 3291 Abrasive products

(G-566)
KEA KITCHEN CABINETRY INC
6310 Walk Cir (33433-7801)
PHONE..............................954 639-6233
Andre J Desouza, *Branch Mgr*
EMP: 18
SALES (corp-wide): 53.7K **Privately Held**
SIC: 2434 Wood kitchen cabinets
PA: Kea Kitchen Cabinetry Inc
5523 N Military Trl # 121
Boca Raton FL

(G-567)
KELLSTROM AEROSPACE GROUP INC (HQ)
2500 N Military Trl Ste 4 (33431-6344)
PHONE..............................954 538-2482
Jeff Lund, *President*
Oscar Torres, *COO*
John McKirdy, *Senior VP*
EMP: 21 EST: 2015
SALES (est): 48.1MM
SALES (corp-wide): 1B **Privately Held**
WEB: www.aeroequity.com
SIC: 3369 3324 Aerospace castings, nonferrous: except aluminum; aerospace investment castings, ferrous
PA: Ae Industrial Partners, Lp
2500 N Military Trl Ste 4
Boca Raton FL 33431
561 372-7820

(G-568)
KETER NORTH AMERICA LLC (HQ)
901 W Yamato Rd Ste 180 (33431-4409)
PHONE..............................765 298-6800
Amy Kropp, *Vice Pres*
Dolores Davalos, *Accountant*

Orgad Shapiro, *Mng Member*
Michael Goodman, *Manager*
Elliott Smith, *Manager*
▲ EMP: 5 EST: 2007
SALES (est): 7MM **Privately Held**
SIC: 2392 2519 Household furnishings; lawn & garden furniture, except wood & metal

(G-569)
KINETICS USA INC
Also Called: Real Time Labratories
990 S Rogers Cir Ste 5 (33487-2836)
PHONE..............................561 988-8826
Bob Knabe, *President*
▲ EMP: 36 EST: 1999
SALES (est): 6.3MM **Privately Held**
SIC: 3823 3492 Fluidic devices, circuits & systems for process control; fluid power valves & hose fittings
HQ: Kinetics Ltd.

Airport City 70199

(G-570)
KNEX LTD PARTNERSHIP GROUP
301 E Yamato Rd Ste 4200 (33431-4933)
PHONE..............................215 997-7722
Michael Araten, *CEO*
◆ EMP: 84 EST: 2006
SALES (est): 5MM **Privately Held**
SIC: 3944 Games, toys & children's vehicles

(G-571)
KOOL LEDZ LLC
21238 Stonewood Dr (33428-1014)
PHONE..............................561 212-5843
Elaine Kuter, *Treasurer*
Angela Herrera,
Camille Filoramo,
EMP: 7 EST: 2007
SQ FT: 4,000
SALES (est): 695K **Privately Held**
SIC: 3499 Novelties & giftware, including trophies

(G-572)
KRS GLOBAL BIOTECHNOLOGY INC
Also Called: Krs Global Biotechnology Mfg
791 Park Of Commerce Blvd # 600 (33487-3633)
PHONE..............................888 502-2050
Charles P Richardson, *CEO*
Riccardo Roscetti, *General Mgr*
Kelsey McDaniel, *Production*
Mirtha Fonte-Okunski, *CFO*
Viviana Rodriguez, *CFO*
▲ EMP: 40 EST: 2001
SALES (est): 11.7MM **Privately Held**
WEB: www.krsbio.com
SIC: 2834 5122 Pharmaceutical preparations; drugs, proprietaries & sundries
PA: Cleveland Diabetes Care, Inc.
10752 Deerwood Park Blvd
Jacksonville FL 32256
904 394-2620

(G-573)
KULFI LLC
1100 Holland Dr (33487-2701)
PHONE..............................855 488-4273
Syed Shah, *CEO*
Fred Hassan, *Chairman*
Ed Henricks, *Controller*
Patrick Corsino, *Exec Dir*
EMP: 30 EST: 2013
SALES (est): 4.5MM **Privately Held**
WEB: www.nestlehealthscience.us
SIC: 2099 8049 Food preparations; dietician; nutritionist

(G-574)
LASER PHOTO-TOOLING SVCS INC
Also Called: Lps
5081 N Dixie Hwy (33431-4922)
PHONE..............................561 393-4710
John Leyva, *CEO*
Steven Angona, *Vice Pres*
Jeff Ankenney, *Engineer*
EMP: 12 EST: 1987
SQ FT: 5,000

SALES (est): 5.4MM **Privately Held**
WEB: www.l-p-s.com
SIC: 3672 Printed circuit boards

(G-575)
LATITUDE CLEAN TECH GROUP INC
190 Nw Spanish River Blvd # 101 (33431-4217)
PHONE..............................561 417-0687
EMP: 11
SALES (est): 732.3K **Privately Held**
SIC: 3589 Mfg Service Industry Machinery

(G-576)
LAUNDROMART
23182 Sandalfoot Plaza Dr (33428-6627)
PHONE..............................561 487-4343
Lawerence Percipo, *Principal*
EMP: 8 EST: 2006
SALES (est): 156K **Privately Held**
SIC: 2499 Hampers, laundry

(G-577)
LEOPARD BRANDS INC
6800 E Rogers Cir (33487-2651)
PHONE..............................954 794-0007
Harris Pollock, *President*
Peter Antonacci, *Treasurer*
▲ EMP: 7 EST: 2010
SALES (est): 969.7K **Privately Held**
WEB: www.leopardbrands.com
SIC: 2252 Socks

(G-578)
LEXINGTON INTERNATIONAL LLC
Also Called: Hairmax Lasercomb
1040 Holland Dr (33487-2759)
PHONE..............................800 973-4769
Leonard Stillman, *Vice Pres*
Grant Gunderson, *Sales Staff*
Greg Riofrio, *Sales Staff*
Chris Latorre, *Manager*
David Michaels, *Manager*
▲ EMP: 30 EST: 2000
SALES (est): 5MM **Privately Held**
WEB: www.hairmax.com
SIC: 3845 Laser systems & equipment, medical

(G-579)
LF OF AMERICA CORP
7700 Congress Ave # 1120 (33487-1352)
PHONE..............................561 988-0303
Ferrari Giovanni, *Vice Pres*
Diego Bulgarelli, *Sales Staff*
▲ EMP: 5 EST: 2002
SQ FT: 40,000
SALES (est): 522.9K **Privately Held**
WEB: www.lfofamerica.com
SIC: 2844 2834 Cosmetic preparations; proprietary drug products

(G-580)
MAFEKS INTERNATIONAL LLC
4755 Tech Way Ste 208 (33431)
PHONE..............................561 997-2080
Susan Morgan, *Traffic Mgr*
Natasha Craig, *Sales Staff*
Frieda Foster, *Sales Staff*
Howard McCall Jr,
▼ EMP: 16 EST: 2003
SQ FT: 3,500
SALES (est): 895.9K **Privately Held**
SIC: 3531 Railway track equipment

(G-581)
MAGELLAN AVIATION GROUP LLLP
1100 Holland Dr (33487-2701)
PHONE..............................561 266-0845
Larry Grogan, *Partner*
Linda Manfre, *Accountant*
EMP: 90 **Privately Held**
WEB: www.magellangroup.net
SIC: 3724 Aircraft engines & engine parts
HQ: Magellan Aviation Group Lllp
2345 Township Rd Ste B
Charlotte NC 28273
704 504-9204

(G-582)
MALEMA ENGINEERING CORPORATION (DH)
Also Called: Malema Flow Sensors
1060 S Rogers Cir (33487-2815)
PHONE.............................561 995-0595
Anand Malani, CEO
Deepak B Malani, President
Rahul Malani, Principal
Mannan Bandukwala, Vice Pres
Kalash Jhamb, QC Mgr
▲ EMP: 10 EST: 1981
SQ FT: 10,500
SALES (est): 10.3MM
SALES (corp-wide): 7.9B Publicly Held
WEB: www.malema.com
SIC: 3823 3625 Industrial instrmnts msrmnt display/control process variable; flow actuated electrical switches
HQ: Dover Pumps & Process Solutions Segment, Inc.
3005 Highland Pkwy # 200
Downers Grove IL 60515
630 541-1540

(G-583)
MARITIME REPLICAS USA LLC
70 Dorset B (33434-3006)
PHONE.............................305 921-9690
Warren R Samut,
EMP: 25 EST: 2014
SALES (est): 694.7K Privately Held
WEB: www.maritimereplicas.com
SIC: 3944 Boat & ship models, toy & hobby

(G-584)
MARK BENTON
Also Called: Enforty
900 N Federal Hwy (33432-2755)
PHONE.............................754 203-9377
Mark Benton, Owner
EMP: 30 EST: 2020
SALES (est): 1.1MM Privately Held
WEB: www.enforty.com
SIC: 2254 Shorts, shirts, slips & panties (underwear): knit

(G-585)
MARKETSHARE LLC
6790 E Rogers Cir (33487-2649)
PHONE.............................631 273-0598
Nancy Mantell, Principal
Steven Zaken, Co-Owner
David Guarnieri, Vice Pres
Jennifer Boudreau, Manager
Monique Greene, Manager
EMP: 5 EST: 2003
SALES (est): 434.5K Privately Held
SIC: 2752 3991 Playing cards, lithographed; toothbrushes, except electric

(G-586)
MARLO ELECTRONICS INC
2412 Nw 35th St (33431-5412)
PHONE.............................561 477-0856
Mark Goddard, President
Steven Goddard, Admin Sec
EMP: 23 EST: 1966
SQ FT: 35,000
SALES (est): 1.9MM Privately Held
SIC: 3672 Printed circuit boards

(G-587)
MASC ASPEN PARTNERS LLC
17639 Lake Estates Dr (33496-1425)
PHONE.............................212 545-1076
Martin L Markowitz, Mng Member
EMP: 7 EST: 2005
SALES (est): 83.9K Privately Held
SIC: 2752 Commercial printing, lithographic

(G-588)
MCCORMICK RESTAURANT SERVICES
7682 Solimar Cir (33433-1035)
PHONE.............................561 706-5554
EMP: 8 EST: 2001
SALES (est): 125.1K Privately Held
SIC: 2099 Spices, including grinding

(G-589)
MCMILL LLC
4800 N Federal Hwy 302d (33431-3414)
PHONE.............................561 279-3232
Linda McGuffie, Principal
EMP: 8 EST: 2013
SALES (est): 247.6K Privately Held
SIC: 2652 Setup paperboard boxes

(G-590)
MEDATTEND LLC
1200 Clint Moore Rd Ste 5 (33487-2731)
PHONE.............................561 465-2735
Gregory Kis, Mng Member
EMP: 10 EST: 2016
SALES (est): 767K Privately Held
SIC: 3669 Emergency alarms

(G-591)
MEDFARE LLC
6560 W Rogers Cir Ste 13 (33487-2746)
PHONE.............................561 998-9444
Amy Lee, Opers Staff
Gary Lorenz, Mng Member
EMP: 10 EST: 1974
SALES (est): 1.3MM Privately Held
WEB: www.medfare.com
SIC: 2752 Commercial printing, offset

(G-592)
MEDIAOPS INC
751 Park Of Commerce Dr # 108 (33487-3622)
PHONE.............................516 857-7409
Alan Shimel, CEO
Saleem Padani, COO
Parker Yates, Officer
EMP: 30 EST: 2013
SALES (est): 2.6MM Privately Held
SIC: 7372 Prepackaged software

(G-593)
MERIDIAN CENTRE
6531 Park Of Commerce Blv (33487-8299)
PHONE.............................253 620-4542
Jeff Dixon, General Mgr
Eric Chirinsky, Manager
EMP: 7 EST: 2011
SALES (est): 114.5K Privately Held
SIC: 2421 Building & structural materials, wood

(G-594)
MERIDIAN LIFE SCIENCE INC
1121 Holland Dr Ste 27 (33487-2736)
PHONE.............................561 241-0223
Debbie Colombo, Branch Mgr
EMP: 10
SALES (corp-wide): 317.9MM Publicly Held
WEB: www.meridianbioscience.com
SIC: 2835 Microbiology & virology diagnostic products
HQ: Meridian Life Science, Inc.
60 Industrial Park Rd
Saco ME 04072
207 283-6500

(G-595)
METRITEK GROUP LLC
370 Camino Gardens Blvd (33432-5816)
PHONE.............................561 995-2414
Robert Jablin, Mng Member
Edward Meyer,
EMP: 5 EST: 2019
SALES (est): 313.1K Privately Held
SIC: 2221 Textile mills, broadwoven: silk & manmade, also glass

(G-596)
MICA PDTS & WD BOCA RATON INC
150 Glades Rd (33432-1605)
PHONE.............................561 395-4686
Gregory Heinmiller, President
David L Risley, Vice Pres
EMP: 40 EST: 1974
SQ FT: 5,000
SALES (est): 4.2MM Privately Held
WEB: www.micaproductsandwood.com
SIC: 2434 Wood kitchen cabinets

(G-597)
MICROCOMPUTER SERVICES
1200 S Rogers Cir Ste 8 (33487-5703)
PHONE.............................561 988-7000
Cobden Lyn, Managing Prtnr
Brian Davies, Partner
EMP: 5 EST: 1993
SALES (est): 519K Privately Held
WEB: www.mcscompany.com
SIC: 2759 7379 7331 Commercial printing; data processing consultant; direct mail advertising services

(G-598)
MIDWAY LABS USA LLC
6401 Congress Ave Ste 100 (33487-2841)
P.O. Box 480573, Delray Beach (33448-0573)
PHONE.............................561 571-6252
Wilton Colle, President
Catherine Colle, Vice Pres
Peter Giallorenzo, CFO
Christine Hassel, Executive Asst
▼ EMP: 10 EST: 2006
SQ FT: 4,000
SALES (est): 2.1MM Privately Held
WEB: www.midwaylabsusa.com
SIC: 2833 Medicinals & botanicals

(G-599)
MILANO WORLDWIDE CORP
222 W Yamato Rd Ste 106 (33431-4704)
PHONE.............................561 266-0201
Paula Kruger, CEO
Flavia Milano, President
▲ EMP: 5 EST: 2005
SQ FT: 900
SALES (est): 456.3K Privately Held
WEB: www.milanoworldwide.com
SIC: 3229 Art, decorative & novelty glassware

(G-600)
MISFIT GAMING
6401 Congress Ave (33487-2843)
PHONE.............................954 347-0906
Ben Spoont, CEO
EMP: 99 EST: 2016
SALES (est): 3.5MM Privately Held
SIC: 3944 Electronic game machines, except coin-operated

(G-601)
MMP-BOCA RATON LLC
Also Called: Nml
1609 Nw 2nd Ave (33432-1654)
PHONE.............................561 392-8626
Michael Orr,
EMP: 11 EST: 2008
SALES (est): 967.7K Privately Held
SIC: 2752 Commercial printing, offset

(G-602)
MOBILEHELP LLC (HQ)
5050 Conference Way N # 125 (33431-4462)
PHONE.............................561 347-6255
Robert S Flippo, CEO
Dennis V Boyle, President
Elias Janetis, Principal
Scott H Adams, Chairman
Ellen Declaire, Vice Pres
▲ EMP: 70 EST: 2006
SQ FT: 45,000
SALES (est): 51.6MM
SALES (corp-wide): 12.8B Privately Held
WEB: www.mobilehelp.com
SIC: 3841 Biopsy instruments & equipment; diagnostic apparatus, medical; medical instruments & equipment, blood & bone work; instruments, microsurgical: except electromedical
PA: Advocate Aurora Health Inc.
3075 Highland Pkwy Fl 6
Downers Grove IL 60515
630 572-9393

(G-603)
MODERNIZING MEDICINE INC (PA)
Also Called: Modmed
4850 Network Way Ste 200 (33431)
PHONE.............................561 880-2998
Daniel Cane, CEO
Joe Harpaz, President
Patrick Deangelo, Senior VP
Nicki Anders, Vice Pres
Dan Dalton, Vice Pres
EMP: 127 EST: 2010
SALES (est): 118.4MM Privately Held
WEB: www.modmed.com
SIC: 7372 Application computer software

(G-604)
MODERNZING MDCINE GSTRNTRLOGY
Also Called: Gmed
4850 Network Way Ste 200 (33431)
PHONE.............................561 880-2998
Daniel Cane, CEO
Joe D Rubinsztain, President
Samuel Rubinsztain, President
Gabrielle Rubinsztain, Corp Secy
Samuel Flicki, COO
EMP: 125 EST: 1997
SQ FT: 7,500
SALES (est): 24.4MM
SALES (corp-wide): 118.4MM Privately Held
WEB: www.modmed.com
SIC: 7372 8099 Application computer software; medical services organization
PA: Modernizing Medicine, Inc.
4850 Network Way Ste 200
Boca Raton FL 33431
561 880-2998

(G-605)
MONIER LIFETILE INC
135 Nw 20th St (33431-7901)
PHONE.............................561 338-8200
EMP: 7 EST: 2019
SALES (est): 178.7K Privately Held
SIC: 2952 Asphalt felts & coatings

(G-606)
MULTITRODE INC
6560 E Rogers Cir (33487-2655)
PHONE.............................561 737-1210
Craig S Parkinson, Principal
EMP: 23 EST: 2019
SALES (est): 5.1MM Publicly Held
SIC: 3561 Pumps & pumping equipment
PA: Xylem Inc.
1 International Dr
Rye Brook NY 10573

(G-607)
N E D LLC
902 Clint Moore Rd # 206 (33431-2800)
PHONE.............................610 442-1017
Nick Riccione, Principal
EMP: 9 EST: 2010
SALES (est): 304.1K Privately Held
SIC: 3841 Surgical & medical instruments

(G-608)
NABI
5800 Pk Of Commerce Blvd (33487-8221)
PHONE.............................561 989-5800
Michael Ramroth, Principal
Mike Kulas, Technician
EMP: 14 EST: 2008
SALES (est): 1MM Privately Held
SIC: 2834 Pharmaceutical preparations

(G-609)
NATURECITY LLC
990 S Rogers Cir Ste 11 (33487-2835)
PHONE.............................800 593-2563
Beth Geller, Vice Pres
Beth Giller, Vice Pres
Scott Greenberg, Vice Pres
Carl M Pradelli, Mng Member
Vincent Degiaimo, Mng Member
EMP: 9 EST: 2002
SALES (est): 1.7MM Privately Held
WEB: www.naturecity.com
SIC: 2023 Dietary supplements, dairy & non-dairy based

(G-610)
NATURES BOUNTY CO
1297 Clint Moore Rd (33487-2718)
PHONE.............................800 327-0908
Jeff Wellenbusher, Controller
EMP: 53
SALES (corp-wide): 92.3B Privately Held
WEB: www.bountifulcompany.com
SIC: 2833 Medicinals & botanicals

HQ: The Nature's Bounty Co
110 Orville Dr
Bohemia NY 11716
631 200-2000

(G-611)
NAVINTA III INC
1003 Clint Moore Rd (33487-2826)
PHONE..................................561 997-6959
Mahendra Patel, *CEO*
EMP: 7 **EST:** 2016
SALES (est): 8MM **Privately Held**
WEB: www.navinta.com
SIC: 2834 Druggists' preparations (pharmaceuticals)

(G-612)
NEURO PHARMALOGICS INC
901 Nw 35th St (33431-6410)
PHONE..................................240 476-4491
David Muth, *President*
Ken Dawson-Scully, *Director*
EMP: 5 **EST:** 2016
SQ FT: 2,000
SALES (est): 367.2K **Privately Held**
SIC: 2834 Pills, pharmaceutical

(G-613)
NEW SENTRY MARKETING INC
Also Called: CPD BOTTLING CLOSURE
878 Nafa Dr (33487-1739)
P.O. Box 189, Newtown PA (18940-0189)
PHONE..................................561 982-9599
Daniel Feldman, *President*
Sally Schultz, *Vice Pres*
EMP: 4 **EST:** 2012
SQ FT: 2,700
SALES (est): 5.6MM **Privately Held**
SIC: 3085 Plastics bottles

(G-614)
NEW WORLD GOLD CORPORATION (PA)
Also Called: Nwgc
350 Cmino Grdns Blvd Ste (33432)
PHONE..................................561 962-4139
Robert J Honigford, *CEO*
Robert Talbot, *President*
EMP: 19 **EST:** 2008
SALES (est): 10.7MM **Privately Held**
SIC: 1041 Gold ores processing

(G-615)
NEWBEAUTY MEDIA GROUP LLC
Also Called: Newbeauty Media Group, Lllp
3651 Nw 8th Ave Ste 400 (33431-6489)
PHONE..................................561 961-7600
Adam Sandow, *CEO*
Sarah Eggenberger, *Editor*
Anna Jimenez, *Editor*
Elise Wood, *Vice Pres*
Jennifer Jackolin, *Opers Mgr*
EMP: 50 **EST:** 2004
SQ FT: 30,000
SALES (est): 16MM
SALES (corp-wide): 78.7MM **Privately Held**
SIC: 2759 5122 Publication printing; cosmetics
PA: Sandow Media, Llc
3651 Nw 8th Ave Ste 200
Boca Raton FL 33431
561 961-7749

(G-616)
NEWELL BRANDS INC
2381 Nw Executive Ctr Dr (33431-8560)
PHONE..................................858 729-4138
Rocki Rockingham, *Vice Pres*
Johana Reyes, *Opers Staff*
Daniel Rubia, *QC Mgr*
Jose Betancourt, *Engineer*
Jonathan Davis, *Engineer*
EMP: 53
SALES (corp-wide): 10.5B **Publicly Held**
WEB: www.newellbrands.com
SIC: 3089 Plastic kitchenware, tableware & houseware
PA: Newell Brands Inc.
6655 Pachtree Dunwoody Rd
Atlanta GA 30328
770 418-7000

(G-617)
NICOLETTE MAYER COLLECTION INC
3750 Ne 6th Dr (33431-6114)
PHONE..................................561 241-6906
Nicolette D Mayer, *President*
Jonathan Ostrow, *CFO*
Richard Barnes, *CIO*
◆ **EMP:** 8 **EST:** 2012
SALES (est): 580K **Privately Held**
WEB: www.nicolettemayer.com
SIC: 2679 Wallpaper

(G-618)
NOELL DESIGN GROUP INC
1050 Nw 1st Ave Ste 16 (33432-2603)
PHONE..................................561 391-9942
Mark Noell, *President*
EMP: 7 **EST:** 1995
SQ FT: 18,000
SALES (est): 873.5K **Privately Held**
WEB: www.noelldesigngroup.com
SIC: 2511 Wood household furniture

(G-619)
NORDIC GROUP LLC (PA)
2220 Sw 11th Pl (33486-8511)
PHONE..................................561 789-8676
Kai A Makela, *Manager*
EMP: 6 **EST:** 2015
SALES (est): 502.5K **Privately Held**
WEB: www.nordicgrp.com
SIC: 2339 Women's & misses' outerwear

(G-620)
NORDIC LINE INC (PA)
Also Called: Design NS Leather Furniture
1080 Nw 1st Ave (33432-2608)
PHONE..................................561 338-5545
Aki Makela, *President*
Kai Makela, *Vice Pres*
Vesa Maenanttila, *Manager*
▲ **EMP:** 18 **EST:** 1993
SQ FT: 25,000
SALES (est): 4.8MM **Privately Held**
WEB: www.designns.com
SIC: 2512 5021 Upholstered household furniture; furniture

(G-621)
NOSTALGIC AMERICA INC
102 Ne 2nd St Ste 172 (33432-3908)
P.O. Box 5188, Carefree AZ (85377-5188)
PHONE..................................561 585-1724
Marcia M Berns, *President*
EMP: 10 **EST:** 2001
SALES (est): 610.5K **Privately Held**
WEB: www.nostalgicamerica.com
SIC: 2721 Magazines: publishing only, not printed on site

(G-622)
OAKBROOK SALES INC
2200 Butts Rd Ste 200 (33431-7451)
PHONE..................................800 773-0979
Al Eder, *Treasurer*
EMP: 12 **EST:** 1996
SALES (est): 179.7K **Privately Held**
SIC: 2099 Food preparations

(G-623)
OLLIE PIPPA INTERNATIONAL INC
Also Called: Plantogen Skin Care
21733 Old Bridge Trl (33428-2847)
P.O. Box 970215 (33497-0215)
PHONE..................................888 851-6533
Elda Argenti, *President*
▲ **EMP:** 5 **EST:** 2003
SALES (est): 323K **Privately Held**
SIC: 2844 Cosmetic preparations

(G-624)
OMEGA ONE RESEARCH INC
6458 E Rogers Cir (33487-2653)
PHONE..................................561 995-9611
Carole Hersch, *President*
EMP: 5 **EST:** 2000
SALES (est): 1MM **Privately Held**
WEB: www.omegaoneresearch.com
SIC: 3545 Precision tools, machinists'

(G-625)
OPTOELECTRONICS INC
160 W Camino Real (33432-5942)
PHONE..................................954 642-8997
Linda Hufft, *President*
EMP: 11 **EST:** 1974
SQ FT: 13,000
SALES (est): 1.2MM **Privately Held**
WEB: www.optoelectronics.com
SIC: 3825 3823 Test equipment for electronic & electrical circuits; industrial instrmnts msrmnt display/control process variable

(G-626)
OSMI INC (PA)
7777 Glades Rd Ste 200 (33434-4150)
PHONE..................................561 330-9300
Bernard Mintz, *CEO*
David Mintz, *President*
Neil Mintz, *COO*
Ted Hagberg, *VP Bus Dvlpt*
Perry Slaughter, *Sales Mgr*
◆ **EMP:** 11 **EST:** 1990
SQ FT: 80,000
SALES (est): 13.2MM **Privately Held**
SIC: 3297 Nonclay refractories

(G-627)
OTTICA DANTE AMERICAS LLC
10890 Haydn Dr (33498-6750)
PHONE..................................561 322-0186
Massimo Armiraglio,
Laura Ferrario,
Fabio Massetta,
EMP: 8 **EST:** 2014
SALES (est): 286.4K **Privately Held**
WEB: www.otticadante.com
SIC: 3851 7389 Frames & parts, eyeglass & spectacle;

(G-628)
PACIFIC COAST FEATHER LLC (PA)
901 W Yamato Rd Ste 250 (33431-4415)
PHONE..................................206 624-1057
Alex Blanco, *Vice Pres*
Scott Carlson, *Vice Pres*
Pedro Pena, *Plant Mgr*
James Elnathan, *Opers Staff*
Elana Aberge, *VP Finance*
◆ **EMP:** 150 **EST:** 2017
SALES (est): 257MM **Privately Held**
WEB: www.pacificcoast.com
SIC: 2392 Cushions & pillows; comforters & quilts: made from purchased materials

(G-629)
PALLET HOLDINGS LLC (PA)
1200 N Federal Hwy # 207 (33432-2803)
PHONE..................................561 367-0009
Marc Steinberg,
David Davidson,
EMP: 65 **EST:** 2003
SALES (est): 10.8MM **Privately Held**
SIC: 2448 Wood pallets & skids

(G-630)
PARAFLOW ENERGY SOLUTIONS LLC
6501 Congress Ave Ste 100 (33487-2840)
PHONE..................................713 239-0336
Jeff Edwards, *President*
EMP: 25 **EST:** 2015
SALES (est): 2.6MM
SALES (corp-wide): 10.8MM **Privately Held**
SIC: 2843 Surface active agents; emulsifiers, except food & pharmaceutical
PA: Verdant Specialty Solutions Us Llc
811 Main St Fl 18
Houston TX 77002
708 259-1364

(G-631)
PARAMOUNT ELECTRONIC MFG CO
Also Called: Pemco
1551 Sw 6th Ter (33486-7005)
PHONE..................................954 781-3755
Michael De Grandchamp, *President*
EMP: 25 **EST:** 1982

SALES (est): 412K
SALES (corp-wide): 4.1MM **Privately Held**
SIC: 3679 Harness assemblies for electronic use: wire or cable
PA: Paramount Industries Inc
1020 Sw 10th Ave Ste 6
Pompano Beach FL 33069
954 781-3755

(G-632)
PARIS INK INC
Also Called: Speedpro Imaging
1020 Holland Dr Ste 119 (33487-5719)
PHONE..................................561 990-1194
Daniel J Paris, *President*
Nathaniel Paris, *Principal*
EMP: 9 **EST:** 2017
SALES (est): 485.9K **Privately Held**
WEB: www.speedpro.com
SIC: 2759 Posters, including billboards: printing

(G-633)
PHOENIX MEDIA NETWORK INC
Also Called: Produce Business Magazine
6531 Pk Of Commerce Blvd (33487-8299)
P.O. Box 810425 (33481-0425)
PHONE..................................561 994-1118
Jim Prevor, *CEO*
Jim Bartelson, *Vice Pres*
E Shaunn Alderman, *Marketing Staff*
Kate Grace, *Marketing Staff*
Lori Schlossberg, *Manager*
EMP: 20 **EST:** 1993
SALES (est): 3.1MM **Privately Held**
WEB: www.phoenixmedianet.com
SIC: 2721 Magazines: publishing only, not printed on site

(G-634)
PIVOTAL THERAPEUTICS US INC
3651 Fau Blvd Ste 400 (33431-6489)
PHONE..................................905 856-9797
Eugene Bortoluzzi, *CEO*
Rachelle Macsweeney, *President*
EMP: 16 **EST:** 2010
SQ FT: 900
SALES (est): 899.8K **Privately Held**
WEB: www.pivotaltherapeutics.us
SIC: 2834 Vitamin, nutrient & hematinic preparations for human use

(G-635)
PIZZA SPICE PACKET LLC
Also Called: Pizza Packet
170 Ne 2nd St Unit 491 (33429-5020)
PHONE..................................718 831-7036
Itchie Gross, *President*
David New, *Opers Staff*
EMP: 7 **EST:** 2009
SALES (est): 511.2K **Privately Held**
WEB: www.pizzapacket.com
SIC: 2038 5142 5411 5812 Pizza, frozen; packaged frozen goods; frozen food & freezer plans, except meat; pizza restaurants

(G-636)
PLUSHBEDS INC
17076 Boca Club Blvd # 4 (33487-1293)
PHONE..................................888 449-5738
Michael Hughes, *Branch Mgr*
EMP: 7
SALES (corp-wide): 1.1MM **Privately Held**
WEB: www.plushbeds.com
SIC: 2515 5712 Mattresses & bedsprings; mattresses
PA: Plushbeds, Inc
5603 Grey Feather Ct
Westlake Village CA

(G-637)
POLY PLASTIC PACKAGING CO INC
Also Called: Polyplastics
18800 Long Lake Dr (33496-1975)
PHONE..................................561 498-9040
EMP: 25 **EST:** 1951
SQ FT: 20,000
SALES (est): 4.1MM **Privately Held**
SIC: 2673 Mfg Bags-Plastic/Coated Paper

GEOGRAPHIC

(G-638)
POWER POINT GRAPHICS INC
19528 Sedgefield Ter (33498-4643)
PHONE.....................561 351-5599
Leonard Rosenthal, *President*
EMP: 6 **EST:** 1997
SALES (est): 447.9K **Privately Held**
SIC: 2759 7389 Commercial printing;
printing broker

(G-639)
PRACTICAL DESIGN PRODUCTS CO
Also Called: P D P
1101 Holland Dr (33487-2762)
PHONE.....................561 995-4023
Jason Bator, *President*
▲ **EMP:** 15 **EST:** 1993
SQ FT: 4,000
SALES (est): 376.8K **Privately Held**
SIC: 3429 Manufactured hardware (general)

(G-640)
PRETTY VULGAR LLC
17605 Circle Pond Ct (33496-1002)
PHONE.....................561 465-8831
Katherine Garcia, *Manager*
Lewis Farsedakis,
EMP: 8 **EST:** 2015
SALES (est): 1.1MM **Privately Held**
WEB: www.prettyvulgar.com
SIC: 2844 Toilet preparations

(G-641)
PRIVE PORTER LLC
980 N Federal Hwy (33432-2708)
PHONE.....................561 479-9200
Michelle Berk, *Principal*
Jeff Bachand, *Store Mgr*
EMP: 6 **EST:** 2013
SALES (est): 328.8K **Privately Held**
WEB: www.priveporter.com
SIC: 2323 Men's & boys' neckwear

(G-642)
PROJECT MOLD
7666 Cypress Cres (33433-4109)
PHONE.....................561 213-6167
Zev Argov, *Principal*
EMP: 8 **EST:** 2017
SALES (est): 133.8K **Privately Held**
SIC: 3544 Industrial molds

(G-643)
QEP CO INC
Also Called: Roberts Consolidated Inds
1001 Broken Sound Pkwy Nw A
(33487-3532)
PHONE.....................561 994-5550
John Ross, *Branch Mgr*
EMP: 8
SALES (corp-wide): 387.6MM **Privately Held**
WEB: www.qepcorporate.com
SIC: 3423 Hand & edge tools
PA: Q.E.P. Co., Inc.
1001 Broken Sound Pkwy Nw A
Boca Raton FL 33487
561 994-5550

(G-644)
QUARTZ UNLIMITED INC
2255 Glades Rd Ste 324 (33431-8571)
P.O. Box 62019, Sunnyvale CA (94088-2019)
PHONE.....................561 720-7460
Ferenc Ledniczky, *President*
Victoria Gaffney, *Vice Pres*
EMP: 30 **EST:** 1996
SQ FT: 6,000
SALES (est): 522.6K **Privately Held**
SIC: 3679 Quartz crystals, for electronic application

(G-645)
QUARTZ UNLIMITED LLC
5030 Champion Blvd (33496-2473)
PHONE.....................561 306-1243
Ferenc Ledniczky, *Principal*
EMP: 5 **EST:** 2011
SALES (est): 364.3K **Privately Held**
WEB: www.quartzunlimited.com
SIC: 3674 Semiconductors & related devices

(G-646)
RACE PART SOLUTIONS
1181 S Rogers Cir Ste 18 (33487-2726)
PHONE.....................561 999-8911
EMP: 7 **EST:** 2005
SALES (est): 82.1K **Privately Held**
WEB: www.racepartsolutions.com
SIC: 3714 Motor vehicle parts & accessories

(G-647)
RANCHERITOS
8903 Glades Rd Ste A10 (33434-4023)
PHONE.....................561 479-0046
Juan G Maya, *Principal*
EMP: 5 **EST:** 2010
SALES (est): 399.9K **Privately Held**
WEB: www.rancheritosdeboca.com
SIC: 2032 Mexican foods: packaged in cans, jars, etc.

(G-648)
RAYTASH INC (PA)
Also Called: New Choices
1420 Sw 1st St (33486-4470)
PHONE.....................561 347-8863
Ray Tashman, *President*
Myra Tashman, *Vice Pres*
Mona Tashman, *Treasurer*
◆ **EMP:** 5 **EST:** 1982
SALES (est): 550.1K **Privately Held**
SIC: 2511 5021 Wood household furniture; restaurant furniture

(G-649)
REAL-TIME LABORATORIES LLC (DH)
990 S Rogers Cir Ste 5 (33487-2836)
PHONE.....................561 988-8826
Kevin Sigurdsen, *Engineer*
Cletus Glasener, *Treasurer*
Robert Knabe, *Mng Member*
Thomas Tracy, *Contract Mgr*
Chris Puffer, *Admin Sec*
▲ **EMP:** 53 **EST:** 1979
SQ FT: 20,000
SALES (est): 10MM **Privately Held**
WEB: www.realtimelab.com
SIC: 3823 Fluidic devices, circuits & systems for process control

(G-650)
REALM LABS LLC
7700 Congress Ave # 3110 (33487-1357)
PHONE.....................561 549-9099
Richard Mann, *Managing Dir*
Annetta Leggett, *Opers Staff*
Andreia Solett, *Accounts Mgr*
Margo Brown,
EMP: 10 **EST:** 2006
SALES (est): 2.1MM **Privately Held**
WEB: www.realmlabs.net
SIC: 2834 Vitamin, nutrient & hematinic preparations for human use

(G-651)
REFLECTIVE MOMENTS LLC
3152 Saint Annes Dr (33496-2516)
PHONE.....................561 716-2106
Cheryl Runsdorf, *Principal*
EMP: 7 **EST:** 2008
SALES (est): 142.4K **Privately Held**
SIC: 3999 Candles

(G-652)
RM IMAGING INCORPORATED
2499 Glades Rd Ste 206 (33431-7201)
PHONE.....................561 361-8090
Rachael Magro, *President*
Joseph Aucello, *Exec Officer*
Jeffrey Nurge, *Exec Officer*
Elias Robert, *Med Doctor*
EMP: 22 **EST:** 1994
SALES (est): 1MM **Privately Held**
SIC: 3841 8071 Diagnostic apparatus, medical; medical laboratories

(G-653)
ROCKET VENDING INC
Also Called: Vending Company
19234 S Creekshore Ct (33498-6217)
P.O. Box 970724, Coconut Creek (33097-0724)
PHONE.....................561 672-1373
Michael Fischer, *CEO*

Dori Mirkow, *Vice Pres*
EMP: 10 **EST:** 2007
SALES (est): 703.8K **Privately Held**
WEB: domain-for-sale.vereo.com
SIC: 3581 Automatic vending machines

(G-654)
ROKEY CORPORATION
18188 Blue Lake Way (33498-1936)
PHONE.....................561 470-0164
EMP: 5
SALES: 3MM **Privately Held**
SIC: 3429 5199 5961 Mfg /Whol/Ret General Merchandise

(G-655)
RUBINELLI WOODWORK INC
8891 Sw 16th St (33433-7966)
PHONE.....................954 445-0537
Paulo Alves, *Principal*
EMP: 8 **EST:** 2007
SALES (est): 82.1K **Privately Held**
SIC: 2431 Millwork

(G-656)
S M D RESEARCH INC
9151 Pine Springs Dr (33428-1458)
PHONE.....................561 451-9895
Stuart P Oakner, *President*
Mark T Brannick, *Treasurer*
▲ **EMP:** 8 **EST:** 1997
SQ FT: 2,000
SALES (est): 196.4K **Privately Held**
SIC: 2899 Chemical preparations

(G-657)
SAFCO SOFTWARE
7654 Solimar Cir (33433-1035)
PHONE.....................561 750-7879
Steven A Fellman, *Principal*
EMP: 19 **EST:** 2010
SALES (est): 251.6K **Privately Held**
WEB: www.gosafco.com
SIC: 7372 Prepackaged software

(G-658)
SAFETEK INTERNATIONAL INC (PA)
6560 W Rogers Cir (33487-2746)
PHONE.....................702 558-8202
Shmuel Shneibalg, *CEO*
Michael J Krantz, *President*
EMP: 5 **EST:** 1988
SALES (est): 925.9K **Privately Held**
WEB: www.safetekinternational.com
SIC: 3569 Filters

(G-659)
SANDOW MEDIA LLC
3651 Fau Blvd Ste 200 (33431-6489)
PHONE.....................646 805-0200
Juan Lopez, *Exec VP*
Nicholas Wright, *Exec VP*
Janice Browne, *Vice Pres*
Pamela McNally, *Vice Pres*
Alex Cruz, *Opers Staff*
EMP: 10
SALES (corp-wide): 78.7MM **Privately Held**
WEB: www.sandow.com
SIC: 2721 Magazines: publishing only, not printed on site
PA: Sandow Media, Llc
3651 Nw 8th Ave Ste 200
Boca Raton FL 33431
561 961-7749

(G-660)
SANDOW MEDIA LLC (PA)
Also Called: Sandow Media-Airport Linehaul
3651 Nw 8th Ave Ste 200 (33431-6489)
PHONE.....................561 961-7749
Adam I Sandow, *CEO*
Paul Blum, *CEO*
James Dimonekas, *President*
Erica Holborn, *President*
John Gallo, *Publisher*
▲ **EMP:** 100 **EST:** 2002
SQ FT: 15,000
SALES (est): 78.7MM **Privately Held**
WEB: www.sandow.com
SIC: 2721 Magazines: publishing only, not printed on site

(G-661)
SANOMEDICS INC (PA)
7777 Glades Rd Ste 100 (33434-4150)
PHONE.....................305 433-7814
William Lerner, *Ch of Bd*
David C Langle, *President*
Gary J O'Hara, *CTO*
EMP: 3 **EST:** 1938
SQ FT: 1,200
SALES (est): 5.1MM **Publicly Held**
SIC: 3829 Thermometers, including digital: clinical

(G-662)
SANZOGO CORPORATION
Also Called: SANZOGO WINDOW AND WALL
2000 Glades Rd Ste 214 (33431-8504)
PHONE.....................561 334-2138
Elaine Sanzogo, *CEO*
EMP: 6 **EST:** 2013
SALES (est): 1MM **Privately Held**
WEB: www.sanzogo.com
SIC: 2211 1721 5231 2591 Draperies & drapery fabrics, cotton; wallcovering contractors; wallpaper; drapery hardware & blinds & shades; window shades; curtains

(G-663)
SARGEANT MARINE INC
3020 N Military Trl # 100 (33431-1805)
PHONE.....................561 999-9916
Harry J Sargeant, *Ch of Bd*
Daniel Sargeant, *President*
Janet Sargeant, *Corp Secy*
James Sargeant, *Vice Pres*
Suzzane Ghantous, *Bookkeeper*
◆ **EMP:** 15 **EST:** 1984
SALES (est): 2.8MM **Privately Held**
WEB: www.sargeantmarine.com
SIC: 3089 Plastic boats & other marine equipment

(G-664)
SCP COMMERCIAL PRINTING
1100 Holland Dr (33487-2701)
PHONE.....................561 998-0870
Elliot Goldstein, *CEO*
EMP: 10 **EST:** 2000
SALES (est): 162.2K **Privately Held**
WEB: www.scpprinting.com
SIC: 2759 Commercial printing

(G-665)
SENIOR LF CMMNCTIONS GROUP INC
Also Called: Boomer Times & Senior Life
1515 N Federal Hwy # 300 (33432-1911)
PHONE.....................561 392-4550
Anita Finley, *President*
EMP: 10 **EST:** 1988
SALES (est): 1MM **Privately Held**
SIC: 2711 2721 Newspapers: publishing only, not printed on site; periodicals

(G-666)
SENSORMATIC
1110 Sw 18th St (33486-6710)
PHONE.....................561 912-6429
Jaime Ticatic, *Principal*
EMP: 12 **EST:** 2009
SALES (est): 133.1K **Privately Held**
WEB: www.sensormatic.com
SIC: 3812 Search & navigation equipment

(G-667)
SENSORMATIC ELECTRONICS CORP
951 W Yamato Rd (33431-4439)
PHONE.....................561 989-7000
Chris Abbott, *Technical Staff*
EMP: 9 **EST:** 2018
SALES (est): 467.1K **Privately Held**
WEB: www.sensormatic.com
SIC: 3812 Search & navigation equipment

(G-668)
SENSUS HEALTHCARE INC
851 Broken Sound Pkwy Nw (33487-3616)
PHONE.....................561 922-5808
Joseph C Sardano, *Ch of Bd*
Kalman Fishman, *COO*
Richard Golin, *Exec VP*
Stephen Cohen, *Vice Pres*
Hoi-Bun Suen, *Vice Pres*

EMP: 45 EST: 2010
SQ FT: 8,926
SALES (est): 27MM Privately Held
WEB: www.sensushealthcare.com
SIC: 3841 Skin grafting equipment

(G-669)
SEP COMMUNICATIONS LLC
Also Called: Make A Statement Gifts
6001 Park Of Commerce Blv (33487-8234)
PHONE..................................561 998-0870
Marty Harris, Principal
Holly Kaiser, Accounts Exec
EMP: 11 EST: 2014
SALES (est): 3.1MM Privately Held
WEB: www.sepcommunications.com
SIC: 3993 2721 2711 7374 Signs & advertising specialties; periodicals: publishing & printing; commercial printing & newspaper publishing combined; computer graphics service

(G-670)
SFBC LLC
Also Called: Seaboard Folding Box Company
7035 Queenferry Cir (33496-5948)
PHONE..................................978 342-8921
Christopher Morgan, Vice Pres
Kevin Trainor, Vice Pres
James Alansky, Purchasing
Cynthia Lore, Asst Controller
Suzanne Sinnery, Finance
EMP: 18 EST: 2006
SQ FT: 260,000
SALES (est): 4.8MM Privately Held
SIC: 2653 Boxes, corrugated: made from purchased materials

(G-671)
SHILPICO INC
22360 Sands Point Dr (33433-6266)
PHONE..................................561 306-5625
Ravi Shankar, President
EMP: 5 EST: 2007
SALES (est): 374.5K Privately Held
SIC: 3433 Boilers, low-pressure heating: steam or hot water

(G-672)
SIGN PARTNERS INC
1181 S Rogers Cir Ste 3 (33487-2724)
PHONE..................................561 270-6919
Matheus Ostafiuc, President
Henrique De Matos, Exec Dir
EMP: 7 EST: 2015
SALES (est): 1MM Privately Held
WEB: www.sign-partners.com
SIC: 3993 Signs, not made in custom sign painting shops

(G-673)
SIGNATURE COMPUTER SVCS INC
7040 W Palmetto Park Rd (33433-3411)
PHONE..................................954 421-0950
Scott Gutman, President
Vincent C Timphony, Marketing Staff
EMP: 9 EST: 1999
SQ FT: 1,600
SALES (est): 1.3MM Privately Held
WEB: www.signaturecomputer.com
SIC: 3577 Computer peripheral equipment

(G-674)
SIGNIFICANT SOLUTIONS CORP
Also Called: Ai-R.com Got-Leads.com
3003 W Yamato Rd Ste C8 (33434-5337)
PHONE..................................561 703-7703
Christopher Singer, President
◆ EMP: 7 EST: 1993
SQ FT: 2,000
SALES (est): 151.7K Privately Held
WEB: www.got-profits.com
SIC: 3999 Novelties, bric-a-brac & hobby kits

(G-675)
SIGNSATIONS INC
5425 N Dixie Hwy Ste 2 (33487-4923)
PHONE..................................561 989-1900
Jack Glover, President
Mincy Kien, Principal
Roslyn Zimmerman, Vice Pres
Jodi Zimmerman, Treasurer
EMP: 5 EST: 1994
SQ FT: 1,000

SALES (est): 528.9K Privately Held
WEB: www.signsations.com
SIC: 3993 7374 Signs & advertising specialties; computer graphics service

(G-676)
SIMPLEX TIME RECORDER CO
1501 Nw 51st St (33431-4438)
PHONE..................................561 988-7200
Robert F Chauvin, Principal
EMP: 1 EST: 2000
SALES (est): 5.5MM Privately Held
SIC: 3669 Emergency alarms
HQ: Johnson Controls Fire Protection Lp
6600 Congress Ave
Boca Raton FL 33487
561 988-7200

(G-677)
SIMPLEXGRINNELL HOLDINGS LLC (DH)
1501 Nw 51st St (33431-4438)
PHONE..................................978 731-2500
James Spicer, President
Terry Reiter, Opers Mgr
Steven Kelly, Project Engr
Monique Pointer, VP Human Res
Scott Brackett, Human Res Dir
EMP: 3 EST: 1999
SQ FT: 16,000
SALES (est): 2.1B Privately Held
WEB: www.johnsoncontrols.com
SIC: 3579 3669 3699 3822 Time clocks & time recording devices; fire detection systems, electric; fire alarm apparatus, electric; security control equipment & systems; sound signaling devices, electrical; thermostats & other environmental sensors
HQ: Tyco International Management Company, Llc
9 Roszel Rd Ste 2
Princeton NJ 08540
609 720-4200

(G-678)
SIMPLICITY ESPORTS LLC
7000 W Plmtt Prk Rd Ste 5 (33433-3424)
PHONE..................................855 345-9467
Jed Kaplan, CEO
EMP: 14 EST: 2017
SQ FT: 250
SALES (est): 1.1MM
SALES (corp-wide): 3.5MM Privately Held
WEB: www.ggsimplicity.com
SIC: 7372 Application computer software
PA: Simplicity Esports And Gaming Company
7000 W Plmtt Prk Rd Ste 5
Boca Raton FL 33433
855 345-9467

(G-679)
SIMPLICITY ESPORTS & GAMING CO (PA)
7000 W Plmtt Prk Rd Ste 5 (33433-3424)
PHONE..................................855 345-9467
Jed Kaplan, CEO
Donald R Caldwell, Ch of Bd
Roman Franklin, President
Knicks Lau, CFO
EMP: 3 EST: 2017
SQ FT: 250
SALES (est): 3.5MM Privately Held
WEB: www.ggsimplicity.com
SIC: 7372 Application computer software

(G-680)
SIRS PUBLISHING INC (DH)
Also Called: Sirs Commercial Print
5201 Congress Ave Ste 250 (33487-3601)
PHONE..................................800 521-0600
Fax: 561 995-4065
▲ EMP: 98
SQ FT: 50,000
SALES (est): 5.2MM Publicly Held
SIC: 2731 2752 2741 Books-Publishing/Printing Lithographic Commercial Printing Misc Publishing
HQ: Voyager Learning Company
17855 Dallas Pkwy Ste 400
Dallas TX 75287
214 932-9500

(G-681)
SJOSTROM INDUSTRIES INC
Also Called: Sjostrom Electronics
1400 Nw 9th Ave Apt 1 (33486-1324)
PHONE..................................561 368-2000
David K Evans, President
EMP: 10 EST: 1975
SQ FT: 1,000
SALES (est): 679.7K Privately Held
SIC: 3825 Digital test equipment, electronic & electrical circuits

(G-682)
SKY ORGANICS LLC
2901 Clint Moore Rd Ste 2 (33496-2039)
PHONE..................................561 295-1890
Eduard Roosli, CEO
Lisa Nettis, CFO
EMP: 25 EST: 2016
SALES (est): 35MM Privately Held
WEB: www.skyorganics.com
SIC: 2844 Toilet preparations

(G-683)
SLEEPRITE INDUSTRIES INC
Also Called: Restonic/San Francisco
7087 Mandarin Dr (33433-7411)
P.O. Box 814, Burlingame CA (94011-0710)
PHONE..................................650 344-1980
Jeffrey S Karp, President
Elaine Karp, Corp Secy
Randall H Karp, Vice Pres
▼ EMP: 25 EST: 1968
SALES (est): 2.1MM Privately Held
SIC: 2515 Mattresses, containing felt, foam rubber, urethane, etc.; mattresses, innerspring or box spring

(G-684)
SMARTMATIC CORPORATION (DH)
1001 Broken Sound Pkwy Nw D (33487-3532)
PHONE..................................561 862-0747
Antonio Mugica, CEO
Keith Stringfellow, President
David Melville, Principal
Mohamed Mansour, Business Mgr
Roger Pinate, COO
▲ EMP: 10 EST: 2000
SQ FT: 10,000
SALES (est): 21.5MM
SALES (corp-wide): 118.6MM Privately Held
SIC: 3571 3579 7372 Electronic computers; voting machines; prepackaged software
HQ: Smartmatic International Holding B.V.
Hoogoorddreef 11
Amsterdam
207 940-817

(G-685)
SOTA MANUFACTURING INC (PA)
1561 Sw 6th Ave (33486-7001)
PHONE..................................561 368-8007
Noel Gonzales, CEO
Brian Burke, Principal
EMP: 5 EST: 2012
SALES (est): 3MM Privately Held
SIC: 3812 3841 3825 Aircraft/aerospace flight instruments & guidance systems; diagnostic apparatus, medical; electrical energy measuring equipment

(G-686)
SOUTHEAST ENERGY INC
23257 State Road 7 # 107 (33428-5448)
PHONE..................................561 883-1051
EMP: 8
SALES (est): 1MM Privately Held
SIC: 2899 5714 1793 Chemical Preparations, Nec, Nsk

(G-687)
SOUTHEAST WOODCRAFTERS INC
1566 Nw 1st Ave (33432-1706)
PHONE..................................561 392-2929
Timothy J Clemmons, President
▼ EMP: 11 EST: 2003

SALES (est): 647.3K Privately Held
WEB: www.sewoodcrafters.com
SIC: 2434 Wood kitchen cabinets

(G-688)
SOUTHEASTERN PRINTING CO INC
6001 Pk Of Cmmrce Blvd St (33487-8234)
PHONE..................................305 885-8707
EMP: 15
SALES (corp-wide): 50.7MM Privately Held
WEB: www.seprint.com
SIC: 2752 2759 Commercial printing, offset; flexographic printing
PA: Southeastern Printing Co Inc
950 Se 8th St
Hialeah FL 33010
772 287-2141

(G-689)
SOX LLC
Also Called: Sox Erosion Solutions
950 Pnnsula Corp Cir Ste (33487)
PHONE..................................561 501-0057
Brian Fischer, Mng Member
Ryan Leeds,
EMP: 5 EST: 2017
SALES (est): 1.8MM Privately Held
WEB: www.soxerosion.com
SIC: 3999 Permanent wave equipment & machines

(G-690)
SPERANZA THERAPEUTICS CORP
433 Plaza Real Ste 275 (33432-3999)
PHONE..................................844 477-3726
EMP: 11 EST: 2020
SALES (est): 550.8K Privately Held
WEB: www.speranzatherapeutics.com
SIC: 3841 Surgical & medical instruments

(G-691)
SPETT PRINTING CO INC
Also Called: Egmont Press
4115 Georges Way (33434-5345)
PHONE..................................561 241-9758
Michael Spett, President
Lizzie Spett, Treasurer
EMP: 5 EST: 1941
SQ FT: 1,000
SALES (est): 368.5K Privately Held
SIC: 2752 2759 Commercial printing, offset; letterpress printing

(G-692)
SPINNAKER HOLDING COMPANY
Also Called: Minuteman Press
1609 Nw 2nd Ave (33432-1654)
PHONE..................................561 392-8626
Steven Brunk, President
Carlene Brunk, Corp Secy
Lash Hamilton, Marketing Staff
Michael Kochersperger, Graphic Designe
Israel Salcedo, Graphic Designe
EMP: 31 EST: 1976
SQ FT: 7,000
SALES (est): 5.7MM Privately Held
WEB: bocaraton.minutemanpress.com
SIC: 2752 2791 2789 Commercial printing, lithographic; typesetting; bookbinding & related work

(G-693)
SPRINGBIG HOLDINGS INC
621 Nw 53rd St Ste 260 (33487-8281)
PHONE..................................800 772-9172
Jeffrey Harris, CEO
Paul Sykes, CFO
Navin Anand, CTO
EMP: 158 EST: 2020 Privately Held
SIC: 7372 Prepackaged software

(G-694)
STADSON TECHNOLOGY CORPORATION
3651 Fau Blvd Ste 400 (33431-6489)
PHONE..................................561 372-2648
EMP: 24
SALES (corp-wide): 1.2MM Privately Held
SIC: 7372 Application Software

PA: Stadson Technology Corporation
751 Park Of Commerce Dr
Boca Raton FL

(G-695)
STARMAKERS RISING INC (PA)
17239 Boca Club Blvd # 6 (33487-1073)
PHONE....................561 989-8999
Eileen Miller, *President*
EMP: 16 **EST:** 1993
SQ FT: 3,000
SALES (est): 2.4MM **Privately Held**
WEB: www.starmakersrising.com
SIC: 2759 2771 Posters, including billboards: printing; greeting cards

(G-696)
STEM HOLDINGS INC (PA)
2201 Nw Corp Blvd Ste 205 (33431-7337)
PHONE....................561 948-5410
Matthew Cohen, *CEO*
Brian Hayek, *Ch Credit Ofcr*
Robert L B Diener, *Admin Sec*
EMP: 22 **EST:** 2016
SALES (est): 35.7MM **Publicly Held**
WEB: www.stemholdings.com
SIC: 2833 Medicinals & botanicals

(G-697)
STEM HOLDINGS FLORIDA INC
2201 Nw Corp Blvd Ste 205 (33431-7337)
PHONE....................561 948-5410
Steven Hubbard, *President*
Melony Valleau, *Controller*
Angela Letizia, *Director*
EMP: 1 **EST:** 2018
SALES (est): 3MM
SALES (corp-wide): 35.7MM **Publicly Held**
WEB: www.stemholdings.com
SIC: 2833 Medicinals & botanicals
PA: Stem Holdings, Inc.
2201 Nw Corp Blvd Ste 205
Boca Raton FL 33431
561 948-5410

(G-698)
STREAM LINE PUBLISHING INC
Also Called: Fine Art Connoisseur
331 Se Mizner Blvd (33432-6004)
PHONE....................561 655-8778
B Eric Rhoads, *President*
Adam Jacobson, *Chief*
Deborah Parenti, *Exec VP*
Tom Elmo, *Vice Pres*
Bob Hogan, *Vice Pres*
EMP: 12 **EST:** 1995
SALES (est): 3.1MM **Privately Held**
WEB: www.streamlinepublishing.com
SIC: 2721 Magazines: publishing only, not printed on site

(G-699)
STREAMLINE PUBLISHING INC
331 Se Mizner Blvd (33432-6004)
PHONE....................561 655-8778
Eric Rhoads, *President*
Tom Elmo, *Vice Pres*
Bob Hogan, *Vice Pres*
Anne Brown, *Marketing Staff*
Kenneth Whitney, *Creative Dir*
EMP: 9 **EST:** 1987
SQ FT: 5,000
SALES (est): 782.1K **Privately Held**
WEB: www.streamlinepublishing.com
SIC: 2721 Periodicals

(G-700)
SUN INDALEX LLC
5200 Town Center Cir # 470 (33486-1015)
PHONE....................561 394-0550
Timothy R J Stubbs, *President*
EMP: 20 **EST:** 2005
SALES (est): 601.6K **Privately Held**
SIC: 3353 Aluminum sheet, plate & foil

(G-701)
SUN MACKIE LLC
5200 Town Center Cir # 470 (33486-1015)
PHONE....................561 394-0550
Marc J Leder, *CEO*
Rodger R Krouse, *CEO*
Mark Corbidge, *Managing Dir*
Deryl Couch, *Managing Dir*
Antony Levinson, *Senior VP*
◆ **EMP:** 1437 **EST:** 2002

SALES (est): 26.3MM **Privately Held**
SIC: 3651 Audio electronic systems

(G-702)
SUNBEAM AMERICAS HOLDINGS LLC
2381 Nw Executive Ctr Dr (33431-8560)
PHONE....................561 912-4100
Jerry W Levin, *Ch of Bd*
EMP: 38 **EST:** 1990
SQ FT: 27,003
SALES (est): 15.5MM
SALES (corp-wide): 10.5B **Publicly Held**
SIC: 3631 2514 3421 3634 Barbecues, grills & braziers (outdoor cooking); metal lawn & garden furniture; scissors, shears, clippers, snips & similar tools; electric housewares & fans; thermometers & temperature sensors; blood pressure apparatus
HQ: American Household, Inc.
2381 Nw Executive Ctr Dr
Boca Raton FL 33431
561 912-4100

(G-703)
SUNBEAM PRODUCTS INC (HQ)
2381 Nw Executive Ctr Dr (33431-8560)
PHONE....................561 912-4100
Christine Robins, *President*
David Hammer, *President*
Mario Iriarte, *General Mgr*
Rebecca Pangle, *Business Mgr*
Kyle Kaiser, *Senior VP*
◆ **EMP:** 290 **EST:** 1981
SALES (est): 1.9B
SALES (corp-wide): 10.5B **Publicly Held**
WEB: www.sunbeamautotoys.com
SIC: 3631 3634 3089 Barbecues, grills & braziers (outdoor cooking); electric housewares & fans; hair dryers, electric; blenders, electric; food mixers, electric: household; plastic containers, except foam; plastic kitchenware, tableware & houseware
PA: Newell Brands Inc.
6655 Pachtree Dunwoody Rd
Atlanta GA 30328
770 418-7000

(G-704)
SUPER GRAFIX INC
Also Called: Gulf Stream Gear
2889 Nw 24th Ter (33431-6202)
PHONE....................561 585-1519
Michael Chernoff, *President*
EMP: 10 **EST:** 2001
SALES (est): 900.6K **Privately Held**
WEB: www.renegadesupergrafix.com
SIC: 2675 Stencils & lettering materials: die-cut

(G-705)
SURGENTEC LLC
911 Clint Moore Rd (33487-2802)
PHONE....................561 990-7882
Travis Greenhalgh, *Principal*
Lisa Overton, *Opers Staff*
EMP: 9 **EST:** 2016
SALES (est): 1.8MM **Privately Held**
WEB: www.surgentec.com
SIC: 3841 Medical instruments & equipment, blood & bone work

(G-706)
T H STONE
4521 N Dixie Hwy (33431-5029)
PHONE....................561 361-3966
EMP: 6
SALES (est): 1.5MM **Privately Held**
SIC: 3281 5122 Mfg Cut Stone/Products And Cosmetics/Toiletries

(G-707)
TAYLOR & FRANCIS GROUP LLC (DH)
6000 Broken Sound Pkwy Nw # 300 (33487-5704)
PHONE....................561 994-0555
Roger Graham Horton, *President*
Tony Bruce, *Publisher*
Kristine Mednansky, *Editor*
Meredith Norwich, *Editor*
Perry Todd, *Editor*
▲ **EMP:** 150 **EST:** 2004
SQ FT: 36,470

SALES (est): 104.2MM
SALES (corp-wide): 2.4B **Privately Held**
WEB: www.taylorandfrancis.com
SIC: 2721 2731 Periodicals: publishing only; trade journals: publishing only, not printed on site; books: publishing only; textbooks: publishing only, not printed on site

(G-708)
TECHNIFLEX LLC
4400 N Federal Hwy Ste 51 (33431-3426)
PHONE....................561 235-0844
Serhat Unal,
EMP: 25 **EST:** 2016
SALES (est): 678.2K **Privately Held**
SIC: 3999 Atomizers, toiletry

(G-709)
TED CASES INC
2385 Nw Executive Ctr (33431-8579)
PHONE....................561 809-1030
Michael Schiffman, *Principal*
EMP: 8 **EST:** 2017
SALES (est): 268.7K **Privately Held**
SIC: 3523 Farm machinery & equipment

(G-710)
TELSEC CORPORATION
Also Called: E-Tag
1155 Broken Sound Pkwy Nw E (33487-3538)
PHONE....................561 998-9983
Stuart Seidel, *President*
Andrew Gilbert, *Vice Pres*
▲ **EMP:** 6 **EST:** 1994
SQ FT: 6,000
SALES (est): 551.1K **Privately Held**
SIC: 3699 Security control equipment & systems

(G-711)
TENNIER INDUSTRIES INC (PA)
950 Pnnsula Corp Cir Ste (33487)
PHONE....................561 999-9710
Howard Thier, *CEO*
Steven W Eisen, *CFO*
EMP: 3 **EST:** 1976
SALES (est): 109.1MM **Privately Held**
WEB: www.tennierindustries.com
SIC: 2311 Military uniforms, men's & youths': purchased materials

(G-712)
TERRAN ORBITAL CORPORATION (PA)
6800 Broken Sound Pkwy Nw (33487-2721)
PHONE....................561 988-1704
Marc H Bell, *Ch of Bd*
Daniel C Staton, *Vice Ch Bd*
Hilary Hageman, *Exec VP*
Anthony Previte, *Exec VP*
Marco Villa, *Exec VP*
EMP: 15 **EST:** 2020 **Publicly Held**
WEB: www.terranorbital.com
SIC: 3663 3761 Space satellite communications equipment; space vehicles, complete

(G-713)
TERRAN ORBITAL OPERATING CORP (HQ)
Also Called: Terran Orbital Corporation
6800 Broken Sound Pkwy Nw S (33487-2721)
PHONE....................561 988-1704
Marc Bell, *CEO*
Anthony Previte, *Exec VP*
David Caponio, *Vice Pres*
Eric Leeds, *Vice Pres*
Jordi Puig-Suari, *Admin Sec*
EMP: 30 **EST:** 2014
SALES (est): 26.2MM **Publicly Held**
WEB: www.terranorbital.com
SIC: 3761 3764 Space vehicles, complete; guided missiles & space vehicles, research & development; guided missile & space vehicle engines, research & devel.
PA: Terran Orbital Corporation
6800 Broken Sound Pkwy Nw
Boca Raton FL 33487
561 988-1704

(G-714)
THEATER EARS INC
20423 State Road 7 Ste F1 (33498-6774)
PHONE....................561 305-0519
Dan Mangru, *CEO*
EMP: 5 **EST:** 2013
SALES (est): 327.6K **Privately Held**
WEB: www.theaterears.com
SIC: 7372 Application computer software

(G-715)
THERAPEUTICSMD INC (PA)
951 W Yamato Rd Ste 220 (33431-4440)
PHONE....................561 961-1900
Tommy G Thompson, *Ch of Bd*
Hugh O'Dowd, *President*
Brandon Chatkin, *Business Mgr*
James Chestnut, *Business Mgr*
Jennifer Cox, *Business Mgr*
EMP: 91 **EST:** 2008
SQ FT: 56,212
SALES (est): 86.9MM **Publicly Held**
WEB: www.therapeuticsmd.com
SIC: 2834 Pharmaceutical preparations; vitamin, nutrient & hematinic preparations for human use

(G-716)
THINGLOBAL LLC
7700 Congress Ave # 1122 (33487-1352)
PHONE....................561 923-8559
Luiz Serria, *CEO*
Elaine Lignelli, *Mng Member*
Luiz Ferreira, *Manager*
Eliane Lignelli, *Exec Dir*
Kim Huapaya, *Executive*
EMP: 6 **EST:** 2015
SALES (est): 499.8K **Privately Held**
WEB: www.thinglobal.com
SIC: 3577 5734 Computer peripheral equipment; computer peripheral equipment

(G-717)
THOR MANUFACTURING INC
7050 W Plmtt Prk Rd Ste 1 (33433-3426)
PHONE....................866 955-8467
Nicholas Montgomery, *Manager*
EMP: 8 **EST:** 2008
SALES (est): 91.5K **Privately Held**
WEB: www.thorpowerproducts.com
SIC: 3999 Atomizers, toiletry

(G-718)
TODAYS RESTAURANT NEWS INC
6165 Old Court Rd Apt 224 (33433-7830)
PHONE....................561 620-8888
Howard Appell, *Owner*
EMP: 9 **EST:** 2010
SALES (est): 306.7K **Privately Held**
WEB: www.trnusa.com
SIC: 2711 Newspapers, publishing & printing

(G-719)
TOP SALES CO
17047 Boca Club Blvd 141b (33487-1251)
PHONE....................561 852-4311
Stuart Nussbaum, *President*
EMP: 6 **EST:** 1985
SALES (est): 499.1K **Privately Held**
SIC: 3699 Electrical equipment & supplies

(G-720)
TOTALLY PRODUCTS LLC
1101 S Rogers Cir Ste 10 (33487-2748)
PHONE....................786 942-9218
Daniel I Rosenfield, *CEO*
EMP: 5 **EST:** 2009
SALES (est): 592.8K **Privately Held**
SIC: 2833 Vitamins, natural or synthetic: bulk, uncompounded

(G-721)
TRAINOR METAL PRODUCTS INC
171 Nw 16th St (33432-1606)
P.O. Box 1176 (33429-1176)
PHONE....................561 395-5520
Jeff Brader, *President*
EMP: 5 **EST:** 1958
SQ FT: 12,500

▲ = Import ▼=Export
◆ =Import/Export

SALES (est): 446.8K **Privately Held**
WEB: www.trainormetal.com
SIC: 2514 Metal lawn & garden furniture

(G-722)
TRI COUNTY PRINTING CO IN
9070 Kimberly Blvd (33434-2855)
PHONE..................................561 477-8487
Joseph Frank, *Principal*
EMP: 7 **EST:** 2006
SALES (est): 226.8K **Privately Held**
SIC: 2752 Commercial printing, lithographic

(G-723)
TRIGEANT EP LTD
3020 N Military Trl # 100 (33431-1814)
PHONE..................................561 999-9916
Harry Sargeant III, *Partner*
◆ **EMP:** 10 **EST:** 2002
SALES (est): 902.4K **Privately Held**
SIC: 2999 Waxes, petroleum: not produced in petroleum refineries

(G-724)
TRINE INDUSTRIES INC
Also Called: Glamour Goddess Jewelry
2901 Clint Moore Rd (33496-2041)
PHONE..................................561 995-1995
Barbara Golden, *Principal*
EMP: 5 **EST:** 2016
SALES (est): 338.3K **Privately Held**
WEB: www.glamourgoddessjewelry.com
SIC: 3999 Manufacturing industries

(G-725)
TRIPLE CROWN PRINTING
5801 Congress Ave (33487-3603)
PHONE..................................561 939-6440
Neal Heller, *Partner*
Richard Siemans, *Partner*
EMP: 35 **EST:** 2006
SALES (est): 1.6MM **Privately Held**
SIC: 2759 Commercial printing

(G-726)
TWINLAB CNSLD HOLDINGS INC (PA)
Also Called: TCH
4800 T Rex Ave Ste 305 (33431-4479)
PHONE..................................561 443-4301
David L Van Andel, *Ch of Bd*
Anthony Zolezzi, *President*
Gregory Thomas Grochoski, *Exec VP*
Shari Gottesman, *Senior VP*
Carla Goffstein, *CFO*
EMP: 7 **EST:** 2013
SQ FT: 13,000
SALES (est): 72MM **Publicly Held**
WEB: www.tchhome.com
SIC: 2833 2023 Vitamins, natural or synthetic: bulk, uncompounded; dietary supplements, dairy & non-dairy based

(G-727)
TWINLAB CONSOLIDATION CORP
4800 T Rex Ave Ste 350 (33431-4447)
PHONE..................................800 645-5626
Naomi Whittel, *CEO*
Ryan Zackon, *Vice Pres*
Greg Grochoski, *Officer*
Yamit Sadok, *Surgery Dir*
EMP: 5 **EST:** 2017
SALES (est): 4.9MM
SALES (corp-wide): 72MM **Publicly Held**
WEB: twinlab.tlchealth.com
SIC: 2833 Vitamins, natural or synthetic: bulk, uncompounded
PA: Twinlab Consolidated Holdings Inc.
4800 T Rex Ave Ste 305
Boca Raton FL 33431
561 443-4301

(G-728)
TWINLAB CORPORATION
4800 T Rex Ave Ste 305 (33431-4479)
PHONE..................................800 645-5626
Naomi Whittel, *CEO*
Adriane Antoine, *Sales Staff*
Richard Neuwirth, *Officer*
EMP: 5 **EST:** 2003
SQ FT: 5,000

SALES (est): 2.2MM
SALES (corp-wide): 72MM **Publicly Held**
WEB: www.twinlab.com
SIC: 2099 2834 2731 2721 Tea blending; vitamin preparations; books: publishing only; statistical reports (periodicals): publishing only; medicinals & botanicals
PA: Twinlab Consolidated Holdings Inc.
4800 T Rex Ave Ste 305
Boca Raton FL 33431
561 443-4301

(G-729)
TWINLAB HOLDINGS INC (PA)
Also Called: Ideasphere
4800 T Rex Ave Ste 305 (33431-4479)
PHONE..................................800 645-5626
David V Andel, *CEO*
Bill Nicholson, *Vice Ch Bd*
Anthony Robbins, *Vice Ch Bd*
Mark Fox, *President*
Niki Simoneaux, *Senior VP*
EMP: 23 **EST:** 2001
SALES (est): 53.6MM **Privately Held**
WEB: www.twinlab.com
SIC: 2833 2834 5149 2721 Vitamins, natural or synthetic: bulk, uncompounded; pharmaceutical preparations; groceries & related products; periodicals

(G-730)
TWINLAB HOLDINGS INC
2255 Glades Rd Ste 342w (33431-7379)
PHONE..................................800 645-5626
Joseph Sinicropi, *Branch Mgr*
EMP: 62
SALES (corp-wide): 53.6MM **Privately Held**
WEB: www.twinlab.com
SIC: 2833 Medicinals & botanicals
PA: Twinlab Holdings, Inc.
4800 T Rex Ave Ste 305
Boca Raton FL 33431
800 645-5626

(G-731)
ULTIMAXX INC
Also Called: Ultimaxx Health
3651 Fau Blvd Ste 400 (33431-6489)
P.O. Box 5308, Frisco TX (75035-0210)
PHONE..................................877 300-3424
Leonard Lomax, *CEO*
Ron Long, *Vice Pres*
EMP: 10 **EST:** 2008
SALES (est): 996.1K **Privately Held**
WEB: www.ultimaxxhealth.com
SIC: 2833 Medicinals & botanicals

(G-732)
ULTIMAXX HEALTH LLC
3651 Fau Blvd Ste 400 (33431-6489)
PHONE..................................877 300-3424
Lenny Lomax,
EMP: 5 **EST:** 2019
SALES (est): 523.8K **Privately Held**
WEB: www.ultimaxxhealth.com
SIC: 2834 Pharmaceutical preparations

(G-733)
UNICO INTERNATIONAL TRDG CORP
Also Called: A World of Wipes
5499 N Federal Hwy Ste P (33487-4993)
PHONE..................................561 338-3338
AVI Tansman, *President*
Avraham AVI Tansman, *President*
Melinda Tansman, *Vice Pres*
Lisa Carey, *Sales Staff*
Joe Doyle, *Marketing Staff*
▲ **EMP:** 6 **EST:** 1991
SALES: 17.5MM **Privately Held**
WEB: www.aworldofwipes.com
SIC: 2844 Towelettes, premoistened

(G-734)
UNIQUE RECORDING SOFTWARE INC
21218 Saint Andrews Blvd (33433-2435)
PHONE..................................917 854-5403
Nathan Robert, *Principal*
EMP: 5 **EST:** 2004
SALES (est): 322.3K **Privately Held**
WEB: www.ursplugins.com
SIC: 7372 Prepackaged software

(G-735)
UNITED WIRELESS TECH INC
300 Se 5th Ave Apt 8180 (33432-5503)
PHONE..................................561 302-9350
Stephen B Cavayero, *President*
EMP: 14 **EST:** 1993
SQ FT: 20,000
SALES (est): 383.6K **Privately Held**
SIC: 3571 3663 Electronic computers; radio & TV communications equipment; cellular radio telephone

(G-736)
UNIVERSAL TRAINING SFTWR INC
301 Ne 51st St Ste 1240 (33431-4931)
PHONE..................................561 981-6421
Victor Reyes, *Principal*
EMP: 10 **EST:** 1996
SALES (est): 194.6K **Privately Held**
WEB: www.utsintel.com
SIC: 7372 Application computer software

(G-737)
US CHUTES CORP
751 Park Of Commerce Dr # 108 (33487-3622)
PHONE..................................860 567-4000
M John Weber Jr, *President*
EMP: 16 **EST:** 1976
SQ FT: 75,000
SALES (est): 475.2K **Privately Held**
SIC: 3443 Chutes, metal plate

(G-738)
US PAVER CO
22809 Horse Shoe Way (33428-5505)
PHONE..................................954 292-4373
EMP: 7 **EST:** 2007
SALES (est): 234.7K **Privately Held**
WEB: www.uspaverco.com
SIC: 3531 Pavers

(G-739)
US SAMPLE CORP
10386 Stonebridge Blvd (33498-6409)
PHONE..................................954 495-4525
Morton Kader, *President*
▲ **EMP:** 28 **EST:** 1991
SQ FT: 60,000
SALES (est): 1.3MM
SALES (corp-wide): 219.3MM **Privately Held**
SIC: 2782 Sample books
HQ: National Sample Card Company Limited
11500 Boul Armand-Bombardier
Montreal QC

(G-740)
USDIRECTORYCOM LLC
999 Nw 51st St Ste 100 (33431-4478)
PHONE..................................561 989-7400
Robert Oesterlund, *Principal*
EMP: 8 **EST:** 2012
SALES (est): 283.4K **Privately Held**
WEB: www.usdirectory.com
SIC: 2741 Miscellaneous publishing

(G-741)
VALIANT TRANSPORT GROUP LLC
Also Called: Triad Electric Vehicles
5030 Chmpn Blvd Ste G11 (33496)
PHONE..................................855 648-7423
Cory Graves, *Mng Member*
James Mason, *Manager*
Cory Grades,
EMP: 30 **EST:** 2012
SQ FT: 3,500
SALES (est): 980K **Privately Held**
SIC: 3711 Cars, electric, assembly of

(G-742)
VARGAS ENTERPRISES INC
2518 Nw 64th Blvd (33496-2008)
PHONE..................................561 989-0908
Peter Stein, *President*
Susan Stein, *Vice Pres*
EMP: 7 **EST:** 1993
SQ FT: 5,000
SALES (est): 164.9K **Privately Held**
SIC: 2331 Women's & misses' blouses & shirts

(G-743)
VB-S1 ISSUER LLC
750 Park Of Cmn (33487)
PHONE..................................561 948-6367
EMP: 7 **EST:** 2016
SALES (est): 215.5K **Privately Held**
SIC: 3663 Antennas, transmitting & communications

(G-744)
VEHICLE MAINT PROGRAM INC
Also Called: V M P
3595 N Dixie Hwy Ste 7 (33431-5936)
PHONE..................................561 362-6080
Lindi Brooks Cohen, *President*
Lindy Brooks Cohen, *President*
Penny Brooks, *Corp Secy*
ARI Brooks, *Vice Pres*
EMP: 14 **EST:** 1988
SQ FT: 8,000
SALES (est): 5.3MM **Privately Held**
WEB: www.vmpparts.com
SIC: 3429 5012 Motor vehicle hardware; automobiles & other motor vehicles

(G-745)
VERSATUS HPC INC
4700 Nw 2nd Ave (33431-4154)
PHONE..................................561 544-8862
Denis Marcelo P Dos Anjos, *Principal*
EMP: 7 **EST:** 2012
SALES (est): 818.3K **Privately Held**
WEB: www.versatushpc.com.br
SIC: 3571 Electronic computers

(G-746)
VERTICAL BRIDGE TOWERS LLC
750 Park Of Commerce (33487)
P.O. Box 743051, Atlanta GA (30374-3051)
PHONE..................................561 948-6367
Alex Gellman, *CEO*
Michael Belski, *Exec VP*
Jim McCulloch, *Vice Pres*
Buddy Norman, *Vice Pres*
Kimberly White, *Vice Pres*
EMP: 200 **EST:** 2014
SQ FT: 6,000
SALES (est): 22.3MM **Privately Held**
WEB: www.verticalbridge.com
SIC: 3663 Transmitting apparatus, radio or television

(G-747)
VESERCA GROUP LTD INC
Also Called: Embraer
20694 Nw 27th Ave (33434-4366)
PHONE..................................561 210-7400
Alberto Villasmil, *President*
Antonio Dugarte, *Officer*
◆ **EMP:** 19 **EST:** 2005
SALES (est): 240.2K **Privately Held**
SIC: 3721 5599 Aircraft; aircraft dealers

(G-748)
VIP PRTG NIGHT CLB SUPS LLC
1000 Holland Dr Ste 1 (33487-2723)
PHONE..................................561 603-2846
EMP: 7 **EST:** 2017
SQ FT: 4,800
SALES (est): 276.8K **Privately Held**
WEB: www.nightclubshop.com
SIC: 2752 Commercial printing, offset

(G-749)
VPLENISH NUTRITIONALS INC
101 Plaza Real S Apt 306 (33432-4839)
P.O. Box 1100 (33429-1100)
PHONE..................................954 304-4000
Steven Sponder, *President*
▼ **EMP:** 10 **EST:** 2009
SQ FT: 3,000
SALES (est): 461.2K **Privately Held**
WEB: www.vplenishtheworld.org
SIC: 3999 Manufacturing industries

(G-750)
W H L BUSINESS COMMUNICATIONS
Also Called: AlphaGraphics
2880 N Federal Hwy (33431-6802)
PHONE..................................561 361-9202
Wolf H Lehmkuhl, *President*
Alferdo Billings Jr, *General Mgr*
EMP: 8 **EST:** 1998

GEOGRAPHIC

SALES (est): 806.7K **Privately Held**
WEB: www.alphagraphics.com
SIC: 2752 Commercial printing, lithographic

(G-751)
W R GRACE & CO - CONN
6001 Broken Sound Pkwy # 600 (33487-2766)
PHONE..................................561 982-7776
EMP: 10
SALES (corp-wide): 3B **Publicly Held**
SIC: 3086 2819 Mfg Plastic Foam Products Mfg Industrial Inorganic Chemicals
HQ: W. R. Grace & Co. - Conn.
　7500 Grace Dr
　Columbia MD 21044
　410 531-4000

(G-752)
W2E INTERNATIONAL CORP
2200 Nw Corp Blvd Ste 210 (33431-7307)
PHONE..................................561 362-9595
Steven E Honigman Sq, *Principal*
EMP: 8 EST: 2014
SALES (est): 439.8K **Privately Held**
SIC: 1389 Oil & gas field services

(G-753)
WAREHOUSE GOODS LLC
Also Called: Vapeworld
1095 Broken Sound Pkwy Nw # 300 (33487-3503)
PHONE..................................877 865-2260
Eric Hammond, *General Mgr*
Gurpreet Sahani, *Vice Pres*
Zachary Tapp, *CFO*
Mark Lesko, *Asst Controller*
Dimas Correa, *Finance*
▲ EMP: 50 EST: 2007
SQ FT: 2,000
SALES (est): 25.5MM
SALES (corp-wide): 166MM **Publicly Held**
WEB: www.warehousegoods.com
SIC: 3634 2911 5047 5961 Vaporizers, electric: household; aromatic chemical products; medical equipment & supplies; catalog & mail-order houses
PA: Greenlane Holdings, Inc.
　1095 Broken Sound Pkwy Nw # 300
　Boca Raton FL 33487
　877 292-7660

(G-754)
WEIDER PUBLICATIONS LLC
1000 American Media Way (33464-1000)
PHONE..................................561 998-7424
David Pecker,
EMP: 5 EST: 2002
SALES (est): 526.1K **Privately Held**
WEB: www.muscleandfitness.com
SIC: 2741 Miscellaneous publishing

(G-755)
WORLD HLTH ENRGY HOLDINGS INC (PA)
1825 Nw Corp Blvd Ste 110 (33431-8554)
PHONE..................................561 870-0440
Giora Rozensweig, *CEO*
EMP: 10 EST: 1999
SALES (est): 140.1K **Publicly Held**
WEB: www.whengroup.com
SIC: 2869 7372 Glycerin; business oriented computer software

(G-756)
WORLD OF BRIGADEIRO LLC
4240 Oak Cir (33431-4206)
PHONE..................................954 488-4597
Larissa Castro, *CEO*
EMP: 9 EST: 2018
SALES (est): 498.7K **Privately Held**
WEB: www.worldofbrigadeiro.com
SIC: 2051 Bakery: wholesale or wholesale/retail combined

(G-757)
WORLDWIDE MEDIA SVCS GROUP INC
Also Called: AMI
1000 American Media Way (33464-1000)
PHONE..................................212 545-4800
James Robertson, *Editor*
John Greene, *Counsel*
Robert Fenikowski, *VP Prdtn*

Kimberly Watkins, *Production*
Michael Persaud, *Sales Staff*
EMP: 10
SALES (corp-wide): 1.2B **Privately Held**
WEB: www.accelerate360.com
SIC: 2741 2711 Miscellaneous publishing; newspapers: publishing only, not printed on site
PA: Worldwide Media Services Group Inc.
　4 New York Plz Fl 2
　New York NY 10004
　800 929-8274

(G-758)
WORLDWIDE MEDIA SVCS GROUP INC
1000 American Media Way (33464-1000)
PHONE..................................561 989-1342
David Pecker, *Ch of Bd*
Christopher Polimeni, *Exec VP*
Maydee Ehster, *Manager*
Lyndon Perrine, *Manager*
Adam Butterfield, *Producer*
EMP: 222
SALES (corp-wide): 1.2B **Privately Held**
WEB: www.accelerate360.com
SIC: 2711 Newspapers, publishing & printing
PA: Worldwide Media Services Group Inc.
　4 New York Plz Fl 2
　New York NY 10004
　800 929-8274

(G-759)
XELEUM LIGHTING LLC (HQ)
751 Park Of Commerce Dr # 100 (33487-3622)
PHONE..................................954 617-8170
Richard Leaman, *CEO*
Jonathan Cooper, *COO*
Ty Ramsey, *VP Engrg*
Peter Rozendal, *CFO*
▲ EMP: 14 EST: 2011
SALES (est): 9.7MM **Privately Held**
WEB: www.xeleum.com
SIC: 3646 Commercial indusl & institutional electric lighting fixtures

(G-760)
YAREY INC
18840 Mariner Inlet Dr (33498-6366)
PHONE..................................954 520-6015
Alicia Tovar, *President*
EMP: 10 EST: 2007
SALES (est): 519.1K **Privately Held**
SIC: 3281 Marble, building: cut & shaped

(G-761)
YESIL INC
23400 Milano Ct (33433-6936)
P.O. Box 220033, Great Neck NY (11022-0033)
PHONE..................................516 858-0244
Musa Suveyke, *President*
EMP: 10 EST: 2012
SALES (est): 2MM **Privately Held**
SIC: 2299 7389 Recovering textile fibers from clippings & rags;

(G-762)
YUDKIN FUEL CO
7544 Rexford Rd (33434-5144)
PHONE..................................561 487-0418
Myron Eyudkin, *Principal*
EMP: 7 EST: 1998
SALES (est): 207.6K **Privately Held**
SIC: 2869 Fuels

(G-763)
YVEL USA INC
6000 Glades Rd Ste 1153 (33431-7254)
PHONE..................................561 391-5119
Eliaz Gabay, *CEO*
Alexandra Aseraf, *Vice Pres*
Michelle Ip, *Opers Staff*
Nir Shinuk, *Marketing Staff*
EMP: 8 EST: 2015
SALES (est): 445.4K **Privately Held**
WEB: www.yvel.com
SIC: 3172 Cases, jewelry

(G-764)
ZOKOS GROUP INC
Also Called: Jox Sox
6800 E Rogers Cir (33487-2651)
PHONE..................................888 756-9769

Peter Antonacci, *Principal*
Harris Pollock, *Principal*
EMP: 9 EST: 2020
SALES (est): 271.7K **Privately Held**
SIC: 2252 Socks

(G-765)
ZYLOWARE CORPORATION
21214 Via Ventura (33433-2229)
PHONE..................................561 479-4640
Ray Stephens, *Principal*
EMP: 14
SALES (corp-wide): 12MM **Privately Held**
WEB: www.zyloware.com
SIC: 3827 Optical instruments & lenses
PA: Zyloware Corporation
　8 Slater St
　Port Chester NY 10573
　914 708-1200

Bonifay
Holmes County

(G-766)
ARNOLD LUMBER COMPANY INC
3185 Thomas Dr (32425-4239)
PHONE..................................850 547-5733
Joe Jernigan, *CEO*
Stephen Galonski, *Sales Staff*
EMP: 16 EST: 1927
SALES (est): 1.8MM **Privately Held**
SIC: 2491 Wood preserving

(G-767)
BD XTREME HOLDINGS LLC
Also Called: Xtreme Boats
2460 Development Cir (32425-6024)
PHONE..................................850 703-1793
Brian Sandberg, *President*
Michael Campbell, *Plant Mgr*
EMP: 12 EST: 2016
SALES (est): 1MM **Privately Held**
SIC: 3732 Motorized boat, building & repairing

(G-768)
C2C INNOVATED TECHNOLOGY LLC
3371 Highway 90 (32425-6003)
PHONE..................................251 382-2277
Valarian Couch, *Mng Member*
EMP: 5 EST: 2016
SALES (est): 475K **Privately Held**
WEB: www.c2cinnovatedtech.com
SIC: 3825 4911 1731 7622 Network analyzers; ; fiber optic cable installation; computer installation; installation of citizens' band (CB) antennas; computer integrated systems design; computer systems analysis & design; local area network (LAN) systems integrator; value-added resellers, computer systems; software training, computer

(G-769)
CHIPLEY NEWSPAPERS INC
Also Called: Home County Times Advertiser
112 E Virginia Ave (32425-2327)
P.O. Box 67 (32425-0067)
PHONE..................................850 638-0212
Nicole P Barefield, *Principal*
Brenda Taylor, *Office Mgr*
EMP: 7 EST: 2016
SALES (est): 387.2K **Privately Held**
SIC: 2711 Newspapers, publishing & printing

(G-770)
COUNTRY CABINETS
1915 Adolph Whitaker Rd (32425-6515)
PHONE..................................850 547-5477
Neal Reeves, *President*
Barbara Reeves, *Admin Sec*
EMP: 6 EST: 1995
SALES (est): 470.6K **Privately Held**
WEB: www.countrycabinets95.com
SIC: 2434 Wood kitchen cabinets

(G-771)
ENVIRONMENTAL MFG & SUPPLY INC
3255 Highway 90 (32425-6011)
P.O. Box 130 (32425-0130)
PHONE..................................850 547-5287
Stacey Coates, *President*
Kyle Coates, *Vice Pres*
▲ EMP: 19 EST: 1991
SQ FT: 20,000
SALES (est): 5.1MM **Privately Held**
SIC: 3531 Wellpoint systems

(G-772)
HOLMES TOOL & ENGINEERING INC
Also Called: Hte
1019 N Waukesha St (32425-1736)
P.O. Box 95 (32425-0095)
PHONE..................................850 547-4417
Timothy L Steverson, *President*
Brenda G Steverson, *Vice Pres*
Brenda Steverson, *Vice Pres*
Dale Stephens, *Manager*
Rhonda Hayes, *Administration*
EMP: 25 EST: 1978
SQ FT: 9,500
SALES (est): 4.7MM **Privately Held**
WEB: www.holmestool.com
SIC: 3599 7692 Machine shop, jobbing & repair; welding repair

(G-773)
JAMES FLETCHER CNSTR INC
312 W Pennsylvania Ave (32425-2128)
PHONE..................................619 405-9316
James Fletcher, *President*
EMP: 10 EST: 2006
SALES (est): 281.9K **Privately Held**
WEB: www.jamesfletcherconstruction.com
SIC: 1081 Metal mining exploration & development services

(G-774)
NO BOUNDARIES TRANSPORTATION
3330 Highway 2 (32425-3536)
PHONE..................................850 263-1903
William Sellers, *President*
James Monroe, *Vice Pres*
EMP: 5 EST: 2017
SALES (est): 520.7K **Privately Held**
SIC: 3743 Freight cars & equipment

(G-775)
PARK CENTRAL INC
Also Called: Aus Manufacturing
704 W Highway 90 (32425-2526)
PHONE..................................850 547-1660
James Rich, *President*
James Sellers, *Vice Pres*
Lea Bryant, *Admin Sec*
EMP: 20 EST: 2001
SQ FT: 12,500
SALES (est): 314.7K **Privately Held**
WEB: www.ausmanufacturing.com
SIC: 3599 Machine shop, jobbing & repair

(G-776)
PARTS CENTRAL INC
Also Called: Aus Manufacturing
704 W Highway 90 (32425-2526)
P.O. Box 156 (32425-0156)
PHONE..................................850 547-1660
James Rich, *President*
James Sellers, *Vice Pres*
Lea Bryant, *Administration*
EMP: 13 EST: 2001
SALES (est): 2.5MM **Privately Held**
WEB: www.ausmanufacturing.com
SIC: 3433 3599 7692 Burners, furnaces, boilers & stokers; machine shop, jobbing & repair; welding repair

(G-777)
RANDALL BIRGE
2579 Lilly Dr (32425-8403)
PHONE..................................850 373-6131
Randall Birge, *Owner*
EMP: 6 EST: 2010
SALES (est): 404.7K **Privately Held**
SIC: 2411 Logging

2022 Harris Florida
Manufacturers Directory

▲ = Import ▼=Export
◆ =Import/Export

Bonita Springs
Lee County

(G-778)
1ST CHICE HRRCANE PRTCTION LLC
Also Called: 1st Choice Windows and Doors
25241 Bernwood Dr Ste 6 (34135-7886)
PHONE...................................239 325-3400
Lance Lustik,
EMP: 18 **EST:** 2017
SALES (est): 3MM **Privately Held**
WEB:
www.1stchoicehurricaneprotection.com
SIC: 2431 Door shutters, wood

(G-779)
ADVANCED INFRSTRCTURE TECH INC
25110 Bernwood Dr # 101 (34135-7813)
P.O. Box 112126, Naples (34108-0136)
PHONE...................................239 992-1700
Brit E Svobova, *President*
Barry Raeburn, *Vice Pres*
EMP: 11 **EST:** 2009
SQ FT: 950
SALES (est): 504.2K **Privately Held**
WEB: www.aitcomposites.com
SIC: 3531 Construction machinery attachments

(G-780)
AEROX AVI OXGN SYSTEMS LLC (HQ)
12871 Trade Way Dr Ste 8 (34135-7334)
PHONE...................................239 405-6106
Scott Ashton, *CEO*
Lane Morlock, *President*
Ken Ferriabough, *General Mgr*
EMP: 8 **EST:** 1981
SQ FT: 13,000
SALES (est): 2.5MM **Privately Held**
WEB: www.aerox.com
SIC: 3728 Oxygen systems, aircraft

(G-781)
AVAYA INC
25798 Old Gaslight Dr (34135-8894)
PHONE...................................239 498-2737
Kathy Giamballvo, *Manager*
Carl Thorsen, *Manager*
EMP: 16 **Publicly Held**
WEB: www.avaya.com
SIC: 3661 Telephone & telegraph apparatus
HQ: Avaya Inc.
2605 Meridian Pkwy # 200
Durham NC 27713
908 953-6000

(G-782)
BONITA GRANDE MINING LLC
Also Called: Bonita Grande Aggregates
25501 Bonita Grande Dr (34135-6382)
PHONE...................................239 947-6402
Robert Hensley,
EMP: 23 **EST:** 2004
SQ FT: 500
SALES (est): 6.8MM **Privately Held**
SIC: 1442 Sand mining

(G-783)
BONITA PRINTSHOP INC
Also Called: Bonita Print Shop
28210 Old 41 Rd Unit 305 (34135-0839)
PHONE...................................239 992-8522
Mark Montgomery, *President*
Jodi Montgomery, *Vice Pres*
EMP: 5 **EST:** 1981
SQ FT: 2,200
SALES (est): 622.6K
SALES (corp-wide): 1.2MM **Privately Held**
WEB: www.bonitaprintshop.com
SIC: 2752 Commercial printing, offset
PA: I-Partner Group, Inc
28200 Old 41 Rd Unit 204
Bonita Springs FL 34135
239 449-4749

(G-784)
BOOSTANE LLC
10981 Harmony Park Dr # 5 (34135-1806)
PHONE...................................239 908-1615
Iam Lehn, *President*
Kelly Herrmann, *Admin Mgr*
Mark Herrmann,
Dave Wesseldyke,
EMP: 10 **EST:** 2013
SQ FT: 5,000
SALES (est): 1.6MM **Privately Held**
WEB: www.boostane.com
SIC: 2911 7389 Fuel additives;

(G-785)
BOSWELL JM & ASSOCIATES INC
Also Called: Homes & Land Magazine
270 3rd St (34134-7323)
PHONE...................................239 949-2311
James M Boswell II, *President*
EMP: 7 **EST:** 1999
SALES (est): 397.3K **Privately Held**
SIC: 2721 Periodicals

(G-786)
BRIAN SCHATZMAN
Also Called: All About Screens
10111 Sunshine Dr (34135-5038)
PHONE...................................239 398-1798
Brian Schatzman, *Principal*
EMP: 7 **EST:** 2005
SALES (est): 387.9K **Privately Held**
WEB: www.allaboutscreensswf.com
SIC: 3448 Screen enclosures

(G-787)
BURTON JC COMPANIES INC
Also Called: Ott Welding
24241 Production Cir (34135-7058)
P.O. Box 366056 (34136-6056)
PHONE...................................239 992-2377
Jon C Burton, *President*
Jason Dittman, *Business Mgr*
Rita Osullivan, *Office Mgr*
Ryan Ingram, *Manager*
EMP: 8 **EST:** 1967
SQ FT: 3,400
SALES (est): 2.2MM **Privately Held**
WEB: www.ottwelding.com
SIC: 7692 Welding repair

(G-788)
CABINET COLLECTION INC
24830 S Tamiami Trl (34134-7032)
PHONE...................................239 478-0359
Paulette Southwick, *President*
Andrew Gunn, *Vice Pres*
EMP: 7 **EST:** 2015
SALES (est): 361.8K **Privately Held**
WEB: www.thecabinetcollectioninc.com
SIC: 2434 Wood kitchen cabinets

(G-789)
CAMCO CHEMICAL
3635 Bonita Beach Rd # 3 (34134-4157)
PHONE...................................239 992-4100
Brian J Moffatt, *President*
EMP: 5 **EST:** 2014
SALES (est): 969.5K **Privately Held**
WEB: www.camcochemical.com
SIC: 2899 Chemical preparations

(G-790)
CEMEX PACIFIC HOLDINGS LLC
25061 Old 41 Rd (34135-7041)
PHONE...................................239 992-1400
EMP: 60 **Privately Held**
SIC: 3271 Mfg Concrete
HQ: Cemex Pacific Holdings, Llc
7150 Pollock Dr Ste 100
Las Vegas NV 89119
702 260-9900

(G-791)
COASTLAND SPECIALTIES LLC
28340 Trails Edge Blvd (34134-7586)
PHONE...................................239 910-5401
EMP: 7 **EST:** 2010
SALES (est): 438.7K **Privately Held**
SIC: 3629 Electronic generation equipment

(G-792)
COBALT LABORATORIES INC
24840 S Tamiami Trl Ste 1 (34134-7009)
PHONE...................................239 390-0245
Robert Sanzen, *President*
EMP: 12 **EST:** 2005
SQ FT: 2,000
SALES (est): 1.2MM **Privately Held**
WEB: www.cobaltlabs.com
SIC: 2834 Pharmaceutical preparations

(G-793)
CUSTOMER FIRST INC NAPLES
Also Called: Presstige Printing
10940 Harmony Park Dr (34135-1800)
PHONE...................................239 949-8518
Robert Weidenmiller, *President*
Dave Canty, *President*
Jimmy Deleon, *President*
Dana Winchell, *Cust Mgr*
Moe Zimmerman, *Cust Mgr*
EMP: 31 **EST:** 2001
SALES (est): 10.4MM **Privately Held**
SIC: 2752 7336 7334 7331 Commercial printing, offset; commercial art & graphic design; photocopying & duplicating services; direct mail advertising services

(G-794)
DA VINCI CABINETRY LLC
25241 Bernwood Dr Ste 7 (34135-7886)
PHONE...................................239 633-7957
Irmantas O Stiega,
EMP: 12 **EST:** 2006
SALES (est): 1MM **Privately Held**
WEB: www.davincicabinetry.com
SIC: 2434 Wood kitchen cabinets

(G-795)
ERNIES SIGNS
3901 Bonita Beach Rd (34134-4213)
P.O. Box 704 (34133-0704)
PHONE...................................239 992-0800
Joe E Fernandez Jr, *President*
EMP: 7 **EST:** 1972
SQ FT: 1,900
SALES (est): 498.9K **Privately Held**
SIC: 3993 Signs & advertising specialties

(G-796)
FAST SIGNS
Also Called: Fastsigns
28440 Old 41 Rd (34135-7070)
PHONE...................................239 498-7200
Bob Haller Jr, *CEO*
EMP: 8 **EST:** 2015
SALES (est): 182.9K **Privately Held**
WEB: www.fastsigns.com
SIC: 3993 7312 5999 5046 Signs & advertising specialties; outdoor advertising services; banners, flags, decals & posters; commercial equipment

(G-797)
FINAL TOUCH MOLDING CABINETRY
25070 Bernwood Dr (34135-7900)
PHONE...................................239 948-7856
Robert Glownia, *President*
Mike Grenzy, *Business Mgr*
▲ **EMP:** 9 **EST:** 1997
SQ FT: 5,305
SALES (est): 1MM **Privately Held**
WEB: www.finaltouchmc.com
SIC: 2434 Wood kitchen cabinets

(G-798)
FINAL TUCH MLDING CBINETRY INC
25070 Bernwood Dr (34135-7900)
PHONE...................................239 298-0980
Robert W Glownia, *Principal*
EMP: 8 **EST:** 2002
SALES (est): 75.1K **Privately Held**
WEB: www.finaltouchmc.com
SIC: 2434 Wood kitchen cabinets

(G-799)
FLOWERS BKG CO BRADENTON LLC
Also Called: Flowers Baking Company
26240 Old 41 Rd (34135-6634)
PHONE...................................941 758-5656
Chris Peer, *Manager*
EMP: 25
SALES (corp-wide): 4.3B **Publicly Held**
WEB: www.flobradconf.com
SIC: 2051 Bread, cake & related products
HQ: Flowers Baking Co. Of Bradenton, Llc
6490 Parkland Dr
Sarasota FL 34243

(G-800)
GEORGE & COMPANY LLC
28771 S Diesel Dr Ste 3 (34135-1808)
P.O. Box 111898, Naples (34108-0132)
PHONE...................................239 949-3650
Shauna Smilanich, *Sales Mgr*
Peter Smilanich, *Mng Member*
Kerry Bolognese, *Director*
▲ **EMP:** 41 **EST:** 2002
SQ FT: 10,000
SALES (est): 2.2MM **Privately Held**
WEB: www.lcrwild.com
SIC: 3944 Games, toys & children's vehicles

(G-801)
GUEST SERVICE PUBLICATIONS INC
28026 Pisces Ln (34135-8626)
PHONE...................................516 333-3474
Eric Miller, *President*
EMP: 10 **EST:** 1996
SALES (est): 480.7K **Privately Held**
SIC: 2752 2741 Publication printing, lithographic; telephone & other directory publishing

(G-802)
GULF COAST INSTALLERS LLC
28720 S Diesel Dr (34135-1820)
P.O. Box 163 (34133-0163)
PHONE...................................239 273-4663
Gabriel A Bava, *Principal*
EMP: 13 **EST:** 2015
SALES (est): 689.9K **Privately Held**
SIC: 2541 2542 Store & office display cases & fixtures; office & store showcases & display fixtures

(G-803)
I-PARTNER GROUP INC (PA)
Also Called: Bonita Print Shop
28200 Old 41 Rd Unit 204 (34135-0836)
PHONE...................................239 449-4749
Mark Pace, *President*
Albert Arguelles, *Vice Pres*
Marian Hack, *Opers Staff*
Jacob Albion, *Web Dvlpr*
EMP: 5 **EST:** 2012
SALES (est): 1.2MM **Privately Held**
WEB: www.vectradigital.com
SIC: 2399 Banners, pennants & flags

(G-804)
INSTITUTIONAL EYE CARE LLC
27499 Rvrview Ctr Blvd St (34134-4313)
P.O. Box 366550 (34136-6550)
PHONE...................................866 604-2931
EMP: 12
SALES (est): 1.3MM **Privately Held**
SIC: 3851 8042 Mfg Ophthalmic Goods Optometrist's Office

(G-805)
INTERACTYX AMERICAS INC
3461 Bonita Bay Blvd # 2 (34134-4384)
PHONE...................................888 575-2266
Alfred R Novas, *CEO*
John Hillsman, *Business Mgr*
Jodi Harrison, *Vice Pres*
Jodi L Harrison, *Vice Pres*
Michael Mangan, *Manager*
EMP: 29 **EST:** 2006
SQ FT: 2,339
SALES (est): 878.5K **Privately Held**
WEB: www.topyx.com
SIC: 7372 Application computer software

(G-806)
INTRINSIC INTERVENTIONS INC
223 Dolphin Cove Ct (34134-7456)
PHONE...................................614 205-8465
Kelly Burdge, *Branch Mgr*
EMP: 10
SALES (corp-wide): 81.2K **Privately Held**
WEB: www.myvistaflow.com
SIC: 2899

PA: Intrinsic Interventions Inc.
1604 Pecan St
Nokomis FL

(G-807)
JOHNSON BROS PRCSION PRCAST PD
24263 Production Cir (34135-7058)
PHONE..................239 947-6734
David L Johnson, *President*
EMP: 15 EST: 1988
SQ FT: 15,000
SALES (est): 2MM Privately Held
WEB: www.jbprecast.com
SIC: 3272 Concrete products, precast

(G-808)
K-PLEX LLC
Also Called: Coastal Scents
3960 Via Del Ray (34134)
PHONE..................239 963-2280
Reto S Kramer, *President*
Theresa Alfonso, *Human Resources*
▲ EMP: 28 EST: 2005
SQ FT: 2,500
SALES (est): 10.3MM Privately Held
SIC: 2844 5122 Cosmetic preparations; cosmetics

(G-809)
LIBERTY BALLOONS LLC
10401 Morningside Ln (34135-7730)
PHONE..................239 947-3338
EMP: 7 EST: 2018
SALES (est): 443.1K Privately Held
WEB: www.beardeddragongames.com
SIC: 3069 Fabricated rubber products

(G-810)
LOTT QA GROUP INC
27499 Riverview Center Bl (34134-4313)
PHONE..................201 693-2224
Mark Lott, *CEO*
Michele Licausi, *COO*
EMP: 8 EST: 2013
SALES (est): 418K Privately Held
SIC: 7372 7371 7379 Business oriented computer software; application computer software; computer software development & applications; computer related consulting services

(G-811)
MIP-TECHNOLOGY CORP
28100 Bonita Grande Dr # 101 (34135-6220)
PHONE..................239 221-3604
Donald Skelton, *President*
EMP: 6 EST: 2012
SALES (est): 397.5K Privately Held
SIC: 3826 Photometers

(G-812)
PEREZ INDUSTRIES INC
26364 Old 41 Rd (34135-6658)
PHONE..................239 992-2444
Baldemar J Perez, *President*
Christina Perez, *Admin Sec*
EMP: 12 EST: 1988
SQ FT: 4,900
SALES (est): 4.8MM Privately Held
WEB: www.perezindustries.com
SIC: 3353 3444 Aluminum sheet, plate & foil; sheet metalwork

(G-813)
PIZZAROS
24611 Production Cir (34135-7047)
PHONE..................239 390-0349
Daniel Marshall Snow, *Owner*
EMP: 8 EST: 2011
SALES (est): 439.1K Privately Held
WEB: www.pizzarosbonita.com
SIC: 3421 Table & food cutlery, including butchers'

(G-814)
PRESAGE ANALYTICS INC
27500 Rvrview Ctr Blvd St (34134-4325)
PHONE..................800 309-1704
Paul Griswold, *Principal*
EMP: 6 EST: 2019
SALES (est): 323.3K Privately Held
WEB: www.presageanalytics.com
SIC: 2034 Dehydrated fruits, vegetables, soups

(G-815)
PRESTIGE BRANDS INTERNATIONAL
26811 S Bay Dr Ste 300 (34134-4358)
PHONE..................914 524-6800
Matthew M Mannelly, *President*
Jean Boyko, *Senior VP*
John Parkinson, *Senior VP*
Ron Lombardi, *CFO*
Timothy J Connors, *Chief Mktg Ofcr*
EMP: 26 EST: 1999
SALES (est): 6.3MM
SALES (corp-wide): 1B Publicly Held
WEB: www.prestigebrands.com
SIC: 2834 Pharmaceutical preparations
HQ: Prestige Brands, Inc.
660 White Plains Rd # 250
Tarrytown NY 10591
914 524-6800

(G-816)
S & S PRECAST INC
25095 Old 41 Rd (34135-7041)
P.O. Box 366098 (34136-6098)
PHONE..................239 992-8685
Jerry Shannon, *President*
EMP: 14 EST: 2007
SALES (est): 2.6MM Privately Held
WEB: www.s-sprestress.net
SIC: 3272 Concrete products, precast

(G-817)
SHAW DEVELOPMENT LLC (PA)
25190 Bernwood Dr (34135-7846)
PHONE..................239 405-6100
Keith Luomala, *President*
Nancy O'Hara, *Corp Secy*
Robert Beckham, *Mfg Mgr*
David Graham, *Mfg Spvr*
Patrick Greivell, *Engineer*
◆ EMP: 180 EST: 1944
SQ FT: 50,000
SALES (est): 65.4MM Privately Held
WEB: www.shawdev.com
SIC: 3069 3714 3545 Rubber hardware; exhaust systems & parts, motor vehicle; gas tanks, motor vehicle; machine tool accessories

(G-818)
SKIM-A-ROUND INC
28282 Industrial St # 2 (34135-4852)
PHONE..................631 223-5072
Frank Norberto III, *Vice Pres*
EMP: 7 EST: 2015
SALES (est): 62K Privately Held
WEB: www.skim-a-round.com
SIC: 3423 Leaf skimmers or swimming pool rakes

(G-819)
SMARTADVOCATE LLC (PA)
27299 Riverview Center Bl (34134-4322)
PHONE..................239 390-1000
Jerrold Parker, *Principal*
Yana Krasnov, *Engineer*
Allison Rampolla, *VP Sls/Mktg*
Julia Moreland, *VP Sales*
Debra Markell, *Marketing Mgr*
EMP: 22 EST: 2003
SALES (est): 2.6MM Privately Held
WEB: www.smartadvocate.com
SIC: 7372 Business oriented computer software

(G-820)
SOUTHERN PINES INC
26300 Southern Pines Dr (34135-6165)
PHONE..................239 947-1515
Anthony Tesone, *President*
Joseph Tesone, *Vice Pres*
EMP: 5 EST: 1983
SALES (est): 498.1K Privately Held
SIC: 2451 Mobile homes

(G-821)
SPIRITWEAR TODAY
28711 N Diesel Dr Unit 9 (34135-1841)
PHONE..................239 676-7384
Joseph La Rosa, *President*
EMP: 6 EST: 2015
SALES (est): 414.3K Privately Held
WEB: www.heritagespiritwear.com
SIC: 2752 Commercial printing, offset

(G-822)
SPRINT PRINTING COMPANY LLC
28380 Old 41 Rd Ste 4 (34135-6814)
PHONE..................239 947-2221
Louisiana Mena,
Martin J Mena,
EMP: 6 EST: 2010
SALES (est): 712.4K Privately Held
WEB: www.instyprints.com
SIC: 2752 Commercial printing, offset

(G-823)
SUNSHINE SPRAY FOAM INSULATION
10923 K Nine Dr (34135-6853)
PHONE..................239 221-8704
Joceni Sartorio, *President*
EMP: 6 EST: 2019
SALES (est): 448.2K Privately Held
WEB: www.sunshinesprayfoamswfl.com
SIC: 1389 Construction, repair & dismantling services

(G-824)
SWF BONITA BEACH INC
3540 Bonita Beach Rd (34134-4158)
PHONE..................239 466-6600
Tim Anglim, *CEO*
EMP: 55 Privately Held
SIC: 2253 Beachwear, knit
PA: Swf Bonita Beach, Inc
17840 San Carlos Blvd
Fort Myers Beach FL 33931

(G-825)
TEDS SHEDS OF TAMPA
10311 Bonita Beach Rd Se (34135-4810)
PHONE..................239 344-2900
Glenn E Caudill, *President*
EMP: 29 EST: 1974
SQ FT: 23,000
SALES (est): 1MM Privately Held
SIC: 3448 Farm & utility buildings

(G-826)
TIMILON CORPORATION
24301 Walden Center Dr # 101 (34134-4965)
PHONE..................239 330-9650
Bill Sanford, *CEO*
EMP: 16 EST: 2020
SALES (est): 2.2MM Privately Held
WEB: www.timilon.com
SIC: 3564 Air purification equipment

(G-827)
WINDS
Also Called: Mango Bang
4555 Bonita Beach Rd (34134-3985)
PHONE..................239 948-0777
EMP: 10 EST: 2002
SALES (est): 530.8K Privately Held
SIC: 2339 Beachwear: women's, misses' & juniors'

Bowling Green
Hardee County

(G-828)
ABBOTT CITRUS LADDERS INC
4060 State Road 62 (33834-4124)
PHONE..................863 773-6322
Fax: 863 773-6322
EMP: 9
SALES: 800K Privately Held
SIC: 2499 Mfg Wood Products

(G-829)
CESARONI AEROSPACE INC
2280 Commerce Ct (33834-2004)
PHONE..................941 400-1421
Anthony Cesaroni, *President*
Judy V Kiyonaga, *Vice Pres*
Judy Kiyonaga, *Vice Pres*
Tim Green, *Mfg Staff*
Eric Vianna, *Supervisor*
EMP: 40 EST: 1985
SQ FT: 4,000
SALES (est): 4.7MM Privately Held
SIC: 3483 Rockets (ammunition)

(G-830)
LENOC CHEMICAL SOLUTIONS INC
2970 Manuel Rd (33834-3058)
PHONE..................229 499-0665
Bruce J Sperry, *Principal*
EMP: 7 EST: 2016
SALES (est): 139.2K Privately Held
SIC: 2879 Insecticides & pesticides

(G-831)
PROPLUS PRODUCTS INC
149 County Line Rd E (33834-2850)
P.O. Box 426 (33834-0426)
PHONE..................863 375-2487
Christina Lyle, *President*
Holly Lyle, *Office Mgr*
EMP: 12 EST: 2013
SALES (est): 1.9MM Privately Held
WEB: www.proplusproducts.com
SIC: 2873 Fertilizers: natural (organic), except compost

(G-832)
S A FLORIKAN-E LLC
2404 Commerce Ct (33834-2014)
PHONE..................800 322-8666
Kevin Cundiff, *General Mgr*
Donna Osteen, *Production*
Eric Rosenthal, *Mng Member*
John Donegan, *Manager*
Beth Faulkner, *Manager*
EMP: 60
SALES (corp-wide): 69.8MM Privately Held
WEB: www.florikan.com
SIC: 2875 Fertilizers, mixing only
HQ: Florikan-E.S.A Llc
6801 Energy Ct Ste 100
Lakewood Ranch FL 34240
941 379-4048

(G-833)
STREAM2SEA LLC
2498 Commerce Ct (33834-2014)
P.O. Box 907, Wauchula (33873-0907)
PHONE..................866 960-9513
Autumn Blum, *CEO*
Mike Malterre, *Exec VP*
Cat Miller, *Accounts Exec*
Leslie Taylor, *Accounts Exec*
Kate Goldrick, *Director*
EMP: 14 EST: 2014
SALES (est): 1MM Privately Held
WEB: www.stream2sea.com
SIC: 2844 5122 Cosmetic preparations; cosmetics, perfumes & hair products

Boynton Beach
Palm Beach County

(G-834)
3G ENTERPRISES INC
Also Called: 3g Grpahics Design & Printing
1530 Via De Pepi (33426-8240)
P.O. Box 3672 (33424-3672)
PHONE..................754 366-7643
Alexandra Grant, *Principal*
EMP: 14 EST: 2006
SALES (est): 153.6K Privately Held
SIC: 2752 Commercial printing, lithographic

(G-835)
A STEP ABOVE STAIRS RAILS LLC
12254 Colony Preserve Dr (33436-5806)
PHONE..................561 714-0646
Kenneth A Andrews Jr, *Manager*
EMP: 6 EST: 2016
SALES (est): 1.1MM Privately Held
WEB: www.astepabovestairsandrails.com
SIC: 3446 Stairs, staircases, stair treads: prefabricated metal

(G-836)
AD-TAR
26 Bristol Ln (33436-7413)
PHONE..................561 732-2055
Stuart Adelkoff, *Principal*
EMP: 7 EST: 2010
SALES (est): 140.9K Privately Held
SIC: 2865 Tar

▲ = Import ▼=Export
◆ =Import/Export

(G-837)

ADVANCED TRUCK EQUIPMENT INC
1315 Neptune Dr (33426-8403)
PHONE.................................561 424-0442
Kyle J Rathbun, *President*
Deborah A Rathbun, *Corp Secy*
EMP: 46 EST: 1957
SQ FT: 26,000
SALES (est): 1.5MM **Privately Held**
WEB: www.vanguardtrucks.com
SIC: 3713 Truck bodies (motor vehicles)

(G-838)

AMCI TECHNOLOGIES INC
9772 El Clair Ranch Rd (33437-3339)
PHONE.................................561 596-6288
Matthew I Kahn, *Principal*
EMP: 11 EST: 2010
SALES (est): 184.2K **Privately Held**
WEB: www.amcitech.com
SIC: 3823 Industrial instrmnts msrmnt display/control process variable

(G-839)

AMERICAN BOTTLING COMPANY
Southeast-Atlantic
4895 Park Ridge Blvd (33426-8316)
PHONE.................................561 732-7395
Rich Kerner, *Manager*
EMP: 101
SQ FT: 3,000 **Publicly Held**
WEB: www.keurigdrpepper.com
SIC: 2086 Soft drinks: packaged in cans, bottles, etc.
HQ: The American Bottling Company
6425 Hall Of Fame Ln
Frisco TX 75034

(G-840)

AMERICAN MOLDING AND PLAS LLC
870 W Industrial Ave # 8 (33426-3643)
PHONE.................................561 676-1987
Angelo J Christopher, *Mng Member*
EMP: 12 EST: 2012
SALES (est): 4MM **Privately Held**
WEB:
www.americanmoldingandplastics.com
SIC: 3089 Injection molding of plastics

(G-841)

ANTON PAAR QUANTATEC INC
Also Called: Quantachrome Instruments
1900 Corporate Dr (33426-6650)
PHONE.................................561 731-4999
Jakob Santner, *Ch of Bd*
Georg Cortolezis-Supp, *President*
Reinhard Eberl, *Vice Pres*
Josh Young, *Project Mgr*
Mark Contessa, *Opers Mgr*
EMP: 5 EST: 1922
SQ FT: 45,000
SALES (est): 5.4MM
SALES (corp-wide): 452.3MM **Privately Held**
WEB: www.quantachrome.com
SIC: 3826 3829 Analytical instruments; measuring & controlling devices
HQ: Anton Paar Gmbh
Anton-Paar-StraBe 20
Graz 8054
316 257-0

(G-842)

APOGEE SERVICES INC
703 Sw 24th Ave (33435-6752)
PHONE.................................561 441-5354
Joy E Wilkie, *President*
Joy Wilkie, *Marketing Staff*
EMP: 11 EST: 2004
SALES (est): 350K **Privately Held**
SIC: 3531 Airport construction machinery

(G-843)

APPOINTMENT TEAM INC
1530 W Boynton Beach Blvd (33436-4606)
PHONE.................................561 314-5471
Nicholas Atasoy,
EMP: 10 EST: 2018
SALES (est): 641.3K **Privately Held**
SIC: 3699 Security devices

(G-844)

AREWEONLINECOM LLC
1101 N Congress Ave # 202 (33426-3336)
PHONE.................................561 572-0233
Mark Turkel,
James Wright,
EMP: 6 EST: 2010
SALES (est): 300.5K **Privately Held**
WEB: www.areweonline.com
SIC: 3695 Computer software tape & disks: blank, rigid & floppy

(G-845)

ATLAS PEAT & SOIL INC (PA)
9621 S State Road 7 (33472-4609)
PHONE.................................561 734-7300
Brian Lulfs, *President*
Michelle Lancianese, *Corp Secy*
Julie Croteau, *Vice Pres*
Margaret Lulfs, *Vice Pres*
Kathryn Vanreeth, *Vice Pres*
◆ **EMP: 38 EST:** 1965
SQ FT: 6,400
SALES (est): 7.3MM **Privately Held**
WEB: www.atlaspeatandsoil.com
SIC: 3295 Diatomaceous earth, ground or otherwise treated

(G-846)

BOBS QUICK PRTG & COPY CTR
Also Called: Bob's Printing
812 Chapel Hill Blvd (33435-8111)
PHONE.................................561 278-0203
Fax: 561 272-3828
EMP: 8
SQ FT: 4,000
SALES (est): 850K **Privately Held**
SIC: 2752 Offset Printing & Photo Offset

(G-847)

BOUNCE BACK MBL DETAILING LLC ✪
Also Called: Car Wash
200 Knuth Rd Ste 103 (33436-4635)
PHONE.................................561 336-4626
Walter Waitus Pressley III,
EMP: 7 EST: 2021
SALES (est): 439.4K **Privately Held**
SIC: 3589 Car washing machinery

(G-848)

BRADDCK MTLLGL ARSP SER INC
507 Industrial Way (33426-8770)
PHONE.................................561 622-2200
George Gieger, *Principal*
Steve Hutchinson, *Plant Mgr*
EMP: 12 EST: 2008
SALES (est): 1MM **Privately Held**
WEB: www.braddockmt.com
SIC: 3398 Metal heat treating

(G-849)

CC LIGHTING INC
11138 Green Lake Dr (33437-1465)
PHONE.................................805 302-5321
Frank C Cotone, *Principal*
EMP: 10 EST: 2013
SALES (est): 578.4K **Privately Held**
SIC: 3648 Lighting equipment

(G-850)

CECO INC
Also Called: Caribbean Interior Design Ctr
2951 Sw 14th Pl Ste 39 (33426-9005)
P.O. Box 207 (33425-0207)
PHONE.................................561 265-1111
EMP: 10
SQ FT: 1,600
SALES (est): 590K **Privately Held**
SIC: 2591 Manufactures Window Treatments Including Vertical Blinds Mini Blinds And Window Shades

(G-851)

CLEAR COPY INC
Also Called: 33 Wraps
1304 N Federal Hwy (33435-3233)
PHONE.................................561 369-3900
Steve Feldman, *President*
Bob Feldman, *Vice Pres*
Royce Feldman, *Vice Pres*
Mary Anne Feldman, *Manager*
EMP: 29 EST: 1974

SQ FT: 4,000
SALES (est): 1MM **Privately Held**
WEB: www.clearcopyprinting.com
SIC: 2752 Commercial printing, offset

(G-852)

CONDITION CULTURE LLC
Also Called: Featherlocks
123 Harbors Way (33435-2400)
PHONE.................................786 433-8279
Jennifer Donya,
Alexandra Litowitz,
▲ **EMP: 8 EST:** 2011
SALES (est): 703.7K **Privately Held**
WEB: www.conditionculture.com
SIC: 3999 Hair & hair-based products

(G-853)

CUSTOM INSTRUMENTS LLC
711 N Railroad Ave Unit 3 (33435-3817)
PHONE.................................561 735-9971
Edwyn B Pyron,
Lori Pyron,
EMP: 5 EST: 2004
SALES (est): 452.3K **Privately Held**
SIC: 3549 Metalworking machinery

(G-854)

CUSTOM TRUSS LLC
510 Industrial Ave (33426-3645)
PHONE.................................561 266-3451
Iva Kutlova, *President*
EMP: 12 EST: 2008
SALES (est): 2.9MM **Privately Held**
WEB: www.customtrussllc.com
SIC: 2439 Trusses, wooden roof

(G-855)

DELUXE STONE INC
6129 Country Fair Cir (33437-2847)
PHONE.................................561 236-2322
Jimmy Montoya, *Principal*
EMP: 10 EST: 2009
SALES (est): 313.1K **Privately Held**
SIC: 2782 Blankbooks & looseleaf binders

(G-856)

DIGICARE BIOMEDICAL TECH INC
107 Commerce Rd (33426-9365)
PHONE.................................561 689-0408
Eduardo Miranda, *President*
Pedro Miranda, *Software Engr*
Donovan Wright, *Technician*
EMP: 9 EST: 1995
SQ FT: 5,000
SALES (est): 2.4MM **Privately Held**
WEB: www.digicarebiomedical.com
SIC: 3841 Surgical & medical instruments

(G-857)

DOUBLE DS TOBACCCO
700 W Boynton Beach Blvd (33426-3639)
PHONE.................................561 901-9145
Hussein Shehata, *Manager*
EMP: 7 EST: 2011
SALES (est): 132.2K **Privately Held**
SIC: 3999 Cigarette & cigar products & accessories

(G-858)

DOUBLE R PUBLISHING
621 Nw 10th Ct (33426-2972)
PHONE.................................305 525-3573
Rebeca Lamas, *Manager*
EMP: 7 EST: 2013
SALES (est): 412K **Privately Held**
SIC: 2741 Miscellaneous publishing

(G-859)

DRYER VENT WIZARD OF PB
22 Las Flores (33426-8821)
PHONE.................................561 901-3464
Horatio Chiorean, *Owner*
Wai Chan, *Project Mgr*
Mike Tang, *Project Mgr*
Colleen Martin, *Buyer*
Sean Eberhardt, *Engineer*
EMP: 10 EST: 2007
SALES (est): 649.1K **Privately Held**
WEB:
dryerventcleaningbocaraton.blogspot.com
SIC: 3631 Barbecues, grills & braziers (outdoor cooking)

(G-860)

EAGLE ENGRG & LAND DEV INC
302 Sw 3rd Ave (33435-4823)
P.O. Box 990189, Naples (34116-6067)
PHONE.................................913 948-4320
Lori Schulmeister, *President*
Hugh A House Jr, *President*
EMP: 10 EST: 1994
SQ FT: 2,000
SALES (est): 2MM **Privately Held**
WEB: www.eaglesitedev.com
SIC: 1422 1611 1781 1794 Crushed & broken limestone; highway & street construction; water well drilling; excavation & grading, building construction; water distribution or supply systems for irrigation

(G-861)

ECCO DOORS LLC
505 Industrial Way (33426-8770)
PHONE.................................561 392-3533
EMP: 5
SALES (est): 683.6K **Privately Held**
SIC: 2511 Mfg Wood Household Furniture

(G-862)

ECCO DOORS MANUFACTURING LLC
505 Industrial Way (33426-8770)
PHONE.................................561 721-6660
Michael Judes, *Mng Member*
EMP: 11 EST: 2012
SALES (est): 252.2K **Privately Held**
WEB: www.eccodoors.com
SIC: 2511 Wood household furniture

(G-863)

ENDANGERED SPECIES DESIGNS LLC
3469 W Boyntn Bch Blvd (33436-4611)
PHONE.................................954 613-2111
Tyree Jones, *CEO*
EMP: 10 EST: 2018
SALES (est): 110K **Privately Held**
SIC: 2759 Letterpress & screen printing

(G-864)

ERICKSON INTERNATIONAL LLC
161 Commerce Rd Ste 2 (33426-9385)
PHONE.................................702 853-4800
Debbie Lindsay, *Branch Mgr*
EMP: 9
SALES (corp-wide): 13.4MM **Privately Held**
WEB: www.aswf.com
SIC: 3211 Window glass, clear & colored
PA: Erickson International, Llc
3135 Marco St
Las Vegas NV 89115
702 853-4800

(G-865)

FIVE STAR FELD SVCS APPLCHIA L
Also Called: Five Star Measurement
3539 S Federal Hwy Apt L (33435-8689)
PHONE.................................347 446-6816
Douglas Asch, *Mng Member*
William Cook,
Keith Stone,
EMP: 7 EST: 2008
SQ FT: 1,000
SALES (est): 355K **Privately Held**
SIC: 1389 Measurement of well flow rates, oil & gas

(G-866)

FKP
2950 Commerce Park Dr # 6 (33426-8779)
PHONE.................................561 493-0076
Anne Punter, *President*
EMP: 8 EST: 2008
SALES (est): 396.9K **Privately Held**
WEB: www.fkp-us.com
SIC: 3799 Go-carts, except children's

(G-867)

FLAVCITY CORP ✪
3050 Sw 14th Pl Ste 14 (33426-9089)
PHONE.................................413 221-0041
Robert Parrish, *President*
EMP: 8 EST: 2021

SALES (est): 391.1K **Privately Held**
WEB: www.shopflavcity.com
SIC: 2087 5961 Powders, drink;

(G-868)
FLORIDA BEST HEARING
4739 N Congress Ave (33426-7940)
PHONE..................................863 402-0094
Guy Steve Reinshuttle, *Principal*
EMP: 29 **EST:** 2018
SALES (est): 211.3K **Privately Held**
SIC: 3842 8099 Hearing aids; hearing testing service

(G-869)
FRIENDS PROFESSIONAL STY
1521 Neptune Dr (33426-8418)
PHONE..................................561 734-4660
Richard Friend Sr, *President*
Howard Friend, *Corp Secy*
William Friend, *Vice Pres*
EMP: 8 **EST:** 1979
SQ FT: 8,000
SALES (est): 490.9K **Privately Held**
WEB: www.friendsstationery.com
SIC: 2759 Engraving

(G-870)
GATEWAY WRELESS COMMUNICATIONS
3600 S Congress Ave (33426-8488)
PHONE..................................561 732-6444
EMP: 10
SALES (est): 720K **Privately Held**
SIC: 3663 Wireless Communications

(G-871)
GEVAS PCKG CONVERTING TECH LTD
3553 High Ridge Rd (33426-8737)
PHONE..................................561 202-0800
Carlo Gretter, *President*
Thomas Sander, *Partner*
EMP: 5 **EST:** 1997
SQ FT: 12,000
SALES (est): 911.8K **Privately Held**
SIC: 3565 Packaging machinery

(G-872)
GFOODZ LLC
10356 Willow Oaks Trl (33473-4860)
PHONE..................................561 703-4505
Sonali Surve, *Mng Member*
EMP: 7 **EST:** 2016
SALES (est): 100K **Privately Held**
SIC: 2051 5149 Bakery: wholesale or wholesale/retail combined; bakery products

(G-873)
GOLDEN PRINT INC
2701 Sw 6th St (33435-7511)
PHONE..................................561 833-9661
Christopher Lanni, *President*
EMP: 8 **EST:** 2018
SALES (est): 165.3K **Privately Held**
SIC: 2752 Commercial printing, offset

(G-874)
GRAFTON PRODUCTS CORP
Also Called: Grafton Cosmetics
1801 Corporate Dr (33426-6646)
PHONE..................................561 738-2886
Edward Marcus, *President*
Gail Marcus, *Corp Secy*
Steven Marcus, *Vice Pres*
David Carroll, *Opers Staff*
Myra Kenigsman, *Sales Staff*
▲ **EMP:** 24 **EST:** 1962
SQ FT: 17,000
SALES (est): 4.4MM **Privately Held**
WEB: www.shopgraftoncosmetics.com
SIC: 2844 Perfumes, natural or synthetic; cosmetic preparations

(G-875)
GRANITE IMPORTS INC
1500 Gateway Blvd Ste 250 (33426-7245)
PHONE..................................732 500-2549
▲ **EMP:** 1
SQ FT: 1,000
SALES (est): 4MM **Privately Held**
SIC: 1411 Dimension Stone Quarry

(G-876)
H A FRIEND & COMPANY INC
1521 Neptune Dr (33426-8418)
PHONE..................................847 746-1248
Richard W Friend Sr, *Ch of Bd*
Randy Friend, *President*
Richard Friend Jr, *Vice Pres*
EMP: 50 **EST:** 1908
SALES (est): 2.7MM **Privately Held**
WEB: www.friendsstationery.com
SIC: 2759 5112 5021 5044 Embossing on paper; office supplies; office furniture; office equipment

(G-877)
ICE CREAM CLUB INC (PA)
1580 High Ridge Rd (33426-8724)
PHONE..................................561 731-3331
Richard Draper, *CEO*
Tom Jackson, *Exec VP*
Thomas D Jackson, *Vice Pres*
Michael Scott, *Vice Pres*
Mike Scott, *Vice Pres*
▼ **EMP:** 40 **EST:** 1982
SQ FT: 16,500
SALES (est): 7.5MM **Privately Held**
WEB: www.icecreamclub.com
SIC: 2024 Ice cream & frozen desserts

(G-878)
IIS INCORPORATED
3020 High Ridge Rd (33426-8732)
PHONE..................................561 547-4297
Mark A Shymansky, *President*
Catharine Greenman, *Credit Staff*
David Shelfer, *Sales Mgr*
EMP: 7 **EST:** 2007
SALES (est): 781.4K **Privately Held**
SIC: 2394 3089 5039 5199 Canvas awnings & canopies; awnings, fiberglass & plastic combination; awnings; canvas products

(G-879)
INNOVATIVE INDUS SOLUTIONS INC (PA)
Also Called: I I S
3020 High Ridge Rd (33426-8732)
PHONE..................................561 733-1548
Mark Shymansky, *President*
Rodger Wise, *Vice Pres*
Catharine Greenman, *Credit Mgr*
▼ **EMP:** 7 **EST:** 2001
SQ FT: 12,000
SALES (est): 2.7MM **Privately Held**
WEB: www.iisfla.com
SIC: 2394 Canvas & related products

(G-880)
INNOVTIVE WIN CNCPTS DOORS INC
4336 Juniper Ter (33436-3023)
PHONE..................................561 493-2303
EMP: 19
SALES: 3MM **Privately Held**
SIC: 2431 3442 Mfg Millwork Mfg Metal Doors/Sash/Trim

(G-881)
INTERSTATE SIGNCRAFTERS LLC
130 Commerce Rd (33426-9364)
PHONE..................................561 547-3760
Jeff Petersen, *CEO*
Lisa Johnson, *Vice Pres*
Anthony Lipari, *VP Opers*
Valerie Mayer, *VP Finance*
Terri Seldin, *Finance*
▼ **EMP:** 75 **EST:** 1997
SQ FT: 35,000
SALES (est): 9.2MM **Privately Held**
WEB: www.interstatesigncrafters.com
SIC: 3993 1799 Electric signs; sign installation & maintenance

(G-882)
JHN NORTH LLC
3554 Lothair Ave (33436-3122)
PHONE..................................561 294-5613
Juan C Pereyra, *Manager*
EMP: 7 **EST:** 2018
SALES (est): 509.9K **Privately Held**
SIC: 3823 Industrial instrmnts msrmnt display/control process variable

(G-883)
KERRY CONSULTING CORP
30 Lawrence Lake Dr (33436-2020)
PHONE..................................561 364-9969
Joel Sarnow, *President*
Doug Pearsall, *Vice Pres*
Linda Sarnow, *Treasurer*
EMP: 10 **EST:** 2007
SALES (est): 1MM **Privately Held**
WEB: www.kerryconsultingcorp.com
SIC: 2096 Potato chips & similar snacks

(G-884)
LAP OF AMER LSER APPLCTONS LLC
161 Commerce Rd Ste 3 (33426-9385)
PHONE..................................561 416-9250
Peter Van Arkel, *CEO*
Caroly Van Arkel, *General Mgr*
Mamadou Ba, *Engineer*
Michael Olivera, *Engineer*
Hector Serrano, *Engineer*
▲ **EMP:** 7 **EST:** 1996
SQ FT: 1,500
SALES (est): 1.5MM **Privately Held**
WEB: www.lap-america.com
SIC: 3699 5085 Laser systems & equipment; industrial supplies

(G-885)
LEGAR INC
303 E Woolbright Rd # 103 (33435-6010)
PHONE..................................561 635-5882
Michael Basnight, *President*
Arlena Richardson, *Chief Mktg Ofcr*
Michael Hursey, *General Counsel*
EMP: 10 **EST:** 2018
SALES (est): 2MM **Privately Held**
SIC: 2671 Paper coated or laminated for packaging

(G-886)
LIFELINE SOFTWARE INC
161 Commerce Rd Ste 3 (33426-9385)
PHONE..................................866 592-1343
Thomas Simmerer, *CEO*
Craig Laughton, *CEO*
Jim Dube, *President*
Kathie Carrington, *Sales Staff*
David Dube, *Sales Staff*
EMP: 19 **EST:** 1999
SALES (est): 1.4MM **Privately Held**
WEB: www.lifelinesoftware.com
SIC: 7372 Prepackaged software

(G-887)
LJS TOPS & BOTTOMS
Also Called: L J'S Tops & Bottoms
3050 Sw 14th Pl Ste 11 (33426-9020)
PHONE..................................561 736-7868
Lawrence A Walicki, *Partner*
Judy K Walicki, *Partner*
EMP: 24 **EST:** 1993
SQ FT: 4,000
SALES (est): 2.4MM **Privately Held**
WEB: www.ljstopsandbottoms.com
SIC: 3799 3949 Golf carts, powered; sporting & athletic goods

(G-888)
M & S COMPUTER PRODUCTS INC
Also Called: Servers 4 Networks
11419 Wingfoot Dr (33437-1629)
PHONE..................................561 244-5400
Marcia Posen, *President*
◆ **EMP:** 5 **EST:** 1985
SQ FT: 4,000
SALES (est): 451.3K **Privately Held**
SIC: 3571 2844 5999 Electronic computers; tonics, hair; business machines & equipment; telephone & communication equipment

(G-889)
MARK WSSER GRPHIC PRDCTONS INC
Also Called: Mark Weisser Productions
8941 Golden Mountain Cir (33473-3310)
PHONE..................................305 888-7445
Mark Weisser, *President*
EMP: 5 **EST:** 1992
SQ FT: 1,200
SALES (est): 373.3K **Privately Held**
SIC: 2759 Advertising literature: printing

(G-890)
MAXORD LLC
Also Called: Foxhound
10849 Sunset Ridge Cir (33473-4851)
PHONE..................................405 256-2381
Josh Griffin, *Mng Member*
EMP: 10 **EST:** 2019
SALES (est): 100K **Privately Held**
SIC: 7372 Application computer software

(G-891)
MRI SPECIALISTS
1800 W Woolbright Rd # 100 (33426-6398)
PHONE..................................561 369-2144
Richard Bajakian, *President*
Deidra Knevelbaard, *Office Mgr*
Kim Heredia, *Manager*
EMP: 8 **EST:** 2002
SALES (est): 1MM **Privately Held**
WEB: www.mrispecialists.net
SIC: 3845 8071 Magnetic resonance imaging device, nuclear; medical laboratories

(G-892)
MYERS CSTM CABINETS FURN CORP
3151 Sw 14th Pl Ste 7 (33426-9037)
PHONE..................................561 602-0755
Darrin Myers, *Principal*
EMP: 7 **EST:** 2015
SALES (est): 110K **Privately Held**
SIC: 2434 Wood kitchen cabinets

(G-893)
NAMRO INDUSTRIES INC
4336 Juniper Ter (33436-3023)
PHONE..................................561 704-8063
Christine Orman, *Director*
EMP: 8 **EST:** 2005
SALES (est): 305K **Privately Held**
SIC: 3999 Manufacturing industries

(G-894)
NATURAL BEAUTY WOOD PRODUCTS
Also Called: Creative Metal Products
1120 Se 1st St (33435-6013)
PHONE..................................561 732-0224
Joshua Aron, *Vice Pres*
EMP: 10 **EST:** 2000
SQ FT: 1,728
SALES (est): 965.9K **Privately Held**
WEB: www.creativemetals.org
SIC: 2431 Staircases, stairs & railings

(G-895)
PEERLESS WIND SYSTEMS
8681 Hawkwood Bay Dr (33473-7822)
PHONE..................................516 249-6900
Jay Moskowitz, *Owner*
Robert Perless, *Vice Pres*
EMP: 8 **EST:** 2015
SALES (est): 572.2K **Privately Held**
SIC: 3511 3621 Turbines & turbine generator sets; motors & generators

(G-896)
PLOTKOWSKI INC (PA)
Also Called: Delray's Screens
210 Se 12th Ave Ste 1 (33435-6063)
PHONE..................................561 740-2226
Carol Plotkowski, *President*
Michael Plotkowski, *Vice Pres*
EMP: 9 **EST:** 1960
SQ FT: 10,000
SALES (est): 781.3K **Privately Held**
WEB: www.delrayscreen.net
SIC: 3442 3444 Screens, window, metal; screen doors, metal; sheet metalwork

(G-897)
POWERBEES INCORPORATED
1375 Gateway Blvd (33426-8304)
PHONE..................................561 797-5927
John Metz, *Principal*
Rachel Cormier, *Business Mgr*
EMP: 7 **EST:** 2010
SALES (est): 259.8K **Privately Held**
WEB: www.powerbees.com
SIC: 3442 Metal doors, sash & trim

(G-898)
PRECISION PRINTING OF COLUMBUS
11831 Fox Hill Cir (33473-7833)
PHONE.................................561 509-7269
Michael Leaventon, *President*
Marc Leaventon, *General Mgr*
Meridith Solomon, *Treasurer*
Barry Leaventon, *Admin Sec*
EMP: 8 **EST:** 1985
SQ FT: 16,000
SALES (est): 164.6K **Privately Held**
SIC: 2752 2791 Commercial printing, lithographic; typesetting

(G-899)
PREMIER PLASTICS LLC (PA)
1500 Gateway Blvd Ste 250 (33426-7245)
PHONE.................................305 805-3333
Albert Esquenazi,
Morris Esquenazi,
▲ **EMP:** 5 **EST:** 2014
SALES (est): 451.6K **Privately Held**
WEB: www.premierplastics.net
SIC: 3999 2392 3861 Barber & beauty shop equipment; bags, garment storage: except paper or plastic film; reels, film

(G-900)
PREMIUM ABSRBENT DSPSABLES LLC
Also Called: Tite-Dri Industries
3030 Sw 13th Pl Ste A (33426-9086)
PHONE.................................561 737-6377
Carlo Gretter, *Mng Member*
EMP: 47 **EST:** 2005
SALES (est): 11.5MM **Privately Held**
WEB: www.titedri.com
SIC: 2673 Bags: plastic, laminated & coated

(G-901)
PRO MILLWORK INSTALLATIONS
1420 Sw 30th Ave (33426-9062)
PHONE.................................561 302-5869
EMP: 6 **EST:** 2020
SALES (est): 716.3K **Privately Held**
WEB: www.pro-millwork.com
SIC: 2431 Millwork

(G-902)
PRODUCTS BY O2 INC
3020 High Ridge Rd # 300 (33426-8732)
PHONE.................................561 392-1892
Olga Galarza, *President*
EMP: 20 **EST:** 2001
SQ FT: 15,000
SALES (est): 2.5MM **Privately Held**
WEB: www.productsbyo2inc.com
SIC: 2844 Cosmetic preparations

(G-903)
PURADYN FILTER TECH INC
2017 High Ridge Rd (33426-8713)
PHONE.................................561 547-9499
Edward S Vittoria, *CEO*
Joseph V Vittoria, *Ch of Bd*
Kevin G Kroger, *President*
V L Garrity, *Purch Mgr*
Sathish Kannan, *Engineer*
EMP: 20 **EST:** 1988
SQ FT: 25,500
SALES (est): 1.5MM **Privately Held**
WEB: www.puradyn.com
SIC: 3714 Filters: oil, fuel & air, motor vehicle

(G-904)
PYURE COMPANY INC ✪
2055 High Ridge Rd (33426-8713)
PHONE.................................561 735-3701
Jean Francois Huc, *CEO*
EMP: 23 **EST:** 2022
SALES (est): 3.7MM **Privately Held**
WEB: www.pyure.com
SIC: 3634 Air purifiers, portable

(G-905)
QUICKPRINT LINE
2015 Corporate Dr (33426-6653)
P.O. Box 1435, Lake Worth (33460-1435)
PHONE.................................561 740-9930
EMP: 8 **EST:** 2010

SALES (est): 11.6K **Privately Held**
WEB: www.quickprintline.com
SIC: 2752 Commercial printing, offset

(G-906)
RADIAL INC
1903 S Congress Ave # 460 (33426-6559)
P.O. Box 4688 (33424-4688)
PHONE.................................561 737-5151
Theresa Raczkowski, *Consultant*
Dylan Smart, *Consultant*
Kathleen Pastorelli, *Technical Staff*
Daniel Cunningham, *Director*
Susan Haddad, *Recruiter*
EMP: 16
SALES (corp-wide): 2.6B **Privately Held**
WEB: www.radial.com
SIC: 7372 Business oriented computer software
HQ: Radial, Inc.
935 1st Ave
King Of Prussia PA 19406
610 491-7000

(G-907)
RAINBOW PRINTING INC
10699 Cambay Dr (33437-3205)
PHONE.................................561 364-9000
John H Thomas, *President*
Mary Ann Thomas, *Vice Pres*
EMP: 5 **EST:** 1981
SALES (est): 699.2K **Privately Held**
WEB: www.rainbow-printing.com
SIC: 2752 Commercial printing, offset

(G-908)
RED BRICK PUBLISHING LLC
6647 Conch Ct (33437-3648)
PHONE.................................718 208-3600
Jason R Margolin, *Manager*
EMP: 8 **EST:** 2001
SALES (est): 180.4K **Privately Held**
SIC: 2741 Miscellaneous publishing

(G-909)
ROMEO ROSEAU ECOMMERCE
245 Ne 6th Ave (33435-3875)
PHONE.................................561 633-1352
Vladimir Thelisma, *Owner*
EMP: 10 **EST:** 2016
SALES (est): 292.6K **Privately Held**
SIC: 2741

(G-910)
SEAGATE PRODUCTIONS LLC
1162 Rialto Dr (33436-7198)
PHONE.................................561 506-7750
Oswald Imbert, *Principal*
EMP: 6 **EST:** 2019
SALES (est): 485.9K **Privately Held**
WEB: www.seagate.com
SIC: 3572 Computer storage devices

(G-911)
SGS PAVERS INC
5633 Marseilles Port Ln (33472-2463)
PHONE.................................561 436-7276
Edward M Sullivan Jr, *President*
EMP: 12 **EST:** 2005
SALES (est): 187.5K **Privately Held**
SIC: 2951 Asphalt paving mixtures & blocks

(G-912)
SHOWER DOORS UNLIMITED INC
74 Baytree Ln (33436-9146)
PHONE.................................561 547-0702
Linda Sorber, *President*
▼ **EMP:** 7 **EST:** 1997
SALES (est): 433K **Privately Held**
SIC: 3431 3231 Shower stalls, metal; products of purchased glass

(G-913)
SODIKART USA
1025 Gateway Blvd (33426-8348)
PHONE.................................561 493-0290
Peter Bekkers, *Principal*
▲ **EMP:** 8 **EST:** 2013
SALES (est): 516.1K **Privately Held**
WEB: www.sodikartamerica.com
SIC: 3799 Transportation equipment

(G-914)
SOMFY SYSTEMS INC
1200 Sw 35th Ave (33426-8423)
PHONE.................................561 292-3483
Frank Watts, *Manager*
EMP: 13
SALES (corp-wide): 2.6MM **Privately Held**
SIC: 3699 Door opening & closing devices, electrical
HQ: Somfy Systems, Inc.
121 Herrod Blvd
Dayton NJ 08810
609 395-1300

(G-915)
SOUTH FLORIDA STAIRS INC
2019 Corporate Dr (33426-6653)
PHONE.................................561 822-3110
Joshua Cote, *President*
EMP: 15 **EST:** 2013
SALES (est): 5.5MM **Privately Held**
WEB: www.southfloridastairs.com
SIC: 2431 3446 Staircases, stairs & railings; stairs, staircases, stair treads: prefabricated metal

(G-916)
SUNCOAST HEAT TREAT INC (PA)
507 Industrial Way (33426-8770)
PHONE.................................561 776-7763
Robert H Brisell, *CEO*
Jennifer McPeek, *President*
Steve Hutchinson, *Vice Pres*
Jo Gayne, *Treasurer*
EMP: 11 **EST:** 1983
SQ FT: 43,000
SALES (est): 4.3MM **Privately Held**
SIC: 3398 Metal heat treating

(G-917)
T V TRAC LTD
7 Island Dr (33436-6072)
PHONE.................................516 371-1111
EMP: 6
SALES (est): 510K **Privately Held**
SIC: 3699 Mfg Electrical Equipment/Supplies

(G-918)
TACTICAL PRODUCTS GROUP LLC
1914 Corporate Dr (33426-6650)
PHONE.................................561 265-4066
Robert J Leitner, *COO*
Dan T Lounsbury Jr,
▲ **EMP:** 25 **EST:** 1998
SALES (est): 3.6MM **Privately Held**
WEB: www.tacprogroup.com
SIC: 2329 7381 Men's & boys' sportswear & athletic clothing; protective services, guard

(G-919)
TIN-REZ CORP INC
6615 Boynton Beach Blvd (33437-3526)
PHONE.................................561 654-3133
Antony Mitchell, *Principal*
EMP: 13 **EST:** 2012
SALES (est): 607.4K **Privately Held**
SIC: 3356 Tin

(G-920)
TONER TECHNOLOGIES INC
2900 Commerce Park Dr # 11 (33426-8775)
PHONE.................................561 547-9710
Timothy Burnett, *President*
Timothy J Burnett, *President*
Sherry Burnett, *Vice Pres*
Cheryl Burnett, *CFO*
EMP: 5 **EST:** 1989
SQ FT: 1,800
SALES (est): 881.6K **Privately Held**
WEB: www.toner-tech.com
SIC: 3955 5734 5112 5999 Print cartridges for laser & other computer printers; word processing equipment & supplies; stationery & office supplies; photocopying supplies; photocopy machines; photocopy machine repair

(G-921)
TOWER OPTICAL CORPORATION
3600 S Congress Ave Ste J (33426-8488)
PHONE.................................561 740-2525
Mel Kantor, *President*
Don Avritt, *Mfg Dir*
Marty Jennings, *Mktg Dir*
Elizabeth Richardson, *Manager*
EMP: 19 **EST:** 1988
SQ FT: 11,000
SALES (est): 4.2MM **Privately Held**
WEB: www.toweroptical.com
SIC: 3827 Optical instruments & apparatus

(G-922)
VAZKOR TECHNOLOGIES S FLA INC
605 E Boynton Beach Blvd (33435-4199)
PHONE.................................561 357-9029
Aaron Korff, *President*
Shalom Korff, *Administration*
EMP: 7 **EST:** 2000
SALES (est): 838K **Privately Held**
WEB: www.vazkor.com
SIC: 7372 7371 Prepackaged software; computer software systems analysis & design, custom

(G-923)
VEE INDUSTRIES INC
211 Se 9th Ave (33435-5643)
PHONE.................................561 732-1083
Shawn R Aldous, *President*
John G Rubino, *Vice Pres*
Dee Rubino, *Treasurer*
Verena Edler, *Manager*
David A Aldous, *Admin Sec*
▲ **EMP:** 8 **EST:** 1969
SQ FT: 3,600
SALES (est): 1.4MM **Privately Held**
WEB: store.veeindustries.com
SIC: 3643 Current-carrying wiring devices

(G-924)
WINDBRELLA PRODUCTS CORP
2114 Corporate Dr (33426-6655)
PHONE.................................561 734-5222
Glen Kupferman, *President*
Chelsea Heller, *Vice Pres*
▲ **EMP:** 26 **EST:** 1996
SALES (est): 1.4MM **Privately Held**
WEB: www.windbrella.com
SIC: 2211 Umbrella cloth, cotton

(G-925)
WORLDS COLUMBIAN EXONUMIS
802 North Rd (33435-3230)
PHONE.................................561 734-4433
L Tallent-Diddle, *Principal*
EMP: 6 **EST:** 2002
SALES (est): 330.6K **Privately Held**
SIC: 3444 Mail (post office) collection or storage boxes, sheet metal

(G-926)
WORLDWIDE TICKETS & LABELS INC
Also Called: Worldwide Ticketcraft
3606 Quantum Blvd (33426-8637)
P.O. Box 168, Fort Smith AR (72902-0168)
PHONE.................................877 426-5754
Erik Covitz, *CEO*
Captiles Vick, *President*
Mark Loomer, *COO*
George Scher, *CFO*
Natasha Gibson, *Accounts Mgr*
◆ **EMP:** 60 **EST:** 1998
SQ FT: 11,000
SALES (est): 11MM
SALES (corp-wide): 44.8MM **Privately Held**
WEB: www.worldwideticketcraft.com
SIC: 2759 Flexographic printing
PA: Weldon, Williams & Lick, Inc.
711 N A St
Fort Smith AR 72901
479 783-4113

(G-927)
WWSA SOLIDS LLC
2921 Commerce Park Dr (33426-8780)
PHONE.................................561 588-9299
Christian Winkel, *Mng Member*

EMP: 16 **EST:** 2018
SALES (est): 332.4K **Privately Held**
WEB: www.worldwidesolids.com
SIC: 3291 Abrasive products

(G-928)
YKK AP AMERICA INC
8846 Andy Ct Apt C (33436-2489)
PHONE.................................561 736-7808
EMP: 9 **EST:** 2017
SALES (est): 168.3K **Privately Held**
WEB: www.ykkap.com
SIC: 3442 Sash, door or window: metal

(G-929)
YOUMOP LLC
1220 Sw 35th Ave (33426-8425)
PHONE.................................248 343-2013
Mya Johnson, *CEO*
EMP: 9 **EST:** 2020
SALES (est): 523.9K **Privately Held**
WEB: www.youmop.com
SIC: 2392 5961 Mops, floor & dust;

Bradenton
Manatee County

(G-930)
AARON TOOL INC
2819 62nd Ave E (34203-5319)
PHONE.................................941 758-9369
John Gardi, *President*
Tony Vincent, *Executive*
EMP: 24 **EST:** 1978
SQ FT: 18,000
SALES (est): 2.3MM **Privately Held**
WEB: www.aarontool.com
SIC: 3599 Machine shop, jobbing & repair

(G-931)
ACU-GRIND TOOL WORKS INC
2118 58th Ave E (34203-5059)
P.O. Box 68 (34206-0068)
PHONE.................................941 758-6963
Anthony Antony, *President*
Alice Antony, *Vice Pres*
Nick Antony, *Marketing Staff*
EMP: 16 **EST:** 1979
SQ FT: 5,000
SALES (est): 1MM **Privately Held**
WEB: www.acugrind.com
SIC: 3541 Machine tools, metal cutting type

(G-932)
ADEPTUS INDUSTRIES INC
6224 17th St E (34203-5041)
PHONE.................................941 756-7636
Dan L Fraley, *President*
Kenneth Fraley, *Vice Pres*
Patrick Fraley, *Vice Pres*
Richard A Fraley, *Vice Pres*
EMP: 14 **EST:** 1970
SQ FT: 3,500
SALES (est): 556K **Privately Held**
WEB: www.adeptusind.com
SIC: 3599 3444 Machine shop, jobbing & repair; sheet metalwork

(G-933)
ADVANCE CONTROLS INC (PA)
Also Called: A C I
4505 18th St E (34203-3757)
PHONE.................................941 746-3221
Marsha Panuce, *CEO*
David Robertson, *Electrical Engi*
Kenneth J Long, *CFO*
John Garrow, *Admin Sec*
Edward Weiss,
▲ **EMP:** 10 **EST:** 1984
SQ FT: 30,000
SALES (est): 4.8MM **Privately Held**
WEB: www.acicontrols.com
SIC: 3625 5063 Industrial controls: push button, selector switches, pilot; electrical supplies

(G-934)
AER-FLO CANVAS PRODUCTS INC
4455 18th St E (34203-3790)
P.O. Box 1356, Oneco (34264-1356)
PHONE.................................941 747-4151
William W Henning, *President*

Betsy A Henning, *Vice Pres*
Deb Hodge, *Human Resources*
Heather Thrasher, *Manager*
◆ **EMP:** 61 **EST:** 1981
SQ FT: 60,000
SALES (est): 10.6MM **Privately Held**
WEB: www.aerfloenv.com
SIC: 2394 Tarpaulins, fabric: made from purchased materials

(G-935)
ALPINE INDUSTRIES CORPORATION
2908 29th Ave E Ste A (34208-7460)
PHONE.................................941 749-1900
Fax: 941 748-6616
EMP: 10
SQ FT: 10,000
SALES (est): 590K **Privately Held**
SIC: 3552 Mfg Screen Printing Equipment

(G-936)
ALUMATECH MANUFACTURING INC
6063 17th St E (34203-5002)
P.O. Box 115, Oneco (34264-0115)
PHONE.................................941 748-8880
Jeffrey Gilmore, *President*
EMP: 20 **EST:** 1989
SQ FT: 2,000
SALES (est): 2.5MM **Privately Held**
WEB: www.alumatech1.com
SIC: 2519 5712 Lawn & garden furniture, except wood & metal; furniture stores

(G-937)
AMERICAN BOTTLING COMPANY
2919 62nd Ave E (34203-5320)
PHONE.................................941 758-7010
Edward Clain, *Manager*
EMP: 19 **Publicly Held**
WEB: www.keurigdrpepper.com
SIC: 2086 Soft drinks: packaged in cans, bottles, etc.
HQ: The American Bottling Company
6425 Hall Of Fame Ln
Frisco TX 75034

(G-938)
AMERICAN TORCH TIP COMPANY (PA)
6212 29th St E (34203-5304)
PHONE.................................941 753-7557
John D Walters Jr, *President*
Charles Walters, *Vice Pres*
Jeff Walters, *Vice Pres*
John Spara, *Prdtn Mgr*
Juan Solis, *Engineer*
◆ **EMP:** 180 **EST:** 1940
SQ FT: 50,000
SALES (est): 42.2MM **Privately Held**
WEB: www.americantorchtip.com
SIC: 3548 Welding apparatus

(G-939)
ANKO PRODUCTS INC
Also Called: Mityflex
6012 33rd St E (34203-5402)
PHONE.................................941 748-2307
Kent Radovich, *President*
Tim Smith, *Vice Pres*
Stephanie Little, *Materials Mgr*
Cindy Nguyen, *Mfg Spvr*
Patrick Gorman, *Engineer*
◆ **EMP:** 35 **EST:** 1980
SQ FT: 21,000
SALES (est): 4.3MM **Privately Held**
WEB: www.ankoproducts.com
SIC: 3621 3561 Motors & generators; pumps & pumping equipment

(G-940)
AQUATECTONICA LLC
809 Tallgrass Ln (34212-2651)
PHONE.................................941 592-3071
Christopher Nyers,
EMP: 10 **EST:** 2008
SALES (est): 503.3K **Privately Held**
SIC: 3272 3499 Fountains, concrete; fountains (except drinking), metal

(G-941)
ARMS EAST LLC
Also Called: Avro Arms
2335 63rd Ave E Ste M (34203-5017)
PHONE.................................561 293-2915
Walter Lawlor, *Mng Member*
EMP: 6 **EST:** 2014
SALES (est): 490.6K **Privately Held**
WEB: www.armseastusa.com
SIC: 3482 Small arms ammunition

(G-942)
AUTO TAG OF AMERICA INC (PA)
6015 31st St E (34203-5350)
PHONE.................................941 739-8841
Nick S Gigliotti, *President*
EMP: 6 **EST:** 2001
SALES (est): 1MM **Privately Held**
WEB: www.autotagamerica.com
SIC: 2679 Tags, paper (unprinted): made from purchased paper

(G-943)
AVON CABINET CORPORATION
5821 24th St E (34203-5028)
PHONE.................................941 755-2866
Edmond Page, *President*
Jim Hunniford, *Vice Pres*
Mark Page, *Vice Pres*
Todd Page, *Vice Pres*
Joy Coblentz, *Sales Staff*
◆ **EMP:** 120 **EST:** 1981
SQ FT: 140,000
SALES (est): 11.7MM **Privately Held**
WEB: www.avoncabinet.com
SIC: 2434 Vanities, bathroom: wood

(G-944)
BC SALES
3003 29th Ave E (34208-7418)
PHONE.................................941 708-2727
Bill Cournan, *Owner*
EMP: 10 **EST:** 2010
SALES (est): 286.3K **Privately Held**
WEB: www.bcsalesdeco.com
SIC: 2395 Embroidery products, except schiffli machine

(G-945)
BEACH HOUSE ENGINEERING
1625 50th Avenue Dr E (34203-3772)
P.O. Box 79, Oneco (34264-0079)
PHONE.................................941 727-4488
Terri Norwood, *President*
Jan Thompson, *Partner*
Brian Bevan, *Vice Pres*
EMP: 5 **EST:** 1995
SALES (est): 350K **Privately Held**
SIC: 3714 5091 Motor vehicle parts & accessories; boat accessories & parts

(G-946)
BEAUTY PAVERS LLC
3600 Lk Byshore Dr Unit 1 (34205)
PHONE.................................941 720-3655
Elmar D Martinez, *Manager*
EMP: 8 **EST:** 2014
SALES (est): 90.7K **Privately Held**
SIC: 2951 Asphalt paving mixtures & blocks

(G-947)
BEAVERTAIL SKIFFS INC
4601 15th St E (34203-3617)
PHONE.................................941 705-2090
William D Leslie, *President*
Elizabeth Leslie, *Vice Pres*
EMP: 7 **EST:** 2017
SALES (est): 128.5K **Privately Held**
WEB: www.beavertailskiffs.com
SIC: 3732 Boat building & repairing

(G-948)
BEST CHOICE SOFTWARE INC
1117 30th Ave W (34205-6941)
PHONE.................................941 747-5858
Selden F Decker, *President*
Peter H Hoyt, *Vice Pres*
Bret Bottomley, *Prgrmr*
EMP: 10 **EST:** 2001
SALES (est): 265.3K **Privately Held**
WEB: www.bestchoicesoftware.com
SIC: 7372 Prepackaged software

(G-949)
BIBLE ALLIANCE INC (PA)
12108 10th Ave E (34212-2764)
PHONE.................................941 748-3031
Joseph A Aleppo, *President*
Daniel Madison, *Vice Pres*
EMP: 20 **EST:** 1970
SQ FT: 3,500
SALES (est): 1.6MM **Privately Held**
WEB: www.audiobibles.com
SIC: 3652 Magnetic tape (audio): prerecorded

(G-950)
BULLETPROOF HITCHES LLC
3145 Lakewood Ranch Blvd # 106 (34211-5004)
PHONE.................................941 251-8110
Gregory Daniel, *Principal*
EMP: 8 **EST:** 2014
SALES (est): 979.4K **Privately Held**
WEB: www.bulletproofhitches.com
SIC: 3714 Trailer hitches, motor vehicle

(G-951)
C & D INDUSTRIAL MAINT LLC
2208 58th Ave E (34203-5062)
PHONE.................................833 776-5833
Tom Hendon, *CEO*
EMP: 44 **EST:** 2018
SALES (est): 4.3MM **Privately Held**
WEB: www.cdindmaint.com
SIC: 3442 5084 3589 5046 Garage doors, overhead: metal; waste compactors; garbage disposers & compactors, commercial; commercial equipment; industrial & commercial equipment inspection service;

(G-952)
C & H BASEBALL INC (PA)
10615 Tech Ter Ste 100 (34211)
PHONE.................................941 727-1533
Danielle D Huff, *President*
Robert Rex Huff, *Corp Secy*
◆ **EMP:** 8 **EST:** 1946
SQ FT: 6,000
SALES (est): 2.3MM **Privately Held**
WEB: www.chbaseball.com
SIC: 3949 1799 Baseball equipment & supplies, general; welding on site

(G-953)
C PRODUCTS DEFENSE INC
4555 18th St E (34203-3757)
PHONE.................................941 727-0009
Adel Jamil, *CEO*
Marjorie Hart, *President*
Carol Jamil, *General Mgr*
EMP: 20 **EST:** 2011
SALES (est): 2.3MM **Privately Held**
WEB: www.dura-mag.com
SIC: 3484 Guns (firearms) or gun parts, 30 mm. & below

(G-954)
C2 POWDER COATING LLC
6060 28th St E Ste 1 (34203-5303)
PHONE.................................941 404-2671
Christina Reiss, *Principal*
EMP: 6 **EST:** 2015
SALES (est): 480.4K **Privately Held**
WEB: www.c2powdercoating.com
SIC: 3479 Coating of metals & formed products

(G-955)
CABINET DESIGNS SARASOTA INC
Also Called: West Wood Manufacturing
6208 B 17th St E (34203)
PHONE.................................941 739-1607
W Russ Edwards, *President*
EMP: 10 **EST:** 1992
SQ FT: 13,000
SALES (est): 822.2K **Privately Held**
SIC: 2434 Wood kitchen cabinets

(G-956)
CABINETS EXTRAORDINAIRE INC
6150 State Road 70 E # 31 (34203-9712)
PHONE.................................618 925-0515
EMP: 15

SALES (corp-wide): 226.3K **Privately Held**
WEB: www.cabinetsextra.com
SIC: 2434 Wood kitchen cabinets
PA: Cabinets Extraordinaire Inc
    7350 S Tamiami Trl
    Sarasota FL 34231
    941 961-8453

(G-957)
CARBON MINE SUPPLY LLC
11023 Gatewood Dr Ste 103 (34211-4945)
PHONE...........................606 437-9905
EMP: 8
SQ FT: 10,600
SALES (est): 827.1K **Privately Held**
SIC: 3483 Mfg Ammunition-Except Small Arms

(G-958)
CAT 5 HURRICANE PRODUCTS LLC
Also Called: Cat5hp
6112 33rd St E Unit 105 (34203-5401)
PHONE...........................941 752-4692
David E Smith, *Mng Member*
EMP: 11 EST: 2007
SALES (est): 1MM **Privately Held**
WEB: www.cat5hp.com
SIC: 3442 Shutters, door or window: metal

(G-959)
CENTERLINE TOOL & ENGRG INC
3107 29th Ave E Ste A (34208-7456)
PHONE...........................941 749-5519
George H Nason, *President*
Diane Nason, *Corp Secy*
Matt Nason, *IT/INT Sup*
Constance Crawley,
Gregory Nania,
EMP: 15 EST: 1995
SQ FT: 5,000
SALES (est): 1.8MM **Privately Held**
SIC: 3599 Machine shop, jobbing & repair

(G-960)
CENTRAL FLORIDA PRECAST INC
1910 1st Ave E (34208-1502)
PHONE...........................941 730-2158
Eduardo Solorzano, *Principal*
EMP: 7 EST: 2008
SALES (est): 224.6K **Privately Held**
SIC: 3272 Precast terrazo or concrete products

(G-961)
CITY OF BRADENTON
5600 Natalie Way E (34203-5647)
PHONE...........................941 727-6360
Timothy Parks, *Manager*
EMP: 56
SALES (corp-wide): 63.2MM **Privately Held**
WEB: www.realizebradenton.com
SIC: 3589 Water treatment equipment, industrial
PA: Bradenton, City Of (Inc)
    101 12th St W
    Bradenton FL 34205
    941 932-9400

(G-962)
CLINE ALUMINUM DOORS INC
112 32nd Ave W (34205-8909)
PHONE...........................941 746-4104
Cathy Cline, *President*
Robert M Cline, *President*
Rhonda C Zoller, *Corp Secy*
Emma Cline, *Exec VP*
Robert B Ackles, *Vice Pres*
▼ EMP: 20 EST: 1961
SQ FT: 7,000
SALES (est): 3.1MM **Privately Held**
WEB: www.clinedoors.com
SIC: 3442 3354 Metal doors; aluminum extruded products

(G-963)
CONDUIT SPACE RCVERY SYSTEMS L
5204 Lena Rd (34211-9436)
PHONE...........................330 416-0887
Todd Fox, *Chief*

Ron Mason, *Vice Pres*
Kelsey Muller, *Mng Member*
Jorja Allen,
EMP: 15 EST: 2013
SALES (est): 1.4MM **Privately Held**
WEB: www.conduitspacerecovery.com
SIC: 3357 Building wire & cable, nonferrous

(G-964)
CUSTOM CARTS OF SARASOTA LLC
Also Called: Custom Carts of Lakewood Ranch
4515 15th St E (34203-3615)
PHONE...........................941 953-4445
Kurt Didier,
EMP: 45 EST: 2016
SALES (est): 5.5MM **Privately Held**
WEB: www.customcarts.com
SIC: 3949 Driving ranges, golf, electronic

(G-965)
CUSTOM WATERSPORTS EQP INC
1218 50th Avenue Plz W (34207-2538)
PHONE...........................941 753-9949
Julian Shaw, *Principal*
EMP: 12 EST: 2015
SALES (est): 131.2K **Privately Held**
SIC: 3599 Industrial machinery

(G-966)
CUTTING EDGE ARCHTCTRAL MLDNGS
7282 55th Ave E Pmb 176 (34203-8002)
PHONE...........................941 727-1111
Rick D Slawson Mr,
Donald L Greenwood Mr,
Donald J Perella Mr,
EMP: 8 EST: 2004
SQ FT: 12,500
SALES (est): 300K **Privately Held**
WEB: www.cuttingedgemoldings.com
SIC: 3299 Moldings, architectural: plaster of paris

(G-967)
DELUXE EQUIPMENT CO
7817 Alhambra Dr (34209-4834)
P.O. Box 11390 (34282-1390)
PHONE...........................941 753-4184
Sandra E Smith, *President*
Wendy Hayden, *Vice Pres*
EMP: 19 EST: 1984
SQ FT: 22,000
SALES (est): 1MM **Privately Held**
WEB: www.deluxeovens.com
SIC: 3556 Bakery machinery; ovens, bakery

(G-968)
DEPEND-O-DRAIN INC
6012 33rd St E (34203-5402)
PHONE...........................941 756-1710
Kent Radovich, *President*
Patricia Smith, *Master*
◆ EMP: 35 EST: 1966
SQ FT: 20,000
SALES (est): 9.6MM **Privately Held**
WEB: www.dependodrain.com
SIC: 3494 Valves & pipe fittings

(G-969)
DIXIE-SOUTHERN ARKANSAS LLC
9135 58th Dr E (34202-9188)
PHONE...........................479 751-9183
EMP: 8
SALES (est): 1.4MM **Privately Held**
SIC: 3441 Structural Metal Fabrication

(G-970)
DURLACH HOLDINGS INC
6008 28th St E Ste A (34203-5300)
PHONE...........................941 751-1672
Angelo Durlach, *President*
EMP: 11 EST: 2005
SQ FT: 20,000
SALES (est): 288.5K **Privately Held**
WEB: www.precaststair.com
SIC: 3272 Concrete products

(G-971)
DYNOTUNE INC
515 27th St E Ste 4 (34208-1879)
PHONE...........................941 753-8899
Dean Hoffman, *Principal*
EMP: 8 EST: 2014
SALES (est): 734.6K **Privately Held**
WEB: www.dynotunenitrous.com
SIC: 3714 Motor vehicle parts & accessories

(G-972)
EARTECH INC
3904 9th Ave W (34205-1704)
PHONE...........................941 747-8193
Mark A Krywko, *President*
Marja L Krywko, *Vice Pres*
EMP: 8 EST: 1988
SQ FT: 1,500
SALES (est): 936K **Privately Held**
WEB: www.eartechhearingaids.com
SIC: 3842 5999 Hearing aids; autograph supplies

(G-973)
EDMUNDS METAL WORKS INC
6111 15th St E Ste A (34203-7771)
PHONE...........................941 755-4725
Thomas G Edmunds, *President*
Nina E Edmunds, *COO*
Nina Edmunds, *Opers Mgr*
Lisa Kuzniczci, *Purch Agent*
Judy Edmunds, *CFO*
EMP: 26 EST: 1977
SQ FT: 10,000
SALES (est): 5.4MM **Privately Held**
WEB: www.edmundsmetal.com
SIC: 3599 Machine shop, jobbing & repair

(G-974)
ELECTRO MECHANICAL SOUTH INC
8203 Planters Knoll Ter (34201-2074)
PHONE...........................941 342-9111
Richard B Romanoff, *CEO*
Shirley Romanoff, *President*
EMP: 25 EST: 1992
SALES (est): 2.3MM **Privately Held**
WEB: www.ems-fl.com
SIC: 7694 7629 Electric motor repair; rewinding stators; electrical repair shops

(G-975)
ELREHA PRINTED CIRCUITS
7522 Plantation Cir (34201-2062)
PHONE...........................727 244-0130
Patrick Scanlan, *Principal*
EMP: 7 EST: 2010
SALES (est): 121.1K **Privately Held**
SIC: 3672 Circuit boards, television & radio printed

(G-976)
EMERSON PRCESS MGT PWR WTR SLT
1401 Manatee Ave W # 400 (34205-6770)
PHONE...........................941 748-8100
Frank Grywalski, *President*
EMP: 47 EST: 1993
SQ FT: 6,000
SALES (est): 6.7MM
SALES (corp-wide): 18.2B **Publicly Held**
SIC: 7372 Word processing computer software
PA: Emerson Electric Co.
    8000 West Florissant Ave
    Saint Louis MO 63136
    314 553-2000

(G-977)
ENERGY MANAGEMENT PRODUCTS LLC (PA)
Also Called: Led Lighting Solutions
6118 Riverview Blvd (34209-1343)
PHONE...........................410 320-0200
Cara Weisman, *Mng Member*
Kevin Button,
EMP: 5 EST: 2011
SALES (est): 851.3K **Privately Held**
WEB: store.interstateproducts.com
SIC: 3646 3647 3641 Commercial indusl & institutional electric lighting fixtures; vehicular lighting equipment; electric lamps

(G-978)
ETCO INCORPORATED
Also Called: Etco Automotive Products Div
3004 62nd Ave E (34203-5306)
PHONE...........................941 756-8426
Nathan Galla, *Production*
Irina Fridland, *Engineer*
Tom Jacobson, *Sales Mgr*
Paul Richardson, *Sales Mgr*
Fred Bainbridge, *Sales Staff*
EMP: 110
SQ FT: 19,618
SALES (corp-wide): 25.2MM **Privately Held**
WEB: www.etco.com
SIC: 3644 3714 3061 Terminal boards; motor vehicle parts & accessories; mechanical rubber goods
PA: Etco Incorporated
    25 Bellows St
    Warwick RI 02888
    401 467-2400

(G-979)
FIRESIDE HOLDINGS INC
Also Called: American Refrigerants
2053 58th Avenue Cir E (34203-5060)
PHONE...........................941 371-0300
Christopher Mussey, *President*
EMP: 7 EST: 2019
SALES (est): 681.9K **Privately Held**
SIC: 3585 Refrigeration & heating equipment

(G-980)
FLOWERS BKG CO BRADENTON LLC
Also Called: Flowers Baking Company
720 9th St E (34208-2025)
PHONE...........................941 758-5656
Chris Peer, *Manager*
EMP: 25
SALES (corp-wide): 4.3B **Publicly Held**
WEB: www.flobradconf.com
SIC: 2051 Bread, cake & related products
HQ: Flowers Baking Co. Of Bradenton, Llc
    6490 Parkland Dr
    Sarasota FL 34243

(G-981)
GAMMERLERTECH CORPORATION
Also Called: Gammerler US
3135 Lakewood Ranch Blvd # 107 (34211-5006)
PHONE...........................941 803-0150
Gunter Gammerler, *Principal*
Max Frank, *Sales Staff*
Joe Jastrzebski, *Sales Staff*
Tabitha Trotterpowell, *Office Mgr*
Mario Banci, *Manager*
EMP: 19 EST: 2018
SALES (est): 6.1MM **Privately Held**
WEB: www.gammerlertech.com
SIC: 3555 Printing trades machinery

(G-982)
GENIUS CENTRAL SYSTEMS INC
2025 Lakewood Ranch Blvd # 202 (34211-4948)
PHONE...........................800 360-2231
Linda Sheehan, *CEO*
Paul Debonis, *COO*
Peter Ceccacci, *Exec VP*
Gordon Lear, *Exec VP*
Matt Redd, *Exec VP*
EMP: 45 EST: 2013
SALES (est): 11.9MM
SALES (corp-wide): 385.2MM **Publicly Held**
WEB: www.geniuscentral.com
SIC: 7372 Application computer software
PA: Sps Commerce, Inc.
    333 S 7th St Ste 1000
    Minneapolis MN 55402
    612 435-9400

(G-983)
GLOBAL MARKETING CORP
3752 Summerwind Cir (34209-5809)
PHONE...........................973 426-1088
Christopher D Boyhan, *President*
▲ EMP: 52 EST: 1981

SALES (est): 2.5MM **Privately Held**
WEB: www.globalmarketingcorp.com
SIC: 3469 Household cooking & kitchen
utensils, metal; household cooking &
kitchen utensils, porcelain enameled

(G-984)
GLOBAL WRLESS SLTIONS TECH INC
101 Riverfront Blvd # 400 (34205-8812)
PHONE..............................941 744-2511
John Elliott, *President*
Cw Elliott, *Corp Secy*
Joanne Fowkes, *Office Admin*
EMP: 6 **EST:** 2002
SQ FT: 1,500
SALES (est): 683.4K **Privately Held**
SIC: 3663 Radio & TV communications
equipment

(G-985)
GLOBE TRAILERS FLORIDA INC
3101 59th Avenue Dr E (34203-5311)
PHONE..............................941 753-6425
Leonard H Dobala, *President*
Brian Frater, *Plant Mgr*
Dana Spara, *Purch Mgr*
Jeff Walters, *VP Engrg*
Debbie Walters, *Finance*
◆ **EMP:** 40 **EST:** 1985
SQ FT: 60,000
SALES (est): 5.3MM **Privately Held**
WEB: www.globetrailers.com
SIC: 3715 3599 Semitrailers for truck trac-
tors; machine shop, jobbing & repair

(G-986)
GML COATINGS LLC
10315 Technology Ter (34211-4924)
PHONE..............................941 755-2176
Robin Wilson, *Treasurer*
EMP: 14 **EST:** 2008
SALES (est): 3.5MM **Publicly Held**
WEB: www.gmlcoatings.com
SIC: 3479 Coating of metals & formed
products
PA: Primoris Services Corporation
2300 N Field St Ste 1900
Dallas TX 75201

(G-987)
GOODWILL INDUSTRIES S FLA INC
2563 Lakewood Ranch Blvd (34211-4949)
PHONE..............................941 745-8459
EMP: 211
SALES (corp-wide): 92.8MM **Privately Held**
WEB: www.goodwillsouthflorida.org
SIC: 3999 Barber & beauty shop equip-
ment
PA: Goodwill Industries Of South Florida,
Inc.
2121 Nw 21st St
Miami FL 33142
305 325-9114

(G-988)
GRAND BUFFET
4848 14th St W (34207-2017)
PHONE..............................941 752-3388
Haiyan Lu, *President*
EMP: 7 **EST:** 2015
SALES (est): 74.5K **Privately Held**
WEB: www.grandbuffetfl.com
SIC: 2511 5812 Buffets (furniture); eating
places

(G-989)
GUTHMAN SIGNS LLC
4914 Lena Rd Unit 101 (34211-9482)
PHONE..............................941 218-0014
EMP: 6 **EST:** 2019
SALES (est): 966.9K **Privately Held**
WEB: www.guthmansigns.com
SIC: 3993 Signs & advertising specialties

(G-990)
HAWK RACING
6060 28th St E Ste 5 (34203-5303)
PHONE..............................941 209-1790
Cindy Parlin, *Human Resources*
EMP: 7 **EST:** 2010
SALES (est): 81.5K **Privately Held**
WEB: www.hawk-racing.com
SIC: 3751 Bicycles & related parts

(G-991)
HERBERT PAVERS INC
3031 46th Ave E (34203-3923)
PHONE..............................941 447-4909
Hebert A Oliveira, *Principal*
EMP: 7 **EST:** 2011
SALES (est): 771.1K **Privately Held**
SIC: 3531 Pavers

(G-992)
HUDSONS WLDG & FABRICATION INC
10845 Forest Run Dr (34211-9391)
P.O. Box 110096, Lakewood Rch (34211-0002)
PHONE..............................941 355-4858
Kenneth C Hudson, *Vice Pres*
EMP: 7 **EST:** 2011
SALES (est): 213.7K **Privately Held**
SIC: 7692 Welding repair

(G-993)
HURRICANE MEDICAL INC
5315 Lena Rd (34211-9442)
PHONE..............................941 753-1517
Dell Bauslaugh, *President*
David Clapp, *Vice Pres*
G Keith Pike, *Treasurer*
Keith Pike, *Director*
J Craig Pike, *Admin Sec*
▲ **EMP:** 21 **EST:** 1999
SQ FT: 1,700
SALES (est): 4.7MM **Privately Held**
WEB: www.hurricanemedical.com
SIC: 3841 Surgical & medical instruments

(G-994)
IMMUNOTEK BIO CENTERS LLC
825 9th St W (34205-7741)
PHONE..............................337 500-1175
Dmitry Maksimchuck, *Manager*
Jerry Coe, *Supervisor*
EMP: 34
SALES (corp-wide): 27MM **Privately Held**
WEB: www.immunotek.com
SIC: 2836 Blood derivatives
PA: Immunotek Bio Centers, L.L.C.
3900 N Causeway Blvd # 1200
Metairie LA 70002
337 500-1175

(G-995)
INNOVATIVE DESIGNS OF SARASOTA
Also Called: IDI
6224 31st St E Ste 8 (34203-5321)
PHONE..............................941 752-7779
Don Beard, *President*
EMP: 6 **EST:** 1988
SQ FT: 5,400
SALES (est): 467.2K **Privately Held**
SIC: 3841 Ophthalmic instruments & appa-
ratus

(G-996)
INOVART INC
Also Called: Network USA
2304 58th Ave E (34203-5064)
P.O. Box 254, Tallevast (34270-0254)
PHONE..............................941 751-2324
John M Smith, *President*
Mercedez Smith, *Treasurer*
▲ **EMP:** 5 **EST:** 1988
SQ FT: 5,500
SALES (est): 868.8K **Privately Held**
WEB: www.inovart.net
SIC: 2679 Pressed & molded pulp prod-
ucts, purchased material

(G-997)
INTERTAPE POLYMER US INC
3647 Cortez Rd W Ste 102 (34210-3195)
PHONE..............................941 727-5788
Janice Loppe, *President*
Soto Edwin, *Engineer*
Edwin Soto, *Engineer*
Harnois Dave, *Controller*
Dave Lewis, *Natl Sales Mgr*
EMP: 1 **EST:** 2004
SALES (est): 3.5MM
SALES (corp-wide): 232MM **Privately Held**
WEB: www.itape.com
SIC: 2675 Die-cut paper & board

HQ: Ipg (Us) Inc.
100 Paramount Dr Ste 300
Sarasota FL 34232
941 727-5788

(G-998)
ISPG INC
10504 Technology Ter (34211-4927)
PHONE..............................941 896-3999
Maureen F Young, *Corp Secy*
Gerald Luhman, *Vice Pres*
Kyle Cancellieri, *Sales Mgr*
▲ **EMP:** 15 **EST:** 2011
SALES (est): 3.9MM **Privately Held**
WEB: www.ispg.com
SIC: 3841 Surgical & medical instruments

(G-999)
J C INDUSTRIES INC
6105 33rd St E (34203-5414)
P.O. Box 1551, Wauchula (33873-1551)
PHONE..............................863 773-9199
Penny Carlton, *Principal*
EMP: 7 **EST:** 2001
SALES (est): 83.6K **Privately Held**
SIC: 3999 Manufacturing industries

(G-1000)
J L M MACHINE CO INC
2704 29th Ave E (34208-7457)
PHONE..............................941 748-4288
Kelley Graham, *Principal*
Natasha Phifer, *Office Mgr*
EMP: 10 **EST:** 1977
SQ FT: 6,000
SALES (est): 1MM **Privately Held**
WEB: www.jlmmachine.com
SIC: 3599 7692 Machine shop, jobbing &
repair; welding repair

(G-1001)
KINETRONICS CORPORATION
5316 Lena Rd (34211-9438)
PHONE..............................941 951-2432
William N Stelcher, *President*
Carol Stelcher, *Vice Pres*
EMP: 10 **EST:** 1972
SALES (est): 1.5MM **Privately Held**
WEB: www.kinetronics.com
SIC: 3629 Static elimination equipment, in-
dustrial

(G-1002)
LAMBS SIGNS INC
Also Called: Signs Now
4230 26th St W (34205-3516)
PHONE..............................941 792-4453
J Brian Lamb, *Owner*
Debra Lamb, *Owner*
Dave Hassall Jr, *Co-Owner*
EMP: 11 **EST:** 2010
SALES (est): 262.8K **Privately Held**
SIC: 3993 3714 Signs & advertising spe-
cialties; motor vehicle parts & accessories

(G-1003)
LED LGHTING SLUTIONS GLOBL LLC
6118 Riverview Blvd (34209-1343)
PHONE..............................855 309-1702
Carrie Weisman, *CEO*
EMP: 6 **EST:** 2015
SALES (est): 518K **Privately Held**
WEB: www.ledlightingsolutions.com
SIC: 3646 Commercial indusl & institu-
tional electric lighting fixtures

(G-1004)
LEXINGTON CUTTER INC
2951 63rd Ave E (34203-5308)
PHONE..............................941 739-2726
Paul J Enander, *President*
Jim Trammell, *Vice Pres*
Laurie Enander, *Admin Sec*
EMP: 22 **EST:** 1947
SQ FT: 15,000
SALES (est): 5MM **Privately Held**
WEB: www.lexingtoncutter.com
SIC: 3541 5084 3545 Machine tools,
metal cutting type; industrial machinery &
equipment; machine tool accessories

(G-1005)
LIPPERT COMPONENTS INC
Also Called: Sureshade
1900 47th Ter E (34203-3701)
PHONE..............................267 825-0665
EMP: 13
SALES (corp-wide): 4.4B **Publicly Held**
WEB: www.lci1.com
SIC: 3711 Motor vehicles & car bodies
HQ: Lippert Components, Inc.
3501 County Road 6 E
Elkhart IN 46514
574 535-1125

(G-1006)
LIQUID BOTTLES LLC
3165 Lakewood Ranch Blvd (34211-4959)
PHONE..............................888 222-5232
Brandon Young, *Opers Mgr*
Stephanie Fischer, *Marketing Staff*
Jennie Branca, *Manager*
Chad Brown, *Manager*
Tyler McGregor, *Manager*
EMP: 20 **EST:** 2014
SQ FT: 35,000
SALES (est): 13.6MM **Privately Held**
WEB: www.liquidbottles.com
SIC: 2631 5085 Container, packaging &
boxboard; glass bottles

(G-1007)
LIVE WISE NATURALS LLC
13502 4th Plz E (34212-9681)
PHONE..............................866 866-0075
Greg Bulgarelli, *Mng Member*
EMP: 8 **EST:** 2015
SALES (est): 787.7K **Privately Held**
WEB: www.livewisenaturals.com
SIC: 2833 Vitamins, natural or synthetic:
bulk, uncompounded

(G-1008)
LYNX PRODUCTS CORP INC
2424 Manatee Ave W # 203 (34205-4954)
P.O. Box 10977 (34282-0977)
PHONE..............................941 727-9676
Greg Winter, *President*
Debra Winter, *Principal*
▲ **EMP:** 6 **EST:** 1999
SQ FT: 1,500
SALES (est): 819.2K **Privately Held**
WEB: www.lynx-products.com
SIC: 3535 5084 Conveyors & conveying
equipment; industrial machinery & equip-
ment

(G-1009)
M&L CABINETS INC
7320 Manatee Ave W (34209-3441)
PHONE..............................941 761-8100
Clinton C Hoy, *President*
Ryan Nobles, *Vice Pres*
Clint Hoy, *Manager*
EMP: 6 **EST:** 2018
SALES (est): 309.7K **Privately Held**
WEB: www.mlcabinets.com
SIC: 2434 Wood kitchen cabinets

(G-1010)
MANATEE CABINETS INC
Also Called: Cabinets Unlimited
8700 Cortez Rd W (34210-2209)
PHONE..............................941 792-8656
Jan A Manning, *President*
Marcus Hyde, *Vice Pres*
EMP: 5 **EST:** 1969
SQ FT: 19,000
SALES (est): 667K **Privately Held**
WEB: www.cabinets-unlimited.com
SIC: 2434 Wood kitchen cabinets

(G-1011)
MANATEE PRINTERS INC
1007 30th Ave W (34205-6904)
PHONE..............................941 746-9100
Ronald Pickelsimer, *President*
Patricia Pickelsimer, *Vice Pres*
EMP: 20 **EST:** 1964
SQ FT: 6,000
SALES (est): 3.4MM **Privately Held**
WEB: www.manateeprinters.com
SIC: 2752 Commercial printing, offset

(G-1012)
MED X CHANGE LLC (HQ)
Also Called: Med X Change, Inc.
417 8th St W (34205-8623)
PHONE..................................941 746-0538
Craig Scherer, *President*
Jcorey Park, *Project Mgr*
Christie Sharp, *Controller*
Chris Danko, *Director*
U Ghaziabad, *Business Dir*
EMP: 25 **EST:** 2000
SALES (est): 17MM **Publicly Held**
WEB: www.medxchange.com
SIC: 7372 Prepackaged software

(G-1013)
MOJOWAX MEDIA INC
1100 Yale Ave (34207-5250)
PHONE..................................805 550-6013
John J Sullivan, *President*
EMP: 9 **EST:** 2013
SALES (est): 166.8K **Privately Held**
WEB: www.bluesmusicstore.com
SIC: 2759 5961 Publication printing; mag-
azines, mail order

(G-1014)
**MOTIONVIBE INNOVATIONS
LLC**
4031 Caddie Dr E (34203-3429)
PHONE..................................202 285-0235
Nicholas Gerontianos, *CEO*
Jeff Polon, *Research*
EMP: 12
SALES (est): 498K **Privately Held**
WEB: www.motionvibe.com
SIC: 7372 Prepackaged software

(G-1015)
MSH BRICK PAVERS INC
5640 Fountain Lake Cir (34207-3765)
PHONE..................................941 822-6472
Desouza Hiago H, *Principal*
EMP: 12 **EST:** 2014
SALES (est): 903.5K **Privately Held**
SIC: 2951 Asphalt paving mixtures &
blocks

(G-1016)
**NATIONAL POWDR COATING
FLA INC**
6004 31st St E (34203-5309)
PHONE..................................941 756-1322
Steve Campbell, *CEO*
Paul Balliette, *President*
EMP: 8 **EST:** 2005
SALES (est): 873.3K **Privately Held**
WEB: www.nationalpowdercoating.com
SIC: 3479 Coating of metals & formed
products

(G-1017)
NEW ENGLAND MACHINERY
6204 29th St E (34203-5304)
PHONE..................................941 755-5550
EMP: 25
SALES (est): 4.5MM **Privately Held**
SIC: 3565 Packaging Machinery, Nsk

(G-1018)
**NEW ENGLAND MACHINERY
INC**
Also Called: Nem
2820 62nd Ave E (34203-5305)
P.O. Box 20299 (34204-0299)
PHONE..................................941 755-5550
Judith Nickse, *President*
Geza F Bankuty, *Vice Pres*
Aiden Bass, *Project Mgr*
Andrew Butler, *Sales Staff*
Lisa Kowatch, *Sales Staff*
◆ **EMP:** 40 **EST:** 1974
SQ FT: 33,000
SALES (est): 8.6MM **Privately Held**
WEB: www.neminc.com
SIC: 3565 Bottling machinery: filling, cap-
ping, labeling

(G-1019)
**NORTH AMERICA BIO FUEL
CORP**
1767 Lakewood Ranch Blvd # 210
(34211-4906)
PHONE..................................877 877-9279
Winston Turner, *President*

EMP: 9 **EST:** 2015
SALES (est): 396.8K **Privately Held**
SIC: 2869 7389 Fluorinated hydrocarbon
gases;

(G-1020)
NST GLOBAL LLC
Also Called: Sb Tactical
3145 Lakewood Ranch Blvd (34211-5003)
PHONE..................................941 748-2270
Alessandro R Bosco, *CEO*
Jeffry Creamer, *Vice Pres*
Lisa Durello, *CFO*
Amy Pevear, *VP Mktg*
EMP: 26 **EST:** 2008
SALES (est): 2.2MM **Privately Held**
SIC: 3489 5941 Guns or gun parts, over
30 mm.; firearms

(G-1021)
PACEMATE LLC
518 13th St W (34205-7419)
PHONE..................................305 322-5074
Tiffany Higgins, *Partner*
David Harrell, *Vice Pres*
Ken Husted, *Vice Pres*
Noemi Ray, *Vice Pres*
Emily Ramsay, *Corp Comm Staff*
EMP: 6 **EST:** 2016
SALES (est): 1.2MM **Privately Held**
WEB: www.pacemate.com
SIC: 7372 Business oriented computer
software
PA: Biocynetic, Llc
518 13th St W
Bradenton FL 34205
305 322-5074

(G-1022)
PACIFIC PAVERS INC
6326 5th Street Cir E (34203-7613)
PHONE..................................941 238-7854
Julie Nutting, *Principal*
EMP: 7 **EST:** 2010
SALES (est): 111.2K **Privately Held**
WEB: www.pacificpaversfl.com
SIC: 3531 Pavers

(G-1023)
**PAD PRINTING TECHNOLOGY
CORP**
1835 59th Ter E (34203-5019)
PHONE..................................941 739-8667
David Berry, *CEO*
EMP: 9 **EST:** 1995
SALES (est): 797K **Privately Held**
WEB: www.pad-printing.com
SIC: 2752 2759 Commercial printing, off-
set; laser printing

(G-1024)
**PAD PRINTING TECHNOLOGY
GROUP**
1835 59th Ter E (34203-5019)
PHONE..................................941 739-8667
Keith Ekenseair, *CEO*
Tammy Lisko, *Treasurer*
EMP: 10 **EST:** 2019
SALES (est): 510.8K **Privately Held**
WEB: www.pad-printing.com
SIC: 2752 Commercial printing, offset

(G-1025)
**PADGETT MANUFACTURING
INC**
2915 62nd Ave E (34203-5320)
PHONE..................................941 756-8566
Arthur Fowler, *President*
Shirley Fowler, *Corp Secy*
Cleon Fowler, *Vice Pres*
EMP: 68 **EST:** 1970
SQ FT: 14,000
SALES (est): 5.1MM **Privately Held**
WEB: www.padgett-inc.com
SIC: 3535 Conveyors & conveying equip-
ment

(G-1026)
PETLIFT S & B MFG INC
6012 31st St E (34203-5309)
PHONE..................................941 346-2211
Nancy Apatow, *President*
EMP: 9 **EST:** 2016
SALES (est): 294.5K **Privately Held**
SIC: 3537 Forklift trucks

(G-1027)
**PHILLIPS PRINTING SERVICES
LLC**
5103 Lena Rd Unit 107 (34211-9496)
PHONE..................................941 526-6570
Justin H Phillips, *Principal*
EMP: 9 **EST:** 2016
SALES (est): 384.5K **Privately Held**
SIC: 2752 Commercial printing, offset

(G-1028)
PIERCE MANUFACTURING INC
1512 38th Ave E (34208-4652)
PHONE..................................941 748-3900
Dave McAlice, *Vice Pres*
Nancy Krejcarek, *Project Mgr*
Kristina Spang, *Opers Staff*
Rick Kalinski, *Mfg Staff*
Ben Sell, *Mfg Staff*
EMP: 100
SALES (corp-wide): 7.7B **Publicly Held**
WEB: www.piercemfg.com
SIC: 3711 3792 3715 3714 Fire depart-
ment vehicles (motor vehicles), assembly
of; travel trailers & campers; truck trailers;
motor vehicle parts & accessories
HQ: Pierce Manufacturing, Inc.
2600 American Dr
Appleton WI 54914
920 832-3000

(G-1029)
PLASTEC VENTILATION INC
2012 58th Avenue Cir E (34203-5089)
PHONE..................................941 751-7596
Jean-Jacques Gaudiot, *President*
Jean-Jacqu Gaudiot, *President*
▲ **EMP:** 5 **EST:** 2002
SALES (est): 718.1K **Privately Held**
WEB: www.plastecventilation.com
SIC: 3564 Blowers & fans

(G-1030)
PMH HOMES INC
Also Called: Architechtural Foam Systems
14705 21st Ave E (34212-8124)
PHONE..................................941 234-5121
Philip Michael Heuss, *President*
EMP: 9 **EST:** 2008
SALES (est): 1.1MM **Privately Held**
SIC: 3086 Carpet & rug cushions, foamed
plastic

(G-1031)
**POTTRE GARDENING
PRODUCTS LLC**
1115 76th St Nw (34209-1032)
PHONE..................................941 224-8856
Florence C Saldana,
Page Barker,
EMP: 5 **EST:** 2004
SALES (est): 303.4K **Privately Held**
SIC: 3524 5191 Lawn & garden equip-
ment; garden supplies

(G-1032)
**PRECISION DIRECTIONAL DRLG
LLC**
5010 60th Dr E (34203-6333)
PHONE..................................941 320-8308
Carol Gudger, *Branch Mgr*
EMP: 36
SALES (corp-wide): 1.5MM **Privately
Held**
SIC: 1381 Directional drilling oil & gas
wells
PA: Precision Directional Drilling Llc
3027 59th St
Sarasota FL

(G-1033)
PROGRESSIVE CABINETRY
6404 Manatee Ave W Ste N (34209-2360)
PHONE..................................941 866-6975
Victoria Crittenden, *Principal*
EMP: 6 **EST:** 2013
SALES (est): 315.1K **Privately Held**
WEB: www.progressive-cabinetry.com
SIC: 2434 Wood kitchen cabinets

(G-1034)
RAPID SWITCH SYSTEMS LLC
4601 15th St E (34203-3617)
PHONE..................................941 720-7380
William D Leslie, *Manager*

EMP: 9 **EST:** 2018
SALES (est): 1.3MM **Privately Held**
WEB: www.rapidswitchsystems.com
SIC: 3613 Switchgear & switchboard appa-
ratus

(G-1035)
REFTEC INTERNATIONAL INC
10530 Portal Xing Ste 104 (34211-4914)
PHONE..................................800 214-4883
Jeff Moore, *CEO*
Chris Lawrence, *CFO*
William Buckles, *Shareholder*
▲ **EMP:** 36 **EST:** 1997
SALES (est): 1.1MM **Privately Held**
WEB: www.reftec.com
SIC: 3585 Refrigeration & heating equip-
ment

(G-1036)
ROCK RIVER TOOL INC
2953 63rd Ave E (34203-5308)
PHONE..................................941 753-6343
Robert Enander, *President*
Rhonda Stevens, *Mktg Dir*
EMP: 14 **EST:** 1986
SQ FT: 15,000
SALES (est): 1.4MM **Privately Held**
WEB: www.rockrivertool.com
SIC: 3545 5085 Cutting tools for machine
tools; industrial supplies

(G-1037)
ROSCIOLI INTERNATIONAL INC
Also Called: Donzi Yachts By Roscioli
6111 21st St E (34203-5006)
PHONE..................................941 755-7411
Dan Hogan, *Purchasing*
Robert Roscioli, *Branch Mgr*
Rita Acosta, *Director*
EMP: 50
SALES (corp-wide): 4.8MM **Privately
Held**
WEB: www.studio215.com
SIC: 3732 Boat building & repairing
PA: Roscioli International, Inc.
3201 W State Road 84
Fort Lauderdale FL 33312
941 755-7411

(G-1038)
**S & B METAL PRODUCTS S FLA
INC**
6012 31st St E (34203-5309)
PHONE..................................941 727-3669
Steve Adlin, *Manager*
Terri Frank, *Manager*
Marianne King, *Info Tech Mgr*
EMP: 110 **Privately Held**
SIC: 3444 Sheet metalwork
PA: S & B Metal Products Of South Florida,
Inc.
5301 Gateway Blvd
Lakeland FL 33811

(G-1039)
**SAFTRON MANUFACTURING
LLC**
6012 33rd St E (34203-5402)
PHONE..................................305 233-5511
Kent W Radovich, *President*
Donna Sandefur, *Sales Mgr*
▼ **EMP:** 12 **EST:** 2008
SALES (est): 1.2MM **Privately Held**
WEB: www.saftron.com
SIC: 3446 Architectural metalwork

(G-1040)
SARASOTA HERALD-TRIBUNE
8713 State Road 70 E (34202-9408)
PHONE..................................941 745-7808
Patrick Dorsey, *Principal*
EMP: 106
SALES (corp-wide): 278.4MM **Privately
Held**
WEB: www.heraldtribune.com
SIC: 2711 Commercial printing & newspa-
per publishing combined
HQ: Sarasota Herald-Tribune
801 S Tamiami Trl
Sarasota FL 34236
941 953-7755

(G-1041)
SARASOTA KITCHENS CLOSETS INC
Also Called: Finecraft Cabinetry
5822 24th St E (34203-5027)
PHONE..................................941 722-7505
EMP: 6 EST: 2018
SALES (est): 463.3K Privately Held
WEB: www.dreamclosetsllc.com
SIC: 2434 Wood kitchen cabinets

(G-1042)
SAY WHAT SCREEN PRTG & EMB INC
Also Called: Make Your Mark Promo .com
10912 8th Ave E (34212-9776)
PHONE..................................941 745-5822
Marsha Littlefield, CEO
Dan Littlefield, Vice Pres
▼ EMP: 11 EST: 1997
SQ FT: 7,500
SALES (est): 567.8K Privately Held
WEB: www.makeyourmarkpromo.com
SIC: 3953 2395 Screens, textile printing;
embroidery & art needlework

(G-1043)
SCREEN MACHINE
3312 33rd St W (34205-2813)
PHONE..................................941 962-0395
Chris Ladd, Owner
EMP: 8 EST: 2011
SALES (est): 142.8K Privately Held
WEB: www.screenmachine.com
SIC: 2752 Offset & photolithographic printing

(G-1044)
SEASUCKER LLC (PA)
1912 44th Ave E (34203-3798)
PHONE..................................941 586-2664
Genevieve Casagrande, President
Chuck Casagrande, Research
Brian Boyd, Manager
Charles L Casagrande,
EMP: 10 EST: 2008
SALES (est): 6.5MM Privately Held
WEB: www.seasucker.com
SIC: 3949 Sporting & athletic goods

(G-1045)
SIGNING OFF NOW INC
1101 29th Ave W (34205-6931)
PHONE..................................941 747-1000
Charles F Ogle, President
Robert A Dring, Vice Pres
Bill Runyan, Prdtn Mgr
Karen Dring, Office Mgr
Charles Ogle, Executive
EMP: 14 EST: 1955
SQ FT: 13,500
SALES (est): 2.4MM Privately Held
WEB: www.floridasign.com
SIC: 3993 Neon signs

(G-1046)
SLEUTH INC
Also Called: Slueth Bldg Sys Investigations
3988 E State Road 64 (34208-9059)
PHONE..................................941 745-9903
Robert L Bergs, President
John Horton, Vice Pres
EMP: 17 EST: 1982
SQ FT: 790
SALES (est): 4.6MM Privately Held
WEB: www.sleuthleakdetection.com
SIC: 3599 Water leak detectors

(G-1047)
SNAPPLE BEVERAGES
2919 62nd Ave E (34203-5320)
PHONE..................................941 758-7010
Richard Paul, Principal
EMP: 8 EST: 2010
SALES (est): 178.6K Privately Held
SIC: 2086 Soft drinks: packaged in cans,
bottles, etc.

(G-1048)
SNOW-NABSTEDT POWER TRANSMISSI
3007 29th Ave E (34208-7418)
PHONE..................................603 661-5551
Cary Wische, President
▲ EMP: 6 EST: 2013

SALES (est): 751.9K Privately Held
WEB: www.snpt.biz
SIC: 3566 Gears, power transmission, except automotive

(G-1049)
SOUTHERN MCH TL & RBLDRS INC
2923 62nd Ave E (34203-5367)
PHONE..................................941 749-0988
Stephen Wendrick, President
Kathy Wright, Treasurer
EMP: 10 EST: 1979
SQ FT: 10,000
SALES (est): 838.5K Privately Held
SIC: 3599 Machine shop, jobbing & repair

(G-1050)
SOUTHERN REINFORCED PLAS INC
Also Called: S R P
2904 29th Ave E Ste F (34208-7424)
PHONE..................................941 746-8793
Robert Biles, President
Paula Biles, Vice Pres
EMP: 7 EST: 1986
SQ FT: 7,500
SALES (est): 572.7K Privately Held
WEB: www.atokaspeedynet.net
SIC: 3089 Injection molding of plastics

(G-1051)
SPRAYING SYSTEMS CO
Also Called: Herman Group
5107 Lena Rd Unit 110 (34211-9494)
PHONE..................................813 259-9400
Ken Herman, Manager
EMP: 7
SALES (corp-wide): 348.1MM Privately
Held
WEB: www.spray.com
SIC: 3499 Nozzles, spray: aerosol, paint or
insecticide
PA: Spraying Systems Co.
200 W North Ave
Glendale Heights IL 60139
630 665-5000

(G-1052)
STEELE INDUSTRIES INC
10510 Portal Xing Ste 101 (34211-4911)
PHONE..................................800 674-7302
Dominick Steele, CEO
EMP: 11 EST: 2019
SALES (est): 959.4K Privately Held
WEB: www.steeleindustries.com
SIC: 3812 Defense systems & equipment

(G-1053)
STERILINE NORTH AMERICA I
872 62nd Street Cir E (34208-6238)
PHONE..................................941 405-2039
EMP: 6 EST: 2019
SALES (est): 415.6K Privately Held
SIC: 2834 Pharmaceutical preparations

(G-1054)
SUNCOAST ACCRDTED GMLGICAL LAB
4016 Cortez Rd W Ste 1201 (34210-3118)
PHONE..................................941 756-8787
Tom Seguin, President
EMP: 6 EST: 1985
SQ FT: 674
SALES (est): 369.3K Privately Held
SIC: 3915 7631 3911 6531 Diamond cutting & polishing; watch, clock & jewelry repair; jewelry, precious metal; appraiser, real estate

(G-1055)
SUPER TOOL INC
2951 63rd Ave E (34203-5308)
P.O. Box 20849 (34204-0849)
PHONE..................................941 751-9677
Paul Enander, President
Bryan Enander, Mktg Dir
EMP: 15 EST: 1989
SQ FT: 10,000
SALES (est): 1MM Privately Held
WEB: www.supertoolinc.com
SIC: 3541 Machine tools, metal cutting
type

(G-1056)
SUPERIOR ASPHALT INC
4703 15th St E (34203-3619)
Rural Route 2489, Oneco (34264)
PHONE..................................941 755-2850
Craig W Robson, President
Denise Robson, Corp Secy
Alan Mulvey, Vice Pres
Dan Weaver, Project Mgr
Linda Marino, Administration
▲ EMP: 100 EST: 2001
SQ FT: 2,500
SALES (est): 25MM Privately Held
WEB: www.superiorasphaltinc.net
SIC: 2951 1771 Asphalt paving mixtures &
blocks; blacktop (asphalt) work
PA: Modern Construction, U.S.A, Inc.
4703 15th St E
Bradenton FL 34203
941 727-5215

(G-1057)
SZABO POS DISPLAYS INC
1501 63rd St W (34209-4568)
PHONE..................................941 778-0192
Barbara Szabo, CEO
Stephen J Szabo, President
EMP: 7 EST: 1987
SQ FT: 100,000
SALES (est): 101.4K Privately Held
SIC: 3999 2542 3993 3578 Forms: display, dress & show; racks, merchandise
display or storage: except wood; signs &
advertising specialties; calculating & accounting equipment

(G-1058)
TEAM EDITION APPAREL INC
4208 19th Street Ct E (34208-7336)
PHONE..................................941 744-2041
Giovanna Cipriano, Vice Pres
Allen Cotogno, Director
◆ EMP: 225 EST: 1961
SQ FT: 75,000
SALES (est): 64.2MM Publicly Held
SIC: 2329 2396 Athletic (warmup, sweat &
jogging) suits: men's & boys'; screen
printing on fabric articles
PA: Foot Locker, Inc.
330 W 34th St
New York NY 10001

(G-1059)
THOMAS PRODUCTS LLC
503 Pecan Ln (34212-2617)
PHONE..................................563 639-9099
Thomas C Brown Sr, Principal
EMP: 7 EST: 2017
SALES (est): 62.3K Privately Held
WEB: www.thomasproducts.com
SIC: 2048 Prepared feeds

(G-1060)
TMF PLASTIC SOLUTIONS LLC
4690 19th Street Ct E (34203-3768)
PHONE..................................941 748-2946
Gregory Kuppler, Mng Member
Timothy Raymond,
EMP: 24 EST: 2016
SALES (est): 5.5MM Privately Held
SIC: 3089 Injection molding of plastics

(G-1061)
TORTILLERIA LA RANCHERITA
3010 14th St W (34205-6332)
PHONE..................................941 747-7949
Hilda Vega, Principal
EMP: 8 EST: 2005
SALES (est): 338.8K Privately Held
SIC: 2099 Tortillas, fresh or refrigerated

(G-1062)
TRAKKA USA LLC
4725 Lena Rd Unit 103 (34211-9535)
PHONE..................................505 345-0270
Edwin Daniels, CEO
Shawn Mitschelen, Vice Pres
Maryellen Mitschelen, Administration
Peter Rudaizky,
EMP: 6 EST: 2011
SALES (est): 859.3K Privately Held
WEB: www.trakkasystems.com
SIC: 3812 Search & navigation equipment

(G-1063)
TRI C PETROLEUM INC
6442 Shoal Creek St Cir (34202-1711)
PHONE..................................941 756-3370
Charles Coleman, Director
EMP: 7 EST: 2001
SALES (est): 148.6K Privately Held
SIC: 1382 Oil & gas exploration services

(G-1064)
TRI-H METAL PRODUCTS INC
5815 21st St E (34203-5004)
PHONE..................................941 753-7311
Rich Hinkle, President
Will Hinkle, Vice Pres
EMP: 9 EST: 2000
SQ FT: 12,000
SALES (est): 1.9MM Privately Held
SIC: 3444 Sheet metalwork

(G-1065)
TRINITY MANUFACTURING CORP
6205 31st St E Ste A (34203-5388)
P.O. Box 21105 (34204-1105)
PHONE..................................941 727-9595
James A Fitch Jr, President
John Northup, President
Paul Goldich, Vice Pres
Scott Ohearen, Prdtn Mgr
Cheryl Kline, Purchasing
EMP: 29 EST: 2003
SQ FT: 9,500
SALES (est): 5.3MM Privately Held
WEB: www.trinitymfgcorp.com
SIC: 3679 Harness assemblies for electronic use: wire or cable

(G-1066)
TROPICANA MANUFACTURING CO INC
1001 13th Ave E (34208-2699)
PHONE..................................800 237-7799
EMP: 988
SALES (corp-wide): 70.3B Publicly Held
SIC: 2033 Fruit juices: concentrated, hot
pack
HQ: Tropicana Manufacturing Company,
Inc.
433 W Van Buren St Ste 3n
Chicago IL 60607

(G-1067)
TROPICANA PRODUCTS INC (HQ)
1001 13th Ave E (34208-2699)
P.O. Box 338 (34206-0338)
PHONE..................................941 747-4461
Greg Shearson, President
Clay Small, Senior VP
Melinda Brown, Vice Pres
Paul Carr, Plant Mgr
David Schappacher, Opers Staff
◆ EMP: 1800 EST: 1947
SQ FT: 100,000
SALES (est): 1.1B
SALES (corp-wide): 70.3B Publicly Held
WEB: www.tropicana.com
SIC: 2033 2037 2086 2048 Fruit juices:
fresh; fruit juice concentrates, frozen; fruit
drinks (less than 100% juice): packaged
in cans, etc.; citrus seed meal, prepared
as animal feed
PA: Pepsico, Inc.
700 Anderson Hill Rd
Purchase NY 10577
914 253-2000

(G-1068)
TRUE PLUMBING SVC INC
11729 Meadowgate Pl (34211-3712)
PHONE..................................941 296-5123
Micheal Faulconer, Owner
EMP: 8 EST: 2018
SALES (est): 626.9K Privately Held
WEB: www.trueplumbing4u.com
SIC: 3432 Plumbing fixture fittings & trim

(G-1069)
ULTRABOX INC
5827 17th St E (34203-5043)
P.O. Box 21046 (34204-1046)
PHONE..................................941 371-0000
Boldon Jeffrey, Principal
EMP: 9 EST: 2013

2022 Harris Florida
Manufacturers Directory
▲ = Import ▼=Export
◆ =Import/Export

SALES (est): 216.5K **Privately Held**
WEB: www.ultraboxinc.com
SIC: 2653 Boxes, corrugated: made from purchased materials

(G-1070)
UNITED MANUFACTURING SVCS LLC
2908 29th Ave E (34208-7460)
PHONE..................................941 224-1692
Rodney Cole, *Principal*
EMP: 9 EST: 2016
SALES (est): 430.1K **Privately Held**
SIC: 3999 Manufacturing industries

(G-1071)
VANDALAY INDS MANATEE CNTY LLC
6832 14th St W (34207-5866)
PHONE..................................941 756-6028
Roy Killingsworth, *Principal*
EMP: 7 EST: 2010
SALES (est): 176.2K **Privately Held**
SIC: 3999 Manufacturing industries

(G-1072)
VEETHREE ELECTRONICS & MAR LLC
Also Called: Veethree Instruments
2050 47th Ter E (34203-3777)
PHONE..................................941 538-7775
Shekhar Tewatia, *Vice Pres*
Kim Graveline, *Senior Buyer*
Diana Mahle, *Purchasing*
Joe Legerstee, *Sales Mgr*
Kevin Griffioen, *Technology*
◆ EMP: 82 EST: 2009
SQ FT: 50,000
SALES (est): 14.8MM **Privately Held**
WEB: www.veethree.com
SIC: 3629 0919 5088 Electronic generation equipment; cultured pearl production; marine supplies

(G-1073)
W D H ENTERPRISES INC
Also Called: Copy Right Printing
4230 26th St W (34205-3516)
PHONE..................................941 758-6500
Dave Hassall, *Owner*
EMP: 6 EST: 1981
SQ FT: 2,500
SALES (est): 713.4K **Privately Held**
SIC: 2752 7331 2791 2789 Commercial printing, offset; direct mail advertising services; typesetting; bookbinding & related work; commercial printing

(G-1074)
W E W ENTERPRISES INC
Also Called: Woodcrafters, The
6103 28th St E Ste A (34203-5386)
PHONE..................................941 751-6610
William E Wilson III, *President*
EMP: 15 EST: 1980
SQ FT: 7,000
SALES (est): 345.9K **Privately Held**
SIC: 2434 Wood kitchen cabinets

(G-1075)
WAKE UP BEAUTIFUL
6646 Cortez Rd W (34210-2600)
PHONE..................................941 792-6500
Kathy Yeomans, *Owner*
EMP: 9 EST: 2010
SALES (est): 266K **Privately Held**
SIC: 2844 Perfumes & colognes

(G-1076)
WEST COAST CASTINGS INC
1211 44th Ave E (34203-3629)
PHONE..................................941 753-2969
Theodore G Boerger, *President*
Susan Boerger, *Vice Pres*
EMP: 13 EST: 1948
SQ FT: 12,500
SALES (est): 1.6MM **Privately Held**
WEB: www.westcoastcastings.com
SIC: 3365 Aluminum & aluminum-based alloy castings

(G-1077)
WEST COAST SIGNS INC
2071 58th Avenue Cir E (34203-5060)
PHONE..................................941 755-5686

Marc Delisle, *Vice Pres*
EMP: 7 EST: 2007
SALES (est): 76.3K **Privately Held**
SIC: 3993 Signs & advertising specialties

(G-1078)
WHEEL SYSTEMS INTL INC
7645 Tralee Way (34202-6010)
PHONE..................................920 235-9888
Shari Medley, *President*
EMP: 12 EST: 2003
SALES (est): 243.7K **Privately Held**
WEB: www.medleyglobal.com
SIC: 3448 Garages, portable: prefabricated metal

(G-1079)
WOODTECH GLOBAL INC
Also Called: Graber Cabinets
5822 24th St E (34203-5027)
P.O. Box 110258, Lakewood Rch (34211-0004)
PHONE..................................941 371-0392
Scott Spoerl, *President*
EMP: 10 EST: 2016
SALES (est): 941.3K **Privately Held**
SIC: 2434 Wood kitchen cabinets

(G-1080)
Z CANS LLC
1111 Brambling Ct (34212-2919)
PHONE..................................941 748-6688
Mary Zimmerman, *Principal*
EMP: 7 EST: 2007
SALES (est): 207.7K **Privately Held**
WEB: www.zcans.net
SIC: 3089 Garbage containers, plastic

Brandon
Hillsborough County

(G-1081)
A MIL AIR
920 Essex Rd (33510-2735)
PHONE..................................813 417-9114
Joseph P Miller, *Principal*
EMP: 10 EST: 2008
SALES (est): 211.6K **Privately Held**
SIC: 3564 Blowers & fans

(G-1082)
AMERICAN METAL FAB OF CTRL FL
1018 W Brandon Blvd 11b (33511-4101)
PHONE..................................813 653-2788
Roxanna Feldman, *President*
EMP: 5 EST: 1992
SQ FT: 2,400
SALES (est): 774.5K **Privately Held**
SIC: 3441 Fabricated structural metal

(G-1083)
AMETRINE LLC
127 Barrington Dr (33511-6449)
PHONE..................................786 300-7946
Darshan Trivedi, *Branch Mgr*
EMP: 10
SALES (corp-wide): 754.5K **Privately Held**
WEB: www.ametrinesurfaces.com
SIC: 3281 Table tops, marble
PA: Ametrine Llc
201 Se 2nd Ave Apt 2705
Miami FL 33131
800 864-8127

(G-1084)
BOOKS-A-MILLION INC
839 Brandon Town Ctr Mall (33511-4798)
PHONE..................................813 571-2062
Aji Fabi, *Principal*
EMP: 14
SALES (corp-wide): 230.4MM **Privately Held**
WEB: www.booksamillion.com
SIC: 2741 5942 Miscellaneous publishing; book stores
HQ: Books-A-Million, Inc.
402 Industrial Ln
Birmingham AL 35211
205 942-3737

(G-1085)
BORN TO RIDE
1051 E Brandon Blvd (33511-5515)
PHONE..................................813 661-9402
Ronald Galletti, *Branch Mgr*
EMP: 15
SALES (corp-wide): 1.1MM **Privately Held**
WEB: www.borntoride.com
SIC: 2721 Periodicals
PA: Born To Ride
1503 Heritage Dr
Valrico FL 33594
813 661-9402

(G-1086)
CLARI SOLUTIONS LLC
Also Called: Fastsigns
2020 W Brandon Blvd # 17 (33511-4757)
PHONE..................................813 679-4848
Ricardo Cardoso, *Principal*
EMP: 7 EST: 2017
SALES (est): 200.2K **Privately Held**
WEB: www.clari.com
SIC: 3993 Signs & advertising specialties

(G-1087)
COCA COLA BOTTLING CO
599 Lake Kathy Dr (33510-3945)
PHONE..................................813 569-3030
EMP: 16 EST: 2017
SALES (est): 909.8K **Privately Held**
WEB: www.coca-cola.com
SIC: 2086 Bottled & canned soft drinks

(G-1088)
COCA-COLA BTLG CENTL FLA LLC
235 W Brandon Blvd (33511-5103)
PHONE..................................832 260-0462
Steven Johnson, *Finance Dir*
EMP: 10 EST: 2015
SQ FT: 30,000
SALES (est): 5.5MM **Privately Held**
WEB: www.coca-cola.com
SIC: 2086 Bottled & canned soft drinks

(G-1089)
DELTA OIL
823 Bayou Dr (33510)
PHONE..................................813 323-3113
Terry Chaudrey, *President*
EMP: 7 EST: 2004
SALES (est): 245.7K **Privately Held**
SIC: 1311 Crude petroleum production

(G-1090)
ERNIES METAL FABRICATING
406 E Windhorst Rd (33510-2530)
PHONE..................................813 679-0816
Ernest Higgins, *Principal*
EMP: 7 EST: 2017
SALES (est): 509.1K **Privately Held**
SIC: 3499 Fabricated metal products

(G-1091)
EVERSLIM LLC
1429 Oakfield Dr (33511-2801)
PHONE..................................813 265-2100
EMP: 7 EST: 2012
SALES (est): 119K **Privately Held**
SIC: 3949 Dumbbells & other weightlifting equipment

(G-1092)
FAST SIGNS OF BRANDON
Also Called: Fastsigns
2020 Brandon Crossing Cir (33511-3674)
PHONE..................................813 655-9036
EMP: 8 EST: 2015
SALES (est): 143.4K **Privately Held**
WEB: www.fastsigns.com
SIC: 3993 Signs & advertising specialties

(G-1093)
FLORIDA COCA-COLA BOTTLING CO (DH)
521 Lake Kathy Dr (33510-3945)
PHONE..................................813 569-2600
Jay Ard, *Vice Pres*
Curtis Cattanach, *Marketing Staff*
Denise Jamerson, *Supervisor*
Debra Roach, *Supervisor*
Dan Bottie, *Technical Staff*
◆ EMP: 300 EST: 1926

SQ FT: 20,000
SALES (est): 888.1MM
SALES (corp-wide): 33B **Publicly Held**
WEB: www.coca-cola.com
SIC: 2086 Bottled & canned soft drinks
HQ: Coca-Cola Refreshments Usa, Inc.
2500 Windy Ridge Pkwy Se
Atlanta GA 30339
770 989-3000

(G-1094)
GRIP TOOLING TECHNOLOGIES LLC
1202 Telfair Rd (33510-2978)
PHONE..................................813 654-6832
Thomas Kukucka, *Principal*
EMP: 14 EST: 2015
SALES (est): 682.8K **Privately Held**
SIC: 3423 Hand & edge tools

(G-1095)
IDEAL IMAGE BRANDON
1602 Oakfield Dr Ste 105 (33511-0827)
P.O. Box 18191, Tampa (33679-8191)
PHONE..................................813 982-3420
Doh Acebal, *President*
Joe Acebal, *President*
EMP: 6 EST: 2005
SALES (est): 453.7K **Privately Held**
WEB: www.idealimage.com
SIC: 3841 Surgical lasers

(G-1096)
IGUANA GRAPHICS INC
1345 Oakfield Dr (33511-4823)
PHONE..................................813 657-7800
Carlos Arias, *President*
EMP: 6 EST: 2005
SALES (est): 374K **Privately Held**
WEB: www.goiguana.com
SIC: 2752 Commercial printing, offset

(G-1097)
KING PRINTING & GRAPHICS INC
634 Oakfield Dr (33511-5715)
PHONE..................................813 681-5060
Steve Rabstejnek, *President*
Patty Rabstejnek, *Vice Pres*
EMP: 7 EST: 1976
SALES (est): 816.1K **Privately Held**
WEB: www.kingprintingfl.com
SIC: 2752 2759 Commercial printing, offset; commercial printing

(G-1098)
MAGNUM COATINGS INC
802 Lumsden Reserve Dr (33511-5988)
PHONE..................................407 704-0786
Jennifer E Gordon, *Principal*
EMP: 8 EST: 2011
SALES (est): 231.9K **Privately Held**
SIC: 3479 Metal coating & allied service

(G-1099)
PARAMOUNT DIGITAL PUBG LLC
123 W Bloomingdale Ave # 3 (33511-7400)
PHONE..................................813 489-5029
Donald Fawcett, *Mng Member*
EMP: 10 EST: 2011
SALES (est): 495.9K **Privately Held**
SIC: 2741 Miscellaneous publishing

(G-1100)
PATIO PRODUCTS MFG INC
509 S Larry Cir (33511-6040)
PHONE..................................813 681-3806
Al Whitehead, *Principal*
EMP: 8 EST: 2011
SALES (est): 463.4K **Privately Held**
SIC: 3999 Manufacturing industries

(G-1101)
PATRICK GERMAN INDUSTRIES INC
Also Called: Creative Colors International
1302 Wallwood Dr (33510-2242)
PHONE..................................727 251-3015
German Patrick, *Principal*
EMP: 7 EST: 2016
SALES (est): 279.4K **Privately Held**
WEB: www.creativecolorsintl.com
SIC: 3999 7532 Manufacturing industries; top & body repair & paint shops

(G-1102)
PATRIOT PERSON DEFENSE
1604 White Dove Ct (33510-2854)
PHONE..........................813 470-8025
John Thies, *President*
EMP: 7 **EST:** 2017
SALES (est): 239.3K **Privately Held**
SIC: 3812 Defense systems & equipment

(G-1103)
PIECEMAKERS LLC
120 N Knights Ave (33510-4324)
PHONE..........................786 517-1829
Andres Tamayo, *Sales Staff*
Vanessa Larsen, *Office Mgr*
Francisco J Villasante, *Mng Member*
Christopher Villasante, *Mng Member*
EMP: 10 **EST:** 2010
SALES (est): 860.4K **Privately Held**
WEB: www.piece-makers.com
SIC: 3441 Fabricated structural metal

(G-1104)
RJH TECHNICAL SERVICES INC
517 Gornto Lake Rd (33510-3919)
P.O. Box 3658 (33509-3658)
PHONE..........................813 655-7947
Dorothy L Hinderliter, *President*
Robert J Hinderliter, *Principal*
Lee Hinderliter, *Purchasing*
Marcus Hinderliter, *Admin Sec*
EMP: 5 **EST:** 1992
SALES (est): 718.6K **Privately Held**
WEB: www.rjhtechnicalservicesinc.com
SIC: 3825 Internal combustion engine ana-
lyzers, to test electronics

(G-1105)
SAMTECK INC
1005 Croydonwood Cir (33510-2610)
PHONE..........................813 210-6784
Samuel Almonte, *Principal*
EMP: 9 **EST:** 2011
SALES (est): 1MM **Privately Held**
SIC: 3679 Electronic circuits

(G-1106)
SEATTLE ENGRAVING CENTER
LLC
1073 E Brandon Blvd (33511-5515)
PHONE..........................813 330-7620
Reem Gamil, *Exec Dir*
EMP: 7 **EST:** 2014
SALES (est): 583.2K **Privately Held**
WEB: www.seattleengravingcenter.com
SIC: 2759 3949 Currency: engraved;
sporting & athletic goods

(G-1107)
SIENTRA INC
1302 Guiles Hill Ct (33511-7612)
PHONE..........................813 751-7576
EMP: 8 **EST:** 2017
SALES (est): 132.6K **Privately Held**
WEB: www.sientra.com
SIC: 3842 Surgical appliances & supplies

(G-1108)
SIGNS NOW OF BRANDON INC
1947 W Brandon Blvd (33511-4813)
PHONE..........................813 684-0047
EMP: 8 **EST:** 2020
SALES (est): 233.6K **Privately Held**
SIC: 3993 Signs & advertising specialties

(G-1109)
SOCRATIC SOLUTIONS INC
220 W Brandon Blvd # 207 (33511-5100)
P.O. Box 414, Lithia (33547-0414)
PHONE..........................813 324-7018
Ryan Lampel, *CEO*
Jennifer Lampel, *Vice Pres*
EMP: 5 **EST:** 2019
SALES (est): 475.4K **Privately Held**
WEB: www.socraticsolutions.us
SIC: 2833 5499 Medicinals & botanicals;
tea

(G-1110)
TABLE GOLF LLC
667 W Lumsden Rd (33511-5911)
P.O. Box 3290 (33509-3290)
PHONE..........................813 435-6111
EMP: 7
SQ FT: 2,000

SALES: 85K **Privately Held**
SIC: 3944 Mfg Games/Toys

Branford
Suwannee County

(G-1111)
BARNES & SONS WOOD
PRODUCERS
105 Suwannee Ave Nw (32008-3273)
PHONE..........................386 935-2229
Larry Barnes, *President*
Wesley Barnes, *Vice Pres*
EMP: 5 **EST:** 1970
SQ FT: 3,000
SALES (est): 486K **Privately Held**
SIC: 2411 Pulpwood contractors engaged
in cutting

(G-1112)
HATCH ENTERPRISES INC
8199 Us Highway 27 (32008-2680)
P.O. Box 238 (32008-0238)
PHONE..........................386 935-1419
EMP: 5
SQ FT: 2,500
SALES (est): 559.9K **Privately Held**
SIC: 1411 0191 Dolomite Demension-
Quarrying And General Farm Primarily
Crop

(G-1113)
JOHN LACQUEY ENTERPRISES
INC
8125 264th St (32008-2645)
PHONE..........................386 935-1705
John Lacquey, *President*
EMP: 10 **EST:** 2001
SALES (est): 449.4K **Privately Held**
SIC: 2353 Harvest hats, straw

(G-1114)
PINE TOP LOGGING LLC
27687 65th Rd (32008-2510)
PHONE..........................386 365-0857
Donald J Harrison, *Owner*
EMP: 6 **EST:** 2014
SALES (est): 320K **Privately Held**
SIC: 2411 Logging camps & contractors

(G-1115)
TW BYRDS SONS INC
11860 E Us 27 (32008-8315)
PHONE..........................386 935-1544
T Jack Byrd, *President*
Paul Byrd, *Vice Pres*
J W Byrd, *Treasurer*
Earl Byrd, *Admin Sec*
Benita Byrd, *Asst Sec*
EMP: 34 **EST:** 1945
SQ FT: 2,500
SALES (est): 2.8MM **Privately Held**
WEB: www.byrdsdepot.com
SIC: 2411 Logging camps & contractors

Bristol
Liberty County

(G-1116)
APALACHEE POLE COMPANY
INC
18601 Nw County Road 379a (32321)
P.O. Box 610 (32321-0610)
PHONE..........................850 643-2121
David Powell, *Manager*
Jason Daniels, *Manager*
EMP: 30
SALES (corp-wide): 4.2MM **Privately
Held**
WEB: www.rex-lumber.com
SIC: 2411 2491 Poles, wood: untreated;
poles & pole crossarms, treated wood
PA: Apalachee Pole Company, Inc.
1820 Highway 2
Graceville FL 32440
850 263-4457

(G-1117)
C & G TIMBER HARVESTERS
INC
10213 Nw Dan Jacobs Ln (32321-3508)
PHONE..........................850 643-1340
Patricia Whitfield, *Principal*
EMP: 7 **EST:** 2003
SALES (est): 97.4K **Privately Held**
SIC: 2411 Logging camps & contractors

(G-1118)
FLORIDA NORTH LUMBER CO
INC
Hwy 12 S (32321)
PHONE..........................850 643-2238
C Finley Mc Rae, *President*
Robert F Mc Rae Jr, *Vice Pres*
Tom Smith, *Manager*
EMP: 73 **EST:** 1982
SQ FT: 100,000
SALES (est): 5.5MM **Privately Held**
WEB: www.rex-lumber.com
SIC: 2421 Lumber: rough, sawed or planed

(G-1119)
FLORIDA NORTH LUMBER INC
18601 Nw County Road 12 (32321-4176)
P.O. Box 7, Graceville (32440-0007)
PHONE..........................850 263-4457
C Finley McRae, *President*
EMP: 34 **EST:** 1980
SALES (est): 3.3MM **Privately Held**
WEB: www.rex-lumber.com
SIC: 2421 Sawmills & planing mills, gen-
eral

(G-1120)
JOHN HARVEY GREEN
Also Called: Johnny Green Logging
301 1st St (32321)
P.O. Box 633 (32321-0633)
PHONE..........................850 643-2544
John H Green, *Owner*
John Green, *Owner*
EMP: 5 **EST:** 1950
SALES (est): 505.5K **Privately Held**
SIC: 2411 Logging

(G-1121)
JOHNNY SELLERS LOGGING
INC
Turkey Creek Rd (32321)
P.O. Box 582 (32321-0582)
PHONE..........................850 643-5214
Johnny Sellers, *President*
EMP: 9 **EST:** 1995
SALES (est): 892.1K **Privately Held**
SIC: 2411 Logging camps & contractors

(G-1122)
LIBERTY CALHOUN JOURNAL
INC
11493 Nw Summers Rd (32321-3364)
P.O. Box 536 (32321-0536)
PHONE..........................850 643-3333
Johnny Eubanks, *President*
Theresa Eubanks, *Vice Pres*
EMP: 9 **EST:** 1981
SALES (est): 784K **Privately Held**
WEB: www.libertycountyflorida.com
SIC: 2711 2791 Newspapers, publishing &
printing; typesetting

(G-1123)
MCMILLAN LOGGING INC
15405 Nw Pea Ridge Rd (32321-3660)
P.O. Box 8 (32321-0008)
PHONE..........................850 643-4819
James S McMillan, *President*
EMP: 12 **EST:** 2007
SQ FT: 2,542
SALES (est): 792.2K **Privately Held**
SIC: 2411 Logging camps & contractors

(G-1124)
MICHAEL P WAHLQUIST
13036 Nw Freeman Rd (32321-3026)
PHONE..........................850 643-5139
Michael P Wahlquist, *Owner*
EMP: 7 **EST:** 2005
SALES (est): 255K **Privately Held**
SIC: 3589 Water filters & softeners, house-
hold type

(G-1125)
NORTH FLORIDA WOODLANDS
INC
Also Called: North Florida Lumber
18601 Nw County Road 12 (32321-4176)
P.O. Box 610 (32321-0610)
PHONE..........................850 643-2238
Ken Betts, *Manager*
EMP: 18
SALES (corp-wide): 2.2MM **Privately
Held**
WEB: www.rex-lumber.com
SIC: 2421 Sawmills & planing mills, gen-
eral
PA: North Florida Woodlands, Inc
1820 Highway 2
Graceville FL 32440
850 263-4457

(G-1126)
REX LUMBER LLC
Highway 12 S (32321)
PHONE..........................850 643-2172
Derik Blesky, *Manager*
EMP: 18
SALES (corp-wide): 51.9MM **Privately
Held**
WEB: www.rex-lumber.com
SIC: 2421 Sawmills & planing mills, gen-
eral
HQ: Rex Lumber, Graceville, Llc
5299 Alabama St
Graceville FL 32440
850 263-2056

(G-1127)
RUBY VANRUM
Also Called: Varnums Rest Home
12167 Nw Freeman Rd (32321-3019)
P.O. Box 6 (32321-0006)
PHONE..........................850 643-5155
Ruby Varnum, *Owner*
EMP: 7 **EST:** 1985
SALES (est): 390.5K **Privately Held**
SIC: 2512 Living room furniture: uphol-
stered on wood frames

Brooksville
Hernando County

(G-1128)
ACCUFORM GLOBAL INC
16228 Flight Path Dr (34604-6875)
PHONE..........................800 237-1001
Rob Ogilbee, *President*
EMP: 12 **EST:** 2011
SALES (est): 371.3K **Privately Held**
WEB: www.accuform.com
SIC: 3993 Signs & advertising specialties

(G-1129)
ACCUFORM MANUFACTURING
INC
Also Called: Accuform Signs
16228 Flight Path Dr (34604-6875)
PHONE..........................352 799-5434
Wayne D Johnson, *CEO*
Rob Ogilbee, *President*
David B Johnson, *COO*
Rebecca Baker, *Assistant*
◆ **EMP:** 270 **EST:** 1976
SQ FT: 100,000
SALES (est): 55.3MM **Privately Held**
WEB: www.accuform.com
SIC: 3993 Signs, not made in custom sign
painting shops

(G-1130)
ADAMS ARMS HOLDINGS LLC
21228 Powell Rd (34604-6723)
PHONE..........................727 853-0550
Jason East, *President*
EMP: 35 **EST:** 2019
SALES (est): 3.8MM **Privately Held**
WEB: www.adamsarms.net
SIC: 3484 Guns (firearms) or gun parts, 30
mm. & below

(G-1131)
AIRDYNE AEROSPACE INC
3160 Premier Dr (34604-8299)
PHONE..........................352 593-4163
Ross Neyedly, *President*

▲ = Import ▼=Export
◆ =Import/Export

Mike Hillestad, *Vice Pres*
Sammy Sedita, *Accountant*
Anselma Roman, *Credit Staff*
Bill Hargraves, *Sales Mgr*
EMP: 29 **EST:** 2010
SALES (est): 5.3MM **Privately Held**
WEB: www.airdyne-aero.com
SIC: 3728 Aircraft parts & equipment

(G-1132)
AL COVELL ELECTRIC INC
600 S Main St (34601-3764)
P.O. Box 294, Nobleton (34661-0294)
PHONE.............................352 544-0680
James Covell, *President*
Anna Liisa Covell, *Vice Pres*
Bryon Covell, *Director*
EMP: 5 **EST:** 1992
SQ FT: 3,600
SALES (est): 499.4K **Privately Held**
WEB: www.covellservices.com
SIC: 7694 1731 5999 Electric motor re-
pair; electrical work; motors, electric

(G-1133)
AMAX WELDING &
FABRICATION
19496 Fort Dade Ave (34601-2414)
P.O. Box 1871 (34605-1871)
PHONE.............................352 544-8484
Brenda J Smith, *President*
Roger D Smith, *Vice Pres*
EMP: 5 **EST:** 2008
SALES (est): 447K **Privately Held**
WEB: amax-welding-fabrication-inc.hub.biz
SIC: 7692 Welding repair

(G-1134)
AME TRITON LLC
Also Called: AME International
2347 Circuit Way (34604-0622)
PHONE 352 799-1111
Kyle Sparkman, *Opers Staff*
Kirk Kramer, *Sales Staff*
Justin Meyer, *Sales Staff*
Shane Wiley, *Sales Staff*
Brittany Yunka, *Marketing Staff*
▲ **EMP:** 23 **EST:** 2007
SQ FT: 19,000
SALES (est): 4.2MM **Privately Held**
SIC: 3429 Motor vehicle hardware

(G-1135)
AMERICAN INJECTABLES INC
15261 Telcom Dr (34604-0718)
PHONE.............................813 435-6014
Vern Allen, *CEO*
EMP: 12 **EST:** 2020
SALES (est): 2.6MM **Privately Held**
WEB: www.americaninj.com
SIC: 2834 Pharmaceutical preparations

(G-1136)
AMERICAN SILICA HOLDINGS
LLC
24060 Deer Run Rd (34601-4548)
P.O. Box 68 (34605-0068)
PHONE.............................352 796-8855
EMP: 5
SALES (est): 608.7K **Privately Held**
SIC: 1389 5082 Oil/Gas Field Services
Whol Construction/Mining Equipment

(G-1137)
ANTHONY SPAGNA SVC &
MAINT INC
3335 Mustang Dr (34604-8113)
P.O. Box 15316 (34604-0116)
PHONE.............................352 796-2109
Anthony Spagna, *President*
EMP: 6 **EST:** 2004
SQ FT: 3,000
SALES (est): 934.1K **Privately Held**
SIC: 3441 Fabricated structural metal

(G-1138)
AVALANCHE CORPORATION
Also Called: Monster Transmission & Prfmce
17109 Old Ayers Rd (34604-6808)
PHONE.............................800 708-0087
Curtis Thomas, *Treasurer*
Eva Thomas, *Office Mgr*
▼ **EMP:** 75 **EST:** 2003

SALES (est): 9.4MM **Privately Held**
SIC: 3714 7539 Rebuilding engines &
transmissions, factory basis; torque converter repair, automotive

(G-1139)
BARRETTE OUTDOOR LIVING
INC
Also Called: Alumi-Guard
2401 Corporate Blvd (34604-0623)
PHONE.............................352 754-8555
Chip Howison, *Vice Pres*
Tom Cozza, *Safety Dir*
John Holcomb, *Plant Mgr*
Laura Holcomb, *Materials Mgr*
Jon Constantino, *Production*
EMP: 98
SALES (corp-wide): 30.9B **Privately Held**
WEB: www.barretteoutdoorliving.com
SIC: 3446 Ornamental metalwork
HQ: Barrette Outdoor Living, Inc.
7830 Freeway Cir
Middleburg Heights OH 44130
440 891-0790

(G-1140)
BET ER MIX INC
21101 Cortez Blvd (34601-5645)
PHONE.............................352 799-5538
Chuck Jackson, *President*
EMP: 7 **EST:** 2017
SALES (est): 182.1K **Privately Held**
WEB: www.betermix.com
SIC: 3273 Ready-mixed concrete

(G-1141)
BLACK DIAMOND COATINGS
INC
6036 Nature Coast Blvd (34602-8286)
PHONE.............................800 270-4050
David Warren, *CEO*
Heather Warren, *Vice Pres*
EMP: 21 **EST:** 2013
SALES (est): 2.8MM **Privately Held**
WEB: www.blackdiamondcoatings.com
SIC: 2851 Paints & allied products

(G-1142)
BREINER MACHINE CO INC
15373 Flight Path Dr (34604-6862)
PHONE.............................352 544-0463
James Breiner, *President*
EMP: 12 **EST:** 1985
SALES (est): 1.9MM **Privately Held**
WEB: www.breinermachineinc.com
SIC: 3444 3599 Sheet metalwork; ma-
chine shop, jobbing & repair

(G-1143)
BROOKSVILLE PRINTING INC
712 S Main St (34601-3745)
PHONE.............................352 848-0016
Carl Brady, *President*
C J Brady, *Vice Pres*
EMP: 5 **EST:** 1973
SQ FT: 1,500
SALES (est): 484K **Privately Held**
SIC: 2752 Commercial printing, offset

(G-1144)
CHASCO MACHINE &
MANUFACTURING
5071 Cedar Ridge Dr (34601-6535)
PHONE.............................727 815-3510
Jeffrey A Roth, *President*
EMP: 6 **EST:** 1999
SALES (est): 633.1K **Privately Held**
SIC: 3599 3469 Catapults; metal stamp-
ings

(G-1145)
CHASCO MACHINE & MFG INC
5071 Cedar Ridge Dr (34601-6535)
PHONE.............................352 678-4188
Jeff Roth, *President*
Jeffrey A Roth, *Principal*
▲ **EMP:** 30 **EST:** 2004
SALES (est): 4.6MM **Privately Held**
WEB: www.ictcpm.com
SIC: 3469 5084 Machine parts, stamped
or pressed metal; machine tools & acces-
sories

(G-1146)
CMF TRUSS INC
13521 Ponce De Leon Blvd (34601-8650)
PHONE.............................352 796-5805
Pat Owens, *President*
EMP: 37 **EST:** 1992
SQ FT: 512
SALES (est): 1.6MM **Privately Held**
SIC: 2439 Trusses, wooden roof

(G-1147)
COASTAL MFG & FABRICATION
INC
16208 Cortez Blvd (34601-8911)
P.O. Box 15815 (34604-0124)
PHONE.............................352 799-8706
Darrell L Witt, *President*
Roxanne M Witt, *Vice Pres*
EMP: 6 **EST:** 2005
SALES (est): 932.3K **Privately Held**
SIC: 3441 2431 Fabricated structural
metal; staircases, stairs & railings

(G-1148)
COMPLIANCESIGNS LLC
16228 Flight Path Dr (34604-6875)
P.O. Box 208363, Dallas TX (75320-8363)
PHONE.............................800 578-1245
Doug Waugaman,
EMP: 8 **EST:** 2016
SALES (est): 33.8K **Privately Held**
WEB: www.compliancesigns.com
SIC: 3993 Signs, not made in custom sign
painting shops

(G-1149)
COUNTY OF HERNANDO
Also Called: Lykes Memorial Co Library
238 Howell Ave (34601-2040)
PHONE.............................352 754-4042
Barbara Shiflett, *Manager*
EMP: 10
SQ FT: 15,763
SALES (corp-wide): 229.8MM **Privately**
Held
WEB: www.hernandocounty.us
SIC: 2782 Library binders, looseleaf
PA: County Of Hernando
15470 Flight Path Dr
Brooksville FL 34604
352 754-4201

(G-1150)
D A B CONSTRUCTORS INC
3300 Northeast Pkwy (34609)
PHONE.............................352 797-3537
Debrah Bachsmidt, *President*
EMP: 8 **EST:** 2001
SALES (est): 1MM **Privately Held**
SIC: 3531 Asphalt plant, including gravel-
mix type

(G-1151)
DAY METAL PRODUCTS LLC
119 E Dr M L King Jr Blvd (34601-4043)
P.O. Box 176 (34605-0176)
PHONE.............................352 799-9258
Alan R Day, *Manager*
EMP: 5 **EST:** 2011
SALES (est): 810.6K **Privately Held**
SIC: 3444 Sheet metalwork

(G-1152)
DELAMERE INDUSTRIES INC
19370 Oliver St (34601-5532)
PHONE.............................813 929-0841
Paul B Hughes, *President*
Rebecca Dickerson, *Project Mgr*
EMP: 39 **EST:** 2016
SALES (est): 2.7MM **Privately Held**
WEB: www.delamereindustriesinc.com
SIC: 3446 Railings, prefabricated metal

(G-1153)
DFA DAIRY BRANDS FLUID LLC
16235 Aviation Loop Dr (34604-6805)
PHONE.............................352 754-1750
Kevin Lampe, *Branch Mgr*
EMP: 8
SALES (corp-wide): 19.3B **Privately Held**
SIC: 2026 5143 Milk processing (pasteur-
izing, homogenizing, bottling); milk

HQ: Dfa Dairy Brands Fluid, Llc
1405 N 98th St
Kansas City KS 66111
816 801-6455

(G-1154)
ERRATIC OAKS VINEYARD INC
6222 Zirkels Cir (34601-8576)
PHONE.............................206 233-0683
EMP: 7 **EST:** 2016
SALES (est): 411.5K **Privately Held**
WEB: www.citationwine.com
SIC: 2084 Wines

(G-1155)
EXCALIBUR MANUFACTURING
CORP (PA)
16186 Flight Path Dr (34604-6845)
PHONE.............................352 544-0055
Douglas Schneider, *President*
Wade Thomas, *Corp Secy*
Ellen Schneider, *Vice Pres*
▲ **EMP:** 16 **EST:** 1989
SQ FT: 7,200
SALES (est): 1.5MM **Privately Held**
WEB: www.seawayplastics.com
SIC: 3089 Injection molding of plastics

(G-1156)
FATHER & SON FENCE SUPPLY
LLC
Also Called: Fencing - Retail
16300 Wiscon Rd (34601-8819)
P.O. Box 430, Homosassa Springs (34447-
0430)
PHONE.............................352 848-3180
John May, *President*
EMP: 10 **EST:** 2002
SALES (est): 2.4MM **Privately Held**
SIC: 3089 3312 3315 5039 Fences,
gates & accessories: plastic; fence posts,
iron & steel; chain link fencing; fence
gates posts & fittings: steel; wire fence,
gates & accessories; fencing

(G-1157)
FLORIDA LIVING LLC
7410 Dent St (34601-8922)
P.O. Box 10374 (34603-0374)
PHONE.............................352 556-9691
Ronald D McCabe, *Principal*
EMP: 7 **EST:** 2008
SALES (est): 235.6K **Privately Held**
WEB: www.mysinkholerepair.com
SIC: 2741 Miscellaneous publishing

(G-1158)
FSP-GES INC
Also Called: Flagstone Pavers
9070 Old Cobb Rd (34601-8700)
PHONE.............................352 799-7933
Geoff Bond, *President*
Russ Young, *General Mgr*
Christine Wright, *Sales Mgr*
Jessica Hurd, *Sales Staff*
Elizabeth Jones, *Sales Staff*
◆ **EMP:** 25 **EST:** 1999
SQ FT: 20,300
SALES (est): 5.3MM **Privately Held**
WEB: www.flagstonepavers.com
SIC: 3272 Concrete products

(G-1159)
GOTG LLC
Also Called: Florida Container Depot
19182 Powell Rd 1 (34604-7059)
PHONE.............................800 381-4684
Annette Cenal, *General Mgr*
Michael McCafrey,
EMP: 5 **EST:** 2009
SALES (est): 484K **Privately Held**
SIC: 3629 4225 5039 Inverters, nonrotat-
ing: electrical; power conversion units,
a.c. to d.c.: static-electric; warehousing,
self-storage;

(G-1160)
HERNANDO LITHOPRINTING INC
Also Called: Hernando Litho Printing
969 Hale Ave (34601-3931)
PHONE.............................352 796-4136
Philip James Myrea, *President*
Barbara Myrea, *Vice Pres*
EMP: 5 **EST:** 1974
SQ FT: 1,200

SALES (est): 316.6K **Privately Held**
SIC: 2752 Commercial printing, offset

(G-1161)
HITECH TRUSS INC
Also Called: Hitek Truss
6179 Nature Coast Blvd (34602-8243)
PHONE..................................352 797-0877
Derrick Rushnell, *President*
EMP: 17 **EST:** 2020
SALES (est): 1.4MM **Privately Held**
SIC: 2439 Trusses, wooden roof

(G-1162)
HITEK PROPERTY LLC
6179 Nature Coast Blvd (34602-8243)
PHONE..................................352 797-0877
Joseph Pastore, *Mng Member*
Robert Eaton,
EMP: 12 **EST:** 2004
SQ FT: 5,000
SALES (est): 2.1MM **Privately Held**
WEB: www.hitektruss.com
SIC: 2439 Trusses, wooden roof

(G-1163)
INDUSTRIAL WELDING & MAINT
10080 Cobb Rd (34601-8710)
P.O. Box 1404 (34605-1404)
PHONE..................................352 799-3432
Curtis B Cannon, *President*
Scott E Dennison, *Vice Pres*
Vera L Cannon, *Treasurer*
EMP: 8 **EST:** 1981
SQ FT: 6,250
SALES (est): 888.9K **Privately Held**
WEB: www.lemasteriwm.com
SIC: 3441 Fabricated structural metal

(G-1164)
INTERCONNECT CABLE TECH CORP
Also Called: Ictc USA
16090 Flight Path Dr (34604-6824)
PHONE..................................352 796-1716
Sareet Majumdar, *President*
Rick Osgood, *Export Mgr*
Erich Brandt, *Engineer*
Henry Gaither, *Engineer*
Paul Sochacki, *Sales Staff*
▲ **EMP:** 101 **EST:** 1988
SQ FT: 45,000
SALES (est): 51.3MM **Privately Held**
WEB: www.ictcusa.com
SIC: 3679 3643 3678 5065 Harness assemblies for electronic use: wire or cable; current-carrying wiring devices; electronic connectors; electronic parts & equipment

(G-1165)
INTREPID MACHINE INC
2305 Circuit Way (34604-0622)
PHONE..................................352 540-9919
Tim M Tabor, *President*
Mike Belle, *Admin Sec*
EMP: 30 **EST:** 1995
SQ FT: 9,000
SALES (est): 3.9MM **Privately Held**
WEB: www.intrepidmachine.com
SIC: 3599 Machine shop, jobbing & repair

(G-1166)
JONI INDUSTRIES INC
16230 Aviation Loop Dr (34604-6804)
PHONE..................................352 799-5456
Gustav Guadagnino, *President*
EMP: 19 **EST:** 1988
SQ FT: 11,000
SALES (est): 2.4MM **Privately Held**
WEB: www.jonipromotionals.com
SIC: 3552 3999 3993 2396 Silk screens for textile industry; novelties, bric-a-brac & hobby kits; signs & advertising specialties; automotive & apparel trimmings; pleating & stitching; screen printing

(G-1167)
KEYLON LIGHTING SERVICES INC
6931 Remington Rd (34602-7443)
PHONE..................................352 279-3249
Kenneth Keylon, *President*
Danny Keylon, *Principal*
EMP: 7 **EST:** 2001

SALES (est): 732K **Privately Held**
SIC: 3646 Commercial indusl & institutional electric lighting fixtures

(G-1168)
KINCAID PLASTICS INC
2400 Corporate Blvd (34604-0621)
PHONE..................................352 754-9979
Jerry L Kincaid, *President*
Jerry Kincaid, *General Mgr*
Maurine Kincaid, *Vice Pres*
David Kincaid, *Manager*
EMP: 61 **EST:** 1967
SQ FT: 23,500
SALES (est): 15.3MM **Privately Held**
WEB: www.kincaidplastics.com
SIC: 3089 Molding primary plastic; injection molding of plastics

(G-1169)
KINEMATICS AND CONTROLS CORP
15151 Technology Dr (34604-0690)
PHONE..................................352 796-0300
John Rakucewicz, *President*
Anne Rakucewicz, *Comptroller*
EMP: 8 **EST:** 1969
SQ FT: 9,600
SALES (est): 1.4MM **Privately Held**
WEB: www.kcontrols.com
SIC: 3625 3565 Relays & industrial controls; packaging machinery

(G-1170)
LASER INTERCEPTOR USA LLC
18260 Mason Smith Rd (34604-9052)
PHONE..................................352 688-0708
Clifford M Crane, *Principal*
EMP: 7 **EST:** 2009
SALES (est): 245.7K **Privately Held**
WEB: www.laser-interceptorusa.com
SIC: 3699 Electrical equipment & supplies

(G-1171)
LEE MCCULLOUGH INC
Also Called: McCullough Bottled Water
Hud (34606)
P.O. Box 909, Ocala (34478-0909)
PHONE..................................352 796-7100
Fax: 352 351-4468
EMP: 8
SALES: 650K **Privately Held**
SIC: 2086 Mfg Bottled/Canned Soft Drinks

(G-1172)
LEGACY VULCAN LLC
14556 Ponce De Leon Blvd (34601-8422)
P.O. Box 427 (34605-0427)
PHONE..................................352 796-5690
Steve Salantai, *Principal*
Jake Sauer, *Executive*
EMP: 10 **Publicly Held**
SIC: 3273 5032 Ready-mixed concrete; limestone
HQ: Legacy Vulcan, Llc
1200 Urban Center Dr
Vestavia AL 35242
205 298-3000

(G-1173)
LEGACY WDM LLC
16228 Flight Path Dr (34604-6875)
PHONE..................................352 799-5434
Wayne Johnson, *Manager*
EMP: 8 **EST:** 2007
SALES (est): 168.4K **Privately Held**
WEB: www.ceoaccu4m.com
SIC: 3552 Textile machinery

(G-1174)
LHOIST NORTH AMERICA ALA LLC
Also Called: Brooksville Terminal Us11
10245 Cement Plant Rd (34601-8634)
P.O. Box 10448 (34603-0448)
PHONE..................................352 585-3488
Hanspeter Dietiker, *Terminal Mgr*
John Patzner, *Sales Staff*
EMP: 8
SALES (corp-wide): 2.6MM **Privately Held**
SIC: 3274 Lime
HQ: Lhoist North America Of Alabama, Llc
5600 Clearfork Main St # 300
Fort Worth TX 76109
817 732-8164

(G-1175)
LOOPER SPORTS CONNECTION INC
19225 Cortez Blvd (34601-3028)
PHONE..................................352 796-7974
Edward Looper, *CEO*
Jennifer Looper, *Vice Pres*
EMP: 5 **EST:** 2004
SALES (est): 316.6K **Privately Held**
WEB: www.loopersports.com
SIC: 2759 5941 5949 5999 Screen printing; sporting goods & bicycle shops; sewing & needlework; trophies & plaques

(G-1176)
LORI ROBERTS PRINT SHOP I
20332 Ayers Rd (34604-7002)
PHONE..................................813 882-8456
Lorelei Roberts, *Principal*
EMP: 7 **EST:** 2005
SALES (est): 135K **Privately Held**
SIC: 2752 Commercial printing, offset

(G-1177)
MASTER OVERLAND LLC
16214 Aviation Loop Dr (34604-6804)
PHONE..................................727 255-3764
Josh Stallings, *Mng Member*
EMP: 6 **EST:** 2020
SALES (est): 349.7K **Privately Held**
SIC: 3716 Recreational van conversion (self-propelled), factory basis

(G-1178)
MCR AMRCAN PHARMACEUTICALS INC
16255 Aviation Loop Dr (34604-6805)
PHONE..................................352 754-8587
David Ambrose, *CEO*
Gary Dutton, *President*
Robert Davis, *Director*
EMP: 40 **EST:** 1991
SQ FT: 2,000
SALES (est): 5.9MM **Publicly Held**
SIC: 2834 Pharmaceutical preparations
PA: Natural Hitech Petroleum, Inc.
1 Penn Plz Ste 1503
New York NY 10119

(G-1179)
MED-NAP LLC
Also Called: Acme
301 Marianne St (34601-3412)
PHONE..................................352 796-6020
Pierre Sanfacon, *General Mgr*
▲ **EMP:** 12 **EST:** 2013
SQ FT: 10,000
SALES (est): 2.4MM
SALES (corp-wide): 182MM **Publicly Held**
WEB: www.mednap.us
SIC: 2844 Towelettes, premoistened
PA: Acme United Corporation
1 Waterview Dr Ste 200
Shelton CT 06484
203 254-6060

(G-1180)
MICRO MATIC USA INC
15111 Dispense Ln (34604-6879)
PHONE..................................352 799-6331
EMP: 8
SALES (corp-wide): 226MM **Privately Held**
WEB: www.micromatic.com
SIC: 3585 Refrigeration & heating equipment
HQ: Micro Matic Usa, Inc.
2386 Simon Ct
Brooksville FL 34604
352 544-1081

(G-1181)
MICRO MATIC USA INC (HQ)
2386 Simon Ct (34604-0751)
PHONE..................................352 544-1081
Peter J Muzzonigro, *President*
Leah Haab, *COO*
Matthew Claridge, *Prdtn Mgr*
Glen Metzger, *Opers Staff*
Chuck Pederson, *Mfg Staff*
◆ **EMP:** 44 **EST:** 1984
SQ FT: 18,000

SALES (est): 28.5MM
SALES (corp-wide): 226MM **Privately Held**
WEB: www.micromatic.com
SIC: 3491 5087 3585 Industrial valves; liquor dispensing equipment & systems; soda fountain & beverage dispensing equipment & parts
PA: Micro Matic A/S
Holkebjergvej 48
Odense Sv 5250
631 742-17

(G-1182)
MILLWORK AND DESIGN INC
22309 Rodeo Dr (34602-9173)
PHONE..................................352 544-0444
Wayne G Benedict, *President*
John Lovering, *Vice Pres*
Deborah K Benedict, *Admin Sec*
EMP: 9 **EST:** 1987
SQ FT: 10,000
SALES (est): 259K **Privately Held**
SIC: 2431 5211 1796 Millwork; millwork & lumber; installing building equipment

(G-1183)
MONITOR PRODUCTS INC
15400 Flight Path Dr (34604-6823)
PHONE..................................352 544-2620
Carl H Sunden, *President*
John McClure, *Prdtn Mgr*
EMP: 70 **EST:** 1979
SQ FT: 27,000
SALES (est): 10.7MM **Privately Held**
WEB: www.monitorpro.com
SIC: 3443 Heat exchangers, plate type

(G-1184)
MR GS FOODS
Also Called: Eggplant and Dough
15402 Aviation Loop Dr (34604-6856)
PHONE..................................352 799-1806
Mike Guarino, *Owner*
EMP: 11 **EST:** 2009
SALES (est): 1.1MM **Privately Held**
WEB: www.mrgsfoods.com
SIC: 2051 Bakery: wholesale or wholesale/retail combined

(G-1185)
NEUBERT AERO CORP
16110 Flight Path Dr (34604-6845)
P.O. Box 320467, Tampa (33679-2467)
PHONE..................................352 345-4828
Timothy W Neubert, *President*
▲ **EMP:** 7 **EST:** 1998
SQ FT: 10,000
SALES (est): 911.9K **Privately Held**
WEB: www.airportnac.com
SIC: 3829 3612 3648 1611 Measuring & controlling devices; lighting transformers, street & airport; airport lighting fixtures: runway approach, taxi or ramp; airport runway construction

(G-1186)
OMNI DISPLAYS LLC
15261 Telcom Dr (34604-0718)
PHONE..................................352 799-9997
EMP: 25
SQ FT: 20,000
SALES (est): 2.3MM **Privately Held**
SIC: 2653 Mfg Corrugated & Solid Fiber Boxes

(G-1187)
PAVERS INC
Also Called: Sun Coast Pavers
14497 Ponce De Leon Blvd (34601-8418)
PHONE..................................352 754-3875
Francisco Fleites, *President*
EMP: 5 **EST:** 2007
SALES (est): 495.3K **Privately Held**
WEB: www.suncoastpavers.com
SIC: 3531 Pavers

(G-1188)
PED-STUART CORPORATION
Also Called: Stuart Promotional Products
15351 Flight Path Dr (34604-6862)
P.O. Box 15550 (34604-0120)
PHONE..................................352 754-6001
Stuart Walasek, *President*
Terry Walasek, *Vice Pres*
EMP: 20 **EST:** 1982

▲ = Import ▼=Export
◆ =Import/Export

SQ FT: 30,000
SALES (est): 2.2MM **Privately Held**
WEB: www.ped-stuart.com
SIC: 3999 3841 3081 Identification badges & insignia; identification tags, except paper; surgical & medical instruments; unsupported plastics film & sheet

(G-1189)
PEM-AIR TURBINE ENG SVCS LLC
16300 Flight Path Dr (34604-6885)
PHONE.................................954 900-9956
Juan Robles, *Purchasing*
Virgil Pizer,
EMP: 10 EST: 2013
SALES (est): 2.5MM **Privately Held**
WEB: www.pem-airturbine.com
SIC: 3724 Turbines, aircraft type

(G-1190)
PLAYERS MEDIA GROUP INC
5267 Zenith Garden Loop (34601-6651)
PHONE.................................509 254-4949
Collin Castellaw, *Partner*
EMP: 15 EST: 2019
SALES (est): 1.5MM **Privately Held**
SIC: 2836 Culture media

(G-1191)
PQ PHARMACY LLC
15215 Technology Dr (34604-0690)
PHONE.................................352 477-8977
Angela Kassay, *President*
EMP: 9 EST: 2020
SALES (est): 610.6K **Privately Held**
SIC: 2834 Pharmaceutical preparations

(G-1192)
PRINT SHACK
210 W Jefferson St (34601-2523)
PHONE.................................352 799-2972
Jennie Drummond, *Owner*
EMP: 6 EST: 1985
SALES (est): 371.1K **Privately Held**
WEB: www.printshacknc.com
SIC: 2759 2396 Screen printing; automotive & apparel trimmings

(G-1193)
PRO STAIR & TRIM INC
9322 Highpoint Blvd (34613-5567)
PHONE.................................407 415-2566
Bennie S Marsala, *President*
EMP: 7 EST: 2005
SALES (est): 147.4K **Privately Held**
SIC: 3446 Stairs, staircases, stair treads: prefabricated metal

(G-1194)
RINKER MATERIALS CORP
10311 Cement Plant Rd (34601-8657)
PHONE.................................352 799-7881
EMP: 7 EST: 2019
SALES (est): 173.1K **Privately Held**
WEB: www.rinkerpipe.com
SIC: 3273 Ready-mixed concrete

(G-1195)
ROGERS SIGN CORP
701 S Lemon Ave (34601-3742)
PHONE.................................352 799-1923
Robert F Rogers, *President*
EMP: 16 EST: 1988
SQ FT: 10,062
SALES (est): 600K **Privately Held**
WEB: www.rogerssigncorp.com
SIC: 3993 1799 5085 Electric signs; sign installation & maintenance; signmaker equipment & supplies

(G-1196)
RUSCO INC
13360 Chambord St (34613-6812)
PHONE.................................352 597-2522
Michael Klump, *President*
EMP: 15 EST: 1983
SALES (est): 1.1MM **Privately Held**
WEB: www.rusco.com
SIC: 3677 Filtration devices, electronic

(G-1197)
SEATING CONSTRUCTORS USA INC
2347 Circuit Way (34604-0622)
P.O. Box 15258 (34604-0115)
PHONE.................................813 505-7560
Phil Vanderhider, *Owner*
Yvette Vanderhider, *Vice Pres*
EMP: 14 EST: 2001
SALES (est): 488.4K **Privately Held**
WEB: www.seatingusa.com
SIC: 2531 Stadium seating

(G-1198)
SEAWAY PLASTICS ENGRG LLC
16186 Flight Path Dr (34604-6845)
PHONE.................................352 799-3167
Russell Catchpole, *Opers Staff*
Kristen Rubio, *QC Mgr*
Matthew Claridge, *Engineer*
Lori Rhoden, *Accountant*
Chuck Waidler, *Finance*
EMP: 33
SALES (corp-wide): 1.3B **Privately Held**
WEB: www.seawayplastics.com
SIC: 3089 Injection molding of plastics
HQ: Seaway Plastics Engineering Llc
6006 Siesta Ln
Port Richey FL 34668

(G-1199)
SHIRLEY L JORDAN COMPANY INC
Also Called: Esco Equipment Supply Co
15270 Flight Path Dr (34604-6849)
PHONE.................................352 754-1117
Jeff Jobe, *CEO*
Michael Tammaro, *Purch Mgr*
William Fisher Jr, *Consultant*
Chris Manfre, *Info Tech Mgr*
◆ EMP: 12 EST: 1984
SQ FT: 22,000
SALES (est): 2.4MM **Privately Held**
SIC: 3559 Automotive related machinery

(G-1200)
SHO ME NUTRICEUTICALS INC
Also Called: Sho ME Natural Products
15431 Flight Path Dr (34604-6851)
PHONE.................................352 797-9600
Chris Reckner, *President*
Theodore C Irving, *Vice Pres*
Theodore Irving, *Vice Pres*
▲ EMP: 48 EST: 1998
SQ FT: 11,000
SALES (est): 1.3MM **Privately Held**
SIC: 2834 Vitamin, nutrient & hematinic preparations for human use

(G-1201)
SIMS MACHINE & CONTROLS INC
15538 Aviation Loop Dr (34604-6801)
PHONE.................................352 799-2405
Robert Jones, *President*
EMP: 23 EST: 1975
SQ FT: 48,000
SALES (est): 670.2K **Privately Held**
WEB: www.simsmachine.com
SIC: 3569 Robots, assembly line: industrial & commercial

(G-1202)
SJG MACHINE INC
316 Marianne St (34601-3411)
PHONE.................................352 345-3656
Scott Gray, *Principal*
EMP: 9 EST: 2007
SALES (est): 273.5K **Privately Held**
SIC: 3599 Machine shop, jobbing & repair

(G-1203)
SOUTHERN WOOD SERVICES LLC
6288 California St (34604-8310)
P.O. Box 531, Freeport (32439-0531)
PHONE.................................352 279-3208
Mike Cusic, *Sales Staff*
Andy Mudd, *Bd of Directors*
John Paff,
EMP: 5 EST: 2008

SALES (est): 431.8K **Privately Held**
SIC: 2411 2421 2611 4212 Timber, cut at logging camp; driving & booming timber; sawdust, shavings & wood chips; pulp mills, mechanical & recycling processing; lumber & timber trucking

(G-1204)
SOUTHWEST EQP FOR HRNANDO CNTY
13484 Chambord St (34613-4865)
PHONE.................................352 596-5142
Paul Arcona, *President*
EMP: 6 EST: 2003
SALES (est): 670.6K **Privately Held**
SIC: 3555 7699 Printing presses; aircraft & heavy equipment repair services

(G-1205)
SPARTRONICS BROOKSVILLE LLC (DH)
30167 Power Line Rd (34602-8299)
PHONE.................................352 799-6520
Paul Fraipont, *President*
EMP: 100 EST: 2013
SALES (est): 31.8MM
SALES (corp-wide): 810.8MM **Privately Held**
WEB: www.spartronics.com
SIC: 3674 Microprocessors
HQ: Spartronics, Llc
2333 Reach Rd
Williamsport PA 17701
763 703-4321

(G-1206)
SPARTRONICS BROOKSVILLE LLC
Also Called: Sparton Electronics
30167 Power Line Rd (34602-8299)
PHONE.................................352 799-6520
Jason Craft, *Branch Mgr*
Christine Cartwright, *Executive Asst*
EMP: 253
SALES (corp-wide): 810.8MM **Privately Held**
WEB: www.spartronics.com
SIC: 3674 3812 Semiconductors & related devices; warfare counter-measure equipment
HQ: Spartronics Brooksville, Llc
30167 Power Line Rd
Brooksville FL 34602
352 799-6520

(G-1207)
SPRING OAKS LLC
725 Desoto Ave (34601-2813)
PHONE.................................352 592-1150
David C Jones,
EMP: 18 EST: 2005
SALES (est): 3.4MM **Privately Held**
WEB: www.seniorlifestyle.com
SIC: 2512 Living room furniture: upholstered on wood frames

(G-1208)
SUNSHINE NYLON PRODUCTS INC
16101 Flight Path Dr (34604-6846)
PHONE.................................352 754-9932
Helen Reynolds, *President*
EMP: 6 EST: 1979
SQ FT: 7,000
SALES (est): 380.3K **Privately Held**
SIC: 3999 2221 Pet supplies; broadwoven fabric mills, manmade

(G-1209)
TAMPA BAY TIMES
13045 Cortez Blvd (34613-4838)
PHONE.................................352 754-6100
EMP: 7 EST: 2019
SALES (est): 210.1K **Privately Held**
WEB: www.tampabay.com
SIC: 2711 Newspapers, publishing & printing

(G-1210)
TG UNITED INC
16255 Aviation Loop Dr (34604-6805)
PHONE.................................888 627-9139
Andrew Wittman II, *CEO*
David Ambrose, *President*
Robert Davis, *Business Dir*

▼ EMP: 6 EST: 2004
SQ FT: 12,000
SALES (est): 1MM **Privately Held**
WEB: www.tgunited.com
SIC: 2834 Adrenal pharmaceutical preparations

(G-1211)
THUNDER BAY ENTERPRISES INC
5130 Broad St (34601-5814)
P.O. Box 10186 (34603-0186)
PHONE.................................352 796-9551
Sharon Carty, *Vice Pres*
EMP: 40 EST: 2008
SALES (est): 5.3MM **Privately Held**
SIC: 3715 Truck trailers

(G-1212)
TOPLINE HY-LIFT JOHNSON INC (PA)
2251 Topline Way (34604-6892)
PHONE.................................352 799-4668
Chester Staron, *President*
EMP: 10 EST: 2004
SQ FT: 300,000
SALES (est): 5.1MM **Privately Held**
SIC: 3764 3519 Engines & engine parts, guided missile; internal combustion engines; parts & accessories, internal combustion engines

(G-1213)
TROY THOMPSON INC
20255 Denny Dr (34601-1257)
PHONE.................................813 716-1598
EMP: 5 EST: 1994
SQ FT: 2,500
SALES (est): 533.6K **Privately Held**
SIC: 3599 Machine shop, jobbing & repair

(G-1214)
TYCO MACHINE INC
1400 Ponce De Leon Blvd (34601-1670)
P.O. Box 1235 (34605-1235)
PHONE.................................352 544-0210
Michael Ray, *President*
EMP: 6 EST: 1999
SQ FT: 5,000
SALES (est): 813K **Privately Held**
SIC: 3531 3599 Construction machinery; machine shop, jobbing & repair

(G-1215)
UNBRIDLED TECHNOLOGIES LLC
Also Called: U Tech
21125 Cortez Blvd (34601-5645)
P.O. Box 344 (34605-0344)
PHONE.................................888 334-8402
Joseph Salway, *CEO*
Christina Walz, *Admin Asst*
Cristian Benitez, *Technician*
EMP: 8 EST: 2015
SQ FT: 1,800
SALES (est): 1MM **Privately Held**
WEB: www.utechcnc.com
SIC: 3541 Machine tools, metal cutting type

(G-1216)
UNIVERSAL MICROWAVE CORP (PA)
6036 Nature Coast Blvd (34602-8286)
PHONE.................................352 754-2200
David Lyle, *President*
Mark Lyle, *Vice Pres*
Lisa Lyle, *Admin Sec*
EMP: 28 EST: 1998
SQ FT: 20,000
SALES (est): 7.9MM **Privately Held**
WEB: www.vco1.com
SIC: 3612 3825 Voltage regulators, transmission & distribution; instruments to measure electricity

(G-1217)
VAN-ESS MANUFACTURING INC
15311 Flight Path Dr (34604-6862)
PHONE.................................352 799-1015
Ralph Esposito, *President*
Eugene Van Nostrand, *Corp Secy*
EMP: 5 EST: 1982
SQ FT: 3,400

SALES (est): 764.1K **Privately Held**
WEB: www.vanessmanufacturing.com
SIC: 3599 Machine shop, jobbing & repair

(G-1218)
VC DISPLAYS INC
Also Called: Vc Technology
15250 Flight Path Dr (34604-6849)
PHONE................352 796-0060
Gregory Potter, *President*
Chen James, *General Mgr*
Gregorypotter, *Principal*
Robert Bauer, *Vice Pres*
Jana Blair, *CFO*
▲ **EMP:** 25 **EST:** 2004
SQ FT: 20,000
SALES (est): 8.1MM **Privately Held**
WEB: www.vcdisplays.com
SIC: 3679 5065 Liquid crystal displays
(LCD); electronic parts & equipment

(G-1219)
VENDAPIN LLC (PA)
16381 Cherokee Rd (34601-4202)
PHONE................352 796-2693
Darrell Rademacher,
Diane Rademacher,
▲ **EMP:** 10 **EST:** 1999
SQ FT: 1,200
SALES (est): 1.2MM **Privately Held**
WEB: www.vendapin.com
SIC: 3581 Automatic vending machines

(G-1220)
VUFLOW FILTERS CO INC
13370 Chambord St (34613-6812)
PHONE................352 597-2607
Thomas R Welte, *President*
Mary Latin, *Admin Sec*
EMP: 5 **EST:** 1978
SALES (est): 398K **Privately Held**
WEB: www.vuflow.com
SIC: 3569 Filters, general line: industrial

(G-1221)
WAYNE DIXON LLC
27340 Popiel Rd (34602-7107)
PHONE................352 279-6886
Wayne Dixon, *Manager*
EMP: 8 **EST:** 2005
SALES (est): 412.8K **Privately Held**
SIC: 2451 Mobile homes

(G-1222)
WITTMAN PHARMA INC (PA)
16206 Flight Path Dr (34604-6875)
PHONE................352 799-9813
Andrew Wittman, *CEO*
Jannet Sands, *Manager*
EMP: 22 **EST:** 2006
SALES (est): 1.3MM **Privately Held**
WEB: www.tgunited.com
SIC: 2032 Canned specialties

(G-1223)
WOODCRAFTS BY ANGEL INC
Also Called: Tools & More
15400 Shady St (34604-8543)
PHONE................352 754-9335
Peggy Niles, *President*
Mark Miles, *Vice Pres*
EMP: 9 **EST:** 1991
SALES (est): 1.4MM **Privately Held**
SIC: 2511 2499 Wood household furniture;
wood desks, bookcases & magazine
racks; wood lawn & garden furniture; dec-
orative wood & woodwork

(G-1224)
WOODYS ACRES LLC
4000 Crum Rd (34604-7611)
PHONE................352 345-8145
Steven Johnson, *Principal*
EMP: 7 **EST:** 2016
SALES (est): 303.9K **Privately Held**
SIC: 3714 Motor vehicle parts & acces-
sories

Bryceville
Nassau County

(G-1225)
A&L HALL INVESTMENTS INC
Also Called: (FORMALY NICHOLS TRUCK
BODIES, INC.)
1384 Cortez Rd (32009-1304)
PHONE................904 781-5080
Arthur H Hall Jr, *President*
Clarence Suggs, *General Mgr*
Linda N Hall, *Corp Secy*
EMP: 22 **EST:** 1954
SQ FT: 19,500
SALES (est): 3.6MM **Privately Held**
SIC: 3713 5012 3441 Truck bodies (motor
vehicles); truck bodies; fabricated struc-
tural metal

Bunnell
Flagler County

(G-1226)
BEUTLICH PHARMACEUTICALS LLC (PA)
7775 S Us Highway 1 H (32110-3827)
PHONE................386 263-8860
Frederic J Beutlich, *General Ptnr*
Heather Wagner, *Sales Mgr*
Jennifer Dilascia, *Sales Staff*
Erlene Thomas, *Mng Member*
Ivone Raposo, *Supervisor*
EMP: 17 **EST:** 1954
SQ FT: 10,000
SALES (est): 3.6MM **Privately Held**
WEB: www.beutlich.com
SIC: 2834 Druggists' preparations (phar-
maceuticals)

(G-1227)
BLANE E TAYLOR WELDING INC
75 County Road 125 (32110-8703)
PHONE................386 931-1242
Blane E Taylor, *Principal*
EMP: 7 **EST:** 2012
SALES (est): 240.2K **Privately Held**
SIC: 7692 Welding repair

(G-1228)
BUILT RGHT KTCHENS OF PALM CAS
7755 S Us Highway 1 (32110-3807)
PHONE................386 437-7077
Don Gordon, *Owner*
EMP: 7 **EST:** 1997
SQ FT: 3,000
SALES (est): 922.8K **Privately Held**
WEB: www.brkitchens.com
SIC: 2434 Wood kitchen cabinets

(G-1229)
KING MOBILE WELDING ANDREW
1645 County Road 302 (32110-7922)
P.O. Box 2425 (32110-2425)
PHONE................386 437-1007
Andrew King, *President*
EMP: 5 **EST:** 2008
SALES (est): 418.7K **Privately Held**
SIC: 7692 Welding repair

(G-1230)
M & L TIMBER INC
Sr 11 (32110)
PHONE................386 437-0895
M Mitchell Henry, *President*
Doug Henry, *Vice Pres*
EMP: 10 **EST:** 1988
SQ FT: 1,500
SALES (est): 243.4K **Privately Held**
SIC: 2411 Logging camps & contractors

(G-1231)
MCNEILL SIGNS INC
400 Ninth St (32110-6932)
P.O. Box 1093 (32110-1093)
PHONE................386 586-7100
Jay McNeil, *President*
EMP: 8

SALES (corp-wide): 3.2MM **Privately Held**
WEB: www.mcneillsigns.com
SIC: 3993 Neon signs; electric signs; ad-
vertising artwork
PA: Mcneill Signs Inc
555 S Dixie Hwy E
Pompano Beach FL 33060
561 737-6304

(G-1232)
RAILINGS PLUS INC
1150 State Rd 11 Ste 201 (32110)
PHONE................386 437-4501
Mike Adkins, *General Mgr*
Dawn Spoly, *Principal*
EMP: 9 **EST:** 2007
SALES (est): 2.4MM **Privately Held**
WEB: www.railingsplusinc.com
SIC: 3743 Railroad equipment

(G-1233)
RALPH SANTORE & SONS INC
2546 County Road 305 (32110-5350)
P.O. Box 70 (32110-0070)
PHONE................386 437-2242
Ralph Santore Jr, *President*
Lloyd Sponenburgh, *General Mgr*
Anthony Santore Jr, *Vice Pres*
Irene Nielsen, *Admin Asst*
◆ **EMP:** 24 **EST:** 1974
SQ FT: 910
SALES (est): 4.5MM **Privately Held**
WEB: www.santorepyro.com
SIC: 2899 7999 Fireworks; fireworks dis-
play service

(G-1234)
SIZEMORE WELDING INC
Also Called: Sizemore Ultimate Food Trucks
205 N Bay St (32110-4444)
P.O. Box 1772 (32110-1772)
PHONE................386 437-4073
Duane Sizemore, *President*
EMP: 25 **EST:** 1985
SQ FT: 40,000
SALES (est): 4MM **Privately Held**
WEB: www.sizemorewelding.com
SIC: 3714 3599 Motor vehicle parts & ac-
cessories; machine shop, jobbing & repair

(G-1235)
T-BRAND FERTILIZER INC
801 N Bay St (32110)
P.O. Box 266 (32110-0266)
PHONE................386 437-2970
John W Stone, *President*
Thomas Bratcher, *Vice Pres*
Tommie Bennett, *Office Mgr*
EMP: 8 **EST:** 1983
SQ FT: 5,000
SALES (est): 931.2K **Privately Held**
SIC: 2873 Nitrogenous fertilizers

(G-1236)
TRUSS SYSTEMS OF VLSIA FLGLER
3615 S Us Highway 1 (32110-3824)
P.O. Box 291250, Port Orange (32129-
1250)
PHONE................386 255-3009
Lynn Mc Carthy, *President*
James Paytas, *Corp Secy*
Ian Halliday, *Vice Pres*
EMP: 12 **EST:** 1986
SQ FT: 1,600
SALES (est): 1.1MM **Privately Held**
SIC: 2439 2452 Trusses, wooden roof;
prefabricated wood buildings

(G-1237)
TUMBLING PINES INC
10987 State Road 11 (32110-5782)
PHONE................386 437-2668
Morgan Henry, *President*
Laurel Henry, *Corp Secy*
EMP: 13 **EST:** 1987
SALES (est): 896.2K **Privately Held**
SIC: 2411 4212 Logging camps & contrac-
tors; local trucking, without storage

(G-1238)
WORLD CLASS MACHINING INC
Also Called: Holeshot Performance Wheels
6650 S Us Highway 1 (32110-6806)
PHONE................386 437-7036

Marlene D Morton, *President*
EMP: 10 **EST:** 1993
SQ FT: 2,500
SALES (est): 1.1MM **Privately Held**
WEB: www.worldclassmachining.com
SIC: 3599 7692 Machine shop, jobbing &
repair; welding repair

(G-1239)
WORLD PLATE
2323 N State St Unit 55 (32110-4395)
PHONE................386 597-7832
Suzette Negron-Wicklund, *President*
EMP: 7 **EST:** 2017
SALES (est): 303.8K **Privately Held**
WEB: world-plate.business.site
SIC: 3471 Plating & polishing

Bushnell
Sumter County

(G-1240)
BUSHNELL SAWMILL INC
5178 W C 48 (33513-8370)
P.O. Box 1240 (33513-0075)
PHONE................352 793-2740
Mark Elliott, *President*
Marsha Garcia, *Vice Pres*
EMP: 8 **EST:** 1978
SQ FT: 1,065
SALES (est): 720.6K **Privately Held**
WEB: www.bushnellsawmill.com
SIC: 2421 2426 2411 Lumber: rough,
sawed or planed; hardwood dimension &
flooring mills; logging

(G-1241)
BUSHNELL TRUSS ENTERPRISES LLC
5240 W C 476 (33513-8558)
P.O. Box 773 (33513-0047)
PHONE................352 793-6090
James W Malloy, *President*
Mike Reed, *Plant Mgr*
Claire Malloy, *Treasurer*
EMP: 10 **EST:** 1978
SQ FT: 15,000
SALES (est): 1MM **Privately Held**
WEB: www.bushnelltruss.com
SIC: 2439 5211 Trusses, wooden roof;
lumber products

(G-1242)
COUNTY OF SUMTER
Also Called: Sumter Planning Department
910 N Main St Ste 308 (33513-5006)
PHONE................352 689-4460
Brad Cornelius, *Director*
EMP: 9
SALES (corp-wide): 172.4MM **Privately
Held**
WEB: www.sumtercountyfl.gov
SIC: 3553 Planing mill machinery
PA: County Of Sumter
7375 Powell Rd Ste 200
Wildwood FL 34785
352 689-4400

(G-1243)
FLORIDA CRUSHED STONE CO
3919 Cr 673 (33513-8357)
PHONE................352 799-7460
Ralph Burdin, *Principal*
EMP: 5 **EST:** 2002
SALES (est): 393.1K **Privately Held**
SIC: 1241 3281 Coal mining services;
stone, quarrying & processing of own
stone products

(G-1244)
FULL CIRCLE DIRECTIONAL INC
2161 Sw 83rd Pl (33513-5705)
P.O. Box 1465 (33513-0079)
PHONE................352 568-0639
George P Mauldin, *CEO*
Kristi Mauldin, *President*
EMP: 5 **EST:** 2009
SALES (est): 889.1K **Privately Held**
SIC: 1381 Directional drilling oil & gas
wells

▲ = Import ▼=Export
◆ =Import/Export

(G-1245)
KNIGHTS FARM FRESH FEEDS INC
5376 Cr 316a (33513-8115)
P.O. Box 670 (33513-0046)
PHONE...................352 793-2242
Michael R Knight, *President*
Paula S Knight, *Corp Secy*
EMP: 6 **EST:** 1984
SQ FT: 4,000
SALES (est): 817K **Privately Held**
WEB: www.knightsfeed.com
SIC: 2048 Cereal-, grain-, & seed-based feeds

(G-1246)
MEMCO INC
Also Called: Memco Enviro Safe
1789 Ec 48 (33513)
P.O. Box 519, Center Hill (33514-0519)
PHONE...................352 241-2302
Michael S Evans, *President*
Steve Holt, *Project Mgr*
Samveg Turakhia, *Engineer*
◆ **EMP:** 29 **EST:** 1995
SQ FT: 48,000
SALES (est): 10.4MM **Privately Held**
WEB: www.memcostaffing.com
SIC: 3795 Tanks & tank components

(G-1247)
METAL INDUSTRIES INC
Also Called: US Aire
400 Walker Ave (33513-4423)
PHONE...................352 793-8610
Steve Brush, *Manager*
Jud Dietz, *Manager*
Tonya Jackson, *Manager*
EMP: 93
SALES (corp-wide): 1.2B **Privately Held**
WEB: www.mihvac.com
SIC: 3585 3564 3446 3433 Refrigeration & heating equipment; blowers & fans; architectural metalwork; heating equipment, except electric
HQ: Metal Industries, Inc.
1985 Carroll St
Clearwater FL 33765
727 441-2651

(G-1248)
RVCC OF FLORIDA
2540 W C 48 (33513-8386)
PHONE...................352 569-5870
Armando Salinas, *Director*
EMP: 11 **EST:** 2011
SALES (est): 349.2K **Privately Held**
WEB: catalog.raritanval.edu
SIC: 3799 Trailer hitches

(G-1249)
SOUTHERN PRE CAST STRUCTURES L
4457 Cr 542h (33513-5536)
P.O. Box 1543 (33513-0080)
PHONE...................352 569-1128
Danny Hall, *Principal*
EMP: 5 **EST:** 2005
SALES (est): 384.9K **Privately Held**
SIC: 3272 Precast terrazo or concrete products

Callahan
Nassau County

(G-1250)
A & R MATERIAL HANDLING INC
540439 Us Highway 1 (32011-7868)
P.O. Box 1359 (32011-1359)
PHONE...................904 879-6957
Jack Anders, *President*
EMP: 23 **EST:** 1998
SQ FT: 44,000
SALES (est): 1.2MM **Privately Held**
SIC: 3537 Lift trucks, industrial: fork, platform, straddle, etc.

(G-1251)
AARONS EQUIPMENT REPAIR INC
Also Called: Aaron's Welding & Repair
45417 Zidell Rd (32011-3691)
PHONE...................904 879-3249

Franklin A Bell, *President*
Dana R Bell, *Admin Sec*
EMP: 7 **EST:** 2014
SALES (est): 213.5K **Privately Held**
SIC: 7692 Welding repair

(G-1252)
J Q BELL & SONS
44247 Bell Ln (32011-7645)
PHONE...................904 879-1597
Richard Musgrove, *Partner*
Janie B Musgrove, *Partner*
EMP: 7 **EST:** 1950
SALES (est): 728.5K **Privately Held**
SIC: 2411 Pulpwood contractors engaged in cutting

(G-1253)
JAX TRUSS INC
450526 State Road 200 (32011-4409)
PHONE...................904 710-8198
Scott Nicholson, *Principal*
EMP: 7 **EST:** 2019
SALES (est): 330.4K **Privately Held**
WEB: www.jaxtruss.com
SIC: 3441 Fabricated structural metal

(G-1254)
JUSTIN BELL LOGGING INC
44001 Bell Ln (32011-7646)
PHONE...................904 759-9006
EMP: 7 **EST:** 2019
SALES (est): 116.1K **Privately Held**
SIC: 2411 Logging

(G-1255)
NASSAU PRINTING & OFF SUP INC
542028 Us Highway 1 (32011-8108)
P.O. Box 812 (32011-0812)
PHONE...................904 879-2305
Jo Ann Thompson, *President*
EMP: 7 **EST:** 1976
SQ FT: 6,072
SALES (est): 879.1K **Privately Held**
WEB: www.nassauprinting.com
SIC: 2752 5943 Commercial printing, offset; office forms & supplies

(G-1256)
RBJ TIMBER INC
44247 Bell Ln (32011-7645)
PHONE...................904 879-1597
Richard B Musgrove Sr, *President*
Joshua R Musgrove, *Vice Pres*
Janie Musgrove, *Admin Sec*
EMP: 8 **EST:** 2005
SALES (est): 939.2K **Privately Held**
SIC: 2411 7389 Timber, cut at logging camp; business services

(G-1257)
RELIABLE SITE SOLUTIONS LLC
Also Called: Transportation
55050 Bartram Trl (32011-3563)
PHONE...................904 238-3113
Michael Horton, *Mng Member*
EMP: 5 **EST:** 2020
SALES (est): 1.2MM **Privately Held**
SIC: 1442 7389 Construction sand & gravel;

(G-1258)
SOUTHERN COMPANY ENTP INC
Also Called: Florida Sun Printing
54024 Cravey Rd (32011-4600)
P.O. Box 627 (32011-0627)
PHONE...................904 879-2101
Mark Thompson, *President*
David Vickers, *President*
Delores Hagan, *Bookkeeper*
Christie Anglea,
EMP: 25 **EST:** 1963
SQ FT: 25,000
SALES (est): 3MM **Privately Held**
WEB: www.flasunprinting.com
SIC: 2752 Commercial printing, offset

Campbellton
Jackson County

(G-1259)
BARBER FERTILIZER COMPANY
Also Called: Campbellton Farm Service
5221 Highway 231 (32426-6831)
P.O. Box 234 (32426-0234)
PHONE...................850 263-6324
Ronald Barber, *Manager*
EMP: 21
SALES (corp-wide): 23.1MM **Privately Held**
SIC: 2873 5191 2875 Fertilizers: natural (organic), except compost; feed; fertilizer & fertilizer materials; fertilizers, mixing only
PA: Barber Fertilizer Company
1011 Airport Rd
Bainbridge GA 39817
229 246-7412

Canal Point
Palm Beach County

(G-1260)
FIVE STONES MINE LLC (PA)
Also Called: Mayaca Materials
18500 Us Highway 441 (33438-9580)
PHONE...................813 967-2123
Dennis McClelland, *General Mgr*
Peter V De Sanctis, *CPA*
Michael Rendina, *Mng Member*
EMP: 11 **EST:** 2009
SALES (est): 2.6MM **Privately Held**
SIC: 1411 Limestone, dimension-quarrying

Candler
Marion County

(G-1261)
TOWNLEY ENGRG & MFG CO INC (PA)
Also Called: Townley Engineering & Mfg Co
10551 Se 110th St Rd (32111)
P.O. Box 221 (32111-0221)
PHONE...................352 687-3001
J O Townley Jr, *President*
Steven Colquitt, *Vice Pres*
Sarah T Dean, *Vice Pres*
Sara Townley Hall, *Vice Pres*
Kurt Olandt, *Vice Pres*
▲ **EMP:** 199 **EST:** 1963
SQ FT: 7,500
SALES (est): 49.4MM **Privately Held**
WEB: www.townley.net
SIC: 3532 3561 3531 3498 Mining machinery; pumps & pumping equipment; construction machinery; fabricated pipe & fittings

(G-1262)
TOWNLEY FOUNDRY & MCH CO INC
10551 Se 110th St Rd (32111)
P.O. Box 221 (32111-0221)
PHONE...................352 687-3001
J O Townley Jr, *President*
Helen Townley, *Corp Secy*
Sara Townley Dean, *Vice Pres*
Parnell Townley, *Vice Pres*
Martin Harris, *Business Dir*
▲ **EMP:** 56 **EST:** 1982
SQ FT: 7,500
SALES: 15.6MM
SALES (corp-wide): 49.4MM **Privately Held**
WEB: www.townley.net
SIC: 3532 Mining machinery
PA: Townley Engineering And Manufacturing Company, Inc.
10551 Se 110th St Rd
Candler FL 32111
352 687-3001

Campbellton
Jackson County

Cantonment
Escambia County

(G-1263)
ALPHA COATINGS INC
3040 Ashfield Estates Rd (32533-8195)
PHONE...................850 324-9454
Steven Eggart, *Principal*
EMP: 7 **EST:** 2011
SALES (est): 91.9K **Privately Held**
SIC: 3479 Coating of metals & formed products

(G-1264)
ASCEND PERFORMANCE MTLS INC
3000 Old Chemstrand Rd (32533-8900)
P.O. Box 68, Gonzalez (32560-0068)
PHONE...................850 968-7000
Matt Hamilton Pmp, *Project Mgr*
Michael Scheibe, *Opers Staff*
Ralph McCallister, *Buyer*
Gregg Scott, *Engineer*
Marshall McGaw, *Finance Mgr*
EMP: 359
SALES (corp-wide): 1.4B **Privately Held**
WEB: www.ascendmaterials.com
SIC: 2821 Plastics materials & resins
HQ: Ascend Performance Materials Inc.
1010 Travis St Ste 900
Houston TX 77002
713 315-5700

(G-1265)
ASCEND PRFMCE MTLS OPRTONS LLC
3000 Old Chemstrand Rd (32533-8900)
P.O. Box 68, Gonzalez (32560-0068)
PHONE...................850 968-7000
Richard Briere, *Plant Mgr*
Andrew Hosmer, *Export Mgr*
Doug Foust, *Engineer*
Kenneth Krueger, *Engineer*
Connor Manthey, *Engineer*
EMP: 600
SQ FT: 6,244
SALES (corp-wide): 1.4B **Privately Held**
WEB: www.ascendmaterials.com
SIC: 2824 5169 2821 5131 Organic fibers, noncellulosic; chemicals & allied products; plastics materials & resins; synthetic fabrics
HQ: Ascend Performance Materials Operations Llc
1010 Travis St Ste 900
Houston TX 77002

(G-1266)
CEREX ADVANCED FABRICS INC
610 Chemstrand Rd (32533-6857)
PHONE...................850 968-0100
James T Walker, *CEO*
James Boston, *Vice Pres*
Jim Bostwick, *Vice Pres*
James Crews, *Prdtn Mgr*
Sheldon Ford, *Mfg Staff*
▼ **EMP:** 80 **EST:** 1994
SALES (est): 15.4MM **Privately Held**
WEB: www.cerex.com
SIC: 2297 Nonwoven fabrics

(G-1267)
COUCH READY MIX USA INC
3008 S Highway 95a (32533-5800)
PHONE...................850 236-9042
EMP: 25
SALES (est): 6.1MM **Privately Held**
SIC: 3273 Mfg Ready-Mixed Concrete

(G-1268)
CUSTOM CONTROL SOLUTIONS INC
1520 Power Blvd (32533-5102)
PHONE...................850 937-8902
Manfred Laner, *President*
Glenn Miller, *Vice Pres*
EMP: 50 **EST:** 2004
SQ FT: 8,000
SALES (est): 15.9MM **Privately Held**
WEB: www.ccsinc-florida.com
SIC: 3613 Control panels, electric

GEOGRAPHIC

(G-1269)
INSULATION DESIGN & DIST LLC
1879 Ziglar Rd (32533-8586)
P.O. Box 67 (32533-0067)
PHONE..................................850 332-7312
William R Ingram, *Mng Member*
EMP: 7 EST: 2010
SQ FT: 20,000
SALES (est): 314.5K **Privately Held**
SIC: 3498 Fabricated pipe & fittings

(G-1270)
INTERNATIONAL PAPER COMPANY
375 Muscogee Rd (32533-1422)
P.O. Box 87 (32533-0087)
PHONE..................................850 968-2121
Brent Griffin, *Engineer*
Stan Shaw, *Human Res Mgr*
Nicki Sousser, *Manager*
Wesley Greeson, *Manager*
Chad Kaunitz, *Maintence Staff*
EMP: 267
SALES (corp-wide): 19.3B **Publicly Held**
WEB: www.internationalpaper.com
SIC: 2621 Book, bond & printing papers
PA: International Paper Company
6400 Poplar Ave
Memphis TN 38197
901 419-7000

(G-1271)
NINE MILE RACEWAY INC
1281 Lear Ct (32533-5742)
PHONE..................................850 937-1845
Mohammed H Hoque, *President*
EMP: 8 EST: 2017
SALES (est): 289.4K **Privately Held**
SIC: 3644 Raceways

(G-1272)
ONEILL INDUSTRIES INTL INC (PA)
8 E Quintette Rd Ste B (32533-7213)
PHONE..................................850 754-0312
David O'Neill, *President*
Alexander O'Neill, *Treasurer*
EMP: 8 EST: 2017
SQ FT: 11,000
SALES (est): 835.3K **Privately Held**
SIC: 1382 Oil & gas exploration services

(G-1273)
SERF INC
Also Called: Systems Engrg RES & Facilities
3065 S Highway 29 (32533-8562)
PHONE..................................850 476-8203
Jack W Sparks, *President*
Cheri Sparks, *Corp Secy*
Jeremy Sparks, *Safety Dir*
Jim Jimgilmore, *Sales Engr*
◆ EMP: 50 EST: 1972
SQ FT: 12,000
SALES (est): 8.8MM **Privately Held**
WEB: www.serfinc.com
SIC: 3569 8711 7692 3561 Assembly machines, non-metalworking; engineering services; welding repair; pumps & pumping equipment; valves & pipe fittings; fabricated plate work (boiler shop)

(G-1274)
SOUTHEASTERN PIPE PRECAST INC
2900 N Highway 95a (32533-7190)
PHONE..................................850 587-7473
EMP: 35
SALES (est): 6.1MM **Privately Held**
SIC: 3272 Mfg Concrete Products

(G-1275)
SOUTHERN ALUMINUM AND STL INC
2501 S Highway 29 (32533-5811)
PHONE..................................850 484-4700
Dj Kusterer, *President*
EMP: 5 EST: 1998
SQ FT: 5,140
SALES (est): 737.3K **Privately Held**
SIC: 3441 Fabricated structural metal

Cape Canaveral
Brevard County

(G-1276)
AMERICAN BOOM AND BARRIER INC
Also Called: Abbco
720 Mullet Rd Ste M (32920-4520)
PHONE..................................321 784-2110
Randall O'Brien, *President*
Pat Rooney, *Vice Pres*
◆ EMP: 23 EST: 1977
SQ FT: 42,000
SALES (est): 2MM **Privately Held**
WEB: www.acmeboom.com
SIC: 3589 3531 Sewage & water treatment equipment; marine related equipment

(G-1277)
BATECH INC
Also Called: Sunshine Welding
760 Mullet Rd (32920-4504)
PHONE..................................321 784-4838
James L Smith, *President*
David Bragdon, *Vice Pres*
Brandon Smith, *Vice Pres*
David Pearson, *QC Mgr*
Darrell Hunt, *Admin Sec*
▼ EMP: 40 EST: 1972
SALES (est): 4.5MM **Privately Held**
WEB: www.sunshinewelding.com
SIC: 3429 Marine hardware

(G-1278)
BLINDS SIDE
5801 N Atlantic Ave (32920-3972)
PHONE..................................888 610-8366
EMP: 7 EST: 2018
SALES (est): 61.7K **Privately Held**
WEB: www.theblindsside.com
SIC: 2591 Window blinds

(G-1279)
BOEING COMPANY
Hanger Rd Bldg A-0 (32920)
P.O. Box 833 (32920-0833)
PHONE..................................321 853-6647
Pete Montgomery, *Manager*
EMP: 300
SALES (corp-wide): 62.2B **Publicly Held**
WEB: www.boeing.com
SIC: 3721 3761 3764 4225 Aircraft; guided missiles & space vehicles; guided missile & space vehicle propulsion unit parts; general warehousing & storage
PA: The Boeing Company
929 Long Bridge Dr
Arlington VA 22202
703 414-6338

(G-1280)
CANAVERAL CUSTOM BOATS INC
774 Mullet Rd (32920-4504)
PHONE..................................321 783-3536
▼ EMP: 7
SALES: 1MM **Privately Held**
SIC: 3732 Boatbuilding/Repairing

(G-1281)
CEMEX CNSTR MTLS FLA LLC
Also Called: Port Canaveral FL Canaveral Rm
209 George King Blvd (32920)
PHONE..................................321 636-5121
Larry Jenkins, *Branch Mgr*
Scott Campbell, *Manager*
Brian Carroll, *Manager*
EMP: 8 **Privately Held**
SIC: 3273 Ready-mixed concrete
HQ: Cemex Construction Materials Florida, Llc
1501 Belvedere Rd
West Palm Beach FL 33406

(G-1282)
DENVER ELEVATOR SYSTEMS INC
7073 N Atlantic Ave (32920-3711)
PHONE..................................800 633-9788
Walter Burns, *President*
EMP: 6 EST: 1981
SQ FT: 1,600

SALES (est): 643.3K **Privately Held**
WEB: www.eciamerica.com
SIC: 3672 7629 Printed circuit boards; circuit board repair

(G-1283)
ENVIRO-USA AMERICAN MFR LLC
151 Center St Ste 101 (32920-3727)
PHONE..................................321 222-9551
Susan Austin, *Purch Mgr*
Jennifer A Vargas, *CFO*
Jennifer Vargas, *CFO*
Jamie Meade, *Sales Mgr*
Luis Vargas, *Sales Staff*
◆ EMP: 21 EST: 2009
SALES (est): 4.9MM **Privately Held**
WEB: www.enviro-usa.com
SIC: 3589 3531 Sewage & water treatment equipment; marine related equipment

(G-1284)
EXCELL COATINGS INC
745 Scallop Dr (32920-4550)
PHONE..................................321 868-7968
Robert Tampa, *President*
Frederick Distasio, *Treasurer*
EMP: 20 EST: 1991
SQ FT: 27,000
SALES (est): 3MM **Privately Held**
WEB: www.excellcoatings.com
SIC: 3479 Coating of metals & formed products; painting, coating & hot dipping

(G-1285)
HANSON LEHIGH CEMENT
575 Cargo Rd (32920-4415)
PHONE..................................800 665-6006
EMP: 6 EST: 2015
SALES (est): 626.9K **Privately Held**
SIC: 3273 Ready-mixed concrete

(G-1286)
IMAGE PRINTING & GRAPHICS LLC
Also Called: Jet Press
8649 Villanova Dr (32920-4328)
PHONE..................................321 783-5555
Nick Laspina, *Marketing Staff*
Cheryl Emmons,
Amanda Emmons,
EMP: 6 EST: 2004
SALES (est): 860.7K **Privately Held**
SIC: 2752 Commercial printing, offset

(G-1287)
INDIAN RIVER BREWERY CORP
Also Called: Indian Rver Brwing C/Flrida Be
200 Imperial Blvd (32920-4245)
P.O. Box 523 (32920-0523)
PHONE..................................321 728-4114
James Webb, *CEO*
Oscar Cabarcas, *Plant Engr*
Caroline Magnolia, *Sales Staff*
EMP: 17 EST: 2013
SALES (est): 5.1MM **Privately Held**
WEB: www.caribbreweryusa.com
SIC: 2082 Beer (alcoholic beverage)

(G-1288)
L3HARRIS INTERSTATE ELEC CORP
Air Force Sta Bldg 54815 (32920)
PHONE..................................321 730-0119
Larry Fitzgerald, *Systems Mgr*
EMP: 66
SQ FT: 3,200
SALES (corp-wide): 17.8B **Publicly Held**
WEB: www.l3harris.com
SIC: 3825 3812 3663 Test equipment for electronic & electric measurement; search & navigation equipment; radio & TV communications equipment
HQ: L3harris Interstate Electronics Corporation
602 E Vermont Ave
Anaheim CA 92805
714 758-0500

(G-1289)
LEHIGH CEMENT COMPANY LLC
9012 Marlin St (32920-3308)
PHONE..................................321 323-5039
Gary Milla, *Branch Mgr*

EMP: 10
SALES (corp-wide): 21.1B **Privately Held**
WEB: www.lehighhanson.com
SIC: 3273 Ready-mixed concrete
HQ: Lehigh Cement Company Llc
300 E John Carpenter Fwy
Irving TX 75062
877 534-4442

(G-1290)
LOCKHEED MARTIN CORPORATION
Pier Rd (32920)
P.O. Box 246 (32920-0246)
PHONE..................................321 853-5194
James Gower, *Engineer*
Ronald Ivey, *Manager*
Brian Ewanyk, *Software Engr*
EMP: 13 **Publicly Held**
WEB: www.gyrocamsystems.com
SIC: 3761 3812 8734 Guided missiles & space vehicles; space vehicle guidance systems & equipment; testing laboratories
PA: Lockheed Martin Corporation
6801 Rockledge Dr
Bethesda MD 20817

(G-1291)
MOON EXPRESS INC
Also Called: Moonex
100 Space Port Way (32920-4000)
PHONE..................................650 241-8577
Robert D Richards, *CEO*
Jim Cantrell, *General Mgr*
Daven Maharaj, *COO*
Julie Arnold, *Treasurer*
EMP: 30 EST: 2010
SALES (est): 4.8MM **Privately Held**
WEB: www.moonexpress.com
SIC: 3761 Guided missiles & space vehicles

(G-1292)
MORTON SALT INC
450 Cargo Rd (32920-4406)
PHONE..................................321 868-7136
Nicole Turner, *Vice Pres*
Tim McKean, *CFO*
Mike Markley, *Branch Mgr*
EMP: 238
SALES (corp-wide): 701.2MM **Privately Held**
WEB: www.mortonsalt.com
SIC: 2899 Salt
HQ: Morton Salt, Inc.
444 W Lake St Ste 3000
Chicago IL 60606

(G-1293)
SPACE EXPLORATION TECH CORP
Cape Cnaveral A Force Sta (32920)
PHONE..................................310 363-6000
Rory Mulcahy, *Engineer*
Christopher Wallden, *Senior Mgr*
James Wisnom, *Technology*
Dustin Ferguson, *IT/INT Sup*
Michael Kuhman, *Officer*
EMP: 583
SALES (corp-wide): 2B **Privately Held**
WEB: www.spacex.com
SIC: 3761 Rockets, space & military, complete
PA: Space Exploration Technologies Corp.
1 Rocket Rd
Hawthorne CA 90250
310 363-6000

(G-1294)
SYNERGY COMMUNICATION MGT LLC (PA)
400 Imperial Blvd (32920-4213)
P.O. Box 657 (32920-0657)
PHONE..................................800 749-3160
William R Mays,
Berchet R Mays,
EMP: 15 EST: 2013
SALES (est): 19MM **Privately Held**
SIC: 3661 Communication headgear, telephone; headsets, telephone

Cape Coral
Lee County

(G-1295)
ABC SCREEN MASTERS INC
1110 Ne Pine Island Rd # 23 (33909-2188)
PHONE.................................239 772-7336
Robert Bobay, *President*
EMP: 6 EST: 1990
SALES (est): 500K **Privately Held**
WEB: www.abcscreenmasters.com
SIC: 3448 1799 5039 5211 Screen enclo-
sures; screening contractor: window,
door, etc.; prefabricated structures;
screens, door & window

(G-1296)
**ACTION MANUFACTURING &
SUP INC (PA)**
Also Called: Pegasus Water Systems
2602 Ne 9th Ave (33909-2933)
PHONE.................................239 574-3443
Richard Shepard, *President*
Carolyn Eulena Pilgrim, *Vice Pres*
Nick Painter, *Warehouse Mgr*
Eva Williams, *Technology*
▼ EMP: 14 EST: 1980
SQ FT: 10,000
SALES (est): 5.9MM **Privately Held**
WEB: www.actionmfg.com
SIC: 3589 Water purification equipment,
household type; water filters & softeners,
household type

(G-1297)
ADVERMARKET CORP
954 Country Club Blvd (33990-3074)
PHONE.................................239 541-1144
Benjamin Kiesinger, *President*
EMP: 7 EST: 2017
SALES (est): 482.4K **Privately Held**
WEB: www.hi-defprinting.com
SIC: 2752 Commercial printing, offset

(G-1298)
ADVERMARKET CORP
4720 Se 15th Ave Ste 205 (33904-9600)
PHONE.................................239 542-1020
Benjamin Kiesinger, *President*
EMP: 6 EST: 2005
SALES (est): 525.4K **Privately Held**
WEB: www.hi-defprinting.com
SIC: 2752 Commercial printing, offset

(G-1299)
AGI-VR/WESSON INC
2673 Ne 9th Ave (33909-2917)
PHONE.................................239 573-5132
Thomas A Fliss, *President*
Todd Grabow, *Vice Pres*
Steve Scott, *Vice Pres*
Linda S Fliss, *Treasurer*
▼ EMP: 27 EST: 1990
SQ FT: 15,000
SALES (est): 4.6MM **Privately Held**
WEB: www.vrwesson.com
SIC: 3541 3545 Machine tools, metal cut-
ting type; cutting tools for machine tools

(G-1300)
AMD ORNAMENTAL INC
918 Se 9th Ln Unit A (33990-3120)
PHONE.................................239 458-7437
Mark Christian, *President*
EMP: 8 EST: 2008
SALES (est): 693.3K **Privately Held**
WEB: www.amdornamental.com
SIC: 3446 Ornamental metalwork

(G-1301)
**AMERICAN QUALITY
EMBROIDERY**
1830 Del Prado Blvd S # 1 (33990-4575)
PHONE.................................239 772-8687
Donna Gibbons, *President*
EMP: 62 **Privately Held**
WEB: www.aqembroidery.net
SIC: 2284 Thread mills
PA: American Quality Embroidery Inc
1546 Ocean Ave Ste 6
Bohemia NY 11716

(G-1302)
ANCHOR & DOCKING INC
830 Ne 24th Ln Unit G (33909-2939)
PHONE.................................239 770-2030
Rune Ilerod, *President*
EMP: 8 EST: 2015
SQ FT: 7,000
SALES (est): 651.8K **Privately Held**
SIC: 3462 Anchors, forged

(G-1303)
APPLIANCES TO GO USA LLC
741 Del Prado Blvd N # 160 (33909-2291)
PHONE.................................239 278-0811
Mickey Rosabo,
EMP: 5 EST: 2008
SQ FT: 10,000
SALES (est): 650.1K **Privately Held**
WEB: www.appliancestogousa.us
SIC: 3639 Major kitchen appliances, ex-
cept refrigerators & stoves

(G-1304)
**APPLIED COOLING
TECHNOLOGY LLC**
75 Mid Cape Ter 23 (33991-2012)
PHONE.................................239 217-5080
Heather Dutescu, *Engineer*
Nicholas Welford,
Peter Jackson,
◆ EMP: 5 EST: 2007
SQ FT: 12,000
SALES (est): 865.1K **Privately Held**
WEB: www.appliedcool.com
SIC: 3443 Finned tubes, for heat transfer

(G-1305)
**AQUINO TRUCKS CENTER
CORP ✪**
Also Called: Pork and Shake
31 Nw 13th Ave (33993-7732)
PHONE.................................239 327-9708
Jessica Silva, *CEO*
EMP: 10 EST: 2022
SALES (est): 413.1K **Privately Held**
SIC: 2599 7389 Food wagons, restaurant;

(G-1306)
**ARCHITCTRAL MTAL
FLASHINGS LLC**
2659 Ne 9th Ave (33909-2917)
PHONE.................................239 221-0123
Scott Bonk,
EMP: 13 EST: 2016
SALES (est): 6.6MM **Privately Held**
WEB: www.architecturalmetalflashings.com
SIC: 3354 Aluminum extruded products

(G-1307)
**ART STAIRCASE & WOODWORK
LLC**
4229 Sw 14th Pl (33914-5682)
PHONE.................................239 440-6591
Gregory Ziemba, *Principal*
EMP: 10 EST: 2017
SALES (est): 353.7K **Privately Held**
SIC: 2431 Millwork

(G-1308)
ATLAS BOAT WORKS INC
2404 Andalusia Blvd (33909-2901)
P.O. Box 150205 (33915-0205)
PHONE.................................239 574-2628
Thomas Gamso, *President*
Stan Gamso, *Shareholder*
▼ EMP: 7 EST: 1985
SQ FT: 3,000
SALES (est): 505.7K **Privately Held**
WEB: www.acadia25.com
SIC: 3732 Boats, fiberglass: building & re-
pairing

(G-1309)
ATM PAVERS INC
2710 Del Prado Blvd S (33904-5788)
PHONE.................................239 322-7010
Marcos V De Medeiros, *President*
Jim Adams, *Marketing Staff*
EMP: 7 EST: 2010
SALES (est): 142K **Privately Held**
SIC: 3531 Pavers

(G-1310)
BACC COATINGS LLC
926 Se 9th St (33990-6204)
PHONE.................................239 424-8843
Celia Turner, *Owner*
EMP: 7 EST: 2015
SALES (est): 257.3K **Privately Held**
SIC: 3479 Metal coating & allied service

(G-1311)
BENCHMARK METALS INC
1003 Se 12th Ave Unit 2 (33990-3018)
PHONE.................................239 699-0802
Jason M Guy, *Principal*
EMP: 7 EST: 2019
SALES (est): 513K **Privately Held**
WEB: www.benchmark-metals.com
SIC: 1081 Metal mining exploration & de-
velopment services

(G-1312)
BETHEL PRODUCTS LLC
926 Se 9th St (33990-6204)
P.O. Box 100884 (33910-0884)
PHONE.................................954 636-2645
Jason Turner, *CEO*
John Delmonte, *Prdtn Mgr*
Celia Turner,
EMP: 14 EST: 2005
SQ FT: 9,000
SALES (est): 2.5MM **Privately Held**
WEB: www.bpcoils.com
SIC: 3621 3479 Coils, for electric motors
or generators; coating of metals & formed
products

(G-1313)
**BEVERAGE EQUIPMENT REPAIR
CO**
Also Called: Berco
1020 Ne Pine Island Rd # 201
(33909-2104)
PHONE.................................239 573-0683
Michael Depasquale, *President*
Greg Blakely, *Technician*
EMP: 10 EST: 1996
SQ FT: 1,500
SALES (est): 2.1MM **Privately Held**
WEB: www.beveragerepair.com
SIC: 3585 Refrigeration & heating equip-
ment

(G-1314)
BIOBOTANICAL LLC
889 Ne 27th Ln (33909-2957)
PHONE.................................239 458-4534
Christopher Mitchell, *Principal*
EMP: 9 EST: 2015
SALES (est): 451.6K **Privately Held**
SIC: 2833 Medicinals & botanicals

(G-1315)
BRAVO INC
Also Called: Bravo Construction Materials
1811 Se 5th Ave (33990-2204)
PHONE.................................239 471-8127
Stephen Berge, *President*
Ricco Longo, *Manager*
EMP: 1 EST: 2016
SALES (est): 3.5MM **Privately Held**
WEB: www.bravomaterials.com
SIC: 3523 3524 3531 3537 Cabs, trac-
tors & agricultural machinery; lawn & gar-
den tractors & equipment; backhoes,
tractors, cranes, plows & similar equip-
ment; trucks, tractors, loaders, carriers &
similar equipment; clamps, surgical

(G-1316)
BREEZE CORPORATION (DH)
Also Called: Fort Meyers Beach Bulletin
2510 Del Prado Blvd S (33904-5750)
P.O. Box 151306 (33915-1306)
PHONE.................................239 574-1110
George Ogden Nutting, *President*
Raymond Eckenrode, *Publisher*
Michael Pistella, *Editor*
Robert M Nutting, *Vice Pres*
Henry Keim, *Opers Staff*
EMP: 24 EST: 1890
SQ FT: 13,000
SALES (est): 29.6MM **Privately Held**
WEB: www.breezenewspapers.com
SIC: 2711 Newspapers: publishing only,
not printed on site

HQ: The Ogden Newspapers Inc
1500 Main St
Wheeling WV 26003
304 233-0100

(G-1317)
BREEZE NEWSPAPERS
2510 Del Prado Blvd S (33904-5750)
PHONE.................................239 574-1110
Jim Konig, *Director*
EMP: 7 EST: 2003
SALES (est): 179.2K **Privately Held**
WEB: www.breezenewspapers.com
SIC: 2711 Newspapers: publishing only,
not printed on site

(G-1318)
CABINET GENIES
815 Se 47th Ter (33904-9004)
PHONE.................................239 458-8563
EMP: 7 EST: 2020
SALES (est): 1.1MM **Privately Held**
WEB: www.cabinetgenies.com
SIC: 2434 Wood kitchen cabinets

(G-1319)
CABINETS PLUS INC
Also Called: Cabinetsplusfl.com
1056 Ne Pine Island Rd G (33909-2183)
PHONE.................................239 574-7020
Phillip Baumstark, *President*
Vicki Baumstark, *Corp Secy*
EMP: 22 EST: 1992
SQ FT: 2,500
SALES (est): 6MM **Privately Held**
WEB: www.cabinetsplusfl.com
SIC: 2541 2434 Cabinets, lockers & shelv-
ing; wood kitchen cabinets

(G-1320)
CALNAT INTERNATIONAL INC
2118 Se 1st St (33990-1401)
PHONE.................................239 839-2581
Calvin Smith Sr, *President*
Natisha L Smith, *Vice Pres*
EMP: 5 EST: 2005
SALES (est): 2MM **Privately Held**
WEB: calnat.ucanr.edu
SIC: 3312 Tubes, steel & iron; plate, steel;
stainless steel; forgings, iron & steel

(G-1321)
**CAMPBELLS ORNAMENTAL
CONCRETE**
Also Called: Campbells Ornamental & Con
1930 Ne Pine Island Rd (33909-1728)
PHONE.................................239 458-0800
Paul Campbell, *President*
EMP: 5 EST: 1970
SQ FT: 450
SALES (est): 389.9K **Privately Held**
WEB: www.campbellsiron.com
SIC: 3299 5999 Statuary: gypsum, clay,
papier mache, metal, etc.; monuments &
tombstones

(G-1322)
CAPE CANVAS INC
1036 Ne Pine Island Rd # 10 (33909-2184)
PHONE.................................239 772-0300
Raymond G Siegman, *Principal*
EMP: 7 EST: 2003
SALES (est): 46.5K **Privately Held**
SIC: 2211 Canvas

(G-1323)
CAPE SPIRITS INC
131 Sw 3rd Pl (33991-2011)
PHONE.................................239 242-5244
Joann Curtin Elardo, *President*
EMP: 5 EST: 2011
SALES (est): 436.3K **Privately Held**
SIC: 2085 Distilled & blended liquors

(G-1324)
CK PRIME INVESTMENTS INC
Also Called: Action Craft Boats
830 Ne 24th Ln Unit C (33909-2939)
PHONE.................................239 574-7800
Chad Kovarik, *Owner*
David Spurlin, *Principal*
EMP: 9 EST: 2015
SALES (est): 952.5K **Privately Held**
SIC: 3732 Motorized boat, building & re-
pairing

(G-1325)
COLLECTIBLES OF SW FLORIDA
Also Called: Magnetic Bookmarks
1502 Ne 11th Ter (33909-1547)
PHONE..............................239 332-2344
Gaby Peden, *President*
Glenn Peden, *Vice Pres*
▲ EMP: 7 EST: 1999
SALES (est): 388.6K **Privately Held**
SIC: 3999 Novelties, bric-a-brac & hobby kits

(G-1326)
COLOSSUS PAVERS LLC
2118 Sw 39th St (33914-5429)
PHONE..............................239 601-5230
Hector Vara-Monje, *Principal*
EMP: 7 EST: 2014
SALES (est): 153.1K **Privately Held**
SIC: 2951 Asphalt paving mixtures & blocks

(G-1327)
CORN-E-LEE WOODCRAFTS
1201 Se 9th Ter (33990-3006)
PHONE..............................239 574-2414
Vaughn Cornelle, *President*
EMP: 5 EST: 1972
SQ FT: 9,300
SALES (est): 600K **Privately Held**
WEB: www.corneleewoodcraft.com
SIC: 2434 2541 Wood kitchen cabinets; wood partitions & fixtures

(G-1328)
CREATIVE COLORS INTERNATIONAL
Also Called: H & W Creative Colors
1221 Se 9th Ter (33990-3078)
PHONE..............................239 573-8883
Wally Reece, *Partner*
Linda Lakes, *Partner*
EMP: 10 EST: 1996
SALES (est): 156.2K **Privately Held**
WEB: www.wecanfixthat.com
SIC: 3199 7549 Desk sets, leather; automotive maintenance services

(G-1329)
CUSTOM BUILT SCREEN ENCLOSURES
765 Ne 19th Pl Unit 2 (33909-7803)
PHONE..............................239 242-0224
David Hemed, *CEO*
EMP: 12 EST: 1996
SALES (est): 498K **Privately Held**
WEB: www.cbseinc.com
SIC: 3448 Screen enclosures

(G-1330)
DATA BUOY INSTRUMENTATION LLC
75 Mid Cape Ter Ste 8 (33991-2012)
PHONE..............................239 849-7063
Jeffrey Wingenroth, *Mng Member*
Anthony Harness,
Kahu Trust,
◆ EMP: 5 EST: 2011
SQ FT: 4,000
SALES (est): 672.1K **Privately Held**
SIC: 3826 7389 Laser scientific & engineering instruments;

(G-1331)
DEKORON UNITHERM LLC (DH)
1531 Commerce Creek Blvd (33909-6502)
PHONE..............................800 633-5015
Paul Brezovsky, *President*
Shane Hehir, *Vice Pres*
Keith Peels, *Controller*
◆ EMP: 34 EST: 2004
SQ FT: 30,000
SALES (est): 13.6MM
SALES (corp-wide): 354.6B **Publicly Held**
WEB: www.unithermcc.com
SIC: 3357 Nonferrous wiredrawing & insulating
HQ: Marmon Group Llc
181 W Madison St Ste 3900
Chicago IL 60602
312 372-9500

(G-1332)
DETAILED SERVICES INC
Also Called: Arthur Printing
1518 Se 46th Ln (33904-8635)
PHONE..............................239 542-2452
Robert F Welsh, *President*
Lois M Welsh, *Vice Pres*
Tony Rumreich, *Manager*
EMP: 13 EST: 1976
SQ FT: 3,000
SALES (est): 993.9K **Privately Held**
SIC: 2752 Commercial printing, offset

(G-1333)
DIMENSION MACHINE ENGRG LLC
5201 Sw 28th Pl (33914-6016)
PHONE..............................586 948-3600
Hans Lohr,
Charles Arent,
EMP: 10 EST: 1997
SQ FT: 15,000
SALES (est): 196.5K **Privately Held**
SIC: 3544 Special dies, tools, jigs & fixtures

(G-1334)
DIMENSION MACHINE TOOL INC
5201 Sw 28th Pl (33914-6016)
PHONE..............................586 948-3600
Hans Lohr, *President*
EMP: 15 EST: 1983
SQ FT: 24,000
SALES (est): 233.4K **Privately Held**
SIC: 3599 3544 Machine shop, jobbing & repair; custom machinery; special dies, tools, jigs & fixtures

(G-1335)
DIRECT IMPRESSIONS INC
1335 Miramar St (33904-9734)
PHONE..............................239 549-4484
Robert Boye, *CEO*
Steve Delaney, *President*
Richard Boye, *Mktg Dir*
EMP: 40 EST: 1992
SQ FT: 12,000
SALES (est): 10.2MM **Privately Held**
WEB: www.directimpressions.com
SIC: 2752 7331 Commercial printing, offset; direct mail advertising services

(G-1336)
ECOLOGICAL LABORATORIES INC
2525 Ne 9th Ave (33909-2917)
P.O. Box 24, Matlacha (33993-0024)
PHONE..............................239 573-6650
Nick Simone, *Vice Pres*
Scott Berke, *Sales Mgr*
EMP: 40
SALES (corp-wide): 11.5MM **Privately Held**
WEB: www.microbelift.com
SIC: 2899 5169 2836 Water treating compounds; chemicals & allied products; biological products, except diagnostic
PA: Ecological Laboratories Inc.
4 Waterford Rd
Island Park NY 11558
516 823-3441

(G-1337)
ENERGY HARNESS CORPORATION (PA)
Also Called: Energy Harness Led Lighting
71 Mid Cape Ter Ste 8 (33991-2010)
PHONE..............................239 790-3300
Michael J Fischer, *President*
Peter Lehrer, *Vice Pres*
Dustin Fischer, *Opers Mgr*
Cristiano Rodrigues, *Sales Staff*
Mid Ter, *Sales Staff*
▲ EMP: 4 EST: 2010
SALES (est): 3.7MM **Privately Held**
WEB: www.energyharness.com
SIC: 3646 Commercial indusl & institutional electric lighting fixtures

(G-1338)
EPOXY2U OF FLORIDA INC
922 Se 14th Pl (33990-3021)
PHONE..............................239 772-0899
Erlan Araujo, *President*
EMP: 11 EST: 2018

SALES (est): 785.7K **Privately Held**
WEB: www.epoxy2ufl.com
SIC: 2851 Epoxy coatings

(G-1339)
EURO TRIM INC
17200 Primavera Cir (33909-3024)
PHONE..............................239 574-6646
Peter Geresdi, *Principal*
EMP: 10 EST: 2008
SALES (est): 181.6K **Privately Held**
WEB: www.eurotriminc.info
SIC: 3089 Injection molding of plastics

(G-1340)
EVERYTHING PRINTING INC
Also Called: Pioneer Printing and Signs
202 Se 44th St (33904-8426)
PHONE..............................239 541-2679
Robert L Ratcliff, *President*
EMP: 5 EST: 2015
SALES (est): 368.5K **Privately Held**
SIC: 2752 Commercial printing, offset

(G-1341)
EXTREME CARE INC
11997 Princess Grace Ct (33991-7536)
PHONE..............................239 898-3709
Maureen Kaufmann, *President*
EMP: 5 EST: 2004
SALES (est): 386.1K **Privately Held**
WEB: extreme-care-inc.business.site
SIC: 2844 Toilet preparations

(G-1342)
FABWORX LLC
848 Se 9th St (33990-3219)
PHONE..............................239 573-9353
Eric Wirgin,
EMP: 15 EST: 1999
SALES (est): 1.7MM **Privately Held**
SIC: 3355 Aluminum rail & structural shapes

(G-1343)
FLATSMASTER MARINE LLC
Also Called: Action Craft
830 Ne 24th Ln Unit C (33909-2939)
PHONE..............................239 574-7800
Paul Guard, *Mng Member*
▼ EMP: 7 EST: 2009
SQ FT: 34,000
SALES (est): 347.8K **Privately Held**
SIC: 3732 Boat building & repairing

(G-1344)
FLORIDA SW DRONES LLC
1425 Sw 43rd Ter (33914-5665)
PHONE..............................239 785-8337
Gregory Lagrand, *Principal*
EMP: 7 EST: 2016
SALES (est): 160.6K **Privately Held**
SIC: 3721 Motorized aircraft

(G-1345)
FORCON PRECISION PRODUCTS LLC
1110 Ne Pine Island Rd (33909-2126)
PHONE..............................239 574-4543
Paul Saalmuller, *Mng Member*
Dale Wheeling,
EMP: 13 EST: 1986
SQ FT: 2,800
SALES (est): 800K **Privately Held**
WEB: www.forconprecisionproducts.com
SIC: 3451 Screw machine products

(G-1346)
GATOR POLYMERS LLC
3302 Se 22nd Ave (33904-4421)
PHONE..............................866 292-7306
John R Rasmussen, *Manager*
EMP: 8 EST: 2005
SALES (est): 80.9K **Privately Held**
WEB: www.gatorpolymers.com
SIC: 3089 Injection molding of plastics

(G-1347)
GENERATIONS METIER INC
883 Ne 27th Ln (33909-2953)
PHONE..............................239 458-8127
Stephen Morrow, *Manager*
EMP: 20 **Privately Held**
WEB: www.generationsmetier.com
SIC: 3553 Cabinet makers' machinery

PA: Generations Metier, Inc.
2818 Nw 43rd Pl
Cape Coral FL 33993

(G-1348)
GIRALDO & DONALISIO CORP
3909 Ne 19th Ave (33909-3123)
P.O. Box 4132, Fort Myers (33918-4132)
PHONE..............................239 567-2206
Donalisio Cristiano, *President*
Giraldo Paola, *Director*
▲ EMP: 13 EST: 2005
SALES (est): 278.5K **Privately Held**
SIC: 3541 3915 Machine tools, metal cutting type; diamond cutting & polishing

(G-1349)
GOLDEN WOOD WORKS LLC
2529 Sw 26th Pl (33914-3827)
PHONE..............................239 677-8540
Timothy Golden, *Manager*
EMP: 7 EST: 2012
SALES (est): 257.3K **Privately Held**
SIC: 2431 Millwork

(G-1350)
GREYLOR DYNESCO CO INC
2340 Andalusia Blvd (33909-2901)
PHONE..............................239 574-2011
Michael J Becher, *President*
Amy Chase, *Office Mgr*
▲ EMP: 8 EST: 1948
SQ FT: 4,500
SALES (est): 1.2MM **Privately Held**
WEB: www.greylor.com
SIC: 3561 5084 Industrial pumps & parts; pumps & pumping equipment

(G-1351)
GULFSHORE CUSTOM WOODWORKS LLC
1012 Nw 36th Ave (33993-9426)
PHONE..............................239 205-0777
Alan Hiebing, *Owner*
EMP: 8 EST: 2011
SALES (est): 553.5K **Privately Held**
WEB: www.gulfshorewoodworks.com
SIC: 2431 Millwork

(G-1352)
HANGER PRSTHTICS ORTHOTICS INC
Also Called: Hanger Clinic
323 Del Prado Blvd S (33990-1747)
PHONE..............................239 772-4510
Sam Liang, *President*
EMP: 10 EST: 2010
SALES (est): 542.6K **Privately Held**
SIC: 3842 Orthopedic appliances

(G-1353)
HIGH TEMP INDUSTRIES
3808 Sw 6th Ter (33991-1611)
PHONE..............................215 794-0864
Jerold L Bloom, *Principal*
EMP: 8 EST: 2012
SALES (est): 216.2K **Privately Held**
SIC: 3999 Manufacturing industries

(G-1354)
HOME IMPROVER INC
1732 Se 47th Ter (33904-8717)
PHONE..............................239 549-6901
Sean C Campbell, *President*
Ralph Harris, *COO*
EMP: 11 EST: 2002
SQ FT: 1,300
SALES (est): 251.4K **Privately Held**
SIC: 2721 Magazines: publishing only, not printed on site

(G-1355)
HOMEMAG INC
1732 Se 47th Ter (33904-8717)
PHONE..............................239 549-6960
Sean Campbell, *President*
Chris Goebel, *President*
EMP: 42 EST: 2003
SALES (est): 4.9MM **Privately Held**
WEB: www.thehomemag.com
SIC: 2721 Magazines: publishing only, not printed on site

(G-1356)
HOMEWOOD HOLDINGS LLC
Also Called: Acne Seal Coating and Paving
745 Ne 19th Pl Ste E (33909-7807)
P.O. Box 511543, Punta Gorda (33951-1543)
PHONE................................941 740-3655
David C Plummer,
Jennifer D Keese,
EMP: 15 **EST:** 2016
SQ FT: 1,500
SALES (est): 1.5MM **Privately Held**
WEB: www.acmepaving.net
SIC: 3531 Pavers

(G-1357)
HUMAN SIGN
1830 Del Prado Blvd S (33990-4575)
PHONE................................239 573-4292
Paul Watson, *Principal*
EMP: 8 **EST:** 2007
SALES (est): 524K **Privately Held**
WEB: www.humansignsllc.com
SIC: 3993 Signs & advertising specialties

(G-1358)
JB WOOD WERKS LLC
2550 Sw 27th Ave (33914-3833)
PHONE................................239 314-4462
Bradley Walker, *Principal*
EMP: 7 **EST:** 2010
SALES (est): 145.2K **Privately Held**
WEB: www.jbwoodwerks.com
SIC: 2431 Millwork

(G-1359)
JDL SURFACE INNOVATIONS INC
922 Se 14th Pl (33990-3021)
PHONE................................239 772-0077
Roberta Sloat, *Treasurer*
EMP: 15 **EST:** 2010
SALES (est): 2.4MM **Privately Held**
WEB: www.jdlsurfaceinnovations.com
SIC: 3531 1771 7359 Surfacers, concrete grinding; flooring contractor; floor maintenance equipment rental

(G-1360)
JSM CREATIONS INC
16260 Saddlewood Ln (33991-7514)
PHONE................................239 229-8746
Justin S Mullen, *Principal*
EMP: 8 **EST:** 2013
SALES (est): 472.3K **Privately Held**
SIC: 3648 Decorative area lighting fixtures

(G-1361)
KELTOUR US INC
71 Mid Cape Ter Unit 1/2 (33991-2010)
PHONE................................239 424-8901
David Jakob, *President*
EMP: 12 **EST:** 2014
SALES (est): 3MM **Privately Held**
WEB: www.keltour.com
SIC: 3569 1731 Liquid automation machinery & equipment; electrical work

(G-1362)
MARINE CONCEPTS
2443 Sw Pine Island Rd (33991-1282)
PHONE................................239 283-0800
John Bower, *Program Mgr*
Del Sturdivant, *Manager*
EMP: 16 **EST:** 2008
SALES (est): 7.5MM **Privately Held**
WEB: www.dcmc-us.com
SIC: 1446 Molding sand mining

(G-1363)
MATTEO GRAPHICS INC
160 Hunter Blvd Ste A1 (33909-2846)
PHONE................................239 652-1002
Joseph C Trunkett, *President*
Carmen Trunkett, *Vice Pres*
Angela Trunkett, *Officer*
EMP: 9 **EST:** 1989
SALES (est): 1.3MM **Privately Held**
WEB: www.matteographics.com
SIC: 2339 2393 2331 Sportswear, women's; textile bags; women's & misses' blouses & shirts

(G-1364)
MAXXFI LLC
3428 Sw 25th Pl (33914-4875)
PHONE................................513 289-6521
John Reynolds, *Mng Member*
EMP: 10 **EST:** 2016
SQ FT: 2,500
SALES (est): 528K **Privately Held**
WEB: www.maxxfi.com
SIC: 3663 3812 3748 Television antennas (transmitting) & ground equipment; antennas, transmitting & communications; ; antennas, radar or communications; telecommunications consultant

(G-1365)
MERCHANT CENTRAL PLAZA
159 Hancock Bridge Pkwy (33990-4015)
PHONE................................239 574-7166
Eddie Ardire, *Principal*
EMP: 7 **EST:** 2006
SALES (est): 134.9K **Privately Held**
SIC: 2844 Manicure preparations

(G-1366)
MOST VALUABLE PAVERS
224 Sw 22nd Pl (33991-1352)
PHONE................................239 590-5217
Shaun Haag, *President*
EMP: 8 **EST:** 2006
SALES (est): 268.8K **Privately Held**
SIC: 2951 Asphalt paving mixtures & blocks

(G-1367)
NEW LIFE PUBLISHING INC
4103 Sw 27th Ave (33914-5480)
PHONE................................239 549-9152
Vickie G Bradley, *Director*
EMP: 7 **EST:** 2005
SALES (est): 116.4K **Privately Held**
WEB: www.newlifepublishing.co.uk
SIC: 2741 Miscellaneous publishing

(G-1368)
NOUMENON CORPORATION
1616 Cape Coral Pkwy W (33914-6979)
PHONE................................302 296-5460
Linda Higinbotham, *Principal*
EMP: 5 **EST:** 2016
SALES (est): 431.9K **Privately Held**
SIC: 1311 Crude petroleum & natural gas

(G-1369)
NXGEN BRANDS INC (PA)
2322 Se 8th St (33990-2795)
PHONE................................954 329-2205
Carlos Hurtado, *President*
EMP: 30 **EST:** 2003
SALES (est): 2.1MM **Privately Held**
SIC: 3812 Defense systems & equipment

(G-1370)
OLDCASTLE INFRASTRUCTURE INC
2140 Pondella Rd (33909-5134)
PHONE................................239 574-8896
Mike Kovalick, *General Mgr*
EMP: 29
SALES (corp-wide): 30.9B **Privately Held**
WEB: www.oldcastleinfrastructure.com
SIC: 3272 Concrete products
HQ: Oldcastle Infrastructure, Inc.
7000 Central Pkwy Ste 800
Atlanta GA 30328
770 270-5000

(G-1371)
ONLINE GERMAN PUBLISHER LLC
1000 Nw 37th Pl (33993-9305)
PHONE................................239 344-8953
Jens Struck, *President*
EMP: 7 **EST:** 2018
SALES (est): 77.2K **Privately Held**
WEB: www.germanonlinepublisher.com
SIC: 2741 Miscellaneous publishing

(G-1372)
PATRICK INDUSTRIES INC
2443 Sw Pine Island Rd (33991-1282)
PHONE................................239 283-0800
Andy L Nemeth, *Branch Mgr*
EMP: 90

SALES (corp-wide): 4B **Publicly Held**
WEB: www.patrickind.com
SIC: 3429 Marine hardware
PA: Patrick Industries, Inc.
107 W Franklin St
Elkhart IN 46516
574 294-7511

(G-1373)
PAULAS DVES SIGN TS OTHER PRTG
1122 Se 21st Ln (33990-4614)
PHONE................................239 673-8923
Dave King, *Owner*
Paula King, *Partner*
EMP: 8 **EST:** 1990
SALES (est): 150K **Privately Held**
SIC: 2752 Commercial printing, lithographic

(G-1374)
PREMIER MANUFACTURING PDTS LLC
730 Ne 19th Pl (33909-5176)
PHONE................................239 542-0260
Mark Baits, *Principal*
EMP: 12 **EST:** 2018
SALES (est): 1MM **Privately Held**
WEB: www.premiermp.com
SIC: 2396 Automotive & apparel trimmings

(G-1375)
PRIMARY METALS INTL LLC
4637 Vincennes Blvd Ste 2 (33904-9109)
PHONE................................800 243-1923
Richard Phillips, *President*
Erika Phillips,
EMP: 2 **EST:** 2016
SALES (est): 4.1MM **Privately Held**
WEB: www.heattransferdivision.com
SIC: 3317 5051 Steel pipe & tubes; metals service centers & offices

(G-1376)
PROJECT AND CNSTR WLDG INC
Also Called: IMS
2603 Andalusia Blvd (33909-2922)
PHONE................................239 772-9299
Rolf Nilsen, *President*
Eve Roe, *Bookkeeper*
◆ **EMP:** 15 **EST:** 1987
SALES (est): 2MM **Privately Held**
WEB: www.imsgroups.com
SIC: 3312 Forgings, iron & steel

(G-1377)
RAY ELECTRIC OUTBOARDS INC
908 Ne 24th Ln Unit 6 (33909-2915)
PHONE................................239 574-1948
Morton Ray, *President*
▲ **EMP:** 5 **EST:** 1971
SQ FT: 4,000
SALES (est): 738.9K **Privately Held**
WEB: www.rayeo.com
SIC: 3621 5551 Motors, electric; boat dealers

(G-1378)
RIK ENTERPRISES INC
954 Ne Pine Island Rd G (33909-2506)
PHONE................................239 772-9485
Richard Dahlberg, *President*
EMP: 9 **EST:** 2000
SQ FT: 6,000
SALES (est): 1MM **Privately Held**
WEB: www.rikgraniteshop.com
SIC: 3281 1751 Granite, cut & shaped; cabinet & finish carpentry

(G-1379)
S4J MANUFACTURING SERVICES INC
2685 Ne 9th Ave (33909-2917)
PHONE................................239 574-9400
Douglas Gyure, *CEO*
Steven E Gyure, *President*
Douglas S Gyure, *Vice Pres*
EMP: 14 **EST:** 1965
SQ FT: 15,000
SALES (est): 2.2MM **Privately Held**
WEB: www.s4jmfg.com
SIC: 3841 Surgical & medical instruments

(G-1380)
SANDY LENDER INC
2200 Nw 5th St (33993-7591)
PHONE................................239 272-8613
Sandra Lender, *Principal*
Sandy Lender, *Editor*
Cara Owings, *Sales Staff*
EMP: 9 **EST:** 2011
SALES (est): 70.9K **Privately Held**
SIC: 2721 7389 Magazines: publishing only, not printed on site;

(G-1381)
SATELLITE NOW INC
411 Sw 34th Ter (33914-7824)
PHONE................................239 945-0520
Suzanne Prytherch, *President*
EMP: 8 **EST:** 2005
SALES (est): 591.9K **Privately Held**
SIC: 3663 Space satellite communications equipment

(G-1382)
SCREENPRINT PLUS INC
1336 Se 47th St (33904-9636)
PHONE................................239 549-7284
H M Williamson Jr, *President*
Donna Williamson, *Corp Secy*
H M Williamson III, *Vice Pres*
EMP: 62 **EST:** 1986
SQ FT: 15,000
SALES (est): 1.2MM **Privately Held**
WEB: www.screenprintplus.com
SIC: 2261 2397 Screen printing of cotton broadwoven fabrics; schiffli machine embroideries

(G-1383)
SEND IT SWEETLY LLC
1309 Se 47th Ter (33904-9674)
PHONE................................239 850-5500
Anita R Grant, *Principal*
EMP: 7 **EST:** 2013
SALES (est): 475.5K **Privately Held**
WEB: www.senditsweetly.com
SIC: 2064 Candy & other confectionery products

(G-1384)
SET UP INC
170 Sw 51st St (33914-7126)
PHONE................................239 542-4142
Jean Bersch, *President*
EMP: 6 **EST:** 1977
SALES (est): 464.6K **Privately Held**
WEB: www.thesetup.com
SIC: 2791 Typesetting

(G-1385)
SIGN ON LLC
4519 Del Prado Blvd S B (33904-7525)
PHONE................................239 800-9454
Gabriel Jacobs, *CEO*
Jacobs Kristian, *Principal*
EMP: 11 **EST:** 2015
SALES (est): 582.5K **Privately Held**
WEB: www.signsandleds.com
SIC: 3993 Signs & advertising specialties

(G-1386)
SILVER ENTERPRISES ASSOC INC
1417 Sw 52nd Ter (33914-7416)
PHONE................................239 542-0068
Robert McGuire, *Principal*
EMP: 9 **EST:** 2002
SALES (est): 108.5K **Privately Held**
WEB: www.slvx.com
SIC: 3743 Railroad equipment

(G-1387)
SOURCE SUP IN PLYURETHANES INC
2645 Ne 9th Ave Unit 12 (33909-2929)
P.O. Box 7127, Fort Myers (33919-0127)
PHONE................................239 573-3637
Bart J Derosso, *Principal*
EMP: 3 **EST:** 1993
SALES (est): 8.4MM **Privately Held**
WEB: www.sosfoams.com
SIC: 3086 Packaging & shipping materials, foamed plastic

(G-1388)
SOUTHERN ALUMINUM INC
677 Stonecrest Ln (33909-2308)
PHONE..................................239 275-3367
Matt Myers, *President*
Stacie Brice, *General Mgr*
Coy Brown, *Purch Mgr*
Shawn Tuggle, *Engineer*
Daniel Watson, *Controller*
EMP: 16 **EST:** 2007
SALES (est): 4.9MM **Privately Held**
WEB: www.southern-aluminum.com
SIC: 3446 Ornamental metalwork

(G-1389)
SOUTHWEST CHOPPERS INC
2123 Ne 3rd Ter (33909-2849)
PHONE..................................239 242-1101
Dave Zink, *General Mgr*
Chris Wallen, *Principal*
EMP: 8 **EST:** 2007
SALES (est): 68.4K **Privately Held**
SIC: 3751 Motorcycles & related parts

(G-1390)
SOUTHWEST FLA NEWSPAPERS INC
308 Se 25th Ter (33904-2763)
PHONE..................................239 574-9733
Karen P Moore, *Principal*
EMP: 7 **EST:** 2013
SALES (est): 88.7K **Privately Held**
WEB: www.breezenewspapers.com
SIC: 2711 Newspapers: publishing only, not printed on site

(G-1391)
SOUTHWEST STEEL GROUP INC
3405 Yucatan Pkwy (33993-9450)
PHONE..................................239 283-8980
EMP: 9
SALES (est): 1.3MM **Privately Held**
SIC: 3441 Structural Metal Fabrication

(G-1392)
SPOSEN SIGNATURE HOMES LLC
2311 Santa Barbara Blvd # 111 (33991-4394)
PHONE..................................239 244-8886
EMP: 14 **EST:** 2019
SALES (est): 2.7MM **Privately Held**
SIC: 3993 Signs & advertising specialties

(G-1393)
STONE HARBOR HOMES LLC
5225 Sw 22nd Pl (33914-6834)
PHONE..................................239 672-7687
Pia Powell, *Principal*
EMP: 5 **EST:** 2015
SALES (est): 363.2K **Privately Held**
WEB: www.stoneharbor4.com
SIC: 2451 Mobile homes, personal or private use

(G-1394)
SUPERIOR FIRE & LF SAFETY INC
1709 Sw 15th Ave (33991-3240)
PHONE..................................850 572-0265
Richard M King, *President*
EMP: 12 **EST:** 2012
SALES (est): 1.1MM **Privately Held**
WEB: www.summitfiresecurity.com
SIC: 3669 Fire alarm apparatus, electric

(G-1395)
SWFL HURRICANE SHUTTERS INC
422 Sw 2nd Ter Ste 214 (33991-1949)
PHONE..................................239 454-4944
Richard Jones, *Principal*
EMP: 9 **EST:** 2007
SALES (est): 93.2K **Privately Held**
SIC: 3442 5023 Shutters, door or window: metal; window furnishings

(G-1396)
SWIFT PRINT SERVICE INC
1431 Se 10th St Unit B (33990-3630)
PHONE..................................239 458-2212
Jerry Kuhen, *President*
Mike Shough, *Mfg Staff*

Victoria Kuhn, *Purchasing*
EMP: 5 **EST:** 1994
SALES (est): 467.2K **Privately Held**
WEB: www.floridaprinter.com
SIC: 2752 Commercial printing, offset

(G-1397)
T & E PAVERS INC
1319 Sw 10th Pl (33991-2912)
PHONE..................................239 243-6229
Tarcilla Vianna, *Principal*
EMP: 7 **EST:** 2009
SALES (est): 86.7K **Privately Held**
SIC: 3531 Pavers

(G-1398)
TDT MANUFACTURING LLC (PA)
2137 Se 19th Pl (33990-3112)
PHONE..................................239 573-7498
Dennis F Walsh, *Manager*
EMP: 7 **EST:** 2018
SALES (est): 93.1K **Privately Held**
SIC: 3999 Manufacturing industries

(G-1399)
THINK OUTLOUD PRINTING
613 Sw Pine Island Rd (33991-1992)
PHONE..................................239 800-3219
EMP: 7 **EST:** 2015
SALES (est): 357.3K **Privately Held**
SIC: 2759 Screen printing

(G-1400)
TRADEWIND CUSTOM CABINETRY LLC
1213 Cape Coral Pkwy E (33904-9604)
PHONE..................................239 257-3295
Paul Beattie, *Principal*
Mark Zinn, *Broker*
Jill Jones, *Sales Staff*
Heather Metsch, *Sales Staff*
EMP: 7 **EST:** 2014
SALES (est): 276.3K **Privately Held**
SIC: 2434 Wood kitchen cabinets

(G-1401)
TROPIX MARBLE COMPANY
17121 Primavera Cir (33909-3026)
PHONE..................................239 334-2371
Sean W Hassett, *President*
EMP: 13 **EST:** 1958
SALES (est): 439.8K **Privately Held**
SIC: 3281 5032 Bathroom fixtures, cut stone; brick, stone & related material

(G-1402)
TURBINE GENERATOR MAINT INC (PA)
125 Sw 3rd Pl Ste 300 (33991-2029)
PHONE..................................239 573-1233
David Branton, *CEO*
Robert W Davis, *Finance Dir*
Michael Lake, *Sales Dir*
◆ **EMP:** 25 **EST:** 2007
SQ FT: 8,000
SALES (est): 21.6MM **Privately Held**
WEB: www.turbinegenerator.com
SIC: 3511 Turbines & turbine generator sets

(G-1403)
VEGA
447 Ne 8th Ter (33909-1969)
PHONE..................................239 574-1798
Deborah Vega, *Principal*
EMP: 7 **EST:** 2012
SALES (est): 251K **Privately Held**
WEB: www.euphoria4two.com
SIC: 3497 Metal foil & leaf

(G-1404)
VITERRA AFFORDABLE SHUTTERS
1104 Se 46th Ln Ste 2 (33904-8882)
PHONE..................................239 738-6364
Terry Mc Dermott, *Principal*
EMP: 8 **EST:** 2008
SALES (est): 147.4K **Privately Held**
SIC: 3089 Shutters, plastic

(G-1405)
W E CONNERY BOAT BUILDERS
5787 Sw 9th Ct (33914-8004)
PHONE..................................239 549-8014
Edwin Connery, *Owner*

EMP: 7 **EST:** 1991
SALES (est): 382.8K **Privately Held**
SIC: 3732 3089 Boats, fiberglass: building & repairing; plastic boats & other marine equipment

(G-1406)
WALTZING WATERS INC
1410 Se 10th St (33990-3604)
PHONE..................................239 574-5181
Michael Przystawik, *President*
EMP: 8 **EST:** 1971
SQ FT: 8,000
SALES (est): 1.6MM **Privately Held**
WEB: www.liquidfireworks.com
SIC: 3499 Fountains (except drinking), metal

(G-1407)
WICKED DOLPHIN DISTILLERY
131 Sw 3rd Pl (33991-2011)
PHONE..................................239 565-7947
EMP: 7 **EST:** 2017
SALES (est): 70.4K **Privately Held**
WEB: www.wickeddolphin.com
SIC: 2085 Distilled & blended liquors

(G-1408)
WILDNER SIGN & PAINT CO
17 Nicholas Pkwy W (33991-2879)
PHONE..................................239 997-5155
Gary Wildner, *Director*
EMP: 7 **EST:** 2006
SALES (est): 150K **Privately Held**
SIC: 3993 Signs & advertising specialties

Carrabelle
Franklin County

(G-1409)
CARRABELLE BEACH AN RVC
1843 Highway 98 W (32322-3006)
PHONE..................................850 697-8813
Andrew F Cates, *President*
EMP: 7 **EST:** 2017
SALES (est): 235.8K **Privately Held**
WEB: www.carrabellebeachrv.com
SIC: 2875 Fertilizers, mixing only

(G-1410)
DONALD SMITH LOGGING INC
127 Cora Mae Rd (32322-2064)
PHONE..................................850 697-3975
Shirley T Chason, *President*
EMP: 9 **EST:** 1988
SALES (est): 442.4K **Privately Held**
WEB: www.kulinarykingscatering.com
SIC: 2411 4212 Logging; local trucking, without storage

Casselberry
Seminole County

(G-1411)
CALVERT MANUFACTURING INC
Also Called: Calvert Solutions
228 Colombo Dr (32707-3308)
PHONE..................................407 331-5522
Dana Tucker, *CEO*
Albert A Rollins Jr, *Vice Pres*
Albert Rollins, *Vice Pres*
EMP: 25 **EST:** 1976
SQ FT: 6,000
SALES (est): 1MM **Privately Held**
SIC: 3553 8711 Veneer mill machines; consulting engineer

(G-1412)
CHEM GUARD INC
3964 Buglers Rest Pl (32707-4709)
PHONE..................................407 402-2798
David McCullough, *President*
EMP: 10 **EST:** 2008
SALES (est): 84.7K **Privately Held**
SIC: 2899 Chemical preparations

(G-1413)
CLADDAH CORP
Also Called: Olde Hearth Bread Company
207 Reece Way Ste 1625 (32707-3880)
PHONE..................................407 834-8881
Shannon Talty, *President*
David Talty, *Partner*
Janice Brahm, *Vice Pres*
EMP: 11 **EST:** 1998
SALES (est): 901.2K **Privately Held**
WEB: www.oldehearthbreadcompany.com
SIC: 2051 5461 Bread, all types (white, wheat, rye, etc): fresh or frozen; bakeries

(G-1414)
DARMERICA LLC
198 Wilshire Blvd (32707-5352)
P.O. Box 219, Goldenrod (32733-0219)
PHONE..................................321 219-9111
Wayne Maccinis,
EMP: 8 **EST:** 2016
SALES (est): 810.7K **Privately Held**
WEB: www.darmerica.com
SIC: 2834 Pharmaceutical preparations

(G-1415)
DELRAY PIN FACTORY INTL INC
1009 Howell Harbor Dr (32707-5810)
PHONE..................................561 994-1680
Martin Fox, *President*
Barbara Fox, *Vice Pres*
EMP: 5 **EST:** 1990
SALES (est): 409.8K **Privately Held**
WEB: www.delraypin.com
SIC: 3961 3993 Pins (jewelry), except precious metal; advertising novelties

(G-1416)
FLORIDA NATURAL FLAVORS INC
170 Lyman Rd (32707-2803)
P.O. Box 181125 (32718-1125)
PHONE..................................407 834-5979
Dave Erdman, *President*
David A Erdman, *President*
Jeffrey Smail, *General Mgr*
Garry L Erdman, *Vice Pres*
Scott Munson, *Purchasing*
▼ **EMP:** 35 **EST:** 1983
SQ FT: 32,500
SALES (est): 6.9MM **Privately Held**
WEB: www.floridanaturalflavors.com
SIC: 2087 Flavoring extracts & syrups

(G-1417)
H & H GYPSUM LLC
371 Oleander Way Ste 1325 (32707-3273)
PHONE..................................321 972-5571
Curtis House, *President*
EMP: 8 **EST:** 2017
SALES (est): 257.8K **Privately Held**
WEB: www.hhgypsum.com
SIC: 3275 Gypsum products

(G-1418)
HARRIS AERIAL LLC (PA)
1043 Seminola Blvd (32707-3516)
PHONE..................................407 725-7886
Benjamin Harris, *CEO*
Patrick Burton, *Principal*
Ethan Wash, *Principal*
EMP: 10 **EST:** 2014
SALES (est): 1.7MM **Privately Held**
WEB: www.harrisaerial.com
SIC: 3861 3721 Aerial cameras; aircraft

(G-1419)
INSTANT LOCATE INC
Also Called: Big League Cards
920 State Road 436 (32707-5633)
PHONE..................................800 431-0812
Alan P Narzissenfeld RES, *President*
EMP: 7 **EST:** 2013
SALES (est): 165.4K **Privately Held**
WEB: www.thenarzgroup.com
SIC: 2752 Commercial printing, lithographic

(G-1420)
J CUBE INC
180 E Trade Winds Rd (32708-3521)
PHONE..................................407 699-6866
Joe Casalese, *Branch Mgr*
EMP: 13

SALES (corp-wide): 109.1K **Privately Held**
WEB: www.j-cube.jp
SIC: 3721 Airplanes, fixed or rotary wing
PA: J Cube Inc
12260 Pescara Ln
Orlando FL

(G-1421)
JET-SET PRINTING INC
130 N Cypress Way (32707-3216)
PHONE....................407 339-1900
Mary Stanley, *President*
EMP: 5 **EST:** 1976
SQ FT: 5,000
SALES (est): 448.2K **Privately Held**
WEB: www.jetsetprintingorlando.com
SIC: 2759 2791 2789 2752 Screen printing; typesetting; bookbinding & related work; commercial printing, lithographic

(G-1422)
LILES OIL COMPANY
201 Kraft Dr (32707-5746)
PHONE....................407 739-2083
David L Liles, *President*
David Liles, *Owner*
EMP: 10 **EST:** 1990
SALES (est): 580.1K **Privately Held**
WEB: www.lilesoilco.com
SIC: 2869 Fuels

(G-1423)
MAGIC FABRICATORS INC
320 Commercial St (32707-3207)
PHONE....................407 332-0722
Mateen Qadri, *President*
▼ **EMP:** 10 **EST:** 1991
SQ FT: 5,000
SALES (est): 979.7K **Privately Held**
WEB: www.magicfabricators.com
SIC: 3441 Fabricated structural metal

(G-1424)
MAGNOLIA MILLWORK INTL INC
231 Plaza Oval (32707-2934)
PHONE....................407 585-3470
David Chauvin, *President*
Charles Palmer, *CFO*
EMP: 7 **EST:** 2014
SALES (est): 130.4K **Privately Held**
SIC: 2431 5211 Millwork; millwork & lumber

(G-1425)
MF INDUSTRIES LLC
Also Called: Franczak Roofing
1215 Guinevere Dr (32707-4543)
PHONE....................407 457-7531
Matt Franczak, *Principal*
EMP: 7 **EST:** 2018
SALES (est): 259.1K **Privately Held**
SIC: 3999 Manufacturing industries

(G-1426)
NEV INTERNATIONAL INC
1211 State Road 436 # 141 (32707-6442)
P.O. Box 181428 (32718-1428)
PHONE....................407 671-0045
▲ **EMP:** 15
SQ FT: 15,000
SALES: 2MM **Privately Held**
SIC: 3711 Mfg Motor Vehicle/Car Bodies

(G-1427)
PERFORMANCE PUMPS INC
321 Oleander Way (32707-3244)
PHONE....................407 339-6700
Jonathan Kenney, *President*
Michael Hase, *President*
Bradley Share, *Treasurer*
EMP: 23 **EST:** 1994
SALES (est): 1MM **Privately Held**
SIC: 3561 5084 Pumps & pumping equipment; industrial machinery & equipment

(G-1428)
PIPETTE SOLUTIONS LLC
1749 Grand Rue Dr (32707-2427)
PHONE....................877 974-7388
EMP: 7 **EST:** 2008
SALES (est): 331K **Privately Held**
WEB: www.thepipettesolution.com
SIC: 3826 Analytical instruments

(G-1429)
PLASMA BIOLIFE SERVICES L P
1385 State Road 436 (32707-6503)
PHONE....................407 388-1052
EMP: 9 **Privately Held**
WEB: www.biolifeplasma.com
SIC: 2836 Plasmas
HQ: Biolife Plasma Services L.P.
1200 Lakeside Dr
Bannockburn IL 60015
224 940-2000

(G-1430)
PLATINUM SIGNS AND DESIGN LLC
352 W Melody Ln (32707-3279)
PHONE....................407 971-3640
Tony Warren, *Office Mgr*
Jayeshbhai Patel, *Mng Member*
EMP: 8 **EST:** 2005
SQ FT: 4,500
SALES (est): 1.5MM **Privately Held**
WEB: www.platinum-signs.com
SIC: 3993 7389 Signs & advertising specialties; advertising, promotional & trade show services; sign painting & lettering shop

(G-1431)
R C SPECIALIZED INTERNATIONAL
1436 State Road 436 (32707-6572)
PHONE....................407 681-5905
Robert A Michael, *President*
EMP: 7 **EST:** 2007
SALES (est): 131.7K **Privately Held**
SIC: 3714 Motor vehicle parts & accessories

(G-1432)
SAFETY INTL BAGS & STRAPS INC
160 Lyman Rd (32707-2801)
PHONE....................407 830-0888
Henry Sanders, *President*
Bonnie Manjura, *Chairman*
◆ **EMP:** 14 **EST:** 1989
SQ FT: 17,000
SALES (est): 832K **Privately Held**
SIC: 2393 3842 Canvas bags; restraints, patient

(G-1433)
SIGN-O-SAURUS INC
3008 S Us Highway 17/92 (32707-2911)
PHONE....................407 677-8965
Alan Migliorato, *Principal*
EMP: 8 **EST:** 2008
SALES (est): 874.3K **Privately Held**
WEB: www.sign-o-saurus.com
SIC: 3993 Signs, not made in custom sign painting shops

(G-1434)
T & C GODBY ENTERPRISES INC
Also Called: Fastsigns
915 State Road 436 (32707-5632)
PHONE....................407 831-6334
Timm A Godby, *President*
EMP: 18 **EST:** 1992
SQ FT: 2,150
SALES (est): 856.5K **Privately Held**
WEB: www.fastsigns.com
SIC: 3993 Signs & advertising specialties

(G-1435)
THERMOCARBON INC (PA)
391 W Melody Ln (32707-3259)
P.O. Box 181220 (32718-1220)
PHONE....................407 834-7800
John Boucher, *President*
David Bajune, *Vice Pres*
Irene Miller, *Technical Staff*
EMP: 33 **EST:** 1978
SQ FT: 14,000
SALES (est): 4MM **Privately Held**
WEB: www.dicing.com
SIC: 3545 Diamond cutting tools for turning, boring, burnishing, etc.

(G-1436)
WESOL DISTRIBUTION LLC
1486 Seminola Blvd Unit 1 (32707-3640)
PHONE....................407 921-9248

Gerald A Wesol, *Mng Member*
EMP: 5 **EST:** 2007
SQ FT: 1,600
SALES (est): 431.5K **Privately Held**
WEB: www.wesoldistribution.com
SIC: 2389 Men's miscellaneous accessories

Cedar Key
Levy County

(G-1437)
1842 DAILY GRIND & MERCANTILE
598 2nd St (32625-5120)
P.O. Box 565 (32625-0565)
PHONE....................352 543-5004
Terry E Williams, *Principal*
EMP: 6 **EST:** 2016
SALES (est): 306.1K **Privately Held**
SIC: 3599 Grinding castings for the trade

Celebration
Osceola County

(G-1438)
KEMPHARM INC (PA)
1180 Celebration Blvd # 10 (34747-4950)
PHONE....................321 939-3416
Travis D Mickle, *Ch of Bd*
Richard W Pascoe, *Ch of Bd*
Sven Guenther, *Exec VP*
Andrew Barrett, *Vice Pres*
Nichol Ochsner, *Vice Pres*
EMP: 5 **EST:** 2006
SQ FT: 17,000
SALES (est): 28.6MM **Publicly Held**
WEB: www.kempharm.com
SIC: 2834 Pharmaceutical preparations

(G-1439)
ORION TRAVEL TECHNOLOGIES INC (PA)
200 Celebration Pl # 840 (34747-5483)
PHONE....................407 574-6649
Gary German, *CEO*
EMP: 10 **EST:** 2015
SQ FT: 2,000
SALES (est): 3.2MM **Privately Held**
WEB: www.oriontraveltechnologies.com
SIC: 7372 Business oriented computer software

Center Hill
Sumter County

(G-1440)
CENTRAL BEEF IND LLC
Also Called: Chernin Beef Industries
571 W Kings Hwy (33514-4001)
PHONE....................352 793-3671
Ida Raye Chernin, *Managing Prtnr*
Randy Bertrand, *Purch Agent*
Adam Chernin,
Alex Chernin,
EMP: 225 **EST:** 1945
SQ FT: 60,000
SALES (est): 21.5MM **Privately Held**
SIC: 2011 Beef products from beef slaughtered on site

(G-1441)
FCS HOLDINGS INC
530 W Kings Hwy (33514-4002)
PHONE....................352 793-5151
John B Collins, *Manager*
EMP: 38 **Privately Held**
SIC: 1481 Nonmetallic mineral services
PA: Fcs Holdings, Inc.
8500 Us Highway 441
Leesburg FL 34788

Century
Escambia County

(G-1442)
CENTURY MILLWORKS
6082 Industrial Blvd (32535-3312)
P.O. Box 248 (32535-0248)
PHONE....................850 256-2565
Don Dockens, *President*
Sandra Dockens, *Treasurer*
EMP: 10 **EST:** 1984
SQ FT: 5,000
SALES (est): 434K **Privately Held**
WEB: www.centurymillworks.com
SIC: 2431 2434 Doors, wood; wood kitchen cabinets

Chiefland
Levy County

(G-1443)
AMERICAN TRUSS
6760 Nw 138th Pl (32626-8280)
PHONE....................352 493-9700
Terry Hassell, *Partner*
EMP: 7 **EST:** 2007
SALES (est): 169.6K **Privately Held**
SIC: 2439 Structural wood members

(G-1444)
AMERICAN TRUSS CHIEFLAND LL
6750 Nw 138th Pl (32626-8280)
PHONE....................352 493-9700
Michael Martin, *Principal*
EMP: 9 **EST:** 2007
SALES (est): 321.7K **Privately Held**
WEB: www.americantrussofchiefland.com
SIC: 2439 Trusses, wooden roof

(G-1445)
ANDERSON COLUMBIA CO INC
Also Called: Anderson Materials
8191 Nw 160th St (32626)
P.O. Box 2209 (32644-2209)
PHONE....................352 463-6342
Diana Stevens, *Manager*
EMP: 8
SALES (corp-wide): 168.7MM **Privately Held**
WEB: www.andersoncolumbia.com
SIC: 3273 5211 3272 Ready-mixed concrete; cement; concrete products, precast
PA: Anderson Columbia Co., Inc.
871 Nw Guerdon St
Lake City FL 32055
386 752-7585

(G-1446)
B SQUARED OF CHIEFLAND LLC
710 Nw 17th Ave (32626-1736)
P.O. Box 582 (32644-0582)
PHONE....................352 507-2195
Bradlee Bruner, *Principal*
EMP: 7 **EST:** 2012
SALES (est): 229.4K **Privately Held**
SIC: 2711 Newspapers, publishing & printing

(G-1447)
CHIEFLAND CRAB COMPANY INC
1606 Sw 4th Pl (32626-0260)
P.O. Box 174, Steinhatchee (32359-0174)
PHONE....................352 493-4887
EMP: 25
SQ FT: 5,000
SALES (est): 3.3MM **Privately Held**
SIC: 2092 Mfg Fresh/Frozen Packaged Fish

(G-1448)
MARCUS V HALL
14271 Nw 66th Ave (32626-2211)
PHONE....................352 490-9694
Marcus V Hall, *Owner*
▲ **EMP:** 6 **EST:** 1997
SALES (est): 524.2K **Privately Held**
SIC: 3272 Steps, prefabricated concrete

(G-1449)
PRINT SHOP OF CHIEFLAND INC
Also Called: Print Shop, The
208 N Main St (32626-0802)
P.O. Box 606 (32644-0606)
PHONE.....................................352 493-0322
Richard Pelletir, *CEO*
Linda Pelletire, *President*
EMP: 5 **EST:** 1989
SALES (est): 487.4K **Privately Held**
WEB: www.printshopofchiefland.com
SIC: 2752 5999 2759 Commercial printing, offset; rubber stamps; visiting cards (including business): printing

(G-1450)
SHEPS WELDING INC
9791 Nw County Road 345 (32626-7545)
P.O. Box 296 (32644-0296)
PHONE.....................................352 493-1730
Derwood Sheppard, *President*
Susan Sheppard, *Admin Sec*
EMP: 5 **EST:** 1975
SQ FT: 6,000
SALES (est): 599.9K **Privately Held**
WEB: www.shepswelding.net
SIC: 7692 Welding repair

(G-1451)
USHER LAND & TIMBER INC
6551 Nw 100th St (32626-4229)
P.O. Box 843 (32644-0843)
PHONE.....................................352 493-4221
Ken Griner, *President*
Lynetta Usher Griner, *Corp Secy*
John Fisher, *Vice Pres*
Lynetta Griner, *Admin Sec*
EMP: 40 **EST:** 1950
SQ FT: 2,500
SALES (est): 1.3MM **Privately Held**
WEB: www.usherlandtimber.com
SIC: 2411 4212 Logging; local trucking, without storage

Chipley
Washington County

(G-1452)
ABC FENCE SYSTEMS INC (PA)
963 Industrial Dr (32428-6314)
P.O. Box 119 (32428-0119)
PHONE.....................................850 638-8876
Kelly Brock, *President*
Marlene Brock, *Vice Pres*
Vann Brock, *Vice Pres*
EMP: 13 **EST:** 1982
SQ FT: 560
SALES (est): 4MM **Privately Held**
WEB: www.abcfencesystems.com
SIC: 2499 5411 Fencing, wood; grocery stores

(G-1453)
BACK LORY LEE
Also Called: Medical Concepts
403 Cutchins Mill Rd (32428-4397)
PHONE.....................................850 638-5430
Lory L Back, *Owner*
Douglas Back, *Owner*
EMP: 8 **EST:** 1993
SQ FT: 1,200
SALES (est): 150K **Privately Held**
WEB: www.medicalconceptschipley.com
SIC: 3841 Surgical & medical instruments

(G-1454)
CORBIN SAND AND CLAY INC
1177 Jackson Ave (32428-2004)
PHONE.....................................850 638-8462
Travis Corbin, *CEO*
EMP: 5 **EST:** 2001
SALES (est): 377.6K **Privately Held**
WEB: www.corbinautosales.com
SIC: 1442 Construction sand & gravel

(G-1455)
D & S LOGGING INC
261 Highway 273 (32428-4209)
P.O. Box 935 (32428-0935)
PHONE.....................................850 638-5500
Dwayne Taylor, *Principal*
Barry McGaughey, *Vice Pres*

Rex Dwayne Taylor, *Director*
David Morris, *Director*
EMP: 6 **EST:** 1997
SALES (est): 719.1K **Privately Held**
WEB: www.panhandleforestry.net
SIC: 2411 3272 Logging camps & contractors; poles & posts, concrete

(G-1456)
EZY-GLIDE INC
715 7th St (32428-1932)
PHONE.....................................850 638-4403
Bobby Padgett, *President*
Bobby R Padgett, *President*
Stephen Padgett, *Officer*
Tyler Padgett, *Officer*
▲ **EMP:** 7 **EST:** 1981
SQ FT: 4,800
SALES (est): 600K **Privately Held**
WEB: www.ezyglide.com
SIC: 3714 Steering mechanisms, motor vehicle; motor vehicle steering systems & parts

(G-1457)
RANDY MORRIS LOGGING INC
4259 Highway 77 (32428-4910)
PHONE.....................................850 773-9010
EMP: 12
SQ FT: 3,300
SALES (est): 1.5MM **Privately Held**
SIC: 2411 Logging Contractor

(G-1458)
WASHINGTON COUNTY NEWS (DH)
1364 N Railroad Ave (32428-1456)
PHONE.....................................850 638-4242
Nicole Barefield, *Principal*
EMP: 16 **EST:** 1924
SQ FT: 7,000
SALES (est): 10MM
SALES (corp-wide): 3.2B **Publicly Held**
WEB: www.washingtoncounty.news
SIC: 2711 Commercial printing & newspaper publishing combined; newspapers, publishing & printing
HQ: Panama City News Herald
501 W 11th St
Panama City FL 32401
850 747-5000

(G-1459)
WEST POINT STEVENS
1414 Main St (32428-6952)
PHONE.....................................850 638-9421
John Martin, *General Mgr*
Steve Harr, *Engineer*
EMP: 6 **EST:** 2014
SALES (est): 359.5K **Privately Held**
WEB: www.westpointhome.com
SIC: 2211 Broadwoven fabric mills, cotton

(G-1460)
WESTPOINT HOME INC
1056 Commerce Ave (32428-6395)
PHONE.....................................850 415-4100
Terry Ellis, *Engineer*
Vinta Yon, *Human Res Mgr*
Normand Savaria, *Mng Member*
Kristopher Graham, *Manager*
EMP: 273 **Publicly Held**
WEB: www.westpointhome.com
SIC: 2211 Sheets, bedding & table cloths: cotton
HQ: Westpoint Home, Inc.
777 3rd Ave Fl 7
New York NY 10017
212 930-2000

(G-1461)
WESTPOINT HOME INC
Also Called: Home Fashion Source
1414 Main St (32428-6952)
P.O. Box 625 (32428-0625)
PHONE.....................................850 415-4100
Steve Harr, *Engineer*
Terry Ellis, *Manager*
Courtney Hoard, *Manager*
EMP: 818 **Publicly Held**
WEB: www.westpointhome.com
SIC: 2211 2392 2391 Broadwoven fabric mills, cotton; household furnishings; curtains & draperies

HQ: Westpoint Home, Inc.
777 3rd Ave Fl 7
New York NY 10017
212 930-2000

Christmas
Orange County

(G-1462)
FERRERA EMBROIDERY & PRTG SER
21709 Hobby Horse Ln (32709-9275)
PHONE.....................................786 667-2680
Lenin Ferrera, *Principal*
EMP: 6 **EST:** 2016
SALES (est): 393.3K **Privately Held**
SIC: 2759 Screen printing

Chuluota
Seminole County

(G-1463)
ALICIA DIAGNOSTIC INC
150 W 11th St (32766-9454)
PHONE.....................................407 365-8498
Hassan Soltani, *President*
John Tobin, *Vice Pres*
EMP: 10 **EST:** 1989
SQ FT: 5,000
SALES (est): 902.2K **Privately Held**
SIC: 3841 Surgical & medical instruments

(G-1464)
BEFORE WIND BLOWS LLC
282 Osprey Lakes Cir (32766-6664)
PHONE.....................................407 977-4833
EMP: 7
SALES (est): 736.5K **Privately Held**
SIC: 3442 Mfg Metal Doors/Sash/Trim

(G-1465)
JSL ENTERPRISES OF ORLANDO
Also Called: Glass Works
1434 Circle Ln (32766-9283)
PHONE.....................................386 767-9653
Steven Lovell, *President*
Harry Waltz, *Vice Pres*
▲ **EMP:** 11 **EST:** 1987
SQ FT: 12,500
SALES (est): 350.1K **Privately Held**
SIC: 3231 5231 3211 Products of purchased glass; glass, leaded or stained; flat glass

Citra
Marion County

(G-1466)
A L BAXLEY & SONS INC
1542 E Highway 329 (32113-4238)
P.O. Box 180, Sparr (32192-0180)
PHONE.....................................352 629-5137
Daniel Baxley, *Vice Pres*
Tonya Baxley, *Vice Pres*
Glen Davis, *Treasurer*
EMP: 16 **EST:** 1977
SALES (est): 1MM **Privately Held**
WEB: www.albaxleyandsons.com
SIC: 2411 2426 2421 Logging camps & contractors; hardwood dimension & flooring mills; sawmills & planing mills, general

(G-1467)
MEI COMPANIES INC
12150 Ne 7th Ave (32113-4258)
P.O. Box 1672, Anthony (32617-1672)
PHONE.....................................352 361-6895
Christopher N Bowden, *CEO*
EMP: 8 **EST:** 2017
SALES (est): 653.2K **Privately Held**
SIC: 1389 Construction, repair & dismantling services

(G-1468)
SCKY INDUSTRIES INC
855 W Highway 318 (32113-2145)
PHONE.....................................352 595-7782
Allen Perry, *Principal*

EMP: 7 **EST:** 2006
SALES (est): 102.6K **Privately Held**
SIC: 3999 Manufacturing industries

Clearwater
Pinellas County

(G-1469)
180BYTWO
600 Cleveland St (33755-4151)
PHONE.....................................202 403-7097
Travis Thomas, *Manager*
Alana Hallquist, *Director*
Onna Harrigan, *Director*
Eric Shaffer, *Administration*
EMP: 8 **EST:** 2017
SALES (est): 1.5MM **Privately Held**
WEB: www.anteriad.com
SIC: 7372 Prepackaged software

(G-1470)
AAR MANUFACTURING INC
Also Called: AAR Composites
14201 Myerlake Cir (33760-2824)
PHONE.....................................727 539-8585
Michael Pentedemos, *President*
Erica Barrett, *Business Mgr*
Andy Coomer, *Business Mgr*
Melissa Logan, *Business Mgr*
Dan Fitzpatrick, *VP Opers*
EMP: 53
SALES (corp-wide): 1.8B **Publicly Held**
WEB: www.aarcorp.com
SIC: 3728 Aircraft assemblies, subassemblies & parts
HQ: Aar Manufacturing, Inc.
1100 N Wood Dale Rd
Wood Dale IL 60191
630 227-2000

(G-1471)
ACCON MARINE INC
13665 Automobile Blvd (33762-3843)
PHONE.....................................727 572-9202
Bernd Czipri, *President*
▲ **EMP:** 13 **EST:** 1980
SQ FT: 19,000
SALES (est): 2.1MM **Privately Held**
WEB: www.acconmarine.com
SIC: 3429 Marine hardware

(G-1472)
ACE MECHANICAL INC
14455 Myerlake Cir (33760-2840)
PHONE.....................................727 304-6277
Pamela Thompson, *Controller*
EMP: 6 **EST:** 2019
SALES (est): 405.5K **Privately Held**
SIC: 3317 Tubing, mechanical or hypodermic sizes: cold drawn stainless

(G-1473)
ACTRON ENTITIES INC
Also Called: Actron Engineering
13089 60th St N (33760-3915)
PHONE.....................................727 531-5871
John Staszewski, *President*
Alana Dergham, *Exec VP*
Heather Eicher, *Buyer*
Tina Mam, *Sales Staff*
EMP: 60 **EST:** 2006
SQ FT: 28,500
SALES (est): 10.4MM **Privately Held**
WEB: www.actronengineering.com
SIC: 3444 Sheet metal specialties, not stamped

(G-1474)
ADAMAS INSTRUMENT CORPORATION
13247 38th St N Ste B (33762-4234)
P.O. Box 17558 (33762-0558)
PHONE.....................................727 540-0033
Thomas C Smith, *Managing Dir*
EMP: 10 **EST:** 1988
SALES (est): 890.7K **Privately Held**
SIC: 3915 3841 3559 Jewel preparing: instruments, tools, watches & jewelry; diamond cutting & polishing; jewel cutting, drilling, polishing, recutting or setting; ophthalmic instruments & apparatus; semiconductor manufacturing machinery

(G-1475)
ADVANCED ENGINE TECH LLC
Also Called: A E T
3087 Cherry Ln (33759-4306)
PHONE..........................727 744-2935
Rck Pelfrey, *President*
Dale Pelfrey,
EMP: 5 **EST:** 2006
SALES (est): 391.2K **Privately Held**
WEB: www.aetco.com
SIC: 2992 3463 3519 Lubricating oils &
greases; oils & greases, blending & compounding; engine or turbine forgings, non-ferrous; parts & accessories, internal
combustion engines

(G-1476)
ADVANCED METAL WORKS INC
1780 Calumet St (33765-1142)
PHONE..........................727 449-9353
Patrick Bogart, *President*
Terri Haire, *Admin Sec*
EMP: 10 **EST:** 1992
SQ FT: 8,000
SALES (est): 2MM **Privately Held**
WEB: www.exometalfab.com
SIC: 3699 Electron beam metal cutting,
forming or welding machines

(G-1477)
ADVER-T SCREEN PRINTING INC
408 S Saturn Ave (33755-6550)
PHONE..........................727 443-5525
William Peluso, *President*
Scott Walker, *Vice Pres*
Brian Peluso, *Sales Mgr*
EMP: 14 **EST:** 1978
SQ FT: 4,600
SALES (est): 1.5MM **Privately Held**
WEB: www.advertscreenprinting.com
SIC: 2759 Screen printing

(G-1478)
AEROSONIC LLC
1212 N Hercules Ave (33765-1920)
PHONE..........................727 461-3000
Joe Grote, *President*
Kwanghee H Han, *Regional Mgr*
Scott Sweet, *Vice Pres*
Alaine Ferreira, *Production*
Justin Banchy, *Engineer*
EMP: 150 **EST:** 2013
SALES (est): 64MM
SALES (corp-wide): 4.8B **Publicly Held**
WEB: www.aerosonic.com
SIC: 3728 Aircraft parts & equipment
HQ: Transdigm, Inc.
1301 E 9th St Ste 300
Cleveland OH 44114

(G-1479)
AGORA SALES INC
Also Called: Agora Leather Products
4215 E Bay Dr Apt 802 (33764-6970)
PHONE..........................727 490-0499
Tom Ayers, *Sales Mgr*
EMP: 93
SALES (corp-wide): 30.6MM **Privately
Held**
WEB: www.agoraedge.com
SIC: 3161 Cases, carrying
PA: Agora Sales, Inc.
2101 28th St N
Saint Petersburg FL 33713
727 321-0707

(G-1480)
AIR AUTHORITIES OF TAMPA INC
4810 110th Ave N Ste 1a (33762-4935)
PHONE..........................727 525-1575
EMP: 5
SALES (est): 674.3K **Privately Held**
SIC: 3822 Mfg Environmental Controls

(G-1481)
AJ ASSOC MFG & ENGRG CO INC
Also Called: Aj Associates
5300 115th Ave N (33760-4830)
PHONE..........................727 258-0994
Josephine Zdzierak, *Ch of Bd*
Andrew Zdzierak, *President*
EMP: 13 **EST:** 1991

SQ FT: 2,800
SALES (est): 4.3MM **Privately Held**
WEB: www.ajflorida.com
SIC: 3728 Aircraft parts & equipment

(G-1482)
AJ ASSOCIATES
11346 53rd St N (33760-4821)
PHONE..........................727 258-0994
Fax: 727 539-0904
EMP: 13
SALES (est): 2.7MM **Privately Held**
SIC: 3728 Mfg Aircraft Parts/Equipment

(G-1483)
AK U TEC MACHINE & TOOL INC
13191 Automobile Blvd (33762-4105)
PHONE..........................727 573-5211
Thomas P McDonald, *President*
Thomas P Mc Donald, *President*
EMP: 5 **EST:** 1989
SQ FT: 3,500
SALES (est): 488.5K **Privately Held**
SIC: 3599 Machine shop, jobbing & repair

(G-1484)
ALEX ROBERT SILVERSMITH INC
625 Pinellas St Unit C (33756-3351)
PHONE..........................727 442-7333
Robert Alex, *President*
EMP: 6 **EST:** 1980
SALES (est): 363.1K **Privately Held**
SIC: 3471 Plating of metals or formed
products

(G-1485)
ALL BRGHT ELECTROPOLISHING INC
5100 Ulmerton Rd Ste 7 (33760-4016)
PHONE..........................727 449-9353
Dustin Colina, *President*
Patrick Bogart, *Principal*
EMP: 5 **EST:** 1997
SQ FT: 4,000
SALES (est): 450.6K **Privately Held**
WEB: www.all-bright.com
SIC: 3471 Electroplating of metals or
formed products

(G-1486)
ALL SOUTHERN FABRICATORS INC
5010 126th Ave N (33760-4607)
P.O. Box 658, Pinellas Park (33780-0658)
PHONE..........................727 573-4846
Manuel Santana Jr, *President*
EMP: 43 **EST:** 1967
SQ FT: 40,000
SALES (est): 5.9MM **Privately Held**
WEB: www.allsouthern.com
SIC: 3469 3444 Household cooking &
kitchen utensils, metal; sheet metalwork

(G-1487)
ALLEN INDUSTRIES INC
11351 49th St N (33762-4808)
PHONE..........................727 573-3076
David Allen, *Owner*
Jeff Morrow, *Plant Mgr*
Steve Byrd, *Project Mgr*
Zachary Cesternino, *Project Mgr*
Christopher Cummings, *Project Mgr*
EMP: 60
SALES (corp-wide): 76.8MM **Privately
Held**
WEB: www.allenindustries.com
SIC: 3993 Signs, not made in custom sign
painting shops
PA: Allen Industries, Inc.
6434 Burnt Poplar Rd
Greensboro NC 27409
336 668-2791

(G-1488)
ALPHA INDUSTRIES INC
701 N Mlk Jr Ave (33755-4210)
PHONE..........................727 443-2673
Loleta Magers, *President*
EMP: 5 **EST:** 1971
SALES (est): 318.5K **Privately Held**
SIC: 3841 Medical instruments & equipment, blood & bone work

(G-1489)
ALTTEC CORPORATION
Also Called: Digital Control Company
4260 114th Ter N (33762-4905)
PHONE..........................727 547-1622
John D Cattel, *President*
EMP: 7 **EST:** 2005
SQ FT: 5,600
SALES (est): 952.2K **Privately Held**
SIC: 3625 Relays & industrial controls

(G-1490)
AMERICAN INTERNATIONAL MTR SVC
5150 Ulmerton Rd Ste 5 (33760-4013)
PHONE..........................727 573-9501
Dennis D Keihl, *President*
EMP: 6 **EST:** 1979
SQ FT: 4,800
SALES (est): 441.8K **Privately Held**
SIC: 7694 Electric motor repair

(G-1491)
AMERICAN PLASTIC SUP & MFG INC (PA)
Also Called: Design Cncpts By Amrcn Plitics
11601 56th Ct N (33760-4805)
PHONE..........................727 573-0636
Robbin Belzer, *President*
Bob Belzer, *President*
Leslie Fields, *Manager*
▲ **EMP:** 20 **EST:** 1985
SQ FT: 12,000
SALES (est): 4.3MM **Privately Held**
WEB: www.americanplasticsupply.com
SIC: 3082 5162 3089 3732 Rods, unsupported plastic; tubes, unsupported plastic;
plastics sheets & rods; plastics basic
shapes; injection molding of plastics;
boats, rigid: plastics; forms (molds), for
foundry & plastics working machinery

(G-1492)
AMERICAN TECHNICAL MOLDING INC
Also Called: A T M
1700 Sunshine Dr (33765-1331)
PHONE..........................727 447-7377
Emilia G Opoulos, *CEO*
Emilia Giannakopoulos, *CEO*
Demetre Loulourgas, *President*
Penelope Loulourgas, *Vice Pres*
Victor Cohen, *Engineer*
◆ **EMP:** 91 **EST:** 1978
SQ FT: 140,000
SALES (est): 9.6MM **Privately Held**
WEB: www.atmmolding.com
SIC: 3089 Injection molding of plastics

(G-1493)
AMERICAN TOOL & MOLD INC
Also Called: American Technical Molding
1700 Sunshine Dr (33765-1331)
PHONE..........................727 447-7377
Emilia Loulourgas-Giannakopoul, *CEO*
Demetre Loulourgas, *President*
Tabitha Davis, *President*
Penelope Loulourgas, *Vice Pres*
Mark Tardif, *Plant Mgr*
◆ **EMP:** 180 **EST:** 1978
SQ FT: 150,000
SALES (est): 29.2MM **Privately Held**
WEB: www.a-t-m.com
SIC: 3089 Injection molding of plastics

(G-1494)
AMTECO MACHINE & MANUFACTURING
4652 107th Cir N (33762-5005)
PHONE..........................727 573-0993
Dennis Pavluk, *President*
EMP: 11 **EST:** 1978
SQ FT: 10,000
SALES (est): 156.1K **Privately Held**
WEB: www.rcamachine.com
SIC: 3599 Machine shop, jobbing & repair

(G-1495)
ANZIO IRONWORKS CORP
14605 49th St N Ste 8 (33762-2810)
PHONE..........................727 895-2019
Mike Remo, *President*
David Lydel, *Principal*
EMP: 5 **EST:** 1993

SALES (est): 440K **Privately Held**
WEB: www.anzioironworks.com
SIC: 3949 Sporting & athletic goods

(G-1496)
APYX MEDICAL CORPORATION (PA)
5115 Ulmerton Rd (33760-4004)
PHONE..........................727 384-2323
Charles D Goodwin, *CEO*
Andrew Makrides, *Ch of Bd*
John Andres, *Vice Ch Bd*
Todd Hornsby, *Exec VP*
Moshe Citronowicz, *Senior VP*
EMP: 203 **EST:** 1982
SQ FT: 60,000
SALES (est): 48.5MM **Publicly Held**
WEB: www.apyxmedical.com
SIC: 3841 Surgical & medical instruments

(G-1497)
ARCHITECTURAL GRAPHICS INC
5500 Rio Vista Dr (33760-3140)
PHONE..........................757 427-1900
Jason Chalaire, *Project Mgr*
EMP: 16
SALES (corp-wide): 212.5MM **Privately
Held**
WEB: www.agi.net
SIC: 3993 Signs, not made in custom sign
painting shops
PA: Architectural Graphics, Inc.
2655 International Pkwy
Virginia Beach VA 23452
800 877-7868

(G-1498)
ARDEN PHOTONICS LLC
4500 140th Ave N Ste 101 (33762-3848)
PHONE..........................727 478-2651
David Robinson, *President*
Lesley Allison, *Sales Staff*
Roger Frampton, *Manager*
Alistair Robinson, *Manager*
EMP: 10 **EST:** 2015
SQ FT: 300
SALES (est): 569.2K **Privately Held**
WEB: www.ardenphotonics.com
SIC: 3661 Fiber optics communications
equipment

(G-1499)
ARROWHEAD GLOBAL LLC
22033 Us Highway 19 N (33765-2362)
PHONE..........................727 497-7340
Chad Hill, *General Mgr*
Tiffani Hunley, *Manager*
Tara Potter, *Manager*
Tony Frasca, *Officer*
David W Rittenhouse,
EMP: 14 **EST:** 2013
SQ FT: 1,900
SALES (est): 3.7MM **Privately Held**
WEB: www.arrowheadglobal.com
SIC: 3728 5063 7373 3678 Research &
dev by manuf., aircraft parts & auxiliary
equip; lugs & connectors, electrical; computer integrated systems design; electronic connectors; fasteners; bolts, nuts,
rivets & washers

(G-1500)
ARTISTIC PAVERS LLC
12700 Automobile Blvd (33762-4719)
PHONE..........................727 573-0918
Robert B Welch, *President*
Sally Welch,
EMP: 11 **EST:** 2017
SALES (est): 2.3MM **Privately Held**
WEB: www.artistic-pavers.com
SIC: 3531 Pavers

(G-1501)
ASAP SIGNS & GRAPHICS OF FLA
509 D St (33756-3337)
PHONE..........................727 443-4878
EMP: 5
SALES: 450K **Privately Held**
SIC: 3993 Signs And Advertising Specialties

GEOGRAPHIC

(G-1502)
ASCO POWER TECHNOLOGIES LP
14550 58th St N (33760-2805)
PHONE..................................727 450-2730
Jose Cuevas, *District Mgr*
David Enfield, *Mfg Staff*
Mark Williams, *Engineer*
Andy Malcolm, *Branch Mgr*
Dana Papalardo, *Manager*
EMP: 8
SALES (corp-wide): 177.9K **Privately Held**
SIC: 3699 Electrical equipment & supplies
HQ: Asco Power Technologies, L.P.
　　160 Park Ave
　　Florham Park NJ 07932

(G-1503)
AVT TECHNOLOGY SOLUTIONS LLC
5350 Tech Data Dr (33760-3122)
PHONE..................................727 539-7429
Robert M Dutkowsky, *CEO*
Kimberly Freeman, *Opers Staff*
Cyndi Hash, *Manager*
EMP: 131 **EST:** 2016
SALES (est): 10.8MM
SALES (corp-wide): 31.6B **Publicly Held**
SIC: 7372 Prepackaged software
HQ: Tech Data Corporation
　　5350 Tech Data Dr
　　Clearwater FL 33760
　　727 539-7429

(G-1504)
AXIOM SERVICES INC (PA)
Also Called: Axiom International
1805 Drew St (33765-2918)
PHONE..................................727 442-7774
David Greenbaum, *CEO*
Ed Clark, *President*
Catherine Rossi, *Partner*
Hetha Chelin, *Exec VP*
Brendan Haggerty, *Exec VP*
EMP: 39 **EST:** 1984
SQ FT: 10,000
SALES (est): 9.9MM **Privately Held**
WEB: www.axiomint.com
SIC: 7372 7371 Prepackaged software;
　　computer software development

(G-1505)
AYANNA PLASTICS & ENGRG INC
4701 110th Ave N (33762-4912)
PHONE..................................727 561-4329
Daniel R Redmond Jr, *President*
Tammy E Redmond, *Vice Pres*
▲ **EMP:** 32 **EST:** 2001
SQ FT: 12,000
SALES (est): 5.9MM **Privately Held**
WEB: www.ayannaplastics.com
SIC: 3089 Injection molding of plastics

(G-1506)
AZIMUTH COMMUNICATIONS CORP
12770 44th St N (33762-4713)
PHONE..................................727 573-5735
D Peterson, *Adv Dir*
EMP: 7 **EST:** 2018
SALES (est): 223.9K **Privately Held**
SIC: 3663 Radio & TV communications
　　equipment

(G-1507)
B & R SALES CORPORATION
11551 43rd St N (33762-4925)
PHONE..................................727 571-2231
William Evans, *President*
EMP: 6 **EST:** 2001
SQ FT: 10,000
SALES (est): 739K **Privately Held**
WEB: www.clearwatermachining.com
SIC: 3089 Injection molding of plastics

(G-1508)
BACKTOCAD TECHNOLOGIES LLC
601 Cleveland St Ste 310 (33755-4164)
PHONE..................................727 303-0383
Andreas Kazmierczak, *CEO*
EMP: 6 **EST:** 2009

SALES (est): 1.4MM
SALES (corp-wide): 587.7K **Privately Held**
WEB: solutions.backtocad.com
SIC: 7372 7373 Prepackaged software;
　　computer-aided system services; com-
　　puter-aided design (CAD) systems serv-
　　ice; computer-aided engineering (CAE)
　　systems service
PA: Kazmierczak Software Gmbh
　　Raiffeisenstr. 30
　　Filderstadt BW 70794
　　711 518-6692

(G-1509)
BASEWEST INC
4240 116th Ter N (33762-4971)
PHONE..................................727 573-2700
Gary Leegate, *President*
Richard Barnes, *Vice Pres*
Tom Jurlina, *Vice Pres*
David Stanton, *Vice Pres*
Jim Leblanc, *QC Mgr*
EMP: 44 **EST:** 1991
SQ FT: 12,000
SALES (est): 6.9MM **Privately Held**
WEB: www.basewest.com
SIC: 3647 Vehicular lighting equipment;
　　aircraft lighting fixtures

(G-1510)
BASS AUTO INDUSTRIES LLC
2084 Range Rd (33765-2123)
PHONE..................................727 446-4051
EMP: 6 **EST:** 2018
SALES (est): 405.6K **Privately Held**
SIC: 3999 Manufacturing industries

(G-1511)
BATTERY POWER SOLUTIONS INC
936 Cleveland St Ste A (33755-4500)
PHONE..................................727 446-8400
Charles Van Breemen, *President*
EMP: 5 **EST:** 2005
SALES (est): 350.8K **Privately Held**
WEB: www.batterypowersolutions.net
SIC: 3694 Engine electrical equipment

(G-1512)
BAUSCH & LOMB INCORPORATED
21 N Park Place Blvd (33759-3917)
PHONE..................................727 724-6600
Lilian Eshem, *Mfg Mgr*
Tania Collazo, *Mfg Staff*
Wesley Wood, *Technical Mgr*
Lorenzo Salvatori, *Engineer*
Bryan Williams, *Engineer*
EMP: 174
SALES (corp-wide): 8.6B **Privately Held**
WEB: www.bausch.com
SIC: 3851 5048 Intraocular lenses; opto-
　　metric equipment & supplies
HQ: Bausch & Lomb Incorporated
　　400 Somerset Corp Blvd
　　Bridgewater NJ 08807
　　585 338-6000

(G-1513)
BAUSCH LOMB SURGICAL INC
21 N Park Place Blvd (33759-3917)
PHONE..................................727 724-6600
Jason Smith, *Vice Pres*
EMP: 13 **EST:** 2020
SALES (est): 1.3MM **Privately Held**
SIC: 3851 Ophthalmic goods

(G-1514)
BAYCARE HOME CARE INC
Also Called: Bay Area Prosthetics
1237 S Myrtle Ave (33756-3469)
PHONE..................................727 461-5878
EMP: 10
SALES (corp-wide): 463.9MM **Privately Held**
SIC: 3842 Mfg Surgical Appliances/Sup-
　　plies
HQ: Baycare Home Care, Inc.
　　8452 118th Ave
　　Largo FL 33773

(G-1515)
BEACHCHIP TECHNOLOGIES LLC
2655 Ulmerton Rd (33762-3337)
PHONE..................................727 643-8106
Peter Weyant, *Manager*
EMP: 6 **EST:** 2003
SQ FT: 400
SALES (est): 819.1K **Privately Held**
WEB: www.beachchip.com
SIC: 3559 5045 7379 Electronic compo-
　　nent making machinery; computer soft-
　　ware;

(G-1516)
BELQUETTE INC
3634 131st Ave N (33762-4262)
PHONE..................................727 329-9483
Brett Weibel, *CEO*
Mark Mombourquette, *Principal*
EMP: 6 **EST:** 2007
SALES (est): 894.6K **Privately Held**
WEB: www.coldesi.com
SIC: 3826 8711 Laser scientific & engi-
　　neering instruments; acoustical engineer-
　　ing

(G-1517)
BERRY GLOBAL INC
2940 Bay Meadow Ct (33761-3304)
PHONE..................................727 447-8845
Tim Leasure, *Vice Pres*
Gary Abraham, *VP Opers*
David Ashton, *Prdtn Mgr*
Robert Jenkins, *Production*
Donald Sharp, *Production*
EMP: 9 **Publicly Held**
WEB: www.berryglobal.com
SIC: 3089 Plastic containers, except foam
HQ: Berry Global, Inc.
　　101 Oakley St
　　Evansville IN 47710

(G-1518)
BHF PUBLISHING INC
14835 49th St N (33762-2806)
PHONE..................................727 536-2245
Freddie S Dixon Jr, *President*
EMP: 9 **EST:** 2005
SALES (est): 140.9K **Privately Held**
SIC: 2741 Miscellaneous publishing

(G-1519)
BIC CORPORATION
Also Called: Bic Graphic USA
14421 Myerlake Cir (33760-2840)
P.O. Box 23088, Tampa (33623-2088)
PHONE..................................727 536-7895
Gerard Krief, *VP Opers*
Cameron Koch, *Project Mgr*
Jeremy Miller, *Mfg Mgr*
Nick Undis, *Mfg Mgr*
Mike Mashburn, *Mfg Spvr*
EMP: 800
SALES (corp-wide): 742.7MM **Privately Held**
WEB: us.bic.com
SIC: 3951 3952 Pens & mechanical pen-
　　cils; lead pencils & art goods
HQ: Bic Corporation
　　1 Bic Way Ste 1 # 1
　　Shelton CT 06484
　　203 783-2000

(G-1520)
BIO CEPS INC
15251 Roosevelt Blvd # 204 (33760-3560)
PHONE..................................727 669-7544
EMP: 30
SALES (est): 1.7MM **Privately Held**
SIC: 3841 Mfg Surgical/Medical Instru-
　　ments

(G-1521)
BL BIO LAB LLC
2021 Sunnydale Blvd # 14 (33765-1202)
PHONE..................................727 900-2707
Marian Kapusta,
EMP: 10 **EST:** 2018
SALES (est): 1.8MM **Privately Held**
WEB: www.blbiolab.com
SIC: 2023 Dietary supplements, dairy &
　　non-dairy based

(G-1522)
BODEN CO INC
Also Called: Adjust-A-Brush
10445 49th St N Ste B (33762-5036)
PHONE..................................727 571-1234
Duane H Newville, *President*
Eric Newville, *Vice Pres*
Marillyn Newville, *CFO*
Kurt Newville, *Executive*
▲ **EMP:** 27 **EST:** 1960
SQ FT: 27,000
SALES (est): 1.3MM **Privately Held**
WEB: www.greenblade.org
SIC: 3991 Brushes, household or industrial

(G-1523)
BOEING COMPANY
14100 Roosevelt Blvd (33762-3805)
PHONE..................................562 797-9131
EMP: 7 **EST:** 2017
SALES (est): 136.3K **Privately Held**
WEB: www.boeing.com
SIC: 3721 Aircraft

(G-1524)
BOYD INDUSTRIES INC
12900 44th St N (33762-4729)
PHONE..................................727 561-9292
Adrian E Latrace, *CEO*
Brian Vitoritt, *Project Mgr*
Mark Dietrich, *Opers Mgr*
Aferdit Vinca, *Buyer*
Gloria Herrera, *Engineer*
◆ **EMP:** 75 **EST:** 1957
SQ FT: 63,000
SALES (est): 16.7MM **Privately Held**
WEB: www.boydindustries.com
SIC: 3843 Dental chairs

(G-1525)
BREN TUCK INC
12929 44th St N (33762-4731)
PHONE..................................727 561-7697
Mark Tucker, *President*
▲ **EMP:** 13 **EST:** 2005
SALES (est): 2.4MM **Privately Held**
SIC: 3643 Lightning protection equipment

(G-1526)
BRITO BRICK & PAVERS CORP
6262 142nd Ave N (33760-2757)
PHONE..................................727 214-8760
Robison De Oliveira, *Principal*
EMP: 8 **EST:** 2012
SALES (est): 120.2K **Privately Held**
SIC: 3531 Pavers

(G-1527)
BROTH BOMB LLC
25778 Us Highway 19 N (33763-2039)
PHONE..................................813 278-1912
Andrew Laurent, *CEO*
EMP: 10 **EST:** 2019
SALES (est): 514.3K **Privately Held**
WEB: www.brothbomb.store
SIC: 2099 Seasonings & spices

(G-1528)
BRUCE R ELY ENTERPRISE INC
Also Called: Designers Plastics
12880 Auto Blvd Ste G (33762)
PHONE..................................727 573-1643
Bruce Ely, *President*
Penny Carrigan, *Corp Secy*
EMP: 17 **EST:** 1975
SQ FT: 32,000
SALES (est): 1.9MM **Privately Held**
SIC: 3089 3993 2542 Plastic hardware &
　　building products; signs & advertising
　　specialties; partitions & fixtures, except
　　wood

(G-1529)
BRYAN NELCO INC
15251 Roosevelt Blvd # 202 (33760-3560)
PHONE..................................727 533-8282
Camille Gianetti, *Principal*
▲ **EMP:** 7 **EST:** 2001
SALES (est): 130.1K **Privately Held**
SIC: 3599 5085 Industrial machinery; in-
　　dustrial supplies

(G-1530)
BUCKLEY PALLETS
2409 Laurelwood Dr (33763-1520)
PHONE..................................727 415-4497

Bonnie Elliott, *Principal*
EMP: 8 **EST:** 2011
SALES (est): 600.1K **Privately Held**
WEB: www.buckleypallets.com
SIC: 2448 Pallets, wood

(G-1531)
BUCKLEY PALLETS LLC
14550 62nd St N 2 (33760-2355)
PHONE.................................727 415-4497
Bonnie Buckley,
EMP: 15 **EST:** 2012
SALES (est): 1.7MM **Privately Held**
WEB: www.buckleypallets.com
SIC: 2448 Wood pallets & skids

(G-1532)
BUSINESS CARD EX TAMPA BAY INC
14000 63rd Way N (33760-3618)
PHONE.................................727 535-7768
Eugene Steslicki, *President*
Kathleen Steslicki, *Vice Pres*
Richard Perez, *Info Tech Mgr*
EMP: 80 **EST:** 1986
SQ FT: 10,000
SALES (est): 14.6MM **Privately Held**
SIC: 2754 2761 2759 Visiting cards;
gravure printing; manifold business forms;
commercial printing

(G-1533)
C & E INNOVATIVE MGT LLC
Also Called: Fit Like Foots
2454 N Mcmullen Booth Rd (33759-1353)
PHONE.................................727 408-5146
Kyle Bates, *General Mgr*
EMP: 8 **EST:** 2013
SALES (est): 478.3K **Privately Held**
SIC: 2099 8741 Food preparations; management services

(G-1534)
C Y A POWDER COATING LLC
12099 44th St N (33762-5108)
PHONE.................................727 299-9832
Katrina M Lingenfelter, *Mng Member*
EMP: 5 **EST:** 2007
SQ FT: 20,000
SALES (est): 496K **Privately Held**
WEB: www.cyapowder.com
SIC: 3479 3471 1799 Coating of metals &
formed products; coating, rust preventive;
painting of metal products; finishing, metals or formed products; exterior cleaning,
including sandblasting

(G-1535)
CADCAM SOFTWARE CO
28200 Us Highway 19 N E (33761-2625)
PHONE.................................727 450-6440
Larry Pendelton, *CEO*
EMP: 7 **EST:** 2015
SALES (est): 61.4K **Privately Held**
WEB: www.bobcad.com
SIC: 7372 Prepackaged software

(G-1536)
CARL ZEISS VISION INC
5600 115th Ave N Ste B (33760-4843)
PHONE.................................727 528-8873
Donne David Delle, *Manager*
EMP: 9 **Privately Held**
SIC: 3827 Optical instruments & lenses
HQ: Carl Zeiss Vision Inc.
1040 Worldwide Blvd
Hebron KY 41048

(G-1537)
CELTIC AIRSPARES LLC
28870 Us Highway 19 N # 328
(33761-2596)
PHONE.................................727 431-0482
Annesley R Martin Mr, *Mng Member*
Richard Martin, *Info Tech Mgr*
Ciaran M Moloney,
EMP: 5 **EST:** 2010
SALES (est): 347.4K **Privately Held**
WEB: www.celticairspares.com
SIC: 3721 Aircraft

(G-1538)
CF MOTION INC
4625 E Bay Dr Ste 306 (33764-6868)
PHONE.................................727 458-7092
Israel Menahem, *President*

Sofia Menahem, *Vice Pres*
Mike Menahem, *Admin Sec*
EMP: 8 **EST:** 1998
SALES (est): 998.4K **Privately Held**
WEB: www.cfmotions.com
SIC: 3663 Antennas, transmitting & communications

(G-1539)
CHARIAN MACHINE & MFG INC
4652 107th Cir N (33762-5005)
PHONE.................................727 561-0150
William W Bronson, *President*
Richard Albritton, *Vice Pres*
Bonnie Bronson, *Treasurer*
EMP: 7 **EST:** 1985
SQ FT: 5,000
SALES (est): 965.4K **Privately Held**
WEB: www.rcamachine.com
SIC: 3599 Machine shop, jobbing & repair

(G-1540)
CHASSIS KING LLC
1016 Pnc De Leon Blvd (33756-1073)
PHONE.................................727 585-1500
Donald Pratt, *President*
◆ **EMP:** 7 **EST:** 1997
SQ FT: 30,000
SALES (est): 980.3K **Privately Held**
WEB: www.chassisking.com
SIC: 3715 Truck trailer chassis

(G-1541)
CHEMLINE PRODUCTS INC
3813 126th Ave N Ste 7 (33762-4232)
PHONE.................................727 573-2436
Frank Dibenedetto, *President*
Michelle Helms, *Treasurer*
Pat Dibenedetto, *Admin Sec*
EMP: 5 **EST:** 1994
SQ FT: 3,000
SALES (est): 413.5K **Privately Held**
WEB: www.chemline.net
SIC: 2841 Soap & other detergents

(G-1542)
CLEARWATER ENGINEERING INC
14605 49th St N Ste 19 (33762-2837)
PHONE.................................727 573-2210
Dave Pratt, *President*
▲ **EMP:** 7 **EST:** 1989
SQ FT: 8,320
SALES (est): 675.6K **Privately Held**
WEB: www.clearwatereng.com
SIC: 3826 3823 1623 Environmental testing equipment; industrial instrmnts
msrmnt display/control process variable;
water, sewer & utility lines

(G-1543)
CMZ INDUSTRIES LLC
27232 Us Highway 19 N (33761-2939)
PHONE.................................727 726-1443
Michael A Bansavage, *Branch Mgr*
EMP: 8
SALES (corp-wide): 92.5K **Privately Held**
SIC: 3999 Barber & beauty shop equipment
PA: Cmz Industries Llc
9273 Rustic Pines Blvd E
Seminole FL

(G-1544)
CNC WORKS SERVICE INC
13584 49th St N Ste 5 (33762-3737)
PHONE.................................813 777-8642
Luis Rivera, *Principal*
Donn B Busby, *Purch Mgr*
EMP: 11 **EST:** 2009
SALES (est): 595.8K **Privately Held**
SIC: 3469 Machine parts, stamped or
pressed metal

(G-1545)
COEUR DE LION INC
Also Called: Allied Business Service
1610 N Myrtle Ave (33755-2549)
P.O. Box 1564, Largo (33779-1564)
PHONE.................................727 442-4808
Stanley R Albro, *President*
EMP: 24 **EST:** 1986
SQ FT: 8,000
SALES (est): 1.3MM **Privately Held**
SIC: 2731 Book publishing

(G-1546)
COLE ENTERPRISES INC
Also Called: Florida Research
436 E Shore Dr (33767-2027)
P.O. Box 3129, Clearwater Beach (33767-8129)
PHONE.................................727 441-4101
Robert Cole, *President*
Sandra Cole, *Vice Pres*
EMP: 5 **EST:** 1972
SQ FT: 3,000
SALES (est): 487.3K **Privately Held**
WEB: www.flresearch.com
SIC: 2721 7389 8732 Periodicals: publishing & printing; press clipping service;
commercial nonphysical research

(G-1547)
COLORFAST PRINTING & GRAPHICS
Also Called: Colorfast Coml Prtg Grphics Sv
14114 63rd Way N (33760-3616)
PHONE.................................727 531-9506
Milne Sandra J, *President*
Terry Mohamed, *Owner*
Alwin Chan, *Opers Mgr*
EMP: 5 **EST:** 1991
SALES (est): 500K **Privately Held**
WEB: www.colorfastprint.com
SIC: 2752 Commercial printing, offset

(G-1548)
COMMUNITY PHARMACY SVCS LLC
19387 Us Highway 19 N (33764-3102)
PHONE.................................727 431-8261
Linda L Kaczynski, *Director*
EMP: 8 **EST:** 2012
SALES (est): 221.2K **Privately Held**
SIC: 2834 Pharmaceutical preparations

(G-1549)
CONSOLIDATED POLYMER TECH
4451 110th Ave N (33762-4944)
PHONE.................................727 531-4191
Larry Carpenter, *President*
Rob Klingle, *Corp Secy*
◆ **EMP:** 25 **EST:** 1983
SQ FT: 12,000
SALES (est): 1.3MM **Privately Held**
WEB: www.c-flex-cpt.com
SIC: 3082 3842 Tubes, unsupported plastic; surgical appliances & supplies

(G-1550)
CORERX INC
5733 Myerlake Cir (33760-2952)
PHONE.................................727 259-6950
Mohammed S Shekhani, *Vice Pres*
Hisham Ahmed, *QA Dir*
La-Tonya Rouse, *CFO*
EMP: 16 **Privately Held**
WEB: www.corerxpharma.com
SIC: 2834 Pharmaceutical preparations
PA: Corerx, Inc.
14205 Myerlake Cir
Clearwater FL 33760

(G-1551)
CORERX INC (PA)
14205 Myerlake Cir (33760-2824)
PHONE.................................727 259-6950
Todd R Daviau, *CEO*
Mark J Licarde, *Vice Pres*
Saurabh S Trivedi, *Vice Pres*
James Clark, *Project Mgr*
Cathy Curtis, *Project Mgr*
▲ **EMP:** 199 **EST:** 2006
SQ FT: 9,700
SALES (est): 66.9MM **Privately Held**
WEB: www.corerxpharma.com
SIC: 2834 Pharmaceutical preparations

(G-1552)
CORERX PHARMACEUTICALS INC
14205 Myerlake Cir (33760-2824)
PHONE.................................727 259-6950
Todd Daviau, *CEO*
James Davis, *Vice Pres*
Mark Licarde, *Vice Pres*
Brian McMillan, *Vice Pres*
Bob Berg, *CFO*
EMP: 23 **EST:** 2012

SQ FT: 9,700
SALES (est): 3.9MM **Privately Held**
WEB: www.corerxpharma.com
SIC: 2834 Tablets, pharmaceutical; veterinary pharmaceutical preparations; pills,
pharmaceutical

(G-1553)
COVALENT INDUSTRIES INC
10300 49th St N Ste 434 (33762-5000)
PHONE.................................727 381-2739
Alison Scutte, *Principal*
EMP: 8 **EST:** 2017
SALES (est): 47.9K **Privately Held**
WEB: www.tse-industries.com
SIC: 3999 Manufacturing industries

(G-1554)
CREATING TECH SOLUTIONS LLC (PA)
5250 140th Ave N (33760-3728)
P.O. Box 17840 (33762-0840)
PHONE.................................727 914-3001
Milagros Hofius, *CEO*
Mark Hofius, *President*
John McCusker, *COO*
Melanie Giles, *Vice Pres*
Mark Steele, *Vice Pres*
EMP: 35 **EST:** 2012
SALES (est): 3MM **Privately Held**
WEB: www.crtes.com
SIC: 3692 3629 3825 3691 Primary batteries, dry & wet; battery chargers, rectifying or nonrotating; power conversion
units, a.c. to d.c.: static-electric; instrument relays, all types; batteries, rechargeable

(G-1555)
CREATING TECH SOLUTIONS LLC
Also Called: Technology Research
5250 140th Ave N (33760-3728)
P.O. Box 17840 (33762-0840)
PHONE.................................727 914-3001
Brad Freeman, *Vice Pres*
Roger Tribble, *Research*
David Grafe, *Finance*
Craig Floyd, *Human Res Dir*
Mark Steele, *VP Sales*
EMP: 36
SALES (corp-wide): 3MM **Privately Held**
WEB:
www.creatingtechnologysolutions.com
SIC: 3825 3629 Instrument relays, all
types; power conversion units, a.c. to d.c.:
static-electric
PA: Creating Technology Solutions, Llc
5250 140th Ave N
Clearwater FL 33760
727 914-3001

(G-1556)
CREATING TECH SOLUTIONS LLC
Also Called: Patco Electronics
5250 140th Ave N (33760-3728)
P.O. Box 17840 (33762-0840)
PHONE.................................727 914-3001
Milagros Hofius,
EMP: 36
SALES (corp-wide): 3MM **Privately Held**
WEB:
www.creatingtechnologysolutions.com
SIC: 3692 3691 Primary batteries, dry &
wet; storage batteries; batteries,
rechargeable
PA: Creating Technology Solutions, Llc
5250 140th Ave N
Clearwater FL 33760
727 914-3001

(G-1557)
CUSTOM ATMATED PROSTHETICS LLC
1155 Ne Cleveland St (33755-4815)
PHONE.................................781 279-2771
EMP: 7
SALES (corp-wide): 12.4B **Publicly Held**
WEB: www.henryschein.com
SIC: 3843 Dental materials
HQ: Custom Automated Prosthetics Llc
7 Audubon Rd 101
Wakefield MA 01880
781 279-2771

G
E
O
G
R
A
P
H
I
C

(G-1558)
CUSTOM SIGN & AWNING
4502 107th Cir N Ste D (33762-5038)
PHONE............................727 210-0941
Pedro Corodova, *Principal*
EMP: 10 **EST:** 2006
SALES (est): 427.2K **Privately Held**
SIC: 3993 Signs & advertising specialties

(G-1559)
CUTTING EDGE SGNS GRPHICS OF P
12795 49th St N (33762-4604)
PHONE............................727 546-3700
Jeffery Newburg, *President*
EMP: 5 **EST:** 1996
SALES (est): 637.6K **Privately Held**
WEB: www.thecuttingedgesigns.com
SIC: 3993 2741 7312 Signs, not made in custom sign painting shops; letters for signs, metal; posters: publishing & printing; poster advertising, outdoor

(G-1560)
D & S PALLETS INC
Also Called: D & S Hauling
12195 46th St N (33762-4434)
P.O. Box 18019 (33762-1019)
PHONE............................727 540-0061
EMP: 52
SALES (est): 2MM **Privately Held**
SIC: 2448 4953 1389 0782 Mfg Wood Pallets/Skids Refuse Systems Oil/Gas Field Services Lawn/Garden Services

(G-1561)
D-REP PLASTICS INC
11345 53rd St N (33760-4822)
PHONE............................407 240-4154
Daniel Chalich, *President*
EMP: 7 **EST:** 2012
SALES (est): 160.1K **Privately Held**
SIC: 3089 Injection molding of plastics

(G-1562)
DAVIS CONCRETE INC (PA)
1670 Sunshine Dr (33765-1316)
PHONE............................727 733-3141
EMP: 30 **EST:** 1947
SQ FT: 6,400
SALES (est): 6MM **Privately Held**
WEB: www.davisconcreteinc.com
SIC: 3273 Ready-mixed concrete

(G-1563)
DAVIT MASTER CORP
5560 Ulmerton Rd (33760-4011)
PHONE............................727 573-4414
Cheryl De Abreau, *Principal*
Chris Deabreau, *Purchasing*
Marilyn Thomas, *Treasurer*
Marty McDonald, *Sales Staff*
▼ **EMP:** 18 **EST:** 1977
SQ FT: 8,000
SALES (est): 4.8MM **Privately Held**
WEB: www.davitmaster.com
SIC: 3536 5551 Davits; marine supplies

(G-1564)
DHS ENTERPRISES INC
5150 Ulmerton Rd Ste 14 (33760-4014)
PHONE............................727 572-9470
Andrew Kossowski, *President*
EMP: 8 **EST:** 1990
SQ FT: 8,000
SALES (est): 981.5K **Privately Held**
SIC: 3471 Anodizing (plating) of metals or formed products
PA: Veterans Metal Llc
5150 Ulmerton Rd Ste 14
Clearwater FL 33760
727 572-9470

(G-1565)
DILUTION SOLUTIONS INC
2090 Sunnydale Blvd (33765-1201)
PHONE............................800 451-6628
Pamela M Temko, *President*
Jason Maddox, *Sales Mgr*
EMP: 9 **EST:** 2013
SALES (est): 702.9K **Privately Held**
WEB: www.dilutionsolutions.com
SIC: 3559 Chemical machinery & equipment

(G-1566)
DJ/PJ INC
Also Called: J.W. Appley and Son
13215 38th St N (33762-4229)
PHONE............................813 907-6359
Doug Jennings, *President*
EMP: 26 **EST:** 2003
SQ FT: 17,000
SALES (est): 4.7MM **Privately Held**
WEB: www.djpjlive.com
SIC: 3499 3599 Machine bases, metal; machine & other job shop work; machine shop, jobbing & repair

(G-1567)
DOT GREEN ENERGY INC
100 Hampton Rd Lot 84 (33759-3955)
PHONE............................717 505-8686
Herb Andres, *Exec VP*
Kenneth Brody, *Manager*
Ken Brody, *Director*
EMP: 9 **EST:** 2008
SALES (est): 99.7K **Privately Held**
SIC: 2911 8711 Gasoline; energy conservation engineering

(G-1568)
DOUGLAS MACHINES CORP
Also Called: Cyclone Belt Washer
4500 110th Ave N (33762-4907)
PHONE............................727 461-3477
Paul Claro, *CEO*
David A Ward, *President*
Kevin J Lemen, *Vice Pres*
William J Lever, *Vice Pres*
Susan A Mader, *Vice Pres*
◆ **EMP:** 47 **EST:** 2007
SQ FT: 25,000
SALES (est): 15.8MM
SALES (corp-wide): 129.3MM **Privately Held**
WEB: www.dougmac.com
SIC: 3589 Commercial cleaning equipment
PA: Koda Enterprises Group, Llc
51 Sawyer Rd Ste 420
Waltham MA 02453
781 891-0467

(G-1569)
DOWELS PINS & SHAFTS INC
1975 Calumet St (33765-1108)
P.O. Box 1135, Dunedin (34697-1135)
PHONE............................727 461-1255
Thomas R Mickelson, *President*
Ellen F Mickelson, *Vice Pres*
Bridget Hammond, *Treasurer*
EMP: 18 **EST:** 1977
SQ FT: 13,500
SALES (est): 979.9K **Privately Held**
WEB: www.dowelspinsshafts.com
SIC: 3452 3568 Dowel pins, metal; power transmission equipment

(G-1570)
DOWLING GRAPHICS INC
12920 Automobile Blvd (33762-4714)
PHONE............................727 573-5997
Denise Dowling, *President*
Dave Kaufman, *Sales Staff*
Henry Albritton, *Sales Executive*
EMP: 36 **EST:** 1990
SQ FT: 21,000
SALES (est): 2.5MM **Privately Held**
WEB: www.dowlinggraphics.com
SIC: 2262 2752 7389 Screen printing: manmade fiber & silk broadwoven fabrics; transfers, decalcomania or dry: lithographed; embroidering of advertising on shirts, etc.

(G-1571)
DPS POWDER COATING INC
4980 110th Ave N (33760-4813)
PHONE............................727 573-2797
Art Dorsett, *Owner*
EMP: 8 **EST:** 2005
SALES (est): 600K **Privately Held**
SIC: 3479 Coating of metals & formed products

(G-1572)
DSG CLEARWATER LABORATORY
14333 58th St N (33760-2817)
PHONE............................727 530-9444
Rick Vanmeter, *General Mgr*

James Haeger, *Controller*
EMP: 11 **EST:** 2014
SALES (est): 1.2MM **Privately Held**
SIC: 3843 8072 Dental laboratory equipment; artificial teeth production

(G-1573)
DUNRITE METAL FABRICATORS INC
12099 44th St N (33762-5108)
PHONE............................727 299-9242
David M Lingenfelter, *President*
David Lingenfelter, *President*
EMP: 15 **EST:** 1989
SQ FT: 20,000
SALES (est): 2.8MM **Privately Held**
WEB: www.dunritemetal.com
SIC: 3599 Machine shop, jobbing & repair

(G-1574)
DUPONT PUBLISHING INC (PA)
Also Called: Dupont Registry
4707 140th Ave N Ste 302 (33762-3840)
PHONE............................727 573-9339
Steve Chapman, *CEO*
Thomas L Dupont, *Ch of Bd*
Rosemary Nye, *Partner*
David Warner, *Chief*
Audrey Crowder, *Production*
EMP: 80 **EST:** 1984
SALES (est): 15.7MM **Privately Held**
WEB: advertise.dupontregistry.com
SIC: 2721 Magazines: publishing only, not printed on site

(G-1575)
DURBAL INC
14115 63rd Way N Ste A (33760-3623)
PHONE............................727 531-3040
Markus Voss, *President*
Monika Voss, *Vice Pres*
Rudolf Swoboda, *Admin Sec*
EMP: 8 **EST:** 1981
SALES (est): 725K **Privately Held**
WEB: en.durbal.de
SIC: 3312 Rods, iron & steel: made in steel mills

(G-1576)
ECOATM LLC
27001 Us Highway 19 N # 100
(33761-3402)
PHONE............................858 766-7250
EMP: 70
SALES (corp-wide): 29.2B **Publicly Held**
WEB: www.ecoatm.com
SIC: 3671 Cathode ray tubes, including rebuilt
HQ: Ecoatm, Llc
10121 Barnes Canyon Rd
San Diego CA 92121

(G-1577)
ED PUBLICATIONS INC
2431 Estancia Blvd Bldg B (33761-2608)
PHONE............................727 726-3592
Don Waitt, *President*
David Fairchild, *Vice Pres*
Teresa Tearno, *Manager*
Caroline Ashe, *Information Mgr*
Kevin Pennington, *Art Dir*
EMP: 10 **EST:** 1990
SQ FT: 2,350
SALES (est): 916.7K **Publicly Held**
WEB: www.exoticdancer.com
SIC: 2741 7389 Directories: publishing only, not printed on site; advertising, promotional & trade show services
PA: Rci Hospitality Holdings, Inc.
10737 Cutten Rd
Houston TX 77066

(G-1578)
EIDSCHUN ENGINEERING INC
2899 Heron Pl (33762-3358)
PHONE............................727 647-2300
Charles Eidschun, *President*
EMP: 30 **EST:** 1981
SQ FT: 12,500
SALES (est): 2MM **Privately Held**
WEB: www.cycloneproducts.com
SIC: 3559 5084 Electroplating machinery & equipment; industrial machinery & equipment

(G-1579)
ELECTRALED INC
10990 49th St N (33762-5015)
PHONE............................727 561-7610
Priscilla G Thomas, *President*
Willard Wade Thomas, *Vice Pres*
Jenny Simmons, *Sr Project Mgr*
▲ **EMP:** 18 **EST:** 2002
SQ FT: 27,000
SALES (est): 4.9MM **Privately Held**
WEB: www.electraled.com
SIC: 3646 Commercial indusl & institutional electric lighting fixtures

(G-1580)
ELECTRO TECHNIK INDUSTRIES INC (PA)
Also Called: RES-Net Microwave
5410 115th Ave N (33760-4841)
P.O. Box 18802 (33762-1802)
PHONE............................727 530-9555
Darry K Mayo, *President*
Darryl K Mayo, *President*
Kevin Osborne, *General Mgr*
Geraldine R Mayo, *Corp Secy*
Darryl Mayo, *Vice Pres*
◆ **EMP:** 77 **EST:** 1982
SQ FT: 5,000
SALES (est): 51.7MM **Privately Held**
WEB: www.electrotechnik.com
SIC: 3677 3679 3676 3663 Coil windings, electronic; harness assemblies for electronic use: wire or cable; electronic resistors; radio & TV communications equipment; nonferrous wiredrawing & insulating

(G-1581)
ELECTRO-COMP SERVICES INC
11437 43rd St N (33762-4924)
PHONE............................727 532-4262
▲ **EMP:** 21
SQ FT: 15,000
SALES (est): 3.2MM **Privately Held**
SIC: 3577 Mfg Computer Peripheral Equipment

(G-1582)
ELITE CNC MACHINING INC
6399 142nd Ave N Ste 122 (33760-2728)
PHONE............................727 531-8447
S Arthur Hooper, *CEO*
Jack Lavery, *President*
Yolanda Carter, *Controller*
▼ **EMP:** 38 **EST:** 1994
SQ FT: 45,000
SALES (est): 1MM **Privately Held**
WEB: www.elitecnc.com
SIC: 3599 Machine shop, jobbing & repair

(G-1583)
ELLIOTT DIAMOND TOOL INC
1835 Bough Ave Unit 1 (33760-1541)
P.O. Box 10006, Largo (33773-0006)
PHONE............................727 585-3839
Mark Elliot, *President*
Mary Lou Elliott, *Vice Pres*
EMP: 18 **EST:** 1972
SALES (est): 1.9MM **Privately Held**
WEB: www.elliottdiamond.com
SIC: 3545 3425 3541 Drills (machine tool accessories); saw blades for hand or power saws; machine tools, metal cutting type

(G-1584)
ENDEAVOUR CATAMARAN CORP
3703 131st Ave N (33762-4277)
PHONE............................727 573-5377
Robert L Vincent, *President*
EMP: 11 **EST:** 1991
SQ FT: 52,000
SALES (est): 1.7MM **Privately Held**
WEB: www.endeavourcats.com
SIC: 3732 Yachts, building & repairing

(G-1585)
ENDO-THERAPEUTICS INC
15251 Roosevelt Blvd # 204 (33760-3560)
PHONE............................727 538-9570
Charles Hardy, *CEO*
Peter Sanchirico, *President*
Robert Querido, *President*
Robert Stuba, *Vice Pres*

Kevin Warren, *Opers Staff*
EMP: 55 **EST:** 1992
SQ FT: 5,000
SALES (est): 10.4MM **Privately Held**
WEB: www.endotherapeutics.com
SIC: 3841 Medical instruments & equipment, blood & bone work

(G-1586)
ENGLANDER ENTERPRISES INC
Also Called: Eei Manufacturing Services
703 Grand Central St (33756-3411)
PHONE.................................727 461-4755
C Susan Englander, *President*
Paula Thumma, *Production*
Doreen Natale, *Senior Buyer*
Cang Le, *Engineer*
Paul Markland, *Engineer*
EMP: 47 **EST:** 1993
SQ FT: 18,000
SALES (est): 10.2MM **Privately Held**
WEB: www.eeimfg.com
SIC: 3672 5065 5063 Printed circuit boards; electronic parts & equipment; electrical apparatus & equipment

(G-1587)
ENVIRONMENTAL SERVICES
Also Called: City of Largo
5100 150th Ave N (33760-3502)
PHONE.................................727 518-3080
Rich Mushaben, *Supervisor*
Erwin Katy, *Director*
Ernie Muschner, *Officer*
EMP: 40 **EST:** 1900
SQ FT: 15,344
SALES (est): 5.6MM **Privately Held**
WEB: www.largo.com
SIC: 3589 Sewage treatment equipment

(G-1588)
EQUIPMENT SALES & SERVICE INC (HQ)
12707 44th St N (33762-4725)
PHONE.................................727 572-9197
Robert A Ficocelli, *President*
EMP: 5 **EST:** 1991
SQ FT: 5,000
SALES (est): 1.6MM **Privately Held**
WEB: www.essiwelding.com
SIC: 2813 Industrial gases

(G-1589)
ERA ORGANICS INC
33 N Garden Ave Ste 120 (33755-6616)
PHONE.................................800 579-9817
Tyler Davis, *President*
Linda Clark, *Vice Pres*
Heather Burghorn, *Opers Mgr*
Nikki Davis, *Opers Staff*
▼ **EMP:** 4 **EST:** 2014
SALES (est): 4.2MM **Privately Held**
WEB: www.eraorganics.com
SIC: 2834 Dermatologicals

(G-1590)
ES INVESTMENTS LLC (PA)
Also Called: Sun Microstamping Technologies
14055 Us Highway 19 N (33764-7239)
PHONE.................................727 536-8822
Bryan Clarke, *President*
Steve McKenzie, *Vice Pres*
Phil Ross, *Vice Pres*
John Bartleman, *Mng Member*
Matt Dlugosz, *Director*
▲ **EMP:** 150 **EST:** 2004
SQ FT: 110,000
SALES (est): 45.6MM **Privately Held**
WEB: www.sunmicrostamping.com
SIC: 3469 Stamping metal for the trade

(G-1591)
EZELL PRECISION TOOL CO
Also Called: Legal Components
4733 122nd Ave N (33762-4457)
PHONE.................................727 573-3575
Fax: 727 572-6235
▲ **EMP:** 13
SQ FT: 6,000
SALES (est): 2MM **Privately Held**
SIC: 3544 Mfg Special Dies & Tools

(G-1592)
F K INSTRUMENT CO INC
Also Called: F K Instrument
2134 Sunnydale Blvd (33765-1274)
PHONE.................................727 461-6060
Alfred H Klopfer, *President*
Erich Klopfer, *Vice Pres*
EMP: 59 **EST:** 1952
SQ FT: 37,200
SALES (est): 9.1MM **Privately Held**
WEB: www.fk-instrument.com
SIC: 3599 Machine shop, jobbing & repair

(G-1593)
FABMASTER INC
2100 Palmetto St Ste A (33765-2101)
PHONE.................................727 216-6750
Danh Tran, *President*
John Gray, *Vice Pres*
EMP: 8 **EST:** 2009
SALES (est): 854K **Privately Held**
SIC: 3312 Stainless steel

(G-1594)
FILMFASTENER LLC
12052 49th St N C (33762-4301)
PHONE.................................813 926-8721
Frank Fountas,
EMP: 5 **EST:** 2006
SQ FT: 3,600
SALES (est): 334.2K **Privately Held**
WEB: www.filmfastener.com
SIC: 3429 Keys, locks & related hardware

(G-1595)
FIRST BLOCK LLC
615 Drew St (33755-4109)
PHONE.................................727 462-2526
Jo Beckman, *Accountant*
Fabio Zaniboni, *Manager*
Chiara Basso Zaniboni, *Manager*
EMP: 57 **EST:** 2014
SALES (est): 8.9MM **Privately Held**
SIC: 3648 Lighting equipment

(G-1596)
FK INSTRUMENT CO LLC
2134 Sunnydale Blvd (33765-1274)
PHONE.................................727 472-2003
Erich Klopfer, *Mng Member*
EMP: 70 **EST:** 2019
SALES (est): 5.6MM **Privately Held**
WEB: www.fk-instrument.com
SIC: 3441 Fabricated structural metal

(G-1597)
FLEXIBLE PRTG SOLUTIONS LLC
2070 Weaver Park Dr (33765-2130)
PHONE.................................727 446-3014
Curtis B Miller,
EMP: 10 **EST:** 1999
SQ FT: 6,000
SALES (est): 607.8K **Privately Held**
WEB: www.flexible-solutions.net
SIC: 2752 Commercial printing, lithographic

(G-1598)
FLORIDA AIR CLEANING INC
13584 49th St N Ste 17 (33762-3737)
P.O. Box 17690 (33762-0690)
PHONE.................................727 573-5281
Tom Loudenslagger, *President*
EMP: 6 **EST:** 1997
SALES (est): 385.2K **Privately Held**
SIC: 3564 Air cleaning systems

(G-1599)
FLORIDA CANDY FACTORY INC
721 Lakeview Rd (33756-3422)
PHONE.................................727 446-0024
Gerald S Rehm, *President*
Joanne McDougall, *Office Mgr*
Richard Barnes, *CIO*
EMP: 21 **EST:** 1970
SALES (est): 2.4MM **Privately Held**
WEB: www.angelmint.com
SIC: 2064 7389 Candy & other confectionery products; packaging & labeling services

(G-1600)
FLORIDA FRAMES INC
12880 Auto Blvd Ste B (33762)
PHONE.................................727 572-4064
Greg Brodnick, *President*
Stace Stiverson, *COO*
Debra Brodnick, *Vice Pres*
Holli Miller, *Consultant*
EMP: 14 **EST:** 1979
SALES (est): 1.1MM **Privately Held**
WEB: www.floridaframes.com
SIC: 2499 2431 Picture & mirror frames, wood; millwork

(G-1601)
FLORIDA HYTORC
22131 Hwy Us19 (33765)
PHONE.................................813 990-9470
Jim Reese, *President*
EMP: 10 **EST:** 2017
SALES (est): 404.1K **Privately Held**
WEB: www.floridaprecisiontool.com
SIC: 3541 Machine tools, metal cutting type

(G-1602)
FLORIDA POOL PRODUCTS INC
14550 62nd St N (33760-2355)
P.O. Box 6025 (33758-6025)
PHONE.................................727 531-8913
John C Thomas, *CEO*
James P Eisch, *President*
Fred A Thomas, *Chairman*
▲ **EMP:** 20 **EST:** 1980
SQ FT: 100,000
SALES (est): 807.7K **Privately Held**
WEB: www.floridapoolproducts.com
SIC: 3069 3429 3949 3944 Tubing, rubber; manufactured hardware (general); sporting & athletic goods; games, toys & children's vehicles

(G-1603)
FLYTEONE INC
2687 Westchester Dr N (33761-3026)
PHONE.................................813 421-1410
Alex Atteberry, *CEO*
Diana L Atteberry, *Admin Sec*
EMP: 5 **EST:** 2009
SALES (est): 571.4K **Privately Held**
WEB: www.flyteone.net
SIC: 3592 8742 7363 Valves, aircraft; sales (including sales management) consultant; pilot service, aviation

(G-1604)
FOAM BY DESIGN INC
10606 49th St N (33762-5009)
PHONE.................................727 561-7479
Gustavo Trejos, *President*
Miguel Gransaull, *Sales Staff*
Jenn Fellows, *Office Mgr*
Richard Kelly, *Associate*
EMP: 50 **EST:** 2002
SQ FT: 1,000
SALES (est): 5MM **Privately Held**
WEB: www.foambydesign.com
SIC: 3086 8712 1771 Packaging & shipping materials, foamed plastic; architectural services; concrete work

(G-1605)
FORGE UNLIMITED CO
10880 49th St N (33762-5013)
PHONE.................................727 900-7600
Ergun Baltaci, *CEO*
EMP: 9 **EST:** 2016
SALES (est): 191.7K **Privately Held**
WEB: www.forgeunlimited.com
SIC: 3993 Signs & advertising specialties; letters for signs, metal

(G-1606)
FORMICA PRINT SOLUTIONS LLC ✪
Also Called: Business Card Ex Tampa Bay
14000 63rd Way N (33760-3618)
PHONE.................................800 669-5601
Bob Butler, *Mng Member*
EMP: 40 **EST:** 2022
SALES (est): 2.1MM **Privately Held**
SIC: 2752 Commercial printing, lithographic

(G-1607)
FREEDOM METAL FINISHING INC
5095 113th Ave N (33760-4834)
PHONE.................................727 573-2464
Keith Eidschun, *President*
EMP: 25 **EST:** 1944
SQ FT: 20,000
SALES (est): 3.1MM **Privately Held**
WEB: www.freedommetalfinishing.com
SIC: 3471 Electroplating & plating; plating of metals or formed products

(G-1608)
FULLERTON 799 INC
5300 115th Ave N (33760-4830)
PHONE.................................727 572-7040
Arnold Eichhof, *President*
Beth Flynn, *Corp Secy*
Arne Swanson, *Vice Pres*
▲ **EMP:** 52 **EST:** 1982
SQ FT: 60,000
SALES (est): 1.1MM **Privately Held**
SIC: 3544 3364 Industrial molds; magnesium & magnesium-base alloy die-castings

(G-1609)
GE AVIATION SYSTEMS LLC
14100 Roosevelt Blvd (33762-3805)
PHONE.................................727 532-6370
Diana L Frohn, *Branch Mgr*
EMP: 9
SALES (corp-wide): 74.2B **Publicly Held**
WEB: www.geaerospace.com
SIC: 3812 Aircraft control systems, electronic
HQ: Ge Aviation Systems Llc
1 Aviation Way
Cincinnati OH 45215
937 898-9600

(G-1610)
GE AVIATION SYSTEMS LLC
14200 Roosevelt Blvd (33762-2914)
PHONE.................................727 531-7781
Cesar Castaneda, *Production*
John Aitken, *Engineer*
Kurt Musial, *Engineer*
Tim Wahl, *Engineer*
David Miller, *Branch Mgr*
EMP: 350
SQ FT: 40,000
SALES (corp-wide): 74.2B **Publicly Held**
WEB: www.geaerospace.com
SIC: 3621 3812 Motors & generators; search & navigation equipment
HQ: Ge Aviation Systems Llc
1 Aviation Way
Cincinnati OH 45215
937 898-9600

(G-1611)
GE AVIATION SYSTEMS LLC
14200 Roosevelt Blvd (33762-2914)
P.O. Box 9013 (33758-9013)
PHONE.................................727 539-1631
Kathy Gridley, *Branch Mgr*
Wilma Freamon, *Analyst*
EMP: 40
SALES (corp-wide): 74.2B **Publicly Held**
WEB: www.geaerospace.com
SIC: 3812 Aircraft control systems, electronic
HQ: Ge Aviation Systems Llc
1 Aviation Way
Cincinnati OH 45215
937 898-9600

(G-1612)
GENCA CORP
13805 58th St N (33760-3716)
PHONE.................................727 524-3622
Fax: 727 531-5700
EMP: 37
SALES (est): 3.2MM **Privately Held**
SIC: 3089 Mfg Plastic Products

(G-1613)
GENERAL HYDRULIC SOLUTIONS INC
Also Called: Southcoast Marine Products
10601 47th St N (33762-5003)
PHONE.................................727 561-0719
Kevin Cureton, *President*

Steve Cureton, *Vice Pres*
◆ **EMP:** 6 **EST:** 1999
SALES (est): 843.4K **Privately Held**
WEB: www.ghslift.com
SIC: 3429 Marine hardware

(G-1614)
GENTRY PRINTING COMPANY LLC
2070 Gentry St (33765-2109)
PHONE...................................727 441-1914
Jason Kelly, *President*
Keith Claar,
EMP: 20 **EST:** 1982
SQ FT: 12,000
SALES (est): 4.7MM **Privately Held**
WEB: www.gentryprinting.com
SIC: 2752 Commercial printing, offset

(G-1615)
GOLD EFFECTS INC
13130 56th Ct Ste 609 (33760-4018)
PHONE...................................727 573-1990
Daniel McLaughlin, *President*
EMP: 6 **EST:** 1992
SALES (est): 612.7K **Privately Held**
WEB: www.goldeffects.com
SIC: 3471 Electroplating of metals or formed products

(G-1616)
GOOEE LLC
1444 S Belcher Rd (33764-2826)
PHONE...................................727 510-0663
Simon Coombes, *Chief Engr*
EMP: 12 **EST:** 2015
SALES (est): 247.2K **Privately Held**
SIC: 7372 Business oriented computer software

(G-1617)
GTO USA INC (PA)
805 Court St (33756-5509)
PHONE...................................727 216-6907
Valentina Vaccarone, *President*
▲ **EMP:** 7 **EST:** 2009
SALES (est): 980K **Privately Held**
WEB: www.tampogto.eu
SIC: 3555 Printing trades machinery

(G-1618)
GULF MACHINING INC
5040 110th Ave N (33760-4807)
PHONE...................................727 571-1244
Jerome Peterson, *President*
Jerome A Peterson, *Principal*
Rebecca Lowry, *Vice Pres*
EMP: 11 **EST:** 2013
SALES (est): 1.8MM **Privately Held**
WEB: www.gulfmachining.com
SIC: 3541 Numerically controlled metal cutting machine tools

(G-1619)
GULF PACKAGING CO
1756 Emerald Dr (33756-3665)
PHONE...................................727 441-1117
Jeffrey A Herran, *President*
EMP: 12 **EST:** 1958
SQ FT: 11,000
SALES (est): 1MM **Privately Held**
SIC: 2652 2657 2671 Boxes, newsboard, metal edged: made from purchased materials; paperboard backs for blister or skin packages; packaging paper & plastics film, coated & laminated

(G-1620)
H & H PUBLISHING CO INC
1231 Kapp Dr (33765-2116)
PHONE...................................727 442-7760
Robert D Hackworth, *President*
Mike Eaiy, *IT/INT Sup*
EMP: 6 **EST:** 1978
SQ FT: 2,000
SALES (est): 722.1K **Privately Held**
WEB: www.hhpublishing.com
SIC: 2731 Textbooks: publishing & printing

(G-1621)
HAMMER HAAG STEEL INC
12707 Us Highway 19 N (33764-7213)
PHONE...................................727 216-6903
Constantine Haag, *President*
Denny Fenn, *COO*
Ramon Robles, *Project Mgr*

Slava Moukhov, *CFO*
Amber Allen, *Accounting Dir*
▲ **EMP:** 110 **EST:** 2011
SQ FT: 56,000
SALES (est): 14MM **Privately Held**
WEB: www.hammerhaag.com
SIC: 3599 3441 Machine & other job shop work; building components, structural steel

(G-1622)
HARDER PRCISION COMPONENTS INC
1123 Seminole St (33755-4344)
PHONE...................................727 442-4212
Catherine Katopis, *President*
Cathy Kay, *Executive*
EMP: 23 **EST:** 1960
SQ FT: 6,700
SALES (est): 981.9K **Privately Held**
WEB: www.harderprecision.com
SIC: 3599 Machine shop, jobbing & repair

(G-1623)
HB SEALING PRODUCTS INC (HQ)
Also Called: Hercules Sealing Products
420 Park Place Blvd # 100 (33759-3928)
PHONE...................................727 796-1300
Russell Brown, *CEO*
Ron Garcia, *President*
Russ Petrie, *General Mgr*
Andres Echeverri, *Business Mgr*
Gina Herrera, *COO*
◆ **EMP:** 135 **EST:** 1962
SALES (est): 63.4MM
SALES (corp-wide): 1B **Privately Held**
SIC: 2869 5085 Hydraulic fluids, synthetic base; acetates: amyl, butyl & ethyl; seals, industrial; pistons & valves
PA: Diploma Plc
10-11
London EC1M
207 549-5700

(G-1624)
HENTZEN COATINGS INC
5182 126th Ave N (33760-4615)
PHONE...................................727 572-4474
Nancy Stler, *Admin Mgr*
Ryan Westover, *Technical Staff*
EMP: 10
SALES (corp-wide): 69.5MM **Privately Held**
WEB: www.hentzen.com
SIC: 2851 Lacquer: bases, dopes, thinner; enamels; polyurethane coatings; epoxy coatings
PA: Hentzen Coatings, Inc.
6937 W Mill Rd
Milwaukee WI 53218
414 353-4200

(G-1625)
HOFFSTETTER TOOL & DIE INC
4371 112th Ter N (33762-4930)
PHONE...................................727 573-7775
Ralph Hoffstetter, *President*
Gregory Hoffstetter, *Vice Pres*
Greg Hofstetter, *Vice Pres*
▲ **EMP:** 16 **EST:** 1977
SQ FT: 14,000
SALES (est): 2.1MM **Privately Held**
WEB: www.hoffstettertool.com
SIC: 3469 3544 Metal stampings; special dies, tools, jigs & fixtures

(G-1626)
HOLCOMB INDUSTRIES FLP
2655 Ulmerton Rd 303 (33762-3337)
PHONE...................................480 363-9988
Kyle Weidman, *Principal*
EMP: 8 **EST:** 2016
SALES (est): 53.8K **Privately Held**
WEB: www.tse-industries.com
SIC: 3999 Manufacturing industries

(G-1627)
HONEYWELL INTERNATIONAL INC
13350 Us Highway 19 N (33764-7290)
PHONE...................................727 539-5080
Connie Nelson, *Production*
Neil Balse, *Engineer*
Peter Csorba, *Engineer*

Nicholas Leconte, *Engineer*
Chris Meece, *Engineer*
EMP: 453
SALES (corp-wide): 34.3B **Publicly Held**
WEB: www.honeywell.com
SIC: 3599 3441 Aircraft/aerospace flight instruments & guidance systems; navigational systems & instruments; cabin environment indicators
PA: Honeywell International Inc.
855 S Mint St
Charlotte NC 28202
704 627-6200

(G-1628)
HONEYWELL INTERNATIONAL INC
13350 Us Highway 19 N (33764-7290)
PHONE...................................727 531-4611
Brian Spiegel, *Principal*
Shannon Silva, *Opers Spvr*
Kirk Gerber, *Branch Mgr*
EMP: 700
SALES (corp-wide): 34.3B **Publicly Held**
WEB: www.honeywell.com
SIC: 3812 Aircraft control systems, electronic; aircraft/aerospace flight instruments & guidance systems
PA: Honeywell International Inc.
855 S Mint St
Charlotte NC 28202
704 627-6200

(G-1629)
HONEYWELL INTERNATIONAL INC
13190 56th Ct Ste 403 (33760-4029)
PHONE...................................813 573-1166
Marco Viera, *Engineer*
Ed Gaunt, *Manager*
EMP: 7
SALES (corp-wide): 34.3B **Publicly Held**
WEB: www.honeywell.com
SIC: 3724 Aircraft engines & engine parts
PA: Honeywell International Inc.
855 S Mint St
Charlotte NC 28202
704 627-6200

(G-1630)
HOUSE OF METAL LLC
4161 114th Ter N (33762-4904)
PHONE...................................727 540-0637
Douglas Calibey, *Mng Member*
Melody A Calibey, *Mng Member*
EMP: 5 **EST:** 2005
SALES (est): 428.1K **Privately Held**
WEB: www.houseofmetallc.com
SIC: 7692 Welding repair

(G-1631)
HUTCHINS CO INC
Also Called: S T A Sales
1195 Kapp Dr (33765-2114)
PHONE...................................727 442-6651
Gerry Hutchins, *President*
Rich R Hutchins, *Vice Pres*
Jane Hecht, *Office Mgr*
▼ **EMP:** 15 **EST:** 1957
SQ FT: 17,000
SALES (est): 2.2MM **Privately Held**
WEB: www.com-pacyachts.com
SIC: 3443 3732 Fabricated plate work (boiler shop); boat building & repairing

(G-1632)
HYDREX LLC
627 Pinellas St Unit C (33756-3326)
PHONE...................................727 443-3900
John Green, *Business Mgr*
Sam Williams, *Business Mgr*
Roscelin Vivas, *Office Admin*
Boud Van Rompay,
▲ **EMP:** 9 **EST:** 2008
SQ FT: 1,500
SALES (est): 535.7K **Privately Held**
WEB: www.hydrex.be
SIC: 3731 Shipbuilding & repairing

(G-1633)
HYEND MFG INC
4711 126th Ave N Ste H (33762-4747)
PHONE...................................727 828-0826
Brian Knisley, *Principal*
EMP: 7 **EST:** 2008

SALES (est): 98.1K **Privately Held**
SIC: 3999 Manufacturing industries

(G-1634)
HYMEG CORPORATION
5410 115th Ave N (33762-4841)
P.O. Box 18802 (33762-1802)
PHONE...................................800 322-1953
Darryl Mayo, *CEO*
EMP: 5 **EST:** 2014
SALES (est): 499.3K **Privately Held**
WEB:
SIC: 3625 Resistors & resistor units

(G-1635)
HYTRONICS CORP
Also Called: Hyco
5410 115th Ave N (33760-4841)
P.O. Box 18802 (33762-1802)
PHONE...................................727 535-0413
Darryl K Mayo, *President*
▲ **EMP:** 79 **EST:** 1967
SALES (est): 4.2MM
SALES (corp-wide): 51.7MM **Privately Held**
WEB: www.hytronicscorp.com
SIC: 3677 3829 3643 3621 Coil windings, electronic; measuring & controlling devices; current-carrying wiring devices; motors & generators; transformers, except electric
PA: Electro Technik Industries, Inc.
5410 115th Ave N
Clearwater FL 33760
727 530-9555

(G-1636)
ICMFG & ASSOCIATES INC
3734 131st Ave N Ste 11 (33762-4222)
PHONE...................................727 258-4995
Tom Coghlan, *CEO*
Michael Doyle, *President*
▲ **EMP:** 8 **EST:** 2010
SALES (est): 95.1K **Privately Held**
WEB: www.icm-associates.com
SIC: 3672 Printed circuit boards

(G-1637)
ICPF DEVELOPMENT GROUP LLC (PA)
Also Called: Led Pro Services
514 N Betty Ln (33755-4708)
PHONE...................................727 474-9927
Catalina Banchero, *Principal*
Banchero Catalina, *Principal*
EMP: 5 **EST:** 2011
SALES (est): 1.6MM **Privately Held**
SIC: 3646 Commercial indusl & institutional electric lighting fixtures

(G-1638)
ICS INEX INSPECTION SYSTEMS
13075 Us Highway 19 N (33764-7224)
PHONE...................................727 535-5502
EMP: 11 **EST:** 2019
SALES (est): 385.4K **Privately Held**
WEB: www.inexvision.com
SIC: 3565 Packaging machinery

(G-1639)
ILAN CUSTOM WOODWORK LLC
1630 N Hercules Ave Ste D (33765-1987)
PHONE...................................727 272-5070
Uri Ilan, *Branch Mgr*
EMP: 24
SALES (corp-wide): 145.7K **Privately Held**
SIC: 2431 Millwork
PA: Ilan Custom Woodwork Llc
42 Ventura Dr
Dunedin FL 34698
727 272-5364

(G-1640)
IMAGECARE MAINTENANCE SYSTEMS
14055 46th St N Ste 1108 (33762-3865)
PHONE...................................727 536-8646
Adrienne Slick, *Owner*
Crystal Stiles, *Project Mgr*
Nicole Barber, *Manager*
EMP: 10 **EST:** 2007
SALES (est): 379.6K **Privately Held**
SIC: 3299 Images, small: gypsum, clay or papier mache

▲ = Import ▼=Export
◆ =Import/Export

(G-1641)
IMPACT MOLDING CLEARWATER LLC
2050 Sunnydale Blvd (33765-1201)
PHONE..................................847 718-9300
Philip Kretekos, *Mng Member*
EMP: 45 EST: 2019
SALES (est): 10.2MM
SALES (corp-wide): 134.7MM **Privately Held**
WEB: www.impactmolding.com
SIC: 3069 Floor coverings, rubber
HQ: Thunderbird Parent Plastics Llc
900 Commerce Dr Ste 105
Oak Brook IL

(G-1642)
INDUCTIVE TECHNOLOGIES INC
5410 115th Ave N (33760-4841)
PHONE..................................727 536-7861
John Sellers, *Vice Pres*
EMP: 10 EST: 2010
SALES (est): 106.8K **Privately Held**
WEB: www.inductech.com
SIC: 3612 Transformers, except electric

(G-1643)
INNQUEST CORPORATION
Also Called: Innquest Software
19321 Us Highway 19 N # 407
(33764-3142)
PHONE..................................813 288-4900
Chuck Dunaj, *President*
Ashlyn Staples, *Manager*
EMP: 16 EST: 1997
SALES (est): 3MM
SALES (corp-wide): 185.6K **Privately Held**
WEB: www.innquest.com
SIC: 7372 Prepackaged software
PA: Valsoft Corporation Inc
7405 Rte Transcanadienne Ste 100
Montreal QC H4T 1
514 316-7647

(G-1644)
INSTRUMENT TRANSFORMERS LLC
1907 Calumet St (33765-1190)
P.O. Box 2216, Schenectady NY (12301-2216)
PHONE..................................727 229-0616
John Lu, *Treasurer*
Perry Genovese, *Mng Member*
Bob Criswell, *Info Tech Mgr*
Suzann Lopez, *Info Tech Mgr*
Jeffrey Keogh,
▲ EMP: 642 EST: 1975
SQ FT: 170,000
SALES (est): 143.4MM
SALES (corp-wide): 74.2B **Publicly Held**
WEB: www.instrumenttransformers.com
SIC: 3612 Instrument transformers (except portable)
PA: General Electric Company
5 Necco St
Boston MA 02210
617 443-3000

(G-1645)
INTERGLOBAL CAPITAL INC
Also Called: Chassis King
1016 Pnc De Leon Blvd (33756-1073)
PHONE..................................727 585-1500
Donald Pratt, *President*
John Smith, *Principal*
▼ EMP: 5 EST: 1994
SALES (est): 501.3K **Privately Held**
WEB: www.interglobalcapital.com
SIC: 3715 Truck trailers

(G-1646)
INTERPRINT INCORPORATED (HQ)
Also Called: Interprint Web Printing
12350 Us 19 N (33764-7418)
PHONE..................................727 531-8957
James E Morten, *Ch of Bd*
John Rickerman, *President*
James A Morten, *Vice Pres*
Scott Morten, *Vice Pres*
Daniel McCurdy, *Plant Mgr*
▼ EMP: 76 EST: 1965
SQ FT: 13,000

SALES (est): 13.5MM **Privately Held**
WEB: www.printerusa.com
SIC: 2796 2789 2752 Platemaking services; bookbinding & related work; commercial printing, offset
PA: Morten Enterprises, Inc.
12350 Us Highway 19 N
Clearwater FL 33764
727 531-8957

(G-1647)
INTERSTATE WLDG & FABRICATION
1939 Sherwood St (33765-1932)
PHONE..................................727 446-1449
Charles A Bates Jr, *President*
John C Bates, *Corp Secy*
EMP: 16 EST: 1988
SQ FT: 12,000
SALES (est): 2.7MM **Privately Held**
WEB: www.interstatewf.com
SIC: 3441 7692 3444 Building components, structural steel; welding repair; sheet metalwork

(G-1648)
IPC GLOBAL
1062 Cephas Rd (33765-2107)
PHONE..................................727 470-2134
Norbert Heuser, *Owner*
EMP: 9 EST: 2012
SALES (est): 341.2K **Privately Held**
WEB: www.hienergy.biz
SIC: 3829 Measuring & controlling devices

(G-1649)
IRONHORSE PRESSWORKS INC
Also Called: Harris Letterpress
406 S Jupiter Ave (33755-6517)
PHONE..................................727 462-9988
Earl Harris, *CEO*
Margaret Harris, *Vice Pres*
Troy Harris, *Vice Pres*
Denise McDonald, *Treasurer*
Denise Milano, *Treasurer*
EMP: 9 EST: 1995
SQ FT: 7,000
SALES (est): 727.2K **Privately Held**
SIC: 2752 Commercial printing, offset

(G-1650)
J T WALKER INDUSTRIES INC (PA)
1310 N Hercules Ave Ste A (33765-1940)
PHONE..................................727 461-0501
Peter Desoto, *CEO*
Jay K Poppleton, *President*
Janet L Fasenmyer, *Vice Pres*
Michael Luther, *Vice Pres*
Steve Brush, *Finance Mgr*
◆ EMP: 30 EST: 1997
SQ FT: 15,000
SALES (est): 250.9MM **Privately Held**
WEB: www.mihvac.com
SIC: 3442 3089 3585 5193 Screens, window, metal; window frames & sash, plastic; parts for heating, cooling & refrigerating equipment; nursery stock

(G-1651)
JAKOBSEN TOOL CO INC
805 Pierce St (33756-5525)
PHONE..................................727 447-1143
Norman Brown, *President*
EMP: 8 EST: 1984
SQ FT: 5,300
SALES (est): 568.4K **Privately Held**
SIC: 3599 Machine shop, jobbing & repair

(G-1652)
JAMES REESE ENTERPRISES INC
Also Called: Florida Precision Tool
1714 Misty Plateau Trl (33765-1828)
PHONE..................................727 386-5311
James Reese, *President*
EMP: 10 EST: 2012
SALES (est): 989.4K **Privately Held**
WEB: www.validity.us
SIC: 3423 8742 Wrenches, hand tools; sales (including sales management) consultant

(G-1653)
JIM APPLEYS TRU-ARC INC
5140 110th Ave N (33760-4804)
PHONE..................................727 571-3007
James W Appley II, *President*
Judith H Appley, *Corp Secy*
Larry Macdonald, *Mfg Staff*
EMP: 10 EST: 1978
SQ FT: 12,000
SALES (est): 984K **Privately Held**
WEB: www.jimappleystruarc.com
SIC: 3599 3443 7692 3444 Machine shop, jobbing & repair; fabricated plate work (boiler shop); welding repair; sheet metalwork

(G-1654)
JOHN & BETSY HOVLAND
Also Called: Creative Monogramming
2073 Range Rd (33765-2124)
PHONE..................................727 449-2032
John Hovland, *Partner*
Betsy Hovland, *Partner*
EMP: 7 EST: 1988
SQ FT: 1,250
SALES (est): 452.2K **Privately Held**
SIC: 2284 Embroidery thread

(G-1655)
JORMAC AEROSPACE INC
13130 56th Ct Ste 604 (33760-4018)
PHONE..................................727 549-9600
Steve Jourdenais, *Owner*
Frank Nelson, *General Mgr*
Jerry Koh, *VP Engrg*
Jason Inlow, *Engineer*
Brian Barber, *VP Sls/Mktg*
EMP: 16 EST: 2011
SALES (est): 629.7K **Privately Held**
WEB: www.jormac.com
SIC: 3812 Aircraft/aerospace flight instruments & guidance systems

(G-1656)
JTL ENTERPRISES (DELAWARE)
Also Called: Hydromassage
15395 Roosevelt Blvd (33760-3500)
PHONE..................................727 536-5566
Paul J Lunter, *President*
Fred Seabright, *General Mgr*
Mark Lowder, *Vice Pres*
Tim Shadler, *Plant Mgr*
Jon Roever, *Engineer*
◆ EMP: 35 EST: 1989
SQ FT: 40,000
SALES (est): 9.1MM **Privately Held**
SIC: 3841 Surgical & medical instruments

(G-1657)
JW APPLEY AND SON INC
13215 38th St N (33762-4229)
PHONE..................................727 572-4910
Doug Jennings, *President*
Patricia Pearson, *Purchasing*
Drew Ehehalt, *Sales Executive*
Sue Belmonte, *Admin Sec*
EMP: 30 EST: 1931
SQ FT: 17,000
SALES (est): 5.1MM **Privately Held**
WEB: www.jwappley.com
SIC: 3599 Machine shop, jobbing & repair

(G-1658)
KACOO USA LLC
4500 140th Ave N Ste 101 (33762-3848)
PHONE..................................727 233-8237
Huan Huan Jin,
Gail Holden,
▲ EMP: 6 EST: 2014
SQ FT: 600
SALES (est): 396.7K **Privately Held**
SIC: 2339 Women's & misses' outerwear

(G-1659)
KEMCO SYSTEMS CO LLC (PA)
11500 47th St N (33762-4955)
PHONE..................................727 573-2323
Tom Vanden Heuvel, *President*
Ann Elder, *Engineer*
Tyler Grady, *Engineer*
Joanie Vergo, *CFO*
Anna Sikocinska, *Accountant*
◆ EMP: 57 EST: 1969
SQ FT: 58,000

SALES (est): 12.2MM **Privately Held**
WEB: www.kemcosystems.com
SIC: 3589 3582 Water treatment equipment, industrial; commercial laundry equipment

(G-1660)
KEN CLEARYS TWO LLC
10900 47th St N (33762-5001)
PHONE..................................727 573-0700
Cleary Kenneth J II,
EMP: 17 EST: 2011
SALES (est): 1.8MM **Privately Held**
SIC: 2511 2521 Wood household furniture; wood office furniture

(G-1661)
KINETIC INDUSTRIES LLC
Also Called: Polymatics Plastic Processing
10445 49th St N Ste A (33762-5036)
PHONE..................................727 572-7604
Robert Hoel, *Partner*
Elena Hoel, *Partner*
EMP: 6 EST: 1974
SQ FT: 6,200
SALES (est): 763.5K **Privately Held**
WEB: www.polymatics.com
SIC: 3089 3599 3544 Injection molding of plastics; machine shop, jobbing & repair; special dies, tools, jigs & fixtures

(G-1662)
KLEIDS ENTERPRISES INC
Also Called: Made To Match Clothing Company
22023 Us Highway 19 N (33765-2362)
P.O. Box 2784, Dunedin (34697-2784)
PHONE..................................727 796-7900
Joanne Kleiderman, *President*
Monroe Kleiderman, *Vice Pres*
EMP: 6 EST: 1981
SQ FT: 8,000
SALES (est): 471.5K **Privately Held**
WEB: www.kleids.com
SIC: 2337 2331 Women's & misses' suits & coats; T-shirts & tops, women's: made from purchased materials

(G-1663)
KLOPFER HOLDINGS INC
2134 Sunnydale Blvd (33765-1274)
PHONE..................................727 472-2002
EMP: 70 EST: 1978
SALES (est): 2.4MM **Privately Held**
SIC: 3451 Screw machine products

(G-1664)
KNOTHOLE CREATIONS INC
13205 40th St N (33762-4267)
PHONE..................................727 561-9107
Paul Brown Jr, *President*
David M Brown, *Vice Pres*
David Brown, *Vice Pres*
Anne M Brown, *Treasurer*
Jennifer L Brown, *Admin Sec*
EMP: 5 EST: 1992
SQ FT: 7,824
SALES (est): 582K **Privately Held**
WEB: www.knotholecreations.com
SIC: 2434 Wood kitchen cabinets

(G-1665)
KODIAK SOFTWARE INC
832 Narcissus Ave (33767-1336)
PHONE..................................727 599-8839
Susan Broad, *Director*
EMP: 14 EST: 2001
SALES (est): 87.6K **Privately Held**
WEB: www.kodiak.com
SIC: 7372 Prepackaged software

(G-1666)
KULAGA WILLIAM JOHN
Also Called: Cape Coral Homes Magazine
2080 Envoy Ct (33764-2560)
P.O. Box 8054 (33758-8054)
PHONE..................................727 536-3180
William J Kulaga, *Owner*
EMP: 7 EST: 2007
SALES (est): 40.1K **Privately Held**
SIC: 2741 Miscellaneous publishing

(G-1667)
L & N LABEL COMPANY INC
2051 Sunnydale Blvd (33765-1202)
PHONE..................................727 442-5400

Stephen R Sabadosh, *President*
Julee Sabadosh, *Vice Pres*
Dave Gioia, *Manager*
Shelley Johnson, *Executive*
EMP: 25 **EST:** 1977
SQ FT: 9,000
SALES (est): 3.1MM **Privately Held**
WEB: www.lnlabel.com
SIC: 2759 2752 Labels & seals: printing;
commercial printing, offset

(G-1668)
L E M G INC
Also Called: Sir Speedy
1878 Drew St (33765-2911)
PHONE..................................727 461-5300
Michael G Schratt, *President*
EMP: 5 **EST:** 1977
SQ FT: 3,000
SALES (est): 411.9K **Privately Held**
WEB: www.sirspeedy.com
SIC: 2752 7334 2789 Commercial print-
ing, lithographic; mimeographing; book-
binding & related work

(G-1669)
LABEL PRINTING SERVICE
1245 N Hercules Ave (33765-1921)
PHONE..................................727 820-1226
EMP: 8 **EST:** 2011
SALES (est): 120.6K **Privately Held**
WEB: www.lnlabel.com
SIC: 2752 Commercial printing, litho-
graphic

(G-1670)
LABELPRO INC
Also Called: Grafix
14409 60th St N (33760-2710)
PHONE..................................727 538-2149
Jack Frieder, *President*
EMP: 10 **EST:** 1970
SQ FT: 3,500
SALES (est): 971.8K **Privately Held**
SIC: 3479 3993 2752 2672 Name plates:
engraved, etched, etc.; signs & advertis-
ing specialties; commercial printing, litho-
graphic; coated & laminated paper;
packaging paper & plastics film, coated &
laminated

(G-1671)
LETO LLC
Also Called: Sunglo Paint
14483 62nd St N (33760-2722)
PHONE..................................813 486-8049
Christopher S Leto,
EMP: 5 **EST:** 2020
SALES (est): 504K **Privately Held**
SIC: 3479 Painting of metal products

(G-1672)
LIGHTNING CONNECTING RODS LLC
1630 N Hercules Ave Ste B (33765-1987)
PHONE..................................727 733-2054
Robert S King, *CEO*
EMP: 6 **EST:** 2011
SALES (est): 756.7K **Privately Held**
WEB: www.lightningconnectingrods.com
SIC: 3714 Motor vehicle parts & acces-
sories

(G-1673)
LIGHTNING MASTER CORPORATION
Also Called: Bolt Lightning Protection
2100 Palmetto St Ste A (33765-2101)
PHONE..................................800 749-6800
Bruce Kaiser, *President*
Ramy Malaty, *General Mgr*
Joseph Uhrinek, *General Mgr*
Steven Lenis, *Engineer*
Lori Smith, *Sales Staff*
▼ **EMP:** 40 **EST:** 1984
SQ FT: 30,000
SALES (est): 10.5MM **Privately Held**
WEB: www.lightningmaster.com
SIC: 3629 Electronic generation equipment

(G-1674)
LITHIONICS BATTERY LLC
1770 Calumet St (33765-1137)
PHONE..................................727 726-4204
Reuben Macias, *Prdtn Mgr*
Melissa A Tartaglia, *CFO*

Steven Tartaglia, *Mng Member*
Timothy O Sullivan,
Timothy Sullivan,
▼ **EMP:** 14 **EST:** 2010
SQ FT: 12,000
SALES (est): 2.8MM **Privately Held**
WEB: www.lithionicsbattery.com
SIC: 3691 Storage batteries

(G-1675)
LITHOTEC COMMERCIAL PRINTING
12350 Us Highway 19 N (33764-7418)
PHONE..................................727 541-4614
Barbara Argyros, *President*
William Argyros, *Vice Pres*
EMP: 10 **EST:** 1969
SQ FT: 13,500
SALES (est): 818.7K **Privately Held**
WEB: www.lithotec.net
SIC: 2752 Commercial printing, offset

(G-1676)
LUCKE ENTERPRISES INC
Also Called: Fastsigns
2781 Gulf To Bay Blvd (33759-3904)
PHONE..................................727 797-1177
Michael J Lucke, *President*
EMP: 5 **EST:** 1995
SALES (est): 553.4K **Privately Held**
SIC: 3993 Signs & advertising specialties

(G-1677)
M AND T PRO COATING INC
2200 Euclid Cir N (33764-6814)
PHONE..................................727 272-4620
Mauricio Torres, *President*
EMP: 7 **EST:** 2016
SALES (est): 96.4K **Privately Held**
SIC: 3479 Metal coating & allied service

(G-1678)
M O PRECISION MOLDERS INC
13750 49th St N (33762-3735)
PHONE..................................727 573-4466
EMP: 14
SQ FT: 15,550
SALES (est): 1.8MM **Privately Held**
SIC: 3089 Injection Molding

(G-1679)
MAGIC TILT TRAILER MFG CO INC
Also Called: Magic Trailers
2161 Lions Club Rd (33764-6883)
PHONE..................................727 535-5561
Craig Clawson, *President*
Graham Grainger, *Engineer*
Tony Dippolito, *Regl Sales Mgr*
Robert Lyons, *Manager*
Robert Covert, *Representative*
▼ **EMP:** 50 **EST:** 1955
SQ FT: 48,000
SALES (est): 8.7MM **Privately Held**
WEB: www.magictilt.com
SIC: 3354 3799 Aluminum extruded prod-
ucts; boat trailers

(G-1680)
MAGNATRONIX CORPORATION INC
Also Called: Fetco
5410 115th Ave N (33760-4841)
PHONE..................................727 536-7861
Roger C Mayo, *President*
Roger Mayo, *President*
John Sellers, *COO*
EMP: 13 **EST:** 1980
SALES (est): 776.2K **Privately Held**
SIC: 3612 Specialty transformers

(G-1681)
MAGNIFICAT HOLDINGS LLC
Also Called: Yo Mama's Foods
1125 Eldridge St (33755-4310)
PHONE..................................727 798-0512
David Habib, *Principal*
▼ **EMP:** 5 **EST:** 2018
SALES (est): 500K **Privately Held**
SIC: 2032 Italian foods: packaged in cans,
jars, etc.

(G-1682)
MAGNUM VENUS PLASTECH
5148 113th Ave N (33760-4835)
PHONE..................................727 573-2955
Tom Slay, *Sales Staff*
Dave Miller, *Info Tech Mgr*
EMP: 10 **EST:** 2017
SALES (est): 320.1K **Privately Held**
WEB: www.mvpind.com
SIC: 3296 Mineral wool

(G-1683)
MARINE METAL PRODUCTS CO
2154 Calumet St (33765-1309)
PHONE..................................727 461-5575
Clark M Lea Jr, *President*
Clark M Lea Sr, *Vice Pres*
Mary L Lea, *Treasurer*
Catherine Campbell, *Controller*
Cathy Campbell, *Controller*
▲ **EMP:** 9 **EST:** 1960
SQ FT: 21,000
SALES (est): 1.4MM **Privately Held**
WEB: www.marinemetal.com
SIC: 3949 3561 3523 Buckets, fish & bait;
fishing tackle, general; pumps & pumping
equipment; farm machinery & equipment

(G-1684)
MARPRO MARINE WAYS LLC
1822 N Belcher Rd (33765-1400)
PHONE..................................727 447-4930
George G Pappas, *Principal*
EMP: 7 **EST:** 2011
SALES (est): 210.1K **Privately Held**
SIC: 3732 Boat building & repairing

(G-1685)
MARYSOL TECHNOLOGIES INC
1444c S Belcher Rd 136 (33764-2877)
PHONE..................................727 712-1523
Dan Bar Joseph, *Principal*
EMP: 7 **EST:** 2003
SALES (est): 409.4K **Privately Held**
WEB: www.marysoltechnologies.com
SIC: 3826 3841 Laser scientific & engi-
neering instruments; surgical lasers

(G-1686)
MATHESON TRI-GAS INC
Also Called: Tri Gas 05
12650 49th St N (33762-4601)
PHONE..................................727 572-8737
Robert Richardson, *Branch Mgr*
EMP: 8 **Privately Held**
WEB: www.mathesongas.com
SIC: 2813 5084 Industrial gases; welding
machinery & equipment
HQ: Matheson Tri-Gas, Inc.
3 Mountainview Rd Ste 3 # 3
Warren NJ 07059
908 991-9200

(G-1687)
MATRIX MACHINING & MFG LLC (PA)
1904 Calumet St (33765-1107)
PHONE..................................908 355-1900
Jonathan Barnes, *Partner*
Arun S Samal, *Managing Dir*
Hank Barnes, *Mng Member*
EMP: 10 **EST:** 2014
SQ FT: 6,000
SALES (est): 1.7MM **Privately Held**
WEB: www.matrix-fl.com
SIC: 3599 Machine shop, jobbing & repair

(G-1688)
MAXXIM MEDICAL GROUP INC
4750 118th Ave N (33762-4451)
PHONE..................................727 571-3717
Tron Armstrong, *Principal*
EMP: 11 **EST:** 2000
SALES (est): 203.1K **Privately Held**
SIC: 3841 Surgical instruments & appara-
tus

(G-1689)
MCM INDUSTRIES INC
1721 Penny Ln (33756-3685)
P.O. Box 2567, Largo (33779-2567)
PHONE..................................727 259-9894
Eric Dale Frechette, *Principal*
EMP: 10 **EST:** 2008

SALES (est): 189.4K **Privately Held**
WEB: www.mcmindustries.com
SIC: 3999 Manufacturing industries

(G-1690)
MEDICAL DEVELOPMENTAL RESEARCH
2451 Enterprise Rd (33763-1702)
PHONE..................................727 793-0170
EMP: 7 **EST:** 2019
SALES (est): 126.4K **Privately Held**
SIC: 3851 Ophthalmic goods

(G-1691)
MELITTA NORTH AMERICA INC (DH)
Also Called: Melitta USA
13925 58th St N (33760-3721)
PHONE..................................727 535-2111
Martin T Miller, *President*
Fred Lueck, *Vice Pres*
◆ **EMP:** 100 **EST:** 1996
SQ FT: 104,000
SALES (est): 93.1MM
SALES (corp-wide): 2.3B **Privately Held**
WEB: www.melitta.com
SIC: 2095 3634 5499 Roasted coffee;
coffee makers, electric: household; coffee
HQ: Melitta Group Management Gmbh &
Co. Kg
Marienstr. 88
Minden NW 32425
571 404-60

(G-1692)
MELITTA USA INC (DH)
13925 58th St N (33760-3721)
PHONE..................................727 535-2111
Martin Miller, *President*
Fred Lueck, *CFO*
Phil Wilde, *Controller*
Taylor Burdett, *Business Anlyst*
Ed Mitchell, *Admin Sec*
◆ **EMP:** 55 **EST:** 1963
SQ FT: 104,000
SALES (est): 43MM
SALES (corp-wide): 2.3B **Privately Held**
WEB: www.melitta.com
SIC: 2095 3634 Coffee roasting (except by
wholesale grocers); coffee makers, elec-
tric: household

(G-1693)
MERIDIAN SOUTH AVIATION LLC
15875 Fairchild Dr (33762-3510)
P.O. Box 17882 (33762-0882)
PHONE..................................727 536-5387
Michael L Hauser,
EMP: 5 **EST:** 2006
SQ FT: 2,000
SALES (est): 868.9K **Privately Held**
WEB: www.clpilots.com
SIC: 3721 Aircraft

(G-1694)
METAL CULVERTS INC
2148 Pine Forest Dr (33764-5729)
PHONE..................................727 531-1431
Shawn Hapeman, *Manager*
EMP: 18
SQ FT: 27,837
SALES (corp-wide): 19.5MM **Privately Held**
WEB: www.metalculverts.com
SIC: 3444 3312 3317 Culverts, sheet
metal; blast furnaces & steel mills; steel
pipe & tubes
PA: Metal Culverts, Inc.
711 Heisinger Rd
Jefferson City MO 65109
573 636-7312

(G-1695)
METAL INDUSTRIES INC (HQ)
Also Called: Metal Aire
1985 Carroll St (33765-1909)
PHONE..................................727 441-2651
Jay K Poppleton, *CEO*
Peter Desoto, *CEO*
Grant Tyson, *President*
Mark Paul, *General Mgr*
Janet L Fasenmyer, *Vice Pres*
◆ **EMP:** 200 **EST:** 1949
SQ FT: 700,000

SALES (est): 231.8MM
SALES (corp-wide): 1.2B **Privately Held**
WEB: www.mihvac.com
SIC: 3585 Parts for heating, cooling & re-
frigerating equipment
PA: Greenheck Fan Corporation
1100 Greenheck Dr
Schofield WI 54476
715 359-6171

(G-1696)
METAL INDUSTRIES INC
1310 N Hercules Ave (33765-1940)
PHONE...............................727 441-2651
Barbara Shaloo, *Marketing Mgr*
David Hawkins, *Branch Mgr*
Thomas Gardner, *Manager*
EMP: 51
SALES (corp-wide): 1.2B **Privately Held**
WEB: www.mihvac.com
SIC: 3585 3444 Parts for heating, cooling
& refrigerating equipment; sheet metal-
work
HQ: Metal Industries, Inc.
1985 Carroll St
Clearwater FL 33765
727 441-2651

(G-1697)
MICA VISIONS INC
2650 Enterprise Rd Ste D (33763-1101)
PHONE...............................727 712-3213
James Hazlett II, *President*
Sean Wall, *Vice Pres*
Mike Francisco, *Prdtn Mgr*
EMP: 5 EST: 1989
SQ FT: 5,000
SALES (est): 544K **Privately Held**
WEB: www.micavisions.com
SIC: 2511 Wood household furniture

(G-1698)
MICROSS PRMIER SMCDTR SVCS LLC
Also Called: Micross Components
4400 140th Ave N Ste 140 (33762-3813)
PHONE...............................727 532-1777
Anthony Mastry, *Manager*
EMP: 44 EST: 2013
SALES (est): 3.5MM
SALES (corp-wide): 332.8MM **Privately Held**
WEB: www.micross.com
SIC: 3674 Semiconductors & related de-
vices
HQ: Premier Semiconductor Services Llc
1050 Perimeter Rd Ste 201
Manchester NH 03103
267 954-0130

(G-1699)
MID STATE SCREEN GRAPHICS LLC
13183 38th St N (33762-4228)
PHONE...............................727 573-2299
Richard Hawley, *Vice Pres*
Debbie Sytsma, *Opers Mgr*
Carrie Brightbill,
EMP: 20 EST: 1978
SQ FT: 12,400
SALES (est): 1.2MM
SALES (corp-wide): 54.1MM **Privately Held**
WEB: www.midstatescreengraphics.com
SIC: 2759 Screen printing
PA: Thermopatch Corporation
2204 Erie Blvd E
Syracuse NY 13224
315 446-8110

(G-1700)
MIKE COPE RACE CARS LLC
14152 63rd Way N (33760-3616)
PHONE...............................352 585-2810
Michael S Cope, *Manager*
EMP: 7 EST: 2015
SALES (est): 225.9K **Privately Held**
WEB: www.mikecoperacecars.com
SIC: 3711 Automobile assembly, including
specialty automobiles

(G-1701)
MODERN MAIL PRINT SLUTIONS INC
14201 58th St N (33760-2802)
PHONE...............................727 572-6245
Barbara Cosser, *President*
Rick Cosser, *Vice Pres*
Lisa Giglio, *Accounts Mgr*
Sherie Carlson, *Manager*
EMP: 30 EST: 1976
SQ FT: 19,760
SALES (est): 5.5MM **Privately Held**
WEB: www.modmail.com
SIC: 2752 Commercial printing, offset

(G-1702)
MONIN INC (DH)
Also Called: Monin Gourmet Flavorings
2100 Range Rd (33765-2125)
PHONE...............................727 461-3033
William Lombardo, *CEO*
Olivier Monin, *President*
Christophe Bernardbacot, *Managing Dir*
Catherine Bach, *Business Mgr*
Vittorio Caputi, *Business Mgr*
◆ EMP: 44 EST: 1912
SQ FT: 200,000
SALES (est): 119.5MM **Privately Held**
SIC: 2087 Flavoring extracts & syrups
HQ: Georges Monin Sas
5 Rue Ferdinand De Lesseps
Bourges 18000
248 506-436

(G-1703)
MORTEN ENTERPRISES INC (PA)
12350 Us Highway 19 N (33764-7418)
PHONE...............................727 531-8957
James E Morten, *CEO*
James A Morten, *President*
Scott J Morten, *Vice Pres*
EMP: 15 EST: 1965
SQ FT: 13,228
SALES (est): 13.5MM **Privately Held**
SIC: 2752 Commercial printing, offset

(G-1704)
MORTON PLANT MEASE HEALTH CARE
430 Pinellas St (33756-3365)
PHONE...............................727 462-7052
EMP: 1800
SALES (corp-wide): 18.8B **Privately Held**
WEB: www.mortonplant.com
SIC: 3842 8099 Hearing aids; blood re-
lated health services
HQ: Morton Plant Mease Health Care, Inc.
300 Pinellas St
Clearwater FL 33756

(G-1705)
MR BILLS FINE FOODS
1115 Ponce De Leon Blvd (33756-1040)
PHONE...............................727 581-9850
EMP: 6 EST: 2011
SALES (est): 382.7K **Privately Held**
WEB: www.mrbillsfinefoods.com
SIC: 2099 Food preparations

(G-1706)
MSP INDUSTRIES LLC
Also Called: Model Screw Products
1500 N Belcher Rd (33765-1301)
PHONE...............................727 443-5764
David Knuepfer Jr,
EMP: 128 EST: 2015
SALES (est): 37.4MM **Privately Held**
WEB: www.mspindustriesusa.com
SIC: 3599 3451 Machine shop, jobbing &
repair; screw machine products

(G-1707)
MTS SALES & MARKETING INC
12920 Automobile Blvd (33762-4714)
PHONE...............................727 812-2830
Todd E Seigel, *President*
EMP: 56 EST: 1996
SALES (est): 7.5MM **Publicly Held**
SIC: 3089 Plastic containers, except foam
HQ: Mts Medication Technologies, Inc.
2003 Gandy Blvd N Ste 800
Saint Petersburg FL 33702
727 576-6311

(G-1708)
MY ADVENTURE TO FIT INC
1245 N Hercules Ave (33765-1921)
PHONE...............................727 200-3081
EMP: 10
SALES (corp-wide): 403.5K **Privately Held**
SIC: 2023 Dietary supplements, dairy &
non-dairy based
PA: My Adventure To Fit, Inc.
1497 Main St
Dunedin FL
818 254-6326

(G-1709)
MY FAMILYS SEASONINGS LLC
15301 Roosevelt Blvd # 303 (33760-3561)
P.O. Box 5925, Oceanside CA (92052-
5925)
PHONE...............................863 698-7968
Christine Quinn, *CEO*
EMP: 10 EST: 2005
SALES (est): 1.3MM **Privately Held**
WEB: www.myfamilyseasonings.com
SIC: 2099 5141 Seasonings: dry mixes;
groceries, general line

(G-1710)
N C A MANUFACTURING INC
1985 Carroll St (33765-1909)
PHONE...............................727 441-2651
James R Tatum, *Ch of Bd*
Wayne Binder, *Vice Pres*
Andrew M Simurda, *Vice Pres*
▼ EMP: 64 EST: 1961
SQ FT: 54,000
SALES (est): 12.9MM
SALES (corp-wide): 1.2B **Privately Held**
SIC: 3444 Sheet metalwork
HQ: Metal Industries, Inc.
1985 Carroll St
Clearwater FL 33765
727 441-2651

(G-1711)
NATIONAL SIGN INC
5651 116th Ave N (33760-4812)
PHONE...............................727 572-1503
Dennis D Devine, *President*
EMP: 10 EST: 2003
SALES (est): 675.7K **Privately Held**
SIC: 3993 Signs & advertising specialties

(G-1712)
NATIONAL TRAFFIC SIGNS INC
14521 60th St N (33760-2712)
PHONE...............................727 446-7983
William E Malia, *President*
Barbara Malia, *Treasurer*
Donna Desanto, *Graphic Designe*
Paul Mallett, *Graphic Designe*
EMP: 9 EST: 1962
SQ FT: 5,000
SALES (est): 1.7MM **Privately Held**
WEB: www.ntsigns.com
SIC: 3993 2752 5085 2396 Signs, not
made in custom sign painting shops; de-
cals, lithographed; signmaker equipment
& supplies; automotive & apparel trim-
mings

(G-1713)
NAUSET ENTERPRISES INC
Also Called: Affordable Displays
2120 Calumet St Ste 1 (33765-1325)
PHONE...............................727 443-3469
William Brehm, *President*
Rosemary Brehm, *Vice Pres*
EMP: 9 EST: 1992
SQ FT: 7,500
SALES (est): 1.2MM **Privately Held**
SIC: 2542 2541 3993 Fixtures: display, of-
fice or store: except wood; display fix-
tures, wood; signs & advertising
specialties

(G-1714)
NEAT CLEAN GROUP INC
2523 Marina Key Ln (33763-2162)
PHONE...............................727 459-6079
Zana Lukosiuniene, *Principal*
EMP: 10 EST: 2005
SALES (est): 785.2K **Privately Held**
SIC: 3699 Cleaning equipment, ultrasonic,
except medical & dental

(G-1715)
NELCO PRODUCTS INC
15251 Roosevelt Blvd # 202 (33760-3560)
PHONE...............................727 533-8282
William Mazzio, *General Mgr*
Matt McGuirk, *General Mgr*
William Dalrymple, *Opers Staff*
Bill Mazzio, *Accounts Exec*
Camille Giannetti, *Manager*
EMP: 8
SALES (corp-wide): 10.7MM **Privately Held**
WEB: www.nelcoproducts.com
SIC: 3398 Metal heat treating
PA: Nelco Products, Inc.
22 Riverside Dr
Pembroke MA 02359
781 826-3010

(G-1716)
NEW NAUTICAL COATINGS INC (HQ)
14805 49th St N (33762-2809)
PHONE...............................727 523-8053
Erik Norrie, *CEO*
David Norrie, *President*
Mike Detmer, *COO*
Tommy Craft, *Vice Pres*
Doug Laue, *CFO*
◆ EMP: 30 EST: 1978
SQ FT: 39,000
SALES (est): 14.1MM
SALES (corp-wide): 10.8B **Privately Held**
WEB: www.seahawkpaints.com
SIC: 2851 Marine paints
PA: Akzo Nobel N.V.
Christian Neefestraat 2
Amsterdam
889 697-555

(G-1717)
NEWSPAPER PRINTING COMPANY
12198 44th St N (33762-5109)
PHONE...............................727 572-7488
John Elven, *Owner*
Dick Walsh, *Executive*
EMP: 8 EST: 2013
SALES (est): 102.9K **Privately Held**
SIC: 2711 2759 Commercial printing &
newspaper publishing combined; com-
mercial printing

(G-1718)
NORDQUIST DIELECTRICS INC
Also Called: EMI Filter Company
12750 59th Way N (33760-3906)
PHONE...............................727 585-7990
Ted Nordquist, *President*
Ann Luce, *Vice Pres*
Eric Nordquist, *Vice Pres*
Kevin T Luce, *Manager*
EMP: 25 EST: 1973
SQ FT: 10,000
SALES (est): 2.8MM **Privately Held**
WEB: www.emifiltercompany.com
SIC: 3675 3677 Electronic capacitors; fil-
tration devices, electronic

(G-1719)
NORRIS PRECISION MFG INC
4680 110th Ave N (33762-4951)
P.O. Box 1968, Pinellas Park (33780-1968)
PHONE...............................727 572-6330
Arthur Norris III, *President*
Nancy L Norris, *Corp Secy*
Matt Durfee, *Maint Spvr*
Andrea Just, *Purch Dir*
Richard Nash, *QC Mgr*
EMP: 75 EST: 1978
SQ FT: 52,000
SALES (est): 19.6MM **Privately Held**
WEB: www.norrisprecision.com
SIC: 3724 Aircraft engines & engine parts

(G-1720)
NOTE BIN INC
Also Called: Abyde
29399 Us 19 N Ste 360 (33761-2137)
PHONE...............................727 642-8530
Matt Deblasi, *CEO*
EMP: 12 EST: 2017
SALES (est): 607.9K **Privately Held**
SIC: 7372 Application computer software

(G-1721)
NUENERGY TECHNOLOGIES CORP
601 Cleveland St Ste 501 (33755-4182)
P.O. Box 329 (33757-0329)
PHONE.................................866 895-6838
Hector M Guevara, *President*
Rolando Alcover, *Vice Pres*
EMP: 8 EST: 2009
SALES (est): 416.8K Privately Held
WEB: www.nuenergytech.com
SIC: 3699 Electrical equipment & supplies

(G-1722)
NULAB INC
519 Cleveland St Ste 101 (33755-4009)
PHONE.................................727 446-1126
Hakan Johanson, *Branch Mgr*
EMP: 70 Privately Held
WEB: www.nulabinc.com
SIC: 2833 2048 Vitamins, natural or synthetic: bulk, uncompounded; prepared feeds
PA: Nulab, Inc.
2161 Logan St
Clearwater FL 33765

(G-1723)
NUTRITION LABORATORIES INC
2151 Logan St (33765-1312)
PHONE.................................915 496-7531
Hakan Johanson, *CEO*
Juan Contreras, *Prdtn Mgr*
EMP: 25 EST: 2006
SALES (est): 2MM Privately Held
WEB: www.nutritionlabs.us
SIC: 2023 Dietary supplements, dairy & non-dairy based

(G-1724)
NUTRITION LABORATORIES INC
2141 Logan St (33765-1312)
PHONE.................................727 442-2747
Hakan Johanson, *President*
Hakkan Johanson, *President*
▲ EMP: 20 EST: 2004
SALES (est): 496.6K Privately Held
WEB: www.nutritionlabs.us
SIC: 2834 2087 5149 Vitamin preparations; beverage bases; beverage bases, concentrates, syrups, powders & mixes; beverage concentrates

(G-1725)
OCEANIC ELECTRICAL MFG CO INC
1904 Calumet St (33765-1107)
PHONE.................................908 355-1900
C Hank Barnes, *President*
EMP: 12 EST: 1921
SQ FT: 6,000
SALES (est): 535.5K Privately Held
WEB: www.oceanicelectric.com
SIC: 3641 Electric lamps & parts for specialized applications

(G-1726)
OMNIVORE TECHNOLOGIES INC
13577 Feather Sound Dr # 390 (33762-5547)
PHONE.................................800 293-4058
Mike Wior, *CEO*
Daniel Singer, *COO*
Feras Ghandour, *Vice Pres*
Matt Haselhoff, *Vice Pres*
Danielle Jaksic, *Vice Pres*
EMP: 55 EST: 2013
SQ FT: 3,500
SALES (est): 6MM Privately Held
WEB: www.omnivore.io
SIC: 7372 Business oriented computer software

(G-1727)
ONGOING CARE SOLUTIONS INC
11721 Us Highway 19 N (33764-7405)
PHONE.................................727 526-0707
Richard Nace, *President*
Linda Lee, *Vice Pres*
Brian Trokey, *Purch Mgr*

◆ EMP: 27 EST: 1992
SALES (est): 4.8MM Privately Held
WEB: www.ongoingcare.com
SIC: 3842 Orthopedic appliances; splints, pneumatic & wood

(G-1728)
OPIE CHOICE LLC
Also Called: Futura International
22047 Us Highway 19 N (33765-2363)
PHONE.................................727 726-5157
EMP: 14
SALES (corp-wide): 2MM Privately Held
SIC: 7372 Prepackaged Software Services
PA: Opie Choice Llc
3870 Nw 83rd St
Gainesville FL 32606
352 331-3741

(G-1729)
ORD OF AHEPA CH 356 DAILY & T
2555 Enterprise Rd Ste 10 (33763-1150)
PHONE.................................727 791-1040
John Tsagaris, *Principal*
EMP: 7 EST: 2011
SALES (est): 197.9K Privately Held
SIC: 2711 Newspapers, publishing & printing

(G-1730)
ORIFLOW
2125 Range Rd Ste B (33765-2153)
PHONE.................................727 400-4881
William Bryant, *Principal*
John Gierzak, *Vice Pres*
Tracy Gierzak, *Office Mgr*
EMP: 12 EST: 2010
SALES (est): 1.2MM Privately Held
WEB: www.oriflow.com
SIC: 3829 Liquid leak detection equipment

(G-1731)
ORIGINCLEAR INC (PA)
13575 58th St N Ste 200 (33760-3739)
PHONE.................................323 939-6645
T Riggs Eckelberry, *Ch of Bd*
Tom Marchesello, *COO*
Ken Berenger, *VP Bus Dvlpt*
Kevin Pruett, *Mktg Dir*
Jon Peraza, *Administration*
EMP: 5 EST: 2007
SALES (est): 4.1MM Publicly Held
WEB: www.originclear.com
SIC: 3589 2869 Water treatment equipment, industrial; fuels

(G-1732)
OSBORNE METALS
324 S Madison Ave (33756-5727)
PHONE.................................727 441-1703
Wayne Osborne, *Owner*
Rob Jones, *Vice Pres*
Manish Jaiswal, *Director*
EMP: 5 EST: 1993
SQ FT: 3,000
SALES (est): 487.5K Privately Held
WEB: www.osbornemetals.com
SIC: 3444 3452 Sheet metalwork; bolts, nuts, rivets & washers

(G-1733)
PACE TECH INC
2040 Calumet St (33765-1307)
PHONE.................................727 442-8118
Ilhan Bilgutay, *President*
▲ EMP: 20 EST: 1976
SQ FT: 7,400
SALES (est): 1MM Privately Held
WEB: www.pacetech-med.com
SIC: 3841 Diagnostic apparatus, medical

(G-1734)
PAIR ODICE BREWING CO LLC
4400 118th Ave N Ste 205 (33762-2443)
PHONE.................................727 755-3423
Renee Hurney, *Accounts Mgr*
Julia Rosenthal, *Mng Member*
EMP: 7 EST: 2013
SALES (est): 495.1K Privately Held
WEB: www.pairodicebrewing.com
SIC: 2082 5921 Malt liquors; liquor stores

(G-1735)
PARKER RESEARCH CORPORATION
2642 Enterprise Rd (33763-1105)
P.O. Box 1406, Dunedin (34697-1406)
PHONE.................................727 796-4066
S John Parker, *President*
Donna Parker, *Executive*
EMP: 12 EST: 1963
SALES (est): 1.7MM Privately Held
WEB: www.parkerndt.com
SIC: 3829 Measuring & controlling devices

(G-1736)
PE MANUFACTURING COMPANY FLA
Also Called: Pemco
11400 47th St N Ste A (33762-4901)
PHONE.................................727 823-8172
Kenneth M Elder, *President*
EMP: 20 EST: 2001
SALES (est): 2.2MM Privately Held
SIC: 3559 Screening equipment, electric

(G-1737)
PELICAN INTERNATIONAL INC
Also Called: Badaro Group
6140 Ulmerton Rd (33760-3946)
PHONE.................................727 388-9895
John Ellithorpe, *General Mgr*
Anderson Badaro, *Principal*
Meagan Dozier, *Business Mgr*
Preston Burchette, *Accounts Mgr*
Cody McCarroll, *Accounts Mgr*
▲ EMP: 50 EST: 1974
SQ FT: 80,000
SALES (est): 7.3MM Privately Held
SIC: 3431 Sinks: enameled iron, cast iron or pressed metal; bathroom fixtures, including sinks

(G-1738)
PHASETRONICS INC (PA)
Also Called: Motortronics
1600 Sunshine Dr (33765-1316)
P.O. Box 5988 (33758-5988)
PHONE.................................727 573-1819
James Mitchell, *President*
Leslie Bennet, *Vice Pres*
Leslie Bennett, *Vice Pres*
Joyce Mitchell, *Vice Pres*
Vythach Hoang, *Purchasing*
◆ EMP: 109 EST: 1982
SQ FT: 54,000
SALES (est): 30.1MM Privately Held
WEB: www.phasetronics.com
SIC: 3625 Control equipment, electric

(G-1739)
PIERCE MANUFACTURING INC
Frontline Communications
12770 44th St N (33762-4713)
PHONE.................................727 573-0400
Andy Callaway, *General Mgr*
William Mulford, *Project Mgr*
Chris Custer, *Opers Mgr*
Jody Phillips, *Materials Mgr*
Jeff Dickerson, *Opers Spvr*
EMP: 99
SALES (corp-wide): 7.7B Publicly Held
WEB: www.frontlinecomm.com
SIC: 3713 3711 Truck & bus bodies; motor vehicles & car bodies
HQ: Pierce Manufacturing, Inc.
2600 American Dr
Appleton WI 54914
920 832-3000

(G-1740)
PINELLAS BLIND AND SHUTTER INC
5100 Ulmerton Rd Ste 22 (33760-4031)
PHONE.................................727 481-4461
James Austin, *Principal*
EMP: 7 EST: 2013
SALES (est): 85K Privately Held
SIC: 3442 Shutters, door or window: metal

(G-1741)
PINELLAS ELECTRIC MTR REPR INC
12990 44th St N (33762-4729)
P.O. Box 217, Indian Rocks Beach (33785-0217)
PHONE.................................727 572-0777

Lee C Fletcher, *President*
Christopher Fletcher, *President*
▲ EMP: 6 EST: 1988
SQ FT: 6,500
SALES (est): 687.8K Privately Held
WEB: www.pinellaselectricmotor.com
SIC: 7694 5084 Electric motor repair; industrial machinery & equipment

(G-1742)
PIVOTAL SIGN & GRAPHICS INC
3075 Braeloch Cir W (33761-2709)
PHONE.................................727 462-2266
William M Waszak, *President*
Mary J Waszak, *Vice Pres*
Meagan Faiola, *Sales Mgr*
EMP: 5 EST: 2007
SALES (est): 483.9K Privately Held
WEB: www.pivotalsign.com
SIC: 3993 Signs & advertising specialties

(G-1743)
PNEUMATIC SCALE ANGELUS
Also Called: Pneumatic Scale Clearwater
5320 140th Ave N (33760-3743)
PHONE.................................727 535-4100
Robert H Chapman, *CEO*
William Morgan, *President*
David M Gianini, *Vice Pres*
Michael McLaughlin, *Vice Pres*
Bernie Atkins, *Purchasing*
▲ EMP: 70 EST: 1990
SQ FT: 48,000
SALES (est): 24.4MM Privately Held
WEB: www.psangelus.com
SIC: 3565 Packaging machinery
HQ: Barry-Wehmiller Companies, Inc.
8020 Forsyth Blvd
Saint Louis MO 63105
314 862-8000

(G-1744)
PORTABLE PUMPING SYSTEMS INC
Also Called: Coastal Dewatering
4760 Spring Ave (33762-4435)
P.O. Box 1246, Oldsmar (34677-1246)
PHONE.................................727 518-9191
Don Wendel, *President*
▲ EMP: 9 EST: 1994
SALES (est): 1.2MM Privately Held
WEB: www.portablepumpingsystems.com
SIC: 3561 Pumps & pumping equipment

(G-1745)
POZIN ENTERPRISES INC
Also Called: Sun-Glo Plating Co
14493 62nd St N (33760-2786)
P.O. Box 155, Pinellas Park (33780-0155)
PHONE.................................800 741-1456
Andrew Pozin, *President*
Dave Brackenhamer, *General Mgr*
Bill Farrar, *Purchasing*
EMP: 42 EST: 1986
SQ FT: 30,000
SALES (est): 7.8MM Privately Held
WEB: www.sun-glo.com
SIC: 3471 3479 Finishing, metals or formed products; electroplating & plating; painting of metal products

(G-1746)
PRECAST AND FOAM WORKS LLC
29757 66th Way N (33761-1607)
PHONE.................................727 657-9195
Gabor Szobolodi, *Principal*
EMP: 7 EST: 2014
SALES (est): 435.3K Privately Held
WEB: www.precastandfoam.com
SIC: 3272 Precast terrazo or concrete products

(G-1747)
PRECISION LITHO SERVICE INC
Also Called: Pls Print
4250 118th Ave N (33762-5135)
PHONE.................................727 573-1763
John A Blair, *President*
Terry Olson, *Vice Pres*
Jane Cobb, *Treasurer*
Jane Howell, *Treasurer*
Win Hylton, *Admin Sec*
EMP: 53 EST: 1984
SQ FT: 32,600

SALES (est): 10.9MM **Privately Held**
WEB: www.plsprint.com
SIC: 2752 Commercial printing, offset

(G-1748)
**PRECISION SHAFT
TECHNOLOGY**
Also Called: PST
1717 Overbrook Ave (33755-1935)
PHONE.................................727 442-1711
Mark Veldhuis, *President*
Arlene Veldhuis, *Office Mgr*
▲ EMP: 5 EST: 1996
SQ FT: 3,500
SALES (est): 952.4K **Privately Held**
WEB: www.pstds.com
SIC: 3714 Motor vehicle parts & accessories

(G-1749)
PRECISION TOOL & MOLD INC
12050 44th St N (33762-5107)
PHONE.................................727 573-4441
Sherry Mowery, *President*
Earl C Mowery, *Vice Pres*
William E Mowery, *Vice Pres*
Casey Graham, *Manager*
▲ EMP: 16 EST: 1981
SQ FT: 11,000
SALES (est): 3.4MM **Privately Held**
WEB: www.precisiontoolmoldinc.com
SIC: 3089 Injection molding of plastics

(G-1750)
PREMIUM COATING LLC
10 S Duncan Ave (33755-6405)
PHONE.................................727 270-1173
Sal Contreras, *Principal*
EMP: 7 EST: 2017
SALES (est): 138K **Privately Held**
SIC: 3479 Coating of metals & formed products

(G-1751)
PRESSEX INC
12910 Automobile Blvd (33762-4756)
PHONE.................................727 299-8500
Janelle Gabay, *President*
EMP: 16 EST: 2007
SQ FT: 18,000
SALES (est): 437.5K **Privately Held**
WEB: www.pressexpromo.com
SIC: 2752 Commercial printing, offset

(G-1752)
PREVAIL SOLUTIONS LLC
19321 Us Highway 19 N # 605
(33763-3169)
PHONE.................................727 210-6600
Benjamin E Wieder, *Managing Prtnr*
Daniel J Wieder, *Mng Member*
Noah A Wieder, *Mng Member*
EMP: 5 EST: 2010
SQ FT: 2,000
SALES (est): 413.3K **Privately Held**
SIC: 2844 Toilet preparations

(G-1753)
PRINTS 2 GO INC
24129 Us Highway 19 N (33763-5000)
PHONE.................................727 725-1700
Bahaa Tawsik, *President*
EMP: 8 EST: 2018
SALES (est): 234.2K **Privately Held**
WEB: store.prints2go.us
SIC: 2752 Commercial printing, lithographic

(G-1754)
PRIORITY PRINTING INC
2125 Range Rd Ste B (33765-2153)
PHONE.................................727 446-6605
Fax: 727 446-8514
EMP: 8
SQ FT: 5,000
SALES (est): 1MM **Privately Held**
SIC: 2752 Printing

(G-1755)
PROBALANCE INC
28059 Us Highway 19 N # 300
(33761-2643)
PHONE.................................727 531-8506
Tom Carlin, *CEO*
Robert Kral, *Mng Member*
Kevin McGovern,

Bruce Paddock,
EMP: 10 EST: 2013
SQ FT: 5,000
SALES (est): 751.9K **Privately Held**
WEB: www.theproteinshot.com
SIC: 2087 Beverage bases

(G-1756)
PROCYON CORPORATION (PA)
1300 S Highland Ave (33756-6519)
PHONE.................................727 447-2998
Regina W Anderson, *Ch of Bd*
Justice W Anderson, *President*
James B Anderson, *CFO*
EMP: 8 EST: 1987
SQ FT: 3,800
SALES: 4.8MM **Publicly Held**
WEB: www.procyoncorp.com
SIC: 2834 Pharmaceutical preparations; dermatologicals

(G-1757)
PROTEX INC
10500 47th St N (33762-5017)
PHONE.................................727 573-4665
Christos J Botsolas, *President*
Dana K Botsolas, *Vice Pres*
EMP: 13 EST: 1980
SQ FT: 50,000
SALES (est): 2.1MM **Privately Held**
SIC: 3083 3081 Thermosetting laminates: rods, tubes, plates & sheet; unsupported plastics film & sheet

(G-1758)
PROTO CORP
10500 47th St N (33762-5017)
PHONE.................................727 573-4665
Christos J Botsolas, *President*
Dana K Botsolas, *Vice Pres*
Dana Botsolas, *Vice Pres*
Louis Walton, *Vice Pres*
Ratina Noykathok, *Purchasing*
▼ EMP: 100 EST: 1980
SQ FT: 110,000
SALES (est): 20.2MM **Privately Held**
WEB: www.protocorporation.com
SIC: 3089 Injection molding of plastics

(G-1759)
**PROTOTYPE PLSTIC
EXTRUSION INC**
3637 131st Ave N (33762-4263)
PHONE.................................727 572-0803
Jeffrey Wells, *President*
Duane Wells, *Treasurer*
◆ EMP: 37 EST: 1978
SQ FT: 19,000
SALES (est): 1.5MM **Privately Held**
WEB: www.prototypeplastics.com
SIC: 3089 Mfg Plastic Products

(G-1760)
PURE POSTCARDS INC
1938 Byram Dr (33755-1508)
PHONE.................................877 446-2434
Irma Jeanis, *President*
Dru Jeanis, *Senior VP*
EMP: 11 EST: 2002
SQ FT: 12,400
SALES (est): 237.7K **Privately Held**
SIC: 2752 Promotional printing, lithographic

(G-1761)
QUALITY CREATIONS INC
10550 47th St N (33762-5017)
PHONE.................................727 571-4332
Tiffiny L Barany, *President*
Tiffiny Barany, *President*
EMP: 6 EST: 1993
SALES (est): 526.2K **Privately Held**
WEB: www.quality-creations-inc.com
SIC: 2434 Wood kitchen cabinets

(G-1762)
RANOREX INC
28050 Us Highway 19 N # 303
(33761-2628)
PHONE.................................727 835-5570
Robert Muehlfellner, *President*
Andreas Waschnig, *General Mgr*
Ned Wilbur, *Engineer*
Alex Rodriguez, *Accounts Mgr*
William Silvestri, *Sales Staff*
EMP: 26 EST: 2013

SALES (est): 2.5MM **Privately Held**
SIC: 7372 Application computer software
HQ: Ranorex Gmbh
Untere DonaustraEe 13-15/6. Stock
Wien 1020
316 281-328

(G-1763)
RES-NET MICROWAVE INC
5410 115th Ave N (33760-4841)
P.O. Box 18802 (33762-1802)
PHONE.................................727 530-9555
Roger Mayo, *President*
▲ EMP: 34 EST: 1987
SQ FT: 33,000
SALES: 2.6MM
SALES (corp-wide): 51.7MM **Privately Held**
WEB: www.resnetmicrowave.com
SIC: 3679 3663 Microwave components; television broadcasting & communications equipment
PA: Electro Technik Industries, Inc.
5410 115th Ave N
Clearwater FL 33760
727 530-9555

(G-1764)
**RETAIL CLOUD TECHNOLOGIES
LLC (PA)**
Also Called: Teamwork Commerce
380 Park Place Blvd # 250 (33759-4930)
PHONE.................................727 210-1700
Michael Mauerer, *CEO*
Carmen Mauerer, *VP Finance*
Michael Maurer, *Mng Member*
Chad Willis, *Mng Member*
EMP: 32 EST: 2013
SALES (est): 9.4MM **Privately Held**
WEB: www.teamworkcommerce.com
SIC: 7372 7371 Business oriented computer software; computer software development

(G-1765)
**REVENGE ADVNCED
COMPOSITES LLC**
12705 Daniel Dr (33762-4728)
PHONE.................................727 572-1410
Jon Sadowsky, *Mng Member*
Kevin D Connor, *Mng Member*
Kevin Connor, *Mng Member*
John Dowd, *Mng Member*
David Jones, *Mng Member*
EMP: 16 EST: 2005
SALES (est): 2MM **Privately Held**
SIC: 3732 Boats, fiberglass: building & repairing

(G-1766)
RICH MAID CABINETS INC
Also Called: Innovative Cabinet & Case Work
12706 Daniel Dr (33762-4710)
PHONE.................................727 572-4857
Don Roach, *President*
EMP: 10 EST: 1989
SQ FT: 9,000
SALES (est): 1.3MM **Privately Held**
WEB:
www.richmaidcabinetsclearwater.com
SIC: 2434 Wood kitchen cabinets

(G-1767)
**RICK ERNISSEE WOODWORKS
LLC**
1556 Tilley Ave (33756-2184)
PHONE.................................727 421-7711
Richard Ernissee II, *Principal*
EMP: 7 EST: 2007
SALES (est): 89.2K **Privately Held**
SIC: 2431 Millwork

(G-1768)
RIVA INDUSTRIES INC
Also Called: Florida Machining Center
4986 113th Ave N (33760-4831)
P.O. Box 86003, Saint Petersburg (33738-6003)
PHONE.................................813 573-1601
William Sponheimer, *President*
Mary Ann Sponheimer, *CFO*
EMP: 7 EST: 1984
SQ FT: 5,000
SALES (est): 731.6K **Privately Held**
SIC: 3599 Machine shop, jobbing & repair

(G-1769)
**ROBERTS QUALITY PRINTING
INC**
Also Called: Roberts Printing
2049 Calumet St (33765-1308)
PHONE.................................727 442-4011
Robert T Davis, *President*
J Wayne Nightingale, *Chairman*
Jeanne Davis, *COO*
Renee Davis, *Accounts Exec*
Shani Davis, *Admin Sec*
EMP: 45 EST: 1968
SQ FT: 28,000
SALES (est): 10.7MM **Privately Held**
WEB: www.robpri.com
SIC: 2752 2796 2791 2789 Commercial printing, offset; platemaking services; typesetting; bookbinding & related work; commercial printing

(G-1770)
**ROBOTIC PARKING SYSTEMS
INC**
12812 60th St N (33760-3959)
PHONE.................................727 539-7275
Royce S Monteverdi, *CEO*
Gerhard Haag, *President*
Juergen Bauer, *Chairman*
Ulises Vivanco, *Engineer*
Anne Matoke, *Marketing Staff*
▲ EMP: 12 EST: 1994
SQ FT: 165,133
SALES (est): 3.5MM **Privately Held**
WEB: www.roboticparking.com
SIC: 3559 7389 Parking facility equipment & supplies; design, commercial & industrial

(G-1771)
ROLLSHIELD LLC
1151 Kapp Dr (33765-2114)
PHONE.................................727 441-2243
Larry Sgammato, *Sales Associate*
Gregory Moore,
EMP: 16 EST: 2006
SALES (est): 2.5MM **Privately Held**
WEB: www.rollshield.com
SIC: 3442 1751 Shutters, door or window: metal; window & door installation & erection

(G-1772)
ROOT INTERNATIONAL INC (PA)
Also Called: Cases2go
4910 Creekside Dr Ste B (33760-4042)
PHONE.................................813 265-1808
David W Root, *President*
Chad Albritton, *Technology*
EMP: 10 EST: 1982
SALES (est): 1.2MM **Privately Held**
WEB: www.cases2go.com
SIC: 3086 Packaging & shipping materials, foamed plastic

(G-1773)
RV AIR INC (PA)
628 Cleveland St Apt 1407 (33755-6621)
PHONE.................................309 657-4300
Eddie Rice, *CEO*
Rose Rice, *President*
EMP: 6 EST: 2015
SQ FT: 1,000
SALES (est): 738.4K **Privately Held**
WEB: www.rvair.com
SIC: 3564 5075 Filters, air: furnaces, air conditioning equipment, etc.; air filters

(G-1774)
RXENERGY LLC
2449 N Mcmullen Booth Rd (33759-1314)
PHONE.................................727 726-4204
Steven Tartaglia,
Brian Newton,
Tim O'Sullivan,
EMP: 10 EST: 2010
SALES (est): 472.4K **Privately Held**
WEB: www.rxenergy.com
SIC: 3841 Surgical & medical instruments

(G-1775)
**SAINT-GOBAIN PRFMCE PLAS
CORP**
Also Called: Saint Gobain Performance Plas
4451 110th Ave N (33762-4944)
PHONE.................................727 531-4191

Jerry Stadt, *Branch Mgr*
EMP: 109
SALES (corp-wide): 340.6MM **Privately Held**
WEB: plastics.saint-gobain.com
SIC: 2821 Plastics materials & resins
HQ: Saint-Gobain Performance Plastics Corporation
31500 Solon Rd
Solon OH 44139
440 836-6900

(G-1776)
SAMPLETECH
1953 Whitney Way (33760-1618)
PHONE..............................727 239-7055
Matthew Sweadner, *Owner*
EMP: 5 **EST:** 1996
SQ FT: 2,500
SALES (est): 310K **Privately Held**
SIC: 3822 Auto controls regulating residntl & coml environmt & applncs

(G-1777)
SCRIBE MANUFACTURING INC (PA)
Also Called: Norwood Promotional Products
14421 Myerlake Cir (33760-2840)
PHONE..............................727 524-7482
Emmanuel Bruno, *CEO*
Fareeha S Amin, *Principal*
Lori Bauer, *Vice Pres*
Duke Bjorklund, *Vice Pres*
Todd Gartman, *Vice Pres*
EMP: 18 **EST:** 1999
SALES (est): 17MM **Privately Held**
SIC: 3951 Pens & mechanical pencils

(G-1778)
SCRIBE OPCO INC (PA)
Also Called: Koozie Group
14421 Myerlake Cir (33760-2840)
P.O. Box 23088, Tampa (33623-2088)
PHONE..............................727 536-7895
Jonathan Fox, *President*
Melissa McCaffrey, *Chairman*
Francine Dupuis, *Vice Pres*
Michael Koichopolos, *Vice Pres*
Jeff Ibberson, *Mfg Mgr*
EMP: 28 **EST:** 2017
SALES (est): 25MM **Privately Held**
WEB: www.bicgraphic.eu
SIC: 3951 Pens & mechanical pencils

(G-1779)
SEABOARD MANUFACTURING LLC
13214 38th St N (33762-4268)
PHONE..............................727 497-3572
Shawn McNary, *Managing Prtnr*
Charles Rowland, *Finance Dir*
Tabatha Searles, *Accountant*
Leo J Govoni, *Mng Member*
EMP: 9 **EST:** 2012
SQ FT: 10,000
SALES (est): 1.3MM **Privately Held**
WEB: www.seaboardmfg.com
SIC: 3599 3999 8999 Machine shop, jobbing & repair; atomizers, toiletry; artist

(G-1780)
SENTINEL SQ OFF BLDG MGT & LSG
300 S Duncan Ave Ste 291 (33755-6414)
PHONE..............................727 461-7700
Erika Barrett, *Principal*
EMP: 7 **EST:** 2007
SALES (est): 163.5K **Privately Held**
SIC: 2711 Newspapers, publishing & printing

(G-1781)
SERVO TECH INC
Also Called: Servotech
4785 110th Ave N (33762-4912)
PHONE..............................727 573-7998
Radoslav Prissadachky, *President*
EMP: 6 **EST:** 1985
SALES (est): 449.6K **Privately Held**
WEB: www.servotech.com
SIC: 3599 3549 Machine shop, jobbing & repair; metalworking machinery

(G-1782)
SHADOW-CASTER LED LIGHTING LLC
Also Called: Shadow-Caster Marine
2060 Calumet St (33765-1307)
P.O. Box 82, Dunedin (34697-0082)
PHONE..............................727 474-2877
Steven Uhl, *Opers Staff*
Brian Rogers, *Mng Member*
EMP: 29 **EST:** 2009
SALES (est): 6.8MM **Privately Held**
WEB: www.shadow-caster.com
SIC: 3562 Casters

(G-1783)
SICOMA NORTH AMERICA INC
11300 47th St N (33762-4953)
PHONE..............................800 921-7559
Marianne Johnson, *Principal*
Luca Via Brenta, *Principal*
Michele Via Brenta, *Principal*
Randy Johnson, *Vice Pres*
Gianni Cardoni, *Sales Staff*
▲ **EMP:** 7 **EST:** 2009
SALES (est): 766.6K **Privately Held**
WEB: www.sicomamixers.com
SIC: 3531 Concrete buggies, powered

(G-1784)
SIO CNC MACHINING INC
14241 60th St N (33760-2706)
PHONE..............................727 533-8271
Kouangheu Sio, *President*
Mellissa Malaivanh, *Office Mgr*
EMP: 7 **EST:** 1985
SALES (est): 685.8K **Privately Held**
WEB: www.siomachining.com
SIC: 3599 Machine shop, jobbing & repair

(G-1785)
SKINNY MIXES LLC
Also Called: Gce
2849 Executive Dr Ste 210 (33762-2224)
PHONE..............................727 826-0306
Jordan Engelhardt,
EMP: 9 **EST:** 2009
SALES (est): 2.6MM
SALES (corp-wide): 12.1MM **Privately Held**
WEB: www.skinnymixes.com
SIC: 2087 Flavoring extracts & syrups; beverage bases
PA: Goodwest Industries, Llc
48 Quarry Rd
Douglassville PA 19518
800 948-1922

(G-1786)
SMARTHOME-PRODUCTS INC (PA)
1560 Faulds Rd W (33756-2410)
PHONE..............................727 490-7260
Karl Vantrese, *President*
EMP: 10 **EST:** 2008
SALES (est): 783.8K **Privately Held**
WEB: www.smarthome-products.com
SIC: 3645 Residential lighting fixtures

(G-1787)
SOURCE 1 SOLUTIONS INC
Also Called: Honeywell Authorized Dealer
4904 Creekside Dr (33760-4060)
PHONE..............................727 538-4114
Robert Hessel, *President*
Michael Crawford, *Vice Pres*
Mickey McKeon, *Vice Pres*
Sean Colpoys, *CFO*
Kevin Dommermuth, *Sales Mgr*
EMP: 94 **EST:** 2011
SALES (est): 14.1MM **Privately Held**
WEB: www.source1solutions.com
SIC: 3674 3699 7382 Integrated circuits, semiconductor networks, etc.; security control equipment & systems; security systems services

(G-1788)
SOUTHCOAST MARINE PRODUCTS INC
12550 47th Way N (33762-4441)
PHONE..............................727 573-4821
John R Cureton, *President*
Kevin Cureton, *President*
Richard L Cureton, *Vice Pres*
Steve Cureton, *Vice Pres*

▲ **EMP:** 110 **EST:** 1974
SQ FT: 10,000
SALES (est): 8.8MM **Privately Held**
WEB: www.ghslift.com
SIC: 3429 Marine hardware

(G-1789)
SOUTHERN COATING SYSTEMS INC
880 Mandalay Ave Apt C507 (33767-1214)
P.O. Box 1274, Largo (33779-1274)
PHONE..............................863 712-9900
James D Laudon, *Principal*
EMP: 7 **EST:** 2015
SALES (est): 67.6K **Privately Held**
SIC: 3479 Metal coating & allied service

(G-1790)
SOUTHERN MFG UPHOLSTERY INC
3670 131st Ave N (33762-4262)
PHONE..............................727 573-1006
Matthew J Argue, *President*
Matthew Argue, *President*
Hermes Rivas, *Manager*
EMP: 14 **EST:** 1988
SALES (est): 613.1K **Privately Held**
SIC: 3363 Aluminum die-castings

(G-1791)
SOUTHERNSTONE CABINETS INC
12520 Automobile Blvd (33762-4415)
PHONE..............................727 538-0123
David Baccari, *President*
EMP: 19 **EST:** 1998
SALES (est): 3MM **Privately Held**
WEB: www.southernstonecabinets.com
SIC: 2434 Wood kitchen cabinets

(G-1792)
SPACE MANUFACTURING INC
14271 60th St N (33760-2706)
PHONE..............................727 532-9466
Grace Sokol, *CEO*
Bob Sokol, *President*
EMP: 16 **EST:** 1979
SALES (est): 286.8K **Privately Held**
SIC: 3599 Machine shop, jobbing & repair

(G-1793)
SPACEWERKS INC
13100 56th Ct Ste 711 (33760-4021)
PHONE..............................727 540-9714
Ken Yeager, *President*
EMP: 13 **EST:** 2008
SQ FT: 20,000
SALES (est): 1.2MM **Privately Held**
WEB: www.spacewerksinc.com
SIC: 2431 Moldings, wood: unfinished & prefinished

(G-1794)
SPECTRA CHROME LLC
13130 56th Ct Ste 611 (33760-4018)
PHONE..............................727 573-1990
Daniel A McLaughlin,
▼ **EMP:** 8 **EST:** 2002
SALES (est): 1.4MM **Privately Held**
WEB: www.spectrachrome.com
SIC: 3471 Electroplating of metals or formed products

(G-1795)
SPECTRA METAL SALES INC
Also Called: Alumco
5100 140th Ave N (33760-3753)
P.O. Box 43167, Atlanta GA (30336-0167)
PHONE..............................727 530-5435
Michael Smith, *Manager*
EMP: 10
SALES (corp-wide): 271.2MM **Privately Held**
WEB: www.spectrametals.com
SIC: 3355 5051 5033 Aluminum rolling & drawing; metals service centers & offices; roofing, siding & insulation
PA: Spectra Metal Sales, Inc.
6104 Boat Rock Blvd Sw
Atlanta GA 30336
404 344-4305

(G-1796)
STATEMENT MARINE LLC
12011 49th St N (33762-4302)
PHONE..............................727 525-5235
Craig Barrie, *Principal*
EMP: 10 **EST:** 2008
SALES (est): 693K **Privately Held**
WEB: www.statementmarine.com
SIC: 3732 Boat building & repairing

(G-1797)
STITCH LOGO INC
2165 Sunnydale Blvd Ste H (33765-1211)
PHONE..............................727 446-0228
Christine Lyon, *President*
Cheryl Lyon, *Sales Staff*
Sabrina Lyon, *Corp Comm Staff*
EMP: 7 **EST:** 1999
SQ FT: 1,500
SALES (est): 1MM **Privately Held**
WEB: www.stitchlogo.com
SIC: 2395 Embroidery products, except schiffli machine; embroidery & art needlework

(G-1798)
STRATFORD CORPORATION
1555 Sunshine Dr (33765-1315)
PHONE..............................727 443-1573
Alan Conroy, *President*
EMP: 9 **EST:** 1989
SALES (est): 1.3MM **Privately Held**
WEB: www.stratfordinc.com
SIC: 2842 Specialty cleaning, polishes & sanitation goods

(G-1799)
SUN BUSINESS SYSTEMS INC (PA)
10900 47th St N (33762-5001)
PHONE..............................727 547-6540
Jim Ellis, *President*
EMP: 5 **EST:** 1980
SQ FT: 9,000
SALES (est): 1.1MM **Privately Held**
SIC: 2759 Playing cards: printing

(G-1800)
SUN WORKS PLASTICS INC
15373 Roosevelt Blvd # 202 (33760-3507)
PHONE..............................727 573-2343
Brian Myregaard, *President*
Pamela Myregaard, *Vice Pres*
EMP: 8 **EST:** 1988
SQ FT: 16,000
SALES (est): 956.7K **Privately Held**
WEB: www.sunworksplastics.com
SIC: 3089 Injection molding of plastics

(G-1801)
SUNCOAST TOOL & GAGE INDS INC
11625 54th St N (33760-4852)
PHONE..............................727 572-8000
Michael Powers, *President*
Lee Dove, *Vice Pres*
Doyle Powers, *Vice Pres*
Lloyd Powers, *Vice Pres*
EMP: 13 **EST:** 1982
SQ FT: 15,000
SALES (est): 818K **Privately Held**
WEB: www.suncoasttool.com
SIC: 3829 3824 3545 3544 Aircraft & motor vehicle measurement equipment; gauges for computing pressure temperature corrections; machine tool accessories; special dies, tools, jigs & fixtures

(G-1802)
SUNDOWN MANUFACTURING INC
4505 131st Ave N Ste 26 (33762-4104)
PHONE..............................727 828-0826
Amy Rose, *Principal*
Dan Casaje, *Plant Mgr*
EMP: 10 **EST:** 2008
SALES (est): 532.4K **Privately Held**
WEB: www.sundownmfginc.com
SIC: 3999 Manufacturing industries

(G-1803)
SUNRUI TTNIUM PRCSION PDTS INC
1058 Cephas Rd (33765-2107)
PHONE..............................727 953-7101

▲ = Import ▼=Export
◆ =Import/Export

Blakenship Angela, *Principal*
EMP: 9 **EST:** 2015
SALES (est): 409.3K **Privately Held**
WEB: www.precisiontitaniumproducts.com
SIC: 3356 Titanium

(G-1804)
SUPERIOR ELECTRONICS INC
1140 Kapp Dr (33765-2113)
P.O. Box 2536, Dunedin (34697-2536)
PHONE..................................727 733-0700
Anne Kennedy, *CEO*
Andy Desouza, *President*
Allan Kennedy, *Owner*
Kamill Hilberth, *Principal*
Sherman Desouza, *Vice Pres*
EMP: 22 **EST:** 1986
SALES (est): 2MM **Privately Held**
WEB: www.seimfg.com
SIC: 3643 3672 Current-carrying wiring
devices; printed circuit boards

(G-1805)
SUPLIAEREOS USA LLC
Also Called: Aero Supply USA
21941 Us Highway 19 N (33765-2359)
PHONE..................................727 754-4915
Robert Ramirez, *COO*
William Tyler, *CFO*
Tim Garren, *Accounts Mgr*
Timothy Garren, *Accounts Mgr*
Michelle Ramirez,
EMP: 7 **EST:** 2012
SQ FT: 5,000
SALES (est): 1.2MM **Privately Held**
SIC: 3721 3724 3728 3812 Aircraft; air-
craft engines & engine parts; aircraft parts
& equipment; aircraft/aerospace flight in-
struments & guidance systems; semicon-
ductors & related devices

(G-1806)
SURE-FEED ENGINEERING INC
Also Called: SFE Investments
12050 49th St N (33762-4301)
PHONE..................................727 571-3330
Todd Werner, *President*
Jim Naset, *Vice Pres*
Joe Springer, *CFO*
▲ **EMP:** 99 **EST:** 1998
SQ FT: 100,000
SALES (est): 6.8MM **Privately Held**
SIC: 3554 3579 Paper industries machin-
ery; mailing machines

(G-1807)
SURFACE FINISHING TECH INC
12200 34th St N Ste A (33762-5608)
PHONE..................................727 577-7777
David Weisberg, *President*
Dale Jackson, *Vice Pres*
Kim Gibson, *Buyer*
EMP: 20 **EST:** 1996
SQ FT: 38,000
SALES (est): 11.9MM
SALES (corp-wide): 159.5MM **Privately
Held**
WEB: www.technic.com
SIC: 3559 Electroplating machinery &
equipment
PA: Technic, Inc.
47 Molter St
Cranston RI 02910
401 781-6100

(G-1808)
SYSTEM ENTERPRISES LLC
Also Called: Funsparks
319 Windward Is (33767-2328)
PHONE..................................888 898-3600
Trisha McCabe, *Sales Staff*
Steven T Mueller,
▲ **EMP:** 7 **EST:** 2010
SALES (est): 583.9K **Privately Held**
WEB: www.system-enterprises.com
SIC: 3944 Games, toys & children's vehi-
cles

(G-1809)
T S E INDUSTRIES INC (PA)
5180 113th Ave N (33760-4835)
PHONE..................................727 573-7676
Robert R Klingel Jr, *CEO*
Mark Cucchiara, *President*
Richard K Klingel, *President*
Richard Catalano, *Counsel*

Brad Klingel, *Vice Pres*
◆ **EMP:** 92 **EST:** 1962
SQ FT: 225,000
SALES (est): 59.6MM **Privately Held**
WEB: www.tse-industries.com
SIC: 3089 3061 2891 2822 Molding pri-
mary plastic; mechanical rubber goods;
medical & surgical rubber tubing (ex-
truded & lathe-cut); adhesives; synthetic
rubber

(G-1810)
T S E INDUSTRIES INC
5260 113th Ave N (33760-4838)
PHONE..................................727 540-1368
Marlon Moore, *QC Mgr*
Adam Anderson, *Research*
Joe Barker, *Engineer*
Mary Coots, *Controller*
Radhila Petrovich, *Manager*
EMP: 89
SQ FT: 12,000
SALES (corp-wide): 59.6MM **Privately
Held**
WEB: www.tse-industries.com
SIC: 2821 3089 Thermoplastic materials;
molding primary plastic
PA: T S E Industries Inc.
5180 113th Ave N
Clearwater FL 33760
727 573-7676

(G-1811)
TAMPA BAY GRAND PRIX (PA)
12350 Automobile Blvd (33762-4425)
PHONE..................................727 527-8464
Bertrand Ollier, *Owner*
▲ **EMP:** 5 **EST:** 2005
SALES (est): 977.2K **Privately Held**
WEB: www.tampabaygp.com
SIC: 3799 Go-carts, except children's

(G-1812)
TAMPA BAY PUBLICATIONS INC
Also Called: Tampa Bay Magazine
2531 Landmark Dr Ste 101 (33761-3928)
PHONE..................................727 791-4800
Aaron Fodiman, *President*
Fred Horton, *Vice Pres*
Lew Phillips, *Vice Pres*
Mark Maconi, *Treasurer*
M Rosalie Mahoney, *Controller*
EMP: 18 **EST:** 1986
SQ FT: 1,900
SALES (est): 3.6MM **Privately Held**
WEB: www.tampabaymagazine.com
SIC: 2721 Magazines: publishing only, not
printed on site

(G-1813)
TAMPA MICROWAVE LLC
16255 Bay Vista Dr # 100 (33760-3127)
PHONE..................................813 855-2251
Bob Garvey, *Vice Pres*
Lee Gueffroy, *Vice Pres*
Eric Guerrazzi, *Vice Pres*
Kathy Ward, *Buyer*
Serita Cronin, *Engineer*
EMP: 40 **EST:** 2011
SALES (est): 12.6MM
SALES (corp-wide): 279.3MM **Privately
Held**
WEB: www.tampamicrowave.com
SIC: 3663 Radio & TV communications
equipment
HQ: Thales Defense & Security, Inc.
22605 Gateway Center Dr
Clarksburg MD 20871
240 864-7000

(G-1814)
TAMPA WINES LLC
Also Called: Aspirations Winery
22041 Us Highway 19 N (33765-2363)
PHONE..................................727 799-9463
Bill Linville,
EMP: 7 **EST:** 2005
SALES (est): 532K **Privately Held**
SIC: 2084 Wines

(G-1815)
TAMPA YACHT MANUFACTURING LLC
3671 131st Ave N (33762-4263)
P.O. Box 342033, Tampa (33694-2033)
PHONE..................................813 792-2114

Jeff Reinhold, *Vice Pres*
Mike Martin, *Supervisor*
Robert L Stevens,
Jeff Aguiar,
CJ Lozano,
EMP: 10 **EST:** 2006
SALES (est): 1.5MM **Privately Held**
WEB: www.tampa-yacht.com
SIC: 3732 Yachts, building & repairing

(G-1816)
TARONIS FUELS INC
12707 44th St N (33762-4725)
PHONE..................................727 934-3448
EMP: 158
SALES (corp-wide): 51.8MM **Publicly
Held**
WEB: www.taronisfuels.com
SIC: 2869 2911 5983 Fuels; oils; fuel; fuel
oil dealers
PA: Taronis Fuels, Inc.
24980 N 83rd Ave Unit 100
Peoria AZ 85383
866 370-3855

(G-1817)
TECH DATA EDUCATION INC
5350 Tech Data Dr (33760-3122)
PHONE..................................727 539-7429
Charles V Dannewitz, *Director*
EMP: 19 **EST:** 2018
SALES (est): 1.2MM
SALES (corp-wide): 31.6B **Publicly
Held**
SIC: 7372 Prepackaged software
HQ: Tech Data Corporation
5350 Tech Data Dr
Clearwater FL 33760
727 539-7429

(G-1818)
TECH DATA RESOURCES LLC
5350 Tech Data Dr (33760-3122)
PHONE..................................727 539-7429
EMP: 27 **EST:** 2001
SALES (est): 1.8MM
SALES (corp-wide): 31.6B **Publicly Held**
SIC: 7372 Prepackaged software
HQ: Tech Data Corporation
5350 Tech Data Dr
Clearwater FL 33760
727 539-7429

(G-1819)
TECH DATA TENNESSEE INC
5350 Tech Data Dr (33760-3122)
PHONE..................................727 539-7429
Charles V Dannewitz, *Director*
EMP: 26 **EST:** 1999
SALES (est): 1.9MM
SALES (corp-wide): 31.6B **Publicly Held**
SIC: 7372 Prepackaged software
HQ: Tech Data Corporation
5350 Tech Data Dr
Clearwater FL 33760
727 539-7429

(G-1820)
TECHNAMOLD INC
5190 110th Ave N (33760-4804)
PHONE..................................727 561-0030
Michael Wilfeard, *President*
Kathleen Wilfeard, *Vice Pres*
EMP: 5 **EST:** 1992
SQ FT: 4,000
SALES (est): 654.1K **Privately Held**
SIC: 3544 Industrial molds

(G-1821)
TECHNIFINISH INC
5095 113th Ave N (33760-4834)
PHONE..................................727 576-5955
John S Eidschun, *President*
EMP: 13 **EST:** 2000
SALES (est): 313K **Privately Held**
SIC: 2269 Finishing plants

(G-1822)
TECHNOLOGY RESEARCH LLC (HQ)
Also Called: T R C
4525 140th Ave N Ste 900 (33762-3864)
PHONE..................................727 535-0572
G Gary Yetman, *CEO*
J Kurt Hennelly, *President*
Richard N Burger, *Corp Secy*
J Bradley Freeman, *Vice Pres*

Mark Steele, *Vice Pres*
◆ **EMP:** 92 **EST:** 1981
SQ FT: 43,000
SALES (est): 61.5MM
SALES (corp-wide): 1.7B **Privately Held**
SIC: 3613 Control panels, electric; distribu-
tion boards, electric
PA: Southwire Company, Llc
1 Southwire Dr
Carrollton GA 30119
770 832-4242

(G-1823)
TEEZE INTERNATIONAL INC
2431 Estancia Blvd (33761-2608)
PHONE..................................727 726-3592
Tyler Waitt, *Principal*
EMP: 7 **EST:** 2010
SALES (est): 157.9K **Privately Held**
WEB: www.teezemagazine.com
SIC: 2721 Magazines: publishing only, not
printed on site

(G-1824)
TEKNATOOL USA INC
4499 126th Ave N (33762-4768)
PHONE..................................727 954-3433
George Naruns, *President*
Christopher Wise, *COO*
Tom Rathert, *Vice Pres*
Shannon Barnes, *Marketing Staff*
Brian Latimer, *Director*
▲ **EMP:** 5 **EST:** 2010
SALES (est): 5.2MM **Privately Held**
WEB: www.teknatool.com
SIC: 3553 Woodworking machinery
PA: Teknatool International Limited
7d Dallan Place
Auckland 0632

(G-1825)
TEMPERED GLASS INDUSTRIES INC
11116 47th St N Ste B (33762-4922)
PHONE..................................727 499-0284
Robert C Whitlow, *Principal*
EMP: 24 **EST:** 2006
SALES (est): 1.3MM **Privately Held**
WEB: www.temperedglassindustries.net
SIC: 3231 Tempered glass: made from pur-
chased glass

(G-1826)
TERLYN INDUSTRIES INC
4906 Creekside Dr Ste D (33760-4022)
PHONE..................................727 592-0772
Terence Rushmore, *President*
Lynn Rushmore, *Vice Pres*
Bill Stepp, *Vice Pres*
EMP: 10 **EST:** 1996
SALES (est): 1.8MM **Privately Held**
WEB: www.terlyn.com
SIC: 2899 Water treating compounds

(G-1827)
TESS ENTERPRISES INC
13150 38th St N (33762-4221)
PHONE..................................727 573-9701
Richard A Tess, *President*
Sharon Tess, *Vice Pres*
EMP: 7 **EST:** 1997
SQ FT: 11,880
SALES (est): 572.6K **Privately Held**
WEB: www.tessenterprises.com
SIC: 3949 Sporting & athletic goods

(G-1828)
THOMAS SIGN AND AWNING CO INC
4590 118th Ave N (33762-4405)
PHONE..................................727 573-7757
Priscilla Thomas, *President*
Randall Ryan, *Managing Dir*
W Wade Thomas, *Vice Pres*
Matt Thomas, *VP Opers*
Jessica Goodman, *Project Mgr*
▲ **EMP:** 230 **EST:** 1972
SQ FT: 100,000
SALES (est): 45.1MM **Privately Held**
WEB: www.thomassign.com
SIC: 2394 3993 Awnings, fabric: made
from purchased materials; electric signs

(G-1829)
THREATTRACK SECURITY INC (HQ)
Also Called: Vipre
311 Park Place Blvd # 300 (33759-3994)
P.O. Box 804, Tarpon Springs (34688-0804)
PHONE..................................855 885-5566
John Lyons, *President*
Dipto Chakravarty, *Exec VP*
Heylin Alvarez, *Opers Staff*
Ryan Cook, *Engineer*
Marc Sison, *Engineer*
EMP: 130 **EST:** 1994
SALES (est): 82.9MM
SALES (corp-wide): 1.4B **Publicly Held**
WEB: www.vipre.com
SIC: 7372 Business oriented computer software
PA: Ziff Davis, Inc.
114 5th Ave Fl 15
New York NY 10011
212 503-3500

(G-1830)
THUNDER BAY FOODS CORPORATION
13182 38th St N (33762-4221)
PHONE..................................727 943-0606
Jonathan Key, *President*
Jonathan D Key, *President*
James B Bond, *Vice Pres*
EMP: 18 **EST:** 2017
SALES (est): 1.7MM **Privately Held**
SIC: 2099 Food preparations

(G-1831)
TIMES HOLDING CO
Also Called: Tampa Bay Times
1130 Cleveland St Ste 100 (33755-4834)
PHONE..................................727 445-4249
EMP: 283
SALES (corp-wide): 14.9MM **Privately Held**
WEB: www.poynter.org
SIC: 2711 Newspapers, publishing & printing
HQ: Times Holding Co.
490 1st Ave S
Saint Petersburg FL 33701
727 893-8111

(G-1832)
TITAN TOOLS LLC
2622 Flournoy Cir S # 23 (33764-1411)
PHONE..................................818 984-1001
Athena Singer, *Mng Member*
Daniel Ashburn, *Mng Member*
EMP: 32 **EST:** 2020
SALES (est): 3.6MM **Privately Held**
WEB: www.titan-us.com
SIC: 7372 8299 Application computer software; schools & educational service

(G-1833)
TITANS USA LTD
4371 112th Ter N (33762-4930)
PHONE..................................727 290-9897
Dennis Drew, *President*
Greg Hoffstetter, *Vice Pres*
EMP: 7 **EST:** 2016
SALES (est): 138.9K **Privately Held**
WEB: www.titansusa.com
SIC: 3648 Lighting equipment

(G-1834)
TOM GEORGE YACHT GROUP ○
17166 Us Highway 19 N (33764-7504)
PHONE..................................727 734-8707
Tom George, *President*
EMP: 8 **EST:** 2021
SALES (est): 594K **Privately Held**
WEB: www.tgyg.com
SIC: 3732 7389 Yachts, building & repairing; yacht brokers

(G-1835)
TOPS SOFTWARE
2495 Entp Rd Ste 201 (33763)
PHONE..................................813 960-8300
Teri Perez, *VP Bus Dvlpt*
Sandra Higgins, *Marketing Staff*
Jeffrey Hardy, *Mng Member*
Tricia Berggren, *Manager*
Brianna Sturm, *Manager*
EMP: 8 **EST:** 2017
SALES (est): 555.2K **Privately Held**
WEB: www.topssoft.com
SIC: 7372 Prepackaged software

(G-1836)
TUTHILL CORPORATION
Also Called: Hansen Plastics Division
2050 Sunnydale Blvd (33765-1201)
PHONE..................................727 446-8593
Chris Duncan, *Senior Buyer*
Adam Hanford, *Engineer*
John Mitchell, *Sales Dir*
Richard D Curtin, *Branch Mgr*
EMP: 60
SQ FT: 18,000
SALES (corp-wide): 144.3MM **Privately Held**
WEB: www.tuthill.com
SIC: 3089 Injection molded finished plastic products
PA: Tuthill Corporation
8500 S Madison St
Burr Ridge IL 60527
630 382-4900

(G-1837)
UNILENS CORP USA
21 N Park Place Blvd (33759-3917)
PHONE..................................727 544-2531
Michael Pecora, *President*
Leonard Barker, *Vice Pres*
Alan Frazer, *QA Dir*
EMP: 23 **EST:** 1989
SQ FT: 27,000
SALES (est): 1.7MM **Privately Held**
SIC: 3851 Contact lenses

(G-1838)
UNITED AMERICAN MACHINERY LLC
1717 Overbrook Ave (33755-1935)
PHONE..................................727 442-1711
G Adam Ross, *Mng Member*
EMP: 11 **EST:** 2020
SALES (est): 1.5MM **Privately Held**
SIC: 3089 Automotive parts, plastic

(G-1839)
UNIVERSAL SOFTWARE SOLUTIONS
Also Called: Networking Dynamics
912 Drew St Ste 104 (33755-4523)
PHONE..................................727 298-8877
Daniel F Kingsbury, *CEO*
Donna Dunbar, *President*
Susanne Zimmerling, *Accounting Mgr*
Pamela Anderson, *Sales Staff*
Annette Welton, *Sales Staff*
EMP: 7 **EST:** 1982
SQ FT: 2,500
SALES (est): 1MM **Privately Held**
WEB: www.universalss.com
SIC: 7372 7371 Prepackaged software; custom computer programming services

(G-1840)
UPEXI INC (PA)
17129 Us Highway 19 N (33764-7503)
PHONE..................................701 353-5425
Allan Marshall, *Ch of Bd*
Robert Hackett, *President*
Anthony Bazan, *COO*
Andrew Norstrud, *CFO*
EMP: 0 **EST:** 2018
SALES (est): 44.5MM **Publicly Held**
WEB: www.groveinc.io
SIC: 2833 5122 Medicinals & botanicals; medicinals & botanicals

(G-1841)
VELA RESEARCH LP
13577 Feather Sound Dr # 550 (33762-5527)
PHONE..................................727 507-5300
Mike Reddy, *Partner*
Michele Capps, *Partner*
Kevin Donald, *Partner*
Ken Rubin, *Vice Pres*
Ric Belding, *Engineer*
EMP: 100 **EST:** 1994
SALES (est): 10.2MM **Privately Held**
WEB: www.vela.com
SIC: 3663 Receiver-transmitter units (transceiver)

(G-1842)
VERIFONE INC
300 Park Place Blvd # 100 (33759-4933)
PHONE..................................727 953-4000
Jennifer Miles, *President*
Rich McGin, *General Mgr*
Simcha Gendelman, *General Mgr*
Greg McFaul, *General Mgr*
Morgan Sellen, *Managing Dir*
EMP: 300
SALES (corp-wide): 695.1MM **Privately Held**
WEB: www.verifone.com
SIC: 3578 Point-of-sale devices
HQ: Verifone, Inc.
2744 N University Dr
Coral Springs FL 33065
800 837-4366

(G-1843)
VERIFONE INC
12501 B 562nd St N (33755)
PHONE..................................727 535-9200
Chris Bolson, *Manager*
Bud Waller, *Technical Staff*
Linda Prahl, *Analyst*
William Rosa, *Analyst*
EMP: 200
SALES (corp-wide): 695.1MM **Privately Held**
WEB: www.verifone.com
SIC: 3578 3577 Point-of-sale devices; computer peripheral equipment
HQ: Verifone, Inc.
2744 N University Dr
Coral Springs FL 33065
800 837-4366

(G-1844)
VETERANS METAL LLC (PA)
5150 Ulmerton Rd Ste 14 (33760-4014)
PHONE..................................727 572-9470
Andrew G Kossowski, *President*
EMP: 5 **EST:** 2020
SALES (est): 981.5K **Privately Held**
SIC: 3471 Anodizing (plating) of metals or formed products

(G-1845)
VISIONTECH COMPONENTS LLC
5120 110th Ave N (33760-4804)
PHONE..................................727 547-5466
Shannon Wren,
EMP: 10 **EST:** 2007
SALES (est): 1MM **Privately Held**
SIC: 3674 Integrated circuits, semiconductor networks, etc.

(G-1846)
VITAMINMED LLC
300 S Duncan Ave Ste 263 (33755-6414)
PHONE..................................727 443-7008
James Miller, *CEO*
David Singer,
EMP: 6 **EST:** 2013
SALES (est): 341.1K **Privately Held**
WEB: www.vitaminmed.com
SIC: 2833 Vitamins, natural or synthetic: bulk, uncompounded

(G-1847)
WALKUP ENTERPRISES INC
Also Called: Gulf Machining
5040 110th Ave N (33760-4807)
PHONE..................................727 571-1244
Fred Walkup, *President*
Mary Walkup, *Treasurer*
EMP: 10 **EST:** 1977
SQ FT: 5,000
SALES (est): 955.9K **Privately Held**
SIC: 3451 3669 Screw machine products; intercommunication systems, electric

(G-1848)
WALL BED SYSTEMS INC
Also Called: Closet Systems
5040 140th Ave N (33760-3735)
P.O. Box 2042, Wapakoneta OH (45895-0542)
PHONE..................................419 738-5207
Steven Archer, *President*
Eloise Archer, *Corp Secy*
EMP: 8 **EST:** 1987
SALES (est): 703.1K **Privately Held**
WEB: www.wallbedsmfg.com
SIC: 2514 5712 Beds, including folding & cabinet, household: metal; furniture stores

(G-1849)
WEB OFFSET PRINTING CO INC
12198 44th St N (33762-5109)
PHONE..................................727 572-7488
John L Tevlin Jr, *President*
Don Kennedy, *General Mgr*
John L Tevlin, *Vice Pres*
John Tevlin, *Vice Pres*
EMP: 100 **EST:** 1994
SQ FT: 2,500
SALES (est): 9.7MM **Privately Held**
WEB: www.weboffsetprint.com
SIC: 2752 Commercial printing, offset

(G-1850)
WEST PHARMACEUTICAL SVCS INC
5280 118th Ave N (33760-4300)
PHONE..................................727 546-2402
Tiffany Heier, *Human Resources*
J W Burchfield, *Branch Mgr*
EMP: 7
SALES (corp-wide): 2.8B **Publicly Held**
WEB: www.westpharma.com
SIC: 2834 Pharmaceutical preparations
PA: West Pharmaceutical Services, Inc.
530 Herman O West Dr
Exton PA 19341
610 594-2900

(G-1851)
WHK BIOSYSTEMS LLC
11345 53rd St N (33760-4822)
PHONE..................................727 209-8402
Victoria Bergman, *Engineer*
David J Tottle, *CFO*
Jerry Stadt, *Marketing Staff*
Robert R Klingel Jr, *Mng Member*
EMP: 6 **EST:** 2012
SALES (est): 2.8MM
SALES (corp-wide): 59.6MM **Privately Held**
WEB: www.whkbiosystems.com
SIC: 3829 Medical diagnostic systems, nuclear
PA: T S E Industries Inc.
5180 113th Ave N
Clearwater FL 33760
727 573-7676

(G-1852)
WILCOX STEEL COMPANY LLC
1101 Kapp Dr (33765-2114)
PHONE..................................727 443-0461
Jackie A Wilcox Sr, *Owner*
Susan Wilcox Wagner, *Office Mgr*
EMP: 6 **EST:** 1965
SQ FT: 6,400
SALES (est): 428.3K **Privately Held**
WEB: www.wilcoxsteel.com
SIC: 3446 3441 Architectural metalwork; fabricated structural metal

(G-1853)
WILLETT PRCISION MACHINING INC
11339 43rd St N (33762-4915)
PHONE..................................727 573-9299
Debbie Willett, *President*
Kyle P Willett, *Opers Mgr*
Richard Barnes, *CIO*
EMP: 18 **EST:** 1997
SQ FT: 8,432
SALES (est): 1.1MM **Privately Held**
WEB: www.willettprecision.com
SIC: 3599 Machine shop, jobbing & repair

(G-1854)
WILSON PRINTING USA LLC
1085 Cephas Rd (33765-2108)
PHONE..................................727 536-4173
Thomas R Selenski, *President*
Julie Hale, *COO*
Ella Selenski, *Vice Pres*
Alex Boerma, *Marketing Staff*
Kelsi Hale,
EMP: 7 **EST:** 1969
SALES (est): 971.9K **Privately Held**
WEB: www.wilsonprintingusa.com
SIC: 2752 Commercial printing, offset

▲ = Import ▼=Export
◆ =Import/Export

(G-1855)
WINATIC CORPORATION
5410 115th Ave N (33760-4841)
P.O. Box 18802 (33762-1802)
PHONE..............................727 538-8917
Roger C Mayo, *Chairman*
Geraldine R Mayo, *Treasurer*
EMP: 107 EST: 1951
SQ FT: 16,000
SALES (est): 2MM
SALES (corp-wide): 51.7MM **Privately Held**
WEB: www.winatic.com
SIC: 3677 Coil windings, electronic; transformers power supply, electronic type
PA: Electro Technik Industries, Inc.
   5410 115th Ave N
   Clearwater FL 33760
   727 530-9555

(G-1856)
WORLD INDUS RESOURCES CORP (HQ)
13100 56th Ct Ste 710 (33760-4021)
PHONE..............................727 572-9991
Leslie Unger, *President*
Robert Thompson, *Controller*
Garvin Callaham, *Credit Mgr*
EMP: 25 EST: 1978
SQ FT: 75,000
SALES (est): 123.4MM **Privately Held**
SIC: 3999 2542 5113 2671 Music boxes; fixtures: display, office or store: except wood; industrial & personal service paper; waxed paper: made from purchased material

(G-1857)
XSCREAM INC
1780 Calumet St (33765-1142)
PHONE..............................727 449-9353
Patrick Bogart, *President*
EMP: 5 EST: 2007
SALES (est): 486.4K **Privately Held**
WEB: www.teamxscream.com
SIC: 3799 All terrain vehicles (ATV)

(G-1858)
XUE WU INC
4445 E Bay Dr Ste 302 (33764-6865)
PHONE..............................727 532-4571
Pin Wu, *Principal*
EMP: 7 EST: 2011
SALES (est): 171.2K **Privately Held**
SIC: 3452 Pins

(G-1859)
ZANIBONI LIGHTING LLC
101 N Garden Ave Ste 230 (33755-4197)
PHONE..............................727 213-0410
Chiara Zaniboni, *CEO*
Jo Beckman, *Accountant*
Darin Fowler, *Manager*
▲ EMP: 57 EST: 2014
SALES (est): 4.9MM **Privately Held**
WEB: www.zanibonilighting.com
SIC: 3648 Lighting equipment

Clearwater Beach
Pinellas County

(G-1860)
ICAT RESOURCE LLC
450 S Gulfview Blvd 703s (33767-2558)
PHONE..............................410 908-9369
Todd A Gravois, *President*
EMP: 10 EST: 2008
SALES (est): 108.7K **Privately Held**
WEB: www.icat.com
SIC: 2741 Miscellaneous publishing

Clermont
Lake County

(G-1861)
BLUE EARTH SOLUTIONS INC
13511 Granville Ave (34711-7173)
PHONE..............................352 729-0150
Patricia Cohen, *CEO*
Paul Slufarczyk, *President*
James Cohen Jr, *Vice Pres*

Douglas Vaught, *Vice Pres*
EMP: 25 EST: 2008
SALES (est): 2.2MM **Privately Held**
SIC: 2899 Foam charge mixtures

(G-1862)
CENTER SAND MINE
16375 Hartwood Marsh Rd (34711-8920)
PHONE..............................800 366-7263
EMP: 7 EST: 2007
SALES (est): 95.4K **Privately Held**
SIC: 3281 Stone, quarrying & processing of own stone products

(G-1863)
CIND-AL INC
Also Called: Clasic Fishing Products
13518 Granville Ave (34711-9628)
PHONE..............................863 401-8700
Louie Gibbs, *President*
Damon Albers, *Exec VP*
Dennis C Losey, *CFO*
EMP: 6 EST: 1978
SQ FT: 2,500
SALES (est): 970.9K **Privately Held**
WEB: www.culprit.com
SIC: 3949 3544 Lures, fishing: artificial; special dies, tools, jigs & fixtures
PA: Classic Fishing Products, Inc.
   13518 Granville Ave
   Clermont FL 34711
   407 656-6133

(G-1864)
CLASSIC FISHING PRODUCTS INC (PA)
13518 Granville Ave (34711-9628)
PHONE..............................407 656-6133
Louie Gibbs, *President*
Damon Albers, *Exec VP*
Dennis C Losey, *CFO*
▲ EMP: 25 EST: 1978
SQ FT: 25,000
SALES (est): 4.6MM **Privately Held**
WEB: www.culprit.com
SIC: 3949 5941 Lures, fishing: artificial; sporting goods & bicycle shops

(G-1865)
EXTRA TIME SOLUTIONS
3695 Peaceful Valley Dr (34711-8917)
PHONE..............................407 625-2198
Connie Griggs, *President*
EMP: 9 EST: 2012
SALES (est): 2.4MM **Privately Held**
SIC: 3589 7349 Commercial cleaning equipment; building cleaning service

(G-1866)
FLORIDA ENVIROMENTAL CONS
9734 Crenshaw Cir (34711-5320)
P.O. Box 305, Howey In The Hills (34737-0305)
PHONE..............................407 402-2828
Robert Lee Lightsey, *Principal*
▲ EMP: 9 EST: 2008
SALES (est): 1.1MM **Privately Held**
SIC: 3822 Auto controls regulating residntl & coml environmt & applncs

(G-1867)
FLORIDA MKB HOLDINGS LLC
16212 Sr 50 (34711-6266)
PHONE..............................407 281-7909
Matthew Borisch,
EMP: 25 EST: 2012
SALES (est): 23MM
SALES (corp-wide): 2.5MM **Privately Held**
WEB: www.gettommys.com
SIC: 3732 5551 Boat building & repairing; boat dealers
PA: Mkb Holdings, Llc
   146 Monroe Center St Nw # 820
   Grand Rapids MI 49503
   810 423-7035

(G-1868)
FLORIDA ROCK CONCRETE
15150 Pine Valley Blvd (34711-7602)
PHONE..............................407 877-6180
John Baker, *President*
EMP: 9 EST: 1957
SQ FT: 720

SALES (est): 176.2K **Privately Held**
SIC: 3273 Ready-mixed concrete

(G-1869)
FRESH MARK CORPORATION
12518 El Viento Rd (34711-9339)
PHONE..............................352 394-7746
Michael D Bowers, *President*
Frank Tislaretz, *Sales Staff*
EMP: 17 EST: 1973
SQ FT: 20,000
SALES (est): 250.8K **Privately Held**
WEB: www.freshmark.com
SIC: 2879 3559 Insecticides, agricultural or household; pesticides, agricultural or household; refinery, chemical processing & similar machinery

(G-1870)
GRAPHICS ARTS BINDERY INC
3023 Pinnacle Ct (34711-5942)
P.O. Box 370492, Miami (33137-0492)
PHONE..............................352 394-4077
Jorge Serra, *President*
Josseline Serra, *Corp Secy*
George Serra Jr, *Vice Pres*
EMP: 9 EST: 1976
SQ FT: 10,000
SALES (est): 780K **Privately Held**
SIC: 2789 Binding only: books, pamphlets, magazines, etc.

(G-1871)
HARTMANS CANINE CENTER LLC
6242 Oil Well Rd (34714-9155)
P.O. Box 136146 (34713-6146)
PHONE..............................352 978-6592
Al Hartman, *General Mgr*
Ai V Hartman, *Principal*
EMP: 7 EST: 2017
SALES (est): 154.9K **Privately Held**
WEB: www.hartmank9c.com
SIC: 3231 Cut & engraved glassware: made from purchased glass

(G-1872)
KEEPMEFRESH
614 E Highway 50 Ste 122 (34711-3164)
PHONE..............................502 407-7902
Bradley Tinch, *Owner*
EMP: 5 EST: 2015
SALES (est): 425K **Privately Held**
SIC: 2389 7389 Footlets;

(G-1873)
KINGS FOUR CRNERS AUTO DTLING ✪
940 Us Highway 27 (34714-8909)
PHONE..............................866 886-4383
Paul Campblin, *Mng Member*
EMP: 8 EST: 2021
SALES (est): 562.3K **Privately Held**
SIC: 3589 7389 Car washing machinery;

(G-1874)
LEGACY VULCAN LLC
3310 Green Swamp Rd (34714-7227)
PHONE..............................352 394-6196
Frank C Klein, *Manager*
EMP: 10
SQ FT: 260 **Publicly Held**
SIC: 3273 5032 Ready-mixed concrete; gravel; aggregate
HQ: Legacy Vulcan, Llc
   1200 Urban Center Dr
   Vestavia AL 35242
   205 298-3000

(G-1875)
LIGHT AGE PRESS INC
5660 County Road 561 (34714-9795)
PHONE..............................352 242-4530
Sarah Tirri, *Principal*
EMP: 7 EST: 2007
SALES (est): 96.3K **Privately Held**
SIC: 2741 Miscellaneous publishing

(G-1876)
MARIA DILL INC
17649 Us Highway 27 B3 (34715-9500)
PHONE..............................352 394-0418
Maria C Dill, *CEO*
Dennis Dill, *CFO*
▲ EMP: 8 EST: 2010

SQ FT: 200
SALES (est): 281.6K **Privately Held**
SIC: 3799 Golf carts, powered

(G-1877)
NEWS LEADER INC
Also Called: Sun Publication of Florida
637 8th St (34711-2159)
PHONE..............................352 242-9818
Donna Covert, *President*
EMP: 13 EST: 1983
SQ FT: 1,100
SALES (est): 463.6K **Privately Held**
WEB: static.newsleader.com
SIC: 2711 Newspapers, publishing & printing

(G-1878)
PRESTIGE/AB READY MIX LLC
Also Called: Prestige A B Ready Mix
17600 State Road 50 (34711-7131)
PHONE..............................407 654-3330
Mike Lane, *Manager*
EMP: 42
SALES (corp-wide): 11.2MM **Privately Held**
SIC: 3273 Ready-mixed concrete
PA: Prestige/Ab Ready Mix, Llc
   7228 Westport Pl Ste C
   West Palm Beach FL 33413
   561 478-9980

(G-1879)
R JS BOAT LIFTS INC
18249 E Apshawa Rd (34715-9261)
PHONE..............................352 394-5666
Pam Cavender, *Principal*
EMP: 7 EST: 2014
SALES (est): 702.7K **Privately Held**
WEB: www.rjsboatlifts.com
SIC: 3536 Boat lifts

(G-1880)
RED GIANT ENTERTAINMENT INC (PA)
614 E Hwy 50 Ste 235 (34711-3164)
PHONE..............................877 904-7334
Benny R Powell, *President*
David Dadon, *Vice Chairman*
David Campiti, *COO*
Chris Crosby, *CTO*
Aimee Schoof, *Officer*
EMP: 6 EST: 2005
SALES (est): 627.6K **Publicly Held**
WEB: www.redgiantentertainment.com
SIC: 2731 Books: publishing & printing

(G-1881)
REPUBLIC NEWSPAPERS INC
Also Called: South Lake Press
732 W Montrose St (34711-2122)
PHONE..............................352 394-2183
EMP: 10
SALES (corp-wide): 2MM **Privately Held**
SIC: 2711 Newspaper Publisher
PA: Republic Newspapers, Inc
   11863 Kingston Pike
   Knoxville TN 37934
   865 675-6397

(G-1882)
SEAVIN INC (PA)
Also Called: Lakeridge Winery & Vineyards
19239 Us Highway 27 (34715-9025)
PHONE..............................352 394-8627
Charles G Cox, *President*
Jeanne Burgess, *Vice Pres*
Carmen Napoles, *Opers Staff*
Awn M Enix T, *Treasurer*
Denise McLeod, *Consultant*
▲ EMP: 35 EST: 1990
SQ FT: 22,400
SALES (est): 9.8MM **Privately Held**
WEB: www.lakeridgewinery.com
SIC: 2084 0172 Wines; grapes

(G-1883)
SECURITY ORACLE INC
3614 Solana Cir (34711-5017)
PHONE..............................352 988-5985
Charles Butler, *CEO*
Vontella Kay Kimball, *President*
EMP: 10 EST: 2014

SALES (est): 684.1K **Privately Held**
WEB: www.thesecurityoracle.com
SIC: 7372 7382 1731 Prepackaged software; protective devices, security; safety & security specialization

(G-1884)
TIME IS MONEY CAMPAIGN LLC
16750 Abbey Hill Ct (34711-6353)
PHONE....................................352 255-5273
Denzel Quarterman,
EMP: 12 EST: 2016
SALES (est): 487.8K **Privately Held**
SIC: 3651 Music distribution apparatus

Clewiston
Hendry County

(G-1885)
A & J READY MIX INC
Even Rnge 300 398 W El (33440)
PHONE....................................863 228-7154
Alexander Bentancor, CEO
Juan Bentancor, Principal
EMP: 5 EST: 2018
SALES (est): 357.2K **Privately Held**
SIC: 3273 Ready-mixed concrete

(G-1886)
CLEWISTON WATER BTLG CO LLC
615 Commerce Ct (33440-4501)
PHONE....................................863 902-1317
Ernesto Rodriguez Garrido, Principal
Ferenc Schafer, Principal
Maria Torres, Admin Asst
EMP: 7 EST: 2014
SQ FT: 8,000
SALES (est): 292.5K **Privately Held**
WEB: www.clewiston-fl.gov
SIC: 2086 Mineral water, carbonated: packaged in cans, bottles, etc.

(G-1887)
D & J MACHINERY INC
728 E Trinidad Ave (33440-3924)
PHONE....................................863 983-3171
James G Swindle, President
Jamie Lester, Purch Mgr
Alan Case, Design Engr
Yavor Kantchev, Manager
Joanie L Swindle, Admin Sec
EMP: 40 EST: 1984
SQ FT: 40,000
SALES (est): 7.7MM **Privately Held**
WEB: www.djmachinery.net
SIC: 3599 Machine shop, jobbing & repair

(G-1888)
EVERGLADES MACHINE INC
1816 Red Rd (33440-9507)
PHONE....................................863 983-0133
William E Rudd, President
EMP: 6 EST: 1993
SQ FT: 2,400
SALES (est): 980K **Privately Held**
WEB: www.evergladesmachine.com
SIC: 3599 7699 Machine shop, jobbing & repair; agricultural equipment repair services

(G-1889)
FLORIDA SUGAR FARMERS
111 Ponce De Leon Ave (33440-3032)
PHONE....................................863 983-7276
Charles F Shide, Principal
EMP: 12 EST: 2006
SALES (est): 134.7K **Privately Held**
WEB: www.ussugar.com
SIC: 2062 Cane sugar refining

(G-1890)
GARCIA MINING COMPANY LLC (PA)
6605 Garcia Dr (33440-4309)
PHONE....................................863 902-9777
Joshua Kellam, Mng Member
EMP: 5 EST: 2018
SALES (est): 1.1MM **Privately Held**
SIC: 1442 Sand mining

(G-1891)
HARE LUMBER & READY MIX INC
425 E Haiti Ave (33440-4699)
PHONE....................................863 983-8725
Leroy Hare, President
Sandra Hare, Corp Secy
Sarah D Perkins, Vice Pres
EMP: 12 EST: 1953
SQ FT: 20,000
SALES (est): 2MM **Privately Held**
WEB: www.harereadymixlumber.com
SIC: 3273 5072 5251 Ready-mixed concrete; builders' hardware; builders' hardware

(G-1892)
MAMA BEAR LAWN CARE PRESS
30290 Josie Billie Hwy (33440-9502)
PHONE....................................863 517-5322
EMP: 6 EST: 2019
SALES (est): 535K **Privately Held**
SIC: 2741 Miscellaneous publishing

(G-1893)
MIAMI HANG GLIDING CORP
Also Called: Naples Hang Gliding
12655 E State Road 80 (33440-7595)
PHONE....................................863 805-0440
James Gindle, President
Doug Wielhouwer, Vice Pres
EMP: 6 EST: 2010
SALES (est): 460.1K **Privately Held**
SIC: 3721 8331 Hang gliders; job training & vocational rehabilitation services

(G-1894)
NATURAL4NATURALZ LLC
561 Old Farm Pl (33440-4610)
PHONE....................................561 621-1546
Kio Coffie,
Jesmina Elhirech,
EMP: 7 EST: 2020
SALES (est): 304.1K **Privately Held**
SIC: 2844 Toilet preparations

(G-1895)
SOUTHERN GRDNS CTRUS HLDG CORP (HQ)
111 Ponce De Leon Ave (33440-3032)
PHONE....................................863 983-8121
Robert Buker, CEO
Trist Chapam, President
Ricke A Kress, President
James Terrill, President
Virginia Pena, Principal
◆ EMP: 4 EST: 1990
SQ FT: 40,000
SALES (est): 24.7MM
SALES (corp-wide): 248.3MM **Privately Held**
WEB: www.ussugar.com
SIC: 2037 Fruit juices
PA: United States Sugar Corporation
111 Ponce De Leon Ave
Clewiston FL 33440
863 983-8121

Cocoa
Brevard County

(G-1896)
A & E MACHINE INC
1445 Lake Dr (32922-6284)
P.O. Box 236065 (32923-6065)
PHONE....................................321 636-3110
Art Armellini, President
Teresa Vayda, Manager
EMP: 23 EST: 1982
SQ FT: 3,000
SALES (est): 494.7K **Privately Held**
SIC: 3599 7692 Machine shop, jobbing & repair; welding repair

(G-1897)
ABSOLUTE AUTOMATION & SECURITY
3815 N Highway 1 Ste 101 (32926-5947)
P.O. Box 5687, Titusville (32783-5687)
PHONE....................................321 505-9989
Jason Barati, President

EMP: 8 EST: 2004
SQ FT: 3,200
SALES (est): 1MM **Privately Held**
WEB: www.absoluteautomation.com
SIC: 3699 Security control equipment & systems

(G-1898)
ADRICK MARINE GROUP INC
581 Cidco Rd (32926-5809)
PHONE....................................321 631-0776
Thomas Vassallo, CEO
Susan Vassallo, Corp Secy
Richard Vassallo, Vice Pres
▼ EMP: 12 EST: 1978
SQ FT: 10,000
SALES (est): 1.7MM **Privately Held**
WEB: www.adrickmarine.com
SIC: 3585 Refrigeration & heating equipment

(G-1899)
ADVANCED ALUM CENTL FLA INC
155 N Range Rd Ste 13 (32926-5398)
PHONE....................................321 639-1451
William Johns, President
Paula Carter, Vice Pres
▲ EMP: 5 EST: 1983
SQ FT: 2,000
SALES (est): 500K **Privately Held**
SIC: 3355 Structural shapes, rolled, aluminum

(G-1900)
AGTECK INC
150 N Wilson Ave Ste 101 (32922-7260)
PHONE....................................321 305-5930
Win Everett, President
Raymond Terranova, Analyst
EMP: 20 EST: 2013
SALES (est): 1.8MM **Privately Held**
WEB: www.agteck.net
SIC: 3599 8711 Machine shop, jobbing & repair; engineering services

(G-1901)
AMAZON METAL FABRICATORS INC
Also Called: Dotrailings.com
600 Cox Rd Ste C (32926-4248)
PHONE....................................321 631-7574
Donald Benson, President
Andrew Benson, Vice Pres
Jacominna Benson, Treasurer
EMP: 16 EST: 1984
SQ FT: 8,000
SALES (est): 350K **Publicly Held**
WEB: www.dotrailing.com
SIC: 3446 Architectural metalwork
PA: Amazon.Com, Inc.
410 Terry Ave N
Seattle WA 98109

(G-1902)
AMERICAN BOTTLING COMPANY
1313 W King St (32922-8693)
PHONE....................................321 433-3622
Robert H Paul, Branch Mgr
EMP: 70 **Publicly Held**
WEB: www.keurigdrpepper.com
SIC: 2086 Soft drinks: packaged in cans, bottles, etc.
HQ: The American Bottling Company
6425 Hall Of Fame Ln
Frisco TX 75034

(G-1903)
AMERICAN QUALITY MFG INC
310 Shearer Blvd (32922-7248)
PHONE....................................321 636-3434
David McConnell, President
Andrew McConnell, Vice Pres
▼ EMP: 14 EST: 1991
SQ FT: 8,500
SALES (est): 1.9MM **Privately Held**
WEB: www.highpressuretanningbeds.com
SIC: 3949 Exercise equipment

(G-1904)
ATLANTIC EARTH MATERIALS
2185 W King St (32926-5131)
PHONE....................................321 631-0600
Susan Griffin, President

EMP: 10 EST: 1996
SALES (est): 972.1K **Privately Held**
SIC: 1442 Gravel & pebble mining

(G-1905)
ATLANTIC WIRE AND RIGGING INC
330 Williams Point Blvd A (32927-4606)
P.O. Box 1249, Sharpes (32959-1249)
PHONE....................................321 633-1552
John L Platt Jr, President
Ginger Platt, Corp Secy
▼ EMP: 7 EST: 1992
SQ FT: 10,000
SALES (est): 758.4K **Privately Held**
WEB: www.atlanticwireandrigging.com
SIC: 2298 3312 Slings; rope; wire products, steel or iron

(G-1906)
AYON CYBERSECURITY INC
5155 King St (32926)
PHONE....................................321 953-3033
John H Booher, President
EMP: 27 EST: 2012
SALES (est): 2.9MM
SALES (corp-wide): 7MM **Publicly Held**
WEB: www.videodisplay.com
SIC: 3571 Electronic computers
PA: Video Display Corporation
5155 King St
Cocoa FL 32926
800 241-5005

(G-1907)
BRADEN KITCHENS INC
515 Industry Rd S (32926-5874)
PHONE....................................321 636-4700
Peter Profumo, CEO
Robert Krick, President
Peter Petri, Vice Pres
EMP: 27 EST: 1964
SQ FT: 50,000
SALES (est): 2.6MM **Privately Held**
WEB: www.bradenkitchens.com
SIC: 2521 3299 2541 2821 Cabinets, office: wood; mica products; wood partitions & fixtures; plastics materials & resins; carpentry work; vanities, bathroom: wood

(G-1908)
BRANDFX LLC
605 Townsend Rd (32926-3321)
PHONE....................................321 632-2063
Tim Tierney, Branch Mgr
EMP: 44
SALES (corp-wide): 19.2MM **Privately Held**
WEB: www.brandfxbody.com
SIC: 3524 2879 Lawn & garden equipment; pesticides, agricultural or household
PA: Brandfx, Llc
2800 Golden Triangle Blvd
Fort Worth TX 76177
817 431-1131

(G-1909)
BREVARD ROBOTICS
1485 Cox Rd (32926-4743)
P.O. Box 236651 (32923-6651)
PHONE....................................321 637-0367
George Kellgren, President
EMP: 30 EST: 2001
SQ FT: 17,800
SALES (est): 6.8MM **Privately Held**
SIC: 3599 Machine shop, jobbing & repair

(G-1910)
CABINETS -N- MORE INC
6023 Elgin Rd (32927-9038)
PHONE....................................321 355-9548
Vincent Giusto, Principal
EMP: 8 EST: 2016
SALES (est): 252.7K **Privately Held**
WEB: www.cabinetsnmorefl.com
SIC: 2434 Wood kitchen cabinets

(G-1911)
CEMEX MATERIALS LLC
3365 E Industry Rd (32926-5841)
PHONE....................................321 636-5121
EMP: 147 **Privately Held**
SIC: 3273 Ready-mixed concrete

HQ: Cemex Materials Llc
1720 Centrepark Dr E # 100
West Palm Beach FL 33401
561 833-5555

(G-1912)
COVINGTON PLASTICS INC
427 Shearer Blvd (32922-4211)
PHONE..................................321 632-6775
Gary Mc Murry, *President*
EMP: 14 **EST:** 1975
SQ FT: 14,700
SALES (est): 1.6MM **Privately Held**
WEB: www.covingtonplastics.com
SIC: 3089 3544 Injection molding of plastics; special dies, tools, jigs & fixtures

(G-1913)
CUTTING EDGE MCH FBRCATION LLC
Also Called: Cocoa Customs RC
534 Saint Johns St Bldg C (32922-7241)
PHONE..................................321 626-0588
Martin Richard Van Buren, *Principal*
EMP: 7 **EST:** 2017
SALES (est): 297.6K **Privately Held**
WEB: www.cuttingedgemnf.com
SIC: 3599 Machine shop, jobbing & repair

(G-1914)
D M T INC
817 N Cocoa Blvd (32922-7510)
PHONE..................................321 267-3931
Scott Glover, *President*
Brandon Glover, *President*
EMP: 14 **EST:** 1981
SALES (est): 1MM **Privately Held**
SIC: 3089 3544 Injection molding of plastics; industrial molds

(G-1915)
DIAMONDBACK BARRELS LLC
4135 Pine Tree Pl (32926-3311)
PHONE..................................321 305-5995
Bobby Fleckinger, *Mng Member*
Stephen Scott Broussard,
EMP: 12 **EST:** 2013
SALES (est): 916.7K **Privately Held**
WEB: www.diamondbackbarrels.com
SIC: 2429 Barrels & barrel parts

(G-1916)
DIAMONDBACK CNC LLC
Also Called: Diamondback America
3400 Grissom Pkwy (32926-4543)
PHONE..................................321 305-5995
Faith Denman, *Manager*
Bobby Fleckinger,
Fran Fleckinger,
EMP: 33 **EST:** 2006
SALES (est): 5.8MM **Privately Held**
SIC: 3599 Crankshafts & camshafts, machining
PA: Diamondback Manufacturing, Llc
1060 Cox Rd
Cocoa FL 32926

(G-1917)
DIAMONDBACK FIREARMS LLC
3400 Grissom Pkwy (32926-4543)
PHONE..................................321 305-5995
Bobby Fleckinger, *President*
Faith Denman, *CFO*
Ray Dillingham, *Manager*
EMP: 18 **EST:** 2009
SALES (est): 8.5MM **Privately Held**
WEB: www.diamondbackfirearms.com
SIC: 3484 Guns (firearms) or gun parts, 30 mm. & below
PA: Diamondback Manufacturing, Llc
1060 Cox Rd
Cocoa FL 32926

(G-1918)
DIAMONDBACK MANUFACTURING LLC
1060 Cox Rd Bldg A (32926-4237)
PHONE..................................321 305-5995
Bobby V Fleckinger, *Mng Member*
Faith Denman,
Frances C Fleckinger,
EMP: 17 **EST:** 2012
SALES (est): 132.9K **Privately Held**
WEB: www.diamondbackairboats.com
SIC: 3732 Boat building & repairing

(G-1919)
DIAMONDBACK MANUFACTURING LLC (PA)
Also Called: Diamondback Airboats
1060 Cox Rd (32926-4237)
PHONE..................................321 633-5624
Bobby V Fleckinger, *President*
Frances C Fleckinger, *Mng Member*
▼ **EMP:** 19 **EST:** 1989
SQ FT: 15,000
SALES (est): 17.2MM **Privately Held**
WEB: www.diamondbackairboats.com
SIC: 3732 Boat building & repairing

(G-1920)
DIAMONDBACK TOWERS LLC
1060 Cox Rd Bldg B (32926-4237)
PHONE..................................800 424-5624
Bobby V Fleckinger,
EMP: 29 **EST:** 2010
SALES (est): 3.3MM
SALES (corp-wide): 4B **Publicly Held**
WEB: www.diamondbackmarine.com
SIC: 3949 Water skis
PA: Patrick Industries, Inc.
107 W Franklin St
Elkhart IN 46516
574 294-7511

(G-1921)
DR PEPPER/SEVEN UP INC
1313 W King St (32922-8693)
PHONE..................................321 433-3622
EMP: 17 **Publicly Held**
WEB: www.drpepper.com
SIC: 2086 Soft drinks: packaged in cans, bottles, etc.
HQ: Dr Pepper/Seven Up, Inc.
6425 Hall Of Fame Ln
Frisco TX 75034
972 673-7000

(G-1922)
DUTCHY ENTERPRISES LLC
600 Cox Rd Ste A (32926-4248)
PHONE..................................321 877-0700
Robert Reijm, *Mng Member*
Matthew Sobarzo,
EMP: 7 **EST:** 2016
SQ FT: 2,000
SALES (est): 250K **Privately Held**
WEB: www.dutchyenterprises.com
SIC: 3441 8711 Fabricated structural metal; engineering services

(G-1923)
EAST COAST MACHINE INC
3022 Oxbow Cir (32926-4553)
PHONE..................................321 632-4817
Pereric Tapia, *President*
Frederic Meier, *President*
Eric Tapia, *Principal*
Brenda Meier, *Vice Pres*
Tyler Hamlin, *Production*
EMP: 19 **EST:** 1983
SQ FT: 5,000
SALES (est): 2.1MM **Privately Held**
WEB: www.eastcoastmachine.net
SIC: 3499 3599 Fire- or burglary-resistive products; machine shop, jobbing & repair

(G-1924)
EAST COAST METALWORKS LLC
6615 Bethel St (32927-4220)
PHONE..................................321 698-0624
James C Timberlake III, *Mng Member*
EMP: 6 **EST:** 2013
SALES (est): 382K **Privately Held**
SIC: 3499 7692 7389 Fabricated metal products; welding repair;

(G-1925)
ELASTEC INC
401 Shearer Blvd (32922-7249)
PHONE..................................618 382-2525
Jan Hoven, *Business Mgr*
Tammi Crossett, *Engineer*
Greg Gibbs, *Human Res Dir*
Sharon Behnke, *HR Admin*
Jeff Pearce, *Manager*
EMP: 30 **Privately Held**
WEB: www.elastec.com
SIC: 3999 Massage machines, electric; barber & beauty shops .

PA: Elastec, Inc.
1309 W Main St
Carmi IL 62821

(G-1926)
EQUIPMENT FABRICATORS INC
655 Cidco Rd (32926-5811)
PHONE..................................321 632-0990
Michael Olsen, *President*
Maryann Spellman, *Human Res Dir*
Ginny Bass, *Administration*
EMP: 32 **EST:** 1965
SQ FT: 16,500
SALES (est): 6.4MM **Privately Held**
WEB: www.equipmentfab.com
SIC: 3536 3531 Cranes, overhead traveling; construction machinery

(G-1927)
ETCHART LLC
Also Called: Wallpaper For Windows
3732 N Highway 1 Ste 5 (32926-8782)
PHONE..................................321 504-4060
Larry Cashion,
Renee Combs,
EMP: 5 **EST:** 2004
SALES (est): 472.6K **Privately Held**
WEB: www.wallpaperforwindows.com
SIC: 2591 Drapery hardware & blinds & shades

(G-1928)
FLITE TECHNOLOGY INC
2511 Friday Rd (32926-3423)
PHONE..................................321 631-2050
Leo Burch, *President*
Ron Anderson, *Principal*
▲ **EMP:** 13 **EST:** 1981
SQ FT: 3,000
SALES (est): 1.8MM **Privately Held**
WEB: www.flitetech.com
SIC: 3559 3535 3444 Plastics working machinery; conveyors & conveying equipment; sheet metalwork

(G-1929)
FLORIDA GLSD HOLDINGS INC
Also Called: Ocean Potion
851 Greensboro Rd (32926-4516)
PHONE..................................321 633-4644
Steve Taylor, *CEO*
Gerald Woelcke, *CFO*
▼ **EMP:** 180 **EST:** 1989
SQ FT: 75,000
SALES (est): 21.4MM **Privately Held**
WEB: www.sscrllc.com
SIC: 2844 Suntan lotions & oils

(G-1930)
FUN MARINE INC
Also Called: Fiberglass Fabrication
682 Industry Rd S (32926-5825)
PHONE..................................321 576-1100
Larry Wirtzberger, *President*
Seth Kerzner, *Vice Pres*
EMP: 9 **EST:** 1984
SALES (est): 716.4K **Privately Held**
SIC: 3083 Laminated plastics plate & sheet

(G-1931)
FURNIVAL CABINETRY LLC
7235 Camilo Rd (32927-3040)
PHONE..................................321 638-1223
Ronald E Furnival,
EMP: 9 **EST:** 1999
SALES (est): 914.1K **Privately Held**
WEB: www.furnivalcabinetryllc.com
SIC: 2434 Wood kitchen cabinets

(G-1932)
FURNIVAL CONSTRUCTION LLC
7235 Camilo Rd (32927-3040)
PHONE..................................321 638-1223
Leonard Gallion, *Project Mgr*
Ron Furnival, *Mng Member*
EMP: 10 **EST:** 2014
SALES (est): 809.6K **Privately Held**
SIC: 2434 Wood kitchen cabinets

(G-1933)
GEM INDUSTRIES INC
370 Cox Rd (32926-4280)
PHONE..................................321 302-8985
Ann Jeanette Miner, *President*
Garret S Miner, *General Mgr*
EMP: 45 **EST:** 2004

SALES (est): 7.6MM **Privately Held**
WEB: www.gemindustriesincorporated.com
SIC: 3441 Building components, structural steel

(G-1934)
GUARDIAN IGN INTERLOCK MFG INC
Also Called: Guardian Manufacturing
2971 Oxbow Cir Ste A (32926-4500)
PHONE..................................321 205-1730
Charles E Smith, *President*
Steve Smith, *Vice Pres*
Ken Davis, *Opers Dir*
John Draygos, *Plant Mgr*
Jeff Stewart, *Chief Engr*
▲ **EMP:** 60 **EST:** 1991
SQ FT: 10,000
SALES (est): 24.4MM **Privately Held**
WEB: www.guardianmfg.com
SIC: 3829 Measuring & controlling devices

(G-1935)
HITMAN INDUSTRIES LLC
150 N Wilson Ave (32922-7260)
PHONE..................................321 735-8562
Walter M Falscroft, *Mng Member*
EMP: 15 **EST:** 2016
SALES (est): 4.1MM **Privately Held**
WEB: www.hitmanindustries.net
SIC: 3484 Guns (firearms) or gun parts, 30 mm. & below

(G-1936)
IMMUNOTEK BIO CENTERS LLC
1225 W King St (32922-8619)
PHONE..................................404 345-3570
Jerome Parnell III, *Branch Mgr*
EMP: 15
SALES (corp-wide): 27MM **Privately Held**
WEB: www.immunotek.com
SIC: 2836 Blood derivatives
PA: Immunotek Bio Centers, L.L.C.
3900 N Causeway Blvd # 1200
Metairie LA 70002
337 500-1175

(G-1937)
INFOPIA USA LLC
7160 Bright Ave (32927-8005)
PHONE..................................321 225-3620
James Reynolds, *IT/INT Sup*
Bryan Sowards Sowards,
Bryan Sowards,
EMP: 18 **EST:** 2008
SALES (est): 470.6K **Privately Held**
WEB: www.infopiausa.com
SIC: 3845 Patient monitoring apparatus

(G-1938)
INTERNATIONAL PAINT LLC
3062 Oxbow Cir (32926-4507)
PHONE..................................321 636-9722
EMP: 9
SALES (corp-wide): 10.8B **Privately Held**
WEB: www.akzonobel.com
SIC: 2851 Paints & allied products
HQ: International Paint Llc
535 Marriott Dr Ste 500
Nashville TN 37214
713 684-5839

(G-1939)
KEL-TEC CNC INDUSTRIES INC
Also Called: Keltec
1505 Cox Rd (32926-4741)
P.O. Box 236009 (32923-6009)
PHONE..................................321 631-0068
George Kellgren, *President*
Derek Kellgren, *General Mgr*
Rubi Kellgren, *Corp Secy*
Terrence Stubblefield, *Supervisor*
Adrian Kellgren, *Director*
EMP: 11 **EST:** 1991
SQ FT: 15,000
SALES (est): 2.8MM **Privately Held**
WEB: www.keltecweapons.com
SIC: 3484 Guns (firearms) or gun parts, 30 mm. & below

(G-1940)
MANGO BOTTLING INC
Also Called: Tooter Lingo Liquer
767 Clearlake Rd (32922-5208)
PHONE..................................321 631-1005

Drayton Sproull, *President*
John L Lingo, *President*
Pam McCann, *Office Admin*
Jared Shammah, *Business Dir*
▲ **EMP:** 30 **EST:** 1992
SQ FT: 17,000
SALES (est): 5.4MM **Privately Held**
WEB: www.mangobottling.com
SIC: 3085 5182 Plastics bottles; bottling wines & liquors

(G-1941)
MET-CON INC
465 Canaveral Groves Blvd (32926-4663)
P.O. Box 236129 (32923-6129)
PHONE.................................321 632-4880
Billy E Sheffield, *President*
Brian Greer, *Superintendent*
Dennis Dammann, *Vice Pres*
Jeffrey Gibson, *Vice Pres*
Robert Reijm, *Vice Pres*
▼ **EMP:** 100 **EST:** 1979
SQ FT: 100,000
SALES (est): 15.1MM **Privately Held**
WEB: www.metconinc.com
SIC: 3441 1791 1541 Building compo-
nents, structural steel; structural steel
erection; industrial buildings, new con-
struction

(G-1942)
MID FLORIDA STEEL CORP
870 Cidco Rd (32926-5884)
P.O. Box 236006 (32923-6006)
PHONE.................................321 632-8228
Dale Coxwell, *President*
Greg Homes, *Vice Pres*
Rachel Coxwell, *Treasurer*
EMP: 26 **EST:** 1991
SQ FT: 4,000
SALES (est): 621.6K **Privately Held**
WEB: www.midfloridasteel.com
SIC: 3449 3441 Miscellaneous metalwork;
fabricated structural metal

(G-1943)
MTC ENGINEERING LLC
428 Shearer Blvd (32922-7296)
PHONE.................................321 636-9480
Eric Hochstetler,
▲ **EMP:** 19 **EST:** 1966
SQ FT: 13,000
SALES (est): 4.6MM **Privately Held**
WEB: www.mtceng.com
SIC: 3592 Carburetors, pistons, rings,
valves

(G-1944)
NEELCO INDUSTRIES INC
420 Shearer Blvd (32922-7250)
PHONE.................................321 632-5303
Robert Martin, *President*
Matt Jerry, *Sales Staff*
EMP: 14 **EST:** 1972
SQ FT: 10,000
SALES (est): 2.1MM **Privately Held**
WEB: www.neelco.biz
SIC: 3523 Fertilizing, spraying, dusting &
irrigation machinery

(G-1945)
OB INC (PA)
5020 Scott Rd (32926-2617)
PHONE.................................321 223-0332
Daniel O'Brien, *President*
EMP: 9 **EST:** 1998
SALES (est): 654K **Privately Held**
SIC: 2951 Asphalt paving mixtures &
blocks

(G-1946)
PLATING RESOURCES INC
2845 W King St Ste 108 (32926-4803)
PHONE.................................321 632-2435
Judith E Svenson, *CEO*
Eric C Svenson, *President*
EMP: 16 **EST:** 1990
SQ FT: 12,000
SALES (est): 1.3MM **Privately Held**
WEB: www.plating.com
SIC: 2899 Chemical preparations

(G-1947)
PORTABLE-SHADE USA LLC
428 Shearer Blvd (32922-7250)
PHONE.................................321 704-8100

Eric J Hochstetler, *Mng Member*
EMP: 8 **EST:** 2010
SALES (est): 58.9K **Privately Held**
WEB: www.portable-shade.com
SIC: 2394 Canopies, fabric: made from
purchased materials

(G-1948)
PRECISION FABG & CLG CO INC
3975 E Railroad Ave (32926-5975)
PHONE.................................321 635-2000
Robert Kelly, *President*
Warren Lambert, *Superintendent*
Todd Gray, *Vice Pres*
Casey Cutright, *Foreman/Supr*
Jim Caldwell, *Engineer*
▲ **EMP:** 74 **EST:** 1964
SQ FT: 20,000
SALES (est): 14.2MM **Privately Held**
SIC: 3823 3769 3494 Industrial instrmnts
msrmnt display/control process variable;
guided missile & space vehicle parts &
auxiliary equipment; valves & pipe fittings
PA: Precision Resources, Inc.
3975 E Railroad Ave
Cocoa FL 32926

(G-1949)
PRECISION RESOURCES INC (PA)
3975 E Railroad Ave (32926-5975)
PHONE.................................321 635-2000
Robert W Kelly, *President*
Robert Kelly, *President*
Todd Gray, *Vice Pres*
Alejandra Lopezluna, *Project Mgr*
Jason Shye, *CFO*
EMP: 15 **EST:** 1992
SQ FT: 7,000
SALES (est): 36.4MM **Privately Held**
WEB: www.precisionresource.com
SIC: 3823 1711 8741 Industrial instrmnts
msrmnt display/control process variable;
warm air heating & air conditioning con-
tractor; mechanical contractor; adminis-
trative management

(G-1950)
QUALITY MOLDS USA INC
2402 Cherbourg Rd (32926-5709)
PHONE.................................321 632-6066
William Both, *President*
EMP: 10 **EST:** 2001
SALES (est): 586.2K **Privately Held**
WEB: www.qualitymolds.net
SIC: 3089 Fiberglass doors

(G-1951)
RDS INDUSTRIAL INC
436 Shearer Blvd (32922-7250)
PHONE.................................321 631-0121
Patrick Pacifico, *President*
Fred Garbotz, *President*
Meredith Pacifico, *Executive*
EMP: 18 **EST:** 2009
SQ FT: 10,000
SALES (est): 2.4MM **Privately Held**
WEB: www.rdsindustrial.com
SIC: 3441 3446 Building components,
structural steel; architectural metalwork

(G-1952)
REAL FLEET SOLUTIONS LLC
605 Townsend Rd (32926-3321)
PHONE.................................321 631-2414
Cynthia Smith, *Office Mgr*
James Tierney,
EMP: 34 **EST:** 2017
SQ FT: 22,000
SALES (est): 3.2MM **Privately Held**
WEB: www.realfleetsolutions.com
SIC: 3599 Custom machinery

(G-1953)
REYES STUCCO INC
1515 Peachtree St Lot 3 (32922-8668)
PHONE.................................321 557-1319
Cruz M Cifuentes, *Principal*
EMP: 7 **EST:** 2009
SALES (est): 189.7K **Privately Held**
SIC: 3299 Stucco

(G-1954)
RICKS QUALITY PRTG & SIGNS
Also Called: Rick's Quality Printing & Sign
681 Industry Rd S Ste A (32926-5807)
PHONE.................................321 504-7446
Kay Szucs, *President*
Rick Szucs, *Vice Pres*
EMP: 6 **EST:** 1980
SQ FT: 6,400
SALES (est): 355.5K **Privately Held**
SIC: 3993 Signs & advertising specialties

(G-1955)
ROCKET CRAFTERS LAUNCH LLC
Also Called: Vaya Space
2941 Oxbow Cir (32926-4550)
PHONE.................................321 222-0858
Robert Fabian,
EMP: 15 **EST:** 2018
SALES (est): 879K **Privately Held**
SIC: 3761 Ballistic missiles, complete

(G-1956)
SERVICE CORP INTERNATIONAL
Also Called: SCI
Us Hwy 1 Frontenac (32927)
PHONE.................................321 636-6041
Ralph Sutliff, *Manager*
EMP: 7
SALES (corp-wide): 4.1B **Publicly Held**
WEB: www.sci-corp.com
SIC: 3995 Burial caskets
PA: Service Corporation International
1929 Allen Pkwy
Houston TX 77019
713 522-5141

(G-1957)
SOUTHERN TAPE & LABEL INC
1107 Peachtree St (32922-8638)
P.O. Box 3466 (32924-3466)
PHONE.................................321 632-5275
Robert Ramsey, *President*
Joyce Ramsey, *Corp Secy*
EMP: 19 **EST:** 1978
SQ FT: 11,100
SALES (est): 2.9MM **Privately Held**
WEB: www.labelsstl.com
SIC: 2759 Labels & seals: printing

(G-1958)
SPACE COAST INDUSTRIES INC
700 Cox Rd Ste 1 (32926-4249)
P.O. Box 236875 (32923-6875)
PHONE.................................321 633-9336
Wayne W Clark, *President*
EMP: 5 **EST:** 2008
SALES (est): 491.3K **Privately Held**
WEB: www.spacecoaststeel.com
SIC: 3799 Trailers & trailer equipment

(G-1959)
ST ACTION PRO INC
3815 N Highway 1 Ste 50 (32926-5946)
PHONE.................................321 632-4111
James Stimmell, *President*
Marshall Todd, *Partner*
Eva Stimmell, *General Mgr*
EMP: 5 **EST:** 2001
SQ FT: 725
SALES (est): 488.4K **Privately Held**
WEB: www.stactionpro.com
SIC: 3482 5699 Small arms ammunition;
uniforms & work clothing

(G-1960)
SUNTREE TECHNOLOGIES INC
798 Clearlake Rd Ste 2 (32922-5114)
PHONE.................................321 637-7552
EMP: 14 **Privately Held**
WEB: www.suntreetech.com
SIC: 3822 Auto controls regulating residntl
& coml environmt & applncs
PA: Suntree Technologies, Inc.
798 Clearlake Rd Ste 2
Cocoa FL 32922

(G-1961)
VAPEX ENVIRONMENTAL TECH INC
2971 Oxbow Cir Ste A (32926-4500)
PHONE.................................407 277-0900
Darrel Resch, *CEO*

Greg Fraser, *President*
Patrick Resch, *Technical Staff*
EMP: 6 **EST:** 2002
SQ FT: 5,000
SALES (est): 1.6MM **Privately Held**
WEB: www.vapex.com
SIC: 3589 Water treatment equipment, in-
dustrial

(G-1962)
VIDEO DISPLAY CORPORATION (PA)
5155 King St (32926)
PHONE.................................800 241-5005
Ronald D Ordway, *CEO*
Gregory L Osborn, *CFO*
◆ **EMP:** 20 **EST:** 1975
SALES: 7MM **Publicly Held**
WEB: www.videodisplay.com
SIC: 3671 Cathode ray tubes, including re-
built; television tubes; electron tubes, spe-
cial purpose; electronic tube parts, except
glass blanks

(G-1963)
VIDEO DISPLAY CORPORATION
Also Called: Vdc Display Systems
5155 King St (32926-2339)
PHONE.................................321 784-4427
Charles Acurio, *General Mgr*
Gina Studdard, *General Mgr*
Art Mengel, *Division Pres*
Mary Cairns, *Materials Mgr*
Thomas Funka, *Materials Mgr*
EMP: 60
SALES (corp-wide): 7MM **Publicly Held**
WEB: www.videodisplay.com
SIC: 3671 3663 Electron tubes; radio & TV
communications equipment
PA: Video Display Corporation
5155 King St
Cocoa FL 32926
800 241-5005

Cocoa Beach
Brevard County

(G-1964)
AKMAN INC
2023 N Atl Ave Ste 201 (32931-5096)
PHONE.................................407 948-0562
John Akman, *President*
Beatrice Akman, *Vice Pres*
▼ **EMP:** 5 **EST:** 1983
SQ FT: 4,000
SALES (est): 505.5K **Privately Held**
WEB: www.akman.com
SIC: 3652 Compact laser discs, prere-
corded; magnetic tape (audio): prere-
corded

(G-1965)
CAFM
2023 N Atlantic Ave 223 (32931-5096)
PHONE.................................407 658-6531
Thomas Carney, *Principal*
Dennis Kammerer, *Director*
EMP: 10 **EST:** 2010
SALES (est): 409.8K **Privately Held**
SIC: 7372 Prepackaged software

(G-1966)
CATHODIC PRTECTION TECH OF FLA
Also Called: C P T
2023 N Atl Ave Ste 251 (32931-5096)
PHONE.................................321 799-0046
James Emory, *President*
EMP: 5 **EST:** 1996
SQ FT: 1,500
SALES (est): 444.6K **Privately Held**
SIC: 2851 3671 Shellac (protective coat-
ing); electron tubes

(G-1967)
CITY OF COCOA BEACH
Also Called: Cocoa Bch Wtr Reclamation
Dept
1600 Minutemen Cswy (32931-2010)
PHONE.................................321 868-3342
Charles Billias, *Principal*
EMP: 46

SALES (corp-wide): 31.6MM **Privately Held**
WEB: www.cityofcocoabeach.com
SIC: 3589 Sewage & water treatment equipment
PA: City Of Cocoa Beach
2 S Orlando Ave
Cocoa Beach FL 32931
321 868-3200

(G-1968)
CORE KITES USA
235 W Cocoa Beach Cswy (32931-3538)
PHONE.................................321 302-0693
EMP: 8 EST: 2012
SALES (est): 96.8K **Privately Held**
WEB: www.ridecore.com
SIC: 3944 Kites

(G-1969)
EXPRESS BADGING SERVICES INC
1980 N Atl Ave Ste 525 (32931-3273)
PHONE.................................321 784-5925
Joe French, *President*
Joe L French, *Vice Pres*
Laina French, *CFO*
EMP: 10 EST: 1993
SQ FT: 1,500
SALES (est): 1.4MM **Privately Held**
WEB: www.expressbadging.com
SIC: 3999 5734 7382 2399 Identification badges & insignia; computer software & accessories; protective devices, security; emblems, badges & insignia

(G-1970)
FABRICATD COMPONNTS INC
106 Aucila Rd (32931-2766)
PHONE.................................321 784-3688
David Fout, *Principal*
EMP: 11 EST: 2008
SALES (est): 71.8K **Privately Held**
SIC: 3599 Machine shop, jobbing & repair

(G-1971)
GADGETCAT LLC
465 North Shore Dr (32931-2813)
PHONE.................................802 238-3671
Jane Zurn,
EMP: 6 EST: 2013
SALES (est): 414.6K **Privately Held**
WEB: www.gadgetcat.com
SIC: 3699 8711 5999 5961 Teaching machines & aids, electronic; electrical or electronic engineering; educational aids & electronic training materials; computer equipment & electronics, mail order

(G-1972)
GARCO MANUFACTURING CO INC
1400 S Orlando Ave (32931-2334)
PHONE.................................321 868-3778
Gary D Cobb, *President*
Alison Capers, *Admin Sec*
EMP: 6 EST: 1997
SALES (est): 525.3K **Privately Held**
WEB: www.garcomfg.com
SIC: 2299 Ramie yarn, thread, roving & textiles

(G-1973)
L3HARRIS INTERSTATE ELEC CORP
Cape Cnvral Ar Bldg 54815 (32932)
PHONE.................................321 730-0119
Bob Huffman, *President*
Mark Butner, *Finance*
EMP: 25
SALES (corp-wide): 17.8B **Publicly Held**
WEB: www.l3harris.com
SIC: 3825 Instruments to measure electricity
HQ: L3harris Interstate Electronics Corporation
602 E Vermont Ave
Anaheim CA 92805
714 758-0500

(G-1974)
MORGANS ELC MTR & PUMP SVC
Also Called: Morgans Elc Mtr & Pump Svc
157 N Orlando Ave (32931-2973)
PHONE.................................321 960-2209
B Morgan Weglein, *President*
EMP: 10 EST: 1994
SALES (est): 278.8K **Privately Held**
SIC: 7694 7699 5261 Electric motor repair; pumps & pumping equipment repair; hydroponic equipment & supplies

Coconut Creek
Broward County

(G-1975)
AERO UNO LLC
2403 Antigua Cir Apt B1 (33066-1005)
PHONE.................................561 767-5597
Lucio Montenegro, *CEO*
EMP: 5 EST: 2016
SALES (est): 486.9K **Privately Held**
WEB: www.aerouno.com
SIC: 3674 5065 Solid state electronic devices; capacitors, electronic

(G-1976)
AIR & POWER SOLUTIONS INC
6810 Lyons Tech Pkwy # 125 (33073-4367)
PHONE.................................954 427-0019
Dale T Keitz, *President*
Marcos Diaz, *Products*
▼ EMP: 6 EST: 2003
SALES (est): 545.2K **Privately Held**
WEB: www.airandpowersolutions.com
SIC: 3585 1731 Heating & air conditioning combination units; computer power conditioning

(G-1977)
ALLLIANCE PRECIOUS MTLS GROUP
6820 Lyons Tech Pkwy (33073-4314)
PHONE.................................954 480-8676
Cindy Vandeveer, *Principal*
EMP: 8 EST: 2008
SALES (est): 130K **Privately Held**
SIC: 3339 Precious metals

(G-1978)
ATLANTIC JET SUPPORT INC
4801 Johnson Rd Ste 11 (33073-4359)
PHONE.................................954 360-7549
Zlata Archy, *President*
Sarunas Rackauskas, *CFO*
EMP: 8 EST: 2004
SQ FT: 5,600
SALES (est): 3.1MM **Privately Held**
WEB: www.ajsupport.com
SIC: 3728 Aircraft parts & equipment

(G-1979)
BOCADELRAY LIFE MAGAZINE
4611 Johnson Rd (33073-4361)
P.O. Box 970335 (33097-0335)
PHONE.................................954 421-9797
Mindi Rudan, *Publisher*
Geraldine Caramat, *Accounting Mgr*
EMP: 9 EST: 2006
SALES (est): 167.5K **Privately Held**
SIC: 2721 Magazines: publishing only, not printed on site

(G-1980)
BUCHELLI GLASS INC
5417 Nw 50th Ct (33073-3301)
PHONE.................................954 695-8067
Albert A Berchiolli, *Director*
EMP: 7 EST: 2004
SALES (est): 71.3K **Privately Held**
SIC: 3231 Products of purchased glass

(G-1981)
COBEX RECORDERS INC
6601 Lyons Rd Ste F8 (33073-3622)
PHONE.................................954 425-0003
Matthew Levine, *President*
▲ EMP: 12 EST: 1994

SALES (est): 1.7MM **Privately Held**
WEB: www.cobexrecorders.com
SIC: 3823 Temperature measurement instruments, industrial

(G-1982)
CREATIVE PRTG & GRAPHICS INC
4402 Nw 51st Ct (33073-2909)
PHONE.................................954 242-2562
Gay Woodruff, *President*
EMP: 7 EST: 2010
SALES (est): 108.4K **Privately Held**
SIC: 2752 Commercial printing, offset

(G-1983)
DASS LOGISTICS INC
6601 Lyons Rd Ste H1 (33073-3632)
PHONE.................................954 837-8339
Alan Codlin, *President*
Joseph Sellers, *Treasurer*
EMP: 16 EST: 1997
SQ FT: 6,400
SALES (est): 3MM **Privately Held**
WEB: www.jollyplace.com
SIC: 3728 Aircraft parts & equipment
PA: Dass & Associates, L.L.C.
2309 Roosevelt Dr Ste A
Arlington TX 76016

(G-1984)
ELITE ALUMINUM CORPORATION
Also Called: Elite Panel Products
4650 Lyons Tech Pkwy (33073-4360)
PHONE.................................954 949-3200
Michael Anoti, *Ch of Bd*
Peter Zadok, *President*
Will Boehmer, *Prdtn Mgr*
Richard Stedding, *Human Resources*
◆ EMP: 80 EST: 1982
SQ FT: 76,000
SALES (est): 26.5MM **Privately Held**
WEB: www.elitealuminum.com
SIC: 3089 Panels, building: plastic; windows, plastic

(G-1985)
EUROPA MANUFACTURING INC
4900 Lyons Tech Pkwy # 7 (33073-4357)
PHONE.................................954 426-2965
Richard Spagna, *President*
Anthony Garofalo, *Engineer*
EMP: 11 EST: 2017
SALES (est): 2.9MM **Privately Held**
WEB: www.europamanufacturing.com
SIC: 3444 Sheet metalwork
PA: Sentech Eas Corporation
4900 Lyons Tech Pkwy # 7
Coconut Creek FL 33073

(G-1986)
FIRE TECHNOLOGIES CORP
2302 Lucaya Ln Apt D1 (33066-1117)
PHONE.................................305 592-1914
Juan Carlos Guilbe, *CEO*
Robledo Aybar, *General Mgr*
Carmen D Rodriguez, *Vice Pres*
Lina Garrido, *Controller*
EMP: 6 EST: 2006
SALES (est): 5.9MM **Privately Held**
SIC: 3499 Fire- or burglary-resistive products
PA: Fire Technologies S.R.L.
Calle Mauricio Baez #262
Santo Domingo

(G-1987)
FORTS SERVICES LLC
4650 Lyons Tech Pkwy (33073-4360)
PHONE.................................786 942-4389
Jesse Lapin-Bertone, *Director*
Eliott Rimon, *Officer*
Daniel Rimon,
Sarita Zadok, *Administration*
EMP: 10 EST: 2018
SALES (est): 1.6MM **Privately Held**
WEB: www.fortsservices.com
SIC: 3448 Buildings, portable: prefabricated metal

(G-1988)
GREENWISE BANKCARD
4400 W Sample Rd (33073-3470)
PHONE.................................954 673-0406
Charles Cardona, *Principal*

EMP: 8 EST: 2010
SALES (est): 965.1K **Privately Held**
WEB: www.greenwisebankcard.com
SIC: 3578 Banking machines

(G-1989)
INFINITY MANUFACTURING LLC
4811 Lyons Tech Pkwy (33073-4346)
PHONE.................................954 531-6918
Tyler Howard,
Jim Howard,
EMP: 7 EST: 2015
SALES (est): 494K **Privately Held**
SIC: 2842 Sanitation preparations, disinfectants & deodorants

(G-1990)
INGEANT FLORIDA LLC
5163 Woodfield Way (33073-2233)
PHONE.................................954 868-2879
Luis Parra, *General Mgr*
EMP: 7 EST: 2011
SALES (est): 167.7K **Privately Held**
SIC: 3661 Communication headgear, telephone

(G-1991)
INNOMED TECHNOLOGIES INC (DH)
6601 Lyons Rd Ste B1 (33073-3605)
PHONE.................................800 200-9842
Ron F Richard, *CEO*
Markus Asch, *Accounting Mgr*
▲ EMP: 6 EST: 2001
SALES (est): 4.7MM
SALES (corp-wide): 118.5MM **Privately Held**
WEB: www.sun-med.com
SIC: 3841 Surgical & medical instruments
HQ: Salter Labs, Llc
2710 Northridge Dr Nw A
Grand Rapids MI 49544
847 739-3224

(G-1992)
INNOVATIVE FASTENERS LLC
6601 Lyons Rd Ste I5 (33073-3631)
PHONE.................................561 542-2152
Cid Roberto, *Branch Mgr*
EMP: 15
SALES (corp-wide): 175.6K **Privately Held**
WEB: www.innovativefasteners.com
SIC: 3965 Fasteners
PA: Innovative Fasteners, L.L.C
3495 N Dixie Hwy
Boca Raton FL 33431
561 235-5746

(G-1993)
INTERNATIONAL PRINTING & COPYI
5379 Lyons Rd (33073-2810)
PHONE.................................954 295-5239
Carrie A Sacca, *Principal*
EMP: 7 EST: 2007
SALES (est): 256.5K **Privately Held**
SIC: 2752 Commercial printing, offset

(G-1994)
INTERNTNAL DRECTIONAL DRLG INC ✪
Also Called: Idd
6601 Lyons Rd Ste A5 (33073-3637)
PHONE.................................954 890-1331
Danny Fournel, *CEO*
EMP: 11 EST: 2021
SALES (est): 1.2MM **Privately Held**
SIC: 1381 1623 1731 Directional drilling oil & gas wells; water, sewer & utility lines; gas main construction; underground utilities contractor; fiber optic cable installation

(G-1995)
JW MARKETING AND CONSULTING
Also Called: Battery On The Go
6574 N State Road 7 # 27 (33073-3625)
PHONE.................................866 323-0001
Jamie Sasso, *President*
EMP: 8 EST: 2009
SALES (est): 193.4K **Privately Held**
WEB: www.batteryonthego.com
SIC: 3692 Primary batteries, dry & wet

(G-1996)
KO ORTHOTICS INC
5130 Heron Ct (33073-2409)
PHONE..................................954 570-8096
Kristin Orta, *Principal*
EMP: 7 EST: 2016
SALES (est): 156.1K **Privately Held**
SIC: 3842 Orthopedic appliances

(G-1997)
MAMA ASIAN NOODLE BAR
4437 Lyons Rd (33073-4387)
PHONE..................................954 973-1670
Robert Kaufman, *Principal*
EMP: 11 EST: 2010
SALES (est): 739.1K **Privately Held**
WEB: www.promenadeatcoconutcreek.com
SIC: 2098 Noodles (e.g. egg, plain & water), dry

(G-1998)
MICHIGAN GROUP INC
5481 Wiles Rd (33073-4259)
PHONE..................................954 328-6341
Ariel Giglio, *President*
EMP: 6 EST: 2016
SALES (est): 321.5K **Privately Held**
WEB: www.michigangroup.us
SIC: 3531 Construction machinery

(G-1999)
MOBILE SIGN SERVICE INC
4381 Nw 4th St (33066-1721)
PHONE..................................954 579-8628
Timothy Bucaro, *Director*
EMP: 6 EST: 2001
SALES (est): 405.4K **Privately Held**
SIC: 3993 Signs & advertising specialties

(G-2000)
PARODI GENERAL GROUP CORP
5431 Nw 50th Ct (33073-3301)
PHONE..................................954 306-1098
Jose Parodi, *Principal*
EMP: 7 EST: 2007
SALES (est): 115.9K **Privately Held**
SIC: 3548 Electric welding equipment

(G-2001)
PERMASAFE PRTCTIVE CATINGS LLC
6855 Lyons Tech Cir Ste 1 (33073-4374)
PHONE..................................866 372-9622
Jay Lighter, *Mng Member*
EMP: 25 EST: 2018
SALES (est): 1.2MM **Privately Held**
SIC: 2842 2879 Disinfectants, household or industrial plant; pesticides, agricultural or household

(G-2002)
POLARIS TRADING CORP
Also Called: Wholesale Foreign Products Brk
2205 Nw 45th Ave (33066-2008)
PHONE..................................954 956-6999
Mamdouh Skeik, *CEO*
Faisel M Skeik, *President*
EMP: 8 EST: 2017
SALES (est): 1.2MM **Privately Held**
SIC: 2096 2052 7389 Potato chips & similar snacks; pretzels; business services

(G-2003)
SENTECH EAS CORPORATION (PA)
4900 Lyons Tech Pkwy # 7 (33073-4357)
PHONE..................................954 426-2965
Richard J Spagna, *President*
Ricky Spagna, *Opers Mgr*
Paul Spagna, *Buyer*
Anthony Garofalo, *Engineer*
Lukas A Geiges, *Director*
▲ EMP: 9 EST: 1990
SALES (est): 6.4MM **Privately Held**
WEB: www.sentecheas.com
SIC: 3812 Detection apparatus: electronic/magnetic field, light/heat

(G-2004)
SERGEANT BRETTS COFFEE LLC
Also Called: Sgt. Bretts Healthy Lifestyles
1991 Nw 38th Ter (33066-3006)
PHONE..................................561 451-0048
EMP: 5 EST: 2006
SALES: 900K **Privately Held**
SIC: 2095 4971 2086 3589 Mfg Roasted Coffee Irrigation Systems Mfg Soft Drinks Mfg Svc Industry Mach Water Supply Service

(G-2005)
SIMPSON
7137 Pinecreek Ln (33073-2705)
PHONE..................................954 804-0829
Paul A Simpson, *Principal*
EMP: 10 EST: 2012
SALES (est): 321.1K **Privately Held**
WEB: www.simpsondoor.com
SIC: 2431 Millwork

(G-2006)
SMARTBEAR SOFTWARE
4611 Johnson Rd Unit 4 (33073-4361)
PHONE..................................954 312-0188
Douglas McNary, *Principal*
EMP: 10 EST: 2013
SALES (est): 519.5K **Privately Held**
WEB: www.smartbear.com
SIC: 7372 Prepackaged software

(G-2007)
STEEL COMPONENTS INC
4701 Johnson Rd Ste 1 (33073-4340)
PHONE..................................954 427-6820
Sammy Shemtov, *President*
Howard Feldsher, *Vice Pres*
Margaret Wong, *Admin Sec*
◆ EMP: 18 EST: 1997
SALES (est): 2.2MM **Privately Held**
WEB: www.steelcomponentsinc.net
SIC: 3441 Fabricated structural metal

(G-2008)
TRUMETER COMPANY INC (DH)
6601 Lyons Rd Ste H7 (33073-3632)
PHONE..................................954 725-6699
Fred Hickey, *President*
Ron Smith, *Managing Dir*
Ron Kendzior, *Vice Pres*
Sean McNaughton, *VP Opers*
Regina Hickey, *Human Res Mgr*
▲ EMP: 3 EST: 1994
SALES (est): 8.5MM
SALES (corp-wide): 11.6MM **Privately Held**
WEB: www.trumeter.com
SIC: 3812 3824 3545 Distance measuring equipment; mechanical & electromechanical counters & devices; precision measuring tools
HQ: Trumeter Technologies Limited
Floor 4 Pilot Mill
Bury LANCS BL9 9
161 674-0960

(G-2009)
VAL DOR APPAREL LLC (PA)
Also Called: Valdor Apparel
6820 Lyons Tech Cir # 220 (33073-4323)
PHONE..................................954 363-7340
Robert Rothbaum, *Mng Member*
Marcy Rosen, *Director*
Martin Granoff,
Marc Odrobina,
◆ EMP: 8 EST: 2006
SQ FT: 2,200
SALES (est): 58.9MM **Privately Held**
WEB: www.valdorapparel.com
SIC: 2322 2329 2331 2339 Men's & boys' underwear & nightwear; men's & boys' sportswear & athletic clothing; T-shirts & tops, women's: made from purchased materials; women's & misses' outerwear; women's & children's undergarments

(G-2010)
VICTORY COATINGS INC
4742 Lago Vista Dr (33073-4930)
PHONE..................................954 708-4388
Kristina A Krslovic, *Principal*
EMP: 7 EST: 2016

SALES (est): 108.8K **Privately Held**
SIC: 3479 Metal coating & allied service

(G-2011)
WELL MADE BUS SOLUTIONS LLC
5671 Nw 40th Ter (33073-4057)
PHONE..................................754 227-7268
EMP: 7
SQ FT: 3,800
SALES (est): 675K **Privately Held**
SIC: 3955 5112 Mfg Cartridges & Whol Office Supplies

(G-2012)
WEMERGE INC
3620 W Hillsboro Blvd (33073-2104)
PHONE..................................561 305-2070
Dwayne M Adams, *Principal*
Wemerge Magazine, *Creative Dir*
EMP: 8 EST: 2009
SALES (est): 47.2K **Privately Held**
WEB: www.wemerge.com
SIC: 2741 Miscellaneous publishing

(G-2013)
XTREME PALLETS INC
5440 Nw 55th Blvd Apt 108 (33073-3789)
PHONE..................................954 302-8915
Silver J Mendez, *Principal*
EMP: 7 EST: 2008
SALES (est): 71.5K **Privately Held**
SIC: 2448 Pallets, wood & wood with metal

Coconut Grove
Miami-Dade County

(G-2014)
SPECIAL NUTRIENTS LLC
2766 Sw 37th Ave (33133-2749)
PHONE..................................305 857-9830
Fernando Tamames III, *CEO*
Jesus Martinez, *Manager*
EMP: 18 EST: 2018
SQ FT: 3,000
SALES (est): 1.9MM **Privately Held**
WEB: www.specialnutrients.com
SIC: 2048 Feed supplements

Cooper City
Broward County

(G-2015)
ABC COMPONENTS INC
8963 Stirling Rd Ste 5 (33328-5113)
PHONE..................................954 249-6286
Mine Gulec, *President*
Ender Ozelcaglayan, *Sales Mgr*
EMP: 14 EST: 2009
SALES (est): 2.3MM **Privately Held**
WEB: www.abccomponents.com
SIC: 3812 3679 Aircraft/aerospace flight instruments & guidance systems; recording & playback apparatus, including phonograph

(G-2016)
ALWAYS FUN INC
Also Called: America Mia
5660 Sw 99th Ln (33328-5720)
PHONE..................................954 258-4377
Ernesto Ochoa, *President*
EMP: 7 EST: 2009
SALES (est): 293.8K **Privately Held**
SIC: 2721 Periodicals

(G-2017)
ATMOSPHERIC WTR SOLUTIONS INC
12260 Sw 53rd St Ste 603 (33330-3354)
PHONE..................................954 306-6763
Doug Marcille, *CEO*
Howard Ullman, *President*
Reid Goldstein, *Exec VP*
◆ EMP: 16 EST: 2011
SQ FT: 3,000
SALES (est): 1MM **Privately Held**
WEB: www.atmosphericwatersolutions.com
SIC: 3589 Water purification equipment, household type

(G-2018)
AUTOMOTIVE ADVERTISING ASSOC
13024 Spring Lake Dr (33330-2669)
PHONE..................................954 389-6500
Fred Stangle, *Principal*
EMP: 8 EST: 2016
SALES (est): 278.5K **Privately Held**
WEB: www.automotiveadvertisingassociates.com
SIC: 3993 Signs & advertising specialties

(G-2019)
BETROCK INFO SYSTEMS INC
Also Called: Plantfinder
12330 Sw 53rd St Ste 712 (33330-3355)
P.O. Box 848759, Hollywood (33084-0759)
PHONE..................................954 981-2821
Irving Betrock, *President*
Bette Betrock, *Vice Pres*
▲ EMP: 33 EST: 1972
SQ FT: 4,000
SALES (est): 5MM **Privately Held**
WEB: www.betrock.com
SIC: 2721 7379 Magazines: publishing only, not printed on site; trade journals: publishing & printing; computer related consulting services

(G-2020)
DUKE CUSTOM FABRICATION LLC
5846 S Flamingo Rd (33330-3237)
PHONE..................................954 707-1722
Terrell I Duke II, *Manager*
EMP: 7 EST: 2017
SALES (est): 442.9K **Privately Held**
SIC: 7692 Welding repair

(G-2021)
HAPPY MIX LLC
8747 Stirling Rd (33328-5932)
PHONE..................................954 880-0160
Carlos Sabater,
Nannette Sabater,
EMP: 8 EST: 2008
SALES (est): 258K **Privately Held**
SIC: 2024 Ice cream & ice milk

(G-2022)
SKYMO LLC
12260 Sw 53rd St Ste 609 (33330-3320)
PHONE..................................305 676-6739
Raul Santoya, *President*
Reyniel Santoya, *CFO*
EMP: 5 EST: 2016
SALES (est): 402.4K **Privately Held**
WEB: www.skymo.net
SIC: 2841 2842 5087 2911 Soap & other detergents; detergents, synthetic organic or inorganic alkaline; degreasing solvent; janitors' supplies; solvents; solvents, organic

(G-2023)
SOUTH FLORIDA FABRICATORS LLC
Also Called: All Star Pvc Products
4960 Sw 91st Ter (33328-3524)
PHONE..................................954 802-6782
William Roberson, *Principal*
EMP: 6 EST: 2016
SALES (est): 424.6K **Privately Held**
SIC: 3999 Manufacturing industries

Coral Gables
Miami-Dade County

(G-2024)
ACI WORLDWIDE INC (PA)
2811 Ponce De Leon Blvd (33134-6910)
PHONE..................................305 894-2200
Odilon Almeida, *President*
Alex Kutovoy, *Chief*
Ajmal Syed, *Chief*
Evanthia C Aretakis, *Exec VP*
Kuhl David, *Exec VP*
EMP: 399 EST: 1993
SALES (est): 1.3B **Publicly Held**
WEB: www.aciworldwide.com
SIC: 7372 5045 Business oriented computer software; computer software

(G-2025)
AERSALE 23440 LLC
255 Alhambra Cir Ste 435 (33134-7409)
PHONE................................305 764-3200
Nicholas Finazzo, *CEO*
Michael Henrickson, *Owner*
Robert Nichols, *COO*
EMP: 1 **EST:** 2011
SALES (est): 5.1MM
SALES (corp-wide): 208.9MM **Publicly Held**
SIC: 3724 Aircraft engines & engine parts
HQ: Aersale, Inc.
    255 Alhambra Cir Ste 435
    Coral Gables FL 33134

(G-2026)
AERSALE 26346 LLC
255 Alhambra Cir Ste 435 (33134-7409)
PHONE................................305 764-3200
Nicolas Finazzo, *Mng Member*
Michael Henrickson, *Manager*
Doug Meyer,
Robert Nichols,
EMP: 66 **EST:** 1997
SALES (est): 14.7MM
SALES (corp-wide): 208.9MM **Publicly Held**
SIC: 3728 Bodies, aircraft
HQ: Aersale, Inc.
    255 Alhambra Cir Ste 435
    Coral Gables FL 33134

(G-2027)
ALVEAN AMERICAS INC
2525 Ponce De Leon Blvd (33134-6037)
PHONE................................305 606-0770
Julie Decaudin, *Principal*
Megan Conkey, *Associate*
EMP: 8 **EST:** 2015
SALES (est): 197.3K **Privately Held**
WEB: www.alvean.com
SIC: 2061 3556 Raw cane sugar; sugar plant machinery

(G-2028)
AMERICAN ROOFING SERVICES LLC
95 Merrick Way Ste 514 (33134-5310)
PHONE................................305 250-7115
Mauro Iurman, *Mng Member*
Marga Degwitz,
Henry Iurman,
◆ **EMP:** 8 **EST:** 2006
SALES (est): 2.9MM **Privately Held**
WEB: www.naroofing.com
SIC: 2952 Roofing materials

(G-2029)
APAKUS INC
75 Valencia Ave Ste 701 (33134-6132)
PHONE................................305 403-2603
Vladimir Zhamgotsev, *President*
EMP: 9 **EST:** 2004
SALES (est): 401.2K **Privately Held**
SIC: 2671 2011 Packaging paper & plastics film, coated & laminated; meat packing plants

(G-2030)
APPGATE INC (HQ)
2 Alhambra Plz Ste Ph-1b (33134-5202)
PHONE................................866 524-4782
Barry Field, *CEO*
EMP: 8 **EST:** 2007
SQ FT: 6,000
SALES (est): 45.3MM **Publicly Held**
SIC: 7372 Prepackaged software
PA: Sis Holdings Lp
    2333 Ponce De Leon Blvd
    Coral Gables FL 33134
    855 699-8372

(G-2031)
AUTOMUNDO PRODUCTIONS INC
Also Called: Automundo Magazine
2520 Coral Way Ste 2 (33145-3431)
PHONE................................305 541-4198
Jorge Koechlin, *President*
EMP: 6 **EST:** 1983
SALES (est): 546.6K **Privately Held**
SIC: 2721 Magazines: publishing & printing

(G-2032)
BAKERLY LLC (HQ)
2600 S Douglas Rd Ste 410 (33134-6134)
PHONE................................786 539-5888
Julien Caron, *CEO*
Fabian Milon, *COO*
Tugdual Denis, *Vice Pres*
Amber Bachman, *Plant Mgr*
Tess Fagan, *Project Mgr*
EMP: 9 **EST:** 2015
SQ FT: 100
SALES (est): 7.7MM
SALES (corp-wide): 1.2MM **Privately Held**
WEB: www.bakerly.com
SIC: 2051 Bakery: wholesale or wholesale/retail combined
PA: Norac
    2 A 3
    Rennes 35000
    299 652-932

(G-2033)
BEES BROTHERS LLC
2990 Ponce De Leon Blvd # 202 (33134-6803)
P.O. Box 141071 (33114-1071)
PHONE................................305 529-5789
JP Baggini, *General Mgr*
Juan P Baggini, *Mng Member*
Rodrigo Alberton,
Joaquin Mantovani,
▲ **EMP:** 7 **EST:** 2011
SQ FT: 2,000
SALES (est): 618.7K **Privately Held**
WEB: www.beesbrothersllc.com
SIC: 2099 Honey, strained & bottled

(G-2034)
BLUE LEAF HOSPITALITY INC
2332 Galiano St 2 (33134-5402)
PHONE................................305 668-3000
Stan C Shockley, *President*
Anamaria Jimenez, *Project Mgr*
Yvette Perea, *Office Mgr*
Rachel Penabella, *Sr Project Mgr*
Solanch Mejia, *Manager*
▲ **EMP:** 10 **EST:** 2002
SALES (est): 1.6MM **Privately Held**
WEB: www.blueleafmiami.com
SIC: 2599 Hotel furniture

(G-2035)
BLUE STONE USA LLC
1172 S Dixie Hwy 301 (33146-2918)
PHONE................................305 494-1141
Alex Daian, *Principal*
EMP: 7 **EST:** 2009
SALES (est): 63.6K **Privately Held**
WEB: www.bluestoneusa.com
SIC: 2099 Food preparations

(G-2036)
BSK USA LLC
201 Alhambra Cir Ste 603 (33134-5199)
PHONE................................786 328-5395
Jose A Caraballo, *Administration*
EMP: 7 **EST:** 2016
SALES (est): 265.7K **Privately Held**
SIC: 3432 Plumbing fixture fittings & trim

(G-2037)
BUTTERCREAM CPCAKES COF SP INC
1411 Sunset Dr (33143-5824)
PHONE................................305 669-8181
Kristine E Graulich, *President*
Jose F Cuellar, *Vice Pres*
EMP: 10 **EST:** 2007
SQ FT: 400
SALES (est): 747.7K **Privately Held**
WEB: www.buttercreamcupcakes.com
SIC: 2051 5812 Bakery: wholesale or wholesale/retail combined; coffee shop

(G-2038)
CATALYST PHARMACEUTICALS INC (PA)
355 Alhambra Cir Ste 801 (33134-5075)
PHONE................................305 420-3200
Patrick J McEnany, *Ch of Bd*
Steven R Miller, *COO*
Jeff D Carmen, *Senior VP*
Jeff Del Carmen, *Senior VP*
Brian Elsbernd, *Senior VP*
EMP: 20 **EST:** 2002
SQ FT: 5,200
SALES (est): 140.8MM **Publicly Held**
WEB: www.catalystpharma.com
SIC: 2834 Pharmaceutical preparations

(G-2039)
CHUXCO INC
Also Called: Ameritek U.S.A.
1 Alhambra Plz Ste Ph (33134-5227)
PHONE................................305 470-9595
Charles Galan, *President*
EMP: 10 **EST:** 1976
SQ FT: 5,000
SALES (est): 1.5MM **Privately Held**
WEB: www.chuxco.com
SIC: 3492 7699 5047 3841 Valves, hydraulic, aircraft; hydraulic equipment repair; patient monitoring equipment; medical equipment & supplies; medical instruments & equipment, blood & bone work; confinement surveillance systems maintenance & monitoring

(G-2040)
CLEAN ENERGY ESB INC
600 Biltmore Way Apt 508 (33134-7530)
PHONE................................202 905-6726
Andrea P Irarrazaval, *CEO*
EMP: 24 **EST:** 2018
SQ FT: 1,100
SALES (est): 500MM **Privately Held**
SIC: 2911 5261 Diesel fuels; fertilizer

(G-2041)
COMMUNICATIONS SURVEILLANCE INC
4000 Ponce De Leon Blvd (33146-1431)
P.O. Box 771373, Miami (33177-0023)
PHONE................................305 377-1211
Jose M Noy, *President*
Jose Noy, *General Mgr*
Nathaly C Noy, *Senior VP*
Miguel A Noy, *Vice Pres*
EMP: 10 **EST:** 1992
SQ FT: 2,000
SALES (est): 1.1MM **Privately Held**
SIC: 3699 Security control equipment & systems

(G-2042)
CONDE NAST AMERICAS (DH)
Also Called: Vogue Latinoamerica
800 S Douglas Rd Ste 835 (33134-3188)
P.O. Box 141799 (33114-1799)
PHONE................................305 371-9393
Farid Aouragh, *President*
Rafael Schuck, *Finance*
Christine Iliffe, *Manager*
▲ **EMP:** 3 **EST:** 1998
SALES (est): 3.3MM
SALES (corp-wide): 2.8B **Privately Held**
SIC: 2721 Magazines: publishing & printing

(G-2043)
CORAL GABLES LIVING
400 University Dr Fl 2 (33134-7114)
P.O. Box 140249, Miami (33114-0249)
PHONE................................786 552-6464
Joellen Phillips, *Principal*
EMP: 9 **EST:** 2005
SALES (est): 217.1K **Privately Held**
WEB: www.palacecoralgables.com
SIC: 2721 Periodicals: publishing only

(G-2044)
CUSTOM BEACH HUTS LLC
800 S Douglas Rd Ste 300 (33134-3160)
PHONE................................305 439-3991
Thomas Bache-Wiig, *Principal*
EMP: 10 **EST:** 2014
SALES (est): 332.4K **Privately Held**
WEB: www.custombeach.com
SIC: 2511 Wood household furniture

(G-2045)
DADE ENGINEERING CORP
Also Called: Daeco
6855 Edgewater Dr Apt 1e (33133-7038)
PHONE................................305 885-2766
Joanne Goodstein, *President*
◆ **EMP:** 11 **EST:** 1953
SALES (est): 600.3K **Privately Held**
WEB: www.dadecoolers.com
SIC: 3448 Panels for prefabricated metal buildings

(G-2046)
DANIEL BUSTAMANTE
1210 Placetas Ave (33146-3243)
PHONE................................305 779-7777
Daniel Bustamante, *Principal*
EMP: 7 **EST:** 2017
SALES (est): 168.4K **Privately Held**
SIC: 3082 Unsupported plastics profile shapes

(G-2047)
DEL MONTE FRESH PRODUCE NA INC (DH)
241 Sevilla Ave (33134-6622)
P.O. Box 149222, Miami (33114-9222)
PHONE................................305 520-8400
Mohammad Abu-Ghazaleh, *CEO*
Hani El Naffy, *President*
Kevin Hobbs, *General Mgr*
Anthony Luongo, *General Mgr*
James Senich, *Regional Mgr*
◆ **EMP:** 50 **EST:** 1952
SQ FT: 48,000
SALES (est): 658.8MM **Privately Held**
WEB: www.freshdelmonte.com
SIC: 2033 5148 Fruits & fruit products in cans, jars, etc.; fruits, fresh
HQ: Del Monte Fresh Produce Company
    241 Sevilla Ave Ste 200
    Coral Gables FL 33134
    305 520-8400

(G-2048)
DIAGEO NORTH AMERICA INC
396 Alhambra Cir (33134-5045)
PHONE................................305 476-7761
Chris Sherrill, *Sales Staff*
EMP: 37
SALES (corp-wide): 18B **Privately Held**
SIC: 2085 Distilled & blended liquors
HQ: Diageo North America Inc.
    3 World Trade Ctr
    New York NY 10007
    212 202-1800

(G-2049)
DISTRIVALTO USA INC
2020 Ponce De Leon Blvd # 1004 (33134-4476)
PHONE................................305 715-0366
Jose Valera, *President*
Jose Luis Valera, *President*
Nalvis Torres De Valera, *Vice Pres*
Vanessa V Nolte, *Treasurer*
Vanessa Valera, *Sales Executive*
◆ **EMP:** 20 **EST:** 1998
SALES (est): 2.4MM **Privately Held**
WEB: www.holsteinhousewares.com
SIC: 3634 5023 Personal electrical appliances; kitchenware

(G-2050)
ECOSAN LLC
Also Called: American Lab Test & Engrg
2520 Coral Way Ste 2 (33145-3431)
PHONE................................954 446-5929
Joseph Prieto, *Principal*
▲ **EMP:** 8 **EST:** 2011
SALES (est): 392.7K **Privately Held**
SIC: 2421 Outdoor wood structural products

(G-2051)
EDCA BAKERY CORPORATION
Also Called: Pinocho Bakery
5236 W Flagler St (33134-1168)
PHONE................................305 448-7843
Carlos Cruz, *President*
Zeus Cruz, *Owner*
EMP: 10 **EST:** 1982
SQ FT: 2,000
SALES (est): 512.8K **Privately Held**
SIC: 2051 5461 Bakery: wholesale or wholesale/retail combined; bakeries

(G-2052)
EDUCATIONAL NETWORKS INC
901 Ponce De Leon Blvd (33134-3073)
PHONE................................866 526-0200
Caitlin Hazelwood, *Project Mgr*
Franziska Hoelzke, *Project Mgr*
Liz Milivio, *Office Mgr*
Kevin Cullinan, *Agent*
Lev Goltseker, *CTO*
EMP: 7

SALES (corp-wide): 2MM **Privately Held**
WEB: www.educationalnetworks.net
SIC: 7372 Educational computer software
PA: Educational Networks, Inc.
104 W 40th St Rm 1810
New York NY 10018
866 526-0200

(G-2053)
EL AMERICAN LLC
420 S Dixie Hwy (33146-2222)
PHONE.....................................305 902-8051
Jorge Granier, *President*
EMP: 40
SALES (est): 1.5MM **Privately Held**
SIC: 2741

(G-2054)
ENKI GROUP INC
11555 Sw 82nd Avenue Rd (33156-4308)
PHONE.....................................305 773-3502
Antonio Ynastrilla, *President*
EMP: 7 EST: 2004
SALES (est): 435.8K **Privately Held**
SIC: 3812 Defense systems & equipment

(G-2055)
EUROINSOLES INCORPORATED
75 Valencia Ave Ste 201 (33134-6162)
PHONE.....................................786 206-6117
Joaquin Santos, *Principal*
EMP: 8 EST: 2010
SALES (est): 531.8K **Privately Held**
SIC: 3842 Orthopedic appliances

(G-2056)
FASTSIGNS
146 Madeira Ave (33134-4552)
PHONE.....................................305 747-7115
EMP: 8 EST: 2016
SALES (est): 156.4K **Privately Held**
WEB: www.fastsigns.com
SIC: 3993 Signs & advertising specialties

(G-2057)
FUSSION INTERNATIONAL INC
446 Loretto Ave (33146-2106)
PHONE.....................................305 662-4848
Stella Crismanich, *Principal*
EMP: 5 EST: 2005
SALES (est): 443K **Privately Held**
SIC: 3161 Luggage

(G-2058)
GABLES ENGINEERING INC
247 Greco Ave (33146-1881)
P.O. Box 140880, Miami (33114-0880)
PHONE.....................................305 774-4400
Gary A Galimidi, *President*
Rene Ramos, *General Mgr*
Lauren Colon, *Vice Pres*
Charles Flores, *Mfg Staff*
Cesar Tricoche, *Mfg Staff*
EMP: 277 EST: 1947
SQ FT: 60,000
SALES (est): 96.6MM **Privately Held**
WEB: www.gableseng.com
SIC: 3812 3365 3369 Aircraft/aerospace
flight instruments & guidance systems;
aerospace castings, aluminum; aero-
space castings, nonferrous: except alu-
minum

(G-2059)
GAMMA INSULATORS CORP
(PA)
2121 Ponce De Leon Blvd (33134-5224)
PHONE.....................................585 302-0878
Christopher Seguin, *Vice Pres*
◆ EMP: 5 EST: 2009
SALES (est): 796.9K **Privately Held**
WEB: www.gammainsulators.com
SIC: 3644 Insulators & insulation materials,
electrical

(G-2060)
GENERAL & DUPLICATING
SERVICES
Also Called: Sir Speedy
3150 Ponce De Leon Blvd (33134-6826)
PHONE.....................................305 541-2116
Leonel Ley, *President*
Rene Ley, *Vice Pres*
▼ EMP: 7 EST: 1981

SALES (est): 500K **Privately Held**
WEB: www.sirspeedy.com
SIC: 2752 Commercial printing, litho-
graphic

(G-2061)
GLOBAL LIFE TECHNOLOGIES
CORP
300 Aragon Ave Ste 214 (33134-5047)
PHONE.....................................301 337-2059
John Willimann, *CEO*
Philippe Touret, *Chairman*
David Hines, *Exec VP*
Kevin Walsh, *Exec VP*
Gregg Wilkinson, *Exec VP*
◆ EMP: 6 EST: 2004
SALES (est): 1.3MM **Privately Held**
WEB: www.nozinpro.com
SIC: 2834 Pharmaceutical preparations

(G-2062)
GLOBAL PRINTING SERVICES
INC
Also Called: Sir Speedy
3150 Ponce De Leon Blvd (33134-6826)
PHONE.....................................305 446-7628
Frank Ley, *President*
Raul Ley, *Vice Pres*
EMP: 5 EST: 1988
SQ FT: 2,100
SALES (est): 618.5K **Privately Held**
WEB: www.sirspeedy.com
SIC: 2752 Commercial printing, litho-
graphic

(G-2063)
GLOBAL RECASH LLC
3191 Coral Way (33145-3213)
PHONE.....................................818 297-4437
Alfred Urcuyo, *Mng Member*
Derick Brol, *Mng Member*
EMP: 80 EST: 2017
SQ FT: 5,000
SALES (est): 7MM **Privately Held**
SIC: 7372 Business oriented computer
software

(G-2064)
GOVERLAN LLC
Also Called: EASYVISTA USA
2655 S Le Jeune Rd # 1001 (33134-5803)
PHONE.....................................888 330-4188
Pascal Bergeot, *CEO*
Judy Lee, *COO*
Josh Wolinski, *Sales Staff*
Eugen Hartmann, *Software Engr*
Sergii Lytvynenko, *Software Dev*
EMP: 26 EST: 1998
SALES (est): 5.5MM
SALES (corp-wide): 9.6MM **Privately**
Held
WEB: www.goverlan.com
SIC: 7372 Prepackaged software
PA: Easyvista Inc.
3 Columbus Cir Fl 15
New York NY 10019
888 398-4876

(G-2065)
GRAPHIC CENTER GROUP
CORP
Also Called: Office Graphic Design
2150 Coral Way Fl 1 (33145-2629)
PHONE.....................................305 961-1649
Oliver Moreno, *CEO*
EMP: 8 EST: 2010
SQ FT: 2,000
SALES (est): 672.9K **Privately Held**
WEB: www.graphiccentergroup.com
SIC: 7372 7336 Prepackaged software;
graphic arts & related design

(G-2066)
GRUPO EDITORIAL EXPANSION
2800 Ponce De Leon Blvd # 1160
(33134-6913)
PHONE.....................................305 374-9003
Dalia Sanchez, *Managing Dir*
German Zimbron, *Director*
EMP: 8 EST: 2004
SQ FT: 2,800
SALES (est): 2.5MM **Privately Held**
SIC: 2721 Magazines: publishing & printing

HQ: Hearst Expansion, S. De R.L. De C.V.
Av. Constituyentes No. 956
Ciudad De Mexico CDMX 11950

(G-2067)
HERA CASES LLC
6901 Edgewater Dr Apt 315 (33133-7035)
PHONE.....................................305 322-8960
Ashley Mouriz, *Manager*
EMP: 6 EST: 2018
SALES (est): 744.7K **Privately Held**
WEB: www.heracases.com
SIC: 3523 Farm machinery & equipment

(G-2068)
HERNOL USA INC
201 Alhambra Cir Ste 6 (33134-5107)
PHONE.....................................786 263-3341
Juan Zurita, *President*
Jose Gabriel Moran, *Vice Pres*
◆ EMP: 30 EST: 2015
SQ FT: 200
SALES (est): 2.8MM **Privately Held**
WEB: www.hernolusa.com
SIC: 3069 Hard rubber & molded rubber
products

(G-2069)
IBD INDUSTRIAL LLC
Also Called: Axxionflex
1825 Ponce De Leon Blvd (33134-4418)
PHONE.....................................786 655-7577
Carlos Martinez, *Mng Member*
EMP: 5 EST: 2016
SALES (est): 349.8K **Privately Held**
SIC: 3492 Hose & tube fittings & assem-
blies, hydraulic/pneumatic

(G-2070)
INK PUBLISHING
CORPORATION
806 S Douglas Rd Ste 300 (33134-3157)
PHONE.....................................786 206-9867
Aracelis Baez, *Human Resources*
Luis Muniz, *Branch Mgr*
EMP: 18
SALES (corp-wide): 30.7MM **Privately**
Held
SIC: 2741 Miscellaneous publishing
HQ: Ink Publishing Corporation
800 Suth Dglas Rd Ste 250
Coral Gables FL 33134

(G-2071)
INK PUBLISHING
CORPORATION (DH)
800 Suth Dglas Rd Ste 250 (33134)
PHONE.....................................786 482-2065
Simon Lesley, *CEO*
Kyra Penn, *Executive*
EMP: 15 EST: 2006
SALES (est): 12.9MM
SALES (corp-wide): 30.7MM **Privately**
Held
SIC: 2741 Miscellaneous publishing
HQ: Esubstance Limited
Blackburn House
London NW6 1
207 625-0700

(G-2072)
INNOVATIVE SURFACES INC
3218 Ponce De Leon Blvd (33134-7239)
PHONE.....................................305 446-9059
Julio Blanco, *President*
EMP: 10 EST: 2000
SALES (est): 539.5K **Privately Held**
WEB: www.innosurfaces.com
SIC: 3253 Ceramic wall & floor tile

(G-2073)
INTERMAS NETS USA INC
2655 S Le Jeune Rd # 810 (33134-5832)
PHONE.....................................305 442-1416
Franois Mouchet, *CEO*
Albert Fort Mauri, *Vice Pres*
EMP: 10 EST: 2013
SALES (est): 349K **Privately Held**
WEB: www.intermasgroup.com
SIC: 2258 3089 Net & netting products;
netting, plastic

(G-2074)
ISA GROUP CORP
1204 Placetas Ave (33146-3243)
PHONE.....................................786 201-8360
Veruska Chalbaud, *Principal*
EMP: 7 EST: 2017
SALES (est): 77.8K **Privately Held**
WEB: www.isagroupca.com
SIC: 3552 Textile machinery

(G-2075)
J M ECONO-PRINT INC
303 Camilo Ave (33134-7208)
PHONE.....................................305 591-3620
EMP: 8
SQ FT: 4,000
SALES (est): 900K **Privately Held**
SIC: 2752 Offset Printing

(G-2076)
KEY BISCAYNE SMOOTHIE
COMPANY
249 Catalonia Ave (33134-6704)
PHONE.....................................305 441-7882
Lawrence J Roberts, *Principal*
EMP: 8 EST: 2008
SALES (est): 176.8K **Privately Held**
SIC: 2037 Frozen fruits & vegetables

(G-2077)
KIMBERLYN INVESTMENTS CO
2828 Coral Way Ste 309 (33145-3214)
PHONE.....................................305 448-6328
Antoniazzi Pablo, *CEO*
EMP: 7 EST: 2007
SALES (est): 611K **Privately Held**
SIC: 2911 Petroleum refining

(G-2078)
KOBALT MUSIC PUBG AMER
INC
2100 Ponce De Leon Blvd (33134-5215)
PHONE.....................................305 200-5682
Willard Ahdritz, *Manager*
EMP: 52
SALES (corp-wide): 519.4MM **Privately**
Held
SIC: 2741 Music book & sheet music pub-
lishing
HQ: Kobalt Music Publishing America, Inc.
2 Gansevoort St Fl 6
New York NY 10014
212 247-6204

(G-2079)
KRAKEN KOFFEE LLC
Also Called: Kimera Koffee
2555 Ponce De Leon Blvd (33134-6010)
PHONE.....................................833 546-3725
Luis F Oviedo, *Mng Member*
Teodoro E Armenteros, *Mng Member*
Alejandro Santoni Fernandez, *Mng Member*
Frank A Pimentel, *Mng Member*
EMP: 8 EST: 2014
SALES (est): 420.3K **Privately Held**
WEB: www.kimerakoffee.com
SIC: 2095 Instant coffee

(G-2080)
LA TROPICAL BREWING CO LLC
1825 Ponce De Leon Blvd (33134-4418)
PHONE.....................................786 362-5429
Manuel J Portuondo, *Manager*
EMP: 5 EST: 1998
SQ FT: 1,000
SALES (est): 352.5K **Privately Held**
SIC: 2085 Distilled & blended liquors

(G-2081)
LAWEX CORPORATION (PA)
Also Called: Trialworks
1550 Madruga Ave Ste 508 (33146-3048)
PHONE.....................................305 259-9755
Robb Steinberg, *President*
Vanessa Steinberg, *Vice Pres*
Luana Patriota, *Manager*
Jeanny Collazo, *Software Dev*
EMP: 10 EST: 1996
SQ FT: 6,000
SALES (est): 2.3MM **Privately Held**
WEB: support.trialworks.com
SIC: 7372 8111 Business oriented com-
puter software; legal services

(G-2082)
LEFAB COMMERCIAL LLC
Also Called: Morelia Paletas Gourmet
76 Miracle Mile (33134-5404)
PHONE..................................305 456-1306
Gilbert Arismendi, *Mng Member*
Fernando Falasca,
Leonardo Romeri-Arrivillaga,
Leonardo Romero,
EMP: 10 EST: 2016
SALES (est): 852.9K Privately Held
WEB: www.paletasmorelia.com
SIC: 2024 5143 5451 Ice cream & frozen
desserts; ice cream & ices; ice cream
(packaged)

(G-2083)
MASSO ESTATE WINERY LLC
(PA)
3150 Sw 38th Ave Ste 1303 (33146-1529)
PHONE..................................305 707-7749
Oscar Piloto,
EMP: 8 EST: 2011
SQ FT: 1,000
SALES (est): 1MM Privately Held
WEB: www.massowinery.com
SIC: 2084 Wines

(G-2084)
MENDEZ FUEL
3201 Coral Way (33145-2233)
PHONE..................................305 227-0470
Michael Mendez, *Principal*
EMP: 9 EST: 2013
SALES (est): 1MM Privately Held
WEB: www.mendez-fuel.com
SIC: 2869 Fuels

(G-2085)
MERKARI GROUP INC
Also Called: Direcly
2222 Ponce De Leon Blvd (33134-5039)
PHONE..................................305 748-3260
Francisco A Garcia, *CEO*
EMP: 12 EST: 2019
SALES (est): 1.8MM Privately Held
WEB: www.direcly.com
SIC: 7372 Application computer software

(G-2086)
MIACUCINA LLC
105 Miracle Mile (33134-5405)
PHONE..................................305 444-7383
Ariel Wainer, *Project Mgr*
Maika Dongellini, *Opers Staff*
Jezabel Cruz, *Sales Staff*
Ivonne Pena, *Sales Staff*
Ivonne Pino, *Sales Staff*
◆ EMP: 16 EST: 2001
SALES (est): 1MM Privately Held
WEB: www.miacucina.com
SIC: 2434 Wood kitchen cabinets

(G-2087)
MINEA USA LLC
1550 S Dixie Hwy Ste 216 (33146-3034)
PHONE..................................800 971-3216
Sylvain Mazloum, *President*
Add Loris Mazloum, *Vice Pres*
EMP: 10 EST: 2008
SALES (est): 9MM Privately Held
WEB: www.mineagroup.com
SIC: 3639 Major kitchen appliances, ex-
cept refrigerators & stoves

(G-2088)
MONARQ AMERICAS LLC
Also Called: Monarq Group
55 Merrick Way Ste 202 (33134-5125)
PHONE..................................305 632-7448
Robert De Monchy, *Mng Member*
EMP: 17 EST: 2011
SALES (est): 1MM Privately Held
WEB: www.monarqgroup.com
SIC: 2084 Wines, brandy & brandy spirits

(G-2089)
MONDELEZ GLOBAL LLC
Also Called: Kraft Foods
396 Alhambra Cir Ste 1000 (33134-5095)
PHONE..................................305 774-6273
Dina Kouvaras, *Business Mgr*
Olga Martinez, *Vice Pres*
Scott McKallagat, *Foreman/Supr*
Sara Evans, *Sales Staff*

Caitlin Clark, *Manager*
EMP: 72 Publicly Held
WEB: www.mondelezinternational.com
SIC: 2022 Processed cheese
HQ: Mondelez Global Llc
905 W Fulton Market # 200
Chicago IL 60607
847 943-4000

(G-2090)
NATIONAL GLASS PDTS &
DISTRS
814 Ponce De Leon Blvd (33134-3049)
PHONE..................................303 762-9768
Bersan Yorgancilar, *Principal*
EMP: 8 EST: 2019
SALES (est): 175.6K Privately Held
SIC: 3211 Laminated glass

(G-2091)
NEXOGY INC
2121 Ponce De Leon Blvd # 200
(33134-5224)
PHONE..................................305 358-8952
Felipe Lahrssen, *COO*
Brian Asher, *Sales Staff*
Jack Vargas, *Manager*
EMP: 65 EST: 2005
SALES (est): 9.5MM
SALES (corp-wide): 12.4MM Publicly
Held
WEB: www.nexogy.com
SIC: 7372 8741 Business oriented com-
puter software; management services
HQ: T3 Communications, Inc.
1610 Royal Palm Ave
Fort Myers FL 33901
239 333-0000

(G-2092)
OPEN INTERNATIONAL LLC
13019 Mar St (33156-6427)
PHONE..................................305 265-0310
William Corredor, *Ch of Bd*
Hernando Parrott, *President*
EMP: 4 EST: 2015
SALES (est): 3.5MM Privately Held
WEB: www.openintl.com
SIC: 7372 Application computer software

(G-2093)
OUHLALA GOURMET CORP
2655 S Le Jeune Rd # 1011 (33134-5803)
PHONE..................................305 774-7332
Jerome Lesur, *CEO*
Fabian Milon, *Vice Pres*
▲ EMP: 16 EST: 2008
SQ FT: 20,000
SALES (est): 768.4K Privately Held
SIC: 2033 Mfg Canned Fruits/Vegetables

(G-2094)
OUTDOOR MEDIA INC
Also Called: Lakeland Outdoor Advertising
3195 Ponce De Leon Blvd # 300
(33134-6801)
P.O. Box 141609 (33114-1609)
PHONE..................................305 529-1400
EMP: 5
SALES (est): 750K Privately Held
SIC: 2752 Advertising Posters Litho-
graphed

(G-2095)
OVERTURE LIFE INC
55 Merrick Way Ste 401 (33134-5126)
PHONE..................................323 420-6343
EMP: 6 EST: 2020
SALES (est): 681.5K Privately Held
WEB: www.overture.life
SIC: 3559 Special industry machinery

(G-2096)
PENTACLES ENERGY GP LLC
1600 Ponce De Leon Blvd (33134-3988)
P.O. Box 140668 (33114-0668)
PHONE..................................786 552-9931
Miguel Otaola, *Opers Staff*
Gustavo Mancera, *Mng Member*
Alvaro Campins, *Mng Member*
Luis Eduardo Guiterrez, *Manager*
EMP: 7 EST: 2010
SALES (est): 1.2MM Privately Held
WEB: www.pentaclesenergy.com
SIC: 2869 Fuels

(G-2097)
PORT HMLTON RFINERY TRNSP
LLLP ✪
2555 Ponce De Leon Blvd (33134-6010)
PHONE..................................305 299-0251
Thomas Eagan,
Charles Chambers,
David Roberts,
EMP: 650 EST: 2022
SALES (est): 69.5MM Privately Held
SIC: 2911 Gasoline

(G-2098)
PREMIER DIE CASTING
COMPANY
47 S Prospect Dr (33133-7003)
PHONE..................................732 634-3000
Leonard Cordaro, *President*
▲ EMP: 60 EST: 1945
SALES (est): 6.3MM Privately Held
WEB: www.diecasting.com
SIC: 3599 Machine shop, jobbing & repair

(G-2099)
PRETEC DIRECTIONAL DRLG
LLC
800 S Douglas Rd Ste 1200 (33134-3165)
PHONE..................................786 220-7667
Robert Apple,
Robert Poteete,
Steven Rooney,
EMP: 9 EST: 2016
SALES (est): 15MM
SALES (corp-wide): 7.9B Publicly Held
WEB: www.pretecdd.com
SIC: 1381 Directional drilling oil & gas
wells
PA: Mastec, Inc.
800 S Douglas Rd Ste 1200
Coral Gables FL 33134
305 599-1800

(G-2100)
PROSTHETIC LABORATORIES
1270 Bird Rd (33146-1110)
PHONE..................................305 250-9900
Pedro Llanes, *President*
EMP: 8 EST: 1940
SALES (est): 1MM Privately Held
SIC: 3842 5999 Prosthetic appliances; or-
thopedic appliances; orthopedic & pros-
thesis applications

(G-2101)
QCI BRITANNIC INC (PA)
1600 Ponce De Leon Blvd # 907
(33134-3991)
P.O. Box 450871, Miami (33245-0871)
PHONE..................................305 860-0102
Ernesto Freund, *President*
Enrique Freund, *Principal*
William Freund, *Principal*
Ricardo Freund, *Vice Pres*
Eduardo Portillo, *CFO*
◆ EMP: 5 EST: 2000
SALES (est): 2.2MM Privately Held
WEB: www.quem.com
SIC: 1481 Nonmetallic mineral services

(G-2102)
RADIATION SHIELD TECH INC
Also Called: R.S.T.
6 Aragon Ave (33134-5300)
P.O. Box 144254 (33114-4254)
PHONE..................................866 733-6766
Ronald Demeo, *President*
Douglas Emery, *Treasurer*
▲ EMP: 12 EST: 2002
SQ FT: 3,000
SALES (est): 1.8MM Privately Held
WEB: www.radshield.com
SIC: 2836 Biological products, except diag-
nostic

(G-2103)
RAW FOODS INTERNATIONAL
LLC
Also Called: Raaw
2600 S Douglas Rd Ste 410 (33134-6134)
PHONE..................................305 856-1991
Simon Decker, *Mng Member*
Paul J Gregg,
EMP: 15 EST: 2009
SQ FT: 5,000

SALES (est): 1.3MM Privately Held
SIC: 2033 5142 2037 Fruit juices: packaged in cans, jars, etc.; fruits & fruit products in cans, jars, etc.; fruit juices, frozen;
fruit juices

(G-2104)
RELMADA THERAPEUTICS INC
2222 Ponce De Leon Blvd (33134-5039)
PHONE..................................646 876-3459
Sergio Traversa, *CEO*
Michael D Becker, *Senior VP*
Danny KAO, *Senior VP*
Marc De Somer Scd, *Senior VP*
Gina Diguglielmo, *Vice Pres*
EMP: 20 EST: 2007 Privately Held
WEB: www.relmada.com
SIC: 2834 Pharmaceutical preparations

(G-2105)
SAGE IMPORTS CORP
232 Andalusia Ave Ste 201 (33134-5914)
PHONE..................................305 962-0631
Diosana Aleman, *President*
EMP: 10 EST: 2011
SALES (est): 269.5K Privately Held
SIC: 2099 Food preparations

(G-2106)
SALCO ELECTRIC SUPPLY
LLC ✪
4000 Ponce De Leon Blvd (33146-1431)
PHONE..................................305 777-0200
Douglas Hasbun Genao,
EMP: 12 EST: 2021
SALES (est): 780K Privately Held
SIC: 3699 Electrical equipment & supplies

(G-2107)
SC GASTRONOMIC CREW INC
127 Miracle Mile (33134-5405)
PHONE..................................786 864-1212
Matias Pagano, *Director*
EMP: 30 EST: 2016
SALES (est): 1.2MM Privately Held
SIC: 2599 Furniture & fixtures

(G-2108)
SIS HOLDINGS LP (PA)
2333 Ponce De Leon Blvd (33134-5422)
PHONE..................................855 699-8372
EMP: 15 EST: 2016
SALES (est): 45.3MM Publicly Held
SIC: 7372 Prepackaged software

(G-2109)
SMR MANAGEMENT INC (PA)
Also Called: Sima Group
1728 Coral Way (33145-2794)
PHONE..................................305 529-2488
Roberto Isaias, *President*
Estefano Isaias, *Shareholder*
William Isaias, *Shareholder*
▲ EMP: 5 EST: 2008
SQ FT: 4,000
SALES (est): 1.5MM Privately Held
SIC: 3714 Motor vehicle parts & acces-
sories

(G-2110)
SONIA LAND INC
5536 Sw 8th St (33134-2220)
PHONE..................................305 798-4912
EMP: 8 EST: 2016
SALES (est): 265.1K Privately Held
SIC: 3861 Motion picture film

(G-2111)
SPS DRILLING EXPLORATION
PROD
1 Alhambra Plz Ste Ph (33134-5227)
PHONE..................................305 777-3553
Manuel E Chinchilla, *President*
Gloria Mayorga, *Buyer*
Rosario Gamez, *Purchasing*
Jenny Pineda, *Director*
EMP: 15 EST: 2012
SALES (est): 2.7MM Privately Held
WEB: www.spsdrilling-ep.com
SIC: 1311 5084 5085 Crude petroleum &
natural gas; industrial machinery & equip-
ment; industrial supplies

(G-2112)
STUDIO BECKER FLORIDA LLC
4216 Ponce De Leon Blvd (33146-1827)
PHONE.....................................305 514-0400
Frank Rosell, *Principal*
EMP: 9 EST: 2016
SALES (est): 472K **Privately Held**
WEB: www.studiobecker.com
SIC: 2434 Wood kitchen cabinets

(G-2113)
SUKALDE INC (PA)
5271 Sw 8th St Apt 213 (33134-2382)
PHONE.....................................786 399-0087
Eduardo J Quintero, *President*
Unai Urtizberea, *Vice Pres*
EMP: 6 EST: 2017
SALES (est): 653.9K **Privately Held**
SIC: 2038 Frozen specialties

(G-2114)
TIN MAN CO
2828 Coral Way Ste 207 (33145-3233)
PHONE.....................................305 365-1926
Michael Netsky, *CEO*
EMP: 4 EST: 2010
SQ FT: 2,000
SALES (est): 72MM **Privately Held**
WEB: www.tinmanco.com
SIC: 3559 8742 Recycling machinery; re-
tail trade consultant

(G-2115)
TITANIC BREWING COMPANY INC
Also Called: Titanic Restaurant & Brewery
5813 Ponce De Leon Blvd (33146-2422)
PHONE.....................................305 668-1742
Kevin Rusk, *President*
EMP: 13 EST: 1995
SQ FT: 4,000
SALES (est): 1MM **Privately Held**
WEB: www.titanicbrewery.com
SIC: 2082 5812 Beer (alcoholic bever-
age); Cajun restaurant

(G-2116)
URAL & ASSOCIATES INC
Also Called: Journal Housing Science
3608 Anderson Rd (33134-7053)
P.O. Box 140525 (33114-0525)
PHONE.....................................305 446-9462
Oktay Ural, *President*
EMP: 6 EST: 1972
SALES (est): 353.9K **Privately Held**
WEB: www.housingsciencejournal.com
SIC: 2721 Trade journals: publishing &
printing

(G-2117)
UREN NORTH AMERICA LLC
2990 Ponce De Leon Blvd (33134-6803)
P.O. Box 140398 (33114-0398)
PHONE.....................................410 924-3478
Paul Jones, *Director*
Julian Wood,
Julie Creese,
Rob Laird,
Ross Stewart,
EMP: 6 EST: 2016
SALES (est): 967.3K **Privately Held**
WEB: www.uren.com
SIC: 2038 Breakfasts, frozen & packaged

(G-2118)
US PRECIOUS METALS INC
Also Called: (AN EXPLORATION STAGE
COMPANY)
1825 Ponce De Leon Blvd (33134-4418)
PHONE.....................................786 814-5804
John Leufray, *CEO*
Michael Green, *CFO*
EMP: 9 EST: 1998
SALES (est): 449.3K **Privately Held**
WEB: www.uspreciousmetals.com
SIC: 1081 1041 1044 1021 Metal mining
exploration & development services; gold
ores; silver ores; copper ores

(G-2119)
WEMI SPORTS
Also Called: World Wide Export Management
156 Giralda Ave (33134-5209)
PHONE.....................................305 446-5178
Raphael Quevedo, *Director*

▲ EMP: 5 EST: 2009
SALES (est): 327.4K **Privately Held**
WEB: www.wemisports.com
SIC: 3949 Sporting & athletic goods

(G-2120)
WORLDCITY INC
Also Called: World City
251 Valencia Ave (33134-5905)
PHONE.....................................305 441-2244
Ken Roberts, *President*
Alison Klapper Leon, *Vice Pres*
Sari Govantes, *Manager*
Tatiana Panzardi, *Director*
Marilys Rios, *Director*
EMP: 8 EST: 1996
SALES (est): 1.8MM **Privately Held**
WEB: www.worldcityweb.com
SIC: 2711 Newspapers

(G-2121)
YELLOW GREEN AEROSPACE INC
Also Called: Ygaero
2525 Ponce De Leon Blvd # 300
(33134-6044)
PHONE.....................................954 599-4161
Vanderlei Van Dias, *President*
Vanderlei Dias, *President*
Remy Alvares, *Regl Sales Mgr*
EMP: 7 EST: 2016
SALES (est): 865K **Privately Held**
WEB: www.ygaero.com
SIC: 3728 Aircraft parts & equipment

Coral Springs
Broward County

(G-2122)
24/7 SOFTWARE INC
12411 Nw 35th St (33065-2413)
PHONE.....................................954 514-8988
Gerald Hwasta, *CEO*
Scott Meyers, *President*
Debbie Popkin, *VP Admin*
Bandana Baid, *Finance*
Cristian Raudales, *Accounts Exec*
EMP: 15 EST: 2007
SQ FT: 4,200
SALES (est): 1.5MM **Privately Held**
WEB: www.247software.com
SIC: 7372 Prepackaged software

(G-2123)
A-1 INDUSTRIES FLORIDA INC (PA)
11555 Heron Bay Blvd # 2 (33076-3360)
PHONE.....................................270 316-9409
Amanda Wethington, *President*
John Herring, *President*
Jan Beck, *Exec VP*
Robert G Lamb, *Vice Pres*
Michael L Ruede, *Vice Pres*
▼ EMP: 15 EST: 1977
SALES (est): 53.5MM **Privately Held**
WEB: www.a1truss.com
SIC: 2439 3448 Trusses, wooden roof;
trusses, except roof: laminated lumber;
trusses & framing: prefabricated metal

(G-2124)
ABB ENTERPRISE SOFTWARE INC
Also Called: A B B Automation Technolgy Div
4300 Coral Ridge Dr (33065-7699)
P.O. Box 91089, Raleigh NC (27675-1089)
PHONE.....................................954 752-6700
Bharat Chopra, *Business Mgr*
Richard Lindo, *Branch Mgr*
Drew Rogers, *Manager*
Mark Thrash, *Manager*
EMP: 170
SALES (corp-wide): 28.9B **Privately Held**
WEB: abb-inc.edan.io
SIC: 3823 3566 3625 3613 Controllers
for process variables, all types; drives,
high speed industrial, except hydrostatic;
relays & industrial controls; switchgear &
switchboard apparatus
HQ: Abb Inc.
305 Gregson Dr
Cary NC 27511

(G-2125)
ACIC PHARMACEUTICALS INC
11772 W Sample Rd Ste 103 (33065-3166)
PHONE.....................................954 341-0795
Luciano Calenti, *President*
Craig Baxter, *Vice Pres*
EMP: 5 EST: 2017
SALES (est): 428.6K **Privately Held**
WEB: www.acic.com
SIC: 2834 Pharmaceutical preparations

(G-2126)
ADVANCED CMMNCATIONS HOLDG INC (DH)
Also Called: Advanced Cable Communica-
tions
12409 Nw 35th St (33065-2413)
PHONE.....................................954 753-0100
Kerry Oslund, *President*
Gary Hoipkemier, *Corp Secy*
Barry Kerr, *Vice Pres*
Bauta Carlos, *Engineer*
Michelle Fitzpatrick, *Mktg Dir*
▲ EMP: 76 EST: 1977
SQ FT: 23,000
SALES (est): 25.7MM
SALES (corp-wide): 2.4B **Publicly Held**
SIC: 2621 2759 2711 2752 Catalog,
magazine & newsprint papers; commer-
cial printing; commercial printing & news-
paper publishing combined; commercial
printing, lithographic
HQ: Schurz Communications, Inc.
1301 E Douglas Rd Ste 200
Mishawaka IN 46545
574 247-7237

(G-2127)
ADVANTAGE MEDICAL ELEC LLC (DH)
Also Called: AMC
11705 Nw 39th St (33065-2511)
PHONE.....................................954 345-9800
Cedric Ragsdale, *CFO*
Kim Davis, *Mng Member*
EMP: 5 EST: 2015
SALES (est): 7.6MM
SALES (corp-wide): 28.3MM **Privately Held**
WEB: www.lifesync.com
SIC: 3841 Surgical & medical instruments
HQ: Lifesync Corporation
11705 Nw 39th St
Coral Springs FL 33065
954 345-9800

(G-2128)
AESINC ADVANCED EQP & SVCS (PA)
Also Called: Advanced Equipment and Svcs
12070 Nw 40th St Ste 2 (33065-7602)
PHONE.....................................954 857-1895
Victor De Sousa, *President*
Patricia Osorio, *Vice Pres*
Carlos Silva, *Project Mgr*
EMP: 9 EST: 2016
SALES (est): 1MM **Privately Held**
WEB: www.advancees.com
SIC: 3589 Water treatment equipment, in-
dustrial

(G-2129)
AIR SPONGE FILTER COMPANY INC
4224 Nw 120th Ave (33065-7603)
PHONE.....................................954 752-1836
Richard Rosen, *Owner*
Elisa Montenero, *Vice Pres*
Moe Adili, *Treasurer*
EMP: 7 EST: 1993
SALES (est): 908.8K **Privately Held**
WEB: www.airsponge.com
SIC: 3564 5075 Filters, air: furnaces, air
conditioning equipment, etc.; air filters

(G-2130)
AL GAREY & ASSOCIATES INC
Also Called: Decimal Engineering
4300 Coral Ridge Dr (33065-7617)
PHONE.....................................954 975-7992
Alan Garey Lee, *President*
Alan Garey, *General Mgr*
Kevin Garey, *Vice Pres*
Mauricio Garzon, *Production*
Wayne Graf, *Production*

▲ EMP: 140 EST: 1980
SALES (est): 23.9MM **Privately Held**
WEB: www.decimal.net
SIC: 3444 3599 Forming machine work,
sheet metal; machine & other job shop
work

(G-2131)
AMETEK POWER INSTRUMENT INC
4050 Nw 121st Ave (33065-7612)
PHONE.....................................954 344-9822
Frank S Hermance, *CEO*
EMP: 86 EST: 1994
SQ FT: 8,400
SALES (est): 7.2MM
SALES (corp-wide): 5.5B **Publicly Held**
SIC: 3823 Industrial instrmnts msrmnt dis-
play/control process variable
PA: Ametek, Inc.
1100 Cassatt Rd
Berwyn PA 19312
610 647-2121

(G-2132)
AW GATES INC
11285 Sw 1st St (33071-8145)
PHONE.....................................954 341-2180
Anthony William Gates, *Owner*
EMP: 9 EST: 2008
SALES (est): 525.8K **Privately Held**
SIC: 2421 Building & structural materials,
wood

(G-2133)
BABY GUARD INC
Also Called: Baby Guard Pool Fence Co
11947 W Sample Rd (33065-3100)
PHONE.....................................954 741-6351
Michael Schatzberg, *President*
Wendy Schatzberg, *Vice Pres*
▲ EMP: 19 EST: 1989
SQ FT: 2,500
SALES (est): 2.4MM **Privately Held**
WEB: www.babyguardfence.com
SIC: 3315 5211 3949 3496 Fencing
made in wiredrawing plants; fencing;
sporting & athletic goods; miscellaneous
fabricated wire products

(G-2134)
BAGINDD PRINTS
1843 Nw 83rd Dr (33071-6243)
PHONE.....................................954 971-9000
Arnold S Reimer, *Partner*
Gloria Reimer, *Partner*
EMP: 10 EST: 1978
SQ FT: 25,000
SALES (est): 535.7K **Privately Held**
SIC: 2262 Screen printing: manmade fiber
& silk broadwoven fabrics

(G-2135)
BAKER-HILL INDUSTRIES INC
3850 Nw 118th Ave (33065-2543)
PHONE.....................................954 752-3090
William Ricci, *President*
Deiter Morlock, *Vice Pres*
John Preiser, *Engineer*
Leigh Livesay, *Manager*
Francisco Pagan, *Manager*
EMP: 33 EST: 1967
SQ FT: 14,400
SALES (est): 7.4MM **Privately Held**
WEB: www.bakerhillindustries.com
SIC: 3599 Machine shop, jobbing & repair

(G-2136)
BELL BROTHERS ELECTRIC LLC
5222 Nw 110th Ave (33076-2758)
PHONE.....................................954 496-0632
Mark A Bell, *Branch Mgr*
EMP: 16
SALES (corp-wide): 301.6K **Privately Held**
WEB: www.bellbrotherselectric.com
SIC: 3699 Bells, electric
PA: Bell Brothers Electric Llc
2436 N Federal Hwy
Lighthouse Point FL

▲ = Import ▼=Export
◆ =Import/Export

(G-2137)
BLACK COLLEGE TODAY INC
4973 Nw 115th Ter (33076-3201)
P.O. Box 25425, Fort Lauderdale (33320-5425)
PHONE..................954 344-4469
Steven Mootry, *President*
EMP: 6 EST: 1991
SALES (est): 530.6K Privately Held
WEB: www.blackcollegetoday.com
SIC: 2721 Magazines: publishing & printing; periodicals: publishing & printing

(G-2138)
BLADES DIRECT LLC
5645 Coral Ridge Dr (33076-3124)
PHONE..................855 225-2337
Robert Slverstone, *Principal*
Kenny Gills, *Regl Sales Mgr*
Joe Carpone, *Sales Staff*
Micheal D Stewart, *Mng Member*
EMP: 15 EST: 2012
SALES (est): 1.1MM Privately Held
WEB: www.bladesdirect.net
SIC: 3425 Saw blades & handsaws

(G-2139)
BR SIGNS INTERNATIONAL IN
5944 Coral Ridge Dr (33076-3300)
PHONE..................954 464-7999
William Reicherter, *President*
EMP: 6 EST: 2017
SALES (est): 443.5K Privately Held
WEB: www.dreamsandvisionsinternational.org
SIC: 3993 Signs & advertising specialties

(G-2140)
CHRISTY LEWIS SHEEK LLC
8761 Forest Hills Blvd (33065-5475)
PHONE..................786 512-2999
Tyree Lewis Sr, *President*
EMP: 7 EST: 2020
SALES (est): 244.6K Privately Held
SIC: 2339 2389 3171 5136 Women's & misses' miscellaneous accessories; men's miscellaneous accessories; purses, women's; apparel belts, men's & boys'; apparel belts, women's & children's

(G-2141)
CNR PRECISION TOOL INC
8480 Nw 29th Ct (33065-5320)
PHONE..................954 426-9650
Rosemarie Thomas, *Owner*
Christopher Thomas, *Co-Owner*
EMP: 6 EST: 1995
SQ FT: 3,100
SALES (est): 474.3K Privately Held
SIC: 3599 Machine shop, jobbing & repair

(G-2142)
COLD STONE CREAMERY-PARKLAND
6230 Coral Ridge Dr # 110 (33076-3386)
PHONE..................954 341-8033
Jerry Kestel, *President*
Daniel Toledano, *General Mgr*
EMP: 9 EST: 2003
SQ FT: 2,000
SALES (est): 494.6K Privately Held
WEB: www.coldstonecreamery.com
SIC: 2024 5812 Ice cream & frozen desserts; ice cream stands or dairy bars

(G-2143)
COLLABORATIVE SFTWR SOLUTIONS
4721 Nw 115th Ave (33076-2154)
PHONE..................954 753-2025
Rickie Ramcharitar, *Principal*
EMP: 5 EST: 2006
SALES (est): 346K Privately Held
WEB: www.collaborativesolutions.com
SIC: 7372 Prepackaged software

(G-2144)
CORE ENTERPRISES INCORPORATED
3650 Coral Ridge Dr # 101 (33065-2558)
PHONE..................954 227-0781
Cornel Opris, *President*
Dennis Cardinale, *Vice Pres*
▲ EMP: 6 EST: 2001
SQ FT: 4,000
SALES (est): 748.5K Privately Held
WEB: www.core-enterprises.com
SIC: 3825 3823 3829 Test equipment for electronic & electric measurement; industrial process measurement equipment; gas detectors

(G-2145)
D GROUP NORTH AMERICA LLC
12486 W Atlantic Blvd (33071-4086)
PHONE..................646 809-0859
Chris Disanto, *President*
EMP: 8 EST: 2006
SALES (est): 745.9K Privately Held
SIC: 3873 Watches, clocks, watchcases & parts

(G-2146)
DA VINCI SYSTEMS INC
124 Th Ave (33065)
PHONE..................954 688-5600
John Peeler, *CEO*
Mark Tremallo, *Corp Secy*
Richard Johnson, *Finance*
EMP: 26 EST: 1990
SQ FT: 8,000
SALES (est): 4.5MM
SALES (corp-wide): 1.2B Publicly Held
WEB: www.blackmagicdesign.com
SIC: 3663 5065 3651 Radio & TV communications equipment; radio & television equipment & parts; household audio & video equipment
HQ: Jdsu Acterna Holdings Llc
   1 Milestone Center Ct
   Germantown MD 20876
   240 404-1550

(G-2147)
DATA PUBLISHERS INC
Also Called: Parklanders
9602 Nw 36th Mnr (33065-2868)
PHONE..................954 752-2332
Trulee Abbondanzio, *President*
EMP: 10 EST: 1996
SALES (est): 562.7K Privately Held
SIC: 2721 Periodicals

(G-2148)
DE LIMA CONSULTANTS GROUP INC (PA)
Also Called: Private Label Express
4216 Nw 120th Ave (33065-7603)
PHONE..................954 933-7030
Robert De Lima, *President*
Peter Cianci, *Business Mgr*
Sam Slama, *Business Anlyst*
Kristy Aldridge, *Marketing Staff*
EMP: 5 EST: 2010
SALES (est): 3.9MM Privately Held
WEB: www.privatelabelexpress.com
SIC: 2833 Vitamins, natural or synthetic: bulk, uncompounded

(G-2149)
DECORAL SYSTEM USA CORPORATION
12477 Nw 44th St (33065-7639)
PHONE..................954 755-6021
Enrico Piva, *CEO*
Francesca Mella, *COO*
Mirta Duarte, *Vice Pres*
William Grunbaum, *VP Business*
Chiara Castagnini, *Controller*
EMP: 23 EST: 2005
SALES (est): 11.7MM
SALES (corp-wide): 69.2MM Privately Held
SIC: 3549 Metalworking machinery
HQ: Decoral System Srl
   Viale Del Lavoro 5
   Arcole VR 37040
   045 763-9101

(G-2150)
DFD LOADERS INC
11820 Nw 37th St (33065-2537)
PHONE..................954 283-8839
David Font, *President*
EMP: 9 EST: 2018
SALES (est): 2MM Privately Held
WEB: www.dfdloaders.com
SIC: 3537 Trucks, tractors, loaders, carriers & similar equipment

(G-2151)
E3 GRAPHICS INC
Also Called: Minuteman Press
9868 W Sample Rd (33065-4006)
PHONE..................954 510-1302
David B Johnson, *Principal*
EMP: 5 EST: 2009
SALES (est): 505.4K Privately Held
WEB: www.minutemanpress.com
SIC: 2752 Commercial printing, lithographic; commercial art & graphic design

(G-2152)
EAST COAST CUSTOM COATINGS INC
2920 Nw 106th Ave (33065-3757)
PHONE..................954 914-6711
Andrew Perkins, *Vice Pres*
EMP: 8 EST: 2017
SALES (est): 69.9K Privately Held
SIC: 3479 Coating of metals & formed products

(G-2153)
FLORIDA MICRO DEVICES INC
4676 Nw 60th Ln (33067-2105)
P.O. Box 970260, Pompano Beach (33097-0260)
PHONE..................954 973-7200
Francisco Miro, *President*
Miiguel Berthin, *Vice Pres*
EMP: 6 EST: 1989
SQ FT: 1,000
SALES (est): 791.3K Privately Held
WEB: www.floridamicro.com
SIC: 3674 Microcircuits, integrated (semiconductor)

(G-2154)
FOOT FUNCTION LAB INC
Also Called: Mr Rach
11540 Wiles Rd Ste 1 (33076-2119)
PHONE..................954 753-2500
Leonard Kerns, *President*
EMP: 5 EST: 1979
SQ FT: 2,100
SALES (est): 358.7K Privately Held
WEB: www.orthotics.net
SIC: 3842 Surgical appliances & supplies

(G-2155)
FORM SCRIPT - FORM PRINT LLC
9101 W Sample Rd Apt 101 (33065-1629)
PHONE..................954 345-3727
Jeffrey Malin, *Mng Member*
EMP: 5 EST: 2018
SALES (est): 442.5K Privately Held
SIC: 2752 Commercial printing, lithographic

(G-2156)
FORTUNE MEDIA GROUP INC
6250 Coral Ridge Dr # 100 (33076-3383)
PHONE..................954 379-4321
P Douglas Scott, *President*
EMP: 10 EST: 2006
SALES (est): 739.5K Privately Held
WEB: www.fortunemediagroupinc.com
SIC: 3663 Radio & TV communications equipment

(G-2157)
FROMKIN ENERGY LLC
4630 N University Dr (33067-4626)
PHONE..................954 683-2509
Lewis Fromkin, *Principal*
EMP: 9 EST: 2008
SALES (est): 229.7K Privately Held
WEB: www.fromkin.energy
SIC: 1311 Crude petroleum & natural gas

(G-2158)
GOLD SHINE LLC ✪
3301 N University Dr # 100 (33065-4164)
PHONE..................561 419-3253
Alfred Phillips, *CEO*
EMP: 20 EST: 2021
SALES (est): 1.1MM Privately Held
SIC: 2842 Automobile polish

(G-2159)
HANDAL FOODS LLC
11822 Nw 30th Ct (33065-3324)
PHONE..................954 753-0649
Abraham Handal, *Principal*
EMP: 6 EST: 2012
SALES (est): 392.9K Privately Held
SIC: 2099 Food preparations

(G-2160)
HC GRUPO INC
2929 N University Dr # 105 (33065-5047)
PHONE..................954 227-0150
Francisco Clavel, *President*
Oscar Clavel, *Vice Pres*
EMP: 5 EST: 2005
SALES (est): 512.8K Privately Held
WEB: www.hc-grupo.com
SIC: 3089 3429 Plastic boats & other marine equipment; marine hardware

(G-2161)
HILTON SOFTWARE LLC
2730 N University Dr (33065-5111)
PHONE..................954 323-2244
Dennis Oliveira, *Engineer*
Brent Werne, *Software Engr*
Hilton Goldstein,
EMP: 17 EST: 2008
SQ FT: 2,730
SALES (est): 2.4MM Privately Held
WEB: www.hiltonsoftware.co
SIC: 7372 Prepackaged software

(G-2162)
HILTRONICS CORPORATION
3979 Nw 126th Ave (33065-7609)
PHONE..................954 341-9100
Stuart Leeman, *President*
Doug Leeman, *Vice Pres*
Stanley Friedman, *Treasurer*
EMP: 7 EST: 1993
SQ FT: 3,400
SALES (est): 883.3K Privately Held
WEB: www.hiltronicscorp.com
SIC: 3679 Electronic circuits

(G-2163)
HISPACOM INC
Also Called: Icco
9900 W Sample Rd Ste 200 (33065-4044)
PHONE..................954 255-2622
Carlos Gonzalez, *President*
Christopher Myers, *Training Spec*
EMP: 15 EST: 1995
SQ FT: 5,000
SALES (est): 369.3K Privately Held
SIC: 7372 7371 Prepackaged software; custom computer programming services

(G-2164)
HUGHES CORPORATION
Also Called: Weschler Instruments
4000 Nw 121st Ave (33065-7612)
PHONE..................954 755-7111
Michael F Dorman, *President*
Rt Houston, *General Mgr*
Matthew Hughes, *Vice Pres*
Howie Schmidt, *Mfg Mgr*
James Rai, *Engineer*
EMP: 39
SQ FT: 24,000
SALES (corp-wide): 26.8MM Privately Held
WEB: www.hughescorporation.com
SIC: 3825 3823 3613 Measuring instruments & meters, electric; industrial instrmnts msrmnt display/control process variable; switchgear & switchboard apparatus
PA: Hughes Corporation
   16900 Foltz Pkwy
   Strongsville OH 44149
   440 238-2550

(G-2165)
HYDES SCREENING INC
3700 Nw 124th Ave Ste 126 (33065-2432)
PHONE..................954 345-6743
Christopher Hyde, *Owner*
EMP: 8 EST: 1988
SALES (est): 876.9K Privately Held
WEB: www.screenpatioenclosures.com
SIC: 3448 1521 1799 Screen enclosures; patio & deck construction & repair; fiberglass work

(G-2166)
INMAN ORTHODONTIC LABS INC
3953 Nw 126th Ave (33065-7609)
PHONE..........................954 340-8477
Donald Paul Inman, *President*
Angela Inmanv, *Vice Pres*
EMP: 17 EST: 1972
SQ FT: 1,000
SALES (est): 1.8MM **Privately Held**
WEB: www.inmanortho.com
SIC: 3843 8072 Orthodontic appliances; dental laboratories

(G-2167)
INTEGRATED LASER SYSTEMS INC
11383 Lakeview Dr (33071-6332)
PHONE..........................954 489-8282
Patricia Reyes, *Principal*
EMP: 8 EST: 2010
SALES (est): 469K **Privately Held**
WEB: www.ils-service.com
SIC: 3699 Laser systems & equipment

(G-2168)
ITS A 10 INC
Also Called: It's A "10" Haircare
4613 N University Dr # 478 (33067-4602)
PHONE..........................954 227-7813
Carolyn Plummer, *CEO*
Scott Scharg, *President*
David Rosenblatt, *Exec VP*
EMP: 2 EST: 2006
SALES (est): 36.7MM **Privately Held**
WEB: www.itsa10haircare.com
SIC: 3999 Hair & hair-based products

(G-2169)
JENSEN SCIENTIFIC PRODUCTS INC
Also Called: Jensen Inert Products
3773 Nw 126th Ave (33065-2400)
PHONE..........................954 344-2006
Stephen R Little, *President*
◆ EMP: 25 EST: 1988
SQ FT: 13,000
SALES (est): 5.6MM **Privately Held**
WEB: www.jenseninert.com
SIC: 3221 5049 3821 3498 Vials, glass; scientific & engineering equipment & supplies; laboratory apparatus & furniture; fabricated pipe & fittings; products of purchased glass

(G-2170)
JNC HABITAT INVESTMENTS INC
Also Called: J N C Investments
645 Nw 112th Way (33071-7950)
PHONE..........................954 249-7469
Maria Veliz, *President*
Gil Veliz, *Vice Pres*
EMP: 9 EST: 1955
SALES (est): 221.6K **Privately Held**
SIC: 2541 Store & office display cases & fixtures

(G-2171)
JNC WELDING & FABRICATING INC
3769 Nw 126th Ave (33065-2424)
PHONE..........................954 227-9424
James R Noel, *President*
James Noel, *President*
Mick Bonifaz, *Vice Pres*
▲ EMP: 18 EST: 1999
SQ FT: 12,000
SALES (est): 3.2MM **Privately Held**
WEB: www.jncwelding.com
SIC: 3441 Fabricated structural metal

(G-2172)
JUST SAY PRINT INC
1500 Nw 112th Way (33071-6466)
PHONE..........................954 254-7793
Christopher D Brown, *Principal*
EMP: 10 EST: 2012
SALES (est): 181.5K **Privately Held**
SIC: 2752 Commercial printing, lithographic

(G-2173)
KERATRONIX INC
4377 Nw 124th Ave (33065-7634)
PHONE..........................954 753-5741
Michael M Anthony, *President*
Michael Anthony, *Principal*
EMP: 12 EST: 2008
SALES (est): 450.3K **Privately Held**
SIC: 2844 Toilet preparations

(G-2174)
KING PHARMACEUTICALS LLC
Also Called: Kings Pharmacy
2814 N University Dr (33065-5010)
PHONE..........................954 575-7085
David Wolman, *Principal*
EMP: 8
SALES (corp-wide): 81.2B **Publicly Held**
SIC: 2834 Pharmaceutical preparations
HQ: King Pharmaceuticals Llc
501 5th St
Bristol TN 37620

(G-2175)
KNOWLES PLASTICS INC
Also Called: Knowles' Mobile Marine
10301 Nw 16th Ct (33071-6518)
PHONE..........................954 232-8756
Jeffrey H Knowles, *President*
Lisa Knowles, *Vice Pres*
EMP: 7 EST: 1996
SALES (est): 93.3K **Privately Held**
SIC: 3732 Boats, fiberglass: building & repairing

(G-2176)
L2D OUTDOORS INC
4300 Nw 120th Ave (33065-7610)
PHONE..........................954 757-6116
Lesleyanne Wolff, *Principal*
EMP: 8 EST: 2018
SALES (est): 307.6K **Privately Held**
SIC: 3489 Ordnance & accessories

(G-2177)
LEAD 2 DESIGN
4302 Nw 120th Ave (33065-7610)
PHONE..........................954 757-6116
Lesley-Anne Wolff, *Co-Owner*
EMP: 8 EST: 2010
SALES (est): 879.9K **Privately Held**
WEB: www.lead2design.com
SIC: 2211 Decorative trim & specialty fabrics, including twist weave

(G-2178)
LEVITA LLC
Also Called: Bedbug Supply
12410 Nw 39th St (33065-2435)
PHONE..........................954 227-7468
Mark Sanders,
Michelle Sanders,
▲ EMP: 6 EST: 2007
SALES (est): 862.4K **Privately Held**
WEB: www.bedbugsupply.com
SIC: 2879 3069 Pesticides, agricultural or household; mattress protectors, rubber

(G-2179)
LEXMARK INTERNATIONAL INC
10866 Nw 14th St (33071-8213)
PHONE..........................954 345-2442
EMP: 159
SALES (corp-wide): 2.5B **Privately Held**
SIC: 3577 Mfg Computer Peripheral Equipment
PA: Lexmark International, Inc.
740 W New Circle Rd
Lexington KY 40511
859 232-2000

(G-2180)
LUPIN RESEARCH INC
4006 Nw 124th Ave (33065-2411)
PHONE..........................800 466-1450
Vinita Gupta, *CEO*
Paul McGarty, *President*
Megan Roberts, *Sales Staff*
Sofia Mumtaz, *Manager*
Jade Ly, *Director*
EMP: 43 EST: 2003
SALES (est): 10.7MM **Privately Held**
SIC: 2834 5122 Pharmaceutical preparations; pharmaceuticals
PA: Lupin Limited
Kalpataru Inspire, 3rd Floor,
Mumbai MH 40005

(G-2181)
MEDIA SYSTEMS INC
Also Called: Jiffi Print
3859 Nw 124th Ave (33065-2406)
PHONE..........................954 427-4411
Raed Bakouni, *President*
Terri Bakouni, *Vice Pres*
EMP: 6 EST: 2013
SQ FT: 2,200
SALES (est): 446.3K **Privately Held**
WEB: www.mediasystems.com
SIC: 2752 Commercial printing, offset

(G-2182)
MEGIN US LLC (PA)
11772 W Sample Rd (33065-3166)
PHONE..........................954 341-2965
Rick Goepfert, *Principal*
Gordon Baltzer, *Mng Member*
Craig Shapero,
EMP: 9 EST: 2020
SALES (est): 1.1MM **Privately Held**
WEB: www.megin.fi
SIC: 3845 7629 Audiological equipment, electromedical; electrical repair shops

(G-2183)
MEI DEVELOPMENT CORPORATION
11772 W Sample Rd Ste 101 (33065-3166)
PHONE..........................954 341-3302
Sam Moti, *President*
Gordon B Baltzer, *Vice Pres*
Richard McLaughlin, *CFO*
EMP: 10 EST: 1997
SALES (est): 1.4MM **Privately Held**
SIC: 3841 Diagnostic apparatus, medical
PA: The Mei Healthcare Group Llc
11772 W Sample Rd
Coral Springs FL 33065

(G-2184)
METAL SPRAY PAINTING POWDER
3701 Nw 126th Ave Ste 4 (33065-2439)
PHONE..........................954 227-2744
Michael C Landi, *President*
EMP: 7 EST: 2013
SALES (est): 875K **Privately Held**
WEB: www.metalspraypainting.com
SIC: 2262 3471 Screen printing: manmade fiber & silk broadwoven fabrics; finishing, metals or formed products

(G-2185)
METHAPHARM INC
11772 W Sample Rd Ste 101 (33065-3166)
PHONE..........................954 341-0795
Luciano Calenti, *President*
Antoniette Walkom, *Vice Pres*
Gordon Baltzer, *Treasurer*
Sharron Brownlee, *Sales Staff*
Brian Frappier, *Sales Staff*
EMP: 5 EST: 2000
SQ FT: 2,000
SALES (est): 3.5MM
SALES (corp-wide): 22.1MM **Privately Held**
WEB: www.methapharm.com
SIC: 2834 Pharmaceutical preparations
HQ: Methapharm Inc
81 Sinclair Blvd
Brantford ON N3S 7
519 751-3602

(G-2186)
METRITEK CORPORATION (PA)
849 Nw 126th Ave (33071-4401)
PHONE..........................561 995-2414
Robert Javelin, *President*
Sheli Lopez, *CFO*
Shelley Lopez, *Executive*
Varda Javelin, *Admin Sec*
◆ EMP: 41 EST: 1986
SALES (est): 7.6MM **Privately Held**
WEB: www.metritek.com
SIC: 2258 Lace, knit

(G-2187)
MICOLE ELECTRIC SIGN COMPANY
10840 Sw 1st Ct (33071-8134)
PHONE..........................954 796-4293
EMP: 5
SALES (est): 423.7K **Privately Held**
SIC: 3993 Mfg Signs/Advertising Specialties

(G-2188)
MICRO CRANE INC
3610 Nw 118th Ave Ste 4 (33065-2552)
PHONE..........................954 755-2225
Charles Helou, *President*
EMP: 9 EST: 1979
SALES (est): 255.5K **Privately Held**
SIC: 3577 Computer peripheral equipment

(G-2189)
MOLD EXPERT
2812 Nw 87th Ave (33065-5342)
PHONE..........................954 829-3102
Manuel Galeano, *Principal*
EMP: 9 EST: 2010
SALES (est): 141.7K **Privately Held**
SIC: 3544 Industrial molds

(G-2190)
MONAR CORPORATION
9825 W Sample Rd Ste 202 (33065-4040)
PHONE..........................954 650-1930
Naraine Seecharan, *Principal*
Ray Chung, *Executive*
EMP: 7 EST: 2004
SALES (est): 840.5K **Privately Held**
WEB: www.monarac.net
SIC: 3585 Air conditioning equipment, complete

(G-2191)
MONROY AEROSPACE
10908 Nw 17th Mnr (33071-6320)
P.O. Box 8217 (33075-8217)
PHONE..........................954 344-4936
Jose Monroy, *President*
EMP: 5 EST: 1986
SALES (est): 492.2K **Privately Held**
WEB: www.monroyaero.com
SIC: 3728 Aircraft assemblies, subassemblies & parts

(G-2192)
MONUMENTAL AIR INC
4333 Nw 64th Ave (33067-3050)
PHONE..........................954 383-9507
Juan Taveras, *Principal*
EMP: 12 EST: 2010
SALES (est): 2.1MM **Privately Held**
SIC: 3272 Monuments & grave markers, except terrazo

(G-2193)
MRN BIOLOGICS LLC
3732 Nw 126th Ave (33065-2408)
PHONE..........................508 989-6090
Robert O McKie,
EMP: 10 EST: 2015
SALES (est): 771K **Privately Held**
SIC: 3821 Clinical laboratory instruments, except medical & dental

(G-2194)
MYRLEN INC
3814 Nw 126th Ave (33065-2450)
P.O. Box 8783 (33075-8783)
PHONE..........................800 662-4762
Paul Rose, *Vice Pres*
EMP: 5 EST: 2000
SQ FT: 1,800
SALES (est): 540.2K **Privately Held**
WEB: www.myrlen.com
SIC: 3443 Bins, prefabricated metal plate; wind & vacuum tunnels

(G-2195)
NEW WAVE SURGICAL CORP
3700 Nw 124th Ave Ste 135 (33065-2433)
PHONE..........................866 346-8883
Elba Lopez, *Principal*
EMP: 11 EST: 2015
SALES (est): 542.9K **Privately Held**
WEB: www.newwavesurgical.com
SIC: 3841 Surgical & medical instruments

(G-2196)
NEWFLO LLC
4613 N University Dr (33067-4602)
PHONE..................................718 795-5691
Matthew Turner, *CEO*
EMP: 5
SALES (est): 304.4K **Privately Held**
SIC: 2211 Apparel & outerwear fabrics, cotton

(G-2197)
NIDEC MOTOR CORPORATION
Also Called: KB Electronics
12095 Nw 39th St (33065-2516)
PHONE..................................954 346-4900
Thomas Dalton, *President*
Omar Blackwood, *Vice Pres*
Christopher Heumann, *Project Mgr*
Michael Ipolyi, *Production*
Guillermo Cruz, *Engineer*
EMP: 174 **Privately Held**
WEB: acim.nidec.com
SIC: 3621 3625 Motors, electric; motor controls & accessories
HQ: Nidec Motor Corporation
8050 West Florissant Ave
Saint Louis MO 63136

(G-2198)
NUTRA PHARMA CORP
4001 Nw 73rd Way (33065-2162)
PHONE..................................954 509-0911
Michael Doherty, *Director*
EMP: 8 EST: 2005
SALES (est): 615.7K **Privately Held**
WEB: www.nutrapharma.com
SIC: 2834 Pharmaceutical preparations

(G-2199)
OPENSKY DRONES LLC
12453 Nw 44th St (33065-7639)
PHONE..................................954 340-9125
Howard Melamed, *Manager*
EMP: 6 EST: 2014
SALES (est): 356.6K **Privately Held**
WEB: www.openskydrones.com
SIC: 3721 Motorized aircraft

(G-2200)
ORKA CABINETS INC
12022 Nw 47th St (33076-3536)
PHONE..................................954 907-2456
Adrian Ortiz Sr, *President*
EMP: 8 EST: 2005
SALES (est): 76.1K **Privately Held**
SIC: 2434 Wood kitchen cabinets

(G-2201)
ORVINO IMPORTS & DISTRG INC
11927 W Sample Rd (33065-3164)
PHONE..................................954 785-3100
John Flora, *President*
▲ EMP: 15 EST: 1995
SALES (est): 1.7MM **Privately Held**
WEB: www.orvinowine.com
SIC: 2084 Wines

(G-2202)
ORYZA PHARMACEUTICALS INC
4117 Nw 124th Ave (33065-7633)
PHONE..................................954 881-5481
Jing LI, *Vice Pres*
Nilobon Podhipleux, *Research*
Kelvin Cui, *CFO*
EMP: 24 EST: 2016
SQ FT: 1,000
SALES (est): 3.4MM **Privately Held**
WEB: www.oryzapharma.com
SIC: 2834 Pharmaceutical preparations

(G-2203)
POMPADOUR PRODUCTS INC
1197 Nw 83rd Ave (33071-6720)
PHONE..................................954 345-2700
◆ EMP: 30
SQ FT: 22,000
SALES: 1.5MM **Privately Held**
SIC: 3089 3061 Mfg Plastic Products Mfg Mechanical Rubber Goods

(G-2204)
PRINTMOR
Also Called: Printmor Large Format Printing
3941 Nw 126th Ave (33065-7609)
PHONE..................................954 247-9405
Jonathan Buchnik, *Principal*
EMP: 13 EST: 2016
SALES (est): 1.1MM **Privately Held**
WEB: www.myprintmor.com
SIC: 2752 Commercial printing, lithographic

(G-2205)
RICHARDS MOBILE WELDING
3541 Nw 73rd Way (33065-2136)
PHONE..................................954 913-0487
Richard Sookoo, *Owner*
EMP: 7 EST: 2016
SALES (est): 242.5K **Privately Held**
SIC: 7692 Welding repair

(G-2206)
ROCHESTER ELECTRO-MEDICAL INC
11711 Nw 39th St (33065-2511)
PHONE..................................813 994-7519
Kim Davis, *President*
John Baccoli, *Manager*
EMP: 20 EST: 1967
SQ FT: 7,500
SALES (est): 5.7MM
SALES (corp-wide): 28.3MM **Privately Held**
WEB: www.rochestersuperstore.com
SIC: 3841 Needles, suture
HQ: Advantage Medical Electronics, Llc
11705 Nw 39th St
Coral Springs FL 33065
954 345-9800

(G-2207)
RPERF TECHNOLOGIES CORP
6584 Nw 56th Dr (33067-3540)
PHONE..................................954 629-2359
Roberto Campos, *Principal*
EMP: 10 EST: 2010
SALES (est): 392K **Privately Held**
WEB: www.rperftech.com
SIC: 7372 7379 Educational computer software; computer related consulting services

(G-2208)
RUNAWARE INC
5440 Nw 108th Way (33076-2742)
PHONE..................................954 907-9052
Tim Keys, *CEO*
EMP: 9 EST: 2005
SALES (est): 73.7K **Privately Held**
WEB: main.runaware.com
SIC: 3652 Pre-recorded records & tapes

(G-2209)
SAUGUS VALLEY CORP
Also Called: Sir Speedy
8716 Nw 54th St (33067-2881)
PHONE..................................954 772-4077
Michael Gaby, *President*
EMP: 9 EST: 1972
SQ FT: 2,100
SALES (est): 993.3K **Privately Held**
WEB: www.sirspeedy.com
SIC: 2752 2791 2789 Commercial printing, lithographic; typesetting; bookbinding & related work

(G-2210)
SCENTSABILITY CANDLES
11480 W Sample Rd (33065-7054)
PHONE..................................954 234-4405
Bonnie Schmidt, *Director*
EMP: 7 EST: 2015
SALES (est): 170.4K **Privately Held**
WEB: www.scentsability.org
SIC: 3999 Candles

(G-2211)
SEEMORE SHIRTS & TEES LLC
1829 N University Dr (33071-6001)
PHONE..................................954 708-1100
A Robert S Forman P, *Principal*
EMP: 7 EST: 2018
SALES (est): 528.2K **Privately Held**
WEB: www.seemoreshirtsandtees.com
SIC: 2759 Screen printing

(G-2212)
SIGN A RAMA
Also Called: Sign-A-Rama
10200 W Sample Rd (33065-3940)
PHONE..................................954 796-1644
Lisa A Finch, *Vice Pres*
EMP: 8 EST: 2010
SALES (est): 291.1K **Privately Held**
WEB: www.signarama.com
SIC: 3993 Signs & advertising specialties

(G-2213)
SPIEGEL PAVERS INC
7761 Nw 42nd Pl 1 (33065-1945)
PHONE..................................954 687-5797
Marcio E Vieira, *President*
EMP: 7 EST: 2005
SALES (est): 72K **Privately Held**
SIC: 2951 Asphalt paving mixtures & blocks

(G-2214)
STARR WHEEL GROUP INC
3659 Nw 124th Ave (33065-2445)
PHONE..................................954 935-5536
Ray A Starr Jr, *President*
◆ EMP: 14 EST: 2005
SQ FT: 12,000
SALES (est): 997K **Privately Held**
WEB: www.warriorimport.com
SIC: 3312 Wheels

(G-2215)
SUPERIOR SHADE & BLIND CO INC
11100 Nw 24th St (33065-3645)
PHONE..................................954 975-8122
Alex Fryburg, *Ch of Bd*
David Fryburg, *President*
Robert Fryburg, *Vice Pres*
▼ EMP: 23 EST: 1981
SALES (est): 1.3MM **Privately Held**
WEB: www.superiorshade.com
SIC: 2591 5131 Blinds vertical; knit fabrics

(G-2216)
SURGIMED CORPORATION
9900 W Sample Rd (33065-4048)
PHONE..................................912 674-7660
Leigh Ann Pettyjohn, *President*
Cira Lavoi, *President*
Luis Arias, *Vice Pres*
Alina Lavoi, *Vice Pres*
◆ EMP: 14 EST: 1981
SQ FT: 54,000
SALES (est): 1.9MM **Privately Held**
WEB: www.surgimedcorp.com
SIC: 3841 Surgical & medical instruments

(G-2217)
SYNERGY THERMAL FOILS INC
12175 Nw 39th St (33065-2518)
PHONE..................................954 420-9553
Amir Bakhtyari, *President*
▼ EMP: 13 EST: 2008
SQ FT: 4,000
SALES (est): 2.4MM **Privately Held**
WEB: www.synergythermofoils.com
SIC: 2431 5031 Planing mill, millwork; millwork

(G-2218)
TEAM INKJET
1440 Coral Ridge Dr 339 (33071-5433)
PHONE..................................954 554-3250
Craig S Brockwell, *Principal*
EMP: 8 EST: 2005
SQ FT: 5,000
SALES (est): 534.6K **Privately Held**
SIC: 3955 Print cartridges for laser & other computer printers

(G-2219)
TECHNIPOWER LLC
Also Called: Unipower
210 N University Dr # 700 (33071-7394)
PHONE..................................954 346-2442
Joe Merino, *Vice Pres*
William Kirk, *CFO*
Tom Johnson, *Manager*
▲ EMP: 10 EST: 1952

SALES (est): 1.9MM
SALES (corp-wide): 21.2MM **Privately Held**
SIC: 3679 3612 3699 3643 Power supplies, all types: static; transformers, except electric; electrical equipment & supplies; current-carrying wiring devices
PA: Unipower, Llc
210 N University Dr # 700
Coral Springs FL 33071
954 346-2442

(G-2220)
TESCO EQUIPMENT LLC
3661 Nw 126th Ave (33065-2426)
PHONE..................................954 752-7994
Joe Ward, *Controller*
Rob Osborn, *Sales Staff*
Robert Osborn,
Bea Osborn,
Doug Robertson,
◆ EMP: 42 EST: 1936
SQ FT: 30,000
SALES (est): 9.2MM **Privately Held**
WEB: www.tescohilift.com
SIC: 3713 3537 3728 Truck & bus bodies; industrial trucks & tractors; aircraft parts & equipment

(G-2221)
THINK EDUCATION SOLUTIONS LLC
5411 N University Dr # 203 (33067-4637)
PHONE..................................954 345-7839
Andrew K Davies, *President*
EMP: 9 EST: 2006
SALES (est): 285.6K **Privately Held**
SIC: 7372 Prepackaged software

(G-2222)
TIDWELLS ORTHOTICS AND PROSTHE
4450 Nw 126th Ave Ste 106 (33065-7604)
PHONE..................................954 346-5402
Chris Tidwell, *Principal*
EMP: 8 EST: 2006
SALES (est): 797.9K **Privately Held**
SIC: 3842 Orthopedic appliances

(G-2223)
UNICOMP CORP OF AMERICA
10101 W Sample Rd Stop 1 (33065-3937)
PHONE..................................954 755-1710
Martin Kaplan, *President*
Laura Seiler, *Manager*
EMP: 5 EST: 1979
SALES (est): 546.9K **Privately Held**
WEB: www.ucoa.com
SIC: 7372 7371 Application computer software; custom computer programming services

(G-2224)
VERIFONE INC (HQ)
2744 N University Dr (33065-5111)
P.O. Box 641536, San Jose CA (95164-1536)
PHONE..................................800 837-4366
Mike Puli, *CEO*
Paul Galant, *Principal*
Michael Cho, *Counsel*
Jonathan Cross, *Counsel*
Alok Bhanot, *Exec VP*
◆ EMP: 190 EST: 1981
SALES (est): 468.8MM
SALES (corp-wide): 695.1MM **Privately Held**
WEB: www.verifone.com
SIC: 3578 7372 3577 3575 Point-of-sale devices; operating systems computer software; application computer software; computer peripheral equipment; printers, computer; computer terminals; engineering services; current-carrying wiring devices
PA: Verifone Systems, Inc.
2744 N University Dr
Coral Springs FL 33065
408 232-7800

(G-2225)
VERIFONE SYSTEMS INC (PA)
2744 N University Dr (33065-5111)
PHONE..................................408 232-7800
Mike Pulli, *CEO*
Vin D'Agostino, *Exec VP*

Albert Liu, *Exec VP*
Glen Robson, *Exec VP*
Suzanne Colvin, *Vice Pres*
▲ **EMP:** 170 **EST:** 1981
SALES (est): 695.1MM **Privately Held**
WEB: www.verifone.com
SIC: 3578 7372 Point-of-sale devices; operating systems computer software; application computer software

(G-2226)
VISTAMATIC LLC
Also Called: Privacy Glass Solutions
11713 Nw 39th St (33065-2511)
PHONE........................866 466-9525
Carlos Betancur, *Vice Pres*
Jamie Knight, *Vice Pres*
Adam Hakimi, *Sales Mgr*
Kevin Roth, *Mng Member*
Mark Nash, *Director*
EMP: 25 **EST:** 2009
SQ FT: 2,100
SALES (est): 2.5MM **Privately Held**
WEB: www.privacyglasssolutions.com
SIC: 3211 Window glass, clear & colored

(G-2227)
YAADIE FIESTA GROUP INC
1293 N University Dr (33071-8315)
PHONE........................562 766-8033
Jason Graham, *President*
EMP: 7 **EST:** 2020
SALES (est): 312.6K **Privately Held**
SIC: 2099 Food preparations

Cottondale
Jackson County

(G-2228)
ENVIVA PELLETS COTTONDALE LLC
2500 Green Circle Pkwy (32431-7450)
PHONE........................850 557-7357
Morten Neraas,
EMP: 30 **EST:** 2015
SALES (est): 9.5MM **Privately Held**
SIC: 2493 Reconstituted wood products

(G-2229)
INGRAMS BACKHOE DUMPTRUCK SVC
2155 Roark Rd (32431-7629)
PHONE........................850 718-6042
Rodney L Ingram, *Principal*
EMP: 9 **EST:** 2014
SALES (est): 199.1K **Privately Held**
SIC: 3531 Backhoes

(G-2230)
VAN NEVEL AEROSPACE LLC
1932 Holley Timber Rd (32431-7754)
PHONE........................337 936-2504
Georges Van Nevel, *President*
EMP: 7 **EST:** 2015
SALES (est): 110K **Privately Held**
WEB: www.vannevelaerospace.com
SIC: 3721 Helicopters

Crawfordville
Wakulla County

(G-2231)
OXYGENIX MOLD AND ODOR LLC
467 Parkside Cir (32327-7418)
PHONE........................850 926-5421
EMP: 5
SALES (est): 426.4K **Privately Held**
SIC: 3544 Mfg Dies/Tools/Jigs/Fixtures

(G-2232)
ST MARKS POWDER INC
7121 Coastal Hwy (32327-2918)
P.O. Box 222, Saint Marks (32355-0222)
PHONE........................850 577-2824
Michael S Wilson, *President*
Guy Cornwell, *Vice Pres*
Jim Dudley, *Engineer*
Chris Beidler, *Project Engr*
Jane Kellett, *Finance*
◆ **EMP:** 340 **EST:** 1998

SALES (est): 90.4MM
SALES (corp-wide): 38.4B **Publicly Held**
SIC: 2869 Industrial organic chemicals
HQ: General Dynamics Ordnance And Tactical Systems, Inc.
100 Carillon Pkwy
Saint Petersburg FL 33716
727 578-8100

(G-2233)
WAKULLA NEWS
3119a Crawfordville Hwy (32327-3148)
P.O. Box 307 (32326-0307)
PHONE........................850 926-7102
Tammie Barfield, *General Mgr*
Eric Stanton, *Production*
EMP: 10 **EST:** 1895
SALES (est): 620.4K **Privately Held**
WEB: www.chronicleonline.com
SIC: 2711 5943 Newspapers: publishing only, not printed on site; office forms & supplies

Crescent City
Putnam County

(G-2234)
AMERICAN RESPIRATORY SOLUTIONS (PA)
1125 N Summit St Ste C (32112-1721)
P.O. Box 608 (32112-0608)
PHONE........................386 698-4446
Warren Fletcher, *President*
EMP: 8 **EST:** 1996
SALES (est): 1.3MM **Privately Held**
WEB: www.arscc.com
SIC: 3578 Billing machines

(G-2235)
CHEZ INDUSTRIES LLC
Also Called: Mel Ray Industries
2167 S Us Highway 17 (32112-3903)
P.O. Box 505 (32112-0505)
PHONE........................386 698-4414
Rita King, *Manager*
Anthony Sanchez,
◆ **EMP:** 11 **EST:** 1987
SQ FT: 56,000
SALES (est): 1.8MM **Privately Held**
WEB: www.melray.com
SIC: 3861 5023 Printing frames, photographic; frames & framing, picture & mirror

(G-2236)
HARTCO INTERNATIONAL
2288 S Us Highway 17 (32112-3900)
PHONE........................386 698-4668
Kelly Hart, *President*
EMP: 9 **EST:** 2002
SALES (est): 500.9K **Privately Held**
WEB: www.hartcoseats.com
SIC: 3751 Saddles & seat posts, motorcycle & bicycle

(G-2237)
SAMS GAS
2680 S Us Highway 17 (32112-5122)
PHONE........................386 698-1033
Randy Sams, *Owner*
EMP: 9 **EST:** 2012
SALES (est): 362.3K **Privately Held**
WEB: www.samsgas.com
SIC: 3569 5172 Gas generators; gases, liquefied petroleum (propane)

(G-2238)
SCOTT BREVARD INC
Also Called: King's Office Supply & Prtg Co
306 Central Ave (32112-2608)
PHONE........................386 698-1121
Scott B King, *Owner*
EMP: 5 **EST:** 1977
SQ FT: 2,400
SALES (est): 519K **Privately Held**
WEB: www.kingsofficeandprint.com
SIC: 2752 5943 Letters, circular or form: lithographed; office forms & supplies

(G-2239)
STAR SIGHT INNOVATIONS
107 Tangelo Ter (32112-4527)
PHONE........................307 786-2911
Natalie Corbett, *Vice Pres*

EMP: 6 **EST:** 2003
SALES (est): 421.5K **Privately Held**
SIC: 3432 Lawn hose nozzles & sprinklers

Crestview
Okaloosa County

(G-2240)
BOEING AROSPC OPERATIONS INC
5486 Fairchild Rd Hngr 3 (32539-8411)
PHONE........................850 682-2746
William Grant, *Site Mgr*
EMP: 18
SALES (corp-wide): 62.2B **Publicly Held**
SIC: 3721 Aircraft
HQ: Boeing Aerospace Operations, Inc.
6001 S A Depo Blvd Ste E
Oklahoma City OK 73150
405 622-6000

(G-2241)
CRESTVIEW READY MIX INC
Also Called: Fort Walton Co
1070 Farmer St (32539-8966)
PHONE........................850 682-6117
James Campbell, *President*
EMP: 10 **EST:** 1981
SALES (est): 874.5K **Privately Held**
WEB: www.crestviewreadymix.com
SIC: 3273 Ready-mixed concrete

(G-2242)
CYGNUS AEROSPACE INCORPORATED
1001 Industrial Dr (32539-6943)
PHONE........................850 612-1618
Barry Green, *Opers Staff*
Don Cleveland, *Branch Mgr*
Rick Ballard, *Manager*
EMP: 28
SALES (corp-wide): 3.3MM **Privately Held**
WEB: www.cygnusworld.com
SIC: 3728 Aircraft parts & equipment
PA: Cygnus Aerospace Incorporated
501 Osigian Blvd Ste B
Warner Robins GA 31088
478 333-6110

(G-2243)
EMERALD COAST SIGNS
4563 Rainbird Rise Rd (32539-8231)
P.O. Box 296 (32536-0296)
PHONE........................850 398-1712
Brad Summers, *CEO*
Bobbie Summers,
EMP: 6 **EST:** 2013
SALES (est): 756.9K **Privately Held**
WEB: www.emeraldcoastsigns.com
SIC: 3993 Signs & advertising specialties

(G-2244)
G2C ENTERPRISES INC
695 Sioux Cir (32536-9516)
PHONE........................850 398-5368
Rodney Greenway, *CEO*
Beth Suttles, *Admin Sec*
EMP: 11 **EST:** 2007
SALES (est): 481.1K **Privately Held**
SIC: 1442 Construction sand & gravel

(G-2245)
G2C ENTERPRISES INC
Also Called: Transand
695 Sioux Cir (32536-9516)
PHONE........................850 585-4166
Rodney Greenway, *President*
EMP: 11 **EST:** 2003
SALES (est): 464.4K **Privately Held**
SIC: 1442 Construction sand & gravel

(G-2246)
GULF COAST WILBERT INC (PA)
Also Called: Gulf Coast Monuments
100 Martin St (32536-5119)
P.O. Box 455 (32536-0455)
PHONE........................850 682-8004
David Chapman, *President*
Denise Chapman, *Vice Pres*
Darren Chapman, *Opers Mgr*
EMP: 3 **EST:** 2001

SQ FT: 13,000
SALES (est): 5MM **Privately Held**
WEB: www.gulfcoastwilbert.com
SIC: 3272 Burial vaults, concrete or precast terrazzo

(G-2247)
HOT DOG SHOPPE LLC
1308 N Ferdon Blvd (32536-1714)
PHONE........................850 682-3649
Robert Vogel, *Principal*
EMP: 5 **EST:** 2007
SALES (est): 391.2K **Privately Held**
SIC: 2013 Sausages from purchased meat

(G-2248)
KACHEMAK BAY FLYING SERVICE
Also Called: Kbfs
5545 John Givens Rd (32539-7019)
PHONE........................850 398-8699
EMP: 15 **EST:** 2007
SALES (est): 184.3K **Privately Held**
WEB: www.s3inc.com
SIC: 3728 Aircraft parts & equipment

(G-2249)
L3 CRESTVIEW AEROSPACE
5486 Fairchild Rd (32539-8410)
PHONE........................850 682-2746
Claude W Tignor, *Principal*
Stacy L Johnson, *CFO*
Kelley Henderson, *Human Res Mgr*
EMP: 5 **EST:** 2011
SALES (est): 5.2MM
SALES (corp-wide): 17.8B **Publicly Held**
SIC: 3812 Search & navigation equipment
HQ: L3 Technologies, Inc.
600 3rd Ave Fl 34
New York NY 10016
321 727-9100

(G-2250)
PHILLIPS ENERGY INC (HQ)
806 W James Lee Blvd (32536-5135)
PHONE........................850 682-5127
Rupert E Phillips, *President*
Debora Link, *Vice Pres*
Debora L Link, *Vice Pres*
Mark Link, *Vice Pres*
Alan Payne, *Treasurer*
EMP: 1 **EST:** 2001
SALES (est): 7.6MM
SALES (corp-wide): 44.9MM **Privately Held**
WEB: www.phillipsenergygroup.com
SIC: 2869 Fuels
PA: Phillips Capital Partners, Inc.
42 Busness Cntre Dr Unitt
Miramar Beach FL 32550
850 460-2601

(G-2251)
RED 7 TEES LLC
189 W Oakdale Ave (32536-3513)
PHONE........................850 612-7007
Christopher Linnel,
EMP: 8 **EST:** 2018
SALES (est): 395.6K **Privately Held**
WEB: www.red7tees.com
SIC: 2759 Screen printing

(G-2252)
SEGERS AEROSPACE CORPORATION
5582 Fairchild Rd (32539-5125)
PHONE........................850 689-2198
Jeremy Hovater, *General Mgr*
Eric Blakeney, *Engineer*
Scarlett Conner, *Sales Staff*
Joe Labean, *Manager*
Gretchen Harshberger, *Director*
EMP: 72 **Privately Held**
SIC: 3812 Search & navigation equipment
PA: Segers Aerospace Corporation
8100 Mcgowin Dr
Fairhope AL 36532

(G-2253)
SIGNS GALORE INC
111 Hammock St (32536-1750)
PHONE........................850 683-8010
Michael Rutledge, *President*
EMP: 8 **EST:** 1998
SQ FT: 6,440

▲ = Import ▼=Export
◆ =Import/Export

SALES (est): 932.9K **Privately Held**
WEB: www.signsgaloreinc.com
SIC: 3993 Electric signs

(G-2254)
SOUTHWIRE COMPANY LLC
5680 John Givens Rd (32539-7018)
PHONE..................................850 423-4680
EMP: 142
SALES (corp-wide): 1.7B **Privately Held**
WEB: www.southwire.com
SIC: 3496 5051 Wire fasteners; wire
PA: Southwire Company, Llc
1 Southwire Dr
Carrollton GA 30119
770 832-4242

(G-2255)
STRIVE DEVELOPMENT CORPORATION
Also Called: Custom Production
3100 Adora Teal Way (32539-7039)
P.O. Box 969 (32536-0969)
PHONE..................................850 689-2124
Elizabeth M Skrovanek, *President*
Michael R Skrovanek, *Vice Pres*
Michael Skrovanek, *Vice Pres*
Stanley Zolek, *Vice Pres*
EMP: 16 EST: 1999
SQ FT: 7,500
SALES (est): 10MM **Privately Held**
WEB: www.customproduction.biz
SIC: 3363 Aluminum die-castings

(G-2256)
WILLIAMS COMMUNICATIONS INC
701 Ashley Dr (32536-9231)
PHONE..................................850 689-6651
Hays Amos, *COO*
Clayton Willis, *Technical Mgr*
Hilarie Geraldi, *Sales Mgr*
Chris Watkins, *Branch Mgr*
Christine Odom, *Manager*
EMP: 7
SALES (corp-wide): 18MM **Privately Held**
WEB: www.wmscom.com
SIC: 3663 Radio & TV communications equipment
PA: Williams Communications Inc
5046 Tenn Capitl Blvd
Tallahassee FL 32303
850 385-1121

(G-2257)
WRONGS WITHOUT WREMEDIES LLC
Also Called: Money Tree Publishing
6256 Bullet Dr (32536-4382)
PHONE..................................850 423-0828
David Gahary, *Principal*
EMP: 7 EST: 2015
SALES (est): 153.4K **Privately Held**
WEB: www.poznervfetzer.com
SIC: 2741 Miscellaneous publishing

Cross City
Dixie County

(G-2258)
CROSS CITY LUMBER LLC
59 Ne 132nd Ave (32628-3419)
PHONE..................................352 578-8078
Robert McKagen, *CEO*
EMP: 10 EST: 2019
SALES (est): 1.3MM **Privately Held**
SIC: 2421 5031 5211 Sawmills & planing mills, general; lumber, plywood & mill-work; millwork & lumber

(G-2259)
CROSS CITY VENEER COMPANY INC
106 Ne 180th St (32628-5866)
PHONE..................................352 498-3226
Bolling Jones IV, *President*
David Cannon, *Vice Pres*
EMP: 60 EST: 1960
SQ FT: 1,200

SALES (est): 2.5MM
SALES (corp-wide): 20.7MM **Privately Held**
SIC: 2436 3496 2441 Plywood, softwood; miscellaneous fabricated wire products; nailed wood boxes & shook
PA: Georgia Crate & Basket Co., Inc.
1200 Parnell St
Thomasville GA 31792
229 226-2541

(G-2260)
DIXIE COUNTY ADVOCATE
174 Ne Highway 351 (32628-3120)
P.O. Box 5030 (32628-5030)
PHONE..................................352 498-3312
Lander Herring, *President*
Dewey Hatcher, *Sheriff*
Joey Lender, *Vice Pres*
EMP: 5 EST: 1920
SQ FT: 2,500
SALES (est): 377.3K **Privately Held**
WEB: www.dixiecountysheriff.com
SIC: 2711 Newspapers: publishing only, not printed on site

(G-2261)
M & R SEAFOOD INC
Also Called: Suwannee River Shellfish
Hwy 351a (32628)
P.O. Box 1600 (32628-1600)
PHONE..................................352 498-5150
Nabeen Rama, *Owner*
Maggie Bieli, *Manager*
EMP: 10
SALES (corp-wide): 4.8MM **Privately Held**
SIC: 2091 5146 2092 Canned & cured fish & seafoods; fish & seafoods; fresh or frozen packaged fish
PA: M & R Seafood, Inc.

Old Town FL
352 543-9395

(G-2262)
REEDS METAL MANUFACTURING INC
16454 Se Highway 19 (32628-3527)
P.O. Box 1690 (32628-1690)
PHONE..................................352 498-0100
Bernard Reed, *President*
Lucas Rollison, *Partner*
EMP: 22 EST: 2017
SALES (est): 2MM **Privately Held**
WEB: www.reedsmetals.com
SIC: 3442 3441 Metal doors, sash & trim; fabricated structural metal

(G-2263)
RESOLUTE CROSS CITY LLC
40 Sw 10th St (32628-3558)
PHONE..................................352 498-3363
Kenneth A Shields, *CEO*
Yuri Lewis, *CFO*
Michael Tate, *VP Finance*
Mike Tate, *VP Finance*
Mikka Dey, *Sales Mgr*
◆ EMP: 8 EST: 2013
SALES (est): 5.3MM
SALES (corp-wide): 2.8B **Privately Held**
SIC: 2426 Dimension, hardwood; flooring, hardwood; lumber, hardwood dimension
PA: Resolute Forest Products Inc
1010 Rue De La Gauchetiere O Bu-reau 400
Montreal QC H3B 2
514 875-2160

(G-2264)
RESOLUTE CROSS CY RE HLDNGS LL
40 Sw 10th St (32628-3558)
PHONE..................................352 498-3363
Charlie Miller, *President*
EMP: 12 EST: 2013
SALES (est): 2.5MM
SALES (corp-wide): 2.8B **Privately Held**
SIC: 2426 Hardwood dimension & flooring mills
PA: Resolute Forest Products Inc
1010 Rue De La Gauchetiere O Bu-reau 400
Montreal QC H3B 2
514 875-2160

(G-2265)
VAN AERNAM LOGGING & TRUCKING
Also Called: Van Aernam Timber Manage-ment
County Rd 351 A (32628)
P.O. Box 2189 (32628-2189)
PHONE..................................352 498-5809
John D Van Aernam, *Partner*
Bobby Van Aernam, *Partner*
Frankin Van Aernam, *Partner*
Karen Van Aernam, *Bookkeeper*
EMP: 16 EST: 1989
SALES (est): 2.4MM **Privately Held**
SIC: 2411 0721 Logging camps & contrac-tors; crop planting & protection

Crystal River
Citrus County

(G-2266)
ANTIQUE CRYSTAL GLASS & PRCLN
126 Ne 2nd St (34429-4114)
PHONE..................................352 220-2666
Smith R Dale, *Principal*
EMP: 7 EST: 2012
SALES (est): 132.9K **Privately Held**
SIC: 3211 Antique glass

(G-2267)
B-SCADA INC (PA)
9030 W Fort Island Trl 9a (34429-8001)
PHONE..................................352 564-9610
Allen Ronald Deserranno, *CEO*
Brian S Thornton, *Vice Pres*
Josephine A Nemmers, *CFO*
Joshua M Weeks, *CTO*
EMP: 9 EST: 2001
SALES (est): 1.9MM **Privately Held**
WEB: www.scada.com
SIC: 7372 Prepackaged software

(G-2268)
CABINET STARTUP LLC
7170 N Ira Martin Ave (34428-6847)
PHONE..................................352 795-2655
Steven Jordan, *Principal*
EMP: 6 EST: 2019
SALES (est): 531.4K **Privately Held**
WEB: www.cabinetstartup.com
SIC: 2434 Wood kitchen cabinets

(G-2269)
CENTRAL MAINTENANCE & WLDG INC
6040 N Suncoast Blvd (34428-6711)
PHONE..................................352 795-2817
Bob Forker, *Branch Mgr*
EMP: 75
SQ FT: 5,280
SALES (corp-wide): 70.8MM **Privately Held**
WEB: www.cmw.cc
SIC: 7692 Welding repair
PA: Central Maintenance And Welding Inc.
2620 E Keysville Rd
Lithia FL 33547
813 229-0012

(G-2270)
CITRUS MOTORSPORTS
7800 W Gulf & Lake Hwy (34429)
PHONE..................................352 564-2453
Charles Allan Pope, *Principal*
Linia Doran, *Manager*
EMP: 10 EST: 2006
SALES (est): 160K **Privately Held**
WEB: www.citrusmotorsports.com
SIC: 3711 Motor vehicles & car bodies

(G-2271)
CITRUS PUBLISHING LLC (DH)
Also Called: Citrus County Chronicle, The
1624 N Meadowcrest Blvd (34429-5760)
P.O. Box 1899, Inverness (34451-1899)
PHONE..................................352 563-6363
Mike Abernathy, *President*
Bradford Bautista, *Editor*
Nancy Kennedy, *Editor*
Brian Lapeter, *Editor*
Ken Melton, *Editor*
EMP: 110 EST: 1891

SQ FT: 45,000
SALES (est): 16.1MM **Privately Held**
WEB: www.chronicleonline.com
SIC: 2711 Newspapers: publishing only, not printed on site
HQ: Landmark Community Newspapers, Llc
601 Taylorsville Rd
Shelbyville KY 40065
502 633-4334

(G-2272)
COLITZ MINING CO INC
Also Called: Crystal River Quarries
7040 N Suncoast Blvd (34428-6726)
PHONE..................................352 795-2409
Frank Colitz, *President*
Edward Colitz, *Vice Pres*
Michelle Colitz, *Vice Pres*
EMP: 12 EST: 1940
SQ FT: 1,500
SALES (est): 849.7K **Privately Held**
SIC: 1422 Limestones, ground

(G-2273)
CRYSTAL RIVER QUARRIES INC
Also Called: Red Level Dolomite
7040 N Suncoast Blvd (34428-6726)
P.O. Box 216 (34423-0216)
PHONE..................................352 795-2828
Frank J Colitz Jr, *President*
Edward Colitz, *Corp Secy*
Michelle Colitz, *Vice Pres*
EMP: 24 EST: 1959
SQ FT: 1,500
SALES (est): 3.9MM **Privately Held**
SIC: 1422 3274 2951 Dolomite, crushed & broken-quarrying; lime; asphalt paving mixtures & blocks

(G-2274)
DEEM CABINETS INC
Also Called: DCI Counter Tops
6843 N Citrus Ave Unit A (34428-6904)
PHONE..................................352 795-1402
John Deem, *Vice Pres*
Eric Griffith, *Purchasing*
EMP: 10 EST: 2003
SALES (est): 691.1K **Privately Held**
WEB: www.godeem.com
SIC: 2434 Wood kitchen cabinets

(G-2275)
ELITE CABINET COATINGS
7170 N Ira Martin Ave (34428-6847)
PHONE..................................352 795-2655
Steven Jordan, *Principal*
EMP: 6 EST: 2016
SALES (est): 491.7K **Privately Held**
SIC: 2434 Wood kitchen cabinets

(G-2276)
FRETTO PRINTS INC
Also Called: Shipyard Dog Prints
255 Se Us Highway 19 # 1 (34429-4890)
PHONE..................................904 687-1985
Michael D Fretto, *Principal*
EMP: 8 EST: 2010
SALES (est): 181.1K **Privately Held**
SIC: 2752 Commercial printing, lithographic

(G-2277)
HOUSE OF CABINETS LTD INC
4107 N Citrus Ave (34428-6021)
PHONE..................................352 795-5300
Richard Hayden, *President*
Jerry Bass, *Vice Pres*
EMP: 6 EST: 1991
SALES (est): 515.9K **Privately Held**
SIC: 2434 Wood kitchen cabinets

(G-2278)
QUANTUM REFLEX INTEGRATION INC
716 Sw Kings Bay Dr (34429-4653)
PHONE..................................352 228-0766
Bruce L Brandes, *Vice Pres*
EMP: 8 EST: 2012
SALES (est): 233.9K **Privately Held**
WEB: www.reflexintegration.net
SIC: 3572 Computer storage devices

(G-2279)
R T INDUSTRIES INC
4926 N Coleus Ter (34428-6359)
PHONE...................................352 427-2632
David Phillips, *Principal*
EMP: 8 EST: 2017
SALES (est): 61.5K **Privately Held**
SIC: 3999 Manufacturing industries

(G-2280)
SIBEX INC (PA)
Also Called: Sibex Systems Division
430 N Suncoast Blvd (34429-5466)
P.O. Box 159, Safety Harbor (34695-0159)
PHONE...................................727 726-4343
Michael J McCarthy, *President*
Glenn Ficco, *Prdtn Mgr*
Mary Drury, *Mfg Spvr*
Wendy Macintyre, *Purch Mgr*
Glenna Mitchell, *Purch Mgr*
EMP: 125 EST: 1983
SQ FT: 120,000
SALES (est): 23.4MM **Privately Held**
WEB: www.powerdesignerssibex.com
SIC: 3672 3679 3699 Printed circuit
   boards; electronic circuits; electrical
   equipment & supplies

Cutler Bay
Miami-Dade County

(G-2281)
A & R KITCHEN CABINET CORP
19100 Sw 106th Ave Unit 5 (33157-7643)
PHONE...................................305 338-3326
Alexei Ruiz, *Principal*
EMP: 8 EST: 2010
SALES (est): 122.8K **Privately Held**
SIC: 2434 Wood kitchen cabinets

(G-2282)
**ADVANCED PHARMA
RESEARCH INC**
10700 Caribbean Blvd # 30 (33189-1232)
PHONE...................................786 234-3709
Jennifer Diaz, *President*
EMP: 12 EST: 2016
SALES (est): 939.6K **Privately Held**
WEB: www.advancedpharmacr.com
SIC: 2834 Pharmaceutical preparations

(G-2283)
ALL PRO INK LLC
10878 Sw 188th St (33157-6745)
PHONE...................................305 252-7644
Johnny Lester, *Owner*
EMP: 8 EST: 2012
SALES (est): 252.1K **Privately Held**
SIC: 2759 Screen printing

(G-2284)
B & R PRODUCTS INC (PA)
18721 Sw 104th Ave (33157-6832)
P.O. Box 970671, Miami (33197-0671)
PHONE...................................305 238-1592
W Robert Millard III, *Exec VP*
Wrobert Millard III, *Vice Pres*
Alodel Gray, *Vice Pres*
Gene Henning, *Vice Pres*
James Ross, *Vice Pres*
▲ EMP: 18 EST: 1977
SQ FT: 15,000
SALES (est): 48.7MM **Privately Held**
WEB: www.brpro.com
SIC: 2844 2899 5169 Hair preparations,
   including shampoos; chemical prepara-
   tions; chemicals & allied products

(G-2285)
CONTAINER MFG SOLUTIONS
Also Called: Cows USA
10460 Sw 186th St (33157-6701)
PHONE...................................888 805-8785
Ana Frank, *CEO*
Ana M Frank, *CEO*
EMP: 20 EST: 2019
SALES (est): 1.1MM **Privately Held**
SIC: 2448 Cargo containers, wood & wood
   with metal

(G-2286)
**CUSTOM CARPENTRY PLUS
LLC**
9801 Bel Aire Dr (33157-7854)
PHONE...................................305 972-3735
Joel Hernandez, *Mng Member*
Maria Carmen Hernandez, *Mng Member*
EMP: 15 EST: 2012
SALES (est): 4MM **Privately Held**
SIC: 2434 7389 Wood kitchen cabinets;

(G-2287)
DANIELS OFFSET PRINTING INC
8541 Franjo Rd (33189-2508)
PHONE...................................305 261-3263
Steve Grimes, *President*
Sue Grimes, *Vice Pres*
EMP: 7 EST: 1949
SQ FT: 6,000
SALES (est): 507.1K **Privately Held**
WEB: www.danielsprinting.net
SIC: 2752 Commercial printing, offset

(G-2288)
DEAKO COATINGS CHEMICAL
10459 Sw 185th Ter (33157-6755)
PHONE...................................305 323-9914
Suzanne Crossland, *Principal*
EMP: 12 EST: 1973
SALES (est): 330.5K **Privately Held**
SIC: 2851 Paints & allied products

(G-2289)
GLOBAL STONE CORP
10780 Sw 188th St (33157-6779)
PHONE...................................786 601-2459
EMP: 10 EST: 2019
SALES (est): 1.5MM **Privately Held**
SIC: 3281 Cut stone & stone products

(G-2290)
**GREEN GLOBAL ENERGY
SYSTEMS**
18868 Sw 80th Ct (33157-7426)
PHONE...................................305 253-3413
Siria Thomas, *President*
Emilio Patrxot, *Exec VP*
Jose Sanchez, *VP Sales*
EMP: 10 EST: 2009
SQ FT: 2,000
SALES (est): 520.1K **Privately Held**
WEB: www.ggesled.com
SIC: 3646 5063 Commercial indusl & insti-
   tutional electric lighting fixtures; lighting
   fixtures

(G-2291)
HONCHIN INC
Also Called: Signs By Design of Miami
10397 Sw 186th St (33157-6824)
PHONE...................................305 235-3800
Honson Chin, *President*
Ingrid Chin, *Vice Pres*
EMP: 7 EST: 1988
SQ FT: 3,000
SALES (est): 483.4K **Privately Held**
WEB: www.signsbydesignofmiami.net
SIC: 3993 Signs & advertising specialties

(G-2292)
**INDUSTRIAL CNVEYOR
SYSTEMS INC**
18693 Sw 103rd Ct (33157-6837)
P.O. Box 972420, Miami (33197-2420)
PHONE...................................305 255-0200
Darrel Padgett, *President*
Diann Padgett, *Admin Sec*
EMP: 10 EST: 1978
SQ FT: 16,000
SALES (est): 2.1MM **Privately Held**
WEB: www.icsmachinery.com
SIC: 3523 3531 Barn, silo, poultry, dairy &
   livestock machinery; soil preparation ma-
   chinery, except turf & grounds; construc-
   tion machinery

(G-2293)
LAMB TEC INC
7755 Sw 193rd Ln (33157-7396)
P.O. Box 566073, Miami (33256-6073)
PHONE...................................305 798-6266
Juan F Cordero, *President*
EMP: 7 EST: 2000

SALES (est): 512.9K **Privately Held**
WEB: www.lambtec.com
SIC: 7372 7389 Business oriented com-
   puter software;

(G-2294)
**LIGHT AND SOUND EQUIPMENT
INC**
Also Called: Lase
10777 Sw 188th St (33157-9001)
PHONE...................................305 233-3737
Robert Wong, *President*
Winston Chin-Quee, *Vice Pres*
Paul Chin-Quee, *Manager*
▼ EMP: 5 EST: 1984
SALES (est): 499.2K **Privately Held**
SIC: 3651 3648 Speaker systems; lighting
   equipment

(G-2295)
MAHAN CABINETS
Also Called: D Mahan Cabinets
10471 Sw 184th Ter (33157-6761)
PHONE...................................305 255-3325
Dennis Mahan, *Owner*
EMP: 5 EST: 1979
SQ FT: 3,600
SALES (est): 477.2K **Privately Held**
SIC: 2434 2541 Wood kitchen cabinets;
   wood partitions & fixtures

(G-2296)
MIAMI ASPHALT STRIPING
10400 Sw 186th Ln (33157-6722)
PHONE...................................305 386-3253
Augustin Rey, *Owner*
EMP: 7 EST: 2002
SALES (est): 61.4K **Privately Held**
SIC: 3999 Manufacturing industries

(G-2297)
MINUTEMAN PRESS
22469 Sw 103rd Ave (33190-1763)
PHONE...................................305 242-6800
Tonya McHugh, *Owner*
EMP: 9 EST: 2009
SALES (est): 142.5K **Privately Held**
WEB: www.minutemanpress.com
SIC: 2752 Commercial printing, litho-
   graphic

(G-2298)
MWG COMPANY INC
10665 Sw 185th Ter (33157-6798)
P.O. Box 971202, Miami (33197-1202)
PHONE...................................305 232-7344
Ned Scheer, *President*
Jean Gwinn, *Principal*
Judy Scheer, *Admin Sec*
EMP: 8 EST: 1984
SQ FT: 1,200
SALES (est): 621K **Privately Held**
WEB: www.mwgco.com
SIC: 3484 Guns (firearms) or gun parts, 30
   mm. & below

(G-2299)
PINTO PALMA SOUND LLC
10665 Sw 190th St # 3103 (33157-7651)
PHONE...................................877 959-1815
Rafael Torres, *Manager*
EMP: 20 EST: 2019
SALES (est): 961.6K **Privately Held**
SIC: 3596 Truck (motor vehicle) scales

(G-2300)
PRO KITCHEN CABINETS CORP
10675 Sw 190th St Ste 110 (33157-7652)
PHONE...................................786 768-4291
Nelson M Guerra, *Principal*
EMP: 8 EST: 2012
SALES (est): 258.5K **Privately Held**
SIC: 2434 Wood kitchen cabinets

(G-2301)
**RONNIES WELDING & MACHINE
INC**
18640 Sw 104th Ct (33157-6704)
PHONE...................................305 238-0972
Carl Wysong, *President*
Ronald Dennis, *Shareholder*
◆ EMP: 7 EST: 1959

SALES (est): 901.3K **Privately Held**
WEB: www.ronniesusa.com
SIC: 3532 5084 3546 3531 Drills &
   drilling equipment, mining (except oil &
   gas); drilling equipment, excluding bits;
   power-driven handtools; construction machinery

(G-2302)
SLEEPY DRAGON STUDIOS INC
22814 Sw 88th Path (33190-1358)
PHONE...................................561 714-6156
Juan Borrero, *CEO*
Alex Martinez, *Principal*
Vanessa Velasquez, *Vice Pres*
EMP: 6 EST: 2012
SALES (est): 330.3K **Privately Held**
SIC: 7372 7371 7812 7389 Home enter-
   tainment computer software; software
   programming applications; motion picture
   & video production; ; commercial art &
   graphic design; creative services to ad-
   vertisers, except writers

(G-2303)
SOLAIR GROUP LLC
10421 Sw 187th Ter (33157-6726)
PHONE...................................786 269-0160
Todd Dauphinais, *CEO*
Wesley Yale Jr, *President*
Dorothy Tilghman, *COO*
Glen Price, *Opers Staff*
Rafael Aguilar, *CFO*
EMP: 28 EST: 2015
SQ FT: 20,000
SALES (est): 2.8MM **Privately Held**
WEB: www.solairgroup.com
SIC: 3728 Aircraft parts & equipment

(G-2304)
SOUTH FLORIDA MARINE
Also Called: Marine Pleasure Craft
19301 Sw 106th Ave Ste 13 (33157-7647)
PHONE...................................305 232-8788
Steven Cefalu, *President*
William Head, *Partner*
EMP: 7 EST: 2005
SALES (est): 500K **Privately Held**
SIC: 3531 3585 1711 7623 Marine re-
   lated equipment; air conditioning equip-
   ment, complete; parts for heating, cooling
   & refrigerating equipment; plumbing,
   heating, air-conditioning contractors; air
   conditioning repair; ice making machinery
   repair service

(G-2305)
**SUN & EARTH MICROBIOLOGY
LLC**
20205 Sw 79th Ct (33189-2173)
PHONE...................................786 354-8894
V G Plasencia, *Principal*
EMP: 5 EST: 2018
SALES (est): 367.6K **Privately Held**
WEB: www.sunearthmicrobiology.com
SIC: 2835 Microbiology & virology diagnos-
   tic products

(G-2306)
TREADSTONE PERFORMANCE
10340 Sw 187th St (33157-6827)
PHONE...................................305 972-9600
Jason Stone, *Principal*
EMP: 12 EST: 2013
SALES (est): 3.7MM **Privately Held**
WEB: www.treadstoneperformance.com
SIC: 3714 Motor vehicle parts & acces-
   sories

(G-2307)
**TREADSTONE PRFMCE ENGRG
INC**
9486 Sw 222nd Ln (33190-1467)
PHONE...................................888 789-4586
Jason Stone, *President*
◆ EMP: 13 EST: 2010
SALES (est): 107.5K **Privately Held**
WEB: www.treadstoneperformance.com
SIC: 3714 Motor vehicle parts & acces-
   sories

(G-2308)
TRUBENDZ TECHNOLOGY INC
18495 S Dixie Hwy Ste 213 (33157-6817)
PHONE...................................305 378-9337
Joshua Kunkowski, *President*

▲ = Import ▼=Export
◆ =Import/Export

EMP: 35
SALES (corp-wide): 620.7K **Privately Held**
WEB: www.trubendz.com
SIC: 3498 Tube fabricating (contract bending & shaping)
PA: Trubendz Technology Inc.
19101 Sw 108th Ave # 19
Cutler Bay FL 33157
305 378-9337

(G-2309)
TRUBENDZ TECHNOLOGY INC (PA)
Also Called: Mandrel Exhaust Systems
19101 Sw 108th Ave # 19 (33157-6797)
PHONE..................................305 378-9337
Joshua Kunkowski, *President*
EMP: 6 **EST:** 2003
SALES (est): 620.7K **Privately Held**
WEB: www.trubendz.com
SIC: 3498 Tube fabricating (contract bending & shaping)

(G-2310)
VERDE SPEED MACHINE SHOP CORP
10780 Sw 190th St (33157-7618)
PHONE..................................305 233-3299
EMP: 7 **EST:** 2018
SALES (est): 414.6K **Privately Held**
SIC: 3599 Machine shop, jobbing & repair

(G-2311)
VIKING KABINETS INC
10445 Sw 186th Ln (33157-6721)
PHONE..................................305 238-9025
Mike Fulford, *President*
Kevin Keenan, *Vice Pres*
▼ **EMP:** 25 **EST:** 1969
SQ FT: 12,000
SALES (est): 2.7MM **Privately Held**
WEB: www.vikingkabinets.com
SIC: 2431 2511 Millwork; wood household furniture

(G-2312)
WILL-RITE INDUSTRIES INC
10853 Sw 188th St (33157-6744)
PHONE..................................305 253-1985
Lyle Glen Willis, *President*
Loreda Willis, *Corp Secy*
Jeffery Willis, *Vice Pres*
EMP: 5 **EST:** 1982
SQ FT: 2,000
SALES (est): 318.2K **Privately Held**
SIC: 2752 Commercial printing, lithographic

Dade City
Pasco County

(G-2313)
ANNA FLORER
20426 Peachtree Ln (33523-1218)
PHONE..................................352 424-2210
Anna Florer, *Principal*
EMP: 7 **EST:** 2002
SALES (est): 133.9K **Privately Held**
WEB: www.jdmachineco.com
SIC: 3499 Fabricated metal products

(G-2314)
CCA INDUSTRIES INC
13010 Us Highway 301 (33525-5419)
PHONE..................................813 601-6238
Timothy Linville, *President*
EMP: 9 **EST:** 2005
SQ FT: 3,904
SALES (est): 359.7K **Privately Held**
SIC: 3999 Manufacturing industries

(G-2315)
CHAMBERS BODY WORKS INC
16556 Old Johnston Rd (33523-7311)
PHONE..................................352 588-3072
Michael Chambers, *President*
EMP: 5 **EST:** 1991
SALES (est): 518.1K **Privately Held**
WEB: www.airflo.net
SIC: 3799 Trailers & trailer equipment

(G-2316)
CLARKWSTERN DTRICH BLDG SYSTEM
38020 Pulp Dr (33523-6013)
PHONE..................................800 543-7140
Bill Courtney, *Branch Mgr*
Mike Gaskins, *Branch Mgr*
EMP: 20 **Privately Held**
WEB: www.clarkdietrich.com
SIC: 3444 Sheet metalwork
HQ: Clarkwestern Dietrich Building Systems Llc
9050 Cntre Pnte Dr Ste 40
West Chester OH 45069

(G-2317)
DELANEY RESOURCES INC
8831 Janmar Rd (33525-0718)
PHONE..................................863 670-5924
John Delaney, *President*
Debra Delaney, *Vice Pres*
EMP: 7 **EST:** 2003
SALES (est): 837.2K **Privately Held**
WEB: www.delaneyresources.com
SIC: 3523 Grading, cleaning, sorting machines, fruit, grain, vegetable

(G-2318)
GENOS CONSTRUCTION INC ✪
12421 Us Highway 301 # 228 (33525-6018)
PHONE..................................234 303-3427
Anthony Geno Martinson, *Principal*
EMP: 62 **EST:** 2021
SALES (est): 1.7MM **Privately Held**
SIC: 1389 Construction, repair & dismantling services

(G-2319)
INK & TONER PLUS
10149 Connerly Rd (33525-1661)
PHONE..................................813 783-1650
Barbara Lycans, *Principal*
EMP: 6 **EST:** 2008
SALES (est): 340.4K **Privately Held**
SIC: 3861 Toners, prepared photographic (not made in chemical plants)

(G-2320)
JIM RINALDOS CABINETRY INC
37828 Sky Ridge Cir (33525-0878)
PHONE..................................813 788-2715
Jim Rinaldo, *President*
EMP: 19 **EST:** 1980
SQ FT: 6,500
SALES (est): 619.6K **Privately Held**
WEB: www.jrcab.com
SIC: 2434 Wood kitchen cabinets

(G-2321)
NEW LINE TRANSPORT LLC
Also Called: Trans - Cem Dade City
9931 Old Lakeland Hwy (33525-0702)
PHONE..................................305 223-9200
John Cooper, *Branch Mgr*
EMP: 27 **Privately Held**
WEB: www.newlinetransport.com
SIC: 3271 Concrete block & brick
HQ: New Line Transport, Llc
1204 Nw 137th Ave
Miami FL 33182
561 833-5555

(G-2322)
REFRESCO BEVERAGES US INC
15340 Citrus Country Dr (33523-6009)
PHONE..................................352 567-2200
Keith Teske, *Branch Mgr*
EMP: 15 **Privately Held**
WEB: www.refresco-na.com
SIC: 2086 Soft drinks: packaged in cans, bottles, etc.
PA: Refresco Beverages Us Inc.
8118 Woodland Center Blvd
Tampa FL 33614

(G-2323)
ROBERTS VAULT CO INC
14621 Roberts Barn Rd (33523-7535)
PHONE..................................352 567-0110
Stephen E Roberts, *President*
C E Roberts, *President*
Craig Roberts, *Vice Pres*
Greg Roberts, *Vice Pres*
Steve Roberts, *Vice Pres*

EMP: 33 **EST:** 1963
SQ FT: 46,000
SALES (est): 6.1MM **Privately Held**
WEB: www.robertsvault.com
SIC: 3272 Burial vaults, concrete or precast terrazzo

(G-2324)
SOUTH PACIFIC TRADING COMPANY
Also Called: Tampa Bay Copack
15340 Citrus Country Dr (33523-6009)
PHONE..................................352 567-2200
William Foley, *CEO*
Lenne Nicklaus, *Vice Pres*
Valerie Hval, *Treasurer*
Andy Powell, *Director*
Deborah L Nicklaus, *Admin Sec*
▲ **EMP:** 40 **EST:** 2001
SQ FT: 76,000
SALES (est): 5.2MM **Privately Held**
WEB: www.southeast-bottling.com
SIC: 2086 Mineral water, carbonated: packaged in cans, bottles, etc.

(G-2325)
YOS BOTTLING LLC
15240 Citrus Country Dr (33523-6003)
PHONE..................................863 258-6820
Ramon Campos, *Mng Member*
EMP: 10 **EST:** 2019
SALES (est): 726.2K **Privately Held**
SIC: 2087 Beverage bases

Dania
Broward County

(G-2326)
ALL AMERICAN BUILDING PRODUCTS
401 Se 10th St (33004-4536)
PHONE..................................786 718-7300
Javier Martinez, *Principal*
EMP: 8 **EST:** 2010
SALES (est): 150K **Privately Held**
WEB: www.aabpinc.com
SIC: 3448 Prefabricated metal buildings

(G-2327)
BONA ENTERPRISES INC (PA)
255 E Dania Beach Blvd (33004-3083)
PHONE..................................954 927-4889
Frank Bona Jr, *President*
John R Bona, *Director*
EMP: 7 **EST:** 1986
SALES (est): 7.5MM **Privately Held**
SIC: 2426 Flooring, hardwood

(G-2328)
BROWARD MACHINE LLC
2070 Tigertail Blvd Ste D (33004-2111)
PHONE..................................954 920-8004
Joseph T Vennaro, *Principal*
EMP: 8 **EST:** 2015
SALES (est): 383.5K **Privately Held**
WEB: www.browardmachine.com
SIC: 3599 Machine shop, jobbing & repair

(G-2329)
BROWARD YARD & MARINE LLC
Also Called: Broward Marine
750 Ne 7th Ave (33004-2502)
PHONE..................................954 927-4119
Pete Snyder, *Purchasing*
Thomas Lewis, *Mng Member*
◆ **EMP:** 98 **EST:** 1948
SALES (est): 2.8MM **Privately Held**
WEB: www.browardmarine.com
SIC: 3732 4493 Yachts, building & repairing; yacht basins

(G-2330)
COMMERCIAL METALS COMPANY
Ft Ladrdale Fab Rnfrcing Stl D
2025 Tigertail Blvd (33004-2106)
PHONE..................................954 921-2500
Steve Parks, *Branch Mgr*
Matt Dykstra, *Director*
EMP: 48

SALES (corp-wide): 8.9B **Publicly Held**
WEB: www.cmc.com
SIC: 3449 3496 Bars, concrete reinforcing: fabricated steel; miscellaneous fabricated wire products
PA: Commercial Metals Company
6565 N Macarthur Blvd # 800
Irving TX 75039
214 689-4300

(G-2331)
EL CUSTOM WOOD CREATIONS INC
2004 Tigertail Blvd (33004-2145)
PHONE..................................786 337-0014
EMP: 6 **EST:** 2018
SALES (est): 342.5K **Privately Held**
WEB: www.elcustomwoodcreations.com
SIC: 2431 Millwork

(G-2332)
HKI SOUNDIGITAL USA LLC
345 Bryan Rd (33004-2363)
PHONE..................................786 600-1056
Diogo Ianaconi, *President*
EMP: 7 **EST:** 2016
SALES (est): 284K **Privately Held**
SIC: 3651 Amplifiers: radio, public address or musical instrument

(G-2333)
INTREPID POWERBOATS INC (HQ)
805 Ne E 3rd St (33004)
PHONE..................................954 324-4196
Charles K Clinton, *President*
Alex Rizo, *Vice Pres*
Doug Denorcy, *Senior Buyer*
Stephen Wedde, *VP Engrg*
Shawn Banks, *QC Mgr*
▲ **EMP:** 46 **EST:** 1992
SQ FT: 120,000
SALES (est): 50MM
SALES (corp-wide): 2B **Publicly Held**
WEB: www.intrepidpowerboats.com
SIC: 3732 Boats, fiberglass: building & repairing
PA: Marinemax, Inc.
2600 Mccormick Dr Ste 200
Clearwater FL 33759
727 531-1700

(G-2334)
IRONCLAD WELDING INC
1205 Sw 4th Ave (33004-3905)
P.O. Box 1868 (33004-1868)
PHONE..................................954 925-7987
William J Stamm, *President*
EMP: 5 **EST:** 1977
SQ FT: 3,000
SALES (est): 442.4K **Privately Held**
WEB: www.ironcladweldinginc.com
SIC: 7692 Welding repair

(G-2335)
MACHINE TOP LLC
720 Sw 4th Ct (33004-3803)
PHONE..................................786 238-8926
Imanuel Hazan, *Principal*
EMP: 11 **EST:** 2014
SALES (est): 674.6K **Privately Held**
WEB: www.machinetopusa.com
SIC: 3599 Machine shop, jobbing & repair

(G-2336)
MARINER INTERNATIONAL TRVL INC
Also Called: Mooring Yacht Brokerage
850 Ne 3rd St Ste 201 (33004-3418)
PHONE..................................954 925-4150
Richard Vass, *Broker*
Dianne Franklin, *Branch Mgr*
Bill Regan, *Consultant*
EMP: 7
SALES (corp-wide): 5.5B **Privately Held**
WEB: www.moorings.com
SIC: 3732 4724 Yachts, building & repairing; travel agencies
HQ: Mariner International Travel, Inc.
93 N Park Place Blvd
Clearwater FL 33759

(G-2337)
MICROMICR CORPORATION
35 Sw 12th Ave Ste 112 (33004-3530)
PHONE......................................954 922-8044
Michael Axelrod, *President*
Chris Schoeller, *COO*
EMP: 20 EST: 1990
SQ FT: 16,600
SALES (est): 1.2MM **Privately Held**
WEB: www.micro-micr.com
SIC: 3955 Print cartridges for laser & other computer printers

(G-2338)
MYDOR INDUSTRIES INC
470 Sw 9th St (33004-3836)
PHONE......................................954 927-1140
Marcel Kon, *President*
Stuart Kaufman, *President*
Doris Kaufman, *Corp Secy*
EMP: 6 EST: 1983
SQ FT: 6,000
SALES (est): 532.3K **Privately Held**
SIC: 2899 3826 2833 Water treating compounds; water testing apparatus; medicinal chemicals

(G-2339)
NEW T MANAGEMENT INC
255 E Dania Beach Blvd # 2 (33004-3083)
PHONE......................................954 927-4889
Frank J Bona Jr, *Principal*
EMP: 8 EST: 2008
SALES (est): 118.2K **Privately Held**
SIC: 2426 Flooring, hardwood

(G-2340)
PAGE ONE LLC
1231 Stirling Rd Ste 107 (33004-3567)
PHONE......................................833 467-2431
Keith Obrien,
EMP: 10 EST: 2019
SALES (est): 508.1K **Privately Held**
WEB: www.page.one
SIC: 2741

(G-2341)
PARK PLUS FLORIDA INC
1111 Old Griffin Rd (33004-2224)
PHONE......................................954 929-7511
Colin Lawrence, *President*
Robert Stone, *Mfg Staff*
Ron Astrup, *CFO*
Aj Jenkins, *Sales Staff*
Abbie Rombaoa, *Administration*
EMP: 10 EST: 2014
SALES (est): 1.5MM **Privately Held**
WEB: www.parkplusinc.com
SIC: 3559 Parking facility equipment & supplies

(G-2342)
RABUD INC
110 N Bryan Rd (33004-2244)
PHONE......................................954 925-4199
Ralph Brown, *President*
Patricia Brown, *Corp Secy*
EMP: 7 EST: 1976
SQ FT: 45,000
SALES (est): 935.1K **Privately Held**
WEB: www.rabud.com
SIC: 3732 Boat building & repairing

(G-2343)
STONEHENGE ARCHITECTURAL CORP
308 Se 5th St (33004-4719)
PHONE......................................954 325-6729
Sigmund Ringoen, *President*
France Gagnge, *Corp Secy*
EMP: 5 EST: 2003
SALES (est): 446.7K **Privately Held**
SIC: 3272 Concrete products, precast; columns, concrete

(G-2344)
TECHNICRAFT PLASTICS INC
1253 Stirling Rd (33004-3555)
PHONE......................................954 927-2575
Ken Kholos, *President*
EMP: 15 EST: 1996
SQ FT: 17,000
SALES (est): 2.4MM **Privately Held**
WEB: www.technicraftplastics.com
SIC: 3089 Injection molding of plastics

(G-2345)
TOTAL WINDOW INC
1249 Stirling Rd Ste 15 (33004-3554)
PHONE......................................954 921-0109
Stephen Stolow, *President*
Cheryl Stolow, *Corp Secy*
Jesse Stolow, *COO*
Ryan Locke, *Assistant*
▼ EMP: 8 EST: 1985
SQ FT: 1,200
SALES (est): 1.4MM **Privately Held**
WEB: www.totalwindow.com
SIC: 2591 5023 Window blinds; venetian blinds

(G-2346)
WINDWARD ASSOCIATES CORP
265 Bryan Rd (33004-2207)
PHONE......................................954 336-8085
Winfield C Austin, *President*
▼ EMP: 10 EST: 2004
SALES (est): 376.6K **Privately Held**
SIC: 2434 Wood kitchen cabinets

(G-2347)
ZEBRA STRIPES INC
915 Nw 7th St (33004-2311)
PHONE......................................561 685-0654
Daniel D Healy, *President*
EMP: 7 EST: 2001
SALES (est): 192K **Privately Held**
WEB: www.zebrastripes.com
SIC: 3993 Signs & advertising specialties

Dania Beach
Broward County

(G-2348)
AMERICAN EPOXY COATINGS LLC
1340 Stirling Rd Ste 1a (33004-3561)
PHONE......................................954 850-1169
Daniel Bowman, *CEO*
EMP: 10 EST: 2017
SALES (est): 781.4K **Privately Held**
SIC: 2821 Epoxy resins

(G-2349)
BOGANTEC CORP
1300 Stirling Rd (33004-3545)
PHONE......................................954 217-0023
Francisco J Bogan Sr, *President*
Juan M Bogan Sr, *Vice Pres*
EMP: 9 EST: 2010
SALES (est): 1.3MM **Privately Held**
WEB: bogantec-corp.hub.biz
SIC: 3531 Marine related equipment

(G-2350)
DANIA CUT HOLDINGS INC
Also Called: Dania Cut Super Yacht Repair
760 Ne 7th Ave (33004-2502)
PHONE......................................954 923-9545
Earl R Macpherson, *President*
Kevin Klar, *Vice Pres*
Bruce Chee, *Opers Staff*
▼ EMP: 12 EST: 2009
SALES (est): 1.6MM **Privately Held**
WEB: www.daniacut.com
SIC: 3732 Yachts, building & repairing

(G-2351)
FLORIDA DERECKTOR INC (PA)
Also Called: Derecktor of Florida
775 Taylor Ln (33004-2536)
PHONE......................................954 920-5756
Cliff Defreitas, *General Mgr*
Mike Wight, *General Mgr*
Eric P Derecktor, *Principal*
Ken Imondi, *COO*
Daniel Cantor, *Project Mgr*
▲ EMP: 124 EST: 1967
SQ FT: 47,000
SALES (est): 22.7MM **Privately Held**
WEB: www.derecktor.com
SIC: 3732 Yachts, building & repairing

(G-2352)
JOHNSON & JOHNSON
1024 Se 3rd Ave Apt 304 (33004-5210)
PHONE......................................954 534-1141
EMP: 80

SALES (corp-wide): 82.5B **Publicly Held**
SIC: 2676 Mfg Consumer Products & Surgical Appliances
PA: Johnson & Johnson
1 Johnson And Johnson Plz
New Brunswick NJ 08933
732 524-0400

(G-2353)
MADAN CORPORATION (PA)
Also Called: Madan Kosher Foods
130 Sw 3rd Ave (33004-3656)
PHONE......................................954 925-0077
Samuel Weiss, *President*
EMP: 9 EST: 1969
SQ FT: 10,000
SALES (est): 848.3K **Privately Held**
SIC: 2038 5812 5084 Frozen specialties; caterers; industrial machinery & equipment

(G-2354)
MARWARE INC
Also Called: Marblue
1206 Stirling Rd Bay 9a-B (33004-3552)
PHONE......................................954 927-6031
Edward W Martin, *CEO*
Maria A Martin, *President*
▲ EMP: 22 EST: 1993
SQ FT: 6,350
SALES (est): 2.3MM **Privately Held**
SIC: 7372 5065 Prepackaged software; electronic parts & equipment

(G-2355)
MASSIMO & UMBERTO INC
Also Called: Mrs. Pasta
132 Sw 3rd Ave (33004-3656)
PHONE......................................954 993-0842
Umberto Costa, *Principal*
EMP: 5 EST: 2010
SALES (est): 358.2K **Privately Held**
SIC: 2099 Noodles, uncooked: packaged with other ingredients

(G-2356)
MAT INDUSTRIES LLC
1815 Griffin Rd Ste 400 (33004-2252)
PHONE......................................847 821-9630
EMP: 56 **Privately Held**
SIC: 3563 Air & gas compressors
HQ: Mat Industries, Llc
6700 Wildlife Way
Long Grove IL 60047

(G-2357)
ORTHOSENSOR INC (HQ)
1855 Griffin Rd Ste A310 (33004-2401)
PHONE......................................954 577-7770
Ivan Delevic, *CEO*
Marty Trabish, *General Mgr*
Eric Christopher, *Business Mgr*
Douglas Leach, *Vice Pres*
Jason McIntosh, *Vice Pres*
EMP: 86 EST: 2007
SALES (est): 24.6MM
SALES (corp-wide): 17.1B **Publicly Held**
WEB: ifu.stryker.com
SIC: 3845 Electrotherapeutic apparatus
PA: Stryker Corporation
2825 Airview Blvd
Portage MI 49002
269 385-2600

(G-2358)
POSEIDON WINDOW TREATMENTS LLC
1942 Tigertail Blvd (33004-2139)
PHONE......................................954 920-1112
Alina Garcia, *President*
Manny Garcia, *VP Opers*
Alex Garcia, *VP Mktg*
EMP: 12 EST: 2012
SQ FT: 9,000
SALES (est): 1.6MM
SALES (corp-wide): 1.7MM **Privately Held**
WEB: www.poseidoninteriors.com
SIC: 2591 Window blinds
PA: Florida International Blind Factory Depot, Inc.
1940 Tigertail Blvd
Dania FL 33004
954 920-1112

(G-2359)
RADIACTION INC ○
1855 Griffin Rd Ste A309 (33004-2291)
PHONE......................................561 351-3697
Jonathan Yifat, *CEO*
Steven Lotz, *Vice Pres*
Nitzan Shalit, *CFO*
EMP: 10 EST: 2021
SALES (est): 166.2K **Privately Held**
SIC: 3841 Surgical & medical instruments
PA: Radiaction Ltd
10 Hanechoshet
Tel Aviv-Jaffa

(G-2360)
US METAL FABRICATORS INC
Also Called: US Marine Supply
800 Old Griffin Rd (33004-2745)
PHONE......................................954 921-0800
Jan R Givskov, *President*
Jens E Sorensen, *Director*
EMP: 15 EST: 2016
SALES (est): 1.2MM **Privately Held**
SIC: 3441 Fabricated structural metal

(G-2361)
WINE PLUM INC
11 Sw 12th Ave Ste 104 (33004-3527)
PHONE......................................844 856-7586
David Koretz, *CEO*
Justin Dopp, *Vice Pres*
Weijing LI, *Vice Pres*
Daniel Emano, *Manager*
Dario Santos, *Supervisor*
EMP: 18 EST: 2015
SALES (est): 2.2MM **Privately Held**
WEB: www.plum.wine
SIC: 3632 Household refrigerators & freezers

Davenport
Polk County

(G-2362)
CEMEX CNSTR MTLS FLA LLC
Also Called: Davenport -Block Manufacturing
100 Lem Carnes Rd (33837-2607)
PHONE......................................863 419-2875
Matt Konjezich, *Branch Mgr*
EMP: 9 **Privately Held**
SIC: 3273 Ready-mixed concrete
HQ: Cemex Construction Materials Florida, Llc
1501 Belvedere Rd
West Palm Beach FL 33406

(G-2363)
DAVID GILL ENTERPRISES
110 Hwy 17 92 (33837)
PHONE......................................863 422-5711
David T Gill, *Owner*
EMP: 9 EST: 2009
SALES (est): 306.7K **Privately Held**
SIC: 3499 Fabricated metal products

(G-2364)
ER JAHNA INDUSTRIES INC
4949 Sand Mine Rd (33897-3414)
PHONE......................................863 424-0730
Eric Cullop, *Branch Mgr*
EMP: 25
SQ FT: 27,014
SALES (corp-wide): 49.2MM **Privately Held**
WEB: www.jahna.com
SIC: 1499 Gemstone & industrial diamond mining
PA: E.R. Jahna Industries, Inc.
202 E Stuart Ave
Lake Wales FL 33853
863 676-9431

(G-2365)
GILL MANUFACTURING INC
110 S Hwy 17 92 (33837)
P.O. Box 769 (33836-0769)
PHONE......................................863 422-5711
David Gill, *President*
Howard Gill, *Vice Pres*
EMP: 10 EST: 1980
SQ FT: 6,000
SALES (est): 1.3MM **Privately Held**
WEB: www.gillmfg.com
SIC: 3441 Fabricated structural metal

(G-2366)
HORSESHOE
150 California Blvd (33897-5601)
PHONE.................................863 438-6632
Ryan D Ault, *Principal*
EMP: 7 **EST:** 2011
SALES (est): 100K **Privately Held**
SIC: 3462 Horseshoes

(G-2367)
J & N STONE INC (PA)
Also Called: Rich Haven Interiors
135 Bargain Barn Rd (33837-7714)
P.O. Box 1199 (33836-1199)
PHONE.................................863 422-7369
Robert Richards, *President*
Barry Rardain, *Safety Dir*
Austin Joiner, *Project Mgr*
Travis Victor, *Accounts Mgr*
Damon Deskins, *Sales Staff*
EMP: 2 **EST:** 1973
SQ FT: 17,600
SALES (est): 5.2MM **Privately Held**
WEB: www.jnstoneveneer.com
SIC: 3281 Cut stone & stone products

(G-2368)
MASCHMEYER CONCRETE CO FLA
4949 Sand Mine Rd (33897-3414)
PHONE.................................863 420-6800
Troy Maschmeyer, *Branch Mgr*
EMP: 23
SALES (corp-wide): 136.2MM **Privately Held**
WEB: www.maschmeyer.com
SIC: 3273 Ready-mixed concrete
PA: Maschmeyer Concrete Company Of Florida
1142 Watertower Rd
Lake Park FL 33403
561 848-9112

(G-2369)
R H QUALITY METAL LLC
1324 Adair Rd (33837-9634)
PHONE.................................407 279-2454
Raul Hernandez, *Principal*
EMP: 7 **EST:** 2017
SALES (est): 390.8K **Privately Held**
SIC: 3499 Fabricated metal products

(G-2370)
SEMG INCORPORATED
225 Aberdeen St (33896-6861)
PHONE.................................407 777-6860
Jose Torrens, *President*
EMP: 7 **EST:** 2019
SALES (est): 270.5K **Privately Held**
SIC: 2851 Paints & paint additives

(G-2371)
STANDARD SAND & SILICA COMPANY (PA)
1850 Us Highway 17 92 N (33837-8608)
P.O. Box 1059 (33836-1059)
PHONE.................................863 422-7100
L Baylis I Carnes, *Chairman*
James L Langford, *Vice Pres*
Kevin Kelley, *Plant Mgr*
Brent Elliott, *CFO*
Lourdes Gomez, *Marketing Staff*
◆ **EMP:** 20 **EST:** 1945
SQ FT: 1,800
SALES (est): 69.8MM **Privately Held**
WEB: www.standardsand.com
SIC: 1446 Industrial sand

(G-2372)
UMBRELLA BUSES INC
Also Called: Umbusa
9800 Us 192 (33897)
PHONE.................................754 457-4004
Zdenek Kozisek, *President*
Melya Tavel, *Principal*
EMP: 7 **EST:** 2019
SALES (est): 535.7K **Privately Held**
SIC: 3829 Fare registers for street cars, buses, etc.

(G-2373)
VERDU-US LLC
741 Caribbean Dr (33897-3940)
PHONE.................................407 776-3017
Hazem Elaeady,

EMP: 10 **EST:** 2017
SALES (est): 589.4K **Privately Held**
WEB: www.verdu-us.com
SIC: 2024 Dairy based frozen desserts

Davie
Broward County

(G-2374)
ABSOLUTE GRAPHICS INC
3721 Sw 47th Ave Ste 302 (33314-2824)
PHONE.................................954 792-3488
Evan R Owen, *President*
▼ **EMP:** 10 **EST:** 1992
SQ FT: 3,000
SALES (est): 1.6MM **Privately Held**
SIC: 2752 2759 Commercial printing, offset; commercial printing

(G-2375)
ACTAVIS LABORATORIES FL INC (DH)
4955 Orange Dr (33314-3902)
PHONE.................................954 585-1400
Sergio Vella, *President*
Deborah Griffin, *Senior VP*
Brian Shanahan, *Vice Pres*
Debra Peterson, *Treasurer*
Thomas Dimitropoulos, *Asst Treas*
EMP: 5 **EST:** 2002
SALES (est): 39.9MM **Privately Held**
SIC: 2834 Pharmaceutical preparations
HQ: Actavis Laboratories Fl, Inc.
5 Giralda Farms
Madison NJ 07940
862 261-7000

(G-2376)
ACTAVIS LABORATORIES FL INC
4955 Orange Dr (33314-3902)
PHONE.................................954 585-1400
Farrah Thelusma, *QA Dir*
James Schwier, *Branch Mgr*
Mike Portalios, *Technical Staff*
Rosi Izquierdo, *Officer*
Lucia Jimenez, *Executive Asst*
EMP: 16 **Privately Held**
WEB: www.actavis.com
SIC: 2834 Pharmaceutical preparations
HQ: Actavis Laboratories Fl, Inc.
5 Giralda Farms
Madison NJ 07940
862 261-7000

(G-2377)
ADLER ANB INC
3721 Sw 47th Ave Ste 306 (33314-2826)
PHONE.................................954 581-2572
Michael Auer, *Manager*
EMP: 8 **EST:** 1998
SALES (est): 967.4K **Privately Held**
SIC: 3732 Yachts, building & repairing

(G-2378)
AERO-TRIM CONTROL SYSTEMS INC
4680 Sw 61st Ave (33314-4406)
PHONE.................................954 321-1936
Elyse S Swalley, *Principal*
EMP: 8 **EST:** 2009
SALES (est): 163.6K **Privately Held**
WEB: www.aerotriminc.com
SIC: 3812 Search & navigation equipment

(G-2379)
AIR FLOW SPECIALISTS
5400 S University Dr 206a (33328-5309)
PHONE.................................954 727-9507
Rodney Fritz, *Principal*
EMP: 5 **EST:** 2012
SALES (est): 333.1K **Privately Held**
WEB: www.airflowspecialists.com
SIC: 3564 Ventilating fans: industrial or commercial

(G-2380)
ALL ABOUT HER
12401 Orange Dr (33330-4341)
PHONE.................................954 559-5175
Errol L Benjamin, *CEO*
EMP: 10 **EST:** 2018

SALES (est): 733.4K **Privately Held**
WEB: www.allabouther.com
SIC: 2676 Feminine hygiene paper products

(G-2381)
ALLPRO FBRICATORS ERECTORS INC
3595 Burris Rd (33314-2221)
PHONE.................................954 797-7300
Robert Singh, *President*
EMP: 5 **EST:** 2009
SQ FT: 4,000
SALES (est): 556.3K **Privately Held**
WEB: www.allprofab.com
SIC: 3441 Fabricated structural metal

(G-2382)
ALLSTAR SCREEN ENCLOSURES & ST
9460 Poinciana Pl Apt 308 (33324-4881)
PHONE.................................954 266-9757
Thomas B Clay, *Principal*
EMP: 7 **EST:** 2009
SALES (est): 157.3K **Privately Held**
WEB: www.coastalhandyman.net
SIC: 3448 Screen enclosures

(G-2383)
ALPHATRON INDUSTRIES INC
3411 Sw 49th Way Ste 3 (33314-2112)
PHONE.................................954 581-1418
Nick Rezai, *President*
EMP: 5 **EST:** 1985
SQ FT: 5,000
SALES (est): 513.8K **Privately Held**
WEB: www.alphatronindustries.com
SIC: 3548 Resistance welders, electric

(G-2384)
AMERICAN FINE WOODWORK LLC
35 Seville Cir (33324-5447)
PHONE.................................954 261-9793
Christian Almonte, *Principal*
EMP: 7 **EST:** 2016
SALES (est): 246.7K **Privately Held**
SIC: 2431 Millwork

(G-2385)
AMERICAN GENERATOR SVCS LLC
14820 Sw 21st St (33326-2004)
PHONE.................................954 965-1210
James E Oberlander, *Manager*
Jim Oberlander, *Manager*
James Oberlander,
EMP: 11 **EST:** 2007
SALES (est): 1.5MM **Privately Held**
WEB:
www.americangeneratorservices.com
SIC: 3621 Motors & generators

(G-2386)
AMMANN AMERICA INC
1125 Sw 101st Rd (33324-4216)
PHONE.................................954 907-5776
EMP: 16 **EST:** 2019
SALES (est): 1.1MM **Privately Held**
WEB: www.ammann.com
SIC: 3531 Construction machinery

(G-2387)
ANDRX CORPORATION (DH)
4955 Orange Dr (33314-3902)
PHONE.................................954 585-1400
Thomas R Giordano, *Senior VP*
Robert J Goldfarb, *Senior VP*
Ian J Watkins, *Senior VP*
Guy Riley, *Maint Spvr*
Janet Vaughn, *Director*
▲ **EMP:** 230 **EST:** 1992
SQ FT: 69,000
SALES (est): 459.7MM **Privately Held**
WEB: www.andrx.com
SIC: 2834 5122 Pharmaceutical preparations; pharmaceuticals
HQ: Actavis Laboratories Fl, Inc.
5 Giralda Farms
Madison NJ 07940
862 261-7000

(G-2388)
ARC ELECTRIC INC
3328 Burris Rd (33314-2215)
PHONE.................................954 583-9800
Omar McFarlane, *President*
Everton Ruddock, *Vice Pres*
Ashley Kay, *Admin Asst*
EMP: 24 **EST:** 2012
SALES (est): 9.6MM **Privately Held**
WEB: www.arcelectricfl.com
SIC: 3699 1731 Electrical equipment & supplies; electrical work

(G-2389)
ARNET PHARMACEUTICAL CORP
Also Called: Natura-Vigor
2525 Davie Rd Ste 330 (33317-7403)
PHONE.................................954 236-9053
Jose Tabacinic, *President*
Carolina Jasmins, *Purch Agent*
Cecilia Turmel, *Buyer*
Liliam Lizazo, *Purchasing*
Ivan Echevarria, *Research*
◆ **EMP:** 350 **EST:** 1972
SQ FT: 46,000
SALES (est): 89.8MM **Privately Held**
WEB: www.arnetusa.com
SIC: 2834 Pharmaceutical preparations

(G-2390)
AUTHENTIC TRADING INC
11107 Sw 15th Mnr (33324-7190)
PHONE.................................347 866-7241
Ariel Rodriguez, *Principal*
EMP: 8 **EST:** 2010
SALES (est): 117.4K **Privately Held**
SIC: 3691 4911 3556 8731 Storage batteries; ; dairy & milk machinery; energy research

(G-2391)
BANASZAK CONCRETE CORP
2401 College Ave (33317-7402)
PHONE.................................954 476-1004
S Howard Banaszak Jr, *President*
S Howard Banaszak Sr, *Vice Pres*
Sarah Lee Banaszak, *Vice Pres*
▼ **EMP:** 14 **EST:** 1964
SALES (est): 606.3K **Privately Held**
WEB: www.banaszakconcrete.com
SIC: 3273 3271 Ready-mixed concrete; blocks, concrete: acoustical

(G-2392)
BNJ NOBLE INC
Also Called: Noble's Jockey Apparel
5408 Stirling Rd (33314-7457)
PHONE.................................954 987-1040
Elizabeth Noble, *President*
EMP: 10 **EST:** 1965
SQ FT: 5,000
SALES (est): 658K **Privately Held**
WEB: www.nobleembroidery.com
SIC: 2253 5699 2397 Jackets, knit; uniforms; schiffli machine embroideries

(G-2393)
C&D CANVAS INC
6110 W Falcons Lea Dr (33331-2981)
PHONE.................................954 924-3433
David Richarson, *Principal*
EMP: 8 **EST:** 2010
SALES (est): 243.4K **Privately Held**
WEB: www.cdcanvasinc.com
SIC: 2394 Canvas & related products

(G-2394)
CABINET GUY 2012 INC
14721 Sw 21st St (33325-4930)
PHONE.................................305 796-5242
Hamid Ahari, *Principal*
EMP: 8 **EST:** 2012
SALES (est): 377.3K **Privately Held**
SIC: 2434 Wood kitchen cabinets

(G-2395)
CBM TRADING INC
10620 Griffin Rd Ste 104 (33328-3213)
P.O. Box 173470, Hialeah (33017-3470)
PHONE.................................954 252-7460
Hanspeter Ehrler, *President*
Peter Edwin, *Owner*
Edward Peters, *Vice Pres*
Doris Brena, *Treasurer*

Persy Sanchez, *Admin Sec*
◆ **EMP:** 5 **EST:** 1998
SQ FT: 1,400
SALES (est): 876.9K **Privately Held**
WEB: www.cbmtrading.net
SIC: 3489 Cannons & howitzers, over 30 mm.

(G-2396)
CELEB LUXURY LLC ✪
6545 Nova Dr Ste 201 (33317-7410)
PHONE..................................954 763-0333
Stacy Gaspard, *Vice Pres*
Tammie Hunt, *Vice Pres*
Howard Sperlein, *Vice Pres*
Peggy Sakki, *Opers Staff*
Leandra Weekes, *Pub Rel Mgr*
EMP: 13 **EST:** 2022
SQ FT: 11,000
SALES (est): 1.1MM **Privately Held**
WEB: www.celebluxury.com
SIC: 2844 Hair preparations, including shampoos

(G-2397)
CERTIFIED MOLD FREE CORP
2881 W Lake Vista Cir (33328-1106)
PHONE..................................954 614-7100
Gary Rosen, *President*
EMP: 6 **EST:** 2003
SALES (est): 1.2MM **Privately Held**
WEB: www.mold-free.org
SIC: 1389 Construction, repair & dismantling services

(G-2398)
COPY-FLOW INC
4727 Orange Dr (33314-3901)
PHONE..................................305 592-0930
Donna Keys, *President*
Jon Keys, *Principal*
Charles Chaddock, *Corp Secy*
EMP: 18 **EST:** 1973
SQ FT: 6,000
SALES (est): 625.9K **Privately Held**
WEB: www.copy-flow.com
SIC: 2752 2789 Commercial printing, offset; promotional printing, lithographic; business form & card printing, lithographic; tag, ticket & schedule printing: lithographic; bookbinding & related work

(G-2399)
CREATIVE COLOR PRINTING INC
3721 Sw 47th Ave Ste 302 (33314-2824)
PHONE..................................954 701-6763
Michael Dubay, *President*
EMP: 8 **EST:** 2013
SALES (est): 173.2K **Privately Held**
SIC: 2752 Commercial printing, offset

(G-2400)
CRYNTEL ENTERPRISES LTD INC
10412 W State Road 84 # 1 (33324-4270)
PHONE..................................954 577-7844
Steven Dreyer, *President*
Joel Dreyer, *Vice Pres*
▲ **EMP:** 7 **EST:** 1988
SALES (est): 955.9K **Privately Held**
WEB: www.cryntel.com
SIC: 2426 Parquet flooring, hardwood

(G-2401)
CURRENT
3301 College Ave Asa105 (33314-7721)
PHONE..................................954 262-8455
Michele Manley, *Director*
EMP: 14 **EST:** 1990
SALES (est): 256.5K **Privately Held**
SIC: 2711 8221 Newspapers, publishing & printing; university

(G-2402)
D & D BUILDING CONTRACTORS INC
Also Called: D & D Millwork Distributors
3380 Sw 50th Ave (33314-2105)
PHONE..................................954 791-2075
David A Green, *President*
Patrick J Brennan, *Vice Pres*
Patrick Brennan, *Vice Pres*
EMP: 8 **EST:** 1986
SQ FT: 1,800

SALES (est): 618.2K **Privately Held**
SIC: 2431 1521 Millwork; single-family housing construction

(G-2403)
DAVIE EMBROIDME
2471 S University Dr (33324-5817)
PHONE..................................954 452-0600
Fernando Corredor, *Principal*
Rachel Sosa, *Sales Staff*
EMP: 9 **EST:** 2006
SALES (est): 442.8K **Privately Held**
SIC: 2759 Screen printing

(G-2404)
DEPENDABLE SHUTTER SERVICE INC
Also Called: Dependable Shutter & Glass
4741 Orange Dr (33314-3901)
PHONE..................................954 583-1411
Wayne C Thompson, *Director*
Mike Waters, *Director*
▼ **EMP:** 35 **EST:** 2001
SALES (est): 6MM **Privately Held**
WEB: www.dependableshutters.com
SIC: 3442 3231 2431 Screen & storm doors & windows; safety glass: made from purchased glass; door shutters, wood

(G-2405)
DOCUVISION INCORPORATED
3650 Hacienda Blvd Ste F (33314-2821)
PHONE..................................954 791-0091
Jim Brodmerkel, *CEO*
John S Leven, *President*
Jackie Leven, *CFO*
Douglas Gonzales, *Supervisor*
EMP: 26 **EST:** 2003
SALES (est): 5.2MM **Privately Held**
WEB: www.docuvis.com
SIC: 2752 Commercial printing, lithographic

(G-2406)
ENERGY CONTROL TECH INC
Also Called: Energycontrol.com
10220 W State Road 84 # 9 (33324-4223)
PHONE..................................954 739-8400
Richard E Combs, *President*
Judith L Combs, *Corp Secy*
Nikhil Dukle, *Vice Pres*
Carissa Garcia, *Opers Mgr*
Judith Combs, *Treasurer*
EMP: 8 **EST:** 1983
SQ FT: 5,000
SALES (est): 1.5MM **Privately Held**
WEB: www.energycontrol.com
SIC: 3825 1711 3823 Electrical energy measuring equipment; plumbing, heating, air-conditioning contractors; industrial instrmnts msrmnt display/control process variable

(G-2407)
ENERGYWARE LLC
17120 Reserve Ct (33331-3526)
PHONE..................................540 809-5902
Tanya Bertamini, *Principal*
EMP: 10 **EST:** 2016
SALES (est): 986.1K **Privately Held**
WEB: www.energywarellc.com
SIC: 3648 Lighting equipment

(G-2408)
EVERGREEN RUSH INDUSTRIES INC
473 Sw 126th Ave (33325-3437)
P.O. Box 266862, Fort Lauderdale (33326-6862)
PHONE..................................954 825-9291
Esther Noltion,
Dethrice Kyles,
Taylor Kyles,
EMP: 15 **EST:** 2019
SALES (est): 565.2K **Privately Held**
SIC: 3999 Manufacturing industries

(G-2409)
EVOLUTION INTRCNNECT SYSTEMS I
11870 W State Road 84 C (33325-3816)
PHONE..................................954 217-6223
Shawn Chalnick, *Vice Pres*
Marcelo Dutra, *Vice Pres*

Suzette Rebull, *Exec Dir*
EMP: 15 **EST:** 1998
SALES (est): 2.9MM **Privately Held**
WEB: www.evoics.com
SIC: 2431 3643 3612 3613 Extension cords; current-carrying wiring devices; electric connectors; contacts, electrical; power & distribution transformers; auto-transformers, electric (power transformers); switchgear & switchboard apparatus

(G-2410)
EXPRESS TOOLS INC
Also Called: Matco Tools
14521 Sw 21st St (33325-4926)
PHONE..................................954 663-4333
Lazaro Salazar, *Principal*
EMP: 8 **EST:** 2016
SALES (est): 685.6K **Privately Held**
WEB: www.matcotools.com
SIC: 3599 Industrial machinery

(G-2411)
FEDS APPAREL
2230 Sw 70th Ave Ste 1 (33317-7131)
PHONE..................................954 932-0685
EMP: 28
SALES (est): 1MM **Privately Held**
SIC: 2353 2321 Mfg Hats/Caps/Millinery Mfg Men's/Boy's Furnishings

(G-2412)
FJH MUSIC COMPANY INC
2525 Davie Rd Ste 360 (33317-7403)
PHONE..................................954 382-6061
Frank J Hackinson, *President*
Phil Groebar, *Editor*
Gail J Hackinson, *Senior VP*
Giorgi Kerry Hackinson, *Vice Pres*
Kevin Hackinson, *Vice Pres*
EMP: 30 **EST:** 1988
SQ FT: 33,000
SALES (est): 5.5MM **Privately Held**
WEB: www.fjhmusic.com
SIC: 2741 Music book & sheet music publishing

(G-2413)
FLORIDA MOLD STOPPERS INC
5520 S University Dr (33328-5333)
PHONE..................................954 445-5560
Earl K Hackworth, *Principal*
EMP: 5 **EST:** 2018
SALES (est): 531.6K **Privately Held**
WEB: www.floridamoldstoppers.com
SIC: 3544 Industrial molds

(G-2414)
FLYER STUDIOS INC
13740 Sw 33rd Ct (33330-4689)
PHONE..................................786 402-9596
Larry M Reyes, *President*
EMP: 7 **EST:** 2017
SALES (est): 313.6K **Privately Held**
WEB: www.flyerstudios.com
SIC: 2752 Commercial printing, offset

(G-2415)
G B WELDING & FABRICATION LLC
2397 College Ave (33317-7155)
PHONE..................................954 967-2573
Garrett Bisogno, *President*
Kimberly Bisogno, *Vice Pres*
Joseph Sclater,
EMP: 12 **EST:** 2011
SALES (est): 1.4MM **Privately Held**
WEB: www.gbweldingandfab.com
SIC: 7692 Welding repair

(G-2416)
G F E INC
3030 Burris Rd (33314-2209)
PHONE..................................954 583-7005
Lori Acvedo, *President*
Lori Acevedo, *President*
EMP: 21 **EST:** 1998
SALES (est): 571.4K **Privately Held**
SIC: 3442 3444 3231 Screen & storm doors & windows; sheet metalwork; products of purchased glass

(G-2417)
GATES CORPORATION
Also Called: Sales & Distribution
15751 Sw 41st St Ste 100 (33331-1520)
PHONE..................................954 926-7823
Joe Serae, *Manager*
EMP: 58
SALES (corp-wide): 3.4B **Publicly Held**
WEB: www.gates.com
SIC: 3052 Rubber belting; rubber hose; automobile hose, rubber; v-belts, rubber
HQ: The Gates Corporation
1144 15th St Ste 1400
Denver CO 80202
303 744-1911

(G-2418)
GATOR DRAIN CLEANING EQUIPMENT
5411 Orange Dr (33314-3816)
PHONE..................................954 584-4441
EMP: 5
SALES (est): 483.4K **Privately Held**
SIC: 3589 Mfg Service Industry Machinery

(G-2419)
GENERAL DEFENSE CORPORATION
4960 Sw 52nd St Ste 413 (33314-5527)
PHONE..................................954 444-0155
Carlos Davidov, *President*
EMP: 5 **EST:** 2006
SALES (est): 482K **Privately Held**
WEB: www.generaldefense.com
SIC: 3489 Ordnance & accessories

(G-2420)
GREEN ROADS OF FLORIDA
5150 Sw 48th Way (33314-5513)
PHONE..................................954 626-0574
EMP: 5 **EST:** 2015
SALES (est): 375K **Privately Held**
SIC: 2834 Mfg Pharmaceutical Preparations

(G-2421)
HAC INTERNATIONAL INC
Also Called: Dynofresh
3911 Sw 47th Ave Ste 914 (33314-2818)
PHONE..................................954 584-4530
Howard Cohen, *President*
Maggie Arvelo, *CFO*
▲ **EMP:** 25 **EST:** 1997
SQ FT: 8,000
SALES (est): 6MM **Privately Held**
SIC: 2819 5169 Chemicals, reagent grade: refined from technical grade; chemicals, industrial & heavy

(G-2422)
HICKS INDUSTRIES INC
2257 Sw 66th Ter (33317-7301)
PHONE..................................954 226-5148
Stephen Hatfield, *Manager*
EMP: 7
SALES (corp-wide): 9.2MM **Privately Held**
WEB: www.hicksindustries.com
SIC: 3272 Burial vaults, concrete or precast terrazzo
PA: Hicks Industries, Inc.
2005 Industrial Park Rd
Mulberry FL 33860
863 425-4155

(G-2423)
HIGH TECH PRECISION MFG LLC
10392 W State Road 84 # 1 (33324-4253)
PHONE..................................954 302-1995
Alejandro Atala, *Administration*
EMP: 8 **EST:** 2015
SALES (est): 77K **Privately Held**
SIC: 3599 Machine shop, jobbing & repair

(G-2424)
HOOPER CORP
6900 Sw 21st Ct (33317-7163)
PHONE..................................954 382-5711
Bob Nichols, *Office Mgr*
EMP: 14 **EST:** 2010
SALES (est): 806.7K **Privately Held**
WEB: www.hoopercorp.com
SIC: 3699 Electrical equipment & supplies

▲ = Import ▼=Export
◆ =Import/Export

(G-2425)
INDUSTRIAL SPRING CORP
3129 Peachtree Cir (33328-6706)
PHONE....................954 524-2558
A W Lidert, *President*
EMP: 12 **EST:** 1969
SALES (est): 775.3K **Privately Held**
WEB: www.industrialspringflorida.com
SIC: 3312 3469 3493 Wire products, steel
or iron; metal stampings; steel springs,
except wire

(G-2426)
IRONCLAD IMPACT WNDOWS DORS LL
3701 Sw 47th Ave Ste 106 (33314-2830)
PHONE....................954 743-4321
David Bitton, *Mng Member*
EMP: 9 **EST:** 2019
SALES (est): 464.8K **Privately Held**
WEB: www.ironcladimpactwindows.com
SIC: 2431 Doors & door parts & trim,
wood; windows, wood

(G-2427)
J&B CMMNICATION SOLUTIONS CORP
6555 Stirling Rd (33314-7117)
PHONE....................786 346-7449
Otilio Alvarado, *President*
EMP: 6 **EST:** 2003
SQ FT: 1,000
SALES (est): 485.5K **Privately Held**
SIC: 3663 Satellites, communications

(G-2428)
KAYCHA TN LLC
4101 Sw 47th Ave (33314-4037)
PHONE....................954 686-0610
James J Horvath, *Manager*
EMP: 9 **EST:** 2019
SALES (est): 607.2K **Privately Held**
SIC: 3999

(G-2429)
KCM MCH SP BROWARD CNTY INC
2394 Sw 66th Ter (33317-7135)
PHONE....................954 475-8732
Feroz Khan, *President*
◆ **EMP:** 13 **EST:** 2008
SQ FT: 9,500
SALES (est): 2.4MM **Privately Held**
WEB: www.kcmmachine.com
SIC: 3549 Metalworking machinery

(G-2430)
KLEEN WHEELS CORPORATION
Also Called: Perma Cap
5000 Oakes Rd Ste H (33314-2119)
PHONE....................954 791-9112
David L Weinberg, *President*
John Herzberg, *Vice Pres*
▲ **EMP:** 7 **EST:** 1989
SQ FT: 7,000
SALES (est): 876.9K **Privately Held**
SIC: 3714 3643 Motor vehicle engines &
parts; motor vehicle brake systems &
parts; current-carrying wiring devices

(G-2431)
KUS USA INC
3350 Davie Rd Ste 203 (33314-1648)
PHONE....................954 463-1075
Yale Huang, *President*
Nataliya Melcher, *Project Mgr*
Arrick Denson, *Prdtn Mgr*
Ciarra Ems, *Sales Engr*
Kerry Weston, *Admin Asst*
▲ **EMP:** 25 **EST:** 1996
SQ FT: 32,500
SALES (est): 5.1MM **Privately Held**
WEB: www.kus-usa.com
SIC: 3812 4226 3824 3823 Nautical in-
struments; liquid storage; liquid meters;
liquid level instruments, industrial process
type

(G-2432)
LAUDERDALE GRAPHICS CORP (PA)
1625 Sw 117th Ave (33325-4648)
PHONE....................954 450-0800
Boon Tirasitipol, *President*
Yoko Tirasitipol, *Vice Pres*

Tony Lopez, *VP Sales*
John Coyle Jr, *Sales Staff*
▲ **EMP:** 30 **EST:** 1988
SALES (est): 2.2MM **Privately Held**
WEB: www.laudgraphics.com
SIC: 2752 2791 2759 Commercial print-
ing, offset; typesetting; commercial print-
ing

(G-2433)
LEHIGH CEMENT COMPANY LLC
Also Called: Continental Concrete Materials
3575 Sw 49th Way (33314-2123)
PHONE....................954 581-2812
Rafael Gonzales, *Branch Mgr*
EMP: 13
SALES (corp-wide): 21.1B **Privately Held**
WEB: www.lehighhanson.com
SIC: 3273 Ready-mixed concrete
HQ: Lehigh Cement Company Llc
300 E John Carpenter Fwy
Irving TX 75062
877 534-4442

(G-2434)
LEXTM3 SYSTEMS LLC
15751 Sw 41st St Ste 300 (33331-1520)
PHONE....................954 888-1024
Lou Bongiovi, *Director*
Nate Lowery,
EMP: 10 **EST:** 2015
SALES (est): 1.4MM **Privately Held**
WEB: www.lexproducts.com
SIC: 3678 3671 3612 3613 Electronic
connectors; electron tubes; transformers,
except electric; switchgear & switchboard
apparatus; relays & industrial controls;
current-carrying wiring devices

(G-2435)
MANUFACTURING BY SKEMA INC
3801 Sw 47th Ave Ste 501 (33314-2816)
PHONE....................954 797-7325
Norberto Grundland, *President*
Patricia Arango, *Vice Pres*
◆ **EMP:** 9 **EST:** 1988
SALES (est): 955.2K **Privately Held**
WEB: www.skemainc.com
SIC: 2511 Wood household furniture

(G-2436)
MARINA MEDICAL INSTRUMENTS INC
8190 W State Road 84 (33324-4611)
PHONE....................954 924-4418
Alexander H Barron, *CEO*
Anthony Zinnanti, *Ch of Bd*
Marina C Zinnanti, *President*
Marina Zinnanti, *Vice Pres*
Laura Connell, *CFO*
▲ **EMP:** 25 **EST:** 1998
SQ FT: 11,303
SALES (est): 3.9MM **Privately Held**
WEB: www.marinamedical.com
SIC: 3841 Surgical & medical instruments

(G-2437)
MCDS PRO LLC
2021 Sw 70th Ave Bay 15 (33317-7314)
PHONE....................954 302-3054
William J Oviedo, *Mng Member*
EMP: 8 **EST:** 2016
SALES (est): 281.1K **Privately Held**
WEB: www.mcdspro.com
SIC: 3441 Fabricated structural metal

(G-2438)
MELMAR CSTM MET FINSHG SVC INC
5990 Sw 42nd Pl (33314-3603)
PHONE....................954 327-5788
Nils Westberg, *Principal*
EMP: 7 **EST:** 2007
SALES (est): 372.2K **Privately Held**
WEB: www.melmarfinishing.com
SIC: 3471 Electroplating of metals or
formed products; plating of metals or
formed products

(G-2439)
MERLIN INDUSTRIES INC
2201 College Ave (33317-7343)
PHONE....................954 472-6891
Larry Maurer, *President*

Jesse Maurer, *Vice Pres*
EMP: 11 **EST:** 1992
SALES (est): 1.5MM **Privately Held**
WEB: www.merlinindustries.net
SIC: 3441 Fabricated structural metal

(G-2440)
MICHELLE ANN LILLO
Also Called: Live Well Cbds
12640 Sw 7th Pl (33325-3410)
PHONE....................954 723-0580
Michelle Lillo, *Principal*
EMP: 7 **EST:** 2017
SALES (est): 141.4K **Privately Held**
SIC: 3999

(G-2441)
MIL-SAT LLC
12555 Orange Dr (33330-4304)
PHONE....................954 862-3613
Mary Ann Richardson, *Branch Mgr*
EMP: 9
SALES (corp-wide): 6.9MM **Privately Held**
WEB: www.mil-sat.com
SIC: 3663 Satellites, communications
PA: Mil-Sat Llc
84 Colonial Trl E Ste B
Surry VA 23883
757 294-9393

(G-2442)
MOHNARK PHARMACEUTICALS INC
5150 Sw 48th Way Ste 604 (33314-5513)
PHONE....................954 607-4559
Donovan Amritt, *CEO*
EMP: 6 **EST:** 2018
SALES (est): 570.3K **Privately Held**
SIC: 2834 Pharmaceutical preparations

(G-2443)
NAIAD DYNAMICS US INC
3750 Hacienda Blvd Ste A (33314-2825)
P.O. Box 292230, Fort Lauderdale (33329-2230)
PHONE....................954 797-7566
Vic Kuzmovich, *Branch Mgr*
EMP: 20 **Privately Held**
WEB: www.naiad.com
SIC: 3731 Shipbuilding & repairing
HQ: Naiad Dynamics Us, Inc.
50 Parrott Dr
Shelton CT 06484

(G-2444)
NATIONAL CHEMICAL SPLY
4151 Sw 47th Ave (33314-4054)
P.O. Box 16785, Fort Lauderdale (33318-6785)
PHONE....................800 515-9938
Phillip Shaffer, *President*
EMP: 10 **EST:** 2001
SALES (est): 1.1MM **Privately Held**
WEB: www.nationalchemicalsupply.com
SIC: 2819 7389 Industrial inorganic chem-
icals; swimming pool & hot tub service &
maintenance

(G-2445)
NB FUEL LLC
10428 Laurel Rd (33328-1358)
PHONE....................954 382-3893
Christy Elsheikh, *Principal*
EMP: 7 **EST:** 2011
SALES (est): 150.7K **Privately Held**
SIC: 2869 Fuels

(G-2446)
NCH MARINE LLC
13325 Sw 28th St (33330-1101)
PHONE....................754 422-4237
Larry Hill, *Principal*
EMP: 7 **EST:** 2011
SALES (est): 309.8K **Privately Held**
SIC: 2842 Specialty cleaning, polishes &
sanitation goods

(G-2447)
NORDIC MADE INC
3801 Sw 47th Ave Ste 503 (33314-2816)
PHONE....................954 651-6208
Michael Rasmussen, *President*
Bettina D Nowak, *Director*
EMP: 13 **EST:** 2012
SQ FT: 3,000

SALES (est): 5.4MM **Privately Held**
WEB: www.tecosolutions.no
SIC: 3731 Shipbuilding & repairing
HQ: Teco Maritime Group As
Lysaker Torg 45
Lysaker 1366

(G-2448)
OCEAN BIO-CHEM LLC (HQ)
4041 Sw 47th Ave (33314-4023)
PHONE....................954 587-6280
Peter G Dornau, *Ch of Bd*
William W Dudman, *COO*
Gregor M Dornau, *Exec VP*
Jeffrey S Barocas, *CFO*
EMP: 22 **EST:** 1973
SQ FT: 12,700
SALES (est): 64.3MM
SALES (corp-wide): 1.2B **Publicly Held**
WEB: www.starbrite.com
SIC: 2842 2992 Polishing preparations &
related products; lubricating oils &
greases
PA: Onewater Marine Inc.
6275 Lanier Islands Pkwy
Buford GA 30518
678 541-6300

(G-2449)
OCEAN TEST EQUIPMENT INC
2021 Sw 70th Ave Ste B1 (33317-7334)
PHONE....................954 474-6603
John Banu, *President*
Gabriela Mirea, *Vice Pres*
▲ **EMP:** 7 **EST:** 1992
SQ FT: 3,000
SALES (est): 895.9K **Privately Held**
WEB: www.oceantestequip.com
SIC: 3812 5049 Nautical instruments; sci-
entific instruments

(G-2450)
ORANGE SUNSHINE GRAPHICS INC
5051 S State Road 7 # 517 (33314-5659)
PHONE....................954 797-7425
Pedro Rivas, *President*
Barbara McCraney, *Corp Secy*
Glenda Rivas, *Vice Pres*
▼ **EMP:** 8 **EST:** 1981
SQ FT: 4,000
SALES (est): 562.3K **Privately Held**
WEB: www.klippedkippahs.com
SIC: 2262 Screen printing: manmade fiber
& silk broadwoven fabrics

(G-2451)
OZINGA SOUTH FLORIDA INC (PA)
2401 College Ave (33317-7402)
PHONE....................786 422-4694
Justin Ozinga, *President*
EMP: 10 **EST:** 2016
SALES (est): 1.6MM **Privately Held**
WEB: www.ozinga.com
SIC: 3273 Ready-mixed concrete

(G-2452)
PALM BEACH TRIM INC
6900 W State Road 84 (33317-7308)
PHONE....................561 588-8746
Fax: 561 588-5855
EMP: 50
SALES (est): 6.6MM **Privately Held**
SIC: 2441 2434 Nonclassified Establish-
ment Mfg Wood Boxes/Shook Mfg Wood
Kitchen Cabinets

(G-2453)
PARADISE CSTM SCREENING & EMB
2180 Sw 71st Ter (33317-7303)
PHONE....................954 566-9096
EMP: 21
SALES (est): 1.6MM **Privately Held**
SIC: 2395 2396 Silk Screening & Embroi-
dery

(G-2454)
PAYO LLC
12481 N Stonebrook Cir (33330-1295)
PHONE....................786 368-8655
Marie Yolete Charles,
▲ **EMP:** 5 **EST:** 2000
SQ FT: 10,000

SALES (est): 356.9K **Privately Held**
SIC: 2051 Bakery: wholesale or wholesale/retail combined

(G-2455)
PEM-AIR LLC
5921 Sw 44th Ct (33314-3640)
PHONE.............................954 321-8726
Virgil D Pizer, *Mng Member*
EMP: 10 EST: 2010
SALES (est): 1.1MM **Privately Held**
WEB: www.pem-air.com
SIC: 3728 Aircraft parts & equipment

(G-2456)
PETIT CUSTOM WOOD WORKS
3673 W Valley Green Dr (33328-2625)
PHONE.............................954 200-3111
Amberlee Petit, *Principal*
EMP: 8 EST: 2016
SALES (est): 58.5K **Privately Held**
SIC: 2499 Laundry products, wood

(G-2457)
PHARMATECH LLC (PA)
4131 Sw 47th Ave Ste 1403 (33314-4036)
P.O. Box 590671, Fort Lauderdale (33359-0671)
PHONE.............................954 581-7881
Raidel I Figueroa, *CEO*
Deylis Cano, *Administration*
Niurbis Aguilera, *Associate*
EMP: 5 EST: 2009
SALES (est): 2.4MM **Privately Held**
WEB: www.pharmatech-llc.com
SIC: 2834 8734 Pharmaceutical preparations; testing laboratories

(G-2458)
PHARMATECH LLC
4131 Sw 47th Ave Ste 1405 (33314-4036)
PHONE.............................954 629-2444
Raidel Figueroa, *Officer*
EMP: 15 **Privately Held**
WEB: www.pharmatech-llc.com
SIC: 2834 Pharmaceutical preparations
PA: Pharmatech Llc
    4131 Sw 47th Ave Ste 1403
    Davie FL 33314

(G-2459)
PL SMOOTHIE LLC
10234 Sw 26th St (33324-7625)
PHONE.............................954 554-0450
Shaukat Umer, *Principal*
EMP: 8 EST: 2010
SALES (est): 336K **Privately Held**
SIC: 2037 Frozen fruits & vegetables

(G-2460)
PRINT-IT USACOM INC
13660 W State Road 84 (33325-5302)
PHONE.............................954 370-2200
Janice Seidner, *President*
Leigh Seidner, *Vice Pres*
EMP: 5 EST: 1992
SALES (est): 493.8K **Privately Held**
WEB: www.printitusa.com
SIC: 2752 Commercial printing, offset

(G-2461)
PRINTING CONNECTION TOO INC
4960 Sw 52nd St Ste 409 (33314-5527)
PHONE.............................954 584-4197
Larry Peterson, *President*
EMP: 5 EST: 1984
SQ FT: 1,650
SALES (est): 456.9K **Privately Held**
WEB: www.pctoo.net
SIC: 2752 Commercial printing, offset

(G-2462)
PURIFY FUELS INC
14113 N Cypress Cove Cir (33325-6736)
PHONE.............................949 842-6159
John Carroll, *CEO*
John Anda, *Ch of Bd*
Pat Gallagher, *Vice Chairman*
Steven Douglas, *COO*
Jay Fountain, *Vice Pres*
EMP: 8 EST: 2016
SALES (est): 244.7K **Privately Held**
WEB: www.purifyfuel.com
SIC: 2911 Fuel additives

(G-2463)
QUALITY ANODIZING INC
5990 Sw 42nd Pl (33314-3603)
PHONE.............................954 791-8711
Morgan Peterson, *Manager*
EMP: 5 EST: 2007
SALES (est): 473.4K **Privately Held**
WEB: www.qualityanodizing.com
SIC: 3471 Electroplating of metals or formed products

(G-2464)
RAINBOW INK PRODUCTS INC
15640 Lancelot Ct (33331-3318)
PHONE.............................954 252-6030
Scott J Lodge, *Principal*
EMP: 7 EST: 2010
SALES (est): 160K **Privately Held**
SIC: 2893 Printing ink

(G-2465)
RAND SEARCH LIGHT ADVERTISING
11330 Sw 17th St (33325-4802)
PHONE.............................954 476-7620
Terrie Rand, *Principal*
Peter Nguyen, *CTO*
EMP: 8 EST: 1999
SALES (est): 676.9K **Privately Held**
WEB: www.randsearchlights.com
SIC: 3648 Searchlights; floodlights

(G-2466)
RED SMITH FOODS INC
4145 Sw 47th Ave (33314-4006)
PHONE.............................954 581-1996
Stephen F Foster, *President*
Mike Hoffman, *General Mgr*
Jonathan Foster, *Vice Pres*
Tim Foster, *Vice Pres*
David Foster, *Treasurer*
EMP: 22 EST: 1973
SQ FT: 12,000
SALES (est): 4.8MM **Privately Held**
WEB: www.redsmithfoods.com
SIC: 2013 Sausages from purchased meat

(G-2467)
RENEW LIFE HOLDINGS CORP
2405 College Ave Unit 105 (33317-7451)
PHONE.............................925 368-9711
Violet Lee, *Manager*
EMP: 31
SALES (corp-wide): 7.1B **Publicly Held**
SIC: 2842 Laundry cleaning preparations
HQ: Renew Life Holdings Corporation
    1221 Broadway Ste 1300
    Oakland CA

(G-2468)
REV OLD INC
Also Called: Reverso
4001 Sw 47th Ave Ste 201 (33314-4030)
PHONE.............................954 523-9396
John Napurano, *President*
Tammy Anstett, *General Mgr*
Dan Bigelow, *Vice Pres*
Heather Kemp, *Buyer*
Richard Dowling, *Engineer*
▲ EMP: 17 EST: 1993
SQ FT: 6,000
SALES (est): 4.4MM **Privately Held**
WEB: www.reversopumps.com
SIC: 3561 Pumps & pumping equipment

(G-2469)
REX THREE INC (PA)
Also Called: Rex 3
15431 Sw 14th St (33326-1937)
PHONE.............................954 452-8301
Julius Miller, *Ch of Bd*
Robert Cannata, *President*
Juan Mendoza, *President*
Stephen H Miller, *President*
Samuel Rautbord, *President*
▼ EMP: 164 EST: 1958
SQ FT: 90,000
SALES (est): 39.4MM **Privately Held**
WEB: www.rex3.com
SIC: 2759 2796 Screen printing; color separations for printing

(G-2470)
RG MECHANICAL USA LLC
12660 Sw 13th St (33325-4400)
PHONE.............................954 835-5287
Sandra Sepulveda, *Exec Dir*
EMP: 8 EST: 2019
SALES (est): 938.6K **Privately Held**
SIC: 1389 1711 Construction, repair & dismantling services; plumbing contractors; mechanical contractor

(G-2471)
ROMCO FUELS INC
10835 Sw 38th Dr (33328-1315)
PHONE.............................954 474-5392
John Romano, *Director*
EMP: 9 EST: 2001
SALES (est): 148.9K **Privately Held**
SIC: 2869 Fuels

(G-2472)
RTC SOLUTIONS INC
4370 Oakes Rd Ste 700 (33314-2225)
PHONE.............................919 439-8680
Todd Saltzman, *President*
EMP: 5 EST: 2008
SQ FT: 1,500
SALES (est): 891.3K **Privately Held**
WEB: www.rtc-solutions.com
SIC: 3625 Relays & industrial controls

(G-2473)
RUSSELL HOME IMPRVMNT CTR INC
3250 Sw 131st Ter (33330-4607)
PHONE.............................954 436-9186
Ralph Russell, *President*
EMP: 8 EST: 1987
SALES (est): 705.7K **Privately Held**
SIC: 3442 Screen & storm doors & windows

(G-2474)
SEMINOLE STATE SIGNS & LTG
5071 S State Road 7 # 717 (33314-5601)
PHONE.............................954 316-6030
Andrew Wyrosdick, *Vice Pres*
EMP: 8 EST: 2015
SALES (est): 229.9K **Privately Held**
SIC: 3993 Signs & advertising specialties

(G-2475)
SHIRTS N THINGS INC
6001 Orange Dr (33314-3609)
PHONE.............................954 434-7480
Steve Chorba, *President*
Renee Chorba, *Corp Secy*
EMP: 5 EST: 1980
SQ FT: 2,900
SALES (est): 488.9K **Privately Held**
WEB: www.shirtsnthings.com
SIC: 2759 Screen printing

(G-2476)
SIGMA NETICS LLC
12644 Sw 8th Ct (33325-5510)
PHONE.............................954 473-2106
Michael A Rosenberg, *Principal*
EMP: 8 EST: 2010
SALES (est): 137.8K **Privately Held**
SIC: 3829 Measuring & controlling devices

(G-2477)
SLAINTE WINES INC (PA)
8958 W State Road 84 (33324-4457)
PHONE.............................954 474-4547
Chris O'Connor, *President*
Erin Landery, *Vice Pres*
Erin Landry, *Vice Pres*
Thelma Condon, *Controller*
EMP: 7 EST: 2004
SALES (est): 1.3MM **Privately Held**
WEB: www.slaintewines.com
SIC: 2084 Wines

(G-2478)
SLATE SOLUTIONS LLC
7060 W State Road 84 # 12 (33317-7365)
PHONE.............................754 200-6752
Michael J Slate, *President*
EMP: 32 EST: 2015
SALES (est): 2.6MM **Privately Held**
WEB: www.slatesolutions.com
SIC: 2389 Men's miscellaneous accessories

(G-2479)
SMART SIGNS INC
4153 Sw 47th Ave Ste 177 (33314-4044)
PHONE.............................754 701-8910
Jason R Matherly, *Principal*
EMP: 7 EST: 2015
SALES (est): 256.9K **Privately Held**
SIC: 3993 Signs & advertising specialties

(G-2480)
SOUTH FLORIDA CORE DISTRS
2030 Sw 71st Ter Ste C6 (33317-7323)
PHONE.............................954 452-9091
William Lowther, *President*
◆ EMP: 5 EST: 1991
SALES (est): 422.3K **Privately Held**
SIC: 3694 Distributors, motor vehicle engine

(G-2481)
STAR-BRITE DISTRIBUTING INC
Also Called: Star Brite
4041 Sw 47th Ave (33314-4031)
PHONE.............................954 587-6280
Peter Dornau, *Ch of Bd*
William Dudman, *Vice Pres*
Dornau Gregor M, *Vice Pres*
Jeff Brocas, *CFO*
◆ EMP: 35 EST: 1973
SQ FT: 300,000
SALES (est): 11.4MM
SALES (corp-wide): 1.2B **Publicly Held**
WEB: www.autoodoreliminator.com
SIC: 2842 Specialty cleaning, polishes & sanitation goods
HQ: Ocean Bio-Chem, Llc
    4041 Sw 47th Ave
    Davie FL 33314
    954 587-6280

(G-2482)
STOLTZ INDUSTRIES INC
9704 E Tree Tops Ct (33328-7105)
PHONE.............................954 792-3270
Carl Stoltz, *President*
▼ EMP: 10 EST: 1976
SALES (est): 1.8MM **Privately Held**
WEB: www.pcourethane.com
SIC: 2821 Plastics materials & resins

(G-2483)
STREET LIGHTING EQUIPMENT CORP
2601 W Abiaca Cir (33328-7137)
PHONE.............................954 961-9140
Barry Levine, *President*
Mary Hallenbeck, *Vice Pres*
Martin Levine, *Admin Sec*
◆ EMP: 15 EST: 1978
SALES (est): 2.8MM **Privately Held**
WEB: www.streetlightingfla.com
SIC: 3648 Street lighting fixtures

(G-2484)
SUN BELT GRAPHICS INC
15431 Sw 14th St (33326-1937)
PHONE.............................954 424-3139
Robert Bernstein, *President*
Jerry Garcia, *Production*
EMP: 16 EST: 1977
SALES (est): 3.3MM **Privately Held**
SIC: 2752 Color lithography

(G-2485)
SUPER COLOR INC
5905 Sw 58th Ct (33314-7313)
PHONE.............................954 964-4656
Doron Shmueli, *President*
Eddie Shmueli, *Vice Pres*
Ilan Shmueli, *Vice Pres*
▼ EMP: 21 EST: 1992
SALES (est): 4MM **Privately Held**
WEB: www.super-color.com
SIC: 2752 Commercial printing, offset

(G-2486)
SUPERMARKET SERVICES INC
4100 Sw 47th Ave (33314-4007)
PHONE.............................954 525-0439
David Johnson, *President*
Maria Johnson, *Treasurer*
▼ EMP: 7 EST: 1968

SALES (est): 739.6K **Privately Held**
WEB: www.smsrecyclingequip.com
SIC: 3569 Baling machines, for scrap metal, paper or similar material

(G-2487)
TECHNICAL DRIVE CTRL SVCS INC
Also Called: T D C S
5081 S State Road 7 (33314-5600)
PHONE.................................954 471-6521
Vivian Martens, *President*
Tony Augusto, *Vice Pres*
EMP: 5 EST: 2003
SQ FT: 1,500
SALES (est): 659.8K **Privately Held**
SIC: 3625 Control circuit devices, magnet & solid state

(G-2488)
TEND SKIN INTERNATIONAL INC
2090 Sw 71st Ter Ste G9 (33317-7322)
PHONE.................................954 382-0800
Steven E Rosen, *President*
Linda Irons, *Opers Mgr*
David Wood, *QC Mgr*
◆ EMP: 16 EST: 1994
SQ FT: 6,000
SALES (est): 2.6MM **Privately Held**
SIC: 2844 5122 5999 7231 Cosmetic preparations; toiletries; toiletries, cosmetics & perfumes; facial salons

(G-2489)
TG OIL SERVICES
14520 Sw 21st St (33325-4925)
PHONE.................................407 576-9571
Carlos Touzan, *Principal*
EMP: 5 EST: 2018
SALES (est): 353.5K **Privately Held**
WEB: www.tgoilservices.com
SIC: 1311 Crude petroleum production

(G-2490)
THERMOVAL SOLENOID VALVES USA
4651 Sw 51st St Ste 808 (33314-5515)
PHONE.................................954 835-5523
EMP: 6 EST: 2018
SALES (est): 378.4K **Privately Held**
WEB: www.thermoval.com.br
SIC: 3491 Solenoid valves

(G-2491)
TONER CITY CORP
4137 Stirling Rd Apt 103 (33314-7562)
PHONE.................................954 945-5392
Vince R Charles, *President*
EMP: 9 EST: 2017
SQ FT: 1,200
SALES (est): 697.2K **Privately Held**
SIC: 3861 Toners, prepared photographic (not made in chemical plants)

(G-2492)
TOTALLY BANANAS LLC
5081 S State Road 7 # 803 (33314-5664)
PHONE.................................954 674-9421
Joel Kornbluth, *Vice Pres*
Charles J Pheterson, *Mng Member*
Mindy Pheterson,
EMP: 12 EST: 2009
SALES (est): 1MM **Privately Held**
WEB: www.totally-bananas.net
SIC: 2037 Fruits, quick frozen & cold pack (frozen)

(G-2493)
TUFLEX MANUFACTURING CO
8421 Sw 28th St (33328-1605)
PHONE.................................954 781-0605
Thomas A Sayward, *President*
Barbara Grasso, *Admin Sec*
EMP: 22 EST: 1964
SALES (est): 3.5MM **Privately Held**
WEB: www.tuflexmfg.com
SIC: 3089 3713 3088 Plastic & fiberglass tanks; truck & bus bodies; plastics plumbing fixtures

(G-2494)
VEEAM SOFTWARE CORPORATION
15137 Sw 36th St (33331-2734)
PHONE.................................614 339-8200
EMP: 68
SALES (corp-wide): 62.3MM **Privately Held**
WEB: www.veeam.com
SIC: 7372 Prepackaged software
HQ: Veeam Software Corporation
8800 Lyra Dr Ste 350
Columbus OH 43240

(G-2495)
W&I PROPERTIES LLC
3400 Davie Rd Apt 515 (33314-1620)
PHONE.................................786 985-1642
Ilan Amar, *Mng Member*
EMP: 6 EST: 2017
SALES (est): 1.5MM **Privately Held**
SIC: 1389 7389 Construction, repair & dismantling services;

(G-2496)
WAYLOOMOTO LLC
7060 W State Road 84 # 8 (33317-7365)
PHONE.................................954 636-1510
EMP: 5
SALES (est): 310K **Privately Held**
SIC: 3949 Mfg Sporting/Athletic Goods

(G-2497)
WEIGHTECH USA LLC
10384 W State Road 84 # 6 (33324-4251)
PHONE.................................954 666-0877
Joao Paulo Pires,
Carlos Alberto Marin,
EMP: 8 EST: 2013
SALES (est): 2.3MM **Privately Held**
WEB: www.weightechusa.com
SIC: 3596 Weighing machines & apparatus

(G-2498)
WILLIS INDUSTRIES INC
5064 S University Dr (33328-4510)
PHONE.................................954 830-6163
Paul Willis, *President*
EMP: 7 EST: 2002
SALES (est): 159.4K **Privately Held**
SIC: 3999 Manufacturing industries

(G-2499)
WINDSTONE DEVELOPMENT INTL LC
Also Called: Fastsigns
7080 W State Road 84 (33317-7368)
PHONE.................................954 370-7201
Howard J Willis,
EMP: 13 EST: 1999
SALES (est): 248K **Privately Held**
WEB: www.fastsigns.com
SIC: 3993 Signs & advertising specialties

(G-2500)
WIREWORLD BY DAVID SALZ INC
Also Called: Wireworld Cable Technology
6545 Nova Dr Ste 204 (33317-7410)
PHONE.................................954 474-4464
David B Salz, *President*
Bernay Bavone, *COO*
Larry Smith, *Natl Sales Mgr*
Martin Harding, *Sales Mgr*
David Salz, *Manager*
◆ EMP: 19 EST: 1992
SQ FT: 2,400
SALES (est): 2.9MM **Privately Held**
WEB: www.wireworldcable.com
SIC: 3651 Household audio & video equipment

(G-2501)
YACHT FURN BY ECLIPSE LLC
7050 W State Road 84 (33317-7364)
PHONE.................................954 792-7339
EMP: 7 EST: 2018
SALES (est): 269.4K **Privately Held**
WEB: www.eclipse-yachtfurnishings.com
SIC: 2394 Canvas & related products

(G-2502)
YUMMY FOODS INC
10408 W State Road 84 # 102 (33324-4264)
P.O. Box 21034, Fort Lauderdale (33335-1034)
PHONE.................................305 681-8437
Niki Chen-Sem, *President*
Dornel C Sem, *President*
Teleckies Gorski, *Vice Pres*
Alfred C Sem, *Treasurer*
Alfred Sem, *Treasurer*
EMP: 5 EST: 1980
SALES (est): 524.5K **Privately Held**
WEB: www.jammyyummy.com
SIC: 2051 Bakery: wholesale or wholesale/retail combined

(G-2503)
ZINC GUY INC (PA)
3811 Sw 47th Ave Ste 617 (33314-2817)
PHONE.................................954 907-2752
Alberto Spinelli, *President*
EMP: 5 EST: 2010
SALES (est): 1.2MM **Privately Held**
WEB: www.thezincguy.com
SIC: 3531 5088 Marine related equipment; marine supplies

Daytona Beach
Volusia County

(G-2504)
88 SOUTH ATLANTIC LLC
835 N Beach St (32114-2233)
PHONE.................................386 253-0105
Pinchas Mamane, *Manager*
EMP: 6 EST: 2018
SALES (est): 492.2K **Privately Held**
SIC: 3479 Metal coating & allied service

(G-2505)
ACHIEVIA DIRECT INC
Also Called: Achievia Optical Solutions
1440 N Nova Rd Unit 311 (32117-3245)
PHONE.................................386 615-8708
Matthew T Banker, *President*
Jeri Putney, *Accounts Mgr*
▲ EMP: 19 EST: 2004
SQ FT: 5,000
SALES (est): 529.2K **Privately Held**
WEB: www.achieviaopticalsolutions.com
SIC: 3851 Ophthalmic goods

(G-2506)
ADSIL INC
1901 Mason Ave Ste 101 (32117-5105)
PHONE.................................386 274-1382
Raymond G Smith, *CEO*
Gordon Miller, *Sales Staff*
EMP: 5 EST: 1998
SQ FT: 12,000
SALES (est): 1MM **Privately Held**
WEB: www.mymicroguard.com
SIC: 2851 Paints & allied products

(G-2507)
AEROJET ROCKETDYNE INC
Also Called: 3dmt
790 Fentress Blvd (32114-1214)
PHONE.................................386 626-0001
Eileen Drake, *Principal*
Tyler Evens, *Principal*
Greg Jones, *Principal*
Arjun Kampani, *Principal*
Paul Lundstrom, *Principal*
EMP: 9 EST: 1945
SALES (est): 740.1K **Privately Held**
WEB: www.rocket.com
SIC: 3728 Aircraft parts & equipment

(G-2508)
AEROSAPIEN TECHNOLOGIES LLC
601 Innovation Way (32114-3865)
PHONE.................................386 361-3838
Chaithanya Cherlopalli, *President*
Sanjay Krishnappa, *Principal*
Vamsi K Konduru,
EMP: 30 EST: 2016

SALES (est): 2.3MM **Privately Held**
WEB: www.aerosapientech.com
SIC: 3365 3357 3724 3728 Aerospace castings, aluminum; aircraft wire & cable, nonferrous; aircraft engines & engine parts; research & dev by manuf., aircraft parts & auxiliary equip; engineering services

(G-2509)
AMERICAN LABEL GROUP INC
705 Fentress Blvd (32114-1213)
PHONE.................................386 274-5234
Timothy K Gleason, *President*
Bill Gall, *General Mgr*
Debbie Fristachi,
EMP: 15 EST: 2004
SALES (est): 2.3MM **Privately Held**
WEB: www.americancaregroupinc.com
SIC: 2679 Tags & labels, paper

(G-2510)
AMERICRAFT ENTERPRISES INC
2800 S Nova Rd Ste H3 (32119-6141)
PHONE.................................386 756-1100
Gene Blake, *President*
EMP: 6 EST: 1989
SALES (est): 442.9K **Privately Held**
WEB: www.americraftboats.com
SIC: 3732 Boat building & repairing

(G-2511)
AO PRECISION MANUFACTURING LLC
1870 Mason Ave (32117-5101)
PHONE.................................386 274-5882
Stephen Koch, *CEO*
Micky Selimovic, *Engineer*
Marc Segal, *Controller*
Tara Higgs, *Accountant*
Kevin Hoisington, *IT/INT Sup*
EMP: 160 EST: 1996
SQ FT: 33,000
SALES (est): 28MM **Privately Held**
WEB: www.aopmfg.com
SIC: 3484 3489 Small arms; ordnance & accessories
PA: Juno Investments Llc
950 3rd Ave Ste 2300
New York NY 10022

(G-2512)
APEX GRINDING INC
817 Swift St Ste 100 (32114-2051)
PHONE.................................386 624-7350
EMP: 5 EST: 2018
SALES (est): 372.9K **Privately Held**
WEB: www.apexgrinding.com
SIC: 3999 Custom pulverizing & grinding of plastic materials

(G-2513)
ARC TRANSITION LLC (DH)
Also Called: 3dmt
790 Fentress Blvd (32114-1214)
PHONE.................................386 626-0001
Jason T Young, *Mng Member*
EMP: 9 EST: 2013
SQ FT: 28,000
SALES (est): 5.1MM
SALES (corp-wide): 2.1B **Publicly Held**
SIC: 3544 3441 Special dies, tools, jigs & fixtures; fabricated structural metal
HQ: Aerojet Rocketdyne, Inc.
2001 Aerojet Rd
Rancho Cordova CA 95742
916 355-4000

(G-2514)
ART-CRETE PRODUCTS INC
1231 S Ridgewood Ave (32114-6127)
PHONE.................................386 252-5118
Ronald Hopkins, *President*
Carol Hopkins, *Corp Secy*
EMP: 10 EST: 1989
SQ FT: 3,000
SALES (est): 940.8K **Privately Held**
WEB: www.discoverdaytona.com
SIC: 3272 5211 Cast stone, concrete; masonry materials & supplies

(G-2515)
ATLANTIC CENTRAL ENTPS INC
336 Lpga Blvd (32117-2820)
PHONE.................................386 255-6227

Steven Traulsen, *President*
EMP: 14 **EST:** 1996
SQ FT: 10,800
SALES (est): 3.3MM **Privately Held**
WEB: www.atlanticcentralsteel.com
SIC: 3441 3499 Fabricated structural metal; friction material, made from powdered metal

(G-2516)
B BRAUN MEDICAL INC
1341 N Clyde Morris Blvd (32117-5528)
PHONE....................................386 274-1837
EMP: 47
SALES (corp-wide): 2.6MM **Privately Held**
WEB: www.bbraunusa.com
SIC: 3841 Surgical & medical instruments
HQ: B. Braun Medical Inc.
　　824 12th Ave
　　Bethlehem PA 18018
　　610 691-5400

(G-2517)
B BRAUN MEDICAL INC
1845 Mason Ave (32117-5102)
PHONE....................................386 888-2000
Jose Mediavilla, *Engineer*
John Bennet, *Branch Mgr*
EMP: 42
SALES (corp-wide): 2.6MM **Privately Held**
WEB: www.bbraun.com
SIC: 3841 Surgical & medical instruments
HQ: B. Braun Medical Inc.
　　824 12th Ave
　　Bethlehem PA 18018
　　610 691-5400

(G-2518)
B BRAUN MEDICAL INC
1830 Holsonback Dr (32117-5112)
PHONE....................................866 388-5120
EMP: 27
SALES (corp-wide): 2.6MM **Privately Held**
WEB: www.bbraunusa.com
SIC: 3841 Surgical & medical instruments
HQ: B. Braun Medical Inc.
　　824 12th Ave
　　Bethlehem PA 18018
　　610 691-5400

(G-2519)
BOBS SPACE RACERS INC
427 Whac A Mole Way (32117-2198)
PHONE....................................386 677-0761
Robert Cassata, *CEO*
John Mendes, *President*
Joyce Cassata, *Vice Pres*
Jack D Cook II, *Vice Pres*
Jack Cook, *Vice Pres*
◆ **EMP:** 120 **EST:** 1968
SALES (est): 21.7MM **Privately Held**
WEB: www.bobsspaceracers.com
SIC: 3599 Amusement park equipment

(G-2520)
BRADDOCK METALLURGICAL GA INC
400 Fentress Blvd (32114-1208)
PHONE....................................386 267-0955
William K Braddock, *Principal*
James Turgeon, *QC Mgr*
Dan Bieller, *Manager*
EMP: 25 **EST:** 2011
SALES (est): 2.4MM **Privately Held**
WEB: www.braddockmt.com
SIC: 3398 Metal heat treating

(G-2521)
BRADDOCK METALLURGICAL MGT LLC
400 Fentress Blvd (32114-1208)
PHONE....................................386 267-0955
George Gieger, *President*
Eric Dvorscak, *General Mgr*
Rachell Cameron, *QC Mgr*
Koko Sztajer, *QC Mgr*
EMP: 15 **EST:** 2010
SALES (est): 844.9K **Privately Held**
WEB: www.braddockmt.com
SIC: 3398 Metal heat treating

(G-2522)
BRADDOCK MTLLRGCAL - DYTONA IN
400 Fentress Blvd (32114-1208)
PHONE....................................386 267-0955
David Adam, *CFO*
▲ **EMP:** 1 **EST:** 2008
SALES (est): 5.2MM
SALES (corp-wide): 27.6MM **Privately Held**
WEB: www.braddockmt.com
SIC: 3398 Metal heat treating
HQ: Braddock Metallurgical, Inc.
　　14600 Duval Pl W
　　Jacksonville FL 32218
　　386 267-0955

(G-2523)
BRADDOCK MTLLURGICAL HOLDG INC (PA)
400 Fentress Blvd (32114-1208)
PHONE....................................386 323-1500
Steven R Braddock, *CEO*
Eric Dvorscak, *General Mgr*
Sabrina Heath, *Accountant*
Josh Hunter, *Manager*
Melissa Robinson, *Manager*
EMP: 6 **EST:** 2005
SALES (est): 27.6MM **Privately Held**
WEB: www.braddockmt.com
SIC: 3398 Metal heat treating

(G-2524)
BRENDA NAUSED
2043 S Atlantic Ave (32118-5007)
PHONE....................................352 344-4729
Brenda Naused, *Chairman*
EMP: 7 **EST:** 2016
SALES (est): 114.5K **Privately Held**
SIC: 2392 Household furnishings

(G-2525)
CABINET FACTORY OUTLET
1595 N Nova Rd Ste A (32117-3000)
PHONE....................................386 323-0778
Ron Daniels, *Owner*
EMP: 5 **EST:** 2008
SALES (est): 364K **Privately Held**
WEB: www.cabinetfactoryfl.com
SIC: 2434 Wood kitchen cabinets

(G-2526)
CARLARON INC
421 Ridgewood Ave (32117-4421)
PHONE....................................386 258-1183
Ronald Cornelius, *President*
Carla Cornelius, *Corp Secy*
EMP: 5 **EST:** 1989
SQ FT: 4,400
SALES (est): 453.3K **Privately Held**
SIC: 3993 7389 7311 5999 Signs & advertising specialties; engraving service; advertising consultant; banners

(G-2527)
CENSYS TECHNOLOGIES CORP
1808 Concept Ct Ste 200 (32114-1281)
PHONE....................................386 314-3599
John Lobdell, *Principal*
Fred Fleszar, *Production*
EMP: 15 **EST:** 2017
SALES (est): 3.2MM **Privately Held**
WEB: www.censystech.com
SIC: 3728 Target drones

(G-2528)
CENTRAL SIGNS LLC
517 Mason Ave Ste 101 (32117-4872)
PHONE....................................386 322-7446
Charles Hutchershon, *CEO*
Charles H Hutchershon, *President*
EMP: 16 **EST:** 2019
SQ FT: 3,930
SALES (est): 1.8MM **Privately Held**
WEB: www.centralsign.net
SIC: 3993 Electric signs

(G-2529)
CLASSIC MAIL CORP
247 Brookline Ave (32118-3327)
PHONE....................................386 290-0309
Lynn Vanginhoven, *President*
EMP: 7 **EST:** 2018

SALES (est): 412.2K **Privately Held**
WEB: www.classicmailcorp.com
SIC: 2741 Miscellaneous publishing

(G-2530)
COASTLINE WHL SGNS LED DISP LL
532 N Segrave St (32114-2618)
PHONE....................................386 238-6200
Nicholas P Florio,
EMP: 10 **EST:** 2013
SALES (est): 560.7K **Privately Held**
WEB: www.coastlinesign.com
SIC: 3993 Electric signs

(G-2531)
COASTLINE WHL SIGNS SVCS LTD
532 N Segrave St (32114-2618)
PHONE....................................386 238-6200
Dan Florio, *Owner*
Nick Florio, *Manager*
EMP: 10 **EST:** 2005
SALES (est): 803.8K **Privately Held**
WEB: www.coastlinesign.com
SIC: 3993 Electric signs

(G-2532)
COCA-COLA BEVERAGES FLA LLC
222 Fentress Blvd (32114-1228)
PHONE....................................386 239-3100
Edward Williams, *Manager*
EMP: 10
SQ FT: 36,574
SALES (corp-wide): 366.5MM **Privately Held**
WEB: www.cocacolaflorida.com
SIC: 2086 Bottled & canned soft drinks
PA: Coca-Cola Beverages Florida, Llc
　　10117 Princess Palm Ave
　　Tampa FL 33610
　　800 438-2653

(G-2533)
COLEO LLC ✪
1198 Champions Dr (32124-2024)
PHONE....................................215 436-0902
Cole Vettraino, *Mng Member*
EMP: 11 **EST:** 2021
SALES (est): 465.7K **Privately Held**
SIC: 2051 Bakery: wholesale or wholesale/retail combined

(G-2534)
COSTA INC (DH)
Also Called: Costa Del Mar
2361 Mason Ave Ste 100 (32117-5163)
PHONE....................................386 274-4000
Chas Macdonald, *CEO*
Eric Thoreux, *President*
Michelle Crockett, *Vice Pres*
Jeffrey J Giguere, *Vice Pres*
Charles S Mellen, *Vice Pres*
◆ **EMP:** 2 **EST:** 1916
SALES (est): 282.9MM
SALES (corp-wide): 1.7MM **Privately Held**
WEB: www.costasunglasses.com
SIC: 3851 Glasses, sun or glare
HQ: Fgx International Inc.
　　500 George Washington Hwy
　　Smithfield RI 02917
　　401 231-3800

(G-2535)
COUNTER PRODUCTIONS INC
Also Called: New Kitchen Concepts
1052 N Beach St (32117-5044)
PHONE....................................386 673-6500
Kenneth A Chiaravalle, *President*
Clinton Tiffany, *President*
Kimberly Tiffany, *Vice Pres*
Kenneth Chiaravalle, *Treasurer*
EMP: 7 **EST:** 2016
SALES (est): 509.3K **Privately Held**
SIC: 2434 Vanities, bathroom: wood

(G-2536)
CRENSHAW DIE & MANUFACTURING
100 Zaharias Cir (32124-2038)
PHONE....................................949 475-5505
EMP: 7 **EST:** 2012

SALES (est): 79.3K **Privately Held**
WEB: www.crenshawdiemfg.com
SIC: 3544 Special dies & tools

(G-2537)
CRICKET MINI GOLF CARTS INC
1575 Avi Ctr Pkwy Ste 432 (32114)
PHONE....................................386 220-3536
Michael Hampton, *President*
EMP: 18 **EST:** 2019
SALES (est): 210K **Privately Held**
WEB: www.cricketminigolfcarts.com
SIC: 3799 Golf carts, powered

(G-2538)
CUBCO INC
605 Commercial Dr (32117-3440)
PHONE....................................386 254-2706
Stephen Jenkins, *President*
Mary Ann Mahnke, *Bookkeeper*
EMP: 18 **EST:** 1987
SQ FT: 6,500
SALES (est): 3.2MM **Privately Held**
WEB: www.cubcoinc.com
SIC: 2261 2395 2759 Screen printing of cotton broadwoven fabrics: pleating & stitching; screen printing

(G-2539)
D & R SIGNS INC
133 Thomasson Ave (32117-4822)
P.O. Box 290656, Port Orange (32129-0656)
PHONE....................................386 252-2777
Darrell King, *President*
Robin King, *Admin Sec*
EMP: 8 **EST:** 1990
SQ FT: 7,500
SALES (est): 902.1K **Privately Held**
WEB: www.drsignsinc.com
SIC: 3993 Signs & advertising specialties

(G-2540)
DASOPS INC
2425 Dodge Dr (32118-5332)
PHONE....................................386 258-6230
Jerry D Tyser, *President*
EMP: 6 **EST:** 1978
SALES (est): 353.8K **Privately Held**
SIC: 2732 Pamphlets: printing only, not published on site

(G-2541)
DAYTONA DOCK & SEAWALL SERVICE
Rebonner Machine Works
862 Terrace Ave (32114-5742)
PHONE....................................386 255-7909
William Bonner, *Manager*
EMP: 8
SALES (corp-wide): 1.2MM **Privately Held**
WEB: www.daytonadockandseawall.com
SIC: 3544 Special dies, tools, jigs & fixtures
PA: Daytona Dock & Seawall Service Inc
　　862 Terrace Ave
　　Daytona Beach FL 32114
　　386 255-7909

(G-2542)
DAYTONA GLASS WORKS LLC
843 Bill France Blvd (32117-5110)
P.O. Box 10690 (32120-0690)
PHONE....................................386 274-2550
Keith Harwood, *Human Res Mgr*
Mel Mathisen, *Mng Member*
Mitch Adams, *Supervisor*
EMP: 13 **EST:** 2014
SALES (est): 1.8MM **Privately Held**
WEB: www.daytonaglass.com
SIC: 3679 Quartz crystals, for electronic application

(G-2543)
DAYTONA MAGIC INC
136 S Beach St (32114-4402)
PHONE....................................386 252-6767
Irving Cook, *President*
Harry Allen Gersh, *Vice Pres*
EMP: 5 **EST:** 1966
SQ FT: 2,000

SALES (est): 526K **Privately Held**
WEB: www.daytonamagic.com
SIC: **3999** 5945 5092 3944 Magic equipment, supplies & props; hobbies; amusement goods; games, toys & children's vehicles

(G-2544)
DAYTONA TROPHY INC
2413 Bellevue Ave (32114-5615)
PHONE.................................386 253-2806
Stuart Sarjeant, *President*
Rachel L Sarjeant, *Vice Pres*
Catherine Sarjeant, *Treasurer*
James A Sarjeant, *Admin Sec*
EMP: 10 EST: 1970
SQ FT: 5,000
SALES (est): 1.1MM **Privately Held**
WEB: www.daytonatrophy.com
SIC: **2261** 5999 3993 Screen printing of cotton broadwoven fabrics; trophies & plaques; signs & advertising specialties

(G-2545)
DAYTONA WELDING & FABRICATION
837 Pinewood St (32114-4573)
P.O. Box 7352 (32116-7352)
PHONE.................................386 562-0093
Michael S Lawhorn Sr, *President*
EMP: 10 EST: 2013
SALES (est): 535.2K **Privately Held**
WEB: www.daytonawelding.com
SIC: **3441** Fabricated structural metal

(G-2546)
DECORTIVE ELECTRO COATINGS INC
501 Kingston Ave (32114-2025)
PHONE.................................386 255-7878
William A Cottrell Jr, *CEO*
Jason Alexan, *Vice Pres*
EMP: 12 EST: 1999
SALES (est): 750.4K **Privately Held**
WEB: www.thecoater.com
SIC: **3479** Coating of metals & formed products

(G-2547)
EAST COAST ORNAMENTAL WLDG INC
1794 State Ave (32117-1748)
PHONE.................................386 672-4340
Terry Howard, *President*
Richard Adjemian, *Vice Pres*
EMP: 15 EST: 2003
SQ FT: 5,000
SALES (est): 1.5MM **Privately Held**
WEB:
www.eastcoastornamentalwelding.com
SIC: **7692** Welding repair

(G-2548)
EDDY STORM PROTECTION
1000 N Nova Rd (32117-4123)
PHONE.................................386 248-1631
James Eddy, *President*
John Eddy, *Manager*
EMP: 9 EST: 2000
SALES (est): 1.3MM **Privately Held**
WEB: www.eddystormprotection.com
SIC: **3442** 1799 2591 Shutters, door or window: metal; awning installation; window shades

(G-2549)
ELTEC INSTRUMENTS INC (PA)
350 Fentress Blvd (32114-1235)
P.O. Box 9610 (32120-9610)
PHONE.................................386 252-0411
Samuel D Mollenkof, *President*
Samuel S Mollenkof, *Chairman*
Douglas Armstrong, *Vice Pres*
Darla Jones, *Vice Pres*
Virginia Ungewitter, *Treasurer*
EMP: 42 EST: 1969
SALES (est): 6MM **Privately Held**
WEB: www.eltecinstruments.com
SIC: **3812** 3823 Infrared object detection equipment; infrared instruments, industrial process type

(G-2550)
ETERNA URN CO INC
126 Carswell Ave (32117-5010)
PHONE.................................386 258-6491
Allan Hannah, *President*
Deborah Hannah, *Corp Secy*
EMP: 5 EST: 1974
SQ FT: 7,500
SALES (est): 440K **Privately Held**
WEB: www.eternaurn.com
SIC: **3281** Urns, cut stone

(G-2551)
FABCO METAL PRODUCTS LLC
1490 Frances Dr (32124-3660)
PHONE.................................386 252-3730
Shane King, *President*
Tracy Thomas, *Vice Pres*
Melissa Sepanek, *Purch Mgr*
Nick Jagos, *Info Tech Mgr*
Tracy Ballew, *Director*
▲ EMP: 75 EST: 1983
SQ FT: 75,000
SALES (est): 21.5MM
SALES (corp-wide): 586.3MM **Privately Held**
WEB: www.fabcometal.com
SIC: **3441** Fabricated structural metal
HQ: Fabsouth Llc
721 Ne 44th St
Oakland Park FL 33334
954 938-5800

(G-2552)
FEDERAL HEATH SIGN COMPANY LLC
1128 Beville Rd Ste E (32114-5769)
PHONE.................................817 685-9075
Nik Patrick, *Marketing Staff*
Mark Symcox, *Branch Mgr*
Michelle Lewis, *Sr Project Mgr*
Rene Trappmann, *Program Mgr*
Rick Foreman, *Manager*
EMP: 20
SALES (corp-wide): 1.8B **Privately Held**
WEB: www.federalheath.com
SIC: **3993** Signs & advertising specialties
HQ: Federal Heath Sign Company, Llc
2300 St Hwy 121
Euless TX 76039

(G-2553)
FLORIDA GRAPHIC PRINTING INC
503 Mason Ave (32117-4811)
PHONE.................................386 253-4532
Patricia Blythe, *President*
Steve Heiden, *Manager*
EMP: 18 EST: 1964
SALES (est): 1MM **Privately Held**
WEB: www.floridagraphicprinting.com
SIC: **2752** 2791 2789 2759 Commercial printing, offset; typesetting; bookbinding & related work; commercial printing; book printing

(G-2554)
FOUNDRY
1384 N Nova Rd (32117-4001)
PHONE.................................904 257-5020
Clarise A Harty, *Principal*
EMP: 7 EST: 2012
SALES (est): 135.7K **Privately Held**
WEB: www.foundrydaytona.com
SIC: **3366** Copper foundries

(G-2555)
GATERMAN PRODUCTS LLC
114 Meadowbrook Cir (32114-1113)
PHONE.................................386 253-1899
Mike Golding, *Marketing Staff*
Deanna Ploederl, *Office Mgr*
William C Gaterman, *Manager*
EMP: 5 EST: 2005
SALES (est): 389.6K **Privately Held**
WEB: www.gatermanproducts.com
SIC: **3714** Motor vehicle parts & accessories

(G-2556)
GILLA INC (PA)
475 Fentress Blvd Ste L (32114-1236)
PHONE.................................416 843-2881
Graham Simmonds, *Ch of Bd*
Ashish Kapoor, *CFO*

Daniel Yuranyi, *EMP*
EMP: 9 EST: 1995
SALES: 4.6MM **Privately Held**
WEB: www.gillainc.com
SIC: **3999** Cigarette & cigar products & accessories

(G-2557)
GRAPHIC SIGN DSIGN CNTL FLA LL
529 Ridgewood Ave (32117-4423)
PHONE.................................386 547-4569
Keith Cook, *Principal*
EMP: 5 EST: 2016
SALES (est): 307.8K **Privately Held**
WEB: www.signsofstone.com
SIC: **3993** Signs & advertising specialties

(G-2558)
HALIFAX MEDIA GROUP LLC (HQ)
2339 Beville Rd (32119-8720)
P.O. Box 11826 (32120-1826)
PHONE.................................386 265-6700
Michael Redding, *CEO*
Rick Martin, *COO*
Bernie Szachara, *Senior VP*
Rob Delaney, *Controller*
Shawna Laethem, *Sales Mgr*
EMP: 300 EST: 2011
SALES (est): 382.2MM
SALES (corp-wide): 3.2B **Publicly Held**
WEB: www.gannett.com
SIC: **2711** Newspapers, publishing & printing
PA: Gannett Co., Inc.
7950 Jones Branch Dr
Mc Lean VA 22102
703 854-6000

(G-2559)
HALIFAX MEDIA HOLDINGS LLC (PA)
901 6th St (32117-3352)
P.O. Box 2831 (32120-2831)
PHONE.................................386 681-2404
Michael Redding, *CEO*
Jackson Farrow Jr, *Manager*
Rupert Phillips, *Manager*
Noel Strauss, *Manager*
Don Rothausen, *Director*
EMP: 38 EST: 2009
SALES (est): 278.4MM **Privately Held**
SIC: **2791** 2711 Typesetting; newspapers, publishing & printing

(G-2560)
HALIFAX PLASTIC INC
Also Called: Southeast Plastics
221 Fentress Blvd (32114-1203)
PHONE.................................386 252-2442
Richard Schwarz, *President*
Stephanie Schwarz, *Treasurer*
◆ EMP: 15 EST: 1981
SQ FT: 35,000
SALES (est): 2.4MM **Privately Held**
SIC: **2759** Screen printing

(G-2561)
HAMSARD USA INC
2330 S Nova Rd Ste A (32119-2574)
PHONE.................................386 761-1830
Iain Whyte, *President*
EMP: 175 EST: 2007
SQ FT: 10,000
SALES (est): 63.7MM
SALES (corp-wide): 351.2K **Privately Held**
SIC: **3272** Bathtubs, concrete
HQ: Hamsard 5037 Limited
Estate House
Redditch WORCS

(G-2562)
HIMGC LIMITED
1301 Beville Rd (32119-9009)
PHONE.................................213 443-8729
EMP: 65 EST: 2018
SALES (est): 250K **Privately Held**
SIC: **7372** Application computer software

(G-2563)
INSPEC SOLUTIONS LLC
2111 Bayless Blvd (32114)
PHONE.................................866 467-7320

Mohamed Yousef, *Mng Member*
EMP: 18
SALES (corp-wide): 3.7MM **Privately Held**
WEB: www.inspectsolutions.com
SIC: **2842** Sanitation preparations, disinfectants & deodorants
PA: Inspec Solutions, Llc
330 Carswell Ave
Holly Hill FL 32117
866 467-7320

(G-2564)
JAY SQUARED LLC
Also Called: Daytona Helmets International
1810 Mason Ave (32117-5101)
PHONE.................................386 677-7700
Ryan Maloney, *General Mgr*
Joseph F Linge, *Principal*
▲ EMP: 10 EST: 1992
SQ FT: 25,500
SALES (est): 1.1MM **Privately Held**
WEB: www.daytonahelmets.com
SIC: **3949** 5571 Helmets, athletic; motorcycle parts & accessories

(G-2565)
KENCO - 2000 INC
1539 Garden Ave (32117-2109)
PHONE.................................386 672-1590
Raymond Kenneth Webb, *President*
Molly McLaughlin, *Office Mgr*
EMP: 19 EST: 1979
SQ FT: 10,000
SALES (est): 918.1K **Privately Held**
WEB: www.kenco2000inc.com
SIC: **3993** 3444 1799 Electric signs; awnings & canopies; sign installation & maintenance

(G-2566)
KT PROPERTIES & DEV INC
500 Walker St (32117-2681)
PHONE.................................386 253-0610
Gregory B Thompson, *President*
EMP: 10 EST: 2010
SALES (est): 262K **Privately Held**
SIC: **3272** Septic tanks, concrete

(G-2567)
L D F SERVICES
1111 State Ave (32117-2700)
PHONE.................................386 947-9256
Danny Funicello, *Principal*
EMP: 19 EST: 2001
SQ FT: 2,000
SALES (est): 4.8MM **Privately Held**
SIC: **3444** Sheet metalwork

(G-2568)
LAMINAR FLOW SYSTEMS INC
1585 Avi Ctr Pkwy Ste 605 (32114)
PHONE.................................386 253-8833
Robin Thomas, *President*
Sandy Norton, *Accountant*
EMP: 12 EST: 1996
SALES (est): 2.9MM **Privately Held**
WEB: www.laminarflowsystems.com
SIC: **3728** Aircraft parts & equipment

(G-2569)
LARSON-BURTON INCORPORATED
1010 N Nova Rd (32117-4123)
PHONE.................................815 637-9500
Jeffrey J Larson, *President*
Dave Burton, *Vice Pres*
EMP: 12 EST: 1998
SQ FT: 15,200
SALES (est): 2.1MM **Privately Held**
WEB: www.larsonburton.com
SIC: **3599** Custom machinery

(G-2570)
M & M ENTERPRISES DAYTONA LLC (PA)
1502 State Ave (32117-2229)
PHONE.................................386 672-1554
John Butterfield, *Mng Member*
Christyna Lynch,
▲ EMP: 5 EST: 1971
SQ FT: 8,000

SALES (est): 733.7K **Privately Held**
WEB:
www.mandmenterprisesofdaytona.com
SIC: 2431 Moldings, wood: unfinished &
prefinished

(G-2571)
MAGELLAN INTL LBRCTION
CHEM TE
Also Called: Manufacturer
317 Carswell Ave (32117-4415)
PHONE..............................386 257-3456
Edward E Parker Sr, *CEO*
EMP: 8 **EST:** 2012
SALES (est): 680.4K **Privately Held**
WEB: www.daytona1.net
SIC: 2992 Lubricating oils & greases

(G-2572)
MAITLAND FURNITURE INC
1711 State Ave (32117-1792)
P.O. Box 9787 (32120-9787)
PHONE..............................386 677-7711
EMP: 5
SALES (est): 380K **Privately Held**
SIC: 3949 Mfg Gaming Furniture

(G-2573)
MAT-VAC TECHNOLOGY INC
410 Arroyo Ln (32114-4808)
PHONE..............................386 238-7017
EMP: 10
SQ FT: 40,000
SALES (est): 2MM **Privately Held**
SIC: 3563 5065 7699 3675 Mfg Air/Gas
Compressors Whol Electronic Parts Re-
pair Services Mfg Electronic Capacitor

(G-2574)
MICRO AUDIOMETRICS
CORPORATION
1901 Mason Ave Ste 104 (32117-5105)
PHONE..............................386 888-7878
Jason Keller, *President*
James Keller, *Vice Pres*
Monica Keller, *Treasurer*
Lance Ralph, *Marketing Mgr*
Kathleen Keller, *Admin Sec*
▲ **EMP:** 8 **EST:** 1980
SALES (est): 1.4MM **Privately Held**
WEB: www.microaud.com
SIC: 3845 Audiological equipment, elec-
tromedical

(G-2575)
MID-FLORIDA SPORTSWEAR
LLC
2415 Bellevue Ave (32114-5615)
PHONE..............................386 258-5632
John Koberg, *President*
Ken Bender, *Vice Pres*
Kenneth Bender, *Vice Pres*
James J Gallagher, *Vice Pres*
Carolyn Russell, *Office Mgr*
EMP: 20 **EST:** 1977
SQ FT: 8,000
SALES (est): 1.8MM **Privately Held**
WEB: www.mfswear.com
SIC: 2261 2395 Screen printing of cotton
broadwoven fabrics; embroidery & art
needlework

(G-2576)
MILLER-LEAMAN INC
800 Orange Ave (32114-4730)
PHONE..............................386 248-0500
Martin Shuster, *President*
Lawrence Call, *General Mgr*
Chris Shuster, *Vice Pres*
Steve Garcia, *Prdtn Mgr*
Judy Letsinger, *Purchasing*
▲ **EMP:** 32 **EST:** 1991
SQ FT: 52,000
SALES (est): 7MM **Privately Held**
WEB: www.millerleaman.com
SIC: 3441 Fabricated structural metal

(G-2577)
MINUTEMAN PRESS
201 N Ridgewood Ave (32114-3243)
PHONE..............................386 255-2767
Patrik Franceschi, *Manager*
EMP: 9 **EST:** 2015

SALES (est): 369.9K **Privately Held**
WEB: www.minutemanpress.com
SIC: 2752 2759 Commercial printing, litho-
graphic; commercial printing

(G-2578)
NEWS-JOURNAL CORPORATION
(PA)
Also Called: New Smyrna Daily Journal
901 6th St (32117-8099)
P.O. Box 2831 (32120-2831)
PHONE..............................386 252-1511
Herbert M Davidson Jr, *President*
Georgia M Kaney, *Vice Pres*
David R Kendall, *Vice Pres*
Marc L Davidson, *Treasurer*
Forrest Scot, *Advt Staff*
▲ **EMP:** 800 **EST:** 1927
SQ FT: 300,000
SALES (est): 68.8MM **Privately Held**
WEB: www.news-journalonline.com
SIC: 2711 Newspapers, publishing & print-
ing

(G-2579)
P & L CREECH INC
Also Called: Godawa Septic Tank Service
2960 S Nova Rd (32119-6106)
PHONE..............................386 547-4182
Paul Creech, *President*
Linda Lee Creech, *Vice Pres*
EMP: 6 **EST:** 1947
SQ FT: 2,000
SALES (est): 1.1MM **Privately Held**
SIC: 3089 7359 7699 Septic tanks, plas-
tic; portable toilet rental; septic tank
cleaning service

(G-2580)
PAPER PUSHERS OF AMERICA
INC
2430 S Atlantic Ave Ste C (32118-5419)
PHONE..............................386 872-7025
Nathaly Encarnacion, *President*
EMP: 7 **EST:** 2019
SALES (est): 290.2K **Privately Held**
WEB: www.mypaperpushers.com
SIC: 2752 Commercial printing, litho-
graphic

(G-2581)
PAVEMAX
1120 Enterprise Ct (32117-2692)
PHONE..............................386 206-3113
Doug Cefalo, *Business Mgr*
EMP: 8 **EST:** 2018
SALES (est): 210K **Privately Held**
WEB: www.pavemax.com
SIC: 2951 Asphalt paving mixtures &
blocks

(G-2582)
PIEDMONT PLASTICS INC
2175 Mason Ave (32117-5147)
PHONE..............................386 274-4627
Marty Sparks, *Sales Staff*
Myra Gercken, *Branch Mgr*
Sal Rapuano, *Branch Mgr*
EMP: 61
SALES (corp-wide): 201.6MM **Privately**
Held
WEB: www.piedmontplastics.com
SIC: 3081 3082 5162 Plastic film & sheet;
rods, unsupported plastic; tubes, unsup-
ported plastic; plastics sheets & rods;
plastics products
PA: Piedmont Plastics, Inc.
5010 W W T Harris Blvd
Charlotte NC 28269
704 597-8200

(G-2583)
PIP PRINTING
133 W Intl Speedway Blvd (32114)
PHONE..............................386 258-3326
EMP: 7 **EST:** 2012
SALES (est): 131.9K **Privately Held**
WEB: www.pip.com
SIC: 2752 Commercial printing, offset

(G-2584)
POWER FLOW SYSTEMS INC
795 Fentress Blvd Ste A (32114-1251)
PHONE..............................386 253-8833
Darren Tilman, *President*
Robin Thomas, *President*

Max Kirby, *Engineer*
Jim Schaeffer, *Sales Mgr*
EMP: 10 **EST:** 1997
SQ FT: 6,000
SALES (est): 1.6MM **Privately Held**
WEB: www.powerflowsystems.com
SIC: 3728 Aircraft parts & equipment

(G-2585)
PRINT ART SCREEN PRINTING
INC
340 Marion St (32114-4834)
PHONE..............................386 258-5186
Okan Avcilar, *President*
Cenk Isjener, *Vice Pres*
EMP: 12 **EST:** 2003
SQ FT: 8,000
SALES (est): 2.1MM **Privately Held**
WEB: www.printartdaytona.com
SIC: 2759 2395 Screen printing; embroi-
dery & art needlework

(G-2586)
PRINTING DEPARTMENT LLC
176 Carswell Ave (32117-5010)
PHONE..............................386 253-7990
David Doak, *Principal*
EMP: 6 **EST:** 2019
SALES (est): 350.7K **Privately Held**
WEB: www.tpdflorida.com
SIC: 2752 Commercial printing, litho-
graphic

(G-2587)
PROFESSIONAL SITE & TRNSPT
INC
3728 W Intl Spwy Blvd (32124-1030)
PHONE..............................386 239-6800
Christopher R Linsley, *President*
Colette M Linsley, *Vice Pres*
EMP: 10 **EST:** 2000
SQ FT: 500
SALES (est): 1.3MM **Privately Held**
SIC: 1442 Construction sand & gravel

(G-2588)
QUALITY PRINTING INC
Also Called: Speedway Press
705 W Intl Speedway Blvd (32114)
PHONE..............................386 255-1565
Craig Solomon, *President*
EMP: 5 **EST:** 1980
SALES (est): 421.5K **Privately Held**
WEB: www.qualityprinting.com
SIC: 2752 Commercial printing, offset

(G-2589)
REPORGRAPHICS UNLIMITED
INC
124 Bay St (32114-3234)
PHONE..............................386 253-7990
Ronnie Hames Jr, *President*
EMP: 9 **EST:** 1997
SQ FT: 1,400
SALES (est): 773.6K **Privately Held**
SIC: 2759 Commercial printing

(G-2590)
REX FOX ENTERPRISES INC
Also Called: Fox Furniture
1966 N Nova Rd (32117-1442)
PHONE..............................386 677-3752
Rex A Fox, *President*
Rick Carter, *Treasurer*
EMP: 11 **EST:** 1968
SQ FT: 18,000
SALES (est): 1.5MM **Privately Held**
WEB: www.foxmattress.com
SIC: 2515 5712 Mattresses & foundations;
furniture stores; mattresses

(G-2591)
ROSIER MANUFACTURING
COMPANY
409 W Intl Speedway Blvd (32114)
P.O. Box 388, Edgewater (32132-0388)
PHONE..............................386 409-7223
Brian Rossiter, *Owner*
Holly Kreitz, *Admin Sec*
EMP: 5 **EST:** 1995
SQ FT: 4,420
SALES (est): 417.4K **Privately Held**
WEB: www.lightningbodies.com
SIC: 3089 Plastics products

(G-2592)
S & B METAL PRODUCTS E FLA
INC
1811 Holsonback Dr (32117-5113)
PHONE..............................386 274-0092
Steven Campbell, *President*
Peter Dierdorf, *Prdtn Mgr*
EMP: 39 **EST:** 2007
SALES (est): 5.1MM **Privately Held**
SIC: 3441 Fabricated structural metal

(G-2593)
SCCY INDUSTRIES LLC
Also Called: Sccy Firearms
1800 Concept Ct (32114-1259)
PHONE..............................386 322-6336
Joseph V Roebuck, *CEO*
Beau Hickman, *COO*
Janine Edwards, *Purchasing*
Daniel Lipinski, *Engineer*
William Riel, *Engineer*
▲ **EMP:** 147 **EST:** 2003
SQ FT: 5,000
SALES (est): 26.6MM **Privately Held**
WEB: www.sccy.com
SIC: 3484 Guns (firearms) or gun parts, 30
mm. & below

(G-2594)
SCHNEIDDER INDUSTRIES LLC
1690 Dunn Ave Apt 408 (32114-1475)
PHONE..............................850 207-0929
Samuel Quinones, *Principal*
EMP: 11 **EST:** 2014
SALES (est): 105.5K **Privately Held**
SIC: 3999 Manufacturing industries

(G-2595)
SEASIDE ALUMINUM LLC
230 Carswell Ave (32117-4918)
PHONE..............................386 252-4940
Bonnie Bannister, *Mng Member*
EMP: 12 **EST:** 2005
SALES (est): 1MM **Privately Held**
WEB: www.seasidealuminum.com
SIC: 3441 Fabricated structural metal

(G-2596)
SENSATEK PROPULSION TECH
INC
1 Aerospace Blvd (32114-3910)
PHONE..............................850 321-5993
Reamonn Soto, *CEO*
Reynaldo Perez, *Engineer*
EMP: 10 **EST:** 2016
SALES (est): 1.3MM **Privately Held**
WEB: www.sensatek.com
SIC: 3764 8731 Guided missile & space
vehicle propulsion unit parts; commercial
physical research

(G-2597)
SHELTAIR DAYTONA BEACH
LLC
Also Called: Daytona Beach Jet Center
561 Pearl Harbor Dr (32114-3845)
PHONE..............................386 255-0471
Gerald Holland,
EMP: 21 **EST:** 1988
SQ FT: 75,000
SALES (est): 2.5MM **Privately Held**
WEB: www.daytonabeach.com
SIC: 2911 Jet fuels

(G-2598)
SHOWCASE MARBLE INC
Also Called: Marble Crafters
405 6th St (32114-4305)
PHONE..............................386 253-6646
Richard C Maugeri, *President*
EMP: 20 **EST:** 1988
SQ FT: 60,000
SALES (est): 974.4K **Privately Held**
SIC: 3281 3949 2434 Marble, building:
cut & shaped; sporting & athletic goods;
wood kitchen cabinets

(G-2599)
SIGNS NOW
1440 N Nova Rd Ste 308 (32117-3245)
PHONE..............................386 238-5507
Nancy Thompson, *Principal*
EMP: 5 **EST:** 2011

▲ = Import ▼=Export
◆ =Import/Export

SALES (est): 303K **Privately Held**
WEB: www.signsnow.com
SIC: 3993 Signs & advertising specialties

(G-2600)
SNAPSPACE SOLUTIONS LLC
626 Landshark Blvd (32124-3726)
PHONE..................................561 756-6610
Chad Walton,
EMP: 25 EST: 2020
SALES (est): 1MM **Privately Held**
WEB: www.snapspacesolutions.com
SIC: 3448 Prefabricated metal buildings

(G-2601)
SOUTHEASTERN LTG SOLUTIONS
821 Fentress Ct (32117-5152)
PHONE..................................386 238-1711
Walton M Cox, *Principal*
EMP: 29 EST: 2003
SALES (est): 4.6MM **Privately Held**
WEB: www.selightingsolutions.com
SIC: 3993 Signs & advertising specialties

(G-2602)
SOUTHEASTERN TRUCK TOPS INC
402 6th St (32117-4306)
PHONE..................................386 761-0002
Bill Varnadore, *President*
Sharon Varnadore, *Admin Sec*
EMP: 15 EST: 1975
SQ FT: 7,496
SALES (est): 2MM **Privately Held**
WEB: www.southeasterntrucktops.com
SIC: 3713 3792 Truck tops; travel trailers & campers

(G-2603)
SPACE COAST DISTRIBUTORS
726 N Segrave St (32114-2020)
PHONE..................................386 239-0305
Ted Bondjuk, *Owner*
EMP: 6 EST: 2007
SALES (est): 439.7K **Privately Held**
SIC: 3052 Rubber hose

(G-2604)
STOVER MANUFACTURING LLC
825 Ballough Rd (32114-2256)
PHONE..................................386 238-3775
Burnett R Random, *Principal*
Nancy Grooms, *CFO*
EMP: 6 EST: 2012
SALES (est): 351.3K **Privately Held**
SIC: 3999 Manufacturing industries

(G-2605)
STRASSER ENTERPRISES
1504 State Ave (32117-2262)
PHONE..................................386 677-5163
Drew Strasser, *Principal*
EMP: 8 EST: 2008
SALES (est): 243.3K **Privately Held**
SIC: 2499 Decorative wood & woodwork

(G-2606)
SUNCOAST HEAT TREAT INC
400 Fentress Blvd (32114-1208)
PHONE..................................386 267-0955
Bruce Sobleski, *Manager*
EMP: 17
SALES (corp-wide): 4.3MM **Privately Held**
SIC: 3398 Metal heat treating
PA: Suncoast Heat Treat, Inc.
507 Industrial Way
Boynton Beach FL 33426
561 776-7763

(G-2607)
TECHNETICS GROUP DAYTONA INC (HQ)
305 Fentress Blvd (32114-1205)
PHONE..................................386 253-0628
Gilles Hudon, *President*
Robert P McKinney, *Vice Pres*
Robert S McLean, *Vice Pres*
Yaakov Abudaram, *Design Engr*
David S Burnett, *Treasurer*
EMP: 138 EST: 2006
SQ FT: 59,172

SALES (est): 98.2MM
SALES (corp-wide): 1.1B **Publicly Held**
SIC: www.technetics.com
SIC: 3577 Computer peripheral equipment
PA: Enpro Industries, Inc.
5605 Carnegie Blvd # 500
Charlotte NC 28209
704 731-1500

(G-2608)
TEL-TRON TECHNOLOGIES CORP (PA)
Also Called: Silversphere Holdings
2570 W Intl Spwy Blvd # 200 (32114-8145)
PHONE..................................386 523-1070
Brian Dawson, *CEO*
Dawson N Rick, *Chairman*
Melinda D Dawson, *Vice Pres*
Rick Taylor, *Vice Pres*
EMP: 50 EST: 1945
SALES (est): 11.9MM **Privately Held**
WEB: www.tel-tron.com
SIC: 3625 Control equipment, electric

(G-2609)
TELEDYNE INSTRUMENTS INC
Also Called: Teledyne Odi
1026 N Williamson Blvd (32114-7113)
PHONE..................................386 236-0780
Francis Dunne, *Vice Pres*
Jason Kordek, *Vice Pres*
Debra Holtzman, *Project Mgr*
John Hawes, *Mfg Mgr*
Jose Herrera, *Production*
EMP: 250
SALES (corp-wide): 4.6B **Publicly Held**
WEB: www.teledyne.com
SIC: 3678 Electronic connectors
HQ: Teledyne Instruments, Inc.
16830 Chestnut St
City Of Industry CA 91748
626 934-1500

(G-2610)
TELEDYNE INSTRUMENTS INC
Also Called: Teledyne Impulse
1026 N Williamson Blvd (32114-7113)
PHONE..................................386 888-0880
Chris Tucket, *Finance*
EMP: 9
SALES (corp-wide): 4.6B **Publicly Held**
WEB: www.teledyne.com
SIC: 3643 Electric connectors
HQ: Teledyne Instruments, Inc.
16830 Chestnut St
City Of Industry CA 91748
626 934-1500

(G-2611)
TELEDYNE TECHNOLOGIES INC
1026 N Williamson Blvd (32114-7113)
PHONE..................................805 373-4545
John Flynn, *Vice Pres*
Tracy Wallace, *Buyer*
Daniel Hawkins, *Engineer*
Matthew Bartell, *Project Engr*
Arnar Steingrimsson, *Sales Staff*
EMP: 111
SALES (corp-wide): 4.6B **Publicly Held**
WEB: www.teledyne.com
SIC: 3679 Electronic circuits
PA: Teledyne Technologies Inc
1049 Camino Dos Rios
Thousand Oaks CA 91360
805 373-4545

(G-2612)
THREE BROTHERS BOARDS
212 S Beach St Ste 100 (32114-4403)
PHONE..................................386 310-4927
Roger Murray Jr, *Principal*
▼ EMP: 7 EST: 2010
SALES (est): 262.8K **Privately Held**
WEB: www.threebrothersboards.com
SIC: 2499 Oars & paddles, wood

(G-2613)
TIFFANY AND ASSOCIATES INC
Also Called: Independent Printing
500 Mason Ave (32117-4812)
PHONE..................................386 252-7351
Tiffany Johnson, *President*
Garry L Tiffany, *President*
▼ EMP: 27 EST: 1943
SQ FT: 10,000

SALES (est): 8.9MM **Privately Held**
WEB: www.printingdaytonabeach.com
SIC: 2752 Lithographing on metal

(G-2614)
TIP TOP PRTG OF VOLUSIA CNTY
1325 Beville Rd (32119-1529)
P.O. Box 1550 (32115-1550)
PHONE..................................386 760-7701
Henry C Winchester Jr, *President*
Bruce Negro, *Business Mgr*
EMP: 6 EST: 1961
SALES (est): 491.5K **Privately Held**
WEB: www.tiptopprinting.com
SIC: 2752 7331 5199 Commercial printing, offset; direct mail advertising services; advertising specialties

(G-2615)
UNION ENGINEERING N AMER LLC
Also Called: Pentair Union Engineering N.A.
2361 Mason Ave Ste 100 (32117-5163)
PHONE..................................386 445-4200
Heidi Jorgensen, *Mng Member*
Kimberle Marquardt, *Officer*
◆ EMP: 15 EST: 1874
SQ FT: 6,000
SALES (est): 5.1MM **Privately Held**
WEB: www.union.dk
SIC: 3569 3556 Gas producers (machinery); brewers' & maltsters' machinery
PA: Pentair Public Limited Company
10 Earlsfort Terrace
Dublin 2

(G-2616)
V I P PRINTING
133 W Intl Speedway Blvd (32114)
PHONE..................................386 258-3326
William Raymond, *Owner*
Angela Raymond-Jones, *Products*
EMP: 7 EST: 1976
SQ FT: 1,000
SALES (est): 750K **Privately Held**
WEB: www.vipprinting.net
SIC: 2752 2791 2789 Commercial printing, offset; typesetting; bookbinding & related work

(G-2617)
VALUE PROVIDERS LLC
2441 Bellevue Ave (32114-5615)
P.O. Box 411985, Melbourne (32941-1985)
PHONE..................................321 567-0919
Marc McCoy, *Manager*
EMP: 7 EST: 2013
SALES (est): 157.2K **Privately Held**
SIC: 3317 Steel pipe & tubes

(G-2618)
VULCAN CONSTRUCTION MTLS LLC
405 Madison Ave (32114-2009)
PHONE..................................386 252-8581
Robert Hable, *Manager*
EMP: 35 **Publicly Held**
WEB: www.vulcanmaterials.com
SIC: 3273 8741 Ready-mixed concrete; management services
HQ: Vulcan Construction Materials, Llc
1200 Urban Center Dr
Vestavia AL 35242
205 298-3000

(G-2619)
WRIGHT PRINTERY INC
735 N Ridgewood Ave (32114-2015)
PHONE..................................386 252-6571
Kim Barker, *President*
Peter Barker, *Vice Pres*
EMP: 5 EST: 1927
SQ FT: 1,200
SALES (est): 442.5K **Privately Held**
WEB: www.wrightprintery.com
SIC: 2752 Commercial printing, offset

De Land
Volusia County

(G-2620)
TECHNETICS GROUP LLC
Also Called: Technetics Group Deland
1700 E Intl Speedway Blvd (32724)
PHONE..................................386 736-7373
Chris Surdo, *Vice Pres*
Jeremy Lawrence, *Engineer*
Stephanie Haley, *Sales Staff*
James Boyd, *Branch Mgr*
Tony Eldridge, *Manager*
EMP: 20
SALES (corp-wide): 1.1B **Publicly Held**
WEB: www.technetics.com
SIC: 3053 3351 Gaskets & sealing devices; copper rolling & drawing
HQ: Technetics Group Llc
5605 Carnegie Blvd # 500
Charlotte NC 28209
704 731-1500

De Leon Springs
Volusia County

(G-2621)
AL-MAR METALS INC
Also Called: Metal Fabricators
1725 Arredondo Grant Rd (32130-3728)
PHONE..................................386 734-3377
Roy Blomquist, *President*
Cynthia Blomquist, *Principal*
Jeremy Blomquist, *Principal*
James Rhodes, *Principal*
EMP: 6 EST: 1995
SALES (est): 759.6K **Privately Held**
WEB: www.almarmetals.net
SIC: 3441 Fabricated structural metal

(G-2622)
ALUMINUM CREATIONS
155 Dawson Brown Rd (32130-3526)
PHONE..................................386 451-0113
N Leon Jones, *Principal*
EMP: 17 EST: 2001
SALES (est): 842.1K **Privately Held**
SIC: 3448 Screen enclosures

(G-2623)
ARCO GLOBAS TRADING LLC
Also Called: Arco Globas International
6111 Lake Winona Rd (32130-3544)
PHONE..................................305 707-7702
Abe Citron, *CEO*
Albert Citron, *Vice Pres*
EMP: 28 EST: 2012
SQ FT: 12,000
SALES (est): 1.1MM **Privately Held**
SIC: 2085 Cordials & premixed alcoholic cocktails

(G-2624)
EO PAINTER PRINTING COMPANY
4900 Us Highway 17 (32130-3199)
P.O. Box 877 (32130-0877)
PHONE..................................386 985-4877
Sidney Johnston, *President*
Jeff Johnston, *Vice Pres*
Mark Johnston, *Treasurer*
EMP: 10 EST: 1878
SALES (est): 885.1K **Privately Held**
WEB: www.eopainterprinting.com
SIC: 2752 Commercial printing, offset

(G-2625)
ERAPSCO
C 0 5612 Johnson Lake Rd (32130)
PHONE..................................386 740-5335
Lynne Moritz, *Principal*
EMP: 9 EST: 2014
SALES (est): 121.6K **Privately Held**
SIC: 3812 Sonar systems & equipment

(G-2626)
PARRISH INC
5498 Aragon Ave (32130-3426)
P.O. Box 1127 (32130-1127)
PHONE..................................386 985-4879
Wesley Parrish, *President*

EMP: 7 EST: 1994
SALES (est): 181.8K **Privately Held**
WEB: www.parrishshadetop.com
SIC: 3444 Awnings & canopies

(G-2627)
SDR SPECIALTIES SERVICES LLC
4511n Us Highway 17 (32130-4302)
P.O. Box 533 (32130-0533)
PHONE..................................386 878-6771
Richard D Slanker,
EMP: 6 EST: 2012
SALES (est): 388.3K **Privately Held**
WEB: www.sdrspecialtiesservice.com
SIC: 7692 7699 Welding repair; nautical repair services

(G-2628)
SPARTON CORPORATION (DH)
5612 Johnson Lake Rd (32130-3657)
PHONE..................................847 762-5800
Joseph McCormack, *CEO*
Steven Korwin, *Senior VP*
Gordon Madlock, *Senior VP*
Michael A Gaul, *Vice Pres*
James M Lackemacher, *Vice Pres*
▲ EMP: 200 EST: 1900
SQ FT: 22,000
SALES: 374.9MM **Privately Held**
WEB: www.sparton.com
SIC: 3672 Printed circuit boards

(G-2629)
SPARTON DELEON SPRINGS LLC (DH)
5612 Johnson Lake Rd (32130-3657)
PHONE..................................386 985-4631
Cary B Wood,
Steve M Korwin,
Michael W Osbourne,
Martin Reilly,
Mark Schlei,
▲ EMP: 138 EST: 1966
SQ FT: 186,000
SALES (est): 57.6MM **Privately Held**
WEB: www.sparton.com
SIC: 3812 3679 3672 Warfare countermeasure equipment; electronic circuits; printed circuit boards
HQ: Sparton Corporation
　　5612 Johnson Lake Rd
　　De Leon Springs FL 32130
　　847 762-5800

Debary
Volusia County

(G-2630)
ANEW INC
32 Cunningham Rd (32713-3168)
PHONE..................................386 668-7785
David Chapman, *President*
Cindy Connolly, *Marketing Staff*
EMP: 7 EST: 1999
SALES (est): 270K **Privately Held**
WEB: www.anewinc.com
SIC: 3841 Medical instruments & equipment, blood & bone work

(G-2631)
ANEW INTERNATIONAL CORPORATION
32 Cunningham Rd (32713-3168)
PHONE..................................386 668-7785
David Chapman, *President*
EMP: 8 EST: 1999
SALES (est): 97.8K **Privately Held**
SIC: 3841 Surgical & medical instruments

(G-2632)
COR LABEL LLC
901 S Chrles Rchard Ball (32713-9793)
PHONE..................................407 402-6633
Bryan G Dolbow,
EMP: 5 EST: 2020
SALES (est): 442.5K **Privately Held**
WEB: www.corlabel.com
SIC: 2759 Commercial printing

(G-2633)
CORNERSTONE FABRICATION LLC
291 Sprngview Commerce Dr (32713-4838)
PHONE..................................386 310-1110
Jim Hedger Jr, *Mng Member*
Kristine Hedger, *Manager*
EMP: 22 EST: 1998
SQ FT: 70,000
SALES (est): 9.2MM **Privately Held**
WEB: www.cornerstonefabrication.com
SIC: 3441 3444 Fabricated structural metal; sheet metal specialties, not stamped

(G-2634)
DYNAMIC ASPECTS INC
108 Fox Chase Ct (32713-4107)
PHONE..................................407 322-1923
James Abbott, *Principal*
Grace Grant, *Manager*
EMP: 8 EST: 2004
SALES (est): 600.1K **Privately Held**
WEB: www.dynamicaspects.net
SIC: 3993 1799 Signs & advertising specialties; sign installation & maintenance

(G-2635)
HILOMAST LLC
402 Chairman Ct Ste 100 (32713-4846)
PHONE..................................386 668-6784
Bruce Sousa, *Principal*
Joe Ostermann, *Engineer*
Barry Gardner,
▲ EMP: 6 EST: 2003
SALES (est): 2.6MM
SALES (corp-wide): 6.7MM **Privately Held**
WEB: www.hilomast.com
SIC: 3663 Radio & TV communications equipment
PA: South Midlands Communications Limited
　　School Close
　　Eastleigh HANTS SO53
　　238 024-6200

(G-2636)
HOFFMAN BROTHERS INC
Also Called: Browning Communications
275 S Chrles Rchard Ball (32713-3718)
PHONE..................................407 563-5004
Dean W O'Brien, *President*
EMP: 39 EST: 1985
SQ FT: 13,500
SALES (est): 1.2MM **Privately Held**
SIC: 2752 Commercial printing, offset

(G-2637)
MASCHMEYER CONCRETE CO FLA
275 Benson Junction Rd (32713-9789)
PHONE..................................386 668-7801
Richard King, *Branch Mgr*
EMP: 23
SALES (corp-wide): 136.2MM **Privately Held**
WEB: www.maschmeyer.com
SIC: 3273 Ready-mixed concrete
PA: Maschmeyer Concrete Company Of Florida
　　1142 Watertower Rd
　　Lake Park FL 33403
　　561 848-9112

(G-2638)
MICRON FIBER - TECH INC
230 Sprngview Commerce Dr (32713-4853)
PHONE..................................386 668-7895
Lixion Lu, *President*
Ning Jiang, *Vice Pres*
▲ EMP: 15 EST: 2001
SALES: 2.7MM **Privately Held**
WEB: www.mft-co.com
SIC: 3433 Gas burners, industrial

(G-2639)
PALM LABS ADHESIVES LLC
3063 Enterprise Rd Ste 31 (32713-2715)
PHONE..................................321 710-4850
Roger A Szafranski,
EMP: 10 EST: 2014

SALES (est): 1.1MM **Privately Held**
WEB: www.palmlabsadhesives.com
SIC: 2891 Adhesives

(G-2640)
RIVER CITY POWERSPORTS LLC
895 Diplomat Dr Unit E (32713-5204)
PHONE..................................386 259-5724
Clint J Furrow, *Principal*
EMP: 9 EST: 2011
SALES (est): 289.5K **Privately Held**
WEB: www.rivercitypowersports.com
SIC: 3799 All terrain vehicles (ATV)

(G-2641)
SEMINOLE PRECAST LLC
331 Benson Junction Rd (32713-9757)
PHONE..................................386 668-7745
EMP: 12 EST: 2020
SALES (est): 554.6K **Privately Held**
WEB: www.seminoleprecast.com
SIC: 3272 Concrete products, precast

(G-2642)
SIGNALVAULT LLC
156 S Charles Richard Bea (32713-3273)
PHONE..................................407 878-6365
Christopher N Gilpin, *Principal*
EMP: 7 EST: 2015
SALES (est): 370.6K **Privately Held**
WEB: www.signal-vault.com
SIC: 3699 Security devices

(G-2643)
SPECIALTY STRUCTURES INC
Also Called: Specilty Strctres Instllations
218 Plumosa Rd (32713-3944)
PHONE..................................386 668-0474
Bernd Rennebeck, *President*
Hernan Naya, *Foreman/Supr*
EMP: 10 EST: 2011
SALES (est): 1.6MM **Privately Held**
WEB: www.specialty-structures.com
SIC: 3441 Fabricated structural metal

(G-2644)
STARKEY PRODUCTS INC ✪
425 Fox Run (32713-4622)
PHONE..................................386 479-3908
Jason Starkey, *Principal*
EMP: 10 EST: 2022
SALES (est): 1.2MM **Privately Held**
WEB: www.starkey-products.com
SIC: 3714 Motor vehicle parts & accessories

(G-2645)
WHITE SIGN COMPANY LLC
909 S Charles Richard Bea (32713-9708)
PHONE..................................407 342-7887
Joel White, *Mng Member*
Jarrod Swinderman, *Manager*
Susan Fisher, *Assistant*
EMP: 5 EST: 2007
SQ FT: 8,000
SALES (est): 1.1MM **Privately Held**
WEB: www.whitesigncompany.com
SIC: 3993 Signs & advertising specialties

(G-2646)
WRAP INSTALLERS INC ✪
915 Diplomat Dr Ste 104 (32713-2792)
PHONE..................................407 404-2914
Tyrone J Sebastien R, *President*
EMP: 5 EST: 2022
SALES (est): 308.3K **Privately Held**
SIC: 3993 Signs & advertising specialties

Deerfield Beach
Broward County

(G-2647)
123 DIET LLC
10 Fairway Dr Ste 225 (33441-1802)
PHONE..................................954 643-2522
Emma Moroni, *Mng Member*
Lawrence F Moroni Jr,
EMP: 5 EST: 2018
SALES (est): 327K **Privately Held**
WEB: www.usa123diet.com
SIC: 2023 Dietary supplements, dairy & non-dairy based

(G-2648)
55 GROUP LLC (PA)
3220 Sw 15th St (33442-8126)
PHONE..................................954 427-8405
Adrian Green, *CEO*
EMP: 8 EST: 2010
SALES (est): 9.4MM **Privately Held**
WEB: www.55-group.com
SIC: 3812 Defense systems & equipment

(G-2649)
55 INDUSTRIES LLC
3220 Sw 15th St (33442-8126)
PHONE..................................954 955-0212
Adrian Green, *Managing Prtnr*
Ofer Klein, *COO*
Arlene Landete, *CFO*
Jack Burstein, *Mng Member*
Amichay Zelcer, *Mng Member*
EMP: 30 EST: 2017
SALES (est): 4.3MM
SALES (corp-wide): 9.4MM **Privately Held**
WEB: www.55-group.com
SIC: 3728 Aircraft body assemblies & parts
PA: 55 Group Llc
　　3220 Sw 15th St
　　Deerfield Beach FL 33442
　　954 427-8405

(G-2650)
55 MANUFACTURING INC
3220 Sw 15th St (33442-8126)
PHONE..................................954 332-2921
Adrian Green, *President*
EMP: 16 EST: 2018
SALES (est): 2.4MM **Privately Held**
WEB: www.ligi.com
SIC: 3599 Machine shop, jobbing & repair

(G-2651)
905 EAST HILLSBORO LLC
Also Called: Aesthetic Mobile Laser Svcs
905 E Hillsboro Blvd (33441-3523)
PHONE..................................954 480-2600
Paul J Miano, *Mng Member*
EMP: 10 EST: 2005
SALES (est): 798.9K **Privately Held**
WEB: www.aestheticmobilelaser.com
SIC: 3699 Laser systems & equipment

(G-2652)
AAA STEEL FABRICATORS INC
1669 Sw 45th Way (33442-9003)
PHONE..................................954 570-7211
Thomas Juliano, *President*
Gary Sheriff, *Vice Pres*
EMP: 6 EST: 1999
SQ FT: 7,500
SALES (est): 975.4K **Privately Held**
WEB: www.aaasteelfabricators.com
SIC: 3441 Fabricated structural metal

(G-2653)
ACCENT CLOSETS INC
3700 Ne 3rd Ave (33064-3526)
PHONE..................................954 561-8800
Ronald Antiliko, *Enginr/R&D Mgr*
EMP: 15 **Privately Held**
WEB: www.accentclosets.com
SIC: 2511 China closets
PA: Accent Closets, Inc.
　　2266 Nw 30th Pl
　　Pompano Beach FL 33069

(G-2654)
ACCUPRINT CORPORATION
Also Called: My Print Shop
1061 Sw 30th Ave (33442-8104)
PHONE..................................954 973-9369
Jeff Pottruck, *President*
Carol Mariano, *Manager*
EMP: 10 EST: 1988
SQ FT: 2,200
SALES (est): 373.2K **Privately Held**
WEB: www.accuprint.us
SIC: 2752 Commercial printing, offset

(G-2655)
ACCUPRINT MY PRINT SHOP
1061 Sw 30th Ave (33442-8104)
PHONE..................................954 973-9369
Jeffery Pottruck, *Owner*
EMP: 11 EST: 1980

▲ = Import ▼=Export
◆ =Import/Export

SALES (est): 155.7K **Privately Held**
WEB: www.myprintshop.com
SIC: 2759 2752 Screen printing; commercial printing, lithographic

(G-2656)
ADVANCED HAIR PRODUCTS INC
1287 E Nwport Ctr Dr Ste (33442)
PHONE.....................561 347-2799
Carmine Gazero, *CEO*
▲ EMP: 8 EST: 1990
SQ FT: 2,800
SALES (est): 655.1K **Privately Held**
WEB: www.innovativehair.com
SIC: 3999 Wigs, including doll wigs, toupees or wiglets

(G-2657)
ADVANCED OUTDOOR CONCEPTS INC
Also Called: Cobb America
3840 W Hillsboro Blvd (33442-9478)
PHONE.....................954 429-1428
EMP: 6 EST: 2006
SQ FT: 3,000
SALES (est): 1.2MM **Privately Held**
SIC: 3631 Mfg Household Cooking Equipment

(G-2658)
ADVANCED PUBLIC SAFETY LLC
Also Called: Centralsquare Technologies
400 Fairway Dr Ste 101 (33441-1808)
PHONE.....................954 354-3000
EMP: 1 EST: 2001
SALES (est): 6.6MM
SALES (corp-wide): 272.3MM **Privately Held**
SIC: 7372 Business oriented computer software
PA: Centralsquare Technologies, Llc
1000 Business Center Dr
Lake Mary FL 32746
800 727-8088

(G-2659)
AESTHETIC MBL LASER SVCS INC
905 E Hillsboro Blvd (33441-3523)
P.O. Box 8550 (33443-8550)
PHONE.....................954 480-2600
Paul J Miano, *President*
Eduardo Bravo-Leon, *Vice Pres*
EMP: 8 EST: 2002
SALES (est): 860.8K **Privately Held**
WEB: www.aestheticmobilelaser.com
SIC: 3841 Surgical lasers

(G-2660)
AIG TECHNOLOGIES INC
5001 Nw 13th Ave Ste B (33064-8649)
PHONE.....................954 433-0618
Stephen Dawes, *President*
Charlene Dawes, *Vice Pres*
Andrea Plante, *Manager*
EMP: 15 EST: 1997
SQ FT: 40,000
SALES (est): 5.2MM **Privately Held**
WEB: www.aigtechnologies.net
SIC: 2844 Hair preparations, including shampoos; shampoos, rinses, conditioners: hair; suntan lotions & oils

(G-2661)
AIR DIMENSIONS INC
Also Called: ADI
1371 W Newport Center Dr # 101 (33442-7700)
PHONE.....................954 428-7333
Gregory English, *President*
Tomas Gunther, *Purchasing*
David W English, *Treasurer*
Greg English, *Train & Dev Mgr*
Elizabeth English, *Personnel*
EMP: 22 EST: 1971
SQ FT: 12,000
SALES (est): 7.1MM **Privately Held**
WEB: www.airdimensions.com
SIC: 3561 Industrial pumps & parts

(G-2662)
ALL IN ONE CMPLETE HNDYMAN SVC
177 Sw 5th Ct (33441-4620)
PHONE.....................954 708-3463
Craig Baldwin,
EMP: 10 EST: 2020
SALES (est): 502.1K **Privately Held**
SIC: 2951 Asphalt paving mixtures & blocks

(G-2663)
ALL PHASE CONSTRUCTION USA LLC
590 Goolsby Blvd (33442-3021)
PHONE.....................754 227-5605
Christopher R Porosky,
EMP: 14 EST: 2017
SALES (est): 1.3MM **Privately Held**
WEB: www.allphaseconstructionfl.com
SIC: 3444 Sheet metalwork

(G-2664)
ALL STAR PRINTING INTL
Also Called: Allstar Printing International
2001 W Sample Rd Ste 100 (33064-1346)
PHONE.....................954 974-0333
Morris Spaszwer, *Owner*
EMP: 5 EST: 2001
SALES (est): 358.4K **Privately Held**
WEB: www.allstarprintinginc.com
SIC: 2752 Commercial printing, offset

(G-2665)
ALLIANCE CABINETS & MILLWORK
3231 Sw 3rd St (33442-2322)
PHONE.....................407 802-9921
Bruno Romano, *President*
EMP: 6 EST: 2010
SALES (est): 476.5K **Privately Held**
WEB: www.alliancewoodworking.com
SIC: 2431 Millwork

(G-2666)
ALLIED AEROSPACE INTERNATIONAL
1022 E Newport Center Dr (33442-7723)
PHONE.....................954 429-8600
Christopher Abukhalaf, *Principal*
EMP: 9 EST: 2016
SALES (est): 203.3K **Privately Held**
WEB: www.alliedaerospaceinc.com
SIC: 3728 Aircraft parts & equipment

(G-2667)
AMERICAN DIESEL AND GAS INC
1911 Nw 40th Ct (33064-8719)
PHONE.....................561 447-8500
Morris Lewitter, *President*
EMP: 15 EST: 2001
SALES (est): 914.1K **Privately Held**
SIC: 3519 Engines, diesel & semi-diesel or dual-fuel

(G-2668)
ANCO PRECISION INC
Also Called: Machine Shop
3191 Sw 11th St Ste 200 (33442-8147)
PHONE.....................954 429-3703
David Velardi, *President*
Andrew Velardi, *President*
Terry Velardi, *Corp Secy*
EMP: 6 EST: 1976
SQ FT: 3,500
SALES (est): 606.7K **Privately Held**
WEB: www.ancoprecision.com
SIC: 3599 Machine shop, jobbing & repair

(G-2669)
AQUALUMA LLC
3251 Sw 13th Dr Ste A (33442-8166)
PHONE.....................954 234-2512
Alexandra Bader, *Vice Pres*
EMP: 9 EST: 2012
SALES (est): 544.6K **Privately Held**
WEB: www.aqualuma.com
SIC: 3674 Light emitting diodes

(G-2670)
ART WOOD CABINETS CORP
1533 Sw 1st Way (33441-6777)
PHONE.....................754 367-0742

Carlos P Lima, *President*
EMP: 10 EST: 2004
SALES (est): 157.5K **Privately Held**
SIC: 2434 Wood kitchen cabinets

(G-2671)
ARTECH SYSTEMS INC
333 Ne 21st Ave (33441-3855)
PHONE.....................954 304-0430
Royi Segal, *Principal*
EMP: 9 EST: 2009
SALES (est): 167.8K **Privately Held**
SIC: 2869 Industrial organic chemicals

(G-2672)
ASHLEY BRYAN INTERNATIONAL INC
1432 E Nwport Ctr Dr Ste (33442)
PHONE.....................954 351-1199
Jerry Isackson, *President*
Bryan Isackson, *Vice Pres*
Sherry Isackson, *Vice Pres*
Michelle Jacob, *Project Mgr*
Mikki Hall, *Treasurer*
◆ EMP: 23 EST: 1988
SALES (est): 3.6MM **Privately Held**
WEB: bryanashley.ofs.com
SIC: 2531 2519 Public building & related furniture; wicker & rattan furniture

(G-2673)
AUDIO INTELLIGENCE DEVICES
637 Jim Moran Blvd (33442-1711)
PHONE.....................954 418-1400
Glen Hower, *President*
William Armour, *CFO*
EMP: 34 EST: 1968
SQ FT: 100,000
SALES (est): 1.2MM **Privately Held**
WEB: www.aid-nia.com
SIC: 3699 Security control equipment & systems

(G-2674)
AUDREY MORRIS COSMT INTL LLC
1601 Green Rd Ste A (33064-1076)
PHONE.....................954 332-2000
Ali Kasi, *CEO*
EMP: 30 EST: 2020
SALES (est): 1.1MM **Privately Held**
WEB: www.audreymorriscosmetics.com
SIC: 2844 5122 7389 Cosmetic preparations; cosmetics, perfumes & hair products; cosmetic kits, assembling & packaging

(G-2675)
BANYAN GAMING LLC
245 Ne 21st Ave Ste 300 (33441-3859)
PHONE.....................954 951-7094
Jason Seelig, *Mng Member*
Daniel Lombana, *Technician*
Charles Bernitz,
▲ EMP: 7 EST: 2015
SQ FT: 6,000
SALES (est): 693.6K **Privately Held**
WEB: www.banyangaming.com
SIC: 3999 Slot machines

(G-2676)
BE POWER TECH INC
1500 S Powerline Rd Ste A (33442-8185)
PHONE.....................954 543-5370
EMP: 16 EST: 2015
SALES (est): 1.2MM **Privately Held**
SIC: 3699 3443 Electrical equipment & supplies; heat exchangers, condensers & components

(G-2677)
BLU SLEEP PRODUCTS LLC (PA)
Also Called: Somni Specialty Sleep
1501 Green Rd Ste B (33064-1077)
PHONE.....................866 973-7614
Erasmo Ciccolelle, *Mng Member*
EMP: 2 EST: 2014
SQ FT: 23,000
SALES (est): 4MM **Privately Held**
WEB: www.myblusleep.com
SIC: 2515 Mattresses & bedsprings

(G-2678)
BOAIR INC
210 S Military Trl (33442-3017)
P.O. Box 266132, Fort Lauderdale (33326-6132)
PHONE.....................954 426-9226
EMP: 6
SQ FT: 3,500
SALES (est): 600K **Privately Held**
SIC: 3564 Mfg Of Electro Static Filters

(G-2679)
BOCA TERRY LLC
3000 Sw 15th St Ste G (33442-8198)
PHONE.....................954 312-4400
Ed Cohen, *CFO*
Jyll Brink, *Accounts Mgr*
Diane Rottner, *Info Tech Mgr*
Edward Cohen,
Bruce Cohen,
▲ EMP: 10 EST: 1997
SALES (est): 1.6MM **Privately Held**
WEB: www.bocaterry.com
SIC: 2384 Robes & dressing gowns

(G-2680)
BRAZILIAN CLSSFIED ADS-CHEI IN
Also Called: Achei USA Newspaper
2001 W Sample Rd Ste 422 (33064-1300)
PHONE.....................954 570-7568
Jose Nunes, *President*
EMP: 7 EST: 2001
SQ FT: 1,000
SALES (est): 557.5K **Privately Held**
WEB: www.acheiusa.com
SIC: 2741 2711 ; newspapers, publishing & printing

(G-2681)
BRITE SHOT INC
600 W Hillsboro Blvd (33441-1609)
PHONE.....................954 418-7125
Peter Ticktin, *President*
Roy McDonald, *Vice Pres*
Irene Conrad, *Treasurer*
Noah Platte, *Manager*
EMP: 10 EST: 2009
SALES (est): 931K **Privately Held**
SIC: 3648 Lighting equipment

(G-2682)
BROWARD CUSTOM WOODWORK LLC
401 Jim Moran Blvd (33442-1707)
PHONE.....................352 376-4732
Bill Koelbel, *President*
EMP: 5 EST: 1988
SALES (est): 506.3K
SALES (corp-wide): 94.6MM **Privately Held**
WEB: www.listindustries.com
SIC: 2434 5021 Wood kitchen cabinets; lockers
PA: List Industries Inc.
401 Jim Moran Blvd
Deerfield Beach FL 33442
954 429-9155

(G-2683)
BRRH CORPORATION
3313 W Hillsboro Blvd # 101 (33442-9423)
PHONE.....................954 427-9665
Brian Altschuler, *Vice Pres*
Mindy Shikiar, *Vice Pres*
Maureen Mann, *Exec Dir*
Brina Watson, *Analyst*
EMP: 56 **Privately Held**
WEB: www.brrh.com
SIC: 3829 Medical diagnostic systems, nuclear
PA: Brrh Corporation
800 Meadows Rd
Boca Raton FL 33486

(G-2684)
BRYAN ASHLEY INC
1432 E Newport Center Dr (33442-7703)
PHONE.....................954 351-1199
Bryan Ashley, *President*
Robert Duban, *Vice Pres*
Sandra Febres, *Vice Pres*
Brittney Williams, *Vice Pres*
Theresa Sauer, *Project Mgr*
EMP: 37 EST: 2017

SALES (est): 3.5MM **Privately Held**
WEB: bryanashley.ofs.com
SIC: **2599** Hotel furniture

(G-2685)
CAPSTONE INDUSTRIES INC
431 Fairway Dr Ste 200 (33441-1823)
PHONE...................................954 570-8889
Stewart Wallach, *CEO*
Reid Goldstein, *President*
Jerry Mc Clinton, *COO*
Jordan Seals, *Marketing Staff*
Aimee Gaudet, *Director*
▲ EMP: 10 EST: 1996
SQ FT: 4,000
SALES (est): 762K
SALES (corp-wide): 685.8K **Publicly Held**
WEB: www.capstoneindustries.com
SIC: **3645** Garden, patio, walkway & yard lighting fixtures: electric
PA: Capstone Companies, Inc.
　　431 Fairway Dr Ste 200
　　Deerfield Beach FL 33441
　　954 252-3440

(G-2686)
CAROLINA WOODWORKS INC
714 Nw 44th Ter Apt 203 (33442-9285)
PHONE...................................954 692-4662
Ecleidivaldo C Araujo, *Principal*
EMP: 8 EST: 2007
SALES (est): 82.7K **Privately Held**
SIC: **2431** Millwork

(G-2687)
CAYMAN MANUFACTURING INC
1301 Sw 34th Ave (33442-8153)
PHONE...................................954 421-1170
Donald H Ferguson, *President*
Josh Ferguson, *Mfg Staff*
EMP: 36 EST: 1989
SQ FT: 20,000
SALES (est): 4MM **Privately Held**
WEB: www.caymanmfg.com
SIC: **2522 2531** Office furniture, except wood; school furniture

(G-2688)
CAYMAN NAT MFG INSTLLATION INC
1301 Sw 34th Ave (33442-8153)
PHONE...................................954 421-1170
Donald H Ferguson, *President*
Margarita Correa, *Project Engr*
Monica Heath, *Manager*
▼ EMP: 75 EST: 2000
SQ FT: 40,000
SALES (est): 7.2MM **Privately Held**
WEB: www.caymanmfg.com
SIC: **2522** Office cabinets & filing drawers: except wood

(G-2689)
CENTRAL CONCRETE SUPERMIX INC
1817 S Powerline Rd (33442-8164)
PHONE...................................954 480-9333
Frank Perez, *Vice Pres*
Tom Figari, *Branch Mgr*
Noel Bueno, *Info Tech Mgr*
EMP: 10
SALES (corp-wide): 43.8MM **Privately Held**
WEB: www.supermix.com
SIC: **3273** Ready-mixed concrete
PA: Central Concrete Supermix Inc
　　4300 Sw 74th Ave
　　Miami FL 33155
　　305 262-3250

(G-2690)
CESAR E RODRIGUEZ
4371 N Dixie Hwy (33064-4245)
PHONE...................................561 305-1312
Cesar E Rodriguez, *Principal*
Hoyt Schmidt, *Senior VP*
Gonzalo Montoya, *Financial Analy*
David Kiefer, *Sales Staff*
Maros Fodor, *Planning*
EMP: 7 EST: 2014
SALES (est): 129.1K **Privately Held**
WEB: www.pbearmor.com
SIC: **3842** Surgical appliances & supplies

(G-2691)
CHECKPOINT CARD GROUP INC
1801 Green Rd (33064-1052)
PHONE...................................954 426-1331
Anthony Gardner, *President*
Ivan Milo, *Vice Pres*
EMP: 9 EST: 2017
SALES (est): 414.9K **Privately Held**
WEB: www.cpcardtech.com
SIC: **3089** Identification cards, plastic

(G-2692)
CHEM-TEC EQUIPMENT CO
Also Called: Chem TEC
3077 Sw 13th Dr (33442-8129)
PHONE...................................954 428-8259
Matthew Donoghue, *President*
Kelly Donoghue, *Admin Sec*
EMP: 11 EST: 1967
SQ FT: 10,000
SALES (est): 1.9MM **Privately Held**
WEB: www.chemtec.com
SIC: **3823 3491** Industrial instrmnts msrmnt display/control process variable; industrial valves

(G-2693)
CIRO MANUFACTURING CORPORATION
692 S Military Trl (33442-3000)
PHONE...................................561 988-2139
Leland Cerasani, *President*
Samantha Williams, *Prgrmr*
▲ EMP: 23 EST: 2002
SALES (est): 2.7MM **Privately Held**
WEB: www.ciromfg.com
SIC: **3084** Plastics pipe

(G-2694)
COSMO INTERNATIONAL CORP (PA)
Also Called: Cosmo International Fragrances
1341 W Newport Center Dr (33442-7734)
PHONE...................................954 798-4500
Marc Blaison, *President*
J Fernando Belmont, *President*
Janine Belmont, *Vice Pres*
Javier Abadia, *Opers Staff*
Duvan Garcia, *Production*
◆ EMP: 50 EST: 1976
SQ FT: 90,000
SALES (est): 51.6MM **Privately Held**
WEB: www.cosmo-fragrances.com
SIC: **2869** Perfume materials, synthetic

(G-2695)
COSMO INTERNATIONAL CORP
Also Called: Cosmo International Fragrances
1341 W Newport Center Dr (33442-7734)
PHONE...................................954 798-4500
EMP: 32
SALES (corp-wide): 58MM **Privately Held**
SIC: **2844** Mfg Toilet Preparations
PA: Cosmo International Corp.
　　2455 E Sunrise Blvd # 720
　　Fort Lauderdale FL 33442
　　954 566-1516

(G-2696)
CRAWFORD GLASS DOOR CO
3301 Sw 13th Dr Ste B (33442-8108)
PHONE...................................954 480-6820
Ralph Crawford, *President*
EMP: 10 EST: 1991
SQ FT: 6,000
SALES (est): 875.7K **Privately Held**
SIC: **3231** Doors, glass: made from purchased glass

(G-2697)
CUSTOM BIOLOGICALS INC
1239 E Nwport Ctr Dr Ste (33442)
PHONE...................................561 998-1699
Thomas Baugh, *President*
Alex Calvo, *Production*
▲ EMP: 9 EST: 2006
SALES (est): 1.6MM **Privately Held**
WEB: www.custombio.com
SIC: **2836** Biological products, except diagnostic

(G-2698)
CUSTOM CABINETS DESIGN INC
5000 Nw 3rd Ave (33064-2425)
PHONE...................................561 210-3423
Alvaro Villalobos, *Principal*
EMP: 7 EST: 2010
SALES (est): 247.5K **Privately Held**
WEB: www.kitchensolvers.com
SIC: **2434** Wood kitchen cabinets

(G-2699)
CUSTOM GRAPHICS INC
1801 Green Rd Ste B (33064-1052)
PHONE...................................954 563-6756
Cathy Cart, *President*
Steven Cart, *Admin Sec*
EMP: 5 EST: 1987
SALES (est): 412.1K **Privately Held**
WEB: www.decalsbycustomgraphics.com
SIC: **2759** Screen printing

(G-2700)
CUSTOM PLASTIC CARD COMPANY
1801 Green Rd Ste A (33064-1052)
P.O. Box 4489 (33064-4489)
PHONE...................................954 426-1331
Tony Gardner, *President*
Ivan Milo, *Opers Mgr*
Arlene Kearney, *Sales Staff*
Deb Devinney, *Advt Staff*
Jordan Manolakis, *Manager*
▲ EMP: 80 EST: 1983
SQ FT: 45,000
SALES (est): 8.8MM **Privately Held**
WEB: www.customplasticcard.com
SIC: **3089** Injection molding of plastics

(G-2701)
CVE REPORTER INC
3501 West Dr (33442-2000)
PHONE...................................954 421-5566
Steven Fine, *Principal*
Kelly Hampton, *Exec Dir*
EMP: 11 EST: 2008
SALES (est): 269.2K **Privately Held**
WEB: www.cvereporter.com
SIC: **2711** Newspapers, publishing & printing

(G-2702)
DAC WOOD WORK INC
428 Se 11th St Apt 202a (33441-6957)
PHONE...................................954 729-9232
Eneias P Costa, *Principal*
EMP: 7 EST: 2011
SALES (est): 72.5K **Privately Held**
SIC: **2431** Millwork

(G-2703)
DAIGLE TOOL & DIE INC
764 Ne 42nd St (33064-4204)
PHONE...................................954 785-9989
Robert V Daigle, *Chairman*
Robert J Daigle, *Vice Pres*
EMP: 7 EST: 1982
SQ FT: 12,000
SALES (est): 520.3K **Privately Held**
SIC: **3542 3089** Machine tools, metal forming type; molding primary plastic

(G-2704)
DESIGN BY YOGI LLC
3413 Sw 14th St (33442-8140)
PHONE...................................954 428-9797
EMP: 9 EST: 2019
SALES (est): 533.6K **Privately Held**
WEB: www.operation32.com
SIC: **2434** Wood kitchen cabinets

(G-2705)
DESIGN-A-RUG INC (PA)
200 N Federal Hwy (33441-3612)
PHONE...................................954 943-7487
Ali R Amjadi, *President*
Fatemeh Amjadi, *Principal*
EMP: 14 EST: 1983
SQ FT: 15,000
SALES (est): 1.2MM **Privately Held**
WEB: www.design-a-rug.com
SIC: **2273 5713** Carpets, hand & machine made; carpets

(G-2706)
DIABETEX CARE
1525 Nw 3rd St (33442-1669)
PHONE...................................954 427-9510
Howard Rich, *Principal*
EMP: 8 EST: 2010
SALES (est): 142.4K **Privately Held**
SIC: **3841** Surgical & medical instruments

(G-2707)
DIZENZO MANUFACTURING INTL INC
4400 Nw 19th Ave Ste J (33064-8703)
PHONE...................................954 978-4624
Frank Dizenzo, *President*
EMP: 7 EST: 1995
SQ FT: 2,400
SALES (est): 800.9K **Privately Held**
SIC: **2591** Window blinds

(G-2708)
DMR CREATIVE MARKETING LLC
321 Goolsby Blvd (33442-3006)
PHONE...................................954 725-3750
Brian Weinman, *President*
Jeffrey Bee, *Exec VP*
Eric Moss, *Controller*
◆ EMP: 5 EST: 2000
SALES (est): 2MM **Privately Held**
WEB: www.dmrcreativem.com
SIC: **2326** Work apparel, except uniforms

(G-2709)
DOORMARK INC
430 Goolsby Blvd (33442-3019)
PHONE...................................954 418-4700
Roy Jacob Van Wyck, *President*
Mark Harmon, *Maint Spvr*
Cindy Vermaas, *Bookkeeper*
Brianna Gendron, *Executive*
◆ EMP: 44 EST: 1994
SALES (est): 7.2MM **Privately Held**
WEB: www.doormark.com
SIC: **2434** Wood kitchen cabinets

(G-2710)
DR JILLS FOOT PADS INC
384 S Military Trl (33442-3007)
PHONE...................................954 573-6557
Jill Scheur, *President*
Jay Scheur, *Vice Pres*
▼ EMP: 10 EST: 2002
SALES (est): 2.1MM **Privately Held**
WEB: www.drjillsfootpads.com
SIC: **3842** Foot appliances, orthopedic

(G-2711)
DYEBAR EXPRESS LTD
3390 Sw 15th St (33442-8126)
PHONE...................................954 298-5171
Stephen Drescher, *CEO*
EMP: 11 EST: 2018
SALES (est): 443.5K **Privately Held**
SIC: **2844** Hair coloring preparations

(G-2712)
DYNASEL INCORPORATED
114 Grantham A (33442-3401)
PHONE...................................972 733-4447
Naomi Levinson, *President*
Robert Levinson, *Treasurer*
▲ EMP: 9 EST: 1963
SALES (est): 108.3K **Privately Held**
SIC: **2673** Plastic bags: made from purchased materials

(G-2713)
E&M INNOVATIVE FORAGER LLC (PA)
Also Called: Sunshine Provisions
736 S Military Trl (33442-3025)
PHONE...................................954 923-0056
Evan S David,
EMP: 24 EST: 2014
SALES (est): 3.3MM **Privately Held**
SIC: **2015 2013** Poultry sausage, luncheon meats & other poultry products; sausages & other prepared meats

(G-2714)
EAGLE PAVERS INC
51 Nw 45th Ave (33442-9393)
PHONE...................................954 822-1137
EMP: 8 EST: 2015

SALES (est): 200.3K **Privately Held**
SIC: 2951 Mfg Asphalt Mixtures/Blocks

(G-2715)
ECHO PLASTIC SYSTEMS
1801 Green Rd Ste B (33064-1052)
PHONE....................................305 655-1300
Norman Mensh, *President*
Tony Garner, *President*
Doug Upton, *Director*
EMP: 12 EST: 1976
SQ FT: 8,500
SALES (est): 879.5K **Privately Held**
SIC: 3083 Laminated plastics plate & sheet

(G-2716)
EDGELINE INDUSTRIES LLC
(PA)
1319 E Hillsboro Blvd # 514 (33441-4225)
PHONE....................................954 727-5272
Hector O Huarte,
Nicolas D Huarte,
Dennis J Watts,
◆ EMP: 6 EST: 2011
SALES (est): 1.8MM **Privately Held**
SIC: 2521 Wood office furniture

(G-2717)
ENDEAVOR MANUFACTURING
INC
510 Goolsby Blvd (33442-3021)
PHONE....................................954 752-6828
Stanley S Noreika, *Principal*
EMP: 12 EST: 2013
SALES (est): 1.3MM **Privately Held**
WEB: www.emfginc.com
SIC: 3999 Manufacturing industries

(G-2718)
ESQUADRO INC
217 Se 1st Ter (33441-3903)
PHONE....................................754 367-3098
Ebrahim Frederico R, *Principal*
EMP: 8 EST: 2014
SALES (est): 293.5K **Privately Held**
SIC: 2434 Wood kitchen cabinets

(G-2719)
FOGMASTER CORPORATION
(PA)
1051 Sw 30th Ave (33442-8104)
PHONE....................................954 481-9975
Thomas M Latta, *President*
Steven Hawkins, *Vice Pres*
▲ EMP: 5 EST: 1982
SQ FT: 21,000
SALES (est): 1.4MM **Privately Held**
WEB: www.fogmaster.com
SIC: 3523 Soil preparation machinery, ex-
cept turf & grounds

(G-2720)
FORNO DE MINAS USA INC
242 Sw 12th Ave (33442-3104)
PHONE....................................954 840-6533
Rosana Parise, *Officer*
Gustavo Salazar, *Officer*
EMP: 10 EST: 2014
SALES (est): 870.9K **Privately Held**
SIC: 2051 Cakes, pies & pastries

(G-2721)
FORUM PUBLISHING GROUP
INC (DH)
Also Called: Choice ADS
1701 Green Rd Ste B (33064-1074)
PHONE....................................954 698-6397
Ken Mitchell, *President*
▲ EMP: 135 EST: 1969
SALES (est): 25.1MM
SALES (corp-wide): 4.6B **Publicly Held**
WEB: www.sun-sentinel.com
SIC: 2711 Newspapers, publishing & print-
ing
HQ: Tribune Media Company
515 N State St Ste 2400
Chicago IL 60654
312 222-3394

(G-2722)
FORUM PUBLISHING GROUP
INC
Also Called: Wellington Forum
333 Sw 12th Ave (33442-3107)
PHONE....................................954 596-5650

Keri Lurtz, *Manager*
EMP: 83
SALES (corp-wide): 4.6B **Publicly Held**
WEB: www.sun-sentinel.com
SIC: 2711 2741 Newspapers: publishing
only, not printed on site; miscellaneous
publishing
HQ: Forum Publishing Group Inc
1701 Green Rd Ste B
Deerfield Beach FL 33064
954 698-6397

(G-2723)
G J SHEET METAL CORP
4710 Ne 2nd Way (33064-3425)
PHONE....................................954 709-9011
Joseph Georges, *Principal*
EMP: 7 EST: 2012
SALES (est): 121.3K **Privately Held**
SIC: 3444 Sheet metalwork

(G-2724)
GBI INTRALOGISTICS
SOLUTIONS
1143 W Newport Center Dr (33442-7732)
PHONE....................................954 596-5000
Jeffrey Spitzer, *COO*
Edgardo Cabrera, *Engineer*
Moshe Raab, *Director*
Bogdan Avasiloae, *Administration*
EMP: 14 EST: 2016
SALES (est): 4.6MM **Privately Held**
WEB: www.gbisorters.com
SIC: 7372 Application computer software

(G-2725)
GEORGE WASH CPITL
PARTNERS LLC (PA) ✪
Also Called: Allied Group, The
1022 E Newport Center Dr (33442-7723)
PHONE....................................786 910-1778
Christopher Abukhalaf, *CEO*
EMP: 3 EST: 2021
SALES (est): 5MM **Privately Held**
SIC: 3812 Aircraft/aerospace flight instru-
ments & guidance systems

(G-2726)
GIOVANNI ART IN CSTM FURN
INC
1478 Sw 1st Way (33441-6754)
PHONE....................................954 698-1008
Jorge Tenutta, *President*
Patricia Tenutta, *Corp Secy*
EMP: 6 EST: 1993
SALES (est): 446.4K **Privately Held**
SIC: 2426 Carvings, furniture: wood

(G-2727)
GLOBAL DIRECTORIES INC
Also Called: Yellow Pages
450 Fairway Dr Ste 204 (33441-1837)
PHONE....................................954 571-8283
EMP: 10
SALES (est): 607K
SALES (corp-wide): 4.9MM **Privately
Held**
SIC: 2741 Misc Publishing
PA: Global Directories, Inc.
6440 Sthpint Pkwy Ste 150
Jacksonville FL 32216
904 899-4400

(G-2728)
GULF ASSOCIATES CONTROL
INC
Also Called: G A C Inc/Gulf Associates
231 Se 1st Ter (33441-3903)
PHONE....................................954 426-0536
James B Martin Jr, *President*
EMP: 28 EST: 1968
SQ FT: 3,750
SALES (est): 566.3K **Privately Held**
SIC: 3433 Heaters, swimming pool: oil or
gas

(G-2729)
H2O INTERNATIONAL INC
3001 Sw 15th St Ste C (33442-8199)
PHONE....................................954 570-3464
Guillermo Guzman, *President*
Ivan Molina, *Technology*
▲ EMP: 15 EST: 1993
SQ FT: 18,000

SALES (est): 2.2MM **Privately Held**
WEB: www.h2ofilter.com
SIC: 3589 5074 Water purification equipment, household type; water purification
equipment

(G-2730)
HANDCRAFT WOODWORKING
INC
1498 Nw 3rd St (33442-1647)
PHONE....................................954 418-6356
Jerry A Rowland, *President*
Charles Wieland, *CFO*
Anthony Bilbao, *Manager*
James Woodburn, *Manager*
EMP: 20 EST: 1991
SQ FT: 11,600
SALES (est): 3.7MM **Privately Held**
WEB: www.handcraftwoodworking.com
SIC: 2431 Millwork

(G-2731)
HEALTH COMMUNICATIONS INC
Also Called: Hci Books
3201 Sw 15th St (33442-8157)
PHONE....................................954 360-0909
Peter Vegso, *President*
◆ EMP: 87 EST: 1976
SQ FT: 100,000
SALES (est): 13.3MM **Privately Held**
WEB: www.hcibooks.com
SIC: 2741 Miscellaneous publishing; globe
covers (maps): publishing & printing

(G-2732)
HENDERSON MACHINE INC
1809 S Powerline Rd # 110 (33442-8196)
PHONE....................................954 419-9789
Daniel Henderson, *President*
Pamela Henderson, *Vice Pres*
EMP: 8 EST: 1977
SQ FT: 5,500
SALES (est): 1.5MM **Privately Held**
WEB: www.hendersonmachine.com
SIC: 3599 Machine shop, jobbing & repair

(G-2733)
HERMES 7 COMMUNICATIONS
LLC
Also Called: Fastsigns
430 W Hillsboro Blvd (33441-1604)
PHONE....................................954 426-1998
Maria Vilas Fraga,
EMP: 13 EST: 2014
SALES (est): 1.5MM **Privately Held**
WEB: www.fastsigns.com
SIC: 3993 Signs & advertising specialties

(G-2734)
HOERBGER AUTO CMFORT
SYSTEMS L
1191 E Nwport Ctr Dr Ste (33442)
PHONE....................................334 321-2292
Gerhard Schoell,
Helmut Kleiber,
◆ EMP: 28 EST: 2001
SQ FT: 18,000
SALES (est): 3.2MM **Privately Held**
SIC: 3714 3511 Motor vehicle engines &
parts; hydraulic turbine generator set
units, complete

(G-2735)
HOERBIGER AMERICA HOLDING
INC (PA)
1432 E Nwport Ctr Dr Ste (33442)
PHONE....................................954 422-9850
Franz Gruber, *President*
Heather Henderson, *Corp Secy*
Anton Petrou, *Vice Pres*
Lisa Freed, *Engineer*
Nicolas Foldes, *Controller*
EMP: 280 EST: 2005
SALES (est): 453.8MM **Privately Held**
SIC: 1389 Gas compressing (natural gas)
at the fields

(G-2736)
HOERBIGER AMERICA HOLDING
INC
Also Called: Corporate It
1191 E Newport Center Dr (33442-7715)
PHONE....................................954 422-9850
Franz Gruber, *President*
EMP: 5002

SALES (corp-wide): 453.8MM **Privately
Held**
SIC: 1389 Gas compressing (natural gas)
at the fields
PA: Hoerbiger America Holding, Inc.
1432 E Nwport Ctr Dr Ste
Deerfield Beach FL 33442
954 422-9850

(G-2737)
HOERBIGER SERVICE INC
Also Called: Hoerbiger Gas Engine Systems
1432 E Nwport Ctr Dr Ste (33442)
PHONE....................................954 422-9850
Darliss Power, *Division Mgr*
EMP: 21
SALES (corp-wide): 453.8MM **Privately
Held**
WEB: www.hoerbigercorp.com
SIC: 3491 Industrial valves
HQ: Hoerbiger Service Inc.
1191 E Nwport Ctr Dr Ste
Deerfield Beach FL 33442
281 955-5888

(G-2738)
HOFMANN & LEAVY INC
Also Called: Tassel Depot
3251 Sw 13th Dr Ste 3 (33442-8166)
PHONE....................................954 698-0000
Roger S Leavy, *President*
April E Leavy, *Vice Pres*
April Leavy, *VP Mktg*
◆ EMP: 100 EST: 1864
SQ FT: 22,000
SALES (est): 8.5MM **Privately Held**
WEB: www.tasseldepot.com
SIC: 2298 5085 2396 2782 Wire rope
centers; rope, cord & thread; apparel find-
ings & trimmings; furniture trimmings, fab-
ric; sample books

(G-2739)
HOME AIDE DIAGNOSTICS INC
1072 S Powerline Rd (33442-8119)
PHONE....................................954 794-0212
Amgad Girgis, *President*
Akram Girgis, *Vice Pres*
▲ EMP: 12 EST: 2006
SALES (est): 1.9MM **Privately Held**
WEB: www.homeaide.us
SIC: 3841 Diagnostic apparatus, medical

(G-2740)
HOOD DEPOT INTERNATIONAL
INC
710 S Powerline Rd Ste H (33442-8176)
PHONE....................................954 570-9860
Donald Lubowicki, *President*
Max Brand, *Principal*
Sam Lubowicki, *Project Mgr*
Richard Jadusingh, *Engineer*
Michael Lubowicki, *Executive*
▼ EMP: 40 EST: 1984
SQ FT: 22,000
SALES (est): 8.8MM **Privately Held**
WEB: www.hooddepot.net
SIC: 3564 3444 Blowers & fans; sheet
metalwork

(G-2741)
HOSE-MCCANN TELEPHONE CO
INC (PA)
Also Called: Hose McCann Communications
1241 W Newport Center Dr (33442-7738)
PHONE....................................954 429-1110
Joan Grande-Butera, *CEO*
Michael Chippolone, *Corp Secy*
Bogen Karlak, *Prdtn Mgr*
Phillip Bester, *Purchasing*
Jim Hebert, *Engineer*
▲ EMP: 37 EST: 1920
SQ FT: 50,000
SALES (est): 12.1MM **Privately Held**
WEB: www.hose-mccann.com
SIC: 3661 3699 Telephones, sound pow-
ered (no battery); electrical equipment &
supplies

(G-2742)
INTERNTNAL SRVILLANCE
TECH INC (PA)
Also Called: National Intelligence Academy
160 Sw 12th Ave (33442-3119)
PHONE....................................954 574-1100

Donald A Difrisco, *Principal*
▼ EMP: 33 EST: 1993
SALES (est): 5.1MM **Privately Held**
WEB: www.istnia.com
SIC: 3716 7532 5099 5065 Recreational van conversion (self-propelled), factory basis; van conversion; video & audio equipment; video equipment, electronic

(G-2743)
ISOFLEX TECHNOLOGIES INTL LLC
3434 Sw 15th St B (33442-8135)
PHONE..................................561 210-5170
EMP: 5 EST: 2017
SALES (est): 305.1K **Privately Held**
WEB: www.isoflextech.com
SIC: 3714 Motor vehicle parts & accessories

(G-2744)
J & P DEERFIELD INC
1191 W Newport Center Dr (33442-7732)
PHONE..................................954 571-6665
Jason Scherr, *President*
Philip Garroway, *Vice Pres*
▲ EMP: 16 EST: 1982
SQ FT: 5,100
SALES (est): 2.2MM **Privately Held**
SIC: 3089 2672 Identification cards, plastic; coated & laminated paper

(G-2745)
JET RESEARCH DEVELOPMENT INC
Also Called: Valve Research & Mfg Co
1215 W Newport Center Dr (33442-7738)
PHONE..................................954 427-0404
Paul L Cruz, *President*
Concepcion Y Cruz, *Vice Pres*
Brad Witkowski, *Mfg Mgr*
Mark Vanzwieten, *Engineer*
Tim Johnson, *Sales Staff*
EMP: 85 EST: 1972
SQ FT: 14,000
SALES (est): 18.2MM **Privately Held**
SIC: 3492 Valves, hydraulic, aircraft; control valves, fluid power: hydraulic & pneumatic

(G-2746)
JIREH WOODWORK INC
3821 Nw 9th Ave (33064-1949)
PHONE..................................954 515-8041
Carlos H Gomes Costa, *Director*
EMP: 9 EST: 2005
SALES (est): 91.8K **Privately Held**
SIC: 2431 Millwork

(G-2747)
K20 OIL LLC
1201 S Military Trl (33442-7632)
PHONE..................................954 421-1735
Lui Alvaro, *Principal*
EMP: 7 EST: 2015
SALES (est): 962.7K **Privately Held**
SIC: 1311 Crude petroleum & natural gas

(G-2748)
KM COATINGS MFG JR
1111 W Newport Center Dr (33442-7732)
PHONE..................................602 253-1168
EMP: 10 EST: 2016
SALES (est): 174.7K **Privately Held**
SIC: 3999 Manufacturing industries

(G-2749)
KOSZEGI INDUSTRIES INC
1801 Green Rd Ste E (33064-1052)
PHONE..................................954 419-9544
Brett M Johnson, *President*
James McKenna, *CFO*
▲ EMP: 31 EST: 1958
SQ FT: 12,000
SALES (est): 3.7MM
SALES (corp-wide): 39MM **Publicly Held**
SIC: 3161 3469 3172 2673 Cases, carrying; briefcases; camera carrying bags; clothing & apparel carrying cases; metal stampings; personal leather goods; bags: plastic, laminated & coated
PA: Forward Industries, Inc.
　　700 Veterans Memorial Hwy # 10
　　Hauppauge NY 11788
　　631 547-3041

(G-2750)
LAMPSHADES OF FLORIDA INC
Also Called: Lampshade Direct
4280 Nw 5th Dr (33442-8032)
PHONE..................................954 491-3377
Morten C Post, *President*
EMP: 12 EST: 1979
SALES (est): 1MM **Privately Held**
WEB: www.allureshadesinc.com
SIC: 3999 Shades, lamp or candle

(G-2751)
LAPOLLA INDUSTRIES LLC
Also Called: Infiniti Paint & Coatings
720 S Military Trl (33442-3025)
PHONE..................................954 379-0241
Jon Palmisciano, *Vice Pres*
EMP: 12
SALES (corp-wide): 95.3MM **Privately Held**
WEB: www.lapolla.com
SIC: 2952 2851 3069 2891 Roofing felts, cements or coatings; paints & paint additives; foam rubber; adhesives & sealants
HQ: Lapolla Industries, Llc
　　3315 E Division St
　　Arlington TX 76011
　　281 219-4100

(G-2752)
LENCO HOLDINGS LLC
1223 Sw 1st Way (33441-6641)
PHONE..................................305 360-0895
Len Brian, *Mng Member*
▲ EMP: 5 EST: 2007
SQ FT: 4,000
SALES (est): 653.6K **Privately Held**
WEB: www.lencoholdings.com
SIC: 3542 Mechanical (pneumatic or hydraulic) metal forming machines

(G-2753)
LIST INDUSTRIES INC (PA)
401 Jim Moran Blvd (33442-1781)
PHONE..................................954 429-9155
Herbert List Jr, *President*
Boyd Bryson, *Regional Mgr*
Thom Champa, *Vice Pres*
Thomas D Champa, *Vice Pres*
Dave Cole, *Vice Pres*
▲ EMP: 117 EST: 1936
SQ FT: 100,000
SALES (est): 94.6MM **Privately Held**
WEB: www.listindustries.com
SIC: 2542 5021 2541 Lockers (not refrigerated): except wood; lockers; lockers, except refrigerated: wood

(G-2754)
LIST MANUFACTURING INC
401 Jim Moran Blvd (33442-1781)
PHONE..................................954 429-9155
Herbert A List Jr, *President*
EMP: 82 EST: 2009
SQ FT: 110,000
SALES (est): 5.8MM
SALES (corp-wide): 94.6MM **Privately Held**
WEB: www.listindustries.com
SIC: 3315 Steel wire & related products
PA: List Industries Inc.
　　401 Jim Moran Blvd
　　Deerfield Beach FL 33442
　　954 429-9155

(G-2755)
LIST PLYMOUTH LLC
401 Jim Moran Blvd (33442-1781)
PHONE..................................954 429-9155
Eric Bello, *CFO*
Alex MAI, *Info Tech Dir*
Herbert A List Jr,
EMP: 52 EST: 2007
SQ FT: 150,000
SALES (est): 5.1MM
SALES (corp-wide): 94.6MM **Privately Held**
SIC: 2542 5021 Lockers (not refrigerated): except wood; lockers
PA: List Industries Inc.
　　401 Jim Moran Blvd
　　Deerfield Beach FL 33442
　　954 429-9155

(G-2756)
LIVING COLOR AQUARIUM CORP
740 S Porwerline Rd Ste E (33442)
PHONE..................................844 522-8265
Daniel Kaufman, *President*
EMP: 20 EST: 2016
SQ FT: 100
SALES (est): 719.4K **Privately Held**
SIC: 3231 Products of purchased glass

(G-2757)
LIVING COLOR ENTERPRISES INC
720 S Powerline Rd Ste D (33442-8156)
PHONE..................................954 970-9511
Michael Feder, *CEO*
Mathew Roy, *CEO*
Mat Roy, *President*
Bill Young, *Vice Pres*
Jose Blanco, *Production*
◆ EMP: 37 EST: 1988
SQ FT: 43,400
SALES (est): 2.1MM **Privately Held**
WEB: www.livingcolor.com
SIC: 3231 Aquariums & reflectors, glass

(G-2758)
M VB INDUSTRIES INC
510 Goolsby Blvd 5 (33442-3021)
P.O. Box 4637 (33442-4637)
PHONE..................................954 480-6448
Gared Von Benecke, *President*
Stan Meacham, *Treasurer*
EMP: 21 EST: 2000
SQ FT: 11,000
SALES (est): 1.4MM **Privately Held**
WEB: www.mvbindustries.com
SIC: 3541 Drilling machine tools (metal cutting)

(G-2759)
MACHITECH AUTOMATION LLC
1199 W Newport Center Dr (33442-7732)
PHONE..................................314 756-2288
Christian Gigeure, *CEO*
Steve Dinsmore, *President*
EMP: 11 EST: 2016
SALES (est): 4.4MM **Privately Held**
WEB: www.machitech.com
SIC: 3541 Plasma process metal cutting machines

(G-2760)
MAGNUM PAVERS CORP
3261 Sw 1st St Apt A (33442-2392)
PHONE..................................754 367-1832
Magno Barboza, *Principal*
EMP: 7 EST: 2013
SALES (est): 128K **Privately Held**
SIC: 2951 Asphalt paving mixtures & blocks

(G-2761)
MAHIGAMING LLC
245 Ne 21st Ave Ste 200 (33441-3859)
PHONE..................................561 504-1534
Neil Moodaliar, *COO*
Seher Basak, *Marketing Staff*
Taun E Masterson, *Manager*
Gabriel Garcia, *Technical Staff*
Ian Owen, *Technical Staff*
EMP: 8 EST: 2017
SALES (est): 2MM **Privately Held**
WEB: www.mahigaming.com
SIC: 3652 Pre-recorded records & tapes

(G-2762)
MAKAI MARINE INDUSTRIES INC
730 S Deerfield Ave Ste 8 (33441-5362)
PHONE..................................954 425-0203
Marc R Kaiser, *President*
EMP: 9 EST: 1982
SALES (est): 29.4K **Privately Held**
SIC: 3563 Air & gas compressors

(G-2763)
MAPEI CORPORATION (DH)
Also Called: North Amrcn Adhesives Coatings
1144 E Newport Center Dr (33442-7725)
PHONE..................................954 246-8888
Luigi Di Geso, *President*
Carlos Rubio, *Plant Mgr*
Brenda Gutierrez, *Export Mgr*
Lusanira Morais, *Export Mgr*

Flavio Becerra, *Maint Spvr*
◆ EMP: 120 EST: 1985
SALES (est): 619.9MM
SALES (corp-wide): 3.6B **Privately Held**
WEB: www.mapei.com
SIC: 2891 5169 Adhesives; chemicals & allied products
HQ: Mapei Spa
　　Viale Edoardo Jenner 4
　　Milano MI 20159
　　023 767-31

(G-2764)
MARTINS PAVERS & POOLS CORP
Also Called: M.T.s Pavers & Pools
220 Nw 40th Ct (33064-2628)
PHONE..................................754 368-4413
Jose C Martins, *Principal*
EMP: 9 EST: 2008
SALES (est): 440.1K **Privately Held**
SIC: 3531 Pavers

(G-2765)
MERGENET MEDICAL INC
1701 W Hillsboro Blvd # 303 (33442-1564)
PHONE..................................561 208-3770
Shara Hernandez, *President*
Charles Lewis, *Director*
Linda Magill, *Director*
EMP: 20 EST: 2004
SALES (est): 1MM
SALES (corp-wide): 2.8MM **Privately Held**
WEB: www.mergenetmedical.com
SIC: 3841 Surgical & medical instruments
PA: Mergenet Solutions, Inc.
　　6601 Lyons Rd Ste B1
　　Coconut Creek FL 33073
　　561 558-0129

(G-2766)
MIAMI TECHNICS LLC
457 Goolsby Blvd (33442-3020)
PHONE..................................754 227-5459
EMP: 11 EST: 2017
SALES (est): 1.4MM **Privately Held**
WEB: www.miamitechnics.com
SIC: 3728 Aircraft parts & equipment

(G-2767)
MICRO QUALITY CORP
438 S Military Trl (33442-3009)
PHONE..................................954 354-5572
Anne M Yowell, *President*
Gordon Yowell, *Vice Pres*
EMP: 5 EST: 2004
SALES (est): 593.6K **Privately Held**
WEB: www.microqualitycorp.com
SIC: 3545 Machine tool accessories

(G-2768)
MISC METAL FABRICATION LLC
3001 Sw 15th St Ste A (33442-8199)
PHONE..................................754 264-1026
Juan Vasquez, *Mng Member*
EMP: 10 EST: 2012
SQ FT: 12,000
SALES (est): 1MM **Privately Held**
SIC: 3441 Fabricated structural metal

(G-2769)
MOBILE RVING
2150 Sw 10th St Ste A (33442-7625)
PHONE..................................954 870-7095
EMP: 7 EST: 2015
SALES (est): 42.4K **Privately Held**
SIC: 2741 Miscellaneous publishing

(G-2770)
MOBILE4LESSUSA CORP
708 Sw 10th St (33441-7810)
PHONE..................................954 706-0582
Raul De Oliveira, *President*
EMP: 8 EST: 2019
SALES (est): 253.6K **Privately Held**
SIC: 2451 Mobile homes

(G-2771)
MORI LEE LLC (PA)
3155 Sw 10th St Ste 6a1 (33442-5948)
PHONE..................................954 418-6165
Suly Yu, *Business Mgr*
Sara Gonzalez, *CFO*
Rick Gross, *Controller*
Vera Shatkovsky, *Credit Mgr*

▲ = Import ▼ = Export
◆ = Import/Export

Mario Ruano, *Credit Staff*
▼ **EMP:** 25 **EST:** 1950
SQ FT: 40,000
SALES (est): 8.8MM **Privately Held**
WEB: www.morilee.com
SIC: 2335 Wedding gowns & dresses

(G-2772)
MWI CORPORATION (PA)
Also Called: Mwi Pumps
33 Nw 2nd St (33441-2013)
PHONE..............................954 426-1500
J David Eller, *Ch of Bd*
Dana J Eller, *President*
John Springer, *General Mgr*
Marc Boudet, *Vice Pres*
Daren J Eller, *Vice Pres*
◆ **EMP:** 50 **EST:** 1927
SQ FT: 60,000
SALES (est): 41.8MM **Privately Held**
WEB: www.mwipumps.com
SIC: 3561 7359 Pumps & pumping equipment; equipment rental & leasing

(G-2773)
MY PRINT SHOP INC
1061 Sw 30th Ave (33442-8104)
PHONE..............................954 973-9369
Jeff Pottruck, *President*
EMP: 13 **EST:** 1981
SQ FT: 3,200
SALES (est): 403.8K **Privately Held**
SIC: 2752 2791 2789 Commercial printing, offset; typesetting; bookbinding & related work

(G-2774)
NEOTECH COMPANY
140 Se 7th St Apt 4 (33441-5486)
PHONE..............................954 570-5833
Panos Giannakos, *Principal*
EMP: 8 **EST:** 2011
SALES (est): 64.2K **Privately Held**
WEB: www.neotech.com
SIC: 3672 Printed circuit boards

(G-2775)
NORES PRECISION INC
44 Se 9th St (33441-5316)
PHONE..............................954 420-0025
James Schlegel, *President*
Rhonda Schlegel, *Vice Pres*
EMP: 38 **EST:** 1945
SQ FT: 8,500
SALES (est): 1.8MM **Privately Held**
WEB: www.noresprecision.com
SIC: 3599 Machine shop, jobbing & repair

(G-2776)
OURO CUSTOM WOODWORK INC
12 Sw 9th St (33441-5346)
P.O. Box 4423 (33442-4423)
PHONE..............................954 428-0735
Mike Ouro, *President*
James J Bugniazet, *Vice Pres*
EMP: 28 **EST:** 2000
SALES (est): 1.3MM **Privately Held**
WEB: www.ourocustomwoodwork.com
SIC: 2431 Millwork

(G-2777)
P S ANALYTICAL INC
1761 W Hillsboro Blvd (33442-1559)
PHONE..............................954 429-1577
Paul Stockwell, *President*
Marsha Micciantuono, *Opers Staff*
Ralph Cochrane, *Sales Mgr*
Vincenzo Fabbricatore, *Manager*
Claude Rogers, *Manager*
EMP: 5 **EST:** 1998
SQ FT: 2,000
SALES (est): 1.2MM **Privately Held**
WEB: www.mercuryanalyser.com
SIC: 3826 Analytical instruments

(G-2778)
P S T COMPUTERS INC
Also Called: PST Computers
2692 Sw 12th St (33442-5912)
PHONE..............................954 566-1600
Patrick Guertin, *President*
Alroger Gomes, *Comp Tech*
EMP: 7 **EST:** 1987

SALES (est): 911.7K **Privately Held**
WEB: www.pstcomputers.com
SIC: 3571 5734 1731 Electronic computers; computer peripheral equipment; computer installation

(G-2779)
PALLET INDUSTRIES INC (DH)
1815 S Powerline Rd (33442-8164)
PHONE..............................954 935-5804
Mitchell Kamps, *President*
Antonio Busto, *Sales Mgr*
EMP: 10 **EST:** 2007
SQ FT: 32,000
SALES (est): 2.8MM
SALES (corp-wide): 1.7B **Privately Held**
WEB: www.palletindustries.com
SIC: 2448 Pallets, wood
HQ: Kamps, Inc.
      2900 Peach Ridge Ave Nw
      Grand Rapids MI 49534
      616 453-9676

(G-2780)
PAVERS SOLUTIONS INC
201 Nw 43rd St (33064-2527)
PHONE..............................754 551-1924
Elvandro F Correa, *Principal*
EMP: 8 **EST:** 2015
SALES (est): 165.4K **Privately Held**
SIC: 2951 Asphalt paving mixtures & blocks

(G-2781)
PAYTON AMERICA INC
Also Called: Payton Group International
1805 S Powerline Rd # 109 (33442-8193)
PHONE..............................954 428-3326
Jim Marinos, *President*
Shareen Wang, *Vice Pres*
David Yativ, *Vice Pres*
Gil Lucas, *Opers Staff*
Amir Yativ, *Director*
▲ **EMP:** 14 **EST:** 1986
SQ FT: 4,400
SALES (est): 4.5MM **Privately Held**
WEB: www.paytongroup.com
SIC: 3612 Power transformers, electric
PA: Payton Industries Ltd.
      3 Haavoda
      Ness Ziona 74031

(G-2782)
PERSONAL BRANDS LLC
508 Sw 12th Ave (33442-3110)
PHONE..............................855 426-7765
Joe Davidson, *President*
Piroov Farshar, *COO*
Rebecca Mariolis, *Vice Pres*
EMP: 20 **EST:** 2017
SALES (est): 1.2MM **Privately Held**
SIC: 2844 Toilet preparations

(G-2783)
POLENGHI USA INC
720 S Powerline Rd Ste C (33442-8156)
PHONE..............................954 637-4900
Marco Polenghi, *Principal*
EMP: 13 **EST:** 2016
SALES (est): 504.8K **Privately Held**
SIC: 2086 Iced tea & fruit drinks, bottled & canned

(G-2784)
POLYGLASS USA INC (DH)
Also Called: Polyglass Roofg Watering Svcs
1111 W Newport Center Dr (33442-7732)
PHONE..............................954 246-8888
Natalino Zanchetta, *CEO*
Robert Hostler, *Plant Mgr*
Richard Anthony, *Prdtn Mgr*
John Cambra, *Prdtn Mgr*
Dan Phelps, *Prdtn Mgr*
◆ **EMP:** 65 **EST:** 1991
SALES (est): 112.3MM
SALES (corp-wide): 3.6B **Privately Held**
WEB: www.polyglass.us
SIC: 2493 2952 Insulation & roofing material, reconstituted wood; roofing felts, cements or coatings
HQ: Polyglass Spa
      Via Dottor Giorgio Squinzi 2
      Ponte Di Piave TV 31047
      042 275-47

(G-2785)
PREBLE ENTERPRISES INC
Also Called: Precision Aluminum Products
1339 Sw 1st Way (33441-6642)
PHONE..............................954 480-6919
Nick Preble, *President*
Laura Preble, *Corp Secy*
Timothy Preble, *Vice Pres*
EMP: 5 **EST:** 1992
SQ FT: 3,000
SALES (est): 886.3K **Privately Held**
WEB: www.acstands.com
SIC: 3585 Air conditioning condensers & condensing units

(G-2786)
PRIME LIFE NTRTN COMPANYLLC
1239 E Nwport Ctr Dr Ste (33442)
PHONE..............................754 307-7137
Thiago Dias, *CEO*
EMP: 5 **EST:** 2018
SALES (est): 341.6K **Privately Held**
SIC: 2023 Dietary supplements, dairy & non-dairy based

(G-2787)
PRINT BASICS INC
Also Called: Dpr Print & Promotional
1059 Sw 30th Ave (33442-8104)
PHONE..............................954 354-0700
Ike Abolafia, *CEO*
Lisa M Tanner, *President*
Marcia Craigie, *Business Mgr*
Craig A Tanner, *Vice Pres*
Brian Vecchio, *Prdtn Mgr*
EMP: 27 **EST:** 2002
SQ FT: 3,050
SALES (est): 6.2MM **Privately Held**
WEB: www.printbasics.com
SIC: 2752 Commercial printing, offset

(G-2788)
PRINT E-SOLUTION INC
Also Called: Print Esolutions
409 Goolsby Blvd (33442-3020)
P.O. Box 1004 (33443-1004)
PHONE..............................954 588-5454
Thomas J Wenzel, *President*
EMP: 6 **EST:** 2011
SALES (est): 971.9K **Privately Held**
WEB: www.printesol.com
SIC: 2752 Commercial printing, offset

(G-2789)
PRIORITY 1 SIGNS
1911 Nw 40th Ct (33064-8719)
PHONE..............................954 971-8689
EMP: 9 **EST:** 2014
SALES (est): 450.7K **Privately Held**
SIC: 3993 Signs & advertising specialties

(G-2790)
PRO PAK ENTERPRISES INC
741 Nw 42nd Way (33442-9221)
PHONE..............................888 375-2275
Ralph Droz, *CEO*
Michael Droz, *Vice Pres*
Debbie Droz, *Director*
EMP: 18 **EST:** 2019
SALES (est): 2.9MM **Privately Held**
SIC: 2673 2674 Plastic bags: made from purchased materials; paper bags: made from purchased materials

(G-2791)
PROCRAFT CABINETRY FLORIDA LLC
1850 S Powerline Rd Ste A (33442-8116)
PHONE..............................754 212-2277
Yao Zhao, *President*
Shu Lin,
Xiguang Tang,
EMP: 15 **EST:** 2015
SALES (est): 484.1K **Privately Held**
WEB: www.procraftflorida.com
SIC: 2434 Wood kitchen cabinets

(G-2792)
PRODECO TECHNOLOGIES LLC
1601 Green Rd (33064-1076)
PHONE..............................954 974-6730
Robert Provost, *CEO*
Daniel D Aguila, *Vice Pres*
▲ **EMP:** 50 **EST:** 2008

SQ FT: 60,000
SALES (est): 4.9MM **Privately Held**
WEB: www.sweetwatercountryhome.com
SIC: 3751 Motorcycles, bicycles & parts

(G-2793)
PROSEGUR EAS USA LLC
598 Hillsboro Tech Dr (33441-7732)
PHONE..............................561 900-2744
Matthew P Sack,
EMP: 23 **EST:** 2020
SALES (est): 10.2MM
SALES (corp-wide): 187.9MM **Privately Held**
SIC: 2679 Tags & labels, paper
PA: Prosegur Services Group, Inc.
      512 Herndon Pkwy Ste A
      Herndon VA 20170
      703 464-4735

(G-2794)
PYLON MANUFACTURING CORP (HQ)
600 W Hillsboro Blvd # 4 (33441-1609)
PHONE..............................800 626-4902
Gary Cohen, *CEO*
Michael Fretwell, *President*
Bart Plaumann, *Principal*
Nicole Shames, *Senior Buyer*
Keith Sennett, *Engineer*
◆ **EMP:** 46 **EST:** 1974
SQ FT: 15,000
SALES (est): 30.4MM
SALES (corp-wide): 81.5MM **Privately Held**
WEB: www.pylonhq.com
SIC: 3714 Wipers, windshield, motor vehicle
PA: Qualitor, Inc.
      1840 Mccullough St
      Lima OH 45801
      248 204-8600

(G-2795)
RAMOS WOODWORK LLC
Also Called: IL Mobile
1955 Sw 15th Pl (33442-6101)
PHONE..............................954 861-7679
Eduardo Coutinho Ramos, *Principal*
EMP: 10 **EST:** 2016
SALES (est): 295K **Privately Held**
SIC: 2431 Millwork

(G-2796)
RASKIN INDUSTRIES LLC
710 S Powerline Rd Ste G (33442-8176)
PHONE..............................561 997-6658
Michael Raskin, *CEO*
John Hunter, *Vice Pres*
Jamie Lampos, *Project Mgr*
William Lapis, *CFO*
Karen Humphries, *Controller*
▲ **EMP:** 13 **EST:** 2011
SALES (est): 1.9MM **Privately Held**
WEB: www.raskinind.com
SIC: 3253 Ceramic wall & floor tile

(G-2797)
REDINGTON COUNTERS INC
702 S Military Trl (33442-3025)
PHONE..............................954 725-6699
Bill Fitzsimmons, *Principal*
Michael Demarco, *COO*
Stefan Ebert, *Vice Pres*
Ron Kendzior, *Vice Pres*
Kenneth Daglio, *Opers Mgr*
EMP: 7 **EST:** 2012
SALES (est): 116K **Privately Held**
SIC: 3829 Measuring & controlling devices

(G-2798)
REGENT LABS INC (PA)
700 W Hillsboro Blvd 2-206 (33441-1695)
PHONE..............................954 426-4889
Eugene RE, *President*
EMP: 6 **EST:** 1979
SQ FT: 8,000
SALES (est): 1.8MM **Privately Held**
WEB: www.regentlabs.com
SIC: 3843 Dental equipment & supplies

(G-2799)
REGENT LABS INC
473 Goolsby Blvd (33442-3020)
PHONE..............................954 426-4889
David Ptak, *Manager*

EMP: 8
SALES (corp-wide): 1.8MM **Privately Held**
WEB: www.regentlabs.com
SIC: 3843 4225 Dental equipment & supplies; general warehousing & storage
PA: Regent Labs, Inc.
　700 W Hillsboro Blvd 2-206
　Deerfield Beach FL 33441
　954 426-4889

(G-2800)
REYNOSO & ASSOCIATES INC
Also Called: Optimum Power & Envmt Fla
434 Sw 12th Ave (33442-3108)
PHONE...................................954 360-0601
Mia China Ling Reynoso, *President*
Christopher Bachman, *Vice Pres*
EMP: 7 EST: 1989
SQ FT: 2,710
SALES (est): 1.1MM **Privately Held**
SIC: 3694 Engine electrical equipment

(G-2801)
SAMS CLOSET INC
1717 Sw 1st Way Ste 28 (33441-6794)
PHONE...................................954 354-8386
EMP: 8 EST: 2006
SALES (est): 483.3K **Privately Held**
WEB: www.customclosetssouthflorida.com
SIC: 2673 Mfg Bags-Plastic/Coated Paper

(G-2802)
SARGEANT BULK ASPHALT INC
321 E Hillsboro Blvd (33441-3539)
PHONE...................................954 763-4796
Daniel Sargeant, *President*
Harry Sargeant Jr, *Director*
EMP: 8 EST: 2014
SALES (est): 610.7K **Privately Held**
WEB: www.sargeantmarine.com
SIC: 2952 Asphalt felts & coatings

(G-2803)
SC ELEARNING LLC
Also Called: Trivantis
400 Fairway Dr Ste 101 (33441-1808)
PHONE...................................561 293-2543
Daniel Bovarnick, *COO*
John Blackmon, *CTO*
EMP: 63 EST: 2016
SALES (est): 1.5MM **Privately Held**
SIC: 7372 Prepackaged software

(G-2804)
SEA BREEZE MARINE CO
1601 Sw 1st Way Ste 16 (33441-6785)
P.O. Box 50165, Lighthouse Point (33074-0165)
PHONE...................................561 368-0463
Henry Garberg III, *President*
EMP: 6 EST: 1980
SALES (est): 454.9K **Privately Held**
WEB: www.seabreezemarine.net
SIC: 3732 Boat building & repairing

(G-2805)
SEATECH FABRICATION INC
101 Se 7th St Unit 5 (33441-5340)
PHONE...................................954 410-0524
Kevin S McNulty Jr, *President*
EMP: 8 EST: 2013
SALES (est): 165.7K **Privately Held**
WEB: www.seatechconstruction.com
SIC: 3441 Fabricated structural metal

(G-2806)
SELECT EUROPE INC
3000 Sw 15th St Ste E (33442-8198)
P.O. Box 668476, Pompano Beach (33066-8476)
PHONE...................................866 204-0899
Tony Varol, *President*
Christina Germakopoulos - Varo, *Vice Pres*
Christina Germakopoulos, *Marketing Staff*
◆ EMP: 10 EST: 2003
SALES (est): 1MM **Privately Held**
WEB: www.selecteuropeinc.com
SIC: 2091 5146 Seafood products: packaged in cans, jars, etc.; fish & seafoods

(G-2807)
SENELCO IBERIA INC
500 Nw 12th Ave (33442-1723)
PHONE...................................561 912-6000
Bob Vanourek, *CEO*

▲ EMP: 682 EST: 1995
SALES (est): 4.5MM **Privately Held**
SIC: 3812 5065 Detection apparatus: electronic/magnetic field, light/heat; security control equipment & systems
HQ: Sensormatic International Inc
　6600 Congress Ave
　Boca Raton FL 33487
　561 912-6000

(G-2808)
SHL PHARMA LLC
588 Jim Moran Blvd (33442-1710)
PHONE...................................954 725-2008
Ken Lahti, *Vice Pres*
Simon Yang, *Project Mgr*
Greg Terranova, *Mfg Mgr*
Thomas Ailsa, *Opers Staff*
Kyle Fitzpatrick, *Engineer*
EMP: 20 EST: 2010
SALES (est): 10.8MM
SALES (corp-wide): 660.4MM **Privately Held**
SIC: 3841 Surgical & medical instruments
PA: Shl Medical Ag
　Gubelstrasse 22
　Zug ZG 6300
　413 680-000

(G-2809)
SIGN GRAPHIX INC
242 S Military Trl (33442-3029)
PHONE...................................954 571-7131
Silvia Lo Monaco, *President*
EMP: 6 EST: 2002
SALES (est): 708.7K **Privately Held**
WEB: www.signgraphix.com
SIC: 3993 Signs & advertising specialties

(G-2810)
SINOBEC RESOURCES LLC
1901 Green Rd Ste E (33064-1059)
PHONE...................................561 409-2205
John Lee,
▲ EMP: 5 EST: 2012
SALES (est): 2.6MM
SALES (corp-wide): 300K **Privately Held**
WEB: www.sinobecresources.com
SIC: 3365 3354 Masts, cast aluminum; aluminum extruded products
HQ: Sinobec Trading Inc.
　4455 Rue Cousens
　Saint-Laurent QC H4S 1
　514 339-9333

(G-2811)
SKI RIXEN - QUIET WATERS INC
Also Called: Ski Rixen USA
401 S Powerline Rd (33442-8182)
PHONE...................................954 429-0215
Brita Schipner, *President*
EMP: 5 EST: 1983
SALES (est): 544.4K **Privately Held**
WEB: www.skirixenusa.com
SIC: 3949 Water skis

(G-2812)
SOLANA REPAIR SERVICES LLC
3220 Sw 15th St (33442-8126)
P.O. Box 1344, Solana Beach CA (92075-7344)
PHONE...................................754 281-8860
Ofer Klein, *Principal*
Brian Raduenz, *Mng Member*
Amy Velver,
EMP: 6 EST: 2016
SQ FT: 50,000
SALES (est): 1MM
SALES (corp-wide): 9.4MM **Privately Held**
WEB: www.55-group.com
SIC: 3724 7699 Aircraft engines & engine parts; aircraft & heavy equipment repair services
PA: 55 Group Llc
　3220 Sw 15th St
　Deerfield Beach FL 33442
　954 427-8405

(G-2813)
SOUTHEAST PUBLICATIONS USA INC
2150 Sw 10th St Ste A (33442-7625)
PHONE...................................954 368-4686
Wally Warrick, *President*

Wayne Morris, *Vice Pres*
Carol Tims, *Sales Associate*
EMP: 37 EST: 1987
SALES (est): 3.2MM **Privately Held**
WEB: www.southeastpublications.com
SIC: 2741 Miscellaneous publishing

(G-2814)
SOUTHEASTERN MKTG ASSOC INC
1522 Se 10th St (33441-7165)
PHONE...................................954 421-7388
William Chupp, *Owner*
EMP: 9 EST: 2002
SALES (est): 282.9K **Privately Held**
SIC: 7372 Prepackaged software

(G-2815)
STERLING MDR INC
741 Nw 42nd Way (33442-9221)
PHONE...................................954 725-2777
Ralph Droz, *President*
Yazmin Carbajal, *Sales Staff*
Lisa Costley, *Sales Associate*
EMP: 14 EST: 2009
SALES (est): 2.4MM **Privately Held**
SIC: 2673 7389 Bags: plastic, laminated & coated;

(G-2816)
SUN-SENTINEL COMPANY LLC
333 Sw 12th Ave (33442-3196)
PHONE...................................954 356-4000
Mansell Jaleel, *Sales Staff*
Charles Ray, *Branch Mgr*
Holly Svekis, *Manager*
EMP: 88 **Privately Held**
WEB: www.sun-sentinel.com
SIC: 2711 2741 Newspapers, publishing & printing; miscellaneous publishing
HQ: Sun-Sentinel Company, Llc
　500 E Broward Blvd # 800
　Fort Lauderdale FL 33394
　954 356-4000

(G-2817)
SUNSHINE ALANCE CABINETS MLLWK
712 S Military Trl (33442-3025)
PHONE...................................954 621-7444
EMP: 15 EST: 2018
SALES (est): 576.7K **Privately Held**
SIC: 2434 Wood kitchen cabinets

(G-2818)
SUSTAINABLE CASEWORK INDS LLC
Also Called: SCI
720 S Deerfield Ave Ste 1 (33441-5385)
PHONE...................................954 980-6506
Jonathan R Kaplan, *Mng Member*
EMP: 7 EST: 2012
SQ FT: 10,000
SALES (est): 146.7K **Privately Held**
SIC: 3999 Chairs, hydraulic, barber & beauty shop

(G-2819)
T & M INDUSTRIES INC
1106 Se 14th Dr (33441-7227)
PHONE...................................954 778-2238
Tanner Strohmenger, *Principal*
EMP: 8 EST: 2018
SALES (est): 54K **Privately Held**
WEB: www.delawarecourt.com
SIC: 3999 Manufacturing industries

(G-2820)
T H L DIAMOND PRODUCTS INC
Also Called: Shark Tools
312 S Powerline Rd (33442-8105)
PHONE...................................954 596-5012
Sean Thompson, *President*
EMP: 7 EST: 1999
SALES (est): 600K **Privately Held**
WEB: www.sharkdiamondblade.com
SIC: 3544 Special dies, tools, jigs & fixtures

(G-2821)
TARMAC FLORIDA INC
455 Fairway Dr (33441-1809)
PHONE...................................954 481-2800
Aris Papadopoulos, *President*
EMP: 16 EST: 1977

SALES (est): 460.3K **Privately Held**
SIC: 3273 Ready-mixed concrete

(G-2822)
TERRA BEAUTY PRODUCTS INC
Also Called: Terra Beauty Bars
440 S Military Trl (33442-3009)
PHONE...................................561 674-2136
Fernanda Gomes, *President*
Luana Gomes Cunha, *Vice Pres*
Jasmine Gomes, *Admin Sec*
EMP: 7 EST: 2017
SALES (est): 517.3K **Privately Held**
WEB: www.terrabeautybars.com
SIC: 2844 Hair preparations, including shampoos; shampoos, rinses, conditioners: hair; lotions, shaving; cosmetic preparations

(G-2823)
TERRY BOCA INC
512 Hillsboro Tech Dr (33441-7732)
PHONE...................................561 893-0333
Jyll Brink, *Accounts Mgr*
Jeffrey Russo, *Sales Executive*
Jennifer Gulliford, *Manager*
Ed Cohen,
Bruce Cohen,
◆ EMP: 8 EST: 1995
SALES (est): 1MM **Privately Held**
WEB: www.bocaterry.com
SIC: 2384 2672 Bathrobes, men's & women's: made from purchased materials; cloth lined paper: made from purchased paper

(G-2824)
TIDES MARINE INC
3251 Sw 13th Dr Ste A (33442-8166)
PHONE...................................954 420-0949
Tom Zaniewski, *President*
◆ EMP: 22 EST: 1990
SQ FT: 10,000
SALES (est): 5MM **Privately Held**
WEB: www.tidesmarine.com
SIC: 3429 Marine hardware

(G-2825)
TIGHTLINE PUBLICATIONS INC
2795 Sw 11th Pl (33442-5909)
P.O. Box 4397 (33442-4397)
PHONE...................................954 570-7174
Vincent Montella, *President*
Anthony Montella, *Vice Pres*
Gail Monteal, *Treasurer*
EMP: 8 EST: 1991
SALES (est): 650.2K **Privately Held**
WEB: www.outdoorcharts.com
SIC: 2741 Miscellaneous publishing

(G-2826)
TITAN AMERICA LLC
Also Called: Tarmac Standard Concrete
455 Fairway Dr Ste 200 (33441-1805)
P.O. Box 8648 (33443-8648)
PHONE...................................954 426-8407
Trey Reese, *Regional Mgr*
Steven Brown, *Vice Pres*
Thomas Cerullo, *Vice Pres*
Don Ingrassano, *Vice Pres*
George Pantazopoulos, *Vice Pres*
EMP: 50
SALES (corp-wide): 177.9K **Privately Held**
WEB: www.titanamerica.com
SIC: 3273 Ready-mixed concrete
HQ: Titan America Llc
　5700 Lake Wright Dr # 300
　Norfolk VA 23502
　757 858-6500

(G-2827)
TRADEMARK SIGNS LLC
2051 Green Rd Ste E (33064-1065)
PHONE...................................954 859-6220
Tom Menshouse, *Manager*
EMP: 7 EST: 2020
SALES (est): 313.3K **Privately Held**
WEB: www.trademarksignllc.com
SIC: 3993 Signs & advertising specialties

▲ = Import ▼=Export
◆ =Import/Export

(G-2828)
TRIVANTIS CORPORATION (HQ)
Also Called: Lectora
400 Fairway Dr Ste 101 (33441-1808)
P.O. Box 1000, Memphis TN (38148-0001)
PHONE.................................513 929-0188
Andrew Scivally, *CEO*
Kenneth Hislop, *Engineer*
Loreine Lea, *Accountant*
Christie Calahan, *Marketing Staff*
Johnattan Barona, *Software Engr*
▲ EMP: 65 EST: 1999
SQ FT: 22,000
SALES (est): 3.3MM Privately Held
WEB: www.elblearning.com
SIC: 7372 7371 Publishers' computer software; custom computer programming services

(G-2829)
TURNER ENVIROLOGIC INC
1140 Sw 34th Ave (33442-8183)
PHONE.................................954 422-9566
Thomas K Turner, *President*
Robert Battleson, *Project Mgr*
Adesh Jaggernauth, *Prdtn Mgr*
EMP: 44 EST: 1981
SQ FT: 18,000
SALES (est): 6.6MM Privately Held
WEB: www.tenviro.com
SIC: 3564 Air purification equipment

(G-2830)
US BUILDING SYSTEMS CORP
401 Fairway Dr Ste 100 (33441-1800)
PHONE.................................954 281-2100
Gary J Rack, *President*
EMP: 22 EST: 1991
SQ FT: 12,400
SALES (est): 1.7MM Privately Held
SIC: 3448 Prefabricated metal buildings

(G-2831)
VINAVIL AMERICAS CORPORATION
1144 E Newport Center Dr (33442-7725)
PHONE.................................954 246-8888
Hemant Shah, *Principal*
▲ EMP: 18 EST: 1997
SALES (est): 243.3K Privately Held
WEB: www.vinavil.com
SIC: 2822 2851 Ethylene-propylene rubbers, EPDM polymers; paints & allied products; vinyl coatings, strippable

(G-2832)
VOLUNTEER CAPITAL LLC
Also Called: Priority One Signs
1911 Nw 40th Ct (33064-8719)
PHONE.................................954 366-6659
William Reicherter, *Mng Member*
EMP: 9 EST: 2014
SALES (est): 442.1K Privately Held
WEB: www.p1signs.com
SIC: 3993 Signs & advertising specialties

(G-2833)
WECANDO PRINT LLC
424 Sw 12th Ave (33442-3108)
PHONE.................................754 222-9144
Thomas C Letourneau, *Principal*
EMP: 8 EST: 2015
SALES (est): 222.6K Privately Held
SIC: 2752 Commercial printing, offset

(G-2834)
WLC WOOD WORKS INC
1340 Nw 48th Pl (33064-1022)
PHONE.................................305 896-6460
Wanderson Campos, *Principal*
EMP: 7 EST: 2016
SALES (est): 71.9K Privately Held
SIC: 2499 Wood products

(G-2835)
WRAP-ART INC
712 S Military Trl (33442-3025)
P.O. Box 6576, Delray Beach (33482-6576)
PHONE.................................954 428-1819
Roberta Tractenberg, *President*
Stanley Tractenberg, *Treasurer*
▲ EMP: 9 EST: 1998
SQ FT: 5,000

SALES (est): 945K Privately Held
WEB: www.wrap-art.com
SIC: 2679 Gift wrap, paper: made from purchased material; novelties, paper: made from purchased material

(G-2836)
WRISTBAND SUPPLY LLC
Also Called: Wristband Specialty
3000 Sw 15th St Ste F (33442-8198)
PHONE.................................954 571-3993
Michael Feingold, *Mng Member*
EMP: 15 EST: 2012
SALES (est): 1.6MM Privately Held
WEB: www.wristbandsupply.com
SIC: 2389 Arm bands, elastic

Defuniak Springs
Walton County

(G-2837)
CHAUTUQUA VINEYARDS WINERY INC (PA)
Also Called: Emerald Coast Wine Cellars
364 Hugh Adams Rd (32435-3429)
P.O. Box 1308 (32435-1308)
PHONE.................................850 892-5887
Paul Owens, *President*
Sharah Curry, *Manager*
EMP: 10 EST: 2005
SALES (est): 1.7MM Privately Held
WEB: www.chautauquawinery.com
SIC: 2084 Wines

(G-2838)
CLASSIC STUCCO & STONE LLC
3148 Rock Hill Rd (32435-8002)
PHONE.................................850 892-1045
William F Carpenter, *Branch Mgr*
EMP: 15
SALES (corp-wide): 116.9K Privately Held
WEB: www.stylestopnepa.com
SIC: 3299 Stucco
PA: Classic Stucco & Stone Llc
    350 16th St Ne
    Winter Haven FL

(G-2839)
FLORIDA TRANSFORMER INC (DH)
Also Called: Emerald Transformer
4509 St Hwy 83 N (32433-3960)
P.O. Box 507 (32435-0507)
PHONE.................................850 892-2711
Stuart Prior, *CEO*
Ben Bodie, *General Mgr*
Travis Carson, *Plant Mgr*
Scott Dees, *Plant Mgr*
Mark Garrett, *Plant Mgr*
◆ EMP: 1 EST: 2006
SQ FT: 100,000
SALES (est): 94.4MM
SALES (corp-wide): 492MM Privately Held
WEB: www.emeraldtransformer.com
SIC: 3612 Transformers, except electric
HQ: Versatile Processing Group, Inc.
    503 Vz County Road 3805
    Wills Point TX 75169
    903 873-3811

(G-2840)
LEGACY VULCAN LLC
Also Called: De Funiak Springs Yard
104 Lee S Pl (32435-7720)
PHONE.................................850 951-0562
Buddy Brown, *Manager*
EMP: 7 Publicly Held
SIC: 3273 Ready-mixed concrete
HQ: Legacy Vulcan, Llc
    1200 Urban Center Dr
    Vestavia AL 35242
    205 298-3000

(G-2841)
ONVOI AVI SUPP AND INSPECT SER
Also Called: Eagle Aviation Maintenance
619 Airpark Rd (32435-4776)
PHONE.................................805 312-3274
Dave Ricker, *Mng Member*
Rich Dobbins, *Mng Member*

EMP: 7 EST: 2019
SALES (est): 476K Privately Held
SIC: 3721 Aircraft

(G-2842)
PROFESSIONAL PRODUCTS INC
Also Called: Ezy Wrap
54 Hugh Adams Rd (32435-3400)
P.O. Box 589 (32435-0589)
PHONE.................................850 892-5731
Bryan E Kilbey, *CEO*
James Miller, *Principal*
Sarah Kilbey, *Corp Secy*
Dean Stanton, *COO*
Terry Drews, *Purch Mgr*
◆ EMP: 170 EST: 1963
SQ FT: 35,000
SALES (est): 21.4MM Privately Held
WEB: www.ezywrap.com
SIC: 3842 5047 Orthopedic appliances; medical equipment & supplies

(G-2843)
SPECTRAFLEX INC
83 Lancelot Rd (32433-6968)
P.O. Box 1225 (32435-1225)
PHONE.................................850 892-3900
Fax: 850 892-3900
▲ EMP: 7
SQ FT: 3,000
SALES (est): 610K Privately Held
SIC: 3679 Mfg Electronic Wire And Cable Harness Assemblies

(G-2844)
SUPERIOR ROOF TILE MFG
50 Hugh Adams Rd (32435-3400)
P.O. Box 487 (32435-0487)
PHONE.................................850 892-2299
Jessie Lynn, *President*
Barbara Ferguson, *Manager*
▼ EMP: 15 EST: 1999
SQ FT: 20,000
SALES (est): 259.2K Privately Held
SIC: 3272 Roofing tile & slabs, concrete

(G-2845)
TIKAL PAVERS INC
5991 Coy Burgess Loop (32435-6362)
PHONE.................................850 892-2207
EMP: 5
SALES (est): 624.8K Privately Held
SIC: 2951 Mfg Asphalt Mixtures/Blocks

Deland
Volusia County

(G-2846)
4FRONT SOLUTIONS LLC
3045 Tech Pkwy (32724)
PHONE.................................814 464-2000
Richard P Ward, *President*
EMP: 60 Privately Held
WEB: www.4frontsolutions.com
SIC: 3672 Printed circuit boards
HQ: 4front Solutions, Llc
    8140 Hawthorne Dr
    Erie PA 16509
    814 464-2000

(G-2847)
ABRAAHAM ROSA SEASONINGS INC
813a Flight Line Blvd (32724-2059)
PHONE.................................386 453-4827
Ana Rosa-Randolph, *CEO*
Ana Cristina Randolph, *Vice Pres*
EMP: 8 EST: 2013
SQ FT: 1,400
SALES (est): 371.5K Privately Held
WEB: www.abrahamrosaseasonings.com
SIC: 2099 Food preparations

(G-2848)
ADVANCED MFG & PWR SYSTEMS INC
Also Called: Amps
1965 Bennett Ave (32724-1928)
PHONE.................................386 822-5565
Chris Ingles, *President*
◆ EMP: 37 EST: 1999
SQ FT: 40,000

SALES (est): 8.7MM Privately Held
WEB: www.amps.cc
SIC: 3621 Electric motor & generator parts

(G-2849)
AERODYNE RESEARCH LLC
1725 Lexington Ave (32724-2148)
PHONE.................................813 891-6300
Debbie Ingling, *Manager*
William Legard, *
EMP: 11 EST: 1990
SALES (est): 1.1MM Privately Held
WEB: www.flyaerodyne.com
SIC: 2399 Parachutes

(G-2850)
AIR LION INCORP
2609 Old Church Pl (32720-1408)
PHONE.................................386 748-9296
Vasyl Levchenko, *Principal*
EMP: 7 EST: 2009
SALES (est): 195.7K Privately Held
WEB: www.airlionturbines.com
SIC: 3724 Aircraft engines & engine parts

(G-2851)
ALTI-2 INC
1200 Flight Line Blvd # 5 (32724-2138)
PHONE.................................386 943-9333
Roger F Allen, *President*
Luann Mann, *Materials Mgr*
Carol White, *Admin Asst*
EMP: 19 EST: 1999
SQ FT: 5,000
SALES (est): 2.4MM Privately Held
WEB: www.alti-2.com
SIC: 3812 Altimeters, standard & sensitive

(G-2852)
ARC ACQUISITION CORP (PA) ✪
Also Called: ARC Group Worldwide
810 Flight Line Blvd (32724-2055)
PHONE.................................386 626-0005
Weston Quasha, *CEO*
Marco Vega, *COO*
Cheryl Reynolds, *CFO*
EMP: 36 EST: 2021
SALES (est): 55MM Privately Held
SIC: 3089 8711 Injection molded finished plastic products; engineering services

(G-2853)
ARC GROUP WORLDWIDE INC (PA)
810 Flight Line Blvd (32724-2055)
PHONE.................................303 467-5236
Drew Kelley, *CEO*
Alan Quasha, *Ch of Bd*
Mike Dini, *General Mgr*
Chris Lak, *Business Mgr*
Sam Vavro, *Business Mgr*
EMP: 28 EST: 1987
SQ FT: 40,000
SALES (est): 82.4MM Privately Held
WEB: www.arcw.com
SIC: 3499 3462 3812 Friction material, made from powdered metal; machine bases, metal; welding tips, heat resistant: metal; flange, valve & pipe fitting forgings, ferrous; antennas, radar or communications

(G-2854)
ARDMORE FARMS LLC
1915 N Woodland Blvd (32720-1799)
PHONE.................................386 734-4634
Kenny Sadai, *Ch of Bd*
James O'Toole, *President*
Thomas A Kolb, *CFO*
▲ EMP: 100 EST: 1951
SQ FT: 78,000
SALES (est): 24.8MM Privately Held
SIC: 2037 2033 Fruit juices, frozen; fruit juice concentrates, frozen; canned fruits & specialties
PA: Country Pure Foods, Inc.
    222 S Main St Ste 401
    Akron OH 44308

(G-2855)
BEST PALLETS OF FL LLC
1830 Patterson Ave Unit D (32724-1962)
PHONE.................................386 624-5575
Constantino Delapaz, *Principal*
EMP: 7 EST: 2013

SALES (est): 173.4K **Privately Held**
WEB: www.bestpalletsoffl.com
SIC: 2448 Pallets, wood

(G-2856)
BP INTERNATIONAL INC
510 W Arizona Ave (32720-4109)
William De Temple, *President*
◆ **EMP:** 53 **EST:** 2003
SALES (est): 4.5MM **Privately Held**
SIC: 3949 2211 2394 Sporting & athletic
goods; gymnasium equipment; canvas &
other heavy coarse fabrics: cotton; canvas & related products

(G-2857)
CEMEX MATERIALS LLC
2170 State Road 472 (32724-9614)
PHONE..............................386 775-0790
Brad Davis, *Branch Mgr*
EMP: 128
SQ FT: 11,467 **Privately Held**
SIC: 3273 5032 5211 Ready-mixed concrete; concrete mixtures; concrete & cinder block
HQ: Cemex Materials Llc
1720 Centrepark Dr E # 100
West Palm Beach FL 33401
561 833-5555

(G-2858)
CONTEMPORARY CARBIDE TECH
1730 Patterson Ave Unit B (32724-1950)
PHONE..............................386 734-0080
Alan Evans, *President*
David Gee, *Vice Pres*
EMP: 17 **EST:** 1997
SQ FT: 5,000
SALES (est): 467.7K **Privately Held**
SIC: 3325 Bushings, cast steel: except investment

(G-2859)
COUNTRY PURE FOODS INC
1915 N Woodland Blvd (32720-1718)
PHONE..............................904 734-4634
EMP: 265
SALES (corp-wide): 4.3B **Privately Held**
SIC: 2037 Mfg Frozen Fruits/Vegetables
HQ: Country Pure Foods, Inc.
681 W Waterloo Rd
Akron OH 44308
330 753-2293

(G-2860)
DAVID SAYNE MASONRY INC
1010 Geryl Way (32724-8063)
PHONE..............................386 873-4696
David Sayne, *President*
Margaret Sayne, *Corp Secy*
EMP: 10 **EST:** 1985
SALES (est): 803.6K **Privately Held**
SIC: 3241 Masonry cement

(G-2861)
DELAND METAL CRAFT COMPANY
300 W Beresford Ave (32720-7397)
PHONE..............................386 734-0828
Edward J Ray, *President*
Brooke Whitaker, *Vice Pres*
EMP: 9 **EST:** 1967
SQ FT: 7,800
SALES (est): 1.3MM **Privately Held**
WEB: www.delandmetalcraft.com
SIC: 3446 5169 Architectural metalwork;
industrial gases

(G-2862)
DELTA MACHINE LLC
1501 Lexington Ave (32724-2117)
PHONE..............................386 738-2204
EMP: 8
SALES (est): 686K **Privately Held**
SIC: 3599 Mfg Industrial Machinery

(G-2863)
DELTA MACHINE & TOOL INC
Also Called: Norco
1212 N Mcdonald Ave (32724-2525)
PHONE..............................386 738-2204
EMP: 20
SQ FT: 5,000

SALES (est): 2.6MM **Privately Held**
SIC: 3542 3089 3544 Mfg Machine Tools-
Forming Mfg Plastic Products Mfg
Dies/Tools/Jigs/Fixtures

(G-2864)
DIEMECH TURBINE SOLUTION INC
Also Called: Turbine Solution Group
1200 Flight Line Blvd # 1 (32724-2138)
PHONE..............................386 804-0179
Christian H Skoppe, *President*
Marvin Kubaszewski, *General Mgr*
▲ **EMP:** 6 **EST:** 2006
SALES (est): 757.1K **Privately Held**
WEB: www.diemechturbinesolution.com
SIC: 3511 Turbines & turbine generator
sets

(G-2865)
DILLCO INC
1842 Patterson Ave (32724-1953)
PHONE..............................386 734-7510
EMP: 16
SQ FT: 2,500
SALES (est): 1.4MM **Privately Held**
SIC: 2759 3089 3499 Contract Screen
Printing & Mfg Plastic Hardware Including
Wall Light Switch Covers & Picture
Frames

(G-2866)
DOBROS INC
803 W New York Ave (32720-5226)
PHONE..............................386 279-0003
Michael Knott, *Owner*
EMP: 8 **EST:** 2011
SALES (est): 724.2K **Privately Held**
WEB: www.dobros.net
SIC: 3421 Table & food cutlery, including
butchers'

(G-2867)
EDC CORPORATION
1701 Lexington Ave (32724-2148)
PHONE..............................386 951-4075
Kurt H Prestegard, *Principal*
Donna Bailey, *Info Tech Mgr*
EMP: 5 **EST:** 2008
SALES (est): 570.4K **Privately Held**
WEB: www.edcpma.com
SIC: 3824 Mechanical measuring meters

(G-2868)
ENVIRO WATER SOLUTIONS LLC
Also Called: Pelican Water Systems
3060 Prfmce Cir Ste 2 (32724)
PHONE..............................877 842-1635
Karl Frykman, *President*
Dan Snellback, *Opers Staff*
Margaret Kearney, *Controller*
Rachel Dixon, *Hum Res Coord*
Michael Leonardi, *Sales Staff*
▼ **EMP:** 79 **EST:** 2013
SALES (est): 10.4MM **Privately Held**
SIC: 3589 5074 Water filters & softeners,
household type; water softeners
PA: Pentair Public Limited Company
10 Earlsfort Terrace
Dublin 2

(G-2869)
F & S CABINETS INC
1307 Yorktown St (32724-2123)
PHONE..............................386 822-9525
Rich Santora, *President*
Murial Santora, *Admin Sec*
EMP: 24 **EST:** 2004
SALES (est): 4.3MM **Privately Held**
SIC: 2521 Cabinets, office: wood

(G-2870)
FABRICO INC
1700 E Intl Speedway Blvd (32724)
PHONE..............................386 736-7373
Patrick Mullane, *President*
Amanda Magee, *CFO*
Bernie Gordon, *Sales Engr*
Mark Lloyd, *Director*
▲ **EMP:** 167 **EST:** 2001
SALES (est): 33.3MM
SALES (corp-wide): 1.1B **Publicly Held**
SIC: 3053 Gaskets & sealing devices

HQ: Technetics Group Llc
5605 Carnegie Blvd # 500
Charlotte NC 28209
704 731-1500

(G-2871)
FILTER SPECIALISTS INC
1750 Filter Dr (32724-2000)
PHONE..............................516 801-9944
EMP: 7 **EST:** 2018
SALES (est): 256.6K **Privately Held**
SIC: 3569 Filters

(G-2872)
FORTERRA PIPE & PRECAST LLC
Also Called: Hanson Pipe & Products
840 West Ave (32720-3528)
P.O. Box 369 (32721-0369)
PHONE..............................386 734-6228
Rebecca Holiday, *Manager*
EMP: 10
SQ FT: 87,860 **Privately Held**
WEB: www.forterrabp.com
SIC: 3272 Concrete products
HQ: Forterra Pipe & Precast, Llc
511 E John Carpenter Fwy
Irving TX 75062
469 458-7973

(G-2873)
GREEN MOUNTAIN SPECIALTIES
2004 Brunswick Ln 5 (32724-2001)
PHONE..............................386 469-0057
Scarlet Marsil, *President*
EMP: 8 **EST:** 2012
SALES (est): 833.1K **Privately Held**
WEB: www.gms-fl.com
SIC: 3315 Steel wire & related products

(G-2874)
HOHOL MARINE PRODUCTS
2741 W New York Ave (32720)
PHONE..............................386 734-0630
Larry Hohol, *Owner*
EMP: 8 **EST:** 2004
SQ FT: 1,000
SALES (est): 164.8K **Privately Held**
WEB: www.theluzernecountyrailroad.com
SIC: 3732 2499 5551 Boat building & repairing; floating docks, wood; boat dealers

(G-2875)
INTELLITEC MOTOR VEHICLES LLC (HQ)
1455 Jacobs Rd (32724-2604)
PHONE..............................386 738-7307
Jennifer Thomas, *Accounting Mgr*
Vincent Pesce, *Marketing Staff*
Chris Benham, *Mng Member*
▲ **EMP:** 2 **EST:** 2004
SALES (est): 11.9MM **Privately Held**
WEB: www.intellitec.com
SIC: 3679 Electronic circuits
PA: Nsi Consulting & Development Inc
24079 Research Dr
Farmington Hills MI 48335
248 987-7180

(G-2876)
ISLAND SHUTTER CO INC
Also Called: Hunter Wood Products
1838 Patterson Ave (32724-1924)
PHONE..............................386 738-9455
Chad Hunter, *President*
Joel Hunter, *Manager*
EMP: 19 **EST:** 1993
SALES (est): 1.1MM **Privately Held**
WEB: www.islandshutter.com
SIC: 2431 5211 2591 7349 Window shutters, wood; lumber & other building materials; drapery hardware & blinds & shades; window cleaning

(G-2877)
J B NOTTINGHAM & CO INC
Also Called: Duraline
1731 Patterson Ave (32724-1943)
PHONE..............................386 873-2990
John Sclafani, *President*
Lisa Pajonas, *Opers Mgr*
Lisa Sclafani, *Opers Staff*
▲ **EMP:** 49 **EST:** 1946

SQ FT: 25,000
SALES (est): 11.1MM **Privately Held**
WEB: www.jbn-duraline.com
SIC: 3643 3699 3646 3548 Current-carrying wiring devices; electrical equipment
& supplies; commercial indusl & institutional electric lighting fixtures; electric
welding equipment; switchgear & switchboard apparatus; mechanical rubber
goods

(G-2878)
JCO METALS INC
Also Called: Parachute Laboratories
1665 Lexington Ave # 106 (32724-2187)
PHONE..............................386 734-5867
Nancy Lariviere, *President*
EMP: 17 **EST:** 1983
SQ FT: 3,000
SALES (est): 384.7K **Privately Held**
WEB: www.jcometals.com
SIC: 3429 Parachute hardware

(G-2879)
JET HELSETH MANUFACTURING INC
1730 Patterson Ave (32724-1950)
PHONE..............................407 324-9001
Andrew Helseth, *CEO*
Jon Thibeault, *COO*
Francine Guillemette, *Project Mgr*
EMP: 32 **EST:** 1995
SQ FT: 12,500
SALES (est): 4MM **Privately Held**
WEB: www.jetmfg.com
SIC: 3599 Machine shop, jobbing & repair

(G-2880)
K & B LANDSCAPE SUPPLIES INC
3900 E State Road 44 (32724-6425)
PHONE..............................800 330-8816
William A Gogel, *President*
EMP: 5 **EST:** 1996
SALES (est): 991.9K **Privately Held**
WEB: www.themulchsoilco.com
SIC: 2499 Mulch, wood & bark

(G-2881)
KINGSPAN INSULATED PANELS INC (DH)
Also Called: Kingspan - Asi
726 Summerhill Dr (32724-2021)
PHONE..............................386 626-6789
Russell Shiels, *President*
Peter Wilson, *Managing Dir*
Ilhan Eser, *Vice Pres*
Carlo Vezza, *Vice Pres*
Simon Cousins, *Plant Mgr*
◆ **EMP:** 39 **EST:** 1961
SQ FT: 109,000
SALES (est): 141.1MM **Privately Held**
SIC: 3448 Prefabricated metal buildings
HQ: Kingspan Insulated Panels Ltd
12557 Coleraine Dr
Bolton ON L7E 3
905 951-5600

(G-2882)
KINGSPAN INSULATED PANELS INC
Also Called: Kingspan Deland Plant
725 Summerhill Dr (32724-2024)
PHONE..............................386 626-6789
EMP: 111 **Privately Held**
WEB: www.kingspan.com
SIC: 3448 Prefabricated metal buildings
HQ: Kingspan Insulated Panels Inc.
726 Summerhill Dr
Deland FL 32724
386 626-6789

(G-2883)
KINGSPAN-MEDUSA INC (HQ)
726 Summerhill Dr (32724-2021)
PHONE..............................386 626-6789
Pat Freeman, *Managing Dir*
Gene M Murtagh, *Principal*
Andrew Williams, *Business Mgr*
Kevin Ogrady, *Opers Dir*
Richard Wenham, *Buyer*
▼ **EMP:** 41 **EST:** 1986
SQ FT: 109,000
SALES (est): 86.7MM **Privately Held**
SIC: 3448 Prefabricated metal buildings

▲ = Import ▼=Export
◆ =Import/Export

(G-2884)
KYP GO INC
1551 Lakeside Dr (32720-3014)
PHONE..............................386 736-3770
Robert J Kyp, *President*
Elisabeth Sanda, *Assistant VP*
▲ EMP: 10 EST: 1964
SQ FT: 10,000
SALES (est): 659.3K **Privately Held**
WEB: www.kyp-go.com
SIC: 3641 Electric lamps

(G-2885)
MIKE PULVER LLC
703 Deerfoot Rd (32720-7933)
PHONE..............................386 747-8951
Michael D Pulver, *Principal*
EMP: 7 EST: 2007
SALES (est): 229.7K **Privately Held**
SIC: 2434 Wood kitchen cabinets

(G-2886)
MIRAGE SYSTEMS INC
1501a Lexington Ave (32724-2117)
P.O. Box 820 (32721-0820)
PHONE..............................386 740-9222
Dan W Thompson, *President*
Dawn M English, *Vice Pres*
EMP: 15 EST: 1996
SQ FT: 5,000
SALES (est): 2.3MM **Privately Held**
WEB: www.miragesys.com
SIC: 3429 3949 5088 Parachute hardware; sporting & athletic goods; aircraft equipment & supplies

(G-2887)
MORGANELLI & ASSOCIATES INC
1401 Saratoga St (32724-2109)
PHONE..............................386 738-3669
Al Morganelli, *President*
Kathy Morganelli, *Corp Secy*
Jenny Malchiodi, *Sales Staff*
EMP: 6 EST: 2000
SQ FT: 7,200
SALES (est): 825.6K **Privately Held**
WEB: www.lightandsirenpros.com
SIC: 3669 Emergency alarms

(G-2888)
MPC CONTAINMENT SYSTEMS LLC (HQ)
880 N Spring Garden Ave (32720-3143)
PHONE..............................773 927-4121
Larry Nunez, *Plant Mgr*
Benjamin Beiler, *Mng Member*
Alan Berman,
Edward E Reicin,
EMP: 65 EST: 1979
SALES (est): 13.6MM **Privately Held**
WEB: www.mpccontainment.com
SIC: 3443 Fabricated plate work (boiler shop)

(G-2889)
MPC GROUP LLC (PA)
880 N Spring Garden Ave (32720-3143)
PHONE..............................773 927-4120
Benjamin Beiler, *CEO*
Doug Roth, *Regl Sales Mgr*
Alan Berman,
Edward Reicin,
EMP: 2 EST: 2006
SALES (est): 29.8MM **Privately Held**
WEB: www.mpcgroupllc.com
SIC: 2394 3089 Canvas & related products; plastic processing

(G-2890)
MT-PROPELLER USA INC
1180 Airport Terminal Dr (32724-2112)
PHONE..............................386 736-7762
Gerd Muhlbauer, *President*
Martin Albrecht, *Vice Pres*
Michael Muhlbauer, *Vice Pres*
Eric Greindl, *Sales Dir*
Hoell Josefine, *Sales Mgr*
EMP: 10 EST: 1997
SQ FT: 1,500
SALES (est): 1.8MM **Privately Held**
WEB: www.mt-propellerusa.com
SIC: 3728 Accumulators, aircraft propeller

(G-2891)
ON SITE SVCS OF MID FL
265 Damascus Rd (32724-6436)
PHONE..............................407 444-2951
Tim McLaughlin, *Manager*
EMP: 6 EST: 1964
SALES (est): 513.3K **Privately Held**
WEB: www.onsiteservicesofmflorida.com
SIC: 7692 Welding repair

(G-2892)
PAIN AWAY LLC
Also Called: Outback Series, The
1515 Detrick Ave (32724-2014)
PHONE..............................800 215-8739
Brandon Godwin, *CEO*
Stacy Godwin, *CFO*
EMP: 12 EST: 2016
SALES (est): 3MM **Privately Held**
SIC: 2833 Medicinals & botanicals

(G-2893)
PALL AEROPOWER CORPORATION
1750 Filter Dr (32724-2000)
PHONE..............................727 849-9999
Nalin Patel, *Engineer*
Terry Flack, *Branch Mgr*
Steve Ebersohl, *Director*
EMP: 458
SALES (corp-wide): 29.4B **Publicly Held**
SIC: 3569 3564 Filters; blowers & fans
HQ: Pall Aeropower Corporation
     10540 Ridge Rd Ste 100
     New Port Richey FL 34654

(G-2894)
PALL FILTRATION AND SEP
Fluid Dynamics
1750 Filter Dr (32724-2000)
PHONE..............................386 822-8000
Max Kuzma, *Opers Staff*
Andrew Gorin, *Sales Dir*
Joe Hahn, *Sales Mgr*
Rick Morris, *Branch Mgr*
Eva Chambers, *Manager*
EMP: 250
SALES (corp-wide): 29.4B **Publicly Held**
SIC: 3677 3564 Filtration devices, electronic; filters, air: furnaces, air conditioning equipment, etc.
HQ: Pall Filtration And Separations Group Inc.
     2120 Greenspring Dr
     Lutherville Timonium MD 21093
     410 252-0800

(G-2895)
PENTAIR LLC
3060 Prfmce Cir Ste 2 (32724)
PHONE..............................386 469-0566
EMP: 8 EST: 2013
SALES (est): 241.5K **Privately Held**
WEB: www.pentair.com
SIC: 3491 Industrial valves

(G-2896)
PERFORMANCE DESIGNS INC
1300 E Intl Speedway Blvd (32724)
PHONE..............................386 738-2224
Tony Yrey, *General Mgr*
John Le Blanc, *Vice Pres*
Katie Barbour, *Purchasing*
Katy Barbour, *Purchasing*
Amanda Festi, *Research*
▲ EMP: 160 EST: 1982
SQ FT: 17,000
SALES (est): 36MM **Privately Held**
WEB: www.performancedesigns.com
SIC: 2399 Parachutes

(G-2897)
REAL GOLD INC
1853 Patterson Ave Unit 4 (32724-1963)
PHONE..............................386 873-4849
Jamie Quick, *President*
Bill Crowley, *Vice Pres*
Tracy Sciulla, *Office Mgr*
EMP: 7 EST: 2013
SALES (est): 1.2MM **Privately Held**
WEB: www.realgoldinc.com
SIC: 3081 3999 Vinyl film & sheet; atomizers, toiletry

(G-2898)
REFLECTIVITY INC
320 S Spring Garden Ave (32720-5038)
PHONE..............................386 738-1008
Kathleen S Truba, *President*
EMP: 13 EST: 2001
SALES (est): 126.7K **Privately Held**
SIC: 3674 Semiconductors & related devices

(G-2899)
RINKER MATERIALS CORP
2170 State Road 472 (32724-9614)
PHONE..............................386 775-0790
Susan Jensen, *Principal*
EMP: 7 EST: 2011
SALES (est): 99.8K **Privately Held**
SIC: 3273 Ready-mixed concrete

(G-2900)
SIEMENS AG
1750 Filter Dr (32724-2000)
PHONE..............................386 822-8000
N Tsounis, *Sales Executive*
EMP: 7 EST: 2013
SALES (est): 192.8K **Privately Held**
WEB: www.siemens.com
SIC: 3661 Telephones & telephone apparatus

(G-2901)
SIMPLICITY ESPORTS
1697 N Woodland Blvd (32720-1834)
PHONE..............................386 479-9091
EMP: 7 EST: 2019
SALES (est): 125.9K **Privately Held**
WEB: www.ggsimplicity.com
SIC: 3944 Games, toys & children's vehicles

(G-2902)
SIMPLY SWEET COMPANY INC (PA)
1431 Orange Camp Rd (32724-7768)
PHONE..............................386 873-6516
Donna Rotondo, *President*
Rotondo Donna, *President*
EMP: 7 EST: 2015
SALES (est): 501.1K **Privately Held**
WEB: www.simplysweeticecream.com
SIC: 2024 Ice cream & frozen desserts

(G-2903)
SLM BOATS INC
1948 Sunset Ct (32720-2366)
PHONE..............................386 738-4425
Richard Langford, *President*
EMP: 6 EST: 1988
SQ FT: 12,000
SALES (est): 350K **Privately Held**
SIC: 3732 Boat building & repairing

(G-2904)
STEADFAST WOODWORKING INC
680 Cumberland Rd (32724-2416)
PHONE..............................386 748-1744
Russell Martini, *Principal*
EMP: 7 EST: 2016
SALES (est): 177.5K **Privately Held**
WEB: www.steadfastwoodworkinginc.com
SIC: 2431 Millwork

(G-2905)
SUNNY HILL INTERNATIONAL INC
901 W New York Ave (32720-5144)
PHONE..............................386 736-5757
William R Murphy, *Director*
Leland M Anderson, *Director*
Hector E Viale, *Director*
▼ EMP: 7 EST: 2004
SALES (est): 2MM **Privately Held**
WEB: www.sunnyhillintl.com
SIC: 2087 Beverage bases

(G-2906)
TCM IMAGINEERING INC
1835 Bennett Ave (32724-1941)
PHONE..............................407 323-6494
Pierre Gauthier, *Executive Asst*
EMP: 17 EST: 2014
SALES (est): 1MM **Privately Held**
SIC: 2542 Partitions & fixtures, except wood

(G-2907)
TEAM PLASTICS INC
2025 Eidson Dr (32724-2029)
PHONE..............................386 740-9555
Michael Allen Agee, *President*
Todd Agee, *General Mgr*
Jim Gierhart, *Prdtn Mgr*
Troy Backman, *Engineer*
Troy Agee, *Maintence Staff*
EMP: 45 EST: 1991
SALES (est): 5MM **Privately Held**
WEB: www.teamplastics.com
SIC: 3089 Injection molding of plastics

(G-2908)
TECHNETICS GROUP LLC
Technetics Group Burbank
1700 E Intl Speedway Blvd (32724)
PHONE..............................386 736-7373
Kelly Ceiler, *Engineer*
Sean Mabry, *Design Engr*
Claudine Andrews, *Manager*
EMP: 417
SALES (corp-wide): 1.1B **Publicly Held**
WEB: www.technetics.com
SIC: 3053 3351 Gaskets & sealing devices; copper rolling & drawing
HQ: Technetics Group Llc
     5605 Carnegie Blvd # 500
     Charlotte NC 28209
     704 731-1500

(G-2909)
TECHNO TRADING MANUFACTURING (PA)
1730 Langley Ave Ste B (32724-2176)
PHONE..............................689 777-0755
Milivoj F Milosevich, *President*
EMP: 8 EST: 2020
SALES (est): 450K **Privately Held**
SIC: 3312 Hot-rolled iron & steel products

(G-2910)
THATCHER CHEMICAL FLORIDA INC (HQ)
Also Called: Thatcher Chemical Company
245 Hazen Rd (32720-3967)
PHONE..............................386 734-3966
Lawrence Thatcher, *CEO*
Craig N Thatcher, *President*
Teri Flanders, *Vice Pres*
Michael Walker, *Analyst*
◆ EMP: 9 EST: 2007
SALES (est): 10.4MM
SALES (corp-wide): 556.6MM **Privately Held**
SIC: 2819 5169 Industrial inorganic chemicals; chemicals & allied products
PA: Thatcher Group, Inc
     1905 W Fortune Rd
     Salt Lake City UT 84104
     801 972-4587

(G-2911)
THREAD GRAPHICS EMBROIDERY
1731 Timber Hills Dr (32724-7980)
PHONE..............................407 688-7026
Kristine Szacik, *President*
EMP: 6 EST: 1997
SQ FT: 3,000
SALES (est): 421.1K **Privately Held**
SIC: 2395 Embroidery products, except schiffli machine

(G-2912)
TITAN SERVICE INDUSTRY LLC
2044 Anchor Ave (32720-2359)
PHONE..............................678 313-4707
Rick Schafrick, *President*
Walter Alvarado,
Richard Schafrick,
EMP: 6 EST: 2015
SALES (est): 474.4K **Privately Held**
WEB: www.tsiweld.com
SIC: 7692 1731 7389 1799 Welding repair; safety & security specialization; safety inspection service; welding on site; ; conveyors & conveying equipment

(G-2913)
TOMI AIRCRAFT INC
1310 Flight Line Blvd (32724-2116)
PHONE..............................863 446-3001
Tad Olmsted, *President*

GEOGRAPHIC

EMP: 7 EST: 2014
SALES (est): 726.6K **Privately Held**
WEB: www.tomiaircraft.com
SIC: 3728 Aircraft parts & equipment

(G-2914)
TRI-DECK LLC (PA)
3402 Black Willow Trl (32724-1100)
PHONE.................................386 748-3239
David C Solar, *Mng Member*
James Wurst Solar,
EMP: 1 **EST:** 2012
SQ FT: 3,500
SALES (est): 50MM **Privately Held**
SIC: 3949 Skateboards

(G-2915)
UNINSRED UNTD PRCHUTE TECH LLC
Also Called: Upt Vector
1645 Lexington Ave (32724-2106)
PHONE.................................386 736-7589
Mark Procos, *General Mgr*
Sheryl Bothwell, *Safety Mgr*
Julia Stone, *QC Mgr*
Hope Cruz, *Controller*
Thiago Gomes, *Human Res Mgr*
EMP: 85 **EST:** 2006
SQ FT: 12,000
SALES (est): 9.2MM **Privately Held**
WEB: www.uptvector.com
SIC: 3429 Parachute hardware

(G-2916)
UNINSURED RELATIVE WORKSHOP
1645 Lexington Ave (32724-2106)
PHONE.................................386 736-7589
William R Booth,
EMP: 13 **EST:** 1976
SQ FT: 11,000
SALES (est): 471.5K **Privately Held**
SIC: 3949 Sporting & athletic goods

(G-2917)
USA VIGIL
1400 Flight Line Blvd (32724-2140)
PHONE.................................386 736-8464
Richard Hall, *Principal*
EMP: 8 **EST:** 2010
SALES (est): 117.2K **Privately Held**
WEB: www.vigil.aero
SIC: 2399 Parachutes

(G-2918)
WARENSFORD WELL DRILLING INC
329 S Blue Lake Ave (32724-6201)
P.O. Box 326 (32721-0326)
PHONE.................................386 738-3257
Kell Warrensford, *CEO*
William Warrens, *CFO*
EMP: 5 **EST:** 2003
SALES (est): 357.6K **Privately Held**
WEB: www.warensfordwelldrilling.com
SIC: 1389 1381 Oil & gas wells: building, repairing & dismantling; drilling oil & gas wells

(G-2919)
WATERFILTERUSA
3060 Prfmce Cir Ste 2 (32724)
PHONE.................................386 469-0138
Robert Prentice, *Principal*
EMP: 8 **EST:** 2010
SALES (est): 180K **Privately Held**
SIC: 3589 Water filters & softeners, household type

(G-2920)
WEST BOLUSIA BEACON
Also Called: Deland Beacon Newspaper
110 W New York Ave (32720-5416)
PHONE.................................386 734-4622
Barbara Shepard, *President*
Coni Tarby, *Advt Staff*
EMP: 14 **EST:** 1992
SALES (est): 2.1MM **Privately Held**
WEB: www.beacononlinenews.com
SIC: 2711 7313 Newspapers: publishing only, not printed on site; newspaper advertising representative

(G-2921)
WOOD ASPECTS
1384 Saratoga St (32724-2186)
PHONE.................................321 800-8875
Eda Abolfathi, *Principal*
EMP: 8 **EST:** 2014
SALES (est): 315.4K **Privately Held**
WEB: www.woodaspects.com
SIC: 2434 Wood kitchen cabinets

Delray Beach
Palm Beach County

(G-2922)
A Z PRINTING DELRAY
645 E Atlantic Ave (33483-5325)
PHONE.................................561 330-4154
Steve Sincoff, *Owner*
EMP: 7 **EST:** 2011
SALES (est): 175.3K **Privately Held**
SIC: 2759 Commercial printing

(G-2923)
AA OLDCO INC (PA)
Also Called: Alfred Angelo Bridals
1625 S Congress Ave # 400 (33445-6301)
PHONE.................................215 659-5300
Vincent E Piccione, *President*
Fred Piccione, *Chairman*
Ron Wible, *COO*
Michael Bruzzese, *Vice Pres*
Joe Weltz, *CFO*
▲ **EMP:** 75 **EST:** 1947
SQ FT: 25,000
SALES (est): 18.2MM **Privately Held**
WEB: locations.alfredangelo.com
SIC: 2335 Wedding gowns & dresses; gowns, formal

(G-2924)
ABC AWNING & CANVAS CO INC
244 Avenue L (33483-4651)
PHONE.................................321 253-1960
Rue McNay, *President*
EMP: 14 **EST:** 1962
SQ FT: 4,950
SALES (est): 997.8K **Privately Held**
SIC: 2394 Awnings, fabric: made from purchased materials

(G-2925)
ADVANCED AUTOMOTIVE DESIGNS
6685 Dana Point Cv (33446-5646)
PHONE.................................561 499-8812
Dov Zucker, *President*
▲ **EMP:** 6 **EST:** 1994
SQ FT: 4,000
SALES (est): 509.4K **Privately Held**
SIC: 3694 3714 Automotive electrical equipment; motor vehicle electrical equipment

(G-2926)
ADVANCED PRCSION MACHINING INC
1035 Nw 17th Ave Ste 3 (33445-2518)
PHONE.................................561 243-4567
Mark Burke, *President*
EMP: 8 **EST:** 1997
SQ FT: 5,000
SALES (est): 971.7K **Privately Held**
WEB: www.advancedprecision.net
SIC: 3599 Machine shop, jobbing & repair

(G-2927)
AFFORDBLE SCREEN ENCLOSURE LLC
5480 Palm Ridge Blvd (33484-1115)
PHONE.................................561 900-8868
Pavel Krutakov, *Principal*
EMP: 8 **EST:** 2016
SALES (est): 866.4K **Privately Held**
SIC: 3448 Screen enclosures

(G-2928)
ALLIED PHARMACY PRODUCTS INC
2905 S Congress Ave Ste A (33445-7337)
PHONE.................................516 374-8862
Stuart Meadow, *Principal*
EMP: 5 **EST:** 2012

SALES (est): 530.7K **Privately Held**
WEB: www.steri-tamp.com
SIC: 2834 5047 Pharmaceutical preparations; medical & hospital equipment

(G-2929)
ALUMINIUM DESIGN PRODUCTS LLC
1055 Sw 15th Ave Ste 1 (33444-1263)
PHONE.................................561 894-8775
Jason Scott Toler, *Vice Pres*
William Toler,
▼ **EMP:** 9 **EST:** 2011
SALES (est): 1.5MM **Privately Held**
WEB: www.aluminumdesignproducts.com
SIC: 3355 Aluminum rolling & drawing

(G-2930)
AMBASSADOR PRINTING COMPANY
Also Called: Ambassador Marketing Group
1025 Nw 17th Ave Ste C (33445-2563)
PHONE.................................561 330-3668
Anthony Gentile, *President*
Mario Gentile, *Principal*
Jerold M Ode, *Vice Pres*
EMP: 9 **EST:** 1994
SALES (est): 1.6MM **Privately Held**
WEB: www.ambassadorprinting.com
SIC: 2752 Commercial printing, offset

(G-2931)
AMERICAN MOLDING & PLAS LLC
3302 Karen Dr (33483-6241)
PHONE.................................561 734-4194
Gregg T Cheverie, *Principal*
Jerry Baker, *QC Mgr*
EMP: 7 **EST:** 2010
SALES (est): 87.9K **Privately Held**
WEB:
www.americanmoldingandplastics.com
SIC: 3089 Injection molding of plastics

(G-2932)
AQUACOMFORT SOLUTIONS LLC
601 N Congress Ave # 311 (33445-4646)
PHONE.................................407 831-1941
EMP: 21
SALES (corp-wide): 2.5MM **Privately Held**
WEB: www.aquacomfort.com
SIC: 3648 Swimming pool lighting fixtures
PA: Aquacomfort Solutions, Llc
7700 High Ridget Rd
Boynton Beach FL 33426
203 265-0100

(G-2933)
ART IN PRINT INC (PA)
Also Called: National Print & Design
8640 Valhalla Dr (33446-9568)
PHONE.................................561 877-0995
David M Ebenstein, *President*
EMP: 10 **EST:** 2015
SQ FT: 12,000
SALES (est): 973.3K **Privately Held**
WEB: www.nationalprintdesign.com
SIC: 2752 Commercial printing, offset

(G-2934)
AXTONNE INC
Also Called: Precision Plastics
350 Se 1st St (33483-4502)
PHONE.................................510 755-7480
Eric Appelblom, *President*
EMP: 10 **EST:** 2018
SALES (est): 472.4K **Privately Held**
WEB: www.axtonne.com
SIC: 3999 Manufacturing industries

(G-2935)
BANYAN HILL
98 Se 6th Ave Ste 2 (33483-5363)
PHONE.................................561 455-9045
Kristen Barrett, *Manager*
Anthony Planas, *Analyst*
EMP: 9 **EST:** 2017
SALES (est): 309.4K **Privately Held**
WEB: www.banyanhill.com
SIC: 2741 Miscellaneous publishing

(G-2936)
BIRDIE PUBLISHING LLC
701 Se 6th Ave Ste 102 (33483-5186)
PHONE.................................561 332-1826
EMP: 6 **EST:** 2019
SALES (est): 391.9K **Privately Held**
WEB: www.birdiepublishing.com
SIC: 2741 Miscellaneous publishing

(G-2937)
BRANDINE WOODCRAFT INC
601 N Congress Ave # 203 (33445-4703)
PHONE.................................561 266-9360
Fax: 561 266-9361
▲ **EMP:** 5
SQ FT: 5,000
SALES (est): 410K **Privately Held**
SIC: 3944 5945 5999 Mfg Games/Toys Ret Hobbies/Toys/Games Ret Misc Merchandise

(G-2938)
BRILL HYGIENIC PRODUCTS INC
601 N Congress Ave (33445-4646)
PHONE.................................561 278-5600
Alan Brill, *CEO*
David Jablow, *Exec VP*
▲ **EMP:** 12 **EST:** 1991
SQ FT: 4,000
SALES (est): 1.7MM **Privately Held**
WEB: www.brillseat.com
SIC: 3089 Fences, gates & accessories: plastic

(G-2939)
BROOKLYN WATER ENTERPRISES INC
1615 S Congress Ave # 103 (33445-6326)
PHONE.................................877 224-3580
Steven Fassberg, *CEO*
David Ross, *President*
Joseph West, *Vice Pres*
Carl Blomgren, *Project Mgr*
EMP: 28 **EST:** 2007
SALES (est): 4.5MM **Privately Held**
WEB: www.brooklynwaterbagel.com
SIC: 2051 Bakery: wholesale or wholesale/retail combined

(G-2940)
CABINETS DIRECT USA
16107 Via Monteverde (33446-2366)
PHONE.................................862 704-6138
EMP: 7 **EST:** 2018
SALES (est): 475.8K **Privately Held**
WEB: www.cabinetsdirectusa.com
SIC: 2434 Wood kitchen cabinets

(G-2941)
CASEY RESEARCH LLC
55 Ne 5th Ave Ste 300 (33483-5461)
PHONE.................................561 455-9043
Mark Arnold, *Mng Member*
EMP: 10 **EST:** 2015
SALES (est): 10MM **Privately Held**
WEB: www.caseyresearch.com
SIC: 2741 Miscellaneous publishing

(G-2942)
CATAPULT LEARNING LL
501 Nw 8th Ave (33444-1701)
PHONE.................................561 573-6025
EMP: 7 **EST:** 2018
SALES (est): 131.9K **Privately Held**
SIC: 3599 Catapults

(G-2943)
CHANNEL LETTER USA CORP
2275 S Federal Hwy # 350 (33483-3337)
PHONE.................................561 243-9699
Shamiroon Little, *Principal*
EMP: 7 **EST:** 2009
SALES (est): 138.6K **Privately Held**
WEB: www.channelletterusa.com
SIC: 3993 Signs & advertising specialties

(G-2944)
CHEM-FREE SYSTEM INC
7168 Cataluna Cir (33446-3176)
PHONE.................................954 258-5415
Edward M Gale, *President*
▼ **EMP:** 8 **EST:** 2011

SALES (est): 564.6K **Privately Held**
WEB: www.chemfreesystemsinc.com
SIC: 2086 Mineral water, carbonated: packaged in cans, bottles, etc.

(G-2945)
CLEAN SKIN LLC
Also Called: Clean Skin Club
1240 Tangelo Ter Ste B11 (33444-1287)
PHONE...................................203 997-2491
Ben Imberman, *Mng Member*
Mor Shnaider,
EMP: 6 EST: 2017
SALES (est): 550.6K **Privately Held**
WEB: www.cleanskinclub.com
SIC: 2621 Toweling tissue, paper

(G-2946)
CLEAR VIEW GLASS & GLAZING
509 Eldorado Ln (33444-1705)
PHONE...................................561 441-7675
Terry Sandfort, *Principal*
EMP: 7 EST: 2004
SALES (est): 133.7K **Privately Held**
SIC: 3231 Products of purchased glass

(G-2947)
COASTAL DOOR & MLLWK SVCS LLC
1300 Sw 10th St (33444-1266)
PHONE...................................561 266-3716
Pat Endres, *Managing Prtnr*
Claudia Arboleda, *Office Mgr*
Pj Hatley, *Mng Member*
EMP: 9 EST: 2014
SALES (est): 376.3K **Privately Held**
WEB: www.coastaldms.com
SIC: 2431 Millwork

(G-2948)
COASTAL SCREEN & RAIL LLC
1127 Poinsettia Dr (33444-1221)
PHONE...................................321 917-4605
Sijifredo Huicochea, *Project Mgr*
R Scott Buchanan, *Mng Member*
▼ EMP: 7 EST: 2006
SQ FT: 14,000
SALES (est): 1.8MM **Privately Held**
WEB: www.coastalscreen.com
SIC: 3448 Screen enclosures

(G-2949)
COMMON SENSE PUBLISHING LLC
55 Ne 5th Ave Ste 100 (33483-5461)
PHONE...................................561 510-1713
Amber Mason,
Ryan Markish,
EMP: 130 EST: 2010
SALES (est): 50.9MM
SALES (corp-wide): 90.5MM **Privately Held**
WEB: www.palmbeachgroup.com
SIC: 2741 7371 7389 Miscellaneous publishing; computer software development & applications;
PA: Monument & Cathedral Holdings, Inc.
14 W Mount Vernon Pl
Baltimore MD 21201
410 783-8499

(G-2950)
CONVERGENT MARKETING LLC
701 Nw 2nd Ave (33444-3909)
PHONE...................................561 270-7081
Michelle R Bidwell, *Principal*
EMP: 9 EST: 2009
SALES (est): 251.7K **Privately Held**
SIC: 3674 Semiconductors & related devices

(G-2951)
CORELLIUM INC
10 Se 1st Ave Ste B (33444-3693)
PHONE...................................561 502-2420
Amanda Gorton, *CEO*
EMP: 20 EST: 2017
SALES (est): 1.2MM **Privately Held**
WEB: www.corellium.com
SIC: 7372 Prepackaged software

(G-2952)
CURVCO STEEL STRUCTURES CORP
14545 S Military Trl H (33484-3781)
PHONE...................................800 956-6341
Shawn Davis, *President*
Paul Kraham, *Vice Pres*
EMP: 12 EST: 2004
SQ FT: 4,000
SALES (est): 1.1MM **Privately Held**
WEB: www.curvcosteelbuildings.com
SIC: 3448 Prefabricated metal buildings

(G-2953)
DAN LIPMAN AND ASSOCIATES
15852 Corintha Ter (33446-9724)
P.O. Box 788, Deerfield Beach (33443-0788)
PHONE...................................561 245-8672
Dan Lipman, *President*
Melissa Lipman, *Exec VP*
EMP: 5 EST: 1994
SALES (est): 485.1K **Privately Held**
WEB: www.danlipman.com
SIC: 3545 Machine tool attachments & accessories

(G-2954)
DELRAY AWNING INC
80 N Congress Ave (33445-3417)
PHONE...................................561 276-5381
Ricky J Day, *President*
Donald Day, *Vice Pres*
EMP: 15 EST: 1959
SQ FT: 4,900
SALES (est): 1.5MM **Privately Held**
WEB: www.delrayawning.com
SIC: 2394 2399 Awnings, fabric: made from purchased materials; banners, made from fabric

(G-2955)
DELRAY TROPIC HOLDINGS INC
Also Called: Gwa Alper
335 E Linton Blvd (33483-5023)
PHONE...................................561 342-1501
Gregg Alper, *President*
Bailee Alper, *Mng Member*
EMP: 8 EST: 2011
SALES (est): 964.5K **Privately Held**
SIC: 3714 Motor vehicle engines & parts

(G-2956)
E1W GAMES LLC ✪
14545 S Military Trl J (33484-3781)
PHONE...................................561 255-7370
Mark Friedlander,
EMP: 10 EST: 2021
SALES (est): 500K **Privately Held**
SIC: 2741

(G-2957)
EL HARLEY INC
2885 S Congress Ave Ste F (33445-7336)
PHONE...................................561 841-9887
Richard Harley, *President*
Craig Harley, *Vice Pres*
▼ EMP: 10 EST: 1948
SALES (est): 1MM **Privately Held**
WEB: www.elharleyinc.com
SIC: 3555 Printing trades machinery

(G-2958)
ENDLESS OCEANS LLC
3125 S Federal Hwy (33483-3221)
PHONE...................................561 274-1990
EMP: 6 EST: 2012
SALES (est): 449.3K **Privately Held**
SIC: 3089 3499 5999 7389 Mfg Plastic Products Mfg Misc Fab Metal Prdts Ret Misc Merchandise Business Services Mfg Prdt-Purchased Glass

(G-2959)
EPIGENETIX INC
1004 Brooks Ln (33483-6508)
PHONE...................................561 543-7569
Joseph W Collard, *Principal*
EMP: 9 EST: 2011
SALES (est): 740.6K **Privately Held**
WEB: www.epigenetix.com
SIC: 2834 Pharmaceutical preparations

(G-2960)
EUROMOTION INC
7194 Skyline Dr (33446-2214)
PHONE...................................954 612-0354
Robin Van Der Putten, *President*
▲ EMP: 5 EST: 2004
SALES (est): 390.2K **Privately Held**
SIC: 3694 Automotive electrical equipment

(G-2961)
F2F INC
10800 Avenida Del Rio (33446-2444)
PHONE...................................561 833-9661
Sherrie Raz, *Principal*
EMP: 8 EST: 2012
SALES (est): 141.3K **Privately Held**
SIC: 2752 Commercial printing, lithographic

(G-2962)
FHS ENTERPRISES LLC
Also Called: Florida Salt Scrubs
2875 S Congress Ave Ste D (33445-7344)
PHONE...................................754 214-9379
Geoffrey Schmidt, *Mng Member*
EMP: 5 EST: 2012
SALES (est): 383.3K **Privately Held**
SIC: 2844 Toilet preparations

(G-2963)
FLICKDIRECT INC
7495 Atl Ave Ste 200-347 (33446)
PHONE...................................561 330-2987
Nathan Rose, *CEO*
Nathan M Rose, *CEO*
Maureen Buccellato, *Director*
EMP: 13 EST: 2008
SALES (est): 120K **Privately Held**
WEB: www.flickdirect.com
SIC: 3663 7372 4832 Television broadcasting & communications equipment; application computer software; news

(G-2964)
FOURNIES ASSOCIATES
1226 Nw 19th Ter (33445-2540)
PHONE...................................561 445-5102
Ferdinand F Fournies, *President*
Sandra Fournies, *Partner*
Elizabeth P Fournies, *Vice Pres*
EMP: 7 EST: 1971
SALES (est): 636.6K **Privately Held**
WEB: www.fournies.com
SIC: 2731 8748 Book publishing; business consulting

(G-2965)
FRESH
4801 Linton Blvd (33445-6503)
PHONE...................................561 330-4345
EMP: 8 EST: 2011
SALES (est): 500K **Privately Held**
SIC: 3421 Mfg Cutlery

(G-2966)
FRESH BLENDS NORTH AMERICA INC
955 Nw 17th Ave Ste J (33445-2516)
PHONE...................................531 665-8200
James Day, *Managing Prtnr*
Marc Lang, *Vice Pres*
Joseph Knauss, *Director*
Mikael Stuart, *Director*
EMP: 10 EST: 2016
SALES (est): 3MM **Privately Held**
WEB: www.freshblends.com
SIC: 2037 Frozen fruits & vegetables

(G-2967)
GB ENERGY TECH
2875 S Congress Ave Ste B (33445-7344)
PHONE...................................561 450-6047
Rafael Gonzalez, *Owner*
EMP: 10 EST: 2014
SALES (est): 563.5K **Privately Held**
WEB: www.gbenergy.com
SIC: 3674 Solar cells

(G-2968)
GELATO PETRINI LLC
1205 Sw 4th Ave (33444-2276)
PHONE...................................561 600-4088
Koby Cohen, *Officer*
Dawn Rachel Petrini,
EMP: 15 EST: 2011

SQ FT: 10,000
SALES (est): 2.1MM **Privately Held**
WEB: www.gelatopetrini.com
SIC: 2024 Ice cream, bulk

(G-2969)
GOODPRESS PUBLISHING LLC
Also Called: Simply The Best Magazine
4731 W Atlantic Ave Ste 5 (33445-3866)
PHONE...................................561 865-8101
Adam Goodkin, *President*
EMP: 5 EST: 1999
SQ FT: 3,000
SALES (est): 513.2K **Privately Held**
SIC: 2721 Magazines: publishing & printing

(G-2970)
GREAT ESCAPE PUBLISHING
101 Se 6th Ave Ste A (33483-5261)
PHONE...................................561 860-8266
EMP: 6 EST: 2019
SALES (est): 511.3K **Privately Held**
WEB: www.greatescapepublishing.com
SIC: 2741 Miscellaneous publishing

(G-2971)
GRIMES AEROSPACE COMPANY
Aircraft Products Div
12807 Lake Drive Ext (33444-3168)
PHONE...................................407 276-6083
Lee Schwartz, *Branch Mgr*
EMP: 88
SQ FT: 10,000
SALES (corp-wide): 34.3B **Publicly Held**
SIC: 3634 Coffee makers, electric: household
HQ: Grimes Aerospace Company
550 State Route 55
Urbana OH 43078
937 484-2000

(G-2972)
GUARDIAN ESSENTIALS LLC
137 Nw 1st Ave (33444-2611)
PHONE...................................817 401-0200
Kilburn Sherman,
Scott James,
Jeremy Office,
EMP: 6 EST: 2016
SQ FT: 2,500
SALES (est): 1MM **Privately Held**
SIC: 2833 Vitamins, natural or synthetic: bulk, uncompounded

(G-2973)
GULFSTREAM GRAPHICS INC
955 S Congress Ave # 103 (33445-4662)
PHONE...................................561 276-0006
Mike Luttino, *Owner*
EMP: 7 EST: 1981
SALES (est): 92.3K **Privately Held**
WEB: www.gulfstreamgraphics.com
SIC: 2752 Commercial printing, lithographic

(G-2974)
HARDRIVES INDUSTRIES INC
2101 S Congress Ave (33445-7307)
PHONE...................................561 278-0456
George T Elmore, *Principal*
Victor Concepcion, *Project Mgr*
Craig Connors, *Project Mgr*
Chris Sherlock, *Manager*
EMP: 16 EST: 2009
SALES (est): 6.7MM **Privately Held**
WEB: www.hardrivespaving.com
SIC: 3999 Manufacturing industries

(G-2975)
INTERCOMP
5910 Morningstar Cir (33484-8571)
PHONE...................................407 637-9766
Laura Michaels, *Principal*
EMP: 7 EST: 2012
SALES (est): 194.2K **Privately Held**
SIC: 3596 Scales & balances, except laboratory

(G-2976)
IRIS INC
955 Nw 17th Ave Ste D (33445-2516)
PHONE...................................561 921-0847
Jean-Marc Fontaine, *President*
Benjamin Bilges, *Partner*
Sally Daflaar, *General Mgr*
Joe Siegal, *Vice Pres*

Mickey Fried, *Project Mgr*
▲ **EMP: 8 EST:** 1997
SALES (est): 4.4MM **Privately Held**
WEB: www.irislink.com
SIC: 7372 Business oriented computer software
HQ: Image Recognition Integrated Systems Group
Rue Du Bosquet 10
Mont-Saint-Guibert
104 513-64

(G-2977)
JEWELNET CORP
Also Called: K & G Creations
72 Se 6th Ave Apt K (33483-5308)
PHONE.................................561 989-8383
Neil Koppel, *President*
▲ **EMP: 9 EST:** 1988
SALES (est): 670.2K **Privately Held**
WEB: www.jewelnet.com
SIC: 3915 Jewelers' materials & lapidary work

(G-2978)
JEWISH BURIAL SOCIETY AMERICA
15310 Strathearn Dr # 11505 (33446-2851)
PHONE.................................954 424-1899
Philip Weinstein, *Principal*
EMP: 7 EST: 2002
SALES (est): 98.1K **Privately Held**
SIC: 3272 Burial vaults, concrete or precast terrazzo

(G-2979)
JOE TAYLOR RESTORATION (PA)
855 Nw 17th Ave Ste C (33445-2520)
P.O. Box 970805, Coconut Creek (33097-0805)
PHONE.................................954 972-5390
Robert Taylor, *Principal*
Annie Russo, *Controller*
Jessica Baxter, *Sales Staff*
Rod Ribeiro, *Branch Mgr*
Glenda Galarza, *Manager*
EMP: 16 EST: 2012
SALES (est): 13.1MM **Privately Held**
WEB: www.jtrestoration.com
SIC: 3442 Molding, trim & stripping

(G-2980)
JTS WOODWORKING INC
75 Nw 18th Ave (33444-1687)
PHONE.................................561 272-7996
Mark Feehan, *President*
EMP: 9 EST: 1981
SQ FT: 10,780
SALES (est): 992.8K **Privately Held**
WEB: www.jtswoodworking.com
SIC: 2499 2521 2511 Decorative wood & woodwork; wood office furniture; wood household furniture

(G-2981)
KC & B CUSTOM INC
Also Called: Kam Tatonetti
2413 N Federal Hwy Unit A (33483-6143)
PHONE.................................561 276-1887
John Kennedy, *President*
John Czulada, *Vice Pres*
EMP: 5 EST: 1988
SALES (est): 500K **Privately Held**
WEB: www.everwoodcabinetandtrim.com
SIC: 2434 5211 1751 Wood kitchen cabinets; cabinets; kitchen; cabinet building & installation

(G-2982)
LAB KINGZ LLC
514 Sw 15th Ter (33444-1446)
PHONE.................................561 808-4216
Eric Wakeley Sr, *Mng Member*
EMP: 5 EST: 2020
SALES (est): 377.6K **Privately Held**
WEB: www.labkingz.com
SIC: 2833 Vitamins, natural or synthetic: bulk, uncompounded

(G-2983)
LUMITEC LLC
1405 Poinsettia Dr Ste 10 (33444-5200)
PHONE.................................561 272-9840
John A Kujawa, *President*
Steve Rotolante, *Electrical Engi*

Karim Kharroubi, *Controller*
Mark Hayward, *Sales Associate*
Michael McDonald, *Marketing Mgr*
◆ **EMP: 34 EST:** 2007
SALES (est): 11.5MM **Privately Held**
WEB: www.lumiteclighting.com
SIC: 3647 3648 8711 Boat & ship lighting fixtures; underwater lighting fixtures; mechanical engineering; electrical or electronic engineering
HQ: Clarience Technologies, Llc
20600 Civic Center Dr
Southfield MI 48076
716 665-6214

(G-2984)
LUXE VINTAGES LLC
14545 S Military Trl J (33484-3781)
PHONE.................................561 558-7399
Peter Staley,
▲ **EMP: 7 EST:** 2007
SALES (est): 632K **Privately Held**
SIC: 2084 Wine cellars, bonded: engaged in blending wines

(G-2985)
MANOTILES LLC ✪
14364 Canalview Dr Apt A (33484-2676)
PHONE.................................954 803-3303
Cynthia Trezona,
EMP: 7 EST: 2021
SALES (est): 96.4K **Privately Held**
SIC: 3253 Mosaic tile, glazed & unglazed: ceramic

(G-2986)
MEDLEYCOM INCORPORATED
Also Called: Adultfriendfinder
1615 S Congress Ave # 10 (33445-6300)
PHONE.................................408 745-5418
Anthony Previte, *CEO*
Gavin Towey, *Administration*
EMP: 22 EST: 2002
SALES (est): 1.1MM **Privately Held**
WEB: www.medley.com
SIC: 2711 Newspapers, publishing & printing

(G-2987)
MESSER LLC
Linde Eco-Snow System
430 S Congress Ave Ste 7 (33445-4701)
PHONE.................................925 606-2000
EMP: 14
SALES (corp-wide): 1.2B **Privately Held**
SIC: 2813 Commerical Cleaning Equipment
HQ: Messer Llc
200 Somerset Corp Blvd # 7000
Bridgewater NJ 08807
908 464-8100

(G-2988)
METAL SUPPLY AND MACHINING INC
1304 Gwenzell Ave Ste B (33444-1268)
PHONE.................................561 276-4941
C William Packer, *President*
Marc Hirsch, *Vice Pres*
▼ **EMP: 16 EST:** 1991
SQ FT: 16,000
SALES (est): 3.6MM **Privately Held**
WEB: www.metalsupplyfl.com
SIC: 3541 5051 3446 3444 Machine tools, metal cutting: exotic (explosive, etc.); metals service centers & offices; architectural metalwork; sheet metalwork; fabricated structural metal

(G-2989)
MM WOOD DESIGNS INC
2859 Cormorant Rd (33444-1068)
PHONE.................................561 602-2775
Manoel L Macedo, *Principal*
EMP: 8 EST: 2016
SALES (est): 223.1K **Privately Held**
WEB: www.mmwooddesigns.com
SIC: 2431 Millwork

(G-2990)
MR MICA WOOD INC
1300 Sw 10th St Ste 3 (33444-1266)
PHONE.................................561 278-5821
John Berube, *President*
Chris Eckert, *Vice Pres*
Dororthy Berube, *Admin Sec*

EMP: 16 EST: 1973
SQ FT: 5,000
SALES (est): 529.7K **Privately Held**
WEB: www.mrmicanwood.com
SIC: 2541 2511 Cabinets, except refrigerated: show, display, etc.: wood; wood household furniture

(G-2991)
MRREAL DEAL BARBQUE LLC ✪
1050 Dotterel Rd Apt 200 (33444-1001)
PHONE.................................561 271-8749
Ronnie Manning,
EMP: 7 EST: 2021
SALES (est): 247.4K **Privately Held**
SIC: 2599 Food wagons, restaurant

(G-2992)
NEW WORLD HOLDINGS INC
Also Called: New World Medicinals
655 Se 1st St (33483-5303)
PHONE.................................561 888-4939
Michelle Larkin, *CEO*
Alan Sporn, *CFO*
EMP: 50 EST: 2017
SALES (est): 5.8MM **Privately Held**
SIC: 2834 6719 3829 5047 Pharmaceutical preparations; holding companies; medical diagnostic systems, nuclear; medical equipment & supplies; medical instruments & equipment, blood & bone work

(G-2993)
PARKSIDE PUBLISHING LLC
1633 W Classical Blvd (33445-1260)
PHONE.................................888 386-1115
EMP: 6 EST: 2019
SALES (est): 443.6K **Privately Held**
SIC: 2741 Miscellaneous publishing

(G-2994)
PEAK PERFORMANCE NUTRIENTS INC
1505 Poinsettia Dr Ste 4 (33444-1272)
PHONE.................................561 266-1038
Jeff Bielec, *President*
Jennifer Bielec, *Vice Pres*
Louella Bielec, *Sales Mgr*
Edward Bielec, *Director*
▲ **EMP: 15 EST:** 1997
SQ FT: 15,000
SALES (est): 2.5MM **Privately Held**
WEB: www.peakperformancenutrients.com
SIC: 2834 Vitamin, nutrient & hematinic preparations for human use

(G-2995)
PETER FOGEL
8108 Summer Shores Dr (33446-3477)
PHONE.................................561 245-5252
Peter Fogel, *Principal*
EMP: 7 EST: 2010
SALES (est): 268.9K **Privately Held**
WEB: www.fogelscorporatecomedy.com
SIC: 3651 Speaker systems

(G-2996)
PHOENIX CUSTOM GEAR LLC
1730 S Federal Hwy # 242 (33483-3309)
PHONE.................................561 808-7181
William Burbank, *Principal*
EMP: 7 EST: 2018
SALES (est): 430.7K **Privately Held**
WEB: www.phoenixcustomgear.com
SIC: 2211 Apparel & outerwear fabrics, cotton

(G-2997)
PLASTI-CARD CORPORATION
7901 Clay Mica Ct (33446-2226)
PHONE.................................305 944-2726
Irwin Feldman, *President*
Steven Feldman, *Vice Pres*
▲ **EMP: 21 EST:** 1981
SALES (est): 2.9MM **Privately Held**
WEB: www.continentalbizmag.com
SIC: 2752 Commercial printing, offset

(G-2998)
PLASTIMOLD PRODUCTS INC
Also Called: Fort Lauderdale Molding
250 N Congress Ave (33445-3415)
PHONE.................................561 869-0183

Joseph Parisi, *President*
Cathy Parisi, *Treasurer*
Sue Kibler, *Manager*
▲ **EMP: 6 EST:** 1991
SQ FT: 8,000
SALES (est): 3.6MM **Privately Held**
WEB: www.plastimoldproducts.com
SIC: 3089 Injection molding of plastics

(G-2999)
PLATINUM GROUP USA INC
Also Called: Www.tpgus.com
75 N Congress Ave (33445-3416)
P.O. Box 6584 (33482-6584)
PHONE.................................561 274-7553
Amer Rustom, *CEO*
Robert R Donofrio, *COO*
Azzam Rustom, *Vice Pres*
EMP: 12 EST: 2003
SALES (est): 614.4K **Privately Held**
WEB: www.platinumgrpinc.com
SIC: 1382 2834 Oil & gas exploration services; pharmaceutical preparations

(G-3000)
PMR GESTION INC
1100 Sw 10th St (33444-1233)
PHONE.................................561 501-5190
Gerald Guy, *Principal*
EMP: 10 EST: 2013
SALES (est): 651.9K **Privately Held**
WEB: www.pmrcc.com
SIC: 3339 Precious metals

(G-3001)
POSITIVEID CORPORATION (PA)
1690 S Congress Ave # 201 (33445-6386)
P.O. Box 880173, Boca Raton (33488-0173)
PHONE.................................561 805-8000
William J Caragol, *Ch of Bd*
Lyle L Probst, *President*
Deborah Szasz, *Office Mgr*
EMP: 5 EST: 2001
SQ FT: 3,000
SALES (est): 5.3MM **Publicly Held**
WEB: www.psidcorp.com
SIC: 2835 In vivo diagnostics

(G-3002)
POWERLINE GROUP INC
8406 Hawks Gully Ave (33446-9678)
PHONE.................................631 828-1183
Patrick Hinchy, *CEO*
EMP: 105 EST: 2016
SALES (est): 4.7MM **Privately Held**
WEB: www.thepowerlinegroup.com
SIC: 7372 Application computer software

(G-3003)
PREMIER STONEWORKS LLC
1455 Sw 4th Ave (33444-2274)
PHONE.................................561 330-3737
Gary Arkin, *Principal*
Ryan Galbreath, *Supervisor*
Glenn Savell, *Director*
◆ **EMP: 52 EST:** 2010
SALES (est): 5.7MM **Privately Held**
WEB: www.premierprecast.com
SIC: 3272 1741 Cast stone, concrete; masonry & other stonework

(G-3004)
PROFESSIONAL CTR AT GARDENS
190 Se 5th Ave (33483-5214)
PHONE.................................561 394-5200
Richard D Gertz, *Principal*
EMP: 10 EST: 2001
SALES (est): 387K **Privately Held**
SIC: 3069 Fabricated rubber products

(G-3005)
PROGRESSIVE PRINTING SOLUTIONS
Also Called: Progressive Printing Services
601 N Congress Ave # 208 (33445-4646)
PHONE.................................800 370-5591
Shawn Samai, *President*
Sara I Martinez, *Vice Pres*
EMP: 6 EST: 1992
SQ FT: 3,000
SALES (est): 517.4K **Privately Held**
SIC: 2752 Commercial printing, offset

▲ = Import ▼=Export
◆ =Import/Export

(G-3006)
PROTEK SYSTEMS INC
1250 Wallace Dr Ste B (33444-4602)
PHONE................................561 395-8155
Dennis Chalas, *President*
Alan Austin, *Vice Pres*
Andrew Aukstikalnis, *Opers Staff*
EMP: 7 **EST:** 1991
SQ FT: 2,500
SALES (est): 904K **Privately Held**
WEB: www.proteksystem.com
SIC: 3441 Fabricated structural metal

(G-3007)
PROTEXT MOBILITY INC (PA)
55 Se 2nd Ave (33444-3615)
PHONE................................435 881-3611
Roger Baylis-Duffield, *CEO*
EMP: 6 **EST:** 2001
SALES (est): 809.1K **Privately Held**
WEB: www.protextm.co
SIC: 7372 7382 Prepackaged software; security systems services

(G-3008)
PSC BUILDING GROUP INC
Also Called: Precision Stone
900 Sw 15th Ave (33444-1322)
PHONE................................561 756-6811
Guy Paterra, *Principal*
EMP: 22 **EST:** 2006
SQ FT: 800
SALES (est): 1MM **Privately Held**
WEB: www.precisionstonecorp.com
SIC: 3281 Cut stone & stone products

(G-3009)
QUALITY SOFTWARE LLC
55 Se 2nd Ave 1 (33444-3615)
PHONE................................561 714-2314
Ryan Armstrong, *President*
Ryan F Morrissey, *Principal*
EMP: 24 **EST:** 2013
SALES (est): 1.3MM **Privately Held**
WEB: www.qualitysoftwarepartners.com
SIC: 7372 Prepackaged software

(G-3010)
RAMSTAR CORPORATION
5304 Ventura Dr (33484-8386)
PHONE................................561 499-8488
Michael Reale, *Principal*
EMP: 7 **EST:** 2009
SALES (est): 193K **Privately Held**
SIC: 3599 Machine shop, jobbing & repair

(G-3011)
RANDOLPH CNSTR GROUP INC
1191 N Federal Hwy Ste 1 (33483-5800)
PHONE................................954 276-2889
Dwayne Randolph, *President*
Remona Rey, *Vice Pres*
EMP: 6 **EST:** 2019
SALES (est): 654K **Privately Held**
WEB: www.randolph-cg.com
SIC: 1389 Construction, repair & dismantling services

(G-3012)
RAVE LLC (HQ)
Also Called: Internano
430 S Congress Ave Ste 7 (33445-4701)
PHONE................................561 330-0411
Barry Hopkins, *President*
Rick Greece, *CFO*
Crystal Brazzel, *Admin Sec*
EMP: 32 **EST:** 1996
SQ FT: 7,500
SALES (est): 13MM
SALES (corp-wide): 2.4B **Publicly Held**
WEB: www.ravellc.com
SIC: 3826 Analytical instruments
PA: Bruker Corporation
40 Manning Rd
Billerica MA 01821
978 663-3660

(G-3013)
ROYAL ATLANTIC VENTURES LLC
Also Called: Channel Letter USA
1505 Poinsettia Dr H-9 (33444-1272)
PHONE................................561 243-9699
Jason Ditkofsky, *Mng Member*
EMP: 9 **EST:** 2017

SALES (est): 379.1K **Privately Held**
SIC: 3993 Signs & advertising specialties

(G-3014)
SEA SIDE SPECIALTIES
Also Called: Tyler Fabricators
1200 S Swinton Ave (33444-2296)
PHONE................................561 276-6518
Mico Klingler, *President*
Kelly Klingler, *Vice Pres*
▼ **EMP:** 7 **EST:** 1975
SALES (est): 1.5MM **Privately Held**
SIC: 3312 Blast furnaces & steel mills

(G-3015)
SHAKA ENERGY EXPLORATION INC
1118 Island Dr (33483-7122)
PHONE................................561 279-1379
EMP: 7 **EST:** 2011
SALES (est): 150K **Privately Held**
SIC: 1382 Oil/Gas Exploration Services

(G-3016)
SHASHI LLC
6926 Royal Orchid Cir (33446-4342)
PHONE................................561 447-8800
Natalie L Sudit, *Mng Member*
EMP: 8 **EST:** 2009
SQ FT: 500
SALES (est): 394.6K **Privately Held**
SIC: 2252 Socks

(G-3017)
SIW SOLUTIONS LLC
975 S Congress Ave (33445-4661)
PHONE................................561 274-9392
Yida A Lopez, *Principal*
EMP: 150 **Privately Held**
SIC: 2431 Doors, wood
HQ: Siw Solutions, Llc
401 State Ave N
Warroad MN 56763
888 537-7828

(G-3018)
SKILL-METRIC MACHINE & TL INC
1424 Gwenzell Ave 3c (33444-1267)
PHONE................................561 454-8900
Miguel Leon, *Engineer*
EMP: 25 **EST:** 1978
SQ FT: 11,000
SALES (est): 5.1MM **Privately Held**
WEB: www.skill-metric.com
SIC: 3724 3541 Aircraft engines & engine parts; machine tools, metal cutting type

(G-3019)
SNEIDS INC
Also Called: Sign-A-Rama
2905 S Congress Ave Ste E (33445-7337)
PHONE................................561 278-7446
Michael Sneiderman, *President*
David Sneiderman, *Vice Pres*
Michelle Laskowski, *Sales Executive*
EMP: 8 **EST:** 1994
SQ FT: 1,600
SALES (est): 651.2K **Privately Held**
WEB: www.sneids.com
SIC: 3993 Signs & advertising specialties

(G-3020)
SOUTHERN BUSINESS CARD INC
7901 Clay Mica Ct (33446-2226)
PHONE................................305 944-2931
Steven Feldman, *President*
Ann Feldman, *Corp Secy*
EMP: 8 **EST:** 1973
SALES (est): 247.8K **Privately Held**
SIC: 2752 2396 Commercial printing, offset; automotive & apparel trimmings

(G-3021)
SPLINTER WOODWORKING INC
738 Dotterel Rd (33444-2087)
PHONE................................305 731-9334
EMP: 5 **EST:** 2015
SALES (est): 416.1K **Privately Held**
SIC: 2431 5999 Millwork; miscellaneous retail stores

(G-3022)
STRAW GIANT COMPANY
Also Called: Mask Giant
10290 W Atlantic Ave (33448-6901)
P.O. Box 481295 (33448-1295)
PHONE................................561 430-0729
Gregg Fredman, *CEO*
EMP: 8 **EST:** 2019
SALES (est): 614.1K **Privately Held**
SIC: 3842 Clothing, fire resistant & protective

(G-3023)
SULLIVAN PENNY WOODWORKING
2 Abbey Ln Apt 104 (33446-1621)
PHONE................................561 860-1163
Matthew Penny, *Principal*
EMP: 7 **EST:** 2016
SALES (est): 171.2K **Privately Held**
SIC: 2431 Millwork

(G-3024)
SUNCOAST STONE INC
151 Nw 18th Ave (33444-1685)
PHONE................................561 364-2061
Roger Smith, *CEO*
Dave Koevort, *Accountant*
▼ **EMP:** 20 **EST:** 2005
SALES (est): 2.3MM **Privately Held**
WEB: www.suncoast-stone.com
SIC: 3281 Cut stone & stone products

(G-3025)
THRIV INDUSTRIES LLC
402 W Atlantic Ave 65 (33444-2554)
PHONE................................404 436-3230
Joseph Pritchett,
EMP: 12 **EST:** 2017
SALES (est): 357K **Privately Held**
SIC: 3999 Manufacturing industries

(G-3026)
TIBOR INC
Also Called: Juracsik, Ted Tool & Die
255 N Congress Ave (33445-3418)
PHONE................................561 272-0770
Ted Juracsik Sr, *President*
Wilma Juracsik, *Corp Secy*
Ted Juracsik Jr, *Vice Pres*
EMP: 40 **EST:** 1960
SQ FT: 20,000
SALES (est): 4.6MM **Privately Held**
WEB: www.tiborreel.com
SIC: 3544 3949 3444 Special dies & tools; reels, fishing; sheet metalwork

(G-3027)
TITAN AMERICA LLC
1300 S Swinton Ave (33444-2242)
PHONE................................800 396-3434
Johnny Santano, *Branch Mgr*
EMP: 12
SALES (corp-wide): 177.9K **Privately Held**
WEB: www.titanamerica.com
SIC: 3273 3271 Ready-mixed concrete; blocks, concrete or cinder: standard
HQ: Titan America Llc
5700 Lake Wright Dr # 300
Norfolk VA 23502
757 858-6500

(G-3028)
TROPICAL AWNING FLORIDA INC
335 Se 1st Ave Ste A (33444-3581)
PHONE................................561 276-1144
Monna Simpson, *President*
Robert Scott Simpson, *Corp Secy*
EMP: 10 **EST:** 1952
SQ FT: 8,000
SALES (est): 1MM **Privately Held**
WEB: www.tropicalawning.net
SIC: 2394 Awnings, fabric: made from purchased materials

(G-3029)
TRU CRAFT WOODWORKS LLC
1865 Sw 4th Ave Ste D9 (33444-7998)
PHONE................................561 441-2742
William A Canty, *Mng Member*
EMP: 8 **EST:** 2009
SALES (est): 54.1K **Privately Held**
SIC: 2431 Millwork

(G-3030)
TRUCRAFT SPECIALTIES INC
1503 Hummingbird Dr (33444-3324)
PHONE................................561 441-2742
William A Canty, *President*
EMP: 8 **EST:** 2001
SALES (est): 128.2K **Privately Held**
SIC: 2431 Millwork

(G-3031)
VANBERT CORPORATION
1855 Sw 4th Ave Ste B3 (33444-7937)
PHONE................................561 945-5856
Constantin Chiriac, *CEO*
▲ **EMP:** 6 **EST:** 2013
SALES (est): 900K **Privately Held**
WEB: www.vanbertdesign.com
SIC: 2434 Wood kitchen cabinets

(G-3032)
VARIOUS INC (PA)
Also Called: Friendfinder.com
1615 S Congress Ave # 103 (33445-6326)
PHONE................................561 900-3691
Jonathan Buckheit, *CEO*
Anthony Previte, *CEO*
Jason Collins, *Project Mgr*
Marc Glissman, *Project Mgr*
Rich Coughlin, *Engineer*
EMP: 49 **EST:** 2010
SALES (est): 30.7MM **Privately Held**
WEB: www.various.com
SIC: 2711 Newspapers

(G-3033)
VENGA LLC
955 Nw 17th Ave (33445-2516)
PHONE................................561 665-8200
Jamie Day, *Managing Prtnr*
James L Day, *Principal*
Mamadi Niknejad, *Director*
EMP: 7 **EST:** 2007
SALES (est): 171.8K **Privately Held**
SIC: 2086 Bottled & canned soft drinks

(G-3034)
VERITEQ ACQUISITION CORP
220 Congress Park Dr # 200 (33445-4670)
PHONE................................561 805-8007
Scott R Silverman, *CEO*
EMP: 6 **EST:** 2011
SQ FT: 5,000
SALES (est): 1MM
SALES (corp-wide): 5.9MM **Privately Held**
SIC: 3851 Ophthalmic goods
PA: Veriteq Corporation
11211 S Military Trl # 32
Boynton Beach FL 33436

(G-3035)
VERSAILLES LIGHTING INC
1305 Poinsettia Dr Ste 6 (33444-1251)
PHONE................................561 945-5744
Maurine Locke, *CEO*
Max Guedj, *President*
EMP: 12 **EST:** 1982
SQ FT: 15,000
SALES (est): 575.2K **Privately Held**
SIC: 3645 3646 5063 Residential lighting fixtures; commercial indusl & institutional electric lighting fixtures; lighting fixtures

(G-3036)
VX TECHNOLOGIES ✿
Also Called: Vxpass
2541 Southridge Rd (33444-8114)
PHONE................................608 774-5221
Michael Willis, *CEO*
Justin Pauly, *President*
EMP: 14 **EST:** 2021
SALES (est): 513.7K **Privately Held**
SIC: 7372 Prepackaged software

(G-3037)
WAY BEYOND BAGELS INC
16850 S Jog Rd Ste 108 (33446-2384)
PHONE................................561 638-1320
Marcy Speranza, *Manager*
EMP: 9 **EST:** 2001
SALES (est): 498.8K **Privately Held**
WEB: www.waybeyondbagels.com
SIC: 2051 5461 Bakery: wholesale or wholesale/retail combined; bakeries

(G-3038)
WORRELL WATER TECHNOLOGIES LLC
Also Called: Goodwater Albemarle Co
14 S Swinton Ave (33444-3654)
PHONE......................................434 973-6365
Steven J Keeler,
EMP: 7 EST: 2006
SALES (est): 869.9K Privately Held
SIC: 1389 Impounding & storing salt water, oil & gas field

Deltona
Volusia County

(G-3039)
A/C CAGES
890 Merrimac St (32725-5776)
PHONE......................................407 446-9259
Brandi N Baker, Principal
EMP: 8 EST: 2008
SALES (est): 128.8K Privately Held
WEB: www.snydercontractingny.com
SIC: 3441 Fabricated structural metal

(G-3040)
BKS BAKERY INC
2531 Dumas Dr (32738-5112)
PHONE......................................386 216-0540
Margaret Granito, Co-Owner
Theresa Granito, Co-Owner
EMP: 8 EST: 2012
SQ FT: 1,805
SALES (est): 464.4K Privately Held
SIC: 2051 5142 Bakery, for home service delivery; bakery products, frozen

(G-3041)
BRIAN RECK VALENZUELA
Also Called: Freon & Fabric
2885 W Huron Dr (32738-1662)
PHONE......................................386 801-5096
Brian Reck Valenzuela, Owner
EMP: 7 EST: 2017
SALES (est): 362.6K Privately Held
SIC: 2869 Freon

(G-3042)
CLUPPER LLC
2386 Pavillion Ter (32738-8731)
PHONE......................................386 956-6396
Robert J Clupper III, Principal
EMP: 11 EST: 2005
SALES (est): 487.9K Privately Held
SIC: 3448 Screen enclosures

(G-3043)
CUSTOM MOLDING & CASEWORK INC
1650 Travers Ln (32738-5044)
PHONE......................................407 709-7377
Joseph D Hubbard, Vice Pres
EMP: 7 EST: 2013
SALES (est): 91.2K Privately Held
SIC: 3089 Molding primary plastic

(G-3044)
FGMG INTERNATIONAL
2820 Lightwood St (32738-9185)
PHONE......................................305 988-7436
Demetris Hardy, CEO
EMP: 10 EST: 2017
SALES (est): 100K Privately Held
SIC: 3651 Music distribution apparatus

(G-3045)
GBC INTERIORS LLC
958 Roberts Blvd (32725-5761)
PHONE......................................386 624-8294
Gloria Burgos-Cotroneo, Principal
EMP: 7 EST: 2012
SALES (est): 94.7K Privately Held
SIC: 2653 Corrugated & solid fiber boxes

(G-3046)
JORDAN WELD FABRICATION
3300 Sky St (32738-5395)
PHONE......................................386 789-3606
Larry Bruce Jordan, Principal
EMP: 7 EST: 2007
SALES (est): 106.5K Privately Held
SIC: 7692 Welding repair

(G-3047)
LNL LOGISTICS LLC ✪
915 Doyle Rd Ste 303-150 (32725-8254)
PHONE......................................386 977-9276
Lashunda N Lewis, Principal
Lashunda Lewis, Principal
EMP: 8 EST: 2021
SALES (est): 299.2K Privately Held
SIC: 3799 Transportation equipment

(G-3048)
M J BOTURLA INDUSTRIES INC
1885 S Lehigh Dr (32738-8645)
PHONE......................................386 574-0811
Phyllis E Boturla, President
EMP: 8 EST: 2001
SALES (est): 272.8K Privately Held
SIC: 3999 Manufacturing industries

(G-3049)
NATIONWIDE PUBLISHING COMPANY (PA)
Also Called: Claims Pages
537 Deltona Blvd (32725-8017)
PHONE......................................352 253-0017
D Scott Plakon, President
Phillip J Imbrenda, Exec VP
Melissa Hoffler, Vice Pres
Alison Post, Opers Mgr
EMP: 30 EST: 1997
SQ FT: 7,000
SALES (est): 10.3MM Privately Held
SIC: 2741 Telephone & other directory publishing

(G-3050)
PATRIOT STAIRS LLC
736 Red Coach Ave (32725-7125)
PHONE......................................407 489-6248
Hazen A Poulin, Principal
EMP: 7 EST: 2015
SALES (est): 131.4K Privately Held
SIC: 3446 Stairs, staircases, stair treads: prefabricated metal

(G-3051)
PRECISION CABINETRY LLC
2240 E Old Mill Dr (32725-2826)
PHONE......................................386 218-3340
Stephen Theisen, Manager
EMP: 7 EST: 2014
SALES (est): 78.3K Privately Held
WEB: www.precisioncabinetry.com
SIC: 2434 Wood kitchen cabinets

(G-3052)
PREMIUM POWDER COATING
1872 Sweetwater Bnd (32738-3522)
PHONE......................................386 789-0216
Dana Lehman, Principal
EMP: 7 EST: 2012
SALES (est): 146.3K Privately Held
WEB: www.premiumpowdercoating.com
SIC: 3479 Coating of metals & formed products

(G-3053)
SERENITY HAIR EXTENSIONS LLC ✪
1235 Providence Blvd R10 (32725-7363)
P.O. Box 11335, Daytona Beach (32120-1335)
PHONE......................................407 917-1788
Marquita Fish, Mng Member
EMP: 10 EST: 2021
SALES (est): 469.6K Privately Held
SIC: 3999 Hair & hair-based products

(G-3054)
SUMMIT HOLSTERS LLC
843 Superior St (32725-5586)
PHONE......................................386 383-4090
Michael Salimbene, Manager
EMP: 8 EST: 2015
SALES (est): 266.6K Privately Held
SIC: 3199 Holsters, leather

(G-3055)
TRIUMPHANT MAGAZINE LLC
2651 Arcadia St (32738-9190)
PHONE......................................407 549-5443
Theresa Jordan, Manager
EMP: 7 EST: 2015

SALES (est): 90.2K Privately Held
WEB: www.triumphantmagazine.com
SIC: 2711 Newspapers

(G-3056)
VOLUSIA WASTE INC
1455 Brayton Cir (32725-5684)
PHONE......................................386 878-3322
Gladys E Quiles, Principal
EMP: 12 EST: 2005
SALES (est): 196.6K Privately Held
SIC: 3089 Garbage containers, plastic

(G-3057)
XPRESS FINANCE INC (PA)
807 S Orlando Ave Ste B (32738)
PHONE......................................407 629-0095
David Rasmussen, Director
EMP: 7 EST: 2005
SALES (est): 321.9K Privately Held
WEB: www.xpressfinanceinc.com
SIC: 2741 Miscellaneous publishing

Destin
Okaloosa County

(G-3058)
ARMADA SYSTEMS INC (PA)
Also Called: Asi
508 Mountain Dr (32541-2332)
P.O. Box 307, Mary Esther (32569-0307)
PHONE......................................850 664-5197
Phillip F Robbins, President
Tina Smith, Admin Sec
▼ EMP: 5 EST: 1992
SQ FT: 10,000
SALES (est): 1.4MM Privately Held
WEB: www.armadahull.com
SIC: 3541 Machine tools, metal cutting type

(G-3059)
AUTHENTIC PAVERS LLC
709 Elise Ln (32541-1954)
PHONE......................................850 687-1678
EMP: 7 EST: 2015
SALES (est): 198.6K Privately Held
SIC: 2951 Mfg Asphalt Mixtures/Blocks

(G-3060)
BOTE PADDLE BOARDS
383 Harbor Blvd (32541-2323)
PHONE......................................850 460-2250
Corey Cooper, Principal
Seth Coffey, Sales Mgr
EMP: 13 EST: 2013
SALES (est): 1MM Privately Held
WEB: www.boteboard.com
SIC: 3949 Surfboards

(G-3061)
CARPEDIEM LLC
618 Gulf Shore Dr (32541-3128)
PHONE......................................229 230-1453
David Penney, Mng Member
EMP: 18 EST: 2019
SALES (est): 2MM Privately Held
SIC: 7372 Business oriented computer software

(G-3062)
COASTAL PROMOTIONS INC
128 Indian Bayou Dr (32541-4415)
PHONE......................................850 460-2270
Patricia L Bramlet, President
Douglas McWhorter, Vice Pres
EMP: 8 EST: 1993
SALES (est): 894.2K Privately Held
WEB: www.tasteofl.com
SIC: 2087 Beverage bases; fruit juices: concentrated for fountain use

(G-3063)
DESTIN MACHINE INC
600 Fourth St (32541-1629)
PHONE......................................850 837-7114
Wayne E Lung, President
Norma L Lung, Corp Secy
EMP: 5 EST: 1980
SQ FT: 3,040
SALES (est): 568.1K Privately Held
WEB: www.burnhamford.com
SIC: 3599 3544 Machine shop, jobbing & repair; special dies, tools, jigs & fixtures

(G-3064)
DESTINATION BVI II INC
36120 Emerald Coast Pkwy (32541-4705)
PHONE......................................850 699-9551
Tim Creehan, Principal
Tim Wellborn, Principal
EMP: 6 EST: 2010
SALES (est): 431.9K Privately Held
SIC: 2035 Seasonings, seafood sauces (except tomato & dry)

(G-3065)
DIGICRIB LLC
Also Called: E-Commerce
34990 Emerald Coast Pkwy (32541-8416)
PHONE......................................833 932-8800
Josef N Quiroz, Mng Member
EMP: 7 EST: 2015
SALES (est): 299.1K Privately Held
WEB: www.digicrib.com
SIC: 2741

(G-3066)
ENCORE ANALYTICS LLC
86 Shirah St (32541-3513)
P.O. Box 2247, Santa Rosa Beach (32459-2247)
PHONE......................................866 890-4331
Gary W Toop, Principal
Brittany Hayes, Analyst
James Price,
EMP: 8 EST: 2009
SALES (est): 949.2K Privately Held
WEB: www.encore-analytics.com
SIC: 7372 Application computer software

(G-3067)
GIBSON WLDG SHETMETAL VENT INC
335 Mountain Dr (32541-2335)
PHONE......................................850 837-6141
Dean Gibson, President
Tina Henschen, Corp Secy
EMP: 8 EST: 1993
SALES (est): 938.7K Privately Held
WEB: www.gwsmv.com
SIC: 3444 Booths, spray: prefabricated sheet metal

(G-3068)
HART S CERAMIC & STONE INC
981 Highway 98 E Ste 3 (32541-2525)
PHONE......................................850 217-6145
John C Hart, Principal
EMP: 7 EST: 2010
SALES (est): 80.5K Privately Held
SIC: 3269 Pottery products

(G-3069)
HAYLEY CARSON ODOM CORDRAYS
4508 Pottery Pl (32541-3426)
PHONE......................................850 830-8270
Hayley Odom, Principal
EMP: 7 EST: 2011
SALES (est): 152.8K Privately Held
SIC: 3545 Milling cutters

(G-3070)
HIMES SIGNS INC
4 Commerce Dr Ste 4 # 4 (32541-7350)
P.O. Box 5324 (32540-5324)
PHONE......................................850 837-1159
John Himes, President
EMP: 13 EST: 1982
SALES (est): 956.2K Privately Held
WEB: www.himessigns.com
SIC: 3993 Electric signs

(G-3071)
INFINITE LASERS LLC
Also Called: Destin Engraving
45 Harbor Blvd (32541-2309)
PHONE......................................850 424-3759
Drew Cooper, Principal
EMP: 7 EST: 2012
SALES (est): 247.1K Privately Held
WEB: www.infinitelasersllc.com
SIC: 3423 Engravers' tools, hand

(G-3072)
INNOVATION PAVERS LLC
559 Kelly St (32541-1723)
PHONE......................................850 687-2864
Alessandro Pugin, Principal

▲ = Import ▼=Export
◆ =Import/Export

EMP: 9 EST: 2013
SALES (est): 127.1K **Privately Held**
SIC: 2951 Asphalt paving mixtures & blocks

(G-3073)
LINX DEFENSE LLC
4507 Furling Ln Ste 205 (32541-5342)
PHONE..................................805 233-2472
Steve Olson, *Owner*
EMP: 10 EST: 2017
SALES (est): 394.7K **Privately Held**
WEB: www.psgglobal.net
SIC: 3812 Defense systems & equipment

(G-3074)
NORTHSIDE PHARMACY LLC
36474c Emerald Coast Pkwy (32541-6700)
PHONE..................................256 398-7500
Jeff South, *Mng Member*
EMP: 9 EST: 2013
SALES (est): 478.9K **Privately Held**
SIC: 2834 Pharmaceutical preparations

(G-3075)
PEGASUS AEROSPACE
290 Vinings Way Blvd # 6103
(32541-6803)
PHONE..................................850 376-0991
Eugen Toma, *Principal*
EMP: 7 EST: 2017
SALES (est): 199.5K **Privately Held**
WEB: www.pegasp.com
SIC: 3721 Aircraft

(G-3076)
QUINTESSENTIAL HOME SVCS LLC
503 Second Ave (32541-1705)
PHONE..................................850 259-5064
Roy Q Rector, *Mng Member*
EMP: 8 EST: 2016
SALES (est): 2.5MM **Privately Held**
SIC: 1389 7389 Construction, repair & dismantling services; business services

(G-3077)
RB CABINETRY LLC
408 Evergreen Dr Ste A (32541-2202)
P.O. Box 22 (32540-0022)
PHONE..................................850 685-5316
Ronald C Banks, *Branch Mgr*
EMP: 22 **Privately Held**
SIC: 2434 Wood kitchen cabinets
PA: Rb Cabinetry Llc
140 Azalea Dr Ste B
Destin FL

(G-3078)
SAAS TRANSPORTATION INC
3551 Scenic Highway 98 (32541-5748)
PHONE..................................850 650-7709
Ken Pehanick, *President*
EMP: 10 EST: 2011
SALES (est): 507.2K **Privately Held**
WEB: web.saastransportation.com
SIC: 7372 Application computer software

(G-3079)
SKATER SOCKS
516 Mountain Dr Ste 104 (32541-7370)
PHONE..................................850 424-6764
EMP: 8 EST: 2012
SALES (est): 172.2K **Privately Held**
WEB: www.skatersocks.com
SIC: 2252 Socks

(G-3080)
TIMBER CREEK DISTILLING LLC
146 Country Club Dr W (32541-4418)
PHONE..................................408 439-0973
EMP: 8 EST: 2015
SALES (est): 474.9K **Privately Held**
WEB: www.timbercreekdistillery.com
SIC: 2085 Distilled & blended liquors

(G-3081)
WATERHOUSE PRESS LLC
4481 Legendary Dr Ste 200 (32541-5381)
PHONE..................................781 975-6191
Fuchsia McInerney, *Principal*
Yvonne Ellis, *Prdtn Mgr*
Scott Saunders, *Manager*
Haley Byrd, *Producer*

Kurt Vachon, *Info Tech Dir*
EMP: 8 EST: 2016
SALES (est): 922.1K **Privately Held**
WEB: www.waterhousepress.com
SIC: 2741 Miscellaneous publishing

(G-3082)
WEIDENHAMER CORPORATION
Also Called: S O S Printing & Office Supply
808 Wild Oak Ave (32541-2646)
P.O. Box 1786 (32540-1786)
PHONE..................................850 837-3190
Thomas Weidenhamer, *President*
Nancy Weidenhamer, *Vice Pres*
EMP: 7 EST: 1982
SALES (est): 361.7K **Privately Held**
WEB: www.sos-products.com
SIC: 2752 5943 Commercial printing, offset; office forms & supplies

Destin
Walton County

(G-3083)
BETTER BUILT GROUP INC
66 N Holiday Rd (32550-6936)
PHONE..................................850 803-4044
Rupert E Phillips, *President*
Harold D Daws, *Vice Pres*
James N Perry, *Vice Pres*
Alan Payne, *Treasurer*
Sandra K Phillips, *Admin Sec*
EMP: 9 EST: 1995
SALES (est): 154K **Privately Held**
SIC: 2711 Newspapers

Doral
Miami-Dade County

(G-3084)
3-DIMENSION GRAPHICS INC
8031 Nw 14th St (33126-1611)
PHONE..................................305 599-3277
Jaime Cadena, *Principal*
▼ EMP: 30 EST: 2000
SQ FT: 15,000
SALES (est): 4.7MM **Privately Held**
WEB: www.threedg.com
SIC: 2752 Commercial printing, offset

(G-3085)
3NSTAR INC
10813 Nw 30th St Ste 100 (33172-2191)
PHONE..................................786 233-7011
Socorro Viayrada, *President*
Anna Cerna, *VP Opers*
Jeronimo Urbina, *Director*
EMP: 10 EST: 2013
SALES (est): 1MM **Privately Held**
WEB: www.3nstar.com
SIC: 3571 2678 Computers, digital, analog or hybrid; mainframe computers; tablets & pads

(G-3086)
7 HOLDINGS GROUP LLC
10450 Nw 29th Ter (33172-2527)
PHONE..................................754 200-1365
Wynn Housel, *CFO*
Lucius French,
EMP: 50 EST: 2020
SALES (est): 1.7MM **Privately Held**
SIC: 3829 Thermometers, including digital; clinical

(G-3087)
A & A SHEETMETAL CONTR CORP
3067 Nw 107th Ave (33172-2134)
PHONE..................................305 592-2217
Angel Santos, *President*
Juan Vergara, *Project Mgr*
Lissette Santos, *Admin Sec*
EMP: 60 EST: 1985
SQ FT: 10,000
SALES (est): 5.8MM **Privately Held**
WEB: www.aasheetmetal.net
SIC: 3444 Sheet metalwork

(G-3088)
A & S EQUIPMENT CO
1900 Nw 95th Ave (33172-2349)
P.O. Box 228043, Miami (33222-8043)
PHONE..................................305 436-8207
Andrew S Ferrera Jr, *President*
EMP: 18 EST: 1996
SALES (est): 2MM **Privately Held**
SIC: 3537 Forklift trucks

(G-3089)
A A SHEET METAL CORP
3067 Nw 107th Ave (33172-2134)
PHONE..................................305 592-2217
EMP: 7 EST: 2020
SALES (est): 224.1K **Privately Held**
WEB: www.aasheetmetal.net
SIC: 3444 Sheet metalwork

(G-3090)
A&C MICROSCOPES LLC
7925 Nw 12th St Ste 112 (33126-1820)
PHONE..................................786 514-3967
Joe Salgado, *Exec VP*
Michael Lopez,
EMP: 10 EST: 2014
SALES (est): 950.8K **Privately Held**
WEB: www.acmicroscopes.com
SIC: 3827 Microscopes, except electron, proton & corneal

(G-3091)
ABZ MARKETING SOLUTIONS CORP
9716 Nw 29th St (33172-1071)
PHONE..................................305 340-1887
Luis Alzate, *CEO*
EMP: 30 EST: 2020
SALES (est): 500K **Privately Held**
SIC: 3699 Security control equipment & systems

(G-3092)
ACER LATIN AMERICA INC
3750 Nw 87th Ave Ste 450 (33178-2430)
PHONE..................................305 392-7000
Mario Teuffer, *General Mgr*
◆ EMP: 9 EST: 1989
SQ FT: 2,000
SALES (est): 2.1MM **Privately Held**
WEB: acla.acer.com
SIC: 3571 Minicomputers; personal computers (microcomputers)
HQ: Gateway, Inc.
7565 Irvine Center Dr # 150
Irvine CA 92618
949 471-7000

(G-3093)
ACOLITE CLAUDE UNTD SIGN INC (PA)
Also Called: Acusigns
2555 Nw 102nd Ave Ste 216 (33172-2131)
P.O. Box 522517, Miami (33152-2517)
PHONE..................................305 362-3333
Paul Yesbeck, *President*
Chet Diffenderfer, *Vice Pres*
Andrew Merrillfacio, *Sales Staff*
Ralph Moreno, *Sales Staff*
Gunther Schopfer, *Officer*
EMP: 23 EST: 1993
SALES (est): 5.8MM **Privately Held**
SIC: 3993 Electric signs

(G-3094)
ACOLITE SIGN COMPANY INC
2555 Nw 102nd Ave Ste 216 (33172-2131)
PHONE..................................305 362-3333
Chester Diffenderfer Jr, *President*
Jim Glober, *Vice Pres*
EMP: 7 EST: 1938
SALES (est): 436.1K **Privately Held**
SIC: 3993 Electric signs

(G-3095)
ACOUSTIC COMMUNICATIONS LLC (PA)
5049 Nw 114th Ct (33178-3529)
PHONE..................................305 463-9485
Michael E Reilly,
EMP: 5 EST: 2009
SALES (est): 349.5K **Privately Held**
WEB: www.acousticcomm.com
SIC: 3669 8711 Intercommunication systems, electric; acoustical engineering

(G-3096)
AENOVA DORAL MANUFACTURING INC (HQ)
10400 Nw 29th Ter (33172-2527)
PHONE..................................305 463-2270
Ramon Torres, *President*
Otto Prange, *President*
Sue Hammil, *Principal*
Dietmar Rohleder, *Vice Pres*
EMP: 4 EST: 2015
SQ FT: 85,000
SALES (est): 4.2MM
SALES (corp-wide): 726.4K **Privately Held**
SIC: 2834 Pharmaceutical preparations
PA: Health Care Invest Gmbh
Hermann-Graf-Str. 5
Eisenberg (Pfalz) RP 67304
635 112-7919

(G-3097)
AENOVA DORAL MANUFACTURING INC
10655 Nw 29th Ter (33172-2197)
PHONE..................................305 463-2263
Prange Otto, *President*
EMP: 114
SALES (corp-wide): 726.4K **Privately Held**
SIC: 2834 Pharmaceutical preparations
HQ: Aenova Doral Manufacturing, Inc.
10400 Nw 29th Ter
Doral FL 33172
305 463-2270

(G-3098)
AG PARTS CORPORATION
10375 Nw 30th Ter (33172-5049)
PHONE..................................305 670-6227
EMP: 8 EST: 2010
SALES (est): 94.9K **Privately Held**
SIC: 3465 Mfg Automotive Stampings

(G-3099)
AGRO & CNSTR SOLUTIONS INC
3630 Nw 115th Ave (33178-1863)
PHONE..................................305 593-7011
Lucas Noriega, *CEO*
Pedro Molina, *Vice Pres*
Malcolm Andrade, *Sales Executive*
Monica Molina, *Manager*
◆ EMP: 11 EST: 2009
SQ FT: 6,409
SALES (est): 2.3MM **Privately Held**
WEB: www.agrosolutions.us
SIC: 3523 Farm machinery & equipment

(G-3100)
AGS ENTERPRISES INC
10305 Nw 41st St Ste 210 (33178-2976)
PHONE..................................305 716-7660
Carlos R Perez, *President*
▼ EMP: 5 EST: 2003
SQ FT: 1,500
SALES (est): 591.2K **Privately Held**
WEB: www.agsenterprisesinc.com
SIC: 3357 Fiber optic cable (insulated)

(G-3101)
AIR-O-MATIC CORP
1992 Nw 95th Ave (33172-2349)
PHONE..................................786 364-6960
Eddy Gomez, *President*
EMP: 3 EST: 2013
SALES (est): 7MM **Privately Held**
WEB: www.airomaticcorp.com
SIC: 3564 Air cleaning systems

(G-3102)
ALABAMA MARBLE CO INC
3435 Nw 79th Ave (33122-1017)
PHONE..................................305 718-8000
▲ EMP: 15
SQ FT: 45,845
SALES (est): 2.3MM **Privately Held**
SIC: 3261 Mfg Marble Window Items

(G-3103)
ALCO ADVANCED TECHNOLOGIES
10773 Nw 58th St Ste 3707 (33178-2801)
PHONE..................................305 333-0831
Alberto Surijon, *CEO*
EMP: 5 EST: 1998

SALES (est): 490K **Privately Held**
WEB: www.alcogroup-la.com
SIC: **3699** Security control equipment &
systems

(G-3104)
ALDANA LASER MIAMI INC
10201 Nw 58th St Ste 308 (33178-2737)
PHONE......................................786 681-7752
Aldana J Guillermo, *President*
EMP: 8 EST: 2016
SALES (est): 479.1K **Privately Held**
WEB: www.aldanalasermiami.com
SIC: **3827** Optical instruments & lenses

(G-3105)
ALECTRON INC
8810 Nw 24th Ter (33172-2418)
PHONE......................................786 397-6827
Juan Amortegui, *President*
Juan D Montoya, *Vice Pres*
Sandra M Restrepo, *Admin Sec*
EMP: 7 EST: 2012
SALES (est): 588K **Privately Held**
WEB: www.alectron.co
SIC: **3699** Electrical equipment & supplies
PA: Almacenes Electron S A S
   Calle 12 B Sur 51 54
   Medellin

(G-3106)
ALEPH GRAPHICS INC
Also Called: Www.alephgraphics.com
1723 Nw 82nd Ave (33126-1015)
PHONE......................................305 994-9933
Gonzalo D Novas, *President*
Loisa Manitto, *Vice Pres*
Elida Barreiro, *Admin Sec*
◆ EMP: 6 EST: 1996
SALES (est): 776.5K **Privately Held**
WEB: www.alephgraphics.com
SIC: **2752** Commercial printing, litho-
graphic

(G-3107)
ALLIED AEROSPACE INC
2223 Nw 79th Ave (33122-1618)
PHONE......................................786 616-8484
Max H Kraushaar, *Principal*
Claudio Kraushaar, *Vice Pres*
EMP: 12 EST: 2017
SALES (est): 2.4MM **Privately Held**
WEB: www.alliedaerospaceinc.com
SIC: **3728** Aircraft parts & equipment

(G-3108)
ALP INDUSTRIES INC
Also Called: American Lifting Products
1828 Nw 82nd Ave (33126-1014)
PHONE......................................786 845-8617
Frank Hill, *General Mgr*
▲ EMP: 26 EST: 2008
SALES (est): 677.2K **Privately Held**
SIC: **3496** Miscellaneous fabricated wire
products

(G-3109)
ALPHATEC COMMUNICATIONS
10570 Nw 27th St Ste 102 (33172-2105)
PHONE......................................518 580-0520
Gary Webster, *President*
EMP: 8 EST: 2011
SALES (est): 416.2K **Privately Held**
WEB: www.chenaccountinggroup.com
SIC: **3663** Satellites, communications

(G-3110)
ALVITA PHARMA USA INC
8180 Nw 36th St Ste 100 (33166-6650)
PHONE......................................305 961-1623
Sajan P Unnithan, *Vice Pres*
EMP: 8 EST: 2012
SALES (est): 131.3K **Privately Held**
SIC: **2834** Pharmaceutical preparations

(G-3111)
AMC DEVELOPMENT GROUP
LLC
Also Called: High Export
10825 Nw 33rd St (33172-2188)
PHONE......................................305 597-8641
Claudia Gomez, *Manager*
◆ EMP: 17 EST: 2002
SALES (est): 1MM **Privately Held**
SIC: **3577** Encoders, computer peripheral
equipment

(G-3112)
AMERICAN TECH NETWRK
CORP (PA)
Also Called: American Technologies Network
2400 Nw 95th Ave (33172-2348)
PHONE......................................800 910-2862
Marc Vayn, *CEO*
John Borja, *Regional Mgr*
Jonathan Borja, *Regional Mgr*
James Munn, *COO*
Krassimir Gentchev, *Production*
▲ EMP: 48 EST: 1995
SALES (est): 12.7MM **Privately Held**
WEB: www.atncorp.com
SIC: **3827** Optical instruments & lenses;
aiming circles (fire control equipment)

(G-3113)
AMERICAN WELDING SOCIETY
INC (PA)
Also Called: Aws
8669 Nw 36th St Ste 130 (33166-6672)
PHONE......................................305 443-9353
Gary Konarska II, *CEO*
John Bruskotter, *President*
Andrew Davis, *Managing Dir*
Tim Hirthe, *Vice Chairman*
Cassie Burrell, *COO*
▼ EMP: 94 EST: 1919
SQ FT: 32,000
SALES (est): 43.8MM **Privately Held**
WEB: www.aws.org
SIC: **2721** **8611** Magazines: publishing
only, not printed on site; trade associa-
tions

(G-3114)
AMPER USA LLC
4447 Nw 98th Ave (33178-3361)
PHONE......................................305 717-3101
Ariel Lara, *Principal*
▲ EMP: 7 EST: 2010
SALES (est): 271.9K **Privately Held**
WEB: www.amper-usa.com
SIC: **3691** **3621** Storage batteries; genera-
tors for storage battery chargers

(G-3115)
AMTEL SECURITY SYSTEMS
INC
1691 Nw 107th Ave (33172-2707)
P.O. Box 490808, Key Biscayne (33149-
0808)
PHONE......................................305 591-8200
Suresh Gajwani, *President*
Andy Smith, *Engineer*
◆ EMP: 25 EST: 1982
SQ FT: 18,000
SALES (est): 2.3MM **Privately Held**
WEB: www.amtelasps.com
SIC: **3699** **1731** **7382** Security control
equipment & systems; safety & security
specialization; security systems services

(G-3116)
ANIMAL AIR SERVICE INC
1952 Nw 93rd Ave (33172-2925)
PHONE......................................305 218-1759
John Ebert, *President*
Rique Valdivieso, *President*
Michael Williams, *Vice Pres*
Brandon Valdivieso, *Treasurer*
EMP: 33 EST: 1966
SALES (est): 2.9MM **Privately Held**
WEB: www.animalairmia.com
SIC: **3496** **0751** **3523** **2441** Cages; wire;
livestock services, except veterinary; farm
machinery & equipment; nailed wood
boxes & shook

(G-3117)
APICAL PHARMACEUTICAL
CORP
10460 Nw 37th Ter (33178-4200)
PHONE......................................786 331-7200
Bill Bamford, *President*
EMP: 8 EST: 2000
SALES (est): 111.2K **Privately Held**
SIC: **2834** Pharmaceutical preparations

(G-3118)
APTUM TECHNOLOGIES (USA)
INC
2300 Nw 89th Pl (33172-2431)
PHONE......................................877 504-0091
David Alfaro, *Accounts Mgr*
Michael Rivera, *Sales Staff*
Alex SOO, *Sales Staff*
Jonathan Richardson, *Technology*
EMP: 64
SALES (corp-wide): 41.3MM **Privately**
Held
WEB: www.aptum.com
SIC: **7372** Business oriented computer
software
PA: Aptum Technologies (Usa) Inc.
   106 Jefferson St Ste 300
   San Antonio TX 78205
   604 683-7747

(G-3119)
ARGO CRATES & CONTAINERS
10461 Nw 26th St (33172-2181)
PHONE......................................786 487-4607
Alberto Gomez, *President*
EMP: 5 EST: 1999
SALES (est): 422K **Privately Held**
SIC: **2653** Solid fiber boxes, partitions, dis-
play items & sheets

(G-3120)
ASENCOEX LLC
10400 Nw 69th Ter (33178-3249)
PHONE......................................305 433-7260
Natalia I Constain, *Principal*
EMP: 7 **Privately Held**
WEB: www.asencoex.com
SIC: **2542** Postal lock boxes, mail racks &
related products
PA: Asencoex, Llc
   10850 Nw 21st St Ste 210
   Miami FL 33172

(G-3121)
ASTERION BEVERAGES INC
Also Called: Kamsa
3357 Nw 97th Ave (33172-1105)
PHONE......................................866 335-2672
Nicolas Bonilla, *President*
EMP: 8 EST: 2016
SALES (est): 546.8K **Privately Held**
WEB: www.drinkkamsa.com
SIC: **2086** Carbonated beverages, nonal-
coholic: bottled & canned

(G-3122)
ASTROTED INC
3320 Nw 67th Ave Unit 980 (33122-2267)
PHONE......................................786 220-5898
Felipe Tedesco, *Principal*
EMP: 9 EST: 2001
SALES (est): 497.1K **Privately Held**
WEB: www.astroted.com
SIC: **3999** Manufacturing industries

(G-3123)
ATEEI INTERNATIONAL CORP
(PA)
8284 Nw 56th St (33166-4018)
PHONE......................................305 597-6408
Luiz D Pereira Ferreira, *President*
EMP: 5 EST: 2013
SALES (est): 472.7K **Privately Held**
WEB: www.ateei.com.br
SIC: **3672** Printed circuit boards

(G-3124)
ATG SPECIALTY PRODUCTS
CORP
Also Called: Breakthrough Clean Tech
1725 Nw 97th Ave (33172-2301)
PHONE......................................888 455-5499
Erick Navarro, *President*
Tara Yager, *Marketing Mgr*
EMP: 6 EST: 2013
SALES (est): 585.6K **Privately Held**
WEB: www.breakthroughclean.com
SIC: **3949** Shooting equipment & supplies,
general

(G-3125)
ATRIA INDUSTRY
1866 Nw 82nd Ave (33126-1014)
PHONE......................................786 334-6621
Nicola Atria, *Principal*

EMP: 7 EST: 2016
SALES (est): 491K **Privately Held**
WEB: www.atriaindustries.com
SIC: **3999** Manufacturing industries

(G-3126)
AXZES LLC
3401 Nw 82nd Ave Ste 370 (33122-1052)
PHONE......................................786 626-1611
EMP: 6 EST: 2019
SALES (est): 315.8K **Privately Held**
WEB: www.axzes.com
SIC: **3652** Pre-recorded records & tapes

(G-3127)
B/E AEROSPACE INC
9835 Nw 14th St (33172-2756)
PHONE......................................305 471-8800
Tony Garcia, *Sales Staff*
Luis Munoz, *Branch Mgr*
EMP: 60
SALES (corp-wide): 64.3B **Publicly Held**
WEB: www.beaerospace.com
SIC: **3728** Aircraft parts & equipment
HQ: B/E Aerospace, Inc.
   1400 Corporate Center Way
   Wellington FL 33414
   410 266-2048

(G-3128)
BAGS EXPRESS INC
1555 Nw 97th Ave (33172-2815)
PHONE......................................305 500-9849
Alberto Loo, *President*
EMP: 7 EST: 1998
SQ FT: 11,000
SALES (est): 666.6K **Privately Held**
WEB: www.polybagsexpress.com
SIC: **2673** Plastic bags: made from pur-
chased materials

(G-3129)
BARU AGENCY INCORPORATED
Also Called: 5 Cents T-Shirt Design
8400 Nw 36th St Ste 450 (33166-6606)
PHONE......................................305 259-8800
Sebastian Jaramillo, *CEO*
EMP: 7 EST: 2014
SALES (est): 1.1MM **Privately Held**
SIC: **2396** **7336** Screen printing on fabric
articles; graphic arts & related design

(G-3130)
BEARING SPECIALIST INC
1908 Nw 94th Ave (33172-2330)
PHONE......................................305 796-3415
EMP: 6 EST: 2002
SALES (est): 538.4K **Privately Held**
WEB: www.bspecialist.com
SIC: **3562** Ball & roller bearings

(G-3131)
BELLA VISTA BAKERY INC
Also Called: Tqmuch
2220 Nw 82nd Ave (33122-1509)
PHONE......................................954 759-1920
Christian Pinto, *President*
Alejandra Rocha, *Vice Pres*
Manuel Rivero, *Sales Mgr*
EMP: 50 EST: 2010
SALES (est): 4MM **Privately Held**
SIC: **2051** Breads, rolls & buns

(G-3132)
BELLAK COLOR CORPORATION
Also Called: Foilmania
9730 Nw 25th St (33172-2201)
P.O. Box 227656, Miami (33222-7656)
PHONE......................................305 854-8525
Manuel S Fernandez, *President*
Oscar Gonzalez, *President*
Manuel J Fernandez, *Vice Pres*
Neil Fernandez, *Vice Pres*
Armando Caballero, *Production*
▼ EMP: 45 EST: 1961
SQ FT: 3,000
SALES (est): 9MM **Privately Held**
WEB: www.bellak.com
SIC: **2752** **2796** Commercial printing, off-
set; color lithography; platemaking serv-
ices

(G-3133)
BELZONA INC
2000 Nw 88th Ct (33172-2627)
PHONE......................................305 512-3200

▲ = Import ▼=Export
◆ =Import/Export

Ron Campbell, *Managing Dir*
Joel Svendsen, *Branch Mgr*
EMP: 47
SALES (corp-wide): 47.2MM **Privately Held**
WEB: www.belzona.com
SIC: 3732 Boat building & repairing
HQ: Belzona, Inc.
2000 Nw 88th Ct
Doral FL 33172

(G-3134)
BELZONA INC (HQ)
2000 Nw 88th Ct (33172-2627)
PHONE..............................305 594-4994
Joel Svendsen, *President*
Andrew Lamb, *Business Mgr*
Laura Mendrek, *Business Mgr*
Xi Chen, *Vice Pres*
Hamsely Mirre, *Vice Pres*
◆ **EMP:** 25 **EST:** 1952
SQ FT: 43,000
SALES (est): 26MM
SALES (corp-wide): 47.2MM **Privately Held**
WEB: www.belzonaboats.com
SIC: 2899 5169 Chemical preparations; industrial chemicals
PA: Belzona International Limited
Claro Road
Harrogate HG1 4
142 356-7641

(G-3135)
BEV-CO ENTERPRISES INC
9533 Nw 41st St (33178-2371)
PHONE..............................786 953-7109
Enoc S Martinez, *Branch Mgr*
EMP: 46
SALES (corp-wide): 320.1K **Privately Held**
SIC: 2087 Beverage bases
PA: Bev-Co Enterprises, Inc.
2761 Nw 82nd Ave
Miami FL 33122
786 362-6368

(G-3136)
BG EXPO GROUP LLC
11231 Nw 20th St Unit 140 (33172-1865)
PHONE..............................305 428-3576
Ruben Santamaria, *Mng Member*
EMP: 8 **EST:** 2008
SALES (est): 382.1K **Privately Held**
WEB: www.appledisplays.com
SIC: 2741 7336 ; graphic arts & related design

(G-3137)
BIG WOOD MILLWORK SALES INC
10842 Nw 27th St (33172-5907)
PHONE..............................305 471-1155
Rene Picanes, *President*
Lourdes Picanes, *Vice Pres*
EMP: 8 **EST:** 2003
SALES (est): 775.4K **Privately Held**
WEB: www.bigwoodmillwork.com
SIC: 2431 Doors & door parts & trim, wood

(G-3138)
BINCA LLC
10680 Nw 37th Ter (33178-4207)
PHONE..............................305 698-8883
Alexandra Garavito, *Principal*
Dennis Llama, *Sales Staff*
Michel Nudelman, *Sales Staff*
EMP: 10 **EST:** 2013
SALES (est): 2.3MM **Privately Held**
WEB: www.bincaimaging.com
SIC: 3993 Signs & advertising specialties

(G-3139)
BIOMAR PRODUCTS LLC
9441 Nw 47th Ter (33178-2084)
PHONE..............................800 216-2080
Eduardo Munoz, *Mng Member*
Luz Diana Vasquez, *Mng Member*
EMP: 8 **EST:** 2006
SALES (est): 185.4K **Privately Held**
WEB: www.biomarproducts.com
SIC: 2834 Chlorination tablets & kits (water purification)

(G-3140)
BISCHOFF AERO LLC
8130 Nw 58th St (33166-3405)
PHONE..............................305 883-4410
Michael Bischoff,
EMP: 12 **EST:** 2006
SALES (est): 882.2K **Privately Held**
SIC: 3728 Aircraft parts & equipment

(G-3141)
BL BRANDHOUSE LLC
8375 Nw 30th Ter (33122-1916)
PHONE..............................305 600-7181
Jose A Beguiristain, *Administration*
EMP: 8 **EST:** 2016
SALES (est): 275.1K **Privately Held**
WEB: www.blbrandhouse.com
SIC: 2759 Screen printing

(G-3142)
BLIX CORPORATE IMAGE LLC
Also Called: Blix Graphics
1352 Nw 78th Ave (33126-1606)
PHONE..............................305 572-9001
Diego Bussano, *President*
German Bussano, *Project Mgr*
Diego L Bussano, *Mng Member*
German N Bussano, *Mng Member*
▼ **EMP:** 10 **EST:** 2005
SALES (est): 1MM **Privately Held**
WEB: www.blixgraphics.com
SIC: 2752 Commercial printing, lithographic

(G-3143)
BLU SENSE
7855 Nw 29th St (33122-1142)
PHONE..............................786 616-8628
Luciano Tartarini, *Owner*
EMP: 5 **EST:** 2014
SALES (est): 308.3K **Privately Held**
SIC: 3645 Fluorescent lighting fixtures, residential

(G-3144)
BLUE CHIP GROUP LLC
Also Called: Vacation Vault
3400 Nw 113th Ct (33178-1836)
PHONE..............................305 863-9094
Robert Perlman, *Mng Member*
EMP: 5 **EST:** 2003
SALES (est): 484.4K **Privately Held**
WEB: www.bluechipgroup.us
SIC: 3499 Safes & vaults, metal

(G-3145)
BONNE SANTE NATURAL MFG INC
Also Called: Millenium Natural Health Pdts
10575 Nw 37th Ter (33178-4209)
PHONE..............................305 594-4990
Darren Minton, *CEO*
Alfonso Cervantes, *President*
Ray Martinez, *Vice Pres*
Edgard Castellanos, *Opers Staff*
Yeni Abreu, *Purchasing*
▼ **EMP:** 33 **EST:** 1998
SQ FT: 16,000
SALES (est): 2.1MM
SALES (corp-wide): 9MM **Publicly Held**
WEB: www.milleniumnatural.com
SIC: 2834 Vitamin, nutrient & hematinic preparations for human use
PA: Smart For Life, Inc.
990 Biscayne Blvd # 1203
Miami FL 33132
786 749-1221

(G-3146)
BOSTIC STEEL INC
7740 Nw 34th St (33122-1110)
PHONE..............................305 592-7276
Judith D Bostic, *President*
Michael Belcher, *General Mgr*
Dean D Agati, *Exec VP*
Dean D 'agati, *Exec VP*
Guy Cusano, *Vice Pres*
EMP: 100 **EST:** 1991
SQ FT: 21,000
SALES (est): 15.4MM **Privately Held**
WEB: www.bosticsteel.com
SIC: 3441 Fabricated structural metal

(G-3147)
BPJ INTERNATIONAL LLC
11091 Nw 27th St Ste 204 (33172-5010)
PHONE..............................305 507-8971
EMP: 7
SALES (est): 275K **Privately Held**
SIC: 2844 Mfg Toilet Preparations

(G-3148)
BRICKLSER ENGRV MONUMENTS CORP
7964 Nw 14th St (33126-1614)
PHONE..............................786 806-0672
Alexis Butler, *President*
Cody Evans, *President*
James Dixon, *Admin Sec*
EMP: 11 **EST:** 2018
SQ FT: 12,000
SALES (est): 995.8K **Privately Held**
SIC: 3479 6798 5999 Etching & engraving; real estate investment trusts; monuments & tombstones

(G-3149)
BROMIDE MINING LLC
2335 Nw 107th Ave Ste 127 (33172-2165)
PHONE..............................786 477-6229
Kristin Timberlake, *Mng Member*
Oren Goldgraber,
Yehuda Goldgraber,
EMP: 10 **EST:** 2008
SALES (est): 888.8K **Privately Held**
SIC: 1041 Gold ores mining

(G-3150)
BUENAVIDA IMPORTS LLC
3508 Nw 114th Ave Ste 205 (33178-1841)
PHONE..............................305 988-5992
Maximiliano Martirena, *Mng Member*
EMP: 5 **EST:** 2019
SALES (est): 361.7K **Privately Held**
WEB: www.buenavidaimports.com
SIC: 2084 Wines, brandy & brandy spirits

(G-3151)
BUILDING MANAGEMENT GROUP
2451 Nw 109th Ave Unit 5 (33172-2003)
PHONE..............................305 440-9101
Miguel Suarez, *Principal*
Milagros Suarez, *Co-Owner*
EMP: 7 **EST:** 2016
SQ FT: 2,000
SALES (est): 800K **Privately Held**
SIC: 3824 Mechanical & electromechanical counters & devices

(G-3152)
CAPRA GRAPHICS INC
Also Called: Stedi Press
1625 Nw 79th Ave (33126-1105)
PHONE..............................305 418-4582
George Capra, *President*
Adriana Capra, *Vice Pres*
EMP: 6 **EST:** 1990
SALES (est): 892.9K **Privately Held**
SIC: 2752 Commercial printing, offset

(G-3153)
CARBEL LLC
2323 Nw 82nd Ave (33122-1512)
PHONE..............................305 599-0832
Francisco J Torrens, *Principal*
Gressia Perez, *Regional Mgr*
EMP: 200 **EST:** 2004
SQ FT: 150,000
SALES (est): 23.6MM **Privately Held**
WEB: www.carbel-wd.com
SIC: 3694 Distributors, motor vehicle engine

(G-3154)
CARIBBEAN EMBLEMS
3555 Nw 79th Ave (33122-1019)
PHONE..............................305 593-8183
Alfredo J Gomez, *President*
Lydia Gomez, *Admin Sec*
EMP: 5 **EST:** 1991
SQ FT: 8,800
SALES (est): 382.9K **Privately Held**
WEB: www.caribbeanemblems.com
SIC: 2395 Embroidery products, except schiffli machine

(G-3155)
CARIBBEAN PAINT COMPANY INC
5295 Nw 79th Ave (33166-4715)
P.O. Box 522550, Miami (33152-2550)
PHONE..............................305 594-4500
George F Sixto, *President*
Ernesto Milian, *Vice Pres*
Silvia R Milian, *Treasurer*
George Sixto, *Office Mgr*
▼ **EMP:** 7 **EST:** 1976
SQ FT: 10,000
SALES (est): 1MM **Privately Held**
WEB: caribbean-paint-company-inc.sbcontract.com
SIC: 2851 Enamels; paints & paint additives; stains: varnish, oil or wax; lacquers, varnishes, enamels & other coatings

(G-3156)
CASTONE CREATIONS INC
Also Called: Cast-One
8309 Nw 70th St (33166-2622)
PHONE..............................305 599-3367
Ariel Gonzales, *President*
EMP: 22 **EST:** 2003
SQ FT: 10,000
SALES (est): 2.5MM **Privately Held**
SIC: 3272 Concrete products, precast

(G-3157)
CCM CLLLAR CNNECTION MIAMI INC
1825 Nw 79th Ave (33126-1114)
P.O. Box 228387, Miami (33222-8387)
PHONE..............................305 406-1656
Karim Ben Yahia, *President*
Pascale Vanclee, *Vice Pres*
▲ **EMP:** 21 **EST:** 1995
SALES (est): 1.1MM **Privately Held**
WEB: www.ccmmobile.com
SIC: 3661 Telephones & telephone apparatus

(G-3158)
CENTRAL INK INTERNATIONAL
8107 Nw 33rd St (33122-1005)
PHONE..............................786 747-8411
Amber Cordoba, *Office Mgr*
EMP: 8 **EST:** 2017
SALES (est): 98.5K **Privately Held**
WEB: www.rendicgs.com
SIC: 2752 Commercial printing, offset

(G-3159)
CENTRAL TURBOS CORP (PA)
1951 Nw 97th Ave (33172-2305)
PHONE..............................305 406-3933
Antonio Tilkian, *President*
Carlos Tilkian, *Vice Pres*
Nina Montiel, *Sales Staff*
Carlos Rudge, *Branch Mgr*
Luie Krum, *Manager*
◆ **EMP:** 9 **EST:** 2001
SQ FT: 6,000
SALES (est): 2.9MM **Privately Held**
WEB: www.centralturbos.com
SIC: 3694 3612 Distributors, motor vehicle engine; transformers, except electric

(G-3160)
CHECKSUM SOFTWARE LLC
7979 Nw 21st St (33122-1630)
P.O. Box 25331, Miami (33102-5331)
PHONE..............................786 375-8091
Van Glass,
Leo Salas, *Admin Sec*
EMP: 9 **EST:** 2001
SALES (est): 3MM
SALES (corp-wide): 8.5MM **Privately Held**
SIC: 7372 Prepackaged software
PA: Advanced Systems Concepts, Inc.
1180 Hdqters Plz W Towe F
Morristown NJ 07960
973 539-2660

(G-3161)
CIM USA INC
10813 Nw 30th St Ste 108 (33172-2191)
PHONE..............................305 369-1040
Alberto Mucelli, *President*
Mads Petersen, *Exec VP*
Sandro Mucelli, *Vice Pres*
▲ **EMP:** 5 **EST:** 1999

SQ FT: 7,000
SALES (est): 5.2MM
SALES (corp-wide): 355.8K **Privately Held**
WEB: www.cim-usa.com
SIC: 3579 Embossing machines for store & office use
HQ: Mf Group Srl
Localita' Braine 54/A
Monzuno BO
051 677-6511

(G-3162)
CIRVEN USA LLC
9681 Nw 45th Ln (33178-4017)
PHONE..........................305 815-2545
Gerardo Serriao, *CEO*
Orlando Diaz, *CFO*
◆ **EMP:** 5 **EST:** 2010
SALES (est): 1.4MM **Privately Held**
SIC: 3569 Lubricating systems, centralized

(G-3163)
CISCO SYSTEMS INC
8200 Nw 41st St Ste 400 (33166-6206)
PHONE..........................305 718-2600
Jose Garrido, *Partner*
Santiago Serrano, *Principal*
Armando Matute, *Business Mgr*
Perry Herndon, *Counsel*
Catherine Gomez-Mcpherson, *Project Mgr*
EMP: 14
SALES (corp-wide): 51.5B **Publicly Held**
WEB: www.cisco.com
SIC: 3577 5065 5045 Data conversion equipment, media-to-media: computer; electronic parts & equipment; computers, peripherals & software
PA: Cisco Systems, Inc.
170 W Tasman Dr
San Jose CA 95134
408 526-4000

(G-3164)
CITY CLORS DGITAL PRTG CTR INC
1470 Nw 79th Ave (33126-1610)
PHONE..........................305 471-0816
Roberto J Infante, *President*
Maria E Infante, *Vice Pres*
EMP: 17 EST: 1998
SALES (est): 2.5MM **Privately Held**
WEB: www.citycolors.com
SIC: 2752 Commercial printing, offset

(G-3165)
CLIMAX INC
Also Called: Mechanical Air Concepts
10401 Nw 28th St (33172-2100)
PHONE..........................786 264-6082
Victor Gomez, *President*
EMP: 8 EST: 2002
SALES (est): 1MM **Privately Held**
SIC: 3585 Refrigeration & heating equipment

(G-3166)
COFRAN INTERNATIONAL CORP
1540 Nw 94th Ave (33172-2846)
PHONE..........................305 592-2644
Yann Pacreau, *CEO*
Frederick Mas, *President*
▲ **EMP:** 25 **EST:** 1983
SQ FT: 14,000
SALES (est): 4.8MM **Privately Held**
WEB: www.cofrancorp.com
SIC: 2844 7389 Cosmetic preparations; packaging & labeling services

(G-3167)
COJALI USA INC
2200 Nw 102nd Ave Ste 4b (33172-2225)
PHONE..........................305 960-7651
Alberca Venancio, *President*
Carlos Rivas, *Senior Mgr*
EMP: 8 EST: 2013
SALES (est): 1.4MM **Privately Held**
WEB: www.cojaliusa.com
SIC: 2835 In vitro & in vivo diagnostic substances

(G-3168)
CONCURRENT MFG SOLUTIONS LLC (DH)
10773 Nw 58th St Ste 100 (33178-2801)
PHONE..........................512 637-2540

Gustavo Balleza, *Supervisor*
Tim Ogrady,
▲ **EMP:** 50 **EST:** 2006
SQ FT: 100,000
SALES (est): 20MM **Privately Held**
WEB: www.concurrentmfg.com
SIC: 3679 Electronic circuits
HQ: Cypress Holdings Ltd.
8027 Exchange Dr
Austin TX 78754
512 637-2540

(G-3169)
CONSTRUMINING INC
10885 Nw 89th Ter Unit 20 (33178-2123)
PHONE..........................786 217-3146
Erick Marquez, *Vice Pres*
EMP: 7 EST: 2017
SALES (est): 103.9K **Privately Held**
SIC: 1041 Open pit gold mining

(G-3170)
CONVERLOGIC INTER LLC (PA)
Also Called: Converlogic Americas
2254 Nw 93rd Ave (33172-4801)
PHONE..........................786 623-4747
Jose Luis Horna,
▲ **EMP:** 5 **EST:** 2014
SALES (est): 1.5MM **Privately Held**
WEB: www.converlogic.com
SIC: 3661 Telephone & telegraph apparatus

(G-3171)
COOLTECH HOLDING CORP (HQ)
2100 Nw 84th Ave (33122-1517)
PHONE..........................786 675-5236
Mauricio Diaz, *CEO*
Rein Boigt, *COO*
Alfredo Carrasco, *CFO*
Carlos Padilla, *Controller*
Felipe Rezk, *Chief Mktg Ofcr*
EMP: 4 EST: 2016
SALES (est): 4.1MM **Publicly Held**
WEB: www.cooltech.co
SIC: 7372 Prepackaged software

(G-3172)
COQUI RDO PHARMACEUTICALS CORP
Also Called: Coqui Pharma
3125 Nw 84th Ave (33122-1994)
PHONE..........................787 685-5046
Carmen Bigles, *CEO*
EMP: 5 EST: 2009
SALES (est): 630.3K **Privately Held**
SIC: 2834 7389 Pharmaceutical preparations;

(G-3173)
CORPORATE SIGNS INC
1375 Nw 97th Ave Ste 12 (33172-2855)
PHONE..........................305 500-9313
James Zuniga, *President*
EMP: 6 EST: 1998
SALES (est): 530K **Privately Held**
WEB: www.corporatesignsinc.com
SIC: 3993 Electric signs

(G-3174)
CORPORATE SIGNS INC
5960 Nw 99th Ave Unit 8 (33178-2712)
PHONE..........................305 500-9313
EMP: 7 EST: 2017
SALES (est): 312.5K **Privately Held**
WEB: www.corporatesignsinc.com
SIC: 3993 Signs & advertising specialties

(G-3175)
COSMETICS & CLEANERS INTL LLC
Also Called: C&C Industries
6000 Nw 97th Ave Unit 9 (33178-1639)
PHONE..........................305 592-5504
Andy Boutros, *CEO*
Nakia Thompson, *Asst Controller*
Boutros Andy, *Mng Member*
▼ **EMP:** 30 **EST:** 2010
SQ FT: 50,000
SALES (est): 6.1MM **Privately Held**
WEB: www.cncinds.com
SIC: 2844 Cosmetic preparations

(G-3176)
COTTONIMAGESCOM INC
Also Called: Cotton Images
10481 Nw 28th St (33172-2152)
PHONE..........................305 251-2560
Sandra K Hertzbach, *President*
Ramon Martinez, *COO*
Scott Hertzbach, *Vice Pres*
Isaac Diaz, *Accounting Mgr*
Lissette Herrera, *Manager*
▲ **EMP:** 45 **EST:** 2002
SALES (est): 6.8MM **Privately Held**
WEB: www.cottonimages.com
SIC: 2262 2711 Screen printing: manmade fiber & silk broadwoven fabrics; commercial printing & newspaper publishing combined

(G-3177)
CREATIVE HOME AND KITCHEN LLC
Also Called: Kitchenest
2000 Nw 97th Ave Ste 112 (33172-2347)
PHONE..........................786 233-8621
Brokerage Tomahawk, *Mng Member*
EMP: 18 EST: 2013
SALES (est): 3.1MM **Privately Held**
WEB: www.creativehomeandkitchen.com
SIC: 3631 Household cooking equipment

(G-3178)
CREATIVE MOLDING CORP
2949 Nw 97th Ct (33172-1099)
PHONE..........................786 251-4241
Gerardo Villegas, *President*
EMP: 11 EST: 2005
SALES (est): 314.3K **Privately Held**
SIC: 3089 Molding primary plastic

(G-3179)
CURALLUX LLC
1715 Nw 82nd Ave (33126-1015)
PHONE..........................786 888-1875
Carlos Pina, *CEO*
Ray Del Pino, *Purchasing*
Barry Pintar, *Accounts Exec*
Fernando Bermudez, *Sales Staff*
Frances Brea, *Chief Mktg Ofcr*
EMP: 50 EST: 2012
SQ FT: 21,257
SALES (est): 5.9MM **Privately Held**
WEB: www.capillus.com
SIC: 3845 Electrotherapeutic apparatus

(G-3180)
CUT SERVICES LLC
8264 Nw 58th St (33166-3407)
PHONE..........................305 560-0905
Amedeo Muscelli, *Mng Member*
EMP: 6 EST: 2016
SALES (est): 520.5K **Privately Held**
WEB: www.cutservices.com
SIC: 2426 Carvings, furniture: wood

(G-3181)
D & L AUTO & MARINE SUPPLIES
5601 Nw 79th Ave (33166-3532)
PHONE..........................305 593-0560
Eleodoro Aguero, *President*
Deborah Aguero, *Shareholder*
▲ **EMP:** 5 **EST:** 1980
SQ FT: 4,000
SALES (est): 694.8K **Privately Held**
WEB: www.dnlauto.com
SIC: 3694 5013 3625 Automotive electrical equipment; automotive supplies & parts; relays & industrial controls

(G-3182)
D&W FINE PACK LLC
7740 Nw 55th St (33166-4112)
PHONE..........................305 592-4329
Ariel Soler, *President*
EMP: 24
SALES (corp-wide): 900.4MM **Privately Held**
WEB: www.dwfinepack.com
SIC: 3089 Plastic kitchenware, tableware & houseware
HQ: D&W Fine Pack Llc
777 Mark St
Wood Dale IL 60191

(G-3183)
DAISY CRAZY INC
3902 Estepona Ave (33178-2926)
PHONE..........................305 300-5144
Deisy Contreras, *Principal*
▲ **EMP:** 5 **EST:** 2009
SALES (est): 309K **Privately Held**
SIC: 2339 2331 2253 Jeans: women's, misses' & juniors'; women's & misses' blouses & shirts; T-shirts & tops, knit

(G-3184)
DAJE INDUSTRIES INC
6020 Nw 99th Ave (33178-2725)
PHONE..........................305 592-7711
Duglay Zavala, *Principal*
EMP: 8 EST: 2008
SALES (est): 160.6K **Privately Held**
WEB: www.daje-usa.com
SIC: 3999 Barber & beauty shop equipment

(G-3185)
DANAS SAFTY SUPPLY INC
1622 Nw 82nd Ave (33126-1018)
PHONE..........................305 639-6024
EMP: 15
SALES (est): 2.1MM **Privately Held**
SIC: 3669 Mfg Communications Equipment

(G-3186)
DAYTONA RUBBER COMPANY INC
Also Called: Daytona Cooling Systems
10460 Nw 29th Ter (33172-2527)
PHONE..........................305 513-4105
Rafael Lorenzo, *President*
◆ **EMP:** 10 **EST:** 2010
SALES (est): 359.8K **Privately Held**
SIC: 2822 Synthetic rubber

(G-3187)
DDY MARTINEZ LLC
3105 Nw 107th Ave Ste 400 (33172-2215)
PHONE..........................786 263-2672
Yoanner Martinez,
EMP: 10 EST: 2020
SALES (est): 750K **Privately Held**
SIC: 1389 Construction, repair & dismantling services

(G-3188)
DECO ABRUSCI INTERNATIONAL LLC
8485 Nw 29th St (33122-1919)
PHONE..........................305 406-3401
Gregorio Abrusci, *President*
Johnnie Abrusci,
EMP: 12 EST: 2014
SALES (est): 1.2MM **Privately Held**
WEB: www.decoabrusci.us
SIC: 2591 8743 Drapery hardware & blinds & shades; sales promotion

(G-3189)
DELTANA ENTERPRISES INC
10820 Nw 29th St (33172-2149)
PHONE..........................305 592-8188
Philip Wong, *President*
Paul Wong, *Principal*
Stewart Donnarae, *CFO*
◆ **EMP:** 20 **EST:** 1977
SQ FT: 60,000
SALES (est): 2.5MM **Privately Held**
WEB: www.deltana.net
SIC: 3441 Fabricated structural metal

(G-3190)
DELUXE SHADES INC
8314 Nw 56th St (33166-4020)
PHONE..........................786 355-0086
Marco Murcia, *Principal*
EMP: 7 EST: 2016
SALES (est): 89.1K **Privately Held**
SIC: 2782 Blankbooks & looseleaf binders

(G-3191)
DIAMOND AIRCRAFT LOGISCTICS
11003 Nw 33rd St (33172-5021)
PHONE..........................305 456-8400
Danny Carchi, *CEO*
▲ **EMP:** 5 **EST:** 2012

▲ = Import ▼=Export
◆ =Import/Export

SALES (est): 500K **Privately Held**
SIC: 3721 Aircraft

(G-3192)
DIGITAL OUTDOOR LLC
Also Called: Lightking Outdoor
8405 Nw 29th St (33122-1924)
PHONE...................................305 944-7945
Timur Colak, *President*
Will Wang, *COO*
EMP: 20 EST: 2012
SALES (est): 1.9MM **Privately Held**
SIC: 3993 Electric signs

(G-3193)
DILOREN INC
8800 Nw 13th Ter (33172-3003)
PHONE...................................786 618-9671
Raul Di Lorenzo, *Manager*
EMP: 7 EST: 2015
SALES (est): 198.5K **Privately Held**
WEB: www.diloren-composites.com
SIC: 3721 Aircraft

(G-3194)
DIMENSIONAL AMERICAS INC
10411 Nw 28th St Ste C103 (33172-2168)
PHONE...................................786 417-9370
EMP: 6 EST: 2000
SALES (est): 347.2K **Privately Held**
WEB: www.dimensionalamericas.com
SIC: 3993 Signs & advertising specialties

(G-3195)
DOLE
10055 Nw 12th St (33172-2761)
PHONE...................................305 925-7900
John Schouten, *Principal*
Alexis Barrios, *Accounts Mgr*
EMP: 8 EST: 2014
SALES (est): 198.1K **Privately Held**
SIC: 2099 Food preparations

(G-3196)
DORAL BUILDING SUPPLY CORP
5095 Nw 79th Ave (33166-4711)
PHONE...................................305 471-9797
Cesar F Arellano Jr, *President*
▼ EMP: 15 EST: 1985
SQ FT: 52,000
SALES (est): 2.3MM **Privately Held**
WEB: www.doralbldgsupply.com
SIC: 3444 5032 Studs & joists, sheet metal; drywall materials

(G-3197)
DORAL DGTAL REPROGRAPHICS CORP
5701 Nw 79th Ave (33166-3535)
PHONE...................................305 704-3194
Giancarlo Annitto, *President*
Jose Alvarez, *Principal*
Morgan Gregory, *Vice Pres*
Beatrice Berrera, *Sales Mgr*
Beatriz Pereira, *Sales Mgr*
EMP: 6 EST: 2006
SALES (est): 2.7MM **Privately Held**
WEB: www.ddrepro.com
SIC: 2752 7336 2759 Commercial printing, lithographic; art design services; commercial printing; promotional printing; magazines: printing; menus: printing

(G-3198)
DORAL FAMILY JOURNAL LLC
10773 Nw 58th St Ste 96 (33178-2801)
PHONE...................................305 300-4594
Ettore Sabatella, *Manager*
EMP: 7 EST: 2016
SALES (est): 103.3K **Privately Held**
WEB: www.doralfamilyjournal.com
SIC: 2711 Newspapers, publishing & printing

(G-3199)
DOTAMED LLC
6332 Nw 99th Ave (33178-2721)
PHONE...................................786 594-0144
Francisco J Franco Velez, *Manager*
Gladys H Largo De Franco, *Manager*
Angelina Da Silva Suarez, *Manager*
John J Franco Velez, *Manager*
▲ EMP: 7 EST: 2007

SALES (est): 499.4K **Privately Held**
WEB: www.dtmusa.net
SIC: 3843 Dental equipment & supplies

(G-3200)
DS HEALTHCARE GROUP INC (DH)
Also Called: Ds Laboratories
1850 Nw 84th Ave Ste 108 (33126-1027)
PHONE...................................888 829-4212
Fernando Tamez Gutierrez, *CEO*
Carlos Luzuriaga Castro, *COO*
Fernando Tamez, *COO*
Mauricio Gomez-Mont Gavito, *CFO*
John Eberhardt, *Sales Dir*
EMP: 29 EST: 2007
SQ FT: 50,000
SALES (est): 25.8MM
SALES (corp-wide): 37.3MM **Privately Held**
WEB: www.dslaboratories.com
SIC: 2844 Hair preparations, including shampoos
HQ: Medilogistics Corp
1451 Brickell Ave # 2701
Miami FL 33131
786 856-8311

(G-3201)
DUY DRUGS INC
1730 Nw 79th Ave (33126-1111)
PHONE...................................305 594-3667
Maria Elorzuy, *President*
▲ EMP: 10 EST: 2004
SALES (est): 773K **Privately Held**
SIC: 2834 Pharmaceutical preparations

(G-3202)
EARTH & SEA WEAR LLC
Also Called: Cover Style
8785 Nw 13th Ter (33172-3013)
PHONE...................................786 332-2236
Augusto Hanimian, *President*
EMP: 40 EST: 1993
SQ FT: 12,000
SALES (est): 6.9MM **Privately Held**
SIC: 2339 Bathing suits: women's, misses' & juniors'; sportswear, women's

(G-3203)
EASI 360 CORP
10975 Nw 65th St (33178-2853)
PHONE...................................305 213-6346
Luz Roman, *President*
EMP: 7 EST: 2016
SALES (est): 126.1K **Privately Held**
SIC: 3822 Energy cutoff controls, residential or commercial types

(G-3204)
ECS AMERICA LLC
Also Called: Locksmith Killers
3555 Nw 79th Ave (33122-1019)
PHONE...................................305 798-3825
Jose Romero, *President*
EMP: 5 EST: 2015
SALES (est): 825.7K **Privately Held**
WEB: www.locksmithkeyless.com
SIC: 3429 Keys, locks & related hardware

(G-3205)
EEM TECHNOLOGIES CORP (PA)
9590 Nw 40th Street Rd (33178-2971)
PHONE...................................786 606-5993
Ricardo Solorzano, *President*
Eliana Toledo, *Vice Pres*
Juan Soto, *Sales Staff*
EMP: 5 EST: 2016
SALES (est): 1.1MM **Privately Held**
WEB: www.eemtechnologies.com
SIC: 3593 3594 7389 3492 Fluid power actuators, hydraulic or pneumatic; fluid power pumps; personal service agents, brokers & bureaus; control valves, fluid power: hydraulic & pneumatic

(G-3206)
EL TRIGAL INTERNATIONAL
10740 Nw 74th St (33178-1504)
PHONE...................................305 594-6610
EMP: 6 EST: 2010
SALES (est): 353.4K **Privately Held**
SIC: 2051 Cakes, bakery: except frozen

(G-3207)
ELIPTER CORP
3900 Nw 79th Ave Ste 482 (33166-6548)
PHONE...................................305 593-8355
Angelo Espinoza, *Principal*
EMP: 9 EST: 2010
SALES (est): 112K **Privately Held**
SIC: 3699 Security control equipment & systems

(G-3208)
EMPIRE CORP KIT OF
2846 Nw 79th Ave (33122-1033)
PHONE...................................800 432-3028
Henri Bertuch, *Principal*
EMP: 7 EST: 2012
SALES (est): 132.3K **Privately Held**
SIC: 2752 Commercial printing, offset

(G-3209)
ESPERANTO INC
Also Called: Market Logic
8725 Nw 18th Ter Ste 312 (33172-2610)
P.O. Box 228505, Miami (33222-8505)
PHONE...................................305 513-8980
Marcelo Castro, *President*
▲ EMP: 15 EST: 1994
SQ FT: 2,500
SALES (est): 2MM **Privately Held**
SIC: 2731 Books: publishing only

(G-3210)
EVEREST INDUSTRIES LLC
9600 Nw 25th St Ste 4e (33172-1416)
PHONE...................................786 210-0662
Sebastian Perdigon, *Principal*
EMP: 7 EST: 2017
SALES (est): 80.5K **Privately Held**
WEB: www.everestref.com
SIC: 3999 Manufacturing industries

(G-3211)
EXTREME WOOD WORKS S FLA INC
1520 Nw 79th Ave (33126-1104)
PHONE...................................305 463-8614
Martha Hernandez, *Administration*
EMP: 10 EST: 2006
SALES (est): 1MM **Privately Held**
WEB: www.extremewoodworks.com
SIC: 2541 Wood partitions & fixtures; display fixtures, wood

(G-3212)
FASTKIT CORP
11250 Nw 25th St Ste 100 (33172-1820)
PHONE...................................305 599-0839
Jose Fernandez Jr, *President*
Denisse Martinez, *General Mgr*
David Barjun, *COO*
Lidia Fernandez, *Vice Pres*
Yosmar Barrios, *Production*
▲ EMP: 38 EST: 1986
SALES (est): 8.6MM **Privately Held**
WEB: www.fastkit.com
SIC: 2782 Blankbooks & looseleaf binders

(G-3213)
FCA NORTH AMERICA HOLDINGS LLC
Also Called: Planet Fiat of West Miami
9975 Nw 12th St (33172-2762)
PHONE...................................305 597-2222
EMP: 7 **Privately Held**
WEB: www.stellantis.com
SIC: 3714 Motor vehicle parts & accessories
HQ: Fca Us Llc
1000 Chrysler Dr
Auburn Hills MI 48326

(G-3214)
FELDENKREIS HOLDINGS LLC (PA)
3000 Nw 107th Ave (33172-2133)
PHONE...................................305 592-2830
Oscar Feldenkreis, *President*
George Feldenkreis, *Vice Pres*
Tim Garrett, *VP Sales*
Amarilys Carpio, *Manager*
Carlos Guerra, *Manager*
EMP: 83 EST: 2018
SALES (est): 874.8MM **Privately Held**
WEB: www.pery.com
SIC: 2321 Men's & boys' furnishings

(G-3215)
FINE SURFACES AND MORE INC
8850 Nw 15th St (33172-3028)
PHONE...................................305 691-5752
Gabriel Segret, *President*
Pablo Lorenzo, *Vice Pres*
EMP: 13 EST: 2009
SALES (est): 1.6MM **Privately Held**
WEB: www.finesurfacesandmore.com
SIC: 3281 Granite, cut & shaped

(G-3216)
FIPLEX COMMUNICATIONS INC (PA)
2101 Nw 79th Ave (33122-1611)
PHONE...................................305 884-8991
Ron Pitcock, *CEO*
Marta Braun, *Ch of Bd*
Bob Joslin, *Vice Pres*
Francesco Floridia, *Engineer*
Augusto Montoya, *Engineer*
▲ EMP: 42 EST: 1985
SQ FT: 2,000
SALES (est): 11MM **Privately Held**
WEB: www.fiplex.com
SIC: 3663 Radio & TV communications equipment

(G-3217)
FK IRONS INC
1771 Nw 79th Ave (33126-1112)
PHONE...................................855 354-7667
Gaston A Siciliano Sr, *President*
Lewins Cisneros, *Software Engr*
Ivan Rodrigueztellah, *Graphic Designe*
EMP: 35 EST: 2009
SQ FT: 20,000
SALES (est): 4.3MM **Privately Held**
WEB: www.fkirons.com
SIC: 3399 Metal fasteners

(G-3218)
FLOWERS BAKING CO MIAMI LLC
2681 Nw 104th Ct (33172-2172)
PHONE...................................305 599-8457
Willie Prince, *Manager*
EMP: 22
SALES (corp-wide): 4.3B **Publicly Held**
SIC: 2051 Bakery: wholesale or wholesale/retail combined
HQ: Flowers Baking Co. Of Miami, Llc
17800 Nw Miami Ct
Miami FL 33169
305 652-3416

(G-3219)
FLUID HANDLING SUPPORT CORP
6030 Nw 99th Ave Unit 409 (33178-2731)
PHONE...................................786 623-2105
Manuel Escobar, *Branch Mgr*
▼ EMP: 12
SALES (corp-wide): 1MM **Privately Held**
WEB: www.fluid-handling.com
SIC: 2026 Fluid milk
PA: Fluid Handling Support, Corp
11139 Nw 122nd St Unit 6
Medley FL 33178
786 623-2105

(G-3220)
FREEZETONE PRODUCTS LLC
7986 Nw 14th St (33126-1614)
PHONE...................................305 961-1116
Luis M Latour Jr, *Mng Member*
▼ EMP: 18 EST: 1978
SALES (est): 8.3MM **Privately Held**
WEB: www.freezetoneglobal.com
SIC: 2899 2842 Chemical preparations; specialty cleaning, polishes & sanitation goods

(G-3221)
FRESENIUS KABI USA LLC
1733 Nw 79th Ave (33191-1101)
PHONE...................................847 550-2300
EMP: 35
SALES (corp-wide): 42.4B **Privately Held**
WEB: www.fresenius-kabi.com
SIC: 2834 Pharmaceutical preparations

HQ: Fresenius Kabi Usa, Llc
3 Corporate Dr
Lake Zurich IL 60047
847 550-2300

(G-3222)
FUEL CELL INC
7841 Nw 56th St (33166-3523)
PHONE....................................954 776-7555
EMP: 5 **EST:** 2019
SALES (est): 436.7K **Privately Held**
WEB: www.thefuelcell.com
SIC: 3728 Aircraft parts & equipment

(G-3223)
GALIX BMEDICAL INSTRUMENTATION
8205 Nw 30th Ter (33122-1913)
PHONE....................................305 534-5905
EMP: 15
SALES (est): 1.8MM **Privately Held**
SIC: 3841 5047 Mfg Surgical/Medical Instruments Whol Medical/Hospital Equipment

(G-3224)
GEM AEROSPACE
10300 Nw 19th St (33172-2538)
PHONE....................................786 464-5900
Eradin Dejesus, *General Mgr*
Julio Ramirez, *Vice Pres*
Armando Noy, *Opers Mgr*
Olessia Silakova, *Asst Controller*
Osbelto Barroso, *Cust Mgr*
EMP: 9 **EST:** 2012
SALES (est): 312.6K **Privately Held**
WEB: www.global-engine.com
SIC: 3519 Jet propulsion engines

(G-3225)
GENECELL INTERNATIONAL LLC
2664 Nw 97th Ave (33172-1400)
PHONE....................................305 382-6737
Jose Cirino, *Opers Staff*
Aixa Cortez, *Mktg Dir*
Eduardo Cortez, *Mng Member*
EMP: 10 **EST:** 2010
SALES (est): 1.3MM **Privately Held**
WEB: www.genecell.com
SIC: 3821 Autoclaves, laboratory

(G-3226)
GENEL/LANDEC INC
10845 Nw 29th St (33172-5909)
P.O. Box 142161, Miami (33114-2161)
PHONE....................................305 591-9990
James Talamas, *President*
Jim Talamas, *Opers Mgr*
EMP: 6 **EST:** 1980
SQ FT: 2,500
SALES (est): 886K **Privately Held**
WEB: www.genel-landec.com
SIC: 7372 5045 Educational computer software; business oriented computer software; computers

(G-3227)
GENERAL MILLS INC
8400 Nw 36th St Ste 310 (33166-6657)
PHONE....................................305 591-1771
Ericson Mark, *Manager*
Amanda TSO, *Planning*
EMP: 22
SALES (corp-wide): 18.9B **Publicly Held**
WEB: www.generalmills.com
SIC: 2043 2041 2045 2099 Wheat flakes: prepared as cereal breakfast food; oats, rolled: prepared as cereal breakfast food; corn flakes: prepared as cereal breakfast food; rice: prepared as cereal breakfast food; flour: prepared flour mixes & doughs; dessert mixes & fillings
PA: General Mills, Inc.
1 General Mills Blvd
Minneapolis MN 55426
763 764-7600

(G-3228)
GENERAL POWER LIMITED INC
9930 Nw 21st St Fl 1 (33172-2212)
PHONE....................................800 763-0359
Luis Lopez, *President*
John Cortiella, *Partner*
Carmen C Moreno De Lopez, *Vice Pres*
Melissa Lopez, *Marketing Staff*

Laura Lopez, *Admin Asst*
◆ **EMP:** 16 **EST:** 1999
SQ FT: 11,000
SALES (est): 4.5MM **Privately Held**
WEB: www.genpowerusa.com
SIC: 3621 Power generators

(G-3229)
GENERAL WELDING SVC ENTPS INC
8115 Nw 56th St (33166-4016)
P.O. Box 227668, Miami (33222-7668)
PHONE....................................305 592-9483
Jose Antonio Cid, *President*
Nancy Cid, *Corp Secy*
Pedro Cid, *Vice Pres*
Juan Cid, *Asst Sec*
EMP: 8 **EST:** 1972
SQ FT: 11,000
SALES (est): 878.2K **Privately Held**
SIC: 7692 Welding repair

(G-3230)
GENFLOOR LLC
Also Called: General Floors
6312 Nw 99th Ave (33178-2721)
PHONE....................................305 477-1557
Jose E Calvino,
▲ **EMP:** 7 **EST:** 2010
SQ FT: 8,000
SALES (est): 672.2K **Privately Held**
WEB: www.genfloor.net
SIC: 3589 Floor washing & polishing machines, commercial

(G-3231)
GENSCO LABORATORIES LLC
Also Called: Gensco Pharma
8550 Nw 33rd St Ste 200 (33122-1941)
PHONE....................................754 263-2898
Carlos Alfaras, *President*
Paul Meek, *Exec VP*
Lloyd Ramson, *Accounting Mgr*
Lissa Ajmo, *Manager*
David Andry, *Director*
EMP: 14 **EST:** 2009
SALES (est): 2.6MM **Privately Held**
WEB: www.genscopharma.com
SIC: 2834 Zinc ointment

(G-3232)
GEORG FISCHER LLC (HQ)
Also Called: GF Piping Systems
10540 Nw 26th St (33172-5932)
PHONE....................................305 418-9150
James Jackson, *Mng Member*
Max Holloway,
EMP: 5 **EST:** 2007
SALES (est): 12.3MM
SALES (corp-wide): 4B **Privately Held**
WEB: www.gfps.com
SIC: 3498 Piping systems for pulp paper & chemical industries
PA: Georg Fischer Ag
Amsler-Laffon-Strasse 9
Schaffhausen SH 8200
526 311-111

(G-3233)
GLENNY STONE WORKS INC
3000 Nw 77th Ct (33122-1114)
PHONE....................................786 502-3918
Juan C Glenny, *Principal*
Martin Arzani, *Project Mgr*
EMP: 8 **EST:** 2018
SALES (est): 335.9K **Privately Held**
WEB: www.glennystoneworks.com
SIC: 2434 Wood kitchen cabinets

(G-3234)
GLOBAL ALIMENT INC
7791 Nw 46th St Ste 308 (33166-5484)
PHONE....................................786 536-5261
EMP: 2 **EST:** 2016
SALES (est): 11.3MM **Privately Held**
WEB: www.globalaliment.com
SIC: 2092 Seafoods, frozen: prepared

(G-3235)
GLOBAL REACH RX PBF LLC
10560 Nw 27th St Ste 101a (33172-5928)
PHONE....................................786 703-1988
Sergio Ruiz, *CEO*
Wayne J Talamas, *President*
EMP: 15 **EST:** 2014
SQ FT: 5,000

SALES (est): 2.1MM **Privately Held**
SIC: 2834 Pharmaceutical preparations

(G-3236)
GRAPHINK INCORPORATED
8850 Nw 13th Ter Unit 103 (33172-3012)
PHONE....................................305 468-9463
Vanessa Gramatges, *President*
EMP: 8 **EST:** 2014
SQ FT: 6,000
SALES (est): 910.8K **Privately Held**
WEB: www.graphink.com
SIC: 2752 Business form & card printing, lithographic

(G-3237)
GRAZED LLC
9399 Nw 13th St (33172-2807)
PHONE....................................786 534-3975
Homer Luther, *Mng Member*
EMP: 82 **EST:** 2019
SALES (est): 6.5MM **Privately Held**
WEB: www.grazedpet.com
SIC: 2047 Dog & cat food

(G-3238)
GREAT CIR VNTURES HOLDINGS LLC (PA)
Also Called: Tail Activewear
2105 Nw 86th Ave (33122-1527)
PHONE....................................305 638-2650
Jerry Edwards, *CEO*
Cheryl Maurer, *Vice Pres*
Nikki Miller, *VP Sales*
Sherri Balke, *Sales Staff*
Jeanne Craig, *Sales Staff*
◆ **EMP:** 32 **EST:** 2006
SQ FT: 38,000
SALES (est): 10MM **Privately Held**
SIC: 2339 Sportswear, women's

(G-3239)
GREENLAM AMERICA INC
Also Called: Greenlam Laminates
8750 Nw 36th St Ste 635 (33178-2778)
PHONE....................................305 640-0388
Jose Somoza, *Regional Mgr*
Victor Sharma, *COO*
Rohit Kaul, *Vice Pres*
Vaibhav Sharma, *Vice Pres*
Atish Bhattacharya, *Manager*
▲ **EMP:** 12 **EST:** 2008
SALES (est): 2MM **Privately Held**
WEB: www.greenlam.com
SIC: 3589 High pressure cleaning equipment

(G-3240)
GREMED GROUP CORP
8040 Nw 14th St (33126-1612)
PHONE....................................305 392-5331
Felix Perez, *CEO*
Ana Contreras, *Vice Pres*
▲ **EMP:** 17 **EST:** 2004
SQ FT: 16,500
SALES (est): 461.2K **Privately Held**
SIC: 3841 5047 Surgical & medical instruments; instruments, surgical & medical

(G-3241)
GROVE POWER INC
158 (33122)
PHONE....................................305 599-2045
Jeff Flannery, *President*
James Fahrber, *CFO*
EMP: 7 **EST:** 2009
SALES (est): 173K **Privately Held**
SIC: 3621 Motors & generators

(G-3242)
HALCYON AVIATION CAPITAL LLC
8350 Nw 52nd Ter Ste 301 (33166-7708)
PHONE....................................305 615-1575
Patrice Robinet, *Managing Dir*
EMP: 5 **EST:** 2020
SALES (est): 584.5K **Privately Held**
WEB: www.halcyonavcap.com
SIC: 3728 Aircraft parts & equipment

(G-3243)
HAMMER HEAD GROUP INC
Also Called: Deco Wraps
8900 Nw 33rd St Ste 100 (33172-1207)
PHONE....................................305 436-5691

Steven Tchira, *CEO*
Kristie Montez, *Business Mgr*
Lauren Sierra, *Marketing Mgr*
Karen Kaufman, *Graphic Designe*
▲ **EMP:** 30 **EST:** 2016
SALES (est): 4.2MM **Privately Held**
WEB: www.hammerheadcg.com
SIC: 2621 Wrapping & packaging papers

(G-3244)
HANSA OPHTHALMICS LLC
Also Called: United Ophthalmics
4083 Nw 79th Ave (33166-6519)
PHONE....................................305 594-1789
Steven Levesque, *CEO*
EMP: 24 **EST:** 2017
SALES (est): 1MM **Privately Held**
SIC: 3841 Ophthalmic instruments & apparatus

(G-3245)
HERALPIN USA INC
Also Called: Petroheral
10570 Nw 27th St Ste H101 (33172-2105)
PHONE....................................305 218-0174
Rafael Betancourt, *President*
▼ **EMP:** 5 **EST:** 2002
SALES (est): 536.2K **Privately Held**
WEB: www.heralpinusa.com
SIC: 3272 5012 5399 6799 Tanks, concrete; truck tractors; Army-Navy goods; commodity contract trading companies

(G-3246)
HERMES TECHNICAL INTL INC
8227 Nw 54th St (33166-4008)
PHONE....................................305 477-8993
Manuel Ugas, *President*
Nadia Ugas, *Vice Pres*
Vicky Ramirez, *Purchasing*
Sue Arroyo, *Sales Mgr*
Gabriela Cabanillas, *Sales Staff*
▼ **EMP:** 7 **EST:** 1986
SQ FT: 5,000
SALES (est): 1.6MM **Privately Held**
WEB: www.hermestechnical.com
SIC: 3728 Aircraft parts & equipment; brakes, aircraft

(G-3247)
HERNANDEZ ORNAMENTAL INC
1910 Nw 96th Ave (33172-2319)
PHONE....................................305 592-7296
Barbara Hernandez, *President*
Jorge F Hernandez, *President*
Felix Hernandez, *Vice Pres*
EMP: 8 **EST:** 1980
SQ FT: 2,400
SALES (est): 803.3K **Privately Held**
SIC: 3446 Ornamental metalwork

(G-3248)
HIGH STANDARD AVIATION INC
5900 Nw 97th Ave Unit 3 (33178-1642)
PHONE....................................305 599-8855
Villasante Francisco, *President*
Alina Villasante, *President*
Francisco Villasante, *Chairman*
Villasante Alina, *Vice Pres*
▲ **EMP:** 38 **EST:** 1991
SQ FT: 25,000
SALES (est): 19.8MM
SALES (corp-wide): 5.5B **Publicly Held**
WEB: www.ametekmro.com
SIC: 3721 4581 3728 Aircraft; aircraft maintenance & repair services; aircraft parts & equipment
PA: Ametek, Inc.
1100 Cassatt Rd
Berwyn PA 19312
610 647-2121

(G-3249)
HIMMEL LOSUNGEN GROUP HLG LLC
4711 Nw 79th Ave Ste 12l (33166-5443)
PHONE....................................786 631-5531
Jefferson Zambrano Angel, *Mng Member*
◆ **EMP:** 5 **EST:** 2015
SQ FT: 625
SALES (est): 1.5MM **Privately Held**
SIC: 3728 Aircraft parts & equipment

(G-3250)
HMD INVESTMENT GROUP LLC
Also Called: Ejuice Depo
7753 Nw 53rd St (33166-4101)
PHONE..................................305 244-1290
EMP: 7 **EST:** 2016
SALES (est): 434.6K **Privately Held**
SIC: 3999 Cigarette & cigar products & accessories

(G-3251)
HS STONE GALLERY LLC
1660 Nw 82nd Ave (33126-1018)
PHONE..................................305 200-5810
EMP: 5 **EST:** 2018
SALES (est): 489.2K **Privately Held**
SIC: 1411 Quartzite, dimension-quarrying

(G-3252)
I C T S AMERICA INC
8400 Nw 36th St Ste 450 (33166-6606)
PHONE..................................786 307-2993
Rafael Gonzalez, *President*
Cesar Maraver, *Director*
EMP: 8 **EST:** 2015
SQ FT: 1,200
SALES (est): 223K **Privately Held**
SIC: 1389 Gas field services

(G-3253)
IAMGOLD PURCHASING SVCS INC
Also Called: Rosebel Gold Mines NV
2000 Nw 97th Ave Ste 114 (33172-2347)
PHONE..................................713 671-5973
Gordon Stothart, *President*
Steve Letwin, *President*
L Steve Wagner, *Admin Sec*
◆ **EMP:** 3 **EST:** 1987
SQ FT: 3,000
SALES (est): 5.9MM
SALES (corp-wide): 1B **Privately Held**
SIC: 1041 Gold ores mining
PA: Iamgold Corporation
401 Bay St Suite 3200
Toronto ON M5H 2
416 360-4710

(G-3254)
IDEA DESIGN STUDIO INC
8562 Nw 56th St (33166-3329)
PHONE..................................305 823-6008
Fabian Forero, *President*
EMP: 10 **EST:** 2006
SQ FT: 500
SALES (est): 800K **Privately Held**
WEB: www.ideadstudio.com
SIC: 2821 7389 Acrylic resins; design, commercial & industrial

(G-3255)
IMAGIK INTERNATIONAL CORP
8390 Nw 25th St (33122-1504)
PHONE..................................786 631-5003
Pablo Vadillo, *President*
Jorge Garcia, *Agent*
▲ **EMP:** 15 **EST:** 1994
SALES (est): 5.3MM **Privately Held**
WEB: www.imagikcorp.com
SIC: 3663 Radio & TV communications equipment

(G-3256)
IMC STORAGE
3955 Adra Ave (33178-2907)
PHONE..................................305 418-0069
Agosto Tabana, *President*
Willy Herrera, *Business Mgr*
Engels Jarquin, *Engineer*
John Florez, *Manager*
EMP: 5 **EST:** 2012
SALES (est): 343.8K **Privately Held**
WEB: www.imcstorage.com
SIC: 3572 Computer auxiliary storage units

(G-3257)
IMPEXPAR LLC
10540 Nw 26th St Ste G302 (33172-5934)
PHONE..................................786 238-5700
Rafael Parisi, *Mng Member*
Gabriel Parisi,
EMP: 6 **EST:** 2019
SALES (est): 697.4K **Privately Held**
SIC: 3646 Commercial indusl & institutional electric lighting fixtures

(G-3258)
INFINITI DIGITAL EQUIPMENT INC
10500 Nw 29th Ter (33172-2526)
PHONE..................................305 477-6333
Ming Xu, *President*
▲ **EMP:** 8 **EST:** 2005
SALES (est): 686.8K **Privately Held**
SIC: 3823 Digital displays of process variables

(G-3259)
INTERNTNAL TECH SLTONS SUP LLC
Also Called: Trugard
2636 Nw 97th Ave (33172-1400)
P.O. Box 226575, Miami (33222-6575)
PHONE..................................305 364-5229
Leonardo J Brito, *Mng Member*
Nataly Bermudez, *Administration*
EMP: 5 **EST:** 2009
SALES (est): 547.4K **Privately Held**
SIC: 1382 5139 Oil & gas exploration services; boots

(G-3260)
INVERSNES WLLDEL ASOCIADOS INC
8250 Nw 58th St (33166-3407)
PHONE..................................305 591-0931
William Delgado, *Branch Mgr*
EMP: 70
SALES (corp-wide): 1.1MM **Privately Held**
SIC: 3441 Railroad car racks, for transporting vehicles: steel
PA: Inversiones Willdel & Asociados, Inc.
4700 Nw 72nd Ave
Miami FL 33166
305 591-0118

(G-3261)
ITALIAN MOONSHINERS INC
8300 Nw 53rd St Ste 350 (33166-7712)
PHONE..................................954 687-4500
Carlo A Lazzari, *Principal*
Marco Grilli, *Relations*
EMP: 7 **EST:** 2010
SALES (est): 96.6K **Privately Held**
WEB: www.italianmoonshiners.com
SIC: 2085 2084 Vodka (alcoholic beverage); wines, brandy & brandy spirits

(G-3262)
ITALKRAFT LLC (PA)
2900 Nw 77th Ct (33122-1113)
PHONE..................................305 406-1301
Orlando Rodriguez, *Project Mgr*
Panos Symvoulidis, *Project Mgr*
Cody Hansen, *Sr Project Mgr*
Adam Ka, *Manager*
Carlos Peirallo, *Director*
EMP: 16 **EST:** 2011
SQ FT: 24,645
SALES (est): 6.4MM **Privately Held**
WEB: www.italkraft.com
SIC: 2511 5712 Vanity dressers: wood; cabinet work, custom

(G-3263)
IVAN & IVAN LLC
Also Called: Inversiones Medicas SIS
1465 Nw 97th Ave (33172-2819)
PHONE..................................305 507-8793
Ivan A Fernandez, *Mng Member*
Krina Fernandez,
EMP: 6 **EST:** 2010
SQ FT: 100
SALES (est): 785K **Privately Held**
WEB: www.needlefreesystem.com
SIC: 3841 Surgical & medical instruments

(G-3264)
J D M CORP
Also Called: Modern Display
1551 Nw 93rd Ave (33172-2910)
PHONE..................................305 947-5876
David Milgrom, *President*
Lee Sack, *Vice Pres*
Abraham Bochman, *Treasurer*
▲ **EMP:** 8 **EST:** 1968
SQ FT: 3,000
SALES (est): 936.4K **Privately Held**
SIC: 3993 Electric signs

(G-3265)
J&D OIL FIELD INTL INC
Also Called: J&D Oilfield International
3785 Nw 82nd Ave Ste 206 (33166-6630)
PHONE..................................305 436-0024
Argimiro Malave Leon, *President*
Jose V Rivera, *Vice Pres*
Jose Rivera, *Vice Pres*
Victor A Alezones Rivero, *Vice Pres*
Isabel Verde, *Manager*
EMP: 5 **EST:** 2005
SALES (est): 1.5MM **Privately Held**
SIC: 1389 Oil field services

(G-3266)
JAT POWER LLC
Also Called: Aksa's Generator
8000 Nw 29th St (33122-1077)
PHONE..................................305 592-0103
Joe Niswanger, *CEO*
Rudolph N Niswanger, *Mng Member*
◆ **EMP:** 10 **EST:** 2012
SALES (est): 560.7K **Privately Held**
WEB: www.jatpower.com
SIC: 3621 Generators & sets, electric

(G-3267)
JC TOYS GROUP INC
2841 Nw 107th Ave (33172-2130)
PHONE..................................305 592-3541
Juan L Cerda, *President*
Richard Cerda, *Vice Pres*
Janet Marquez, *Sales Mgr*
Laura Cerda, *Marketing Staff*
◆ **EMP:** 10 **EST:** 1993
SQ FT: 40,000
SALES (est): 2.1MM **Privately Held**
WEB: www.jctoys.com
SIC: 3942 3944 Dolls & stuffed toys; games, toys & children's vehicles

(G-3268)
JERS GROUP
Also Called: Abam Export
8625 Nw 54th St (33166-3324)
PHONE..................................786 953-6419
Cesar Bolivar, *Owner*
EMP: 5 **EST:** 2014
SALES (est): 662K **Privately Held**
SIC: 3089 Automotive parts, plastic
PA: Serviseguros C.A
Centro Gerencial Mohedano,
Caracas D.F.

(G-3269)
JLG INDUSTRIES INC
10974 Nw 63rd St (33178-2852)
PHONE..................................786 558-8909
Martin Lacks, *Branch Mgr*
EMP: 10
SALES (corp-wide): 7.7B **Publicly Held**
WEB: www.jlg.com
SIC: 3531 Construction machinery
HQ: Jlg Industries, Inc.
1 Jlg Dr
Mc Connellsburg PA 17233
717 485-5161

(G-3270)
JMP MARINE LLC
Also Called: Jmp USA
2000 Nw 84th Ave Ste 244 (33122-1520)
P.O. Box 162955, Miami (33116-2955)
PHONE..................................305 599-0009
EMP: 27
SALES (est): 2.6MM **Privately Held**
SIC: 3523 Mfg Farm Machinery/Equipment

(G-3271)
KAYVA DISTRIBUTION LLC
Also Called: Blue Sun International
2201 Nw 102nd Pl Ste 4a (33172-2521)
PHONE..................................305 428-2816
Nadia Perez, *Opers Mgr*
Alexander Bliziotis, *Accounts Mgr*
Fu Zhou, *Accounts Mgr*
Victor Alvarez, *Mng Member*
▲ **EMP:** 7 **EST:** 2009
SALES (est): 756.5K **Privately Held**
SIC: 2844 5122 Toilet preparations; cosmetics, perfumes & hair products

(G-3272)
KENDOO TECHNOLOGY INC
1950 Nw 94th Ave Lowr (33172-2324)
PHONE..................................305 592-9688
Harry Chang, *President*
▲ **EMP:** 7 **EST:** 1998
SQ FT: 3,000
SALES (est): 555.9K **Privately Held**
WEB: www.kendoo.com
SIC: 3691 Batteries, rechargeable

(G-3273)
KITKO CORP
10773 Nw 58th St Ste 87 (33178-2801)
PHONE..................................786 287-8900
EMP: 8
SQ FT: 7,000
SALES (est): 557.4K **Privately Held**
SIC: 3086 Mfg Plastic Foam Products

(G-3274)
KLIMAIRE PRODUCTS INC
2190 Nw 89th Pl (33172-2427)
PHONE..................................305 593-8358
Korkmaz Iltekin, *President*
Idania Sosa, *Sales Staff*
Walter Bolivar, *Department Mgr*
Richard Barnes, *CIO*
◆ **EMP:** 15 **EST:** 1989
SQ FT: 24,000
SALES (est): 2.7MM **Privately Held**
WEB: www.klimaire.com
SIC: 3585 Air conditioning equipment, complete

(G-3275)
KLYO MEDICAL SYSTEMS INC
1464 Nw 82nd Ave (33126-1508)
PHONE..................................305 330-5025
Luis Torres, *CEO*
Alejandra Cervantes, *Marketing Staff*
EMP: 15 **EST:** 2015
SQ FT: 10,000
SALES (est): 1.9MM **Privately Held**
WEB: www.klyomedical.com
SIC: 3841 Surgical & medical instruments

(G-3276)
KOVER CORP
1375 Nw 97th Ave Ste 12 (33172-2855)
PHONE..................................305 888-0146
Gabriel Conti, *President*
Alejandro Burrone, *Vice Pres*
Anais Ramirez, *Sales Mgr*
EMP: 6 **EST:** 2010
SALES (est): 356.6K **Privately Held**
SIC: 2759 Commercial printing

(G-3277)
KR SOLUTIONS GROUP US LLC
1500 Nw 89th Ct Ste 115 (33172-2640)
PHONE..................................305 307-8353
Kristhian Rincon,
EMP: 5 **EST:** 2020
SALES (est): 500K **Privately Held**
SIC: 1389 Construction, repair & dismantling services

(G-3278)
KREATIVE DRIVE INC
8953 Nw 23rd St (33172-2404)
PHONE..................................786 845-8605
Rita M Valdes, *Principal*
Rita Valdes, *Principal*
Jose Otero, *Manager*
EMP: 6 **EST:** 2009
SALES (est): 426.2K **Privately Held**
WEB: www.kreativedrive.com
SIC: 2754 Stationery & invitation printing, gravure

(G-3279)
L C LA FINESTRA
2790 Nw 104th Ct (33172-2175)
PHONE..................................305 599-8093
Bruno Salvoni, *Mng Member*
◆ **EMP:** 20 **EST:** 2001
SQ FT: 13,000
SALES (est): 1.9MM **Privately Held**
WEB: www.lafinestra.us
SIC: 3442 Metal doors

(G-3280)
LA ESQUINA DEL LE BILLTO
Also Called: La Esquina Del Lechon
8601 Nw 58th St Unit 101 (33166-3312)
PHONE..................................305 477-4225
La Esquina Del Lechon, *Principal*
EMP: 26

GEOGRAPHIC

SALES (corp-wide): 2.5MM **Privately Held**
WEB: secure.esquinalechon.com
SIC: **2013** 5812 Prepared pork products from purchased pork; Mexican restaurant
PA: La Esquina Del Lechon, L.L.C.
7900 Nw 36th St
Doral FL 33166
305 640-3041

(G-3281)
LEATHERWORKS INC
9631 Nw 33rd St (33172-1100)
PHONE...........................305 471-4430
Michael Turkanis, *President*
Doris Dubay, *COO*
▲ EMP: 5 EST: 1985
SQ FT: 8,000
SALES (est): 1MM **Privately Held**
WEB: www.leatherwks.com
SIC: **3199** Equestrian related leather articles

(G-3282)
LED NATION CORP
7859 Nw 15th St (33126-1109)
PHONE...........................888 590-1720
Joaquin Gutierrez, *Principal*
EMP: 7 EST: 2020
SALES (est): 103.6K **Privately Held**
WEB: www.lednationusa.com
SIC: **3674** Semiconductors & related devices

(G-3283)
LENNOX GLOBAL LTD (HQ)
Also Called: Lgl Latin America Operations
2335 Nw 107th Ave Ste 132 (33172-2219)
PHONE...........................305 718-2921
Victor Mora, *Managing Dir*
◆ EMP: 44 EST: 1980
SALES (est): 26MM
SALES (corp-wide): 4.1B **Publicly Held**
SIC: **3585** Refrigeration & heating equipment
PA: Lennox International Inc.
2140 Lake Park Blvd
Richardson TX 75080
972 497-5000

(G-3284)
LOCKHEED MARTIN CORPORATION
7925 Nw 12th St (33126-1827)
PHONE...........................305 599-3004
Charles Holzler, *Principal*
Rigoberto Roche, *Engineer*
EMP: 435 **Publicly Held**
WEB: www.gyrocamsystems.com
SIC: **3721** Aircraft
PA: Lockheed Martin Corporation
6801 Rockledge Dr
Bethesda MD 20817

(G-3285)
LOPEZ & COMPANY INC
Also Called: Lopco Aviation
10773 Nw 58th St Ste 250 (33178-2801)
PHONE...........................305 302-3045
Jose E Lopez, *Branch Mgr*
EMP: 21
SALES (corp-wide): 737.4K **Privately Held**
SIC: **3724** Aircraft engines & engine parts
PA: Lopez & Company, Inc.
2221 Ne 164th St
Miami FL 33160
305 302-3045

(G-3286)
LORINA INC
8750 Nw 36th St Ste 260 (33178-2499)
PHONE...........................305 779-3085
Jean Pierre Barjon, *President*
Bouchra El Mansour, *Finance*
Caroline Dupoizat, *Marketing Staff*
James Grimes, *Manager*
▲ EMP: 13 EST: 2000
SALES (est): 7.9MM
SALES (corp-wide): 355.8K **Privately Held**
WEB: www.lorina.com
SIC: **2086** Lemonade: packaged in cans, bottles, etc.

HQ: Etablissements Geyer Freres
Route De Sarre Union
Munster 57670
387 016-201

(G-3287)
LTB AEROSPACE LLC
2250 Nw 102nd Pl (33172-2516)
PHONE...........................954 251-1141
Raul M Garcia, *Principal*
EMP: 9 EST: 2019
SALES (est): 2.2MM **Privately Held**
WEB: www.ltbaerospace.com
SIC: **3728** Aircraft parts & equipment

(G-3288)
LUBRICATION GLOBAL LLC
8450 Nw 56th St (33166-3327)
PHONE...........................954 239-9522
Jorge Ramos, *Mng Member*
July Ramos,
Daniel Romero,
EMP: 10 EST: 2018
SALES (est): 1.8MM **Privately Held**
WEB: www.lubricationglobal.com
SIC: **2992** Lubricating oils & greases

(G-3289)
MAMBO LLC
Also Called: Wgentv
1800 Nw 94th Ave (33172-2329)
PHONE...........................305 860-2544
Olga Echeverri, *General Mgr*
Mauricio Cruz, *Finance Mgr*
EMP: 22 EST: 2008
SALES (est): 2.1MM **Privately Held**
SIC: **3663** Radio & TV communications equipment

(G-3290)
MARAJO DIESEL POWER CORP
1950 Nw 93rd Ave (33172-2925)
PHONE...........................786 212-1485
Elias Novoa, *President*
Ana Beatriz Novoa Silva, *Vice Pres*
EMP: 7 EST: 2014
SALES (est): 816.7K **Privately Held**
WEB: www.mdpusa.com
SIC: **3511** Turbines & turbine generator set units, complete

(G-3291)
MARATHON TECHNOLOGY CORP
Also Called: Maracom Marine
8280 Nw 56th St (33166-4018)
PHONE...........................305 592-1340
Robert M Hewitt, *President*
Christine Hewitt, *Treasurer*
EMP: 11 EST: 1980
SQ FT: 6,000
SALES (est): 280.1K **Privately Held**
WEB: www.26miles.com
SIC: **3829** 5064 Thermometers & temperature sensors; radios

(G-3292)
MASAKA LLC
3105 Nw 107th Ave Ste 601 (33172-2221)
PHONE...........................786 800-8337
Alfonzo Bolivar, *CEO*
Carolina Prince, *Principal*
Carlena Prince, *Manager*
EMP: 10 EST: 2013
SALES (est): 942.6K **Privately Held**
WEB: www.masakatractors.com
SIC: **3462** 3531 Construction or mining equipment forgings, ferrous; construction machinery attachments

(G-3293)
MCCLATCHY SHARED SERVICES CTR
3511 Nw 91st Ave (33172-1243)
PHONE...........................305 740-8800
Patrick J Talamantes, *CEO*
Gary B Pruitt, *Ch of Bd*
Christian A Hendricks, *Vice Pres*
Karole M Prager, *Vice Pres*
EMP: 21 EST: 1985
SALES (est): 1.7MM **Privately Held**
SIC: **2711** Newspapers, publishing & printing

(G-3294)
MEDIA DIGITTAL LLC
8410 Nw 53rd Ter Ste 107 (33166-4540)
PHONE...........................305 506-0470
EMP: 7
SQ FT: 3,000
SALES (est): 293K **Privately Held**
SIC: **2741** 7311 7313 Internet Publishing And Broadcasting Advertising Agency Advertising Representative

(G-3295)
MEDICAL DEFENSE COMPANY INC
1300 Nw 84th Ave (33126-1500)
PHONE...........................954 614-3266
Daniel Niefeld, *Principal*
EMP: 10 EST: 2020
SALES (est): 657.5K **Privately Held**
SIC: **3069** Medical sundries, rubber

(G-3296)
MEDTRONIC USA INC
9850 Nw 41st St Ste 450 (33178-2993)
PHONE...........................786 709-4200
Randy Bright, *District Mgr*
Ruben Lopez, *Controller*
Genny Lawrence, *Sales Staff*
Michele Lucisano, *Marketing Staff*
James Hogan, *Branch Mgr*
EMP: 2510 **Privately Held**
WEB: www.medtronic.com
SIC: **3841** Surgical & medical instruments
HQ: Medtronic Usa, Inc.
710 Medtronic Pkwy
Minneapolis MN 55432
763 514-4000

(G-3297)
MERCAEREO INC
6346 Nw 99th Ave (33178-2721)
PHONE...........................305 307-0672
Mauricio Camacho, *President*
◆ EMP: 5 EST: 2001
SALES (est): 495.7K **Privately Held**
WEB: www.mercaereo.com.co
SIC: **3812** Aircraft/aerospace flight instruments & guidance systems

(G-3298)
MIAMI HERALD
3500 Nw 89th Ct (33172-1203)
PHONE...........................800 843-4372
Alexandra Villoch, *President*
Andres Oppenheimer, *Editor*
EMP: 7 EST: 2014
SALES (est): 147.8K **Privately Held**
SIC: **2711** Newspapers, publishing & printing

(G-3299)
MIAMI INDUSTRIAL MOTOR INC
8252 Nw 58th St (33166-3407)
PHONE...........................305 593-2370
Mario Garcia Jr, *President*
Ana Carolina Garcia, *Treasurer*
◆ EMP: 9 EST: 1983
SQ FT: 4,000
SALES (est): 909.5K **Privately Held**
WEB: www.miamiindustrialmotors.com
SIC: **7694** Electric motor repair

(G-3300)
MIAMI NEWS 24 INC
6874 Nw 113th Pl (33178-4547)
PHONE...........................786 331-8141
Tulio Capriles, *Principal*
EMP: 7 EST: 2015
SALES (est): 78.2K **Privately Held**
WEB: www.miaminews24.com
SIC: **2711** Newspapers: publishing only, not printed on site

(G-3301)
MIAMI OLIVEOIL & BEYOND LLC
1783 Nw 79th Ave (33126-1112)
PHONE...........................954 632-2762
Samuel Sasson, *Opers Staff*
Miguel Fernandez, *Mng Member*
EMP: 7 EST: 2014
SALES (est): 367.7K **Privately Held**
WEB: www.miaoliveoil.com
SIC: **2099** 2079 Vinegar; olive oil

(G-3302)
MIAMI TBR LLC
Also Called: Bessie Barnie
1919 Nw 82nd Ave (33126-1011)
PHONE...........................786 275-4773
Theodor Rozenberg, *Mng Member*
EMP: 9 EST: 2017
SALES (est): 411.2K **Privately Held**
WEB: www.bessieandbarnie.com
SIC: **3999** 5199 5999 Pet supplies; pet supplies; pet supplies

(G-3303)
MILANS MACHINE SHOP & WLDG SVC
8052 Nw 56th St (33166-4015)
PHONE...........................305 592-2447
Milan Baranek, *President*
Eva Baranek, *Admin Sec*
◆ EMP: 28 EST: 1974
SQ FT: 14,000
SALES (est): 2.1MM **Privately Held**
WEB: www.milansmachineshop.com
SIC: **3599** 7692 Machine shop, jobbing & repair; welding repair

(G-3304)
MIRAFLEX CORPORATION
7950 Nw 53rd St Ste 324 (33166-4791)
PHONE...........................786 380-4494
Peter J Montana, *CEO*
EMP: 5 EST: 2011
SALES (est): 422.1K **Privately Held**
WEB: www.miraflexglass.com
SIC: **3851** Eyeglasses, lenses & frames

(G-3305)
MIRAMAR COSMETIC INC
Also Called: Miramar Labs
2301 Nw 107th Ave Ste 101 (33172-2242)
PHONE...........................305 455-5016
Victor Ramirez, *CEO*
Mary Rodriguez, *Admin Sec*
▲ EMP: 10 EST: 2003
SALES (est): 864.1K **Privately Held**
WEB: www.miramarlab.com
SIC: **2844** Face creams or lotions

(G-3306)
MK AVIATION LLC
9471 Nw 12th St (33172-2803)
PHONE...........................305 825-4810
Katrina Ruiz, *Principal*
EMP: 8 EST: 2015
SALES (est): 3.1MM **Privately Held**
WEB: www.mkaviationllc.com
SIC: **3728** Aircraft parts & equipment

(G-3307)
MOOG
1525 Nw 82nd Ave (33126-1019)
PHONE...........................305 471-0444
EMP: 10 EST: 2017
SALES (est): 359.8K **Privately Held**
WEB: www.moog.com
SIC: **3812** Search & navigation equipment

(G-3308)
MORRIS VALVES INC
5590 Nw 84th Ave Ste C (33166-3335)
PHONE...........................305 477-6525
William Mogollon, *President*
Miriam Escalante, *Vice Pres*
EMP: 7 EST: 2010
SALES (est): 386.5K **Privately Held**
WEB: www.morrisvalve.com
SIC: **3491** Industrial valves
PA: Morris Industrial Supplier, C.A.
Carrera Caura, Torre Nekuina
Puerto Ordaz

(G-3309)
MVR COPIADORAS DIGITALES
9649 Nw 33rd St (33172-1100)
PHONE...........................786 366-1842
Luis A Rueda, *Owner*
EMP: 5 EST: 2013
SALES (est): 483.8K **Privately Held**
SIC: **3571** Computers, digital, analog or hybrid

(G-3310)
NAVISTAR INC
8600 Nw 36th St Ste 304 (33166-6651)
PHONE...........................305 513-2255

2022 Harris Florida
Manufacturers Directory

▲ = Import ▼=Export
◆ =Import/Export

Cesar Longo, *Sales Staff*
Jackie Farinas, *Manager*
EMP: 16
SALES (corp-wide): 283.1B **Privately Held**
WEB: www.internationaltrucks.com
SIC: 3711 Truck & tractor truck assembly
HQ: Navistar, Inc.
2701 Navistar Dr
Lisle IL 60532
331 332-5000

(G-3311)
NEW CONCEPTS DISTRS INTL LLC
Also Called: Ncdi
2315 Nw 107th Ave Ste 1b5 (33172-2164)
P.O. Box 227847, Miami (33222-7847)
PHONE...................................305 463-8735
Janice Santiago, *Mng Member*
EMP: 10 **EST:** 2010
SQ FT: 5,000
SALES (est): 982.1K **Privately Held**
WEB: www.ncdiusa.com
SIC: 2342 2339 2251 5137 Bras, girdles & allied garments; foundation garments, women's; women's & misses' athletic clothing & sportswear; women's hosiery, except socks; women's & children's lingerie & undergarments

(G-3312)
NOBEL AEROSPACE LLC
1532 Nw 89th Ct (33172-2647)
PHONE...................................786 210-0716
Juan Benitez, *Manager*
EMP: 8 **EST:** 2014
SALES (est): 824.5K **Privately Held**
WEB: www.nobaero.com
SIC: 3721 Aircraft

(G-3313)
NOVAGROUP LLC (PA)
3470 Nw 82nd Ave Ste 790 (33122-1043)
PHONE...................................305 471-4824
Jorge Nieves, *COO*
Luis Oliveros, *Purch Mgr*
▼ **EMP:** 6 **EST:** 2012
SQ FT: 5,000
SALES (est): 1.8MM **Privately Held**
SIC: 3357 Communication wire

(G-3314)
NUPRESS OF MIAMI INC
2050 Nw 94th Ave (33172-2331)
PHONE...................................305 594-2100
Enrique F De La Vega, *President*
Leslie Perez, *Manager*
Henry Reynoso, *Manager*
Greg Rosen, *Manager*
Ricky Vega, *Info Tech Mgr*
▼ **EMP:** 50 **EST:** 1995
SQ FT: 45,000
SALES (est): 11.5MM **Privately Held**
WEB: www.nupress.com
SIC: 2752 Commercial printing, offset

(G-3315)
O MUSTAD & SON USA INC
2315 Nw 107th Ave Ste 88 (33172-2117)
PHONE...................................206 284-7871
Lars Lemhag, *President*
Edward Galka, *General Mgr*
◆ **EMP:** 39 **EST:** 1969
SQ FT: 56,000
SALES (est): 2.2MM **Privately Held**
SIC: 3949 Hooks, fishing
PA: O Mustad & Son As
Raufossvegen 40
Gjovik 2821

(G-3316)
OCTAMETRO LLC
8539 Nw 56th St (33166-3328)
PHONE...................................305 715-9713
Fernando Rodriguez, *Office Mgr*
William Rodriguez, *Office Mgr*
Fernando Rodrguez, *Manager*
Jose Aylagas,
▲ **EMP:** 7 **EST:** 2007
SQ FT: 2,030
SALES (est): 1MM **Privately Held**
WEB: www.octametro.com
SIC: 2599 Furniture & fixtures

(G-3317)
OMZ INDUSTRIES LLC
6010 Nw 99th Ave Unit 102 (33178-2723)
PHONE...................................786 210-6763
Omar Zemmama, *Branch Mgr*
EMP: 14
SALES (corp-wide): 400.5K **Privately Held**
WEB: www.hzindustry.us
SIC: 3999 Barber & beauty shop equipment
PA: Omz Industries Llc
3363 Sheridan St Ste 214
Hollywood FL

(G-3318)
ON-BOARD MEDIA INC
Also Called: Onboard Media
8400 Nw 36th St Ste 500 (33166-6620)
PHONE...................................305 673-0400
Marissa Cosculluela, *President*
Rina Alvarado, *Opers Staff*
Tim Kern, *Human Res Mgr*
Kristy Masters, *VP Sales*
Nyla Christian, *Sales Mgr*
◆ **EMP:** 90 **EST:** 1990
SQ FT: 13,000
SALES (est): 11.9MM
SALES (corp-wide): 503.8MM **Privately Held**
WEB: www.onboard.com
SIC: 2721 4724 7819 2731 Magazines: publishing only, not printed on site; travel agencies; services allied to motion pictures; book publishing
PA: Lvmh Moet Hennessy Louis Vuitton
22 Avenue Montaigne
Paris 75008
962 177-144

(G-3319)
ORIGINAL PNGUIN DRECT OPRTIONS
3000 Nw 107th Ave (33172-2133)
PHONE...................................305 592-2830
John Griffin, *Principal*
EMP: 11 **EST:** 2010
SALES (est): 440.9K **Privately Held**
WEB: www.originalpenguin.com
SIC: 2325 5621 5944 Men's & boys' trousers & slacks; women's clothing stores; watches

(G-3320)
OZINGA SOUTH FLORIDA INC
Also Called: Ozingaready Mix
3905 Nw 107th Ave Ste 106 (33178-2785)
PHONE...................................305 594-2828
EMP: 46
SALES (corp-wide): 1.6MM **Privately Held**
WEB: www.ozinga.com
SIC: 3273 Ready-mixed concrete
PA: Ozinga South Florida, Inc.
2401 College Ave
Davie FL 33317
786 422-4694

(G-3321)
PARAMOUNT DEPOT LLC
7975 Nw 56th St (33166-4012)
PHONE...................................786 275-0107
Rafael Dominguez, *CEO*
Paramount-Yud Gonzalez, *General Mgr*
Sandra Porras, *Vice Pres*
James C Kennedy, *CFO*
◆ **EMP:** 19 **EST:** 2005
SALES (est): 2.7MM **Privately Held**
WEB: www.paramountdepot.com
SIC: 1411 5031 3088 3646 Granite dimension stone; flagstone mining; quartzite, dimension-quarrying; lumber, plywood & millwork; kitchen cabinets; plastics plumbing fixtures; fluorescent lighting fixtures, commercial

(G-3322)
PARINTO GLOBAL ENTERPRISES LLC
Also Called: Tres Leches Factory & Beyond
5213 Nw 79th Ave (33166-4715)
PHONE...................................305 606-3107
Cesar A Liccardo,
Luisa V Liccardo,
Jose C Ortiz,

EMP: 7 **EST:** 2008
SALES (est): 520.8K **Privately Held**
SIC: 2051 Bakery: wholesale or wholesale/retail combined

(G-3323)
PARKER DAVIS HVAC INTL INC
Also Called: Highseer.com
3250 Nw 107th Ave (33172-2137)
PHONE...................................305 513-4488
Baran Gokce, *CEO*
EMP: 50 **EST:** 2000
SALES (est): 6.7MM **Privately Held**
WEB: www.pdhvac.com
SIC: 3585 5075 Air conditioning equipment, complete; air conditioning units, complete: domestic or industrial; heat pumps, electric; heating & air conditioning combination units; air conditioning & ventilation equipment & supplies

(G-3324)
PERKINS POWER CORP
Also Called: Southeast Diesel
5820 Nw 84th Ave (33166-3313)
PHONE...................................904 278-9919
Thomas J Tracy III, *CEO*
Chuck Scott, *General Mgr*
Alexander Colon Sr, *CFO*
Jason Miller, *Sales Mgr*
Jerry Rose, *Manager*
◆ **EMP:** 19 **EST:** 1978
SALES (est): 5.4MM **Privately Held**
SIC: 3621 Motors & generators
PA: Southeast Power Group, Inc.
5820 Nw 84th Ave
Doral FL 33166

(G-3325)
PERRY ELLIS INTERNATIONAL INC (HQ)
3000 Nw 107th Ave (33172-2133)
PHONE...................................305 592-2830
Oscar Feldenkreis, *President*
Luis Avila, *General Mgr*
Bility Yim, *Managing Dir*
Dawna Ryan, *Area Mgr*
Bradley Arkin, *Exec VP*
EMP: 350 **EST:** 1967
SQ FT: 240,000
SALES (est): 874.8MM **Privately Held**
WEB: www.pery.com
SIC: 2325 2339 2337 5611 Men's & boys' trousers & slacks; men's & boys' dress slacks & shorts; women's & misses' outerwear; women's & misses' suits & coats; men's & boys' clothing stores; women's clothing stores; men's & boys' dress shirts
PA: Feldenkreis Holdings Llc
3000 Nw 107th Ave
Doral FL 33172
305 592-2830

(G-3326)
PHELPS DODGE INTL CORP (DH)
9850 Nw 41st St Ste 200 (33178-2987)
P.O. Box 942286, Miami (33194-2286)
PHONE...................................305 648-7888
Mathias Sandoval, *President*
Chris Kesl, *Vice Pres*
Keith Macintosh, *Vice Pres*
Walter Barinaga, *Purch Dir*
Juan Arizpe, *Human Res Mgr*
◆ **EMP:** 30 **EST:** 1956
SQ FT: 12,000
SALES (est): 46.1MM **Privately Held**
WEB: www.dodge.com
SIC: 3357 3315 8742 Nonferrous wire-drawing & insulating; steel wire & related products; industrial consultant
HQ: Prysmian Cables And Systems Usa, Llc
4 Tesseneer Dr
Highland Heights KY 41076
859 572-8000

(G-3327)
PHOENIX JEWELRY MFG INC
Also Called: Pjm
1499 Nw 79th Ave (33126-1609)
PHONE...................................305 477-2515
Ira Nusbaum, *Corp Secy*
Fred Nusbaum, *Purch Dir*
Fred Nausbaum, *Director*

EMP: 10 **EST:** 1992
SQ FT: 5,000
SALES (est): 1.6MM **Privately Held**
SIC: 3911 5094 Jewelry, precious metal; jewelry

(G-3328)
PIECEMAKERS LLC
5521 Nw 78th Ave (33166-4119)
PHONE...................................786 517-1829
Andres Tamayo, *Purch Mgr*
Francisco Villasante Jr, *Mng Member*
Llobal Alonso,
Alfredo Hernandez,
Jose Mayorga,
EMP: 10 **EST:** 2010
SALES (est): 1MM **Privately Held**
WEB: www.piece-makers.com
SIC: 3441 Fabricated structural metal

(G-3329)
PILKINGTON NORTH AMERICA INC
8850 Nw 24th Ter (33172-2418)
PHONE...................................305 470-1813
Jason Alonson, *Branch Mgr*
EMP: 7 **Privately Held**
WEB: www.pilkington.com
SIC: 3211 Flat glass
HQ: Pilkington North America, Inc.
811 Madison Ave Fl 3
Toledo OH 43604
419 247-3731

(G-3330)
PMF TECH CORP
11411 Nw 74th Ter (33178-1579)
PHONE...................................786 636-7021
Paolo D Francini, *Principal*
EMP: 7 **EST:** 2013
SALES (est): 284.7K **Privately Held**
WEB: www.pmftechcorp.com
SIC: 3221 5999 Bottles for packing, bottling & canning: glass; packaging materials: boxes, padding, etc.

(G-3331)
POTTER ROEMER LLC
8306 Nw 14th St (33126-1504)
PHONE...................................786 845-0842
Romer Potter, *Principal*
EMP: 18
SALES (corp-wide): 85MM **Privately Held**
WEB: www.potterroemer.com
SIC: 3669 Emergency alarms
HQ: Potter Roemer, Llc
17451 Hurley St
City Of Industry CA 91744
626 855-4890

(G-3332)
POWERPUMP LLC
11447 Nw 34th St (33178-1831)
PHONE...................................305 514-3030
Ben Yahia, *Mng Member*
EMP: 23
SALES (est): 939.1K **Privately Held**
SIC: 3694 Battery charging generators, automobile & aircraft

(G-3333)
PPG INDUSTRIES INC
1376 Nw 78th Ave (33126-1606)
PHONE...................................305 477-0541
EMP: 24
SALES (corp-wide): 15.3B **Publicly Held**
SIC: 2851 Mfg Misc Products
PA: Ppg Industries, Inc.
1 Ppg Pl
Pittsburgh PA 15272
412 434-3131

(G-3334)
PRECISION MACHINE TECH LLC
4083 Nw 79th Ave (33166-6519)
PHONE...................................305 594-1789
Wolfgang Reimann,
EMP: 11 **EST:** 2011

GEOGRAPHIC

SALES (est): 757.9K **Privately Held**
WEB: www.pmt-industries.com
SIC: **3599** 3841 3484 Machine shop, jobbing & repair; electrical discharge machining (EDM); surgical & medical instruments; instruments, microsurgical: except electromedical; guns (firearms) or gun parts, 30 mm. & below

(G-3335)
PRECISION MOLD TECH INC
4083 Nw 79th Ave (33166-6519)
P.O. Box 667748, Miami (33166-9405)
PHONE....................305 594-1789
Enrique Dobrilla, *President*
Govita Dobrilla, *Vice Pres*
EMP: 9 EST: 1987
SQ FT: 6,000
SALES (est): 833.7K **Privately Held**
WEB: www.precisionmoldremoval.com
SIC: **3089** Laminating of plastic

(G-3336)
PRESTRESSED SYSTEMS INC
11405 Nw 112th Ct (33178-2163)
PHONE....................305 556-6699
Vega Emilio R, *Principal*
EMP: 14 EST: 2015
SALES (est): 1.1MM **Privately Held**
WEB: www.spimiami.com
SIC: **3272** Prestressed concrete products

(G-3337)
PRINT MOTION INC
8000 Nw 31st St Ste 4 (33122-1050)
PHONE....................786 212-1817
EMP: 9
SALES (corp-wide): 279.4K **Privately Held**
WEB: www.printmotion.us
SIC: **2752** Commercial printing, offset
PA: Print Motion Inc
180 State St Ste 225
Southlake TX 76092
305 851-7206

(G-3338)
PRISION BREWING CO LLC
8302 Nw 14th St (33126-1504)
PHONE....................305 487-2780
Juan Pipkin, *CEO*
EMP: 14 EST: 2020
SALES (est): 1MM **Privately Held**
WEB: www.prisionpals.com
SIC: **2082** Beer (alcoholic beverage)

(G-3339)
PROFESSIONAL PET PRODUCTS INC
Also Called: P P P
1873 Nw 97th Ave (33172-2303)
PHONE....................305 592-1992
John Plant, *President*
Donna Plant, *Corp Secy*
▼ EMP: 30 EST: 1983
SQ FT: 7,000
SALES (est): 3.4MM **Privately Held**
WEB: www.professionalpetproducts.com
SIC: **3999** 3841 Pet supplies; surgical & medical instruments

(G-3340)
PURE SOURCE LLC
Also Called: Pure Source, The
9750 Nw 17th St (33172-2753)
PHONE....................305 477-8111
Manny Garcia, *CFO*
Jared Meyerson, *Manager*
Joel Meyerson,
EMP: 35 EST: 2015
SALES (est): 11.6MM **Privately Held**
WEB: www.thepuresource.com
SIC: **2844** Cosmetic preparations

(G-3341)
QUAD INTL INCORPORATED
Also Called: Score Group, The
1629 Nw 84th Ave (33126-1031)
P.O. Box 558150, Miami (33255-8150)
PHONE....................305 662-5959
John Fox, *President*
Rafael Trinidad, *Software Dev*
Daniel Wade, *Technician*
EMP: 36 EST: 1993
SQ FT: 20,000

SALES (est): 4.4MM **Privately Held**
WEB: www.scorepass.com
SIC: **2741** 2721 Miscellaneous publishing; periodicals

(G-3342)
QUICK LIFT INC
8491 Nw 54th St (33166-3320)
PHONE....................305 471-0147
Salvador Piles, *President*
Maria Piles, *Vice Pres*
▼ EMP: 6 EST: 1995
SQ FT: 5,000
SALES (est): 897.6K **Privately Held**
WEB: www.quicklift.com
SIC: **3536** Davits

(G-3343)
R S APPAREL INC
8454 Nw 58th St (33166-3302)
PHONE....................305 599-4939
Rudolph Depass, *President*
Audrey Degen, *Director*
◆ EMP: 10 EST: 1997
SALES (est): 938.2K **Privately Held**
WEB: www.rsapparel.com
SIC: **2221** Apparel & outerwear fabric, manmade fiber or silk

(G-3344)
RADICA LLC
10471 Nw 36th St (33178-4367)
PHONE....................954 383-0089
Cristina Barreto, *President*
EMP: 8 EST: 2017
SALES (est): 330.8K **Privately Held**
SIC: **2431** Doors & door parts & trim, wood

(G-3345)
RAMI TECHNOLOGY USA LLC
Also Called: Raltron Electronics
10400 Nw 33rd St Ste 290 (33172-5904)
PHONE....................305 593-6033
Ross Weiss, *Vice Pres*
Richard Knecht, *CFO*
Alexandre Wolloch,
EMP: 6 EST: 2012
SALES (est): 2.3MM **Privately Held**
WEB: www.raltron.com
SIC: **3679** Electronic circuits

(G-3346)
REDERICK METAL INDUSTRIES
9550 Nw 12th St Ste 12 (33172-2831)
PHONE....................305 396-3396
Guillermo R Thomas, *Branch Mgr*
EMP: 21
SALES (corp-wide): 288.6K **Privately Held**
SIC: **3999** Barber & beauty shop equipment
PA: Rederick Metal Industries Corp
1933 Nw 21st Ter
Miami FL 33142
305 396-3396

(G-3347)
REPWIRE LLC
5500 Nw 106th Ct (33178-6635)
PHONE....................786 486-1823
Bernardo Pigna, *Mng Member*
Josefina Ruan,
EMP: 2 EST: 2014
SALES (est): 9MM **Privately Held**
SIC: **3315** Wire & fabricated wire products

(G-3348)
RESTIFO INVESTMENTS LLC
Also Called: Unlimited Impressions
1424 Nw 82nd Ave (33126-1508)
PHONE....................305 468-0013
Eligio Restifo,
Reinaldo Restifo,
EMP: 10 EST: 2009
SALES (est): 948.7K **Privately Held**
WEB: www.uiprints.com
SIC: **2754** Commercial printing, gravure

(G-3349)
ROBERLO USA INC
8501 Nw 17th St Ste 103 (33126-1099)
PHONE....................786 334-6191
Jaume Juher, *President*
George Trach, *Area Mgr*
Sergi Balbin, *Warehouse Mgr*
Jaume Bermudez, *Director*

EMP: 16 EST: 2011
SALES (est): 5.2MM
SALES (corp-wide): 1MM **Privately Held**
WEB: en.roberlo.us
SIC: **2851** Paints & allied products
HQ: Roberlo Sa
Carretera Nacional Ii (Paratge L Hostal Nou), Km 706,5
Riudellots De La Selva 17457
972 478-060

(G-3350)
RONTAN NORTH AMERICA INC
7859 Nw 46th St Ste 5b (33166-5470)
P.O. Box 226362, Miami (33222-6362)
PHONE....................305 599-2974
EMP: 20
SALES (est): 2.9MM **Privately Held**
SIC: **3647** Mfg Vehicle Lighting Equipment

(G-3351)
ROSUCA INTERNATIONAL LLC
5639 Nw 113th Ct (33178-3856)
PHONE....................305 332-5572
Roman Rodriguez, *Mng Member*
EMP: 6 EST: 2017
SALES (est): 470.9K **Privately Held**
WEB: www.rosucainternational.com
SIC: **3462** 4731 Gear & chain forgings; foreign freight forwarding

(G-3352)
ROVER AEROSPACE INC
Also Called: Altima Technology Devices
2254 Nw 94th Ave (33172-2333)
PHONE....................305 594-7799
George Delapaz, *President*
Gio Fagueroa, *Admin Sec*
EMP: 7 EST: 2000
SALES (est): 787.7K **Privately Held**
SIC: **3812** Acceleration indicators & systems components, aerospace; aircraft/aerospace flight instruments & guidance systems

(G-3353)
ROYAL ANCIENT SUPERFOODS
10530 Nw 37th Ter (33178-4209)
PHONE....................305 600-1747
Daniel Blanco, *Owner*
EMP: 7 EST: 2016
SALES (est): 103.1K **Privately Held**
SIC: **2068** Seeds: dried, dehydrated, salted or roasted

(G-3354)
RUBYQUARTZ TECHNOLOGY LLC
10400 Nw 33rd St Ste 290 (33172-5904)
PHONE....................305 406-0211
Alexander Wolloch, *Mng Member*
EMP: 12 EST: 2010
SALES (est): 1.4MM **Privately Held**
WEB: www.rubyquartz.com
SIC: **3559** Electronic component making machinery

(G-3355)
RVR USA LLC
Also Called: Rvr Elettronica
7782 Nw 46th St 20 (33166-5460)
PHONE....................305 471-9091
Valentino Biavati, *President*
Angel Ylisastigui, *Director*
▲ EMP: 5 EST: 2000
SALES (est): 430.2K **Privately Held**
WEB: www.rvrusa.com
SIC: **3663** Radio & TV communications equipment

(G-3356)
SANCHELIMA INTERNATIONAL INC
1783 Nw 93rd Ave (33172-2921)
PHONE....................305 591-4343
Juan Sanchelima, *President*
Estelle Sanchelima, *Treasurer*
Armando Suarez, *Technology*
◆ EMP: 14 EST: 1980
SQ FT: 5,400

SALES (est): 3.6MM **Privately Held**
WEB: www.sanchelimainternational.com
SIC: **3523** 5083 3556 Barn, silo, poultry, dairy & livestock machinery; dairy machinery & equipment; dairy & milk machinery; homogenizing machinery: dairy, fruit, vegetable; pasteurizing equipment, dairy machinery

(G-3357)
SAZON INC
2000 Nw 92nd Ave (33172-2928)
PHONE....................305 591-9785
Jose A Ortega, *President*
Frank R Unanue Jr, *Vice Pres*
Joseph Unanue, *Vice Pres*
Hiram Carlo, *Plant Mgr*
Javier Madrigal, *Purchasing*
▼ EMP: 29 EST: 1983
SQ FT: 37,500
SALES (est): 8.6MM **Privately Held**
WEB: www.sazonhp.com
SIC: **2099** Spices, including grinding

(G-3358)
SDKC CORP
Also Called: Certapro Painters Centl Miami
9624 Nw 47th Ter (33178-2087)
PHONE....................305 469-7578
Villani-Vertesch Carla, *Principal*
EMP: 11 EST: 2014
SALES (est): 667.6K **Privately Held**
SIC: **3732** Boat building & repairing

(G-3359)
SEGUTRONIC INTERNATIONAL INC
11042 Nw 72nd Ter (33178-3663)
PHONE....................305 463-8551
Fax: 305 463-8552
EMP: 7 EST: 1989
SALES: 1MM **Privately Held**
SIC: **3699** Mfg Electrical Equipment/Supplies

(G-3360)
SEPRONET INC
11042 Nw 72nd Ter (33178-3663)
PHONE....................305 463-8551
EMP: 12
SALES (est): 1.1MM **Privately Held**
SIC: **3699** Mfg Electrical Equipment/Supplies

(G-3361)
SEVEN DEFENSES CORPORATION
10550 Nw 74th St Unit 202 (33178-2475)
PHONE....................786 448-5701
Suarez Diaz, *Principal*
EMP: 10 EST: 2015
SALES (est): 130.7K **Privately Held**
SIC: **3812** Defense systems & equipment

(G-3362)
SEVEN GROUP USA INC
1681 Nw 79th Ave (33126-1105)
PHONE....................305 392-9193
Mariela B Aparicio, *President*
EMP: 8 EST: 2017
SALES (est): 145.3K **Privately Held**
SIC: **3086** Packaging & shipping materials, foamed plastic

(G-3363)
SHIELD PRODUCTS INC
6010 Nw 99th Ave Unit 110 (33178-2723)
PHONE....................904 880-6060
Juan P Saenz PHD, *Principal*
EMP: 8 EST: 2015
SALES (est): 676.1K **Privately Held**
WEB: www.shieldproducts.com
SIC: **2899** Chemical preparations

(G-3364)
SHIMA GROUP CORP
10836 Nw 27th St (33172-5907)
PHONE....................305 463-0288
Fax: 305 262-2155
EMP: 7
SQ FT: 3,000
SALES (est): 790K **Privately Held**
SIC: **2752** Lithographic Commercial Printing

(G-3365)
SI AEROSPACE GROUP INC
10877 Nw 33rd St (33172-2188)
PHONE.................................786 384-2338
EMP: 7 EST: 2015
SALES (est): 117.6K Privately Held
SIC: 3721 Aircraft

(G-3366)
SIKE USA INC
3004 Nw 82nd Ave (33122-1042)
PHONE.................................786 331-4020
Jorge E Tovar, President
Juana I Tovar, Admin Sec
EMP: 8 EST: 2012
SALES (est): 678.8K Privately Held
WEB: www.sikeusa.com
SIC: 3999 5191 Grasses, artificial & pre-
served; seeds: field, garden & flower

(G-3367)
SILIGOM USA LLC
5930 Nw 99th Ave Unit 9 (33178-2710)
PHONE.................................786 406-6262
Juan J Portela Zardetto, Mng Member
Maria L Francetich,
▲ EMP: 8 EST: 2006
SALES (est): 237.4K Privately Held
WEB: www.siligom.com
SIC: 3452 5085 Washers; gaskets

(G-3368)
SOLE INC
8029 Nw 54th St (33166-4004)
PHONE.................................305 513-2603
Gabriel Cardenas, President
▲ EMP: 5 EST: 2000
SALES (est): 510K Privately Held
WEB: www.soleinc.net
SIC: 2519 Garden furniture, except wood,
metal, stone or concrete

(G-3369)
SOUTH FLORIDA PALLETS DIST
1951 Nw 89th Pl Ste 100 (33172-2606)
PHONE.................................305 330-7663
Joel Gil, Principal
EMP: 12 EST: 2017
SALES (est): 347.3K Privately Held
WEB: www.sfpallets.com
SIC: 2448 Pallets, wood

(G-3370)
**SOUTHEAST POWER GROUP
INC (PA)**
Also Called: Perkins Power
5820 Nw 84th Ave (33166-3313)
PHONE.................................305 592-9745
Thomas J Tracy III, President
Steve Cathels, Prdtn Mgr
Rick Mendez, Warehouse Mgr
Juan Monreal, Sales Dir
Mike Braswell, Sales Staff
◆ EMP: 60 EST: 1976
SQ FT: 40,000
SALES (est): 32.6MM Privately Held
WEB: www.deere.com
SIC: 3494 3621 5084 5013 Pipe fittings;
generators & sets, electric; industrial ma-
chinery & equipment; motor vehicle sup-
plies & new parts

(G-3371)
SPANISH PERI & BK SLS INC
Also Called: Publicaciones Internacional
2105 Nw 102nd Ave (33172-2243)
PHONE.................................305 592-3919
Arthur Gelfand, President
Joe Bohorques, Exec VP
Daniel Gelfand, Vice Pres
▼ EMP: 75 EST: 1974
SQ FT: 30,000
SALES (est): 4.2MM Privately Held
SIC: 2721 5192 Magazines: publishing
only, not printed on site; magazines

(G-3372)
**SPECIALTY FOOD GROUP LLC
(HQ)**
9835 Nw 14th St (33172-2756)
PHONE.................................305 392-5000
Wissam Amoudi,
▲ EMP: 2 EST: 2009

SALES (est): 27.2MM
SALES (corp-wide): 144.9MM Privately
Held
SIC: 2096 Corn chips & other corn-based
snacks
PA: Sam's Group Of Companies, Inc.
9835 Nw 14th St
Doral FL 33172
305 392-5000

(G-3373)
SPLIFFPUFF LLC
6961 Nw 111th Ave (33178-3716)
PHONE.................................786 493-4529
Sebastian Arenas,
EMP: 10 EST: 2019
SALES (est): 283.1K Privately Held
SIC: 3999 Tobacco pipes, pipestems & bits

(G-3374)
SSEMIAMI CORPORATION
Also Called: Severstal Export Miami Corp.
8350 Nw 52nd Ter Ste 408 (33166-7709)
PHONE.................................305 322-1890
Adalberto Torres, President
EMP: 18 EST: 2009
SALES (est): 592.2K Privately Held
SIC: 1081 Metal mining services
PA: Severstal, Pao
D. 30 Ul. Mira
Cherepovets 16260

(G-3375)
STARLOCK INC
Also Called: Elc Security Products
8252 Nw 30th Ter (33122-1914)
PHONE.................................305 477-2303
Alberto L Castro, President
▲ EMP: 8 EST: 2000
SALES (est): 1.3MM Privately Held
WEB: www.elc.com.br
SIC: 2673 2677 2754 Bags: plastic, lami-
nated & coated; envelopes; seals:
gravure printing

(G-3376)
**STELLAR GROUP OF SOUTH
FLORIDA**
5574 Nw 79th Ave (33166-4124)
PHONE.................................305 715-7246
Robin A Watkin, Principal
EMP: 7 EST: 2012
SALES (est): 69K Privately Held
WEB: www.stellar305.com
SIC: 3651 Household audio & video equip-
ment

(G-3377)
STONE CRAFT MASTERS LLC
7975 Nw 54th St (33166-4027)
PHONE.................................786 401-7060
Yoel Cruz, Mng Member
Christian Carlesi,
EMP: 11 EST: 2019
SQ FT: 15,000
SALES (est): 1.8MM Privately Held
WEB: www.stonecraftmasters.com
SIC: 3281 Cut stone & stone products

(G-3378)
STONEXCHANGE INC
9605 Nw 13th St (33172-2813)
PHONE.................................305 513-9795
Volkan O Yazici, President
◆ EMP: 12 EST: 2005
SALES (est): 513.3K Privately Held
WEB: www.windowsills.com
SIC: 3272 Thresholds, precast terrazzo

(G-3379)
STRENA MEDICAL LLC
3016 Nw 82nd Ave (33122-1042)
PHONE.................................305 406-3931
EMP: 7 EST: 2017
SALES (est): 79.9K Privately Held
WEB: www.strenamedical.com
SIC: 3841 Surgical & medical instruments

(G-3380)
**STRUCTRAL PRESTRESSED
INDS INC**
Also Called: SPI
11405 Nw 112th Ct (33178-2163)
PHONE.................................305 556-6699
Emilio R Vega, President

Oswaldo Nordelo, Prdtn Mgr
Jorge Hernandez, Opers Staff
Edmundo Bendana, Engineer
Michelle Riera, Comptroller
◆ EMP: 100 EST: 1996
SALES (est): 13.2MM Privately Held
WEB: www.spimiami.com
SIC: 3272 Joists, concrete

(G-3381)
STUART-DEAN CO INC
2279 Nw 102nd Pl (33172-2523)
PHONE.................................305 652-9595
Eric Dwyer, Sales Staff
Mitchell Figueroa, Sales Staff
Mary Ann Degan, Branch Mgr
EMP: 33
SALES (corp-wide): 65.4MM Privately
Held
WEB: www.stuartdean.com
SIC: 3471 Finishing, metals or formed
products
PA: Stuart-Dean Co. Inc.
4350 10th St
Long Island City NY 11101
800 322-3180

(G-3382)
SUN ORCHARD LLC (PA)
8600 Nw 36th St Ste 250 (33166-6651)
PHONE.................................786 646-9200
Marc Isaacs, President
Jean-Marc Rotsaert, Chairman
Deena Pitzele, Vice Pres
Kevin Mason, Purch Mgr
Kim Hansen, QC Mgr
▲ EMP: 35 EST: 1988
SALES (est): 65.2MM Privately Held
WEB: www.sunorchard.com
SIC: 2033 2037 Fruit juices: fresh; fruit
juices, frozen

(G-3383)
SUN PAPER COMPANY
7925 Nw 12th St Ste 321 (33126-1846)
PHONE.................................305 887-0040
Jose R Salgado Sr, President
Carlos M Salgado, Vice Pres
Graciela Salgado, Vice Pres
Jose Salgado Jr, Vice Pres
Rita Rodriguez, Treasurer
▼ EMP: 45 EST: 1990
SQ FT: 65,000
SALES (est): 11.5MM Privately Held
WEB: www.royalpaper.us
SIC: 2621 Napkin stock, paper; tissue
paper; toweling tissue, paper

(G-3384)
SUNSHINE BOTTLING CO
Also Called: Ironbeer Soft Drink
8447 Nw 54th St (33166-3320)
PHONE.................................305 592-4366
Carlos R Blanco, President
Teresa Trujillo, Vice Pres
Olga Fornet, Finance
Richard Barnes, CIO
Myra Blanco, Admin Sec
◆ EMP: 29 EST: 1992
SALES (est): 6.7MM Privately Held
WEB: www.sunshinebottling.com
SIC: 2086 Soft drinks: packaged in cans,
bottles, etc.; fruit drinks (less than 100%
juice): packaged in cans, etc.

(G-3385)
**SUPERIOR TRUSS SYSTEMS
INC**
8500 Nw 58th St (33166-3304)
P.O. Box 558247, Miami (33255-8247)
PHONE.................................305 591-9918
Juan Duarte, President
Armelio Gomez, Vice Pres
Patrick Gomez, Manager
EMP: 70 EST: 1978
SQ FT: 130,000
SALES (est): 9.8MM Privately Held
WEB: www.superiortrusses.com
SIC: 2439 Trusses, wooden roof

(G-3386)
**SUPREME INTERNATIONAL LLC
(DH)**
Also Called: Rafaella
3000 Nw 107th Ave (33172-2133)
P.O. Box 21562, Louisville KY (40221-
0562)
PHONE.................................305 592-2830
William V Roberti, President
George Narino, Senior VP
Ronald G Threadgill, Senior VP
Terri Gonzalez, Vice Pres
Moises Kurny, Natl Sales Mgr
◆ EMP: 712 EST: 2002
SQ FT: 190,000
SALES (est): 271.7MM
SALES (corp-wide): 874.8MM Privately
Held
WEB: www.pery.com
SIC: 2331 2325 Women's & misses'
blouses & shirts; men's & boys' trousers &
slacks; shorts (outerwear): men's, youths'
& boys'; jeans: men's, youths' & boys'
HQ: Perry Ellis International Inc
3000 Nw 107th Ave
Doral FL 33172
305 592-2830

(G-3387)
SURVEY SUPPLIES INC
1779 Nw 79th Ave (33126-1112)
PHONE.................................305 477-1555
Charles F Brian, President
▼ EMP: 6 EST: 1954
SQ FT: 5,000
SALES (est): 705.8K Privately Held
WEB: www.surveying.com
SIC: 3829 Measuring & controlling devices

(G-3388)
SURVIVOR INDUSTRIES INC
9399 Nw 13th St (33172-2807)
PHONE.................................805 385-5560
Howard Wallace, President
Linda Wallace, Corp Secy
▲ EMP: 35 EST: 1983
SALES (est): 1.8MM Privately Held
SIC: 2099 Food preparations

(G-3389)
**SYSTEMONE TECHNOLOGIES
INC (PA)**
8305 Nw 27th St Ste 107 (33122-1934)
PHONE.................................305 593-8015
Paul I Mansur, President
◆ EMP: 6 EST: 1990
SQ FT: 62,000
SALES (est): 1.6MM Privately Held
WEB: www.systemonetechnologies.com
SIC: 3559 Degreasing machines, automo-
tive & industrial

(G-3390)
TAK PAPER CORP
10773 Nw 58th St Ste 651 (33178-2801)
PHONE.................................786 287-8900
EMP: 8
SALES (est): 400K Privately Held
SIC: 2674 Mfg Bags-Uncoated Paper

(G-3391)
TAP EXPRESS INC
9625 Nw 33rd St (33172-1100)
PHONE.................................305 468-0038
Michael Walther, President
◆ EMP: 5 EST: 1984
SQ FT: 4,000
SALES (est): 712.5K Privately Held
WEB: www.supertap.eu
SIC: 3131 Heel parts for shoes; top lifts,
shoe & boot

(G-3392)
TECHNET CORP
10595 Nw 43rd Ter (33178-2265)
PHONE.................................305 582-5369
Andreas Jena, President
EMP: 7 EST: 2009
SALES (est): 238.5K Privately Held
WEB: www.technetllc.com
SIC: 3621 Electric motor & generator parts

G
E
O
G
R
A
P
H
I
C

(G-3393)
TECHNO CABINETS INC
1681 Nw 97th Ave (33172-2817)
PHONE..305 910-9929
Jesus L Govea, *President*
EMP: 7 EST: 2015
SALES (est): 375.6K **Privately Held**
WEB: www.technocabinets305.com
SIC: 2434 5211 1751 Wood kitchen cabinets; tile, ceramic; window & door installation & erection

(G-3394)
TECKNO CORP
8640 Nw 101st Pl (33178-2626)
PHONE..305 677-3487
Alejandro Paliz, *President*
EMP: 8 EST: 2010
SALES (est): 224.1K **Privately Held**
SIC: 3494 Pipe fittings

(G-3395)
TEKTROL INC
11013 Nw 30th St (33172-5070)
PHONE..305 305-0937
William F Astbury, *President*
EMP: 11 EST: 2000
SALES (est): 154.2K **Privately Held**
SIC: 2759 Embossing on paper

(G-3396)
TERRAFERMA USA CORPORATION
2201 Nw 93rd Ave (33172-4802)
PHONE..305 994-7892
Gianni Meneghini, *President*
◆ **EMP: 15 EST:** 2009
SALES (est): 259.2K **Privately Held**
WEB: www.terrafermausa.com
SIC: 3231 Decorated glassware: chipped, engraved, etched, etc.

(G-3397)
TM USA INC
1628 Nw 82nd Ave (33126-1018)
PHONE..954 801-4649
Jin Park, *President*
EMP: 5 EST: 2015
SQ FT: 10,000
SALES (est): 300K **Privately Held**
SIC: 3674 Light emitting diodes

(G-3398)
TRACKING SOLUTIONS CORP
Also Called: TSO Mobile
7791 Nw 46th St Ste 306 (33166-5484)
PHONE..877 477-2922
Juan Olano, *President*
Briglg Ruiz, *Accounting Mgr*
Briglig Ruiz, *Manager*
Douglas Frain, *Technology*
EMP: 25 EST: 2002
SALES (est): 3.3MM
SALES (corp-wide): 10.8MM **Privately Held**
WEB: www.tsomobile.com
SIC: 7372 Prepackaged software
PA: Gpstrackit Holdings, Llc
　1080 Holcomb Bridge Rd
　Roswell GA 30076
　951 296-1316

(G-3399)
TRADEWINDS CLIMATE SYSTEM LLC ✪
10300 Nw 19th St Ste 105 (33172-2538)
PHONE..855 452-0005
EMP: 372 EST: 2021
SALES (est): 1.6MM
SALES (corp-wide): 6.2B **Publicly Held**
SIC: 3585 Parts for heating, cooling & refrigerating equipment
PA: Watsco, Inc.
　2665 S Byshr Dr Ste 901
　Miami FL 33133
　305 714-4100

(G-3400)
TRADEWINDS POWER CORP (HQ)
Also Called: John Deere Authorized Dealer
5820 Nw 84th Ave (33166-3313)
PHONE..305 592-9745
Thomas J Tracy III, *CEO*
Jeff Beard, *General Mgr*
Daniel Santos, *Export Mgr*
Ramiro Quintana, *Purch Agent*
Jorge Rodriguez, *Engineer*
◆ **EMP: 65 EST:** 1985
SQ FT: 40,000
SALES (est): 27.1MM **Privately Held**
WEB: www.tradewindspower.com
SIC: 3621 3585 5013 Generators & sets, electric; pipe fittings; industrial machinery & equipment; motor vehicle supplies & new parts

(G-3401)
TRANE TECHNOLOGIES COMPANY LLC
2660 Nw 89th Ct (33172-1615)
PHONE..305 592-0672
EMP: 7 **Privately Held**
WEB: www.ingersollrand.com
SIC: 3563 Air & gas compressors
HQ: Trane Technologies Company Llc
　800 Beaty St Ste E
　Davidson NC 28036
　704 655-4000

(G-3402)
TRI-COUNTY AEROSPACE INC
2080 Nw 96th Ave (33172-2319)
PHONE..305 639-3356
Emilio M Brown, *President*
Santiago Rodriguez, *General Mgr*
Janet Bishop, *Vice Pres*
Lacey Conolly, *Engineer*
Astrid Brown, *Office Mgr*
EMP: 16 EST: 2003
SALES (est): 2.4MM **Privately Held**
WEB: www.tcaerospace.com
SIC: 7694 Rewinding services

(G-3403)
TROPICAL PAPER BOX
1401 Nw 78th Ave (33126-1616)
PHONE..305 592-5520
Herb Quartin, *Owner*
EMP: 8 EST: 2010
SALES (est): 287.2K **Privately Held**
SIC: 2652 Setup paperboard boxes

(G-3404)
TROY INDUSTRIES INC
2100 Nw 102nd Pl (33172-2525)
PHONE..305 324-1742
Steve Shapiro, *CEO*
Bernice Shapiro, *President*
Steven Shapiro, *President*
Howard Wilson, *Controller*
◆ **EMP: 40 EST:** 1947
SALES (est): 5MM **Privately Held**
WEB: www.troyindustries.com
SIC: 2392 2842 5099 Polishing cloths, plain; specialty cleaning, polishes & sanitation goods; safety equipment & supplies

(G-3405)
UNICORNIO BAKERY LLC
8255 Lake Dr (33166-7819)
PHONE..786 665-1602
Nestor Ferreiro,
EMP: 10 EST: 2019
SALES (est): 430.1K **Privately Held**
SIC: 2051 Bakery products, partially cooked (except frozen)

(G-3406)
UNISCAN LLC
10913 Nw 30th St Ste 101 (33172-5029)
PHONE..305 322-7669
Hector Redroban,
Elizabeth Benavides,
EMP: 8 EST: 2020
SALES (est): 968.4K **Privately Held**
WEB: www.uniscanamerica.com
SIC: 3577 Magnetic ink & optical scanning devices; bar code (magnetic ink) printers

(G-3407)
UNISIGNS USA INC
5526 Nw 79th Ave (33166-4124)
PHONE..305 509-5232
Karla Barquero, *President*
EMP: 7 EST: 2016
SALES (est): 229.8K **Privately Held**
WEB: www.unisignsusa.com
SIC: 3993 Signs & advertising specialties

(G-3408)
UNNO TEKNO LLC
6451 Nw 102nd Ave Unit 4 (33178-4745)
PHONE..786 536-5992
Walter Katsef, *Mng Member*
EMP: 6 EST: 2017
SALES (est): 478.4K **Privately Held**
SIC: 3679 Electronic components

(G-3409)
USA AND INTERNATIONAL RES INC ✪
1200 Nw 78th Ave Ste 112 (33126-1816)
PHONE..786 558-5115
Felix Perez, *CEO*
EMP: 7 EST: 2021
SALES (est): 320.4K **Privately Held**
SIC: 2834 Pharmaceutical preparations

(G-3410)
USVI PHARMACEUTICALS LLC
1301 Nw 84th Ave Ste 101 (33126-1516)
PHONE..305 643-8841
Rick Nielsen, *Principal*
EMP: 12 EST: 2006
SQ FT: 5,000
SALES (est): 20.4K **Privately Held**
SIC: 2834 Pharmaceutical preparations

(G-3411)
VALOR LATIN GROUP INC
8320 Nw 14th St (33126-1504)
PHONE..305 791-5255
Jose Maleh, *President*
EMP: 5 EST: 2016
SALES (est): 444.7K **Privately Held**
WEB: www.valorlg.com
SIC: 3571 Computers, digital, analog or hybrid

(G-3412)
VFM AEROSYSTEMS LLC
10050 Nw 44th Ter Apt 301 (33178-3331)
PHONE..786 567-2348
Valery Mesa, *Director*
EMP: 7 EST: 2015
SALES (est): 615K **Privately Held**
SIC: 3724 Aircraft engines & engine parts

(G-3413)
VISION CONCEPTS INK INC
8953 Nw 23rd St (33172-2404)
PHONE..305 463-8003
Diane G Sardinas, *President*
Manuel Sardinas, *Vice Pres*
EMP: 10 EST: 2006
SQ FT: 9,400
SALES (est): 2.2MM **Privately Held**
WEB: www.vcink.com
SIC: 2752 Commercial printing, lithographic; commercial printing, offset

(G-3414)
VISION SOLUTION TECHNOLOGY LL
10367 Nw 41st St (33178-2305)
PHONE..305 477-4480
Carlos Romero, *Owner*
EMP: 6 EST: 2005
SALES (est): 792.8K **Privately Held**
SIC: 3827 5048 Optical instruments & lenses; optometric equipment & supplies

(G-3415)
VISTA COLOR CORPORATION
Also Called: Commercial Printer Phrm Prtr
1401 Nw 78th Ave Ste 201 (33126-1616)
PHONE..305 635-2000
Jesus E Serrano, *CEO*
Enrique Serrano, *President*
Gene Gonzalez, *Vice Pres*
Jesus L Hernandez, *Vice Pres*
Maria Hernandez, *Vice Pres*
▼ **EMP: 92 EST:** 1966
SQ FT: 12,500
SALES (est): 12MM **Privately Held**
WEB: www.vistacolor.com
SIC: 2752 Commercial printing, offset

(G-3416)
VOSSEN WHEELS INC
1598 Nw 82nd Ave (33126-1020)
PHONE..305 463-7778
Raul Goffredo, *Production*
EMP: 9 EST: 2018
SALES (est): 642.9K **Privately Held**
WEB: www.vossenwheels.com
SIC: 3011 Automobile tires, pneumatic

(G-3417)
VYP SERVICES LLC
Also Called: Caribbean Embroidery Designs
3555 Nw 79th Ave (33122-1019)
PHONE..305 593-8183
Pages Garcia, *Principal*
EMP: 7 EST: 2012
SALES (est): 227.9K **Privately Held**
SIC: 2395 Embroidery products, except schiffli machine

(G-3418)
WBN LLC
Also Called: AC Dob Led
1630 Nw 82nd Ave (33126-1022)
PHONE..786 870-4172
Jin Park, *Mng Member*
EMP: 5 EST: 2017
SQ FT: 10,000
SALES (est): 300K **Privately Held**
SIC: 3674 Light emitting diodes

(G-3419)
WELCH ALLYN INC
2500 Nw 107th Ave Ste 300 (33172-5924)
PHONE..305 669-9003
Nicole Gibson, *Sales Staff*
Jason Hermansen, *Sales Staff*
Steven Bakalar, *Manager*
Franca Candela,
◆ **EMP: 44**
SALES (corp-wide): 12.7B **Publicly Held**
WEB: www.hillrom.com
SIC: 3841 Diagnostic apparatus, medical
HQ: Welch Allyn Inc
　4341 State Street Rd
　Skaneateles Falls NY 13153
　315 685-4100

(G-3420)
WEST PALM INSTALLERS INC
5141 Nw 79th Ave Unit 1 (33166-4756)
PHONE..305 406-3575
Louis Montalbo, *General Mgr*
EMP: 13 EST: 2000
SQ FT: 10,000
SALES (est): 1MM **Privately Held**
WEB: www.brandernet.com
SIC: 3442 Shutters, door or window: metal

(G-3421)
WORLD CONTAINER SERVICES LLC
3341 Nw 82nd Ave (33122-1025)
P.O. Box 520275, Miami (33152-0275)
PHONE..305 400-4850
Alberto Benitez, *CEO*
Roman Benitez, *Managing Dir*
Patrick Gordon, *CFO*
Jose Aguila, *Mng Member*
EMP: 32 EST: 2009
SQ FT: 1,200
SALES (est): 3MM **Privately Held**
WEB: www.worldcontainerservices.com
SIC: 3731 Cargo vessels, building & repairing

(G-3422)
WORLD FUEL CX LLC
9800 Nw 41st St Ste 400 (33178-2980)
PHONE..305 428-8000
Michael J Kasbar, *CEO*
Michael Crosby, *Exec VP*
John P Rau, *Exec VP*
Amy Abraham, *Senior VP*
R Alexander Lake, *Senior VP*
EMP: 10 EST: 2013
SALES (est): 4.5MM
SALES (corp-wide): 31.3B **Publicly Held**
SIC: 2869 Fuels
PA: World Fuel Services Corp
　9800 Nw 41st St Ste 400
　Doral FL 33178
　305 428-8000

(G-3423)
XTS CORP
8870 Nw 18th Ter (33172-2642)
PHONE..305 863-7779
Augusto Perez, *President*
▲ **EMP: 14 EST:** 2006
SQ FT: 2,500

▲ = Import ▼=Export
◆ =Import/Export

SALES (est): 551.5K **Privately Held**
WEB: www.xtscorp.com
SIC: 3699 Security devices

(G-3424)
ZUMEX USA INC
1573 Nw 82nd Ave (33126-1019)
PHONE...................................305 591-0061
Victor Bertolin, *President*
Sergio Davo, *Vice Pres*
▲ EMP: 4 EST: 2007
SQ FT: 3,500
SALES (est): 3MM
SALES (corp-wide): 22MM **Privately Held**
WEB: www.zumex.com
SIC: 3556 Juice extractors, fruit & vegetable: commercial type
PA: Zumex Group, Sa
Calle Moli (Pol. Industrial Moncada Iii)
2
Moncada 46113
961 301-251

Dover
Hillsborough County

(G-3425)
AARON RICE
5203 Downing St (33527-5028)
PHONE...................................813 752-3820
Aaron Rice, *Principal*
EMP: 7 EST: 2017
SALES (est): 88.3K **Privately Held**
SIC: 3634 Electric housewares & fans

(G-3426)
ALPHA OMEGA MBL WLDG SVCS INC
2421 Mcintosh Rd (33527-5982)
PHONE...................................813 629-5777
Laneesha N Castrejon, *President*
EMP: 6 EST: 2017
SALES (est): 401.4K **Privately Held**
WEB: www.aomwelding.com
SIC: 7692 Welding repair

(G-3427)
BINGHAM ON SITE PORTABLES LLC
3640 Sumner Rd (33527-4222)
P.O. Box 749 (33527-0749)
PHONE...................................813 659-0003
Anthony D Bingham, *Mng Member*
Dwayne Bingham Jr,
Linda J Bingham,
EMP: 7 EST: 2011
SQ FT: 1,000
SALES (est): 951.7K **Privately Held**
SIC: 3089 Toilets, portable chemical: plastic

(G-3428)
BINGHAM ON-SITE SEWERS INC
3640 Sumner Rd (33527-4222)
PHONE...................................813 659-0003
Amos Dewayne Bingham Sr, *President*
Linda Jean Bingham, *Corp Secy*
Amos Bingham Jr, *Vice Pres*
Anthony Bingham, *Vice Pres*
Daniel Gildea, *Vice Pres*
EMP: 66 EST: 1965
SQ FT: 8,400
SALES (est): 11MM **Privately Held**
WEB: www.binghamseptic.com
SIC: 3272 1711 7699 4959 Septic tanks, concrete; septic system construction; septic tank cleaning service; sanitary services

(G-3429)
DEANS CSTM SHTMTL FBRCTION IN
5106 Varnadore Ln (33527-5409)
PHONE...................................813 757-6270
Dean Varnadore, *President*
Robin Varnadore, *Vice Pres*
James Register, *Treasurer*
EMP: 9 EST: 1985
SQ FT: 7,000
SALES (est): 1.2MM **Privately Held**
SIC: 3444 1799 Sheet metalwork; welding on site

(G-3430)
FRAZIERS FBRICATION PRFMCE LLC
4730 Durant Rd (33527-6304)
PHONE...................................813 928-1449
Ryan P Frazier, *Manager*
EMP: 7 EST: 2015
SALES (est): 261.4K **Privately Held**
WEB: www.ffpcustoms.com
SIC: 3999 Manufacturing industries

(G-3431)
MARY SYMON
13206 Emerald Acres Ave (33527-3527)
PHONE...................................813 986-4676
Mary P Symon, *Principal*
EMP: 7 EST: 2010
SALES (est): 116.6K **Privately Held**
SIC: 3644 Raceways

Duette
Manatee County

(G-3432)
MOODY CONSTRUCTION SVCS INC
12450 County Road 39 (34219-6835)
PHONE...................................941 776-1542
Matthew Moody, *President*
EMP: 32 EST: 1991
SQ FT: 10,000
SALES (est): 5.8MM **Privately Held**
WEB:
www.moodyconstructionservicesinc.com
SIC: 3441 1541 1542 Fabricated structural metal; renovation, remodeling & repairs: industrial buildings; commercial & office buildings, renovation & repair

(G-3433)
SOUTHSTERN INDUS FBRCATORS LLC
Also Called: Dixie Southern
12650 County Road 39 (34219-6836)
PHONE...................................941 776-1211
David Batts, *Project Mgr*
Jason Howell, *CFO*
Pascal Logue, *Marketing Mgr*
David Howell,
Jonathan Howell,
EMP: 40 EST: 2017
SALES (est): 12MM **Privately Held**
WEB: www.dixiesouthern.com
SIC: 3317 3443 3511 Steel pipe & tubes; industrial vessels, tanks & containers; bins, prefabricated metal plate; hoppers, metal plate; missile silos & components, metal plate; hydraulic turbines

---

Dundee
Polk County

(G-3434)
CHILIPRINT LLC
28597 Hwy 27 (33838-4282)
PHONE...................................863 547-6930
Christopher Chilton, *Principal*
EMP: 8 EST: 2010
SALES (est): 288.9K **Privately Held**
SIC: 3993 Signs & advertising specialties

(G-3435)
MAXIJET INC
8400 Lake Trask Rd (33838-4700)
P.O. Box 1849 (33838-1849)
PHONE...................................863 439-3667
Susan S Thayer, *President*
Thomas A Thayer Jr, *Treasurer*
Virginia Thayer Dunson, *Admin Sec*
EMP: 32 EST: 1981
SQ FT: 30,000
SALES (est): 6MM **Privately Held**
WEB: www.maxijet.com
SIC: 3523 Irrigation equipment, self-propelled
PA: Thayer Industries Inc
5600 Lake Trask Rd
Dundee FL 33838
813 719-6597

(G-3436)
PHANTOM USA LLC
101 Shepard Ave (33838-4381)
PHONE...................................863 353-5972
Doug Wilson, *Principal*
EMP: 9 EST: 2015
SALES (est): 565K **Privately Held**
WEB: www.artattackfx.com
SIC: 2752 Commercial printing, lithographic

(G-3437)
PRATT INDUSTRIES INC
Also Called: Corrugating Division
331 W Frederick Ave (33838-4257)
P.O. Box 1900 (33838-1900)
PHONE...................................863 439-4184
Steven Roberts, *Design Engr*
John Rice, *Sales Mgr*
Philip Savarese, *Sales Mgr*
Juli Hickey, *Accounts Mgr*
Ken Seymour, *Sales Staff*
EMP: 9 **Privately Held**
WEB: www.prattindustries.com
SIC: 2653 Boxes, corrugated: made from purchased materials
PA: Pratt Industries, Inc.
1800 Sarasot Bus Pkwy Ne S
Conyers GA 30013

(G-3438)
THAYER INDUSTRIES INC (PA)
Also Called: Thayer Citrus
5600 Lake Trask Rd (33838-4701)
P.O. Box 1849 (33838-1849)
PHONE...................................813 719-6597
Thomas Thayer Sr, *President*
Susan S Thayer, *Vice Pres*
Thomas Thayer Jr, *Vice Pres*
Virginia Thayer Dunson, *Treasurer*
Ann S Thayer, *Admin Sec*
EMP: 3 EST: 1980
SALES (est): 6MM **Privately Held**
SIC: 3523 0174 7389 5947 Irrigation equipment, self-propelled; citrus fruits; interior designer; gift shop; furniture stores

---

Dunedin
Pinellas County

(G-3439)
ARHOB LLC
Also Called: Dunedin House of Beer
927 Broadway Ste A (34698-5710)
PHONE...................................727 216-6318
Andrew Polce, *Mng Member*
EMP: 13 EST: 2009
SALES (est): 1.4MM **Privately Held**
SIC: 2082 Beer (alcoholic beverage)

(G-3440)
BARTH INDUSTRIES
1701 Hickory Gate Dr S (34698-2413)
PHONE...................................727 787-6392
Harry Barth, *Principal*
EMP: 10 EST: 2008
SALES (est): 126.1K **Privately Held**
WEB: www.barthindustries.com
SIC: 3999 Manufacturing industries

(G-3441)
BIOBAG AMERICAS INC
1059 Broadway Ste F (34698-5756)
P.O. Box 369, Palm Harbor (34682-0369)
PHONE...................................727 789-1646
David J Williams, *President*
Alec Brophy, *Chairman*
Tom Goldy, *Business Mgr*
Bridget Smeltzer, *VP Opers*
Caroline Stone, *Sales Staff*
▲ EMP: 14 EST: 2002
SALES (est): 5MM **Privately Held**
WEB: www.biobagusa.com
SIC: 2673 Plastic bags: made from purchased materials
HQ: Biobag International As
Trogstadveien 9a
Askim 1807

(G-3442)
CAST ART INTERNATIONAL CORP
762 Marjon Ave (34698-7107)
PHONE...................................727 807-3395
Grazia C Caiazza, *President*
EMP: 9 EST: 2010
SALES (est): 108.4K **Privately Held**
SIC: 3272 5211 Silo staves, cast stone or concrete; closets, interiors & accessories

(G-3443)
CATHY MINH LEE
Also Called: Satin Soles
463 Patricia Ave (34698-7872)
PHONE...................................626 827-3214
Cathy Lee, *Principal*
EMP: 5 EST: 2017
SALES (est): 336.5K **Privately Held**
WEB: www.satinsolessalon.com
SIC: 2221 Satins

(G-3444)
CERTEK SOFTWARE DESIGNS INC
507 S Paula Dr (34698-2032)
PHONE...................................727 738-8188
David Roberts, *President*
Kurt Golhardt, *Vice Pres*
Mark Barnes, *CFO*
EMP: 9 EST: 2003
SALES (est): 945.2K **Privately Held**
WEB: www.certek.com
SIC: 7372 Prepackaged software

(G-3445)
CHEVAL COUNTRY CLUB
545 Frederica Ln (34698-5053)
P.O. Box 340465, Tampa (33694-0465)
PHONE...................................813 279-5122
Larry King, *Owner*
Billie Merritt, *Principal*
Itam Antigha, *Personnel*
Ryan Shives, *Director*
EMP: 6 EST: 2012
SALES (est): 499.6K **Privately Held**
WEB: www.playcheval.com
SIC: 3949 7991 Shafts, golf club; athletic club & gymnasiums, membership

(G-3446)
COCA-COLA COMPANY
427 San Christopher Dr (34698-4905)
P.O. Box 979 (34697-0979)
PHONE...................................727 736-7101
Matt Iwanski, *Mfg Staff*
Tim Goodwin, *Opers-Prdtn-Mfg*
Anthony Natal, *Sales Staff*
Tina Davey, *Manager*
EMP: 31
SALES (corp-wide): 33B **Publicly Held**
WEB: www.coca-colacompany.com
SIC: 2086 2033 5142 Bottled & canned soft drinks; canned fruits & specialties; packaged frozen goods
PA: The Coca-Cola Company
1 Coca Cola Plz Nw
Atlanta GA 30313
404 676-2121

(G-3447)
CRUISING GIDE PUBLICATIONS INC
2418 Summerwood Ct (34698-2253)
P.O. Box 1017 (34697-1017)
PHONE...................................727 733-5322
Nancy Scott, *President*
Simon Scott, *Vice Pres*
Ashley Scott, *Production*
Maureen Larroux, *Mktg Dir*
◆ EMP: 5 EST: 1986
SQ FT: 2,000
SALES (est): 529.3K **Privately Held**
WEB: www.cruisingguides.com
SIC: 2741 Atlas, map & guide publishing

(G-3448)
FEWTEK INC
2539 Gary Cir Apt 201 (34698-1748)
PHONE...................................727 736-0533
EMP: 10
SALES: 1.5MM **Privately Held**
SIC: 3824 8721 Mfg Fluid Meter/Counting Devices Accounting/Auditing/Bookkeeping

GEOGRAPHIC

(G-3449)
GATTAS CORP
Also Called: Gattas Marine Services
745 Main St Ste B (34698-5018)
PHONE....................................727 733-5886
Christopher M Gattas, *Director*
EMP: 7 EST: 2005
SALES (est): 175.2K **Privately Held**
SIC: 2397 Schiffli machine embroideries

(G-3450)
GEDDIS INC
2221 Paddock Cir (34698-2428)
PHONE....................................800 844-6792
Dave Geddis, *President*
EMP: 10 EST: 1978
SALES (est): 570.3K **Privately Held**
WEB: www.surgiclean.com
SIC: 3841 3845 3699 Surgical & medical
  instruments; electromedical equipment;
  electrical equipment & supplies

(G-3451)
**IMPACT PROMOTIONAL PUBG
LLC**
1546 Main St (34698-4642)
PHONE....................................727 736-6228
Peter Klein,
EMP: 11 EST: 1996
SALES (est): 715.4K **Privately Held**
WEB: www.impact-i.com
SIC: 2741 Miscellaneous publishing

(G-3452)
**KELLER-NGLILLIS DESIGN MFG
INC**
655 San Christopher Dr (34698-5060)
PHONE....................................727 733-4111
Robert D Keller, *President*
Charles Angelillis, *Corp Secy*
Gerald Keller, *Vice Pres*
Judson Angelillis, *Project Mgr*
Morgan Angelillis, *Admin Mgr*
▼ EMP: 12 EST: 1955
SQ FT: 30,000
SALES (est): 1.4MM **Privately Held**
WEB: www.kellersales.com
SIC: 3535 3443 Conveyors & conveying
  equipment; tanks, lined: metal plate

(G-3453)
KITCHEN SINK EXPRESS LLC
1986 Brae Moor Dr (34698-3250)
PHONE....................................800 888-6604
Alicia Taylor, *Principal*
EMP: 6 EST: 2008
SALES (est): 491.4K **Privately Held**
SIC: 3365 Household utensils, cast alu-
  minum

(G-3454)
MINUTE MAN PRESS
Also Called: Minuteman Press
1425 Main St Ste C (34698-6247)
PHONE....................................727 791-1115
Courtney Tuttle, *Owner*
EMP: 5 EST: 2004
SALES (est): 403.6K **Privately Held**
WEB: www.minutemanpress.com
SIC: 2752 Commercial printing, litho-
  graphic

(G-3455)
NU EARTH LABS LLC
150 Douglas Ave (34698-7908)
PHONE....................................727 648-4787
Chris Estey, *CEO*
Tim Bitterman, *Manager*
Angie Chacon, *Manager*
EMP: 50 EST: 2016
SALES (est): 5MM **Privately Held**
WEB: www.privatelabelskincareflorida.com
SIC: 2869 5999 High purity grade chemi-
  cals, organic; toiletries, cosmetics & per-
  fumes

(G-3456)
**ONE PRICE DRYCLEANERS
TAMPA (PA)**
1850 Main St (34698-5565)
PHONE....................................727 734-3353
James A Robinson, *President*
Tracy Robinson, *Owner*
EMP: 10 EST: 1999

SALES (est): 762.6K **Privately Held**
SIC: 3953 7211 Marking devices; power
  laundries, family & commercial

(G-3457)
PRINT MART INC
1430 Main St (34698-6201)
PHONE....................................727 796-0064
Neil Stein, *President*
EMP: 5 EST: 2014
SALES (est): 316K **Privately Held**
WEB: www.printmart.us
SIC: 2759 Commercial printing

(G-3458)
SINO EAGLE USA INC
1000 Bass Blvd (34698-5801)
PHONE....................................727 259-3570
Jean Raas, *President*
EMP: 18 EST: 2011
SALES (est): 814.9K
SALES (corp-wide): 25.6MM **Privately
Held**
WEB: www.sinoeaglegroup.com
SIC: 3732 Sailboats, building & repairing
PA: Zhejiang Sino-Eagle Holding Group
  Co., Ltd.
  No.81, Gaoerfu Road, Yinhu Sub-Dis-
  trict, Fuya Ng District
  Hangzhou 31140
  571 634-3261

(G-3459)
STIRLING WINERY
461 Main St (34698-4965)
PHONE....................................727 734-4025
Elinor Fox, *Owner*
EMP: 8 EST: 2005
SALES (est): 175.1K **Privately Held**
WEB: www.stirlingwinedunedin.com
SIC: 2084 Wines

(G-3460)
TWO ROADS CONSULTING LLC
469 Limewood Ave (34698-7220)
PHONE....................................305 395-8821
Perry Warren, *Mng Member*
Gable Roby, *Sr Associate*
EMP: 7 EST: 2011
SALES (est): 371.2K **Privately Held**
WEB: www.tworoadsconsulting.com
SIC: 7372 Business oriented computer
  software

Dunnellon
Citrus County

(G-3461)
AIR DISTRIBUTORS INC
Also Called: Metal Shop, The
2541 W Dunnellon Rd (34433-2347)
P.O. Box 1829 (34430-1829)
PHONE....................................352 522-0006
James E Jacobs, *President*
Lynn Jacobs, *Admin Sec*
▲ EMP: 28 EST: 1982
SQ FT: 9,413
SALES (est): 8.9MM **Privately Held**
WEB: www.metalshop.org
SIC: 3444 Sheet metalwork

(G-3462)
DULEY TRUSS INC
2591 W Dunnellon Rd 488 (34433-2347)
P.O. Box 340 (34430-0340)
PHONE....................................352 465-0964
John Duley, *President*
EMP: 22 EST: 1983
SQ FT: 7,000
SALES (est): 3.5MM **Privately Held**
WEB: www.duleytruss.com
SIC: 2439 Trusses, wooden roof

Dunnellon
Marion County

(G-3463)
CARLTON MFG INC (PA)
Also Called: Carlton Mfg Associates
20093 E Penn Ave Ste 3 (34432-6061)
P.O. Box 539, Mount Vernon TX (75457-
0539)
PHONE....................................352 465-2153
Doug Mercier, *President*
Jean Rowe, *Treasurer*
Robert Behymer, *Admin Sec*
▲ EMP: 2 EST: 1976
SQ FT: 126,000
SALES (est): 9.4MM **Privately Held**
SIC: 2512 Living room furniture: uphol-
  stered on wood frames

(G-3464)
D & S STEEL
19450 Sw 5th Pl (34431-2101)
PHONE....................................352 489-8791
Vicky Stancil, *Owner*
EMP: 5 EST: 1997
SQ FT: 4,000
SALES (est): 535.9K **Privately Held**
SIC: 7692 Welding repair

(G-3465)
DONAU CARBON US LCC
551 N Us Highway 41 (34432-1315)
PHONE....................................352 465-5959
Katharina Wiesauer, *Mng Member*
EMP: 25 EST: 2016
SALES (est): 2.5MM **Privately Held**
WEB: www.donau-carbon-us.com
SIC: 2819 Charcoal (carbon), activated

(G-3466)
KASHIBEN SAY LLC
Also Called: Dunnellon Discount Drugs
11150 N Williams St (34432-8363)
PHONE....................................352 489-4960
Tapan J Vora, *Mng Member*
Jittendra Vora,
EMP: 9 EST: 2012
SALES (est): 3.1MM **Privately Held**
WEB: www.dunnellonpharmacy.com
SIC: 2834 5912 Pharmaceutical prepara-
  tions; drug stores

(G-3467)
STANDARD CARBON LLC
Also Called: Standard Purification
551 N Us Highway 41 (34432-1315)
PHONE....................................352 465-5959
James B Sharpe Jr,
Soohyung Kim,
Nicholas Singer,
▲ EMP: 21 EST: 2008
SQ FT: 30,000
SALES (est): 4.8MM **Privately Held**
WEB: www.standardpurification.com
SIC: 2819 Industrial inorganic chemicals

(G-3468)
TRIAD EDM INC
14872 Sw 111th St (34432-4731)
PHONE....................................352 489-5336
Joseph J Hytovick, *President*
Vivian Hytovick, *Corp Secy*
EMP: 6 EST: 1983
SQ FT: 21,000
SALES (est): 525K **Privately Held**
WEB: www.triadedm.com
SIC: 3544 3599 Special dies & tools; elec-
  trical discharge machining (EDM)

(G-3469)
WALKER ELECTRIC INC
9945 Sw 194th Ct (34432-4199)
PHONE....................................941 729-5015
Rose Walker, *Vice Pres*
EMP: 6 EST: 2011
SALES (est): 794.8K **Privately Held**
WEB: www.walkerelectricfl.com
SIC: 3699 1731 Electrical equipment &
  supplies; electrical work

(G-3470)
**WATTS WATER TECHNOLOGIES
INC**
Also Called: Flowmatic
11611 Sw 147th Ct (34432-4759)
PHONE....................................352 465-2000
Renato Trovo, *General Mgr*
Neal Delettre, *Branch Mgr*
Kitae Chang, *Director*
EMP: 20
SALES (corp-wide): 1.8B **Publicly Held**
WEB: www.watts.com
SIC: 3589 Water purification equipment,
  household type
PA: Watts Water Technologies, Inc.
  815 Chestnut St
  North Andover MA 01845
  978 688-1811

East Palatka
Putnam County

(G-3471)
**CAMPBELL CNON CRRAGE
WORKS INC**
431 Federal Point Rd (32134-4359)
PHONE....................................305 304-8528
Lawrence Campbell, *Owner*
EMP: 7 EST: 2014
SALES (est): 252.4K **Privately Held**
WEB: www.campbellcannon.com
SIC: 3366 Bronze foundry

(G-3472)
J M MILLING INC
120 Dog Branch Rd (32131-4161)
PHONE....................................386 546-6826
EMP: 8 EST: 2018
SALES (est): 764.3K **Privately Held**
SIC: 3599 Machine shop, jobbing & repair

(G-3473)
KARNAK CORPORATION
Also Called: Rodents On The Road
147 Pine Tree Rd (32131-4160)
PHONE....................................352 481-4145
Craig Z Sherar, *President*
Jessica R Sherar, *Vice Pres*
EMP: 9 EST: 1984
SALES (est): 638K **Privately Held**
SIC: 2048 7389 Feeds, specialty: mice,
  guinea pig, etc.;

(G-3474)
**PLASTIC MASTERS
INTERNATIONAL**
327 State Road 207 (32131-4106)
PHONE....................................386 312-9775
Lark James, *President*
Steve James, *Corp Secy*
EMP: 13 EST: 1997
SQ FT: 15,000
SALES (est): 2.9MM **Privately Held**
WEB: www.plasticmasters.com
SIC: 2821 Plastics materials & resins

(G-3475)
RYAN MANUFACTURING INC
339b State Road 207 (32131-4106)
PHONE....................................386 325-3644
Mark Ryan, *President*
Marian Ryan, *Manager*
EMP: 10 EST: 1987
SQ FT: 8,000
SALES (est): 1.7MM **Privately Held**
WEB: www.ryanmanufacturing.com
SIC: 3443 3523 Fabricated plate work
  (boiler shop); farm machinery & equip-
  ment

(G-3476)
ST JOHNS TURF CARE LLC
1040 Hstngs Federal Pt Rd (32131-4420)
PHONE....................................352 258-3314
EMP: 11 EST: 2019
SALES (est): 1.4MM **Privately Held**
WEB: www.stjohnsturfcare.com
SIC: 3523 Farm machinery & equipment

(G-3477)
TRUE HOUSE INC
150 State Road 207 (32131-4001)
PHONE....................................386 325-9085

▲ = Import ▼=Export
◆ =Import/Export

Pete Potter, *Principal*
EMP: 110
SALES (corp-wide): 13.6MM **Privately Held**
WEB: www.apextechnology.com
SIC: 2439 Trusses, wooden roof
PA: True House, Inc.
4745 Sutton Park Ct # 501
Jacksonville FL 32224
904 757-7500

(G-3478)
WARWICK LOGGING
Also Called: Warwick, Blane
119 Putnam County Blvd (32131-4020)
P.O. Box 143 (32131-0143)
PHONE..................................386 328-9358
Blane Warwick, *Owner*
EMP: 7 **EST:** 1992
SALES (est): 831.5K **Privately Held**
SIC: 2411 Logging camps & contractors

Edgewater
Volusia County

(G-3479)
B&C SIGNS
2525 Guava Dr (32141-5143)
PHONE..................................386 426-2373
Brendon Cahill, *President*
Tanel Cahill, *Vice Pres*
Brendan Cahill, *Info Tech Mgr*
EMP: 5 **EST:** 1996
SQ FT: 3,740
SALES (est): 437.2K **Privately Held**
WEB: www.bandcsigns.com
SIC: 3993 Electric signs

(G-3480)
BEST IPRODUCTSCOM LLC
111 N Ridgewood Ave (32132-1713)
PHONE..................................386 402-7800
▼ **EMP:** 6 **EST:** 2011
SQ FT: 25,000
SALES: 1MM **Privately Held**
SIC: 3577 Mfg Computer Peripheral Equipment

(G-3481)
BILL MITCHELL PRODUCTS LLC
1726 Hibiscus Dr (32132-3427)
P.O. Box 229344, Glenwood (32722-9344)
PHONE..................................386 957-3009
William Mitchell, *Mng Member*
▼ **EMP:** 11 **EST:** 2017
SALES (est): 1MM **Privately Held**
WEB: www.billmitchellproducts.com
SIC: 3714 Motor vehicle parts & accessories

(G-3482)
BLUE WATER DYNAMICS LLC
Also Called: Dougherty Manufacturing
308 S Old County Rd (32132-1812)
PHONE..................................386 957-5464
Carisa Albrecht, *Vice Pres*
Todd Buck, *QC Mgr*
Yash Mehta, *Engineer*
Sarah N Dougherty, *CFO*
Martin Gatica, *Manager*
EMP: 69 **EST:** 2010
SALES (est): 11.6MM **Privately Held**
SIC: 2821 3089 3448 3469 Plastics materials & resins; prefabricated plastic buildings; buildings, portable: prefabricated metal; ornamental metal stampings; miscellaneous fabricated wire products; tube fabricating (contract bending & shaping)

(G-3483)
BOSTON WHALER INC
100 Whaler Way (32141-7221)
PHONE..................................386 428-0057
John Ward, *President*
Ken Beauregard, *Business Mgr*
Doug Nettles, *Business Mgr*
Anna Collins, *COO*
Jeff Vaughn, *Vice Pres*
◆ **EMP:** 400 **EST:** 1958
SQ FT: 12,000

SALES (est): 100.7MM
SALES (corp-wide): 5.8B **Publicly Held**
WEB: www.bostonwhaler.com
SIC: 3732 Boats, fiberglass: building & repairing
PA: Brunswick Corporation
26125 N Riverwoods Blvd # 500
Mettawa IL 60045
847 735-4700

(G-3484)
BRUNSWICK COMMERCIAL &
100 Whaler Way (32141-7213)
PHONE..................................386 423-2900
Eric Caplan, *President*
Tonia Sawdy, *Administration*
◆ **EMP:** 100 **EST:** 2001
SALES (est): 21MM
SALES (corp-wide): 5.8B **Publicly Held**
WEB: www.brunswickcgp.com
SIC: 3732 Motorized boat, building & repairing
PA: Brunswick Corporation
26125 N Riverwoods Blvd # 500
Mettawa IL 60045
847 735-4700

(G-3485)
C & E CABINETS DESIGN LLC
137 W Marion Ave (32132-3552)
PHONE..................................386 410-4281
EMP: 5 **EST:** 2019
SALES (est): 425.2K **Privately Held**
SIC: 3993 Signs & advertising specialties

(G-3486)
CENTROID PRODUCTS INC
2104 Hibiscus Dr (32141-4008)
PHONE..................................386 423-3574
James Tucker, *President*
EMP: 9 **EST:** 1983
SALES (est): 759.5K **Privately Held**
WEB: www.centroidproducts.com
SIC: 3823 Industrial instrmnts msrmnt display/control process variable

(G-3487)
CHOICE PRODUCTS INC
143 W Palm Way (32132-1817)
PHONE..................................386 426-6450
EMP: 15
SALES (est): 1.1MM **Privately Held**
SIC: 3728 3751 Mfg Aircraft Parts/Equipment Mfg Motorcycles/Bicycles

(G-3488)
CUSTOM TUBE PRODUCTS INC
317 Base Leg Dr (32132-1481)
P.O. Box 936 (32132-0936)
PHONE..................................386 426-0670
David S Love, *President*
Sydney S Love, *CFO*
Jake Baker, *Manager*
John Butler, *Technician*
EMP: 15 **EST:** 2003
SQ FT: 20,000
SALES (est): 4.6MM **Privately Held**
WEB: www.customtubeproducts.com
SIC: 3599 3498 Tubing, flexible metallic; fabricated pipe & fittings

(G-3489)
EDGEWATER POWER BOATS LLC
211 Dale St (32132-1417)
P.O. Box 790 (32132-0790)
PHONE..................................386 426-5457
Daniel Robinson, *Regional Mgr*
Charles Gerlach, *Vice Pres*
David Clements, *Materials Mgr*
Chris Phelps, *Opers Staff*
Bryan Powderly, *Controller*
◆ **EMP:** 65 **EST:** 2004
SQ FT: 66,000
SALES (est): 18.2MM **Privately Held**
WEB: www.ewboats.com
SIC: 3732 Boat building & repairing

(G-3490)
HYDROPLUS
1712 Fern Palm Dr Ste 7 (32132-5500)
PHONE..................................386 341-2768
John Camp, *Principal*
EMP: 7 **EST:** 2010

SALES (est): 487.6K **Privately Held**
SIC: 3829 Pressure & vacuum indicators, aircraft engine

(G-3491)
ILEX ORGANICS LLC ✪
504 Pullman Rd (32132-1465)
PHONE..................................386 566-3826
Bryon White,
EMP: 15 **EST:** 2021
SALES (est): 528.5K **Privately Held**
SIC: 2043 Coffee substitutes, made from grain

(G-3492)
ISLAMORADA BOATWORKS LLC
4501 S Ridgewood Ave (32141-7350)
PHONE..................................786 393-4752
Thomas Gordon, *Mng Member*
Jean Kayat, *Manager*
EMP: 8 **EST:** 2013
SALES (est): 738.9K **Privately Held**
WEB: www.islamoradaboatworks.com
SIC: 3732 Boat building & repairing

(G-3493)
J W GROUP INC (PA)
Also Called: Wennerwear
2004 Sabal Palm Dr (32141-3830)
PHONE..................................386 423-8828
Joyce Wenner, *President*
EMP: 6 **EST:** 1994
SALES (est): 453.7K **Privately Held**
SIC: 2339 2329 5961 Women's & misses' athletic clothing & sportswear; men's & boys' sportswear & athletic clothing; mail order house

(G-3494)
JAS POWDER COATING LLC
1710 Industrial Ave (32132-3561)
PHONE..................................386 410-6675
EMP: 8 **EST:** 2017
SALES (est): 821K **Privately Held**
WEB: www.jaspowdercoating.com
SIC: 3479 Coating of metals & formed products

(G-3495)
JASMINE PURKISS
Also Called: Satchel Group
2526 Hibiscus Dr 108-08 (32141-5004)
PHONE..................................386 244-7726
Jasmine Purkiss, *Principal*
EMP: 11 **EST:** 2020
SALES (est): 306.7K **Privately Held**
SIC: 3161 Satchels

(G-3496)
LEON LEATHER COMPANY INC
Also Called: Desperado Leather
3735 Us Highway 1 (32141-7234)
PHONE..................................386 304-1902
Andrew W Alcantara, *President*
Deborah S Alcantara, *Corp Secy*
▲ **EMP:** 5 **EST:** 1966
SALES (est): 466.2K **Privately Held**
WEB: www.leonleather.com
SIC: 3172 Personal leather goods

(G-3497)
LMN PRINTING CO INC
118 N Ridgewood Ave (32132-1721)
PHONE..................................386 428-9928
Nanette Amalfitano, *President*
Mary Carro, *Corp Secy*
Nora Aly, *Vice Pres*
Noreen Carro, *Vice Pres*
EMP: 15 **EST:** 1990
SQ FT: 2,000
SALES (est): 1MM **Privately Held**
WEB: www.lmn-printing.com
SIC: 2752 2731 Commercial printing, offset; book publishing

(G-3498)
MIL-SPEC METAL FINISHING INC
706 W Park Ave Ste A (32132-1412)
PHONE..................................386 426-7188
Isac Possato, *President*
Ronaldo Possato, *Director*
EMP: 6 **EST:** 1990

SALES (est): 592.3K **Privately Held**
WEB: www.milspecfl.com
SIC: 3471 Decorative plating & finishing of formed products

(G-3499)
R J DOUGHERTY ASSOCIATES LLC
Also Called: Everglades Boats
544 Air Park Rd (32132-3043)
PHONE..................................386 409-2202
Thomas Flocco, *CEO*
Matt Vranich, *Senior VP*
David Brown, *Vice Pres*
Jorge Sotolongo, *Vice Pres*
Keith Santana, *Production*
▼ **EMP:** 250 **EST:** 1997
SQ FT: 115,000
SALES (est): 48.5MM **Privately Held**
WEB: www.evergladesboats.com
SIC: 3732 Boats, fiberglass: building & repairing

(G-3500)
SAPPHIRE EXCHANGE LLC
Also Called: Manufacturing
107 S Ridgewood Ave (32132-1915)
PHONE..................................407 926-8305
Delson Jeanvilma, *CEO*
EMP: 8 **EST:** 2017
SALES (est): 604.2K **Privately Held**
SIC: 2052 1541 Bakery products, dry; food products manufacturing or packing plant construction

(G-3501)
SOUTHERN GRAPHIC MACHINE LLC
3441 Juniper Dr (32141-6811)
PHONE..................................615 812-0778
Jason Black, *President*
EMP: 7 **EST:** 2010
SALES (est): 424.2K **Privately Held**
WEB: www.southerngraphic.com
SIC: 3555 Printing trades machinery

(G-3502)
TARMAC AMERICA INC
200 N Flagler Ave (32132-2152)
PHONE..................................386 427-0438
Kevin Shoemaker, *Principal*
EMP: 10 **EST:** 2001
SALES (est): 372.8K **Privately Held**
SIC: 3531 Mixers, concrete

(G-3503)
VIKING AIRCRAFT ENGINES LLC
735 Air Park Rd 3c (32132-3013)
PHONE..................................386 416-8383
Jan L Eggenfellner, *Principal*
EMP: 5 **EST:** 2012
SALES (est): 626.5K **Privately Held**
WEB: www.vikingaircraftengines.com
SIC: 3728 Aircraft parts & equipment

Eglin Afb
Okaloosa County

(G-3504)
EGLIN AIR FORCE BASE
205 W D Ave Ste 433 (32542-6887)
PHONE..................................850 882-5422
EMP: 188
SALES (corp-wide): 5.4MM **Privately Held**
SIC: 2311 Military uniforms, men's & youths': purchased materials
PA: Eglin Air Force Base
207 W D Ave Ste 125
Eglin Afb FL 32542
850 882-3315

(G-3505)
EGLIN AIR FORCE BASE (PA)
207 W D Ave Ste 125 (32542-6891)
PHONE..................................850 882-3315
Jonas Kemp, *President*
EMP: 7 **EST:** 2020
SALES (est): 5.4MM **Privately Held**
SIC: 2311 Military uniforms, men's & youths': purchased materials

(G-3506)
JAMES TAYLOR
Also Called: Eglin Aero Club
200 W Escambia Rd (32542-5306)
P.O. Box 1588 (32542-0588)
PHONE................................850 882-5148
Gary Steel, *President*
Cindy Larkins, *Principal*
James Taylor, *Manager*
EMP: 10 **EST:** 2020
SALES (est): 367.6K **Privately Held**
WEB: www.eglinaeroclub.com
SIC: 3699 Flight simulators (training aids),
electronic

Elkton
St. Johns County

(G-3507)
MAS HVAC INC
4010 Deerpark Blvd (32033-2060)
PHONE................................904 531-3140
Robert Story, *President*
Mitchell Tatar, *Principal*
Jeremy Bethke, *Opers Mgr*
Samuel Ehling, *Engineer*
Ryan Grey, *Engineer*
EMP: 14 **EST:** 2010
SQ FT: 2,000
SALES (est): 5.8MM **Privately Held**
WEB: www.mas-hvac.com
SIC: 3585 Air conditioning equipment,
complete

(G-3508)
PREFORM LLC
3845 Deerpark Blvd (32033-4063)
PHONE................................888 826-5161
Helmut Makosch, *Vice Pres*
Cat Clark, *Sales Staff*
Judy Welker, *Manager*
Susan Wacha,
EMP: 16 **EST:** 2016
SALES (est): 2.5MM **Privately Held**
WEB: www.preform.us
SIC: 2821 Thermosetting materials

(G-3509)
Q-PAC SYSTEMS INC
4010 Deerpark Blvd (32033-2060)
PHONE................................904 863-5300
Clark Story, *Principal*
Mathew Kent, *Principal*
Mitchell Tatar, *Principal*
EMP: 60 **EST:** 2014
SQ FT: 2,000
SALES (est): 14.9MM **Privately Held**
WEB: www.q-pac.com
SIC: 3564 Blowers & fans

Ellenton
Manatee County

(G-3510)
EASYTURF INC
3203 Us Highway 301 N (34222-2121)
PHONE................................941 753-3312
EMP: 12
SALES (corp-wide): 167.1K **Privately Held**
WEB: www.fieldturflandscape.com
SIC: 3999 0782 1799 Grasses, artificial &
preserved; lawn & garden services; artificial turf installation
HQ: Easyturf, Inc.
175 N Industrial Blvd Ne
Calhoun GA 30701
760 745-7026

(G-3511)
OLIVE ZARZIS OIL LLC
5142 Factory Shops Blvd (34222)
PHONE................................941 284-0291
Lassaad Souiai,
EMP: 10
SALES (est): 394.9K **Privately Held**
SIC: 2079 Olive oil

(G-3512)
PCI COMMUNICATIONS INC
1202 Gary Ave Unit 113 (34222-2012)
P.O. Box 161 (34222-0161)
PHONE................................941 729-5202
Mark Hildabrandt, *President*
Sam Henson, *Manager*
EMP: 5 **EST:** 1973
SQ FT: 4,000
SALES (est): 565.3K **Privately Held**
WEB: www.pci-directories.com
SIC: 2721 2752 Magazines: publishing
only, not printed on site; commercial printing, offset

(G-3513)
SUN CITY BLINDS LLC (PA)
2426 63rd Ter E (34222-2218)
PHONE................................727 522-6695
EMP: 7 **EST:** 2019
SALES (est): 321.8K **Privately Held**
SIC: 2591 Window blinds

Eloise
Polk County

(G-3514)
UNITED FABRICATION & MAINT
622 Snively Ave (33880-5543)
P.O. Box 399, Eagle Lake (33839-0399)
PHONE................................863 295-9000
Don Smith, *President*
EMP: 7 **EST:** 1988
SQ FT: 12,000
SALES (est): 1.4MM **Privately Held**
SIC: 3441 1791 Fabricated structural
metal; structural steel erection

Englewood
Charlotte County

(G-3515)
ADVANCE CTRL MFG JEAN ANNETTE
9161 Cherry Dr (34224-8942)
PHONE................................941 697-0846
Lyn Pack, *President*
Gene Pack, *Admin Sec*
EMP: 6 **EST:** 2016
SALES (est): 500K **Privately Held**
SIC: 3625 Relays & industrial controls

(G-3516)
AERO-MARINE TECHNOLOGIES INC
2800 Placida Rd Ste 103 (34224-5576)
P.O. Box 1209, Hernando (34441-1209)
PHONE................................941 205-5420
Joseph N Vaughn, *President*
Theresa L Vaughn, *Corp Secy*
Ethan Fischer, *Vice Pres*
Andrew Etheridge, *Opers Staff*
Terri Vaughn, *CFO*
EMP: 6 **EST:** 1991
SALES (est): 981.2K **Privately Held**
WEB: www.aero-marinetechnologies.com
SIC: 3599 5088 Machine shop, jobbing &
repair; aeronautical equipment & supplies

(G-3517)
CUSTOM STUCCO INC
1921 Michigan Ave (34224-5424)
PHONE................................941 650-5649
Stephen Heuss, *President*
EMP: 9 **EST:** 2010
SALES (est): 476K **Privately Held**
SIC: 3299 Stucco

(G-3518)
HARTMANS PRINT CENTER INC
2828 S Mccall Rd Ste 37 (34224-9518)
PHONE................................941 475-2220
Jim Hartman, *President*
Pat Hartman, *Vice Pres*
EMP: 5 **EST:** 2000
SALES (est): 465.7K **Privately Held**
WEB: www.hartmansprintcenter.com
SIC: 2752 Commercial printing, offset

(G-3519)
KING HAN INC
Also Called: Kings Han Manufacturing
3725 S Access Rd Ste C (34224-7774)
PHONE................................860 933-8574
Paul Robertson, *President*
Tokcha Robertson, *Owner*
EMP: 5 **EST:** 1997
SQ FT: 2,000
SALES (est): 963K **Privately Held**
WEB: www.kinghaninc.com
SIC: 3825 Frequency meters: electrical,
mechanical & electronic

(G-3520)
OMNI MARINE ENTERPRISES LLC
2640 S Mccall Rd (34224-8499)
PHONE................................941 474-4614
EMP: 7 **EST:** 2019
SALES (est): 369.4K **Privately Held**
WEB: www.omnimarinefl.com
SIC: 7692 Welding repair

(G-3521)
PREMIER TEES
2780 Worth Ave (34224-9159)
PHONE................................941 681-2688
John Mead, *Owner*
EMP: 7 **EST:** 2010
SALES (est): 185.4K **Privately Held**
WEB: www.premierteesfl.com
SIC: 2759 Screen printing

(G-3522)
QUALITY SOCKET SCREW MFG CORP
2790 Worth Ave (34224-9159)
PHONE................................941 475-9585
Jean P Feustel, *President*
Tom Feustel, *Vice Pres*
Nancy Cooper, *Bookkeeper*
Rich Saccoccio, *Manager*
EMP: 15 **EST:** 1970
SQ FT: 10,000
SALES (est): 2.4MM **Privately Held**
WEB: www.qualitysocket.com
SIC: 3452 Screws, metal

(G-3523)
RELIABLE CABINET DESIGNS
6900 San Casa Dr Unit 1 (34224-7929)
PHONE................................941 473-3403
Jerry Weddle, *Owner*
Patti Weddle, *Owner*
Shane Whitmore, *Vice Pres*
EMP: 10 **EST:** 2004
SALES (est): 790K **Privately Held**
WEB: www.reliablecabinetdesigns.com
SIC: 2434 Wood kitchen cabinets

(G-3524)
SOUTHWEST SIGNAL INC
1984 Georgia Ave (34224-5414)
PHONE................................813 621-4949
Kevin Fitzgerald, *President*
Pam Fitzgerald, *Vice Pres*
EMP: 32 **EST:** 2000
SALES (est): 3.6MM **Privately Held**
SIC: 3648 3669 Street lighting fixtures;
traffic signals, electric

(G-3525)
STYLECRAFT CABINETS MFG INC
2780 Ivy St Unit 1 (34224-7773)
PHONE................................941 474-4824
Larry Carvey, *Corp Secy*
EMP: 9 **EST:** 2018
SQ FT: 11,000
SALES (est): 835.7K **Privately Held**
WEB: www.stylecraftcabinetry.com
SIC: 2434 Wood kitchen cabinets

Englewood
Sarasota County

(G-3526)
CABINET GUY OF ENGLEWOOD INC
150 S Mccall Rd (34223-3233)
PHONE................................941 475-9454

Barry Saxman, *President*
EMP: 8 **EST:** 2008
SALES (est): 948K **Privately Held**
SIC: 2434 Wood kitchen cabinets

(G-3527)
CINIDYNE SALES INC
1811 Englewood Rd (34223-1822)
PHONE................................941 473-3914
Edward B Brewer, *Principal*
EMP: 6 **EST:** 2007
SALES (est): 805.6K **Privately Held**
WEB: www.cinidyne.com
SIC: 3861 Photographic equipment & supplies

(G-3528)
CRYSTAL PANEPINTO INC
667 Palomino Trl (34223-3986)
PHONE................................941 475-9235
Dennis Panepinto, *President*
Donna Panepinto, *Vice Pres*
▲ **EMP:** 7 **EST:** 1989
SALES (est): 164.4K **Privately Held**
SIC: 2431 Windows & window parts & trim,
wood

(G-3529)
DRAB TO FAB
136 S Mccall Rd (34223-3251)
PHONE................................941 475-7700
Elizabeth Williams, *Principal*
EMP: 9 **EST:** 2007
SALES (est): 171.4K **Privately Held**
SIC: 2273 Carpets & rugs

(G-3530)
ESSENTIAL OIL UNIVERSITY LLC
Also Called: Perfumery, The
6150 Manasota Key Rd (34223-9253)
PHONE................................502 498-8804
Robert Pappas PHD, *Mng Member*
▲ **EMP:** 6 **EST:** 2001
SALES (est): 716.8K **Privately Held**
WEB: www.essentialoils.org
SIC: 2869 Perfumes, flavorings & food additives

(G-3531)
FLORIDA HARBOR HOMES INC
850 Bayshore Dr (34223-2202)
PHONE................................941 284-8363
Russell W Philbrick, *Principal*
EMP: 12 **EST:** 2008
SALES (est): 355K **Privately Held**
SIC: 2451 Mobile homes, personal or private use

(G-3532)
HARRY CASHATT STUCCO LLC
310 W Cowles St (34223-3107)
PHONE................................941 468-2166
Harry D Cashatt Jr, *Principal*
EMP: 7 **EST:** 2008
SALES (est): 79.7K **Privately Held**
SIC: 3299 Stucco

(G-3533)
IDENTITY STRONGHOLD LLC
563 Paul Morris Dr Unit B (34223-3928)
PHONE................................941 475-8480
Ted Whitaker, *President*
Mike Lampros, *Sales Staff*
Steven Crimaudo, *Marketing Staff*
Walt Augustinowicz,
Mary Fowler. *Admin Asst*
▲ **EMP:** 22 **EST:** 2005
SALES (est): 3.2MM **Privately Held**
WEB: www.idstronghold.com
SIC: 3172 5099 Card cases; cases, carrying

(G-3534)
MILLIKEN & MILLIKEN INC
Also Called: Milliken Industries
101 S Mccall Rd (34223-3227)
PHONE................................941 474-0223
Les Milliken, *CEO*
Shawn Milliken, *President*
Carol M Milliken, *Vice Pres*
▲ **EMP:** 33 **EST:** 1981
SQ FT: 133,000

▲ = Import ▼=Export
◆ =Import/Export

SALES (est): 5.1MM **Privately Held**
SIC: 2394 3993 5999 Awnings, fabric:
made from purchased materials; signs &
advertising specialties; awnings

(G-3535)
R & S MARBLE DESIGNS INC
505 Paul Morris Dr (34223-3961)
PHONE.....................................941 475-3111
Steve Hutchins, *President*
Rebecca Hutchins, *Corp Secy*
EMP: 17 EST: 1991
SQ FT: 12,670
SALES (est): 1.9MM **Privately Held**
SIC: 2493 Marbleboard (stone face hard
board)

(G-3536)
**RENAISSANCE ENTP GROUP
LLC**
155 W Dearborn St (34223-3236)
PHONE.....................................941 284-7854
Trevor E Charnley, *Principal*
EMP: 5 EST: 2008
SALES (est): 489.4K **Privately Held**
SIC: 3272 Columns, concrete

(G-3537)
SHORT STOP PRINT INC
1101 S Mccall Rd Unit A (34223-4233)
PHONE.....................................941 474-4313
Gratia Schroeder, *President*
EMP: 6 EST: 1982
SQ FT: 2,662
SALES (est): 775.6K **Privately Held**
WEB: www.shortstopprinting.com
SIC: 2752 Commercial printing, offset

(G-3538)
SUN COAST MEDIA GROUP INC
Also Called: Englewood Sun Herald
120 W Dearborn St (34223-3237)
PHONE.....................................941 681-3000
Lang Capasso, *Manager*
EMP: 30
SALES (corp-wide): 333.5MM **Privately
Held**
WEB: www.yoursun.com
SIC: 2711 Newspapers, publishing & print-
ing
HQ: Sun Coast Media Group, Inc.
23170 Harborview Rd
Port Charlotte FL 33980
941 206-1300

(G-3539)
TOMSONS INC (PA)
6520 Manasota Key Rd (34223-9211)
PHONE.....................................248 646-0677
Thomas J Connaughton, *President*
Fay E Stuart, *Admin Sec*
▲ EMP: 6 EST: 1981
SALES (est): 24.3MM **Privately Held**
SIC: 3069 3089 2741 Hard rubber &
molded rubber products; injection molding
of plastics; technical manuals: publishing
only, not printed on site

Estero
Lee County

(G-3540)
ARTISTIC LABEL COMPANY INC
20050 Sgrove St Unit 1703 (33928)
PHONE.....................................401 737-0666
Ellen Kaplan, *President*
EMP: 5 EST: 1966
SALES (est): 363K **Privately Held**
WEB: www.artisticlabelcoinc.com
SIC: 2752 Commercial printing, litho-
graphic

(G-3541)
COUNTRYSIDE LOCKS LLC
20020 Barletta Ln # 514 (33928-6352)
PHONE.....................................631 561-5006
Robert Dellasalle, *Manager*
EMP: 5 EST: 2018
SALES (est): 547.9K **Privately Held**
WEB: www.countrysidelocks.com
SIC: 3429 Manufactured hardware (gen-
eral)

(G-3542)
ESTERO FL
23191 Fashion Dr Unit 309 (33928-2596)
PHONE.....................................239 289-9511
EMP: 7 EST: 2017
SALES (est): 101.2K **Privately Held**
WEB: www.estero-fl.gov
SIC: 2079 Olive oil

(G-3543)
**FLORIDA PRECAST INDUSTRIES
INC**
9210 Estero Pk Cmmons Blv (33928)
PHONE.....................................239 390-2868
Robert McCormack, *President*
Todd Backus, *Treasurer*
EMP: 1 EST: 2005
SALES (est): 3MM
SALES (corp-wide): 50.9MM **Privately
Held**
SIC: 3272 Concrete products
PA: The Spancrete Group Inc
N16w23415 Stone Ridge Dr
Waukesha WI 53188
414 290-9000

(G-3544)
FLORIDA WEST POGGENPOHL
10800 Corkscrew Rd # 105 (33928-9426)
PHONE.....................................239 948-9005
Tony Mannoliti, *President*
EMP: 5 EST: 2005
SALES (est): 357K **Privately Held**
SIC: 2434 Wood kitchen cabinets

(G-3545)
FUEL N GO LLC
10351 Corkscrew Rd (33928-9414)
PHONE.....................................239 656-1072
Christian Defilippis, *Owner*
EMP: 9 EST: 2009
SALES (est): 328.7K **Privately Held**
SIC: 2869 Fuels

(G-3546)
IMPORTED YARNS LLC
Also Called: Carotex
21561 Pelican Sound Dr # 101
(33928-8935)
PHONE.....................................239 405-2974
Mike Cooke,
▲ EMP: 7 EST: 1999
SALES (est): 288.7K **Privately Held**
SIC: 2299 7389 Hemp yarn, thread, roving
& textiles; brokers, contract services

(G-3547)
NAPLES HMA LLC
Also Called: Physicians Regional - Pine
24231 Walden Center Dr # 201
(34134-5013)
PHONE.....................................239 390-2174
C Scott Campbell, *CEO*
Timothy R Parry, *Principal*
EMP: 16 EST: 2010
SALES (est): 293.6K **Privately Held**
SIC: 3452 Pins

(G-3548)
PICA SALES AND ENGINEERING
19771 Chapel Trce (33928-1916)
PHONE.....................................239 992-9079
EMP: 6
SALES (est): 2.2MM **Privately Held**
SIC: 3672 Mfg Printed Circuit Boards

(G-3549)
RD ABUKAF 1 INC
Also Called: Marble Club Creamery
8017 Plaza Del Lago Dr # 109
(33928-5304)
PHONE.....................................239 390-8788
Khaled Abukaf, *Principal*
EMP: 7 EST: 2010
SALES (est): 155.2K **Privately Held**
SIC: 2024 Ice cream & frozen desserts

(G-3550)
SHOWERFLOSS INC
20930 Persimmon Pl (33928-2253)
P.O. Box 3121, Peachtree City GA (30269-
7121)
PHONE.....................................239 947-2855
Clyde Stewart, *President*
Jill Bauman, *Manager*

EMP: 9 EST: 1986
SALES (est): 459.5K **Privately Held**
WEB: www.showerfloss.com
SIC: 3843 Dental equipment & supplies

Eustis
Lake County

(G-3551)
A LIVING TESTIMONY LLC
Also Called: La Physique'
2119 Bates Ave (32726-3905)
PHONE.....................................352 406-0249
Rheba C Turnbull, *CEO*
EMP: 6 EST: 2009
SALES (est): 309.2K **Privately Held**
SIC: 2339 5999 Women's & misses' outer-
wear; miscellaneous retail stores

(G-3552)
**ADVANCED PROSTHETICS
AMER INC (HQ)**
Also Called: Advanced Prosthetics America
601 Mount Homer Rd (32726-6261)
PHONE.....................................352 383-0396
Vinit Asar, *CEO*
EMP: 10 EST: 1998
SALES (est): 6.7MM
SALES (corp-wide): 1.1B **Publicly Held**
SIC: 3842 Limbs, artificial
PA: Hanger, Inc.
10910 Domain Dr Ste 300
Austin TX 78758
512 777-3800

(G-3553)
**AERO DOOR INTERNATIONAL
LLC**
2770 Dillard Rd (32726-6281)
PHONE.....................................407 654-0591
Tara Grey, *General Mgr*
Williams F Mathews,
Paul Blake, *Administration*
John Mathews,
EMP: 13 EST: 2011
SALES (est): 1.8MM **Privately Held**
WEB: www.hangardoors.aero
SIC: 3442 Metal doors, sash & trim

(G-3554)
ALL AMERICAN AMPUTEE
601 Mount Homer Rd (32726-6261)
PHONE.....................................352 383-0396
Rod Friedland, *CEO*
EMP: 9 EST: 1998
SALES (est): 97.1K **Privately Held**
SIC: 3842 Prosthetic appliances

(G-3555)
CBD LIFE FLORIDA INC
3109 Kurt St (32726-6528)
PHONE.....................................352 483-8333
Jason C Rein, *Principal*
EMP: 8 EST: 2018
SALES (est): 107.8K **Privately Held**
SIC: 3999

(G-3556)
COUNTER IMPRESSIONS LLC
12 S Bay St (32726-4016)
PHONE.....................................352 589-4966
Matthew Wilson, *Mng Member*
EMP: 10 EST: 2011
SALES (est): 710.4K **Privately Held**
WEB: www.mycounterimpressions.com
SIC: 3131 Counters

(G-3557)
EXCALIBUR CABINETRY LLC
19709 W Eldorado Dr # 32 (32736-8304)
PHONE.....................................248 697-6158
Michael Anderson, *Mng Member*
EMP: 50 EST: 2017
SALES (est): 2.9MM **Privately Held**
SIC: 2541 Cabinets, except refrigerated:
show, display, etc.: wood

(G-3558)
**FLORIDA FOOD PRODUCTS
LLC (PA)**
2231 W County Road 44 # 1 (32726-2628)
P.O. Box 1300 (32727-1300)
PHONE.....................................352 357-4141

Jim Holcrieth, *President*
Pat McCoy, *Exec VP*
Thomas H Brown, *Vice Pres*
Shana Davis, *Safety Mgr*
Derek De Bruyn, *QA Dir*
◆ EMP: 95 EST: 1954
SQ FT: 160,000
SALES (est): 50MM **Privately Held**
WEB: www.floridafood.com
SIC: 2037 2033 Fruit juices, frozen; veg-
etable juices: packaged in cans, jars, etc.

(G-3559)
GREEN FUEL SYSTEMS LLC
24745 Lester Way (32736-8473)
PHONE.....................................352 483-5005
Douglas E Johnson Jr, *Principal*
EMP: 9 EST: 2008
SALES (est): 391.1K **Privately Held**
SIC: 2869 Fuels

(G-3560)
JAMES O CORBETT INC
Also Called: Afab Enterprises
2151 W County Road 44 (32726-2618)
PHONE.....................................352 483-1222
James O Corbett, *President*
Sidney Davis, *Treasurer*
EMP: 8 EST: 1992
SQ FT: 6,000
SALES (est): 1.1MM **Privately Held**
SIC: 3823 7699 3829 Industrial process
control instruments; industrial equipment
services; measuring & controlling devices

(G-3561)
KEVCO BUILDERS INC
Also Called: Trim Spot
2104 S Bay St (32726-6357)
P.O. Box 1267, Tavares (32778-1267)
PHONE.....................................352 308-8025
Kevin Burkholder, *President*
Gloria Burkholder, *Corp Secy*
Ian Kaneshige, *Opers Mgr*
EMP: 12 EST: 1980
SQ FT: 6,000
SALES (est): 1MM **Privately Held**
WEB: www.kevcobuilders.com
SIC: 2431 1521 1751 3442 Doors & door
parts & trim, wood; general remodeling,
single-family houses; carpentry work;
metal doors, sash & trim

(G-3562)
LAKE DOOR AND TRIM INC
1589 Pine Grove Rd (32726-5310)
P.O. Box 449 (32727-0449)
PHONE.....................................352 589-5566
Bobby Green, *President*
Karen Green, *Corp Secy*
Don Allison, *Vice Pres*
EMP: 10 EST: 1982
SQ FT: 18,000
SALES (est): 998K **Privately Held**
WEB: www.trilakeproducts.com
SIC: 2431 3442 Doors, wood; trim, wood;
moldings, wood: unfinished & prefinished;
metal doors

(G-3563)
MFT STAMPS
Also Called: My Favorite Things
132 E Magnolia Ave (32726-3418)
PHONE.....................................352 360-5797
EMP: 8 EST: 2017
SALES (est): 1.1MM **Privately Held**
WEB: www.mftstamps.com
SIC: 3999 Manufacturing industries

(G-3564)
MJR ENTERPRISES INC
1895 Irma Rd (32726-7136)
PHONE.....................................352 483-0735
Michael J Reischmann, *Director*
EMP: 9 EST: 2001
SALES (est): 15.3K **Privately Held**
WEB: www.mjrcorpusa.com
SIC: 3229 5023 Pressed & blown glass;
glassware

(G-3565)
R C D CORPORATION
Also Called: Manufacturer - Distributor
2850 Dillard Rd (32726-6292)
PHONE.....................................352 589-0099
Kevin Brogan, *President*

▼ **EMP:** 9 **EST:** 1958
SQ FT: 12,000
SALES (est): 2.6MM **Privately Held**
WEB: www.rcdmastics.com
SIC: 2891 Adhesives & sealants

(G-3566)
STOLLER CHEMICAL CO OF FLORIDA
1451 Pine Grove Rd (32726-5317)
PHONE.................................352 357-3173
Jerry Stoller, *President*
▲ **EMP:** 10 **EST:** 1965
SQ FT: 1,200
SALES (est): 643.3K **Privately Held**
SIC: 2873 Nitrogenous fertilizers

(G-3567)
TIP TOPS OF AMERICA INC
100 S Bay St (32726-4002)
PHONE.................................352 357-9559
James R Budzynski, *CEO*
EMP: 14 **EST:** 1993
SALES (est): 1.3MM **Privately Held**
WEB: www.tiptops.com
SIC: 2759 Screen printing

(G-3568)
TIPTOPS INC
100 S Bay St (32726-4002)
PHONE.................................352 357-9559
Marilyn Budzynski, *CEO*
EMP: 8 **EST:** 1982
SQ FT: 2,000
SALES (est): 650K **Privately Held**
WEB: www.tiptops.com
SIC: 2396 Screen printing on fabric articles

(G-3569)
US NUTRACEUTICALS INC
Also Called: Valensa International
2751 Nutra Ln (32726-6961)
PHONE.................................352 357-2004
Michael Deese, *Business Mgr*
Bill Donovan, *Senior VP*
Allen Truluck, *Manager*
Anup Chib, *Director*
Muthiah Murugappan, *Director*
▲ **EMP:** 25 **EST:** 1998
SQ FT: 31,000
SALES (est): 8.7MM **Privately Held**
WEB: www.valensa.com
SIC: 2833 Alkaloids & other botanical based products
PA: E.I.D Parry (India) Limited
Dare House, New No.2, Old 234,
Chennai TN 60000

(G-3570)
WICKED WOODWORKS INC
25245 Mcbrady Ln (32736-8495)
PHONE.................................352 455-8402
Seth Begelman, *Branch Mgr*
EMP: 20
SALES (corp-wide): 95.6K **Privately Held**
SIC: 2431 Woodwork, interior & ornamental
PA: Wicked Woodworks Inc
1314 Sw 1st Ave Ste 4
Fort Lauderdale FL 33315
305 714-2209

Fanning Springs
Gilchrist County

(G-3571)
A MATERIALS GROUP INC
Also Called: Trinity Materials
8191 Nw 160th St (32693-7058)
P.O. Box 2209, Trenton (32693-2181)
PHONE.................................352 463-1254
Doug Anderson, *President*
EMP: 65
SQ FT: 784
SALES (corp-wide): 6.3MM **Privately Held**
SIC: 3273 Ready-mixed concrete
PA: A Materials Group, Inc.
871 Nw Guerdon St
Lake City FL 32055
386 758-3164

Felda
Hendry County

(G-3572)
MONSANTO COMPANY
2221 Keri Rd (33930)
P.O. Box 609, Labelle (33975-0609)
PHONE.................................863 673-2157
EMP: 12
SALES (corp-wide): 49.8B **Privately Held**
WEB: www.monsanto.com
SIC: 2879 Agricultural chemicals
HQ: Monsanto Company
800 N Lindbergh Blvd
Saint Louis MO 63167
314 694-1000

(G-3573)
PLANTATION BOTANICALS INC
1401 County Rd Ste 830 (33930)
P.O. Box 128 (33930-0128)
PHONE.................................863 675-2984
Michael Huffman, *CEO*
Eva Huffman, *Vice Pres*
EMP: 26 **EST:** 1964
SALES (est): 1.1MM **Privately Held**
WEB: www.plantationmedicinals.com
SIC: 2833 2048 Botanical products, medicinal: ground, graded or milled; prepared feeds

(G-3574)
PLANTATION MEDICINALS INC
1401 County Rd Ste 830 (33930)
P.O. Box 128 (33930-0128)
PHONE.................................863 675-2984
Michael D Huffman, *President*
Eva Huffman, *Corp Secy*
EMP: 13 **EST:** 1995
SALES (est): 185.8K **Privately Held**
SIC: 2833 Botanical products, medicinal: ground, graded or milled

(G-3575)
SOUTHWEST PRECISION AG INC
14960 S Sr 29 (33930)
P.O. Box 511 (33930-0511)
PHONE.................................863 674-5799
David Rogers, *President*
Leah Nees, *Office Mgr*
EMP: 11 **EST:** 2013
SALES (est): 979.4K **Privately Held**
SIC: 3531 Plows: construction, excavating & grading

Fellsmere
Indian River County

(G-3576)
F T F CONSTRUCTION COMPANY
Also Called: Antiquo Stone By F T F
25 N Myrtle St (32948-7630)
PHONE.................................772 571-1850
Francesco Fornabaio, *President*
Michelle Fornabaio, *Vice Pres*
EMP: 20 **EST:** 1978
SALES (est): 782.1K **Privately Held**
SIC: 3272 1521 3281 Concrete products, precast; single-family housing construction; cut stone & stone products

(G-3577)
GAP ANTENNA PRODUCTS INC
99 N Willow St (32948-5334)
PHONE.................................772 571-9922
Richard Henf, *Owner*
Chris Lane, *MIS Dir*
EMP: 8 **EST:** 1988
SQ FT: 3,000
SALES (est): 864.3K **Privately Held**
WEB: www.gapantenna.com
SIC: 3663 Radio & TV communications equipment

Fern Park
Seminole County

(G-3578)
FLEETBOSS GLOBL PSTNING SLTONS
241 Obrien Rd (32730-2802)
PHONE.................................407 265-9559
Larry Carroll, *CEO*
Brian Carroll, *President*
Floyd Honeycutt, *Vice Pres*
Dan Lee, *Mktg Dir*
EMP: 21 **EST:** 1998
SALES (est): 1.9MM **Privately Held**
WEB: www.fleetboss.com
SIC: 3663

(G-3579)
HERITAGE CNTL FLA JWISH NEWS I
Also Called: Heritage Newspaper
207 Obrien Rd Ste 101 (32730-2838)
P.O. Box 300742, Casselberry (32730-0742)
PHONE.................................407 834-8277
Jeff Gaeser, *President*
EMP: 10 **EST:** 1976
SQ FT: 1,100
SALES (est): 753.8K **Privately Held**
WEB: www.heritagefl.com
SIC: 2752 2711 Newspapers, lithographed only; newspapers, publishing & printing

Fernandina Beach
Nassau County

(G-3580)
ALL POWER PRO INC
995 Egans Creek Ln (32034-5137)
PHONE.................................904 310-3069
Laura Ann Marcin, *Vice Pres*
Marcin Laura Ann, *Vice Pres*
EMP: 6 **EST:** 2013
SALES (est): 464.6K **Privately Held**
WEB: www.all-powerpro.com
SIC: 3621 3585 8741 5084 Motors & generators; refrigeration & heating equipment; management services; engines & parts, diesel; engines, gasoline

(G-3581)
AMELIA ISLAND GRAPHICS
2244 S 8th St (32034-3097)
PHONE.................................904 261-0740
Tony Baia, *Owner*
EMP: 6 **EST:** 1982
SALES (est): 555.2K **Privately Held**
WEB:
www.launchprintingandpromotions.com
SIC: 2759 7336 Commercial printing; graphic arts & related design

(G-3582)
CARIBBEAN BREEZE INC
1438 E Oak St (32034-4726)
P.O. Box 15849 (32035-3115)
PHONE.................................904 261-7831
David Capps, *President*
Carolyn Capps, *Office Mgr*
▼ **EMP:** 8 **EST:** 1992
SALES (est): 2.7MM **Privately Held**
WEB: www.caribbeanbreeze.com
SIC: 2844 Cosmetic preparations; suntan lotions & oils

(G-3583)
COSMETIC CREATIONS INC
1438 E Oak St (32034-4726)
P.O. Box 15849 (32035-3115)
PHONE.................................904 261-7831
Carolyn Capps, *President*
EMP: 7 **EST:** 2014
SALES (est): 479.2K **Privately Held**
WEB: www.cosmeticcreationsspa.com
SIC: 2844 Toilet preparations

(G-3584)
DESIGN IT WRAPS & GRAPHICS LLC
2873 Jamestown Rd (32034-5205)
PHONE.................................904 310-6032

Brent D Knott, *Mng Member*
EMP: 20 **EST:** 2015
SALES (est): 1.1MM **Privately Held**
WEB: www.designitgraphics.com
SIC: 3993 Signs & advertising specialties

(G-3585)
DIVERSIFIED PALLETS INC
1894 S 14th St Ste 2 (32034-4717)
PHONE.................................904 491-6800
Ivey Crump Sr, *Principal*
EMP: 9 **EST:** 2007
SALES (est): 170.2K **Privately Held**
SIC: 2448 Pallets, wood & wood with metal

(G-3586)
EARTH VETS INC
96093 Marsh Lakes Dr (32034-0825)
PHONE.................................352 332-9991
Robert Spiegel, *Owner*
EMP: 7 **EST:** 2007
SALES (est): 121.7K **Privately Held**
SIC: 3841 Veterinarians' instruments & apparatus

(G-3587)
FERNANDINA OBSERVER INC
205 Lighthouse Cir (32034-2533)
PHONE.................................904 261-4372
Susan Hardee Steger, *President*
EMP: 8 **EST:** 2016
SALES (est): 93.8K **Privately Held**
WEB: www.fernandinaobserver.com
SIC: 2711 Newspapers

(G-3588)
ISLAND LIFE GRAPHICS INC (PA)
Also Called: Fastsigns
3114 Egans Bluff Rd (32034-5224)
PHONE.................................904 206-6997
Eric Webb, *Principal*
EMP: 6 **EST:** 2016
SALES (est): 595.1K **Privately Held**
WEB: www.fastsigns.com
SIC: 3993 Signs & advertising specialties

(G-3589)
ISLAND LIFE GRAPHICS INC
Also Called: Fastsigns
1410 E Oak St (32034-4726)
PHONE.................................904 261-0340
Eric W Webb, *President*
EMP: 21
SALES (corp-wide): 595.1K **Privately Held**
WEB: www.fastsigns.com
SIC: 3993 Signs & advertising specialties
PA: Island Life Graphics Inc.
3114 Egans Bluff Rd
Fernandina Beach FL 32034
904 206-6997

(G-3590)
ISLAND MEDIA PUBLISHING LLC
120 N 15th St (32034-3100)
PHONE.................................904 556-3002
Robert Hicks, *Manager*
▲ **EMP:** 7 **EST:** 2010
SALES (est): 213.9K **Privately Held**
SIC: 2741 Miscellaneous publishing

(G-3591)
JOHNSONS MANAGEMENT GROUP INC
1485 S 8th St (32034-3076)
PHONE.................................904 261-4044
Samuel Johnson, *President*
EMP: 7 **EST:** 2003
SQ FT: 1,700
SALES (est): 579.1K **Privately Held**
SIC: 3714 Motor vehicle parts & accessories

(G-3592)
LIGNOTECH FLORIDA LLC
6 Gum St (32034-4280)
P.O. Box 16839 (32035-3131)
PHONE.................................904 577-9077
Peter Morris, *Mng Member*
EMP: 30 **EST:** 2015
SALES (est): 10.3MM
SALES (corp-wide): 1.4B **Publicly Held**
SIC: 2861 Gum & wood chemicals

PA: Rayonier Advanced Materials Inc.
1301 Riverplace Blvd # 23
Jacksonville FL 32207
904 357-4600

(G-3593)
MARLIN & BARREL DISTILLERY LLC
115 S 2nd St (32034-4670)
PHONE...................................321 230-4755
Roger Morenc,
EMP: 5 EST: 2014
SALES (est): 315.1K Privately Held
WEB: www.marlinbarrel.com
SIC: 2085 Distilled & blended liquors

(G-3594)
NELSON RACEWAY LLC
96321 Bay View Dr (32034-6180)
PHONE...................................904 206-1625
Ronald A Nelson, Owner
EMP: 8 EST: 2016
SALES (est): 327.9K Privately Held
SIC: 3644 Raceways

(G-3595)
NETTING PROFESSIONALS LLC
1600 N 14th St (32034-5126)
PHONE...................................904 432-8987
Eli Rogue, Office Mgr
Tyler Hoskins, Asst Office Mgr
EMP: 7 EST: 2015
SALES (est): 1MM Privately Held
WEB: www.nettingpros.com
SIC: 3949 Nets: badminton, volleyball, tennis, etc.

(G-3596)
POPS TURN LLC ✪
Also Called: EZ Turn Signal Kits
4828 Frst Coast Hwy Ste 6 (32034)
PHONE...................................843 725-8890
Jacob Michaelis, President
EMP: 10 EST: 2021
SALES (est): 1.1MM Privately Held
WEB: www.ezturnsignalkits.com
SIC: 3714 Motor vehicle engines & parts

(G-3597)
RAYONIER ADVANCED MTLS INC
10 Gum St (32034-4280)
PHONE...................................904 261-3611
Dorothy Pasik, Project Engr
EMP: 7
SALES (corp-wide): 1.4B Publicly Held
WEB: www.ryamglobal.com
SIC: 2821 Plastics materials & resins
PA: Rayonier Advanced Materials Inc.
1301 Riverplace Blvd # 23
Jacksonville FL 32207
904 357-4600

(G-3598)
SWS SERVICES INC
Also Called: Msm Outdoors
1453 S 8th St (32034-3076)
PHONE...................................904 802-2120
Marina Mattioly, President
EMP: 14 EST: 2017
SALES (est): 2.3MM Privately Held
SIC: 3531 Pavers

(G-3599)
WESTROCK CP LLC
600 N 8th St (32034-3319)
PHONE...................................904 261-5551
Bryan Graves, General Mgr
Al Thompson, General Mgr
Colin Hewett, Safety Mgr
Joe Romeo, Chief Mktg Ofcr
Chad Erwin, Technical Staff
EMP: 110
SALES (corp-wide): 18.7B Publicly Held
WEB: www.westrock.com
SIC: 2653 Boxes, corrugated: made from purchased materials
HQ: Westrock Cp, Llc
1000 Abernathy Rd Ste 125
Atlanta GA 30328

(G-3600)
XL CARTS INC
474415 E State Road 200 (32034-0802)
PHONE...................................904 277-7111

Anthony Douglas, Principal
Kimberly Wilson, Business Mgr
Garrett Wilson,
EMP: 8 EST: 2013
SALES (est): 1.5MM Privately Held
WEB: www.xlcarts.com
SIC: 3369 5088 Castings, except die-castings, precision; transportation equipment & supplies; golf carts

Flagler Beach
Flagler County

(G-3601)
ATHLETIC GUIDE PUBLISHING
509 S Central Ave (32136-3659)
P.O. Box 1050 (32136-1050)
PHONE...................................386 439-2250
Tom Keegan, Owner
EMP: 5 EST: 1995
SALES (est): 331.4K Privately Held
SIC: 2731 Book publishing

(G-3602)
CONSOLDTED MCH TL HOLDINGS LLC (PA)
712 S Ocean Shore Blvd (32136-3602)
PHONE...................................888 317-9990
Richard Hochstuhl, Mfg Staff
Julio Vizuete, Director
Elie Azar,
Ruth Irizarry, Admin Asst
Steve Trowbridge, Maintence Staff
EMP: 13 EST: 2017
SALES (est): 60.4MM Privately Held
WEB: www.cmth.com
SIC: 3599 3451 Machine shop, jobbing & repair; screw machine products

(G-3603)
CONTEMPRARY MCHNREY ENGRG SVCS
551 Roberts Rd (32136-3024)
P.O. Box 7 (32136-0007)
PHONE...................................386 439-0937
James A Smith, President
Julie M Smith, Corp Secy
▲ EMP: 20 EST: 1958
SQ FT: 60,000
SALES (est): 4.6MM Privately Held
SIC: 3743 5084 Railroad equipment; industrial machinery & equipment; controlling instruments & accessories

(G-3604)
REALTY SYSTEMS INC
3165 Old Kings Rd S (32136-4330)
PHONE...................................386 439-0460
EMP: 10 EST: 1994
SALES (est): 716.2K Publicly Held
SIC: 2451 Mfg Mobile Homes
PA: Equity Lifestyle Properties, Inc.
2 N Riverside Plz Ste 800
Chicago IL 60606

(G-3605)
SEA RAY BOATS INC
Also Called: Manufacturing Facility
1958 Unsinkable St (32136-3001)
PHONE...................................386 439-3401
Dan Goddard, Branch Mgr
EMP: 219
SALES (corp-wide): 5.8B Publicly Held
WEB: www.searay.com
SIC: 3732 Boats, fiberglass: building & repairing
HQ: Sea Ray Boats, Inc.
800 S Gay St Ste 1200
Knoxville TN 37929
865 522-4181

(G-3606)
WCM GROUP INC
1516 N Daytona Ave (32136-2909)
P.O. Box 1558 (32136-1558)
PHONE...................................516 238-4261
William Minicozzi, President
Maureen Minicozzi, Admin Sec
EMP: 6 EST: 2014
SALES (est): 622K Privately Held
WEB: www.wcmgroup.com
SIC: 3999 Barber & beauty shop equipment

Fleming Island
Clay County

(G-3607)
ASPEN PRODUCTS INC
1857 Inlet Cove Ct (32003-7275)
PHONE...................................904 579-4366
George Odonoghue, Principal
EMP: 437
SALES (corp-wide): 379.2MM Privately Held
WEB: www.aspenpro.com
SIC: 2674 Bags: uncoated paper & multiwall
PA: Aspen Products, Inc.
4231 Clary Blvd
Kansas City MO 64130
816 921-0234

(G-3608)
BARRON BOYZ AUTO ✪
1324 Fairway Village Dr (32003-8398)
PHONE...................................229 403-2656
Antonio Barron, Owner
EMP: 10 EST: 2021
SALES (est): 150K Privately Held
SIC: 3711 Automobile assembly, including specialty automobiles

(G-3609)
ELITE MANUFACTURING US LLC
1860 Indian River Dr (32003-7941)
PHONE...................................904 516-4796
EMP: 8 EST: 2017
SALES (est): 250.5K Privately Held
WEB: www.elitemanufacturingus.com
SIC: 3599 Machine shop, jobbing & repair

Florahome
Putnam County

(G-3610)
PAVEWAY SYSTEMS INC
114 Indian Lakes Ln (32140-3614)
PHONE...................................386 659-1316
Tiffany Albright, President
Annie Hope, Business Dir
EMP: 10 EST: 2011
SALES (est): 1MM Privately Held
WEB: www.pavewaysystems.com
SIC: 3999 Manufacturing industries

Floral City
Citrus County

(G-3611)
INSTANT PRINTING SERVICES INC
Also Called: I P S
8885 E Haines Ct (34436-4261)
PHONE...................................727 546-8036
Dan Conroy, President
Patty Conroy, Vice Pres
EMP: 13 EST: 1974
SALES (est): 874.3K Privately Held
WEB: www.instantprintinginc.com
SIC: 2752 7334 2791 2789 Commercial printing, offset; photocopying & duplicating services; typesetting; bookbinding & related work; commercial printing

Florida City
Miami-Dade County

(G-3612)
SOUTHERN PACKAGING MCHY CORP
Also Called: Spmc
550 Nw 3rd Ave (33034-3351)
P.O. Box 349197, Homestead (33034-9197)
PHONE...................................305 245-3045
David Raska, President
EMP: 27 EST: 1975
SQ FT: 16,500

SALES (est): 6.7MM Privately Held
WEB: www.spmc.biz
SIC: 3565 5084 Packaging machinery; industrial machinery & equipment

Fort Denaud
Hendry County

(G-3613)
AUSTIN POWDER COMPANY
6051 Fort Denaud Rd (33935-0445)
PHONE...................................863 674-0504
Ben Marquez, Master
EMP: 9
SALES (corp-wide): 734.5MM Privately Held
WEB: www.austinpowder.com
SIC: 2892 Explosives
HQ: Austin Powder Company
25800 Science Park Dr # 300
Cleveland OH 44122
216 464-2400

Fort Lauderdale
Broward County

(G-3614)
1800FLOWERSCOM
5350 Nw 35th Ter (33309-6334)
PHONE...................................954 683-1246
EMP: 7 EST: 2019
SALES (est): 262.6K Privately Held
WEB: www.1800flowers.com
SIC: 3999 Artificial flower arrangements; flowers, artificial & preserved

(G-3615)
21ST CENTURY CHEMICAL INC (PA)
2960 Sw 23rd Ter Ste 108 (33312-4936)
PHONE...................................954 689-7111
Bryan Hacht, President
EMP: 9 EST: 2011
SQ FT: 2,000
SALES (est): 1.8MM Privately Held
WEB: www.21stcenturychemical.com
SIC: 2899 Chemical preparations

(G-3616)
925 NUEVOS CUBANOS INC
925 N Andrews Ave (33311-7440)
PHONE...................................954 806-8375
Luis Valdes, Vice Pres
EMP: 9 EST: 2011
SALES (est): 289.3K Privately Held
WEB: www.925nuevoscubanos.com
SIC: 2711 Newspapers, publishing & printing

(G-3617)
AAA ABLE APPLIANCE SERVICE INC
Also Called: A A A Able Air Conditioning
430 N Andrews Ave (33301-3214)
PHONE...................................954 791-5222
Robert Murphy, Owner
Denise Murphy, Co-Owner
EMP: 8 EST: 2000
SQ FT: 4,000
SALES (est): 1.6MM Privately Held
WEB: www.aaaable.com
SIC: 3585 7623 5722 Refrigeration & heating equipment; refrigeration service & repair; household appliance stores

(G-3618)
AAXON LAUNDRY SYSTEMS LLC
6100 Powerline Rd (33309-2016)
PHONE...................................954 772-7100
Frank D'Annunzio, Author
EMP: 11 EST: 2013
SALES (est): 1.6MM Privately Held
WEB: www.aaxon.com
SIC: 3559 Special industry machinery

(G-3619)
ABC IMAGING OF WASHINGTON
714 N Federal Hwy (33304-2733)
PHONE...................................954 759-2037
Jennifer Daddio, Regl Sales Mgr

Leon Powell, *Branch Mgr*
EMP: 17
SALES (corp-wide): 127.2MM **Privately Held**
WEB: www.abcimaging.com
SIC: 2759 Publication printing
PA: Abc Imaging Of Washington, Inc
　　5290 Shawnee Rd Ste 300
　　Alexandria VA 22312
　　202 429-8870

(G-3620)
ACE BLUEPRINTING INC
1770 Nw 64th St Ste 500 (33309-1853)
PHONE......................954 771-0104
Ronald Chin, *President*
Karen Chin, *Vice Pres*
EMP: 10 **EST:** 1983
SALES (est): 488.3K **Privately Held**
WEB: www.ourplanroom.com
SIC: 2752 Commercial printing, offset

(G-3621)
ACR ELECTRONICS INC (DH)
5757 Ravenswood Rd (33312-6603)
PHONE......................954 981-3333
Gerald Angeli, *President*
Vance Cook, *Vice Pres*
Amporn Ortu, *Production*
Salvador Sanchez, *Production*
Pat Scarpelli, *Senior Buyer*
▲ **EMP:** 64 **EST:** 1989
SQ FT: 65,000
SALES (est): 58.7MM **Privately Held**
WEB: www.acrartex.com
SIC: 3663 3648 Receiver-transmitter units (transceiver); lighting equipment; flashlights
HQ: Acr Holdings Llc
　　5757 Ravensrood Rd
　　Fort Lauderdale FL 33312
　　954 981-3333

(G-3622)
ACRYLUX PAINT MFG CO INC
6010 Powerline Rd (33309-2014)
PHONE......................954 772-0300
Janet Riedesel, *President*
Andrew Berry, *Opers Mgr*
Trish Davis, *Credit Staff*
Patrick Berry, *Admin Sec*
▼ **EMP:** 11 **EST:** 1959
SQ FT: 14,000
SALES (est): 2.3MM **Privately Held**
WEB: www.acrylux.com
SIC: 2851 5231 Paints, waterproof; paints: oil or alkyd vehicle or water thinned; paint

(G-3623)
ACUDERM INC
6555 Powerline Rd Ste 114 (33309-7018)
PHONE......................954 733-6935
Charles R Yeh, *President*
James Foster, *Plant Mgr*
Edward Shaw, *Purch Mgr*
Alan Hartstein, *Controller*
Jaime Kroop, *Cust Mgr*
EMP: 65 **EST:** 1982
SALES (est): 11.2MM **Privately Held**
WEB: www.acuderm.com
SIC: 3069 2836 Medical & laboratory rubber sundries & related products; culture media

(G-3624)
ADD HELIUM
3590 Nw 54th St Ste 1 (33309-6366)
PHONE......................239 300-0913
Yvonne Lessmann, *Principal*
Melody Hearndon, *Marketing Mgr*
EMP: 5 **EST:** 2009
SALES (est): 393K **Privately Held**
WEB: www.addhelium.com
SIC: 2813 Helium

(G-3625)
ADVANCED MECHANICAL ENTPS INC
217 Sw 28th St (33315-3131)
PHONE......................954 764-2678
Richard Merhige, *President*
Fred Blockland, *Project Mgr*
Christine Battles, *Officer*
Peter Charbonnet, *Technician*
Jorge Garcia, *Technician*
◆ **EMP:** 20 **EST:** 1991

SQ FT: 4,200
SALES (est): 3.2MM **Privately Held**
WEB: www.amesolutions.com
SIC: 3731 Shipbuilding & repairing

(G-3626)
ADVANCED SEWING
3619 Nw 19th St (33311-4120)
PHONE......................954 484-2100
Elliot Levontin, *President*
EMP: 5 **EST:** 1986
SQ FT: 3,000
SALES (est): 322.5K **Privately Held**
SIC: 2393 3999 5021 7389 Cushions, except spring & carpet: purchased materials; garden umbrellas; outdoor & lawn furniture; sewing contractor

(G-3627)
AERCAP INC
100 Ne 3rd Ave Ste 800 (33301-1156)
PHONE......................954 760-7777
Aengus Kelly, *CEO*
Colin Merry, *Managing Dir*
Wouter Den Dikken, *COO*
Tuulia Rajamki, *VP Legal*
Betsy Chatterson, *Assistant VP*
EMP: 51 **EST:** 2014
SALES (est): 6.3MM **Privately Held**
WEB: www.aercap.com
SIC: 3721 7359 8711 Aircraft; aircraft rental; aviation &/or aeronautical engineering

(G-3628)
AERCAP GROUP SERVICES INC (HQ)
Also Called: Wings Aircraft Finance
100 Ne 3rd Ave Ste 800 (33301-1156)
PHONE......................954 760-7777
Anil Mehta, *President*
David Southard, *Counsel*
David Torres, *Senior VP*
Scot Kennedy, *VP Legal*
Gus Merizalde, *Assistant VP*
EMP: 10 **EST:** 1999
SALES (corp-wide): 19.3MM
SALES (corp-wide): 1B **Privately Held**
WEB: www.aercap.com
SIC: 3721 7359 Aircraft; aircraft rental
PA: Aercap Holdings N.V.
　　Onbekend Nederlands Adres
　　Onbekend
　　353 163-6065

(G-3629)
AERION CORP (PA)
500 Nw 62nd St Ste 400 (33309-6156)
PHONE......................775 337-6682
Tom Vice, *President*
Douglas Coleman, *Exec VP*
Michael Hinderberger, *Vice Pres*
Hal Martin, *Vice Pres*
Jeff Miller, *Vice Pres*
EMP: 9 **EST:** 2002
SALES (est): 6MM **Privately Held**
WEB: www.aerionsupersonic.com
SIC: 3721 Airplanes, fixed or rotary wing

(G-3630)
AGA MACHINE SHOP INC
277 Sw 33rd St (33315-3327)
PHONE......................954 522-1108
Adolfo Gomez, *President*
EMP: 6 **EST:** 2006
SALES (est): 691K **Privately Held**
WEB: www.agamachineshop.com
SIC: 3599 Machine shop, jobbing & repair

(G-3631)
AGM INDUSTRIES INC
1560 Nw 23rd Ave (33311-5149)
PHONE......................954 486-1112
Carmine Parente, *President*
Guido Parente, *Corp Secy*
◆ **EMP:** 14 **EST:** 1986
SQ FT: 16,000
SALES (est): 2.9MM **Privately Held**
WEB: www.acdelete.com
SIC: 3231 Mirrored glass; doors, glass: made from purchased glass

(G-3632)
AIRLINE SUPPORT GROUP INC
2700 W Cypress Creek Rd (33309-1744)
PHONE......................954 971-4567

Joseph Custy, *President*
EMP: 17 **EST:** 1999
SALES (est): 1.7MM **Privately Held**
WEB: www.airlinesupportgroup.net
SIC: 3728 Aircraft parts & equipment

(G-3633)
AIRMARK COMPONENTS INC
2701 Sw 2nd Ave (33315-3129)
PHONE......................954 522-5370
Louis Moritz, *President*
Kirk Alexander, *Vice Pres*
Yvonne Silva, *Purchasing*
Brian Nee, *Sales Staff*
William Baumann, *Marketing Staff*
EMP: 44 **EST:** 1985
SQ FT: 22,000
SALES (est): 5.7MM **Privately Held**
WEB: www.airmarkcomponents.com
SIC: 3728 Aircraft parts & equipment

(G-3634)
AIRMARK OVERHAUL INC
Also Called: Airmark Engines, Inc.
6001 Nw 29th Ave (33309-1731)
PHONE......................954 970-3200
David Williams, *President*
William Milburn, *President*
Ernest Moritz, *Treasurer*
◆ **EMP:** 9 **EST:** 1975
SQ FT: 20,000
SALES (est): 736.9K **Privately Held**
WEB: www.airmarkoverhaul.com
SIC: 3724 Aircraft engines & engine parts

(G-3635)
AJ ORIGINALS INC
1710 Ne 63rd Ct (33334-5128)
PHONE......................954 563-9911
EMP: 8
SALES (est): 1.6MM **Privately Held**
SIC: 2434 2511 2599 2426 Mfg Furniture/Fixtures Mfg Wood Household Furn Mfg Wood Kitchen Cabinet Hdwd Dimension/Flr Mill

(G-3636)
ALCAS USA CORP
5347 Nw 35th Ave (33309-6315)
PHONE......................305 591-3325
EMP: 7 **EST:** 2015
SALES (est): 484.1K **Privately Held**
SIC: 2024 Ice Cream And Frozen Desserts, Nsk

(G-3637)
ALL AMERICAN BARRICADES
2300 Sw 41st Ave (33317-6927)
PHONE......................305 685-6124
Ruben G Santos, *President*
Monique Santos, *Vice Pres*
Ali Garces, *Office Mgr*
EMP: 8 **EST:** 1998
SQ FT: 3,000
SALES (est): 1.5MM **Privately Held**
WEB: www.barricades.com
SIC: 3499 Barricades, metal

(G-3638)
ALL LIQUID ENVMTL SVCS LLC
Also Called: Johnson Environmental Services
4600 Powerline Rd (33309-3838)
PHONE......................800 767-9594
Albert Panzarella, *Principal*
Allan Lange, *Opers Staff*
Dione Dixon, *Administration*
EMP: 34 **EST:** 1933
SALES (est): 11.8MM **Privately Held**
WEB: www.johnsones.com
SIC: 3089 5039 4953 7699 Septic tanks, plastic; septic tanks; liquid waste, collection & disposal; catch basin cleaning

(G-3639)
ALL POINTS BOATS INC
Also Called: Manufacturing
900 Sw 21st Ter (33312-3121)
PHONE......................954 767-8255
Jerry Clark, *CEO*
Nathan Goodwin, *President*
EMP: 55 **EST:** 1996

SALES (est): 6.6MM **Privately Held**
WEB: www.apb1.com
SIC: 3441 7699 7389 3999 Fabricated structural metal for ships; boat repair; metal cutting services; atomizers, toiletry; commercial cargo ships, building & repairing; construction machinery

(G-3640)
ALLIED AEROFOAM PRODUCTS LLC
1883 W State Road 84 # 106 (33315-2232)
PHONE......................731 660-2705
Billy Rust, *Branch Mgr*
EMP: 19
SALES (corp-wide): 45.8MM **Privately Held**
WEB: www.alliedaerofoam.com
SIC: 3086 Plastics foam products
HQ: Allied Aerofoam Products, Llc
　　1883 W State Road 84 # 106
　　Fort Lauderdale FL 33315
　　813 626-0090

(G-3641)
ALLIED AEROFOAM PRODUCTS LLC (HQ)
1883 W State Road 84 # 106 (33315-2232)
PHONE......................813 626-0090
Kevin M Pocongan, *CEO*
Bill Carrington, *President*
Lambert Willett, *General Mgr*
Angela Murphy, *Purch Dir*
Jeff Aguiar, *CFO*
◆ **EMP:** 70 **EST:** 2002
SALES (est): 45.8MM **Privately Held**
WEB: www.alliedaerofoam.com
SIC: 3086 Plastics foam products

(G-3642)
ALLIED DECALS-FLA INC
Also Called: Allied Binders
5225 Nw 35th Ave (33309-3303)
PHONE......................800 940-2233
Bruce Landis, *President*
Heidi Landis, *Vice Pres*
▼ **EMP:** 13 **EST:** 1978
SQ FT: 11,000
SALES (est): 588K **Privately Held**
SIC: 2759 2782 Screen printing; decals: printing; looseleaf binders & devices

(G-3643)
ALLIED INSULATED PANELS INC
6451 N Federal Hwy # 1204 (33308-1402)
PHONE......................800 599-3905
Michael D Lassner, *President*
EMP: 7 **EST:** 2018
SALES (est): 550.2K **Privately Held**
WEB: www.alliedbuildings.com
SIC: 3448 Prefabricated metal buildings

(G-3644)
ALLIED STEEL BUILDINGS INC
6451 N Federal Hwy # 1202 (33308-1402)
PHONE......................800 508-2718
Sergio Plaza, *Vice Pres*
John Barnes, *Prdtn Mgr*
Ursulla Milla, *Human Resources*
Collin Burich, *Accounts Mgr*
Lassner Michael, *Branch Mgr*
EMP: 23 **Privately Held**
WEB: www.alliedbuildings.com
SIC: 3448 Prefabricated metal buildings
PA: Allied Steel Buildings Inc.
　　6451 N Federal Hwy # 411
　　Fort Lauderdale FL 33308

(G-3645)
ALLIED-360 LLC
101 Ne 3rd Ave Ste 300 (33301-1128)
PHONE......................954 590-4940
Michael Lassner, *President*
Catherine Soto, *General Mgr*
Alex Andersen, *Business Mgr*
Guy Susi, *Vice Pres*
Sergio Plaza, *VP Opers*
EMP: 30 **EST:** 2010
SALES (est): 2.4MM **Privately Held**
SIC: 3441 Fabricated structural metal

▲ = Import ▼=Export
◆ =Import/Export

(G-3646)
ALLSTEEL PROCESSING LC
1250 Nw 23rd Ave (33311-5243)
PHONE................................954 587-1900
Maria Esquilin, *Human Res Mgr*
Will Snyder, *Sales Mgr*
Glenn Markus, *Mng Member*
Vanessa Parrilla, *Manager*
Richard Abbott, *Manager*
EMP: 15 **EST:** 1996
SALES (est): 1.9MM **Privately Held**
WEB: www.allsteelproducts.com
SIC: 3317 Steel pipe & tubes

(G-3647)
ALM GLOBAL LLC
Also Called: Miami Daily Business Review
633 S Andrews Ave Ste 100 (33301-2843)
PHONE................................954 468-2600
Shirley Cohen, *Manager*
Maria Mesa, *Legal Staff*
Nadine Modestil, *Clerk*
EMP: 13
SALES (corp-wide): 202.2MM **Privately
Held**
WEB: www.alm.com
SIC: 2711 Newspapers
HQ: Alm Global, Llc
150 E 42nd St
New York NY 10017
212 457-9400

(G-3648)
AMERICAN CHANGER CORP
Also Called: Hoffman Mint
1400 Nw 65th Pl (33309-1902)
PHONE................................954 917-3009
Wayne Snihur, *President*
Harry Steinbok, *Principal*
Armando Mendez, *Controller*
◆ **EMP:** 58 **EST:** 2001
SQ FT: 43,000
SALES (est): 11.3MM **Privately Held**
WEB: www.americanchanger.com
SIC: 3578 Change making machines

(G-3649)
**AMERICAN DIAMOND
DISTRIBUTORS**
Also Called: Beverely's
3600 W Coml Blvd Ste 101 (33309)
PHONE................................954 485-7808
Jeff Malvin, *President*
Mark Malvin, *Vice Pres*
EMP: 8 **EST:** 1985
SALES (est): 152.4K **Privately Held**
SIC: 3911 Jewelry, precious metal

(G-3650)
**AMERICAN PRTECTIVE
COATING INC**
Also Called: American Powder Coating
6795 Nw 17th Ave (33309-1521)
PHONE................................954 561-0999
Robert Symington, *President*
EMP: 19 **EST:** 1990
SQ FT: 10,000
SALES (est): 1.6MM **Privately Held**
WEB: www.apcfl.net
SIC: 3479 Coating of metals & formed
products

(G-3651)
AND-DELL CORPORATION
245 Sw 33rd St (33315-3397)
PHONE................................954 523-6478
Jon A Lobdell, *President*
Beverly Lobdell, *Treasurer*
Mike Stein, *Marketing Staff*
Ric Colson, *Consultant*
▲ **EMP:** 30 **EST:** 1966
SQ FT: 14,000
SALES (est): 2.9MM **Privately Held**
WEB: www.dellheatrix.com
SIC: 3634 Heating units, electric (radiant
heat): baseboard or wall

(G-3652)
**ANDREWS WAREHOUSE
PARTNERSHIP**
1512 E Broward Blvd (33301-2122)
PHONE................................954 524-3330
Edward D Stone Jr, *Partner*
Joseph J Lalli, *Partner*
EMP: 7 **EST:** 1985

SQ FT: 4,000
SALES (est): 635.6K **Privately Held**
SIC: 2512 Wood upholstered chairs &
couches

(G-3653)
**APPLE PRINTING & ADVG SPC
INC**
5055 Nw 10th Ter (33309-3167)
PHONE................................954 524-0493
Sean Donato, *President*
Kevin Donato, *Vice Pres*
Randolph Bastein, *Production*
EMP: 20 **EST:** 1970
SQ FT: 8,500
SALES (est): 3.3MM **Privately Held**
WEB: www.appleprinting.com
SIC: 2752 2791 2789 Commercial print-
ing, offset; typesetting; bookbinding & re-
lated work

(G-3654)
ARCHIMAZE LOGISTICS INC
1776 Nw 38th Ave (33311-4117)
PHONE................................954 615-7485
Evan Graham, *Principal*
EMP: 9 **EST:** 2012
SALES (est): 394.6K **Privately Held**
WEB: www.forkliftfrenzy.com
SIC: 3061 3559 3462 Automotive rubber
goods (mechanical); automotive related
machinery; degreasing machines, auto-
motive & industrial; automotive forgings,
ferrous: crankshaft, engine, axle, etc.

(G-3655)
ARGOTEC INC (PA)
2432 Ne 27th Ave (33305-2719)
PHONE................................954 491-6550
Paul Novakovic, *President*
EMP: 15 **EST:** 1980
SALES (est): 1.3MM **Privately Held**
SIC: 3699 Underwater sound equipment

(G-3656)
ARKAY DISTRIBUTING INC
401 E Las Olas Blvd # 1400 (33301-2210)
PHONE................................954 536-8413
Eynald Grattagliano R, *President*
Reynald Grattagliano, *Corp Secy*
Monique Force, *Vice Pres*
Jair Dos Santos Pereira, *Vice Pres*
EMP: 8 **EST:** 2013
SALES (est): 177.1K **Privately Held**
SIC: 2086 Carbonated beverages, nonal-
coholic: bottled & canned

(G-3657)
ARMOUR GROUP INC
6700 Powerline Rd (33309-2154)
PHONE................................954 767-2030
G Robert Tatum, *CEO*
Martine Miller, *President*
EMP: 21 **EST:** 2010
SALES (est): 661.4K **Privately Held**
WEB: www.thearmourgroup.com
SIC: 3711 Cars, armored, assembly of

(G-3658)
**ARRIBAS BINDERY SERVICES
INC**
6701 Nw 15th Way B (33309-1527)
PHONE................................954 978-8886
Ramon Arriba, *President*
EMP: 5 **EST:** 1999
SALES (est): 477.1K **Privately Held**
SIC: 2789 Binding only: books, pamphlets,
magazines, etc.

(G-3659)
ART SIGN CO INC
Also Called: Art Sign & Neon
835 Nw 6th Ave (33311-7222)
PHONE................................954 763-4410
Joe Dillard, *President*
Tina Mastandrea, *Sales Executive*
Kristina O 'brien, *Mktg Dir*
Fred Shuaibi, *Graphic Designe*
◆ **EMP:** 80 **EST:** 1947
SQ FT: 2,500
SALES (est): 9.6MM **Privately Held**
WEB: www.artsignfl.com
SIC: 3993 Electric signs; displays &
cutouts, window & lobby

(G-3660)
**ASBURY MANUFACTURING CO
LLC**
3355 Entp Ave Ste 160 (33331)
PHONE................................954 202-7419
Christopher Klingensmith, *Engineer*
Oscar Neal Asbury, *Mng Member*
◆ **EMP:** 30 **EST:** 1955
SQ FT: 46,285
SALES (est): 7MM
SALES (corp-wide): 208MM **Privately
Held**
SIC: 3585 Ice making machinery
PA: Greenfield World Trade, Inc.
3355 Entp Ave Ste 160
Fort Lauderdale FL 33331
954 202-7419

(G-3661)
ASSA ABLOY HOSPITALITY INC
Also Called: Vingcard
5601 Powerline Rd Ste 305 (33309-2831)
PHONE................................954 920-0772
Clive Marshall, *Manager*
EMP: 7
SALES (corp-wide): 10.3B **Privately Held**
WEB: www.assaabloyglobalsolutions.com
SIC: 3429 Locks or lock sets
HQ: Assa Abloy Global Solutions, Inc.
631 Interntl Pkwy Ste 100
Richardson TX 75081
972 907-2273

(G-3662)
ATKINSON MARINE INC
235 Sw 32nd Ct (33315-3333)
PHONE................................954 763-1652
Fred Collins, *Principal*
EMP: 7 **EST:** 2011
SALES (est): 105K **Privately Held**
SIC: 3429 Manufactured hardware (gen-
eral)

(G-3663)
ATLAS EMBROIDERY LLC
Also Called: Atlas Embroidery & Screen Prtg
2300 Sw 34th St (33312-5061)
PHONE................................954 625-2411
Mitchell Lombard, *President*
Alex Lombard, *Vice Pres*
Jacki Murray, *Human Res Mgr*
Karen Johnson, *Department Mgr*
Jeremy Feinberg, *Director*
▼ **EMP:** 95 **EST:** 2002
SQ FT: 16,000
SALES (est): 12.1MM **Privately Held**
WEB: www.atlasembroidery.com
SIC: 2395 Embroidery products, except
schiffli machine; embroidery & art needle-
work

(G-3664)
ATLAS MARINE SYSTEMS INC
1801 S Perimeter Rd # 150 (33309-7139)
PHONE................................954 735-6767
Mark Loring, *President*
Ray Beutel, *Chairman*
Andrew Ford, *Prdtn Mgr*
Bob Saxon, *Treasurer*
Dennis Braun, *Sales Mgr*
EMP: 19 **EST:** 2002
SALES (est): 1.4MM **Privately Held**
WEB: www.atlasmarinesystems.com
SIC: 3679 Electronic loads & power sup-
plies

(G-3665)
ATTACK COMMUNICATIONS INC
Also Called: Vick Houston
1314 E Las Olas Blvd (33301-2334)
PHONE................................954 300-2716
Steven Vickers, *President*
EMP: 7 **EST:** 1997
SALES (est): 1MM **Privately Held**
WEB: www.attack.ac
SIC: 3651 Household audio & video equip-
ment

(G-3666)
**AUDIO STORAGE
TECHNOLOGIES**
Also Called: Audacity Audio
1540 Ne 60th St (33334-5989)
PHONE................................954 229-5050
Fred L Clark, *President*

Tom Harrah, *Vice Pres*
EMP: 5 **EST:** 2001
SALES (est): 315.2K **Privately Held**
WEB: www.audiost.com
SIC: 7372 Operating systems computer
software

(G-3667)
**AUTOMATED PARKING
CORPORATION**
6555 Nw 9th Ave Ste 106 (33309-2048)
PHONE................................754 200-8441
Marco Radonic, *CEO*
Paula Voss, *Marketing Staff*
EMP: 7 **EST:** 2016
SALES (est): 908K **Privately Held**
WEB: www.apcpark.com
SIC: 3535 Conveyors & conveying equip-
ment

(G-3668)
AVALON AVIATION INC
1323 Se 17th St Unit 344 (33316-1707)
PHONE................................954 655-0256
Kevin Maguire, *President*
EMP: 5 **EST:** 2010
SQ FT: 1,600
SALES (est): 466.7K **Privately Held**
SIC: 3728 8711 Aircraft body assemblies
& parts; aviation &/or aeronautical engi-
neering

(G-3669)
AWAB LLC
245 Sw 32nd St (33315-3323)
P.O. Box 22248 (33335-2248)
PHONE................................954 763-3003
J Denny Turner, *President*
Kellie Bucchiere, *General Mgr*
Whitney Turner, *General Mgr*
Valerie Bressler, *Manager*
▼ **EMP:** 5 **EST:** 2000
SALES (est): 542.9K **Privately Held**
WEB: www.awabllc.com
SIC: 3492 Hose & tube fittings & assem-
blies, hydraulic/pneumatic

(G-3670)
**B&SDELICIOUS
DESSERTS&CUPCAKES**
865 Nw 27th Ter (33311-6657)
PHONE................................954 557-8350
Shontel Burke, *Principal*
EMP: 7 **EST:** 2013
SALES (est): 140.5K **Privately Held**
SIC: 2051 Bread, cake & related products

(G-3671)
BALLISTA TACTICAL SYSTEMS
2881 E Oakland Park Blvd (33306-1813)
PHONE................................954 260-0765
Shawn Johnson, *CEO*
EMP: 8 **EST:** 2011
SALES (est): 654.8K **Privately Held**
WEB: www.ballistatactical.com
SIC: 3484 3489 Small arms; guns or gun
parts. over 30 mm.

(G-3672)
**BALPRO POWDER COATING
INC**
1624 Nw 38th Ave (33311-4137)
PHONE................................954 797-0520
EMP: 15
SALES (corp-wide): 265.9K **Privately
Held**
WEB: www.balpropowdercoating.com
SIC: 3479 Coating of metals & formed
products
PA: Balpro Powder Coating, Inc.
6800 Nw 45th St
Lauderhill FL

(G-3673)
BANDART ENTERPRISES INC
Also Called: PIP Printing
5303 Nw 35th Ter (33309-6328)
PHONE................................954 564-1224
Jan Geller, *President*
Linda Geller, *Vice Pres*
EMP: 17 **EST:** 2000
SQ FT: 5,400
SALES (est): 2.1MM **Privately Held**
WEB: www.pip.com
SIC: 2752 Commercial printing, offset

(G-3674)
BARNACLE KING LLC
1701 Ne 14th Ave Unit 2 (33305-3334)
PHONE.....................................954 952-9140
Richard M Bassett, *CEO*
EMP: 5 EST: 2019
SALES (est): 463.9K **Privately Held**
WEB: www.barnacleking.com
SIC: 3731 Shipbuilding & repairing

(G-3675)
BAS PLASTICS INC
1000 Nw 56th St (33309-2833)
PHONE.....................................954 202-9080
Micolas Bara, *President*
▲ EMP: 5 EST: 1996
SALES (est): 721.4K **Privately Held**
WEB: www.basplastics.com
SIC: 3089 Molding primary plastic

(G-3676)
BAUFORMAT SOUTH-EAST LLC
1413 Nw 5th Ave (33311-6053)
PHONE.....................................201 693-6635
Lothar Birkenfeld, *Principal*
EMP: 9 EST: 2017
SALES (est): 397.2K **Privately Held**
SIC: 2434 Wood kitchen cabinets

(G-3677)
BAY STATE MILLING COMPANY
Also Called: Bakers Element
3270 Sw 11th Ave (33315-2962)
PHONE.....................................630 427-3400
EMP: 10
SALES (corp-wide): 131.8MM **Privately Held**
WEB: www.baystatemilling.com
SIC: 2041 Flour & other grain mill products
PA: Bay State Milling Company
100 Congress St Ste 2
Quincy MA 02169
617 328-4400

(G-3678)
BAYSIDE CNVAS YCHT INTRORS INC
2830 W State Road 84 # 11 (33312-4826)
PHONE.....................................954 792-8535
Sally Moran, *President*
▼ EMP: 8 EST: 1996
SALES (est): 575.1K **Privately Held**
WEB: www.baysidecanvas.com
SIC: 2394 Canvas & related products

(G-3679)
BBX SWEET HOLDINGS LLC (HQ)
401 E Las Olas Blvd # 800 (33301-4284)
PHONE.....................................954 940-4000
Kevin Coen, *CEO*
Rick Harris, *President*
Alan Levan,
EMP: 15 EST: 2013
SALES (est): 15.1MM
SALES (corp-wide): 313.6MM **Publicly Held**
WEB: www.bbxcapital.com
SIC: 2064 5441 Chocolate candy, except solid chocolate; candy
PA: Bbx Capital, Inc.
201 E Las Olas Blvd # 1900
Fort Lauderdale FL 33301
954 940-4900

(G-3680)
BCT INTERNATIONAL INC (HQ)
Also Called: B C T
2810 E Oklnd Prk Blvd # 308 (33306-1801)
PHONE.....................................305 563-1224
William Wilkerson, *CEO*
Peter Posk, *President*
Ben Fretti, *Senior VP*
Bob Dolan, *Vice Pres*
Gary Hiltbrand, *Vice Pres*
▲ EMP: 30 EST: 1981
SALES (est): 8MM **Privately Held**
WEB: www.evoprint.com
SIC: 2752 6794 Commercial printing, lithographic; franchises, selling or licensing
PA: Phoenix Group Of Florida, Inc.
3000 Ne 30th Pl Fl 5
Fort Lauderdale FL 33306
954 563-1224

(G-3681)
BEMA INC
Also Called: Minuteman Press
2301 S Andrews Ave (33316-3947)
PHONE.....................................954 761-1919
Dan Kornfield, *President*
EMP: 5 EST: 1977
SQ FT: 1,800
SALES (est): 785.3K **Privately Held**
WEB: www.minutemanpress.com
SIC: 2752 Commercial printing, lithographic

(G-3682)
BERGERON SAND & ROCK MIN INC (PA)
Also Called: Bergeron Properties & Inv
19612 Sw 69th Pl (33332-1618)
PHONE.....................................954 680-6100
Ronald M Bergeron, *President*
Ted Hojara, *Project Mgr*
Phil Desai, *Treasurer*
EMP: 33 EST: 1968
SALES (est): 10.7MM **Privately Held**
SIC: 1442 Common sand mining; gravel mining

(G-3683)
BETAWAVE LLC ☉
2968 Nw 60th St (33309-1735)
PHONE.....................................954 223-8298
Robert Babik, *Mng Member*
EMP: 15 EST: 2021
SALES (est): 528.8K **Privately Held**
SIC: 3841 Medical instruments & equipment, blood & bone work

(G-3684)
BI-ADS INC
Also Called: West Side Gazette
545 Nw 7th Ter (33311-8140)
P.O. Box 5304 (33310-5304)
PHONE.....................................954 525-1489
Levi Henry Jr, *President*
Henry Yvonne, *Vice Pres*
Sonia Henry, *Treasurer*
EMP: 15 EST: 1971
SQ FT: 3,170
SALES (est): 1MM **Privately Held**
WEB: www.thewestsidegazette.com
SIC: 2711 2752 Newspapers, publishing & printing; commercial printing, lithographic

(G-3685)
BIG EAGLE LLC
3051 W State Road 84 (33312-4821)
PHONE.....................................305 586-8766
EMP: 8 EST: 2004
SALES (est): 174.2K **Privately Held**
SIC: 3732 Yachts, building & repairing

(G-3686)
BIGHAM INSULATION & SUP CO INC
2816 Sw 3rd Ave (33315-3110)
PHONE.....................................954 522-2887
Robert E Bryant, *President*
James P Collier Jr, *Vice Pres*
Martin Krutz, *Accountant*
Dominick Palleschi, *Director*
◆ EMP: 31 EST: 1960
SQ FT: 36,000
SALES (est): 3.5MM **Privately Held**
WEB: www.bighamsparta.com
SIC: 3296 Mineral wool insulation products; fiberglass insulation

(G-3687)
BIMBO BAKERIES USA
6783 Nw 17th Ave (33309-1521)
PHONE.....................................954 968-7684
EMP: 10 EST: 2019
SALES (est): 460.8K **Privately Held**
WEB: www.bimbobakeriesusa.com
SIC: 2051 Bakery: wholesale or wholesale/retail combined

(G-3688)
BIO-TECH MEDICAL SOFTWARE INC
Also Called: Biotrackthc
6750 N Andrews Ave # 325 (33309-2142)
PHONE.....................................800 797-4711
Patrick Vo, *CEO*
Moe Afaneh, *COO*
Gary Greenwood, *Exec VP*
Cody Stiffler, *Vice Pres*
Jenna Smeryage, *Project Mgr*
EMP: 62 EST: 2007
SQ FT: 3,000
SALES (est): 14.6MM **Privately Held**
WEB: www.bioscriptrx.com
SIC: 7372 Business oriented computer software

(G-3689)
BJB MARINE WELDING & SVCS INC
2700 Sw 25th Ter (33312-4858)
PHONE.....................................954 909-4967
Warren C Edwards, *Vice Pres*
EMP: 10 EST: 2014
SALES (est): 424.9K **Privately Held**
WEB: www.bjbmarine.com
SIC: 7692 Automotive welding

(G-3690)
BLINDSOURCE LLC
100 Davie Blvd (33315-1517)
PHONE.....................................954 455-1965
Lani Guluk, *Mng Member*
Michael Guluk, *Mng Member*
Rik Vanduinen, *Mng Member*
Cody Guluk,
EMP: 6 EST: 2012
SALES (est): 492.5K **Privately Held**
WEB: www.blindsource.com
SIC: 2591 Window blinds

(G-3691)
BLUE CHIP SERVICING INC
Also Called: Blue Chip Srvcing Fster Fnding
515 E Las Olas Blvd Ste 1 (33301-2296)
PHONE.....................................844 607-2029
Paul Damiano, *President*
EMP: 11 EST: 2016
SALES (est): 581K **Privately Held**
SIC: 1389 Roustabout service

(G-3692)
BLUE MARLIN TOWERS INC
3100 W State Road 84 # 20 (33312-4876)
PHONE.....................................954 530-9140
Edward R Milo, *Director*
EMP: 9 EST: 1993
SQ FT: 2,500
SALES (est): 339.7K **Privately Held**
SIC: 3441 Fabricated structural metal for ships

(G-3693)
BLUE OCEAN PRESS INC
6299 Nw 27th Way (33309-1728)
PHONE.....................................954 973-1819
Tom Mounce, *President*
Gregory Von Hausch, *President*
Mary A McKay, *Prdtn Mgr*
Mary McKay, *Prdtn Mgr*
Kevin Murray, *Production*
▲ EMP: 46 EST: 1984
SQ FT: 30,000
SALES (est): 12.2MM **Privately Held**
WEB: www.blueoceanpress.com
SIC: 2752 7336 7389 2262 Promotional printing, lithographic; graphic arts & related design; apparel pressing service; screen printing: manmade fiber & silk broadwoven fabrics; embroidery products, except schiffli machine; catalog & mail-order houses

(G-3694)
BLUEOCEAN MARINE SERVICES LLC
Also Called: Broward Armature and Generator
340 Sw 21st Ter (33312-1427)
PHONE.....................................954 583-9888
Michael L Brochu Sr, *CEO*
Michael W Brochu Jr, *President*
▼ EMP: 13 EST: 1995
SQ FT: 5,000
SALES (est): 891.3K **Privately Held**
SIC: 7694 Electric motor repair

(G-3695)
BLUEWATER CHAIRS INC
240 Sw 33rd Ct (33315-3306)
PHONE.....................................954 318-0840
Thomas Ackel, *CEO*
Joe Schwab, *President*
▲ EMP: 15 EST: 1987
SQ FT: 16,000
SALES (est): 1.7MM **Privately Held**
WEB: www.bluewaterchairs.com
SIC: 2511 Chairs, household, except upholstered: wood

(G-3696)
BMC SERVICES INC
2351 Sw 34th St (33312-5046)
PHONE.....................................954 587-6337
Ricardo Mejia, *President*
Isabelle Mejia, *Vice Pres*
EMP: 10 EST: 2011
SQ FT: 10,000
SALES (est): 833.3K **Privately Held**
SIC: 2599 1751 Ship furniture; carpentry work

(G-3697)
BOAT ENERGY LLC
714 Nw 57th St (33309-2825)
PHONE.....................................954 501-2628
Linda Bernhardt, *VP Sales*
EMP: 6 EST: 2013
SALES (est): 518K **Privately Held**
WEB: www.boatenergy.com
SIC: 3519 Marine engines

(G-3698)
BOAT INTERNATIONAL MEDIA INC
Also Called: Duck Walk
1800 Se 10th Ave Ste 340 (33316-2984)
PHONE.....................................954 522-2628
Leonardo Careddu, *Publisher*
Stewart Campbell, *Editor*
Lee Franklin, *Editor*
Nick Kisch, *Editor*
Risa Merl, *Editor*
▲ EMP: 3 EST: 1997
SALES (est): 3MM
SALES (corp-wide): 11.1MM **Privately Held**
WEB: www.dockwalk.com
SIC: 2721 Magazines: publishing only, not printed on site
HQ: Boat International Media Limited
Hartfield House
London SW19

(G-3699)
BOCATECH INC
4101 Ravenswood Rd # 219 (33312-5352)
PHONE.....................................954 397-7070
Abram Ackerman, *President*
Arlene McMachen, *Principal*
Brian Shaw, *Principal*
▲ EMP: 5 EST: 2005
SALES (est): 846.9K **Privately Held**
WEB: www.bocatechswitches.com
SIC: 3679 3675 3677 3678 Electronic circuits; condensers, electronic; electronic transformers; electronic connectors

(G-3700)
BOMBARDIIER
Also Called: Bombardier Aircraft Services
4100 Sw 11th Ter (33315-3504)
PHONE.....................................954 622-1200
Melissa Bertrand, *Project Mgr*
Joseph Scarfone, *Finance Mgr*
Steve Garrett, *Supervisor*
Cristiane Maia, *Admin Asst*
Zachary Lilly, *Technician*
EMP: 11
SALES (corp-wide): 6B **Privately Held**
WEB: www.bombardier.com
SIC: 3721 Aircraft
PA: Bombardier Inc
400 Ch De La Cote-Vertu
Dorval QC H4S 1
514 855-5000

(G-3701)
BONNIER CORPORATION
705 Sw 16th St (33315-1628)
PHONE.....................................954 830-4460
Natasha Lloyd, *Principal*
Doug Olander, *Chief*
Leslie Acevedo, *Opers Staff*
Kelly Weekley, *Production*
Missie Prichard, *Sales Staff*
EMP: 19 **Privately Held**
WEB: www.bonniercorp.com

▲ = Import ▼=Export
◆ =Import/Export

SIC: 2721 Magazines: publishing only, not printed on site
HQ: Bonnier Corporation
480 N Orlando Ave Ste 236
Winter Park FL 32789

(G-3702)
BRADFORD YACHT LIMITED INC
3051 W State Road 84 (33312-4821)
PHONE..................................954 791-3800
Dieter Cosman, *Ch of Bd*
Kathy Nitabach, *Vice Pres*
Colin Lord, *Project Mgr*
◆ EMP: 165 EST: 1966
SALES (est): 11.6MM Privately Held
WEB: www.bradford-marine.com
SIC: 3732 Yachts, building & repairing

(G-3703)
BRIGHT MANUFACTURING LLC (PA)
Also Called: Power Bright Technologies
2933 W Cypress Creek Rd # 202 (33309-1777)
PHONE..................................954 603-4950
Guil Hetzroni, *Sales Staff*
Jose Guzman, *Manager*
Kim Nguyen, *Executive Asst*
Daniel Hetzroni,
▲ EMP: 5 EST: 2008
SALES (est): 1.1MM Privately Held
WEB: www.brightmfg.com
SIC: 3612 Power transformers, electric

(G-3704)
BROWARD CASTING FOUNDRY INC
Also Called: Gatto Furniture
2240 Sw 34th St (33312-5049)
PHONE..................................954 584-6400
Ronald J Gatto, *President*
Ronald J Gatto Jr, *President*
Denise Gatto-Trissel, *Vice Pres*
Lynn Zophres, *Treasurer*
Dawn Brooks, *Admin Sec*
▼ EMP: 30 EST: 1963
SQ FT: 22,000
SALES (est): 7.3MM Privately Held
WEB: www.browardcasting.com
SIC: 3365 Aluminum foundries

(G-3705)
BROWARD POWER TRAIN CO INC
5300 Nw 12th Ave Ste 3 (33309-3164)
PHONE..................................954 772-0881
Lee Minyard, *President*
Charles Minyeard, *Vice Pres*
Sue Minyard, *Treasurer*
Joy Minyard, *Admin Sec*
EMP: 24 EST: 1980
SQ FT: 2,000
SALES (est): 2.2MM Privately Held
WEB: www.browardpowertrain.com
SIC: 3714 Drive shafts, motor vehicle

(G-3706)
BROWARD SIGNS
1901 S Federal Hwy (33316-3500)
PHONE..................................954 320-9903
Donna A Richards P, *Principal*
EMP: 5 EST: 2010
SALES (est): 448.4K Privately Held
WEB: www.browardsigns.com
SIC: 3993 Electric signs

(G-3707)
BUDDY CUSTARD INC
1451 W Cypress Creek Rd (33309-1961)
PHONE..................................561 715-3785
Robert Schlien, *CEO*
Katherine Schlien, *President*
Paul R Smith, *Treasurer*
EMP: 8 EST: 2017
SALES (est): 963.1K Privately Held
WEB: www.buddycustard.com
SIC: 2048 Prepared feeds

(G-3708)
BUILDERS NOTICE CORPORATION
Also Called: Construction Collections
708 S Andrews Ave (33316-1032)
PHONE..................................954 764-1322

James A Carmel, *CEO*
Kenneth Deangelis, *President*
Regina Durand, *Vice Pres*
Francesca Durand, *Marketing Staff*
EMP: 7 EST: 1975
SQ FT: 2,000
SALES (est): 943.5K Privately Held
WEB: www.buildersnotice.com
SIC: 2741 7389 Newsletter publishing; process serving service

(G-3709)
BUKKEHAVE INC
6750 N Andrews Ave # 200 (33309-2180)
P.O. Box 13143 (33316-0100)
PHONE..................................954 525-9788
Christian Haar, *CEO*
Morten Frederiksen, *President*
Mark Combs, *Vice Pres*
Rohit Damodar, *Vice Pres*
Bo Dybbro, *CFO*
◆ EMP: 7 EST: 1996
SALES (est): 6.9MM
SALES (corp-wide): 226.3K Privately Held
WEB: www.bukkehave.com
SIC: 1389 5013 Cementing oil & gas well casings; automotive supplies & parts
PA: B1925 Aps
Troensevej 29
Svendborg
632 121-21

(G-3710)
C P VEGETABLE OIL INC
Also Called: CP Vegetable Oil
601 Sw 21st Ter Ste 1 (33312-2278)
PHONE..................................954 584-0420
Christian Pellerin, *CEO*
EMP: 11 EST: 1998
SALES (est): 6.4MM
SALES (corp-wide): 18.3MM Privately Held
SIC: 2076 Vegetable oil mills
PA: Distributions Christian Pellerin Inc
719 Boul Industriel Bureau 101
Blainville QC J7C 3
450 434-4641

(G-3711)
C-MIX CORP
5600 Nw 12th Ave Ste 306 (33309-6600)
PHONE..................................954 670-0208
Fred Rosenfield, *Director*
EMP: 13 EST: 2005
SALES (est): 445.4K Privately Held
SIC: 3273 Ready-mixed concrete

(G-3712)
CAMBRIDGE DIAGNOSTIC PDTS INC
6880 Nw 17th Ave (33309-1524)
PHONE..................................954 971-4040
Roy Gold, *CEO*
Jack H Gold, *CEO*
Gary Gold, *President*
Marc Gold, *Principal*
Jane Walk, *Master*
EMP: 10 EST: 1953
SQ FT: 20,000
SALES (est): 2.2MM Privately Held
WEB: www.ecamco.com
SIC: 2835 2841 In vitro diagnostics; soap & other detergents

(G-3713)
CAPITAL CONTRACTING & DESIGN (PA)
817 Sw 10th St (33315-1224)
P.O. Box 1333, Plainfield NJ (07061-1333)
PHONE..................................908 561-8411
Donald W Finley, *President*
Mark McQuillan, *Vice Pres*
Silvio Montesdeoca, *CFO*
Scott Angelica, *Sales Executive*
Michele Reese, *Office Mgr*
EMP: 18 EST: 1979
SALES (est): 3MM Privately Held
WEB: www.captlfix.com
SIC: 2541 2542 Display fixtures, wood; fixtures: display, office or store: except wood

(G-3714)
CAPTAINS FASTENERS CORP
3706 Sw 30th Ave (33312-6707)
PHONE..................................954 533-9259

JC Betancor Santos, *Exec Dir*
EMP: 7 EST: 2010
SALES (est): 2.7MM Privately Held
WEB: www.captainsfasteners.com
SIC: 3965 Fasteners

(G-3715)
CAYAGO AMERICAS INC
Also Called: Seabob
1881 W State Road 84 # 104 (33315-2208)
PHONE..................................754 216-4600
Claus Gruner, *CEO*
Alex Sarris, *Business Mgr*
Danilo Tejada, *Warehouse Mgr*
Kevin Couvillon, *Marketing Staff*
Gary Babbitt, *Manager*
EMP: 10 EST: 2016
SALES (est): 6.4MM
SALES (corp-wide): 1.7MM Privately Held
WEB: www.seabob.com
SIC: 3949 Water sports equipment
HQ: Cayago Ag
Flachter Str. 32
Stuttgart BW 70499
711 993-3970

(G-3716)
CBD LLC
Also Called: Diamond Cbd
3531 Griffin Rd Ste 100 (33312-5444)
PHONE..................................305 615-1194
Ricardo Mandini, *Marketing Staff*
Adam Lowry, *Manager*
EMP: 17 EST: 2017
SALES (est): 5.1MM Privately Held
WEB: www.diamondcbd.com
SIC: 3999

(G-3717)
CD GREETING LLC
3260 Ne 32nd St (33308-7102)
PHONE..................................954 530-1301
EMP: 5
SALES (est): 453.3K Privately Held
SIC: 2335 Mfg Women's/Misses' Dresses

(G-3718)
CEMENT-IT INC
2455 E Sunrise Blvd # 11 (33304-3118)
PHONE..................................954 565-7875
Peter Krokstedt, *President*
Jonas Ekberg, *Vice Pres*
◆ EMP: 5 EST: 1999
SQ FT: 2,000
SALES (est): 1.1MM Privately Held
WEB: www.cement-it.com
SIC: 3273 Ready-mixed concrete

(G-3719)
CEMEX MATERIALS LLC
29 Sw 33rd St (33315-3300)
PHONE..................................954 523-9978
David Packard, *Branch Mgr*
EMP: 69 Privately Held
SIC: 3273 5032 5211 Ready-mixed concrete; concrete mixtures; concrete & cinder block
HQ: Cemex Materials Llc
1720 Centrepark Dr E # 100
West Palm Beach FL 33401
561 833-5555

(G-3720)
CENTRIFUGAL REBABBITTING INC
234 Sw 29th St (33315-3134)
PHONE..................................954 522-3003
Oliver W Street Jr, *President*
EMP: 10 EST: 1985
SQ FT: 10,000
SALES (est): 1MM Privately Held
WEB: www.centrifugalinc.com
SIC: 3562 7699 Ball bearings & parts; roller bearings & parts; nautical repair services

(G-3721)
CF BOATWORKS INC
3340 Sw 2nd Ave (33315-3302)
PHONE..................................954 325-6007
Carol Coffman, *President*
William Coffman, *Vice Pres*
EMP: 5 EST: 2007

SALES (est): 441.1K Privately Held
WEB: www.cfboats.com
SIC: 3732 Boat building & repairing

(G-3722)
CG BURGERS (PA)
1732 N Federal Hwy (33305-2543)
PHONE..................................954 618-6450
Shone Sullizan, *Owner*
EMP: 9 EST: 2011
SALES (est): 1.2MM Privately Held
WEB: www.cgburgers.com
SIC: 2599 Food wagons, restaurant

(G-3723)
CHAMPION CONTROLS INC (PA)
811 Nw 57th Pl (33309-2031)
PHONE..................................954 318-3090
Chantal Wedderburn, *CEO*
Marcel V Wedderburn, *Vice Pres*
Shady Al, *Engineer*
Miguel Cedeno, *Engineer*
Abel Gonzalez, *Engineer*
▼ EMP: 35 EST: 2003
SALES (est): 14MM Privately Held
WEB: www.championcontrols.com
SIC: 3613 5063 Control panels, electric; panelboards

(G-3724)
CHARLES & CO LLC
909 Nw 10th Ter (33311-7119)
PHONE..................................404 592-1190
Charles Kline, *Mng Member*
EMP: 12 EST: 2012
SALES (est): 1.6MM Privately Held
SIC: 3634 Hair curlers, electric

(G-3725)
CHROM INDUSTRIES LLC
3131 Sw 42nd St (33312-6802)
PHONE..................................954 400-5135
Jonas Carreon, *CFO*
Rishi Kukreja,
EMP: 30 EST: 2014
SALES (est): 2.6MM Privately Held
SIC: 3089 Blow molded finished plastic products

(G-3726)
CHROMALLOY COMPONENT SVCS INC
3600 Nw 54th St (33309-2400)
PHONE..................................954 378-1999
Dillon Huffsmith, *Engineer*
Jeffery Kiech, *Engineer*
Rico Metellus, *Engineer*
Gilbert Mora, *Engineer*
Jeff Wang, *Engineer*
EMP: 135
SALES (corp-wide): 8.7B Publicly Held
WEB: www.chromalloy.com
SIC: 3724 Aircraft engines & engine parts
HQ: Chromalloy Component Services, Inc.
303 Industrial Park Rd
San Antonio TX 78226
210 331-2300

(G-3727)
CHROMALLOY MTL SOLUTIONS LLC
3600 Nw 54th St (33309-2400)
PHONE..................................954 378-1999
Jim Guillano, *President*
James Langelotti, *Treasurer*
Catherine Nairn, *Controller*
Bert Gonzalez, *Sales Mgr*
Donald Findeson, *Technical Staff*
EMP: 42 EST: 2010
SALES (est): 15.8MM
SALES (corp-wide): 8.7B Publicly Held
WEB: www.chromalloy.com
SIC: 3511 Turbines & turbine generator sets & parts
HQ: Chromalloy Gas Turbine Llc
4100 Rca Blvd
Palm Beach Gardens FL 33410
561 935-3571

(G-3728)
CIRCUITRONIX LLC (PA)
3131 Sw 42nd St (33312-6802)
PHONE..................................786 364-4458
John Clarke, *Business Mgr*

Sandra Danielson, *Business Mgr*
Paul Silverthorn, *Opers Staff*
Joel Magat, *Engineer*
Eric Shumway, *VP Sls/Mktg*
▲ **EMP:** 84 **EST:** 2002
SALES (est): 44.9MM **Privately Held**
WEB: www.circuitronix.com
SIC: 3672 Circuit boards, television & radio printed

(G-3729)
CITRIX SYSTEMS INC (PA)
851 W Cypress Creek Rd (33309-2040)
PHONE..................954 267-3000
Robert M Calderoni, *Ch of Bd*
Dinesh Katariya, *Chief*
Jaja Dela Cruz, *Business Mgr*
Ken Greene, *Business Mgr*
Ashikul Islam, *Business Mgr*
EMP: 600 **EST:** 1989
SQ FT: 320,000
SALES (est): 3.2B **Publicly Held**
WEB: www.citrix.com
SIC: 7372 Prepackaged software; business oriented computer software

(G-3730)
CLARKWSTERN DTRICH BLDG SYSTEM
1001 Nw 58th Ct (33309-1944)
PHONE..................954 772-6300
EMP: 21 **Privately Held**
SIC: 3441 Structural Metal Fabrication
HQ: Clarkwestern Dietrich Building Systems Llc
9050 Cntre Pnte Dr Ste 40
West Chester OH 45069

(G-3731)
CLASSIC YACHT REFINISHING INC
1881 W State Road 84 # 10 (33315-2208)
PHONE..................954 760-9626
Ian McDonald, *President*
William Gould, *Project Mgr*
◆ **EMP:** 12 **EST:** 1989
SALES (est): 289.2K **Privately Held**
WEB: www.premieryachtrefinishing.com
SIC: 3732 Yachts, building & repairing

(G-3732)
CLEANCOR EQP SOLUTIONS LLC (DH)
2200 Eller Dr (33316-3069)
PHONE..................954 523-2200
Jeff Woods, *CEO*
EMP: 2 **EST:** 2014
SALES (est): 3.4MM
SALES (corp-wide): 753.8MM **Privately Held**
WEB: www.cleancor.energy
SIC: 1311 Gas & hydrocarbon liquefaction from coal
HQ: Cleancor Energy Solutions Llc
2200 Eller Dr
Fort Lauderdale FL 33316
954 523-2200

(G-3733)
CMA INTERACTIVE CORPORATION
5011 Neptune Ln (33312-5218)
PHONE..................954 336-6403
Cesar A Cifuentes, *CEO*
EMP: 16 **EST:** 2001
SALES (est): 592K **Privately Held**
WEB: www.cmainteractive.com
SIC: 7372 Prepackaged software

(G-3734)
COGSWELL INNOVATIONS INC
2000 E Oklnd Prk Blvd # 106 (33306-1120)
PHONE..................954 245-8877
David L Cogswell, *President*
Corinne Adams, *COO*
Maureen Burke, *Admin Sec*
EMP: 5 **EST:** 2012
SALES (est): 369K **Privately Held**
WEB: www.cogswellinnovations.com
SIC: 2842 Sanitation preparations, disinfectants & deodorants

(G-3735)
COHEN CAPITAL LLC
3020 E Commercial Blvd (33308-4312)
PHONE..................954 661-8270
Jason Cohen,
EMP: 9 **EST:** 2020
SALES (est): 500K **Privately Held**
SIC: 1389 Construction, repair & dismantling services

(G-3736)
COLAIANNI ITALIAN FLR TILE MFG
Also Called: Italfloor Tile
700 Sw 21st Ter (33312-2234)
PHONE..................954 321-8244
Cosimo Colaianni, *President*
EMP: 5 **EST:** 1986
SQ FT: 1,500
SALES (est): 447.9K **Privately Held**
SIC: 3253 Wall tile, ceramic

(G-3737)
COLOR-CHROME TECHNOLOGIES INC
Also Called: Wow Innovations
2345 Sw 34th St (33312-5004)
PHONE..................954 335-0127
Alan Weizman, *President*
EMP: 6 **EST:** 2005
SQ FT: 5,000
SALES (est): 623.1K **Privately Held**
WEB: www.wow-innovations.com
SIC: 2899 8999 Chemical preparations; chemical consultant

(G-3738)
COMMERCIAL PRINTERS INC (PA)
6600 Nw 15th Ave (33309-1503)
PHONE..................954 781-3737
Jeffery Runde, *President*
Jeffrey W Runde, *President*
William Runde, *President*
Joe Siess, *President*
Elizabeth I Runde, *Corp Secy*
▼ **EMP:** 55 **EST:** 1970
SQ FT: 18,000
SALES (est): 12.3MM **Privately Held**
WEB: www.commercialprintersinc.com
SIC: 2752 2791 2789 2759 Commercial printing, offset; typesetting; bookbinding & related work; commercial printing

(G-3739)
COMMONWEALTH BRANDS INC (HQ)
5900 N Andrews Ave Ste 11 (33309-2367)
PHONE..................800 481-5814
Kevin Freudenthal, *President*
Russ Mantuso, *President*
Rob Wilkey, *Principal*
Jose Rubiralta, *Regional Mgr*
Pauline Autret, *Vice Pres*
◆ **EMP:** 200 **EST:** 1991
SQ FT: 11,880
SALES (est): 81.7MM **Privately Held**
SIC: 2111 2131 2621 Cigarettes; smoking tobacco; paper mills

(G-3740)
COMPLETE METAL SOLUTIONS INTL
107 Nw 5th Ave (33311-9141)
P.O. Box 178 (33302-0178)
PHONE..................954 560-0583
Thomas P McDonough, *President*
EMP: 7 **EST:** 2016
SALES (est): 354.9K **Privately Held**
WEB: www.completemetalsolutions.com
SIC: 3441 Fabricated structural metal

(G-3741)
CONALI EXPRESS CORP
3281 Nw 65th St (33309-1617)
PHONE..................954 531-9573
Conrado Fernandez, *President*
Alina Fraguela, *Vice Pres*
EMP: 8 **EST:** 2008
SALES (est): 103.8K **Privately Held**
SIC: 2095 Coffee roasting (except by wholesale grocers)

(G-3742)
CONSOLIDATED CIGR HOLDINGS INC
5900 N Andrews Ave Ste 11 (33309-2367)
PHONE..................954 772-9000
Gary R Ellis, *President*
James M Parnofiello, *CFO*
◆ **EMP:** 1410 **EST:** 1993
SQ FT: 19,000
SALES (est): 82.1MM **Privately Held**
SIC: 2121 Cigars; cigarillos
HQ: Altadis Holdings U.S.A. Inc.
5900 N Andrews Ave # 600
Fort Lauderdale FL 33309
954 772-9000

(G-3743)
CONSTRUCTION SOFTWARE INC
515 E Las Olas Blvd Ste 1 (33301-2296)
P.O. Box 21024, West Palm Beach (33416-1024)
PHONE..................888 801-0675
Monai Dupree, *President*
Kelvin Brady, *Manager*
Katherine Dunkley, *Manager*
EMP: 5 **EST:** 1991
SALES (est): 1MM **Privately Held**
SIC: 7372 7389 Prepackaged software; business services

(G-3744)
CONTAINER OF AMERICA LLC
6278 N Federal Hwy # 615 (33308-1916)
PHONE..................954 772-5519
J R Marquard, *CEO*
EMP: 10 **EST:** 2014
SALES (est): 6.5MM **Privately Held**
WEB: www.containerofamerica.com
SIC: 3412 5085 Barrels, shipping: metal; bins & containers, storage

(G-3745)
CONTINENTAL SERVICES GROUP INC
2901 W Broward Blvd (33312-1249)
PHONE..................954 327-0809
Cherry D Wheeler-Capik, *CEO*
EMP: 8
SALES (corp-wide): 6.4MM **Privately Held**
WEB: www.continentalbloodbank.com
SIC: 2835 In vitro & in vivo diagnostic substances
PA: Continental Services Group, Inc.
1300 Nw 36th St
Miami FL 33142
305 633-7700

(G-3746)
CONTROL INVESTMENTS INC (PA)
6001 Ne 14th Ave (33334-5007)
PHONE..................954 491-6660
Matthew W Jones, *President*
Matthew Jones, *General Mgr*
David Jones, *Founder*
C David Jones, *Vice Pres*
Scott Barchuk, *Project Mgr*
EMP: 19 **EST:** 1990
SALES (est): 14.2MM **Privately Held**
SIC: 3699 Security control equipment & systems

(G-3747)
CUSTOM CAB DOORS & MORE INC
1538 Nw 23rd Ave (33311-5149)
PHONE..................954 318-1881
Svetlana Elfimova, *President*
EMP: 12 **EST:** 2004
SALES (est): 904.1K **Privately Held**
WEB:
www.customcabinetdoorsnadmore.com
SIC: 2434 Wood kitchen cabinets

(G-3748)
CUSTOM CRATE & LOGISTICS CO
280 Sw 33rd St (33315-3328)
PHONE..................954 527-5742
Scott Janello, *Vice Pres*
Don Janello, *Treasurer*
◆ **EMP:** 9 **EST:** 1968

SQ FT: 10,000
SALES (est): 1.2MM **Privately Held**
WEB: www.customcratflorida.com
SIC: 2441 4731 Packing cases, wood: nailed or lock corner; freight forwarding

(G-3749)
CYALUME TECH HOLDINGS INC (HQ)
910 Se 17th St Ste 300 (33316-2968)
PHONE..................954 315-4939
Thomas G Rebar, *Ch of Bd*
Yaron Eitan, *Vice Ch Bd*
Zivi Nedivi, *President*
Dale Baker, *COO*
Andrea Settembrino, *CFO*
▲ **EMP:** 8 **EST:** 2008
SQ FT: 8,500
SALES (est): 41.2MM **Privately Held**
WEB: www.cyalume.com
SIC: 3648 Lighting equipment
PA: Cps Performance Materials Corp.
100 W Main St
Bound Brook NJ 08805
732 469-7760

(G-3750)
CYCLING QUARTERLY LLC
1007 N Federal Hwy 383 (33304-1422)
PHONE..................786 367-2497
Michael Gale, *Principal*
EMP: 20 **EST:** 2018
SALES (est): 601.3K **Privately Held**
WEB: www.cyclingquarterly.com
SIC: 2741 Miscellaneous publishing

(G-3751)
D & D MBL WLDG FABRICATION INC (PA)
Also Called: D & D Welding
222 Sw 21st Ter (33312-1425)
PHONE..................954 791-3385
Edmund O Massa, *President*
Diane Jackson, *Exec VP*
Daniel Massa, *Vice Pres*
EMP: 11 **EST:** 1983
SQ FT: 4,000
SALES (est): 6.7MM **Privately Held**
WEB: www.ddwelding.com
SIC: 7692 3441 Welding repair; fabricated structural metal

(G-3752)
D & D WLDG & FABRICATION LLC (PA)
222 Sw 21st Ter (33312-1425)
PHONE..................954 791-3385
Daniel Massa, *Vice Pres*
EMP: 14 **EST:** 2007
SALES (est): 20MM **Privately Held**
WEB: www.ddwelding.com
SIC: 3441 Fabricated structural metal

(G-3753)
DAKOTA PLUMBING PRODUCTS LLC (PA)
800 Nw 65th St Ste B (33309-2006)
PHONE..................954 987-3430
Jeff Hughes, *Marketing Staff*
David Kaye, *Mng Member*
Nick Borg, *Manager*
▲ **EMP:** 10 **EST:** 2010
SQ FT: 10,000
SALES (est): 2MM **Privately Held**
WEB: www.dakotasinks.com
SIC: 3432 Plumbing fixture fittings & trim

(G-3754)
DARKHORSE INC (PA)
5470 Nw 10th Ter (33309-2808)
PHONE..................954 849-4440
EMP: 7 **EST:** 2019
SALES (est): 252.1K **Privately Held**
WEB: www.darkhorsemiami.com
SIC: 3993 Signs & advertising specialties

(G-3755)
DASHCLICKS LLC
2901 Stirling Rd Ste 210 (33312-6531)
PHONE..................866 600-3369
Chanuka Kodary, *Principal*
Billy Peery, *Manager*
Marc Frankel, *Director*
EMP: 9 **EST:** 2018

▲ = Import ▼ =Export
◆ =Import/Export

SALES (est): 459.2K **Privately Held**
WEB: www.dashclicks.com
SIC: 7372 Prepackaged software

(G-3756)
DATA PHONE WIRE & CABLE CORP
3420 Sw 14th St (33312-3600)
PHONE..................954 761-7171
Gary Gunter, *President*
George Burke, *Vice Pres*
EMP: 13 EST: 1990
SALES (est): 608.9K **Privately Held**
SIC: 3643 1731 Current-carrying wiring devices; voice, data & video wiring contractor

(G-3757)
DATACORE SOFTWARE CORPORATION (PA)
1901 W Cypress Creek Rd # 200 (33309-1864)
PHONE..................954 377-6000
Dave Zabrowski, *CEO*
Ziya Aral, *Chairman*
George Teixeira, *Chairman*
Amit Baranwal, *Vice Pres*
Amanda Bedborough, *Vice Pres*
▼ EMP: 65 EST: 1998
SALES (est): 71.9MM **Privately Held**
WEB: www.datacore.com
SIC: 3695 7372 Computer software tape & disks: blank, rigid & floppy; prepackaged software

(G-3758)
DAYTON-GRANGER INC
Also Called: D G
3299 Sw 9th Ave (33315-3000)
P.O. Box 350550 (33335-0550)
PHONE..................954 463-3451
Gibbons D Cline, *President*
Kristin K Cline, *Corp Secy*
Kristen Cline, *Vice Pres*
Sigrun U Cline, *Vice Pres*
Louis Lergier, *Traffic Mgr*
▲ EMP: 250 EST: 2007
SQ FT: 105,000
SALES (est): 54.3MM **Privately Held**
WEB: www.daytongranger.com
SIC: 3812 3663 3643 Aircraft/aerospace flight instruments & guidance systems; airborne radio communications equipment; current-carrying wiring devices

(G-3759)
DEB PRINTING & GRAPHICS INC
6500 Nw 15th Ave Ste 100 (33309-1948)
PHONE..................954 968-0060
Dave Eichner, *Owner*
David Eichner, *Owner*
Richard Barnes, *CIO*
EMP: 5 EST: 1999
SALES (est): 752K **Privately Held**
WEB: www.debprinting.com
SIC: 2752 Commercial printing, offset

(G-3760)
DELTA METAL FINISHING INC
101 Ne 3rd Ave Ste 1500 (33301-1181)
P.O. Box 11376, Saint Petersburg (33733-1376)
PHONE..................954 953-9898
James Humphrey, *President*
Marilyn Humphrey, *Vice Pres*
James Humphry Jr, *Vice Pres*
Steve Humphry, *Vice Pres*
Kimberly Humphry, *Manager*
EMP: 22 EST: 1987
SALES (est): 1.7MM **Privately Held**
WEB: deltametalfinishing.business.site
SIC: 3471 Electroplating of metals or formed products

(G-3761)
DESIGNER SIGN SYSTEMS INC
3540 Nw 56th St Ste 201 (33309-2260)
PHONE..................954 972-0707
Paul Peirson, *President*
Anthony Barbieri, *President*
Judith Barbieri, *Treasurer*
EMP: 7 EST: 1990
SQ FT: 5,000
SALES (est): 914.8K **Privately Held**
WEB: www.dssfla.com
SIC: 3993 Signs & advertising specialties

(G-3762)
DESIGNERS SPECIALTY CAB CO INC (PA)
Also Called: Designer's Specialty Millwork
1320 Nw 65th Pl (33309-1901)
PHONE..................954 868-3440
Gladys G Harrison, *President*
EMP: 44 EST: 1994
SQ FT: 39,000
SALES (est): 12MM **Privately Held**
WEB: www.designersspecialty.com
SIC: 2431 Interior & ornamental woodwork & trim; woodwork, interior & ornamental; ornamental woodwork: cornices, mantels, etc.; exterior & ornamental woodwork & trim

(G-3763)
DEVATIS INC
2800 W State Road 84 # 11 (33312-4813)
PHONE..................954 316-4844
EMP: 7 EST: 2018
SALES (est): 348.9K **Privately Held**
WEB: www.devatis.com
SIC: 2834 Pharmaceutical preparations

(G-3764)
DIAMOND WELLNESS HOLDINGS INC (PA)
3531 Griffin Rd (33312-5444)
PHONE..................800 433-0127
Gary Blum, *Ch of Bd*
Lee Lefkowitz, *President*
Kyle L Pritz, *Vice Pres*
EMP: 5 EST: 1996
SALES (est): 9.6MM **Privately Held**
WEB: www.potnetworkholding.com
SIC: 2833 5122 5521 Medicinals & botanicals; medicinals & botanicals; automobiles, used cars only

(G-3765)
DILLON YARN CORPORATION (PA)
3250 W Coml Blvd Ste 320 (33309)
PHONE..................973 684-1600
William Cohen, *CEO*
Mitchel Weinberger, *President*
Christopher Jarosz, *Vice Pres*
Michelle Oneill, *Controller*
Deirdre Gallenagh, *Human Res Dir*
◆ EMP: 56 EST: 1880
SQ FT: 20,000
SALES (est): 25MM **Privately Held**
WEB: www.dillonyarn.com
SIC: 2221 2282 Textile warping, on a contract basis; textured yarn

(G-3766)
DIMAR USA INC (PA)
1332 W Mcnab Rd (33309-1120)
PHONE..................954 590-8573
Anthony Dehart, *CEO*
Ilan Shneor, *Director*
▲ EMP: 5 EST: 2011
SQ FT: 8,000
SALES (est): 721.7K **Privately Held**
SIC: 3553 Woodworking machinery

(G-3767)
DIRECT SALES AND DESIGN INC
1140 Ne 7th Ave Unit 3 (33304-2018)
PHONE..................954 522-5477
Omar Fernandez, *Owner*
EMP: 15
SALES (corp-wide): 607.8K **Privately Held**
WEB: www.directsalesanddesign.com
SIC: 3465 Body parts, automobile: stamped metal
PA: Direct Sales And Design Inc
2448 Ne 26th Ter
Fort Lauderdale FL
954 564-0721

(G-3768)
DJ ROOF AND SOLAR SUPPLY LLC
2009 Admirals Way (33316-3643)
PHONE..................954 557-1992
Daryl Hudson,
EMP: 2 EST: 2018
SQ FT: 2,000

SALES (est): 24MM **Privately Held**
SIC: 2952 5033 Roofing materials; roofing & siding materials

(G-3769)
DK INTERNATIONAL ASSOC INC
Also Called: Dkia
1417 Sw 1st Ave (33315-1555)
PHONE..................954 828-1256
Daryl E Soderman, *Principal*
Miller Randy, *Sales Staff*
Daryl Soderman, *Sales Executive*
Katherine H Soderman, *Director*
Kathy Soderman, *Executive*
EMP: 35 EST: 2002
SQ FT: 8,000
SALES (est): 5.6MM **Privately Held**
WEB: www.dkia.net
SIC: 3441 Fabricated structural metal

(G-3770)
DMSO STORE INC
3580 Sw 30th Ave (33312-6716)
PHONE..................954 616-5699
Bryan Hacht, *President*
EMP: 5 EST: 2016
SALES (est): 442.1K **Privately Held**
WEB: www.dmsostore.com
SIC: 2023 Dietary supplements, dairy & non-dairy based

(G-3771)
DOLL MARINE METAL FABRICA
6800 Nw 15th Way (33309-1501)
PHONE..................954 941-5093
EMP: 5 EST: 2020
SALES (est): 453.4K **Privately Held**
SIC: 3499 Fabricated metal products

(G-3772)
DONS CUSTOM SERVICE INC
Also Called: D C S
900 Ne 3rd Ave (33304-1940)
PHONE..................954 491-4043
Sandra Potts, *CEO*
Christopher Potts, *Vice Pres*
EMP: 5 EST: 1992
SALES (est): 488.4K **Privately Held**
SIC: 3356 Welding rods

(G-3773)
DRAPERY CONTROL SYSTEMS INC (PA)
Also Called: Brambier's Windows & Walls
5545 Nw 35th Ave D (33309-6309)
PHONE..................305 653-1712
Robert Brambier, *President*
Lyle Brambier, *Vice Pres*
Keith Lemmon, *Warehouse Mgr*
Allan Slater, *Sales Mgr*
Leeann Stephenson, *Executive Asst*
▼ EMP: 16 EST: 1973
SALES (est): 2.5MM **Privately Held**
WEB: www.ver-tex.com
SIC: 2221 Upholstery, tapestry & wall covering fabrics

(G-3774)
DUBHOUSE INC
404 Se 15th St (33316-1942)
PHONE..................954 524-3658
Michael Pardo, *President*
EMP: 9 EST: 1997
SQ FT: 1,000
SALES (est): 844.3K **Privately Held**
WEB: www.thedubhouse.net
SIC: 3652 Compact laser discs, prerecorded

(G-3775)
DYNALCO CONTROLS CORPORATION (DH)
5450 Nw 33rd Ave Ste 104 (33309-6353)
PHONE..................323 589-6181
Nizar Elias, *President*
EMP: 40 EST: 1988
SQ FT: 44,400
SALES (est): 17.7MM
SALES (corp-wide): 3.1B **Privately Held**
SIC: 3829 3694 3823 3825 Measuring & controlling devices; engine electrical equipment; industrial instrmnts msrmnt display/control process variable; instruments to measure electricity; fluid power cylinders & actuators; relays & industrial controls

(G-3776)
DYNAMIC GLUCOSE HLTH CTRS LLC
515 E Las Olas Blvd Ste 1 (33301-2296)
PHONE..................800 610-6422
Dr John M Magac, *Principal*
Heather Jobe, *Principal*
EMP: 5 EST: 2017
SALES (est): 355.9K **Privately Held**
WEB: www.dynamicglucose.com
SIC: 7372 Application computer software

(G-3777)
E & A INDUSTRIES INC
16 Ne 4th St Ste 110e (33301-3262)
P.O. Box 350303 (33335-0303)
PHONE..................954 278-2428
Terrance Ward, *Principal*
Oz Chowdhry, *Business Anlyst*
EMP: 12 EST: 2011
SALES (est): 930.4K **Privately Held**
SIC: 3999 Manufacturing industries

(G-3778)
EARL PARKER YACHT REFINISHING
1915 Sw 21st Ave (33312-3113)
PHONE..................954 791-1811
J Earl Parker, *President*
EMP: 15 EST: 1978
SALES (est): 1.4MM **Privately Held**
SIC: 3732 Boat building & repairing

(G-3779)
EASTMAN PERFORMANCE FILMS LLC
Also Called: Suntek Window Films
5553 Ravenswood Rd # 104 (33312-6655)
PHONE..................954 920-2001
Hilary Thomas, *Manager*
EMP: 7 **Publicly Held**
SIC: 3442 Window & door frames
HQ: Eastman Performance Films, Llc
4210 The Great Rd
Fieldale VA 24089
276 627-3000

(G-3780)
EBWAY LLC
6600 Nw 21st Ave Ste A (33309-1821)
PHONE..................954 971-4911
Edward Bennett, *President*
Tom Walker, *Manager*
▼ EMP: 27 EST: 1961
SQ FT: 43,000
SALES (est): 8MM **Privately Held**
WEB: www.ebway.com
SIC: 3544 3549 3469 Die sets for metal stamping (presses); metalworking machinery; metal stampings

(G-3781)
EBWAY LLC
6601 Nw 20th Ave (33309-1500)
PHONE..................954 971-4911
Catherine E Bennett, *Manager*
EMP: 100 EST: 2015
SALES (est): 6MM **Privately Held**
WEB: www.ebway.com
SIC: 3544 Die sets for metal stamping (presses)

(G-3782)
ECI PHARMACEUTICALS LLC (PA)
5311 Nw 35th Ter (33309-6328)
PHONE..................954 486-8181
Bob Franks, *General Mgr*
Ellen Gettenberg, *Vice Pres*
Dusty Snoeberg, *Vice Pres*
Lewis Soars, *Vice Pres*
Jonathan Villalobos, *Maint Spvr*
EMP: 23 EST: 2010
SQ FT: 20,000
SALES (est): 10.7MM **Privately Held**
WEB: www.ecipharma.com
SIC: 2834 Pharmaceutical preparations

(G-3783)
ECI TELECOM INC (DH)
5100 Nw 33rd Ave Ste 150 (33309-6362)
PHONE..................954 772-3070
Gerald Degrace, *President*
Lili Globman, *President*
David Robinson, *General Mgr*

Ron Levin, *Vice Pres*
Denise Marr, *Mfg Staff*
EMP: 45 **EST:** 1982
SALES (est): 26.9MM **Privately Held**
SIC: 3661 7373 Telephone & telegraph apparatus; computer integrated systems design

(G-3784)
ECO WORLD WATER CORP
150 N Federal Hwy Ste 200 (33301-1172)
PHONE..................954 599-3672
Scott Worley, *CEO*
EMP: 6 **EST:** 2017
SALES (est): 2MM **Privately Held**
WEB: www.ecowatertechnologies.com
SIC: 3589 Sewage & water treatment equipment

(G-3785)
EDGEWATER TECHNOLOGIES INC
Also Called: Paradox Marine
1200 Ne 7th Ave Ste 4 (33304-2021)
PHONE..................954 565-9898
Joseph Patrick Keenan II, *CEO*
Marc Curreri, *COO*
Nicole Lorenzi, *Opers Mgr*
Erin West Keenan, *CFO*
Brian Kane, *CTO*
▲ **EMP:** 10 **EST:** 2005
SQ FT: 1,400
SALES (est): 1.9MM **Privately Held**
WEB: www.edgewatertechnologies.com
SIC: 3699 5065 Security control equipment & systems; security control equipment & systems

(G-3786)
EDIBLE FLAIR INC
220 Florida Ave (33312-1136)
PHONE..................954 321-3608
Kriss Carlson, *Principal*
EMP: 7 **EST:** 2010
SALES (est): 83K **Privately Held**
SIC: 2899 Flares

(G-3787)
EDISONECOENERGYCOM CORPORATION
528 Sw 5th Ave Apt 3 (33315-1057)
PHONE..................954 417-5326
Fred Ford, *President*
EMP: 8 **EST:** 2009
SALES (est): 448.5K **Privately Held**
WEB: www.edisonecoenergy.com
SIC: 3612 Transformers, except electric

(G-3788)
EES DESIGN LLC
2801 Nw 55th Ct Ste 5e (33309-2501)
PHONE..................954 541-2660
Eric E Small, *General Mgr*
Maxanne Loew, *General Mgr*
EMP: 17 **EST:** 2011
SALES (est): 2.5MM **Privately Held**
WEB: www.eesdesignllc.com
SIC: 3499 Aerosol valves, metal

(G-3789)
ELECTROLUX PROFESSIONAL LLC
3225 Sw 42nd St (33312-6810)
PHONE..................954 327-6778
John Babila, *Branch Mgr*
EMP: 10
SALES (corp-wide): 858.6MM **Privately Held**
WEB: www.electroluxprofessional.com
SIC: 3585 3524 Air conditioning units, complete: domestic or industrial; lawn & garden equipment
HQ: Electrolux Professional, Llc
   20445 Emerald Pkwy
   Cleveland OH 44135
   980 236-2000

(G-3790)
ELEMENT SOLUTIONS INC (PA)
500 E Broward Blvd # 1860 (33394-3030)
PHONE..................561 207-9600
Benjamin Gliklich, *CEO*
Martin E Franklin, *Ch of Bd*
John E Capps, *Exec VP*
Vic Michels, *Vice Pres*

Patricia A Mount, *Vice Pres*
EMP: 96 **EST:** 1922
SALES (est): 2.4B **Publicly Held**
WEB: www.elementsolutionsinc.com
SIC: 2899 2869 Chemical preparations; hydraulic fluids, synthetic base

(G-3791)
ELEMENTUS MINERALS LLC
2400 E Coml Blvd Ste 810 (33308)
PHONE..................561 815-2617
Joe Carrabba, *CEO*
Jessica Garvey, *Principal*
EMP: 15 **EST:** 2020
SALES (est): 2.8MM **Privately Held**
SIC: 2819 Industrial inorganic chemicals

(G-3792)
EMBRACE TELECOM INC
Also Called: Blackbox Gps
333 Las Olas Way Cu1 (33301-2363)
PHONE..................866 933-8986
Martin Moller, *CEO*
EMP: 14 **EST:** 2008
SQ FT: 4,000
SALES (est): 662.9K **Privately Held**
WEB: www.embracetelecom.com
SIC: 3829 Meteorologic tracking systems

(G-3793)
EMBRAER SERVICES INC
276 Sw 34th St (33315-3603)
PHONE..................954 359-3700
Gary Spulak, *CEO*
Gary J Spulak, *COO*
Eric Leblanc, *Engineer*
Gary Kertz, *Controller*
Jack Benabib, *Technology*
▲ **EMP:** 600 **EST:** 1997
SQ FT: 2,000
SALES (est): 100.5MM **Privately Held**
WEB: www.embraer.com
SIC: 3721 Aircraft
HQ: Embraer Aircraft Holding, Inc.
   276 Sw 34th St
   Fort Lauderdale FL 33315

(G-3794)
ENG GROUP LLC
Also Called: Eng Group LLC Teg , The
5309 Sw 34th Ave (33312-5566)
PHONE..................954 323-2024
Hedi Enghelberg,
▲ **EMP:** 5 **EST:** 2004
SQ FT: 1,000
SALES (est): 702K **Privately Held**
WEB: www.engautomotivegroup.com
SIC: 3714 4812 2992 Motor vehicle parts & accessories; radio telephone communication; lubricating oils & greases; brake fluid (hydraulic): made from purchased materials; transmission fluid: made from purchased materials; oils & greases, blending & compounding

(G-3795)
ENGINEERED YACHT SOLUTIONS INC
2025 Sw 20th St (33315-1892)
PHONE..................954 993-6989
Thomas McGowan, *President*
Aksel King, *Vice Pres*
EMP: 75 **EST:** 2015
SALES (est): 6.8MM **Privately Held**
WEB: www.eyswelding.com
SIC: 3732 Boat building & repairing

(G-3796)
ERB ROBERTS TILLAGE LLC
401 E Las Olas Blvd Ste 1 (33301-2210)
PHONE..................352 376-4888
Devansh Mehta,
◆ **EMP:** 6 **EST:** 2011
SALES (est): 569.3K **Privately Held**
SIC: 3523 Farm machinery & equipment

(G-3797)
EUROSIGN METALWERKE INC
5301 Nw 35th Ave (33309-6315)
PHONE..................954 717-4426
Alfred M Bulkan, *President*
Andrew R Bulkan, *Corp Secy*
Jerome R Bulkan, *Finance*
◆ **EMP:** 8 **EST:** 1987
SQ FT: 15,680

SALES (est): 1.2MM **Privately Held**
WEB: www.euro-sign.com
SIC: 3469 Automobile license tags, stamped metal

(G-3798)
EVE UAM LLC ✪
276 Sw 34th St (33315-3603)
PHONE..................954 359-3700
Gary Spulak,
Luis Carlos Affonso,
Daniel Moczydlower,
EMP: 5 **EST:** 2021
SALES (est): 313.4K **Publicly Held**
SIC: 3812 Search & navigation equipment
PA: Eve Holding, Inc.
   25101 Chagrin Blvd # 350
   Cleveland OH 44122
   216 292-0200

(G-3799)
EVENTTRACKER SECURITY LLC
100 W Cypress Creek Rd (33309-2181)
PHONE..................410 953-6776
Theresa Kuemmer, *Business Mgr*
Jagat Shah, *CTO*
Deepak Jha, *Info Tech Mgr*
Narinder Bhambra, *Webmaster*
Ramesh Thampi, *Director*
EMP: 71 **EST:** 2016
SQ FT: 5,376
SALES (est): 18.4MM **Privately Held**
WEB: www.netsurion.com
SIC: 7372 7371 Business oriented computer software; computer software development & applications
PA: Netsurion Llc
   100 W Cypress Creek Rd
   Fort Lauderdale FL 33309

(G-3800)
EVERGLADES ENVELOPE CO INC
6650 Nw 15th Ave (33309-1503)
PHONE..................954 783-7920
William G Runde, *President*
Paul Royka, *Info Tech Dir*
EMP: 10 **EST:** 1990
SQ FT: 4,000
SALES (est): 5.4MM
SALES (corp-wide): 12.3MM **Privately Held**
WEB: www.evergladesenvelope.com
SIC: 2677 Envelopes
PA: Commercial Printers, Inc.
   6600 Nw 15th Ave
   Fort Lauderdale FL 33309
   954 781-3737

(G-3801)
EVOLIS INC (DH)
3201 W Coml Blvd Ste 110 (33309)
PHONE..................954 777-9262
Emmanuel Picot P, *CEO*
Gerardo Talavera, *Managing Dir*
Olivier Chevance, *Business Mgr*
Michelle Fourmond, *Buyer*
Radhika Maheshwari, *Human Resources*
▲ **EMP:** 11 **EST:** 2004
SQ FT: 1,900
SALES (est): 8.1MM
SALES (corp-wide): 2.3MM **Privately Held**
WEB: www.evolis.com
SIC: 3577 Printers, computer; tape print units, computer

(G-3802)
EW PUBLISHING LLC
2820 Ne 30th St Apt 10 (33306-1942)
PHONE..................305 358-1100
Ellen M White,
EMP: 7 **EST:** 2008
SALES (est): 118.2K **Privately Held**
SIC: 2741 Miscellaneous publishing

(G-3803)
EWHITE LLC
2633 Bayview Dr (33306-1765)
PHONE..................954 530-3382
Yohann Guarracino, *Principal*
▲ **EMP:** 7 **EST:** 2013
SALES (est): 760.8K **Privately Held**
WEB: www.easy-whitening.com
SIC: 2844 Toilet preparations

(G-3804)
EXALOS INC
824 Se 12th St (33316-2008)
P.O. Box 460007 (33346-0007)
PHONE..................215 669-4488
Eugene Covell, *President*
Bettina Lambrechts, *Corp Secy*
Philippe Crepelliere, *Manager*
Udo Oehri, *Director*
Christian Velez, *Director*
EMP: 33 **EST:** 2015
SALES (est): 5MM
SALES (corp-wide): 13.1MM **Privately Held**
WEB: www.exalos.com
SIC: 3674 Semiconductors & related devices
PA: Exalos Ag
   Wagisstrasse 21
   Schlieren ZH 8952
   434 446-090

(G-3805)
EXCLUSIVE APPAREL LLC
2598 E Sunrise Blvd # 2104 (33304-3230)
PHONE..................800 859-6260
Naziha Mustafa,
EMP: 13 **EST:** 2016
SQ FT: 800
SALES (est): 414.8K **Privately Held**
SIC: 2389 Men's miscellaneous accessories

(G-3806)
EXIST INC
Also Called: Exist Clothing & Embroidery
1650 Nw 23rd Ave Ste A (33311-4539)
PHONE..................954 739-7030
Joshua Glickman, *President*
Shaul Ashkenazy, *Vice Pres*
Hava Austin, *CFO*
Stephen Feldschuh, *CFO*
Meyer Coen, *Sales Staff*
◆ **EMP:** 100 **EST:** 1995
SQ FT: 100,000
SALES (est): 14.5MM **Privately Held**
WEB: www.existusa.com
SIC: 2329 5621 Men's & boys' sportswear & athletic clothing; women's clothing stores

(G-3807)
EXODUS MANAGEMENT LLC
Also Called: Exodus Aviation
6750 N Andrews Ave Ste 20 (33309-2173)
PHONE..................954 995-4407
Juliet Gonzalez, *CEO*
Chris Santana, *Sales Staff*
EMP: 5 **EST:** 2016
SALES (est): 1.1MM **Privately Held**
WEB: www.exodusaviation.com
SIC: 3728 5088 Research & dev by manuf., aircraft parts & auxiliary equip; aircraft & parts; aircraft engines & engine parts; aircraft & space vehicle supplies & parts; aeronautical equipment & supplies

(G-3808)
F&J USA LLC (PA)
Also Called: Dr. Botanicals
601 Sw 21st Ter (33312-2278)
PHONE..................800 406-6190
Richard Walker, *President*
David Ledezma, *Vice Pres*
EMP: 17 **EST:** 2017
SALES (est): 7MM **Privately Held**
SIC: 2844 Cosmetic preparations

(G-3809)
FABRICATION FLORIDA VENTR LLC
1201 Nw 65th Pl (33309-1942)
PHONE..................954 388-5014
Jop Vos, *Principal*
EMP: 10 **EST:** 2016
SALES (est): 259.9K **Privately Held**
SIC: 3599 Machine shop, jobbing & repair

(G-3810)
FAST LANE AUTOSHOP LLC
813 Nw 1st St (33311-9003)
PHONE..................954 835-5728
Frederick Pantin, *Principal*
EMP: 7 **EST:** 2018

▲ = Import ▼=Export
◆ =Import/Export

SALES (est): 202.7K **Privately Held**
WEB: www.fastlaneautoshop.com
SIC: 3599 Industrial machinery

(G-3811)
FASTSIGNS
3328 Griffin Rd (33312-5519)
PHONE..................954 404-8341
EMP: 7 EST: 2018
SALES (est): 185.7K **Privately Held**
WEB: www.fastsigns.com
SIC: 3993 Signs & advertising specialties

(G-3812)
FCT-COMBUSTION INC
5049 Sw 35th Ter Tce (33312-8264)
PHONE..................610 725-8840
EMP: 8 EST: 2016
SALES (est): 311.5K **Privately Held**
WEB: www.fctcombustion.com
SIC: 3823 Industrial instrmnts msrmnt display/control process variable

(G-3813)
FEDERAL EASTERN INTL INC
3516 W Broward Blvd (33312-1012)
PHONE..................954 533-4506
EMP: 14 **Privately Held**
WEB: www.fedeastintl.com
SIC: 3569 Filters
PA: Federal Eastern International, Llc
1523 Chaffee Rd S Unit 12
Jacksonville FL 32221

(G-3814)
FEDERAL MILLWORK CORP
3300 Se 6th Ave (33316-4118)
PHONE..................954 522-0653
Richard A Ungerbuehler, *President*
◆ EMP: 28 EST: 1939
SQ FT: 55,000
SALES (est): 3.8MM **Privately Held**
WEB: www.federalmillwork.com
SIC: 2431 Ornamental woodwork: cornices, mantels, etc.

(G-3815)
FIIK SKATEBOARDS LLC
5300 Powerline Rd Ste 209 (33309-3187)
PHONE..................561 405-9541
EMP: 15
SALES (corp-wide): 301.3K **Privately Held**
WEB: www.fiik.com
SIC: 3949 Skateboards
PA: Fiik Skateboards Llc
7050 W Palmetto Park Rd
Boca Raton FL 33433
561 316-8234

(G-3816)
FINE ARCHTCTRAL MLLWK SHUTTERS
800 Nw 57th Pl (33309-2032)
PHONE..................954 491-2055
Richard T Svopa Jr, *President*
EMP: 17 EST: 1996
SALES (est): 304K **Privately Held**
SIC: 2431 2511 2439 2434 Millwork; wood household furniture; structural wood members; wood kitchen cabinets

(G-3817)
FIRST IMPRSEESION SOUTH FLO
1509 Sw 1st Ave (33315-1710)
PHONE..................954 525-0342
Margaret Russell, *Principal*
EMP: 7 EST: 2011
SALES (est): 350.8K **Privately Held**
WEB: www.firstimpressionftl.com
SIC: 2752 Commercial printing, offset

(G-3818)
FIRST LOOK INC
757 Se 17th St 986 (33316-2960)
PHONE..................954 240-0530
Herbert Magney, *Director*
EMP: 8 EST: 2005
SALES (est): 86.5K **Privately Held**
SIC: 3629 Electrical industrial apparatus

(G-3819)
FIVE STAR QUALITY MFG CORP
Also Called: Five Star Shutters
2200 Ne 62nd Ct (33308-2210)
PHONE..................954 972-4772
David H Ceccofiglio, *Principal*
◆ EMP: 7 EST: 2010
SALES (est): 160.4K **Privately Held**
SIC: 3999 Manufacturing industries

(G-3820)
FLIGHT SOURCE LLC
2011 S Perimeter Rd (33309-7135)
PHONE..................954 249-8449
Joseph Miller, *Manager*
EMP: 8 EST: 2019
SALES (est): 277.1K **Privately Held**
WEB: www.flightsourcepa.com
SIC: 3724 Aircraft engines & engine parts

(G-3821)
FLORIDA FUNERAL SHIPPING CNTRS
Also Called: Flite Rite Industries
1321c Nw 65th Pl Ste C (33309-1991)
PHONE..................954 957-9259
Robert Gurin, *President*
Irene Gurin, *Corp Secy*
▼ EMP: 6 EST: 1987
SQ FT: 5,000
SALES (est): 936.6K **Privately Held**
SIC: 2448 3281 Cargo containers, wood; burial vaults, stone

(G-3822)
FLORIDA ORDNANCE CORPORATION
4740 Nw 15th Ave (33309-7210)
PHONE..................954 493-8691
Israel Schnabel, *President*
▲ EMP: 15 EST: 1976
SQ FT: 15,000
SALES (est): 2.2MM **Privately Held**
SIC: 3795 Specialized tank components, military

(G-3823)
FLORIDA PACKG & GRAPHICS INC
Also Called: F P G
6680 Nw 16th Ter (33309-1514)
PHONE..................954 781-1440
Frances L Long, *President*
John Long, *Vice Pres*
Paul Rivera, *Warehouse Mgr*
Suzanne Simmons, *Accounts Mgr*
EMP: 17 EST: 1972
SQ FT: 28,000
SALES (est): 2.5MM **Privately Held**
WEB: www.flpginc.com
SIC: 2653 Boxes, corrugated: made from purchased materials

(G-3824)
FLORIDA SHUTTER FACTORY INC
3069 Nw 26th St (33311-2057)
PHONE..................954 687-4793
Mark N Simons, *Principal*
EMP: 11 EST: 2010
SALES (est): 807.1K **Privately Held**
WEB: www.flshutterfactory.com
SIC: 3442 Louvers, shutters, jalousies & similar items

(G-3825)
FLORIDA SILICA SAND COMPANY
Also Called: Eldorado Stone
2962 Trivium Cir Ste 105 (33312-4656)
PHONE..................954 923-8323
Betty Pegram, *CEO*
EMP: 9
SALES (corp-wide): 15MM **Privately Held**
WEB: www.eldoradostone.com
SIC: 3272 Concrete products, precast
PA: Florida Silica Sand Company
2962 Trivium Cir Ste 106
Fort Lauderdale FL 33312
954 923-8323

(G-3826)
FOAM & PSP INC
3325 Griffin Rd Ste 208 (33312-5500)
PHONE..................954 816-5648
Paul Goken, *President*
EMP: 8 EST: 2000
SQ FT: 5,000
SALES (est): 550.5K **Privately Held**
SIC: 3086 Plastics foam products

(G-3827)
FORECAST TRADING CORPORATION
Also Called: Forecast Products
2760 Nw 63rd Ct (33309-1712)
PHONE..................954 979-1120
Jeff Olefson, *President*
Fredric Olefson, *Chairman*
Jessica Olefson, *Corp Secy*
Jefferson Holmes, *Warehouse Mgr*
◆ EMP: 50 EST: 1974
SQ FT: 45,000
SALES (est): 10.7MM
SALES (corp-wide): 1.3B **Publicly Held**
WEB: www.forecastparts.com
SIC: 3714 Motor vehicle parts & accessories
PA: Standard Motor Products, Inc.
3718 Northern Blvd # 600
Long Island City NY 11101
718 392-0200

(G-3828)
FORTRESS IMPACT WNDOWS DORS LL
6788 Nw 17th Ave (33309-1522)
PHONE..................954 621-2395
Mike Betancourt,
Hector Jordan,
EMP: 7 EST: 2016
SALES (est): 706.9K **Privately Held**
SIC: 3442 Screen & storm doors & windows

(G-3829)
FOUNDRY-MILL LTD
425 N Andrews Ave Ste 1 (33301-3268)
PHONE..................954 467-0287
Alan C Hooper, *Principal*
EMP: 7 EST: 2008
SALES (est): 276.5K **Privately Held**
SIC: 3993 Signs & advertising specialties

(G-3830)
FRAMETASTIC INC
Also Called: Foundation Art Services
5470 Nw 10th Ter (33309-2808)
PHONE..................954 567-2800
Nicholas A Doherty, *President*
Katherine Doherty, *Treasurer*
▲ EMP: 14 EST: 2002
SQ FT: 24,000
SALES (est): 2MM **Privately Held**
SIC: 2499 Picture & mirror frames, wood

(G-3831)
FRANK MURRAY & SONS INC
Also Called: Murray Products
1515 Se 16th St (33316-1713)
PHONE..................561 845-1366
Vincent Murray, *President*
Lynn Murray-Shea, *Corp Secy*
Michael Murray, *Vice Pres*
▲ EMP: 18 EST: 1982
SQ FT: 9,000
SALES (est): 1.2MM **Privately Held**
WEB: www.frankcmurray.ie
SIC: 2298 3732 Fishing lines, nets, seines: made in cordage or twine mills; boat building & repairing

(G-3832)
FREEDOM STEEL BUILDING CORP
1883 W State Road 84 # 106 (33315-2232)
PHONE..................561 330-0447
Sean Hackner, *CEO*
Michael Hackner, *Sales Mgr*
▼ EMP: 30 EST: 1989
SALES (est): 4.9MM **Privately Held**
WEB: www.freedomsteel.com
SIC: 3449 Curtain walls for buildings, steel

(G-3833)
FT LAUDERDALE WAX
Also Called: Euroteam Wax Center
1912 N Sederal Hwy (33305)
PHONE..................954 256-9291
Annemarie Healy, *Owner*
EMP: 8 EST: 2013
SALES (est): 370.9K **Privately Held**
SIC: 2842 Wax removers

(G-3834)
G S PRINTERS INC
Also Called: Gold Star Printers
1239 N Flagler Dr (33304-2131)
PHONE..................305 931-2755
Curt Kreisler, *President*
Sabrina Shores, *Sales Mgr*
Renee Yeoman, *Manager*
EMP: 7 EST: 1974
SALES (est): 919.5K **Privately Held**
SIC: 2752 7334 2741 2791 Commercial printing, offset; photocopying & duplicating services; miscellaneous publishing; typesetting; bookbinding & related work; commercial printing

(G-3835)
GA FD SVCS PINELLAS CNTY LLC
Also Called: G A Food Services
1750 W Mcnab Rd (33309-1011)
PHONE..................954 972-8884
Larry Kotkin, *Manager*
Uriel Arroyo, *Manager*
Arnaldo Gonzalez, *Manager*
Debra Green, *Supervisor*
Carol Lovell, *IT/INT Sup*
EMP: 51
SALES (corp-wide): 151.6MM **Privately Held**
WEB: www.sunmeadow.com
SIC: 2038 5812 5142 Frozen specialties; contract food services; packaged frozen goods
PA: G.A. Food Services Of Pinellas County, Llc
12200 32nd Ct N
Saint Petersburg FL 33716
727 573-2211

(G-3836)
GAAB LOCKS LLC
21014 Sheridan St (33332-2310)
PHONE..................305 788-8515
James Gagel,
Miguel Calancha,
Mariela V De Lellis,
EMP: 5 EST: 2019
SALES (est): 332.5K **Privately Held**
SIC: 3429 Keys, locks & related hardware

(G-3837)
GENESIS II SYSTEMS INC
2425 E Coml Blvd Ste 101 (33308)
PHONE..................954 489-1124
Walter E Apple, *President*
Michelle L Apple, *Admin Sec*
EMP: 10 EST: 1994
SQ FT: 1,500
SALES (est): 169.3K **Privately Held**
SIC: 2875 Compost

(G-3838)
GERMKLEEN LLC
1160 N Federal Hwy # 916 (33304-1436)
PHONE..................954 947-5602
David Demerau,
EMP: 5 EST: 2020
SALES (est): 313K **Privately Held**
SIC: 2833 Medicinal chemicals

(G-3839)
GIGLIOLA INC
3341 E Oakland Park Blvd (33308-7216)
PHONE..................954 564-7871
Roberto Pacella, *Principal*
EMP: 8 EST: 2010
SALES (est): 99.9K **Privately Held**
SIC: 2051 Cakes, bakery: except frozen

(G-3840)
GK INC (PA)
2724 Ne 35th Dr (33308-6316)
PHONE..................215 223-7207
William Kowalchuk, *President*

Walter Cavalcanti, *Vice Pres*
Karen Bixler, *Representative*
EMP: 22 **EST:** 1923
SALES (est): 2MM **Privately Held**
SIC: 2514 2522 Medicine cabinets & vanities: metal; office furniture, except wood

(G-3841)
GLOBAL SATELLITE PRPTS LLC
1901 S Andrews Ave (33316-2858)
PHONE.................954 459-3000
Martin Fierstone, *CEO*
Jeffery Palmer, *Managing Dir*
Khadija Fierstone, *COO*
Scott Walters, *Manager*
EMP: 9 **EST:** 2010
SALES (est): 496.4K **Privately Held**
WEB: www.globalsatellite.us
SIC: 3663 Satellites, communications

(G-3842)
GLOBAL TECH LED LLC
1883 W State Road 84 # 106 (33315-2232)
PHONE.................877 748-5533
Gary Mart Jr, *Partner*
Luis Ivon, *Finance*
Jeffrey Newman,
Ivon Padilla,
▲ **EMP:** 40 **EST:** 2008
SALES (est): 5MM **Privately Held**
WEB: www.globaltechled.com
SIC: 3646 Commercial indusl & institutional electric lighting fixtures

(G-3843)
GRAPEVINE USA INC
333 Las Olas Way (33301-2363)
PHONE.................786 510-9122
EMP: 6 **EST:** 2018
SALES (est): 346.6K **Privately Held**
WEB: www.theinsidersnet.com
SIC: 2741 Miscellaneous publishing

(G-3844)
GRAPHIC DYNAMICS INC
735 Nw 7th Ter (33311-7312)
PHONE.................954 728-8452
Ken Cooper, *President*
Karen Cooper, *CFO*
EMP: 5 **EST:** 1992
SQ FT: 7,000
SALES (est): 478.8K **Privately Held**
WEB: www.graphdyn.com
SIC: 2752 Commercial printing, offset

(G-3845)
GRATE IDEAS OF AMERICA LLC
1417 Sw 1st Ave (33315-1555)
PHONE.................844 292-6044
Chuck Wobby, *Managing Prtnr*
Charles J Wobby, *Director*
Daryl Soderman,
▼ **EMP:** 9 **EST:** 2010
SALES (est): 597.3K **Privately Held**
WEB: www.grate-ideas.com
SIC: 3429 Fireplace equipment, hardware: andirons, grates, screens

(G-3846)
GREAT VIRTUALWORKS LLC
4100 Sw 28th Way (33312-5200)
PHONE.................800 606-6518
Ken Meares, *Mng Member*
Richard Thompson, *Analyst*
EMP: 17 **EST:** 2013
SALES (est): 1MM **Privately Held**
WEB: www.greatvirtualworks.com
SIC: 2741 Miscellaneous publishing
PA: Great Healthworks, Inc.
    4150 Sw 28th Way
    Fort Lauderdale FL 33312

(G-3847)
GREEK ISLAND SPICE INC
2905 Sw 2nd Ave (33315-3121)
PHONE.................954 761-7161
Joanne Theodore, *President*
Jackie Jeffrey, *Office Mgr*
▼ **EMP:** 8 **EST:** 1997
SQ FT: 4,500
SALES (est): 927.9K **Privately Held**
WEB: www.greekislandspice.com
SIC: 2099 Seasonings & spices

(G-3848)
GREEN APPLICATIONS LLC
Also Called: Star Led
3233 Sw 2nd Ave Ste 200 (33315-3335)
PHONE.................954 900-2290
Charlie Blanco, *Principal*
Phillip Kloc, *Marketing Staff*
EMP: 40 **EST:** 2016
SALES (est): 1.8MM **Privately Held**
SIC: 3646 5063 Commercial indusl & institutional electric lighting fixtures; lighting fixtures

(G-3849)
GREENTREE MARKETING SVCS INC
1828 Sw 24th Ave (33312-4530)
P.O. Box 460458 (33346-0458)
PHONE.................800 557-9567
EMP: 8
SALES (corp-wide): 3MM **Privately Held**
WEB: www.gtmsus.com
SIC: 2711 8742 Commercial printing & newspaper publishing combined; marketing consulting services
PA: Greentree Marketing Services, Inc.
    1451 W Cypress Creek Rd
    Fort Lauderdale FL 33309
    800 557-9567

(G-3850)
GREENWAVE BIODIESEL LLC
420 W Mcnab Rd (33309-2144)
PHONE.................239 682-7700
Eric N Lesperance,
Jon C Solin,
EMP: 2 **EST:** 2008
SQ FT: 17,000
SALES (est): 3MM **Privately Held**
WEB: www.greenwavebiodiesel.com
SIC: 2869 Fuels

(G-3851)
GT INDUSTRIES INC
3109 Stirling Rd Ste 200 (33312-6558)
PHONE.................954 962-9700
Walter Hollander, *Principal*
EMP: 9 **EST:** 2018
SALES (est): 47.3K **Privately Held**
WEB: www.gtindustries.com
SIC: 3999 Manufacturing industries

(G-3852)
GUARDIA LLC (PA)
Also Called: Carrier & Tech Solutions LLC
5900 N Andrews Ave Ste 10 (33309-2367)
PHONE.................954 670-2900
John J Rearer, *CEO*
David G Hampson, *Security Dir*
EMP: 6 **EST:** 2011
SALES (est): 2.6MM **Privately Held**
WEB: www.ctsholdings.com
SIC: 7372 Business oriented computer software

(G-3853)
GUARDIAN INDUSTRIES COR
3060 Sw 2nd Ave (33315-3310)
PHONE.................954 525-3481
EMP: 7 **EST:** 2019
SALES (est): 249.4K **Privately Held**
SIC: 3211 Flat glass

(G-3854)
GULFSTREAM MEDIA GROUP INC
Also Called: Treasure Coastline
1401 E Broward Blvd # 206 (33301-2118)
PHONE.................954 462-4488
Mark Mc Cormick, *President*
Bernard McCormick, *Vice Pres*
Brian Beach, *Prdtn Mgr*
Mike Romano, *Opers Staff*
Laura Zele, *Sales Staff*
EMP: 20 **EST:** 1965
SQ FT: 1,900
SALES (est): 2.5MM **Privately Held**
WEB: www.gulfstreammediagroup.com
SIC: 2721 Magazines: publishing only, not printed on site

(G-3855)
H M J CORPORATION
81 Bay Colony Dr (33308-2001)
PHONE.................954 229-1873

Howard Bedick, *President*
EMP: 10 **EST:** 1978
SQ FT: 6,500
SALES (est): 150.9K **Privately Held**
SIC: 2331 Women's & misses' blouses & shirts

(G-3856)
HAILEY CIAN LLC
201 Sw 2nd St (33301-1821)
PHONE.................954 895-7143
Wesley Gleeson, *Principal*
EMP: 8 **EST:** 2012
SALES (est): 354.7K **Privately Held**
SIC: 2893 Printing ink

(G-3857)
HALL FOUNTAINS INC
5500 Nw 22nd Ave (33309-2715)
PHONE.................954 484-8530
Scott Hall, *President*
Stewart Hall, *Vice Pres*
Brian Hall, *Treasurer*
Todd Hall, *Prgrmr*
Tanya Hall, *Admin Sec*
◆ **EMP:** 17 **EST:** 1965
SQ FT: 20,000
SALES (est): 2.9MM **Privately Held**
WEB: www.hallfountains.com
SIC: 3272 Concrete products

(G-3858)
HAMNER PARKING LOT SERVICE
2151 Ne 55th St (33308-3154)
PHONE.................954 328-3216
Paul S Wilner, *President*
EMP: 6 **EST:** 1973
SQ FT: 1,000
SALES (est): 653.8K **Privately Held**
SIC: 3272 1629 1611 Cast stone, concrete; tennis court construction; highway & street construction

(G-3859)
HAMWORTHY INC (DH)
2900 Sw 42nd St (33312-6811)
PHONE.................305 597-7520
▲ **EMP:** 6
SQ FT: 2,000
SALES (est): 10.3MM **Privately Held**
SIC: 3561 Mfg Pumps/Pumping Equipment

(G-3860)
HAPPY KIDS FOR KIDS INC
1380 W Mcnab Rd (33309-1120)
PHONE.................954 730-7922
Bella Ahoron, *President*
Shmaul Ahoron, *Vice Pres*
Eddie Glikc, *Prdtn Mgr*
◆ **EMP:** 15 **EST:** 1997
SALES (est): 3.8MM **Privately Held**
WEB: www.happykidsforkids.com
SIC: 2339 Women's & misses' outerwear

(G-3861)
HARDWARE ONLINE STORE
4343 N Andrews Ave (33309-4743)
PHONE.................954 565-5678
Corey Golden, *President*
EMP: 8 **EST:** 2015
SALES (est): 215.4K **Privately Held**
WEB: www.floridapropertysupply.com
SIC: 3429 4813 Manufactured hardware (general);

(G-3862)
HAWTHORNE & SON INDUSTRIES LLC
2630 W Broward Blvd # 203 (33312-1315)
PHONE.................954 980-8427
Sidney Hawthorne, *CEO*
EMP: 8 **EST:** 2019
SALES (est): 629.5K **Privately Held**
SIC: 3999 Manufacturing industries

(G-3863)
HEADHUNTER INC
3380 Sw 11th Ave (33315-2902)
PHONE.................954 462-5953
Mel Mellinger, *Ch of Bd*
Mark Mellinger, *Vice Pres*
Paul C Mellinger, *Vice Pres*
Jane Mellinger, *Shareholder*
Max Vidaurre, *Internal Med*

◆ **EMP:** 40 **EST:** 1983
SQ FT: 45,000
SALES (est): 6MM **Privately Held**
WEB: www.headhunterinc.com
SIC: 3429 5551 Marine hardware; marine supplies

(G-3864)
HEADHUNTER SPEARFISHING CO
1140 Ne 7th Ave Unit 6 (33304-2018)
PHONE.................954 745-0747
Bradley Thornbrough, *Principal*
EMP: 7 **EST:** 2015
SALES (est): 225.2K **Privately Held**
WEB: www.headhunterspearfishing.com
SIC: 3949 Sporting & athletic goods

(G-3865)
HID GLOBAL CORPORATION
600 Corporate Dr Ste 310 (33334-3604)
PHONE.................954 990-2782
Stephan Widing, *Branch Mgr*
EMP: 41
SALES (corp-wide): 10.3B **Privately Held**
WEB: www.hidglobal.com
SIC: 3825 Radio frequency measuring equipment
HQ: Hid Global Corporation
    611 Center Ridge Dr
    Austin TX 78753

(G-3866)
HIGH SIERRA TERMINALING LLC
1200 Se 20th St (33316-3596)
PHONE.................954 764-8818
Joshua Patterson, *Vice Pres*
Lindy R Jones, *Treasurer*
Glenn R Jones, *Mng Member*
John C Wilkinson, *Admin Sec*
John Lynn,
EMP: 18 **EST:** 2006
SQ FT: 20,400
SALES (est): 2.2MM **Privately Held**
SIC: 2952 Asphalt felts & coatings

(G-3867)
HOLLY SARGENT
1000 Se 4th St Apt 315 (33301-2370)
PHONE.................954 560-6973
Holly Sargent, *Principal*
EMP: 7 **EST:** 2008
SALES (est): 91.8K **Privately Held**
SIC: 3699 Electrical equipment & supplies

(G-3868)
HOOVER CANVAS PRODUCTS CO (PA)
844 Nw 9th Ave (33311-7210)
PHONE.................954 764-1711
James E Carroll Jr, *President*
Lucie Fabien, *Corp Secy*
Matt Carroll, *Vice Pres*
Justin Hagelberg, *Prdtn Mgr*
Lucie Spratlin, *Controller*
▼ **EMP:** 35 **EST:** 1960
SALES (est): 9.4MM **Privately Held**
WEB: www.hooverap.com
SIC: 2394 Awnings, fabric: made from purchased materials

(G-3869)
HOWMEDICA OSTEONICS CORP
505 Nw 65th Ct Ste 102 (33309-6120)
PHONE.................954 714-7933
Frank Russo, *Manager*
EMP: 115
SALES (corp-wide): 17.1B **Publicly Held**
SIC: 3841 Surgical & medical instruments
HQ: Howmedica Osteonics Corp.
    325 Corporate Dr
    Mahwah NJ 07430
    201 831-5000

(G-3870)
HOWMEDICA OSTEONICS CORP
Also Called: Stryker Spine
2944 Trivium Cir (33312-4659)
PHONE.................954 791-6078
Nicolas Lluch, *Manager*
EMP: 115
SALES (corp-wide): 17.1B **Publicly Held**
SIC: 3841 Surgical instruments & apparatus

HQ: Howmedica Osteonics Corp.
325 Corporate Dr
Mahwah NJ 07430
201 831-5000

(G-3871)
HUNTER AEROSPACE SUPPLY LLC
3331 Nw 55th St (33309-6306)
P.O. Box 22178 (33335-2178)
PHONE....................................954 321-8848
John Pergolini,
Richard Kosachiner,
Richard Smith,
EMP: 6 EST: 2015
SQ FT: 2,500
SALES (est): 493.7K Privately Held
WEB: www.hunter.aero
SIC: 3452 3451 Bolts, nuts, rivets & washers; screw machine products

(G-3872)
IBI SYSTEMS INC
6842 Nw 20th Ave (33309-1513)
PHONE....................................954 978-9225
Daljeet Singh, President
EMP: 6 EST: 1987
SQ FT: 4,200
SALES (est): 714.4K Privately Held
WEB: www.ibi-systems.com
SIC: 3571 Electronic computers

(G-3873)
ICARECOM LLC
401 E Las Olas Blvd Ste 1 (33301-2210)
PHONE....................................954 768-7100
James Riley, CEO
▼ EMP: 19 EST: 2012
SQ FT: 8,000
SALES (est): 881.4K Privately Held
WEB: www.icare.com
SIC: 7372 Application computer software

(G-3874)
IMS PUBLISHING INC
Also Called: Yacht International Magazine
1850 Se 17th St Ste 107 (33316-3051)
PHONE....................................954 761-8777
Michel Karsenti, President
EMP: 9 EST: 1997
SQ FT: 2,500
SALES (est): 826.9K Privately Held
SIC: 2721 Magazines: publishing only, not printed on site

(G-3875)
INDUCTOWELD TUBE CORP
3350 Ne 33rd Ave (33308-7134)
PHONE....................................646 734-7094
Michele Rella, Principal
EMP: 9 EST: 2016
SALES (est): 498.4K Privately Held
SIC: 3312 Blast furnaces & steel mills

(G-3876)
INDUSTRIAL SHADEPORTS INC
6600 Nw 12th Ave Ste 220 (33309-1147)
PHONE....................................954 755-0661
Stanley D Breitweiser, President
Agnee E Breitweiser, Admin Sec
EMP: 5 EST: 2016
SALES (est): 737.4K Privately Held
WEB: www.shadeports.com
SIC: 2394 Canvas covers & drop cloths

(G-3877)
INSPECTECH AEROSERVICE INC
902 Sw 34th St (33315-3403)
PHONE....................................954 359-6766
James P Lang, President
EMP: 16 EST: 1993
SQ FT: 3,500
SALES (est): 565.5K Privately Held
WEB: www.inspectech.net
SIC: 3369 Aerospace castings, nonferrous: except aluminum

(G-3878)
INSPIRE ME BRACELETS
3333 Ne 16th Pl (33305-3716)
PHONE....................................404 644-7771
William D Waldbueser, Owner
EMP: 11 EST: 2017

SALES (est): 581.9K Privately Held
WEB: www.inspirationco.com
SIC: 3961 Bracelets, except precious metal

(G-3879)
INTERMEDIX CORPORATION (DH)
6451 N Federal Hwy # 1000 (33308-1424)
PHONE....................................954 308-8700
Joel Portice, CEO
Nicole Cawley, General Mgr
Clint Farquhar, Business Mgr
Ken Cooke, COO
Kenneth Cooke, COO
EMP: 70 EST: 2005
SALES (est): 328.6MM
SALES (corp-wide): 1.4B Publicly Held
SIC: 7372 Business oriented computer software
HQ: Intermedix Holdings, Inc.
401 N Michigan Ave # 2700
Chicago IL 60611
312 324-7820

(G-3880)
INTERNATIONAL QUIKSIGNS INC
804 Se 17th St (33316-2930)
PHONE....................................954 462-7446
Paul Rabinowitz, President
Brett Selwitz, Admin Sec
▼ EMP: 11 EST: 1990
SALES (est): 422.8K Privately Held
WEB: www.quiksignsftl.com
SIC: 3993 5999 Signs, not made in custom sign painting shops; banners

(G-3881)
INTERNATIONAL SHIPYARDS ANCONA
1850 Se 17th St Ste 200 (33316-3050)
PHONE....................................305 371-7722
Edward Sacks, Principal
Brian Jupp, Chief Acct
Kathleen Deppe, Human Resources
Per Bjornsen, Director
EMP: 14 EST: 2014
SALES (est): 698.3K Privately Held
SIC: 3731 Shipbuilding & repairing

(G-3882)
INTERNI CUCINE LLC
Also Called: Interni Cucine Itln Cabinetry
1783 Nw 38th Ave (33311-4138)
PHONE....................................954 486-7000
Marco Maset,
EMP: 5 EST: 2018
SALES (est): 473.2K Privately Held
WEB: www.internicucine.com
SIC: 2434 Wood kitchen cabinets

(G-3883)
IRON BRIDGE TOOLS INC
101 Ne 3rd Ave Ste 1800 (33301-1252)
PHONE....................................954 596-1090
Hardy Haenisch, CEO
Alissa Robinson, COO
EMP: 5 EST: 2006
SALES (est): 1MM Privately Held
WEB: www.ironbridgetools.com
SIC: 3423 Hand & edge tools

(G-3884)
ISLAND JOYS
3679 Nw 19th St (33311-4120)
PHONE....................................561 201-6005
EMP: 7 EST: 2018
SALES (est): 356.9K Privately Held
SIC: 2085 Distilled & blended liquors

(G-3885)
ISLANDOOR COMPANY
951 Nw 9th Ave (33311-7211)
PHONE....................................954 524-3667
A J Schwencke, President
Rebecca Cabanaugh, Controller
EMP: 6 EST: 1989
SQ FT: 20,000
SALES (est): 713K Privately Held
SIC: 2431 3442 Doors, wood; metal doors

(G-3886)
ITEG LLC
333 Las Olas Way Cu1 (33301-2363)
PHONE....................................305 399-2510
Sergio Lotero, Mng Member
Jose Ayala,
EMP: 10 EST: 2013
SALES (est): 2MM Privately Held
SIC: 2621 Parchment, securites & bank note papers

(G-3887)
ITG CIGARS INC (HQ)
Also Called: Altadis USA
5900 N Andrews Ave Ste 11 (33309-2367)
PHONE....................................954 772-9000
Gary R Ellis, CEO
Rob Wilkey, President
Javier Estades, General Mgr
Donnie Felts, Regional Mgr
Teresa Wadhams, District Mgr
◆ EMP: 95 EST: 1920
SQ FT: 38,000
SALES (est): 216.2MM Privately Held
WEB: www.altadisusa.com
SIC: 2121 Cigars

(G-3888)
ITW BLDING CMPONENTS GROUP INC
Also Called: ITW Alpine
6451 N Federal Hwy # 101 (33308-1402)
PHONE....................................954 781-3333
Dave Dunbar, General Mgr
Andy Thomas, Design Engr
Diane Stanton, Human Resources
Christine Pierda, Branch Mgr
Kevin Kraft, Manager
EMP: 41
SALES (corp-wide): 14.4B Publicly Held
SIC: 3443 3446 3444 3441 Truss plates, metal; architectural metalwork; sheet metalwork; fabricated structural metal
HQ: Itw Building Components Group, Inc.
13389 Lakefront Dr
Earth City MO 63045
314 344-9121

(G-3889)
J & G EXPLOSIVES LLC
413 Idlewyld Dr (33301-2730)
PHONE....................................407 883-0734
John W Angelini, Principal
EMP: 8 EST: 2016
SALES (est): 992.1K Privately Held
SIC: 2892 Explosives

(G-3890)
J R WHEELER CORPORATION
Also Called: Structurz Exhibits & Graphics
3748 Sw 30th Ave (33312-6708)
PHONE....................................954 585-8950
Jim Wheeler, President
Jarre Mesadieu, Vice Pres
EMP: 6 EST: 1997
SQ FT: 3,222
SALES (est): 469.3K Privately Held
WEB: www.structurz.com
SIC: 3993 Signs & advertising specialties

(G-3891)
JAMES D NALL CO INC (PA)
Also Called: Aqua-Air Manufacturing
1883 W State Road 84 # 106 (33315-2232)
PHONE....................................305 884-8363
James D Nall, President
John O'Brien, Vice Pres
Marilyn Nall, Treasurer
◆ EMP: 30 EST: 1941
SALES (est): 6.2MM Privately Held
WEB: www.aquaair.net
SIC: 3585 3429 Air conditioning units, complete: domestic or industrial; manufactured hardware (general)

(G-3892)
JANINE OF LONDON INC
45 Fort Royal Is (33308-6013)
PHONE....................................954 772-3593
Janine Dunn, President
Janine Lesley Shamy, Principal
Ezra Shamy, Vice Pres
▲ EMP: 5 EST: 1986

SALES (est): 326.9K Privately Held
WEB: www.janineoflondonfashions.net
SIC: 2335 Women's, juniors' & misses' dresses

(G-3893)
JAS POWDER COATING LLC
219 Sw 21st Ter (33312-1424)
PHONE....................................954 916-7711
Ellen F Reinig, Mng Member
EMP: 7 EST: 2011
SQ FT: 12,000
SALES (est): 1.6MM Privately Held
WEB: www.jaspowdercoating.com
SIC: 3479 Etching & engraving

(G-3894)
JAVALUTION COFFEE COMPANY
2485 E Sunrise Blvd # 20 (33304-3100)
PHONE....................................954 568-1747
David Briskie, CEO
Scott Pumper, President
Anthony Sanzari, COO
Mike Randolph, Vice Pres
Maritza Beck, Accounts Mgr
EMP: 14 EST: 2003
SQ FT: 8,000
SALES (est): 1.1MM Privately Held
WEB: www.javalution.com
SIC: 2095 Roasted coffee

(G-3895)
JEFCO MANUFACTURING INC
718 Nw 1st St (33311-9000)
P.O. Box 14843 (33302-4843)
PHONE....................................954 527-4220
Steve Karden, President
Allan Karden, Vice Pres
EMP: 20 EST: 1976
SQ FT: 12,000
SALES (est): 2.9MM Privately Held
WEB: www.jefcomfg.com
SIC: 3429 Manufactured hardware (general)

(G-3896)
JESUS IN TRENCHES INC
1314 E Las Olas Blvd (33301-2334)
PHONE....................................800 865-8274
Gregory McCloud, President
EMP: 10 EST: 2019
SALES (est): 661.2K Privately Held
SIC: 2211 Apparel & outerwear fabrics, cotton

(G-3897)
JON PAUL INC
Also Called: Jon Paul Jewelers
3353 Galt Ocean Dr 55 (33308-7002)
PHONE....................................954 564-4221
Paul Schroeders, President
Mathew Schroeders, Corp Secy
EMP: 9 EST: 1969
SQ FT: 2,700
SALES (est): 795K Privately Held
WEB: www.jonpauljewelers.com
SIC: 3911 5944 Jewelry, precious metal; jewelry, precious stones & precious metals

(G-3898)
JRG SYSTEMS INC
Also Called: Grant Printing
1239 N Flagler Dr (33304-2131)
PHONE....................................954 962-1020
Jim Grant, President
Kim Sozio, General Mgr
Chad Rodgers, Principal
▼ EMP: 10 EST: 1978
SALES (est): 1.3MM Privately Held
WEB: www.grantprintinginc.com
SIC: 2752 2732 2759 Commercial printing, offset; books: printing only; pamphlets: printing only, not published on site; visiting cards (including business): printing

(G-3899)
KAI LIMITED
1650 W Mcnab Rd (33309-1009)
PHONE....................................954 957-8586
Scott Zucker, CEO
James Pederson, President
Robert Crigler, Vice Pres
▲ EMP: 250 EST: 1998

SQ FT: 37,000
SALES (est): 14.9MM **Privately Held**
WEB: www.kailimited.com
SIC: 3679 5065 3357 Electronic circuits; connectors, electronic; nonferrous wire-drawing & insulating

(G-3900)
KARNAK SOUTH INC
1010 Se 20th St (33316-3594)
P.O. Box 13137 (33316-0100)
PHONE......................................954 761-7606
Sima Jelin, *Ch of Bd*
James D Hannah, *President*
Sarah Jelin, *Vice Pres*
Chris Salazar, *Vice Pres*
Robert Andrews, *CFO*
▼ **EMP:** 10 **EST:** 1985
SQ FT: 65,000
SALES (est): 1.1MM **Privately Held**
SIC: 2952 3354 2951 Roofing materials; aluminum extruded products; asphalt paving mixtures & blocks

(G-3901)
KB AEROSPACE CO
401 E Las Olas Blvd (33301-2210)
PHONE......................................754 366-9194
Gregory T Dunn, *Principal*
EMP: 7 **EST:** 2010
SALES (est): 529.3K **Privately Held**
WEB: www.kbaerospace.com
SIC: 3721 Aircraft

(G-3902)
KC MARINE SERVICES INC
213 Sw 21st St (33315-2526)
PHONE......................................954 766-8100
Kelly Carver, *President*
EMP: 6 **EST:** 1998
SALES (est): 350K **Privately Held**
WEB: www.kcmarineservices.net
SIC: 3732 7699 Yachts, building & repairing; boat repair

(G-3903)
KEMET CORPORATION (HQ)
1 E Broward Blvd Ste 200 (33301-1872)
P.O. Box 5928, Greenville SC (29606-5928)
PHONE......................................954 766-2800
William M Lowe Jr, *CEO*
Per Olof Loof, *CEO*
R James Assaf, *Senior VP*
Phillip M Lessner, *Senior VP*
Chris Hall, *Vice Pres*
▲ **EMP:** 103 **EST:** 1919
SALES (est): 1.2B **Privately Held**
WEB: www.kemet.com
SIC: 3675 Electronic capacitors

(G-3904)
KENCO HOSPITALITY INC
1000 Nw 56th St (33309-2833)
PHONE......................................954 921-5434
Gary Kenney, *President*
Judy Mau, *Bookkeeper*
◆ **EMP:** 62 **EST:** 1994
SQ FT: 17,000
SALES (est): 8.6MM **Privately Held**
WEB: www.kencohospitality.com
SIC: 2392 2391 Bedspreads & bed sets: made from purchased materials; curtains & draperies

(G-3905)
KENCO QUILTING & TEXTILES INC
1000 Nw 56th St (33309-2833)
PHONE......................................954 921-5434
Gary Kenney, *President*
EMP: 15 **EST:** 1971
SQ FT: 17,000
SALES (est): 574.3K **Privately Held**
WEB: www.kencohospitality.com
SIC: 2392 5131 Bedspreads & bed sets: made from purchased materials; comforters & quilts: made from purchased materials; drapery material, woven

(G-3906)
KERNO LLC
20958 Sheridan St (33332-2311)
PHONE......................................954 261-5854
Hugo Conde, *Mng Member*
Maite Blanco Fombon,

EMP: 9 **EST:** 2015
SALES (est): 967.1K **Privately Held**
WEB: www.kerno-usa.com
SIC: 3471 Decorative plating & finishing of formed products

(G-3907)
KIZABLE LLC
1125 Ne 16th Ter (33304-2320)
P.O. Box 235, Clearwater (33757-0235)
PHONE......................................727 600-3469
Brian Schroeder, *Exec Dir*
EMP: 8 **EST:** 2011
SALES (est): 715.2K **Privately Held**
SIC: 2064 Fruit & fruit peel confections

(G-3908)
KRON DESIGNS LLC
Also Called: Good Gal Storage G.G.s
6818 Nw 20th Ave (33309-1513)
PHONE......................................954 941-0800
Vanessa Maria Genet,
Veronica Michelle Illsen,
◆ **EMP:** 7 **EST:** 2009
SQ FT: 3,500
SALES (est): 681.7K **Privately Held**
WEB: www.krondesigns.com
SIC: 3231 2531 2599 Furniture tops, glass: cut, beveled or polished; public building & related furniture; library furniture; school furniture; hotel furniture

(G-3909)
KSM ELECTRONICS INC (PA)
6301 Nw 5th Way Ste 1500 (33309-6176)
PHONE......................................954 642-7050
Stephen Benjamin, *President*
Sergio Santiago, *Business Mgr*
Josh Salcedo, *COO*
Richard Huott, *Mfg Dir*
Ana Oliveira, *Production*
◆ **EMP:** 80 **EST:** 1975
SALES (est): 57.7MM **Privately Held**
WEB: www.ksmelectronics.com
SIC: 3679 3629 Harness assemblies for electronic use: wire or cable; static elimination equipment, industrial

(G-3910)
LAGACI INC
Also Called: Lagaci Sport
2201 Stirling Rd Ste 101 (33312-6626)
PHONE......................................954 929-1395
Yuval Lugassy, *CEO*
Shay Y Lugassy, *Vice Pres*
David Lougassy, *Treasurer*
Sela Jonathan, *Info Tech Mgr*
◆ **EMP:** 12 **EST:** 1998
SQ FT: 7,000
SALES (est): 2.1MM **Privately Held**
WEB: www.lagaci.com
SIC: 2339 2325 Women's & misses' outerwear; men's & boys' trousers & slacks

(G-3911)
LAJOIE INVESTMENT CORP
Also Called: Leo Manufacturing
819 Nw 7th Ter (33311-7201)
PHONE......................................954 463-3271
Fax: 954 463-7123
EMP: 10
SQ FT: 15,500
SALES (est): 1.4MM **Privately Held**
SIC: 3444 3585 Mfg Sheet Metalwork Mfg Refrigeration/Heating Equipment

(G-3912)
LASTRADA FURNITURE INC (PA)
Also Called: Lastrada Furniture & Interiors
1785 Nw 38th Ave (33311-4138)
PHONE......................................954 485-6000
Eli Mordehay, *President*
Eric Denoun, *Executive Asst*
EMP: 18 **EST:** 1995
SQ FT: 50,000
SALES (est): 3.6MM **Privately Held**
SIC: 3553 7389 Furniture makers' machinery, woodworking; interior design services

(G-3913)
LATHAM MARINE INC
280 Sw 32nd Ct (33315-3347)
PHONE......................................954 462-3055
Robert P Latham, *President*
Kathleen Latham, *CFO*

Latham Robert, *Director*
Tom Gongola, *Technician*
EMP: 20 **EST:** 1973
SQ FT: 11,000
SALES (est): 2.5MM **Privately Held**
WEB: www.lathammarine.com
SIC: 3429 3714 3441 3312 Marine hardware; motor vehicle parts & accessories; fabricated structural metal; blast furnaces & steel mills; folding paperboard boxes

(G-3914)
LD TELECOMMUNICATIONS INC
Also Called: Nexogy Sac
2101 W Commercial Blvd (33309-3071)
PHONE......................................954 628-3029
EMP: 56
SALES (corp-wide): 19.6MM **Privately Held**
WEB: www.ldtelecom.com
SIC: 7372 Application computer software
PA: Ld Telecom, Inc
     2121 Ponce De Leon Blvd # 200
     Coral Gables FL 33134
     305 358-8952

(G-3915)
LE PUBLICATIONS INC
Also Called: Life Extension
3600 W Commercial Blvd (33309-3338)
PHONE......................................954 766-8433
Renee Price, *President*
Alexandra Maldonado, *Art Dir*
EMP: 8 **EST:** 2004
SALES (est): 195.7K **Privately Held**
SIC: 2741 Miscellaneous publishing

(G-3916)
LEAN GREEN ENTERPRISES LLC
2125 S Andrews Ave (33316-3431)
PHONE......................................954 525-2971
Scott Frybarger, *Mng Member*
Andrew Portano, *Manager*
Michael Burgio,
EMP: 5 **EST:** 2009
SALES (est): 426.4K **Privately Held**
SIC: 3639 Trash compactors, household

(G-3917)
LENNOX LETTS
801 Nw 1st St (33311-9003)
PHONE......................................954 630-5989
Lennox Letts, *President*
EMP: 7 **EST:** 2013
SALES (est): 171.9K **Privately Held**
SIC: 3585 Refrigeration & heating equipment

(G-3918)
LIFESTYLE MEDIA GROUP LLC
3511 W Commercial Blvd (33309-3331)
PHONE......................................954 377-9470
Jeffrey Dinetz, *Publisher*
Michelle Simon, *Publisher*
Beth Tache, *Publisher*
Michelle Solomon, *Editor*
Dan Fudge, *Vice Pres*
EMP: 17 **EST:** 2013
SALES (est): 2.3MM **Privately Held**
SIC: 2721 Magazines: publishing & printing

(G-3919)
LIONS GATE PUBLISHING PROD LLC
1720 Nw 26th Ter (33311-4426)
PHONE......................................954 733-9576
Amos Benefield, *Principal*
EMP: 7 **EST:** 2016
SALES (est): 104.6K **Privately Held**
SIC: 2741 Miscellaneous publishing

(G-3920)
LIQUIGUARD TECHNOLOGIES INC
5807 N Andrews Way (33309-2359)
PHONE......................................954 566-0996
Abbas Sadriwalla, *President*
EMP: 20 **EST:** 2004
SALES (est): 2MM **Privately Held**
WEB: www.liquiguard.com
SIC: 3069 Medical & laboratory rubber sundries & related products

(G-3921)
LONGBOW MARINE INC
1305 Sw 1st Ave (33315-1503)
PHONE......................................954 616-5737
Simon Addrison, *Principal*
EMP: 7 **EST:** 2014
SALES (est): 1.4MM **Privately Held**
WEB: www.longbowmarine.com
SIC: 3429 Aircraft & marine hardware, inc. pulleys & similar items

(G-3922)
LOW CODE IP HOLDING LLC
Also Called: Blazedpath
401 E Las Olas Blvd Ste 1 (33301-2210)
PHONE......................................833 260-2151
Gustavo Merchan, *Mng Member*
EMP: 8 **EST:** 2016
SALES (est): 563.7K **Privately Held**
SIC: 7372 Prepackaged software

(G-3923)
LPS LATH PLST & STUCCO INC
513 Nw 16th Ave (33311-8851)
PHONE......................................954 444-3727
Eddie Brown, *Principal*
EMP: 10 **EST:** 2008
SALES (est): 146.3K **Privately Held**
SIC: 3541 Lathes

(G-3924)
LYNN ELECTRONICS LLC (PA)
936 Nw 1st St (33311-8902)
PHONE......................................215 355-8200
Mike Boulanger, *President*
James Gioconda, *Managing Dir*
Eileen Jacob, *COO*
Elizabeth Strzelecki, *Opers Mgr*
Dana Walls, *Sales Staff*
◆ **EMP:** 55 **EST:** 1964
SQ FT: 38,000
SALES (est): 20.9MM **Privately Held**
WEB: www.lynnelec.com
SIC: 3679 3643 Harness assemblies for electronic use: wire or cable; connectors & terminals for electrical devices

(G-3925)
M AUSTIN FORMAN
888 Se 3rd Ave Ste 501 (33316-1159)
PHONE......................................954 763-8111
Austin M Forman, *Principal*
EMP: 73 **EST:** 2008
SALES (est): 1MM **Privately Held**
SIC: 3324 Commercial investment castings, ferrous
PA: Town Of Davie
     6591 Orange Dr
     Davie FL 33314
     954 797-1000

(G-3926)
MADDYS PRINT SHOP LLC
5450 Nw 33rd Ave Ste 108 (33309-6353)
PHONE......................................954 749-0440
Steven Lopata,
Maddy Lopata,
EMP: 8 **EST:** 1985
SQ FT: 3,500
SALES (est): 1MM **Privately Held**
WEB: www.maddysprintshop.com
SIC: 2752 5699 7374 5999 Commercial printing, offset; T-shirts, custom printed; computer graphics service; banners

(G-3927)
MAGENAV INC
Also Called: Statgear
3530 Nw 53rd Ave (33309-6340)
PHONE......................................718 551-1815
Avraham Goldstein, *President*
▲ **EMP:** 8 **EST:** 2011
SALES (est): 851.4K **Privately Held**
WEB: www.statgeartools.com
SIC: 3569 5961 Firefighting apparatus & related equipment; fishing, hunting & camping equipment & supplies: mail order

(G-3928)
MAJOR CANVAS PRODUCTS INC
Also Called: Hoover Canvas Products
844 Nw 9th Ave (33311-7210)
PHONE......................................954 764-1711
James Caroli Jr, *President*

▲ = Import ▼=Export
◆ =Import/Export

Jim Carroll, *Vice Pres*
Lucy Spratlin, *Treasurer*
EMP: 11 **EST:** 1963
SALES (est): 191.3K **Privately Held**
SIC: 2394 Awnings, fabric: made from purchased materials; canopies, fabric: made from purchased materials

(G-3929)
MANAGEMENT INTERNATIONAL INC
1828 Se 1st Ave (33316-2802)
PHONE..................954 763-8811
Joan McNulty, *President*
Barbara McNulty, *Vice Pres*
Bill McNulty, *Vice Pres*
EMP: 17 **EST:** 1969
SALES (est): 460.2K **Privately Held**
SIC: 2731 2741 Books: publishing only; miscellaneous publishing

(G-3930)
MANNING COMPANY
Also Called: TMC
223 Sw 28th St (33315-3131)
PHONE..................954 523-9355
Richard V Manning, *President*
EMP: 7 **EST:** 1997
SQ FT: 9,000
SALES (est): 1.1MM **Privately Held**
WEB: www.themanningco.com
SIC: 3444 3441 2522 Sheet metalwork; fabricated structural metal; office furniture, except wood

(G-3931)
MANSFIELD INTERNATIONAL INC
3561 N 55th (33301)
PHONE..................954 632-3280
Craig Mansfield, *President*
▼ **EMP:** 7 **EST:** 2004
SALES (est): 130K **Privately Held**
SIC: 2241 Cotton narrow fabrics

(G-3932)
MAPEI CORPORATION
1851 Nw 22nd St (33311-2940)
PHONE..................954 485-8637
Roger Pratt, *Business Mgr*
Mike Zalusky, *Maint Spvr*
Francesco Cappi, *Engineer*
Scott Benavent, *Sales Staff*
Robert Piapek, *Manager*
EMP: 67
SALES (corp-wide): 3.6B **Privately Held**
WEB: www.mapei.com
SIC: 2891 2899 Adhesives; chemical preparations
HQ: Mapei Corporation
1144 N Newport Center Dr
Deerfield Beach FL 33442
954 246-8888

(G-3933)
MAS ENTRPRSES OF FT LAUDERDALE
Also Called: Consolidated Box
1883 W State Road 84 # 10 (33315-2232)
PHONE..................904 356-9606
Mariano Arranz Jr, *President*
Robert Arranz, *Vice Pres*
Mike Trout, *Technology*
Judith Arranz, *Admin Sec*
▼ **EMP:** 31 **EST:** 1978
SQ FT: 50,000
SALES (est): 1.6MM **Privately Held**
SIC: 2653 Boxes, corrugated: made from purchased materials

(G-3934)
MEDIA CREATIONS INC
Also Called: Llumina Press
7101 W Coml Blvd Ste 4e (33319)
PHONE..................954 726-0902
Deborah Greenspan, *President*
EMP: 8 **EST:** 1997
SALES (est): 732K **Privately Held**
WEB: www.mediacreations.net
SIC: 2741 Miscellaneous publishing

(G-3935)
MEDIC HEALTHCARE LLC
6750 N Andrews Ave # 200 (33309-2180)
PHONE..................954 336-1776

Osullivan James, *Mng Member*
EMP: 7 **EST:** 2009
SQ FT: 1,500
SALES (est): 488K **Privately Held**
SIC: 3841 Surgical & medical instruments

(G-3936)
MEDICAL MAGNETICS INC
Also Called: Bioflex Medical Magnetics, Inc
5970 Sw 32nd Ter (33312-6325)
PHONE..................954 565-8500
Charles Zablotsky, *CEO*
Theodore Zablotsky, *President*
Willy Moses, *CFO*
▲ **EMP:** 10 **EST:** 1991
SALES (est): 1.2MM
SALES (corp-wide): 2.1MM **Privately Held**
WEB: www.bioflexmedicalmagnetics.com
SIC: 3841 Surgical & medical instruments
PA: Relevium Technologies Inc.
1000 Rue Sherbrooke O Bureau 2700
Montreal QC H3A 3
514 824-8559

(G-3937)
MEGAWATTAGE LLC (PA)
Also Called: Megawattage.com Generators
850 Sw 21st Ter (33312-2236)
PHONE..................954 328-0232
Michael Jansen, *President*
Lisa Puffer, *Supervisor*
Allen Brenner,
EMP: 10 **EST:** 2006
SQ FT: 10,000
SALES (est): 5.2MM **Privately Held**
WEB: www.megawattage.com
SIC: 3519 3621 7629 1731 Diesel, semi-diesel or duel-fuel engines, including marine; power generators; electrical equipment repair services; electric power systems contractors; industrial & commercial equipment inspection service; industrial machinery & equipment repair

(G-3938)
MERIT INVESTMENTS INC
6400 N Andrews Ave # 200 (33309-2114)
PHONE..................877 997-8335
Michael Lassner, *President*
Larry Lassner, *CFO*
Mike Stock, *Sr Project Mgr*
EMP: 14 **EST:** 2003
SALES (est): 353.9K **Privately Held**
SIC: 3441 Fabricated structural metal

(G-3939)
METROPOLIS CORP
2455 E Sunrise Blvd # 909 (33304-3112)
PHONE..................954 951-1011
David Brown, *President*
Stacey Sterling, *Comms Mgr*
Rebecca Mouncevalletti, *Technical Staff*
EMP: 50 **EST:** 2017
SALES (est): 2.1MM **Privately Held**
WEB: www.metropolis.com
SIC: 3999 Manufacturing industries

(G-3940)
MICRO PRINTING INC
2571 Nw 4th Ct (33311-8626)
PHONE..................954 676-5757
Alex Buelvas, *President*
Eva Falcone, *Manager*
▼ **EMP:** 10 **EST:** 1987
SQ FT: 2,000
SALES (est): 250K **Privately Held**
WEB: www.micro-printing.com
SIC: 2752 Commercial printing, offset

(G-3941)
MICROSOFT CORPORATION
6750 N Andrews Ave # 400 (33309-2180)
PHONE..................425 882-8080
Kon Ieong, *Partner*
Persio Afonso, *Business Mgr*
Robert Ivanschitz, *Counsel*
Maria Saenz, *Opers Staff*
Siddhant Gupta, *Engineer*
EMP: 200
SALES (corp-wide): 198.2B **Publicly Held**
WEB: www.microsoft.com
SIC: 7372 Application computer software

PA: Microsoft Corporation
1 Microsoft Way
Redmond WA 98052
425 882-8080

(G-3942)
MODERN HAPPY HOME LLC
1201 E Sunrise Blvd # 305 (33304-2880)
PHONE..................954 436-0055
Carlos Moratinos, *Mng Member*
EMP: 5 **EST:** 2011
SALES (est): 331.5K **Privately Held**
WEB: www.modernhappyhome.com
SIC: 2512 Upholstered household furniture

(G-3943)
MONDOLFO LLC
1145 S Federal Hwy (33316-1228)
PHONE..................954 523-1115
EMP: 12 **EST:** 2012
SALES (est): 560.3K **Privately Held**
SIC: 3421 Mfg Cutlery

(G-3944)
MONTESINO INTERNATIONAL CORP
1816 N Dixie Hwy (33305-3849)
PHONE..................954 767-6185
Mitchell D Ousley, *Principal*
Dan Crilly,
▲ **EMP:** 9 **EST:** 2006
SALES (est): 845.3K **Privately Held**
WEB: www.marazullarimar.com
SIC: 3911 Bracelets, precious metal

(G-3945)
MOTUS GI LLC
Also Called: Motus Gi, Inc.
1301 E Broward Blvd # 31 (33301-2152)
PHONE..................954 541-8000
Timothy Moran, *Principal*
David Guzman, *Principal*
Jeff Hutchison, *Vice Pres*
EMP: 7 **EST:** 2015
SALES (est): 62.2K
SALES (corp-wide): 391K **Publicly Held**
WEB: www.motusgi.com
SIC: 3841 Surgical & medical instruments
PA: Motus Gi Holdings, Inc.
1301 E Broward Blvd Fl 3
Fort Lauderdale FL 33301
954 541-8000

(G-3946)
MOTUS GI HOLDINGS INC (PA)
1301 E Broward Blvd Fl 3 (33301-2152)
PHONE..................954 541-8000
Timothy P Moran, *CEO*
David Hochman, *Ch of Bd*
Mark Pomeranz, *President*
Scott C Aldrich, *Vice Pres*
Steven M Bosrock, *Vice Pres*
EMP: 12 **EST:** 2016
SQ FT: 4,554
SALES (est): 391K **Publicly Held**
WEB: www.motusgi.com
SIC: 3841 3845 Surgical & medical instruments; electromedical apparatus; colonascopes, electromedical

(G-3947)
MURPHY BED USA INC (PA)
4330 N Federal Hwy (33308-5208)
PHONE..................954 493-9001
Jack B Hulse, *President*
Ralph Cascone, *Vice Pres*
▼ **EMP:** 24 **EST:** 1991
SALES (est): 2.8MM **Privately Held**
WEB: www.murphybedusa.com
SIC: 2514 2515 Beds, including folding & cabinet, household: metal; mattresses & bedsprings

(G-3948)
MVP GROUP LLC
3560 Nw 56th St (33309-2240)
PHONE..................786 600-4687
Fabrizio Busso-Campana, *Vice Pres*
Michael Bromberg, *Mng Member*
◆ **EMP:** 68 **EST:** 2012

SALES (est): 13.7MM
SALES (corp-wide): 6.7MM **Privately Held**
WEB: www.mvpgroupcorp.com
SIC: 3556 3589 Meat, poultry & seafood processing machinery; grinders, commercial, food; commercial cooking & food-warming equipment
HQ: Mvp Group Corporation
5659 Av Royalmount
Mont-Royal QC H4P 2
514 737-9701

(G-3949)
N23D SERVICES LLC ✪
20974 Sheridan St (33332-2311)
PHONE..................754 217-3362
Richard Wissinger, *Vice Pres*
Paul Mira,
EMP: 7 **EST:** 2021
SQ FT: 1,000
SALES (est): 554.6K **Privately Held**
WEB: www.n23dservices.com
SIC: 3728 Aircraft parts & equipment

(G-3950)
NACE AIRCRAFT CABINETRY INC
1701 Nw 22nd St (33311-2942)
PHONE..................754 366-5799
Paul L Nace, *Principal*
EMP: 7 **EST:** 2014
SALES (est): 68.9K **Privately Held**
SIC: 2434 Wood kitchen cabinets

(G-3951)
NANAS ORIGINAL STROMBOLI INC
5421 Ne 14th Ave (33334-4928)
PHONE..................954 771-6262
Kenneth J Ventura, *President*
Cynthia J Ventura, *Corp Secy*
EMP: 5 **EST:** 2009
SALES (est): 489.9K **Privately Held**
WEB: www.nanasoriginalstromboli.com
SIC: 2032 Italian foods: packaged in cans, jars, etc.

(G-3952)
NARDIS ENTERPRISES LLC
2831 Ne 56th Ct (33308-2713)
PHONE..................954 529-0691
Angela M Naridis,
EMP: 8 **EST:** 2006
SALES (est): 481.6K **Privately Held**
WEB: www.bakersstongo.com
SIC: 3411 Food & beverage containers

(G-3953)
NASCO INDUSTRIES INC
Also Called: Industrial Products Div
3541 Nw 53rd St (33309-6391)
PHONE..................954 733-8665
Jason Petrucci, *President*
Ed Brenner, *President*
◆ **EMP:** 23 **EST:** 1959
SQ FT: 17,000
SALES (est): 1.6MM **Privately Held**
WEB: www.nascoindust.com
SIC: 3545 5085 3546 3423 Machine tool attachments & accessories; industrial supplies; power-driven handtools; hand & edge tools

(G-3954)
NATIONAL MULTIPLE LISTING INC (PA)
6511 Bay Club Dr Apt 2 (33308-1806)
PHONE..................954 772-8880
Harris A Small Jr, *President*
▲ **EMP:** 26 **EST:** 1947
SQ FT: 42,000
SALES (est): 3MM **Privately Held**
WEB: www.printitondemand.com
SIC: 2752 Commercial printing, offset

(G-3955)
NAUTICAL SPECIALISTS INC
2841 Ne 36th St (33308-5817)
PHONE..................954 761-7130
Robert Miles, *Principal*
EMP: 5 **EST:** 2007

SALES (est): 910.5K **Privately Held**
WEB: www.nauticalspecialists.com
SIC: **3822** Air conditioning & refrigeration controls

(G-3956)
NAV-X LLC
Also Called: Fortress Marine Anchors
1386 W Mcnab Rd (33309-1132)
PHONE..........................954 978-9988
Don M Hallerberg, *Principal*
Alicia Hallerberg, *Corp Secy*
EMP: 20 EST: 1986
SQ FT: 12,000
SALES (est): 3.3MM **Privately Held**
WEB: www.fortressanchors.com
SIC: **3463** 3462 3369 3354 Aluminum forgings; iron & steel forgings; nonferrous foundries; aluminum extruded products

(G-3957)
NBL1 INC
280 Sw 6th St (33301-2822)
PHONE..........................954 524-3616
Randy Whitesides, *CEO*
Kirstie Vernese, *VP Opers*
Karan Bhat, *Engineer*
Kurt Edwins, *Sales Staff*
▼ EMP: 29 EST: 2007
SQ FT: 10,000
SALES (est): 4MM **Privately Held**
SIC: **3536** Boat lifts

(G-3958)
NEUTRAL GUARD LLC
1401 Sw 34th Ave (33312-3659)
PHONE..........................954 249-6600
Larry Konzy, *Principal*
EMP: 7 EST: 2010
SALES (est): 185.7K **Privately Held**
WEB: www.thecellphonechipstore.com
SIC: **3842** Surgical appliances & supplies

(G-3959)
NEW RIVER CABINET & FIX INC
750 Nw 57th Ct (33309-2028)
PHONE..........................954 938-9200
Joanne R Triviz, *President*
Joannne R Triviz, *President*
Dan Ptak, *COO*
Salvadore Garcia, *Vice Pres*
Christine Rodriguez, *Admin Sec*
▲ EMP: 39 EST: 1984
SQ FT: 93,000
SALES (est): 1MM **Privately Held**
SIC: **2541** 2542 Cabinets, except refrigerated: show, display, etc.: wood; cabinets: show, display or storage: except wood

(G-3960)
NEW YOU MEDIA LLC
4150 Sw 28th Way (33312-5201)
PHONE..........................800 606-6518
Ken Meares, *Mng Member*
EMP: 10 EST: 2011
SALES (est): 1MM **Privately Held**
WEB: www.newyou.com
SIC: **2741** Miscellaneous publishing
PA: Great Healthworks, Inc.
4150 Sw 28th Way
Fort Lauderdale FL 33312

(G-3961)
NEWMIL INC
2029 Sw 20th St (33315-1881)
PHONE..........................954 444-4471
Sauer Van Den Berg, *President*
EMP: 12 EST: 2000
SQ FT: 1,600
SALES (est): 641.2K **Privately Held**
WEB: www.newmilmarine.com
SIC: **2431** Woodwork, interior & ornamental

(G-3962)
NFJB INC
60 Nw 60th St (33309-2332)
PHONE..........................954 771-1100
John T Connelly Jr, *President*
Nicole Savino, *Project Mgr*
Joakim Hjornhede, *Prdtn Mgr*
Ryan Reynolds, *Purchasing*
Krystal Vega, *Purchasing*
◆ EMP: 22 EST: 1974
SQ FT: 6,480

SALES (est): 5.1MM **Privately Held**
SIC: **2511** 5932 2434 Wood household furniture; used merchandise stores; wood kitchen cabinets

(G-3963)
NOTICE FOUR LLC
2775 Nw 62nd St (33309-1750)
PHONE..........................954 652-1168
Melissa A Notice Ms, *Principal*
EMP: 9 EST: 2002
SQ FT: 10,160
SALES (est): 199.1K **Privately Held**
SIC: **3674** Semiconductors & related devices

(G-3964)
NUTOP INTERNATIONAL LLC
2601 E Oklnd Prk Blvd # 205 (33306-1658)
PHONE..........................954 909-0010
Wolf M Gerhard, *Mng Member*
Flavio Rego,
EMP: 6 EST: 2015
SALES (est): 500K **Privately Held**
SIC: **2833** Vitamins, natural or synthetic: bulk, uncompounded
PA: Nutop Produtos Funcionais Ltda.
Estr. Marica Marques 1055
Santana Do Parnaiba SP

(G-3965)
NYRSTAR US INC
350 E Las Olas Blvd # 800 (33301-4211)
PHONE..........................954 400-6464
Michael Morley, *President*
Dan Harrell, *Superintendent*
Julien De Wilde, *Chairman*
Kevin McCullough, *Maint Spvr*
Mark Schroeder, *Chief Engr*
EMP: 100 EST: 2007
SALES (est): 17.8MM **Privately Held**
WEB: www.nyrstar.com
SIC: **1081** Metal mining services
HQ: Nyrstar Sales & Marketing Ag
Rue De Jargonnant 1
Genf GE 1207

(G-3966)
OHM AMERICAS LLC
Also Called: OHM Power Solutions
3736 Sw 30th Ave (33312-6708)
PHONE..........................800 467-7275
Allen Licht,
EMP: 10 EST: 2012
SALES (est): 1.7MM **Privately Held**
WEB: www.ohmps.com
SIC: **3679** 3677 3612 8711 Electronic loads & power supplies; electronic coils, transformers & other inductors; power & distribution transformers; electrical or electronic engineering; power conversion units, a.c. to d.c.: static-electric

(G-3967)
OMT LLC
3848 Sw 30th Ave (33312-6824)
PHONE..........................954 327-1447
Monique Traad, *President*
Daisy Pagang, *Manager*
EMP: 10 EST: 2004
SALES (est): 963.8K **Privately Held**
WEB: www.omtmedical.com
SIC: **3069** Medical & laboratory rubber sundries & related products

(G-3968)
OP YACHT SERVICES CORP
2015 Sw 20th St Ste 220 (33315-1883)
PHONE..........................954 451-3677
Alessandra Lamarca, *Principal*
EMP: 10 EST: 2015
SALES (est): 449.6K **Privately Held**
WEB: www.opyachtservices.com
SIC: **3732** Yachts, building & repairing

(G-3969)
ORBUSNEICH MEDICAL INC
5363 Nw 35th Ave (33309-6315)
PHONE..........................954 730-0711
Alfred Novak, *Ch of Bd*
Bruce Wayne Johnson, *President*
Joe Velarde, *General Mgr*
Robert Cottone, *Vice Pres*
Dennis Liong, *Opers Staff*
EMP: 30 EST: 1996
SQ FT: 11,000

SALES (est): 11.7MM **Privately Held**
WEB: www.orbusneich.com
SIC: **3841** Surgical & medical instruments
HQ: Orbusneich Medical Company Limited
Rm 303&305 3/F Bldg 20 Hong Kong Science Park
Sha Tin NT

(G-3970)
OTIS ELEVATOR COMPANY
5381 Nw 33rd Ave Ste 103 (33309-6345)
PHONE..........................305 816-5740
Carlos Maristany, *Branch Mgr*
EMP: 215
SALES (corp-wide): 14.3B **Publicly Held**
WEB: www.otis.com
SIC: **3534** 1796 7699 Elevators & equipment; installing building equipment; miscellaneous building item repair services
HQ: Otis Elevator Company
1 Carrier Pl
Farmington CT 06032
860 676-6000

(G-3971)
PALMLAND PAPER CO INC
708 Ne 2nd Ave (33304-2616)
P.O. Box 550848 (33355-0848)
PHONE..........................954 764-6910
Bernard Beauregard, *Ch of Bd*
Todd Beauregard, *President*
EMP: 8 EST: 1959
SQ FT: 7,500
SALES (est): 840K **Privately Held**
SIC: **2679** Paper products, converted

(G-3972)
PANOFF PUBLISHING INC
Also Called: Ppi Group
6261 Nw 6th Way Ste 100 (33309-6103)
PHONE..........................954 377-7777
▲ EMP: 60
SQ FT: 2,000
SALES (est): 819.3K **Privately Held**
SIC: **2741** Misc Publishing

(G-3973)
PANTROPIC POWER INC
Also Called: Caterpillar Authorized Dealer
1881 W State Road 84 # 103 (33315-2208)
PHONE..........................954 797-7972
Daniel Berrios, *Engineer*
Doug Hughes, *Manager*
EMP: 73
SALES (corp-wide): 59.9MM **Privately Held**
WEB: www.pantropic.com
SIC: **3531** 5082 Construction machinery; construction & mining machinery
PA: Pantropic Power, Inc.
8205 Nw 58th St
Doral FL 33166
305 477-3329

(G-3974)
PARADIGM PRECISION LLC
2400 E Commercial Blvd (33308-4030)
PHONE..........................954 634-8012
EMP: 8 EST: 2014
SALES (est): 244.3K **Privately Held**
WEB: www.paradigmprecision.com
SIC: **3599** Machine shop, jobbing & repair

(G-3975)
PARAMOUNT MOLD LLC
1701 W Cypress Creek Rd (33309-1805)
PHONE..........................954 772-2333
Andrew Shelton, *President*
Adrianne D'Antonio, *Human Res Dir*
EMP: 31 EST: 2011
SALES (est): 4.2MM **Privately Held**
SIC: **3089** Injection molding of plastics

(G-3976)
PARAMOUNT MOLDED PRODUCTS INC
1701 W Cypress Creek Rd (33309-1805)
PHONE..........................954 772-2333
Robert H Petrucci, *President*
Richard A Bonopane, *Vice Pres*
Evelyn B Petrucci, *Treasurer*
Joan A Bonopane, *Admin Sec*
▲ EMP: 29 EST: 1979
SQ FT: 20,000
SALES (est): 6.3MM **Privately Held**
SIC: **3089** Injection molding of plastics

(G-3977)
PARKER BOATWORKS INC
617 Nw 7th Ave (33311-7306)
PHONE..........................954 585-1059
Brian Parker, *President*
EMP: 10 EST: 2015
SALES (est): 374.8K **Privately Held**
WEB: www.parkerboatworks.com
SIC: **3732** Boat building & repairing

(G-3978)
PARKSON CORPORATION (HQ)
Also Called: Schreiber
1401 W Cypress Creek Rd # 100 (33309-1969)
PHONE..........................954 974-6610
Michael Hill, *President*
Dianne Kaplan, *Principal*
Stephen Young, *Regional Mgr*
Clare Peeters, *COO*
Jeff Fangman, *Vice Pres*
◆ EMP: 4 EST: 1962
SQ FT: 25,000
SALES (est): 50.6MM
SALES (corp-wide): 635.3MM **Privately Held**
WEB: www.parkson.com
SIC: **3589** Water treatment equipment, industrial
PA: Axel Johnson Inc.
155 Spring St Fl 6
New York NY 10012
646 291-2445

(G-3979)
PARKSTONE INTERNATIONAL INC
110 E Broward Blvd # 170 (33301-3503)
PHONE..........................954 205-0075
Enrique L Mong, *President*
EMP: 8 EST: 2005
SALES (est): 81.3K **Privately Held**
WEB: www.parkstone-international.com
SIC: **2741** Miscellaneous publishing

(G-3980)
PEGASUS CLEAN AIR MTR CARS INC
2400 W Cypress Creek Rd (33309-1824)
PHONE..........................954 682-2000
Jack Trotman, *President*
EMP: 11 EST: 2010
SALES (est): 265.4K **Privately Held**
SIC: **3711** Motor vehicles & car bodies

(G-3981)
PERFECT PAVERS SOUTH FLA LLC
5809 N Andrews Way (33309-2359)
PHONE..........................954 779-1855
John C Lewis, *Principal*
EMP: 12 EST: 2011
SALES (est): 2.9MM **Privately Held**
WEB: www.perfectpavers.com
SIC: **3531** Pavers

(G-3982)
PHARMAMED USA INC
Also Called: Pharmamed Global Distributors
3778 Sw 30th Ave (33312-6701)
PHONE..........................954 533-4462
Julian Lopera, *CEO*
Claudio Oliveira, *Vice Pres*
Paula Morato, *CFO*
Andres Otalvaro, *Sales Mgr*
Amy Lee, *Admin Asst*
EMP: 6 EST: 2013
SALES (est): 1.7MM **Privately Held**
WEB: www.pharmamed.us
SIC: **2834** Pharmaceutical preparations

(G-3983)
PHARMATECH PHARMATECH LLC
3597 Nw 19th St (33311-4260)
PHONE..........................954 583-8778
EMP: 7 EST: 2017
SALES (est): 80.3K **Privately Held**
WEB: www.pharmatech-llc.com
SIC: **2834** Pharmaceutical preparations

▲ = Import ▼=Export
◆ =Import/Export

(G-3984)
PHLEBOTOMISTS ON WHEELS INC
1451 W Cypress Creek Rd # 300 (33309-1961)
PHONE........................954 873-7591
Tamika Shontal Williams, *Principal*
EMP: 8 **EST:** 2008
SALES (est): 120.3K **Privately Held**
SIC: 3312 Blast furnaces & steel mills

(G-3985)
PHOENIX GROUP FLORIDA INC (PA)
3000 Ne 30th Pl Fl 5 (33306-1957)
PHONE........................954 563-1224
William Wilkerson, *Ch of Bd*
Peter Posk, *President*
◆ **EMP:** 2 **EST:** 2003
SALES (est): 8MM **Privately Held**
WEB: www.evoprint.com
SIC: 2752 Commercial printing, lithographic

(G-3986)
PICKLED ART INC
1495 N Federal Hwy (33304-1472)
PHONE........................954 635-7370
Kaylin M Parrish, *Principal*
EMP: 7 **EST:** 2010
SALES (est): 89.4K **Privately Held**
SIC: 2035 Pickled fruits & vegetables

(G-3987)
PIPE WELDERS INC (PA)
2965 W State Road 84 (33312-4867)
PHONE........................954 587-8400
George M Irvine Jr, *Ch of Bd*
John Winters, *Vice Pres*
Scot M Coller, *VP Finance*
Shelly Green, *Human Res Mgr*
Bryan Ahrens, *Manager*
EMP: 79 **EST:** 1977
SQ FT: 50,000
SALES (est): 23.4MM **Privately Held**
WEB: www.billfishmarina.com
SIC: 3441 3732 2394 Fabricated structural metal for ships; boats, fiberglass; building & repairing; canvas & related products

(G-3988)
PIPEWELDERS MARINE INC
2965 W State Road 84 (33312-4867)
PHONE........................954 587-8400
George Irvine Jr, *Ch of Bd*
George M Irvine III, *President*
EMP: 97 **EST:** 1986
SALES (est): 15.6MM
SALES (corp-wide): 23.4MM **Privately Held**
WEB: www.pipewelders.com
SIC: 3429 5551 3444 3441 Marine hardware; boat dealers; sheet metalwork; fabricated structural metal
PA: Pipe Welders, Inc.
2965 W State Road 84
Fort Lauderdale FL 33312
954 587-8400

(G-3989)
PIXELOPTICS INC
6750 N Andrews Ave (33309-2173)
PHONE........................954 376-1542
Gary Davis, *CEO*
EMP: 6 **EST:** 2007
SALES (est): 307.8K **Privately Held**
SIC: 3851 Frames, lenses & parts, eyeglass & spectacle

(G-3990)
POWERFICIENT LLC
6250 Nw 27th Way (33309-1729)
PHONE........................800 320-2535
Gerald P Quindlen, *Principal*
Joseph Pizzella, *Vice Pres*
John Nixdorf, *CFO*
EMP: 32 **EST:** 2015

SALES (est): 2.5MM **Privately Held**
WEB: www.powerficient.com
SIC: 3679 3825 3612 3613 Electronic loads & power supplies; meters, power factor & phase angle; electrical power measuring equipment; voltage regulating transformers, electric power; switches, electric power except snap, push button, etc.

(G-3991)
POWERS INDUSTRIES LLC
3800 Galt Ocean Dr Ph 1 (33308-7619)
PHONE........................954 706-6001
Pamela Powers, *Branch Mgr*
EMP: 14
SALES (corp-wide): 99.8K **Privately Held**
SIC: 3999 Barber & beauty shop equipment
PA: Powers Industries, Llc
2715 Ne 6th Ln
Wilton Manors FL 33334
786 444-3616

(G-3992)
PRECISION PADDLEBOARDS
429 Seabreeze Blvd 214 (33316-1621)
PHONE........................954 616-8046
Joshua Vajda, *Principal*
▼ **EMP:** 6 **EST:** 2010
SALES (est): 420.5K **Privately Held**
WEB: www.precisionpaddleboards.com
SIC: 3949 Sporting & athletic goods

(G-3993)
PREGE
1475 W Cypress Creek Rd (33309-1930)
PHONE........................954 908-1535
Ruben Molina, *Manager*
EMP: 8 **EST:** 2016
SALES (est): 163K **Privately Held**
WEB: www.pregelamerica.com
SIC: 2099 Food preparations

(G-3994)
PREMIER COATINGS LLC
Also Called: Tailored Living
450 Nw 27th Ave (33311-8600)
PHONE........................954 797-9275
Balsa Baletic,
John Jurlich,
EMP: 20 **EST:** 2006
SALES (est): 1.9MM **Privately Held**
WEB: www.premiercoatingsfl.com
SIC: 2541 1799 Cabinets, lockers & shelving; home/office interiors finishing, furnishing & remodeling

(G-3995)
PREMIER LUXURY GROUP LLC
2860 W State Road 84 Ste (33312-4808)
P.O. Box 846, Dania Beach (33004-0846)
PHONE........................954 358-9885
C J Butler, *Mng Member*
M Butler,
EMP: 28 **EST:** 2012
SALES (est): 1.9MM **Privately Held**
SIC: 3731 5199 7514 1522 Commercial cargo ships, building & repairing; general merchandise, non-durable; passenger car rental; residential construction; commercial & office building, new construction

(G-3996)
PREMIER PRINTING SOLUTIONS INC
6600 Nw 15th Ave (33309-1503)
PHONE........................305 490-0244
Stephen F Rothenberg, *President*
Jennifer O'Neill, *Vice Pres*
EMP: 7 **EST:** 1999
SALES (est): 785.6K **Privately Held**
WEB: www.printpremier.com
SIC: 2752 Commercial printing, offset

(G-3997)
PRESS GOURMET SANDWICHES
6206 N Federal Hwy (33308-1904)
PHONE........................954 440-0422
Christopher Del Prete, *Owner*
EMP: 10 **EST:** 2015
SALES (est): 512.3K **Privately Held**
WEB: www.pressgourmetsandwiches.com
SIC: 2741 Miscellaneous publishing

(G-3998)
PRINCESS PRESERVE INC
Also Called: Ritter's Printing
1660 W Mcnab Rd (33309-1001)
PHONE........................954 771-7204
Steven Ritter, *President*
Enrique Andino, *President*
Rosalind Ritter, *Vice Pres*
Scott Pearson, *Engineer*
Michael Ritter, *Treasurer*
EMP: 25 **EST:** 1981
SQ FT: 15,000
SALES (est): 3.7MM **Privately Held**
WEB: www.rittersprinting.com
SIC: 2711 7331 Commercial printing & newspaper publishing combined; mailing service

(G-3999)
PRINT DYNAMICS
1223 N Flagler Dr (33304-2131)
PHONE........................954 524-9294
Robert Kesities, *President*
Ashley Keshigian, *Vice Pres*
Eddy Ruiz, *Controller*
Pery Canan, *Accounts Exec*
Michael Feinstein, *Accounts Exec*
EMP: 10 **EST:** 2009
SALES (est): 503.5K **Privately Held**
WEB: www.printdynamics.com
SIC: 2752 Commercial printing, offset

(G-4000)
PUMA AERO MARINE INC
622 Ne 14th Ave Apt 10 (33304-2869)
PHONE........................904 638-5888
Robert EBY, *President*
Charles Rowsell Jr, *CFO*
EMP: 5 **EST:** 2011
SALES (est): 394.3K **Privately Held**
WEB: www.pumamarine.com
SIC: 3731 3721 Shipbuilding & repairing; aircraft

(G-4001)
PURE BRIGHT LIGHTING LLC
711 Bayshore Dr Apt 302 (33304-3964)
PHONE........................954 780-8700
Bill Balkou, *CEO*
EMP: 6 **EST:** 2013
SALES (est): 578.4K **Privately Held**
WEB: www.purebrightlighting.com
SIC: 3648 Lighting equipment

(G-4002)
PURITAIR LLC
1320 Nw 65th Pl Ste 201 (33309-1901)
PHONE........................954 281-5105
Alex Techoueyres, *Vice Pres*
EMP: 10
SALES (est): 409.5K **Privately Held**
SIC: 2842 Specialty cleaning, polishes & sanitation goods

(G-4003)
Q INDUSTRIES INC
401 E Las Olas Blvd # 130 (33301-2210)
PHONE........................954 689-2263
John Moser, *President*
EMP: 9 **EST:** 2003
SALES (est): 308K **Privately Held**
SIC: 3563 Air & gas compressors

(G-4004)
QUALITEST USA LC
401 E Las Olas Blvd Ste 1 (33301-2210)
PHONE........................877 884-8378
Arash Behzadi, *President*
EMP: 15 **EST:** 2001
SALES (est): 2.2MM **Privately Held**
WEB: www.worldoftest.com
SIC: 3829 3824 Fatigue testing machines, industrial: mechanical; mechanical measuring meters

(G-4005)
QUALITY BAKERY PRODUCTS LLC (DH)
888 E Las Olas Blvd # 700 (33301-2272)
PHONE........................954 779-3663
David Finch, *Mng Member*
EMP: 6 **EST:** 2010

SALES (est): 17.6MM **Privately Held**
WEB: www.qualitybakeryproducts.net
SIC: 2099 Bread crumbs, not made in bakeries

(G-4006)
QUALITY CMPONENTS ASSEMBLY INC
440 Nw 27th Ave (33311-8600)
PHONE........................954 792-5151
John Maschin, *President*
Allison Maschin, *Office Mgr*
EMP: 6 **EST:** 1991
SQ FT: 6,000
SALES (est): 700K **Privately Held**
SIC: 3599 Machine shop, jobbing & repair

(G-4007)
QUANTUM ENVMTL SLUTIONS ST INC
2699 Stirling Rd Ste C (33312-6517)
PHONE........................800 975-8721
Stephen N Rosenthal, *President*
Tim Morley, *Vice Pres*
Anne Rosenthal, *Vice Pres*
Neal Rudder, *Treasurer*
Alexandra Zionts, *Admin Sec*
EMP: 6 **EST:** 2010
SQ FT: 2,500
SALES (est): 389.1K **Privately Held**
SIC: 2842 Degreasing solvent

(G-4008)
QUANTUM LIMIT PARTNERS LLC (PA)
1037 Se 2nd Ct (33301-3627)
PHONE........................954 849-3720
Glenn C Rice, *CEO*
EMP: 5 **EST:** 2012
SALES (est): 600K **Privately Held**
SIC: 3572 Computer storage devices

(G-4009)
QUEUELOGIX LLC
1200 E Las Olas Blvd # 201 (33301-2365)
PHONE........................404 721-3928
Chris Ragland, *Vice Pres*
EMP: 9 **EST:** 2017
SALES (est): 313.1K **Privately Held**
WEB: www.queuelogix.com
SIC: 7372 Prepackaged software

(G-4010)
QUICK PRINTS LLC
3145 Davie Blvd (33312-2728)
PHONE........................954 526-9013
William Exemar, *CEO*
EMP: 7 **EST:** 2014
SALES (est): 761.7K **Privately Held**
WEB: www.quickprints.org
SIC: 2752 Commercial printing, offset

(G-4011)
QUICKSERIES PUBLISHING INC
5100 Nw 33rd Ave Ste 247 (33309-6382)
PHONE........................954 584-1606
Roger G Ledoux, *President*
Steve Arless, *Vice Pres*
Adam Wasserman, *Vice Pres*
Caroline Dussault, *Finance*
Matthew Cybulski, *Accounts Mgr*
EMP: 52 **EST:** 1993
SQ FT: 26,000
SALES (est): 5MM **Privately Held**
WEB: www.quickseries.com
SIC: 2741 Miscellaneous publishing

(G-4012)
RAY EATON YACHT SERVICE INC
2311 Sw 33rd Ter (33312-4337)
PHONE........................954 583-8762
Ray Eaton, *President*
Shirley Eaton, *Vice Pres*
EMP: 5 **EST:** 1974
SALES (est): 400.3K **Privately Held**
SIC: 3732 Yachts, building & repairing

(G-4013)
RDT BUSINESS ENTERPRISES INC
3333 Se 14th Ave (33316-4212)
PHONE........................954 525-1133
Richard D Ticktin, *President*
◆ **EMP:** 15 **EST:** 1992

GEOGRAPHIC

SQ FT: 50,000
SALES (est): 556.6K **Privately Held**
SIC: 3999 Pet supplies

(G-4014)
RELU CO
Also Called: Pdr of The Gables
1885 W State Road 84 # 103 (33315-2243)
PHONE..........................786 717-5665
Edison Recinos, *President*
Ofelia Lucas, *Vice Pres*
EMP: 20 **EST:** 2014
SALES (est): 2.8MM **Privately Held**
SIC: 2842 1521 1541 Sanitation preparations, disinfectants & deodorants; repairing fire damage, single-family houses; renovation, remodeling & repairs: industrial buildings

(G-4015)
REMCO INDUSTRIES INTERNATIONAL
Also Called: Remco Specialty Products Co
917 Nw 8th Ave (33311-7207)
PHONE..........................954 462-0000
Roman Moretth III, *President*
Susan J Moretth, *Admin Sec*
EMP: 16 **EST:** 1992
SQ FT: 18,000
SALES (est): 2.4MM **Privately Held**
WEB: www.remcousa.com
SIC: 3556 Food products machinery

(G-4016)
RENOVATEC ENTERPRISE INC
2590 Nw 4th Ct (33311-8627)
PHONE..........................954 444-8694
Michel Beaulieu, *President*
EMP: 9 **EST:** 1999
SALES (est): 881.6K **Privately Held**
SIC: 2431 Staircases, stairs & railings

(G-4017)
RESCUE METAL FRAMING LLC
2601 Delmar Pl (33301-1577)
PHONE..........................561 660-5945
Drew Rosen, *President*
Bill Ryan, *CFO*
EMP: 12 **EST:** 2018
SQ FT: 130,680
SALES (est): 1.8MM **Privately Held**
SIC: 3442 Metal doors, sash & trim

(G-4018)
RESOURCES IN RARE MINING
800 E Broward Blvd # 700 (33301-2008)
PHONE..........................954 800-5251
Michael Bellhorn, *Owner*
EMP: 8 **EST:** 2013
SALES (est): 108K **Privately Held**
SIC: 1499 Miscellaneous nonmetallic minerals

(G-4019)
RIVERHEAD HOUSING INC
3044 Sw 42nd St (33312-6809)
PHONE..........................630 688-6791
Samuel Sosa, *Principal*
Samuel P Sosa, *Principal*
EMP: 7 **EST:** 2012
SALES (est): 131.9K **Privately Held**
SIC: 2452 Prefabricated buildings, wood

(G-4020)
RIVERSTONE SNCTARY - CBD - INC
Also Called: Closets By Design
2101 W Coml Blvd Ste 3500 (33309)
PHONE..........................954 473-1254
Ronald Linares, *CEO*
EMP: 9 **EST:** 2012
SQ FT: 11,000
SALES (est): 114.5K **Privately Held**
WEB: www.closetsbydesign.com
SIC: 2511 Wood household furniture

(G-4021)
RL SCHREIBER INC (PA)
2745 W Cypress Creek Rd (33309-1721)
PHONE..........................954 972-7102
Tom Schreiber, *President*
Chris Carson, *Managing Dir*
Kathleen S Peterson, *Exec VP*
Mary S Massengale, *Vice Pres*
Mary Massengale, *Vice Pres*

◆ **EMP:** 95 **EST:** 1925
SQ FT: 52,000
SALES (est): 27.5MM **Privately Held**
WEB: www.rlschreiber.com
SIC: 2099 2034 2035 2032 Spices, including grinding; soup mixes; pickles, sauces & salad dressings; canned specialties

(G-4022)
ROAD MASTER
203 W State Road 84 (33315-2544)
PHONE..........................561 479-6450
David Benmoha, *Principal*
EMP: 9 **EST:** 2010
SALES (est): 305.9K **Privately Held**
WEB: www.roadmastersf.com
SIC: 3714 Motor vehicle parts & accessories

(G-4023)
ROBERT PETRUCCI INC
1701 W Cypress Creek Rd (33309-1805)
PHONE..........................954 772-2333
Robert Petrucci, *President*
Evelyn Petrucci, *Corp Secy*
EMP: 10 **EST:** 1973
SQ FT: 2,500
SALES (est): 861.3K **Privately Held**
SIC: 3544 Industrial molds

(G-4024)
ROPE WORKS INC
262 Sw 33rd St (33315-3328)
PHONE..........................954 525-6575
Bob Nance, *President*
Roger Underwood, *Vice Pres*
Micheal Burrelle, *Director*
▼ **EMP:** 10 **EST:** 2000
SALES (est): 657.3K **Privately Held**
WEB: www.ropeinc.com
SIC: 2298 Ropes & fiber cables

(G-4025)
ROS HOLDING CORPORATION
3201 W State Road 84 (33312-4817)
PHONE..........................954 581-9200
Robert Roscioli, *President*
Sharon Roscioli, *Corp Secy*
EMP: 27 **EST:** 1989
SQ FT: 600
SALES (est): 681K **Privately Held**
SIC: 3732 5551 4493 7389 Fishing boats: lobster, crab, oyster, etc.: small; marine supplies & equipment; boat yards, storage & incidental repair; yacht brokers

(G-4026)
ROSCIOLI INTERNATIONAL INC (PA)
Also Called: Donzi Yachts
3201 W State Road 84 (33312-4869)
PHONE..........................941 755-7411
Robert Roscioli, *President*
Sharon Roscioli, *Corp Secy*
Shawn Schmoll, *Plant Mgr*
EMP: 30 **EST:** 1987
SQ FT: 26,000
SALES (est): 4.8MM **Privately Held**
WEB: www.studio215.com
SIC: 3732 Boat building & repairing

(G-4027)
ROSSAM INDUSTRIES INC
811 Nw 57th Pl (33309-2031)
PHONE..........................305 493-5111
William T Frattalone, *President*
Ross John Petrie, *President*
▼ **EMP:** 40 **EST:** 1983
SQ FT: 12,000
SALES (est): 3.6MM **Privately Held**
SIC: 3669 Emergency alarms

(G-4028)
ROTAB INC
20950 Sheridan St (33332-2311)
PHONE..........................954 447-7746
Roy Rolle, *Principal*
▼ **EMP:** 13 **EST:** 2010
SALES (est): 1.9MM **Privately Held**
WEB: www.rotab1.com
SIC: 3465 Body parts, automobile: stamped metal

(G-4029)
ROTH SOUTHEAST LIGHTING LLC
Also Called: Roth Lighting
204 Sw 21st Ter (33312-1425)
PHONE..........................954 423-6640
Marty Capogreco, *Exec VP*
Bic Vest, *Project Mgr*
Michelle Nicastro, *Controller*
Tom Buchanan, *Sales Staff*
Sheldon Mashburn, *Sales Executive*
EMP: 8 **EST:** 2015
SQ FT: 12,000
SALES (est): 2.8MM **Privately Held**
WEB: www.rothsoutheast.com
SIC: 3648 5063 Lighting equipment; light bulbs & related supplies

(G-4030)
ROXY LADY LLC
1904 Nw 16th Ct (33311-4639)
PHONE..........................954 706-6735
Rockelle Charleswell, *Manager*
EMP: 10
SALES (est): 451.9K **Privately Held**
WEB: www.roxyladyllc.net
SIC: 2099 7389 Food preparations;

(G-4031)
ROYAL PRESTIGE
5221 Nw 33rd Ave (33309-6302)
PHONE..........................813 464-9872
Semenia Poblete, *Principal*
EMP: 30 **EST:** 2013
SALES (est): 3MM **Privately Held**
SIC: 3469 Household cooking & kitchen utensils, metal

(G-4032)
RT22 CREATIONS INC
5438 Nw 10th Ter (33309-2830)
PHONE..........................954 254-8258
EMP: 5 **EST:** 2018
SALES (est): 400.3K **Privately Held**
WEB: www.rt22creations.com
SIC: 2434 Wood kitchen cabinets

(G-4033)
RTJ GROUP INC
1451 Nw 62nd St Ste 300 (33309-1953)
PHONE..........................954 999-4060
Shirley Auxais, *CEO*
EMP: 5 **EST:** 2020
SALES (est): 317.8K **Privately Held**
SIC: 7372 8299 8748 8111 Educational computer software; educational service, nondegree granting: continuing educ.; educational consultant; legal services

(G-4034)
RX FOR FLEAS INC
Also Called: Fleabusters
6555 Powerline Rd Ste 412 (33309-2051)
PHONE..........................954 351-9244
Melvin Yarmouth, *President*
Jeffrey Bleile, *General Mgr*
Charles Bayles, *Exec VP*
Robert Yarmuth, *Exec VP*
EMP: 18 **EST:** 1987
SQ FT: 3,000
SALES (est): 2.9MM **Privately Held**
WEB: www.fleabusters.com
SIC: 2834 2879 Powders, pharmaceutical; agricultural chemicals

(G-4035)
SAFE BANKS AND LOCK
2870 Ne 55th Ct (33308-3454)
PHONE..........................954 762-3565
Richard Dragin, *President*
EMP: 7 **EST:** 2007
SALES (est): 500.8K **Privately Held**
WEB: www.bankssafeco.com
SIC: 3499 7382 5044 7699 Locks, safe & vault: metal; security systems services; vaults & safes; lock & key services

(G-4036)
SANDY FINISHED WOOD INC
3163 Sw 13th Ct (33312-2714)
PHONE..........................954 615-7271
Julio Camacho, *Principal*
EMP: 30
SALES (corp-wide): 77.3K **Privately Held**
SIC: 2499 Laundry products, wood

PA: Sandy Finished Wood Inc
18451 Nw 37th Ave Apt 152
Miami Gardens FL 33056
786 623-8431

(G-4037)
SCI ARCHITECTURAL WDWRK INC
2801 Nw 55th Ct Ste 1w (33309-2501)
PHONE..........................954 247-9601
Alexandre Segura, *President*
Gaston S Galella, *Vice Pres*
Stanton W Reich, *Treasurer*
EMP: 12 **EST:** 2007
SQ FT: 1,500
SALES (est): 374.4K **Privately Held**
WEB: www.sciwoodwork.com
SIC: 2431 Millwork

(G-4038)
SCIENTIFIC RESEARCH PRODUCTS
1850 W Mcnab Rd (33309-1012)
PHONE..........................954 971-0600
Frank F Ferola, *President*
Tom Dambrosio, *Vice Pres*
EMP: 40 **EST:** 1996
SALES (est): 2.7MM **Privately Held**
SIC: 2844 Hair preparations, including shampoos

(G-4039)
SCOTTISH SPIRITS IMPORTS INC
3101 N Federal Hwy # 301 (33306-1018)
PHONE..........................954 332-1116
EMP: 12 **EST:** 2011
SQ FT: 3,200
SALES (est): 810K **Privately Held**
SIC: 2085 Mfg Distilled/Blended Liquor

(G-4040)
SCRIBE INC
3758 Sw 30th Ave (33312-6708)
PHONE..........................215 336-5094
EMP: 10 **Privately Held**
WEB: www.scribenet.com
SIC: 2731 Book publishing
PA: Scribe Inc.
765 S Front St
Philadelphia PA 19147

(G-4041)
SDM ACQUISITION CORPORATION
Also Called: S D Modular Displays
590 Sw 9th St Ste 9 (33315-3848)
PHONE..........................954 462-1919
George Braeunig, *President*
▲ **EMP:** 8 **EST:** 1983
SALES (est): 179.9K **Privately Held**
SIC: 3993 Displays & cutouts, window & lobby

(G-4042)
SEACOR MARINE LLC
2200 Eller Dr (33316-3069)
P.O. Box 13038 (33316-0101)
PHONE..........................954 523-2200
Oivind Lorentzen, *CEO*
John Gellert, *President*
Charles Fabrikant, *Chairman*
Robert Clemons, *COO*
Jess Llorca, *Exec VP*
EMP: 82 **EST:** 1982
SALES (est): 13.8MM
SALES (corp-wide): 170.9MM **Publicly Held**
WEB: www.seacormarine.com
SIC: 1382 Oil & gas exploration services
PA: Seacor Marine Holdings Inc.
12121 Wickchester Ln # 500
Houston TX 77079
346 980-1700

(G-4043)
SELF MADE DYNASTY LLC ✪
4811 E Pcf View Ter Fl 33 Flr 333 (33309)
PHONE..........................754 303-3134
Marvens Metellus,
EMP: 7 **EST:** 2021
SALES (est): 491K **Privately Held**
SIC: 3663 Studio equipment, radio & television broadcasting

(G-4044)
SEN-DURE PRODUCTS INC
6785 Nw 17th Ave (33309-1521)
PHONE...................................954 973-1260
Winston Shutt, *President*
Walter H Shutt III, *President*
Richard Shutt, *Vice Pres*
Winston W Shutt, *Vice Pres*
Stefanie Fitzpatrick, *Executive*
▼ EMP: 61 EST: 1928
SQ FT: 20,000
SALES (est): 8.4MM Privately Held
WEB: www.sen-dureproducts.com
SIC: 3443 3519 5013 Heat exchangers, condensers & components; marine engines; automotive engines & engine parts

(G-4045)
SHREDDED TIRE INC
6680 Nw 17th Ave (33309-1520)
PHONE...................................954 970-8565
Richard Spreen, *President*
Andrey Glispie, *Finance*
Randy Charnin, *Sales Dir*
EMP: 10 EST: 2016
SALES (est): 673.6K Privately Held
WEB: www.shreddedtire.com
SIC: 3069 Roofing, membrane rubber

(G-4046)
SIGNAL DYNAMICS CORPORATION
Also Called: Backoff Products
6500 Nw 21st Ave Ste 1 (33309-1867)
PHONE...................................904 342-4008
Walter Jakobowski, *President*
Mike Johnson, *Vice Pres*
EMP: 9 EST: 1990
SQ FT: 18,000
SALES (est): 167.5K Privately Held
WEB: www.signaldynamics.com
SIC: 3714 Motor vehicle parts & accessories

(G-4047)
SIGNARAMA DWNTWN FORT LDERDALE
1422 Se 17th St (33316-1710)
PHONE...................................954 990-4749
Shonagh Baigent, *Principal*
EMP: 10 EST: 2020
SALES (est): 330.2K Privately Held
SIC: 3993 Signs & advertising specialties

(G-4048)
SIGNSOURSE USA INCORPORATED
2500 E Oakland Park Blvd (33306-1601)
PHONE...................................954 561-1234
Marjorie Collins, *Principal*
EMP: 7 EST: 2007
SALES (est): 113.6K Privately Held
SIC: 3993 5099 Signs & advertising specialties; signs, except electric

(G-4049)
SIMPLY45 LLC
Also Called: Gosimplyconnect
3490 Sw 30th Ave (33312-6700)
PHONE...................................954 982-2017
EMP: 8 EST: 2019
SALES (est): 440.3K Privately Held
WEB: www.simply45.com
SIC: 2511 Stools, household: wood

(G-4050)
SINGING MACHINE COMPANY INC (PA)
6301 Nw 5th Way Ste 2900 (33309-6191)
PHONE...................................954 596-1000
Gary Atkinson, *CEO*
▲ EMP: 17 EST: 1982
SQ FT: 6,500
SALES: 47.5MM Publicly Held
WEB: www.singingmachine.com
SIC: 3651 3652 5735 Household audio equipment; tape recorders: cassette, cartridge or reel: household use; pre-recorded records & tapes; records, audio discs & tapes

(G-4051)
SINOCARE MEDITECH INC
2400 Nw 55th Ct (33309-2672)
PHONE...................................800 342-7226

Scott Verner, *President*
EMP: 16 EST: 2016
SALES (est): 1.9MM Privately Held
SIC: 3841 8731 Eye examining instruments & apparatus; medical research, commercial
HQ: Trividia Health, Inc.
2400 Nw 55th Ct
Fort Lauderdale FL 33309
954 677-8201

(G-4052)
SINTAVIA LLC (PA)
2500 Sw 39th St (33312-5104)
PHONE...................................954 474-7800
Brian Neff, *CEO*
Doug Hedges, *President*
Christopher Arcia, *Mfg Staff*
Alex Bencomo, *QC Mgr*
Rebecca Amorim, *Engineer*
EMP: 1 EST: 2012
SALES (est): 13.5MM Privately Held
WEB: www.sintavia.com
SIC: 3471 Finishing, metals or formed products

(G-4053)
SOFT TECH AMERICA INC (PA)
401 E Las Olas Blvd # 1400 (33301-2218)
PHONE...................................954 563-3198
Phillip Thompson, *CEO*
Darryl Huber, *Vice Pres*
EMP: 10 EST: 1985
SALES (est): 10.8MM Privately Held
WEB: www.softtech.com
SIC: 7372 Prepackaged software

(G-4054)
SOGOFISHING LLC
1542 Nw 15th Ave (33311-5467)
PHONE...................................800 308-0259
Thomas Glasco, *CEO*
EMP: 5 EST: 2019
SALES (est): 318.8K Privately Held
WEB: www.sogofishing.com
SIC: 3949 Sporting & athletic goods; lures, fishing: artificial

(G-4055)
SOLIDEXPERTS INC
2005 W Cypress Creek Rd (33309-1878)
PHONE...................................954 772-1903
Michael P Pomper, *President*
Neil Bourgeois, *Vice Pres*
Amos Avery, *Engineer*
Maureen Pomper, *Office Mgr*
James Harrison, *Manager*
EMP: 12 EST: 2005
SALES (est): 2.5MM Privately Held
WEB: www.thesolidexperts.com
SIC: 7372 Prepackaged software; application computer software; business oriented computer software; word processing computer software

(G-4056)
SOPHIO SOFTWARE INC (PA)
6300 Ne 1st Ave Ste 201 (33334-1901)
PHONE...................................323 446-2172
Michael B Birnholz, *President*
EMP: 14 EST: 1999
SQ FT: 2,000
SALES (est): 1.9MM Privately Held
WEB: www.sophio.com
SIC: 7372 Business oriented computer software

(G-4057)
SOUTH FLORIDA GRAPHICS CORP
Also Called: AlphaGraphics
1770 Nw 64th St Ste 500 (33309-1853)
PHONE...................................954 917-0606
Salamon Ojalvo, *President*
Dorita Ojalvo, *Vice Pres*
▼ EMP: 9 EST: 1996
SALES (est): 955.9K Privately Held
WEB: www.ourplanroom.com
SIC: 2752 Commercial printing, offset

(G-4058)
SOUTH FLORIDA PETRO SVCS LLC
2550 Eisenhower Blvd # 11 (33316-3078)
PHONE...................................561 793-2102
Todd Tad, *Director*

Christopher S Vecellio,
Todd Cannon,
▼ EMP: 9 EST: 2005
SALES (est): 1.3MM Privately Held
SIC: 1311 Crude petroleum & natural gas

(G-4059)
SOUTH FLORIDA WOODWORKERS INC
2873 Sw 16th St (33312-3989)
PHONE...................................954 868-5043
Donald Fenstermaker, *Principal*
EMP: 8 EST: 2001
SALES (est): 100.3K Privately Held
SIC: 2431 Millwork

(G-4060)
SOUTHERN CROSS BOATWORKS INC
2019 Sw 20th St Ste 111 (33315-1862)
PHONE...................................954 467-5801
Pablo Munoz, *President*
Este Faia Urso, *Vice Pres*
▲ EMP: 16 EST: 1966
SALES (est): 1.4MM Privately Held
WEB: www.southerncrossboatworks.com
SIC: 3732 Boats, fiberglass: building & repairing

(G-4061)
SOUTHLAND POWER & ENRGY CO LLC
Also Called: SP&e
5215 Nw 35th Ave (33309-3303)
PHONE...................................800 217-6040
Kenneth E Sidler, *President*
EMP: 11 EST: 2010
SALES (est): 275.6K Privately Held
WEB: www.southlandpower.com
SIC: 3433 Heating equipment, except electric

(G-4062)
SPEER LABORATORIES LLC
4950 W Prospect Rd (33309-3050)
PHONE...................................954 586-8700
Ian Jones, *Opers Staff*
Amberly Vogelsang, *Natl Sales Mgr*
Amy E Nicolo, *Mng Member*
Nicolo Amy, *Mng Member*
Matthew Nicolo, *CIO*
EMP: 18 EST: 2012
SALES (est): 5.9MM Privately Held
WEB: www.speerlaboratories.com
SIC: 2834 Proprietary drug products

(G-4063)
SPICE ISLAND BOAT WORKS INC
505 Se 18th St (33316-2821)
P.O. Box 350504 (33335-0504)
PHONE...................................954 632-9453
Brenda J Moorethomas, *Principal*
EMP: 7 EST: 2010
SALES (est): 80K Privately Held
SIC: 3732 Boat building & repairing

(G-4064)
SPRAYMATION DEVELOPMENT CORP
4180 Nw 10th Ave (33309-7014)
PHONE...................................954 484-9700
Grant M Fitzwilliam, *CEO*
Jim McMillen, *Vice Pres*
Michael P Moran, *Vice Pres*
EMP: 21 EST: 2019
SALES (est): 4.9MM Privately Held
WEB: www.spraymation.com
SIC: 3563 Spraying outfits: metals, paints & chemicals (compressor)

(G-4065)
STANDARD REGISTER INC
4710 Nw 15th Ave (33309-3785)
PHONE...................................954 492-9986
EMP: 19
SALES (corp-wide): 3.8B Privately Held
SIC: 2759 Commercial Printing Lithograph Offset
HQ: Standard Register, Inc.
600 Albany St
Dayton OH
937 221-1000

(G-4066)
STANRON CORPORATION
Also Called: Stanron Steel Specialties Div
2770 Nw 63rd Ct (33309-1712)
PHONE...................................954 974-8050
George Tio, *Opers Mgr*
Barbara Ciechowski, *Bookkeeper*
Rick Dunaj, *Manager*
EMP: 35
SQ FT: 12,200
SALES (corp-wide): 18MM Privately Held
WEB: www.stanron.com
SIC: 3469 3444 Stamping metal for the trade; sheet metalwork
PA: Stanron Corporation
5050 W Foster Ave
Chicago IL 60630
773 777-2600

(G-4067)
STAR PHARMACEUTICALS LLC
2881 E Oakland Park Blvd # 221 (33306-1813)
PHONE...................................800 845-7827
Roseanne Branciforte, *Mng Member*
Gene Branciforte,
EMP: 5 EST: 2007
SQ FT: 650
SALES (est): 500.1K Privately Held
WEB: www.starpharm.com
SIC: 2834 Pharmaceutical preparations

(G-4068)
STAR-SEAL OF FLORIDA INC
2740 Nw 55th Ct (33309-2543)
PHONE...................................954 484-8402
Cynthia Thompson, *President*
Alfred Brode, *Principal*
Belinda Broido, *Vice Pres*
Linda Brode, *Treasurer*
◆ EMP: 15 EST: 1981
SQ FT: 10,000
SALES (est): 1.8MM Privately Held
WEB: www.starsealfl.com
SIC: 2951 7699 5169 Coal tar paving materials (not from refineries); industrial equipment services; coal tar products, primary & intermediate

(G-4069)
STONEHARDSCAPES INTL INC
5755 Powerline Rd (33309-2001)
PHONE...................................954 989-4050
David Bond, *President*
Arthur H Bond, *Vice Pres*
James S Bond, *Vice Pres*
Michele M Bond, *Treasurer*
Johanna Harrison, *Manager*
EMP: 10 EST: 2011
SALES (est): 1.6MM Privately Held
WEB: www.stonehardscapes.com
SIC: 3272 Building stone, artificial: concrete

(G-4070)
STUART MAGAZINE
1401 E Broward Blvd # 206 (33301-2116)
PHONE...................................954 332-3214
Tracy Auken, *Principal*
Joan Tessmer, *Controller*
Patty Beck, *Manager*
Sowmya Malla, *Manager*
Mark McCormick, *Assoc Editor*
EMP: 13 EST: 2010
SALES (est): 570.7K Privately Held
WEB: www.magazinemanager.com
SIC: 2721 Magazines: publishing only, not printed on site

(G-4071)
STYLEPOINT US LLC
1401 Ne 9th St Apt 39 (33304-4412)
PHONE...................................954 990-6778
Frits Van Der Werff, *Principal*
▲ EMP: 7 EST: 2010
SALES (est): 162.6K Privately Held
WEB: stylepoint.us.com
SIC: 2899 Frit

(G-4072)
SUITS STLTTOS LPSTICK FNDTION
1995 E Oklnd Prk Blvd (33306-1147)
PHONE...................................954 903-9426
Altagracia D Salas, *Principal*

EMP: 8 **EST:** 2015
SALES (est): 323.6K **Privately Held**
WEB: www.sslwomen.org
SIC: 2844 Lipsticks

(G-4073)
SUN-SENTINEL COMPANY LLC (DH)
Also Called: News & Sun Sentinel Company
500 E Broward Blvd # 800 (33394-3018)
PHONE..................................954 356-4000
Howard Greenberg, *President*
Victoria Ballard, *Editor*
David Selig, *Editor*
Douglas Lyons, *Chairman*
Robyn Motley, *Chairman*
▲ **EMP:** 456 **EST:** 1925
SQ FT: 90,000
SALES (est): 163.4MM **Privately Held**
WEB: www.sun-sentinel.com
SIC: 2711 Newspapers, publishing & printing
HQ: Tribune Publishing Company
560 W Grand Ave
Chicago IL 60654
312 222-9100

(G-4074)
SUN-SENTINEL COMPANY INC
3585 Nw 54th St (33309-6358)
PHONE..................................954 735-6414
Charles Hare, *Manager*
EMP: 10
SQ FT: 10,480 **Privately Held**
WEB: www.sun-sentinel.com
SIC: 2711 Newspapers, publishing & printing
HQ: Sun-Sentinel Company, Llc
500 E Broward Blvd # 800
Fort Lauderdale FL 33394
954 356-4000

(G-4075)
SUNSHINE HEALTH PRODUCTS INC
6245 Powerline Rd Ste 106 (33309-2047)
PHONE..................................954 493-5469
Ida Cathie Rhames, *President*
Ralf Morton, *Vice Pres*
▲ **EMP:** 18 **EST:** 2001
SALES (est): 1.3MM **Privately Held**
WEB: www.sunshinehealthproducts.net
SIC: 3843 Dental materials

(G-4076)
SUPER CLEANING WOMAN SERVICES
1528 N Andrews Ave (33311-5560)
PHONE..................................954 670-7527
Carline Lubin, *President*
EMP: 8 **EST:** 2019
SALES (est): 146.6K **Privately Held**
WEB:
www.supercleaningwomanservices.com
SIC: 2842 Specialty cleaning, polishes & sanitation goods

(G-4077)
SUPERIOR AVIONICS INC
2700 W Cypress Creek Rd (33309-1744)
PHONE..................................954 917-9194
Timothy N Hankins, *President*
EMP: 5 **EST:** 1989
SQ FT: 1,500
SALES (est): 1.1MM **Privately Held**
SIC: 3728 Aircraft parts & equipment

(G-4078)
SUPPLY NETWORK INC
3436 Sw 22nd St (33312-4316)
PHONE..................................954 791-2287
John M Olsen, *Branch Mgr*
EMP: 9
SALES (corp-wide): 2.6MM **Privately Held**
WEB: www.vikinggroupinc.com
SIC: 3444 Sheet metalwork
HQ: Supply Network, Inc.
5150 Beltway Dr Se
Caledonia MI 49316
269 945-9501

(G-4079)
SURIPARTS CORP
21020 Sheridan St (33332-2310)
PHONE..................................954 639-7700
Rafael J Falcon, *President*
▼ **EMP:** 5 **EST:** 2004
SALES (est): 806.4K **Privately Held**
WEB: www.suriparts.com
SIC: 3812 Aircraft control instruments

(G-4080)
SUZANO PULP & PAPER
550 W Cypress Creek Rd # 420
(33309-6168)
PHONE..................................954 772-7716
Gerry O'Connor, *Owner*
▲ **EMP:** 6 **EST:** 2006
SALES (est): 498.7K **Privately Held**
SIC: 2611 2621 Pulp mills; paper mills

(G-4081)
SYNERGY LABS INC
888 Se 3rd Ave Ste 301 (33316-1159)
PHONE..................................954 525-1133
Lyle J Canida, *President*
Louise Krupp, *Vice Pres*
Richard Falero, *Mfg Mgr*
Kim Gale, *Purchasing*
Franklin Villasmil, *Accounts Mgr*
▼ **EMP:** 32 **EST:** 1992
SALES (est): 8.4MM **Privately Held**
WEB: www.synergylabs.com
SIC: 2047 Dog food

(G-4082)
SYNERGYLABS LLC
888 Se 3rd Ave Ste 301 (33316-1159)
PHONE..................................954 525-1133
Rick Klein, *Vice Pres*
Fred Jean, *Mfg Mgr*
Megan Gouge, *QC Mgr*
Philip Menard, *Controller*
Elena Azzarita, *Human Res Dir*
◆ **EMP:** 45 **EST:** 2014
SALES (est): 5MM **Privately Held**
WEB: www.synergylabs.com
SIC: 2834 3999 Veterinary pharmaceutical preparations; pet supplies

(G-4083)
T-WIZ PRTG & EMB DESIGNS LLC
464 W Melrose Cir (33312-1805)
PHONE..................................954 280-8949
Davidson Pierre, *CEO*
EMP: 32 **EST:** 2018
SALES (est): 1.1MM **Privately Held**
SIC: 2395 2759 Embroidery & art needlework; commercial printing

(G-4084)
TECH COMM INC
511 Se 32nd Ct (33316-4134)
PHONE..................................954 712-7777
Gersald O'Hearn, *President*
EMP: 10 **EST:** 1981
SQ FT: 10,000
SALES (est): 1.7MM **Privately Held**
WEB: www.techcommdf.com
SIC: 3663 Radio broadcasting & communications equipment

(G-4085)
TECNOGRAFIC INC
1010 Nw 51st Pl (33309-3140)
PHONE..................................954 928-1714
Marc Belhoste, *President*
Diane Belhoste, *Vice Pres*
EMP: 20 **EST:** 1983
SQ FT: 12,000
SALES (est): 1MM **Privately Held**
WEB: www.tecnografic.com
SIC: 3531 3732 Marine related equipment; boat building & repairing

(G-4086)
TELLABS INTERNATIONAL INC
1000 Corporate Dr Ste 300 (33334-3688)
PHONE..................................954 492-0120
EMP: 30
SALES (corp-wide): 77.5K **Privately Held**
SIC: 3661 Mfg Telephone/Telegraph Apparatus

HQ: Tellabs International Inc
1415 W Diehl Rd
Naperville IL 60515
630 798-8800

(G-4087)
TESS LLC (DH)
Also Called: T E S S Electrical Sales & Svc
2900 Sw 2nd Ave (33315-3122)
P.O. Box 8564 (33310-8564)
PHONE..................................954 583-6262
Hilda Fleming, *Office Mgr*
Paul Salinex, *Mng Member*
▲ **EMP:** 14 **EST:** 2006
SQ FT: 1,300
SALES (est): 7.4MM **Privately Held**
WEB: www.tessllc.us
SIC: 3613 Switchgear & switchboard apparatus
HQ: Rh Marine Netherlands B.V.
Jan Evertsenweg 2
Schiedam 3115
104 871-911

(G-4088)
TESTMAXX SERVICES CORPORATION
6330 N Andrews Ave 312 (33309-2130)
PHONE..................................954 946-7100
Michael G Ames, *President*
EMP: 10 **EST:** 1987
SALES (est): 817.8K **Privately Held**
SIC: 3825 8748 Test equipment for electronic & electric measurement; testing services

(G-4089)
TEXTRON GROUND SUPPORT EQP INC
1800 Sw 34th St (33315-3410)
PHONE..................................954 359-5730
David Tennant, *Sales Staff*
Benjamin Richards, *Branch Mgr*
EMP: 8
SALES (corp-wide): 12.3MM **Publicly Held**
WEB: textrongse.txtsv.com
SIC: 3537 Trucks, tractors, loaders, carriers & similar equipment; tractors, used in plants, docks, terminals, etc.: industrial
HQ: Textron Ground Support Equipment Inc.
41 Busch Dr Ne Ste 100
Cartersville GA 30121
770 422-7230

(G-4090)
THREE D PRODUCTS CORP
6889 Nw 28th Way (33309-1325)
PHONE..................................954 971-6511
Lydia Lopes Woods, *President*
George Woods, *Vice Pres*
Deborah Wood, *Shareholder*
Denise Wood, *Shareholder*
Diana Wood, *Shareholder*
EMP: 5 **EST:** 1995
SALES (est): 303.3K **Privately Held**
SIC: 3251 Ceramic glazed brick, clay

(G-4091)
THROW RAFT LLC
1202 Ne 8th Ave (33304-2002)
PHONE..................................954 366-8004
Troy Faletra, *Mng Member*
EMP: 6 **EST:** 2012
SALES (est): 1.2MM **Privately Held**
WEB: www.throwraft.com
SIC: 3069 5099 5999 Life jackets, inflatable: rubberized fabric; lifesaving & survival equipment (non-medical); alarm & safety equipment stores

(G-4092)
TITAN AMERICA LLC
2500 Sw 2nd Ave (33315-3114)
PHONE..................................954 523-9790
Darlene Studenmund, *Branch Mgr*
EMP: 59
SQ FT: 43,516
SALES (corp-wide): 177.9K **Privately Held**
WEB: www.titanamerica.com
SIC: 3273 3281 3271 1442 Ready-mixed concrete; cut stone & stone products; concrete block & brick; construction sand & gravel

HQ: Titan America Llc
5700 Lake Wright Dr # 300
Norfolk VA 23502
757 858-6500

(G-4093)
TLC RECOVERY CENTER S FLA LLC
465 Sw 20th Ave (33312-7694)
PHONE..................................954 533-0783
EMP: 7
SALES (corp-wide): 7.5MM **Privately Held**
WEB: www.evolutionstreatment.com
SIC: 3842 Prosthetic appliances
PA: Tlc Recovery Center Of South Florida Llc
2901 W Cypress Creek Rd # 123
Fort Lauderdale FL 33309
954 915-7444

(G-4094)
TM MARKETING GROUP LLC
3200 S Andrews Ave # 100 (33316-4121)
PHONE..................................954 848-9955
Anthony Munoz, *Mng Member*
EMP: 7 **EST:** 2005
SQ FT: 875
SALES (est): 330.3K **Privately Held**
SIC: 2721 8742 Magazines: publishing only, not printed on site; marketing consulting services

(G-4095)
TOP QUALITY YACHT REFINISHING
1513 Sw 18th Ave (33312-4125)
PHONE..................................954 522-5232
Thanh Van Le, *President*
Binh Le, *Vice Pres*
EMP: 10 **EST:** 1985
SALES (est): 972.2K **Privately Held**
WEB: www.tqyllc.com
SIC: 3732 Yachts, building & repairing

(G-4096)
TRAC ECOLOGICAL AMERICA INC
3400 Sw 26th Ter Ste A3 (33312-5068)
PHONE..................................954 583-4922
Kevin Greene, *CEO*
Patrick Leclerc, *President*
▲ **EMP:** 6 **EST:** 2001
SALES (est): 1.2MM **Privately Held**
WEB: www.trac-online.com
SIC: 2819 Industrial inorganic chemicals

(G-4097)
TRI-FECTA SOLUTIONS LLC
3900 W Commercial Blvd (33309-3328)
PHONE..................................954 908-1669
Hassan Latoiya, *Principal*
EMP: 6 **EST:** 2016
SALES (est): 326.3K **Privately Held**
WEB: www.trifecta-pharma.com
SIC: 2834 Pharmaceutical preparations

(G-4098)
TRITON STONE HOLDINGS LLC (PA)
800 Nw 65th St (33309-2006)
PHONE..................................219 669-4890
Josh Kessler, *Mng Member*
Eric Kimmerling,
Randy Mathis,
Sandy McCarter,
Joe Saulkenbery,
▲ **EMP:** 2 **EST:** 2014
SQ FT: 35,000
SALES (est): 51.2MM **Privately Held**
WEB: www.tritonfooddivision.com
SIC: 3281 5032 1752 3253 Granite, cut & shaped; brick, stone & related material; floor laying & floor work; ceramic wall & floor tile

(G-4099)
TRIVECTA PHARMACEUTICALS INC
1 E Broward Blvd Ste 700 (33301-1876)
PHONE..................................561 856-0842
Lina Garcia, *Principal*
EMP: 12 **EST:** 2017
SALES (est): 874.1K **Privately Held**
SIC: 2834 Pharmaceutical preparations

▲ = Import ▼=Export
◆ =Import/Export

(G-4100)
TRIVIDIA MEDITECH LLC
2400 Nw 55th Ct (33309-2672)
PHONE..................................954 677-9201
Scott Verner, *Manager*
EMP: 12 **EST:** 2019
SALES (est): 1.1MM **Privately Held**
WEB: www.trividiahealth.com
SIC: 3999 Manufacturing industries

(G-4101)
TWIN UPHOLSTERY & FURN MFG
1868 Nw 38th Ave 3 (33311-4119)
PHONE..................................954 791-0744
Maurice Contrears, *President*
Edgar Contrears, *Vice Pres*
EMP: 10 **EST:** 1996
SQ FT: 6,060
SALES (est): 290.1K **Privately Held**
WEB: www.twinsupholstery.com
SIC: 2512 Upholstered household furniture

(G-4102)
TWO BROTHERS CULTIVATION LLC
Also Called: Gorilla Boost
817 Se 2nd Ave Apt 518 (33316-1064)
P.O. Box 460193 (33346-0193)
PHONE..................................954 478-2402
Marc Morrow, *Mng Member*
EMP: 26 **EST:** 2014
SALES (est): 2.7MM **Privately Held**
SIC: 2824 Organic fibers, noncellulosic

(G-4103)
UNDERWATER LIGHTS USA LLC
3406 Sw 26th Ter Ste 5 (33312-5010)
PHONE..................................954 760-4447
Ian McDonald, *Mng Member*
Nicole Lippuner, *Manager*
Randal Rash,
EMP: 14 **EST:** 2001
SALES (est): 2.4MM **Privately Held**
WEB: www.underwaterlightsusa.com
SIC: 3646 Commercial indusl & institutional electric lighting fixtures

(G-4104)
UNIFI AVIATION LLC
50 Terminal Dr (33315-3601)
PHONE..................................954 377-2724
Angela Jones, *Branch Mgr*
EMP: 2003
SALES (corp-wide): 652.1MM **Privately Held**
WEB: www.unifiservice.com
SIC: 3448 Ramps: prefabricated metal
HQ: Unifi Aviation, Llc
950 E Paces Ferry Rd Ne # 2000
Atlanta GA 30326
404 715-4300

(G-4105)
UNION CHEMICAL INDUSTRIES CORP
Also Called: UCI Paints
1320 Nw 23rd Ave (33311-5244)
PHONE..................................954 581-6060
Richard Devick, *President*
Melissa Goupee, *Vice Pres*
Melissa Patterson Goupe, *VP Opers*
Mike Clevens, *Plant Mgr*
Sam Devick, *Sales Staff*
EMP: 16 **EST:** 1973
SQ FT: 28,000
SALES (est): 3.9MM **Privately Held**
SIC: 2851 Paints & paint additives

(G-4106)
UNIQUE ORIGINALS INC
19205 Sw 66th St (33332-1641)
PHONE..................................305 634-2274
Gregory Milu, *President*
▼ **EMP:** 23 **EST:** 1973
SALES (est): 865.8K **Privately Held**
SIC: 2512 2211 2431 Upholstered household furniture; broadwoven fabric mills, cotton; panel work, wood

(G-4107)
UNITED ADVG PUBLICATIONS
3313 W Coml Blvd Ste 130 (33309)
PHONE..................................954 730-9700
Terry Slattey, *Post Master*
EMP: 8 **EST:** 2009
SALES (est): 116.9K **Privately Held**
SIC: 2741 Miscellaneous publishing

(G-4108)
UNITED SHIP SERVICE CORP (PA)
1341 Sw 21st Ter (33312-3116)
PHONE..................................954 583-4588
Erik Engebretsen, *President*
◆ **EMP:** 9 **EST:** 2000
SALES (est): 1.2MM **Privately Held**
WEB: www.uss-us.com
SIC: 3731 Shipbuilding & repairing

(G-4109)
UNITY MARINE INC
2860 W State Road 84 # 118 (33312-4808)
PHONE..................................954 321-1727
Dennis J Cummings, *President*
▲ **EMP:** 11 **EST:** 2007
SALES (est): 129.5K **Privately Held**
SIC: 3086 Packaging & shipping materials, foamed plastic

(G-4110)
UNIVERSAL SIGNS
6045 Nw 31st Ave (33309-2209)
PHONE..................................954 366-1535
EMP: 8 **EST:** 2015
SALES (est): 46K **Privately Held**
WEB: www.universalsignsfl.com
SIC: 3993 Signs & advertising specialties

(G-4111)
UNIWELD PRODUCTS INC (PA)
2850 Ravenswood Rd (33312-4994)
P.O. Box 8427 (33310-8427)
PHONE..................................954 584-2000
David Pearl, *Ch of Bd*
David Foster, *Managing Dir*
David Pearl II, *Exec VP*
Douglas Pearl, *Vice Pres*
Martha Garcia, *Export Mgr*
◆ **EMP:** 250 **EST:** 1949
SQ FT: 100,000
SALES (est): 41.3MM **Privately Held**
WEB: www.uniweld.com
SIC: 3548 3823 Gas welding equipment; welding & cutting apparatus & accessories; pressure gauges, dial & digital

(G-4112)
USA MARINE ENGINES
2600 Sw 3rd Ave (33315-3106)
PHONE..................................954 614-4810
Jason Buchanan, *Principal*
EMP: 10 **EST:** 2019
SALES (est): 2MM **Privately Held**
WEB: www.usamarineengines.com
SIC: 3519 Marine engines

(G-4113)
USA MARITIME ENTERPRISES INC
2600 Eshnwer Blvd Lhigh C Lehigh Cement (33308)
P.O. Box 22723 (33335-2723)
PHONE..................................954 764-8360
Antonio J Orejuela, *President*
Augusto Maldonado, *Vice Pres*
Claudia P Osorio, *Treasurer*
Valerie T Maldonado, *Admin Sec*
EMP: 6 **EST:** 1984
SALES (est): 475.1K **Privately Held**
WEB: www.usamaritime.us
SIC: 3731 4731 Landing ships, building & repairing; agents, shipping

(G-4114)
V P PRESS INC
Also Called: Discount Printing
3934 Davie Blvd (33312-3406)
PHONE..................................954 581-7531
Vincent Cefalu, *President*
Pamela Cefalu, *Treasurer*
Frank Ramirez, *Admin Sec*
EMP: 10 **EST:** 1980
SQ FT: 2,400
SALES (est): 1.5MM **Privately Held**
WEB: www.vp-press.com
SIC: 2752 2791 2789 Commercial printing, offset; typesetting; bookbinding & related work

(G-4115)
VALLEYMEDIA INC
Also Called: Cioreview
600 S Andrews Ave Ste 405 (33301-2846)
PHONE..................................510 565-7559
Harvi Sachar, *President*
Dan Smith, *Research*
Katherine Jones, *Sales Mgr*
EMP: 26 **EST:** 2015
SALES (est): 2.4MM **Privately Held**
SIC: 2721 Magazines: publishing only, not printed on site

(G-4116)
VAN TIBOLLI BEAUTY CORP
Also Called: GK Hair
4800 Nw 15th Ave Unit E (33309-3781)
PHONE..................................305 390-0044
Vanderlei Tibolli, *President*
Martin Mosley, *COO*
Faisal Kamal, *CFO*
Shannon Tibbitts, *Sales Staff*
▲ **EMP:** 25 **EST:** 2009
SALES (est): 2.9MM **Privately Held**
WEB: www.vantibolli.com
SIC: 2844 3634 Tonics, hair; hair curlers, electric

(G-4117)
VERITAS FARMS INC (PA)
1512 E Broward Blvd # 300 (33301-2147)
PHONE..................................561 288-6603
Alexander M Salgado, *CEO*
Dave Smith, *COO*
Erduis Sanabria, *Exec VP*
Spencer Fuller, *Vice Pres*
Rianna Meyer, *Vice Pres*
EMP: 10 **EST:** 2011
SQ FT: 2,145
SALES (est): 3MM **Publicly Held**
WEB: www.theveritasfarms.com
SIC: 2833 Medicinals & botanicals

(G-4118)
VERTIV IT SYSTEMS INC
550 W Cypress Creek Rd # 200 (33309-6169)
PHONE..................................954 746-9000
Melanie Whelan, *President*
Erica Gomez, *General Mgr*
Marco Gonzalez, *General Mgr*
Craig Hook, *General Mgr*
Victor Medina, *Business Mgr*
EMP: 873
SALES (corp-wide): 5B **Publicly Held**
WEB: www.vertiv.com
SIC: 3577 Computer peripheral equipment
HQ: Vertiv It Systems, Inc.
4991 Corporate Dr Nw
Huntsville AL 35805
256 430-4000

(G-4119)
VITAPAK LLC
21070 Sheridan St (33332-2310)
PHONE..................................954 661-0390
Nick Mariano,
EMP: 7 **EST:** 2020
SALES (est): 635.5K **Privately Held**
SIC: 2023 Dietary supplements, dairy & non-dairy based

(G-4120)
WALRUSS ENTERPRISES INC
Also Called: First Impression Graphic Svcs
1509 Sw 1st Ave (33315-1710)
PHONE..................................954 525-0342
Margaret Russell, *President*
EMP: 9 **EST:** 2011
SALES (est): 309.7K **Privately Held**
SIC: 2759 Commercial printing

(G-4121)
WARDEN ENTERPRISES INC (PA)
Also Called: Clutch House
807 Nw 7th St (33311-7304)
PHONE..................................954 463-4404
Paul Fontanella, *President*
EMP: 6 **EST:** 1975
SQ FT: 10,000
SALES (est): 766.1K **Privately Held**
SIC: 3714 Clutches, motor vehicle

(G-4122)
WARFIGHTER FCSED LOGISTICS INC
936 Nw 1st St (33311-8902)
PHONE..................................740 513-4692
Darrell Kem, *CEO*
Ron Wilson, *Vice Pres*
EMP: 15
SQ FT: 1,500
SALES (corp-wide): 2.5MM **Privately Held**
WEB: www.warfighterfocusedlogistics.com
SIC: 3069 3429 Rubber hardware; aircraft & marine hardware, inc. pulleys & similar items; motor vehicle hardware; aircraft hardware; marine hardware
PA: Warfighter Focused Logistics Inc.
936 Nw 1st St
Fort Lauderdale FL 33311
740 513-4692

(G-4123)
WATERMAKERS INC
2233 S Andrews Ave (33316-3400)
PHONE..................................954 467-8920
Toll Free:..................................888 -
Joseph Hocher, *President*
Harry D 'oyley, *Vice Pres*
Harry Doyley, *Vice Pres*
David Hocher, *Vice Pres*
Dave Henderson, *Purchasing*
◆ **EMP:** 15 **EST:** 1984
SQ FT: 6,000
SALES (est): 3.4MM **Privately Held**
WEB: www.watermakers.com
SIC: 3589 8111 Water purification equipment, household type; water treatment equipment, industrial; legal services

(G-4124)
WATTERA LLC
3131 Sw 42nd St (33312-6802)
PHONE..................................954 400-5135
Rishi Kukreja,
EMP: 20 **EST:** 2012
SQ FT: 3,500
SALES (est): 3.3MM **Privately Held**
SIC: 3089 Injection molding of plastics

(G-4125)
WAYLOO INC
2700 W Cypress Creek Rd (33309-1744)
P.O. Box 668665, Pompano Beach (33066-8665)
PHONE..................................954 914-3192
Nancy Nagamatsu-Silverman, *CEO*
Wayne St James, *Exec VP*
▲ **EMP:** 8 **EST:** 1992
SQ FT: 10,000
SALES (est): 1MM **Privately Held**
SIC: 2326 2752 7319 2393 Work uniforms; commercial printing, lithographic; distribution of advertising material or sample services; textile bags; men's miscellaneous accessories

(G-4126)
WE BRONZE WHOLESALE LLC
2736 N Federal Hwy (33306-1424)
PHONE..................................954 922-8826
Ed Maslanka,
William Aribu,
▲ **EMP:** 5 **EST:** 2004
SALES (est): 782.3K **Privately Held**
WEB: www.webronze.com
SIC: 3366 Bronze foundry

(G-4127)
WEBVOIP INC
6400 N Andrews Ave # 490 (33309-2114)
PHONE..................................305 793-2061
David J Rachiele, *President*
EMP: 5 **EST:** 2002
SALES (est): 2MM **Privately Held**
SIC: 7372 Application computer software

(G-4128)
WHEELS A MILLION
1100 Nw 54th St (33309-2819)
PHONE..................................754 444-2869
Clodoaldo Neto, *Principal*
EMP: 6 **EST:** 2014
SALES (est): 842.2K **Privately Held**
WEB: www.wheelsamillion.com
SIC: 3714 Motor vehicle parts & accessories

(G-4129)
WHOLE ENCHLADA FRESH MXCAN GRI
4115 N Federal Hwy (33308-5530)
PHONE...................................954 561-4040
David Cardaci, *Principal*
EMP: 10 EST: 2006
SALES (est): 341.6K **Privately Held**
WEB: www.twefreshmex.com
SIC: 2032 Mexican foods: packaged in cans, jars, etc.

(G-4130)
WHR HOLDINGS LLC (PA)
Also Called: Wilkenson Hi-Rise
3402 Sw 26th Ter Ste 10 (33312-5071)
PHONE...................................954 342-4342
Chad George, *CEO*
Michael Bracken, *President*
Michael J Malo,
Michael Malo,
Stormy Hicks, *Advisor*
▼ EMP: 32 EST: 2006
SALES (est): 10.1MM **Privately Held**
SIC: 2842 Sanitation preparations, disinfectants & deodorants

(G-4131)
WICKED WOODWORKS INC (PA)
1314 Sw 1st Ave Ste 4 (33315-1500)
PHONE...................................305 714-2209
Bruce Geddes, *CEO*
EMP: 7 EST: 2020
SALES (est): 95.6K **Privately Held**
SIC: 2431 Millwork

(G-4132)
WILKINSON HI-RISE LLC
3402 Sw 26th Ter Ste 10 (33312-5071)
PHONE...................................954 342-4400
Alejandro Tobon, *Opers Mgr*
Michael Bracken, *Mng Member*
Dennis Donohue,
EMP: 120 EST: 2001
SALES (est): 10.5MM **Privately Held**
WEB: www.whrise.com
SIC: 3444 5084 3559 Metal housings, enclosures, casings & other containers; processing & packaging equipment; recycling machinery

(G-4133)
WILO USA LLC
Also Called: Scot Pump Company
3001 Sw 3rd Ave Ste 7 (33315-3315)
PHONE...................................954 524-6776
Steve Wilkerson, *Branch Mgr*
EMP: 59
SALES (corp-wide): 144.1K **Privately Held**
WEB: www.wilo.com
SIC: 3561 Pumps & pumping equipment
HQ: Wilo Usa Llc
   9550 W Higgins Rd Ste 300
   Rosemont IL 60018

(G-4134)
WILSON CUSTOM CABINETS
810 Nw 45th St (33309-3947)
PHONE...................................954 296-1095
Bobette Wilson, *Principal*
EMP: 7 EST: 2013
SALES (est): 154.6K **Privately Held**
WEB: www.wilsoncustomcabinets.com
SIC: 2434 Wood kitchen cabinets

(G-4135)
WIRE PRODUCTS INC OF FLORIDA (PA)
4300 Nw 10th Ave (33309-4603)
PHONE...................................954 772-1477
Thomas J Bourg Jr, *President*
Susan Day, *Corp Secy*
Doug Schleenbaker, *Vice Pres*
Raul Blanco, *Sales Staff*
Derrick D Holmes, *Sales Staff*
◆ EMP: 20 EST: 1957
SQ FT: 30,000
SALES (est): 5.7MM **Privately Held**
WEB: www.wireproducts.us
SIC: 3496 3315 Concrete reinforcing mesh & wire; wire & fabricated wire products

(G-4136)
WOOL WHOLESALE PLUMBING SUPPLY
Also Called: Pipco
1321 Ne 12th Ave (33304-1898)
PHONE...................................954 763-3632
Carl Wool, *President*
Shirley Wool, *Corp Secy*
▼ EMP: 71 EST: 1975
SALES (est): 10MM
SALES (corp-wide): 71MM **Privately Held**
WEB: www.woolsupply.com
SIC: 3432 3431 3261 5074 Plumbing fixture fittings & trim; metal sanitary ware; plumbing fixtures, vitreous china; plumbing & hydronic heating supplies
PA: Wool Wholesale Plumbing Supply, Inc.
   4340 Sw 74th Ave
   Miami FL 33155
   305 266-7111

(G-4137)
WORLD WIDE FROZEN FOODS LLC
800 W Cypress Creek Rd (33309-2075)
PHONE...................................954 266-8500
Daniel R Pollak, *Mng Member*
Rigo Ugarte,
▲ EMP: 4 EST: 2017
SQ FT: 3,300
SALES (est): 6MM **Privately Held**
SIC: 2037 Frozen fruits & vegetables

(G-4138)
WRITE STUFF ENTERPRISES LLC
1001 S Andrews Ave # 120 (33316-1015)
PHONE...................................954 462-6657
Sandy Cruz, *Vice Pres*
Jeffrey L Rodengen,
Marianne Roberts,
EMP: 20 EST: 1996
SQ FT: 10,000
SALES (est): 3.9MM **Privately Held**
WEB: www.writestuffbooks.com
SIC: 2731 2752 2721 Books: publishing only; calendar & card printing, lithographic; magazines: publishing only, not printed on site

(G-4139)
YACHT 10 INC
Also Called: Megafend Mooring Products
3001 Sw 3rd Ave Ste 1 (33315-3315)
PHONE...................................954 759-9929
Garry L Gassew, *President*
Nathan Marsack, *Sales Staff*
▲ EMP: 6 EST: 1986
SQ FT: 2,200
SALES (est): 730.1K **Privately Held**
WEB: www.knot10.com
SIC: 3732 Yachts, building & repairing

(G-4140)
YACHT-MATE PRODUCTS INC
3200 S Andrews Ave Ste 10 (33316-4100)
PHONE...................................954 527-0112
Sandra H Handrahan, *Principal*
EMP: 8 EST: 2015
SALES (est): 1.7MM **Privately Held**
WEB: www.yachtmate.com
SIC: 3589 Water treatment equipment, industrial

(G-4141)
YOLO LAS OLAS LLC
200 Sw 2nd St (33301-1822)
PHONE...................................954 522-3002
Timothy Petrillo, *Manager*
EMP: 13 EST: 2007
SALES (est): 712.6K **Privately Held**
WEB: www.lasolasboulevard.com
SIC: 3421 Table & food cutlery, including butchers'

(G-4142)
YOUNGER YOU INC (PA)
Also Called: Nutra-Lift Skin Care
5961 Bayview Dr (33308-2739)
PHONE...................................954 924-4462
Robert Trovato, *President*
EMP: 5 EST: 1996
SQ FT: 3,000
SALES (est): 848.3K **Privately Held**
SIC: 2844 Face creams or lotions

(G-4143)
ZEDORA INC
Also Called: Zed Promo's
110 E Broward Blvd (33301-3503)
PHONE...................................954 332-3322
Alex Reed, *CEO*
EMP: 20 EST: 2002
SALES (est): 1.7MM **Privately Held**
SIC: 3911 Bracelets, precious metal

(G-4144)
ZENITH ROLLERS LLC
764 Nw 57th Ct (33309-2028)
PHONE...................................954 493-6484
Sashi Ravada,
Shiva Sistla,
▲ EMP: 7 EST: 2005
SALES (est): 922.7K **Privately Held**
WEB: www.zenithrollersus.com
SIC: 3555 Printing trades machinery

(G-4145)
ZENO FURNITURE & MAT MFG CO
Also Called: Zeno Mattress and Furn Mfg Co
671 Nw 4th Ave (33311-7322)
PHONE...................................954 764-1212
Joseph Zeno, *President*
EMP: 9 EST: 1960
SQ FT: 15,000
SALES (est): 1.2MM **Privately Held**
WEB: www.zenomattress.com
SIC: 2515 5712 Mattresses, innerspring or box spring; mattresses

(G-4146)
ZEPPELIN PRODUCTS INC
Also Called: Zep-Pro
3744 Sw 30th Ave (33312-6708)
PHONE...................................954 989-8808
Alon Granovsky, *CEO*
Lebedin German, *President*
German Lebedin, *Data Proc Staff*
◆ EMP: 13 EST: 1994
SALES (est): 1.2MM **Privately Held**
WEB: www.zeppro.com
SIC: 2387 3144 3143 2389 Apparel belts; sandals, women's; sandals, men's; men's miscellaneous accessories

(G-4147)
ZOYA INC
641 Sw 3rd Ave (33315-1005)
PHONE...................................954 523-6531
Zoya Hajianpour, *President*
EMP: 5 EST: 2001
SQ FT: 1,500
SALES (est): 684.5K **Privately Held**
WEB: www.zoyainc.com
SIC: 3999 Atomizers, toiletry

Fort Mc Coy
Marion County

(G-4148)
CIRCLE S MANUFACTURING CO INC
13650 Ne 110th St (32134-7877)
P.O. Box 1440 (32134-1440)
PHONE...................................352 236-3580
Earla Sogan, *President*
Bruce Sogan, *Vice Pres*
Michael Sogan, *Vice Pres*
Maria Carter, *Treasurer*
Gail Sogan, *Admin Sec*
EMP: 7 EST: 1979
SQ FT: 3,200
SALES (est): 226K **Privately Held**
WEB: circle-s-manufacturing-co-inc.business.site
SIC: 3599 Machine shop, jobbing & repair

(G-4149)
FM MEAT PRODUCTS LTD PARTNR
19798 Ne Highway 315 (32134-7601)
P.O. Box 450 (32134-0450)
PHONE...................................352 546-3000
Frank Stronach, *Partner*
Corban Russell, *Partner*
EMP: 48 EST: 2013
SALES (est): 9.2MM **Privately Held**
WEB: www.adenafarms.com
SIC: 2011 Meat packing plants

Fort Meade
Polk County

(G-4150)
KOMATSU MINING CORP
1321 State Road 630 W (33841-9404)
PHONE...................................863 804-0131
Glen Zielinski, *Branch Mgr*
EMP: 32 **Privately Held**
WEB: www.mining.komatsu
SIC: 3532 Mining machinery
HQ: Komatsu Mining Corp.
   311 E Greenfield Ave
   Milwaukee WI 53204
   414 670-8454

(G-4151)
NOVAPHOS INC
3200 County Rte 630 W (33841)
PHONE...................................863 285-8607
Theodore Fowler, *President*
David Blake, *Vice Pres*
EMP: 43 EST: 2013
SALES (est): 8.2MM **Privately Held**
WEB: www.novaphos.com
SIC: 2874 Phosphates

Fort Myers
Lee County

(G-4152)
5571 HALIFAX INC
5571 Halifax Ave (33912-4403)
PHONE...................................239 454-4999
Daniel R Harper, *President*
Shawn Harper, *Vice Pres*
Ronald E Inge, *Treasurer*
EMP: 30 EST: 1999
SQ FT: 10,651
SALES (est): 1MM **Privately Held**
WEB: www.dssrecycle.com
SIC: 7692 Welding repair

(G-4153)
A QUALLITY PALLET COMPANY
5896 Enterprise Pkwy (33905-5030)
P.O. Box 50975 (33994-0975)
PHONE...................................239 245-0900
Daniel Crismon, *Principal*
EMP: 7 EST: 2007
SALES (est): 137.2K **Privately Held**
SIC: 2448 Pallets, wood

(G-4154)
ABSOLUTE PLASTIC SOLUTIONS INC
2178 Andrea Ln (33912-1986)
PHONE...................................239 313-7779
Barry J Bowen Jr, *Principal*
EMP: 10 EST: 2012
SALES (est): 2MM **Privately Held**
SIC: 3089 Injection molding of plastics

(G-4155)
ACE METALWORKS & MFG INC
11821 Palm Beach Blvd (33905-5908)
PHONE...................................239 666-1103
Diana Rogers, *President*
EMP: 20
SALES (est): 832.8K **Privately Held**
SIC: 3549 Metalworking machinery

(G-4156)
ACE PRESS INC
2133 Broadway (33901-3634)
PHONE...................................239 334-1118
Tom Jackson, *President*
Stephen Cooper, *CTO*
EMP: 8 EST: 1963
SQ FT: 12,000
SALES (est): 642.3K **Privately Held**
WEB: www.ace-press.com
SIC: 2752 Commercial printing, offset

▲ = Import ▼=Export
◆ =Import/Export

(G-4157)
ADVANCED PRECISION MCH US INC
3791 Edison Ave (33916-4705)
PHONE..............................239 332-2841
Thomas L Pancoast, *Principal*
EMP: 10 **EST:** 2010
SALES (est): 829K **Privately Held**
WEB: www.apmachineshop.com
SIC: 3599 Machine shop, jobbing & repair

(G-4158)
AERO-MACH TCO MANUFACTURING
604 Danley Dr (33907-1529)
PHONE..........................,....239 936-7570
Jason White, *President*
EMP: 9 **EST:** 1974
SQ FT: 4,000
SALES (est): 933.2K
SALES (corp-wide): 11.9MM **Privately Held**
WEB: www.tcomanufacturing.com
SIC: 3663 Radio & TV communications equipment
PA: Aero-Mach Laboratories, Inc.
7707 E Funston St
Wichita KS 67207
316 682-7707

(G-4159)
AIRO INDUSTRIES INC
2837 Fowler St (33901-6314)
PHONE..............................239 229-5273
Mark Pruskauer, *President*
Patricia Lamentia, *Vice Pres*
EMP: 7 **EST:** 2012
SQ FT: 10,500
SALES (est): 880.9K **Privately Held**
WEB: www.airoind.com
SIC: 3699 Electrical equipment & supplies

(G-4160)
AKJ INDUSTRIES INC (PA)
10175 6 Mile Cypress Pkwy (33966-6993)
PHONE..............................239 939-1696
Kenneth Bumside, *President*
Jerry Nelesen, *Exec VP*
Daniel Deer, *Vice Pres*
William McHale, *Opers Staff*
Nina Verios, *Admin Asst*
◆ **EMP:** 9 **EST:** 1981
SQ FT: 3,000
SALES (est): 9.1MM **Privately Held**
WEB: www.akjindustries.com
SIC: 2899 3559 Carbon removing solvent; degreasing machines, automotive & industrial; refinery, chemical processing & similar machinery

(G-4161)
ALICO METAL FABRICATORS LLC
Also Called: Metropolis Iron By Design
16750 Link Ct Ste 205 (33912-5907)
PHONE..............................239 454-4766
Andrew N Aiken, *Mng Member*
Andrew Aiken Jr, *Mng Member*
EMP: 5 **EST:** 2009
SALES (est): 465.7K **Privately Held**
WEB: www.alicometalfabricators.com
SIC: 3441 Fabricated structural metal

(G-4162)
ALL CUT INC NO SELECTION
2910 Hunter St (33916-7608)
PHONE..............................239 789-1748
EMP: 7 **EST:** 2018
SALES (est): 254.7K **Privately Held**
WEB: www.allcut.com
SIC: 3599 Machine shop, jobbing & repair

(G-4163)
ALLEGRA FORT MYERS
12140 Metro Pkwy Ste C (33966-8364)
PHONE..............................239 275-5797
Terry P Fortney, *Principal*
Fernando Portugal, *Graphic Designe*
EMP: 7 **EST:** 2012
SALES (est): 881.7K **Privately Held**
WEB: www.allegramarketingprint.com
SIC: 2752 Commercial printing, offset

(G-4164)
ALLENSTEEL INC
16281 Pine Ridge Rd (33908-2689)
PHONE..............................239 454-1331
Tony Allen, *Owner*
EMP: 11 **EST:** 2003
SQ FT: 81,100
SALES (est): 145.9K **Privately Held**
SIC: 3441 Fabricated structural metal

(G-4165)
ALLI CATS INC
Also Called: Fastsigns
12211 S Cleveland Ave (33907-3746)
PHONE..............................239 274-0744
Paul Hill, *President*
Paul J Hill, *President*
EMP: 5 **EST:** 2002
SALES (est): 500K **Privately Held**
WEB: www.fastsigns.com
SIC: 3993 Signs & advertising specialties

(G-4166)
ALLOY CLADDING COMPANY LLC
16170 Old Us 41 (33912-2286)
PHONE..............................561 625-4550
EMP: 15 **EST:** 2008
SALES (est): 142.3K **Privately Held**
SIC: 3548 Welding apparatus

(G-4167)
ALLSTAIR
7800 Drew Cir Ste 15 (33967-6075)
PHONE..............................239 313-5574
Christopher D Adams, *Principal*
EMP: 7 **EST:** 2013
SALES (est): 115.5K **Privately Held**
SIC: 2431 Millwork

(G-4168)
ALTERNATIVE LABORATORIES LLC (PA)
4740 S Cleveland Ave (33907-1311)
PHONE..............................239 692-9160
Kevin Thomas, *CEO*
Jennifer Cooper, *President*
Dawn Hollander, *Purchasing*
Bill Boettcher, *Manager*
Mary Ann Crabtree, *Director*
▲ **EMP:** 43 **EST:** 2009
SALES (est): 18.1MM **Privately Held**
WEB: www.alternativelabs.com
SIC: 2834 Vitamin, nutrient & hematinic preparations for human use

(G-4169)
AMAZON SHEDS AND GAZEBOS INC (PA)
17300 Jean St (33967-6067)
PHONE..............................239 498-5558
Filiberto Rodriguez, *President*
Zoe Branca, *Sales Mgr*
EMP: 7 **EST:** 2006
SALES (est): 3.7MM **Privately Held**
WEB: www.amazonsheds.com
SIC: 2452 3448 Prefabricated wood buildings; prefabricated metal buildings

(G-4170)
AMD AERO INC
14230 Jetport Loop W (33913-7712)
PHONE..............................239 561-8622
James H Cline, *President*
Barbara Cline, *Corp Secy*
EMP: 14 **EST:** 1991
SQ FT: 10,000
SALES (est): 1.1MM **Privately Held**
SIC: 3829 Fuel system instruments, aircraft; fuel totalizers, aircraft engine

(G-4171)
AMERICAN BOTTLING COMPANY
Also Called: Southeast-Atlantic
2236 Hemingway Dr (33912-1917)
PHONE..............................239 489-0838
Jeff Sutherland, *Manager*
EMP: 51 **Publicly Held**
WEB: www.keurigdrpepper.com
SIC: 2086 Soft drinks: packaged in cans, bottles, etc.
HQ: The American Bottling Company
6425 Hall Of Fame Ln
Frisco TX 75034

(G-4172)
AMERICAN TRACTION SYSTEMS INC
Also Called: A T S
10030 Amberwood Rd Ste 1 (33913-8521)
PHONE..............................239 768-0757
Bonne Posma, *President*
Anthony Davis, *Vice Pres*
Juan Pinzon, *Vice Pres*
Car Wilcox, *Vice Pres*
Steve Beeson, *Engineer*
EMP: 20 **EST:** 2008
SALES (est): 5.1MM **Privately Held**
WEB: www.americantraction.com
SIC: 3621 Control equipment for electric buses & locomotives

(G-4173)
AMERICAN WINDOWS SHUTTERS INC
Also Called: Croci North America
11600 Adelmo Ln (33966-8400)
PHONE..............................239 278-3066
Cesare Croci, *President*
Spencer Bass, *Sales Staff*
Cindy Rhoton, *Admin Asst*
◆ **EMP:** 30 **EST:** 1993
SQ FT: 120,000
SALES (est): 11.6MM
SALES (corp-wide): 7.9MM **Privately Held**
WEB: www.crocinorthamerica.com
SIC: 3354 Aluminum extruded products
PA: Croci Italia Srl
Via Emilia 732
Bertinoro FC 47032
054 346-3911

(G-4174)
AMERICUT OF FLORIDA INC
1941 Custom Dr (33907-2101)
PHONE..............................800 692-2187
Michael Harris, *President*
Kevin Sorrell, *Vice Pres*
EMP: 14 **EST:** 2013
SALES (est): 690.9K **Privately Held**
WEB: www.americut.com
SIC: 3541 Sawing & cutoff machines (metalworking machinery)

(G-4175)
AMERITECH POWDER COATING INC
502 South Rd Unit D (33907-2454)
PHONE..............................239 274-8000
Ovidio Chavez, *President*
Johnathan Kob, *Vice Pres*
EMP: 10 **EST:** 2002
SALES (est): 1MM **Privately Held**
WEB: www.ameritechpc.com
SIC: 3479 Coating of metals & formed products

(G-4176)
AMSWFL INC
4700 Laredo Ave (33905-4909)
PHONE..............................239 334-7433
Brian Egner, *President*
EMP: 19
SALES (est): 1MM **Privately Held**
SIC: 3354 Aluminum extruded products

(G-4177)
ANNA ANDRES
Also Called: USA Today
2442 Dr M L King Blvd Martin (33901)
PHONE..............................239 335-0233
Anna Andres, *Principal*
EMP: 16 **EST:** 1997
SALES (est): 388.3K **Privately Held**
WEB: www.2395404884.com
SIC: 2711 Newspapers, publishing & printing

(G-4178)
ANYTHING DISPLAY
6225 Presidential Ct (33919-3566)
PHONE..............................239 433-9738
Chris Andrews, *Division Mgr*
EMP: 8 **EST:** 2011
SALES (est): 828.4K **Privately Held**
WEB: www.anythingdisplay.com
SIC: 3993 Signs & advertising specialties

(G-4179)
ARCHITECTURAL METALS S W FL
4700 Laredo Ave (33905-4909)
PHONE..............................239 334-7433
Chris Mills, *President*
EMP: 25 **EST:** 1994
SQ FT: 9,600
SALES (est): 3.7MM **Privately Held**
WEB: www.archmetalsfl.com
SIC: 3444 Sheet metalwork

(G-4180)
ARIZONA BEVERAGE COMPANY LLC
1685 Target Ct Ste 18 (33905-4926)
PHONE..............................516 812-0303
Thomas Deluca, *Manager*
EMP: 10
SALES (corp-wide): 284.6MM **Privately Held**
SIC: 2086 Iced tea & fruit drinks, bottled & canned
HQ: Arizona Beverage Company Llc
60 Crossways Park Dr W # 400
Woodbury NY 11797
516 812-0300

(G-4181)
AROMA COFFEE SERVICE INC
2168 Andrea Ln (33912-1901)
PHONE..............................239 481-7262
Karen Long, *President*
Brian Long, *Vice Pres*
Jared Dupre, *Opers Mgr*
Phil Lessor, *Branch Mgr*
EMP: 5 **EST:** 1986
SQ FT: 1,500
SALES (est): 1.4MM **Privately Held**
WEB: www.aromacoffee.net
SIC: 2095 5149 5499 Roasted coffee; coffee, green or roasted; coffee

(G-4182)
ATLANTIC BEV GROUP USA INC
2711 1st St Apt 102 (33916-1843)
PHONE..............................239 334-3016
Albert J Degutis, *President*
Paul F Dumas, *Treasurer*
EMP: 6 **EST:** 2002
SALES (est): 394.8K **Privately Held**
SIC: 2087 Concentrates, drink

(G-4183)
ATLANTIC DRINKING WATER SYSTMS
2700 Parker Ave (33905-1958)
PHONE..............................252 255-1110
Joel Walker, *President*
Karen Walker, *Principal*
EMP: 7 **EST:** 1985
SALES (est): 258.7K **Privately Held**
SIC: 3589 Water filters & softeners, household type

(G-4184)
AXI INTERNATIONAL (PA)
5400 Division Dr Ste 1 (33905-5016)
PHONE..............................239 690-9589
Bruwer Wessel Van Tonder, *CEO*
Islam Nahdi, *President*
Ernest Neafsey, *General Mgr*
Bernard W Keizer, *Corp Secy*
Christian Smith, *COO*
◆ **EMP:** 20 **EST:** 1998
SQ FT: 7,000
SALES (est): 9.6MM **Privately Held**
WEB: www.axi-international.com
SIC: 3823 5169 Combustion control instruments; compressed gas

(G-4185)
BAMM MANUFACTURING INC
Also Called: Handcrafted Pewter
1222 Hemingway Dr (33912-1926)
PHONE..............................239 277-0776
Angie Winebrenner, *President*
Bonnie Mason, *Vice Pres*
▲ **EMP:** 5 **EST:** 2002
SALES (est): 369K **Privately Held**
SIC: 3499 Novelties & giftware, including trophies

(G-4186)
BARON LLC
4784 Skates Cir (33905-7326)
PHONE 239 691-5783
Cindy Young, *Manager*
EMP: 8 **EST:** 2005
SALES (est): 182.5K **Privately Held**
SIC: 3728 Aircraft parts & equipment

(G-4187)
BAYSHORE PRECAST CONCRETE INC
Also Called: Bayshore Concrete & Ldscp Mtls
8100 Bayshore Rd (33917-3627)
P.O. Box 51410 (33994-1410)
PHONE 239 543-3001
Willem Dedeugd, *President*
EMP: 7 **EST:** 1984
SALES (est): 1MM
SALES (corp-wide): 4.1MM **Privately Held**
WEB: www.bayshoreconcrete.net
SIC: 3272 Concrete products
PA: Tricircle Pavers, Inc.
2709 Jeffcott St
Fort Myers FL 33901
239 332-2325

(G-4188)
BF ONE LLC
5661 Independence Cir (33912-4419)
PHONE 239 939-5251
Mary Belindan, *Engineer*
Donald D Brooks, *Manager*
EMP: 11 **EST:** 2006
SALES (est): 244.2K **Privately Held**
SIC: 3011 Tires & inner tubes

(G-4189)
BOAT LIFT PROS OF SW FLA INC
2559 4th St (33901-2507)
PHONE 239 339-7080
Vincent T Forte, *Principal*
EMP: 10 **EST:** 2019
SALES (est): 1.3MM **Privately Held**
WEB: www.theboatliftpros.com
SIC: 3536 Boat lifts

(G-4190)
BOAT LIFTS BY SYNERGY LLC
15864 Brothers Ct Ste B (33912-2248)
PHONE 641 676-4785
Brandon Graham, *Mng Member*
EMP: 6 **EST:** 2020
SALES (est): 514K **Privately Held**
SIC: 3536 Boat lifts

(G-4191)
BOAT MASTER ALUMINUM TRAILERS
Also Called: Jdci Enterprises
11950 Amedicus Ln Unit 2 (33907-4062)
PHONE 239 768-2224
Joseph K Isley Jr, *President*
John Kraft, *Purch Mgr*
EMP: 8 **EST:** 1983
SQ FT: 5,000
SALES (est): 1.7MM **Privately Held**
SIC: 3799 Boat trailers

(G-4192)
BOBS BARRICADES INC
8031 Mainline Pkwy (33912-5931)
PHONE 239 656-1183
David Feise, *Manager*
EMP: 18
SALES (corp-wide): 37.2MM **Privately Held**
WEB: www.bobsbarricades.com
SIC: 3499 Barricades, metal
PA: Bob's Barricades, Inc.
921 Shotgun Rd
Sunrise FL 33326
954 423-2627

(G-4193)
BONITA DAILY NEWS
Also Called: Naple Daily News, The
4415 Metro Pkwy Ste 300 (33916-9425)
PHONE 239 213-6060
Corbin Wyant, *Principal*
EMP: 25 **EST:** 1990

SALES (est): 1.4MM **Privately Held**
WEB: www.enzosofbonita.com
SIC: 2711 2741 Newspapers, publishing & printing; miscellaneous publishing

(G-4194)
BRADEN & SON CONSTRUCTION INC
6730 Circle Dr (33905-7624)
PHONE 239 694-8600
Charles Richter, *Owner*
EMP: 7 **EST:** 2016
SALES (est): 83.6K **Privately Held**
SIC: 3577 Computer peripheral equipment

(G-4195)
BREEZE NEWSPAPERS
14051 Jetport Loop (33913-7705)
PHONE 239 574-1116
Scott Blonde, *Principal*
Beth Zedeck, *Advt Staff*
Sonia Santiago, *Executive*
Dede Stuart, *Graphic Designe*
EMP: 11 **EST:** 2010
SALES (est): 295.4K **Privately Held**
WEB: www.breezenewspapers.com
SIC: 2711 Newspapers: publishing only, not printed on site

(G-4196)
BURMA SPICE INC
31 Georgetown (33919-1016)
PHONE 863 254-0960
Edward Brakus Jr, *President*
EMP: 6 **EST:** 2014
SALES (est): 565.8K **Privately Held**
WEB: www.burmaspice.com
SIC: 2099 Seasonings & spices

(G-4197)
C M C STEEL FABRICATORS INC
2665 Prince St (33916-5527)
PHONE 239 337-3480
Bryan Porter, *Branch Mgr*
EMP: 7
SALES (corp-wide): 8.9B **Publicly Held**
SIC: 3441 Fabricated structural metal
HQ: C M C Steel Fabricators, Inc.
1 Steel Mill Dr
Seguin TX 78155
830 372-8200

(G-4198)
CABINET KINGS LLC
11595 Kelly Rd Ste 322 (33908-2572)
PHONE 239 288-6740
Christopher Snow, *Mng Member*
EMP: 7 **EST:** 2011
SALES (est): 492.3K **Privately Held**
WEB: www.thecabinetkings.com
SIC: 2434 Wood kitchen cabinets

(G-4199)
CALOREX USA LLC
Also Called: Aquatherm Heat Pumps
2213 Andrea Ln Ste 110 (33912-1934)
PHONE 239 482-0606
Ed Hall, *Vice Pres*
Reed Wilson,
EMP: 9 **EST:** 1977
SQ FT: 10,000
SALES (est): 258.6K **Privately Held**
WEB: www.aquathermheatpumps.com
SIC: 3585 Heat pumps, electric

(G-4200)
CARBON PRESS LLC
1635 Hendry St (33901-2909)
PHONE 239 689-4406
Patrick Wilke, *President*
EMP: 11 **EST:** 2017
SALES (est): 382.1K **Privately Held**
WEB: www.carbonpress.com
SIC: 2741 Miscellaneous publishing

(G-4201)
CARFORE LTD
Also Called: Shapley
11650 Chitwood Dr (33908-3258)
PHONE 239 415-2275
Cindy S Carfore, *President*
Carol Yorkson, *Buyer*
▼ **EMP:** 6 **EST:** 1938
SQ FT: 4,000

SALES (est): 1MM **Privately Held**
SIC: 2844 Cosmetic preparations

(G-4202)
CARTER SIGNS INC
Also Called: Carter Signs Scott
6350 Slater Mill Way (33917-6645)
P.O. Box 3648 (33918-3648)
PHONE 239 543-4004
Scott Carter, *President*
EMP: 9 **EST:** 1956
SALES (est): 779.1K **Privately Held**
WEB: www.carteroutdoor.com
SIC: 3993 Signs & advertising specialties

(G-4203)
CE SAFES AND SEC PDTS INC
5650 Zip Dr (33905-5028)
PHONE 239 561-1260
Elizabeth Trice, *Branch Mgr*
EMP: 10
SQ FT: 7,200
SALES (corp-wide): 1.5MM **Privately Held**
WEB: www.cesafes.com
SIC: 3499 Safes & vaults, metal
PA: C.E. Safes And Security Products, Inc.
730 S Powerline Rd
Deerfield Beach FL 33442
954 977-8499

(G-4204)
CEMENT INDUSTRIES INC
2925 Hanson St (33916-7507)
PHONE 239 332-1440
Gay R Thompson, *President*
W Brown Thompson III, *Senior VP*
Vickie Dragich, *CFO*
Sharon Thompson, *Treasurer*
Carmi Terrell, *Admin Sec*
EMP: 60 **EST:** 1953
SQ FT: 3,500
SALES (est): 13.4MM **Privately Held**
WEB: www.cementindustries.com
SIC: 3272 5032 Concrete products, precast; brick, stone & related material

(G-4205)
CEMEX MATERIALS LLC
2040 Ortiz Ave (33905-3721)
PHONE 239 332-0135
Peter Dalenberg, *Branch Mgr*
EMP: 88 **Privately Held**
SIC: 3273 Ready-mixed concrete
HQ: Cemex Materials Llc
1720 Centrepark Dr E # 100
West Palm Beach FL 33401
561 833-5555

(G-4206)
CHARLES THAGGARD INC
1951 Collier Ave Ste A (33901-7931)
PHONE 239 936-8059
Charles E Thaggard, *Director*
EMP: 5 **EST:** 2002
SQ FT: 2,418
SALES (est): 365.8K **Privately Held**
SIC: 3993 Signs & advertising specialties

(G-4207)
CHURRICO FACTORY LLC
4125 Cleveland Ave # 1370 (33901-9046)
PHONE 239 989-7616
Christian Monroe, *CEO*
EMP: 5 **EST:** 2014
SALES (est): 352.3K **Privately Held**
SIC: 2051 Cakes, bakery: except frozen

(G-4208)
CIANOS TILE & MARBLE INC
Also Called: Cambria
5680 Halifax Ave (33912-4417)
PHONE 239 267-8453
Paul Ciano, *President*
Mary Kay Sablotny, *Vice Pres*
EMP: 36 **EST:** 1993
SQ FT: 12,500
SALES (est): 2.2MM **Privately Held**
SIC: 2541 1752 2434 Counter & sink tops; floor laying & floor work; wood kitchen cabinets

(G-4209)
CINTAS CORPORATION
Also Called: Cintas Fire Protection
12771 Westlinks Dr Ste 1 (33913-8074)
PHONE 239 693-8722
Jeff Playter, *General Mgr*
Steve Taylor, *Principal*
Jared Krempels, *Sales Staff*
Anthony Lisak, *Sales Staff*
EMP: 7
SQ FT: 1,000
SALES (corp-wide): 7.8B **Publicly Held**
WEB: www.cintas.com
SIC: 2326 7382 2337 7218 Work uniforms; burglar alarm maintenance & monitoring; fire alarm maintenance & monitoring; uniforms, except athletic: women's, misses' & juniors'; industrial uniform supply; wiping towel supply; treated equipment supply: mats, rugs, mops, cloths, etc.; safety equipment
PA: Cintas Corporation
6800 Cintas Blvd
Cincinnati OH 45262
513 459-1200

(G-4210)
CLEVER PAVERS INC
2727 Clnl Blvd Apt 204 (33907)
PHONE 239 633-7048
Stephanie Raggi, *Vice Pres*
EMP: 7 **EST:** 2005
SALES (est): 77.1K **Privately Held**
SIC: 2951 Asphalt paving mixtures & blocks

(G-4211)
CLINICON CORPORATION
Also Called: Clinical Refractions Perfected
3949 Evans Ave Ste 107 (33901-9341)
PHONE 239 939-1345
Fax: 239 939-3675
EMP: 11
SQ FT: 2,000
SALES (est): 790K **Privately Held**
SIC: 3841 8071 Mfg Opthalmology Equipment

(G-4212)
COASTAL CANVAS AND AWNING CO
5761 Independence Cir # 1 (33912-4416)
PHONE 239 433-1114
John Desesa, *President*
Danny Martin, *Sales Mgr*
EMP: 15 **EST:** 1975
SALES (est): 2MM **Privately Held**
WEB: www.coastalcanvasandawning.com
SIC: 2394 Awnings, fabric: made from purchased materials

(G-4213)
COASTAL CONCRETE PRODUCTS LLC
Also Called: Coastal Site Development
7742 Alico Rd (33912-6021)
PHONE 239 208-4079
David E Torres,
EMP: 30 **EST:** 2010
SALES (est): 6.5MM **Privately Held**
WEB: www.coastalconcreteprod.com
SIC: 3272 1771 1623 1611 Concrete products, precast; concrete work; underground utilities contractor; highway & street construction; highway & street paving contractor

(G-4214)
COASTAL ELECTRIC
5760 Youngquist Rd Ste 9 (33912-2267)
PHONE 239 245-7396
EMP: 7 **EST:** 2016
SALES (est): 88.3K **Privately Held**
WEB: www.coastalelectriccooperative.com
SIC: 3699 1731 Electrical equipment & supplies; electrical work

(G-4215)
COASTLINE CBNTRY CSTM MLLWK LL
6440 Metro Plantation Rd (33966-1266)
PHONE 239 208-2876
Carl B Maxner, *Mng Member*
Brian J Beaudet,
Danny E Cox,

▲ = Import ▼=Export
◆ =Import/Export

EMP: 14 **EST:** 2013
SALES (est): 1.6MM **Privately Held**
WEB: www.coastlinecabinetry.com
SIC: 2434 Wood kitchen cabinets

(G-4216)
COMPUTERS AT WORK INC
Also Called: Vtech Io
3033 Winkler Ave Ste 210 (33916-9522)
PHONE.................................239 571-1050
David W Peterson, *President*
Marsha Bewersdorf, *CFO*
Terry Timmins, *Accounts Mgr*
Ruhl Shawn, *Maintence Staff*
EMP: 31 **EST:** 2001
SALES (est): 13MM **Privately Held**
WEB: www.vtechio.com
SIC: 3572 5734 Computer storage devices; computer & software stores

(G-4217)
CONRIC HOLDINGS LLC
Also Called: Conric PR & Marketing
8770 Paseo De Valencia St (33908-9657)
PHONE.................................239 690-9840
Connie Ramos-Williams, *CEO*
Rick Williams, *Exec VP*
Kirsten O Donnell, *Vice Pres*
Frederick R Williams Jr, *CFO*
Josh Milton, *Mktg Coord*
EMP: 10 **EST:** 2010
SALES (est): 1.1MM **Privately Held**
WEB: www.conricpr.com
SIC: 2721 8743 7311 Magazines: publishing only, not printed on site; public relations services; advertising agencies

(G-4218)
CORNERSTONE KITCHENS INC
Also Called: Cornerstone Builders S W Fla
3150 Old Metro Pkwy (33916-7517)
PHONE.................................239 332-3020
Anthony Leeber, *President*
▲ **EMP:** 113 **EST:** 1988
SQ FT: 9,000
SALES (est): 12.3MM **Privately Held**
WEB: www.cornerstonebuilderswfl.com
SIC: 2431 5211 Doors & door parts & trim, wood; lumber & other building materials

(G-4219)
CREATIVE ARCHTCTRAL RESIN PDTS
3080 Warehouse Rd (33916-7615)
PHONE.................................239 939-0034
Marilyn Santiago, *President*
Michael Kupper, *Director*
EMP: 7 **EST:** 2014
SALES (est): 814.7K **Privately Held**
WEB: www.carpusa.com
SIC: 3089 Synthetic resin finished products

(G-4220)
CREATIVE CABINET CONCEPTS INC
Also Called: Creative Solid Surfacing
7947 Drew Cir (33967-6005)
PHONE.................................239 939-1313
Stephen Ruffino, *President*
EMP: 25 **EST:** 1982
SQ FT: 20,000
SALES (est): 4.7MM **Privately Held**
SIC: 2541 2434 Cabinets, except refrigerated: show, display, etc.: wood; wood kitchen cabinets

(G-4221)
CREATIVE CARBIDE INC (PA)
7880 Interstate Ct Unit A (33917-2131)
PHONE.................................239 567-0041
Tom Shoecraft Jr, *President*
Rick Brockway, *Data Proc Dir*
EMP: 15 **EST:** 1993
SALES (est): 2.9MM **Privately Held**
WEB: www.creativecarbide.com
SIC: 2819 3568 3545 Carbides; power transmission equipment; machine tool accessories

(G-4222)
CREATIVE MARINE
6261 Arc Way (33966-1352)
PHONE.................................239 437-1010
Bobbi Land, *Office Mgr*
Weston Beckwith, *Art Dir*
Nia Joseph, *Creative Dir*

EMP: 7 **EST:** 2019
SALES (est): 603.9K **Privately Held**
WEB: www.this-creative.com
SIC: 3732 Boat building & repairing

(G-4223)
CRUMBLISS MANUFACTURING CO
Also Called: Crumbliss Test Equipment
5812 Enterprise Pkwy (33905-5001)
PHONE.................................239 693-8588
Ronald Crumbliss, *President*
EMP: 10 **EST:** 1933
SQ FT: 13,000
SALES (est): 692.1K **Privately Held**
WEB: www.crumbliss.com
SIC: 3825 3829 Instruments to measure electricity; measuring & controlling devices

(G-4224)
CRYSTEK CRYSTALS CORPORATION
16850 Oriole Rd Ste 3 (33912-2544)
P.O. Box 60135 (33906-6135)
PHONE.................................239 561-3311
Anthony Mastropole, *CEO*
James J Browne, *Vice Pres*
Luiz Oricchio, *Sales Staff*
Maria Guerra, *Marketing Staff*
James D Hohman, *Admin Sec*
EMP: 30 **EST:** 1996
SQ FT: 25,000
SALES (est): 5.1MM **Privately Held**
WEB: www.crystek.com
SIC: 3679 3825 Crystals & crystal assemblies, radio; instruments to measure electricity

(G-4225)
CUMMINS POWER GENERATION INC
Also Called: Onan Gasoline Engines
2671 Edison Ave (33916-5305)
PHONE.................................239 337-1211
Tim Alban, *Sales Mgr*
EMP: 30
SQ FT: 15,090
SALES (corp-wide): 24B **Publicly Held**
WEB: www.cummins.com
SIC: 3621 Generators & sets, electric
HQ: Cummins Power Generation Inc.
   1400 73rd Ave Ne
   Minneapolis MN 55432
   763 574-5000

(G-4226)
CURTIS K FOULKS
Also Called: Foulks Forest
2240 Hemingway Dr Ste J (33912-1979)
PHONE.................................239 454-9663
Curtis K Foulks, *Owner*
EMP: 6 **EST:** 1985
SALES (est): 465.8K **Privately Held**
SIC: 2434 Wood kitchen cabinets

(G-4227)
CUSTOM CABINETS SW FLORIDA LLC
5929 Youngquist Rd (33912-2294)
PHONE.................................239 415-3350
Terrence Tripp, *Mng Member*
EMP: 8 **EST:** 2010
SALES (est): 632.8K **Privately Held**
WEB: www.customcabinetsofsouthwestflorida.com
SIC: 2434 1751 5712 Wood kitchen cabinets; cabinet & finish carpentry; cabinet work, custom

(G-4228)
D & D MACHINE & HYDRAULICS INC
10945 Metro Pkwy (33966-1202)
PHONE.................................239 275-7177
W Jack J Harlan, *President*
Bob Hess, *President*
D Todd McGee, *Corp Secy*
William F Ballantine, *Director*
Bruce Bartholomew, *Director*
▼ **EMP:** 34 **EST:** 1969
SQ FT: 55,000
SALES (est): 6.4MM **Privately Held**
WEB: www.ddpumps.com
SIC: 3561 Pumps & pumping equipment

(G-4229)
D AND S SUPERIOR COATINGS INC
6150 Metro Plantation Rd (33966-1200)
PHONE.................................360 388-6099
Harrison Hubschman, *Administration*
EMP: 7 **EST:** 2016
SALES (est): 179.5K **Privately Held**
SIC: 3479 Coating of metals & formed products

(G-4230)
DBI SERVICES LLC
5893 Entp Pkwy Ste A (33905)
PHONE.................................239 218-5204
Paul D Deangelo, *Mng Member*
Joseph G Ferguson, *Admin Sec*
Neal A Deangelo,
EMP: 33 **EST:** 2007
SALES (est): 4MM **Privately Held**
SIC: 3679 Electronic circuits

(G-4231)
DEAN DAIRY HOLDINGS LLC
3579 Work Dr (33916-7535)
PHONE.................................239 334-1114
Rick Oneill, *Manager*
Kevin Cross, *Supervisor*
EMP: 51
SQ FT: 9,280 **Publicly Held**
WEB: www.mcarthurdairy.com
SIC: 2024 5143 Ice cream & frozen desserts; dairy products, except dried or canned
HQ: Dean Dairy Holdings, Llc
   6851 Ne 2nd Ave
   Miami FL 33138
   305 795-7700

(G-4232)
DEAN STEEL BUILDINGS INC (PA)
2929 Industrial Ave (33901-6437)
PHONE.................................239 334-1051
Nan Dean, *President*
John Amann, *Vice Pres*
Michelle Boyer, *Vice Pres*
William A Clark, *Vice Pres*
Charlotte Edwards, *Vice Pres*
◆ **EMP:** 80 **EST:** 1955
SQ FT: 100,000
SALES (est): 14.2MM **Privately Held**
WEB: www.deansteelbuildings.com
SIC: 3448 1542 Prefabricated metal buildings; commercial & office building, new construction

(G-4233)
DEKSCAPE
17051 Alico Commerce Ct # 3 (33967-8510)
P.O. Box 61421 (33906-1421)
PHONE.................................239 278-3325
Jason Fowler, *President*
EMP: 9 **EST:** 2014
SALES (est): 894.1K **Privately Held**
SIC: 2851 1771 Lacquers, varnishes, enamels & other coatings; flooring contractor

(G-4234)
DIEMOLD MACHINE COMPANY INC
2350 Bruner Ln (33912-1970)
PHONE.................................239 482-1400
Ulrich K Boehnke, *President*
Karin Franchuk, *Manager*
EMP: 27 **EST:** 1962
SQ FT: 30,000
SALES (est): 5.5MM **Privately Held**
WEB: www.diemoldmachine.com
SIC: 3089 3544 Injection molding of plastics; industrial molds

(G-4235)
DIXIE METALCRAFT INCORPORATED
3050 Warehouse Rd (33916-7615)
PHONE.................................239 337-4299
Gene C Sutton, *President*
Ron Kinchen, *Corp Secy*
Bruce E Bordeaux, *Vice Pres*
EMP: 17 **EST:** 1985
SQ FT: 5,000

SALES (est): 904.6K **Privately Held**
SIC: 3444 Sheet metalwork

(G-4236)
DIXIE STRUCTURES & MAINTENANCE (PA)
1216 Hopedale Dr (33919-1619)
PHONE.................................205 274-4525
Gwen Blackwell, *President*
Bryan Blackwell, *Senior VP*
EMP: 15 **EST:** 1997
SQ FT: 20,000
SALES (est): 1MM **Privately Held**
WEB: www.dixiestructures.com
SIC: 3312 Structural shapes & pilings, steel

(G-4237)
DNE POT SBOB INC
Also Called: Bob's Top End
11000 Metro Pkwy Ste 10 (33966-1210)
PHONE.................................239 936-8880
Robert Foster, *President*
Georgia Foster, *Vice Pres*
EMP: 10 **EST:** 1978
SQ FT: 2,000
SALES (est): 819.1K **Privately Held**
WEB: www.bobstopend.com
SIC: 2759 Screen printing

(G-4238)
DOLPHIN BOAT LIFTS INC
6440 Topaz Ct (33966-8310)
PHONE.................................239 936-1782
Robert Shenkel, *President*
Joanne Shenkel, *Vice Pres*
EMP: 6 **EST:** 1988
SQ FT: 7,100
SALES (est): 977.6K **Privately Held**
WEB: www.dolphinboatlifts.com
SIC: 3429 1629 Marine hardware; dams, waterways, docks & other marine construction

(G-4239)
DRAKE INC
2920 Rockfill Rd (33916-4886)
PHONE.................................239 590-9199
Terry Drake, *Principal*
EMP: 12 **EST:** 2006
SALES (est): 476.4K **Privately Held**
SIC: 3273 Ready-mixed concrete

(G-4240)
DRAKE READY MIX INC
2920 Rockfill Rd (33916-4886)
PHONE.................................239 590-9199
Annie Drake, *President*
EMP: 52 **EST:** 2005
SALES (est): 10.8MM **Privately Held**
WEB: www.drakereadymix.com
SIC: 3273 Ready-mixed concrete

(G-4241)
E-Z METALS INC
Also Called: Suncoast Industries of Florida
6133 Idlewild St (33966-1217)
PHONE.................................239 936-7887
Jonathan L Dean, *President*
Rusty Billger, *Vice Pres*
Sharon Hackett, *Treasurer*
Kenneth Berdick, *Shareholder*
Judith Leishure, *Admin Sec*
▲ **EMP:** 27 **EST:** 1987
SQ FT: 32,500
SALES (est): 5.1MM **Privately Held**
SIC: 3441 Fabricated structural metal

(G-4242)
EAGLE READY MIX LLC
16576 Gator Rd (33912-5938)
PHONE.................................239 693-1500
Kevin R Eisenbath, *Mng Member*
Doug Mennemeier,
EMP: 17 **EST:** 2007
SQ FT: 1,879
SALES (est): 2MM **Privately Held**
SIC: 3273 Ready-mixed concrete

(G-4243)
EAR-TRONICS INC (PA)
7181 College Pkwy Ste 14 (33907-5642)
P.O. Box 60151 (33906-6151)
PHONE.................................239 275-7655
Robert Hooper, *President*
Terri Hooper, *Treasurer*

Wendy Kuo, *Accountant*
Gale Fagan, *Office Mgr*
Peggy Thomas, *Office Mgr*
EMP: 9 **EST:** 1980
SALES (est): 2.4MM **Privately Held**
WEB: www.eartronics.com
SIC: 3842 5999 8049 Hearing aids; hearing aids; audiologist

(G-4244)
EIDOLON ANALYTICS INC
Also Called: J&C Equipment
2487 N Airport Rd (33907-1401)
PHONE.................................239 288-6951
Gina Hyon, *President*
Francisco Colon, *Vice Pres*
Minette La Croix, *CFO*
EMP: 10 **EST:** 2011
SQ FT: 19,000
SALES (est): 938.5K **Privately Held**
WEB: www.unisourcesigns.com
SIC: 3993 Signs & advertising specialties

(G-4245)
ELECTRNIC SYSTEMS SUTHEAST LLC
5840 Halifax Ave (33912-4418)
PHONE.................................561 955-9006
Michael Monteiro, *Sales Staff*
John Ludwig, *Manager*
Steve Brody,
EMP: 10 **EST:** 2002
SALES (est): 276.2K **Privately Held**
SIC: 3629 Electronic generation equipment

(G-4246)
EMCYTE CORP
4331 Veronica S Shoemaker (33916-2233)
PHONE.................................239 481-7725
Patrick Pennie, *President*
Marcia James, *Vice Pres*
Jeanette Acker, *Production*
Glendal S Romanini, *Finance*
Peter Everts, *Officer*
EMP: 20 **EST:** 2008
SALES (est): 2.8MM **Privately Held**
WEB: www.emcyte.com
SIC: 3841 Surgical & medical instruments

(G-4247)
ENTERTAINMENT METALS INC
Also Called: Entertainment Mfg Group
13351 Saddle Rd Ste 205 (33913-9054)
PHONE.................................800 817-2683
Ryan Bringardner, *CEO*
Kevin Kirchner, *President*
John Irvin, *CFO*
Brinley Mazza, *Marketing Staff*
EMP: 32 **EST:** 2009
SQ FT: 13,393
SALES (est): 4.7MM **Privately Held**
WEB: www.emfgrp.com
SIC: 3441 Fabricated structural metal

(G-4248)
ETERNITY CABINETS
17000 Alico Commerce Ct (33967-8503)
PHONE.................................239 482-7172
Attira Ila, *Owner*
EMP: 10 **EST:** 2013
SALES (est): 532.7K **Privately Held**
WEB: www.cabinetsforswfl.com
SIC: 2434 Wood kitchen cabinets

(G-4249)
EV PILOTCAR INC
16121 Lee Rd Ste 107 (33912-2512)
PHONE.................................239 243-8023
Ali Mete Timur, *President*
Sukru Ozkilic, *Vice Pres*
EMP: 7 **EST:** 2019
SALES (est): 629.1K **Privately Held**
WEB: www.pilotcarev.com
SIC: 3711 Cars, electric, assembly of

(G-4250)
EV RIDER LLC
6410 Arc Way Ste A (33966-1413)
PHONE.................................239 278-5054
Juan Rivera, *Mng Member*
Ana Rivera,
◆ **EMP:** 8 **EST:** 2006
SALES (est): 1.2MM **Privately Held**
WEB: www.evrider.com
SIC: 3944 Scooters, children's

(G-4251)
EVERLAST INDUSTRIES CORP
Also Called: Everlast Marine Products Co.
7981 Mainline Pkwy (33912-5921)
PHONE.................................239 689-3837
Steve Dinkel, *Pres*
EMP: 9 **EST:** 2002
SALES (est): 6.6K **Privately Held**
WEB: www.everlast.com
SIC: 3999 Manufacturing industries

(G-4252)
FBI INDUSTRIES INC
11020 Yellow Poplar Dr (33913-8882)
PHONE.................................239 462-1176
Ryan D Beavers, *Principal*
EMP: 8 **EST:** 2016
SALES (est): 247.7K **Privately Held**
SIC: 3999 Manufacturing industries

(G-4253)
FF SYSTEMS INC
2840 Hunter St (33916-7617)
PHONE.................................239 288-4255
Benno Forstner, *Principal*
Friedrich Heindl, *Vice Pres*
Kimberly Quintero, *Office Mgr*
◆ **EMP:** 7 **EST:** 2010
SQ FT: 13,500
SALES (est): 1MM **Privately Held**
WEB: www.ffsystems.com
SIC: 3613 Control panels, electric

(G-4254)
FLEXSTAKE INC
2150 Andrea Ln (33912-1901)
PHONE.................................239 481-3539
Robert K Hughes Jr, *President*
Jim Zadrozny, *General Mgr*
John W Hughes, *Vice Pres*
▼ **EMP:** 20 **EST:** 1988
SQ FT: 21,550
SALES (est): 1.8MM **Privately Held**
WEB: www.flexstake.com
SIC: 3231 5091 Reflector glass beads, for highway signs or reflectors; golf equipment

(G-4255)
FLORIDA ROCK INDUSTRIES
Also Called: Vulcan Materials Company
14341 Alico Rd (33913-8231)
P.O. Box 380607, Birmingham AL (35238-0607)
PHONE.................................239 454-2831
Lisa Kingsbury, *Branch Mgr*
Curt Zimmerman, *Manager*
EMP: 12 **Publicly Held**
WEB: www.flarock.com
SIC: 3999 Barber & beauty shop equipment
HQ: Florida Rock Industries
4707 Gordon St
Jacksonville FL 32216
904 355-1781

(G-4256)
FLORIDA SALES & MARKETING
11840 Metro Pkwy (33966-8384)
PHONE.................................239 274-3103
Charles Hurt, *Principal*
John Bilvich, *Sales Staff*
Timothy Steger, *Representative*
◆ **EMP:** 20 **EST:** 2004
SALES (est): 3.5MM **Privately Held**
WEB: www.floridamarketingandsales.com
SIC: 3334 Primary aluminum

(G-4257)
FLORIDA STYLE ALUMINUM INC
15481 Old Wedgewood Ct (33908-7208)
PHONE.................................239 689-8662
Andrew McCurdy, *President*
Carol McCurdy, *Vice Pres*
EMP: 12 **EST:** 1994
SQ FT: 6,900
SALES (est): 282.1K **Privately Held**
WEB: www.florida-style.com
SIC: 3231 Scientific & technical glassware: from purchased glass

(G-4258)
FLORIDA WEEKLY
2891 Center Pointe Dr # 300 (33916-9458)
PHONE.................................239 333-2135
Angela Schivinski, *Publisher*
Michele Foley, *Accounts Exec*
Cori Higgins, *Executive*
EMP: 10 **EST:** 2019
SALES (est): 648.9K **Privately Held**
WEB: www.floridaweekly.com
SIC: 2711 Newspapers, publishing & printing

(G-4259)
FLORIDAS FINEST INDUSTRIES
5294 Summerlin (33907)
PHONE.................................239 333-1777
Annalisa Xioutas, *President*
Sheri Aws, *Bookkeeper*
EMP: 11 **EST:** 2009
SALES (est): 1.2MM **Privately Held**
SIC: 3999 Manufacturing industries

(G-4260)
FOCUS ON WATER INC
10160 Mcgregor Blvd (33919-1039)
PHONE.................................239 275-1880
Robert L Farnsworth, *President*
Gayle Farnsworth, *Vice Pres*
EMP: 8 **EST:** 2014
SALES (est): 123.3K **Privately Held**
SIC: 3589 Water purification equipment, household type; water treatment equipment, industrial

(G-4261)
FORESTRY RESOURCES LLC (PA)
Also Called: Mulch and Soil Company, The
4325 Michigan Link (33905)
PHONE.................................239 332-3966
John W Cauthen, *President*
Glen Davis, *CFO*
EMP: 40 **EST:** 1983
SQ FT: 6,500
SALES (est): 15MM **Privately Held**
WEB: www.fri-eco.com
SIC: 2499 2875 Mulch, wood & bark; potting soil, mixed

(G-4262)
FORT MYERS DIGITAL LLC
6381 Corp Pk Cir Ste 2 (33966)
PHONE.................................239 482-3086
Dorothy P Kres,
EMP: 8 **EST:** 2012
SALES (est): 556.1K **Privately Held**
WEB: www.fortmyersdigital.com
SIC: 2752 2851 Commercial printing, offset; vinyl coatings, strippable

(G-4263)
FRESCO GROUP INC
Also Called: Styleview Industries
13300 S Clevlnd Ave Ste 5 (33907-3871)
PHONE.................................239 936-8055
Lynn B Myers, *President*
P Fred Biery, *Vice Pres*
P Biery, *Vice Pres*
EMP: 26 **EST:** 1984
SQ FT: 7,150
SALES (est): 2.7MM **Privately Held**
SIC: 3444 1521 Awnings, sheet metal; patio & deck construction & repair

(G-4264)
FUSION INDUSTRIES LLC
16710 Gator Rd (33912-5926)
PHONE.................................239 415-7554
Stevens Jeff, *Mng Member*
Brooke Hendrix, *Admin Asst*
EMP: 16 **EST:** 2011
SALES (est): 3.8MM **Privately Held**
WEB: www.fusionindustriesllc.com
SIC: 3999 Hair & hair-based products

(G-4265)
FUSION INDUSTRIES INTL LLC
16710 Gator Rd (33912-5926)
PHONE.................................239 415-7554
Jeffrey Stevens, *President*
EMP: 6 **EST:** 2014
SALES (est): 893.3K **Privately Held**
WEB: www.fusionindustriesllc.com
SIC: 3281 Curbing, granite or stone

(G-4266)
FUSION WELDING
15865 Brothers Ct (33912-2253)
PHONE.................................239 288-6530
Lisa Beaner, *Principal*
Darin Beaner, *Vice Pres*
EMP: 15 **EST:** 2011
SALES (est): 2.2MM **Privately Held**
WEB: www.fusion-welding.com
SIC: 7692 Welding repair

(G-4267)
G & F MANUFACTURING INC
Also Called: G&F Mnfctring Mfr Glfstream He
7902 Interstate Ct (33917-2112)
PHONE.................................239 939-7446
Dan Goldberg, *President*
Bill Fields, *Vice Pres*
Jim Fields, *Treasurer*
Eric Watters, *Natl Sales Mgr*
Brian Goldberg, *Admin Sec*
EMP: 12 **EST:** 2003
SQ FT: 10,200
SALES (est): 2.6MM **Privately Held**
WEB: www.gulfstreamheatpump.com
SIC: 3561 Industrial pumps & parts

(G-4268)
GA FD SVCS PINELLAS CNTY LLC
5501 Division Dr (33905-5017)
PHONE.................................239 693-5090
Larry Page, *Controller*
Terry White, *Sales Staff*
Abe Pacheco, *Manager*
EMP: 34
SALES (corp-wide): 151.6MM **Privately Held**
WEB: www.sunmeadow.com
SIC: 2038 5812 2099 Frozen specialties; contract food services; food preparations
PA: G.A. Food Services Of Pinellas County, Llc
12200 32nd Ct N
Saint Petersburg FL 33716
727 573-2211

(G-4269)
GO MOBILE SIGNS
13468 Palm Beach Blvd C (33905-2168)
PHONE.................................239 245-7803
Joseph H Baker Jr, *President*
EMP: 5 **EST:** 2009
SALES (est): 374.1K **Privately Held**
WEB: www.gomobile-signs.com
SIC: 3993 Signs, not made in custom sign painting shops

(G-4270)
GOLD PLATING SPECIALTIES
17560 Allentown Rd (33967-2961)
PHONE.................................239 851-9323
Jill Stulak, *Principal*
EMP: 5 **EST:** 2001
SALES (est): 331K **Privately Held**
SIC: 3471 Plating of metals or formed products

(G-4271)
GRAPHIX BY FRAN INC
12541 Metro Pkwy Ste 10 (33966-8348)
PHONE.................................239 939-3125
EMP: 7 **EST:** 2019
SALES (est): 734.9K **Privately Held**
WEB: www.graphixbyfran.com
SIC: 2759 Screen printing

(G-4272)
GRATE FIREPLACE & STONE SHOPPE
16611 S Tamiami Trl (33908-4504)
PHONE.................................239 939-7187
William J Stasko Sr, *President*
Susan Stasko, *Vice Pres*
Diane Key, *Treasurer*
Helen Stasko, *Admin Sec*
EMP: 24 **EST:** 1982
SQ FT: 3,000
SALES (est): 743.2K **Privately Held**
WEB: www.gratefireplace.com
SIC: 3272 5719 Fireplaces, concrete; fireplace equipment & accessories

▲ = Import ▼=Export
◆ =Import/Export

(G-4273)
GREG VALENTINE LLC
Also Called: Valentines Glass & Metal
3590 Old Metro Pkwy (33916-7539)
P.O. Box 60272 (33906-6272)
PHONE....................................239 332-0855
Gregory Valentine, *Principal*
Tim Stewmon, *Principal*
EMP: 30 **EST:** 2014
SALES (est): 2.2MM **Privately Held**
WEB: www.vgmholdings.com
SIC: 3446 1793 Gates, ornamental metal;
glass & glazing work

(G-4274)
**GULF COAST CABINETS
CARPENTRY**
11824 Rosalinda Ct (33912-8998)
PHONE....................................239 222-2994
Gary Cohen, *President*
EMP: 7 **EST:** 2000
SALES (est): 136.1K **Privately Held**
SIC: 2434 Wood kitchen cabinets

(G-4275)
**GULF COAST NON EMERGENCY
TRANS**
17531 Boat Club Dr (33908-4465)
PHONE....................................239 825-1350
EMP: 8
SALES (est): 679.6K **Privately Held**
SIC: 3842 Surgical Appliances And Sup-
plies, Nsk

(G-4276)
GULF COAST PRECAST INC
2506 Precast Ct (33916-4898)
PHONE....................................239 337-0021
James Gorrell, *President*
Bjarni Jonsson, *General Mgr*
Joe D Cavage, *Vice Pres*
EMP: 19 **EST:** 1998
SQ FT: 3,900
SALES (est): 4.5MM **Privately Held**
WEB: www.gulfcoastprecast.com
SIC: 3272 Concrete products

(G-4277)
GULF COAST PRINTING
Also Called: Allez Partnership
11000 Panther Printing Wa (33908-3480)
PHONE....................................239 482-5555
Joe Andersen, *Partner*
EMP: 20 **EST:** 2006
SALES (est): 1.2MM **Privately Held**
WEB: www.pantherprinting.net
SIC: 2759 Commercial printing

(G-4278)
**HALL INDUSTRIES
INCORPORATED**
11850 Regional Ln Unit 6 (33913-8874)
PHONE....................................239 768-0372
Alfred Steinberg, *Branch Mgr*
EMP: 9
SALES (corp-wide): 26.2MM **Privately
Held**
WEB: www.hallindustries.com
SIC: 3999 Barber & beauty shop equip-
ment
PA: Hall Industries, Incorporated
514 Mecklem Ln
Ellwood City PA 16117
724 752-2000

(G-4279)
HF SCIENTIFIC INC
16260 Arprt Pk Dr Ste 140 (33913)
PHONE....................................888 203-7248
A Suellen Torregrosa, *CEO*
Srinivas K Bagepalli, *President*
Munish Nanda, *President*
Roberto Vengoechea, *President*
Kenneth R Lepage, *Vice Pres*
▲ **EMP:** 40 **EST:** 1964
SALES (est): 10.6MM
SALES (corp-wide): 1.8B **Publicly Held**
SIC: 3821 3625 3826 3823 Laboratory
apparatus & furniture; electric controls &
control accessories, industrial; analytical
instruments; industrial instrmnts msrmnt
display/control process variable

PA: Watts Water Technologies, Inc.
815 Chestnut St
North Andover MA 01845
978 688-1811

(G-4280)
HINES BENDING SYSTEMS INC
Also Called: Manufctring Sls Pipe Bnding Eq
6441 Metro Plantation Rd (33966-1257)
PHONE....................................239 433-2132
James Hynes, *President*
▲ **EMP:** 16 **EST:** 1975
SQ FT: 1,600
SALES (est): 1.3MM **Privately Held**
WEB: www.hinesbending.com
SIC: 3498 Fabricated pipe & fittings

(G-4281)
HINSILBLON LTD INC
Also Called: Hinsilblon Laboratories
12381 S Cleveland Ave (33907-3893)
PHONE....................................239 418-1133
Richard Hindin, *President*
Tim Planker, *Vice Pres*
EMP: 7 **EST:** 1990
SQ FT: 2,500
SALES (est): 672.3K **Privately Held**
WEB: www.hinsilblon.com
SIC: 2842 Deodorants, nonpersonal

(G-4282)
HJ GERMAN CORNER LLC
3674 Cleveland Ave (33901-7906)
PHONE....................................239 672-8462
EMP: 7 **EST:** 2019
SALES (est): 161.7K **Privately Held**
WEB:
handjgermancorner.godaddysites.com
SIC: 2024 Ice cream & frozen desserts

(G-4283)
HOMES MAGAZINE INC
Also Called: Homes Real Estate Magazine
2133 Broadway (33901-3634)
PHONE....................................239 334-7168
Robert Kaye, *President*
EMP: 10 **EST:** 1973
SALES (est): 599.3K **Privately Held**
WEB: www.homesmagazine.net
SIC: 2741 Directories: publishing only, not
printed on site

(G-4284)
**HUDSON CABINETS &
MILLWORK LLC**
6261 Metro Plantation Rd (33966-1213)
PHONE....................................239 218-0451
Mark Hudson, *Manager*
EMP: 10 **EST:** 2010
SALES (est): 830.5K **Privately Held**
WEB: www.hudsoncabinets.com
SIC: 2434 Wood kitchen cabinets

(G-4285)
HUGHES FABRICATION
2304 Bruner Ln Ste 1 (33912-2077)
PHONE....................................239 481-1376
EMP: 5
SALES (est): 302.3K **Privately Held**
SIC: 3999 Mfg Misc Products

(G-4286)
IMC-HEARTWAY LLC (PA)
Also Called: Heartway USA
5681 Independence Cir A (33912-4457)
PHONE....................................239 275-6767
Young Ho, *CEO*
Yi-Ting Wang, *President*
▲ **EMP:** 5 **EST:** 2001
SQ FT: 8,500
SALES (est): 891.5K **Privately Held**
SIC: 3842 5047 Wheelchairs; orthopedic
equipment & supplies

(G-4287)
IMM SURVIVOR INC
17030 Alico Center Rd (33967-6063)
PHONE....................................239 454-7020
George Becker, *President*
Mike Nanda, *Sales Staff*
EMP: 11 **EST:** 1982
SQ FT: 12,000
SALES (est): 933.1K **Privately Held**
SIC: 3536 Boat lifts

(G-4288)
IMPACT EDUCATION INC
18180 Old Dominion Ct (33908-4677)
PHONE....................................239 482-0202
Adam Hall, *CEO*
Leonard Hall, *President*
EMP: 9 **EST:** 2000
SALES (est): 455.5K **Privately Held**
SIC: 7372 Educational computer software

(G-4289)
IMPERIAL KITCHENS INC
12541 Metro Pkwy Ste 14 (33966-8349)
PHONE....................................239 208-9359
EMP: 7 **EST:** 2018
SALES (est): 334.8K **Privately Held**
WEB: www.imperialkitchensinc.com
SIC: 2434 Wood kitchen cabinets

(G-4290)
INDUSTRIAL TECHNOLOGY LLC
Also Called: Comtronix US
6310 Techster Blvd Ste 3 (33966-4710)
PHONE....................................877 224-5534
Jimmy Haugen, *Vice Pres*
EMP: 10 **EST:** 2018
SALES (est): 819.8K **Privately Held**
WEB: www.comtronixus.com
SIC: 3571 Electronic computers

(G-4291)
INSECO INC
2897 South St (33916-5515)
PHONE....................................239 939-1072
Michael Daikos, *CEO*
▲ **EMP:** 10 **EST:** 1995
SALES (est): 1MM **Privately Held**
WEB: www.woodrx.com
SIC: 2851 Paints & allied products

(G-4292)
**ISLAND PARK CUSTOM
WOODWORKING**
16270 Old Us 41 (33912-2254)
PHONE....................................239 437-9670
John Hayden, *President*
Joe Preel, *Vice Pres*
EMP: 5 **EST:** 1996
SQ FT: 8,000
SALES (est): 575.4K **Privately Held**
SIC: 2431 Doors & door parts & trim,
wood; windows & window parts & trim,
wood

(G-4293)
J & J CUSTOM MICA INC
1361 Canterbury Dr (33901-8760)
PHONE....................................239 433-2828
Lynn A Dunlavey, *President*
EMP: 19 **EST:** 1989
SALES (est): 950K **Privately Held**
SIC: 2434 2541 2517 Wood kitchen cabi-
nets; wood partitions & fixtures; wood tel-
evision & radio cabinets

(G-4294)
**J & J LITHO ENTERPRISES INC
(PA)**
Also Called: Kwik Kopy Printing
6835 Intl Ctr Blvd Ste 9 (33912-7149)
PHONE....................................239 433-2311
Scott Laden, *President*
Christopher J O'Hern, *Vice Pres*
EMP: 16 **EST:** 1983
SALES (est): 2MM **Privately Held**
SIC: 2759 Thermography

(G-4295)
J D ALUMINUM
18161 Sandy Pines Cir (33917-4713)
PHONE....................................239 543-3558
John Deschenes, *Owner*
EMP: 8 **EST:** 1993
SALES (est): 519.8K **Privately Held**
WEB: www.campbellcraneservice.com
SIC: 3448 Screen enclosures

(G-4296)
JBJB HOLDINGS LLC
Also Called: Sign-A-Rama
14110 Clear Water Ln (33907-4711)
PHONE....................................239 267-1975
Jeffery Bayer,
Judith Bayer,
EMP: 5 **EST:** 2001

SQ FT: 2,150
SALES (est): 498K **Privately Held**
WEB: www.signarama.com
SIC: 3993 Signs & advertising specialties

(G-4297)
JDCI ENTERPRISES INC
Also Called: Boatmaster/J D C I Enterprises
11950 Amedicus Ln Unit 2 (33907-4062)
PHONE....................................239 768-2292
Seth Hartt, *Sales Staff*
Marty Adams, *IT Specialist*
Joseph K Isley III, *Director*
▼ **EMP:** 25 **EST:** 1982
SQ FT: 10,000
SALES (est): 5MM **Privately Held**
WEB: www.boat-trailers.com
SIC: 3799 3548 Boat trailers; welding &
cutting apparatus & accessories

(G-4298)
JFLISZO INDUSTRIES INC
17051 Alico Commerce Ct # 3
(33967-8510)
P.O. Box 61421 (33906-1421)
PHONE....................................239 215-6965
EMP: 7 **EST:** 2018
SALES (est): 389.3K **Privately Held**
SIC: 3999 Manufacturing industries

(G-4299)
JML PAVERS LLC
18657 Holly Rd (33967-3626)
PHONE....................................239 240-0082
Juan Maldonado-Loredo, *President*
EMP: 7 **EST:** 2015
SALES (est): 363.9K **Privately Held**
SIC: 2951 Asphalt paving mixtures &
blocks

(G-4300)
**JOHN MADER ENTERPRISES
INC**
Also Called: Mader Electric Motors
18161 N Tamiami Trl (33903-1301)
PHONE....................................239 731-5455
Jeremy D Mader, *President*
EMP: 31 **EST:** 1984
SQ FT: 12,000
SALES (est): 5.1MM **Privately Held**
SIC: 7694 7699 3463 3561 Electric
motor repair; pumps & pumping equip-
ment repair; pump, compressor, turbine &
engine forgings, except auto; pumps &
pumping equipment; pumps, oil well &
field; pumps, domestic: water or sump; in-
dustrial pumps & parts

(G-4301)
**JONATHAN MARIOTTI ENTPS
LLC**
Also Called: Abaxial Elevator
608 Danley Dr Unit C (33907-1538)
P.O. Box 61361 (33906-1361)
PHONE....................................855 353-8280
EMP: 6
SQ FT: 2,000
SALES (est): 580K **Privately Held**
SIC: 3534 Mfg Elevators/Escalators

(G-4302)
JUPITER INDUSTRIES LLC
9373 Laredo Ave (33905-4633)
PHONE....................................239 225-9041
Rick Mendez, *Opers Staff*
James E Phillips, *Mng Member*
Buddy Yates, *Manager*
Cliff Yates, *Manager*
◆ **EMP:** 8 **EST:** 2008
SALES (est): 1MM **Privately Held**
WEB: www.jupiter-industries.com
SIC: 3354 Aluminum extruded products

(G-4303)
K N M FOOD STORE
2441 Hanson St (33901-7343)
PHONE....................................239 334-7699
Jad Awaab, *Principal*
EMP: 7 **EST:** 2009
SALES (est): 115.6K **Privately Held**
SIC: 3578 Automatic teller machines (ATM)

(G-4304)
KDD INC (PA)
Also Called: Mr Shower Door
16431 Domestic Ave (33912-6008)
PHONE..................................239 689-8402
Keith W Daubmann, *President*
Doug Daubmann, *Corp Secy*
William Daubmann, *Senior VP*
▲ EMP: 10 EST: 2003
SALES (est): 5.8MM **Privately Held**
SIC: 3088 Shower stalls, fiberglass & plastic

(G-4305)
KING BRANDS LLC
9910 Bavaria Rd (33913-8509)
PHONE..................................239 313-2057
Mark Hetzel, *Plant Mgr*
Mark Kent, *Prdtn Mgr*
Amy Geszler, *CFO*
John King, *Mng Member*
Jason King,
▲ EMP: 50 EST: 2007
SALES (est): 9.7MM **Privately Held**
WEB: www.kingsbrand.com
SIC: 2037 Fruit juices

(G-4306)
KLOCKE OF AMERICA INC
16260 Arprt Pk Dr Ste 125 (33913)
PHONE..................................239 561-5800
Donald W Hopta, *CEO*
Carsten Klocke, *President*
Eden Sheffield, *Treasurer*
Marie Springsteen, *Admin Sec*
EMP: 60 EST: 1996
SALES (est): 2.5MM **Privately Held**
WEB: www.klockeamerica.com
SIC: 3399 Primary metal products

(G-4307)
KRAFT HEINZ FOODS COMPANY
5521 Division Dr (33905-5017)
PHONE..................................239 694-3663
Todd Shuttleworth, *Prdtn Mgr*
Joe Garrard, *Manager*
EMP: 40
SQ FT: 2,700
SALES (corp-wide): 26B **Publicly Held**
WEB: www.kraftheinzcompany.com
SIC: 2033 Canned fruits & specialties
HQ: Kraft Heinz Foods Company
1 Ppg Pl Ste 3400
Pittsburgh PA 15222
412 456-5700

(G-4308)
LANAI LIGHTS LLC
3411 Hanson St Unit A (33916-6509)
PHONE..................................239 415-2561
David Fiorillo, *Principal*
EMP: 7 EST: 2010
SALES (est): 580.9K **Privately Held**
WEB: www.lanailights.com
SIC: 3648 Lighting equipment

(G-4309)
LCF PAVERS INC
1825 Linhart Ave Lot 25 (33901-6028)
PHONE..................................239 826-8177
Luiz C Faria, *Principal*
EMP: 7 EST: 2013
SALES (est): 226.6K **Privately Held**
SIC: 2951 Asphalt paving mixtures & blocks

(G-4310)
LEE COUNTY FUELS INC
16272 Cutters Ct (33908-3092)
PHONE..................................239 349-5322
John Stephens, *President*
EMP: 5 EST: 2007
SALES (est): 578.7K **Privately Held**
WEB: www.leecountyfuels.com
SIC: 2869 Fuels

(G-4311)
LEE DESIGNS LLC
3300 Palm Ave (33901-7430)
PHONE..................................239 278-4245
Jeff White, *General Mgr*
Elisha White, *Sr Project Mgr*
Bill Wallace, *Manager*
Kip Thomas,
Michael Johnston,
EMP: 17 EST: 1993

SQ FT: 12,000
SALES (est): 2.1MM **Privately Held**
WEB: 198051.group1.sites.hubspot.net
SIC: 3993 Electric signs

(G-4312)
LIST DISTILLERY LLC
3680 Evans Ave (33901-8315)
PHONE..................................239 208-7214
Thomas List, *Principal*
Chelsie Graddy, *Prdtn Mgr*
Tania Fahnemann,
Thomas Fahnemann,
Renate List,
EMP: 11 EST: 2015
SALES (est): 1.8MM **Privately Held**
WEB: www.listdistillery.com
SIC: 2085 Distilled & blended liquors

(G-4313)
M D NUTRA-LUXE LLC
12801 Commwl Dr Ste 1 (33913)
PHONE..................................239 561-9699
Peter Von Berg,
▲ EMP: 10 EST: 2003
SQ FT: 2,800
SALES (est): 1.5MM **Privately Held**
WEB: www.nutraluxemd.com
SIC: 2844 Cosmetic preparations

(G-4314)
M SEVEN HOLDINGS LLC
Also Called: Mark 7 Reloading LLC
11750 Metro Pkwy Ste A (33966-8305)
PHONE..................................888 462-7577
Jay C Hirshberg,
Martin Stark,
EMP: 12 EST: 2016
SQ FT: 6,000
SALES (est): 2.1MM
SALES (corp-wide): 34.4MM **Privately Held**
WEB: www.markvii-loading.com
SIC: 3559 Ammunition & explosives, loading machinery
PA: Lyman Products Corporation
475 Smith St
Middletown CT 06457
860 632-2020

(G-4315)
MAGIC PRINT COPY CENTER
2133 Broadway (33901-3634)
PHONE..................................239 332-4456
John Totzeke, *Partner*
Jennifer Totzeke, *Partner*
EMP: 8 EST: 1982
SQ FT: 1,800
SALES (est): 590.9K **Privately Held**
SIC: 2752 Commercial printing, offset

(G-4316)
MAJIC WHEELS CORP (PA)
Also Called: Dumpster Company
1950 Custom Dr (33907-2102)
PHONE..................................239 313-5672
Denise Houghtaling, *President*
Mark Houghtaling, *Admin Sec*
EMP: 5 EST: 2007
SALES (est): 483.5K **Privately Held**
SIC: 3944 Games, toys & children's vehicles

(G-4317)
MARK MCMANUS INC
Also Called: McManus Superboats
15821 Chief Ct (33912-2261)
PHONE..................................239 454-1300
Mark McManus, *President*
Kelli Thurman, *Vice Pres*
▼ EMP: 10 EST: 1989
SQ FT: 15,000
SALES (est): 1.4MM **Privately Held**
WEB: www.apachepowerboats.com
SIC: 3732 Boats, fiberglass: building & repairing

(G-4318)
MASTER KITCHEN CABINETS
12960 Commerce Lk Dr # 8 (33913-8660)
PHONE..................................239 225-9668
Guillermo Rivera,
EMP: 8 EST: 2013
SALES (est): 415.4K **Privately Held**
WEB: www.masterkitchencabinets.com
SIC: 2434 Wood kitchen cabinets

(G-4319)
MEDIAWRITE LLC
6835 Intl Ctr Blvd Ste 9 (33912-7149)
PHONE..................................239 344-9988
Lee Lake, *Prdtn Mgr*
Tammy Joy O'Dell,
Dale Odell,
EMP: 6 EST: 2014
SALES (est): 357.4K **Privately Held**
WEB: www.mediawrite.com
SIC: 3999 Advertising display products

(G-4320)
MERITS HEALTH PRODUCTS INC
4245 Evans Ave (33901-9311)
PHONE..................................239 772-0579
Chung-Lun Liu, *CEO*
Jonathan Cheng, *Vice Pres*
Rohan Smith, *Prdtn Mgr*
John Gadue, *Production*
Josh Haynes, *Research*
◆ EMP: 26 EST: 1993
SALES (est): 8.7MM **Privately Held**
WEB: www.meritsusa.com
SIC: 3842 5047 Wheelchairs; medical & hospital equipment
PA: Merits Health Products Co., Ltd.
No. 18, Jingke Rd., T.P.M.T Park,
Taichung City 40852

(G-4321)
MERMAID MFG SOUTHWEST FLA INC
Also Called: Mermaid Marine Air
2651 Park Windsor Dr # 203 (33901-8319)
P.O. Box 60205 (33906-6205)
PHONE..................................239 418-0535
William Banfield, *President*
Marilyn Banfield, *Principal*
▲ EMP: 15 EST: 1983
SQ FT: 8,000
SALES (est): 3.5MM **Privately Held**
WEB: www.mmair.com
SIC: 3585 3429 Air conditioning units, complete: domestic or industrial; manufactured hardware (general)

(G-4322)
MFJR PAVERS LLC
1621 Red Cedar Dr (33907-7645)
PHONE..................................239 440-2580
Martin Franco Jr, *Principal*
EMP: 7 EST: 2013
SALES (est): 97.9K **Privately Held**
SIC: 2951 Asphalt paving mixtures & blocks

(G-4323)
MICHAEL L LARVIERE INC
17537 Braddock Rd (33967-2970)
PHONE..................................239 267-2738
Michael L Lariviere, *President*
EMP: 9 EST: 2001
SALES (est): 373.4K **Privately Held**
SIC: 1389 Construction, repair & dismantling services

(G-4324)
MICHAEL VALENTINES INC
10660 Clear Lake Loop # 234
(33908-2374)
PHONE..................................239 332-0855
Michael Valentine, *President*
EMP: 18 EST: 1992
SALES (est): 1.2MM **Privately Held**
SIC: 3441 1793 Fabricated structural metal; glass & glazing work

(G-4325)
MICRO CONTROL SYSTEMS INC
5580 Enterprise Pkwy (33905-5022)
PHONE..................................239 694-0089
Brian W Walterick, *President*
Ronnie Andersen, *Vice Pres*
Robert Toney, *Vice Pres*
John Walterick, *Vice Pres*
Chris Hadsock, *Research*
▲ EMP: 37 EST: 1994
SQ FT: 9,000

SALES (est): 7.4MM **Privately Held**
WEB: www.mcscontrols.com
SIC: 3674 3822 3625 Microprocessors; auto controls regulating residntl & coml environmt & applncs; relays & industrial controls

(G-4326)
MID-STATE MACHINE COMPANY LLC
4516 Longboat Ln (33919-4641)
PHONE..................................704 636-7029
Larry Schwoeri, *CEO*
Gerald Williams Sr, *Mng Member*
Tim Williams,
EMP: 17 EST: 2007
SQ FT: 87,000
SALES (est): 2.1MM **Privately Held**
WEB: www.midstatemachine.com
SIC: 3549 Machine Shop

(G-4327)
MOBIUS BUSINESS GROUP INC
Also Called: Coastal and Mainland Cabinets
1961 Dana Dr (33907-2103)
PHONE..................................239 274-8900
Todd Lesley, *President*
Karen Lesley, *Treasurer*
EMP: 10 EST: 1985
SQ FT: 9,500
SALES (est): 1MM **Privately Held**
WEB: www.mobiusconnect.com
SIC: 2541 2511 2434 Cabinets, except refrigerated: show, display, etc.: wood; wood household furniture; wood kitchen cabinets

(G-4328)
MOLD BE GONE PLUS
14120 Carlotta St (33905-8621)
PHONE..................................239 672-5321
Luis Alvarez, *Principal*
EMP: 7 EST: 2016
SALES (est): 100.6K **Privately Held**
WEB: www.moldbegoneplus.com
SIC: 3544 Industrial molds

(G-4329)
MOREY MACHINING & MFG INC
9350 Workmen Way (33905-5212)
PHONE..................................239 693-8699
Timothy Morey, *President*
Tim Morey, *Engineer*
EMP: 25 EST: 2001
SQ FT: 5,400
SALES (est): 2.3MM **Privately Held**
WEB: www.moreymachining.com
SIC: 3599 Machine shop, jobbing & repair

(G-4330)
MOTAZ INC
2441 Hanson St (33901-7343)
PHONE..................................239 334-7699
Jad Awadallah, *Principal*
EMP: 7 EST: 2010
SALES (est): 79.7K **Privately Held**
SIC: 3578 Automatic teller machines (ATM)

(G-4331)
MOTOROLA SOLUTIONS
13891 Jetport Loop Ste 9 (33913-7716)
PHONE..................................239 939-7717
EMP: 10 EST: 2019
SALES (est): 3.5MM **Privately Held**
WEB: www.motorolasolutions.com
SIC: 3663 Radio & TV communications equipment

(G-4332)
MR FOAMY SOUTHWEST FL LLC
Also Called: Mr Foamy
3411 Hanson St Unit A (33916-6509)
PHONE..................................239 461-3110
Karen Fiorillo, *President*
Jeffrey Hebert, *Admin Sec*
EMP: 16 EST: 2000
SQ FT: 4,000
SALES (est): 2.7MM **Privately Held**
WEB: www.mrfoamy.com
SIC: 2431 Exterior & ornamental woodwork & trim

(G-4333)
MUNTERS CORPORATION
108 6th St (33907-1554)
PHONE..................................239 936-1555

▲ = Import ▼=Export
◆ =Import/Export

Erik Reese, *Regional Mgr*
Hansi Kruger, *Vice Pres*
John Labarre, *Production*
Mike Sadosky, *Regl Sales Mgr*
Priscilla Long, *Marketing Staff*
EMP: 9
SALES (corp-wide): 802.4MM **Privately Held**
WEB: www.munters.us
SIC: 3585 Refrigeration & heating equipment
HQ: Munters Corporation
79 Monroe St
Amesbury MA 01913

(G-4334)
MUTUAL INDUSTRIES NORTH INC
2940 Walpear St Unit 1 (33916-7549)
PHONE.................................239 332-2400
John Gregory, *Manager*
EMP: 63
SALES (corp-wide): 48.6MM **Privately Held**
WEB: www.mutualindustries.com
SIC: 2221 3496 2297 Specialty broadwoven fabrics, including twisted weaves; miscellaneous fabricated wire products; nonwoven fabrics
PA: Mutual Industries North, Inc.
707 W Grange Ave Ste 1
Philadelphia PA 19120
215 927-6000

(G-4335)
MWI CORPORATION
Also Called: John Deere Authorized Dealer
4945 Kim Ln (33905-3714)
PHONE.................................239 337-4747
David Berggren, *Manager*
EMP: 10
SQ FT: 3,560
SALES (corp-wide): 41.8MM **Privately Held**
WEB: www.mwipumps.com
SIC: 3594 7359 5082 Pumps, hydraulic power transfer; equipment rental & leasing; construction & mining machinery
PA: Mwi Corporation
33 Nw 2nd St
Deerfield Beach FL 33441
954 426-1500

(G-4336)
MY SHOWER DOOR TAMPA LLC (PA)
16431 Domestic Ave (33912-6008)
PHONE.................................239 337-3667
William C Daubmann, *Principal*
EMP: 6 **EST:** 2012
SALES (est): 1.1MM **Privately Held**
WEB: www.myshowerdoor.com
SIC: 3089 Fiberglass doors

(G-4337)
NATURE MEDRX INC
1342 Clnl Blvd Unit C20 (33907)
PHONE.................................239 215-8557
Vincent Cataldi, *President*
EMP: 12 **EST:** 2015
SQ FT: 2,000
SALES (est): 1.1MM **Privately Held**
SIC: 2834 Vitamin, nutrient & hematinic preparations for human use

(G-4338)
NETEXPRESSUSA INC (PA)
Also Called: Reliabilityweb.com
8991 Daniels Center Dr # 105 (33912-0317)
P.O. Box 425, Blair NE (68008-0425)
PHONE.................................888 575-1245
Terrence J O Hanlon, *President*
Kelly I O Hanlon, *Vice Pres*
Mary Grubisich, *Accountant*
Maura Abad, *Manager*
Crystal Ward, *Manager*
EMP: 6 **EST:** 2003
SQ FT: 9,000
SALES (est): 1MM **Privately Held**
WEB: www.reliabilityweb.com
SIC: 2721 2731 2741 4813 Magazines: publishing only, not printed on site; books: publishing only; newsletter publishing; ; professional membership organizations

(G-4339)
NFI MASKS LLC
16140 Lee Rd Unit 120 (33912-2520)
PHONE.................................239 990-6546
Todd Raines,
EMP: 30 **EST:** 2020
SALES (est): 1.1MM **Privately Held**
SIC: 3821 Incubators, laboratory

(G-4340)
NITE-BRIGHT SIGN COMPANY INC
Also Called: Toucanvas
16061 Pine Ridge Rd (33908-2634)
PHONE.................................239 466-2616
David W Mathey Jr, *President*
David W Mathey III, *Vice Pres*
Linda H Mathey, *Vice Pres*
Lyn Bradford, *Treasurer*
Roland Castonguay, *Sales Staff*
EMP: 23 **EST:** 1945
SQ FT: 30,000
SALES (est): 2.7MM **Privately Held**
WEB: www.nitebright.com
SIC: 3993 Signs, not made in custom sign painting shops

(G-4341)
NOFLOOD INC
17061 Alico Commerce Ct # 107 (33967-2512)
PHONE.................................239 776-1671
Richard Downare, *President*
Karen Downare, *Co-Owner*
Ashtin Downare, *Vice Pres*
EMP: 5 **EST:** 2017
SALES (est): 492.9K **Privately Held**
WEB: www.noflood.com
SIC: 3569 Filters

(G-4342)
NORTHPOINTE BANK
8660 College Pkwy Ste 150 (33919-5816)
PHONE.................................239 308-4532
EMP: 7 **EST:** 2019
SALES (est): 128.9K **Privately Held**
WEB: www.northpointe.com
SIC: 7372 Prepackaged software

(G-4343)
NOVA SOLID SURFACES INC
12350 Crystal Commerce Lo (33966-1097)
PHONE.................................239 888-0975
Monique Pedrosa, *Principal*
EMP: 9 **EST:** 2015
SALES (est): 321K **Privately Held**
SIC: 3999 Manufacturing industries

(G-4344)
NOVUS CLIP SIGNS & VIDEO PROD
12771 Metro Pkwy Ste 1 (33966-1369)
PHONE.................................239 471-5639
Nelson Diaz, *Principal*
EMP: 7 **EST:** 2014
SALES (est): 247.6K **Privately Held**
SIC: 3993 Signs & advertising specialties

(G-4345)
OAI ENTERPRISES LLC
12960 Commerce Lakes Dr (33913-8659)
PHONE.................................239 225-1350
Robert C Irion, *Principal*
EMP: 13 **EST:** 2012
SALES (est): 508K **Privately Held**
SIC: 3599 Machine shop, jobbing & repair

(G-4346)
OFFSHORE PERFORMANCE SPC INC
15881 Chief Ct (33912-2262)
PHONE.................................239 481-2768
Donald D Carter, *President*
Mary Davenport, *General Mgr*
Donald Carter III, *Vice Pres*
Donnie Carter, *Vice Pres*
Mandi Dettmering, *Executive Asst*
▼ **EMP:** 16 **EST:** 1987
SQ FT: 10,000
SALES (est): 2.5MM **Privately Held**
WEB: www.offshoreperformance.com
SIC: 3519 5561 7699 Marine engines; recreational vehicle parts & accessories; marine engine repair

(G-4347)
OGRADY TOOL COMPANY
Also Called: Precision Manufacturing
7721 Hidden Pond Ln (33917-4525)
P.O. Box 3485 (33918-3485)
PHONE.................................239 560-3395
EMP: 17 **EST:** 1946
SALES (est): 3.4MM **Privately Held**
SIC: 3545 7389 Mfg Machine Tool Accessories

(G-4348)
OLDE WORLD CRAFTSMEN INC
15970 Lake Candlewood Dr (33908-1790)
PHONE.................................239 229-3806
George Coffey, *Principal*
EMP: 5 **EST:** 2008
SALES (est): 325.7K **Privately Held**
SIC: 3272 Concrete products

(G-4349)
OLIVE NAPLES OIL COMPANY
7101 Cypress Lake Dr (33907-6523)
PHONE.................................239 275-5100
EMP: 11 **Privately Held**
WEB: www.naplesoliveoilcompany.com
SIC: 2079 Olive oil
PA: Olive Naples Oil Company
2368 Immokalee Rd
Naples FL 34110

(G-4350)
OMAX HOME INC
1946 Dana Dr (33907-2104)
PHONE.................................239 980-2755
Linas Liaukus, *Principal*
EMP: 11 **EST:** 2017
SALES (est): 495.6K **Privately Held**
WEB: www.omaxcabinets.com
SIC: 2434 Wood kitchen cabinets

(G-4351)
ONE SRCE PRPERTY SOLUTIONS INC
Also Called: Landscape/Irrigation
7139 N Brentwood Rd (33919-6801)
PHONE.................................239 800-9771
Matthew Gillispie, *President*
EMP: 5 **EST:** 2015
SALES (est): 1.2MM **Privately Held**
WEB: www.onesourcewfl.com
SIC: 1389 0782 1629 0721 Construction, repair & dismantling services; landscape contractors; land reclamation; irrigation system operation, not providing water; business services

(G-4352)
ORNAMENTAL COLUMNS STATUES INC
16179 S Tamiami Trl (33908-4306)
PHONE.................................239 482-3911
Alain Colas, *President*
Bobby Colas, *Vice Pres*
EMP: 16 **EST:** 1978
SQ FT: 1,600
SALES (est): 1.6MM **Privately Held**
WEB: www.ornamentalcolumnsandstatues.com
SIC: 3272 Columns, concrete

(G-4353)
P B C H INCORPORATED
Also Called: High Performance Boats & Cars
7941 Mercantile St (33917-2115)
PHONE.................................239 567-5030
Trond Schou, *President*
▲ **EMP:** 30 **EST:** 1986
SQ FT: 6,000
SALES (est): 4.1MM **Privately Held**
WEB: www.nortechboats.com
SIC: 3732 Motorboats, inboard or outboard: building & repairing

(G-4354)
PACE ENCLOSURES INC
12101 Crystal Condo Rd (33966-8363)
PHONE.................................239 275-3818
Dexter Seriao, *President*
EMP: 21 **EST:** 1999
SALES (est): 3MM **Privately Held**
SIC: 3448 Screen enclosures

(G-4355)
PALM PRNTING/PRINTERS INK CORP
5900 Enterprise Pkwy (33905-5003)
PHONE.................................239 332-8600
Kimberly L Darrow, *Principal*
Randy S Darrow, *Principal*
Randy Darrow, *Mng Member*
EMP: 23 **EST:** 2001
SALES (est): 2.5MM **Privately Held**
SIC: 2752 3555 2741 7334 Commercial printing, offset; printing presses; art copy: publishing & printing; photocopying & duplicating services

(G-4356)
PALM PRTG STRGC SOLUTIONS LLC
2306 Dr Mrtn Luther King (33901-3624)
PHONE.................................239 332-8600
Kim Darrow, *Managing Prtnr*
Kimberly L Darrow, *Mng Member*
Randy S Darrow, *Vice Pres*
EMP: 8 **EST:** 2001
SQ FT: 6,000
SALES (est): 750.7K **Privately Held**
SIC: 2752 Commercial printing, offset

(G-4357)
PANTHER PRINTING INC
Also Called: Strategy Marketing Group
11580 Marshwood Ln (33908-3206)
PHONE.................................239 936-5050
Hannah Yolin, *President*
Jennifer Namour, *Principal*
EMP: 21 **EST:** 1996
SALES (est): 5.2MM **Privately Held**
WEB: www.pantherprinting.net
SIC: 2752 Commercial printing, offset

(G-4358)
PAPER FISH PRINTING INC
17251 Alico Center Rd # 5 (33967-6025)
PHONE.................................239 481-3555
Peter Heerwagen, *President*
EMP: 6 **EST:** 1990
SQ FT: 2,500
SALES (est): 901.7K **Privately Held**
WEB: www.paperfish.com
SIC: 2752 2791 Commercial printing, offset; typesetting

(G-4359)
PAPER MACHINE SERVICES INC
9010 Old Hickory Cir (33912-6844)
PHONE.................................608 365-8095
Duane Steinert, *President*
Cindy Steinert, *Vice Pres*
EMP: 5 **EST:** 2000
SALES (est): 421.5K **Privately Held**
SIC: 2621 Paper mills

(G-4360)
PARKWAY PRINTING INC
6371 Arc Way Ste 1 (33966-1416)
PHONE.................................239 936-6970
Ethel Barbosa, *President*
Steven Barbosa, *General Mgr*
Donna Meridith, *Corp Secy*
EMP: 5 **EST:** 1987
SQ FT: 4,000
SALES (est): 443.4K **Privately Held**
WEB: www.parkwayprinting.biz
SIC: 2752 Commercial printing, offset

(G-4361)
PEPSI-COLA BOTTLING CO TAMPA
3625 Mrtin Lther King Blv (33916-4650)
PHONE.................................239 337-2011
Don Cossairt, *Manager*
Matt Cornelius, *Admin Sec*
EMP: 261
SQ FT: 1,239
SALES (corp-wide): 70.3B **Publicly Held**
WEB: www.pepsico.com
SIC: 2086 Carbonated soft drinks, bottled & canned
HQ: Pepsi-Cola Bottling Company Of Tampa
11315 N 30th St
Tampa FL 33612
813 971-2550

(G-4362)
PINNACLE CBINETS BY DESIGN INC
2550 Edison Ave (33901-5302)
PHONE.................................239 440-2950
Linford Stiles, *Vice Pres*
EMP: 7 EST: 2019
SALES (est): 298.4K **Privately Held**
WEB: www.pinnaclecabinetsbydesign.com
SIC: 2434 Wood kitchen cabinets

(G-4363)
PLAYA PERFECTION INC ✪
Also Called: Apexbuilt
5686 Youngquist Rd (33912-2259)
PHONE.................................440 670-8154
Graham Conron, *President*
EMP: 25 EST: 2022
SALES (est): 624.7K **Privately Held**
SIC: 2396 Automotive & apparel trimmings

(G-4364)
POLSON TRANSPORTATION LLC
9032 Pomelo Rd W (33967-3722)
PHONE.................................614 733-9677
Andre G Polson, *CEO*
EMP: 7 EST: 2020
SALES (est): 85K **Privately Held**
SIC: 3537 Trucks, tractors, loaders, carriers & similar equipment

(G-4365)
POLYGON SOLUTIONS INC
6461 Metro Plantation Rd (33966-1257)
PHONE.................................239 628-4800
Steven M Derbin, *President*
EMP: 7 EST: 2010
SQ FT: 4,000
SALES (est): 1MM **Privately Held**
WEB: www.polygonsolutions.com
SIC: 3545 Machine tool attachments & accessories

(G-4366)
POSEIDON BOAT MANUFACTURING
5826 Corporation Cir (33905-5026)
PHONE.................................239 362-3736
Osbel Diaz Pacheco, *Principal*
EMP: 9 EST: 2010
SALES (est): 252.5K **Privately Held**
WEB: www.poseidon2boats.com
SIC: 3999 Manufacturing industries

(G-4367)
POVIA PAINTS INC (PA)
2897 South St (33916-5515)
PHONE.................................239 791-0011
Michael Doikos, *President*
George Doikos, *Vice Pres*
Kostas Doikos, *Vice Pres*
William Doikos, *Shareholder*
EMP: 8 EST: 1968
SQ FT: 4,000
SALES (est): 2.6MM **Privately Held**
WEB: www.poviapaints.com
SIC: 2851 5198 5231 Paints & paint additives; paints; paint; paint brushes, rollers, sprayers & other supplies

(G-4368)
PRESS PRINTING ENTERPRISES INC
Also Called: Press Printing Company
3601 Hanson St (33916-6537)
P.O. Box 220 (33902-0220)
PHONE.................................239 598-1500
Larry Luettich, *President*
Carl Luettich, *Corp Secy*
EMP: 20 EST: 1964
SQ FT: 23,000
SALES (est): 1.2MM **Privately Held**
WEB: www.pressprinting.com
SIC: 2752 2796 Commercial printing, offset; platemaking services

(G-4369)
PROJECT PROS WOODWORKING INC
17051 Jean St Ste 12 (33967-6066)
PHONE.................................239 454-6800
John Presanzano, *President*
EMP: 7 EST: 2005

SALES (est): 252K **Privately Held**
WEB: www.projectproswoodworking.com
SIC: 2434 Wood kitchen cabinets

(G-4370)
PROPRINT OF NAPLES INC (PA)
Also Called: Print Shop, The
5900 Enterprise Pkwy (33905-5003)
PHONE.................................239 775-3553
Ron Eikens, *President*
Frank C Tibbetts, *Vice Pres*
Melissa Steindler, *Marketing Staff*
Staci Hamilton, *Manager*
Orvel Bicking, *Admin Sec*
EMP: 15 EST: 1985
SALES (est): 3.1MM **Privately Held**
SIC: 2752 7336 Commercial printing, offset; commercial art & graphic design

(G-4371)
PULSADERM LLC
12801 Commwl Dr Ste 2 (33913)
PHONE.................................877 474-4038
Yvonne Von Berg, *Mng Member*
EMP: 9 EST: 2016
SALES (est): 925.6K **Privately Held**
WEB: www.pulsaderm.com
SIC: 2844 Cosmetic preparations

(G-4372)
Q SQUARED DESIGN LLC
19064 Marquesa Dr (33913-9396)
PHONE.................................212 686-8860
Nancy Mosny, *Mng Member*
Rudolf Mosny, *CIO*
◆ EMP: 14 EST: 2008
SALES (est): 2MM **Privately Held**
WEB: www.shopqhome.com
SIC: 3089 2392 Tableware, plastic; household furnishings

(G-4373)
QUALITY CABINETS & COUNTERS
7869 Drew Cir Unit 1 (33967-6087)
PHONE.................................239 948-5364
Mary Reynolds, *President*
James Brunco, *Vice Pres*
John Reynolds, *Vice Pres*
Sue Ellen Brunco, *Director*
EMP: 14 EST: 2000
SQ FT: 6,049
SALES (est): 2.2MM **Privately Held**
WEB:
www.qualitycabinetsandcounters.com
SIC: 2434 Wood kitchen cabinets

(G-4374)
QUALITY RESCREENING
17221 Alico Center Rd # 2 (33967-6019)
P.O. Box 510473, Punta Gorda (33951-0473)
PHONE.................................941 625-9765
Kirk Bruns, *Owner*
EMP: 8 EST: 2001
SALES (est): 121.4K **Privately Held**
SIC: 3448 Screen enclosures

(G-4375)
RANGER PLASTIC EXTRUSIONS INC
Also Called: Rpe
15320 Blue Bay Cir (33913-9706)
P.O. Box 5443, Arlington TX (76005-5443)
PHONE.................................817 640-6067
John M Earnest, *President*
Gordon Jacobson, *Treasurer*
Bob Hestes, *Admin Sec*
Robert Hestes, *Admin Sec*
EMP: 22 EST: 1986
SALES (est): 1.5MM **Privately Held**
WEB: www.rangerplastics.com
SIC: 3089 Injection molding of plastics

(G-4376)
RAPID PRINT SOUTHWEST FLA INC
12244 Treeline Ave Ste 4 (33913-8503)
PHONE.................................239 590-9797
Craig Nelson, *President*
Erin Nelson, *Vice Pres*
EMP: 5 EST: 1999
SALES (est): 661K **Privately Held**
WEB: www.rapidprintswfl.com
SIC: 2752 Commercial printing, offset

(G-4377)
REGENCY CUSTOM CABINETS INC
8207 Katanga Ct (33916-7541)
PHONE.................................239 332-7977
Wayne M Jurick, *President*
Ralph Sites, *Vice Pres*
EMP: 11 EST: 1981
SQ FT: 9,100
SALES (est): 315.4K **Privately Held**
SIC: 2599 5031 2434 Cabinets, factory; kitchen cabinets; wood kitchen cabinets

(G-4378)
REGENT CABINETRY AND MORE INC
5610 Zip Dr (33905-5028)
PHONE.................................239 693-2207
Kasey Hill, *President*
EMP: 7 EST: 2008
SALES (est): 176.9K **Privately Held**
WEB: www.regentcabinets.com
SIC: 2434 Wood kitchen cabinets

(G-4379)
RESOURCE MANAGEMENT ASSOCIATES
Also Called: R M A
1675 Temple Ter Ste 2 (33917-3949)
P.O. Box 4363 (33918-4363)
PHONE.................................239 656-0818
William Rose, *President*
Dave Bartz, *Corp Secy*
Michael Gillern, *Vice Pres*
EMP: 9 EST: 2003
SALES (est): 548.6K **Privately Held**
SIC: 3589 Sewage treatment equipment

(G-4380)
RIANI PAVERS INC
1735 Brantley Rd Apt 2015 (33907-3921)
PHONE.................................239 321-1875
Kesios Z De Araujo, *President*
EMP: 7 EST: 2013
SALES (est): 203.9K **Privately Held**
SIC: 2951 Asphalt paving mixtures & blocks

(G-4381)
ROAD BLOCK FABRICATION INC
16140 Lee Rd Unit 100 (33912-2520)
PHONE.................................708 417-6091
Daniel J Martindale, *Principal*
EMP: 7 EST: 2020
SALES (est): 319.5K **Privately Held**
WEB: www.roadblockfabrication.com
SIC: 3444 Sheet metalwork

(G-4382)
ROCKET MARINE INC
Also Called: Rocket International
2360 Crystal Rd (33907-4061)
PHONE.................................239 275-0880
Paul Lockwood, *President*
EMP: 18 EST: 1984
SALES (est): 1.2MM **Privately Held**
WEB: www.rockettrailers.com
SIC: 3799 Boat trailers

(G-4383)
ROCKET SIGN SUPPLIES LLC
3587 Vrnica S Shmker Blvd (33916-2274)
PHONE.................................239 995-4684
Rayford A Betts, *Principal*
EMP: 5 EST: 2012
SALES (est): 343.7K **Privately Held**
WEB: www.rocketsignsuppliesllc.com
SIC: 3993 Signs & advertising specialties

(G-4384)
ROLLERTECH CORP
5845 Corporation Cir (33905-5014)
PHONE.................................239 645-6698
Carlos A Leon, *President*
▲ EMP: 9 EST: 2008
SALES (est): 243.4K **Privately Held**
SIC: 3442 Shutters, door or window: metal

(G-4385)
ROLSAFE LLC
12801 Commwl Dr Ste 7 (33913)
P.O. Box 51619 (33994-1619)
PHONE.................................239 225-2487
Kirsten Tjosaas, *Controller*
Vernon E Collins, *Mng Member*

EMP: 12 EST: 2004
SQ FT: 50,000
SALES (est): 1.5MM **Privately Held**
WEB: www.rolsafe.com
SIC: 3442 Storm doors or windows, metal; shutters, door or window: metal

(G-4386)
RYAN TIRE & PETROLEUM INC
Also Called: Ryan Petroleum
2650 Edison Ave (33916-5306)
PHONE.................................239 334-1351
Bruce Ryan, *President*
Candy Ryan, *Vice Pres*
EMP: 8 EST: 1973
SQ FT: 500
SALES (est): 2.3MM **Privately Held**
SIC: 1389 Construction, repair & dismantling services

(G-4387)
RYDER ORTHOPEDICS INC (PA)
1500 Royal Palm Square Bl (33919-1058)
PHONE.................................239 939-0009
Laura Ryder, *President*
Josh C Ryder, *Vice Pres*
Pat Owen, *Manager*
EMP: 7 EST: 1987
SALES (est): 950.1K **Privately Held**
WEB: www.ryderortho.com
SIC: 3842 Limbs, artificial

(G-4388)
S A FEATHER CO INC
Also Called: S.A. Feather Co., Inc. Florida
5852 Enterprise Pkwy (33905-5001)
PHONE.................................239 693-6363
Darren Samuel, *President*
Kay Isserman, *Corp Secy*
Tamara Stroh-Samuel, *Vice Pres*
▲ EMP: 11 EST: 1906
SQ FT: 8,000
SALES (est): 484.2K **Privately Held**
WEB: www.safeathercompany.com
SIC: 3999 Feathers & feather products

(G-4389)
S T WOOTEN CORPORATION
Also Called: Fort Myers Asphalt Plant
16560 Mass Ct (33912-5942)
PHONE.................................239 337-9486
Scott Wooten, *President*
Robert Peterson, *Manager*
EMP: 32
SALES (corp-wide): 319.8MM **Privately Held**
WEB: www.stwcorp.com
SIC: 3531 Asphalt plant, including gravel-mix type
PA: S. T. Wooten Corporation
3801 Black Creek Rd Se
Wilson NC 27893
252 291-5165

(G-4390)
SAMINCO INC (PA)
10030 Amberwood Rd Ste 5 (33913-8521)
PHONE.................................239 561-1561
Bonne Posma, *President*
Patrick Deweese, *General Mgr*
Cari Wilcox, *Vice Pres*
Michael Rigsby, *Project Mgr*
Robert Lockhart, *Engineer*
▲ EMP: 35 EST: 1992
SQ FT: 18,000
SALES (est): 11.8MM **Privately Held**
WEB: www.saminoinc.com
SIC: 3625 Motor controls & accessories

(G-4391)
SANIBEL PRINT & GRAPHICS
15630 Mcgregor Blvd Ste 1 (33908-2553)
PHONE.................................239 454-1001
Lilburn Horton, *Partner*
David Horton, *Partner*
David Rockifeller, *Partner*
EMP: 5 EST: 1976
SALES (est): 317.5K **Privately Held**
WEB: sanibel-print-graphics.hub.biz
SIC: 2752 Commercial printing, offset

(G-4392)
SCHWING BIOSET
12290 Treeline Ave (33913-8513)
PHONE.................................239 237-2174
John Brown, *Sales Staff*

2022 Harris Florida
Manufacturers Directory

▲ = Import ▼=Export
◆ =Import/Export

Treavor Eaton, *Sales Staff*
EMP: 10 **EST:** 2017
SALES (est): 282.8K **Privately Held**
WEB: www.schwingbioset.com
SIC: 3561 Pumps & pumping equipment

(G-4393)
SCOTT FISCHER ENTERPRISES LLC (PA)
12730 Commwl Dr Ste 2 (33913)
PHONE...................................844 749-2363
Scott Fischer, *President*
Kimberly Haskins, *CFO*
Sarah Mutka, *Sales Mgr*
Taylor Loethen, *Corp Comm Staff*
Dustin Hughes, *Info Tech Dir*
EMP: 40 **EST:** 2010
SALES (est): 13.3MM **Privately Held**
WEB: www.sfe-us.com
SIC: 3751 Motorcycle accessories

(G-4394)
SCREEN ENCLOSURE SERVICES INC
502 South Rd Unit A (33907-2454)
PHONE...................................239 334-6528
Mark Hansen, *President*
Charles Morgan, *Vice Pres*
EMP: 7 **EST:** 1984
SQ FT: 2,000
SALES (est): 730.7K **Privately Held**
WEB: www.myscreendoctor.com
SIC: 3448 Screen enclosures

(G-4395)
SCREENS FAST
1435 Terra Palma Dr (33901-8845)
PHONE...................................239 565-1211
Kurt Meyer, *President*
EMP: 7 **EST:** 2005
SALES (est): 87.5K **Privately Held**
WEB: screens-fast.business.site
SIC: 3448 Prefabricated metal buildings

(G-4396)
SEA KING KANVAS & SHADE INC
Also Called: Sea King Canvas & Shade
15581 Pine Ridge Rd Ste A (33908-2798)
PHONE...................................239 481-3535
Lesley G Beers, *President*
EMP: 5 **EST:** 1988
SQ FT: 5,000
SALES (est): 499.6K **Privately Held**
WEB: www.seakingkanvas.com
SIC: 2394 5999 Shades, canvas: made from purchased materials; canvas products

(G-4397)
SEABREZE CMMNCATIONS GROUP INC
Also Called: Seabreeze Publications
5630 Halifax Ave (33912-4417)
PHONE...................................239 278-4222
Terrence Reid, *President*
Jacquelyn Reid, *Corp Secy*
Sherry Whalon, *Director*
EMP: 10 **EST:** 1985
SQ FT: 2,700
SALES (est): 1MM **Privately Held**
WEB: www.seabreezecommunications.com
SIC: 2721 6531 2711 Magazines: publishing only, not printed on site; real estate agents & managers; newspapers

(G-4398)
SEP NATIONAL LOGISTICS LLC
15050 Elderberry Ln (33907-8504)
PHONE...................................239 439-2239
Sean Pischeda,
EMP: 6
SALES (est): 520.4K **Privately Held**
SIC: 3537 Trucks: freight, baggage, etc.: industrial, except mining

(G-4399)
SIGNCRAFT PUBLISHING CO INC
Also Called: Signcraft Magazine
3950 Ellis Rd (33905-6400)
P.O. Box 60031 (33906-6031)
PHONE...................................239 939-4644
William G McIltrot, *President*
John K Mc Iltrot, *Vice Pres*

Thomas D Mc Iltrot, *Treasurer*
Michelle Digiacomo, *Advt Staff*
Dennis P Mc Iltrot, *Admin Sec*
EMP: 13 **EST:** 1980
SALES (est): 1.5MM **Privately Held**
WEB: www.signcraft.com
SIC: 2721 3993 2731 Trade journals: publishing & printing; signs & advertising specialties; book publishing

(G-4400)
SMART TRACKS INC
6182 Idlewild St (33966-1216)
PHONE...................................239 938-1000
Brian D Rist, *Principal*
EMP: 12 **EST:** 2008
SALES (est): 238.2K **Privately Held**
SIC: 3442 Louvers, shutters, jalousies & similar items

(G-4401)
SOMERO ENTERPRISES INC (PA)
14530 Global Pkwy (33913-8888)
P.O. Box 309, Houghton MI (49931-0309)
PHONE...................................906 482-7252
Jack Cooney, *President*
John Yuncza, *President*
Lawrence Horsch, *Chairman*
Vincenzo Licausi, *Vice Pres*
Alan Schmitt, *Purch Mgr*
◆ **EMP:** 93 **EST:** 1986
SALES (est): 23MM **Privately Held**
WEB: www.somero.com
SIC: 3559 Concrete products machinery

(G-4402)
SOUTHPOINTE PRECISION
12960 Commerce Lk Dr # 10 (33913-8660)
PHONE...................................239 225-1350
Robert Irion, *Owner*
EMP: 5 **EST:** 2000
SALES (est): 560.2K **Privately Held**
WEB: www.southpointeprecision.com
SIC: 3544 Special dies & tools

(G-4403)
SOUTHWEST STRL SYSTEMS INC
5774 Corporation Cir (33905-5008)
PHONE...................................239 693-6000
Randy Whalin, *President*
EMP: 29 **EST:** 1987
SQ FT: 35,000
SALES (est): 2.6MM **Privately Held**
SIC: 2439 Trusses, wooden roof

(G-4404)
SPECIALTIES UNLIMITED
14726 Calusa Palms Dr # 101 (33919-7795)
PHONE...................................239 482-8433
Howard J Weisberg, *Principal*
EMP: 7 **EST:** 2007
SALES (est): 219.4K **Privately Held**
SIC: 3089 Plastics products

(G-4405)
SPECTRUM ENGINEERING INC
1342 Clnl Blvd Ste D31 (33907)
PHONE...................................239 277-1182
R J Ward, *President*
EMP: 5 **EST:** 1987
SALES (est): 410.3K **Privately Held**
WEB: www.spectrumengineering.net
SIC: 3312 8711 Blast furnaces & steel mills; acoustical engineering

(G-4406)
STREAMLINE ALUMINUM INC
12651 Metro Pkwy Ste 1 (33966-1306)
PHONE...................................239 561-7200
Robert H Boehm Jr, *President*
Kenneth R Boehm, *Vice Pres*
Donna Boehm, *Manager*
EMP: 10 **EST:** 1997
SQ FT: 6,000
SALES (est): 999.9K **Privately Held**
WEB: www.streamlinealuminum.com
SIC: 3334 1761 Primary aluminum; roofing, siding & sheet metal work

(G-4407)
STRETCH BLOW SYSTEMS LLC
5237 Smmrlin Commons Blvd (33907-2158)
PHONE...................................239 275-2207
Rodney Kuntz, *Owner*
EMP: 8 **EST:** 2011
SALES (est): 190.5K **Privately Held**
SIC: 3085 Plastics bottles

(G-4408)
STUART BUILDING PRODUCTS LLC
3601 Work Dr (33916-7552)
PHONE...................................239 461-3100
Stacey Mower, *Manager*
EMP: 77
SALES (corp-wide): 26MM **Privately Held**
SIC: 3316 Bars, steel, cold finished, from purchased hot-rolled
PA: Stuart Building Products, Llc
  1341 Nw 15th St
  Pompano Beach FL 33069
  954 971-7264

(G-4409)
STUMP INDUSTRIES LLC
1300 Lee St (33901-2823)
PHONE...................................239 940-5754
Joshua Stump, *Manager*
EMP: 99 **EST:** 2019
SALES (est): 2.4MM **Privately Held**
SIC: 3999 Manufacturing industries

(G-4410)
SUNCOAST ALUMINUM FURN INC
6291 Thomas Rd (33912-2269)
PHONE...................................239 267-8300
Rajiv Varshney, *President*
Rajiv P Varshney, *President*
Raj D Varshney, *Corp Secy*
Prakash C Varshney, *Vice Pres*
Trina Oxendine, *Accounting Mgr*
◆ **EMP:** 35 **EST:** 1983
SQ FT: 125,000
SALES (est): 8.9MM **Privately Held**
WEB: www.suncoastfurniture.com
SIC: 2514 Metal household furniture

(G-4411)
SUNCOAST IDENTIFICATION TECH
Also Called: Suncoast Lmntion Idntification
13300 S Clevlnd Ave Ste 5 (33907-3871)
PHONE...................................239 277-9922
Frank Savage, *President*
EMP: 8 **EST:** 1988
SALES (est): 1.1MM **Privately Held**
SIC: 3083 7389 7389 3577 Plastic finished products, laminated; gifts & novelties; laminating service; computer peripheral equipment; coated & laminated paper

(G-4412)
SUNCOAST IDNTFCTION SLTONS LLC
618 Danley Dr (33907-1530)
PHONE...................................239 277-9922
Pat Tinajero,
Cori Savage,
EMP: 10 **EST:** 2004
SALES (est): 1MM **Privately Held**
WEB: www.idsource.com
SIC: 3999 Identification badges & insignia

(G-4413)
SUNSET PAVERS INC
8210 Katanga Ct (33916-7541)
PHONE...................................239 208-7293
EMP: 7 **EST:** 2016
SALES (est): 153.3K **Privately Held**
SIC: 2951 Asphalt paving mixtures & blocks

(G-4414)
SUPER SWIM CORP
10711 Deer Run Farms Rd (33966-1048)
PHONE...................................239 275-7600
Dave Bellerive, *CEO*
Donald Bellerive, *President*
Daniel Bellerive, *Director*
EMP: 5 **EST:** 1986

SALES (est): 482.3K **Privately Held**
WEB: www.superswim.com
SIC: 3949 7389 Exercise equipment;

(G-4415)
SURVIVAL ARMOR INC
12621 Corp Lakes Dr Ste 8 (33913)
PHONE...................................239 210-0891
James L McCraney, *President*
Bobbie S Epright, *Principal*
Kenneth Mueller, *Vice Pres*
Kurt Osborne, *Vice Pres*
Chad Childers, *Engineer*
▼ **EMP:** 23 **EST:** 2006
SALES (est): 6MM **Privately Held**
WEB: www.survivalarmor.com
SIC: 3462 Armor plate, forged iron or steel

(G-4416)
SWEETLIGHT SYSTEMS
1506 Alhambra Dr (33901-6607)
PHONE...................................239 245-8159
John Snow, *General Mgr*
EMP: 6 **EST:** 2013
SALES (est): 368.2K **Privately Held**
WEB: www.sweetlightsystems.com
SIC: 3648 Stage lighting equipment

(G-4417)
TAG MEDIA GROUP LLC
Also Called: Gulf Coast Aluminum
16751 Link Ct (33912-5913)
PHONE...................................239 288-0499
Thomas Davis, *Principal*
EMP: 14 **EST:** 2017
SALES (est): 1.5MM **Privately Held**
SIC: 2431 3442 5211 Door screens, metal covered wood; screens, window, metal; screens, door & window

(G-4418)
TANTASIA
5100 S Cleveland Ave # 312 (33907-2189)
PHONE...................................239 274-5455
Jim Florig, *President*
EMP: 5 **EST:** 1997
SALES (est): 460K **Privately Held**
SIC: 3648 Sun tanning equipment, incl. tanning beds

(G-4419)
TAYLOR L MAX L C
Also Called: Dioxyme
12751 S Cleveland Ave (33907-7732)
PHONE...................................833 346-9963
Marc Schneider, *Director*
Bennett T Schneider,
Madison Schneider,
◆ **EMP:** 5 **EST:** 2014
SALES (est): 614.6K **Privately Held**
WEB: www.dioxyme.com
SIC: 2834 5122 Vitamin preparations; vitamins & minerals

(G-4420)
THOMAS C GIBBS CUSTOM CABINETS
12141 Clover Dr (33905-6802)
PHONE...................................239 872-6279
Thomas Gibbs, *Principal*
EMP: 7 **EST:** 2005
SALES (est): 253.4K **Privately Held**
WEB: www.gibbscabinets.com
SIC: 2434 Wood kitchen cabinets

(G-4421)
THOMAS MIX KITCHENS BATHS INC
18070 S Tamiami Trl # 13 (33908-4602)
PHONE...................................239 229-4323
Thomas Mix, *Principal*
EMP: 5 **EST:** 2009
SALES (est): 507.6K **Privately Held**
WEB: www.tmkbinc.com
SIC: 3553 Cabinet makers' machinery

(G-4422)
THOMAS UNITED INC
Also Called: Signs By Tomorrow
12700 Metro Pkwy Ste 3 (33966-1303)
PHONE...................................239 561-7446
Michael Thomas, *President*
Robert Thomas, *President*
Deborah Thomas, *Treasurer*
EMP: 8 **EST:** 1997

SQ FT: 2,400
SALES (est): 872.7K **Privately Held**
WEB: www.signsbytomorrow.com
SIC: 3993 5999 7532 Signs & advertising
  specialties; banners; lettering, automotive

(G-4423)
THOMPSON MANUFACTURING INC
2700 Evans Ave Unit 1 (33901-5303)
PHONE..................239 332-0446
EMP: 8
SALES (est): 875.6K **Privately Held**
SIC: 3999 Mfg Misc Products

(G-4424)
THOMPSON SALES GROUP INC
2700 Evans Ave Unit 1 (33901-5303)
PHONE..................239 332-0446
EMP: 20
SQ FT: 2,000
SALES: 2MM **Privately Held**
SIC: 3272 Mfg Concrete Products

(G-4425)
TITAN MFG INC
6381 Metro Plantation Rd (33966-1289)
PHONE..................239 939-5152
Thomas J McAtee Jr, *President*
Tom McAtee, *President*
Linda McAtee, *Vice Pres*
EMP: 10 **EST:** 2001
SQ FT: 4,000
SALES (est): 964.6K **Privately Held**
SIC: 7692 Welding repair

(G-4426)
TOP TRTMENT CSTOMES ACCESORIES
50 Mildred Dr Unit A (33901-9190)
PHONE..................239 936-4600
Jean Bess, *President*
EMP: 9 **EST:** 1991
SQ FT: 2,500
SALES (est): 828.5K **Privately Held**
SIC: 2591 1799 7641 2392 Window
  blinds; blinds vertical; venetian blinds;
  window shades; window treatment instal-
  lation; upholstery work; household fur-
  nishings; curtains & draperies

(G-4427)
TORTILLERIA AMERICA INC
2853 Work Dr Ste 1-2 (33916-6524)
PHONE..................239 462-2175
EMP: 9
SQ FT: 5,000
SALES: 725K **Privately Held**
SIC: 2099 Mfg Food Preparations

(G-4428)
TORTILLERIA SANTA ROSA
18067 Constitution Cir (33967-3012)
PHONE..................239 839-0832
Maria J Hernandez, *Principal*
EMP: 7 **EST:** 2006
SALES: 230K **Privately Held**
SIC: 2099 Tortillas, fresh or refrigerated

(G-4429)
TOTAL OF FLORIDA
12881 Metro Pkwy (33966-8342)
PHONE..................239 768-9400
Ken Traaium, *Owner*
EMP: 7 **EST:** 2007
SALES (est): 100.4K **Privately Held**
SIC: 3585 5075 Air conditioning equip-
  ment, complete; air conditioning & ventila-
  tion equipment & supplies

(G-4430)
TPI ALUMINUM
5612 6th Ave (33907-2915)
P.O. Box 51074 (33994-1074)
PHONE..................239 332-3900
Timothy W Persinger, *President*
EMP: 7 **EST:** 2010
SALES (est): 245K **Privately Held**
WEB: www.tpialum.com
SIC: 3499 Fabricated metal products

(G-4431)
TRAFFIC CONTROL PDTS FLA INC
4020 Edison Ave (33916-4830)
PHONE..................813 621-8484
Bruce Goncalo, *Division Mgr*
Joel Hawkins, *General Mgr*
Orlando Nunez, *Superintendent*
Richard Barnes, *CIO*
Keri Brusa, *Assistant*
EMP: 30
SALES (corp-wide): 15.5MM **Privately Held**
WEB: www.trafficcontrolproducts.org
SIC: 3499 7359 Barricades, metal; work
  zone traffic equipment (flags, cones, bar-
  rels, etc.)
PA: Traffic Control Products Of Florida, Inc.
  5514 Carmack Rd
  Tampa FL 33610
  813 621-8484

(G-4432)
TRANE US INC
14241 Jtport Loop W Ste 1 (33913)
PHONE..................239 277-0344
EMP: 8 **Privately Held**
WEB: www.trane.com
SIC: 3585 Refrigeration & heating equip-
  ment
HQ: Trane U.S. Inc.
  800 Beaty St Ste E
  Davidson NC 28036
  704 655-4000

(G-4433)
TRASH EXPRESS SW INC
3040 Oasis Grand Blvd # 2104
(33916-1607)
PHONE..................239 340-5291
George Kavouras, *President*
EMP: 5 **EST:** 2013
SALES (est): 410.1K **Privately Held**
SIC: 3443 Dumpsters, garbage

(G-4434)
TROPIC SEAL INDUSTRIES INC
1745 Coral Way (33917-2531)
PHONE..................239 543-8069
Richard P Dietrich, *President*
EMP: 8 **EST:** 2004
SALES (est): 485K **Privately Held**
WEB: www.tropicseal.com
SIC: 3479 Metal coating & allied service

(G-4435)
US SIGN AND MILL INC
Also Called: U S Sign and Mill
7981 Mainline Pkwy (33912-5921)
PHONE..................239 936-9154
Steve Dinkel, *President*
Rene Kilbourne, *Vice Pres*
EMP: 25 **EST:** 1987
SQ FT: 18,213
SALES (est): 3.4MM **Privately Held**
WEB: www.ussignandmill.com
SIC: 3993 Signs & advertising specialties

(G-4436)
USA SHUTTER COMPANY LLC
Also Called: Maestroshield
2141 Flint Dr (33916-4811)
PHONE..................239 596-8883
Marie Kallstrom, *CFO*
Christer Kallstrom, *Mng Member*
EMP: 6 **EST:** 2005
SALES (est): 1MM **Privately Held**
SIC: 3089 5211 Shutters, plastic; door &
  window products

(G-4437)
UTILITIES STRUCTURES INC
2700 Evans Ave Unit 2 (33901-5303)
P.O. Box 9303 (33902-9303)
PHONE..................239 334-7757
W Brown Thompson III, *President*
Carmi Thompson, *Principal*
T Nathan Thompson, *Vice Pres*
Gay Rebel Thompson, *Treasurer*
Robin Thompson, *Bookkeeper*
EMP: 19 **EST:** 1988
SQ FT: 4,000
SALES (est): 2.5MM **Privately Held**
WEB: www.utilitiesstructures.com
SIC: 3272 Poles & posts, concrete

(G-4438)
VAULT STRUCTURES INC
Also Called: VSI
3640 Work Dr (33916-7534)
PHONE..................239 332-3270
Kevin P McNamara, *CEO*
Howard T Ankney, *President*
Lukens Alisca, *Asst Controller*
◆ **EMP:** 50 **EST:** 1986
SQ FT: 44,000
SALES (est): 13.6MM **Privately Held**
WEB: www.vaultstructures.com
SIC: 3499 Safes & vaults, metal

(G-4439)
VELMAXXX ENTERPRISES INC
Also Called: No No-See-Um
10941 Gladiolus Dr Unit 9 (33908-2685)
P.O. Box 71, Sanibel (33957-0071)
PHONE..................239 689-4343
Caroline Semerjian, *Principal*
Kip Buntrock, *Sales Staff*
Kimberly Chaffin, *Sales Staff*
EMP: 6 **EST:** 2009
SALES (est): 710.3K **Privately Held**
WEB: www.velmaxxx.net
SIC: 2879 Insecticides & pesticides

(G-4440)
VIANNY CORPORATION
6860 Daniels Pkwy (33912-1571)
PHONE..................239 888-4536
David Aranda, *CEO*
EMP: 10 **EST:** 2015
SALES (est): 495.5K **Privately Held**
SIC: 2844 5122 Toilet preparations; toilet
  preparations

(G-4441)
VISIONARE LLC
12251 Towne Lake Dr (33913-8012)
PHONE..................305 989-7271
Irineu Vitor Leite,
Marina Adami, *Administration*
Geninho Thome,
EMP: 7 **EST:** 2013
SALES (est): 552.8K **Privately Held**
WEB: www.visionare.us
SIC: 3842 Orthopedic appliances

(G-4442)
VISIONS MILLWORK INC
15674 Spring Line Ln (33905-2450)
PHONE..................239 390-0811
Kim Rose, *President*
John McCallum, *Vice Pres*
Barbara Rose, *Admin Sec*
EMP: 10 **EST:** 2003
SALES (est): 854.9K **Privately Held**
SIC: 2431 5099 5251 Interior & ornamen-
  tal woodwork & trim; locks & lock sets;
  door locks & lock sets

(G-4443)
VISTA SERV CORP
2346 Winkler Ave (33901-9264)
PHONE..................239 275-1973
Laurie Andersen, *Principal*
EMP: 7 **EST:** 2007
SALES (est): 96.1K **Privately Held**
SIC: 2499 2599 3089 5046 Food handling & processing products, wood;
  restaurant furniture, wood or metal; plastic kitchenware, tableware & houseware;
  restaurant equipment & supplies

(G-4444)
W C H ENTERPRISES INC
17640 Holly Oak Ave (33967-5141)
PHONE..................239 267-7549
Cynthia Heisler, *President*
EMP: 5 **EST:** 1997
SALES (est): 328K **Privately Held**
SIC: 2431 Window shutters, wood

(G-4445)
WATER BOY INC
1520 Lee St (33901-2915)
PHONE..................239 461-0860
Scott McLaughlin, *Principal*
EMP: 11

SALES (corp-wide): 8.7MM **Privately Held**
WEB: www.waterboyinc.com
SIC: 2086 5499 Water, pasteurized: packaged in cans, bottles, etc.; water: distilled
  mineral or spring
PA: Water Boy, Inc.
  4454 19th Street Ct E
  Bradenton FL 34203
  941 744-9249

(G-4446)
WEAR FUND LLC
93 Mildred Dr Ste B (33901-9044)
PHONE..................239 313-3907
Samuel S Lewis, *Principal*
Jake Smith, *Supervisor*
EMP: 15 **EST:** 2018
SALES (est): 449.5K **Privately Held**
WEB: www.wearthefund.com
SIC: 2759 Screen printing

(G-4447)
WESTERN FABRICATING LLC
17061 Alico Commerce Ct (33967-2512)
PHONE..................239 676-5382
EMP: 9 **EST:** 2019
SALES (est): 1.4MM **Privately Held**
WEB: www.westernfabricating.com
SIC: 3441 Fabricated structural metal

(G-4448)
WHEELHOUSE DIRECT LLC
17595 S Tamiami Trl # 125 (33908-4570)
PHONE..................239 246-8788
Arlene Milner, *Opers Mgr*
EMP: 7 **EST:** 2018
SALES (est): 351.2K **Privately Held**
WEB: www.wheelhousedirect.com
SIC: 2721 Periodicals

(G-4449)
WINE AND CANVAS DEV LLC
6351 Emerald Bay Ct (33908-5080)
PHONE..................239 980-9138
Melissa Loerwald, *Instructor*
EMP: 8
SALES (corp-wide): 1.1MM **Privately Held**
WEB: www.wineandcanvas.com
SIC: 2211 Canvas
PA: Wine And Canvas Development Llc
  1760 Cholla Ter
  Indianapolis IN 46240
  317 345-1567

(G-4450)
WOODYS HEATING & AC LLC
14250 A And W Bulb Rd (33908-2307)
PHONE..................651 829-4570
Dustin Wood, *President*
EMP: 7 **EST:** 2012
SALES (est): 195.8K **Privately Held**
WEB: www.woodysheating.com
SIC: 3585 Heating & air conditioning com-
  bination units

(G-4451)
YOUNGQUIST BROTHERS ROCK INC
15401 Alico Rd (33913-8232)
PHONE..................239 267-6000
Tim G Youngquist, *President*
Richard Friday, *CFO*
Andy Marquez, *Manager*
EMP: 60 **EST:** 1996
SALES (est): 16.1MM **Privately Held**
WEB: www.youngquistbrothers.com
SIC: 1411 Trap rock, dimension-quarrying

(G-4452)
ZBC CABINETRY
3593 Vrnica S Shmker Blvd (33916-2274)
PHONE..................239 332-2940
Zac Carpenter, *Principal*
EMP: 9 **EST:** 2015
SALES (est): 522.1K **Privately Held**
WEB: www.zbccabinetry.com
SIC: 2434 Wood kitchen cabinets

▲ = Import ▼ =Export
◆ =Import/Export

Fort Myers Beach
Lee County

(G-4453)
DIVERSIFIED YACHT SERVICES INC
751 Fishermans Wharf (33931-2203)
PHONE..............................239 765-8700
Richard H Levi, *President*
Ryan Levi, *Exec VP*
Pamela Benad, *Vice Pres*
Greg Collins, *Vice Pres*
EMP: 30 EST: 2007
SQ FT: 60,000
SALES (est): 5MM
SALES (corp-wide): 110.1MM **Privately Held**
WEB: www.dysinc.com
SIC: 3732 4493 Yachts, building & repairing; boat yards, storage & incidental repair
PA: Levi Ray & Shoup Inc
2401 W Monroe St
Springfield IL 62704
217 793-3800

(G-4454)
GRAVITY PRODUCE LLC
4401 Bay Beach Ln Apt 844 (33931-5918)
PHONE..............................269 471-9463
Rockie Rick, *Owner*
Jeffrey Hischke, *Senior Mgr*
EMP: 5 EST: 2005
SALES (est): 492.5K **Privately Held**
WEB: www.gravitywine.com
SIC: 2084 Wines

(G-4455)
JUVENT MEDICAL INC
3111 Shell Mound Blvd (33931-3629)
PHONE..............................732 748-8866
John Moroney, *President*
EMP: 9 EST: 2003
SQ FT: 12,000
SALES (est): 255.9K **Privately Held**
SIC: 3842 Cotton & cotton applicators

(G-4456)
SKIP ONE SEAFOOD INC
17650 San Carlos Blvd (33931-3033)
PHONE..............................239 463-8788
EMP: 6
SALES (est): 571.4K **Privately Held**
SIC: 2092 Mfg Fresh/Frozen Packaged Fish

Fort Pierce
St. Lucie County

(G-4457)
A B SURVEY SUPPLY ENTPS INC
2603 Industrial Avenue 2 (34946-8644)
PHONE..............................772 464-9500
Anwar Bacchus, *President*
Christopher Golding, *Vice Pres*
EMP: 6 EST: 1982
SQ FT: 2,400
SALES (est): 575.9K **Privately Held**
SIC: 2499 5049 8713 Surveyors' stakes, wood; scientific & engineering equipment & supplies; surveying services

(G-4458)
A-1 ROOF TRUSSES LTD COMPANY
Also Called: A1 Building Components
4451 Saint Lucie Blvd (34946-9035)
PHONE..............................772 409-1010
John Hering, *Branch Mgr*
EMP: 110
SALES (corp-wide): 53.5MM **Privately Held**
WEB: www.a1truss.com
SIC: 2439 Trusses, wooden roof
PA: A-1 Industries Of Florida, Inc.
11555 Heron Bay Blvd # 2
Coral Springs FL 33076
270 316-9409

(G-4459)
ADVANCED MACHINE AND TOOL INC
3900 Selvitz Rd (34981-4709)
PHONE..............................772 465-6546
Lloyd D Riley, *President*
Jerry Jacques, *General Mgr*
John Drumm, *Purchasing*
Clay Becton, *Sales Mgr*
◆ EMP: 65 EST: 1979
SQ FT: 32,000
SALES (est): 11.2MM **Privately Held**
WEB: www.amtfl.com
SIC: 3599 7692 3544 Machine shop, jobbing & repair; welding repair; special dies, tools, jigs & fixtures

(G-4460)
AERO SHADE TECHNOLOGIES INC
Also Called: AST
3106 Industrial Avenue 3 (34946-8662)
PHONE..............................772 562-2243
John Manchec, *President*
▲ EMP: 5 EST: 1998
SALES (est): 643.5K **Privately Held**
WEB: www.aero-shade.com
SIC: 2591 Window shades

(G-4461)
AIRFRAME INTERNATIONAL INC
3150 Airmans Dr (34946-9131)
PHONE..............................218 461-9305
Larry Calabrese, *CEO*
Carlos Byrne, *President*
▲ EMP: 14 EST: 1998
SQ FT: 22,000
SALES (est): 1MM **Privately Held**
SIC: 3728 Aircraft parts & equipment

(G-4462)
AMERACAT INC
3340 N Us Highway 1 Ste 1 (34946-8478)
PHONE..............................772 882-9186
Stephen Meitner, *CEO*
Scott Meitner, *President*
EMP: 7 EST: 2009
SALES (est): 433.6K **Privately Held**
WEB: www.ameracat.com
SIC: 3732 Boat building & repairing

(G-4463)
AMERICAN BOTTLING COMPANY
Also Called: Canada Dry of Florida
3700 Avenue F (34947-5832)
PHONE..............................772 461-3383
Don Castle, *Sales/Mktg Mgr*
EMP: 70
SQ FT: 30,000 **Publicly Held**
WEB: www.keurigdrpepper.ca
SIC: 2086 Soft drinks: packaged in cans, bottles, etc.
HQ: The American Bottling Company
6425 Hall Of Fame Ln
Frisco TX 75034

(G-4464)
AMERICAN CONCRETE INDS INC
350 N Rock Rd (34945-3437)
PHONE..............................772 464-1187
Robert L Snowe, *President*
▲ EMP: 25 EST: 1987
SQ FT: 28,750
SALES (est): 4.8MM **Privately Held**
WEB: american-concrete-industries.business.site
SIC: 3272 Concrete products, precast

(G-4465)
AMERICAST PRECAST GENERATOR
3204 Ohio Ave (34947-4673)
PHONE..............................772 971-1958
Charles Pitt, *Manager*
EMP: 8 EST: 2018
SALES (est): 368.9K **Privately Held**
WEB: www.ameri-casting.com
SIC: 3272 Concrete products

(G-4466)
ANCIENT MOSAIC STUDIOS LLC
4106 Mariah Cir (34947-1771)
PHONE..............................772 460-3145
Stuart A Horowitz, *President*
◆ EMP: 21 EST: 2002
SQ FT: 27,000
SALES (est): 1MM **Privately Held**
WEB: www.stoneyardinc.com
SIC: 3281 Table tops, marble

(G-4467)
APPLE MACHINE & SUPPLY CO
5900 Orange Ave (34947-1550)
P.O. Box 68 (34954-0068)
PHONE..............................772 466-9353
James R Turner, *President*
EMP: 26 EST: 1984
SQ FT: 12,000
SALES (est): 4.2MM **Privately Held**
WEB: www.appleindustrialsupply.com
SIC: 3599 Machine shop, jobbing & repair

(G-4468)
AUTOMATED SERVICES INC
Also Called: A S I
2700 Industrial Avenue 3 (34946-8663)
P.O. Box 650889, Vero Beach (32965-0889)
PHONE..............................772 461-3388
EMP: 17
SQ FT: 22,000 **Privately Held**
SIC: 3479 2759 2821 2396 Coating/Engraving Svcs Commercial Printing Mfg Plstc Material/Resin Mfg Auto/Apparel Trim

(G-4469)
BEE ELECTRONICS INC
2733 Peters Rd (34945-2613)
PHONE..............................772 468-7477
Robert Lunn, *President*
Andrew Lunn, *Manager*
EMP: 100 EST: 1996
SALES (est): 9.3MM **Privately Held**
WEB: www.beecase.com
SIC: 3161 5099 Cases, carrying; cases, carrying
PA: U.S. Communications Industries Inc
2733 Peters Rd
Fort Pierce FL 34945
772 468-7477

(G-4470)
BEST INDUSTRIES INC
15860 W Park Ln (34945-4232)
PHONE..............................772 460-8310
Otto G Wild, *President*
Luis Gil, *Project Mgr*
▼ EMP: 10 EST: 2003
SQ FT: 4,000
SALES (est): 1.3MM **Privately Held**
WEB: www.bestindustries.net
SIC: 3441 Fabricated structural metal

(G-4471)
BOOTH MANUFACTURING COMPANY
Also Called: Auto Labe
3101 Industrial Ave Ste 2 (34946)
PHONE..............................772 465-4441
Roy Shepherd, *CEO*
Mark Birchall, *Chairman*
◆ EMP: 30 EST: 1967
SQ FT: 25,000
SALES (est): 8.2MM **Privately Held**
WEB: www.autolabe.com
SIC: 3565 Labeling machines, industrial

(G-4472)
CARIB SEA INC
3434 Industrial 31st St (34946-8613)
P.O. Box 13359 (34979-3359)
PHONE..............................772 461-1113
Richard M Greenfield Jr, *President*
Nancy P Greenfield, *Corp Secy*
Betsey Greenfiled-Moore, *Vice Pres*
Jud McCracken, *Sales Mgr*
Shannon Greenfield, *Analyst*
◆ EMP: 30 EST: 1971
SQ FT: 50,000
SALES (est): 5.5MM **Privately Held**
WEB: www.caribsea.com
SIC: 3231 Aquariums & reflectors, glass

(G-4473)
CEI LIQUIDATION INC
Also Called: Red Phoenix Extracts
3495 S Us Highway 1 Ste A (34982-6651)
PHONE..............................281 541-2444
Steven L Sample, *CEO*
Gwendolyn G Sample, *Admin Sec*
◆ EMP: 9 EST: 2008
SALES (est): 232.1K **Privately Held**
SIC: 3556 Mixers, commercial, food

(G-4474)
CEMEX CNSTR MTLS FLA LLC
Also Called: Agg Trading-W Ft Pierce Term
Glades Cut Off Rd (34981)
PHONE..............................800 992-3639
EMP: 25 **Privately Held**
SIC: 3273 Ready-mixed concrete
HQ: Cemex Construction Materials Florida, Llc
1501 Belvedere Rd
West Palm Beach FL 33406

(G-4475)
CEMEX CNSTR MTLS FLA LLC
Also Called: East Ft. Pierce FL Readymix
514 S 3rd St (34950-1525)
PHONE..............................772 461-7102
Charles Carew, *Branch Mgr*
EMP: 7 **Privately Held**
SIC: 3273 Ready-mixed concrete
HQ: Cemex Construction Materials Florida, Llc
1501 Belvedere Rd
West Palm Beach FL 33406

(G-4476)
CHAMBERS TRUSS INC (PA)
3105 Oleander Ave (34982-6496)
PHONE..............................772 465-2012
Robert J Becht, *President*
Phyllis Chambers, *Corp Secy*
Arvin L Rieger, *Vice Pres*
Branden Baird, *Sales Staff*
Heidi Baird, *Info Tech Mgr*
▼ EMP: 90 EST: 1968
SALES (est): 9MM **Privately Held**
WEB: www.chamberstruss.com
SIC: 2439 Trusses, wooden roof

(G-4477)
CITRUS EXTRACTS LLC
3495 S Us Highway 1 Ste A (34982-6651)
P.O. Box 394, Johnston IA (50131-0394)
PHONE..............................772 464-9800
Al Koch, *CEO*
William Howe, *President*
EMP: 15 EST: 2015
SALES (est): 2.6MM **Privately Held**
WEB: www.allthingscitrus.com
SIC: 2836 Extracts

(G-4478)
CUSTOM METAL CREATIONS LLC
3106 S Brocksmith Rd (34945-4411)
PHONE..............................772 807-0000
Christopher Day,
EMP: 7 EST: 2014
SALES (est): 910.2K **Privately Held**
SIC: 3446 Ornamental metalwork

(G-4479)
D & D MBL WLDG FABRICATION INC
Also Called: D & D Welding
5300 Steel Blvd (34946-9129)
PHONE..............................772 489-7900
Martine Vaughn, *Branch Mgr*
EMP: 57
SQ FT: 3,000
SALES (corp-wide): 6.7MM **Privately Held**
WEB: www.ddwelding.com
SIC: 3446 3441 Architectural metalwork; fabricated structural metal
PA: D & D Mobile Welding And Fabrication, Inc.
222 Sw 21st Ter
Fort Lauderdale FL 33312
954 791-3385

(G-4480)
DELTA REGIS TOOLS INC
7370 Commercial Cir (34951-4109)
PHONE.................................772 465-4302
Thomas G Deadman, *President*
Bob Deadman, *Vice Pres*
James Deadman, *Sales Staff*
Mark Kotiesen, *Sales Staff*
▲ EMP: 20 EST: 1996
SALES (est): 4.4MM
SALES (corp-wide): 419.3K **Privately Held**
WEB: www.deltaregis.com
SIC: 3546 5085 7629 Power-driven hand-tools; industrial tools; electrical repair shops
PA: Deadman Holdings Inc
4120 Ridgeway Dr Unit 23
Mississauga ON L5L 5

(G-4481)
DERECKTOR SHIP YARD
101 Port Ave (34950-1000)
PHONE.................................772 595-9326
Peter Smykowski, *CFO*
EMP: 9 EST: 2019
SALES (est): 363K **Privately Held**
WEB: www.derecktor.com
SIC: 3731 Shipbuilding & repairing

(G-4482)
ELEMENT 26 LLC
1810 S Ocean Dr (34949-3361)
PHONE.................................413 519-1146
Philip J Gauthier, *Principal*
EMP: 8 EST: 2018
SALES (est): 1.4MM **Privately Held**
WEB: www.element26.co
SIC: 2819 Elements

(G-4483)
EM ADAMS INC
7496 Commercial Cir (34951-4111)
P.O. Box 12160 (34979-2160)
PHONE.................................772 468-6550
Richard K Donahue, *President*
Rich Donahue, *Vice Pres*
Richard Donahue, *Vice Pres*
Clifford Snow, *Sales Staff*
◆ EMP: 65 EST: 1958
SALES (est): 8.4MM **Privately Held**
WEB: www.emadamsco.com
SIC: 3841 5047 Surgical & medical instruments; orthopedic equipment & supplies; therapy equipment

(G-4484)
EP6 GROUP INC
1150 Bell Ave (34982-6581)
PHONE.................................772 332-9100
Leanna Evans, *President*
EMP: 9 EST: 2018
SALES (est): 697.6K **Privately Held**
WEB: www.ep6group.com
SIC: 2621 Building & roofing paper, felts & insulation siding

(G-4485)
FASCO EPOXIES INC
2550 N Us Highway 1 (34946-8963)
PHONE.................................772 464-0808
Daniel Delo, *President*
EMP: 11 EST: 2015
SALES (est): 2.1MM **Privately Held**
WEB: www.fascoepoxies.com
SIC: 2891 Epoxy adhesives

(G-4486)
FAUX EFFECTS INTERNATIONAL INC
Also Called: Aqua Finishing Solutions
2701 Industrial Avenue 2 (34946-8665)
PHONE.................................800 270-8871
Raymond P Sandor, *President*
Jane Koehler, *Vice Pres*
Joan Rooney, *Office Mgr*
Bill James, *Technology*
Scot Povlin, *Director*
◆ EMP: 25 EST: 1986
SALES (est): 4.2MM **Privately Held**
WEB: www.fauxfx.com
SIC: 2851 Paints & allied products

(G-4487)
FLORIDA COCA-COLA BOTTLING CO
3939 Saint Lucie Blvd (34946-9025)
PHONE.................................772 461-3636
Bob Johnson, *Manager*
EMP: 1025
SALES (corp-wide): 33B **Publicly Held**
WEB: www.coca-cola.com
SIC: 2086 Bottled & canned soft drinks
HQ: Florida Coca-Cola Bottling Company
521 Lake Kathy Dr
Brandon FL 33510
813 569-2600

(G-4488)
FORZA X1 INC ●
3101 S Us Highway 1 (34982-6337)
PHONE.................................772 202-8039
Joseph Visconti, *President*
EMP: 75 EST: 2021
SALES (est): 1.4MM **Publicly Held**
SIC: 3732 Motorized boat, building & repairing
PA: Twin Vee Powercats, Inc.
3101 S Us Highway 1
Fort Pierce FL 34982

(G-4489)
GEM FRESHCO LLC
3586 Oleander Ave (34982-6509)
P.O. Box 15009 (34979-5009)
PHONE.................................772 595-0070
EMP: 60
SALES (est): 3.9MM **Privately Held**
SIC: 2033 5142 Canned Fruits And Specialties

(G-4490)
GLOBAL STONE COLLECTION LLC
1800 N Us Highway 1 (34946-1453)
PHONE.................................772 467-1924
EMP: 21
SALES (corp-wide): 1.3MM **Privately Held**
WEB: www.globalstonecollection.com
SIC: 2541 Table or counter tops, plastic laminated
PA: Global Stone Collection Llc
1405 N Us Highway 1
Fort Pierce FL 34950
772 467-1924

(G-4491)
GLOBAL STONE COLLECTION LLC (PA)
1405 N Us Highway 1 (34950-1418)
PHONE.................................772 467-1924
Yesid Medina, *Manager*
EMP: 6 EST: 2008
SALES (est): 1.3MM **Privately Held**
WEB: www.globalstonecollection.com
SIC: 2541 Table or counter tops, plastic laminated

(G-4492)
GLOMASTER SIGNS INC
4141 Bandy Blvd (34981-4732)
PHONE.................................772 464-0718
James M Hart, *President*
Rebecca Hart, *Admin Sec*
EMP: 6 EST: 1965
SQ FT: 3,000
SALES (est): 818.1K **Privately Held**
WEB: www.glomastersigns.com
SIC: 3993 Signs, not made in custom sign painting shops

(G-4493)
GRAVITYSTORM INC
7402 Fort Walton Ave (34951-1429)
PHONE.................................772 519-3009
Nicholas Barson, *Principal*
EMP: 12 EST: 2014
SALES (est): 265.4K **Privately Held**
WEB: www.gravitystorm.us
SIC: 2431 Storm windows, wood

(G-4494)
HALL METAL CORP
4700 Magnum Dr (34981-4839)
PHONE.................................772 460-0706
Peter D Hall, *President*
EMP: 5 EST: 1935
SQ FT: 4,000
SALES (est): 710.1K **Privately Held**
WEB: www.hallmetals.net
SIC: 3441 Building components, structural steel

(G-4495)
HOMETOWN NEWS LC (PA)
Also Called: Martin County Hometown News
1102 S Us Highway 1 (34950-5132)
P.O. Box 850 (34954-0850)
PHONE.................................772 465-5656
David Crain, *General Mgr*
Lee Mooty, *General Mgr*
Mercedes Paquette, *Prdtn Mgr*
Lee Mootym, *CFO*
Carol Deprey, *Sales Staff*
▲ EMP: 45 EST: 2002
SQ FT: 5,000
SALES (est): 16MM **Privately Held**
WEB: www.hometowngiftcertificates.com
SIC: 2711 Newspapers, publishing & printing

(G-4496)
IMMUNOTEK BIO CENTERS LLC
2710 S Us Highway 1 (34982-5919)
PHONE.................................772 577-7194
Erica Reid, *QC Mgr*
John Bonczak, *Manager*
EMP: 32
SALES (corp-wide): 27MM **Privately Held**
WEB: www.immunotek.com
SIC: 2836 Blood derivatives
PA: Immunotek Bio Centers, L.L.C.
3900 N Causeway Blvd # 1200
Metairie LA 70002
337 500-1175

(G-4497)
INDIAN RIVER ARMATURE INC
120 Lakes End Dr Apt A (34982-6747)
PHONE.................................772 461-2067
Richard M Mc Arthur, *President*
Lela McArthur, *Corp Secy*
EMP: 7 EST: 1958
SQ FT: 4,800
SALES (est): 303.7K **Privately Held**
SIC: 7694 5063 Electric motor repair; motors, electric

(G-4498)
ISLAND STYLE HOMES INC
4275 Mariah Cir (34947-1707)
PHONE.................................772 464-6259
Gordon Mock, *President*
Susan Mock, *Vice Pres*
▼ EMP: 6 EST: 1990
SQ FT: 4,000
SALES (est): 892.3K **Privately Held**
WEB: www.islandstylehomes.com
SIC: 2452 Modular homes, prefabricated, wood

(G-4499)
KYOCERA DCMENT SLTONS STHAST L
480 Okeechobee Rd Ste 101 (34947)
PHONE.................................772 562-0511
Barry Rokaw, *Manager*
EMP: 13
SALES (corp-wide): 17.9MM **Privately Held**
SIC: 3555 7378 5044 Copy holders, printers'; computer maintenance & repair; office equipment
PA: Kyocera Document Solutions Southeast, Llc
3401 Wd Judge Dr Ste 140
Orlando FL 32808
407 841-2932

(G-4500)
LAS & JB INC
Also Called: Beltran Construction
4840 S Us Highway 1 (34982-7013)
PHONE.................................772 672-5315
Jony Beltran, *President*
Gregg Bozenbury, *Principal*
EMP: 7 EST: 2005
SQ FT: 1,500
SALES (est): 868.3K **Privately Held**
WEB: www.lasjbgranite.com
SIC: 3281 5032 1741 Granite, cut & shaped; granite building stone; masonry & other stonework

(G-4501)
LOST FABRICATION LLC
3811 Crossroads Pkwy (34945-2703)
PHONE.................................772 971-3467
Craig E Blazer,
Michael L Barson,
EMP: 9 EST: 2014
SALES (est): 530.5K **Privately Held**
WEB: www.lostfab.com
SIC: 3441 Fabricated structural metal

(G-4502)
LP AUTO & HOME GLASS
2471 Se Sapelo Ave (34952-6770)
PHONE.................................772 335-3697
Harold Gerber, *Principal*
EMP: 10 EST: 1998
SALES (est): 547.6K **Privately Held**
SIC: 3231 Enameled glass

(G-4503)
MARTINEZ BUILDERS SUPPLY LLC
Also Called: East Coast Truss
5285 Saint Lucie Blvd (34946-9051)
PHONE.................................772 466-2480
Charlie Martinez, *President*
Raymond Grady, *Contractor*
EMP: 60 EST: 2010
SALES (est): 5.3MM **Privately Held**
SIC: 2439 Trusses, wooden roof

(G-4504)
MAVERICK BOAT GROUP INC
4551 Saint Lucie Blvd (34946-9002)
PHONE.................................772 465-0631
EMP: 185
SALES (corp-wide): 1.2B **Publicly Held**
WEB: www.maverickboats.com
SIC: 3732 Boat building & repairing
HQ: Maverick Boat Group, Inc.
3207 Industrial 29th St
Fort Pierce FL 34946
772 465-0631

(G-4505)
MAVERICK BOAT GROUP INC (HQ)
3207 Industrial 29th St (34946-8642)
PHONE.................................772 465-0631
Douglas Deal, *President*
Joseph Lyshon, *General Mgr*
Jim Leffew, *VP Mfg*
Debbie Spencer, *Purchasing*
Mark Mergott, *Engineer*
▼ EMP: 155 EST: 1984
SQ FT: 103,000
SALES (est): 59.5MM
SALES (corp-wide): 1.2B **Publicly Held**
WEB: www.maverickboats.com
SIC: 3732 Fishing boats: lobster, crab, oyster, etc.: small; skiffs, building & repairing
PA: Malibu Boats, Inc.
5075 Kimberly Way
Loudon TN 37774
865 458-5478

(G-4506)
MCCAIN SALES OF FLORIDA INC
Also Called: Universal Signs & Accessories
3001 Orange Ave (34947-3634)
PHONE.................................772 461-0665
Dixon Mc Cain, *President*
Pete Wells, *General Mgr*
Steven Mc Cain, *Corp Secy*
Rui Mc Cain, *Vice Pres*
Pam Cowger, *CFO*
▲ EMP: 22 EST: 1962
SQ FT: 18,000
SALES (est): 3.9MM **Privately Held**
WEB: www.universalsignsfl.com
SIC: 3993 Signs, not made in custom sign painting shops

(G-4507)
MIAMI FILTER LLC
Also Called: Miami Tank
7384 Commercial Cir (34951-4109)
PHONE.....................772 466-1440
Jeremy Mulvey, *General Mgr*
Ron Masse, *Project Mgr*
James D Miller, *Mng Member*
Kevin Mulvey, *Mng Member*
◆ **EMP:** 27 **EST:** 1958
SQ FT: 50,000
SALES (est): 6MM **Privately Held**
WEB: www.miamifilter.com
SIC: 3569 Filters, general line: industrial

(G-4508)
MORGAN TECHNICAL SERVICES
5512 Silver Oak Dr (34982-7464)
PHONE.....................772 466-5757
Ron Morgan, *Owner*
EMP: 5 **EST:** 1990
SALES (est): 331.9K **Privately Held**
SIC: 3571 Electronic computers

(G-4509)
MOSAICS LIQUIDATION CO INC
901 N 3rd St (34950-5172)
PHONE.....................772 468-8453
Rickey L Farrell, *Principal*
EMP: 8 **EST:** 1989
SALES (est): 66.7K **Privately Held**
SIC: 3253 Ceramic wall & floor tile

(G-4510)
MSA AIRCRAFT PRODUCTS
3106 Industrial Avenue 3 (34946-8662)
PHONE.....................772 562-2243
John Manchec, *Principal*
Hector Jimenez, *Manager*
EMP: 10 **EST:** 2016
SALES (est): 2.5MM **Privately Held**
WEB: www.msaaircraft.com
SIC: 3728 Aircraft parts & equipment

(G-4511)
NILFISK PRESSURE-PRO LLC
7300 Commercial Cir (34951-4109)
PHONE.....................772 672-3697
Dale Reed, *President*
Jeff Barna, *Vice Pres*
Mike Cecchini, *Design Engr*
Alexis White, *Sales Staff*
EMP: 87 **EST:** 2005
SALES (est): 14.8MM
SALES (corp-wide): 2.1B **Privately Held**
WEB: www.pressure-pro.com
SIC: 3589 High pressure cleaning equipment
PA: Nkt A/S
Vibeholms Alle 20
Brondby
434 820-00

(G-4512)
OFFICE OF MEDICAL EXAMINER
2500 S 35th St (34981-5573)
PHONE.....................772 464-7378
Charles Diggs, *Owner*
EMP: 7 **EST:** 1991
SALES (est): 545.8K **Privately Held**
SIC: 2711 Newspapers, publishing & printing

(G-4513)
ORACLE CORPORATION
2100 Nebraska Ave (34950-4704)
PHONE.....................772 466-0704
Colleen Varana, *Surgery Dir*
EMP: 302
SALES (corp-wide): 42.4B **Publicly Held**
WEB: www.oracle.com
SIC: 7372 Prepackaged software
PA: Oracle Corporation
2300 Oracle Way
Austin TX 78741
737 867-1000

(G-4514)
ORCHID ISLAND JUICE CO INC
Also Called: Natalies Orchid Island Juice
330 N Us Highway 1 (34950-4207)
PHONE.....................772 465-1122
Marygrace Sexton, *CEO*
John Martinelli, *Exec VP*

William Martinelli, *Vice Pres*
Jim Zurbey, *Opers Staff*
Christine Roberts, *CFO*
▼ **EMP:** 85 **EST:** 1990
SQ FT: 65,000
SALES (est): 25.9MM **Privately Held**
WEB: www.orchidislandjuice.com
SIC: 2037 Fruit juices

(G-4515)
PATRIOT BUILDING & CNSTR INC
11175 Muller Rd (34945-2322)
PHONE.....................863 634-8489
Francis Alsdorf, *Principal*
EMP: 7 **EST:** 2010
SALES (est): 115.6K **Privately Held**
SIC: 3541 Lathes

(G-4516)
PB HOLDCO LLC
Also Called: Pursuit Boats
3901 Saint Lucie Blvd (34946-9025)
PHONE.....................772 465-6006
Neal Hager, *Business Mgr*
Kevin Keyes, *Project Mgr*
Cory Rettenmaier, *Project Mgr*
Stephen Troisi, *Opers Mgr*
Donna Panchyshyn, *Materials Mgr*
EMP: 450
SALES (corp-wide): 1.2B **Publicly Held**
SIC: 3732 Fishing boats: lobster, crab, oyster, etc.: small
HQ: Pb Holdco, Llc
5075 Kimberly Way
Loudon TN 37774
865 458-5478

(G-4517)
PEPSI-COLA METRO BTLG CO INC
Also Called: Pepsico
3620 Crossroads Pkwy (34945-2709)
PHONE.....................772 464-6150
M Reprints, *Managing Dir*
Ken Willis, *Principal*
Julie Thomas, *QC Mgr*
Latoya Campbell, *Sales Staff*
Karen Baker, *Clerk*
EMP: 142
SALES (corp-wide): 70.3B **Publicly Held**
WEB: www.pepsico.com
SIC: 2086 Carbonated soft drinks, bottled & canned
HQ: Pepsi-Cola Metropolitan Bottling Company, Inc.
700 Anderson Hill Rd
Purchase NY 10577
914 767-6000

(G-4518)
PHOENIX METAL PRODUCTS INC
3000 Industrial Avenue 3 (34946-8609)
PHONE.....................772 595-6386
Philip Price III, *President*
William J Wilcox, *Vice Pres*
▼ **EMP:** 24 **EST:** 1995
SQ FT: 14,000
SALES (est): 5.1MM **Privately Held**
WEB: www.phoenixgse.com
SIC: 3441 Fabricated structural metal

(G-4519)
PIONEER AG-CHEM INC (PA)
Also Called: Diamond R Fertilizer
4100 Glades Cut Off Rd (34981-4711)
P.O. Box 12489 (34979-2489)
PHONE.....................772 464-9300
Mike Mikles, *President*
John Minton, *Principal*
Wayne Carlton, *Principal*
Roy Childs, *Principal*
Ken Scott, *Chairman*
◆ **EMP:** 40 **EST:** 1973
SQ FT: 21,000
SALES (est): 109.3MM **Privately Held**
SIC: 2873 5191 Nitrogen solutions (fertilizer); fertilizers & agricultural chemicals

(G-4520)
PREMIER FABRICATORS LLC
7413 Commercial Cir (34951-4112)
PHONE.....................772 323-2042
Kenneth A Geremia Jr, *President*

Sherry Curtale, *General Mgr*
Terry W Sloan, *Vice Pres*
EMP: 7 **EST:** 2009
SALES (est): 1.7MM **Privately Held**
WEB: www.premierfabricators.net
SIC: 3441 Fabricated structural metal

(G-4521)
PRESTIGE/AB READY MIX LLC
4190 Selvitz Rd (34981-4728)
PHONE.....................772 468-4666
EMP: 20 **Privately Held**
SIC: 3273 Mfg Ready-Mixed Concrete
HQ: Prestige/Ab Ready Mix, Llc
7228 Westport Pl Ste C
West Palm Beach FL 33413
561 478-9980

(G-4522)
RAYMOND NEWKIRK
Also Called: Rays Pallets
920 Angle Rd (34947-1702)
PHONE.....................772 359-0237
Raymond Newkirk, *Principal*
EMP: 7 **EST:** 2010
SALES (est): 98.3K **Privately Held**
SIC: 2448 Pallets, wood & wood with metal

(G-4523)
RE-BUS LLC
5015 Saint Lucie Blvd (34946-9047)
PHONE.....................772 418-7711
Keith Moody, *Mng Member*
EMP: 6 **EST:** 2015
SALES (est): 575.5K **Privately Held**
WEB: www.re-bus.net
SIC: 3585 Air conditioning, motor vehicle

(G-4524)
REDDY ICE CORPORATION
2901 Industrial Avenue 2 (34946-8647)
PHONE.....................772 461-5046
Ronald Forgham, *Treasurer*
EMP: 9 **Privately Held**
WEB: www.reddyice.com
SIC: 2097 Manufactured ice
HQ: Reddy Ice Llc
5710 Lbj Fwy Ste 300
Dallas TX 75240
214 526-6740

(G-4525)
ROCLA CONCRETE TIE INC
600 S 3rd St (34950-1525)
PHONE.....................772 800-1855
Dana Head, *Branch Mgr*
EMP: 124
SALES (corp-wide): 1MM **Privately Held**
WEB: www.vossloh-north-america.com
SIC: 3272 Ties, railroad: concrete
HQ: Rocla Concrete Tie, Inc
1819 Denver West Dr # 450
Lakewood CO 80401

(G-4526)
SCULPTURE HOUSE INC
3804 Crossroads Pkwy (34945-2704)
PHONE.....................609 466-2986
Bruner Barrie, *President*
▲ **EMP:** 10 **EST:** 1918
SQ FT: 10,000
SALES (est): 1.7MM **Privately Held**
WEB: www.sculpturehouse.com
SIC: 3952 Artists' equipment

(G-4527)
SEA CAST CURB ADPTORS CRBS LLC
2601 Industrial Avenue 3 (34946-8624)
PHONE.....................772 466-2400
John V Langel, *Administration*
EMP: 13 **EST:** 2017
SALES (est): 986.2K **Privately Held**
WEB: www.curbsfast.com
SIC: 3441 Building components, structural steel

(G-4528)
SEACOAST AIR CONDITIONING & SH
3108 Industrial 31st St (34946-8610)
PHONE.....................772 466-2400
EMP: 12 **EST:** 2020

SALES (est): 3.8MM **Privately Held**
WEB: www.seacoastair.com
SIC: 3444 Sheet metalwork

(G-4529)
SONIC BOATWORKS LLC ✪
309 Angle Rd (34947-2502)
PHONE.....................561 631-6071
Anna Gore,
EMP: 10 **EST:** 2022
SALES (est): 413.1K **Privately Held**
SIC: 3732 Boat building & repairing

(G-4530)
SOUTHEAST ELEVATOR LLC
811 Edwards Rd (34982-6286)
PHONE.....................772 461-0030
Charles McGee, *President*
Stephanie Perdue, *Project Mgr*
Lynn Pellegrino, *Office Mgr*
David Zane, *Admin Sec*
◆ **EMP:** 75 **EST:** 1995
SALES (est): 7MM **Privately Held**
WEB: www.seelevator.com
SIC: 3534 Elevators & moving stairways

(G-4531)
SOUTHERN TRUSS COMPANIES INC
2590 N Kings Hwy (34951-4019)
PHONE.....................772 464-4160
John C Byers, *President*
Burak Askin, *Engineer*
EMP: 90 **EST:** 2004
SALES (est): 11MM **Privately Held**
WEB: www.southerntrusscompanies.com
SIC: 2439 Trusses, wooden roof

(G-4532)
SPECTRA COMPOSITES EAST FLA
7445 Commercial Cir (34951-4112)
PHONE.....................772 461-7747
Ginger Moore, *Branch Mgr*
EMP: 7 **EST:** 2012
SALES (est): 675.1K **Privately Held**
WEB: www.spectracomposites.com
SIC: 3229 Glass fiber products

(G-4533)
ST LUCIE SIGNS LLC
1147 Hernando St (34949-3347)
PHONE.....................772 971-6363
James M Nole, *Manager*
EMP: 8 **EST:** 2017
SALES (est): 372.3K **Privately Held**
SIC: 3993 Signs & advertising specialties

(G-4534)
STANDARD CLAY MINES
3804 Crossroads Pkwy (34945-2704)
PHONE.....................609 466-2986
EMP: 9
SALES: 1MM **Privately Held**
SIC: 3952 Mfg Lead Pencils/Art Goods

(G-4535)
SUNNYLAND USA INC
600 Citrus Ave Ste 200 (34950-4280)
PHONE.....................772 293-0293
Abbasgholi Bayat, *President*
◆ **EMP:** 11 **EST:** 2008
SQ FT: 1,000
SALES (est): 335.5K **Privately Held**
SIC: 2037 Frozen fruits & vegetables

(G-4536)
SUPERMIX CONCRETE
4550 Glades Cut Off Rd (34981-4715)
PHONE.....................305 265-4465
EMP: 92
SALES (corp-wide): 12.3MM **Privately Held**
SIC: 3273 Ready-mixed concrete
PA: Supermix Concrete
4300 Sw 74th Ave
Miami FL 33155
954 858-0780

(G-4537)
TEC AIR INC
2195 N Kings Hwy (34951-4018)
PHONE.....................772 335-8220
Barbara A Macwilliam, *President*
EMP: 6 **EST:** 2008

SALES (est): 493.2K **Privately Held**
WEB: www.tecairllc.com
SIC: 3089 Injection molding of plastics

(G-4538)
TIG TECHNOLOGIES INC
4250 Bandy Blvd (34981-4733)
PHONE.............................561 691-3633
Roy McKee, *President*
Janis McKee, *Vice Pres*
EMP: 6 EST: 1994
SQ FT: 5,600
SALES (est): 415.8K **Privately Held**
WEB: www.tigtechnologies.com
SIC: 7692 Welding repair

(G-4539)
TITAN AMERICA LLC
4199 Selvitz Rd (34981-4729)
PHONE.............................772 467-2101
Craig Phillips, *Branch Mgr*
EMP: 17
SQ FT: 4,896
SALES (corp-wide): 177.9K **Privately Held**
WEB: www.titanamerica.com
SIC: 3273 Ready-mixed concrete
HQ: Titan America Llc
5700 Lake Wright Dr # 300
Norfolk VA 23502
757 858-6500

(G-4540)
TRANSITION OF SLC INC
7300 Commercial Cir (34951-4109)
PHONE.............................772 461-4486
Dale Reed, *President*
Shaun Spring, *Production*
Bill Mathews, *Engineer*
John Cooper, *Sales Staff*
Bob Gruetzmacher, *Sales Staff*
EMP: 42 EST: 1995
SALES (est): 11.7MM
SALES (corp-wide): 1.1B **Privately Held**
WEB: www.pressure-pro.com
SIC: 3589 High pressure cleaning equipment
HQ: Nilfisk Ltd.
Unit 18-19
Penrith CA11
176 886-8995

(G-4541)
TRICEN TECHNOLOGIES FLA LLC (PA)
500 Farmers Market Rd # 6 (34982-6663)
PHONE.............................866 620-9407
Christopher Hale, *CEO*
▲ EMP: 14 EST: 2009
SALES (est): 5.4MM **Privately Held**
WEB: www.tricen.net
SIC: 1389 7389 Pipe testing, oil field service; inspection & testing services; industrial & commercial equipment inspection service; petroleum refinery inspection service; pipeline & power line inspection service

(G-4542)
TROPICANA PRODUCTS INC
6500 Glades Cut Off Rd (34981-4399)
PHONE.............................772 465-2030
Dick Lineberger, *Engineer*
Tim Kelly, *Branch Mgr*
EMP: 17
SALES (corp-wide): 70.3B **Publicly Held**
WEB: www.tropicana.com
SIC: 2033 2037 Fruit juices: packaged in cans, jars, etc.; fruit juice concentrates, frozen
HQ: Tropicana Products, Inc.
1001 13th Ave E
Bradenton FL 34208
941 747-4461

(G-4543)
TRUE STONE CORP
7324 Commercial Cir (34951-4109)
PHONE.............................772 334-9797
Leanardo Sanchez, *President*
Sean Yeoman, *Prdtn Mgr*
EMP: 36 EST: 2000
SALES (est): 1.3MM **Privately Held**
WEB: www.truestonemasonry.com
SIC: 3272 Stone, cast concrete

(G-4544)
TRUE STONE MASONRY LLC
7324 Commercial Cir (34951-4109)
PHONE.............................772 334-9797
Julie Smith, *CEO*
Troy Smith, *President*
EMP: 11 EST: 2015
SALES (est): 1.3MM **Privately Held**
WEB: www.truestonemasonry.com
SIC: 3272 1741 Cast stone, concrete; masonry & other stonework

(G-4545)
TURNER MACHINE & SUPPLY CO
5000 Orange Ave (34947-1303)
PHONE.............................772 464-4550
David Turner, *President*
Charles Turner, *Corp Secy*
EMP: 8 EST: 1944
SQ FT: 12,600
SALES (est): 996.7K **Privately Held**
SIC: 3599 3561 3523 Machine shop, jobbing & repair; pumps & pumping equipment; farm machinery & equipment

(G-4546)
TWIN VEE CATAMARANS INC
3101 S Us Highway 1 (34982-6337)
PHONE.............................772 429-2525
Donna Dunshee, *President*
▼ EMP: 15 EST: 2010
SQ FT: 77,300
SALES (est): 2.8MM **Privately Held**
WEB: www.twinvee.com
SIC: 3732 Motorized boat, building & repairing

(G-4547)
TWO WAY RADIO GEAR INC
3245 Okeechobee Rd (34947-4618)
PHONE.............................800 984-1534
David Lloyd, *CEO*
Linda Lloyd, *Principal*
Benny Permuy, *Manager*
Edward Wirsing, *Info Tech Mgr*
▲ EMP: 16 EST: 2011
SALES (est): 2.4MM **Privately Held**
WEB: www.twowayradiogear.com
SIC: 3669 5045 Intercommunication systems, electric; computer peripheral equipment

(G-4548)
UNCLE CARLOS GELATOS
141 Melody Ln (34950-4402)
PHONE.............................810 523-8506
EMP: 8
SALES (est): 720.1K **Privately Held**
SIC: 2024 Mfg Ice Cream/Frozen Desert

(G-4549)
UNIQUE TOOL & DIE LLC
3343 S Us Highway 1 Ste 4 (34982-6664)
PHONE.............................772 464-5006
William Gates, *President*
Fred St John, *Vice Pres*
EMP: 14 EST: 2005
SALES (est): 1.2MM **Privately Held**
WEB: www.utdllc.com
SIC: 3544 Special dies & tools

(G-4550)
UNITED STATES FILTER CORP
7374 Commercial Cir (34951-4109)
PHONE.............................772 466-5955
Doug Hicks, *President*
EMP: 7 EST: 2002
SALES (est): 98.5K **Privately Held**
SIC: 3569 Filters

(G-4551)
US COMMUNICATIONS INDUSTRIES (PA)
2733 Peters Rd (34945-2613)
PHONE.............................772 468-7477
Robert A Lunn, *President*
EMP: 50 EST: 1981
SALES (est): 9.3MM **Privately Held**
SIC: 3161 7389 Cases, carrying; telephone answering service

(G-4552)
UTILITY SERVICES AUTHORITY LLC
275 W Coker Rd (34945-2114)
PHONE.............................772 344-9339
Allen Wishon, *Business Mgr*
Brian Bunton, *Branch Mgr*
EMP: 41
SALES (corp-wide): 10.7MM **Privately Held**
WEB: www.usallc.net
SIC: 3812 Horizon flight indicators
PA: Utility Services Authority, Llc
6001 Schooner St
Van Buren Twp MI 48111
734 481-0872

(G-4553)
WARREN HEIM CORP
3107 Industrial 25th St (34946-8620)
PHONE.............................772 466-8265
Nancy Heim, *President*
Chuck Heim, *Vice Pres*
William Heim, *Vice Pres*
EMP: 19 EST: 1927
SQ FT: 10,000
SALES (est): 1.6MM **Privately Held**
WEB: www.warrenheimcorp.com
SIC: 2393 2381 Canvas bags; fabric dress & work gloves

(G-4554)
WHEELER LUMBER LLC
Also Called: Southern Covert
1031 Digiorgio Rd (34982-6447)
PHONE.............................772 464-4400
Zerion Simpson, *Manager*
EMP: 10
SALES (corp-wide): 75.3MM **Privately Held**
WEB: www.wheeler-con.com
SIC: 3272 3444 3441 2821 Culvert pipe, concrete; sheet metalwork; fabricated structural metal; plastics materials & resins
HQ: Wheeler Lumber, L.L.C.
9531 W 78th St Ste 100
Eden Prairie MN 55344
952 929-7854

(G-4555)
WHEELS FOR YOU INC
5701 Pinetree Dr (34982-3200)
PHONE.............................772 485-0162
Michael D Gelter, *Principal*
EMP: 7 EST: 2010
SALES (est): 98.9K **Privately Held**
SIC: 3312 Blast furnaces & steel mills

(G-4556)
WOODWORKX UNLIMITED INC
103 N 13th St (34950-8829)
PHONE.............................772 882-4197
EMP: 7 EST: 2018
SALES (est): 213.3K **Privately Held**
WEB: www.woodworkxunlimited.com
SIC: 2434 Wood kitchen cabinets

(G-4557)
WORLD INDUSTRIAL EQUIPMENT INC
Also Called: Stamm Manufacturing
4850 Orange Ave (34947-3413)
PHONE.............................772 461-6056
John G Stamm, *President*
Raul Cepero, *Sales Staff*
Tom Johns, *Admin Sec*
◆ EMP: 25 EST: 1994
SQ FT: 23,859
SALES (est): 5.4MM **Privately Held**
WEB: www.stamm-mfg.com
SIC: 3713 3537 Truck bodies & parts; industrial trucks & tractors

Fort Walton Beach
Okaloosa County

(G-4558)
ABLE RAILING & WELDING LLC
170 Park Dr (32548-3517)
PHONE.............................850 243-5444
EMP: 7

SALES (est): 97.6K **Privately Held**
SIC: 7692 Welding Repair

(G-4559)
ANCHOR SCREEN PRINTING LLC
808 South Dr (32547-2253)
PHONE.............................850 243-4200
April Wade, *Principal*
EMP: 6 EST: 2012
SALES (est): 764.2K **Privately Held**
WEB: www.anchorscreenprint.com
SIC: 2759 Screen printing

(G-4560)
AND SERVICES
410 Racetrack Rd Ne (32547-2504)
PHONE.............................850 805-6455
EMP: 7 EST: 2020
SALES (est): 264.4K **Privately Held**
WEB: www.andservices.com
SIC: 2842 1711 Specialty cleaning, polishes & sanitation goods; plumbing, heating, air-conditioning contractors

(G-4561)
APPAREL EXPRESSIONS LLC
209b Lang Rd (32547-3120)
P.O. Box 487 (32549-0487)
PHONE.............................850 314-0100
Bret Berglund, *General Mgr*
Sarah J Berglund,
Bret D Berglund,
EMP: 7 EST: 2005
SQ FT: 2,000
SALES (est): 976.2K **Privately Held**
WEB: www.promoaxp.com
SIC: 2395 Embroidery products, except schiffli machine; embroidery & art needlework

(G-4562)
ARMSTRONGS PRTG & GRAPHICS INC (PA)
30 Walter Martin Rd Ne (32548-4960)
PHONE.............................850 243-6923
Fostine Armstrong, *President*
Bill Kirby, *General Mgr*
Jim Armstrong, *Vice Pres*
EMP: 7 EST: 1984
SALES (est): 607.3K **Privately Held**
WEB: www.armstrongsprint.com
SIC: 2752 2791 2789 Commercial printing, offset; typesetting; bookbinding & related work

(G-4563)
BAE SYSTEMS TECH SLTONS SVCS I
557 Mary Esther Cut Off N (32548-4038)
PHONE.............................850 664-6070
Eric Terry, *Superintendent*
Ronald Desharnais, *Principal*
Dennis Morrissette, *Principal*
Devin Runyan, *Business Mgr*
Stephanie Chandonnet, *COO*
EMP: 35
SALES (corp-wide): 26B **Privately Held**
SIC: 3812 Search & navigation equipment
HQ: Bae Systems Technology Solutions & Services Inc.
520 Gaither Rd
Rockville MD 20850
703 847-5820

(G-4564)
BAE SYSTEMS TECH SLTONS SVCS I
715 Hollywood Blvd Nw (32548-3863)
PHONE.............................850 244-6433
Brad West, *Sales Mgr*
Tanya Whitfield, *Sales Mgr*
Ed Pitkus, *Technical Staff*
Kristin Soto, *Analyst*
EMP: 76
SALES (corp-wide): 26B **Privately Held**
SIC: 3812 Search & navigation equipment
HQ: Bae Systems Technology Solutions & Services Inc.
520 Gaither Rd
Rockville MD 20850
703 847-5820

2022 Harris Florida
Manufacturers Directory

▲ = Import ▼=Export
◆ =Import/Export

(G-4565)
BAE SYSTEMS TECH SLTONS SVCS I
70 Ready Ave Nw (32548-3857)
PHONE..................................850 344-0832
Austin Stevens, *Branch Mgr*
EMP: 7
SALES (corp-wide): 26B **Privately Held**
SIC: 3812 Search & navigation equipment
HQ: Bae Systems Technology Solutions & Services Inc.
   520 Gaither Rd
   Rockville MD 20850
   703 847-5820

(G-4566)
BOEING
20 Hill Ave Nw (32548-3858)
PHONE..................................850 301-6635
Randall Calloway, *Production*
Kevin Swearingen, *Engineer*
Daniel Tompkins, *Engineer*
Phillip Conrey, *Accountant*
Vicki Lanter, *Finance*
EMP: 35 **EST:** 2016
SALES (est): 1.4MM **Privately Held**
WEB: www.boeing.com
SIC: 3721 Aircraft

(G-4567)
BOTE BOARDS
630 Anchors St Nw (32548-3861)
PHONE..................................850 855-4046
EMP: 7 **EST:** 2018
SALES (est): 249.8K **Privately Held**
WEB: www.boteboard.com
SIC: 3949 Surfboards

(G-4568)
BRAZILIAN BRICKPAVERS INC
200 Racetrack Rd Ne (32547-1805)
PHONE..................................850 699-7833
Bruno D Suares, *Principal*
EMP: 8 **EST:** 2008
SALES (est): 296.5K **Privately Held**
WEB: www.brazilianbrickpavers.net
SIC: 3531 Pavers

(G-4569)
CANVAS SPC CSTM MAR FBRCTION I
Also Called: Canvas Specialties & Uphl
18 Hollywood Blvd Sw (32548-4848)
PHONE..................................850 664-6200
EMP: 6 **EST:** 1990
SALES (est): 418.4K **Privately Held**
WEB: www.canvas-specialties.com
SIC: 2394 2392 Canvas & related products; canvas boat seats; sails: made from purchased materials; boat cushions

(G-4570)
COBHAM MISSION SYSTEM CORP
706 Anchors St Nw (32548-3867)
PHONE..................................850 226-6717
Dennis Shindel, *Principal*
EMP: 8 **EST:** 2011
SALES (est): 748.2K **Privately Held**
WEB: www.cobham.com
SIC: 3812 Search & navigation equipment

(G-4571)
COTERIE CARE INC
701 Ferguson Dr (32547-2025)
PHONE..................................850 325-0422
Chase Newton, *Chairman*
Betty Allen, *Manager*
Cierra Allen, *Manager*
EMP: 14 **EST:** 2018
SALES (est): 1MM **Privately Held**
SIC: 2833 Medicinals & botanicals

(G-4572)
CRANE ELECTRONICS INC
84 Hill Ave Nw (32548-3858)
PHONE..................................850 244-0043
Carol Cassidy, *Principal*
Charles Jewett, *Business Mgr*
Glynis Richardson, *Buyer*
Bethany Grace, *Purchasing*
Keith Colvard, *QC Mgr*
EMP: 99

SALES (corp-wide): 3.1B **Privately Held**
WEB: www.craneae.com
SIC: 3728 Aircraft parts & equipment
HQ: Crane Electronics, Inc.
   16700 13th Ave W
   Lynnwood WA 98037
   425 882-3100

(G-4573)
DRS ADVANCED ISR LLC
654 Anchors St Nw Ste 1 (32548-3861)
PHONE..................................850 226-4888
Chris Bloomfield, *Principal*
Korey Bales, *Principal*
Dana Mortensen, *Manager*
EMP: 11
SALES (corp-wide): 16B **Privately Held**
WEB: www.leonardodrs.com
SIC: 3812 Search & navigation equipment
HQ: Drs Icas, Llc
   2601 Mssion Pt Blvd Ste 2
   Beavercreek OH 45431

(G-4574)
DRS C3 SYSTEMS INC
645 Anchors St Nw (32548-3803)
PHONE..................................850 302-3909
Alan Dietrich, *President*
Nikhil Junankar, *Network Enginr*
EMP: 24 **EST:** 1966
SALES (est): 487.6K **Privately Held**
WEB: www.leonardodrs.com
SIC: 3812 Search & navigation equipment

(G-4575)
DRS CONSOLIDATED CONTROLS
645 Anchors St Nw (32548-3803)
PHONE..................................850 302-3000
William Lynn III, *CEO*
Wade Havlat, *Engineer*
EMP: 19 **EST:** 2010
SALES (est): 2.6MM **Privately Held**
WEB: www.leonardodrs.com
SIC: 3812 Search & navigation equipment

(G-4576)
DRS LEONARDO INC
645 Anchors St Nw (32548-3803)
PHONE..................................850 302-3000
William J Lynn III, *Branch Mgr*
EMP: 106
SALES (corp-wide): 16B **Privately Held**
WEB: www.leonardodrs.com
SIC: 3812 Search & navigation equipment
HQ: Leonardo Drs, Inc.
   2345 Crystal Dr Ste 1000
   Arlington VA 22202
   703 416-8000

(G-4577)
DRS LEONARDO INC
640 Lovejoy Rd Nw (32548-3832)
PHONE..................................850 302-3514
EMP: 53
SALES (corp-wide): 16B **Privately Held**
WEB: www.leonardodrs.com
SIC: 3812 Search & navigation equipment
HQ: Leonardo Drs, Inc.
   2345 Crystal Dr Ste 1000
   Arlington VA 22202
   703 416-8000

(G-4578)
DRS TRAINING CTRL SYSTEMS LLC (DH)
Also Called: Drs Technologies
645 Anchors St Nw (32548-3803)
PHONE..................................850 302-3000
William J Lynn III, *CEO*
Edwin R Epstein, *President*
Jim Scott, *President*
Robert Viviano, *President*
Larry Azelle, *General Mgr*
EMP: 50 **EST:** 1957
SQ FT: 72,000
SALES (est): 100.2MM
SALES (corp-wide): 16B **Privately Held**
WEB: www.leonardodrs.com
SIC: 3812 8713 Radar systems & equipment;
HQ: Leonardo Drs, Inc.
   2345 Crystal Dr Ste 1000
   Arlington VA 22202
   703 416-8000

(G-4579)
E BENTON GRIMSLEY INC
909 Mar Walt Dr (32547-6635)
PHONE..................................850 863-4064
E Benton Grimsley, *Principal*
EMP: 7 **EST:** 2010
SALES (est): 68.7K **Privately Held**
SIC: 3999 Manufacturing industries

(G-4580)
EMERALD COAST COATINGS LLC
705 Anchors St Nw (32548-3868)
PHONE..................................850 424-5244
Kevin Harvey, *President*
EMP: 10 **EST:** 2017
SALES (est): 530.9K **Privately Held**
WEB: www.emeraldcoastcoatings.com
SIC: 3479 Metal coating & allied service

(G-4581)
EMERGENCY STANDBY POWER LLC
Also Called: John Deere Authorized Dealer
17 Duval St (32547-2478)
PHONE..................................850 259-2304
Jennifer Diener, *Office Mgr*
Charles R Jacopetti,
Barbara Jacopetti,
EMP: 9 **EST:** 2007
SALES (est): 2.4MM **Privately Held**
WEB: www.espgenerators.com
SIC: 3621 5082 Generators & sets, electric; construction & mining machinery

(G-4582)
EXPLOTRAIN LLC
26 Eglin Pkwy Se Ste 2 (32548-5474)
PHONE..................................850 862-5344
Dean Preston, *President*
EMP: 7 **EST:** 1998
SALES (est): 1MM **Privately Held**
WEB: www.explotrain.com
SIC: 3699 Electrical equipment & supplies

(G-4583)
FORT WALTON CONCRETE CO
Also Called: Crestview Ready Mix
26 Industrial St Nw (32548-4814)
P.O. Box 655 (32549-0655)
PHONE..................................850 243-8114
James E Campbell, *President*
Tim Campbell, *Vice Pres*
EMP: 19 **EST:** 1975
SQ FT: 1,500
SALES (est): 1.2MM **Privately Held**
WEB: fort-walton-concrete-fwb-fl.business.site
SIC: 3273 Ready-mixed concrete

(G-4584)
FORT WALTON MACHINING INC
635 Anchors St Nw (32548-3803)
PHONE..................................800 223-0881
EMP: 28
SALES (corp-wide): 18MM **Privately Held**
WEB: www.fwmachining.com
SIC: 3599 Machine shop, jobbing & repair
PA: Fort Walton Machining, Inc.
   43 Jet Dr Nw
   Fort Walton Beach FL 32548
   850 244-9095

(G-4585)
FORT WALTON MACHINING INC (PA)
43 Jet Dr Nw (32548-4807)
PHONE..................................850 244-9095
Ken Hill, *CEO*
Jan McDonald, *Chairman*
Timothy M McDonald, *Corp Secy*
Chad Weisenburger, *Prdtn Mgr*
Douglas Huber, *Materials Mgr*
EMP: 103 **EST:** 1987
SQ FT: 105,000
SALES (est): 18MM **Privately Held**
WEB: www.fwmachining.com
SIC: 3599 Machine shop, jobbing & repair

(G-4586)
GLOBAL SUPPLY SOLUTIONS LLC
Also Called: Gss Gear
1988 Lewis Turner Blvd # 1 (32547-5262)
PHONE..................................757 227-6757
Emily Whittaker, *Branch Mgr*
EMP: 17
SALES (corp-wide): 13.8MM **Privately Held**
WEB: www.gssgear.com
SIC: 3812 Defense systems & equipment
PA: Global Supply Solutions, Llc
   1988 Lewis Turner Blvd # 1
   Fort Walton Beach FL 32547
   757 227-6757

(G-4587)
GRAHAMS WELDING FABRICATION
622 Fairway Ave Ne (32547-1708)
PHONE..................................850 865-0899
Charles F Graham, *President*
Teresa Graham, *Corp Secy*
EMP: 6 **EST:** 1997
SQ FT: 3,000
SALES (est): 333.1K **Privately Held**
SIC: 7692 Welding repair

(G-4588)
GREVAN ARTISTIC VENTURES INC (PA)
Also Called: Artistic Stoneworks
622 Lovejoy Rd Nw (32548-7005)
PHONE..................................850 243-8111
Hanley P Gramillion Jr, *President*
Joel Vanderlick, *Vice Pres*
EMP: 17 **EST:** 2014
SQ FT: 15,000
SALES (est): 1.8MM **Privately Held**
WEB: www.artisticstoneworksinc.com
SIC: 3281 5211 Granite, cut & shaped; cabinets, kitchen

(G-4589)
GS GELATO AND DESSERTS INC
1785 Fim Blvd (32547-1152)
PHONE..................................850 243-5455
Guido Tremolini, *President*
Michelle Popp, *Business Mgr*
Simona Faroni, *Vice Pres*
Maria Pizarro, *QC Mgr*
Cameron Lewis, *Research*
▲ **EMP:** 50 **EST:** 1998
SALES (est): 17.8MM **Privately Held**
WEB: www.gsgelato.com
SIC: 2024 Ice cream & frozen desserts

(G-4590)
GULF COAST BUSINESS WORLD INC
3 Racetrack Rd Nw (32547-1601)
PHONE..................................850 864-1511
Richard Moore, *President*
EMP: 10 **EST:** 1988
SQ FT: 8,800
SALES (est): 550K **Privately Held**
SIC: 2752 5943 3993 2791 Commercial printing, offset; office forms & supplies; signs & advertising specialties; typesetting; bookbinding & related work

(G-4591)
GULF SOUTH DISTRIBUTORS INC
Also Called: Kitchen Design Center
707 Anchors St Nw (32548-3868)
PHONE..................................850 244-1522
Richard V Nivens, *President*
EMP: 15 **EST:** 1980
SQ FT: 12,000
SALES (est): 1MM **Privately Held**
WEB: www.gulfsouthkitchendesign.com
SIC: 2599 2542 2511 Cabinets, factory; partitions & fixtures, except wood; wood household furniture

(G-4592)
HOME ROBOT LLC
53 Ferry Rd Ne (32548-5170)
PHONE..................................850 826-8720
Maxim Zlobin, *Manager*
EMP: 7 **EST:** 2017

SALES (est): 67.6K **Privately Held**
WEB: www.hobot.us
SIC: 3651 7389 Household audio & video equipment;

(G-4593)
JOHN R CAITO
Also Called: Delta Industries
91 Ready Ave Nw (32548-3848)
PHONE.................................850 612-0179
John R Caito, *Owner*
EMP: 8 **EST:** 2003
SALES (est): 158.9K **Privately Held**
SIC: 3446 5999 Stairs, staircases, stair treads: prefabricated metal; awnings

(G-4594)
KITCHEN & BATH CENTER INC (PA)
Also Called: Marble Works Kit & Bath Ctr
20 Ready Ave Nw (32548-3857)
PHONE.................................850 244-3996
Toll Free:..............................888　-
Ron Fisher, *President*
Ann Hanna, *General Mgr*
Kara Lunsford, *Project Mgr*
Bridget Talbot, *Project Mgr*
Ruby Bullock, *Office Admin*
EMP: 35 **EST:** 1985
SQ FT: 36,000
SALES (est): 10.6MM **Privately Held**
WEB: www.kitchenandbathcenter.net
SIC: 3272 5211 Art marble, concrete; bathroom fixtures, equipment & supplies; cabinets, kitchen; counter tops

(G-4595)
MAGNA MANUFACTURING INC
Also Called: Loboy
85 Hill Ave Nw (32548-3846)
P.O. Box 279 (32549-0279)
PHONE.................................850 243-1112
Paul D Owens Jr, *President*
Medla Greg, *COO*
Kenny Watkins, *Vice Pres*
Brian Claycomb, *Financial Exec*
Myleto Stewart, *Sales Staff*
◆ **EMP:** 27 **EST:** 1984
SQ FT: 60,000
SALES (est): 6.6MM **Privately Held**
WEB: www.loboy.com
SIC: 3086 Packaging & shipping materials, foamed plastic; ice chests or coolers (portable), foamed plastic

(G-4596)
MICRO SYSTEMS INC (HQ)
35 Hill Ave Nw (32548-3852)
PHONE.................................850 244-2332
Eric M Demarco, *President*
Michael Fink, *Vice Pres*
Stephen Kesegich, *Prdtn Mgr*
Chip Wells, *Purch Dir*
Glen Larmore, *Engineer*
EMP: 135 **EST:** 1976
SQ FT: 19,758
SALES (est): 34.7MM **Publicly Held**
WEB: www.kratosdefense.com
SIC: 3812 3663 3721 3728 Search & navigation equipment; radio & TV communications equipment; aircraft; aircraft parts & equipment; guided missiles & space vehicles; guided missile & space vehicle parts & auxiliary equipment

(G-4597)
MONEY TREE ATM MFG LLC
130 Staff Dr Ne (32548-5051)
P.O. Box 4247 (32549-4247)
PHONE.................................850 244-5543
EMP: 5
SQ FT: 15,000
SALES (est): 803.3K
SALES (corp-wide): 1.7MM **Privately Held**
SIC: 3578 7629 Mfg Calculating Equipment Electrical Repair
PA: Integrated Financial Systems Llc
130 Staff Dr Ne
Fort Walton Beach FL 32548
850 244-5543

(G-4598)
NORTHROP GRUMMAN SYSTEMS CORP
Also Called: TSC
1992 Lewis Turner Blvd (32547-1255)
PHONE.................................850 863-8000
Glenn Pruszinski, *Manager*
EMP: 54 **Publicly Held**
WEB: www.northropgrumman.com
SIC: 3812 8731 7374 Search & navigation equipment; commercial physical research; data processing & preparation
HQ: Northrop Grumman Systems Corporation
2980 Fairview Park Dr
Falls Church VA 22042
703 280-2900

(G-4599)
NORTHWEST FLORIDA DAILY NEWS (DH)
2 Eglin Pkwy Ne (32548-4915)
P.O. Box 2949 (32549-2949)
PHONE.................................850 863-1111
James Hutto, *Sales Engr*
Tracy Conner, *Manager*
Roger Underwood, *Director*
EMP: 26 **EST:** 1999
SALES (est): 4.3MM
SALES (corp-wide): 3.2B **Publicly Held**
WEB: www.nwfdailynews.com
SIC: 2711 Newspapers, publishing & printing
HQ: Gatehouse Media, Llc
175 Sullys Trl Ste 203
Pittsford NY 14534
585 598-0030

(G-4600)
PALANJIAN ENTERPRISES INC
Also Called: Bon Appetit French Bakery
420 Mary Esther Cut Off N (32548-4023)
PHONE.................................850 244-2848
Vasken Palanjian, *President*
Janice Palanjian, *Corp Secy*
Arous Palanjian, *Vice Pres*
EMP: 18 **EST:** 1983
SQ FT: 3,751
SALES (est): 1MM **Privately Held**
SIC: 2051 Bakery: wholesale or wholesale/retail combined

(G-4601)
PANAMA CITY NEWS HERALD
Also Called: Northwest Florida Daily News
2 Eglin Pkwy Ne (32548-4915)
P.O. Box 2949 (32549-2949)
PHONE.................................850 863-1111
Tom Conner, *Principal*
EMP: 475
SQ FT: 36,923
SALES (corp-wide): 3.2B **Publicly Held**
WEB: www.newsherald.com
SIC: 2711 Newspapers, publishing & printing
HQ: Panama City News Herald
501 W 11th St
Panama City FL 32401
850 747-5000

(G-4602)
PITTS FABRICATION LLC
617 James Lee Rd (32547-2319)
PHONE.................................850 259-4548
Joseph M Pitts Sr, *Manager*
EMP: 7 **EST:** 2018
SALES (est): 501.3K **Privately Held**
SIC: 3499 Fabricated metal products

(G-4603)
PROBOTIX
628 Lovejoy Rd Nw Unit 3e (32548-7023)
PHONE.................................844 472-9262
EMP: 7 **EST:** 2017
SALES (est): 333.2K **Privately Held**
SIC: 3699 Electrical equipment & supplies

(G-4604)
R4 INTEGRATION INC
45 Beal Pkwy Ne (32548-4818)
PHONE.................................850 226-6913
Vishnu Nathu, *CEO*
John Parsley, *President*
David Felker, *Engineer*
Tommy Ruiz, *Technical Staff*

EMP: 25 **EST:** 2008
SALES (est): 2.9MM **Privately Held**
WEB: www.r4-integration.com
SIC: 3721 3728 7373 8711 Aircraft; aircraft parts & equipment; systems engineering, computer related; aviation &/or aeronautical engineering

(G-4605)
RMC EWELL INC
1787 F I M Rd (32547)
PHONE.................................850 863-5040
EMP: 8
SALES (corp-wide): 15.4B **Privately Held**
SIC: 3273 3272 Manufactures Ready Mix Concrete And Concrete Pipe
HQ: Ewell Rmc Inc
801 Mccue Rd
Lakeland FL
863 688-5787

(G-4606)
ROCKY BAYOU ENTERPRISES INC
Also Called: Breeze Boat Lifts
630 Lovejoy Rd Nw (32548-3832)
P.O. Box 226, Niceville (32588-0226)
PHONE.................................850 244-4567
Gregory Teman, *Principal*
Kathleen Teman, *Officer*
EMP: 8 **EST:** 1991
SALES (est): 984K **Privately Held**
SIC: 3536 5551 Boat lifts; marine supplies

(G-4607)
ROGUE INDUSTRIES LLC
217 Miracle Strip Pkwy Se (32548-5819)
PHONE.................................850 797-9228
EMP: 8 **EST:** 2018
SALES (est): 1MM **Privately Held**
SIC: 3999 Manufacturing industries

(G-4608)
ROLIN INDUSTRIES INC
94 Ready Ave Nw Unit A1 (32548-3523)
P.O. Box 1017 (32549-1017)
PHONE.................................850 654-1704
Linda K Ross, *President*
EMP: 9 **EST:** 1991
SQ FT: 5,000
SALES (est): 1MM **Privately Held**
WEB: www.rolinindustries.com
SIC: 2399 3728 Automotive covers, except seat & tire covers; research & dev by manuf., aircraft parts & auxiliary equip

(G-4609)
SERIGRAPHIA INC
223 Troy St Ne (32548-4483)
PHONE.................................850 243-9743
Greg Keith, *President*
Wendy Aplin, *Office Mgr*
EMP: 15 **EST:** 1979
SQ FT: 23,000
SALES (est): 432.7K **Privately Held**
WEB: www.serigraphia.com
SIC: 2396 Screen printing on fabric articles

(G-4610)
SUN COAST CONVERTERS INC
Also Called: Suncoast Diesel
631 Anchors St Nw (32548-3803)
PHONE.................................850 864-2361
Ronald W Wolverton, *President*
Joan M Webb, *President*
Joe F Penn Jr, *Vice Pres*
Luther Taylor, *Manager*
Ron Wolverton, *Administration*
▲ **EMP:** 8 **EST:** 1989
SALES (est): 1.5MM **Privately Held**
WEB: www.suncoastdiesel.com
SIC: 3714 Rebuilding engines & transmissions, factory basis

(G-4611)
TCS ELECTRICAL CO
302 Sudduth Cir Ne (32548-5125)
PHONE.................................844 827-1040
Thomas Alexander, *President*
EMP: 13 **EST:** 2016
SALES (est): 3MM **Privately Held**
WEB: www.tcselectrical.com
SIC: 3825 Electrical power measuring equipment

(G-4612)
TECHNICAL SERVICE LABS INC
Also Called: Tsl-Reico
95 Ready Ave Nw (32548-3800)
PHONE.................................850 243-3722
Andrew J Corbin, *President*
Julia G Gordon, *Corp Secy*
Petropoulos Peter, *Director*
EMP: 28 **EST:** 1971
SQ FT: 12,000
SALES (est): 1.2MM **Privately Held**
WEB: www.tslinc.com
SIC: 3679 Electronic circuits

(G-4613)
TECHNOLOGIES DRS UNMANNED INC
645 Anchors St Nw (32548-3803)
PHONE.................................850 302-3909
Mark Newman, *President*
Joe Hart, *Vice Pres*
Nina L Dunn, *Admin Sec*
EMP: 76 **EST:** 1998
SQ FT: 191,000
SALES (est): 6.7MM
SALES (corp-wide): 16B **Privately Held**
WEB: www.leonardodrs.com
SIC: 3812 Search & navigation equipment
HQ: Leonardo Drs, Inc.
2345 Crystal Dr Ste 1000
Arlington VA 22202
703 416-8000

(G-4614)
UTILIS USA LLC
36 Tupelo Ave Se (32548-5435)
PHONE.................................850 226-7043
Thomas Eggers,
Danny Jura,
EMP: 6 **EST:** 2006
SQ FT: 13,000
SALES (est): 574.5K **Privately Held**
WEB: www.uts-systems.com
SIC: 2394 Canvas & related products

(G-4615)
UTS SYSTEMS LLC
36 Tupelo Ave Se Ste A (32548-5435)
PHONE.................................850 226-4301
Aaron Williams, *Production*
Thomas Eggers,
EMP: 7 **EST:** 2014
SALES (est): 2.1MM **Privately Held**
WEB: www.uts-systems.com
SIC: 2394 7373 8733 3721 Tents: made from purchased materials; computer integrated systems design; noncommercial research organizations; biotechnical research, noncommercial; research & development on aircraft by the manufacturer; commercial physical research

(G-4616)
VER-VAL ENTERPRISES INC
Also Called: Vve
646 Anchors St Nw Ste 8 (32548-7002)
P.O. Box 4550 (32549-4550)
PHONE.................................850 244-7931
Nathaniel Smith Jr, *President*
Rufus Willis, *General Mgr*
Jannie V Smith, *Corp Secy*
Leroy H Harris, *Opers Mgr*
▲ **EMP:** 10 **EST:** 1979
SQ FT: 10,000
SALES (est): 1.9MM **Privately Held**
WEB: www.verval.biz
SIC: 3444 3429 7699 3535 Sheet metal specialties, not stamped; aircraft hardware; aircraft & heavy equipment repair services; conveyors & conveying equipment; aircraft parts & equipment; trailers & trailer equipment

(G-4617)
WALIN TOOLS LLC
642a Anchors St Nw (32548-3861)
PHONE.................................850 226-8632
Michael Neau, *Manager*
Linda Swadling,
EMP: 6 **EST:** 2008
SALES (est): 498.9K **Privately Held**
WEB: www.walintools.com
SIC: 3541 Machine tools, metal cutting type

Fort White
Columbia County

(G-4618)
ADVENT GLASS WORKS INC
242 Sw George Gln (32038-8280)
P.O. Box 174 (32038-0174)
PHONE.................................386 497-2050
EMP: 5 **EST:** 1974
SALES: 350K **Privately Held**
SIC: 3231 Mfg Products-Purchased Glass

(G-4619)
CRACKER MACHINING INC
340 Sw Murdock Ct (32038-3232)
PHONE.................................386 497-1335
Frederick M Beaumont, *President*
EMP: 7 **EST:** 2005
SALES (est): 135.6K **Privately Held**
SIC: 3599 Machine shop, jobbing & repair

(G-4620)
ENGEDI SPECIALITIES INC
429 Sw Greenwood Ter (32038-8855)
PHONE.................................386 497-1010
EMP: 5
SALES (est): 559.2K **Privately Held**
SIC: 3353 Mfg Aluminum Sheet/Foil

Freeport
Walton County

(G-4621)
ARSENAL DEMOCRACY LLC
48 Commerce Ln Ste 7 (32439-4557)
PHONE.................................850 296-2122
James P Pechi, *Mng Member*
EMP: 10 **EST:** 2013
SALES (est): 223.2K **Privately Held**
WEB: www.arsenaldemocracy.us
SIC: 3484 Machine guns & grenade
launchers; guns (firearms) or gun parts,
30 mm. & below

(G-4622)
FLAMINGO PAVERS INC
289 Tropical Way (32439-4789)
PHONE.................................850 974-0094
Alberto M Soares Jr, *President*
EMP: 16 **EST:** 2005
SALES (est): 864.8K **Privately Held**
SIC: 2951 Asphalt paving mixtures &
blocks

(G-4623)
FREEPORT TRUSS COMPANY INC
16676 Us Highway 331 S (32439-4101)
PHONE.................................850 835-4541
Keven O Logan, *President*
A O Logan, *Vice Pres*
EMP: 9 **EST:** 1984
SQ FT: 1,600
SALES (est): 208.3K **Privately Held**
SIC: 2439 Trusses, wooden roof; trusses,
except roof: laminated lumber

(G-4624)
G & S BOATS INC
143 Yacht Dr (32439-3508)
PHONE.................................850 835-7700
Curtis Gentry, *President*
Steve Sauer, *Vice Pres*
Marcy Graves, *Manager*
EMP: 10 **EST:** 1973
SQ FT: 11,999
SALES (est): 679.6K **Privately Held**
WEB: www.gandsboats.com
SIC: 3732 5551 Yachts, building & repair-
ing; boat dealers

(G-4625)
GREEN AIR GROUP LLC
Also Called: Green Air Controls
902 State Highway 20 E # 104
(32439-3912)
PHONE.................................850 608-3065
Jonathan Michael Green, *Principal*
EMP: 60 **EST:** 2015

SALES (est): 7.9MM **Privately Held**
WEB: www.greenairgroup.com
SIC: 3585 Refrigeration & heating equip-
ment

(G-4626)
GULFSTREAM SHIPBUILDING LLC
116 Shipyard Rd (32439-4091)
PHONE.................................850 835-5125
Stuart Reeves, *Mng Member*
EMP: 7 **EST:** 2013
SALES (est): 317.3K **Privately Held**
WEB: www.gulfstreamshipyard.net
SIC: 3731 Shipbuilding & repairing

(G-4627)
HI-TEC LABORATORIES INC
9646 State Highway 20 W (32439-2122)
P.O. Box 7068, Destin (32540-7068)
PHONE.................................850 835-6822
John J Magee, *President*
EMP: 44 **EST:** 1993
SQ FT: 10,000
SALES (est): 2.4MM **Privately Held**
SIC: 2819 5169 Industrial inorganic chem-
icals; chemicals & allied products

(G-4628)
PROLINE CHEMICAL & PLASTICS LL
9646 State Highway 20 W (32439-2122)
PHONE.................................850 835-6822
EMP: 9 **EST:** 2017
SALES (est): 731.9K **Privately Held**
SIC: 2899 Chemical preparations

(G-4629)
SEQUEL INDUSTRIES INC
360 Juniper Dr (32439-6726)
PHONE.................................850 517-6088
Daniel Cassidy, *Branch Mgr*
EMP: 11
SALES (corp-wide): 39.6K **Privately Held**
SIC: 3999 Atomizers, toiletry
PA: Sequel Industries Inc.
2 Marina Cove Dr
Niceville FL

(G-4630)
SOUTHLAND SERVICES LLC
4828 State Highway 20 E (32439-6038)
P.O. Box 670 (32439-0670)
PHONE.................................850 393-2444
Karen Miller, *Partner*
Herbert L Miller Jr,
EMP: 5 **EST:** 2008
SALES (est): 409K **Privately Held**
SIC: 3531 Construction machinery

(G-4631)
VERONICAS HEALTH CRUNCH LLC
88 Fanny Ann Way (32439-7607)
PHONE.................................352 409-1124
Veronica L Geist, *Principal*
Veronica Geist, *Mng Member*
EMP: 9 **EST:** 2011
SALES (est): 278.3K **Privately Held**
WEB: www.veronicashealthcrunch.com
SIC: 2068 Salted & roasted nuts & seeds

(G-4632)
WOODWARDS CABINETS INC
Also Called: Woodwards Custom Cabinets
17921 Us Highway 331 S (32439-9810)
PHONE.................................850 835-0071
Scott Woodward, *Owner*
EMP: 6 **EST:** 1988
SQ FT: 3,000
SALES (est): 505.6K **Privately Held**
WEB: www.woodwardcabinetsinc.com
SIC: 2434 Wood kitchen cabinets

Frostproof
Polk County

(G-4633)
BEN HILL GRIFFIN INC (PA)
Also Called: GRIFFIN FERTILIZER CO
700 S Scenic Hwy Fl 33843 (33843-2443)
P.O. Box 127 (33843-0127)
PHONE.................................863 635-2281

Ben Hill Griffin III, *Ch of Bd*
Ben Hill Griffin IV, *President*
Eugene Mooney, *Exec VP*
Mike Roberts, *Vice Pres*
Steve Moore, *Plant Mgr*
▲ **EMP:** 40 **EST:** 1943
SQ FT: 100,000
SALES (est): 71MM **Privately Held**
WEB: www.griffinfertilizer.com
SIC: 2875 0174 2033 Fertilizers, mixing
only; citrus fruits; fruits: packaged in cans,
jars, etc.

(G-4634)
BEN HILL GRIFFIN INC
Griffin Fertilizer Co
72 North Ave (33843-2527)
P.O. Box 188 (33843-0188)
PHONE.................................863 635-2281
Stuart Hurst, *CFO*
Jesse Wooten, *Manager*
EMP: 100
SQ FT: 43,156
SALES (corp-wide): 71MM **Privately Held**
WEB: www.griffinfertilizer.com
SIC: 2875 2879 2873 Fertilizers, mixing
only; agricultural chemicals; nitrogenous
fertilizers
PA: Ben Hill Griffin, Inc.
700 S Scenic Hwy Fl 33843
Frostproof FL 33843
863 635-2281

(G-4635)
COOK MANUFACTURING GROUP INC
100 E 7th St (33843)
P.O. Box 1175 (33843-1175)
PHONE.................................863 546-6183
Charles Cook, *President*
Vicki Cook, *Vice Pres*
Seth W Turlington, *Vice Pres*
Keith A Cremerius, *Project Engr*
Joe Hale, *Senior Engr*
◆ **EMP:** 15 **EST:** 1986
SALES (est): 4.7MM **Privately Held**
WEB: www.cookmanufacturing.com
SIC: 3585 Evaporative condensers, heat
transfer equipment

(G-4636)
CORNELIUS WELDING INC
Also Called: Cwi Industrial Services
221 N Scenic Hwy (33843-2119)
P.O. Box 1104 (33843-1104)
PHONE.................................863 635-3668
Donald L Cornelius, *President*
EMP: 18 **EST:** 1997
SQ FT: 2,700
SALES (est): 2MM **Privately Held**
WEB: www.cwi-industrial.com
SIC: 7692 Welding repair

(G-4637)
D C INC PRTBLE WLDG FBRICATION
3971 Mammoth Grove Rd (33843)
PHONE.................................863 533-4483
Don Dumire, *President*
Charlotte Dumire, *Vice Pres*
EMP: 6 **EST:** 1996
SQ FT: 10,000
SALES (est): 794.8K **Privately Held**
WEB: www.dcportablewelding.com
SIC: 3444 1799 Sheet metalwork; welding
on site

(G-4638)
LEMON-X CORPORATION
Also Called: Bevolution Group
500 S Lake Reedy Blvd (33843-2340)
PHONE.................................863 635-8400
James Grassi, *Ch of Bd*
Sonia Grassi, *Corp Secy*
Robert Londono, *Plant Mgr*
Carl Szypula, *Plant Mgr*
Rachel Spradley, *Production*
◆ **EMP:** 7 **EST:** 1972
SALES (est): 4.4MM **Privately Held**
WEB: www.bevolutiongroup.com
SIC: 2087 Cocktail mixes, nonalcoholic

(G-4639)
NUCOR STEEL FLORIDA INC
22 Nucor Dr (33843)
PHONE.................................863 546-5800
David A Sumoski, *President*
Tomas A Miller, *Vice Pres*
Brian L Barbery, *Treasurer*
Rae A Eagle, *Admin Sec*
EMP: 5 **EST:** 2018
SALES (est): 6MM
SALES (corp-wide): 36.4B **Publicly Held**
WEB: www.nucor.com
SIC: 3312 Blast furnaces & steel mills
PA: Nucor Corporation
1915 Rexford Rd Ste 400
Charlotte NC 28211
704 366-7000

(G-4640)
QUALITY PETROLEUM CORP
301 Hwy 630 E (33843-1739)
PHONE.................................863 635-6708
Shane Weeks, *Owner*
EMP: 7 **EST:** 2011
SALES (est): 158.9K **Privately Held**
WEB: qualitypetroleum.tripod.com
SIC: 2911 Petroleum refining

Fruitland Park
Lake County

(G-4641)
HOME-ART CORPORATION
2408 Us Highway 441/27 (34731-2128)
P.O. Box 637 (34731-0637)
PHONE.................................352 326-3337
Gregory L Kimes, *President*
Jeffrey L Myers, *Corp Secy*
EMP: 20 **EST:** 1982
SQ FT: 12,790
SALES (est): 1MM **Privately Held**
WEB: www.homeartcabinets.com
SIC: 2512 2434 Upholstered household
furniture; vanities, bathroom: wood

(G-4642)
SIGN WIZARD
3195 Us Highway 441/27 (34731-4476)
PHONE.................................352 365-6922
Bruce Collett, *Owner*
EMP: 7 **EST:** 2010
SALES (est): 272.2K **Privately Held**
WEB: www.signwizardinc.com
SIC: 3993 Signs & advertising specialties

Gainesville
Alachua County

(G-4643)
352INK CORP
Also Called: Allegra Gainesville
327 Nw 23rd Ave Ste 1-4 (32609-8615)
PHONE.................................352 373-7547
Donald Bailey, *President*
Donald W Bailey, *President*
Karen D Bailey, *Vice Pres*
Karen Bailey, *Vice Pres*
Karen D Bailey, *Vice Pres*
EMP: 5 **EST:** 1984
SQ FT: 3,000
SALES (est): 509.1K **Privately Held**
SIC: 2752 7334 Commercial printing, off-
set; photocopying & duplicating services

(G-4644)
ACTIONABLE QUALITY ASSURANCE
747 Sw 2nd Ave Ste 170 (32601-7160)
PHONE.................................352 562-0005
John King, *COO*
Bruce Perkin, *Consultant*
Yuly Virviescas, *Director*
EMP: 8 **EST:** 2017
SALES (est): 164.5K **Privately Held**
WEB: www.actionableqa.com
SIC: 7372 Prepackaged software

GEOGRAPHIC

(G-4645)
AESTHETIC PRINT & DESIGN INC
2618 Ne 18th Ter (32609-3263)
PHONE.....................352 278-3714
Jonathan M Hamilton, *Director*
EMP: 8 EST: 2005
SALES (est): 270.9K Privately Held
WEB: www.aestheticprint.com
SIC: 2752 Commercial printing, offset

(G-4646)
AGAROSE UNLIMITED INC
707 Nw 13th St (32601-4918)
P.O. Box 817, Alachua (32616-0817)
PHONE.....................800 850-0659
EMP: 5
SALES (est): 350K Privately Held
SIC: 2899 Suppliers Of Multipurpose Molecular Biology Grade Agarose

(G-4647)
AKIRA WOOD INC
619 S Main St Ste A (32601-6700)
PHONE.....................352 375-0691
Hoch Shitama, *President*
Paul Goble, *Project Mgr*
Chip Sawyer, *Design Engr*
Gale Clark, *Treasurer*
Ben Shitama, *Manager*
EMP: 35 EST: 1977
SQ FT: 32,000
SALES (est): 7.3MM Privately Held
WEB: www.akirawood.com
SIC: 2431 Millwork

(G-4648)
ALTA SYSTEMS INC
6825 Nw 18th Dr (32653-1613)
PHONE.....................352 372-2534
Jane Er Nesbit, *President*
Reginald Johnson, *President*
Richard B Nesbit, *Vice Pres*
Alan Chaset, *Project Dir*
Richard Nesbit, *CFO*
▼ EMP: 42 EST: 1983
SQ FT: 14,900
SALES (est): 7.5MM Privately Held
WEB: www.altainc.com
SIC: 2752 2791 Commercial printing, offset; typesetting

(G-4649)
AMERICAN OPTIMAL DECISIONS INC
4014 Sw 98th Ter (32608-4662)
PHONE.....................352 278-2034
Stan Uryasev, *President*
EMP: 7 EST: 2008
SALES (est): 342.1K Privately Held
WEB: www.aorda.com
SIC: 7372 Prepackaged software

(G-4650)
ARGOS
924 S Main St (32601-2025)
PHONE.....................352 376-6491
Matt Carcaba, *President*
EMP: 15 EST: 2015
SALES (est): 1.5MM Privately Held
WEB: www.argos-us.com
SIC: 3273 Ready-mixed concrete

(G-4651)
ARMALASER INC
5200 Nw 43rd St (32606-4484)
PHONE.....................800 680-5020
Mary Lou Price, *Owner*
Richard Hovsepian, *Founder*
EMP: 15 EST: 2016
SALES (est): 1.2MM Privately Held
WEB: www.armalaser.com
SIC: 3949 Sporting & athletic goods

(G-4652)
ASAP SCREEN PRINTING INC
4641 Nw 6th St Ste A (32609-1700)
PHONE.....................352 505-7574
Larry E Watts, *Principal*
Scott Ronn, *Vice Pres*
EMP: 6 EST: 2006
SALES (est): 557.5K Privately Held
WEB: www.screenprintingasap.com
SIC: 2759 Screen printing

(G-4653)
ASCENDANTS PUBLISHING LLC
626 Se 2nd Pl Apt 3 (32601-6876)
PHONE.....................813 391-2745
Vijaya Seixas, *Principal*
EMP: 7 EST: 2016
SALES (est): 41.3K Privately Held
SIC: 2741 Miscellaneous publishing

(G-4654)
ATKINS TECHNICAL INC
6911 Nw 22nd St Ste B (32653-1253)
PHONE.....................860 349-3473
Carol P Wallace, *President*
Carol Duplessis, *Admin Sec*
EMP: 31 EST: 1957
SALES (est): 625K Privately Held
WEB: www.cooper-atkins.com
SIC: 3823 Temperature instruments: industrial process type; humidity instruments, industrial process type

(G-4655)
ATRIS TECHNOLOGY LLC
3417 Nw 97th Blvd Ste 30 (32606-7376)
PHONE.....................352 331-3100
Lon Davis, *CEO*
Michael Simmons, *Accounts Exec*
Dan Roberts, *Info Tech Dir*
Mauricio Goez, *Technology*
Mark Bernard, *Technical Staff*
EMP: 12 EST: 1995
SALES (est): 1.2MM Privately Held
WEB: www.atris.com
SIC: 7372 7371 Application computer software; custom computer programming services

(G-4656)
BALLS ROD & KUSTOM LLC
5118 Nw 24th Dr (32605-6227)
PHONE.....................888 446-2191
Jun A Evangelista, *Principal*
EMP: 7 EST: 2008
SALES (est): 343.8K Privately Held
WEB: www.ballsrodandkustom.com
SIC: 3714 Motor vehicle parts & accessories

(G-4657)
BARR SYSTEMS LLC
4961 Nw 8th Ave Ste B (32605-4775)
PHONE.....................352 491-3100
Anthony Barr,
EMP: 30 EST: 2006
SALES (est): 3.8MM Privately Held
WEB: www.barrsystems.com
SIC: 3429 3695 Cabinet hardware; computer software tape & disks: blank, rigid & floppy

(G-4658)
BATH JUNKIE OF GAINESVILLE
7529 Nw 136th St (32653-2474)
PHONE.....................352 331-3012
Cindy Futral, *CEO*
EMP: 5 EST: 2006
SALES (est): 496.8K Privately Held
SIC: 3087 Custom compound purchased resins

(G-4659)
BEAR ARCHERY INC
4600 Sw 41st Blvd (32608-4999)
PHONE.....................352 376-2327
Walt Glazer, *CEO*
Dan Massimillo, *Production*
Liz Petree, *Production*
Joseph Benjamin, *Purch Mgr*
Annette Paramore, *Buyer*
◆ EMP: 200 EST: 2003
SALES (est): 45.1MM
SALES (corp-wide): 313.6MM Publicly Held
WEB: www.beararchery.com
SIC: 3949 Archery equipment, general
PA: Escalade, Incorporated
   817 Maxwell Ave
   Evansville IN 47711
   812 467-1358

(G-4660)
BIGG WILLS WHEELS LLC
125 Nw 23rd Ave Ste D (32609-8611)
PHONE.....................352 222-6170
William Henderson, *Mng Member*

EMP: 5 EST: 2012
SALES (est): 536.4K Privately Held
WEB: www.bwwcustoms.com
SIC: 3312 Wheels

(G-4661)
BLACK COLLEGE MONTHLY INC
901 Se 18th Ter (32641-9429)
PHONE.....................352 335-5771
Charles Goston, *Founder*
EMP: 7 EST: 1983
SALES (est): 111.6K Privately Held
SIC: 2721 Magazines: publishing & printing

(G-4662)
BLUAZU LLC
101 Se 2nd Pl Ste 201b (32601-6591)
PHONE.....................386 697-3743
Richard Allen, *CEO*
James Davis, *Vice Pres*
Jon Stevens, *Senior Engr*
EMP: 12 EST: 2013
SALES (est): 1.3MM Privately Held
SIC: 3663 Radio & TV communications equipment;

(G-4663)
BUSINESS REPORT OF N CNTRL FL
1314 S Main St (32601-7921)
PHONE.....................352 275-9469
Scott Schroeder, *Principal*
EMP: 7 EST: 2014
SALES (est): 139.3K Privately Held
WEB: www.gainesvillebizreport.com
SIC: 2711 Newspapers, publishing & printing

(G-4664)
CADUCEUS INTERNATIONAL PUBG
100 Sw 75th St Ste 206 (32607-5777)
PHONE.....................866 280-2900
Ryan Fagerberg, *President*
Seigfred Fagerberg, *Vice Pres*
Andrew Huston, *Vice Pres*
Laura Fields, *Controller*
Kristin Polhill, *Accounts Mgr*
EMP: 10 EST: 2004
SALES (est): 1.6MM Privately Held
WEB: www.cipcourses.com
SIC: 2741 7371 Miscellaneous publishing; computer software development & applications

(G-4665)
CAMPUS COMMUNICATIONS INC
Also Called: Independent Florida Alligator
1105 W University Ave (32601-5111)
P.O. Box 14257 (32604-2257)
PHONE.....................352 376-4482
Patricia Carey, *President*
Christopher Timson, *Accounts Exec*
April Rubin, *Manager*
Patricia Cuadra, *Internal Med*
Lily Girton, *Assistant*
EMP: 125 EST: 1906
SQ FT: 16,000
SALES (est): 600.3K Privately Held
WEB: www.alligator.org
SIC: 2711 Newspapers, publishing & printing

(G-4666)
CARBONXT INC
3951 Nw 48th Ter Ste 111 (32606-7229)
PHONE.....................352 378-4950
David Mazyck, *CEO*
Jack Drwiega, *Opers Dir*
Gabrielle Giampietro, *Research*
Lindsey Zachow, *Finance Mgr*
Spencer Martin, *Manager*
EMP: 38 EST: 2009
SALES (est): 9.9MM Privately Held
WEB: www.cglimited.com.au
SIC: 2819 Charcoal (carbon), activated

(G-4667)
CARDINAL SIGNS INC
6342 Nw 18th Dr Ste 1 (32653-1680)
PHONE.....................352 376-8494
Paul Randall, *Principal*
EMP: 7 EST: 2006

SALES (est): 257.9K Privately Held
WEB: www.cardinalsigns.net
SIC: 3993 Signs & advertising specialties

(G-4668)
CEMENT PRECAST PRODUCTS INC
2033 Ne 27th Ave (32609-3379)
PHONE.....................352 372-0953
Michael Harper, *President*
Pat Clark, *Principal*
Jeff Stanford, *Manager*
EMP: 22 EST: 1958
SALES (est): 2.8MM Privately Held
WEB: www.precastfl.com
SIC: 3272 3446 3442 Concrete products, precast; architectural metalwork; metal doors, sash & trim

(G-4669)
CONRAD YELVINGTON DISTRS INC
7605 Nw 13th St (32653-1114)
PHONE.....................352 336-5049
Jeff Wells, *Principal*
EMP: 16
SALES (corp-wide): 109.9MM Privately Held
WEB: www.cydi.com
SIC: 3295 5261 5032 Perlite, aggregate or expanded; sod; sand, construction
PA: Conrad Yelvington Distributors, Inc.
   2328 Bellevue Ave
   Daytona Beach FL 32114
   386 257-5504

(G-4670)
CONVERGENT ENGINEERING INC
100 Sw 75th St Ste 106 (32607-5775)
PHONE.....................352 378-4899
Neil R Euliano, *Director*
Thomas Heimann, *Administration*
EMP: 13 EST: 2004
SALES (est): 2.5MM Privately Held
WEB: www.conveng.com
SIC: 3674 Semiconductors & related devices

(G-4671)
CORDAROYS WHOLESALE INC (PA)
3421 W University Ave (32607-2402)
PHONE.....................352 332-1837
Byron Young, *President*
Jerry Lewicki, *CFO*
Dan Yoder, *Manager*
John Gassert, *Admin Sec*
▲ EMP: 5 EST: 2000
SQ FT: 6,000
SALES (est): 2.5MM Privately Held
WEB: www.cordaroys.com
SIC: 2519 5712 ; furniture stores

(G-4672)
CORPORATE ONE HUNDRED INC
Also Called: Tel Test
605 Nw 53rd Ave Ste A17 (32609-1020)
PHONE.....................352 335-0901
Ezequiel Zetien, *President*
EMP: 26 EST: 1974
SQ FT: 6,000
SALES (est): 4.4MM Privately Held
SIC: 3825 8711 Engine electrical test equipment; engineering services

(G-4673)
CROM CORPORATION (PA)
Also Called: Crom Corporation of America
250 Sw 36th Ter (32607-2889)
PHONE.....................352 372-3436
James D Copley Jr, *President*
Stephen Crawford, *President*
Jeffrey Pomeroy, *General Mgr*
Evan Burton, *Superintendent*
Buddy Williams, *Superintendent*
▼ EMP: 445 EST: 1930
SQ FT: 13,000
SALES (est): 94.8MM Privately Held
WEB: www.cromcorp.com
SIC: 3272 Concrete products

(G-4674)
CYPRESS & GROVE BREWING CO LLC
1001 Nw 4th St (32601-4256)
PHONE...................................352 376-4993
Patrick Burger,
Gary Heil,
Anna Heineman,
EMP: 15 EST: 2014
SALES (est): 640.8K **Privately Held**
WEB: www.cypressandgrove.com
SIC: 2082 Beer (alcoholic beverage)

(G-4675)
DAILY GREEN
436 Se 2nd St (32601-6772)
PHONE...................................352 226-8288
EMP: 7 EST: 2013
SALES (est): 129.2K **Privately Held**
WEB: www.dailygreendowntown.org
SIC: 2711 Newspapers, publishing & printing

(G-4676)
DATAGRID INC
4111 Nw 6th St Ste D (32609-0730)
PHONE...................................352 371-7608
Bo Gustafson, President
EMP: 6 EST: 1999
SQ FT: 3,000
SALES (est): 559.9K **Privately Held**
WEB: www.datagrid-gnss.com
SIC: 3829 Surveying instruments & accessories

(G-4677)
DIGI-NET TECHNOLOGIES INC (PA)
Also Called: Digichat
4420 Nw 36th Ave Ste A (32606-7222)
PHONE...................................352 505-7450
Robert Parker, President
Todd Chase, COO
R Todd Johnson, Vice Pres
EMP: 33 EST: 1999
SQ FT: 8,000
SALES (est): 3.9MM **Privately Held**
WEB: www.digi-net.com
SIC: 7372 4813 Prepackaged software;

(G-4678)
DOCKSIDE AT HORSESHOE BEACH L
6809 Nw 48th Ln (32653-3953)
PHONE...................................352 377-4616
Frank Darabi, Principal
EMP: 8 EST: 2005
SALES (est): 118.9K **Privately Held**
SIC: 3462 Horseshoes

(G-4679)
DOUBLE ENVELOPE CORPORATION
Also Called: BSC Ventures
2500 Ne 39th Ave (32609-2098)
PHONE...................................352 375-0738
Brian Sass, CEO
Fred G Tucker Jr, President
Dalton Miller, Senior VP
William Britts, Vice Pres
Mike Rubyor, Accounts Exec
EMP: 315 EST: 1927
SQ FT: 85,000
SALES (est): 50.2MM
SALES (corp-wide): 126.1MM **Privately Held**
WEB: www.double-envelope.com
SIC: 2677 Envelopes
HQ: Bsc Ventures Llc
7702 Plantation Rd
Roanoke VA 24019
540 362-3311

(G-4680)
DOWNTOWN PROJECTS I LLC
702 Nw 12th Ave (32601-4118)
PHONE...................................352 226-8288
Adam Reinhard, Principal
EMP: 7 EST: 2013
SALES (est): 237.7K **Privately Held**
SIC: 2711 Newspapers: publishing only, not printed on site

(G-4681)
DRAGONFLY GRAPHICS INC
319 Sw 3rd Ave (32601-6561)
PHONE...................................352 375-2144
Joy L Revels, President
Joy Revels, President
EMP: 6 EST: 1978
SQ FT: 2,700
SALES (est): 921K **Privately Held**
WEB: www.dragonflygraphics.com
SIC: 2759 Screen printing

(G-4682)
DRSINGH TECHNOLOGIES INC
1912 Nw 67th Pl (32653-1649)
PHONE...................................352 334-7270
Deepika Singh, President
Rajiv K Singh, President
Sarah Wilson, Business Mgr
Joel Alford, Mfg Staff
Lisa Skeete Tatum,
EMP: 15 EST: 2000
SQ FT: 6,000
SALES (est): 4MM **Privately Held**
SIC: 7372 Business oriented computer software

(G-4683)
EASYDRIFT LLC
13100 Nw 50th Ave (32606-3561)
PHONE...................................352 318-3683
Louis Callard, Manager
▲ EMP: 10 EST: 2009
SALES (est): 601.9K **Privately Held**
SIC: 3999 Education aids, devices & supplies

(G-4684)
EJCO INC
Also Called: Xerographic Copy Center
927 Nw 13th St (32601-4141)
PHONE...................................352 375-0797
Eric Hall, President
Eric Hill, President
Carolyne Salt, Sales Staff
Jamie Ault, Admin Sec
EMP: 6 EST: 2002
SQ FT: 2,100
SALES (est): 857.1K **Privately Held**
WEB: www.xerographicgainesville.com
SIC: 2752 Commercial printing, offset

(G-4685)
ELISA TECHNOLOGIES INC
2501 Nw 66th Ct (32653-1693)
PHONE...................................352 337-3929
Natalie Rosskopf, Vice Pres
Bickford Justin, Treasurer
Mary Davidson, Marketing Staff
Justin Bickford, Director
EMP: 12 EST: 1990
SQ FT: 4,800
SALES (est): 2.2MM **Privately Held**
WEB: www.elisa-tek.com
SIC: 2899 8734 Food contamination testing or screening kits; food testing service

(G-4686)
ETECTRX INC
747 Sw 2nd Ave Ste 365t (32601-7163)
PHONE...................................352 262-8054
Eric Buffkin, CEO
Susan L Baumgartner, Vice Pres
Tony Carnes, Vice Pres
Neil Euliano, Engineer
Judd Sheets, Engineer
EMP: 15 EST: 2017
SALES (est): 1.6MM **Privately Held**
WEB: www.etectrx.com
SIC: 3821 Clinical laboratory instruments, except medical & dental

(G-4687)
EXACTECH INC (HQ)
2320 Nw 66th Ct (32653-1630)
PHONE...................................352 377-1140
William Petty, Ch of Bd
Darin Johnson, President
Ray Langenberg, Managing Dir
Jeffrey R Binder, Chairman
Gary J Miller, Exec VP
▲ EMP: 62 EST: 1985
SQ FT: 206,000
SALES (est): 189.3MM
SALES (corp-wide): 257.5MM **Privately Held**
WEB: www.exac.com
SIC: 3842 Surgical appliances & supplies; implants, surgical; orthopedic appliances; trusses, orthopedic & surgical
PA: Osteon Holdings, Inc.
301 Commerce St Ste 3300
Fort Worth TX 76102
817 871-4000

(G-4688)
EXPLORATION SERVICES LLC
4440 Ne 41st Ter (32609-1684)
PHONE...................................352 505-3578
Craig Bell, Mng Member
Randal Ferrell, Manager
EMP: 6 EST: 2009
SALES (est): 999.4K **Privately Held**
WEB: www.explorationservicesllc.com
SIC: 1382 8999 Oil & gas exploration services; search & rescue service

(G-4689)
FABCO-AIR INC
Also Called: Bennett Company
3716 Ne 49th Ave (32609-1686)
P.O. Box 5159 (32627-5159)
PHONE...................................352 373-3578
William R Schmidt, President
Jeremiah Schmidt, Plant Mgr
Robbie Severance, Prdtn Mgr
Clayton Kight, Maint Spvr
Mike Legrow, QC Mgr
▲ EMP: 95 EST: 1962
SQ FT: 61,000
SALES (est): 23.8MM
SALES (corp-wide): 3.3B **Privately Held**
WEB: www.fabco-air.com
SIC: 3542 3546 3491 Riveting machines; power-driven handtools; automatic regulating & control valves
HQ: Festo Corporation
1377 Motor Pkwy Ste 310
Islandia NY 11749
800 993-3786

(G-4690)
FAGERBERG INDUSTRIES LLC
100 Sw 75th St Ste 206 (32607-5777)
PHONE...................................352 318-2254
Ryan Fagerberg, Principal
EMP: 8 EST: 2009
SALES (est): 241.7K **Privately Held**
WEB: www.cipcourses.com
SIC: 3999 Manufacturing industries

(G-4691)
FAULKNER MEDIA LLC
Also Called: Faulkner Press
3324 W University Ave (32607-2540)
PHONE...................................855 393-3393
Dungan Keith, CEO
EMP: 33
SALES (corp-wide): 539.1K **Privately Held**
WEB: www.faulknerpress.com
SIC: 2741 Miscellaneous publishing
PA: Faulkner Media Llc
623 Sw 27th St
Gainesville FL 32607
352 378-0003

(G-4692)
FLORICAL SYSTEMS INC (PA)
4500 Nw 27th Ave Ste B1 (32606-7042)
PHONE...................................352 372-8326
Jim Moneyhun, President
James Moneyhun, President
Shawn Maynard, Vice Pres
Russ Brannon, Engineer
Jonathan Prescott, Engineer
EMP: 49 EST: 1977
SQ FT: 8,400
SALES (est): 4.8MM **Privately Held**
WEB: www.florical.com
SIC: 3663 Television broadcasting & communications equipment

(G-4693)
FLORIDA NORTH HEARING SOLUTION
Also Called: Miralear
2228 Nw 44th Pl (32605-1761)
PHONE...................................386 466-0902
Greg Leon, Vice Pres
Deep Bhatt, Project Engr
Chad Zandstra, Project Engr
Kelly Urata, Controller
David Acrell, Sr Project Mgr
EMP: 7 EST: 2011
SALES (est): 108.6K **Privately Held**
SIC: 3842 Hearing aids

(G-4694)
FLORIDA PROBE CORPORATION
3700 Nw 91st St Ste C100 (32606-7307)
PHONE...................................352 372-1142
Charles Gibbs, President
John Hirschfeld, Vice Pres
Ron Joos, Vice Pres
Samuel B Low, Vice Pres
Chris Gibbs, Treasurer
EMP: 7 EST: 1987
SQ FT: 1,500
SALES (est): 1MM **Privately Held**
WEB: www.floridaprobe.com
SIC: 3843 5047 Dental tools; dental equipment & supplies

(G-4695)
FOCAL POINT PUBLISHING LLC
4131 Nw 13th St Ste 200 (32609-1863)
PHONE...................................877 469-9530
Olivia Jannis,
EMP: 8 EST: 2018
SALES (est): 200K **Privately Held**
SIC: 2741 Miscellaneous publishing

(G-4696)
FREEMAN PALLETS INC
3530 Se Hawthorne Rd (32641-8858)
PHONE...................................352 328-9326
David Freeman, President
EMP: 8 EST: 2007
SALES (est): 520.6K **Privately Held**
WEB: www.freemanpallets.com
SIC: 2448 Pallets, wood

(G-4697)
GAINESVILLE
8039 Sw 67th Rd (32608-7566)
PHONE...................................352 339-0294
Amy Hackett, Principal
EMP: 8 EST: 2017
SALES (est): 181.5K **Privately Held**
WEB: www.gainesville.com
SIC: 2711 Newspapers, publishing & printing

(G-4698)
GAINESVILLE ICE COMPANY
Also Called: GI
508 Se 11th Ave (32601-8078)
PHONE...................................352 378-2604
Richard Bunch, President
Nancy Bunch, Vice Pres
EMP: 19 EST: 1973
SQ FT: 2,500
SALES (est): 5.3MM **Privately Held**
WEB: www.gainesvilleice.com
SIC: 2097 Manufactured ice

(G-4699)
GAINESVILLE IRON WORKS INC
Also Called: Gainesville Ironworks
2341 Nw 66th Ct (32653-1664)
PHONE...................................352 373-4004
Vicki Lowry, President
Dean Lowry, Corp Secy
EMP: 7 EST: 1984
SQ FT: 7,500
SALES (est): 804.2K **Privately Held**
WEB: www.gainesvilleironworks.com
SIC: 3446 Stairs, staircases, stair treads: prefabricated metal

(G-4700)
GAINESVILLE SUN
2700 Sw 13th St (32608-2015)
PHONE...................................352 374-5000
Mickie Anderson, Editor
Darrell Hartman, Editor
Terry Tramell, Director
EMP: 14 EST: 2010
SALES (est): 1.5MM **Privately Held**
WEB: www.gainesville.com
SIC: 2679 Paper products, converted

(G-4701)
GAINESVILLE SUN PUBLISHING CO (HQ)
2700 Sw 13th St (32608-2015)
PHONE..................................352 378-1411
John Fitzwater, *Publisher*
Mickie Anderson, *Editor*
Alan Festo, *Editor*
Kimberly Kanemoto, *Sales Staff*
EMP: 275 **EST:** 1876
SQ FT: 71,000
SALES (est): 36.9MM
SALES (corp-wide): 278.4MM **Privately Held**
WEB: www.gainesville.com
SIC: 2711 Commercial printing & newspaper publishing combined; newspapers, publishing & printing
PA: Halifax Media Holdings, Llc
　901 6th St
　Daytona Beach FL 32117
　386 681-2404

(G-4702)
GAINESVILLE WLDG & FABRICATION
Also Called: Florida Handrail & Fabrication
2327 Ne 19th Dr (32609-3320)
P.O. Box 141985 (32614-1985)
PHONE..................................352 373-0384
Greg Upshaw, *Owner*
EMP: 6 **EST:** 1997
SQ FT: 6,000
SALES (est): 732.4K **Privately Held**
SIC: 3441 Building components, structural steel

(G-4703)
GLEIM PUBLICATIONS INC
4201 Nw 95th Blvd (32606-3741)
P.O. Box 12848 (32604-0848)
PHONE..................................352 375-0772
Irvin N Gleim, *President*
Joe Lyden, *General Mgr*
Vince Ferguson, *Business Mgr*
Andrew Johnson, *Research*
Andrew Schreiber, *Research*
◆ **EMP:** 94 **EST:** 1980
SQ FT: 10,000
SALES (est): 11.4MM **Privately Held**
WEB: www.gleim.com
SIC: 2731 8249 7372 8299 Books: publishing only; aviation school; prepackaged software; airline training; catalog & mail-order houses

(G-4704)
GREENTECHNOLOGIES LLC (PA)
3926 Nw 34th Dr (32605-1475)
P.O. Box 357905 (32635-7905)
PHONE..................................352 379-7780
Marla Buchanan, *COO*
Dr Amir Varshovi, *Mng Member*
Marla K Buchanan,
▲ **EMP:** 6 **EST:** 1999
SALES (est): 2.3MM **Privately Held**
WEB: www.green-edge.com
SIC: 2873 8731 Fertilizers: natural (organic), except compost; environmental research

(G-4705)
GUERRILLA PRESS
314 Ne 10th St Apt 201 (32601-5740)
PHONE..................................352 281-7420
Jason Page, *Principal*
EMP: 7 **EST:** 2008
SALES (est): 86.1K **Privately Held**
WEB: www.guerrillapress.net
SIC: 2741 Miscellaneous publishing

(G-4706)
HIGHROLLER FISHING LURE CO LLC
4630 Nw 30th St (32605-1120)
PHONE..................................352 215-2925
Terry J Jertberg, *Owner*
EMP: 7 **EST:** 1999
SQ FT: 1,500
SALES (est): 525.6K **Privately Held**
WEB: www.highrollerlures.com
SIC: 3949 Lures, fishing: artificial

(G-4707)
HONDURAS FOOD SERVICES INC
2337 Sw Archer Rd Apt 302 (32608-1005)
PHONE..................................310 940-2071
Carlos Adrian R Roman, *Branch Mgr*
EMP: 24
SALES (corp-wide): 87.1K **Privately Held**
WEB: www.hondurasfoodservice.com
SIC: 2599 Food wagons, restaurant
PA: Honduras Food Services, Inc.
　540 Brickell Key Dr # 14
　Miami FL

(G-4708)
HYGREEN INC
3630 Sw 47th Ave Ste 100 (32608-7756)
PHONE..................................352 327-9747
Craig Davehport, *President*
Richard J Melker MD PHD, *CTO*
EMP: 13 **EST:** 2009
SQ FT: 6,000
SALES (est): 348.6K **Privately Held**
WEB: www.hygreen.com
SIC: 3841 5047 Surgical & medical instruments; medical & hospital equipment

(G-4709)
ICM PRINTING CO INC
5510 Sw 41st Blvd Ste 101 (32608-4976)
P.O. Box 141046 (32614-1046)
PHONE..................................352 377-7468
EMP: 12
SQ FT: 20,000
SALES (est): 1.2MM **Privately Held**
SIC: 2752 2791 2789 2759 Lithographic Coml Print Typesetting Services Bookbinding/Related Work Commercial Printing

(G-4710)
IGBO NETWORK LLC
5021 Nw 34th Blvd Ste D (32605-1191)
PHONE..................................352 727-4113
Victor Okorochukw, *Mng Member*
EMP: 10 **EST:** 2012
SALES (est): 219.4K **Privately Held**
SIC: 2741

(G-4711)
INNOVATIVE MACHINE INC
Also Called: IMI
6115 Nw 123rd Pl (32653-7999)
PHONE..................................386 418-8880
Gary Gillespie, *President*
Keith Monroe, *Vice Pres*
EMP: 10 **EST:** 1999
SQ FT: 5,000
SALES (est): 1.8MM **Privately Held**
WEB: www.imisolutions.com
SIC: 3599 Machine shop, jobbing & repair

(G-4712)
INSTABOOK CORP
12300 Nw 56th Ave (32653-3551)
PHONE..................................352 332-1311
Victor Celorio, *President*
EMP: 5 **EST:** 1997
SQ FT: 2,184
SALES (est): 445.9K **Privately Held**
WEB: www.instabook.net
SIC: 3555 Bookbinding machinery

(G-4713)
INVIVO CORPORATION (DH)
3545 Sw 47th Ave (32608-7691)
PHONE..................................301 525-9683
Stephen Lorenc, *CEO*
Brian Harmon, *Buyer*
John Armstrong, *Engineer*
Stephan Hohmuth, *Engineer*
Larry Kibler, *Engineer*
▲ **EMP:** 300 **EST:** 1964
SQ FT: 3,000
SALES (est): 113.9MM
SALES (corp-wide): 133.6MM **Privately Held**
WEB: usa.philips.com
SIC: 3841 3829 Diagnostic apparatus, medical; measuring & controlling devices
HQ: Philips Medical Systems Mr, Inc
　450 Old Niskayuna Rd
　Latham NY 12110
　518 782-1122

(G-4714)
INVIVO CORPORATION
3600 Sw 47th Ave (32608-7555)
PHONE..................................352 336-0010
Randy Duensing, *Branch Mgr*
EMP: 35
SALES (corp-wide): 133.6MM **Privately Held**
WEB: usa.philips.com
SIC: 3826 3845 Magnetic resonance imaging apparatus; electromedical equipment
HQ: Invivo Corporation
　3545 Sw 47th Ave
　Gainesville FL 32608
　301 525-9683

(G-4715)
IRVING PUBLICATIONS LLC
Also Called: Giggle Magazine
5745 Sw 75th St Unit 286 (32608-5504)
PHONE..................................352 219-4688
Nicole Irving, *Publisher*
Nicole B Irving, *Vice Pres*
Shane Irving, *Exec VP*
EMP: 14 **EST:** 2011
SALES (est): 1.5MM **Privately Held**
WEB: www.irvingpublications.com
SIC: 2741 Miscellaneous publishing

(G-4716)
JOHN W HOCK COMPANY
Also Called: Hock, John W Co
7409 Nw 23rd Ave (32606-6315)
PHONE..................................352 378-3209
Deborah H Focks, *President*
Dana Focks, *Vice Pres*
John Hock, *Vice Pres*
EMP: 6 **EST:** 1974
SQ FT: 2,000
SALES (est): 882.7K **Privately Held**
WEB: www.johnwhock.com
SIC: 3496 3523 Wire cloth & woven wire products; farm machinery & equipment

(G-4717)
KEVIN JEFFERS INC
Also Called: Jeffcoat Signs
1611 S Main St (32601-8608)
PHONE..................................352 377-2322
Kevin Jeffers, *President*
EMP: 9 **EST:** 1998
SALES (est): 717.7K **Privately Held**
WEB: www.jeffcoatsigns.com
SIC: 3993 7389 Electric signs; sign painting & lettering shop

(G-4718)
LARRYS MOBILCRETE INC
1104 Nw 50th Ave Ste A (32609-0728)
PHONE..................................352 336-2525
EMP: 7
SALES (est): 520K **Privately Held**
SIC: 3273 Mfg Ready-Mixed Concrete

(G-4719)
LARSON INDUSTRIES INCORPORATED (PA)
409 Sw 4th Ave (32601-6551)
P.O. Box 14715 (32604-4715)
PHONE..................................352 262-0566
Tim Larson, *President*
EMP: 6 **EST:** 2012
SALES (est): 909K **Privately Held**
SIC: 2095 Coffee extracts

(G-4720)
LEGACY VULCAN LLC
924 S Main St (32601-2025)
P.O. Box 4667, Ocala (34478-4667)
PHONE..................................352 376-2182
Rick Monghane, *Manager*
EMP: 7
SQ FT: 1,176 **Publicly Held**
SIC: 3273 Ready-mixed concrete
HQ: Legacy Vulcan, Llc
　1200 Urban Center Dr
　Vestavia AL 35242
　205 298-3000

(G-4721)
LENNOX INTERNATIONAL INC
605 Nw 53rd Ave Ste A4 (32609-1019)
PHONE..................................352 379-9630
Sanjeev Hingorani, *Manager*

EMP: 9
SALES (corp-wide): 4.1B **Publicly Held**
WEB: www.lennoxinternational.com
SIC: 3585 Refrigeration & heating equipment
PA: Lennox International Inc.
　2140 Lake Park Blvd
　Richardson TX 75080
　972 497-5000

(G-4722)
LITTLE RIVER MARINE
250 Se 10th Ave (32601-7143)
PHONE..................................352 378-5025
William Larson, *Owner*
◆ **EMP:** 8 **EST:** 1977
SALES (est): 943K **Privately Held**
WEB: www.littlerivermarine.com
SIC: 3732 5551 Boats, fiberglass: building & repairing; boat dealers

(G-4723)
M C H JOURNAL SERVICES INC
8430 Sw 55th Pl (32608-4315)
PHONE..................................352 336-4215
Maurice Hopper, *President*
EMP: 7 **EST:** 1992
SALES (est): 212.2K **Privately Held**
SIC: 2711 Newspapers, publishing & printing

(G-4724)
MAUPIN HOUSE PUBLISHING INC
2300 Nw 71st Pl (32653-1622)
PHONE..................................800 524-0634
Julia C Graddy, *President*
Robert H Graddy, *Vice Pres*
▲ **EMP:** 5 **EST:** 1988
SQ FT: 13,800
SALES (est): 648.7K **Privately Held**
SIC: 2731 Books: publishing only

(G-4725)
MCCALLUM CABINETS INC
3004 Ne 21st Way (32609-3341)
PHONE..................................352 372-2344
Thomas C McCallum, *President*
Gene McCallum, *Shareholder*
EMP: 11 **EST:** 1982
SQ FT: 5,000
SALES (est): 902.5K **Privately Held**
WEB: www.mccallumcabinets.com
SIC: 2521 2541 2517 2511 Wood office furniture; wood partitions & fixtures; wood television & radio cabinets; wood household furniture; wood kitchen cabinets

(G-4726)
MCCLUNEYS ORTHPD PRSTHETIS SVC
Also Called: McCluneys Orthpd Prsthtic Srvi
2930 Nw 16th Ave (32605-3733)
PHONE..................................352 373-5754
T Howard Mc Cluney, *President*
Janie Mc Cluney, *Vice Pres*
EMP: 5 **EST:** 1982
SQ FT: 2,000
SALES (est): 449.9K **Privately Held**
SIC: 3842 Orthopedic appliances

(G-4727)
MEDIA EDGE COMMUNICATIONS LLC
Also Called: Media Edge Publishing
3951 Nw 48th Ter Ste 219 (32606-7230)
PHONE..................................352 313-6700
Kevin Brown,
Riquan Liu, *Admin Asst*
EMP: 8 **EST:** 2004
SALES (est): 1MM
SALES (corp-wide): 7MM **Privately Held**
WEB: www.mecgnv.com
SIC: 2741 Miscellaneous publishing
PA: Media Edge Communications Inc
　2001 Sheppard Ave E Suite 500
　North York ON M2J 4
　416 512-8186

(G-4728)
MEGA BOOK INC
Also Called: Megabooks
2937 Ne 19th Dr (32609-3373)
P.O. Box 358659 (32635-8659)
PHONE..................................352 378-4567

▲ = Import ▼=Export
◆ =Import/Export

Glenda Hogg, *Manager*
EMP: 5 **EST:** 1993
SALES (est): 460.5K **Privately Held**
WEB: www.muscleanatomybook.com
SIC: 2731 Book publishing

(G-4729)
MERCURY SYSTEMS INC
800 Sw 2nd Ave Ste 300 (32601-6295)
PHONE................................352 371-2567
Stuart Audley, *Branch Mgr*
EMP: 23
SALES (corp-wide): 988.2MM **Publicly Held**
WEB: www.mrcy.com
SIC: 3674 7371 7372 7379 Semiconductors & related devices; custom computer programming services; prepackaged software; computer related consulting services; commercial physical research
PA: Mercury Systems, Inc.
50 Minuteman Rd
Andover MA 01810
978 256-1300

(G-4730)
MICAWORKS CABINETRY INC
Also Called: Mica Works Cabinetry
4440 Sw 35th Ter (32608-7596)
PHONE................................352 336-1707
John R Pedersen, *President*
EMP: 9 **EST:** 1996
SALES (est): 1.2MM **Privately Held**
WEB: www.micaworks.com
SIC: 2434 Wood kitchen cabinets

(G-4731)
MILLIKEN & COMPANY
Sivance Plant
5002 Ne 54th Pl (32609-1694)
PHONE................................352 244-2267
EMP: 7
SALES (corp-wide): 1.6B **Privately Held**
WEB: www.milliken.com
SIC: 2273 Floor coverings, textile fiber
PA: Milliken & Company
920 Milliken Rd
Spartanburg SC 29303
864 503-2020

(G-4732)
MIRAGE MANUFACTURING INC
3001 Ne 20th Way (32609-3396)
PHONE................................352 377-4146
Kenneth James Fickett, *President*
Dennis Keller, *Vice Pres*
Rebecca Fickett, *Treasurer*
Eric Kraft, *Sales Dir*
EMP: 65 **EST:** 1973
SQ FT: 25,000
SALES (est): 5.2MM **Privately Held**
WEB: www.mirage-mfg.com
SIC: 3732 Boats, fiberglass: building & repairing

(G-4733)
MOLDSBIZ
4579 Nw 6th St Ste B (32609-6303)
PHONE................................352 327-2720
Harry Robinson, *Principal*
EMP: 7 **EST:** 2010
SALES (est): 105.2K **Privately Held**
SIC: 3544 Industrial molds

(G-4734)
MONTEOCHA COATINGS INC
2607 Ne 56th Ter (32609-5603)
PHONE................................352 367-3136
Gary Washington, *Principal*
EMP: 7 **EST:** 2013
SALES (est): 165.6K **Privately Held**
SIC: 3479 Metal coating & allied service

(G-4735)
MPH INDUSTRIES INC
Also Called: Boone Welding
2406 Ne 19th Dr (32609-3319)
PHONE................................352 372-9533
Carl K Bussard Jr, *President*
EMP: 15 **EST:** 1945
SQ FT: 2,500
SALES (est): 1.8MM **Privately Held**
WEB: www.boonewelding.com
SIC: 3498 7692 3441 Fabricated pipe & fittings; welding repair; fabricated structural metal

(G-4736)
MUNRO INTERNATIONAL INC
Also Called: Molly & Friends
1030 Sw 4th St (32601-8004)
PHONE................................352 337-1535
Thomas M Grant, *President*
Tom Grant, *Sales Executive*
EMP: 20 **EST:** 2000
SQ FT: 3,000
SALES (est): 2.5MM **Privately Held**
SIC: 3999 Pet supplies

(G-4737)
NELSON AND AFFILIATES INC
3324 W University Ave (32607-2540)
PHONE................................352 316-5641
Rick Nelson, *Branch Mgr*
EMP: 25 **Privately Held**
WEB: www.nelsonandaffiliates.com
SIC: 3443 Farm storage tanks, metal plate
PA: Nelson And Affiliates, Inc.
4025 Nw Passage
Tallahassee FL 32303

(G-4738)
NEXTOWER LLC
11895 Sw 33rd Ln (32608-8815)
PHONE................................407 907-7984
David H Hudson Boeff, *Owner*
EMP: 6 **EST:** 2014
SALES (est): 901.4K **Privately Held**
WEB: www.nextower.net
SIC: 3441 Tower sections, radio & television transmission

(G-4739)
NORTH AMRCN SIGNAL SYSTEMS LLC
605 Nw 53rd Ave Ste A17 (32609-1020)
PHONE................................352 376-8341
Ezequiel Zetien, *Mng Member*
EMP: 9 **EST:** 2009
SALES (est): 848.2K **Privately Held**
WEB: www.nasignal.com
SIC: 3669 Traffic signals, electric

(G-4740)
OCALA STAR BANNER CORPORATION
2700 Sw 13th St (32608-2015)
PHONE................................352 867-4010
Bruce Gaultney, *President*
Amy Deckerflingos, *Cust Mgr*
Reynolds Larry, *Sales Staff*
John Gavel, *Manager*
EMP: 200 **EST:** 1980
SALES (est): 11.7MM
SALES (corp-wide): 278.4MM **Privately Held**
WEB: www.ocala.com
SIC: 2711 Newspapers, publishing & printing
PA: Halifax Media Holdings, Llc
901 6th St
Daytona Beach FL 32117
386 681-2404

(G-4741)
OCEAN KITCHEN CABINETS
4445 Sw 35th Ter Ste 200 (32608-8477)
PHONE................................352 745-7110
Rene Arango, *Principal*
EMP: 8 **EST:** 2015
SALES (est): 215.2K **Privately Held**
WEB: ocean-kitchen-cabinets.negocio.site
SIC: 2434 Wood kitchen cabinets

(G-4742)
OLDCASTLE BUILDING PRODUC
Also Called: Old Castle Coastal
3302 Ne 2nd St (32609-2333)
PHONE................................352 377-1699
Martin Maulden, *President*
EMP: 6 **EST:** 2013
SALES (est): 503.2K **Privately Held**
WEB: www.oldcastlecoastal.com
SIC: 3272 Concrete products

(G-4743)
OPIE CHOICE LLC (PA)
Also Called: Opie Choice Network
3870 Nw 83rd St (32606-5601)
PHONE................................352 331-3741
Priya Rudradas, *COO*
Brook Waddell, *QA Dir*

Chris Vigilante, *Engineer*
Paul Prusakowski, *Mng Member*
Samantha Dickensheets, *Manager*
EMP: 8 **EST:** 2014
SALES (est): 1.7MM **Privately Held**
WEB: www.opiesoftware.com
SIC: 7372 Application computer software

(G-4744)
ORTHOTIC PRSTHTIC RHBLTTION AS
Also Called: M & M Rehabilitation
6608 Nw 9th Blvd (32605-4207)
PHONE................................352 331-3399
Frank Vero, *President*
Mark Phelps, *Vice Pres*
EMP: 7 **EST:** 1996
SALES (est): 656.8K **Privately Held**
WEB: www.midflpros.com
SIC: 3842 5999 Limbs, artificial; orthopedic & prosthesis applications

(G-4745)
OXENDINE PUBLISHING INC
412 Nw 16th Ave (32601-4203)
PHONE................................352 373-6907
W H Oxendine Jr, *President*
EMP: 20 **EST:** 1983
SQ FT: 4,000
SALES (est): 931.8K **Privately Held**
WEB: www.studentleader.com
SIC: 2721 Magazines: publishing only, not printed on site

(G-4746)
PAUL WALES INC
Also Called: Atlas Screen Printing
131 Se 10th Ave (32601-7998)
PHONE................................352 371-2120
Paul Wales, *President*
Glenda Grosnick, *Sales Mgr*
Annie Orlando, *Admin Sec*
EMP: 21 **EST:** 1976
SQ FT: 14,000
SALES (est): 2MM **Privately Held**
WEB: www.wildcotton.com
SIC: 2759 Screen printing

(G-4747)
PENNGEAR LLC
1134 Old Dominion Rd (32612-0001)
P.O. Box 727, Washington Crossing PA (18977-0727)
PHONE................................215 968-2403
Craig Stranahan,
EMP: 5 **EST:** 2016
SALES (est): 500K **Privately Held**
SIC: 3566 7389 Speed changers, drives & gears; business services

(G-4748)
PEPSI-COLA METRO BTLG CO INC
6335 Nw 18th Dr (32653-1643)
PHONE................................352 376-8276
Karen Connelly, *Human Resources*
Johanna Reyes, *Manager*
EMP: 14
SQ FT: 28,200
SALES (corp-wide): 70.3B **Publicly Held**
WEB: www.pepsico.com
SIC: 2086 5149 Carbonated soft drinks, bottled & canned; groceries & related products
HQ: Pepsi-Cola Metropolitan Bottling Company, Inc.
700 Anderson Hill Rd
Purchase NY 10577
914 767-6000

(G-4749)
PRECISION TL ENGRG GNSVLLE INC
2709 Ne 20th Way (32609-3314)
PHONE................................352 376-2533
Bette J Thibault, *President*
William C Thibault, *Vice Pres*
EMP: 20 **EST:** 1966
SQ FT: 19,000
SALES (est): 1MM **Privately Held**
WEB: ptefl.blogspot.com
SIC: 3549 3599 3728 3544 Metalworking machinery; machine shop, jobbing & repair; aircraft parts & equipment; special dies, tools, jigs & fixtures

(G-4750)
PREMIER PARTIES ENTERTAINMENT
805 Nw 13th St (32601-2904)
PHONE................................352 375-6122
Eric Manin, *President*
Anthony Hernandez, *Vice Pres*
▲ **EMP:** 31 **EST:** 1994
SQ FT: 2,200
SALES (est): 1.4MM **Privately Held**
SIC: 2759 7929 7299 7311 Commercial printing; entertainers & entertainment groups; party planning service; advertising agencies

(G-4751)
PS & QS CUSTOM PRINTS LLC
4024 Ne 1st Dr (32609-1702)
PHONE................................352 231-3961
Patrickk W McDonald, *Branch Mgr*
EMP: 15
SALES (corp-wide): 69K **Privately Held**
SIC: 2752 Commercial printing, lithographic
PA: P's & Q's Custom Prints, Llc
4609 Buchanan Dr
Fort Pierce FL 34982
772 626-7434

(G-4752)
PURE LABORATORIES LLC
5909 Nw 18th Dr (32653-1639)
PHONE................................888 425-6649
EMP: 106
SALES (corp-wide): 30.2MM **Privately Held**
WEB: www.purelabs.com
SIC: 3634 Electric housewares & fans
PA: Pure Laboratories, Llc
5909 Nw 18th Dr
Gainesville FL 32653
888 425-6649

(G-4753)
QUICK-MED TECHNOLOGIES INC
902 Nw 4th St (32601-4285)
PHONE................................352 379-0611
Bernd Liesenfeld, *President*
William Toreki, *Vice Pres*
Susan Leander, *Research*
Paul Jenssen, *CFO*
Gerald M Olderman, *Director*
EMP: 7 **EST:** 1997
SQ FT: 3,200
SALES (est): 1MM **Privately Held**
WEB: www.quickmedtech.com
SIC: 3841 8731 Surgical & medical instruments; medical research, commercial

(G-4754)
R & J MFG OF GAINESVILLE
Also Called: Air-Trac
2001 Ne 31st Ave (32609-2506)
PHONE................................352 375-3130
Loyce Osteen, *President*
James F Osteen, *Vice Pres*
EMP: 6 **EST:** 1974
SQ FT: 20,000
SALES (est): 690.3K **Privately Held**
WEB: www.air-trac.com
SIC: 3822 3585 3564 3433 Air flow controllers, air conditioning & refrigeration; refrigeration & heating equipment; blowers & fans; heating equipment, except electric

(G-4755)
RAD WEAR INC
2135 Nw 40th Ter Ste A (32605-5802)
PHONE................................352 727-4498
Jennifer Ruland, *President*
Radley Ruland, *Vice Pres*
EMP: 8 **EST:** 2010
SALES (est): 1.1MM **Privately Held**
WEB: www.radweardesigns.com
SIC: 2211 Apparel & outerwear fabrics, cotton

(G-4756)
RAFFERTY HOLDINGS LLC
Also Called: Rafferty Machine and Tool
2722 Nw 74th Pl (32653-1201)
PHONE................................352 248-0906
Conway Tomlinson,
Celia Gtomlinson,

EMP: 20 EST: 1972
SQ FT: 10,000
SALES (est): 1.6MM Privately Held
SIC: 3544 3599 Special dies & tools; machine shop, jobbing & repair

(G-4757)
RIDGWAY ROOF TRUSS COMPANY
235 Sw 11th Pl (32601-7939)
PHONE.................................352 376-4436
Wells S The Losen, *President*
Keith Dewing, *General Mgr*
Jeff Lincoln, *Principal*
Karl The Losen, *Vice Pres*
Wells Losen, *Vice Pres*
EMP: 100 EST: 1957
SQ FT: 10,000
SALES (est): 16.3MM Privately Held
WEB: www.ridgwaytruss.com
SIC: 2439 Trusses, wooden roof

(G-4758)
SCAN TECHNOLOGY INC (PA)
10305 Nw 4th Pl (32607-1350)
PHONE.................................931 723-0304
Paul A Flowers, *CEO*
Michael Flowers, *Treasurer*
Stephen Flowers, *Admin Sec*
▼ EMP: 6 EST: 1979
SQ FT: 1,400
SALES (est): 1.3MM Privately Held
WEB: www.scantec.com
SIC: 3577 3643 7389 Magnetic ink recognition devices; readers, sorters or inscribers, magnetic ink; optical scanning devices; current-carrying wiring devices; packaging & labeling services

(G-4759)
SCF PROCESSING LLC
1604 Nw 8th Ave (32603-1004)
PHONE.................................352 377-0858
Siobhan Matthews, *Principal*
EMP: 7 EST: 2010
SALES (est): 78.7K Privately Held
SIC: 3089 Injection molding of plastics

(G-4760)
SEL WEST COAST INC
817 Ne Waldo Rd (32641-4674)
PHONE.................................352 373-6354
Russ Keaton, *Branch Mgr*
EMP: 21
SALES (corp-wide): 9.5MM Privately Held
SIC: 3312 Blast furnaces & steel mills
PA: Sel West Coast, Inc.
    7005 E 14th Ave
    Tampa FL 33619

(G-4761)
SILKMASTERS INC
1911 Sw 80th Dr (32607-3499)
PHONE.................................904 372-8958
Shirley Bonamie, *President*
Julie Bonamie, *Corp Secy*
Clifford Bonamie, *Vice Pres*
EMP: 8 EST: 1986
SQ FT: 7,800
SALES (est): 658.1K Privately Held
WEB: www.silkmasters.com
SIC: 2759 Screen printing

(G-4762)
SINMAT COMMERCIAL LLC
1912 Nw 67th Pl (32653-1649)
PHONE.................................352 334-7270
Sarah Wilson, *Business Mgr*
Deepika Singh,
Rajiv Singh,
EMP: 15 EST: 2012
SQ FT: 22,500
SALES (est): 4.3MM Privately Held
WEB: www.entegris.com
SIC: 2819 Industrial inorganic chemicals

(G-4763)
SIRA
912 Nw 13th St (32601-4140)
PHONE.................................352 377-4947
Kathy Grotto, *Exec Dir*
EMP: 7 EST: 2019
SALES (est): 122K Privately Held
WEB: www.siragainesville.com
SIC: 2499 Decorative wood & woodwork

(G-4764)
SIVANCE LLC (HQ)
5002 Ne 54th Pl (32609-1694)
P.O. Box 1466 (32627-1466)
PHONE.................................352 376-8246
William Carpenter, *Safety Mgr*
Craig Stafford, *Mng Member*
Amy Sweeney, *Manager*
James R Richeson,
◆ EMP: 56 EST: 2009
SALES (est): 99.5MM
SALES (corp-wide): 1.6B Privately Held
SIC: 2819 Industrial inorganic chemicals
PA: Milliken & Company
    920 Milliken Rd
    Spartanburg SC 29303
    864 503-2020

(G-4765)
SIVANCE LLC
Also Called: Clariant
4404 Ne 53rd Rd (32609-1661)
P.O. Box 1466 (32627-1466)
PHONE.................................352 376-8246
Kenneth Handley, *Principal*
Mike Brummitt, *Director*
EMP: 21
SALES (corp-wide): 1.6B Privately Held
SIC: 2869 Industrial organic chemicals
HQ: Sivance, Llc
    5002 Ne 54th Pl
    Gainesville FL 32609
    352 376-8246

(G-4766)
STORTERCHILDS PRINTING CO INC
1540 Ne Waldo Rd (32641-4629)
PHONE.................................352 376-2658
Joe R Davis, *CEO*
Shariq Siraj, *President*
David A Cheadle, *Treasurer*
Sharon Murphy, *Controller*
Dave Hendryx, *Accounts Mgr*
EMP: 24 EST: 1949
SQ FT: 21,000
SALES (est): 5MM
SALES (corp-wide): 4.9B Privately Held
SIC: 2759 Commercial printing
HQ: Consolidated Graphics, Inc.
    5858 Westheimer Rd # 200
    Houston TX 77057
    713 787-0977

(G-4767)
STOUT DEFENSE PA
5215 Sw 91st Ter (32608-7125)
PHONE.................................352 665-9266
Adam P Stout, *Principal*
EMP: 5 EST: 2017
SALES (est): 468.6K Privately Held
WEB: www.stoutdefense.com
SIC: 3812 Defense systems & equipment

(G-4768)
STREAMLINE NUMERICS INC
3221 Nw 13th St Ste A (32609-2189)
PHONE.................................352 271-8841
Siddhart Thakur, *President*
EMP: 7 EST: 1999
SALES (est): 568K Privately Held
WEB: www.snumerics.com
SIC: 3812 Search & navigation equipment

(G-4769)
STRICTLY ECOMMERCE
5210 Ne 49th Ter (32609-1630)
PHONE.................................352 672-6566
Shannon Flesner, *President*
EMP: 5 EST: 2007
SALES (est): 346.4K Privately Held
WEB: www.strictlytoolboxes.com
SIC: 3999 Atomizers, toiletry

(G-4770)
STRICTLY TOOLBOXES
4820 Ne 49th Rd (32609-1624)
PHONE.................................352 672-6566
Shannon Flesner, *President*
EMP: 7 EST: 2013
SALES (est): 799.9K Privately Held
WEB: www.strictlytoolboxes.com
SIC: 3469 Metal stampings

(G-4771)
SWI PUBLISHING INC
116 Sw 40th Ter (32607-2755)
PHONE.................................352 538-1438
Lisa D Wilkinson, *Principal*
EMP: 9 EST: 2010
SALES (est): 170.3K Privately Held
SIC: 2741 Miscellaneous publishing

(G-4772)
T E M INC
8930 Nw 13th St (32653-1033)
PHONE.................................352 371-3898
Paul Bergsma, *Owner*
Marcus Muir, *Admin Sec*
EMP: 5 EST: 1996
SQ FT: 1,600
SALES (est): 455K Privately Held
WEB: www.mtetooling.com
SIC: 3599 Machine shop, jobbing & repair

(G-4773)
TAPESOUTH INC
1626 Nw 55th Pl (32653-2109)
PHONE.................................904 642-1800
Melissa Norman, *CEO*
Susan S Norman, *President*
Norman Woody, *CFO*
▲ EMP: 8 EST: 1993
SQ FT: 15,400
SALES (est): 1.9MM Privately Held
WEB: www.tapesouth.com
SIC: 2672 Adhesive papers, labels or tapes: from purchased material

(G-4774)
TARGET COPY GAINESVILLE INC
3422 Sw Archer Rd (32608-2409)
P.O. Box 13955 (32604-1955)
PHONE.................................352 372-1171
Jennifer Ford, *Manager*
EMP: 14
SALES (corp-wide): 9.8MM Privately Held
WEB: www.target-copy.com
SIC: 2789 7389 7334 2759 Bookbinding & related work; laminating service; blueprinting service; commercial printing
PA: Target Copy Of Gainesville, Inc.
    4130 Nw 16th Blvd
    Gainesville FL 32605
    352 372-2233

(G-4775)
THEISSEN TRAINING SYSTEMS INC
3705 Sw 42nd Ave Ste 2 (32608-2599)
P.O. Box 141917 (32614-1917)
PHONE.................................352 490-8020
Tilman Rumpf, *President*
Omar Silva, *Vice Pres*
Rymond Shepherd, *Program Mgr*
Katie Bryan, *Admin Asst*
Mark Price, *Technician*
▲ EMP: 56 EST: 2001
SALES (est): 11.3MM
SALES (corp-wide): 2MM Privately Held
WEB: www.theissentraining.com
SIC: 3499 Fire- or burglary-resistive products
HQ: T.T.S. Theissen Training Systems Gmbh
    Schuchardstr. 3
    Dusseldorf NW 40595
    211 975-040

(G-4776)
THREAD PIT INC
2708 Ne Waldo Rd (32609-3323)
PHONE.................................352 505-0065
EMP: 6
SALES (est): 716.2K Privately Held
SIC: 2759 Commercial Printing

(G-4777)
TOWER PUBLICATIONS INC
Also Called: Senior Times Magazine
4400 Nw 36th Ave (32606-7215)
PHONE.................................352 372-5468
Carlos Delatorre, *President*
Ericka Winterrowd, *Chief*
Bonita D Delatorre, *Vice Pres*
Helen Mincey, *Representative*
Nancy Short, *Representative*

EMP: 15 EST: 1999
SQ FT: 3,300
SALES (est): 1.4MM Privately Held
WEB: www.towerpublications.com
SIC: 2741 Miscellaneous publishing

(G-4778)
TRENDY ENTERTAINMENT INC
4910 Sw 78th Ln (32608-5196)
PHONE.................................814 384-7123
Marco Dusse, *CEO*
Eric Petrie, *QA Dir*
Linda Hoyles, *CFO*
EMP: 28 EST: 2010
SALES (est): 1.8MM Privately Held
WEB: www.chromatic.games
SIC: 7372 Prepackaged software

(G-4779)
TRIUMPH GROUP CONSULTING
1720 Nw 122nd St (32606-5341)
PHONE.................................352 213-3007
Becky Burns, *Principal*
EMP: 7 EST: 2016
SALES (est): 265.3K Privately Held
WEB: www.triumphgroup.com
SIC: 3728 Aircraft parts & equipment

(G-4780)
TROXEL AEROSPACE INDS INC
2023 Ne 55th Blvd (32641-2786)
PHONE.................................720 626-0454
Ian Troxel, *CEO*
Claire Troxel, *COO*
EMP: 10 EST: 2015
SALES (est): 1.4MM Privately Held
WEB: www.troxelaerospace.com
SIC: 3761 3764 3812 5088 Guided missiles & space vehicles, research & development; guided missile & space vehicle engines, research & devel.; acceleration indicators & systems components, aerospace; space propulsion units & parts

(G-4781)
TWO TREE INC
24 Nw 33rd Ct Ste A (32607-2556)
PHONE.................................352 284-1763
Thomas L Thompson, *Director*
EMP: 7 EST: 2001
SALES (est): 106.9K Privately Held
WEB: www.flanaturecoast.com
SIC: 3822 Auto controls regulating residntl & coml environmt & apolncs

(G-4782)
US SPARS INC
Also Called: Z Spars
6320 Nw 123rd Pl (32653-1069)
PHONE.................................386 462-3760
Mike Wukotich, *President*
Rick Pantall, *Manager*
◆ EMP: 9 EST: 1997
SQ FT: 160,000
SALES (est): 1.5MM Privately Held
WEB: www.usspars.com
SIC: 2394 3732 Sails: made from purchased materials; boat building & repairing
HQ: Z Diffusion
    Avenue Louis Lumiere
    Perigny 17180
    546 442-088

(G-4783)
VERTAEON LLC
747 Sw 2nd Ave Ste 349 (32601-6284)
PHONE.................................404 823-6232
Rekha Menon-Varma,
EMP: 8 EST: 2018
SALES (est): 428K Privately Held
WEB: www.vertaeon.com
SIC: 7372 Prepackaged software

(G-4784)
VOS SYSTEMS LLC
304 W University Ave (32601-5208)
PHONE.................................352 317-2954
Omar Ghazzaoui,
EMP: 16 EST: 2020
SALES (est): 2.6MM Privately Held
WEB: www.vosiq.com
SIC: 3699 Electrical equipment & supplies

(G-4785)
XHALE INC (PA)
3630 Sw 47th Ave Ste 100 (32608-7756)
PHONE.................................352 371-8488
Richard R Allen, *CEO*
Thomas Bigger, *President*
Andrew Kersey, *President*
John F Harper, *Chairman*
Lori Herman, *Counsel*
EMP: 8 **EST:** 2005
SALES (est): 802.7K **Privately Held**
WEB: www.xhale.com
SIC: 3841 Surgical & medical instruments

Geneva
Seminole County

(G-4786)
CWP SHEET METAL INC
1661 Bandit Way (32732-8520)
PHONE.................................407 349-0926
EMP: 26
SALES (est): 3.1MM **Privately Held**
SIC: 3444 Mfg Sheet Metalwork

(G-4787)
EVOLUTION WOODWORKING
670 Coffee Trl (32732-7279)
PHONE.................................407 221-5031
Stephen Chrismore Hamblin, *Owner*
EMP: 7 **EST:** 2010
SALES (est): 95.5K **Privately Held**
SIC: 2431 Millwork

(G-4788)
F & S MILL WORKS
522 Cemetery Rd (32732-8921)
PHONE.................................407 349-9948
Leon H Flowers, *Principal*
EMP: 7 **EST:** 2003
SALES (est): 155.3K **Privately Held**
SIC: 2434 Wood kitchen cabinets

(G-4789)
FLORIDA STEAM SERVICES INC
349 Whitcomb Dr (32732-9254)
PHONE.................................407 247-8250
David Segrest, *Principal*
Sally Segrest, *Admin Sec*
EMP: 6 **EST:** 1991
SQ FT: 1,400
SALES (est): 490.6K **Privately Held**
SIC: 3317 Welded pipe & tubes

(G-4790)
SUNS EYE INC
2098 Tall Pine Trl (32732-9138)
P.O. Box 39 (32732-0039)
PHONE.................................407 519-4904
Ashley Stollings, *President*
EMP: 6 **EST:** 2013
SALES (est): 706.2K **Privately Held**
WEB: www.sunseye.com
SIC: 2899 5169 Oils & essential oils; essential oils

(G-4791)
WOPS HOPS BREWING LLC (PA)
Also Called: Wop's Hops Brewing Company
510 S Cochran Rd (32732-8977)
PHONE.................................407 927-8929
Gregory J Piecora,
EMP: 5 **EST:** 2013
SALES (est): 988.2K **Privately Held**
WEB: www.wopshopsbrewing.com
SIC: 2082 Malt beverages

Gibsonton
Hillsborough County

(G-4792)
A-FABCO INC
11550 S Us Highway 41 (33534-5209)
P.O. Box 2097 (33534-2097)
PHONE.................................813 677-8790
Robert Harburg, *CEO*
Jerry Harburg, *President*
Dave Barkley, *General Mgr*
Joel Christy, *Sales Staff*
Ken Kennedy, *Sales Staff*
▲ **EMP:** 25 **EST:** 1970

SQ FT: 17,250
SALES (est): 4MM **Privately Held**
WEB: www.afabxray.com
SIC: 3443 5072 Nuclear shielding, metal plate; builders' hardware

(G-4793)
ALL STEEL BLDNGS CMPONENTS INC
10159 S Us Highway 41 (33534-4016)
PHONE.................................813 671-8044
Bobby Ramey, *President*
Henry Suggs, *Sales Executive*
▼ **EMP:** 36 **EST:** 2001
SQ FT: 21,600
SALES (est): 8.8MM **Privately Held**
WEB: www.allsteel-buildings.com
SIC: 3448 Prefabricated metal buildings

(G-4794)
BACKYARD CANVAS & SIGNS INC
11225 Restwood Dr (33534-4735)
P.O. Box 1131 (33534-1131)
PHONE.................................813 672-2660
Carter William W, *Principal*
EMP: 7 **EST:** 2017
SALES (est): 232.8K **Privately Held**
WEB: www.backyardcanvas.com
SIC: 3993 Signs & advertising specialties

(G-4795)
BELAMOUR LOGISTICS LLC ✪
9727 Cypress Harbor Dr (33534-5141)
PHONE.................................813 540-2199
Elizabeth Francois,
EMP: 7 **EST:** 2021
SALES (est): 100K **Privately Held**
SIC: 3537 Trucks: freight, baggage, etc.: industrial, except mining

(G-4796)
BIG BEND FUEL INC
6912 Big Bend Rd (33534-5832)
PHONE.................................727 946-8727
Richard Elkhoury, *Principal*
EMP: 10 **EST:** 2010
SALES (est): 625.2K **Privately Held**
SIC: 2869 Fuels

(G-4797)
GOLD BOND BUILDING PDTS LLC
12949 S Us Highway 41 (33534-5826)
PHONE.................................813 672-8269
EMP: 10
SALES (corp-wide): 91.2MM **Privately Held**
WEB: www.nationalgypsum.com
SIC: 2621 Paper mills
HQ: Gold Bond Building Products, Llc
2001 Rexford Rd
Charlotte NC 28211
704 365-7300

(G-4798)
INNOVATIVE STEEL TECH INC
12620 S Us Highway 41 (33534-5812)
PHONE.................................813 767-1746
Richard D Biddle, *President*
EMP: 16 **EST:** 2007
SALES (est): 385.3K **Privately Held**
SIC: 3312 Blast furnaces & steel mills

(G-4799)
PROFORM FINISHING PRODUCTS LLC
Also Called: National Gypsum
12949 S Us Highway 41 (33534-5826)
PHONE.................................813 672-8269
Eric Anderson, *Plant Engr*
Jeff McChesney, *Manager*
Sally Holden, *Manager*
Susan Kinnamon, *Manager*
EMP: 46
SALES (corp-wide): 795.8MM **Privately Held**
WEB: www.nationalgypsum.com
SIC: 3275 Building board, gypsum
HQ: Proform Finishing Products, Llc
2001 Rexford Rd
Charlotte NC 28211

(G-4800)
SANTIAGO CHOPPER LLC (PA)
10935 Sonora Dr (33534-5456)
PHONE.................................813 671-9097
Christine Bernard, *Principal*
EMP: 5 **EST:** 2011
SALES (est): 332.5K **Privately Held**
WEB: www.santiagochopper.com
SIC: 3714 Motor vehicle parts & accessories

(G-4801)
TAMPA TANK & WELDING INC
12781 S Us Highway 41 (33534-5829)
PHONE.................................813 241-0123
Kevin Sigl, *General Mgr*
Calvin H Reed, *Vice Pres*
John M Malcolm, *Safety Mgr*
Albert Brian, *Controller*
Deborah Hayden, *Controller*
EMP: 15
SQ FT: 22,332 **Privately Held**
WEB: www.tti-fss.com
SIC: 3446 3443 3441 Architectural metalwork; fabricated plate work (boiler shop); fabricated structural metal
HQ: Tampa Tank & Welding, Inc.
2710 E 5th Ave
Tampa FL 33605
813 623-2675

(G-4802)
TURN KEY INDUSTRIES
9901 Alafia River Ln (33534-4635)
P.O. Box 1306, Riverview (33568-1306)
PHONE.................................813 671-3446
Claudia Haupt, *Owner*
Donny Guedry, *Production*
Dan Belore, *Sales Staff*
Timothy Lewis, *Manager*
EMP: 8 **EST:** 2001
SALES (est): 346.3K **Privately Held**
WEB: www.tkind.com
SIC: 3999 Manufacturing industries

(G-4803)
W R WILLIAMS ENTERPRISES INC
Also Called: Dock Builders Supply
6202 Powell Rd (33534-5800)
P.O. Box 3450, Apollo Beach (33572-1003)
PHONE.................................813 677-2000
William R Williams Jr, *President*
Richard A Tahela, *Vice Pres*
◆ **EMP:** 8 **EST:** 1998
SALES (est): 1.3MM **Privately Held**
WEB: www.dockbuilders.com
SIC: 2499 5072 5251 Floating docks, wood; builders' hardware; builders' hardware

Glen Saint Mary
Baker County

(G-4804)
NATIONAL PIPE WELDING INC
9473 Smokey Rd (32040-5335)
P.O. Box 1661 (32040-1661)
PHONE.................................904 588-2589
Michelle Fish, *Mng Member*
Lamar Fish,
EMP: 10 **EST:** 2011
SALES (est): 3.2MM **Privately Held**
SIC: 7692 Welding repair

(G-4805)
SOUTHERN FUEL INC
7028 E Mount Vernon St (32040-5066)
PHONE.................................904 545-5163
Lynn Driskell, *Principal*
EMP: 6 **EST:** 2010
SALES (est): 509K **Privately Held**
SIC: 2869 Fuels

Gotha
Orange County

(G-4806)
BLUETOAD INC
2225 Lake Nally Woods Dr (34734-4902)
PHONE.................................407 992-8744

Paul Dehart, *CEO*
EMP: 30 **EST:** 2007
SQ FT: 4,700
SALES (est): 5.5MM **Privately Held**
WEB: www.bluetoad.com
SIC: 2741 Miscellaneous publishing

Graceville
Jackson County

(G-4807)
APALACHEE POLE COMPANY INC (PA)
1820 Highway 2 (32440-4124)
P.O. Box 7 (32440-0007)
PHONE.................................850 263-4457
C Finley McRae, *President*
Robert McRae Jr, *Vice Pres*
EMP: 2 **EST:** 1986
SQ FT: 6,000
SALES (est): 4.2MM **Privately Held**
WEB: www.rex-lumber.com
SIC: 2421 Sawmills & planing mills, general

(G-4808)
REX LUMBER GRACEVILLE LLC (HQ)
5299 Alabama St (32440-2105)
P.O. Box 7 (32440-0007)
PHONE.................................850 263-2056
Jason Gulledge, *General Mgr*
Anthony Hanson, *General Mgr*
Matt Pelham, *Project Mgr*
Jason Daniels, *Opers Mgr*
Michelle Collier, *Engineer*
EMP: 115 **EST:** 1926
SALES (est): 40.8MM
SALES (corp-wide): 51.9MM **Privately Held**
WEB: www.rex-lumber.com
SIC: 2421 Sawmills & planing mills, general
PA: Rex Lumber, Llc
5299 Alabama St
Graceville FL 32440
850 263-2056

(G-4809)
REX LUMBER LLC (PA)
5299 Alabama St (32440-2105)
PHONE.................................850 263-2056
Joshua Triplett, *Maint Spvr*
Frank Bondurant, *Mng Member*
Tommy Wheeler, *Supervisor*
Pam Griffin, *Technician*
Shawn Norris, *Maintence Staff*
EMP: 17 **EST:** 2018
SALES (est): 51.9MM **Privately Held**
WEB: www.rex-lumber.com
SIC: 2421 Sawmills & planing mills, general

Grandin
Putnam County

(G-4810)
LEGACY VULCAN LLC
1 Mile W On Hwy 100 (32138)
PHONE.................................386 659-2477
Mitchell Johns, *Manager*
EMP: 10 **Publicly Held**
SIC: 3273 Ready-mixed concrete
HQ: Legacy Vulcan, Llc
1200 Urban Center Dr
Vestavia AL 35242
205 298-3000

Grant
Brevard County

(G-4811)
CARBONARA LABS INC
4550 S Us Highway 1 (32949-4909)
PHONE.................................321 952-1303
John Carpenter, *President*
Bill Carpenter, *General Mgr*
Robert Rapp Jr, *Vice Pres*
▲ **EMP:** 10 **EST:** 1974

GEOGRAPHIC

SALES (est): 798.2K **Privately Held**
WEB: www.carpindustries.com
SIC: **3812** Search & navigation equipment

(G-4812)
JGA LIGHTING LLC
Also Called: JEAN ARCHIBALD DBA JGA
ASSOC
3869 Garden Wood Cir (32949)
PHONE.................................772 408-8224
Jean G Archibald,
Douglas W Archibald,
EMP: 6 EST: 2013
SALES (est): 462.7K **Privately Held**
WEB: www.bulbwizards.com
SIC: **3229** Bulbs for electric lights

(G-4813)
TRIPLE SEVEN HOME LLC
3385 Grant Rd (32949-8126)
PHONE.................................321 652-5151
Jessica L Lelievre, Principal
EMP: 6 EST: 2015
SALES (est): 464.3K **Privately Held**
WEB: www.triplesevenhome.com
SIC: **3648** Lighting fixtures, except electric:
residential

Green Cove Springs
Clay County

(G-4814)
**AMERICAN TRFFIC SFETY MTLS
INC**
1272 Harbor Rd (32043-8729)
P.O. Box 1449, Orange Park (32067-1449)
PHONE.................................904 284-0284
Sandi Ricketts, CEO
Roberta Seay Soldner, President
EMP: 21 EST: 1997
SQ FT: 5,000
SALES (est): 981.4K **Privately Held**
WEB: www.atsminc.com
SIC: **2824** Vinyl fibers

(G-4815)
AMMCON CORP
1503 County Road 315 # 204
(32043-8773)
P.O. Box 890, North Plains OR (97133-0890)
PHONE.................................904 863-3196
Josh Grow, Principal
Chris Whitlock, Nursing Mgr
EMP: 7
SALES (corp-wide): 11.8MM **Privately
Held**
WEB: www.ammcon.com
SIC: **3599** Machine shop, jobbing & repair
PA: Ammcon Corp.
21450 Nw West Union Rd
Hillsboro OR 97124
503 645-5206

(G-4816)
ARTEMIS HOLDINGS LLC (HQ)
Also Called: Pyramid Mouldings
4630 County Road 209 S (32043-8182)
PHONE.................................904 284-5611
Ray Hammons, President
Gordon Davis, CFO
EMP: 1 EST: 2014
SALES (est): 38.9MM
SALES (corp-wide): 120.2MM **Privately
Held**
WEB: www.rollerdie.com
SIC: **3441** Fabricated structural metal
PA: Roller Die And Forming Company, Inc.
1172 Industrial Blvd
Louisville KY 40219
502 969-1327

(G-4817)
ASHLEY F WARD INC
Also Called: Ashley Ward
3525 Enterprise Way (32043-9334)
PHONE.................................904 284-2848
Brian Storey, Manager
EMP: 10
SQ FT: 50,000
SALES (corp-wide): 3.3K **Privately Held**
WEB: www.ashleyward.com
SIC: **3451** Screw machine products

PA: Ashley F. Ward, Inc.
7490 Easy St
Mason OH 45040
513 398-1414

(G-4818)
B & B TIMBER COMPANY
4880 Highway 17 S (32043-8139)
PHONE.................................904 284-5541
Merrill Batten, Partner
Melvin Batten, Partner
EMP: 7 EST: 1977
SALES (est): 843.3K **Privately Held**
SIC: **2411** Timber, cut at logging camp

(G-4819)
CALLOWAY BARGE LINES INC
967 Bulkhead Rd Pier 5 (32043-8340)
P.O. Box 188 (32043-0188)
PHONE.................................904 284-0503
Latham Smith, President
EMP: 11 EST: 2001
SALES (est): 286.5K **Privately Held**
SIC: **3441** Boat & barge sections, prefabricated metal

(G-4820)
CAPT LATHAM LLC
967 Bulkhead Rd (32043-8340)
PHONE.................................904 483-6118
Latham Smith, Principal
EMP: 7 EST: 2016
SALES (est): 94.6K **Privately Held**
SIC: **3731** Shipbuilding & repairing

(G-4821)
**CHARDONNAY BOAT WORKS
LLC**
411 Walnut St (32043-3443)
PHONE.................................703 981-6339
Scott Berg, Principal
EMP: 5 EST: 2010
SALES (est): 466.8K **Privately Held**
SIC: **3732** Boat building & repairing

(G-4822)
**COMMERCIAL ENERGY
SERVICES**
1528 Virgils Way Ste 14 (32043-3781)
PHONE.................................904 589-1059
Shannon Cascarelli, President
Tracy Huff, Vice Pres
EMP: 10 EST: 2008
SALES (est): 976.4K **Privately Held**
SIC: **3646** Commercial indusl & institutional electric lighting fixtures

(G-4823)
**ED-GAR LEASING COMPANY
INC**
1306 Idlewild Ave (32043-3805)
P.O. Box 726 (32043-0726)
PHONE.................................904 284-1900
Garland Deel, President
Edna Deel, Vice Pres
Edmond Deel, Treasurer
EMP: 10 EST: 1999
SQ FT: 1,260
SALES (est): 341K **Privately Held**
SIC: **1389** Lease tanks, oil field: erecting,
cleaning & repairing

(G-4824)
FOX EQUIPMENT LLC (PA)
965 Bunker Ave (32043-8346)
PHONE.................................904 531-3150
William Holthaus, Plant Mgr
Kevin Simpson, Engineer
Eric W Fox, Mng Member
Jason Davidson, Manager
Jim Garrett, Manager
EMP: 25 EST: 2003
SALES (est): 8.7MM **Privately Held**
WEB: www.foxequipment.com
SIC: **3441** Expansion joints (structural
shapes), iron or steel

(G-4825)
FOX MANUFACTURING LLC
965 Bunker Ave (32043-8346)
PHONE.................................904 531-3150
Eric Fox, Mng Member
EMP: 9 EST: 2011
SALES (est): 572.6K **Privately Held**
SIC: **3999** Manufacturing industries

(G-4826)
GENEVA SYSTEMS INC
712 Simmons Trl (32043-9567)
PHONE.................................352 235-2990
Robert J McMullen, Principal
EMP: 7 EST: 2008
SALES (est): 233.3K **Privately Held**
WEB: www.genevaservice.com
SIC: **3699** Cleaning equipment, ultrasonic,
except medical & dental

(G-4827)
**H&R WELDING EQUIPMENT
REPR INC**
937 Bulkhead Rd (32043-8340)
PHONE.................................904 487-9829
James R Tharp, President
Michelle Tharp, Vice Pres
James Tharp, Treasurer
EMP: 7 EST: 2015
SALES (est): 44.4K **Privately Held**
WEB: www.weldingequipment.repair
SIC: **7692** Automotive welding

(G-4828)
HBP PIPE & PRECAST LLC
4210 Highway 17 S Us (32043-8137)
PHONE.................................904 529-8228
EMP: 36
SALES (corp-wide): 15.6B **Privately Held**
SIC: **3272** Mfg Concrete Products
HQ: Hbp Pipe & Precast Llc
300 E John Carpenter Fwy
Irving TX 75062
972 653-5500

(G-4829)
HERITAGE SIGNS
1282 Energy Cove Ct (32043-4308)
PHONE.................................904 529-7446
Denise Mankinen, Principal
Jonathan Knight, Opers Staff
Mary Knight, Sales Staff
Chuck Knight, Sales Executive
EMP: 6 EST: 2008
SALES (est): 532.1K **Privately Held**
WEB: www.heritagesignsfl.com
SIC: **3993** Signs & advertising specialties

(G-4830)
**HUMIC GROWTH SOLUTIONS
INC**
938 Hall Park Rd (32043-4934)
PHONE.................................904 329-1012
Kevin Merritt, President
EMP: 9
SALES (corp-wide): 10MM **Privately
Held**
WEB: www.humicgrowth.com
SIC: **2879** Soil conditioners
PA: Humic Growth Solutions, Inc.
709 Eastport Rd
Jacksonville FL 32218
904 392-7201

(G-4831)
**NEW WORLD ENCLOSURES
INC**
1350 Riviera Dr (32043-8764)
PHONE.................................904 334-4752
Wendy Serrentino, Principal
EMP: 11 EST: 2007
SALES (est): 465.6K **Privately Held**
WEB: www.newworldenclosures.com
SIC: **3448** Screen enclosures

(G-4832)
**PREMIER SPECIALTY SERVICE
LLC**
Also Called: Premier Gas and Grills
3293 Highway 17 (32043-9372)
PHONE.................................904 531-9315
Todd Alton Knowles,
EMP: 8 EST: 2016
SALES (est): 524.1K **Privately Held**
SIC: **3631** Barbecues, grills & braziers
(outdoor cooking)

(G-4833)
**PROFORM FINISHING
PRODUCTS LLC**
1767 Wildwood Rd (32043-8319)
PHONE.................................904 284-0221
Larry Adams, Manager

EMP: 21
SALES (corp-wide): 795.8MM **Privately
Held**
WEB: www.nationalgypsum.com
SIC: **2891** 3275 3496 3272 Cement;
linoleum & tile; gypsum products; miscellaneous fabricated wire products; concrete products
HQ: Proform Finishing Products, Llc
2001 Rexford Rd
Charlotte NC 28211

(G-4834)
ROLLER DIE + FORMING
4630 County Road 209 S (32043-8182)
PHONE.................................502 804-5571
Brian Wesley, Business Mgr
Cathy Deckard, Controller
Jeff Hallstrom, Manager
EMP: 15 EST: 2016
SALES (est): 10.6MM **Privately Held**
WEB: www.rollerdie.com
SIC: **3544** Special dies & tools

(G-4835)
RYAN SCIENTIFIC LLC
4035a Reynolds Blvd (32043-8360)
PHONE.................................904 284-6025
Nisa Ryan, Mng Member
Dale Ryan, Mng Member
EMP: 19 EST: 2013
SALES (est): 800K **Privately Held**
SIC: **3296** 5063 5999 Fiberglass insulation; electrical supplies; fiberglass materials, except insulation

(G-4836)
**RYMAN HOSPITALITY PRPTS
INC**
625 Oak St (32043-4313)
PHONE.................................904 284-2770
Richard Loftus, Branch Mgr
EMP: 1040
SALES (corp-wide): 939.3MM **Privately
Held**
WEB: www.rymanhp.com
SIC: **3949** Lures, fishing: artificial
PA: Ryman Hospitality Properties, Inc.
1 Gaylord Dr
Nashville TN 37214
615 316-6000

(G-4837)
**SHARK TOOTH ENTERPRISES
INC**
Also Called: R & J Enterprises
981 Martin Ave (32043-8354)
PHONE.................................904 449-8247
Steven W Tyler, President
EMP: 15 EST: 2008
SQ FT: 28,000
SALES (est): 3.4MM **Privately Held**
WEB: www.homeinspectionadvisory.com
SIC: **3231** Aquariums & reflectors, glass

(G-4838)
TAPE TECHNOLOGIES INC
Also Called: Coating Laminating Converting
1272 Harbor Rd (32043-8729)
P.O. Box 56 (32043-0056)
PHONE.................................904 284-0284
Samuel R Phillips, President
Sindy Goldsborough, Purch Agent
Rocky Holland, Engineer
Sergio Sandoval, Sales Mgr
Dana Kominski, Regl Sales Mgr
◆ EMP: 45 EST: 1986
SQ FT: 43,000
SALES (est): 5.3MM **Privately Held**
WEB: www.tapetechnologies.com
SIC: **3081** Unsupported plastics film &
sheet

(G-4839)
TRINITY FABRICATORS INC
825 Corporate Sq (32043-3748)
P.O. Box 1826 (32043-1826)
PHONE.................................904 284-9657
Merrill C Westfall, President
Damon A Westfall, Corp Secy
Daniel M Westfall, Vice Pres
Kalena Bishop, Production
EMP: 46 EST: 1984
SQ FT: 45,000
SALES (est): 9.3MM **Privately Held**
SIC: **3441** Fabricated structural metal

▲ = Import ▼=Export
◆ =Import/Export

(G-4840)
U2 CLOUD LLC
1300 Cooks Ln (32043-8988)
PHONE...................................888 370-5433
Joe Solsona, *COO*
Diane Wood, *Bookkeeper*
Amanda Juneau, *Accounts Exec*
Joe F Solsona, *Mng Member*
EMP: 15 **EST:** 2010
SQ FT: 8,000
SALES (est): 970.6K **Privately Held**
WEB: www.u2cloud.com
SIC: 7372 Application computer software

(G-4841)
VAC-CON INC (HQ)
969 Hall Park Rd (32043-4940)
PHONE...................................904 284-4200
Darrell Lesage, *President*
Mark Wardlaw, *Regional Mgr*
Greg Hamilton, *Corp Secy*
Todd Masley, *Exec VP*
Alexandra Acevedo-Yates, *Opers Staff*
◆ **EMP:** 271 **EST:** 1987
SALES (est): 118.8MM
SALES (corp-wide): 730.1MM **Privately
Held**
WEB: www.vac-con.com
SIC: 3711 3589 Motor vehicles & car bod-
ies; motor trucks, except off-highway, as-
sembly of; sewer cleaning equipment,
power
PA: Holden Industries, Inc.
500 Lake Cook Rd Ste 400
Deerfield IL 60015
847 940-1500

(G-4842)
**VIRGINIA ELECTRONIC & LTG
CORP (PA)**
Also Called: Velcorp Gems Vels
1293 Energy Cove Ct (32043-4302)
PHONE...................................904 230-2840
Gregory Stepp, *CEO*
Ray Stephens, *Treasurer*
▲ **EMP:** 5 **EST:** 1994
SQ FT: 1,000
SALES (est): 794.9K **Privately Held**
WEB: www.velcorpgems.com
SIC: 3648 5023 7629 7389 Airport light-
ing fixtures: runway approach, taxi or
ramp; lamps: floor, boudoir, desk; electri-
cal repair shops; design services

(G-4843)
WORTH METALS INC
4135 Highway 17 S (32043-8137)
PHONE...................................904 626-1434
Timothy P Worth, *President*
EMP: 12 **EST:** 2007
SALES (est): 3.3MM **Privately Held**
WEB: www.worthmetalsincfl.com
SIC: 3448 3499 Prefabricated metal build-
ings; fabricated metal products

Greenacres
Palm Beach County

(G-4844)
**BLAST CTINGS
POWDERCOATING LLC (PA)**
1745 Sawgrass Cir (33413-3038)
PHONE...................................561 301-9538
Matias Sprindys, *Manager*
EMP: 8 **EST:** 2016
SALES (est): 277.6K **Privately Held**
SIC: 3479 Coating of metals & formed
products

(G-4845)
CONCRAFT INC (PA)
Also Called: Concraft Patio Products
353 Swain Blvd (33463-3341)
PHONE...................................561 689-0149
Neil Stegall, *President*
Eric Stegall, *Vice Pres*
EMP: 6 **EST:** 1957
SQ FT: 7,500
SALES (est): 993.9K **Privately Held**
WEB: www.concraft.com
SIC: 3272 5999 Concrete products, pre-
cast; concrete products, pre-cast

(G-4846)
**ESSENTIAL PUBLISHING
GROUP LLC**
5319 Lake Worth Rd (33463-3353)
PHONE...................................561 570-7165
EMP: 7
SALES (corp-wide): 456.5K **Privately
Held**
WEB: www.essentialpublishinggroup.com
SIC: 2741 Miscellaneous publishing
PA: Essential Publishing Group Llc
1140 Holland Dr Ste 21
Boca Raton FL 33487
410 440-5777

(G-4847)
**FM PUBLICATIONS ENTERPRISE
INC**
6742 Forest Hill Blvd (33413-3321)
PHONE...................................561 670-7205
Frantz Marcelin, *Principal*
EMP: 7 **EST:** 2016
SALES (est): 237.1K **Privately Held**
SIC: 2741 Miscellaneous publishing

(G-4848)
**GOLD BUYERS OF AMERICA
LLC**
2001 20th Ln (33463-4259)
PHONE...................................877 721-8033
EMP: 184 **Privately Held**
SIC: 3356 Nonferrous Rolling/Drawing
PA: Gold Buyers Of America, Llc
2790 Windham Ct
Delray Beach FL 33445

(G-4849)
IMMUNOTEK BIO CENTERS LLC
4560 Lake Worth Rd (33463-3450)
PHONE...................................561 270-6712
Alison Comegys, *Controller*
Rendi Dillard, *Manager*
EMP: 29
SALES (corp-wide): 27MM **Privately
Held**
WEB: www.immunotek.com
SIC: 2836 Blood derivatives
PA: Immunotek Bio Centers, L.L.C.
3900 N Causeway Blvd # 1200
Metairie LA 70002
337 500-1175

(G-4850)
KID GROUP INC
4010 S 57th Ave Ste 104 (33463-4301)
PHONE...................................888 805-8851
Keren Aydogan, *President*
EMP: 5 **EST:** 2010
SALES (est): 966.2K **Privately Held**
WEB: www.sepconn.com
SIC: 3679 Electronic circuits

(G-4851)
LIFEGATE PUBLISHING LLC
1110 Parkside Green Dr (33415-1506)
PHONE...................................561 602-0089
Evette Lawton, *Administration*
EMP: 7 **EST:** 2014
SALES (est): 133.8K **Privately Held**
WEB: www.lifegate.com
SIC: 2741 Miscellaneous publishing

(G-4852)
RELCOM INDUSTRIES INC
3900 Woodlake Blvd # 200 (33463-3044)
PHONE...................................561 304-7717
Allan Liebowitz, *Vice Pres*
EMP: 5 **EST:** 2005
SALES (est): 526.1K **Privately Held**
WEB: www.relcominc.com
SIC: 3679 Electronic circuits

(G-4853)
SAPPHIRE LLC
6432 Melaleuca Ln (33463-3807)
PHONE...................................561 346-7449
Patrick Adams, *Principal*
EMP: 7 **EST:** 2013
SALES (est): 312.8K **Privately Held**
SIC: 3993 Signs & advertising specialties

Greenville
Madison County

(G-4854)
FLORIDA PLYWOODS INC
1228 Nw Us 221 (32331-4268)
P.O. Box 458 (32331-0458)
PHONE...................................850 948-2211
John Maultsby Jr, *President*
Charles Maultsby, *President*
Arthur Maultsby, *Executive*
EMP: 75 **EST:** 1956
SQ FT: 100,000
SALES (est): 7.2MM **Privately Held**
WEB: www.flply.com
SIC: 2434 2493 Wood kitchen cabinets;
particleboard products

Greenwood
Jackson County

(G-4855)
L W TIMBER CO INC
3830 Highway 69 (32443-2150)
PHONE...................................850 592-2597
Charles M Leslie, *Director*
EMP: 6 **EST:** 2001
SALES (est): 424.1K **Privately Held**
SIC: 2411 Timber, cut at logging camp

Gretna
Gadsden County

(G-4856)
CDS MANUFACTURING INC
106 Charles Hayes Sr Dr (32332-2406)
PHONE...................................850 875-4651
Melanie D Sembler, *CEO*
Clayton H Sembler, *President*
Angel Majors, *Controller*
EMP: 52 **EST:** 1999
SALES (est): 9.9MM **Privately Held**
WEB: www.cdsmanufacturing.net
SIC: 3272 Precast terrazo or concrete
products; concrete products, precast; pre-
stressed concrete products

Groveland
Lake County

(G-4857)
ACCU TECH LLC
1506 Max Hooks Rd Ste E (34736-8037)
PHONE...................................407 446-6676
Gary D Akers, *Principal*
EMP: 8 **EST:** 2012
SALES (est): 896.3K **Privately Held**
SIC: 3089 Injection molding of plastics

(G-4858)
**ACR FAMILY COMPONENTS
LLC**
19900 Independence Blvd (34736-8535)
PHONE...................................352 243-0307
Arthur V Raney,
EMP: 29 **EST:** 2006
SALES (est): 9.4MM **Privately Held**
SIC: 3679 Electronic circuits

(G-4859)
DOGLIPS LOGISTICS LLC ✪
471 Kestrel Dr (34736-8053)
PHONE...................................407 704-0097
Richard Gabriel, *Mng Member*
EMP: 7 **EST:** 2021
SALES (est): 347.1K **Privately Held**
SIC: 3743 Freight cars & equipment

(G-4860)
GJCB SIGNS GRAPHICS INC
Also Called: Jds Uniforms
136 S Main Ave (34736-2554)
PHONE...................................352 429-0803
Charles G Thompson, *President*
Jennifer S Thompson, *Vice Pres*
EMP: 10 **EST:** 2014

SALES (est): 487.6K **Privately Held**
WEB: www.linkprintingcf.com
SIC: 3993 Signs & advertising specialties

(G-4861)
GTM MANUFACTURING INC
14350 Eastside St (34736-8438)
PHONE...................................407 654-6598
Dale Strange, *President*
EMP: 6 **EST:** 2017
SALES (est): 490.6K **Privately Held**
WEB: www.qwikchute.com
SIC: 3999 Manufacturing industries

(G-4862)
ICON INDUSTRIES
3015 Shady Oak Pl (34736-8425)
PHONE...................................352 988-3895
Benjamin Edward Golub, *Owner*
EMP: 7 **EST:** 2017
SALES (est): 50.7K **Privately Held**
WEB: www.iconindustries.com
SIC: 3999 Manufacturing industries

(G-4863)
**INTERNL STERILIZATION LAB
LLC**
Also Called: Isl
217 Sampey Rd (34736-3305)
PHONE...................................352 429-3200
Yasushi Kuki, *President*
Lori Swisher, *Manager*
EMP: 9 **EST:** 1996
SQ FT: 12,080
SALES (est): 917.1K **Privately Held**
WEB: www.isl-fl.com
SIC: 3842 Sterilizers, hospital & surgical

(G-4864)
JAYSHREE HOLDINGS INC
18830 State Road 19 (34736-8658)
P.O. Box 397 (34736-0397)
PHONE...................................352 429-1000
Sudhir Bhagani, *President*
Jayshree Bhagani, *Vice Pres*
Nitesh Bhagani, *Sales Staff*
EMP: 17 **EST:** 1989
SQ FT: 8,000
SALES (est): 472.3K **Privately Held**
WEB: www.jayshree.com
SIC: 2099 0139 Seasonings & spices;
herb or spice farm

(G-4865)
MAJESTIC WOODWORKS
156 Groveland Farms Rd (34736-2026)
PHONE...................................352 429-2520
Laurie Summers Tueros, *Principal*
EMP: 8 **EST:** 2014
SALES (est): 353.8K **Privately Held**
WEB: www.majesticcustomwood.com
SIC: 2434 Wood kitchen cabinets

(G-4866)
MARITEC INDUSTRIES INC
Also Called: Gambler Bass Boats
20150 Independence Blvd (34736-8528)
PHONE...................................352 429-8888
Thurston R Ackerbloom Jr, *President*
Leonard D Jones, *Vice Pres*
EMP: 55 **EST:** 1986
SQ FT: 45,000
SALES (est): 10.4MM **Privately Held**
WEB: www.gamblerboats.com
SIC: 3732 Fishing boats: lobster, crab, oys-
ter, etc.: small

(G-4867)
NOVELTY CRYSTAL CORP
Also Called: Ncc Promotional
21005 Obrien Rd (34736-9590)
PHONE...................................352 429-9036
EMP: 20
SALES (corp-wide): 11.6MM **Privately
Held**
SIC: 3089 Mfg Plastic Products
PA: Novelty Crystal Corp.
3015 48th Ave
Long Island City NY 32819
718 458-6700

(G-4868)
QUIET FLEX
7730 American Way (34736-8649)
PHONE...................................352 429-3286
EMP: 10 **EST:** 2017

SALES (est): 1.6MM **Privately Held**
WEB: www.quietflex.com
SIC: 3296 Mineral wool

(G-4869)
ROYAL SCREEN ENCLOSURES INC
18241 Sky Top Ln (34736-8591)
PHONE....................................407 970-0864
Willard Keene Jr, *Branch Mgr*
EMP: 11 **Privately Held**
SIC: 3448 Screen enclosures
PA: Royal Screen Enclosures Inc
　　10030 Tween Waters St
　　Clermont FL 34715

(G-4870)
SCOTTS COMPANY LLC
20605 State Road 19 (34736-9030)
PHONE....................................352 429-0066
Howard Burger, *Branch Mgr*
Randy Swanks, *Manager*
EMP: 60
SQ FT: 5,000
SALES (corp-wide): 4.9B **Publicly Held**
WEB: www.scotts.com
SIC: 2873 2875 Plant foods, mixed: from plants making nitrog. fertilizers; fertilizers, mixing only
HQ: The Scotts Company Llc
　　14111 Scottslawn Rd
　　Marysville OH 43040
　　937 644-0011

(G-4871)
SHIFTED INDUSTRIES
6930 Swamp Dr (34736-8437)
PHONE....................................561 302-8915
Caleb Rennekamp, *Principal*
EMP: 7 EST: 2018
SALES (est): 317.7K **Privately Held**
WEB: www.shiftedind.com
SIC: 3999 Manufacturing industries

(G-4872)
SNOOKTON INC
146 E Broad St (34736-4003)
PHONE....................................352 429-1133
James J Baumann, *Principal*
EMP: 8 EST: 2010
SALES (est): 113.7K **Privately Held**
SIC: 2741 Miscellaneous publishing

(G-4873)
SUNCOAST PROJECTS LLC
Also Called: Hub Steel
7500 Republic Dr (34736-8670)
P.O. Box 140761, Orlando (32814-0761)
PHONE....................................407 581-0665
John Meacham, *Manager*
EMP: 30 EST: 2010
SQ FT: 5,000
SALES (est): 4.9MM **Privately Held**
WEB: www.gohubsteel.com
SIC: 3441 Fabricated structural metal

Gulf Breeze
Santa Rosa County

(G-4874)
A PLUS MARINE SUPPLY INC (PA)
212 Mcclure Dr (32561-7401)
PHONE....................................850 934-3890
Eric W Duntz, *President*
Dana Gonzales, *Corp Secy*
◆ EMP: 5 EST: 1989
SQ FT: 2,500
SALES (est): 691K **Privately Held**
WEB: www.aplusmarine.com
SIC: 3949 5091 Skin diving equipment, scuba type; diving equipment & supplies

(G-4875)
ALOHA SCREEN PRINTING INC
2635 Gulf Breeze Pkwy (32563-3023)
PHONE....................................850 934-4716
Rodney Lopaka Robello, *President*
Chad Kaipo Robello, *Vice Pres*
EMP: 5 EST: 1994
SQ FT: 900

SALES (est): 346.2K **Privately Held**
WEB: www.alohascreenprinting.com
SIC: 2396 2759 Screen printing on fabric articles; screen printing

(G-4876)
ASCEND PRFMCE MTLS OPRTONS LLC
200 Pensacola Beach Rd B3 (32561-4840)
PHONE....................................734 819-0656
Chong Kim, *Branch Mgr*
EMP: 209
SALES (corp-wide): 1.4B **Privately Held**
WEB: www.ascendmaterials.com
SIC: 2821 Plastics materials & resins
HQ: Ascend Performance Materials Operations Llc
　　1010 Travis St Ste 900
　　Houston TX 77002

(G-4877)
AVALEX TECHNOLOGIES LLC
2665 Gulf Breeze Pkwy (32563-3023)
PHONE....................................850 470-8464
Jurgen R Ihns, *President*
Paul Stephens, *Business Mgr*
Kevin Hatch, *COO*
Tony Hatten, *Vice Pres*
David Phillips, *Mfg Mgr*
▼ EMP: 105 EST: 1992
SQ FT: 1,500
SALES (est): 26.2MM
SALES (corp-wide): 988.2MM **Publicly Held**
WEB: www.mrcy.com
SIC: 3812 Aircraft control systems, electronic
PA: Mercury Systems, Inc.
　　50 Minuteman Rd
　　Andover MA 01810
　　978 256-1300

(G-4878)
COASTAL PADDLE CO LLC
848 Gulf Breeze Pkwy (32561-4723)
PHONE....................................850 916-1600
Randy Cook Jr, *Mng Member*
EMP: 9 EST: 2010
SALES (est): 431.2K **Privately Held**
WEB: www.coastalpaddlecompany.com
SIC: 2499 2339 Oars & paddles, wood; women's & misses' accessories

(G-4879)
DARK HORSE SIGNS AND PRTG LLC
6476 Starfish Cv (32563-9079)
PHONE....................................850 684-3833
Caleb Rogers, *Principal*
EMP: 7 EST: 2017
SALES (est): 378.2K **Privately Held**
WEB: www.darkhorsesignsandprinting.com
SIC: 2752 Commercial printing, lithographic

(G-4880)
DONALDSON ENTERPRISES
5041 Lantana Dr (32563-8933)
PHONE....................................850 934-5030
EMP: 7 EST: 2016
SALES (est): 104.4K **Privately Held**
WEB: www.donaldson.com
SIC: 3599 Industrial machinery

(G-4881)
FISHGUM
1830 Cowen Rd (32563-9579)
PHONE....................................256 394-2760
Tony Faggioni, *Manager*
EMP: 9
SALES (corp-wide): 83.7K **Privately Held**
SIC: 3949 Bait, artificial: fishing
PA: Fishgum
　　2040 Jamaica Dr
　　Navarre FL 32566
　　256 394-2761

(G-4882)
GULF BREEZE NEWS INC
913 Gulf Breeze Pkwy # 35 (32561-4729)
P.O. Box 1414 (32562-1414)
PHONE....................................850 932-8986
Lisa Newell, *President*
Franklin Hayes, *Editor*
Claire Musmansky, *Manager*
Laura Lane, *Director*

Gregory Papajohn, *Director*
EMP: 5 EST: 2001
SALES (est): 806.1K **Privately Held**
WEB: www.gulfbreezenews.com
SIC: 2711 Newspapers, publishing & printing

(G-4883)
GULF COAST SHADES & BLINDS LLC
714 Roanoke Ct (32561-4509)
PHONE....................................850 332-2100
Joseph D Selogy, *Principal*
EMP: 13 EST: 2018
SALES (est): 2.8MM **Privately Held**
WEB: www.gcshadesandblinds.com
SIC: 2591 Window blinds

(G-4884)
HOGENKAMP RESEARCH INC
308 Plantation Hill Rd (32561-4818)
PHONE....................................850 677-1072
James D Doyle, *Owner*
▲ EMP: 10 EST: 1990
SALES (est): 903.9K **Privately Held**
WEB: www.hogenkampresearch.com
SIC: 2611 Pulp manufactured from waste or recycled paper

(G-4885)
INTEGRATED SURROUNDINGS INC
4333 Gulf Breeze Pkwy (32563-9152)
PHONE....................................850 932-0848
Roy Pedersen, *President*
David Gray, *COO*
Derek Elmore, *Vice Pres*
EMP: 14 EST: 2008
SALES (est): 2.4MM **Privately Held**
WEB: www.integratedsurroundings.com
SIC: 3699 1731 Security control equipment & systems; energy management controls

(G-4886)
MORRISSY & CO
204 Fairpoint Dr (32561-4308)
P.O. Box 1434 (32562-1434)
PHONE....................................850 934-4243
EMP: 5
SALES (est): 300K **Privately Held**
SIC: 7372 Prepackaged Software Services

(G-4887)
NORTH AMERICA WIRELINE LLC
6057 Clay Cir (32563-9715)
PHONE....................................870 365-5401
EMP: 7 EST: 2019
SALES (est): 1.9MM **Privately Held**
WEB: www.northamericawireline.com
SIC: 1389 Oil field services

(G-4888)
NORTH W FLA CNCIL OF BLIND COR
2807 Sandy Ridge Rd (32563-2603)
PHONE....................................850 982-7867
Barbara Reeves, *Principal*
EMP: 7 EST: 2018
SALES (est): 84.2K **Privately Held**
SIC: 2591 Window blinds

(G-4889)
PERFORMANCE COATINGS INC
3749 Gulf Breeze Pkwy (32563-5717)
PHONE....................................850 733-0082
Alan K Eason, *Principal*
EMP: 12 EST: 2010
SALES (est): 95.4K **Privately Held**
SIC: 3479 Metal coating & allied service

(G-4890)
SANDPAPER PUBLISHING INC
7502 Harvest Village Ct (32566-7319)
PHONE....................................850 939-8040
Sandra Kemp, *President*
EMP: 9 EST: 1997
SQ FT: 2,400
SALES (est): 991.6K **Privately Held**
WEB: www.navarrepress.com
SIC: 2741 Miscellaneous publishing

(G-4891)
SEPARATION SYSTEMS INC
100 Nightingale Ln A (32561-4300)
PHONE....................................850 932-1433
Joaquin Lubkowitz, *President*
Adela Lubkowitz, *Vice Pres*
Bob Belair, *Sales Staff*
EMP: 10 EST: 1990
SQ FT: 1,300
SALES (est): 2.1MM **Privately Held**
WEB: www.separationsystems.com
SIC: 3826 Gas chromatographic instruments

(G-4892)
SQUARED MACHINE & TOOL INC A
1851 Cowen Rd Unit F (32563-4109)
PHONE....................................678 988-2477
Chris Wysoczynski, *Principal*
EMP: 9 EST: 2017
SALES (est): 286.7K **Privately Held**
WEB: www.asquaredmachineandtool.com
SIC: 3599 Machine shop, jobbing & repair

(G-4893)
T SALS SHIRT CO
1161 Oriole Beach Rd (32563-3260)
PHONE....................................850 916-9229
Becky Serio, *Owner*
EMP: 10 EST: 1972
SALES (est): 984.5K **Privately Held**
WEB: www.salstshirts.com
SIC: 2759 Screen printing

(G-4894)
TASTE OF THAI LLC
3475 Gulf Breeze Pkwy (32563-1402)
PHONE....................................850 581-3340
Viparat B Pippin,
EMP: 5 EST: 2012
SALES (est): 500.7K **Privately Held**
WEB: www.tasteofthaillc.com
SIC: 3421 Table & food cutlery, including butchers'

(G-4895)
TOWN STREET PRINT SHOP INC
Also Called: Tmt Printing & Mailing
1142 Bayview Ln (32563-3302)
P.O. Box 18630, Pensacola (32523-8630)
PHONE....................................850 432-8300
Linda Traweek, *Vice Pres*
Dennis Malloy, *Manager*
Angela Tarweek, *Admin Sec*
EMP: 5 EST: 1972
SQ FT: 5,000
SALES (est): 483.1K **Privately Held**
SIC: 2752 7331 2791 2789 Commercial printing, offset; mailing service; typesetting; bookbinding & related work

(G-4896)
VINYL BROS
5668 Gulf Breeze Pkwy # 4 (32563-9524)
PHONE....................................850 396-5977
Cory Malesa, *President*
EMP: 7 EST: 2017
SALES (est): 354.6K **Privately Held**
WEB: www.vinylbrosfl.com
SIC: 3993 Signs & advertising specialties

Gulfport
Pinellas County

(G-4897)
FULL BORE DIRECTIONAL INC
4921 15th Ave S (33707-4317)
PHONE....................................727 327-7784
EMP: 5
SQ FT: 900
SALES (est): 500K **Privately Held**
SIC: 1381 Oil/Gas Well Drilling

(G-4898)
GULFCOAST GABBER INC
1419 49th St S (33707-4301)
PHONE....................................727 321-6965
Ken Reichart, *President*
EMP: 6 EST: 1986

SALES (est): 613.5K **Privately Held**
WEB: www.thegabber.com
SIC: **2711** Newspapers, publishing & printing

(G-4899)
GULFPORT GRIND INC
5825 20th Ave S (33707-4049)
PHONE....................................727 343-2785
Theodore Kehoe, *Principal*
EMP: 8 EST: 2012
SALES (est): 98.6K **Privately Held**
WEB: www.mygulfport.us
SIC: **3599** Grinding castings for the trade

(G-4900)
PFA PUBLISHING
6020 Shore Blvd S (33707-5801)
PHONE....................................727 512-5814
Vernon Fitch, *Principal*
EMP: 8 EST: 2007
SALES (est): 97.8K **Privately Held**
WEB: www.pinkfloydarchives.com
SIC: **2741** Miscellaneous publishing

Haines City
Polk County

(G-4901)
AERCON FLORIDA LLC
3701 State Road 544 E (33844-8898)
PHONE....................................863 422-6360
Mike Quaka, *General Mgr*
Michael McCormick, *Sales Executive*
Chris Green, *Info Tech Mgr*
◆ EMP: 66 EST: 2002
SQ FT: 95,000
SALES (est): 12.1MM **Privately Held**
WEB: www.aerconaac.com
SIC: **3272** Concrete products, precast

(G-4902)
CENTRAL ELECTRIC MOTOR SVC INC
313 N 12th St (33844-4403)
P.O. Box 696 (33845-0696)
PHONE....................................863 422-4721
Joey Rulli, *President*
EMP: 10 EST: 1969
SQ FT: 6,435
SALES (est): 491.3K **Privately Held**
SIC: **7694 7699 1731 1623** Electric motor repair; pumps & pumping equipment repair; electrical work; pumping station construction

(G-4903)
COST CAST INC
1301 W Commerce Ave (33844-3292)
PHONE....................................863 422-5617
Gary Kallmeyer, *President*
Jason Kallmeyer, *Engineer*
Alex Wilding, *Engineer*
EMP: 17 EST: 2017
SALES (est): 1.8MM **Privately Held**
WEB: www.costcast.com
SIC: **3599** Machine shop, jobbing & repair

(G-4904)
COST CAST ALUMINUM CORP
1301 W Commerce Ave (33844-3292)
PHONE....................................863 422-5617
Gary Kallmeyer, *President*
EMP: 33 EST: 1966
SQ FT: 9,380
SALES (est): 2.6MM **Privately Held**
WEB: www.costcast.com
SIC: **3365 3543 3369** Aluminum foundries; industrial patterns; nonferrous foundries

(G-4905)
CROMER PRINTING INC
Also Called: Cromer International Press
24 N 6th St (33844-4206)
P.O. Box 1268 (33845-1268)
PHONE....................................863 422-8651
Bobbi C Freeman, *President*
James Robert Freeman, *Manager*
Sharon Lepsic, *Manager*
Margie Wells, *Manager*
EMP: 20 EST: 1971

SALES (est): 4.7MM
SALES (corp-wide): 5.4MM **Privately Held**
WEB: www.cromerprinting.com
SIC: **2752** Commercial printing, offset
PA: The Pamatian Group Inc
997 W Kennedy Blvd Ste A1
Orlando FL 32810
407 291-8387

(G-4906)
ER JAHNA INDUSTRIES INC
Also Called: Haines City Mine
4910 State Road 544 E (33844-8739)
PHONE....................................863 422-7617
Brian Corley, *Sales Staff*
Emil R Jahna, *Marketing Staff*
Dalton Jahna, *Branch Mgr*
Kirk Davis, *Director*
Jake Simmons, *Director*
EMP: 7
SALES (corp-wide): 49.2MM **Privately Held**
WEB: www.jahna.com
SIC: **1442** Construction sand & gravel
PA: E.R. Jahna Industries, Inc.
202 E Stuart Ave
Lake Wales FL 33853
863 676-9431

(G-4907)
FLOYD FABRICATION LLC
2821 Sanderling St (33844-8444)
PHONE....................................330 289-7351
Ben Floyd, *Principal*
EMP: 7 EST: 2019
SALES (est): 221.1K **Privately Held**
WEB: www.floydfabrication.com
SIC: **7692** Welding repair

(G-4908)
ITW BLDING CMPONENTS GROUP INC
ITW Alpine
1950 Marley Dr 3 (33844-9202)
PHONE....................................863 422-8685
Charlie Hoover, *Branch Mgr*
EMP: 38
SALES (corp-wide): 14.4B **Publicly Held**
SIC: **3443 3446 3441 3312** Truss plates, metal; architectural metalwork; fabricated structural metal; blast furnaces & steel mills; miscellaneous metalwork
HQ: Itw Building Components Group, Inc.
13389 Lakefront Dr
Earth City MO 63045
314 344-9121

(G-4909)
JAIN IRRIGATION HOLDINGS CORP
3777 State Road 544 E (33844-8898)
P.O. Box 3546 (33845-3546)
PHONE....................................863 422-4000
Sherry Davis, *Manager*
EMP: 260
SALES (corp-wide): 13.3MM **Privately Held**
WEB: www.jainsusa.com
SIC: **3523** Irrigation equipment, self-propelled
PA: Jain Irrigation Holdings Corporation
5965 S 900 E Ste 450
Murray UT 84121
909 395-5200

(G-4910)
MARTIN & VLEMINCKX RIDES LLC
31096 Us Hwy 27 N (33844-7318)
PHONE....................................407 566-0036
Charles Bingham, *Partner*
Pierre Cloutier, *Vice Pres*
David Welsh, *Project Mgr*
Gerry Gosine, *VP Sales*
Eve Melanson, *Marketing Staff*
EMP: 7 EST: 2003
SALES (est): 2.2MM
SALES (corp-wide): 836.1K **Privately Held**
WEB: www.martin-vleminckx.com
SIC: **3441** Fabricated structural metal

PA: Martin, G. & A. Vleminckx Amusement Ltd
1255 Boul Laird Bureau 215
Mont-Royal QC H3P 2
514 733-0060

(G-4911)
OLDCASTLE APG SOUTH INC
1980 Marley Dr (33844-9202)
PHONE....................................863 421-7422
▲ EMP: 10 EST: 2013
SALES (est): 949.1K **Privately Held**
WEB: www.oldcastlecoastal.com
SIC: **3272** Concrete products

(G-4912)
POWER WTHIN CNSLING CNSLTN LLC
280 Patterson Rd Ste 1 (33844-6261)
PHONE....................................863 242-3023
Cheryl Cyr,
EMP: 5 EST: 2018
SALES (est): 335K **Privately Held**
WEB: www.powerwithcc.com
SIC: **3844** Therapeutic X-ray apparatus & tubes

(G-4913)
PRE-TECH INC
3052 Us Highway 17 92 N (33844-9541)
PHONE....................................863 422-5079
Larry E Witherington, *President*
Kathleen Witherington, *Admin Sec*
EMP: 5 EST: 1981
SQ FT: 8,000
SALES (est): 451.7K **Privately Held**
WEB: www.pre-tech.net
SIC: **3599** Machine shop, jobbing & repair

(G-4914)
QUALITY METAL WORX LLC
1306 Melbourne Ave (33844-4810)
PHONE....................................863 353-6638
Todd Dunnahoe, *Principal*
EMP: 10 EST: 2016
SALES (est): 915.8K **Privately Held**
WEB: quality-metal-worx.business.site
SIC: **3441 7692** Fabricated structural metal; welding repair

(G-4915)
QUALITY TOOL INC
659 Copeland Dr (33844-9657)
PHONE....................................386 265-1492
Peter Sweeney, *Principal*
EMP: 10 EST: 2017
SALES (est): 62K **Privately Held**
WEB: www.qualitytool.com
SIC: **3599** Machine shop, jobbing & repair

(G-4916)
STANDARD SAND & SILICA COMPANY
2 Us Highway 17 92 N (33844-4826)
P.O. Box 1240, Davenport (33836-1240)
PHONE....................................863 419-9673
Brynn Summerlin, *Manager*
EMP: 7
SALES (corp-wide): 69.8MM **Privately Held**
WEB: www.standardsand.com
SIC: **3471 1446** Sand blasting of metal parts; abrasive sand mining
PA: Standard Sand & Silica Company
1850 Us Highway 17 92 N
Davenport FL 33837
863 422-7100

(G-4917)
STANDARD TRUSS & ROOF SUP INC
608 N 12th St (33844-4471)
PHONE....................................863 422-8293
James Mc Intee, *President*
David Mc Intee, *Vice Pres*
Steven Mc Intee, *Treasurer*
Sheryl Wolkenhauer, *Admin Sec*
EMP: 22 EST: 1978
SQ FT: 23,640
SALES (est): 3.2MM **Privately Held**
SIC: **2439** Trusses, wooden roof

(G-4918)
SUN ORCHARD LLC
1200 S 30th St (33845-9099)
P.O. Box 2008 (33845-2008)
PHONE....................................863 422-5062
Jose Vargas, *Production*
Duane Walker, *Engineer*
Jean-Marc Rotsaert, *Branch Mgr*
EMP: 100
SALES (corp-wide): 65.2MM **Privately Held**
WEB: www.sunorchard.com
SIC: **2033** Canned fruits & specialties
PA: Sun Orchard, Llc
8600 Nw 36th St Ste 250
Doral FL 33166
786 646-9200

Hallandale
Broward County

(G-4919)
AQUATIC FABRICATORS OF S FLA
Also Called: Aquatic Wetsuits
2930 Sw 30th Ave Ste A (33009-5142)
PHONE....................................954 458-0400
Gene Sonnabend, *President*
Connie Sonnabend, *Admin Sec*
EMP: 6 EST: 1991
SQ FT: 2,500
SALES (est): 709K **Privately Held**
WEB: www.wetwear.com
SIC: **3069** Wet suits, rubber

(G-4920)
ATLANTIC SHIP SUPPLY INC
2050 Sw 31st Ave (33009-2027)
PHONE....................................954 961-8885
Adam Notis, *President*
▼ EMP: 9 EST: 2004
SALES (est): 339.6K **Privately Held**
SIC: **2674** Shipping & shopping bags or sacks

(G-4921)
CHIPTECH INC (PA)
Also Called: Vertical Cable
2885 Sw 30th Ave (33009-3801)
PHONE....................................954 454-3554
Majid Sattarzadeh, *President*
Mahsa Sattarzadeh, *Business Mgr*
Sam Jazayri, *Vice Pres*
Jenny Maloney, *Accounting Mgr*
Shervin Shahrdar, *Sales Staff*
◆ EMP: 11 EST: 1989
SQ FT: 22,000
SALES (est): 13.2MM **Privately Held**
SIC: **2298** Cable, fiber

(G-4922)
CORONA PRINTING COMPANY INC
1833 Sw 31st Ave (33009-2020)
PHONE....................................754 263-2914
EMP: 6 EST: 2018
SALES (est): 323.8K **Privately Held**
SIC: **2752** Commercial printing, lithographic

(G-4923)
DANDY MEDIA CORPORATION
Also Called: Dandyprint.com
2031 Sw 31st Ave (33009-2031)
PHONE....................................954 616-6800
William T Clegg, *President*
Juan E Soriano, *Vice Pres*
Juan Soriano, *Vice Pres*
John Melendez, *Treasurer*
EMP: 10 EST: 2012
SALES (est): 404.6K **Privately Held**
SIC: **2759** Commercial printing

(G-4924)
EDDY FLOOR SCRAPER INC
1806 Sw 31st Ave (33009-2024)
PHONE....................................954 981-0715
Stephane Tailly, *CEO*
◆ EMP: 5 EST: 1999
SQ FT: 9,000

SALES (est): 430.7K **Privately Held**
WEB: www.eddyfloortools.com
SIC: **3544** Special dies, tools, jigs & fixtures

(G-4925)
ELEGANT HOUSE INTL LLC
1960 Sw 30th Ave (33009-2005)
PHONE..................................954 457-8836
▲ EMP: 5
SQ FT: 20,000
SALES (est): 460.2K **Privately Held**
SIC: **2392 2517 2512 2511** Mfg Household Furnishing Mfg Wd Tv/Radio Cabinets Mfg Uphls Household Furn Mfg Wood Household Furn

(G-4926)
JM OCEAN MAR CANVAS & UPHL INC
1825 Sw 31st Ave (33009-2020)
PHONE..................................786 473-7143
Michael E Pelier P, *Principal*
EMP: 9 EST: 2017
SALES (est): 717.8K **Privately Held**
SIC: **2211** Canvas

(G-4927)
MYTON INDUSTRIES INC
1981 S Park Rd (33009-2013)
PHONE..................................954 989-0113
Raymond Leone, *President*
▼ EMP: 12 EST: 1974
SQ FT: 10,000
SALES (est): 1.6MM **Privately Held**
WEB: www.mytonindustries.com
SIC: **3089** Plastic containers, except foam

(G-4928)
PLASMA CUTTING LLC
3140 W Hllandale Bch Blvd (33009-5100)
PHONE..................................954 558-1371
Andres G A C Gonzalez Sr, *Owner*
EMP: 7 EST: 2017
SALES (est): 450.9K **Privately Held**
SIC: **2836** Plasmas

(G-4929)
PRINTEX WORLDWIDE INC
2037 Sw 31st Ave (33009-2031)
PHONE..................................954 518-0722
Gary Walko, *President*
EMP: 6 EST: 2002
SALES (est): 513.7K **Privately Held**
WEB: www.printexusa.com
SIC: **2759** Screen printing

(G-4930)
TROPICAL ASPHALT LLC
1904 Sw 31st Ave (33009-2022)
PHONE..................................954 983-3434
Richard Zegelbone, *Branch Mgr*
EMP: 15
SALES (corp-wide): 9.7MM **Privately Held**
WEB: www.tropicalroofingproducts.com
SIC: **2952** Asphalt felts & coatings
PA: Tropical Asphalt, Llc
14435 Macaw St
La Mirada CA 90638
714 739-1408

(G-4931)
UNLIMITED CABINET DESIGNS INC
1798 Sw 31st Ave (33009-2023)
PHONE..................................954 923-3269
Gerardo Bernal, *President*
EMP: 10 EST: 1988
SQ FT: 100,000
SALES (est): 698.9K **Privately Held**
SIC: **2511 2541** Wood household furniture; cabinets, lockers & shelving

Hallandale Beach
Broward County

(G-4932)
AAA INDEX TABS LLC
201 Ansin Blvd (33009-3116)
PHONE..................................954 457-7777
Richard Hughes, *Principal*
EMP: 7 EST: 2009

SALES (est): 185.4K **Privately Held**
SIC: **3577** Printers, computer

(G-4933)
ABSOLUTE WOOD CREATIONS LLC
200 S Dixie Hwy (33009-5436)
PHONE..................................954 251-2202
AVI Avni,
Rochell Avni,
EMP: 9 EST: 2004
SALES (est): 1.1MM **Privately Held**
SIC: **2434** Wood kitchen cabinets

(G-4934)
ALAMO USA INC
1117 Ne 10th St (33009-2683)
PHONE..................................954 774-3747
Alexander Aralov, *President*
EMP: 9 EST: 2015
SALES (est): 88.6K **Privately Held**
WEB: www.alamo.com
SIC: **3519** Controls, remote, for boats

(G-4935)
AMERICAN IMPACT MEDIA CORP
413 Se 1st Ave (33009-6406)
P.O. Box 1266, Hallandale (33008-1266)
PHONE..................................954 457-9003
Jeffrey Eichner, *President*
Donna Eichner, *Vice Pres*
Dina Saman, *Office Mgr*
EMP: 17 EST: 1989
SQ FT: 2,500
SALES (est): 3.3MM **Privately Held**
WEB: www.americanimpact.com
SIC: **3661 7922** Message concentrators; radio producers

(G-4936)
ARNO BELO INC
Also Called: Manufacturer
221 W Hllndale Bch Blvd P (33009-5441)
PHONE..................................800 734-2356
Manuel Garrido, *CFO*
Arno Inc, *Administration*
EMP: 6 EST: 2016
SALES (est): 401.7K **Privately Held**
WEB: www.arnobelo.com
SIC: **2325 2339 3949 2329** Jeans: men's, youths', men's & boys'; jeans: women's, misses & juniors'; sporting & athletic goods; men's & boys' sportswear & athletic clothing

(G-4937)
ATLANTIC VENDING INC (PA)
224 Nw 6th Ave (33009-4022)
PHONE..................................954 605-6046
Irwin M Egert, *President*
EMP: 6 EST: 1995
SALES (est): 3.2MM **Privately Held**
WEB: www.atlanticvendingnj.com
SIC: **3581** Mechanisms & parts for automatic vending machines

(G-4938)
BIO-PHARM LLC
409 W Hallandale Beach Bl (33009-5301)
PHONE..................................973 223-7163
Amit Shah, *Principal*
EMP: 5 EST: 2015
SQ FT: 300
SALES (est): 415K **Privately Held**
SIC: **2834** Pharmaceutical preparations

(G-4939)
BLUUM LAB LLC
470 Ansin Blvd Ste Aa (33009-3106)
PHONE..................................877 341-3339
Yehuda Gabay, *Mng Member*
Elad Barda,
EMP: 16 EST: 2015
SALES (est): 1.1MM **Privately Held**
WEB: www.bluumdistribution.com
SIC: **3999**

(G-4940)
CALIFORNO CORP
217 Nw 2nd Ave (33009-4008)
PHONE..................................855 553-6766
Shali Zanzuri, *President*
EMP: 8 EST: 2016

SALES (est): 400K **Privately Held**
WEB: www.californo.co
SIC: **3556** Ovens, bakery

(G-4941)
CELLPHONE PARTS EXPRESS LLC
2633 Park Ln (33009-3812)
PHONE..................................954 635-5525
Abderrahmane Guennouni,
EMP: 8 EST: 2017
SALES (est): 1.3MM **Privately Held**
WEB: www.cpp-express.com
SIC: **3661** Telephone & telegraph apparatus

(G-4942)
CONRAD PLASTICS LLC
1904 S Ocean Dr Apt 1703 (33009-5962)
PHONE..................................954 391-9515
Javier Solis,
Mariela Zampini,
EMP: 6 EST: 2019
SALES (est): 482.1K **Privately Held**
WEB: www.conradplasticsllc.com
SIC: **3089** Plastic processing

(G-4943)
DAVILA WOODWORKING INC
214 Nw 1st Ave (33009-4002)
PHONE..................................954 458-0460
Carlos Davila Sr, *Partner*
EMP: 6 EST: 1985
SALES (est): 511.2K **Privately Held**
WEB: www.davilawoodwork.com
SIC: **2511** Wood household furniture

(G-4944)
FIERO ENTERPRISES INC
203 Nw 5th Ave (33009-4019)
PHONE..................................954 454-5004
Joseph Fiero, *President*
EMP: 10 EST: 1971
SQ FT: 19,000
SALES (est): 603.7K **Privately Held**
SIC: **3993** Displays & cutouts, window & lobby

(G-4945)
FINGER MATE INC
Also Called: National Jewellers
2500 E Hallandale Beach B (33009-4833)
P.O. Box 607, Hallandale (33008-0607)
PHONE..................................954 458-2700
Howard Kelrick, *President*
Robert Brooks, *Vice Pres*
Alan Wildstein, *Production*
Kathy Brooks, *Shareholder*
EMP: 21 EST: 1964
SQ FT: 2,500
SALES (est): 2MM **Privately Held**
WEB: www.fingermate.com
SIC: **3911 5944 3915** Jewelry apparel; jewelry stores; jewelers' materials & lapidary work

(G-4946)
FIRST CASE CASH LLC
225 Holiday Dr (33009-6515)
PHONE..................................954 200-5374
Dmitry Fateev, *Principal*
EMP: 8 EST: 2019
SALES (est): 736.5K **Privately Held**
SIC: **3523** Farm machinery & equipment

(G-4947)
FITLETIC SPORTS LLC
1049 Nw 1st Ct (33009-3903)
PHONE..................................305 907-6663
Shifra Pomerantz,
Uri Sharabi,
EMP: 7 EST: 2008
SQ FT: 4,000
SALES (est): 1.1MM **Privately Held**
WEB: www.fitletic.com
SIC: **2339 2329** Sportswear, women's; men's & boys' sportswear & athletic clothing

(G-4948)
FIVE STAR SPORTS TICKETS
1755 E Hallandale Bch (33009-4684)
PHONE..................................440 899-2000
Sherry Sabe, *President*
Brian Blume, *Vice Pres*
Bonnie Blume, *Treasurer*

EMP: 10 EST: 1990
SQ FT: 1,200
SALES (est): 781.8K **Privately Held**
SIC: **2711 2759 2752** Newspapers; commercial printing; commercial printing, lithographic

(G-4949)
GREENTEX AMERICA LLC
520 S Dixie Hwy Ofc 120 (33009-6332)
PHONE..................................305 908-8580
Leon Amitai Liberman, *Mng Member*
Leon Liberman, *Mng Member*
Karen Sutton Neirus,
EMP: 10 EST: 2018
SALES (est): 469.8K **Privately Held**
WEB: www.greentexamerica.com
SIC: **2759** Publication printing

(G-4950)
HYCOMB USA INC
311 W Ansin Blvd (33009-3114)
PHONE..................................954 251-1691
John Bartos, *President*
Dan Slain, *Director*
▲ EMP: 10 EST: 2013
SALES (est): 738.1K **Privately Held**
WEB: www.hycombusa.com
SIC: **3469** Porcelain enameled products & utensils

(G-4951)
INTEGRITY ENGINEERING CORP
Also Called: Integrity Marine
301 W Ansin Blvd (33009-3114)
PHONE..................................954 458-0500
Sixto Gonzalez, *President*
EMP: 8 EST: 2006
SALES (est): 1.3MM **Privately Held**
WEB: www.integritymarineusa.com
SIC: **3731** Shipbuilding & repairing

(G-4952)
INTERNATIONAL DOCK PDTS INC
Also Called: S King Fulton Div
3101 Sw 25th St Ste 106 (33009-3096)
PHONE..................................954 964-5315
Elliot Turk, *President*
Rita Turk, *Corp Secy*
Frank Turk, *Executive*
◆ EMP: 15 EST: 1991
SQ FT: 6,000
SALES (est): 1.8MM **Privately Held**
WEB: www.dockproducts.com
SIC: **3999 3444 3429** Dock equipment & supplies, industrial; sheet metalwork; manufactured hardware (general)

(G-4953)
ITQLICK INC
2100 E Hlnd Bch Blvd # 203 (33009-3765)
PHONE..................................855 487-5425
Shlomo Lavi, *Principal*
EMP: 7 EST: 2017
SALES (est): 70.8K **Privately Held**
WEB: www.itqlick.com
SIC: **7372** Prepackaged software

(G-4954)
JADA FOODS LLC
Also Called: Krunchy Melts
3126 John P Curci Dr # 1 (33009-3827)
PHONE..................................305 319-0263
Moises Mizrahi, *Partner*
Daniel Ginsberg, *Managing Dir*
EMP: 15 EST: 2011
SQ FT: 4,950
SALES (est): 2.3MM **Privately Held**
WEB: www.jadafoods.com
SIC: **2052** Cookies

(G-4955)
JPL ASSOCIATES INC
Also Called: Promotional Concepts Team
1250 E Hallandale Beach B (33009-4634)
PHONE..................................954 929-6024
John Lombardo, *President*
Cindy Lombardo, *Vice Pres*
EMP: 10 EST: 2003
SALES (est): 1.1MM **Privately Held**
WEB: www.jpl-associates.com
SIC: **3993 7311** Signs & advertising specialties; advertising agencies

(G-4956)
KASULIK II LLC
Also Called: Ragalta
1170 E Hllndale Bch Blvd (33009-4437)
PHONE..........................786 629-8978
Paul Hariton, *CEO*
Ricardo Shneiderman,
▲ **EMP:** 16 **EST:** 2009
SQ FT: 65,000
SALES (est): 1.9MM **Privately Held**
SIC: 3089 5023 Plastic kitchenware, table-
ware & houseware; home furnishings

(G-4957)
LAKAY VITA LLC
419 N Federal Hwy Apt 209 (33009-3499)
PHONE..........................786 985-7552
Wency Germinal, *CEO*
Sacha Hernandez,
EMP: 5 **EST:** 2019
SALES (est): 505K **Privately Held**
SIC: 2131 5199 Smoking tobacco; general
merchandise, non-durable

(G-4958)
**LEGACY CNSTR RMDLG CLG
SVCS LL**
500 N Federal Hwy Ste 631 (33009-2405)
PHONE..........................800 638-9646
Edison Jules,
EMP: 40 **EST:** 2019
SALES (est): 1.1MM **Privately Held**
SIC: 1389 Construction, repair & disman-
tling services

(G-4959)
**LILLYS GSTRNMIA ITLANA FLA
INC**
Also Called: Lillys Gastronomia Italiana FL
370 Ansin Blvd (33009-3107)
PHONE..........................305 655-2111
Fred Botta, *Vice Pres*
EMP: 5 **EST:** 1994
SQ FT: 5,000
SALES (est): 400K **Privately Held**
SIC: 2099 2098 2038 Packaged combina-
tion products: pasta, rice & potato; maca-
roni & spaghetti; frozen specialties

(G-4960)
MABELS PLACE CORP
Also Called: Mabel's Quality Products
370 Ansin Blvd 370 # 370 (33009-3107)
PHONE..........................786 355-0435
Victor Alvarez, *Principal*
EMP: 8 **EST:** 2019
SALES (est): 180.1K **Privately Held**
SIC: 2099 Food preparations

(G-4961)
MIRACLES FOR FUN INC
Also Called: Better Sourcing Worldwide
1835 E Hllndale Bch Blvd (33009-4619)
PHONE..........................561 702-8217
Danny Hui, *CEO*
Greg Sanders, *President*
▲ **EMP:** 12 **EST:** 2006
SQ FT: 5,000
SALES (est): 489.8K **Privately Held**
WEB: www.miracles4funusa.com
SIC: 3229 Glassware, art or decorative

(G-4962)
MN TRADES INC
200 Leslie Dr Ofc (33009-7344)
PHONE..........................954 455-9320
Joao Montoro, *President*
Leandro Montoro, *Vice Pres*
Neuza Montoro, *Treasurer*
EMP: 6 **EST:** 1996
SALES (est): 846.9K **Privately Held**
SIC: 3679 Electronic circuits

(G-4963)
NATURES GIFT CBD
320 Ne 12th Ave Apt 506 (33009-4507)
PHONE..........................954 405-1000
Gratziela Lazarov, *Principal*
EMP: 7 **EST:** 2017
SALES (est): 118.3K **Privately Held**
SIC: 3999

(G-4964)
NVAULTED ENTERPRISES INC
2080 S Ocean Dr Apt 306 (33009-6679)
PHONE..........................305 632-0525
Antonio C Dimarco, *CEO*
EMP: 8 **EST:** 2007
SALES (est): 504.1K **Privately Held**
SIC: 7372 Application computer software

(G-4965)
**ON DEMAND SPCLTY
ENVELOPE CORP**
917 Sw 10th St (33009-6819)
PHONE..........................305 681-5345
Joanne Heller-Mahoney, *President*
Gerry Mahoney, *Vice Pres*
EMP: 11 **EST:** 2011
SQ FT: 10,700
SALES (est): 268.6K **Privately Held**
SIC: 2732 Book printing

(G-4966)
PREMIER PLASTICS LLC
500 S Federal Hwy # 2715 (33009-6435)
PHONE..........................305 805-3333
Albert Esquenazi, *Branch Mgr*
EMP: 35
SALES (corp-wide): 451.6K **Privately
Held**
WEB: www.premierplastics.net
SIC: 3999 Barber & beauty shop equip-
ment
PA: Premier Plastics, Llc
1500 Gateway Blvd Ste 250
Boynton Beach FL 33426
305 805-3333

(G-4967)
QSRR CORPORATION
Also Called: Bemeals
3126 John P Curci Dr # 4 (33009-3884)
PHONE..........................305 322-9867
Michael Esrubilsky, *CEO*
EMP: 7 **EST:** 2017
SALES (est): 415.7K **Privately Held**
SIC: 2099 7371 Food preparations; com-
puter software development & applica-
tions

(G-4968)
R-LINES LLC
201 Ansin Blvd (33009-3116)
PHONE..........................954 457-7777
Diana McNally, *Mng Member*
◆ **EMP:** 7 **EST:** 1995
SQ FT: 25,000
SALES (est): 865.7K **Privately Held**
WEB: www.rlines.com
SIC: 2086 Soft drinks: packaged in cans,
bottles, etc.

(G-4969)
RENOVASHIP INC
2700 S Park Rd (33009-3833)
PHONE..........................954 342-9062
Dennis P Carbee, *President*
Dennis Rodriguez, *Treasurer*
Oscar Medina, *Admin Sec*
▲ **EMP:** 5 **EST:** 2005
SALES (est): 545.5K **Privately Held**
WEB: renovaship-inc.hallandalebeachdi-
rect.info
SIC: 3312 Structural shapes & pilings,
steel

(G-4970)
**SERVICES ON DEMAND PRINT
INC**
Also Called: On Demand Envelopes
917 Sw 10th St (33009-6819)
PHONE..........................305 681-5345
Jose Rosario, *Vice Pres*
David Voyasy, *Manager*
▼ **EMP:** 13 **EST:** 1995
SQ FT: 10,000
SALES (est): 402.2K **Privately Held**
WEB: www.ondemandenvelope.com
SIC: 2759 2752 2677 Envelopes: printing;
commercial printing, lithographic; en-
velopes

(G-4971)
SERVISION INC
2100 E Hallandale Beach B (33009-3770)
PHONE..........................305 900-4999

Gidon Tahan, *CEO*
Yaniv Ben, *Vice Pres*
Tamir Alush, *Director*
Brett Schor, *Director*
EMP: 1 **EST:** 2003
SQ FT: 600
SALES (est): 4.6MM **Privately Held**
WEB: www.servision.net
SIC: 3699 Security devices
HQ: Servision Ltd
1 Eitan
Rishon Lezion 75703

(G-4972)
SMILEFY INC
221 W Hallandale B106 (33009)
PHONE..........................302 465-6606
Tatjana Georg, *General Mgr*
Ralph Georg, *Principal*
EMP: 10 **EST:** 2017
SALES (est): 283.2K **Privately Held**
WEB: www.smilefy.com
SIC: 2741 8742 ; marketing consulting
services

(G-4973)
**SOUTH BEACH SKIN CARE INC
(PA)**
Also Called: Lifecell
701 N Federal Hwy Ste 400 (33009-2452)
PHONE..........................954 606-5057
Chris Suarez, *President*
Httpswwwlinke Levitt, *Sales Staff*
Lauren Baszczewski, *Manager*
Sherry Powers, *Manager*
Httpswwwlinke Monroe, *Consultant*
▲ **EMP:** 10 **EST:** 2009
SALES (est): 5.1MM **Privately Held**
WEB: www.lifecellskin.com
SIC: 2844 Cosmetic preparations

(G-4974)
SOUTH BROWARD BRACE INC
Also Called: Petti, Vince
1920 E Hallandale Bch 702 (33009-4725)
PHONE..........................954 458-0656
Vince Petti, *President*
EMP: 10 **EST:** 1986
SALES (est): 502.5K **Privately Held**
SIC: 3842 Prosthetic appliances

(G-4975)
SOUTH FLORIDA DIGEST INC
Also Called: South Florida Suntimes
305 Nw 10th Ter (33009-3103)
PHONE..........................954 458-0635
Cecile Hiles, *Vice Pres*
EMP: 17 **EST:** 2004
SALES (est): 1MM **Privately Held**
WEB: www.southfloridasuntimes.com
SIC: 2711 Newspapers, publishing & print-
ing

(G-4976)
SUNGRAF INC
325 W Ansin Blvd (33009-3114)
P.O. Box 260397, Pembroke Pines (33026-
7397)
PHONE..........................954 456-8500
Joseph D Cesarotti Jr, *President*
Marianne Cesarotti, *Vice Pres*
EMP: 8 **EST:** 1956
SQ FT: 30,000
SALES (est): 159.7K **Privately Held**
SIC: 3993 3081 3083 2522 Electric
signs; plastic film & sheet; laminated plas-
tics plate & sheet; office furniture, except
wood; metal household furniture; wood
kitchen cabinets

(G-4977)
TAGS & LABELS PRINTING INC
520 Ne 1st Ave (33009-2417)
PHONE..........................954 455-2867
Peter Applebaum, *President*
Angie Sundar, *Officer*
Brenda Ayotte,
EMP: 21 **EST:** 1976
SQ FT: 10,200
SALES (est): 3.1MM **Privately Held**
WEB: www.tagsandlabels.net
SIC: 2752 Commercial printing, offset;
tags, lithographed

(G-4978)
TAN PRINTING INC
2211 John P Lyons Ln (33009-2173)
PHONE..........................954 986-9869
Henk Tan, *President*
Lilly Lifter, *Vice Pres*
▼ **EMP:** 6 **EST:** 1992
SQ FT: 9,000
SALES (est): 724K **Privately Held**
WEB: www.tanprinting.com
SIC: 2752 Commercial printing, offset

(G-4979)
TITANUS TECHNOLOGIES LLC
2876 S Park Rd (33009-3819)
PHONE..........................888 378-2673
Jose Seisdedos, *Mng Member*
David Rodriguez,
EMP: 8 **EST:** 2013
SALES (est): 1.1MM **Privately Held**
WEB: www.titancomputers.com
SIC: 3571 Electronic computers

(G-4980)
TM CABINETRY LLC
313 Ansin Blvd (33009-3108)
PHONE..........................954 639-1725
Tomer Mesika, *Principal*
EMP: 5 **EST:** 2016
SALES (est): 473.2K **Privately Held**
WEB: www.tmcabinetry.com
SIC: 2434 Wood kitchen cabinets

(G-4981)
US PATRIOT INDUSTRIES INC
100 Golden Isles Dr (33009-5885)
PHONE..........................954 802-7402
William Carney, *Mng Member*
Mike Giallombardo, *Director*
Jesse Kearney, *Director*
Tim Masshardt, *Director*
Rob Polumbo, *Director*
EMP: 7 **EST:** 2018
SALES (est): 351.6K **Privately Held**
SIC: 3999 Manufacturing industries

(G-4982)
USA ALUMINUM
1880 S Ocean Dr (33009-7610)
PHONE..........................305 303-9121
Claudia Menemdez,
EMP: 6 **EST:** 2006
SQ FT: 5,000
SALES (est): 684K **Privately Held**
SIC: 3442 Shutters, door or window: metal

(G-4983)
USA PRINTING LLC
26 Se 3rd Ave (33009-5515)
PHONE..........................754 275-5048
EMP: 9
SALES (est): 356.2K **Privately Held**
SIC: 2752 7389 Commercial printing, litho-
graphic;

(G-4984)
UZZI AMPHIBIOUS GEAR LLC
205 Ansin Blvd (33009-3116)
PHONE..........................954 777-9595
Elan Barshean, *Owner*
EMP: 9 **EST:** 2015
SALES (est): 656.8K **Privately Held**
WEB: www.uzzi.com
SIC: 2339 2326 Service apparel, wash-
able: women's; service apparel (baker,
barber, lab, etc.), washable: men's

(G-4985)
**WINSTED THERMOGRAPHERS
INC**
917 Sw 10th St (33009-6898)
PHONE..........................305 944-7862
Lester Jacobowitz, *President*
Gary Jacobowitz, *Vice Pres*
◆ **EMP:** 19 **EST:** 1971
SQ FT: 20,000
SALES (est): 2.8MM **Privately Held**
WEB: www.winsted-thermo.com
SIC: 2759 2677 Thermography; envelopes

Hampton
Bradford County

(G-4986)
MCCLELLAN LOGGING INC
State Rd 325 (32044)
P.O. Box 108 (32044-0108)
PHONE.................................352 468-1856
Margie McClellan, *President*
Dewey McClellan, *Vice Pres*
EMP: 5 **EST:** 1963
SALES (est): 397.2K **Privately Held**
SIC: 2411 Logging camps & contractors

Harmony
Osceola County

(G-4987)
PHOENIX NAVTECH LLC
6943 Beargrass Rd (34773-9182)
PHONE.................................407 285-4536
Charles G Smith, *Principal*
EMP: 7 **EST:** 2014
SALES (est): 341.1K **Privately Held**
SIC: 3812 Search & navigation equipment

Hastings
St. Johns County

(G-4988)
HARWIL FIXTURES INC
103 W Saint Johns Ave (32145-4125)
P.O. Box 788 (32145-0788)
PHONE.................................904 692-1051
Louis F Cici, *President*
Don Smyth, *Opers Staff*
Bridgitte Cici, *Treasurer*
EMP: 15 **EST:** 1978
SQ FT: 50,000
SALES (est): 3.7MM **Privately Held**
WEB: www.harwilgroup.net
SIC: 2541 Store & office display cases & fixtures; cabinets, except refrigerated: show, display, etc.: wood

(G-4989)
R SMITH PRINTING INC
4820 Joseph St (32145-6316)
PHONE.................................518 827-7700
Robert Smith, *President*
Linda L Quinn, *CFO*
EMP: 6 **EST:** 2005
SQ FT: 8,500
SALES (est): 411.2K **Privately Held**
SIC: 2752 Commercial printing, offset

Havana
Gadsden County

(G-4990)
APPLIED FIBER HOLDINGS LLC
25 Garrett Dr (32333-3316)
PHONE.................................850 539-7720
Richard Campbell, *Mng Member*
EMP: 30 **EST:** 2003
SALES (est): 2.7MM **Privately Held**
WEB: www.applied-fiber.com
SIC: 2298 Cable, fiber

(G-4991)
APPLIED FIBER MFG LLC
25 Garrett Dr (32333-3316)
PHONE.................................850 539-7720
John Steadman, *COO*
Paul Badeau, *VP Bus Dvlpt*
Casey Davis, *Controller*
Richard Campbell, *Mng Member*
▲ **EMP:** 20 **EST:** 2003
SALES (est): 8.6MM **Privately Held**
WEB: www.applied-fiber.com
SIC: 2298 Cable, fiber

(G-4992)
ARUKI SERVICES LLC
102 Sw 3rd St (32333-1612)
P.O. Box 1228 (32333-1298)
PHONE.................................850 364-5206

Jeffery A Snyder,
EMP: 10 **EST:** 2008
SALES (est): 863.9K **Privately Held**
WEB: www.arukiservices.com
SIC: 3567 5074 Heating units & devices, industrial: electric; heating equipment (hydronic)

(G-4993)
BIG BEND ICE CREAM CO
138 Staghorn Trl (32333-5545)
PHONE.................................850 539-7778
Laurie Shaffer, *President*
EMP: 7 **EST:** 2003
SALES (est): 112.3K **Privately Held**
SIC: 2024 5451 5947 5812 Ice cream & frozen desserts; ice cream (packaged); gifts & novelties; caterers

(G-4994)
BIG BEND TRUSS COMPONENTS INC
52 Salem Rd (32333-6834)
P.O. Box 962 (32333-0962)
PHONE.................................850 539-5351
Keith Jones, *President*
Travis Jones, *Vice Pres*
EMP: 15 **EST:** 1971
SQ FT: 2,120
SALES (est): 1.5MM **Privately Held**
SIC: 2439 8711 Trusses, wooden roof; engineering services

(G-4995)
BOISE CASCADE COMPANY
8007 Fl Ga Hwy (32333-6382)
PHONE.................................800 359-6432
Jim Pattillo, *Branch Mgr*
EMP: 9
SALES (corp-wide): 7.9B **Publicly Held**
WEB: www.bc.com
SIC: 2435 Hardwood veneer & plywood
PA: Boise Cascade Company
1111 W Jefferson St # 100
Boise ID 83702
208 384-6161

(G-4996)
COASTAL FOREST RESOURCES CO (PA)
Also Called: Coastal Timberlands
8007 Fl Ga Hwy (32333-6382)
PHONE.................................850 539-6432
J Travis Bryant, *President*
James Randolph Light, *Chairman*
Ryan Daniels, *Vice Pres*
Thomas Evans, *Vice Pres*
Dillon Forbes, *VP Sales*
◆ **EMP:** 300 **EST:** 1937
SALES (est): 131.7MM **Privately Held**
SIC: 2436 2491 0811 0851 Plywood, softwood; structural lumber & timber; treated wood; timber tracts; forestry services

(G-4997)
COASTAL PLYWOOD LLC
Also Called: Coastal Plywood Company
8007 Fl Ga Hwy (32333-6382)
P.O. Box 1128 (32333-1128)
PHONE.................................800 359-6432
Jim Pattillo, *President*
Travis Bryant, *President*
Libby Sumner, *Production*
Donnie Vickers, *Sales Mgr*
David Norman, *Manager*
▼ **EMP:** 354 **EST:** 2003
SALES (est): 43MM
SALES (corp-wide): 131.7MM **Privately Held**
WEB: www.coastalplywood.com
SIC: 2435 Hardwood veneer & plywood
PA: Coastal Forest Resources Company
8007 Fl Ga Hwy
Havana FL 32333
850 539-6432

(G-4998)
COASTAL TREATED PRODUCTS LLC
8007 Fl Ga Hwy (32333-6382)
PHONE.................................850 539-6432
EMP: 9 **EST:** 2008

SALES (est): 65.4K **Privately Held**
WEB: www.coastalplywood.com
SIC: 2491 Flooring, treated wood block; millwork, treated wood

(G-4999)
CORRY CABINET COMPANY INC
811 N Main St (32333-1209)
P.O. Box 944 (32333-0944)
PHONE.................................850 539-6455
Henry C Corry Jr, *President*
EMP: 20 **EST:** 1992
SQ FT: 20,295
SALES (est): 2.6MM **Privately Held**
WEB: www.corrycabinets.com
SIC: 2541 Cabinets, except refrigerated: show, display, etc.: wood

(G-5000)
DELEVOES LOBBY LLC
10850 Fl Ga Hwy (32333-8405)
PHONE.................................305 906-0475
Patrice Delevoe, *CEO*
EMP: 10 **EST:** 2016
SALES (est): 529K **Privately Held**
SIC: 3911 Jewelry, precious metal

(G-5001)
FREEDOM FABRICATION INC
815 N Main St Ste B (32333-1243)
PHONE.................................850 539-4194
Anthony Wickman, *President*
EMP: 10 **EST:** 1992
SQ FT: 6,000
SALES (est): 871.8K **Privately Held**
WEB: www.freedomfabrication.com
SIC: 3842 Orthopedic appliances

(G-5002)
PRIME TECHNOLOGICAL SVCS LLC
Also Called: Teligentems
102 Technology Way (32333-2000)
PHONE.................................850 539-2500
Christopher Eldred, *Branch Mgr*
EMP: 100 **Privately Held**
WEB: www.prime-ems.com
SIC: 3672 8711 Printed circuit boards; electrical or electronic engineering
PA: Prime Technological Services, Llc
2925 Shawnee Industrial W
Suwanee GA 30024

(G-5003)
TMS ENTERPRISES LLC
Also Called: Plant 2
102 Technology Way (32333-2000)
PHONE.................................850 539-2500
Duncan Coke, *Production*
Jeff Hearn, *Production*
Donna Walker, *Engineer*
Mike A Wallace, *VP Bus Dvlpt*
Lillie Jackson, *Accountant*
EMP: 500 **EST:** 2002
SALES (est): 52.2MM **Privately Held**
WEB: www.teligentems.com
SIC: 3672 Printed circuit boards

Haverhill
Palm Beach County

(G-5004)
WEARABLE NALIA LLC
5081 Palo Verde Pl (33415-1273)
PHONE.................................561 629-5804
Kenya L Glenn, *Principal*
EMP: 7 **EST:** 2008
SALES (est): 246K **Privately Held**
WEB: www.wearablenalia.com
SIC: 2395 Embroidery & art needlework

Hawthorne
Alachua County

(G-5005)
ADVANCED METALS LLC
158 Hour Glass Cir (32640-4224)
PHONE.................................352 494-2476
Richard Mahoney, *Owner*
Sherri Sable, *Production*
EMP: 8 **EST:** 2011

SALES (est): 805.9K **Privately Held**
WEB: www.advancedmetalsmachining.com
SIC: 3444 Ducts, sheet metal

(G-5006)
ALL FLORIDA ENGRAVING
17728 S County Road 325 (32640-8301)
PHONE.................................352 213-4572
Louis Wise, *Principal*
Susan Wise, *Manager*
EMP: 8 **EST:** 2014
SALES (est): 285.7K **Privately Held**
WEB: www.allfloridaengraving.com
SIC: 2759 Screen printing

(G-5007)
FLORIDA SEPTIC INC
5757 Se 211th St (32640-3695)
P.O. Box 545 (32640-0545)
PHONE.................................352 481-2455
Susan Allen, *President*
Joan Ellen Vause, *President*
Dulcie Vause, *Corp Secy*
Susan Gail Vause Palmer, *Vice Pres*
Susan Palmer, *Vice Pres*
EMP: 48 **EST:** 1961
SQ FT: 1,000
SALES (est): 7.5MM **Privately Held**
WEB: www.flsepticinc.com
SIC: 3272 Septic tanks, concrete

(G-5008)
INTERLACHEN CABINETS INC
2010 State Road 20 (32640-5407)
PHONE.................................352 481-6078
Gene Quimby, *President*
EMP: 8 **EST:** 2008
SALES (est): 369.6K **Privately Held**
SIC: 2434 Wood kitchen cabinets

Hernando
Citrus County

(G-5009)
MERIT SCREW
Also Called: Merit Screw Products
3484 E Hartley Ct (34442-5009)
PHONE.................................352 344-3744
Jack Briscoe, *Partner*
EMP: 5 **EST:** 1973
SQ FT: 4,000
SALES (est): 494.7K **Privately Held**
WEB: www.meritscrew.com
SIC: 3451 3599 Screw machine products; machine shop, jobbing & repair

(G-5010)
TURBINE BROACH COMPANY
521 E Overdrive Cir (34442-9602)
P.O. Box 280, Holder (34445-0280)
PHONE.................................352 795-1163
Timothy Short, *President*
Jeanne Short, *Treasurer*
George Marks, *Manager*
EMP: 17 **EST:** 1972
SQ FT: 16,688
SALES (est): 2.4MM **Privately Held**
WEB: www.turbinebroach.com
SIC: 3545 Broaches (machine tool accessories)

Hernando Beach
Hernando County

(G-5011)
AFLG INVSTMNTS-INDUSTRIALS LLC
Hidralmac USA
5000 Calienta St (34607-2900)
PHONE.................................813 443-8203
Doug Joseph, *Managing Dir*
EMP: 10
SALES (corp-wide): 6MM **Privately Held**
WEB: www.aflgholdings.com
SIC: 3542 3569 Mechanical (pneumatic or hydraulic) metal forming machines; liquid automation machinery & equipment
PA: Aflg Investments-Industrials, Llc
701 Suth Hward Ave 106
Tampa FL 33606
813 443-8203

▲ = Import ▼=Export
◆ =Import/Export

(G-5012)
SON LIFE PRSTHTICS ORTHTICS IN (PA)
4138 Daisy Dr (34607-3339)
PHONE..................................352 596-2257
David Goris, *President*
EMP: 11 **EST:** 1987
SALES (est): 1.5MM **Privately Held**
WEB: www.sonlifeprosthetics.com
SIC: 3842 5999 5661 Prosthetic appliances; orthopedic appliances; artificial limbs; shoes, orthopedic

---

Hialeah
Miami-Dade County

(G-5013)
3 STARS KITCHEN CABINETS CORP
529 W 28th St (33010-1325)
PHONE..................................786 285-7147
Nelson Monzon, *President*
▲ **EMP:** 7 **EST:** 2013
SALES (est): 276.2K **Privately Held**
WEB: www.3starkitchencabinet.com
SIC: 2434 Wood kitchen cabinets

(G-5014)
5301 REALTY LLC
Also Called: Franklin Trade Graphics
950 Se 8th St (33010-5740)
PHONE..................................305 633-9779
Peter Dunne,
Geronimo Alvarez,
Michael Barber,
Robert Dunne,
▼ **EMP:** 149 **EST:** 2002
SQ FT: 70,000
SALES (est): 15.6MM **Privately Held**
SIC: 2752 Commercial printing, lithographic

(G-5015)
A & V REFRIGERATION CORP
997 Se 12th St (33010-5904)
PHONE..................................305 883-0733
Jacob Essenfeld, *President*
Servando Cougil, *Vice Pres*
Alfredo Rodriguez, *Director*
◆ **EMP:** 7 **EST:** 1990
SQ FT: 4,500
SALES (est): 1MM **Privately Held**
WEB: www.av-refrigeration.com
SIC: 3585 7623 Ice making machinery; refrigeration repair service

(G-5016)
A L CUSTOM WOOD CORP
950 W 22nd St (33010-2012)
PHONE..................................305 557-2434
EMP: 8 **EST:** 2019
SALES (est): 389K **Privately Held**
SIC: 2431 Millwork

(G-5017)
A SUPERIOR GARAGE DOOR COMPANY
12195 Nw 98th Ave (33018-2941)
PHONE..................................305 556-6624
Joe Berger, *Partner*
Tiffeny Roque, *Manager*
Edgy Vargas, *Manager*
Richard Barnes, *CIO*
EMP: 45 **EST:** 1997
SALES (est): 2.3MM **Privately Held**
SIC: 3442 Garage doors, overhead: metal

(G-5018)
A&C SIGNS SOLUTIONS CORP
1745 W 37th St (33012-4677)
PHONE..................................786 953-5600
Armando J Antelo, *Principal*
EMP: 12 **EST:** 2019
SALES (est): 630.1K **Privately Held**
SIC: 3993 Signs & advertising specialties

(G-5019)
A-1 SPORTSWEAR INC
18820 Nw 84th Ave (33015-5347)
PHONE..................................305 773-7028
Kar Lei Cheung, *President*
Patrick Lei, *Vice Pres*
EMP: 9 **EST:** 1987

SQ FT: 8,000
SALES (est): 110.9K **Privately Held**
SIC: 2339 Athletic clothing: women's, misses' & juniors'

(G-5020)
A1A ELECTRIC SIGNS & NEON INC
Also Called: A1a Signs & Svc.
1640 W 32nd Pl (33012-4510)
PHONE..................................305 757-6950
Jorge Bravo, *President*
EMP: 10 **EST:** 1992
SALES (est): 1MM **Privately Held**
SIC: 3993 Neon signs

(G-5021)
AARG STAIRS & RAILLINGS CORP
2384 W 80th St Ste 7 (33016-5689)
PHONE..................................786 545-6465
Ruben Gonzalez, *Principal*
EMP: 8 **EST:** 2012
SALES (est): 128.6K **Privately Held**
SIC: 3446 Stairs, staircases, stair treads: prefabricated metal

(G-5022)
ABALUX INC
8000 W 26th Ave (33016-2743)
PHONE..................................305 698-9192
Juan D Cabral, *CEO*
EMP: 14 **EST:** 2006
SALES (est): 497.5K **Privately Held**
WEB: www.abaluxgraphics.com
SIC: 3993 Signs & advertising specialties

(G-5023)
AC GRAPHICS INC
1056 E 24th St (33013-4394)
P.O. Box 133220 (33013-0220)
PHONE..................................305 691-3778
Augusto R Casamayor, *President*
Augusto G Casamayor, *COO*
Cliff Conchak, *Vice Pres*
◆ **EMP:** 33 **EST:** 1979
SQ FT: 6,000
SALES (est): 7.8MM **Privately Held**
WEB: www.acgraphics.com
SIC: 2752 Commercial printing, offset

(G-5024)
AC PLASTICS LLC
1627 W 31st Pl (33012-4505)
PHONE..................................305 826-6333
EMP: 7
SALES (est): 530K **Privately Held**
SIC: 3085 Mfg Plastic Bottles

(G-5025)
ACAI INVESTMENTS LLC
Also Called: Dievac Plastics
7803 W 25th Ct (33016-2758)
PHONE..................................305 821-8872
Andres Marino,
EMP: 6 **EST:** 2007
SALES (est): 538.1K **Privately Held**
SIC: 3089 Injection molding of plastics

(G-5026)
ACTIVE LINE CORP
Also Called: Miami Sublimation
915 W 18th St (33010-2322)
PHONE..................................786 766-1944
Boris Litvinov, *President*
◆ **EMP:** 10 **EST:** 1994
SQ FT: 5,000
SALES (est): 728.5K **Privately Held**
SIC: 2395 Embroidery & art needlework

(G-5027)
ADAPTO STORAGE PRODUCTS
625 E 10th Ave (33010-4641)
PHONE..................................305 887-9563
Joe Caridnan, *President*
Jenny Nunez, *Admin Sec*
▼ **EMP:** 32 **EST:** 1999
SQ FT: 106,000
SALES (est): 1.2MM **Privately Held**
WEB: www.adapto.com
SIC: 2542 Shelving, office & store: except wood

(G-5028)
ADEC METAL FABRICATION INC
455 W 28th St (33010-1323)
PHONE..................................305 401-5073
John M Ariza, *Principal*
EMP: 7 **EST:** 2010
SALES (est): 100K **Privately Held**
SIC: 3499 Fabricated metal products

(G-5029)
ADVANCE PLASTICS UNLIMITED
905 W 19th St (33010-2308)
PHONE..................................305 885-6266
Abraham Kolker, *President*
Elena Kolker, *Treasurer*
◆ **EMP:** 21 **EST:** 1969
SQ FT: 45,000
SALES (est): 3.3MM **Privately Held**
WEB: www.advanceplasticsindustries.com
SIC: 3085 Plastics bottles

(G-5030)
ADVANCED METAL FAB INC
2247 W 77th St (33016-1867)
PHONE..................................305 557-2008
Olga L Gordillo, *President*
Edward Gordillo Jr, *Vice Pres*
EMP: 10 **EST:** 1986
SQ FT: 5,000
SALES (est): 900K **Privately Held**
SIC: 3599 Machine shop, jobbing & repair

(G-5031)
ADVANCED PRINTING FINSHG INC
Also Called: Boxrus.com
1061 E 32nd St (33013-3523)
PHONE..................................305 836-8581
Omar Martinez, *President*
EMP: 16 **EST:** 2007
SALES (est): 1.6MM **Privately Held**
WEB: advanced-printing-finishing-inc.hub.biz
SIC: 2675 Die-cut paper & board

(G-5032)
AEROWEST MFG CORP
8835 Nw 117th St (33018-1949)
PHONE..................................786 367-6948
Daily Boffill Montano, *CEO*
Daily Boffill-Montano, *General Mgr*
EMP: 5 **EST:** 2006
SALES (est): 897.3K **Privately Held**
WEB: www.aerowestmfg.com
SIC: 3728 3541 Aircraft parts & equipment; drilling machine tools (metal cutting)

(G-5033)
AFFORDABLE METAL INC
3522 E 10th Ct (33013-2916)
PHONE..................................305 691-8082
Silbio Monrable, *President*
Ville Corta, *Vice Pres*
Eduardo Villacorta, *Vice Pres*
▼ **EMP:** 16 **EST:** 2001
SALES (est): 4.6MM **Privately Held**
WEB: www.affordablemetal.com
SIC: 3444 Sheet metal specialties, not stamped

(G-5034)
AGUSTIN REYES INC
2307 W 77th St (33016-1869)
PHONE..................................305 558-8870
Agustin Reyes III, *President*
Ana Maria Reyes, *Vice Pres*
◆ **EMP:** 12 **EST:** 1927
SQ FT: 2,750
SALES (est): 507.1K **Privately Held**
WEB: www.agustinreyes.com
SIC: 2844 Cosmetic preparations

(G-5035)
AIRGUIDE MANUFACTURING LLC
795 W 20th St (33010-2429)
PHONE..................................305 888-1631
Douglas Marty Jr, *Sales Mgr*
Adonais Posada, *Office Mgr*
Charles Robinson,
◆ **EMP:** 150 **EST:** 2003
SQ FT: 52,000

SALES (est): 24.9MM **Privately Held**
WEB: www.airguidemfg.com
SIC: 3446 Architectural metalwork

(G-5036)
ALEXANDER INDUSTRIES INC
905 W 23rd St (33010-2013)
P.O. Box 502, Vernon (32462-0502)
PHONE..................................305 888-9840
George Alexander, *President*
Mary Ann Alexander, *Vice Pres*
Nery Alexander, *Vice Pres*
▲ **EMP:** 6 **EST:** 1972
SQ FT: 10,000
SALES (est): 688.2K **Privately Held**
WEB: www.alexanderindustries.net
SIC: 3556 Food products machinery

(G-5037)
ALL BINDERS & INDEXES INC
Also Called: Delran Business Products
860 W 20th St (33010-2311)
PHONE..................................305 889-9983
Juan Carlos Cruz, *President*
EMP: 14 **EST:** 1993
SQ FT: 7,000
SALES (est): 897.1K **Privately Held**
WEB: www.delran.com
SIC: 2789 Binding only: books, pamphlets, magazines, etc.

(G-5038)
ALL MOLDINGS INC
7950 W 26th Ave (33016-2728)
PHONE..................................305 556-6171
EMP: 6
SALES (est): 630K **Privately Held**
SIC: 2491 Wood Preserving

(G-5039)
ALL PRO CHELO CORP
11750 Nw 87th Pl (33018-1974)
PHONE..................................786 317-3914
Magnaset Martinez, *President*
EMP: 7 **EST:** 2011
SALES (est): 181K **Privately Held**
SIC: 2431 5211 Garage doors, overhead: wood; garage doors, sale & installation

(G-5040)
ALLAY PHARMACEUTICAL LLC (PA)
16600 Nw 54th Ave Unit 23 (33014-6109)
PHONE..................................954 336-1136
Rosy Sultana, *CEO*
Maroof H Choudhur, *President*
Abdul M Bhuiyan, *COO*
Abdul Bhuiyan, *COO*
EMP: 7 **EST:** 2006
SQ FT: 13,500
SALES (est): 2.5MM **Privately Held**
WEB: www.allay.us
SIC: 2834 Pharmaceutical preparations

(G-5041)
ALUMINUM EXPRESS INC
2745 W 78th St (33016-2772)
PHONE..................................954 868-2628
Fax: 305 825-4932
EMP: 5
SALES (est): 410K **Privately Held**
SIC: 2741 Misc Publishing

(G-5042)
ALUMINUM POWDER COATING
16200 Nw 49th Ave (33014-6315)
PHONE..................................305 628-4155
Michael J Buzzella, *Principal*
EMP: 8 **EST:** 2010
SALES (est): 265.3K **Privately Held**
WEB: www.aluminumpowdercoating.com
SIC: 3479 Coating of metals & formed products

(G-5043)
ALUMINUM POWDER COATING LC
16200 Nw 49th Ave (33014-6315)
PHONE..................................305 628-4155
Joseph Buzzella,
Michael Buzzella,
EMP: 10 **EST:** 2002
SQ FT: 24,000

SALES (est): 663.2K **Privately Held**
WEB: www.aluminumpowdercoating.com
SIC: **3479** Coating of metals & formed products

(G-5044)
AMERICAN ARCHTCTRAL MTLS GL LL
Also Called: Aamg
16201 Nw 49th Ave (33014-6314)
PHONE....................................305 688-8778
Donna Rosenberg,
EMP: 7 EST: 2009
SALES (est): 993K **Privately Held**
WEB: www.aamg.us
SIC: **3441** 5231 Fabricated structural metal; glass

(G-5045)
AMERICAN ELASTIC & TAPE INC
1675 E 11th Ave (33010-3309)
PHONE....................................305 888-0303
Frank R Zampieri, *President*
Valentin Zampieri, *Vice Pres*
▲ EMP: 8 EST: 1999
SQ FT: 7,500
SALES (est): 933.3K **Privately Held**
WEB: www.americanelastic.com
SIC: **2241** Narrow fabric mills

(G-5046)
AMERICAN FENCE SHOP LLC
4790 E 11th Ave (33013-2130)
PHONE....................................305 681-3511
Isaac Henriquez, *Mng Member*
◆ EMP: 12 EST: 1995
SQ FT: 5,000
SALES (est): 2.1MM **Privately Held**
WEB: www.americanfenceshop.com
SIC: **3315** 7692 Fence gates posts & fittings: steel; welding repair

(G-5047)
AMERICAN FORCE WHEELS INC
2310 W 76th St (33016-1843)
PHONE....................................786 345-6301
Alireza Shadravan, *President*
Albert Diaz, *Sales Staff*
Nick Chin, *Mktg Dir*
▲ EMP: 15 EST: 1995
SALES (est): 4MM **Privately Held**
WEB: www.americanforce.com
SIC: **3312** Wheels

(G-5048)
AMERICAN MARINE COVERINGS INC
1065 Se 9th Ct (33010-5815)
PHONE....................................305 889-5355
Philip Lavista, *President*
▼ EMP: 10 EST: 1972
SQ FT: 2,200
SALES (est): 254.2K **Privately Held**
WEB: www.american-marine.com
SIC: **2394** 3429 2512 Canvas & related products; manufactured hardware (general); upholstered household furniture

(G-5049)
AMERICAN MARINE MFG INC
2637 W 76th St (33016-5615)
PHONE....................................305 497-7723
Guillermo Santoya, *President*
Byron Carbonell, *Purch Mgr*
EMP: 5 EST: 2016
SALES (est): 434K **Privately Held**
WEB: www.americanmarinewindows.com
SIC: **3731** 3442 Lighters, marine: building & repairing; patrol boats, building & repairing; towboats, building & repairing; storm doors or windows, metal

(G-5050)
AMERICAN S-SHORE PLTING STTCHI
Also Called: Trim Rite Trimmings and Lace
1085 E 31st St (33013-3521)
PHONE....................................305 978-9934
Ike Cortes, *President*
EMP: 8 EST: 1972
SQ FT: 12,500

SALES (est): 662.1K **Privately Held**
WEB: www.americanseashore.com
SIC: **2395** Embroidery & art needlework

(G-5051)
AMERICAN VINYL COMPANY (PA)
Also Called: Avc Plastics
600 W 83rd St (33014-3612)
PHONE....................................305 687-1863
Eric J Wiborg II, *President*
Ryan Wiborg, *General Counsel*
▲ EMP: 20 EST: 2002
SALES (est): 9.6MM **Privately Held**
WEB: www.avcplastics.com
SIC: **2821** Vinyl resins

(G-5052)
AMERIFAX ACQUISITION CORP
Also Called: Ameri-Fax
7290 W 18th Ln (33014-3704)
PHONE....................................305 828-1701
Lambert Thom, *President*
George Manur, *Vice Pres*
◆ EMP: 7 EST: 1989
SQ FT: 12,000
SALES (est): 733.1K **Privately Held**
WEB: www.posconcepts.com
SIC: **2679** Paper products, converted

(G-5053)
AMERIGLASS ENGINEERING INC
2246 W 79th St (33016-5520)
PHONE....................................305 558-6227
Samuel F Verdecia, *President*
EMP: 17 EST: 2005
SALES (est): 838.2K **Privately Held**
WEB: www.ameriglassinc.com
SIC: **3231** Products of purchased glass

(G-5054)
AMERIKOOLER LLC
575 E 10th Ave (33010-4639)
PHONE....................................305 884-8384
Renato M Alonso, *Chairman*
Juan Madariaga, *COO*
Renato Alonso, *Vice Pres*
Alejandro Canela, *Engineer*
Yoelmir Santana, *Engineer*
◆ EMP: 140 EST: 1986
SQ FT: 210,000
SALES (est): 57MM **Privately Held**
WEB: www.amerikooler.com
SIC: **3585** Room coolers, portable

(G-5055)
APPLIED FIBER CONCEPTS INC
2425 W 8th Ln (33010-2031)
PHONE....................................754 581-2744
Alejandro F Cejas, *President*
EMP: 7 EST: 2015
SQ FT: 5,000
SALES (est): 1.5MM **Privately Held**
WEB: www.afcarmor.com
SIC: **3423** Tools or equipment for use with sporting arms

(G-5056)
ARCA KNITTING INC (PA)
1060 E 23rd St (33013-4322)
PHONE....................................305 836-0155
Jorge Canals Jr, *President*
Matilde M Canals, *Admin Sec*
EMP: 100 EST: 1981
SQ FT: 180,000
SALES (est): 11.4MM **Privately Held**
WEB: www.arcaknitting.com
SIC: **2261** Dyeing cotton broadwoven fabrics; decorative finishing of cotton broadwoven fabrics; embossing cotton broadwoven fabrics

(G-5057)
ARTCRAFT ENGRAVING & PRTG INC
7921 W 26th Ave (33016-2729)
PHONE....................................305 557-9449
Frederick R Narup, *President*
William L Sayers, *Vice Pres*
William Sayers, *Treasurer*
Erinn Schnur, *Sales Staff*
Brenda Betancourt, *Technology*
EMP: 19 EST: 1989
SQ FT: 15,000

SALES (est): 3.9MM **Privately Held**
WEB: www.artcraftengraving.com
SIC: **2752** Commercial printing, offset

(G-5058)
ARTEC MANUFACTURING LLC
699 W 17th St (33010-2414)
PHONE....................................305 888-4375
Roy Bustillo, *Mng Member*
EMP: 10 EST: 2011
SALES (est): 498.8K **Privately Held**
SIC: **3999** Manufacturing industries

(G-5059)
ARTEC METAL FABRICATION INC
699 W 17th St (33010-2414)
PHONE....................................305 888-4375
Ramon Trujillo, *CEO*
▲ EMP: 8 EST: 2007
SQ FT: 4,400
SALES (est): 943K **Privately Held**
WEB: www.artecmf.com
SIC: **3441** Fabricated structural metal

(G-5060)
ARTISTIC FENCE CORPORATION
1070 Se 9th Ter Ste B (33010-5832)
P.O. Box 111088 (33011-1088)
PHONE....................................305 805-1976
Ernesto Alvarez, *President*
EMP: 6 EST: 1991
SQ FT: 7,485
SALES (est): 600K **Privately Held**
SIC: **3272** 1741 3496 Concrete products, precast; foundation & retaining wall construction; miscellaneous fabricated wire products

(G-5061)
ASEMBLU INC
18520 Nw 67th Ave 208 (33015-3302)
PHONE....................................800 827-4419
EMP: 15
SALES (est): 522.5K **Privately Held**
SIC: **2599** Mfg Furniture/Fixtures

(G-5062)
ASP ALARM & ELEC SUPS INC
7535 W 20th Ave (33014-3728)
PHONE....................................305 556-9047
Mitchell A Delgado, *President*
EMP: 6 EST: 2004
SALES (est): 696.8K **Privately Held**
SIC: **3669** Emergency alarms

(G-5063)
ASSOCTION HSPNIC HRITG FSTIVAL
3430 E 1st Ave (33013-2602)
PHONE....................................305 885-5613
Eloy Vazquez, *Principal*
EMP: 7 EST: 2006
SALES (est): 190K **Privately Held**
SIC: **2836** Culture media

(G-5064)
ATLAS PAPER MILLS LLC
3725 E 10th Ct (33013-2900)
PHONE....................................305 835-8046
Juan Michelena, *Vice Pres*
EMP: 149
SALES (corp-wide): 2.8B **Privately Held**
WEB: www.atlaspapermills.com
SIC: **2621** 5113 Toilet tissue stock; industrial & personal service paper
HQ: Atlas Paper Mills, Llc
    3301 Nw 107th St
    Miami FL 33167
    800 562-2860

(G-5065)
B & D PRECISION TOOLS INC
2367 W 8th Ln (33010-2029)
PHONE....................................305 885-1583
Heliodoro Duran, *President*
▼ EMP: 31 EST: 1978
SQ FT: 24,000
SALES (est): 2.5MM **Privately Held**
SIC: **3544** 3949 2591 3089 Dies & die holders for metal cutting, forming, die casting; industrial molds; sporting & athletic goods; drapery hardware & blinds & shades; injection molding of plastics

(G-5066)
B LINE APPAREL INC
4671 E 11th Ave (33013-2115)
P.O. Box 530671, Miami (33153-0671)
PHONE....................................305 953-8300
Fax: 305 953-7909
▼ EMP: 12
SQ FT: 20,000
SALES (est): 3.4MM **Privately Held**
SIC: **3552** Mfg Textile Machinery

(G-5067)
BARO GRANITE INC
2775 W 79th St Unit 6 (33016-2761)
PHONE....................................786 663-2514
Pablo Baro, *CEO*
EMP: 7 EST: 2017
SALES (est): 62.6K **Privately Held**
SIC: **3281** Cut stone & stone products

(G-5068)
BASS INDUSTRIES INC
Also Called: Bass Bulletin and Directory
604 W 18th St (33010-2423)
PHONE....................................305 751-2716
Robert Baron, *President*
Paul Baron, *Vice Pres*
Ruth Mayorga, *Sales Staff*
Anne Baron, *Admin Sec*
◆ EMP: 33 EST: 1961
SQ FT: 19,600
SALES (est): 2.6MM **Privately Held**
WEB: www.bassind.com
SIC: **3993** 2542 2519 Displays & cutouts, window & lobby; partitions & fixtures, except wood; furniture, household: glass, fiberglass & plastic

(G-5069)
BAYLEE & COMPANY LLC
Also Called: Baylee Nasco
605 W 17th St (33010-2414)
PHONE....................................305 333-6464
Alina Nasco,
EMP: 5 EST: 2016
SQ FT: 13,000
SALES (est): 333.1K **Privately Held**
WEB: www.bayleenasco.com
SIC: **3552** Card clothing, textile machinery

(G-5070)
BEAUTIFUL MAILBOX CO
2360 W 76th St (33016-1843)
PHONE....................................305 403-4820
Andrew Corsetti, *President*
Sherri Corsetti, *Vice Pres*
Seth Valancy, *Controller*
Sheri Corsetti, *VP Sales*
Eliana Molina, *Sales Staff*
EMP: 38 EST: 1988
SQ FT: 30,000
SALES (est): 6MM **Privately Held**
WEB: www.beautifulmailbox.com
SIC: **3444** 3993 Sheet metalwork; signs & advertising specialties

(G-5071)
BELLA LUNA INC
3650 E 10th Ct (33013-2918)
PHONE....................................305 696-0310
Amelia Costa, *President*
Theresa Costa, *Partner*
Nicolas Trujillo, *Partner*
◆ EMP: 23 EST: 1995
SQ FT: 15,000
SALES (est): 3.1MM **Privately Held**
WEB: www.lunabella.com
SIC: **3648** 3641 Lighting fixtures, except electric: residential; electric lamps

(G-5072)
BENITEZ FORKLIFT CORP
18820 Nw 57th Ave Apt 301 (33015-7012)
PHONE....................................786 307-3872
Yeymi Sardubas, *Principal*
▼ EMP: 7 EST: 2010
SALES (est): 607.9K **Privately Held**
WEB: www.benitezforklift.com
SIC: **3537** Forklift trucks

(G-5073)
BERNARD CAP LLC
620 W 27th St (33010-1214)
PHONE....................................305 822-4800
Lawrence Weinstein, *CEO*
Jack Cendros, *Vice Pres*

Barry L Showalter, *Treasurer*
Barry Showalter, *Treasurer*
Leo Fonseca, *Human Res Mgr*
◆ **EMP:** 140 **EST:** 1974
SQ FT: 60,000
SALES (est): 19.5MM **Privately Held**
WEB: www.bernardcap.com
SIC: 2353 Hats & caps

(G-5074)
BEST POWDER COATINGS INC
3970 E 10th Ct (33013-2924)
PHONE................................305 836-9460
Omar Romero Jr, *President*
EMP: 21 **EST:** 1999
SQ FT: 7,500
SALES (est): 2.6MM **Privately Held**
WEB: www.bestpowdercoatings.com
SIC: 3479 Coating of metals & formed
products

(G-5075)
BEST PRODUCTS MIX INC
17541 Nw 89th Ct (33018-6693)
PHONE................................305 512-9920
Luis M Gutierrez, *President*
Maria B Gutierrez, *Vice Pres*
▼ **EMP:** 8 **EST:** 1993
SQ FT: 10,000
SALES (est): 823.8K **Privately Held**
SIC: 3299 Stucco; plaques: clay, plaster or
papier mache

(G-5076)
BIOSCULPTOR CORPORATION
2480 W 82nd St Unit 1 (33016-2735)
PHONE................................305 823-8300
Alan Finnieston, *President*
Karen Finnieston, *Vice Pres*
EMP: 5 **EST:** 1994
SALES (est): 997.5K **Privately Held**
WEB: www.biosculptor.com
SIC: 3695 3575 7372 3842 Computer
software tape & disks: blank, rigid &
floppy; computer terminals; prepackaged
software; surgical appliances & supplies;
manufactured hardware (general)

(G-5077)
BISCAYNE BEDDING INTL LLC
3925 E 10th Ct (33013-2923)
PHONE................................305 633-4634
Alan Mandell, *President*
Jean Mandell, *Corp Secy*
Stephen Mandell, *Vice Pres*
▼ **EMP:** 25 **EST:** 1949
SQ FT: 15,000
SALES (est): 5.3MM **Privately Held**
WEB: www.biscaynebedding.com
SIC: 2515 Mattresses, innerspring or box
spring; box springs, assembled

(G-5078)
BOTANICA ODOMIWALE CORP
1301 Palm Ave (33010-3463)
PHONE................................305 381-5834
Ramon B Ruiz Sr, *Principal*
EMP: 9 **EST:** 2015
SALES (est): 138.4K **Privately Held**
SIC: 2833 Medicinals & botanicals

(G-5079)
BROS WILLIAMS PRINTING
4716 E 10th Ct (33013-2122)
PHONE................................305 769-9925
Fax: 305 769-9927
EMP: 9
SQ FT: 5,000
SALES: 380K **Privately Held**
SIC: 2759 5199 Commercial Printing Whol
Nondurable Goods

(G-5080)
BROS WILLIAMS PRINTING INC
Also Called: Williams Specialities
4716 E 10th Ct (33013-2122)
PHONE................................305 769-9925
Mario Williams Jr, *President*
Mario J Williams Jr, *President*
EMP: 9 **EST:** 1981
SQ FT: 5,000

SALES (est): 708.1K **Privately Held**
WEB: www.williamsspecialties.com
SIC: 2752 2791 2789 2759 Commercial
printing, offset; typesetting; bookbinding &
related work; commercial printing; die-cut
paper & board

(G-5081)
**BUILDING ENVELOPE SYSTEMS
INC**
3121 E 11th Ave (33013-3513)
PHONE................................305 693-0683
▲ **EMP:** 4
SQ FT: 15,000
SALES: 3MM **Privately Held**
SIC: 3442 Mfg Metal Doors/Sash/Trim

(G-5082)
BUILT RIGHT INSTALLERS INTL
7930 W 26th Ave Unit 2 (33016-2718)
PHONE................................305 362-6010
George Martinez, *CEO*
EMP: 10 **EST:** 1993
SALES (est): 920.1K **Privately Held**
WEB: www.builtrightinstallers.com
SIC: 3535 1796 Unit handling conveying
systems; installing building equipment

(G-5083)
BULLET LINE LLC (DH)
Also Called: BI Acquisition
6301 E 10th Ave Ste 110 (33013-0008)
PHONE................................305 623-9223
David Nicholson, *President*
Mark Weiss, *Vice Pres*
Christie Blanco, *Opers Staff*
Deenna Fajardo, *Opers Staff*
Maria Morenodelfosse, *Opers Staff*
◆ **EMP:** 146 **EST:** 2006
SQ FT: 250,000
SALES (est): 100.8MM **Privately Held**
WEB: www.humphreyline.com
SIC: 3993 Advertising novelties

(G-5084)
BUSINESS CLINIC INC
1475 W Okeechobee Rd # 3 (33010-2860)
PHONE................................786 473-4573
Antonio Diaz, *Principal*
Tony Diaz, *Consultant*
EMP: 7 **EST:** 2018
SALES (est): 351.9K **Privately Held**
WEB: the-business-clinic-
inc.myshopify.com
SIC: 2752 Commercial printing, litho-
graphic

(G-5085)
**CABRERAS SPANISH
SAUSAGES LLC**
765 W 27th St (33010-1215)
PHONE................................305 882-1040
Rodolfo Cabrera,
Rafael Cabrera,
Joanna Desten,
▲ **EMP:** 9 **EST:** 2013
SALES (est): 665.4K **Privately Held**
SIC: 2013 Sausages from purchased
meat; ham, canned: from purchased meat

(G-5086)
**CARGILL MEAT SOLUTIONS
CORP**
Also Called: Cargill Food Distribution
4220 W 91st Pl Unit 100 (33018-3903)
PHONE................................305 826-3699
Jerry Mullins, *Branch Mgr*
EMP: 58
SALES (corp-wide): 42.9B **Privately Held**
WEB: www.cargill.com
SIC: 2011 Meat packing plants
HQ: Cargill Meat Solutions Corp
825 E Douglas Ave
Wichita KS 67202
316 291-2500

(G-5087)
**CARIBBEAN FOAM PRODUCTS
INC**
480 W 84th St Ste 109 (33014-3601)
PHONE................................786 431-5024
Alberto Da Silva, *President*
Carlos Da Silva, *Vice Pres*
Patricia C Da Silva, *Treasurer*
Victoria Castro-Iglesias, *Admin Sec*

▲ **EMP:** 10 **EST:** 2013
SALES (est): 181.8K **Privately Held**
SIC: 3086 Plastics foam products

(G-5088)
**CBM PRINTING WORLDWIDE
INC**
1061 E 23rd St (33013-4321)
PHONE................................786 531-1834
Enrique Carpinteiro, *Principal*
EMP: 7 **EST:** 2017
SALES (est): 83.9K **Privately Held**
SIC: 2752 Commercial printing, litho-
graphic

(G-5089)
CG QUALITY WOODWORKS INC
7530 W 19th Ct (33014-3725)
PHONE................................305 231-3480
Carlos Gomez, *President*
EMP: 7 **EST:** 1998
SALES (est): 973.5K **Privately Held**
WEB: www.cgqualitywoodworks.com
SIC: 2431 Millwork

(G-5090)
CHARLESTON ALUMINUM LLC
1150 Nw 159th Dr (33016)
PHONE................................305 628-4014
EMP: 11
SALES (corp-wide): 40MM **Privately
Held**
SIC: 3334 Primary Aluminum Producer
PA: Charleston Aluminum, Llc
480 Frontage Rd
Gaston SC 29053
803 939-4600

(G-5091)
CHEMSEAL INC
7891 W 25th Ct (33016-2758)
PHONE................................305 433-8362
Carlos Simanca, *Principal*
EMP: 6 **EST:** 2011
SALES (est): 1.3MM **Privately Held**
WEB: www.chemsealinc.net
SIC: 3491 Industrial valves
PA: Chemseal, C.A.
Avenida Aragua Oeste # 15
Maracay

(G-5092)
CIRON CUSTOM WELDING INC
2954 W 84th St (33018-4914)
PHONE................................786 259-7589
Ana R Rodriguez, *President*
Ciro Verdecia, *Vice Pres*
EMP: 7 **EST:** 2016
SALES (est): 105.8K **Privately Held**
SIC: 7692 Welding repair

(G-5093)
**CNC-PRECISION MACHINING
CORP**
1055 E 26th St (33013-3717)
PHONE................................786 452-9575
Lucio Castillo, *President*
EMP: 6 **EST:** 1996
SQ FT: 10,000
SALES (est): 864.5K **Privately Held**
WEB: www.cnc-precision.com
SIC: 3599 Machine shop, jobbing & repair

(G-5094)
COLOR EXPRESS INC
7990 W 25th Ct (33016-2701)
PHONE................................305 558-2061
Lee Mc Call, *President*
EMP: 8 **EST:** 1979
SQ FT: 5,000
SALES (est): 872.5K **Privately Held**
WEB: www.colorexpressprinting.com
SIC: 2752 2791 2789 Commercial print-
ing, offset; typesetting; bookbinding & re-
lated work

(G-5095)
**CONDO ELECTRIC MOTOR
REPR CORP**
3615 E 10th Ct (33013-2917)
PHONE................................305 691-5400
Hector Gomez, *President*
Mohamed Hallaj, *Principal*
Jose G Espinola, *Vice Pres*
Hector Gomez Jr, *Treasurer*

Amos Rojas, *Controller*
◆ **EMP:** 30 **EST:** 1976
SQ FT: 20,000
SALES (est): 6.3MM **Privately Held**
WEB: www.condoelectric.com
SIC: 7694 Electric motor repair

(G-5096)
**CONTROL AND AUTOMTN CONS
INC**
11300 Nw 87th Ct Ste 125 (33018-4518)
P.O. Box 171825 (33017-1825)
PHONE................................305 823-8670
Wilky Gonzalez, *President*
Sadiye Gonzalez, *Vice Pres*
Wilky N Gonzales, *Manager*
EMP: 8 **EST:** 1992
SQ FT: 3,600
SALES (est): 927.8K **Privately Held**
WEB: www.controlandautomation.com
SIC: 3699 Security control equipment &
systems

(G-5097)
CORAL CLUB TEE SHIRTS INC
3192 W 81st St (33018-5808)
PHONE................................305 828-6939
Morton Blake, *President*
▼ **EMP:** 9 **EST:** 1990
SQ FT: 8,000
SALES (est): 861.5K **Privately Held**
SIC: 2253 2759 T-shirts & tops, knit;
screen printing

(G-5098)
CORDOBA FOODS LLC
4477 E 11th Ave (33013-2534)
PHONE................................305 733-4768
Karina Mena, *President*
David Mena, *Mng Member*
Karina F Porritiello,
EMP: 20 **EST:** 2004
SQ FT: 1,000
SALES (est): 4.7MM **Privately Held**
WEB: www.cordobafoods.com
SIC: 2033 Barbecue sauce: packaged in
cans, jars, etc.

(G-5099)
CORELITE INC (PA)
1060 E 30th St (33013-3520)
PHONE................................305 921-4292
Pascual Del Cioppo, *President*
Mariella Vazquez, *Vice Pres*
Domenica Del Cioppo, *Treasurer*
Elsa Axelsdottir, *Manager*
Giancarlo Del Cioppo, *Admin Sec*
▲ **EMP:** 11 **EST:** 2011
SQ FT: 25,000
SALES (est): 9MM **Privately Held**
WEB: www.corelitecomposites.com
SIC: 2436 Softwood veneer & plywood

(G-5100)
CORP COMFORT FINISHER MR
2501 W 80th St Unit 1 (33016-2719)
PHONE................................786 332-3655
Reynaldo Almaguer, *Owner*
EMP: 5 **EST:** 2012
SALES (est): 408K **Privately Held**
SIC: 3821 Laboratory apparatus & furniture

(G-5101)
CREATIVE MILLWORK INC
7635 W 28th Ave Bay 3 (33016-5107)
PHONE................................305 885-5474
William Rodriguez, *President*
EMP: 5 **EST:** 1997
SQ FT: 700
SALES (est): 467K **Privately Held**
WEB: www.creative-millwork.com
SIC: 2431 Millwork

(G-5102)
CURV-A-TECH CORP
930 W 23rd St (33010-2014)
PHONE................................305 888-9631
Ernesto F Sarabia, *President*
Mayra Sarabia, *Corp Secy*
▼ **EMP:** 10 **EST:** 1986
SQ FT: 15,000
SALES (est): 930.3K **Privately Held**
SIC: 3442 Sash, door or window: metal

(G-5103)
CUSTOM CONTROLS TECHNOLOGY INC
Also Called: CCT
2230 W 77th St (33016-1866)
PHONE...................................305 805-3700
Sheila Gallo, *President*
Gerardo Gallo, *Vice Pres*
Gordon Myers, *Vice Pres*
EMP: 26 EST: 1987
SQ FT: 15,000
SALES (est): 9.2MM **Privately Held**
WEB: www.cct-inc.com
SIC: 3625 Relays & industrial controls

(G-5104)
CUSTOM MICA FURNITURE INC
575 W 28th St (33010-1325)
PHONE...................................305 888-8480
Fax: 305 885-2284
EMP: 6
SQ FT: 8,000
SALES (est): 470K **Privately Held**
SIC: 2511 Kitchen Cabinets/Cultured Marble/Granite

(G-5105)
D T WOODCRAFTERS CORP
1677 W 31st Pl (33012-4505)
PHONE...................................305 556-3771
David Thibaudeau, *President*
George Miller, *Plant Mgr*
Maickel Plaza, *Plant Mgr*
Wendy Ackerman, *Controller*
EMP: 17 EST: 1989
SQ FT: 16,000
SALES (est): 3.5MM **Privately Held**
WEB: www.dtwoodcrafters.com
SIC: 2541 2434 Store & office display cases & fixtures; cabinets, except refrigerated: show, display, etc.: wood; wood kitchen cabinets

(G-5106)
D TURIN & COMPANY INC
8045 W 26th Ct (33016-2797)
PHONE...................................305 825-2004
Ronald Plask, *President*
Robert Edelman, *Vice Pres*
David Plask, *Vice Pres*
Kenny Plask, *Vice Pres*
Barbara Spivack, *Vice Pres*
▲ EMP: 24 EST: 1926
SQ FT: 7,200
SALES (est): 2MM **Privately Held**
WEB: www.dturin.com
SIC: 2353 3911 2752 3961 Hats, caps & millinery; jewelry, precious metal; commercial printing, lithographic; costume jewelry

(G-5107)
DADE DOORS INC
1707 W 32nd Pl (33012-4511)
PHONE...................................305 556-8980
Wilfredo Gonsalez, *President*
▼ EMP: 10 EST: 1999
SQ FT: 2,000
SALES (est): 1MM **Privately Held**
WEB: www.dadedoors.com
SIC: 2434 Wood kitchen cabinets

(G-5108)
DADE MADE
478 W 28th St (33010-1324)
PHONE...................................305 846-9482
L Michael Underwood Jr, *President*
EMP: 7 EST: 2017
SALES (est): 475.5K **Privately Held**
WEB: www.dademadefab.com
SIC: 7692 Welding repair

(G-5109)
DAVID VIERA LLC
7828 W 29th Ln Apt 101 (33018-5166)
PHONE...................................305 218-3401
David Viera, *Manager*
EMP: 6 EST: 2004
SALES (est): 476.8K **Privately Held**
WEB: www.dvmiamistairsrailing.com
SIC: 3446 Architectural metalwork

(G-5110)
DB MOTORING GROUP INC
Also Called: Traklite Wheels
8075 W 20th Ave (33014-3230)
PHONE...................................305 685-0707
Gustavo Baldor, *President*
◆ EMP: 8 EST: 2009
SALES (est): 1MM **Privately Held**
WEB: www.dbmotoringgroup.com
SIC: 3011 5014 Tires & inner tubes; tires & tubes

(G-5111)
DEBWAY CORPORATION
2343 W 76th St (33016-1842)
PHONE...................................305 818-6353
Gesualdo Vitale, *President*
Rosanna Vitale, *Vice Pres*
Patrizia Vitlae, *Treasurer*
Mariana Vitale, *Admin Sec*
◆ EMP: 6 EST: 1991
SQ FT: 9,600
SALES (est): 840.7K **Privately Held**
WEB: www.debwaycorp.com
SIC: 3562 Ball & roller bearings

(G-5112)
DECO SHADES SOLUTIONS INC
3155 W Okeechobee Rd (33012-4519)
PHONE...................................305 558-9800
Enrique Perez, *Principal*
▼ EMP: 6 EST: 2012
SALES (est): 371.2K **Privately Held**
SIC: 2591 Drapery hardware & blinds & shades

(G-5113)
DELCONTE PACKAGING INC
757 W 26th St (33010-1211)
PHONE...................................305 885-2800
William Block, *President*
▲ EMP: 15 EST: 1995
SQ FT: 10,000
SALES (est): 2.3MM **Privately Held**
WEB: www.delcontepackaging.com
SIC: 3089 3993 Plastic containers, except foam; signs & advertising specialties

(G-5114)
DERM-BURO INC
Also Called: G-Forces Div
4675 E 10th Ct (33013-2107)
PHONE...................................305 953-4025
Derrick Visla, *Manager*
EMP: 41
SALES (corp-wide): 3.4MM **Privately Held**
WEB: www.gforces.com
SIC: 3841 Surgical & medical instruments
PA: Derm-Buro, Inc.
229 Newtown Rd
Plainview NY 11803
516 694-8300

(G-5115)
DESIGNER FILMS INC
7485 W 19th Ct (33014-3722)
PHONE...................................305 828-0605
Monica Anderson, *President*
Eduardo Temkin, *Principal*
▲ EMP: 17 EST: 2010
SQ FT: 15,000
SALES (est): 1MM **Privately Held**
WEB: www.designerfilms.com
SIC: 3081 Plastic film & sheet

(G-5116)
DHF MARKETING INC
685 W 25th St (33010-2148)
PHONE...................................305 884-8077
Barry J Richman, *President*
EMP: 15 EST: 2003
SQ FT: 28,255
SALES (est): 502.1K **Privately Held**
SIC: 2211 Draperies & drapery fabrics, cotton

(G-5117)
DIAZ BROTHERS CORP
7750 W 24th Ave (33016-5786)
PHONE...................................305 364-4911
Nelson Y Diaz Mendez, *Principal*
EMP: 10 EST: 2009
SALES (est): 169.8K **Privately Held**
WEB: www.bandmpaving.com
SIC: 2515 Mattresses & bedsprings

(G-5118)
DILAN ENTERPRISES INC
2339 W 9th Ct (33010-2003)
PHONE...................................305 887-3051
▼ EMP: 36
SQ FT: 4,000
SALES (est): 1.5MM **Privately Held**
SIC: 2339 2369 Mfg Women's/Misses' Outerwear Mfg Girl/Youth Outerwear

(G-5119)
DIVITAE INC
570 E 65th St (33013-1161)
PHONE...................................786 585-5556
Gabriel Kohen, *CEO*
EMP: 7 EST: 2019
SALES (est): 1.2MM **Privately Held**
SIC: 2869 Industrial organic chemicals

(G-5120)
DJ CABINET FACTORY INC
2552 W 3rd Ct (33010-1457)
PHONE...................................786 483-8868
Jose Luis Lopez, *President*
EMP: 9 EST: 2006
SALES (est): 285.4K **Privately Held**
SIC: 2434 Vanities, bathroom: wood

(G-5121)
DOBBS & BRODEUR BOOKBINDERS
Also Called: D & B Bookbinders
1030 E 14th St (33010-3312)
PHONE...................................305 885-5215
Edward Lloret, *President*
Anthony Lloret, *Vice Pres*
Jorge Lloret, *Treasurer*
EMP: 11 EST: 1975
SQ FT: 8,000
SALES (est): 900.9K **Privately Held**
SIC: 2789 2796 2782 2759 Binding only: books, pamphlets, magazines, etc.; platemaking services; blankbooks & looseleaf binders; commercial printing

(G-5122)
DON INDUSTRIAL GROUP LLC
7760 W 20th Ave Ste 7 (33016-1829)
PHONE...................................305 290-4237
Reinier Hernandez, *Mng Member*
Melanie Garcia, *Administration*
EMP: 10 EST: 2010
SALES (est): 1.3MM **Privately Held**
WEB: www.donindustrialgroup.com
SIC: 3728 Aircraft parts & equipment

(G-5123)
DRT EXPRESS INC
7855 W 2nd Ct Ste 4 (33014-4333)
PHONE...................................305 827-5005
Pok Hao Truong, *Principal*
EMP: 8 EST: 2009
SALES (est): 927.4K **Privately Held**
WEB: www.drtexpress.com
SIC: 3312 Wheels

(G-5124)
DTI DESIGN TREND INC
496 W 18th St (33010-2419)
PHONE...................................954 680-8370
Jack Wiener, *President*
EMP: 10 EST: 2004
SQ FT: 11,000
SALES (est): 106K **Privately Held**
SIC: 2399 2221 Emblems, badges & insignia; draperies & drapery fabrics, manmade fiber & silk; bedspreads, silk & manmade fiber

(G-5125)
DUCT DESIGN CORPORATION
7850 W 22nd Ave Unit 1 (33016-1873)
PHONE...................................305 827-0110
Rolando Ors, *President*
Maria Ors, *Corp Secy*
Jorge Galvez, *Engineer*
Gianni Jimenez, *Project Engr*
EMP: 33 EST: 1992
SQ FT: 2,000
SALES (est): 4.9MM **Privately Held**
WEB: www.ductdesign.com
SIC: 3444 Ducts, sheet metal

(G-5126)
DYNABILT TECHNOLOGIES CORP
180 W 22nd St (33010-2208)
P.O. Box 726, Hallandale (33008-0726)
PHONE...................................305 919-9800
Fax: 954 455-9911
EMP: 15
SQ FT: 10,000
SALES: 3MM **Privately Held**
SIC: 3441 Structural Metal Fabrication

(G-5127)
DYNACOLOR GRAPHICS INC
950 Se 8th St (33010-5740)
P.O. Box 699037, Miami (33269-9037)
PHONE...................................305 625-5388
Donald M Duncanson, *President*
Harry Duncanson, *Vice Pres*
▼ EMP: 23 EST: 1971
SQ FT: 41,000
SALES (est): 696.8K **Privately Held**
WEB: www.dynacolor.com
SIC: 2752 Commercial printing, offset

(G-5128)
E & D KITCHEN CABINET INC
6790 W 6th Ct (33012-6534)
PHONE...................................786 343-8558
Elio Montero, *Principal*
EMP: 7 EST: 2010
SALES (est): 335.6K **Privately Held**
SIC: 2434 Wood kitchen cabinets

(G-5129)
E & E WOODCRAFT CORP
1619 W 33rd Pl (33012-4513)
PHONE...................................305 556-1443
Diosmede Cano, *President*
EMP: 10 EST: 2005
SALES (est): 426.5K **Privately Held**
WEB: www.eandemillwork.net
SIC: 2431 Millwork

(G-5130)
EAST COAST METALS INC
Also Called: Manufacturing
7905 W 20th Ave (33014-3229)
PHONE...................................305 885-9991
Tom Castellanos, *President*
▼ EMP: 32 EST: 1996
SQ FT: 9,000
SALES (est): 5.4MM **Privately Held**
WEB: www.eastcoast-metals.com
SIC: 3999 Barber & beauty shop equipment

(G-5131)
EASTERN SIGNS LLC
13408 Nw 38th Ct (33014)
PHONE...................................305 542-8274
Jorge L Quintero, *Principal*
EMP: 7 EST: 2016
SALES (est): 320.4K **Privately Held**
SIC: 3993 Signs & advertising specialties

(G-5132)
EC CABINETS INC
1511 E 11th Ave (33010-3308)
PHONE...................................305 887-2091
Emilio Cruz, *President*
Yudelka Rosario, *Vice Pres*
EMP: 7 EST: 2002
SQ FT: 20,000
SALES (est): 604.2K **Privately Held**
WEB: www.eccabinets.net
SIC: 2434 Wood kitchen cabinets

(G-5133)
ECONOCHANNEL INC
213 Se 10th Ave (33010-5536)
PHONE...................................305 255-2113
Jose Hernandez, *President*
Leida Hernandez, *Vice Pres*
Jorge Hernandez, *Controller*
Laura Hernandez, *Controller*
▼ EMP: 35 EST: 1997
SALES (est): 4.6MM **Privately Held**
WEB: www.econochannel.com
SIC: 3993 Signs & advertising specialties

(G-5134)
ED STEEL FABRICATOR INC
4807 E 10th Ln (33013-2127)
PHONE...................................305 926-4904

▲ = Import ▼=Export
◆ =Import/Export

EMP: 7 EST: 2015
SALES (est): 587.5K **Privately Held**
WEB: www.edsteelf.com
SIC: 3441 Fabricated structural metal

(G-5135)
EDICIONES ATENEA INC
Also Called: Atenea Maintenance and Repair
15476 Nw 77th Ct Ste 601 (33016-5823)
PHONE..............................305 984-5483
Arelys M Cubero, *Branch Mgr*
EMP: 19
SALES (corp-wide): 202.1K **Privately
Held**
SIC: 2731 5942 8231 Book publishing;
book stores; book rental
PA: Ediciones Atenea, Inc.
6478 Seawolf Ct Apt B2
Naples FL 34112
305 984-5483

(G-5136)
**EDSUN LIGHTING FIXTURES
MFG**
569 W 17th St (33010-2412)
P.O. Box 650861, Miami (33265-0861)
PHONE..............................305 888-8849
Guillermina Garcia, *President*
Roy Garcia, *General Mgr*
Isabelle Moraitis, *Vice Pres*
Johnny Rodriguez, *Sales Mgr*
◆ EMP: 15 EST: 1983
SQ FT: 20,000
SALES (est): 2.1MM **Privately Held**
SIC: 3645 3646 Residential lighting fix-
tures; commercial indusl & institutional
electric lighting fixtures

(G-5137)
**EDYMAR DESIGN CARPENTRY
LLC**
2641 W 76th St (33016-5615)
PHONE..............................954 822-0687
Eduardo Bujato, *Principal*
EMP: 10 EST: 2017
SALES (est): 275.2K **Privately Held**
SIC: 2434 Wood kitchen cabinets

(G-5138)
EGG ROLL SKINS INC
3251 E 11th Ave (33013-3515)
PHONE..............................305 836-0571
Fernando Chang Muy, *President*
Julio Chiong, *Vice Pres*
Wai Chiu Muy, *Vice Pres*
EMP: 10 EST: 1970
SQ FT: 10,000
SALES (est): 152.6K **Privately Held**
SIC: 2051 5812 2099 Rolls, bread type:
fresh or frozen; Chinese restaurant; food
preparations

(G-5139)
ELLIS FAMILY HOLDINGS INC
Also Called: Molded Container
6301 E 10th Ave Ste 110 (33013-0008)
PHONE..............................503 785-7400
Melvin W Ellis, *President*
◆ EMP: 12 EST: 1957
SQ FT: 5,000
SALES (est): 238.6K **Privately Held**
SIC: 3089 3993 Injection molding of plas-
tics; advertising novelties

(G-5140)
EMC REPRESENTATIONS CORP
1198 W 23rd St (33010-1949)
PHONE..............................305 305-1776
Eladio Medina Cabello, *Principal*
EMP: 8 EST: 2016
SALES (est): 94.5K **Privately Held**
WEB: www.emcrepresentaciones.com
SIC: 3572 Computer storage devices

(G-5141)
EMC RESPIRATORY CARE INC
19341 Nw 82nd Ct (33015-5300)
PHONE..............................305 829-5744
Eugenio Castaneda, *Principal*
EMP: 7 EST: 2014
SALES (est): 164.2K **Privately Held**
SIC: 3572 Computer storage devices

(G-5142)
EMJAC INDUSTRIES INC
1075 Hialeah Dr (33010-5551)
PHONE..............................305 883-2194
David Dorta, *President*
Robert Castro, *Business Mgr*
Jeff Cook, *COO*
Kenneth Brown, *Vice Pres*
Terri Dorta, *Vice Pres*
▼ EMP: 96 EST: 1974
SQ FT: 100,000
SALES (est): 11.6MM **Privately Held**
WEB: www.emjacindustries.com
SIC: 2542 3441 Counters or counter dis-
play cases: except wood; fabricated struc-
tural metal

(G-5143)
EMPIRE ENTERPRISES
2980 W 84th St Unit 11 (33018-4916)
PHONE..............................786 373-8003
Erick Martinez, *Principal*
EMP: 5 EST: 2018
SALES (est): 344K **Privately Held**
SIC: 3999 Manufacturing industries

(G-5144)
EMPIRE STONE AND CABINETS
720 W 27th St (33010-1216)
PHONE..............................305 885-7092
Ralph J Granadillo, *President*
Nicole Granadillo, *Vice Pres*
EMP: 21 EST: 2016
SALES (est): 2.5MM **Privately Held**
SIC: 2434 Wood kitchen cabinets

(G-5145)
**EMPIRE TRNSPT SOLUTIONS
CORP**
228 W 18th St (33010-2527)
PHONE..............................305 439-5677
Adolfo A Rumbaut Guzman, *President*
EMP: 6 EST: 2017
SALES (est): 300K **Privately Held**
SIC: 3537 Trucks, tractors, loaders, carri-
ers & similar equipment

(G-5146)
**ENVIRONMENTAL
CONTRACTORS INC**
Also Called: E C I
2648 W 78th St (33016-2745)
PHONE..............................305 556-6942
Kelly Moran, *President*
EMP: 12 EST: 1985
SQ FT: 6,064
SALES (est): 2.8MM **Privately Held**
WEB: www.hannahindustries.com
SIC: 1481 1541 4212 Overburden re-
moval, nonmetallic minerals; industrial
buildings & warehouses; hazardous
waste transport

(G-5147)
EXCLUSIVE BATS LLC
10930 Nw 138th St Unit 1 (33018-1139)
PHONE..............................305 450-3858
Roberto Maya, *Principal*
EMP: 8 EST: 2016
SALES (est): 511.5K **Privately Held**
WEB: www.exclusivebats.com
SIC: 3949 Sporting & athletic goods

(G-5148)
EXPRESS VISION CARE INC
1550 W 84th St Ste 15 (33014-3368)
PHONE..............................786 587-7404
Raul Lopez, *Manager*
EMP: 8 EST: 2012
SALES (est): 1MM **Privately Held**
WEB: www.expressvisioncare.com
SIC: 3851 Contact lenses

(G-5149)
**F & R GENERAL INTERIORS
CORP**
480 W 20th St (33010-2426)
PHONE..............................305 635-4747
Ruben Rodriguez, *President*
Chris Rodriguez, *Vice Pres*
▼ EMP: 13 EST: 1984
SALES (est): 2MM **Privately Held**
WEB: www.fandrgeneralinteriors.com
SIC: 2531 2491 Chairs, table & arm; mill-
work, treated wood

(G-5150)
FALCONPRO INDUSTRIES INC
1690 W 40th St (33012-7043)
PHONE..............................305 556-4456
John Carlos, *President*
Juan Rivero, *Director*
Anna Gonzalez, *Admin Sec*
▼ EMP: 6 EST: 1983
SQ FT: 4,000
SALES (est): 653.7K **Privately Held**
WEB: www.falconpro.com
SIC: 2842 Deodorants, nonpersonal

(G-5151)
**FASHION CONNECTION MIAMI
INC**
Also Called: Classic Uniforms
900 W 19th St (33010-2309)
PHONE..............................305 882-0782
Sergio Urquiza Jr, *President*
Joseph Urquiza, *Vice Pres*
Maria Urquiza, *Treasurer*
EMP: 9 EST: 1977
SQ FT: 15,000
SALES (est): 835.1K **Privately Held**
SIC: 2389 Uniforms & vestments

(G-5152)
FAST FUEL CORP
2274 W 80th St Unit 4 (33016-5550)
PHONE..............................786 251-0373
Ricardo Rivero, *Principal*
EMP: 8 EST: 2007
SALES (est): 199.6K **Privately Held**
SIC: 2869 Fuels

(G-5153)
FAULKNER INC OF MIAMI
Also Called: Faulkner Plastics
7275 W 20th Ave (33014-3707)
PHONE..............................305 885-4731
Joseph E McCabe, *President*
Tami L McCabe, *Vice Pres*
Rick Allen, *Opers Mgr*
Vanessa Fleitas, *Manager*
Jame Gonzalez, *Manager*
▼ EMP: 14 EST: 1966
SQ FT: 14,000
SALES (est): 4.9MM **Privately Held**
WEB: www.plasticproductsinc.com
SIC: 3089 Injection molding of plastics

(G-5154)
FDC PRINT LLC
Also Called: Franklin Dodd Communications
950 Se 8th St (33010-5740)
PHONE..............................305 885-8707
Donald Mader, *President*
Maryjo Lynch, *Prdtn Mgr*
Elizabeth Cal, *Engineer*
Robert Cooler, *Engineer*
Ken Justilien, *Accounts Exec*
▼ EMP: 71 EST: 2011
SALES (est): 15.7MM
SALES (corp-wide): 50.7MM **Privately
Held**
WEB: www.franklindodd.com
SIC: 2759 Commercial printing
PA: Southeastern Printing Co Inc
950 Se 8th St
Hialeah FL 33010
772 287-2141

(G-5155)
FEDAN CORP
Also Called: Fedan Tire Co
2280 W 1st Ave (33010-2202)
PHONE..............................305 885-5415
Felix Sanchez Sr, *President*
Mireya Sanchez, *Corp Secy*
Felix J Sanchez Jr, *Vice Pres*
◆ EMP: 8 EST: 1979
SQ FT: 8,000
SALES (est): 2.5MM **Privately Held**
WEB: www.fedantire.com
SIC: 3011 5531 5014 7534 Retreading
materials, tire; automotive tires; tires &
tubes; tire retreading & repair shops

(G-5156)
**FLORIDA DRAGLINE
OPERATION**
3163 W 81st St (33018-5807)
PHONE..............................305 824-9755
David White, *Manager*

▲ EMP: 10 EST: 1995
SALES (est): 750.2K **Privately Held**
SIC: 3531 Excavators: cable, clamshell,
crane, derrick, dragline, etc.

(G-5157)
FLORIDA FLEXIBLE
2681 W 81st St (33016-2716)
PHONE..............................305 512-2222
Armando Corbett, *President*
EMP: 8 EST: 2014
SALES (est): 593.2K **Privately Held**
WEB: www.floridaflex.com
SIC: 2759 Screen printing

(G-5158)
**FLORIDA KIT CBNETS AMERCN
CORP**
9325 W Okeechobee Rd (33016-2183)
PHONE..............................305 828-2830
Carlos Cabrera, *Principal*
EMP: 7 EST: 2005
SALES (est): 172.6K **Privately Held**
SIC: 2434 Wood kitchen cabinets

(G-5159)
FLORIDA THREAD & TRIMMING
7395 W 18th Ln (33014-3739)
PHONE..............................954 240-2474
Erwin Fein, *President*
Robert Fein, *Corp Secy*
Alan Fein, *Vice Pres*
▼ EMP: 10 EST: 1968
SQ FT: 10,000
SALES (est): 194.9K **Privately Held**
SIC: 2284 5131 Thread from manmade
fibers; notions

(G-5160)
FOREVER SIGNS INC
2400 W 3rd Ct (33010-1439)
PHONE..............................305 885-3411
Arturo Dizcaiano, *President*
Dailyn Gonzalez, *Admin Sec*
▲ EMP: 19 EST: 2006
SALES (est): 2.5MM **Privately Held**
WEB: www.foreversignsusa.net
SIC: 3993 Electric signs

(G-5161)
FRIENDLY WELDING INC
4600 E 10th Ln (33013-2112)
PHONE..............................786 953-8413
EMP: 11 **Privately Held**
SIC: 7692 Welding Repair
PA: Friendly Welding Inc
17051 Ne 23rd Ave Apt 1k
North Miami Beach FL

(G-5162)
G PRINT INC
2392 W 80th St Ste 1 (33016-5687)
PHONE..............................305 316-2266
Gilbert A Gutierrez, *President*
EMP: 9 EST: 2016
SALES (est): 542K **Privately Held**
SIC: 2752 Commercial printing, litho-
graphic

(G-5163)
G S SERVICORE CORP
3630 E 10th Ct (33013-2918)
PHONE..............................305 888-0189
Victor Medina, *President*
Karlos Medina, *Opers Staff*
Samuel Ospina, *Sales Staff*
Jorge Ruiz, *Manager*
Ronald Sanchez, *Manager*
◆ EMP: 22 EST: 2001
SQ FT: 18,000
SALES (est): 2.6MM **Privately Held**
WEB: www.sgsequipment.com
SIC: 3621 4581 7699 Motors & genera-
tors; airport terminal services; industrial
equipment services

(G-5164)
G-CAR INC (PA)
235 W 75th Pl (33014-4340)
PHONE..............................305 883-8223
Gerardo Cabrera, *President*
Carlos Cabrera, *Corp Secy*
▲ EMP: 60 EST: 1985
SQ FT: 35,000

SALES (est): 5.1MM **Privately Held**
SIC: 3714 Steering mechanisms, motor vehicle

(G-5165)
GAMA TEC CORPORATION
2208 W 79th St (33016-5520)
PHONE...................................305 362-0456
Claudio Gatto, *President*
EMP: 6 **EST:** 1991
SQ FT: 3,000
SALES (est): 677.6K **Privately Held**
SIC: 3544 Industrial molds

(G-5166)
GARCIA DELUXE SERVICES CORP
1240 W 34th St (33012-4810)
PHONE...................................786 291-4329
Mijail Garcia, *President*
EMP: 7 **EST:** 2018
SALES (est): 144.9K **Privately Held**
SIC: 2782 Blankbooks & looseleaf binders

(G-5167)
GARCIA IRON WORKS
365 W 21st St (33010-2518)
PHONE...................................305 888-0080
Martin Garcia, *Owner*
Alena Garcia, *Opers-Prdtn-Mfg*
EMP: 6 **EST:** 1995
SALES (est): 654.6K **Privately Held**
WEB: www.garciaironwork.com
SIC: 3312 5712 Hot-rolled iron & steel products; furniture stores

(G-5168)
GENERAL IMPACT GL WINDOWS CORP
290 W 78th Rd (33014-4302)
PHONE...................................305 558-8103
Jose Gunida, *President*
Jose Ruiz, *Sales Staff*
▼ **EMP:** 16 **EST:** 2001
SALES (est): 3.2MM **Privately Held**
SIC: 3442 Shutters, door or window: metal

(G-5169)
GENERAL PILLOWS & FIBER INC
Also Called: Hygenator Pillow Service
605 W 17th St (33010-2414)
PHONE...................................305 884-8300
Alina G Nasco, *President*
Miguel A Nasco Jr, *Vice Pres*
Alina Nasco, *CFO*
EMP: 9 **EST:** 2005
SALES (est): 943.6K **Privately Held**
WEB: www.pillowsandfibers.com
SIC: 2392 Cushions & pillows

(G-5170)
GENERAL STAIR CORPORATION
Also Called: G S C
690 W 83rd St (33014-3612)
PHONE...................................305 769-9900
Saby Behar, *President*
Moises Vaninstein, *Treasurer*
Alejandro Davila, *Finance Mgr*
Rachel Martinez, *Sales Staff*
Jaime Shapiro, *Director*
EMP: 32 **EST:** 1986
SQ FT: 23,000
SALES (est): 4.4MM **Privately Held**
WEB: www.generalstair.com
SIC: 2431 Staircases & stairs, wood

(G-5171)
GESS TECHNOLOGIES LLC
7292 W 20th Ave (33016-1854)
PHONE...................................305 231-6322
Johnny Ferreira, *CEO*
EMP: 13 **EST:** 2003
SALES (est): 984.1K **Privately Held**
WEB: www.gess-inc.com
SIC: 3699 Security devices

(G-5172)
GILDA INDUSTRIES INC
2525 W 4th Ave (33010-1339)
PHONE...................................305 887-8286
Juan Blazquez, *President*
Jeannice Blazquez, *Vice Pres*
Carmen E Blazquez, *Director*
◆ **EMP:** 97 **EST:** 1967

SQ FT: 40,000
SALES (est): 13.6MM **Privately Held**
WEB: www.gildaindustries.com
SIC: 2052 Crackers, dry

(G-5173)
GLOBAL INTL INVESTMENTS LLC
6175 Nw 167th St Ste G32 (33015-4362)
PHONE...................................305 825-2288
Dorelis La Capruccia, *Vice Pres*
Pamela Hermoza, *Sales Staff*
EMP: 6 **EST:** 2010
SALES (est): 811.9K **Privately Held**
WEB: www.giillc.net
SIC: 3728 Aircraft parts & equipment

(G-5174)
GOLD NETWORK OF MIAMI INC
17620 Nw 63rd Ct (33015-4484)
PHONE...................................305 343-7355
George Smith, *Principal*
EMP: 9 **EST:** 2011
SALES (est): 181.6K **Privately Held**
SIC: 3571 Personal computers (microcomputers)

(G-5175)
GOURMET 3005 INC
2315 W 77th St (33016-1869)
PHONE...................................786 334-6250
Mario Marquez, *President*
Robinson Avila, *Vice Pres*
EMP: 6 **EST:** 2011
SALES (est): 300K **Privately Held**
WEB: www.eternalwaterheater.com
SIC: 2011 Bacon, slab & sliced from meat slaughtered on site

(G-5176)
GQ INVESTMENTS LLC
Also Called: Fine Art Lamps
3840 W 104th St Unit 20 (33018-1230)
PHONE...................................305 821-3850
Bill Gearhart, *Controller*
Melissa Roman, *Sales Staff*
Laura Goldblum,
Aymee Zayas, *Graphic Designe*
Rene Quintana,
EMP: 140 **EST:** 2018
SQ FT: 125,000
SALES (est): 25MM **Privately Held**
SIC: 3645 Wall lamps; table lamps; desk lamps

(G-5177)
GREGG TOOL & DIE CO INC
4725 E 10th Ct (33013-2121)
PHONE...................................305 685-6309
Gregg Jones, *President*
Edith Jones, *Corp Secy*
EMP: 5 **EST:** 1970
SQ FT: 15,000
SALES (est): 610.4K **Privately Held**
WEB: www.greggtool.com
SIC: 3544 3469 Special dies & tools; metal stampings

(G-5178)
GROUP STEEL INC (PA)
3492 W 84th St (33018-4930)
PHONE...................................786 319-1222
Erick Gonzalez, *President*
Angelica Bustamante, *Treasurer*
EMP: 6 **EST:** 2010
SALES (est): 1.5MM **Privately Held**
SIC: 3441 Fabricated structural metal

(G-5179)
GUIMAR INC
Also Called: Sir Speedy
1224 E 4th Ave (33010-3502)
PHONE...................................305 888-1547
Maria Noguera, *President*
Maurice Noguera, *Vice Pres*
Mauricio Noguera, *Vice Pres*
Rosa Osorio, *Manager*
David Robidoux, *Executive*
EMP: 14 **EST:** 1980
SQ FT: 3,200
SALES (est): 2.5MM **Privately Held**
WEB: www.sirspeedy.com
SIC: 2752 Commercial printing, lithographic

(G-5180)
GUNDERLIN LTD INC
3625 E 11th Ave (33013-2929)
PHONE...................................305 696-6071
Jay Bass, *President*
Lynn Kislack, *Corp Secy*
Russ Marot, *Vice Pres*
Charlie Sammarco, *Vice Pres*
▼ **EMP:** 95 **EST:** 1954
SQ FT: 100,000
SALES (est): 14.2MM **Privately Held**
WEB: www.gunderlin.com
SIC: 3534 Elevators & equipment

(G-5181)
H GOICOECHEA INC
Also Called: Best Supplier
695 E 10th Ave (33010-4641)
PHONE...................................305 805-3333
Hugo Goicoechea, *President*
▲ **EMP:** 15 **EST:** 2010
SALES (est): 269.7K **Privately Held**
SIC: 2673 Bags: plastic, laminated & coated

(G-5182)
HAMBURG HOUSE INC
6157 Nw 167th St Ste F20 (33015-4360)
PHONE...................................305 557-9913
Peter Auerbach, *President*
▲ **EMP:** 19 **EST:** 1933
SALES (est): 1.3MM **Privately Held**
WEB: www.hamburghouse.com
SIC: 2299 2395 Linen fabrics; embroidery products, except schiffli machine

(G-5183)
HG TRADING CIA INC
1055 Se 9th Ter (33010-5804)
PHONE...................................305 986-5702
Hector Gahaleano, *President*
◆ **EMP:** 9 **EST:** 1997
SALES (est): 16.7K **Privately Held**
SIC: 3251 5032 Brick & structural clay tile; brick, stone & related material

(G-5184)
HIALEAH DISTRIBUTION CORP
Also Called: Beverage Depot
270 W 25th St (33010-1528)
PHONE...................................786 200-2498
Marc Gueron, *CEO*
Viktor Razon, *General Mgr*
EMP: 26 **EST:** 1970
SQ FT: 6,000
SALES (est): 564.9K **Privately Held**
WEB: www.hialeahfl.gov
SIC: 2097 5149 Manufactured ice; soft drinks

(G-5185)
HIALEAH PLATING
4335 E 10th Ave (33013-2513)
PHONE...................................305 953-4143
EMP: 8 **EST:** 2018
SALES (est): 936.9K **Privately Held**
WEB: www.alliedplating.com
SIC: 3471 Electroplating of metals or formed products

(G-5186)
HIALEAH POWDER COATING CORP
1690 W 33rd Pl (33012-4514)
PHONE...................................786 275-4107
Jimmy J Hernandez, *President*
EMP: 12 **EST:** 2014
SALES (est): 421.6K **Privately Held**
SIC: 3479 Etching & engraving

(G-5187)
HIGH END DEFENSE SOLUTIONS LLC
8080 W 26th Ct (33016-2730)
PHONE...................................305 647-2597
Carmen Consuegra, *Manager*
▲ **EMP:** 7 **EST:** 2009
SALES (est): 966.9K **Privately Held**
SIC: 3489 Guns, howitzers, mortars & related equipment

(G-5188)
HOLPACK CORP
Also Called: Best Bubble Mailers
3840 W 104th St Unit 7 (33018-1230)
PHONE...................................786 565-3969
Benjamin Wainberg, *President*
EMP: 12 **EST:** 2018
SALES (est): 1MM **Privately Held**
WEB: www.holpack.com
SIC: 3089 Blister or bubble formed packaging, plastic

(G-5189)
HOME DESIGN GROUP CORP
220 W 21st St (33010-2517)
PHONE...................................305 888-5836
Javier Barrera, *President*
Dianne Camps, *Admin Sec*
EMP: 6 **EST:** 2003
SALES (est): 339.8K **Privately Held**
SIC: 2434 Wood kitchen cabinets

(G-5190)
HYBRID IMPRESSIONS INC (PA)
8020 W 30th Ct (33018-3853)
PHONE...................................305 392-5029
John Braceras, *President*
▼ **EMP:** 12 **EST:** 2005
SALES (est): 2.6MM **Privately Held**
WEB: www.hybridimpressions.com
SIC: 2752 Commercial printing, lithographic

(G-5191)
IC INDUSTRIES INC
1101 E 33rd St Fl 2 (33013-3528)
P.O. Box 139075 (33013-9075)
PHONE...................................305 696-8330
Harvey Rothstein, *Ch of Bd*
Joel Bachelor, *President*
Wendy Rothstein, *Exec VP*
Matthew Rothstein, *Vice Pres*
◆ **EMP:** 85 **EST:** 1990
SQ FT: 20,000
SALES (est): 23MM
SALES (corp-wide): 818.9MM **Privately Held**
WEB: www.icind.com
SIC: 2653 Boxes, corrugated: made from purchased materials
HQ: Supplyone, Inc.
11 Campus Blvd Ste 150
Newtown Square PA 19073
484 582-5005

(G-5192)
ICE BUNKER A&M CORP
717 W 27th St (33010-1215)
PHONE...................................786 368-0924
Yeicsa R Mucarsel, *Principal*
EMP: 10 **EST:** 2018
SALES (est): 456.5K **Privately Held**
SIC: 3999 Manufacturing industries

(G-5193)
INSTANT GARDEN INC
7751 W 28th Ave Unit 2 (33016-5113)
PHONE...................................305 815-1090
Valentina Alvarez, *President*
EMP: 7 **EST:** 2013
SALES (est): 233.7K **Privately Held**
SIC: 2752 Commercial printing, lithographic

(G-5194)
INTEGRATED COMPONENTS CORP
2592 W 78th St (33016-2773)
PHONE...................................305 824-0484
Juan P Rodriguez, *President*
◆ **EMP:** 18 **EST:** 1993
SQ FT: 11,000
SALES (est): 2.3MM **Privately Held**
SIC: 3089 Injection molded finished plastic products

(G-5195)
INTERNATIONAL IRON WORKS LLC (PA)
3585 E 10th Ct (33013-2915)
PHONE...................................305 835-0190
Juana Ramos,
EMP: 5 **EST:** 2007

▲ = Import ▼=Export
◆ =Import/Export

SALES (est): 1.1MM **Privately Held**
SIC: **3312** Structural shapes & pilings, steel

(G-5196)
INTERNATIONAL SOUND CORP
Also Called: Teleview Racing Patrol
1550 W 35th Pl (33012-4626)
PHONE...................305 556-1000
Ron Sellitto, *Branch Mgr*
Mauricio Morello, *IT/INT Sup*
Darrell Calhoun, *Executive*
Amanda Rush, *Executive*
EMP: 105
SALES (corp-wide): 14MM **Privately Held**
WEB: www.isctv.com
SIC: **3663** Television broadcasting & communications equipment
PA: International Sound Corporation
7130 Milford Indus Rd
Pikesville MD 21208
410 484-2244

(G-5197)
INTERTEK INTERNATIONAL CORP
Also Called: Intertek Auto-Sun-Shade
401 Se 11th Ave (33010-5737)
PHONE...................305 883-8700
Ezra David Eskandry, *President*
▲ EMP: 42 EST: 1985
SQ FT: 20,000
SALES (est): 5.2MM **Privately Held**
SIC: **3714** Motor vehicle parts & accessories

(G-5198)
IVERICA INDUSTRIAL INC
1044 E 29th St (33013-3518)
PHONE...................305 691-1659
EMP: 10
SQ FT: 6,476
SALES: 500K **Privately Held**
SIC: **2426 2542** Hardwood Dimension/Floor Mill Mfg Partitions/Fixtures-Nonwood

(G-5199)
J C S ENGINEERING & DEV
211 W 22nd St (33010-1593)
PHONE...................305 888-7911
EMP: 10
SQ FT: 10,000
SALES (est): 1MM **Privately Held**
SIC: **3495 5085 3544 3493** Mfg Wire Springs Whol Industrial Supplies Mfg Dies/Tools/Jigs/Fixt Mfg Steel Spring-Nonwire

(G-5200)
JAFFER WLL DRLLNG A DIV OF AC
1451 Se 9th Ct (33010-5944)
PHONE...................954 523-6669
Eugene C Friedlander, *Partner*
William J Mc Cluskey, *Partner*
Caroline Urtiaga, *Partner*
EMP: 10 EST: 2010
SALES (est): 217.9K **Privately Held**
WEB: www.acschultes.com
SIC: **1381 1711** Directional drilling oil & gas wells; plumbing, heating, air-conditioning contractors

(G-5201)
JAIBA CABINETS INC
8125 W 20th Ave (33014-3231)
PHONE...................305 364-3646
EMP: 5
SQ FT: 7,000
SALES (est): 542.7K **Privately Held**
SIC: **2434** Mfg Wood Kitchen Cabinets

(G-5202)
JAM CABINETS & INVESTMENTS LLC
Also Called: Cary's Kitchen Cabinets
2795 W 78th St (33016-2772)
PHONE...................305 823-9020
Jorge Merida, *Mng Member*
Miguel Ferreiro,
Clara D Merida,
EMP: 12 EST: 1981
SQ FT: 16,572

SALES (est): 1.3MM **Privately Held**
WEB: www.caryskitchen.com
SIC: **2434** Wood kitchen cabinets

(G-5203)
JANORO FIXTURE MFG CORP
249 W 29th St (33012-5705)
PHONE...................305 887-2524
James G Sobie, *President*
Rebecca Sobie, *Vice Pres*
Helen Sobie, *Admin Sec*
EMP: 6 EST: 1978
SQ FT: 10,000
SALES (est): 561.5K
SALES (corp-wide): 1.4MM **Privately Held**
SIC: **3646 3645** Commercial indusl & institutional electric lighting fixtures; residential lighting fixtures
PA: H L H Sobyco Electrical Supplies Corp
275 W 29th St
Hialeah FL 33012
305 887-2524

(G-5204)
JEB THERMOFOIL OF SOUTH FLA
1065 E 16th St (33010-3315)
PHONE...................305 887-6214
Antonio Garlovo, *President*
EMP: 9 EST: 2017
SALES (est): 372.5K **Privately Held**
WEB: florida.intercreditreport.com
SIC: **2431** Doors & door parts & trim, wood

(G-5205)
JESUS CABINETS CORP
1701 W 42nd Pl (33012-8403)
PHONE...................786 285-1088
Jesus R Piloto, *Principal*
EMP: 8 EST: 2010
SALES (est): 116.9K **Privately Held**
SIC: **2434** Wood kitchen cabinets

(G-5206)
JONEL KNITTING MILLS INC
7130 W 12th Ln (33014-4513)
PHONE...................305 887-7333
Jonel Jankuc, *President*
Donna Jankuc, *Vice Pres*
Jeffrey Jankuc, *Vice Pres*
EMP: 25 EST: 1987
SALES (est): 500K **Privately Held**
WEB: www.jonelknittingmills.com
SIC: **2253** Knit outerwear mills

(G-5207)
JOSE LEAL ENTERPRISES INC
705 W 20th St (33010-2429)
PHONE...................305 887-9611
Jose M Leal, *President*
Christina Leal, *Project Mgr*
Stephanie Leal, *Project Mgr*
Sandra Leal, *Opers Staff*
◆ EMP: 65 EST: 1968
SQ FT: 40,000
SALES (est): 8.6MM **Privately Held**
WEB: www.wwdrape.com
SIC: **2211 7641** Bedspreads, cotton; draperies & drapery fabrics, cotton; furniture upholstery repair

(G-5208)
JP COSMETICS INC
1687 W 32nd Pl (33012-4509)
PHONE...................305 231-4963
Eudel Morales, *President*
Juan M Dominguez, *Vice Pres*
Lorenzo C Morales, *Treasurer*
▲ EMP: 12 EST: 2005
SALES (est): 225.1K **Privately Held**
WEB: www.corlys.com
SIC: **2844** Face creams or lotions

(G-5209)
JUAN RODRIGUEZ CABINETRY CORP
221 W 41st St (33012-4345)
PHONE...................305 467-3878
Juan Rodriguez, *President*
EMP: 8 EST: 2015
SALES (est): 371.3K **Privately Held**
SIC: **2434** Wood kitchen cabinets

(G-5210)
KIBBY FOODS LLC
2315 W 77th St (33016-1869)
PHONE...................305 456-3635
Samir Mourra, *Mng Member*
Olga M Mourra,
EMP: 9 EST: 2007
SALES (est): 560.2K **Privately Held**
WEB: www.kibbyfoods.com
SIC: **2038** Frozen specialties

(G-5211)
KIT RESIDENTIAL DESIGNS INC
5921 Nw 176th St Unit 2 (33015-5133)
PHONE...................305 796-5940
Louis Gonzales, *President*
EMP: 5 EST: 2003
SALES (est): 475.8K **Privately Held**
SIC: **2514 5031** Kitchen cabinets: metal; kitchen cabinets

(G-5212)
KNIGHTSBRIDGE STEEL LLC
507 W 17th St (33010-2412)
PHONE...................786 532-0290
Shir Keidan,
EMP: 8 EST: 2016
SALES (est): 234.2K **Privately Held**
SIC: **3272** Building materials, except block or brick: concrete

(G-5213)
KOKI INTERIORS FURN MFG INC
7680 W 7th Ave (33014-4116)
PHONE...................305 558-6573
Jose Pelaez, *President*
Magda Pelaez, *Treasurer*
◆ EMP: 11 EST: 1977
SQ FT: 43,000
SALES (est): 560.5K **Privately Held**
SIC: **2512** Living room furniture: upholstered on wood frames

(G-5214)
KRISTINE WINDOW TREATMENTS LLC
15998 Nw 49th Ave (33014-6309)
PHONE...................305 623-8302
Howard Rothman,
EMP: 18 EST: 2015
SQ FT: 5,000
SALES (est): 1.2MM **Privately Held**
SIC: **2591** Window blinds; venetian blinds; mini blinds; micro blinds

(G-5215)
L AND C SCIENCE AND TECH INC
2205 W 80th St Ste 1 (33016-5759)
PHONE...................305 200-3531
Agustin F Venero, *President*
Yaima Suarez, *Purch Mgr*
Marcelo Mancheno, *Engineer*
Agustin Venero, *Director*
EMP: 7 EST: 1990
SALES (est): 800K **Privately Held**
WEB: www.landcscience.com
SIC: **3844 3826 7389** X-ray apparatus & tubes; analytical instruments; spectrometers; design services

(G-5216)
L C CH INTERNATIONAL INC
Also Called: La Caja China
7395 W 18th Ln (33014-3739)
PHONE...................305 888-1323
Roberto Guerra, *President*
Berta Guerra, *Admin Sec*
▼ EMP: 9 EST: 2000
SQ FT: 20,200
SALES (est): 1.9MM **Privately Held**
SIC: **3631** Barbecues, grills & braziers (outdoor cooking)

(G-5217)
L C NPEE
Also Called: National Police Ammunition
451 E 10th Ct (33010-5152)
PHONE...................888 316-3718
David Moose, *Office Mgr*
Erik Agazim,
EMP: 30 EST: 2009
SALES (est): 5MM **Privately Held**
SIC: **3482** Small arms ammunition

(G-5218)
LA AUTENTICA
2294 W 78th St (33016-5525)
PHONE...................786 409-3779
Manuel Diaz, *President*
Luis N Medina, *General Mgr*
Alejandro Perez, *Vice Pres*
EMP: 8 EST: 1991
SQ FT: 4,000
SALES (est): 550K **Privately Held**
SIC: **2053** Pastries (danish): frozen

(G-5219)
LA AUTENTICA FOODS INC
2294 W 78th St (33016-5525)
PHONE...................305 888-6727
Fabrice Riviere, *President*
▲ EMP: 15 EST: 1997
SQ FT: 45,000
SALES (est): 1.2MM **Privately Held**
WEB: www.laautenticafood.com
SIC: **2099 5141** Tortillas, fresh or refrigerated; groceries, general line

(G-5220)
LARRY JOHNSON INC
Also Called: Miami Wall
701 W 25th St (33016-2150)
P.O. Box 28109 (33002-8109)
PHONE...................305 888-2300
Keith Johnson, *President*
Frank Ortega, *Vice Pres*
EMP: 19 EST: 1990
SALES (est): 397K **Privately Held**
SIC: **3442** Window & door frames

(G-5221)
LASER CNSTR & RESTORATION
Also Called: LASER RESTORATION
6043 Nw 167th St Ste A8 (33015-4322)
PHONE...................786 536-2065
Alfredo Alejos, *President*
EMP: 5 EST: 2013
SALES (est): 2MM **Privately Held**
SIC: **1389 1522** Construction, repair & dismantling services; remodeling, multi-family dwellings

(G-5222)
LEO FASHIONS INC
230 W 23rd St (33010-1524)
PHONE...................305 887-1032
Evelio Villa, *President*
Herminia Villia, *Treasurer*
EMP: 11 EST: 1977
SALES (est): 485.5K **Privately Held**
SIC: **2331 2321** Shirts, women's & juniors': made from purchased materials; men's & boys' furnishings

(G-5223)
LIEBHERR CRANES INC
Also Called: Liebherr Nenzing Crane
15101 Nw 112th Ave (33018-3709)
PHONE...................305 817-7500
Winston Ziegler, *Sales Staff*
Deutsch Helmut, *Manager*
Katerin Rangel, *Administration*
EMP: 8
SALES (corp-wide): 12.8B **Privately Held**
WEB: www.liebherr.com
SIC: **3531 5082** Cranes, ship; construction & mining machinery
HQ: Liebherr Cranes, Inc.
4100 Chestnut Ave
Newport News VA 23607
757 928-2505

(G-5224)
LISA BAKERY INC
2460 W 1st Ave (33010-1718)
PHONE...................305 888-8431
Alberto Diaz, *President*
Albert Diaz, *President*
EMP: 8 EST: 2000
SALES (est): 497.3K **Privately Held**
SIC: **2051** Bakery: wholesale or wholesale/retail combined

(G-5225)
LIZA GOLD CORP
9 E 20th St (33010-2725)
PHONE...................305 885-0731
Luis Estrada, *President*
EMP: 9 EST: 1974
SQ FT: 5,000

SALES (est): 710K **Privately Held**
SIC: 3911 3961 Necklaces, precious metal; costume jewelry

(G-5226)
LOS LATINOS MAGAZINE INC
138 Hialeah Dr (33010-5250)
PHONE..............................305 882-9074
Hercules A Vilchez, *President*
Luis Bilchez, *Vice Pres*
Hercules D Vilchez, *Vice Pres*
Luis E Vilchez, *Treasurer*
Luz Falkowski, *Admin Sec*
EMP: 10 EST: 1991
SALES (est): 790K **Privately Held**
SIC: 2721 Magazines: publishing only, not printed on site

(G-5227)
LOVE IS IN THE AIR CORP
Also Called: Wholesalers
2284 W 77th St (33016-1866)
PHONE..............................305 828-8181
Alexander Longa, *President*
Luis Christian Longa, *Vice Pres*
◆ **EMP: 5 EST:** 1996
SALES (est): 654.6K **Privately Held**
WEB: www.loveisintheair.net
SIC: 2899 5169 5999 Incense; essential oils; candle shops

(G-5228)
LRA ARCHITECTURAL WD WORK INC
915 W 72nd St (33014-5225)
PHONE..............................305 801-5573
Lucas R Arrieta, *Principal*
EMP: 7 EST: 2016
SALES (est): 77.6K **Privately Held**
SIC: 2431 Millwork

(G-5229)
LUFEMOR INC
Also Called: Quick Print Center
5392 W 16th Ave (33012-2165)
PHONE..............................305 557-2162
Luis Morales, *President*
▼ **EMP: 7 EST:** 1982
SQ FT: 1,800
SALES (est): 581.7K **Privately Held**
SIC: 2752 Commercial printing, offset

(G-5230)
LUXURY WOODWORKING SOLUTI
3468 W 84th St Unit 108 (33018-4927)
PHONE..............................786 398-1785
EMP: 9 EST: 2019
SALES (est): 567.6K **Privately Held**
SIC: 2431 Millwork

(G-5231)
M & E KITCHEN CABINETS INC
7237 W 29th Ln (33018-5361)
PHONE..............................786 346-9987
Nivaldo Sosa, *Principal*
EMP: 7 EST: 2013
SALES (est): 121.4K **Privately Held**
WEB: m-ekitchencabinets.business.site
SIC: 2434 Wood kitchen cabinets

(G-5232)
M & H ENTERPRISES INC
589 W 27th St (33010-1321)
PHONE..............................305 885-5945
Fax: 305 885-5989
EMP: 9
SQ FT: 4,000
SALES: 450K **Privately Held**
SIC: 2241 5199 Narrow Fabric Mill Whol Nondurable Goods

(G-5233)
MAC D&D INC
Also Called: Alicia Studio
971 W 53rd St (33012-2418)
PHONE..............................305 821-9452
John David Machleid Jr, *President*
Dianne Machleid, *Corp Secy*
EMP: 7 EST: 1960
SQ FT: 3,750
SALES (est): 486.3K **Privately Held**
SIC: 2392 Bedspreads & bed sets: made from purchased materials

(G-5234)
MAG WORKS INC
7725 W 2nd Ct (33014-4307)
P.O. Box 668226, Miami (33166-9413)
PHONE..............................305 823-4440
▼ **EMP:** 22
SQ FT: 35,000
SALES (est): 2.3MM **Privately Held**
SIC: 2514 Mfg Metal Household Furniture

(G-5235)
MAJESTY FOODS LLC
Also Called: Majestic Foods
2740 W 81st St (33016-2732)
PHONE..............................305 817-1888
Colin Chang,
Carl Barnett,
Gary Tie-Shue,
Henry Tie-Shue,
Steven Whittingham,
EMP: 31 EST: 2018
SALES (est): 9.7MM **Privately Held**
WEB: www.majestyfoods.com
SIC: 2041 Bread & bread-type roll mixes
PA: Gracekennedy Limited
73 Harbour Street
Kingston

(G-5236)
MAJOR LEAGUE SIGNS INC
9103 Nw 171st Ln (33018-6650)
PHONE..............................954 600-5505
Hilda Noriega, *Principal*
EMP: 7 EST: 2019
SALES (est): 260.4K **Privately Held**
WEB: www.miamisignandwraps.com
SIC: 3993 Signs & advertising specialties

(G-5237)
MANNYS STONE DEPOT CORP
2200 W 8th Ave (33010-2017)
PHONE..............................954 744-2506
Manuel Estevez Hernandez, *President*
EMP: 9 EST: 2014
SALES (est): 67.7K **Privately Held**
SIC: 3281 Cut stone & stone products

(G-5238)
MANUFACTURING INC SP
2200 W 77th St (33016-1866)
PHONE..............................305 362-0456
EMP: 10 EST: 2020
SALES (est): 1.5MM **Privately Held**
SIC: 3999 Manufacturing industries

(G-5239)
MARAMED PRECISION CORPORATION
Also Called: Maramed Orthopedic Systems
2480 W 82nd St Unit 1 (33016-2735)
PHONE..............................305 823-8300
Alan Finnieston, *President*
Mark Mazloff, *Vice Pres*
EMP: 32 EST: 1973
SQ FT: 19,200
SALES (est): 1.1MM **Privately Held**
WEB: www.maramed.com
SIC: 3842 Prosthetic appliances; orthopedic appliances

(G-5240)
MARCOS PROFESSIONAL CABINETS C
1412 W 39th Pl (33012-4752)
PHONE..............................305 962-4378
Marcos J Fernandez, *Principal*
EMP: 7 EST: 2006
SALES (est): 58.8K **Privately Held**
SIC: 2434 Wood kitchen cabinets

(G-5241)
MARIA E ACOSTA
4004 W 11th Ln (33012-7743)
PHONE..............................305 231-5543
Maria E Acosta, *Principal*
EMP: 8 EST: 2000
SALES (est): 211.6K **Privately Held**
SIC: 2024 Ice cream & frozen desserts

(G-5242)
MARINE MANUFACTURING INC
295 W 23rd St (33010-1523)
PHONE..............................305 885-3493
Phil Thun, *President*
Kenneth Murray, *President*

▼ **EMP: 5 EST:** 1974
SQ FT: 10,000
SALES (est): 426.8K **Privately Held**
WEB: www.marinemanufacturing.com
SIC: 3429 Marine hardware

(G-5243)
MARITIME REPLICAS AMERICA INC
Also Called: Liners of Legend
1275 W 47th Pl Ste 423 (33012-3453)
PHONE..............................305 386-1958
Warren Sanut, *President*
John Kennedy, *Exec VP*
Rocio Davila, *Vice Pres*
▼ **EMP: 5 EST:** 1983
SALES (est): 301.4K **Privately Held**
WEB: www.maritimereplicas.com
SIC: 3999 Boat models, except toy

(G-5244)
MERENGUITOSCOM LLC
4847 E 10th Ct (33013-2123)
PHONE..............................305 685-2709
Luis Aular, *President*
Ada Tapia, *Principal*
Marisol Osorio, *Administration*
EMP: 8 EST: 2011
SALES (est): 154.4K **Privately Held**
SIC: 2051 Bread, cake & related products

(G-5245)
METALCO MFG INC
700 W 20th St (33010-2430)
PHONE..............................305 592-0704
Jesus L Ameijeiras, *Principal*
EMP: 13 EST: 2006
SALES (est): 423.2K **Privately Held**
WEB: www.metalcomfg.com
SIC: 3444 Sheet metalwork

(G-5246)
METALWORKS ENGINEERING CORP
1745 W 32nd Pl (33012-4511)
PHONE..............................305 223-0011
Michael A Silva, *President*
Ivan Jerak, *Vice Pres*
Igor Kotlyar, *Opers Staff*
Oscar Borrelli, *Engineer*
Karel Jerak, *Treasurer*
EMP: 10 EST: 2011
SALES (est): 1.9MM **Privately Held**
WEB: www.metalworkscorp.com
SIC: 3444 Sheet metalwork

(G-5247)
MIA PRODUCTS COMPANY
71 W 22nd St Apt 9 (33010-2297)
PHONE..............................786 479-4021
Angel Lopez, *Branch Mgr*
EMP: 22
SALES (corp-wide): 1.1B **Publicly Held**
SIC: 2024 Ice cream & frozen desserts
HQ: Mia Products Company
4 Rocky Glen Rd
Avoca PA 18641
570 457-7431

(G-5248)
MIAMI CELLOPHANE INC
7485 W 19th Ct (33014-3722)
PHONE..............................786 293-2212
Eduardo Temkin, *President*
◆ **EMP: 21 EST:** 1989
SQ FT: 9,000
SALES (est): 831.6K **Privately Held**
SIC: 3081 Unsupported plastics film & sheet

(G-5249)
MIAMI EPIC TEES CORP
10990 Nw 138th St Unit 16 (33018-1233)
PHONE..............................305 224-3465
Fabian Soto, *Owner*
EMP: 7 EST: 2018
SALES (est): 330.3K **Privately Held**
SIC: 2759 Screen printing

(G-5250)
MIAMI FOODS DISTRS USA INC
Also Called: El Equisteo Sabor
2761 W 77th Pl (33016-5635)
PHONE..............................305 512-3246
Fernando Fernandes, *President*

Maria Gomez, *Principal*
▲ **EMP: 14 EST:** 2004
SQ FT: 5,770
SALES (est): 3.2MM **Privately Held**
WEB: www.elexquisitosabor.com
SIC: 2024 5143 Yogurt desserts, frozen; frozen dairy desserts

(G-5251)
MIAMI GRANDSTAND ENTRMT CORP
2330 W 79th St (33016-5516)
PHONE..............................305 636-9665
Felipe Perbomo, *President*
▲ **EMP: 5 EST:** 1997
SALES (est): 396.3K **Privately Held**
WEB: www.grandstandmiami.com
SIC: 2531 Bleacher seating, portable

(G-5252)
MIAMI METAL ROOFING LLC
Also Called: Miami Metal Deck
16000 Nw 49th Ave A (33014-6311)
PHONE..............................305 749-6356
Gabriel Villabon, *General Mgr*
Dan Dasilva, *Vice Pres*
Tahiry Wilhelm, *Regl Sales Mgr*
Peter Muskovac, *Marketing Staff*
Nelson R Parra Perdomo,
EMP: 15 EST: 2014
SALES (est): 4.8MM **Privately Held**
WEB: www.mmdeck.com
SIC: 2952 Roofing materials

(G-5253)
MIAMI TAPE INC
6175 Nw 167th St Ste G38 (33015-4362)
PHONE..............................305 558-9211
Carlos A Garcia Jr, *Vice Pres*
Carlos Garcia, *Vice Pres*
Roberto Page, *Vice Pres*
Antonio Moreno, *Treasurer*
Dario Gonzalez, *Admin Sec*
EMP: 10 EST: 1974
SQ FT: 25,300
SALES (est): 991K **Privately Held**
WEB: www.miamitape.com
SIC: 3652 Magnetic tape (audio): prerecorded; compact laser discs, prerecorded

(G-5254)
MIAMI TECH INC
1725 W 39th Pl (33012-7016)
P.O. Box 126040 (33012-1600)
PHONE..............................786 354-1115
Jose Behar, *Principal*
EMP: 10 EST: 2009
SALES (est): 302.7K **Privately Held**
WEB: www.miamitech.com
SIC: 3444 Sheet metalwork

(G-5255)
MIAMI WALL SYSTEMS INC
701 W 25th St (33010-2150)
PHONE..............................305 888-2300
Larry D Johnson, *CEO*
Keith A Johnson, *President*
Jorge Valdes Pe, *General Mgr*
Francisco Ortega, *Vice Pres*
Keith Johnson, *Manager*
◆ **EMP: 110 EST:** 1974
SQ FT: 30,000
SALES (est): 17.2MM **Privately Held**
WEB: www.miamiwallsystems.com
SIC: 3442 Window & door frames; sash, door or window: metal

(G-5256)
MIGUEL CASA CORP
2005 W 4th Ave (33010-2404)
PHONE..............................305 887-0098
Laude M Pena, *President*
EMP: 10 EST: 2009
SALES (est): 336.4K **Privately Held**
SIC: 3421 Table & food cutlery, including butchers'

(G-5257)
MIKES PRECISION INC
1929 W 76th St (33014-3269)
PHONE..............................305 558-6421
EMP: 8
SQ FT: 3,000
SALES: 471.8K **Privately Held**
SIC: 3599 3089 Machine Shop And Injection Molding

▲ = Import ▼=Export
◆ =Import/Export

(G-5258)
MILLENIUM ENGINE PLATING INC
600 W 84th St (33014-3617)
PHONE..............................305 688-0098
Juan G Yanes, *President*
Leonardo Cowley, *Technical Staff*
EMP: 8 **EST:** 2005
SALES (est): 1.2MM **Privately Held**
WEB: www.meplating.com
SIC: 3471 Electroplating of metals or formed products

(G-5259)
MINI CIRCUITS LAB INC
2160 W 80th St (33016-1846)
PHONE..............................305 558-6381
Harvey Kaylie, *President*
Gloria Kaylie, *Admin Sec*
EMP: 35 **EST:** 1977
SALES (est): 1.2MM **Privately Held**
SIC: 3679 Electronic switches

(G-5260)
MIO GOURMENT PRODUCTS LLC
616 W 27th St (33010-1214)
PHONE..............................305 219-0253
Iristel Reyes, *Managing Prtnr*
Orlando Cordoves, *Managing Prtnr*
Magaly Vangelder, *Managing Prtnr*
EMP: 10 **EST:** 2015
SALES (est): 677.8K **Privately Held**
SIC: 2096 Potato chips & similar snacks

(G-5261)
MIPE CORP
3960 W 16th Ave Ste 208 (33012-7029)
PHONE..............................305 825-1195
Laude Miguel Pena, *President*
EMP: 8 **EST:** 2011
SALES (est): 303K **Privately Held**
SIC: 2086 Carbonated beverages, nonalcoholic: bottled & canned

(G-5262)
MISHY SPORTSWEAR
7305 W 19th Ct (33014-3720)
PHONE..............................305 819-7556
Sandy Lipson, *President*
Sonia Lipson, *Treasurer*
EMP: 30 **EST:** 1984
SQ FT: 20,000
SALES (est): 1.8MM **Privately Held**
SIC: 2339 2369 Sportswear, women's; girls' & children's outerwear

(G-5263)
MISTER CABINET DELUXE INC
Also Called: Mobica Center
2280 W 77th St (33016-1866)
PHONE..............................305 205-3601
Silvio Barreiro, *Principal*
EMP: 11 **EST:** 2016
SALES (est): 434.7K **Privately Held**
WEB: www.mistercabinet.com
SIC: 2434 Wood kitchen cabinets

(G-5264)
MJM CABINET INC
226 W 23rd St (33010-1524)
PHONE..............................786 953-5000
Carlos M Toledo, *President*
Jessie L Rosario, *CFO*
EMP: 6 **EST:** 2009
SQ FT: 50,000
SALES (est): 448.2K **Privately Held**
WEB: www.mjmcabinet.com
SIC: 2434 Wood kitchen cabinets

(G-5265)
MONTEDANA FUELS
2090 Palm Ave (33010-2620)
PHONE..............................305 887-6754
Henry Izquierdo, *President*
EMP: 8 **EST:** 2014
SALES (est): 586.3K **Privately Held**
SIC: 2869 Fuels

(G-5266)
MORALMAR KITCHEN CABINETS
3130 W 15th Ave (33012-4799)
PHONE..............................305 819-8402
Eduardo Moreno, *President*

Noelia Moreno, *Corp Secy*
Andres Baez, *Vice Pres*
EMP: 42 **EST:** 1975
SQ FT: 60,000
SALES (est): 1MM **Privately Held**
WEB: www.moralmar.com
SIC: 2434 Wood kitchen cabinets

(G-5267)
MORAN TRANSPORT
9829 Nw 129th Ter (33018-7410)
PHONE..............................305 824-3366
Jorge Moran, *Owner*
EMP: 7 **EST:** 2000
SALES (est): 309.9K **Privately Held**
SIC: 3799 Cars, off-highway: electric

(G-5268)
MULTIFIX CBD LLC
3740 E 10th Ct (33013-2920)
PHONE..............................786 487-0792
Felipe E Lopez, *Principal*
EMP: 7 **EST:** 2018
SALES (est): 309.9K **Privately Held**
SIC: 3999

(G-5269)
MWS DRAPERY INC
496 W 18th St (33010-2419)
PHONE..............................305 794-3811
Michael Weiss, *President*
EMP: 23 **EST:** 1961
SALES (est): 715.8K **Privately Held**
WEB: www.mwsdrapery.com
SIC: 2391 Curtains & draperies

(G-5270)
MY FOCUS INC
3514 W 94th St (33018-2076)
PHONE..............................305 826-4480
Chenny WEI Chen, *President*
EMP: 7 **EST:** 2004
SALES (est): 497.7K **Privately Held**
SIC: 3161 Traveling bags

(G-5271)
MYRIAM INTERIORS INC (PA)
16301 Nw 49th Ave (33014-6316)
PHONE..............................305 626-9898
Myriam Gebara, *President*
Robert Gebara, *Vice Pres*
◆ **EMP:** 8 **EST:** 1976
SALES (est): 1.4MM **Privately Held**
WEB: www.myriaminteriorssouth.com
SIC: 2591 5714 Blinds vertical; draperies

(G-5272)
NATURAL FRUIT CORP
770 W 20th St (33010-2430)
PHONE..............................305 887-7525
Simon Bravo, *President*
Jorge Bravo, *Vice Pres*
Angelo Delia, *Opers Staff*
Maggie Solana, *Office Mgr*
Gustavo Escobar, *Manager*
◆ **EMP:** 50 **EST:** 1986
SQ FT: 20,000
SALES (est): 14.3MM **Privately Held**
WEB: www.nfc-fruti.com
SIC: 2037 Frozen fruits & vegetables

(G-5273)
NATURAL WOOD WORKS LLC
2382 W 77th St (33016-1868)
PHONE..............................954 445-1493
Juan Martell, *Principal*
EMP: 7 **EST:** 2010
SALES (est): 85.2K **Privately Held**
SIC: 2431 Millwork

(G-5274)
NEARLY NATURAL LLC
3870 W 108th St Unit 20 (33018-1266)
PHONE..............................800 711-0544
Robbie Singer, *President*
Nick Kong, *Vice Pres*
Anita Singer, *Vice Pres*
Dennis Singer, *Vice Pres*
George Blews, *CFO*
◆ **EMP:** 12 **EST:** 2002
SALES (est): 5.2MM **Privately Held**
WEB: www.nearlynatural.com
SIC: 3999 5193 Artificial flower arrangements; artificial flowers

(G-5275)
NEON WORKFORCE TECHNOLOGIES
2300 W 84th St Ste 601 (33016-5773)
PHONE..............................305 458-8244
G Michael McCullars, *President*
EMP: 7 **EST:** 2015
SALES (est): 97.5K **Privately Held**
SIC: 2813 Neon

(G-5276)
NEW MARCO FOODS INC
3251 E 11th Ave (33013-3515)
PHONE..............................305 836-0571
Qing Chen, *Vice Pres*
Jia Zhao, *Director*
EMP: 14 **EST:** 2008
SALES (est): 480.6K **Privately Held**
SIC: 2051 Bread, cake & related products

(G-5277)
NEW STYLE KIT CABINETS CORP
2735 W 61st St Apt 104 (33016-5946)
PHONE..............................305 989-9665
Oscar Espinosa, *President*
EMP: 6 **EST:** 2012
SALES (est): 341.7K **Privately Held**
WEB: www.newstylekitchencabinets.com
SIC: 2431 7389 Millwork;

(G-5278)
NEXT DOOR COMPANY
4005 E 10th Ct (33013-2925)
PHONE..............................954 772-6666
Justin Schechter, *President*
James Schechter, *Vice Pres*
Karen Brock, *Sales Staff*
Fray Gomez, *Manager*
Steve Velligan, *Manager*
◆ **EMP:** 40 **EST:** 1993
SALES (est): 9MM **Privately Held**
WEB: www.nextdoorco.com
SIC: 3442 Metal doors; window & door frames; sash, door or window: metal

(G-5279)
NIEFELD GROUP LLC
Also Called: Beautiko
2420 W 80th St Unit 5 (33016-2783)
PHONE..............................786 587-7423
Daniel Niefeld, *Manager*
Bruce Niefeld,
EMP: 7 **EST:** 2016
SQ FT: 2,500
SALES (est): 275.5K **Privately Held**
SIC: 2381 Gloves, work: woven or knit, made from purchased materials

(G-5280)
NISSI ELASTIC CORP
961 E 17th St (33010-3353)
PHONE..............................305 968-3812
Jose H Mejia, *President*
Maria D Mejia, *Senior VP*
EMP: 8 **EST:** 2002
SALES (est): 136.5K **Privately Held**
SIC: 2241 Yarns, elastic: fabric covered

(G-5281)
NOGUERA HOLDINGS LLC
Also Called: NOGHOLD
1635 W 32nd Pl (33012-4509)
PHONE..............................305 846-9144
Michele Reinel, *Administration*
EMP: 8 **EST:** 2013
SALES (est): 452.9K **Privately Held**
SIC: 3711 3842 Cars, armored, assembly of; bulletproof vests

(G-5282)
NOVELTEX MIAMI INC
151 E 10th Ave (33010-5140)
P.O. Box 112791 (33011-2791)
PHONE..............................305 887-8191
Dimis A Maratos, *President*
Anton Maratos, *Sales Pres*
◆ **EMP:** 37 **EST:** 1953
SQ FT: 20,000
SALES (est): 2.9MM **Privately Held**
WEB: www.noveltexmiami.com
SIC: 3089 2499 Plastic processing; decorative wood & woodwork

(G-5283)
NU-VUE INDUSTRIES INC
1055 E 29th St (33013-3517)
PHONE..............................305 694-0397
Maria Guardado, *President*
EMP: 25 **EST:** 1993
SQ FT: 23,000
SALES (est): 6.5MM **Privately Held**
WEB: www.nu-vueindustries.com
SIC: 3479 Galvanizing of iron, steel or endformed products; aluminum coating of metal products

(G-5284)
NUTRA SCIENCES WORLD INC
8125 W 8th Ct (33014-3503)
PHONE..............................305 302-8870
Nestor Peralta, *Principal*
EMP: 7 **EST:** 2012
SALES (est): 83.8K **Privately Held**
SIC: 2834 Pharmaceutical preparations

(G-5285)
NUTRICORP LLC
671 W 18th St (33010-2422)
PHONE..............................305 680-4896
EMP: 11
SALES (corp-wide): 844.9K **Privately Held**
SIC: 2834 Medicines, capsuled or ampuled
PA: Nutricorp Llc
11801 Nw 100th Rd
Medley FL 33178
305 215-0571

(G-5286)
OFFICE FURNITURE BY TEMPO INC
4136 E 10th Ln (33013-2506)
PHONE..............................305 685-3077
Carlos Perez, *President*
Jesus Perez, *Administration*
EMP: 16 **EST:** 1976
SQ FT: 3,000
SALES (est): 1.9MM **Privately Held**
WEB: www.ofbtempo.com
SIC: 2521 Wood office furniture

(G-5287)
ONCA GEAR LLC
2372 W 77th St (33016-1868)
PHONE..............................857 253-8207
Marco Carrizosa, *Mng Member*
EMP: 6 **EST:** 2016
SQ FT: 18,000
SALES (est): 650K
SALES (corp-wide): 165.2K **Privately Held**
WEB: www.oncagear.com
SIC: 2329 Men's & boys' sportswear & athletic clothing
PA: Likentex Sl.
Calle De La Perfumeria (Pol Industria); 21 - Nav 8
Colmenar Viejo
918 473-971

(G-5288)
ONSITE RLBLE FORKLIFT SVCS INC
714 E 28th St (33013-3616)
PHONE..............................305 305-8638
Mayelin Perez, *Vice Pres*
EMP: 9 **EST:** 2013
SALES (est): 829.8K **Privately Held**
SIC: 3537 Forklift trucks

(G-5289)
OPTICAL HONG KONG
6073 Nw 167th St Ste C20 (33015-4346)
PHONE..............................305 200-5522
Adriel Ovadia,
EMP: 11 **EST:** 2016
SALES (est): 336.9K **Privately Held**
SIC: 3089 Lenses, except optical: plastic

(G-5290)
ORNAMNTAL METAL SPECIALIST INC
7889 Nw 173rd St (33015-3854)
PHONE..............................786 360-5727
Ileana Burns, *President*
Wayne Burns, *Vice Pres*
EMP: 6 **EST:** 2008

SALES (est): 397.1K **Privately Held**
SIC: 3446 Architectural metalwork

(G-5291)
PANELTRONICS INCORPORATED
11960 Nw 87th Ct Ste 1 (33018-1972)
PHONE.............................305 823-9777
Pedro R Pelaez Sr, *President*
Pedro R Pelaez Jr, *Vice Pres*
Pedro J Pelaez, *Vice Pres*
Marcel Padilla, *Engineer*
Jose Verdecia, *Engineer*
EMP: 70 EST: 1979
SQ FT: 21,000
SALES (est): 15.4MM **Privately Held**
WEB: www.paneltronics.com
SIC: 3613 Control panels, electric

(G-5292)
PATTY KING INC
Also Called: Patty King Production Plant
2740 W 81st St (33016-2732)
PHONE.............................305 817-1888
Gary Chin, *President*
Colin Chang, *Vice Pres*
Warren Chung, *Vice Pres*
Gary Tieshue, *Vice Pres*
◆ EMP: 31 EST: 1997
SQ FT: 10,000
SALES (est): 3.7MM **Privately Held**
WEB: www.majestyfoods.com
SIC: 2038 5812 Ethnic foods, frozen; ethnic food restaurants

(G-5293)
PETER PRINTER INC
1355 W 49th St (33012-3223)
PHONE.............................305 558-0147
George Pappas, *President*
Gregory Pappas, *Admin Sec*
EMP: 9 EST: 1983
SQ FT: 4,000
SALES (est): 632K **Privately Held**
SIC: 2752 Commercial printing, offset

(G-5294)
PETROLEUM EQUIPMENT AND MFG CO
Also Called: Pemco
2185 W 76th St (33016-1838)
PHONE.............................305 558-9573
Juan H Tamayo, *President*
Iran Tamayo, *Vice Pres*
Ivan Tamayo, *Vice Pres*
Jorge Tamayo, *Treasurer*
Joseph Petix, *Sales Mgr*
◆ EMP: 19 EST: 1985
SQ FT: 53,000
SALES (est): 5.2MM **Privately Held**
WEB: www.pemcofl.com
SIC: 3491 Gas valves & parts, industrial

(G-5295)
PLACETAS PALLET CORP
195 W 19th St (33010-2640)
PHONE.............................305 633-4262
Orlando F Mesa, *Principal*
EMP: 8 EST: 2010
SALES (est): 169.1K **Privately Held**
SIC: 2448 Pallets, wood

(G-5296)
POLYMERSAN LLC
1181 Se 9th Ter Ste B (33010-5814)
PHONE.............................305 887-3824
Tayfun Oktem, *Principal*
EMP: 6 EST: 2018
SALES (est): 596.2K **Privately Held**
WEB: www.polymersan.com
SIC: 2821 Plastics materials & resins

(G-5297)
POLYUMAC INC
1060 E 30th St (33013-3520)
PHONE.............................305 691-9093
Mariella Vazquez, *President*
◆ EMP: 30 EST: 1996
SQ FT: 36,000
SALES (est): 5.9MM **Privately Held**
WEB: www.polyumac.com
SIC: 3559 Plastics working machinery

(G-5298)
PRADERE MANUFACTURING CORP
Also Called: Pradere Office Products
7655 W 20th Ave (33014-3226)
PHONE.............................305 823-0190
Jose Pradere, *President*
Maria Victoria Pradere, *Vice Pres*
Ileana Pradere, *Treasurer*
Michelle Pradere, *IT/INT Sup*
▼ EMP: 10 EST: 1972
SQ FT: 21,500
SALES (est): 2.6MM **Privately Held**
WEB: www.pradereoffice.com
SIC: 2431 2521 Millwork; chairs, office: padded, upholstered or plain: wood

(G-5299)
PRECISION CONCEPTS (MIAMI) LLC
7300 W 18th Ln (33014-3715)
PHONE.............................305 825-5244
Arnold Coburn, *CEO*
Manuel Gomez, *COO*
Uriel Lanzas, *Admin Mgr*
EMP: 73 EST: 2007
SQ FT: 30,000
SALES (est): 14.4MM **Privately Held**
WEB: www.cgpacks.com
SIC: 3089 3085 Plastic processing; plastics bottles

(G-5300)
PRECISION MTAL FBRICATIONS INC
3600 E 10th Ct 20 (33013-2918)
PHONE.............................305 691-0616
John Sanchez, *President*
EMP: 6 EST: 1998
SALES (est): 487.5K **Privately Held**
SIC: 3441 Fabricated structural metal

(G-5301)
PREMIER BLINDS & VERTICALS
881 Ne 1st Pl (33010-5102)
PHONE.............................305 244-0598
Lino Pleites, *Principal*
EMP: 7 EST: 2004
SALES (est): 140K **Privately Held**
SIC: 2591 Drapery hardware & blinds & shades

(G-5302)
PREMIER DISTRIBUTOR OF MIAMI
1635 W 40th St (33012-7065)
P.O. Box 126970 (33012-1616)
PHONE.............................305 821-9671
Cesar Zorrilla, *President*
Nancy Zorrilla, *Admin Sec*
EMP: 5 EST: 1991
SQ FT: 4,600
SALES (est): 432.1K **Privately Held**
SIC: 2035 Pickles, sauces & salad dressings

(G-5303)
PRICE KING 2 LLC
495 W 29th St (33012-5700)
PHONE.............................786 337-8801
Miguel Sanchez, *Principal*
EMP: 8 EST: 2010
SALES (est): 72.6K **Privately Held**
SIC: 3421 Table & food cutlery, including butchers'

(G-5304)
PRIME ENTERPRISES LLC
Also Called: Prime Matter Labs
16363 Nw 49th Ave (33014-6316)
PHONE.............................305 625-4929
Mohamed Barakat, *President*
Maged Barakat, *Vice Pres*
Francisco Linares, *Vice Pres*
Jorge Perdomo, *Purch Agent*
Carla Goffstein, *CFO*
◆ EMP: 65 EST: 1983
SQ FT: 75,000
SALES (est): 27.6MM **Privately Held**
WEB: www.primematterlabs.com
SIC: 2844 Cosmetic preparations; shampoos, rinses, conditioners: hair; deodorants, personal; perfumes, natural or synthetic

(G-5305)
PRIME PACKAGING INC
16363 Nw 49th Ave (33014-6316)
PHONE.............................305 625-6737
Mohamad Barakat, *President*
Jorge Perdomo, *Purchasing*
Aaron Paas, *Officer*
EMP: 20 EST: 2000
SALES (est): 1.5MM **Privately Held**
SIC: 2844 Cosmetic preparations

(G-5306)
PRIME TOPCO LLC
16363 Nw 49th Ave (33014-6316)
PHONE.............................305 625-4929
Mohamed Barakat, *Mng Member*
EMP: 5 EST: 2020
SALES (est): 323.6K **Privately Held**
SIC: 2844 Toilet preparations

(G-5307)
PRINT BIG INC
1680 W 33rd Pl (33012-4514)
PHONE.............................305 398-8898
Amarilys Curbelo, *President*
EMP: 7 EST: 2008
SALES (est): 650K **Privately Held**
WEB: www.printbigmiami.com
SIC: 2752 Commercial printing, offset

(G-5308)
PRINT SOLUTION DIGITAL LLC
6540 W 20th Ave Unit 3 (33016-2672)
PHONE.............................305 819-7420
Jairo Palacio, *Principal*
EMP: 6 EST: 2003
SALES (est): 382K **Privately Held**
SIC: 2752 Commercial printing, offset

(G-5309)
PRINTHOUSEUSACOM INC
450 W 28th St Ste 2 (33010-1317)
PHONE.............................305 231-0202
Alex Montano, *President*
Raul Montano, *Vice Pres*
EMP: 7 EST: 2006
SQ FT: 18,000
SALES (est): 1MM **Privately Held**
WEB: www.printhouseusa.com
SIC: 2759 Commercial printing

(G-5310)
PRINTING EXPRESS
1608 W 68th St (33014-4435)
PHONE.............................305 512-0900
Rafael H Gomez, *Principal*
EMP: 7 EST: 2008
SALES (est): 262.3K **Privately Held**
WEB: www.printgoodprice.com
SIC: 2752 Commercial printing, offset

(G-5311)
PROFESSIONAL KITCHEN CABINETS
1035 E 13th St (33010-3752)
PHONE.............................305 888-5660
Jose Valdivia, *President*
EMP: 6 EST: 1977
SQ FT: 4,200
SALES (est): 464.8K **Privately Held**
WEB: www.professionalkitchencabinet.com
SIC: 2434 Wood kitchen cabinets

(G-5312)
PROFESSNAL MTAL INNOVATION INC
3492 W 84th St Unit 110 (33018-4930)
PHONE.............................786 354-3091
EMP: 7 EST: 2019
SALES (est): 259.8K **Privately Held**
SIC: 3999 Manufacturing industries

(G-5313)
PROLABEL INC
621 W 20th St (33010-2432)
PHONE.............................305 620-2202
Ramon Fernandez, *President*
Tony Sierra, *Vice Pres*
Becky Peffer, *Executive*
▼ EMP: 11 EST: 1995
SQ FT: 15,000
SALES (est): 3MM **Privately Held**
WEB: www.prolabelinc.com
SIC: 2759 Labels & seals: printing

(G-5314)
PROMEX LLC
1415 E 11th Ave (33010-3307)
P.O. Box 630716, Miami (33163-0716)
PHONE.............................305 884-2400
Yolanda Eustaquio, *Mng Member*
Alexander Avila,
Priscilla Avila,
EMP: 9 EST: 2005
SALES (est): 691.4K **Privately Held**
WEB: www.promexllc.com
SIC: 2844 Toilet preparations

(G-5315)
PTE SYSTEMS INTERNATIONAL LLC (PA)
1950 W 8th Ave (33010-2328)
PHONE.............................305 863-3409
Kenneth Antonelli, *Project Mgr*
Gloria Molina, *Project Mgr*
Maria Sanchez, *Project Mgr*
Alejandro Tejada, *Project Mgr*
Gustavo Nava, *Production*
EMP: 9 EST: 2013
SALES (est): 11.9MM **Privately Held**
WEB: www.ptestrand.com
SIC: 3315 Steel wire & related products

(G-5316)
PUPPET WORKSHOP INC (PA)
295 E 10th Ct (33010-5148)
P.O. Box 398077, Miami Beach (33239-8077)
PHONE.............................305 666-2655
Ronnie Burns, *President*
Jerald Burns, *Vice Pres*
Gerald Burns, *Treasurer*
◆ EMP: 222 EST: 1977
SQ FT: 75,000
SALES (est): 21.7MM **Privately Held**
WEB: www.puppetworkshop.com
SIC: 2369 Girls' & children's outerwear

(G-5317)
PURA VIDA DAIRY INC
Also Called: Yogurico
3130 W 84th St U1 (33018-4977)
PHONE.............................305 817-1762
Lilliana Murillo, *President*
Roman Alvarez, *Vice Pres*
Victor Fermin, *Manager*
▲ EMP: 13 EST: 2008
SQ FT: 3,000
SALES (est): 4.1MM **Privately Held**
WEB: www.puravidadairy.com
SIC: 2026 Yogurt

(G-5318)
PUROX BRANDS CORP
5801 E 10th Ave Unit 108 (33013-1758)
PHONE.............................305 392-0738
Faisal Khan, *CEO*
Isaac Khan, *Marketing Staff*
EMP: 10 EST: 2016
SALES (est): 698.5K **Privately Held**
SIC: 2841 Soap & other detergents

(G-5319)
QUALITY 1 APPRAISAL INC
18831 Nw 78th Pl (33015-5272)
PHONE.............................786 859-4085
Jose A Gutierrez Jr, *President*
Janet Mincey, *Treasurer*
Sharon Townsend, *Admin Sec*
EMP: 9 EST: 2006
SALES (est): 259K **Privately Held**
SIC: 2431 Millwork

(G-5320)
QUALITY ARTS LCP LLC
7880 W 25th Ct (33016-2757)
PHONE.............................305 735-2310
Leandro C Perini, *Principal*
EMP: 6 EST: 2017
SALES (est): 319.3K **Privately Held**
SIC: 2752 Commercial printing, lithographic

(G-5321)
QUALITY PRECISION PDTS CO INC
678 W 27th St (33010-1214)
PHONE.............................305 885-4596
Pedro Capote, *President*
Elida Pascual, *Treasurer*

EMP: 13 **EST:** 1972
SQ FT: 11,312
SALES (est): 276.6K **Privately Held**
WEB: www.qualityprecisionproducts.com
SIC: 3451 Screw machine products

(G-5322)
QUALITY RAILINGS MIAMI CORP
460 W 18th St (33010-2419)
PHONE..................786 400-0462
Alberto Cancio, *CEO*
EMP: 9 **EST:** 2015
SALES (est): 671.8K **Privately Held**
WEB: www.qualityrailingsmiami.com
SIC: 2431 3446 Staircases, stairs & railings; railings, prefabricated metal

(G-5323)
QUALITY STINLESS STL WORKS INC
873 W 48th St (33012-3541)
PHONE..................305 519-0142
EMP: 8 **EST:** 2010
SALES (est): 110K **Privately Held**
SIC: 3312 Blast Furnace-Steel Works

(G-5324)
R & R DOORS CORP
1660 W 33rd Pl (33012-4514)
PHONE..................305 982-8106
Rogelio Garcia, *President*
EMP: 7 **EST:** 2010
SQ FT: 5,000
SALES (est): 899.8K **Privately Held**
WEB: www.rrdoors.com
SIC: 2434 Wood kitchen cabinets

(G-5325)
RALPH & LLERENA PALLETS INC
495 E 47th St (33013-1863)
PHONE..................305 446-2651
Rafael A Ruiz, *Principal*
EMP: 9 **EST:** 2010
SALES (est): 152.3K **Privately Held**
SIC: 2448 Pallets, wood

(G-5326)
RC INVESTMENT CASTING
4570 E 11th Ave (33013-2114)
PHONE..................305 801-9088
Ronaldo Cruz, *Principal*
EMP: 5 **EST:** 2009
SALES (est): 398.9K **Privately Held**
SIC: 3365 Aluminum & aluminum-based alloy castings

(G-5327)
RCS WOOD CRAFTERS LLC
Also Called: Rcs Woodcrafters
1051 E 24th St (33013-4323)
PHONE..................305 836-0120
Robert Santos, *Mng Member*
Carlos Santos,
Ivonne Santos,
EMP: 8 **EST:** 2009
SQ FT: 17,000
SALES (est): 988.9K **Privately Held**
WEB: www.rcswood.com
SIC: 2434 Wood kitchen cabinets

(G-5328)
REACH INTERNATIONAL INC
Also Called: Reach Cooling Group
625 E 10th Ave (33010-4641)
P.O. Box 667765, Medley (33166-9405)
PHONE..................305 863-6360
Jun Lou, *President*
Luo Jun, *President*
D I C K Chen, *Exec VP*
Connie Chen, *Vice Pres*
Chris Philpott, *Sales Mgr*
◆ **EMP:** 32 **EST:** 1999
SQ FT: 30,800
SALES (est): 10.9MM **Privately Held**
WEB: www.reachcooling.com
SIC: 3714 Motor vehicle parts & accessories

(G-5329)
RESOLUTE TISSUE SALES
3725 E 10th Ct (33013-2919)
PHONE..................800 562-2860
Humberto Falcon, *Purchasing*
Roberto De Leon, *Manager*

EMP: 210 **EST:** 2019
SALES (est): 11.7MM **Privately Held**
SIC: 2621 Tissue paper

(G-5330)
RHINO TOOLS INC
18844 Nw 89th Ct (33018-6278)
PHONE..................305 332-7750
Gilberto Aguilar, *Owner*
EMP: 10 **EST:** 2004
SALES (est): 526.7K **Privately Held**
WEB: www.rhinotool.com
SIC: 3545 Machine tool accessories

(G-5331)
RHONDA CLANTON
6133 Nw 181st Ter Cir S (33015-5627)
PHONE..................305 502-7050
Rhonda Clanton, *Principal*
EMP: 8 **EST:** 1995
SALES (est): 465.3K **Privately Held**
SIC: 2024 Ice cream & frozen desserts

(G-5332)
RICKS PALLET CO INC
2420 W 3rd Ave (33010-1437)
PHONE..................305 884-4896
Rick Scarbary, *President*
April Scarbary, *Vice Pres*
▲ **EMP:** 7 **EST:** 1993
SALES (est): 650K **Privately Held**
SIC: 2448 Pallets, wood

(G-5333)
RICOS TOSTADITOS INC
Also Called: Ricos Candy Snack & Bakery
740 W 28th St (33010-1220)
PHONE..................305 885-7392
Albertina Padron, *President*
Hilda Lopez, *Corp Secy*
Alfred Padron, *Vice Pres*
EMP: 10 **EST:** 1968
SQ FT: 4,200
SALES (est): 499.4K **Privately Held**
SIC: 2064 2052 Candy & other confectionery products; cookies & crackers

(G-5334)
RIKA BAKERIES INC
1025 E 24th St (33013-4323)
PHONE..................305 691-5673
Manuel Sendina, *President*
Roberto Sanchez, *Corp Secy*
EMP: 16 **EST:** 1964
SQ FT: 7,500
SALES (est): 444.8K **Privately Held**
SIC: 2052 Crackers, dry

(G-5335)
ROD BISCAYNE MANUFACTURING
425 E 9th St (33010-4547)
PHONE..................305 884-0808
Eddie M Carman, *President*
Kenneth S Carman, *Vice Pres*
Joseph K Carman, *Shareholder*
Mary Jo Carman, *Admin Sec*
▼ **EMP:** 5 **EST:** 1948
SQ FT: 3,500
SALES (est): 380.1K **Privately Held**
WEB: www.biscaynerod.com
SIC: 3949 Rods & rod parts, fishing

(G-5336)
ROLU WOODCRAFT INC
4733 E 11th Ave (33013-2129)
PHONE..................305 685-0914
Roberto Palenzuela Sr, *President*
Juana Palenzuela, *Vice Pres*
Luis Palenzuela, *Vice Pres*
EMP: 12 **EST:** 1969
SQ FT: 14,500
SALES (est): 967.9K **Privately Held**
SIC: 2434 2521 2511 2431 Wood kitchen cabinets; wood office furniture; wood household furniture; millwork

(G-5337)
ROMAX INDUSTRIES INC
8620 Nw 190th Ter (33015-5384)
PHONE..................305 773-6657
Robert Fernandez, *President*
EMP: 8 **EST:** 2001
SALES (est): 150K **Privately Held**
SIC: 3999 Manufacturing industries

(G-5338)
S P MANUFACTURING LLC
2208 W 79th St (33016-5520)
PHONE..................305 362-0456
Claudio U Gatto, *Principal*
EMP: 8 **EST:** 2007
SALES (est): 978.1K **Privately Held**
SIC: 3999 Barber & beauty shop equipment

(G-5339)
S&S GLOBAL SUPPLY LLC
730 W 38th Pl (33012)
PHONE..................786 529-4799
Juma M Salem, *Mng Member*
Hani Salem, *Mng Member*
Sami Salem, *Mng Member*
EMP: 7 **EST:** 2015
SALES (est): 207.2K **Privately Held**
WEB: www.ssglobalsupply.com
SIC: 2515 5021 2512 Mattresses, containing felt, foam rubber, urethane, etc.; furniture; upholstered household furniture

(G-5340)
SAFE PRO INC
1650 W 33rd Pl (33012-4514)
PHONE..................954 494-5768
Pravin Borkar, *Principal*
EMP: 7 **EST:** 2016
SQ FT: 4,000
SALES (est): 637.9K **Privately Held**
WEB: www.safeprousa.net
SIC: 3089 Awnings, fiberglass & plastic combination

(G-5341)
SALSA CUBA INC
1275 W 49th St (33012-3220)
PHONE..................305 993-9757
Angel Pellicier, *Principal*
EMP: 7 **EST:** 2016
SALES (est): 114.8K **Privately Held**
SIC: 2099 Dips, except cheese & sour cream based

(G-5342)
SCHWARZ PRTNERS PCKG MIAMI LLC
1101 E 33rd Pl (33013-3528)
PHONE..................305 693-1399
Barbara Perez, *Human Res Mgr*
Jack W Schwarz, *Mng Member*
Alan Lankenau, *Manager*
Ruben Torresdey, *Maintence Staff*
◆ **EMP:** 2 **EST:** 2007
SALES (est): 3MM **Privately Held**
SIC: 2653 Boxes, corrugated: made from purchased materials

(G-5343)
SELECT ENGINEERED SYSTEMS INC
Also Called: S E S
7991 W 26th Ave (33016-2799)
PHONE..................305 823-5410
John Sheppard Sr, *President*
Susan Hancock, *COO*
Rick Muller, *Exec VP*
Charles Brennan, *Engineer*
Sandy Tsairis, *CFO*
▲ **EMP:** 20 **EST:** 1976
SQ FT: 11,000
SALES (est): 3.4MM **Privately Held**
WEB: www.selectses.com
SIC: 3699 3829 3661 3643 Security control equipment & systems; measuring & controlling devices; telephone & telegraph apparatus; current-carrying wiring devices; relays & industrial controls; computer peripheral equipment

(G-5344)
SEMINOLE PRINTING INC
2310 W 78th St (33016-5526)
PHONE..................305 823-7204
Stephanie Pintado, *President*
EMP: 7 **EST:** 2006
SQ FT: 5,100
SALES (est): 100K **Privately Held**
SIC: 2752 Commercial printing, offset

(G-5345)
SEMPRUN & MORALES CORPORATION
Also Called: Minuteman Press
3418 W 84th St Ste 100 (33018-4936)
PHONE..................305 698-2554
Ana T Morales, *President*
▼ **EMP:** 8 **EST:** 2010
SALES (est): 377.1K **Privately Held**
WEB: www.minutemanpress.com
SIC: 2752 Commercial printing, lithographic

(G-5346)
SEVILLA CABINETS INC
1550 W 34th Pl (33012-4622)
PHONE..................305 888-2174
Omar Cepero, *President*
EMP: 10 **EST:** 1998
SQ FT: 30,000
SALES (est): 824.3K **Privately Held**
SIC: 2434 Wood kitchen cabinets

(G-5347)
SHARING THREE INC
575 E 10th Ave (33010-4639)
PHONE..................305 884-8384
Renato Alonso, *President*
Danny Acosta, *Accounts Mgr*
Xenia Borges, *Accounts Mgr*
Virginia Freyre, *Accounts Mgr*
Gilbert Lebron, *Sales Staff*
EMP: 14 **EST:** 2001
SALES (est): 252.3K **Privately Held**
SIC: 3585 Refrigeration & heating equipment

(G-5348)
SIGN ONE INC
760 E 51st St (33013-1630)
PHONE..................305 888-6565
George Thalman, *President*
EMP: 5 **EST:** 1992
SQ FT: 3,400
SALES (est): 460.9K **Privately Held**
WEB: www.signoneinc.com
SIC: 3993 Electric signs

(G-5349)
SILCAR CORP
1475 W 82nd St (33014-3359)
PHONE..................305 557-8391
Carlos Zayas, *Principal*
EMP: 9 **EST:** 2010
SALES (est): 105.1K **Privately Held**
SIC: 3089 Injection molding of plastics

(G-5350)
SKYLITE SIGNS & SERVICES INC
1640 W 32nd Pl (33012-4510)
PHONE..................305 362-5015
George Bravo, *President*
EMP: 10 **EST:** 2006
SALES (est): 711.5K **Privately Held**
WEB: www.skylitesignsfl.com
SIC: 3993 Signs & advertising specialties

(G-5351)
SLICK DESIGNS & AP MIAMI INC
3710 E 10th Ct (33013-2920)
PHONE..................305 836-7950
Sasson Jacoby, *President*
◆ **EMP:** 11 **EST:** 2000
SQ FT: 30,000
SALES (est): 188.6K **Privately Held**
SIC: 2759 Screen printing

(G-5352)
SOBRINO CUSTOM CABINETS INC
2220 W 10th Ct (33010-1911)
PHONE..................786 564-2699
Darney Suarez, *Principal*
EMP: 9 **EST:** 2013
SALES (est): 240.1K **Privately Held**
WEB: sobrinocustomcabinet.wixsite.com
SIC: 2434 Wood kitchen cabinets

(G-5353)
SOS SERVICES ON PRTG CORP
2738 W 68th Pl (33016-5476)
PHONE..................305 225-6000
Brenda Ardua, *Principal*
EMP: 7 **EST:** 2010

SALES (est): 99.8K **Privately Held**
SIC: 2752 Commercial printing, lithographic

(G-5354)
SOUTH FLORIDA CUTTING
3965 E 10th Ct (33013-2923)
PHONE...................................305 693-6711
EMP: 12
SALES (est): 934.1K **Privately Held**
SIC: 2299 2399 Mfg Textile Goods Mfg Fabricated Textile Products

(G-5355)
SOUTH FLORIDA PAVERS CORP
18506 Nw 67th Ave (33015-3304)
PHONE...................................786 517-9100
Mariana E Lorente MD, *Principal*
EMP: 7 **EST:** 2012
SALES (est): 379.6K **Privately Held**
SIC: 3531 Pavers

(G-5356)
SOUTH FLORIDA TECH SVCS INC
Also Called: Florida Emrgncy Eqp Upfitters
2333 W 3rd Ct (33010-1431)
PHONE...................................786 286-2882
Stephen Crowe, *CEO*
EMP: 10 **EST:** 2006
SALES (est): 606.4K **Privately Held**
SIC: 3999 Badges, metal: policemen, firemen, etc.

(G-5357)
SOUTHEASTERN PRINTING CO INC (PA)
950 Se 8th St (33010-5740)
PHONE...................................772 287-2141
Donald N Mader, *President*
Lawrence Reger, *Chairman*
Suzanne Z Kenik, *Project Mgr*
Diana Gannon, *CFO*
Rob Cawthon, *Controller*
▼ **EMP:** 102 **EST:** 1924
SQ FT: 60,000
SALES (est): 50.7MM **Privately Held**
WEB: www.seprint.com
SIC: 2752 2759 2789 2732 Commercial printing, offset; flexographic printing; bookbinding & related work; book printing

(G-5358)
SOUTHERN WELDING & MECHANICS
592 W 28th St (33010-1326)
PHONE...................................305 772-0961
Luis R Fernandez, *President*
Josbel Fernandez, *Vice Pres*
EMP: 15 **EST:** 2011
SQ FT: 3,000
SALES (est): 5MM **Privately Held**
WEB: www.southernwm.com
SIC: 7692 1711 Welding repair; mechanical contractor

(G-5359)
SOUTHWEST TURBINE INC
4550 E 10th Ct (33013-2106)
PHONE...................................305 769-1765
Lourdes Hermoso, *President*
Maria Bolnoes, *General Mgr*
George Castro, *CFO*
EMP: 9 **EST:** 2002
SALES (est): 97.9K **Privately Held**
WEB: www.southwestturbine.com
SIC: 3511 Turbines & turbine generator sets

(G-5360)
ST JUDAS TADEUS FOUNDRY INC
Also Called: Saint Judas Tadeus Foundry
2160 W 10th Ct (33010-1909)
PHONE...................................305 512-3612
Ildefonso Vega, *President*
Alfonso Vega, *General Mgr*
EMP: 8 **EST:** 1964
SALES (est): 711.5K **Privately Held**
SIC: 3365 3496 Masts, cast aluminum; miscellaneous fabricated wire products

(G-5361)
STAR BEDDING MFG CORP
1053 E 14th St (33010-3311)
PHONE...................................305 887-5209
Richard D Morales, *President*
Maria Morales, *Vice Pres*
Gabriel Morales, *CFO*
▼ **EMP:** 25 **EST:** 1969
SQ FT: 11,200
SALES (est): 502.6K **Privately Held**
WEB: www.starbeddingmfg.com
SIC: 2515 Box springs, assembled; mattresses, innerspring or box spring

(G-5362)
STAR ENVIROTECH INC
1010 E 31st St (33013-3522)
PHONE...................................714 427-1244
Jim Saffie, *President*
▲ **EMP:** 12 **EST:** 2000
SQ FT: 15,000
SALES (est): 220.6K **Privately Held**
SIC: 3559 Automotive maintenance equipment

(G-5363)
STITCH BY STITCH
1675 W 49th St (33012-2935)
PHONE...................................305 979-2275
EMP: 6 **EST:** 2013
SALES (est): 327.6K **Privately Held**
SIC: 2395 Embroidery & art needlework

(G-5364)
STREAMLINE PERFORMANCE BOATS C
7711 W 22nd Ave (33016-5518)
PHONE...................................305 393-8848
EMP: 15 **EST:** 2020
SALES (est): 1MM **Privately Held**
WEB: www.streamlineboats.com
SIC: 3732 Boat building & repairing

(G-5365)
STRUCTURE GLASS SOLUTIONS LLC
13202 Nw 107th Ave Unit 8 (33018-1289)
PHONE...................................954 499-9450
Flavio Schonholz, *Principal*
Norma Schonholz, *Mng Member*
EMP: 12 **EST:** 2015
SALES (est): 1.6MM **Privately Held**
WEB: www.structuregs.com
SIC: 3211 Structural glass

(G-5366)
STS APPAREL CORP
325 W 74th Pl (33014-5024)
PHONE...................................305 628-4000
Marty Tacher, *CEO*
Marco Tiapago, *President*
Scott Valancy, *Vice Pres*
EMP: 14 **EST:** 1999
SALES (est): 712.3K **Privately Held**
WEB: www.stsmiami.com
SIC: 2395 5699 Emblems, embroidered; T-shirts, custom printed

(G-5367)
SUNNMAN INC
2475 W 8th Ln (33010-2031)
PHONE...................................305 505-6615
Enriqueta M Saldarriaga, *Principal*
EMP: 8 **EST:** 2010
SALES (est): 264.8K **Privately Held**
SIC: 3999 Manufacturing industries

(G-5368)
SUNSHINE AVIONICS LLC
963 W 81st Pl (33014-3515)
PHONE...................................954 517-1294
Leon Gonzalez, *President*
Thomas Irwin, *Treasurer*
Elizabeth Letendre, *Admin Sec*
Judith Vetter, *Asst Sec*
EMP: 6 **EST:** 2008
SALES (est): 6.6MM **Publicly Held**
SIC: 3724 Aircraft engines & engine parts
HQ: Heico Aerospace Corporation
3000 Taft St
Hollywood FL 33021
954 987-6101

(G-5369)
SUNSHINE PACKAGING INC
880 W 19th St (33010-2307)
PHONE...................................305 887-8141
Santos Flores, *President*
Eva Monzon, *CFO*
Francisca Flores, *Treasurer*
Eva Flores, *Admin Sec*
▼ **EMP:** 26 **EST:** 1972
SALES (est): 4.2MM **Privately Held**
WEB: www.sunshinepkg.com
SIC: 2653 2657 Boxes, corrugated: made from purchased materials; folding paperboard boxes

(G-5370)
SUNSHINE WINDOWS MFG INC
1785 W 33rd Pl (33012-4515)
PHONE...................................305 364-9952
Jaime Puerto, *President*
Carolina Sendon, *Vice Pres*
Jose Nunez, *Admin Sec*
◆ **EMP:** 72 **EST:** 1988
SQ FT: 34,500
SALES (est): 10.1MM **Privately Held**
WEB: www.sunshinewindows.com
SIC: 3442 3231 Louvers, shutters, jalousies & similar items; doors, glass: made from purchased glass

(G-5371)
SUNSOF INC (PA)
Also Called: Tomasa Healthy Passion
5821 E 10th Ave (33013-1759)
PHONE...................................305 691-1875
Edgardo Armando, *President*
James Jaroscak, *Vice Pres*
Mayra Gonzalez, *Mfg Staff*
Javier Castillo, *Production*
Federico Armando, *CFO*
▲ **EMP:** 26 **EST:** 2004
SQ FT: 15,000
SALES (est): 6.5MM **Privately Held**
WEB: www.sunsof.com
SIC: 2053 7389 Frozen bakery products, except bread; packaging & labeling services

(G-5372)
SUPERFORMANCE MFG INC
Also Called: Unlimited Marine Mfg
2637 W 76th St (33016-5615)
PHONE...................................305 420-6034
Guillermo Hechevarria, *President*
EMP: 5 **EST:** 2020
SALES (est): 321.5K **Privately Held**
WEB: www.superformancejet.com
SIC: 3731 Shipbuilding & repairing

(G-5373)
SUPERIOR QUALITY CONTRACTORS
17240 Nw 64th Ave Apt 206 (33015-6304)
PHONE...................................786 371-7991
Nicholas Perez, *Principal*
EMP: 8 **EST:** 2018
SALES (est): 96.7K **Privately Held**
WEB: www.superiordoorsfl.com
SIC: 3442 2431 5031 Storm doors or windows, metal; doors & door parts & trim, wood; windows & window parts & trim, wood; doors & windows

(G-5374)
SUPERIOR SLEEP TECHNOLOGY INC
705 E 10th Ave (33010-4643)
PHONE...................................305 888-0953
Jesus Lopez Teresa, *President*
EMP: 11 **EST:** 2012
SALES (est): 444.5K **Privately Held**
WEB: www.superiorhd.net
SIC: 2392 Cushions & pillows

(G-5375)
SURF LIGHTING INC
210 W 24th St (33010-1526)
P.O. Box 441894, Miami (33144-1894)
PHONE...................................305 888-7851
Geraldine Ossakow, *President*
▲ **EMP:** 16 **EST:** 1960
SQ FT: 35,000

SALES (est): 802.5K **Privately Held**
WEB: www.surflighting.com
SIC: 3646 3699 3641 Fluorescent lighting fixtures, commercial; electrical equipment & supplies; electric lamps

(G-5376)
SYNERGY CUSTOM FIXTURES CORP
215 Se 10th Ave (33010-5536)
PHONE...................................305 693-0055
Alexander Giron, *President*
Peter Garro, *COO*
Luis Flores, *CFO*
Peter Hernandez, *Manager*
EMP: 150 **EST:** 2010
SQ FT: 60,000
SALES (est): 27.2MM **Privately Held**
WEB: www.synergycustomfixtures.com
SIC: 2541 2542 Store fixtures, wood; office & store showcases & display fixtures; fixtures, store: except wood

(G-5377)
T & Y CABINETS INC
7380 W 20th Ave Ste 102 (33016-5541)
PHONE...................................305 512-0802
Jorge Rivero, *Principal*
EMP: 7 **EST:** 2006
SALES (est): 253.6K **Privately Held**
WEB: t-y-cabinets-inc.hub.biz
SIC: 2434 Wood kitchen cabinets

(G-5378)
TEJEDA SHEET METAL & ALUMINUM
651 W 43rd Pl (33012-3852)
PHONE...................................305 609-5477
Aleido Tejeda, *Principal*
EMP: 7 **EST:** 2013
SALES (est): 138.9K **Privately Held**
SIC: 3444 Sheet metalwork

(G-5379)
TERRADES CUSTOM WOODWORKS INC
219 W 27th St (33010-1511)
PHONE...................................305 316-2908
Sergio Terrades, *President*
EMP: 7 **EST:** 2015
SALES (est): 105.1K **Privately Held**
SIC: 2431 Millwork

(G-5380)
TIGER BUSINESS FORMS INC
Also Called: Tiger/Southland
7765 W 20th Ave (33014-3227)
PHONE...................................305 888-3528
Mike Pina, *President*
Millie Pina, *Vice Pres*
▼ **EMP:** 23 **EST:** 1988
SQ FT: 25,000
SALES (est): 3.6MM **Privately Held**
WEB: www.tigerprintingsolutions.com
SIC: 2752 2761 Commercial printing, offset; manifold business forms

(G-5381)
TRIM-LINE OF MIAMI INC
2755 W 81st St (33016-2733)
PHONE...................................305 556-6210
Randell V Hulan, *President*
◆ **EMP:** 9 **EST:** 1978
SQ FT: 8,000
SALES (est): 507.2K **Privately Held**
WEB: www.trimlinegraphicsusa.com
SIC: 2759 7336 Screen printing; commercial art & graphic design

(G-5382)
TROPICAL MFG INC
783 W 18th St (33010-2424)
PHONE...................................305 394-6280
Anna K Janania, *President*
▼ **EMP:** 7 **EST:** 2010
SALES (est): 588.2K **Privately Held**
WEB: www.tropicalmfg.com
SIC: 3999 Manufacturing industries

(G-5383)
TROPICAL TEXTILES INTL INC
6073 Nw 167th St Ste C17 (33015-4392)
PHONE...................................305 364-4595
Jose A Rego, *President*
EMP: 7 **EST:** 2017

SALES (est): 321.6K **Privately Held**
SIC: 2211 Dress fabrics, cotton

(G-5384)
TTS FOOD LLC
Also Called: Venfood Disrtibutors
15990 Nw 49th Ave (33014-6309)
PHONE..................................305 622-2726
Tomas Gonzalez, *Mng Member*
Lorelvy M Hurtado,
▲ EMP: 6 EST: 2011
SQ FT: 5,000
SALES (est): 893.9K **Privately Held**
WEB: www.venfooddistributors.com
SIC: 2051 Breads, rolls & buns

(G-5385)
TURIN EM INC
8045 W 26th Ct (33016-2731)
PHONE..................................305 825-2004
Martin Mendelson, *President*
Robert Edelman, *Vice Pres*
Ronald Plask, *Treasurer*
EMP: 10 EST: 1989
SQ FT: 2,000
SALES (est): 664.3K **Privately Held**
SIC: 2395 Embroidery & art needlework

(G-5386)
TUUCI LLC
1000 Se 8th St Ste A (33010-5781)
PHONE..................................305 634-5116
Dougan H Clarke, *CEO*
David Schutte, *President*
Jose Castillo, *QC Mgr*
Peter Nunez, *Design Engr*
Charles Munroe, *CFO*
◆ EMP: 300 EST: 2008
SALES (est): 45.7MM **Privately Held**
WEB: www.tuuci.com
SIC: 2514 Backs & seats for metal house-
hold furniture
PA: Tuuci Worldwide, Llc
2900 Nw 35th St
Miami FL 33142

(G-5387)
TUUCI WORLDWIDE
1000 Se 8th St (33010-5780)
PHONE..................................305 634-5116
EMP: 8 EST: 2018
SALES (est): 380.9K **Privately Held**
WEB: www.tuuci.com
SIC: 2514 Metal household furniture

(G-5388)
TUUCI WORLDWIDE LLC
Also Called: Pavilion Furniture
16200 Nw 49th Ave (33014-6315)
PHONE..................................305 823-3480
Ward Usmar, *Branch Mgr*
EMP: 348 **Privately Held**
WEB: www.tuuci.com
SIC: 2514 Metal household furniture
PA: Tuuci Worldwide, Llc
2900 Nw 35th St
Miami FL 33142

(G-5389)
U S HOLDINGS INC (PA)
Also Called: Eagle Manufacturing Group
3200 W 84th St (33018-4908)
PHONE..................................305 885-0301
Alex Debogory Jr, *President*
Lee Fortney, *General Mgr*
Alex L Bogory, *COO*
David H Brunswick, *Vice Pres*
John Debogory, *Vice Pres*
◆ EMP: 3 EST: 1937
SQ FT: 210,000
SALES (est): 157.6MM **Privately Held**
SIC: 3321 3543 Gray iron castings;
foundry patternmaking

(G-5390)
ULTIMATE UMBRELLA
COMPANY INC (PA)
Also Called: Tuuci
1000 Se 8th St Ste A (33010-5781)
PHONE..................................305 634-5116
Dougan Clarke, *CEO*
Thomas Parker, *President*
Alexander Kromidas, *Regional Mgr*
Patrick N Troy, *Vice Pres*
Edward Usmar, *Vice Pres*
◆ EMP: 28 EST: 1998

SALES (est): 49.6MM **Privately Held**
SIC: 3999 Umbrellas, canes & parts

(G-5391)
UNION PVC INDUSTRIES INC
295 W 27th St (33010-1511)
PHONE..................................305 883-1640
Manuel J Lopez, *Principal*
EMP: 7 EST: 2016
SALES (est): 47.3K **Privately Held**
WEB: www.unionpvcindustries.com
SIC: 3999 Manufacturing industries

(G-5392)
UNITED BEDDINGS CORP
421 W 28th St (33010-1323)
PHONE..................................786 333-4795
Edel Sosa, *President*
EMP: 14 EST: 2011
SALES (est): 534.7K **Privately Held**
WEB: united-beddings-corp.business.site
SIC: 2515 Mattresses, containing felt, foam
rubber, urethane, etc.

(G-5393)
UNITED CABINETS CORP
867 W 30th St (33012-5001)
PHONE..................................305 887-5050
Edelso Riveron Jr, *President*
Telma Riveron, *Admin Sec*
EMP: 5 EST: 1983
SALES (est): 390.1K **Privately Held**
WEB: www.unitedcabinets.com
SIC: 2434 Wood kitchen cabinets

(G-5394)
UNIVERSAL ALUM WINDOWS &
DOORS
1675 W 31st Pl (33012-4505)
PHONE..................................305 825-7900
Jose Fernandez, *President*
EMP: 13 EST: 1984
SQ FT: 16,500
SALES (est): 701.8K **Privately Held**
SIC: 3442 3231 Sash, door or window:
metal; products of purchased glass

(G-5395)
UNIVERSAL CON & RDYMX
CORP
10505 W Okeechobee Rd # 10
(33018-1979)
PHONE..................................305 512-3400
Juan Alvarez, *President*
EMP: 38 EST: 1983
SQ FT: 2,800
SALES (est): 5MM **Privately Held**
SIC: 3273 Ready-mixed concrete

(G-5396)
UNLIMITED MARINE MFG INC
2637 W 76th St (33016-5615)
PHONE..................................305 420-6034
Lida Munoz, *CEO*
EMP: 7 EST: 2020
SALES (est): 250K **Privately Held**
WEB: www.unlimitedmarinemfg.com
SIC: 3731 Marine rigging

(G-5397)
UP2SPEED PRINTING INC
8081 W 28th Ave (33016-5101)
PHONE..................................850 508-2620
Orlando Valdes, *Principal*
EMP: 16 EST: 2003
SALES (est): 1MM **Privately Held**
WEB: www.up2speedprinting.com
SIC: 2752 Commercial printing, offset

(G-5398)
US MANUFACTURING COMPANY
Also Called: US Foundry
3200 W 84th St (33018-4908)
PHONE..................................305 556-1661
Paula Cavache, *Exec VP*
Diana Vanegas, *Purch Agent*
Juan Mejia, *QC Mgr*
Rick Terrill, *Manager*
Angelo Vega, *Executive*
EMP: 10
SALES (corp-wide): 157.6MM **Privately**
Held
SIC: 3321 3441 Gray iron castings; fabri-
cated structural metal

HQ: Us Manufacturing Company
8351 Nw 93rd St
Medley FL 33166
305 885-0301

(G-5399)
US PRECAST CORP
3200 W 84th St (33018-4908)
PHONE..................................305 364-8253
Debra Cloudie, *President*
Ana Sierra, *Human Res Mgr*
Angelo Vega, *Branch Mgr*
Hugo Fernandez, *Executive*
EMP: 33 EST: 1916
SALES (est): 1.8MM **Privately Held**
SIC: 3272 Precast terrazo or concrete
products

(G-5400)
USA SHEET METAL INC
650 W 18th St (33010-2423)
PHONE..................................786 517-3482
Carlos E Rosa, *President*
Lazaro Reinoso, *Vice Pres*
EMP: 7 EST: 2006
SQ FT: 2,000
SALES (est): 1.1MM **Privately Held**
SIC: 3444 Sheet metalwork

(G-5401)
USF FABRICATION INC (PA)
3200 W 84th St (33018-4908)
PHONE..................................305 556-1661
Alexander De Bogory Jr, *President*
Valdez Robert, *Vice Pres*
Jamie Rubin, *Vice Pres*
Grant Finlinson, *Opers Mgr*
Ralph Jimenez, *Production*
▼ EMP: 200 EST: 1996
SQ FT: 90,000
SALES (est): 51.7MM **Privately Held**
WEB: www.usffab.com
SIC: 3441 Fabricated structural metal

(G-5402)
V & G INDUSTRIES INC
4965 E 10th Ct (33013-1731)
PHONE..................................786 853-1265
Enio Guerrero, *Principal*
EMP: 9 EST: 2013
SALES (est): 285.1K **Privately Held**
WEB: vandginc.business.site
SIC: 3999 Manufacturing industries

(G-5403)
V A ELECTRICAL MOTORS CTR
INC
4011 W 18th Ave (33012-7054)
PHONE..................................305 825-3327
Horacio Valdes, *Partner*
Margarita Valdes, *Partner*
▼ EMP: 5 EST: 1986
SALES (est): 349.9K **Privately Held**
SIC: 7694 Electric motor repair; rebuilding
motors, except automotive

(G-5404)
V G CARPENTRY LLC
4855 E 10th Ct (33013-2123)
PHONE..................................786 531-7824
EMP: 9 EST: 2018
SALES (est): 428.8K **Privately Held**
SIC: 2434 Wood kitchen cabinets

(G-5405)
V P R ART LLC
Also Called: USA Hemp Solutions
2630 W 81st St (33016-2755)
PHONE..................................786 205-4526
Kevin Tellado, *Mng Member*
EMP: 30 EST: 2013
SALES (est): 2.5MM **Privately Held**
SIC: 2844 Toilet preparations

(G-5406)
VECELLIO & GROGAN INC
White Rock Quarries Division
18300 Nw 122nd Ave (33018)
P.O. Box 667776, Miami (33166-9405)
PHONE..................................305 822-5322
Eddie Allsopp, *Vice Pres*
Eric Jackson, *Project Engr*
Alba Padilla, *Credit Mgr*
Raymond Maddy, *Branch Mgr*
Earon Lee, *Planning*
EMP: 100

SALES (corp-wide): 596.1MM **Privately**
Held
WEB: www.vecelliogrogan.com
SIC: 1422 1442 Limestones, ground; con-
struction sand & gravel
HQ: Vecellio & Grogan, Inc.
2251 Robert C Byrd Dr
Beckley WV 25801
304 252-6575

(G-5407)
VEGGIESPETIT POIS INC
2202 W 78th St (33016-5525)
PHONE..................................305 826-7867
Rafael Gabeiras, *President*
Viviana Gabeiras, *Vice Pres*
EMP: 30 EST: 1999
SQ FT: 6,000
SALES (est): 4.9MM **Privately Held**
WEB: www.mypetitpois.com
SIC: 2339 Athletic clothing: women's,
misses' & juniors'

(G-5408)
VERONICA KNITS INC
490 W 18th St (33010-2419)
PHONE..................................305 887-7333
Jonel Jankuc, *President*
Jeffrey Jankuc, *Vice Pres*
▼ EMP: 11 EST: 1990
SQ FT: 12,000
SALES (est): 271.8K **Privately Held**
WEB: veronica-knits.business.site
SIC: 2253 Skirts, knit

(G-5409)
VET SONIC INC
1099 E 47th St (33013-2139)
PHONE..................................305 681-4486
Eva Engler, *President*
EMP: 8 EST: 1963
SALES (est): 107.9K **Privately Held**
SIC: 3843 Dental equipment

(G-5410)
VICTORS CSTM QLTING
BDSPREAD I
2765 W 78th St (33016-2741)
PHONE..................................305 362-1990
Victor Chao, *President*
▼ EMP: 8 EST: 1977
SALES (est): 699.8K **Privately Held**
SIC: 2392 Household furnishings

(G-5411)
VICTORS DIE CUTTING INC
1385 Se 9th Ave (33010-5907)
PHONE..................................305 599-0255
Victor Rodriguez, *President*
Juan Rodriguez, *Vice Pres*
EMP: 5 EST: 1989
SALES (est): 462.1K **Privately Held**
WEB: www.victorsdiecut.com
SIC: 3544 Dies, steel rule

(G-5412)
VITAL GRAPHICS AND SIGNS
INC
2131 W 60th St (33016-2602)
PHONE..................................305 557-8181
Luis Gonzalez, *President*
Luis E Gonzalez, *Principal*
Alberto Cabrera, *Vice Pres*
EMP: 5 EST: 2010
SQ FT: 3,600
SALES (est): 495.3K **Privately Held**
WEB: www.vital-graphics.com
SIC: 2752 Commercial printing, offset

(G-5413)
VITAL PHARMA RESEARCH INC
2300 W 84th St Ste 303 (33016-5772)
PHONE..................................786 666-0592
Luis Canete, *Principal*
EMP: 6 EST: 2014
SALES (est): 412K **Privately Held**
WEB: www.vprfl.org
SIC: 2834 Pharmaceutical preparations

(G-5414)
VOICE PUBLISHING CO INC
Also Called: La Voz De La Calle
4696 E 10th Ct (33013-2108)
P.O. Box 133187 (33013-0187)
PHONE..................................305 687-5555

Vincent Rodriguez, *President*
Juan Suarez, *General Mgr*
Zenaida Moreno, *Editor*
EMP: 7 **EST:** 1982
SQ FT: 1,500
SALES (est): 598.6K **Privately Held**
WEB: www.lavozdelacalle.net
SIC: 2711 Newspapers

(G-5415)
VP CAST STONE CORP
Also Called: Vp Castone
879 E 25th St 899 (33013-3401)
PHONE.................................305 691-9306
Amanda Munoz Garcia, *President*
Alfredo Estevan, *Vice Pres*
◆ **EMP:** 5 **EST:** 2007
SALES (est): 313.9K **Privately Held**
WEB: www.vpcaststone.com
SIC: 3272 Cast stone, concrete

(G-5416)
VSF CORP
Also Called: Infinity Embroidery
4241 W 108th St Unit 1 (33018-1292)
PHONE.................................305 769-2202
Joseph Friedman, *President*
Lior Friedman, *Vice Pres*
Orit Olshansky, *Controller*
▲ **EMP:** 30 **EST:** 1999
SALES (est): 4.2MM **Privately Held**
WEB: www.infinityapparelgroup.com
SIC: 2395 Embroidery products, except schiffli machine

(G-5417)
WALTER HAAS GRAPHICS INC
123 W 23rd St (33010-2211)
PHONE.................................305 883-2257
Patrick Haas, *President*
Chrisitne Lohmeyer, *Vice Pres*
David Lohmeyer, *Treasurer*
Christopher Haas, *Department Mgr*
Marianne Haas, *Director*
▼ **EMP:** 25 **EST:** 1972
SQ FT: 20,000
SALES (est): 3.3MM **Privately Held**
WEB: www.haasprint.com
SIC: 2759 2396 2752 Screen printing; fabric printing & stamping; commercial printing, lithographic

(G-5418)
WARREN TECHNOLOGY INC
Also Called: Warren Manufacturing
2050 W 73rd St (33016-1816)
P.O. Box 5347 (33014-1347)
PHONE.................................305 556-6933
Winfield L Kelley, *President*
Patricia L Parnell, *Corp Secy*
Taylor Hamilton, *Purchasing*
Frank Zavala, *Accounts Mgr*
Scott Hamilton, *Sales Engr*
▲ **EMP:** 200 **EST:** 1986
SQ FT: 40,000
SALES (est): 44.9MM **Privately Held**
WEB: www.warrenhvac.com
SIC: 3585 3564 Air conditioning equipment, complete; ventilating fans; industrial or commercial

(G-5419)
WASTE PETRO RECOVER
4680 W 13th Ln Apt 316 (33012-3237)
PHONE.................................305 345-4199
Rudy Santana, *Principal*
EMP: 7 **EST:** 2008
SALES (est): 140.3K **Privately Held**
SIC: 2819 Industrial inorganic chemicals

(G-5420)
WILLIAMS SPECIALTIES INC
4716 E 10th Ct (33013-2122)
PHONE.................................305 769-9925
Mario Williams Jr, *President*
EMP: 8 **EST:** 2016
SALES (est): 536.8K **Privately Held**
SIC: 2396 Printing & embossing on plastics fabric articles

(G-5421)
WINSTON MANUFACTURING CORP
1745 W 32nd Pl Ste 55 (33012-4511)
PHONE.................................305 822-3344
Bill Newnan, *CEO*

Larry Goldstein, *President*
▲ **EMP:** 11 **EST:** 1993
SQ FT: 18,000
SALES (est): 527.3K **Privately Held**
SIC: 3172 Personal leather goods

(G-5422)
WORLD OF AWNINGS INC
151 W 21st St (33010-2615)
PHONE.................................305 884-6699
Ignasio Sotolongo, *President*
◆ **EMP:** 10 **EST:** 1992
SALES (est): 818.7K **Privately Held**
WEB: www.aworldofawnings.com
SIC: 2431 2394 Awnings, blinds & shutters, wood; canvas & related products

(G-5423)
WORLDWIDE DRAPERIES WEST LLC
705 W 20th St (33010-2429)
PHONE.................................305 887-9611
Sandra Leal, *Opers Staff*
Jose Manuel Leal, *Manager*
Sandra Lina Leal, *Manager*
EMP: 9 **EST:** 2015
SALES (est): 149.8K **Privately Held**
WEB: www.wwdrape.com
SIC: 2591 Shade, curtain & drapery hardware; curtain & drapery rods, poles & fixtures

(G-5424)
XPRESS PRECISION PRODUCTS INC
4432 E 10th Ct (33013-2523)
PHONE.................................305 685-2127
Leonel Montepeque, *President*
EMP: 6 **EST:** 1996
SALES (est): 897.6K **Privately Held**
SIC: 3599 7692 Machine shop, jobbing & repair; welding repair

(G-5425)
Y&D MACHINE SHOP INC
748 E 51st St (33013-1630)
PHONE.................................786 717-6356
Sandra Delgado, *Vice Pres*
EMP: 9 **EST:** 2018
SALES (est): 203.8K **Privately Held**
SIC: 3599 Machine shop, jobbing & repair

(G-5426)
YOSNIEL FINISHING INC
1171 W 28th St Apt 8 (33010-1185)
PHONE.................................305 890-3287
Yosniel Penton Suarez, *President*
EMP: 7 **EST:** 2017
SALES (est): 80K **Privately Held**
SIC: 3471 Electroplating of metals or formed products

(G-5427)
YOUR DREAMS CABINETS CORP
7635 W 28th Ave (33016-5107)
PHONE.................................305 305-3729
Vanler R Napoles, *President*
Madelaine Napoles, *Vice Pres*
EMP: 6 **EST:** 2008
SALES (est): 781.1K **Privately Held**
WEB: www.kitchencabinetsformiami.com
SIC: 2434 Wood kitchen cabinets

(G-5428)
ZAYAS FASHIONS INC (PA)
665 W 33rd St (33012-5112)
PHONE.................................305 823-1438
Daniel Zayas, *Ch of Bd*
Carlos Zayas, *President*
Lilliam Llanos, *Vice Pres*
Haydee Zayas, *Vice Pres*
EMP: 27 **EST:** 1968
SQ FT: 6,000
SALES (est): 1.9MM **Privately Held**
WEB: www.zayasfashions.com
SIC: 2326 5632 Men's & boys' work clothing; apparel accessories

(G-5429)
ZERONS METAL DESIGNERS INC
115 117 W 24th St (33010)
PHONE.................................305 688-2240
Jose A Zeron, *President*

EMP: 13 **EST:** 2004
SALES (est): 1MM **Privately Held**
WEB: www.zeronsmetaldesigners.com
SIC: 3499 3312 Bank chests, metal; stainless steel

Hialeah Gardens
Miami-Dade County

(G-5430)
AMERICAN PROFESSIONAL IR WORK
8320 Nw 103rd St (33016-4657)
PHONE.................................305 556-9522
Mauricio Rivera, *Principal*
EMP: 9 **EST:** 2015
SALES (est): 253.1K **Privately Held**
SIC: 3462 Iron & steel forgings

(G-5431)
BENGIS SIGNS INC
9821 Nw 80th Ave Unit 5t (33016-2366)
PHONE.................................305 592-3860
Joel Serkes, *President*
Janet Serkes, *Vice Pres*
EMP: 15 **EST:** 1991
SQ FT: 14,500
SALES (est): 575.4K **Privately Held**
SIC: 3993 Electric signs; neon signs

(G-5432)
BEST ROLLING MANUFACTURER INC
Also Called: Best Door
9780 Nw 79th Ave (33016-2514)
PHONE.................................305 821-4276
Santiago Suarez, *President*
▼ **EMP:** 60 **EST:** 1999
SALES (est): 11.3MM **Privately Held**
WEB: www.bestdoor.us
SIC: 3442 Garage doors, overhead: metal; rolling doors for industrial buildings or warehouses, metal; hangar doors, metal

(G-5433)
BETWELL OIL & GAS COMPANY (PA)
8083 Nw 103rd St (33016-2201)
P.O. Box 22577, Hialeah (33002-2577)
PHONE.................................305 821-8300
Lowell S Dunn II, *President*
EMP: 5 **EST:** 1981
SQ FT: 10,000
SALES (est): 1.6MM **Privately Held**
SIC: 1381 Directional drilling oil & gas wells

(G-5434)
BIODEGRADABLE PACKAGING CORP
9775 Nw 80th Ave (33016-2315)
PHONE.................................305 824-1164
Frades Sanchez Sr, *President*
Frades Sanchez Jr, *Vice Pres*
Diane Sanchezm, *Manager*
EMP: 17 **EST:** 1989
SQ FT: 14,000
SALES (est): 3.9MM **Privately Held**
SIC: 2631 2653 Paperboard mills; corrugated & solid fiber boxes

(G-5435)
DONOSO PRINTING CORP
9811 Nw 80th Ave (33016-2347)
PHONE.................................786 508-9426
Carlos Donoso, *Principal*
EMP: 9 **EST:** 2014
SALES (est): 364.4K **Privately Held**
WEB: www.tshirtprintingabc.com
SIC: 2752 Commercial printing, offset

(G-5436)
FLORIDA TRUCK PARTS
13115 W Okeechobee Rd # 101 (33018-6056)
PHONE.................................786 251-8614
Nubia Conner, *President*
Nubia Miranda, *Admin Sec*
EMP: 8 **EST:** 2012
SALES (est): 606.6K **Privately Held**
SIC: 3713 Truck bodies & parts

(G-5437)
FRUITFUL LLC
Also Called: Fruitful International
10030 Nw 79th Ave Hleahg (33016-2408)
PHONE.................................954 534-9828
Angel Rodriguez, *CEO*
Mario Arrue, *President*
EMP: 5 **EST:** 2018
SALES (est): 498.4K **Privately Held**
SIC: 2844 Toilet preparations

(G-5438)
IESC DIESEL CORP
Also Called: Hd Kit
13202 Nw 107th Ave Unit 4 (33018-1289)
PHONE.................................305 470-9306
Laura Paret, *President*
Jose Paret, *Vice Pres*
Stan Rodriguez, *Sales Staff*
◆ **EMP:** 5 **EST:** 2003
SQ FT: 2,000
SALES (est): 888.9K **Privately Held**
WEB: www.heavydutykits.com
SIC: 3714 Motor vehicle parts & accessories

(G-5439)
JTF VENTURES LLC
Also Called: Advak Techologies
7889 Nw 98th St (33016-2428)
P.O. Box 171034, Hialeah (33017-1034)
PHONE.................................305 556-5156
Tania Garza, *CEO*
Simon Pineda, *General Mgr*
EMP: 7 **EST:** 1994
SQ FT: 10,000
SALES (est): 1MM **Privately Held**
SIC: 3089 Injection molding of plastics

(G-5440)
LA EXPERIENCIA CRANKSHAFT
9910 Nw 80th Ave Unit 2m (33016-2322)
PHONE.................................305 823-6161
Jacobo Ulloa, *President*
EMP: 7 **EST:** 2000
SALES (est): 458.1K **Privately Held**
SIC: 3714 Crankshaft assemblies, motor vehicle

(G-5441)
LED ARE US LLC (PA)
9840 Nw 77th Ave (33016-2421)
PHONE.................................305 823-2803
Norton Hinojosa, *Project Mgr*
Fabiola Verri, *Purch Mgr*
Armando Garcia, *Sales Staff*
James Knips, *Mng Member*
▼ **EMP:** 8 **EST:** 2011
SALES (est): 5MM **Privately Held**
WEB: www.ledareus.com
SIC: 3674 5063 Light emitting diodes; lighting fixtures; light bulbs & related supplies

(G-5442)
LUMINOSO LLC
Also Called: Led Lighting
9800 Nw 78th Ave (33016-2402)
PHONE.................................305 364-8099
James Knips, *Manager*
EMP: 6 **EST:** 2013
SALES (est): 658.5K **Privately Held**
WEB: www.luminosoled.com
SIC: 3674 Light emitting diodes

(G-5443)
MARBLE LITE PRODUCTS CORP
9920 Nw 79th Ave (33016-2406)
PHONE.................................305 557-8766
Nestor Perez, *President*
Juan Miguel Blanco, *Vice Pres*
Magda Larrauri, *Vice Pres*
Gustavo Perez, *Vice Pres*
Tony Riestra, *Vice Pres*
◆ **EMP:** 28 **EST:** 1978
SQ FT: 16,000
SALES (est): 4.3MM **Privately Held**
WEB: www.marblelite.com
SIC: 3281 Marble, building: cut & shaped

(G-5444)
NUNEZ MACHINE SHOP INC
9809 Nw 80th Ave (33016-2333)
PHONE.................................786 615-4261
Eugene Nunez, *President*
EMP: 14 **EST:** 2015

▲ = Import ▼=Export
◆ =Import/Export

SALES (est): 837K **Privately Held**
SIC: 3599 Machine shop, jobbing & repair

(G-5445)
OCC MY STONE LLC
10090 Nw 80th Ct Apt 1238 (33016-2239)
PHONE.................................786 352-1567
Oscar Castillo, *Mng Member*
EMP: 8 EST: 2013
SALES (est): 2MM **Privately Held**
SIC: 1411 Granite dimension stone

(G-5446)
PAN AMERICAN GRAPHIC INC
9745 Nw 80th Ave (33016-2315)
P.O. Box 524149, Miami (33152-4149)
PHONE.................................305 885-1962
Martin Roca, *President*
Elba Roca, *Vice Pres*
Dan Lincoln, *Accounts Exec*
Danielle Roca, *Sales Staff*
Magda Luna, *Admin Asst*
◆ EMP: 26 EST: 1976
SQ FT: 4,000
SALES (est): 7.2MM **Privately Held**
WEB: www.panamgraphic.com
SIC: 2752 Commercial printing, offset

(G-5447)
PETRUJ CHEMICAL CORP
8055 Nw 98th St (33016-2319)
PHONE.................................305 556-1271
Raul Perez-Trujillo, *President*
Casandra Perez-Trujillo, *Vice Pres*
Adrian Garcia, *Manager*
Al Morgan, *Software Dev*
◆ EMP: 10 EST: 1979
SQ FT: 5,000
SALES (est): 1.9MM **Privately Held**
SIC: 2842 Degreasing solvent

(G-5448)
POWER SUSPENSION & PARTS LLC
13550 Nw 107th Ave Unit D (33018-1176)
PHONE.................................305 986-2235
Luis San Martin, *Mng Member*
EMP: 7 EST: 2020
SALES (est): 2.3MM **Privately Held**
SIC: 3714 Motor vehicle parts & accessories

(G-5449)
ROLLING SHIELD INCORPORATED
9875 Nw 79th Ave (33016-2424)
PHONE.................................305 436-6661
Jose A Delgado, *President*
Daniel Hazinski, *Production*
Faustino Mora, *Controller*
Yaris Ovalles, *Clerk*
◆ EMP: 23 EST: 1993
SQ FT: 50,000
SALES (est): 4.6MM **Privately Held**
WEB: www.rollingshield.com
SIC: 3442 3354 3444 Shutters, door or window: metal; aluminum extruded products; awnings, sheet metal

(G-5450)
ROLLING SHIELD PARTS INC
Also Called: Rollingshield
9875 Nw 79th Ave (33016-2424)
PHONE.................................305 436-6661
Jose Delgado, *President*
◆ EMP: 18 EST: 1995
SALES (est): 3.5MM **Privately Held**
WEB: www.rollingshield.com
SIC: 3442 3444 5999 Shutters, door or window: metal; awnings, sheet metal; awnings

(G-5451)
SOS FOOD LAB LLC (PA)
14802 Nw 107th Ave Unit 5 (33018-1238)
PHONE.................................305 594-9933
Jessica Brack, *CEO*
Stella Koniecpolski, *President*
Ludwig Kahn, *Principal*
Beatrice Ableton, *Vice Pres*
Immanuel Decastro, *Purchasing*
▲ EMP: 24 EST: 1984
SQ FT: 10,000

SALES (est): 5MM **Privately Held**
WEB: www.sosfoodlab.com
SIC: 2099 2086 Food preparations; water, pasteurized: packaged in cans, bottles, etc.

(G-5452)
SPACE FLYERS INC
11115 W Okeechobee Rd # 1 (33018-4277)
PHONE.................................305 219-6990
EMP: 8 EST: 2016
SALES (est): 97.7K **Privately Held**
WEB: www.spaceflyers.com
SIC: 2752 Commercial printing, offset

(G-5453)
UNIVERSAL WELDING SERVICE CO
9921 Nw 80th Ave Unit 1u (33016-2363)
PHONE.................................305 898-9130
EMP: 8 EST: 2018
SALES (est): 546.9K **Privately Held**
SIC: 3441 Fabricated structural metal

High Springs
Alachua County

(G-5454)
COMMERCIAL GATES AND ELC LLC
Also Called: Greg Pyle Enterprises
27317 Nw 78th Ave (32643-9754)
PHONE.................................386 454-2329
Greg Tyle, *Owner*
EMP: 10 EST: 2014
SALES (est): 2MM **Privately Held**
WEB:
www.commercialgatesandelectric.com
SIC: 3699 1731 Electrical equipment & supplies; electronic controls installation

(G-5455)
HALCYON MANUFACTURING INC
24587 Nw 178th Pl (32643-2305)
PHONE.................................386 454-0811
Jarrod Jablonski, *President*
Mary Townsend, *Vice Pres*
Ken Charlesworth, *Sales Mgr*
Orie Braun, *Sales Staff*
Corey Jablonski, *Executive*
◆ EMP: 30 EST: 1999
SALES (est): 5.8MM **Privately Held**
WEB: www.halcyon.net
SIC: 3949 Skin diving equipment, scuba type

(G-5456)
THEMEWORKS INCORPORATED
17594 High Sprng Main St (32643-0529)
PHONE.................................386 454-7500
Robert S Gill, *President*
Ryan Kremser, *Vice Pres*
Joe Gazdun, *Foreman/Supr*
Heather Tchou, *Purch Agent*
EMP: 104 EST: 1995
SQ FT: 54,000
SALES (est): 12.2MM **Privately Held**
WEB: www.themeworks.com
SIC: 3999 Theatrical scenery

(G-5457)
WOOD SCAPES INTERIORS
26509 W Us Highway 27 (32643-2096)
PHONE.................................386 454-1540
Petra Johnson, *Owner*
EMP: 6 EST: 2015
SALES (est): 397.2K **Privately Held**
WEB: www.woodscapesinteriors.com
SIC: 2434 Wood kitchen cabinets

(G-5458)
ZENITHTECH INDUSTRIES INC
27124 Nw 203rd Pl (32643-1600)
PHONE.................................386 454-7630
EMP: 8 EST: 2008
SALES (est): 490K **Privately Held**
SIC: 3999 Mfg Misc Products

Highland Beach
Palm Beach County

(G-5459)
ARFONA PRINTING LLC
1121 Bel Air Dr Apt 4 (33487-4229)
PHONE.................................312 339-0215
Justin Marks, *Principal*
Clay Teufel, *Principal*
Mark Teufel, *Manager*
EMP: 8 EST: 2020
SALES (est): 431.9K **Privately Held**
SIC: 2752 Commercial printing, lithographic

(G-5460)
GMX TECHNOLOGIES LLC
Also Called: Kgs Agro Group
1111 Russell Dr Apt A (33487-4278)
PHONE.................................917 697-0211
Arnold Simon, *CEO*
EMP: 8 EST: 2013
SALES (est): 2MM **Privately Held**
SIC: 2879 8731 Agricultural chemicals; biotechnical research, commercial

(G-5461)
IMPRESS3D LLC
1121 Bel Air Dr Apt 4 (33487-4229)
PHONE.................................312 339-0215
Mark Teufel,
EMP: 8 EST: 2020
SALES (est): 750K **Privately Held**
WEB: www.impress3d.com
SIC: 3843 Dental equipment & supplies

(G-5462)
PGH INDUSTRIES LTD
1016 Bel Air Dr (33487-4206)
PHONE.................................847 849-0800
Paul Herskovitz, *Administration*
EMP: 7 EST: 2016
SALES (est): 137.7K **Privately Held**
SIC: 3999 Manufacturing industries

Hilliard
Nassau County

(G-5463)
G HADDOCK ROWLAND INC
376488 Kings Ferry Rd (32046-6372)
PHONE.................................904 845-2725
Rowland G Haddock, *President*
EMP: 8 EST: 1996
SQ FT: 1,305
SALES (est): 733.4K **Privately Held**
SIC: 2411 7389 Logging;

(G-5464)
GEIGER LOGGING INC
28714 Yellow Rose Ln (32046-2339)
P.O. Box 1050 (32046-1050)
PHONE.................................904 845-7534
Zenous R Geiger Jr, *President*
Karyn N Geiger, *Vice Pres*
EMP: 25 EST: 1997
SQ FT: 1,000
SALES (est): 3MM **Privately Held**
WEB: geiger-logging-inc.business.site
SIC: 2411 Logging camps & contractors

(G-5465)
GREG FRANKLIN ENTERPRISES INC
Also Called: Franklin Equipment
551797 Us Highway 1 (32046-8821)
P.O. Box 809 (32046-0809)
PHONE.................................904 675-9129
Gregory W Franklin, *President*
Carrol E Franklin, *Admin Sec*
EMP: 14 EST: 2014
SALES (est): 1.8MM **Privately Held**
SIC: 3524 5231 Blowers & vacuums, lawn; paint brushes, rollers, sprayers & other supplies

(G-5466)
HARRY PICKETT
Also Called: Pickett Logging
37752 Kings Ferry Rd (32046-6526)
PHONE.................................904 845-4643

Harry Pickett, *President*
Julie Pickett, *Vice Pres*
EMP: 8 EST: 2002
SQ FT: 2,717
SALES (est): 994.5K **Privately Held**
SIC: 2411 Logging camps & contractors

(G-5467)
HOBBS TRUCKING LLC
15616 County Road 108 (32046-5202)
PHONE.................................904 463-5681
Benjamin F Hobbs, *Principal*
EMP: 7 EST: 2017
SALES (est): 280.1K **Privately Held**
SIC: 2411 Logging

(G-5468)
JOHNS & CONNER INC
15924 County Road 108 (32046-6700)
P.O. Box 1319 (32046-1319)
PHONE.................................904 845-4430
Charles E Johns, *Principal*
EMP: 6 EST: 2011
SALES (est): 785.5K **Privately Held**
SIC: 2411 Logging camps & contractors

(G-5469)
JOHNS & CONNER LOGGING INC
15924 County Road 108 (32046-6700)
P.O. Box 1319 (32046-1319)
PHONE.................................904 845-4430
Charles E Johns, *President*
EMP: 9 EST: 1970
SALES (est): 229.2K **Privately Held**
SIC: 2411 Logging camps & contractors

(G-5470)
JOHNS & CONNOR INC
28244 Pond View Cir (32046-7254)
PHONE.................................904 845-4541
Charles E Johns, *President*
Donald B Connor, *Vice Pres*
Donald Connor, *Vice Pres*
EMP: 10 EST: 1972
SALES (est): 210.6K **Privately Held**
WEB: www.johnsconner.com
SIC: 2411 Logging camps & contractors

(G-5471)
LARRY C CRIBB
28145 Enterprise Dr (32046-2316)
PHONE.................................904 845-2804
Larry C Cribb, *Principal*
EMP: 8 EST: 2010
SALES (est): 160.4K **Privately Held**
SIC: 2491 Structural lumber & timber, treated wood

(G-5472)
P & S LOGGING INC
15864 County Road 108 (32046-6711)
P.O. Box 969 (32046-0969)
PHONE.................................904 845-4256
Timothy R Pickett, *President*
Susan Pickett, *Admin Sec*
EMP: 9 EST: 2002
SALES (est): 480.3K **Privately Held**
SIC: 2411 Logging camps & contractors

(G-5473)
R & M LOGGING INC
17313 Bell Rd (32046-5232)
PHONE.................................904 813-4877
Ricky L Hodges, *President*
EMP: 7 EST: 2003
SALES (est): 149.6K **Privately Held**
SIC: 2411 Logging camps & contractors

(G-5474)
REMAS DRAPERIES ETC INC
27777 Conner Nelson Rd (32046-7607)
PHONE.................................904 845-9300
Latrelle Murphy, *Owner*
Ann Combs, *Manager*
EMP: 7 EST: 1958
SQ FT: 5,000
SALES (est): 494.6K **Privately Held**
SIC: 2221 5714 2392 2391 Draperies & drapery fabrics, manmade fiber & silk; draperies; household furnishings; curtains & draperies

G E O G R A P H I C

(G-5475)
RIVERLAND LOGGING INC
25190 County Road 121 (32046-5368)
PHONE..................................904 845-4326
Mike Van Zant, *President*
EMP: 6 EST: 2003
SALES (est): 979.4K **Privately Held**
WEB: www.riverlandlogging.com
SIC: 2411 Logging camps & contractors

(G-5476)
SMITH MACHINE SERVICES INC
552121 Us Highway 1 (32046-2326)
P.O. Box 339 (32046-0339)
PHONE..................................904 845-2002
Barry D Smith, *CEO*
EMP: 7 EST: 1990
SQ FT: 2,000
SALES (est): 605.5K **Privately Held**
SIC: 3549 Metalworking machinery

(G-5477)
STELLAR ON-SITE LLC
27167 Betina Dr (32046-3500)
PHONE..................................904 945-1908
Charles R Carroll Sr, *Manager*
EMP: 15 EST: 2018
SALES (est): 3MM **Privately Held**
WEB: www.stellaronsite.com
SIC: 2611 Pulp mills, mechanical & recycling processing

(G-5478)
VAN ZANT TIMBER INCORPORATED
373120 Kings Ferry Rd (32046-6617)
PHONE..................................904 845-4661
John Van Zant, *CEO*
Mary Van Zant, *Corp Secy*
EMP: 6 EST: 2002
SQ FT: 2,667
SALES (est): 348.8K **Privately Held**
SIC: 2411 Logging

Hobe Sound
Martin County

(G-5479)
ARONS TOWING & RECOVERY INC
12872 Se Suzanne Dr (33455-9713)
P.O. Box 2391, Stuart (34995-2391)
PHONE..................................772 220-1151
Aron Dames, *President*
EMP: 9 EST: 1987
SALES (est): 1.1MM **Privately Held**
WEB: www.aronstowingandrecovery.com
SIC: 3711 7549 1629 Wreckers (tow truck), assembly of; towing service, automotive; land clearing contractor

(G-5480)
C MIKE ROACH INC
4847 Se Longleaf Pl (33455-8108)
PHONE..................................864 882-1101
Clyde Roach, *President*
Annie Smith, *Manager*
EMP: 10 EST: 2012
SQ FT: 15,000
SALES (est): 834.4K **Privately Held**
SIC: 3432 Lawn hose nozzles & sprinklers

(G-5481)
COUNTY CARDBOARD LLC
8970 Se Bridge Rd (33455-5311)
PHONE..................................772 546-1983
Jed Brownie, *Principal*
EMP: 7 EST: 2014
SALES (est): 74.3K **Privately Held**
SIC: 2631 Cardboard

(G-5482)
EASTGATE PUBLISHING INC
9015 Se Athena St (33455-5501)
PHONE..................................772 286-0101
Robert Ritter, *President*
EMP: 6 EST: 1997
SALES (est): 304.4K **Privately Held**
WEB: www.eastgate.com
SIC: 2741 Newsletter publishing

(G-5483)
SIMPLEPIN LLC
8954 Se Bridge Rd (33455-5311)
PHONE..................................800 727-4136
Metod Popolnik, *Mng Member*
EMP: 10 EST: 2020
SALES (est): 1MM **Privately Held**
WEB: www.simplepin.com
SIC: 7372 Application computer software

(G-5484)
TEES PLEASE INC
9278 Se Sharon St (33455-6920)
PHONE..................................857 472-3391
Barbara McLaughlin, *Principal*
EMP: 9 EST: 2018
SALES (est): 259K **Privately Held**
WEB: tees-please-fla.myshopify.com
SIC: 2759 Screen printing

(G-5485)
TREASURE COAST SEALING CO
8949 Se Bridge Rd (33455-5312)
PHONE..................................772 834-5014
Steve Middleton, *Principal*
EMP: 8 EST: 2006
SALES (est): 985.7K **Privately Held**
SIC: 2911 Asphalt or asphaltic materials, made in refineries

(G-5486)
ULTRA TUFF MANUFACTURING INC
8845 Se Robwyn St (33455-5326)
PHONE..................................970 252-9457
▼ EMP: 9 EST: 1999
SALES (est): 987.9K **Privately Held**
SIC: 2851 Paints & allied products

Holiday
Pasco County

(G-5487)
ADMIRAL PRINTING INC
Also Called: Fantasy Escapes
5412 Provost Dr Unit 12 (34690-2904)
PHONE..................................727 938-9589
Leonore Sitton, *President*
Melanie Land, *Production*
Steven Riddle, *Sales Mgr*
Anthony El-Ghoul, *Accounts Exec*
Nate Touchberry, *Accounts Exec*
EMP: 6 EST: 1993
SALES (est): 524.9K **Privately Held**
WEB: admiral.win.net
SIC: 2759 Screen printing

(G-5488)
AGM PUBLISHING INC
3049 Coldwell Dr (34691-4842)
PHONE..................................727 934-9993
Alfred G Messina, *President*
EMP: 7 EST: 2005
SALES (est): 72.5K **Privately Held**
SIC: 2741 Miscellaneous publishing

(G-5489)
ARTEX PUBLISHING INC
3130 Westridge Dr (34691-2538)
PHONE..................................727 944-4117
Les Zielinski, *President*
EMP: 6 EST: 1985
SALES (est): 350.4K **Privately Held**
SIC: 2731 Books: publishing only

(G-5490)
B224 USA CO
2508 Baywood Dr (34690-3801)
PHONE..................................786 598-8805
Stella Valerie Sampsonidi, *President*
EMP: 5 EST: 2020
SALES (est): 500K **Privately Held**
WEB: www.b224perfumes.com
SIC: 2844 Perfumes & colognes

(G-5491)
BUZZ POP COCKTAILS CORPORATION (PA)
4407 Buena Vista Ln (34691-5454)
PHONE..................................727 275-9848
Joseph Isaacs, *CEO*
Christos Argeras, *Accounts Mgr*
EMP: 12 EST: 2016

SQ FT: 1,850
SALES (est): 1.5MM **Privately Held**
SIC: 2085 2024 Cocktails, alcoholic; sorbets, non-dairy based

(G-5492)
BXD ENTERPRISES INC
4148 Louis Ave (34691-5612)
PHONE..................................727 937-4100
Robin Selby, *President*
Gail Selby, *Vice Pres*
▲ EMP: 7 EST: 1998
SALES (est): 1.3MM
SALES (corp-wide): 14MM **Privately Held**
SIC: 3053 Oil seals, rubber
HQ: Premiere Seals Holdings, Llc
4148 Louis Ave
Holiday FL 34691
727 937-4100

(G-5493)
E-SEA RIDER LLC
Also Called: E-Sea Rider Marine Bean Bags
4054 Louis Ave (34691-5600)
PHONE..................................727 863-3333
Patrick M Bennett,
▼ EMP: 6 EST: 2004
SQ FT: 5,000
SALES (est): 650K **Privately Held**
WEB: www.e-searider.com
SIC: 2519

(G-5494)
GREAT BAY DISTRIBUTORS INC
2310 Starkey Rd (34690)
PHONE..................................727 584-8626
Scott Penland, *Vice Pres*
Sandy Ho, *Human Res Dir*
Brian Costanza, *Accounts Mgr*
Karl Fratilla, *Accounts Mgr*
Jeffrey Patterson, *Accounts Mgr*
EMP: 200
SALES (corp-wide): 61.6MM **Privately Held**
WEB: www.greatbaybud.com
SIC: 2082 Beer (alcoholic beverage)
PA: Great Bay Distributors, Inc.
2750 Eagle Ave N
Saint Petersburg FL 33716
727 584-8626

(G-5495)
GUARDIAN SOLAR LLC
4366 Louis Ave Ste 106 (34691-5661)
PHONE..................................727 504-2790
Glen D Upchurch, *President*
▲ EMP: 15 EST: 2007
SALES (est): 2.9MM **Privately Held**
WEB: www.guardiansolar.com
SIC: 3674 Solar cells

(G-5496)
H & F INDUSTRIES CORP
3341 Wiltshire Dr (34691-1351)
PHONE..................................727 271-4974
Sally E Hunter, *Principal*
EMP: 7 EST: 2016
SALES (est): 65.1K **Privately Held**
SIC: 3999 Manufacturing industries

(G-5497)
HARBERSON RV PINELLAS LLC
2112 Us Highway 19 (34691-4347)
PHONE..................................727 937-6176
Mark Hollan, *Manager*
EMP: 23
SALES (corp-wide): 11.9MM **Privately Held**
WEB: www.harbersonrv-pinellas.com
SIC: 3365 7538 5561 Aluminum foundries; general automotive repair shops; recreational vehicle dealers
PA: Harberson Rv Pinellas Llc
17028 Us Highway 19 N
Clearwater FL 33764
727 539-8714

(G-5498)
HARBORTECH PLASTICS LLC
3151 Grand Blvd (34690-2244)
PHONE..................................727 944-2425
Bill D Price, *Engineer*
Billy Price, *Engineer*
Chris Tubergen, *Sales Staff*
EMP: 10 EST: 2007

SALES (est): 982.1K **Privately Held**
WEB: www.harbortechplastics.com
SIC: 3089 Injection molding of plastics

(G-5499)
HIGH NOON UNLIMITED INC
Also Called: High Noon Holsters
4339 Buena Vista Ln (34691-5404)
P.O. Box 1923, Tarpon Springs (34688-1923)
PHONE..................................727 939-2701
Claire V Inabinet, *President*
George B Inabinet III, *COO*
EMP: 8 EST: 1997
SQ FT: 4,500
SALES (est): 570K **Privately Held**
WEB: www.highnoonholsters.com
SIC: 3199 Holsters, leather; dog furnishings: collars, leashes, muzzles, etc.: leather

(G-5500)
INFINITE PRINT LLC
1014 Us Highway 19 # 114 (34691-5634)
PHONE..................................727 942-2121
EMP: 5 EST: 2017
SALES (est): 456.8K **Privately Held**
WEB: www.infiniteprint.com
SIC: 2752 Commercial printing, offset

(G-5501)
INSTANT PRINTING & COPY CENTER
3307 Us Highway 19 (34691-1847)
PHONE..................................727 849-1199
Robert Wagner, *President*
EMP: 5 EST: 2003
SALES (est): 395.1K **Privately Held**
SIC: 2752 Commercial printing, offset

(G-5502)
MARY LAME WROUGHT IRON & ALUM
1022 Us Highway 19 (34691-5635)
PHONE..................................727 934-2879
Richard Price, *President*
Sharon Price, *Treasurer*
Steven Katona, *Admin Sec*
EMP: 9 EST: 1952
SQ FT: 10,000
SALES (est): 673.8K **Privately Held**
WEB: www.marylame.com
SIC: 3446 3334 3354 Architectural metalwork; primary aluminum; aluminum extruded products

(G-5503)
PEPSI-COLA BOTTLING CO TAMPA
5406 Whippoorwill Dr (34690-2162)
PHONE..................................727 942-3664
Theodore Soper, *Engineer*
Tomek Targosz, *Engineer*
John Torres, *Sales Associate*
Berry Joyce, *Manager*
EMP: 241
SALES (corp-wide): 70.3B **Publicly Held**
WEB: www.pepsico.com
SIC: 2086 Carbonated soft drinks, bottled & canned
HQ: Pepsi-Cola Bottling Company Of Tampa
11315 N 30th St
Tampa FL 33612
813 971-2550

(G-5504)
SUN PRINT MANAGEMENT LLC
5441 Provost Dr (34690-2939)
PHONE..................................727 945-0255
Nikolle Smith, *VP Opers*
Laura Jones, *Accounts Mgr*
Bruce Rushton, *Accounts Exec*
Chelsea Schlimm, *Accounts Exec*
Peter Wagner, *Mng Member*
EMP: 49 EST: 2006
SALES (est): 12.6MM **Privately Held**
WEB: www.sunprint.com
SIC: 2752 3955 7699 5112 Commercial printing, lithographic; print cartridges for laser & other computer printers; photocopy machine repair; laserjet supplies; business machine & electronic equipment rental services

(G-5505)
SUNCOAST TONER CARTRIDGE INC
5441 Provost Dr (34690-2939)
PHONE....................727 945-0255
Peter Wagner, *President*
Jack Thompson, *Corp Secy*
Stephen Miklos, *Vice Pres*
Steve Miklos, *Vice Pres*
EMP: 10 EST: 1995
SQ FT: 3,000
SALES (est): 232.1K **Privately Held**
SIC: 3955 Print cartridges for laser & other computer printers

(G-5506)
VICTORY CUSTOM CABINETRY
2623 Grand Blvd (34690-3002)
PHONE....................727 937-2284
Victor Samulian, *Principal*
EMP: 7 EST: 2004
SALES (est): 53K **Privately Held**
SIC: 2434 Wood kitchen cabinets

(G-5507)
WROBEL INDUSTRIES INC
1004 Us Highway 19 # 202 (34691-5632)
PHONE....................727 560-6850
Hayden Wrobel, *President*
EMP: 7 EST: 2007
SALES (est): 104.1K **Privately Held**
SIC: 3999 Manufacturing industries

Hollister
Putnam County

(G-5508)
KEY LOGGING
229 Lynn Dr (32147)
P.O. Box 486 (32147-0486)
PHONE....................386 328-6984
Randall Key Jr, *President*
EMP: 6 EST: 2001
SALES (est): 742.3K **Privately Held**
SIC: 2411 Logging camps & contractors

Holly Hill
Volusia County

(G-5509)
AMERICAN TECHNICAL FURN LLC
831 Carswell Ave (32117-3513)
PHONE....................866 239-4204
John Ashman, *COO*
Greg Schmidt, *Sales Mgr*
Heath Jones, *Marketing Staff*
Dayna Slater, *Clerk*
EMP: 5 EST: 2012
SALES (est): 6MM **Privately Held**
WEB: www.americantechnicalfurniture.com
SIC: 2599 Factory furniture & fixtures

(G-5510)
AMERITECH ENERGY CORPORATION
1115 Enterprise Ct Ste L (32117-2683)
PHONE....................610 730-1733
Warren Ellis Fondrie, *President*
Stephen Searfoss Sr, *Corp Secy*
Warren Ellis, *CTO*
▲ EMP: 8 EST: 2014
SALES (est): 643K **Privately Held**
WEB: www.ameritechenergy.com
SIC: 3648 5074 7699 Lighting equipment; outdoor lighting equipment; heating equipment & panels, solar; battery service & repair

(G-5511)
AQUARIAN BATH INC
46 High Ridge Rd (32117-1875)
PHONE....................310 919-0220
Cory Trusty, *Principal*
EMP: 8 EST: 2012
SALES (est): 255.1K **Privately Held**
WEB: www.aquarianbath.com
SIC: 2844 Toilet preparations

(G-5512)
CC MACHINE INC (PA)
Also Called: Custom Wheel
618 Ridgewood Ave Ste B (32117-3604)
PHONE....................888 577-0144
John Purner, *President*
▲ EMP: 17 EST: 1992
SQ FT: 8,000
SALES (est): 2.7MM **Privately Held**
SIC: 3714 Motor vehicle parts & accessories

(G-5513)
ENCORE STONE PRODUCTS LLC
Also Called: Paramount Stoneworks
711 Commercial Dr (32117-3442)
PHONE....................352 428-1542
Brett Maugeri,
▲ EMP: 22 EST: 2011
SALES (est): 2.5MM **Privately Held**
WEB: www.encorestone.com
SIC: 3272 Paving materials, prefabricated concrete

(G-5514)
INSPEC SOLUTIONS LLC (PA)
330 Carswell Ave (32117-4416)
P.O. Box 730732, Ormond Beach (32173-0732)
PHONE....................866 467-7320
Timothy Alderson, *Business Mgr*
Mohamed Yousef, *Manager*
Kimberly Brown, *Manager*
EMP: 17 EST: 2017
SALES (est): 3.7MM **Privately Held**
WEB: www.inspecsolutions.com
SIC: 2844 5999 Toilet preparations; cosmetics

(G-5515)
KENCO SIGNS AWNING LLC
1538 Garden Ave (32117-2110)
PHONE....................386 672-1590
Raymond Webb, *Owner*
EMP: 15 EST: 2003
SQ FT: 1,900
SALES (est): 2.5MM **Privately Held**
WEB: www.kenco2000inc.com
SIC: 3993 Electric signs

(G-5516)
MOTORSPORT MARKETING INC
Also Called: Classic Motor Sport
915 Ridgewood Ave (32117-3519)
PHONE....................386 239-0523
Timothy P Suddard, *President*
Marjorie J Suddard, *Vice Pres*
Kevin Maffett, *Sales Dir*
Nicole Suddard, *Mktg Coord*
Rick Goolsby, *Manager*
▼ EMP: 40 EST: 1984
SQ FT: 4,800
SALES (est): 4.6MM **Privately Held**
WEB: www.grassrootsmotorsports.com
SIC: 2721 Magazines: publishing only, not printed on site

(G-5517)
NORTH AMERICAN DIAGNOSTICS LLC
Also Called: Manufacturing
618 Ridgewood Ave Ste 100 (32117-3604)
PHONE....................855 752-6879
Elizabeth Lashinsky, *Manager*
EMP: 125 EST: 2020
SALES (est): 5.3MM **Privately Held**
SIC: 3841 Medical instruments & equipment, blood & bone work

(G-5518)
TOWNSEND SIGNS INC
515 Lpga Blvd (32117-2626)
PHONE....................386 255-1955
Alan Townsend, *President*
John Townsend, *Vice Pres*
Tom Townsend, *Vice Pres*
Dena Townsend, *Admin Sec*
EMP: 8 EST: 1980
SQ FT: 4,500
SALES (est): 990.5K **Privately Held**
WEB: www.signsbytownsend.com
SIC: 3993 3444 Electric signs; displays & cutouts, window & lobby; sheet metalwork

Hollywood
Broward County

(G-5519)
A-1 CUSTOM MICA INC
5805 Plunkett St (33023-2347)
PHONE....................954 893-0063
Michael Bencivenga, *President*
Harry Malles, *Vice Pres*
EMP: 5 EST: 1987
SQ FT: 2,000
SALES (est): 500.4K **Privately Held**
WEB: www.a1custommica.com
SIC: 2434 Wood kitchen cabinets

(G-5520)
AB ELECTRIC MOTORS & PUMPS
6013 Johnson St (33024-6027)
PHONE....................954 322-6900
Domingo Garcia, *President*
Jesus Garcia, *Sales Staff*
EMP: 27 EST: 2001
SALES (est): 2.3MM **Privately Held**
WEB: www.abemap.com
SIC: 3621 Electric motor & generator parts

(G-5521)
AGISUPREME LLC
2252 Hayes St (33020-3438)
PHONE....................818 232-6699
Irit Bruchim,
EMP: 9 EST: 2017
SALES (est): 745K **Privately Held**
SIC: 3441 Fabricated structural metal

(G-5522)
AIR MARSHALL INC
2870 Stirling Rd Ste 110 (33020-1113)
PHONE....................954 843-0991
Donald Marshall Jr, *President*
Karen Cruz, *Controller*
Camille Urquhart, *Sales Staff*
EMP: 14 EST: 1989
SQ FT: 25,000
SALES (est): 3.2MM **Privately Held**
WEB: www.air-marshall.com
SIC: 3724 Aircraft engines & engine parts

(G-5523)
AIRCRAFT TECHNOLOGY INC
Also Called: ATI
3000 Taft St (33021-4441)
PHONE....................954 744-7602
Ryan Sadonis, *Engineer*
Thomas Irwin, *CFO*
Carlos Ibanez, *Director*
Elizabeth Letendre, *Admin Sec*
EMP: 40 EST: 1985
SQ FT: 25,000
SALES (est): 10.4MM **Publicly Held**
WEB: www.heico.com
SIC: 3724 Aircraft engines & engine parts
HQ: Heico Aerospace Holdings Corp.
3000 Taft St
Hollywood FL 33021
954 987-4000

(G-5524)
ALICO LIGHTING GROUP INC
140 S Dixie Hwy Unit 101 (33020-7332)
PHONE....................305 542-2648
EMP: 6 EST: 2006
SQ FT: 2,400
SALES (est): 2MM **Privately Held**
SIC: 3643 Mfg Conductive Wiring Devices

(G-5525)
ALL GREEN RECYCLING INC
811 Se 16th St Ste 105 (33024)
PHONE....................754 204-3707
Carlos Moreno, *President*
EMP: 8 EST: 2010
SALES (est): 78.5K **Privately Held**
WEB: www.allgreenrecycling.com
SIC: 2611 Pulp manufactured from waste or recycled paper

(G-5526)
ALLEGRA PRINT SIGNS MAIL
5846 Stirling Rd (33021-1527)
PHONE....................954 963-3886
EMP: 7 EST: 2014
SALES (est): 336.5K **Privately Held**
WEB: www.allegramarketingprint.com
SIC: 3993 2752 Signs & advertising specialties; commercial printing, offset

(G-5527)
ALMI INTL PLASTIC INDS INC
2227 N Federal Hwy (33020-2229)
PHONE....................954 920-6836
Abraham Lalo, *CEO*
▼ EMP: 6 EST: 1982
SQ FT: 6,000
SALES (est): 762.1K **Privately Held**
SIC: 2671 Plastic film, coated or laminated for packaging

(G-5528)
ANNETTE M WELLINGTON-HALL INC
5830 Sheridan St (33021-3253)
PHONE....................954 437-9880
Annette M Wellington, *Principal*
EMP: 14 EST: 2008
SALES (est): 319.9K **Privately Held**
SIC: 2511 Wood household furniture

(G-5529)
ARCO COMPUTER PRODUCTS LLC
Also Called: Data Protection Solutions
3100 N 29th Ct Ste 100 (33020-1321)
PHONE....................954 925-2688
Itzik Levy, *Mng Member*
EMP: 5 EST: 1989
SQ FT: 3,000
SALES (est): 712.2K **Privately Held**
WEB: www.ezd2d.com
SIC: 3577 Computer peripheral equipment

(G-5530)
ARTWORKS PRINTING ENTPS INC
5922 Liberty St (33021-3843)
PHONE....................954 893-7984
Sergio Pellecer, *President*
Gloria Pellecer, *Vice Pres*
EMP: 5 EST: 1991
SALES (est): 431.3K **Privately Held**
WEB: www.artworksprinting.com
SIC: 2752 2759 5199 Commercial printing, offset; screen printing; advertising specialties

(G-5531)
ATI BY SEA CO
11251 Rockinghorse Rd (33026-1355)
PHONE....................954 483-0526
Mohammed A Hussain, *Principal*
EMP: 8 EST: 2008
SALES (est): 263.5K **Privately Held**
SIC: 3312 Stainless steel

(G-5532)
ATK SALES CORP
121 S 61st Ter Ste B (33023-1376)
PHONE....................954 701-0465
Kravatz Alane, *Principal*
EMP: 7 EST: 2014
SALES (est): 78.8K **Privately Held**
SIC: 3764 Propulsion units for guided missiles & space vehicles

(G-5533)
AUDIOSHARK INC
2635 Sherman St (33020-1948)
PHONE....................954 591-9252
Robert Harvey, *Principal*
EMP: 7 EST: 2007
SALES (est): 98K **Privately Held**
SIC: 3651 Household audio & video equipment

(G-5534)
AUTOMATED PAPER CONVERTERS
400 S Dixie Hwy (33020-4914)
PHONE....................954 925-0721
Placido Barbeite, *President*
William Chouinard, *Sales Staff*
Larry Lipsitz, *Sales Staff*
Robert L Blumfield, *Admin Sec*
EMP: 7 EST: 1988
SALES (est): 857.7K **Privately Held**
WEB: www.apcinc.net
SIC: 2679 Paper products, converted

GEOGRAPHIC

(G-5535)
AWNINGS OF HOLLYWOOD INC
Also Called: American Made Awnings
5828 Washington St (33023-1947)
PHONE..................................954 963-7717
Gerald Thompson, *President*
Chris Thompson, *Vice Pres*
Lori Roman, *Human Res Mgr*
Brent Lalor, *Department Mgr*
Jerry Thompson, *Executive*
▼ EMP: 30 EST: 1972
SALES (est): 6.4MM **Privately Held**
WEB: www.thompsonarchitecturalproducts.com
SIC: 3446 2394 Stairs, fire escapes, balconies, railings & ladders; shades, canvas: made from purchased materials

(G-5536)
BABY FOOD CHEF LLC
Also Called: Soapy Chef, The
2905 W Aviary Dr (33026-3635)
PHONE..................................305 335-5990
Leanna Blacher, *Principal*
EMP: 6 EST: 2012
SALES (est): 375.2K **Privately Held**
WEB: www.babyfoodchef.com
SIC: 2099 Food preparations

(G-5537)
BACH DIAMONDS
2910 Oakwood Blvd (33020-7122)
PHONE..................................954 921-4069
Ted Olson, *Manager*
EMP: 7 EST: 1996
SALES (est): 125.4K **Privately Held**
SIC: 3915 Diamond cutting & polishing

(G-5538)
BAPTIST COMMUNICATIONS MISSION (HQ)
3400 Raleigh St (33021-3122)
PHONE..................................954 981-2271
Phil Brown, *Director*
Arthur Edgar, *Director*
Mickey Searcy, *Director*
EMP: 18 EST: 1975
SALES (est): 3.6MM
SALES (corp-wide): 110.9MM **Privately Held**
SIC: 2731 7812 Pamphlets: publishing & printing; audio-visual program production
PA: The International Mission Board Of The Southern Baptist Convention
3806 Monument Ave
Richmond VA 23230
804 353-0151

(G-5539)
BELT CORP
4032 N 29th Ave (33020-1012)
PHONE..................................954 505-7400
EMP: 10 EST: 2019
SALES (est): 1MM **Privately Held**
WEB: www.belt.com.co
SIC: 3312 Blast furnaces & steel mills

(G-5540)
BEST MANUFACTURING COMPANY
3282 N 29th Ct (33020-1320)
PHONE..................................954 922-1443
Eugene J Monsignore, *President*
Nancy Monsignore, *Corp Secy*
Eugene Monsignore Sr, *Shareholder*
◆ EMP: 10 EST: 1954
SQ FT: 20,000
SALES (est): 965.8K **Privately Held**
WEB: bestmanufacturing.8m.com
SIC: 3496 5031 Lath, woven wire; woven wire products; building materials, exterior; building materials, interior

(G-5541)
BLUE RIBBON TAG & LABEL CORP (PA)
4035 N 29th Ave (33020-1011)
PHONE..................................954 922-9292
Daniel Ferreiro, *President*
Dan Ferreiro, *Vice Pres*
Secundino Ferreiro, *Treasurer*
▼ EMP: 30 EST: 1980
SQ FT: 30,000
SALES (est): 6MM **Privately Held**
WEB: www.blueribbonlabel.com
SIC: 2672 2752 Labels (unprinted), gummed: made from purchased materials; tags, lithographed

(G-5542)
BLUE RIBBON TAG & LABEL OF PR
4035 N 29th Ave (33020-1011)
PHONE..................................787 858-5300
Robert Schwartztol, *President*
Secundino Ferreiro, *Vice Pres*
Victor Torres, *Vice Pres*
EMP: 10 EST: 1988
SQ FT: 12,000
SALES (est): 1.4MM
SALES (corp-wide): 6MM **Privately Held**
WEB: www.blueribbonlabel.com
SIC: 2759 Tags: printing; labels & seals: printing
PA: Blue Ribbon Tag & Label Corp.
4035 N 29th Ave
Hollywood FL 33020
954 922-9292

(G-5543)
BOMBASTIC GROUP INC
2029 Tyler St (33020-4518)
PHONE..................................754 232-2932
Michael L Patman Sr, *CEO*
EMP: 8 EST: 2018
SALES (est): 292.5K **Privately Held**
SIC: 1389 Construction, repair & dismantling services

(G-5544)
BUSINESS FORWARD INC
Also Called: Signs Now
3286 N 29th Ct (33020-1320)
PHONE..................................954 967-6730
Alan Bleiweiss, *President*
Elizabeth Fairchild, *Opers Dir*
EMP: 5 EST: 2004
SALES (est): 366.1K **Privately Held**
WEB: www.signsnow.com
SIC: 3993 Signs & advertising specialties

(G-5545)
CAAMACOSTA INC
5400 N 35th St (33021-2324)
PHONE..................................954 987-5895
Daniel Caamano, *Principal*
EMP: 7 EST: 2012
SALES (est): 100.9K **Privately Held**
SIC: 2051 Bread, all types (white, wheat, rye, etc): fresh or frozen

(G-5546)
CARD USA INC
201 N Ocean Dr Ste 200 (33019-1784)
PHONE..................................954 862-1300
Marc Rochman, *CEO*
Samuel Fridman, *President*
Samuel Guy Fridman, *COO*
Samuel G Fridman, *COO*
Janissa Khal, *Marketing Staff*
▼ EMP: 15 EST: 1996
SQ FT: 6,300
SALES (est): 2MM **Privately Held**
WEB: www.cardusa.com
SIC: 3089 5199 Identification cards, plastic; cards, plastic: unprinted

(G-5547)
CARDIOVASULAR INNOVATION INC
4000 Hollywood Blvd Ste 5 (33021-6751)
PHONE..................................512 517-7761
Michelle Noll, *President*
EMP: 7 EST: 2014
SALES (est): 109.5K **Privately Held**
SIC: 2834 Drugs acting on the cardiovascular system, except diagnostic

(G-5548)
CARLO MORELLI
Also Called: All Spring Manufacturing Inds
1926 Hollywood Blvd (33020-4532)
PHONE..................................954 241-1426
Carlo Moreilli, *Owner*
Carlo Morelli, *Owner*
EMP: 6 EST: 2013
SALES (est): 481K **Privately Held**
SIC: 3495 Wire springs

(G-5549)
CGC INDUSTRIES INC
200 N Dixie Hwy (33020-6705)
PHONE..................................954 923-2428
Stefan Pandos, *President*
EMP: 8 EST: 2005
SALES (est): 93.6K **Privately Held**
SIC: 3999 Manufacturing industries

(G-5550)
CITY OF HOLLYWOOD
Also Called: Hollywood Water Trtmnt Plant
3441 Hollywood Blvd Fl 2 (33021-6910)
PHONE..................................954 967-4230
Taylor Calhoun, *Manager*
Carlos Aguilera, *Manager*
EMP: 25 **Privately Held**
WEB: www.hollywoodfl.org
SIC: 3589 4941 Water treatment equipment, industrial; water supply
PA: Hollywood, City Of (Inc)
2600 Hollywood Blvd Ste B
Hollywood FL 33020
954 921-3231

(G-5551)
CKS PACKAGING INC
4020 N 29th Ter (33020-1020)
PHONE..................................954 925-9049
Jim Meyman, *Vice Pres*
John Beasley, *Plant Mgr*
Mike Nance, *Opers Mgr*
Joseph Bernard, *Prdtn Mgr*
James Eberle, *Maint Mgr*
EMP: 100
SALES (corp-wide): 539.6MM **Privately Held**
WEB: www.ckspackaging.com
SIC: 3089 3085 Plastic containers, except foam; plastics bottles
PA: C.K.S. Packaging, Inc.
350 Great Sw Pkwy
Atlanta GA 30336
404 691-8900

(G-5552)
CLASSIC CANVAS & UPHOLSTERY
1934 Cleveland St (33020-3134)
PHONE..................................954 850-4994
Elvin Torres, *Principal*
EMP: 7 EST: 2018
SALES (est): 195.3K **Privately Held**
SIC: 2211 Canvas

(G-5553)
COCA-COLA BEVERAGES FLA LLC
3350 Pembroke Rd (33021-8200)
PHONE..................................954 985-5000
Christina Cullen, *Business Mgr*
Don Droltz, *Branch Mgr*
Asif Ali, *Supervisor*
Steven Russell, *Supervisor*
EMP: 21
SALES (corp-wide): 366.5MM **Privately Held**
WEB: www.cocacolaflorida.com
SIC: 2086 5149 Bottled & canned soft drinks; soft drinks
PA: Coca-Cola Beverages Florida, Llc
10117 Princess Palm Ave
Tampa FL 33610
800 438-2653

(G-5554)
COCA-COLA COMPANY
3350 Pembroke Rd (33021-8200)
PHONE..................................954 985-5000
Rebecca Marquis, *General Mgr*
Melissa Cerda-Richards, *Regional Mgr*
Toris McGhee, *Area Mgr*
Carmen Neri, *Business Mgr*
Tanika Cabral, *Vice Pres*
EMP: 14
SALES (corp-wide): 33B **Publicly Held**
WEB: www.coca-colacompany.com
SIC: 2086 Bottled & canned soft drinks
PA: The Coca-Cola Company
1 Coca Cola Plz Nw
Atlanta GA 30313
404 676-2121

(G-5555)
CONCEPT ONE CUSTOM CABINE
5807 Dawson St (33023-1977)
PHONE..................................954 829-3505
Alphanso Brown, *Principal*
EMP: 7 EST: 2009
SALES (est): 62.9K **Privately Held**
SIC: 2434 Wood kitchen cabinets

(G-5556)
COSMESIS SKINCARE INC
Also Called: Goldfaden Skincare
3816 Hollywood Blvd (33021-6750)
PHONE..................................954 963-5090
Robert Goldfaden, *CEO*
EMP: 5 EST: 2004
SALES (est): 462.5K **Privately Held**
WEB: www.cosmesisskincare.com
SIC: 2844 Face creams or lotions

(G-5557)
CRAINS PRECIOUS METALS LLC
11607 Palmetto Way (33026-1231)
PHONE..................................954 536-8334
Gary A Crain, *Mng Member*
EMP: 7 EST: 2011
SALES (est): 57.6K **Privately Held**
SIC: 3339 Precious metals

(G-5558)
CRYOTHRAPY PAIN RLIEF PDTS INC
3460 Laurel Oaks Ln (33021-8441)
PHONE..................................954 364-8192
Hugo Torres, *President*
Gustavo Romero, *Sales Mgr*
◆ EMP: 6 EST: 2004
SALES (est): 379.8K **Privately Held**
SIC: 2834 Pharmaceutical preparations

(G-5559)
CSI AEROSPACE INC
3000 Taft St (33021-4441)
PHONE..................................954 961-9800
Jon Walkup, *Principal*
EMP: 11 EST: 2017
SALES (est): 3.4MM **Publicly Held**
WEB: www.heico.com
SIC: 3724 Aircraft engines & engine parts
PA: Heico Corporation
3000 Taft St
Hollywood FL 33021

(G-5560)
DALE PHOTO AND DIGITAL INC
2960 Simms St (33020-1511)
PHONE..................................954 925-0103
Elaine Farkas, *CFO*
Juliana Farkas, *Director*
David Farkas, *Director*
EMP: 12 EST: 2010
SALES (est): 1.4MM **Privately Held**
WEB: www.dalephotoanddigital.com
SIC: 3861 Photographic equipment & supplies

(G-5561)
DARNEL INC
Also Called: Crescent Garden
2331 Thomas St (33020-2038)
P.O. Box 10192, Uniondale NY (11555-0192)
PHONE..................................954 929-0085
Eli Papir, *President*
Joanne Papir, *Vice Pres*
◆ EMP: 11 EST: 1974
SALES (est): 3.7MM **Privately Held**
WEB: www.darnelfabrics.com
SIC: 3089 Molding primary plastic

(G-5562)
DAYORIS DOORS
1945 Hayes St (33020-3549)
PHONE..................................954 374-8538
Dan Benica, *Owner*
EMP: 7 EST: 2015
SALES (est): 147.4K **Privately Held**
WEB: www.dayoris.com
SIC: 2431 Door frames, wood

(G-5563)
DEL PRADO HOLDINGS LLC
Also Called: Del Prado Fire and Water
4000 Hollywood Blvd # 55 (33021-6751)
PHONE..................305 680-7425
Robledo Aybar, *Mng Member*
Lina Garrido,
EMP: 6 EST: 2007
SQ FT: 750
SALES (est): 941.6K **Privately Held**
WEB: www.delpradofireandwater.com
SIC: 3491 7382 3561 5085 Automatic
regulating & control valves; security sys-
tems services; pumps & pumping equip-
ment; industrial supplies; commodity
contract trading companies

(G-5564)
DESIGNERS PLUMBING STUDIO INC
3040 N 29th Ave Ste F (33020-1312)
PHONE..................954 920-5997
Maria De Fatima Rodriguez, *Director*
EMP: 8 EST: 2004
SALES (est): 594.8K **Privately Held**
WEB: www.designersplumbingstudio.com
SIC: 3432 Plumbing fixture fittings & trim

(G-5565)
DHSS LLC
Also Called: Sleep Group Solutions
2035 Harding St Ste 200 (33020-2797)
PHONE..................305 830-0327
Frances Reschtszaid, *Principal*
EMP: 25 EST: 2017
SALES (est): 2.6MM **Privately Held**
WEB: health.mo.gov
SIC: 3841 Diagnostic apparatus, medical

(G-5566)
DIAPULSE CORPORATION AMERICA
250 N Dixie Hwy Unit 9 (33020-6736)
PHONE..................516 466-3030
David M Ross, *President*
EMP: 7 EST: 1957
SALES (est): 798.6K **Privately Held**
WEB: www.diapulse.com
SIC: 3845 Electromedical equipment

(G-5567)
DISTINCTIVE CREAT INTR WKSHP I
2126 Pierce St (33020-4412)
PHONE..................954 921-1861
Linda Crawford, *President*
Patricia Vanik, *Vice Pres*
EMP: 13 EST: 1983
SQ FT: 2,500
SALES (est): 1MM **Privately Held**
WEB: www.distinctiveworkroom.com
SIC: 2211 2392 Draperies & drapery fab-
rics, cotton; shade cloth, window: cotton;
upholstery, tapestry & wall coverings: cot-
ton; bedspreads & bed sets: made from
purchased materials

(G-5568)
DK INTERNATIONAL GROUP CORP
Also Called: Americanlite
1930 Harrison St Ste 307 (33020-7828)
PHONE..................954 391-8969
Fabian Kleyman, *President*
Karina Schaechtler, *Vice Pres*
Carlos Portillo, *Manager*
▲ **EMP:** 5 EST: 2005
SALES (est): 538.4K **Privately Held**
WEB: www.americanlite.com
SIC: 3229 Bulbs for electric lights

(G-5569)
ECO CONCEPTS INC
3607 N 29th Ave (33020-1003)
P.O. Box 260850, Pembroke Pines (33026-7850)
PHONE..................954 920-9700
EMP: 13
SALES (est): 3.4MM **Privately Held**
SIC: 2842 2841 Mfg Polishes & Sanitation
Goods Soaps & Other Detergents

(G-5570)
ELECTRA AUTOMOTIVE CORP
1001 N 21st Ave (33020-3536)
PHONE..................941 623-5563
George Burgos, *President*
EMP: 6 EST: 2016
SALES (est): 392.7K **Privately Held**
SIC: 3711 Cars, electric, assembly of

(G-5571)
ELEMENT INTERNATIONAL DIST INC
2815 Evans St (33020-1119)
PHONE..................305 239-9228
Isaac Galazan, *Principal*
EMP: 7 EST: 2018
SALES (est): 150.8K **Privately Held**
SIC: 2819 Industrial inorganic chemicals

(G-5572)
ESTUMKEDA LTD
Also Called: Micco Aircraft Company
6300 Stirling Rd (33024-2153)
PHONE..................954 966-6300
Sandy Miller, *Manager*
Facundo Giacobbe, *Manager*
Rebecca Petrie, *Manager*
Allen Pettigrew, *Exec Dir*
Douglas Zepeda, *Tech/Comp Coord*
EMP: 13 EST: 1994
SQ FT: 40,000
SALES (est): 1.4MM **Privately Held**
WEB: www.semtribe.com
SIC: 3721 Aircraft

(G-5573)
EVERGREEN SWEETENERS INC (PA)
1936 Hollywood Blvd # 20 (33020-4524)
PHONE..................954 381-7776
Arthur Green, *CEO*
Craig Green, *Co-President*
William Green, *Co-President*
Carole Green, *Corp Secy*
Sean Peters, *Warehouse Mgr*
◆ **EMP:** 10 EST: 1985
SQ FT: 4,107
SALES (est): 10.3MM **Privately Held**
WEB: www.esweeteners.com
SIC: 2099 5149 Sugar; sugar, refined

(G-5574)
FACTORY DIRECT CAB REFACING
1060 Scarlet Oak St (33019-4810)
PHONE..................954 445-6635
Perry Blank, *Owner*
EMP: 8 EST: 2012
SALES (est): 236.5K **Privately Held**
WEB: www.factorydirectrenovations.com
SIC: 2434 Wood kitchen cabinets

(G-5575)
FASTSIGNS
2841 Hollywood Blvd (33020-4226)
PHONE..................954 416-3434
Evren Brandao, *Owner*
Edson Brandao, *Sales Staff*
EMP: 9 EST: 2015
SALES (est): 287K **Privately Held**
WEB: www.fastsigns.com
SIC: 3993 5999 Signs & advertising spe-
cialties; banners, flags, decals & posters

(G-5576)
FINISHING GROUP FLORIDA INC
3997 Pembroke Rd (33021-8126)
PHONE..................954 981-2171
John M Hofmann, *President*
EMP: 7 EST: 2017
SALES (est): 230.6K **Privately Held**
SIC: 3471 Plating & polishing

(G-5577)
FULL LF NATURAL HLTH PDTS LLC
1932 Hollywood Blvd (33020-4524)
PHONE..................954 889-4019
Guido Guevara, *Principal*
EMP: 6 EST: 2007
SALES (est): 549.3K **Privately Held**
WEB: www.fulllifedirect.com
SIC: 2023 Dietary supplements, dairy &
non-dairy based

(G-5578)
FULL LIFE DIRECT LLC
1932 Hollywood Blvd (33020-4524)
PHONE..................800 305-3043
Joseph Kalachy,
EMP: 10 EST: 2017
SALES (est): 800K **Privately Held**
WEB: www.fulllifedirect.com
SIC: 2834 Vitamin preparations

(G-5579)
FUNCTION PLEASE LLC (PA)
Also Called: Sleep Please
2001 Tyler St Ste 5 (33020-4566)
PHONE..................305 792-7900
Sandro Starna,
EMP: 4 EST: 2013
SQ FT: 3,000
SALES (est): 11.9MM **Privately Held**
SIC: 2023 5499 Dietary supplements,
dairy & non-dairy based; vitamin food
stores

(G-5580)
G & G PRESSURE WASHERS INC
7331 Branch St (33024-5421)
PHONE..................786 376-1800
Gerald Hernandez, *Principal*
EMP: 7 EST: 2011
SALES (est): 209.5K **Privately Held**
SIC: 3452 Washers

(G-5581)
GAR INDUSTRIES CORP
Also Called: Parker Plastics
10426 Bermuda Dr (33026-4634)
PHONE..................954 456-8088
Alan Roseman, *President*
◆ **EMP:** 10 EST: 1970
SALES (est): 236K **Privately Held**
WEB: www.garindustries.com
SIC: 3171 3172 3161 3949 Handbags,
women's; handbags, regardless of mate-
rial: men's; cases, carrying; sporting &
athletic goods; canvas & related products

(G-5582)
GOURMET PARISIEN INC
Also Called: Chef Philippe
1943 Sherman St (33020-2124)
P.O. Box 331007, Brooklyn NY (11233-7007)
PHONE..................305 778-0756
Fermin Ribes, *President*
Pierre Bahri, *Vice Pres*
Eric Bertoia, *Technician*
▲ **EMP:** 5 EST: 2008
SALES (est): 1.3MM **Privately Held**
SIC: 2024 Ice cream & frozen desserts
HQ: La Compagnie Des Desserts
Zone Industrielle Des Corbieres
Lezignan Corbieres 11200
468 276-288

(G-5583)
GRAPH-PLEX INC
2830 N 28th Ter (33020-1523)
PHONE..................954 920-0905
Carl Schwartz, *President*
Denise Webster, *Corp Secy*
EMP: 16 EST: 1975
SQ FT: 3,000
SALES (est): 2.2MM **Privately Held**
WEB: www.graphplex.com
SIC: 3993 Displays & cutouts, window &
lobby; signs, not made in custom sign
painting shops

(G-5584)
GREEN BULLION FINCL SVCS LLC
3613 N 29th Ave (33020-1003)
PHONE..................954 960-7000
Howard Mofsin,
EMP: 7 EST: 2007
SALES (est): 507K **Privately Held**
SIC: 3911 Jewelry, precious metal

(G-5585)
GREENGOOD ENERGY CORP
Also Called: Cngas Group
3389 Sheridan St Ste 410 (33021-3606)
PHONE..................954 417-6117
Charles Wainer, *CEO*

Humberto Puppo, *COO*
Alejandro Dejtiar, *CTO*
EMP: 9 EST: 2008
SQ FT: 1,000
SALES (est): 796.1K **Privately Held**
SIC: 3563 Air & gas compressors

(G-5586)
GREZZO USA LLC
1109 Pelican Ln (33019-5040)
PHONE..................954 885-0331
Guillermo Rondon, *Principal*
Maria Diaz, *Principal*
EMP: 9 EST: 2019
SALES (est): 537.4K **Privately Held**
SIC: 3144 Women's footwear, except ath-
letic

(G-5587)
GRIFFON GRAPHICS INC
Also Called: Le Soleil De La Floride
2117 Hollywood Blvd (33020-6706)
PHONE..................954 922-1800
Yves Beauchamp, *CEO*
EMP: 7 EST: 1983
SALES (est): 696.5K **Privately Held**
WEB: www.lesoleildelafloride.com
SIC: 2711 Newspapers: publishing only,
not printed on site

(G-5588)
HARVEY BRANKER AND ASSOC PA
Also Called: Harvey Covington Thomas S Fla
3816 Hollywood Blvd # 203 (33021-6750)
PHONE..................954 966-4445
Roderick Harvey, *Partner*
EMP: 25 EST: 2000
SQ FT: 2,000
SALES (est): 1.2MM **Privately Held**
SIC: 2759 8721 Commercial printing; ac-
counting, auditing & bookkeeping

(G-5589)
HEALTHIER CHOICES MGT CORP (PA)
3800 N 28th Way (33020-1114)
PHONE..................305 600-5004
Jeffrey Holman, *Ch of Bd*
Christopher Santi, *President*
John A Ollet, *CFO*
◆ **EMP:** 33 EST: 1987
SQ FT: 10,000
SALES (est): 13.3MM **Publicly Held**
WEB: www.healthiercmc.com
SIC: 2111 5411 Cigarettes; grocery stores

(G-5590)
HEICO AEROSPACE CORPORATION (DH)
3000 Taft St (33021-4441)
PHONE..................954 987-6101
Eric A Mendelson, *CEO*
Luis J Morell, *President*
Prasheel Chaganti, *Business Mgr*
Jeff Biederwolf, *Vice Pres*
Vivian Miller, *Purch Agent*
▲ **EMP:** 31 EST: 1957
SQ FT: 140,000
SALES (est): 203.6MM **Publicly Held**
WEB: www.heico.com
SIC: 3724 3812 Aircraft engines & engine
parts; search & navigation equipment
HQ: Heico Aerospace Holdings Corp.
3000 Taft St
Hollywood FL 33021
954 987-4000

(G-5591)
HEICO AEROSPACE HOLDINGS CORP (HQ)
3000 Taft St (33021-4441)
PHONE..................954 987-4000
Eric Mendelson, *CEO*
Laurans Mendelson, *Principal*
James R Reum, *Exec VP*
Thomas S Irwin, *Treasurer*
Elizabeth R Letendre, *Admin Sec*
▲ **EMP:** 4 EST: 1997
SALES (est): 467.7MM **Publicly Held**
WEB: www.heico.com
SIC: 3724 Aircraft engines & engine parts

(PA)=Parent Co (HQ)=Headquarters (DH)=Div Headquarters
✪ = New Business established in last 2 years

2022 Harris Florida
Manufacturers Directory

205

G E O G R A P H I C

(G-5592)
HEICO CORPORATION (PA)
3000 Taft St (33021-4441)
PHONE...........................954 987-4000
Laurans A Mendelson, *Ch of Bd*
Eric A Mendelson, *President*
Victor H Mendelson, *President*
Juan A Fernandez, *Principal*
Thomas Irwin, *Sr Exec VP*
▲ EMP: 137 EST: 1957
SQ FT: 7,000
SALES (est): 1.8B **Publicly Held**
WEB: www.heico.com
SIC: 3724 3728 7699 Aircraft engines &
engine parts; aircraft training equipment;
aircraft & heavy equipment repair serv-
ices; aircraft flight instrument repair

(G-5593)
**HEICO ELECTRONIC TECH
CORP (HQ)**
Also Called: Heico Electronic Tech Group
3000 Taft St (33021-4441)
PHONE...........................954 987-6101
Laurans A Mendelson, *CEO*
Celia Blanchet, *Engrg Dir*
Clareesa Stehmeier, *Contract Mgr*
Alvaro Soto, *Information Mgr*
EMP: 40 EST: 1996
SQ FT: 5,000
SALES (est): 489.2MM **Publicly Held**
WEB: www.heico.com
SIC: 3724 Aircraft engines & engine parts

(G-5594)
**HEICO FLIGHT SUPPORT CORP
(HQ)**
3000 Taft St (33021-4441)
PHONE...........................954 987-4000
Eric Mendelson, *President*
John Pfohl, *Opers Mgr*
Carlos Macau, *CFO*
Jack Dewitt, *Sales Dir*
John Presley, *Sales Staff*
EMP: 25 EST: 2012
SALES (est): 133.1MM **Publicly Held**
WEB: www.heico.com
SIC: 3724 Aircraft engines & engine parts

(G-5595)
HIGH FIVE INDUSTRIES INC
Also Called: Sakar Zebulun
2719 Hollywood Blvd (33020-4821)
PHONE...........................954 673-1811
Shozana Beckford, *Vice Pres*
Alcy Beckford, *Exec Dir*
EMP: 7 EST: 2016
SALES (est): 68.6K **Privately Held**
SIC: 3999 Manufacturing industries

(G-5596)
HOLLYWOOD LODGING INC
2601 N 29th Ave (33020-1508)
PHONE...........................305 803-7455
Nayan C Patel, *Principal*
EMP: 11 EST: 2015
SALES (est): 383.2K **Privately Held**
SIC: 2499 Wood products

(G-5597)
**HOLLYWOOD MACHINE SHOP
INC**
5835 Rodman St (33023-1939)
PHONE...........................954 893-6103
Carlos A Delascagigas, *President*
EMP: 7 EST: 2009
SALES (est): 420K **Privately Held**
SIC: 3599 Machine shop, jobbing & repair

(G-5598)
HOLLYWOOD WOODWORK INC
2951 Pembroke Rd (33020-5634)
PHONE...........................954 920-5009
Yves Desmarais, *CEO*
Paul Des Marais, *Vice Pres*
Cristina Oparina, *Project Mgr*
Ed Williams, *Project Mgr*
Juan Couto, *Engineer*
◆ EMP: 100 EST: 1968
SQ FT: 52,500
SALES (est): 23.9MM **Privately Held**
WEB: www.hollywoodwoodwork.com
SIC: 2431 Millwork

(G-5599)
HOLLYWOOD WOODWORK LLC
2951 Pembroke Rd (33020-5634)
PHONE...........................954 920-5009
Yves Demsmarais, *Mng Member*
Tony Parkinson,
Robert M Perrotti,
EMP: 13 EST: 2006
SQ FT: 5,000
SALES (est): 493.8K **Privately Held**
WEB: www.hollywoodwoodwork.com
SIC: 2431 Interior & ornamental woodwork
& trim

(G-5600)
**HURST AWNING COMPANY INC
(PA)**
3613 N 29th Ave (33021-1003)
P.O. Box 566330, Miami (33256-6330)
PHONE...........................305 693-0600
Garmendia Magali B, *President*
Frank S Cornelius, *President*
Garcia Jose Luis, *Vice Pres*
Maggie Garmendia, *Treasurer*
▼ EMP: 22 EST: 1957
SQ FT: 60,000
SALES (est): 3.6MM **Privately Held**
WEB: www.amdaluminum.com
SIC: 3444 Awnings, sheet metal; sheet
metal specialties, not stamped

(G-5601)
INFUPHARMA LLC
6720 Tyler St (33024-7526)
PHONE...........................305 301-3389
Michel Rizo, *Principal*
EMP: 5 EST: 2008
SALES (est): 476.3K **Privately Held**
SIC: 2834 Pharmaceutical preparations

(G-5602)
J LEA LLC
Also Called: Grand Band
916 N 20th Ave (33020-3532)
PHONE...........................954 921-1422
Joy Ziefer,
EMP: 7 EST: 2010
SALES (est): 447.3K **Privately Held**
WEB: www.thegrandband.com
SIC: 3172 Wallets

(G-5603)
JA ENGINEERING II CORP (HQ)
3000 Taft St (33021-4441)
PHONE...........................954 744-7560
Thomas S Irwin, *Principal*
EMP: 12 EST: 2010
SALES (est): 54.7MM **Publicly Held**
SIC: 3724 Aircraft engines & engine parts

(G-5604)
JAMES TESTA
Also Called: Testa & Sons Signs
5621 Johnson St (33021-5631)
PHONE...........................954 962-5840
James Testa, *Owner*
▼ EMP: 10 EST: 1969
SQ FT: 4,000
SALES (est): 1.1MM **Privately Held**
WEB: www.testasigns.com
SIC: 3993 Signs, not made in custom sign
painting shops

(G-5605)
JERAE INC
6031 Hollywood Blvd (33024-7935)
PHONE...........................954 989-6665
James Dauria, *Principal*
EMP: 11 EST: 2007
SALES (est): 227.5K **Privately Held**
SIC: 3089 Tires, plastic

(G-5606)
JET AVION CORPORATION
Also Called: Heico Parts Group
3000 Taft St (33021-4441)
PHONE...........................954 987-6101
Rick Stine, *President*
Mike Sego, *Senior VP*
Jack Lewis, *Vice Pres*
Vivian Miller, *Purch Agent*
Joe Randolph, *Project Engr*
▲ EMP: 70 EST: 1970
SQ FT: 140,000

SALES (est): 40.4MM **Publicly Held**
WEB: www.heico.com
SIC: 3724 Aircraft engines & engine parts
HQ: Heico Aerospace Holdings Corp.
3000 Taft St
Hollywood FL 33021
954 987-4000

(G-5607)
JRMETAL ORNAMENTAL
3725 Pembroke Rd Ste A11 (33021-8296)
PHONE...........................954 989-2607
Jose Obando, *Principal*
EMP: 7 EST: 2006
SALES (est): 277.7K **Privately Held**
WEB: www.jrmetalornamental.com
SIC: 3549 Metalworking machinery

(G-5608)
KEYSTONE 75 INC
Also Called: Best Made Flags
5620 Dewey St (33023-1916)
PHONE...........................954 430-1880
Greg Grant, *President*
EMP: 5 EST: 1974
SALES (est): 343K **Privately Held**
WEB: www.southfloridaflags.com
SIC: 2399 5999 Banners, pennants &
flags; flags; banners

(G-5609)
LEDRADIANT LLC
615 N 21st Ave (33020-4049)
PHONE...........................305 901-1313
Alfredo Kiersz, *Mng Member*
▲ EMP: 6 EST: 2014
SALES (est): 605K **Privately Held**
WEB: www.ledradiant.com
SIC: 3646 3229 Commercial indusl & insti-
tutional electric lighting fixtures; bulbs for
electric lights

(G-5610)
LG-TEC CORPORATION
2021 Coolidge St (33020-2427)
PHONE...........................305 770-4005
Gustavo O Fazio, *President*
Hector O Huarte, *President*
◆ EMP: 8 EST: 2007
SQ FT: 7,000
SALES (est): 970.7K **Privately Held**
WEB: www.lg-tec.com
SIC: 2241 Zipper tape

(G-5611)
**LIGHTHOUSE EXPRESS WORLD
INC**
3880 N 28th Ter (33020-1118)
PHONE...........................754 210-6196
Caleb Outten, *President*
EMP: 8 EST: 2016
SALES (est): 234.8K **Privately Held**
WEB: www.lighthouseexpressworld.com
SIC: 2741 Miscellaneous publishing

(G-5612)
LIP TRADING CO
3460 N 34th Ave (33021-2507)
PHONE...........................954 987-0306
William Lipsitz, *President*
Malu Lipsitz, *Treasurer*
▼ EMP: 6 EST: 1975
SQ FT: 4,000
SALES (est): 454.2K **Privately Held**
SIC: 3861 5048 5043 Photographic
equipment & supplies; ophthalmic goods;
photographic equipment & supplies

(G-5613)
LOREN/WTP
3040 N 29th Ave (33020-1311)
PHONE...........................954 846-9800
EMP: 9 EST: 2016
SALES (est): 63.4K **Privately Held**
SIC: 3366 Machinery castings: brass

(G-5614)
LP WATCH GROUP INC
Also Called: Lucien Piccard
101 S State Road 7 # 201 (33023-6736)
PHONE...........................954 985-3827
David Koss, *President*
Sol Friedman, *Chairman*
Elena Koss, *Vice Pres*
Dev Dhar, *CFO*
▲ EMP: 22 EST: 2001

SQ FT: 38,000
SALES (est): 1.1MM **Privately Held**
SIC: 3873 5094 Clocks, assembly of;
watches & parts

(G-5615)
LPI INDUSTRIES CORPORATION
Also Called: L P I
3000 Taft St (33021-4441)
PHONE...........................954 987-4000
James Roubian, *President*
Judith Vetter, *President*
Steve Ray, *Vice Pres*
Tracy Fernandez, *Buyer*
Thomas S Irwin, *Treasurer*
▲ EMP: 67 EST: 1972
SQ FT: 140,000
SALES (est): 60.9MM **Publicly Held**
WEB: www.heico.com
SIC: 3724 Aircraft engines & engine parts
HQ: Heico Aerospace Holdings Corp.
3000 Taft St
Hollywood FL 33021
954 987-4000

(G-5616)
LSJ CORP
2301 N 21st Ave (33020-2114)
PHONE...........................954 920-0905
Carl I Schwartz, *President*
EMP: 7 EST: 2005
SALES (est): 92.8K **Privately Held**
SIC: 3993 Signs & advertising specialties

(G-5617)
**LUCIEN PICCARD/ARNEX
WATCH CO**
101 S State Road 7 # 201 (33023-6736)
PHONE...........................954 241-2745
Alexander Blau, *President*
Sol Mermelstein, *Vice Pres*
▲ EMP: 100 EST: 1983
SALES (est): 5.8MM **Privately Held**
SIC: 3873 Watches & parts, except crys-
tals & jewels

(G-5618)
LUNION LOGISTICS LLC ✪
4000 Hollywood Blvd 555s (33021-6751)
PHONE...........................866 586-4660
Kathy Stfleur, *CEO*
EMP: 10 EST: 2021
SALES (est): 1.1MM **Privately Held**
SIC: 3537 Trucks: freight, baggage, etc.:
industrial, except mining

(G-5619)
**MADISON MILLWORK &
CABINET CO**
5746 Dawson St Ste A (33023-1908)
PHONE...........................954 966-7551
Glenn Hauser, *President*
EMP: 26 EST: 1997
SQ FT: 6,000
SALES (est): 3.3MM **Privately Held**
WEB: www.madisonmillwork.net
SIC: 2511 1751 Wood household furniture;
cabinet & finish carpentry

(G-5620)
MARINIZE PRODUCTS CORP
3986 Pembroke Rd (33021-8127)
PHONE...........................954 989-7990
Martin Panich, *CEO*
Gary Edwards, *Treasurer*
EMP: 7 EST: 1986
SALES (est): 248.8K **Privately Held**
SIC: 2842 Cleaning or polishing prepara-
tions

(G-5621)
MAS EDITORIAL CORP
Also Called: 305 Media Solutions
1596 Trailhead Ter (33021-1410)
PHONE...........................305 748-0124
Martin Rodriguez Gambaro, *President*
EMP: 6 EST: 2015
SALES (est): 336.5K **Privately Held**
SIC: 7372 2721 Publishers' computer soft-
ware; magazines: publishing & printing

(G-5622)
MAXOGEN GROUP LLC
2719 Hollywood Blvd (33020-4821)
PHONE...........................305 814-0734

Eugene Zavolotsky, *CEO*
EMP: 45 **EST:** 2015
SALES (est): 1MM **Privately Held**
WEB: www.maxogengroup.com
SIC: 3824 Mechanical & electromechanical
counters & devices

(G-5623)
**MAYERS JWLY CO HOLLYWOOD
INC (PA)**
Also Called: W C Edge Jewelry Co Division
2002 Grant St (33020-3546)
PHONE.................................954 921-1422
Sam Ziefer, *President*
Martin Gayer, *Corp Secy*
▼ **EMP:** 40 **EST:** 1945
SQ FT: 15,000
SALES (est): 4.5MM **Privately Held**
SIC: 3911 Jewelry, precious metal

(G-5624)
MAYMAAN RESEARCH LLC
3904 N 29th Ave (33020-1010)
PHONE.................................954 374-9376
Eitan Shmueli, *Principal*
EMP: 7 **EST:** 2019
SALES (est): 531.9K **Privately Held**
WEB: www.maymaan.com
SIC: 3621 Motors & generators

(G-5625)
**MERIT DIAMOND
CORPORATION**
1900 Tyler St Fl 3 (33020-4517)
PHONE.................................954 883-3660
Gagi Kaplan, *Ch of Bd*
Neil Bobrow, *COO*
Josef Fraiman, *Exec VP*
Gerson Delgado, *Asst Director*
▲ **EMP:** 30 **EST:** 1981
SQ FT: 15,000
SALES (est): 5MM **Privately Held**
WEB: www.meritdiamond.com
SIC: 3911 Jewelry, precious metal

(G-5626)
METRO SIGNS INC
Also Called: Wrapfink
1220 S State Road 7 (33023-6711)
PHONE.................................954 410-4343
Bruno V Dede, *President*
David Metrosigns, *Sales Executive*
Abbey Freese, *Marketing Staff*
Sofia Christina, *Manager*
EMP: 25 **EST:** 1993
SALES (est): 3.8MM **Privately Held**
WEB: www.metrogroupmiami.com
SIC: 3993 Electric signs

(G-5627)
MILLER SIGNS LLC
2501 N 69th Ave (33024-3750)
PHONE.................................786 395-9420
Rodolfo Baldini, *Principal*
EMP: 7 **EST:** 2016
SALES (est): 261K **Privately Held**
WEB: www.millersignsllc.com
SIC: 3993 Signs & advertising specialties

(G-5628)
MOHAWK INDUSTRIES INC
2500 Sw 32nd Ave (33023-7703)
PHONE.................................918 272-0184
EMP: 8 **EST:** 2019
SALES (est): 277.4K **Privately Held**
WEB: www.mohawkind.com
SIC: 2273 Finishers of tufted carpets &
rugs

(G-5629)
MOLD R US INC
6596 Taft St (33024-4009)
PHONE.................................954 850-6653
Doron Ibgui, *Principal*
EMP: 5 **EST:** 2010
SALES (est): 467.7K **Privately Held**
WEB: www.moldrus.net
SIC: 3544 Industrial molds

(G-5630)
MORENO & SONS INC
2535 Ambassador Ave (33026-4762)
PHONE.................................786 402-8919
Helbi Moreno, *Principal*
EMP: 7 **EST:** 2004

SALES (est): 154.6K **Privately Held**
SIC: 3949 Sporting & athletic goods

(G-5631)
NATURAL HATS AND MORE LLC
5801 Wiley St (33023-2355)
PHONE.................................954 549-0819
EMP: 24
SALES (corp-wide): 64.5K **Privately Held**
SIC: 2353 Hats, caps & millinery
PA: Natural Hats And More Llc
307 Sw 2nd Ave
Dania FL

(G-5632)
NEOCABINET INC
1623 Plunkett St (33020-6443)
PHONE.................................310 927-1008
Georgy Proskuryakov, *Principal*
EMP: 7 **EST:** 2017
SALES (est): 76.2K **Privately Held**
WEB: www.neocabinet.com
SIC: 2434 Wood kitchen cabinets

(G-5633)
NEX-XOS WORLDWIDE LLC (PA)
Also Called: Xmre
3922 Pembroke Rd (33021-8127)
PHONE.................................305 433-8376
Saul Mishkin, *President*
Juan Shehin, *COO*
Ivis Rubero, *Opers Staff*
Harold Rabinowitz, *Controller*
Nani Chlinper, *Sales Mgr*
EMP: 8 **EST:** 2010
SQ FT: 21,250
SALES (est): 5.4MM **Privately Held**
WEB: www.nex-xos.com
SIC: 2099 Packaged combination prod-
ucts: pasta, rice & potato

(G-5634)
NIBA DESIGNS INC (PA)
Also Called: Niba Collections
3609 N 29th Ave (33020-1003)
PHONE.................................305 456-6230
Beth Arrowood, *CEO*
John Berryman, *President*
Maria Costa, *Business Mgr*
Manny Hodak, *CFO*
Melissa Lawhorn, *Cust Mgr*
EMP: 10 **EST:** 2006
SALES (est): 3.7MM **Privately Held**
WEB: www.nibadesigns.com
SIC: 2273 2299 Carpets & rugs; linen fab-
rics

(G-5635)
OCON ENTERPRISE INC
821 N 21st Ave (33020-3505)
P.O. Box 221721 (33022-1721)
PHONE.................................954 920-6700
Don J O'Connell, *President*
A Dawn O'Connell, *CFO*
EMP: 81 **EST:** 1985
SQ FT: 10,000
SALES (est): 7MM **Privately Held**
SIC: 3911 5094 Jewelry, precious metal;
jewelry

(G-5636)
OVERSTITCH INC
4651 Sheridan St Ste 200 (33021-3422)
PHONE.................................954 505-8567
Jared Gamberg, *Principal*
EMP: 7 **EST:** 2017
SALES (est): 132.3K **Privately Held**
WEB: www.overstitch.com
SIC: 2395 Embroidery & art needlework

(G-5637)
PALLADIO BEAUTY GROUP LLC
3912 Pembroke Rd (33021-8127)
PHONE.................................954 922-4311
Philip Solomon, *Mng Member*
EMP: 25 **EST:** 2012
SALES (est): 2.4MM **Privately Held**
WEB: www.palladiobeauty.com
SIC: 2844 5122 Toilet preparations; bath
salts; cosmetics

(G-5638)
PB GROUP LLC
Also Called: Palladio Beauty Group
3912 Pembroke Rd (33021-8127)
PHONE.................................954 922-4311

Philip Solomon, *CEO*
Cristina Martinho, *Vice Pres*
Laura Sucalesca, *Sales Staff*
Lee Khandeece, *Marketing Staff*
Maria Torres, *Manager*
▲ **EMP:** 20 **EST:** 1999
SQ FT: 15,000
SALES (est): 3.7MM **Privately Held**
WEB: www.palladiobeauty.com
SIC: 2844 5199 Toilet preparations; gen-
eral merchandise, non-durable

(G-5639)
**PEERLESS INSTRUMENT CO
INC**
2030 Coolidge St (33020-2428)
PHONE.................................954 921-6006
Thomas Brady, *President*
Martin Ignac, *Vice Pres*
Daniel A Lippiello, *Vice Pres*
Paul Sadhai, *Plant Supt*
Dustin Johnson, *Production*
EMP: 38 **EST:** 1968
SQ FT: 16,000
SALES (est): 4.1MM **Privately Held**
WEB: www.peerlessinstrument.com
SIC: 3599 Machine shop, jobbing & repair

(G-5640)
**PEMBROKE OFFICE
INDUSTRIES LLC**
1500 S 66th Ave (33023-2103)
PHONE.................................954 589-1329
Luiz C Gastaldo, *Director*
EMP: 7 **EST:** 2014
SALES (est): 234.7K **Privately Held**
SIC: 3999 Manufacturing industries

(G-5641)
PERFECTUS PET FOOD LLC
3300 Oakwood Blvd (33020-7104)
PHONE.................................800 774-3296
Donald Radcliffe, *CEO*
Gregory Eastwood, *Vice Pres*
EMP: 5 **EST:** 2019
SQ FT: 3,000
SALES (est): 438.8K **Privately Held**
SIC: 2048 Dry pet food (except dog & cat)

(G-5642)
PHG KENDALL LLC
Also Called: Prime Hotel Group US
4651 Sheridan St Ste 480 (33021-3430)
PHONE.................................954 392-8788
Larry M Abbo, *CEO*
Bob Wilkins, *Purchasing*
Leonardo Benatar, *Project Engr*
Mariano Macchi, *Accounting Mgr*
Danilo Baptista, *Portfolio Mgr*
EMP: 19 **EST:** 2009
SALES (est): 9.5MM **Privately Held**
SIC: 3241 3429 Cement, hydraulic;
builders' hardware

(G-5643)
PLASTIX USA LLC
900 N Federal Hwy Ste 104 (33020-3589)
PHONE.................................305 891-0091
ARI A Birol,
Eda Birol,
▲ **EMP:** 82 **EST:** 2011
SALES (est): 6.4MM **Privately Held**
WEB: www.plastixdunnage.com
SIC: 2673 3086 Plastic bags: made from
purchased materials; packaging & ship-
ping materials, foamed plastic

(G-5644)
PODGO PRINTING LLC
3810 N 29th Ave (33020-1008)
PHONE.................................954 874-9100
Robert Podgorowiez, *President*
Mitchell I Podgorowiez,
EMP: 6 **EST:** 2019
SALES (est): 395.5K **Privately Held**
WEB: www.podgoprinting.com
SIC: 2752 Commercial printing, offset

(G-5645)
PREFERRED SIGNS INC
1906 N Dixie Hwy (33020-2340)
PHONE.................................954 922-0126
Howard Weber, *President*
Mark Weber, *Vice Pres*
EMP: 9 **EST:** 1973
SQ FT: 8,000

SALES (est): 833.4K **Privately Held**
WEB: www.preferredsignsinc.com
SIC: 3993 Electric signs

(G-5646)
PRINTSHAQCOM INC
1654 Jackson St (33020-5110)
PHONE.................................954 678-7286
Annette Filecci, *Principal*
EMP: 7 **EST:** 2011
SALES (est): 119.6K **Privately Held**
WEB: www.printshaq.com
SIC: 2752 Commercial printing, litho-
graphic

(G-5647)
PUBLI SIGNS
250 N Dixie Hwy Unit 5 (33020-6736)
PHONE.................................954 927-4411
Gerard Bensadon, *Principal*
EMP: 5 **EST:** 2007
SALES (est): 412.6K **Privately Held**
WEB: www.publisigns.com
SIC: 3993 Electric signs

(G-5648)
QUALITEL INC
2414 N Federal Hwy (33020-2234)
PHONE.................................954 464-3991
Jeronimo Monteiro, *Principal*
EMP: 11 **EST:** 2009
SALES (est): 219.2K **Privately Held**
WEB: www.qualitel.com
SIC: 3672 Printed circuit boards

(G-5649)
**QUALITY SCREEN ENCLOSURE
LLC**
3800 Hillcrest Dr Apt 210 (33021-7937)
PHONE.................................954 226-1980
Pavel A Lebedev, *Manager*
EMP: 7 **EST:** 2017
SALES (est): 496.2K **Privately Held**
WEB: www.qualityscreenenclosure.com
SIC: 3448 Screen enclosures

(G-5650)
**QUIET TECHNOLOGY
AEROSPACE INC**
4100 N 29th Ter (33020-1022)
PHONE.................................305 687-9808
Fernando Birbragher, *CEO*
Barry Fine, *President*
Ben Brown, *Vice Pres*
Richard Brown, *Vice Pres*
Martha Durand, *Controller*
▲ **EMP:** 47 **EST:** 2000
SQ FT: 50,029
SALES (est): 8.6MM **Privately Held**
WEB: www.qtaerospace.com
SIC: 3728 Aircraft parts & equipment

(G-5651)
R R H INC
Also Called: Advanced Color Graphics Group
5900 Johnson St (33021-5638)
P.O. Box 531518, Miami (33153-1518)
PHONE.................................954 966-1209
Rudy Ambra, *CEO*
Harry Jordan, *President*
EMP: 16 **EST:** 1981
SQ FT: 4,500
SALES (est): 351.2K **Privately Held**
SIC: 2752 Commercial printing, offset

(G-5652)
**RICKEYS WORLD FAMOUS
SAUCE INC**
4799 Hollywood Blvd (33021-6503)
PHONE.................................954 829-9464
Evelyn Mitchell, *CEO*
William Mitchell, *President*
Lisa Solito, *Vice Pres*
◆ **EMP:** 16 **EST:** 1955
SQ FT: 4,000
SALES (est): 674K **Privately Held**
SIC: 2035 Pickles, sauces & salad dress-
ings

(G-5653)
**RODEN INTERNATIONAL INC
(PA)**
3741 N Park Rd (33021-2531)
PHONE.................................954 929-1900
Gabriela Berenstein, *President*

Victor Berenstein, *Treasurer*
▲ **EMP:** 18 **EST:** 1989
SALES (est): 1.2MM **Privately Held**
WEB: www.zackusa.com
SIC: 3914 3469 Stainless steel ware; table tops, porcelain enameled

(G-5654)
SCHEDUALL SCHEDUALL SCHEDUALL
2719 Hollywood Blvd (33020-4821)
PHONE..................................954 334-5400
Isis Thomson, *Human Res Mgr*
Rob Evans, *Products*
EMP: 9 **EST:** 2019
SALES (est): 908.1K **Privately Held**
WEB: www.xytechsystems.com
SIC: 2741 Miscellaneous publishing

(G-5655)
SEA AND SHORE CUSTOM CANVAS UP
3629 Washington St (33021-8215)
PHONE..................................954 983-3060
EMP: 5
SALES (est): 344.5K **Privately Held**
SIC: 2211 Cotton Broadwoven Fabric Mill

(G-5656)
SERV-PAK CORP
5844 Dawson St (33023-1910)
P.O. Box 4563 (33083-4563)
PHONE..................................954 962-4262
Joel Mahler, *President*
◆ **EMP:** 10 **EST:** 1984
SQ FT: 4,000
SALES (est): 986.9K **Privately Held**
WEB: www.serv-pak.com
SIC: 3081 2759 Packing materials, plastic sheet; commercial printing

(G-5657)
SIMULATED ENVMT CONCEPTS INC
Also Called: SEC
3937 Pembroke Rd (33021-8126)
PHONE..................................754 263-3184
Ella Frenkel, *President*
Allen Licht, *COO*
Ilya Spivak, *Vice Pres*
◆ **EMP:** 25 **EST:** 1993
SQ FT: 5,000
SALES (est): 1.9MM **Privately Held**
SIC: 3634 Massage machines, electric, except for beauty/barber shops

(G-5658)
SNAPPY STRUCTURES INC
Also Called: Agg International
2324 Hayes St (33020-3440)
PHONE..................................954 926-6611
Joe Sparacino, *President*
▲ **EMP:** 15 **EST:** 1974
SQ FT: 12,000
SALES (est): 411K **Privately Held**
SIC: 3354 3441 Aluminum extruded products; fabricated structural metal

(G-5659)
SOLUTION ASSET MANAGEMENT LLC
1918 Harrison St (33020-5081)
PHONE..................................786 288-9408
EMP: 8
SALES (est): 602.1K **Privately Held**
SIC: 1389 Oil/Gas Field Services

(G-5660)
SOUTH BROWARD PRINTING INC
Also Called: Sir Speedy
5845 Hollywood Blvd Ste C (33021-6312)
PHONE..................................954 962-1309
Dan Lotford, *President*
Brian Doerner, *Sales Executive*
▼ **EMP:** 5 **EST:** 1972
SALES (est): 357.2K **Privately Held**
WEB: www.sirspeedy.com
SIC: 2752 2791 2789 Commercial printing, lithographic; typesetting; bookbinding & related work

(G-5661)
SOUTHEAST CORN TRADERS LLC
1936 Hollywood Blvd # 20 (33020-4524)
PHONE..................................843 372-4315
Jonathan Sanders, *General Mgr*
Craig Green,
William Green,
Adam Hovermale,
Joe Pryor,
EMP: 5 **EST:** 2020
SALES (est): 502K **Privately Held**
SIC: 2099 Food preparations

(G-5662)
SPA COVER INC
Also Called: Douglas Marine
2310 Hayes St (33020-3440)
PHONE..................................954 923-8801
Judith L Brosseau, *President*
▼ **EMP:** 12 **EST:** 1981
SQ FT: 12,000
SALES (est): 2.7MM **Privately Held**
WEB: www.spacoverinc.net
SIC: 3999 Hot tub & spa covers

(G-5663)
SPARKS CABINETRY
1685 S State Road 7 (33023-6700)
PHONE..................................954 367-2750
Dennis Getsee, *Principal*
EMP: 7 **EST:** 2013
SALES (est): 187.8K **Privately Held**
SIC: 2434 Wood kitchen cabinets

(G-5664)
STANLEY INDUSTRIES OF S FLA (PA)
Also Called: Gallery Industries
3001 S Ocean Dr Apt 1423 (33019-2874)
PHONE..................................954 929-8770
Robert Alexander, *President*
Steven Alexander, *Corp Secy*
Jerome Alexander, *Vice Pres*
◆ **EMP:** 9 **EST:** 1976
SQ FT: 6,000
SALES (est): 654K **Privately Held**
SIC: 2325 2321 2335 2331 Men's & boys' trousers & slacks; men's & boys' furnishings; women's, juniors' & misses' dresses; women's & misses' blouses & shirts; textiles, woven; cloth cutting, bolting or winding

(G-5665)
SUN-ART DESIGNS INC
2806 N 29th Ave Ste 2 (33020-1506)
PHONE..................................954 929-6622
Yoave Bitton, *President*
Shahar Bitton, *Business Anlyst*
▼ **EMP:** 23 **EST:** 1989
SQ FT: 22,000
SALES (est): 1.8MM **Privately Held**
WEB: www.sunartdesign.com
SIC: 3999 7336 Barber & beauty shop equipment; silk screen design

(G-5666)
SUNRAY REFLECTIONS INC
956 Harrison St (33019-1623)
PHONE..................................305 305-6350
Jeffrey Langer, *Director*
EMP: 7 **EST:** 2001
SALES (est): 152.3K **Privately Held**
WEB: www.colorreflections.com
SIC: 3993 Signs & advertising specialties

(G-5667)
SUNSHINE DRIVEWAYS INC
7750 Nw 35th St (33024-2213)
P.O. Box 841123 (33084-3123)
PHONE..................................954 394-7373
Danilo A De Jesus, *President*
EMP: 8 **EST:** 2006
SALES (est): 63.2K **Privately Held**
SIC: 3271 Paving blocks, concrete

(G-5668)
TAIE INC (PA)
Also Called: Minuteman Press
4171 N State Road 7 (33021-1510)
PHONE..................................954 966-0233
Saied Taie Tehrani, *President*
Kevin Taie, *Vice Pres*
Keven Taie Tehrani, *Vice Pres*

Rhea E Taie Tehrani, *Treasurer*
Diane Bryan, *Office Mgr*
EMP: 7 **EST:** 1983
SQ FT: 3,600
SALES (est): 1.9MM **Privately Held**
WEB: www.minuteman.com
SIC: 2752 2789 2759 Commercial printing, lithographic; bookbinding & related work; commercial printing

(G-5669)
TERMINE RAVIOLI MANUFACTURING (PA)
Also Called: Mimi's Ravioli
5714 Johnson St (33021-5634)
PHONE..................................954 983-3711
Frank Billisi, *President*
Linda Billisi, *Co-Owner*
EMP: 10 **EST:** 1972
SQ FT: 10,000
SALES (est): 1.6MM **Privately Held**
WEB: www.mimisravioli.com
SIC: 2098 5499 5149 Macaroni products (e.g. alphabets, rings & shells), dry; gourmet food stores; macaroni

(G-5670)
THUNDER ENERGIES CORPORATION (PA)
8570 Stirling Rd Ste 102 (33024-8204)
PHONE..................................786 855-6190
Yogev Shvo, *Ch of Bd*
Adam Levy, *President*
EMP: 8 **EST:** 2011
SQ FT: 9,525
SALES (est): 7.6MM **Publicly Held**
WEB: www.natureconsulting.com
SIC: 2833 Medicinals & botanicals

(G-5671)
TIAS MILKSHAKES AND MORE
6768 Stirling Rd (33024-1844)
PHONE..................................954 391-8753
Aracelis Caraballo, *Principal*
EMP: 9 **EST:** 2011
SALES (est): 280.8K **Privately Held**
SIC: 2026 Yogurt

(G-5672)
TIZZONI CUCINE INC
2798 Sw 32nd Ave (33023-7702)
PHONE..................................305 698-8889
Salvatore Tizzoni, *Principal*
EMP: 8 **EST:** 2016
SALES (est): 303.2K **Privately Held**
WEB: www.tizzonicucine.com
SIC: 2541 Wood partitions & fixtures

(G-5673)
TREBOR USA CORP
Also Called: Door Shop, The
3901 N 29th Ave (33020-1009)
PHONE..................................954 922-1620
Gratien Proulx, *President*
Micheline Proulx, *President*
Jocelyn Vinet, *Vice Pres*
Marcia Doyle Krutek, *CFO*
Yves Surprenant, *Admin Sec*
◆ **EMP:** 11 **EST:** 1999
SALES (est): 2.4MM **Privately Held**
WEB: www.treborusa.com
SIC: 3442 Metal doors

(G-5674)
TRIARCH INTERNATIONAL INC
Also Called: Triach Industries
4811 Sarazen Dr (33021-2367)
PHONE..................................305 622-3400
Bernard Rogover, *President*
David Labell, *Exec VP*
Howard Rogover, *Vice Pres*
◆ **EMP:** 13 **EST:** 1973
SQ FT: 94,838
SALES (est): 1.4MM **Privately Held**
WEB: www.triarchindustries.com
SIC: 3648 Lighting equipment

(G-5675)
TRIUMPH HOSIERY CORP
4624 Hollywood Blvd # 205 (33021-6526)
PHONE..................................954 929-6021
Ed Solomon, *President*
Ann Solomon, *Chairman*
Gloria Herrera, *Executive Asst*
▲ **EMP:** 8 **EST:** 1990

SALES (est): 1MM **Privately Held**
WEB: www.triumphhosiery.com
SIC: 2251 2252 Women's hosiery, except socks; hosiery

(G-5676)
TROPICAL DVRSONS MRINA MGT INC
3200 N 29th Ave (33020-1313)
PHONE..................................954 922-0387
Douglas Sherron, *Principal*
EMP: 8 **EST:** 2010
SALES (est): 225.7K **Privately Held**
SIC: 3732 Yachts, building & repairing

(G-5677)
TRUTH NUTRITION LLC
4302 Hollywood Blvd # 16 (33021-6635)
PHONE..................................754 400-0382
EMP: 7 **EST:** 2014
SALES (est): 498.8K **Privately Held**
WEB: www.truthnutrition.com
SIC: 2834 Vitamin, nutrient & hematinic preparations for human use

(G-5678)
TURBINE KINETICS INC
3000 Taft St (33021-4441)
PHONE..................................954 744-7526
Victor Mendelson, *President*
Kevin Keating, *Engineer*
EMP: 16 **EST:** 2001
SALES (est): 8.2MM **Publicly Held**
WEB: www.heico.com
SIC: 3724 Aircraft engines & engine parts
HQ: Heico Aerospace Holdings Corp.
3000 Taft St
Hollywood FL 33021
954 987-4000

(G-5679)
UMA HOLDINGS INC
601 S 21st Ave (33020-6905)
PHONE..................................786 587-1349
Juan Villegas, *CEO*
EMP: 47 **EST:** 2005
SALES (est): 516.3K **Privately Held**
SIC: 3711 5012 Automobile assembly, including specialty automobiles; automotive brokers

(G-5680)
URBAN EXTREME LLC
4303 Hayes St (33021-5363)
PHONE..................................954 248-9007
Daniel Shnader, *Manager*
EMP: 10 **EST:** 2015
SALES (est): 876.9K **Privately Held**
SIC: 3949 Playground equipment

(G-5681)
VENCO MARINE INC
2012 Hayes St (33020-3552)
P.O. Box 222526 (33022-2526)
PHONE..................................954 923-0036
Magnar Venoy, *President*
▲ **EMP:** 7 **EST:** 1997
SALES (est): 588.8K **Privately Held**
WEB: www.vencomarine.com
SIC: 2842 3699 Specialty cleaning, polishes & sanitation goods; security control equipment & systems

(G-5682)
VOLVOX INC HOLLYWOOD
Also Called: Erwad Real Estate
537 N Rainbow Dr (33021-6021)
PHONE..................................954 961-4942
Ron Stanish, *President*
Alan Stanish, *President*
Dane Stanish, *Production*
Jean Stanish, *Treasurer*
Andrew Stanish, *Sales Mgr*
EMP: 8 **EST:** 1986
SALES (est): 700K **Privately Held**
SIC: 3949 6531 Fishing equipment; real estate agent, residential

(G-5683)
WALKER GRAPHICS INC
2039 Coolidge St B (33020-2427)
PHONE..................................954 964-1688
Michaell P Walker, *President*
Michael P Walker, *President*
EMP: 9 **EST:** 1982

SALES (est): 801.6K **Privately Held**
WEB: www.walker-graphics.co.uk
SIC: 2796 2791 Platemaking services;
typesetting

(G-5684)
WILLIAM LAROQUE INSTALLERS INC
Also Called: W.L. Installers
5820 Sheridan St (33021-3244)
PHONE..................................305 769-1717
William Laroque, *President*
Claudia Laroque, *Vice Pres*
Pete Laroque, *Vice Pres*
Tim Swett, *Vice Pres*
Jorge Barco, *Manager*
▼ EMP: 23 EST: 1992
SQ FT: 7,000
SALES (est): 2.9MM **Privately Held**
WEB: www.wlinstallers.com
SIC: 3535 5084 Conveyors & conveying
equipment; industrial machinery & equip-
ment

(G-5685)
WORLD EMBLEM INTERNATIONAL INC (PA)
4601 Sheridan St Ste 300 (33021-3433)
PHONE..................................305 899-9006
Randy Carr, *President*
Jamie Carr, *Vice Pres*
Moran Idith, *Vice Pres*
Idith Moran, *Vice Pres*
Tony Morando, *Vice Pres*
EMP: 225 EST: 1993
SQ FT: 35,000
SALES (est): 36.5MM **Privately Held**
WEB: www.worldemblem.com
SIC: 2395 Emblems, embroidered

(G-5686)
WORLDWIDE AUTO SYSTEMS CORP
900 Tallwood Ave Apt 307 (33021-7918)
PHONE..................................954 439-6332
Ana Diaz Duenas, *President*
EMP: 13 EST: 2012
SALES (est): 1.5MM **Privately Held**
SIC: 3711 8011 Ambulances (motor vehi-
cles), assembly of; freestanding emer-
gency medical center

(G-5687)
WORLDWIDE INTL TRADE LLC
601 S 21st Ave (33020-6905)
PHONE..................................305 414-9774
Mary Sangio, *CFO*
Juan Villegas, *Mng Member*
EMP: 47 EST: 2018
SALES (est): 90MM **Privately Held**
SIC: 3751 5012 Motorcycles & related
parts; motorcycles

(G-5688)
ZACHEY DESIGN MARBLE INC
1649 Moffett St 4 (33020-6544)
PHONE..................................754 367-6261
Dumitru Marginean, *President*
EMP: 7 EST: 2005
SALES (est): 130.8K **Privately Held**
SIC: 3281 Marble, building: cut & shaped

(G-5689)
ZHYNO INC
3898 Pembroke Rd (33021-8108)
PHONE..................................844 313-1900
Liliana Ramirez, *President*
EMP: 7 EST: 2016
SALES (est): 695.5K **Privately Held**
SIC: 3578 Point-of-sale devices

Holmes Beach
Manatee County

(G-5690)
MACBONNER INC
Also Called: Macbonner Computer Services
315 58th St Unit J (34217-1555)
PHONE..................................941 778-7978
Bonner Joy, *President*
EMP: 18 EST: 1992

SALES (est): 1.3MM **Privately Held**
WEB: www.islander.org
SIC: 2711 Newspapers: publishing only,
not printed on site

(G-5691)
RED OAK SOFTWARE INC (PA)
528 67th St (34217-1201)
PHONE..................................973 316-6064
George Cummings, *President*
EMP: 5 EST: 1999
SALES (est): 1.7MM **Privately Held**
WEB: www.redoaksw.com
SIC: 7372 Prepackaged software

(G-5692)
TORTILLA BAY
5318 Marina Dr (34217-1709)
PHONE..................................941 778-3663
Perry Pittman, *Owner*
EMP: 7 EST: 2007
SALES (est): 239.8K **Privately Held**
WEB: www.tortilla-bay.com
SIC: 2099 Tortillas, fresh or refrigerated

Holt
Okaloosa County

(G-5693)
PRESTON WORKS INC
Also Called: Creative Metal Works
599 Armistead Blvd (32564-9166)
PHONE..................................850 932-0888
Robert Preston, *Owner*
Michelle Preston, *Office Mgr*
EMP: 8 EST: 2006
SALES (est): 910.5K **Privately Held**
SIC: 3499 Fire- or burglary-resistive prod-
ucts

(G-5694)
TRINITY EXTERIOR SOLUTIONS LLC
4292 Sundance Way (32564-9153)
P.O. Box 4082, Milton (32572-4082)
PHONE..................................850 393-9682
Debra Lorinczy, *Principal*
EMP: 9 EST: 2016
SALES (est): 360K **Privately Held**
SIC: 3299 1742 1771 Stucco; exterior in-
sulation & finish (EIFS) applicator; exte-
rior concrete stucco contractor

Homestead
Miami-Dade County

(G-5695)
A BETTER KITCHEN CABINETS INC
28501 Sw 152nd Ave Lot 21 (33033-1425)
PHONE..................................786 234-1897
Mylene J Romero, *President*
EMP: 7 EST: 2013
SALES (est): 124.4K **Privately Held**
SIC: 2434 Wood kitchen cabinets

(G-5696)
ACC FUELS OPERATION LLC
1498 N Homestead Blvd (33030-5008)
PHONE..................................305 246-8214
Antonio C Carrasco, *Principal*
EMP: 7 EST: 2011
SALES (est): 123.1K **Privately Held**
SIC: 2869 Fuels

(G-5697)
ACDM - PMS INC
Also Called: Princeton Machine Shop
25331 Sw 142nd Ave (33032-5424)
P.O. Box 924459, Princeton (33092-4459)
PHONE..................................305 258-0347
Dallas McGlothin, *Chairman*
Catherine McGlothin, *Administration*
Catherine McGlothin, *Admin Sec*
EMP: 5 EST: 1974
SQ FT: 4,800
SALES (est): 465.9K **Privately Held**
SIC: 3599 Machine shop, jobbing & repair

(G-5698)
ADDISON METAL ADDITIONS INC
20231 Sw 321st St (33030-5118)
PHONE..................................305 245-9860
Mark Addison, *Principal*
EMP: 7 EST: 2007
SALES (est): 519K **Privately Held**
WEB: www.addisonmetal.com
SIC: 3442 Shutters, door or window: metal

(G-5699)
AQUA TECHNOLOGIES
815 N Homestead Blvd (33030-5024)
PHONE..................................305 246-2125
Brian Judge, *Principal*
EMP: 8 EST: 2010
SALES (est): 262.2K **Privately Held**
SIC: 3089 Plastics products

(G-5700)
ARESSCO TECHNOLOGIES INC
15600 Sw 288th St Ste 307 (33033-1223)
PHONE..................................305 245-5854
Robert Houston, *President*
Michael J Marcus, *Vice Pres*
◆ EMP: 8 EST: 1998
SALES (est): 87K
SALES (corp-wide): 272K **Privately Held**
SIC: 3699 Security control equipment &
systems
PA: Hs Gateway Holdings, Inc.
15600 Sw 288th St Ste 307
Homestead FL 33033
305 245-5854

(G-5701)
B & K INSTALLATIONS INC
246 Sw 4th Ave (33030-7077)
PHONE..................................305 245-6968
William E Berzowski, *President*
Joseph M Kurilla, *Vice Pres*
Susan Kurilla, *Marketing Staff*
▼ EMP: 45 EST: 1979
SQ FT: 85,000
SALES (est): 8.5MM **Privately Held**
WEB: www.bkinstall.com
SIC: 3441 3444 3448 3231 Fabricated
structural metal; sheet metalwork; green-
houses: prefabricated metal; products of
purchased glass

(G-5702)
CEMEX CNSTR MTLS FLA LLC
Also Called: Cx1 Miami Mobile Mix
15900 Sw 408th St (33034)
PHONE..................................305 247-3011
EMP: 19 **Privately Held**
SIC: 3273 Ready-mixed concrete
HQ: Cemex Construction Materials Florida,
Llc
1501 Belvedere Rd
West Palm Beach FL 33406

(G-5703)
COMPLETE MOLD REMEDIATORS INC
31800 Sw 195th Ave (33030-5202)
PHONE..................................305 903-8885
Lisa M Brang, *Principal*
EMP: 11 EST: 2015
SALES (est): 877.8K **Privately Held**
SIC: 3544 Industrial molds

(G-5704)
CONTENDER BOATS INC
1820 Se 38th Ave (33035-1345)
PHONE..................................305 230-1600
Joseph Neber, *CEO*
Mike Collins, *General Mgr*
Irving Smith, *COO*
Stephen Cunningham, *Vice Pres*
Michael Behrndt, *Opers Staff*
◆ EMP: 200 EST: 1982
SQ FT: 80,000
SALES (est): 32.6MM **Privately Held**
WEB: www.contenderboats.com
SIC: 3732 Boat building & repairing

(G-5705)
CUSTOMFAB INC
23601 Sw 133rd Ave (33032-2306)
PHONE..................................786 339-9158
EMP: 7 EST: 2016

SALES (est): 85.6K **Privately Held**
WEB: www.customfabusa.com
SIC: 3498 Fabricated pipe & fittings

(G-5706)
DE TODOS TORTILLAS INC
820 N Krome Ave (33030-4407)
PHONE..................................305 248-4402
Borges Edson G Jr, *Principal*
EMP: 8 EST: 2014
SALES (est): 263.5K **Privately Held**
SIC: 2099 Tortillas, fresh or refrigerated

(G-5707)
DECO TRUSS COMPANY INC
13980 Sw 252nd St (33032-5406)
P.O. Box 924868 (33092-4868)
PHONE..................................305 257-1910
Sonia Espineira, *Corp Secy*
Mario R Espineira, *Vice Pres*
Mario Estinera, *Executive*
◆ EMP: 50 EST: 1983
SQ FT: 45,616
SALES (est): 7.8MM **Privately Held**
WEB: www.decotruss.com
SIC: 2439 5072 Trusses, wooden roof;
hardware

(G-5708)
DISCIPLINE MARKETING INC
Also Called: Galileo
21230 Sw 246th St (33031-3653)
PHONE..................................305 793-7358
Michael Whittmeyer, *President*
Mary Whittmeyer, *Vice Pres*
▲ EMP: 13 EST: 1988
SALES (est): 622.8K **Privately Held**
SIC: 3827 Binoculars

(G-5709)
DUENAS MOBILE APPLICATIONS LLC (PA)
Also Called: Vuziq
15600 Sw 288th St Ste 402 (33033-1223)
PHONE..................................305 851-3397
Carlos Duenas, *Mng Member*
Danny Duenas,
EMP: 18 EST: 2012
SALES (est): 820.8K **Privately Held**
SIC: 7372 Application computer software

(G-5710)
ECO PRINT INC
20450 Sw 248th St (33031-1604)
PHONE..................................305 248-1478
Natalie Hew, *Principal*
EMP: 9 EST: 2008
SALES (est): 118.3K **Privately Held**
SIC: 2752 Commercial printing, litho-
graphic

(G-5711)
GO LATINOS MAGAZINE LLC
13345 Sw 264th Ter (33032-7789)
PHONE..................................786 601-7693
Ervin Palacios, *Principal*
EMP: 7 EST: 2015
SALES (est): 132.3K **Privately Held**
WEB: www.golatinos.net
SIC: 2711 Newspapers, publishing & print-
ing

(G-5712)
H&K HOME SUPPLIES DISTRS LLC
10818 Sw 240th St (33032-4309)
PHONE..................................786 308-6024
Keniel Pena,
EMP: 10 EST: 2020
SALES (est): 283.4K **Privately Held**
SIC: 2051 7389 Bakery: wholesale or
wholesale/retail combined;

(G-5713)
HOMESTEAD DIAGNOSTIC CTR INC
650 Ne 22nd Ter Ste 100 (33033-4710)
PHONE..................................305 246-5600
Tomas Gonzales, *President*
EMP: 18 EST: 1999
SALES (est): 2.4MM **Privately Held**
WEB: www.homestead-diagnostic.com
SIC: 3829 8071 Medical diagnostic sys-
tems, nuclear; testing laboratories

(G-5714)
HOMESTEAD NEWSPAPERS INC
Also Called: South Dade News Leader
125 Ne 8th St Ste 2 (33030-4676)
P.O. Box 900340 (33090-0340)
PHONE..............................305 245-2311
Gary K Shorts, *President*
Charles P Smith, *Exec VP*
Shirley C Ellis, *Vice Pres*
Stanley M Ellis, *Vice Pres*
Glenn A Martin, *Vice Pres*
EMP: 1433 **EST:** 1912
SQ FT: 6,000
SALES (est): 5.4MM
SALES (corp-wide): 114.9MM **Privately Held**
SIC: 2711 Newspapers, publishing & printing
PA: Calkins Media Incorporated
8400 Bristol Pike
Levittown PA 19057
215 949-4000

(G-5715)
HORSESHOE PICKING INC
21400 Sw 392nd St (33034-6811)
PHONE..............................305 345-5778
Leonard Talarico, *Principal*
EMP: 9 **EST:** 2007
SALES (est): 213.6K **Privately Held**
SIC: 3462 Horseshoes

(G-5716)
INNOVATIVE HEAT CONCEPTS LLC
127 Sw 5th Ave (33030-7035)
PHONE..............................305 248-4971
Michael Valles, *Principal*
EMP: 8 **EST:** 2010
SALES (est): 122.9K **Privately Held**
WEB: www.innovativeheatconcepts.com
SIC: 3433 Heating equipment, except electric

(G-5717)
INSTITUTIONAL PRODUCTS INC
1011 Nw 6th St (33030-5624)
PHONE..............................305 248-4955
Geymonat Ivan, *CEO*
Ingrid L Crespo, *President*
Ana Maria Moran, *CFO*
▲ **EMP:** 25 **EST:** 1971
SQ FT: 15,000
SALES (est): 4.5MM **Privately Held**
WEB: www.institutionalproductsinc.com
SIC: 3083 1751 Plastic finished products, laminated; cabinet building & installation

(G-5718)
INTELLIGENT HEATER LLC
127 Sw 5th Ave (33030-7035)
P.O. Box 2005, Alpharetta GA (30023-2005)
PHONE..............................305 248-4971
Bosonto Gupta, *Mng Member*
▲ **EMP:** 8 **EST:** 1946
SQ FT: 30,000
SALES (est): 1.5MM **Privately Held**
WEB: www.intelligentheater.com
SIC: 3634 3822 3567 3625 Immersion heaters, electric: household; liquid level controls, residential or commercial heating; oven temperature controls, non-industrial type; electrical furnaces, ovens & heating devices, exc. induction; relays & industrial controls

(G-5719)
ISCHA PRODUCTS LLC ✪
23616 Sw 107th Pl (33032-6122)
PHONE..............................305 609-8244
Thatcher Bernhardt, *Owner*
EMP: 10 **EST:** 2021
SALES (est): 276.1K **Privately Held**
SIC: 2339 7389 5961 Women's & misses' accessories; ;

(G-5720)
J & A CUSTOM CABINETRY INC
15825 Sw 285th St (33033-6108)
PHONE..............................786 255-4181
Joseph Siddons, *Principal*
EMP: 8 **EST:** 2008
SALES (est): 884.3K **Privately Held**
WEB: www.jnacabinetry.com
SIC: 2434 Wood kitchen cabinets

(G-5721)
J & Z PRODUCTION AND PBLCY INC
4045 Ne 15th St (33033-5906)
PHONE..............................786 718-8204
Johnny P Cordova, *Principal*
EMP: 7 **EST:** 2009
SALES (est): 128.6K **Privately Held**
SIC: 2741 Miscellaneous publishing

(G-5722)
KEYSTONE PRECAST & COLUMNS COR
29630 Sw 183rd Ct (33030-3034)
PHONE..............................305 216-5375
Miguel A Dana Sr, *Principal*
EMP: 5 **EST:** 2005
SALES (est): 332.2K **Privately Held**
WEB: www.keystoneprecast.com
SIC: 3272 Concrete products, precast; precast terrazo or concrete products

(G-5723)
KEYSTONE PRODUCTS INC
1414 Nw 3rd Ave (33034-2225)
PHONE..............................305 245-4716
Peter Joseph Santi, *President*
Doug Santi, *Corp Secy*
Jim Santi, *Treasurer*
Vincenzo Santi, *Treasurer*
◆ **EMP:** 17 **EST:** 1976
SQ FT: 3,000
SALES (est): 1.8MM **Privately Held**
WEB: www.keystonecoralproducts.com
SIC: 3281 1411 Stone, quarrying & processing of own stone products; dimension stone

(G-5724)
KONCEPT SYSTEMS LLC
10755 Sw 244th Ter (33032-4686)
PHONE..............................786 610-0122
Ernesto Blanco, *Branch Mgr*
EMP: 24
SALES (corp-wide): 2.6MM **Privately Held**
WEB: www.konceptsystems.com
SIC: 3646 3651 3648 Commercial indusl & institutional electric lighting fixtures; audio electronic systems; speaker systems; stage lighting equipment; arc lighting fixtures
PA: Koncept Systems Llc
15802 Sylvan Lake Dr
Houston TX 77062
800 773-4910

(G-5725)
L AND TW OODWORK LLC
17420 Sw 236th St (33031-3507)
PHONE..............................305 742-4362
Tommy Jimenez, *Principal*
EMP: 5 **EST:** 2019
SALES (est): 427.7K **Privately Held**
SIC: 2431 Millwork

(G-5726)
LANDMARK PRECAST LLC
438 Nw 10th Ave (33030-5764)
P.O. Box 902033 (33090-2033)
PHONE..............................305 242-8888
Roger Tomasiono,
Steven Sproul,
EMP: 10 **EST:** 2004
SALES (est): 1.4MM **Privately Held**
WEB: www.landmarkprecast.com
SIC: 3272 Concrete products

(G-5727)
LEEWARD TECH
815 N Homestead Blvd # 405 (33030-5024)
PHONE..............................305 215-4526
Carlos Mauro, *Principal*
EMP: 9 **EST:** 2008
SALES (est): 453.9K **Privately Held**
SIC: 3679 4513 Electronic components; package delivery, private air

(G-5728)
LUMO PRINT INC
27750 S Dixie Hwy (33032-8222)
PHONE..............................305 246-0003
Moe Mohammed Hakssa, *President*
EMP: 5 **EST:** 1981

SQ FT: 1,200
SALES (est): 470.3K **Privately Held**
WEB: www.lumoprint.com
SIC: 2752 Commercial printing, offset

(G-5729)
MATTIS AEROSPACE
26085 S Dixie Hwy (33032-6613)
PHONE..............................305 910-2377
Melissa Vega, *President*
Kyle Quintero, *Purchasing*
Robert Mattis, *Info Tech Mgr*
EMP: 7 **EST:** 2013
SALES (est): 129.2K **Privately Held**
WEB: www.mattis.aero
SIC: 3728 Aircraft parts & equipment

(G-5730)
MIAMI TRANSFORMERS CORP
13935 Sw 252nd St (33032-5405)
PHONE..............................305 257-1491
Javier O Vila, *President*
Jorge J Vila, *Treasurer*
◆ **EMP:** 17 **EST:** 1995
SQ FT: 7,480
SALES (est): 3.6MM **Privately Held**
WEB: www.miamitransformers.com
SIC: 3612 Transformers, except electric

(G-5731)
MOORE & BODE GROUP LLC
2221 Se 27th Dr (33035-1329)
P.O. Box 140221, Coral Gables (33114-0221)
PHONE..............................786 615-9389
Sharon Moore Bode, *President*
Roberto E Bode, *Vice Pres*
EMP: 8 **EST:** 1984
SALES (est): 186.5K **Privately Held**
WEB: www.mooreandbode.com
SIC: 2121 Cigars

(G-5732)
MR NEXT LEVEL INVESTMENT LLC
25118 Sw 108th Ct (33032-6354)
PHONE..............................786 718-8056
Rene Orellana, *Mng Member*
EMP: 10 **EST:** 2020
SALES (est): 539.6K **Privately Held**
SIC: 2499 3631 7389 Woodenware, kitchen & household; household cooking equipment;

(G-5733)
NATURAL CRVINGS PET TREATS LLC
1100 Nw 7th St (33030-6695)
PHONE..............................786 404-8099
Patrick Caprez, *President*
Lucy Caprez, *Vice Pres*
▼ **EMP:** 5 **EST:** 2014
SALES (est): 984.4K **Privately Held**
WEB: www.naturalcravingsusa.com
SIC: 2047 Dog & cat food

(G-5734)
NEX SOFTWARE LLC
29690 Sw 183rd Ct (33030-3034)
PHONE..............................786 200-3396
Allan Gobin, *Principal*
EMP: 7 **EST:** 2010
SALES (est): 271.5K **Privately Held**
SIC: 7372 Prepackaged software

(G-5735)
PLANT SOLUTIONS INC
15901 Sw 272nd St (33031-3103)
PHONE..............................305 242-3103
Lionelt Marquez, *President*
Margaret Marquez, *President*
◆ **EMP:** 21 **EST:** 1993
SQ FT: 720
SALES (est): 4.1MM **Privately Held**
WEB: www.plantsolutionsinc.com
SIC: 2873 2874 Plant foods, mixed: from plants making nitrog. fertilizers; plant foods, mixed: from plants making phosphatic fertilizer

(G-5736)
RAPID SIGNS AND T SHIRTS
27466 S Dixie Hwy (33032-8213)
PHONE..............................786 486-2804
Olga D Lopez, *President*

EMP: 8 **EST:** 2017
SQ FT: 2,000
SALES (est): 374.4K **Privately Held**
WEB: www.rapidsignsandtshirts.com
SIC: 3993 Signs & advertising specialties

(G-5737)
SAM S ACCRSIO SONS PKG PROD IN
1225 Nw 2nd St (33030-5619)
P.O. Box 901767 (33090-1767)
PHONE..............................305 246-3455
Sam S Accursio Jr, *President*
Phyllis Accursio, *Corp Secy*
EMP: 11 **EST:** 1994
SQ FT: 30,923
SALES (est): 473.1K **Privately Held**
SIC: 2033 Vegetables: packaged in cans, jars, etc.

(G-5738)
SATEN LEAF NURSERY INC
13822 Sw 282nd Ter (33033-5725)
PHONE..............................305 216-5340
Elmer Guandique, *President*
EMP: 12 **EST:** 2005
SALES (est): 674.8K **Privately Held**
SIC: 2221 Satins

(G-5739)
SCHNEBLY REDLANDS WINERY INC
30205 Sw 217th Ave (33030-7601)
PHONE..............................786 247-2060
Peter Schnebly, *President*
Milton Montanez, *Facilities Mgr*
▲ **EMP:** 20 **EST:** 2004
SQ FT: 26,440
SALES (est): 2.9MM **Privately Held**
WEB: www.schneblywinery.com
SIC: 2084 Wines

(G-5740)
SMITTYS BOAT TOPS AND MAR EQP
Also Called: Smittys Boat Tops Sndwner Bats
23701 Sw 212th Ave (33031-1072)
PHONE..............................305 245-0229
William P Crowley, *President*
Robin Crowley, *Vice Pres*
▼ **EMP:** 8 **EST:** 1986
SQ FT: 10,000
SALES (est): 188.3K **Privately Held**
SIC: 2394 2426 2221 3548 Canvas & related products; chair seats, hardwood; glass & fiberglass broadwoven fabrics; welding & cutting apparatus & accessories; welding repair; boat building & repairing

(G-5741)
SOLARBEAM INTERNATIONAL INC
15600 Sw 288th St Ste 307 (33033-1223)
PHONE..............................305 248-8400
Robert Houston, *President*
Robin Marcus, *CFO*
EMP: 7 **EST:** 2007
SALES (est): 572.7K **Privately Held**
WEB: www.solarbeam.com
SIC: 3674 Solar cells

Homosassa
Citrus County

(G-5742)
AEB TECHNOLOGIES INC
Also Called: Lunasea Lighting
9619 W Yulee Dr (34448-4105)
PHONE..............................352 417-0009
Allen Burley, *CEO*
Bill Vengrofski, *Engineer*
Steve Jordan, *Controller*
▲ **EMP:** 7 **EST:** 1982
SQ FT: 12,000
SALES (est): 917.3K **Privately Held**
WEB: www.lunasealighting.com
SIC: 3575 7373 Computer terminals, monitors & components; computer integrated systems design

▲ = Import ▼ =Export
◆ =Import/Export

(G-5743)
CALIBER ELEMENTS LLC
9020 W Veterans Dr (34448-1488)
PHONE....................352 697-1415
Eric Willis,
EMP: 10 **EST:** 2013
SALES (est): 1.8MM **Privately Held**
WEB: www.caliberelements.com
SIC: 2819 Industrial inorganic chemicals

(G-5744)
CAPITAL STEEL INC
6260 S Tex Pt (34448-5922)
PHONE....................352 628-1700
Phil Bailey, *President*
James Gristwood, *Vice Pres*
David A Peters, *Vice Pres*
EMP: 10 **EST:** 2006
SQ FT: 1,000
SALES (est): 3.1MM **Privately Held**
SIC: 3441 Fabricated structural metal

(G-5745)
**CREATIVE CONCEPTS NCJ LLC
(PA)**
4203 S Purslane Dr (34448-3915)
PHONE....................352 302-8100
Nevin C Jenkins, *Mng Member*
EMP: 7 **EST:** 2016
SQ FT: 2,800
SALES (est): 482.3K **Privately Held**
SIC: 3469 Patterns on metal

(G-5746)
CREATIVE CONCEPTS NCJ LLC
7397 S Suncoast Blvd (34446-3406)
PHONE....................352 302-8100
EMP: 37
SALES (corp-wide): 482.3K **Privately
Held**
SIC: 3469 Patterns on metal
PA: Creative Concepts Ncj, Llc
4203 S Purslane Dr
Homosassa FL 34448
352 302-8100

(G-5747)
DIESELSITE INC
7400 W Industrial Ln # 6 (34448-5909)
PHONE....................888 414-3457
Robert T Riley, *Principal*
▲ **EMP:** 7 **EST:** 2012
SALES (est): 907.5K **Privately Held**
WEB: www.dieselsite.com
SIC: 3462 Automotive forgings, ferrous:
crankshaft, engine, axle, etc.

(G-5748)
EASY FOAM INC
4 Calendula Ct W (34446-5933)
P.O. Box 4255, Grand Junction CO (81502-
4255)
PHONE....................970 927-0209
Gregory Larson, *President*
Donald Cochran, *Vice Pres*
EMP: 9 **EST:** 2010
SQ FT: 8,000
SALES (est): 318.9K **Privately Held**
SIC: 2841 Detergents, synthetic organic or
inorganic alkaline

(G-5749)
GULF COAST READY MIX LLC
8778 W Jump Ct (34448-2323)
PHONE....................352 621-3900
Wallace Hindalong,
Crystal Nelson, *Admin Asst*
Pete Nelson, *Admin Asst*
Amber Litle, *Administration*
Lonnie G Gardner,
EMP: 20 **EST:** 2002
SQ FT: 1,700
SALES (est): 4.1MM **Privately Held**
WEB: www.gulfcoastreadymix.com
SIC: 3273 3271 Ready-mixed concrete;
concrete block & brick

(G-5750)
SCREEN MONKEY CORP
5841 W Kime Ln (34448-7330)
PHONE....................352 746-7091
Jeffrey P Scott, *President*
Denise A Scott, *Vice Pres*
EMP: 6 **EST:** 2010

SALES (est): 454.4K **Privately Held**
WEB: www.thescreenmonkey.com
SIC: 2759 1799 Commercial printing;
screening contractor: window, door, etc.

(G-5751)
SPORTS RADAR LTD
7397 S Suncoast Blvd (34446-3406)
PHONE....................352 503-6825
Nevin C Jenkins, *Mng Member*
Rande Newberry, *Mng Member*
▲ **EMP:** 6 **EST:** 1991
SALES (est): 786.2K **Privately Held**
WEB: www.sportsradargun.com
SIC: 3663 3949 3812 Radio broadcasting
& communications equipment; sporting &
athletic goods; search & navigation equip-
ment

(G-5752)
TECH TO SITE
41 Cypress Blvd W (34446-4504)
PHONE....................813 253-9381
Julanda Chree Norton, *Principal*
EMP: 7 **EST:** 2018
SALES (est): 156.8K **Privately Held**
SIC: 3398 Metal heat treating

Horseshoe Beach
Dixie County

(G-5753)
HORSESHOE SHRIMP BOAT LLC
77 Main St (32648-2100)
P.O. Box 383 (32648-0383)
PHONE....................352 356-1982
Donna J Futch, *Manager*
EMP: 7 **EST:** 2016
SALES (est): 282.6K **Privately Held**
SIC: 3462 Horseshoes

Hosford
Liberty County

(G-5754)
CP LOGGING INC
20688 Ne Burlington Rd (32334-2709)
PHONE....................850 379-8698
Gilford E Pullam, *President*
Anne Pullam, *Admin Sec*
EMP: 10 **EST:** 1999
SALES (est): 996K **Privately Held**
SIC: 2411 7389 Logging camps & contrac-
tors;

(G-5755)
G BLACK LOGGING LLC
15698 Ne Moore St (32334-2432)
P.O. Box 106 (32334-0106)
PHONE....................850 379-8747
Gary E Black, *Mng Member*
EMP: 6 **EST:** 2013
SALES (est): 739.8K **Privately Held**
SIC: 2411 Logging

(G-5756)
GEORGIA-PACIFIC LLC
12995 Ne State Road 65 (32334-2221)
PHONE....................850 379-4000
Tim Adams, *Plant Mgr*
Oland Purser, *Technical Staff*
EMP: 63
SALES (corp-wide): 36.9B **Privately Held**
WEB: www.gp.com
SIC: 2621 Paper mills
HQ: Georgia-Pacific Llc
133 Peachtree St Nw
Atlanta GA 30303
404 652-4000

(G-5757)
PAUL WHITE LOGGING INC
65 South (32334)
P.O. Box 113 (32334-0113)
PHONE....................850 379-8651
Kenneth P King, *President*
EMP: 5 **EST:** 1950
SALES (est): 483.4K **Privately Held**
SIC: 2411 4212 Timber, cut at logging
camp; timber trucking, local

Howey In The Hills
Lake County

(G-5758)
**G G MILLWORK CONTRACTOR
INC**
26008 Gaspar Ct (34737-5000)
PHONE....................305 522-6333
EMP: 22 **Privately Held**
SIC: 2431 Millwork
PA: G G Millwork Contractor Inc
300 Atlantic Dr Unit 7
Key Largo FL 33037

(G-5759)
SILVER SPRINGS CITRUS INC
25411 N Mare Ave (34737-3124)
P.O. Box 155 (34737-0155)
PHONE....................352 324-2101
Kenny Sadai, *Ch of Bd*
James O'Toole, *President*
Vince Petrucci, *Vice Pres*
Thomas Kolb, *CFO*
Dennis Parker, *Sales Mgr*
◆ **EMP:** 220 **EST:** 1921
SQ FT: 1,260
SALES (est): 29.6MM **Privately Held**
SIC: 2086 2037 Pasteurized & mineral
waters, bottled & canned; fruit juices,
frozen

(G-5760)
SILVER SPRINGS CITRUS LLC
25411 N Mare Ave (34737-3124)
PHONE....................352 324-2101
Kenichiro Sadai, *Manager*
Sadai Kenichiro, *Manager*
EMP: 18 **EST:** 2017
SALES (est): 453.7K **Privately Held**
SIC: 2086 Pasteurized & mineral waters,
bottled & canned

Hudson
Pasco County

(G-5761)
ADDTAD PARTNERS INC
Also Called: P&L Machine and Tool Co
9704 Katy Dr Ste 2 (34667-4397)
PHONE....................727 863-0847
Alan Dorval, *President*
Trudy Dorval, *Treasurer*
EMP: 6 **EST:** 2014
SQ FT: 4,500
SALES (est): 518.9K **Privately Held**
SIC: 3599 Machine & other job shop work

(G-5762)
ARTVINT CORP
10441 Frierson Lake Dr (34669-3442)
PHONE....................727 856-3565
Amanda J Wisniewski, *President*
▲ **EMP:** 7 **EST:** 2011
SALES (est): 77.8K **Privately Held**
SIC: 2759 7389 5199 5399 Commercial
printing; ; general merchandise, non-
durable; miscellaneous general merchan-
dise

(G-5763)
**AVCO MATERIALS AND SVCS
INC**
Also Called: AVCO MARINE CONSTRUC-
TION
7032 Clark St (34667-1310)
PHONE....................727 233-2043
Edward Avella, *CEO*
EMP: 45 **EST:** 2010
SALES (est): 7MM **Privately Held**
SIC: 1389 Construction, repair & disman-
tling services

(G-5764)
BETTER MIX
9301 Denton Ave (34667-4340)
PHONE....................800 232-6833
Chuck Jackson, *Manager*
EMP: 15 **EST:** 2014
SALES (est): 2.1MM **Privately Held**
WEB: www.betermix.com
SIC: 3273 Ready-mixed concrete

(G-5765)
**CABINET DREAMS & THINGS
INC**
13954 Sand Oak Ct (34669-1367)
PHONE....................727 514-0847
Debra Barker-Sudnik, *Principal*
EMP: 6 **EST:** 2014
SALES (est): 335K **Privately Held**
WEB: www.cabinetdreamsandthings.com
SIC: 2434 Wood kitchen cabinets

(G-5766)
**CLEAR HORIZON VENTURES
COMPANY**
Also Called: Petersen Metals
9410 Eden Ave (34667-5202)
PHONE....................727 372-1100
Paul Schoettelkotte, *President*
Matt Palmer, *Vice Pres*
Shannon Wilson, *Vice Pres*
EMP: 19 **EST:** 2010
SALES (est): 4.6MM **Privately Held**
SIC: 3446 Balconies, metal

(G-5767)
**COASTAL CRAFTSMEN
ALUMINUM INC (PA)**
15046 Labor Pl (34667-3477)
P.O. Box 5606 (34674-5606)
PHONE....................727 868-8802
Bill Woodard, *President*
John Holcomb, *Opers Staff*
John Cotilletta, *Controller*
Pat Shaw, *Sales Staff*
▲ **EMP:** 30 **EST:** 1980
SQ FT: 7,200
SALES (est): 5MM **Privately Held**
WEB: www.coastalcraftsmen.com
SIC: 3448 1799 Screen enclosures; fence
construction

(G-5768)
D & I CARBIDE TOOL CO INC
12104 Parkwood St (34669-3790)
PHONE....................727 848-3356
Fax: 727 848-3374
EMP: 10
SQ FT: 5,000
SALES (est): 800K **Privately Held**
SIC: 3441 Mfg Fabricated Structural Metal
Specializing In Carbide Wear Parts

(G-5769)
**DASHCOVERS PLUS DEPOT
DISTRS**
18304 Oak Way Dr (34667-6335)
PHONE....................954 961-7774
Jane Randolph, *President*
Danny Randolph, *Vice Pres*
▲ **EMP:** 5 **EST:** 2003
SALES (est): 582.5K **Privately Held**
WEB: www.dashcover.com
SIC: 3714 Motor vehicle parts & acces-
sories

(G-5770)
**DONE RIGHT FIRE GEAR REPR
INC**
7621 Maryland Ave (34667-3290)
PHONE....................727 848-9019
Pat Gansert, *President*
Anna Collins, *COO*
Teri Moulton, *CFO*
Renee Costanzo, *Office Mgr*
EMP: 7 **EST:** 2005
SALES (est): 603K **Privately Held**
WEB: www.gearwash.com
SIC: 3569 7699 Firefighting apparatus &
related equipment; fire control (military)
equipment repair

(G-5771)
**DONS CABINETS AND
WOODWORKING**
Also Called: General Cabinets Pasco County
15801 Archer St (34667-3817)
PHONE....................727 863-3404
Donald J Josephik, *President*
EMP: 10 **EST:** 1999
SQ FT: 15,000

GEOGRAPHIC

SALES (est): 1MM **Privately Held**
SIC: 2434 2542 2522 2521 Wood kitchen cabinets; partitions & fixtures, except wood; office furniture, except wood; wood office furniture; wood television & radio cabinets

(G-5772)
FIESTA MARINE PRODUCTS INC
Also Called: Fiesta Pontoon Boats
11016 State Road 52 (34669-3047)
Carl Morahan, *President*
EMP: 12 **EST:** 1996
SQ FT: 10,000
SALES (est): 1.1MM **Privately Held**
WEB: www.fiestaboats.com
SIC: 3732 Pontoons, except aircraft & in-flatable

(G-5773)
FLORIDA ENGINEERED CONSTRU
Also Called: Castcrete
16835 Us Highway 19 (34667-4318)
PHONE................................727 863-7451
Mike Hardy, *Manager*
EMP: 8
SALES (corp-wide): 28.5MM **Privately Held**
WEB: www.castcrete.com
SIC: 3272 Concrete products
PA: Florida Engineered Construction Products Corporation
6324 County Road 579
Seffner FL 33584
813 621-4641

(G-5774)
FLOWERS BKG CO BRADENTON LLC
Also Called: Flowers Baking Company
16721 Us Highway 19 (34667-4316)
PHONE................................941 758-5656
Chris Peer, *Manager*
EMP: 25
SALES (corp-wide): 4.3B **Publicly Held**
WEB: www.flobradconf.com
SIC: 2051 Bread, cake & related products
HQ: Flowers Baking Co. Of Bradenton, Llc
6490 Parkland Dr
Sarasota FL 34243

(G-5775)
GRECO ALUM RAILINGS USA INC
9410 Eden Ave (34667-5202)
PHONE................................727 372-4545
EMP: 73 **EST:** 2002
SALES (est): 10.8MM
SALES (corp-wide): 626.4MM **Publicly Held**
WEB: www.grecorailings.com
SIC: 3446 Railings, prefabricated metal
PA: Csw Industrials, Inc.
5420 Lyndon B Johnson Fwy
Dallas TX 75240
214 884-3777

(G-5776)
GREENWOOD LAKE NEWS INC (PA)
Also Called: Greenwood Lk & W Milford News
13032 Pinnacle Ln (34669-2403)
PHONE................................845 477-2575
Ann Chaimowitz, *President*
EMP: 10 **EST:** 1964
SQ FT: 1,000
SALES (est): 782.3K **Privately Held**
SIC: 2711 Newspapers: publishing only, not printed on site

(G-5777)
GULF VIEW PLASTICS INC
18816 Oak Way Dr (34667-5139)
PHONE................................727 379-3072
Donna Boyle, *Principal*
Russ Boyle, *Accounts Mgr*
EMP: 5 **EST:** 2010
SALES (est): 416.9K **Privately Held**
WEB: www.gulfviewplastics.com
SIC: 3089 Injection molding of plastics

(G-5778)
INNEVAPE LLC
9718 Katy Dr Ste 2 (34667-5207)
PHONE................................631 957-6500
Thomas Klingensmith, *Principal*
EMP: 6 **EST:** 2016
SALES (est): 761.2K **Privately Held**
WEB: www.innevape.com
SIC: 3999 Cigar & cigarette holders

(G-5779)
K L DISTRIBUTING INC
7425 Sailfish Dr (34667-3250)
PHONE................................415 800-2158
Lola Lindon, *Manager*
EMP: 9 **EST:** 1995
SALES (est): 46.5K **Privately Held**
SIC: 2211 Bandages, gauzes & surgical fabrics, cotton

(G-5780)
KINGSTON AUTOMOTIVE & WLDG LLC
8039 Palatine Dr (34667-3545)
PHONE................................727 378-4881
Edwin Kingston, *Principal*
EMP: 7 **EST:** 2019
SALES (est): 449.3K **Privately Held**
WEB: kingston-automotive-and-welding.business.site
SIC: 7692 Automotive welding

(G-5781)
MADE FUR YOU INC
12121 Little Rd (34667-2924)
PHONE................................813 444-7707
Joanna D Lee, *Branch Mgr*
EMP: 10
SALES (corp-wide): 116.6K **Privately Held**
WEB: www.madefuryou.com
SIC: 3999 Furs
PA: Made Fur You Inc.
18112 Thomas Blvd
Hudson FL 34667
813 444-7707

(G-5782)
MARINE ENGINE CONTROLS INC
Also Called: M E C I
9035 Wister Ln (34669-1948)
PHONE................................727 518-8080
Patricia J Smith, *President*
John Smith, *Vice Pres*
EMP: 10 **EST:** 1991
SALES (est): 730.7K **Privately Held**
WEB: www.mecicontrols.com
SIC: 3625 Marine & navy auxiliary controls

(G-5783)
P&L MACHINE & TOOL COMPANY INC
9704 Katy Dr Ste 2 (34667-4397)
PHONE................................727 863-0847
Paul Pataki, *President*
Malinda Pataki, *Corp Secy*
EMP: 5 **EST:** 1974
SQ FT: 3,500
SALES (est): 423.3K **Privately Held**
WEB: www.plmachineinc.com
SIC: 3599 Machine shop, jobbing & repair

(G-5784)
PARKWAY DENTAL SERVICES LLC
9914 State Road 52 (34669-3008)
PHONE................................800 257-0400
John Hall, *General Mgr*
Mandy Hull, *Vice Pres*
Christopher Cooley, *Mng Member*
EMP: 42 **EST:** 1974
SALES (est): 12.5MM **Privately Held**
WEB: www.parkwaydental.com
SIC: 3843 Dental equipment

(G-5785)
PHOENIX TRINITY MFG INC
10620 Harris Loop (34667-6213)
PHONE................................937 619-0172
Brian Williams, *President*
Tiffany Williams, *Treasurer*
EMP: 7 **EST:** 2011
SQ FT: 6,000

SALES (est): 889.8K **Privately Held**
WEB: www.ptrinity.com
SIC: 3443 3599 Metal parts; electrical discharge machining (EDM)

(G-5786)
RACHEL ALLY ❂
9437 Debbie Ln (34669-1832)
PHONE................................727 804-9596
Rachel Ally, *Owner*
EMP: 10 **EST:** 2021
SALES (est): 600K **Privately Held**
SIC: 1389 Construction, repair & dismantling services

(G-5787)
SARASOTA LEATHER GALLERY INC (PA)
15941 Us Highway 19 (34667-3654)
PHONE................................800 741-4336
Bruce Weintraub, *President*
EMP: 5 **EST:** 2014
SALES (est): 1.4MM **Privately Held**
WEB: www.leathergallerysarasota.com
SIC: 3199 Boxes, leather

(G-5788)
TD TRA -DIX SUPPLY INC
Also Called: Hudson Do It Best Hardware
14196 Us Highway 19 (34667-1167)
PHONE................................727 869-8662
EMP: 7 **EST:** 2013
SALES (est): 440.1K **Privately Held**
SIC: 3429 Builders' hardware

(G-5789)
TOM WATSON ENTERPRISES INC
Also Called: Spring Hill Newsletter
9629 Amilia Dr Ste 4 (34667-4371)
PHONE................................352 683-5097
Tom Watson, *President*
Kathryn Watson, *Vice Pres*
EMP: 8 **EST:** 1978
SQ FT: 1,500
SALES (est): 732.2K **Privately Held**
WEB: www.tomwatson.com
SIC: 2711 7948 7299 1611 Newspapers: publishing only, not printed on site; stock car racing; massage parlor; concrete construction: roads, highways, sidewalks, etc.

(G-5790)
TOWN COUNTRY INDUSTRIES
16748 Scheer Blvd (34667-4235)
PHONE................................727 862-5483
EMP: 6 **EST:** 2020
SALES (est): 316.5K **Privately Held**
SIC: 3365 Aluminum foundries

(G-5791)
VINEYARD 101 LLC
12930 Us Highway 19 (34667-1745)
PHONE................................727 819-5300
Anita Castriota, *Principal*
EMP: 7 **EST:** 2015
SALES (est): 99K **Privately Held**
SIC: 2084 Wines, brandy & brandy spirits

Hurlburt Field
Okaloosa County

(G-5792)
L C INDUSTRIES INC
Also Called: LCI-leu
125 Bennett Ave (32544-5705)
PHONE................................850 581-0117
Jim March, *Branch Mgr*
EMP: 17
SALES (corp-wide): 6.7MM **Privately Held**
WEB: www.lcindustries.com
SIC: 2311 Military uniforms, men's & youths': purchased materials
PA: L C Industries Inc.
4500 Emperor Blvd
Durham NC 27703
919 596-8277

Hutchinson Island
St. Lucie County

(G-5793)
RAILTEC CONSTRUCTIONS COMPANY
Also Called: Railtech Construction
4949 N Hwy A1a Apt 182 (34949-8242)
P.O. Box 314, Sykesville MD (21784-0314)
PHONE................................410 795-0712
Bill Kirchoff, *Owner*
EMP: 6 **EST:** 1996
SALES (est): 550.7K **Privately Held**
WEB: www.railtecrailings.com
SIC: 3446 Stairs, staircases, stair treads: prefabricated metal

Hypoluxo
Palm Beach County

(G-5794)
APOLLO WORLDWIDE INC
158 Las Brisas Cir (33462-7072)
PHONE................................561 585-3865
Michael Mc Davitt, *President*
▲ **EMP:** 9 **EST:** 1997
SALES (est): 595.2K **Privately Held**
WEB: www.kirkmorris.com
SIC: 3589 5064 3631 Microwave ovens (cooking equipment), commercial; refrigerators & freezers; microwave ovens, including portable: household

Immokalee
Collier County

(G-5795)
ANDYS WELDING SERVICES INC
1321 Carson Rd (34142-2073)
PHONE................................239 478-4907
Andres Antonio, *Principal*
EMP: 7 **EST:** 2013
SALES (est): 62.9K **Privately Held**
SIC: 7692 Welding repair

(G-5796)
GLOBAL MANUFACTURING TECH INC
160 Airpark Blvd Unit 101 (34142-3806)
PHONE................................239 657-3720
Larry Fox, *President*
EMP: 6 **EST:** 1997
SALES (est): 565.6K **Privately Held**
SIC: 3559 Degreasing machines, automotive & industrial

(G-5797)
GULF CONNECTORS INC
160 Airpark Blvd Unit 104 (34142-3806)
PHONE................................239 657-2986
Adrian Michelle, *CEO*
Minette Langston, *Admin Sec*
EMP: 5 **EST:** 2005
SALES (est): 515.8K **Privately Held**
SIC: 3643 Electric connectors

(G-5798)
IMMOKALEE RANCH
4451 County Road 846 (34142-9659)
PHONE................................239 657-2000
Ronnie Raulerson, *Partner*
Collier Enterprises, *Partner*
EMP: 7 **EST:** 1951
SALES (est): 420.5K **Privately Held**
WEB: www.immokaleecra.com
SIC: 2013 Calf's foot jelly from purchased meat

(G-5799)
MAVERICK NATURAL RESOURCES LLC
909 County Road 846 (34142-9724)
P.O. Box 3236 (34143-3236)
PHONE................................239 657-2171
EMP: 15

▲ = Import ▼=Export
◆ =Import/Export

SALES (corp-wide): 295.4MM **Privately Held**
WEB: www.mavresources.com
SIC: 1382 Oil & gas exploration services
PA: Maverick Natural Resources, Llc
1111 Bagby St Ste 1600
Houston TX 77002
713 437-8000

Indialantic
Brevard County

(G-5800)
A1A RAW LLC
Also Called: Bunkys Raw Bar
2372 N Hwy A1a (32903-2509)
P.O. Box 361017, Melbourne (32936-1017)
PHONE..................................321 777-2526
Douglas F Walker,
EMP: 8 **EST:** 2014
SALES (est): 456K **Privately Held**
SIC: 2599 Bar, restaurant & cafeteria furniture

(G-5801)
ADAMS GLASS CO
116 Melbourne Ave (32903-3216)
PHONE..................................816 842-8686
Glass Adams, Principal
EMP: 8 **EST:** 2004
SALES (est): 170.9K **Privately Held**
WEB: www.adamsglassllc.com
SIC: 3231 Products of purchased glass

(G-5802)
C-NOTE SOLUTIONS INC
334 4th Ave (32903-4214)
PHONE..................................321 952-2490
Gary Parish, CEO
Jim Griffiths, Accountant
Derek Ford, Technical Staff
EMP: 8 **EST:** 2013
SALES (est): 208.7K **Privately Held**
WEB: c-note-solutions.myshopify.com
SIC: 3699 Security devices

(G-5803)
GOLF SHAFT DEALS INC
529 Franklyn Ave (32903-4109)
PHONE..................................321 591-7824
Lee Sanford, Principal
EMP: 7 **EST:** 2010
SALES (est): 112.3K **Privately Held**
SIC: 3949 Shafts, golf club

Indian Harbour Beach
Brevard County

(G-5804)
BULLION INTERNATIONAL INC
Also Called: Highland Mint
4100 N Riverside Dr (32937-4834)
PHONE..................................321 773-2727
Michael Kott, President
Monica Scroggie, Vice Pres
Geet Garg, Opers Staff
EMP: 120 **EST:** 1989
SQ FT: 38,000
SALES (est): 40MM **Privately Held**
WEB: www.highlandmint.com
SIC: 3911 Jewelry, precious metal

(G-5805)
ORCOM LABS INC
131 Tomahawk Dr Ste 9b (32937-1814)
PHONE..................................321 773-0741
Teresa Doherty, President
Bob Kime, Vice Pres
EMP: 7 **EST:** 1991
SQ FT: 600
SALES (est): 321.7K **Privately Held**
WEB: www.orcomtechnologies.com
SIC: 3842 Foot appliances, orthopedic

(G-5806)
PAXEN PUBLISHING LLC (PA)
2194 Highway A1a Ste 208 (32937-4931)
PHONE..................................321 425-3030
Herbert Hilderley, Principal
Richard Semancik, Principal
Deanna Crosson, Vice Pres
Amber Rigney, Vice Pres

Lindsey Alf, CFO
EMP: 7 **EST:** 2017
SALES (est): 1.4MM **Privately Held**
WEB: www.aztecsoftware.com
SIC: 2741 Miscellaneous publishing

(G-5807)
RTA CABINETS & MORE LLC
222 E Eau Gallie Blvd (32937-4874)
PHONE..................................321 288-3068
Robert F Erario, President
EMP: 6 **EST:** 2015
SALES (est): 1.2MM **Privately Held**
WEB: www.cabinetsonthecoast.com
SIC: 2434 5211 Wood kitchen cabinets; cabinets, kitchen

(G-5808)
STEVEN M ROESSLER LLC
Also Called: Printfast & Office Supplies
1859 South Patrick Dr (32937-4377)
PHONE..................................321 773-2300
Steven Roessler,
EMP: 5 **EST:** 1986
SQ FT: 3,000
SALES (est): 386.9K **Privately Held**
SIC: 2752 5943 Commercial printing, offset; office forms & supplies

Indian Rocks Beach
Pinellas County

(G-5809)
SLYCE INC
311 Gulf Blvd Ste 2 (33785-2548)
PHONE..................................727 408-5272
Ken W Gillespie, Principal
Christopher Derry, Manager
Hank Donnay, Software Engr
EMP: 8 **EST:** 2010
SALES (est): 1MM **Privately Held**
WEB: www.slycepizzabar.com
SIC: 3421 Table & food cutlery, including butchers'

Indian Shores
Pinellas County

(G-5810)
GREAT BAY SIGNS INC
19106 Gulf Blvd Unit 302 (33785-2125)
PHONE..................................727 437-1091
Starlyn Fikkert, Principal
Joan Marzi, Administration
EMP: 7 **EST:** 2015
SALES (est): 313.6K **Privately Held**
WEB: tampayborcityfl.image360.com
SIC: 3993 Signs & advertising specialties

Indiantown
Martin County

(G-5811)
ALUMACART INC
19100 Sw Warfield Blvd (34956-9766)
PHONE..................................772 675-2158
Jennifer Knoebel, President
▼ **EMP:** 10 **EST:** 2006
SALES (est): 1.2MM **Privately Held**
WEB: www.alumacart.net
SIC: 3449 3498 3334 3446 Miscellaneous metalwork; fabricated pipe & fittings; primary aluminum; architectural metalwork; aluminum extruded products

(G-5812)
BAY STATE MILLING COMPANY
19150 Sw Warfield Blvd (34956-9766)
P.O. Box 1280 (34956-1280)
PHONE..................................772 597-2056
Dan Collins, Exec VP
Doug J Dewitt, Vice Pres
Walker Humphries, Vice Pres
Len Wunderly, Plant Supt
Sean Costello, Plant Mgr
EMP: 45

SALES (corp-wide): 131.8MM **Privately Held**
WEB: www.baystatemilling.com
SIC: 2041 Flour mills, cereal (except rice)
PA: Bay State Milling Company
100 Congress St Ste 2
Quincy MA 02169
617 328-4400

(G-5813)
GILIBERTI INC
16015 Sw Farm Rd (34956-3526)
PHONE..................................772 597-1870
John F Giliberti Sr, President
John F Giliberti Jr, Vice Pres
▼ **EMP:** 14 **EST:** 1986
SQ FT: 10,000
SALES (est): 2MM **Privately Held**
WEB: www.giliberti.com
SIC: 3711 Automobile assembly, including specialty automobiles

(G-5814)
GUYTON INDUSTRIES LLC
Also Called: Guyton's Custom Design
14601 Sw 168th Ave (34956-3836)
PHONE..................................772 208-3019
Guyton Stone, President
EMP: 20 **EST:** 2017
SALES (est): 1.3MM **Privately Held**
SIC: 2599 2211 2541 5211 Cabinets, factory; furniture denim; cabinets, lockers & shelving; cabinets, kitchen; cabinet work, custom; cabinet building & installation

(G-5815)
SCARB INDUSTRIES INC
15845 Sw Warfield Blvd (34956-3502)
PHONE..................................772 597-3898
Stephen Blake, President
EMP: 10 **EST:** 2003
SALES (est): 330.7K **Privately Held**
SIC: 3999 Barber & beauty shop equipment

Inglis
Levy County

(G-5816)
BUILT-RITE CABINETS INC
18290 Se Highway 19 (34449-4610)
PHONE..................................352 447-2238
Tom Thomas, President
EMP: 8 **EST:** 1977
SALES (est): 908.5K **Privately Held**
WEB: www.builtriteinc.org
SIC: 2434 Wood kitchen cabinets

(G-5817)
GENTEEL COATINGS LLC
10151 Se 195th St (34449-3760)
PHONE..................................772 708-1781
William A Scott III, Principal
EMP: 7 **EST:** 2008
SALES (est): 94.3K **Privately Held**
SIC: 3479 Metal coating & allied service

(G-5818)
GULFSHORE MANUFACTURING INC
Also Called: Young Boats
131 Highway 19 N (34449-9301)
P.O. Box 130 (34449-0130)
PHONE..................................352 447-1330
Robb D Young, President
J Brad Young, Treasurer
Rosemary T Young, Admin Sec
EMP: 12 **EST:** 1997
SQ FT: 5,000
SALES (est): 1.7MM **Privately Held**
WEB: www.youngboats.com
SIC: 3732 Boats, fiberglass: building & repairing

Inlet Beach
Walton County

(G-5819)
OUTPOST 30A LLC
11 N Castle Harbour Dr F (32461-8248)
PHONE..................................850 909-0138

Caitlin Bloodworth, Office Mgr
Mary Clark, Mng Member
EMP: 10 **EST:** 2014
SALES (est): 504.9K **Privately Held**
SIC: 2519 5812 Household furniture, except wood or metal: upholstered; coffee shop

Interlachen
Putnam County

(G-5820)
ROYAL MANOR VINEYARD & WINERY
224 Royal Ave (32148-7267)
PHONE..................................386 684-6270
Thomas J Pasco, Principal
EMP: 7 **EST:** 2008
SALES (est): 207.2K **Privately Held**
WEB: www.royalmanormeadery.com
SIC: 2084 Wines

Inverness
Citrus County

(G-5821)
ADVANCE GREEN ENERGY INC
523 S Us Highway 41 (34450-6027)
PHONE..................................352 765-3850
Peter M Barbee, President
Bradley Dye, Vice Pres
Debra Davis, Executive Asst
EMP: 6 **EST:** 2017
SALES (est): 529.6K **Privately Held**
WEB: www.advancegreenenergy.us
SIC: 1389 Oil consultants

(G-5822)
CMI MICROCLIMATES INC
1720 S Tranquil Ave (34450-5138)
PHONE..................................607 569-2738
Carmen Kramer, Principal
EMP: 11 **EST:** 2018
SALES (est): 512.4K **Privately Held**
SIC: 2655 Fiber cans, drums & similar products

(G-5823)
CONSULTANT MGT GROUP LLC
200 W Main St (34450-4855)
PHONE..................................352 344-4001
Giraldo Alfonso, Owner
Chad W Waller, Mng Member
Shannon Wallen, Manager
Ryan G Waller,
EMP: 9 **EST:** 2011
SQ FT: 1,500
SALES (est): 1.4MM **Privately Held**
WEB: www.cmgutilities.com
SIC: 3568 8741 Power transmission equipment; business management

(G-5824)
CUSTOM MANUFACTURING INC
Also Called: CMI Microclimates
1720 S Tranquil Ave (34450-5138)
PHONE..................................607 569-2738
Carmen J Waters, President
Michael Waters, Vice Pres
▲ **EMP:** 5 **EST:** 1990
SALES (est): 700K **Privately Held**
SIC: 2655 Containers, liquid tight fiber: from purchased material

(G-5825)
DAN FRAME & TRIM INC
7770 E Rustic Trl (34453-1391)
PHONE..................................352 726-4567
EMP: 8
SALES (est): 343.7K **Privately Held**
SIC: 1442 Construction Sand/Gravel

(G-5826)
DLZ HOLDINGS SOUTH INC (PA)
956 S Us Highway 41 (34450-6861)
PHONE..................................352 344-8741
David Ziebarth, President
Keven Fults, Plant Mgr
Karen Wood, Controller
Eric Wood, Marketing Staff
▼ **EMP:** 12 **EST:** 1985

SALES (est): 4.6MM **Privately Held**
SIC: 2851 Lacquers, varnishes, enamels & other coatings

(G-5827)
FLORAL CITY AIRBOAT CO INC (PA)
5098 S Florida Ave (34450-7258)
P.O. Box 292, Floral City (34436-0292)
PHONE..........................352 637-4390
Michael Emrich, *CEO*
Terrie Emrich, *President*
Lisa Calderone, *Manager*
EMP: 11 EST: 1986
SQ FT: 13,500
SALES (est): 1.5MM **Privately Held**
WEB: www.airboatfl.com
SIC: 3732 Boat building & repairing

(G-5828)
GALAXY CUSTOM GRANITE INC
5388 E Jasmine Ln (34453-1069)
PHONE..........................352 220-2822
Jesse O Butzer, *Principal*
Daniel Negrin, *Accounts Mgr*
EMP: 8 EST: 2007
SALES (est): 115.3K **Privately Held**
SIC: 3281 Table tops, marble

(G-5829)
GREEN FOREST PRODUCTS LLC
105 N Apopka Ave (34450-4237)
PHONE..........................352 341-5500
Jeffrey Barnes, *President*
Chay Barnes, *Vice Pres*
◆ EMP: 7 EST: 2000
SQ FT: 1,800
SALES (est): 963.9K **Privately Held**
WEB: www.greenforestprod.com
SIC: 2621 Towels, tissues & napkins: paper & stock

(G-5830)
JANS VENTURES LLC
Also Called: Hemp Pantry
2044 Highway 44 W (34453-3858)
PHONE..........................352 341-1710
Rebekah Potter, *Mng Member*
EMP: 10 EST: 2020
SALES (est): 250K **Privately Held**
SIC: 3999

(G-5831)
JPS DIGITAL LLC
4860 S Marsh Hawk Ter (34452-7847)
PHONE..........................813 501-6040
Susan Janicki, *Branch Mgr*
EMP: 10
SALES (corp-wide): 149.3K **Privately Held**
SIC: 2752 Commercial printing, lithographic
PA: Jps Digital Llc
2231 Elizabeth Dr
Brandon FL
813 600-3077

(G-5832)
KOMMANDER SOFTWARE LLC
2271 E Steven St (34453-9561)
PHONE..........................407 906-2121
William Kicklighter, *CEO*
EMP: 8 EST: 2015
SALES (est): 390.7K **Privately Held**
WEB: www.detailkommander.com
SIC: 7372 Prepackaged software

(G-5833)
PERL INC
Also Called: La Perle Memorials
5009 S Florida Ave (34450-7257)
P.O. Box 447 (34451-0447)
PHONE..........................352 726-2483
David La Perle, *President*
EMP: 10 EST: 1955
SQ FT: 2,000
SALES (est): 1.2MM **Privately Held**
WEB: www.perlgmbh.de
SIC: 3272 7389 Tombstones, precast terrazzo or concrete; crane & aerial lift service

(G-5834)
SINCERE SENTIMENTS INC
8001 E Shannon Ct (34450-2711)
PHONE..........................352 287-1232
Anthony Caponigro, *Principal*
EMP: 8 EST: 2008
SALES (est): 212.9K **Privately Held**
SIC: 2771 Greeting cards

(G-5835)
TIMES PUBLISHING COMPANY
Also Called: Citrus Times Edition
301 W Main St (34450-4743)
PHONE..........................352 567-6660
Andrew Barnes, *Ch of Bd*
EMP: 17
SALES (corp-wide): 14.9MM **Privately Held**
WEB: www.tampabay.com
SIC: 2711 Newspapers, publishing & printing
HQ: Times Publishing Company
490 1st Ave S
Saint Petersburg FL 33701
727 893-8111

Islamorada
Monroe County

(G-5836)
KENTUCKY WELDING LLC
100 Palm Ln (33036-3015)
PHONE..........................305 852-7433
EMP: 7 EST: 2018
SALES (est): 36.9K **Privately Held**
WEB: www.kentuckyweldinginstitute.com
SIC: 7692 Welding repair

(G-5837)
LARGO ALUMINUM INC
86500 Overseas Hwy (33036-3201)
P.O. Box 659, Tavernier (33070-0659)
PHONE..........................305 852-2390
John Kasianowicz, *President*
Michael Powell, *Vice Pres*
EMP: 11 EST: 1978
SQ FT: 6,042
SALES (est): 363.1K **Privately Held**
SIC: 3355 1761 5211 3446 Rails, rolled & drawn, aluminum; roofing contractor; lumber & other building materials; architectural metalwork; sheet metalwork; aluminum extruded products

(G-5838)
S & S PERFORMANCE INC
Also Called: S&S Performance Marine
80460 Overseas Hwy (33036-3750)
PHONE..........................305 951-9846
Erik W Shisler, *President*
EMP: 5 EST: 2015
SALES (est): 316.4K **Privately Held**
WEB: www.ssperformancemarine.com
SIC: 3732 5541 Boat building & repairing; marine service station

Jacksonville
Duval County

(G-5839)
1425 N WASHINGTON STREET LLC
12808 Gran Bay Pkwy W (32258-4468)
PHONE..........................904 680-6600
EMP: 9 EST: 2015
SALES: 7MM
SALES (corp-wide): 749.2MM **Privately Held**
SIC: 7372 Prepackaged software
HQ: Web.Com Group, Inc.
5335 Gate Pkwy Ste 200
Jacksonville FL 32256

(G-5840)
3TISSUE LLC
8286 Wstn Way Cir C9 C10 (32256)
PHONE..........................904 540-4335
Hector Hurtado, *Manager*
Hector Hurtado Sr,
Mario A Hurtado,
▲ EMP: 5 EST: 2015

SQ FT: 6,000
SALES (est): 360.1K **Privately Held**
SIC: 2621 Tissue paper; toweling tissue, paper

(G-5841)
4303 SILVERWOOD LLC
4401 San Jose Ln (32207-6236)
PHONE..........................904 900-1702
Jubeen Vaghefi, *Principal*
EMP: 8 EST: 2016
SALES (est): 257.4K **Privately Held**
SIC: 2499 Wood products

(G-5842)
904 SWEET TREATZ STREET LLC
7643 Gate Pkwy Ste 104 (32256-2893)
PHONE..........................800 889-3298
Marcia Brown, *President*
EMP: 6 EST: 2017
SALES (est): 307.5K **Privately Held**
SIC: 2051 5963 Bakery: wholesale or wholesale/retail combined; bakery goods, house-to-house

(G-5843)
9T TECHNOLOGY LLC
3125 Double Oaks Dr (32226-2086)
PHONE..........................904 703-9214
Charlene Dennis, *Owner*
EMP: 7 EST: 2013
SALES (est): 593.4K **Privately Held**
WEB: www.9ttech.com
SIC: 3571 7389 Electronic computers;

(G-5844)
A & K MACHINE & FAB SHOP INC
3451 W Beaver St (32254-3709)
P.O. Box 14942 (32238-1942)
PHONE..........................904 388-7772
Alice M Stine, *President*
Cynthia L Rhoden, *Corp Secy*
Jenny Smith, *Corp Secy*
Kenneth D Stine, *Vice Pres*
Mary S Horning, *Director*
EMP: 17 EST: 1989
SQ FT: 10,000
SALES (est): 4.9MM **Privately Held**
WEB: www.aandkmachineandfab.com
SIC: 3441 Fabricated structural metal

(G-5845)
A B & B MANUFACTURING INC
2141 Lane Ave N (32254-1531)
P.O. Box 6456 (32236-6456)
PHONE..........................904 378-3350
James T Brooks, *President*
EMP: 14 EST: 1999
SALES (est): 3.1MM **Privately Held**
WEB: www.abandbmachineandfab.com
SIC: 3545 Machine tool accessories

(G-5846)
A CLEAN FINISH INC
Also Called: Property Solutions and Cnstr
8848 Quail Roost Ct (32220-1400)
P.O. Box 6236 (32236-6236)
PHONE..........................407 516-1311
Aleya Wolfla, *President*
Scott Stemper, *Area Mgr*
Charles Wolfla, *Vice Pres*
EMP: 6 EST: 2015
SQ FT: 1,500
SALES (est): 958.4K **Privately Held**
SIC: 3589 1721 3069 1752 High pressure cleaning equipment; painting & paper hanging; flooring, rubber: tile or sheet; access flooring system installation; surfacers, concrete grinding

(G-5847)
A M COPLAN ASSOCIATES
Also Called: Coplan Composition Service
4251 University Blvd S # 201 (32216-4981)
P.O. Box 5545 (32247-5545)
PHONE..........................904 737-6996
Alvin M Coplan, *Owner*
Al Copeland, *Web Proj Mgr*
EMP: 5 EST: 1961
SQ FT: 2,000

SALES (est): 1MM **Privately Held**
SIC: 2711 6162 6163 6512 Newspapers: publishing only, not printed on site; mortgage brokers, using own money; mortgage brokers arranging for loans, using money of others; commercial & industrial building operation

(G-5848)
A PLUS CONSTRUCTION SVCS INC
165 Oakhill St (32227-1817)
PHONE..........................904 612-0597
Chasidy Grubbs, *President*
EMP: 25 EST: 2012
SALES (est): 1.9MM **Privately Held**
SIC: 1389 1521 1542 1541 Construction, repair & dismantling services; single-family housing construction; nonresidential construction; industrial buildings, new construction

(G-5849)
A&W BRICK PAVERS OF NORTH FLA
7901 Baymeadows Cir E # 502 (32256-7685)
PHONE..........................904 672-7112
Ribeiro Souza, *Principal*
EMP: 7 EST: 2016
SALES (est): 383.4K **Privately Held**
SIC: 2951 Asphalt paving mixtures & blocks

(G-5850)
A-1 DOOR SYSTEMS INC
11555 Central Pkwy # 804 (32224-2700)
PHONE..........................904 327-7206
David Eckes, *President*
Doug Stanford, *Vice Pres*
EMP: 12 EST: 2004
SALES (est): 273.7K **Privately Held**
SIC: 2431 1751 Garage doors, overhead: wood; garage door, installation or erection

(G-5851)
AA FIBERGLASS INC
9378 Arlington Expy 358 (32225-8213)
PHONE..........................904 355-5511
Michael A Jackson, *Principal*
EMP: 9 EST: 1985
SALES (est): 122.7K **Privately Held**
WEB: www.aacustomfiberglass.com
SIC: 3083 Laminated plastics plate & sheet

(G-5852)
AA FIBERGLASS INC
521 Copeland St (32204-2721)
PHONE..........................904 355-5511
Michael Jackson, *Owner*
EMP: 9 EST: 2016
SALES (est): 56.3K **Privately Held**
WEB: www.aacustomfiberglass.com
SIC: 2221 Fiberglass fabrics

(G-5853)
AACECORP INC
Also Called: American Assn Clncal Endcrnlgs
245 Riverside Ave Ste 200 (32202-4933)
PHONE..........................904 353-7878
Donald C Jones, *CEO*
EMP: 9 EST: 1996
SQ FT: 3,700
SALES (est): 1.8MM **Privately Held**
SIC: 2721 2759 Periodicals; advertising literature: printing
PA: American Association Of Clinical Endocrinologists, Inc.
245 Riverside Ave Ste 200
Jacksonville FL 32202

(G-5854)
AAR CORP
Also Called: AAR Hngar Jcksnvlle Nval A Stn
Naval A Stn Of Jcksnvlle (32212)
PHONE..........................904 629-2810
Jeffery Fernandez, *Principal*
EMP: 7 EST: 1966
SALES (est): 63.5K **Privately Held**
WEB: www.aarcorp.com
SIC: 3728 Aircraft parts & equipment

(G-5855)
AAR GOVERNMENT SERVICES INC
Also Called: AAR Defense Systems Logistics
8001 Westside Indus Dr (32219-3238)
PHONE....................904 693-7260
Michael Lile, *Manager*
EMP: 10
SALES (corp-wide): 1.8B **Publicly Held**
WEB: www.aarcorp.com
SIC: 3728 Aircraft parts & equipment
HQ: Aar Government Services, Inc.
1100 N Wood Dale Rd
Wood Dale IL 60191
630 227-2000

(G-5856)
ACE FABRICATORS INC
1705 E 30th St (32206-1703)
PHONE....................904 355-3724
Henry Smith, *President*
Joyce Smith, *Treasurer*
EMP: 18 **EST:** 1988
SQ FT: 25,000
SALES (est): 4.3MM **Privately Held**
SIC: 3441 Fabricated structural metal

(G-5857)
ACME BARRICADES LC (PA)
9800 Normandy Blvd (32221-2038)
PHONE....................904 781-1950
Christian Cummings, *General Mgr*
Justin Chancey, *Opers Mgr*
Tony McDonald, *Foreman/Supr*
Scott Campbell, *Opers Staff*
Bucky Wright, *QC Mgr*
▲ **EMP:** 36 **EST:** 1993
SALES (est): 23.7MM **Privately Held**
WEB: www.acmebarricades.com
SIC: 3499 7389 Barricades, metal; flagging service (traffic control)

(G-5858)
AD AMERICA
8679 W Beaver St (32220-2203)
PHONE....................904 781-5900
G Brett Railey, *Owner*
EMP: 7 **EST:** 1972
SQ FT: 2,000
SALES (est): 316.8K **Privately Held**
SIC: 3993 7382 Signs, not made in custom sign painting shops; security systems services

(G-5859)
ADTEC PRODUCTIONS INCORPORATED
Also Called: Adtec Digital
2231 Corporate Sq Blvd (32216-1921)
PHONE....................904 720-2003
Kevin Ancelin, *President*
Anderson Brown, *Engineer*
Danny Dresdner, *Engineer*
Dallas Snider, *Engineer*
Nick Ancelin, *Electrical Engi*
EMP: 12 **Privately Held**
WEB: www.adtecdigital.com
SIC: 3679 3621 Video triggers, except remote control TV devices; generating apparatus & parts, electrical
PA: Adtec Productions, Incorporated
408 Russell St
Nashville TN 37206

(G-5860)
ADVANCED AWNING & DESIGN LLC
2155 Corp Sq Blvd Ste 100 (32216-0323)
PHONE....................904 724-4567
Jackie Smith, *Mng Member*
Todd Smith, *Mng Member*
EMP: 8 **EST:** 1994
SQ FT: 7,500
SALES (est): 1.1MM **Privately Held**
WEB: www.advanced-awning.com
SIC: 2394 Awnings, fabric: made from purchased materials

(G-5861)
ADVANCED COMPOSITE SYSTEMS
10615 New Kings Rd (32219-2129)
PHONE....................904 765-6502
Henry Happy, *President*
Mark L Jones, *President*

Lorraine Happy, *Corp Secy*
Michael Happy, *Vice Pres*
EMP: 11 **EST:** 1997
SQ FT: 20,414
SALES (est): 2.1MM **Privately Held**
WEB: www.teccomposites.com
SIC: 2821 Plastics materials & resins

(G-5862)
ADVANCED DESIGN & PACKG INC
2212 N Pearl St (32206-3647)
PHONE....................904 356-6063
Doug Johnson, *CEO*
EMP: 15 **Privately Held**
SIC: 2653 Boxes, corrugated: made from purchased materials
HQ: Advanced Design & Packaging, Inc.
5090 Mcdougall Dr Sw
Atlanta GA 30336
404 699-1952

(G-5863)
ADVANCED INTELLIGENCE GROUP
4195 Southside Blvd (32216-5403)
PHONE....................904 565-1004
Mike Candell, *Principal*
EMP: 8 **EST:** 2008
SALES (est): 120K **Privately Held**
SIC: 3699 Security control equipment & systems

(G-5864)
ADVANTAGE PRTG LMNTING FLA INC
Also Called: Advantage Prtg Lminating Signs
4618 Sunbeam Rd (32257-6110)
P.O. Box 24140 (32241-4140)
PHONE....................904 737-1613
Troy McGee, *President*
Leanne McGee, *Vice Pres*
Debbie Rittenger, *Graphic Designe*
EMP: 7 **EST:** 2000
SALES (est): 995.7K **Privately Held**
WEB: www.printing.com
SIC: 2759 Commercial printing

(G-5865)
AEI INTERNATIONAL CORP
7709 Alton Ave (32211-7801)
PHONE....................904 724-9771
Lewis Spradlin Jr, *President*
Belinda Spradlin, *Vice Pres*
EMP: 5 **EST:** 1992
SALES (est): 875.6K **Privately Held**
SIC: 3084 5084 1623 Plastics pipe; propane conversion equipment; oil & gas pipeline construction

(G-5866)
AERIAL PRODUCTS CORPORATION
Also Called: Southern Balloon Works
11653 Central Pkwy # 209 (32224-2711)
PHONE....................800 973-9110
Kevin M Hess, *President*
EMP: 11 **EST:** 2007
SALES (est): 495.2K **Privately Held**
WEB: www.aerialproducts.com
SIC: 3721 3069 Aircraft; balloons, advertising & toy: rubber

(G-5867)
AGILE CARGO TRANSPORTATION LLC
1601-1 N Main St (32206-4453)
PHONE....................407 747-0812
Richard F Tavarez, *President*
EMP: 10 **EST:** 2020
SALES (est): 677K **Privately Held**
SIC: 3799 Transportation equipment

(G-5868)
AGILITY PRESS INC
3060 Mercury Rd (32207-7915)
PHONE....................904 731-8989
Ray Farah, *President*
Damon Mattheus, *Manager*
EMP: 16 **EST:** 1999
SQ FT: 10,000
SALES (est): 3.8MM **Privately Held**
WEB: www.agilitypress.net
SIC: 2759 Commercial printing

(G-5869)
AGR FABRICATORS INC
4879 Clydo Rd S Ste 1 (32207-7974)
P.O. Box 10158 (32247-0158)
PHONE....................904 733-9393
George Shami, *President*
Charlie J Shami, *Vice Pres*
Emile Shami, *Treasurer*
▲ **EMP:** 11 **EST:** 1996
SALES (est): 2MM **Privately Held**
WEB: www.agrfabricators.com
SIC: 2541 Counter & sink tops

(G-5870)
AGR OF FLORIDA INC
4879 Clydo Rd S (32207-7957)
PHONE....................904 733-9393
George Shami, *President*
Emile Shami, *Treasurer*
Peter Shami, *Director*
◆ **EMP:** 31 **EST:** 1969
SQ FT: 22,000
SALES (est): 1.4MM **Privately Held**
WEB: www.agrfabricators.com
SIC: 2541 3821 Counter & sink tops; worktables, laboratory

(G-5871)
AIRPRO DIAGNOSTICS LLC
6873 Phillips Ind Blvd (32256-3029)
PHONE....................904 717-1711
Lonnie E Margol, *Principal*
Steve Casella, *Vice Pres*
Mark McCahill, *Human Res Dir*
Rachel Spell, *Manager*
EMP: 16 **EST:** 2016
SALES (est): 1.6MM **Privately Held**
WEB: www.airprodiagnostics.com
SIC: 3829 Measuring & controlling devices

(G-5872)
AKUA RAGE ENTERTAINMENT INC
10960 Beach Blvd Lot 494 (32246-4862)
PHONE....................904 627-5312
Shaun Santos, *CEO*
Peter Whipple, *COO*
EMP: 7 **EST:** 2016
SALES (est): 720K **Privately Held**
SIC: 2741

(G-5873)
ALL METAL FAB INC
2021 Dennis St (32204-1901)
PHONE....................904 570-9772
Dustin W Workman, *President*
Jessica L Workman, *Vice Pres*
EMP: 15 **EST:** 2016
SALES (est): 5MM **Privately Held**
WEB: www.allmetalfabinc.com
SIC: 3444 Sheet metalwork

(G-5874)
ALL METALS FABRICATION LLC
4235 Saint Augustine Rd (32207-6643)
PHONE....................904 862-6885
Michael S Dickens,
Brian H Vick,
EMP: 9 **EST:** 2017
SALES (est): 1.1MM **Privately Held**
WEB: www.amfllc.net
SIC: 3341 Secondary nonferrous metals

(G-5875)
ALL PURPOSE PRTG GRAPHICS INC
3521 Saint Augustine Rd (32207-5526)
P.O. Box 5733 (32247-5733)
PHONE....................904 346-0999
Michael G Amason, *President*
Pamela Woodworth, *Sales Staff*
Sandra Amason, *Admin Sec*
EMP: 10 **EST:** 1999
SQ FT: 10,000
SALES (est): 1.7MM **Privately Held**
WEB: www.appagi.com
SIC: 2759 Screen printing

(G-5876)
ALL-STAR SALES INC
Also Called: Raintree Graphics
5921 Richard St (32216-5926)
P.O. Box 5967 (32247-5967)
PHONE....................904 396-1653
Michael J Seethler, *President*

Michael Seethaler Sr, *Vice Pres*
Manuel Granados, *Project Mgr*
David Harkness, *Accounts Exec*
Jane Fabritius, *Sales Staff*
EMP: 35 **EST:** 1980
SQ FT: 17,000
SALES (est): 7.5MM **Privately Held**
WEB: www.raintreegraphics.com
SIC: 2759 2752 2796 2789 Commercial printing; commercial printing, lithographic; platemaking services; bookbinding & related work

(G-5877)
ALLIED PLASTICS CO INC
2001 Walnut St (32206-3843)
P.O. Box 3125 (32206-0125)
PHONE....................904 359-0386
Gregory Berger, *President*
Dennis Berger, *Vice Pres*
◆ **EMP:** 45 **EST:** 1943
SQ FT: 50,000
SALES (est): 11.6MM **Privately Held**
WEB: www.alliedusa.com
SIC: 2511 2493 2531 2522 Tables, household: wood; particleboard, plastic laminated; public building & related furniture; office furniture, except wood; wood office furniture

(G-5878)
ALLIED PRINTING INC
Also Called: Allied Graphics
7403 Philips Hwy (32256-6807)
P.O. Box 11063, Birmingham AL (35202-1063)
PHONE....................800 749-7683
Dorsey B Thomas Jr, *President*
Richard Muller, *Vice Pres*
Rebecca Duffy, *CFO*
EMP: 58 **EST:** 1958
SQ FT: 15,000
SALES (est): 3MM **Privately Held**
WEB: www.alliedprinting.com
SIC: 2752 Commercial printing, offset

(G-5879)
ALTEC INDUSTRIES INC
2750 Imeson Rd (32220-2458)
PHONE....................904 647-5219
EMP: 9
SALES (corp-wide): 1.2B **Privately Held**
WEB: www.altec.com
SIC: 3531 Construction machinery
HQ: Altec Industries, Inc.
210 Inverness Center Dr
Birmingham AL 35242
205 991-7733

(G-5880)
ALTERNTIVE REPR MCHNING SVCS L
Also Called: Arms
6555 Trade Center Dr (32254-2248)
PHONE....................904 861-3040
Pafford Aimee, *Mfg Staff*
Pafford Jason, *Mfg Staff*
Kevin Hillman, *Engineer*
James Moss, *Engineer*
Aimee D Pafford, *Mng Member*
▼ **EMP:** 20 **EST:** 2011
SALES (est): 6.9MM **Privately Held**
WEB: www.armservicesusa.com
SIC: 3511 Turbines & turbine generator sets

(G-5881)
ALUMINUM PRODUCTS WHL INC
Also Called: Apw Wholesale
6963 Bus Pk Blvd N Ste 2 (32256-2736)
PHONE....................904 268-4895
Mitchell B Shepherd, *President*
EMP: 6 **EST:** 2001
SALES (est): 862.7K **Privately Held**
WEB: aluminum-product-manufacturers.cmac.ws
SIC: 3354 Aluminum extruded products

(G-5882)
AMERICAN BOTTLING COMPANY
Also Called: Seven-Up Snapple Southeast
6001 Bowdendale Ave (32216-6041)
PHONE....................904 739-1000

Robert H Paul III, *Branch Mgr*
EMP: 128　**Publicly Held**
WEB: www.keurigdrpepper.com
SIC: 2086 Soft drinks: packaged in cans, bottles, etc.
HQ: The American Bottling Company
6425 Hall Of Fame Ln
Frisco TX 75034

(G-5883)
AMERICAN COMMODITY EXCH CORP (HQ)
Also Called: Acec
7825 Baymeadows Way No (32256-7557)
PHONE.................................904 687-0588
Paul Cambria, *CEO*
EMP: 6 **EST:** 2004
SQ FT: 1,200
SALES (est): 1.5MM
SALES (corp-wide): 10.4MM **Privately Held**
WEB: www.pcec1896.com
SIC: 3199 Boxes, leather
PA: Pcec (Latin America) Llc
33 E Main St Ste 500
Madison WI 53703
904 687-0588

(G-5884)
AMERICAN PROJECTS BROKERS INC
Also Called: American Prjcts Crprts Stl Bld
5610 Fort Caroline Rd # 7 (32277-1799)
PHONE.................................904 343-5424
David Schomp, *Mng Member*
EMP: 8 **EST:** 2019
SALES (est): 552.6K **Privately Held**
WEB: www.americanprojects.net
SIC: 3448 Prefabricated metal components

(G-5885)
AMERICAN SCREEN PRINT INC
4122 Spring Park Rd (32207-5744)
PHONE.................................904 443-0071
Sara Housend, *President*
EMP: 5 **EST:** 1990
SQ FT: 900
SALES (est): 499.1K **Privately Held**
WEB: www.americanscreenprinting.com
SIC: 2759 Screen printing

(G-5886)
AMERICAN STANDARDS INC
4744 Kingsbury St (32205-5160)
PHONE.................................904 683-2189
Travis Goodale, *Principal*
EMP: 7 **EST:** 2011
SALES (est): 113.7K **Privately Held**
WEB: www.americanstandardair.com
SIC: 3585 Refrigeration & heating equipment

(G-5887)
AMERICAN STOCK LLC
3225 Anniston Rd (32246-4605)
PHONE.................................904 641-2055
A J Johns, *Principal*
EMP: 8 **EST:** 2007
SALES (est): 216.3K **Privately Held**
SIC: 2252 Socks

(G-5888)
ANCHOR GLASS CONTAINER CORP
2121 Huron St (32254-2089)
P.O. Box 6932 (32236-6932)
PHONE.................................904 786-1010
John Rehrer, *General Mgr*
Jerry Brewer, *Warehouse Mgr*
John Burns, *Engineer*
Fritz Hutterli, *Engineer*
Patrick Collins, *Manager*
EMP: 320 **Privately Held**
WEB: www.anchorglass.com
SIC: 3229 3221 Tableware, glass or glass ceramic; glass containers
PA: Anchor Glass Container Corporation
3001 N Rocky Point Dr E # 300
Tampa FL 33607

(G-5889)
ANDRADE PROFESSIONAL PAVERS
10275 Old St Augustne 9 (32257-7687)
PHONE.................................904 504-3257

Elivano Andrade, *Principal*
EMP: 7 **EST:** 2015
SALES (est): 65.5K **Privately Held**
WEB:
www.andradeprofessionalpavers.com
SIC: 2951 Asphalt paving mixtures & blocks

(G-5890)
ANDREWS 1ST CHOICE TRCKG LLC ✪
4532 Lane Ave S (32210-6824)
PHONE.................................205 703-5717
Rhonda Singleton,
EMP: 8 **EST:** 2021
SALES (est): 75K **Privately Held**
SIC: 3799 Transportation equipment

(G-5891)
ANJON INC
4801 Dawin Rd (32207-9512)
PHONE.................................904 730-9373
John Knapik, *President*
Janice Knapik, *Vice Pres*
James Ferrigno, *QC Dir*
James Prather, *Natl Sales Mgr*
Ryan Smetana, *Sales Staff*
EMP: 20 **EST:** 1989
SQ FT: 14,500
SALES (est): 3.4MM **Privately Held**
WEB: www.anjonholdings.com
SIC: 3842 Braces, orthopedic

(G-5892)
ANTIQUE & MODERN CABINETS INC
2384 Vans Ave (32207-6769)
PHONE.................................904 393-9055
Bill Patterson, *President*
Cindy Patterson, *Corp Secy*
Keri Taylor, *Manager*
EMP: 32 **EST:** 1951
SQ FT: 40,000
SALES (est): 2.8MM **Privately Held**
WEB:
www.antiqueandmoderncabinets.com
SIC: 2521 2531 2541 7641 Wood office furniture; public building & related furniture; school furniture; office fixtures, wood; cabinets, except refrigerated: show, display, etc.: wood; shelving, office & store, wood; counters or counter display cases, wood; reupholstery & furniture repair; wood kitchen cabinets

(G-5893)
ANTONYO DENARD LLC ✪
1408 San Marco Blvd (32207-8536)
P.O. Box 9627 (32208-0627)
PHONE.................................904 290-1579
Antonyo Sanders, *CEO*
EMP: 10 **EST:** 2021
SALES (est): 180K **Privately Held**
SIC: 2389 Apparel & accessories

(G-5894)
APS PROMOTIONAL SOLUTIONS INC
7121 Beach Blvd (32216-2832)
PHONE.................................904 721-4977
Ronald Roelse, *President*
Jarret Graff, *Graphic Designe*
EMP: 18 **EST:** 1991
SQ FT: 10,000
SALES (est): 2.8MM **Privately Held**
WEB: www.apstitch.com
SIC: 2759 Screen printing

(G-5895)
APYELEN CURVES LLC
Also Called: Fashion Store
614 Pecan Park Rd (32218-1602)
PHONE.................................904 328-3390
Patrinya Jordan, *CEO*
EMP: 10 **EST:** 2019
SALES (est): 534.7K **Privately Held**
WEB: www.apyelencurvesz.com
SIC: 2331 5999 Women's & misses' blouses & shirts; miscellaneous retail stores

(G-5896)
ARC CREATIVE INC
Also Called: Image 360
2683 St Jhns Bluff Rd S S (32246-3763)
PHONE.................................904 996-7773
Ryan Rippel, *President*
EMP: 6 **EST:** 2008
SQ FT: 2,500
SALES (est): 1MM **Privately Held**
SIC: 3993 Signs & advertising specialties

(G-5897)
ARC-RITE INC
569 Edgewood Ave S (32205-5332)
PHONE.................................386 325-3523
George Battle, *President*
John L Jones, *Vice Pres*
EMP: 21 **EST:** 1982
SQ FT: 16,000
SALES (est): 1.7MM **Privately Held**
WEB: www.arcritecontractorsinc.com
SIC: 3441 7692 3498 3443 Fabricated structural metal; welding repair; fabricated pipe & fittings; tanks, standard or custom fabricated: metal plate; pipe, large diameter: metal plate

(G-5898)
AREA RUGS MFG INC
2068 Gamewell Rd (32211-4768)
PHONE.................................904 398-5481
Kathleen Thomson, *President*
Kimberly Crisp, *Vice Pres*
EMP: 5 **EST:** 1966
SALES (est): 432K **Privately Held**
SIC: 2273 7389 Rugs, hand & machine made; rug binding

(G-5899)
ARGOS
700 Palmetto St (32202-2406)
PHONE.................................678 368-4300
EMP: 15 **EST:** 2015
SALES (est): 3.2MM **Privately Held**
WEB: www.argos-us.com
SIC: 3273 Ready-mixed concrete

(G-5900)
ARIZONA BEVERAGE COMPANY LLC
12721 Gran Bay Pkwy W (32258-4470)
PHONE.................................516 812-0303
Thomas Deluca, *Manager*
EMP: 10
SALES (corp-wide): 284.6MM **Privately Held**
SIC: 2086 Iced tea & fruit drinks, bottled & canned
HQ: Arizona Beverage Company Llc
60 Crossways Park Dr W # 400
Woodbury NY 11797
516 812-0300

(G-5901)
ARLINGTON PRTG STATIONERS INC
Also Called: Apex Color
200 N Lee St (32204-1134)
PHONE.................................904 358-2928
Richard Ghelerter, *President*
Allan Ghelerter, *Vice Pres*
John Vega, *Representative*
EMP: 105 **EST:** 1971
SQ FT: 30,000
SALES (est): 15.1MM **Privately Held**
SIC: 2761 Strip forms (manifold business forms); unit sets (manifold business forms); computer forms, manifold or continuous

(G-5902)
ARMOR ACCESSORIES INC
13386 International Pkwy (32218-2383)
PHONE.................................904 741-1717
Robert R Schiller, *President*
Paul W Cobb Jr, *Admin Sec*
▲ **EMP:** 25 **EST:** 2005
SALES (est): 2.6MM **Privately Held**
WEB: www.safariland.com
SIC: 3699 Security devices

(G-5903)
ARMOR HOLDINGS FORENSICS LLC
Also Called: Nik Public Safety
13386 International Pkwy (32218-2383)
PHONE.................................904 485-1836
Steve Croskey, *CEO*
Jim Seidel, *Vice Pres*
▲ **EMP:** 25 **EST:** 1976
SQ FT: 16,000
SALES (est): 1.1MM **Privately Held**
WEB: www.forensics-intl.com
SIC: 3999 Fingerprint equipment

(G-5904)
ASH SIGNS INC
Also Called: Fastsigns
2141 St Johns Bluff Rd S (32246-2307)
PHONE.................................904 724-7446
Ann K Helfer, *President*
Todd J Helfer, *Vice Pres*
EMP: 8 **EST:** 1995
SALES (est): 1.2MM **Privately Held**
WEB: www.fastsigns.com
SIC: 3993 Signs & advertising specialties

(G-5905)
ATI2 INC
10448 Atlantic Blvd (32225-6771)
PHONE.................................904 396-3766
Edwin Segars, *President*
EMP: 9 **EST:** 2011
SALES (est): 245.7K **Privately Held**
SIC: 3312 Stainless steel

(G-5906)
ATLANTIC COAST ASPHALT CO
10382 Florida Min Blvd E (32257)
PHONE.................................904 268-0274
Randall Bristol, *Principal*
EMP: 10 **EST:** 2009
SALES (est): 112.4K **Privately Held**
SIC: 3531 1622 Asphalt paving blocks (not from refineries); bridge construction

(G-5907)
ATLANTIC DRY DOCK
8500 Heckscher Dr (32226-2434)
PHONE.................................904 251-1545
EMP: 28 **EST:** 2019
SALES (est): 316.6K **Privately Held**
WEB: www.crandalldrydock.com
SIC: 3731 Shipbuilding & repairing

(G-5908)
ATLANTIC INSULATION INC
Also Called: Eagle Insulation Fabrication
325 Dennard Ave (32254-3401)
P.O. Box 37332 (32236-7332)
PHONE.................................904 354-2217
Richard K Whitlock, *President*
Mike Chapman, *Vice Pres*
Robyn Weaver, *Office Mgr*
▲ **EMP:** 85 **EST:** 1985
SQ FT: 12,500
SALES (est): 9.3MM **Privately Held**
WEB: atlantic-insulation-inc.business.site
SIC: 3086 5082 Insulation or cushioning material, foamed plastic; ladders

(G-5909)
ATLANTIC MARBLE COMPANY INC
11303 Bus Pk Blvd Ste 100 (32256-2783)
PHONE.................................904 262-6262
Ronald A Brown, *Ch of Bd*
Robert A Booth, *President*
EMP: 19 **EST:** 1987
SQ FT: 11,000
SALES (est): 1.4MM **Privately Held**
WEB: www.atlanticmarbleco.com
SIC: 3281 2821 Marble, building: cut & shaped; plastics materials & resins

(G-5910)
ATLANTIC MARINE INC
8500 Heckscher Dr (32226-2434)
PHONE.................................904 251-1580
Edward J Fleming Jr. *President*
Byron N Thompson Jr, *Corp Secy*
EMP: 5 **EST:** 1964
SALES (est): 1MM **Privately Held**
WEB: www.atlanticmarinefl.com
SIC: 3731 Shipbuilding & repairing

(G-5911)
ATSG LOGISTIC SUPPORT SERVICE
9526 Argyle Frest Blvd Un (32222)
PHONE..................................904 479-3808
Wesley A Doty, *Principal*
Rodney Housand, *Principal*
Wesley Doty, *Mng Member*
EMP: 24 **EST:** 2011
SALES (est): 2.4MM **Privately Held**
WEB: www.atsgsupport.com
SIC: 3769 8711 8741 8744 Airframe assemblies, guided missiles; engineering services; personnel management; facilities support services

(G-5912)
AUTOMATED PRINTING SERVICES
7124 Glendyne Dr N (32216-5789)
PHONE..................................904 731-3244
Jeffrey D Day, *General Mgr*
Jodi Day, *Vice Pres*
EMP: 5 **EST:** 1971
SALES (est): 384K **Privately Held**
WEB: www.sdn.com
SIC: 2752 Commercial printing, offset

(G-5913)
AVK INDUSTRIES INC
2052 St Johns Bluff Rd S (32246-8783)
PHONE..................................904 998-8400
Andrew J Cherinka, *President*
▼ **EMP:** 10 **EST:** 1990
SQ FT: 3,600
SALES (est): 953.9K **Privately Held**
WEB: www.avkinc.com
SIC: 3829 Testing equipment: abrasion, shearing strength, etc.

(G-5914)
AZ CHEM HOLDINGS LP
4600 Touchton Rd E # 1200 (32246-8299)
PHONE..................................800 526-5294
Kevin M Fogarty, *President*
Kellie D Hardee, *Treasurer*
EMP: 144 **EST:** 2010
SALES (est): 9MM **Privately Held**
SIC: 2861 2911 Gum & wood chemicals; petroleum refining
HQ: Kraton Polymers Llc
15710 John F Kennedy Blvd # 300
Houston TX 77032

(G-5915)
AZAR INDUSTRIES INC
Also Called: Azar & Company
719 E Union St (32206-5606)
P.O. Box 5662 (32247-5662)
PHONE..................................904 358-2354
Sandra Azar, *President*
Philip Azar, *Treasurer*
EMP: 27 **EST:** 1991
SQ FT: 3,800
SALES (est): 3.8MM **Privately Held**
WEB: www.azarsausage.com
SIC: 2011 Meat packing plants

(G-5916)
B & J ATLANTIC INC
5164 Shawland Rd (32254-1651)
PHONE..................................904 338-0088
Minh-Trang Dang, *President*
Thai Q Nguyen, *Vice Pres*
EMP: 25 **EST:** 1998
SQ FT: 15,000
SALES (est): 5.7MM **Privately Held**
WEB: www.bjatlantic.com
SIC: 3613 3728 Cubicles (electric switchboard equipment); aircraft parts & equipment

(G-5917)
BACARDI BOTTLING CORPORATION
12200 N Main St (32218-3819)
PHONE..................................904 757-1290
Mahesh Madhavan, *CEO*
Cheryl Argamasilla, *Opers Staff*
Michael Urick, *Production*
Alan Horton, *Purch Mgr*
Walter Rios, *Treasurer*
◆ **EMP:** 250 **EST:** 1969
SQ FT: 200,000

SALES (est): 68.1MM **Privately Held**
WEB: www.bacardi.com
SIC: 2085 2086 Rum (alcoholic beverage); bottled & canned soft drinks
HQ: Bacardi International Limited
Bacardi Building
Hamilton

(G-5918)
BAE SYSTEMS STHAST SHPYRDS AMH (DH)
8500 Heckscher Dr (32226-2434)
PHONE..................................904 251-3111
Logan Jones, *CEO*
Paul W Cobb Jr, *Vice Pres*
Douglas Coleman, *Vice Pres*
John Marinucci, *Vice Pres*
Dan Welch, *Vice Pres*
◆ **EMP:** 424 **EST:** 1986
SALES (est): 105.9MM
SALES (corp-wide): 26B **Privately Held**
SIC: 3731 Cargo vessels, building & repairing; barges, building & repairing; tankers, building & repairing; tugboats, building & repairing

(G-5919)
BAG-A-NUT LLC
Also Called: Ammo-Up
10601 Theresa Dr (32246-8758)
PHONE..................................904 641-3934
Caleb Dudley, *Managing Prtnr*
Caleb L Dudley, *Managing Prtnr*
Annie Rodriguez, *General Mgr*
Shama Dudley, *Marketing Mgr*
▼ **EMP:** 8 **EST:** 1990
SQ FT: 20,000
SALES (est): 1.3MM **Privately Held**
WEB: www.baganut.com
SIC: 3523 3949 Harvesters, fruit, vegetable, tobacco, etc.; shooting equipment & supplies, general

(G-5920)
BAHRI INDUSTRIES INC
3551 University Blvd N (32277-2422)
PHONE..................................904 744-4472
Andre Bahri, *President*
EMP: 8 **EST:** 2001
SALES (est): 321.5K **Privately Held**
SIC: 3999 Manufacturing industries

(G-5921)
BAKERS SPORTS INC (PA)
Also Called: Baker's Sporting Goods
3600 Beachwood Ct (32224-5705)
PHONE..................................904 388-8126
Josh Baker, *President*
Tiffany Baker, *Vice Pres*
George Girardo, *Sales Mgr*
Jesse Schultz, *Art Dir*
▲ **EMP:** 46 **EST:** 1997
SQ FT: 10,000
SALES (est): 10.9MM **Privately Held**
WEB: www.bakerssport.com
SIC: 2396 2395 5941 2329 Screen printing on fabric articles; emblems, embroidered; sporting goods & bicycle shops; men's & boys' athletic uniforms

(G-5922)
BALLARD PRINTING INC
Also Called: Best Choice Printing
1233 Lane Ave S Ste 11 (32205-6254)
PHONE..................................904 783-4430
Jody Ballard, *President*
Diane Ballard, *Treasurer*
EMP: 6 **EST:** 1983
SALES (est): 498.7K **Privately Held**
WEB: www.ballardprinting.com
SIC: 2752 Commercial printing, offset

(G-5923)
BARBES PUBLISHING INC
Also Called: Beson 4 Media Group
13500 Sutton Park Dr S # 105 (32224-5291)
PHONE..................................904 992-9945
Aj Beson, *President*
Mike Hicks, *Exec VP*
Kayla Brooke, *Accounts Mgr*
Courtney Cooper, *Graphic Designe*
Jason Grim, *Graphic Designe*
EMP: 10 **EST:** 1998
SQ FT: 2,200

SALES (est): 1.6MM **Privately Held**
WEB: www.beson4.com
SIC: 2741 Miscellaneous publishing

(G-5924)
BASTECH INC
3211 Powers Ave (32207-8013)
PHONE..................................904 737-1722
Raymond Basso, *Owner*
Bruce Kissel, *Plant Mgr*
Theresa Freeman, *Purch Mgr*
EMP: 14 **EST:** 2007
SALES (est): 2.5MM **Privately Held**
WEB: www.bastechllc.com
SIC: 2874 Phosphates

(G-5925)
BASTECH LLC
3035 Powers Ave Ste 3 (32207-8033)
PHONE..................................904 737-1722
Thomas S Schafer, *CEO*
Thomas Schafer, *CEO*
Bob Closs, *President*
Bill Graves, *Business Mgr*
John Hines, *Vice Pres*
▲ **EMP:** 32 **EST:** 2007
SQ FT: 8,370
SALES (est): 11.7MM **Privately Held**
WEB: www.bastechllc.com
SIC: 2869 Industrial organic chemicals

(G-5926)
BDT CONCEPTS INC
5105 Philips Hwy Ste 205 (32207-1709)
P.O. Box 600128 (32260-0128)
PHONE..................................904 730-2590
Beverly Williams, *President*
Dan Williams, *Treasurer*
EMP: 9 **EST:** 1991
SALES (est): 1.4MM **Privately Held**
WEB: www.bdtconcepts.com
SIC: 3861 5734 Toners, prepared photographic (not made in chemical plants); computer & software stores

(G-5927)
BEAUTYGE BRANDS USA INC
5344 Overmyer Dr (32254-3645)
PHONE..................................904 693-1200
Lemoyne Metlock, *Branch Mgr*
EMP: 165 **Publicly Held**
SIC: 2844 Hair coloring preparations
HQ: Beautyge Brands Usa, Inc.
1515 Wazee St Ste 200
Denver CO 80202

(G-5928)
BENCHMARK QUALITY GUTTERS INC
9526 Argyle Frest Blvd St (32222)
PHONE..................................904 759-9800
Michael A Katrinic, *President*
EMP: 8 **EST:** 2008
SALES (est): 1MM **Privately Held**
WEB: www.benchmarkqualitygutters.com
SIC: 3444 Gutters, sheet metal

(G-5929)
BENNER CHINA AND GLWR OF FLA
Also Called: Odyssey
5215 Philips Hwy Ste 1-3 (32207-7988)
PHONE..................................904 733-4620
James Y Wang, *President*
Karin Baisden, *Vice Pres*
Scott Mills, *Vice Pres*
Ashley Sakowski, *Bookkeeper*
Scott Wrazin, *Bookkeeper*
▲ **EMP:** 50 **EST:** 1945
SQ FT: 90,000
SALES (est): 8.7MM **Privately Held**
WEB: www.odysseyfl.com
SIC: 2759 Screen printing

(G-5930)
BENNETTS CUSTOM CABINETS INC
9897 Sisson Dr (32218-5542)
PHONE..................................904 751-1455
Brenda A Bennett, *President*
Wesley D Bennett, *Vice Pres*
Barbara Corzo, *Accounts Exec*
Carlos Mitchell, *Manager*
Jairo Serrano, *Supervisor*
EMP: 38 **EST:** 1984

SQ FT: 6,500
SALES (est): 6.1MM **Privately Held**
WEB: www.bennettscustomcabinets.com
SIC: 2434 Wood kitchen cabinets

(G-5931)
BENTON MACHINE WORKS INC
740 Carlton St (32208-4404)
PHONE..................................904 768-9161
Connie Lee, *President*
Connie Evans, *President*
Donna Stallard, *Exec VP*
James E Stallard, *Exec VP*
Alan Stallard, *Accounts Mgr*
EMP: 8 **EST:** 1963
SQ FT: 7,500
SALES (est): 885.6K **Privately Held**
WEB: www.bmw-cnc.com
SIC: 3599 3469 Machine shop, jobbing & repair; machine parts, stamped or pressed metal

(G-5932)
BIG OS STUMP GRINDING
101 Baisden Rd Apt 2 (32218-4193)
PHONE..................................904 945-5900
Phillip R Robinson, *Principal*
EMP: 8 **EST:** 2007
SALES (est): 459.9K **Privately Held**
SIC: 3599 Grinding castings for the trade

(G-5933)
BLACK KNIGHT INC (PA)
601 Riverside Ave (32204-2946)
PHONE..................................904 854-5100
Anthony M Jabbour, *Ch of Bd*
Joseph M Nackashi, *President*
Shannon Stephens, *General Mgr*
Mike Toth, *Managing Dir*
Ashley Chrabot, *Counsel*
EMP: 430 **EST:** 2013
SALES (est): 1.2B **Publicly Held**
WEB: www.blackknightinc.com
SIC: 7372 7373 Prepackaged software; computer integrated systems design

(G-5934)
BLACK KNIGHT FINCL SVCS INC (HQ)
601 Riverside Ave (32204-2946)
PHONE..................................904 854-5100
Tom Sanzone, *President*
Maria Vivas, *Counsel*
Willie Anderson, *Senior VP*
Darrin Bode, *Assistant VP*
Lisa Tran, *Assistant VP*
EMP: 101 **EST:** 2014
SALES (est): 1.4B
SALES (corp-wide): 1.2B **Publicly Held**
WEB: www.blackknightinc.com
SIC: 7372 Prepackaged software
PA: Black Knight, Inc.
601 Riverside Ave
Jacksonville FL 32204
904 854-5100

(G-5935)
BLAIR MACHINE & TOOL INC
1301 Riverplace Blvd # 800 (32207-9047)
PHONE..................................904 731-4377
Grover Blair, *President*
Pearl Blair, *Corp Secy*
Edward Blair, *Vice Pres*
Glen Blair, *Vice Pres*
Janice Mc Dowell, *Vice Pres*
EMP: 18 **EST:** 1972
SQ FT: 35,000
SALES (est): 3.3MM **Privately Held**
WEB: www.blairmachine.com
SIC: 3599 Custom machinery; machine shop, jobbing & repair

(G-5936)
BLAIR MACHINE AND TOOL LLC
8665 Philips Hwy (32256-8298)
PHONE..................................904 731-4377
EMP: 7 **EST:** 2017
SALES (est): 287.9K **Privately Held**
WEB: www.blairmachine.com
SIC: 3599 Machine shop, jobbing & repair

(G-5937)
BLEVINS INC
6740 Broadway Ave Ste H (32254-2725)
PHONE..................................904 562-7428
Dan Dehart, *General Mgr*

Kent Copeland, *Manager*
Paul Moody, *Manager*
EMP: 11
SALES (corp-wide): 153.1MM **Privately Held**
WEB: www.blevinsinc.com
SIC: 2451 Mobile homes
PA: Blevins, Inc.
　　421 Hart Ln
　　Nashville TN 37216
　　615 228-2616

(G-5938)
BLUE EAGLE ALLIANCE INC
4651 Salisbury Rd # 4028 (32256-6107)
PHONE.........................904 322-8067
Carl Thomas, *CEO*
EMP: 8 **EST:** 2010
SALES (est): 339.3K **Privately Held**
SIC: 3578 Calculating & accounting equipment

(G-5939)
BLUE SKY LABS LLC
3811 University Blvd W # 4 (32217-1210)
PHONE.........................901 268-6988
Garland Sullivan, *Owner*
Shane Campbell, *Opers Mgr*
Alex Kiss, *Development*
Max Abre, *Manager*
EMP: 5 **EST:** 2018
SALES (est): 464.7K **Privately Held**
SIC: 2023 Dietary supplements, dairy & non-dairy based

(G-5940)
BLUE WATER INDUSTRIES LLC (PA)
Also Called: Blue Water Industries - FL LLC
200 W Forsyth St Ste 1200 (32202-4326)
PHONE.........................904 512-7706
Ted Baker, *CEO*
Miguel Fernandez, *General Mgr*
Carlos Vergara, *Vice Pres*
Chris Marion, *Plant Mgr*
Mickey Daniels, *Foreman/Supr*
EMP: 18 **EST:** 2016
SALES (est): 67.2MM **Privately Held**
WEB: www.bluewaterindustries.com
SIC: 1422 1423 1611 1442 Crushed & broken limestone; crushed & broken granite; highway & street paving contractor; construction sand & gravel

(G-5941)
BLUEGRASS MATERIALS CO LLC (HQ)
200 W Forsyth St Ste 1200 (32202-4326)
P.O. Box 30013, Raleigh NC (27622-0013)
PHONE.........................919 781-4550
C Howard Nye, *President*
Roselyn R Bar, *Exec VP*
James A J Nickolas, *CFO*
Jeremy Goad, *Sales Mgr*
Edward L Baker, *Mng Member*
EMP: 22 **EST:** 2010
SALES (est): 200MM **Publicly Held**
WEB: www.martinmarietta.com
SIC: 3271 3532 5032 Concrete block & brick; washers, aggregate & sand; concrete & cinder block; aggregate

(G-5942)
BOAT WORKS
1282 Belmont Ter (32207-3218)
PHONE.........................904 389-0090
Jonathan Barron L, *Principal*
EMP: 7 **EST:** 2001
SALES (est): 171.5K **Privately Held**
SIC: 3732 Boat building & repairing

(G-5943)
BOATSWAINS LOCKER INC
4565 Lakeside Dr (32210-3392)
PHONE.........................904 388-0231
Bill J Bransford, *President*
William J Bransford, *President*
Jeanne A Bransford, *Treasurer*
▼ **EMP:** 20 **EST:** 1965
SQ FT: 4,800
SALES (est): 1.9MM **Privately Held**
WEB: www.boatswains-locker.com
SIC: 2394 Convertible tops, canvas or boat: from purchased materials

(G-5944)
BOBS BACKFLOW & PLUMBING CO
4640 Sub Chaser Ct # 113 (32244-3319)
PHONE.........................904 268-8009
Patricia Novak, *President*
Robert A Novak, *Vice Pres*
EMP: 5 **EST:** 1987
SALES (est): 690.7K **Privately Held**
WEB: www.bobsbackflow.com
SIC: 3432 Plumbing fixture fittings & trim

(G-5945)
BOEING COMPANY
6211 Aviation Ave (32221-8113)
P.O. Box 150844 (32215)
PHONE.........................904 317-2490
Troy Ramirez, *Engineer*
Dee Burcham, *Manager*
Atchison Louis, *Manager*
Michael Bozard, *Technical Staff*
EMP: 11
SALES (corp-wide): 62.2B **Publicly Held**
WEB: www.boeing.com
SIC: 3721 Aircraft
PA: The Boeing Company
　　929 Long Bridge Dr
　　Arlington VA 22202
　　703 414-6338

(G-5946)
BOLD CITY BRAVES LLC
3385 Intl Vlg Dr W (32277-0997)
PHONE.........................904 545-3480
Eric Owen, *Principal*
EMP: 7 **EST:** 2017
SALES (est): 57.2K **Privately Held**
WEB: www.boldcitybrewery.com
SIC: 2082 Malt beverages

(G-5947)
BONSAL AMERICAN INC
6659 Highway Ave (32254-3549)
PHONE.........................904 783-0605
Craig Delicato, *Manager*
EMP: 7
SQ FT: 20,040
SALES (corp-wide): 30.9B **Privately Held**
SIC: 3272 Concrete products
HQ: Bonsal American, Inc.
　　625 Griffith Rd Ste 100
　　Charlotte NC 28217
　　704 525-1621

(G-5948)
BORE TECH INC
5333 Skylark Ct (32257-1227)
PHONE.........................904 262-0752
EMP: 5 **EST:** 1995
SALES: 580K **Privately Held**
SIC: 1381 Oil/Gas Well Drilling

(G-5949)
BOX SEAT CLOTHING COMPANY
5555 W 1st St (32254-1670)
PHONE.........................800 787-7792
Heather Cornelius, *Manager*
▲ **EMP:** 5 **EST:** 2011
SALES (est): 318K **Privately Held**
SIC: 2326 Work shirts: men's, youths' & boys'

(G-5950)
BRADDOCK METALLURGICAL INC (HQ)
14600 Duval Pl W (32218-9417)
PHONE.........................386 267-0955
Steve Braddock, *CEO*
George Gieger, *President*
Stephen R Braddock, *Principal*
Bill Braddock, *Exec VP*
William K Braddock, *Exec VP*
EMP: 11 **EST:** 1986
SQ FT: 12,500
SALES (est): 27.6MM **Privately Held**
WEB: www.braddockmt.com
SIC: 3398 Metal heat treating
PA: Braddock Metallurgical Holding Company, Inc.
　　400 Fentress Blvd
　　Daytona Beach FL 32114
　　386 323-1500

(G-5951)
BRAKE-FUNDERBURK ENTPS INC
Also Called: B F E
8383 Baycenter Rd (32256-7415)
PHONE.........................904 730-6788
Eric Nord, *President*
EMP: 25 **EST:** 1971
SQ FT: 30,000
SALES (est): 4.6MM **Privately Held**
WEB: www.bfeinc.net
SIC: 3589 Commercial cooking & food-warming equipment

(G-5952)
BRAND LABEL INC
8295 Western Way Cir (32256-8302)
PHONE.........................904 737-6433
Lemoyne F Matlock, *President*
Robert J Metzger, *Corp Secy*
Ray Hamilton, *Plant Mgr*
Leann Metzger, *CFO*
Nancy Metzger, *Shareholder*
EMP: 35 **EST:** 1970
SQ FT: 16,000
SALES (est): 7.1MM **Privately Held**
WEB: www.brandlabelinc.com
SIC: 2672 Labels (unprinted), gummed: made from purchased materials

(G-5953)
BRANTLEY MACHINE & FABRICATION
4003 N Canal St (32209-3623)
P.O. Box 12268 (32209-0268)
PHONE.........................904 359-0554
William E Taylor, *President*
Pam Walker, *Corp Secy*
EMP: 10 **EST:** 1986
SQ FT: 8,000
SALES (est): 790K **Privately Held**
SIC: 3441 3599 Fabricated structural metal; machine shop, jobbing & repair

(G-5954)
BRC SPORTS LLC
Also Called: Burbank Sports Nets
3600 Beachwood Ct (32224-5705)
PHONE.........................904 388-8126
Lacey Nell, *Principal*
EMP: 9 **EST:** 2016
SALES (est): 525.7K **Privately Held**
SIC: 3949 Sporting & athletic goods

(G-5955)
BREAK-FREE INC
13386 International Pkwy (32218-2383)
PHONE.........................800 347-1200
Jonathan M Spiller, *President*
EMP: 19 **EST:** 1989
SALES (est): 565.1K **Privately Held**
WEB: www.safariland.com
SIC: 2992 3489 Lubricating oils & greases; ordnance & accessories

(G-5956)
BREMER GROUP COMPANY INC
11243-5 Saint Johns (32246)
PHONE.........................904 645-0004
Ross Bremer, *President*
EMP: 10 **EST:** 1994
SQ FT: 4,500
SALES (est): 974.3K **Privately Held**
WEB: www.bremergroup.com
SIC: 3842 Braces, orthopedic

(G-5957)
BRITE LITE SERVICE COMPANY
Also Called: Brite Lite Signs
5300 Shad Rd (32257-2006)
PHONE.........................904 398-5305
Michael Moore, *President*
Bonnie Moore, *Vice Pres*
▲ **EMP:** 17 **EST:** 1972
SQ FT: 35,000
SALES (est): 479.9K **Privately Held**
SIC: 3993 Electric signs

(G-5958)
BRT OAKLEAF PET INC
Also Called: Pet & Feed Store
1619 Leon Rd (32246-8649)
PHONE.........................904 563-1212
Kelong Shi, *President*
Xiaodan Shi, *Principal*

EMP: 8 **EST:** 2013
SALES (est): 215.5K **Privately Held**
SIC: 2048 Prepared feeds

(G-5959)
BRUSS COMPANY
5441 W 5th St (32254-1664)
PHONE.........................904 693-0688
EMP: 179
SALES (corp-wide): 47B **Publicly Held**
WEB: www.tysonfreshmeats.com
SIC: 2011 Beef products from beef slaughtered on site
HQ: The Bruss Company
　　3548 N Kostner Ave
　　Chicago IL 60641
　　773 282-2900

(G-5960)
BRUT PRINTING CO INC
503 Parker St (32202-1199)
PHONE.........................904 354-5055
Adam H Brut Sr, *Ch of Bd*
Adam H Brut Jr, *President*
Dianne Brut, *Corp Secy*
Cliff Summerville, *COO*
Lissley Maddox, *Bookkeeper*
EMP: 38 **EST:** 1966
SQ FT: 20,000
SALES (est): 4.3MM **Privately Held**
WEB: www.brutprinting.com
SIC: 2752 2754 Commercial printing, offset; job printing, gravure

(G-5961)
BUBBA FOODS LLC (PA)
4339 Roosevelt Blvd # 400 (32210-2004)
P.O. Box 2823 (32203-2823)
PHONE.........................904 482-1900
Thomas Pirkle, *Regional Mgr*
William Morris, *Mng Member*
Steven L Coon, *Mng Member*
Clark Schaffer, *Mng Member*
EMP: 49 **EST:** 1993
SQ FT: 55,000
SALES (est): 25MM **Privately Held**
WEB: www.bubbafoods.com
SIC: 2011 Meat packing plants

(G-5962)
BUCHANAN SIGNS SCREEN PROCESS
Also Called: Buchanan Sign & Flag
6755 Beach Blvd (32216-2818)
PHONE.........................904 725-5500
Barbara Buchanan, *President*
Harold G Buchanan, *Vice Pres*
Michael Cross, *CFO*
EMP: 15 **EST:** 1960
SQ FT: 15,000
SALES (est): 1.8MM **Privately Held**
WEB: www.signandflag.com
SIC: 2399 3993 5999 3446 Flags, fabric; signs & advertising specialties; banners, flags, decals & posters; flags; architectural metalwork; automotive & apparel trimmings

(G-5963)
BURBANK TRAWL MAKERS INC
Also Called: Burbank Sport Nets
13913 Duval Rd Ste 100 (32218-0200)
P.O. Box 16198, Fernandina Beach (32035-3120)
PHONE.........................904 321-0976
Josh Baker, *President*
Hunt Er, *Vice Pres*
Hunt Hunter, *Vice Pres*
Josh Kubala, *Project Mgr*
Lacey Nell, *Office Mgr*
EMP: 29 **EST:** 1958
SALES (est): 7.7MM **Privately Held**
SIC: 2258 2399 Net & netting products; fishing nets
PA: Baker's Sports, Inc.
　　3600 Beachwood Ct
　　Jacksonville FL 32224

(G-5964)
BURCH WELDING & FABRICATION
2324 Phoenix Ave (32206-3139)
P.O. Box 28239 (32226-8239)
PHONE.........................904 353-6513
Kenith Burch, *President*
Larry Burch, *Vice Pres*

▲ = Import ▼=Export
◆ =Import/Export

EMP: 9 EST: 1989
SQ FT: 15,000
SALES (est): 884.7K Privately Held
WEB: www.burchwelding.com
SIC: 3441 Fabricated structural metal

(G-5965)
C & H PRINTING INC
11315-1 St Jhns Indus Pkw (32246-6606)
PHONE..................................904 620-8444
Patrick Calder, President
Winston Horton, Vice Pres
Tony Hawk, Prdtn Mgr
Jon Thrasher, Sales Staff
Jill Cavin,
EMP: 8 EST: 1998
SQ FT: 5,200
SALES (est): 1MM Privately Held
WEB: www.candhprinting.com
SIC: 2752 Commercial printing, offset

(G-5966)
CABINETRY MASTERS LLC
4193 Oldfield Crossing Dr (32223-7807)
PHONE..................................954 549-8646
Matthew Herman, Principal
EMP: 6 EST: 2015
SALES (est): 390.7K Privately Held
WEB: www.incrediblekitchens.com
SIC: 2434 Wood kitchen cabinets

(G-5967)
CADRE HOLDINGS INC (PA)
Also Called: Safariland Group, The
13386 International Pkwy (32218-2383)
PHONE..................................904 741-5400
Warren B Kanders, CEO
Brad Williams, President
Jessica Lawlor, Vice Pres
Austin Keaton, Opers Mgr
Blaine Browers, CFO
EMP: 26 EST: 2012
SQ FT: 132,224
SALES (est): 404.6MM Privately Held
SIC: 2311 3842 3199 3069 Military uniforms, men's & youths': purchased materials; policemen's uniforms: made from purchased materials; personal safety equipment; holsters, leather; life jackets, inflatable: rubberized fabric

(G-5968)
CAMPEN COMPANIES
2160 Park St (32204-3812)
PHONE..................................904 388-6000
Ben Campen, Principal
EMP: 6 EST: 2005
SALES (est): 633.2K Privately Held
WEB: www.campenproperties.com
SIC: 2952 Asphalt felts & coatings

(G-5969)
CANAM STEEL CORPORATION
140 Ellis Rd S (32254-3547)
PHONE..................................904 781-0898
Russ Rocco, General Mgr
Rollins Burks, Site Mgr
EMP: 25
SALES (corp-wide): 586.3MM Privately Held
WEB: www.cscsteelusa.com
SIC: 3441 Building components, structural steel
PA: Canam Steel Corporation
4010 Clay St
Point Of Rocks MD 21777
301 874-5141

(G-5970)
CANNONS OF JACK LLC
6150 Richard St (32216-6052)
PHONE..................................904 733-3524
Orren K Phillips, President
EMP: 6 EST: 1958
SQ FT: 6,000
SALES (est): 809.6K Privately Held
WEB: www.cannonsofjax.net
SIC: 7692 Welding repair

(G-5971)
CARIB ENERGY (USA) LLC
9487 Regency Square Blvd (32225-8183)
PHONE..................................904 727-2559
Greg Buffington, President
Rebecca Hamrick, Director
EMP: 1898 EST: 2012

SALES (est): 5.1MM Privately Held
SIC: 3533 Gas field machinery & equipment
HQ: Crowley Petroleum Services, Inc.
9487 Regency Square Blvd
Jacksonville FL 32225
904 727-2200

(G-5972)
CARPENTREE CREATION
11058 Percheron Dr (32257-4724)
PHONE..................................904 300-4008
Michael Gooch, Owner
EMP: 7 EST: 2017
SALES (est): 140K Privately Held
SIC: 2499 Applicators, wood

(G-5973)
CEMEX CNSTR MTLS FLA LLC
Also Called: South Jacksonville - R/M, B/M
14770 Old St Augustine Rd (32258-2464)
PHONE..................................904 880-4958
Steve Kester, Plant Mgr
Brian Bussell, Branch Mgr
EMP: 10 Privately Held
SIC: 3273 Ready-mixed concrete
HQ: Cemex Construction Materials Florida, Llc
1501 Belvedere Rd
West Palm Beach FL 33406

(G-5974)
CEMEX MATERIALS LLC
4807 Collins Rd (32244-9508)
PHONE..................................904 296-2400
Mike Divano, Branch Mgr
EMP: 88 Privately Held
SIC: 3273 Ready-mixed concrete
HQ: Cemex Materials Llc
1720 Centrepark Dr E # 100
West Palm Beach FL 33401
561 833-5555

(G-5975)
CENTRAL STEEL FABRICATORS LLC
2144 Soutel Dr (32208-2177)
P.O. Box 9839 (32208-0839)
PHONE..................................904 503-1660
Ernest Raynor, Mng Member
EMP: 5 EST: 2014
SALES (est): 949.5K Privately Held
SIC: 3441 Fabricated structural metal

(G-5976)
CHANCEY METAL PRODUCTS INC
5130 Sunbeam Rd (32257-6132)
PHONE..................................904 260-6880
Chancey Joseph L Jr, President
Mary G Chancey, Corp Secy
Travis Smith, Project Mgr
EMP: 40 EST: 1986
SQ FT: 24,500
SALES (est): 8.7MM Privately Held
WEB: www.chanceymetals.com
SIC: 3446 Architectural metalwork

(G-5977)
CHICOS PALLETS CORP
7917 W Beaver St (32220-2666)
PHONE..................................904 236-3607
EMP: 9 EST: 2015
SALES (est): 432.1K Privately Held
SIC: 2448 Pallets, wood & wood with metal

(G-5978)
CHILLER MEDIC INC
8933 Western Way Ste 18 (32256-8388)
PHONE..................................904 814-9446
David Lampp, President
EMP: 8 EST: 2012
SALES (est): 1MM Privately Held
WEB: www.chillermedic.com
SIC: 3585 1711 7623 Air conditioning equipment, complete; air conditioning units, complete: domestic or industrial; heating & air conditioning contractors; air conditioning repair

(G-5979)
CHILLY WILLYS HEATING & A INC
8006 Renault Dr (32244-1393)
PHONE..................................904 772-1164

William E Hester, President
EMP: 9 EST: 2009
SALES (est): 151.3K Privately Held
WEB: www.chillywillys.co
SIC: 3564 3823 Air cleaning systems; temperature measurement instruments, industrial

(G-5980)
CLARIOS LLC
Also Called: Johnson Controls
6973 Highway Ave Ste 301 (32254-3430)
PHONE..................................904 786-9161
Shawn Mudd, Division Mgr
Lindsay Gowan, Vice Pres
Robert Riggs, Opers Staff
Jennifer Warren, Buyer
Will Lindsey, Sales Mgr
EMP: 41
SALES (corp-wide): 47.9B Privately Held
WEB: www.clarios.com
SIC: 3691 Storage batteries
HQ: Clarios, Llc
5757 N Green Bay Ave
Milwaukee WI 53209

(G-5981)
CLAWSON CUSTOM CUES INC (PA)
Also Called: Predator Products
7255 Salisbury Rd Ste 1 (32256-6980)
PHONE..................................904 448-8748
John Foster, President
Allan McCarty, President
John Riley, General Mgr
Jessica Fryback, Manager
Paul Costain, Director
▲ EMP: 18 EST: 1994
SQ FT: 1,200
SALES (est): 3.8MM Privately Held
SIC: 3949 Sporting & athletic goods

(G-5982)
CLEAR DISTRIBUTION INC
6611 Sthpint Pkwy Ste C30 (32216)
PHONE..................................904 330-5624
Clifford Martin Jr, CEO
EMP: 6 EST: 2019
SALES (est): 400K Privately Held
SIC: 2051 Bakery: wholesale or wholesale/retail combined

(G-5983)
CLEVELAND DIABETES CARE INC (PA)
10752 Deerwood Park Blvd (32256-4849)
PHONE..................................904 394-2620
Elsa Kerpi, President
EMP: 11 EST: 2018
SALES (est): 11.7MM Privately Held
WEB: www.cdiabetescare.com
SIC: 2834 Pharmaceutical preparations

(G-5984)
CLJ INDUSTRIES INC
6015 Chester Cir Ste 213 (32217-2277)
PHONE..................................562 688-0508
Coridale L Jackson, President
EMP: 8 EST: 2014
SALES (est): 91.9K Privately Held
SIC: 3999 Barber & beauty shop equipment

(G-5985)
CLOROX HEALTHCARE HOLDINGS LLC
Also Called: Healthlink
3611 Saint Johns Ave 1 (32205-9025)
PHONE..................................904 996-7758
Chris Temmons, Branch Mgr
EMP: 25
SALES (corp-wide): 7.1B Publicly Held
WEB: www.thecloroxcompany.com
SIC: 2842 Specialty cleaning, polishes & sanitation goods
HQ: Clorox Healthcare Holdings, Llc
1221 Broadway
Oakland CA

(G-5986)
CMC STEEL US LLC
Also Called: CMC Steel Florida
16770 Rebar Rd (32234-4100)
PHONE..................................904 266-4261
Barbara Smith, Branch Mgr

EMP: 42
SALES (corp-wide): 8.9B Publicly Held
WEB: www.cmc.com
SIC: 3399 Staples, nonferrous metal or wire
HQ: Cmc Steel Us, Llc
6565 N Macarthur Blvd # 8
Irving TX 75039
214 689-4300

(G-5987)
CMF MEDICON SURGICAL INC
11200 St Jhns Indus Pkwy (32246)
PHONE..................................904 642-7500
Joachim Schmid, President
Marian Dipietro, General Mgr
Matthias Alber, Exec VP
Michael Marsiglia, Sales Staff
◆ EMP: 6 EST: 2006
SALES (est): 991.1K Privately Held
WEB: www.medicon.de
SIC: 3841 5047 Surgical & medical instruments; medical equipment & supplies

(G-5988)
CNS SIGNS INC
3539 W Beaver St (32254-3711)
PHONE..................................904 733-4806
Jeanne Bringle, President
Ken Bringle, Vice Pres
Ernest Hammond, Treasurer
EMP: 7 EST: 1990
SALES (est): 890.3K Privately Held
WEB: www.cnssign.com
SIC: 3993 Signs & advertising specialties

(G-5989)
COASTAL FILMS OF FLORIDA
627 Lane Ave N (32254-2822)
PHONE..................................904 786-2031
Robert Barlanti, President
EMP: 95 EST: 1989
SALES (est): 25.3MM Privately Held
SIC: 2673 Bags: plastic, laminated & coated
PA: Alpha Industries Management, Inc.
808 Page Ave
Lyndhurst NJ 07071

(G-5990)
COASTAL INDUSTRIES INC (PA)
3700 St Jhns Indus Pkwy W (32246-7655)
P.O. Box 16091 (32245-6091)
PHONE..................................904 642-3970
Martin Ray Adams, President
William M Cobb, Owner
Mike Hinson, General Mgr
Michele Ford, Principal
Andres Arrubla, Vice Pres
◆ EMP: 167 EST: 1972
SQ FT: 250,000
SALES (est): 32.9MM Privately Held
WEB: www.coastalshowerdoors.com
SIC: 3231 Doors, glass: made from purchased glass

(G-5991)
COCA-COLA BEVERAGES FLA LLC
1411 Huron St (32254-2026)
PHONE..................................904 786-2720
Jerry Reaves, Branch Mgr
EMP: 450
SALES (corp-wide): 366.5MM Privately Held
WEB: www.cocacolaflorida.com
SIC: 2086 5149 Bottled & canned soft drinks; soft drinks
PA: Coca-Cola Beverages Florida, Llc
10117 Princess Palm Ave
Tampa FL 33610
800 438-2653

(G-5992)
CODE 1 INC
14048 Prater Ct (32224-0867)
PHONE..................................786 347-7755
Wilson Santana, President
Brigitte L Santana, Vice Pres
◆ EMP: 3 EST: 1992
SQ FT: 1,900
SALES (est): 3.9MM Privately Held
SIC: 2821 Polyesters

(G-5993)
COM PAC FILTRATION INC
2020 W Beaver St (32209-7533)
P.O. Box 40071 (32203-0071)
PHONE...................................904 356-4003
Dean Atkinson, *President*
Valerie Atkinson, *Admin Sec*
Susan Rodriguez, *Clerk*
▲ EMP: 35 EST: 1987
SQ FT: 8,000
SALES (est): 7.8MM **Privately Held**
WEB: www.com-pac.net
SIC: 3589 3272 Swimming pool filter &
water conditioning systems; fountains,
concrete

(G-5994)
**COMMERCIAL METALS
COMPANY**
9625 E Florida Min Blvd (32257)
PHONE...................................904 262-9770
EMP: 7
SALES (corp-wide): 8.9B **Publicly Held**
WEB: www.cmc.com
SIC: 3441 Fabricated structural metal
PA: Commercial Metals Company
6565 N Macarthur Blvd # 800
Irving TX 75039
214 689-4300

(G-5995)
**COMMERCIAL METALS
COMPANY**
Also Called: CMC Steel Fabricators
10483 General Ave (32220-2103)
P.O. Box 37979 (32236-7979)
PHONE...................................904 781-4780
Rodney Powell, *Branch Mgr*
EMP: 13
SALES (corp-wide): 8.9B **Publicly Held**
WEB: www.cmc.com
SIC: 3312 Blast furnaces & steel mills
PA: Commercial Metals Company
6565 N Macarthur Blvd # 800
Irving TX 75039
214 689-4300

(G-5996)
CONCEALMENT EXPRESS LLC
10066 103rd St Ste 103 (32210-9258)
PHONE...................................888 904-2722
Katrina Boyter, *Opers Staff*
Sang Cho, *Treasurer*
Kane Miguel, *Controller*
Pablo Conde, *Chief Mktg Ofcr*
Benedict Jimenez, *Mng Member*
EMP: 51 EST: 2014
SALES (est): 5.1MM **Privately Held**
WEB: www.roundedgear.com
SIC: 3089 5699 Molding primary plastic;
sports apparel

(G-5997)
**CONFEDERATED SPECIALTY
ASSOC I**
3043 Faye Rd (32226-2336)
PHONE...................................904 751-4754
George Fozzard, *Principal*
EMP: 7 EST: 2010
SALES (est): 98.2K **Privately Held**
SIC: 2899 Chemical preparations

(G-5998)
**CONRAD MARKLE BLDR &
CBNT**
1120 Romney St (32211-5663)
PHONE...................................904 744-4569
Conrad Markle, *Owner*
EMP: 9 EST: 1994
SALES (est): 251.1K **Privately Held**
SIC: 2431 Millwork

(G-5999)
CONSTRUCTION BULLETIN INC
7033 Commwl Ave Ste 1 (32220)
PHONE...................................904 388-0336
Kenneth Heatherman, *CEO*
EMP: 10 EST: 1972
SQ FT: 2,500
SALES (est): 753.2K **Privately Held**
WEB: www.cbids.com
SIC: 2741 2721 Business service newslet-
ters: publishing & printing; periodicals

(G-6000)
**CONTINENTAL CONCRETE
PRODUCTS**
2251 Urban Rd (32210-4239)
PHONE...................................904 388-1390
EMP: 5
SQ FT: 2,500
SALES (est): 370K **Privately Held**
SIC: 3272 1771 Mfg Concrete Products &
Concrete & Foundation Work

(G-6001)
CONTINENTAL PRINTING
3060 Mercury Rd (32207-7915)
PHONE...................................904 731-8989
Ayileka Banke, *Manager*
EMP: 7 EST: 2011
SALES (est): 132.7K **Privately Held**
WEB: www.continentalprintingjax.com
SIC: 2752 Commercial printing, offset

(G-6002)
**CONTINENTAL PRINTING SVCS
INC**
4929 Toproyal Ln (32277-1044)
PHONE...................................904 743-6718
James L Duduit, *President*
Shirley Duduit, *Admin Sec*
▼ EMP: 9 EST: 1972
SQ FT: 9,200
SALES (est): 239.6K **Privately Held**
SIC: 2752 7336 Commercial printing, off-
set; commercial art & graphic design;
graphic arts & related design

(G-6003)
CONTROL SOUTHERN INC
4133 N Canal St (32209-3623)
PHONE...................................904 353-0004
Larry Young, *President*
Andres Espina, *Engineer*
EMP: 31
SALES (corp-wide): 68MM **Privately
Held**
WEB: www.controlsouthern.com
SIC: 3592 Valves
PA: Control Southern Inc.
3850 Lakefield Dr
Suwanee GA 30024
770 495-3100

(G-6004)
COOSA LLC
12811 Helm Dr (32258-2221)
PHONE...................................904 268-1187
Elise P Jones, *Manager*
EMP: 7 EST: 2005
SALES (est): 146.6K **Privately Held**
WEB: www.coosacomposites.com
SIC: 2821 Plastics materials & resins

(G-6005)
**COPELAND WELDING &
MUFFLER SP**
484 Lime St (32204-2777)
PHONE...................................904 355-6383
Raymond R Copeland Jr, *President*
Randy Copeland, *Treasurer*
DOT Copeland, *Admin Sec*
EMP: 6 EST: 1933
SALES (est): 380.5K **Privately Held**
WEB: www.copelandwelding.com
SIC: 7692 Welding repair

(G-6006)
COPY RIGHT BGMD INC
5569 Bowden Rd Ste 6 (32216-0915)
PHONE...................................904 680-0343
Shawn Bass, *President*
Keith Fallon, *Vice Pres*
Kelly Marshall, *Office Mgr*
Ward Huntley, *Director*
Ron Carney, *Graphic Designe*
EMP: 10 EST: 2003
SQ FT: 3,600
SALES (est): 793.5K **Privately Held**
WEB: www.copyrightjax.com
SIC: 2752 Commercial printing, offset

(G-6007)
CORK INDUSTRIES INC
5555 W Beaver St (32254-2916)
PHONE...................................904 695-2400
Stephen Foy, *Sales Staff*
Gerald Clauss, *Marketing Staff*
Mike Cox, *Marketing Staff*
Diana Alexander, *Manager*
Jim Vaccaro, *Director*
EMP: 22
SALES (corp-wide): 10MM **Privately
Held**
WEB: www.corkind.com
SIC: 2851 Paints & allied products
PA: Cork Industries, Inc.
500 Kaiser Dr
Folcroft PA 19032
610 522-9550

(G-6008)
CORROCOAT USA INC
6525 Greenland Rd (32258-2439)
PHONE...................................904 268-4559
Ed Cilli, *Project Mgr*
Clive A Harper, *CFO*
Julie Forte, *Administration*
Jodi Smith, *Administration*
Emily Wainwright, *Administration*
▲ EMP: 12 EST: 2007
SALES (est): 1.2MM
SALES (corp-wide): 20.8MM **Privately
Held**
WEB: www.corrocoatusa.com
SIC: 3479 Coating of metals & formed
products
PA: Corrosioneering Group Limited
Forster Street
Leeds LS10
113 276-0760

(G-6009)
**CORRUGATED CREATIONS BY
ALAN**
12807 Jordan Blair Ct (32225-4166)
PHONE...................................904 683-4347
Alan Beatty, *Principal*
EMP: 7 EST: 2010
SALES (est): 237K **Privately Held**
SIC: 2653 Corrugated & solid fiber boxes

(G-6010)
COSTA BRICK PAVERS INC
12368 Brady Rd (32223-2529)
PHONE...................................904 535-5009
Da Costa Josemar Rodrigues, *Principal*
EMP: 6 EST: 2015
SALES (est): 339.5K **Privately Held**
SIC: 2951 Asphalt paving mixtures &
blocks

(G-6011)
CREATIVE COUNTERTOPS INC
Also Called: Creative Counters
4768 Highway Ave (32254-3788)
PHONE...................................904 387-2800
Ronald Moore, *President*
Jason Rebman, *General Mgr*
Louis Gonzalez, *Vice Pres*
EMP: 13 EST: 1994
SQ FT: 10,000
SALES (est): 2.6MM **Privately Held**
WEB: www.creativecountertops.biz
SIC: 3131 2821 2541 Counters; plastics
materials & resins; wood partitions & fix-
tures

(G-6012)
CREATIVE GLASSWORKS
2062 Saint Martins Dr W (32246-7051)
PHONE...................................904 860-0865
Kirk Reber, *Owner*
▲ EMP: 9 EST: 1993
SALES (est): 453.7K **Privately Held**
SIC: 3231 5231 Stained glass: made from
purchased glass; glass

(G-6013)
**CREATIVE IMAGES
EMBRODIERY**
2989 Philips Hwy (32207-4484)
PHONE...................................904 730-5660
Paul Hahn, *President*
EMP: 8 EST: 1988
SALES (est): 553.1K **Privately Held**
WEB: www.cie-jax.com
SIC: 2395 Embroidery products, except
schiffli machine

(G-6014)
CROWN PLATING INC
5285 Ramona Blvd (32205-4414)
P.O. Box 37675 (32236-7675)
PHONE...................................904 783-6640
Robert E Little, *President*
EMP: 50 EST: 1970
SQ FT: 20,000
SALES (est): 3.1MM **Privately Held**
SIC: 3471 Electroplating of metals or
formed products

(G-6015)
**CROWN PRODUCTS COMPANY
INC (PA)**
6390 Philips Hwy (32216-6092)
PHONE...................................904 737-7144
Peter Tuggle, *Principal*
Linda Hardy, *Principal*
Scott Uhler, *Prdtn Mgr*
Charles Foster, *Sales Staff*
Mallory Odam, *Sales Staff*
▲ EMP: 180 EST: 1964
SQ FT: 90,000
SALES (est): 41.7MM **Privately Held**
WEB: www.crownproductsco.com
SIC: 3444 Flues & pipes, stove or furnace:
sheet metal; ducts, sheet metal

(G-6016)
**CROWN PRODUCTS COMPANY
INC**
Also Called: Crown Building Systems
3545 New Kings Rd (32209-3349)
PHONE...................................904 924-8340
Lisa McGann, *Human Res Dir*
Tad Dalton, *Sales Staff*
Peter S Tuggle, *Manager*
EMP: 55
SALES (corp-wide): 41.7MM **Privately
Held**
WEB: www.crownproductsco.com
SIC: 3444 3585 Sheet metal specialties,
not stamped; refrigeration & heating
equipment
PA: Crown Products Company, Inc.
6390 Philips Hwy
Jacksonville FL 32216
904 737-7144

(G-6017)
CU HOLDINGS LLC
Also Called: Cardinal Straws
5515 W 5th St (32254-1669)
PHONE...................................904 483-5700
Michael Houle, *President*
▲ EMP: 92 EST: 2006
SALES (est): 25.6MM
SALES (corp-wide): 317MM **Privately
Held**
SIC: 2656 Straws, drinking: made from
purchased material
PA: Wincup, Inc.
4640 Lewis Rd
Stone Mountain GA 30083
770 771-5861

(G-6018)
**CUSTOM MARINE
COMPONENTS INC**
13755 Atlantic Blvd (32225-3236)
PHONE...................................904 221-6412
Louis E Leidecker, *President*
Harper Bryan, *Managing Prtnr*
John T Quinlan, *Vice Pres*
John Quinlan, *Vice Pres*
EMP: 21 EST: 1984
SQ FT: 5,000
SALES (est): 4MM **Privately Held**
WEB: www.custommarinecomponents.com
SIC: 3441 5551 3732 Boat & barge sec-
tions, prefabricated metal; boat dealers;
boat building & repairing

(G-6019)
**CUSTOM WOOD PRODUCTS
INC**
3811 University Blvd W # 10 (32217-2234)
PHONE...................................904 737-6906
Danny Hall, *Principal*
EMP: 7 EST: 2002
SALES (est): 991.5K **Privately Held**
WEB: www.customwoodjacksonville.com
SIC: 2434 Wood kitchen cabinets

▲ = Import ▼=Export
◆ =Import/Export

(G-6020)
D J CAMCO CORPORATION
2426 Dennis St (32204-1712)
PHONE..................................904 355-5995
Dennis J Cameron, *President*
EMP: 6 **EST:** 1988
SQ FT: 1,000
SALES (est): 557.3K **Privately Held**
WEB: www.djcamco.com
SIC: 3451 Screw machine products

(G-6021)
D W ALLEN MARINE SVCS INC
1841 Wambolt St (32202-1026)
P.O. Box 3804 (32206-0804)
PHONE..................................904 358-1933
Dan Allen, *President*
Gretchen Williams, *Director*
EMP: 36 **EST:** 1985
SQ FT: 15,000
SALES (est): 4.7MM **Privately Held**
WEB: www.dwallenmarine.com
SIC: 3731 3441 Shipbuilding & repairing;
ship sections, prefabricated metal

(G-6022)
DAGHER & SONS INC
Also Called: DAGHER PRINTING
11775 Marco Beach Dr (32224-7616)
PHONE..................................904 998-0911
Joseph G Dagher, *President*
Salem Dagher, *Vice Pres*
Mouna Khoury, *Treasurer*
EMP: 16 **EST:** 1976
SQ FT: 20,000
SALES (est): 1.6MM **Privately Held**
WEB: www.dagher.com
SIC: 2752 Commercial printing, offset

(G-6023)
DAIKIN COMFORT TECH MFG LP
Also Called: Pioneer Metals
1934 W Beaver St (32209-7531)
PHONE..................................904 355-4520
Rick Rivas, *Manager*
EMP: 9 **Privately Held**
WEB: www.goodmanmfg.com
SIC: 3694 Distributors, motor vehicle en-
gine; alternators, automotive
HQ: Daikin Comfort Technologies Manufac-
turing, L.P.
19001 Kermier Rd
Waller TX 77484
713 861-2500

(G-6024)
DAILYS
9143 Baymeadows Rd (32256-7705)
PHONE..................................904 448-0562
Mike Hall, *General Mgr*
EMP: 18 **EST:** 2014
SALES (est): 627.2K **Privately Held**
WEB: www.dailys.com
SIC: 2711 Newspapers, publishing & print-
ing

(G-6025)
DAILYS
13800 Old St Augustine Rd (32258-2448)
PHONE..................................904 880-4784
EMP: 8 **EST:** 2015
SALES (est): 174.9K **Privately Held**
WEB: www.dailysplace.com
SIC: 2711 Newspapers, publishing & print-
ing

(G-6026)
DAUNTLESS USA INC
9995 Gate Pkwy N Ste 400 (32246-1898)
PHONE..................................904 996-8800
Steven C Koegler, *President*
Lazar S Finker, *Vice Pres*
William E Chattin, *Treasurer*
William Chattin, *Treasurer*
EMP: 20 **EST:** 1994
SALES (est): 3.3MM **Privately Held**
SIC: 1382 Oil & gas exploration services

(G-6027)
DAVIS MAIL SERVICES INC
13464 Grover Rd (32226-1944)
PHONE..................................904 477-7970
Tony E Davis, *President*
Patricia M Davis, *Vice Pres*
Josh Sudduth, *Opers Staff*
EMP: 150 **EST:** 2008

SALES (est): 26.8MM **Privately Held**
SIC: 2542 Locker boxes, postal service:
except wood

(G-6028)
DEALER IT GROUP LLC
5220 Belfort Rd Ste 400 (32256-6018)
PHONE..................................904 518-3379
EMP: 12 **EST:** 2018
SALES (est): 942.8K **Privately Held**
WEB: www.dealeritgroup.com
SIC: 7372 Business oriented computer
software

(G-6029)
DESIGN CONTAINERS INC
Also Called: Design Cores and Tubes
2913 Westside Blvd (32209-2714)
PHONE..................................904 764-6541
Samuel H Vickers, *CEO*
Mike Hott, *CFO*
Samuel Vickers, *Info Tech Dir*
Thomas W Talbot, *Director*
◆ **EMP:** 42 **EST:** 1960
SQ FT: 150,000
SALES (est): 6.3MM **Privately Held**
WEB: www.designcontainers.com
SIC: 2655 1761 2631 Drums, fiber: made
from purchased material; roofing, siding &
sheet metal work; paperboard mills

(G-6030)
DESIGNER LIFESTYLES LLC
619 Cassat Ave (32205-4716)
PHONE..................................904 631-8954
Christopher Mayer, *President*
Christopher J Mayer, *Principal*
EMP: 16 **EST:** 2006
SALES (est): 2.4MM **Privately Held**
WEB: www.designerlifestyles.com
SIC: 2426 5211 1752 1743 Flooring,
hardwood; parquet flooring, hardwood;
flooring, wood; ceramic floor tile installa-
tion; tile installation, ceramic; tiles, cork;
wood flooring

(G-6031)
DEVSCAPE SOFTWARE LLC
5870 Wind Cave Ln (32258-5186)
PHONE..................................904 625-6510
Carrie Monahan, *Marketing Staff*
Lauren Randel, *Marketing Staff*
Sam Macrae, *Officer*
Christine Swartzendruber, *Administration*
EMP: 5 **EST:** 2019
SALES (est): 441.5K **Privately Held**
WEB: www.devscapesoftware.com
SIC: 3652 Pre-recorded records & tapes

(G-6032)
DFA DAIRY BRANDS FLUID LLC
11231 Phillips Ind Blvd E (32256-3016)
PHONE..................................386 775-6700
Randy Vick, *Branch Mgr*
EMP: 15
SALES (corp-wide): 19.3B **Privately Held**
SIC: 2026 Fluid milk
HQ: Dfa Dairy Brands Fluid, Llc
1405 N 98th St
Kansas City KS 66111
816 801-6455

(G-6033)
DIRTRBAGS CHOPPER
2426 Mayport Rd Ste 5 (32233-6818)
PHONE..................................904 725-7600
Jeff Gordon, *CEO*
EMP: 8 **EST:** 2020
SALES (est): 400K **Privately Held**
SIC: 3751 Motorcycle accessories

(G-6034)
**DIVERSIFIED PERFORMANCE
SYSTEM**
6800 N Main St (32208-4726)
PHONE..................................904 765-7181
James Walter Newbold, *Owner*
▲ **EMP:** 8 **EST:** 2002
SALES (est): 243.3K **Privately Held**
WEB: www.onediversified.com
SIC: 3579 Embossing machines for store &
office use

(G-6035)
DIXIE TANK COMPANY
5349 Highway Ave (32254-3634)
PHONE..................................904 781-9500
Chris Eidson, *President*
Chris Crosby, *Superintendent*
Robert Connell, *Safety Dir*
Kim Carter, *Foreman/Supr*
Marty Higdon, *Foreman/Supr*
▼ **EMP:** 50 **EST:** 1943
SQ FT: 59,000
SALES (est): 10MM **Privately Held**
WEB: www.dixietank.com
SIC: 3443 Water tanks, metal plate

(G-6036)
**DKM MACHINE
MANUFACTURING**
3811 University Blvd W # 26 (32217-1210)
PHONE..................................904 733-0103
David Kennedy, *Director*
▲ **EMP:** 10 **EST:** 2012
SALES (est): 485K **Privately Held**
WEB: www.dkmpulpmachines.com
SIC: 3999 Manufacturing industries

(G-6037)
**DOCTORXS ALLERGY
FORMULA**
Also Called: Drs Allergy
2375 St Johns Bluff Rd S (32246-2333)
PHONE..................................904 758-2088
Howard Loff, *Mng Member*
EMP: 7 **EST:** 2013
SALES (est): 254.9K **Privately Held**
WEB: www.doctorsoptimalformula.com
SIC: 2835 In vitro & in vivo diagnostic sub-
stances

(G-6038)
**DORAN MANUFACTURING
CORP FLA**
6261 Powers Ave (32217-2215)
PHONE..................................904 731-3313
Richard Gross, *President*
▲ **EMP:** 7 **EST:** 1975
SQ FT: 36,000
SALES (est): 1MM **Privately Held**
WEB: www.collarstays.com
SIC: 3089 5162 Injection molding of plas-
tics; thermoformed finished plastic prod-
ucts; plastics products

(G-6039)
**DOS AMIGOS BOAT WORKS
LLC**
2913 Westside Blvd (32209-2714)
PHONE..................................904 764-6541
Vickers E Trustee, *Principal*
EMP: 7 **EST:** 2010
SALES (est): 227.5K **Privately Held**
SIC: 3732 Boat building & repairing

(G-6040)
DRESSER INC
12970 Normandy Blvd (32221-2110)
PHONE..................................318 640-2250
Fax: 318 640-6222
▲ **EMP:** 21 **EST:** 1999
SALES (est): 3MM **Privately Held**
SIC: 3491 Mfg Industrial Valves

(G-6041)
DRESSER LLC
Dresser Equipment Group
12970 Normandy Blvd (32221-2110)
PHONE..................................904 781-7071
Richard Fentum, *CEO*
EMP: 300
SALES (corp-wide): 654.8MM **Privately
Held**
WEB: www.dresserutility.com
SIC: 3491 Industrial valves
PA: Dresser, Llc
4425 Westway Park Blvd
Houston TX 77041
262 549-2626

(G-6042)
DRUMMOND PRESS INC (PA)
2472 Dennis St (32204-1757)
P.O. Box 2421 (32203-2421)
PHONE..................................904 354-2818
Robert J Falconetti, *Ch of Bd*
Diane Falconetti, *President*

Brian Baldwin, *Business Mgr*
Andrew Harrow, *Business Mgr*
Stephen Horne, *Business Mgr*
▲ **EMP:** 47 **EST:** 1939
SQ FT: 40,000
SALES (est): 26.7MM **Privately Held**
WEB: www.drummond.com
SIC: 2752 Commercial printing, offset

(G-6043)
DSX PRODUCTS INC
4430 Palmetto Inlt W (32277-1123)
PHONE..................................904 744-3400
Lee Lippert, *Principal*
Leonard Carrion, *Engineer*
Greg Olson, *Design Engr*
Scott Bennett, *Sales Staff*
EMP: 7 **EST:** 2007
SALES (est): 146K **Privately Held**
WEB: www.dsxinc.com
SIC: 3714 Motor vehicle parts & acces-
sories

(G-6044)
**DUKEMANS CUSTOM WDWKG
INC**
Also Called: Dukeman Custom Woodwork
141 N Myrtle Ave Fl 2 (32204-1309)
PHONE..................................904 355-5188
Stan Dukeman, *President*
Kenny Ranpersad, *Principal*
Philip Stein, *Principal*
EMP: 6 **EST:** 1998
SQ FT: 7,000
SALES (est): 824.3K **Privately Held**
WEB:
www.dukemancustomwoodworking.com
SIC: 2434 Wood kitchen cabinets

(G-6045)
DUMPSTERME LLC
13255 Lanier Rd (32226-4505)
PHONE..................................904 647-1945
John J Arwood R, *President*
EMP: 7 **EST:** 2017
SALES (est): 142.3K **Privately Held**
WEB: www.asapsiteservices.com
SIC: 3443 Dumpsters, garbage

(G-6046)
DUOS TECHNOLOGIES INC (PA)
6622 Sthpint Dr S Ste 310 (32216)
PHONE..................................904 652-1601
Chuck Ferry, *CEO*
Gianni B Arcaini, *President*
Larry Strach, *Vice Pres*
Connie L Weeks, *Vice Pres*
Scott Hill, *Electrical Engi*
EMP: 33 **EST:** 1990
SQ FT: 13,000
SALES (est): 30.8MM **Privately Held**
WEB: ir.duostechnologies.com
SIC: 7372 Prepackaged software

(G-6047)
**DUOS TECHNOLOGIES GROUP
INC (PA)**
Also Called: DUOSTECH
6622 Sthpint Dr S Ste 310 (32216)
PHONE..................................904 652-1601
Charles P Ferry, *CEO*
Kenneth Ehrman, *Ch of Bd*
Adrian G Goldfarb, *CFO*
Connie L Weeks,
EMP: 40 **EST:** 1990
SQ FT: 14,603
SALES (est): 8.2MM **Publicly Held**
WEB: www.duostechnologies.com
SIC: 7372 Business oriented computer
software

(G-6048)
DUPUY SILO FACILITY LLC (PA)
1520 Edgewood Ave N (32254-1748)
PHONE..................................904 899-7200
Jeff Hernandez, *Vice Pres*
Joe Waryold, *Vice Pres*
Michael James, *Warehouse Mgr*
Alston Bellflower, *Maint Spvr*
Lane Windham, *Maint Spvr*
EMP: 9 **EST:** 1999
SALES (est): 11.4MM **Privately Held**
WEB: www.dupuygroup.com
SIC: 2095 Coffee extracts

(G-6049)
DUSTSTOP FILTERS INC
Also Called: Duststop Air Filters
1843 Blue Ridge Dr (32246-0601)
PHONE.....................904 725-1001
Ovenie Rodriguez, *President*
EMP: 9 **EST:** 1991
SALES (est): 975.1K **Privately Held**
WEB: www.duststopfilters.com
SIC: 3564 3585 3433 Filters, air: furnaces, air conditioning equipment, etc.; refrigeration & heating equipment; heating equipment, except electric

(G-6050)
DUVAL FIXTURES INC
3600 Saint Augustine Rd (32207-5527)
PHONE.....................904 757-3964
Duane Yoder, *President*
Corey Dawson, *Vice Pres*
Rickie Pittman, *Prdtn Mgr*
EMP: 21 **EST:** 1965
SALES (est): 2.4MM **Privately Held**
WEB: www.duvalfixtures.com
SIC: 2541 Office fixtures, wood

(G-6051)
DWYER PRECISION PRODUCTS INC
266 20th St N (32250-2727)
PHONE.....................904 249-3545
James E Lineberger Jr, *President*
Bert Wechtenhiser, *Vice Pres*
▲ **EMP:** 11 **EST:** 1966
SQ FT: 7,000
SALES (est): 1.2MM **Privately Held**
WEB: www.dwyerprecisionproducts.com
SIC: 3841 Surgical & medical instruments

(G-6052)
DXM MARKETING GROUP LLC
9485 Rgncy Sq Blvd # 460 (32225-8156)
PHONE.....................904 332-6490
David Matchett,
John Brophy,
Ray Owens,
Dencho Vassilev,
EMP: 13 **EST:** 2010
SQ FT: 16,500
SALES (est): 705.3K **Privately Held**
WEB: www.dxmgp.com
SIC: 2759 7331 Advertising literature: printing; direct mail advertising services

(G-6053)
E 3 MAINTENANCE ✪
13720 Old St Agstine Rd S (32258-7414)
PHONE.....................904 708-7208
Edward E Murray, *Owner*
EMP: 23 **EST:** 2021
SALES (est): 1.2MM **Privately Held**
SIC: 1389 Construction, repair & dismantling services

(G-6054)
E G PUMP CONTROLS INC
Also Called: E G Controls
11790 Philips Hwy (32256-1642)
PHONE.....................904 292-0110
Brian Dail, *President*
Alex Chisholm, *General Mgr*
Samuel Jacobson, *Principal*
Tim Howard, *Vice Pres*
Shawna Deesetheobald, *Prdtn Mgr*
EMP: 25 **EST:** 1988
SQ FT: 22,000
SALES (est): 7.6MM **Privately Held**
WEB: www.egcontrols.com
SIC: 3625 Relays & industrial controls

(G-6055)
EAGLE VIEW WINDOWS INC
13340 International Pkwy (32218-2383)
PHONE.....................904 647-8221
William Meyers, *CEO*
Terry Tuten, *COO*
David Detuccio, *Vice Pres*
Derek Neal, *Vice Pres*
Mike Lane, *VP Mfg*
EMP: 14 **EST:** 2013
SALES (est): 1.4MM **Privately Held**
WEB: www.eagleviewwindows.com
SIC: 2431 Window screens, wood frame

(G-6056)
EAGLE-EYE ANESTHESIA INC
Also Called: Anesthesia Service & Equipment
11233 St Jhns Indus Pkwy (32246-6676)
PHONE.....................817 999-9830
Karen Gustafson, *President*
Kenneth Decray, *President*
Nancy Decray, *Vice Pres*
David Mahnken, *Opers Mgr*
Larry Laporte, *Technician*
EMP: 5 **EST:** 1991
SALES (est): 1MM **Privately Held**
WEB: www.eagleeyeanesthesia.com
SIC: 3841 Anesthesia apparatus

(G-6057)
EARTHCORE INDUSTRIES LLC (PA)
6899 Phillips Ind Blvd (32256-3029)
PHONE.....................904 363-3417
Carl R Spadaro, *CEO*
Lou Ramirez, *Regional Mgr*
Ben Whitlock, *Sales Staff*
EMP: 7 **EST:** 2006
SALES (est): 9.8MM **Privately Held**
WEB: www.earthcore.com
SIC: 3272 Fireplace & chimney material: concrete

(G-6058)
EAST COAST COOLING TOWER INC
9850 Interstate Center Dr (32218-5526)
PHONE.....................904 551-5527
Jim Adams, *President*
John Frietz, *Opers Mgr*
John Frietze, *Opers Mgr*
Trish Waters, *Office Mgr*
Terra Strickland, *Manager*
EMP: 12 **EST:** 2008
SQ FT: 11,000
SALES (est): 1.5MM **Privately Held**
WEB: www.eastcoastcoolingtower.com
SIC: 2499 8742 Cooling towers, wood or wood & sheet metal combination; management consulting services

(G-6059)
EAST COAST FIX & MLLWK CO INC
4880 Clydo Rd S (32207-7956)
PHONE.....................904 733-9711
Clyde Knowles, *President*
John Rappold, *Sales Staff*
Elaine Knowles, *Admin Sec*
Shawn McMenis, *Technician*
Melvin Martinez, *Internal Med*
EMP: 7 **EST:** 1966
SQ FT: 7,000
SALES (est): 1MM **Privately Held**
WEB: www.eacoproducts.com
SIC: 2541 2542 3431 3088 Partitions for floor attachment, prefabricated: wood; counters or counter display cases: except wood; metal sanitary ware; plastics plumbing fixtures; wood kitchen cabinets

(G-6060)
EASTERN WIRE PRODUCTS INC
5301 W 5th St (32254-1623)
PHONE.....................904 781-6775
Robert T Yates Jr, *President*
Mark W Yates, *President*
Mark Yates, *Vice Pres*
Scott T Yates, *Vice Pres*
Scott Yates, *Vice Pres*
◆ **EMP:** 38 **EST:** 1971
SQ FT: 80,000
SALES (est): 9.6MM **Privately Held**
WEB: www.eastern-wire.com
SIC: 3496 Miscellaneous fabricated wire products

(G-6061)
EASY RENT INC
Also Called: Fastsigns
8535 Baymeadows Rd Ste 7 (32256-7445)
PHONE.....................904 443-7446
John Ansel, *Owner*
Shawn Layton, *Accounts Mgr*
EMP: 7 **EST:** 1985
SALES (est): 775.4K **Privately Held**
WEB: www.fastsigns.com
SIC: 3993 2759 Signs & advertising specialties; business forms: printing

(G-6062)
ECO RESTORE LLC
Also Called: Construction
7563 Philips Hwy Ste 305 (32256-6858)
PHONE.....................904 226-9265
Joshua Bridgeman, *Mng Member*
EMP: 30 **EST:** 2018
SALES (est): 2.4MM **Privately Held**
WEB: www.ecorestorellc.com
SIC: 1389 1761 Construction, repair & dismantling services; roofing contractor

(G-6063)
ECO SOLAR TECHNOLOGY
12334 Hidden Hills Ln (32225-1702)
PHONE.....................904 219-0807
David Jolicoeur, *Principal*
EMP: 7 **EST:** 2010
SALES (est): 103.3K **Privately Held**
SIC: 3433 Solar heaters & collectors

(G-6064)
ECONOMY DNTRES JCKSONVILLE LLC
1680 Dunn Ave Ste 6 (32218-4788)
PHONE.....................904 696-6767
Leroy R Polite, *President*
Leroy Polite, *President*
Helen Polite, *Vice Pres*
Harold Polite,
EMP: 22 **EST:** 2008
SALES (est): 480.7K **Privately Held**
SIC: 3843 Dental equipment & supplies

(G-6065)
ECONOMY PRINTING CO
14413 Christen Dr S (32218-0854)
P.O. Box 2281 (32203-2281)
PHONE.....................904 786-4070
Robert D Strickland Jr, *President*
Tim Strickland, *Corp Secy*
Joseph Strickland, *Vice Pres*
EMP: 13 **EST:** 1932
SALES (est): 1.4MM **Privately Held**
WEB: www.economyprinting.net
SIC: 2761 2752 Manifold business forms; commercial printing, lithographic

(G-6066)
EDWARDS ORNAMENTAL IRON INC
Also Called: Gate Access Systems
1252 W Beaver St (32204-1410)
PHONE.....................904 354-4282
Michael Thurman, *President*
James Thurman, *President*
Lloyd Thurman, *Project Mgr*
EMP: 15 **EST:** 1947
SQ FT: 30,000
SALES (est): 2.1MM **Privately Held**
WEB: www.edwardsornamental.com
SIC: 3446 Ornamental metalwork

(G-6067)
EF ENTERPRISES OF NORTH FLA
4381 Gadsden Ct (32207-6218)
P.O. Box 550987 (32255-0987)
PHONE.....................904 739-5995
Frank Wallmeyer, *President*
EMP: 8 **EST:** 2007
SALES (est): 155.4K **Privately Held**
SIC: 2754 2759 Business forms: gravure printing; business forms: printing

(G-6068)
EHUD INDUSTRIES INC
9782 Nimitz Ct S (32246-3608)
PHONE.....................904 803-0873
Rebekah Hudnall, *President*
Brenda Hudnall, *Vice Pres*
EMP: 7 **EST:** 2014
SALES (est): 360.1K **Privately Held**
WEB: www.taxcheckinc.com
SIC: 3089 Injection molded finished plastic products; injection molding of plastics; molding primary plastic

(G-6069)
ELEMENTAL MOBILE SERVICES LLC
3435 Japonica Rd N (32209-2056)
PHONE.....................904 768-9840
Letecia Newman, *Principal*
EMP: 6 **EST:** 2018

SALES (est): 326.7K **Privately Held**
SIC: 2819 Industrial inorganic chemicals

(G-6070)
ELTON FOIL EMBOSSING INC
3414 Galilee Rd (32207-4718)
PHONE.....................904 399-1510
Floyd Houser, *Principal*
EMP: 9 **EST:** 2001
SALES (est): 182.9K **Privately Held**
SIC: 2759 Embossing on paper

(G-6071)
ELYSE INSTALLATIONS LLC
1848 Ector Rd (32211-4705)
PHONE.....................904 322-4754
Joshua Harvey,
EMP: 20 **EST:** 2020
SALES (est): 420K **Privately Held**
SIC: 1389 Construction, repair & dismantling services

(G-6072)
EMBRAER DEFENSE AND SEC INC
2110 Cole Flyer Rd (32218-2390)
PHONE.....................954 359-3700
Norman Ramby, *President*
Jon Spisak, *Prdtn Mgr*
Klaus Cipi, *Engineer*
Christopher Copeland, *Engineer*
Greta Williams, *Engineer*
▲ **EMP:** 1 **EST:** 2013
SALES (est): 41MM **Privately Held**
WEB: defense.embraer.com
SIC: 3721 Aircraft
HQ: Embraer Aircraft Holding, Inc.
276 Sw 34th St
Fort Lauderdale FL 33315

(G-6073)
EMERSON ELECTRIC CO
Also Called: Emerson Process Management
13350 International Pkwy # 102
(32218-2397)
PHONE.....................904 741-6800
EMP: 43
SALES (corp-wide): 24.6B **Publicly Held**
SIC: 3823 Mfg Process Control Instruments
PA: Emerson Electric Co.
8000 W Florissant Ave
Saint Louis MO 63136
314 553-2000

(G-6074)
ENDURIS EXTRUSIONS INC (PA)
7167 Old Kings Rd (32219-3727)
PHONE.....................904 421-3304
John Forbis, *CEO*
John Polidan, *President*
Brad Hillman, *CFO*
▲ **EMP:** 44 **EST:** 1998
SQ FT: 68,000
SALES (est): 9.1MM **Privately Held**
WEB: www.enduris.com
SIC: 3083 Plastic finished products, laminated

(G-6075)
ENGINEER SERVICE CORPORATION
2950 Halcyon Ln Ste 601 (32223-6691)
P.O. Box 23511 (32241-3511)
PHONE.....................904 268-0482
Alva C Atkins Jr, *President*
Charlene Atkins, *Admin Sec*
EMP: 6 **EST:** 1974
SQ FT: 1,000
SALES (est): 824.9K **Privately Held**
WEB: www.escscada.com
SIC: 3823 Water quality monitoring & control systems

(G-6076)
ENGLAND TRADING COMPANY LLC
Also Called: Industry West
4660 Pow Mia Mem Pkwy Ste
(32221-8201)
PHONE.....................888 969-4190
Shannon Stewart, *Chairman*
Amy Reese, *COO*
Rocco Paone, *Sales Staff*
Jordan England, *Mng Member*

Ellie Boline, *Manager*
▲ **EMP:** 36 **EST:** 2013
SALES (est): 10MM **Privately Held**
SIC: 2599 Factory furniture & fixtures; cabinets, factory

(G-6077)
ENVIROSAFE TECHNOLOGIES INC
11201 St Johns Indstrl Pk (32246)
PHONE...............................904 646-3456
John Wing, *Principal*
EMP: 7 **EST:** 2016
SALES (est): 152.9K **Privately Held**
SIC: 3089 Plastics products

(G-6078)
ENVIROVAULT LLC
Also Called: Phoenix Tanks
1727 Bennett St (32206-5415)
PHONE...............................904 354-1858
Doug Aiosa,
EMP: 17 **EST:** 2004
SALES (est): 264K **Privately Held**
WEB: www.phoenixprods.com
SIC: 3443 Fuel tanks (oil, gas, etc.): metal plate

(G-6079)
EPIC HARVESTS LLC
5215 Philips Hwy Ste 3 (32207-7990)
PHONE...............................904 503-5143
EMP: 25
SALES: 3MM **Privately Held**
SIC: 2053 Mfg Frozen Bakery Products

(G-6080)
EVERYTHING BLOCKCHAIN INC
12574 Flagler Center Blvd (32258-2614)
PHONE...............................904 454-2111
Eric C Jaffe, *CEO*
Michael W Hawkins, *Ch of Bd*
Toney E Jennings, *COO*
William C Regan, *CFO*
EMP: 20 **EST:** 2017
SQ FT: 800
SALES: 2.4MM **Privately Held**
WEB: www.everythingblockchain.io
SIC: 7372 Prepackaged software

(G-6081)
EVOLUTION SIGNS AND PRINT INC
11672 Philips Hwy Ste 3 (32256-2782)
PHONE...............................904 634-5666
EMP: 8 **EST:** 2018
SALES (est): 489.3K **Privately Held**
WEB: www.evojax.com
SIC: 2752 Commercial printing, lithographic

(G-6082)
EXACT INC
5285 Ramona Blvd (32205-4414)
P.O. Box 61087 (32236-1087)
PHONE...............................904 783-6640
W Wallace Buzz Allen III, *President*
Frank Hajosch, *President*
Jacob Perrotti, *Business Mgr*
William W Allen IV, *Vice Pres*
Karali Fedor, *Production*
EMP: 115 **EST:** 1964
SQ FT: 112,000
SALES (est): 24MM **Privately Held**
WEB: www.exactinc.com
SIC: 7692 3471 3469 3444 Welding repair; plating & polishing; metal stampings; sheet metal specialties, not stamped

(G-6083)
EXIDE BATTERY
600 Suemac Rd Ste 1 (32254-2796)
PHONE...............................904 783-1224
Ron Johnson, *Principal*
EMP: 5 **EST:** 2007
SALES (est): 352K **Privately Held**
SIC: 3691 5063 Storage batteries; batteries

(G-6084)
EXPERT TS OF JACKSONVILLE
711 Cassat Ave (32205-4859)
PHONE...............................904 387-2500
Denise Fisher, *President*
Steven Fisher, *Vice Pres*

EMP: 10 **EST:** 1991
SQ FT: 4,300
SALES (est): 983.7K **Privately Held**
WEB: www.experttsjax.com
SIC: 2396 5699 Screen printing on fabric articles; T-shirts, custom printed

(G-6085)
EXPRESS PRINTING & OFFICE SUPS
9840 Interstate Center Dr (32218-5528)
PHONE...............................904 765-9696
Michael Benso, *President*
John Benso, *Vice Pres*
EMP: 6 **EST:** 1983
SQ FT: 7,000
SALES (est): 499.4K **Privately Held**
WEB: www.expressprintingjax.com
SIC: 2752 5943 2791 Commercial printing, offset; office forms & supplies; typesetting

(G-6086)
FAM INDUSTRIES INC
7039 Mirabelle Dr (32258-8466)
PHONE...............................281 779-0650
Frank D Mays, *Principal*
EMP: 10 **EST:** 2007
SALES (est): 448.3K **Privately Held**
SIC: 3999 Barber & beauty shop equipment

(G-6087)
FANATICS MOUNTED MEMORIES INC
8100 Nations Way (32256-4405)
PHONE...............................866 578-9115
Ross Tannenbaum, *President*
David M Greene, *Senior VP*
Scott Widelitz, *Vice Pres*
Mark Cassuto, *Sales Staff*
Jeff Rabinowitz, *Sales Staff*
EMP: 37 **EST:** 1998
SALES (est): 5.1MM **Privately Held**
WEB: www.sportsmemorabilia.com
SIC: 2499 5199 Novelties, wood fiber; gifts & novelties

(G-6088)
FAST LABELS
8680 Bandera Cir S (32244-5947)
PHONE...............................904 626-0508
Susan Sermons, *General Mgr*
Michael Sermons, *Exec Dir*
EMP: 7 **EST:** 2001
SALES (est): 404.6K **Privately Held**
SIC: 2759 Labels & seals: printing

(G-6089)
FASTGLAS
Also Called: Island Tops
12819 Fenwick Island Ct E (32224-8613)
PHONE...............................904 765-2222
Gary Crull, *Owner*
EMP: 8 **EST:** 1998
SALES (est): 887K **Privately Held**
SIC: 2221 Fiberglass fabrics

(G-6090)
FINCANTIERI MARINE REPAIR LLC ✪
9485 Rgncy Sq Blvd # 101 (32225-8111)
PHONE...............................904 990-5869
Ryan W Smith,
Sandra Armstrong,
Shawn Johnston,
Paolo Pezzulo,
EMP: 30 **EST:** 2021
SALES (est): 2.9MM **Privately Held**
WEB: www.fincantierimarinesystems.com
SIC: 3731 Shipbuilding & repairing

(G-6091)
FINNS BRASS AND SILVER POLSG
2025 Hamilton St (32210-2045)
PHONE...............................904 387-1165
Michael R Finn, *President*
Kathy Finn, *Vice Pres*
EMP: 6 **EST:** 1972
SQ FT: 6,151

SALES (est): 481.1K **Privately Held**
WEB: www.finnsbrass.com
SIC: 3479 3592 3471 Coating of metals & formed products; antiques; plating & polishing

(G-6092)
FIRST CAST STRPPING MBL SNDBLS
4846 Philips Hwy (32207-7270)
PHONE...............................904 733-5915
R Jay Miller, *President*
Lisa Miller, *Vice Pres*
EMP: 5 **EST:** 1992
SALES (est): 581.1K **Privately Held**
SIC: 3471 Sand blasting of metal parts

(G-6093)
FIRST COAST CARGO INC
7643 Gate Pkwy Ste 104-31 (32256-3092)
PHONE...............................844 774-7711
Kyle Bailey, *CEO*
Ashley Bailey, *CEO*
EMP: 10 **EST:** 2019
SALES (est): 659.3K **Privately Held**
WEB: www.1stcoastcargo.com
SIC: 3537 Trucks: freight, baggage, etc.: industrial, except mining

(G-6094)
FIRST COAST CONCRETE PUMPING
6115 Earline Cir N (32258-1645)
PHONE...............................904 262-6488
Tammy A McDaniels, *President*
EMP: 8 **EST:** 2001
SALES (est): 87.7K **Privately Held**
SIC: 3272 Concrete products

(G-6095)
FIRST COAST GRANITE & MBL INC
6860 Phillips Ind Blvd (32256-3028)
PHONE...............................904 388-1217
Timothy Deck, *President*
EMP: 18 **EST:** 2001
SALES (est): 1.1MM **Privately Held**
SIC: 3281 Cut stone & stone products

(G-6096)
FIRST COAST TEE SHIRT CO INC
5971 Powers Ave Ste 104 (32217-2246)
PHONE...............................904 737-1985
Michael D Arthur, *President*
Craig L Melton, *Vice Pres*
EMP: 9 **EST:** 1994
SQ FT: 6,000
SALES (est): 780K **Privately Held**
WEB: www.firstcoasttees.com
SIC: 2759 Screen printing

(G-6097)
FIS AVANTGARD LLC (DH)
Also Called: Sungard
347 Riverside Ave (32202-4909)
PHONE...............................484 582-2000
Jl Alarcon, *General Mgr*
Leslie Harlow, *Vice Pres*
Judy Cho, *Manager*
Jose Fajardo, *Director*
Alain Fraiberger,
EMP: 42 **EST:** 2006
SALES (corp-wide): 13.8B **Publicly Held**
SIC: 7372 7378 7379 Business oriented computer software; computer maintenance & repair; computer related consulting services
HQ: Fis Capital Markets Us Llc
347 Riverside Ave
Jacksonville FL 32202
877 776-3706

(G-6098)
FIS KIODEX LLC
601 Riverside Ave (32204-2946)
PHONE...............................904 438-6000
EMP: 18 **EST:** 2000
SALES: 1.7MM
SALES (corp-wide): 13.8B **Publicly Held**
SIC: 7372 Business oriented computer software

PA: Fidelity National Information Services, Inc.
601 Riverside Ave
Jacksonville FL 32204
904 438-6000

(G-6099)
FITZLORD INC
Also Called: Vulcan Steel
650 E 27th St (32206-2347)
PHONE...............................904 731-2041
Thomas E Fitzpatrick, *CEO*
Davis H Hopper, *President*
Nancy M Fitzpatrick, *Principal*
EMP: 65 **EST:** 1974
SQ FT: 55,000
SALES (est): 3.1MM **Privately Held**
SIC: 3441 1791 Fabricated structural metal; structural steel erection

(G-6100)
FLAGSHIPMD LLC
7800 Belfort Pkwy Ste 230 (32256-6983)
PHONE...............................904 302-6160
Aishwarya Nallapillai, *Vice Pres*
Manivannan M Nallapillai,
EMP: 8 **EST:** 2007
SALES (est): 509.4K **Privately Held**
WEB: www.flagshipmd.com
SIC: 7372 Business oriented computer software

(G-6101)
FLAMM INDUSTRIES INC
Also Called: Wco Enterprises
1313 Haines St (32206-6035)
PHONE...............................904 356-2876
Martin Flamm, *President*
Roger McCoy, *Plant Mgr*
EMP: 5 **EST:** 1978
SQ FT: 28,000
SALES (est): 861.7K **Privately Held**
WEB: www.flammindustries.com
SIC: 2653 Boxes, corrugated: made from purchased materials

(G-6102)
FLAT GLASS DISTRIBUTORS LLC
5355 Shawland Rd (32254-1649)
P.O. Box 41146 (32203-1146)
PHONE...............................904 354-5413
Thomas Lee, *General Mgr*
Roger Steinke, *General Mgr*
Wanda Williamson, *Manager*
Rusty Melcom,
JD Moeller,
EMP: 16 **EST:** 2016
SALES (est): 4.4MM **Privately Held**
WEB: www.flatglassdistributors.com
SIC: 3229 1793 Glassware, industrial; glass & glazing work

(G-6103)
FLORIDA CMC REBAR
1395 Chaffee Rd S 2 (32221-1117)
PHONE...............................407 518-5101
Tania Murciano, *Principal*
EMP: 7 **EST:** 2016
SALES (est): 172.2K **Privately Held**
WEB: www.cmc.com
SIC: 3441 Fabricated structural metal

(G-6104)
FLORIDA E COAST HOLDINGS CORP
Also Called: Florida East Coast Railway
6140 Philips Hwy (32216-5921)
PHONE...............................904 279-3152
Linda Horn, *Opers Staff*
Alonso Rodriguez, *Manager*
EMP: 25 **Publicly Held**
WEB: www.fecrwy.com
SIC: 3531 Railway track equipment
HQ: Florida East Coast Holdings Corp.
7150 Philips Hwy
Jacksonville FL 32256

(G-6105)
FLORIDA FLOATS INC (HQ)
Also Called: B M I Properties
1813 Dennis St (32204-2009)
P.O. Box 8, Bellingham WA (98227-0008)
PHONE...............................904 358-3362
J Everett Babbitt, *President*
J Everett Babbit, *President*

Paul Chapman, *Vice Pres*
Stan Reimer, *Vice Pres*
Kevin Thompson, *Vice Pres*
▲ **EMP:** 25 **EST:** 1969
SQ FT: 5,000
SALES (est): 11.2MM
SALES (corp-wide): 69.6MM **Privately Held**
WEB: www.bellingham-marine.com
SIC: 3448 1629 Docks: prefabricated metal; marine construction
PA: Bellingham Marine Industries Acquisition, Inc.
　　1323 Lincoln St Ste 102
　　Bellingham WA 98229
　　360 676-2800

(G-6106)
FLORIDA JACKSONVILLE FORKLIFT
1063 Haines St (32206-6029)
PHONE.................................904 674-6898
EMP: 8 **EST:** 2017
SALES (est): 301K **Privately Held**
WEB: www.floridaforklift.com
SIC: 3537 Forklift trucks

(G-6107)
FLORIDA ROCK CONCRETE INC
700 Palmetto St (32202-2406)
PHONE.................................904 355-1781
EMP: 0
SALES (est): 14.4MM
SALES (corp-wide): 2.9B **Publicly Held**
SIC: 3273 Stone Clay Glass Products
HQ: Legacy Vulcan, Llc
　　1200 Urban Center Dr
　　Shoal Creek AL 35242
　　205 298-3000

(G-6108)
FLORIDA ROCK INDUSTRIES (HQ)
Also Called: Vulcan Mtls Co Vestavia Al
4707 Gordon St (32216-4037)
P.O. Box 4667 (32201-4667)
PHONE.................................904 355-1781
Thompson Baker II, *President*
Hill J T, *President*
Michael P Oates, *Vice Pres*
Wallace A Patzke Jr, *Vice Pres*
John D Milton Jr, *CFO*
◆ **EMP:** 140 **EST:** 1931
SQ FT: 60,000
SALES (est): 391.4MM **Publicly Held**
WEB: www.flarock.com
SIC: 1422 Lime rock, ground

(G-6109)
FLORIDA ROCK INDUSTRIES
Also Called: Concrete Group
10151 Deerwood Park Blvd # 10 (32256-0566)
P.O. Box 4667 (32201-4667)
PHONE.................................904 355-1781
John Baker, *President*
EMP: 15 **Publicly Held**
WEB: www.flarock.com
SIC: 3273 Ready-mixed concrete
HQ: Florida Rock Industries
　　4707 Gordon St
　　Jacksonville FL 32216
　　904 355-1781

(G-6110)
FLORIDA STAR INC
Also Called: Florida Star & News
1257 Edgewood Ave W (32208-2741)
P.O. Box 40629 (32203-0629)
PHONE.................................904 766-8834
Clara Criswell, *President*
EMP: 10 **EST:** 1951
SQ FT: 1,300
SALES (est): 730.6K **Privately Held**
WEB: www.thefloridastar.com
SIC: 2711 Newspapers, publishing & printing

(G-6111)
FLORIDA TRAILER RANCH LLC
14714 Normandy Blvd (32234-2400)
PHONE.................................904 289-7710
Harry Horton, *President*
Shane McKeel, *Vice Pres*
Larry Petrozi, *Treasurer*
Carl Frankich, *Admin Sec*

▼ **EMP:** 10 **EST:** 1991
SALES (est): 936.8K **Privately Held**
WEB: www.florida-trailer.com
SIC: 3799 Horse trailers, except fifth-wheel type

(G-6112)
FLORIDA WILBERT INC (PA)
5050 New Kings Rd (32209-2737)
P.O. Box 40485 (32203-0485)
PHONE.................................904 765-2641
William H Maddox Jr, *President*
▼ **EMP:** 5 **EST:** 1945
SQ FT: 8,000
SALES (est): 3MM **Privately Held**
WEB: www.floridawilbert.com
SIC: 3272 1791 Burial vaults, concrete or precast terrazzo; concrete reinforcement, placing of

(G-6113)
FLOTECH LLC (HQ)
Also Called: Tube Services-Division
136 Eastport Rd (32218-3906)
P.O. Box 26829 (32226-6829)
PHONE.................................904 358-1849
Joe Ferranti, *VP Opers*
Kevin Perrigo, *Opers Staff*
Mark Umphress, *Opers Staff*
Charlie Santana, *Engineer*
Joao Vaz, *CFO*
◆ **EMP:** 100 **EST:** 1982
SQ FT: 26,000
SALES (est): 26.3MM
SALES (corp-wide): 573.9MM **Privately Held**
WEB: www.flotechinc.com
SIC: 3494 7699 3339 3341 Valves & pipe fittings; valve repair, industrial; primary nonferrous metals; secondary nonferrous metals; sheet metalwork; nonferrous foundries
PA: Floworks International Llc
　　3750 Hwy 225
　　Pasadena TX 77503
　　713 672-2222

(G-6114)
FLOWERS BKG JACKSONVILLE LLC (DH)
Also Called: Sunbeam Bread
2261 W 30th St (32209-3606)
P.O. Box 12579 (32209-0579)
PHONE.................................904 354-3771
Rick McCombs, *President*
Bruce Rupert, *General Mgr*
Robert White, *Vice Pres*
▼ **EMP:** 80 **EST:** 1944
SQ FT: 100,000
SALES (est): 13MM
SALES (corp-wide): 4.3B **Publicly Held**
SIC: 2051 Bakery: wholesale or wholesale/retail combined
HQ: Flowers Baking Co. Of Thomasville, Inc.
　　1919 Flowers Cir
　　Thomasville GA 31757
　　229 226-9110

(G-6115)
FLUIDRA USA LLC
Also Called: Commercial Division
8525 Mallory Rd (32220-2358)
PHONE.................................904 378-4486
Joan Llop, *Manager*
EMP: 15 **Privately Held**
WEB: www.fluidrausa.com
SIC: 3589 Swimming pool filter & water conditioning systems
PA: Fluidra Usa, Llc
　　2882 Whiptail Loop # 100
　　Carlsbad CA 92010

(G-6116)
FLYING W PLASTICS FL INC
109 Stevens St (32254-3656)
PHONE.................................904 800-2451
Douglas Morris, *CEO*
Candice Bailey, *Manager*
EMP: 14 **EST:** 2020
SALES (est): 1.9MM **Privately Held**
SIC: 2821 Polyethylene resins

(G-6117)
FOLEY AIR LLC
Also Called: Air2 G2 Machine
136 Ellis Rd N (32254-2835)
PHONE.................................904 379-2243
Glen Black, *President*
EMP: 11 **EST:** 2020
SALES (est): 2.2MM
SALES (corp-wide): 12.1MM **Privately Held**
SIC: 3523 Farm machinery & equipment
PA: Foley Company, Llc
　　1750 Ryden Rd
　　Prescott WI 54021
　　800 225-9810

(G-6118)
FRASCOLD USA CORPORATION
5343 Bowden Rd 2 (32216-5945)
PHONE.................................855 547-5600
Kristian Ellefsen, *CEO*
Bina Ellefsen, *Human Res Mgr*
▲ **EMP:** 6 **EST:** 2014
SALES (est): 1.8MM **Privately Held**
WEB: www.frascold.it
SIC: 3585 Compressors for refrigeration & air conditioning equipment

(G-6119)
FRASER MILLWORKS INC
9424 Sisson Dr (32218-6064)
PHONE.................................904 768-7710
Chris M Fraser, *President*
Sharon Fraser, *Treasurer*
EMP: 7 **EST:** 1978
SQ FT: 10,000
SALES (est): 849.7K **Privately Held**
WEB: www.frasermillworks.com
SIC: 2431 Millwork

(G-6120)
FRASER WEST INC
6640 County Road 218 (32234-3047)
PHONE.................................904 289-7261
Chip Osteen, *Manager*
EMP: 126
SALES (corp-wide): 10.5B **Privately Held**
SIC: 2431 Millwork
HQ: West Fraser, Inc.
　　1900 Exeter Rd Ste 105
　　Germantown TN 38138
　　901 620-4200

(G-6121)
FRATTLE STAIRS & RAILS INC
465 Tresca Rd (32225-6566)
PHONE.................................904 384-3495
Don Frattle, *President*
Troy Pagnotto, *Opers Mgr*
EMP: 17 **EST:** 2000
SQ FT: 40,000
SALES (est): 4.4MM **Privately Held**
WEB: www.frattle.com
SIC: 3446 Balconies, metal; railings, bannisters, guards, etc.: made from metal pipe; railings, prefabricated metal; stairs, staircases, stair treads: prefabricated metal

(G-6122)
FRESH THREAD LLC
2823 State Road A1a (32233-2843)
PHONE.................................904 677-9505
Jerry Rodriguez, *Principal*
EMP: 13 **EST:** 2012
SALES (est): 490.3K **Privately Held**
WEB: www.mfgmerch.com
SIC: 2752 5136 Commercial printing, lithographic; men's & boys' clothing

(G-6123)
FT ACQUISITION COMPANY LLC
Also Called: Fabtech Supply
6600 Suemac Pl 2 (32254-2773)
P.O. Box 23325 (32241-3325)
PHONE.................................904 367-0095
Alan Ennis, *CEO*
Scott Lapierre, *Engineer*
EMP: 29 **EST:** 1992
SALES (est): 5MM **Privately Held**
SIC: 3444 Metal housings, enclosures, casings & other containers

(G-6124)
FUTCH PRINTING & MAILING INC
4606 Shirley Ave (32210-1934)
PHONE.................................904 388-3995
Shuford M Futch III, *President*
Agata Futch, *Vice Pres*
EMP: 12 **EST:** 1922
SQ FT: 10,000
SALES (est): 1MM **Privately Held**
WEB: www.futchprint.com
SIC: 2759 7331 Letterpress printing; direct mail advertising services

(G-6125)
FUTURE HOUSE
11201 Ponset Rd (32218-6325)
PHONE.................................904 683-9177
Troy Flowers, *Principal*
EMP: 8 **EST:** 2015
SALES (est): 624.4K **Privately Held**
WEB: www.future.loans
SIC: 2711 Newspapers

(G-6126)
G6 EMBROIDERY LLC
6001 Argyle Frest Blvd St (32244)
PHONE.................................904 729-1191
EMP: 6 **EST:** 2018
SALES (est): 444K **Privately Held**
SIC: 2395 Embroidery products, except schiffli machine

(G-6127)
GATE PETROLEUM COMPANY
11040 Mccormick Rd (32225-1821)
PHONE.................................904 998-7126
EMP: 9
SALES (corp-wide): 708.1K **Privately Held**
WEB: www.gatepetro.com
SIC: 3052 Rubber belting
PA: Gate Petroleum Company
　　9540 San Jose Blvd
　　Jacksonville FL 32257
　　904 737-7220

(G-6128)
GATE PETROLEUM COMPANY
4100 Heckscher Dr (32226-3030)
PHONE.................................904 396-0517
Earl Shimp, *President*
Lindsey Love, *Manager*
Eugene Thomas, *Asst Mgr*
EMP: 9
SQ FT: 5,984
SALES (corp-wide): 708.1K **Privately Held**
WEB: www.gatepetro.com
SIC: 3272 Concrete products
PA: Gate Petroleum Company
　　9540 San Jose Blvd
　　Jacksonville FL 32257
　　904 737-7220

(G-6129)
GATE PRECAST COMPANY
402 Zoo Pkwy (32226-2604)
PHONE.................................904 520-5795
Donald Davis, *Vice Pres*
Todd Petty, *Vice Pres*
Jay Givens, *Project Mgr*
Robert Bowen, *Purch Mgr*
Lisa Neuman, *Purch Agent*
EMP: 220
SALES (corp-wide): 708.1K **Privately Held**
WEB: www.gateprecast.com
SIC: 3272 Precast terrazo or concrete products
HQ: Gate Precast Company
　　9540 San Jose Blvd
　　Jacksonville FL 32257
　　904 732-7668

(G-6130)
GATE PRECAST COMPANY (HQ)
9540 San Jose Blvd (32257-5432)
P.O. Box 23627 (32241-3627)
PHONE.................................904 732-7668
Dean Gwin, *CEO*
Jane Martin, *General Mgr*
Earl N Shimp, *Senior VP*
Mark Ledkins, *Vice Pres*
Joseph Luke, *Vice Pres*
◆ **EMP:** 9 **EST:** 1996

SALES (est): 221.3K
SALES (corp-wide): 708.1K **Privately Held**
WEB: www.gateprecast.com
SIC: 3272 Concrete stuctural support & building material
PA: Gate Petroleum Company
9540 San Jose Blvd
Jacksonville FL 32257
904 737-7220

(G-6131)
GATE PRECAST ERECTION CO
9540 San Jose Blvd (32257-5432)
P.O. Box 23627 (32241-3627)
PHONE...................................904 737-7220
Joseph C Luke, *Director*
Jack C Lueders Jr, *Director*
Jeremy P Smith Jr, *Director*
EMP: 66 EST: 1978
SALES (est): 6.4MM
SALES (corp-wide): 708.1K **Privately Held**
WEB: www.gateprecast.com
SIC: 3272 Concrete stuctural support & building material
PA: Gate Petroleum Company
9540 San Jose Blvd
Jacksonville FL 32257
904 737-7220

(G-6132)
GAUKAUPA RACEWAY
8405 Beach Blvd (32216-3130)
PHONE...................................904 483-3473
Raj Patel, *Principal*
EMP: 7 EST: 2009
SALES (est): 145.3K **Privately Held**
SIC: 3644 Raceways

(G-6133)
GBC SOLUTIONS LLC
6982 Roundleaf Dr (32258-5505)
PHONE...................................904 705-2415
Greg Borys, *Principal*
EMP: 7 EST: 2015
SALES (est): 105.8K **Privately Held**
SIC: 2653 Corrugated & solid fiber boxes

(G-6134)
GE
12079 Normandy Blvd (32221-1820)
PHONE...................................904 570-3151
Jason Duran, *Production*
Lisa Marchand, *Manager*
Dana Deye, *Senior Mgr*
EMP: 9 EST: 2015
SALES (est): 104.8K **Privately Held**
WEB: www.ge.jobs
SIC: 3511 Turbines & turbine generator sets

(G-6135)
GE CONSUMER CORPORATION
Also Called: GE Consumer Distribution
600 Whittaker Rd (32218-5781)
PHONE...................................904 696-9775
Steve Holton, *General Mgr*
EMP: 50
SALES (corp-wide): 74.2B **Publicly Held**
WEB: www.appliancege.com
SIC: 3632 Household refrigerators & freezers
HQ: Ge Consumer Corporation
140 Whittington Pkwy
Louisville KY 40222
203 373-2211

(G-6136)
GEM ASSET ACQUISITION LLC
Also Called: Gemseal Pvments Pdts - Jackson
9556 Historic Kings Rd.S (32257-2009)
PHONE...................................904 268-6063
Jason Adair, *Store Mgr*
EMP: 35
SALES (corp-wide): 19.3MM **Privately Held**
SIC: 2951 Asphalt paving mixtures & blocks
PA: Gem Asset Acquisition Llc
1855 Lindbergh St Ste 500
Charlotte NC 28208
704 225-3321

(G-6137)
GENERAL BUSINESS SERVICES
12412 San Jose Blvd # 101 (32223-8620)
PHONE...................................904 260-1099
Tom Carroll, *Owner*
EMP: 6 EST: 2000
SALES (est): 470.9K **Privately Held**
SIC: 3578 Calculating & accounting equipment

(G-6138)
GENERAL ELECTRIC COMPANY
12854 Kenan Dr Ste 201 (32258-7402)
P.O. Box 2320 (32203-2320)
PHONE...................................203 796-1000
Tom Cratem, *Engineer*
Joe Clark, *Electrical Engi*
Vanessa Santiago, *Finance Mgr*
Paul Bossidy, *Manager*
Anthony Smiley, *Technician*
EMP: 213
SALES (corp-wide): 74.2B **Publicly Held**
WEB: www.ge.com
SIC: 3699 Electrical equipment & supplies
PA: General Electric Company
5 Necco St
Boston MA 02210
617 443-3000

(G-6139)
GENERAL METALS & PLASTICS INC
2727 Waller St (32205-5631)
PHONE...................................904 354-8224
Fred Broadwell Jr, *President*
Joyce Broadwell, *Vice Pres*
EMP: 5 EST: 1965
SQ FT: 5,500
SALES (est): 780.9K **Privately Held**
WEB: www.generalmetalsandplastics.com
SIC: 3444 3448 Awnings & canopies; screen enclosures; carports: prefabricated metal

(G-6140)
GENERAL SIGN SERVICE INC
1940 Spearing St (32206-3942)
PHONE...................................904 355-5630
Randall Ginzig, *President*
Carol Ginzig, *Admin Sec*
Randy Ginzig, *Admin Sec*
EMP: 10 EST: 1973
SALES (est): 883.3K **Privately Held**
WEB: www.generalsignservice.com
SIC: 3993 1731 Electric signs; general electrical contractor

(G-6141)
GILSON INC
730 Trinidad Rd (32216-9342)
PHONE...................................904 725-7612
Curtis Carter, *Principal*
EMP: 7 EST: 2009
SALES (est): 87.2K **Privately Held**
WEB: www.gilson.com
SIC: 3826 Analytical instruments

(G-6142)
GLASFLOSS INDUSTRIES INC
1310 Tradeport Dr (32218-2485)
PHONE...................................904 741-9922
Doug Lange, *District Mgr*
Mark Filewood, *Vice Pres*
Cheryl Manrique, *Vice Pres*
Bill McKnight, *Vice Pres*
Charles Watts, *Vice Pres*
EMP: 29
SQ FT: 74,952
SALES (corp-wide): 49.5MM **Privately Held**
WEB: www.glasfloss.com
SIC: 3564 Filters, air: furnaces, air conditioning equipment, etc.
PA: Glasfloss Industries, Inc.
420 E Danieldale Rd
Desoto TX 75115
740 687-1100

(G-6143)
GLASSFLAKE INTERNATIONAL INC
6525 Greenland Rd (32258-2439)
PHONE...................................904 268-4000
Clive Harper, *President*
▲ EMP: 6 EST: 1972

SQ FT: 10,000
SALES (est): 623.3K **Privately Held**
WEB: www.glassflake.com
SIC: 3479 2273 Coating of metals & formed products; floor coverings, textile fiber

(G-6144)
GLOBAL PUBLISHING INC
9799 Old St Augustine Rd (32257-8974)
PHONE...................................904 262-0491
Ronald Legrand, *President*
Debbie Waters, *Mktg Dir*
Jon Duck, *Manager*
Brian Albertson, *Technology*
Kenneth Pressley, *Advisor*
EMP: 35 EST: 1999
SQ FT: 25,000
SALES (est): 5.8MM **Privately Held**
WEB: www.ronlegrand.com
SIC: 2741 Miscellaneous publishing

(G-6145)
GLODEA STORE CORP
Also Called: Glodea Kitchens
521 Copeland St (32204-2721)
PHONE...................................888 400-4937
Ignacio L Santos, *President*
Santos Jose Ignacio L, *President*
Patrick Cherix, *Vice Pres*
▲ EMP: 5 EST: 2013
SQ FT: 800
SALES (est): 614.4K **Privately Held**
WEB: www.glodea.com
SIC: 2511 5021 Wood household furniture; household furniture

(G-6146)
GOODRICH CORPORATION
Engineered Polymer Products
6061 Goodrich Blvd (32226-3402)
PHONE...................................904 757-3660
Mike Smith, *General Mgr*
Drew Wannamaker, *General Mgr*
Keith Reed, *Plant Mgr*
Tom Lynn, *Purchasing*
EMP: 120
SALES (corp-wide): 64.3B **Publicly Held**
WEB: www.collinsaerospace.com
SIC: 3812 8711 3429 3493 Sonar systems & equipment; engineering services; manufactured hardware (general); steel springs, except wire; wire springs; synthetic rubber
HQ: Goodrich Corporation
2730 W Tyvola Rd
Charlotte NC 28217
704 423-7000

(G-6147)
GOSAN USA INC
1926 Spearing St (32206-3942)
P.O. Box 600920 (32260-0920)
PHONE...................................904 356-4181
Rocio Santin, *President*
Francisco Javi Esteban, *Managing Dir*
▲ EMP: 12 EST: 2007
SALES (est): 425.1K **Privately Held**
WEB: www.jcrenfroe.com
SIC: 3537 Trucks, tractors, loaders, carriers & similar equipment

(G-6148)
GRAHAM & COMPANY LLC
9440 Philips Hwy Ste 1 (32256-1339)
PHONE...................................904 281-0003
Leslie Williamson, *Chief Engr*
Thomas Michael, *Engineer*
Tana Welch, *Accountant*
EMP: 8
SALES (corp-wide): 11.2MM **Privately Held**
WEB: www.grahamcompany.com
SIC: 3563 Vacuum pumps, except laboratory
PA: Graham & Company, Llc
1801 5th Ave N Ste 300
Birmingham AL 35203
205 871-7100

(G-6149)
GREAT ATLANTIC OUTFITTERS
803 North St (32211-5727)
PHONE...................................904 722-0196
Bob Morris, *CEO*
Andrew Lassiter, *Info Tech Mgr*

EMP: 5 EST: 2005
SALES (est): 531.7K **Privately Held**
WEB: www.greatatlanticoutfitters.com
SIC: 2759 Screen printing

(G-6150)
GREAT NORTHERN CORPORATION
Also Called: Laminations Southeast
1420 Vantage Way S # 100 (32218-2398)
PHONE...................................920 739-3671
Warren Bobyk, *Business Mgr*
Jeffrey Phillips, *Opers Mgr*
Bill Voss, *Production*
Tim Richardson, *VP Sales*
Chris Sauceda, *Branch Mgr*
EMP: 44
SALES (corp-wide): 406.9MM **Privately Held**
WEB: www.greatnortherncorp.com
SIC: 2631 2671 Container, packaging & boxboard; packaging paper & plastics film, coated & laminated
PA: Great Northern Corporation
395 Stroebe Rd
Appleton WI 54914
920 739-3671

(G-6151)
GREEN ENERGY ENTERPRISES INC
9300 Normandy Blvd # 502 (32221-5562)
PHONE...................................904 207-6503
EMP: 11 **Privately Held**
WEB: www.greenenergyent.com
SIC: 3812 3721 Aircraft/aerospace flight instruments & guidance systems; aircraft
PA: Green Energy Enterprises, Inc.
9300 Normandy Blvd # 511
Jacksonville FL 32221

(G-6152)
GREEN ENERGY ENTERPRISES INC (PA)
9300 Normandy Blvd # 511 (32221-5562)
PHONE...................................904 309-8993
Jeffrey Landreth, *CEO*
Joshua Henderson, *President*
Lisa Betros, *COO*
Gene Johnson, *CFO*
EMP: 12 EST: 2004
SALES (est): 6.3MM **Privately Held**
SIC: 3812 Aircraft/aerospace flight instruments & guidance systems

(G-6153)
GREEN POWER SYSTEMS LLC
4155 Lakeside Dr (32210-3303)
PHONE...................................904 545-1311
Ingo Krieg,
Dick Basford,
Richard Breitmoser,
EMP: 6 EST: 2004
SQ FT: 6,500
SALES (est): 373.9K **Privately Held**
WEB: www.greenpowersystems.com
SIC: 7372 Utility computer software

(G-6154)
GREEN SHADES SOFTWARE INC
7020 A C Skinner Pkwy (32256-6961)
PHONE...................................904 807-0160
Welles Housh, *President*
Carly Pleines, *Partner*
April Camerlengo, *Opers Staff*
April Shanbari, *Technical Mgr*
Kelly Faust, *Engineer*
EMP: 10 EST: 1985
SALES (est): 2.2MM **Privately Held**
WEB: go.greenshades.com
SIC: 7372 Business oriented computer software

(G-6155)
GREG ALLENS INC (PA)
7071 Davis Creek Rd (32256-3027)
PHONE...................................904 262-8912
Gregory J Allen Jr, *President*
Cynthia J Allen, *Admin Sec*
EMP: 33 EST: 1986
SQ FT: 18,000

SALES (est): 5.7MM **Privately Held**
WEB: www.gregallens.com
SIC: 2759 5112 Commercial printing; stationery & office supplies

(G-6156)
GREG CLARK WELDING INC
6108 Arlington Rd (32211-5420)
PHONE...................................904 226-2952
Gregory A Clark, *Principal*
EMP: 5 **EST:** 2008
SALES (est): 363.4K **Privately Held**
SIC: 7692 Welding repair

(G-6157)
GRIFFIN & HOLMAN INC
1855 Cassat Ave Ste 8 (32210-1635)
P.O. Box 60332 (32236-0332)
PHONE...................................904 781-4531
Pam Holman, *President*
EMP: 9 **EST:** 1984
SALES (est): 286.3K **Privately Held**
WEB: www.holman-inc.com
SIC: 2531 School furniture

(G-6158)
GRISWOLD READY MIX CON INC
11660 Camden Rd (32218-3902)
P.O. Box 28310 (32226-8310)
PHONE...................................904 751-3796
Sherry Griswold, *President*
Larry Griswold Jr, *Vice Pres*
Mabrine H Griswold, *Admin Sec*
EMP: 17 **EST:** 1989
SQ FT: 300
SALES (est): 1.5MM **Privately Held**
WEB: www.griswoldconcrete.com
SIC: 3273 Ready-mixed concrete

(G-6159)
GTG-JAX LLC
Also Called: Global Tissue Group Jax
11801 Central Pkwy (32224-2637)
PHONE...................................904 861-3290
Phillip Shaoul, *Mng Member*
Vincent Tria, *Manager*
Ehsan Elnaghave,
EMP: 30 **EST:** 2007
SALES (est): 16.6MM
SALES (corp-wide): 25.8MM **Privately Held**
SIC: 2621 Tissue paper
PA: Global Tissue Group, Inc.
870 Expressway Dr S
Medford NY 11763
631 924-3019

(G-6160)
GTGJFE LLC
Also Called: Joint Force Enterprises
5570 Fl Min Blvd S Ste 1 (32257-3246)
PHONE...................................904 800-6333
Robert Bright, *President*
EMP: 6 **EST:** 2015
SQ FT: 4,500
SALES (est): 696.8K **Privately Held**
SIC: 3484 Small arms

(G-6161)
GUANABANA & CO LLC
Also Called: Guanabana Artisan Ice Pops
8802 Corporate Square Ct # 306
(32216-1984)
PHONE...................................904 891-5256
Oliver Mosqueda,
EMP: 11 **EST:** 2014
SALES (est): 523.3K **Privately Held**
WEB: www.guanabanaicepops.com
SIC: 2024 Juice pops, frozen

(G-6162)
GYRX LLC
11222 St Johns Indus Pkwy (32246-6675)
PHONE...................................904 641-2599
EMP: 12
SALES (est): 930K **Privately Held**
SIC: 3841 Mfg Surgical/Medical Instruments

(G-6163)
H & M STEEL
9843 Evans Rd (32208-7512)
PHONE...................................904 765-3465
Rudolph Murray, *Owner*
EMP: 5 **EST:** 1974

SALES (est): 301.8K **Privately Held**
SIC: 3312 Pipes, iron & steel

(G-6164)
H2 HOME COLLECTION INC
1601-1 N Main St # 3159 (32206-4453)
PHONE...................................714 916-9513
Deanna Hodges, *President*
EMP: 19 **EST:** 2020
SALES (est): 1MM **Privately Held**
SIC: 2299 Broadwoven fabrics: linen, jute, hemp & ramie

(G-6165)
HANS-MILL CORP
5406 W 1st St (32254-1648)
P.O. Box 660, New Vernon NJ (07976-0660)
PHONE...................................904 395-2288
Hong Yuan Han, *President*
Janice LI, *Vice Pres*
Todd Beasley, *Opers Staff*
Jeremy Ewing, *Engineer*
Xiao Yang, *CFO*
▲ **EMP:** 155 **EST:** 2016
SQ FT: 125,000
SALES (est): 27.6MM **Privately Held**
SIC: 3089 Plastic kitchenware, tableware & houseware

(G-6166)
HARRIS MANUFACTURING INC
Also Called: Harris Lighting
9143 Philips Hwy Ste 420 (32256-1381)
PHONE...................................877 204-7540
Bertha Calkins, *Vice Pres*
George Wilson, *Vice Pres*
Scott Green, *CFO*
Greg Green, *Manager*
◆ **EMP:** 56 **EST:** 1968
SQ FT: 106,000
SALES (est): 3.2MM
SALES (corp-wide): 124.3MM **Publicly Held**
SIC: 3646 Commercial indusl & institutional electric lighting fixtures
PA: Orion Energy Systems, Inc.
2210 Woodland Dr
Manitowoc WI 54220
920 892-9340

(G-6167)
HARTCO INC
Also Called: Sir Speedy
25 E Beaver St (32202-3020)
PHONE...................................904 353-5259
Michael A Hartley, *President*
Susan Hartley, *Vice Pres*
EMP: 8 **EST:** 1974
SQ FT: 4,000
SALES (est): 2.2MM **Privately Held**
WEB: www.hartco.com
SIC: 2752 2791 Commercial printing, lithographic; typesetting

(G-6168)
HARTLEY PRESS INC
4250 Saint Augustine Rd (32207-6694)
PHONE...................................904 398-5141
Mike Hartley, *President*
Diane McConaughey, *Vice Pres*
Don Patton, *Warehouse Mgr*
Kerri Corriea, *Human Resources*
Kelly Banning, *Sales Staff*
▲ **EMP:** 100 **EST:** 1968
SQ FT: 50,000
SALES (est): 16.6MM **Privately Held**
WEB: www.hartleyprint.com
SIC: 2752 Commercial printing, offset

(G-6169)
HCR SOFTWARE SOLUTIONS INC
13400 Sutton Park Dr S # 1101
(32224-0236)
PHONE...................................904 638-6177
James B Davis, *President*
Rachel Cottle, *Manager*
Melissa Downes, *Consultant*
Shannon Laszlo, *Consultant*
Matthew Davis, *Director*
EMP: 25 **EST:** 2007
SQ FT: 2,400
SALES (est): 5.4MM **Privately Held**
WEB: www.compensationxl.com
SIC: 7372 Application computer software

(G-6170)
HEALTHY SCHOOLS LLC
3546 Saint Johns Bluff Rd (32224-2714)
PHONE...................................904 887-4540
Tony Boselli, *Mng Member*
EMP: 106 **EST:** 2013
SQ FT: 2,200
SALES (est): 8.7MM **Privately Held**
WEB: www.schoolcare.com
SIC: 2836 Vaccines & other immunizing products

(G-6171)
HECHT RUBBER CORPORATION
6161 Philips Hwy (32216-5982)
PHONE...................................904 731-3401
Larry Hecht, *President*
Sylvia Hecht, *Corp Secy*
Jacob Hecht, *Vice Pres*
Stuart Hecht, *CFO*
Ric Fleming, *Manager*
EMP: 53 **EST:** 1944
SQ FT: 75,000
SALES (est): 5.2MM **Privately Held**
WEB: www.hechtrubber.com
SIC: 3052 Rubber & plastics hose & beltings

(G-6172)
HEMP CBD DAILY INC
13724 Shady Woods St N (32224-4822)
PHONE...................................904 672-7623
Jason Brandner, *Principal*
EMP: 7 **EST:** 2018
SALES (est): 115.4K **Privately Held**
SIC: 3999

(G-6173)
HENLEY METAL LLC
Also Called: Eligius Metal Works
6593 Powers Ave Ste 23 (32217-2853)
PHONE...................................904 353-4770
Melody Henley,
George Henley,
EMP: 10 **EST:** 2009
SQ FT: 10,000
SALES (est): 1.8MM **Privately Held**
SIC: 3441 Fabricated structural metal

(G-6174)
HENRYS HICKORY HOUSE INC
249 Copeland St (32204-1836)
P.O. Box 2823 (32203-2823)
PHONE...................................904 493-4420
William Morris, *President*
EMP: 73 **EST:** 1966
SQ FT: 40,000
SALES (est): 1MM **Privately Held**
WEB: leisurecare.teleflora.com
SIC: 2011 2013 Pork products from pork slaughtered on site; sausages & other prepared meats

(G-6175)
HERFF JONES LLC
12086 Fort Caroline Rd # 201
(32225-2689)
PHONE...................................904 641-4060
Kevin Whitlow, *Owner*
EMP: 8
SALES (corp-wide): 2B **Privately Held**
WEB: www.yearbookdiscoveries.com
SIC: 2752 Commercial printing, lithographic
HQ: Herff Jones, Llc
4501 W 62nd St
Indianapolis IN 46268
317 297-3741

(G-6176)
HERITAGE PUBLISHING INC
8130 Bymdws Cir W Ste 101 (32256-1812)
PHONE...................................904 296-1304
Marzoug Al-Amad, *President*
Zeng Hua Lu, *Vice Pres*
Judeh Handoush, *CFO*
Theresamae Teri Ortega, *Manager*
Nour Matrahji, *Graphic Designe*
EMP: 14 **EST:** 1996
SALES (est): 2.1MM **Privately Held**
WEB: www.heritagepublishinginc.com
SIC: 2741 Telephone & other directory publishing

(G-6177)
HISCO PUMP SOUTH LLC
2664 Robert St (32207-9500)
PHONE...................................904 786-4488
Julie Dubois, *Owner*
Cato Rogers, *Sales Mgr*
Matthew J Montineri,
Joseph M Montineri,
Joseph A Montineri,
EMP: 13 **EST:** 2007
SALES (est): 2.9MM **Privately Held**
WEB: www.hiscopumpsouth.com
SIC: 3561 3563 5085 Pumps & pumping equipment; vacuum pumps, except laboratory; gaskets

(G-6178)
HNC ENTERPRISES INC
Also Called: Hairnet Company, The
1624 Talbot Ave (32205-8429)
PHONE...................................904 448-9387
John Hassenzahl, *President*
▲ **EMP:** 8 **EST:** 2007
SALES (est): 23.4K **Privately Held**
SIC: 3069 Hairpins, rubber

(G-6179)
HOGAN ASSESSMENT SYSTEMS INC
13500 Sutton Park Dr S # 401
(32224-5291)
PHONE...................................904 992-0302
EMP: 7
SALES (est): 490.9K **Privately Held**
SIC: 2741 8742 Job Training Services
PA: Hogan Assessment Systems, Inc.
11 S Greenwood Ave
Tulsa OK 74120

(G-6180)
HOLLAND CREATIVE SERVICES INC
Also Called: Printing.com
2736 University Blvd W # 1 (32217-2170)
PHONE...................................904 732-4932
Jennifer Holland, *President*
EMP: 5 **EST:** 1998
SALES (est): 715.1K **Privately Held**
WEB: www.hollandhelix.com
SIC: 2759 Commercial printing

(G-6181)
HOLLAND PUMP COMPANY
2720 Lane Ave N (32254-1228)
PHONE...................................904 880-0010
William W Blodgett, *Principal*
EMP: 7
SALES (corp-wide): 20.1MM **Privately Held**
WEB: www.hollandpump.com
SIC: 3561 7359 Pumps & pumping equipment; equipment rental & leasing
PA: Holland Pump Company
7312 Westport Pl
West Palm Beach FL 33413
561 697-3333

(G-6182)
HOLLAND WELDING LLC
7014 Abbot Ct (32216-9003)
PHONE...................................904 675-6106
William M Holland, *Principal*
EMP: 7 **EST:** 2017
SALES (est): 46K **Privately Held**
WEB: www.hollandco.com
SIC: 7692 Welding repair

(G-6183)
HOLMES STAMP COMPANY (PA)
Also Called: Hsc
2021 Saint Augustine Rd E (32207-4144)
P.O. Box 5274 (32247-5274)
PHONE...................................904 396-2291
Bryan Croft, *CEO*
Bob Croft, *President*
Steve Fernandez, *Vice Pres*
Coleman Lisa, *Vice Pres*
Marcoldin Rials, *Opers Mgr*
EMP: 25 **EST:** 1954
SQ FT: 3,000

▲ = Import ▼=Export
◆ =Import/Export

SALES (est): 6.9MM **Privately Held**
WEB: www.hcbrands.com
SIC: 3089 3953 3993 2759 Engraving of
plastic; cancelling stamps, hand: rubber
or metal; signs & advertising specialties;
commercial printing; packaging paper &
plastics film, coated & laminated

(G-6184)
HOPPIN POP KETTLE STOP LLC
(PA)
Also Called: Nutty Scoopz
1850 Emerson St (32207-6108)
PHONE...................................502 220-2372
Tina Parks, *Mng Member*
EMP: 5 **EST:** 2018
SALES (est): 548.6K **Privately Held**
WEB:
www.edibleblessingscustomcakes.com
SIC: 3556 Food products machinery

(G-6185)
HOWARD PUBLICATIONS INC
(HQ)
Also Called: American Shipper
501 W Bay St Ste 200 (32202-4418)
PHONE...................................904 355-2601
Craig Fuller, *CEO*
EMP: 9 **EST:** 1954
SALES (est): 5.3MM
SALES (corp-wide): 12.9MM **Privately
Held**
SIC: 2721 Magazines: publishing only, not
printed on site
PA: Freightwaves, Inc.
405 Cherry St
Chattanooga TN 37402
423 205-3001

(G-6186)
HUCKINS YACHT
CORPORATION
3482 Lake Shore Blvd (32210-5391)
PHONE...................................904 389-1125
Dale B Purcell, *President*
Margaret C Purcell, *Corp Secy*
Ricardo Lopez, *Purch Mgr*
Randy Marchman, *Purch Mgr*
Pj Rogers, *Manager*
▲ **EMP:** 30 **EST:** 1928
SQ FT: 32,000
SALES (est): 4.6MM **Privately Held**
WEB: www.huckinsyacht.com
SIC: 3732 Yachts, building & repairing

(G-6187)
HUGHES CONSOLIDATED
SERVICES
4712 Royal Ave (32205-4954)
PHONE...................................904 438-5710
David Hughes, *Partner*
Glenda Hughes, *Partner*
EMP: 5 **EST:** 1988
SQ FT: 3,800
SALES (est): 322.8K **Privately Held**
SIC: 2752 Commercial printing, offset

(G-6188)
HUMIC GROWTH SOLUTIONS
INC (PA)
709 Eastport Rd (32218-3915)
PHONE...................................904 392-7201
Kevin Merritt, *President*
Ryan Merritt, *Exec VP*
Ryan S Merritt, *Vice Pres*
▼ **EMP:** 15 **EST:** 2013
SQ FT: 60,000
SALES (est): 10MM **Privately Held**
WEB: www.humicgrowth.com
SIC: 2879 Soil conditioners

(G-6189)
HYDROLEC INC
5050 Stepp Ave (32216-6054)
PHONE...................................904 730-3766
Kim Kawasaki, *President*
Khoa Le, *Production*
Joe Grooms, *Purchasing*
Prabin Thapamagar, *Engineer*
▲ **EMP:** 30 **EST:** 1978
SQ FT: 100,000
SALES (est): 8.4MM **Privately Held**
WEB: www.hydrolecinc.com
SIC: 3561 3594 Pumps & pumping equip-
ment; motors: hydraulic, fluid power or air

(G-6190)
HYPERION MANAGING LLC
2751-2 Larsen Rd (32207-7233)
PHONE...................................904 612-3987
EMP: 9 **EST:** 2015
SALES (est): 400K **Privately Held**
SIC: 2044 Brewers' rice

(G-6191)
I ABC CORP
11711 Marco Beach Dr (32224-7616)
PHONE...................................904 645-6000
EMP: 7 **EST:** 2013
SALES (est): 173K **Privately Held**
SIC: 2381 Fabric dress & work gloves

(G-6192)
IFF CHEMICAL HOLDINGS INC
2051 Lane Ave N (32254-1529)
PHONE...................................904 783-2180
Richard O'Leary, *President*
Anne Chwat, *Vice Pres*
Tom Rollins, *Engineer*
Robert Anderson, *Treasurer*
▲ **EMP:** 71 **EST:** 2001
SQ FT: 76,890
SALES (est): 44.3MM
SALES (corp-wide): 8.7MM **Publicly Held**
SIC: 2869 Industrial organic chemicals
HQ: International Flavors & Fragrances Inc.
521 W 57th St
New York NY 10019
212 765-5500

(G-6193)
IMPACT DESIGN GROUP INC
Also Called: Quality Images
4613 Philips Hwy Ste 207 (32207-7290)
PHONE...................................904 636-8989
Alex Pecci Jr, *President*
Chris Brunner, *Vice Pres*
Kate Donalson, *Art Dir*
Samantha Back, *Creative Dir*
EMP: 21 **EST:** 1986
SQ FT: 11,000
SALES (est): 1.8MM **Privately Held**
WEB: www.qualityimages.com
SIC: 2791 2796 2759 Typesetting;
platemaking services; commercial printing

(G-6194)
IMPULSE AIR INC
2126 W 21st St (32209-4110)
P.O. Box 12273 (32209-0273)
PHONE...................................904 475-1822
Bruce R Hampton, *President*
Edward Guertin, *Vice Pres*
Bruce Hampton, *Executive*
EMP: 22 **EST:** 1991
SQ FT: 26,000
SALES (est): 2.5MM **Privately Held**
WEB: www.impulseairspiral.com
SIC: 3444 Ducts, sheet metal

(G-6195)
INDUSTRIAL MARINE INC
7259 Old Plank Rd (32254-2754)
P.O. Box 37292 (32236-7292)
PHONE...................................904 781-4707
Charles Hawkins Jr, *President*
Robert Combs, *Opers Staff*
Vincent French, *Manager*
EMP: 10 **EST:** 1976
SQ FT: 25,000
SALES (est): 2.1MM **Privately Held**
WEB: www.industrialmarineinc.com
SIC: 3471 3599 1721 3589 Sand blasting
of metal parts; machine shop, jobbing &
repair; industrial painting; ship painting;
sandblasting equipment; painting of metal
products

(G-6196)
INDUSTRIAL MOBILE
HYDRAULICS
Also Called: Imh
1180 Lane Ave N (32254-2228)
P.O. Box 65518, Orange Park (32065-
0009)
PHONE...................................904 866-7592
Brian G Sowers, *President*
Donald Presley, *Principal*
Laura Presley, *Principal*
Trudy T Sowers, *Vice Pres*
EMP: 9 **EST:** 2008
SQ FT: 6,000

SALES (est): 1.6MM **Privately Held**
WEB: www.imhinc.com
SIC: 3492 Control valves, fluid power: hy-
draulic & pneumatic

(G-6197)
INKY FINGERS PRINTING INC
4613 Philips Hwy Ste 207 (32207-7290)
PHONE...................................904 384-1900
Randy Madison, *President*
Melissa Russell, *Vice Pres*
EMP: 8 **EST:** 1990
SALES (est): 635.5K **Privately Held**
WEB: www.inkyfingers.biz
SIC: 2752 Commercial printing, offset

(G-6198)
INNOVATIVE CNSTR GROUP LLC
(HQ)
5216 Shad Rd (32257-2006)
PHONE...................................904 398-5690
Ryan Melin, *President*
Todd Sheldon, *Mng Member*
EMP: 21 **EST:** 2019
SALES (est): 52.7MM
SALES (corp-wide): 13.9B **Publicly Held**
WEB: www.icgbuilds.com
SIC: 2421 Building & structural materials,
wood
PA: Pultegroup, Inc.
3350 Peachtree Rd Ne # 1500
Atlanta GA 30326
404 978-6400

(G-6199)
INNOVATIVE MFG SOLUTIONS
LLC
7949 Atl Blvd Unit 209 (32211)
PHONE...................................904 647-5300
Randall Bahr,
Linda Wade-Bahr,
EMP: 5 **EST:** 2008
SALES (est): 621.5K **Privately Held**
WEB: www.imfgsol.com
SIC: 3841 3842 Surgical & medical instru-
ments; fixation appliances, internal; bone
plates & screws; implants, surgical

(G-6200)
INNOVTIVE CABINETS CLOSETS
INC
5772 Mining Ter (32257-3227)
PHONE...................................904 475-2336
David Brent, *President*
Richard Stobe, *CFO*
EMP: 14 **EST:** 2017
SALES (est): 8.5MM **Privately Held**
WEB: www.inncorp.com
SIC: 2434 Wood kitchen cabinets

(G-6201)
INSTRUMENT & VALVE
SERVICES CO
Also Called: Emerson Instr & Valve Svcs
13350 Intl Pkwy Ste 102 (32218-2395)
PHONE...................................904 741-6800
Greg Dawes, *Manager*
EMP: 8
SALES (corp-wide): 18.2B **Publicly Held**
SIC: 3823 Industrial instrmnts msrmnt dis-
play/control process variable
HQ: Instrument & Valve Services Company
205 S Center St
Marshalltown IA 50158

(G-6202)
INTERNATIONAL BALER CORP
5400 Rio Grande Ave (32254-1352)
PHONE...................................904 358-3812
D Roger Griffin, *CEO*
Ronald L McDaniel, *Ch of Bd*
Curtis Adkins, *Purch Agent*
Donald Johnson, *Purch Agent*
Dani Galski, *Engineer*
EMP: 49 **EST:** 1945
SQ FT: 62,000
SALES (est): 10MM **Privately Held**
WEB: www.intl-baler.com
SIC: 3569 5084 Baling machines, for
scrap metal, paper or similar material; in-
dustrial machinery & equipment

(G-6203)
INTERNTNAL FLVORS
FRGRNCES INC
Also Called: I F F
2051 Lane Ave N (32254-1529)
PHONE...................................904 783-2180
James Nakkash, *Mktg Dir*
Neil Wheeler, *Branch Mgr*
John Williams, *Assistant*
Kenyata Addison, *Associate*
EMP: 75
SALES (corp-wide): 8.7MM **Publicly Held**
WEB: ir.iff.com
SIC: 2869 Industrial organic chemicals
HQ: International Flavors & Fragrances Inc.
521 W 57th St
New York NY 10019
212 765-5500

(G-6204)
INTERNTNAL FLVORS
FRGRNCES INC
Also Called: I F F Augusta
2051 Lane Ave N (32254-1529)
P.O. Box 250, Augusta GA (30903-0250)
PHONE...................................706 796-2800
Tom O'Rourke, *Manager*
EMP: 58
SALES (corp-wide): 8.7MM **Publicly Held**
WEB: ir.iff.com
SIC: 2869 Perfumes, flavorings & food ad-
ditives
HQ: International Flavors & Fragrances Inc.
521 W 57th St
New York NY 10019
212 765-5500

(G-6205)
INTERRAIL ENGINEERING INC
12443 San Jose Blvd # 1103 (32223-8657)
PHONE...................................904 268-6411
Chryol A Kelley, *President*
Brad Slover, *Exec VP*
Dana Fender, *Engineer*
Dee IEM, *Engineer*
Adam Kelley, *Engineer*
EMP: 50 **EST:** 2001
SALES (est): 6.6MM **Privately Held**
WEB: www.interrail-signal.com
SIC: 3669 Railroad signaling devices, elec-
tric

(G-6206)
INTERRAIL POWER INC
12443 San Jose Blvd (32223-8646)
PHONE...................................904 268-6411
Leta Kelley, *Finance Dir*
Jessica Anderson, *Admin Sec*
EMP: 10 **EST:** 2016
SALES (est): 1MM **Privately Held**
WEB: www.interrail-signal.com
SIC: 3699 Electrical equipment & supplies

(G-6207)
ISLAND DREAM ITLN ICE
DSSRTS L
9501 Arlington Expy Fc4 (32225-8200)
PHONE...................................904 778-6839
Brittany Sinclair, *Mng Member*
EMP: 10 **EST:** 2019
SALES (est): 200K **Privately Held**
SIC: 2024 Ice cream & frozen desserts

(G-6208)
IT SMELLS GOOD
1705 W 4th St (32209-6002)
PHONE...................................904 899-2818
Lesley Redmond, *Principal*
EMP: 7 **EST:** 2010
SALES (est): 121.7K **Privately Held**
SIC: 2844 Perfumes, natural or synthetic

(G-6209)
ITS TECHNOLOGIES LOGISTICS
LLC
Also Called: Conglobal Industries
8831 Moncrief Dinsmore Rd (32219-2464)
P.O. Box 7092, Lawrence KS (66044-7092)
PHONE...................................904 751-1300
Allen Dutra, *Principal*
EMP: 295 **Privately Held**
SIC: 3999 Barber & beauty shop equip-
ment

GEOGRAPHIC

PA: Intermodal Acquisition, Llc
8205 Cass Ave Ste 115
Darien IL 60561

(G-6210)
J AND L ARTISTRY
8166 Jamaica Rd S (32216-3268)
PHONE...................................904 701-3070
Well Jeffrey Lawrence Bed, *Principal*
EMP: 7 **EST:** 2019
SALES (est): 103.9K **Privately Held**
WEB: www.jandlartistry.com
SIC: 3554 Paper industries machinery

(G-6211)
J2B INDUSTRIAL LLC
5941 Richard St Unit 19 (32216-5926)
PHONE...................................904 574-8919
Scott Baldwin, *President*
EMP: 15 **EST:** 2018
SALES (est): 2.4MM **Privately Held**
WEB: www.j2bindustrial.com
SIC: 3441 Fabricated structural metal

(G-6212)
**JACKSNVLLE ADVNCED
MCHNING LLC**
9655 Fl Min Blvd W (32257-2031)
PHONE...................................904 292-2999
EMP: 8
SQ FT: 6,800
SALES: 1.1MM **Privately Held**
SIC: 3545 Mfg Machine Tool Accessories

(G-6213)
JACKSON EQUIPMENT INC
2310 Shipwreck Cir W (32224-1126)
PHONE...................................904 845-3696
Bill Schuetz, *President*
EMP: 8 **EST:** 1971
SALES (est): 829.9K **Privately Held**
SIC: 7692 Welding repair

(G-6214)
**JACKSONVILLE BOX &
WOODWORK CO**
5011 Buffalo Ave (32206-1573)
P.O. Box 3447 (32206-0447)
PHONE...................................904 354-1441
Jennings B King Jr, *President*
Jason Kittrell, *General Mgr*
Ernie Stuckey, *Opers Mgr*
Chip King, *Manager*
◆ **EMP:** 10 **EST:** 1948
SQ FT: 1,700
SALES (est): 2.5MM **Privately Held**
WEB: www.jaxbox.com
SIC: 2448 Pallets, wood

(G-6215)
JACKSONVILLE FREE PRESS
1122 Edgewood Ave W (32208-3419)
P.O. Box 43580 (32203-3580)
PHONE...................................904 634-1993
Rita Perry, *Owner*
EMP: 10 **EST:** 1986
SQ FT: 1,276
SALES (est): 702K **Privately Held**
WEB: www.jacksonvillefreepress.com
SIC: 2711 Newspapers, publishing & printing

(G-6216)
**JACKSONVILLE STEEL PDTS
INC**
6085 Greenland Rd (32258-2405)
PHONE...................................904 268-3364
Janie Vonhofen, *President*
Christopher Roblow, *Vice Pres*
EMP: 9 **EST:** 1996
SQ FT: 2,000
SALES (est): 1.9MM **Privately Held**
SIC: 3443 3441 Fabricated plate work (boiler shop); fabricated structural metal

(G-6217)
**JACKSONVILLE TIRE RESCUE
INC**
Also Called: Jax Tire Rescue
7010 Lenox Ave (32205-6866)
P.O. Box 6931 (32236-6931)
PHONE...................................904 783-1296
Maryalice Lundy, *President*
EMP: 10 **EST:** 2005

SALES (est): 499.5K **Privately Held**
WEB: www.jaxtirerescue.com
SIC: 3011 7534 Tires & inner tubes; tire repair shop

(G-6218)
**JADE SOFTWARE
CORPORATION USA**
10151 Deerwood Park Blvd (32256-0566)
PHONE...................................904 677-5133
Mark Cadman, *Software Dev*
Ian Cornelius, *Exec Dir*
EMP: 12 **EST:** 2016
SALES (est): 3.3MM
SALES (corp-wide): 1.1B **Privately Held**
WEB: www.jadeworld.com
SIC: 7372 Prepackaged software
HQ: Jade Software Corporation Limited
5 Sir Gil Simpson Drive
Christchurch 8053

(G-6219)
JAMES HINES PRINTING
1650 Art Museum Dr Ste 18 (32207-2188)
PHONE...................................904 398-5110
James Hines, *Owner*
EMP: 6 **EST:** 2007
SALES (est): 315.5K **Privately Held**
WEB: www.hinesprinting.com
SIC: 2759 Screen printing

(G-6220)
JAX ENTERPRISES LLC
Also Called: Metal Building Erection
7042 Wiley Rd (32210-2736)
P.O. Box 37064 (32236-7064)
PHONE...................................904 786-6909
John R Collins, *Mng Member*
EMP: 8 **EST:** 2007
SALES (est): 848.9K **Privately Held**
SIC: 3448 7389 Prefabricated metal buildings;

(G-6221)
JAX METALS LLC
6600 Suemac Pl 2 (32254-2773)
PHONE...................................904 731-4655
Alan T Ennis, *Manager*
EMP: 7 **EST:** 2018
SALES (est): 483.4K **Privately Held**
SIC: 3444 Sheet metalwork

(G-6222)
JCI JONES CHEMICALS INC
1433 Talleyrand Ave (32206-5435)
PHONE...................................904 355-0779
Ken Lucas, *Vice Pres*
EMP: 19
SALES (corp-wide): 196.9MM **Privately Held**
WEB: www.jcichem.com
SIC: 2812 2819 Chlorine, compressed or liquefied; industrial inorganic chemicals
PA: Jci Jones Chemicals, Inc.
1765 Ringling Blvd # 200
Sarasota FL 34236
941 330-1537

(G-6223)
JEPSEN TOOL COMPANY INC
6864 Phillips Pkwy Dr S (32256-1564)
PHONE...................................904 262-2793
Henry D Speckhahn, *President*
Michael Speckhahn, *Vice Pres*
Ingeborg S Speckhahn, *Treasurer*
EMP: 10 **EST:** 1979
SALES (est): 1MM **Privately Held**
WEB: www.jepsentool.com
SIC: 3841 3535 Surgical & medical instruments; conveyors & conveying equipment

(G-6224)
JJJ & H INC
Also Called: Vizergy
4237 Salisbury Rd Ste 200 (32216-0906)
P.O. Box 551459 (32255-1459)
PHONE...................................904 389-1130
Joseph R Hyman, *President*
Steve E Million,
Michael D Murray, *Admin Sec*
EMP: 36 **EST:** 1996
SQ FT: 10,800
SALES (est): 4.1MM **Privately Held**
WEB: www.vizergy.com
SIC: 2741

(G-6225)
JKS RESIDUAL ASSETS LLC
1431 Riverplace Blvd # 910 (32207-9028)
PHONE...................................904 346-3200
Mitchell W Legler, *Principal*
EMP: 8 **EST:** 2015
SALES (est): 182.2K **Privately Held**
SIC: 2911 Residues

(G-6226)
JMG COUNTERS LLC
5120 W Beaver St (32254-2909)
PHONE...................................904 551-7006
Jose M Garcia, *Mng Member*
EMP: 18 **EST:** 2011
SALES (est): 1.4MM **Privately Held**
WEB: www.jmgcountersllc.com
SIC: 3131 Counters

(G-6227)
JOB NEWS
Also Called: United Metro Media
6620 S Sthpnt Dr Ste 300 (32256)
PHONE...................................904 296-3006
Michael Talbot, *CEO*
Leonilda Jamieson, *CFO*
EMP: 17 **EST:** 1994
SALES (est): 521.9K **Privately Held**
WEB: www.jobnewsjax.com
SIC: 2711 Newspapers: publishing only, not printed on site

(G-6228)
**JOHN STEWART ENTERPRISES
INC**
Also Called: River Printing
502 N Hogan St (32202-4106)
PHONE...................................904 356-9392
Van Stewart, *President*
Van Janet Stewart, *President*
John Stewart, *Vice Pres*
EMP: 10 **EST:** 1977
SQ FT: 8,000
SALES (est): 902.6K **Privately Held**
WEB: www.riverprinting.com
SIC: 2761 2752 Computer forms, manifold or continuous; lithographing on metal

(G-6229)
**JOHNS MANVILLE
CORPORATION**
Also Called: NRG Barrriers South
5510 W 12th St (32254-1653)
PHONE...................................904 786-0298
Brian Zall, *Counsel*
Cedrick Downer, *Plant Mgr*
Brian Olson, *Manager*
Ricardo Santos, *Technical Staff*
EMP: 53
SALES (corp-wide): 354.6B **Publicly Held**
WEB: www.jm.com
SIC: 3296 Mineral wool
HQ: Johns Manville Corporation
717 17th St Ste 800
Denver CO 80202
303 978-2000

(G-6230)
**JOHNSON JHNSON VISION
CARE INC (HQ)**
Also Called: Vistakon
7500 Centurion Pkwy (32256-0517)
P.O. Box 10157 (32247-0157)
PHONE...................................904 443-1000
Ashley McEvoy, *Ch of Bd*
Bill Abbott, *Area Mgr*
Madonna M Malin, *Vice Pres*
James Cowart, *Opers Staff*
Charles Chavers, *Mfg Staff*
◆ **EMP:** 1200 **EST:** 1962
SQ FT: 150,000
SALES (est): 663.4MM
SALES (corp-wide): 93.7B **Publicly Held**
WEB: www.jjvision.com
SIC: 3851 Contact lenses; eyes, glass & plastic
PA: Johnson & Johnson
1 Johnson And Johnson Plz
New Brunswick NJ 08933
732 524-0400

(G-6231)
**JOHNSTON ARCHTCTRAL
SYSTEMS IN**
Also Called: Delta Fountains
11494 Columbia Park Dr W (32258-1742)
PHONE...................................904 886-9030
Joseph W Petry, *President*
Dixon Scott Johnston, *Corp Secy*
James W J Turner, *Vice Pres*
James Turner, *Vice Pres*
Tyson Newkirk, *Project Mgr*
EMP: 35 **EST:** 1994
SQ FT: 53,100
SALES (est): 6.5MM **Privately Held**
WEB: www.deltafountains.com
SIC: 3499 3641 3561 3432 Fountains (except drinking); metal; electric lamps; pumps & pumping equipment; plumbing fixture fittings & trim

(G-6232)
JT ENTERPRISES GROUP LLC
6100 Philips Hwy (32216-5980)
PHONE...................................904 551-2680
EMP: 18
SALES (corp-wide): 5.5MM **Privately Held**
WEB: www.jturner.com
SIC: 2519 Furniture, household: glass, fiberglass & plastic
PA: Jt Enterprises Group Llc
280 Village Main St
Ponte Vedra Beach FL 32082
904 803-9338

(G-6233)
K & G BOX INC
Also Called: Stronghaven
2212 N Pearl St (32206-3647)
P.O. Box 40104 (32203-0104)
PHONE...................................904 356-6063
Doug Johnson, *CEO*
Rob Macpherson, *Vice Pres*
Charrie Henderson, *Admin Asst*
EMP: 55 **EST:** 1957
SQ FT: 92,000
SALES (est): 8.9MM **Privately Held**
SIC: 2653 Boxes, corrugated: made from purchased materials; display items, solid fiber: made from purchased materials

(G-6234)
K & I CREATIVE PLAS & WD LLC
582 Nixon St (32204-3010)
PHONE...................................904 923-0409
Albert R Trotter,
EMP: 8 **EST:** 2013
SALES (est): 569.5K **Privately Held**
SIC: 3089 Injection molding of plastics

(G-6235)
K & I PLASTICS INC
582 Nixon St (32204-3010)
PHONE...................................904 387-0438
Bonnie Osterman, *President*
EMP: 7 **EST:** 1958
SQ FT: 11,000
SALES (est): 400K **Privately Held**
SIC: 3089 3993 Plastic containers, except foam; signs & advertising specialties

(G-6236)
**KAMAN AEROSPACE
CORPORATION**
Integrted Strctres Mtllics Div
227 Gun Club Rd (32218-5779)
PHONE...................................904 485-1410
Ian K Walsh, *CEO*
Paul V Boenish, *Prdtn Mgr*
Edward Varga, *Engineer*
EMP: 255
SALES (corp-wide): 708.9MM **Publicly Held**
WEB: www.kaman.com
SIC: 3721 3728 3769 Aircraft; aircraft parts & equipment; guided missile & space vehicle parts & auxiliary equipment
HQ: Kaman Aerospace Corporation
1332 Blue Hills Ave
Bloomfield CT 06002
860 242-4461

▲ = Import ▼=Export
◆ =Import/Export

(G-6237)
KAMAN AEROSPACE CORPORATION
9410 Parker Ave (32218-5764)
PHONE...................................904 751-5369
EMP: 9
SALES (corp-wide): 708.9MM Publicly Held
WEB: www.kaman.com
SIC: 3721 3728 Aircraft; aircraft parts & equipment
HQ: Kaman Aerospace Corporation
1332 Blue Hills Ave
Bloomfield CT 06002
860 242-4461

(G-6238)
KARRY INDUSTRIES INC
4007 Saint Augustine Rd (32207-6640)
P.O. Box 5810 (32247-5810)
PHONE...................................904 398-4007
Brice R Holladay, President
EMP: 7 EST: 1987
SQ FT: 5,300
SALES (est): 300K Privately Held
WEB: www.karryindustries.com
SIC: 3599 Machine shop, jobbing & repair

(G-6239)
KATCHERI DAVIS SERVICES LLC
10365 Jolynn Ct E (32225-6759)
PHONE...................................754 222-4464
Sarrah Davis, CEO
EMP: 8 EST: 2020
SALES (est): 284.6K Privately Held
SIC: 2844 3999 5999 Hair preparations, including shampoos; hair & hair-based products; hair care products

(G-6240)
KELLY FOODS
2240 Dennis St (32204-1808)
PHONE...................................904 354-7600
Kenneth Kelly, Vice Pres
Cammie J Lane, Executive
EMP: 9 EST: 2014
SALES (est): 991.9K Privately Held
WEB: www.kellysfoods.com
SIC: 2011 Meat packing plants

(G-6241)
KEYSTONE INDUSTRIES LLC (PA)
Also Called: Keystone Development
1915 Wigmore St (32206-1732)
PHONE...................................239 337-7474
Philip Hetzner, Finance
Nicole Biunno, Sales Staff
Chris Briginshaw, Sales Staff
Tom L Scholl, Mng Member
Tony L Scholl, Mng Member
◆ EMP: 11 EST: 1864
SALES (est): 17.8MM Privately Held
WEB: www.keystoneindustries.com
SIC: 1241 5052 Coal mining exploration & test boring; coal

(G-6242)
KIGHTS PRINTING & OFFICE PDTS
8505-1 Baymeadows Rd (32256-7421)
PHONE...................................904 731-7990
William E Kight, President
David Kight, President
Arlene S Kight, Vice Pres
Sue Harms, Admin Sec
EMP: 8 EST: 1968
SQ FT: 17,000
SALES (est): 248.3K Privately Held
WEB: www.kights-printing.com
SIC: 2752 2791 2789 2759 Commercial printing, offset; typesetting; bookbinding & related work; commercial printing

(G-6243)
KINCO LTD (DH)
5245 Old Kings Rd (32254-1191)
P.O. Box 6429 (32236-6429)
PHONE...................................904 355-1476
Dearen Gates, Manager
EMP: 325 EST: 1971

SALES (est): 41.2MM
SALES (corp-wide): 5.5B Privately Held
WEB: www.kinco.com
SIC: 3442 Metal doors, sash & trim
HQ: Atrium Windows And Doors, Inc.
9001 Ambassador Row
Dallas TX 75247
214 583-1840

(G-6244)
KITCHEN USA INC
6965 Philips Hwy (32216-6037)
PHONE...................................904 714-1970
Kai Zheng, President
▲ EMP: 7 EST: 2008
SALES (est): 961.7K Privately Held
WEB: www.kitchenusa.net
SIC: 2434 Wood kitchen cabinets

(G-6245)
KME AMRICA MAR TUBE FTTING LLC
3440 Evergreen Ave (32206-2327)
PHONE...................................904 265-4001
John Shay, President
Curt Jackson, Exec Dir
EMP: 85 EST: 2014
SALES (est): 9.5MM Privately Held
SIC: 3351 Copper & copper alloy pipe & tube

(G-6246)
KNOPF & SONS BINDERY INC (PA)
Also Called: Atlantic Book Bindery
1817 Florida Ave (32206-3971)
PHONE...................................904 353-5115
R Ed Knopf Jr, President
Ronald Knopf, Vice Pres
Ralph Knopf, Treasurer
Cynthia Knopf, Admin Asst
EMP: 30 EST: 1964
SQ FT: 55,000
SALES (est): 3.5MM Privately Held
WEB: www.knopfbindery.com
SIC: 2789 Binding only: books, pamphlets, magazines, etc.

(G-6247)
KNOPF & SONS BINDERY INC
Atlantic East Coast Bindery
1817 Florida Ave (32206-3971)
PHONE...................................904 355-4411
Ronald Knopf, Manager
EMP: 13
SQ FT: 18,850
SALES (corp-wide): 3.5MM Privately Held
WEB: www.knopfbindery.com
SIC: 2789 2759 2675 Rebinding books, magazines or pamphlets; commercial printing; die-cut paper & board
PA: Knopf & Sons Bindery, Inc.
1817 Florida Ave
Jacksonville FL 32206
904 353-5115

(G-6248)
KRAFT HEINZ FOODS COMPANY
Kraft Foods
735 E Bay St (32202-2303)
PHONE...................................904 632-3400
Mitchel Rickman, Maint Spvr
Darrell Larsen, Sales Mgr
Joe Waryold, Manager
Lisa Buzby, Supervisor
John Wingard, Maintence Staff
EMP: 143
SALES (corp-wide): 26B Publicly Held
WEB: www.kraftheinzcompany.com
SIC: 2095 Coffee roasting (except by wholesale grocers); coffee, ground: mixed with grain or chicory
HQ: Kraft Heinz Foods Company
1 Ppg Pl Ste 3400
Pittsburgh PA 15222
412 456-5700

(G-6249)
KRAFT HEINZ FOODS COMPANY
Portion Pac
7500 Forshee Dr (32219-5303)
PHONE...................................904 695-1300
Ryan Baker, Plant Mgr
Robert Lopez, Mfg Mgr
EMP: 65

SALES (corp-wide): 26B Publicly Held
WEB: www.kraftheinzcompany.com
SIC: 2035 2033 Pickles, sauces & salad dressings; jams, jellies & preserves: packaged in cans, jars, etc.
HQ: Kraft Heinz Foods Company
1 Ppg Pl Ste 3400
Pittsburgh PA 15222
412 456-5700

(G-6250)
KRATON CHEMICAL LLC (DH)
Also Called: Arizona Chemical
4600 Touchton Rd E # 1200 (32246-8299)
PHONE...................................904 928-8700
Kevin M Fogarty, President
April Cullen, Business Mgr
Charles Nelson, Senior VP
Carl Bilgrien, Vice Pres
Joe Chan, Vice Pres
◆ EMP: 106 EST: 1930
SQ FT: 29,000
SALES (est): 525.2MM Privately Held
WEB: www.kraton.com
SIC: 2861 2911 Wood distillation products; fractionation products of crude petroleum, hydrocarbons

(G-6251)
KWIKPRINT MANUFACTURING CO INC
4868 Victor St (32207-1702)
P.O. Box 23055 (32241-3055)
PHONE...................................904 737-3755
Jay D Cann Jr, President
Michael Bulger, COO
Nancy Cann, Treasurer
Lynn R Cann, Admin Sec
▼ EMP: 9 EST: 1926
SQ FT: 12,000
SALES (est): 1.8MM Privately Held
WEB: www.kwik-print.com
SIC: 3469 Stamping metal for the trade

(G-6252)
KYOCERA AVX CMPNNTS JCKSNVLLE
Also Called: American Tchncal Crmics Fla In
2201 Corporate Sq Blvd (32216-1921)
PHONE...................................904 724-2000
Richard Monsorno, Vice Pres
Jay Infield, Vice Pres
Steve Rabe, Vice Pres
Kurt P Cummings, CFO
Evan Slavitt, Admin Sec
EMP: 75 EST: 1979
SALES (est): 4.6MM Privately Held
SIC: 3675 Electronic capacitors
HQ: Kyocera Avx Components Corporation
1 Avx Blvd
Fountain Inn SC 29644
864 967-2150

(G-6253)
LAWKO INC
5126 Ortega Blvd (32210-8306)
PHONE...................................904 389-2850
Dan Lawless, President
Kelly Culber, Vice Pres
EMP: 7 EST: 1980
SQ FT: 18,500
SALES (est): 198.4K Privately Held
SIC: 2511 Unassembled or unfinished furniture, household: wood

(G-6254)
LEE NET SERVICES INC
8216 Cheryl Ann Ln (32244-1224)
PHONE...................................904 777-4833
Jimmie Smith, Principal
EMP: 7 EST: 2005
SALES (est): 527.5K Privately Held
WEB: www.netleeservices.com
SIC: 3825 Network analyzers

(G-6255)
LEGGETT & PLATT INCORPORATED
Leggett & Platt 0a01
925 Lane Ave N (32254-2828)
P.O. Box 6607 (32236-6607)
PHONE...................................904 786-0750
EMP: 77

SALES (corp-wide): 4.2B Publicly Held
WEB: www.leggett.com
SIC: 2515 Mattresses & bedsprings
PA: Leggett & Platt, Incorporated
1 Leggett Rd
Carthage MO 64836
417 358-8131

(G-6256)
LFTD PARTNERS INC (PA)
4227 Habana Ave (32217-4048)
PHONE...................................847 915-2446
Gerard M Jacobs, Ch of Bd
William C Jacobs, President
Nicholas S Warrender, COO
EMP: 11 EST: 1986
SALES (est): 31.6MM Publicly Held
WEB: www.lftdpartners.com
SIC: 3999 5122 5999 ; medicinals & botanicals;

(G-6257)
LIDDYS MACHINE SHOP INC
Also Called: Industrial Repair
7621 Holiday Rd S (32216-3247)
PHONE...................................904 354-0134
Ted Gollnick, President
Chris Gollnick, Vice Pres
Douglas Gollnick, Vice Pres
Keith Yake, Foreman/Supr
EMP: 20 EST: 1929
SALES (est): 2.4MM Privately Held
WEB: www.liddysmachineshop.com
SIC: 3599 Machine shop, jobbing & repair

(G-6258)
LIGHTER THAN AIR SYSTEMS CORP (HQ)
Also Called: Drone Aviation
11651 Central Pkwy # 118 (32224-2708)
PHONE...................................904 834-4400
Marty Chandler, Opers Staff
Art Hughes, Engineer
EMP: 12 EST: 2009
SALES (est): 1.3MM
SALES (corp-wide): 12.6MM Publicly Held
WEB: www.ltascorp.com
SIC: 3721 Aircraft
PA: Comsovereign Holding Corp.
5000 Quorum Dr Ste 400
Dallas TX 75254
904 834-4400

(G-6259)
LIMAS PAVERS AND SERVICES INC
7901 Bymdws Cir E Ste 44 (32256-7677)
PHONE...................................904 314-7719
Adriana Lima, Principal
EMP: 7 EST: 2013
SALES (est): 117.4K Privately Held
SIC: 2951 Asphalt paving mixtures & blocks

(G-6260)
LIPSCOMB FINCH CO
Also Called: Lipscomb and Finch
7750 Belfort Pkwy Apt 737 (32256-6991)
PHONE...................................904 415-4265
Arnita Lewis, President
Arnita Lipscomb Lewis, Corp Secy
Joseph Lipscomb Lewis, CFO
EMP: 10 EST: 2014
SQ FT: 10,000
SALES (est): 333.1K Privately Held
SIC: 2389 2311 2337 7389 Men's miscellaneous accessories; men's & boys' suits & coats; women's & misses' suits & coats; textile & apparel services

(G-6261)
LIT TV NETWORK LLC ✪
7901 Baymeadows Way Ste 8 (32256-8535)
PHONE...................................904 274-0732
Edward C Weston, CEO
EMP: 8 EST: 2021
SALES (est): 381K Privately Held
SIC: 3663 Television broadcasting & communications equipment

(G-6262)
LOAD KING MANUFACTURING
14001 Atlantic Blvd (32225-3242)
PHONE...................................904 633-7352

Marlena Sopira, *Project Mgr*
Carella Ken, *Mfg Staff*
Alicia Hackney, *Buyer*
Sharon Oliver, *Sr Project Mgr*
Kim Highsmith, *Manager*
EMP: 7 **EST:** 2016
SALES (est): 114K **Privately Held**
SIC: 3999 Manufacturing industries

(G-6263)
**LOAD KING MANUFACTURING
CO (PA)**
Also Called: Lk Industries
1357 W Beaver St (32209-7694)
PHONE....................904 354-8882
Charles O Chupp, *President*
James M Chupp Sr, *Founder*
Tanner Franklin, *Vice Pres*
David Strathmann, *Vice Pres*
Franklin Tanner, *Vice Pres*
EMP: 199 **EST:** 1972
SQ FT: 280,000
SALES (est): 53.4MM **Privately Held**
WEB: www.loadking.com
SIC: 2542 2541 3569 3496 Counters or
counter display cases: except wood; store
fixtures, wood; baling machines, for scrap
metal, paper or similar material; grocery
carts, made from purchased wire; carts,
restaurant equipment

(G-6264)
LOUIS SHERRY COMPANY LLC
Also Called: Louis Chocolates
4339 Rosevlt Blvd Ste 400 (32210-2000)
PHONE....................904 482-1900
William Morris, *CEO*
Timothy Tippin, *President*
Jeffery Smith, *COO*
EMP: 5 **EST:** 2013
SQ FT: 500
SALES (est): 311.3K **Privately Held**
SIC: 2026 2064 Milk, chocolate; candy
bars, including chocolate covered bars;
chocolate candy, except solid chocolate

(G-6265)
LUCAS 5135 INC
Also Called: Cue & Case
8130 Bymdws Way W Ste 10 (32256-4409)
P.O. Box 889, Evansville IN (47706-0889)
PHONE....................800 835-7665
James O Lucas III, *President*
Dorothea Lucas, *Corp Secy*
Cavin Kubala, *Sales Mgr*
◆ **EMP:** 1 **EST:** 1990
SALES (est): 9.4MM
SALES (corp-wide): 313.6MM **Publicly
Held**
SIC: 3949 Sporting & athletic goods
PA: Escalade, Incorporated
817 Maxwell Ave
Evansville IN 47711
812 467-1358

(G-6266)
LYRIC CHOIR GOWN COMPANY
6801 Beach Blvd (32216-2820)
P.O. Box 10990 (32247-0990)
PHONE....................904 725-7977
Fax: 904 725-7924
EMP: 7 **EST:** 1960
SQ FT: 1,000
SALES (est): 600K **Privately Held**
SIC: 2384 Mfg Choir Gowns

(G-6267)
M & M SIGNS
524 Stockton St (32204-2535)
PHONE....................904 381-7353
Ww Gay, *President*
Andy Patrick, *Manager*
EMP: 25 **EST:** 1994
SALES (est): 1.3MM **Privately Held**
WEB: www.wwgmc.com
SIC: 3993 Signs & advertising specialties

(G-6268)
M/V MARINE INC
609 Talleyrand Ave (32202-1032)
PHONE....................904 633-7992
Michael Gurliaccio, *President*
Vicki Gurliaccio, *Vice Pres*
EMP: 19 **EST:** 1997
SQ FT: 12,000

SALES (est): 2.4MM **Privately Held**
WEB: www.mvmarine.com
SIC: 3731 5699 Shipbuilding & repairing;
military goods & regalia

(G-6269)
MAC PAPER CONVERTERS LLC
Also Called: Mac Papers Envelope Convert-
ers
8370 Philips Hwy (32256-8204)
P.O. Box 5369 (32247-5369)
PHONE....................800 334-7026
David S McGehee, *CEO*
Sutton McGehee, *President*
Thomas R McGehee, *Senior VP*
Darnell M Babbit, *Vice Pres*
Robert Tees, *Vice Pres*
EMP: 213 **EST:** 1971
SQ FT: 156,000
SALES (est): 34.4MM **Privately Held**
WEB: www.macenvelopes.com
SIC: 2677 Envelopes

(G-6270)
MACHINE ENGINEERS INC
651 E 8th St (32206-3976)
PHONE....................904 353-8289
Earl Sarrells, *President*
Jacey Sarrells, *Corp Secy*
Jt Nobels, *Vice Pres*
EMP: 11 **EST:** 1953
SQ FT: 10,000
SALES (est): 1MM **Privately Held**
WEB: www.machineengineersinc.com
SIC: 3599 Machine shop, jobbing & repair

(G-6271)
MADDEN MILLWORKS
1650 Margaret St 116 (32204-3868)
PHONE....................310 514-2640
EMP: 5
SALES (est): 539.2K **Privately Held**
SIC: 2499 Mfg Wood Products

(G-6272)
**MAIN & SIX BREWING
COMPANY LLC**
2922 Madrid Ave E (32217-2764)
PHONE....................904 673-0144
Dennis Espinosa, *Mng Member*
Cindy Lasky,
EMP: 7 **EST:** 2016
SALES (est): 486.8K **Privately Held**
WEB: www.mainandsixbrewing.com
SIC: 2082 Malt beverages

(G-6273)
**MAJESTIC MACHINE & ENGRG
INC**
570 Us Highway 90 E (32234-1908)
P.O. Box 4 (32234-0004)
PHONE....................904 257-9115
Linda G Nettles, *President*
Steve Cooley, *Vice Pres*
Thomas L Nettles, *Vice Pres*
EMP: 10 **EST:** 2004
SQ FT: 8,000
SALES (est): 2.4MM **Privately Held**
WEB: www.majesticmachine.com
SIC: 3599 Machine shop, jobbing & repair

(G-6274)
MANIFEST DISTILLING LLC
960 E Forsyth St (32202-2222)
PHONE....................904 619-1479
Jim Webb, *General Mgr*
Hana Ferguson, *Manager*
EMP: 12 **EST:** 2019
SALES (est): 745.9K **Privately Held**
WEB: www.manifestdistilling.com
SIC: 2085 Distilled & blended liquors

(G-6275)
**MANUFACTURING MARTIN LLC
KLS**
11228 St Jhns Indus Pkwy (32246-7651)
PHONE....................904 641-0421
Thomas S Johnston Jr, *President*
EMP: 11 **EST:** 2017
SALES (est): 1.1MM **Privately Held**
SIC: 3999 Atomizers, toiletry

(G-6276)
**MARGO OUTDOOR LIVING INC
(HQ)**
Also Called: Margo State Line, Inc.
2562 Cabot Commerce Dr (32226-5602)
PHONE....................912 496-2999
Michael J Spector, *Ch of Bd*
Orlando Diaz, *General Mgr*
Randall Herndon, *CFO*
◆ **EMP:** 17 **EST:** 2005
SALES (est): 14.2MM
SALES (corp-wide): 25MM **Publicly Held**
SIC: 2499 2875 Mulch, wood & bark; pot-
ting soil, mixed
PA: Margo Caribe Inc.
Carr 690 Km 5/8 St Ca
Vega Alta PR 00692
787 883-2570

(G-6277)
**MARTIN MARIETTA MATERIALS
INC**
Also Called: Jacksonville Rail Yard
5942 Soutel Dr (32219-3740)
PHONE....................904 596-0230
EMP: 8 **Publicly Held**
WEB: www.martinmarietta.com
SIC: 1422 3291 Crushed & broken lime-
stone; stones, abrasive
PA: Martin Marietta Materials Inc
4123 Parklake Ave
Raleigh NC 27612

(G-6278)
MASTER MARINE
14255 Beach Blvd (32250-1576)
PHONE....................904 329-1541
Morris Hackett, *Owner*
Candice Macvicar, *Purch Mgr*
EMP: 7 **EST:** 2009
SALES (est): 723.7K **Privately Held**
SIC: 3732 Boat building & repairing

(G-6279)
**MASTERCRAFT SHTTERS
BLINDS LLC**
1700 E Church St (32202-1120)
PHONE....................904 379-7544
Ivan Dusevic, *Principal*
EMP: 9 **EST:** 2019
SALES (est): 1.1MM **Privately Held**
WEB:
www.mastercraftshuttersandblinds.com
SIC: 2591 Window blinds

(G-6280)
MATTRESS MAKERS USA INC ✪
7660 Gainesville Ave (32208-3232)
PHONE....................904 906-2793
Josh Swenson, *President*
Shane Saltink, *Vice Pres*
Christian Miller, *CFO*
EMP: 30 **EST:** 2021
SALES (est): 1.4MM **Privately Held**
WEB: www.mattressmakers.us
SIC: 2515 Mattresses & bedsprings

(G-6281)
MAXVILLE LLC
Also Called: Gilman Building Products
6640 County Road 218 (32234-3047)
PHONE....................904 289-7261
William H Davis, *President*
Bernard D Bergreen, *Chairman*
Dominick Sorrentino, *Senior VP*
Victor Garrett, *Vice Pres*
Natalie P Moody, *Vice Pres*
EMP: 154 **EST:** 1973
SALES (est): 18.2MM
SALES (corp-wide): 10.5B **Privately Held**
SIC: 2421 Building & structural materials,
wood
HQ: Gilman Building Products, Llc
2900 Saint Marys Rd
Saint Marys GA 31558
912 576-0300

(G-6282)
MAYO CLINIC
Also Called: Mayo Clnic Pet Rdchmstry Fclty
14225 Zumbro Dr (32224-8803)
PHONE....................904 953-2000
Jeff Brunette, *Administration*
EMP: 8

SALES (corp-wide): 16.3B **Privately Held**
SIC: 2834 Pharmaceutical preparations
HQ: Mayo Clinic Jacksonville (A Nonprofit
Corporation)
4500 San Pablo Rd S
Jacksonville FL 32224
904 953-2000

(G-6283)
MAYO CLINIC
Also Called: Mayo Clnic Pet Rdchmstry Fclty
4500 San Pablo Rd S (32224-1865)
PHONE....................904 953-2000
Hancheng Cai, *Branch Mgr*
EMP: 8
SALES (corp-wide): 16.3B **Privately Held**
SIC: 2834 Pharmaceutical preparations
HQ: Mayo Clinic Jacksonville (A Nonprofit
Corporation)
4500 San Pablo Rd S
Jacksonville FL 32224
904 953-2000

(G-6284)
MCGEE ENTERPRISES INC
8535 Baymeadows Rd Ste 28
(32256-7445)
PHONE....................904 328-3226
Ryan McGee, *President*
EMP: 7 **EST:** 2015
SQ FT: 2,000
SALES (est): 177K **Privately Held**
SIC: 2396 2732 2752 Fabric printing &
stamping; pamphlets: printing only, not
published on site; commercial printing,
lithographic; business form & card printing, lithographic; calendar & card printing,
lithographic

(G-6285)
**MCLAREN INDUSTRIES INC
(PA)**
9985 103rd St (32210-8623)
PHONE....................310 212-1333
Richardson Doyle, *CEO*
George Valev, *CFO*
Anita Cannon, *Accounts Exec*
Ron Colvin, *Sales Staff*
◆ **EMP:** 25 **EST:** 1997
SALES (est): 6.3MM **Privately Held**
WEB: www.mclarenindustries.com
SIC: 3011 Automobile tires, pneumatic

(G-6286)
MDK ENTERPRISES INC
Also Called: Premiere Plastering
11623 Columbia Park Dr E (32258-2491)
PHONE....................904 288-6855
Mark D Kozak, *President*
Mark Kozak, *President*
Linda Hanna, *Manager*
EMP: 12 **EST:** 2005
SQ FT: 4,873
SALES (est): 249.8K **Privately Held**
SIC: 3299 Stucco

(G-6287)
ME THOMPSON INC (PA)
Also Called: Dandee Sandwich
2178 W 21st St (32209-4110)
PHONE....................904 356-6258
Jerry A Thompson, *President*
EMP: 1 **EST:** 1956
SQ FT: 10,000
SALES (est): 10.2MM **Privately Held**
SIC: 2099 Sandwiches, assembled &
packaged: for wholesale market

(G-6288)
MEDIA WORKS INC
Also Called: Printing.com
1451 Louisa St (32207-8317)
PHONE....................904 398-5518
Fax: 904 398-6747
EMP: 17
SQ FT: 8,000
SALES (est): 2.1MM **Privately Held**
SIC: 2759 Commercial Printing

(G-6289)
MEDIWARE INFO SYSTEMS INC
Also Called: Mediware BCT
7800 Belfort Pkwy Ste 291 (32256-6969)
PHONE....................904 281-0467
EMP: 10

▲ = Import ▼=Export
◆ =Import/Export

SALES (corp-wide): 113.5MM **Privately Held**
SIC: 7372 8742 Prepackaged Software Services Management Consulting Services
PA: Mediware Information Systems, Inc.
11711 W 79th St
Lenexa KS 66210
913 307-1000

(G-6290)
MEDTRNIC SOFAMOR DANEK USA INC
10245 Centurion Pkwy N (32256-2808)
PHONE............................904 645-6925
Kashif Zakir, *Buyer*
Kevin Porter, *Branch Mgr*
EMP: 8 **Privately Held**
WEB: www.medtronic.com
SIC: 3841 Surgical & medical instruments
HQ: Medtronic Sofamor Danek Usa, Inc.
4340 Swinnea Rd
Memphis TN 38118
901 396-3133

(G-6291)
MEDTRONIC INC
6743 Southpoint Dr N (32216-6218)
PHONE............................904 296-9600
Amanda Fischler, *Engineer*
Dave Hodge, *Manager*
Steve Knight, *Technical Staff*
EMP: 13 **Privately Held**
WEB: www.medtronic.com
SIC: 3841 Surgical & medical instruments
HQ: Medtronic, Inc.
710 Medtronic Pkwy
Minneapolis MN 55432
763 514-4000

(G-6292)
MEDTRONIC USA INC
6743 Southpoint Dr N (32216-6218)
PHONE............................702 308-1302
Brian L Banks, *Director*
EMP: 1506 **Privately Held**
WEB: www.medtronic.com
SIC: 3841 3842 Surgical & medical instruments; surgical appliances & supplies
HQ: Medtronic Usa, Inc.
710 Medtronic Pkwy
Minneapolis MN 55432
763 514-4000

(G-6293)
MEDTRONIC XOMED INC (DH)
6743 Southpoint Dr N (32216-6218)
PHONE............................904 296-9600
Mark J Fletcher, *President*
Bob Blankemeyer, *Principal*
Nathan Fowler, *District Mgr*
Amy Newbern, *Business Mgr*
Mike Darragh, *Vice Pres*
EMP: 650 **EST:** 1996
SALES (est): 120.2MM **Privately Held**
WEB: www.solan.com
SIC: 3842 3841 Implants, surgical; instruments, microsurgical: except electromedical
HQ: Medtronic, Inc.
710 Medtronic Pkwy
Minneapolis MN 55432
763 514-4000

(G-6294)
MEDTRONIC XOMED INC
4102 Southpoint Blvd (32216-0929)
PHONE............................904 296-9600
EMP: 282 **Privately Held**
WEB: www.solan.com
SIC: 3842 3841 Implants, surgical; instruments, microsurgical: except electromedical
HQ: Medtronic Xomed, Inc.
6743 Southpoint Dr N
Jacksonville FL 32216

(G-6295)
MEDWAY HALL DEV GROUP INC (PA)
Also Called: Ejcon
590 Beautyrest Ave (32254-3605)
P.O. Box 61266 (32236-1266)
PHONE............................904 786-0622
J Franklin Stallwood, *President*
Randy Sheppard, *VP Sales*

EMP: 15 **EST:** 1991
SQ FT: 12,000
SALES (est): 4.6MM **Privately Held**
WEB: www.ejcon.com
SIC: 3499 Aerosol valves, metal

(G-6296)
MERCHANTS METALS LLC
5918-1 Lane Cir S (32254-2244)
PHONE............................904 781-3920
Matt Jansen, *Manager*
EMP: 72
SALES (corp-wide): 1B **Privately Held**
WEB: www.merchantsmetals.com
SIC: 3496 Miscellaneous fabricated wire products
HQ: Merchants Metals Llc
3 Ravinia Dr Ste 1750
Atlanta GA 30346
770 741-0300

(G-6297)
METAL CONTAINER CORPORATION
1100 Ellis Rd N (32254-2200)
PHONE............................904 695-7600
Dave Olecki, *Opers-Prdtn-Mfg*
Cesar Vargas, *Officer*
Kelvin Highsmith, *Maintence Staff*
EMP: 158
SALES (corp-wide): 1.2B **Privately Held**
WEB: www.metal-containers.com
SIC: 3411 3354 Metal cans; aluminum extruded products
HQ: Metal Container Corporation
3636 S Geyer Rd Ste 100
Saint Louis MO 63127
314 577-2000

(G-6298)
METAL SALES MANUFACTURING CORP
7110 Stuart Ave (32254-3421)
PHONE............................904 783-3660
Rick Edwards, *Sales Staff*
Eric Leonetti, *Branch Mgr*
EMP: 25
SQ FT: 68,866
SALES (corp-wide): 347.3MM **Privately Held**
WEB: metalsales.us.com
SIC: 3444 Sheet metalwork
HQ: Metal Sales Manufacturing Corporation
545 S 3rd St Ste 200
Louisville KY 40202
502 855-4300

(G-6299)
METALCRAFTERS LLC
10759 Grayson St (32220-1890)
PHONE............................904 257-9036
Christopher Goodman, *Administration*
EMP: 11 **EST:** 2017
SALES (est): 526.8K **Privately Held**
SIC: 3444 Sheet metalwork

(G-6300)
METALPLATE GALVANIZING LP
7123 Moncrief Rd W (32219-3313)
PHONE............................904 768-6330
Marcus Palacios, *Plant Supt*
Grant Hauth, *Plant Mgr*
Melanie Gamble, *Info Tech Mgr*
EMP: 60
SQ FT: 14,172
SALES (corp-wide): 95.2MM **Privately Held**
WEB: www.metalplate.com
SIC: 3479 3547 Galvanizing of iron, steel or end-formed products; galvanizing lines (rolling mill equipment)
PA: Metalplate Galvanizing, L.P.
1120 39th St N
Birmingham AL 35234
205 595-4700

(G-6301)
METAVANTE HOLDINGS LLC (HQ)
601 Riverside Ave (32204-2946)
PHONE............................904 438-6000
Gary Norcross, *President*
Michael Gravelle, *Vice Pres*
Keneitha Gross, *Project Mgr*
Gail Duran, *Manager*

Amy Klapper, *Manager*
▼ **EMP:** 4 **EST:** 2009
SALES (est): 249.3MM
SALES (corp-wide): 13.8B **Publicly Held**
SIC: 3578 5049 7374 Banking machines; bank equipment & supplies; data processing & preparation
PA: Fidelity National Information Services, Inc.
601 Riverside Ave
Jacksonville FL 32204
904 438-6000

(G-6302)
METRO MACHINE CORP
Also Called: General Dynmics Nassco Mayport
599 Wonderwood Dr (32233-4613)
PHONE............................904 249-7772
Karl Haroldsonn, *Branch Mgr*
Andrea Tanner, *Info Tech Mgr*
EMP: 65
SALES (corp-wide): 38.4B **Publicly Held**
WEB: www.nassconorfolk.com
SIC: 3731 Shipbuilding & repairing
HQ: Metro Machine Corp.
200 Ligon St
Norfolk VA 23523
757 543-6801

(G-6303)
MICRO-ANT LLC
7898 Baymeadows Way (32256-7512)
PHONE............................904 683-8394
Michael Blefko, *General Mgr*
Ganga Hurakadli, *COO*
Evan Decosta, *Engineer*
Philip Koh, *Engineer*
Clyde Schlabach, *Engineer*
◆ **EMP:** 75 **EST:** 2008
SALES (est): 25MM **Privately Held**
WEB: www.micro-ant.com
SIC: 3679 Antennas, satellite: household use

(G-6304)
MICROTEK MEDICAL INC
Also Called: Isolyser
13500 Tradeport Cir E (32218-2504)
PHONE............................904 741-2964
J M Mabry, *Exec VP*
Joe Carr, *Branch Mgr*
EMP: 275
SALES (corp-wide): 12.7B **Publicly Held**
SIC: 3841 Surgical & medical instruments
HQ: Microtek Medical Inc.
13000 Drfeld Pkwy Ste 300
Alpharetta GA 30004
662 327-1863

(G-6305)
MILLENNIUM METALS INC
10200 Eastport Rd (32218-2229)
PHONE............................904 358-8366
Scott Gramling, *CEO*
Tanya Cogan, *Vice Pres*
Tonya Steele, *Vice Pres*
Becky Fitchett, *Human Res Dir*
▼ **EMP:** 41 **EST:** 1999
SQ FT: 32,500
SALES (est): 9.9MM **Privately Held**
WEB: www.mmi2000.net
SIC: 3444 Siding, sheet metal

(G-6306)
MILLER CREATIVE GRAPHICS
Also Called: Printing.com
8725 Youngerman Ct # 101 (32244-6692)
PHONE............................904 771-5855
David Miller, *CEO*
Mike Lear, *Project Mgr*
EMP: 6 **EST:** 2005
SALES (est): 500.4K **Privately Held**
WEB: www.mcg247.com
SIC: 2759 Commercial printing

(G-6307)
MILLER CREATIVE WORKS INC
710 9th Ave N (32250-4652)
PHONE............................904 504-3212
Brian J Miller, *President*
EMP: 5 **EST:** 2005
SALES (est): 422.5K **Privately Held**
WEB: www.millercreative.com
SIC: 2335 Wedding gowns & dresses

(G-6308)
MILLERKNOLL INC
1015 Kings Ave (32207-8311)
PHONE............................904 858-9918
John Greenwald, *Principal*
EMP: 26
SALES (corp-wide): 3.9B **Publicly Held**
WEB: www.hermanmiller.com
SIC: 2521 Wood office furniture
PA: Millerknoll, Inc.
855 E Main Ave
Zeeland MI 49464
616 654-3000

(G-6309)
MINUTEMAN PRESS
1370 Marsh Harbor Dr (32225-2643)
PHONE............................904 733-5578
EMP: 8 **EST:** 2012
SALES (est): 192.1K **Privately Held**
WEB: www.mmpjax.com
SIC: 2752 Commercial printing, lithographic

(G-6310)
MLXL PRODUCTIONS INX
2935 Dawn Rd (32207-7903)
P.O. Box 60428 (32236-0428)
PHONE............................904 350-0048
Michael Brown, *CEO*
Peter Malloy, *Vice Pres*
Elizabeth Yates, *Vice Pres*
▲ **EMP:** 7 **EST:** 2004
SQ FT: 11,329
SALES (est): 574.2K **Privately Held**
WEB: www.mlxlpro.com
SIC: 2759 Screen printing

(G-6311)
MODULAR LIFE SOLUTIONS LLC
6622 Sthpint Dr S Ste 250 (32216)
PHONE............................904 900-7965
Doug Recker,
EMP: 8 **EST:** 2017
SALES (est): 609.2K **Privately Held**
WEB: www.modularlifesolutions.com
SIC: 3448 Prefabricated metal buildings

(G-6312)
MOLD REMEDIATION SERVICES INC
Also Called: All US Mold Rmval Jcksnvlle FL
7643 Gate Pkwy 104-57 (32256-3092)
PHONE............................904 574-5266
EMP: 7 **EST:** 2001
SALES (est): 79.9K **Privately Held**
WEB: www.allusmoldremoval.com
SIC: 3589 Asbestos removal equipment

(G-6313)
MOLONEY DIE COMPANY
Also Called: Moloney Wire Dies
5002 Palmer Ave (32210-3245)
PHONE............................904 388-3654
Tom Moloney, *President*
Becky Moloney, *President*
Ruth Ann Moloney, *Treasurer*
EMP: 6 **EST:** 1985
SQ FT: 1,019
SALES (est): 446.6K **Privately Held**
SIC: 3544 Special dies & tools

(G-6314)
MONISON PALLETS INC
3160 W 45th St (32209-2726)
PHONE............................904 359-0235
Joe Brown, *Principal*
EMP: 11 **EST:** 2009
SALES (est): 426.2K **Privately Held**
WEB: www.monisonpallets.net
SIC: 2448 Pallets, wood

(G-6315)
MONTGOMERY INDUSTRIES INTL
2017 Thelma St (32206-4240)
P.O. Box 3687 (32206-0687)
PHONE............................904 355-4055
Robert C Montgomery, *President*
Jonathan Montgomery, *Exec VP*
Jonathan C Montgomery, *Vice Pres*
Robert C Montgomrey Jr, *Treasurer*
▼ **EMP:** 20 **EST:** 1925
SQ FT: 36,600

SALES (est): 3.2MM **Privately Held**
WEB: www.montgomeryindustries.com
SIC: 3532 Crushing, pulverizing & screening equipment

(G-6316)
MS MOBILE WLDG & FABRICATION
5314 Long Branch Rd (32234-3083)
PHONE....................904 591-1488
Gary M Suggs, *Principal*
EMP: 8 EST: 2009
SALES (est): 216.9K **Privately Held**
WEB: www.msmobilewelding.com
SIC: 7692 Welding repair

(G-6317)
N-VIRO INC
7259 Old Plank Rd (32254-2754)
PHONE....................904 781-4707
Charles Hawkins Jr, *President*
Jr C Hawkins, *Admin Sec*
EMP: 5 EST: 1994
SQ FT: 15,000
SALES (est): 501.9K **Privately Held**
SIC: 3589 Sandblasting equipment

(G-6318)
NAPAC INC
5355 Ramona Blvd (32205-4414)
PHONE....................904 766-4470
Alfred A Young, *Principal*
Patricia Melick, *Accounting Mgr*
EMP: 8 EST: 2006
SALES (est): 435.5K **Privately Held**
WEB: www.napacinc.com
SIC: 3494 Pipe fittings

(G-6319)
NATIONAL CARBURETORS INC
2461 Rolac Rd (32207-7916)
PHONE....................904 636-9400
Edward L Obi Jr, *President*
▼ **EMP: 25 EST:** 1996
SALES (est): 3.9MM **Privately Held**
WEB: www.nationalcarburetors.com
SIC: 3714 5013 Fuel systems & parts, motor vehicle; motor vehicle supplies & new parts

(G-6320)
NAVMAR APPLIED SCIENCES CORP
7254 Golden Wings Rd (32244-3321)
PHONE....................904 423-0927
Clinton Fitch, *Engineer*
Charles Lee, *Engineer*
Tiffany Penge, *Engineer*
Guy Spencer, *Engineer*
Alvin Cabato, *Electrical Engi*
EMP: 111
SALES (corp-wide): 50.6MM **Privately Held**
WEB: www.nasc.com
SIC: 3721 Motorized aircraft
PA: Navmar Applied Sciences Corporation
65 W Street Rd Ste C
Warminster PA 18974
215 675-4900

(G-6321)
NB PRODUCTS INC
1551 Atl Blvd Ste 105 (32207)
PHONE....................904 807-0140
Arthur Wotiz, *President*
EMP: 30 EST: 2012
SALES (est): 2.1MM **Privately Held**
SIC: 3841 Surgical & medical instruments

(G-6322)
NCP SOLUTIONS LLC
841 Prudential Dr # 1200 (32207-8329)
PHONE....................205 849-5200
Bobby Helms, *President*
Jeffrey Booker, *Vice Pres*
Joseph Tetstone, *Vice Pres*
Jeff England, *Inv Control Mgr*
Jane Scholl, *Controller*
EMP: 60
SALES (corp-wide): 539MM **Privately Held**
WEB: www.ncpsolutions.com
SIC: 2752 7331 Business form & card printing, lithographic; direct mail advertising services

HQ: Ncp Solutions, Llc
5200 E Lake Blvd
Birmingham AL 35217
205 849-5200

(G-6323)
NEPTUNE TECH SERVICES INC (PA)
Also Called: Neptune Precision Composites
11657 Central Pkwy # 405 (32224-2661)
PHONE....................904 646-2700
Joseph Rocchi, *President*
Marge Pitts, *Human Res Mgr*
Mark Wilson, *Manager*
EMP: 35 EST: 1994
SQ FT: 21,000
SALES (est): 5.2MM **Privately Held**
WEB: www.neptuneprecision.com
SIC: 3083 8711 7374 Plastic finished products, laminated; engineering services; data processing & preparation

(G-6324)
NESSMITH DYE CUTTING & FINSHG
536 E 4th St (32206-4657)
P.O. Box 10527 (32247-0527)
PHONE....................904 353-6317
Wayne Elton, *President*
EMP: 7 EST: 1963
SQ FT: 3,128
SALES (est): 439.7K **Privately Held**
SIC: 3423 Cutting dies, except metal cutting

(G-6325)
NEW & IMPROVED SERVICES LLC
2438 Automobile Dr (32209-5832)
PHONE....................904 323-2348
Elon Dickey, *Vice Pres*
Andrea Dickey, *Mng Member*
Traci Smith, *Mng Member*
EMP: 11 EST: 2019
SALES (est): 796.3K **Privately Held**
WEB: www.newandimprovedservices.com
SIC: 3743 7299 7389 1521 Freight cars & equipment; handyman service; notary publics; single-family home remodeling, additions & repairs; commercial & office buildings, renovation & repair

(G-6326)
NEW IEM POWER SYSTEMS LLC
3600 Prt Jcksnvl Pkwy (32226-4780)
PHONE....................904 365-4444
Edward Herman, *CEO*
Clayton Such, *COO*
Dan O'Callaghan, *Vice Pres*
Aaron Hargraves, *Project Mgr*
Mike Peterson, *Electrical Engi*
EMP: 223 EST: 2014
SQ FT: 187,000
SALES (est): 49.4MM
SALES (corp-wide): 250MM **Privately Held**
SIC: 3613 Switchgear & switchboard apparatus
PA: Iem Holdings Group Inc.
48205 Warm Springs Blvd
Fremont CA 94539
510 656-1600

(G-6327)
NEW IMAGE PRINTING PROMOTION
9556 Historic Kings Rd S (32257-2009)
PHONE....................904 240-1516
Melinda Anchel, *CEO*
EMP: 8 EST: 2012
SALES (est): 865K **Privately Held**
WEB: www.newimageppd.com
SIC: 2759 Promotional printing

(G-6328)
NEW MIX PRODUCTS
4465 Crooked Oak Ct (32257-6482)
PHONE....................904 292-1920
George Pannell, *Owner*
EMP: 7 EST: 2013
SALES (est): 248.2K **Privately Held**
SIC: 2844 Shampoos, rinses, conditioners: hair

(G-6329)
NEW VBB LLC
Also Called: Village Bread & Bagells
3044 Mercury Rd S (32207-7976)
PHONE....................904 631-5978
L Ward Huntley, *Mng Member*
▲ **EMP: 45 EST:** 2014
SQ FT: 18,000
SALES (est): 3.7MM **Privately Held**
SIC: 2051 Bakery: wholesale or wholesale/retail combined

(G-6330)
NEW WORLD PUBLICATIONS INC
1861 Cornell Rd (32207-7780)
PHONE....................904 737-6558
Edward L Deloach, *President*
Eric Riesch, *Managing Dir*
Paul H Humann, *Vice Pres*
Ned Deloach, *Author*
Paul Humann, *Author*
◆ **EMP: 6 EST:** 1989
SALES (est): 750K **Privately Held**
WEB: www.fishid.com
SIC: 2731 Books: publishing only

(G-6331)
NEW YORK NAILS
5869 University Blvd W (32216-0804)
PHONE....................904 448-6040
Tommy Lopez, *Manager*
EMP: 5 EST: 2002
SALES (est): 372.9K **Privately Held**
WEB: www.newyorknails.ie
SIC: 3399 7231 Nails: aluminum, brass or other nonferrous metal or wire; beauty shops

(G-6332)
NGWEB SOLUTIONS LLC
Also Called: Next Gen Web Solutions
6821 Sthpint Dr N Ste 220 (32216)
PHONE....................904 332-9001
Jim Grace, *Manager*
Taige Haines,
EMP: 7 EST: 2008
SQ FT: 660
SALES (est): 2.8MM
SALES (corp-wide): 1.5B **Publicly Held**
WEB: www.ngwebsolutions.com
SIC: 7372 Educational computer software
PA: Nelnet, Inc.
121 S 13th St Ste 201
Lincoln NE 68508
402 458-2370

(G-6333)
NICHOLS TRUCK BODIES LLC
1168 Cahoon Rd S (32221-6166)
PHONE....................904 781-5080
Clarence Suggs, *General Mgr*
Kevin Bachhofer, *General Mgr*
Michele Johnson, *Office Mgr*
Clay Suggs, *Manager*
EMP: 11 EST: 2016
SALES (est): 1.2MM **Privately Held**
WEB: www.nicholstruckbodies.com
SIC: 3713 3446 7699 Dump truck bodies; stake, platform truck bodies; utility truck bodies; lintels light gauge steel; industrial truck repair

(G-6334)
NINE ENTERPRISES INC
3633 Southside Blvd (32216-4635)
PHONE....................904 998-8880
Laura J Ninesling, *Principal*
EMP: 7 EST: 2018
SALES (est): 471.6K **Privately Held**
SIC: 3993 Signs & advertising specialties

(G-6335)
NIVEL HOLDINGS LLC (PA)
Also Called: Nivel Parts Manufacturing
3510 Pt Jacksonville Park (32226)
PHONE....................904 741-6161
William Bugg, *Mng Member*
James Kerley, *Maintence Staff*
▲ **EMP: 1 EST:** 2004
SALES (est): 101.2MM **Privately Held**
WEB: www.nivelparts.com
SIC: 3799 5088 Golf carts, powered; golf carts

(G-6336)
NIVEL PARTS & MFG CO LLC (HQ)
3510-1 Port Jcksnvlle Pkw (32226)
PHONE....................904 741-6161
Brett Hankey, *CEO*
Dustin Ashley, *Business Mgr*
John Brenholt, *Corp Secy*
Alina Alvarez, *Vice Pres*
Aric Singletary, *Vice Pres*
◆ **EMP: 50 EST:** 1968
SQ FT: 30,348
SALES (est): 52MM **Privately Held**
WEB: www.nivelparts.com
SIC: 3799 5088 Golf carts, powered; golf carts

(G-6337)
NOAHS MBL TIRE AUTO SOLUTIONS
2060 W 21st St (32209-4746)
PHONE....................904 250-1502
Corey Lundy, *CEO*
EMP: 10 EST: 2017
SALES (est): 200K **Privately Held**
SIC: 3011 Tire & inner tube materials & related products

(G-6338)
NORTH FL CUSTOM COATINGS INC
2896 Cortez Rd (32246-3718)
PHONE....................904 251-4462
Kyle L Tibbetts, *Principal*
EMP: 8 EST: 2015
SALES (est): 444.6K **Privately Held**
WEB: www.northflcustomcoatings.com
SIC: 3479 Metal coating & allied service

(G-6339)
NPACT AMERICA INC
14476 Duval Pl W Ste 109 (32218-9404)
PHONE....................904 755-6259
Sigmund C Mayerlen, *President*
Harold White, *Vice Pres*
Tommie J Hall, *Admin Sec*
EMP: 5 EST: 2010
SALES (est): 457.3K **Privately Held**
WEB: www.npact.com
SIC: 3826 Analytical instruments

(G-6340)
NUFLO INC
3440 Evergreen Ave Ste 1 (32206-2327)
P.O. Box 3251 (32206-0251)
PHONE....................904 265-4001
John Licausi, *President*
John Conderman, *CFO*
Ann Eadie, *Controller*
Thomas C Goelz, *Director*
William T Goelz, *Director*
▲ **EMP: 50 EST:** 2002
SQ FT: 15,000
SALES (est): 8.2MM **Privately Held**
WEB: www.nufloinc.com
SIC: 3494 3356 3272 Pipe fittings; nickel & nickel alloy pipe, plates, sheets, etc.; cylinder pipe, prestressed or pretensioned concrete

(G-6341)
ONESOURCE OF FLORIDA INC
6720 Arlington Expy (32211-7234)
PHONE....................904 620-0003
Paul Lepore, *President*
EMP: 6 EST: 2004
SALES (est): 407.5K **Privately Held**
SIC: 2752 Commercial printing, lithographic

(G-6342)
ORION ENERGY SYSTEMS INC
Also Called: Orion Engineered Systems
9143 Philips Hwy Ste 420 (32256-1381)
PHONE....................920 892-5825
Mike Altschaefl, *CEO*
Rob Spann, *Manager*
EMP: 21
SALES (corp-wide): 124.3MM **Publicly Held**
WEB: www.orionlighting.com
SIC: 3646 Commercial indusl & institutional electric lighting fixtures

PA: Orion Energy Systems, Inc.
2210 Woodland Dr
Manitowoc WI 54220
920 892-9340

(G-6343)
ORION POWER SYSTEMS INC (PA)
2939 W Beaver St (32254-3169)
PHONE....................877 385-1654
Robert E Bridenbaugh, *President*
Ivette Bridenbaugh, *Vice Pres*
Conne Bridenbaugh, *Treasurer*
Richard Shaw, *Manager*
▲ EMP: 5 EST: 2011
SALES (est): 2MM **Privately Held**
WEB: www.orionpowersystems.com
SIC: 3568 Chain, power transmission

(G-6344)
OUR SENIORS GUIDECOM INC
14286-19 Bch Blvd Ste 335 (32246)
PHONE....................904 655-2130
Brenda Elizabeth Badger, *President*
EMP: 7 EST: 2018
SALES (est): 191.7K **Privately Held**
WEB: www.elykinnovation.com
SIC: 2721 Periodicals: publishing only

(G-6345)
OUTLINE TECHNOLOGIES INC
Also Called: Renovation Concrete
9920 Blakeford Mill Rd (32256-3434)
PHONE....................904 858-9933
Richard S Still, *President*
Chuck Pitman, *Vice Pres*
EMP: 6 EST: 2000
SALES (est): 428.6K **Privately Held**
WEB: www.outlinetechnologies.com
SIC: 3545 Scales, measuring (machinists' precision tools)

(G-6346)
OWENS CORNING SALES LLC
1035 Talleyrand Ave (32206-6019)
PHONE....................904 353-7361
Kim Joseph, *Buyer*
Ryan Smith, *Sales Staff*
Walter Joba, *Branch Mgr*
Amanda Moore, *Maintence Staff*
Albert Ring, *Maintence Staff*
EMP: 77 **Publicly Held**
WEB: www.owenscorning.com
SIC: 2951 2952 Asphalt paving mixtures & blocks; asphalt felts & coatings
HQ: Owens Corning Sales, Llc
1 Owens Corning Pkwy
Toledo OH 43659
419 248-8000

(G-6347)
P D I S INC
2801 Rosselle St (32205-5685)
PHONE....................561 243-8442
Robert Schenk, *CEO*
John W Wilson II, *CEO*
EMP: 19 EST: 1995
SALES (est): 2.5MM **Privately Held**
SIC: 3599 Custom machinery

(G-6348)
P3 FLEET LLC
11950 New Kings Rd (32219-1714)
PHONE....................904 549-5500
Mark Padgtte, *President*
EMP: 19 EST: 2016
SALES (est): 5.7MM **Privately Held**
WEB: www.p3fleet.com
SIC: 3531 Construction machinery

(G-6349)
PACKAGING CORPORATION AMERICA
Also Called: Pca/Jacksonville 336
659 Eastport Rd (32218-3952)
PHONE....................904 757-8140
Tom Portz, *General Mgr*
Dan Nelson, *General Mgr*
Don Pope, *General Mgr*
Silken McClain, *Accountant*
EMP: 104
SQ FT: 163,654
SALES (corp-wide): 7.7B **Publicly Held**
WEB: www.packagingcorp.com
SIC: 2653 Boxes, corrugated: made from purchased materials

PA: Packaging Corporation Of America
1 N Field Ct
Lake Forest IL 60045
847 482-3000

(G-6350)
PAL-KING INC
1300 W Beaver St (32209-7633)
P.O. Box 442264 (32222-0051)
PHONE....................904 334-8797
Bonnie Quasnick, *General Mgr*
Dan Quasnick, *Vice Pres*
EMP: 23 EST: 1977
SQ FT: 12,000
SALES (est): 3.7MM **Privately Held**
WEB: www.palking.com
SIC: 2448 Pallets, wood

(G-6351)
PALLET DOCTOR INC
221 N Hogan St Ste 371 (32202-4201)
PHONE....................904 444-2514
Eric Andrews, *President*
EMP: 6 EST: 2001
SQ FT: 5,000
SALES (est): 509.4K **Privately Held**
SIC: 2448 Pallets, wood

(G-6352)
PALLET EX JACKSONVILLE INC
7779 Hammond Blvd (32220-3379)
PHONE....................904 781-2500
Michael Oliveira, *CEO*
Matthew Oliveira, *President*
Brian Keegan, *Vice Pres*
EMP: 23 EST: 2006
SQ FT: 50,000
SALES (est): 719.7K **Privately Held**
SIC: 2448 5031 7699 Pallets, wood; pallets, wood; pallet repair

(G-6353)
PALLET EXPRESS OF JKVL INC
7779 Hammond Blvd (32220-3379)
PHONE....................904 781-2500
Michael Oliveira, *CEO*
EMP: 13 EST: 2012
SALES (est): 263.3K **Privately Held**
SIC: 2448 Pallets, wood

(G-6354)
PAPA JOHNS PEANUTS INC
2555 W Beaver St (32254-3242)
PHONE....................904 389-2511
Dwight Champion, *President*
EMP: 19 EST: 1998
SQ FT: 7,000
SALES (est): 1.4MM **Privately Held**
WEB: www.papajohnspeanuts.biz
SIC: 2068 Salted & roasted nuts & seeds

(G-6355)
PARKER MACHINERY CO INC
424 Copeland St (32204-2720)
PHONE....................904 356-5038
Hugh Parker III, *President*
EMP: 5 EST: 1981
SQ FT: 3,500
SALES (est): 437.2K **Privately Held**
WEB: www.parkermachinery.net
SIC: 3599 Machine shop, jobbing & repair

(G-6356)
PAS REFORM NORTH AMERICA LLC
Also Called: Natureform Hatchery Systems
2550 Cabot Commerce Dr (32226-5607)
PHONE....................904 358-0355
Ellis R Warren, *Corp Secy*
Scott Conley, *Vice Pres*
Terry Doss, *Vice Pres*
Jack Hubbell, *Vice Pres*
Cliff Maycott, *Plant Mgr*
◆ EMP: 33 EST: 1981
SQ FT: 40,000
SALES (est): 3MM **Privately Held**
WEB: www.pasreform.com
SIC: 3523 Incubators & brooders, farm

(G-6357)
PAVERS PROFESSIONAL INC
4086 Stillwood Dr (32257-8919)
PHONE....................239 878-6989
Fabiano R De Souza, *Principal*
EMP: 8 EST: 2012

SALES (est): 197.8K **Privately Held**
WEB: www.paversprofessionaljax.com
SIC: 2951 Asphalt paving mixtures & blocks

(G-6358)
PAW INC
Also Called: Diversified Products Mfg
8330 Atlantic Blvd (32211-8736)
PHONE....................904 724-0310
Daniel Beilfuss, *President*
Paw II Lc, *Shareholder*
Claudia Beilfuss, *Admin Sec*
EMP: 40 EST: 1963
SALES (est): 7.1MM **Privately Held**
WEB: www.pawinc.org
SIC: 3714 Motor vehicle parts & accessories

(G-6359)
PAYLESS BRICK PAVERS LLC
8719 Derry Dr (32244-7124)
PHONE....................904 629-7436
Renato Machado, *Principal*
EMP: 7 EST: 2012
SALES (est): 450.6K **Privately Held**
WEB: www.plbpavers.com
SIC: 3531 Pavers

(G-6360)
PEARL ACADEMY LLC
450 Busch Dr Unit 6 (32218-8543)
PHONE....................904 619-6419
Nacole Guyton, *Director*
Prasanna Baruah, *Professor*
Pavni Gupta, *Assoc Prof*
EMP: 5 EST: 2011
SALES (est): 660.9K **Privately Held**
WEB: www.pearlacademykids.com
SIC: 3641 Electric lamps

(G-6361)
PEDANO CUSTOM FURNITURE INC
10617 Coleman Rd (32257-1199)
PHONE....................904 704-9329
Thomas Pedano Jr, *President*
EMP: 5 EST: 2003
SQ FT: 8,000
SALES (est): 323.8K **Privately Held**
SIC: 2434 Wood kitchen cabinets

(G-6362)
PEDICRAFT INC
4134 Saint Augustine Rd (32207-6600)
P.O. Box 5969 (32247-5969)
PHONE....................904 348-3170
Doug Maynard, *President*
Myers Margaret, *Vice Pres*
Rita Freeman, *Mfg Dir*
Patty Langone, *Mktg Dir*
Bobbie Nord, *Admin Sec*
EMP: 13 EST: 1966
SQ FT: 10,000
SALES (est): 1.9MM **Privately Held**
WEB: www.pedicraft.com
SIC: 3841 Surgical & medical instruments

(G-6363)
PEDRONIS CAST STONE INC
5169 Edgewood Ct (32254-3601)
PHONE....................904 783-1690
Craig Pedroni, *President*
Pat Pedroni, *Vice Pres*
EMP: 41 EST: 1984
SQ FT: 850
SALES (est): 2.7MM **Privately Held**
SIC: 3272 Cast stone, concrete

(G-6364)
PENGUIN DOOR HOLDING CO LLC
Also Called: Penguin Door Company
2903 Burke St (32254-4014)
PHONE....................904 540-4450
Peter Osgard, *President*
EMP: 25 EST: 2016
SALES (est): 2.3MM **Privately Held**
WEB: www.penguindoor.com
SIC: 3999 Manufacturing industries

(G-6365)
PENSTRIPE GRAPHICS
4251 University Blvd S # 402 (32216-4923)
PHONE....................904 726-0200

Sid Stiles, *Owner*
Jackie Stiles, *Co-Owner*
EMP: 7 EST: 1988
SALES (est): 400.6K **Privately Held**
WEB: www.penstripe.com
SIC: 2752 Commercial printing, offset

(G-6366)
PENTAIR FLOW TECHNOLOGIES
8952 Western Way (32256-0316)
PHONE....................904 538-0894
EMP: 7 EST: 2016
SALES (est): 27.9K **Privately Held**
WEB: www.pentair.com
SIC: 3491 Industrial valves

(G-6367)
PEPSI-COLA METRO BTLG CO INC
Also Called: Pepsico
5829 Pepsi Pl (32216-6162)
PHONE....................904 733-1627
Letitia Griffin, *Regional Mgr*
Kevin Munder, *Business Mgr*
Andrew Dacunto, *Opers Staff*
Selena Blount, *Production*
Ron Cobb, *Sales Staff*
EMP: 250
SALES (corp-wide): 70.3B **Publicly Held**
WEB: www.pepsico.com
SIC: 2086 5149 Carbonated soft drinks, bottled & canned; groceries & related products
HQ: Pepsi-Cola Metropolitan Bottling Company, Inc.
700 Anderson Hill Rd
Purchase NY 10577
914 767-6000

(G-6368)
PETROLEUM CONTAINMENT INC
8873 Western Way (32256-0367)
PHONE....................904 358-1700
Robert W Arn, *President*
Samuel J Arn, *Vice Pres*
Janet Arn, *Treasurer*
Janet L Arn, *Treasurer*
Donna J Arn, *Admin Sec*
EMP: 23 EST: 1984
SQ FT: 20,000
SALES (est): 5.8MM **Privately Held**
WEB: www.petroleum-containment.com
SIC: 3089 2655 Synthetic resin finished products; fiber cans, drums & containers

(G-6369)
PHASE INTEGRATION LLC
815 S Main St (32207-9050)
PHONE....................877 778-8885
Barbara S Strickland, *Manager*
Stephen M Suddath,
Barry S Vaughn,
EMP: 5 EST: 2020
SALES (est): 326.2K **Privately Held**
WEB: www.phaseintegration.com
SIC: 7372 Application computer software

(G-6370)
PILLAR INC
2232 Corporate Sq Blvd (32216-1922)
PHONE....................904 545-4993
Griffith Michael S, *Principal*
EMP: 8 EST: 2014
SALES (est): 275.3K **Privately Held**
SIC: 3567 Industrial furnaces & ovens

(G-6371)
PINNACLE CENTRAL COMPANY INC (PA)
103 Bryan St (32202-1307)
PHONE....................904 354-5746
Toll Free:....................888 -
Steve Archibald, *President*
Rick Asbury, *Sales Staff*
▼ EMP: 11 EST: 1999
SQ FT: 4,000
SALES (est): 6.6MM **Privately Held**
WEB: www.pinnaclecentral.com
SIC: 3621 7629 Generator sets: gasoline, diesel or dual-fuel; generator repair

G
E
O
G
R
A
P
H
I
C

(G-6372)
PINNACLE CMMNCATIONS GROUP LLC
Also Called: PCG
7949 Atl Blvd Unit 201 (32211)
PHONE.............................904 910-0444
Sonya Morales, *CEO*
Marissa Marchisillo, *COO*
Amara Marchisillo, *Mktg Dir*
EMP: 11 EST: 2020
SALES (est): 172.4K **Privately Held**
SIC: 3663 3825 3812 Radio broadcasting & communications equipment; radio frequency measuring equipment; antennas, radar or communications

(G-6373)
PIONEER DREDGE INC
8515 Baymeadows Way # 201 (32256-1214)
PHONE.............................904 732-2151
Thomas H Kroeger, *Opers Staff*
Tom H Kroeger, *Opers Staff*
Suzette Allen, *Finance Dir*
Michel Allen, *Director*
Bob Sutton, *Admin Sec*
EMP: 9 EST: 2013
SALES (est): 749K **Privately Held**
WEB: www.pioneerdredge.com
SIC: 3561 Industrial pumps & parts

(G-6374)
PLAN B MANUFACTURING INC
1636 Wambolt St (32202-1419)
PHONE.............................904 633-7888
Paul Kamke, *President*
EMP: 5 EST: 2009
SALES (est): 545.2K **Privately Held**
WEB: www.planbmfg.com
SIC: 3444 Sheet metalwork

(G-6375)
PLASTIC CONCEPTS & DESIGNS INC
880 Us Highway 301 S # 1 (32234-2902)
PHONE.............................904 396-7500
Carl A Ackerman, *President*
EMP: 5 EST: 1989
SQ FT: 4,000
SALES (est): 962.2K **Privately Held**
WEB: www.plasticconcepts.com
SIC: 3089 Injection molded finished plastic products; injection molding of plastics

(G-6376)
POET LLC
4373 Marsh Hawk Dr S (32218-9137)
PHONE.............................904 619-6901
Bennett Chavis, *Principal*
EMP: 7 EST: 2016
SALES (est): 23.2K **Privately Held**
WEB: www.poet.com
SIC: 2869 Ethyl alcohol, ethanol

(G-6377)
POLYHISTOR INTERNATIONAL INC
11200 Saint Johns (32246)
PHONE.............................904 646-5666
Peter Schonning, *President*
Dennis Herdegen, *Opers Mgr*
Timothy Dehof, *Engineer*
Michelle Forwood, *Admin Asst*
EMP: 5 EST: 1999
SALES (est): 1MM **Privately Held**
WEB: www.phi2.com
SIC: 3841 8711 3069 3812 Surgical & medical instruments; engineering services; rubber automotive products; defense systems & equipment

(G-6378)
POLYTECH INTERNATIONAL LLC
6635 Highway Ave (32254-3519)
PHONE.............................904 354-9355
James Velliky, *President*
John Richards, *COO*
EMP: 10 EST: 2012
SQ FT: 1,600
SALES (est): 1.7MM **Privately Held**
WEB: www.danalysis.com
SIC: 3353 Coils, sheet aluminum

(G-6379)
PRECIOUS METAL GROUP LLC
5410 Blanding Blvd (32244-1901)
PHONE.............................904 219-8358
EMP: 8 EST: 2011
SALES (est): 476.3K **Privately Held**
SIC: 3339 Precious metals

(G-6380)
PRECISION LEAK DETECTION INC
84 Autumn Springs Ct W (32225-3164)
PHONE.............................904 996-9290
Scott R Monnoyer, *Principal*
EMP: 7 EST: 2007
SALES (est): 522.5K **Privately Held**
SIC: 3829 Liquid leak detection equipment

(G-6381)
PRECISION SVCS JCKSONVILLE INC
5201 W Beaver St (32254-2910)
PHONE.............................904 781-3770
Robert B Coleman, *President*
EMP: 10 EST: 2007
SQ FT: 500
SALES (est): 824.4K **Privately Held**
WEB: www.precisionjax.com
SIC: 7692 Welding repair

(G-6382)
PREMIER CORPORATE PRINTING
3414 Galilee Rd (32207-4718)
PHONE.............................305 378-8480
Isaac R Camargo, *President*
Joseph Hammond, *Principal*
Shirley Camargo, *Vice Pres*
EMP: 5 EST: 2014
SALES (est): 717K **Privately Held**
WEB: www.premiercorporateprinting.com
SIC: 2752 Commercial printing, offset

(G-6383)
PREMIER CORPORATE PRINTING LLC
3414 Galilee Rd (32207-4718)
PHONE.............................305 378-8480
Blake Houser, *President*
EMP: 10 EST: 2020
SALES (est): 400K **Privately Held**
WEB: www.premiercorporateprinting.com
SIC: 2752 Commercial printing, offset

(G-6384)
PREMIER WATER & ENRGY TECH INC
11481 Columbia Park Dr W (32258-4404)
PHONE.............................904 268-1152
Thomas F Brandvold, *President*
Amanda Geist, *Accountant*
Chuck Brandvold, *Sales Dir*
Josh Albert, *Consultant*
Tyler Cooper, *Consultant*
◆ EMP: 28 EST: 1973
SQ FT: 9,500
SALES (est): 5.3MM **Privately Held**
WEB: www.premierwater.com
SIC: 3589 2899 Water treatment equipment, industrial; water treating compounds

(G-6385)
PRESTIGE CONSTRUCTION JAX LLC
1114 Las Robida Dr (32211-8828)
PHONE.............................904 334-4772
John Budnik, *Principal*
EMP: 5 EST: 2006
SALES (est): 306.4K **Privately Held**
SIC: 2851 Paints & allied products

(G-6386)
PRINT EXPRESS
1889 Southampton Rd (32207-8777)
PHONE.............................904 737-6641
Bill Weaver, *Partner*
Debby K Weaver, *Partner*
EMP: 8 EST: 1988
SALES (est): 649.7K **Privately Held**
WEB:
printexpressjacksonville.wordpress.com
SIC: 2752 Commercial printing, offset

(G-6387)
PRINT RESOURCES
3728 Philips Hwy Ste 11 (32207-6840)
PHONE.............................904 316-0373
Brian Holcomb, *President*
EMP: 7 EST: 2017
SALES (est): 547.1K **Privately Held**
WEB: www.printjax.com
SIC: 2752 Commercial printing, offset

(G-6388)
PRINTED SYSTEMS INC
Also Called: PSI Printing
1309 Saint Johns Bluff Rd (32225-8396)
PHONE.............................904 281-0909
Michael Lee Dunaway, *President*
EMP: 8 EST: 1986
SQ FT: 1,500
SALES (est): 986.7K **Privately Held**
SIC: 2752 5112 Commercial printing, offset; business forms

(G-6389)
PRINTING EDGE INC
2205 Emerson St (32207-9208)
PHONE.............................904 399-3343
Ruth A Murr, *President*
Karla Newell, *Manager*
EMP: 6 EST: 1994
SQ FT: 2,880
SALES (est): 907.1K **Privately Held**
WEB: www.eprintingedge.com
SIC: 2752 Commercial printing, offset

(G-6390)
PROCORP LLC
8535 Baymeadows Rd Ste 58 (32256-7445)
PHONE.............................904 477-6762
Fred Ewan,
Bob Ozmik,
EMP: 8 EST: 2005
SALES (est): 622.7K **Privately Held**
SIC: 2759 Commercial printing

(G-6391)
PROFESSNAL REPRODUCTION OF JAX
Also Called: Rapid Print
7029 Commonwealth Ave (32220-2859)
PHONE.............................904 389-4141
Beverly Aldridge, *President*
Kent Aldridge, *Vice Pres*
EMP: 5 EST: 1975
SALES (est): 518.6K **Privately Held**
SIC: 2752 Commercial printing, offset

(G-6392)
PROGRESS RAIL SERVICES CORP
420 Agmac Ave (32254-2863)
PHONE.............................904 783-1143
Del King, *Manager*
EMP: 10
SQ FT: 25,282
SALES (corp-wide): 50.9B **Publicly Held**
WEB: www.progressrail.com
SIC: 3743 Railroad equipment
HQ: Progress Rail Services Corporation
1600 Progress Dr
Albertville AL 35950
256 505-6421

(G-6393)
PROGRESSIVE POWER PRODUCTS INC
4062 N Liberty St (32206-1410)
P.O. Box 24905 (32241-4905)
PHONE.............................904 354-1819
Nancy Kates, *President*
Larry Kates, *Vice Pres*
▲ EMP: 8 EST: 1989
SQ FT: 9,000
SALES (est): 1MM **Privately Held**
WEB: www.ppallison.com
SIC: 3714 Power transmission equipment, motor vehicle

(G-6394)
PROGRESSIVE PRINTING CO INC
4505 Lexington Ave (32210-2037)
PHONE.............................904 388-0746
Fax: 904 388-1330
EMP: 15 EST: 1977

SQ FT: 7,113
SALES: 1.2MM **Privately Held**
SIC: 2752 Offset Printing

(G-6395)
PROLIFIC CABINETRY & MORE INC
7660 Philips Hwy Ste 5 (32256-6819)
PHONE.............................904 448-6575
Steven E Brust, *President*
EMP: 5 EST: 2006
SALES (est): 876.9K **Privately Held**
WEB: www.prolificcabinetry.com
SIC: 2434 Wood kitchen cabinets

(G-6396)
PROSERVICES SUPPLY LLC
12620 Beach Blvd Ste 3304 (32246-7131)
PHONE.............................858 254-4415
Gary Phillips, *Mng Member*
EMP: 12 EST: 2020
SALES (est): 1MM **Privately Held**
SIC: 3585 Air conditioning equipment, complete

(G-6397)
PUZZLED CATERPILLARS INC
5230 Anisa Ct (32209-3058)
PHONE.............................904 379-9219
Frances McMiller, *Principal*
EMP: 7 EST: 2017
SALES (est): 564.3K **Privately Held**
SIC: 3531 Construction machinery

(G-6398)
QUADRAMED CORPORATION
Tempus Software
225 Water St Ste 2250 (32202-5185)
PHONE.............................904 355-2900
Sasha Gribov, *Partner*
Keith Dipirro, *District Mgr*
Pat Garrison, *Business Mgr*
Tom Ferrone, *Counsel*
Erik Phelps, *Exec VP*
EMP: 12
SALES (corp-wide): 5.1B **Privately Held**
WEB: www.quadramed.com
SIC: 7372 7371 Business oriented computer software; computer software development
HQ: Quadramed Corporation
2429 Military Rd Ste 300
Niagara Falls NY 14304
571 267-3928

(G-6399)
QUALITY NEON SIGN COMPANY (PA)
Also Called: Harbinger
5300 Shad Rd (32257-2006)
PHONE.............................904 268-4681
Roger S Williams II, *CEO*
Roger S Williams, *Ch of Bd*
Sherry Bishop, *Vice Pres*
Julie Bain, *Project Mgr*
Steve Margolese, *Project Mgr*
EMP: 42 EST: 1963
SQ FT: 25,000
SALES (est): 17MM **Privately Held**
SIC: 3993 Electric signs; neon signs

(G-6400)
QUALITY STONES R US LLC
10475 Fortune Pkwy St (32256-3585)
PHONE.............................904 551-5619
Pratik Shah, *President*
EMP: 8 EST: 2008
SALES (est): 1.8MM **Privately Held**
WEB: www.qualitystonesjax.com
SIC: 1411 Granite dimension stone

(G-6401)
R & K MARKETING INC
Also Called: Aim
11657 Central Pkwy # 401 (32224-2661)
P.O. Box 350489 (32235-0489)
PHONE.............................904 745-0022
David Harrison, *President*
Julie Harrison, *Vice Pres*
Inaldis Sibilia, *Manager*
EMP: 7 EST: 1991
SQ FT: 2,000
SALES (est): 1MM **Privately Held**
WEB: www.aimhere.net
SIC: 3579 5044 Duplicating machines; photocopy machines

▲ = Import ▼=Export
◆ =Import/Export

(G-6402)
R A PRINTING INC
Also Called: Minuteman Press
4185 Sunbeam Rd Ste 100 (32257-2424)
PHONE..904 733-5578
Arch Copeland, *President*
Rosemary Copeland, *Vice Pres*
EMP: 7 EST: 1994
SQ FT: 4,000
SALES (est): 866.5K Privately Held
SIC: 2752 Commercial printing, lithographic

(G-6403)
R T PUBLISHING INC
12443 San Jose Blvd # 403 (32223-8646)
PHONE..904 886-4919
David L Taus, *Treasurer*
Rebecca Thomson, *Creative Dir*
EMP: 5 EST: 2001
SALES (est): 463.5K Privately Held
WEB: www.rtpublishinginc.com
SIC: 2721 Magazines: publishing only, not printed on site

(G-6404)
RAKILINE LLC
6180 Fort Caroline Rd (32277-2095)
PHONE..904 800-2632
Zsofia Villarreal, *CEO*
EMP: 7 EST: 2018
SALES (est): 466.7K Privately Held
SIC: 2759 5699 Commercial printing; uniforms & work clothing

(G-6405)
RAYONIER A M PRODUCTS INC (HQ)
1301 Riverplace Blvd (32207-9047)
PHONE..904 357-9100
Paul Gerard Boynton, *President*
Michael R Herman, *Senior VP*
Charles H Hood, *Senior VP*
Frank A Ruperto, *Senior VP*
Erin M Byers, *Vice Pres*
EMP: 100 EST: 2008
SALES (est): 183.4MM
SALES (corp-wide): 1.4B Publicly Held
WEB: www.ryamglobal.com
SIC: 2821 Plastics materials & resins
PA: Rayonier Advanced Materials Inc.
1301 Riverplace Blvd # 23
Jacksonville FL 32207
904 357-4600

(G-6406)
RAYONIER ADVANCED MTLS INC (PA)
1301 Riverplace Blvd # 23 (32207-9047)
PHONE..904 357-4600
Lisa M Palumbo, *Ch of Bd*
De Lyle W Bloomquist, *President*
Daniel Howard, *Superintendent*
Stacey Williams, *Superintendent*
Paul Boynton, *Vice Chairman*
EMP: 243 EST: 1926
SALES (est): 1.4B Publicly Held
WEB: www.ryamglobal.com
SIC: 2823 2821 Cellulosic manmade fibers; cellulose derivative materials

(G-6407)
RAYONIER AM SALES AND TECH INC (DH)
Also Called: Rayonier Advanced Materials
1301 Riverplace Blvd # 23 (32207-9047)
PHONE..904 357-4600
Paul G Boynton, *President*
◆ **EMP: 34 EST: 2013**
SALES (est): 32.4MM
SALES (corp-wide): 1.4B Publicly Held
WEB: www.ryamglobal.com
SIC: 2821 2822 Cellulose derivative materials; ethylene-propylene rubbers, EPDM polymers
HQ: Rayonier A.M. Products Inc.
1301 Riverplace Blvd
Jacksonville FL 32207
904 357-9100

(G-6408)
REDDI SIGN CORPORATION
107 Mott St (32254-4030)
P.O. Box 28846 (32226-8846)
PHONE..904 757-0680
Wendy J Dobson, *Principal*
EMP: 9 EST: 2010
SALES (est): 309.4K Privately Held
WEB: www.reddi-sign.com
SIC: 3993 Signs, not made in custom sign painting shops

(G-6409)
REDDY ICE CORPORATION
5849 Commonwealth Ave (32254-2205)
P.O. Box 60099 (32236-0099)
PHONE..904 388-2653
Fred Day, *Division Mgr*
Alendwa Mallya, *General Mgr*
Lee Hatch, *Manager*
Troy Winkler, *Manager*
Praveen Edwin, *Senior Mgr*
EMP: 13 Privately Held
WEB: www.reddyice.com
SIC: 2097 Manufactured ice
HQ: Reddy Ice Llc
5710 Lbj Fwy Ste 300
Dallas TX 75240
214 526-6740

(G-6410)
REDWIRE CORPORATION (HQ)
8226 Philips Hwy Ste 101 (32256-1230)
PHONE..650 701-7722
Peter Cannito, *Ch of Bd*
Andrew Rush, *President*
Nathan O'Konek, *Exec VP*
Jonathan Baliff, *CFO*
William Read, *CFO*
EMP: 11 EST: 2010
SALES (est): 137.6MM
SALES (corp-wide): 161.3MM Publicly Held
WEB: www.genesis-park.com
SIC: 3761 Guided missiles & space vehicles
PA: Red Ae Holdings Llc
669 Forest St
Marlborough MA 01752
561 372-7820

(G-6411)
REFRESHING SMOOTHIE
9550 Baymeadows Rd (32256-0710)
PHONE..904 549-5366
Ming Hui Yang, *Principal*
EMP: 8 EST: 2015
SALES (est): 146.1K Privately Held
SIC: 2037 Frozen fruits & vegetables

(G-6412)
REGENCY CAP & GOWN COMPANY
Also Called: Sia Swimwear
7534 Atlantic Blvd (32211-8714)
P.O. Box 8988 (32239-0988)
PHONE..904 724-3500
David K Crisp, *President*
Bob Walkord, *Owner*
Robert E Walkord, *Treasurer*
Robert Walkord, *Treasurer*
EMP: 18 EST: 1981
SQ FT: 36,000
SALES (est): 1.1MM Privately Held
WEB: www.rcgown.com
SIC: 2389 2339 Academic vestments (caps & gowns); bathing suits: women's, misses' & juniors'

(G-6413)
REGIONAL TRAILER REPAIR INC
1048 Escambia St (32208-4319)
P.O. Box 3900, Savannah GA (31414-3900)
PHONE..912 484-7729
William Brantley, *President*
Marc Scheurer, *Vice Pres*
Samuel Adams, *Shareholder*
EMP: 15 EST: 2003
SQ FT: 10,000
SALES (est): 333.7K Privately Held
WEB: regional-trailer-repair.business.site
SIC: 2448 Pallets, wood

(G-6414)
REINS INC
5357 Winrose Falls Dr (32258-2582)
PHONE..904 868-3381
Ameera Sayeed, *CEO*
EMP: 10 EST: 2020
SALES (est): 460K Privately Held
WEB: www.reinsapp.com
SIC: 7372 7389 Application computer software;

(G-6415)
RELIOX CORPORATION
8475 Western Way Ste 155 (32256-0351)
PHONE..904 729-5097
Eric Johnson, *CEO*
Cristina Knapp, *Vice Pres*
Kurt Walchle, *Sales Staff*
Sam McConnell, *Director*
Dawn Tetreault, *Director*
EMP: 5 EST: 2012
SALES (est): 855.8K Privately Held
WEB: www.reliox-clo2.com
SIC: 2842 Disinfectants, household or industrial plant; industrial plant disinfectants or deodorants

(G-6416)
RESIDENT CMNTY NEWS GROUP INC
1650 Margaret St 31 (32204-3868)
PHONE..904 962-6876
Percy Rosenbloom Jr, *Principal*
Kate Hallock, *Manager*
EMP: 10 EST: 2009
SALES (est): 386.1K Privately Held
WEB: www.residentnews.net
SIC: 2711 Newspapers, publishing & printing

(G-6417)
RESILIENT GROUP INC
3114 Double Oaks Dr (32226-2085)
PHONE..518 434-4414
EMP: 21
SALES (corp-wide): 86.9K Privately Held
WEB: www.resilientpma.com
SIC: 3732 Boat building & repairing
PA: The Resilient Group Inc
3408 Foxmeadow Ct
Longwood FL
800 604-2443

(G-6418)
REVERE MANUFACTURED PDTS INC
323 Hwy Ave (32254)
PHONE..904 503-9733
Andrew C Kaufmann, *President*
Howard Kaufmann, *Vice Pres*
Howard W Kaufmann, *Vice Pres*
EMP: 9 EST: 2005
SALES (est): 153.1K Privately Held
SIC: 3069 Hard rubber & molded rubber products

(G-6419)
REVERE SURVIVAL INC
5323 Highway Ave (32254-3634)
PHONE..904 503-9733
Andrew Richards, *CEO*
Nicholas Howland, *President*
Kini Bowers, *Vice Pres*
Thomas Mastrella, *Vice Pres*
Michelle Snow, *Opers Staff*
EMP: 18 EST: 2014
SQ FT: 35,000
SALES (est): 3.9MM Privately Held
WEB: www.reveresurvival.com
SIC: 3732 Boat kits, not models

(G-6420)
REVLON INC
540 Beautyrest Ave (32254-3605)
PHONE..904 693-1254
George Adams, *Engineer*
Patricia Cazcarro, *Engineer*
EMP: 28 Publicly Held
WEB: www.revlon.com
SIC: 2844 Cosmetic preparations
HQ: Revlon, Inc.
1 New York Plz Fl 49
New York NY 10004

(G-6421)
REVLON CONSUMER PRODUCTS CORP
5344 Overmyer Dr (32254-3645)
PHONE..904 378-4167
Brian Kalch, *Opers Staff*
Sean Dupuis, *Manager*
Henrique Vianna, *Manager*
EMP: 25 Publicly Held
WEB: www.revlon.com
SIC: 2844 Cosmetic preparations
HQ: Revlon Consumer Products Corporation
1 New York Plz
New York NY 10004

(G-6422)
RFL & FIGLIO LLC
Also Called: US Body Source
12819 Fenwick Island Ct E (32224-8613)
PHONE..904 765-2222
Christine Zoyhofski,
EMP: 10 EST: 2014
SALES (est): 548.8K Privately Held
SIC: 2221 Broadwoven fabric mills, manmade

(G-6423)
RING POWER CORPORATION
Phoenix Products
1544 E 8th St (32206-5453)
PHONE..904 354-1858
Ron Roy, *Manager*
EMP: 105
SALES (corp-wide): 1B Privately Held
WEB: www.ringpower.com
SIC: 3443 3448 3613 Tanks, standard or custom fabricated: metal plate; panels for prefabricated metal buildings; regulators, power
HQ: Ring Power Corporation
500 World Commerce Pkwy
Saint Augustine FL 32092
904 201-7400

(G-6424)
RITCHIE
8477 Graybar Dr (32221-1672)
PHONE..904 783-0416
Sven Ritchie, *Principal*
EMP: 9 EST: 2010
SALES (est): 232.5K Privately Held
WEB: www.ritchienavigation.com
SIC: 3812 Search & navigation equipment

(G-6425)
RIVER CITY ADVG OBJECTIONAL
3514 Morton St (32217-2547)
PHONE..904 731-3452
John Wondracek, *Principal*
Theresa Wondracek, *Admin Sec*
EMP: 8 EST: 1992
SQ FT: 2,000
SALES (est): 500K Privately Held
SIC: 3993 5099 Signs & advertising specialties; signs, except electric

(G-6426)
RIVER CITY STUCCO INC
117 Magnolia Ave (32218-2606)
PHONE..904 234-9526
Vance Fiedler, *Principal*
EMP: 7 EST: 2008
SALES (est): 108.3K Privately Held
WEB: rivercitystucco.business.site
SIC: 3299 Stucco

(G-6427)
RIVERCITY CUSTOM CABINETRY INC
1863 Mayport Rd (32233-1919)
PHONE..904 247-0807
Damon Rebhahn, *President*
Chad Handy, *Engineer*
EMP: 12 EST: 1994
SQ FT: 7,954
SALES (est): 2.2MM Privately Held
WEB: www.rivercitycustomcabinetry.com
SIC: 2434 1751 Wood kitchen cabinets; cabinet & finish carpentry

(G-6428)
RIVERVIEW MILLWORKS INC
9157 Lem Turner Rd (32208-2293)
PHONE..904 764-9571
Charles A Nichols Jr, *President*
Danny R Raulerson, *Vice Pres*
Danny Raulerson, *Vice Pres*
Garry Du'bois, *Project Mgr*
Bryon Nobles, *Manager*
EMP: 6 EST: 1936
SQ FT: 27,000

SALES (est): 888.4K **Privately Held**
WEB: www.riverviewmillworks.com
SIC: 2431 Millwork

(G-6429)
RIW OF JACKSONVILLE INC
608 Carmen St (32206-3951)
PHONE..........................904 356-5635
EMP: 10 EST: 1919
SQ FT: 23,000
SALES (est): 950K **Privately Held**
SIC: 3443 3599 Mfg Fabricated Plate
　Work Mfg Industrial Machinery

(G-6430)
RLC NETWORKS INC
14678 Longview Dr S (32223-2660)
PHONE..........................904 262-0587
Richard L Carter Jr, *Principal*
EMP: 8 EST: 2010
SALES (est): 121.8K **Privately Held**
SIC: 3651 Household audio & video equip-
　ment

(G-6431)
RM BRANDS INC
Also Called: Property Armor
2910 W Beaver St (32254-3170)
PHONE..........................904 356-0092
Robert Michell, *President*
Robert F Michell, *President*
EMP: 9 EST: 2003
SALES (est): 1.2MM **Privately Held**
WEB: www.hapcohvac.com
SIC: 3441 3699 Fabricated structural
　metal; security devices

(G-6432)
**ROBERT JAMES CSTM MET
FABG LLC**
2900 N Canal St (32209-4630)
PHONE..........................772 214-0996
James R Reitz, *Manager*
EMP: 12 EST: 2005
SALES (est): 1.1MM **Privately Held**
SIC: 3499 Fabricated metal products

(G-6433)
RONCO MACHINE INC
2100 Dennis St (32204-1806)
P.O. Box 31, Lake Winola PA (18625-0031)
PHONE..........................904 827-9795
Bradley Reeves, *President*
Gina L Polseno, *Admin Sec*
EMP: 8 EST: 2013
SQ FT: 30,000
SALES (est): 796K **Privately Held**
WEB: www.roncomachine.com
SIC: 3554 Paper industries machinery

(G-6434)
ROYAL FOAM US LLC
Also Called: Www.royalfoam.us
4225 James E Casey Dr (32219-3084)
PHONE..........................904 345-5400
Valentyn Kulbaka, *CEO*
EMP: 50 EST: 2019
SALES (est): 1.4MM **Privately Held**
SIC: 3993 7389 5023 Advertising artwork;
　design, commercial & industrial; decora-
　tive home furnishings & supplies

(G-6435)
RPD MANAGEMENT LLC
Also Called: Intuition Ale Works
720 King St (32204-3440)
PHONE..........................904 710-8911
▲ EMP: 7
SALES (est): 969.6K **Privately Held**
SIC: 2082 Malt Beverages, Nsk

(G-6436)
RUBIN IRON WORKS LLC
608 Carmen St (32206-3951)
P.O. Box 3333 (32206-0333)
PHONE..........................904 356-5635
Charles P Berman, *CEO*
Rochelle B Stoddard, *Admin Sec*
Eric Berman,
▼ EMP: 14 EST: 2004
SALES (est): 2MM **Privately Held**
WEB: www.bermanbros.com
SIC: 3441 Fabricated structural metal

(G-6437)
RUBIX FOODS LLC
13203 Flagler Center Blvd (32258-2666)
PHONE..........................904 268-8999
Andrew M Block, *CEO*
Midd McManus, *President*
Jeffrey Block, *Exec VP*
Mark Rones, *Research*
William Block, *CFO*
EMP: 45 EST: 1981
SQ FT: 7,000
SALES (est): 14.5MM **Privately Held**
WEB: www.rubixfoods.com
SIC: 2026 2024 5143 Fermented & cul-
　tured milk products; ice cream & frozen
　desserts; dairy products, except dried or
　canned

(G-6438)
**RUSH TO EXCELLENCE PRTG
INC**
4204 Spring Park Rd (32207-6956)
PHONE..........................904 367-0100
William Poarch Sr, *President*
EMP: 6 EST: 1992
SQ FT: 2,000
SALES (est): 489.8K **Privately Held**
WEB: www.rushtoexcellenceprinting.com
SIC: 2752 Commercial printing, offset

(G-6439)
RZ SERVICE GROUP LLC
12574 Flagler Center Blvd (32258-2614)
PHONE..........................904 402-2313
Joseph Newkirk, *CEO*
Wali Murphy, *COO*
Joseph R Newkirk,
EMP: 6 EST: 2015
SALES (est): 1.2MM **Privately Held**
WEB: www.recoveryz.com
SIC: 3569 1799 8742 1629 Generators:
　steam, liquid oxygen or nitrogen; con-
　struction site cleanup; materials mgmt.
　(purchasing, handling, inventory) consult-
　ant; dams, waterways, docks & other ma-
　rine construction; waste water & sewage
　treatment plant construction; water treat-
　ment equipment, industrial; nitrogen

(G-6440)
**S & S METAL AND PLASTICS
INC**
6600 Suemac Pl 2 (32254-2773)
PHONE..........................904 731-4655
Cynthia L Strickland, *President*
Nancy Dearmas, *Corp Secy*
EMP: 32 EST: 1962
SALES (est): 6.3MM **Privately Held**
WEB: www.ssmetal.com
SIC: 3993 3499 Signs, not made in cus-
　tom sign painting shops; furniture parts,
　metal

(G-6441)
S GAGER INDUSTRIES INC
11436 Philips Hwy (32256-1636)
PHONE..........................904 268-6727
Forest Gager, *President*
George Gager, *Vice Pres*
Linda Gager, *Treasurer*
EMP: 30 EST: 1969
SQ FT: 20,000
SALES (est): 2.7MM **Privately Held**
WEB: sgagerindustries.wixsite.com
SIC: 3089 Injection molding of plastics

(G-6442)
**S&P USA VNTILATION SYSTEMS
LLC**
6393 Powers Ave (32217-2217)
PHONE..........................904 731-4711
Mark Bojarzin, *CEO*
Eugene Scotcher, *CEO*
Patrick Williams III, *President*
Patrick M Williams, *President*
Patrick Williams Jr, *Chairman*
◆ EMP: 86 EST: 1974
SQ FT: 65,000
SALES (est): 30.3MM **Privately Held**
WEB: www.solerpalau-usa.com
SIC: 3564 Blowing fans: industrial or com-
　mercial; exhaust fans: industrial or com-
　mercial; ventilating fans: industrial or
　commercial

(G-6443)
SAFARI PROGRAMS INC (PA)
8010 Westside Indus Dr (32219-3290)
PHONE..........................305 621-1000
Alexandre M Pariente, *CEO*
Christina Pariente, *President*
Jorge Alvarado, *Managing Prtnr*
Elizabeth Cruz, *Accountant*
Christina Hartman, *Sales Mgr*
◆ EMP: 58 EST: 1981
SALES (est): 13.1MM **Privately Held**
WEB: www.safariltd.com
SIC: 3944 5092 Craft & hobby kits & sets;
　toys & games

(G-6444)
SAFARILAND LLC
3041 Faye Rd (32226-2336)
PHONE..........................904 741-5400
EMP: 19 EST: 2016
SALES (est): 4.8MM **Privately Held**
WEB: www.safariland.com
SIC: 3842 Surgical appliances & supplies

(G-6445)
SAFARILAND LLC
Also Called: Rogers Holster Co
3041 Faye Rd (32226-2336)
PHONE..........................904 646-0141
Warren Kanders, *CEO*
Jaime Marini, *Program Mgr*
Tim West, *Manager*
EMP: 46
SALES (corp-wide): 404.6MM **Privately
Held**
WEB: www.safariland.com
SIC: 3089 Blow molded finished plastic
　products
HQ: Safariland, Llc
　13386 International Pkwy
　Jacksonville FL 32218
　904 741-5400

(G-6446)
SAFARILAND LLC (HQ)
Also Called: Safariland Group
13386 International Pkwy (32218-2383)
PHONE..........................904 741-5400
Warren Kanders, *CEO*
Brad E Williams, *President*
Jacqueline Beasley, *General Mgr*
Wanda Moody, *General Mgr*
Scott T O'Brien, *Chairman*
▲ EMP: 73 EST: 1997
SALES (est): 308.5MM
SALES (corp-wide): 404.6MM **Privately
Held**
WEB: www.safariland.com
SIC: 3199 5099 Holsters, leather; safety
　equipment & supplies
PA: Cadre Holdings, Inc.
　13386 International Pkwy
　Jacksonville FL 32218
　904 741-5400

(G-6447)
SAFARILAND LLC
4101 Bulls Bay Hwy (32219-3233)
PHONE..........................904 741-5400
EMP: 30
SALES (corp-wide): 404.6MM **Privately
Held**
WEB: www.safariland.com
SIC: 3842 Surgical appliances & supplies
HQ: Safariland, Llc
　13386 International Pkwy
　Jacksonville FL 32218
　904 741-5400

(G-6448)
SAFE PASSAGE HOME INC
9 Hopson Rd (32250-2611)
PHONE..........................904 241-4211
Joseph S McCoy, *President*
EMP: 7 EST: 2005
SALES (est): 149.6K **Privately Held**
SIC: 7372 Prepackaged software

(G-6449)
SAFETY CLAMPS INC
233 Santa Barbara Ave (32254-3589)
PHONE..........................904 781-2809
Scott Griffin, *President*
EMP: 12 EST: 1962
SQ FT: 9,000

SALES (est): 2.2MM **Privately Held**
WEB: www.safetyclamps.com
SIC: 3429 Clamps, metal

(G-6450)
**SAN MARCO PLACE CONDO
ASSN**
1478 Riverplace Blvd (32207-1831)
PHONE..........................504 812-0352
Jim Ralph, *Vice Pres*
EMP: 6 EST: 2015
SALES (est): 462.5K **Privately Held**
SIC: 2752 Commercial printing, litho-
　graphic

(G-6451)
**SAPUTO DAIRY FOODS USA
LLC**
2198 W Beaver St (32209-7405)
PHONE..........................904 354-0406
Hassan Malih, *Manager*
EMP: 8
SALES (corp-wide): 3.7B **Privately Held**
WEB: www.saputo.com
SIC: 2023 Cream substitutes
HQ: Saputo Dairy Foods Usa, Llc
　2711 N Haskell Ave # 370
　Dallas TX 75204
　214 863-2300

(G-6452)
SARGENT SEAT COVER CO INC
Also Called: Sargent Cycle Upholstery
44 E 1st St (32206-5006)
PHONE..........................904 355-2529
Marion E Todd, *CEO*
Mike Todd, *President*
Margaret Todd, *Corp Secy*
Mark Todd, *Vice Pres*
▲ EMP: 25 EST: 1955
SQ FT: 20,000
SALES (est): 2.5MM **Privately Held**
WEB: www.sargentupholstery.com
SIC: 2399 7532 Seat covers, automobile;
　top & body repair & paint shops

(G-6453)
SAWGRASS NUTRA LABS LLC
7018 A C Skinner Pkwy # 230
(32256-6935)
PHONE..........................844 688-7244
Scott Teagle, *Mng Member*
John Devries,
EMP: 35 EST: 2018
SALES (est): 3MM **Privately Held**
WEB: www.sawgrassnutralabs.com
SIC: 2023 Dietary supplements, dairy &
　non-dairy based

(G-6454)
SCHUR & COMPANY LLC
Also Called: Schurco Slurry Pumps
9410 Florida Min Blvd E (32257)
P.O. Box 2369 (32203-2369)
PHONE..........................904 353-8075
Lisa S Schur, *President*
Nicholas J Schur, *Corp Secy*
Nick Schur, *Plant Mgr*
◆ EMP: 51 EST: 2002
SQ FT: 25,000
SALES (est): 9.5MM **Privately Held**
WEB: www.schurco.com
SIC: 3599 3568 Custom machinery;
　shafts, flexible

(G-6455)
SCIF SOLUTIONS INC (PA)
11518 Normandy Blvd (32221-1811)
PHONE..........................904 298-0631
Bruce Paquin Sr, *CEO*
Bruce Paquin Jr, *COO*
Mathangi Sivaraman, *Engineer*
Rebecca Manuel, *CFO*
Joel McDaniel, *Sales Staff*
EMP: 10 EST: 2004
SQ FT: 15,000
SALES (est): 2.5MM **Privately Held**
WEB: www.scifsolutions.com
SIC: 3448 Prefabricated metal buildings;
　buildings, portable: prefabricated metal;
　panels for prefabricated metal buildings

▲ = Import ▼=Export
◆ =Import/Export

(G-6456)
SCOTT INDUSTRIAL SYSTEMS INC
4130 N Canal St (32209-3668)
PHONE..............................904 693-3318
EMP: 18
SALES (corp-wide): 43.8MM **Privately Held**
WEB: www.scottindustrialsystems.com
SIC: 3594 Fluid power pumps & motors
PA: Scott Industrial Systems Inc
    4433 Interpoint Blvd
    Dayton OH 45424
    937 233-8146

(G-6457)
SCREEN PROCESS PRINTERS INC
101 S Myrtle Ave (32204-2174)
P.O. Box 2511 (32203-2511)
PHONE..............................904 354-8708
Smith Easton, *CEO*
James M Sullivan, *President*
EMP: 5 EST: 1979
SALES (est): 446.6K **Privately Held**
WEB: www.screenprocessprinters.com
SIC: 2759 3993 Screen printing; signs & advertising specialties

(G-6458)
SEA PRODUCTS INC (PA)
Also Called: Southeastern Aluminum
4925 Bulls Bay Hwy (32219-3250)
P.O. Box 6427 (32236-6427)
PHONE..............................904 781-8200
Patrick Dussinger, *President*
William K Jackson Jr, *President*
Jeffrey E Dowd, *Vice Pres*
Courtney Hughes, *Vice Pres*
Joseph T Jackson, *Vice Pres*
◆ EMP: 95 EST: 1952
SALES (est): 27MM **Privately Held**
WEB: www.southeasternaluminum.com
SIC: 3442 3231 3088 Sash, door or window: metal; doors, glass: made from purchased glass; shower stalls, fiberglass & plastic

(G-6459)
SEACURE INC
9485 Regency Square Blvd # 110 (32225-8194)
PHONE..............................904 353-5353
Warren P Powers, *Principal*
EMP: 10 EST: 2006
SALES (est): 740.4K **Privately Held**
SIC: 3089 Plastic boats & other marine equipment

(G-6460)
SENTRY FOOD SOLUTIONS LLC
4339 Roosevelt Blvd # 400 (32210-2004)
PHONE..............................904 482-1900
William Morris, *President*
EMP: 7 EST: 2014
SQ FT: 55,000
SALES (est): 459.8K **Privately Held**
SIC: 2099 Food preparations

(G-6461)
SG BLOCKS INC (PA)
5011 Gate Pkwy Bldg 100s (32256-0830)
PHONE..............................646 240-4235
Paul M Galvin, *Ch of Bd*
▼ EMP: 5 EST: 1993
SALES (est): 38.3MM **Publicly Held**
WEB: www.sgblocks.com
SIC: 2448 5032 8711 8741 Cargo containers, wood & metal combination; building blocks; engineering services; construction management

(G-6462)
SHARK SIGNS OF NE FL INC
5317 Shen Ave (32205-4757)
PHONE..............................904 766-6222
Donny Cagle, *President*
Christopher Miller, *General Mgr*
EMP: 9 EST: 2014
SALES (est): 983.8K **Privately Held**
WEB: www.sharksignsofnefl.com
SIC: 3993 Electric signs

(G-6463)
SHAWS STHERN BLLE FRZ FODS IN
821 Virginia St (32208-4950)
P.O. Box 28620 (32226-8620)
PHONE..............................904 768-1591
Howard Shaw, *President*
John R Shaw Jr, *Exec VP*
Joanne Zimmerman, *CFO*
▲ EMP: 100 EST: 1934
SQ FT: 105,000
SALES (est): 21MM
SALES (corp-wide): 51.9MM **Privately Held**
SIC: 2092 5963 8742 Seafoods, fresh: prepared; direct selling establishments; management consulting services
PA: Southern Belle Frozen Foods Inc
    821 Virginia St
    Jacksonville FL 32208
    904 768-1591

(G-6464)
SHERMANS WELDING & MAINTENCE
6299 Powers Ave Ste 3 (32217-2287)
PHONE..............................904 731-3460
Art Sherman, *President*
Alice Sherman, *President*
Craig Sherman, *Vice Pres*
EMP: 10 EST: 1981
SALES (est): 283.3K **Privately Held**
WEB: swm.inc.angelfire.com
SIC: 7692 Welding repair

(G-6465)
SHIPPING + BUSINESS SVCS LLC
Also Called: SBS Promotional Solutions
12627 San Jose Blvd Ste 5 (32223-2662)
P.O. Box 54593 (32245-4593)
PHONE..............................904 240-1737
Randall Smith,
EMP: 9 EST: 2008
SALES (est): 257K **Privately Held**
WEB: www.shippingplus.biz
SIC: 3993 7389 7313 Signs & advertising specialties; embroidering of advertising on shirts, etc.; printed media advertising representatives; poster advertising service, except outdoor; poster advertising, outdoor

(G-6466)
SHORELINE PLASTICS LLC
7167 Old Kings Rd (32219-3727)
PHONE..............................904 696-2981
Mark A Porter,
Mark Porter,
▼ EMP: 20 EST: 2006
SQ FT: 30,000
SALES (est): 7.9MM **Privately Held**
WEB: www.shorelineplastics.com
SIC: 3089 Extruded finished plastic products

(G-6467)
SHRIJI SWAMI LLC
Also Called: Monument Pharmacy
1301 Monument Rd Ste 22 (32225-6462)
PHONE..............................904 727-3434
M Patel,
EMP: 8 EST: 2010
SALES (est): 817.2K **Privately Held**
WEB: www.monumentrx.com
SIC: 2834 5122 Pharmaceutical preparations; pharmaceuticals

(G-6468)
SIGN A RAMA INC
Also Called: Sign-A-Rama
3633 Southside Blvd (32216-4635)
PHONE..............................904 998-8880
Cheri Vianello, *Principal*
▲ EMP: 5 EST: 2008
SALES (est): 499.7K **Privately Held**
WEB: www.signarama.com
SIC: 3993 Signs & advertising specialties

(G-6469)
SIGN PRO AMERICA
3811 University Blvd W # 37 (32217-1210)
PHONE..............................412 908-9832
EMP: 10 EST: 2011

SALES (est): 517.3K **Privately Held**
WEB: www.signproamerica.com
SIC: 3993 Signs & advertising specialties

(G-6470)
SIGNSHARKS SIGN SERVICE
7030 N Main St (32208-4730)
PHONE..............................904 766-6222
Donny Cagle, *President*
Christopher Miller, *General Mgr*
Amber Raulerson, *Info Tech Mgr*
EMP: 9 EST: 1997
SQ FT: 2,282
SALES (est): 551K **Privately Held**
WEB: www.sharksignsofnefl.com
SIC: 3993 Electric signs

(G-6471)
SILVERMAN FENCE MFG INC
4698 Dusk Ct (32207-7951)
PHONE..............................904 730-0882
Lynda Silverman, *President*
EMP: 8 EST: 1984
SQ FT: 10,000
SALES (est): 848.7K **Privately Held**
WEB: www.silvermanfence.com
SIC: 2499 1799 Fencing, wood; fence construction

(G-6472)
SILVERSHORE PARTNERS LLC
Also Called: Profilegorilla
10175 Fortune Pkwy # 60 (32256-6746)
PHONE..............................904 562-0812
Edward Baldwin, *Partner*
Edward B Baldwin, *Principal*
Ariel Tveraas, *Manager*
EMP: 10 EST: 2012
SALES (est): 1.2MM **Privately Held**
SIC: 7372 Business oriented computer software

(G-6473)
SIMMONDS PRECISION PDTS INC
Also Called: UTC Aerospace Systems
6061 Goodrich Blvd (32226-3402)
PHONE..............................904 757-3660
Justin Robert Keppy, *President*
Jacob Boynton, *Engineer*
Trevor Hall, *Engineer*
Colleen Lott, *Treasurer*
Candace A Kronholm, *Director*
EMP: 17 EST: 2013
SALES (est): 1.7MM **Privately Held**
SIC: 3728 3724 Aircraft assemblies, subassemblies & parts; engine mount parts, aircraft

(G-6474)
SIMPSON SCREENS INC
11458 Harlan Dr (32218-4052)
PHONE..............................904 757-1498
EMP: 10
SALES (est): 976.4K **Privately Held**
SIC: 3442 Mfg Metal Doors/Sash/Trim

(G-6475)
SIPP TECHNOLOGIES LLC
5245 Old Kings Rd (32254-1126)
PHONE..............................904 374-5606
Brooks Andrew, *Engineer*
Daniel Sawyer, *Engineer*
Hector Colon, *Senior Engr*
Brian Augustine, *CFO*
Kent Weisenberg,
EMP: 30 EST: 2016
SQ FT: 140,000
SALES (est): 4.5MM **Privately Held**
WEB: www.sipptech.com
SIC: 3531 Construction machinery

(G-6476)
SKIPPER WRIGHT INC
Also Called: I R Bowen & Sons
634 Dyal St (32206-3916)
PHONE..............................904 354-4381
Benjamin W Wright, *President*
▲ EMP: 22 EST: 1992
SQ FT: 10,000
SALES (est): 501.2K **Privately Held**
WEB: www.irbowen.com
SIC: 3312 Wheels, locomotive & car: iron & steel

(G-6477)
SMART STREAM INC
13500 Sutton Park Dr S # 7 (32224-5251)
PHONE..............................904 223-1511
John Thompson, *Officer*
EMP: 16 EST: 1999
SALES (est): 359.8K **Privately Held**
SIC: 2024 Ice cream & frozen desserts

(G-6478)
SOLAR ENTERPRISES INC
Also Called: Brown Enterprises
8841 Corporate Square Ct (32216-1981)
P.O. Box 8241 (32239-0241)
PHONE..............................904 724-2262
Ed Brown, *President*
Nancy R Brown, *Corp Secy*
Linda J Brown, *Vice Pres*
Pam Ricard, *Vice Pres*
Tyson Witt, *Store Mgr*
EMP: 33 EST: 1969
SQ FT: 10,000
SALES (est): 3.1MM **Privately Held**
SIC: 3993 Signs & advertising specialties

(G-6479)
SONSHINE DIGITAL GRAPHICS INC
Also Called: Minuteman Press
4613 Philips Hwy Ste 207 (32207-7290)
PHONE..............................904 858-1000
M Lee Curtis, *President*
Jon Curtis, *Vice Pres*
Jonathan D Curtis, *Vice Pres*
EMP: 15 EST: 2013
SALES (est): 1.2MM **Privately Held**
WEB: www.minutemanjax.com
SIC: 2752 7336 Commercial printing, lithographic; commercial art & graphic design

(G-6480)
SOUTHASTERN SPECIALTY COATINGS
33 W 55th St (32208-4628)
PHONE..............................904 616-9186
Adams Duane, *Principal*
EMP: 7 EST: 2015
SALES (est): 141.6K **Privately Held**
SIC: 3479 Metal coating & allied service

(G-6481)
SOUTHEAST ATLANTIC BEV CORP
6001 Bowdendale Ave (32216-6041)
PHONE..............................904 731-3644
Robert H Paul III, *Ch of Bd*
Christpher Y Paul, *President*
Guy Jackson, *CFO*
◆ EMP: 176 EST: 1939
SQ FT: 4,200
SALES (est): 10.5MM **Publicly Held**
WEB: www.seabev.com
SIC: 2086 Soft drinks: packaged in cans, bottles, etc.
HQ: Dr Pepper/Seven Up, Inc.
    6425 Hall Of Fame Ln
    Frisco TX 75034
    972 673-7000

(G-6482)
SOUTHEAST CLINICAL RES LLC
6817 Sthpint Pkwy Ste 902 (32216)
PHONE..............................904 296-3260
Tammy Parrott,
Karen Johnson,
EMP: 10 EST: 2006
SALES (est): 877.4K **Privately Held**
WEB: www.southeastclinicalresearch.com
SIC: 3821 Clinical laboratory instruments, except medical & dental

(G-6483)
SOUTHEAST INTL CHEM CO INC
221 N Hogan St 230 (32202-4201)
PHONE..............................904 992-4007
Ken Mattiace, *President*
◆ EMP: 6 EST: 2014
SALES (est): 652.1K **Privately Held**
SIC: 2899 Insulating compounds

(PA)=Parent Co (HQ)=Headquarters (DH)=Div Headquarters
✿ = New Business established in last 2 years

2022 Harris Florida
Manufacturers Directory

237

GEOGRAPHIC

(G-6484)
SOUTHEAST PACKG SANITATION LLC
Also Called: SPS
2899 Powers Ave Ste 4 (32207-8039)
P.O. Box 1024, Auburndale (33823-1024)
PHONE..........................904 634-7911
Paula Camp, *Vice Pres*
Jay B Javetz, *Mng Member*
Thomas W Chambers,
Stephen C Saterbo,
EMP: 9 **EST:** 2012
SALES (est): 845.9K **Privately Held**
SIC: 2672 2429 3089 2671 Adhesive papers, labels or tapes: from purchased material; shavings & packaging, excelsior; blister or bubble formed packaging, plastic; paper coated or laminated for packaging; plastic film, coated or laminated for packaging; tags & labels, paper

(G-6485)
SOUTHEAST WINDOW COVERINGS
6900 Philips Hwy Ste 46 (32216-6060)
PHONE..........................904 372-0326
Chase Sams, *Executive*
EMP: 8 **EST:** 2009
SALES (est): 63.1K **Privately Held**
WEB: www.southeastwindowcoverings.com
SIC: 2591 Drapery hardware & blinds & shades

(G-6486)
SOUTHEASTERN ALUMINUM PDTS LLC
4925 Bulls Bay Hwy (32219-3250)
P.O. Box 6427 (32236-6427)
PHONE..........................800 243-8200
Patrick Dussinger, *Mng Member*
EMP: 9 **EST:** 1952
SALES (est): 96.9K **Privately Held**
WEB: www.southeasternaluminum.com
SIC: 3231 Doors, glass: made from purchased glass

(G-6487)
SOUTHEASTERN PALLETS INC
2203 W Beaver St (32209-7404)
P.O. Box 92 (32234-0092)
PHONE..........................904 783-8363
Brett Griffis, *Vice Pres*
EMP: 7 **EST:** 2004
SQ FT: 2,474
SALES (est): 754.2K **Privately Held**
SIC: 2448 Pallets, wood

(G-6488)
SOUTHEASTERN PEG BD PRTRS INC
Also Called: Pegbroad Data System
2750 Dawn Rd (32207-7904)
PHONE..........................904 731-0357
Steve Edenfield, *President*
EMP: 5 **EST:** 1971
SQ FT: 14,000
SALES (est): 665.5K **Privately Held**
SIC: 2761 5044 Unit sets (manifold business forms); accounting machines, excluding machine program readable type

(G-6489)
SOUTHERN BALLOON WORKS INC
11653 Central Pkwy # 209 (32224-2710)
PHONE..........................727 388-8360
Tom Macnaughton, *President*
EMP: 5 **EST:** 1993
SQ FT: 1,800
SALES (est): 434K **Privately Held**
WEB: www.southernballoonworks.com
SIC: 2211 Balloon cloth, cotton

(G-6490)
SOUTHERN FIBERGLASS INC
41 Spring St (32254-4087)
PHONE..........................904 387-2246
James R Rowand, *President*
James Rowand, *President*
Don A Rowand, *Vice Pres*
EMP: 10 **EST:** 1971
SQ FT: 7,000

SALES (est): 693.9K **Privately Held**
WEB: www.southernfiberglass.com
SIC: 3599 3732 3728 3523 Machine shop, jobbing & repair; boat building & repairing; aircraft parts & equipment; farm machinery & equipment; laminated plastics plate & sheet

(G-6491)
SOUTHERN LBR & TREATING CO INC
1433 Lane Cir E (32254-2239)
P.O. Box 7450 (32238-0450)
PHONE..........................904 695-0784
William Sumner, *President*
EMP: 11 **EST:** 1988
SQ FT: 7,000
SALES (est): 1.7MM **Privately Held**
WEB: www.southern-lumber.com
SIC: 2491 Wood preserving

(G-6492)
SOUTHERN RECREATION INC
4060 Edison Ave (32254-4108)
PHONE..........................904 387-4390
Terry Rogers, *President*
Tim Norton, *Vice Pres*
Sue Box, *Office Mgr*
EMP: 10 **EST:** 1985
SQ FT: 4,000
SALES (est): 1MM **Privately Held**
WEB: www.southernrecreation.com
SIC: 3949 1799 Playground equipment; playground construction & equipment installation

(G-6493)
SOUTHERN SURGICAL CONSULTANTS
11653 Central Pkwy # 201 (32224-2711)
PHONE..........................904 296-7828
Kent Adams, *President*
EMP: 5 **EST:** 1996
SALES (est): 362.5K **Privately Held**
SIC: 3842 Foot appliances, orthopedic

(G-6494)
SOUTHERN TECHNOLOGIES
Also Called: Honeywell Authorized Dealer
270 Us Highway 90 E (32234-1902)
PHONE..........................904 266-2100
Marty Hanks, *Owner*
EMP: 19 **EST:** 2009
SALES (est): 4.8MM **Privately Held**
SIC: 3585 Parts for heating, cooling & refrigerating equipment

(G-6495)
SOUTHERN WHEEL & RIM INC
1044 Lane Ave S (32205-4709)
P.O. Box 37028 (32236-7028)
PHONE..........................904 786-7542
Olin P Joiner, *President*
Roy Hawkins, *Treasurer*
Mike Wilson, *Consultant*
▲ **EMP:** 18 **EST:** 1979
SQ FT: 15,000
SALES (est): 1.7MM **Privately Held**
WEB: www.southernwheel-rim.com
SIC: 3714 Wheels, motor vehicle

(G-6496)
SOUTHSTERN STNLESS FBRCTORS IN
Also Called: Florida Georgia Welding Supply
634 Dyal St (32206-3916)
PHONE..........................904 354-4381
Teresa Moore, *President*
Douglas Moore, *Director*
Larry Rolfe, *Director*
EMP: 10 **EST:** 2004
SQ FT: 10,000
SALES (est): 1.7MM **Privately Held**
WEB: www.irbowen.com
SIC: 3441 Fabricated structural metal

(G-6497)
SPACELABS HEALTHCARE INC
Also Called: Statcorp Medical
14476 Duval Pl W Ste 303 (32218-9414)
PHONE..........................904 786-5113
EMP: 35

SALES (corp-wide): 906.7MM **Publicly Held**
SIC: 3841 Surgical And Medical Instruments
HQ: Spacelabs Healthcare, Inc.
35301 Se Center St
Snoqualmie WA 98065
425 396-3302

(G-6498)
SPECIAL TOOL SOLUTIONS INC
11699 Camden Rd (32218-3901)
P.O. Box 40585 (32203-0585)
PHONE..........................904 356-5671
John Snead, *President*
EMP: 47 **EST:** 2000
SQ FT: 10,000
SALES (est): 9.2MM **Privately Held**
SIC: 3599 Custom machinery

(G-6499)
SPECIALTY DEF SYSTEMS KY INC
13386 International Pkwy (32218-2383)
PHONE..........................904 741-5400
EMP: 8 **EST:** 2015
SALES (est): 261.1K **Privately Held**
SIC: 3842 Surgical appliances & supplies

(G-6500)
SPECIALTY TANK AND EQP CO
857 Robinson Ave (32209-7559)
P.O. Box 2370 (32203-2370)
PHONE..........................904 353-8761
▼ **EMP:** 7 **EST:** 1940
SQ FT: 30,000
SALES (est): 1.2MM **Privately Held**
SIC: 3443 Mfg Fabricated Plate Work

(G-6501)
SPLASH OF COLOR LLC
2885 Starshire Cv (32257-5801)
PHONE..........................732 735-3090
Natalie Dayan, *Branch Mgr*
EMP: 23
SALES (corp-wide): 73.2K **Privately Held**
SIC: 2759 Screen printing
PA: Splash Of Color Llc
14701 Bartrm Pk Blvd
Jacksonville FL

(G-6502)
ST JOHNS BKY & GOURMET FD CO (PA)
Also Called: Truffles Coffee House & Bakery
6301 Powers Ave (32217-2217)
PHONE..........................813 727-3528
Peter A Podes, *President*
Angelo P Podes, *Principal*
Susan W Podes, *Exec VP*
EMP: 17 **EST:** 1993
SQ FT: 4,800
SALES (est): 1.1MM **Privately Held**
SIC: 2051 Bakery: wholesale or wholesale/retail combined

(G-6503)
STAMPCO INC
2930 Mercury Rd (32207-7913)
PHONE..........................904 737-6144
Kenneth L Parmenter, *President*
Dorothy Decker, *Corp Secy*
James A Parmenter, *Vice Pres*
EMP: 10 **EST:** 1973
SQ FT: 18,000
SALES (est): 1.7MM **Privately Held**
SIC: 3444 5063 Sheet metalwork; wire & cable

(G-6504)
STANDARD PRECAST INC
12300 Presidents Ct (32220-3225)
P.O. Box 61839 (32236-1839)
PHONE..........................904 268-0466
Barbara L Peterson, *President*
Roger Cole, *General Mgr*
Russell A Smith, *Vice Pres*
▲ **EMP:** 80 **EST:** 1965
SALES (est): 17.2MM
SALES (corp-wide): 30.9B **Privately Held**
WEB: www.oldcastleinfrastructure.com
SIC: 3272 Manhole covers or frames, concrete; sewer pipe, concrete

HQ: Oldcastle Infrastructure, Inc.
7000 Central Pkwy Ste 800
Atlanta GA 30328
770 270-5000

(G-6505)
STAR FABRICATORS
989 Imeson Park Blvd (32218-4903)
PHONE..........................904 899-6569
Peter Wu, *Principal*
EMP: 7 **EST:** 2010
SALES (est): 120.4K **Privately Held**
SIC: 3441 Fabricated structural metal

(G-6506)
STENNER PUMP COMPANY INC (PA)
3174 Desalvo Rd (32246-3733)
PHONE..........................904 641-1666
Ben Ware, *Partner*
Ralph Baynes, *Prdtn Mgr*
Brian Schubert, *Engineer*
Michael Kincid, *CFO*
Cindy Burgholzer, *Human Res Mgr*
▲ **EMP:** 84 **EST:** 1957
SQ FT: 55,000
SALES (est): 28MM **Privately Held**
WEB: www.stenner.com
SIC: 3561 3586 Pump jacks & other pumping equipment; measuring & dispensing pumps

(G-6507)
STEPHENS ADVERTISING INC
7029 Commwl Ave Ste 9 (32220)
PHONE..........................904 354-7004
Ruth Ann Hicks, *President*
EMP: 5 **EST:** 1978
SQ FT: 15,000
SALES (est): 478.7K **Privately Held**
WEB: www.stephensjax.com
SIC: 3993 Electric signs

(G-6508)
STERITOOL INC
2376 Lake Shore Blvd (32210-4026)
PHONE..........................904 388-3672
Stephen Rountree, *President*
Adam Rountree, *Vice Pres*
◆ **EMP:** 10 **EST:** 2005
SQ FT: 30,000
SALES (est): 1MM **Privately Held**
WEB: www.steritool.com
SIC: 3423 Hand & edge tools

(G-6509)
STITCHEZ LLC
13714 Longs Landing Rd W (32225-5423)
PHONE..........................904 221-9148
Sebastian Stanciu, *Principal*
EMP: 7 **EST:** 2016
SALES (est): 95.5K **Privately Held**
SIC: 2395 Embroidery & art needlework

(G-6510)
STITCHING HEART LLC
8174 Lexington Dr (32208-2843)
PHONE..........................904 379-7990
Chris Davis, *Principal*
EMP: 7 **EST:** 2013
SALES (est): 261.2K **Privately Held**
SIC: 2395 Embroidery & art needlework

(G-6511)
STORMFORCE JACKSONVILLE LLC
6111 Gazebo Park Pl N # 21 (32257-1302)
PHONE..........................904 288-6639
Becky Manderson, *CFO*
Keith Manderson, *Sales Staff*
Dillon Mavrich, *Sales Staff*
Rebecca Manderson, *Mng Member*
Debbie Barket, *Recruiter*
EMP: 6 **EST:** 2011
SALES (est): 1.8MM **Privately Held**
WEB: www.stormforce.com
SIC: 2952 Roofing felts, cements or coatings

(G-6512)
STRATTON INC DM
7653 Bayard Blvd (32256-2406)
PHONE..........................904 268-6052
Dillon M Stratton, *President*
EMP: 6 **EST:** 1988

SALES (est): 597.9K **Privately Held**
SIC: 2411 Pulpwood contractors engaged
in cutting

(G-6513)
STRYKER ORTHOPEDICS
7014 A C Skinner Pkwy (32256-6959)
PHONE..................................904 296-6000
John Bowers, *President*
M Kathryn Kat Fink, *Vice Pres*
Dana McMahon, *Vice Pres*
George Knoblach, *Regl Sales Mgr*
David Dubish, *Sales Staff*
EMP: 7 **EST:** 1986
SQ FT: 1,600
SALES (est): 1MM **Privately Held**
SIC: 3841 Surgical & medical instruments

(G-6514)
STYLORS INC
640 W 41st St (32206-6235)
PHONE..................................904 765-4453
Michael A Kersun, *President*
Sam Kersun, *Corp Secy*
Mirian Kersun, *Vice Pres*
EMP: 19 **EST:** 1935
SQ FT: 29,000
SALES (est): 1.1MM **Privately Held**
WEB: www.stylors.com
SIC: 3999 2844 2221 Hair curlers, de-
signed for beauty parlors; home perma-
nent kits; shampoos, rinses, conditioners:
hair; broadwoven fabric mills, manmade

(G-6515)
SUN SCREEN PRINT INC
4849 Dawin Rd Ste 3 (32207-9528)
PHONE..................................904 674-0520
David E Fitzsimmons, *President*
Melissa Long, *Vice Pres*
EMP: 6 **EST:** 2005
SALES (est): 509.5K **Privately Held**
WEB: www.sunscreenprint.com
SIC: 2752 Commercial printing, offset

(G-6516)
**SUNOPTIC TECHNOLOGIES LLC
(PA)**
6018 Bowdendale Ave (32216-6042)
PHONE..................................877 677-2832
Bryant Thigpen, *Opers Mgr*
Closson Brandon, *Purch Agent*
Janice Lee, *QA Dir*
William Broyles, *Engineer*
Jose Galarza, *Engineer*
◆ **EMP:** 98 **EST:** 1978
SALES (est): 11.7MM **Privately Held**
WEB: www.sunopticsurgical.com
SIC: 3827 3841 3823 3843 Optical in-
struments & lenses; surgical & medical in-
struments; industrial instrmnts msrmnt
display/control process variable; dental
equipment & supplies; products of pur-
chased glass; medical & hospital equip-
ment

(G-6517)
SUNRISE FOODS LLC
4520 Swilcan Bridge Ln N (32224-5617)
PHONE..................................904 613-4756
Bradley R Dermond, *Principal*
EMP: 6 **EST:** 2012
SALES (est): 592.4K **Privately Held**
SIC: 2099 Food preparations

(G-6518)
SUNSET POWER INC
Also Called: Solarenergy.com
5191 Shawland Rd (32254-1649)
PHONE..................................866 485-2757
◆ **EMP:** 16
SQ FT: 25,000
SALES (est): 2.4MM **Privately Held**
SIC: 3433 5074 Mfg Heating Equipment-
Nonelectric Whol Plumbing
Equipment/Supplies

(G-6519)
**SUNSHINE ORGANICS
COMPOST LLC**
Also Called: Compost Jax
6478 Buffalo Ave (32208-4810)
PHONE..................................904 900-3072
Mike Kelcourse, *Principal*
Michael Kelcourse, *Principal*
EMP: 5 **EST:** 2019

SALES (est): 437.7K **Privately Held**
WEB:
www.sunshineorganicsandcompost.com
SIC: 2875 Fertilizers, mixing only

(G-6520)
**SUNSHINE PACKING & NOODLE
CO**
Also Called: Chen, Chao Ming Company
57 Cantee St (32204-1701)
PHONE..................................904 355-7561
Chao Chen, *President*
Bill H Chen, *Vice Pres*
EMP: 8 **EST:** 1982
SALES (est): 848.5K **Privately Held**
SIC: 2099 Sauces: dry mixes; spices, in-
cluding grinding

(G-6521)
**SUPERIOR MILLWORK
COMPANY INC**
501 E 27th St (32206-2212)
P.O. Box 3321 (32206-0321)
PHONE..................................904 355-5676
Francis Polly III, *President*
Jennifer Polly, *Admin Sec*
EMP: 15 **EST:** 1941
SQ FT: 16,560
SALES (est): 2.2MM **Privately Held**
WEB: www.superiormillworkcompany.com
SIC: 2431 Woodwork, interior & ornamen-
tal

(G-6522)
**SUPERIOR PAVERS AND STONE
LLC**
731 Duval Station Rd # 107 (32218-0800)
PHONE..................................904 887-7831
Rex Williams, *Principal*
EMP: 6 **EST:** 2008
SALES (est): 520.9K **Privately Held**
SIC: 3531 Pavers

(G-6523)
**SWISHER INTERNATIONAL INC
(DH)**
459 E 16th St (32206-3025)
P.O. Box 2230 (32203-2230)
PHONE..................................904 353-4311
Peter J Ghiloni, *President*
Kyle Nugent, *Regional Mgr*
Tim Neas, *Dept Chairman*
Lou Caldropoli, *Vice Pres*
Louis A Caldropoli, *Vice Pres*
◆ **EMP:** 1 **EST:** 1966
SALES (est): 118.6MM **Privately Held**
WEB: www.swisher.com
SIC: 2121 Cigars
HQ: Swisher International Group Inc.
20 Thorndal Cir
Darien CT 06820
203 656-8000

(G-6524)
SWISHER INTL GROUP INC
14425 Duval Rd (32218-2473)
PHONE..................................904 353-4311
Carl Trammell, *Branch Mgr*
EMP: 11 **Privately Held**
WEB: www.swisher.com
SIC: 2131 Smoking tobacco
HQ: Swisher International Group Inc.
20 Thorndal Cir
Darien CT 06820
203 656-8000

(G-6525)
SY-KLONE COMPANY LLC
Also Called: Sy-Klone International
4390 Imeson Rd (32219-5314)
PHONE..................................904 448-6563
Brandon Cooper, *Principal*
Mary Barrington, *Vice Pres*
Dana Cain, *Purchasing*
Rich Uhrie, *Engineer*
Rebecca Manuel, *Controller*
EMP: 44 **EST:** 2017
SQ FT: 62,587
SALES (est): 5MM **Privately Held**
WEB: www.sy-klone.com
SIC: 3599 3564 Machine & other job shop
work; blowers & fans

(G-6526)
SYMRISE INC
Also Called: Aroma Chemicals
601 Crestwood St (32208-4476)
PHONE..................................904 768-5800
Jason Whitelocke, *Superintendent*
Jackie Ortiz, *Export Mgr*
Kalid Assali, *Engineer*
Michael Klamm, *Branch Mgr*
Anali Carr, *Technician*
EMP: 150 **Privately Held**
WEB: www.symrise.com
SIC: 2869 Industrial organic chemicals
HQ: Symrise Inc.
300 North St
Teterboro NJ 07608
201 288-3200

(G-6527)
T-SHIRT EXPRESS
8286 Western Way Cir (32256-0369)
PHONE..................................904 448-3761
Tom Ryan, *Owner*
EMP: 6 **EST:** 2005
SALES (est): 436.5K **Privately Held**
WEB: www.printsrus.com
SIC: 2759 5199 5651 5949 Screen print-
ing; nondurable goods; family clothing
stores; sewing & needlework

(G-6528)
TACTICAL AIR SUPPORT INC
13401 Aerospace Way # 945 (32221-8107)
PHONE..................................229 563-7502
Rolland Thompson, *CEO*
Andrew Gamble, *Vice Pres*
Rocklyn Schweser, *CFO*
EMP: 206 **EST:** 2005
SALES (est): 11.4MM **Privately Held**
WEB: www.tacticalairsupport.com
SIC: 3721 3812 3429 8711 Aircraft; air-
craft/aerospace flight instruments & guid-
ance systems; aircraft hardware;
engineering services

(G-6529)
TAKERIA MIX INC
6680 Powers Ave Ste 108 (32217-8807)
PHONE..................................904 338-9157
Martha L Navarro, *Vice Pres*
EMP: 15 **EST:** 2005
SALES (est): 374.4K **Privately Held**
WEB: takeria-mix-jacksonville.business.site
SIC: 3273 Ready-mixed concrete

(G-6530)
TALENT ASSESSMENT INC
Also Called: Borden, Ben Talent Assessment
6838 Phillips Pkwy Dr S (32256-1564)
P.O. Box 5087 (32247-5087)
PHONE..................................904 260-4102
Ben P Borden, *President*
David Cloninger, *Natl Sales Mgr*
Betty Playdon, *Sales Staff*
Randy Clayton, *Director*
Jamie Coker, *Representative*
EMP: 7 **EST:** 1980
SQ FT: 8,100
SALES (est): 600K **Privately Held**
WEB: www.talentassessment.com
SIC: 3999 Education aids, devices & sup-
plies

(G-6531)
TAMPA ARMATURE WORKS INC
Also Called: Taw Jacksonville Service Ctr
10520 Busch Dr N (32218-5604)
PHONE..................................904 757-7790
Caroline Turner, *Vice Pres*
Rocco Day, *Project Mgr*
Chris Durrance, *Project Mgr*
George Guillen, *Opers Mgr*
John Reid, *Prdtn Mgr*
EMP: 80
SQ FT: 66,788
SALES (corp-wide): 169.6MM **Privately
Held**
WEB: www.tawinc.com
SIC: 7694 5063 Electric motor repair; mo-
tors, electric
PA: Tampa Armature Works, Inc.
6312 S 78th St
Riverview FL 33578
813 621-5661

(G-6532)
TAMPA FORK LIFT INC
7033 Commonwealth Ave (32220-2851)
PHONE..................................904 674-6899
EMP: 10
SALES (corp-wide): 14.1MM **Privately
Held**
WEB: www.floridaforklift.com
SIC: 3537 Forklift trucks
PA: Tampa Fork Lift, Inc.
3221 N 40th St
Tampa FL 33605
813 623-5251

(G-6533)
TANGLE CORPORATION
1535 Blair Rd (32221-2012)
PHONE..................................904 712-0042
Kristie Usher, *Principal*
EMP: 7 **EST:** 2019
SALES (est): 111.1K **Privately Held**
WEB: www.tanglecreations.com
SIC: 3944 Games, toys & children's vehi-
cles

(G-6534)
TAYLOR SIGN & DESIGN INC
4162 Saint Augustine Rd (32207-6618)
PHONE..................................904 396-4652
Randy Taylor, *President*
Ken May, *General Mgr*
Damon Katsikas, *Sales Staff*
Chris Taylor, *Sales Associate*
Guy Browning, *Info Tech Mgr*
EMP: 19 **EST:** 1928
SQ FT: 2,500
SALES (est): 2.7MM **Privately Held**
WEB: www.taylorsignco.com
SIC: 3993 Electric signs

(G-6535)
TAYLOR-COTTON-RIDLEY INC
4873 Victor St (32207-7971)
PHONE..................................904 733-8373
James L Ridley Jr, *Branch Mgr*
Julie Rich, *Admin Asst*
EMP: 58
SQ FT: 10,080
SALES (corp-wide): 15.6MM **Privately
Held**
WEB: www.taylorcottonridley.com
SIC: 2431 Door frames, wood
PA: Taylor-Cotton-Ridley, Inc.
4410 Sw 35th Ter
Gainesville FL 32608
352 378-1608

(G-6536)
TEAPOSH NATURALS LLC
9501 Arlington Expy # 135 (32225-8240)
PHONE..................................904 683-2099
Keith Nelson, *CEO*
EMP: 12 **EST:** 2016
SALES (est): 737.4K **Privately Held**
WEB: www.teaposhnaturals.com
SIC: 2599 2099 Bar, restaurant & cafeteria
furniture; food preparations

(G-6537)
TEC COMPOSITES INC
10615 New Kings Rd (32219-2129)
PHONE..................................904 765-6502
EMP: 9 **EST:** 2019
SALES (est): 1MM **Privately Held**
WEB: www.teccomposites.com
SIC: 2821 Plastics materials & resins

(G-6538)
**TECHNCAL PNTG
JACKSONVILLE INC**
1401 Wheels Rd Bldg 3 (32218-9408)
PHONE..................................904 652-1129
Shoji Mori, *Principal*
Toshiji Yamanaka, *Vice Pres*
Takanori Mori, *Admin Sec*
EMP: 66 **EST:** 2003
SQ FT: 23,000
SALES (est): 4MM **Privately Held**
SIC: 2851 Undercoatings, paint
PA: Totsuka Sogyo Co.,Ltd.
6400-15, Nishiobuchi
Kakegawa SZO 437-1

(G-6539)
TECHNLOGY INTEGRATION SVCS LLC
4600 Touchton Rd E # 1150 (32246-8299)
PHONE........................904 565-4050
Tim Stickelmaier, *Mng Member*
EMP: 6 **EST:** 2010
SALES (est): 635.1K **Privately Held**
WEB: www.tecisusa.com
SIC: 3357 Building wire & cable, nonferrous

(G-6540)
TECTRON
546 Ellis Rd S (32254-3555)
PHONE........................904 355-5512
Michael Jackson, *Owner*
EMP: 10 **EST:** 2007
SALES (est): 524.7K **Privately Held**
WEB: www.tectron.net
SIC: 3599 Bellows, industrial: metal

(G-6541)
TECTRON ENGINEERING COMPANY (PA)
Also Called: Tectron Metal Detection
5820 Commonwealth Ave (32254-2206)
PHONE........................904 394-0683
Michael Jackson, *President*
Michael A Jackson, *President*
▲ **EMP:** 10 **EST:** 1968
SQ FT: 11,200
SALES (est): 2.3MM **Privately Held**
WEB: www.tectron.net
SIC: 3669 3829 Metal detectors; measuring & controlling devices

(G-6542)
TEHGOL INDUSTRIES LLC
25 N Market St Ste 121 (32202-2802)
P.O. Box 78, Orange Park (32067-0078)
PHONE........................904 439-5623
Rapheal Dabney, *CEO*
EMP: 8 **EST:** 2018
SALES (est): 510K **Privately Held**
WEB: www.tehgol.com
SIC: 3999 Manufacturing industries

(G-6543)
TELEIOS MANUFACTURING INC
8940 Western Way Ste 15 (32256-0329)
PHONE........................904 490-0600
EMP: 9 **EST:** 2019
SALES (est): 1.3MM **Privately Held**
WEB: www.teleiosmfg.com
SIC: 3812 Aircraft/aerospace flight instruments & guidance systems

(G-6544)
TERRA NOVA PVERS HRDSCAPE SLTO
7095 Stonelion Cir (32256-6048)
PHONE........................904 662-2999
Rodrigo C Herreros, *President*
EMP: 7 **EST:** 2012
SALES (est): 247.8K **Privately Held**
SIC: 2951 Asphalt paving mixtures & blocks

(G-6545)
TERRAFUSE USA INC ❂
14476 Duval Pl W Ste 206 (32218-9414)
PHONE........................904 207-9564
Steve Breithaupt,
Stephen Breithaupt,
Debbie Novello,
EMP: 5 **EST:** 2021
SALES (est): 963.9K **Privately Held**
WEB: www.terrafuse.com
SIC: 3272 Concrete products

(G-6546)
THERMAL CONVERSION TECH INC
101 Copeland St (32204-1803)
PHONE........................904 358-3720
Steven K Gorman, *CEO*
▼ **EMP:** 26 **EST:** 1979
SALES (est): 1.4MM **Privately Held**
SIC: 3433 Solar heaters & collectors

(G-6547)
THOMPSON AWNING & SHUTTER CO
2036 Evergreen Ave (32206-3978)
P.O. Box 3478 (32206-0478)
PHONE........................904 355-1616
Bob O'Brien, *President*
Carol O'Brien, *Vice Pres*
EMP: 16 **EST:** 1920
SQ FT: 7,000
SALES (est): 1MM **Privately Held**
WEB: www.thompsonawning.com
SIC: 2591 2394 3444 Blinds vertical; venetian blinds; awnings, fabric: made from purchased materials; awnings, sheet metal

(G-6548)
THOMPSON REPAIRS INC
4857 Dignan St (32254-3791)
P.O. Box 37922 (32236-7922)
PHONE........................904 384-5175
Stephen Thompson III, *President*
Nina L Thompson, *Corp Secy*
EMP: 7 **EST:** 1987
SQ FT: 12,000
SALES (est): 912.9K **Privately Held**
WEB: www.thompsonrepairs.com
SIC: 3599 Machine shop, jobbing & repair

(G-6549)
THREE CAY G LLC
5121 Bowden Rd Ste 107 (32216-5929)
PHONE........................904 930-4554
Barbara Johnson, *Principal*
EMP: 8 **EST:** 2018
SALES (est): 540.7K **Privately Held**
WEB: www.3cayg.com
SIC: 2844 Toilet preparations

(G-6550)
THREEZ COMPANY LLC (PA)
1225 W Beaver St Ste 123 (32204-1415)
PHONE........................904 422-9224
Hanan Furqan, *CEO*
Zakee Furqan, *COO*
▼ **EMP:** 5 **EST:** 2011
SQ FT: 1,000
SALES (est): 3.9MM **Privately Held**
WEB: www.threezsupplies.com
SIC: 2676 5099 5087 Towels, napkins & tissue paper products; safety equipment & supplies; cleaning & maintenance equipment & supplies; restaurant supplies

(G-6551)
TIER5 TECHNICAL SERVICES
Also Called: Jacksonville Cyber Defense
16167 Kayla Cove Ct (32218-0109)
PHONE........................904 435-3484
Christopher Boyle,
EMP: 7 **EST:** 2016
SALES (est): 445.7K **Privately Held**
WEB: www.tier5-tech.com
SIC: 3661 5064 7371 1731 Telephones & telephone apparatus; multiplex equipment, telephone & telegraph; answering machines, telephone; custom computer programming services; telephone & telephone equipment installation

(G-6552)
TIME PRINTING CO INC
Also Called: Ink Master Graphics
3504 Saint Augustine Rd (32207-5525)
P.O. Box 5643 (32247-5643)
PHONE........................904 396-9967
Ronald Smith, *President*
Hazel E Smith, *Corp Secy*
EMP: 5 **EST:** 1965
SQ FT: 7,500
SALES (est): 483.6K **Privately Held**
WEB: www.cryptotabbrowser.com
SIC: 2752 Commercial printing, offset

(G-6553)
TIMUS INC
8131 Baymeadows Cir (32256-2012)
PHONE........................904 614-4342
Russell E Cain Jr, *President*
EMP: 5 **EST:** 1999
SALES (est): 594.2K **Privately Held**
WEB: www.timus.com
SIC: 7372 Business oriented computer software

(G-6554)
TITAN AMERICA LLC
6557 Greenland Rd (32258-2439)
PHONE........................800 520-2083
Terry Merrion, *General Mgr*
Dean Dimaio, *Manager*
EMP: 13
SALES (corp-wide): 177.9K **Privately Held**
WEB: www.titanamerica.com
SIC: 3273 Ready-mixed concrete
HQ: Titan America Llc
5700 Lake Wright Dr # 300
Norfolk VA 23502
757 858-6500

(G-6555)
TITAN AMERICA LLC
1220 Eastport Rd (32218-2216)
PHONE........................904 296-0609
Tim Bilotta, *Manager*
EMP: 12
SALES (corp-wide): 177.9K **Privately Held**
WEB: www.titanamerica.com
SIC: 3273 Ready-mixed concrete
HQ: Titan America Llc
5700 Lake Wright Dr # 300
Norfolk VA 23502
757 858-6500

(G-6556)
TITAN AMERICA LLC
Also Called: Tarmac Florida
7330 Philips Hwy (32256-6806)
P.O. Box 24825 (32241-4825)
PHONE........................904 296-0609
Jim Cook, *Branch Mgr*
EMP: 13
SQ FT: 13,126
SALES (corp-wide): 177.9K **Privately Held**
WEB: www.titanamerica.com
SIC: 3273 Ready-mixed concrete
HQ: Titan America Llc
5700 Lake Wright Dr # 300
Norfolk VA 23502
757 858-6500

(G-6557)
TKS PRINTING & PROMO PRODUCTS
3107 Spring Glen Rd Ste 2 (32207-5916)
PHONE........................904 469-0968
Zachary Robinson, *CEO*
EMP: 84 **EST:** 2017
SALES (est): 2.8MM **Privately Held**
SIC: 2752 Commercial printing, lithographic

(G-6558)
TOMS INSTANT PRINTING INC
Also Called: Tom's Instant Printing
3100 Beach Blvd (32207-3796)
PHONE........................904 396-0686
Tom Tomaski, *President*
Suzanne Tomaski, *Vice Pres*
EMP: 7 **EST:** 1971
SQ FT: 1,500
SALES (est): 554.5K **Privately Held**
SIC: 2752 2791 8743 Commercial printing, offset; typesetting; promotion service

(G-6559)
TOO MANY IDEAS INC
Also Called: TMI
1716 Hendricks Ave (32207-3112)
PHONE........................904 396-9245
Guy Beard, *President*
Linda Beard, *Corp Secy*
EMP: 8 **EST:** 1992
SALES (est): 522K **Privately Held**
SIC: 3911 Jewelry apparel

(G-6560)
TOP NOTCH DIECUTTING FOIL STA
4246 Saint Augustine Rd (32207-6644)
PHONE........................904 346-3511
Michael D Hartley, *President*
Clint McConnaughey, *General Mgr*
Diane M McConnaughey, *Vice Pres*
EMP: 5 **EST:** 1999
SQ FT: 9,000

SALES (est): 476.3K **Privately Held**
SIC: 3469 2675 Metal stampings; paper die-cutting

(G-6561)
TOP SPEC US INC
1650 Margaret St (32204-3868)
PHONE........................904 345-0814
Ronald Shinall, *Principal*
EMP: 7 **EST:** 2010
SALES (est): 203.8K **Privately Held**
WEB: www.topspecus.com
SIC: 3949 Sporting & athletic goods

(G-6562)
TRAFFIC CONTROL PDTS FLA INC
5639 Witten Rd (32254-1534)
PHONE........................352 372-7088
Orlando Nunez, *Superintendent*
Robert Stone, *Manager*
EMP: 30
SALES (corp-wide): 15.5MM **Privately Held**
WEB: www.trafficcontrolproducts.org
SIC: 3499 3669 1799 3993 Barricades, metal; transportation signaling devices; parking lot maintenance; signs & advertising specialties
PA: Traffic Control Products Of Florida, Inc.
5514 Carmack Rd
Tampa FL 33610
813 621-8484

(G-6563)
TRAILMATE INC
6620 Suemac Pl (32254-2773)
PHONE........................941 739-5743
Harry Bakker, *President*
▲ **EMP:** 25 **EST:** 1977
SALES (est): 4.3MM **Privately Held**
WEB: www.trailmate.com
SIC: 3524 3751 Lawnmowers, residential: hand or power; bicycles & related parts

(G-6564)
TRANE US INC
8929 Western Way Ste 1 (32256-8391)
PHONE........................904 538-8600
John Foret, *Project Mgr*
Curtis Humphrey, *Branch Mgr*
Casey Hazen, *Manager*
Brent Reitz, *Manager*
EMP: 84 **Privately Held**
WEB: www.trane.com
SIC: 3585 Refrigeration & heating equipment
HQ: Trane U.S. Inc.
800 Beaty St Ste E
Davidson NC 28036
704 655-4000

(G-6565)
TREMRON LLC (PA)
Also Called: Tremron Group
2885 Saint Clair St (32254-1863)
PHONE........................904 359-5900
Jeff Kirtley, *Sales Staff*
Thomas Williams, *Technician*
EMP: 5 **EST:** 2016
SALES (est): 36.1MM **Privately Held**
WEB: www.tremron.com
SIC: 3531 Pavers

(G-6566)
TREMRON LLC
9440 Philips Hwy (32256-1357)
PHONE........................904 886-1970
EMP: 59
SALES (corp-wide): 36.1MM **Privately Held**
WEB: www.tremron.com
SIC: 3281 Curbing, paving & walkway stone
PA: Tremron, Llc
2885 Saint Clair St
Jacksonville FL 32254
904 359-5900

(G-6567)
TREND OFFSET PRINTING SVCS INC
Also Called: Mittera
10301 Busch Dr N (32218-5635)
PHONE........................562 598-2446
Ricky Carter, *President*

▲ = Import ▼=Export
❂ =Import/Export

Steven Poliks, *General Mgr*
Rich Clark, *Regional Mgr*
Lewis Story, *COO*
Steve Furlong, *Vice Pres*
EMP: 100
SALES (corp-wide): 656.1MM **Privately Held**
WEB: www.mittera.com
SIC: 2752 Commercial printing, offset
HQ: Trend Offset Printing Services, Inc.
3701 Catalina St
Los Alamitos CA 90720
562 598-2446

(G-6568)
TRUE HOUSE INC (PA)
Also Called: True Truss
4745 Sutton Park Ct # 501 (32224-0251)
PHONE.....................904 757-7500
Barry E Dixon, *President*
Rebecca Harrison, *COO*
Oliver L Dixon, *Vice Pres*
Edie D Dixon, *Admin Sec*
EMP: 10 **EST:** 1997
SQ FT: 20,000
SALES (est): 13.6MM **Privately Held**
WEB: www.apextechnology.com
SIC: 2439 Trusses, except roof: laminated
lumber; trusses, wooden roof

(G-6569)
TURNING POINT PROPELLERS INC
11762 Marco Beach Dr # 2 (32224-5677)
P.O. Box 59299, Schaumburg IL (60159-0299)
PHONE.....................904 900-7739
Eben Chen, *President*
Liheng Chen, *COO*
Dickson Kendall, *Vice Pres*
James Nickels, *Director*
▲ **EMP:** 6 **EST:** 1982
SALES (est): 577.3K **Privately Held**
WEB: www.turningpointpropellers.com
SIC: 3366 5551 5088 Propellers; boat
dealers; marine crafts & supplies

(G-6570)
TURTLE PUBLISHING CO
1034 Hendricks Ave (32207-8308)
PHONE.....................904 568-1484
Katherine Lee, *Principal*
EMP: 7 **EST:** 2016
SALES (est): 293.7K **Privately Held**
SIC: 2741 Miscellaneous publishing

(G-6571)
U S A COATINGS INC
2361 Edwards Ave (32254-4071)
PHONE.....................904 477-0916
Steven Tyrrel, *Principal*
EMP: 12 **EST:** 2009
SALES (est): 94.3K **Privately Held**
SIC: 3479 Metal coating & allied service

(G-6572)
ULTIMATE CARGO SERVICES LLC
10752 Deerwood Park Blvd (32256-4849)
PHONE.....................954 251-1680
EMP: 13
SALES (est): 2MM **Privately Held**
SIC: 3715 4424 5088 Mfg Truck Trailers
Domestic Sea Freight Transportation
Whol Transportation Equipment

(G-6573)
ULTRATECH INTERNATIONAL INC (PA)
11542 Davis Creek Ct (32256-3003)
PHONE.....................904 292-9019
Mark D Shaw, *CEO*
J Tad Heyman, *President*
Dale Shaw, *Vice Pres*
Sonja Day, *Project Mgr*
Ken Strange, *Purch Agent*
◆ **EMP:** 20 **EST:** 1987
SQ FT: 9,000
SALES (est): 5.7MM **Privately Held**
WEB: www.spillcontainment.com
SIC: 3089 Plastic containers, except foam

(G-6574)
UNDERWOOD BUTCHER BLOCK CO INC
51 Nitram St Ste 500 (32211-7686)
PHONE.....................904 338-2348
Ken O Underwood, *President*
Kristina Underwood, *Vice Pres*
EMP: 10 **EST:** 2012
SALES (est): 909.8K **Privately Held**
WEB: www.underwoodbutcherblock.com
SIC: 2434 2411 Wood kitchen cabinets;
wooden logs

(G-6575)
UNILEVER
12200 Presidents Ct (32220-3220)
PHONE.....................904 378-0298
Diane Angevine, *Business Mgr*
Sara Bertram, *Business Mgr*
Melissa Witsil, *Counsel*
Kevin Bednarz, *Mfg Mgr*
Doug Banes, *Opers Staff*
▼ **EMP:** 20 **EST:** 2013
SALES (est): 11.6MM **Privately Held**
WEB: www.unileverusa.com
SIC: 2844 Toilet preparations

(G-6576)
UNISON INDUSTRIES LLC (DH)
7575 Baymeadows Way (32256-7525)
PHONE.....................904 739-4000
Tom Hoferer, *President*
Andi Bartz, *General Mgr*
Chad Harris, *General Mgr*
Kevin Prindable, *Opers Dir*
Samath Sieng, *Plant Mgr*
EMP: 600 **EST:** 1980
SQ FT: 135,000
SALES (est): 390.9MM
SALES (corp-wide): 74.2B **Publicly Held**
WEB: www.unisonindustries.com
SIC: 3728 Aircraft parts & equipment
HQ: Ge Engine Services, Llc
1 Aviation Way
Cincinnati OH 45215
513 243-2000

(G-6577)
UNITED RAIL INC
13500 Sutton Park Dr S # 601
(32224-5290)
P.O. Box 1162, Ponte Vedra Beach (32004-1162)
PHONE.....................904 503-9757
Norwin K Voegeli, *CEO*
Paul Campbell, *Principal*
Bob Walker, *Vice Pres*
Brad McLelland, *Director*
EMP: 10 **EST:** 2012
SALES (est): 757.1K **Privately Held**
WEB: www.global-ingress.com
SIC: 3669 5051 8711 Railroad signaling
devices, electric; rails & accessories; en-
gineering services

(G-6578)
UNITED STATE POSTAL SERVICE
1815 Silver St (32206-3665)
P.O. Box 40005 (32203-0005)
PHONE.....................904 783-7145
P Dobbins MD, *Principal*
◆ **EMP:** 21 **EST:** 2014
SALES (est): 2.6MM **Privately Held**
SIC: 2542 Mail racks & lock boxes, postal
service: except wood

(G-6579)
UNITED STATES GYPSUM COMPANY
6825 Evergreen Ave (32208-4996)
P.O. Box 9579 (32208-0579)
PHONE.....................904 768-2501
Tony Setera, *Foreman/Supr*
Jim Parnell, *Plant Engr*
Kenneth Jenkins, *Manager*
Darrell Denmark, *Supervisor*
Hugh McMillan, *Supervisor*
EMP: 99
SALES (corp-wide): 12.4B **Privately Held**
WEB: www.usg.com
SIC: 3275 Gypsum products

HQ: United States Gypsum Company
550 W Adams St Ste 1300
Chicago IL 60661
312 606-4000

(G-6580)
UNIVERSAL CNTACT LENSES OF FLA
3840 Williamsburg Pk Blvd (32257-9227)
PHONE.....................904 731-3410
Juanita Padgett, *President*
James F Beeler, *President*
EMP: 7 **EST:** 1982
SQ FT: 2,000
SALES (est): 929.4K **Privately Held**
SIC: 3851 Contact lenses

(G-6581)
UNIVERSAL METAL WORKS INC
14600 Duval Pl W Ste 52 (32218-9418)
PHONE.....................904 765-2600
Larry C Bruce, *President*
Shelia Peters, *Treasurer*
EMP: 7 **EST:** 1993
SQ FT: 22,000
SALES (est): 550K **Privately Held**
WEB: www.comcastbiz.net
SIC: 3443 Fabricated plate work (boiler
shop)

(G-6582)
UP - N - ATOM
3443 Maiden Voyage Cir S (32257-6318)
PHONE.....................904 716-5431
Steven A Kerwick, *Principal*
EMP: 8 **EST:** 2006
SALES (est): 383.2K **Privately Held**
WEB: www.up-n-atom.com
SIC: 3553 Cabinet makers' machinery

(G-6583)
US 1 TRUCK SALES LLC
10126 New Kings Rd (32219-2412)
PHONE.....................904 545-1233
Dagmar K Cvek, *Principal*
Alois Cvek, *Principal*
▼ **EMP:** 7 **EST:** 2011
SALES (est): 223.9K **Privately Held**
WEB: www.us1trucksales.com
SIC: 3596 Truck (motor vehicle) scales

(G-6584)
V-BLOX CORPORATION
Also Called: Florida Power Systems
3653 Regent Blvd Ste 408 (32224-6511)
PHONE.....................904 425-4908
David T Mulvaney, *President*
John Boggs, *Vice Pres*
Scott Hartley, *Vice Pres*
Doug Overvold, *Vice Pres*
Paul Dubriske, *Regl Sales Mgr*
▲ **EMP:** 9 **EST:** 1998
SQ FT: 35,000
SALES (est): 1.8MM **Privately Held**
WEB: www.v-blox.com
SIC: 3679 Electronic crystals

(G-6585)
VALLEY PROTEINS (DE) INC
6142 Old Soutel Ct (32219-3793)
PHONE.....................704 718-6568
EMP: 31
SALES (corp-wide): 473.5MM **Privately Held**
WEB: www.valleyproteins.com
SIC: 2077 Animal & marine fats & oils
PA: Valley Proteins (De), Inc.
151 Valpro Dr
Winchester VA 22603
540 877-2533

(G-6586)
VANITY FAIR BRANDS LP
10300 Southside Blvd (32256-0770)
PHONE.....................904 538-0288
John Turner, *Branch Mgr*
EMP: 28
SALES (corp-wide): 354.6B **Publicly Held**
WEB: www.fotlinc.com
SIC: 2341 Nightgowns & negligees:
women's & children's
HQ: Vanity Fair Brands, Lp
1 Fruit Of The Loom Dr
Bowling Green KY 42103
270 781-6400

(G-6587)
VANITY FURS OF AVONDALE LLC
4555 Saint Johns Ave # 6 (32210-1858)
PHONE.....................904 387-9900
Dawn M Parker, *Principal*
EMP: 8 **EST:** 2010
SALES (est): 339.6K **Privately Held**
SIC: 3999 Furs

(G-6588)
VEGAN SUCKERS LLC ✪
11111 San Jose Blvd Ste 5 (32223-7274)
PHONE.....................904 265-5263
Adrien Ham, *CEO*
EMP: 10 **EST:** 2021
SALES (est): 748.5K **Privately Held**
SIC: 2024 Ice cream & frozen desserts

(G-6589)
VENUS MANUFACTURING CO INC
Also Called: Vm
11711 Marco Beach Dr (32224-7616)
PHONE.....................904 645-3187
Patricia Reifensnyder, *General Mgr*
George Christ Mavrantzas, *Vice Pres*
Kerstin Pittman, *Project Mgr*
Robin Sheffler, *Controller*
Henry Ferris, *Marketing Staff*
EMP: 60 **Privately Held**
WEB: www.venusmanufacturing.com
SIC: 2339 Bathing suits: women's, misses'
& juniors'
PA: Venus Manufacturing Co Inc
349 Lakeview Dr
Dexter NY 13634

(G-6590)
VICTORY VALET SERVICES LLC
5549 Fort Caroline Rd # 107 (32277-1748)
PHONE.....................904 521-6517
Wylie Watkins, *President*
EMP: 10 **EST:** 2017
SALES (est): 409.5K **Privately Held**
SIC: 2842 Sanitation preparations, disin-
fectants & deodorants

(G-6591)
VIDEOLINQ STREAMING SVCS LLC
Also Called: Streaming Store, The
4651 Salisbury Rd (32256-6107)
PHONE.....................904 330-1026
Eyal Menin, *Manager*
EMP: 7 **EST:** 2019
SALES (est): 267.9K **Privately Held**
SIC: 2741

(G-6592)
VISTA PRODUCTS INC (DH)
8801 Corporate Square Ct (32216-1981)
PHONE.....................904 725-2242
Marv Hopkins, *CEO*
Jim Singer, *President*
James E Singer, *President*
Carmen Singer, *Corp Secy*
Ajit Mehra, *Exec VP*
▲ **EMP:** 100 **EST:** 1980
SQ FT: 40,000
SALES (est): 28.6MM **Privately Held**
WEB: www.vistaproducts.com
SIC: 2591 Blinds vertical; mini blinds; win-
dow shades
HQ: Hunter Douglas Inc.
1 Blue Hill Plz Ste 1569
Pearl River NY 10965
845 664-7000

(G-6593)
VISTAKON PHARMACEUTICALS LLC
7500 Centurion Pkwy # 100 (32256-0517)
PHONE.....................904 443-1000
EMP: 5 **EST:** 2004
SALES (est): 4MM
SALES (corp-wide): 93.7B **Publicly Held**
SIC: 2834 Pharmaceutical preparations
HQ: Johnson & Johnson Vision Care, Inc.
7500 Centurion Pkwy
Jacksonville FL 32256
904 443-1000

(G-6594)
VIVID IMAGES USA INC
240 Talleyrand Ave A (32202-1228)
PHONE..................................904 620-0303
Kenneth D Tapper, *President*
Karen Tapper, *Vice Pres*
EMP: 10 EST: 1997
SALES (est): 901.9K Privately Held
WEB: www.vividimagesusa.com
SIC: 2759 3993 2396 2395 Screen printing; signs & advertising specialties; automotive & apparel trimmings; pleating & stitching

(G-6595)
VIZTEK INC
6491 Powers Ave (32217-2821)
PHONE..................................904 448-9936
EMP: 10 EST: 2019
SALES (est): 846.9K Privately Held
SIC: 3841 Surgical & medical instruments

(G-6596)
VOSS BINDERY INC
2565 Philips Hwy (32207-3553)
PHONE..................................904 396-3330
Alan Weaver, *President*
EMP: 9 EST: 2006
SQ FT: 2,970
SALES (est): 174.8K Privately Held
SIC: 2789 Binding only: books, pamphlets, magazines, etc.

(G-6597)
WALKER WOOD PRODUCTS INC
6112 Quattlebaum Rd (32217-2233)
PHONE..................................904 448-5202
John Walker, *President*
EMP: 5 EST: 1986
SQ FT: 4,000
SALES (est): 386.8K Privately Held
SIC: 2434 Wood kitchen cabinets

(G-6598)
WEBCOM GROUP INC (HQ)
5335 Gate Pkwy Ste 200 (32256-3071)
PHONE..................................904 680-6600
David L Brown, *President*
Roseann Duran, *Exec VP*
James Moore, *Senior VP*
Helen Rowan, *Senior VP*
Nicole Cassis, *Vice Pres*
▲ EMP: 250 EST: 1999
SQ FT: 112,306
SALES: 749.2MM Privately Held
WEB: www.web.com
SIC: 7372 7374 Prepackaged software; computer graphics service
PA: Parker Private Holdings Ii, Llc
601 Lexington Ave Fl 59
New York NY 10022
212 231-0095

(G-6599)
WEDDINGS BY TINA
4720 Salisbury Rd (32256-6101)
PHONE..................................904 235-3740
Tina M Payne, *Principal*
EMP: 7 EST: 2008
SALES (est): 430.4K Privately Held
WEB: www.weddingsbytina.com
SIC: 2335 Wedding gowns & dresses

(G-6600)
WELLS LEGAL SUPPLY INC
Also Called: Wells & Drew Companies, The
3414 Galilee Rd (32207-4718)
P.O. Box 10554 (32247-0554)
PHONE..................................904 399-1510
Steven R Houser, *President*
Linda Wells Houser, *Corp Secy*
Robyn Rossi, *Cust Mgr*
Roger Davis, *Accounts Exec*
Robyn Owens, *Manager*
EMP: 37 EST: 1982
SQ FT: 12,000
SALES (est): 5.6MM Privately Held
WEB: www.wellsdrew.com
SIC: 2754 2752 5943 Seals: gravure printing; commercial printing, offset; office forms & supplies

(G-6601)
WEST FRASER INC
109 Halsema Rd S (32220-1657)
PHONE..................................904 786-4155
Allan Stearns, *Project Mgr*
Brenda Kersey, *Human Res Mgr*
Hardy Maloch, *Branch Mgr*
EMP: 162
SALES (corp-wide): 10.5B Privately Held
SIC: 2421 2426 2411 Sawmills & planing mills, general; hardwood dimension & flooring mills; logging
HQ: West Fraser, Inc.
1900 Exeter Rd Ste 105
Germantown TN 38138
901 620-4200

(G-6602)
WEST TEXAS PROTEIN INC
601 Riverside Ave (32204-2946)
PHONE..................................806 250-5959
Gary Norcross, *CEO*
Charles Toledo, *President*
Manuel Toledo, *General Mgr*
James Woody, *CFO*
EMP: 10 EST: 2009
SQ FT: 125,000
SALES (est): 784.9K Privately Held
SIC: 3999 4222 7389 8999 Pet supplies; warehousing, cold storage or refrigerated; ; scientific consulting; banking school, training

(G-6603)
WESTERN MICROSYSTEMS INC (PA)
Also Called: Desert Micro
4230 Pablo Pro Ct Ste 200 (32224-3223)
PHONE..................................800 547-7082
Barry J Grahek, *President*
Evan Schwartz, *CTO*
EMP: 20 EST: 1988
SALES (est): 2.5MM Privately Held
SIC: 3577 7371 7372 Computer peripheral equipment; custom computer programming services; prepackaged software

(G-6604)
WESTROCK CP LLC
2002 E 18th St (32206-3419)
PHONE..................................904 356-5611
Fax: 904 798-0238
EMP: 112
SALES (corp-wide): 14.1B Publicly Held
SIC: 2653 Corrugated Container Plant
HQ: Westrock Cp, Llc
504 Thrasher St
Norcross GA 30328

(G-6605)
WESTROCK CP LLC
9469 Eastport Rd (32218-2261)
P.O. Box 26998 (32226-6998)
PHONE..................................904 714-7151
Del Brooks, *Manager*
EMP: 200
SALES (corp-wide): 18.7B Publicly Held
WEB: www.westrock.com
SIC: 2631 Container board; boxboard
HQ: Westrock Cp, Llc
1000 Abernathy Rd Ste 125
Atlanta GA 30328

(G-6606)
WESTROCK RKT LLC
1660 Prudential Dr # 202 (32207-8197)
P.O. Box 100084, Duluth GA (30096-9373)
PHONE..................................904 714-1643
Art Renfro, *Controller*
Paul Powers, *Maintence Staff*
Roy Hughes, *Master*
EMP: 161
SALES (corp-wide): 18.7B Publicly Held
WEB: www.westrock.com
SIC: 2653 Boxes, corrugated: made from purchased materials
HQ: Westrock Rkt, Llc
1000 Abernathy Rd Ste 125
Atlanta GA 30328
770 448-2193

(G-6607)
WHATS WRONG PUBLISHING CO
2641 Park St (32204-4519)
PHONE..................................904 388-3494
John V Rossi, *Principal*
EMP: 7 EST: 2008
SALES (est): 56K Privately Held
SIC: 2741 Miscellaneous publishing

(G-6608)
WHERTEC INC (DH)
Also Called: Boiler Inspection Services
5409 Highway Ave (32254-3636)
PHONE..................................904 278-6503
Pete Castiglione, *President*
Ed Lloyd, *General Mgr*
Mark Smith, *Vice Pres*
Edward Lloyd, *Opers Mgr*
William Nixon, *Opers Mgr*
▼ EMP: 36 EST: 1996
SQ FT: 2,700
SALES (est): 25.4MM
SALES (corp-wide): 308.7MM Privately Held
WEB: www.castolin.com
SIC: 3398 Metal heat treating
HQ: Eutectic Corporation
N94w14355 Garwin Mace Dr
Menomonee Falls WI 53051
262 532-4677

(G-6609)
WHERTEC TECHNOLOGIES INC
5409 Highway Ave (32254-3636)
PHONE..................................866 207-6503
EMP: 5
SALES (est): 494.1K Privately Held
SIC: 3822 Mfg Environmental Controls

(G-6610)
WHITE PUBLISHING CO INC
Also Called: Jacksonville Magazine
1531 Osceola St (32204-4305)
PHONE..................................904 389-3622
James L White III, *President*
Amy Robertson, *Publisher*
Debbie Fewell, *Principal*
Vanessa Raola, *Accounts Exec*
Mandy Niesen, *Advt Staff*
EMP: 13 EST: 1985
SALES (est): 1.6MM Privately Held
SIC: 2721 5812 Magazines: publishing only, not printed on site; eating places

(G-6611)
WILKINSON STEEL SUPPLY LLC
3210 Faye Rd (32226-2383)
PHONE..................................904 757-1522
Mike Zipp, *Sales Staff*
Charles H Denny IV, *Mng Member*
Rhonda Dunn, *Mng Member*
Dan Dunn,
EMP: 8 EST: 2009
SALES (est): 2.1MM Privately Held
WEB: www.wilkinsonsteelsupply.com
SIC: 3441 Fabricated structural metal

(G-6612)
WILLIAM MARIE LLC
Also Called: Gifting Goodies
8271 Haverhill St (32211-5173)
PHONE..................................904 536-9542
Ann Ruble, *Mng Member*
EMP: 7 EST: 2016
SALES (est): 663.8K Privately Held
SIC: 3537 Trucks, tractors, loaders, carriers & similar equipment

(G-6613)
WILLIAMS INDUSTRIAL SVCS LLC
11380 Island Dr 1 (32226-4484)
PHONE..................................904 696-9994
Herb Deaton, *Regional Mgr*
Megan Horgan, *Counsel*
Loren Monty, *Vice Pres*
Jeremy Williams, *Project Dir*
Alvin Young, *Project Mgr*
EMP: 124

SALES (corp-wide): 304.9MM Publicly Held
WEB: live-us-wisg.pantheonsite.io
SIC: 1389 Construction, repair & dismantling services
HQ: Williams Industrial Services, Llc
200 Ashford Ctr N
Atlanta GA 30338
770 879-4165

(G-6614)
WINGARD LLC
Also Called: Printing.com 5point
76 S Laura St Ste 1501 (32202-3420)
PHONE..................................904 387-2570
EMP: 13
SALES (est): 1.8MM Privately Held
SIC: 2759 8742 Commercial Printing Management Consulting Services

(G-6615)
WIRE MESH CORP
4034 Faye Rd (32226-2347)
PHONE..................................706 922-5179
Luis Barrenechea, *CEO*
Hector Lopez, *Plant Mgr*
Joaquin Hernandez, *Opers Staff*
Jose Aguirre, *Credit Staff*
Rusty Smith, *Regl Sales Mgr*
EMP: 19 EST: 2002
SALES (est): 10.6MM
SALES (corp-wide): 201.4MM Privately Held
WEB: www.wmc-us.com
SIC: 3496 Wire winding
HQ: Wmc Holdings, Lp
25219 Kuykendahl Rd Ste 2
The Woodlands TX 77375
904 751-4301

(G-6616)
WJS PRINTING PARTNERS INC
Also Called: Complete Printing Solutions
2750 Dawn Rd (32207-7904)
PHONE..................................904 731-0357
William S Edenfield, *Principal*
EMP: 7 EST: 2014
SALES (est): 240K Privately Held
WEB: www.completeprintingsolutionsjax.com
SIC: 2752 Commercial printing, offset

(G-6617)
WONDERLAND PRODUCTS INC
5772 Lenox Ave (32205-6374)
P.O. Box 6074 (32236-6074)
PHONE..................................904 786-0144
Robert L Ponsler Jr. *President*
James A Ponsler, *Vice Pres*
Joseph Ponsler, *Vice Pres*
Robert Ponsler III, *Vice Pres*
EMP: 7 EST: 1950
SQ FT: 5,000
SALES (est): 674.6K Privately Held
WEB: www.wonderlandproducts.com
SIC: 3446 Ornamental metalwork

(G-6618)
WOODWORKS CABINETRY INC
4541 Saint Augustine Rd (32207-9524)
PHONE..................................904 924-5300
Arron Ramroop, *Principal*
EMP: 7 EST: 2014
SALES (est): 258.9K Privately Held
WEB: www.woodworksjax.com
SIC: 2434 Wood kitchen cabinets

(G-6619)
WORKING DRONES INC
Also Called: Apellix
2180 Emerson St (32207-5544)
PHONE..................................904 647-4511
Robert Dahlstrom, *CEO*
Jeff McCutcheon, *CFO*
◆ EMP: 9 EST: 2017
SALES (est): 1.5MM Privately Held
WEB: www.apellix.com
SIC: 3728 Target drones

(G-6620)
WWF OPERATING COMPANY LLC
Also Called: Whitewave Foods
2198 W Beaver St (32209-7405)
P.O. Box 2768 (32203-2768)
PHONE..................................904 354-0406

Bobby Hayden, *Controller*
Nick Dobransky, *Manager*
Erquail Collier, *CIO*
Sidney Rath, *Technician*
James Janssen,
EMP: 79
SALES (corp-wide): 718.6MM **Privately Held**
SIC: 2026 Milk processing (pasteurizing, homogenizing, bottling)
HQ: Wwf Operating Company, Llc
12002 Airport Way
Broomfield CO 80021

(G-6621)
WYLA INC (PA)
Also Called: Wyla Laces
6920 Phillips Ind Blvd (32256-3007)
P.O. Box 600549 (32260-0549)
PHONE..................904 886-4338
Joseph D Wiener, *President*
John G Benis, *Corp Secy*
Charlene C Wilkins, *Vice Pres*
Charlene Wilkins, *Vice Pres*
Emilie Ibanez, *Admin Asst*
▲ **EMP:** 17 **EST:** 1971
SQ FT: 40,000
SALES (est): 2.3MM **Privately Held**
WEB: www.wyla.com
SIC: 2258 Lace & lace products

(G-6622)
YOUR ID GUARD
4811 Beach Blvd Ste 433 (32207-4825)
PHONE..................904 354-8989
Laurence F Lee III, *Principal*
Anne Teel, *Accounts Mgr*
Keith Hayes, *Manager*
EMP: 9 **EST:** 2008
SALES (est): 270.5K **Privately Held**
WEB: www.yigadmin.com
SIC: 3089 Identification cards, plastic

(G-6623)
ZIMMER BIOMET CMF THORACIC LLC
Also Called: Biomet Microfixation, LLC
1520 Tradeport Dr (32218-2480)
P.O. Box 708, Warsaw IN (46581-0708)
PHONE..................574 267-6639
Adam Johnson, *President*
David Joseph, *President*
Brian Hatcher, *General Mgr*
Gary Blackall, *Vice Pres*
Aure Bruneau, *Vice Pres*
EMP: 235 **EST:** 1991
SQ FT: 82,000
SALES (est): 57.2MM
SALES (corp-wide): 7.8B **Publicly Held**
WEB: www.zimmerbiomet.com
SIC: 3841 5047 Surgical instruments & apparatus; surgical equipment & supplies
HQ: Biomet, Inc.
345 E Main St
Warsaw IN 46580
574 267-6639

Jacksonville
St. Johns County

(G-6624)
ABC BOOK PUBLISHERS INC
4940 Blackhawk Dr (32259-2170)
PHONE..................904 230-0737
Kimberly S Benton, *Principal*
EMP: 7 **EST:** 2010
SALES (est): 70.5K **Privately Held**
WEB: www.abcbookpublishers.com
SIC: 2741 Miscellaneous publishing

(G-6625)
GRAY SEISMIC MONITORING LLC
Also Called: GSM
2220 County Road 210 W # 10 (32259-4058)
PHONE..................904 728-3299
Adam Gray,
EMP: 10 **EST:** 2010
SALES (est): 568.1K **Privately Held**
SIC: 3829 Measuring & controlling devices

(G-6626)
MTG DESIGNS INC
Also Called: Howard & Mary Glavin
1249 Cunningham Creek Dr (32259-8963)
PHONE..................904 923-1620
Mary Glavin, *President*
EMP: 7 **EST:** 1991
SALES (est): 192.7K **Privately Held**
SIC: 3231 Stained glass: made from purchased glass

Jacksonville Beach
Duval County

(G-6627)
ADVANCED SOFTWARE INC
1902 2nd Ave N (32250-2734)
PHONE..................215 369-7800
Joseph Hentz, *President*
Julie Hentz, *Treasurer*
Paul Evenson, *Director*
John Loeb, *Administration*
EMP: 18 **EST:** 1991
SALES (est): 1MM **Privately Held**
WEB: www.advancedcpc.com
SIC: 7372 5734 5045 Business oriented computer software; computer software & accessories; computers

(G-6628)
AMXS CORP
524 Patricia Ln (32250-4760)
PHONE..................904 568-1416
Kenneth Mangione, *Exec Dir*
EMP: 21 **EST:** 2020
SALES (est): 1MM **Privately Held**
SIC: 3721 Aircraft

(G-6629)
APEX METAL FABRICATION INC
4204 Duval Dr (32250-5816)
P.O. Box 1421, Palatka (32178-1421)
PHONE..................386 328-2564
Keven Walker, *President*
Walter Walker, *President*
Donald Walker, *Chairman*
EMP: 12 **EST:** 1980
SALES (est): 2.9MM **Privately Held**
WEB: www.apexmetalfabrication.com
SIC: 3441 Building components, structural steel

(G-6630)
BENCHMARK DESIGN GROUP INC (PA)
Also Called: Benchmark Contract Furniture
456 Osceola Ave (32250-4078)
PHONE..................904 246-5060
Mark Carroll, *President*
Melissa A Compton, *Principal*
Homer Edmonson, *Vice Pres*
Paul H Haser, *Vice Pres*
Paul Haser, *Vice Pres*
▲ **EMP:** 19 **EST:** 1996
SALES (est): 5.2MM **Privately Held**
WEB:
www.benchmarkcontractfurniture.com
SIC: 2531 Public building & related furniture

(G-6631)
CLASSIC IRON DECOR INC
1004 10th Ave S (32250-3306)
PHONE..................904 241-5022
Slade Richardson, *President*
EMP: 10 **EST:** 1994
SQ FT: 10,000
SALES (est): 1.5MM **Privately Held**
WEB: www.classicirondecor.com
SIC: 3446 Architectural metalwork

(G-6632)
CUPCAKE GIRLS DESSERT COMPANY
1516 3rd St N (32250-7352)
PHONE..................904 372-4579
Behrouz Y Arabi, *Principal*
EMP: 8 **EST:** 2009
SALES (est): 469.7K **Privately Held**
WEB: www.cupcakegirlsdessert.com
SIC: 2051 Cakes, bakery: except frozen

(G-6633)
GORUCK LLC (HQ)
415 Pablo Ave Ste 140 (32250-5530)
PHONE..................904 708-2081
Christian Sbailo, *Opers Mgr*
Michael Vaulx, *Opers Staff*
Dakota Habel, *Asst Controller*
Jason McCarthy, *Mng Member*
Kendra Mills, *Manager*
▲ **EMP:** 1 **EST:** 2008
SQ FT: 3,000
SALES (est): 9.4MM **Privately Held**
WEB: www.goruck.com
SIC: 2389 Costumes
PA: Goruck Holdings, Llc
415 Pablo Ave Ste 140
Jacksonville Beach FL 32250
904 708-2081

(G-6634)
GORUCK HOLDINGS LLC (PA)
415 Pablo Ave Ste 140 (32250-5530)
PHONE..................904 708-2081
Jason J McCarthy, *Principal*
Robert Lovely, *Controller*
Kurt Smith, *CTO*
EMP: 8 **EST:** 2011
SALES (est): 9.4MM **Privately Held**
WEB: www.goruck.com
SIC: 2389 Costumes

(G-6635)
GSW STUCCO LLC
827 20th St N (32250-2786)
PHONE..................904 246-0783
Grant Wilson, *Principal*
EMP: 7 **EST:** 2008
SALES (est): 11.6K **Privately Held**
SIC: 3299 Stucco

(G-6636)
JD PAVERS INC
1304 8th St N (32250-4739)
PHONE..................904 245-9183
Joshua Dubberly, *Principal*
EMP: 8 **EST:** 2012
SALES (est): 202.7K **Privately Held**
WEB: www.jdpaversjax.com
SIC: 2951 Asphalt paving mixtures & blocks

(G-6637)
LEE PRINTING INC (PA)
2653 Isabella Blvd Unit 4 (32250-3841)
PHONE..................904 396-5715
Darral Lee, *President*
Andrew Lee, *Vice Pres*
Donald Lee, *Treasurer*
Brad Robinson, *Manager*
June Lee, *Admin Sec*
EMP: 12 **EST:** 1964
SQ FT: 38,000
SALES (est): 2.5MM **Privately Held**
WEB: www.perfectdomain.com
SIC: 2752 Commercial printing, offset

(G-6638)
LEVITECH SERVICES LLC
Also Called: Onnow.fm
112 5th Ave S Apt 301 (32250-6795)
PHONE..................904 576-0562
John Fasciana,
EMP: 10 **EST:** 2020
SALES (est): 275.3K **Privately Held**
WEB: www.levitechservices.com
SIC: 7372 7379 Business oriented computer software; computer related consulting services

(G-6639)
MOFFITT CORPORATION INC (PA)
1351 13th Ave S Ste 130 (32250-3237)
PHONE..................904 241-9944
John D Moffitt, *President*
Larry Thompson, *Superintendent*
Kimberly Dove, *Vice Pres*
Taylor Harrington, *Project Mgr*
Jeremy Slater, *Project Mgr*
EMP: 13 **EST:** 1961
SQ FT: 7,000
SALES (est): 11MM **Privately Held**
WEB: www.moffittcorp.com
SIC: 3564 Blowers & fans

(G-6640)
MOFFITT FAN CORPORATION
1351 13th Ave S Ste 130 (32250-3237)
PHONE..................585 768-7010
John Moffitt, *Ch of Bd*
Terence R Wirth II, *President*
EMP: 17 **EST:** 1993
SALES (est): 1.6MM **Privately Held**
WEB: www.moffittcorp.com
SIC: 3564 Blowers & fans

(G-6641)
OCEAN WAVES INC
525 3rd St N Ste 105 (32250-7042)
PHONE..................904 372-4743
Kevin Carlson, *President*
Kelly Carlson, *General Mgr*
Dale Moore, *Accounts Mgr*
Brad Corwin, *Admin Sec*
EMP: 19 **EST:** 1980
SQ FT: 6,400
SALES (est): 1.5MM **Privately Held**
WEB: www.oceanwaves.com
SIC: 3851 2339 Glasses, sun or glare; women's & misses' outerwear

(G-6642)
R S S PARTNERS INC
1301 1st St S Apt 1501 (32250-6434)
PHONE..................904 241-6144
Edward A Oertli, *President*
Denise Oertli, *Treasurer*
▲ **EMP:** 10 **EST:** 2000
SALES (est): 305.5K **Privately Held**
SIC: 3578 3824 7389 Calculating & accounting equipment; tally counters; business services

(G-6643)
REEF PAVERS INC
604 Barbara Ln (32250-4758)
PHONE..................904 471-0859
Charles S Jones III, *Principal*
EMP: 5 **EST:** 2011
SALES (est): 493.4K **Privately Held**
WEB: www.reefpavers.com
SIC: 3531 Pavers

(G-6644)
SALT LIFE LLC
240 3rd St S (32250-6717)
PHONE..................904 595-5370
Edward Steelmon, *Vice Pres*
Kristin Chase, *Store Mgr*
Parker Hussong, *Store Mgr*
Iris Davis, *Purchasing*
Diana Rumsey, *Sales Associate*
EMP: 9
SALES (corp-wide): 436.7MM **Publicly Held**
WEB: www.saltlife.com
SIC: 3949 2353 2339 5091 Sporting & athletic goods; hats, caps & millinery; women's & misses' outerwear; sporting & recreation goods
HQ: Salt Life, Llc
24 12th St
Columbus GA 31901

Jasper
Hamilton County

(G-6645)
ASCENT PRECISION GEAR CORP
12180 Se County Road 137 (32052-3803)
PHONE..................386 792-3215
Debbie Murray, *President*
Chuck Murray, *Vice Pres*
EMP: 6 **EST:** 1998
SQ FT: 4,000
SALES (est): 501.2K **Privately Held**
WEB: www.ascentgear.com
SIC: 3599 Machine shop, jobbing & repair

(G-6646)
PACKAGING CORPORATION AMERICA
Also Called: Pca/Valdosta 645a
5939 Se Us Highway 41 (32052-3816)
P.O. Box 248 (32052-0248)
PHONE..................386 792-0810
David Allie, *Accounts Exec*

David George, *Manager*
Greg Nolan, *Supervisor*
EMP: 8
SALES (corp-wide): 7.7B **Publicly Held**
WEB: www.packagingcorp.com
SIC: 2653 Boxes, corrugated: made from purchased materials
PA: Packaging Corporation Of America
1 N Field Ct
Lake Forest IL 60045
847 482-3000

Jay
Santa Rosa County

(G-6647)
AIRPLANE SERVICES INC
1817 Mineral Springs Rd (32565-9571)
PHONE....................850 675-1252
Ellis Stuart, *President*
▼ **EMP:** 5 **EST:** 1982
SALES (est): 350K **Privately Held**
SIC: 3728 Aircraft assemblies, subassemblies & parts

(G-6648)
BAXLEY SERVICES INC
13451 Highway 89 (32565-9131)
P.O. Box 828 (32565-0828)
PHONE....................850 675-4459
Larry Baxley, *President*
Joyce Baxley, *Vice Pres*
EMP: 5 **EST:** 1972
SQ FT: 2,000
SALES (est): 894.4K **Privately Held**
SIC: 7692 Welding repair

(G-6649)
BREITBURN OPERATING LP
5415 Oil Plant Rd (32565-1683)
PHONE....................850 675-1704
Halbert S Washburn, *CEO*
EMP: 177 **EST:** 2006
SALES (est): 4.2MM
SALES (corp-wide): 295.4MM **Privately Held**
SIC: 1311 Crude petroleum & natural gas production
PA: Maverick Natural Resources, Llc
1111 Bagby St Ste 1600
Houston TX 77002
713 437-8000

Jennings
Hamilton County

(G-6650)
FKA RACING INC
Also Called: Sims Promotions
3994 Nw 36th Loop (32053-2670)
PHONE....................386 938-4211
Jimmy Sims, *President*
Judy Sims, *Vice Pres*
▲ **EMP:** 9 **EST:** 1982
SQ FT: 5,000
SALES (est): 725.3K **Privately Held**
SIC: 3519 Gasoline engines

Jensen Beach
Martin County

(G-6651)
AMERICAN RECYCLING SYSTEMS INC
1125 Ne Savannah Oaks Way (34957-3737)
PHONE....................772 225-8072
EMP: 8
SQ FT: 3,000
SALES (est): 520K **Privately Held**
SIC: 3569 Mfg General Industrial Machinery

(G-6652)
AQUATIC TECHNOLOGIES INC
1820 Ne Jensen Beach Blvd (34957-7212)
PHONE....................772 225-4389
Dennis Hardy, *President*
Sean Hardy, *Vice Pres*

EMP: 13 **EST:** 1996
SALES (est): 947.1K **Privately Held**
SIC: 2851 Epoxy coatings

(G-6653)
DUCK IN TRUCK PUPPETS INC
1649 Ne Sunview Ter (34957-3908)
PHONE....................772 334-3022
David Opasik, *President*
EMP: 7 **EST:** 1997
SALES (est): 350.2K **Privately Held**
SIC: 3999 Puppets & marionettes

(G-6654)
ENVIRO PETROLEUM INC
10072 S Ocean Dr Apt 7n (34957-2556)
PHONE....................713 896-6996
Roger Sahni, *President*
▲ **EMP:** 9 **EST:** 1995
SALES (est): 202.3K **Privately Held**
SIC: 3533 5172 Oil & gas field machinery; petroleum products

(G-6655)
HAMILTON PRINTING INC
779 Ne Dixie Hwy (34957-6176)
P.O. Box 376 (34958-0376)
PHONE....................772 334-0151
Leonard A Hamilton, *President*
Vince Hamilton, *Vice Pres*
Tiffany Linch, *Vice Pres*
Nancy Hamilton, *Treasurer*
EMP: 5 **EST:** 1985
SQ FT: 1,700
SALES (est): 420.9K **Privately Held**
SIC: 2752 Commercial printing, offset

(G-6656)
MANUCCI WINERY INC
Also Called: Wild Coyote Winery
4060 Ne Breakwater Dr (34957-4233)
PHONE....................805 239-4770
Gianni Manucci, *President*
EMP: 7 **EST:** 2000
SALES (est): 656.1K **Privately Held**
WEB: www.manucciwinery.com
SIC: 2084 7011 Wines; bed & breakfast inn

(G-6657)
MORNING STAR INDUSTRIES INC
630 Ne Jensen Beach Blvd (34957-4750)
P.O. Box 1266 (34958-1266)
PHONE....................800 440-6050
Kathleen Peruski, *President*
Steven J Peruski, *Vice Pres*
Kelly A Brill, *Treasurer*
Casey J Peruski, *Admin Sec*
EMP: 25 **EST:** 1996
SQ FT: 120,000
SALES (est): 5.2MM **Privately Held**
WEB: www.morningstarusa.com
SIC: 3646 5169 5063 Commercial indusl & institutional electric lighting fixtures; industrial chemicals; electrical apparatus & equipment

(G-6658)
ONAN GENERATORS & ENGINES
883 Ne Dixie Hwy (34957-6187)
PHONE....................772 334-8282
George Dietz, *Owner*
EMP: 5 **EST:** 2005
SALES (est): 362.2K **Privately Held**
SIC: 3569 Generators: steam, liquid oxygen or nitrogen

(G-6659)
WILL SHUTTER U INC
2087 Nw Marsh Rabbit Ln (34957-3524)
PHONE....................772 285-3600
Cameron Corn, *Principal*
EMP: 7 **EST:** 2005
SALES (est): 86K **Privately Held**
SIC: 3442 Shutters, door or window: metal

Juno Beach
Palm Beach County

(G-6660)
BLUE SUMMIT WIND LLC (DH)
700 Universe Blvd (33408-2657)
PHONE....................561 691-7171
Tj Tuscai, *Principal*
▲ **EMP:** 2 **EST:** 2012
SALES (est): 11.8MM
SALES (corp-wide): 17B **Publicly Held**
SIC: 3621 6719 Windmills, electric generating; investment holding companies, except banks
HQ: Esi Energy, Llc
700 Universe Blvd
Juno Beach FL 33408
561 691-7171

(G-6661)
BRU BOTTLING INC
1507 Villa Juno Dr N (33408-2258)
PHONE....................561 324-5053
Gerard George, *Principal*
EMP: 10 **EST:** 2016
SALES (est): 296.1K **Privately Held**
SIC: 2037 Fruit juices

(G-6662)
CLEAN CUT INTL LLC
14255 Us Highway 1 (33408-1490)
PHONE....................866 599-7066
Winfield S Anderson Jr, *Mng Member*
Sharon Haas, *Manager*
Tom Little,
▲ **EMP:** 10 **EST:** 2009
SQ FT: 1,000
SALES (est): 1.3MM **Privately Held**
SIC: 3634 3639 Electric housewares & fans; major kitchen appliances, except refrigerators & stoves

(G-6663)
EIQ MOBILITY INC
700 Universe Blvd (33408-2657)
PHONE....................561 691-7171
John Ketchum, *CEO*
EMP: 9 **EST:** 2018
SALES: 283.6K
SALES (corp-wide): 17B **Publicly Held**
WEB: www.eiqmobility.com
SIC: 2451 Mobile homes
HQ: Nextera Energy Resources, Llc
700 Universe Blvd
Juno Beach FL 33408
561 691-7171

(G-6664)
GEXA ENERGY CALIFORNIA LLC
700 Universe Blvd (33408-2657)
PHONE....................561 691-7171
James Keener, *Vice Pres*
EMP: 1 **EST:** 2010
SALES (est): 3.1MM
SALES (corp-wide): 17B **Publicly Held**
SIC: 1389 Gas field services
HQ: Nextera Energy Services, Llc
13 Executive Park Dr
Halfmoon NY 12065

(G-6665)
NEXTERA FIBERNET LLC
700 Universe Blvd (33408-2657)
PHONE....................866 787-2637
Carmen Perez, *President*
EMP: 561 **EST:** 2010
SALES (est): 4.7MM
SALES (corp-wide): 17B **Publicly Held**
SIC: 3661 Fiber optics communications equipment
HQ: Nextera Energy Capital Holdings, Inc.
700 Universe Blvd
Juno Beach FL 33408
561 691-7171

(G-6666)
PHEASANT RUN WIND LLC
700 Universe Blvd (33408-2657)
PHONE....................561 691-7171
John W Ketchum, *Principal*
EMP: 1 **EST:** 2013

SALES (est): 5.3MM
SALES (corp-wide): 17B **Publicly Held**
SIC: 3621 Windmills, electric generating
HQ: Pheasant Run Wind Holdings, Llc
700 Universe Blvd
Juno Beach FL 33408
561 691-7171

(G-6667)
TBC RETAIL GROUP INC
Also Called: Big O Tires
823 Donald Ross Rd (33408-1605)
PHONE....................702 395-2100
EMP: 8
SALES (corp-wide): 35.1B **Privately Held**
SIC: 3011 7538 Mfg Tires/Inner Tubes General Auto Repair
HQ: Tbc Retail Group, Inc.
4280 Prof Ctr Dr Ste 400
Palm Beach Gardens FL 33410
561 383-3000

(G-6668)
TUSCOLA WIND II LLC
700 Universe Blvd (33408-2657)
PHONE....................561 691-7171
Tj Tuscai, *Principal*
EMP: 1 **EST:** 2012
SALES (est): 6.3MM
SALES (corp-wide): 17B **Publicly Held**
SIC: 3621 4911 Windmills, electric generating; distribution, electric power
HQ: Esi Energy, Llc
700 Universe Blvd
Juno Beach FL 33408
561 691-7171

(G-6669)
VASCO WINDS LLC
700 Universe Blvd (33408-2657)
PHONE....................561 691-7171
Tj Tuscai, *Principal*
EMP: 1 **EST:** 2011
SALES (est): 4.6MM
SALES (corp-wide): 17B **Publicly Held**
SIC: 3621 4911 Windmills, electric generating; electric services
HQ: Esi Energy, Llc
700 Universe Blvd
Juno Beach FL 33408
561 691-7171

(G-6670)
WHITE OAK ENERGY BACKLEVERAGE (DH)
700 Universe Blvd (33408-2657)
PHONE....................561 691-7171
T J Tuscai, *Mng Member*
EMP: 1 **EST:** 2011
SALES (est): 3.1MM
SALES (corp-wide): 17B **Publicly Held**
SIC: 3621 4911 Windmills, electric generating; electric services
HQ: Esi Energy, Llc
700 Universe Blvd
Juno Beach FL 33408
561 691-7171

(G-6671)
WHITE OAK ENERGY HOLDINGS LLC
700 Universe Blvd (33408-2657)
PHONE....................561 691-7171
T J Tuscai, *President*
Ryan Jones, *Manager*
EMP: 1 **EST:** 2010
SALES (est): 7.6MM
SALES (corp-wide): 17B **Publicly Held**
WEB: www.whiteoakenergy.com
SIC: 3621 Windmills, electric generating
HQ: Esi Energy, Llc
700 Universe Blvd
Juno Beach FL 33408
561 691-7171

(G-6672)
WILTON WIND II LLC
700 Universe Blvd (33408-2657)
PHONE....................561 691-7171
T J Tuscai, *President*
Dean Gosselin, *Vice Pres*
Charles S Schultz, *Admin Sec*
EMP: 1 **EST:** 2008

SALES (est): 5MM
SALES (corp-wide): 17B **Publicly Held**
SIC: 3621 4911 Windmills, electric generating; electric services
HQ: Esi Energy, Llc
 700 Universe Blvd
 Juno Beach FL 33408
 561 691-7171

Jupiter
Palm Beach County

(G-6673)
6 PORTS LLC
Also Called: In-O-Vate Technologies
250 S Central Blvd # 207 (33458-8812)
PHONE............................561 743-8696
James Ortiz, *Vice Pres*
Jackie Lopopolo, *Opers Staff*
Missy Clark, *Cust Mgr*
Richard J Harpenau,
Karen A Harpenau,
◆ EMP: 12 EST: 2019
SQ FT: 1,000
SALES (est): 2.7MM **Privately Held**
WEB: www.dryerbox.com
SIC: 3499 Metal household articles

(G-6674)
A AND J SHEET METAL INC
1567 Cypress Dr (33469-3137)
PHONE............................561 746-4048
Kari E Neville, *CEO*
Suki Atwal, *Vice Pres*
Zenelia Aguilar, *Manager*
EMP: 6 EST: 1997
SQ FT: 5,900
SALES (est): 925.5K **Privately Held**
WEB: www.ajsheetmetals.com
SIC: 3699 1761 1531 Laser welding, drilling & cutting equipment; roofing, siding & sheet metal work;

(G-6675)
A MOBILE TECH LLC
9363 Whippoorwill Trl (33478-6373)
PHONE............................561 631-4563
Michael T Bull, *Manager*
EMP: 7 EST: 2018
SALES (est): 112.6K **Privately Held**
WEB: www.mtechmobility.com
SIC: 3731 Shipbuilding & repairing

(G-6676)
A TEK STEEL INDUSTRIES INC
3 Turtle Creek Dr (33469-1593)
PHONE............................561 745-2858
Bryan McIntyre, *Principal*
EMP: 8 EST: 2004
SALES (est): 212.7K **Privately Held**
SIC: 3479 Metal coating & allied service

(G-6677)
ACUCALL LLC
1475 Park Ln S Ste 5 (33458-8094)
PHONE............................855 799-7905
Rafael Egiazarian, *Chief Engr*
Alec Snow, *Sales Engr*
Kurt Goodridge, *CIO*
Stephen Ward, *Executive*
EMP: 11 EST: 2011
SALES (est): 1.3MM **Privately Held**
WEB: www.acucall.com
SIC: 7372 Application computer software

(G-6678)
AERO-FLEX CORP ✪
3147 Jupiter Park Cir # 2 (33458-6027)
PHONE............................561 745-2534
Joshua Deakter, *Principal*
Brian Uccellini, *Sales Executive*
Eric Hobart, *Program Mgr*
EMP: 20 EST: 2022
SALES (est): 8.4MM **Privately Held**
WEB: www.aero-flex.aero
SIC: 3728 Aircraft parts & equipment

(G-6679)
AEROJET ROCKETDYNE INC
15270 Endeavor Dr (33478-6447)
P.O. Box 109680, Palm Beach Gardens (33410-9680)
PHONE............................561 796-2000
Tyler Evans, *Senior VP*

Greg Jones, *Vice Pres*
Rick Bonek, *Mfg Staff*
Matthew Bullivant, *Engineer*
Louis Chan, *Engineer*
EMP: 400 EST: 2013
SALES (est): 43.1MM **Privately Held**
WEB: www.rocket.com
SIC: 3764 Guided missile & space vehicle propulsion unit parts

(G-6680)
AEROJET ROCKETDYNE DE INC
Pratt & Whitney
17900 Bee Line Hwy (33478-6414)
P.O. Box 109600, West Palm Beach (33410-9600)
PHONE............................561 882-5150
Patricia Mills, *Business Mgr*
Gary Halker, *Project Mgr*
Roger Lawrence, *Senior Buyer*
Brett Austin, *Engineer*
Corey Brown, *Engineer*
EMP: 200
SALES (corp-wide): 2.1B **Publicly Held**
WEB: www.rocket.com
SIC: 2869 3724 Rocket engine fuel, organic; aircraft engines & engine parts
HQ: Inc Aerojet Rocketdyne Of De
 8900 De Soto Ave
 Canoga Park CA 91304
 818 586-1000

(G-6681)
AGPB LLC
Also Called: AlphaGraphics
800 W Indiantown Rd (33458-7501)
PHONE............................561 935-4147
Timothy J Kerbs, *Mng Member*
Jenn Kerbs,
EMP: 12 EST: 2006
SALES (est): 2.9MM **Privately Held**
WEB: www.alphagraphics.com
SIC: 2752 Commercial printing, lithographic

(G-6682)
AGROSOURCE INC
166 Beacon Ln (33469-3504)
P.O. Box 3091, Tequesta (33469-1000)
PHONE............................908 251-3500
Taw Richardson, *President*
Rene Amundson, *Opers Staff*
EMP: 12 EST: 2015
SALES (est): 1.1MM **Privately Held**
SIC: 2879 Insecticides, agricultural or household; pesticides, agricultural or household

(G-6683)
ALLOY CLADDING
15850 Guild Ct (33478-6436)
PHONE............................561 625-4550
Robert Burns, *Principal*
Dewayne Carver, *Vice Pres*
Robert Macdonald, *Vice Pres*
Cecil Feagin, *Supervisor*
EMP: 48 EST: 2008
SALES (est): 5.8MM **Privately Held**
WEB: www.alloycladding.com
SIC: 3842 Welders' hoods

(G-6684)
ANDREW MJ INC
10152 Indiantown Rd (33478-4707)
PHONE............................561 575-6032
Jane Miller, *Principal*
EMP: 8 EST: 2008
SALES (est): 188K **Privately Held**
SIC: 3651 Household audio & video equipment

(G-6685)
ASSOCATE CBINETMAKERS PALM BCH
134 Toney Penna Dr (33458-5751)
PHONE............................561 743-9566
Michael Odell, *President*
EMP: 5 EST: 1992
SQ FT: 1,250
SALES (est): 439.6K **Privately Held**
WEB: www.associatedcabinetspalm-beach.com
SIC: 2434 Wood kitchen cabinets

(G-6686)
AVSTAR FUEL SYSTEMS INC
1365 Park Ln S (33458-8042)
PHONE............................561 575-1560
Ronald Weaver, *President*
Katia Fuentes, *Buyer*
Jacqueline Weaver, *Human Resources*
Stephen Bennett, *Manager*
Eric Weaver, *Director*
EMP: 8 EST: 2007
SALES (est): 2.6MM **Privately Held**
WEB: www.avstardirect.com
SIC: 3724 Aircraft engines & engine parts

(G-6687)
AYLYNN MARITIME LLC (PA)
400 Ocean Trail Way (33477-5523)
PHONE............................954 564-6134
Jerry D Palfenier, *President*
EMP: 5 EST: 2014
SALES (est): 1.9MM **Privately Held**
SIC: 3519 Marine engines

(G-6688)
BARON INTERNATIONAL LLC
Also Called: Baron Sign Manufacturing
17180 Innovation Dr (33478-6445)
PHONE............................800 531-9558
Kimberly G Nemic,
Tom Nemic,
EMP: 11 EST: 2018
SALES (est): 2.5MM **Privately Held**
WEB: www.baronsign.com
SIC: 3993 Signs & advertising specialties

(G-6689)
BEACON PHRM JUPITER LLC
210 Military Trl (33458-5786)
PHONE............................212 991-8988
Philippe Gastone, *CEO*
Nancy Torres Kaufman, *Ch of Bd*
Martin Weisberg,
EMP: 50 EST: 2019
SALES (est): 2.6MM **Privately Held**
SIC: 2834 8731 Pharmaceutical preparations; commercial physical research

(G-6690)
BELL COMPOSITES INC (PA)
23 Oak Ridge Ln (33469-2623)
PHONE............................561 575-9175
Michael Bell, *Owner*
EMP: 7 EST: 2003
SALES (est): 200.2K **Privately Held**
WEB: www.offshorecatamarans.com
SIC: 3732 Boat building & repairing

(G-6691)
BERMAN PRODUCTS LLC
19558 Red Gum Trl (33458-2473)
PHONE............................561 743-5197
Robert S Berman MD,
EMP: 10 EST: 2009
SALES (est): 843.6K **Privately Held**
WEB: www.bermanresearch.org
SIC: 2834 Pharmaceutical preparations

(G-6692)
BEVERLY ACQUISITIONS INC (PA)
Also Called: Schrappers Fine Cabinetry
240 W Indiantown Rd # 101 (33458-3548)
PHONE............................561 746-3827
Beverly Levine, *President*
Keith Levine, *Vice Pres*
Brad Rosenberg, *Prdtn Mgr*
EMP: 11 EST: 1976
SQ FT: 8,000
SALES (est): 3MM **Privately Held**
SIC: 2434 Vanities, bathroom: wood

(G-6693)
BEYONDCLEAN LLC
601 Heritage Dr Ste 422 (33458-2777)
PHONE............................561 799-5710
Helen P Troup, *Mng Member*
Lloyd Hanson, *CTO*
EMP: 10 EST: 2004
SALES (est): 696.7K **Privately Held**
WEB: www.gobeyondclean.com
SIC: 2842 Specialty cleaning preparations

(G-6694)
BIO-REVIVAL LLC
661 Maplewood Dr Ste 21 (33458-5569)
PHONE............................561 667-3990
Liudmila Karimova, *President*
Eugene Richter, *Vice Pres*
EMP: 10 EST: 2015
SQ FT: 1,800
SALES (est): 540K **Privately Held**
WEB: www.bio-revival.com
SIC: 2099 Food preparations

(G-6695)
BIOCHEM MANUFACTURING INC
15074 Pk Of Commerce Blvd (33478-6424)
PHONE............................561 799-1590
Jorge Cepeda, *President*
Nely Cepeda, *Vice Pres*
Violeta Cepeda, *Vice Pres*
▲ EMP: 18 EST: 2012
SALES (est): 983.2K **Privately Held**
SIC: 2879 Agricultural disinfectants

(G-6696)
BIOCHEMICAL MANUFACTURING INC
15074 Pk Of Commerce Blvd (33478-6424)
PHONE............................561 799-1590
George Cepeda, *President*
EMP: 7 EST: 2011
SALES (est): 363.8K **Privately Held**
SIC: 3999 Manufacturing industries

(G-6697)
BLUE HOLE HELICOPTERS INC
3161 Se Chandelle Rd (33478-1909)
PHONE............................561 723-0378
Brian T Parker Sr, *Principal*
EMP: 10 EST: 2007
SALES (est): 121.2K **Privately Held**
SIC: 3721 Helicopters

(G-6698)
BRITE LITE TRIBE
840 Jupiter Park Dr (33458-8947)
PHONE............................561 250-6824
EMP: 7 EST: 2019
SALES (est): 508.3K **Privately Held**
WEB: www.britelitetribe.com
SIC: 3993 Signs & advertising specialties

(G-6699)
CAMCO CORP
1829 Park Ln S Ste 9 (33458-8086)
PHONE............................561 427-0433
Barbara Roginski, *Principal*
EMP: 8 EST: 2004
SALES (est): 168K **Privately Held**
WEB: www.camcohealthcare.com
SIC: 3442 Shutters, door or window: metal

(G-6700)
CARLING TECHNOLOGIES INC
120 Intracoastal Cir # 100 (33469-2709)
PHONE............................561 745-0405
Richard Sorenson, *Principal*
EMP: 30
SALES (corp-wide): 2B **Publicly Held**
WEB: www.carlingtech.com
SIC: 3699 Electrical equipment & supplies
HQ: Carling Technologies, Inc.
 60 Johnson Ave
 Plainville CT 06062
 860 793-9281

(G-6701)
CBD BRANDS INC
725 N Highway A1a C106 (33477-4565)
PHONE............................561 325-0482
EMP: 8
SALES (est): 342.4K **Privately Held**
SIC: 2844 Toilet preparations

(G-6702)
CEMEX CNSTR MTLS FLA LLC
Also Called: Materials Div-Jupiter Lab
1557 Jupiter Park Dr # 1 (33458-8083)
PHONE............................561 745-5240
Mike Epifano, *Branch Mgr*
EMP: 10 **Privately Held**
SIC: 3273 Ready-mixed concrete

HQ: Cemex Construction Materials Florida, Llc
1501 Belvedere Rd
West Palm Beach FL 33406

(G-6703)
CEMEX MATERIALS LLC
282 Old Dixie Hwy (33469-2753)
P.O. Box 3331 (33469-1005)
PHONE...................................561 746-4556
Floyd Gallow, *Branch Mgr*
EMP: 128 **Privately Held**
SIC: 3271 3273 3272 3444 Concrete block & brick; ready-mixed concrete; concrete products; sheet metalwork; cut stone & stone products
HQ: Cemex Materials Llc
1720 Centrepark Dr E # 100
West Palm Beach FL 33401
561 833-5555

(G-6704)
CEMEX MATERIALS LLC
1001 Jupiter Park Dr # 108 (33458-6002)
PHONE...................................561 743-4039
Jesse Deurer, *Branch Mgr*
EMP: 128 **Privately Held**
SIC: 3271 3273 3272 1422 Blocks, concrete or cinder: standard; ready-mixed concrete; concrete products used to facilitate drainage; crushed & broken limestone
HQ: Cemex Materials Llc
1720 Centrepark Dr E # 100
West Palm Beach FL 33401
561 833-5555

(G-6705)
CSA INTERNATIONAL INC
759 Parkway (33477-4505)
PHONE...................................561 746-7946
EMP: 30
SALES (est): 3.2MM **Privately Held**
SIC: 3531 Mfg Construction Machinery

(G-6706)
CSC RACING CORPORATION
Also Called: Rjs Racing Equipment
15819 Guild Ct B (33478-6436)
PHONE...................................248 548-5727
Robert Farmer, *President*
Cheryl Pemberton, *Vice Pres*
▲ **EMP:** 16 **EST:** 1959
SQ FT: 15,000
SALES (est): 1.2MM **Privately Held**
SIC: 2399 2326 Seat belts, automobile & aircraft; men's & boys' work clothing

(G-6707)
CUSTOM CABINET DESIGNS INC
128 Timber Ln (33458-7707)
PHONE...................................561 781-3251
Miahcel Gildemeyer, *Director*
Babette Gildemeyer, *Director*
Elizabeth Hales, *Director*
EMP: 7 **EST:** 2018
SALES (est): 410.8K **Privately Held**
WEB: www.customcabinetdesignsinc.com
SIC: 2434 Wood kitchen cabinets

(G-6708)
CV TECHNOLOGY INC
15852 Mercantile Ct # 100 (33478-6437)
PHONE...................................561 694-9588
David Cvetas, *CEO*
Marty Cvetas, *President*
Bob Cudnik, *Vice Pres*
Jillian Gruss, *Engineer*
Nicholas Kowalewski, *Engineer*
EMP: 36 **EST:** 1994
SQ FT: 29,000
SALES (est): 10.3MM **Privately Held**
WEB: www.cvtechnology.com
SIC: 3823 8748 1731 Infrared instruments, industrial process type; industrial process control instruments; environmental consultant; fire detection & burglar alarm systems specialization

(G-6709)
DB TUCKER LLC
126 S Village Way (33458-7828)
PHONE...................................561 301-4974
Dolores Dioguardi, *President*
EMP: 7 **EST:** 2015

SALES (est): 272.9K **Privately Held**
SIC: 3634 5072 Housewares, excluding cooking appliances & utensils; hand tools

(G-6710)
DL MYERS CORP
5500 Military Trl Ste 22 (33458-2871)
PHONE...................................609 698-8800
Darren L Myers, *President*
EMP: 10 **EST:** 2005
SALES (est): 968.8K **Privately Held**
SIC: 3443 Fuel tanks (oil, gas, etc.): metal plate

(G-6711)
DOLPHIN SHEET METAL INC
142 Jupiter St (33458-4929)
PHONE...................................561 744-0242
Rachelle Wood, *President*
Bradley Wood, *Contractor*
EMP: 19 **EST:** 1987
SQ FT: 3,900
SALES (est): 343.9K **Privately Held**
WEB: www.dolphinsheetmetal.com
SIC: 3444 Awnings, sheet metal

(G-6712)
DONALD ROSS GAS INC
225 Skylark Pt (33458-8307)
PHONE...................................561 776-1324
Jay Goldwasser, *President*
EMP: 11 **EST:** 2005
SALES (est): 328.8K **Privately Held**
SIC: 2911 Gases & liquefied petroleum gases

(G-6713)
DYADIC INTERNATIONAL INC (PA)
140 Intrcostal Pt Dr # 404 (33477-5094)
PHONE...................................561 743-8333
Mark A Emalfarb, *President*
Matthew S Jones, *Managing Dir*
Ronen Tchelet, *Vice Pres*
Ping W Rawson, *CFO*
Joe Hazelton, *Officer*
▲ **EMP:** 5 **EST:** 1979
SQ FT: 2,000
SALES (est): 2.4MM **Publicly Held**
WEB: www.dyadic.com
SIC: 2836 Biological products, except diagnostic

(G-6714)
DYADIC INTERNATIONAL USA INC (HQ)
Also Called: Dyadic Industries Intl
140 Intrcostal Pt Dr # 404 (33477-5094)
PHONE...................................561 743-8333
Harry Rosengart, *Ch of Bd*
David Hooper, *COO*
◆ **EMP:** 5 **EST:** 1979
SALES (est): 592.2K
SALES (corp-wide): 2.4MM **Publicly Held**
WEB: www.dyadic.com
SIC: 2842 2899 5169 5032 Fabric softeners; chemical preparations; industrial chemicals; stone, crushed or broken; cut stone & stone products; brick & structural clay tile
PA: Dyadic International, Inc.
140 Intrcostal Pt Dr # 404
Jupiter FL 33477
561 743-8333

(G-6715)
DYN-O-MAT INC
1201 Jupiter Park Dr # 1 (33458-8140)
PHONE...................................561 747-2301
Mike Yourwicz, *Sales Mgr*
EMP: 7 **EST:** 2017
SALES (est): 46.5K **Privately Held**
SIC: 2273 Carpets & rugs

(G-6716)
DYNOMAT INC
Also Called: Environmental Aborbent Pdts
1201 Jupiter Park Dr (33458-8084)
PHONE...................................561 747-2301
Peter Cordani, *CEO*
Michael Cordani, *COO*
EMP: 35 **EST:** 1994
SQ FT: 1,450
SALES (est): 2MM **Privately Held**
SIC: 2273 Carpets & rugs

(G-6717)
ECOLAB INC
1201 Jupiter Park Dr # 1 (33458-8084)
PHONE...................................800 931-8911
EMP: 15
SALES (corp-wide): 11.7B **Publicly Held**
SIC: 3999 2841 3432 Mfg Misc Products Mfg Soap/Other Detergents Mfg Plumbing Fixture Fittings
PA: Ecolab Inc.
1 Ecolab Pl
Saint Paul MN 55102
800 232-6522

(G-6718)
EDWARD THOMAS COMPANY
Also Called: Smartcolor Graphics
185 E Indiantown Rd # 114 (33477-5071)
PHONE...................................561 746-1441
Tom Beckett, *President*
EMP: 7 **EST:** 1987
SQ FT: 2,700
SALES (est): 869K **Privately Held**
WEB: www.edwardthomasco.com
SIC: 2752 2791 Commercial printing, offset; typesetting

(G-6719)
ELK CREEK WINE
4392 Nicole Cir (33469-2572)
PHONE...................................561 529-2822
Curtis Sigretto, *Principal*
EMP: 7 **EST:** 2013
SALES (est): 209.9K **Privately Held**
WEB: www.elkcreekvineyards.com
SIC: 2084 Wines

(G-6720)
ELLISON GRAPHICS CORP
1400 W Indiantown Rd (33458-7998)
P.O. Box 937 (33468-0937)
PHONE...................................561 746-9256
Nicholas E Litwin, *President*
Robert Herlin, *Vice Pres*
EMP: 14 **EST:** 1972
SQ FT: 21,000
SALES (est): 500.8K **Privately Held**
WEB: www.ellisongraphics.com
SIC: 2752 Commercial printing, offset

(G-6721)
ELLISONS PREMIER MAR SVCS LLC
1508 Cypress Dr (33469-3142)
PHONE...................................561 570-9807
Scott Ellison, *Manager*
EMP: 7 **EST:** 2019
SALES (est): 174.2K **Privately Held**
WEB: www.ellisonspremiermarine.com
SIC: 3731 Shipbuilding & repairing

(G-6722)
ENVOY THERAPEUTICS INC
555 Heritage Dr Ste 150 (33458-5290)
PHONE...................................561 210-7705
EMP: 7 **EST:** 2019
SALES (est): 895.5K **Privately Held**
SIC: 2834 Pharmaceutical preparations

(G-6723)
EXHAUST TECHNOLOGIES INC
851 Jupiter Park Ln (33458-8959)
PHONE...................................561 744-9500
Barton Swank, *President*
Robert E Sterling, *President*
William A Sutherland, *Corp Secy*
▲ **EMP:** 8 **EST:** 1998
SALES (est): 2.4MM
SALES (corp-wide): 53.5MM **Publicly Held**
SIC: 3714 Motor vehicle parts & accessories
HQ: Florida Pneumatic Manufacturing Corporation
851 Jupiter Park Ln Ste A
Jupiter FL 33458
561 744-9500

(G-6724)
EZ NEON INC
12179 179th Ct N (33478-4610)
PHONE...................................561 262-7813
James Mackey, *President*
EMP: 8 **EST:** 2011

SALES (est): 98.6K **Privately Held**
SIC: 2813 Neon

(G-6725)
F L F CORP
810 Saturn St Ste 28 (33477-4456)
PHONE...................................561 747-7077
Richard Reina, *Principal*
EMP: 7 **EST:** 2008
SALES (est): 192.1K **Privately Held**
SIC: 2741 Miscellaneous publishing

(G-6726)
FASHION POOL USA INC
6111 Linton St (33458-6745)
PHONE...................................970 367-4797
Hans Taubenberger, *President*
EMP: 5 **EST:** 2009
SALES (est): 907K
SALES (corp-wide): 2.2MM **Privately Held**
SIC: 2339 2329 5136 5137 Women's & misses' outerwear; men's & boys' leather, wool & down-filled outerwear; men's & boys' outerwear; women's & children's outerwear
PA: Fashion Pool Gmbh Textilagentur & Vertrieb
St.-Ottilien-Weg 11
Grasbrunn BY 85630
810 637-7883

(G-6727)
FASULO GRANITE & MARBLE INC
368 River Edge Rd (33477-9344)
PHONE...................................561 371-5410
Laura Fasulo, *President*
John Fasulo, *Vice Pres*
EMP: 8 **EST:** 2004
SALES (est): 79.7K **Privately Held**
SIC: 3281 Granite, cut & shaped

(G-6728)
FIMCO MANUFACTURING INC
15795 Corporate Rd N (33478-6421)
P.O. Box 300 (33468-0300)
PHONE...................................561 624-3308
Roger D Slagel, *President*
Donna Slagel, *Corp Secy*
Gunther Albert, *Vice Pres*
Janet Albert, *Admin Sec*
EMP: 7 **EST:** 1962
SQ FT: 10,000
SALES (est): 986.4K **Privately Held**
WEB: www.fimcomfg.com
SIC: 3089 Injection molding of plastics

(G-6729)
FINDEXCOM INC (PA)
1097 Jupiter Park Ln (33458-8907)
PHONE...................................561 328-6488
Steven Malone, *CEO*
EMP: 5 **EST:** 1999
SQ FT: 8,560
SALES: 334.3K **Publicly Held**
WEB: www.findex.com
SIC: 2851 Lacquers, varnishes, enamels & other coatings; removers & cleaners

(G-6730)
FIRST CLASS MEDIA INC
1003 Jupiter Park Ln # 5 (33458-8909)
PHONE...................................561 719-3433
Daniel Moody, *Principal*
EMP: 6 **EST:** 2007
SALES (est): 341.5K **Privately Held**
SIC: 2711 Newspapers

(G-6731)
FLORIDA EMBROIDERED PATCH &
1095 Jupiter Park Dr # 8 (33458-8972)
PHONE...................................561 748-9356
▲ **EMP:** 18
SALES (est): 891.3K **Privately Held**
SIC: 2395 Pleating/Stitching Services

(G-6732)
FLORIDA TURBINE TECH INC (HQ)
1701 Military Trl Ste 110 (33458-6331)
PHONE...................................561 427-6400
Shirley Brostmeyer, *President*
Dean Johnson, *Dean*

Jesse Eng, *Chief Engr*
Dan Davies, *Engineer*
Bob Felker, *Engineer*
EMP: 5 **EST:** 1998
SQ FT: 63,000
SALES (est): 48.4MM **Publicly Held**
WEB: www.kratosdefense.com
SIC: 3724 8711 Aircraft engines & engine parts; consulting engineer

(G-6733)
GDP CONSULTING INC (PA)
15074 Park Of Commerce Bl (33478-6426)
PHONE...................................561 401-9195
Gina Hartley, *President*
◆ **EMP:** 5 **EST:** 2013
SALES (est): 535.9K **Privately Held**
WEB: brandedproducts.espwebsite.com
SIC: 2759 7389 7319 5199 Promotional printing; laser printing; advertising, promotional & trade show services; distribution of advertising material or sample services; advertising specialties

(G-6734)
GE MEDCAL SYSTEMS INFO TECH IN
100 Marquette Dr (33458-7101)
PHONE...................................561 575-5000
Jerry Lentz, *General Mgr*
Doug Van Epps, *Research*
EMP: 52
SALES (corp-wide): 74.2B **Publicly Held**
SIC: 3845 8744 7629 Patient monitoring apparatus; facilities support services; electrical repair shops
HQ: Ge Medical Systems Information Technologies, Inc.
9900 W Innovation Dr
Wauwatosa WI 53226
262 544-3011

(G-6735)
GELTECH SOLUTIONS INC
1460 Park Ln S Ste 1 (33458-8079)
PHONE...................................561 427-6144
Michael Reger, *Ch of Bd*
Gerry Kaiser, *Vice Pres*
Matthew Struzziero, *Vice Pres*
Michael Hull, *CFO*
Matt Struzziero, *Sales Staff*
EMP: 20 **EST:** 2006
SALES (est): 4.5MM **Privately Held**
WEB: www.geltechsolutions.com
SIC: 2899 Fire retardant chemicals

(G-6736)
GLOBAL PHARMA ANALYTICS LLC
225 Chimney Corner Ln # 30 (33458-4803)
PHONE...................................701 491-7770
Theresa Crawford, *Controller*
S Chandrasekhar,
EMP: 9 **EST:** 2013
SALES (est): 476.9K **Privately Held**
WEB: www.globalpharmaanalytics.com
SIC: 2834 Pharmaceutical preparations

(G-6737)
GOLD COFFEE ROASTERS INC
1425 Park Ln S (33458-8081)
P.O. Box 719 (33468-0719)
PHONE...................................561 746-8110
John Parry, *President*
Jessie Parry, *Treasurer*
EMP: 10 **EST:** 1999
SQ FT: 2,000
SALES (est): 386.4K **Privately Held**
SIC: 2095 Coffee roasting (except by wholesale grocers); instant coffee; coffee extracts

(G-6738)
GRAFLEX INC
15855 Assembly Loop # 100 (33478-6431)
PHONE...................................561 691-5959
Paul Ganther, *President*
HB Brad Ganther, *President*
Jennifer Ganther, *Vice Pres*
Angela C Ganther, *Treasurer*
Jaimie Heard, *Info Tech Mgr*
EMP: 6 **EST:** 1993
SQ FT: 6,000

SALES (est): 1.4MM **Privately Held**
WEB: www.graflex.com
SIC: 3827 Lenses, optical: all types except ophthalmic; sighting & fire control equipment, optical

(G-6739)
HARDSCAPECOM LLC
15132 Pk Of Cmmrce Blvd S (33478-6438)
PHONE...................................561 998-5000
EMP: 8 **EST:** 2018
SALES (est): 326.4K **Privately Held**
WEB: www.hardscape.com
SIC: 3253 3469 Ceramic wall & floor tile; architectural panels or parts, porcelain enameled

(G-6740)
HEALTHLIGHT LLC
110 Front St Ste 300 (33477-5095)
PHONE...................................224 231-0342
Warren Graber, *President*
Jonathan Stewart, *Opers Mgr*
Christopher Johl, *Opers Staff*
Donald Baldwin, *CFO*
Barbara Rhodessherrill, *Office Mgr*
EMP: 11 **EST:** 2015
SALES (est): 1.8MM **Privately Held**
WEB: www.healthlightllc.com
SIC: 3845 Electromedical apparatus

(G-6741)
HEMARUS LLC-JCKSNVLE PLSMA CTR
601 Heritage Dr 118 (33458-2777)
PHONE...................................904 642-1005
Chigurupati Jayaram, *Manager*
EMP: 5 **EST:** 2010
SALES (est): 319.4K **Privately Held**
WEB: www.hemarusplasma.us
SIC: 2836 Plasmas

(G-6742)
HOLTEC INTERNATIONAL (PA)
1001 N Us Highway 1 (33477-4482)
PHONE...................................561 745-7772
Kris Singh, *President*
Pankaj Chaudry, *Senior VP*
Pierre Paul Oneid, *Senior VP*
Savit Sinha, *Project Mgr*
Robert R Galvin, *CFO*
◆ **EMP:** 100 **EST:** 1986
SQ FT: 38,000
SALES (est): 681.4MM **Privately Held**
WEB: www.holtecinternational.com
SIC: 2819 8711 Nuclear fuel scrap, reprocessing; engineering services

(G-6743)
HOWARD SCRIPTS INC
Also Called: Jupiter Courier
800 W Indiantown Rd (33458-7501)
P.O. Box 9009, Stuart (34995-9009)
PHONE...................................561 746-5111
Ken Lowe, *President*
EMP: 15 **EST:** 2001
SALES (est): 945K **Privately Held**
SIC: 2711 2741 Newspapers: publishing only, not printed on site; miscellaneous publishing

(G-6744)
IMAGINATION CREATIONS INC
2895 Jupiter Park Dr # 300 (33458-6038)
PHONE...................................561 744-7802
Kathy K Link, *President*
Donna Kurtz, *Vice Pres*
Jackie Link, *Opers Mgr*
EMP: 20 **EST:** 1992
SQ FT: 3,800
SALES (est): 1.5MM **Privately Held**
WEB: www.imaginationcreationsinc.com
SIC: 2353 Hats, caps & millinery

(G-6745)
IN THE BITE
342 Toney Penna Dr (33458-5774)
PHONE...................................561 529-3940
Dale Wills, *Principal*
EMP: 11 **EST:** 2016
SALES (est): 327.1K **Privately Held**
WEB: www.inthebite.com
SIC: 2721 Periodicals: publishing only

(G-6746)
INTEGRITY TECHNOLOGIES LLC
Also Called: Integrity Medical
5270 Pennock Point Rd (33458-3446)
PHONE...................................561 768-9023
Christopher Walsh, *President*
EMP: 9 **EST:** 2010
SALES (est): 424.9K **Privately Held**
WEB: www.seadev.us
SIC: 3069 Medical & laboratory rubber sundries & related products

(G-6747)
INTER CELL TECHNOLOGIES INC
Also Called: Art and Orchid Gallery, The
6671 W Indiantown Rd # 56439 (33458-3991)
PHONE...................................561 575-6868
EMP: 8
SQ FT: 1,400
SALES (est): 100K **Privately Held**
SIC: 2836 2865 2835 2834 Mfg Biological Products Mfg Cyclic Crudes/Intrmd Mfg Diagnostic Substance

(G-6748)
J-COAST WOODWORKS LLC
1312 Commerce Ln (33458-5685)
PHONE...................................561 262-6144
EMP: 7 **EST:** 2019
SALES (est): 510.7K **Privately Held**
SIC: 2431 Millwork

(G-6749)
JENOPTIK NORTH AMERICA INC (HQ)
16490 Innovation Dr (33478-6449)
PHONE...................................561 881-7400
Jay Kumler, *President*
Eric Smith, *General Mgr*
Marc Himel, *Business Mgr*
Rob Brown, *Project Mgr*
David Stewart, *Prdtn Mgr*
EMP: 250 **EST:** 2009
SQ FT: 80,000
SALES (est): 191.8MM
SALES (corp-wide): 849.6MM **Privately Held**
WEB: www.jenoptik.com
SIC: 3827 Optical instruments & lenses
PA: Jenoptik Ag
Carl-Zeiss-Str. 1
Jena TH 07743
364 165-0

(G-6750)
JENOPTIK OPTICAL SYSTEMS LLC (DH)
16490 Innovation Dr Ste A (33478-6449)
PHONE...................................561 881-7400
Ralf Kuschnnereit, *Ch of Bd*
Marvin Loveless, *General Mgr*
Thomas Goundry, *Business Mgr*
Sujeet Sudhir, *Business Mgr*
Ying Zhao, *Business Mgr*
▲ **EMP:** 169 **EST:** 1991
SQ FT: 45,000
SALES (est): 55.4MM
SALES (corp-wide): 849.6MM **Privately Held**
WEB: www.jenoptik.com
SIC: 3827 Optical instruments & lenses

(G-6751)
JUPITER PETROLEUM INC
5490 Military Trl (33458-2862)
PHONE...................................561 622-1276
Nuruddin Sheikh, *Manager*
EMP: 8 **EST:** 2017
SALES (est): 205.4K **Privately Held**
SIC: 2911 Petroleum refining

(G-6752)
JUPITER WELDING LLC
Also Called: Jupiter Weld & Repair
1525 Cypress Dr (33469-3137)
PHONE...................................561 801-3585
Daniel Measelle, *Mng Member*
EMP: 5 **EST:** 2015
SALES (est): 308.4K **Privately Held**
WEB: www.jupiterwelding.com
SIC: 7692 Welding repair

(G-6753)
JUST ENGINES
209 Circle W (33458-7517)
PHONE...................................561 575-2681
Stephen P Gropp, *Owner*
EMP: 7 **EST:** 2013
SALES (est): 289.7K **Privately Held**
SIC: 3519 Internal combustion engines

(G-6754)
KN MACHINE & TOOLS INC
3125 Jupiter Park Cir # 4 (33458-6028)
PHONE...................................561 748-3035
Khoa V Nguyen, *President*
EMP: 13 **EST:** 2000
SQ FT: 5,000
SALES (est): 3.3MM **Privately Held**
WEB: www.knmachine.com
SIC: 3599 Machine shop, jobbing & repair

(G-6755)
LARTER & SONS
83 River Dr (33469-1950)
PHONE...................................732 290-1515
Stephen G Schutz, *CEO*
EMP: 85 **EST:** 1865
SALES (est): 5.7MM **Privately Held**
SIC: 3911 Medals, precious or semi-precious metal; jewel settings & mountings, precious metal; earrings, precious metal; rings, finger: precious metal

(G-6756)
LIGHTHOUSE BOATWORKS INC
512 N Hepburn Ave (33458-4956)
PHONE...................................561 667-7382
Thomas Land, *Principal*
EMP: 7 **EST:** 2016
SALES (est): 99K **Privately Held**
SIC: 3732 Boat building & repairing

(G-6757)
LIONHEART PRINTERS LLC
1312 Commerce Ln Ste A15 (33458-5640)
PHONE...................................561 781-8300
Enrique Sasson, *Mng Member*
Sasha Dash, *Mng Member*
EMP: 6 **EST:** 2018
SALES (est): 574.8K **Privately Held**
WEB: www.lhprinters.com
SIC: 2752 Commercial printing, lithographic

(G-6758)
M & M STUDIOS INC
1445 Jupiter Park Dr # 1 (33458-8936)
PHONE...................................561 744-2754
Marilyn Welch, *President*
EMP: 6 **EST:** 1972
SQ FT: 3,000
SALES (est): 523.9K **Privately Held**
WEB: www.mandmstudios.com
SIC: 3952 2759 Frames for artists' canvases; business forms: printing

(G-6759)
MADDOX INDUSTRIES INC
16401 134th Ter N (33478-6520)
PHONE...................................561 529-2165
Stephan Maddox, *President*
EMP: 7 **EST:** 2013
SALES (est): 256.9K **Privately Held**
WEB: www.maddoxindustriesinc.com
SIC: 3999 Manufacturing industries

(G-6760)
MAR-CO GAS SERVICES INC
11138 161st St N (33478-6188)
PHONE...................................561 745-0085
Mark Scoville, *President*
EMP: 6 **EST:** 2004
SALES (est): 509.5K **Privately Held**
WEB: www.marcogasservices.com
SIC: 1321 Natural gas liquids

(G-6761)
MARLIN GRAPHICS INC
1251 Jupiter Park Dr # 7 (33458-8074)
PHONE...................................561 743-5220
Joseph Gonzalez Jr, *President*
EMP: 7 **EST:** 1991
SQ FT: 2,500

SALES (est): 493.4K Privately Held
WEB: www.marlingraphics.com
SIC: 2759 5943 5699 Commercial printing; office forms & supplies; customized clothing & apparel

(G-6762)
MARS TALENT AGENCY
18406 Se Lakeside Dr (33469-8117)
PHONE..............................561 748-6566
Adam W Rhys, *Branch Mgr*
EMP: 8
SALES (corp-wide): 91.7K Privately Held
WEB: www.marstalent.com
SIC: 3931 Musical instruments
PA: Mars Talent Agency
5715 Se Canyata Ct
Hobe Sound FL 33455
561 748-6566

(G-6763)
MATHESON TRI-GAS INC
18000 Bee Line Hwy (33478-6412)
P.O. Box 10 (33468-0010)
PHONE..............................561 615-3000
Larry Anguish, *Branch Mgr*
EMP: 33 Privately Held
WEB: www.mathesongas.com
SIC: 2813 5084 Industrial gases; welding machinery & equipment
HQ: Matheson Tri-Gas, Inc.
3 Mountainview Rd Ste 3 # 3
Warren NJ 07059
908 991-9200

(G-6764)
MAVERICK COMPOSITES INC
6105 Francis St (33458-6750)
PHONE..............................561 601-3393
Philip La Spina, *Principal*
EMP: 6 EST: 2014
SALES (est): 544.4K Privately Held
WEB: www.maverickcomposites.com
SIC: 3728 Aircraft parts & equipment

(G-6765)
MMATS INC
Also Called: Mmats Professional Audio
15132 Pk Of Commerce Blvd (33478-6438)
PHONE..............................561 842-0600
Kathryn Speranza, *President*
Suzanne Hoffman, *Vice Pres*
▲ EMP: 20 EST: 1976
SQ FT: 15,000
SALES (est): 4MM Privately Held
WEB: www.mmatsproaudio.com
SIC: 3823 Computer interface equipment for industrial process control

(G-6766)
MODE MARIMBA INC
19960 Earlwood Dr (33458-1867)
PHONE..............................561 512-5001
EMP: 7 EST: 2016
SALES (est): 233K Privately Held
WEB: www.modemarimba.com
SIC: 3931 Marimbas

(G-6767)
MULTI PARTS SUPPLY USA INC (PA)
Also Called: Multiparts
1649 Park Ln S (33458-8076)
PHONE..............................561 748-1515
Brian S Cohn, *President*
Jeff Stankard, *President*
Barry Cohn, *Chairman*
Seaman Fang, *Opers Staff*
Nannette Cassidy, *CFO*
▲ EMP: 24 EST: 2005
SQ FT: 15,000
SALES (est): 5.4MM Privately Held
WEB: www.multiparts.net
SIC: 3714 Brake drums, motor vehicle; clutches, motor vehicle

(G-6768)
MZ MACHINE INC
3046 Jupiter Park Cir (33458-6011)
PHONE..............................561 744-2791
Mario Zola, *President*
Linda Zola, *Vice Pres*
EMP: 9 EST: 1987
SQ FT: 6,000

SALES (est): 1.3MM Privately Held
WEB: www.mzmachine.com
SIC: 3599 Machine shop, jobbing & repair

(G-6769)
NANO SAFE COATINGS INC
5500 Military Trl Ste 22 (33458-2871)
PHONE..............................561 747-5758
Joseph Raich, *Vice Pres*
EMP: 12 EST: 2014
SALES (est): 508.3K Privately Held
SIC: 3479 Metal coating & allied service

(G-6770)
NEW TECHNOLOGY PRECISION MACHI
15300 Pk Of Commerce Blvd (33478-6407)
PHONE..............................561 624-3830
Kateryna Larsen, *CEO*
John Larsen, *President*
EMP: 12 EST: 1977
SALES (est): 2.4MM Privately Held
WEB: www.newtechprecision.com
SIC: 3599 Machine shop, jobbing & repair

(G-6771)
NITEO PRODUCTS LLC
Also Called: Cyclo Industries
902 S Us Highway 1 (33477-6404)
PHONE..............................561 745-1812
Doug Salazar, *Vice Pres*
Eric Mowls, *Marketing Staff*
EMP: 7
SALES (corp-wide): 194MM Privately Held
WEB: www.niteoproducts.com
SIC: 3523 Farm machinery & equipment
HQ: Niteo Products, Llc
5949 Sherry Ln Ste 540
Dallas TX 75225
214 245-5000

(G-6772)
NITROGEN JUPITER LLC
6779 W Indiantown Rd (33458-4654)
PHONE..............................561 662-2150
John Ford, *Principal*
EMP: 7 EST: 2015
SALES (est): 454.8K Privately Held
SIC: 2813 Nitrogen

(G-6773)
NORTH ERIE ELECTRONICS INC
Also Called: Western Reserve Tool Machine
1001 N Us Highway 1 # 506 (33477-4305)
PHONE..............................561 839-8127
William Anderson, *President*
EMP: 11 Privately Held
WEB: www.northerie.com
SIC: 3679 Power supplies, all types: static
PA: Erie North Electronics Inc
1001 N Us Highway 1 # 506
Jupiter FL 33477

(G-6774)
NUTRAMEDIX LLC
2885 Jupiter Park Dr # 1600 (33458-6045)
PHONE..............................561 745-2917
Timothy J Eaton, *President*
Mark Toothman, *General Mgr*
Bruce Hodge, *Vice Pres*
Lisa Rojas, *Asst Controller*
Jon Gaydosh, *Sales Staff*
▲ EMP: 14 EST: 1994
SQ FT: 6,700
SALES (est): 2.9MM Privately Held
WEB: www.nutramedix.com
SIC: 2834 5122 Vitamin, nutrient & hematinic preparations for human use; drugs, proprietaries & sundries

(G-6775)
OPREME BEVERAGE CORP
5151 Corporate Way (33458-3101)
PHONE..............................954 699-0669
Ryan El-Hosseiny, *President*
Adam El-Hosseiny, *Director*
EMP: 8 EST: 2012
SALES (est): 525.9K Privately Held
SIC: 2086 Bottled & canned soft drinks

(G-6776)
P&G PAVERS INC
6671 W Indiantown Rd 50-2 (33458-3991)
PHONE..............................561 716-5113
Nathalie Gelinas, *Principal*
EMP: 7 EST: 2013
SALES (est): 3.1MM Privately Held
WEB: www.pandgpavers.com
SIC: 2951 Asphalt paving mixtures & blocks

(G-6777)
PIXOTINE PRODUCTS INC
1095 Jupiter Park Dr # 12 (33458-8972)
PHONE..............................305 479-1335
Evan Grossman, *CEO*
Melissa Grossman, *President*
Justin Merrell, *Principal*
Chris Miquel, *Principal*
EMP: 6 EST: 2013
SQ FT: 1,500
SALES (est): 1MM Privately Held
WEB: www.pixotine.com
SIC: 2499 Toothpicks, wood

(G-6778)
POWER SYSTEMS INC
1440 W Indiantown Rd # 200 (33458-7925)
PHONE..............................561 354-1100
Valerie Slagle, *Human Res Mgr*
Jason Eason, *Sales Mgr*
Kathryn Maclane, *Cust Mgr*
Fergus Ahern, *Sales Staff*
Christy Browning, *Marketing Staff*
EMP: 57 EST: 2001
SALES (est): 4MM Privately Held
SIC: 3511 Gas turbine generator set units, complete

(G-6779)
POWER SYSTEMS MFG LLC
Also Called: PSM
1440 W Indiantown Rd # 200 (33458-7925)
PHONE..............................561 354-1100
Alexander Hoffs, *CEO*
Charles M Biondo, *Vice Pres*
Chuck Biondo, *Vice Pres*
Tim Te Riele, *Vice Pres*
David Marr, *Project Mgr*
◆ EMP: 400 EST: 2003
SQ FT: 200,000
SALES (est): 131.7MM Privately Held
WEB: www.psm.com
SIC: 3511 8711 Gas turbines, mechanical drive; hydraulic turbines; steam engines; engineering services
PA: Hanwha Corporation
86 Cheonggyecheon-Ro, Jung-Gu
Seoul 04541

(G-6780)
POWERPHASE LLC
1001 N Us Highway 1 # 206 (33477-4482)
PHONE..............................561 299-3970
Plazi Ricklin, *Engineer*
Bob Kraft,
James Kraft,
Peter Perr,
EMP: 12 EST: 2012
SQ FT: 2,400
SALES (est): 1.5MM Privately Held
WEB: www.powerphase.com
SIC: 3511 Gas turbine generator set units, complete

(G-6781)
PRATT & WHITNEY
15270 Endeavor Dr (33478-6447)
PHONE..............................561 796-6701
Jayne Nye, *President*
Alex Sylvain, *Project Mgr*
Brian Sams, *Opers Mgr*
Mario Saavedra, *Prdtn Mgr*
Leo Arel, *Materials Mgr*
EMP: 27 EST: 2014
SALES (est): 6.4MM Privately Held
SIC: 3812 Aircraft/aerospace flight instruments & guidance systems

(G-6782)
PRISM VENTURE PARTNERS LLC
675 W Indiantown Rd # 103 (33458-7555)
PHONE..............................561 427-6565
Timothy Anderson, *Principal*
EMP: 7 EST: 2006

SALES (est): 386.7K Privately Held
SIC: 7372 Prepackaged software

(G-6783)
PROFESSOR SOFTWARE COMPANY
268 Barbados Dr (33458-2917)
PHONE..............................561 691-5455
R F McDonough, *Principal*
EMP: 7 EST: 2008
SALES (est): 163.6K Privately Held
SIC: 7372 Prepackaged software

(G-6784)
QUIK SHRED
1070 E Indiantown Rd # 308 (33477-5148)
PHONE..............................561 841-1822
Louise Sacco, *CEO*
EMP: 9 EST: 2008
SALES (est): 780K Privately Held
SIC: 3559 Tire shredding machinery

(G-6785)
RACERINK LLC
1515 Cypress Dr (33469-3144)
PHONE..............................239 470-0872
EMP: 5 EST: 2020
SALES (est): 386.1K Privately Held
WEB: www.racerink.com
SIC: 2759 Screen printing

(G-6786)
RAYTHEON TECHNOLOGIES CORP
Pratt & Whitney
17900 Bee Line Hwy (33478-6414)
P.O. Box 109600, Palm Beach Gardens (33410-9600)
PHONE..............................860 565-4321
EMP: 650
SALES (corp-wide): 64.3B Publicly Held
WEB: www.rtx.com
SIC: 3511 8611 3812 3728 Gas turbines, mechanical drive; business associations; search & navigation equipment; aircraft parts & equipment; aircraft engines & engine parts; blowers & fans
PA: Raytheon Technologies Corporation
1000 Wlson Blvd Arlngton Arlington Va
Arlington VA 22209
781 522-3000

(G-6787)
REXPRO SERVICES
1097 Jupiter Park Ln # 8 (33458-8907)
PHONE..............................561 328-6488
Steven Malone, *Principal*
John Kuehne, *Principal*
Micki Malone, *Principal*
Michael Membrado, *Principal*
Donald Schoenfeld, *Principal*
EMP: 6 EST: 2019
SALES (est): 456.1K Privately Held
SIC: 2851 Paints & allied products

(G-6788)
ROEBIC LABORATORIES INC
1213 Ocean Dunes Cir (33477-9130)
PHONE..............................561 799-3380
Hedy Bush, *COO*
Dale Schmidt, *Vice Pres*
John Peters, *Branch Mgr*
EMP: 13
SALES (corp-wide): 6.8MM Privately Held
WEB: www.roebic.com
SIC: 2842 Specialty cleaning, polishes & sanitation goods
PA: Roebic Laboratories, Inc.
25 Connair Rd
Orange CT 06477
203 795-1283

(G-6789)
ROYAL CONCRETE CONCEPTS INC (PA)
1410 Park Ln S Ste 2 (33458-8078)
P.O. Box 2486, Greenville SC (29602-2486)
PHONE..............................561 689-5398
Wallace D Sanger, *CEO*
Dean Locke, *Chairman*
Dean J Locke, *COO*
Eric R Engstrom, *CFO*
Ronald Moffett, *Manager*

▼ EMP: 50 **EST:** 1997
SQ FT: 11,000
SALES (est): 7.4MM **Privately Held**
WEB: www.royalconcreteconcepts.com
SIC: 3272 3271 Concrete products, pre-cast; concrete block & brick

(G-6790)
S P SHEET METAL CO INC
5500 Military Trl Ste 22 (33458-2871)
PHONE....................609 698-8800
Darren Myers, *President*
Clara Dominguez, *Principal*
EMP: 17 **EST:** 1962
SALES (est): 474.5K **Privately Held**
SIC: 3444 Sheet metal specialties, not stamped

(G-6791)
SASCO MACHINING INC
904 Penn Trl (33458-4330)
PHONE....................561 746-8233
Gregory E Stephen, *President*
Libby Van Deusen, *Vice Pres*
Louis Vandeusen, *Vice Pres*
EMP: 10 **EST:** 1978
SALES (est): 722.2K **Privately Held**
WEB: www.100dollarclub.com
SIC: 3599 Machine shop, jobbing & repair

(G-6792)
SCHRAPPERS FINE CABINETRY INC
240 W Indiantown Rd # 101 (33458-3548)
PHONE....................561 746-3827
Keith Levine, *President*
Beverly Levine, *Vice Pres*
Michelle Egan, *Production*
EMP: 10 **EST:** 2008
SALES (est): 751.4K **Privately Held**
WEB: www.schrappers.com
SIC: 2541 5712 Cabinets, lockers & shelving; cabinet work, custom

(G-6793)
SEABREEZE PUBLICATION CENTL FL
Also Called: Seabreeze Publications
1102 W Indiantown Rd # 5 (33458-6813)
PHONE....................561 741-7770
Sean Reid, *President*
EMP: 6 **EST:** 1990
SALES (est): 513.9K **Privately Held**
WEB: www.seabreezepublications.com
SIC: 2759 Commercial printing

(G-6794)
SEATBELT SOLUTIONS LLC
15835 Corporate Rd N (33478-6422)
PHONE....................855 642-3964
Glenn Davis, *Manager*
Jeffery L Biegun,
▲ EMP: 28 **EST:** 2006
SQ FT: 10,000
SALES (est): 7MM **Privately Held**
WEB: www.seatbeltsolutions.com
SIC: 2399 Seat belts, automobile & aircraft

(G-6795)
SHINY PRINTS
143 Juno St (33458-4941)
PHONE....................561 200-2872
William George Heinitz, *Principal*
EMP: 10 **EST:** 2016
SALES (est): 578.4K **Privately Held**
WEB: www.shinyprints.com
SIC: 2752 Commercial printing, lithographic

(G-6796)
SHUTTER LUBRICATION & SERVICE
1821 W 10th St Ste 3 (33469)
P.O. Box 32474, West Palm Beach (33420-2474)
PHONE....................561 745-8956
Tracy Trefzer, *President*
Paul Trefzer, *Vice Pres*
EMP: 11 **EST:** 2003
SALES (est): 477.6K **Privately Held**
SIC: 3442 Shutters, door or window: metal

(G-6797)
SHYFT GROUP INC
15335 Pk Of Commerce Blvd (33478-6452)
PHONE....................954 946-9955
EMP: 24
SALES (corp-wide): 991.7MM **Publicly Held**
WEB: www.theshyftgroup.com
SIC: 3711 Chassis, motor vehicle
PA: The Shyft Group Inc
41280 Bridge St
Novi MI 48375
517 543-6400

(G-6798)
SIGNATURE ATHLETICS INC
1025 W Indiantown Rd # 10 (33458-6852)
PHONE....................561 212-9284
Daniel Soviero, *CEO*
Madeline Lewis, *Manager*
Lance Stone, *Director*
EMP: 6 **EST:** 2016
SALES (est): 2.5MM **Privately Held**
WEB: www.signaturelacrosse.com
SIC: 3949 Baseball, softball & cricket sports equipment

(G-6799)
SIKORSKY AIRCRAFT CORPORATION
Also Called: Development Flight Center
17900 Bee Line Hwy (33478-6414)
PHONE....................561 775-5142
EMP: 12 **Publicly Held**
WEB: www.gyrocamsystems.com
SIC: 3721 Helicopters
HQ: Sikorsky Aircraft Corporation
6900 Main St
Stratford CT 06614

(G-6800)
SNEAKZ LLC
Also Called: Sneakz Organic
2895 Jupiter Park Dr # 500 (33458-6049)
P.O. Box 1998 (33468-1998)
PHONE....................201 693-5695
Jeff Robbins, *Mng Member*
Reese Costa, *Manager*
Jim Costa,
EMP: 6 **EST:** 2012
SQ FT: 3,000
SALES (est): 3MM **Privately Held**
WEB: www.sneakz.com
SIC: 2026 Milk drinks, flavored

(G-6801)
SOFTWARETEACHER INC
300 N Highway A1a H104 (33477-9510)
PHONE....................954 593-3333
David Reid, *Principal*
EMP: 8 **EST:** 2001
SALES (est): 284.5K **Privately Held**
SIC: 7372 Prepackaged software

(G-6802)
SOUTHEAST MARKETING CONCEPTS
Also Called: Country Tees
801 Maplewood Dr Ste 11 (33458-8800)
PHONE....................561 747-7010
Greg Olson, *President*
Gregg Olson, *COO*
EMP: 8 **EST:** 1988
SQ FT: 3,500
SALES (est): 808.1K **Privately Held**
SIC: 2759 3953 Screen printing; screens, textile printing

(G-6803)
SOUTHEASTERN DOOR COMPANY LLC
1505 Commerce Ln (33458-8837)
P.O. Box 794 (33468-0794)
PHONE....................561 746-5493
Charles Austin, *Purchasing*
William Weizer,
▼ EMP: 12 **EST:** 1970
SQ FT: 10,500
SALES (est): 2.4MM **Privately Held**
WEB: www.southeasterndoor.com
SIC: 3442 Screen doors, metal; screens, window, metal

(G-6804)
SPRING LOADED INC
Also Called: J & R Metal Fabrications
315 Commerce Way Ste 1 (33458-8841)
PHONE....................561 747-8785
Karen B Kinberger, *President*
Charles R Kinberger, *Vice Pres*
EMP: 5 **EST:** 1987
SQ FT: 2,000
SALES (est): 650.9K **Privately Held**
WEB: www.springloadedtechnology.com
SIC: 3441 Fabricated structural metal

(G-6805)
STEWART MATERIALS INC (PA)
2875 Jupiter Park Dr # 1100 (33458-6058)
PHONE....................561 972-4517
Nick T Stewart, *President*
Oneil Gardner, *Safety Mgr*
Laura Perham, *Finance Dir*
Mike Dodson, *Finance*
Jackson Stewart, *Business Anlyst*
EMP: 3 **EST:** 1981
SQ FT: 400
SALES (est): 8.1MM **Privately Held**
WEB: www.stewartmaterials.com
SIC: 1442 Construction sand & gravel

(G-6806)
TECHTRAN LENSES INC
601 Heritage Dr Ste 118 (33458-2777)
PHONE....................561 623-5490
Chigurupati Jayaram, *Principal*
EMP: 11 **EST:** 2012
SALES (est): 236.2K **Privately Held**
SIC: 3851 Ophthalmic goods
PA: Techtran Polylenses Limited
S -7 Ida Technocrat Industrial Estate
Hyderabad TG 50003

(G-6807)
TEQUESTA COMMUNITY HEALTH CTR
470 Tequesta Dr (33469-2585)
PHONE....................561 713-0798
Leticia Arroyo, *CEO*
EMP: 9 **EST:** 2010
SALES (est): 592.2K **Privately Held**
SIC: 3841 Surgical & medical instruments

(G-6808)
THERMAL BRAZE INC
231 Venus St (33458-4967)
PHONE....................561 746-6640
Ivan Batchelder, *President*
David Wise, *Vice Pres*
EMP: 7 **EST:** 1980
SQ FT: 1,500
SALES (est): 471.2K **Privately Held**
WEB: www.thermalbraze.com
SIC: 7692 3398 Brazing; metal heat treating

(G-6809)
TIBA ENTERPRISES INC
Also Called: Minuteman Press
1601 Commerce Ln Ste 102 (33458-8818)
PHONE....................561 575-3037
Barbara Watson, *President*
Timothy R Watson, *Vice Pres*
EMP: 6 **EST:** 2000
SQ FT: 1,500
SALES (est): 815.5K **Privately Held**
WEB: www.minutemanpress.com
SIC: 2752 Commercial printing, lithographic

(G-6810)
TITANS PROTECTIVE COATINGS LLC
150 Evernia St (33458-4954)
PHONE....................561 370-2085
Andrea Taslidzic, *Manager*
EMP: 8 **EST:** 2016
SALES (est): 730.7K **Privately Held**
SIC: 3479 Metal coating & allied service

(G-6811)
TRAFFIPAX LLC
16490 Innovation Dr (33478-6449)
PHONE....................561 881-7400
Stewart Mackiernan, *CEO*
Albert Miranda, *President*
Jeri Anderson, *Treasurer*
▲ EMP: 417 **EST:** 1999

SQ FT: 6,000
SALES (est): 3.6MM
SALES (corp-wide): 849.6MM **Privately Held**
SIC: 3669 Traffic signals, electric
HQ: Jenoptik North America, Inc.
16490 Innovation Dr
Jupiter FL 33478

(G-6812)
TRIATOMIC ENVIRONMENTAL INC
1838 Park Ln S (33458-8077)
P.O. Box 1867 (33468-1867)
PHONE....................561 748-4864
Christopher Willette, *President*
Chad Knapp, *VP Opers*
Dale Harrison, *Technical Mgr*
Marissa Granados, *Train & Dev Mgr*
Tim Steinmetz, *Sales Mgr*
▼ EMP: 10 **EST:** 1996
SQ FT: 1,500
SALES (est): 2.5MM **Privately Held**
WEB: www.freshaireuv.com
SIC: 3564 Air cleaning systems

(G-6813)
TROPICAL STENCIL PCB INC
1530 Cypress Dr Ste E (33469-3184)
PHONE....................561 972-5133
Barbara McGlynn, *President*
Priscilla McGlynn, *COO*
James McGlynn, *Vice Pres*
Bob McGlynn, *Human Resources*
William Bishop, *Sales Staff*
EMP: 13 **EST:** 2010
SALES (est): 2.3MM **Privately Held**
WEB: www.tropicalstencil.com
SIC: 3672 Printed circuit boards

(G-6814)
TROPICHEM RESEARCH LABS LLC
Also Called: Vetio Dev't & Mfg Plant
15335 Pk Of Cmmrce Blvd S (33478-6452)
PHONE....................561 804-7603
Christine Marriott, *Controller*
Maureen Lalonde, *Manager*
Erin Burns, *Office Admin*
EMP: 90 **Privately Held**
WEB: www.vetio.com
SIC: 2844 2834 3999 Shampoos, rinses, conditioners: hair; pharmaceutical preparations; pet supplies
PA: Tropichem Research Labs, Llc
15843 Guild Ct
Jupiter FL 33478

(G-6815)
TROPICHEM RESEARCH LABS LLC (PA)
Also Called: Vetio Animal Health
15843 Guild Ct (33478-6436)
PHONE....................314 686-4614
John Kane,
▲ EMP: 36 **EST:** 1989
SALES (est): 20.8MM **Privately Held**
WEB: www.vetio.com
SIC: 2844 3999 2834 Shampoos, rinses, conditioners: hair; cosmetic preparations; pet supplies; pharmaceutical preparations

(G-6816)
TRUE LINE INDUSTRIES INC
13841 151st Ln N (33478-3541)
PHONE....................561 745-4828
Randall C Chew, *Principal*
EMP: 8 **EST:** 2003
SALES (est): 616.2K **Privately Held**
SIC: 3999 Manufacturing industries

(G-6817)
ULTRACLENZ LLC
1201 Jupiter Park Dr # 1 (33458-8084)
PHONE....................800 931-8911
▲ EMP: 15
SQ FT: 8,500
SALES (est): 1.5MM **Privately Held**
SIC: 3999 2841 3432 Mfg Misc Products Mfg Soap/Other Detergents Mfg Plumbing Fixture Fittings

(G-6818)
US MOLD INC
612 N Orange Ave Ste A4 (33458-5021)
PHONE..............................561 748-2223
Mike Fadell, *Manager*
EMP: 5 EST: 2007
SALES (est): 498.8K **Privately Held**
WEB: www.usmold.com
SIC: 3544 Industrial molds

(G-6819)
VENTEX TECHNOLOGY INC (PA)
1201 Jupiter Park Dr (33458-8140)
PHONE..............................561 354-6300
John S Boyd, *President*
Morgan Crook, *General Mgr*
Jim Sloan, *Vice Pres*
Richard Ogden, *CFO*
◆ EMP: 12 EST: 1993
SQ FT: 14,924
SALES (est): 1MM **Privately Held**
WEB: www.ventextech.com
SIC: 3612 Specialty transformers

(G-6820)
VENUE ADVERTISING INC
Also Called: Venue Marketing Group
815 S Us Highway 1 # 103 (33477-6006)
PHONE..............................561 844-1778
Denise Carter, *Editor*
Mike Albanese, *Chairman*
Shelli Lockhart, *Pub Rel Mgr*
Adam Rosmarin, *Marketing Staff*
Cameron Crotts, *Creative Dir*
EMP: 21 EST: 1984
SALES (est): 2.2MM **Privately Held**
WEB: www.venueadv.com
SIC: 2796 7311 2759 Color separations
for printing; advertising agencies; com-
mercial printing

(G-6821)
VITSUR INDUSTRIES INC
130 Evernia St Ste 3 (33458-4913)
PHONE..............................561 744-1290
John Vitsur, *President*
Victoria Vitsur, *Vice Pres*
EMP: 5 EST: 1982
SQ FT: 2,000
SALES (est): 412.5K **Privately Held**
WEB: www.motivateddesign.com
SIC: 3429 Marine hardware

(G-6822)
VULCAN STEEL
326 Jupiter Lakes Blvd # 2 (33458-7102)
PHONE..............................561 945-1259
EMP: 7 EST: 2017
SALES (est): 175.6K **Privately Held**
WEB: www.vulcansteel.com
SIC: 3441 Fabricated structural metal

(G-6823)
WASTE ADVANTAGE CORPORATION
Also Called: Waste Advantage Magazine
230 Tresana Blvd Unit 64 (33478-5438)
P.O. Box 30126, Palm Beach Gardens
(33420-0126)
PHONE..............................800 358-2873
Angelina Ruiz, *Publisher*
Elisa Weil, *Accounting Mgr*
Noreen Cocron, *Sales Mgr*
Sean Earley, *Accounts Exec*
EMP: 8 EST: 2017
SALES (est): 1MM **Privately Held**
WEB: www.wasteadvantagemag.com
SIC: 2721 Periodicals: publishing only

(G-6824)
WATER BAGEL BOCA EAST LLLP
201 N Us Highway 1 Ste C5 (33477-5106)
PHONE..............................347 661-7171
Anne Dangelo, *Principal*
EMP: 8 EST: 2013
SALES (est): 103K **Privately Held**
SIC: 3589 Water treatment equipment, in-
dustrial

(G-6825)
WEISS GROUP LLC (PA)
15430 Endeavor Dr Ste 101 (33478-6402)
PHONE..............................561 627-3300
Thomas J Clarke Jr, *CEO*

Cynthia Canterberry, *President*
Jeffrey Rano, *CFO*
Ionel Roiban, *Manager*
Italo Silveria, *Prgrmr*
EMP: 150 EST: 1994
SQ FT: 54,000
SALES (est): 26.5MM **Privately Held**
WEB: www.weissratings.com
SIC: 2721 Magazines: publishing only, not
printed on site

(G-6826)
WEISS RESEARCH INC
Also Called: Safe Money Report
15430 Endeavor Dr Ste 101 (33478-6400)
PHONE..............................561 627-3300
Tracey L Butz, *President*
Sharon A Daniels, *Vice Pres*
Jeffrey Rano, *CFO*
Martin Weiss, *Director*
EMP: 150 EST: 1971
SQ FT: 190,000
SALES (est): 15.4MM **Privately Held**
WEB: www.weissratings.com
SIC: 2721 6282 Magazines: publishing
only, not printed on site; investment ad-
vice
PA: Weiss Group, Llc
15430 Endeavor Dr Ste 101
Jupiter FL 33478

(G-6827)
WELDCORP INDUSTRIES
15188 Pk Of Cmmrce Blvd S (33478-6406)
PHONE..............................561 339-7713
Alfredo Nicholas, *Principal*
EMP: 40 EST: 2020
SALES (est): 1MM **Privately Held**
WEB: www.weldcorpindustries.com
SIC: 1389 Construction, repair & disman-
tling services

(G-6828)
WORLD FOODS & FLAVORS USA LLC
4245 E Main St (33458-5314)
PHONE..............................561 619-3655
Jordi Esteve Riera, *CEO*
Curtis Lezama, *CFO*
EMP: 11 EST: 2013
SALES: 18.9MM **Privately Held**
SIC: 2087 Concentrates, flavoring (except
drink)

(G-6829)
ZEROC INC
4425 Military Trl Ste 209 (33458-4817)
PHONE..............................561 283-1480
Marc Laukien, *President*
Benard Normier, *Vice Pres*
Bernard Nornier, *Vice Pres*
Michelle George, *Accounts Mgr*
Benoit Foucher, *Software Engr*
EMP: 5 EST: 2002
SALES (est): 687.4K **Privately Held**
WEB: www.zeroc.com
SIC: 7372 Application computer software

Kennedy Space Center
Brevard County

(G-6830)
ASRC AEROSPACE CORP
Bldg M6-744 (32899-0001)
PHONE..............................321 867-1462
EMP: 298
SALES (corp-wide): 2.7B **Privately Held**
SIC: 3812 7371 7373 5088 Search &
navigation equipment; custom computer
programming services; computer inte-
grated systems design; transportation
equipment & supplies
HQ: Asrc Aerospace Corp
7000 Muirkirk Meadows Dr # 100
Beltsville MD 20705
301 837-5500

(G-6831)
BOEING COMPANY
Nasa Cswy (32815)
P.O. Box 21233 (32815-0233)
PHONE..............................321 867-7380
Bruce Melnik, *Manager*
EMP: 14

SALES (corp-wide): 62.2B **Publicly Held**
WEB: www.boeing.com
SIC: 3721 Aircraft
PA: The Boeing Company
929 Long Bridge Dr
Arlington VA 22202
703 414-6338

Kenneth City
Pinellas County

(G-6832)
OLAS FOODS SPECIALTY MKT INC
5791 54th Ave N (33709-2005)
PHONE..............................813 447-5127
Ola Yusuf, *Branch Mgr*
EMP: 18
SALES (corp-wide): 146.8K **Privately Held**
WEB: www.olasfoods.com
SIC: 2032 Canned specialties
PA: Ola's Foods Specialty Market, Inc.
1908 W Dr Mrtn Lther King
Tampa FL 33607
813 200-7202

Key Biscayne
Miami-Dade County

(G-6833)
ARGOS GLOBAL PARTNER SVCS LLC (PA)
Also Called: Lc Alliances
240 Crandon Blvd Ste 230 (33149-1624)
PHONE..............................305 365-1096
Uciana Ciuchini, *President*
Luciana Ciuchini, *General Mgr*
Thomas Alonso, *Accountant*
◆ EMP: 7 EST: 2005
SALES: 10.9MM **Privately Held**
WEB: www.argosus.com
SIC: 3728 3714 5199 5065 Aircraft parts
& equipment; motor vehicle body compo-
nents & frame; general merchandise,
non-durable; electronic parts & equip-
ment; automotive supplies & parts; agri-
cultural machinery & equipment

(G-6834)
ASI GLOBAL
240 Crandon Blvd Ste 242 (33149-1620)
PHONE..............................786 703-7155
EMP: 7 EST: 2019
SALES (est): 85.1K **Privately Held**
WEB: www.asiglobal.site
SIC: 3085 Plastics bottles

(G-6835)
BUENA CEPA WINES LLC
951 Crandon Blvd (33149-3400)
PHONE..............................310 621-2566
Sebastian E Bustamante, *Mng Member*
Joseph A Foley,
Lisa D Weeks,
▲ EMP: 9 EST: 2008
SALES (est): 544.3K **Privately Held**
SIC: 2084 Wines

(G-6836)
LINKPOINT LLC
137 E Enid Dr (33149-2204)
PHONE..............................305 903-9191
Peter Hoffmann, *Mng Member*
Erika Hoffmann,
▼ EMP: 16 EST: 2009
SALES (est): 2.1MM **Privately Held**
SIC: 2821 Plastics materials & resins

(G-6837)
MILCA BOTTLING COMPANY
620 Harbor Cir (33149-1703)
PHONE..............................305 365-0044
Ramiro Cardenal, *Principal*
EMP: 10 EST: 2010
SALES (est): 416K **Privately Held**
SIC: 2086 Bottled & canned soft drinks

(G-6838)
ORGANIC AMAZON CORP
Also Called: Acai To Go
104 Crandon Blvd (33149-1526)
PHONE..............................305 365-7811
Michael Simon, *CEO*
Jayson Fittipaldi,
Rodrigo Lima,
EMP: 9 EST: 2013
SALES (est): 593.9K **Privately Held**
WEB: www.acaitogo.com
SIC: 2099 5499 Food preparations; health
foods

(G-6839)
SAMARA PUBLISHING
Also Called: Islander
104 Crandon Blvd Ste 301 (33149-1556)
PHONE..............................305 361-3333
Anne Owens, *President*
◆ EMP: 7 EST: 1966
SQ FT: 1,400
SALES (est): 1.6MM **Privately Held**
SIC: 2711 Newspapers: publishing only,
not printed on site

(G-6840)
UPAYA HOLDINGS INC
350 Grapetree Dr Apt 405 (33149-2750)
PHONE..............................850 261-9203
Dan Riner, *Principal*
EMP: 11 EST: 2020
SALES (est): 590.3K **Privately Held**
WEB: www.upayahealth.com
SIC: 3999

(G-6841)
WAU USA CORP
240 Crandon Blvd Ste 278 (33149-1623)
PHONE..............................305 361-6110
Edmond Saade, *President*
Reynaldo Acosta, *President*
EMP: 15 EST: 2008
SALES (est): 500.3K **Privately Held**
SIC: 3577 Data conversion equipment,
media-to-media: computer

Key Largo
Monroe County

(G-6842)
AUTOMATED PRODUCTION EQP APE
Also Called: A P E
2 N Blackwater Ln (33037-2900)
PHONE..............................631 654-1197
William Scheu, *Ch of Bd*
Jose Vilar, *Opers Mgr*
Barbara Scheu, *Admin Sec*
EMP: 10 EST: 1969
SQ FT: 24,200
SALES (est): 927.9K **Privately Held**
WEB: www.ape.com
SIC: 3559 3548 3423 Electronic compo-
nent making machinery; welding appara-
tus; hand & edge tools

(G-6843)
AUTOMATED PRODUCTION EQP APE
Also Called: Ape South
2 N Blackwater Ln (33037-2900)
PHONE..............................305 451-4722
Casey Scheu, *President*
Bobbie Scheu, *Vice Pres*
Casey K Scheu, *Information Mgr*
EMP: 8 EST: 1991
SQ FT: 13,000
SALES (est): 1.9MM **Privately Held**
WEB: www.ape.com
SIC: 3599 Machine & other job shop work

(G-6844)
CROSS KEY MARINE CANVAS INC
Also Called: Key Largo Canvas
103761 Overseas Hwy (33037-2832)
P.O. Box 371865 (33037-1865)
PHONE..............................305 451-1302
Robert A Cullin, *President*
Deborah Cullin, *Admin Sec*
EMP: 7 EST: 1980
SQ FT: 5,000

▲ = Import ▼=Export
◆ =Import/Export

SALES (est): 997.5K **Privately Held**
WEB: www.keylargocanvas.com
SIC: 2394 3354 Awnings, fabric: made
from purchased materials; aluminum extruded products

(G-6845)
FBO KEY LARGO LLC
14 Rainbow Dr (33037-3209)
PHONE...............................305 451-3018
Robert Stoky, *Mng Member*
EMP: 6 EST: 2020
SALES (est): 528.4K **Privately Held**
SIC: 2211 Apparel & outerwear fabrics,
cotton

(G-6846)
**FLORIDA KEYS KEYLIME
PRODUCTS**
95231 Overseas Hwy (33037-3897)
P.O. Box 9305, Fort Myers (33902-9305)
PHONE...............................305 853-0378
John McCarthy, *President*
▲ EMP: 6 EST: 1995
SQ FT: 1,800
SALES (est): 666K **Privately Held**
WEB: www.keylimeproducts.com
SIC: 2844 5947 7231 Face creams or lo-
tions; gift, novelty & souvenir shop; facial
salons

(G-6847)
**G G MILLWORK CONTRACTOR
INC (PA)**
300 Atlantic Dr Unit 7 (33037-4320)
P.O. Box 9688, Tavernier (33070-9688)
PHONE...............................305 852-1718
George Gargiulo, *President*
EMP: 6 EST: 2006
SALES (est): 367.3K **Privately Held**
SIC: 2431 Millwork

(G-6848)
**KEYS DECK & DOCK SUPPLIES
INC**
100151 Overseas Hwy (33037-4422)
PHONE...............................305 451-8001
Daniel Hoffman, *President*
EMP: 7 EST: 2012
SALES (est): 135.2K **Privately Held**
WEB: www.keysdecksanddocks.com
SIC: 3999 Dock equipment & supplies, in-
dustrial

(G-6849)
SINCLAIR INDUSTRIES LLC (PA)
101691 Overseas Hwy (33037-4585)
PHONE...............................305 215-0990
Ronald A Skrumbellos, *Manager*
EMP: 6 EST: 2017
SALES (est): 304.7K **Privately Held**
SIC: 3999 Manufacturing industries

(G-6850)
SPEEDSOURCE INC
4 South Dr (33037-2921)
PHONE...............................954 578-7071
EMP: 8
SQ FT: 12,000
SALES (est): 1.6MM **Privately Held**
SIC: 3711 Motor Vehicles And Car Bodies

(G-6851)
TIKI WATER SPORTS INC
94.5 Ocean Side (33037)
PHONE...............................305 852-9298
Robert Chester, *President*
Ted Tumbale, *Vice Pres*
Chip Short, *Sales Staff*
Daniel Delo, *Director*
▼ EMP: 8 EST: 1983
SQ FT: 7,000
SALES (est): 1.3MM **Privately Held**
WEB: www.tikiwatersports.com
SIC: 3089 5999 Plastic & fiberglass tanks;
fiberglass materials, except insulation

(G-6852)
VIVONEX LLC
24 Dockside Ln (33037-5267)
PHONE...............................210 695-9244
EMP: 61

SALES (corp-wide): 276.8K **Privately Held**
WEB: www.nexdosemtm.com
SIC: 3841 Surgical & medical instruments
PA: Vivonex, Llc
4000 Ponce De Leon Blvd
Coral Gables FL 33146
305 367-3606

Key West
Monroe County

(G-6853)
**ANCHOR ALUMINUM
PRODUCTS SOUTH**
2807 Staples Ave (33040-4040)
PHONE...............................305 293-7965
EMP: 5
SALES (est): 557.7K **Privately Held**
SIC: 3446 3442 3354 Mfg Architectural
Metalwork Mfg Metal Doors/Sash/Trim
Mfg Aluminum Extruded Products

(G-6854)
APPS 47 INC
1118 Catherine St (33040-3306)
PHONE...............................413 200-7533
Adrain Laza, *CEO*
EMP: 17 EST: 2017
SALES (est): 655.3K **Privately Held**
SIC: 1389 Construction, repair & disman-
tling services

(G-6855)
BABYS COFFEE LLC
3178 Us Highway 1 (33040-6124)
P.O. Box 6558 (33041-6558)
PHONE...............................305 744-9866
Gary Teplitsky, *President*
Mary Broman, *General Mgr*
Olga Teplitsky, *Admin Sec*
EMP: 5 EST: 1991
SQ FT: 2,800
SALES (est): 563.2K **Privately Held**
WEB: www.babyscoffee.com
SIC: 2095 5499 5149 Roasted coffee;
beverage stores; coffee & tea

(G-6856)
BARRETT & COMPANY
3201 Flagler Ave Ste 501 (33040-4693)
PHONE...............................305 293-4501
EMP: 6
SALES (est): 895.6K **Privately Held**
SIC: 3577 Mfg Computer Peripheral Equip-
ment
PA: Local Enterprises, Inc.
3201 Flagler Ave Ste 501
Key West FL 33040

(G-6857)
CARPE DIEM ICE CREAM LLC
Also Called: Carpe Diem Ice Cream Key West
300 Front St (33040-6629)
PHONE...............................305 504-4469
Julie Cruchet, *Principal*
Patrick Cruchet, *Principal*
EMP: 7 EST: 2014
SALES (est): 248K **Privately Held**
SIC: 2024 2052 Ice cream & frozen
desserts; cones, ice cream

(G-6858)
**CAYO HUESO ENTERPRISES
INC**
Also Called: Hanson and Bringle Cabinets
5750 2nd Ave (33040-5950)
PHONE...............................305 747-0020
Steve Bringle, *President*
Norma Bringle, *Treasurer*
Ross Brown, *Admin Sec*
EMP: 25 EST: 1978
SQ FT: 2,700
SALES (est): 1.7MM **Privately Held**
WEB: www.hansenandbringle.com
SIC: 2434 Wood kitchen cabinets

(G-6859)
CHEF DISTILLED LLC
107 Simonton St (33040-6626)
PHONE...............................305 747-8236
William P Cormack, *Director*
EMP: 7 EST: 2013

SALES (est): 519.9K **Privately Held**
WEB: www.keywestlegalrum.com
SIC: 2085 Distilled & blended liquors

(G-6860)
**COOKE COMMUNICATIONS FLA
LLC (PA)**
Also Called: Key West Citizen
3140 Flagler Ave (33040-4602)
P.O. Box 1800 (33041-1800)
PHONE...............................305 292-7777
John Cooke Jr, *Publisher*
Kevin Downey, *Adv Dir*
Ernestine Balin, *Advt Staff*
Glenn Brandt, *Advt Staff*
Melissa Fernandez, *Advt Staff*
EMP: 100 EST: 2000
SALES (est): 16.5MM **Privately Held**
WEB: www.keysnews.com
SIC: 2711 Commercial printing & newspa-
per publishing combined

(G-6861)
CURRY & SONS INC
Also Called: Curry & Sons Prtg & Off Sup
3201 Flagler Ave Ste 504 (33040-4693)
PHONE...............................305 296-8781
Scott Curry, *President*
EMP: 5 EST: 1972
SQ FT: 2,800
SALES (est): 658.8K **Privately Held**
WEB: www.curryandsonsprinting.com
SIC: 2752 Commercial printing, offset; lith-
ographing on metal; visiting cards, litho-
graphed; business forms, lithographed

(G-6862)
DION FUELS LLC (PA)
5300 Overseas Hwy 2 (33040-4327)
PHONE...............................305 296-2000
Steven M Uphoff, *CEO*
John J Cary, *President*
Linda Uphoff, *Corp Secy*
EMP: 15 EST: 2016
SALES (est): 2.4MM **Privately Held**
SIC: 2911 Gasoline blending plants

(G-6863)
FISHERS OF KEYS INC
5700 4th Ave (33040-6038)
P.O. Box 2601 (33045-2601)
PHONE...............................305 296-8671
Alan H Kirby, *President*
EMP: 7 EST: 2011
SALES (est): 68.2K **Privately Held**
WEB: www.keysnews.com
SIC: 2711 Commercial printing & newspa-
per publishing combined

(G-6864)
FURY SURF SHACK
201 Front St Ste 109 (33040-8346)
PHONE...............................305 747-0799
Peter Norquoy, *President*
EMP: 7 EST: 2007
SALES (est): 174K **Privately Held**
SIC: 2211 Apparel & outerwear fabrics,
cotton

(G-6865)
GLE HOLDINGS INC
3255 Flagler Ave Ste 301 (33040-4646)
PHONE...............................305 295-7585
Patrick Labrada, *Partner*
EMP: 7 EST: 1991
SALES (est): 623.1K **Privately Held**
WEB: www.goallineembroidery.com
SIC: 2395 Embroidery products, except
schiffli machine

(G-6866)
**HEMINGWAY RUM COMPANY
LLC (PA)**
201 Simonton St (33040-6628)
P.O. Box 783486, Winter Garden (34778-
3486)
PHONE...............................305 414-8754
Jessie Behar, *Marketing Staff*
Eric Lear, *Mng Member*
Shawn Martin, *Manager*
EMP: 8 EST: 2012
SALES (est): 2.8MM **Privately Held**
WEB: www.papaspilar.com
SIC: 2085 Rum (alcoholic beverage)

(G-6867)
ISLAND BOTTLES
718 Emma St (33040-7381)
PHONE...............................305 304-7673
Sandra Guthrie, *Principal*
EMP: 7 EST: 2010
SALES (est): 206.9K **Privately Held**
SIC: 3085 Plastics bottles

(G-6868)
KEY WEST PRINTING LLC
5585 2nd Ave Ste 1 (33040-5932)
P.O. Box 809 (33041-0809)
PHONE...............................305 517-6711
Richard C Davis,
EMP: 5 EST: 2017
SALES (est): 650K **Privately Held**
WEB: store.keywestprinting.net
SIC: 2752 2711 2621 Commercial print-
ing, offset; newspapers, publishing &
printing; book, bond & printing papers

(G-6869)
**KEY WEST WLDG FABRICATION
INC**
5650 1st Ave (33040-5999)
P.O. Box 2658 (33045-2658)
PHONE...............................305 296-5555
Steve Condella, *President*
EMP: 6 EST: 1970
SQ FT: 15,000
SALES (est): 1MM **Privately Held**
WEB:
www.keywestweldingandfabrication.com
SIC: 7692 7353 Welding repair; cranes &
aerial lift equipment, rental or leasing

(G-6870)
KEYS BLINDS INC
1103 Truman Ave (33040-3371)
George R Newman, *Principal*
EMP: 8 EST: 2019
SALES (est): 127.5K **Privately Held**
WEB: www.keysblinds.com
SIC: 2591 Mfg Drapery Hardware/Blinds

(G-6871)
KINO SANDALS INC
Also Called: Kino Shoe Factory
107 Fitzpatrick St (33040-6514)
PHONE...............................305 294-5044
Robert Lopez Jr, *President*
Christina Ruiz, *Vice Pres*
Anna Sariegl, *Vice Pres*
Magot Lopez, *Shareholder*
EMP: 17 EST: 1966
SALES (est): 2MM **Privately Held**
WEB: www.kinosandals.com
SIC: 3089 3144 3143 Boot or shoe prod-
ucts, plastic; women's footwear, except
athletic; men's footwear, except athletic

(G-6872)
LANDMARK AVIATION
3471 S Roosevelt Blvd (33040-5234)
PHONE...............................305 296-5422
EMP: 7 EST: 2016
SALES (est): 249.1K **Privately Held**
SIC: 3721 Aircraft

(G-6873)
LOCAL ENTERPRISES INC
Also Called: Category 5 Design
3201 Flagler Ave Ste 501 (33040-4693)
PHONE...............................305 295-0026
Mike Marrero, *Principal*
EMP: 7 EST: 2010
SALES (est): 78.3K **Privately Held**
SIC: 2759 Screen printing

(G-6874)
MATTHEESSONS
106 Duval St (33040-6506)
PHONE...............................305 296-1616
Yakov Blives, *Principal*
EMP: 7 EST: 2010
SALES (est): 104.5K **Privately Held**
WEB: www.mattskeywest.com
SIC: 2024 Ice cream, bulk

(G-6875)
MCCONNELL CORP
Also Called: Flamingo Crossing
1107 Duval St (33040-3127)
PHONE...............................305 296-6124

Eleanor McConnell, *President*
Daniel McConnell, *Treasurer*
EMP: 5 **EST:** 1987
SALES (est): 563.2K **Privately Held**
SIC: 2024 5451 Ice cream, bulk; ice cream (packaged)

(G-6876)
MONROE CONCRETE PRODUCTS INC
155 Overseas Hwy (33040-5475)
P.O. Box 1149 (33041-1149)
PHONE...................................305 296-5606
Frank P Toppino, *President*
Edward Toppino Sr, *Corp Secy*
EMP: 70 **EST:** 1997
SQ FT: 4,000
SALES (est): 5.5MM **Privately Held**
WEB: www.charleytoppinoandsons.com
SIC: 3272 Concrete products

(G-6877)
MULTIHULL TECHNOLOGIES INC
Also Called: Key West Multihull
6811 Shrimp Rd (33040-5481)
P.O. Box 5372 (33045-5372)
PHONE...................................305 296-2773
Walter Schurtenberger, *President*
Sara C Smiley, *Vice Pres*
EMP: 8 **EST:** 1993
SQ FT: 5,400
SALES (est): 430.7K **Privately Held**
WEB: www.constellationyachts.com
SIC: 3732 5551 Yachts, building & repairing; boat dealers

(G-6878)
NEPTUNE DESIGNS INC
301 Duval St (33040-6509)
PHONE...................................305 294-8131
Jay Pfahl, *President*
Carmenza Pfahl, *Vice Pres*
EMP: 6 **EST:** 1976
SQ FT: 1,400
SALES (est): 530.5K **Privately Held**
WEB: www.neptunedesignskeywest.com
SIC: 3911 5944 Jewelry, precious metal; jewelry, precious stones & precious metals

(G-6879)
OVERSEAS RADIO LLC
Also Called: Mile Marker News
3732 Flagler Ave (33040-4529)
PHONE...................................305 296-1630
Guy Deboer, *President*
EMP: 7 **EST:** 2009
SALES (est): 213.3K **Privately Held**
WEB: www.konkam.com
SIC: 2711 7383 Newspapers, publishing & printing; news reporting services for newspapers & periodicals

(G-6880)
SANTIAGO OF KEY WEST INC
1301 United St (33040-3411)
PHONE...................................305 304-6063
Ramona L Santiago, *Principal*
EMP: 9 **EST:** 2014
SALES (est): 103.9K **Privately Held**
SIC: 2711 Commercial printing & newspaper publishing combined

(G-6881)
SPIRES EMPIRE LLC
1106 Grinnell St (33040-3206)
PHONE...................................305 797-0622
Angelo Morrison,
EMP: 5 **EST:** 2017
SALES (est): 300K **Privately Held**
SIC: 3161 Clothing & apparel carrying cases

(G-6882)
WHIZ BANG LLC
Also Called: Absolutely Amazing Ebooks
926 Truman Ave (33040-6431)
PHONE...................................305 296-0160
Albert L Kelley, *Manager*
EMP: 11 **EST:** 2010
SALES (est): 571.4K **Privately Held**
SIC: 2741 Miscellaneous publishing

Keystone Heights
Clay County

(G-6883)
AAT OMEGA LLC
6670 Spring Lake Rd (32656-8684)
PHONE...................................352 473-6673
EMP: 46 **EST:** 2014
SALES (est): 7.7MM **Privately Held**
WEB: www.aatomega.com
SIC: 3441 Fabricated structural metal

(G-6884)
CROFT PUBLISHING INC
5006 County Road 214 (32656-9796)
PHONE...................................352 473-3159
Sylvia Croft, *Principal*
EMP: 7 **EST:** 2002
SALES (est): 77.2K **Privately Held**
SIC: 2741 Miscellaneous publishing

(G-6885)
FABRICATING TECHNOLOGIES LLC
6670 Spring Lake Rd (32656-8684)
PHONE...................................352 473-6673
EMP: 9 **EST:** 2014
SALES (est): 445.4K **Privately Held**
SIC: 3441 Fabricated structural metal

(G-6886)
G & A MANUFACTURING INC
6045 State Road 21 (32656-9703)
PHONE...................................352 473-6882
Deborah Hoffman, *President*
John Hoffman, *Director*
EMP: 18 **EST:** 2005
SALES (est): 2.2MM **Privately Held**
WEB: www.gamanufacturing.com
SIC: 3441 Fabricated structural metal

(G-6887)
MANUFACTURERS INV GROUP LLC
Also Called: Mrl Industries
6670 Spring Lake Rd (32656-8684)
PHONE...................................630 285-0800
Andrew Sandberg, *CEO*
James Soderquist, *President*
▼ **EMP:** 13 **EST:** 1964
SQ FT: 40,000
SALES (est): 522K **Privately Held**
SIC: 3499 Magnetic shields, metal

(G-6888)
S & J CUSTOM FABRICATION INC
5955 Indian Trl (32656-9775)
PHONE...................................352 246-1462
Shane F Baker, *Principal*
EMP: 10 **EST:** 2012
SALES (est): 919.7K **Privately Held**
SIC: 3499 Novelties & giftware, including trophies

Kinard
Calhoun County

(G-6889)
FLOWERS LOGGING CO INC
5644 Sw Odeen Flowers Rd (32449-2506)
PHONE...................................850 639-2856
EMP: 8
SALES (est): 689.6K **Privately Held**
SIC: 2411 Logging

Kissimmee
Osceola County

(G-6890)
5TH ELEMENT INC
3848 Shoreview Dr (34744-0001)
PHONE...................................321 331-7028
Berith Nielsen, *Principal*
EMP: 7 **EST:** 2012
SALES (est): 146.4K **Privately Held**
WEB: www.my5thelement.com
SIC: 2819 Industrial inorganic chemicals

(G-6891)
AARDVARK SGNS PRPERTY SVCS LLC
304 W Oak St (34741-4422)
PHONE...................................407 348-7446
Lynn M Ingersoll, *Principal*
EMP: 6 **EST:** 2015
SALES (est): 811K **Privately Held**
WEB: www.aardvarksignsofkissimmee.com
SIC: 3993 Signs & advertising specialties

(G-6892)
ABBY PRESS INC
Also Called: PIP Printing
929 W Oak St (34741-4941)
PHONE...................................407 847-5565
Jacqueline Bohman, *President*
Frank Petrellis, *President*
Clarice Petrellis, *Corp Secy*
EMP: 36 **EST:** 1984
SQ FT: 4,800
SALES (est): 5.4MM **Privately Held**
WEB: www.pip.com
SIC: 2791 2789 2759 2752 Typesetting; bookbinding & related work; commercial printing; commercial printing, offset; signs & advertising specialties

(G-6893)
ACCURATE METAL FABRICATORS
3718 Grissom Ln (34741-4602)
PHONE...................................407 933-2666
Roger N Shorey, *President*
Brenda Shorey, *Treasurer*
EMP: 18 **EST:** 1985
SQ FT: 20,000
SALES (est): 1.2MM **Privately Held**
WEB: www.accuratemetal.net
SIC: 3469 Kitchen fixtures & equipment: metal, except cast aluminum

(G-6894)
AMERICAN STAINLESS & ALUM PDTS
315 Industrial Way (34746)
PHONE...................................423 472-4832
Michael Gray, *President*
Linda Gray, *Vice Pres*
EMP: 8 **EST:** 1969
SQ FT: 5,000
SALES (est): 580.9K **Privately Held**
WEB: www.americanstainless.net
SIC: 3443 Tanks, standard or custom fabricated: metal plate

(G-6895)
AUTOMATED MACHINE PRODUCTS INC
109 Acadia Ter (34747-5003)
PHONE...................................715 256-9575
Michael Berry, *President*
Greg J Berry, *Vice Pres*
EMP: 15 **EST:** 1950
SALES (est): 565.7K **Privately Held**
SIC: 3599 Machine shop, jobbing & repair

(G-6896)
BARSTOOL COMFORTS LLC
623 Front St Apt 5305 (34747-5467)
PHONE...................................610 737-5856
Stephanie Bertha, *Mng Member*
EMP: 8 **EST:** 2018
SALES (est): 1.3MM **Privately Held**
WEB: www.barstoolcomforts.com
SIC: 2521 Wood office chairs, benches & stools

(G-6897)
BASTINELLI CREATIONS LLC
109 Hangar Rd (34741-4505)
PHONE...................................407 572-8073
France Coves, *Principal*
EMP: 12 **EST:** 2017
SALES (est): 630K **Privately Held**
WEB: www.bastinelliknives.com
SIC: 3914 Cutlery, stainless steel

(G-6898)
BEST ENGINEERED SURFC TECH LLC (PA)
Also Called: Windsor Metal Finishing
1820 Avenue A (34758-2001)
P.O. Box 421210 (34742-1210)
PHONE...................................407 932-0008
Jack Sweeney, *General Mgr*
William Faucett,
▲ **EMP:** 65 **EST:** 1991
SQ FT: 33,000
SALES (est): 9.5MM **Privately Held**
WEB: www.1stchoicewindsor.com
SIC: 3479 3471 Coating of metals & formed products; finishing, metals or formed products

(G-6899)
BEST PRICE MOBILITY INC
941 Armstrong Blvd Ste B (34741-4619)
PHONE...................................321 402-5955
Robert Odell, *President*
Konni Odell, *Admin Sec*
EMP: 17 **EST:** 2008
SQ FT: 4,200
SALES (est): 1.6MM **Privately Held**
WEB: www.bpmobility.com
SIC: 3842 5012 5999 Wheelchairs; motor scooters; baby carriages & strollers

(G-6900)
BREATH LIFE MUSIC PUBLISHING
142 White Birch Dr (34743-8618)
PHONE...................................407 350-4669
Sandra M Darosa, *Principal*
EMP: 7 **EST:** 2011
SALES (est): 101.2K **Privately Held**
SIC: 2741 Miscellaneous publishing

(G-6901)
BRIAN BELITZ
3130 Winding Trl (34746-2807)
P.O. Box 1345, Geneva (32732-1345)
PHONE...................................407 924-5543
Brian Belitz, *Principal*
Brian L Belitz, *Principal*
EMP: 7 **EST:** 2012
SALES (est): 247.4K **Privately Held**
WEB: www.propertyclean.net
SIC: 3088 Shower stalls, fiberglass & plastic

(G-6902)
BUILDING BLOCKS GFRC LLC
1150 Joelson Rd (34744-1400)
PHONE...................................312 243-9960
Kevin Miske, *Mng Member*
EMP: 60 **EST:** 2017
SALES (est): 11.4MM **Privately Held**
WEB: www.buildingblocks.com
SIC: 3272 Concrete products, precast

(G-6903)
BUILDING BLOCKS MANAGEMENT INC
1150 Joelson Rd (34744-1400)
PHONE...................................214 289-9737
EMP: 13 **EST:** 2017
SALES (est): 2.4MM **Privately Held**
WEB: www.buildingblocks.com
SIC: 3089 Spouting, plastic & glass fiber reinforced

(G-6904)
CAM BROC SPORTS INC
Also Called: Cambroc Sports
3726 Grissom Ln (34741-4615)
PHONE...................................407 933-6524
Roger Paul Jones, *President*
Betty Ann Jones, *Vice Pres*
EMP: 6 **EST:** 1991
SQ FT: 3,500
SALES (est): 483.3K **Privately Held**
SIC: 2759 Screen printing

(G-6905)
CARGILL INCORPORATED
1845 Avenue A (34758-2002)
PHONE...................................407 846-4169
Jonathan Lindestrom, *Manager*
EMP: 36
SQ FT: 43,956

▲ = Import ▼=Export
◆ =Import/Export

SALES (corp-wide): 42.9B **Privately Held**
WEB: www.cargill.com
SIC: 2048 2047 Poultry feeds; livestock feeds; dog & cat food
PA: Cargill, Incorporated
  15407 Mcginty Rd W
  Wayzata MN 55391
  952 742-7575

(G-6906)
CHEMLINE INC
Also Called: SCI-Chem
1662 Broad St (34746-4282)
P.O. Box 422352 (34742-2352)
PHONE....................407 847-4181
Greg Livingston, *Principal*
Cheryl Ann Livingston, *Principal*
EMP: 7 **EST:** 1985
SQ FT: 6,000
SALES (est): 983.9K **Privately Held**
WEB: www.chemlineinc.com
SIC: 2899 Water treating compounds

(G-6907)
CHHAYA CORPORATION
Also Called: Ventura Cleaners
1988 E Osceola Pkwy (34743-8600)
PHONE....................407 348-9400
Sonal S Patel, *President*
EMP: 8 **EST:** 2004
SALES (est): 385.8K **Privately Held**
WEB: www.chhayacdc.org
SIC: 2842 Laundry cleaning preparations

(G-6908)
CONWAY BLDG CSTM WOODWORKS LLC
3001 Viscount Cir (34747-1620)
PHONE....................407 738-9266
Peter R Conway, *Manager*
EMP: 8 **EST:** 2010
SALES (est): 11.1K **Privately Held**
WEB: www.cbcw.us
SIC: 2431 Millwork

(G-6909)
CRAIN VENTURES INC
Also Called: Osceola Press
2775 Old Dixie Hwy Ste C (34744-1470)
P.O. Box 450245 (34745-0245)
PHONE....................407 933-1820
Kevin Crain, *President*
Melanie Crain, *Treasurer*
EMP: 5 **EST:** 1993
SQ FT: 2,400
SALES (est): 795.6K **Privately Held**
WEB: www.osceolapress.com
SIC: 2759 2752 Letterpress printing; screen printing; commercial printing, off-set

(G-6910)
CUSTOM PLASTIC DEVELOPMENTS
2710 N John Young Pkwy (34741-1266)
P.O. Box 422406 (34742-2406)
PHONE....................407 847-3054
Richard L Hord, *President*
Louise Hord, *Treasurer*
▲ **EMP:** 58 **EST:** 1962
SQ FT: 52,000
SALES (est): 9.2MM **Privately Held**
WEB: www.cpdfl.com
SIC: 3089 Injection molding of plastics

(G-6911)
DEEJA FOODS INC
1770 Business Center Ln (34758-1800)
PHONE....................321 402-8300
Hefazul Hakh, *CEO*
Ikbal Samad, *Director*
Mohamed S Mohamad, *Admin Sec*
◆ **EMP:** 9 **EST:** 2011
SALES (est): 875.3K **Privately Held**
SIC: 2044 Rice milling

(G-6912)
DENNYS WELDING SERVICE CORP
1533 Tina Ln (34744-5029)
P.O. Box 451488 (34745-1488)
PHONE....................321 494-2608
Dennys Ramirez, *Principal*
EMP: 7 **EST:** 2008

SALES (est): 89.7K **Privately Held**
SIC: 7692 Welding repair

(G-6913)
DEVCLAN INC
808 N Main St (34744-4564)
PHONE....................407 933-8212
Joshua Peters, *President*
Phillip Jackson, *Vice Pres*
Ray Peters, *Admin Sec*
Michael J Barber,
EMP: 8 **EST:** 2012
SALES (est): 401.7K **Privately Held**
WEB: www.devclan.com
SIC: 7372 Educational computer software

(G-6914)
E B CUSTOM CABINETS LLC
2756 Michigan Ave (34744-1557)
PHONE....................407 927-2346
Eliziah Bullock, *Principal*
EMP: 7 **EST:** 2010
SALES (est): 112.5K **Privately Held**
SIC: 2431 Millwork

(G-6915)
E G COATINGS LLC
1751 Covey Ct (34744-4082)
PHONE....................407 624-2615
Esteban J Guzman, *Manager*
EMP: 11 **EST:** 2013
SALES (est): 586.5K **Privately Held**
WEB: www.egcoatings.com
SIC: 3479 Coating of metals & formed products

(G-6916)
EASY FOODS INC
1965 Avenue A (34758-2003)
PHONE....................321 300-1104
Juan Pablo Viejo, *Branch Mgr*
Lisa Govind, *Manager*
EMP: 177 **Privately Held**
WEB: www.easyfoodsinc.com
SIC: 2099 Food preparations
PA: Easy Foods Inc.
  1728 Coral Way Ste 900
  Miami FL 33145

(G-6917)
EDEN FAST FROZEN DESSERT LLC
107 Broadway (34741-5713)
PHONE....................787 375-0826
Janette Alvarez, *Mng Member*
EMP: 10 **EST:** 2018
SALES (est): 675.3K **Privately Held**
SIC: 2024 Ice cream & frozen desserts

(G-6918)
EVEREST AIR CORP
3830 Golden Feather Way (34746-1918)
PHONE....................407 319-6204
Bibi Rahim, *Principal*
EMP: 18 **EST:** 2010
SALES (est): 537.1K **Privately Held**
SIC: 3585 1711 7623 Air conditioning equipment, complete; air conditioning units, complete: domestic or industrial; heating & air conditioning contractors; air conditioning repair

(G-6919)
FERIA DE ARTESANIA PARA TI
5425 Calla Lily Ct (34758-1909)
PHONE....................407 545-0909
Ismael Perez, *Principal*
EMP: 7 **EST:** 2015
SALES (est): 92.3K **Privately Held**
SIC: 2752 Commercial printing, litho-graphic

(G-6920)
FLORIDA GOLD FOODS LLC
1770 Business Center Ln (34758-1800)
PHONE....................347 595-1983
Ashishkumar Khandge, *Principal*
EMP: 10 **EST:** 2019
SALES (est): 1.1MM **Privately Held**
WEB: www.floridagoldfoods.com
SIC: 2044 Rice milling

(G-6921)
FLORIDA ROCK INDUSTRIES
49 Neptune Rd (34744-5238)
PHONE....................407 847-6457
EMP: 9 **Publicly Held**
WEB: www.flarock.com
SIC: 1422 Lime rock, ground
HQ: Florida Rock Industries
  4707 Gordon St
  Jacksonville FL 32216
  904 355-1781

(G-6922)
FLOWERS BKG CO BRADENTON LLC
Also Called: Flowers Baking Company
4990 S Orange Blossom Trl (34758-2039)
PHONE....................941 758-5656
Chris Peer, *Manager*
EMP: 25
SALES (corp-wide): 4.3B **Publicly Held**
WEB: www.flobradconf.com
SIC: 2051 Bread, cake & related products
HQ: Flowers Baking Co. Of Bradenton, Llc
  6490 Parkland Dr
  Sarasota FL 34243

(G-6923)
GATE PRECAST COMPANY
Also Called: Gate Precast Concrete
1018 Sawdust Trl (34744-1418)
PHONE....................407 847-5285
Bryant Luke, *Vice Pres*
Lisa Neuman, *Purch Agent*
Dawn Shaw, *Controller*
Hagan Lambert, *Manager*
EMP: 150
SALES (corp-wide): 708.1K **Privately Held**
WEB: www.gateprecast.com
SIC: 3272 Concrete products, precast
HQ: Gate Precast Company
  9540 San Jose Blvd
  Jacksonville FL 32257
  904 732-7668

(G-6924)
GEONOVA GAMING LLC
2989 Siesta View Dr (34744-4136)
PHONE....................908 414-5874
George Quijano, *CEO*
EMP: 7 **EST:** 2020
SALES (est): 259.1K **Privately Held**
WEB: www.geonova-gaming.com
SIC: 7372 Prepackaged software

(G-6925)
HYDROGEN DIESEL PRFMCE INC
2410 Sabra Ct (34744-2784)
PHONE....................407 847-6064
Charlene Birch, *CFO*
EMP: 5 **EST:** 2009
SALES (est): 310K **Privately Held**
SIC: 3621 Motors & generators

(G-6926)
INNOVATIVE PDT SOLUTIONS LLC
2710 N John Young Pkwy (34741-1266)
P.O. Box 421265 (34742-1265)
PHONE....................407 933-2029
Richard W Hord,
Michael Bloemker,
EMP: 10 **EST:** 2002
SALES (est): 918.1K **Privately Held**
WEB: www.gotohmg.com
SIC: 3089 Air mattresses, plastic

(G-6927)
INSPIRATION FOAM INC
2860 Nicole Ave (34744-3808)
PHONE....................407 498-0040
Linda C Fuest, *Principal*
EMP: 10 **EST:** 2006
SALES (est): 162.1K **Privately Held**
SIC: 3069 Foam rubber

(G-6928)
J HERBERT CORPORATION
1751 S John Young Pkwy (34741-6392)
PHONE....................407 846-0588
Mary M Selbach, *President*
John Selbach, *Exec VP*
Tyler Bouchard, *Sales Staff*

Rosiland Selbach, *Manager*
◆ **EMP:** 17 **EST:** 1978
SQ FT: 9,200
SALES (est): 3.9MM **Privately Held**
WEB: www.jherbertcorp.com
SIC: 3536 Cranes & monorail systems
PA: Pm Enterprises Holdings, Llc
  1751 S John Young Pkwy
  Kissimmee FL 34741
  407 846-0588

(G-6929)
JAYDAD LLC
2734 Dixie Ln (34744-2782)
PHONE....................407 508-6267
Ruth Esperance, *CEO*
EMP: 9 **EST:** 2019
SALES (est): 253K **Privately Held**
SIC: 3999 Hair, dressing of, for the trade

(G-6930)
JCS CONTRACTING INC
731 Duncan Ave (34744-1916)
PHONE....................407 348-4555
Eric Litteral, *Admin Sec*
EMP: 5 **EST:** 2008
SALES (est): 450K **Privately Held**
SIC: 3271 Concrete block & brick

(G-6931)
JELD-WEN INC
Jeld-Wen Doors
1700 Avenue A (34758-2013)
PHONE....................407 343-8596
Keith Lewallen, *General Mgr*
EMP: 92 **Publicly Held**
SIC: 2431 5031 Doors, wood; doors & windows
HQ: Jeld-Wen, Inc.
  2645 Silver Crescent Dr
  Charlotte NC 28273
  800 535-3936

(G-6932)
JULIO GARCIA SATELLITE
1248 S John Young Pkwy (34741-6389)
PHONE....................407 414-3223
Julio Garcia, *President*
EMP: 8 **EST:** 2009
SALES (est): 160.3K **Privately Held**
SIC: 3663 Space satellite communications equipment

(G-6933)
KING CONSTRUCTION & GLASS LLC
1414 Grandview Blvd (34744-6689)
PHONE....................407 508-6286
James R Arneson, *Manager*
EMP: 8 **EST:** 2015
SALES (est): 250.4K **Privately Held**
SIC: 3211 Construction glass

(G-6934)
KISSIMMEE IRON WORKS INC
2741 Old Dixie Hwy (34744-1411)
PHONE....................407 870-8872
Alberto Vega, *President*
Wanda Vega, *Vice Pres*
EMP: 5 **EST:** 1998
SQ FT: 5,000
SALES (est): 809.5K **Privately Held**
SIC: 3312 Rods, iron & steel: made in steel mills

(G-6935)
KISSIMMEE PRINTING
1230 Simpson Rd (34744-4602)
PHONE....................407 518-2514
Fredy Peralta, *President*
EMP: 9 **EST:** 2011
SALES (est): 92.2K **Privately Held**
WEB: www.osceolapress.com
SIC: 2752 Commercial printing, offset

(G-6936)
KITE TECHNOLOGY GROUP LLC
2642 Michigan Ave Ste C (34744-1911)
PHONE....................407 557-0512
Rafael Perez, *Principal*
EMP: 12 **EST:** 2015
SALES (est): 490.7K **Privately Held**
WEB: www.kitetechnologygroup.com
SIC: 3944 Kites

(G-6937)
LEADAIR INC
113 Hangar Rd (34741-4505)
PHONE....................................407 343-7571
Jean P Barriere, *President*
Shirley Meyers, *Admin Mgr*
James Burditt, *Technician* ·
EMP: 21 **EST:** 2001
SALES (est): 5MM **Privately Held**
WEB: www.trackair.us
SIC: 3829 Surveying instruments & accessories

(G-6938)
LENTUS PRODUCTS LLC
215 Celebration Pl # 520 (34747-5400)
PHONE....................................203 913-7600
Dennis Walls, *CEO*
EMP: 7 **EST:** 2014
SALES (est): 616.4K **Privately Held**
WEB: www.lentusllc.com
SIC: 3531 Pavers

(G-6939)
LOGIC ILLUMINATION LLC
Also Called: Led Supply, The
3600 Commerce Blvd 102b (34741-4678)
PHONE....................................407 906-0126
Carlos Torres, *President*
Frank Veliz, *COO*
Christian Torres, *Vice Pres*
EMP: 10 **EST:** 2016
SALES (est): 828.2K **Privately Held**
WEB: www.logicillumination.com
SIC: 3648 3645 Outdoor lighting equipment; public lighting fixtures; residential lighting fixtures

(G-6940)
LOS COQUITOS
1319 E Vine St (34744-3642)
PHONE....................................407 289-9315
Elizabeth Braunschneider, *Principal*
EMP: 8 **EST:** 2007
SALES (est): 152.4K **Privately Held**
SIC: 2024 Ice cream & frozen desserts

(G-6941)
LOV INDUSTRIES INC
742 Royal Palm Dr (34743-9517)
PHONE....................................407 406-8221
Vanessa Gonzalez, *Branch Mgr*
EMP: 18
SALES (corp-wide): 71K **Privately Held**
SIC: 3999 Atomizers, toiletry
PA: Lov Industries Inc
  14200 Avonlea Ct
  Orlando FL

(G-6942)
METAL BUILDING SUPPLIES LLC
800 E Donegan Ave (34744-1939)
PHONE....................................407 935-9714
Scott J Prossen, *Mng Member*
EMP: 12 **EST:** 2000
SQ FT: 10,000
SALES (est): 1.6MM **Privately Held**
WEB: www.mbsmetals.com
SIC: 3448 Panels for prefabricated metal buildings

(G-6943)
MIX IT AT LOOP
2617 W Osceola Pkwy (34741-0766)
PHONE....................................407 201-8948
Brian Melaney, *Vice Pres*
EMP: 10 **EST:** 2010
SALES (est): 562.5K **Privately Held**
SIC: 2024 Ice cream, bulk

(G-6944)
MK BROTHERS INC
2790 Michigan Ave Ste 318 (34744-1558)
PHONE....................................407 847-9547
Mohammad Khan, *Principal*
EMP: 6 **EST:** 2008
SALES (est): 468K **Privately Held**
SIC: 2253 T-shirts & tops, knit

(G-6945)
NURSERY SUPPLIES INC
2050 Avenue A (34758-2407)
PHONE....................................407 846-9750
Audrey Schultz, *Buyer*

Michelle Boudreau, *Sales Staff*
Cory Butler, *Sales Staff*
Skye Sawyer, *Sales Staff*
David Conney, *Manager*
EMP: 360
SALES (corp-wide): 78.2MM **Privately Held**
WEB: www.nurserysupplies.com
SIC: 3089 Flower pots, plastic
PA: Nursery Supplies, Inc.
  1415 Orchard Dr
  Chambersburg PA 17201
  717 263-7780

(G-6946)
ORGANIZACION MARKETING MIX LLC
1006 Verona St (34741-5453)
PHONE....................................407 924-2709
Maria T Story, *Principal*
EMP: 8 **EST:** 2010
SALES (est): 213.8K **Privately Held**
SIC: 3273 Ready-mixed concrete

(G-6947)
ORION DNTL SLS TRNING REPR LLC
Also Called: Orion Repair
4721 Rockvale Dr (34758-3361)
PHONE....................................888 674-6657
Amanda Laird, *Principal*
EMP: 6 **EST:** 1995
SALES (est): 505.9K **Privately Held**
WEB: www.orionrepair.com
SIC: 3843 Autoclaves, dental; burs, dental; drills, dental; hand pieces & parts, dental

(G-6948)
OSCEOLA STAR
921 Emmett St (34741-5435)
PHONE....................................407 933-0174
Bill Hansen, *Owner*
EMP: 6 **EST:** 1993
SALES (est): 498.9K **Privately Held**
WEB: www.elosceolastar.com
SIC: 2711 Newspapers: publishing only, not printed on site

(G-6949)
OSCEOLA WOMAN NEWSPAPER LLC
111 E Monu Ave Unit 401 (34741)
PHONE....................................407 891-9771
Gregg Blain, *Owner*
EMP: 6 **EST:** 2007
SALES (est): 450.3K **Privately Held**
WEB: www.osceolawoman.com
SIC: 2711 Commercial printing & newspaper publishing combined; newspapers, publishing & printing

(G-6950)
PEEKS MOBILE APP CORP
3955 Golden Finch Way (34746-2007)
PHONE....................................407 931-3878
Estefania Tejada, *Branch Mgr*
EMP: 15
SALES (corp-wide): 158.1K **Privately Held**
SIC: 7372 Application computer software
PA: Peeks Mobile App Corp
  611 N Mills Ave
  Orlando FL

(G-6951)
PEPSICO INC
1650 S Poinciana Blvd (34758-2046)
PHONE....................................407 933-5542
John Carriero, *Regional Mgr*
Heather Hoytink, *Vice Pres*
David Price, *Production*
Keith Thompson, *Technical Mgr*
Daniel Dorman, *Finance*
EMP: 24
SALES (corp-wide): 70.3B **Publicly Held**
WEB: www.pepsico.com
SIC: 2033 2086 Fruit juices: packaged in cans, jars, etc.; bottled & canned soft drinks
PA: Pepsico, Inc.
  700 Anderson Hill Rd
  Purchase NY 10577
  914 253-2000

(G-6952)
PM ENTERPRISES HOLDINGS LLC (PA)
1751 S John Young Pkwy (34741-6392)
PHONE....................................407 846-0588
Peter A Scheckenhofer, *Mng Member*
EMP: 3 **EST:** 2019
SALES (est): 3.9MM **Privately Held**
SIC: 3536 Cranes & monorail systems

(G-6953)
PNC MANUFACTURING LEATHER
4107 S Orange Blossom Trl (34746-7265)
PHONE....................................407 201-2069
Jose Guzman, *Principal*
EMP: 7 **EST:** 2014
SALES (est): 329.6K **Privately Held**
SIC: 3999 Manufacturing industries

(G-6954)
POINCIANA MILLING COMPLEX INC
1770 Business Center Ln (34758-1800)
PHONE....................................407 587-5525
Omawattie Badley, *CEO*
Mohindra Persaud, *Director*
Rajendra Persaud, *Director*
◆ **EMP:** 7 **EST:** 2013
SALES (est): 111K **Privately Held**
WEB: www.poincianamillingcomplex.com
SIC: 2044 Rice milling

(G-6955)
PRECISION MOLD & TOOL INC
2780 N John Young Pkwy (34741-1222)
PHONE....................................407 847-5687
Jerry Longbrake, *President*
Joseph W Longbrake, *Corp Secy*
Mark E Longbrake, *Vice Pres*
Jennifer Dipaula, *Office Mgr*
▼ **EMP:** 33 **EST:** 1961
SQ FT: 20,000
SALES (est): 7.2MM **Privately Held**
SIC: 3089 Injection molding of plastics

(G-6956)
PRO DUMPSTERS INC
3864 Wood Thrush Dr (34744-9156)
PHONE....................................407 910-6341
Freddy Pena, *Principal*
EMP: 16 **EST:** 2017
SALES (est): 604.8K **Privately Held**
WEB: www.produmpsterorlando.com
SIC: 3443 Dumpsters, garbage

(G-6957)
QUAKER OATS COMPANY
1650 S Poinciana Blvd (34758-2046)
PHONE....................................407 846-5926
Roger Dicky, *General Mgr*
EMP: 233
SALES (corp-wide): 70.3B **Publicly Held**
SIC: 2086 Bottled & canned soft drinks
HQ: The Quaker Oats Company
  555 W Monroe St Fl 1
  Chicago IL 60661
  312 821-1000

(G-6958)
QUANTEM FBO GROUP KSSIMMEE LLC
3950 Merlin Dr (34741-4551)
PHONE....................................407 846-8001
Frank Pisano, *Vice Pres*
Ansel Richardson, *Opers Mgr*
EMP: 8 **EST:** 2015
SALES (est): 563.5K **Privately Held**
WEB: www.quantemfbo.com
SIC: 3572 Computer storage devices

(G-6959)
SANDPIPER TURBINE LLC
3955 Merlin Dr (34741-4551)
PHONE....................................407 377-7220
William M Whelan,
EMP: 10 **EST:** 2018
SALES (est): 610.2K **Privately Held**
WEB: www.sandpiperturbine.com
SIC: 3511 Turbines & turbine generator sets & parts

(G-6960)
SCHIMMBROS INC
3726 Grissom Ln (34741-4615)
PHONE....................................407 796-8361
Randy E Schimmelpfennig, *Principal*
EMP: 7 **EST:** 2015
SALES (est): 486.7K **Privately Held**
WEB: www.schimmbros.com
SIC: 2759 Screen printing

(G-6961)
SUN PUBLICATIONS FLORIDA INC
Also Called: Osceola Shopper
108 Church St (34741-5055)
PHONE....................................321 402-0257
Jim Zajas, *General Mgr*
Bill Hoar, *Sales Mgr*
Paula Stark, *Manager*
Kathy Beckham, *Manager*
Rochelle Stidham, *Manager*
EMP: 90
SALES (corp-wide): 13.7MM **Privately Held**
WEB: www.sunpubfla.com
SIC: 2741 6531 Guides: publishing only, not printed on site; shopping news: publishing only, not printed on site; real estate agents & managers
HQ: Sun Publications Of Florida, Inc.
  7060 Havertys Way
  Lakeland FL 33805

(G-6962)
SUNRISE PRINTING & SIGNS
1218 Dyer Blvd (34741-3723)
PHONE....................................321 284-3803
EMP: 8 **EST:** 2016
SALES (est): 141.9K **Privately Held**
SIC: 2752 Commercial printing, lithographic

(G-6963)
SYMBOL MATTRESS FLORIDA INC
5000 Mercantile Ln (34758-2401)
P.O. Box 3233, Fort Worth TX (76113-3233)
PHONE....................................407 343-4626
Eric Rhea, *CEO*
Charles H Neal, *Ch of Bd*
Ronald L Clevenger, *President*
Michael J McQuiston, *Exec VP*
George Coffey, *Manager*
▼ **EMP:** 7 **EST:** 2005
SALES (est): 495.8K **Privately Held**
SIC: 2515 Sleep furniture

(G-6964)
TECHTRONICS LLC
Also Called: 12 Volt USA
2450 Smith St Ste A (34744-2301)
PHONE....................................407 738-4680
Anthony S Marasco, *CEO*
EMP: 7 **EST:** 2007
SALES (est): 190.1K **Privately Held**
SIC: 3679 Electronic circuits

(G-6965)
TEDDY MOUNTAIN LLC (PA)
1901 S John Young Pkwy # 104 (34741-0601)
PHONE....................................877 480-2327
Patrick M Shirkey, *President*
▲ **EMP:** 8 **EST:** 2012
SALES (est): 1.3MM **Privately Held**
WEB: direct.teddymountain.com
SIC: 3942 Dolls & stuffed toys

(G-6966)
TF DEFENSE LLC
147 Toluca Dr (34743-7027)
PHONE....................................321 961-7596
EMP: 6 **EST:** 2018
SALES (est): 559.1K **Privately Held**
SIC: 3812 Defense systems & equipment

(G-6967)
U GOT RECOVERY INC
3406 W Vine St (34741-4637)
P.O. Box 420627 (34742-0627)
PHONE....................................407 343-9919
Eric R Escobales, *Principal*
EMP: 9 **EST:** 2006

2022 Harris Florida
Manufacturers Directory

▲ = Import ▼=Export
◆ =Import/Export

SALES (est): 410.4K **Privately Held**
SIC: 3531 Automobile wrecker hoists

(G-6968)
UFP TECHNOLOGIES INC
United Foam Plastic
2175 Partin Settlement Rd (34744-4956)
PHONE..................................407 933-4880
John Waddington, *Plant Mgr*
Gwenael Busnel, *Plant Mgr*
Tony Johnson, *Mfg Mgr*
EMP: 40
SALES (corp-wide): 206.3MM **Publicly Held**
WEB: www.ufpmedtech.com
SIC: 3086 Packaging & shipping materials, foamed plastic
PA: Ufp Technologies, Inc.
100 Hale St
Newburyport MA 01950
978 352-2200

(G-6969)
UNIVERSAL KIT CABINETS CLOSETS
2905 Welcome Cir (34746-3007)
PHONE..................................305 406-9096
Jorge Escobar, *Principal*
EMP: 7 EST: 2016
SALES (est): 210.4K **Privately Held**
WEB: www.universalcabinetsfl.com
SIC: 2434 Wood kitchen cabinets

(G-6970)
UTILYTECH COMPANY
630 Baldwin Dr (34758-4100)
PHONE..................................813 778-6952
Kenneth Leff, *Owner*
EMP: 10 EST: 2000
SALES (est): 504.5K **Privately Held**
SIC: 3823 Industrial instrmnts msrmnt display/control process variable

(G-6971)
VEATIC
2450 Smith St Ste P (34744-2305)
PHONE..................................888 474-2999
Dario Camacho, *President*
EMP: 6 EST: 2014
SALES (est): 490.4K **Privately Held**
WEB: www.veatic.com
SIC: 3441 Fabricated structural metal

(G-6972)
WELSHMAN INVESTMENT CORP
Also Called: Specialty Wood Manufacturing
1570 Kelley Ave Ste 2 (34744-3305)
PHONE..................................407 933-4444
David Wood, *President*
▼ EMP: 8 EST: 1989
SQ FT: 8,000
SALES (est): 658.4K **Privately Held**
SIC: 2434 2499 1751 Wood kitchen cabinets; decorative wood & woodwork; cabinet & finish carpentry

(G-6973)
YESCO ORLANDO SOUTH
929 W Oak St (34741-4941)
PHONE..................................407 922-5856
EMP: 7 EST: 2019
SALES (est): 140.6K **Privately Held**
WEB: www.yesco.com
SIC: 3993 Signs & advertising specialties

(G-6974)
Z & N MANUFACTURING CORP
1732 Kelley Ave (34744-3300)
PHONE..................................407 518-1114
Yolanda Zambrano, *Principal*
EMP: 7 EST: 2007
SALES (est): 240.4K **Privately Held**
SIC: 3999 Manufacturing industries

Kissimmee
Polk County

(G-6975)
CND EXPRESS SCOOTERS LLC
721 Pincon Ln (34759-3807)
PHONE..................................407 633-1079
Dayvid Derat,
EMP: 7

SALES (est): 302.2K **Privately Held**
SIC: 2519 7389 Household furniture;

(G-6976)
DON SIGNS INC (PA)
766 Camel Ct (34759-4315)
PHONE..................................407 344-9444
Jorge Ferrera, *Principal*
EMP: 6 EST: 2007
SALES (est): 400.2K **Privately Held**
WEB: www.donsigns.com
SIC: 3993 Signs & advertising specialties

(G-6977)
MATRY GROUP LLC ✪
10 S Flag Dr (34759-3319)
PHONE..................................407 461-9797
Jeff R Bernal, *CEO*
EMP: 10 EST: 2021
SALES (est): 300K **Privately Held**
SIC: 3999 Pet supplies

(G-6978)
WILLIE MAES PIES LLC
843 Cypress Pkwy 253 (34759-3408)
P.O. Box 581329 (34758-0017)
PHONE..................................407 655-9360
Sophia Brown, *Principal*
EMP: 8 EST: 2008
SALES (est): 400K **Privately Held**
SIC: 2051 Bakery: wholesale or wholesale/retail combined

La Belle
Hendry County

(G-6979)
ER JAHNA INDUSTRIES INC
Ortona Sand Company
Highway 78 E (33935)
P.O. Box 786, Labelle (33975-0786)
PHONE..................................863 675-3942
Giddel Gallardo, *Branch Mgr*
EMP: 10
SALES (corp-wide): 49.2MM **Privately Held**
WEB: www.jahna.com
SIC: 1442 Common sand mining
PA: E.R. Jahna Industries, Inc.
202 E Stuart Ave
Lake Wales FL 33853
863 676-9431

Labelle
Hendry County

(G-6980)
CENTERLINE DRCTNAL DRLG SVC IN
Also Called: Centerline Drctnal Drlg Srvcin
900 S Elm St (33935-4620)
P.O. Box 2705 (33975-2705)
PHONE..................................863 674-0913
Lauro Aceveado, *President*
EMP: 42 EST: 2011
SALES (est): 6.2MM **Privately Held**
SIC: 1381 Directional drilling oil & gas wells

(G-6981)
KENTON INDUSTRIES LLC
1477 Forestry Division Rd (33935-3001)
PHONE..................................863 675-8233
Robert Spencer, *Treasurer*
Kenneth A Wallace,
EMP: 5 EST: 2007
SALES (est): 420.9K **Privately Held**
WEB: www.kentonindustries.com
SIC: 3271 Concrete block & brick

(G-6982)
LABELLE BRICK PAVERS TILE LLC
Also Called: Gulf Coast Pavers
1515 Forestry Division Rd (33935-3003)
PHONE..................................863 230-3100
Daniel Hinthorn,
Dan Hinthorn,
▲ EMP: 15 EST: 2006

SALES (est): 1.2MM **Privately Held**
SIC: 3271 3531 Blocks, concrete: drystack interlocking; pavers

(G-6983)
MIMS WELDING INCORPORATED
90 Evans Rd (33935-9135)
P.O. Box 3235, Immokalee (34143-3235)
PHONE..................................863 612-9819
Alton L Mims, *President*
Preston T Mims, *Vice Pres*
EMP: 9 EST: 1962
SQ FT: 13,000
SALES (est): 603.5K **Privately Held**
SIC: 7692 Automotive welding

(G-6984)
NEW ENERGY FUELS LLC
259 Ford Ave (33935-4642)
PHONE..................................281 205-0153
Nick Dunbar, *Mng Member*
Robert Dascal,
EMP: 8 EST: 2008
SALES (est): 139.7K **Privately Held**
SIC: 2911 Diesel fuels

(G-6985)
OVIPOST INC
635 A Rd (33935-9454)
PHONE..................................707 776-6108
Trina Chiasson, *CEO*
EMP: 10 EST: 2017
SALES (est): 1MM **Privately Held**
WEB: www.ovipost.com
SIC: 3523 Farm machinery & equipment

(G-6986)
SOUTH WEST ADVENTURE TEAM LLC
Also Called: Pool Cleaning Service
505 W Hickpochee Ave # 2001 (33935-4735)
PHONE..................................903 288-4739
James Beecham, *CEO*
EMP: 5 EST: 2017
SALES (est): 318.1K **Privately Held**
SIC: 3589 1799 5091 5999 Swimming pool filter & water conditioning systems; swimming pool construction; swimming pools, equipment & supplies; swimming pool chemicals, equipment & supplies; swimming pool & hot tub service & maintenance; swimming pool, non-membership

(G-6987)
SUNCREST SHEDS INC (PA)
1451 Commerce Dr (33935-3002)
PHONE..................................863 675-8600
Brian Quinn, *President*
▼ EMP: 7 EST: 1999
SALES (est): 2.4MM **Privately Held**
WEB: www.suncrestsheds.com
SIC: 2452 Prefabricated buildings, wood

(G-6988)
TROPIC MANUFACTURING INC
1451 Commerce Dr (33935-3002)
PHONE..................................863 673-3179
Brian K Quinn, *Principal*
EMP: 7 EST: 2012
SALES (est): 122.2K **Privately Held**
SIC: 3999 Manufacturing industries

Lady Lake
Lake County

(G-6989)
CAROLINA COMPANY USA LLC (PA)
1019 Nell Way (32159-2331)
PHONE..................................401 487-2749
Carri Barr,
EMP: 6 EST: 2017
SALES (est): 396.7K **Privately Held**
SIC: 2295 3949 2992 Coated fabrics, not rubberized; sporting & athletic goods; lubricating oils & greases

(G-6990)
DOUG BLOODWORTH ENTERPRISES
3211 Lake Griffin Rd (32159-3432)
PHONE..................................407 247-9728
Doug Bloodworth, *President*
EMP: 6 EST: 1993
SALES (est): 373.8K **Privately Held**
SIC: 3993 7532 Signs & advertising specialties; lettering & painting services

(G-6991)
HARTSOCK SAWMILL INC
2939 Hartsock Sawmill Rd (32159-5249)
PHONE..................................352 753-3581
Diane L Murray, *Principal*
EMP: 7 EST: 2010
SALES (est): 138.5K **Privately Held**
SIC: 2421 Lumber: rough, sawed or planed

(G-6992)
LOR-ED ENTERPRISES LLC
309 Lagrande Blvd (32159-2386)
PHONE..................................352 750-1999
Francis Neuzil Jr,
EMP: 8 EST: 2008
SQ FT: 3,500
SALES (est): 176.2K **Privately Held**
SIC: 3841 5047 Inhalators, surgical & medical; oxygen therapy equipment

(G-6993)
TOTAL NTRTN & THERAPEUTICS PA
809 Highway 466 Ste 202c (32159-3909)
PHONE..................................352 259-5190
Lori Esarey, *President*
EMP: 9 EST: 2007
SALES (est): 832.5K **Privately Held**
WEB: www.totalnutritionandtherapeutics.com
SIC: 2834 Vitamin, nutrient & hematinic preparations for human use

Lady Lake
Sumter County

(G-6994)
ATLANTECH PROCESS TECHNOLOGY
1953 Lake Miona Dr (32162-6404)
PHONE..................................352 751-4286
Hans H Thiemann, *President*
David Thiemann, *Director*
Karen L Thiemann, *Admin Sec*
EMP: 8 EST: 2017
SALES (est): 225.1K **Privately Held**
WEB: www.atlantechprocess.com
SIC: 3069 Brushes, rubber

Lake Alfred
Polk County

(G-6995)
GROWERS FERTILIZER CORPORATION (PA)
312 N Buena Vista Dr (33850-2006)
P.O. Box 1407 (33850-1407)
PHONE..................................863 956-1101
Brent W Sutton, *President*
Rick O Steen, *Corp Secy*
Harvey B Snively, *Vice Pres*
John Strang, *Vice Pres*
David White, *Sales Staff*
EMP: 48 EST: 1934
SQ FT: 30,000
SALES (est): 27.7MM **Privately Held**
WEB: www.growersfertilizer.com
SIC: 2874 2879 2873 Phosphatic fertilizers; insecticides, agricultural or household; nitrogenous fertilizers

(G-6996)
MIZKAN AMERICA INC
445 N Dakota Ave (33850-2127)
PHONE..................................863 956-0391
Jack Kichura, *Business Mgr*
Tim Carrigan, *Vice Pres*
Craig Cotton, *Plant Mgr*
Timothy Hakimi, *Plant Mgr*

Nicholas Richards, *Plant Mgr*
EMP: 18 **Privately Held**
WEB: www.mizkan.com
SIC: 2099 2035 Vinegar; dressings; salad: raw & cooked (except dry mixes); mustard, prepared (wet)
HQ: Mizkan America, Inc.
1661 Feehanville Dr 100a
Mount Prospect IL 60056
847 590-0059

(G-6997)
THE FORKLIFT COMPANY INC
290 W Harbord St (33850-3339)
PHONE................................863 595-8156
EMP: 15
SALES: 266K **Privately Held**
SIC: 3537 Mfg Industrial Trucks/Tractors

Lake Buena Vista
Orange County

(G-6998)
BUENA VISTA CONSTRUCTION CO
3291 Wed Way (32830)
PHONE................................407 828-2104
Greg Ruse, *Vice Pres*
EMP: 45 **EST:** 1972
SALES (est): 10MM
SALES (corp-wide): 67.4B **Publicly Held**
SIC: 1389 Construction, repair & dismantling services
HQ: Walt Disney Parks And Resorts U.S., Inc.
1375 E Buena Vista Dr # 4
Lake Buena Vista FL 32830
407 824-2222

(G-6999)
JFH TECHNOLOGIES LLC
Also Called: Field Service Office
1500 W Buena Vista Dr (32830)
PHONE................................407 938-9336
Julie Fantauzzo, *Branch Mgr*
EMP: 23
SALES (corp-wide): 1.8MM **Privately Held**
SIC: 3679 Power supplies, all types: static
PA: Jfh Technologies, Llc
13506 Smmrport Vlg Pkwy
Windermere FL 34786
407 938-9336

Lake Butler
Union County

(G-7000)
FRASER WEST INC
9022 Se 186th Pl (32054-4965)
P.O. Box 68 (32054-0068)
PHONE................................904 290-6460
EMP: 148
SALES (corp-wide): 10.5B **Privately Held**
SIC: 2431 0831 Millwork; forest products
HQ: West Fraser, Inc.
1900 Exeter Rd Ste 105
Germantown TN 38138
901 620-4200

(G-7001)
HYPER-SUB PLATFORM TECH INC
4661 W State Road 238 (32054-5353)
P.O. Box 471, Lake City (32056-0471)
PHONE................................386 365-6021
Reynolds Marion, *Ch of Bd*
EMP: 10 **EST:** 2018
SALES (est): 601.8K **Privately Held**
WEB: www.hypersub.com
SIC: 3812 1629 Defense systems & equipment; marine construction

(G-7002)
JOHN L SHADD ENTERPRISES
Us Hwy 121 (32054)
P.O. Box 506 (32054-0506)
PHONE................................386 496-3989
John L Shadd, *Owner*
EMP: 22 **EST:** 1956
SQ FT: 5,000

SALES (est): 289.9K **Privately Held**
WEB: www.shaddtrucking.us
SIC: 2411 Logging

(G-7003)
KIRKLAND INDUSTRIES LLC
4638 Sw 150th Rd (32054-8102)
PHONE................................386 496-3491
Amy Kirkland, *Principal*
EMP: 7 **EST:** 2014
SALES (est): 256.9K **Privately Held**
SIC: 3999 Barber & beauty shop equipment

(G-7004)
PEARCE LOGGING LLC
9335 Nw 148th Trl (32054-4159)
PHONE................................386 365-1880
Nathan Pearce, *Principal*
EMP: 7 **EST:** 2016
SALES (est): 328K **Privately Held**
SIC: 2411 Logging

(G-7005)
SAPHIRE SERVICES LLC
Also Called: Saphire Disinfection Products
250 Sw 9th Ave (32054-1415)
PHONE................................386 247-1048
Jody Read, *CEO*
Francis Read, *Principal*
EMP: 5 **EST:** 2016
SALES (est): 400.8K **Privately Held**
WEB: www.sapphiredisinfection.com
SIC: 2842 Sanitation preparations, disinfectants & deodorants

(G-7006)
SOUTHERN DOOR TECHNOLOGIES
9124 S County Road 231 (32054-7736)
PHONE................................386 496-3844
Ezra Eugene Mock, *President*
Ezra Mock, *Vice Pres*
EMP: 5 **EST:** 2000
SQ FT: 2,400
SALES (est): 309.4K **Privately Held**
SIC: 2431 Door frames, wood

Lake City
Columbia County

(G-7007)
A 2 Z OF LAKE CITY INC
628 Se Allison Ct (32025-6101)
PHONE................................386 755-0235
Dave Mangrum, *Principal*
EMP: 7 **EST:** 2010
SALES (est): 64.7K **Privately Held**
SIC: 2899 Salt

(G-7008)
A MATERIALS GROUP INC (PA)
871 Nw Guerdon St (32055-4346)
PHONE................................386 758-3164
Brian P Schreiber, *CEO*
Joe H Anderson Jr, *Ch of Bd*
Jim Maples, *President*
Douglas M Anderson, *Vice Pres*
Cindy Childers, *Treasurer*
EMP: 21 **EST:** 2002
SALES (est): 6.3MM **Privately Held**
SIC: 3273 Ready-mixed concrete

(G-7009)
A MINING GROUP LLC
871 Nw Guerdon St (32055-4346)
P.O. Box 1829 (32056-1829)
PHONE................................386 752-7585
Joe H Anderson III,
Dan Johnson,
Brian P Schreiber,
Shawn Snyder,
EMP: 23 **EST:** 2004
SALES (est): 1.1MM **Privately Held**
SIC: 1422 Crushed & broken limestone

(G-7010)
ACTION SIGNS & GRAPHICS INC
4180 S Us Highway 441 (32025-0304)
PHONE................................386 752-0121
Lindsay Laxton, *President*
Lashaun Perry, *President*
Larry Perry Jr, *Vice Pres*

EMP: 6 **EST:** 1998
SQ FT: 5,000
SALES (est): 637.5K **Privately Held**
WEB: www.actionsignsfl.com
SIC: 3993 Signs & advertising specialties

(G-7011)
AMERICAN METAL PROCESSORS INC
Also Called: Ampco
186 Se Newell Dr (32025-1985)
PHONE................................386 754-9367
James Prevatt, *President*
Jessica Langley, *Admin Sec*
EMP: 16 **EST:** 2000
SALES (est): 343K **Privately Held**
SIC: 3398 Tempering of metal

(G-7012)
ANDERSON TRUSS LLC
1730 Nw Oakland Ave (32055-4318)
PHONE................................386 752-3103
Shawn Anderson,
EMP: 22 **EST:** 1985
SQ FT: 6,000
SALES (est): 435.5K **Privately Held**
WEB: www.andersontrusscompany.com
SIC: 2439 Trusses, wooden roof

(G-7013)
BUGGY BAGG INC
248 Sw Webbs Gln (32024-0234)
PHONE................................386 758-5836
Shirley Rogers, *President*
Michael Rogers, *Superintendent*
Sharla Coles, *Vice Pres*
Elizabeth Rogers, *Admin Sec*
▲ **EMP:** 5 **EST:** 2000
SALES (est): 488.3K **Privately Held**
SIC: 2673 Plastic bags: made from purchased materials

(G-7014)
COLUMBIA READY MIX CONCRETE (PA)
516 Nw Waldo St (32055-4357)
P.O. Box 2101 (32056-2101)
PHONE................................386 755-2458
Renny B Eadie III, *President*
Theda Eadie, *Corp Secy*
Robert M Eadie, *Vice Pres*
EMP: 14 **EST:** 1977
SQ FT: 2,000
SALES (est): 4.8MM **Privately Held**
WEB: sell.sawbrokers.com
SIC: 3273 Ready-mixed concrete

(G-7015)
COMMUNITY NEWS PAPERS INC
Also Called: Lake City Reporter
180 E Duval St (32055-4085)
P.O. Box 1709 (32056-1709)
PHONE................................386 752-1293
Tom Wood, *Ch of Bd*
W H Dink Ne Smith, *President*
Michael Philips, *Editor*
Vince Brown, *Prdtn Dir*
Sharlyn Elmore, *Sales Staff*
EMP: 25 **EST:** 1874
SQ FT: 18,000
SALES (est): 2.3MM
SALES (corp-wide): 53.1MM **Privately Held**
WEB: www.lakecityreporter.com
SIC: 2711 Newspapers, publishing & printing
PA: Community Newspapers, Inc.
2365 Prince Ave A
Athens GA 30606
706 548-0010

(G-7016)
CUSTOM POWDER COATING LLC
1129 Se Ormond Witt Rd (32025-2750)
PHONE................................386 758-3973
Mary Witt T, *Principal*
EMP: 8 **EST:** 2010
SALES (est): 93K **Privately Held**
SIC: 3479 Metal coating & allied service

(G-7017)
D R NICKELSON & COMPANY INC
229 Nw Wilks Ln Ste 1 (32055-8373)
P.O. Box 1744 (32056-1744)
PHONE................................386 755-6565
Dale R Nickelson, *President*
Mark Nickelson, *General Mgr*
David Schlimmer, *Project Mgr*
Scott Nickelson, *Opers Staff*
Diane Steele, *Office Mgr*
EMP: 15 **EST:** 2001
SQ FT: 35,000
SALES (est): 2.8MM **Privately Held**
WEB: www.drnickelson.com
SIC: 2431 2434 Doors, wood; wood kitchen cabinets

(G-7018)
FEAGLE LOGGING LLC
805 Ne Indigo Dr (32055-6858)
PHONE................................386 365-2689
EMP: 8 **EST:** 2019
SALES (est): 495.9K **Privately Held**
SIC: 2411 Logging

(G-7019)
FURST-MCNESS COMPANY
3830 Nw Brown Rd (32055-7508)
P.O. Box 168, Wellborn (32094-0168)
PHONE................................386 755-5605
Mike Casey, *Manager*
Ted Ladue, *Manager*
Bob Simon, *Technical Staff*
EMP: 8 **Privately Held**
WEB: www.mcness.com
SIC: 2048 Prepared feeds
HQ: Furst-Mcness Company
120 E Clark St
Freeport IL 61032
800 435-5100

(G-7020)
GRAYS PORTABLE BUILDINGS INC
Also Called: Bam Building and More
792 Sw Bascom Norris Dr (32025-1365)
PHONE................................386 755-6449
Kevin Gray, *President*
EMP: 6 **EST:** 2011
SALES (est): 768.9K **Privately Held**
WEB: www.buildingsandmore.com
SIC: 3448 Prefabricated metal buildings

(G-7021)
GREAT SOUTH TIMBER & LBR INC
1135 Se State Road 100 (32025-1463)
P.O. Box 2249 (32056-2249)
PHONE................................386 752-3774
Roland Bales, *Manager*
EMP: 43
SALES (corp-wide): 9.5MM **Privately Held**
WEB: www.gstl.us
SIC: 2421 Lumber: rough, sawed or planed
PA: Great South Timber & Lumber, Inc.
517 Se Baya Dr
Lake City FL 32025
386 755-3046

(G-7022)
GREAT SOUTH TIMBER & LBR INC (PA)
517 Se Baya Dr (32025-6031)
P.O. Box 2249 (32056-2249)
PHONE................................386 755-3046
W K Cook, *Ch of Bd*
Roland Stern, *President*
Mike Dennard, *General Mgr*
Chad Stalnaker, *Mill Mgr*
Robert Cook, *Treasurer*
EMP: 15 **EST:** 1985
SQ FT: 3,000
SALES (est): 9.5MM **Privately Held**
WEB: www.gstl.us
SIC: 2421 Sawmills & planing mills, general

(G-7023)
GRECIAN & COMPANY INC
2988 Nw Us Highway 41 (32055-8189)
P.O. Box 2947 (32056-2947)
PHONE................................386 344-1967
Grecian Paul, *President*

EMP: 8 **EST:** 2010
SALES (est): 523.7K **Privately Held**
SIC: 3421 Table & food cutlery, including butchers'

(G-7024)
GRIZZLY MANUFACTURING INC
Also Called: Quality Mills
174 Ne Cortez Ter (32055-1439)
PHONE.................................386 755-0220
Jeff Stotrz, *CEO*
Floyd Messer, *President*
EMP: 25 **EST:** 1972
SQ FT: 19,000
SALES (est): 5MM
SALES (corp-wide): 13.6MM **Privately Held**
WEB: www.grizzlysprockets.com
SIC: 3568 3541 3462 Sprockets (power transmission equipment); machine tools, metal cutting type; iron & steel forgings
PA: Quality Industries Of America, Inc.
3631 E Us Highway 90
Lake City FL 32055
386 755-0220

(G-7025)
IDAHO TIMBER LLC
176 Sw Midtown Pl Ste 101 (32025-0782)
PHONE.................................386 758-8111
Tom Griffith, *Traffic Mgr*
Chris McSwain, *Branch Mgr*
EMP: 75
SALES (corp-wide): 8.1B **Publicly Held**
SIC: 2421 Planing mills
HQ: Products Forest Llc Coushatta
3540 E Longwing Ln # 270
Meridian ID 83646
208 377-3000

(G-7026)
LAKE CITY MEDIPLEX LLC
162 Nw Birdie Pl (32055-8665)
PHONE.................................386 752-2209
Minesh Patel, *Owner*
EMP: 8 **EST:** 2009
SALES (est): 234.2K **Privately Held**
SIC: 2899 Salt

(G-7027)
LAMARTEK INC
Also Called: Dive Rite
175 Nw Washington St (32055-2862)
PHONE.................................386 752-1087
Lamar Hires, *President*
Jared Hires, *General Mgr*
Lee Ann Hires, *Admin Sec*
Lee Hires, *Admin Sec*
◆ **EMP:** 25 **EST:** 1980
SQ FT: 4,500
SALES (est): 4.4MM **Privately Held**
WEB: www.diverite.com
SIC: 3949 5091 Skin diving equipment, scuba type; diving equipment & supplies

(G-7028)
LINMAN INC
Also Called: Clayton Industries
Us Hwy 100 (32055)
P.O. Box 1059 (32056-1059)
PHONE.................................904 755-6800
Robert Chaplin III, *President*
Barbara Chaplin, *Vice Pres*
Milburn E Rich, *Vice Pres*
Debra R Williams, *Admin Sec*
EMP: 267 **EST:** 1987
SQ FT: 95,000
SALES (est): 20MM **Privately Held**
SIC: 2451 Mobile homes, except recreational

(G-7029)
LIVILITI HEALTH PRODUCTS CORP
2140 Sw Main Blvd (32025-0027)
PHONE.................................888 987-0744
Caleb Umstead, *President*
Mickala Emery, *Marketing Mgr*
EMP: 5 **EST:** 2020
SALES (est): 302.7K **Privately Held**
WEB: www.liviliti.com
SIC: 3841 5047 Surgical & medical instruments; medical equipment & supplies

(G-7030)
LOLLIPOP CHILDREN CENTER INC
416 Se Ermine Ave (32025-0801)
PHONE.................................386 755-3953
Joanne George, *President*
EMP: 8 **EST:** 2017
SALES (est): 518.9K **Privately Held**
SIC: 2064 Lollipops & other hard candy

(G-7031)
NEW MLLENNIUM BLDG SYSTEMS LLC
1992 Nw Bascom Norris Dr (32055-4888)
PHONE.................................386 466-1300
Jeff Coker, *General Mgr*
Bob Hudson, *General Mgr*
Francisco Sanchez, *General Mgr*
Chris Graham, *Vice Pres*
Doug Rees-Evans, *QC Mgr*
EMP: 148 **Publicly Held**
WEB: www.newmill.com
SIC: 3441 Joists, open web steel: long-span series
HQ: New Millennium Building Systems Llc
7575 W Jefferson Blvd
Fort Wayne IN 46804
260 969-3500

(G-7032)
NORTH CENTRAL ADVERTISER INC
358 Nw Main Blvd (32055-3309)
PHONE.................................386 755-2917
Thomas J Ricketson, *Principal*
EMP: 7 **EST:** 2009
SALES (est): 677.2K **Privately Held**
WEB: www.allthingsvisual.com
SIC: 2711 Newspapers

(G-7033)
NORTH FLORIDA AG SERVICES INC
3151 Sw Custom Made Cir (32024-1372)
PHONE.................................352 494-3978
Michael Emery, *President*
Cindy A Payne, *Principal*
Austin Emory, *Vice Pres*
Austin Ty Hiers, *Vice Pres*
EMP: 6 **EST:** 2017
SALES (est): 882.4K **Privately Held**
SIC: 2879 Pesticides, agricultural or household

(G-7034)
NORTH FLORIDA VAULT LLC
561 Nw Hilton Ave (32055-2710)
PHONE.................................386 303-2267
Christopher M Charles, *Principal*
EMP: 9 **EST:** 2015
SALES (est): 827.8K **Privately Held**
SIC: 3272 Concrete products

(G-7035)
OMI OF LAKE CITY LLC
4066 Nw Wisteria Dr (32055-4889)
PHONE.................................386 288-5632
Darshana Patel, *Principal*
EMP: 7 **EST:** 2010
SALES (est): 88.5K **Privately Held**
SIC: 2899 Salt

(G-7036)
OPTIMA ASSOCIATES INC
Also Called: Bag of Ice
2469 W Us Highway 90 # 130 (32055-4740)
PHONE.................................877 371-1555
Michelle Dedeo, *President*
Michelle R Dedeo, *President*
EMP: 10 **EST:** 2009
SQ FT: 6,960
SALES (est): 1.9MM **Privately Held**
SIC: 3581 Automatic vending machines

(G-7037)
PANDA MONI YUM LAKE CITY LL
2888 W Us Highway 90 (32055-4760)
PHONE.................................352 494-5193
Larry K Thompson, *Principal*
EMP: 7 **EST:** 2008
SALES (est): 120.4K **Privately Held**
SIC: 2899 Salt

(G-7038)
PRINT THIS AND THAT LLC
231 Nw Burk Ave Ste 101 (32055-3704)
PHONE.................................386 344-4420
Joshua Johnson, *Principal*
EMP: 21
SALES (corp-wide): 96.4K **Privately Held**
SIC: 2752 Commercial printing, lithographic
PA: Print This And That, Llc
167 Sw Mossy Oak Way
Lake City FL 32024
386 752-5905

(G-7039)
QUAIL HEIGHT GOLF CLUB
161 Sw Quail Heights Ter (32025-1427)
PHONE.................................386 752-3339
Chet Carter, *General Mgr*
Todd Carter, *Superintendent*
Carter Robert, *Principal*
Jill Huesman, *Executive*
EMP: 11 **EST:** 2012
SALES (est): 571.7K **Privately Held**
WEB: www.quailheightscc.com
SIC: 3949 Shafts, golf club

(G-7040)
QUALITY FBRCTION MCH WORKS INC
3631 E Us Highway 90 (32055-1436)
PHONE.................................386 755-0220
Dale Dryden, *President*
Jeffery Stortz, *President*
Guy Musser, *Vice Pres*
James Brown III, *CFO*
EMP: 11 **EST:** 1972
SQ FT: 22,000
SALES (est): 2.1MM
SALES (corp-wide): 13.6MM **Privately Held**
SIC: 3443 3441 3553 3535 Fabricated plate work (boiler shop); fabricated structural metal; woodworking machinery; conveyors & conveying equipment; mining machinery
PA: Quality Industries Of America, Inc.
3631 E Us Highway 90
Lake City FL 32055
386 755-0220

(G-7041)
QUALITY INDUSTRIES AMERICA INC (PA)
Also Called: Quality Fabrication Mch Works
3631 E Us Highway 90 (32055-1436)
PHONE.................................386 755-0220
Edward D Dryden, *Ch of Bd*
Jeffery Stortz, *President*
Guy D Messer, *Principal*
James Brown III, *Corp Secy*
Dale N Dryden, *Vice Pres*
EMP: 4 **EST:** 1972
SQ FT: 78,000
SALES (est): 13.6MM **Privately Held**
WEB: www.qiagroup.com
SIC: 3568 3441 1791 5085 Sprockets (power transmission equipment); fabricated structural metal; structural steel erection; mill supplies; steel

(G-7042)
REDBUD ENTERPRISES INC
1435 Nw County Road 25a (32055-4955)
P.O. Box 1118 (32056-1118)
PHONE.................................386 752-5696
Warren E Nail, *President*
Steve Nail, *Vice Pres*
EMP: 26 **EST:** 1976
SQ FT: 17,000
SALES (est): 4.7MM **Privately Held**
SIC: 3083 Plastic finished products, laminated

(G-7043)
ROADSAFE TRAFFIC SYSTEMS INC
2118 Nw County Road 25a (32055-4904)
P.O. Box 2027 (32056-2027)
PHONE.................................386 755-0140
Jack R Keiter, *Manager*
EMP: 22
SQ FT: 11,250 **Privately Held**
WEB: www.roadsafetraffic.com
SIC: 3531 Construction machinery

PA: Roadsafe Traffic Systems, Inc.
8750 W Bryn Mawr Ave
Chicago IL 60631

(G-7044)
SIGNCRAFT & MORE INC
1554 E Duval St (32055-4118)
PHONE.................................386 755-4754
James E Frazier, *President*
EMP: 8 **EST:** 2017
SALES (est): 223.7K **Privately Held**
WEB: www.signcraftandmoreinc.com
SIC: 3993 Signs & advertising specialties

(G-7045)
SIGNSITECOM INC
Also Called: Speedysignsusa.com,
162 Sw Spencer Ct Ste 106 (32024-0366)
PHONE.................................386 487-0265
Laura A Willems, *President*
Shane D Willems, *Vice Pres*
Tyler Rolfe, *Manager*
Laura Willems, *Info Tech Mgr*
Danielle Bullock, *Representative*
EMP: 5 **EST:** 2006
SALES (est): 1.1MM **Privately Held**
WEB: www.signsite.com
SIC: 3993 Signs & advertising specialties

(G-7046)
SPEEDYSIGNS COM INC
Also Called: Speedy Sign
162 Sw Spencer Ct Ste 101 (32024-0366)
PHONE.................................386 755-2006
Shane D Willems, *President*
Laura A Willems, *Corp Secy*
Alex Kirsch, *Vice Pres*
EMP: 22 **EST:** 1996
SQ FT: 12,000
SALES (est): 1MM **Privately Held**
WEB: www.speedysigns.com
SIC: 3993 Signs & advertising specialties

(G-7047)
STARTECH LAKE CITY INC
109 Nw Spring Hill Ct (32055-7512)
PHONE.................................386 466-1969
Bryant Jennings, *Principal*
EMP: 10 **EST:** 2009
SALES (est): 446.6K **Privately Held**
WEB: www.computerserviceslakecity.com
SIC: 2899 Salt

(G-7048)
TEEKO GRAPHICS INC
2018 Sw Main Blvd (32025-0025)
PHONE.................................386 754-5600
Rob Summerall, *President*
Milas Summerall, *Principal*
EMP: 5 **EST:** 1999
SALES (est): 911.5K **Privately Held**
WEB: www.teeko.com
SIC: 2759 Screen printing

(G-7049)
TRAUMAONE HELICOPTER BASE
3792 E Us Highway 90 (32055-1406)
PHONE.................................386 755-9294
Chris Kick, *Owner*
EMP: 8 **EST:** 2005
SALES (est): 86.9K **Privately Held**
SIC: 3721 Helicopters

Lake Hamilton
Polk County

(G-7050)
GOLD GRANITE & MARBLE
930 Robert Rd Unit 47 (33851)
PHONE.................................863 439-9794
Luis Mondragon, *Principal*
EMP: 10 **EST:** 2006
SALES (est): 268.6K **Privately Held**
WEB: www.goldenmarblegranite.com
SIC: 3281 Marble, building: cut & shaped

(G-7051)
NWL INC
4701 Crump Rd (33851)
PHONE.................................800 742-5695
EMP: 84

G
E
O
G
R
A
P
H
I
C

SALES (corp-wide): 103.4MM **Privately Held**
WEB: www.nwl.com
SIC: 3612 Power transformers, electric
HQ: Nwl, Inc.
　312 Rising Sun Rd
　Bordentown NJ 08505
　609 298-7300

(G-7052)
R & K WELDING AND FABRICATION
4709 Crump Rd (33851)
P.O. Box 912 (33851-0912)
PHONE.................................863 422-8728
Kevin Giles, *President*
EMP: 5 **EST:** 2005
SALES (est): 418.5K **Privately Held**
WEB: www.rkwelding.com
SIC: 7692 Welding repair

(G-7053)
WOODYS HEDGING LLC
225 Water Tank Rd (33851)
P.O. Box 885 (33851-0885)
PHONE.................................863 557-4525
Calvin Ford,
EMP: 5 **EST:** 2010
SALES (est): 311.1K **Privately Held**
SIC: 3524 Hedge trimmers, electric

Lake Harbor
Palm Beach County

(G-7054)
CALCIUM SILICATE CORP INC
601 Watson Farm Rd (33459)
P.O. Box 405 (33459-0405)
PHONE.................................863 902-0217
Mark Elizer, *President*
EMP: 11 **Privately Held**
WEB: www.calsil.com
SIC: 3295 5191 Slag, crushed or ground;
　fertilizers & agricultural chemicals
PA: Calcium Silicate Corp., Inc.
　2656 Harlan Farm Rd
　Columbia TN

Lake Helen
Volusia County

(G-7055)
TST INDUSTRIES LLC
623 Pleasant St (32744-3523)
PHONE.................................386 868-2011
Bart P Rogowski, *Administration*
Bart Rogowski, *Administration*
EMP: 8 **EST:** 2017
SALES (est): 1MM **Privately Held**
WEB: www.tstindustries.com
SIC: 3999 Manufacturing industries

Lake Mary
Seminole County

(G-7056)
ABB INC
Also Called: ABB Power Distribution
680 Century Pt (32746-2294)
PHONE.................................407 732-2000
Edgard Rodriguez, *Sr Project Mgr*
Bruce Wittbrodt, *Manager*
EMP: 477
SALES (corp-wide): 28.9B **Privately Held**
WEB: www.abb.com
SIC: 3613 3625 3675 3612 Switchgear &
　switchboard apparatus; distribution
　boards, electric; generator control & me-
　tering panels; relays & industrial controls;
　electronic capacitors; power & distribution
　transformers
HQ: Abb Inc.
　305 Gregson Dr
　Cary NC 27511

(G-7057)
AIRFLOWBALANCE LLC
4273 Regal Town Ln (32746-2062)
PHONE.................................386 871-8136

Craig Gordon, *Opers Staff*
Ryan Gordon, *Mng Member*
EMP: 10 **EST:** 2013
SALES (est): 150K **Privately Held**
SIC: 3822 Air flow controllers, air condition-
　ing & refrigeration

(G-7058)
ALACRIANT HOLDINGS LLC
1051 Sand Pond Rd Ste 101 (32746-3341)
PHONE.................................330 233-0523
Nicholas Dvorak, *Principal*
EMP: 25 **EST:** 2008
SALES (est): 10.6MM
SALES (corp-wide): 39.4MM **Privately
Held**
WEB: www.alacriant.com
SIC: 3444 Sheet metalwork
PA: Alacriant Inc.
　1760 Miller Pkwy
　Streetsboro OH 44241
　330 562-7191

(G-7059)
AMAG TECHNOLOGY INC
858 Bright Meadow Dr (32746-4861)
PHONE.................................407 549-3882
Gordon Beatty, *Principal*
EMP: 6 **EST:** 2010
SALES (est): 576.8K **Privately Held**
WEB: www.amag.com
SIC: 3577 Computer peripheral equipment
HQ: G4s Technology Limited
　International Drive
　Tewkesbury GLOS GL20

(G-7060)
ARCHER ELLISON INC
7025 County Road 46a # 1071
(32746-4721)
PHONE.................................800 449-4095
Allen D'Angelo, *CEO*
Kimberly D'Angelo, *Vice Pres*
EMP: 7 **EST:** 2002
SQ FT: 2,700
SALES (est): 733.5K **Privately Held**
WEB: www.archerellison.com
SIC: 2731 8741 8748 Books: publishing
　only; management services; business
　consulting

(G-7061)
AUREL PARTNERS LLC
7025 County Road 46a # 1071380
(32746-4721)
PHONE.................................203 300-7470
William Black,
EMP: 40 **EST:** 2017
SALES (est): 1.1MM **Privately Held**
SIC: 3999 Manufacturing industries

(G-7062)
AXIS PHRM PARTNERS LLC
550 Technology Park (32746-7131)
PHONE.................................407 936-2949
Mark C Montgomery, *Principal*
EMP: 8 **EST:** 2011
SALES (est): 115.1K **Privately Held**
SIC: 2834 Pharmaceutical preparations

(G-7063)
BLACKCLOAK INC
7025 Cty Rd 46a Ste 1071 46 A (32746)
PHONE.................................833 882-5625
Chris Pierson, *CEO*
Christine Schaefer, *Marketing Staff*
Kerry Tary, *Executive*
Scott Urquhart, *Administration*
EMP: 11 **EST:** 2018
SALES (est): 1.4MM **Privately Held**
WEB: www.blackcloak.io
SIC: 7372 Application computer software

(G-7064)
CENTRAL FLORIDA BOX CORP
Also Called: Cfb Display Group
2950 Lake Emma Rd # 1000 (32746-3702)
PHONE.................................407 936-1277
Jeffrey T Ramsey, *President*
Joseph Magliaro, *Opers Staff*
Angela Ramsey, *VP Sls/Mktg*
Alisa Hoskins, *Consultant*
▲ **EMP:** 40 **EST:** 1979
SQ FT: 190,000

SALES (est): 12MM
SALES (corp-wide): 18.7B **Publicly Held**
WEB: www.centralfloridabox.com
SIC: 2653 Boxes, corrugated: made from
　purchased materials
HQ: Westrock Paper And Packaging, Llc
　1000 Abernathy Rd
　Atlanta GA 30328

(G-7065)
CHARISMA MEDIA
Also Called: Plus Communication
1051 Sand Pond Rd (32746-3341)
PHONE.................................407 333-0600
Steven Strang, *CEO*
Maureen Eha, *Editor*
Joyce Strang, *CFO*
Dicksie Carroll, *Accounting Mgr*
Brenda Santiago, *Sales Staff*
EMP: 84 **EST:** 2012
SALES (est): 10.6MM **Privately Held**
WEB: www.charismamedia.com
SIC: 2711 7311 Newspapers; advertising
　consultant

(G-7066)
COLONIAL INDUSTRIES CENTL FLA
462 Mohave Ter (32746-7010)
PHONE.................................407 484-5239
John T Davy, *Director*
EMP: 8 **EST:** 2001
SALES (est): 528.2K **Privately Held**
WEB: www.colonialindustriesfl.us
SIC: 3999 Manufacturing industries

(G-7067)
CREATIVE DATA SOLUTIONS INC
1540 Intl Pkwy Ste 2000 (32746)
PHONE.................................407 333-4770
Lisa L Morris, *President*
Rex H Arnold, *Vice Pres*
EMP: 13 **EST:** 1992
SALES (est): 673.3K **Privately Held**
WEB: www.cdscourts.com
SIC: 7372 Prepackaged software

(G-7068)
DEALERUPS INC
4185 W Lake Mary Blvd # 2 (32746-2400)
PHONE.................................407 557-5368
Theodore Rubin, *President*
David Lampert, *Vice Pres*
EMP: 18 **EST:** 2000
SQ FT: 2,000
SALES (est): 300K **Privately Held**
SIC: 7372 Prepackaged software

(G-7069)
DIEBOLD NIXDORF INCORPORATED
735 Primera Blvd Ste 215 (32746-2150)
PHONE.................................407 549-2000
Glenn Rowe, *Principal*
Randy Deabenderfer, *Project Mgr*
EMP: 18
SALES (corp-wide): 3.9B **Publicly Held**
WEB: www.dieboldnixdorf.com
SIC: 3578 5049 Automatic teller machines
　(ATM); bank equipment & supplies
PA: Diebold Nixdorf, Incorporated
　50 Executive Pkwy
　Hudson OH 44236
　330 490-4000

(G-7070)
DIXON TICONDEROGA COMPANY (DH)
615 Crscent Exec Ct Ste 5 (32746)
PHONE.................................407 829-9000
James Schmitz, *CEO*
Massimo Candela, *President*
Cody Agaard, *Exec VP*
Luis Pedro, *Exec VP*
Tony Rufo, *Exec VP*
◆ **EMP:** 90 **EST:** 1978
SALES (est): 154.5MM **Privately Held**
WEB: www.dixonwriting.com
SIC: 3952 3951 Pencils & leads, including
　artists'; artists' materials, except pencils &
　leads; crayons: chalk, gypsum, charcoal,
　fusains, pastel, wax, etc.; pencils & pencil
　parts, mechanical; ball point pens & parts;
　markers, soft tip (felt, fabric, plastic, etc.)

HQ: F.I.L.A Fabbrica Italiana Lapis Ed Affini
　Spa
　Via Xxv Aprile 5
　Pero MI 20016
　023 810-51

(G-7071)
EMERGING MFG TECH INC
108 Commerce St Ste 102 (32746-6218)
P.O. Box 952828 (32795-2828)
PHONE.................................407 341-3476
EMP: 7 **EST:** 2011
SALES (est): 84.7K **Privately Held**
SIC: 3999 Manufacturing industries

(G-7072)
EVOLUTION ORTHOTICS INC
156 Harston Ct (32746-6973)
PHONE.................................407 688-2860
▲ **EMP:** 22
SALES (est): 1.3MM **Privately Held**
SIC: 3842 Mfg Surgical Appliances/Sup-
　plies

(G-7073)
EXPLORATION RESOURCES INTN GEO
1130 Business Center Dr (32746-7617)
PHONE.................................601 747-0726
Seth Broadfoot, *Mng Member*
EMP: 5 **EST:** 2012
SALES (est): 302.8K **Privately Held**
SIC: 3699 8711 3829 7389 Electrical
　equipment & supplies; engineering serv-
　ices; measuring & controlling devices;

(G-7074)
FARO TECHNOLOGIES INC
125 Technology Park (32746-6230)
PHONE.................................800 736-0234
John Sutton, *Business Mgr*
Kevin Beadle, *Vice Pres*
Arnold Torres, *Production*
David Sistrunk, *Technical Mgr*
Nicholas Nicou, *Engineer*
EMP: 21 **Publicly Held**
WEB: www.faro.com
SIC: 3699 Laser systems & equipment
PA: Faro Technologies, Inc.
　250 Technology Park
　Lake Mary FL 32746

(G-7075)
FARO TECHNOLOGIES INC (PA)
250 Technology Park (32746-7115)
PHONE.................................407 333-9911
John Donofrio, *Ch of Bd*
Michael D Burger, *President*
Dirk Marks, *General Mgr*
Brooke Blake, *Vice Pres*
Ann Hewitt, *Vice Pres*
▲ **EMP:** 293 **EST:** 1982
SQ FT: 46,500
SALES (est): 337.8MM **Publicly Held**
WEB: www.faro.com
SIC: 3829 Medical diagnostic systems, nu-
　clear

(G-7076)
FICAP
705 Remington Oak Dr (32746-5710)
P.O. Box 4075, Milton (32572-4075)
PHONE.................................407 302-3316
Tony Nguyenthang, *Opers Dir*
Brad Coolidge, *Treasurer*
Terry Reynolds, *Sales Staff*
Michael Smith, *Manager*
Wayne Willis, *Manager*
EMP: 10 **EST:** 2008
SALES (est): 591.1K **Privately Held**
WEB: www.ficap.org
SIC: 3531 Mixers, concrete

(G-7077)
FINASTRA USA CORPORATION
744 Primera Blvd Ste 2000 (32746-2230)
PHONE.................................800 989-9009
Ryan Hengehold, *Partner*
Travis Benn, *Counsel*
Danica Pettit, *Project Mgr*
Brad Blust, *Opers Staff*
Sheri Williams, *Opers Staff*
EMP: 173
SALES (corp-wide): 1.6B **Privately Held**
WEB: www.finastra.com
SIC: 7372 Prepackaged software

▲ = Import ▼=Export
◆ =Import/Export

HQ: Finastra Usa Corporation
555 Sw Morrison St # 300
Portland OR 97204
407 804-6600

(G-7078)
FLORIDA CANDY BUFFETS LLC
3279 Safe Harbor Ln (32746-1807)
PHONE..............................407 529-5880
Wazir Farida, *Manager*
EMP: 8 **EST:** 2019
SALES (est): 444.3K **Privately Held**
WEB: www.floridacandybuffets.com
SIC: 2024 Ice cream & frozen desserts

(G-7079)
FLORIDA FROYO INC
725 Primera Blvd (32746-2125)
PHONE..............................407 977-4911
Brian K Linden, *Principal*
EMP: 8 **EST:** 2009
SALES (est): 226.2K **Privately Held**
SIC: 2024 Yogurt desserts, frozen

(G-7080)
FLORIDA PRTCTIVE CTNGS CONS IN
482 Cardinal Oaks Ct (32746-3972)
PHONE..............................407 322-1243
Michael R Kendig, *President*
Michael R Stensrud, *Vice Pres*
EMP: 7 **EST:** 1986
SALES (est): 824.9K **Privately Held**
SIC: 2851 Paints & allied products

(G-7081)
GAP IMAGING INTL LLC
2558 Dwyer Ln (32746-1809)
PHONE..............................407 268-9746
Abass Bouniady, *Principal*
Kim Bouniady,
EMP: 5 **EST:** 2005
SALES (est): 455.2K **Privately Held**
WEB: www.gapimaging.com
SIC: 3845 Electromedical equipment

(G-7082)
HALLDALE MEDIA INC
4300 W Lake Mary Blvd # 1 (32746-2060)
PHONE..............................407 322-5605
Andy Smith, *President*
Lori Ponoroff, *Editor*
Holly Foster, *Business Mgr*
Michelle Viens, *Business Mgr*
David Malley, *Prdtn Mgr*
EMP: 20 **EST:** 2002
SALES (est): 3.5MM **Privately Held**
WEB: www.halldale.com
SIC: 2741 Miscellaneous publishing

(G-7083)
HAZMAT SOFTWARE LLC
760 Heather Glen Cir (32746-6128)
PHONE..............................407 416-5434
Luis Zambrana,
EMP: 19 **EST:** 2001
SALES (est): 1MM **Privately Held**
WEB: www.hazmatsoftware.com
SIC: 7372 Prepackaged software

(G-7084)
IGOVSOLUTIONS LLC
1307 S Intl Pkwy Ste 2061 (32746)
PHONE..............................407 574-3056
Prasad Valay,
EMP: 27 **EST:** 2014
SALES (est): 2.7MM **Privately Held**
WEB: www.igovsolution.com
SIC: 7372 7371 Business oriented computer software; computer software development & applications; computer software systems analysis & design, custom; computer software development

(G-7085)
INFORMATION BUILDERS INC
300 Primera Blvd Ste 300 (32746-2145)
PHONE..............................407 804-8000
Fax: 407 804-8023
EMP: 25
SALES (corp-wide): 575.4MM **Privately Held**
SIC: 7372 7371 Prepackaged Software Services Custom Computer Programing

PA: Information Builders, Inc.
2 Penn Plz Fl 28
New York NY 10001
212 736-4433

(G-7086)
INTERNATIONAL GUIDELINES CTR
Also Called: Guideline Central
106 Commerce St Ste 105 (32746-6217)
PHONE..............................407 878-7606
Charles Kennedy, *President*
Mark Altenburger, *VP Bus Dvlpt*
Tom Tracy, *Manager*
Paul Almodovar, *Software Dev*
William Reithmeyer, *Software Dev*
EMP: 6 **EST:** 2002
SALES (est): 1.3MM **Privately Held**
WEB: www.guidelinecentral.com
SIC: 2721 Magazines: publishing only, not printed on site

(G-7087)
JJAZ ENTERPRISES INC
Also Called: AlphaGraphics
1061 S Sun Dr Ste 1033 (32746-6170)
PHONE..............................407 330-0245
Joshua Field, *President*
Joshua A Field, *President*
Andrew Destefano, *Mng Member*
EMP: 5 **EST:** 2018
SALES (est): 694.3K **Privately Held**
WEB: www.alphagraphics.com
SIC: 2752 Commercial printing, lithographic

(G-7088)
JST POWER EQUIPMENT INC
30 Skyline Dr (32746-6201)
PHONE..............................844 631-9046
LI Zhiyuan, *Ch of Bd*
Ling Xiangsheng, *Vice Ch Bd*
Richard Wolff, *VP Bus Dvlpt*
Mark Du, *CFO*
Emerson Mosquera, *Sales Staff*
▲ **EMP:** 56 **EST:** 1998
SALES (est): 9.4MM **Privately Held**
WEB: www.jstpower.com
SIC: 3677 Coil windings, electronic

(G-7089)
KENEXA LEARNING INC
100 Colonial Center Pkwy # 1 (32746-4767)
PHONE..............................407 548-0434
John Alonso, *Senior Partner*
Roger Surprenant, *Regional Mgr*
EMP: 9
SALES (corp-wide): 57.3B **Publicly Held**
WEB: www.outstart.com
SIC: 7372 7379 4813 Business oriented computer software; computer related consulting services;
HQ: Kenexa Learning, Inc.
650 E Swedesford Rd 2nd
Wayne PA 19087
610 971-9171

(G-7090)
MAGICAL CREAMERY LLC
965 Helmsley Ct Apt 101 (32746-2010)
PHONE..............................407 719-6866
Abdiel De Jesus, *Principal*
EMP: 7 **EST:** 2010
SALES (est): 94.1K **Privately Held**
WEB: www.mccateringorlando.com
SIC: 2021 Creamery butter

(G-7091)
MARY LAKE LIFE MAG INC
881 Silversmith Cir (32746-4975)
PHONE..............................407 324-2644
Chip Colandreo, *Publisher*
Dennie Heidemann, *Principal*
Penny O 'connell, *Advt Staff*
EMP: 8 **EST:** 2011
SALES (est): 167.1K **Privately Held**
WEB: www.lakemarylife.com
SIC: 2721 Magazines: publishing only, not printed on site

(G-7092)
MARY LAKE LIFE MAGAZINE INC
3232 W Lake Mary Blvd # 1420 (32746-3582)
PHONE..............................407 324-2644
Sheila Kramer, *President*
Judith Topper, *Vice Pres*
Michael Kramer, *Admin Sec*
EMP: 16 **EST:** 2003
SALES (est): 2.5MM **Privately Held**
WEB: www.lakemarylife.com
SIC: 2721 Magazines: publishing only, not printed on site

(G-7093)
MEASUREMENTS INTERNATIONAL INC
343 Clermont Ave (32746-3629)
PHONE..............................315 393-1323
Duane Brown, *President*
Mike Frisz, *Sales Mgr*
EMP: 25 **EST:** 1998
SALES (est): 1.3MM **Privately Held**
WEB: www.mintl.com
SIC: 3825 Instruments to measure electricity

(G-7094)
MICROSEMI CORP
Also Called: Rfis Security Solutions
1064 Greenwood Blvd # 124 (32746-5419)
PHONE..............................407 965-5687
EMP: 12
SALES (est): 1.9MM
SALES (corp-wide): 1.1B **Publicly Held**
SIC: 3699 Mfg Electrical Equipment/Supplies
PA: Microsemi Corporation
1 Enterprise
Aliso Viejo CA 92841
949 380-6100

(G-7095)
MICROVISION TECHNOLOGY CORP
Also Called: Logic Springs Technologies
43 Skyline Dr Ste 3051 (32746-7117)
P.O. Box 950728 (32795-0728)
PHONE..............................407 333-2943
Efren Yero, *President*
Jeremiah Cline, *Engineer*
Nathaniel Dennis, *Engineer*
Lance Stratton, *Engineer*
EMP: 16 **EST:** 1993
SQ FT: 8,500
SALES (est): 3MM **Privately Held**
WEB: www.logicsprings.com
SIC: 7372 7379 Business oriented computer software; computer related consulting services

(G-7096)
MITSUBISHI POWER AMERICAS INC (DH)
Also Called: Mitsubshi Htchi Pwr Systems Am
400 Colonial Center Pkwy # 500 (32746-7683)
PHONE..............................407 688-6100
William A Newsom Jr, *President*
Tom Brittain, *General Mgr*
Mark Passino, *General Mgr*
Sam Suttle, *General Mgr*
Bill Newsom, *Exec VP*
◆ **EMP:** 100 **EST:** 2001
SALES (est): 870.1MM **Privately Held**
WEB: www.mhi.com
SIC: 3511 3629 7389 Gas turbines, mechanical drive; steam turbines; thermoelectric generators; patrol of electric transmission or gas lines

(G-7097)
NATIONAL NEWSPAPER PLACEM
766 N Sun Dr Ste 2090 (32746-2566)
PHONE..............................866 404-5913
EMP: 8
SALES (est): 650.3K **Privately Held**
SIC: 2711 Newspapers-Publishing/Printing

(G-7098)
ORLANDO SHUTTERS LLC (PA)
Also Called: Orlando Shutters Blinds & More
4300 W Lake Mary Blvd # 1 (32746-2060)
PHONE..............................407 495-5250
Lala Beals, *Manager*
EMP: 7 **EST:** 2018
SALES (est): 283K **Privately Held**
WEB: www.orlandoshuttersblindsand-more.com
SIC: 3442 2591 2431 Shutters, door or window: metal; drapery hardware & blinds & shades; blinds vertical; window shutters, wood; awnings, blinds & shutters, wood; blinds (shutters), wood

(G-7099)
PAYLOCITY HOLDING CORPORATION
615 Crescent Executive Ct (32746-2116)
PHONE..............................407 878-6585
Tracey Gridley, *Partner*
Chris Westfall, *Chairman*
Jeff Franklin, *District Mgr*
Holly Fulp, *Vice Pres*
Ted Gaty, *Vice Pres*
EMP: 679
SALES (corp-wide): 561.3MM **Publicly Held**
WEB: www.paylocity.com
SIC: 7372 Prepackaged software
PA: Paylocity Holding Corporation
1400 American Ln
Schaumburg IL 60173
847 463-3200

(G-7100)
PLUS COMMUNICATIONS INC (PA)
Also Called: Strang Communications
600 Rinehart Rd (32746-4803)
P.O. Box 951420 (32795-1420)
PHONE..............................407 333-0600
Stephen E Strang, *CEO*
Joy F Strang, *Corp Secy*
Frank Hefeli, *Vice Pres*
Marcos Perez, *Vice Pres*
Rebecca McInnis, *Human Res Dir*
▲ **EMP:** 44 **EST:** 1975
SQ FT: 60,000
SALES (est): 34.9MM **Privately Held**
WEB: www.charismamedia.com
SIC: 2731 2721 Books: publishing & printing; magazines: publishing & printing

(G-7101)
PLUS COMMUNICATIONS INC
Casa Creacion
600 Rinehart Rd (32746-4803)
PHONE..............................407 333-0600
Steve Strang, *Branch Mgr*
EMP: 38
SALES (corp-wide): 34.9MM **Privately Held**
WEB: www.charismamedia.com
SIC: 2731 Book publishing
PA: Plus Communications, Inc.
600 Rinehart Rd
Lake Mary FL 32746
407 333-0600

(G-7102)
PREMIERETRADE FOREX LLC
103 Commerce St Ste 140 (32746-6237)
PHONE..............................407 287-4149
Ralph J Brunton, *Mng Member*
Tyler Benzel, *Manager*
EMP: 5 **EST:** 2004
SALES (est): 646.9K **Privately Held**
WEB: www.premieretrade.com
SIC: 7372 Business oriented computer software

(G-7103)
PROJSTREAM LLC
1540 Intl Pkwy 2000 (32746)
PHONE..............................407 476-1084
James Spear, *COO*
Jim Speer, *COO*
Rory Parkinson, *Project Mgr*
Andrew Smith, *Director*
Jeff Lutton, *Business Dir*
EMP: 11 **EST:** 2009
SQ FT: 1,000

SALES (est): 2.7MM **Privately Held**
SIC: **7372** Business oriented computer
software

(G-7104)
QUALITY MANUFACTURING SVCS INC
400 Caring Dr Ste 1010 (32746-2558)
PHONE..................................407 531-6000
Jeffrey Cox, *CEO*
Sam Hanna, *President*
David Deborde, *Principal*
Josh King, *Production*
Carol Maxey, *Production*
▲ EMP: 98 EST: 1995
SQ FT: 45,000
SALES (est): 28.2MM **Privately Held**
WEB: www.qmscfl.com
SIC: **3672** Printed circuit boards

(G-7105)
QUANTUM TECHNOLOGY INC
108 Commerce St Ste 101 (32746-6225)
PHONE..................................407 333-9348
Sanjay R Adhav, *President*
EMP: 5 EST: 1968
SALES (est): 600K **Privately Held**
WEB: www.quantumtech.com
SIC: **3674** Semiconductors & related devices

(G-7106)
SMART ACCESS INC
2950 Lake Emma Rd # 1030 (32746-3702)
PHONE..................................407 331-4724
M Mehdi Daryadel, *President*
Hadi Daryadel, *Vice Pres*
EMP: 9 EST: 1985
SQ FT: 3,000
SALES (est): 245K **Privately Held**
SIC: **3699** Security control equipment & systems

(G-7107)
SPECTRUM BRIDGE INC
110 Timberlachen Cir # 1012 (32746-3338)
PHONE..................................407 792-1570
Rod Dir, *President*
Peter Stanforth, *Vice Pres*
EMP: 13 EST: 2007
SALES (est): 303.7K **Privately Held**
WEB: www.192168ll.onl
SIC: **3825** Spectrum analyzers

(G-7108)
STOCKDALE TECHNOLOGIES INC
104 Commerce St (32746-6206)
PHONE..................................407 323-5121
Blake Guiles, *President*
EMP: 75 EST: 1983
SQ FT: 14,900
SALES (est): 4.3MM **Privately Held**
SIC: **3089** Thermoformed finished plastic products

(G-7109)
SUPERION LLC
Also Called: Centralsquare Technologies
1000 Business Center Dr (32746-5585)
PHONE..................................407 304-3235
Todd Schulte, *COO*
Robert Valvano, *CFO*
Lisa Neumann, *Controller*
Dale Loyd, *Accounts Mgr*
Teri Crockett, *Sales Staff*
EMP: 800 EST: 2017
SQ FT: 90,000
SALES (est): 136MM
SALES (corp-wide): 272.3MM **Privately Held**
WEB: www.centralsquare.com
SIC: **7372** Prepackaged software
PA: Centralsquare Technologies, Llc
1000 Business Center Dr
Lake Mary FL 32746
800 727-8088

(G-7110)
SWAMI FOODS LLC ✪
1617 Kersley Cir (32746-1925)
PHONE..................................888 697-9264
Graeme Duncan,
EMP: 10 EST: 2021

SALES (est): 448.6K **Privately Held**
SIC: **2051** Bakery: wholesale or wholesale/retail combined

(G-7111)
TEAM CYMRU INC
901 Intrntl Pkwy Ste 30 (32746-4703)
PHONE..................................847 378-3300
Robert Thomas, *CEO*
Jeremy Katzman, *Partner*
Awsccp Mark Stevenson, *Engineer*
Bounds Darren, *CFO*
Matthew Lopez, *Controller*
EMP: 105 EST: 2011
SALES (est): 10.5MM **Privately Held**
WEB: www.team-cymru.com
SIC: **7372** Prepackaged software

(G-7112)
TOTALLY STORAGE INC
Also Called: Micro Design International
59 Skyline Dr Ste 1550 (32746-7113)
PHONE..................................407 472-6000
M Geoffrey Legat, *President*
EMP: 19 EST: 1999
SQ FT: 6,000
SALES (est): 324.7K **Privately Held**
WEB: www.mdi.com
SIC: **3572** Computer storage devices

(G-7113)
TREASURED PHOTO GIFTS LLC
Also Called: Printerpix
107 Commerce St (32746-6206)
PHONE..................................407 324-4816
Roshanali Daya, *Mng Member*
▲ EMP: 18 EST: 2011
SALES (est): 7.8MM **Privately Held**
WEB: www.printerpix.com
SIC: **2759** Commercial printing

(G-7114)
UNITED BIOSOURCE LLC (UBC)
680 Century Pt (32746-2294)
PHONE..................................877 599-7748
Patricia Mosher, *Vice Pres*
Courtney Graham, *Sales Staff*
Ellen Baty, *Analyst*
EMP: 8 EST: 2019
SALES (est): 1.2MM **Privately Held**
WEB: www.ubc.com
SIC: **2834** Pharmaceutical preparations

(G-7115)
VISHAY AMERICAS INC
735 Primera Blvd (32746-2112)
PHONE..................................407 804-2567
David Valletta, *Exec VP*
EMP: 854
SALES (corp-wide): 3.2B **Publicly Held**
SIC: **3676** Electronic resistors
HQ: Vishay Americas, Inc.
1 Greenwich Pl
Shelton CT 06484
203 452-5648

(G-7116)
VISUAL COMM SPECIALISTS INC
707 Platinum Pt Ste 2001 (32746-5702)
PHONE..................................407 936-7300
Cheryl Walker, *CEO*
EMP: 5 EST: 1996
SALES (est): 374.7K **Privately Held**
WEB: www.viscomspec.com
SIC: **3663** Radio & TV communications equipment

(G-7117)
WESTROCK LAKE MARY
2950 Lake Emma Rd (32746-3702)
PHONE..................................407 936-1277
EMP: 6 EST: 2019
SALES (est): 529.1K **Privately Held**
SIC: **3999** Manufacturing industries

(G-7118)
ZENIT SERVICE LLC
309 Grand Valley Dr (32746-6287)
PHONE..................................407 878-7840
Ivan Stoyanov, *Manager*
EMP: 8 EST: 2012
SALES (est): 2.4MM **Privately Held**
WEB: www.zenitservice.com
SIC: **3585** Air conditioning units, complete: domestic or industrial

---

Lake Panasoffkee
Sumter County

(G-7119)
GREAT SOUTHERN WOOD PRSV INC
194 Cr 527a (33538-6504)
P.O. Box 759 (33538-0759)
PHONE..................................352 793-9410
Sean Odell, *Plant Mgr*
Danny Trabue, *Sales Staff*
Linda Thornton, *Office Mgr*
Mike French, *Branch Mgr*
Mark Callender, *Manager*
EMP: 36
SALES (corp-wide): 337.5MM **Privately Held**
WEB: www.yellawood.com
SIC: **2491** Wood preserving
PA: Great Southern Wood Preserving, Incorporated
1100 Us Highway 431 S
Abbeville AL 36310
334 585-2291

(G-7120)
UNITED AG SVCS AMER INC
534 Cr Ste 529a (33538)
PHONE..................................352 793-1682
Mark Pecsenka, *President*
Lajos Pecsenka, *Vice Pres*
Gyorgy V Pecsenka, *Treasurer*
Hilda Pecsenka, *Admin Sec*
▲ EMP: 23 EST: 1994
SQ FT: 10,000
SALES (est): 4.9MM **Privately Held**
WEB: www.cropmaster.com
SIC: **2875** 2873 Potting soil, mixed; fertilizers: natural (organic), except compost

---

Lake Park
Palm Beach County

(G-7121)
ALL TENNIS LLC
1434 10th St (33403-2037)
PHONE..................................561 842-0070
Perry E Carrell, *Principal*
EMP: 6 EST: 2009
SALES (est): 444.9K **Privately Held**
WEB: www.alltennisstore.com
SIC: **3949** Tennis equipment & supplies

(G-7122)
BIG DIGITAL GRAPHICS LLC
1335 Old Dixie Hwy Unit 4 (33403-1967)
PHONE..................................561 844-4708
Cat Estes, *Office Mgr*
Patrick Ward,
EMP: 6 EST: 2007
SALES (est): 671.6K **Privately Held**
WEB: www.bigdigitalgraphics.com
SIC: **3993** Signs & advertising specialties

(G-7123)
ECOSMART
1313 S Killian Dr (33403-1918)
PHONE..................................561 328-6488
Brian Ireland, *Principal*
Micki Malone, *Controller*
EMP: 9 EST: 2012
SALES (est): 185K **Privately Held**
SIC: **2851** Paints & allied products

(G-7124)
EMERGENCY VEHICLES INC (PA)
705 13th St (33403-2303)
PHONE..................................561 848-6652
Ernst E Temme, *President*
Barbara Temme, *Principal*
Dave M Taliercio, *Vice Pres*
Chris Temme, *Prdtn Mgr*
Michael Cox, *VP Sales*
◆ EMP: 18 EST: 1988
SQ FT: 35,000
SALES (est): 6.9MM **Privately Held**
WEB: www.evi-fl.com
SIC: **3711** Automobile assembly, including specialty automobiles

---

(G-7125)
FLORIDA AERO PRECISION INC (HQ)
120 Reed Rd (33403-3015)
PHONE..................................561 848-6248
James K Rice, *President*
Maria Duke, *Human Res Dir*
Scott Burfield, *Personnel Exec*
Linda Graham, *Office Mgr*
EMP: 30 EST: 1981
SQ FT: 10,000
SALES (est): 9.2MM
SALES (corp-wide): 344.8MM **Privately Held**
WEB: www.floridaaeroprecisioninc.com
SIC: **3724** 4581 Aircraft engines & engine parts; aircraft servicing & repairing
PA: Meyer Tool, Inc.
3055 Colerain Ave
Cincinnati OH 45225
513 681-7362

(G-7126)
FLORIDA RDWAY GRDRAIL SGNS INC ✪
1137 Silver Beach Rd (33403-3025)
PHONE..................................561 719-7478
Debra Ricci, *President*
EMP: 8 EST: 2021
SALES (est): 318.3K **Privately Held**
WEB: www.floridaroadway.com
SIC: **3993** Signs & advertising specialties

(G-7127)
FLORIDA ROADWAY SIGNS INC
1137 Silver Beach Rd (33403-3025)
PHONE..................................561 722-4067
Debra Ricci, *President*
Brittani Ricci, *Vice Pres*
EMP: 9 EST: 2018
SALES (est): 302K **Privately Held**
SIC: **3993** Signs & advertising specialties

(G-7128)
GC CABINET EXPRESS LLC
1335 Old Dixie Hwy # 20 (33403-1966)
PHONE..................................561 662-0369
Ronald M Conner, *Manager*
EMP: 11 EST: 2016
SALES (est): 795K **Privately Held**
WEB: gc-cabinet-express-llc.business.site
SIC: **2434** Wood kitchen cabinets

(G-7129)
HARD CHROME ENTERPRISES INC
220 10th St (33403-3150)
PHONE..................................561 844-2529
William Onuska, *President*
William M Onuska Jr, *Vice Pres*
EMP: 9 EST: 1971
SQ FT: 5,000
SALES (est): 1MM **Privately Held**
WEB: www.hceplating.com
SIC: **3471** Electroplating of metals or formed products

(G-7130)
JUNO IRONCRAFT
1233 Old Dixie Hwy (33403-2347)
PHONE..................................561 352-0471
Shea John, *Principal*
EMP: 5 EST: 2016
SALES (est): 780.5K **Privately Held**
WEB: www.junoiron.com
SIC: **3441** Fabricated structural metal

(G-7131)
MASCHMEYER CONCRETE CO FLA (PA)
1142 Watertower Rd (33403-2397)
PHONE..................................561 848-9112
Troy W Maschmeyer Jr, *President*
Mark Arbuckle, *Vice Pres*
Gary Riley, *Plant Mgr*
Renee Williams, *Project Mgr*
Mac McCurry, *Opers Mgr*
▲ EMP: 46 EST: 1985
SQ FT: 1,800
SALES (est): 136.2MM **Privately Held**
WEB: www.maschmeyer.com
SIC: **3273** 3312 Ready-mixed concrete; wire products, steel or iron

---

▲ = Import ▼ =Export
◆ =Import/Export

(G-7132)
PALM BEACH BTRY VENTURES LLC (PA)
Also Called: Batteries Plus
1250 Northlake Blvd (33403-2050)
PHONE................................561 881-8900
Brenda Phipps, *Vice Pres*
Richard L Phipps Jr,
EMP: 8 EST: 2012
SQ FT: 1,600
SALES (est): 2.4MM **Privately Held**
SIC: 3691 5531 Storage batteries; batteries, automotive & truck

(G-7133)
PRESSURE WASHERS USA
1440 10th Ct Bay A (33403-2007)
PHONE................................561 848-7970
Lewis Paul, *Director*
EMP: 7 EST: 2011
SALES (est): 321.6K **Privately Held**
WEB: www.pressurewashersusa.com
SIC: 3452 Washers

(G-7134)
STREET SIGNS USA INC
1137 Silver Beach Rd (33403-3025)
PHONE................................561 848-1411
Alan Weissman, *Principal*
EMP: 5 EST: 2007
SALES (est): 453.5K **Privately Held**
SIC: 3993 Signs & advertising specialties

(G-7135)
WEST POINT INDUSTRIES INC
1300 Old Dixie Hwy # 101 (33403-1925)
PHONE................................561 848-8381
Robert Greaves, *President*
EMP: 6 EST: 1988
SQ FT: 5,000
SALES (est): 798.6K **Privately Held**
WEB: www.westpointindustries.com
SIC: 7692 3544 3441 Welding repair; special dies, tools, jigs & fixtures; building components, structural steel

(G-7136)
WOOD DRAMS INC OF PALM BEACHES
1137 Silver Beach Rd (33403-3025)
PHONE................................561 842-9814
Fax: 561 842-5307
EMP: 6
SQ FT: 6,000
SALES (est): 430K **Privately Held**
SIC: 2511 Mfg Wall Units

Lake Placid
Highlands County

(G-7137)
APPLIED DESIGN & FABRICATION
3525 Northern Blvd (33852-7595)
PHONE................................954 524-6619
Lisa Ludwig, *President*
EMP: 7 EST: 1993
SALES (est): 550K **Privately Held**
SIC: 3548 Welding & cutting apparatus & accessories

(G-7138)
C & C TOOL & MOLD
3417 Paso Fino Dr (33852-5204)
PHONE................................863 699-5337
Harold N Crews, *Owner*
EMP: 5 EST: 1983
SQ FT: 2,400
SALES (est): 383.2K **Privately Held**
SIC: 3599 3544 Machine shop, jobbing & repair; industrial molds

(G-7139)
C C LEAD INC
127 Ranier Dr (33852-2404)
PHONE................................863 465-6458
Clifton H Canter Jr, *President*
Phyllis Canter, *Admin Sec*
EMP: 14 EST: 1981
SQ FT: 4,150

SALES (est): 564.8K **Privately Held**
SIC: 3356 3842 3444 3339 Lead & lead alloy: rolling, drawing or extruding; surgical appliances & supplies; sheet metalwork; primary nonferrous metals; asphalt felts & coatings

(G-7140)
GENPAK LLC
55 Pine Ridge Dr (33852-7095)
PHONE................................863 243-1068
Paula Neville, *Principal*
EMP: 8 EST: 2016
SALES (est): 146.3K **Privately Held**
WEB: www.genpak.com
SIC: 3089 Plastic containers, except foam

(G-7141)
HEARTLAND METALS INC
Also Called: Pure Lead Products
127 Ranier Dr (33852-2404)
PHONE................................863 465-7501
Mike P Hoy, *President*
Jack B Edgemon, *Vice Pres*
Jack Edgemon, *Vice Pres*
Kathleen P Edgemon, *Vice Pres*
Troy Ragan, *Sales Mgr*
EMP: 38 EST: 2003
SALES (est): 17.1MM **Privately Held**
WEB: www.pureleadproducts.com
SIC: 3356 Nonferrous rolling & drawing

(G-7142)
HENSCRATCH FARMS INC
Also Called: Henscratch Farms Winery
980 Henscratch Rd (33852-8220)
PHONE................................863 699-2060
Brooke Bundy, *President*
Sylvia Lauchman, *President*
Drew Jones, *Vice Pres*
EMP: 7 EST: 1998
SQ FT: 1,391
SALES (est): 518.1K **Privately Held**
WEB: www.henscratchfarms.com
SIC: 2084 Wines

(G-7143)
JM CABINETS INCORP
1212 County Road 621 E (33852-8657)
PHONE................................863 699-2888
Jerry Morton, *Owner*
EMP: 5 EST: 2007
SALES (est): 300.3K **Privately Held**
WEB: www.jmcabinets.com
SIC: 2434 Wood kitchen cabinets

(G-7144)
KEYSTONE WATER COMPANY LLC
200 Turner Rd (33852-5440)
PHONE................................863 465-1932
Christopher Rapp, *Mng Member*
Darren Keller, *Mng Member*
Ryan Hurlbut,
Chris Rapp,
▼ EMP: 17 EST: 2008
SQ FT: 86,000
SALES (est): 2.4MM **Privately Held**
WEB: www.keystonewatercompany.com
SIC: 2086 7389 5963 Water, pasteurized: packaged in cans, bottles, etc.; labeling bottles, cans, cartons, etc.; bottled water delivery

(G-7145)
PAUL WONG
1475 Jersey St Ne (33852-3684)
PHONE................................863 465-1114
Paul Wong, *Principal*
EMP: 7 EST: 2010
SALES (est): 162K **Privately Held**
SIC: 3482 Small arms ammunition

(G-7146)
PERFORMANCE SALES AND SVC INC
1130 Us Highway 27 N (33852-5684)
PHONE................................863 465-2814
Darin L Whitaker, *President*
EMP: 6 EST: 1974
SQ FT: 2,400

SALES (est): 805.2K **Privately Held**
WEB: www.performancesalesandservice.com
SIC: 3599 5551 4493 3732 Machine shop, jobbing & repair; outboard boats; outboard motors; marine supplies; marinas; boat building & repairing

(G-7147)
RAVENSWOOD IMPORT EXPORT LTD L
204 S Main Ave Ste 5 (33852-1810)
P.O. Box 1849 (33862-1849)
PHONE................................863 800-0210
Greg Gustum, *President*
Angel R Alonso, *Partner*
Angel Rodriguez Alonso R, *Chairman*
Patricia Savanella, *Exec VP*
Alexander Ferguson, *CTO*
EMP: 5 EST: 2013
SQ FT: 900
SALES (est): 779.8K **Privately Held**
WEB: www.ravenswood-usa.com
SIC: 2833 8748 Vegetable oils, medicinal grade: refined or concentrated; business consulting

(G-7148)
SMITHS WOODWORKS INC
3005 Waterway Dr (33852-2308)
PHONE................................863 381-6564
Timothy Smith, *Principal*
EMP: 8 EST: 1995
SALES (est): 376.5K **Privately Held**
WEB: www.niceknobs.com
SIC: 2431 Millwork

(G-7149)
WEDGWORTHS INC
211 Sr 70 W (33852-8716)
PHONE................................561 996-2076
EMP: 8 EST: 1952
SALES (est): 71.5K **Privately Held**
WEB: www.wedgworth.com
SIC: 2034 Dried & dehydrated vegetables

Lake Suzy
Desoto County

(G-7150)
WINSLOW MARINE PRODUCTS CORP
Also Called: Winslow Life Raft Co
11700 Sw Winslow Dr (34269-1902)
PHONE................................941 613-6666
David Gitlin, *President*
Wendy Ledoux, *General Mgr*
▼ EMP: 85 EST: 2002
SQ FT: 35,000
SALES (est): 10.9MM
SALES (corp-wide): 64.3B **Publicly Held**
WEB: www.winslowliferaft.com
SIC: 3069 Life rafts, rubber
PA: Raytheon Technologies Corporation
1000 Wlson Blvd Arlngton Arlington Va
Arlington VA 22209
781 522-3000

Lake Wales
Polk County

(G-7151)
ACCOMMODATING SERVICES INC
19456 State Road 60 E (33898-7185)
PHONE................................863 528-3231
J R Furko, *President*
EMP: 7 EST: 2004
SALES (est): 775.4K **Privately Held**
SIC: 3589 Microwave ovens (cooking equipment), commercial

(G-7152)
ASI CHEMICAL INC
Also Called: Hand 2 Hand Sanitizer
1901 State Road 60 W (33859-8286)
P.O. Box 712 (33859-0712)
PHONE................................863 678-1814
Michael Diaz, *President*
Miguel Diaz, *President*
Raul J Diaz, *President*

Felix V Vassallo, *Vice Pres*
Cindy Diaz, *Manager*
◆ EMP: 11 EST: 2000
SQ FT: 40,000
SALES (est): 2.4MM **Privately Held**
WEB: www.asichemical.com
SIC: 2842 2841 Degreasing solvent; automobile polish; soap & other detergents

(G-7153)
AUTOMATED METAL PRODUCTS INC
16070 Hwy 27 (33859-2512)
P.O. Box 3426 (33859-3426)
PHONE................................863 638-4404
Mary B Kregl, *President*
John Kregl, *Corp Secy*
EMP: 6 EST: 1997
SQ FT: 8,000
SALES (est): 883.8K **Privately Held**
WEB: www.automatedmetalproducts.com
SIC: 3441 Fabricated structural metal

(G-7154)
CEMEX MATERIALS LLC
Also Called: Rinker Materials
534 Story Rd (33898-9265)
P.O. Box 24731, West Palm Beach (33416-4731)
PHONE................................863 678-3945
EMP: 45 **Privately Held**
SIC: 3273 Ready-mixed concrete
HQ: Cemex Materials Llc
1720 Centrepark Dr E # 100
West Palm Beach FL 33401
561 833-5555

(G-7155)
CITRUS WORLD INC (PA)
Also Called: Florida's Natural Growers
20205 Hwy 27 (33853-3080)
P.O. Box 1111 (33859-1111)
PHONE................................863 676-1411
Stephen M Caruso, *CEO*
Joe L Davis Jr, *Ch of Bd*
Dennis Broadaway, *President*
Ed Hendricks, *Business Mgr*
Todd Jones, *Business Mgr*
◆ EMP: 740 EST: 1934
SQ FT: 1,000,000
SALES (est): 188.1MM **Privately Held**
WEB: www.citrusworldinc.com
SIC: 2037 Fruit juice concentrates, frozen

(G-7156)
CITRUS WORLD SERVICES INC
20205 Hwy 27 (33853-3080)
PHONE................................863 676-1411
Stephen Caruso, *Principal*
EMP: 10 EST: 2011
SALES (est): 427.7K **Privately Held**
WEB: www.citrusworldinc.com
SIC: 2037 Citrus pulp, dried

(G-7157)
COSNER MANUFACTURING LLC
511 N Scenic Hwy (33853-3203)
P.O. Box 152 (33859-0152)
PHONE................................863 676-2579
Michael Ciferri Jr, *Mng Member*
Michelle Upchurch, *Manager*
EMP: 10 EST: 1966
SQ FT: 12,000
SALES (est): 588.1K **Privately Held**
WEB: www.cosnermfg.com
SIC: 2394 2673 Tarpaulins, fabric: made from purchased materials; bags: plastic, laminated & coated

(G-7158)
DURA-CAST PRODUCTS INC
16160 Hwy 27 (33859-2528)
PHONE................................863 638-3200
Bruce Orcutt, *President*
David Orcutt, *Vice Pres*
Peter Villa, *Engineer*
Amber Baldi, *Office Mgr*
Timothy McBride, *Manager*
▼ EMP: 90 EST: 1956
SQ FT: 50,000
SALES (est): 16.6MM **Privately Held**
WEB: www.duracast.com
SIC: 3089 Injection molding of plastics

PA: Tank Holding Corp.
6940 O St Ste 100
Lincoln NE 68510

(G-7159)
ELLISON RBM INC
4865 State Road 60 E (33898-9390)
P.O. Box 2422 (33859-2422)
PHONE..............................863 679-5283
Woodrow Ellison, *President*
Vicki Ellison, *Manager*
EMP: 5 **EST:** 2002
SALES (est): 772K **Privately Held**
WEB: www.designcreations2011.com
SIC: 2911 Road materials, bituminous

(G-7160)
FLINTS WRECKER SERVICE INC
6442 State Road 60 E (33898-9721)
PHONE..............................863 676-1318
James Flint, *President*
Victoria Flint, *Corp Secy*
EMP: 5 **EST:** 1958
SQ FT: 1,600
SALES (est): 436.7K **Privately Held**
SIC: 3711 7539 Wreckers (tow truck), assembly of; automotive sound system service & installation

(G-7161)
FLORIDAS NATURAL FOOD SVC INC
20205 Hwy 27 (33853-2428)
PHONE..............................888 657-6600
Richard A Fort Jr, *Principal*
Christopher Groom, *Vice Pres*
Scott Smith, *Vice Pres*
David Castle, *Production*
Terica Turlington, *Production*
EMP: 26 **EST:** 2012
SALES (est): 1.1MM **Privately Held**
WEB: www.floridasnaturalfoodservice.com
SIC: 2037 Frozen fruits & vegetables

(G-7162)
FREEDOM BRICK PAVERS LLC
2625 Shiner Dr (33898-8822)
PHONE..............................863 224-6008
Scott Rian, *Principal*
EMP: 7 **EST:** 2013
SALES (est): 838.5K **Privately Held**
WEB: www.freedombrickpaversllc.com
SIC: 2951 Asphalt paving mixtures & blocks

(G-7163)
GRIFFIN SAWMILL & WOODWORKING
845 W Lake Wales Rd N (33859-8272)
PHONE..............................863 241-5180
Jerrod T Griffin, *President*
EMP: 8 **EST:** 2014
SALES (est): 266.6K **Privately Held**
WEB: www.griffinsawmill.com
SIC: 2421 Specialty sawmill products; flitches (veneer stock), made in sawmills

(G-7164)
HEATH CORPORATION
1303 Meyers Rd (33859-2531)
P.O. Box 72 (33859-0072)
PHONE..............................863 638-1819
Willard Heath Jr, *President*
EMP: 6 **EST:** 1986
SQ FT: 10,000
SALES (est): 764K **Privately Held**
SIC: 3541 Machine tools, metal cutting type

(G-7165)
INNOVATIVE CARBIDE INC
6403 Park Ln Unit 1 (33898-9503)
PHONE..............................863 696-7999
Allen D Davis, *Principal*
Bethany Wardropper, *Exec VP*
Ronald Geckle, *Vice Pres*
Joel Wardropper, *Vice Pres*
Thomas Adams, *Human Res Mgr*
EMP: 19
SALES (corp-wide): 9.7MM **Privately Held**
WEB: www.innovativecarbide.com
SIC: 3544 Special dies & tools

PA: Innovative Carbide, Inc.
11040 Parker Dr
Irwin PA 15642
412 751-6900

(G-7166)
LIQUI-BOX CORPORATION
Also Called: Liquid Packaging Systems
104 S Scenic Hwy (33853-3823)
PHONE..............................863 676-7602
Greg Skinner, *Manager*
EMP: 22
SQ FT: 12,000
SALES (corp-wide): 370.1MM **Privately Held**
WEB: www.liquibox.com
SIC: 3085 3089 Plastics bottles; blow molded finished plastic products
PA: Liqui-Box Corporation
901 E Byrd St Ste 1105
Richmond VA 23219
804 325-1400

(G-7167)
LTSC LLC
28 W Park Ave (33853-4132)
PHONE..............................863 678-0011
Mark Warda, *President*
EMP: 6 **EST:** 2012
SALES (est): 362.5K **Privately Held**
WEB: www.floridalandtrust.com
SIC: 2741 Miscellaneous publishing

(G-7168)
MIDGARD INC
6402 State Road 60 E (33898-9721)
PHONE..............................863 696-1224
Brian Byrd, *Vice Pres*
Brian Bird, *Vice Pres*
Cheryl Rathbun, *Safety Dir*
Dale Andrew, *Manager*
Debbie Steedley, *Manager*
EMP: 59
SALES (corp-wide): 15MM **Privately Held**
WEB: www.midgardplastics.com
SIC: 2821 3559 3089 Polycarbonate resins; plastics working machinery; plastic processing
PA: Midgard, Inc
1255 Nursery Rd
Green Lane PA 18054
215 536-3174

(G-7169)
PETERSEN INDUSTRIES INC
4000 State Road 60 W (33898-8201)
PHONE..............................863 676-1493
Woodrow Casey Hardy, *President*
Bob Beasock, *General Mgr*
Nancy Rathbun, *Trustee*
Sam Petersen, *Vice Pres*
Samuel S Petersen, *Vice Pres*
EMP: 104 **EST:** 1948
SQ FT: 10,000
SALES (est): 26MM **Privately Held**
WEB: www.petersenind.com
SIC: 3523 Farm machinery & equipment

(G-7170)
PIPELINE FABRICATORS INC
Also Called: Pfi
733 Carlton Ave (33853-4236)
PHONE..............................863 678-0977
Perry D Batson, *President*
EMP: 10 **EST:** 1997
SALES (est): 846.2K **Privately Held**
SIC: 3498 Fabricated pipe & fittings

(G-7171)
R & R LIVESTOCK SOLUTIONS INC
7 Lincoln Ave (33853-3279)
PHONE..............................863 223-8443
Richard S Batson, *President*
EMP: 7 **EST:** 2017
SALES (est): 174K **Privately Held**
SIC: 3496 3315 Mesh, made from purchased wire; cages, wire; fence gates posts & fittings; steel

(G-7172)
ROYAL WESTLAKE ROOFING LLC
Also Called: Lifetile
200 Story Rd (33898-9230)
PHONE..............................863 676-9405
Shawn White, *Opers Staff*
Don Tracewell, *Manager*
EMP: 15 **Publicly Held**
SIC: 2952 5033 3272 Asphalt felts & coatings; roofing, asphalt & sheet metal; roofing tile & slabs, concrete
HQ: Royal Westlake Roofing Llc
7575 Irvine Center Dr # 10
Irvine CA 92618
949 756-1605

(G-7173)
SPIN MAGNETICS
22501 Us Highway 27 (33859-6863)
P.O. Box 752 (33859-0752)
PHONE..............................863 676-9333
Howard Spence, *President*
Jim Graham, *Vice Pres*
Deanna Spence, *Opers Staff*
Maya Wiisanen, *CFO*
Margaret Alford, *Admin Sec*
▲ **EMP:** 32 **EST:** 1989
SALES (est): 3.4MM **Privately Held**
WEB: www.spinmagnetics.com
SIC: 3677 3612 5999 Electronic coils, transformers & other inductors; transformers, except electric; electronic parts & equipment

(G-7174)
SPINCONTROL GEARING LLC
4535 Tiger Creek Trl (33898-5552)
PHONE..............................863 241-9055
Eric Carrier, *General Mgr*
EMP: 7 **EST:** 2009
SALES (est): 506.3K **Privately Held**
SIC: 3566 Speed changers, drives & gears

(G-7175)
STORY CITRUS INC
20205 Hwy 27 (33853-2428)
P.O. Box 1221 (33859-1221)
PHONE..............................863 638-1619
Victor Story, *President*
EMP: 21 **EST:** 2001
SALES (est): 1.4MM **Privately Held**
WEB: www.storycompanies.com
SIC: 2034 Dehydrated fruits, vegetables, soups

(G-7176)
SUZANNE CHALET FOODS INC
Also Called: Chalet Suzanne Rest Cntry Inn
3800 Chalet Suzanne Dr (33859-7763)
PHONE..............................863 676-6011
Vita Hinshaw, *President*
Eric Hinshaw, *Treasurer*
EMP: 6 **EST:** 1956
SALES (est): 540.7K **Privately Held**
SIC: 2032 5812 2035 Soups, except seafood: packaged in cans, jars, etc.; eating places; pickles, sauces & salad dressings

(G-7177)
TAYLORS INDUS COATINGS INC
108 Drive J A Wltshire Av (33853)
PHONE..............................800 932-3049
Greg Taylor, *President*
Reamonn McRae, *General Mgr*
Scott McRae, *Vice Pres*
Scott Taylor, *Vice Pres*
Tracey Reddick, *Office Mgr*
EMP: 19 **EST:** 1984
SQ FT: 10,000
SALES (est): 4.9MM **Privately Held**
WEB: www.tic-coatings.com
SIC: 3479 Coating of metals & formed products

(G-7178)
TRIFECTA PUBLISHING
3900 Chalet Suzanne Dr (33859-6881)
PHONE..............................863 676-6311
Eric Farewell, *Principal*
EMP: 7 **EST:** 2009
SALES (est): 51K **Privately Held**
SIC: 2741 Miscellaneous publishing

(G-7179)
WATTS WELDING INC
18400 County Road 630 (33898-5818)
PHONE..............................863 978-3371
Brandon Watts, *Principal*
EMP: 8 **EST:** 2018
SALES (est): 27.6K **Privately Held**
WEB: www.watts.com
SIC: 7692 Welding repair

Lake Worth
Palm Beach County

(G-7180)
ACCU RIGHT INC
1012 7th Ave S Ste 1 (33460-4973)
PHONE..............................561 586-5368
William W Vogler Jr, *President*
William W Vogler Sr, *Vice Pres*
EMP: 5 **EST:** 1987
SALES (est): 498.8K **Privately Held**
WEB: www.accuright.com
SIC: 3599 Machine shop, jobbing & repair

(G-7181)
ACRYLICO INC
2633 Lantana Rd Ste 6 (33462-2477)
PHONE..............................561 304-2921
Carlos Cavanagh, *President*
EMP: 5 **EST:** 2004
SALES (est): 497.9K **Privately Held**
WEB: www.acrylico.com
SIC: 3732 Motorized boat, building & repairing

(G-7182)
AERIALIFE INC
1319 S L St Fl 334 (33460-5618)
PHONE..............................561 990-9299
Bin Liu, *Ch of Bd*
EMP: 8 **EST:** 2020
SALES (est): 300K **Privately Held**
SIC: 2869 Silicones

(G-7183)
ALL AMERICAN LUBE
5865 S State Road 7 (33449-5429)
PHONE..............................561 432-0476
EMP: 5
SQ FT: 42,186
SALES (est): 340K **Privately Held**
SIC: 2911 Petroleum Refiner

(G-7184)
ANC SHUTTERS LLC
3386 Pony Run (33449-8005)
PHONE..............................561 966-8336
Adrian Hernandez, *President*
EMP: 14 **EST:** 2006
SALES (est): 987K **Privately Held**
SIC: 3442 Shutters, door or window: metal

(G-7185)
AROUND HOUSE PUBLISHING INC
3760 Country Vista Way (33467-2442)
PHONE..............................561 969-7412
EMP: 19 **EST:** 1997
SALES (est): 1.3MM **Privately Held**
WEB: www.athpublishing.com
SIC: 2721 Magazines: publishing only, not printed on site

(G-7186)
AUSSIE BOOMERANG BAR ON AVE IN
249 N Country Club Dr (33462-1113)
PHONE..............................561 436-9741
Rod Regan, *Principal*
EMP: 8 **EST:** 2011
SALES (est): 248.1K **Privately Held**
SIC: 3949 Boomerangs

(G-7187)
BIKEKEEPER LLC
Also Called: Whole Trade
8461 Lake Worth Rd # 173 (33467-2474)
PHONE..............................561 209-6863
Juho Sillanpaa,
EMP: 5 **EST:** 2016
SALES (est): 491.4K **Privately Held**
WEB: www.bikekeeper.com
SIC: 3429 Bicycle racks, automotive

▲ = Import ▼=Export
◆ =Import/Export

(G-7188)
BILLET TECHNOLOGY
714 S East Coast St (33460-4962)
PHONE..................................561 582-6171
EMP: 9 EST: 2017
SALES (est): 307.8K Privately Held
WEB: www.billettechnology.com
SIC: 3714 Motor vehicle parts & accessories

(G-7189)
CANVAS CLINICAL RESEARCH (PA)
3898 Via Poinciana (33467-2951)
PHONE..................................561 229-0002
Ezequiel Perez, President
EMP: 6 EST: 2013
SALES (est): 306.1K Privately Held
WEB: www.canvascr.com
SIC: 2211 Canvas

(G-7190)
CARAVAGGIO CABINETRY INC
119 S H St (33460-4430)
PHONE..................................561 609-3355
Anthony J Lauria, Principal
EMP: 12 EST: 2015
SALES (est): 277.8K Privately Held
WEB: www.caravaggiocabinetry.com
SIC: 2434 Wood kitchen cabinets

(G-7191)
CLARKS ELECTRICAL SIGNS & SVCS
108 W Cypress Rd (33467-4816)
PHONE..................................561 248-5932
A Clark, Principal
EMP: 7 EST: 2001
SALES (est): 87.2K Privately Held
SIC: 3993 Signs & advertising specialties

(G-7192)
COASTAL SHEET MTALOF S FLA LLC
8927 Hypoluxo Rd Ste A4 (33467-5249)
PHONE..................................561 718-6044
David Wall,
EMP: 20 EST: 2012
SALES (est): 1.2MM Privately Held
SIC: 3441 Fabricated structural metal

(G-7193)
COLOR MSTR PRESSURE WASHER INC
7800 Springfield Lake Dr (33467-7895)
PHONE..................................561 366-7747
Guilherme Coimbra, Principal
EMP: 7 EST: 2010
SALES (est): 215K Privately Held
SIC: 3452 Washers

(G-7194)
D & D PLASTERING & LATH INC
1707 Katherine Ct (33461-6106)
PHONE..................................561 312-7256
Cesar D Vasquez, Principal
EMP: 8 EST: 2016
SALES (est): 54.1K Privately Held
SIC: 3541 Lathes

(G-7195)
DOORWAY PROJECTS INC
6484 Kirsten Way (33467-8703)
PHONE..................................561 523-2040
Michael L Schooley, Principal
Robert Schooley, Vice Pres
EMP: 7 EST: 2014
SALES (est): 472.5K Privately Held
WEB: www.doorwayprojects.com
SIC: 3728 Aircraft parts & equipment

(G-7196)
DPDM INC
10444 White Pinto Ct (33449-5492)
PHONE..................................561 327-4150
Isaac Taylor, Principal
EMP: 8 EST: 2012
SALES (est): 131.5K Privately Held
SIC: 2752 Commercial printing, offset

(G-7197)
DR SPIRITS COMPANY LLC
604 Lake Ave (33460-3811)
PHONE..................................561 349-5005
Daniel De Liege,
EMP: 5 EST: 2019
SALES (est): 311.3K Privately Held
SIC: 2085 Distilled & blended liquors

(G-7198)
DRIVESHAFT POWER INC
10101 Lantana Rd Ste K (33449-5475)
PHONE..................................561 433-0022
Ollie Jones, Principal
EMP: 9 EST: 2006
SALES (est): 385.9K Privately Held
WEB: www.driveshaftpower.com
SIC: 3317 Tubes, seamless steel

(G-7199)
E & M RECYCLING INC
630 S Palmway (33460-4937)
PHONE..................................561 718-1092
Matthew Pickering, President
Elizabeth Pickering, Admin Sec
EMP: 7 EST: 1999
SALES (est): 983K Privately Held
SIC: 2499 Mulch or sawdust products, wood; mulch, wood & bark

(G-7200)
EAGLE METAL PRODUCTS INC
100 N Country Club Blvd (33462-1030)
PHONE..................................561 964-4192
Lester W Hensley, President
EMP: 5 EST: 2008
SALES (est): 785.8K Privately Held
WEB: www.eaglemetal.com
SIC: 3441 Fabricated structural metal

(G-7201)
FUTURE FOODS LLC
Also Called: Oumph
1005 Lake Ave (33460-3709)
PHONE..................................786 390-5226
Patrik Waxin,
Steve Cohen,
John Resigl,
EMP: 5 EST: 2016
SALES (est): 453.6K Privately Held
WEB: www.oumph.us
SIC: 2013 5141 Sausages & other prepared meats; food brokers

(G-7202)
GOLD COAST AERO ACCESSORIES
2633 Lantana Rd Ste 23 (33462-2480)
PHONE..................................561 965-7767
Dorothy E O'Neill, President
EMP: 7 EST: 2006
SALES (est): 126.2K Privately Held
SIC: 3728 Aircraft parts & equipment

(G-7203)
GUY GASKET INC
4446 Carver St (33461-2723)
P.O. Box 31, Ardsley NY (10502-0031)
PHONE..................................561 703-1774
Moshe Schneider, President
Avner Harel, Vice Pres
Barak Levy, Vice Pres
Karen Schneider, Admin Sec
▲ EMP: 20 EST: 2001
SQ FT: 2,500
SALES (est): 569.1K Privately Held
SIC: 3053 Gaskets & sealing devices

(G-7204)
HYDROFOILS INCORPORATED
4151 Lake Worth Rd (33466-5001)
P.O. Box 6006 (33466-6006)
PHONE..................................561 964-6399
EMP: 7
SALES (est): 460K Privately Held
SIC: 3732 Mfg Boats Custom Made

(G-7205)
INDIAN RVER HM PRFSSIONALS INC ✪
3306 Fargo Ave (33467-1051)
PHONE..................................561 906-3881
Ronald J Trickel, President
EMP: 7 EST: 2021
SALES (est): 108.3K Privately Held
SIC: 3732 Boat building & repairing

(G-7206)
INSTATECH INDUSTRIES INC
9835 Lake Worth Rd Ste 16 (33467-2370)
PHONE..................................954 415-4392
Aleksandr Fesenko, Principal
EMP: 6 EST: 2012
SALES (est): 430.6K Privately Held
WEB: www.instatech.com
SIC: 3999 Manufacturing industries

(G-7207)
J & H SUPPLY CO INC
825 N Dixie Hwy (33460-2528)
PHONE..................................561 582-3346
Curt R Harvey, President
Janice E Harvey, Vice Pres
EMP: 5 EST: 1962
SQ FT: 3,600
SALES (est): 469.1K Privately Held
SIC: 2221 5131 Upholstery fabrics, man-made fiber & silk; upholstery fabrics, woven

(G-7208)
J A CUSTOM FABRICATORS INC
Also Called: A Custom Fabrication
1230 Wingfield St (33460-5586)
PHONE..................................561 615-4680
George Angel, Owner
EMP: 10 EST: 2007
SALES (est): 1.1MM Privately Held
WEB: www.jacustomfab.com
SIC: 3499 8712 8711 Fire- or burglary-resistive products; architectural services; engineering services

(G-7209)
JC 323 MEDIA PUBG GROUP INC
7186 Ontario Shores Pl (33467-7790)
PHONE..................................772 940-3510
Donnetta Alansari, CEO
EMP: 7 EST: 2017
SALES (est): 252.4K Privately Held
SIC: 2741 Miscellaneous publishing

(G-7210)
JEWM INC
Also Called: Tablecloth Co
4834 Exeter Estate Ln (33449-8107)
PHONE..................................973 942-1555
Judith Metzger, President
Michael Kramer, Exec VP
Mary Kerr, Vice Pres
Bernie Kramer, Vice Pres
▼ EMP: 12 EST: 1980
SALES (est): 364.8K Privately Held
WEB: www.tablecloth.com
SIC: 2392 5949 Tablecloths: made from purchased materials; sewing, needlework & piece goods

(G-7211)
JODAN TECHNOLOGY INC
7708 Coral Colony Way (33467-6960)
PHONE..................................561 515-5556
Stanley Jasne, President
Joe Thoman, Vice Pres
EMP: 11 EST: 1997
SALES (est): 227.9K Privately Held
SIC: 2851 Epoxy coatings

(G-7212)
K M I INTERNATIONAL INC
2501 Park St (33460-6139)
PHONE..................................561 588-5514
Carlos Rodriguez, President
Ed Fryns, General Mgr
◆ EMP: 25 EST: 1988
SQ FT: 18,200
SALES (est): 4MM Privately Held
WEB: www.kmiinternational.us
SIC: 2431 1751 Doors, wood; finish & trim carpentry

(G-7213)
LABEL GRAPHICS INC
11298 Roselynn Way (33449-8451)
PHONE..................................561 798-8180
Kathy Robinson, President
Robert Robinson, Vice Pres
Shannon Reynolds, Administration
EMP: 6 EST: 1991
SQ FT: 5,000
SALES (est): 460.6K Privately Held
WEB: www.labelgraphicsinc.com
SIC: 2759 2671 Labels & seals: printing; packaging paper & plastics film, coated & laminated

(G-7214)
LAKE WORTH HERALD PRESS INC
Also Called: Coastal Observer
1313 Central Ter (33460-1835)
P.O. Box 191 (33460-0191)
PHONE..................................561 585-9387
Mark J Easton, President
Bruce Easton, Vice Pres
EMP: 13 EST: 1912
SQ FT: 5,200
SALES (est): 843.4K Privately Held
WEB: www.lwherald.com
SIC: 2711 2752 2791 2789 Job printing & newspaper publishing combined; lithographing on metal; typesetting; bookbinding & related work

(G-7215)
MAGGAC CORPORATION
Also Called: Precision Woodcraft
7629 Santee Ter (33467-7866)
PHONE..................................561 439-2707
Micheal Clark, President
Anita Johnson, Vice Pres
EMP: 5 EST: 1981
SALES (est): 443.2K Privately Held
SIC: 2426 2511 2434 Furniture dimension stock, hardwood; wood household furniture; wood kitchen cabinets

(G-7216)
MICROWAVE ELECTRONICS
6314 Dornich Ln (33463-6529)
PHONE..................................561 432-8511
Mitch Kulick, Owner
EMP: 5 EST: 2007
SALES (est): 337.9K Privately Held
SIC: 3679 Microwave components

(G-7217)
MIDDS INC
Also Called: Banyan Printing
128 S Dixie Hwy (33460-4133)
PHONE..................................561 586-6220
Roger B Manning Mr, Principal
EMP: 11 EST: 1977
SALES (est): 175.5K Privately Held
SIC: 2752 Commercial printing, offset

(G-7218)
MILLERS CUSTOM METALS INC
1224 Pope Ln (33460-6146)
PHONE..................................561 540-6263
John Miller, President
Gina Miller, Vice Pres
◆ EMP: 11 EST: 1993
SQ FT: 5,000
SALES (est): 1.9MM Privately Held
WEB: www.millerscustommetals.com
SIC: 3446 Stairs, staircases, stair treads: prefabricated metal

(G-7219)
MINUTEMAN PRESS
6677 Lake Worth Rd (33467-1507)
PHONE..................................954 804-8304
EMP: 9 EST: 2018
SALES (est): 748.2K Privately Held
WEB: www.minutemanpress.com
SIC: 2752 Commercial printing, lithographic

(G-7220)
N Y I INDUSTRIES INC
926 Lehto Ln (33461-5047)
PHONE..................................561 248-6760
Nelson Martinez, Principal
EMP: 7 EST: 2018
SALES (est): 39.6K Privately Held
SIC: 3999 Manufacturing industries

(G-7221)
NATIONAL ASSEMBLERS INC
6586 Hypoluxo Rd Ste 145 (33467-7678)
PHONE..................................877 915-5505
Jeri Castrillon, Principal
Jenny Schneider, Opers Staff
Nathalie Makepeace, Business Anlyst
Debbie Schneider, Recruiter

Nancy O'Brien, *Clerk*
EMP: 28 EST: 2014
SALES (est): 4.7MM **Privately Held**
WEB: v5.teamnai.com
SIC: 3732 Boat building & repairing

(G-7222)
NATURES CLEAR LLC
2328 10th Ave N Ste 501d (33461-6615)
PHONE.................................561 503-1751
Anivain Marius, *Principal*
EMP: 5 EST: 2020
SALES (est): 332.7K **Privately Held**
WEB: www.naturesclear.com
SIC: 2833 Medicinals & botanicals

(G-7223)
NUTRITORCH
8073 Pelican Harbour Dr (33467-6845)
PHONE.................................561 777-9079
Alkey Noel, *CEO*
EMP: 9 EST: 2018
SALES (est): 504K **Privately Held**
SIC: 2023 Dietary supplements, dairy &
non-dairy based

(G-7224)
ORKAN18
9835 Lake Worth Rd Ste 16 (33467-2370)
PHONE.................................855 675-2618
Hanan Assayag, *Principal*
EMP: 6 EST: 2015
SALES (est): 365.8K **Privately Held**
SIC: 3565 Packaging machinery

(G-7225)
PALM BEACH JUNIOR CLG PRNT SHP
4200 S Congress Ave (33461-4705)
PHONE.................................561 969-0122
▼ **EMP: 15 EST:** 1988
SALES (est): 266.2K **Privately Held**
WEB: www.palmbeachstate.edu
SIC: 2752 Commercial printing, offset

(G-7226)
PAPER CHASE
6626 Via Rienzo (33467-5915)
PHONE.................................561 641-5319
Steven Askinazi, *Principal*
EMP: 7 EST: 2005
SALES (est): 132.2K **Privately Held**
WEB: www.paperchaseboca.net
SIC: 2621 Paper mills

(G-7227)
PLASTIC KINGDOM INC
407 N Dixie Hwy (33460-3037)
PHONE.................................561 586-9300
Eligiusz Baska, *President*
Joanna Baska, *Vice Pres*
EMP: 5 EST: 1996
SALES (est): 556.5K **Privately Held**
SIC: 3089 Injection molding of plastics

(G-7228)
POLO PLAYERS EDITION
Also Called: Rizzo Management
9011 Lake Worth Rd B (33467-3617)
PHONE.................................561 968-5208
Gwen Rizzo, *Principal*
Cristina Fernandez, *Marketing Staff*
Maggie Mitchell, *Manager*
EMP: 5 EST: 1996
SALES (est): 420.6K **Privately Held**
WEB: www.poloplayersedition.com
SIC: 2721 Magazines: publishing only, not
printed on site

(G-7229)
PRISON LEGAL NEWS
Also Called: Human Rights Defense Center
1013 Lucerne Ave Ste 206 (33460-3741)
P.O. Box 1151 (33460-1151)
PHONE.................................561 360-2523
Dan Axtell, *Principal*
Kathrine Browne, *Manager*
EMP: 16 EST: 2011
SALES (est): 1.1MM **Privately Held**
WEB: www.prisonlegalnews.org
SIC: 2711 Newspapers, publishing & print-
ing

(G-7230)
QUALITY SHAVINGS SOUTH FLORIDA
10191 Lantana Rd (33449-5443)
PHONE.................................561 433-9955
Giuseppe J Lebisernia, *Branch Mgr*
EMP: 35
SALES (corp-wide): 162.3K **Privately
Held**
SIC: 2399 Horse blankets
PA: Quality Shavings Of South Florida
7800 N University Dr
Tamarac FL

(G-7231)
REBUILD GLOBALLY INC
Also Called: Deux Mains
810 S K St (33460-5046)
PHONE.................................407 801-9936
Julie Colombino, *CEO*
Bridget Healy, *President*
Leslie Hielema, *President*
Laurent Prosper, *Vice Pres*
Joshua Johnson, *Treasurer*
EMP: 32 EST: 2010
SALES (est): 213K **Privately Held**
WEB: www.rebuildglobally.org
SIC: 3021 Sandals, rubber

(G-7232)
SFA SYSTEMS INC
Also Called: South Florida Aluminum
1230 Wingfield St (33460-5586)
PHONE.................................561 585-5927
Robert W Miller, *President*
Harry F Leeser Jr, *Vice Pres*
EMP: 26 EST: 1965
SQ FT: 15,000
SALES (est): 2.7MM **Privately Held**
WEB: www.southfloridaaluminum.com
SIC: 3444 3312 2851 3446 Canopies;
sheet metal; rails, steel or iron; under-
coatings, paint; architectural metalwork

(G-7233)
SOUTHERN AWNING INC (PA)
313 S H St (33460-4434)
PHONE.................................561 586-0464
Mitch Lewis, *President*
Richard Trobaugh, *Vice Pres*
Joanne Trobaugh, *Treasurer*
Janice Lewis, *Admin Sec*
EMP: 21 EST: 1992
SQ FT: 5,400
SALES (est): 2.4MM **Privately Held**
WEB: www.southernawning.com
SIC: 2394 7692 5999 Canvas awnings &
canopies; welding repair; awnings

(G-7234)
SWEET AND VICIOUS LLC
1512 N Lakeside Dr (33460-1922)
PHONE.................................772 907-3030
Melba Thompson, *Branch Mgr*
▲ **EMP:** 13
SALES (corp-wide): 1.2MM **Privately
Held**
WEB: www.sweet-vicious.com
SIC: 2254 Knit underwear mills
PA: Sweet And Vicious Llc
111 Ne 21st St
Miami FL 33137
305 576-0012

(G-7235)
TECHNICO
507 S G St (33460-4370)
PHONE.................................561 588-8300
John Maher, *Manager*
EMP: 11 EST: 1985
SALES (est): 652.7K **Privately Held**
WEB: www.technicofl.com
SIC: 3822 Auto controls regulating residntl
& coml environmt & applncs

(G-7236)
TIENDA MAYA
6082 S Congress Ave (33462-2318)
PHONE.................................561 965-0900
Juan Tomas, *Principal*
EMP: 7 EST: 2009
SALES (est): 193K **Privately Held**
WEB: www.krockstarz.com
SIC: 3643 Outlets, electric: convenience

(G-7237)
TPL MANUFACTURING INC
8854 Pinion Dr (33467-1186)
PHONE.................................954 783-3400
Koule Lyras, *President*
EMP: 9 EST: 2001
SALES (est): 976.3K **Privately Held**
WEB: www.tplmanufacturing.com
SIC: 2511 Wood household furniture

(G-7238)
TRI-EDGE INDUSTRIES LLC
6586 Hypoluxo Rd (33467-7678)
PHONE.................................561 703-5961
EMP: 5 EST: 2016
SALES (est): 505.1K **Privately Held**
WEB: www.tri-edge.com
SIC: 3999 Manufacturing industries

(G-7239)
TRS INDUSTRIES INC
6845 Finamore Cir (33467-8727)
PHONE.................................561 880-0031
Francis Waite, *President*
Brian Waite, *Vice Pres*
▼ **EMP: 7 EST:** 2006
SALES (est): 488.9K **Privately Held**
WEB: www.trsindustries.com
SIC: 3951 7389 Markers, soft tip (felt, fab-
ric, plastic, etc.);

(G-7240)
ULTIMATE DOOR PALM BEACH INC
2800 2nd Ave N (33461-4114)
PHONE.................................561 642-2828
Roger Warwick, *President*
Cal Morris, *Vice Pres*
▲ **EMP: 16 EST:** 1994
SQ FT: 10,000
SALES (est): 1.1MM **Privately Held**
WEB: www.ultimatedoor.com
SIC: 2431 3442 Doors, wood; metal
doors, sash & trim

(G-7241)
UNDERSEA BREATHING SYSTEMS
2565 N Dixie Hwy (33460-6250)
PHONE.................................561 588-7698
William H Delp II, *President*
Dick Rutkowski, *Shareholder*
Morgan J Wells, *Shareholder*
◆ **EMP: 6 EST:** 1994
SQ FT: 4,000
SALES (est): 442.3K **Privately Held**
WEB: www.dnax.com
SIC: 3949 5091 Skin diving equipment,
scuba type; diving equipment & supplies

(G-7242)
VERTEX PRECISION INC
Also Called: V P I
714 S East Coast St (33460-4962)
PHONE.................................561 582-6171
Heidi Tetzlaff, *President*
EMP: 16 EST: 1997
SQ FT: 5,000
SALES (est): 3.3MM **Privately Held**
WEB: www.custombilletstore.net
SIC: 3532 Mining machinery

(G-7243)
VIRGO AEROSPACE LLC
6180 Royal Birkdale Dr (33463-6526)
PHONE.................................954 816-3455
Sandra Vergara, *Principal*
Sandra P Vergara, *Principal*
EMP: 7 EST: 2010
SALES (est): 248K **Privately Held**
SIC: 3721 Aircraft

(G-7244)
WALLACE INDUSTRIES INC
906 N Dixie Hwy (33460-2531)
PHONE.................................561 301-0811
Paul R Kludt, *Principal*
EMP: 9 EST: 2012
SALES (est): 255K **Privately Held**
WEB: www.ksmachineinc.com
SIC: 3999 Manufacturing industries

(G-7245)
XTREME ELECTRONIC DESIGNS INC
1432 S Lakeside Dr Apt 9 (33460-5732)
PHONE.................................561 557-3667
John C McKeeman, *President*
Owen Dewar, *Engineer*
EMP: 5 EST: 2005
SALES (est): 460.4K **Privately Held**
WEB: www.xedi.us
SIC: 3672 Printed circuit boards

Lake Worth Beach
Palm Beach County

(G-7246)
ALL COUNTY SHEET METAL INC
1930 7th Ct N (33461-3302)
PHONE.................................561 588-0099
Ronald L Davis, *President*
James Trasport, *Vice Pres*
Kathleen J Davis, *Admin Sec*
EMP: 9 EST: 1982
SQ FT: 2,950
SALES (est): 882.3K **Privately Held**
WEB: www.allcountysheetmetal.com
SIC: 3444 Sheet metal specialties, not
stamped

(G-7247)
ALL-PRO ACCNTING BKKEEPING LLC
1947 10th Ave N (33461-3309)
PHONE.................................561 212-8418
Rene D Sexton, *Principal*
EMP: 7 EST: 2014
SALES (est): 203.6K **Privately Held**
SIC: 2782 Account books

(G-7248)
ARC STONE III LLC
1800 4th Ave N Unit A (33461-3874)
PHONE.................................561 478-8805
Micheal Coiro, *Mng Member*
▲ **EMP: 10 EST:** 1998
SQ FT: 50,000
SALES (est): 3.2MM **Privately Held**
WEB: www.arcstonegranite.com
SIC: 1411 Limestone & marble dimension
stone

(G-7249)
ARTISTIC DOORS INC
2223 2nd Ave N (33461-3212)
PHONE.................................561 582-0348
Luis E Masson, *President*
EMP: 6 EST: 2008
SALES (est): 425.7K **Privately Held**
SIC: 2431 Millwork

(G-7250)
BENCHMARK ENTERTAINMENT LC
Also Called: Benchmark Games
2201 4th Ave N (33461-3835)
PHONE.................................561 588-5200
Ivan Viau, *Purch Mgr*
Yvon Viau, *Senior Buyer*
Grazzy Delong, *Sales Staff*
Anthony Medina, *Sales Staff*
Alexander F Kress, *Mng Member*
◆ **EMP: 20 EST:** 1993
SALES (est): 5.1MM **Privately Held**
WEB: www.benchmarkgames.com
SIC: 3944 Electronic games & toys

(G-7251)
BENCHMARK GAMES INTL LLC
2201 4th Ave N (33461-3835)
PHONE.................................561 588-5200
Anthony Maniscalco, *Exec VP*
Yvon Viau, *Purch Dir*
Jeffrey Delong, *QA Dir*
Joshua Seidel, *Controller*
Tiffany Lomax, *Manager*
EMP: 85 EST: 2017
SALES (est): 15MM **Privately Held**
WEB: www.benchmarkgames.com
SIC: 3944 Electronic games & toys

(G-7252)
BLAST CTINGS
POWDERCOATING LLC
1847 Aragon Ave Unit 2 (33461-2620)
PHONE................................561 635-7605
Matias D Sprindys, *Branch Mgr*
EMP: 14 **Privately Held**
SIC: 3479 Etching & engraving
PA: Blast Coatings Powdercoating Llc
1745 Sawgrass Cir
Greenacres FL 33413

(G-7253)
CAPZERPHARMA
MANUFACTURING LLC
3677 23rd Ave S Ste B107 (33461-3264)
PHONE................................561 493-4000
Abdul Naim, *Mng Member*
Mohammad Mamun, *Mng Member*
EMP: 5 EST: 2017
SALES (est): 403.9K **Privately Held**
WEB: www.capzerpharmaceuticals.com
SIC: 2834 Tablets, pharmaceutical

(G-7254)
DS POWDER COATING INC
1800 4th Ave N Unit B (33461-3874)
PHONE................................561 660-7835
Kristen Dal Santo, *President*
EMP: 7 EST: 2017
SALES (est): 453.7K **Privately Held**
WEB: www.dspowdercoatings.com
SIC: 3479 Coating of metals & formed
products

(G-7255)
DURA-WELD INC
3599 23rd Ave S Ste 9 (33461-3291)
PHONE................................561 586-0180
Russell Wanser, *President*
Marilyn Prommel, *Office Mgr*
▼ EMP: 5 EST: 1994
SQ FT: 1,000
SALES (est): 452.8K **Privately Held**
WEB: www.dura-weld.com
SIC: 3089 Plastic & fiberglass tanks; plas-
tic processing

(G-7256)
ICE LINK 2018 LLC
1963 10th Ave N (33461-3361)
PHONE................................305 988-4023
Ash Howell,
EMP: 5 EST: 2017
SALES (est): 307.4K **Privately Held**
SIC: 3585 Ice making machinery

(G-7257)
JABS INVESTORS CORP
1815 10th Ave N Ste A (33461-3365)
PHONE................................561 540-2693
Jaime A Bolivar, *President*
EMP: 16 EST: 2003
SALES (est): 258.2K **Privately Held**
SIC: 2493 Marbleboard (stone face hard
board)

(G-7258)
MIDDS INC
Also Called: Banyan Printing
1937 10th Ave N (33461-3309)
PHONE................................561 586-6220
Roger Manning, *President*
Stacie Bailey, *Engineer*
Dawn Roth, *Sales Staff*
EMP: 44 EST: 1977
SALES (est): 5.2MM **Privately Held**
SIC: 2752 7389 2789 2672 Commercial
printing, offset; printers' services: folding,
collating; bookbinding & related work;
coated & laminated paper

(G-7259)
MILCOM SERVICES INC
1963 10th Ave N (33461-3361)
PHONE................................561 907-6816
Ursula White Lemmens, *President*
Kurt Freiter, *Vice Pres*
EMP: 5 EST: 1984
SQ FT: 6,000
SALES (est): 454.9K **Privately Held**
WEB: www.milcomservices.com
SIC: 3199 Harness or harness parts

(G-7260)
PATTEN CO INC
Also Called: Patten Group
1803 Madrid Ave (33461-3395)
PHONE................................707 826-2887
Fred Kaplan, *President*
EMP: 38 EST: 1974
SQ FT: 38,000
SALES: 10MM
SALES (corp-wide): 59.3MM **Privately
Held**
WEB: www.pattencompany.com
SIC: 3069 Life rafts, rubber
HQ: Wing Inflatables, Inc.
1220 5th St
Arcata CA 95521

(G-7261)
SOLID PRINT SOLUTIONS INC
1961 10th Ave N (33461-3361)
PHONE................................561 670-4391
EMP: 9 EST: 2019
SALES (est): 296.1K **Privately Held**
WEB: www.solidprintsolutions.com
SIC: 2752 Commercial printing, offset

(G-7262)
SOUTHERN CUSTOM IRON &
ART LLC
3787 Boutwell Rd (33461-3803)
PHONE................................561 586-8400
Ashleigh R Hernandez, *Mng Member*
EMP: 30 EST: 2014
SALES (est): 1.7MM **Privately Held**
WEB: www.southerncustomiron.com
SIC: 3441 Fabricated structural metal

(G-7263)
VAN LINDA IRON WORKS INC
3787 Boutwell Rd (33461-3893)
PHONE................................561 586-8400
Ashleigh Hernandez, *President*
Dave Drewery, *Vice Pres*
▼ EMP: 30 EST: 1949
SQ FT: 47,500
SALES (est): 8.5MM **Privately Held**
WEB: www.vanlinda.com
SIC: 3441 3599 Fabricated structural
metal; machine & other job shop work

(G-7264)
VITAL PRINTING CORPORATION
1983 10th Ave N (33461-3361)
PHONE................................561 659-2367
William J Vitale, *President*
EMP: 10 EST: 1980
SALES (est): 908.4K **Privately Held**
WEB: www.vitalprinting.com
SIC: 2752 Commercial printing, offset

Lakeland
Polk County

(G-7265)
ADEMERO INC
4685 E County Road 540a (33813-4407)
PHONE................................863 937-0272
Sam Fulwider, *Opers Staff*
Daniel Snell, *Research*
Ian Goodman, *Engineer*
Michael Ludden, *VP Sales*
Susana Reilly, *Sales Staff*
EMP: 15 EST: 2014
SALES (est): 1.6MM **Privately Held**
WEB: www.ademero.com
SIC: 7372 7371 Prepackaged software;
custom computer programming services

(G-7266)
ADVANCED ALUM POLK CNTY
INC
Also Called: Permatile Roofing
2941 Parkway St (33811-1391)
P.O. Box 5075 (33807-5075)
PHONE................................863 648-5787
James E Smith, *President*
Marjorie J Smith, *Corp Secy*
EMP: 20 EST: 1991
SQ FT: 55,000
SALES (est): 3.5MM **Privately Held**
WEB: www.advaluminum.com
SIC: 3448 3444 Prefabricated metal build-
ings; sheet metalwork

(G-7267)
ADVANCED OVERHEAD
SYSTEMS INC
3510 Craftsman Blvd (33803-7307)
P.O. Box 2645, Eaton Park (33840-2645)
PHONE................................863 667-3757
David W Roberts, *General Mgr*
William Y Harrell, *Vice Pres*
John Haney, *Sales Staff*
Lou Harrell, *Admin Sec*
Mary Harrell, *Admin Sec*
EMP: 23 EST: 1993
SALES (est): 7.6MM **Privately Held**
WEB:
www.advancedoverheadsystems.com
SIC: 3536 Hoists, cranes & monorails

(G-7268)
AETHER MEDIA USA INC
Also Called: Sir Speedy
4175 S Pipkin Rd Ste 108 (33811-1699)
PHONE................................863 647-5500
Julian Robins, *President*
John Robins, *Vice Pres*
Darwin Eicher, *Manager*
EMP: 7 EST: 1982
SALES (est): 611.2K **Privately Held**
WEB: www.sirspeedy.com
SIC: 2752 2791 Commercial printing, litho-
graphic; typesetting

(G-7269)
ALABAMA METAL INDUSTRIES
CORP
1033 Pine Chase Ave (33815-3139)
PHONE................................863 688-9256
Robert Poar, *Branch Mgr*
EMP: 59
SQ FT: 86,360
SALES (corp-wide): 1.3B **Publicly Held**
WEB: www.amicoglobal.com
SIC: 3446 Open flooring & grating for con-
struction
HQ: Alabama Metal Industries Corporation
3245 Fayette Ave
Birmingham AL 35208
205 787-2611

(G-7270)
ALL-AMERICAN SIGNS INC
206 N Eastside Dr (33801-2608)
P.O. Box 697, Highland City (33846-0697)
PHONE................................863 665-7161
Andrew Alach, *President*
EMP: 6 EST: 1971
SQ FT: 12,500
SALES (est): 833.9K **Privately Held**
WEB: www.aa-signs.net
SIC: 3993 1799 Neon signs; sign installa-
tion & maintenance

(G-7271)
AMEGA SCIENCES INC
6550 New Tampa Hwy Ste A (33815-3146)
PHONE................................863 937-9792
Julie I Bowey, *President*
David Sparks, *Research*
Gene Baldwin, *Natl Sales Mgr*
▲ EMP: 6 EST: 2005
SALES (est): 1.3MM **Privately Held**
WEB: www.amegasciencesusa.com
SIC: 3523 Soil preparation machinery, ex-
cept turf & grounds

(G-7272)
AMERICAN BOTTLING
COMPANY
Also Called: Southeast Atlantic
3520 Waterfield Rd (33803-9741)
PHONE................................863 665-6128
Randy Vaxley, *Manager*
EMP: 82 **Publicly Held**
WEB: www.keurigdrpepper.com
SIC: 2086 Soft drinks: packaged in cans,
bottles, etc.
HQ: The American Bottling Company
6425 Hall Of Fame Ln
Frisco TX 75034

(G-7273)
AMERICAN-MARSH PUMPS LLC
2805 Badger Rd (33811-1370)
PHONE................................863 646-5689
EMP: 9

SALES (corp-wide): 37K **Privately Held**
SIC: 3561 Pumps And Pumping Equipment, Nsk
HQ: American-Marsh Pumps Llc
550 E South St
Collierville TN 38017
800 888-7167

(G-7274)
AMERICOAT CORPORATION
2935 Barneys Pumps Pl (33812-4209)
P.O. Box 2228, Eaton Park (33840-2228)
PHONE................................863 667-1035
Shrikant V Desai, *President*
EMP: 5 EST: 1995
SALES (est): 549K **Privately Held**
WEB: www.ameri-coat.com
SIC: 3479 Coating of metals & formed
products

(G-7275)
AREA LITHO INC
238 N Wabash Ave (33815-7371)
PHONE................................863 687-4656
Gerald Winchester, *CEO*
Stanley Sheafer, *Ch of Bd*
EMP: 6 EST: 1981
SQ FT: 4,000
SALES (est): 527.9K **Privately Held**
WEB: www.unitedlitho.com
SIC: 2752 Promotional printing, litho-
graphic; commercial printing, offset

(G-7276)
ARGENAL CABINETS INC
911 Hammock Shade Dr (33809-4644)
PHONE................................863 670-7973
Alejandra Argenal, *Owner*
EMP: 7 EST: 2016
SALES (est): 90.6K **Privately Held**
WEB: www.argenalcabinets.com
SIC: 2434 Wood kitchen cabinets

(G-7277)
ARGOS USA
2300 Mershon St (33815-3532)
PHONE................................863 687-1898
EMP: 8 EST: 2015
SALES (est): 121.9K **Privately Held**
WEB: www.argos-us.com
SIC: 3273 Ready-mixed concrete

(G-7278)
AVERETT SEPTIC TANK CO INC
2610 Longhorn Ave (33801-6425)
P.O. Box 266, Eaton Park (33840-0266)
PHONE................................863 665-1748
Sam A Averett, *President*
Suzanne Britt, *Vice Pres*
Ida Averett, *Shareholder*
EMP: 38 EST: 1958
SQ FT: 1,500
SALES (est): 6.8MM **Privately Held**
WEB: www.averettseptic.com
SIC: 3272 1711 7699 3432 Septic tanks,
concrete; septic system construction; sep-
tic tank cleaning service; plumbing fixture
fittings & trim

(G-7279)
B H BUNN COMPANY
2730 Drane Field Rd (33811-1325)
PHONE................................863 647-1555
John R Bunn, *President*
◆ EMP: 15 EST: 1907
SQ FT: 18,000
SALES (est): 2.4MM **Privately Held**
WEB: www.bunntyco.com
SIC: 3565 Packaging machinery

(G-7280)
BATTERY USA INC (PA)
Also Called: Imperial Motor Parts-Division
1840 S Combee Rd (33801-6852)
PHONE................................863 665-6317
Robert Thomas Standifer II, *President*
Jeff Gray, *Regional Mgr*
Jim Lawless, *Vice Pres*
Byron Smith, *Opers Mgr*
Merelyn Olivera, *Sales Staff*
▲ EMP: 40 EST: 1970
SQ FT: 20,000

SALES (est): 17MM **Privately Held**
WEB: www.batteryusa.com
SIC: 3714 5531 5013 7699 Motor vehicle parts & accessories; batteries, automotive & truck; automotive batteries; battery service & repair; motor vehicle parts, used

(G-7281)
BATTERY USA INC
Also Called: Imperial Motor Parts
1930 S Combee Rd (33801-6854)
PHONE..................................863 665-5401
Kevin Layton, *Manager*
EMP: 7
SALES (corp-wide): 17MM **Privately Held**
WEB: www.batteryusa.com
SIC: 3714 Motor vehicle parts & accessories
PA: Battery Usa, Inc.
1840 S Combee Rd
Lakeland FL 33801
863 665-6317

(G-7282)
BIO-LAB INC
3125 Drane Field Rd # 10 (33811-1398)
PHONE..................................863 709-1411
Bill Gilberti, *Director*
EMP: 10
SALES (corp-wide): 2.1B **Privately Held**
WEB: www.kikcorp.com
SIC: 2819 2869 2812 Industrial inorganic chemicals; alcohols, industrial: denatured (non-beverage); alkalies & chlorine
HQ: Bio-Lab, Inc.
1725 N Brown Rd
Lawrenceville GA 30043
678 502-4000

(G-7283)
BLUE PLANET HOLDINGS LLC (PA)
1738 Clarendon Pl (33803-2567)
PHONE..................................863 559-1236
Scott McBride, *Principal*
EMP: 12 **EST:** 2013
SALES (est): 14.4MM **Privately Held**
SIC: 2013 Smoked meats from purchased meat

(G-7284)
BOBS WLDG FBRCATION MAINT INC
542 S Combee Rd (33801-6310)
P.O. Box 1557, Eaton Park (33840-1557)
PHONE..................................863 665-0135
Cameron Honeycutt, *President*
Robert L Honeycutt, *President*
Robert B Honeycutt, *Corp Secy*
Cameron B Honeycutt, *Vice Pres*
EMP: 14 **EST:** 1986
SALES (est): 770.7K **Privately Held**
WEB: www.bobs-welding.net
SIC: 3599 7692 Machine shop, jobbing & repair; welding repair

(G-7285)
BREW HUB LLC
Also Called: Brew Hub, The
3900 Frontage Rd S (33815-3205)
PHONE..................................863 698-7600
Timothy Schoen, *CEO*
Jerry Mullane, *President*
Jessica Bowey, *General Mgr*
Baye Perry, *General Mgr*
Bryan Amaral, *Facilities Mgr*
▲ **EMP:** 45 **EST:** 2012
SALES (est): 13.5MM **Privately Held**
WEB: www.brewhub.com
SIC: 2082 Brewers' grain

(G-7286)
BROTHERS PALLETS
2410 Mcjunkin Rd (33803-7318)
P.O. Box 689, Eaton Park (33840-0689)
PHONE..................................863 944-5278
Jose C Garcia, *Owner*
EMP: 6 **EST:** 2000
SALES (est): 522.9K **Privately Held**
WEB: www.doodlekit.com
SIC: 2448 Pallets, wood

(G-7287)
C&D SIGN AND LIGHTING SVCS LLC
Also Called: Sign-A-Rama
2175 E Edgewood Dr (33803-3603)
PHONE..................................863 937-9323
Greg Cameron, *Owner*
EMP: 7 **EST:** 2008
SALES (est): 883.8K **Privately Held**
WEB: www.signarama.com
SIC: 3993 2752 2389 5999 Signs & advertising specialties; commercial printing, lithographic; apparel & accessories; banners

(G-7288)
CARPENTER CO
5100 Frontage Rd S (33815-0901)
PHONE..................................863 687-9494
Tracy Lane, *Manager*
EMP: 66
SQ FT: 30,000
SALES (corp-wide): 1.8B **Privately Held**
WEB: www.carpenter.com
SIC: 3086 1311 2869 2821 Insulation or cushioning material, foamed plastic; carpet & rug cushions, foamed plastic; padding, foamed plastic; crude petroleum & natural gas; industrial organic chemicals; plastics materials & resins; insulation material, building; insulation materials
PA: Carpenter Co.
5016 Monument Ave
Richmond VA 23230
804 359-0800

(G-7289)
CATAPULT LAKELAND INC
226 N Kentucky Ave (33801-4963)
PHONE..................................863 687-3788
Ira Anderson, *President*
EMP: 9 **EST:** 2017
SALES (est): 4.3MM **Privately Held**
WEB: www.catapultlakeland.com
SIC: 3599 Catapults

(G-7290)
CEMEX MATERIALS LLC
801 Mccue Rd (33815-3236)
PHONE..................................863 688-2306
Jeffrey Toennies, *Accounts Mgr*
Eric Hagerman, *Branch Mgr*
EMP: 10
SQ FT: 3,752 **Privately Held**
SIC: 3273 Ready-mixed concrete
HQ: Cemex Materials Llc
1720 Centrepark Dr E # 100
West Palm Beach FL 33401
561 833-5555

(G-7291)
CHICAGO SOFT LTD
1820 E Edgewood Dr # 105 (33803-3420)
PHONE..................................863 940-2066
Eileen Krause, *President*
Joai Broughton, *Opers Mgr*
Carol Brown, *Accountant*
Mando Reyes, *Natl Sales Mgr*
Stephanie Patterson, *Administration*
EMP: 10 **EST:** 1982
SQ FT: 800
SALES (est): 1.6MM **Privately Held**
WEB: www.chicago-soft.com
SIC: 7372 Prepackaged software

(G-7292)
CITY OF LAKELAND
Utilities Finance Div
1140 E Parker St (33801-2066)
PHONE..................................863 834-6780
EMP: 12 **Privately Held**
SIC: 3087 Custom Compounding-Purchased Resins
PA: City Of Lakeland
228 S Massachusetts Ave
Lakeland FL 33801
863 834-6000

(G-7293)
COATINGS SMPLES SLTONS ETC LLC
5515 Summerland Hills Dr (33812-6375)
PHONE..................................863 398-8513
Timothy Franklin, *Mng Member*
EMP: 9 **EST:** 2016

SALES (est): 780.2K **Privately Held**
SIC: 2952 Asphalt felts & coatings

(G-7294)
COCA-COLA BEVERAGES FLA LLC
1770 Interstate Dr (33805-2602)
PHONE..................................863 499-6300
EMP: 10
SALES (corp-wide): 366.5MM **Privately Held**
WEB: www.cocacolaflorida.com
SIC: 2086 Bottled & canned soft drinks
PA: Coca-Cola Beverages Florida, Llc
10117 Princess Palm Ave
Tampa FL 33610
800 438-2653

(G-7295)
COMPUTATIONAL SYSTEMS INC
5030 Gateway Blvd Ste 11 (33811-2708)
PHONE..................................863 648-9044
Greg Dawes, *Manager*
EMP: 129
SALES (corp-wide): 18.2B **Publicly Held**
SIC: 3823 Industrial instrmnts msrmnt display/control process variable
HQ: Computational Systems, Incorporated
8000 West Florissant Ave
Saint Louis MO 63136
314 553-2000

(G-7296)
CONIBEAR EQUIPMENT CO INC (PA)
Also Called: Conibear Recreational Vehicles
8910 Us Highway 98 N (33809-1013)
P.O. Box 90215 (33804-0215)
PHONE..................................863 858-4414
Robert Conibear, *President*
Joanne A Conibear, *Corp Secy*
Donald D Mills, *Exec VP*
Dale Burges, *Vice Pres*
Judith C Mills, *Vice Pres*
EMP: 8 **EST:** 1940
SQ FT: 1,200
SALES (est): 1.6MM **Privately Held**
WEB: www.conibearequipmentinc.com
SIC: 3523 Fertilizing machinery, farm

(G-7297)
CORNERSTONE INTERLOCKING INC
5915 Walt Loop Rd (33809-6637)
PHONE..................................863 944-1609
Keith Davis, *Owner*
EMP: 7 **EST:** 2003
SALES (est): 91.3K **Privately Held**
SIC: 3272 Concrete products

(G-7298)
CREATIVE LIGHTING & POWER LLC
Also Called: Creative Lighting & Solar
330 Winston Creek Pkwy G (33810-2856)
PHONE..................................407 967-0957
Richelle Ortiz, *Principal*
Candice Clark, *COO*
EMP: 17 **EST:** 2014
SALES (est): 6.3MM **Privately Held**
WEB: www.creativelightingandpower.com
SIC: 3648 Lighting equipment

(G-7299)
CRH AMERICAS INC
Also Called: Oldcastle Lawn & Garden
500 S Florida Ave Ste 240 (33801-5252)
PHONE..................................843 672-5553
George Driver, *Principal*
EMP: 639
SALES (corp-wide): 30.9B **Privately Held**
WEB: www.crhamericas.com
SIC: 3273 Ready-mixed concrete
HQ: Crh Americas, Inc.
900 Ashwood Pkwy Ste 600
Atlanta GA 30338
770 804-3363

(G-7300)
CRICHLOW DATA SCIENCES INC
2500 Drane Feld Rd Ste 10 (33811)
PHONE..................................863 616-1222
Richard H Crichlow, *Ch of Bd*
Robert C Crichlow III, *President*
◆ **EMP:** 9 **EST:** 1983

SQ FT: 16,000
SALES (est): 1.2MM **Privately Held**
WEB: www.thegeneralstore.com
SIC: 7372 Business oriented computer software

(G-7301)
CROWN PRINTING INC
1303 E Main St (33801-5714)
PHONE..................................863 682-4881
Mark Rust, *President*
Edith Rust, *Vice Pres*
EMP: 18 **EST:** 1967
SQ FT: 17,500
SALES (est): 1.9MM **Privately Held**
WEB: www.crownprint.net
SIC: 2752 Commercial printing, offset

(G-7302)
D E E CUSTOM FABRICATORS INC
3545 Waterfield Pkwy (33803-9735)
P.O. Box 1798, Highland City (33846-1798)
PHONE..................................863 667-1850
Gary Bruce McWhirter, *CEO*
Ethan McWhirter, *Opers Mgr*
Erik McWhirter, *Sales Mgr*
EMP: 20 **EST:** 1999
SALES (est): 1.7MM **Privately Held**
WEB: www.deecustom.com
SIC: 3993 Signs & advertising specialties

(G-7303)
D I R INC
Also Called: Rob Dinic Interiors
3430 Flightline Dr (33811-2836)
PHONE..................................863 661-5360
Rob Dinicolantonio, *President*
EMP: 9 **EST:** 2004
SQ FT: 6,000
SALES (est): 169.9K **Privately Held**
SIC: 3429 Aircraft hardware

(G-7304)
D J TRUSSES UNLIMITED INC
3125 Reynolds Rd (33803-8328)
PHONE..................................863 687-4796
Gerald B Chipps, *President*
David Snell, *Vice Pres*
Dan Mitola, *Opers Staff*
Gary Roth, *Sales Mgr*
EMP: 16 **EST:** 1993
SQ FT: 2,000
SALES (est): 3.3MM **Privately Held**
WEB: www.djtrussesunlimited.com
SIC: 2439 Trusses, wooden roof

(G-7305)
DCP HOLDINGS
3502 Dmg Dr Ste 102 (33811-1003)
PHONE..................................863 644-0030
Ryan Delliveniri, *President*
Dan Snyder, *Principal*
Brenda Dell, *Vice Pres*
EMP: 42 **EST:** 1994
SALES (est): 2.4MM **Privately Held**
SIC: 3993 Signs & advertising specialties

(G-7306)
DCR FABRICATION INC
4101 Holden Rd (33811-1338)
PHONE..................................863 709-1121
Dale C Rossman, *President*
Ronald E Jordan, *Corp Secy*
Shelly Prickett, *Admin Asst*
EMP: 35 **EST:** 1991
SQ FT: 70,000
SALES (est): 10.1MM
SALES (corp-wide): 27.4MM **Privately Held**
WEB: www.dcrfabinc.com
SIC: 3444 Pipe, sheet metal
PA: Dcr Services, Inc.
2830 Parkway St
Lakeland FL 33811

(G-7307)
DEC SHEET METAL INC
Also Called: Dec Metals
3015 Waterfield Cir (33803-9733)
P.O. Box 580, Highland City (33846-0580)
PHONE..................................863 669-0707
Cory Maxwell, *CEO*
David Maxwell, *President*
Eric Maxwell, *President*
Karen Maxwell, *Vice Pres*

▲ = Import ▼=Export
◆ =Import/Export

EMP: 13 **EST:** 1980
SQ FT: 7,500
SALES (est): 5.2MM **Privately Held**
WEB: www.decmetals.com
SIC: 3441 Fabricated structural metal

(G-7308)
DEMOSS CABINETRY LLC
3003 Brooks St Ste 1 (33803-8386)
PHONE.............................863 738-0080
Thomas E Sharrett, *Mng Member*
EMP: 8 **EST:** 2005
SALES (est): 390.5K **Privately Held**
WEB: www.demosscabinetry.com
SIC: 2434 Wood kitchen cabinets

(G-7309)
DIG IN ANCHORS LLC
535 Hardenoak Blvd (33813-1500)
PHONE.............................386 308-7745
Grady Michael, *Principal*
EMP: 6 **EST:** 2012
SALES (est): 324.4K **Privately Held**
WEB: www.diginanchors.com
SIC: 3732 Boat building & repairing

(G-7310)
DIGITAL TECH OF LAKELAND INC
Also Called: Digitech Graphics Group
3020 Winter Lake Rd (33803-9707)
PHONE.............................863 668-8770
Alfredo Balingit, *President*
David Butfiloski, *Director*
Barbara Balingit, *Admin Sec*
EMP: 10 **EST:** 1990
SALES (est): 1.4MM **Privately Held**
WEB: www.dtechgraphics.com
SIC: 3993 Signs & advertising specialties

(G-7311)
DIXIE SIGNS INC
2930 Drane Field Rd (33811-1329)
PHONE.............................863 644-3521
Roger Snyder, *President*
Patrick Snyder, *Opers Staff*
John R Douglass, *Treasurer*
Keely Chestnut, *Accounting Mgr*
EMP: 21 **EST:** 1939
SQ FT: 15,500
SALES (est): 4.1MM **Privately Held**
WEB: www.dixiesignsinc.com
SIC: 3993 Electric signs

(G-7312)
DOUGLASS SCREEN PRINTERS INC
Also Called: Dprint
2710 New Tampa Hwy (33815-3463)
PHONE.............................863 687-8545
Lisa K Hickey, *Ch of Bd*
Lane Hickey-Wiggins, *President*
Michael Hickey, *Vice Pres*
Stephanie McDonald, *Accounts Exec*
Steve Hurley, *Supervisor*
EMP: 28 **EST:** 1964
SQ FT: 28,000
SALES (est): 5.8MM **Privately Held**
WEB: www.mydprint.com
SIC: 2759 Screen printing

(G-7313)
DRAKEN INTERNATIONAL LLC
3330 Flightline Dr (33811-2851)
PHONE.............................863 644-1832
Joe Ford, *CEO*
EMP: 25 **EST:** 2019
SALES (est): 1MM **Privately Held**
SIC: 3721 Aircraft

(G-7314)
EAGLE PNEUMATIC INC
3902 Industry Blvd (33811-1341)
PHONE.............................863 644-4870
Karl Q Kondolf, *President*
Helen Kondolf, *Corp Secy*
Patrick C Evans, *Vice Pres*
David Sirkin, *Electrical Engi*
Jerry Kondolf, *Manager*
EMP: 25 **EST:** 1977
SQ FT: 28,000
SALES (est): 5.3MM **Privately Held**
WEB: www.eaglepneumatic.com
SIC: 3535 3494 Pneumatic tube conveyor systems; valves & pipe fittings

(G-7315)
EASTERN METAL SUPPLY INC
4675 Drane Field Rd (33811-1253)
PHONE.............................863 682-6660
James Price, *Opers Mgr*
Norberto Salinas, *Mfg Mgr*
Jesse Cruz, *Mfg Staff*
Matt Stubblefield, *Production*
Larry Hubbard, *Purch Mgr*
EMP: 17
SALES (corp-wide): 162.6MM **Privately Held**
WEB: www.easternmetal.com
SIC: 3334 5051 Primary aluminum; aluminum bars, rods, ingots, sheets, pipes, plates, etc.
PA: Eastern Metal Supply, Inc.
3600 23rd Ave S
Lake Worth Beach FL 33461
561 533-6061

(G-7316)
ENERSYS
4740 Lklnd Comrce Pkwy # 8 (33805-7670)
PHONE.............................863 577-3900
Greg Deckerman, *General Mgr*
Kevin Case, *Production*
Sarah Ajaeb, *Senior Engr*
Ethirajulu Dayalan, *Technical Staff*
EMP: 8
SALES (corp-wide): 3.3B **Publicly Held**
WEB: www.enersys.com
SIC: 3621 Generators for storage battery chargers
PA: Enersys
2366 Bernville Rd
Reading PA 19605
610 208-1991

(G-7317)
ESCO INDUSTRIES INC
2001 Lasso Ln (33801-9732)
PHONE.............................863 666-3696
Bill Ellis, *President*
EMP: 12
SALES (corp-wide): 26.7MM **Privately Held**
WEB: www.escoindustries.com
SIC: 2435 Plywood, hardwood or hardwood faced
PA: Esco Industries, Inc.
185 Sink Hole Rd
Douglas GA 31533
912 384-1417

(G-7318)
EVOLUTIONARY SCREEN PRINTING L
3521 Waterfield Pkwy (33803-9735)
PHONE.............................863 248-2692
Michael D Frankow, *Principal*
EMP: 6 **EST:** 2007
SALES (est): 507.5K **Privately Held**
WEB: www.evolutionaryscreenprinting.com
SIC: 2759 Screen printing

(G-7319)
EXCELL SOLUTIONS LLC
5115 N Socrum Loop Rd (33809-4288)
PHONE.............................407 615-9330
Retina Holt, *Principal*
EMP: 7 **EST:** 2018
SALES (est): 148K **Privately Held**
WEB: www.excellsol.com
SIC: 3599 Machine shop, jobbing & repair

(G-7320)
EYE SPECIALISTS MID FLORIDA PA
2004 E County Road 540a (33813-3739)
PHONE.............................863 937-4515
EMP: 12 **EST:** 1960
SALES (est): 367.5K **Privately Held**
WEB: www.eyesfl.com
SIC: 3827 Optical instruments & lenses

(G-7321)
FERRERA TOOLING INC
3960 Air Park Dr (33811-1270)
PHONE.............................863 646-8500
Brian Herrera, *President*
Derrick Fearnow, *President*
EMP: 12 **EST:** 2005

SALES (est): 2.3MM **Privately Held**
WEB: www.ferreratooling.com
SIC: 3448 Prefabricated metal components

(G-7322)
FIRMENICH INCORPORATED
4330 Drane Field Rd (33811-1211)
PHONE.............................863 292-7456
Pierre-Yves Firmenich, *Director*
Donnie Willis, *Maintence Staff*
EMP: 19
SALES (corp-wide): 4.7B **Privately Held**
WEB: www.firmenich.com
SIC: 2899 Essential oils
HQ: Firmenich Incorporated
250 Plainsboro Rd
Plainsboro NJ 08536
609 452-1000

(G-7323)
FIRMENICH INCORPORATED
4300 Drane Field Rd (33811-1211)
PHONE.............................863 646-0165
Patrick Firmenich, *President*
Craig Savage, *Sr Project Mgr*
Miriam Coria, *Manager*
Dara Sandberg, *Manager*
EMP: 47
SQ FT: 43,851
SALES (corp-wide): 4.7B **Privately Held**
WEB: www.firmenich.com
SIC: 2087 Flavoring extracts & syrups
HQ: Firmenich Incorporated
250 Plainsboro Rd
Plainsboro NJ 08536
609 452-1000

(G-7324)
FIRMENICH INCORPORATED
3919 Kidron Rd (33811-1293)
PHONE.............................863 646-0165
Peary Marro, *Vice Pres*
James Clifton, *Facilities Mgr*
Jeffrey Dodson, *Mfg Staff*
Rob Hastings, *Manager*
Bred Ferrol, *Director*
EMP: 122
SALES (corp-wide): 4.7B **Privately Held**
WEB: www.firmenich.com
SIC: 2869 2899 Perfumes, flavorings & food additives; flavors or flavoring materials, synthetic; essential oils
HQ: Firmenich Incorporated
250 Plainsboro Rd
Plainsboro NJ 08536
609 452-1000

(G-7325)
FIRMENICH LAKELAND
3919 Kidron Rd (33811-1293)
PHONE.............................863 646-0165
EMP: 10 **EST:** 2017
SALES (est): 199.3K **Privately Held**
WEB: www.firmenich.com
SIC: 2844 Perfumes & colognes

(G-7326)
FL CENTRAL CNSTR & RMDLG
8120 Timberidge Loop W (33809-2357)
P.O. Box 90044 (33804-0044)
PHONE.............................863 701-3548
Thomas R Hughes, *Mng Member*
EMP: 8 **EST:** 2012
SALES (est): 229.9K **Privately Held**
SIC: 2434 2514 1799 Wood kitchen cabinets; kitchen cabinets: metal; kitchen & bathroom remodeling

(G-7327)
FLARE CLOTHING INC
3800 Us Highway 98 N # 746 (33809-3833)
PHONE.............................863 859-1800
Basheer Alsharif, *Principal*
EMP: 7 **EST:** 2015
SALES (est): 244.3K **Privately Held**
SIC: 2899 Flares

(G-7328)
FLORIDA AMICO
1033 Pine Chase Ave (33815-3139)
PHONE.............................863 688-9256
Ashley Carver, *Branch Mgr*
EMP: 6 **EST:** 2010

SALES (est): 516.2K **Privately Held**
SIC: 3089 3281 5032 Plastic hardware & building products; building stone products; concrete & cinder building products

(G-7329)
FLORIDA CENTAL LOGGING INC
7328 Us Highway 98 N (33809-5323)
P.O. Box 94, Polk City (33868-0094)
PHONE.............................863 272-5364
Teresa White, *Principal*
EMP: 11 **EST:** 2010
SALES (est): 402.4K **Privately Held**
SIC: 2411 Logging

(G-7330)
FLORIDA COOL RING COMPANY
2220 Gator Creek Ranch Rd (33809-0909)
PHONE.............................863 858-2211
Joel F Butler, *Owner*
EMP: 10 **EST:** 2003
SALES (est): 340K **Privately Held**
WEB: www.thecoolring.com
SIC: 3269 Pottery products

(G-7331)
FLORIDA NUTRI LABS LLC
2715 Badger Rd (33811-1348)
PHONE.............................863 607-6708
Ron Novak, *Mng Member*
EMP: 10 **EST:** 2002
SALES (est): 956.2K **Privately Held**
WEB: www.wemakevitamins.com
SIC: 2834 Vitamin preparations

(G-7332)
FLORIDA REFRESCO INC
2090 Bartow Rd (33801-6557)
PHONE.............................863 665-5515
David Moller, *President*
J Michael Grady, *Principal*
John P Grady, *Chairman*
Terry Simmers, *COO*
Keith Bishop, *Vice Pres*
◆ **EMP:** 180 **EST:** 1967
SQ FT: 210,000
SALES (est): 42.2MM **Privately Held**
SIC: 2033 2086 Fruit juices: packaged in cans, jars, etc.; tea, iced: packaged in cans, bottles, etc.
HQ: Refresco Us, Inc.
6655 S Lewis Ave
Tulsa OK 74136

(G-7333)
FLOWERS BKG CO BRADENTON LLC
Also Called: Flowers Baking Company
2610 Mine And Mill Rd 4-9 (33801-7002)
PHONE.............................941 758-5656
Chris Peer, *Manager*
EMP: 20
SALES (corp-wide): 4.3B **Publicly Held**
WEB: www.flobradconf.com
SIC: 2051 Bread, cake & related products
HQ: Flowers Baking Co. Of Bradenton, Llc
6490 Parkland Dr
Sarasota FL 34243

(G-7334)
GENESIS CARIBBEAN CUISINE LLC
304 E Pine St (33801-4969)
PHONE.............................718 503-4308
Nathaniel Smith, *Administration*
EMP: 5 **EST:** 2020
SALES (est): 370.2K **Privately Held**
SIC: 2499 Food handling & processing products, wood

(G-7335)
GENIE PUBLISHING
5111 Fernbrook Ln (33811-1653)
PHONE.............................863 937-7769
Gay N Finkelman, *Owner*
EMP: 9 **EST:** 2009
SALES (est): 373.2K **Privately Held**
WEB: www.geniepub.com
SIC: 2741 Miscellaneous publishing

(G-7336)
GIVAUDAN FRAGRANCES CORP
Also Called: Givaudan Roure Flavors
4705 Us Highway 92 E (33801-9584)
PHONE.............................863 667-0821

Chris Rimes, *Maint Spvr*
Mike Taylor, *Branch Mgr*
Kristy McKinney, *Planning Mgr*
Maria Torres, *Analyst*
EMP: 48
SALES (corp-wide): 7.2B **Privately Held**
SIC: 2869 2087 Industrial organic chemicals; flavoring extracts & syrups
HQ: Givaudan Fragrances Corporation
　　1199 Edison Dr Ste 1-2
　　Cincinnati OH 45216
　　513 948-8000

(G-7337)
GKWF INC
Also Called: Con Serv Manufacturing
520 W Brannen Rd (33813-2726)
P.O. Box 6160 (33807-6160)
PHONE..............................863 644-6925
Dwight Royal, *CEO*
David S Royal Jr, *President*
Kristine Burnett, *Office Mgr*
EMP: 5 **EST:** 1997
SQ FT: 10,000
SALES (est): 752.5K **Privately Held**
SIC: 3823 Industrial instrmnts msrmnt display/control process variable

(G-7338)
GMF INDUSTRIES INC
Also Called: G M F
4600 Drane Field Rd (33811-1216)
P.O. Box 6688 (33807-6688)
PHONE..............................863 646-5081
Vincent Larry Norman, *President*
Spencer A Norman, *Vice Pres*
Stuart A Norman, *Vice Pres*
Jason Hall, *Sales Mgr*
Pamela Lsecreta Norman, *Admin Sec*
EMP: 90 **EST:** 1982
SQ FT: 136,000
SALES (est): 13.8MM **Privately Held**
WEB: www.gmfsteel.com
SIC: 3449 3599 Miscellaneous metalwork; machine shop, jobbing & repair

(G-7339)
GRAPHIC INSTALLERS INC
4403 Holden Rd (33811-2849)
P.O. Box 7017 (33807-7017)
PHONE..............................863 646-5543
Andrew Gutentag, *President*
Susan Gutentag, *Vice Pres*
▲ **EMP:** 8 **EST:** 1990
SQ FT: 8,000
SALES (est): 990.8K **Privately Held**
WEB: www.graphicinstallers.com
SIC: 3993 Signs & advertising specialties

(G-7340)
GSE AMERICA LLC (PA)
3928 Anchuca Dr Ste 3 (33811-1859)
PHONE..............................863 583-4343
Michael Miner,
EMP: 5 **EST:** 2017
SALES (est): 1MM **Privately Held**
WEB: www.gse-america.com
SIC: 3728 Aircraft parts & equipment

(G-7341)
HARRELLS LLC (HQ)
5105 New Tampa Hwy (33815-3262)
P.O. Box 807, Atlanta GA (30301-0807)
PHONE..............................863 687-2774
Jack Harrell Jr, *CEO*
David Schermerhorn, *President*
Alex Barcia, *Vice Pres*
Rick Helpingstine, *Vice Pres*
Brad Bolyard, *Opers Mgr*
◆ **EMP:** 48 **EST:** 2007
SALES (est): 220MM
SALES (corp-wide): 243.4MM **Privately Held**
WEB: www.harrells.com
SIC: 2875 5191 Fertilizers, mixing only; fertilizers & agricultural chemicals
PA: Harrell's Inc.
　　5105 New Tampa Hwy
　　Lakeland FL 33815
　　863 687-2774

(G-7342)
HEMINGWAY RUM COMPANY LLC
5300 Gateway Blvd (33811-1852)
PHONE..............................863 937-8107

EMP: 12
SALES (corp-wide): 2.8MM **Privately Held**
WEB: www.papaspilar.com
SIC: 2085 Distilled & blended liquors
PA: Hemingway Rum Company, Llc
　　201 Simonton St
　　Key West FL 33040
　　305 414-8754

(G-7343)
HEXION INC
2525 S Combee Rd (33801-6865)
PHONE..............................863 669-2565
Harold Moore, *Principal*
Paul Moore, *Principal*
EMP: 30
SALES (corp-wide): 2.5B **Privately Held**
WEB: www.hexion.com
SIC: 2821 Thermosetting materials
HQ: Hexion Inc.
　　180 E Broad St
　　Columbus OH 43215
　　614 225-4000

(G-7344)
HIGH PERFORMANCE HOLDINGS LTD
Also Called: Createch Machine & Design
625 Mccue Rd Ste 1 (33815-3202)
PHONE..............................815 874-9421
Larry Bull, *President*
Jim Wood, *Sales Dir*
EMP: 16 **EST:** 2007
SALES (est): 2.7MM **Privately Held**
SIC: 3541 Machine tools, metal cutting type; drilling machine tools (metal cutting)

(G-7345)
HOSE POWER USA
3110 Winter Lake Rd (33803-9708)
PHONE..............................863 669-9333
Jeff Hill, *Manager*
▼ **EMP:** 7 **EST:** 2013
SALES (est): 235.6K **Privately Held**
WEB: www.hosepower.com
SIC: 3492 3491 Fluid power valves & hose fittings; industrial valves

(G-7346)
HUNT ENTERPRISES INC
Also Called: True Bloods Colonial Printing
1224 E Lime St (33801-5754)
PHONE..............................863 682-6187
Charles N Hunt, *President*
Jesse M Thrower, *Vice Pres*
Dorene Hunt, *Treasurer*
▼ **EMP:** 5 **EST:** 1966
SQ FT: 1,320
SALES (est): 708.4K **Privately Held**
WEB: www.truebloods.com
SIC: 2752 Commercial printing, offset

(G-7347)
ILLINOIS TOOL WORKS INC
Also Called: ITW Professional Auto Pdts
3606 Craftsman Blvd (33803-7398)
PHONE..............................863 665-3338
William Crowe, *General Mgr*
Laura Blalock, *Lab Dir*
EMP: 100
SALES (corp-wide): 14.4B **Publicly Held**
WEB: www.itw.com
SIC: 2899 5169 2992 2842 Chemical preparations; chemicals & allied products; lubricating oils & greases; specialty cleaning, polishes & sanitation goods
PA: Illinois Tool Works Inc.
　　155 Harlem Ave
　　Glenview IL 60025
　　847 724-7500

(G-7348)
INDUSTRIAL BRUSH CORPORATION
4000 Drane Field Rd (33811-1208)
PHONE..............................863 647-5643
Tony Jensen, *Purch Agent*
Gary A Messier, *Manager*
Chuck Richardson, *Manager*
EMP: 10
SALES (corp-wide): 11.6MM **Privately Held**
WEB: www.industrialbrush.com
SIC: 3991 Brooms & brushes

PA: Industrial Brush Corporation
　　763 E Commerce Dr
　　St George UT 84790
　　909 591-9341

(G-7349)
INDUSTRIAL CMPSITE SYSTEMS LLC
Also Called: Industrial Plastic Systems
4225 Drane Field Rd (33811-1292)
PHONE..............................863 646-8551
Michael Brown, *President*
EMP: 18 **EST:** 2013
SQ FT: 15,000
SALES (est): 2.4MM **Privately Held**
WEB: www.ips-frp.com
SIC: 3089 Plastic & fiberglass tanks; ducting, plastic; fittings for pipe, plastic

(G-7350)
INDUSTRIAL CONSTRUCTION & WLDG
3341 Blueberry Dr (33811-1929)
PHONE..............................863 644-6124
Graidy T Gunn, *President*
Jeffrey T Gunn, *Treasurer*
EMP: 7 **EST:** 1984
SQ FT: 840
SALES (est): 111.9K **Privately Held**
WEB: www.cwi-industrial.com
SIC: 7692 1541 Welding repair; industrial buildings & warehouses

(G-7351)
INDUSTRIAL PLASTIC SYSTEMS INC
Also Called: Ips
4225 Drane Field Rd (33811-1292)
P.O. Box 6280 (33807-6280)
PHONE..............................863 646-8551
Barron Burhans, *President*
Doug Wolcott, *Opers Mgr*
EMP: 20 **EST:** 1975
SALES (est): 3MM **Privately Held**
WEB: www.ips-frp.com
SIC: 3089 Plastic containers, except foam

(G-7352)
INNOVATIER INC
2769 New Tampa Hwy (33815-3462)
PHONE..............................863 688-4548
Lawrence J Keim, *CFO*
EMP: 6 **EST:** 2004
SALES (est): 503.5K **Privately Held**
WEB: www.innovatier.com
SIC: 3083 Laminated plastics plate & sheet

(G-7353)
INTEGRATED METAL PRODUCTS INC
2923 Old Tampa Hwy (33803-1674)
PHONE..............................863 687-4110
Wayne Albritton, *President*
Eva Albritton, *Vice Pres*
Dewayne Watford, *Controller*
Blair Kinney, *Manager*
Kenia Luna, *Assistant*
EMP: 70 **EST:** 2001
SQ FT: 78,000
SALES (est): 16.5MM **Privately Held**
WEB: www.integratedmetal.com
SIC: 3444 Sheet metalwork

(G-7354)
INTERACTIVE CARDS INC
2787 New Tampa Hwy (33815-3462)
PHONE..............................863 688-4548
Michael Scruggs, *CEO*
David Patterson, *President*
Robert Singleton, *COO*
Lisa Blue, *Mng Member*
Mike Scruggs, *Director*
EMP: 17 **EST:** 2009
SALES (est): 3.1MM **Privately Held**
WEB: www.iacards.com
SIC: 3559 Electronic component making machinery

(G-7355)
INTERCIT INC
4330 Drane Field Rd (33811-1211)
PHONE..............................863 646-0165
Beverly Bateman, *President*
Don Hendrix, *Vice Pres*
Peary Marro, *Vice Pres*

Eric Jorgensen, *Treasurer*
Lisa Alexander, *Admin Sec*
◆ **EMP:** 320 **EST:** 1970
SQ FT: 10,000
SALES (est): 29.1MM
SALES (corp-wide): 4.7B **Privately Held**
SIC: 2899 Oils & essential oils
HQ: Firmenich Incorporated
　　250 Plainsboro Rd
　　Plainsboro NJ 08536
　　609 452-1000

(G-7356)
INTERLAKE INDUSTRIES INC
1022 County Line Rd (33815-3177)
PHONE..............................863 688-5665
Jeff Groenstein, *Manager*
Mark Groenstein, *Manager*
EMP: 17
SALES (corp-wide): 25.3MM **Privately Held**
WEB: www.interlakestamping.com
SIC: 3469 Stamping metal for the trade
PA: Interlake Industries, Inc.
　　4732 E 355th St
　　Willoughby OH 44094
　　440 942-0800

(G-7357)
INTERLAKE STAMPING FLORIDA INC
1022 County Line Rd (33815-3177)
PHONE..............................863 688-5665
Lisa Habe, *Principal*
Laura Whitt, *Admin Asst*
EMP: 81 **EST:** 1985
SALES (est): 5.5MM
SALES (corp-wide): 25.3MM **Privately Held**
WEB: www.interlakestamping.com
SIC: 3469 Stamping metal for the trade
PA: Interlake Industries, Inc.
　　4732 E 355th St
　　Willoughby OH 44094
　　440 942-0800

(G-7358)
INTOUCH GPS LLC
439 S Florida Ave 100b (33801-5212)
PHONE..............................877 593-2981
Jon Jarell, *President*
Rob Case, *Opers Mgr*
Selina Campbell, *Manager*
Angela Stivers, *Director*
Tia Warren, *Executive*
EMP: 41 **EST:** 1978
SQ FT: 3,500
SALES (est): 5.5MM
SALES (corp-wide): 10.8MM **Privately Held**
WEB: www.intouchgps.com
SIC: 7372 Prepackaged software
PA: Gpstrackit Holdings, Llc
　　1080 Holcomb Bridge Rd
　　Roswell GA 30076
　　951 296-1316

(G-7359)
JBT FOODTECH CITRUS SYSTEMS
Also Called: Jbt Food Tech
400 Fairway Ave (33801-2468)
PHONE..............................863 683-5411
John T Gremp, *CEO*
Thomas W Giacomini, *President*
Paul Sternlieb, *President*
Bryant Lowery, *Vice Pres*
Younes Benkabbou, *Engineer*
◆ **EMP:** 67 **EST:** 2008
SALES (est): 22.2MM **Privately Held**
SIC: 3556 Food products machinery

(G-7360)
JC MACHINE INC
Also Called: J C M I
3620 Airport Rd (33811-1002)
P.O. Box 5027 (33807-5027)
PHONE..............................863 644-2815
John Creasy Creasy, *President*
Chelci Hughes, *Accounts Mgr*
Marsha Coelho, *Administration*
EMP: 10 **EST:** 1984
SQ FT: 4,000
SALES (est): 2.7MM **Privately Held**
WEB: www.jcmi-usa.com
SIC: 3599 Machine shop, jobbing & repair

(G-7361)
JOHN BEAN TECHNOLOGIES CORP
Also Called: Jbt Foodtech
400 Fairway Ave (33801-2468)
PHONE..................863 683-5411
Halejendro Huidobro, *Principal*
Vijay Kurmapu, *Technical Mgr*
Ian Houston, *Engineer*
Bobbie Spahr, *Engineer*
Sean Casey, *Finance Dir*
EMP: 200 **Publicly Held**
WEB: www.jbtc.com
SIC: 3556 Food products machinery
PA: John Bean Technologies Corporation
70 W Madison St Ste 4400
Chicago IL 60602

(G-7362)
JVL PRODUCE INC
4633 Musket Dr (33810-0171)
PHONE..................813 862-6155
Victor Lucas, *Manager*
EMP: 46
SALES (corp-wide): 833.6K **Privately Held**
SIC: 2542 Postal lock boxes, mail racks & related products
PA: Jvl Produce Inc
702 W Sam Allen Rd
Plant City FL 33565
813 862-6155

(G-7363)
K-TECHNOLOGIES INC
4306 Wallace Rd (33812-6379)
P.O. Box 5377 (33807-5377)
PHONE..................863 940-4815
Thomas Baroody, *CEO*
Wes Berry, *Vice Pres*
EMP: 8 **EST:** 1987
SQ FT: 12,000
SALES (est): 1.1MM **Privately Held**
WEB: www.ktech-inc.com
SIC: 2819 Industrial inorganic chemicals

(G-7364)
KELLER MANUFACTURING INC
4442 Holden Rd (33811-2850)
PHONE..................863 937-8928
EMP: 13 **EST:** 2011
SALES (est): 831K **Privately Held**
WEB: www.keller-mfg.com
SIC: 3999 Manufacturing industries

(G-7365)
KEMIRA WATER SOLUTIONS INC
808 E Main St (33801-5127)
PHONE..................863 533-5990
Lawrence Hjersted, *Branch Mgr*
EMP: 21
SALES (corp-wide): 3B **Privately Held**
WEB: www.kemirawater.ca
SIC: 2899 Chemical preparations
HQ: Kemira Water Solutions, Inc.
1000 Parkwood Cir Se # 500
Atlanta GA 30339

(G-7366)
KEY AUTOMOTIVE FLORIDA LLC
Also Called: Joyson Safety Systems
5300 Allen K Breed Hwy (33811-1130)
PHONE..................863 668-6000
Matthew C Cohn, *President*
William McLeod, *Engineer*
Natalia Zarycky, *Treasurer*
Steve Parrish, *Manager*
Marsha A Fershtman, *Admin Sec*
▲ **EMP:** 350 **EST:** 1990
SQ FT: 195,000
SALES (est): 44.7MM
SALES (corp-wide): 7.1B **Privately Held**
SIC: 3714 Motor vehicle parts & accessories
HQ: Joyson Safety Systems Acquisition Llc
2025 Harmon Rd
Auburn Hills MI 48326
248 373-8040

(G-7367)
KEY SAFETY SYSTEMS INC
5300 Allen K Breed Hwy (33811-1130)
PHONE..................863 668-6000
John Reiss, *President*
Brian Freeburg, *Engineer*
Kurt Kastelic, *Engineer*
Heriberto Valle, *Human Res Dir*
Anthony Penner, *Manager*
EMP: 185
SALES (corp-wide): 7.1B **Privately Held**
SIC: 2399 3714 Seat belts, automobile & aircraft; motor vehicle parts & accessories
HQ: Key Safety Systems, Inc.
2025 Harmon Rd
Auburn Hills MI 48326
586 726-3800

(G-7368)
KEYMARK CORPORATION FLORIDA
2540 Knights Station Rd (33810-2505)
PHONE..................863 858-5500
William L Keller III, *President*
Joe Crenna, *Vice Pres*
James Keller, *Vice Pres*
Shawn Slton, *Plant Mgr*
Leo Slecton, *Plant Mgr*
▲ **EMP:** 115 **EST:** 1997
SALES (est): 28.5MM **Privately Held**
WEB: www.keymarkcorp.com
SIC: 3354 Aluminum extruded products

(G-7369)
KINGS & QUEENS CABINETS
841 Windsor St (33803-3713)
PHONE..................863 646-6972
Ronald D Gadd, *Owner*
EMP: 8 **EST:** 1976
SALES (est): 219.3K **Privately Held**
SIC: 2434 2521 Wood kitchen cabinets; wood office furniture

(G-7370)
KNIGHT INDUSTRIAL EQP INC
3701 Airfield Dr W (33811-1244)
PHONE..................863 646-2997
Bob Knight, *President*
Ray Foucher, *Vice Pres*
Dorothy Gribble, *Manager*
EMP: 8 **EST:** 1984
SQ FT: 6,000
SALES (est): 1.5MM **Privately Held**
WEB: www.knightindustrial.net
SIC: 3532 5084 Mining machinery; industrial machinery & equipment

(G-7371)
KONECRANES INC
Also Called: Crane Pro Services
3633 Century Blvd Ste 2 (33811-1798)
PHONE..................813 707-0086
Isabelle Grandemange, *Export Mgr*
Mike Schleehauf, *Opers Staff*
Caroline Bennett, *Human Res Dir*
Nathan Beane, *Sales Staff*
David Caro, *Sales Staff*
EMP: 32 **Privately Held**
WEB: www.konecranes.com
SIC: 3536 Hoists, cranes & monorails
HQ: Konecranes, Inc.
4401 Gateway Blvd
Springfield OH 45502

(G-7372)
L C ACME BARRICADES
8135 Tomkow Rd (33809-1700)
PHONE..................863 816-5874
John Simms, *Branch Mgr*
EMP: 9 **Privately Held**
WEB: www.acmebarricades.com
SIC: 3499 7389 Barricades, metal; flagging service (traffic control)
PA: Acme Barricades, L.C.
9800 Normandy Blvd
Jacksonville FL 32221

(G-7373)
LAKELAND LURES INC
955 Oak Ln (33811-2348)
PHONE..................863 644-3127
Jan Bully, *President*
Vivian Rogers, *General Mgr*
EMP: 11 **EST:** 1981
SQ FT: 3,000
SALES (est): 120.2K **Privately Held**
SIC: 3069 Hard rubber & molded rubber products

(G-7374)
LANE CONSTRUCTION CORPORATION
3350 Reynolds Rd (33803-7325)
P.O. Box 2684, Eaton Park (33840-2684)
PHONE..................863 665-0457
Gary Jerabeck, *Manager*
EMP: 70
SALES (corp-wide): 6.7B **Privately Held**
WEB: www.laneconstruct.com
SIC: 3272 Building materials, except block or brick; concrete
HQ: The Lane Construction Corporation
90 Fieldstone Ct
Cheshire CT 06410
203 235-3351

(G-7375)
LASALLE BRISTOL CORPORATION
Lasalle Hvac Supply
5030 Great Oak Dr (33815-3122)
PHONE..................863 680-1729
Frank Alter, *Manager*
Christopher Marshall, *Supervisor*
EMP: 15
SALES (corp-wide): 4B **Publicly Held**
WEB: www.lasallebristol.com
SIC: 3585 5075 Refrigeration & heating equipment; warm air heating equipment & supplies
HQ: Lasalle Bristol Corporation
601 County Road 17
Elkhart IN 46516
574 295-8400

(G-7376)
LEDGER (HQ)
Also Called: Ledger Publishing Company
300 W Lime St (33815-4649)
P.O. Box 408 (33802-0408)
PHONE..................863 802-7000
Toll Free:..................888 -
Nancy Graham Jump, *Editor*
Arthur Ochs Sulzberger, *Chairman*
Linda Hieber, *Accountant*
Patricia Martin, *Adv Mgr*
Don Rothausen, *Adv Dir*
EMP: 353 **EST:** 1989
SALES (est): 52.6MM
SALES (corp-wide): 278.4MM **Privately Held**
WEB: www.theledger.com
SIC: 2759 2711 Commercial printing; newspapers, publishing & printing
PA: Halifax Media Holdings, Llc
901 6th St
Daytona Beach FL 32117
386 681-2404

(G-7377)
LEGACY VULCAN LLC
2300 Mershon St (33815-3532)
PHONE..................863 687-7625
Harvie Blebins, *Branch Mgr*
EMP: 9 **Publicly Held**
SIC: 3273 Ready-mixed concrete
HQ: Legacy Vulcan, Llc
1200 Urban Center Dr
Vestavia AL 35242
205 298-3000

(G-7378)
LEGGETT & PLATT INCORPORATED
Also Called: Lakeland Box Spring 0026
2715 Crystal Lk Acres Dr (33801-9729)
PHONE..................863 666-8999
Morris Montgomery, *Branch Mgr*
Petra Reyes, *Administration*
EMP: 20
SALES (corp-wide): 4.2B **Publicly Held**
WEB: www.leggett.com
SIC: 2515 Box springs, assembled
PA: Leggett & Platt, Incorporated
1 Leggett Rd
Carthage MO 64836
417 358-8131

(G-7379)
LINCOLN SMITH VENTURES LLC
Also Called: Minuteman Press
2058 E Edgewood Dr (33803-3632)
PHONE..................863 337-6670
Patrick L Lincoln,
EMP: 7 **EST:** 2017
SALES (est): 564.8K **Privately Held**
WEB: www.minutemanpress.com
SIC: 2752 Commercial printing, lithographic

(G-7380)
LOCKHEED MARTIN CORPORATION
Also Called: Lockheed Martin Government
1040 S Pkwy Frontage Rd (33813-1400)
PHONE..................863 647-0100
Shari Foret, *Vice Pres*
Leo S Mackay, *Vice Pres*
Steven Hinchee, *Mfg Spvr*
Josue Barrantes, *Engineer*
Mark Dailey, *Engineer*
EMP: 99 **Publicly Held**
WEB: www.lockheedmartin.com
SIC: 3812 Search & navigation equipment
PA: Lockheed Martin Corporation
6801 Rockledge Dr
Bethesda MD 20817

(G-7381)
LOCKHEED MARTIN CORPORATION
1040 S Pkwy Frontage Rd (33813-1400)
P.O. Box 33064 (33807-3064)
PHONE..................863 647-0100
Jody Pregent, *Senior Mgr*
EMP: 12 **Publicly Held**
WEB: www.gyrocamsystems.com
SIC: 3812 Search & navigation equipment
PA: Lockheed Martin Corporation
6801 Rockledge Dr
Bethesda MD 20817

(G-7382)
LOCKHEED MARTIN CORPORATION
1040 South Blvd (33803-1352)
P.O. Box 33017 (33807-3017)
PHONE..................863 647-0558
Greg Bosey, *Manager*
EMP: 400 **Publicly Held**
WEB: www.gyrocamsystems.com
SIC: 3812 Search & navigation equipment
PA: Lockheed Martin Corporation
6801 Rockledge Dr
Bethesda MD 20817

(G-7383)
LOCKHEED MARTIN CORPORATION
1040 S Pkwy Frontage Rd (33813-1400)
P.O. Box 33037 (33807-3037)
PHONE..................863 647-0100
EMP: 9 **Publicly Held**
WEB: www.lockheedmartin.com
SIC: 3812 Search & navigation equipment
PA: Lockheed Martin Corporation
6801 Rockledge Dr
Bethesda MD 20817

(G-7384)
LOCKHEED MARTIN CORPORATION
Also Called: Aeronics Customer Support Ctr
1040 S Pkwy Frontage Rd (33813-1400)
PHONE..................863 647-0303
Hulda Raybon, *Manager*
EMP: 15 **Publicly Held**
WEB: www.lockheedmartin.com
SIC: 3812 Search & navigation equipment
PA: Lockheed Martin Corporation
6801 Rockledge Dr
Bethesda MD 20817

(G-7385)
M & N PLASTICS
5579 Summerland Hills Dr (33812-6375)
PHONE..................863 646-0208
Alan Gilmer, *Sales Staff*
Brian Beatty, *Manager*
Jones Finch, *Manager*
Richard Barnes, *CIO*
EMP: 8 **EST:** 2001
SALES (est): 124K **Privately Held**
SIC: 3089 Injection molding of plastics

(G-7386)
M P N INC
Also Called: Active Radiator Supply Company
815 Pear St (33815-1333)
PHONE..................................863 606-5999
Monica Rivers, *Branch Mgr*
EMP: 10 **Privately Held**
WEB: www.activeradiator.com
SIC: 3714 Motor vehicle parts & accessories
PA: M. P. N., Inc.
    3675 Amber St
    Philadelphia PA 19134

(G-7387)
MACLAN CORPORATION INC (PA)
1808 S Combee Rd (33801-6852)
P.O. Box 1906, Eaton Park (33840-1906)
PHONE..................................863 665-4814
Phillip M Lane Sr, *President*
Michael A Lane, *Treasurer*
Wallace Maegan, *Sales Staff*
Dawn Peters, *Admin Asst*
Sterling Crump, *Analyst*
EMP: 36 EST: 1975
SQ FT: 80,000
SALES (est): 6.9MM **Privately Held**
WEB: www.maclan.com
SIC: 2822 3312 Synthetic rubber; blast furnaces & steel mills

(G-7388)
MANGO PUBLICATIONS
715 S New York Ave (33815-4747)
PHONE..................................863 583-4773
EMP: 7
SALES (est): 320K **Privately Held**
SIC: 2759 Commercial Printing

(G-7389)
MAR COR PURIFICATION INC
5001 Gateway Blvd Ste 21 (33811-2715)
PHONE..................................484 991-0220
Patrick Schilling, *Branch Mgr*
EMP: 20
SALES (corp-wide): 1.4B **Publicly Held**
WEB: www.mcpur.com
SIC: 3589 Water treatment equipment, industrial
HQ: Mar Cor Purification, Inc.
    4450 Township Line Rd
    Skippack PA 19474
    800 633-3080

(G-7390)
MARK/TRECE INC
Also Called: Mark Trece
5385 Gateway Blvd (33811-1785)
PHONE..................................863 647-4372
EMP: 17
SALES (corp-wide): 33.5MM **Privately Held**
WEB: www.marktrece.com
SIC: 3555 Printing trades machinery
PA: Mark/Trece, Inc.
    2001 Stockton Rd
    Joppa MD 21085
    410 879-0060

(G-7391)
MAX TORQUE LLC
3360 Flightline Dr (33811)
PHONE..................................863 701-8000
EMP: 15
SALES (corp-wide): 12MM **Privately Held**
SIC: 3721 Aircraft, Nsk
PA: Max Torque, Llc
    10000 Manchester St Ste H
    Houston TX
    800 696-7272

(G-7392)
MAX-PAK INC (DH)
Also Called: Maxpak
2808 New Tampa Hwy (33815-3438)
PHONE..................................863 682-0123
Robert K Beswick, *President*
Scott J McBride, *Vice Pres*
Rhonda G Beswick, *Treasurer*
Julie L McBride, *Admin Sec*
◆ EMP: 36 EST: 1984
SQ FT: 150,000

SALES (est): 53.2MM
SALES (corp-wide): 573.3MM **Privately Held**
WEB: www.maxpak.cc
SIC: 2653 Boxes, corrugated: made from purchased materials
HQ: Schwarz Partners Packaging, Llc
    10 W Carmel Dr Ste 300
    Carmel IN 46032
    317 290-1140

(G-7393)
ME THOMPSON INC
Also Called: Dandee Foods
1840 Fairbanks St (33805-2542)
PHONE..................................863 667-3732
Alan Berry, *Manager*
EMP: 66
SALES (corp-wide): 10.2MM **Privately Held**
SIC: 2099 5149 Sandwiches, assembled & packaged: for wholesale market; groceries & related products
PA: M.E. Thompson, Inc.
    2178 W 21st St
    Jacksonville FL 32209
    904 356-6258

(G-7394)
MGL ENGINEERING INC
2740 Parkway St (33811-1343)
P.O. Box 7701 (33807-7701)
PHONE..................................863 648-0320
Harry Love, *President*
Richard Grant, *Corp Secy*
Barry Mc Keown, *Vice Pres*
Andrew Bridges, *Engineer*
Margo Allen, *Office Mgr*
◆ EMP: 40 EST: 1998
SALES (est): 9.2MM **Privately Held**
WEB: www.mglengineering.com
SIC: 3312 8711 Structural shapes & pilings, steel; engineering services

(G-7395)
MID-STATE MACHINE & FABG CORP (PA)
Also Called: Mid State Machine & Fabg
2730 Mine And Mill Rd (33801-7006)
PHONE..................................863 665-6233
Harold E Kersey, *CEO*
Jeff E Clyne, *President*
Kevin Spivey, *Superintendent*
Paul Thomassee, *Superintendent*
Mark Freeman, *Business Mgr*
EMP: 201 EST: 1972
SQ FT: 60,000
SALES (est): 82.9MM **Privately Held**
WEB: www.midstateindustrialcorp.com
SIC: 3443 3599 7692 3441 Fabricated plate work (boiler shop); machine & other job shop work; welding repair; sheet metalwork

(G-7396)
MINUTEMAN PRESS
2058 E Edgewood Dr Ste C (33803-3632)
PHONE..................................863 337-6670
Patrick Lee Lincoln II, *Principal*
EMP: 9 EST: 2016
SALES (est): 128.1K **Privately Held**
WEB: www.minutemanpress.com
SIC: 2752 Commercial printing, lithographic

(G-7397)
MMT TECHNOLOGIES INC
4302 Holden Rd (33811-2854)
PHONE..................................863 619-2926
Otho N Fletcher Jr, *President*
Samantha M Pratt, *Admin Sec*
EMP: 7 EST: 1995
SALES (est): 129K **Privately Held**
SIC: 2869 Glycol ethers

(G-7398)
MOBILE HOME REBUILDERS LLC
3618 Deborah Dr (33810-0703)
P.O. Box 1348 (33802-1348)
PHONE..................................863 838-9547
Michael D Howington, *Manager*
Michael Howington, *Manager*
EMP: 7 EST: 2005
SALES (est): 243K **Privately Held**
SIC: 2451 Mobile homes

(G-7399)
MOSAIC
5810 Deer Flag Dr (33811-4008)
PHONE..................................863 860-1328
Robert Fredere, *General Mgr*
Chris Hagemo, *General Mgr*
Nevin Maga, *General Mgr*
Phil Maxey, *Superintendent*
Jeanne Pierson, *Business Mgr*
EMP: 61
SALES (corp-wide): 281.6MM **Privately Held**
WEB: www.mosaicinfo.org
SIC: 1241 Coal mining services
PA: Mosaic
    4980 S 118th St
    Omaha NE 68137
    402 896-3884

(G-7400)
MPC COMPANY INC
4300 Steward Rd (33815-3240)
PHONE..................................863 802-1722
Carol Beaty, *Branch Mgr*
EMP: 7
SALES (corp-wide): 37.9MM **Privately Held**
SIC: 2449 2653 Wood containers; corrugated & solid fiber boxes
PA: Mpc Company, Inc.
    3752 Riverside Rd
    Riverside MI 49084
    269 849-1722

(G-7401)
NARRAMORE MACHINE SHOP LLC
2770 Industrial Park Dr (33801-7108)
PHONE..................................863 667-1004
Christopher S Narramore R, *Manager*
EMP: 9 EST: 2019
SALES (est): 806.2K **Privately Held**
WEB: www.narramoremachineshopllc.com
SIC: 3599 Machine shop, jobbing & repair

(G-7402)
NEXSTAR BROADCASTING INC
Also Called: Tampa Tribune
223 S Florida Ave (33801-4621)
PHONE..................................863 683-6531
EMP: 15
SALES (corp-wide): 2.4B **Publicly Held**
SIC: 2711 7313 Newspapers-Publishing/Printing Advertising Representative
HQ: Wood Television Llc
    120 College Ave Se
    Grand Rapids MI 49503
    616 456-8888

(G-7403)
OMNIA INC
3125 Drane Feld Rd Ste 29 (33811)
PHONE..................................863 619-8100
William Marcy, *Principal*
Christine Buchanan, *Sales Staff*
Keith Wong, *Sales Staff*
EMP: 8 EST: 2012
SALES (est): 660.1K **Privately Held**
WEB: www.omniasalesinc.com
SIC: 3728 Aircraft assemblies, subassemblies & parts

(G-7404)
OMNIA INCORPORATED
3125 Drane Feld Rd Ste 29 (33811)
PHONE..................................863 619-8100
Cynthia B Maddox, *President*
Neu A Lawrence, *Vice Pres*
Roger Lack, *Manager*
EMP: 28 EST: 1984
SALES (est): 2.6MM **Privately Held**
WEB: www.omniainc.com
SIC: 3843 Dental equipment & supplies

(G-7405)
PALLET DEPOT LLC
6300 New Tampa Hwy (33815-3144)
PHONE..................................863 686-6245
Brian E O'Donnell,
Bethann O'Donnell,
Mark L Schulcz,
EMP: 22 EST: 2008
SALES (est): 1.4MM **Privately Held**
WEB: www.palletdepotfl.com
SIC: 2448 Pallets, wood

(G-7406)
PARKINSON ENTERPRISES INC
Also Called: Innovative Ink
1840 Harden Blvd (33803-1827)
PHONE..................................863 688-7900
Charles Parkinson, *President*
Chuck Parkinson, *Accounts Mgr*
Carrie Anderson, *Graphic Designe*
EMP: 21 EST: 1985
SQ FT: 4,500
SALES (est): 3.2MM **Privately Held**
SIC: 2752 2791 2789 Commercial printing, offset; typesetting; bookbinding & related work

(G-7407)
PATTERSON PUBLISHING LLC
214 Traders Aly (33801-4986)
P.O. Box 41 (33802-0041)
PHONE..................................863 701-2707
Curtis A Patterson, *Principal*
Debra K Patterson, *Vice Pres*
EMP: 14 EST: 2003
SALES (est): 538.3K **Privately Held**
SIC: 2741 Miscellaneous publishing

(G-7408)
PEPSI BOTTLING GROUP INC
Also Called: Pepsi-Cola
4100 Frontage Rd S (33815-3201)
PHONE..................................863 687-7605
Eric J Foss, *CEO*
Michael Fichera, *Vice Pres*
Thomas M Lardieri, *Vice Pres*
Steven M Rapp, *Vice Pres*
Alfred H Drewes, *CFO*
EMP: 6 EST: 2000
SALES (est): 1.3MM **Privately Held**
WEB: www.pepsico.com
SIC: 2086 Carbonated soft drinks, bottled & canned

(G-7409)
PLASTIC TRADING INTL INC
3612 Ventura Dr E (33811-1229)
PHONE..................................863 688-1983
Brian T Brandt, *President*
Mark Bacon, *Opers Staff*
Jesse Ritter, *Regl Sales Mgr*
Stephanie Fuller, *Marketing Staff*
Nicole Ackerman, *Office Mgr*
EMP: 23 EST: 2012
SQ FT: 25,000
SALES: 5.7MM **Privately Held**
WEB: www.plastictradingint.org
SIC: 2821 Plastics materials & resins

(G-7410)
PM CRAFTSMAN
Also Called: T & C Creations
3525 Craftsman Blvd (33803-7397)
PHONE..................................863 665-0815
Robert F Schofield Jr, *President*
Linda J Schofield, *Vice Pres*
Linda Schofield, *Vice Pres*
Derek Schofield, *Treasurer*
EMP: 25 EST: 1911
SQ FT: 55,000
SALES (est): 2.5MM **Privately Held**
WEB: www.pmcraftsman.com
SIC: 3499 5199 3366 Novelties & giftware, including trophies; gifts & novelties; copper foundries

(G-7411)
POLK AIR FILTER SALES INC
1851 E Gary Rd (33801-2295)
PHONE..................................863 688-4436
Gene Hyman, *President*
Sid Hyman, *Manager*
EMP: 7 EST: 1971
SQ FT: 15,000
SALES (est): 577K **Privately Held**
SIC: 3564 Filters, air: furnaces, air conditioning equipment, etc.

(G-7412)
PORTER PIZZA BOX FLORIDA INC (PA)
6094 Us Highway 98 S (33812-4347)
P.O. Box 1795, Highland City (33846-1795)
PHONE..................................800 626-0828
Halden L Porter, *President*
Jack Robinson, *Principal*
Linda G Porter, *Vice Pres*
Grant Porter, *Manager*

▼ **EMP:** 20 **EST:** 1991
SQ FT: 6,000
SALES (est): 6.5MM **Privately Held**
SIC: 2631 Corrugating medium

(G-7413)
PRO-AD MEDIA INC
115 Allamanda Dr (33803-2925)
P.O. Box 864 (33802-0864)
PHONE.....................863 802-5043
Wes Craven, *President*
James Holloway, *Vice Pres*
EMP: 8 **EST:** 1996
SQ FT: 1,700
SALES (est): 807.1K **Privately Held**
WEB: www.eldercareguide.com
SIC: 3993 Displays & cutouts, window & lobby

(G-7414)
PURINA ANIMAL NUTRITION LLC
2815 Drane Field Rd (33811-1851)
PHONE.....................863 262-4332
Kevin Sheridan, *Branch Mgr*
EMP: 13
SALES (corp-wide): 2.8B **Privately Held**
WEB: www.purinamills.com
SIC: 2048 Prepared feeds
HQ: Purina Animal Nutrition Llc
100 Danforth Dr
Gray Summit MO 63039

(G-7415)
QGIV INC
207 Bartow Rd (33801-5106)
PHONE.....................888 855-9595
Todd Baylis, *President*
Stephen W Baylis, *Principal*
Chris Morata, *Vice Pres*
Ross Garinger, *Engineer*
Trevor Hillsgrove, *Software Engr*
EMP: 39 **EST:** 2005
SALES (est): 5.1MM **Privately Held**
WEB: www.qgiv.com
SIC: 7372 Business oriented computer software

(G-7416)
QUALITY AEROSPACE COATINGS LLC
3610 Airport Rd (33811-1002)
PHONE.....................863 619-2628
John Creasy, *Principal*
EMP: 7 **EST:** 2008
SALES (est): 224.5K **Privately Held**
WEB: www.quality-aero.com
SIC: 3479 Coating of metals & formed products

(G-7417)
QUIKRETE COMPANIES LLC
4230 Maine Ave (33801-9785)
P.O. Box 778, Eaton Park (33840-0778)
PHONE.....................863 665-5127
Danette One, *Office Mgr*
Brian Cronin, *Branch Mgr*
Donald Long, *Director*
Felicia Kennedy, *Admin Asst*
EMP: 55
SQ FT: 19,960 **Privately Held**
WEB: www.quikrete.com
SIC: 3272 Concrete products
HQ: The Quikrete Companies Llc
5 Concourse Pkwy Ste 1900
Atlanta GA 30328
404 634-9100

(G-7418)
RAPID METAL PRODUCTS INC
4257 Holden Rd (33811-2837)
PHONE.....................863 701-0058
Kirk D Balliette, *President*
Terry Wisniewski, *General Mgr*
Douglas M Foust, *Vice Pres*
Terry L Wisniewski, *Vice Pres*
EMP: 35 **EST:** 1998
SQ FT: 18,000
SALES (est): 6.3MM **Privately Held**
WEB: www.rapidmetalproducts.com
SIC: 3444 Sheet metalwork

(G-7419)
REDEAGLE INTERNATIONAL LLC
Also Called: Redeag Le
5143 S Lakeland Dr Ste 4 (33813-2589)
PHONE.....................863 682-6698
Rhett Atkins, *General Mgr*
Bala Marimuthu, *Business Dir*
Yingxue Yu,
▲ **EMP:** 9 **EST:** 2008
SALES (est): 1.4MM **Privately Held**
WEB: www.redeagleinternational.com
SIC: 2879 Agricultural disinfectants

(G-7420)
RESTORATION MEDICAL LLC
5235 Nichols Dr E (33812-4077)
PHONE.....................863 272-0250
Kurt Stefan,
EMP: 5 **EST:** 2015
SALES (est): 1.4MM **Privately Held**
WEB: www.restorationmedical.com
SIC: 3842 Surgical appliances & supplies

(G-7421)
RING POWER CORPORATION
Also Called: Ring Lift
3425 Reynolds Rd (33803-8331)
PHONE.....................863 606-0512
Chris Hobbs, *Branch Mgr*
EMP: 8
SALES (corp-wide): 1B **Privately Held**
WEB: www.ringpower.com
SIC: 3537 5084 Forklift trucks; materials handling machinery
HQ: Ring Power Corporation
500 World Commerce Pkwy
Saint Augustine FL 32092
904 201-7400

(G-7422)
ROBINSON FANS INC
3955 Drane Field Rd (33811-1289)
PHONE.....................724 452-6121
Dustin Moskal, *Editor*
Mike Arblaster, *Vice Pres*
Josh Tillotson, *Vice Pres*
Jorge Martinez, *Project Mgr*
Tim Velte, *Prdtn Mgr*
EMP: 86 **Privately Held**
WEB: www.robinsonfans.com
SIC: 3564 Blowers & fans
HQ: Robinson Fans, Inc.
400 Robinson Dr
Zelienople PA 16063
863 646-5270

(G-7423)
ROCKFORD ETTCO PROCUNIER INC
304 Winston Creek Pkwy (33810-2866)
PHONE.....................863 688-0071
Mary Bull, *President*
William S Mele, *Vice Pres*
Ben Hall, *Materials Mgr*
Susan Caldwell, *Admin Sec*
EMP: 16 **EST:** 1917
SQ FT: 30,000
SALES (est): 2.4MM **Privately Held**
WEB: www.createch-design.com
SIC: 3541 Tapping machines; drilling machine tools (metal cutting)

(G-7424)
RUBINGERS MANUFACTURING CO
2626 Mine And Mill Ln (33801-7607)
P.O. Box 1381, Eaton Park (33840-1381)
PHONE.....................863 665-1599
John R Nightlinger Jr, *President*
Ruby Nightlinger, *Corp Secy*
Christopher R Nightlinger, *Vice Pres*
John Nightlinger, *VP Engrg*
EMP: 10 **EST:** 1979
SQ FT: 21,000
SALES (est): 1.6MM **Privately Held**
WEB: www.rubingers.com
SIC: 3599 Machine shop, jobbing & repair

(G-7425)
RYANS CUSTOM COATINGS
7096 Remington Oaks Loop (33810-4788)
PHONE.....................863 669-3310
Ryan Harwood, *Principal*
EMP: 9 **EST:** 2013

SALES (est): 86.8K **Privately Held**
SIC: 3479 Metal coating & allied service

(G-7426)
S & B METAL PRODUCTS S FLA INC (PA)
5301 Gateway Blvd (33811-1735)
PHONE.....................941 727-3669
Paul R Balliette, *CEO*
Stephen R Campbell, *President*
Ethan Maskolunas, *General Mgr*
Joseph Pateos, *General Mgr*
Larry Hager, *Engineer*
EMP: 40 **EST:** 1991
SQ FT: 15,000
SALES (est): 41.5MM **Privately Held**
SIC: 3444 Sheet metalwork

(G-7427)
SAFETY ZONE SPECIALISTS INC
2318 Old Combee Rd 107 (33805-7520)
P.O. Box 90764 (33804-0764)
PHONE.....................863 984-1385
David Vespa, *President*
EMP: 6 **EST:** 1992
SALES (est): 885.7K **Privately Held**
WEB: www.gotchen.com
SIC: 3499 3699 Barricades, metal; trouble lights

(G-7428)
SAMSON METAL AND MACHINE INC
3145 Us Highway 92 E (33801-9234)
P.O. Box 1586 (33802-1586)
PHONE.....................863 665-0283
Barak Samson, *President*
Samson Dan, *Vice Pres*
Wesley Samson, *Vice Pres*
Carolyn Stewart, *Vice Pres*
Nathan Samson, *Safety Mgr*
EMP: 35 **EST:** 1947
SQ FT: 100,000
SALES (est): 3.7MM **Privately Held**
WEB: www.samsonmetal.com
SIC: 3599 Machine shop, jobbing & repair

(G-7429)
SANITUBE LLC (PA)
180 Contractors Way (33801-6356)
P.O. Box 2447, Eaton Park (33840-2447)
PHONE.....................863 606-5960
Houston Sigmund, *Prdtn Mgr*
Haz Crawn, *QC Mgr*
Tanya Wilson, *General Mgr*
Marty Coggins, *Natl Sales Mgr*
Todd Wilson, *VP Sales*
EMP: 9 **EST:** 2010
SQ FT: 100,000
SALES (est): 10MM **Privately Held**
WEB: www.sanitube.us
SIC: 3317 Steel pipe & tubes

(G-7430)
SCHWARZ PARTNERS PACKAGING LLC
Maxpak
2808 New Tampa Hwy (33815-3438)
PHONE.....................863 682-0123
Kevin Bailey, *General Mgr*
EMP: 135
SALES (corp-wide): 573.3MM **Privately Held**
WEB: www.sppmia.com
SIC: 2653 Boxes, corrugated: made from purchased materials
HQ: Schwarz Partners Packaging, Llc
10 W Carmel Dr Ste 300
Carmel IN 46032
317 290-1140

(G-7431)
SERVICE MODERN TRADE LLC
4108 Prima Lago Cir (33810-3061)
PHONE.....................708 942-9154
Jamil Rathore,
EMP: 10
SALES (est): 283.4K **Privately Held**
SIC: 2099 7389 Spices, including grinding;

(G-7432)
SHAIKH RIZWAN
Also Called: Leatherjacket4
316 N Canal Ave (33801-2460)
PHONE.....................202 740-9796

Rizwan Shaikh, *Owner*
Anna Jolie, *Sales Mgr*
EMP: 5 **EST:** 2019
SALES (est): 500K **Privately Held**
WEB: www.leatherjacket4.com
SIC: 2386 Leather & sheep-lined clothing

(G-7433)
SHED4LESS LLC
3147 Us Highway 98 S (33803-7372)
PHONE.....................863 660-7300
Alicia B Wood, *Principal*
EMP: 8 **EST:** 2015
SALES (est): 1.1MM **Privately Held**
WEB: www.shed4less.com
SIC: 3448 Prefabricated metal buildings

(G-7434)
SHOWCASE PUBLICATIONS INC
Also Called: Auto Shopper
1211 E Main St (33801-5773)
PHONE.....................863 687-4377
Fax: 863 682-5098
EMP: 50
SALES (est): 5.1MM
SALES (corp-wide): 7.7MM **Privately Held**
SIC: 2721 7313 Periodicals-Publishing/Printing Advertising Representative
PA: Showcase Publications, Inc.
90 Irons St
Toms River NJ
732 349-1134

(G-7435)
SLAPPEY COMMUNICATIONS LLC
Also Called: Presidium
624 Midflorida Dr (33813-4901)
PHONE.....................863 619-5600
EMP: 9
SALES (corp-wide): 5MM **Privately Held**
SIC: 7372 Prepackaged software
PA: Slappey Communications, Llc
1800 Mcfarland Blvd N
Tuscaloosa AL 35406
205 970-4209

(G-7436)
SMC DIVERSIFIED SERVICES INC
Also Called: Florida Applied Films
7120 Regent Dr (33810-4710)
PHONE.....................863 698-9696
Shayne Cheney, *President*
EMP: 9 **EST:** 1995
SALES (est): 784.2K **Privately Held**
WEB: www.floridaappliedfilms.com
SIC: 2752 Decals, lithographed

(G-7437)
SMITH CHALLENGER MFG SVCS INC
3434 Waterfield Rd (33803-9703)
PHONE.....................863 248-2624
Betty J Smith, *President*
Loni Smith, *Treasurer*
EMP: 15 **EST:** 2009
SALES (est): 2.6MM **Privately Held**
WEB: www.smithchallenger.com
SIC: 3531 Construction machinery

(G-7438)
SMITH EQUIPMENT & SUPPLY CO
3825 Maine Ave (33801-9779)
PHONE.....................863 665-4904
James H Smith, *Ch of Bd*
Ginger L Smith, *President*
Keith E Smith, *Senior VP*
Karey J Smith, *Vice Pres*
Dawn Oeters, *Manager*
▲ **EMP:** 37 **EST:** 1965
SQ FT: 26,000
SALES (est): 7.3MM **Privately Held**
WEB: www.smith-equipment.com
SIC: 3991 3589 Brooms & brushes; dirt sweeping units, industrial

(G-7439)
SOLARA INDUSTRIES INC
Also Called: Remodeling Guys, The
4190 Waring Rd (33811-2857)
PHONE...................................863 688-3330
Edward G Bloom, *President*
Charlotte M Bloom, *Corp Secy*
▲ EMP: 20 EST: 2013
SALES (est): 2.2MM **Privately Held**
WEB: www.solaraindustries.com
SIC: 3446 8748 Balconies, metal; business consulting

(G-7440)
SOLID START INC
2801 Saluda Rd (33801-6335)
PHONE...................................863 937-9297
Amber Lerrall Kossak, *President*
Crystal Matthews, *President*
Fred Pascarella, *Vice Pres*
Freddy Pascarella, *Vice Pres*
Jason Whitaker, *Plant Mgr*
EMP: 20 EST: 2010
SALES (est): 2.6MM **Privately Held**
WEB: www.solidstart.com
SIC: 3559 Automotive maintenance equipment

(G-7441)
SOUTHEASTERN PAPER GROUP INC
7080 Havertys Way (33805-1413)
PHONE...................................864 574-0440
Mitchell Harris, *Opers Staff*
Gordon Back, *Sales Staff*
Jennifer Richmond, *Sales Staff*
Louis Miller, *Manager*
EMP: 172 **Privately Held**
WEB: info.sepg.com
SIC: 3554 Paper industries machinery
HQ: Southeastern Paper Group, Llc
50 Old Blackstock Rd
Spartanburg SC 29301
800 858-7230

(G-7442)
SOUTHERN AUTOMATED SYSTEMS INC
2415 W Socrum Loop Rd (33810-0393)
PHONE...................................863 815-7444
George Aycock, *President*
Teresa Aycock, *Treasurer*
EMP: 5 EST: 2000
SALES (est): 697.9K **Privately Held**
WEB: www.sasoncall.com
SIC: 3625 Electric controls & control accessories, industrial

(G-7443)
SOUTHERN BAKERIES INC (HQ)
Also Called: Butterkrust Bakeries
3355 W Memorial Blvd (33815-1084)
P.O. Box 1707 (33802-1707)
PHONE...................................863 682-1155
Doug Wimberly, *President*
Rob Hancock, *Vice Pres*
Teresa Bass, *Director*
Shea Brock, *Executive*
EMP: 250 EST: 1950
SALES (est): 65.8MM
SALES (corp-wide): 4.3B **Publicly Held**
WEB: www.lakelandedc.com
SIC: 2051 5149 Bread, all types (white, wheat, rye, etc): fresh or frozen; bakery products
PA: Flowers Foods, Inc.
1919 Flowers Cir
Thomasville GA 31757
229 226-9110

(G-7444)
SOUTHERN SOFTWOODS INC
2425 Lasso Ln (33801-9733)
PHONE...................................863 666-1404
Shakir Wissa, *President*
Karen Park, *Admin Sec*
▼ EMP: 50 EST: 1991
SALES (est): 4.6MM **Privately Held**
SIC: 2499 Mulch, wood & bark

(G-7445)
SOUTHERN-BARTLETT INTL LLC
4070 S Pipkin Rd (33811-1849)
PHONE...................................407 374-1613

Christopher Vitito, *President*
EMP: 17 EST: 2009
SALES (est): 502.4K **Privately Held**
SIC: 3199 Aprons: welders', blacksmiths', etc.: leather

(G-7446)
SPECIALTY FABRICATION LLC
4015 Drane Field Rd (33811-1290)
PHONE...................................863 683-0708
Samantha Morgan, *Project Mgr*
Clayton Cook, *Manager*
Hosler L Wall,
Kevin Hissem,
EMP: 34 EST: 2017
SALES (est): 9.7MM **Privately Held**
WEB: www.specialtyfabllc.com
SIC: 3449 Miscellaneous metalwork

(G-7447)
SPECIALTY MAINTENANCE & CONSTR
4121 Drane Field Rd (33811-1291)
PHONE...................................863 644-8432
EMP: 6 EST: 2019
SALES (est): 846.5K **Privately Held**
SIC: 3498 Fabricated pipe & fittings

(G-7448)
STEEL TECHNOLOGY & DESIGN
401 Howard Ave Apt C (33815-3400)
PHONE...................................863 665-2525
Daniel Perkins, *President*
Tom Davis, *Vice Pres*
Dave Keen, *Purchasing*
▼ EMP: 14 EST: 1989
SALES (est): 511.3K **Privately Held**
WEB: www.steeltechnologyanddesign.com
SIC: 3448 Trusses & framing: prefabricated metal

(G-7449)
STERIPACK (USA) LIMITED LLC
4255 S Pipkin Rd (33811-1442)
PHONE...................................863 648-2333
Tony Paolino, *President*
Gary Leonard, *VP Opers*
Eric Lundy, *Opers Staff*
Marlena Dworzecka, *Purchasing*
Robert Del Mastro, *CFO*
◆ EMP: 50 EST: 2012
SQ FT: 40,000
SALES (est): 13.7MM
SALES (corp-wide): 13.3MM **Privately Held**
WEB: www.steripackgroup.com
SIC: 3841 5047 Medical instruments & equipment, blood & bone work; hospital equipment & supplies
HQ: Nelipak Healthcare Packaging Ireland Limited
Kilbeggan Road
Clara R35 F

(G-7450)
STONE CENTER INC
2205 E Edgewood Dr (33803-3605)
P.O. Box 1115, Eaton Park (33840-1115)
PHONE...................................863 669-0292
David Beck, *President*
EMP: 10 EST: 1991
SALES (est): 962.5K **Privately Held**
WEB: stonecenterinc.vpweb.com
SIC: 1411 Dimension stone

(G-7451)
STYLE CREST PRODUCTS
5001 Gateway Blvd Ste 14 (33811-2715)
PHONE...................................863 709-8735
Tom Kern, *President*
EMP: 7 EST: 1986
SALES (est): 706.8K **Privately Held**
WEB: www.stylecrestinc.com
SIC: 3714 Transmission housings or parts, motor vehicle

(G-7452)
SUN PUBLICATIONS FLORIDA INC (HQ)
Also Called: Osceola Shopper
7060 Havertys Way (33805-1413)
PHONE...................................863 583-1202
Dennis Wilkinson, *COO*
Maurice Maisonville, *Plant Mgr*
Ken Penrod, *Plant Mgr*
Chris A Tiffer, *CFO*

Roger Vanegas, *Manager*
EMP: 50 EST: 2003
SQ FT: 40,000
SALES (est): 13.7MM **Privately Held**
WEB: www.sunpubfla.com
SIC: 2741 Miscellaneous publishing
PA: Lakeway Publishers Of Florida, Inc
1609 W 1st North St
Morristown TN 37814
423 581-5630

(G-7453)
SUNSHINE CAP COMPANY
1142 W Main St (33815-4362)
PHONE...................................863 688-8147
Jordan Cokee, *President*
Matthew Cokee, *Vice Pres*
EMP: 9 EST: 1977
SQ FT: 14,000
SALES (est): 291.6K **Privately Held**
SIC: 2353 Caps: cloth, straw & felt

(G-7454)
SUREWELD WELDING INC
3050 W Socrum Loop Rd (33810-0328)
PHONE...................................813 918-1857
Melissa Coe, *CEO*
EMP: 20 EST: 1998
SALES (est): 1.1MM **Privately Held**
SIC: 7692 Welding repair

(G-7455)
T&S KITCHEN AND BBQ LLC
4798 S Florida Ave 235 (33813-2181)
PHONE...................................863 608-6223
Terrance Howell, *CEO*
Sonja F Howel, *Mng Member*
EMP: 6 EST: 2020
SALES (est): 311K **Privately Held**
SIC: 2099 Food preparations

(G-7456)
TASTE ADVANTAGE LLC
3135 Drane Feld Rd Ste 22 (33811)
PHONE...................................863 619-8101
Donald Dawson, *Office Mgr*
Tony Willard,
Henry Todd Sr,
EMP: 6 EST: 2006
SALES (est): 967.1K
SALES (corp-wide): 10.2MM **Privately Held**
WEB: www.natadv.com
SIC: 2087 Flavoring extracts & syrups
PA: Natural Advantage, Llc
1050 Cypress Creek Rd
Oakdale LA 71463
318 215-1456

(G-7457)
TASTEFUL DELIGHT LLC ✪
1919 W 10th St Apt 43 (33805-3389)
PHONE...................................305 879-6487
Tanisha Hobbs,
EMP: 10 EST: 2021
SALES (est): 90K **Privately Held**
WEB: atastefuldelightllc.setmore.com
SIC: 2099 Food preparations

(G-7458)
TEAM HAMMER SCREEN PRINTING
2328 E Main St (33801-2666)
PHONE...................................863 666-1108
Ed Hammerbuger, *President*
EMP: 5 EST: 1991
SQ FT: 4,500
SALES (est): 386.1K **Privately Held**
WEB: www.teamhammerfl.com
SIC: 2211 Print cloths, cotton

(G-7459)
TECHNICAL COMPONENTS INC (PA)
3901 Industry Blvd Ste 6 (33811-1387)
P.O. Box 7178 (33807-7178)
PHONE...................................863 646-3253
Robert K Henning, *President*
Robert J Shemansky, *Vice Pres*
EMP: 5 EST: 1988
SQ FT: 2,800
SALES (est): 638.5K **Privately Held**
WEB: www.techcomponents.com
SIC: 3599 Machine shop, jobbing & repair

(G-7460)
THERMO COMPACTION SYSTEMS INC
5001 Gateway Blvd Ste 22 (33811-2715)
PHONE...................................863 370-3799
William C Major, *President*
EMP: 7 EST: 2009
SALES (est): 145K **Privately Held**
WEB: moose-herring-ffhe.squarespace.com
SIC: 2821 Plastics materials & resins

(G-7461)
THOMAS SMITH & COMPANY INC
3828 Knights Station Rd (33810-2548)
PHONE...................................863 858-2199
Thomas C Smith, *President*
EMP: 26 EST: 1953
SQ FT: 760
SALES (est): 2.8MM **Privately Held**
SIC: 3444 1761 1721 Metal roofing & roof drainage equipment; roofing & gutter work; residential painting; commercial painting

(G-7462)
TITANIUM REAL ESTATE LLC
1543 Lakeland Hills Blvd (33805-3246)
PHONE...................................863 808-0445
Kerry J Nice Jr, *Principal*
Kerry Nice, *Broker*
EMP: 6 EST: 2018
SALES (est): 563.6K **Privately Held**
SIC: 3356 Titanium

(G-7463)
TOM BURKE SERVICES
6244 Troi Ln (33813-3752)
PHONE...................................863 940-4504
Thomas Burke, *Principal*
EMP: 8 EST: 2006
SALES (est): 294.5K **Privately Held**
SIC: 3545 Drilling machine attachments & accessories

(G-7464)
TOOGLE INDUSTRIES LLC
127 N Lake Parker Ave (33801-2164)
PHONE...................................863 688-8975
Anthony Escapa, *Mng Member*
EMP: 5 EST: 2019
SALES (est): 395.7K **Privately Held**
SIC: 3999 7539 Manufacturing industries; automotive repair shops

(G-7465)
TRENWA INC
1920 Longhorn Ave (33801-9770)
PHONE...................................863 666-1680
Austin Riggs, *Project Mgr*
Elliott Schurr, *Project Mgr*
Dan Key, *Opers-Prdtn-Mfg*
Rebecca Whitaker, *QC Mgr*
Jay Wahlbrink, *Sales Engr*
EMP: 16
SALES (corp-wide): 10.3MM **Privately Held**
WEB: www.trenwa.com
SIC: 3272 5211 Concrete products, precast; masonry materials & supplies
PA: Trenwa, Inc.
1419 Alexandria Pike
Fort Thomas KY 41075
859 781-0831

(G-7466)
TRIUMPH TRANSPORT INC
1104 Bartow Rd Apt 173 (33801-5866)
PHONE...................................863 226-7276
Young Laster Jr, *Owner*
EMP: 8 EST: 2019
SALES (est): 263.9K **Privately Held**
SIC: 3799 Transportation equipment

(G-7467)
TWS CABINETS LLC
2947 Vermont Ave (33803-8348)
PHONE...................................863 614-4693
Timmy W Sanquenetti, *Branch Mgr*
EMP: 15
SALES (corp-wide): 72.1K **Privately Held**
SIC: 2434 Wood kitchen cabinets

▲ = Import ▼=Export
◆ =Import/Export

PA: Tws Cabinets Llc
910 E Memorial Blvd # 1303
Lakeland FL 33801
812 201-3201

(G-7468)
UNIVERSAL DIE SERVICES INC
2646 Lasso Ln (33801-9769)
PHONE................................863 665-6092
Scott A Farrington, President
▼ **EMP:** 5 **EST:** 2005
SALES (est): 410.3K **Privately Held**
SIC: 3544 Special dies & tools

(G-7469)
VALIANT PRODUCTS INC
939 Quincy St (33815-1337)
P.O. Box 405 (33802-0405)
PHONE................................863 688-7998
Robert F English, CEO
Byron English, General Mgr
Jason Turner, General Mgr
John Harris, Engineer
Joel Watkins, Engineer
EMP: 32 **EST:** 1978
SQ FT: 20,000
SALES (est): 7.6MM **Privately Held**
WEB: www.valiantproductsinc.com
SIC: 2542 3443 Chutes, metal
plate; lockers (not refrigerated): except
wood; shutters, door or window: metal

(G-7470)
VIP SOFTWARE CORPORATION
6000 S Florida Ave # 6832 (33807-8001)
P.O. Box 531826, Saint Petersburg (33747-
1826)
PHONE................................813 837-4347
James Makris, President
Josh Nelson, CFO
Nathan Gieseke, Manager
EMP: 12 **EST:** 2013
SQ FT: 2,500
SALES (est): 885.3K **Privately Held**
WEB: www.vipsoftware.com
SIC: 7372 7371 Business oriented com-
puter software; computer software devel-
opment & applications

(G-7471)
**WASTEQUIP MANUFACTURING
CO LLC**
2624 Mine And Mill Ln (33801-7607)
PHONE................................704 900-4654
Bill Haynes, Vice Pres
Thomas Kaltenbaugn, Manager
EMP: 56
SQ FT: 8,000 **Privately Held**
WEB: www.wastequip.com
SIC: 3443 Dumpsters, garbage
HQ: Wastequip Manufacturing Company
Llc
6525 Carnegie Blvd # 300
Charlotte NC 28211

(G-7472)
WE MAKE VITAMINS LLC
2715 Badger Rd (33811-1348)
PHONE................................863 607-6708
Cameron Novak, CEO
EMP: 9 **EST:** 2018
SALES (est): 1.1MM **Privately Held**
WEB: www.wemakevitamins.com
SIC: 2833 Vitamins, natural or synthetic:
bulk, uncompounded

(G-7473)
**WILKERSON INSTRUMENT CO
INC**
2915 Parkway St (33811-1391)
P.O. Box 6986 (33807-6986)
PHONE................................863 647-2000
Rick Huffman, President
Bill Wilkerson, President
Ted Marshall, Accounting Mgr
Leslie Cox, Manager
Cecil Johnson, Technician
EMP: 16 **EST:** 1983
SQ FT: 14,000
SALES (est): 2.4MM **Privately Held**
WEB: www.wici.com
SIC: 3823 Industrial instrmnts msrmnt dis-
play/control process variable

(G-7474)
WILLIAM BURNS
Also Called: Radiant Printing
1800 Via Lago Dr (33810-2341)
PHONE................................877 462-5872
William Burns, Owner
Jonathan Reyes, Creative Dir
EMP: 9 **EST:** 2015
SALES (est): 477.5K **Privately Held**
SIC: 2752 Commercial printing, offset

Lakewood Ranch
Manatee County

(G-7475)
AMERICAN ACCOUNTING ASSN
9009 Town Center Pkwy # 104
(34202-4257)
PHONE................................941 921-7747
Stephanie Austin, Managing Dir
Jim Farr, Accountant
Connie O 'brien, Accountant
James Rock, Accountant
Michelle Russak, Accountant
▼ **EMP:** 25 **EST:** 1916
SQ FT: 5,000
SALES (est): 10.3MM **Privately Held**
WEB: www.aaahq.org
SIC: 2721 2731 Magazines: publishing
only, not printed on site; books: publishing
only

(G-7476)
**BIG MAN FRIENDLY TRNSP
LLC** ✪
11161 State Road 70 E # 1 (34202-9407)
PHONE................................941 229-3454
George Hegamin,
EMP: 7 **EST:** 2021
SALES (est): 559.1K **Privately Held**
SIC: 3537 Trucks: freight, baggage, etc.:
industrial, except mining

(G-7477)
ENOZO TECHNOLOGIES INC
8470 Enterprise Cir (34202-4102)
PHONE................................512 944-7772
Wayne Lieberman, CEO
Matthew Robuck, VP Sales
EMP: 8 **EST:** 2020
SALES (est): 423.6K **Privately Held**
WEB: www.enozo.com
SIC: 2842 Specialty cleaning, polishes &
sanitation goods

(G-7478)
FIRSTLINE PRODUCTS INC
7036 Twin Hills Ter (34202-2400)
PHONE................................401 219-0378
Robert Mollicone, President
EMP: 7 **EST:** 1983
SQ FT: 16,000
SALES (est): 154.3K **Privately Held**
SIC: 3961 Costume jewelry, ex. precious
metal & semiprecious stones

(G-7479)
INTERNATIONAL VAULT INC
16227 Daysailor Trl (34202-5617)
PHONE................................941 390-4505
Stephen G Lask, CEO
EMP: 40 **EST:** 2018
SALES (est): 2.8MM **Privately Held**
WEB: www.internationalvault.com
SIC: 3499 Fabricated metal products

(G-7480)
MANATEE SMOOTHIES LLC
1161 E State Road 70 (34202)
PHONE................................985 640-3088
Christopher A Thomas, Principal
EMP: 6 **EST:** 2012
SALES (est): 409.4K **Privately Held**
SIC: 2037 Frozen fruits & vegetables

Lakewood Ranch
Sarasota County

(G-7481)
ADS-TEC ENERGY INC ✪
5343 Paylor Ln Ste 200 (34240-2213)
PHONE................................941 358-7445
Wolfgang Breme, President
EMP: 17 **EST:** 2021
SALES (est): 1.1MM **Privately Held**
SIC: 3694 Battery charging generators, au-
tomobile & aircraft

(G-7482)
CARBON RESOURCES INC
5206 Paylor Ln (34240-2204)
PHONE................................941 746-8089
Fred Murrell, Principal
EMP: 7 **EST:** 2007
SALES (est): 631.9K **Privately Held**
SIC: 1241 Coal mining services

(G-7483)
**DISCOVERY TECHNOLOGY INTL
INC (DH)**
6700 Professional Pkwy (34240-8444)
PHONE................................941 907-4444
Mark Broderick, President
Nic Copley, VP Bus Dvlpt
Valentin Zhelyaskov, Development
EMP: 4 **EST:** 2004
SALES (est): 5.1MM
SALES (corp-wide): 265.7K **Publicly
Held**
WEB: www.discovtech.com
SIC: 3621 Motors, electric
HQ: Piezo Motion Corp.
6700 Professional Pkwy
Lakewood Ranch FL 34240
941 907-4444

(G-7484)
INVO BIOSCIENCE INC (PA)
5582 Broadcast Ct (34240-8471)
PHONE................................978 878-9505
Steven M Shum, CEO
Michael J Campbell, COO
Inger Carlsson, Vice Pres
Chris Myer, VP Bus Dvlpt
Andrea Goren, CFO
EMP: 5 **EST:** 2005
SQ FT: 1,223
SALES (est): 4.1MM **Publicly Held**
WEB: www.invobioscience.com
SIC: 3841 Surgical & medical instruments

(G-7485)
LUMOS DIAGNOSTICS INC
7040 Prof Pkwy Ste B (34240)
PHONE................................941 556-1850
Sacha Dopheide, CEO
David McCourt, Project Mgr
Kerrianne Casado, Mfg Staff
Srikanth Jandhyala, Engineer
Randall Ross, Finance
EMP: 31 **Privately Held**
WEB: www.lumosdiagnostics.com
SIC: 2835 In vitro diagnostics
HQ: Lumos Diagnostics, Inc.
2724 Loker Ave W
Carlsbad CA 92010
760 683-5374

(G-7486)
**SASQUATCH CABINET
COMPANY**
6841 Energy Ct (34240-8523)
PHONE................................941 365-4950
Lawrence M Hankin, President
EMP: 8 **EST:** 2001
SALES (est): 118.3K **Privately Held**
SIC: 2434 Wood kitchen cabinets

(G-7487)
STEWART-HEDRICK INC
Also Called: Palm Printing
6001 Business Blvd (34240-8410)
PHONE................................941 907-0090
Randy J Hedrick, President
Larry Weisenberger, Vice Pres
Nicole Hedrick, CFO
Renee Phinney, VP Sales
Charles Zweil, VP Sales

▲ **EMP:** 26 **EST:** 1988
SQ FT: 15,000
SALES (est): 4.2MM **Privately Held**
SIC: 2752 Commercial printing, offset

Land O Lakes
Pasco County

(G-7488)
**ARCHITCTRAL SGNAGE
SYSTEMS INC**
6812 Land O Lakes Blvd (34638-3227)
PHONE................................813 996-6777
Jonathan Fischer, Principal
Heather Kearney, Production
EMP: 5 **EST:** 1984
SQ FT: 3,551
SALES (est): 496.9K **Privately Held**
WEB: www.signsbyasap.com
SIC: 3993 Signs & advertising specialties

(G-7489)
ARTECH
5323 Swallow Dr (34639-3817)
PHONE................................813 929-0754
Lorena Cabedzas, Principal
EMP: 9 **EST:** 2001
SALES (est): 71.5K **Privately Held**
WEB: www.artech.com
SIC: 3993 Signs & advertising specialties

(G-7490)
CEMEX
11121 Ehren Cutoff (34639-8123)
PHONE................................813 995-0396
EMP: 7 **EST:** 2020
SALES (est): 545K **Privately Held**
SIC: 3273 Ready-mixed concrete

(G-7491)
DESIGN SERVICES INC
2200 Knight Rd (34639-5107)
P.O. Box 1789 (34639-1789)
PHONE................................813 949-4748
Jane Cetrangolo, President
Dave Cetrangolo, Vice Pres
Liberty Puckett, Asst Sec
▲ **EMP:** 8 **EST:** 1984
SQ FT: 4,000
SALES (est): 1.1MM **Privately Held**
WEB: www.industrialgeneralstore.com
SIC: 3953 5131 Stencils, painting & mark-
ing; ribbons

(G-7492)
**EXPRESS PRINTING CENTER
INC**
2355 Raden Dr (34639-5137)
PHONE................................813 909-1085
John Towson, President
Betty Whitaker, Officer
EMP: 10 **EST:** 1983
SQ FT: 5,000
SALES (est): 1.8MM **Privately Held**
WEB: www.expprinting.com
SIC: 2752 2759 Commercial printing, off-
set; business forms; printing

(G-7493)
IN THE LOOP BREWING INC
3338 Land O Lakes Blvd (34639-4408)
PHONE................................813 857-0111
Peter Abreut, Principal
EMP: 8 **EST:** 2016
SALES (est): 372.7K **Privately Held**
WEB: www.intheloopbrewingcompany.com
SIC: 2082 Malt beverages

(G-7494)
IT IS FINISHED INC
24851 Ravello St (34639-6316)
PHONE................................813 598-9585
Vernon Butler, Vice Pres
EMP: 5 **EST:** 2005
SALES (est): 496.5K **Privately Held**
WEB: www.itisfinishednow.com
SIC: 2426 Flooring, hardwood

(G-7495)
JAG STUCCO INC
4047 Marlow Loop (34639-4071)
PHONE................................813 210-6577
Kimberly Orr, Principal

EMP: 7 **EST:** 2009
SALES (est): 242.4K **Privately Held**
SIC: 3299 Stucco

(G-7496)
LAND O LAKES WINERY LLC
3901 Land O Lakes Blvd (34639-4421)
PHONE...................................813 995-9463
Susan Hardy,
Corey Kempton,
EMP: 6 **EST:** 2015
SQ FT: 3,200
SALES (est): 354.3K **Privately Held**
WEB: www.landolakeswinery.com
SIC: 2084 Wines

(G-7497)
M30 FREEDOM INC
Also Called: Real Producers
4018 Stornoway Dr (34638-7801)
PHONE...................................813 433-1776
Donald Hill, *Principal*
EMP: 9 **EST:** 2017
SALES (est): 267.4K **Privately Held**
WEB: www.realproducersmag.com
SIC: 2741 Miscellaneous publishing

(G-7498)
MANATEE MEDIA INC
Also Called: Community News Publications
3632 Land O Lakes Blvd (34639-4405)
P.O. Box 479, Lutz (33548-0479)
PHONE...................................813 909-2800
Diane Kortus, *President*
Diane Mathes, *President*
Mark Mathes, *Vice Pres*
EMP: 12 **EST:** 1999
SALES (est): 1MM **Privately Held**
WEB: www.manateemedia.com
SIC: 2741 Miscellaneous publishing

(G-7499)
MERRITT MFG LLC
2347 Foggy Ridge Pkwy (34639-5414)
PHONE...................................407 481-1074
Al Erturk, *President*
Deborah Erturk, *Admin Sec*
EMP: 7 **EST:** 2007
SALES (est): 132.6K **Privately Held**
WEB: www.merrittmfg.com
SIC: 3564 Blowers & fans

(G-7500)
PRODUCT MAX GROUP INC
Also Called: Body Action Products
8011 Land O Lakes Blvd (34638-5802)
P.O. Box 1188 (34639-1188)
PHONE...................................813 949-5061
Joey L Jennings, *President*
Christine A Altigilbers, *Vice Pres*
EMP: 5 **EST:** 1999
SALES (est): 505.2K **Privately Held**
WEB: www.pinkprivates.org
SIC: 2844 Face creams or lotions

(G-7501)
PROSHOWMAKER INC
2310 Foggy Ridge Pkwy (34639-5411)
PHONE...................................813 765-2676
Tim Pickens, *Principal*
EMP: 10 **EST:** 2010
SALES (est): 123.7K **Privately Held**
SIC: 3088 Tubs (bath, shower & laundry),
plastic

(G-7502)
ROAN MANUFACTURING INC
23791 Oaks Blvd (34639-5577)
PHONE...................................813 510-4929
Greg Roan, *President*
EMP: 8 **EST:** 2005
SALES (est): 986.4K **Privately Held**
SIC: 3599 Machine shop, jobbing & repair

(G-7503)
S G F INC
3018 Joan Ct (34639-4608)
P.O. Box 1999 (34639-1999)
PHONE...................................813 996-2528
William Fotopoulos, *President*
EMP: 8 **EST:** 1992
SQ FT: 2,800
SALES (est): 104.3K **Privately Held**
SIC: 3949 Bows, archery

(G-7504)
SANDS MOLDING INC
23324 Gracewood Cir (34639-4947)
PHONE...................................813 345-8646
Jacqueline M Campbell, *Principal*
EMP: 8 **EST:** 2008
SALES (est): 82.6K **Privately Held**
SIC: 3089 Molding primary plastic

(G-7505)
STRONG PUBLICATIONS LLC
3809 Tristram Loop (34638-3014)
PHONE...................................813 362-8224
Rickey W George, *Branch Mgr*
EMP: 43
SALES (corp-wide): 264.8K **Privately
Held**
WEB: www.myhardwear.com
SIC: 2741 Miscellaneous publishing
PA: Strong Publications Llc
13046 Race Track Rd
Tampa FL 33626
813 852-9933

(G-7506)
TEAREPAIR INC
2223 Knight Rd (34639-5111)
P.O. Box 1879 (34639-1879)
PHONE...................................813 948-6898
David Cetrangolo, *Principal*
Jane Cetrangolo, *Vice Pres*
EMP: 27 **EST:** 1998
SALES (est): 4.2MM **Privately Held**
WEB: tearepair.openfos.com
SIC: 3089 Kits, plastic

(G-7507)
TRXADE INC
3840 Land O Lakes Blvd (34639-4418)
P.O. Box 1186 (34639-1186)
PHONE...................................727 230-1915
Suren Ajjarapu, *President*
Jariel Morales, *Vice Pres*
Sarah Caldwell, *Accounts Mgr*
Kelsey Wesley, *Manager*
Heidy Gonzalez, *Bd of Directors*
EMP: 9 **EST:** 2013
SALES (est): 4MM
SALES (corp-wide): 9.8MM **Publicly Held**
WEB: rx.trxade.com
SIC: 2834 Pharmaceutical preparations
PA: Trxade Group, Inc.
3840 Land O Lakes Blvd
Land O Lakes FL 34639
800 261-0281

Lantana
Palm Beach County

(G-7508)
CARMAN CABINETS
7800 Coral St (33462-6102)
PHONE...................................561 202-9871
William Carman, *Owner*
EMP: 7 **EST:** 2004
SALES (est): 240K **Privately Held**
SIC: 2434 Wood kitchen cabinets

(G-7509)
CATEGORY 5 MANUFACTURING INC
7150 Seacrest Blvd (33462-5190)
PHONE...................................561 777-2491
EMP: 10 **EST:** 2010
SALES (est): 446.5K **Privately Held**
WEB: www.category5manufacturing.com
SIC: 3999 Manufacturing industries

(G-7510)
EAST COAST MEDAL
860 N 8th St (33462-1637)
PHONE...................................561 619-6753
EMP: 8 **EST:** 2013
SALES (est): 131.7K **Privately Held**
WEB: www.eastcoastmetals.net
SIC: 3441 Fabricated structural metal

(G-7511)
EAST COAST METAL DECKS INC
620 Whitney Ave (33462-1642)
PHONE...................................561 433-8259
Tami Allmon, *President*

Chip Post, *Vice Pres*
Scott Carmichael, *Project Mgr*
Luis Diaz, *Project Mgr*
Steven McBreairty, *Project Mgr*
▼ **EMP:** 49 **EST:** 1984
SQ FT: 2,000
SALES (est): 9.7MM **Privately Held**
WEB: www.eastcoastmetals.net
SIC: 3441 Fabricated structural metal

(G-7512)
EMBROIDERY PLUS
824 W Lantana Rd (33462-1509)
PHONE...................................561 439-8943
Tom Fazor, *Owner*
EMP: 8 **EST:** 2015
SALES (est): 273.1K **Privately Held**
SIC: 2395 Embroidery products, except
schiffli machine

(G-7513)
EVERY THING ALUMINUM
615 Whitney Ave Ste 15 (33462-1645)
P.O. Box 542002, Lake Worth (33454-
2002)
PHONE...................................561 202-9900
Clifton Duckworth, *Owner*
EMP: 6 **EST:** 2005
SALES (est): 409.4K **Privately Held**
SIC: 3479 Aluminum coating of metal prod-
ucts

(G-7514)
FLORIDA PWDR CTING SHTTERS INC
854 N Dixie Hwy (33462-1817)
PHONE...................................561 588-2410
EMP: 12
SQ FT: 47,000
SALES (est): 940K **Privately Held**
SIC: 3479 5023 Powder Coating And
Whol Shutters

(G-7515)
SUNDOWN LIGHTING
417 Se Atlantic Dr (33462-1905)
PHONE...................................561 254-3738
Andrej Benesz, *Officer*
EMP: 7 **EST:** 2005
SALES (est): 76.6K **Privately Held**
SIC: 3648 Lighting equipment

(G-7516)
TAGALONG INC
5485 Old Spanish Trl (33462-5121)
PHONE...................................561 585-7400
EMP: 5 **EST:** 1993
SALES (est): 662.5K **Privately Held**
SIC: 2824 Mfg Nylon Products

(G-7517)
WILDAS JEAN-JOSEPH
Also Called: Down From Hven Silk Screen Prt
701 Miner Rd (33462-6158)
PHONE...................................561 929-1907
Joseph Wildas, *Principal*
EMP: 7 **EST:** 2011
SALES (est): 133.3K **Privately Held**
SIC: 2752 Commercial printing, litho-
graphic

Largo
Pinellas County

(G-7518)
3FDM INC
10600 Endeavour Way (33777-1621)
PHONE...................................727 877-3336
S Pres Parvataneni, *Owner*
Philip Berg, *Marketing Staff*
EMP: 10 **EST:** 2017
SALES (est): 1.1MM **Privately Held**
WEB: www.3fdm.com
SIC: 3999 Manufacturing industries

(G-7519)
AABC INC
Also Called: Roll-A-Guard
12722 62nd St Ste 206 (33773-1818)
PHONE...................................727 434-4444
Andrew J Ayers, *President*
EMP: 15 **EST:** 2006

SALES (est): 2.6MM **Privately Held**
WEB: www.rollaguard.com
SIC: 3442 Shutters, door or window: metal

(G-7520)
ACCENT WOODWORKING INC
2233 34th Way (33771-3902)
PHONE...................................727 522-2700
Richard P Carnevali, *President*
Janet L Carnevali, *Vice Pres*
EMP: 7 **EST:** 1990
SQ FT: 6,000
SALES (est): 753.1K **Privately Held**
WEB: www.accentwoodworking.com
SIC: 2431 Millwork

(G-7521)
ADR POWER SYSTEMS INC (PA)
6545 125th Ave (33773-3604)
PHONE...................................813 241-6999
Andrew Hudgins, *President*
David Arata, *Principal*
Will Odling, *Manager*
EMP: 6 **EST:** 2015
SALES (est): 6.8MM **Privately Held**
SIC: 3714 Motor vehicle parts & acces-
sories

(G-7522)
ADVANCED IMPACT TECH INC
Also Called: Ait Group
2310 Starkey Rd (33771-3852)
PHONE...................................727 287-4620
Jeffrey E Besse, *President*
Christopher Kapiloff, *Vice Pres*
Christine Besse, *Office Mgr*
Jeffrey Wilson, *Director*
Peter Kapiloff, *Admin Sec*
EMP: 19 **EST:** 1984
SALES (est): 3.2MM **Privately Held**
WEB: www.advanced-impact.com
SIC: 3211 Laminated glass

(G-7523)
ADVENT AEROSPACE INC (PA)
11221 69th St (33773-5504)
PHONE...................................727 549-9600
Steve Jourdenais, *President*
Todd Hart, *Director*
EMP: 15 **EST:** 2006
SALES (est): 11.5MM **Privately Held**
WEB: www.adventaerospace.com
SIC: 3728 Aircraft parts & equipment

(G-7524)
AFC CABLE SYSTEMS INC
2000 Tall Pines Dr (33771-3845)
PHONE...................................813 539-0588
EMP: 8 **EST:** 2017
SALES (est): 240.1K **Privately Held**
WEB: www.afcweb.com
SIC: 3644 Noncurrent-carrying wiring serv-
ices

(G-7525)
AJAX PAVING INDUSTRIES FLA LLC
1550 Starkey Rd (33771-3116)
PHONE...................................727 584-3329
EMP: 219 **Privately Held**
SIC: 2911 Asphalt or asphaltic materials,
made in refineries
HQ: Ajax Paving Industries Of Florida Llc
1 Ajax Dr
North Venice FL 34275
941 486-3600

(G-7526)
AL STEIN INDUSTRIES LLC
Also Called: Asieei
6911 Bryan Dairy Rd # 280 (33777-1641)
PHONE...................................727 329-8755
Allen Stein, *President*
▼ **EMP:** 14 **EST:** 2008
SQ FT: 10,000
SALES (est): 1.6MM **Privately Held**
WEB: www.asieei.com
SIC: 3559 Anodizing equipment; electro-
plating machinery & equipment; metal fin-
ishing equipment for plating, etc.; metal
pickling equipment

▲ = Import ▼=Export
◆ =Import/Export

(G-7527)
ALAKAI DEFENSE SYSTEMS INC
8285 Bryan Dairy Rd # 125 (33777-1350)
P.O. Box 10405 (33773-0405)
PHONE................................727 541-1600
Ed Dottery, *President*
Edwin Dottery, *General Mgr*
Keahi Renaud, *Engineer*
Timothy Molner, *Electrical Engi*
Ryan Robins, *Electrical Engi*
EMP: 18 **EST:** 2009
SALES (est): 2.9MM **Privately Held**
WEB: www.alakaidefense.com
SIC: 3812 Search & navigation equipment

(G-7528)
ALEXANDER PUBLICATIONS LLC
10322 Barry Dr (33774-5441)
PHONE................................727 596-4544
Richard A Ewald II, *Principal*
EMP: 8 **EST:** 2011
SALES (est): 71.1K **Privately Held**
WEB: www.alexanderpublications.com
SIC: 2741 Miscellaneous publishing

(G-7529)
ALPINE TOOL INC
13070 90th St (33773-1327)
PHONE................................727 587-0407
Norma Lopez, *President*
Mario Lopez, *Vice Pres*
Antonio Diaz, *Mfg Staff*
EMP: 5 **EST:** 1996
SQ FT: 3,000
SALES (est): 550K **Privately Held**
WEB: www.alpineprecisiontools.com
SIC: 3312 Tool & die steel & alloys

(G-7530)
AMERI FOOD & FUEL INC
790 East Bay Dr (33770-3724)
PHONE................................727 584-0120
Zyad Qusini, *Principal*
EMP: 10 **EST:** 2010
SALES (est): 638K **Privately Held**
SIC: 2869 Fuels

(G-7531)
AMERICAN ACRYLIC ADHESIVES LLC
2020 Wild Acres Rd Unit D (33771-3885)
PHONE................................877 422-4583
Jeffrey Smith, *Principal*
EMP: 9 **EST:** 2017
SALES (est): 1.9MM **Privately Held**
WEB: www.aaaglue.com
SIC: 2891 Adhesives

(G-7532)
AMERICAN ADHESIVES LLC
12350 Belcher Rd S 1b (33773-3045)
PHONE................................877 422-4583
Stuart Young, *Manager*
EMP: 6 **EST:** 2017
SALES (est): 360K **Privately Held**
WEB: www.aaaglue.com
SIC: 2891 Adhesives

(G-7533)
AMERICAN VET SCIENCES LLC
6911 Bryan Dairy Rd (33777-1641)
PHONE................................727 471-0850
Mihir Taneja, *Vice Pres*
EMP: 5 **EST:** 2012
SQ FT: 40,000
SALES (est): 956.1K **Privately Held**
SIC: 2834 Veterinary pharmaceutical preparations

(G-7534)
AMETEK INC
Ametek Msrment Clibration Tech
8600 Somerset Dr (33773-2700)
PHONE................................800 527-9999
Lisa Simpson, *Buyer*
Jimmy Kane, *Engineer*
Dan Musinski, *Engineer*
Chris Elliott, *Design Engr*
Mike Kern, *Branch Mgr*
EMP: 90

SALES (corp-wide): 5.5B **Publicly Held**
SIC: 3823 Industrial instrmnts msrmnt display/control process variable
PA: Ametek, Inc.
1100 Cassatt Rd
Berwyn PA 19312
610 647-2121

(G-7535)
ANVIL PAINTS & COATINGS INC
Also Called: Anvil Paints and Coating
1255 Starkey Rd Ste A (33771-3198)
PHONE................................727 535-1411
Thomas Saeli, *President*
Shawn Sny, *President*
David Wade, *Opers Staff*
Cory Gergar, *CFO*
Tom Sampson, *Natl Sales Mgr*
▼ **EMP:** 19 **EST:** 1967
SQ FT: 55,000
SALES (est): 4.4MM **Privately Held**
WEB: www.anvilpaints.com
SIC: 2851 5231 Paints & paint additives; coating, air curing; paint

(G-7536)
AQUATECH LLC
3448 Avocado Rd (33770-4552)
PHONE................................727 559-8084
Thomas L Lauttenbach, *Manager*
EMP: 8 **EST:** 2013
SALES (est): 205K **Privately Held**
WEB: www.aquatech.com
SIC: 3589 Water treatment equipment, industrial

(G-7537)
ARC DIMENSIONS INC
7545 124th Ave Unit Stef (33773-3016)
P.O. Box 6242, Clearwater (33758-6242)
PHONE................................727 524-6139
Robert E Pope, *President*
David E Kulak, *Vice Pres*
Paul K Boucher, *Treasurer*
EMP: 5 **EST:** 1995
SALES (est): 392.8K **Privately Held**
WEB: www.arcdimensionsinc.com
SIC: 7692 Welding repair

(G-7538)
ARCHITCTRAL MLLWK SLUTIONS INC
Also Called: Doors and Hardware Tampa Bay
13090 Starkey Rd (33773-1415)
PHONE................................727 441-1409
Daniel J Nash, *CEO*
Richard Souza, *Vice Pres*
EMP: 5 **EST:** 2008
SQ FT: 5,000
SALES (est): 488.5K **Privately Held**
WEB: www.doorsandhardwareoftampabay.com
SIC: 2431 5211 5251 Doors & door parts & trim, wood; door & window products; door locks & lock sets

(G-7539)
ATLANTIC TOOL & MFG CORP S
12600 Belcher Rd S # 10 (33773-1656)
PHONE................................727 546-2250
Donald Schneider, *President*
Eric Schneider, *Vice Pres*
Nicolas Schneider, *Vice Pres*
▼ **EMP:** 15 **EST:** 1963
SQ FT: 12,000
SALES (est): 1.8MM **Privately Held**
SIC: 3469 Stamping metal for the trade

(G-7540)
AUTEK SPRAY BOOTHS
6145 126th Ave Unit E (33773-1855)
PHONE................................727 709-4373
EMP: 6
SALES (est): 900K **Privately Held**
SIC: 2851 Mfg Paints/Allied Products

(G-7541)
AXLEY BROTHERS SAW MILL INC
6350 123rd Ave (33773-3605)
PHONE................................727 531-8724
Bill Axley, *President*
EMP: 7 **EST:** 1963

SALES (est): 71.9K **Privately Held**
WEB: www.axleybros.com
SIC: 2499 Wood products

(G-7542)
B & B SIGNS & AWNINGS INC
12305 62nd St Unit B (33773-3716)
PHONE................................727 507-0600
Jack Z Borys, *President*
EMP: 7 **EST:** 2001
SALES (est): 74.1K **Privately Held**
WEB: www.bandbsigns.com
SIC: 3993 Signs & advertising specialties

(G-7543)
B & L CREMATION SYSTEMS INC
7205 114th Ave Ste A (33773-5140)
PHONE................................727 541-4666
Steve Looker, *President*
John Rawl, *COO*
Gary Ruhlman, *Purch Agent*
Danie Phelps, *Purchasing*
Tabitha Watts, *Human Resources*
▼ **EMP:** 55 **EST:** 1985
SQ FT: 30,000
SALES (est): 16.1MM **Privately Held**
WEB: www.blcremationsystems.com
SIC: 3569 Cremating ovens

(G-7544)
BARE BOARD GROUP INC (PA)
8565 Somerset Dr Ste B (33773-2723)
PHONE................................727 549-2200
Adrienne Ridley, *Managing Prtnr*
Kelsen W Liu, *Opers Staff*
Armanda Duross, *Accounts Mgr*
Marie Hill, *Sales Staff*
Jason Liu, *Mng Member*
▲ **EMP:** 16 **EST:** 2002
SQ FT: 9,600
SALES (est): 3.1MM **Privately Held**
WEB: www.ncabgroup.com
SIC: 3672 Circuit boards, television & radio printed

(G-7545)
BARE BOARD GROUP INTL LLC
8565 Somerset Dr Ste B (33773-2723)
PHONE................................727 549-2200
EMP: 11 **EST:** 2012
SALES (est): 349.5K
SALES (corp-wide): 3.1MM **Privately Held**
SIC: 3672 Printed circuit boards
PA: The Bare Board Group Inc
8565 Somerset Dr Ste B
Largo FL 33773
727 549-2200

(G-7546)
BAXTER HEALTHCARE CORPORATION
7511 114th Ave (33773-5129)
P.O. Box 1230, Pinellas Park (33780-1230)
PHONE................................727 544-5050
John Bedingfield, *Principal*
Susan Pulling, *Principal*
Alex Yu, *Principal*
Rui Conceicao, *Engineer*
Maurice Dobbins, *Engineer*
EMP: 281
SALES (corp-wide): 12.7B **Publicly Held**
WEB: www.baxter.com
SIC: 3841 Surgical instruments & apparatus
HQ: Baxter Healthcare Corporation
1 Baxter Pkwy
Deerfield IL 60015
224 948-2000

(G-7547)
BELCHER HOLDINGS INC (PA)
Also Called: Belcher Pharm Acquisition
12393 Belcher Rd S # 420 (33773-3097)
PHONE................................727 530-1585
George Stuart, *CEO*
Joseph Mastronardy, *President*
▲ **EMP:** 28 **EST:** 2001
SALES (est): 9.1MM **Privately Held**
SIC: 2834 Pharmaceutical preparations

(G-7548)
BELCHER HOLDINGS INC
6911 Bryan Dairy Rd (33777-1641)
PHONE................................727 471-0850

Prejith Jayakumar, *Engineer*
Arun Kapoor, *VP Bus Dvlpt*
Kotha Sekharam, *Branch Mgr*
Prabhu Peesapati, *Manager*
Harry Bedi, *CIO*
EMP: 122
SALES (corp-wide): 9.1MM **Privately Held**
WEB: www.belcherpharma.com
SIC: 2834 Pharmaceutical preparations
PA: Belcher Holdings, Inc.
12393 Belcher Rd S # 420
Largo FL 33773
727 530-1585

(G-7549)
BELCHER PHARMACEUTICALS LLC
6911 Bryan Dairy Rd # 210 (33777-1641)
PHONE................................727 471-0850
Jugal Taneja, *Chairman*
Mandeep Taneja, *Vice Pres*
Mihir Taneja, *Vice Pres*
Judy Bartell Goodman, *CFO*
Manju Taneja, *Mng Member*
EMP: 106 **EST:** 2010
SQ FT: 25,000
SALES (est): 7.4MM **Privately Held**
SIC: 2834 Pharmaceutical preparations

(G-7550)
BIODERM INC
12320 73rd Ct (33773-3011)
PHONE................................727 507-7655
Gary Damkoehler, *Ch of Bd*
Gaet Tyranski, *President*
John Debella, *COO*
Shawn Stone, *VP Opers*
Marc Garofani, *CFO*
▲ **EMP:** 54 **EST:** 1990
SQ FT: 8,500
SALES (est): 10.3MM **Privately Held**
WEB: www.bioderminc.com
SIC: 3841 Surgical & medical instruments

(G-7551)
BLUE HAWAIIAN PRODUCTS INC (PA)
Also Called: Blue Hawaiian Fiberglass Pools
2055 Blue Hawaiian Dr (33771)
PHONE................................727 535-5677
Roger W Erdelac, *President*
▼ **EMP:** 40 **EST:** 1988
SQ FT: 36,000
SALES (est): 9.1MM **Privately Held**
WEB: www.lathampool.com
SIC: 3949 Swimming pools, plastic

(G-7552)
BLUESKY MAST INC
Also Called: Bluesky Innovations
2080 Wild Acres Rd (33771-3818)
PHONE................................877 411-6278
Scott Vanover, *President*
Crystal Freund, *Accountant*
◆ **EMP:** 11 **EST:** 2003
SALES (est): 2.4MM **Privately Held**
WEB: www.blueskymast.com
SIC: 3812 Antennas, radar or communications

(G-7553)
BONATO & PIRES LLC
Also Called: Prestige Machine, and Tool
13091 92nd St Unit 502 (33773-1312)
PHONE................................727 581-1220
Andre Bonato, *President*
Juliana Bonato, *Vice Pres*
EMP: 7 **EST:** 2011
SQ FT: 4,000
SALES (est): 691.3K **Privately Held**
SIC: 3469 3541 Machine parts, stamped or pressed metal; machine tool replacement & repair parts, metal cutting types

(G-7554)
BPI LABS LLC
12393 Belcher Rd S # 450 (33773-3097)
PHONE................................727 471-0850
Jugal Taneja, *CEO*
Shyam Busireddy, *COO*
Mandeep Taneja, *Vice Pres*
Lana Radowick, *CFO*
Mihir Taneja, *VP Sales*
EMP: 106 **EST:** 2012

SALES (est): 24.2MM **Privately Held**
WEB: www.bpi-labs.com
SIC: 2834 Pharmaceutical preparations

(G-7555)
BRAWLEY DISTRIBUTING CO INC
Also Called: National Saw Company
7162 123rd Cir (33773-3041)
PHONE..................................727 539-8500
Terrance Brawley, *President*
Tom Lewis, *Vice Pres*
Annett Brawley, *Treasurer*
▲ **EMP:** 11 **EST:** 1945
SQ FT: 6,000
SALES (est): 2.1MM **Privately Held**
WEB: www.brawleydistributing.com
SIC: 3991 Paint brushes; paint rollers

(G-7556)
BREEZE PRODUCTS INC
7207 114th Ave Ste B (33773-5132)
PHONE..................................727 521-4482
Mike Lemle, *President*
Robert Dowdell, *Vice Pres*
Sandy Akl, *Treasurer*
Ashley Croyle, *Sales Executive*
Tania Lentine, *Senior Mgr*
EMP: 33 **EST:** 1999
SQ FT: 11,000
SALES (est): 2.6MM **Privately Held**
WEB: www.breezeproducts.com
SIC: 2844 Suntan lotions & oils

(G-7557)
BRIGHTFISH LABEL LLC
8222 118th Ave Ste 615 (33773-5054)
PHONE..................................727 521-7900
Robert Castles Jr, *President*
Jamie Castles, *Project Mgr*
EMP: 8 **EST:** 2007
SALES (est): 967.8K **Privately Held**
WEB: www.brightfishlabel.com
SIC: 2759 Labels & seals: printing

(G-7558)
BUCKEYE USED OFFICE FURN INC
Also Called: Buckeye Office Intrors Instllt
6166 126th Ave (33773-1854)
PHONE..................................727 457-5287
Dominic J De Marte, *President*
Nicholas Pasquine, *Principal*
EMP: 6 **EST:** 1995
SQ FT: 10,000
SALES (est): 500K **Privately Held**
SIC: 2522 Office furniture, except wood

(G-7559)
BUILDERS AUTOMTN MCHY CO LLC
12775 Starkey Rd Ste B (33773-1436)
PHONE..................................727 538-2180
Robert J Mitvalsky, *Mng Member*
Thomas Schusser,
EMP: 25 **EST:** 1992
SQ FT: 10,500
SALES (est): 4.5MM **Privately Held**
WEB: www.buildersautomation.com
SIC: 3599 Custom machinery

(G-7560)
CABINET MASTERS INC
7168 123rd Cir (33773-3041)
PHONE..................................727 535-0020
David Ogden, *President*
Scott Ellis, *Vice Pres*
EMP: 8 **EST:** 1982
SQ FT: 4,000
SALES (est): 670K **Privately Held**
SIC: 2521 2434 Wood office furniture; wood kitchen cabinets

(G-7561)
CALTI CABINETS INC
11950 67th Way Unit C (33773-3505)
PHONE..................................727 744-7844
Pawel Matejek, *President*
EMP: 7 **EST:** 2010
SALES (est): 174.4K **Privately Held**
WEB: www.calticabinets.com
SIC: 2434 Wood kitchen cabinets

(G-7562)
CATALINA YACHTS INC
7200 Bryan Dairy Rd (33773-1504)
PHONE..................................727 544-6681
Gerry Douglas, *Vice Pres*
Michael Quinn, *Manager*
EMP: 150
SALES (corp-wide): 29.4MM **Privately Held**
WEB: www.catalinayachts.com
SIC: 3732 Sailboats, building & repairing
PA: Catalina Yachts, Inc.
2259 Ward Ave
Simi Valley CA 93065
818 884-7700

(G-7563)
CBD BIOCARE
7381 114th Ave Ste 406 (33773-5125)
PHONE..................................813 380-4376
EMP: 9 **EST:** 2018
SALES (est): 583.1K **Privately Held**
WEB: www.cbdbiocare.com
SIC: 3999

(G-7564)
CLARIOS LLC
Johnson Controls
8575 Largo Lakes Dr (33773-4909)
PHONE..................................727 541-3531
Bob Holoms, *Branch Mgr*
Nancy Freshcorn, *IT/INT Sup*
EMP: 444
SALES (corp-wide): 47.9B **Privately Held**
WEB: www.clarios.com
SIC: 3585 3567 Parts for heating, cooling & refrigerating equipment; industrial furnaces & ovens
HQ: Clarios, Llc
5757 N Green Bay Ave
Milwaukee WI 53209

(G-7565)
CLEARWATER ENVIRO TECH INC
8767 115th Ave (33773-4904)
PHONE..................................727 209-6400
Jeffrey M Conway, *President*
Ryan Duksa, *Sales Executive*
EMP: 22 **EST:** 1994
SQ FT: 12,000
SALES (est): 4.1MM **Privately Held**
WEB: www.clearwaterenviro.com
SIC: 3589 Water purification equipment, household type; water treatment equipment, industrial

(G-7566)
CLONDALKIN LLC
Also Called: Llc, Clondalkin
10950 Belcher Rd S (33777-1438)
PHONE..................................866 545-8703
Aaron Weltz, *General Mgr*
Christine Urdiales, *Vice Pres*
Jerry Mangan, *Purch Mgr*
Kevin Kenjarski, *VP Sales*
Denis Thellab, *Accounts Exec*
◆ **EMP:** 19 **EST:** 2013
SALES (est): 517.1K **Privately Held**
WEB: www.clondalkingroup.com
SIC: 2024 Ice cream, packaged: molded, on sticks, etc.

(G-7567)
COMPUTER FORMS & SUPPLIES
Also Called: One Source Technology
1198 Hickory Dr (33770-4211)
P.O. Box 1830, Pinellas Park (33780-1830)
PHONE..................................727 535-0422
EMP: 7
SQ FT: 3,500
SALES (est): 1MM **Privately Held**
SIC: 3955 5112 Carbon Paper And Inked Ribbons

(G-7568)
CONMED CORPORATION (PA)
11311 Concept Blvd (33773-4908)
PHONE..................................727 392-6464
Curt R Hartman, *Ch of Bd*
Pablo Pineres, *Business Mgr*
Sarah M Oliker, *Counsel*
Heather L Cohen, *Exec VP*
Shanna Cotti-Osmanski, *Exec VP*
◆ **EMP:** 297 **EST:** 1970
SQ FT: 278,000

SALES (est): 1B **Publicly Held**
WEB: www.conmed.com
SIC: 3845 3841 Electromedical apparatus; electrocardiographs; patient monitoring apparatus; surgical instruments & apparatus; trocars; suction therapy apparatus; probes, surgical

(G-7569)
DANCO MACHINE INC
13131 92nd St Ste 608a (33773-1331)
PHONE..................................727 501-0460
Daniel B Mothena, *President*
EMP: 6 **EST:** 2002
SQ FT: 5,000
SALES (est): 429.6K **Privately Held**
WEB: www.dancomachineinc.com
SIC: 3599 3451 Machine shop, jobbing & repair; screw machine products

(G-7570)
DIRECT OPTICAL RESEARCH CO
8725 115th Ave (33773-4904)
PHONE..................................727 319-9000
James T Chivers, *CEO*
EMP: 8 **EST:** 1992
SQ FT: 8,000
SALES (est): 784.7K **Privately Held**
WEB: www.dorc.com
SIC: 3827 Optical test & inspection equipment

(G-7571)
DISCOUNT BOAT TOPS INC
Also Called: Dbt Marine Products
14000 66th St Ste A (33771-4776)
PHONE..................................727 536-4412
Richard Moyse, *President*
EMP: 8 **EST:** 1973
SQ FT: 10,500
SALES (est): 486.3K **Privately Held**
WEB: www.discountboattops.com
SIC: 2394 3732 Convertible tops, canvas or boat: from purchased materials; boat building & repairing

(G-7572)
DISTINCT DSGNS CSTM COML CASE
1135 Starkey Rd (33771-3185)
PHONE..................................727 530-0119
Bill Kratimenos, *President*
Pete Kratimenos, *Director*
EMP: 5 **EST:** 2003
SALES (est): 555.9K **Privately Held**
WEB: www.distinctdesignsfl.com
SIC: 2599 Cabinets, factory

(G-7573)
DOK SOLUTION INC (PA)
12253 62nd St Ste B (33773-3707)
PHONE..................................727 209-1313
John Strauser, *CEO*
Jeanie Strauser, *Vice Pres*
Edwin Young, *Vice Pres*
Tom Strauser, *Sales Mgr*
EMP: 6 **EST:** 2012
SALES (est): 1.2MM **Privately Held**
WEB: www.doksolution.com
SIC: 3931 Musical instruments, electric & electronic

(G-7574)
DRS LAUREL TECHNOLOGIES (DH)
6200 118th Ave (33773-3726)
PHONE..................................727 541-6681
Larry Butera, *General Mgr*
Bob Sleppy, *Technical Staff*
Daniel Skaling, *Director*
EMP: 25 **EST:** 2001
SALES (est): 15.7MM
SALES (corp-wide): 16B **Privately Held**
WEB: www.leonardodrs.com
SIC: 3861 Cameras & related equipment
HQ: Leonardo Drs, Inc.
2345 Crystal Dr Ste 1000
Arlington VA 22202
703 416-8000

(G-7575)
DVC SIGNS LLC
12350 Belcher Rd S 14b (33773-3009)
PHONE..................................727 524-8543

Ralph Kay, *Vice Pres*
Kristopher Kay, *Vice Pres*
Christian Slager, *Creative Dir*
EMP: 6 **EST:** 2014
SALES (est): 340K **Privately Held**
WEB: www.dvcsigns.com
SIC: 3993 Electric signs

(G-7576)
E T I INCORPORATED
10610 75th St (33777-1420)
PHONE..................................727 546-6472
Jim Smith, *President*
EMP: 34 **EST:** 1987
SQ FT: 11,000
SALES (est): 646.8K
SALES (corp-wide): 28MM **Privately Held**
WEB: www.etiincorporated.com
SIC: 2869 Silicones
PA: Molded Rubber & Plastic Corporation
13161 W Glendale Ave
Butler WI 53007
262 781-7122

(G-7577)
E3 FLUID RECOVERY ENG (PA)
13517 65th St (33771-4967)
P.O. Box 41802, Saint Petersburg (33743-1802)
PHONE..................................727 754-9792
EMP: 6 **EST:** 2011
SQ FT: 4,000
SALES (est): 1MM **Privately Held**
SIC: 3677 8711 Mfg Electronic Coils/Transformers Engineering Services

(G-7578)
ELDER & JENKS LLC
12595 71st Ct (33773-3254)
PHONE..................................727 538-5545
Thomas G Typrowicz,
Thomas F Typrowicz,
Stacy Zumwalt,
EMP: 8 **EST:** 2015
SALES (est): 489.2K **Privately Held**
SIC: 3991 Paint & varnish brushes; paint rollers; paint brushes; varnish brushes

(G-7579)
ELDORADO MIRANDA MFG CO INC
1744 12th St Se Ofc Ofc (33771-3754)
PHONE..................................727 586-0707
Andrew Miranda Jr, *President*
Cora Miranda, *Corp Secy*
▼ **EMP:** 5 **EST:** 1981
SQ FT: 7,000
SALES (est): 540.7K **Privately Held**
WEB: www.eldoradomfg.com
SIC: 2599 Restaurant furniture, wood or metal

(G-7580)
FASHIONABLE CANES
7381 114th Ave Ste 402b (33773-5105)
PHONE..................................727 547-8866
Stephen Carroll, *Owner*
Elizabeth Carroll, *Co-Owner*
EMP: 10 **EST:** 2010
SALES (est): 568.7K **Privately Held**
WEB: www.fashionablecanes.com
SIC: 3999 Canes & cane trimmings, except precious metal

(G-7581)
FAST FRONTIER PRINTING
7360 Ulmerton Rd Apt 19d (33771-4543)
PHONE..................................407 538-5621
EMP: 8 **EST:** 2016
SALES (est): 445K **Privately Held**
WEB: www.fastfrontier.co
SIC: 2752 Commercial printing, lithographic

(G-7582)
FDM OF CLEARWATER INC
Also Called: Florida Discharge Machine
10850 75th St (33777-1424)
PHONE..................................727 544-8801
Michael Conte, *President*
Mike Conte, *Executive*
EMP: 10 **EST:** 1971
SQ FT: 10,000

▲ = Import ▼ =Export
◆ =Import/Export

SALES (est): 937.2K **Privately Held**
WEB: www.fdmofclearwater.com
SIC: 3544 Special dies & tools

(G-7583)
FIBRE TECH INC
2323 34th Way (33771-3978)
PHONE................................727 539-0844
Andrew Morris, *President*
▼ **EMP:** 32 **EST:** 1987
SQ FT: 9,000
SALES (est): 4.6MM **Privately Held**
WEB: www.fibretechinc.com
SIC: 2851 7389 Lacquers, varnishes, enamels & other coatings; swimming pool & hot tub service & maintenance

(G-7584)
FILL TECH SOLUTIONS INC 200
11401 Belcher Rd S # 230 (33773-5102)
PHONE................................727 572-8550
Stewart Nelson, *President*
Ron Nelson, *Vice Pres*
Thiago Figueira, *Engineer*
Saysun Phrasikaysone, *Engineer*
Ana Nelson, *CFO*
EMP: 24 **EST:** 2009
SALES (est): 7.8MM **Privately Held**
WEB: www.fill-tech.com
SIC: 3565 Packaging machinery

(G-7585)
FINE WOOD DESIGN INC
12087 62nd St Unit 8 (33773-3709)
PHONE................................727 531-8000
Mark Winter, *President*
EMP: 8 **EST:** 2004
SALES (est): 915.7K **Privately Held**
WEB: www.finewooddesign.net
SIC: 2434 Wood kitchen cabinets

(G-7586)
FLORIDA METAL SERVICES INC
6951 108th Ave (33777-1615)
PHONE................................727 541-6441
John Max Jones, *CEO*
Daryle Jones, *President*
Julie Samsel, *Purch Agent*
EMP: 75 **EST:** 1975
SQ FT: 30,500
SALES (est): 16.1MM **Privately Held**
WEB: www.florida-metal.com
SIC: 3469 Stamping metal for the trade

(G-7587)
FLORIDA SNCAST TRISM PRMTONS I
10750 75th St (33777-1422)
PHONE................................727 544-1212
Drake A Decker, *President*
EMP: 10 **EST:** 1985
SQ FT: 10,000
SALES (est): 947.9K **Privately Held**
WEB: www.floridatourism.com
SIC: 2731 2759 Pamphlets: publishing & printing; commercial printing

(G-7588)
FLORIDA VEEX INC
Also Called: Digital Lightwave
2100 Tall Pines Dr (33771-3809)
PHONE................................727 442-6677
Paul Chang, *President*
EMP: 15 **EST:** 2016
SALES (est): 1MM **Privately Held**
WEB: www.lightwave.com
SIC: 3661 3825 Fiber optics communications equipment; digital test equipment, electronic & electrical circuits; test equipment for electronic & electric measurement

(G-7589)
FORMULATED SOLUTIONS LLC (PA)
11775 Starkey Rd (33773-4727)
PHONE................................727 373-3970
Ray Bodamer, *VP Opers*
Jenna Stephan, *Project Mgr*
Thomas Sharo, *Production*
Philip Gorski, *Buyer*
Ricardo Arcetti, *Engineer*
◆ **EMP:** 88 **EST:** 1999
SQ FT: 177,000

SALES (est): 32.8MM **Privately Held**
WEB: www.formulatedsolutions.com
SIC: 2844 Cosmetic preparations

(G-7590)
FURNITURE CONCEPTS INC
2180 34th Way Ste D (33771-4095)
PHONE................................727 535-0093
Lance Breakwell, *President*
EMP: 5 **EST:** 1997
SALES (est): 658.3K **Privately Held**
WEB: www.furnitureconceptsinc.com
SIC: 2541 Counter & sink tops

(G-7591)
GARELICK MFG CO
7151 114th Ave (33773-5312)
PHONE................................727 545-4571
EMP: 83
SQ FT: 70,000
SALES (corp-wide): 4.3B **Publicly Held**
SIC: 3499 3429 Marine Accessories
HQ: Garelick Mfg. Co.
         644 2nd St
         Saint Paul Park MN 55071
         651 459-9795

(G-7592)
GENESIS ELECTRIC MOTORS INC
6330 118th Ave Unit A (33773-3722)
PHONE................................727 572-1414
David Eskew, *President*
EMP: 6 **EST:** 2000
SQ FT: 4,800
SALES (est): 657.3K **Privately Held**
WEB: www.genesiselectricmotors.com
SIC: 7694 Electric motor repair

(G-7593)
GIOVANNIS BAKERY INC
299 Keene Rd (33771-1729)
PHONE................................727 536-2253
Roberto A Fanzago, *President*
EMP: 12 **EST:** 2000
SQ FT: 4,800
SALES (est): 868.3K **Privately Held**
WEB: www.giovannisbakeryfl.com
SIC: 2051 Bakery: wholesale or wholesale/retail combined

(G-7594)
GJ FRANCOS STAIR CO INC
1079 Woodbrook Dr S (33770-1626)
PHONE................................727 510-4102
Gregory J Franco, *President*
EMP: 7 **EST:** 2004
SALES (est): 63K **Privately Held**
SIC: 3446 Stairs, staircases, stair treads: prefabricated metal

(G-7595)
GLASS WORKS OF LARGO INC
2020 Wild Acres Rd Unit D (33771-3885)
PHONE................................727 535-9808
Kenneth Cruz, *President*
Rhonda Cruz, *Vice Pres*
EMP: 6 **EST:** 1997
SALES (est): 668.2K **Privately Held**
WEB: www.glassworksoflargo.com
SIC: 3089 Molding primary plastic

(G-7596)
GLENNMAR SUPPLY LLC
6265 118th Ave (33773-3727)
PHONE................................727 536-1955
Glenn-Mar Supply, *Sales Staff*
EMP: 9 **EST:** 2016
SALES (est): 2.4MM **Privately Held**
WEB: www.lewismarine.com
SIC: 3465 Body parts, automobile: stamped metal

(G-7597)
GLOBAL IMPRESSIONS INC
1299 Starkey Rd Ste 103 (33771-3101)
PHONE................................727 531-1290
Dean L Stevenson, *President*
Patricia Stevenson, *Treasurer*
EMP: 14 **EST:** 1994
SQ FT: 10,000
SALES (est): 519.4K **Privately Held**
WEB: www.globalimp.com
SIC: 2752 Transfers, decalcomania or dry: lithographed

(G-7598)
GOLDEN RIBBON CORPORATION
Also Called: Marathon Ribbon Co
10321 72nd St (33777-1542)
PHONE................................727 545-4499
Lee Manuel, *President*
EMP: 20 **EST:** 1984
SQ FT: 28,000
SALES (est): 714K **Privately Held**
WEB: www.marathon4imaging.com
SIC: 3955 Ribbons, inked: typewriter, adding machine, register, etc.

(G-7599)
GREAT BAY FABRICATION INC
2111 34th Way (33771-3952)
PHONE................................727 536-1924
John Edwards, *President*
Kenneth Brown, *Treasurer*
Steve Hope, *Sales Staff*
▼ **EMP:** 15 **EST:** 2007
SALES (est): 2.5MM **Privately Held**
WEB: www.secosouth.com
SIC: 2431 Staircases, stairs & railings

(G-7600)
GRINDER WEAR PARTS INC
2062 20th Ave Se (33771-3846)
PHONE................................503 982-0881
Helena Vanderwey, *President*
Wayne Brown, *Exec VP*
Paul Minkler, *Mfg Staff*
Dali Kranzthor, *CFO*
Tom Rice, *CFO*
▲ **EMP:** 23 **EST:** 2010
SALES (est): 4.7MM **Privately Held**
WEB: www.grinderwearparts.com
SIC: 3599 Machine & other job shop work

(G-7601)
GULF ELECTRONICS
12155 Meadowbrook Ln (33774-3141)
P.O. Box 1241 (33779-1241)
PHONE................................727 595-3840
Harry Schlenther, *Owner*
EMP: 10 **EST:** 1994
SALES (est): 567.7K **Privately Held**
WEB: www.shopperonline.com
SIC: 3354 7622 Aluminum extruded products; radio & television repair

(G-7602)
GULF PUBLISHING COMPANY INC (PA)
11470 Oakhurst Rd (33774-3994)
PHONE................................727 596-2863
Edward A Hausdorf, *President*
Karan Hausdorf, *Vice Pres*
EMP: 10 **EST:** 1978
SQ FT: 3,100
SALES (est): 1.1MM **Privately Held**
SIC: 2741 2721 Directories: publishing only, not printed on site; guides: publishing only, not printed on site; periodicals

(G-7603)
HENEFELT PRECISION PDTS INC
8475 Ulmerton Rd (33771-3841)
P.O. Box 1283 (33779-1283)
PHONE................................727 531-0406
William N Henefelt Jr, *President*
Christie M Henefelt, *Vice Pres*
Kathy Henefelt, *Admin Sec*
EMP: 18 **EST:** 1944
SQ FT: 30,000
SALES (est): 1.2MM **Privately Held**
WEB: www.henefelt.com
SIC: 3452 5085 3965 3545 Nuts, metal; industrial supplies; fasteners, buttons, needles & pins; machine tool accessories; copper foundries

(G-7604)
HERMAN CABINETS INC
1000 Belcher Rd S (33771-3321)
PHONE................................727 459-6730
John A Herman, *President*
EMP: 7 **EST:** 2004
SALES (est): 163.8K **Privately Held**
WEB: www.hermancabinetsinc.net
SIC: 2434 Wood kitchen cabinets

(G-7605)
HIT PROMOTIONAL PRODUCTS INC (PA)
7150 Bryan Dairy Rd (33777-1501)
P.O. Box 10200, Saint Petersburg (33733-0200)
PHONE................................727 541-5561
Elizabeth Schmidt, *CEO*
Farah Flores, *President*
Christopher J Schmidt, *President*
Jane Mary, *Editor*
Jennifer Grigorian, *Vice Pres*
◆ **EMP:** 350 **EST:** 1981
SQ FT: 227,000
SALES (est): 229.6MM **Privately Held**
WEB: www.hitpromo.net
SIC: 2759 3993 Promotional printing; signs & advertising specialties

(G-7606)
HONEYWELL INTERNATIONAL INC
13051 66th St (33773-1810)
PHONE................................505 358-0676
Darius Adamczyk, *Ch of Bd*
David Jensen, *Engineer*
Randy Snell, *Director*
EMP: 71
SALES (corp-wide): 34.3B **Publicly Held**
WEB: www.honeywell.com
SIC: 3728 3812 Aircraft parts & equipment; search & navigation equipment
PA: Honeywell International Inc.
         855 S Mint St
         Charlotte NC 28202
         704 627-6200

(G-7607)
HOOK INTERNATIONAL INC
6795 114th Ave (33773-5419)
PHONE................................727 209-0855
Kamal S Juneja, *President*
▲ **EMP:** 8 **EST:** 1993
SALES (est): 799.2K **Privately Held**
SIC: 3536 Hoists

(G-7608)
HOT SHOT WELDING INC
1135 Starkey Rd Ste 10 (33771-3199)
PHONE................................727 585-1900
Stephen Aretz, *President*
EMP: 15 **EST:** 1991
SQ FT: 3,000
SALES (est): 2.1MM **Privately Held**
WEB: www.hotshotwelding.com
SIC: 7692 Welding repair

(G-7609)
HOYA LARGO
12345 Starkey Rd Ste E (33773-2611)
PHONE................................727 531-8964
Donald Behagg, *President*
EMP: 30 **EST:** 1980
SQ FT: 6,000
SALES (est): 4.5MM **Privately Held**
SIC: 3851 3229 Lenses, ophthalmic; pressed & blown glass

(G-7610)
HYPERION MUNITIONS INC
8601 Somerset Dr Ste A (33773-2719)
PHONE................................844 622-8339
Thomas Dane, *Principal*
EMP: 12 **EST:** 2015
SALES (est): 2.4MM **Privately Held**
WEB: www.hyperionmunitions.com
SIC: 3482 Shot, steel (ammunition)

(G-7611)
IMPACT REGISTER INC
1870 Starkey Rd Ste 1 (33771-3105)
PHONE................................727 585-8572
Brad Schmeiser, *President*
Brent Schmeiser, *Vice Pres*
EMP: 5 **EST:** 1940
SQ FT: 3,500
SALES (est): 588.1K **Privately Held**
WEB: www.impactregister.com
SIC: 3829 Accelerometers

(G-7612)
INDUSTRIAL MARKING SVCS INC
10830 Canal St Ste C (33777-1635)
PHONE................................727 541-7622

Charles H Harbold, *President*
Tela Harbold, *Principal*
Carol Davis, *Admin Sec*
EMP: 6 **EST:** 1982
SQ FT: 6,000
SALES (est): 826.7K **Privately Held**
WEB: www.imsink.net
SIC: 2759 Screen printing

(G-7613)
INFINITY MANUFACTURED INDS
12450 Enterprise Blvd (33773-2709)
P.O. Box 10655 (33773-0655)
PHONE.................................727 532-4453
Fred Weisemann, *President*
David Silverstein, *Manager*
EMP: 10 **EST:** 1994
SQ FT: 33,000
SALES (est): 1MM **Privately Held**
WEB: www.imilaser.com
SIC: 3444 Sheet metalwork

(G-7614)
INTERNATIONAL C & C CORP
Also Called: Sign X-Press
10831 Canal St (33777-1636)
PHONE.................................727 249-0675
Xiaojun Liu, *CEO*
William Griffin, *President*
EMP: 40 **EST:** 1990
SQ FT: 2,000
SALES (est): 4.4MM **Privately Held**
WEB: www.signx-press.com
SIC: 3669 Transportation signaling devices; intercommunication systems, electric

(G-7615)
INTERNATIONAL SIGN DESIGN CORP
10831 Canal St (33777-1636)
PHONE.................................727 541-5573
William Griffin, *CEO*
Eric Sekeres, *Vice Pres*
Jordan Grey, *Project Mgr*
Seth F Sekeres, *CFO*
Dana Grey, *Accounting Mgr*
EMP: 47 **EST:** 1972
SQ FT: 54,000
SALES (est): 6.7MM **Privately Held**
WEB: www.intlsign.com
SIC: 3993 Signs & advertising specialties

(G-7616)
INTREPID POWERBOATS INC
11700 Belcher Rd S (33773-5115)
PHONE.................................954 922-7544
EMP: 289
SALES (corp-wide): 2B **Publicly Held**
WEB: www.intrepidpowerboats.com
SIC: 3732 Boat building & repairing
HQ: Intrepid Powerboats, Inc.
805 Ne E 3rd St
Dania FL 33004

(G-7617)
INTUITOS LLC
Also Called: Optek International
2300 Tall Pines Dr # 120 (33771-5342)
P.O. Box 1050, Pinellas Park (33780-1050)
PHONE.................................727 522-2301
Alan Hodges,
EMP: 18 **EST:** 2012
SQ FT: 14,000
SALES (est): 4MM **Privately Held**
WEB: www.optekinternational.com
SIC: 3559 Optical lens machinery

(G-7618)
ISLAND PCKET SAWARD YACHTS LLC
1979 Wild Acres Rd (33771-3815)
PHONE.................................727 535-6431
Leslie Allen, *Managing Prtnr*
Darrell Allen, *Principal*
EMP: 9 **EST:** 2017
SALES (est): 1.2MM **Privately Held**
WEB: www.ipy.com
SIC: 3732 Yachts, building & repairing

(G-7619)
J V G INC
Also Called: Sir Speedy
12509 Ulmerton Rd (33774-3628)
PHONE.................................727 584-7136
Anthony Juliano, *President*

Kelly Kimberlin, *VP Bus Dvlpt*
EMP: 9 **EST:** 1979
SQ FT: 3,800
SALES (est): 983.9K **Privately Held**
WEB: www.sirspeedy.com
SIC: 2752 2791 2789 7334 Commercial printing, lithographic; typesetting; bookbinding & related work; photocopying & duplicating services

(G-7620)
JACKS MAGIC PRODUCTS INC
Also Called: Jack's Magic
12435 73rd Ct (33773-3047)
PHONE.................................727 536-4500
Jack Beane, *President*
Bernard Simon Sr, *Vice Pres*
Michael Davis, *Production*
Joel Gray, *Regl Sales Mgr*
Veronique Couedelo, *Supervisor*
EMP: 18 **EST:** 1989
SQ FT: 25,000
SALES (est): 4.2MM **Privately Held**
WEB: www.jacksmagic.com
SIC: 2899 5999 1799 Water treating compounds; swimming pool chemicals, equipment & supplies; swimming pool construction

(G-7621)
JAMES SPEAR DESIGN INC
12253 62nd St Ste A (33773-3707)
PHONE.................................727 592-9600
James Spear, *President*
EMP: 9 **EST:** 1990
SQ FT: 75,000
SALES (est): 298.8K **Privately Held**
SIC: 2599 2542 Cabinets, factory; partitions & fixtures, except wood

(G-7622)
JEWISH PRESS GROUP OF TMPA BAY
Also Called: Jewish Press Group Tampa Bay
1101 Belcher Rd S Ste H (33771-3356)
P.O. Box 6970, Clearwater (33758-6970)
PHONE.................................727 535-4400
James Dawkins, *Director*
Karen Dawkins, *Director*
EMP: 7 **EST:** 1984
SALES (est): 662.5K **Privately Held**
WEB: www.jewishpresstampabay.com
SIC: 2711 Commercial printing & newspaper publishing combined; newspapers, publishing & printing

(G-7623)
JORMAC AEROSPACE
11221 69th St (33773-5504)
PHONE.................................727 549-9600
Steve Jourdenais, *President*
Tony Mazzuco, *Prdtn Mgr*
Roland Pham, *Inv Control Mgr*
Mina Bassaly, *Engineer*
Matt Palmer, *Engineer*
EMP: 85 **EST:** 1995
SQ FT: 38,500
SALES (est): 28.3MM **Privately Held**
WEB: www.jormac.com
SIC: 3728 Aircraft parts & equipment

(G-7624)
KING & GRUBE ADVG & PRTG LLC
1211 10th St Sw (33770-4420)
PHONE.................................727 327-6033
Merrill King, *President*
Karen King, *Vice Pres*
EMP: 5 **EST:** 2015
SALES (est): 360.7K **Privately Held**
WEB: www.printkg.com
SIC: 2752 Commercial printing, offset

(G-7625)
KING & GRUBE INC
1211 10th St Sw (33770-4420)
PHONE.................................727 327-6033
Merrill King, *President*
Karen King, *Corp Secy*
Donald Grube, *Vice Pres*
EMP: 14 **EST:** 1983
SQ FT: 4,400
SALES (est): 403.7K **Privately Held**
WEB: www.customthreads.com
SIC: 2752 7311 Commercial printing, offset; advertising agencies

(G-7626)
KLA INDUSTRIES
801 West Bay Dr Ste 203 (33770-3200)
PHONE.................................727 315-4719
Karen Sturgeon, *Principal*
EMP: 9 **EST:** 2016
SALES (est): 284.6K **Privately Held**
WEB: www.klaindustries.com
SIC: 3999 Manufacturing industries

(G-7627)
KM INDUSTRIAL RACKING INC
8989 Ulmerton Rd (33771-3814)
PHONE.................................813 900-7457
Keith McKee, *Principal*
EMP: 8 **EST:** 2011
SALES (est): 90.1K **Privately Held**
WEB: www.km-industrial-racking.com
SIC: 2542 Pallet racks: except wood

(G-7628)
KMSS PRODUCTS INC
Also Called: Safe Stride
9225 Ulmerton Rd Ste D (33771-3739)
PHONE.................................800 646-3005
Kathleen Mott, *President*
EMP: 5 **EST:** 1987
SQ FT: 6,000
SALES (est): 433.2K **Privately Held**
SIC: 2842 Specialty cleaning preparations

(G-7629)
KRAMSKI NORTH AMERICA INC
8222 118th Ave Ste 650 (33773-5057)
PHONE.................................727 828-1500
Andreas Kramski, *CEO*
Martin Bischoff, *President*
Wiestaw Kramski, *President*
◆ **EMP:** 16 **EST:** 2002
SQ FT: 33,600
SALES (est): 9.8MM
SALES (corp-wide): 97.5MM **Privately Held**
WEB: www.kramski.de
SIC: 3089 Injection molding of plastics
PA: Kramski Gmbh
Heilbronner Str. 10
Pforzheim BW 75179
723 115-4100

(G-7630)
L & D STEEL USA INC
13240 Belcher Rd S (33773-1600)
PHONE.................................727 538-9917
Charles Carre, *President*
Patrick Dunn, *Vice Pres*
Simon Harnois, *Vice Pres*
Troy Herstine, *Opers Mgr*
Louise Talbot, *Purch Mgr*
EMP: 12 **EST:** 2017
SQ FT: 20,000
SALES (est): 3.5MM **Privately Held**
WEB: www.ldsteelusa.com
SIC: 3441 Fabricated structural metal

(G-7631)
L & S BAIT CO INC
Also Called: Mirrolure
1415 E Bay Dr (33771-1099)
PHONE.................................727 584-7691
William H Le Master, *President*
Jerry Spaulding, *Vice Pres*
Beverly Swata, *Manager*
EMP: 25 **EST:** 1937
SQ FT: 2,000
SALES (est): 1.9MM **Privately Held**
SIC: 3949 5941 Lures, fishing: artificial; sporting goods & bicycle shops

(G-7632)
LED TECHNOLOGIES INCORPORATED
Also Called: Revive Light Therapy
12821 Starkey Rd Ste 4900 (33773-1410)
PHONE.................................800 337-9565
Lloyd Nelson, *President*
Stefanie Longo, *Marketing Mgr*
Cheryl Bradford, *Manager*
John Moretz, *Director*
▲ **EMP:** 18 **EST:** 2004
SQ FT: 5,000
SALES (est): 15MM **Privately Held**
WEB: www.revivelighttherapy.com
SIC: 3841 Surgical & medical instruments

(G-7633)
LINVATEC CORPORATION (HQ)
Also Called: Conmed Linvatec
11311 Concept Blvd (33773-4908)
PHONE.................................727 392-6464
Curt Hartman, *CEO*
Joseph Darling, *President*
Pam Triplett, *President*
Gingerlee Haas, *General Mgr*
Ken Robinson, *General Mgr*
◆ **EMP:** 278 **EST:** 1963
SQ FT: 120,000
SALES (est): 160MM
SALES (corp-wide): 1B **Publicly Held**
SIC: 3842 3841 2821 Surgical appliances & supplies; surgical instruments & apparatus; elastomers, nonvulcanizable (plastics)
PA: Conmed Corporation
11311 Concept Blvd
Largo FL 33773
727 392-6464

(G-7634)
LITE CART CORP
1950 Lake Ave Se Unit A (33771-3719)
PHONE.................................954 659-7671
Henry A Stavinga, *President*
EMP: 8 **EST:** 1975
SQ FT: 16,000
SALES (est): 1.2MM **Privately Held**
WEB: www.litecart.com
SIC: 3537 Industrial trucks & tractors

(G-7635)
LUNDY ENTERPRISES INC
Also Called: Gun Drilling of Florida
6951 114th Ave (33773-5302)
PHONE.................................727 549-1292
David Lundy, *President*
Richard Lundy, *Vice Pres*
EMP: 11 **EST:** 1996
SQ FT: 7,500
SALES (est): 750K **Privately Held**
SIC: 3541 Machine tool replacement & repair parts, metal cutting types

(G-7636)
LUXURABLE KITCHEN & BATH LLC
11601 66th St (33773-5412)
PHONE.................................727 286-8927
Zhong Cao, *Principal*
EMP: 8 **EST:** 2015
SALES (est): 575.5K **Privately Held**
WEB: www.luxurablekitchen.com
SIC: 2434 Wood kitchen cabinets

(G-7637)
MADIERA SERVICE GROUP INC
9225 Ulmerton Rd Ste 318 (33771-3708)
PHONE.................................727 323-3800
Roy Armstrong, *President*
Armstrong Roy, *President*
Linda Armstrong, *Vice Pres*
EMP: 8 **EST:** 1990
SQ FT: 2,500
SALES (est): 2.5MM **Privately Held**
WEB: armstrong-elevator-company.sbcontract.com
SIC: 3534 Automobile elevators; stair elevators, motor powered

(G-7638)
MARTIN-WESTON CO
10860 76th Ct Ste B (33777-1409)
PHONE.................................727 545-8877
Jeff Hunter, *President*
EMP: 10 **EST:** 1989
SQ FT: 5,000
SALES (est): 421.4K **Privately Held**
SIC: 3841 Surgical & medical instruments

(G-7639)
MAVEN MEDICAL MFG INC
2250 Lake Ave Se (33771-3740)
PHONE.................................727 518-0555
Paul Vaughan, *President*
EMP: 39 **EST:** 1992
SQ FT: 12,700
SALES (est): 3.2MM **Privately Held**
WEB: www.maven-medical.com
SIC: 3841 3842 Surgical & medical instruments; surgical appliances & supplies

(G-7640)
MCCABINET INC (PA)
7273 112th Ave N (33773-3146)
PHONE..................................727 608-5929
Kevin McKenzie, *President*
Russell D Drevitson, *Vice Pres*
Eric McKenzie, *Vice Pres*
Brian McKenzie, *Marketing Staff*
Meaghan Gonzalez, *Manager*
EMP: 9 EST: 2003
SQ FT: 9,000
SALES (est): 2.5MM **Privately Held**
WEB: www.mccabinet.com
SIC: 2521 5712 Cabinets, office: wood;
cabinet work, custom

(G-7641)
MEDRX INC
1200 Starkey Rd Ste 105 (33771-3167)
PHONE..................................727 584-9600
Ronald Buck, *President*
Pete Covert, *Chairman*
EMP: 29 EST: 1994
SQ FT: 18,500
SALES (est): 5.1MM **Privately Held**
WEB: www.medrx-diagnostics.com
SIC: 3841 2836 Surgical & medical instru-
ments; veterinary biological products

(G-7642)
MEGA POWER
211 Violet St Ste 100 (33773)
PHONE..................................813 855-6664
▲ EMP: 13
SQ FT: 28,000
SALES (est): 2.2MM **Privately Held**
SIC: 2911 Petroleum Refiner

(G-7643)
MERRITT HOLLOW METAL INC
10822 124th Ave (33778-2716)
PHONE..................................727 656-4380
Randy Merritt, *Principal*
EMP: 8 EST: 2001
SALES (est): 543.3K **Privately Held**
SIC: 3499 Fabricated metal products

(G-7644)
MINUTEMAN PRESS
2475 E Bay Dr Ste A (33771-2472)
PHONE..................................727 535-3800
Corol Polakovich, *Principal*
EMP: 13 EST: 2008
SALES (est): 782.4K **Privately Held**
WEB: www.minutemanpress.com
SIC: 2752 Commercial printing, litho-
graphic

(G-7645)
MITEK INC
Also Called: USP Structural Connectors
11910 62nd St (33773-3705)
PHONE..................................727 536-7891
Jamie Walsh, *Technical Staff*
EMP: 44
SALES (corp-wide): 354.6B **Publicly
Held**
WEB: www.mii.com
SIC: 3469 Stamping metal for the trade
HQ: Mitek Inc.
16023 Swingley Ridge Rd
Chesterfield MO 63017

(G-7646)
MONT EVEREST INC (PA)
Also Called: Mont Krest
6795 114th Ave (33773-5419)
PHONE..................................727 209-0864
Kamal S Juneja, *President*
◆ EMP: 7 EST: 2004
SALES (est): 1.5MM **Privately Held**
WEB: www.montkrest.com
SIC: 3281 Marble, building: cut & shaped;
granite, cut & shaped

(G-7647)
MRO AEROSPACE INC
10530 72nd St Ste 701 (33771-1522)
PHONE..................................727 546-4820
Albert Machtinger, *President*
Sandi Cornett, *General Mgr*
Elaine Thomas, *Controller*
Sue Harrison, *Accounts Mgr*
Ron Zonenblik, *Sales Staff*
EMP: 14 EST: 2001
SQ FT: 10,100

SALES (est): 4.9MM **Privately Held**
WEB: www.mroaerospace.com
SIC: 3728 Aircraft parts & equipment

(G-7648)
MYTEK INDUSTRIES
11910 62nd St (33773-3705)
PHONE..................................727 536-7891
EMP: 15 EST: 2013
SALES (est): 1MM **Privately Held**
WEB: www.mitek-us.com
SIC: 3999 Manufacturing industries

(G-7649)
NATIONAL MOLDING LLC
11311 74th St (33773-5142)
PHONE..................................727 546-7470
John Johnson, *Branch Mgr*
EMP: 38 **Privately Held**
WEB: www.nationalmolding.com
SIC: 3089 Injection molded finished plastic
products
PA: National Molding, Llc
14427 Nw 60th Ave
Miami Lakes FL 33014

(G-7650)
NAUTICAL ACQUISITIONS CORP
Also Called: Nautical Structures
7301 114th Ave (33773-5104)
PHONE..................................727 541-6664
James Glen, *President*
Stuart Pavir, *Chairman*
Joseph Distefano, *Vice Pres*
Christopher Hamilton, *Engineer*
▼ EMP: 100 EST: 1999
SALES (est): 8.7MM
SALES (corp-wide): 46.9MM **Privately
Held**
WEB: www.nautical-structures.com
SIC: 3536 5551 5091 Cranes, overhead
traveling; boat dealers; boats, canoes,
watercrafts & equipment
PA: County Plastics Corp.
361 Neptune Ave
West Babylon NY 11704
631 422-8300

(G-7651)
**NAUTICAL STRUCTURES INDS
INC (PA)**
7301 114th Ave (33773-5104)
PHONE..................................727 541-6664
Robert E Bolline, *President*
Rick Thomas, *Vice Pres*
Scott Milford, *Prdtn Mgr*
Sunthorn Ingersoll, *Engineer*
John Prentice, *Engineer*
▲ EMP: 48 EST: 1987
SALES (est): 16.3MM **Privately Held**
WEB: www.nautical-structures.com
SIC: 3441 3443 3444 Fabricated struc-
tural metal; metal parts; sheet metalwork

(G-7652)
**OHANRAHAN CONSULTANTS
INC**
Also Called: Ohmac Chemical Group
6414 125th Ave (33773-3601)
P.O. Box 5301, Clearwater (33758-5301)
PHONE..................................727 531-3375
Edward J O'Hanrahan Jr, *President*
Sandra M Pisano, *Vice Pres*
Sandra Pisano, *Vice Pres*
Sandi Subrize, *Accountant*
Ed O'Hanrahan, *Manager*
EMP: 40 EST: 1960
SQ FT: 9,000
SALES (est): 3.4MM **Privately Held**
WEB: www.sunseal.com
SIC: 2841 5087 2842 Detergents, syn-
thetic organic or inorganic alkaline; car-
wash equipment & supplies; deodorants,
nonpersonal

(G-7653)
**OMEGA PROF BRICK PAVERS
INC**
3679 141st Ave Apt B (33771-4022)
PHONE..................................727 243-4659
Josafa S Alves, *Principal*
EMP: 7 EST: 2015
SALES (est): 233.3K **Privately Held**
SIC: 2951 Asphalt paving mixtures &
blocks

(G-7654)
ONICON INCORPORATED (HQ)
11451 Belcher Rd S (33773-5110)
PHONE..................................727 447-6140
Marvin J Feldman, *President*
Ian Peterson, *Buyer*
Parthiban Elavarasan, *Engineer*
Alec Nickerson, *Engineer*
Vince Stanziani, *Engineer*
◆ EMP: 42 EST: 1987
SALES (est): 49.9MM
SALES (corp-wide): 1.2B **Privately Held**
WEB: www.onicon.com
SIC: 3823 Industrial instrmnts msrmnt dis-
play/control process variable
PA: Harbour Group Ltd.
7733 Forsyth Blvd Fl 23
Saint Louis MO 63105
314 727-5550

(G-7655)
PARTI LINE INTERNATIONAL INC
Also Called: Ffutter Fetti
9219 133rd Ave Unit 1e (33773-1314)
PHONE..................................504 522-0300
Ronee Holmes, *CEO*
◆ EMP: 10 EST: 2007
SALES (est): 1.6MM **Privately Held**
WEB: www.flutterfetti.com
SIC: 2679 Confetti: made from purchased
material

(G-7656)
PCM AND S L PLOTA CO LLC
8016 118th Ave (33773-5044)
PHONE..................................727 547-6277
Larry Earl,
Mike Penhallegon,
EMP: 14 EST: 2008
SQ FT: 3,000
SALES (est): 326.2K **Privately Held**
SIC: 3845 3694 3559 3089 Medical
cleaning equipment, ultrasonic; genera-
tors, automotive & aircraft; automotive re-
lated machinery; automotive parts, plastic

(G-7657)
PHARMALINK INC
8285 Bryan Dairy Rd # 200 (33777-1350)
PHONE..................................800 257-3527
Thierry C Beckers, *President*
Patricia Fitzgerald, *Vice Pres*
Conley Hicks, *Sales Staff*
Henry Montes, *Sales Staff*
Adalberto Rivera, *Sales Staff*
EMP: 150 EST: 2000
SQ FT: 50,000
SALES (est): 25.3MM **Privately Held**
WEB: www.pharmalinkinc.com
SIC: 2834 Pharmaceutical preparations

(G-7658)
PHILLIP ROY INC
13200 106th Ave (33774-5500)
P.O. Box 130, Indian Rocks Beach (33785-
0130)
PHONE..................................727 593-2700
Ruth Bragman, *President*
Phil Tadol, *Vice Pres*
EMP: 6 EST: 1988
SQ FT: 5,000
SALES (est): 681.5K **Privately Held**
WEB: www.philliproy.com
SIC: 2731 Textbooks: publishing only, not
printed on site

(G-7659)
**PINELLAS CUSTOM CABINETS
INC**
8800 126th Ave (33773-1508)
PHONE..................................727 864-4263
William A Clore, *President*
Linda L Clore, *Vice Pres*
EMP: 8 EST: 1974
SQ FT: 6,000
SALES (est): 678.7K **Privately Held**
WEB: www.pinellascustomcabinets.com
SIC: 2434 2521 2511 Wood kitchen cabi-
nets; wood office furniture; wood house-
hold furniture

(G-7660)
PLASTIC SOLUTIONS INC
801 West Bay Dr Ste 308 (33770-3264)
PHONE..................................727 202-6815
EMP: 7 EST: 2016

SALES (est): 81.8K **Privately Held**
SIC: 3089 Injection molding of plastics

(G-7661)
PMC NORTH AMERICA INC
2060 34th Way (33771-3960)
PHONE..................................727 530-0714
EMP: 14
SQ FT: 12,000
SALES: 2MM **Privately Held**
SIC: 3566 3519 Mfg Speed Changers/Dri-
ves Mfg Internal Combustion Engines

(G-7662)
PRECISE TECHNOLOGIES INC
12395 75th St (33773-3033)
PHONE..................................727 535-5594
David Schwanke, *President*
Jim Lyngholm, *General Mgr*
Jeff Messick, *Vice Pres*
Tara M Schwanke, *Admin Sec*
EMP: 15 EST: 1999
SQ FT: 6,000
SALES (est): 4.1MM **Privately Held**
WEB: www.precise-largo.com
SIC: 3599 3769 3429 Machine shop, job-
bing & repair; guided missile & space ve-
hicle parts & auxiliary equipment;
manufactured hardware (general)

(G-7663)
PRESS EX INC
8601 Somerset Dr (33773-2719)
PHONE..................................727 532-4177
Janelle Gabay, *President*
▲ EMP: 17 EST: 2002
SQ FT: 42,000
SALES (est): 443K **Privately Held**
SIC: 2752 Commercial printing, offset

(G-7664)
**PULSAR PROCESS
MEASUREMENT INC**
11451 Belcher Rd S (33773-5110)
P.O. Box 5177, Niceville (32578-5177)
PHONE..................................850 279-4882
Jeffrey Roberts, *President*
Stephen Burton, *Admin Sec*
EMP: 6 EST: 2009
SALES (est): 2.1MM
SALES (corp-wide): 1.2B **Privately Held**
WEB: www.pulsarmeasurement.com
SIC: 3823 Industrial process measurement
equipment
HQ: Pulsar Process Measurement Limited
Cardinal Building
Malvern WORCS WR14

(G-7665)
Q E M INC
Also Called: Pharmacy Automation Systems
6513 116th Ave (33773-3735)
PHONE..................................727 545-8833
Norman Knoth, *President*
Linda Knoth, *Vice Pres*
▲ EMP: 32 EST: 1989
SQ FT: 7,000
SALES (est): 6.2MM **Privately Held**
WEB: www.qem.biz
SIC: 3599 Machine shop, jobbing & repair

(G-7666)
**QUALITY CMPNENTS TAMPA
BAY LLC**
6801 114th Ave (33773-5308)
PHONE..................................727 623-4909
Ivan Dotzinski,
◆ EMP: 9 EST: 1997
SQ FT: 10,000
SALES (est): 2MM **Privately Held**
SIC: 2452 Prefabricated wood buildings

(G-7667)
RAYOVAC CORP
7636 91st St (33777-4028)
PHONE..................................727 393-0966
EMP: 6
SALES (est): 641.5K **Privately Held**
SIC: 3692 5063 5531 Mfg Primary Batter-
ies Whol Electrical Equipment Ret
Auto/Home Supplies

(G-7668)
RAYTHEON COMPANY
7887 Bryan Dairy Rd # 110 (33777-1455)
P.O. Box 2920 (33779-2920)
PHONE..............................310 647-9438
Mitchell Lee, *Principal*
Hiram Legrand, *Principal*
Evenel Bonhomme, *Engineer*
Jason Greer, *Engineer*
Jim Holder, *Engineer*
EMP: 200
SALES (corp-wide): 64.3B **Publicly Held**
WEB: www.rtx.com
SIC: 3812 3674 3661 3651 Sonar systems & equipment; semiconductors & related devices; telephone & telegraph apparatus; household audio & video equipment
HQ: Raytheon Company
　　　870 Winter St
　　　Waltham MA 02451
　　　781 522-3000

(G-7669)
RAYTHEON COMPANY
7887 Bryan Dairy Rd # 110 (33777-1455)
P.O. Box 2920 (33779-2920)
PHONE..............................727 768-8468
Kyle Hoyt, *Engineer*
Luis Izquierdo, *Exec Dir*
Michael Campisi, *Director*
EMP: 27
SALES (corp-wide): 64.3B **Publicly Held**
WEB: www.rtx.com
SIC: 3812 3663 3651 Radar systems & equipment; sonar systems & equipment; radio & TV communications equipment; household audio & video equipment
HQ: Raytheon Company
　　　870 Winter St
　　　Waltham MA 02451
　　　781 522-3000

(G-7670)
REFTEC INTL SYSTEMS LLC
6950 112th Cir (33773-5209)
PHONE..............................727 290-9830
Jeff Moore, *President*
Tim Naylor, *VP Sales*
Greg D Veltman,
William G Buckles,
EMP: 12 EST: 2008
SQ FT: 9,000
SALES (est): 3MM **Privately Held**
WEB: www.reftec.com
SIC: 3585 Refrigeration & heating equipment

(G-7671)
REPCO EQUIPMENT LEASING INC
1550 Starkey Rd (33771-3116)
P.O. Box 607, Ozona (34660-0607)
PHONE..............................727 584-3329
Raymond E Purcell, *President*
EMP: 11 EST: 1994
SALES (est): 675.1K **Privately Held**
SIC: 2911 7353 Asphalt or asphaltic materials, made in refineries; heavy construction equipment rental

(G-7672)
ROUZBEH INC
Also Called: Frida's Bakery and Cafe
9700 Ulmerton Rd (33771-3603)
PHONE..............................727 587-7077
Jafar Alipour, *President*
Frida Alipour, *Treasurer*
Melissa Crapsey, *Manager*
EMP: 17 EST: 1991
SQ FT: 5,955
SALES (est): 1.2MM **Privately Held**
WEB: www.fridascafe.com
SIC: 2051 Bakery: wholesale or wholesale/retail combined

(G-7673)
ROYAL CANES
12399 Belcher Rd S # 160 (33773-3053)
PHONE..............................727 474-0792
EMP: 7 EST: 2017
SALES (est): 99.8K **Privately Held**
WEB: www.royalcanes.com
SIC: 3999 Manufacturing industries

(G-7674)
RYTEX INDUSTRIES INC
12855 Belcher Rd S (33773-1657)
PHONE..............................727 557-7450
Patrick J McBride, *Principal*
EMP: 15 EST: 2013
SQ FT: 10,000
SALES (est): 508.6K **Privately Held**
WEB: www.rytexindustries.com
SIC: 3999 Barber & beauty shop equipment

(G-7675)
SAINT-GOBAIN PRFMCE PLAS CORP
Also Called: Saint Gobain
8615 126th Ave Ste 650 (33773-1510)
PHONE..............................727 373-1299
EMP: 98
SALES (corp-wide): 340.6MM **Privately Held**
WEB: www.sheergard.com
SIC: 3089 Thermoformed finished plastic products
HQ: Saint-Gobain Performance Plastics Corporation
　　　31500 Solon Rd
　　　Solon OH 44139
　　　440 836-6900

(G-7676)
SCHOONER PRINTS INC
8632 115th Ave (33773-4901)
PHONE..............................727 397-8572
Patrick Bluett, *President*
Chris Arrison,
◆ EMP: 52 EST: 1979
SQ FT: 70,000
SALES (est): 6.6MM **Privately Held**
WEB: www.schoonerprints.com
SIC: 2759 2789 2221 Screen printing; bookbinding & related work; upholstery, tapestry & wall covering fabrics; wall covering fabrics, manmade fiber & silk

(G-7677)
SCOTT-DOUGLAS DESIGN INC
6275 147th Ave (33770)
PHONE..............................727 535-7900
Scott Garrison, *President*
Page Garrison, *Vice Pres*
EMP: 6 EST: 1975
SALES (est): 450.2K **Privately Held**
WEB: www.scott-douglasdesign.com
SIC: 2431 Staircases & stairs, wood

(G-7678)
SEA LINK HOLDINGS LLC
13151 66th St (33773-1812)
PHONE..............................727 523-8660
Tara Dunfield, *VP Sls/Mktg*
Victor Saab, *Program Mgr*
Seth Weisberg, *Director*
EMP: 8 EST: 2018
SALES (est): 186.5K **Privately Held**
WEB: www.sealinkinternational.com
SIC: 3089 Automotive parts, plastic

(G-7679)
SEA LINK INTERNATIONAL IRB INC (PA)
13151 66th St (33773-1812)
PHONE..............................727 523-8660
Eric Showalter, *President*
Susan McFarland, *Vice Pres*
John Newton, *CFO*
Victor Saab, *Program Mgr*
Lisa Beegles, *Admin Asst*
◆ EMP: 17 EST: 1992
SQ FT: 5,300
SALES (est): 49.3MM **Privately Held**
WEB: www.sealinkinternational.com
SIC: 3647 3172 Automotive lighting fixtures; sewing cases

(G-7680)
SEA SYSTEMS GROUP INC
10631 Whittington Ct (33773-1870)
PHONE..............................434 374-9553
Barbara McKinney, *President*
Richard McKinney, *Treasurer*
EMP: 9 EST: 1995
SALES (est): 570.1K **Privately Held**
SIC: 3714 Motor vehicle parts & accessories

(G-7681)
SF&KF ENTERPRISES LLC
13801 Walsingham Rd Ste B (33774-3237)
PHONE..............................727 614-9902
Calvin Smith, *Branch Mgr*
EMP: 19
SALES (corp-wide): 145K **Privately Held**
SIC: 3651 Household audio & video equipment
PA: Sf&Kf Enterprises Llc
　　　5501 Rttlsnake Hmmock Rd
　　　Naples FL 34113
　　　239 774-7073

(G-7682)
SIGLO HOLDINGS LLC
8285 Bryan Dairy Rd (33777-1350)
PHONE..............................727 369-5220
EMP: 175
SALES (est): 12.3MM **Privately Held**
SIC: 3648 Mfg Lighting Equipment

(G-7683)
SIGNS NOW
12350 Belcher Rd S 14a (33773-3009)
PHONE..............................727 524-8500
Travis R Masters, *President*
Kris Kay, *Vice Pres*
EMP: 10 EST: 1991
SQ FT: 3,000
SALES (est): 709.4K **Privately Held**
WEB: www.signsnow.com
SIC: 3993 Signs & advertising specialties

(G-7684)
SMARTSAT INC
8222 118th Ave Ste 600 (33773-5054)
PHONE..............................727 535-6880
David Akers, *President*
Heidi L Akers, *Vice Pres*
Heidi Akers, *CFO*
Richard Barnes, *CIO*
▼ EMP: 15 EST: 1996
SQ FT: 5,000
SALES (est): 2.2MM **Privately Held**
WEB: www.smartsat.com
SIC: 3825 8711 Instruments to measure electricity; electrical or electronic engineering

(G-7685)
SMOKERSVAPORCOM INCORPORATED
1129 Woodbrook Dr (33770-1625)
PHONE..............................727 258-4942
Barry D Gray, *Principal*
EMP: 7 EST: 2011
SALES (est): 122.3K **Privately Held**
SIC: 3911 Cigar & cigarette accessories

(G-7686)
SODA SERVICE OF FLORIDA LLC
14184 Mark Dr (33774-5112)
PHONE..............................727 595-7632
Lisa A Bialaski, *Manager*
EMP: 6 EST: 2006
SALES (est): 928.2K **Privately Held**
WEB: www.floridasodaservice.com
SIC: 3585 Refrigeration & heating equipment

(G-7687)
SOLIDAR EXPRESS COATINGS LLC
12912 91st St N (33773-1313)
PHONE..............................727 585-2192
Daniel Plante, *President*
Abe Azar, *Vice Pres*
Zach Thacker, *Technician*
▲ EMP: 8 EST: 2009
SALES (est): 949.1K **Privately Held**
WEB: www.solidarexpress.com
SIC: 3851 Ophthalmic goods

(G-7688)
SOUTHWEST FLORIDA REGIONAL
Also Called: H C A
12901 Starkey Rd (33773-1435)
PHONE..............................615 344-9551
Jack Bovinder, *President*
John Battista, *Principal*
Gregory James, *Principal*
Ayaz Virji, *Principal*

EMP: 169 EST: 2006
SALES (est): 30.6MM **Privately Held**
SIC: 3842 6035 Ligatures, medical; savings institutions, federally chartered

(G-7689)
SOUTHWIRE COMPANY LLC
Also Called: Technology RES A Southwire Co
11211 69th St (33773-5504)
PHONE..............................727 535-0572
EMP: 31 EST: 2014
SALES (est): 8.2MM **Privately Held**
SIC: 3613 Power circuit breakers

(G-7690)
ST MARY PHARMACY LLC
Also Called: Good Neighbor Pharmacy
1290 West Bay Dr (33770-2204)
PHONE..............................727 585-1333
Albert Shaker,
John Shaker,
Marko Shaker,
EMP: 11 EST: 2009
SALES (est): 1MM **Privately Held**
WEB: www.mygnp.com
SIC: 2834 5912 Pharmaceutical preparations; drug stores

(G-7691)
STRAIGHT POLARITY WELDING INC
Also Called: Honeywell Authorized Dealer
12855 Belcher Rd S Ste 19 (33773-1638)
PHONE..............................727 530-7224
EMP: 5
SQ FT: 3,500
SALES (est): 350K **Privately Held**
SIC: 7692 Welding Shop

(G-7692)
SUN COAST PAPER & ENVELOPE INC
Also Called: Gulf Shore Printing
2050 Tall Pines Dr Ste A (33771-3813)
PHONE..............................727 545-9566
Elaine M Lewis, *President*
Lori A Wardell, *Corp Secy*
Denise Vanmeter, *Manager*
EMP: 14 EST: 1986
SQ FT: 32,000
SALES (est): 426.9K **Privately Held**
SIC: 2754 Envelopes: gravure printing

(G-7693)
SUNCOAST MOLDERS INC
Also Called: S M I
10760 76th Ct (33777-1440)
PHONE..............................727 546-0041
William E Simmers, *President*
EMP: 13 EST: 1990
SQ FT: 20,000
SALES (est): 2.3MM **Privately Held**
SIC: 3089 Injection molding of plastics

(G-7694)
SUNSHINE FILTERS PINELLAS INC
12415 73rd Ct (33773-3047)
PHONE..............................727 530-3884
Fred Cooklin, *President*
Horace Baker, *Vice Pres*
Carmine Cardone, *Vice Pres*
EMP: 21 EST: 1985
SQ FT: 21,000
SALES (est): 3.8MM **Privately Held**
WEB: www.sunshinefilters.com
SIC: 3599 3564 Air intake filters, internal combustion engine, except auto; blowers & fans

(G-7695)
THAT SOFTWARE GUY INC
12825 Pineforest Way W (33773-1723)
PHONE..............................727 533-8109
Scott C Wilson, *Principal*
EMP: 5 EST: 2003
SALES (est): 350.9K **Privately Held**
WEB: www.thatsoftwareguy.com
SIC: 7372 Prepackaged software

(G-7696)
TIMBERLAND DOOR LLC
12555 Entp Blvd Ste 102 (33773)
PHONE..............................727 539-8600
Gregory Reynolds, *Opers Staff*

▲ = Import ▼=Export
◆ =Import/Export

Todd Mahon, *Sales Staff*
Keith Norder,
Sal Alfaqeer, *Analyst*
EMP: 30 **EST:** 2006
SQ FT: 46,000
SALES (est): 8MM **Privately Held**
WEB: www.timberlanddoor.com
SIC: 2431 Doors & door parts & trim, wood

(G-7697)
TROLLEY BOATS
9470 Ulmerton Rd Ste 6b (33771-3700)
PHONE................................727 588-1100
David Beagle, *Manager*
▲ **EMP:** 8 **EST:** 2014
SALES (est): 264K **Privately Held**
WEB: www.trolleyboats.net
SIC: 3732 Boat building & repairing

(G-7698)
TRY WINE INC
11812 143rd St (33774-2948)
PHONE................................727 898-9463
Oliver R Motschmann, *Principal*
EMP: 7 **EST:** 2013
SALES (est): 95.2K **Privately Held**
SIC: 2084 Wines, brandy & brandy spirits

(G-7699)
TTC-THE TRADING COMPANY INC (PA)
Also Called: Trading Company, The
2062 20th Ave Se (33771-3846)
PHONE................................503 982-0880
Helena Vanderwey, *President*
Patience Bernstein, *Accounts Exec*
▲ **EMP:** 22 **EST:** 2004
SALES (est): 4.6MM **Privately Held**
SIC: 3599 Machine & other job shop work

(G-7700)
TUBOS INC
718 4th Ave Ne (33770-5020)
PHONE................................727 504-0633
Kevin M Morris, *Vice Pres*
EMP: 8 **EST:** 2008
SALES (est): 173.3K **Privately Held**
WEB: www.tubos.biz
SIC: 3296 Mineral wool

(G-7701)
UNIVERSAL PRECISION INDS INC
1876 Lake Ave Se Ste A (33771-3799)
PHONE................................727 581-7097
John Sessa, *President*
EMP: 6 **EST:** 1997
SQ FT: 4,000
SALES (est): 777K **Privately Held**
WEB: www.upi-largo.com
SIC: 3625 Motor controls, electric

(G-7702)
VGI MEDICAL LLC
Also Called: V G I
11651 87th St (33774-4917)
PHONE................................727 565-1235
Dan Grayson, *CEO*
Ryne Willard, *Sales Staff*
Tony Caputo, *Manager*
Scott Ely, *Manager*
Lori Longo, *Manager*
EMP: 12 **EST:** 2007
SALES (est): 1.4MM **Privately Held**
WEB: www.vgimedical.com
SIC: 3841 Surgical & medical instruments

(G-7703)
VILLAGE SCRIBE PRINTING CO
Also Called: Monthly Media
1548 Shirley Pl (33770-2218)
PHONE................................727 585-7388
Kurt E Beard, *President*
Catherine L Beard, *Admin Sec*
EMP: 10 **EST:** 1975
SQ FT: 1,400
SALES (est): 992K **Privately Held**
WEB: www.monthly-media.com
SIC: 2752 Commercial printing, offset; publication printing, lithographic

(G-7704)
VISION ENGINEERING LABS
Also Called: Amglo Halogen
8787 Enterprise Blvd (33773-2702)
PHONE................................727 812-2000
Larry A Kerchenfaut, *Principal*
EMP: 43
SALES (corp-wide): 273K **Privately Held**
WEB: www.amglo.com
SIC: 3641 Electric lamps
PA: Vision Engineering Laboratories, Inc
215 Gateway Rd
Bensenville IL 60106
630 350-9470

(G-7705)
VISION ENGINEERING LABS
Also Called: Amglo Kemlite Laboratories
8787 Enterprise Blvd (33773-2702)
PHONE................................727 812-2035
James Hyland, *President*
Isabela Veigel, *Vice Pres*
Calvin Zhu, *CFO*
Larry A Kerchenfaut, *Treasurer*
Cathy De Carli, *Sales Associate*
▲ **EMP:** 53 **EST:** 1985
SQ FT: 3,000
SALES (est): 8.8MM
SALES (corp-wide): 33.3MM **Privately Held**
WEB: www.amglo.com
SIC: 3677 3679 3646 Electronic transformers; power supplies, all types: static; commercial indusl & institutional electric lighting fixtures
PA: Amglo Kemlite Laboratories, Inc.
215 Gateway Rd
Bensenville IL 60106
630 238-3031

(G-7706)
VISTAPHARM INC
7265 Ulmerton Rd (33771-4809)
PHONE................................727 530-1633
Judith Rodriguez, *Vice Pres*
Francisco Cosme, *Project Mgr*
Marcos Rosado, *QA Dir*
Alex Ramirez, *Engineer*
Juan Rubio, *Senior Engr*
EMP: 25
SQ FT: 34,016
SALES (corp-wide): 98.2MM **Privately Held**
WEB: www.vistapharm.com
HQ: Vistapharm, Llc
20 Waterview Blvd Ste 303
Parsippany NJ 07054
908 376-1622

(G-7707)
VISTAPHARM INC
13707 66th St (33771-4902)
PHONE................................727 530-1633
Erin Casto, *Finance*
Brett Johns, *Manager*
Nilied Baez, *Consultant*
Richard Barnes, *CIO*
Fernando Montini, *Director*
EMP: 20
SQ FT: 55,220
SALES (corp-wide): 98.2MM **Privately Held**
WEB: www.vistapharm.com
SIC: 2834 2833 Proprietary drug products; drugs & herbs: grading, grinding & milling
HQ: Vistapharm, Llc
20 Waterview Blvd Ste 303
Parsippany NJ 07054
908 376-1622

(G-7708)
WEBB-MASON INC
12397 Belcher Rd S # 240 (33773-3054)
PHONE................................727 531-1112
Mark Smith, *Vice Pres*
Chris Berexa, *Vice Pres*
EMP: 7 **Privately Held**
WEB: www.webbmason.com
SIC: 2752 Commercial printing, offset; business form & card printing, lithographic
PA: Webb-Mason, Inc.
10830 Gilroy Rd
Hunt Valley MD 21031

(G-7709)
WINDWARD COMMUNICATIONS INC
2401 West Bay Dr Ste 414 (33770-1941)
P.O. Box 1750 (33779-1750)
PHONE................................727 584-7191
William Vanbeuning, *President*
Andria Vanbeuning, *General Mgr*
EMP: 8 **EST:** 1989
SQ FT: 1,500
SALES (est): 702.7K **Privately Held**
SIC: 2741 Miscellaneous publishing

(G-7710)
ZEUS INDUSTRIES
12545 Creekside Dr (33773-2708)
PHONE................................727 530-4373
Franco Fraine, *Manager*
EMP: 8 **EST:** 2002
SALES (est): 185.8K **Privately Held**
SIC: 3089 Plastics products

Laud By Sea
Broward County

(G-7711)
REFLECTIONS BEACH&RESORTWEAR
104 Commercial Blvd (33308-3681)
PHONE................................954 776-1230
Elli Mordoch Sr, *Principal*
EMP: 7 **EST:** 2010
SALES (est): 92.6K **Privately Held**
SIC: 2253 Bathing suits & swimwear, knit

Lauderdale Lakes
Broward County

(G-7712)
DELAROSA REAL FOODS LLC
Also Called: De La Rosa
2648 Nw 31st Ave (33311-2708)
PHONE................................718 333-0333
EMP: 54
SALES (est): 4MM **Privately Held**
SIC: 2032 2099 5411 Mfg Canned Specialties Mfg Food Preparations Ret Groceries

(G-7713)
DRINKABLE AIR INC
2944 Nw 27th St Bldg 14 (33311-2039)
PHONE................................954 533-6415
Steven J Kairis, *President*
Jeff Szur, *Project Mgr*
Reece Carvalho, *Production*
Japheth Grayson, *Sales Dir*
Joseph Mule, *Mktg Dir*
▲ **EMP:** 16 **EST:** 2010
SQ FT: 15,000
SALES (est): 2.3MM **Privately Held**
WEB: www.drinkableair.tech
SIC: 3585 Refrigeration & heating equipment

(G-7714)
DSAS AIR INC
4509 Nw 39th St (33319-4759)
PHONE................................954 673-5385
Daniel R Silburn, *Principal*
EMP: 9 **EST:** 2011
SALES (est): 2.4MM **Privately Held**
WEB: www.dsasair.com
SIC: 3822 Air conditioning & refrigeration controls

(G-7715)
GSG GROUP INC
Also Called: Paradise Embroidery
2918 Nw 28th St (33311-2028)
P.O. Box 16576, Fort Lauderdale (33318-6576)
PHONE................................954 733-8219
Shamir Yaron, *President*
Zvika Mayrom, *Corp Secy*
Ronen Givon, *Vice Pres*
EMP: 30 **EST:** 1995
SQ FT: 10,000
SALES (est): 2.5MM **Privately Held**
SIC: 2339 Women's & misses' athletic clothing & sportswear

(G-7716)
HUGH ROBINSON INC
2718 Nw 31st Ave (33311-2034)
P.O. Box 5543, Fort Lauderdale (33310-5543)
PHONE................................954 484-0660
John S Robinson, *President*
Richard Robinson, *Vice Pres*
Thomas Robinson, *Vice Pres*
EMP: 6 **EST:** 1975
SQ FT: 13,000
SALES (est): 879.2K **Privately Held**
WEB: www.robinsonwalls.com
SIC: 2541 Partitions for floor attachment, prefabricated: wood

(G-7717)
KAMTEX USA INCORPORATED
2916 Nw 28th St (33311-2028)
PHONE................................954 733-1044
▲ **EMP:** 8 **EST:** 2007
SALES (est): 1MM **Privately Held**
SIC: 2331 2341 2342 5137 Mfg Women/Misses Blouses Mfg Women/Miss Underwear Mfg Bra/Girdles Whol Women/Child Clothng

(G-7718)
MOBILE 1 INC
3680 W Oakland Park Blvd (33311-1148)
PHONE................................954 283-8100
Mustafa Natour, *Principal*
EMP: 9 **EST:** 2010
SALES (est): 187.8K **Privately Held**
SIC: 2911 Oils, lubricating

(G-7719)
SHORR ENTERPRISES INC
Also Called: New Design Furniture Mfg
3033 Nw 28th St (33311-2029)
PHONE................................954 733-9840
Linda Shorr, *President*
EMP: 16 **EST:** 2001
SQ FT: 12,000
SALES (est): 1.5MM **Privately Held**
SIC: 3429 7641 Furniture builders' & other household hardware; reupholstery

(G-7720)
STITCH INK INC
2684 Nw 31st Ave (33311-2708)
PHONE................................954 203-0868
Maria V Laverde Alvarez, *Principal*
EMP: 8 **EST:** 2017
SALES (est): 259.6K **Privately Held**
SIC: 2395 Embroidery & art needlework

(G-7721)
TROPIC SHIELD INC
Also Called: Exotic Interiors
3031 Nw 28th St (33311-2029)
PHONE................................954 731-5553
William Holiday, *President*
Jeffrey Holiday, *Vice Pres*
Michael Holiday, *Vice Pres*
EMP: 16 **EST:** 1977
SQ FT: 10,000
SALES (est): 481.9K **Privately Held**
SIC: 3442 5211 2591 5719 Shutters, door or window: metal; windows, storm: wood or metal; blinds vertical; vertical blinds; carpets; home improvement & renovation contractor agency

(G-7722)
WEST HARBOUR WOODWORKING LLC
2543 Nw 49th Ave Apt 203 (33313-3347)
PHONE................................954 822-7543
Vaughan McKenzie, *Principal*
EMP: 8 **EST:** 2013
SALES (est): 270.2K **Privately Held**
WEB: www.westharbourwoodworking.com
SIC: 2431 Millwork

Lauderhill
Broward County

(G-7723)
24HOUR PRINTING INC
7431 Nw 57th St (33319-2101)
PHONE................................954 247-9575
EMP: 9 **EST:** 2018

SALES (est): 349K **Privately Held**
SIC: 2752 Commercial printing, offset

(G-7724)
ADD-V LLC
Also Called: Sugart
1801 Nw 38th Ave Ste H (33311-4144)
PHONE....................305 496-2445
Valeria Garavaglia, *Mng Member*
Julian Baluk,
EMP: 5 EST: 2015
SQ FT: 2,000
SALES (est): 500K **Privately Held**
SIC: 2061 Dry cane sugar products, except refining

(G-7725)
ALLURE SHADES INC
3714 Nw 16th St (33311-4132)
PHONE....................954 543-6259
Mark Vanwettering, *President*
Sofia V Sanchez, *Vice Pres*
▲ EMP: 12 EST: 2008
SALES (est): 1.5MM **Privately Held**
WEB: www.allureshadesinc.com
SIC: 3645 Lamp & light shades

(G-7726)
BIG STAR SYSTEMS LLC
2061 Nw 47th Ter Apt 200 (33313-4159)
PHONE....................954 243-7209
Rebecca Castanon,
EMP: 5 EST: 2017
SALES (est): 300K **Privately Held**
WEB: www.bigstarsystems.com
SIC: 7372 7389 Prepackaged software; business services

(G-7727)
BLACKSTONE LEGAL SUPPLIES INC (PA)
Also Called: Blackstone Legal Supply
3732 Nw 16th St (33311-4148)
PHONE....................305 945-3450
Leslie Heyman, *President*
EMP: 10 EST: 1978
SALES (est): 971.1K **Privately Held**
WEB: www.blackstonelegal.com
SIC: 2752 2761 Commercial printing, offset; manifold business forms

(G-7728)
COLOR TOUCH INC
3701 Nw 16th St (33311-4135)
PHONE....................954 444-1999
Nathan Kurliker, *President*
Moshe Kurliker, *Vice Pres*
EMP: 10 EST: 1997
SQ FT: 15,000
SALES (est): 3MM **Privately Held**
SIC: 2253 Dyeing & finishing knit outerwear, excl. hosiery & glove

(G-7729)
CREATIVE BIZ CENTER INC
7860 W Commercial Blvd (33351-4324)
PHONE....................954 918-7322
Apolonio I Cedeno, *Vice Pres*
EMP: 7 EST: 2016
SALES (est): 220.8K **Privately Held**
SIC: 2752 Commercial printing, lithographic

(G-7730)
DAILY THERAPY SERVICES INC
8040 Nw 54th St (33351-5069)
PHONE....................954 649-3620
Albert J Daley, *Principal*
EMP: 9 EST: 2008
SALES (est): 96.2K **Privately Held**
SIC: 2711 Newspapers, publishing & printing

(G-7731)
FASSMER SERVICE AMERICA LLC (HQ)
3650 Nw 15th St (33311-4133)
PHONE....................305 557-8875
Maija Marzougui, *Opers Mgr*
Kathy Villalba, *Opers Mgr*
Vincent Francis, *Engineer*
Tom Donnangelo, *Senior Engr*
Daniel Ramirez, *Senior Engr*
◆ EMP: 21 EST: 2008

SALES (est): 10MM
SALES (corp-wide): 262.4MM **Privately Held**
WEB: www.fassmerusa.com
SIC: 3731 Shipbuilding & repairing
PA: Gebr. Fassmer Ag
Industriestr. 2
Berne NI 27804
440 694-20

(G-7732)
FOOT PRINT TO SCCESS CLBHUSE I
3521 W Broward Blvd # 10 (33312-1048)
P.O. Box 221261, West Palm Beach (33422-1261)
PHONE....................954 657-8010
Barbara Harmon, *President*
EMP: 10 EST: 2010
SQ FT: 5,000
SALES (est): 726.5K **Privately Held**
SIC: 2752 Commercial printing, lithographic

(G-7733)
GRAPHIC DIFFERENCE INC A
Also Called: Image360 - Lauderhill
7362 W Commercial Blvd (33319-2128)
PHONE....................954 748-6990
Brian Meister, *President*
Susan Meister, *Vice Pres*
▼ EMP: 12 EST: 2004
SQ FT: 4,000
SALES (est): 1.9MM **Privately Held**
SIC: 3993 Signs & advertising specialties

(G-7734)
KEE KREATIVE LLC
3405 Nw 14th Ct (33311-8447)
PHONE....................954 931-2579
Kurtis Eiben, *Principal*
EMP: 7 EST: 2016
SALES (est): 316.5K **Privately Held**
SIC: 2752 Commercial printing, lithographic

(G-7735)
MACIAS GABIONS INC
3801 Environ Blvd Apt 519 (33319-4292)
PHONE....................850 910-8000
Jorge Macias, *President*
Olga L Quintero, *Vice Pres*
EMP: 7 EST: 2013
SALES (est): 79.7K **Privately Held**
SIC: 3315 Steel wire & related products

(G-7736)
MIRANDAS WOODCRAFT LLC
3764 Nw 16th St (33311-4132)
PHONE....................954 306-3568
EMP: 6
SALES (est): 382.1K **Privately Held**
SIC: 2491 1751 Wood Preserving Carpentry Contractor

(G-7737)
OPIF- OUR PLSTIC IS FNTSTIC
698 1/2 Nw 16 Stunits E F (33311)
PHONE....................954 636-4228
Esther Tepper Barak, *Mng Member*
Zevi Barak,
EMP: 6 EST: 2012
SALES (est): 367.2K **Privately Held**
SIC: 3089 Plastic containers, except foam

(G-7738)
P S RESEARCH CORP
3702 Nw 16th St (33311-4132)
PHONE....................954 558-8727
Gary Mandel, *President*
Dale Cormier, *Vice Pres*
Dean Koslofsky, *Vice Pres*
Mel Mandel, *Shareholder*
EMP: 8 EST: 1989
SQ FT: 5,000
SALES (est): 384K **Privately Held**
SIC: 2819 2899 2891 2851 Industrial inorganic chemicals; chemical preparations; adhesives & sealants; paints & allied products

(G-7739)
RAYS MOBILE SERVICE LLC
4846 N University Dr (33351-4510)
PHONE....................754 204-5816
Stacey Mills, *Mng Member*

EMP: 5 EST: 2017
SALES (est): 304.9K **Privately Held**
SIC: 3463 Mechanical power transmission forgings, nonferrous

(G-7740)
SESAME FLYERS OF SOUTH FLORIDA
6781 Nw 45th St (33319-4073)
PHONE....................954 274-7233
Andy Ansola, *CFO*
EMP: 5 EST: 2001
SALES (est): 317.2K **Privately Held**
SIC: 1442 Construction sand & gravel

(G-7741)
SHEAR ELEMENTS LLC
8741 Nw 50th St (33351-5403)
PHONE....................954 678-8528
Tamara Green-Smith, *Principal*
EMP: 6 EST: 2018
SALES (est): 518.9K **Privately Held**
WEB: www.shearelements.org
SIC: 2819 Industrial inorganic chemicals

(G-7742)
SPARKLES AND SUSPENDERS FL
5405 Nw 67th Ave (33319-7298)
PHONE....................754 701-4528
Samuel Y Andrusier, *Principal*
EMP: 6 EST: 2018
SALES (est): 359K **Privately Held**
WEB: www.sparklesandsuspenders.com
SIC: 2389 Suspenders

(G-7743)
STONE SYSTEMS SOUTH FLA LLC
3501 Nw 16th St (33311-4157)
PHONE....................954 584-4058
Jesus Garcia, *Manager*
Kurt Thiemer,
▼ EMP: 13 EST: 2006
SQ FT: 4,000
SALES (est): 2.6MM **Privately Held**
WEB: www.silestone.com
SIC: 1411 Dimension stone

(G-7744)
THALERS PRINTING CENTER INC
Also Called: Thaler's Printing Cetner
4970 N University Dr (33351-5748)
PHONE....................954 741-6522
Gary Thaler, *President*
Morton Thaler, *Trustee*
Warren Thaler, *Vice Pres*
EMP: 8 EST: 1979
SQ FT: 3,700
SALES (est): 729.1K **Privately Held**
SIC: 2752 5943 2791 2789 Commercial printing, offset; office forms & supplies; typesetting; bookbinding & related work

Lawtey
Bradford County

(G-7745)
CRAWFORDS CUSTOM WOODWORK
21535 Us Highway 301 N (32058-4237)
PHONE....................904 782-1375
John Crawford, *Principal*
EMP: 8 EST: 2017
SALES (est): 59.5K **Privately Held**
WEB:
www.crawfordscustomwoodworks.com
SIC: 2431 Millwork

(G-7746)
PROFESSIONAL COATING SYSTEMS
2187 Nw 247th St (32058-3106)
PHONE....................904 477-7138
William Price, *Principal*
Morgan Price, *Principal*
EMP: 6 EST: 2019
SALES (est): 527.8K **Privately Held**
SIC: 3731 Shipbuilding & repairing

(G-7747)
TATUM BROTHERS LUMBER CO INC
22796 Nw County Road 200a (32058-4212)
P.O. Box A (32058-0701)
PHONE....................904 782-3690
Charles W Tatum, *President*
John Tatum, *Vice Pres*
Thomas W Tatum Jr, *Vice Pres*
Thomas W Tatum III, *Vice Pres*
Linda Tatum, *Treasurer*
EMP: 35 EST: 1963
SQ FT: 1,000
SALES (est): 1.1MM **Privately Held**
SIC: 2421 Sawdust & shavings

Lecanto
Citrus County

(G-7748)
BRUCE COMPONENT SYSTEMS INC
3409 W Pennington Ct (34461-8854)
P.O. Box 730 (34460-0730)
PHONE....................352 628-0522
Ret Bruce, *President*
EMP: 17 EST: 1985
SALES (est): 4.5MM **Privately Held**
SIC: 2439 Trusses, wooden roof

(G-7749)
CAVALLO ESTATE WINERY LLC
8123 S Lecanto Hwy (34461-9072)
PHONE....................352 500-9463
Katie Wright, *COO*
Philip J Bomhoff Jr, *Mng Member*
Pien Bomhoff,
EMP: 7 EST: 2016
SALES (est): 446.2K **Privately Held**
WEB: www.cavalloestatewinery.com
SIC: 2084 7389 Wines;

(G-7750)
CEMEX CNSTR MTLS FLA LLC
Also Called: Lecanto Ready Mix Con Plant
2975 S Lecanto Hwy (34461-9022)
PHONE....................352 746-0136
Jerry Hays, *Branch Mgr*
EMP: 7 **Privately Held**
SIC: 3273 Ready-mixed concrete
HQ: Cemex Construction Materials Florida, Llc
1501 Belvedere Rd
West Palm Beach FL 33406

(G-7751)
DMA CABINETS INC
1653b W Gulf To Lake Hwy (34461-7723)
PHONE....................352 249-8147
David J Beccia, *Principal*
EMP: 9 EST: 2016
SALES (est): 283.3K **Privately Held**
WEB: dma-cabinets-inc.business.site
SIC: 2434 Wood kitchen cabinets

(G-7752)
GILMANS CUSTOM FURN & CABINETS
Also Called: Gilman's Cabinets
4625 W Homosassa Trl (34461-9107)
PHONE....................352 746-3532
Lloyd F Gilman, *President*
Patricia Gilman, *Corp Secy*
EMP: 10 EST: 1973
SQ FT: 7,400
SALES (est): 732K **Privately Held**
WEB: www.gilmanscabinets.com
SIC: 2511 2521 2434 Wood household furniture; wood office furniture; wood kitchen cabinets

(G-7753)
JWN FAMILY PARTNERS LP LTD
Also Called: All-Bright Signs
6198 S Lecanto Hwy (34461-9057)
PHONE....................352 628-4910
John W Nemeth, *Partner*
John T Nemeth, *Partner*
Judy Nemeth, *Partner*
EMP: 5 EST: 1983
SALES (est): 410K **Privately Held**
SIC: 3993 Signs & advertising specialties

▲ = Import ▼=Export
◆ =Import/Export

(G-7754)
KCI
24 S Ponder Ave (34461-8030)
PHONE..................................352 572-2873
EMP: 9 **EST:** 2014
SALES (est): 129.6K **Privately Held**
WEB: www.kci.com
SIC: 2599 Hospital beds

Lee
Madison County

(G-7755)
C F WEBB AND SONS LOGGING LLC
625 Se Old Logging Trl (32059-6264)
PHONE..................................850 971-5565
Coye Webb, *Administration*
EMP: 10 **EST:** 2014
SALES (est): 570.1K **Privately Held**
SIC: 2411 Logging camps & contractors

Leesburg
Lake County

(G-7756)
AERO FUEL LLC
9595 Silver Lake Dr (34788-3406)
PHONE..................................352 728-2018
Lester A Coggins Jr, *Principal*
EMP: 7 **EST:** 2009
SALES (est): 160.4K **Privately Held**
WEB: www.umatillaaero.com
SIC: 2869 Fuels

(G-7757)
AKERS MEDIA GROUP INC
108 S 5th St Ste 201 (34748-5856)
P.O. Box 490088 (34749-0088)
PHONE..................................352 787-4112
Michael Akers, *President*
Debra Hodges, *Editor*
Doug Akers, *Vice Pres*
Tim McRae, *Vice Pres*
Judi Murphy, *Accounts Mgr*
EMP: 31 **EST:** 2008
SALES (est): 5.4MM **Privately Held**
WEB: www.akersmediagroup.com
SIC: 2721 Magazines: publishing & printing

(G-7758)
AMTEX-NMS HOLDINGS INC (PA)
2500 Industrial St (34748-3609)
PHONE..................................352 728-2930
Jim Ginas, *President*
David Meyer, *Chairman*
Les Berczy, *COO*
EMP: 13 **EST:** 1999
SALES (est): 88.3MM **Privately Held**
SIC: 3448 Prefabricated metal buildings

(G-7759)
ANCHOR COATINGS LEESBURG INC
2280 Talley Rd (34748-3316)
PHONE..................................352 728-0777
Gary Tutor, *President*
Amanda Schick, *Vice Pres*
Debbie Tutor, *Treasurer*
EMP: 20 **EST:** 1989
SQ FT: 15,000
SALES (est): 3.1MM **Privately Held**
WEB: www.anchorcoatings.com
SIC: 2851 2891 2821 Paints & paint additives; lacquers, varnishes, enamels & other coatings; adhesives & sealants; plastics materials & resins

(G-7760)
ARCHITECTURAL MASTERS LLC
2319 Griffin Rd (34748-3307)
PHONE..................................239 290-2250
David Ashenbrener, *Principal*
EMP: 7 **EST:** 2016
SALES (est): 242K **Privately Held**
SIC: 3272 Concrete products

(G-7761)
BAILEY INDUSTRIES INC (PA)
1107 Thomas Ave (34748-3631)
P.O. Box 490090 (34749-0090)
PHONE..................................352 326-2898
Elijah J Bailey, *President*
Patricia A Kiser, *Vice Pres*
▲ **EMP:** 40 **EST:** 1992
SQ FT: 15,000
SALES (est): 56.9MM **Privately Held**
WEB: www.baileyind.com
SIC: 2434 Vanities, bathroom: wood

(G-7762)
CENTRAL PROCESSING CORP
304 Richey Rd (34748-7165)
P.O. Box 435, Astatula (34705-0435)
PHONE..................................352 787-3004
John Sonnentag, *Principal*
EMP: 7 **EST:** 2008
SALES (est): 153.5K **Privately Held**
SIC: 3589 Water treatment equipment, industrial

(G-7763)
COLUMBIA PARCAR CORP
2505 Industrial St (34748-3608)
P.O. Box 493744 (34749-3744)
PHONE..................................352 753-0244
Ron Sheldon, *Manager*
EMP: 10 **Privately Held**
WEB: www.columbiavehicles.com
SIC: 3799 Golf carts, powered
HQ: Columbia Vehicle Group, Inc.
    1115 Commercial Ave
    Reedsburg WI 53959
    608 524-8888

(G-7764)
CONSOLIDATED MINERALS INC (PA)
Also Called: CMI
8500 Us Highway 441 (34788-4017)
P.O. Box 490180 (34749-0180)
PHONE..................................352 365-6522
Frederick B Gregg, *Ch of Bd*
Fred J Houton, *President*
Joshua Herter, *QC Mgr*
Gary L Jones, *CFO*
Sharon Mills, *Info Tech Mgr*
◆ **EMP:** 10 **EST:** 2000
SQ FT: 20,000
SALES (est): 51.2MM **Privately Held**
WEB: www.cmineralsinc.com
SIC: 3272 Concrete products

(G-7765)
CUTRALE CITRUS JUICES USA INC
Also Called: Foods Div
11 Cloud St (34748-5306)
PHONE..................................352 728-7800
Jim Fitzgerald, *Vice Pres*
Cathia Pizetta, *Plant Mgr*
Raul Martinez, *Production*
Dean Evans, *Buyer*
Susan Stenlund, *Buyer*
EMP: 662
SQ FT: 68,840 **Privately Held**
WEB: www.cutrale.com
SIC: 2037 2086 2033 Fruit juices; bottled & canned soft drinks; fruit juices: packaged in cans, jars, etc.
HQ: Cutrale Citrus Juices Usa, Inc.
    602 Mckean St
    Auburndale FL 33823

(G-7766)
DIP-A-DEE DONUTS
1376 W North Blvd (34748-3900)
PHONE..................................352 460-4266
Sandy Kurtis, *President*
Kevin J Robson, *President*
Val Robson, *Vice Pres*
EMP: 20 **EST:** 1986
SQ FT: 1,200
SALES (est): 1.9MM **Privately Held**
SIC: 2051 5461 4225 Doughnuts, except frozen; doughnuts; general warehousing & storage

(G-7767)
DONUT KING OF LEESBURG LLC
708 S 14th St (34748-5619)
PHONE..................................352 250-8487
Lance Johnston,
EMP: 6 **EST:** 2018
SALES (est): 302.3K **Privately Held**
WEB: www.donutking.com.au
SIC: 2051 Doughnuts, except frozen

(G-7768)
DUCKSTEINS SERVICES
3 Morgan Ave (34748-8912)
PHONE..................................352 449-5678
Brittany Duckstein, *Owner*
EMP: 6 **EST:** 2018
SALES (est): 300K **Privately Held**
WEB: www.ducksteins.com
SIC: 1389 Construction, repair & dismantling services

(G-7769)
DURA-STRESS INC (PA)
Also Called: Allendale Hunting Management
11325 County Road 44 (34788-2615)
P.O. Box 490779 (34749-0779)
PHONE..................................352 787-1422
G Kent Fuller, *President*
Ryan Wiles, *Project Mgr*
Jeff Gerger, *Foreman/Supr*
Charlie Baker, *Chief Engr*
Ken Kepley, *CFO*
▲ **EMP:** 170 **EST:** 1950
SQ FT: 11,970
SALES (est): 49.7MM **Privately Held**
WEB: www.durastress.com
SIC: 3272 Prestressed concrete products

(G-7770)
DYNAMIC ALLOY
1018 W North Blvd Ste A (34748-5057)
PHONE..................................352 728-7600
EMP: 12
SALES (est): 57.2K **Privately Held**
SIC: 3398 Metal Treating Of Metals

(G-7771)
ELITE ENCLOSURES
2505 Industrial St (34748-3608)
PHONE..................................352 323-6005
William R Sauey, *Principal*
EMP: 9 **EST:** 2012
SALES (est): 224.1K **Privately Held**
SIC: 3799 3711 Golf carts, powered; personnel carriers (motor vehicles), assembly of
PA: Nordic Group Of Companies Ltd.
    715 Lynn Ave Ste 100
    Baraboo WI 53913

(G-7772)
FCS HOLDINGS INC (PA)
8500 Us Highway 441 (34788-4017)
PHONE..................................352 787-0608
Frederick Browne Gregg, *President*
S Randolph Simpson III, *CFO*
Gary L Jones, *Treasurer*
William Reid Darnell, *Admin Sec*
EMP: 4 **EST:** 1993
SQ FT: 20,000
SALES (est): 5.2MM **Privately Held**
SIC: 1422 3241 4911 Crushed & broken limestone; cement, hydraulic; electric services

(G-7773)
FFO LEESBURG LLC
9917 Us Highway 441 (34788-3922)
PHONE..................................352 315-0783
Thomas A Marino, *President*
EMP: 7 **EST:** 2015
SALES (est): 225K **Privately Held**
SIC: 3069 Flooring, rubber: tile or sheet

(G-7774)
FLATWOODS FOREST PRODUCTS INC
240 State Road 44 (34748-9488)
PHONE..................................352 787-1161
Charles K Sellars, *President*
Darrell C Sellars, *Principal*
EMP: 18 **EST:** 2003
SQ FT: 3,500

SALES (est): 538.3K **Privately Held**
SIC: 2411 Logging camps & contractors; timber, cut at logging camp

(G-7775)
FLC MACHINES INC
8010 Us Highway 441 (34788-8243)
P.O. Box 863, Coffeyville KS (67337-0863)
PHONE..................................352 728-2303
Frederick Froelich, *President*
Onzelle Froelich, *Admin Sec*
EMP: 22 **EST:** 1968
SQ FT: 12,000
SALES (est): 1.4MM **Privately Held**
WEB: www.flcmachines.com
SIC: 3599 Custom machinery

(G-7776)
FLYING COLORS AIR PARTS
2727 W Main St (34748-4630)
PHONE..................................352 728-1900
EMP: 9 **EST:** 2016
SALES (est): 510.5K **Privately Held**
WEB: www.flyingcolorsairparts.com
SIC: 3728 Aircraft parts & equipment

(G-7777)
FORD PRESS INC
305 S Canal St (34748-5903)
P.O. Box 490480 (34749-0480)
PHONE..................................352 787-4650
Richard Kelley, *President*
Dean Simmons, *Vice Pres*
Kassie Cozart, *Manager*
Kaylyn Harrell,
Jerry Grisham, *Representative*
EMP: 18 **EST:** 1957
SQ FT: 7,000
SALES (est): 2.3MM **Privately Held**
WEB: www.fordpress.com
SIC: 2752 2791 Commercial printing, offset; typesetting

(G-7778)
GBC BY GLEN BERGQUIST LLC
2101 Edgewood Ave (34748-5517)
PHONE..................................352 348-7957
Glens Bergquist, *Principal*
EMP: 7 **EST:** 2008
SALES (est): 89.2K **Privately Held**
SIC: 2653 Corrugated & solid fiber boxes

(G-7779)
HAMMOND ENTERPRISES
1460 William St (34748-3811)
PHONE..................................386 575-2402
Les Hammond, *Principal*
EMP: 7 **EST:** 2000
SALES (est): 115.7K **Privately Held**
WEB: www.hammondenterprises.com
SIC: 2711 Newspapers

(G-7780)
HARBORPOINT MEDIA LLC (PA)
Also Called: Daily Commercial
212 E Main St (34748-5227)
P.O. Box 490007 (34749-0007)
PHONE..................................352 365-8200
Michael Redding, *CEO*
Jordan Walker, *Accounts Exec*
Joanne French, *Representative*
EMP: 116 **EST:** 2004
SALES (est): 8.3MM **Privately Held**
WEB: www.dailycommercial.com
SIC: 2711 Newspapers, publishing & printing

(G-7781)
JAY BERRY SIGNS
125 Montclair Rd Ste 1 (34748-9773)
P.O. Box 491620 (34749-1620)
PHONE..................................352 805-4050
EMP: 9 **EST:** 2018
SALES (est): 352.2K **Privately Held**
WEB: www.jayberrysigns.com
SIC: 3993 Signs & advertising specialties

(G-7782)
LEESBURG CONCRETE COMPANY INC
1335 Thomas Ave (34748-3223)
PHONE..................................352 787-4177
Lannie M Thomas, *President*
Shawn Thomas, *Vice Pres*
April Accor, *Sales Engr*
Susan Kindle, *Sales Staff*

Katherine Manning, *Sales Staff*
EMP: 50 **EST:** 1983
SQ FT: 4,500
SALES (est): 9.5MM **Privately Held**
WEB: www.leesburgconcrete.com
SIC: 3499 3272 Metal ladders; concrete products

(G-7783)
LEESBURG PRINTING COMPANY
3606 Parkway Blvd (34748-9744)
P.O. Box 491140 (34749-1140)
PHONE..............................352 787-3348
Michael P Mason, *President*
Amy Mason, *Vice Pres*
EMP: 10 **EST:** 1966
SQ FT: 6,600
SALES (est): 1.1MM **Privately Held**
WEB: www.aplusprintingzone.com
SIC: 2752 Commercial printing, offset

(G-7784)
M S AMTEX-N INC
Also Called: Southeast Modular Mfg
2500 Industrial St (34748-3609)
PHONE..............................352 326-9729
Jim Ginas, *President*
David Meyer, *Chairman*
Les Berczy, *COO*
Barbara Hicks, *Sales Staff*
John Marzicola, *Sales Staff*
EMP: 150 **EST:** 1975
SQ FT: 65,000
SALES (est): 49.4MM
SALES (corp-wide): 88.3MM **Privately Held**
SIC: 3448 Buildings, portable: prefabricated metal
PA: Amtex-Nms Holdings, Inc.
2500 Industrial St
Leesburg FL 34748
352 728-2930

(G-7785)
MASON-FLORIDA LLC
2415 Griffin Rd (34748-3201)
P.O. Box 59226, Birmingham AL (35259-9226)
PHONE..............................352 638-9003
Allen Applebee,
EMP: 13 **EST:** 2002
SALES (est): 730K **Privately Held**
SIC: 2394 Canopies, fabric: made from purchased materials

(G-7786)
MINUTEMAN PRESS
1417 E Main St (34748-5377)
PHONE..............................352 728-6333
EMP: 8 **EST:** 2018
SALES (est): 257.1K **Privately Held**
WEB: www.minutemanpress.com
SIC: 2752 Commercial printing, lithographic

(G-7787)
MOBILE POWER GENERATORS LLC
Also Called: Power Technology Southeast
634 State Road 44 (34748-8103)
P.O. Box 490133 (34749-0133)
PHONE..............................352 365-2777
Christopher Gray, *CFO*
EMP: 33
SALES (est): 4.5MM **Privately Held**
WEB: www.powertechgenerators.com
SIC: 3621 Generator sets: gasoline, diesel or dual-fuel

(G-7788)
PREMIER WATER TANKS LLC ✪
425 Flatwoods Rd (34748-4345)
PHONE..............................352 910-0188
EMP: 11 **EST:** 2021
SALES (est): 1MM **Privately Held**
SIC: 3443 Water tanks, metal plate

(G-7789)
PTSE HOLDING INC
Also Called: Powertech Generators
634 State Road 44 (34748-8103)
P.O. Box 490133 (34749-0133)
PHONE..............................800 760-0027
Gerald Hayman, *President*
Jim Fudge, *Corp Secy*

Chris Gray, *CFO*
Bill Dauley, *Sales Mgr*
▲ **EMP:** 33 **EST:** 1989
SQ FT: 19,000
SALES (est): 6.6MM **Privately Held**
SIC: 3621 Generator sets: gasoline, diesel or dual-fuel

(G-7790)
QUALITY CUSTOM CABINET DESIGN
2215 Griffin Rd (34748-3305)
P.O. Box 491117 (34749-1117)
PHONE..............................352 728-4292
Mark Daigneau, *President*
EMP: 8 **EST:** 1980
SQ FT: 7,550
SALES (est): 200K **Privately Held**
SIC: 2434 5064 5032 5039 Wood kitchen cabinets; electrical appliances, major; marble building stone; structural assemblies, prefabricated: non-wood

(G-7791)
SEAHILL PRESS INC
214 N 3rd St Ste A (34748-5141)
PHONE..............................805 845-8636
Gregory Sharp, *Principal*
EMP: 7 **EST:** 2018
SALES (est): 286.4K **Privately Held**
WEB: www.seahillpress.com
SIC: 2741 Miscellaneous publishing

(G-7792)
SHAR FAMILY ENTERPRISES LLC
2207 Aitkin Loop (34748-2964)
PHONE..............................352 365-6988
Htun Tin Shar, *Principal*
EMP: 7 **EST:** 2009
SALES (est): 169K **Privately Held**
SIC: 3356 Nonferrous rolling & drawing

(G-7793)
SIGN DESIGN OF FLORIDA INC
Also Called: Mid Florida Signs
3602 Parkway Blvd Ste 2 (34748-8591)
PHONE..............................352 787-3882
Richard Hayes, *President*
Matthew Taylor, *Project Mgr*
Chris Singh, *Opers Mgr*
EMP: 24 **EST:** 1941
SQ FT: 6,000
SALES (est): 2.9MM **Privately Held**
WEB: www.midflsigns.com
SIC: 3993 7389 Signs & advertising specialties; sign painting & lettering shop

(G-7794)
SIGNCRAFTERS OF CENTRAL FLA
1134 E North Blvd (34748-5350)
PHONE..............................352 323-1862
Dennis Martin, *President*
Brad Riley, *Manager*
EMP: 18 **EST:** 2007
SQ FT: 6,000
SALES (est): 2.2MM **Privately Held**
WEB: www.signcraftersflorida.com
SIC: 3993 Electric signs

(G-7795)
SOUTH CAROLINA MINERALS INC (PA)
8500 Us Highway 441 (34788-4017)
P.O. Box 490180 (34749-0180)
PHONE..............................352 365-6522
Fred Horton Jr, *President*
Mike Gentry, *Plant Mgr*
EMP: 5 **EST:** 2012
SALES (est): 1.2MM **Privately Held**
WEB: www.cmineralsinc.com
SIC: 1429 Grits mining (crushed stone)

(G-7796)
SUNSHINE CANVAS INC
240 State Road 44 (34748-9488)
PHONE..............................352 787-4436
Russell D Sellars, *President*
EMP: 10 **EST:** 2017
SALES (est): 284.8K **Privately Held**
SIC: 2211 Canvas

(G-7797)
TECHNICUFF CORP
2525 Industrial St (34748-3608)
PHONE..............................352 326-2833
William L Yandell, *President*
Caroline Dyken, *Vice Pres*
Julie Yandell, *Vice Pres*
Scott Van Dyken, *Marketing Staff*
EMP: 10 **EST:** 1992
SQ FT: 5,000
SALES (est): 1.1MM **Privately Held**
WEB: www.technicuff.com
SIC: 3841 5047 Blood pressure apparatus; medical equipment & supplies

(G-7798)
TOP LINE INSTALLATION INC
Also Called: Connectsure
2134 Aitkin Loop (34748-2960)
PHONE..............................352 636-4192
Andre Desforges, *Principal*
EMP: 7 **EST:** 2010
SALES (est): 242.2K **Privately Held**
SIC: 3822 7382 Building services monitoring controls, automatic; security systems services

(G-7799)
TOTAL NUTRITION TECHNOLOGY LLC
Also Called: TNT Supplements
154 Park Center St Ste A (34748-4640)
PHONE..............................352 435-0050
Lourdes McAgy, *President*
Lou Fernandez, *Plant Mgr*
Steve Nault, *Mktg Dir*
▲ **EMP:** 20 **EST:** 2006
SQ FT: 4,000
SALES (est): 5.8MM **Privately Held**
WEB: www.totalnutritiontech.com
SIC: 2099 Food preparations

(G-7800)
TUCKERS MACHINE & STL SVC INC
400 County Road 468 (34748-8548)
P.O. Box 492810 (34749-2810)
PHONE..............................352 787-3157
B Murraytucker III, *President*
Matthew C Tucker, *Corp Secy*
Bascom M Tucker Jr, *Director*
Charles B Tucker, *Director*
▼ **EMP:** 58 **EST:** 1991
SQ FT: 10,000
SALES (est): 9.6MM **Privately Held**
WEB: www.tuckerbilt.com
SIC: 3441 3599 Fabricated structural metal; machine shop; jobbing & repair

(G-7801)
WALLING CRATE COMPANY
507 N 14th St (34748-4252)
PHONE..............................352 787-5211
Robert Walling, *President*
Mark Sullivan, *Sales Staff*
EMP: 19 **EST:** 1917
SQ FT: 35,000
SALES (est): 254.9K **Privately Held**
SIC: 2448 2449 Pallets, wood; fruit crates, wood: wirebound

(G-7802)
YOUR CABINET SOURCE INC
2606 South St Ste 4 (34748-8704)
PHONE..............................352 728-3806
Jimmy Griffith, *Director*
EMP: 8 **EST:** 2019
SALES (est): 252.7K **Privately Held**
WEB: www.yourcabinetsourceinc.com
SIC: 2434 Wood kitchen cabinets

Lehigh Acres
Lee County

(G-7803)
A MORRIS INDUSTRIES LLC
3824 23rd St W (33911-7571)
PHONE..............................239 308-2199
Alfredo Morris, *Principal*
EMP: 10 **EST:** 2017
SALES (est): 272.8K **Privately Held**
WEB: www.morris-industries.com
SIC: 3999 Manufacturing industries

(G-7804)
AIR DOCTOR OF SWFL LLC
1020 Jackson Ave (33972-3522)
PHONE..............................239 285-8774
Abraham Cortez, *CEO*
EMP: 6 **EST:** 2017
SALES (est): 585.1K **Privately Held**
WEB: www.airdoctorofswfl.com
SIC: 3585 7623 Air conditioning units, complete: domestic or industrial; air conditioning repair

(G-7805)
CAHILL CONSTRUCTION SERVICES
212 Lake Dr (33936-7020)
PHONE..............................239 369-9290
Micheal Cahill, *President*
Nemorio Ruiz, *Vice Pres*
EMP: 7 **EST:** 2002
SALES (est): 680.6K **Privately Held**
WEB: www.cahillconstructionservices.com
SIC: 3292 Pipe covering (heat insulating material), except felt

(G-7806)
CHACHO CUSTOMS
2401 Gretchen Ave S F (33973-3713)
PHONE..............................239 369-4664
Ezequiel Garcia, *Principal*
EMP: 8 **EST:** 2005
SALES (est): 116.8K **Privately Held**
SIC: 3089 Tires, plastic

(G-7807)
CHARLES SCREENING & ALUM LLC
848 Theodore Vail St E (33974-9769)
P.O. Box 1648 (33970-1648)
PHONE..............................239 369-0551
Mark Charles, *Owner*
EMP: 5 **EST:** 2002
SALES (est): 499.8K **Privately Held**
WEB: www.charlesscreening.com
SIC: 3448 Screen enclosures

(G-7808)
EASY PICKER GOLF PRODUCTS INC
415 Leonard Blvd N (33971-6302)
PHONE..............................239 368-6600
Giles Meyer, *President*
Scott Meyer, *General Mgr*
George Hedlund, *Exec VP*
Brett Graham, *Vice Pres*
Angel Fernandez, *Mfg Mgr*
◆ **EMP:** 29 **EST:** 1984
SQ FT: 45,000
SALES (est): 5.9MM **Privately Held**
WEB: www.easypicker.com
SIC: 3949 Driving ranges, golf, electronic

(G-7809)
GOOD TIMES SPORTS BAR AND GRIL
700 Leeland Hts Blvd W (33936-6660)
PHONE..............................239 369-7000
EMP: 6
SALES (est): 525.1K **Privately Held**
SIC: 2599 Mfg Furniture/Fixtures

(G-7810)
INDUSTRIAL REPAIR INC
551 Westgate Blvd Ste 111 (33971-6315)
P.O. Box 1896 (33970-1896)
PHONE..............................239 368-7435
Jim Miller,
Frank R Miller,
EMP: 12 **EST:** 2004
SALES (est): 458.4K **Privately Held**
SIC: 7692 Welding repair

(G-7811)
JEANIUS PUBLISHING LLC
108 Airview Ave (33936-6972)
P.O. Box 1562 (33970-1562)
PHONE..............................239 560-5229
Pierre Jeanty, *Principal*
EMP: 5 **EST:** 2016
SALES (est): 312.6K **Privately Held**
WEB: www.jeaniuspublishing.com
SIC: 2741 Miscellaneous publishing

▲ = Import ▼ =Export
◆ =Import/Export

(G-7812)
JOE TAYLOR RESTORATION
216 Waldo Ave (33971-6303)
PHONE.................................888 814-1455
Joe Taylor, *Branch Mgr*
EMP: 9
SALES (corp-wide): 13.1MM **Privately Held**
WEB: www.jtrestoration.com
SIC: 3442 Molding, trim & stripping
PA: Joe Taylor Restoration
855 Nw 17th Ave Ste C
Delray Beach FL 33445
954 972-5390

(G-7813)
LEALS TIRES & WHEELS
1585 Gretchen Ave S # 1 (33973-2616)
PHONE.................................239 491-2214
Leal Epimenio, *Principal*
EMP: 7 EST: 2011
SALES (est): 312.2K **Privately Held**
WEB: lealstiresandwheels.webs.com
SIC: 3312 Wheels

(G-7814)
LEHIGH ACRS FRE CNRL & RSCUE
636 Thomas Sherwin Ave S (33974-0555)
PHONE.................................239 303-5300
Donald Adams, *Principal*
Anita Kressel, *Finance Mgr*
Tim Mace, *Technology*
Katie Heck, *Officer*
EMP: 32 EST: 2008
SALES (est): 5.3MM **Privately Held**
WEB: www.lehighfd.com
SIC: 3699 Fire control or bombing equipment, electronic

(G-7815)
LIBERTY ALUMINUM CO
5613a 6th St W (33971-6323)
PHONE.................................239 369-3000
James E Lowndes, *President*
James D Guerin, *Vice Pres*
Wayne Rafalski, *Project Mgr*
Yvette Worthington, *Opers Staff*
Maureen Grosso, *Controller*
▲ EMP: 50 EST: 1993
SQ FT: 7,500
SALES (est): 9.2MM **Privately Held**
WEB: www.libertyaluminum.com
SIC: 3446 1799 3444 3354 Architectural metalwork; screening contractor: window, door, etc.; sheet metalwork; aluminum extruded products

(G-7816)
MARATHON ENGINEERING CORP
Also Called: Specialty Contractor
5615 2nd St W (33971-6332)
PHONE.................................239 303-7378
George Hrunka, *President*
EMP: 30 EST: 1974
SQ FT: 7,800
SALES (est): 4.8MM **Privately Held**
WEB: www.goldmedalsafetypadding.com
SIC: 3069 Rubber floor coverings, mats & wallcoverings; wallcoverings, rubber

(G-7817)
MIL-TEC INCORPORATED
5578 6th St W (33971-6327)
PHONE.................................239 369-2880
David Povich, *Principal*
John Forest, *Vice Pres*
Todd Smith, *Plant Mgr*
EMP: 16 EST: 2003
SALES (est): 1.5MM **Privately Held**
WEB: www.miltecusa.com
SIC: 3599 Machine shop, jobbing & repair

(G-7818)
ODARA KANVAS COSMETICS
1126 Homer Ave S (33973-2095)
PHONE.................................239 785-8013
James A Laumont, *CEO*
EMP: 10 EST: 2017
SALES (est): 326.4K **Privately Held**
SIC: 2844 Toilet preparations

(G-7819)
PAPER FREE TECHNOLOGY INC
10626 Windsmont Ct (33936-7267)
PHONE.................................515 270-1505
Samuel W Warren, *President*
EMP: 8 EST: 1994
SALES (est): 702.2K **Privately Held**
SIC: 7372 7338 7389 Prepackaged software; secretarial & typing service;

(G-7820)
PARADISE POOL CARE & CO LLC (PA)
2605 27th St Sw (33976-4074)
PHONE.................................239 338-7715
Hensley Paul,
EMP: 9 EST: 2020
SALES (est): 890.3K **Privately Held**
WEB: www.paradisepoolcareco.com
SIC: 3589 Swimming pool filter & water conditioning systems

(G-7821)
POOF GAME LLC
4209 9th St Sw (33976-2704)
PHONE.................................239 245-2957
Roodely Forvil, *Administration*
EMP: 30 EST: 2017
SALES (est): 1MM **Privately Held**
SIC: 2389 2211 Apparel & accessories; apparel & outerwear fabrics, cotton

(G-7822)
PREMIER SIGN & SERVICE INC
7716 6th Pl (33936-2241)
PHONE.................................239 258-6979
Abner Altamar, *President*
EMP: 9 EST: 2014
SALES (est): 410K **Privately Held**
SIC: 3993 Signs & advertising specialties

(G-7823)
PS CABINET WORKS INC
217 Jefferson Ave (33936-1633)
PHONE.................................239 850-2162
Patrick Sakitis, *President*
EMP: 7 EST: 2005
SALES (est): 175.6K **Privately Held**
SIC: 2434 Wood kitchen cabinets

(G-7824)
RPM GRAPHICS INC
508 Owen Ave N (33971-6316)
PHONE.................................239 275-3278
John H Bowman, *President*
Sheila Skeel, *Manager*
EMP: 5 EST: 2008
SQ FT: 1,200
SALES (est): 310K **Privately Held**
SIC: 3993 Signs & advertising specialties

Lighthouse Point
Broward County

(G-7825)
ASTRO PURE INCORPORATED
Also Called: Astro-Pure Water Purifiers
2121 Ne 29th St (33064-7622)
PHONE.................................954 422-8966
Roger L Stefl, *President*
Mary Munn, *Vice Pres*
EMP: 10 EST: 1970
SALES (est): 683.3K **Privately Held**
SIC: 3589 Water purification equipment, household type; water treatment equipment, industrial

(G-7826)
COMFORT BRACE LLC
1971 Ne 31st St (33064-7643)
PHONE.................................954 899-1563
William Diedwardo,
EMP: 7 EST: 2009
SALES (est): 409K **Privately Held**
SIC: 3842 Surgical appliances & supplies

(G-7827)
NORTH COAST MACHINING INC
2311 Ne 26th St (33064-8350)
PHONE.................................954 942-6943
Paul Maloney, *President*
Deborah Maloney, *Treasurer*
EMP: 6 EST: 1983
SQ FT: 20,000
SALES (est): 419.2K **Privately Held**
SIC: 3599 Machine shop, jobbing & repair

(G-7828)
NORTH SHORE HLDNGS LGHTHUSE PT
4130 Ne 24th Ave (33064-8028)
PHONE.................................954 785-1055
Joseph Giaquinto, *CEO*
Gil Harmon, *VP Sales*
◆ EMP: 30 EST: 1994
SALES (est): 9.9MM **Privately Held**
SIC: 3842 Abdominal supporters, braces & trusses
PA: Modular Thermal Technologies, Llc
1520 Sw 5th Ct
Pompano Beach FL 33069
954 785-1055

(G-7829)
ZAHN BUILDERS INC
4628 N Federal Hwy (33064-6511)
PHONE.................................718 885-2202
Suzy Zahn, *Assistant*
EMP: 7 EST: 2019
SALES (est): 935.1K **Privately Held**
WEB: www.zahnbuilders.net
SIC: 3443 Fabricated plate work (boiler shop)

Lithia
Hillsborough County

(G-7830)
AMERICAN SPERIOR COMPOUNDS INC
17409 Chelsea Downs Cir (33547-4942)
PHONE.................................716 873-1209
▲ EMP: 8
SQ FT: 500
SALES (est): 520K **Privately Held**
SIC: 2821 Mfg Plastic Materials/Resins

(G-7831)
CENTRAL MAINTENANCE & WLDG INC (PA)
Also Called: C M W
2620 E Keysville Rd (33547-1605)
PHONE.................................813 229-0012
Conrad Varnum, *President*
Scott M Varnum, *Corp Secy*
Randy Coates, *COO*
Arthur Davenport, *Project Mgr*
Daryl Peterson, *QC Mgr*
EMP: 200 EST: 1966
SQ FT: 4,100
SALES (est): 70.8MM **Privately Held**
WEB: www.cmw.cc
SIC: 3443 1791 7692 Heat exchangers, condensers & components; structural steel erection; welding repair

(G-7832)
COMPLETE INSTRMNTTION CNTRLS I
11524 Hammock Oaks Ct (33547-1947)
PHONE.................................813 340-8545
David L Harris, *Principal*
EMP: 5 EST: 2014
SALES (est): 692.9K **Privately Held**
WEB: www.completeiandc.com
SIC: 3823 Industrial instrmnts msrmnt display/control process variable

(G-7833)
DYNAMIC PRINTING OF BRANDON
6014 Tealside Ct (33547-3872)
PHONE.................................813 664-6880
David Waring, *President*
Charles M Moore, *Vice Pres*
EMP: 9 EST: 1979
SQ FT: 6,100
SALES (est): 331.2K **Privately Held**
SIC: 2752 Commercial printing, offset

(G-7834)
FLORIDA OIL SERVICE INC
16220 Ternglade Dr (33547-5845)
PHONE.................................813 655-4753
Layne Williams, *Principal*
EMP: 17 EST: 2002
SALES (est): 546.7K **Privately Held**
SIC: 3559 7549 Automotive maintenance equipment; automotive services

(G-7835)
MOSAIC CROP NUTRITION LLC
13830 Circa Crossing Dr (33547-3953)
PHONE.................................813 500-6800
Linda D Weber, *Branch Mgr*
EMP: 98 **Publicly Held**
SIC: 2874 Phosphatic fertilizers
HQ: Mosaic Crop Nutrition, Llc
3033 Campus Dr
Minneapolis MN 55441
763 577-2700

(G-7836)
MOSAIC FERTILIZER LLC (HQ)
13830 Circa Crossing Dr (33547-3953)
PHONE.................................813 500-6300
James T Prokopanko, *CEO*
Jason Vanvleet, *Principal*
Richard L Mack, *Exec VP*
Gary Bo Davis, *Senior VP*
Erica Gibson, *Vice Pres*
◆ EMP: 700 EST: 2004
SQ FT: 8,288
SALES (est): 1.2B **Publicly Held**
SIC: 2874 Phosphatic fertilizers

(G-7837)
PREFERRED STITCHING INC
10552 Lithia Pinecrest Rd (33547-2679)
PHONE.................................813 737-3996
Damon E Hunter, *Principal*
EMP: 8 EST: 2010
SALES (est): 109.1K **Privately Held**
SIC: 2395 Embroidery & art needlework

(G-7838)
SOUTHERN FABRICATING MACHINERY
10417 S County Road 39 (33547-2864)
PHONE.................................813 966-3983
Bill Bursik, *Sales Staff*
EMP: 7 EST: 2019
SALES (est): 1.1MM **Privately Held**
WEB: www.southernfabsales.com
SIC: 3559 Special industry machinery

(G-7839)
TITANIUM GYMNASTICS & CHEER
7017 Lithia Pinecrest Rd (33547-1885)
PHONE.................................813 689-2200
Jessica Charbonneau, *President*
EMP: 6 EST: 2014
SALES (est): 455.6K **Privately Held**
WEB: www.titaniumgymandcheer.com
SIC: 3356 Titanium

(G-7840)
UNIVERSAL ERECTORS INC
5668 Fshhawk Crssing Blvd (33547)
PHONE.................................813 621-8111
Jonathan W Hobbs, *Principal*
EMP: 6 EST: 2015
SALES (est): 386.1K **Privately Held**
WEB: www.universalerectorsinc.com
SIC: 3441 Fabricated structural metal

Live Oak
Suwannee County

(G-7841)
ADVANTA ASPHALT INC
Also Called: Anderson Advanta Asphalt
1400 Howard St E (32064-3505)
PHONE.................................386 362-5580
Samuel Skierski, *President*
EMP: 8 EST: 2011
SALES (est): 1.1MM **Privately Held**
WEB: www.advantaasphalt.com
SIC: 2951 Concrete, asphaltic (not from refineries)

(G-7842)
BOWEN MEDICAL SERVICES INC
709 Industrial Ave Sw (32064-4997)
PHONE.................................386 362-1345

Tom Bowen, *President*
Teresa Bowen, *Vice Pres*
EMP: 6 **EST:** 1985
SQ FT: 1,000
SALES (est): 498.4K **Privately Held**
WEB: www.bowenmed.com
SIC: 3841 Surgical & medical instruments

(G-7843)
CHECKS YOUR WAY INC
621 Ohio Ave N (32064-1853)
PHONE..................................386 362-4044
Miles Peaven, *Manager*
EMP: 5 **EST:** 2000
SALES (est): 329.4K **Privately Held**
WEB: www.checksyourway.com
SIC: 3579 Check writing, endorsing or signing machines

(G-7844)
CUSTOM ILLUSIONZ
319 Howard St E (32064-3237)
PHONE..................................386 330-5245
Diane Allen, *Owner*
EMP: 6 **EST:** 2002
SALES (est): 335.3K **Privately Held**
WEB: www.custom-illusionz.com
SIC: 3993 Signs, not made in custom sign painting shops

(G-7845)
DENALI INVESTMENTS INC
140 Palm St Ne (32064-4823)
P.O. Box 327 (32064-0327)
PHONE..................................386 364-2979
Wayne Beaver, *President*
Susan Beaver, *Vice Pres*
EMP: 8 **EST:** 1998
SALES (est): 956.1K **Privately Held**
SIC: 1411 Limestone, dimension-quarrying

(G-7846)
ELITE METAL MANUFACTURING LLC
10121 88th Trce (32060-7701)
PHONE..................................386 364-0777
Kevin B Greene,
EMP: 6 **EST:** 2020
SALES (est): 623.9K **Privately Held**
SIC: 3441 Fabricated structural metal

(G-7847)
ELITE OUTDOOR BUILDINGS LLC
2008 Ohio Ave N (32064-4858)
PHONE..................................386 364-1364
Kevin B Greene, *Mng Member*
EMP: 7 **EST:** 2016
SALES (est): 799K **Privately Held**
WEB: www.eliteoutdoorbuildings.com
SIC: 3448 Prefabricated metal buildings

(G-7848)
FARMERS COOPERATIVE INC (PA)
1841 Howard St W (32064-4326)
P.O. Box 610 (32064-0610)
PHONE..................................386 362-1459
William T Carte, *President*
Barry Long, *Division Mgr*
Todd Lawrence, *Treasurer*
Robert Sap, *Manager*
EMP: 22 **EST:** 1946
SQ FT: 42,500
SALES (est): 13.3MM **Privately Held**
WEB: www.farmerscooperative.org
SIC: 2875 5191 5984 5699 Fertilizers, mixing only; farm supplies; liquefied petroleum gas dealers; western apparel

(G-7849)
KEENS PORTABLE BUILDINGS INC
620 Howard St W (32064-2211)
PHONE..................................386 364-7995
Kevin Keen, *President*
EMP: 10 **EST:** 2000
SQ FT: 600
SALES (est): 1MM **Privately Held**
WEB: www.keensbuildings.com
SIC: 3448 Buildings, portable: prefabricated metal

(G-7850)
NORTH FLORIDA PRINTING INC
109 Tuxedo Ave Ne (32064-2469)
P.O. Box 850 (32064-0850)
PHONE..................................386 362-1080
Edward Howell, *President*
Coy Howell, *General Mgr*
Joanne Howell, *Treasurer*
EMP: 9 **EST:** 1967
SQ FT: 5,000
SALES (est): 500K **Privately Held**
WEB: www.nfpci.com
SIC: 2752 Commercial printing, offset

(G-7851)
PILGRIMS PRIDE CORPORATION
Also Called: Live Oak Feed Mill
1306 Howard St W (32064-2005)
P.O. Box 789 (32064-0789)
PHONE..................................386 362-4171
Hyman Frier, *Purchasing*
Ali Perry, *Sales Mgr*
Doug Chezma, *Manager*
EMP: 62 **Publicly Held**
WEB: www.pilgrims.com
SIC: 2015 Poultry slaughtering & processing
HQ: Pilgrim's Pride Corporation
1770 Promontory Cir
Greeley CO 80634
970 506-8000

(G-7852)
PRECISION TURNING CORPORATION
715 Goldkist Blvd Sw (32064-4995)
PHONE..................................386 364-5788
Cindy W Swann, *Corp Secy*
Charles L Swann, *Administration*
EMP: 19 **EST:** 1996
SQ FT: 9,000
SALES (est): 3.1MM **Privately Held**
WEB: www.precisionturning.net
SIC: 3451 3541 Screw machine products; screw machines, automatic

(G-7853)
RAINBOW STORAGE
7434 County Road 795 (32060-8486)
PHONE..................................386 362-1171
Jack Flowers, *President*
EMP: 10 **EST:** 2005
SALES (est): 560.1K **Privately Held**
SIC: 3691 Storage batteries

(G-7854)
RECYCLING CENTER
700 Houston Ave Nw (32064-4702)
PHONE..................................386 364-5865
Alfred Linton, *President*
EMP: 6 **EST:** 2008
SALES (est): 785.1K **Privately Held**
WEB: www.biggreenball.org
SIC: 3559 Metal finishing equipment for plating, etc.

(G-7855)
SHEDS GALORE AND MORE LLC
1410 Howard St E (32064-3505)
PHONE..................................386 362-1786
EMP: 6 **EST:** 2016
SALES (est): 398.2K **Privately Held**
WEB: www.shedsgaloreandmore.com
SIC: 3448 Prefabricated metal buildings

(G-7856)
SMITH STEPS INC
Also Called: Manufacturer
6944 Us Highway 90 (32060-7155)
P.O. Box 1210 (32064-1210)
PHONE..................................386 963-5655
William Ward, *President*
Lynn Ward, *Treasurer*
EMP: 6 **EST:** 2003
SALES (est): 528.8K **Privately Held**
WEB: www.smithsteps.com
SIC: 3272 Steps, prefabricated concrete

Lloyd
Jefferson County

(G-7857)
LEGACY VULCAN LLC
2792 Gamble Rd (32337)
P.O. Box 305 (32337-0305)
PHONE..................................850 997-1490
Dennis Smith, *Manager*
EMP: 7 **Publicly Held**
SIC: 3273 Ready-mixed concrete
HQ: Legacy Vulcan, Llc
1200 Urban Center Dr
Vestavia AL 35242
205 298-3000

Longboat Key
Manatee County

(G-7858)
LONGBOAT KEY NEWS INC
5370 Gulf Of Mexico Dr (34228-2070)
P.O. Box 8001 (34228-8001)
PHONE..................................941 387-2200
Stephen L Reid, *President*
Melissa L Reid, *Vice Pres*
Aaron Kleiner, *Executive*
EMP: 11 **EST:** 2003
SALES (est): 327.8K **Privately Held**
WEB: www.lbknews.com
SIC: 2711 Newspapers, publishing & printing

(G-7859)
RESOLVER GROUP INC
20 Lighthouse Point Dr (34228-3917)
PHONE..................................941 387-7410
Peter M Simonson, *Principal*
Jay Zhang, *Engineer*
Julie Garcia, *Accounts Mgr*
Scott James, *Manager*
Mary Shiffer, *Manager*
EMP: 21 **EST:** 2008
SALES (est): 739.5K **Privately Held**
SIC: 3621 Resolvers

(G-7860)
SPECIALTY FIN CONSULTING CORP (PA)
5541 Gulf Of Mexico Dr (34228-1903)
PHONE..................................717 246-1661
Carl W Cheek, *CEO*
John Forrey Jr, *President*
EMP: 450 **EST:** 2001
SALES (est): 49.6MM **Privately Held**
SIC: 2653 2679 3672 2675 Sheets, corrugated: made from purchased materials; paper products, converted; printed circuit boards; die-cut paper & board

Longwood
Seminole County

(G-7861)
35 TECHNOLOGIES GROUP INC
2280 N Ronald Reagan Blvd (32750-3519)
PHONE..................................407 402-2119
Ann Norelli, *President*
Joseph Norelli, *Vice Pres*
Judith Norelli, *Director*
Nicholas Norelli, *Director*
▼ **EMP:** 26 **EST:** 2007
SQ FT: 15,500
SALES (est): 2.3MM **Privately Held**
SIC: 3699 Electric sound equipment

(G-7862)
7 PLASTICS INC
1680 Timocuan Way (32750-3729)
PHONE..................................407 321-5441
Eduardo Gomez, *President*
Bill Morgan, *Engineer*
Oswald Guzman, *Manager*
EMP: 14 **EST:** 2001
SALES (est): 1MM **Privately Held**
WEB: www.7plastics.com
SIC: 3089 Injection molding of plastics

(G-7863)
ACCU-SPAN TRUSS CO
1891 High St (32750-3721)
PHONE..................................407 321-1440
Emile W Skura, *President*
Gary Pierpont, *General Mgr*
Gerald Mackall, *Corp Secy*
Walter McCall, *Vice Pres*
Linda McCall, *Manager*
EMP: 50 **EST:** 1982
SQ FT: 30,000
SALES (est): 7.3MM **Privately Held**
WEB: www.accuspan.com
SIC: 2439 5039 Trusses, wooden roof; joists

(G-7864)
ALL ELEMENTS MECHANICAL CORP (PA)
776 Bennett Dr Unit 101 (32750-6392)
PHONE..................................866 306-0359
Ronald K Haupt, *President*
Gary Carmack, *Principal*
EMP: 7 **EST:** 2008
SALES (est): 1.5MM **Privately Held**
WEB: www.allelementsmechanical.com
SIC: 2819 Industrial inorganic chemicals

(G-7865)
ALLSTAR LIGHTING & SOUND INC
Also Called: Advanced Powder Coating Fla
754 Fleet Fin Ct Ste 102 (32750-2610)
PHONE..................................407 767-0111
Sandra L Krieger-Bond, *President*
Paula Masselli, *Office Mgr*
Michelle Le Leux, *Manager*
EMP: 10 **EST:** 1991
SQ FT: 10,000
SALES (est): 914.8K **Privately Held**
SIC: 3479 Painting of metal products; painting, coating & hot dipping

(G-7866)
ALTAMONTE OFFICE SUPPLY INC
1983 Corporate Sq # 101 (32750-3627)
PHONE..................................407 339-6911
EMP: 9
SQ FT: 9,000
SALES (est): 1.5MM **Privately Held**
SIC: 3555 5712 Mfg Printing Trades Machinery Ret Furniture

(G-7867)
AMERICAN MENTALITY INC
Also Called: Ugp
210 E Palmetto Ave (32750-4241)
PHONE..................................407 599-7255
Ronald Bonner Jr, *President*
Ronald Bonner Sr, *Vice Pres*
▲ **EMP:** 9 **EST:** 1986
SQ FT: 5,000
SALES (est): 1MM **Privately Held**
WEB: www.sparkysdistribution.com
SIC: 2261 2759 Screen printing of cotton broadwoven fabrics; screen printing

(G-7868)
ANALOG MODULES INC
126 Baywood Ave (32750-3416)
PHONE..................................407 339-4355
Ian Drummond Crawford, *President*
Elizabeth R Letendre, *Principal*
Carlos L Macau, *CFO*
Judith W Vetter, *Admin Sec*
EMP: 70 **EST:** 1980
SQ FT: 21,000
SALES (est): 13.7MM **Publicly Held**
WEB: www.analogmodules.com
SIC: 3663 3674 Amplifiers, RF power & IF; modules, solid state
HQ: Heico Electronic Technologies Corp.
3000 Taft St
Hollywood FL 33021
954 987-6101

(G-7869)
ARCHITECTURAL OPENINGS INC
1975 Corporate Sq (32750-3536)
PHONE..................................407 260-7110
Robert Bussart, *President*
Chris Bussart, *Director*
EMP: 15 **EST:** 1976

SQ FT: 13,600
SALES (est): 3.5MM **Privately Held**
WEB: www.architecturalopeningsinc.com
SIC: 3442 Metal doors; window & door frames

(G-7870)
ARGOTEC INC
225 Pineda St Unit 103 (32750-6452)
P.O. Box 520760 (32752-0760)
PHONE.................................407 331-9372
EMP: 7
SALES (corp-wide): 2.2MM **Privately Held**
SIC: 3699 Mfg Electrical Equipment/Supplies
PA: Argotec Inc
4750 N Dixie Hwy Ste 4
Oakland Park FL 33305
954 491-6550

(G-7871)
ATLANTIC STEEL INC
131 Sheridan Ct (32750-3956)
PHONE.................................407 599-3822
Barry McCullen, *President*
John W Grant, *Vice Pres*
EMP: 38 **EST:** 2000
SQ FT: 12,000
SALES (est): 7.1MM **Privately Held**
WEB: www.atlanticsteelinc.com
SIC: 3441 5039 Fabricated structural metal; structural assemblies, prefabricated: non-wood

(G-7872)
AUDINA HEARING INSTRUMENTS INC
165 E Wildmere Ave (32750-5455)
PHONE.................................407 331-0077
Marc McLarnon, *President*
Frank J Robilotta, *Vice Pres*
EMP: 85 **EST:** 1989
SQ FT: 12,000
SALES (est): 8.9MM **Privately Held**
WEB: www.audina.net
SIC: 3842 5999 5047 Hearing aids; hearing aids; hearing aids

(G-7873)
AXON CIRCUIT INC
155 National Pl Unit 105 (32750-6432)
PHONE.................................407 265-7980
Manish Patel, *Manager*
James Thomas, *Manager*
EMP: 15 **Privately Held**
WEB: www.axoncircuit.com
SIC: 3672 5063 Printed circuit boards; switchboards
PA: Axon Circuit, Inc.
424 S Ware Blvd Ste A
Tampa FL 33619

(G-7874)
BAY MEADOW ARCHITECTURAL MLLWK
400 Bay Meadow Rd (32750-3430)
PHONE.................................407 332-7992
Edgar Fernandez, *President*
Pedro Fernandez, *Vice Pres*
▼ **EMP:** 23 **EST:** 1992
SQ FT: 9,600
SALES (est): 973.6K **Privately Held**
WEB: www.baymeadowmillwork.com
SIC: 2431 5211 Millwork; millwork & lumber

(G-7875)
BELL PERFORMANCE INC
1340 Bennett Dr (32750-7503)
PHONE.................................407 831-5021
Ola R Williams, *President*
Dan Bordui, *Partner*
Glenn Williams, *Vice Pres*
Maria Holder Davis, *Opers Staff*
Jim Parry, *Controller*
EMP: 16 **EST:** 1909
SQ FT: 3,000
SALES (est): 2.8MM **Privately Held**
WEB: www.bellperformance.com
SIC: 2992 2899 Oils & greases, blending & compounding; fuel treating compounds

(G-7876)
BOLT SIGNS & MARKETING LLC
2660 Bent Hickory Cir (32779-3666)
PHONE.................................407 865-7446
Craig R Lamphere, *Branch Mgr*
EMP: 15
SALES (corp-wide): 137.6K **Privately Held**
WEB: www.myboltsigns.com
SIC: 3993 Signs & advertising specialties
PA: Bolt Signs & Marketing, Llc
151 Smran Cmmrce Pl Ste A
Apopka FL 32703
407 865-7446

(G-7877)
BRIESA INC
Also Called: 2020 EMBROIDERY
1335 Bennett Dr Unit 173 (32750-7605)
PHONE.................................407 830-5307
Brian Blaufox, *President*
Janice Zacharkan, *Accounts Mgr*
EMP: 9 **EST:** 2008
SALES (est): 720.7K **Privately Held**
SIC: 2395 7389 Embroidery products, except schiffli machine; embroidering of advertising on shirts, etc.

(G-7878)
C B PRECIOUS METALS LLC
1237 Bella Vista Cir (32779-5867)
PHONE.................................407 790-1585
Dipak Parekh, *Principal*
EMP: 10 **EST:** 2011
SALES (est): 938.6K **Privately Held**
SIC: 3339 Precious metals

(G-7879)
C W PRODUCTS INTERNATIONAL
1340 Bennett Dr (32750-7503)
PHONE.................................407 831-4966
Ola Williams, *President*
Glen Williams, *Vice Pres*
EMP: 5 **EST:** 1985
SQ FT: 3,000
SALES (est): 838.4K **Privately Held**
WEB: www.bellperformance.com
SIC: 2899 Chemical preparations

(G-7880)
CANVAS LAND SURVEYING LLC
1650 Oak Valley Dr (32750-6263)
PHONE.................................321 689-5330
Roxanna Fulford, *Principal*
EMP: 6 **EST:** 2019
SALES (est): 300K **Privately Held**
WEB: www.canvaslandsurveying.com
SIC: 2211 Canvas

(G-7881)
COINWEEK LLC
306 N Swetwater Cove Blvd (32779-2318)
P.O. Box 916909 (32791-6909)
PHONE.................................407 786-5555
Scott Purvis,
EMP: 7 **EST:** 2010
SALES (est): 296.3K **Privately Held**
WEB: www.coinweek.com
SIC: 2711 Commercial printing & newspaper publishing combined

(G-7882)
CONSOLIDATED FOREST PDTS INC (PA)
375 Commerce Way (32750-7633)
PHONE.................................407 830-7723
William Stlaurent, *President*
EMP: 18 **EST:** 1982
SQ FT: 200
SALES (est): 2.7MM **Privately Held**
WEB: www.consolidatedforestproducts.com
SIC: 2869 2499 Fuels; fencing, wood

(G-7883)
CREATIVE CONCEPTS ORLANDO INC
1650 Forest Ave Ste 100 (32750-6423)
PHONE.................................407 260-1435
Wayne Bishop, *President*
Cooper Thacker, *Manager*
Joann Arndt, *Director*
Timothy Arndt, *Director*
EMP: 50 **EST:** 1997

SQ FT: 35,000
SALES (est): 7.5MM **Privately Held**
WEB: www.creativeconceptsorl.com
SIC: 2434 2521 2431 Wood kitchen cabinets; wood office furniture; millwork

(G-7884)
CUSTOM GRAPHICS AND PLATES INC
782 Big Tree Dr Unit 100 (32750-3528)
PHONE.................................407 696-5448
Robert Spering, *President*
Anthony Spering, *Vice Pres*
Robert Spring, *Manager*
EMP: 15 **EST:** 1997
SQ FT: 7,000
SALES (est): 522.2K **Privately Held**
WEB: www.platecrafters.com
SIC: 2752 Commercial printing, offset

(G-7885)
CUSTOM MASTERS INC
Also Called: Flo King Filter Systems
401 Lake Bennett Ct (32750-7670)
PHONE.................................407 331-4634
Allen Horvath, *President*
Valerie Parks, *Vice Pres*
EMP: 20 **EST:** 1985
SQ FT: 8,000
SALES (est): 4.2MM **Privately Held**
WEB: www.floking.com
SIC: 3561 3569 8742 3564 Pumps & pumping equipment; filters, general line: industrial; management consulting services; blowers & fans

(G-7886)
CYBORTRACK SOLUTIONS INC
657 Florida Central Pkwy (32750-6345)
PHONE.................................805 904-5677
EMP: 5
SQ FT: 1,000
SALES (est): 3MM **Privately Held**
SIC: 3674 Mfg Semiconductors/Related Devices

(G-7887)
DAPP EMBROIDERY INC
1075 Fla Cntl Pkwy Ste 25 (32750)
PHONE.................................407 260-1600
Stephen Sutphin, *CEO*
EMP: 5 **EST:** 2006
SQ FT: 2,300
SALES (est): 516K **Privately Held**
WEB: www.dappembroidery.com
SIC: 2395 Embroidery products, except schiffli machine; embroidery & art needlework

(G-7888)
DESIGN PRO SCREENS INC
1287 S Oleander St (32750-5424)
PHONE.................................407 831-6541
Jeffrey Cheffer, *Owner*
EMP: 6 **EST:** 1991
SALES (est): 413.1K **Privately Held**
WEB: www.designproscreensinc.com
SIC: 3448 Screen enclosures

(G-7889)
DONALD ART COMPANY INC
713 Industry Rd (32750-3629)
PHONE.................................407 831-2525
Andrea Wallace, *President*
EMP: 7 **EST:** 2001
SALES (est): 76.8K **Privately Held**
WEB: www.donaldartco.com
SIC: 2752 Commercial printing, lithographic

(G-7890)
ERIC LEMOINE
Also Called: Black Aces Tactical
1355 Bennett Dr Unit 129 (32750-7587)
PHONE.................................407 919-9783
Eric Lemoine, *Owner*
EMP: 5 **EST:** 2016
SALES (est): 706K **Privately Held**
SIC: 3484 Small arms

(G-7891)
EXIT TEN INC
Also Called: Southern Ordnance
100 Highline Dr Unit 116 (32750-5192)
PHONE.................................407 574-2433
Larry Newberry, *President*

Megan Simara, *Director*
Vladimir Simara, *Director*
▲ **EMP:** 7 **EST:** 2002
SQ FT: 2,300
SALES (est): 691K **Privately Held**
WEB: www.southord.com
SIC: 3423 Masons' hand tools

(G-7892)
EXPRESS LABEL CO INC
1955 Corp Sq Ste 1001 (32750)
PHONE.................................407 332-4774
Michael Sisinni, *President*
EMP: 20 **EST:** 1987
SQ FT: 10,000
SALES (est): 3.6MM **Privately Held**
WEB: www.expresslabel.net
SIC: 2672 2679 2241 Labels (unprinted), gummed: made from purchased materials; labels, paper: made from purchased material; labels, woven

(G-7893)
EXXELIA USA INC (HQ)
1221 N Us Highway 17 92 (32750-3739)
PHONE.................................407 695-6562
Paul Massioner, *CEO*
Lynn Hartley, *Buyer*
Robert Testa, *Manager*
Duane Covington, *Technician*
Brigith Pardo, *Clerk*
EMP: 21 **EST:** 2019
SALES (est): 23.6MM
SALES (corp-wide): 89.9MM **Privately Held**
WEB: www.exxelia.com
SIC: 3612 3677 3675 5063 Transformers, except electric; electronic coils, transformers & other inductors; filtration devices, electronic; electronic capacitors; transformers, electric

(G-7894)
F W I INC
Also Called: Florida Wood
1388 S Ronald Reagan Blvd (32750-6419)
PHONE.................................407 509-9739
Charles D Poole, *President*
James Piegls, *General Mgr*
EMP: 12 **EST:** 1974
SQ FT: 11,000
SALES (est): 353.8K **Privately Held**
SIC: 2431 Millwork

(G-7895)
FALCO INDUSTRIES INC
1550 Dixon Rd (32779-2759)
PHONE.................................407 956-0045
Ileana Dimario, *President*
▲ **EMP:** 8 **EST:** 2007
SQ FT: 1,200
SALES (est): 382.9K **Privately Held**
SIC: 3999 Manufacturing industries

(G-7896)
FIRST IMPRSSONS PRTG CMMNCTONS
851 E State Road 434 (32750-5386)
PHONE.................................407 831-6100
Erika Williams, *President*
EMP: 6 **EST:** 1982
SALES (est): 419.5K **Privately Held**
SIC: 2752 2791 2789 Commercial printing, offset; typesetting; bookbinding & related work

(G-7897)
FLORIDA MARKING PRODUCTS LLC
1205 Sarah Ave Ste 171 (32750-6564)
PHONE.................................407 834-3000
Kevin Bennett, *General Mgr*
Aaron Sanborn, *Production*
Bertram Kennedy,
Sandra Balsamo, *Administration*
Michael Kennedy,
EMP: 22 **EST:** 2010
SALES (est): 3.4MM
SALES (corp-wide): 27.4MM **Privately Held**
WEB: www.kennedygrp.com
SIC: 2269 Labels, cotton: printed
PA: The Kennedy Group Incorporated
38601 Kennedy Pkwy
Willoughby OH 44094
440 951-7660

(G-7898)
FOUR G ENTERPRISES INC
Also Called: BCT
1150 Florida Central Pkwy (32750-6348)
PHONE..................................407 834-4143
Gary A Grieger, *President*
Martha Grieger, *Vice Pres*
Caroline Lavender, *Accounting Mgr*
EMP: 45 **EST:** 1981
SALES (est): 7.5MM **Privately Held**
WEB: www.evoprint.com
SIC: 2752 3953 2741 2759 Commercial
printing, lithographic; marking devices;
typesetting; commercial printing; packaging paper & plastics film, coated & laminated

(G-7899)
GOOD REP INC
100 Bay Hammock Ln (32779-3401)
PHONE..................................407 869-6531
Mary E Gary, *Director*
EMP: 7 **EST:** 2001
SALES (est): 77.2K **Privately Held**
SIC: 2451 Mobile homes

(G-7900)
GREYSON CORP
Also Called: Sign King
726 N Us Highway 17 92 (32750-3293)
PHONE..................................407 830-7443
Micheal Gray, *President*
Scott M Grey, *Vice Pres*
Carla Grey, *Treasurer*
Stephanie Tolles, *Sales Associate*
EMP: 13 **EST:** 1976
SALES (est): 1MM **Privately Held**
WEB: www.greyson.com
SIC: 3993 Signs & advertising specialties

(G-7901)
HOLIDAY ICE INC
Also Called: Arctic-Temp Ice Makers
204 Short Ave (32750-5130)
P.O. Box 520606 (32752-0606)
PHONE..................................407 831-2077
Raymond Armstrong, *President*
Ray Armstrong, *General Mgr*
Walter Nicholas, *Purchasing*
Nick Creanza, *Sales Staff*
Rich Bush, *CIO*
◆ **EMP:** 22 **EST:** 1959
SQ FT: 7,000
SALES (est): 4.9MM **Privately Held**
WEB: www.holiday-ice.com
SIC: 3585 7359 Ice making machinery;
equipment rental & leasing

(G-7902)
I C PROBOTICS INC
122 E Lake Ave (32750-5441)
P.O. Box 520669 (32752-0669)
PHONE..................................407 339-8298
EMP: 60
SQ FT: 4,000
SALES (est): 551.6K **Privately Held**
SIC: 3825 3823 3643 Mfg Electrical
Measuring Instruments Mfg Process Control Instruments Mfg Conductive Wiring
Devices

(G-7903)
IMPREMEDIA LLC
Also Called: La Prensa
685 S Ronald Reagan Blvd (32750-6435)
PHONE..................................407 767-0070
Dora Detoro, *Manager*
EMP: 10
SALES (corp-wide): 94.2MM **Privately
Held**
WEB: www.impremedia.com
SIC: 2711 Newspapers, publishing & printing
PA: Impremedia, Llc
41 Flatbush Ave Ste 1
Brooklyn NY 11217
212 807-4600

(G-7904)
INK BROS PRINTING LLC
1372 Bennett Dr Unit 164 (32750-7564)
PHONE..................................407 494-9585
Diego R Milan, *Manager*
EMP: 7 **EST:** 2019

SALES (est): 384.1K **Privately Held**
WEB: www.inkbros.com
SIC: 2752 Commercial printing, lithographic

(G-7905)
**INTERNATIONAL SIGNS & LTG
INC**
714 Commerce Cir (32750-3608)
PHONE..................................407 332-9663
Morgan Voke, *President*
Paul C Riccard, *President*
Maria L Riccard, *Treasurer*
EMP: 16 **EST:** 2008
SALES (est): 2.2MM **Privately Held**
WEB: www.islsigns.com
SIC: 3993 Electric signs

(G-7906)
IRON-ART & FENCE INC
731 N Us Highway 17 92 # 201
(32750-3639)
PHONE..................................407 699-1734
Lou Guglielmello, *President*
Marilyn Guglielmello, *Director*
EMP: 10 **EST:** 1989
SQ FT: 6,000
SALES (est): 776.7K **Privately Held**
SIC: 3446 Fences or posts, ornamental
iron or steel; gates, ornamental metal

(G-7907)
**IT BUSNESS SOLUTIONS
GROUP INC**
Also Called: Minuteman Press
800 Waterway Pl (32750-3535)
PHONE..................................407 260-0116
Michael Wise, *President*
Bill Potter, *President*
EMP: 18 **EST:** 2000
SQ FT: 5,800
SALES (est): 2.6MM **Privately Held**
WEB: www.itbsg.com
SIC: 2752 Commercial printing, lithographic

(G-7908)
JD TOOLS LLC
786 Big Tree Dr (32750-3539)
PHONE..................................407 767-5175
John Deac, *Mng Member*
EMP: 18 **EST:** 2007
SALES (est): 1.3MM **Privately Held**
WEB: www.jdtoolshop.com
SIC: 3599 Machine shop, jobbing & repair

(G-7909)
JM COATINGS INC
1910 Longwood Lk Mary Rd (32750-4619)
PHONE..................................407 312-1115
Miguel Marzcuk, *Principal*
EMP: 9 **EST:** 2007
SALES (est): 240.6K **Privately Held**
SIC: 3479 Metal coating & allied service

(G-7910)
KIDS WOOD
714 Commerce Cir (32750-3608)
PHONE..................................407 332-9663
Kevin Webb, *President*
Julie Webb, *Vice Pres*
EMP: 10 **EST:** 1995
SALES (est): 380.6K **Privately Held**
SIC: 3993 Signs & advertising specialties

(G-7911)
KITCHENS CRAFTERS INC
302 Black Gum Trl (32779-2529)
PHONE..................................407 788-0560
James Knowles Jr, *President*
EMP: 6 **EST:** 1989
SQ FT: 1,800
SALES (est): 708.5K **Privately Held**
WEB: www.kitchencrafters.net
SIC: 2434 Wood kitchen cabinets

(G-7912)
KRAFT HEINZ FOODS COMPANY
2180 W State Road 434 # 2112
(32779-5041)
PHONE..................................407 786-8157
Mark Matthews, *Principal*
EMP: 7

SALES (corp-wide): 26B **Publicly Held**
WEB: www.kraftheinzcompany.com
SIC: 2032 Canned specialties
HQ: Kraft Heinz Foods Company
1 Ppg Pl Ste 3400
Pittsburgh PA 15222
412 456-5700

(G-7913)
**KUSTOM INDUSTRIAL
FABRICATORS**
265 Hunt Park Cv (32750-7567)
PHONE..................................407 965-1940
Andrew Zavodney, *President*
Jim Guenther, *Project Mgr*
Jim Howell, *Project Mgr*
Dan Noyce, *Project Mgr*
Kirk Zachrich, *Project Mgr*
EMP: 16 **EST:** 2008
SALES (est): 1.3MM **Privately Held**
SIC: 3444 Sheet metalwork

(G-7914)
KUSTOM US INC (PA)
640 E State Road 434 # 1000
(32750-5389)
PHONE..................................407 965-1940
Andrew L Zavodney Jr, *President*
Donnie Jordan, *Managing Prtnr*
Travis Christensen, *General Mgr*
Jason Kohlscheen, *General Mgr*
Jeff Louis, *General Mgr*
EMP: 18 **EST:** 1968
SALES (est): 34.3MM **Privately Held**
WEB: www.kustom.us
SIC: 3444 1761 1799 Sheet metalwork;
roofing, siding & sheet metal work; post-
disaster renovations

(G-7915)
LA PARADA CRIOLLA INC
254 W State Road 434 (32750-5114)
PHONE..................................321 207-7100
Elizabeth Ocasio, *Principal*
EMP: 8 **EST:** 2011
SALES (est): 453.9K **Privately Held**
SIC: 3421 Table & food cutlery, including
butchers'

(G-7916)
**LDS VACUUM PRODUCTS INC
(PA)**
773 Big Tree Dr (32750-3513)
PHONE..................................407 862-4643
Greer Russo, *President*
Cindy Reed, *Sales Staff*
Charles Price, *Manager*
▲ **EMP:** 25 **EST:** 1973
SQ FT: 11,000
SALES (est): 5.1MM **Privately Held**
WEB: www.ldsvacuumshopper.com
SIC: 3589 3829 Vacuum cleaners &
sweepers, electric: industrial; gas detectors

(G-7917)
LEE CHEMICAL CORPORATION
Also Called: Hotsy Cleaning Systems
460 W State Road 434 # 128 (32750-4920)
PHONE..................................407 843-6950
Robley Hackley II, *President*
Mary C Hackley, *Corp Secy*
James Dunn, *Mktg Coord*
Jim Dunn, *Mktg Coord*
Sandy Fielding, *Office Mgr*
EMP: 5 **EST:** 1964
SALES (est): 460.2K **Privately Held**
WEB: leechemical.alkotadistributors.com
SIC: 2842 5084 Industrial plant disinfectants or deodorants; industrial machinery
& equipment

(G-7918)
LIGHT INTEGRATION INC
477 Commerce Way Ste 105 (32750-7571)
P.O. Box 141503, Orlando (32814-1503)
PHONE..................................407 681-0072
Robert Temple, *President*
Gary Gunter, *Treasurer*
◆ **EMP:** 6 **EST:** 2000
SQ FT: 3,000
SALES (est): 683.6K **Privately Held**
WEB: www.namestore.com
SIC: 3647 Vehicular lighting equipment

(G-7919)
MACROCAP LABS INC (PA)
975 Bennett Dr (32750-6352)
PHONE..................................321 234-6282
Chris Wagner, *CEO*
Troy Weyman, *Vice Pres*
Mike Murphy, *QA Dir*
David Castro, *Supervisor*
EMP: 22 **EST:** 2010
SALES (est): 8.4MM **Privately Held**
WEB: www.macrocaplabs.com
SIC: 2833 Medicinals & botanicals

(G-7920)
MARK WAYNE ADAMS INC
490 Wekiva Cove Rd (32779-5666)
P.O. Box 916392 (32791-6392)
PHONE..................................407 756-5862
Mark Adams, *Principal*
EMP: 9 **EST:** 2007
SALES (est): 561.5K **Privately Held**
WEB: www.markwayneadams.com
SIC: 2741 Miscellaneous publishing

(G-7921)
**MASCHMEYER CONCRETE CO
FLA**
1601 S Ronald Reagan Blvd (32750-6420)
PHONE..................................407 339-5311
Jessie James, *Vice Pres*
Mike Merrell, *Controller*
Suzy Wittman, *Manager*
Jerri J Harris, *Director*
EMP: 23
SALES (corp-wide): 136.2MM **Privately
Held**
WEB: www.maschmeyer.com
SIC: 3273 Ready-mixed concrete
PA: Maschmeyer Concrete Company Of
Florida
1142 Watertower Rd
Lake Park FL 33403
561 848-9112

(G-7922)
**MERIT FASTENER
CORPORATION (PA)**
2510 N Ronald Reagan Blvd (32750-3703)
PHONE..................................407 331-4815
Gene Romagna, *CEO*
Donna J Best, *President*
Ritch Stevens, *Corp Secy*
Linda Sprinkle Anderson, *Vice Pres*
Laura Napoleon, *Vice Pres*
◆ **EMP:** 20 **EST:** 1977
SQ FT: 15,000
SALES (est): 5.6MM **Privately Held**
WEB: www.meritfasteners.com
SIC: 3599 5085 Machine & other job shop
work; fasteners, industrial: nuts, bolts,
screws, etc.

(G-7923)
METAL ESSENCE INC
910 Waterway Pl (32750-3545)
PHONE..................................407 478-8480
Yvonne Stimac, *President*
Alfredo Stimac, *Vice Pres*
▼ **EMP:** 6 **EST:** 1986
SQ FT: 7,800
SALES (est): 1MM **Privately Held**
WEB: www.metalessence.com
SIC: 3444 3599 Sheet metalwork; machine shop, jobbing & repair

(G-7924)
**MOHAWK MANUFACTURING
COMPANY**
963 N Ronald Reagan Blvd (32750-3011)
PHONE..................................407 849-0333
Darrell Leidigh, *President*
Betty S Leidigh, *Corp Secy*
EMP: 19 **EST:** 1964
SALES (est): 1.1MM **Privately Held**
WEB: www.mohawk-mfg.com
SIC: 3469 Stamping metal for the trade

(G-7925)
MRI DEPOT INC
1075 Fla Cntl Pkwy Ste 20 (32750)
PHONE..................................407 696-9822
Richard J Henderson, *President*
Mark R Henderson, *Vice Pres*
Mark Henderson, *Vice Pres*
Rick Henderson, *Finance Mgr*

EMP: 7 **EST:** 1996
SQ FT: 5,200
SALES (est): 1MM **Privately Held**
WEB: www.mridepot.com
SIC: 3845 3829 Ultrasonic scanning devices, medical; ultrasonic testing equipment

(G-7926)
NAVA PETS INC
400 North St Unit 184 (32750-7566)
P.O. Box 679226, Orlando (32867-9226)
PHONE....................407 982-7256
Janel Young, *Principal*
EMP: 10 **EST:** 2013
SALES (est): 741.4K **Privately Held**
WEB: www.petcult.com
SIC: 3999 Pet supplies

(G-7927)
NELSON PLASTICS INC
578 North St (32750-7646)
PHONE....................407 339-3570
Richard Bradford, *President*
Becky Kesselring, *Vice Pres*
Rebecca Kesselring, *Office Mgr*
EMP: 25 **EST:** 1992
SQ FT: 12,000
SALES (est): 3.6MM **Privately Held**
WEB: www.nelsonplastics.com
SIC: 3089 Injection molding of plastics

(G-7928)
NEXUS ALLIANCE CORP
160 Vista Oak Dr (32779-3009)
PHONE....................321 945-4283
George Habash, *Principal*
EMP: 8 **EST:** 2012
SALES (est): 132.3K **Privately Held**
SIC: 2834 Pharmaceutical preparations

(G-7929)
NUTRAKEY LLC
975 Bennett Dr (32750-6352)
PHONE....................321 234-6282
Christopher Wagner, *CEO*
Troy Weyman, *COO*
Lex Kovacs, *Natl Sales Mgr*
EMP: 52 **EST:** 2016
SALES (est): 7MM
SALES (corp-wide): 8.4MM **Privately Held**
SIC: 2834 Medicines, capsuled or ampuled
PA: Macrocap Labs, Inc.
975 Bennett Dr
Longwood FL 32750
321 234-6282

(G-7930)
PAGEANTRY TLENT ENTRMT SVCS IN
Also Called: Pageantry Magazine
1855 W State Road 434 (32750-5069)
P.O. Box 160307, Altamonte Springs (32716-0307)
PHONE....................407 260-2262
Carl Dunn, *CEO*
Betty W Dunn, *President*
Charles Dunn, *Publisher*
EMP: 6 **EST:** 1992
SQ FT: 1,300
SALES (est): 1.1MM **Privately Held**
WEB: www.pageantrymagazine.com
SIC: 2721 8111 Magazines: publishing only, not printed on site; legal services

(G-7931)
PALLET LOGIX CORP
1655 Jackson St (32750-6210)
PHONE....................407 834-2336
Alan A Aden, *President*
EMP: 8 **EST:** 2011
SALES (est): 27.3K **Privately Held**
SIC: 2448 Pallets, wood

(G-7932)
PANEL ARMOR PRODUCTS LLC
1970 Corporate Sq Unit B (32750-3520)
PHONE....................407 960-5946
Gene Piscopo, *Principal*
EMP: 7 **EST:** 2014
SALES (est): 261K **Privately Held**
WEB: www.panelarmorproducts.com
SIC: 3999 Manufacturing industries

(G-7933)
PAVERSEALINGCOM CORP
1225 Windsor Ave (32750-6825)
PHONE....................407 951-6437
George T Sandland, *Principal*
EMP: 8 **EST:** 2010
SALES (est): 106.4K **Privately Held**
WEB: www.paversealing.com
SIC: 2951 Asphalt paving mixtures & blocks

(G-7934)
PEMBERTON INC
103 Highline Dr (32750-4939)
P.O. Box 521000 (32752-1000)
PHONE....................407 831-6688
Todd N Pemberton, *President*
Bruce Pemberton, *Vice Pres*
Tony Kaiser, *Sales Associate*
W Bruce Pemberton, *Shareholder*
▲ **EMP:** 50 **EST:** 1968
SQ FT: 4,000
SALES (est): 14.2MM **Privately Held**
WEB: www.pembertonattachments.com
SIC: 3531 Construction machinery attachments

(G-7935)
PERFORMANCE POWDER COATING
416 Commerce Way (32750-7659)
PHONE....................407 339-4000
Heath Walters, *Mng Member*
Robert Hiii Bledsoe, *Manager*
EMP: 18 **EST:** 2013
SALES (est): 2MM **Privately Held**
WEB:
www.performancepowdercoating.com
SIC: 3479 Coating of metals & formed products

(G-7936)
PFI INC
607 Savage Ct (32750-5151)
PHONE....................407 822-4499
Joseph Gurley, *President*
James C Gurley, *President*
Ruth Ann Gurley, *Vice Pres*
◆ **EMP:** 9 **EST:** 1980
SALES (est): 1.9MM **Privately Held**
WEB: www.pfipcb.com
SIC: 3699 Electrical equipment & supplies

(G-7937)
PHANTOM TECHNOLOGIES INC
2280 N Ronald Reagan Blvd # 103 (32750-3519)
PHONE....................407 265-2567
Joseph Norelli, *President*
EMP: 24 **EST:** 2000
SALES (est): 4.4MM **Privately Held**
WEB: www.phantomtec.com
SIC: 3679 Electronic circuits

(G-7938)
PIRANHA BOATWORKS LLC
1210 Sarah Ave (32750-5488)
PHONE....................619 417-3592
EMP: 10 **EST:** 2019
SALES (est): 284.7K **Privately Held**
WEB: www.piranhaboatworks.com
SIC: 3732 Boat building & repairing

(G-7939)
PLATECRAFTERS CORPORATION
782 Big Tree Dr (32750-3528)
PHONE....................215 997-1990
Robert Spering, *President*
EMP: 10 **EST:** 2018
SALES (est): 276.7K **Privately Held**
WEB: www.platecrafters.com
SIC: 2759 Commercial printing

(G-7940)
PRECISION LABORATORIES INC
165 E Wildmere Ave (32750-5455)
P.O. Box 609500, Orlando (32860-9500)
PHONE....................407 774-4261
William V Lassiter, *President*
Donna Lassiter, *Vice Pres*
EMP: 20 **EST:** 1991
SALES (est): 5.2MM **Privately Held**
WEB: www.precisionweb.com
SIC: 3842 Hearing aids

(G-7941)
RANGER ASSOCIATES INC
Also Called: Ranger Prtg & Promotional Pdts
688 Florida Central Pkwy (32750-6344)
PHONE....................407 869-0024
Sharon Lane, *CEO*
William Lane, *President*
Rob Lane, *CFO*
EMP: 6 **EST:** 1979
SQ FT: 2,400
SALES (est): 1MM **Privately Held**
WEB: www.rangeronline.com
SIC: 2759 2752 Screen printing; commercial printing, lithographic

(G-7942)
RELIABLE CUSTOM IMPRINTS CORP
448 Commerce Way Unit 100 (32750-6384)
PHONE....................407 834-0571
Bill Melise, *President*
EMP: 6 **EST:** 2000
SALES (est): 525.4K **Privately Held**
WEB: www.rciapparel.com
SIC: 2395 2396 Embroidery & art needlework; screen printing on fabric articles

(G-7943)
ROLLADEN INC
1328 Bennett Dr (32750-7503)
PHONE....................954 454-4114
Robert Hoffman, *President*
EMP: 10
SALES (corp-wide): 8.1MM **Privately Held**
WEB: www.rolladen.com
SIC: 3442 5211 Storm doors or windows, metal; door & window products
PA: Rolladen, Inc.
3146 John P Curci Dr # 5
Hallandale Beach FL 33009
954 454-4114

(G-7944)
SAMJAY MEDIA GROUP ORLANDO LLC
Also Called: Home Mag, The
187 Sabal Palm Dr Ste 200 (32779-2595)
PHONE....................407 865-7526
John Jericiau,
EMP: 6 **EST:** 2008
SALES (est): 569K **Privately Held**
SIC: 2731 Book publishing

(G-7945)
SELECTWO MACHINE COMPANY INC
1695 Ee Williamson Rd (32779-2839)
PHONE....................407 788-3102
Elizabeth Reyes, *CEO*
Gary Skrobiak, *Principal*
EMP: 6 **EST:** 1978
SQ FT: 2,000
SALES (est): 734.4K **Privately Held**
WEB: www.selectwo.com
SIC: 3599 3545 Machine shop, jobbing & repair; precision tools, machinists'

(G-7946)
SENTINEL CMMNCTONS NEWS VNTRES
210 Pembrook Pl (32779-4523)
PHONE....................407 420-6229
Mike Griffin, *Principal*
EMP: 9
SALES (corp-wide): 4.6B **Publicly Held**
SIC: 2711 Newspapers, publishing & printing
HQ: Sentinel Communications News Ventures Inc.
633 N Orange Ave
Orlando FL 32801
407 420-5000

(G-7947)
SERVOS AND SIMULATION INC
Also Called: Engineering
421 Meadowridge Cv (32750-7126)
PHONE....................407 807-0208
Rachel Baker, *President*
Phil Hutchings, *Executive*
EMP: 5 **EST:** 1980

SALES (est): 554.9K **Privately Held**
WEB: www.servosandsimulation.com
SIC: 3699 3825 8748 7371 Flight simulators (training aids), electronic; test equipment for electronic & electrical circuits; systems analysis or design; computer software development; computer software systems analysis & design, custom

(G-7948)
SOURGLASS BREWING
480 S Ronald Reagan Blvd (32750-5498)
PHONE....................407 262-0056
EMP: 7 **EST:** 2019
SALES (est): 122.8K **Privately Held**
WEB: www.hourglassbrewing.com
SIC: 2082 Malt beverages

(G-7949)
SPRAY-TECH STAINING INC
569 Darby Way (32779-3389)
PHONE....................407 443-4239
Martin Feinen IV, *President*
Rosalie Feinen, *Admin Sec*
EMP: 10 **EST:** 2000
SALES (est): 583K **Privately Held**
SIC: 2499 Fencing, wood

(G-7950)
STARBOARD CONSULTING LLC
2170 W State Road 434 (32779-4957)
PHONE....................407 622-6414
Todd Carson, *Project Mgr*
Tony Sanchez, *Project Mgr*
Samuel McKinney, *Sales Executive*
Alicia Hilliard, *Office Mgr*
Doug Carrington, *Manager*
EMP: 22 **EST:** 2007
SALES (est): 4.4MM **Privately Held**
WEB: www.starboard-consulting.com
SIC: 7372 7371 Application computer software; computer software development & applications

(G-7951)
SUN BARRIER PRODUCTS INC
159 Baywood Ave (32750-3449)
PHONE....................407 830-9085
Charles T Donaldson, *President*
Charles Donaldson, *Med Doctor*
▼ **EMP:** 11 **EST:** 1988
SQ FT: 3,500
SALES (est): 772.3K **Privately Held**
WEB: www.sunbarrierproducts.com
SIC: 3442 5211 Shutters, door or window: metal; door & window products

(G-7952)
TIFFANY QUILTING & DRAPERY
206 E Palmetto Ave (32750-4241)
PHONE....................407 834-6386
Benjamin Magaldino, *President*
Michael P Magaldino, *Vice Pres*
EMP: 15 **EST:** 1977
SQ FT: 7,000
SALES (est): 1.2MM **Privately Held**
SIC: 2392 2391 2395 Bedspreads & bed sets: made from purchased materials; comforters & quilts: made from purchased materials; draperies, plastic & textile: from purchased materials; pleating & stitching

(G-7953)
TREASURE CHEST OF SWEETWATER
2901 W State Road 434 # 121 (32779-4883)
P.O. Box 915102 (32791-5102)
PHONE....................407 788-0020
Ginny Ellison, *President*
EMP: 5 **EST:** 1979
SALES (est): 380.6K **Privately Held**
WEB: www.treasurechestsw.com
SIC: 2711 Newspapers, publishing & printing

(G-7954)
TRU DIMENSIONS PRINTING INC
2100 N R Reagan Blvd 10 (32750)
PHONE....................407 339-3410
Mary E Jett, *President*
Charles Jett, *Treasurer*
EMP: 9 **EST:** 1985
SQ FT: 4,000

SALES (est): 667.4K **Privately Held**
WEB: www.techmerc.com
SIC: **2759** 7334 5199 Commercial printing; photocopying & duplicating services;
advertising specialties

(G-7955)
**TTC PERFORMANCE
PRODUCTS INC**
Also Called: Black Aces Tactical
1355 Bennett Dr Unit 129 (32750-7587)
PHONE..............................407 630-9359
Eric Lemoine, *President*
▲ EMP: 11 EST: 2005
SALES (est): 536.8K **Privately Held**
SIC: **3484** Shotguns or shotgun parts, 30
mm. & below

(G-7956)
UNI-PAK CORP
1015 N Ronald Reagan Blvd (32750-3013)
P.O. Box 522168 (32752-2168)
PHONE..............................407 830-9300
Jeffrey A Coutant, *President*
Christopher T Coutant, *Vice Pres*
Stephen J Coutant, *Vice Pres*
John Garvis, *Cust Mgr*
Jean Olsen, *Info Tech Dir*
◆ EMP: 30 EST: 1970
SQ FT: 40,000
SALES (est): 6.2MM **Privately Held**
WEB: www.unipak.com
SIC: **3535** Unit handling conveying sys-
tems

(G-7957)
VJ PUBLICATIONS INC
1551 W Marvin St (32750-6761)
P.O. Box 915804 (32791-5804)
PHONE..............................407 461-0707
EMP: 7 EST: 2006
SALES (est): 201K **Privately Held**
WEB: www.vjpinc.com
SIC: **2741** Miscellaneous publishing

(G-7958)
VMAK CORP
Also Called: Sir Speedy
131 Applewood Dr (32750-3450)
PHONE..............................407 260-1199
Patricia Brown, *President*
Betty Chesser, *Vice Pres*
Vicente Cruz, *Director*
EMP: 10 EST: 1999
SALES (est): 2MM **Privately Held**
WEB: www.sirspeedy.com
SIC: **2752** 2791 2789 Commercial print-
ing, lithographic; typesetting; bookbinding
& related work

(G-7959)
WATERBOX USA LLC (PA)
Also Called: Waterbox Aquariums
320 W Sabal Palm Pl # 10 (32779-3639)
PHONE..............................800 674-2608
Richard Gilliland, *President*
EMP: 5 EST: 2018
SALES (est): 1.2MM **Privately Held**
SIC: **3231** 5999 Aquariums & reflectors,
glass; aquarium supplies

(G-7960)
WINTEL
1051 Bennett Dr Ste 101 (32750-7588)
PHONE..............................407 834-1188
Angie Rivera, *General Mgr*
EMP: 14 EST: 1971
SQ FT: 18,000
SALES (est): 3.4MM **Privately Held**
WEB: www.wintelphones.com
SIC: **3661** 7629 Telephone & telegraph
apparatus; telecommunication equipment
repair (except telephones)

(G-7961)
XOTHERMIC INC
311 Riverbend Blvd (32779-2307)
PHONE..............................407 951-8008
James Nabors, *Principal*
EMP: 8 EST: 2016
SALES (est): 929.1K **Privately Held**
WEB: www.xothermicinc.com
SIC: **3823** Industrial instrmnts msrmnt dis-
play/control process variable

(G-7962)
XPERIENT LLC
250 W Church Ave Ste 100 (32750-5900)
PHONE..............................407 265-8000
Jason McCormick, *Mng Member*
Frances Maldonadomartin,
Karen Ryan,
▼ EMP: 8 EST: 2003
SALES (est): 1MM **Privately Held**
WEB: www.xperient.com
SIC: **2752** Commercial printing, offset

Lorida
Highlands County

(G-7963)
CAPTAIN RUSTYS
Also Called: Captain Rustys Smoked Fish Dip
1958 Us Highway 98 (33857-9724)
PHONE..............................813 244-2799
Rusty West, *Principal*
EMP: 8 EST: 2015
SALES (est): 202.8K **Privately Held**
WEB: www.captainrustysseafood.com
SIC: **2091** 5421 Fish, smoked; fish &
seafood markets; seafood markets

Loxahatchee
Palm Beach County

(G-7964)
**ACE MIRROR & GLASS WORKS
INC**
Also Called: Ace Window & Door
14083 85th Rd N (33470-4353)
PHONE..............................561 792-7478
Jason Louis Higgins, *President*
EMP: 9 EST: 2002
SALES (est): 998.5K **Privately Held**
SIC: **3231** Ornamental glass: cut, en-
graved or otherwise decorated

(G-7965)
**ACET JOINT VENTURE (AJV)
LLC**
Also Called: Defense Technology Systems
891 Sweetgrass St (33470-6096)
PHONE..............................240 509-1360
Patricia Bird, *Principal*
Claudia Rivas, *Principal*
EMP: 5 EST: 2018
SALES (est): 456.2K **Privately Held**
SIC: **3812** Defense systems & equipment

(G-7966)
AMERICAN ALL
16079 70th St N (33470-3445)
PHONE..............................561 401-0885
EMP: 7 EST: 2013
SALES (est): 153.9K **Privately Held**
WEB: www.allamericanlandclearing.net
SIC: **3674** Semiconductors & related de-
vices

(G-7967)
AMERICAN MOLD REMOVAL INC
17462 37th Pl N (33470-5408)
PHONE..............................561 575-7757
Donal Dillon, *Principal*
EMP: 7 EST: 2012
SALES (est): 148.6K **Privately Held**
SIC: **3544** Industrial molds

(G-7968)
DANIBELLA INC
7040 Seminole Pratt Whtn (33470-5714)
PHONE..............................561 307-9274
Karina Prado, *Principal*
EMP: 8 EST: 2011
SALES (est): 100.2K **Privately Held**
SIC: **2844** Cosmetic preparations

(G-7969)
**FLORIDA ROOFING & SHTMTL
LLC**
17975 89th Pl N (33470-2672)
PHONE..............................561 517-9675
EMP: 7 EST: 2020
SALES (est): 381.1K **Privately Held**
SIC: **3444** Sheet metalwork

(G-7970)
FLOWMASTER INC
14231 83rd Ln N (33470-4377)
PHONE..............................561 249-1145
Joseph T Hennessey Vp, *Principal*
EMP: 9 EST: 2014
SALES (est): 103.8K **Privately Held**
SIC: **3714** Motor vehicle parts & acces-
sories

(G-7971)
JOSHUA THROCKMORTON
2000 Lion Cntry Safari Rd (33470-3976)
PHONE..............................561 236-3349
Joshua Throckmorton, *Principal*
EMP: 7 EST: 2002
SALES (est): 126.5K **Privately Held**
SIC: **2431** Door trim, wood

(G-7972)
**LOXAHATCHEE MOBILE
EQUIPMENT R**
17506 37th Pl N (33470-5410)
PHONE..............................561 723-6378
James E Laclair, *President*
EMP: 7 EST: 2004
SALES (est): 93.1K **Privately Held**
SIC: **3537** Industrial trucks & tractors

(G-7973)
**LOXAHATCHEE SHUTTER &
ALUM INC**
16758 67th Ct N (33470-3331)
PHONE..............................561 513-9581
Sidney Garcia, *President*
EMP: 9 EST: 2018
SALES (est): 373.6K **Privately Held**
SIC: **3442** Shutters, door or window: metal

(G-7974)
**PALM BEACH AGGREGATES
LLC**
20125 Southern Blvd (33470-9259)
P.O. Box 700 (33470-0700)
PHONE..............................561 795-6550
Sam Klein, *Ch of Bd*
Enrique Tomeu, *President*
Ben R Turner, *Exec VP*
John Bates, *Opers Mgr*
R Patrick McMullen, *CFO*
▲ EMP: 43 EST: 1900
SQ FT: 12,000
SALES (est): 17MM **Privately Held**
WEB: www.palmbeachag.com
SIC: **3281** 0181 0133 Stone, quarrying &
processing of own stone products; sod
farms; sugarcane farm

(G-7975)
ROY SMITH S SCREEN
16648 71st Ln N (33470-3382)
PHONE..............................561 792-3381
Roy Smith, *Principal*
EMP: 11 EST: 2009
SALES (est): 738.5K **Privately Held**
WEB: roysmithscreensandshutters.yola-
site.com
SIC: **2431** Door shutters, wood

(G-7976)
**TROPICAL PCB DESIGN SVCS
INC**
7960 Banyan Blvd (33470-3030)
PHONE..............................561 784-9536
Sam Burton, *President*
EMP: 10 EST: 1998
SQ FT: 500
SALES (est): 423.4K **Privately Held**
WEB: www.tropicalpcb.com
SIC: **3577** 8711 Computer peripheral
equipment; engineering services

Lulu
Columbia County

(G-7977)
**CASONS QUALITY CARE SVCS
LLC**
226 Se Lee Dr (32061-7548)
PHONE..............................386 365-1016
Erin Cason, *Principal*
EMP: 7 EST: 2013

SALES (est): 419K **Privately Held**
SIC: **2431** Millwork

Lutz
Hillsborough County

(G-7978)
A A A SIGNS INC
1911 Passero Ave (33559-7352)
PHONE..............................813 949-8397
David M Smith, *President*
EMP: 8 EST: 1991
SQ FT: 4,000
SALES (est): 569.1K **Privately Held**
SIC: **3993** Electric signs

(G-7979)
A C REPAIRS INC
1519 Camphor Cove Dr (33549-5831)
PHONE..............................813 909-0809
John Daniel, *Principal*
EMP: 8 EST: 2006
SALES (est): 789.4K **Privately Held**
WEB: www.acrepairstampa.com
SIC: **3585** Air conditioning equipment,
complete

(G-7980)
**ABOUT FACE CABINETRY &
REFACIN**
110 Crenshaw Lake Rd (33548-6101)
PHONE..............................813 777-4088
Christopher C Robinson, *President*
EMP: 11 EST: 2008
SALES (est): 493.1K **Privately Held**
WEB: www.aboutfacecabinetry.com
SIC: **2434** Wood kitchen cabinets

(G-7981)
**ACCESS WRLESS DATA
SLTIONS LLC**
21756 State Road 54 # 101 (33549-2905)
PHONE..............................813 751-2039
Becky Messenger, *Project Mgr*
Laurann Flynn, *Opers Staff*
Loretta Lau, *Purchasing*
Michelle Hart, *Accounts Mgr*
Megan Lynch, *Accounts Mgr*
EMP: 8 EST: 2008
SQ FT: 1,000
SALES (est): 1.7MM **Privately Held**
WEB: www.accesswds.com
SIC: **3669** Intercommunication systems,
electric

(G-7982)
**ADVANCED COMPONENTS
SOLUTIONS**
22652 Laureldale Dr (33549-8787)
PHONE..............................813 884-1600
Eric Levenson, *President*
EMP: 5 EST: 2003
SALES (est): 330K **Privately Held**
SIC: **3089** Lamp bases & shades, plastic

(G-7983)
APPLE SIGN & AWNING LLC
1635 Dale Mabry Hwy Ste 7 (33548-3000)
PHONE..............................813 948-2220
Madeline C Rogers, *Mng Member*
EMP: 10 EST: 1991
SALES (est): 794.2K **Privately Held**
WEB: www.applesignandawning.info
SIC: **3993** Electric signs

(G-7984)
COAST TO COAST SOLAR INC
19209 N Us Highway 41 (33549-4262)
PHONE..............................813 406-6501
Jeff Saitta, *Owner*
Gary McDonald, *Principal*
Scott Tucker, *Sales Staff*
Coast Melissa, *Med Doctor*
Melissa McDonald, *Manager*
EMP: 15 EST: 2012
SALES (est): 4.2MM **Privately Held**
WEB: www.coasttocoastsolar.com
SIC: **3433** Solar heaters & collectors

▲ = Import ▼=Export
◆ =Import/Export

(G-7985)
COLORPROOF SOFTWARE INC
Also Called: Colorbyte Software
234 Crystal Grove Blvd (33548-6460)
PHONE......................813 963-0241
Mark M Dale, *CEO*
John Pannozzo, *President*
EMP: 5 EST: 1994
SQ FT: 3,000
SALES (est): 564.4K **Privately Held**
WEB: www.colorbytesoftware.com
SIC: 7372 Application computer software

(G-7986)
COMMUNITY NEWS PUBLICATIONS
Also Called: Riverview Community News
3632 Land O Lkes Blvd Ste (33549)
P.O. Box 479 (33548-0479)
PHONE......................813 909-2800
Diane Kortus, *Owner*
B Manion, *Editor*
EMP: 10 EST: 1999
SALES (est): 251.1K **Privately Held**
WEB: www.lakerlutznews.com
SIC: 2721 2711 Periodicals; newspapers

(G-7987)
CROSS CONSTRUCTION SVCS INC
25221 Wesley Chapel Blvd (33559-7201)
PHONE......................813 907-1013
Russell E Arney, *President*
Tony Hanson, *Senior VP*
Carlos Castro, *Project Mgr*
EMP: 52 EST: 1978
SALES (est): 7.8MM **Privately Held**
WEB: www.crossconstructionservices.net
SIC: 3531 Construction machinery

(G-7988)
CYTO DYNCORP INC
110 Crenshaw Lake Rd (33548-6101)
PHONE......................813 527-6969
Kenneth J Van Ness, *CEO*
EMP: 7 EST: 2012
SALES (est): 153K **Privately Held**
SIC: 2834 Pharmaceutical preparations

(G-7989)
DOORKNOB DISCOUNT CENTER LLC
18404 Bittern Ave (33558-2738)
PHONE......................813 963-3104
Bob Bardel, *CEO*
EMP: 7 EST: 2010
SALES (est): 231K **Privately Held**
SIC: 3429 5961 Builders' hardware; cabinet hardware; door locks, bolts & checks; tools & hardware, mail order

(G-7990)
GIBBONS INDUSTRIES INC
Also Called: Comprehensive Grants MGT
1927 Passero Ave (33559-7352)
PHONE......................352 330-0294
Cereta M Gibbons, *President*
EMP: 9 EST: 2017
SALES (est): 207.6K **Privately Held**
SIC: 3999 Barber & beauty shop equipment

(G-7991)
GMA-FOOD LLC
24756 State Road 54 (33559-6245)
PHONE......................646 469-8599
Mohamed Ismail,
Abdelrahman Abdaltattah,
Sherif Ismail,
Mahamed Masoud,
EMP: 7 EST: 2019
SALES (est): 100K **Privately Held**
WEB: www.gmafood.com
SIC: 2033 Canned fruits & specialties

(G-7992)
GRIND IT LLC
17002 Hanna Rd (33549-5665)
PHONE......................813 310-9710
Dillon J Harris, *Owner*
EMP: 7 EST: 2014
SALES (est): 1MM **Privately Held**
WEB: www.grinditstumpremoval.com
SIC: 3599 Grinding castings for the trade

(G-7993)
HANTERI ENTERPRISES CORP
Also Called: Designs In Rugs
1915 Vandervort Rd (33549-5758)
PHONE......................813 949-8729
Henry J Molesky, *President*
EMP: 11 EST: 2004
SALES (est): 311.5K **Privately Held**
SIC: 2273 Carpets & rugs

(G-7994)
HIGHWAY SYSTEMS INCORPORATED
4450 Pet Ln (33559-6307)
PHONE......................813 907-7512
EMP: 7 EST: 2013
SALES (est): 199.3K **Privately Held**
WEB: www.arcosatrafficstructures.com
SIC: 3441 Fabricated structural metal

(G-7995)
IN DIVERSIFIED PLANT SERVICES
22528 Laureldale Dr (33549-8785)
P.O. Box 931 (33548-0931)
PHONE......................813 453-7025
Denny Langworthy, *President*
Mark A Ogden, *Treasurer*
Steve Boleyn, *Shareholder*
Dante Dalere, *Shareholder*
Joy Vallieril, *Shareholder*
EMP: 12 EST: 2008
SALES (est): 1.4MM **Privately Held**
WEB: www.dpsfla.com
SIC: 1446 Blast sand mining

(G-7996)
INTEC PRINTING SOLUTIONS CORP
16011 N Nebraska Ave (33549-6158)
PHONE......................813 949-7799
Ian Melville, *President*
Michael Sparbeck, *COO*
Helen Sims, *Purchasing*
Steve Heads, *Technical Mgr*
Todd Tedesco, *Engineer*
▲ EMP: 6 EST: 2011
SALES (est): 941.5K **Privately Held**
WEB: www.intecprinters.com
SIC: 2752 Commercial printing, offset

(G-7997)
JAB-B-INC
18125 N Us Highway 41 # 104
(33549-6455)
PHONE......................813 803-3995
Marie L Blaxton, *President*
Bill Falin, *Vice Pres*
EMP: 5 EST: 2016
SQ FT: 1,200
SALES (est): 5.6MM **Privately Held**
SIC: 1389 1522 Construction, repair & dismantling services; remodeling, multi-family dwellings

(G-7998)
JDT SERVICING LLC
24310 Breezy Oak Ct (33559-7924)
PHONE......................813 909-8640
Ashley Wilhelm, *Principal*
EMP: 6 EST: 2015
SALES (est): 551.3K **Privately Held**
WEB: www.jdtservicing.com
SIC: 1389 Roustabout service

(G-7999)
LEAN DESIGN & MFG INC
19412 Livingston Ave (33559-4011)
PHONE......................727 415-3504
Tarek Chbeir, *CEO*
Michael Bacher, *President*
EMP: 12 EST: 2013
SALES (est): 634K **Privately Held**
SIC: 3089 Engraving of plastic

(G-8000)
LOWE GEAR PRINTING
15510 N Nebraska Ave B (33549-6107)
PHONE......................866 714-9965
Cotton Lowe, *Principal*
▲ EMP: 6 EST: 2011
SALES (est): 724.5K **Privately Held**
WEB: www.lowegear.com
SIC: 2759 Screen printing

(G-8001)
MAILING & BINDERY SYSTEMS INC
3959 Van Dyke Rd (33558-8025)
PHONE......................813 416-8965
Brian Walders, *Principal*
EMP: 5 EST: 2010
SALES (est): 351.6K **Privately Held**
WEB: www.mailingandbinderysystems.com
SIC: 2789 Bookbinding & related work

(G-8002)
MARSIG GROUP INC
23100 State Road 54 # 18 (33549-6933)
PHONE......................813 840-3714
Richard A Marsiglio, *Principal*
EMP: 9 EST: 2008
SALES (est): 85.1K **Privately Held**
SIC: 2493 Insulation & roofing material, reconstituted wood

(G-8003)
MEDITEK-ICOT INC
Also Called: Lutz Radiology
1916 Highland Oaks Blvd (33559-7323)
PHONE......................813 909-7476
Thomas G Winter, *President*
David E Six, *Vice Pres*
Richard R Six, *Med Doctor*
EMP: 12 EST: 1992
SQ FT: 3,600
SALES (est): 312.4K **Privately Held**
SIC: 3845 Laser systems & equipment, medical

(G-8004)
METICULOUS DETAIL INC
16418 N Florida Ave (33549-6133)
PHONE......................813 310-6440
Matthew A Calay, *Principal*
EMP: 8 EST: 2012
SALES (est): 348.9K **Privately Held**
WEB: www.detail7.com
SIC: 2842 Automobile polish

(G-8005)
MHMS CORP
142 Whitaker Rd Ste A (33549-5767)
PHONE......................813 948-0504
Vincent Menendez, *President*
EMP: 45 EST: 1986
SALES (est): 2.7MM **Privately Held**
SIC: 2389 2673 Disposable garments & accessories; plastic bags: made from purchased materials

(G-8006)
NANO LIQUITEC LLC
5627 Terrain De Golf Dr (33558-2864)
PHONE......................813 447-1742
Julie Manley, *Branch Mgr*
EMP: 10
SALES (corp-wide): 133.1K **Privately Held**
WEB: www.nanoliquitec.com
SIC: 2819 Catalysts, chemical
PA: Nano Liquitec, Llc
2202 N West Shore Blvd # 2
Tampa FL

(G-8007)
NOWVISION TECHNOLOGIES INC
618 De Buel Rd Bldng A (33549)
PHONE......................813 943-4639
Dan S Lawrence, *COO*
EMP: 9 EST: 2000
SQ FT: 3,000
SALES (est): 561.6K **Privately Held**
WEB: www.nowvision.com
SIC: 3651 Household audio & video equipment

(G-8008)
OPINICUS TEXTRON INC
1827 Northpointe Pkwy (33558-0101)
PHONE......................813 792-9300
Mark G Budd, *CEO*
James R Takats, *President*
Patricia Elmer, *Vice Pres*
Troy Fey, *Vice Pres*
Jodi Noah, *CFO*
▲ EMP: 75 EST: 1988
SALES (est): 28.1K
SALES (corp-wide): 12.3MM **Publicly Held**
SIC: 3699 Flight simulators (training aids), electronic
PA: Textron Inc.
40 Westminster St
Providence RI 02903
401 421-2800

(G-8009)
PERPETUAL MARKETING ASSOC INC (PA)
25126 State Road 54 (33559-6256)
PHONE......................813 949-9385
Jaime Wood, *President*
Diane Putt, *CFO*
EMP: 5 EST: 1981
SALES (est): 423.8K **Privately Held**
SIC: 3651 5099 Household audio & video equipment; video & audio equipment

(G-8010)
PRECISE PRINT FLORIDA
410 W Chapman Rd (33548-6100)
PHONE......................813 960-4958
Donna Christine Sutton, *Principal*
EMP: 7 EST: 2009
SALES (est): 192.2K **Privately Held**
SIC: 2752 Commercial printing, lithographic

(G-8011)
PREFERRED MATERIALS INC (DH)
4636 Scarborough Dr (33559-8506)
PHONE......................904 288-0244
Darryl Fales, *President*
Sherman Matt, *Area Mgr*
Gregory Baier, *Vice Pres*
David Cerniglia, *Vice Pres*
Tony Dipietro, *Vice Pres*
EMP: 25 EST: 2007
SALES (est): 111MM
SALES (corp-wide): 30.9B **Privately Held**
SIC: 3273 Ready-mixed concrete

(G-8012)
PSYCHLGCAL ASSSSMENT RSRCES IN (PA)
Also Called: Par
16204 N Florida Ave (33549-8119)
PHONE......................813 968-3003
R Bob I Smith, *Chairman*
Travis G White, *Exec VP*
Serje Seminoff, *Vice Pres*
Catherine Smith, *Vice Pres*
Carrie Morera, *Project Dir*
EMP: 61 EST: 1978
SQ FT: 15,000
SALES (est): 14.2MM **Privately Held**
WEB: www.parinc.com
SIC: 2741 Miscellaneous publishing

(G-8013)
SAFECRAFT RSTRAINT SYSTEMS INC
3959 Van Dyke Rd (33558-8025)
PHONE......................813 758-3571
Charles Espenlaub, *Branch Mgr*
EMP: 11
SALES (corp-wide): 287.7K **Privately Held**
WEB: www.safecraftracing.com
SIC: 3799 Automobile trailer chassis
PA: Safecraft Restraint Systems, Inc.
304 S Plant Ave
Tampa FL 33606
813 758-3571

(G-8014)
SAR WHOLESALE SIGN FACTORY
1903 Passero Ave (33559-7352)
PHONE......................813 949-8397
Roberto Hiller, *Principal*
EMP: 17 EST: 2013
SALES (est): 1.5MM **Privately Held**
SIC: 3993 Electric signs

(G-8015)
SIGNS OF TAMPA BAY LLC
Also Called: Sign-A-Rama
1903 Passero Ave (33559-7352)
PHONE......................813 526-0484

James Charos, *General Mgr*
Roberto Hiller, *COO*
David West, *Sales Staff*
Beatriz E Cardona,
EMP: 31 **EST:** 2010
SQ FT: 15,000
SALES (est): 2.5MM **Privately Held**
WEB: www.signarama.com
SIC: 3993 Signs & advertising specialties

(G-8016)
SOUND CONNECTIONS INTL
Also Called: Vampire Wire
611 Chancellar Dr (33548-4510)
PHONE..............................813 948-2707
Stuart Marcus, *President*
▲ **EMP:** 6 **EST:** 1979
SALES (est): 496.2K **Privately Held**
SIC: 3679 Harness assemblies for electronic use: wire or cable

(G-8017)
SYMMETRY PAVERS INC
2407 Vandervort Rd (33549-5706)
PHONE..............................813 340-0724
Robert Counts, *Principal*
EMP: 8 **EST:** 2014
SALES (est): 147.9K **Privately Held**
SIC: 2951 Asphalt paving mixtures & blocks

(G-8018)
TRADEMARK COMPONENTS INC
21432 Keating Way (33549-8757)
PHONE..............................813 948-2233
Debra Coslov, *President*
Arlyn Shane, *Vice Pres*
EMP: 8 **EST:** 2004
SALES (est): 528.1K **Privately Held**
WEB: www.trademarkcomponents.com
SIC: 3679 Electronic components

(G-8019)
VALIDSOFT
19103 Centre Rose Blvd (33558-9015)
PHONE..............................813 334-9745
Steven Gersten, *Vice Pres*
Tom Hohman, *Vice Pres*
EMP: 8 **EST:** 2009
SALES (est): 588.6K **Privately Held**
WEB: www.validsoft.com
SIC: 3699 Security control equipment & systems

(G-8020)
VOLT LIGHTING
16011 N Nebraska Ave # 102 (33549-6158)
PHONE..............................813 978-3700
Alan Brynjolfsson, *CEO*
John Dinardi, *President*
Josh Barter, *Marketing Mgr*
Ekaterina Capatides, *Marketing Staff*
Griffin Brynjolfsson, *Manager*
◆ **EMP:** 17 **EST:** 2010
SALES (est): 5.9MM **Privately Held**
SIC: 3648 Lighting equipment

(G-8021)
XCAPE SOLUTIONS INC (PA)
207 Crystal Grove Blvd # 101 (33548-6409)
P.O. Box 213, Odessa (33556-0213)
PHONE..............................813 369-5261
David Ellis, *President*
Leslie Ellis, *Vice Pres*
EMP: 19 **EST:** 2004
SQ FT: 3,500
SALES (est): 2.9MM **Privately Held**
WEB: www.xcapesolutions.net
SIC: 7372 Prepackaged software

(G-8022)
YORK BRIDGE CONCEPTS INC
2423 Brunello Trce (33558-7800)
PHONE..............................813 482-0613
James York, *President*
Brian Bullock, *Project Mgr*
Rachel Marshall, *Opers Staff*
Vivian Lenoble, *Controller*
Lelia Preiser, *Controller*
EMP: 40 **EST:** 1985
SALES (est): 9MM **Privately Held**
WEB: www.ybc.com
SIC: 2491 Bridges & trestles, treated wood

Lynn Haven
Bay County

(G-8023)
ACMT SOUTH LLC
Also Called: Aerospace Manufacturing
1006 Arthur Dr (32444-1683)
PHONE..............................860 645-0592
Michael Polo, *CEO*
EMP: 13 **EST:** 2015
SQ FT: 14,000
SALES (est): 1.4MM **Privately Held**
WEB: www.acmt.aero
SIC: 3724 3728 Aircraft engines & engine parts; roto-blades for helicopters

(G-8024)
AMERICAN CARBONS INC
104 New York Ave (32444-1347)
PHONE..............................850 265-4214
M D Bowen, *President*
Eric A Newsom, *Corp Secy*
EMP: 5 **EST:** 1978
SALES (est): 301.1K **Privately Held**
SIC: 2869 2819 Fuels; charcoal (carbon), activated

(G-8025)
B AND B ROOF AND FLOOR TRUSSES
1808 Tennessee Ave (32444-4223)
PHONE..............................850 265-4119
James Barnhill, *President*
EMP: 6 **EST:** 1989
SQ FT: 7,000
SALES (est): 750.3K **Privately Held**
SIC: 2439 Trusses, wooden roof

(G-8026)
BOARDWALK DESIGNS INC
1312 Louisiana Ave (32444-2742)
P.O. Box 747 (32444-0747)
PHONE..............................850 265-0988
Joseph Paffoon, *President*
Sandy Paffoon, *Vice Pres*
Jo Maxhimer, *Office Mgr*
Cassandra Paffoon, *Admin Sec*
EMP: 9 **EST:** 1992
SQ FT: 3,600
SALES (est): 991.1K **Privately Held**
WEB: www.boardwalkdesigns.com
SIC: 3993 Signs, not made in custom sign painting shops

(G-8027)
CAMERA2CANVAS LLC
2500 Minnesota Ave (32444-4801)
PHONE..............................850 276-6990
Chris Moseley, *Principal*
EMP: 8 **EST:** 2015
SALES (est): 315.7K **Privately Held**
WEB: www.mycamera2canvas.com
SIC: 2211 Canvas

(G-8028)
HARLEN S WOODWORKING
1709 Tennessee Ave (32444-4220)
PHONE..............................850 774-2224
Lawrence A Harlen, *Principal*
EMP: 7 **EST:** 2009
SALES (est): 77.5K **Privately Held**
SIC: 2431 Millwork

(G-8029)
INTERNET MARKETING PRESS
818 Radcliff Ave (32444-3041)
PHONE..............................850 271-4333
Lisa Oshesky, *Principal*
EMP: 8 **EST:** 2008
SALES (est): 85K **Privately Held**
SIC: 2741 Miscellaneous publishing

(G-8030)
MERRICK INDUSTRIES INC
10 Arthur Dr (32444-1685)
PHONE..............................850 265-3611
Joseph K Tannehill Jr, *CEO*
Kathy Gower, *President*
Ed Boardway, *Vice Pres*
Grady W McDaniel, *Vice Pres*
Charlene Garrett, *Purchasing*
◆ **EMP:** 115 **EST:** 1977
SQ FT: 40,000

SALES (est): 25.8MM **Privately Held**
WEB: www.merrick-inc.com
SIC: 3596 Weighing machines & apparatus
PA: Tannehill International Industries, Inc.
10 Arthur Dr
Lynn Haven FL 32444

(G-8031)
RINEHART CORP
Also Called: Off The Wall Screen Printing
1515 Ohio Ave (32444-3744)
PHONE..............................850 271-5600
Bronze Lee Rinehart, *President*
Rielly Rinehart, *Vice Pres*
EMP: 5 **EST:** 1994
SQ FT: 3,500
SALES (est): 536.4K **Privately Held**
SIC: 2759 Screen printing

(G-8032)
SHWINCO INDUSTRIES INC
400 Aberdeen Loop (32444)
P.O. Box 1496 (32444-6296)
PHONE..............................850 271-8900
Fax: 850 271-3050
EMP: 40 **EST:** 1989
SQ FT: 11,000
SALES (est): 4.2MM **Privately Held**
SIC: 3089 Mfg Plastic Products

(G-8033)
TANNEHILL INTL INDS INC (PA)
10 Arthur Dr (32444-1685)
PHONE..............................850 265-3611
Joe K Tannehill Sr, *Chairman*
Grady W McDaniel, *Vice Pres*
Jene Roberson, *Foreman/Supr*
A Giridhar, *Opers Staff*
Steve Rhinehart, *Purch Mgr*
EMP: 120 **EST:** 1991
SQ FT: 57,000
SALES (est): 29.9MM **Privately Held**
SIC: 3596 Weighing machines & apparatus

(G-8034)
THE NATURAL LIGHT INC
Also Called: Natural Light, The
1020 Arthur Dr (32444-1683)
P.O. Box 16449, Panama City (32406-6449)
PHONE..............................850 265-0800
Harvey Hollingsworth, *President*
Joann Hollingsworth, *Admin Sec*
◆ **EMP:** 50 **EST:** 1978
SQ FT: 40,000
SALES (est): 8.9MM **Privately Held**
WEB: www.thenaturallight.com
SIC: 3645 5712 Table lamps; chandeliers, residential; furniture stores

Macclenny
Baker County

(G-8035)
APEX FABRICATION INC
710 Griffin Ct (32063-4629)
P.O. Box 366 (32063-0366)
PHONE..............................904 259-4666
Kirby L O'Steen III, *President*
John Linsley, *Vice Pres*
Casey Woron, *QC Mgr*
David Richardson, *Director*
EMP: 19 **EST:** 1999
SQ FT: 3,638
SALES (est): 2.5MM **Privately Held**
WEB: www.apexfab.com
SIC: 3441 Fabricated structural metal

(G-8036)
BAKER COUNTY PRESS INC
104 S 5th St (32063-2304)
P.O. Box 598 (32063-0598)
PHONE..............................904 259-2400
James Charles Mc Gauley, *President*
James Mc Gauley, *Publisher*
Joel Addington, *Editor*
Brianna Bartlett, *Editor*
Margaret E Mc Gauley, *Vice Pres*
EMP: 5 **EST:** 1968
SQ FT: 1,800

SALES (est): 994.1K **Privately Held**
WEB: www.bakercountypress.com
SIC: 2711 5112 5943 2752 Newspapers: publishing only, not printed on site; office supplies; office forms & supplies; commercial printing, lithographic; gift shop

(G-8037)
GW CREAMERY LLC
1458 S 6th St (32063-4623)
PHONE..............................904 509-6202
Joseph A Graham, *Principal*
EMP: 7 **EST:** 2011
SALES (est): 73.6K **Privately Held**
SIC: 2021 Creamery butter

(G-8038)
MAX GRAPHIX LLC
583 S 6th St (32063-2605)
PHONE..............................904 408-1543
EMP: 7 **EST:** 2019
SALES (est): 238.5K **Privately Held**
WEB: www.maxgraphix904.com
SIC: 3993 Signs & advertising specialties

Madeira Beach
Pinellas County

(G-8039)
A SANBORN CORPORATION
Also Called: Sanbornwebdesigns.com
15019 Madeira Way (33738-1900)
P.O. Box 86747, Saint Petersburg (33738-6747)
PHONE..............................727 397-3073
Ann Sanborn, *President*
EMP: 21 **EST:** 2000
SALES (est): 1MM **Privately Held**
WEB: www.sanbornwebdesigns.com
SIC: 3229 7374 Art, decorative & novelty glassware; glassware, art or decorative; computer graphics service

(G-8040)
JOHNS PASS WINERY
12945 Village Blvd (33708-2656)
PHONE..............................727 362-0008
Diane Downs, *Manager*
EMP: 5 **EST:** 2004
SALES (est): 474K **Privately Held**
WEB: www.thefloridawinery.com
SIC: 2084 Wines

(G-8041)
SPORT AMERICA MAGAZINE
248 144th Ave (33708-2108)
PHONE..............................727 391-3099
Allan Dill, *President*
EMP: 8 **EST:** 1978
SALES (est): 395.9K **Privately Held**
SIC: 2721 Magazines: publishing only, not printed on site

Madison
Madison County

(G-8042)
GRAY LOGGING LLC
811 Ne Oats Ave (32340-3648)
PHONE..............................850 973-3863
Jerry Gray, *Mng Member*
EMP: 7 **EST:** 2002
SQ FT: 800
SALES (est): 466.8K **Privately Held**
WEB: www.graylogging.com
SIC: 2411 Logging camps & contractors

(G-8043)
GRAY LOGGING LLC
665 Sw Harvey Greene Dr (32340-4429)
PHONE..............................850 973-3863
Jerry Gray, *Mng Member*
EMP: 8 **EST:** 2012
SALES (est): 1.2MM **Privately Held**
WEB: www.graylogging.com
SIC: 2411 Logging camps & contractors

▲ = Import ▼=Export
◆ =Import/Export

(G-8044)
GREENE PUBLISHING INC
1695 S State Road 53 (32340-3331)
P.O. Box 772 (32341-0772)
PHONE..................................850 973-6397
Emerald Greene, *President*
Emerald Kinsley, *President*
Cheltsie Holbrook, *Office Mgr*
Mary E Greene, *Admin Sec*
EMP: 28 **EST:** 1964
SQ FT: 1,000
SALES (est): 2.6MM **Privately Held**
WEB: www.greenepublishing.com
SIC: 2711 Newspapers, publishing & print-
ing

(G-8045)
JIMBOB PRINTING INC
482 Sw Range Ave (32340-2209)
P.O. Box 633 (32341-0633)
PHONE..................................850 973-2633
James Williams, *President*
Sylvia Williams, *Treasurer*
EMP: 10 **EST:** 1968
SQ FT: 2,100
SALES (est): 668.2K **Privately Held**
SIC: 2752 Commercial printing, offset

(G-8046)
PRG PACKING CORP (PA)
Also Called: Ferris Stahl-Meyers Packing
294 Sw Harvey Greene Dr (32340-4266)
P.O. Box 1538, Fort Lee NJ (07024-8038)
PHONE..................................201 242-5500
Guillermo Gonzalez, *Ch of Bd*
Christina Gonzalez, *VP Sls/Mktg*
Ana Gonzalez, *Controller*
Louie Miller, *Manager*
EMP: 39 **EST:** 1997
SALES (est): 21.8MM **Privately Held**
WEB: www.stahlmeyer.com
SIC: 2011 Meat packing plants

(G-8047)
SWAPPER
115 Se Madison St (32340-2715)
P.O. Box 422 (32341-0422)
PHONE..................................850 973-6653
Wilmer Strickland, *Owner*
EMP: 6 **EST:** 1986
SALES (est): 370.5K **Privately Held**
WEB: www.madisonswapper.com
SIC: 2721 2711 Magazines: publishing
only, not printed on site; newspapers:
publishing only, not printed on site

Maitland
Orange County

(G-8048)
3N2 LLC
Also Called: 3n2 Sports
111 Atlantic Annex Pt # 1 (32751-3369)
PHONE..................................407 862-3622
Sean Murphy, *CEO*
Marty Graham, *Vice Pres*
Leroy Santos, *Graphic Designe*
▲ **EMP:** 6 **EST:** 2007
SALES (est): 1MM **Privately Held**
WEB: www.3n2sports.com
SIC: 3949 Sporting & athletic goods

(G-8049)
ABBOTT PRINTING CO
Also Called: Abbott Communications Group
110 Atlantic Dr Ste 110 # 110 (32751-3300)
PHONE..................................407 831-2999
Arthur R Abbott, *President*
George Adorno, *President*
Casey Webb, *Business Mgr*
Kathy Trail, *Assistant VP*
David W Abbott, *Vice Pres*
EMP: 54 **EST:** 1977
SQ FT: 23,000
SALES (est): 14.8MM **Privately Held**
WEB: www.abbottcg.com
SIC: 2752 Commercial printing, offset

(G-8050)
**BAYSHORE CON
PRDCTS/CHSPAKE IN**
2600 Mtland Ctr Pkwy Ste (32751)
P.O. Box 230, Cape Charles VA (23310-
0230)
PHONE..................................757 331-2300
John Gray, *President*
John Chandler, *Vice Pres*
EMP: 95 **EST:** 1989
SALES (est): 2.6MM
SALES (corp-wide): 15.7B **Privately Held**
SIC: 3272 Concrete products
HQ: Bayshore Concrete Products Corpora-
tion
2600 Mtland Ctr Pkwy Ste
Maitland FL 32751
757 331-2300

(G-8051)
**BAYSHORE CONCRETE PDTS
CORP (DH)**
2600 Mtland Ctr Pkwy Ste (32751)
PHONE..................................757 331-2300
John Gray, *President*
John D Chandler, *Corp Secy*
Wade Watson, *Project Dir*
Wayne Bell, *Safety Mgr*
▲ **EMP:** 250 **EST:** 1961
SALES (est): 94.1MM
SALES (corp-wide): 15.7B **Privately Held**
SIC: 3272 Prestressed concrete products
HQ: Skanska Usa Civil Southeast Inc.
2600 Mtland Ctr Pkwy Ste
Maitland FL 32751
757 420-4140

(G-8052)
BCA TECHNOLOGIES INC
1051 Winderley Pl Ste 310 (32751-7266)
PHONE..................................407 659-0653
Brian Cumming, *President*
Craig Scurlock, *Engineer*
Lollie Marcelin, *Sales Executive*
Danny Saladiakanda, *Manager*
Keith Szirmay, *Software Dev*
EMP: 12 **EST:** 1997
SALES (est): 2MM **Privately Held**
WEB: www.bcatech.com
SIC: 7372 8711 7373 7371 Business ori-
ented computer software; engineering
services; systems software development
services; computer software development
& applications; computer software devel-
opment

(G-8053)
BOTANICAL INNOVATIONS INC
Also Called: Tree Innovations
100 Candace Dr Unit 120 (32751-3359)
PHONE..................................407 332-8733
James N Wilke, *President*
EMP: 7 **EST:** 1982
SQ FT: 5,000
SALES (est): 123.1K **Privately Held**
SIC: 3999 Artificial trees & flowers; plants,
artificial & preserved; flowers, artificial &
preserved

(G-8054)
COMP U NETCOM INC
331 N Maitland Ave D10 (32751-4762)
PHONE..................................407 539-1800
Edgar Aya, *Principal*
EMP: 9 **EST:** 2001
SALES (est): 470.9K **Privately Held**
SIC: 7372 Prepackaged software

(G-8055)
**CREATIVE VTRAN
PRODUCTIONS LLC**
2400 Mtland Ctr Pkwy Ste (32751)
PHONE..................................407 656-2743
Joshua Lively, *Principal*
James Noble, *Principal*
Randy Noble, *Vice Pres*
Kevin Schmitt, *Manager*
David Wellons, *Manager*
EMP: 18 **EST:** 2007
SALES (est): 2.5MM **Privately Held**
WEB: www.creativevet.com
SIC: 7372 Prepackaged software

(G-8056)
CUPCAKE INC
105 Candace Dr Unit 109 (32751-3327)
PHONE..................................407 644-7800
William J Murphy, *President*
EMP: 7 **EST:** 2010
SALES (est): 215.4K **Privately Held**
SIC: 2051 Bread, cake & related products

(G-8057)
ENGAGE SURGICAL KNEE LLC
201 Wood Lake Dr (32751-3155)
PHONE..................................614 915-2960
Ronald Webster, *Mng Member*
EMP: 5 **EST:** 2020
SALES (est): 1.1MM
SALES (corp-wide): 5.2B **Privately Held**
SIC: 2834 Pharmaceutical preparations
PA: Smith & Nephew Plc
Building 5, Croxley Park
Watford HERTS WD18
800 015-7573

(G-8058)
FIREHOUSE PROMOTIONS INC
2450 Maitland Center Pkwy (32751-4140)
PHONE..................................407 990-1600
Sylvanio Perino, *President*
Anthony Perino, *Vice Pres*
Lee Drayton, *Director*
Sarah Morrison, *Admin Sec*
EMP: 7 **EST:** 2013
SALES (est): 245.6K **Privately Held**
SIC: 2752 Advertising posters, litho-
graphed

(G-8059)
FURRYTAILS LLC
555 Winderley Pl Ste 300 (32751-7133)
P.O. Box 1039, Ocoee (34761-1039)
PHONE..................................407 654-1465
Steve Ellis, *Managing Prtnr*
▲ **EMP:** 10 **EST:** 1992
SALES (est): 794.3K **Privately Held**
WEB: www.furrytails.com
SIC: 3944 Games, toys & children's vehi-
cles

(G-8060)
GLUCORELL INC
Also Called: Insulow
130 White Oak Cir (32751-4827)
P.O. Box 470794, Lake Monroe (32747-
0794)
PHONE..................................407 384-3388
Laurence Berube, *President*
Jerel Scott Ferguson, *Vice Pres*
Ursula Berube, *Treasurer*
EMP: 10 **EST:** 2000
SALES (est): 770.9K **Privately Held**
WEB: www.glucorell.com
SIC: 2834 Vitamin preparations

(G-8061)
GRAND CYPRESS GROUP INC
Also Called: Brandcomet
151 N Maitland Ave (32751-5515)
P.O. Box 947819 (32794-7819)
PHONE..................................407 622-1993
Sandal Scarborough, *CEO*
James Esch, *President*
EMP: 6 **EST:** 2001
SQ FT: 1,000
SALES (est): 671.7K **Privately Held**
WEB: www.brandcomet.com
SIC: 2759 8743 8742 Screen printing;
promotion service; marketing consulting
services

(G-8062)
JAYCO SIGNS INC
149 Atlantic Dr (32751-3323)
PHONE..................................407 339-5252
Gregory Yoder, *President*
Gregory L Yoder, *President*
▲ **EMP:** 10 **EST:** 1972
SQ FT: 100,000
SALES (est): 446.7K **Privately Held**
WEB: www.jaycosigns.net
SIC: 3993 7389 1799 Electric signs;
crane & aerial lift service; sign installation
& maintenance

(G-8063)
KBF DESIGN GALLERY INC
1295 S Orlando Ave (32751-6412)
PHONE..................................407 830-7703
Keith J Vellequette, *President*
Meredith Barnes, *Consultant*
EMP: 5 **EST:** 2003
SALES (est): 791.2K **Privately Held**
WEB: www.kbfdesigngallery.com
SIC: 2434 Wood kitchen cabinets

(G-8064)
KENEXA LEARNING INC
601 S Lake Destiny Rd # 30 (32751-7226)
PHONE..................................407 562-1905
Masood Zarrabian, *Branch Mgr*
EMP: 8
SALES (corp-wide): 57.3B **Publicly Held**
WEB: www.outstart.com
SIC: 7372 7379 Business oriented com-
puter software; computer related consult-
ing services
HQ: Kenexa Learning, Inc.
650 E Swedesford Rd 2nd
Wayne PA 19087
610 971-9171

(G-8065)
L4 DESIGN LLC (PA)
Also Called: Oakley Signs
2701 Mtland Ctr Pkwy Ste (32751)
PHONE..................................407 262-8200
Kenneth D Levitt, *President*
Tom Symonanis, *COO*
Brett M Levitt, *Vice Pres*
Brett Levitt, *Vice Pres*
Keith R Levitt, *Vice Pres*
▼ **EMP:** 20 **EST:** 2003
SALES (est): 10.2MM **Privately Held**
WEB: www.oakleysign.com
SIC: 3993 Signs, not made in custom sign
painting shops

(G-8066)
L4 DESIGN LLC
2701 Mtland Ctr Pkwy Ste (32751)
PHONE..................................224 612-5045
Kenneth D Levitt, *Branch Mgr*
Jason Vetter, *Supervisor*
EMP: 15
SALES (corp-wide): 10.2MM **Privately
Held**
WEB: www.oakleysign.com
SIC: 3993 Signs & advertising specialties
PA: L4 Design, Llc
2701 Mtland Ctr Pkwy Ste
Maitland FL 32751
407 262-8200

(G-8067)
MAP & GLOBE LLC (PA)
Also Called: Map and Globe Store, The
113 Candace Dr Ste 3 (32751-3330)
PHONE..................................407 898-0757
Jane Bond,
Greg Bond,
EMP: 5 **EST:** 1989
SQ FT: 4,677
SALES (est): 1.2MM **Privately Held**
WEB: www.mgstore.com
SIC: 2741 5999 Maps: publishing only, not
printed on site; maps & charts

(G-8068)
P3D CREATIONS LLC
105 Candace Dr Unit 121 (32751-3327)
PHONE..................................407 801-9126
Katherine G Palmer, *Principal*
Nickolas Polanosky, *Mng Member*
EMP: 10 **EST:** 2015
SALES (est): 947.4K **Privately Held**
WEB: www.p3dcreations.com
SIC: 3599 7389 Machine shop, jobbing &
repair; metal cutting services

(G-8069)
PHOCAS SOFTWARE
235 S Maitland Ave (32751-5677)
PHONE..................................863 738-9107
Jamie Brooks, *Partner*
Mike Hills, *General Mgr*
Myles Glashier, *Principal*
Evan Tennyson, *Business Mgr*
Peter Jenkins, *Sales Executive*
EMP: 22 **EST:** 2014

SALES (est): 2.6MM **Privately Held**
WEB: www.phocsoftware.com
SIC: 7372 Business oriented computer software

(G-8070)
PROPEL BUILDERS INC
111 S Maitland Ave # 200 (32751-5637)
PHONE.............................407 960-5116
Walter Olejarski, *Production*
Ashley Cornell, *Office Mgr*
Kimberly Carter, *Manager*
Brandy Rizzo, *Admin Asst*
EMP: 14 **EST:** 2016
SALES (est): 849.2K **Privately Held**
WEB: www.propelbuilders.com
SIC: 3731 Shipbuilding & repairing

(G-8071)
RESELL MFG LLC
2600 Maitland Center Pkwy (32751-7221)
PHONE.............................407 478-8181
John K Butz, *Principal*
EMP: 5 **EST:** 2015
SALES (est): 464.3K **Privately Held**
WEB: www.auction.resellcnc.com
SIC: 3999 Manufacturing industries

(G-8072)
SAINT-GOBAIN VETROTEX AMER INC
110 Atlantic Annex Pt (32751-3314)
PHONE.............................407 834-8968
EMP: 169
SALES (corp-wide): 340.6MM **Privately Held**
WEB: www.saint-gobain-northamerica.com
SIC: 3089 Spouting, plastic & glass fiber reinforced
HQ: Saint-Gobain Vetrotex America, Inc.
20 Moores Rd
Valley Forge PA 19482

(G-8073)
SIGNPOST LLC
Also Called: Signposts
1236 Trust Ln (32751-4258)
PHONE.............................813 334-7678
Randall Chan-A-Shing, *Manager*
EMP: 9 **EST:** 2014
SALES (est): 255.1K **Privately Held**
WEB: www.signpost.com
SIC: 3993 Signs & advertising specialties

(G-8074)
SOUTHERN HVAC CORPORATION (HQ)
Also Called: Honeywell Authorized Dealer
485 N Keller Rd Ste 515 (32751-7506)
PHONE.............................407 917-1800
Bryan Benak, *President*
Dena Jalbert, *CFO*
EMP: 5 **EST:** 2016
SALES (est): 9.7MM **Privately Held**
WEB: www.southernhomeservices.com
SIC: 3585 Air conditioning units, complete: domestic or industrial

(G-8075)
TEKTRONIX INC
151 Southhall Ln Ste 170 (32751-7486)
PHONE.............................407 660-2727
EMP: 14
SALES (corp-wide): 19.1B **Publicly Held**
SIC: 3825 Mfg Computers And Computer Software & Service Center
HQ: Tektronix, Inc.
14150 Sw Karl Braun Dr
Beaverton OR 97005
800 833-9200

(G-8076)
THE NANOSTEEL COMPANY LLC (HQ)
485 N Keller Rd Ste 100 (32751-7507)
PHONE.............................407 838-1427
Harald Lemke, *Vice Pres*
Robert C Marini Jr, *Vice Pres*
David Paratore,
EMP: 7 **EST:** 2002
SQ FT: 3,600
SALES (est): 2.3MM
SALES (corp-wide): 4MM **Privately Held**
SIC: 3479 Galvanizing of iron, steel or end-formed products

PA: Military Commercial Technologies, Inc.
750 S Orlando Ave Ste 200
Winter Park FL 32789
407 659-0443

(G-8077)
US IMPLANT SOLUTIONS LLC
Also Called: I.T.S. USA
1778 N Park Ave Ste 200 (32751-6504)
PHONE.............................407 971-8054
Dustin Dittmer, *COO*
EMP: 9 **EST:** 2004
SALES (est): 5.3MM **Privately Held**
WEB: www.its-implant.com
SIC: 3842 Implants, surgical

(G-8078)
VMAX VISION INC
2600 Mtland Ctr Pkwy Ste (32751)
PHONE.............................321 972-1823
Christy Barnes, *Office Mgr*
Xantha Real, *Director*
EMP: 5 **EST:** 2007
SQ FT: 2,500
SALES (est): 1.2MM **Privately Held**
WEB: www.vmaxvision.com
SIC: 3841 Eye examining instruments & apparatus

(G-8079)
WESTCOAST BRACE & LIMB INC
341 N Maitland Ave # 210 (32751-4783)
PHONE.............................407 502-0024
Greg Bauer, *Principal*
EMP: 75 **EST:** 1981
SALES (est): 2MM **Privately Held**
WEB: www.wcbl.com
SIC: 3842 Surgical appliances & supplies

(G-8080)
ZERION GROUP LLC
235 S Maitland Ave # 100 (32751-5677)
P.O. Box 940411 (32794-0411)
PHONE.............................877 872-1726
Joel Gordon, *Marketing Staff*
Steve Gonter, *Consultant*
Libby Juarez, *Consultant*
Mark Murph, *Consultant*
Christy Tucker, *Consultant*
EMP: 10 **EST:** 2005
SALES (est): 693.2K **Privately Held**
WEB: www.zeriongroup.com
SIC: 7372 Business oriented computer software

Malabar
Brevard County

(G-8081)
DWI INC
1960 Howell Ln (32950-7017)
P.O. Box 500283 (32950-0283)
PHONE.............................321 508-9833
Douglas E Weaver, *Principal*
EMP: 9 **EST:** 2008
SALES (est): 470K **Privately Held**
SIC: 3443 Industrial vessels, tanks & containers

(G-8082)
HALO FISHING LLC
520 Atz Rd (32950-3625)
PHONE.............................321 373-2055
Lionel Botha, *CEO*
Lesley Botha,
▲ **EMP:** 6 **EST:** 2012
SALES (est): 1MM **Privately Held**
WEB: www.americanbaitworks.com
SIC: 3949 Rods & rod parts, fishing

(G-8083)
JOHNSON WOODWORKING
3470 Leghorn Rd (32950-4017)
PHONE.............................772 473-1404
Craig Johnson, *Owner*
EMP: 9 **EST:** 1983
SALES (est): 458.8K **Privately Held**
SIC: 2431 Millwork

(G-8084)
K K WOODWORKING
2300 Kahler Ln (32950-4009)
PHONE.............................321 724-1298
Kim Kahler, *Owner*
EMP: 8 **EST:** 2000
SALES (est): 546.4K **Privately Held**
WEB: www.k-kwoodworking.com
SIC: 2499 Decorative wood & woodwork

(G-8085)
KRIEGER PUBLISHING CO INC
1725 Krieger Ln (32950-3323)
PHONE.............................321 724-9542
Robert E Krieger, *CEO*
Donald Krieger, *President*
Maxine D Krieger, *Vice Pres*
Shel Cohen, *Sales Dir*
Carol Krieger, *Manager*
▲ **EMP:** 13 **EST:** 1969
SQ FT: 40,000
SALES (est): 2MM **Privately Held**
WEB: www.krieger-publishing.com
SIC: 2741 Miscellaneous publishing

(G-8086)
L3HARRIS TECHNOLOGIES INC
2800 Jordan Blvd (32950-4536)
PHONE.............................321 768-4660
Bill Brown, *CEO*
Brian Warkentine, *Manager*
EMP: 57
SALES (corp-wide): 17.8B **Publicly Held**
WEB: www.l3harris.com
SIC: 3812 3663 Search & navigation equipment; radio & TV communications equipment
PA: L3harris Technologies, Inc.
1025 W Nasa Blvd
Melbourne FL 32919
321 727-9100

Mangonia Park
Palm Beach County

(G-8087)
AMERICAN METAL FABRICATORS INC
Also Called: AMF Building Products
1501 53rd St (33407-2210)
PHONE.............................561 790-5799
David T Zajac, *President*
◆ **EMP:** 40 **EST:** 2008
SALES (est): 9.1MM **Privately Held**
WEB: www.amfbuildingproducts.com
SIC: 3444 Sheet metalwork

(G-8088)
AUTOMATED MFG SYSTEMS INC
5700 Columbia Cir (33407-2217)
P.O. Box 31731, West Palm Beach (33420-1731)
PHONE.............................561 833-9898
Richard Bell, *President*
Brandon Bell, *Sales Executive*
EMP: 7 **EST:** 1993
SALES (est): 1.7MM **Privately Held**
WEB: www.ams-plasticextrusions.com
SIC: 3089 Injection molding of plastics

(G-8089)
BAHAMA BOAT WORKS LLC
5490 Dexter Way (33407-2219)
PHONE.............................561 882-4069
Amy Kirk, *Purchasing*
John Mooney, *Purchasing*
Derek Rawnsley, *Sales Staff*
Robert Sparks, *Mng Member*
EMP: 10 **EST:** 2005
SALES (est): 1.8MM **Privately Held**
WEB: www.bahamaboatworks.com
SIC: 3732 Boats, fiberglass: building & repairing

(G-8090)
BOGUE EXECUTIVE ENTERPRISES
Also Called: Dexter Tool 94
1501 53rd St (33407-2210)
PHONE.............................561 842-5336
Carrie A Bogue, *President*
Dennis Jones, *Vice Pres*
Ms Chris De Souza, *Controller*

EMP: 18 **EST:** 1965
SQ FT: 25,000
SALES (est): 1.6MM **Privately Held**
SIC: 3724 3589 1799 7389 Aircraft engines & engine parts; rocket motors, aircraft; sewage & water treatment equipment; welding on site; inspection & testing services

(G-8091)
BRICK MARKERS USA INC
4430 W Tiffany Dr Ste 2 (33407-3239)
PHONE.............................561 842-1338
Sharon Rieck, *President*
Albert S Rieck, *Vice Pres*
Kellie Wallace, *Sales Staff*
EMP: 14 **EST:** 1996
SQ FT: 7,500
SALES (est): 1.9MM **Privately Held**
WEB: www.brickmarkers.com
SIC: 3251 Brick & structural clay tile

(G-8092)
HOOVER CANVAS PRODUCTS CO
Also Called: Datum Metal Products
5107 N Australian Ave (33407-2313)
PHONE.............................954 541-9745
Jo Montenegro, *Manager*
EMP: 13
SALES (corp-wide): 9.4MM **Privately Held**
WEB: www.hooverap.com
SIC: 2394 Awnings, fabric: made from purchased materials
PA: Hoover Canvas Products, Co.
844 Nw 9th Ave
Fort Lauderdale FL 33311
954 764-1711

(G-8093)
HOOVER CANVAS PRODUCTS CO
5107 N Australian Ave (33407-2313)
PHONE.............................561 844-4444
Eric Garey, *Prdtn Mgr*
Chad Zimmermann, *Engineer*
Jennifer Walter, *Manager*
Tim Whipps, *Director*
EMP: 13
SALES (corp-wide): 9.4MM **Privately Held**
WEB: www.hooverap.com
SIC: 2394 Awnings, fabric: made from purchased materials
PA: Hoover Canvas Products, Co.
844 Nw 9th Ave
Fort Lauderdale FL 33311
954 764-1711

(G-8094)
JM CUSTOM MILLWORKS INC
1113 48th St Ste 2 (33407-2367)
PHONE.............................561 582-5600
Jeremy J Mulligan, *Principal*
EMP: 16 **EST:** 2012
SALES (est): 1.2MM **Privately Held**
SIC: 2431 Millwork

(G-8095)
JM CUSTOM WOODWORKING
1113 48th St Ste 2 (33407-2367)
PHONE.............................561 582-5600
Jeremy J Mulligan, *President*
EMP: 17 **EST:** 2008
SALES (est): 2.4MM **Privately Held**
SIC: 2431 Millwork

(G-8096)
KEMP SIGNS INC
1740 Hill Ave (33407-2237)
PHONE.............................561 840-6382
Steven Kemp, *President*
Stephen Kemp, *President*
Gilbert Strelec Jr, *Vice Pres*
▼ **EMP:** 10 **EST:** 1995
SQ FT: 2,000
SALES (est): 1.5MM **Privately Held**
WEB: www.kempsigns.net
SIC: 3993 Signs, not made in custom sign painting shops

(G-8097)
PALM BEACH CSTM WOODWORKS LLC
Also Called: Pbcw Shutters and More
1315 53rd St Ste 5 (33407-2245)
PHONE...................561 575-5335
Perez Victor, *Mng Member*
EMP: 18 **EST:** 2013
SALES (est): 1.7MM **Privately Held**
WEB:
www.palmbeachcustomwoodworks.com
SIC: 2431 Millwork

(G-8098)
PALM BEACH WOODWORK CO INC
1101 53rd Ct S Ste B (33407-2384)
PHONE...................561 844-8818
Bradley T Haylett, *President*
Tom Haylett, *Senior VP*
Bartley R Haylett, *Vice Pres*
Thomas D Haylett, *Vice Pres*
EMP: 6 **EST:** 1934
SQ FT: 8,000
SALES (est): 909.6K **Privately Held**
WEB: www.palmbeachwoodwork.com
SIC: 2431 Ornamental woodwork: cornices, mantels, etc.

(G-8099)
PRIME TECH COATINGS INC
Also Called: Prime Technical Coatings
1135 53rd Ct N (33407-2347)
PHONE...................561 844-2312
Pete J Luther, *President*
Sherry M Luther, *Vice Pres*
▼ **EMP:** 7 **EST:** 1971
SQ FT: 10,000
SALES (est): 984.5K **Privately Held**
WEB: www.primetechcoatings.com
SIC: 3479 Coating of metals & formed products

(G-8100)
SCIENTIFIC INSTRUMENTS INC
4400 W Tiffany Dr (33407-3294)
PHONE...................561 881-8500
Leigh Ann Hoey, *President*
Joan Hoey, *Principal*
Deanna Szpendyk, *Purch Mgr*
Romeo Cuvin, *QC Mgr*
Dwaine Hessing, *Research*
▼ **EMP:** 40 **EST:** 1967
SQ FT: 12,000
SALES (est): 9.2MM **Privately Held**
WEB: www.scientificinstruments.com
SIC: 3829 3823 3674 3625 Measuring & controlling devices; industrial instrmnts msrmnt display/control process variable; semiconductors & related devices; relays & industrial controls

(G-8101)
STERLING STEEL FABRICATIONS
1139 53rd Ct N (33407-2347)
PHONE...................561 366-8600
Patricia A Fye, *President*
Allen Auman, *Opers Mgr*
EMP: 20 **EST:** 2004
SQ FT: 16,200
SALES (est): 3.8MM **Privately Held**
WEB: www.sterlingsteelfabrications.com
SIC: 3441 Fabricated structural metal

(G-8102)
TERRY D TRIPLETT INC
Also Called: House of Wood
1103 53rd Ct S Ste B (33407-2329)
P.O. Box 17559, West Palm Beach (33416-7559)
PHONE...................561 251-3641
Terry D Triplett, *President*
EMP: 7 **EST:** 1993
SALES (est): 698.9K **Privately Held**
SIC: 2431 Moldings, wood: unfinished & prefinished

(G-8103)
TITAN AMERICA LLC
1453 53rd St (33407-2208)
PHONE...................561 842-5309
Tyron Roberson, *General Mgr*
EMP: 10
SQ FT: 28,794

SALES (corp-wide): 177.9K **Privately Held**
WEB: www.titanamerica.com
SIC: 3273 Ready-mixed concrete
HQ: Titan America Llc
5700 Lake Wright Dr # 300
Norfolk VA 23502
757 858-6500

(G-8104)
ZELLERMAYER SUPPLY CORP (PA)
1231 52nd St Ste B (33407-2267)
P.O. Box 13026, West Palm Beach (33408-7026)
PHONE...................561 848-0057
Gerald Singer, *President*
Myrna Singer, *Vice Pres*
David Singer, *Treasurer*
Eric Singer, *Admin Sec*
EMP: 12 **EST:** 1938
SALES (est): 1.4MM **Privately Held**
SIC: 2211 Bags & bagging, cotton

Marathon
Monroe County

(G-8105)
AIR ALLIANCE INC
13369 Overseas Hwy (33050-3550)
PHONE...................305 735-4864
Michael Moore, *CEO*
Lynn Moore, *CFO*
EMP: 7 **EST:** 2020
SALES (est): 800.1K **Privately Held**
WEB: www.airalliance.co
SIC: 3724 Aircraft engines & engine parts

(G-8106)
BROADSWORD SOLUTIONS CORP
2020 Manor Ln (33050-2462)
PHONE...................248 341-3367
Jeffrey Dalton, *President*
Jill Mannaioni, *Partner*
Amy Wilson, *Marketing Staff*
Patricia Dalton, *Director*
Michelle Rauch, *Sr Consultant*
EMP: 10 **EST:** 2004
SALES (est): 452.2K **Privately Held**
WEB: www.broadswordsolutions.com
SIC: 7372 Business oriented computer software

(G-8107)
JONES MEDIAAMERICA INC
11399 Overseas Hwy 5sw (33050-3403)
PHONE...................305 289-4524
Gwen Jones, *President*
Robert W Hampton, *Vice Pres*
Gary Schonfeld, *Vice Pres*
Lorri Ellis, *Treasurer*
Mark Lane, *Admin Sec*
EMP: 134 **EST:** 1987
SALES (est): 324.7K **Privately Held**
SIC: 3825 Network analyzers
PA: Triton Media Group, Llc
15303 Ventura Blvd # 1500
Sherman Oaks CA 91403

(G-8108)
KEYNOTER PUBLISHING CO INC
Also Called: Florida Keys Keynoter
3015 Overseas Hwy (33050-2236)
P.O. Box 500158 (33050-0158)
PHONE...................305 743-5551
Wayne Markem, *Vice Pres*
Robert Singleton, *Vice Pres*
Larry Levin, *Treasurer*
Mary Lou Sollberger, *Finance Dir*
EMP: 15 **EST:** 1953
SQ FT: 4,000
SALES (est): 3.8MM
SALES (corp-wide): 709.5MM **Privately Held**
WEB: www.keysinfonet.com
SIC: 2711 Newspapers, publishing & printing
HQ: Jck Legacy Company
1601 Alhambra Blvd # 100
Sacramento CA 95816
916 321-1844

(G-8109)
WEEKLY NEWSPAPER
9709 Overseas Hwy (33050-3342)
PHONE...................305 743-0844
Jason Koler, *Owner*
Lesley Aaron, *Marketing Staff*
EMP: 10 **EST:** 2007
SALES (est): 1.3MM **Privately Held**
WEB: www.keysweekly.com
SIC: 2711 5994 Newspapers, publishing & printing; newsstand

(G-8110)
WOHLERS PUBLISHING INC
10701 6th Avenue Gulf (33050-2919)
P.O. Box 504462 (33050-4462)
PHONE...................305 289-1644
Tressa L Wohlers, *President*
EMP: 7 **EST:** 2010
SALES (est): 175.4K **Privately Held**
WEB: www.wohlerspublishing.com
SIC: 2741 Miscellaneous publishing

Marco Island
Collier County

(G-8111)
EVOLVE TECHNOLOGIES INC
Also Called: Evolve E-Learning Solutions
950 N Collier Blvd # 400 (34145-2722)
PHONE...................239 963-8037
Preston Stiner, *President*
Jeanine Delaney, *Sales Staff*
EMP: 5 **EST:** 2001
SALES (est): 410.1K **Privately Held**
WEB: www.evolveeelearning.com
SIC: 7372 Prepackaged software

(G-8112)
HYDRAPOWER INTERNATIONAL INC
950 N Collier Blvd # 202 (34145-2725)
P.O. Box 2649 (34146-2649)
PHONE...................239 642-5379
Robin F Wissing, *President*
Carol A Wissing, *Admin Sec*
▲ **EMP:** 1100 **EST:** 1973
SQ FT: 3,100
SALES (est): 37.7MM **Privately Held**
WEB: www.hydrapower-intl.com
SIC: 3542 Shearing machines, power; press brakes; presses: hydraulic & pneumatic, mechanical & manual

(G-8113)
TEAM SERVICE CORP NEW YORK
1040 Coronado Ct (34145-4520)
PHONE...................410 365-1574
James Huber, *Branch Mgr*
EMP: 30
SALES (corp-wide): 9.8MM **Privately Held**
SIC: 7694 5063 Electric motor repair; motors, electric
PA: T.E.A.M. Service Corporation Of New York
1400 Rome Rd
Baltimore MD 21227
410 536-4488

(G-8114)
WHITMAN INDUSTRIES LLC
1825 Dogwood Dr (34145-6718)
PHONE...................239 216-6171
Robert J Whitman,
EMP: 8 **EST:** 2008
SALES (est): 860.9K **Privately Held**
WEB: www.whitmanindustries.com
SIC: 3999 Manufacturing industries

Margate
Broward County

(G-8115)
AC PHARMA CORP
3241 Holiday Springs Blvd (33063-5468)
PHONE...................954 773-9735
Mohamed Shafeek, *President*
Naeema Lodhi, *Exec Sec*
EMP: 5 **EST:** 2013

SQ FT: 3,000
SALES (est): 500K **Privately Held**
WEB: www.acpharmacorp.com
SIC: 2834 Pharmaceutical preparations

(G-8116)
ADVANCED CNC MACHINING INC
6135 Nw 20th Ct (33063-2346)
PHONE...................954 478-8369
Peter Paulovich, *President*
EMP: 6 **EST:** 1996
SQ FT: 4,000
SALES (est): 508.9K **Privately Held**
SIC: 3599 Machine shop, jobbing & repair

(G-8117)
ADVANCED PALLETS INC
2151 N State Road 7 (33063-5713)
P.O. Box 51629, Lighthouse Point (33074-1629)
PHONE...................954 785-1215
Michael K McBride, *President*
EMP: 21 **EST:** 1996
SALES (est): 1.4MM **Privately Held**
SIC: 2448 Pallets, wood

(G-8118)
AHC VENTURES CORP
Also Called: Cryoderm
5415 Nw 24th St Ste 103 (33063-7730)
PHONE...................954 978-9290
Lloyd List, *CEO*
Laura Allen, *Vice Pres*
Alyse M List, *CFO*
▼ **EMP:** 11 **EST:** 2000
SQ FT: 10,000
SALES (est): 1.7MM **Privately Held**
WEB: www.cryoderm.com
SIC: 3841 Surgical & medical instruments

(G-8119)
AJ AZ WOODWORK INC
1917 Mears Pkwy (33063-3702)
PHONE...................561 859-4963
Everton Reid, *Principal*
EMP: 8 **EST:** 2010
SALES (est): 209.8K **Privately Held**
SIC: 2431 Millwork

(G-8120)
AMERICAN COATINGS CORPORATION
1457 Banks Rd (33063-3960)
PHONE...................954 970-7820
Herbert Weisberg, *President*
EMP: 5 **EST:** 1979
SQ FT: 6,300
SALES (est): 930.7K **Privately Held**
WEB: www.goamerco.com
SIC: 3292 2842 2851 5085 Asbestos products; specialty cleaning preparations; lacquers, varnishes, enamels & other coatings; industrial supplies; chemicals, industrial & heavy

(G-8121)
ASSIS MASTER PAINT CORP
511 Sw 62nd Ter (33068-1740)
PHONE...................786 797-6106
Francis De Assis, *Director*
EMP: 7 **EST:** 2003
SALES (est): 47.2K **Privately Held**
SIC: 2851 Paints & allied products

(G-8122)
AVW INC
Also Called: Blow Off
541 S State Road 7 Ste 2 (33068-1711)
P.O. Box 9962, Fort Lauderdale (33310-0962)
PHONE...................954 972-3338
Michael Fishman, *President*
▼ **EMP:** 24 **EST:** 1992
SQ FT: 4,000
SALES (est): 25MM **Privately Held**
SIC: 2813 5065 3822 Aerosols; electronic parts & equipment; auto controls regulating residntl & coml environmt & applncs

(G-8123)
BRANDANO DISPLAYS INC (PA)
1473 Banks Rd (33063-3960)
PHONE...................954 956-7266
John D Brandano, *Principal*

Patrick Brandano, *Exec VP*
EMP: 20 **EST:** 1976
SQ FT: 50,000
SALES (est): 5MM **Privately Held**
WEB: www.brandanodisplays.com
SIC: 3496 3999 Miscellaneous fabricated wire products; advertising display products

(G-8124)
COLLINS MEDIA & ADVG LLC
5453 Nw 24th St Ste 2 (33063-7776)
PHONE....................................954 688-9758
Elitsa Hristova,
EMP: 11 **EST:** 2015
SALES (est): 1.2MM **Privately Held**
SIC: 3993 7812 2754 7313 Signs & advertising specialties; video production; commercial printing, gravure; printed media advertising representatives

(G-8125)
COMPASS PRINTING AND MARKETING
5218 Nw 15th St (33063-3783)
PHONE....................................954 856-8331
Jose Vasquez, *Principal*
EMP: 7 **EST:** 2015
SALES (est): 148.6K **Privately Held**
SIC: 2752 Commercial printing, offset

(G-8126)
CONTRACTORS CABINET COMPANY
5512 W Sample Rd (33073-3468)
PHONE....................................786 492-7118
Hal Berner, *President*
Jan Hoffman, *Vice Pres*
EMP: 7 **EST:** 1993
SQ FT: 1,400
SALES (est): 801K **Privately Held**
WEB: www.cabinetsmargatefl.com
SIC: 2434 5211 Wood kitchen cabinets; cabinets, kitchen

(G-8127)
DAVIS-WICK TALENT MGT LLC
5400 Nw 27th Ct (33063-1602)
PHONE....................................407 369-1614
Janelle Brice, *CEO*
Brian Brice, *Director*
EMP: 36 **EST:** 2013
SALES (est): 1.1MM **Privately Held**
SIC: 2389 8741 7922 7929 Men's miscellaneous accessories; business management; entertainment promotion; entertainment group

(G-8128)
EXCELL WOODWORK CORP
1917 Mears Pkwy (33063-3702)
PHONE....................................954 461-0465
Yngrid Silva, *Principal*
EMP: 8 **EST:** 2017
SALES (est): 290.2K **Privately Held**
SIC: 2431 Millwork

(G-8129)
EXECUTIVE LABEL INC
5447 Nw 24th St Ste 5 (33063-7773)
PHONE....................................954 978-6983
Richard Preiser, *President*
Kevin Longuiel, *Vice Pres*
Peggy Preiser, *Production*
Preiser Peggy, *Treasurer*
Jason Raye, *Sales Staff*
◆ **EMP:** 12 **EST:** 1989
SQ FT: 10,000
SALES (est): 3.7MM **Privately Held**
WEB: www.executivelabel.com
SIC: 2759 Labels & seals: printing

(G-8130)
FIT CANVAS INC
870 Sw 50th Ave (33068-3135)
PHONE....................................954 258-9352
Valencia Jiovani, *Principal*
EMP: 7 **EST:** 2014
SALES (est): 89.7K **Privately Held**
WEB: www.fit-canvas.com
SIC: 2211 Canvas

(G-8131)
GLO CONSUMER SVCS & PRTG CO
6223 Nw 15th Ct (33063-2706)
PHONE....................................954 977-5450
Joseph Ondo, *President*
EMP: 7 **EST:** 2010
SALES (est): 94.6K **Privately Held**
SIC: 2752 Commercial printing, lithographic

(G-8132)
GOLD COAST PLST & STUCCO INC
1815 Nw 64th Way (33063-2326)
PHONE....................................954 275-9132
Jim A Kriz, *President*
EMP: 12 **EST:** 2001
SALES (est): 365.5K **Privately Held**
SIC: 3299 Stucco

(G-8133)
GOLDEN CENTURY INC
1935 Banks Rd (33063-7716)
PHONE....................................954 933-2911
Hwan K Yoon, *President*
EMP: 5 **EST:** 1984
SQ FT: 1,600
SALES (est): 433.3K **Privately Held**
WEB: www.goldencenturycasting.com
SIC: 3911 Jewelry, precious metal

(G-8134)
GRAPHIC DATA INC
7378 W Atlantic Blvd (33063-4214)
PHONE....................................954 493-8003
David Tomlin, *President*
EMP: 5 **EST:** 1995
SQ FT: 4,260
SALES (est): 597.5K **Privately Held**
SIC: 3577 5045 Computer peripheral equipment; computers, peripherals & software

(G-8135)
HURRICANE ROOFING & SHTMTL INC
1905 Mears Pkwy (33063-3702)
PHONE....................................954 968-8155
Eduardo B Valle Sr, *President*
EMP: 9 **EST:** 2012
SALES (est): 94.5K **Privately Held**
SIC: 3444 Sheet metalwork

(G-8136)
JAMBCO MILLWORK INC
101 S State Road 7 (33068-5722)
PHONE....................................954 977-4998
Don Gladis, *President*
Jane Jolliff, *Administration*
EMP: 12 **EST:** 1989
SQ FT: 22,000
SALES (est): 1.3MM **Privately Held**
WEB: www.jambcomillwork.com
SIC: 2431 3442 3431 3231 Doors, wood; metal doors, sash & trim; metal sanitary ware; products of purchased glass

(G-8137)
JPM IMPORT LLC
7350 Nw 1st St Apt 207 (33063-7519)
PHONE....................................800 753-3009
Joseph Maas, *President*
EMP: 35
SALES (corp-wide): 128.4K **Privately Held**
SIC: 3714 Wheels, motor vehicle
PA: Jpm Import Llc
5935 W Park Rd
Hollywood FL 33021
800 753-3009

(G-8138)
KAY PEAK GROUP INC
6510 W Atlantic Blvd (33063-5135)
PHONE....................................754 307-5400
Yves Laurent, *President*
EMP: 6 **EST:** 2017
SALES (est): 300K **Privately Held**
SIC: 2066 Chocolate

(G-8139)
KOVA LABORATORIES INC
1711 Banks Rd (33063-7744)
PHONE....................................954 978-8730

Kirk Sakai, *President*
EMP: 8 **EST:** 1986
SQ FT: 2,000
SALES (est): 988.7K **Privately Held**
SIC: 2834 Pharmaceutical preparations

(G-8140)
LANDMARK FINGERPRINTING
1855 N State Road 7 (33063-5707)
PHONE....................................754 205-6505
Robert Savin, *Owner*
EMP: 7 **EST:** 2014
SALES (est): 176.5K **Privately Held**
WEB: www.landmarkfingerprinting.com
SIC: 2752 Commercial printing, lithographic

(G-8141)
LATIN QUARTERS LLC (PA)
5100 Sw 6th St (33068-3012)
PHONE....................................954 470-8034
Yovana Navarro, *Manager*
EMP: 9 **EST:** 2016
SALES (est): 134.2K **Privately Held**
SIC: 3131 Footwear cut stock

(G-8142)
LOCAL WOODWORK LLC
5491 Nw 15th St (33063-3779)
PHONE....................................954 551-1515
EMP: 5 **EST:** 2018
SALES (est): 426.4K **Privately Held**
SIC: 2431 Millwork

(G-8143)
MAX AVW PROFESSIONAL LLC
441 S State Road 7 Ste 4 (33068-1967)
P.O. Box 5501, Fort Lauderdale (33310-5501)
PHONE....................................954 972-3338
Michael Fishman, *Mng Member*
Niel Markus,
EMP: 13 **EST:** 2010
SQ FT: 10,000
SALES (est): 754.6K **Privately Held**
SIC: 2834 5122 Pharmaceutical preparations; pharmaceuticals

(G-8144)
MYERS ENGINEERING INTL INC
Also Called: Antennas.us
5425 Nw 24th St Ste 202 (33063-7731)
PHONE....................................954 975-2712
Steven Myers, *President*
Christine Coyle, *Administration*
EMP: 28 **EST:** 1990
SQ FT: 6,000
SALES (est): 3.1MM **Privately Held**
WEB: www.myerseng.com
SIC: 3663 7373 Antennas, transmitting & communications; computer integrated systems design

(G-8145)
P & G PRINTING GROUP INC
Also Called: Yovino Printing
2034 Mears Pkwy (33063-3753)
PHONE....................................954 971-2511
George Paparelli, *President*
Patricia Paparelli, *Vice Pres*
EMP: 11 **EST:** 1985
SQ FT: 1,600
SALES (est): 281K **Privately Held**
SIC: 2752 Commercial printing, offset

(G-8146)
PHI CHI FOUNDATION INC
740 Sw 50th Ter (33068-3042)
PHONE....................................561 526-3401
Nzinga N Myton, *President*
Neville Myton, *Publisher*
William Myton, *Vice Pres*
Nastassia Myton, *Treasurer*
Paulette Myton, *Admin Sec*
EMP: 8 **EST:** 2013
SALES (est): 99.3K **Privately Held**
WEB: www.chiphi.org
SIC: 2759 2396 5111 2269 Fashion plates: printing; printing & embossing on plastics fabric articles; printing paper; printing of narrow fabrics; community service employment training program

Kirk Sakai, *President*

(G-8147)
PICK-A-LOAD DISPATCH LLC ✪
6812 Nw 4th St (33063-5022)
PHONE....................................954 907-8245
Stecie Desamours,
EMP: 7 **EST:** 2022
SALES (est): 305.4K **Privately Held**
SIC: 3537 7389 Trucks, tractors, loaders, carriers & similar equipment;

(G-8148)
POMS ENTERPRISES INC
5425 Nw 24th St Ste 210 (33063-7731)
PHONE....................................954 358-1359
Carol Musto, *President*
Anthony Musto, *Vice Pres*
Donna Hicks, *Admin Sec*
EMP: 6 **EST:** 1992
SQ FT: 6,000
SALES (est): 584.7K **Privately Held**
WEB: www.datahorse.net
SIC: 2759 Commercial printing

(G-8149)
PRINCETON INDUSTRIES INC (PA)
Also Called: Princeton Custom Cabinetry
1790 Mears Pkwy (33063-3749)
PHONE....................................954 344-9155
Brad W Brewster, *President*
Marc B Kaye, *Corp Secy*
Mona Fleri, *Sales Staff*
Brent Brewster, *Director*
Sue Kaye, *Director*
EMP: 30 **EST:** 1987
SQ FT: 7,200
SALES (est): 2.9MM **Privately Held**
WEB: www.princetonkb.com
SIC: 2511 2541 5211 1751 Wood household furniture; wood partitions & fixtures; cabinets, kitchen; cabinet & finish carpentry; vanities, bathroom: wood

(G-8150)
PRO WATER TREATMENT INC
1935 Mears Pkwy Frnt (33063-3702)
PHONE....................................954 650-1955
William Avellanet Sr, *Manager*
EMP: 6 **EST:** 2002
SALES (est): 498.1K **Privately Held**
WEB: www.prowaterfl.net
SIC: 3589 Water treatment equipment, industrial

(G-8151)
PRO WELD OF SOUTH FLORIDA INC
3101 Vista Del Mar (33063-9304)
PHONE....................................954 984-0104
Effie Darshan, *President*
EMP: 7 **EST:** 1999
SALES (est): 229.3K **Privately Held**
SIC: 7692 Welding repair

(G-8152)
RBS WOODWORK CORP
1621 Banks Rd (33063-7743)
PHONE....................................754 214-7682
EMP: 19
SALES (corp-wide): 225.4K **Privately Held**
SIC: 2431 Millwork
PA: Rbs Woodwork Corp
378 Nw 153rd Ave
Pembroke Pines FL 33028
754 214-7682

(G-8153)
SAM WEISS WOODWORKING INC
5195 Nw 15th St (33063-3714)
PHONE....................................954 975-8158
Sam Weiss, *President*
Linda Weiss, *Vice Pres*
Kevin Weiss, *Treasurer*
EMP: 5 **EST:** 1981
SQ FT: 11,000
SALES (est): 964.7K **Privately Held**
WEB: www.samweisswoodwork.com
SIC: 2541 3993 2542 Store & office display cases & fixtures; signs & advertising specialties; partitions & fixtures, except wood

(G-8154)
SIGN DESIGN AND CREATIONS
5000 Nw 17th St Ste 3 (33063-3707)
PHONE.................................954 724-2884
Regis M Sassaki, *President*
EMP: 6 EST: 2013
SALES (est): 598.7K **Privately Held**
WEB: www.signdesignandcreations.com
SIC: 3993 Signs & advertising specialties

(G-8155)
STUDIO M LLC
225 Nw 79th Ter (33063-4731)
PHONE.................................954 918-8528
Shamar Ansby, *Branch Mgr*
EMP: 12
SALES (corp-wide): 112.6K **Privately Held**
WEB: www.studiomus.com
SIC: 7372 7389 Home entertainment computer software; business services
PA: Studio M L.L.C.
    4851 Nw 103rd Ave
    Sunrise FL

(G-8156)
THINKTECH CORPORATION
1840 Vista Way (33063-1206)
PHONE.................................954 501-3034
Antonio Mendez, *President*
Cliff Toma, *Engineer*
EMP: 10 EST: 2003
SALES (est): 641.4K **Privately Held**
WEB: www.thinktech.us
SIC: 3577 Computer peripheral equipment

(G-8157)
TRADING POST OF CENTRAL FLA
Also Called: Orlando Post
7626 Nw 25th St (33063-8132)
PHONE.................................954 675-2149
Robert Ericson, *President*
Mary Lowerey, *Admin Sec*
EMP: 9 EST: 1985
SQ FT: 2,000
SALES (est): 251.4K **Privately Held**
SIC: 2741 Shopping news: publishing & printing

(G-8158)
V L PAVERS CORP
3055 Palm Pl (33063-7041)
PHONE.................................954 605-0061
Lomeu Mauro Donato, *Principal*
EMP: 7 EST: 2014
SALES (est): 112.4K **Privately Held**
SIC: 2951 Asphalt paving mixtures & blocks

(G-8159)
VINYLOT OF FLORIDA INC
Also Called: Vinylot Signs & Graphics
2048 Mears Pkwy (33063-3753)
PHONE.................................954 978-8424
Albert L Scungio, *President*
Gwendolyn Scungio, *Vice Pres*
EMP: 5 EST: 1983
SALES (est): 652.3K **Privately Held**
WEB: www.vinylot.com
SIC: 2752 Commercial printing, lithographic

(G-8160)
WILLSON & SON INDUSTRY INC
Also Called: W.S.I.
2000 Banks Rd Ste H1 (33063-7732)
PHONE.................................954 972-5073
Les Willson Jr, *President*
Hannelore Willson, *Vice Pres*
EMP: 7 EST: 1975
SQ FT: 7,000
SALES (est): 499K **Privately Held**
WEB: willson-son-industry-inc.business.site
SIC: 2511 Wood household furniture

Marianna
Jackson County

(G-8161)
ACG MATERIALS
5160 Vermont Rd (32448-7473)
PHONE.................................405 366-9500

EMP: 6 EST: 2019
SALES (est): 323.2K **Privately Held**
WEB: www.arcosaspecialtymaterials.com
SIC: 1499 Miscellaneous nonmetallic minerals

(G-8162)
CATALYST FABRIC SOLUTIONS LLC
3595 Industrial Park Dr (32446-8092)
PHONE.................................850 396-4325
Rufus Honeycutt, *Technical Staff*
Charles Smith,
EMP: 50 EST: 2016
SQ FT: 235,000
SALES (est): 7.4MM **Privately Held**
WEB: www.catalystfabricsolutions.com
SIC: 2396 Apparel & other linings, except millinery

(G-8163)
DOLOMITE INC
1321 Highway 71 (32448-5399)
P.O. Box 1568 (32447-5568)
PHONE.................................850 482-4962
David Sloan, *President*
Kathy Sloan, *Vice Pres*
EMP: 15 EST: 1972
SQ FT: 1,000
SALES (est): 3.7MM
SALES (corp-wide): 8.5MM **Privately Held**
WEB: www.dolomitefl.com
SIC: 1422 Dolomite, crushed & broken-quarrying
PA: Baxter's Asphalt And Concrete, Inc.
    4049 Lafayette St
    Marianna FL 32446
    850 482-4621

(G-8164)
EMAC INC (PA)
4518 Lafayette St (32446-3418)
PHONE.................................850 526-4111
Timothy Mowrey, *President*
Nolan Coumbe, *Vice Pres*
Laura Mowrey, *Treasurer*
EMP: 40 EST: 1976
SQ FT: 480,000
SALES (est): 5.7MM **Privately Held**
WEB: emac-bar.business.site
SIC: 3534 Elevators & equipment

(G-8165)
HARRISON GYPSUM LLC
5160 Vermont Rd (32448-7473)
PHONE.................................850 762-4315
Fred Webb, *Branch Mgr*
EMP: 30
SALES (corp-wide): 2B **Publicly Held**
WEB: www.arcosaspecialtymaterials.com
SIC: 1499 4213 Gypsum mining; trucking, except local
HQ: Harrison Gypsum, Llc
    1550 Double C Dr
    Norman OK 73069
    405 366-9500

(G-8166)
HOME SOURCE MANUFACTURING INC
3595 Industrial Park Dr (32446-8092)
PHONE.................................404 663-0647
Keith Sorgeloos, *CEO*
Mike Beard, *CFO*
EMP: 23 EST: 1995
SQ FT: 275,000
SALES (est): 583K **Privately Held**
SIC: 2392 Household furnishings

(G-8167)
KENNETH JAKE LINTON
4430 Magnolia Rd (32448-7410)
P.O. Box 189 (32447-0189)
PHONE.................................850 526-0121
Kenneth J Linton, *Principal*
EMP: 7 EST: 2011
SALES (est): 126.7K **Privately Held**
SIC: 3699 Cleaning equipment, ultrasonic, except medical & dental

(G-8168)
LARRY WOLEYS TRIM CABINETS LLC
3440 Larkspur Cir (32446-2106)
PHONE.................................850 526-3974
Larry Wooley, *Principal*
EMP: 7 EST: 2012
SALES (est): 241.3K **Privately Held**
SIC: 2434 Wood kitchen cabinets

(G-8169)
LMS MANUFACTURING LLC
4430 Magnolia Rd (32448-7410)
P.O. Box 189 (32447-0189)
PHONE.................................850 526-0121
Leslie Linton, *Finance Dir*
Kenneth Linton,
Greg Self,
EMP: 10 EST: 1982
SALES (est): 1MM **Privately Held**
WEB: www.lmsmanufacturing.com
SIC: 3599 Machine shop, jobbing & repair

(G-8170)
MARIANNA LIME PRODUCTS INC
3333 Valley View Rd (32446-5664)
P.O. Box 1505 (32447-5505)
PHONE.................................850 526-3580
Leon Brooks, *President*
EMP: 8 EST: 1979
SQ FT: 20,000
SALES (est): 678.1K **Privately Held**
WEB: www.southfieldcarton.com
SIC: 1422 3274 Agricultural limestone, ground; lime

(G-8171)
MARIANNA LIMESTONE LLC
3333 Valley View Rd (32446-5664)
PHONE.................................954 581-1220
M Austin Forman, *Mng Member*
Leon Brooks,
Gilbert Spenser,
EMP: 13 EST: 2005
SQ FT: 12,000
SALES (est): 2.3MM **Privately Held**
SIC: 1422 3274 Agricultural limestone, ground; agricultural lime

(G-8172)
MARIANNA TRUSS INC
3644 Highway 71 (32446-8074)
P.O. Box 833 (32447-0833)
PHONE.................................850 594-5420
Garry Gochenaur, *President*
Debra Gochenaur, *Corp Secy*
EMP: 17 EST: 1985
SQ FT: 21,000
SALES (est): 802.6K **Privately Held**
WEB: www.mariannatruss.com
SIC: 2439 2448 Trusses, wooden roof; trusses, except roof: laminated lumber; wood pallets & skids

(G-8173)
METAL PRODUCTS COMPANY LC
3787 Industrial Park Dr (32446-8096)
P.O. Box 6429 (32447-6429)
PHONE.................................850 526-5593
Billy Taylor, *COO*
Gary Pinson,
Marcie Pinson,
EMP: 22 EST: 2000
SALES (est): 2.6MM **Privately Held**
SIC: 3469 3444 Metal stampings; sheet metalwork

(G-8174)
ROLLS RITE TRAILERS INC
3741 Industrial Park Dr (32446-8096)
PHONE.................................850 526-2290
Richard Dunlap, *President*
EMP: 16 EST: 1998
SQ FT: 21,000
SALES (est): 4.2MM **Privately Held**
WEB: www.rollsrite.com
SIC: 3715 3537 Truck trailers; industrial trucks & tractors

(G-8175)
SPANISH TRAIL LUMBER CO LLC
6112 Old Spanish Trl (32448-7598)
PHONE.................................850 592-8512
Ross Jackson, *General Mgr*
Jay Rees, *General Mgr*
Ross D Jackson, *Mng Member*
EMP: 126 EST: 2003
SALES (est): 19.2MM **Privately Held**
WEB: www.spanishtraillumber.com
SIC: 2421 Lumber: rough, sawed or planed

(G-8176)
WOODY HATCHER
Also Called: Jackson County Times
2866 Madison St (32448-4610)
PHONE.................................850 526-1501
Linda Hatcher, *President*
EMP: 9 EST: 2005
SALES (est): 111.6K **Privately Held**
WEB: www.jacksoncountytimes.net
SIC: 2711 Newspapers, publishing & printing

Mary Esther
Okaloosa County

(G-8177)
IMAGE PRTG & DIGITAL SVCS INC
Also Called: Insty-Prints
315 E Hollywood Blvd # 3 (32569-1915)
PHONE.................................850 244-3380
McCain J Young, *President*
Gill McLane, *Vice Pres*
EMP: 8 EST: 1986
SQ FT: 2,000
SALES (est): 633K **Privately Held**
WEB: www.instyprints.com
SIC: 2752 2791 Commercial printing, offset; typesetting

(G-8178)
NAVARRE 3D PRINTING LLC (PA)
300 Mary Esther Blvd # 66 (32569-1676)
PHONE.................................850 281-6780
EMP: 7 EST: 2018
SALES (est): 119.1K **Privately Held**
WEB: www.navarre3dprinting.com
SIC: 2752 Commercial printing, lithographic

(G-8179)
PFMC BAYER LIMITED PARTNERSHIP
257 W Miracle Strip Pkwy (32569-1971)
PHONE.................................850 244-1310
Peter F Bayer, *Principal*
EMP: 11 EST: 2008
SALES (est): 135.7K **Privately Held**
SIC: 2834 Pharmaceutical preparations

(G-8180)
TRIO ENVMTL SOLUTIONS LLC
301 Friar Tuck Rd (32569-2213)
PHONE.................................850 543-9125
Deborah R Hammett, *CEO*
Caren Schau, *Controller*
EMP: 15 EST: 2009
SALES (est): 1.9MM **Privately Held**
WEB: www.trioenvironmentalsolutions.com
SIC: 2655 4213 Wastebaskets, fiber: made from purchased material; automobiles, transport & delivery

Mascotte
Lake County

(G-8181)
ALL MODULAR SERVICE INC
861 W Myers Blvd (34753-9727)
P.O. Box 516, Groveland (34736-0516)
PHONE.................................352 429-0868
Kevin J Pearson, *President*
EMP: 21 EST: 1987
SQ FT: 1,000

SALES (est): 935.2K **Privately Held**
SIC: 2452 Modular homes, prefabricated, wood

Mayo
Lafayette County

(G-8182)
AGRI METAL SUPPLY INC
232 Se Indus Pk Cir Ste C (32066-5629)
PHONE..............................386 294-1720
Moises Rodriguez, *President*
EMP: 7 **EST:** 2005
SALES (est): 826.3K **Privately Held**
SIC: 3446 Architectural metalwork

(G-8183)
MAYO PLASTICS MFG INC
232 Se Indus Cir S B (32066)
P.O. Box 248 (32066-0248)
PHONE..............................386 294-1049
Robin C Shiver Sr, *President*
Robin C Shiver Jr, *Corp Secy*
Vera L Shiver, *Vice Pres*
EMP: 10 **EST:** 1991
SQ FT: 40,000
SALES (est): 463K **Privately Held**
SIC: 3949 Lures, fishing: artificial

(G-8184)
MAYO TRUSS CO INC
845 E Us 27 (32066-5730)
PHONE..............................386 294-3988
Wayne Hamlin, *President*
EMP: 16 **EST:** 1996
SALES (est): 4.7MM **Privately Held**
SIC: 2439 Trusses, wooden roof

(G-8185)
PEARSONS READY-MIX CON INC
968 S State Road 51 (32066-6611)
PHONE..............................386 294-3637
Tommy Pearson, *President*
Troy Pearson, *Vice Pres*
Kyle Pearson, *Treasurer*
Kristopher Pearson, *Admin Sec*
EMP: 15 **EST:** 2008
SALES (est): 1.2MM **Privately Held**
SIC: 3273 8741 Ready-mixed concrete; management services

(G-8186)
PERRY PRECAST INC
232 Se Industrial Pk Cir (32066-5200)
PHONE..............................386 294-2710
EMP: 5
SALES (est): 509.5K **Privately Held**
SIC: 3272 Mfg Concrete Products

Mc Alpin
Suwannee County

(G-8187)
BUBBLEMAC INDUSTRIES INC
11932 156th St (32062-2242)
P.O. Box 51 (32062-0051)
PHONE..............................352 396-8043
Cathie L Mach, *Principal*
EMP: 6 **EST:** 2014
SALES (est): 454.4K **Privately Held**
WEB: www.bubblemacairdiffusers.com
SIC: 3999 Manufacturing industries

(G-8188)
COMPETITION SPECIALTIES INC
Also Called: Csr Performance Products
16936 County Road 252 (32062-2048)
PHONE..............................386 776-1476
Rowland W Wood, *President*
Kim Wood, *Principal*
EMP: 15 **EST:** 1989
SQ FT: 22,000
SALES (est): 2.4MM **Privately Held**
WEB: www.csr-performance.com
SIC: 3714 3694 Motor vehicle parts & accessories; engine electrical equipment

(G-8189)
PETERSON ENTERPRISES LLC
12502 158th Ter (32062-2333)
PHONE..............................386 456-3400
Douglas Peterson, *Principal*
EMP: 7 **EST:** 2011
SALES (est): 106.9K **Privately Held**
SIC: 3524 5261 7699 Lawn & garden tractors & equipment; lawn & garden mowers & accessories; lawn & garden equipment; lawn mower repair shop

Mc David
Escambia County

(G-8190)
WEST FRASER INC
401 Champion (32568-2676)
PHONE..............................850 587-1000
Allen Smith, *Manager*
EMP: 158
SALES (corp-wide): 10.5B **Privately Held**
SIC: 2426 2421 2621 Hardwood dimension & flooring mills; sawmills & planing mills, general; paper mills
HQ: West Fraser, Inc.
1900 Exeter Rd Ste 105
Germantown TN 38138
901 620-4200

Medley
Miami-Dade County

(G-8191)
AAR LANDING GEAR LLC
Also Called: AAR Landing Gear Services
9371 Nw 100th St (33178-1420)
PHONE..............................305 883-1511
Mike Kritch, *Vice Pres*
Brian Sartain, *Vice Pres*
Shane Laakso, *Mfg Staff*
Eidel Ochoa, *QC Mgr*
Bevon Dobney, *Engineer*
▲ **EMP:** 27 **EST:** 2011
SALES (est): 9.9MM
SALES (corp-wide): 1.8B **Publicly Held**
WEB: www.aarcorp.com
SIC: 3728 Aircraft parts & equipment
HQ: Aar Airlift Group, Inc.
2301 Commerce Park Dr Ne # 11
Palm Bay FL 32905
321 837-2345

(G-8192)
ACCURATE METALS SPINNING INC
9001 Nw 97th Ter Ste K (33178-1460)
PHONE..............................305 885-9988
Alfredo Perez, *President*
Teresa Perez, *Vice Pres*
EMP: 7 **EST:** 1995
SQ FT: 7,250
SALES (est): 673.7K **Privately Held**
WEB: www.accuratemetalspinning.com
SIC: 3443 3469 Heat exchangers, condensers & components; spinning metal for the trade

(G-8193)
ALLSTONE CASTING
6900 Nw 77th Ter (33166-2540)
PHONE..............................305 528-1677
EMP: 11 **EST:** 2015
SALES (est): 275.4K **Privately Held**
WEB: www.allstonecasting.com
SIC: 3272 Concrete products

(G-8194)
ALPINE SYSTEMS ASSOCIATES INC
11725 Nw 100th Rd Ste 1 (33178-1013)
PHONE..............................305 262-3263
Petra Peters, *President*
EMP: 8 **EST:** 1996
SALES (est): 1.6MM **Privately Held**
WEB: www.alpinehandlingsystems.com
SIC: 3537 Containers (metal), air cargo

(G-8195)
AMIGO PALLETS INC
7650 Nw 69th Ave (33166-2521)
PHONE..............................305 631-2452
Raul Alfonso, *CEO*
David Lopez, *CFO*
EMP: 6 **EST:** 2018
SALES (est): 803.8K **Privately Held**
WEB: www.amigopallets.com
SIC: 2448 Pallets, wood

(G-8196)
ANTHEM SOUTH LLC
9710 Nw 110th Ave Unit 10 (33178-2549)
PHONE..............................973 779-1982
Raj Prakash, *Mng Member*
◆ **EMP:** 36 **EST:** 2018
SALES (est): 15MM
SALES (corp-wide): 52.4MM **Privately Held**
WEB: www.anthemusb.com
SIC: 2676 Cleansing tissues: made from purchased paper
PA: Disposable Hygiene Llc
1225 Mcbride Ave Ste 213
Woodland Park NJ 07424
973 779-1982

(G-8197)
ARCTIC INDUSTRIES LLC
9731 Nw 114th Way (33178-1178)
PHONE..............................305 883-5581
Brian Murphy, *CEO*
Donald Goodstein, *President*
David Grife, *COO*
Lucy Deltoro, *Vice Pres*
Janet De, *Sales Staff*
◆ **EMP:** 85 **EST:** 1978
SQ FT: 50,000
SALES (est): 17.1MM **Privately Held**
WEB: www.arcticwalkins.com
SIC: 3585 Refrigeration equipment, complete

(G-8198)
ARGEN FOODS
9220 Nw 102nd St (33178-1315)
PHONE..............................305 884-0037
EMP: 6
SALES (est): 415.3K **Privately Held**
SIC: 2099 Mfg Food Preparations

(G-8199)
ARMOR SUPPLY METALS LLC
Also Called: Amb Trucks
12690 Nw South River Dr (33178-1198)
PHONE..............................305 640-9901
Jimmy Dos Reis, *Mng Member*
EMP: 6 **EST:** 2016
SALES (est): 522.2K **Privately Held**
SIC: 3713 7692 Dump truck bodies; welding repair

(G-8200)
ARTE BRONCE MONUMENTS INC
Also Called: AB Transportation
8600 Nw S Rver Dr Ste 109 (33166)
PHONE..............................305 477-0813
Miguel Lozano Pampillon, *President*
Maria Josefa Espinosa, *Vice Pres*
EMP: 10 **EST:** 2002
SALES (est): 599.9K **Privately Held**
WEB: www.artebroncemonuments.com
SIC: 3366 Bronze foundry

(G-8201)
ARTEMISA ESCOBAR BROTHERS INC
10147 Nw 87th Ave (33178-1343)
PHONE..............................786 286-1493
EMP: 8 **EST:** 2019
SALES (est): 810.5K **Privately Held**
SIC: 3553 Cabinet makers' machinery

(G-8202)
ASSOCIATED PAINT INC
10160 Nw South River Dr (33178-1324)
PHONE..............................305 885-1964
Lee Hackmeyer, *Vice Pres*
Mark Hackmeyer, *Treasurer*
◆ **EMP:** 14 **EST:** 1953
SQ FT: 10,000
SALES (est): 1.9MM **Privately Held**
WEB: www.associatedpaint.com
SIC: 2851 Paints & paint additives

(G-8203)
ATLANTIC MODELS INC
10631 Nw 123rd Street Rd (33178-3166)
PHONE..............................305 883-2012
Carol Jarman, *President*
Roger Jarman, *Vice Pres*
EMP: 25 **EST:** 1982
SALES (est): 1.1MM **Privately Held**
WEB: www.atlantic-models.com
SIC: 3944 Airplane models, toy & hobby

(G-8204)
AZTLAN FOODS CORP
9110 Nw 106th St (33178-1204)
PHONE..............................786 202-8301
Mariana Saul, *President*
EMP: 16 **EST:** 2010
SALES (est): 763.3K **Privately Held**
WEB: www.aztlanfoods.com
SIC: 2099 Food preparations

(G-8205)
B E AEROSPACE
9100 Nw 105th Cir (33178-1305)
PHONE..............................305 459-7000
Kevin K Kim, *President*
Kristin Longmire, *Buyer*
Alex Micu, *Engineer*
William Quintana, *Engineer*
Steven Shull, *Engineer*
EMP: 30 **EST:** 1995
SQ FT: 23,000
SALES (est): 8.4MM
SALES (corp-wide): 64.3B **Publicly Held**
WEB: www.beaerospace.com
SIC: 3728 Aircraft parts & equipment
HQ: B/E Aerospace, Inc.
1400 Corporate Center Way
Wellington FL 33414
410 266-2048

(G-8206)
BAILA CON MICHO INC
7911 Nw 72nd Ave (33166-2227)
PHONE..............................786 953-8566
Michel Valdes, *President*
EMP: 6 **EST:** 2017
SALES (est): 521.9K **Privately Held**
WEB: www.bailaconmicho.com
SIC: 3661 Modems

(G-8207)
BARJO PRINTING AND SIGN
7911 Nw 72nd Ave (33166-2227)
PHONE..............................786 332-2661
Renny Gamez, *Administration*
EMP: 12 **EST:** 2016
SALES (est): 534.7K **Privately Held**
WEB: www.barjoprintshop.com
SIC: 2759 Commercial printing

(G-8208)
BEN KAUFMAN SALES CO INC
10025 Nw 116th Way Ste 14 (33178-1173)
PHONE..............................305 688-2144
Benjamin Kaufman, *President*
EMP: 27
SALES (corp-wide): 13.3MM **Privately Held**
WEB: www.benkaufmansales.com
SIC: 2395 5023 Embroidery products, except schiffli machine; home furnishings
PA: Ben Kaufman Sales Co., Inc.
9265 Nw 101st St
Medley FL 33178
305 688-2144

(G-8209)
BERRY GLOBAL INC
9016 Nw 105th Way (33178-1218)
PHONE..............................305 887-2040
Wendy Wildenberg, *Sales Staff*
Tony Iannazzone, *Manager*
EMP: 8 **Publicly Held**
WEB: www.berryglobal.com
SIC: 3089 Bottle caps, molded plastic
HQ: Berry Global, Inc.
101 Oakley St
Evansville IN 47710

▲ = Import ▼=Export
◆ =Import/Export

(G-8210)
BONUS AEROSPACE INC
8545 Nw 79th Ave (33166-2166)
P.O. Box 669203, Miami (33166-9429)
PHONE....................................305 887-6778
Vincent Benoit, *CEO*
Jeffrey Kuhn, *Principal*
Vladimir V Pereira, *Principal*
▲ EMP: 5 EST: 2002
SALES (est): 713.2K Privately Held
SIC: 3724 Aircraft engines & engine parts

(G-8211)
BONUS TECH INC
8575 Nw 79th Ave Ste 4d (33166-2188)
PHONE....................................786 251-4232
Jeffrey Kuhn, *President*
Vladimir Pereira, *Vice Pres*
EMP: 12 EST: 2000
SQ FT: 6,400
SALES (est): 1.1MM Privately Held
WEB: www.bonus-tech.com
SIC: 3724 Aircraft engines & engine parts

(G-8212)
BROADBAND INTERNATIONAL INC (PA)
11650 Nw 102nd Rd (33178-1026)
PHONE....................................305 882-0505
Edward Perez, *President*
Lynn Newsom, *Vice Pres*
Angela Spyredes, *Purchasing*
Jennifer Tyrrel, *Sales Staff*
Marcia Delgado, *Business Anlyst*
◆ EMP: 7 EST: 1997
SALES (est): 3.2MM Privately Held
WEB: www.broadbandinternational.com
SIC: 3643 Plugs, electric

(G-8213)
BROADCAST TECH INC (PA)
10100 Nw 116th Way Ste 6 (33178-1154)
PHONE....................................786 351-4227
Roquel Garcia, *President*
EMP: 7 EST: 2004
SALES (est): 260.4K Privately Held
WEB: www.broadcast-tech.com
SIC: 2741

(G-8214)
CEMEX CONCRETE COMPANY
11100 Nw 138th St (33178-3110)
PHONE....................................305 558-0255
Ramiro Lanzis, *Principal*
EMP: 10 EST: 2010
SALES (est): 1.3MM Privately Held
WEB: www.cemexusa.com
SIC: 3273 Ready-mixed concrete

(G-8215)
CEMEX MATERIALS LLC
13292 Nw 118th Ave (33178-3106)
PHONE....................................305 821-5661
Frank Prieto, *Sales Staff*
Danny Blomme, *Branch Mgr*
EMP: 88 Privately Held
SIC: 3273 Ready-mixed concrete
HQ: Cemex Materials Llc
1720 Centrepark Dr E # 100
West Palm Beach FL 33401
561 833-5555

(G-8216)
CEMEX MATERIALS LLC
FEC Quary
13292 Nw 118th Ave (33178-3106)
PHONE....................................305 818-4941
Roderick B Martin, *Branch Mgr*
Manuel Dovales, *Manager*
EMP: 177 Privately Held
WEB: www.cemex.com
SIC: 3273 Ready-mixed concrete
HQ: Cemex Materials Llc
1720 Centrepark Dr E # 100
West Palm Beach FL 33401
561 833-5555

(G-8217)
CIENFUEGOS PALLETS CORP
7781 Nw 73rd Ct (33166-2201)
PHONE....................................786 703-3686
Zoila Hernandez, *President*
EMP: 9 EST: 2016

SALES (est): 415.1K Privately Held
WEB: www.cienfuegospallet.com
SIC: 2448 Pallets, wood

(G-8218)
CLARIOS LLC
Also Called: Johnson Controls
10801 Nw 97th St Ste 21 (33178-2540)
PHONE....................................305 805-5600
Rosaro Rodriguiz, *Branch Mgr*
EMP: 88
SALES (corp-wide): 47.9B Privately Held
WEB: www.clarios.com
SIC: 3822 Building services monitoring controls, automatic
HQ: Clarios, Llc
5757 N Green Bay Ave
Milwaukee WI 53209

(G-8219)
CLIMB YOUR MOUNTAIN INC
11345 Nw 122nd St (33178-3176)
PHONE....................................571 571-8623
Ana Marma Duque, *Ch of Bd*
▲ EMP: 50 EST: 2011
SQ FT: 3,400
SALES (est): 8.6MM Privately Held
SIC: 2023 Dry, condensed, evaporated dairy products

(G-8220)
CONCHITA FOODS INC (PA)
10051 Nw 99th Ave Ste 3 (33178-1161)
P.O. Box 520156, Miami (33152-0156)
PHONE....................................305 888-9703
Sixto L Ferro, *President*
Andrea Barrail, *Founder*
Alex Alves, *Area Mgr*
Carlos Ferro, *Vice Pres*
Teresita F Menendez, *Vice Pres*
◆ EMP: 55 EST: 1987
SQ FT: 45,000
SALES (est): 8.6MM Privately Held
WEB: www.conchita-foods.com
SIC: 2033 2032 5149 2077 Fruits: packaged in cans, jars, etc.; beans, with meat: packaged in cans, jars, etc.; groceries & related products; animal & marine fats & oils; rice milling; dehydrated fruits, vegetables, soups

(G-8221)
CONVERPACK INC
6891 Nw 74th St (33166-2528)
PHONE....................................786 304-1680
Guillermo Roversi, *President*
Luis G Roversi, *Vice Pres*
Ranza Armas, *Accountant*
◆ EMP: 6 EST: 2010
SALES (est): 2.7MM Privately Held
WEB: www.conver-pack.com
SIC: 2656 Paper cups, plates, dishes & utensils

(G-8222)
CORESLAB STRUCTURES MIAMI INC
10501 Nw 121st Way (33178-1011)
PHONE....................................305 823-8950
Mario Francisosa, *President*
Ted Wolfsthal, *General Mgr*
Sidney Speigel, *Corp Secy*
Frank Franciosa, *Vice Pres*
William Whitcher, *Vice Pres*
▼ EMP: 280 EST: 1955
SQ FT: 10,000
SALES (est): 68.3MM
SALES (corp-wide): 27.3MM Privately Held
WEB: www.coreslab.com
SIC: 3272 Concrete products, precast; prestressed concrete products
HQ: Coreslab Holdings U S Inc
332 Jones Rd Suite 1
Stoney Creek ON
905 643-0220

(G-8223)
COSMETIC CORP OF AMERICA INC
9750 Nw 91st Ct (33178-1427)
PHONE....................................305 883-8434
Jesus Rodriguez, *President*
Eric Bedenbaugh, *CFO*
EMP: 21 EST: 1996

SALES (est): 2.4MM Privately Held
WEB: www.cosmeticcorpamerica.com
SIC: 2844 Cosmetic preparations

(G-8224)
CREACTION INDUSTRY LLC
Also Called: Creaction Organize
8710 Nw 100th St (33178-1454)
PHONE....................................305 779-4851
Pierre Amezcua, *CEO*
EMP: 17 EST: 2011
SQ FT: 17,500
SALES (est): 1.7MM Privately Held
WEB: www.creaction.co
SIC: 2541 Store & office display cases & fixtures; display fixtures, wood; store fixtures, wood

(G-8225)
CROSSTAC CORPORATION
12605 Nw 115th Ave B-104 (33178-3190)
PHONE....................................406 522-9300
Sean Osman, *Manager*
EMP: 7
SALES (corp-wide): 1.1MM Privately Held
WEB: www.crosstac.com
SIC: 3484 Small arms
PA: Crosstac Corporation
1010 S Lincoln Ave # 100
Loveland CO 80537
406 522-9300

(G-8226)
CRP MACHINE SHOP INC
11294 Nw South River Dr (33178-1137)
PHONE....................................305 824-7450
Ramon Perdomo, *Principal*
EMP: 7 EST: 2015
SALES (est): 89.6K Privately Held
SIC: 3599 Machine shop, jobbing & repair

(G-8227)
CUSTOM BUILDING PRODUCTS LLC
8850 Nw 79th Ave (33166-2122)
PHONE....................................305 885-3444
Fred Gomez, *Plant Mgr*
Hector Arteaga, *Manager*
EMP: 114 Privately Held
WEB: www.custombuildingproducts.com
SIC: 3273 Ready-mixed concrete
HQ: Custom Building Products Llc
7711 Center Ave Ste 500
Huntington Beach CA 92647
800 272-8786

(G-8228)
CUSTOM MANUFACTURING CORP
9324 Nw 102nd St (33178-1334)
PHONE....................................305 863-1001
David Wilpon, *President*
Sharon L Wilpon, *Vice Pres*
EMP: 18 EST: 1999
SQ FT: 15,000
SALES (est): 3.7MM Privately Held
WEB: www.custom-mfg.com
SIC: 2844 Cosmetic preparations

(G-8229)
DAUER MANUFACTURING CORP
10100 Nw 116th Way Ste 1 (33178-1154)
PHONE....................................800 883-2590
Craig Klomparens, *President*
Joaquin Obeso, *Vice Pres*
▲ EMP: 8 EST: 2012
SALES (est): 953.5K Privately Held
WEB: www.dauermanufacturing.com
SIC: 3646 3645 Commercial indusl & institutional electric lighting fixtures; residential lighting fixtures

(G-8230)
DEL ROSARIO ENTERPRISES INC
7339 Nw 79th Ter (33166-2211)
PHONE....................................786 547-6812
Emanuel Fernandez, *President*
EMP: 12 EST: 2019
SALES (est): 715K Privately Held
WEB: www.delrosariomiami.com
SIC: 2092 5147 Fresh or frozen packaged fish; meats & meat products

(G-8231)
DOORS 4 U INC
7322 Nw 79th Ter (33166-2212)
PHONE....................................786 400-2298
Sardinas S Gendry, *Principal*
EMP: 12 EST: 2014
SALES (est): 367.3K Privately Held
SIC: 2431 Door frames, wood

(G-8232)
DOR-A-LUM CORPORATION
Also Called: Doralum
7040 Nw 77th Ter (33166-2542)
PHONE....................................305 884-3922
Victorina Pino, *President*
Vicky Pino, *Office Mgr*
Richard Gallart, *Manager*
▼ EMP: 12 EST: 1996
SALES (est): 250K Privately Held
WEB: www.doralum.com
SIC: 3442 Metal doors; store fronts, prefabricated, metal

(G-8233)
ECO CUSTOM FILTERS INC
7725 Nw 75th Ave (33166-7508)
PHONE....................................786 536-6764
Jesus O Astaiza, *President*
EMP: 7 EST: 2018
SALES (est): 271.1K Privately Held
WEB: ecocustomfilters.business.site
SIC: 3564 Blowers & fans

(G-8234)
ECO WINDOW SYSTEMS LLC
8502 Nw 80th St Unit 103 (33166-2137)
PHONE....................................305 885-5299
Jeff Jackson, *President*
Paola Gomez, *Sales Mgr*
Mike Vilarino, *Manager*
David Dominguez, *IT/INT Sup*
▼ EMP: 1018 EST: 2008
SALES (est): 23MM
SALES (corp-wide): 1.1B Publicly Held
WEB: www.ecowindowsystems.com
SIC: 2431 Storm windows, wood; window frames, wood; window sashes, wood; windows, wood
PA: Pgt Innovations, Inc.
1070 Technology Dr
North Venice FL 34275
941 480-1600

(G-8235)
ELECTRONIC SIGN SUPPLY CORP
12601 Nw 115th Ave 106a (33178-3184)
PHONE....................................305 477-0555
Marcela Veloz, *Principal*
◆ EMP: 6 EST: 2009
SALES (est): 1.3MM Privately Held
WEB: www.electronicsignsupply.com
SIC: 3993 Signs & advertising specialties
PA: Sign Solution S A S
Via Parque Agroindustrial De La Sabana Bg 35 Km 18
Mosquera

(G-8236)
EPIC ELEMENTS LLC
8348 Nw 74th Ave (33166-7450)
PHONE....................................305 388-1384
Camilo Ernesto Lemus Gomez, *Principal*
EMP: 7 EST: 2013
SALES (est): 171.6K Privately Held
SIC: 2819 Industrial inorganic chemicals

(G-8237)
EUROPE COATING INDUSTRIES LLC
8213 Nw 74th Ave (33166-7403)
PHONE....................................786 535-4143
EMP: 7 EST: 2017
SALES (est): 251K Privately Held
SIC: 3999 Manufacturing industries

(G-8238)
EUSA GLOBAL LLC
Also Called: Ecleris
11801 Nw 100th Rd Ste 17 (33178-1046)
PHONE....................................786 483-7490
Henry E Sand Casali, *Mng Member*
EMP: 9 EST: 2013
SALES (est): 896.6K Privately Held
SIC: 3841 Surgical & medical instruments

(G-8239)
EXPRESSWAY OIL CORP
7391 Nw 78th St (33166-2207)
PHONE................................786 302-9534
Jose Ochoa, *Owner*
EMP: 5 **EST:** 2012
SALES (est): 404K Privately Held
SIC: 1389 Oil & gas field services

(G-8240)
FAMATEL USA LLC
Also Called: Easylife Tech
9800 Nw 100th Rd 1 (33178-1239)
PHONE................................754 217-4841
Carlos Latre, *Director*
EMP: 5 **EST:** 2017
SALES (est): 400K
SALES (corp-wide): 355.8K Privately
Held
WEB: www.famatelusa.com
SIC: 3699 3264 3469 Electrical equipment & supplies; insulators, electrical: porcelain; furniture components, porcelain enameled
HQ: Fabricacion De Material Electrico Sa
Carretera A-1223 (Km 8)
Peralta De Alcofea 22210
938 634-640

(G-8241)
FLORIDA AA PALLETS INC
7611 Nw 74th Ave (33166-2424)
PHONE................................305 805-1522
Leonardo Acosta, *President*
EMP: 7 **EST:** 2007
SQ FT: 10,000
SALES (est): 1MM Privately Held
WEB: www.aafloridapallets.com
SIC: 2448 Pallets, wood; pallets, wood & wood with metal

(G-8242)
FLORIDA LIFT STATIONS CORP
9498 Nw South River Dr (33166-2004)
PHONE................................305 887-8485
Alex De Bogory Jr, *President*
David Brunswick, *CFO*
EMP: 7 **EST:** 1976
SQ FT: 5,000
SALES (est): 578.5K Privately Held
SIC: 3272 Concrete products

(G-8243)
FRIEDMAN BROS DCRTIVE ARTS INC
9015 Nw 105th Way (33178-1217)
PHONE................................800 327-1065
Bernard Singer, *President*
Marilyn Singer, *Vice Pres*
◆ **EMP:** 70 **EST:** 1903
SQ FT: 30,000
SALES (est): 7.7MM Privately Held
WEB: www.friedmanmirrors.com
SIC: 3231 Mirrored glass; ornamental glass: cut, engraved or otherwise decorated

(G-8244)
G & S MACHINE SHOP CORP
7715 Nw 74th Ave (33166-7501)
PHONE................................305 863-7866
Gregorio Martin, *President*
Nelsey Perez, *Vice Pres*
Alberto D Armas, *Admin Sec*
EMP: 9 **EST:** 1996
SALES (est): 646.7K Privately Held
SIC: 3599 Machine shop, jobbing & repair

(G-8245)
GAR-P INDUSTRIES INC
10890 Nw South River Dr (33178-1129)
PHONE................................305 888-7252
Peter Garcia Jr, *President*
◆ **EMP:** 45 **EST:** 1975
SALES (est): 5.5MM Privately Held
WEB: www.gar-p.com
SIC: 3713 5013 7532 3711 Truck bodies (motor vehicles); truck parts & accessories; body shop, trucks; motor vehicles & car bodies

(G-8246)
GEM PAVER SYSTEMS INC (PA)
9845 Nw 118th Way (33178-1043)
PHONE................................305 805-0000

Jorge Fernandez, *President*
Jurek Kocik, *Corp Secy*
◆ **EMP:** 26 **EST:** 1989
SQ FT: 20,000
SALES (est): 8.8MM Privately Held
WEB: www.gempavers.com
SIC: 3255 Brick, clay refractory

(G-8247)
GENERAL MRO AEROSPACE INC
10990 Nw 92nd Ter (33178-2515)
PHONE................................305 482-9903
Cristian Munoz, *President*
Lester Kamberger, *President*
Lonnie Brownell, *Exec Officer*
Patricia Colaiacovo, *Purch Mgr*
Sebastian Nardo, *Purch Agent*
EMP: 3 **EST:** 2006
SALES (est): 3.5MM Privately Held
WEB: www.generalmroaerospace.com
SIC: 3728 Aircraft parts & equipment

(G-8248)
GEORGES WELDING SERVICES INC
Also Called: George's Metal Fab
11400 Nw 134th St (33178-3113)
PHONE................................305 822-2445
Jorge Amador Sr, *CEO*
Angelica Amador, *Vice Pres*
Jorge Amador Jr, *Vice Pres*
Andres Acuna, *Project Engr*
Luz Amador, *Treasurer*
◆ **EMP:** 60 **EST:** 1984
SQ FT: 32,000
SALES (est): 9MM Privately Held
WEB: www.georgeswelding.com
SIC: 3441 Fabricated structural metal

(G-8249)
GLOBAL TURBINE SERVICES INC
9374 Nw 102nd St (33178-1334)
PHONE................................786 476-2166
Jack A Tanner, *Vice Pres*
David Rodriguez, *Vice Pres*
EMP: 12 **EST:** 2012
SQ FT: 25,000
SALES (est): 2.9MM Privately Held
WEB: www.gtsaviation.com
SIC: 3724 Aircraft engines & engine parts

(G-8250)
GONDIA MACHINE SHOP INC
9452 Nw 109th St (33178-1223)
PHONE................................305 763-7494
Louis Diaz, *President*
EMP: 9 **EST:** 1989
SALES (est): 604K Privately Held
WEB: www.medleymachine.com
SIC: 3599 Machine shop, jobbing & repair

(G-8251)
HARBOR LINEN LLC (HQ)
Also Called: 1concier
10800 Nw 106th St Ste 12 (33178-1261)
PHONE................................305 805-8085
Chris Nelson, *CEO*
Ron Brozo, *Vice Pres*
Gary Geiger, *Vice Pres*
Lou Gostino, *Vice Pres*
Lamar Tomlin, *Vice Pres*
◆ **EMP:** 100 **EST:** 1973
SQ FT: 87,000
SALES (est): 44.7MM
SALES (corp-wide): 193MM Privately
Held
WEB: www.1concier.com
SIC: 2299 5023 Linen fabrics; linens & towels; bedspreads; draperies; linens, table
PA: Lion Equity Holdings Ii, Llc
260 Josephine St Ste 220
Denver CO 80206
303 847-4100

(G-8252)
HITACHI RAIL STS USA INC
11150 Nw 122nd St (33178-3456)
PHONE................................415 397-7010
Giancarlo Fantappie, *Branch Mgr*
EMP: 60 Privately Held
SIC: 3743 Train cars & equipment, freight or passenger

HQ: Hitachi Rail Sts Usa, Inc.
1000 Technology Dr
Pittsburgh PA 15219
412 688-2400

(G-8253)
HOBBY PRESS INC
Also Called: Executive Printers of Florida
8001 Nw 74th Ave (33166-7507)
PHONE................................305 887-4333
Jo A Gardner, *CEO*
David Gardner, *President*
Ryan Gardner, *Vice Pres*
Elena Gardner, *Opers Staff*
Carly Gardner, *CFO*
▼ **EMP:** 34 **EST:** 1972
SQ FT: 11,000
SALES (est): 4.8MM Privately Held
WEB: www.executiveprinters.com
SIC: 2752 7334 Commercial printing, offset; photocopying & duplicating services

(G-8254)
HOMETOWN FOODS USA LLC
Also Called: Tribute Baking Company
11800 Nw 102nd Rd Ste 6 (33178-1030)
PHONE................................305 887-5200
Troy Schwartzberg, *President*
Ed Eberts, *COO*
Gary J Schwartzberg, *Exec VP*
Janet Martin, *Vice Pres*
Bryan Schwartzberg, *Vice Pres*
◆ **EMP:** 200 **EST:** 1931
SQ FT: 85,000
SALES (est): 30MM Privately Held
WEB: www.tributebaking.com
SIC: 2053 2051 Frozen bakery products, except bread; bagels, fresh or frozen

(G-8255)
HONTUS LTD (PA)
Also Called: Hontus, Ltd., Inc.
11450 Nw 122nd St Ste 100 (33178-3259)
PHONE................................786 322-3022
Haroon Sheikh, *President*
Kayla Crawford, *Sales Staff*
EMP: 9 **EST:** 2014
SALES (est): 2MM Privately Held
WEB: www.hontus.com
SIC: 3161 Wardrobe bags (luggage)

(G-8256)
IDA SOLUTIONS ✪
Also Called: Marvelous Mushrooms
10302 Nw S Rver Dr Ste 15 (33178)
PHONE................................305 603-9835
Alessandro Farana, *CEO*
EMP: 8 **EST:** 2021
SALES (est): 607.2K Privately Held
WEB: www.idasolutions.net
SIC: 2033 Mushrooms: packaged in cans, jars, etc.

(G-8257)
IMPEX OF DORAL INC
7850 Nw 80th St (33166-2104)
PHONE................................305 470-0041
Giancarlo Di Mella, *CEO*
Giovanni Di Mella, *Ch of Bd*
◆ **EMP:** 50 **EST:** 1994
SQ FT: 80,000
SALES (est): 13.2MM Privately Held
WEB: www.impexofdoral.com
SIC: 2676 Diapers, paper (disposable): made from purchased paper; feminine hygiene paper products
PA: Zaimella Del Ecuador S.A.
Ave Juan De Dios Morales Lt.1
Quito

(G-8258)
INTERNATIONAL CLOSET CENTER
7330 Nw 79th Ter (33166-2212)
PHONE................................305 883-6551
Paola I Frewa, *President*
Elia Frewa, *Admin Sec*
▼ **EMP:** 6 **EST:** 2006
SALES (est): 849.7K Privately Held
WEB: www.internationalcabinetcontractors.com
SIC: 2421 Sawmills & planing mills, general

(G-8259)
INTRADECO APPAREL INC (HQ)
9500 Nw 108th Ave (33178-2517)
PHONE................................305 264-8888
Felix Siman, *CEO*
Jaime Miguel, *President*
Terry Trofholz, *Exec VP*
Jose Siman, *CFO*
Eti Ashkenazi, *Controller*
◆ **EMP:** 22 **EST:** 1982
SQ FT: 15,000
SALES (est): 75.5MM
SALES (corp-wide): 101.2MM Privately
Held
WEB: www.intradecoapparel.com
SIC: 2254 3161 Underwear, knit; clothing & apparel carrying cases
PA: Intradeco, Inc.
9500 Nw 108th Ave
Medley FL 33178
305 264-6022

(G-8260)
IRON METAL USA CORP
8572 Nw 93rd St (33166-2005)
PHONE................................786 757-3263
Pedro E Montilla, *President*
EMP: 9 **EST:** 2011
SALES (est): 231.5K Privately Held
WEB: www.ironmetalusa.com
SIC: 3441 Fabricated structural metal

(G-8261)
IVORY INTERNATIONAL INC (DH)
5090 Nw 108th Ave (33178-2517)
P.O. Box 569, Waynesville NC (28786-0569)
PHONE................................305 687-2244
Robert J Lodge, *CEO*
Sandy Lipson, *President*
Wilbur O Hopper, *CFO*
Joseph I J Lodge, *Shareholder*
◆ **EMP:** 102 **EST:** 1976
SQ FT: 60,000
SALES (est): 22.2MM
SALES (corp-wide): 101.2MM Privately
Held
SIC: 2326 2339 2369 Service apparel (baker, barber, lab, etc.), washable: men's; women's & misses' outerwear; girls' & children's outerwear
HQ: Intradeco Apparel, Inc.
9500 Nw 108th Ave
Medley FL 33178
305 264-8888

(G-8262)
J & J STEEL SERVICES CORP
9401 Nw 109th St Unit 5 (33178-1226)
PHONE................................305 878-8929
EMP: 9 **EST:** 2014
SALES (est): 483.5K Privately Held
SIC: 3441 3444 Fabricated structural metal; sheet metalwork

(G-8263)
J&N KEYSTONE OF FLORIDA
6900 Nw 77th Ter (33166-2540)
PHONE................................305 528-1677
Jose Delgado, *Principal*
EMP: 7 **EST:** 2008
SALES (est): 885K Privately Held
SIC: 3369 Nonferrous foundries

(G-8264)
JAMO INC
8850 Nw 79th Ave (33166-2197)
PHONE................................305 885-3444
Thomas R Peck Sr, *President*
Michael Bilek, *Vice Pres*
◆ **EMP:** 58 **EST:** 1967
SQ FT: 17,000
SALES (est): 9.4MM Privately Held
WEB: www.jamoproducts.com
SIC: 3273 3255 2899 2891 Ready-mixed concrete; clay refractories; chemical preparations; adhesives & sealants
HQ: Custom Building Products Llc
7711 Center Ave Ste 500
Huntington Beach CA 92647
800 272-8786

(G-8265)
JOHNSON CONTROLS INC
9960 Nw 116th Way Ste 4 (33178-1174)
PHONE..................................305 883-3760
Norm Sted, *Branch Mgr*
Ana De Cavaliere, *Manager*
EMP: 23 **Privately Held**
WEB: www.johnsoncontrols.com
SIC: 2531 Seats, automobile
HQ: Johnson Controls, Inc.
5757 N Green Bay Ave
Glendale WI 53209
414 524-1200

(G-8266)
KONUS USA CORPORATION
7530 Nw 79th St (33166-7537)
PHONE..................................305 884-7618
Giuseppe Alberti, *President*
Stefano Alberti, *Vice Pres*
Patricia Torres, *Bookkeeper*
Patricia L Torres, *Comptroller*
▲ **EMP:** 6 **EST:** 1998
SALES (est): 999.6K **Privately Held**
WEB: www.konuspro.com
SIC: 3827 Aiming circles (fire control equipment)

(G-8267)
LAWSON INDUSTRIES INC (PA)
8501 Nw 90th St (33166-2187)
PHONE..................................305 696-8660
Harold Bailey, *President*
Ronald Bailey, *Vice Pres*
Joe Thiry, *Opers Staff*
Carolina Campillo, *Purch Mgr*
Eric Martinez, *Purch Mgr*
◆ **EMP:** 300 **EST:** 1965
SQ FT: 300,000
SALES (est): 31.1MM **Privately Held**
WEB: www.lawson-industries.com
SIC: 3231 3442 Doors, glass: made from purchased glass; metal doors, sash & trim

(G-8268)
LIGHT SOLUTIONS INC
8795 Nw 100th St (33178-1455)
PHONE..................................305 884-3468
▲ **EMP:** 7 **EST:** 2008
SALES (est): 224.1K **Privately Held**
SIC: 3641 5719 Electric lamps; lighting, lamps & accessories

(G-8269)
LOCUST USA INC
Also Called: Locust Power
8312 Nw 74th Ave (33166-7406)
PHONE..................................305 889-5410
Kirk Warshaw, *President*
Rene Borroto, *Mfg Staff*
Frigerio Fred, *Engineer*
EMP: 18 **EST:** 1999
SALES (est): 1.9MM **Privately Held**
WEB: www.locustusa.com
SIC: 3511 Turbines & turbine generator sets

(G-8270)
MADSON INC
Also Called: Madson Meat
10925 Nw South River Dr (33178-1132)
PHONE..................................305 863-7390
John Maderal, *President*
Stacy Maderal, *Corp Secy*
Francisco Maderal, *Vice Pres*
EMP: 10 **EST:** 1974
SQ FT: 8,000
SALES (est): 1MM **Privately Held**
SIC: 2011 7692 3599 Meat packing plants; welding repair; machine & other job shop work

(G-8271)
MANN+HUMMEL FILTRATION TECHNOL
10505 Nw 112th Ave Ste 22 (33178-1000)
PHONE..................................305 499-5100
EMP: 101
SALES (corp-wide): 4.7B **Privately Held**
SIC: 3714 Motor vehicle brake systems & parts
HQ: Mann+Hummel Filtration Technology Group Inc.
1 Wix Way
Gastonia NC 28054
704 869-3300

(G-8272)
MARQUEZ BROTHERS INC
9115 Nw 93rd St (33178-1440)
PHONE..................................305 888-0090
Andres A Marquez, *Ch of Bd*
Lidia Marquez, *President*
Olga Lidia Marquez, *Vice Pres*
Olga Marquez, *Admin Sec*
▼ **EMP:** 12 **EST:** 1987
SQ FT: 9,000
SALES (est): 2.4MM **Privately Held**
WEB: www.mbrothersdumpbody.com
SIC: 3465 Body parts, automobile: stamped metal

(G-8273)
MARTINEZ TRUSS COMPANY INC
9280 Nw S River Dr (33166-2110)
PHONE..................................305 883-6261
Jorge L Martinez, *President*
Marta C Martinez, *Vice Pres*
Jason Quinones, *Sales Staff*
▼ **EMP:** 18 **EST:** 1984
SQ FT: 7,000
SALES (est): 2.4MM **Privately Held**
WEB: www.martineztruss.net
SIC: 2439 Trusses, wooden roof

(G-8274)
MCM FOOD CORP
7385 Nw 78th St (33166-2207)
PHONE..................................305 885-9254
Clara I Lenis, *President*
Adeliks Villareal, *Vice Pres*
EMP: 6 **EST:** 2004
SALES (est): 1MM **Privately Held**
WEB: www.mcmfoodcorp.com
SIC: 2099 Food preparations

(G-8275)
MCMASTER CONCRETE PRODUCTS LLC
Also Called: Florida Block
8720 Nw 91st St (33178-1858)
PHONE..................................305 863-8854
Thomas McMaster, *Mng Member*
Delinda McMaster,
EMP: 17 **EST:** 2014
SALES (est): 2.5MM **Privately Held**
WEB:
www.mcmasterconcreteproducts.com
SIC: 3271 1771 Concrete block & brick; concrete work

(G-8276)
MDT TECHNOLOGIES INC
10619 Nw 122nd St (33178-3186)
PHONE..................................305 308-2902
EMP: 6 **EST:** 2005
SALES (est): 528.1K **Privately Held**
WEB: www.mdttechnologiesfl.com
SIC: 3651 Household audio & video equipment

(G-8277)
MEDLEY MACHINE SHOP INC
Also Called: Gondia Machine Shop
9452 Nw 109th St (33178-1223)
PHONE..................................305 884-3200
Luis Diaz, *President*
Luis Alaniz, *VP Sales*
Raquel Ball, *Asst Mgr*
EMP: 10 **EST:** 1994
SALES (est): 1.4MM **Privately Held**
WEB: www.medleymachine.com
SIC: 3599 Machine shop, jobbing & repair

(G-8278)
MELT-TECH POLYMERS INC
7570 Nw 79th St (33166-7537)
PHONE..................................305 887-6148
Juan A Bravo, *Director*
EMP: 7 **EST:** 2015
SALES (est): 105.5K **Privately Held**
SIC: 3089 5162 Extruded finished plastic products; plastics materials

(G-8279)
MELTPOINT PLASTICS INTL INC
7570 Nw 79th St (33166-7537)
PHONE..................................305 887-8020
Carlos Bravo, *President*
John Bravo, *Marketing Staff*
◆ **EMP:** 27 **EST:** 2000

SQ FT: 13,000
SALES (est): 6.4MM **Privately Held**
WEB: www.meltpointplastics.com
SIC: 3089 Injection molding of plastics

(G-8280)
METRO ROOF TILE INC
9845 Nw 118th Way (33178-1043)
PHONE..................................863 467-0042
Fernando Arias, *President*
Arias Fernando M, *Principal*
James Bertelson, *Sales Staff*
Kelly McElwee, *Sales Staff*
◆ **EMP:** 19 **EST:** 1984
SQ FT: 2,000
SALES (est): 349K **Privately Held**
SIC: 3259 3272 2952 Roofing tile, clay; concrete products; asphalt felts & coatings

(G-8281)
MEW AUTOMATION LLC
12630 Nw 115th Ave (33178-3179)
PHONE..................................305 319-9199
Cesare Cardinale, *Manager*
EMP: 7 **EST:** 2020
SALES (est): 102.4K **Privately Held**
SIC: 3541 Electrical discharge erosion machines

(G-8282)
MIAMI NDT INC
8050 Nw 90th St (33166-2114)
P.O. Box 14213, Fort Lauderdale (33302-4213)
PHONE..................................305 599-9393
Jose Perez, *President*
Jessie Cardena, *Vice Pres*
Jesus Rojas, *Vice Pres*
Victor Campos, *Technical Staff*
▼ **EMP:** 10 **EST:** 2008
SALES (est): 2.3MM **Privately Held**
WEB: www.miamindt.aero
SIC: 3724 Aircraft engines & engine parts

(G-8283)
MODUSLINK CORPORATION
10990 Nw 92nd Ter (33178-2515)
PHONE..................................305 888-8091
Charlie Cartaya, *Branch Mgr*
EMP: 30
SALES (corp-wide): 613.7MM **Publicly Held**
WEB: www.moduslink.com
SIC: 7372 Prepackaged software
HQ: Moduslink Corporation
2000 Midway Ln
Smyrna TN 37167
615 267-6100

(G-8284)
MOTORS PUMPS AND ACCESSORIES
7530 Nw 77th St (33166-7525)
PHONE..................................305 883-3181
Fernando Higuera, *Principal*
EMP: 6 **EST:** 2001
SALES (est): 750.5K **Privately Held**
SIC: 3594 Fluid power pumps & motors

(G-8285)
MR WINTER INC
Also Called: ISO Panel
8800 Nw 77th Ct (33166-2105)
P.O. Box 126460, Hialeah (33012-1607)
PHONE..................................800 327-3371
Manny Mijares, *President*
Manuel Mijares, *President*
David Mijares, *Vice Pres*
Jennifer Ghacham, *Sales Staff*
Javier Martinez, *Sales Staff*
◆ **EMP:** 48 **EST:** 1976
SQ FT: 54,000
SALES (est): 11.3MM **Privately Held**
WEB: www.mrwinterinc.net
SIC: 3585 Refrigeration equipment, complete

(G-8286)
NETS DEPOT INC
9949 Nw 89th Ave Unit 13 (33178-1466)
PHONE..................................305 215-5579
Jean-Michel Fethiere, *President*
Antonio Suergiu, *Vice Pres*
Ralph Rouzier, *Admin Sec*
EMP: 10 **EST:** 2015

SALES (est): 507.2K **Privately Held**
WEB: www.netsdepot.com
SIC: 2298 Blasting mats, rope

(G-8287)
NEW AGE WINDOWS & DOORS CORP
7196 Nw 77th Ter (33166-2544)
PHONE..................................305 889-0703
Jose Bosch, *President*
◆ **EMP:** 10 **EST:** 1994
SQ FT: 16,150
SALES (est): 1.5MM **Privately Held**
WEB: www.newagewindow.com
SIC: 2431 3442 Doors & door parts & trim, wood; windows & window parts & trim, wood; metal doors, sash & trim

(G-8288)
NEW GENERATION AEROSPACE INC
8004 Nw 90th St (33166-2114)
PHONE..................................305 882-1410
Orlando Fernandez, *President*
Amauri Izquierdo, *Vice Pres*
Ivon Fernandez, *Director*
EMP: 6 **EST:** 2010
SALES (est): 1MM **Privately Held**
WEB: www.ngaerospace.com
SIC: 3812 7694 Aircraft/aerospace flight instruments & guidance systems; armature rewinding shops; rewinding services; coil winding service; rewinding stators

(G-8289)
NEWLINK CABLING SYSTEMS INC (PA)
11701 Nw 102nd Rd Ste 21 (33178-1016)
PHONE..................................305 477-8063
Jorge Villegas, *President*
Pacheco Fernando, *Vice Pres*
◆ **EMP:** 12 **EST:** 1994
SQ FT: 10,000
SALES (est): 2.3MM **Privately Held**
WEB: www.newlink-usa.com
SIC: 3357 2298 Fiber optic cable (insulated); cable, fiber

(G-8290)
NORTH AMERICAN MINING
10025 Nw 116th Way Ste 1 (33178-1197)
PHONE..................................305 824-3181
EMP: 12 **EST:** 2019
SALES (est): 3.1MM **Privately Held**
WEB: www.nacoal.com
SIC: 1241 Coal mining services

(G-8291)
NUSFC LLC ✪
Also Called: US Foundry
8351 Nw 93rd St (33166-2025)
P.O. Box 8351 Nw 93rd St (33166)
PHONE..................................920 725-7000
Tom Slabe, *Mng Member*
EMP: 170 **EST:** 2021
SALES (est): 119MM **Privately Held**
SIC: 3321 Gray & ductile iron foundries

(G-8292)
OLDCASTLE INFRASTRUCTURE INC
7311 Nw 77th St (33166-2205)
PHONE..................................305 887-3527
Carolina Hurtado, *Plant Mgr*
Michael Palij, *Mfg Spvr*
David Piterski, *Manager*
EMP: 30
SQ FT: 22,969
SALES (corp-wide): 30.9B **Privately Held**
WEB: www.oldcastleinfrastructure.com
SIC: 3272 Concrete products
HQ: Oldcastle Infrastructure, Inc.
7000 Central Pkwy Ste 800
Atlanta GA 30328
770 270-5000

(G-8293)
OSKO INC
8085 Nw 90th St (33166-2113)
PHONE..................................305 599-7161
Jinsu Do, *President*
Cesar Sotomayor, *Marketing Staff*
Jeonghoon Hyun,
Kukchin Yang, *Director*
EMP: 19 **EST:** 2013

SALES (est): 8.1MM **Privately Held**
WEB: www.oskomedical.com
SIC: 3844 X-ray apparatus & tubes
PA: Rayence Co., Ltd.
14 Samsung 1-Ro 1-Gil
Hwaseong 18449

(G-8294)
PALM FURNITURE SYSTEMS INC
8181 Nw 91st Ter Ste 2 (33166-2135)
PHONE..........................305 888-7009
Nelson Cortes, *President*
Lucy Rispa, *Sales Staff*
EMP: 5 **EST:** 1981
SQ FT: 20,000
SALES (est): 332.2K **Privately Held**
WEB: www.palmfurnituresystems.com
SIC: 2512 Upholstered household furniture

(G-8295)
PAN AMERICAN CNSTR PLANT
8000 Nw 74th St (33166-2318)
PHONE..........................305 477-5058
Bob Pritchard, *Principal*
EMP: 10 **EST:** 2001
SALES (est): 24.2K **Privately Held**
SIC: 2951 Asphalt paving mixtures & blocks

(G-8296)
PANAPASTRY LLC
9001 Nw 97th Ter Ste M (33178-1460)
PHONE..........................305 883-1557
Maria E Del Rio,
EMP: 5 **EST:** 2007
SALES (est): 480.6K **Privately Held**
WEB: www.panapastry.com
SIC: 2051 Pastries, e.g. danish: except frozen

(G-8297)
PEPSICO INC
Also Called: Pepsi-Cola
8701 Nw 93rd St (33178-2103)
PHONE..........................305 593-7500
Blake Clair, *Opers Mgr*
Elizabeth Pinol, *Sales Staff*
Robert Smythe, *Sales Staff*
Alejandra Negrin, *Marketing Staff*
John Nickels, *Branch Mgr*
EMP: 54
SALES (corp-wide): 70.3B **Publicly Held**
WEB: www.pepsico.com
SIC: 2086 5149 3565 Carbonated soft drinks, bottled & canned; soft drinks; packaging machinery
PA: Pepsico, Inc.
700 Anderson Hill Rd
Purchase NY 10577
914 253-2000

(G-8298)
PERRI BROTHERS AND ASSOCIATES
9001 Nw 97th Ter (33178-1460)
PHONE..........................305 887-8686
EMP: 7 **EST:** 2019
SALES (est): 359.4K **Privately Held**
WEB: www.perribros.com
SIC: 2511 Wood household furniture

(G-8299)
PINOS WINDOW CORPORATION
6860 Nw 75th St (33166-2549)
PHONE..........................305 888-9903
Mario Pino, *President*
Mercy Blanco, *Vice Pres*
George Pino, *Vice Pres*
Julio Rodriguez, *CFO*
▼ **EMP:** 18 **EST:** 1965
SQ FT: 26,000
SALES (est): 2.9MM **Privately Held**
WEB: www.pinoswindowcorp.com
SIC: 3442 1751 Window & door frames; window & door installation & erection

(G-8300)
PLASTIC COMPONENTS INC (PA)
Also Called: Plastic International
9051 Nw 97th Ter (33178-1430)
PHONE..........................305 885-0561
Thomas Stark, *President*
Jon Jay, *Production*

Michael Molling, *CFO*
Audrey English, *Accountant*
Herman Guervara, *Natl Sales Mgr*
◆ **EMP:** 34 **EST:** 1976
SQ FT: 40,000
SALES (est): 9.4MM **Privately Held**
WEB: www.plasticcomponents.com
SIC: 3089 Plastic hardware & building products

(G-8301)
POLIMIX USA LLC
11750 Nw South River Dr (33178-1117)
PHONE..........................305 888-4752
Tarik Andrade, *President*
Luis Gabriel Munoz, *General Mgr*
EMP: 18 **EST:** 2014
SQ FT: 174,240
SALES (est): 3.8MM **Privately Held**
WEB: www.polimixusa.com
SIC: 3273 Ready-mixed concrete

(G-8302)
PRECAST DEPOT INC
11002 Nw South River Dr (33178-1133)
PHONE..........................305 885-2530
Jose Zarraluqui, *President*
Walter Lista, *Vice Pres*
EMP: 49 **EST:** 2001
SALES (est): 5.1MM **Privately Held**
SIC: 3272 Concrete products, precast

(G-8303)
PRO-CHEMICALS USA CORP
7575 Nw 82nd St (33166-7412)
PHONE..........................305 885-7922
Enrique Herrero, *President*
Gabriel Herrero, *Corp Secy*
Bibiana Herrero, *Vice Pres*
EMP: 5 **EST:** 1998
SALES (est): 688.5K **Privately Held**
SIC: 3471 Cleaning, polishing & finishing

(G-8304)
PRO-MIX INC
11405 Nw 138th St (33178-3111)
PHONE..........................305 556-6699
Emilio R Vega, *President*
EMP: 7 **EST:** 2005
SALES (est): 322.9K **Privately Held**
SIC: 3273 Ready-mixed concrete

(G-8305)
PROBAG INC
9955 Nw 88th Ave (33178-1450)
PHONE..........................305 883-3266
Ignacio Rivero, *President*
Paul La Fontaine, *Vice Pres*
Sergio Jilmnez, *Treasurer*
EMP: 15 **EST:** 2010
SALES (est): 1.9MM **Privately Held**
WEB: www.probag.biz
SIC: 2621 Bag paper

(G-8306)
QUEST MANUFACTURING CORP
11200 Nw 138th St (33178-3157)
PHONE..........................305 513-8583
Armando Ujueta, *President*
Nestor Novo, *Vice Pres*
Hernan Salcedo, *Treasurer*
Michael Convissar, *Admin Sec*
EMP: 14 **EST:** 2001
SALES (est): 429.2K **Privately Held**
WEB: www.questtechnologyintl.com
SIC: 3399 1731 Iron ore recovery from open hearth slag; voice, data & video wiring contractor

(G-8307)
RAM INVESTMENTS SOUTH FLA INC (PA)
Also Called: Sea Enterprise Adventures
11102 Nw South River Dr (33178-1135)
PHONE..........................305 759-6419
Ariel Parad, *President*
Elizabeth Gomez, *Business Mgr*
Moises Rodrigues, *Treasurer*
Ivania Martinez, *Human Res Mgr*
Rocmay Chaviano, *Department Mgr*
▼ **EMP:** 50 **EST:** 1993
SALES (est): 21.8MM **Privately Held**
SIC: 3732 5551 Motorized boat, building & repairing; boat dealers

(G-8308)
RAVIC TECHNOLOGIES LLC
7939 Nw 84th St Ste 101 (33166-2107)
PHONE..........................954 237-3241
Alberto Ravachi Arza,
Sandra Victoria,
▼ **EMP:** 6 **EST:** 2000
SQ FT: 5,000
SALES (est): 600.2K **Privately Held**
WEB: www.stumplaw.net
SIC: 3663 Cable television equipment

(G-8309)
RED HOT TRENDS INC
7911 Nw 72nd Ave Ste 107 (33166-2221)
P.O. Box 562073, Miami (33256-2073)
PHONE..........................305 888-6951
John A McAlister, *President*
Albert Zamora, *Vice Pres*
Dalila Gomez, *Admin Sec*
▼ **EMP:** 6 **EST:** 1989
SQ FT: 3,500
SALES (est): 485.3K **Privately Held**
WEB: www.redhottrends.com
SIC: 2759 Screen printing

(G-8310)
REVOLUTION BRANDS INTL LLC (PA) ✪
10801 Nw 97th St (33178-2540)
PHONE..........................786 571-3876
Mauricio Diaz, *Mng Member*
Federico Urdaneta,
EMP: 7 **EST:** 2021
SALES (est): 276.2K **Privately Held**
SIC: 3714 Motor vehicle parts & accessories

(G-8311)
RFG CONSULTING SERVICES INC
7214 Nw 78th Ter (33166-2219)
PHONE..........................832 298-5696
Jose G Guevara, *President*
Anthony C Fernandes, *Vice Pres*
Ernesto L Guevara, *Director*
EMP: 7 **EST:** 2011
SALES (est): 112.9K **Privately Held**
SIC: 1389 7299 3599 Acidizing wells; turkish bath; amusement park equipment

(G-8312)
RICOMA INTERNATIONAL CORP
11555 Nw 124th St (33178-3193)
PHONE..........................305 418-4421
Guofeng MA, *President*
WEI Cheng, *Vice Pres*
Wenrui MA, *Vice Pres*
◆ **EMP:** 7 **EST:** 2008
SALES (est): 3.3MM
SALES (corp-wide): 17.5MM **Privately Held**
WEB: www.ricoma.com
SIC: 3552 Textile machinery
PA: Ricoma (Shenzhen) Co.,Ltd.
201, Bldg. A, Bailian Qimengcheng Industrial Zone, No. 11, Shuit
Shenzhen 51811
755 536-6999

(G-8313)
RINKER MATERIALS
13100 Nw 118th Ave (33178-3105)
PHONE..........................305 345-4127
David Clarke, *CEO*
EMP: 18 **EST:** 2015
SALES (est): 2.4MM **Privately Held**
SIC: 3272 Concrete products

(G-8314)
RINKER MATERIALS CORP CON
12155 Nw 136th St (33178-3109)
PHONE..........................305 818-4952
Johnny Arellano, *Manager*
Dan Brown, *Director*
EMP: 6 **EST:** 2009
SALES (est): 453.7K **Privately Held**
SIC: 1422 Crushed & broken limestone

(G-8315)
RIOS CON PMPG & RENTL INC
Also Called: Rio's Concrete Equipment
8750 Nw 93rd St (33178-1412)
PHONE..........................305 888-7909
Serafin Del Rio, *President*

Olga Del Rio, *Vice Pres*
Barbara Delrio, *Opers Staff*
Amado Del Rio, *Human Resources*
Bargo Del Rio, *Manager*
▼ **EMP:** 40 **EST:** 1975
SQ FT: 5,000
SALES (est): 4.3MM **Privately Held**
WEB: www.riosequipmentsales.com
SIC: 3273 5084 Ready-mixed concrete; industrial machinery & equipment

(G-8316)
ROYAL HEADWEAR & EMB INC
7675 Nw 80th Ter (33166-7538)
PHONE..........................305 889-8480
Dominic Amendolia, *President*
◆ **EMP:** 12 **EST:** 1987
SQ FT: 15,000
SALES (est): 399.6K **Privately Held**
SIC: 2353 5136 5137 2395 Hats: cloth, straw & felt; hats, men's & boys'; hats: women's, children's & infants'; embroidery products, except schiffli machine; schiffli machine embroideries

(G-8317)
ROYAL TRUSS CORP
10900 Nw South River Dr (33178-1131)
PHONE..........................786 222-1100
Edward J Davies, *President*
Hector Llado, *Corp Secy*
EMP: 10 **EST:** 1978
SALES (est): 933.6K **Privately Held**
WEB: www.royaltrusscorp.com
SIC: 2439 Trusses, wooden roof

(G-8318)
SALTAGE INC
9092 Nw S River Dr Ste 61 (33166-2128)
PHONE..........................305 462-8960
Sam Fitzpatrick, *CEO*
EMP: 5 **EST:** 2019
SALES (est): 2.2MM **Privately Held**
SIC: 3648 Outdoor lighting equipment

(G-8319)
SAUL SIGNS INC
10631 Nw 123rd Street Rd (33178-3166)
PHONE..........................305 266-8484
Jose Hernandez, *President*
Leida Hernandez, *Vice Pres*
EMP: 11 **EST:** 1981
SQ FT: 20,000
SALES (est): 737.2K **Privately Held**
SIC: 3993 Signs & advertising specialties

(G-8320)
SOLAR ERECTORS US INC
10501 Nw 121st Way (33178-1028)
PHONE..........................305 823-8950
Luiqi Francisosa, *President*
Robert Spiegel, *Principal*
Sidney Spiegel, *Principal*
Mario Franciosa, *Vice Pres*
EMP: 10 **EST:** 2003
SALES (est): 267.5K **Privately Held**
WEB: www.solarerectors.com
SIC: 3272 Concrete stuctural support & building material

(G-8321)
SOUTH FLORIDA CONCRETE & RDYMX
Also Called: S F C
9500 Nw 109th St (33178-1230)
PHONE..........................305 888-0420
Neida Suarez, *President*
Sergio Suarez, *General Mgr*
Lilia Verde, *General Mgr*
Lily Verde, *Office Mgr*
EMP: 28 **EST:** 1981
SQ FT: 1,190
SALES (est): 5.7MM **Privately Held**
WEB: www.sfcrmix.com
SIC: 3273 Ready-mixed concrete

(G-8322)
SOUTHAST AUTO ACQUISITION CORP
Also Called: Southeast Worldwide
7575 Nw 74th Ave (33166-2422)
PHONE..........................305 885-8689
Bernardo Davila, *CEO*
◆ **EMP:** 33 **EST:** 1981
SQ FT: 49,500

▲ = Import ▼ =Export
◆ =Import/Export

SALES (est): 987.5K Privately Held
WEB: www.unagota.com
SIC: **3089** 5013 Automotive parts, plastic; automotive supplies & parts

(G-8323)
SOUTHPOINT SPORTSWEAR LLC
11525 Nw 124th St (33178-3193)
PHONE..................................305 885-3045
Branko Zunjic, *Mng Member*
Allison Rosen, *Manager*
Gale S Crawford,
◆ **EMP: 5 EST:** 2002
SALES (est): 1MM Privately Held
WEB: www.southpointsportswear.com
SIC: **2339** Sportswear, women's

(G-8324)
SPANISH HOUSE INC
Also Called: Editorial Unilit
8167 Nw 84th St (33166-2111)
PHONE..................................305 503-1191
David Ecklebarger, *President*
Catherine Ecklebarger, *Vice Pres*
Myriam Macri, *Sales Dir*
◆ **EMP: 43 EST:** 1977
SQ FT: 16,000
SALES (est): 5.2MM Privately Held
SIC: **2731** 5192 7812 2721 Books: publishing only; books; music video production; periodicals

(G-8325)
STANDARD KEGS LLC
Also Called: Standard Kegs & Equipment
9106 Nw 106th St (33178-1204)
PHONE..................................305 454-9721
Zhi Yang, *General Mgr*
Zhilong Yang,
▲ **EMP: 9 EST:** 2015
SALES (est): 2.8MM Privately Held
WEB: www.standardkegs.com
SIC: **3412** Metal barrels, drums & pails

(G-8326)
STORE IT COLD LLC
9731 Nw 114th Way (33178-1178)
PHONE..................................720 456-1178
Brian Murphy, *Mng Member*
Ryan Berk, *Manager*
Michael Dworkis, *Manager*
EMP: 8 EST: 2015
SALES (est): 865.2K Privately Held
WEB: www.storeitcold.com
SIC: **3585** Refrigeration & heating equipment

(G-8327)
STOROPACK INC
11825 Nw 100th Rd Ste 5 (33178-1034)
PHONE..................................305 805-9696
Mike Osgood, *Owner*
EMP: 9
SALES (corp-wide): 590.9MM Privately Held
WEB: www.storopack.us
SIC: **3086** 5199 2671 Packaging & shipping materials, foamed plastic; packaging materials; packaging paper & plastics film, coated & laminated
HQ: Storopack, Inc.
4758 Devitt Dr
West Chester OH 45246
513 874-0314

(G-8328)
SUINPLA LLC
12605 Nw 115th Ave # 106 (33178-3191)
PHONE..................................786 747-4829
Maria C Toro,
Jaime M Ferreira,
EMP: 12 EST: 2016
SALES (est): 2.3MM Privately Held
WEB: www.suinpla.com
SIC: **3569** 3599 Filters; filters, general line: industrial; gasoline filters, internal combustion engine, except auto; air intake filters, internal combustion engine, except auto

(G-8329)
SUNSHINE MARINE TANKS INC
8045 Nw 90th St (33166-2113)
PHONE..................................305 805-9898
Lucy Maciaz, *President*

▼ **EMP: 8 EST:** 1984
SQ FT: 7,190
SALES (est): 1.2MM Privately Held
WEB: www.sunshinemarinetanks.com
SIC: **3443** Tanks, standard or custom fabricated: metal plate

(G-8330)
THE SOBE GROUP INC
8125 Nw 74th Ave Unit 3 (33166-7489)
PHONE..................................305 884-4008
Frank Wright, *Manager*
EMP: 8
SALES (corp-wide): 831.2K Privately Held
SIC: **2752** Commercial printing, offset
PA: The Sobe Group Inc
7503 W 34th Ln
Hialeah FL

(G-8331)
TIRE EXPERTS LLC
10903 Nw 122nd St (33178-3168)
PHONE..................................305 663-3508
Silvano Buttaci,
Carlos A Buttaci,
Tiberio Buttaci,
Nunzia Costanzo De Buttaci,
▲ **EMP: 8 EST:** 2011
SALES (est): 1.1MM Privately Held
SIC: **3011** Tire & inner tube materials & related products

(G-8332)
TITAN AMERICA LLC
11955 Nw 102nd Rd (33178-1014)
PHONE..................................305 761-1944
John Taut, *Branch Mgr*
EMP: 32
SALES (corp-wide): 177.9K Privately Held
WEB: www.titanamerica.com
SIC: **3273** Ready-mixed concrete
HQ: Titan America Llc
5700 Lake Wright Dr # 300
Norfolk VA 23502
757 858-6500

(G-8333)
TITAN AMERICA LLC
Tarmac Block Division
10100 Nw 121st Way (33178-1010)
PHONE..................................954 481-2800
George Pantaz, *Vice Pres*
Terry Merrion, *Branch Mgr*
Carlos Odriozola, *Supervisor*
Frank Alonso, *Maintence Staff*
EMP: 10
SALES (corp-wide): 177.9K Privately Held
WEB: www.titanamerica.com
SIC: **3273** Ready-mixed concrete
HQ: Titan America Llc
5700 Lake Wright Dr # 300
Norfolk VA 23502
757 858-6500

(G-8334)
TITAN AMERICA LLC
Also Called: Titan Florida
10100 Nw 121st Way (33178-1010)
PHONE..................................305 364-2200
Alberto Hernandez, *Principal*
Carlos Gonzalez, *Project Mgr*
Curtis Leonard, *Manager*
EMP: 180
SALES (corp-wide): 177.9K Privately Held
WEB: www.titanamerica.com
SIC: **3241** 3273 3271 4213 Cement, hydraulic; ready-mixed concrete; blocks, concrete or cinder: standard; trucking, except local
HQ: Titan America Llc
5700 Lake Wright Dr # 300
Norfolk VA 23502
757 858-6500

(G-8335)
TITAN FLORIDA LLC
10100 Nw 121st Way (33178-1010)
PHONE..................................800 588-3939
Aris Papadopoulos, *Mng Member*
◆ **EMP: 774 EST:** 2000

SALES (est): 83.7MM
SALES (corp-wide): 177.9K Privately Held
WEB: www.titanamerica.com
SIC: **3273** Ready-mixed concrete
HQ: Titan America Llc
5700 Lake Wright Dr # 300
Norfolk VA 23502
757 858-6500

(G-8336)
TOP KITCHEN CABINETS
12650 Nw 107th Ave (33178-3127)
PHONE..................................305 392-9938
Gilbert Cover, *Principal*
▼ **EMP: 8 EST:** 2013
SALES (est): 322.9K Privately Held
WEB: www.topskitchen.com
SIC: **2434** Wood kitchen cabinets

(G-8337)
TREADMILL PARTS ZONE
11401 Nw 122nd St (33178-3182)
PHONE..................................305 336-5600
Treadmill Parts Zone, *Principal*
EMP: 8 EST: 2011
SALES (est): 190.4K Privately Held
WEB: www.treadmillpartszone.com
SIC: **3949** Treadmills

(G-8338)
TREMRON INC (DH)
11321 Nw 138th St (33178-3101)
PHONE..................................305 825-9000
Michelle Caron, *President*
Jacques Tremblay, *Vice Pres*
Edilio Pacitti, *Manager*
Alli Pappas, *Manager*
Francisco Leite, *Supervisor*
◆ **EMP: 16 EST:** 1990
SQ FT: 2,000
SALES (est): 11.6MM
SALES (corp-wide): 2.1MM Privately Held
WEB: www.tremron.com
SIC: **3271** Blocks, concrete: drystack interlocking
HQ: Groupe Caron & Caron Inc
800 Boul Pierre-Tremblay
Saint-Jean-Sur-Richelieu QC J2X 4
450 545-7174

(G-8339)
TRITON SEAFOOD CO
7301 Nw 77th St (33166-2205)
PHONE..................................305 888-8999
Alfredo Alvarez, *CEO*
Yvonne M Conde, *President*
Rady M Alvarez, *Treasurer*
EMP: 15 EST: 1987
SALES (est): 2.2MM Privately Held
WEB: www.tritonsfd.com
SIC: **2099** Food preparations

(G-8340)
TRUSSCORP INTERNATIONAL INC
9590 Nw 89th Ave (33178-1406)
PHONE..................................305 882-8826
Oscar Tabares, *President*
EMP: 37 EST: 1991
SQ FT: 2,500
SALES (est): 2.6MM Privately Held
WEB: trusscorp-international-inc.business.site
SIC: **2439** Trusses, wooden roof

(G-8341)
ULTIMA DESIGN SOUTH FLA INC
11305 Nw 128th St (33178-3118)
PHONE..................................305 477-9300
Victoria Hallett, *President*
Vicky Hallett, *Vice Pres*
Sofia Liebster, *Manager*
◆ **EMP: 14 EST:** 1993
SQ FT: 15,000
SALES (est): 4.6MM Privately Held
WEB: www.ultimadesign.com
SIC: **2599** Factory furniture & fixtures

(G-8342)
UNITED CONCRETE PRODUCTS LLC (HQ)
8351 Nw 93rd St (33166-2025)
PHONE..................................786 402-3536
Alex L Debugory Jr,

Thomas Bond,
▼ **EMP: 4 EST:** 2012
SALES (est): 7.7MM
SALES (corp-wide): 157.6MM Privately Held
WEB: www.frsprestress.com
SIC: **3272** Precast terrazo or concrete products
PA: U. S. Holdings, Inc.
3200 W 84th St
Hialeah FL 33018
305 885-0301

(G-8343)
UNIVERSAL CONCRETE & READY MIX
11790 Nw South River Dr (33178-1117)
PHONE..................................305 888-4101
Juan Alvarez, *President*
EMP: 16 EST: 1986
SQ FT: 6,140
SALES (est): 312.2K Privately Held
SIC: **3273** Ready-mixed concrete

(G-8344)
UNIVERSAL TRANSACTIONS INC
Also Called: Universal Packaging Co
12870 Nw South River Dr (33178-1108)
PHONE..................................305 887-4677
Larry Epstein, *President*
◆ **EMP: 14 EST:** 1979
SQ FT: 6,000
SALES (est): 2.5MM Privately Held
SIC: **2812** 2899 Alkalies & chlorine; chemical preparations

(G-8345)
US DEFIB MEDICAL TECH LLC
7831 Nw 72nd Ave (33166-2215)
PHONE..................................305 887-7552
Amanda Felix, *CEO*
Marco Aurelio M Felix, *Mng Member*
▲ **EMP: 7 EST:** 2011
SQ FT: 5,000
SALES (est): 862.3K Privately Held
WEB: www.usdefib.com
SIC: **3845** Defibrillator

(G-8346)
US MANUFACTURING COMPANY (HQ)
Also Called: United States Fndry & Mfg Corp
8351 Nw 93rd St (33166-2025)
PHONE..................................305 885-0301
Alex Lane De Bogory, *Ch of Bd*
Alex Debogory Jr, *President*
Robert Marr, *General Mgr*
Bill Vanness, *General Mgr*
Dave Owens, *Vice Pres*
▼ **EMP: 200 EST:** 1916
SALES (est): 104.4MM
SALES (corp-wide): 157.6MM Privately Held
SIC: **3321** 3441 3322 Gray iron castings; fabricated structural metal; malleable iron foundries
PA: U. S. Holdings, Inc.
3200 W 84th St
Hialeah FL 33018
305 885-0301

(G-8347)
US PRECAST CORPORATION
8351 Nw 93rd St (33166-2096)
P.O. Box 918720, Orlando (32891-0001)
PHONE..................................305 885-8471
Alexander De Bogory Jr, *President*
Barbara Degregory, *Principal*
David Brunswick, *CFO*
Alex S Debogory, *Treasurer*
Jorge Landrian, *Manager*
▼ **EMP: 1 EST:** 1965
SALES (est): 12.1MM
SALES (corp-wide): 157.6MM Privately Held
SIC: **3272** Concrete products
PA: U. S. Holdings, Inc.
3200 W 84th St
Hialeah FL 33018
305 885-0301

(G-8348)
VAZKO LLC
10957 Nw 123rd St (33178-3192)
PHONE.....................................786 521-0808
Arys L Gargallo, *Administration*
EMP: 6 EST: 2016
SALES (est): 326.4K **Privately Held**
SIC: 2033 Vegetables: packaged in cans, jars, etc.

(G-8349)
VIDCO INDUSTRIES INC
Also Called: Delta Doors
7500 Nw 69th Ave Frnt Ste (33166-2525)
PHONE.....................................305 888-0077
Jesus Martinez, *President*
◆ EMP: 27 EST: 1996
SQ FT: 40,000
SALES (est): 2.6MM **Privately Held**
SIC: 3442 Metal doors; store fronts, prefabricated, metal

(G-8350)
WALL WAY CORPORATION
Also Called: Wall Way USA of Florida
9001 Nw 97th Ter Ste F (33178-1460)
PHONE.....................................305 484-7600
Amir Massoumi, *President*
Mohammed Dadullah, *Treasurer*
▲ EMP: 17 EST: 1988
SQ FT: 10,000
SALES (est): 3MM **Privately Held**
WEB: www.wallwayusa.com
SIC: 3272 Concrete products

(G-8351)
WDC MIAMI INC
9721 Nw 114th Way (33178-1178)
PHONE.....................................305 884-2800
Richard Worthy, *President*
EMP: 7 EST: 2013
SALES (est): 180.4K **Privately Held**
SIC: 3825 Instruments to measure electricity

(G-8352)
YORK INTERNATIONAL CORPORATION
Also Called: Johnson Controls
10801 Nw 97th St Ste 21 (33178-2540)
PHONE.....................................305 805-5600
Rosaro Rodriguez, *Manager*
EMP: 18 **Privately Held**
WEB: www.shumakerwilliams.com
SIC: 3585 Refrigeration & heating equipment
HQ: York International Corporation
631 S Richland Ave
York PA 17403
800 481-9738

Melbourne
Brevard County

(G-8353)
ABS STRUCTURAL CORP
700 E Melbourne Ave (32901-5507)
PHONE.....................................321 768-2067
Frank Kingston, *President*
Helen Kingston, *Corp Secy*
Heather Chambers, *Vice Pres*
EMP: 11 EST: 1985
SQ FT: 4,653
SALES (est): 1.9MM **Privately Held**
WEB: www.abs-structural.com
SIC: 3312 Structural shapes & pilings, steel

(G-8354)
ACT USA INTERNATIONAL LLC
Also Called: Act USA Int'l
3962 W Eau Gallie Blvd C (32934-3294)
PHONE.....................................321 725-4200
Jerry Gerard, *President*
Sharlene Edlin, *Vice Pres*
Jack Gemmell, *Opers Mgr*
Patrick Higgins, *Technical Mgr*
Adam Tennant, *Accounts Mgr*
▲ EMP: 18 EST: 1994
SALES (est): 2.9MM **Privately Held**
WEB: www.act-usa.com
SIC: 3672 Printed circuit boards

(G-8355)
ADVANCED MAGNET LAB INC
1604 S Hbr Cy Blvd Ste 10 (32901)
PHONE.....................................321 728-7543
Rainer Meinka, *President*
Mark Senti, *Vice Pres*
Matthew McDowell, *Research*
EMP: 12 EST: 1995
SALES (est): 2.4MM **Privately Held**
WEB: www.amlsuperconductivity.com
SIC: 3357 Magnet wire, nonferrous

(G-8356)
AEROBASE GROUP INC (PA)
Also Called: A B G
145 East Dr Ste B (32904-1007)
PHONE.....................................321 802-5889
Lisette Corrao, *Principal*
Thomas Corrao, *Principal*
Jason Lyczkowski, *Purchasing*
Alexina Cyr, *Accounts Mgr*
Robert Frungillo, *Accounts Mgr*
EMP: 23 EST: 2013
SALES (est): 5.3MM **Privately Held**
WEB: www.aerobasegroup.com
SIC: 3728 Aircraft parts & equipment

(G-8357)
AIRCRAFT TBULAR COMPONENTS INC
3939 Dow Rd (32934-9221)
PHONE.....................................321 757-9020
Rodney Simon, *President*
Jeffrey Simon, *Vice Pres*
Jeffrey W Simon, *Vice Pres*
Robert C Simon, *Vice Pres*
Jeff Simon, *VP Mfg*
EMP: 27 EST: 1991
SQ FT: 23,000
SALES (est): 5.3MM **Privately Held**
WEB: www.airtube.net
SIC: 3469 Machine parts, stamped or pressed metal

(G-8358)
AIRON CORPORATION
751 North Dr Ste 6 (32934-9289)
PHONE.....................................321 821-9433
G Eric Gjerde, *President*
Pamela Kay Fry, *Vice Pres*
Manish Jindal, *Engineer*
Marcus Cain, *Sales Staff*
◆ EMP: 8 EST: 1997
SQ FT: 2,300
SALES (est): 1.6MM **Privately Held**
WEB: www.aironusa.com
SIC: 3841 Surgical & medical instruments

(G-8359)
ALERTGY INC
2401 S Harbor City Blvd (32901-5530)
PHONE.....................................321 914-3199
Marc Rippen, *President*
John Hubert, *Vice Pres*
Craig Nelson, *Officer*
Anton Stiernelofgullb, *Technician*
EMP: 5 EST: 2017
SALES (est): 669.9K **Privately Held**
WEB: www.alertgy.com
SIC: 3829 Measuring & controlling devices

(G-8360)
ALL SERVICE GRAPHICS INC
1020 W Eau Gallie Blvd I (32935-5874)
PHONE.....................................321 259-8957
William Smith, *President*
Donald E Gust, *Vice Pres*
Linda Finley, *Comptroller*
Herry Allen, *Persnl Mgr*
EMP: 17 EST: 1987
SQ FT: 11,500
SALES (est): 3.1MM **Privately Held**
WEB: www.asgprinting.com
SIC: 2752 Commercial printing, offset

(G-8361)
ALLGEO & YERKES ENTPS INC
Also Called: Tropical Designs
397 Pineda Ct (32940-7508)
PHONE.....................................321 255-9030
William Yerkes, *President*
William Allgeo, *Vice Pres*
▲ EMP: 10 EST: 1990
SQ FT: 10,000
SALES (est): 1.4MM **Privately Held**
SIC: 2759 Screen printing

(G-8362)
ALSTOM SIGNALING OPERATION LLC
Also Called: Real Solutions
1990 W Nasa Blvd (32904-2309)
PHONE.....................................781 740-8111
EMP: 200
SALES (corp-wide): 1.6B **Privately Held**
SIC: 3669 Mfg Electronic Systems
PA: Alstom Signaling Operation, Llc
2901 E Lake Rd Bldg 122
Erie PA 64029
800 825-3178

(G-8363)
ALTERNATIVE CNSTR TECH INC (PA)
Also Called: Act
2910 Bush Dr (32935-2156)
PHONE.....................................321 421-6601
Anthony J Francel, *Ch of Bd*
John S Wittler, *CFO*
Leigh Cerke, *Manager*
Gina Bennett, *Officer*
Thomas G Amon, *Admin Sec*
EMP: 7 EST: 2004
SALES (est): 12.9MM **Privately Held**
SIC: 2451 1799 1521 1751 Mobile homes; safe or vault installation; single-family housing construction; framing contractor; architectural engineering; panels for prefabricated metal buildings; trusses & framing: prefabricated metal

(G-8364)
AMERICAN MOULDING CORPORATION
710 Atlantis Rd (32904-2317)
PHONE.....................................321 676-8929
Robert Sicoli, *President*
Chris Bryant, *Owner*
John Sicoli, *Admin Sec*
EMP: 14 EST: 2002
SALES (est): 3.5MM **Privately Held**
WEB: www.americanmouldingllc.com
SIC: 3089 Molding primary plastic

(G-8365)
ANDREW MARTIN SWIFT
Also Called: Sgmc Microwave
620 Atlantis Rd Ste A (32904-2341)
PHONE.....................................321 409-0509
Andrew Swift, *Owner*
EMP: 6 EST: 2000
SALES (est): 415.9K **Privately Held**
SIC: 3559 Electronic component making machinery

(G-8366)
ANUVA MANUFACTURING SVCS INC
7801 Ellis Rd Ste 101 (32904-1190)
PHONE.....................................321 821-4900
Vinu Patel, *CEO*
Jim Davis, *Vice Pres*
Kathy Horvath, *Info Tech Mgr*
EMP: 25 EST: 2010
SALES (est): 4.3MM **Privately Held**
WEB: www.anuva.com
SIC: 3661 5063 Telephone sets, all types except cellular radio; electrical apparatus & equipment

(G-8367)
APIS COR INC
3060 Venture Ln Ste 101 (32934-8103)
PHONE.....................................347 404-1481
Anna Cheniutai, *CEO*
Nikita Cheniutai, *Director*
EMP: 24 EST: 2019
SALES (est): 1.1MM **Privately Held**
WEB: www.apis-cor.com
SIC: 2759 Commercial printing

(G-8368)
APPLIED SYSTEMS INTEGRATOR INC
746 North Dr Ste B (32934-9252)
P.O. Box 411471 (32941-1471)
PHONE.....................................321 259-6106
Kanitha Hay, *President*
EMP: 6 EST: 1997
SQ FT: 10,000
SALES (est): 970.1K **Privately Held**
WEB: applied-systems-integrator-inc1.sb-contract.com
SIC: 3663 7373 Satellites, communications; computer systems analysis & design

(G-8369)
ATLANTIC JET CENTER INC
1401 Gen Avi Dr (32935)
PHONE.....................................321 255-7111
Spence Edwards, *President*
Kim Brose, *General Mgr*
EMP: 6 EST: 1990
SQ FT: 40,000
SALES (est): 670K **Privately Held**
WEB: www.atlanticjetcenter.com
SIC: 2911 5172 6512 5599 Jet fuels; gasoline; aircraft fueling services; commercial & industrial building operation; aircraft, self-propelled

(G-8370)
AURORA STONE & GRAVEL LLC
2699 Aurora Rd (32935-2854)
PHONE.....................................321 253-4808
Saul Ventura, *Mng Member*
EMP: 6 EST: 2009
SALES (est): 548K **Privately Held**
WEB: www.aurorastoneandgravel.com
SIC: 1442 Construction sand & gravel

(G-8371)
AVASAR CORP
435 West Dr (32904-1035)
PHONE.....................................321 723-3456
EMP: 30
SQ FT: 11,000
SALES (est): 3.6MM **Privately Held**
SIC: 3489 Mfg Ordnance & Accessories

(G-8372)
AVIDYNE CORPORATION (PA)
710 North Dr (32934-9286)
PHONE.....................................321 751-8520
Dan Schwinn, *CEO*
Steve Jacobson, *Senior VP*
Roger Mitchell, *Senior VP*
Kenneth Toney, *Senior Buyer*
WEI Guo, *Engineer*
EMP: 95 EST: 1994
SQ FT: 30,000
SALES (est): 65.6MM **Privately Held**
WEB: www.avidyne.com
SIC: 3812 Aircraft/aerospace flight instruments & guidance systems

(G-8373)
B & K DISCOUNT CABINETS LLC (PA)
Also Called: Bk Cabinets
280 N Wickham Rd (32935-8650)
PHONE.....................................321 254-2322
Karen Livingood,
Dina Mae Whipple,
EMP: 9 EST: 2018
SALES (est): 252.1K **Privately Held**
WEB: www.melbournecabinets.com
SIC: 2434 Wood kitchen cabinets

(G-8374)
BARRETT CUSTOM DESIGNS LLC
6430 Anderson Way Ste A (32940-7407)
PHONE.....................................321 242-2002
Jeffrey G Barrett, *Mng Member*
▼ EMP: 5 EST: 2011
SALES (est): 776.8K **Privately Held**
WEB: www.barrettcustomdesigns.com
SIC: 3441 1799 3444 Fabricated structural metal; ornamental metal work; sheet metalwork

(G-8375)
BARTMAN ENTERPRISES INC
2735 Center Pl Ste 101 (32940-7181)
PHONE.....................................321 259-4898
Dave Bartman, *President*
Gloria Jeanne Bartman, *Vice Pres*
EMP: 5 EST: 1986
SQ FT: 40,000
SALES (est): 561.1K **Privately Held**
WEB: www.bartmanenterprises.com
SIC: 2395 Embroidery products, except schiffli machine; embroidery & art needlework

(G-8376)
BEST CIRCUITS INC
300 North Dr Ste 106 (32934-9273)
PHONE...................................321 425-6725
Daniel Dina, *President*
Isaac Gratzian, *Manager*
EMP: 22 **EST:** 2001
SALES (est): 1.7MM **Privately Held**
WEB: www.bestcircuits.com
SIC: 3679 Electronic circuits

(G-8377)
BEST LIDAR CORPORATION ✪
300 North Dr Ste 106 (32934-9273)
PHONE...................................321 425-6725
Daniel Dina, *President*
EMP: 50 **EST:** 2021
SALES (est): 1.7MM **Privately Held**
WEB: www.bestlidar.us
SIC: 3571 Computers, digital, analog or hybrid

(G-8378)
BIOFUSE MEDICAL TECH INC
200 S Hbr Cy Blvd Ste 402 (32901)
PHONE...................................877 466-2434
Ralph Zipper MD Facog, *CEO*
Vik Malik, *CEO*
Ralph Zipper, *President*
Guy Hoagland, *Principal*
Charles Federico, *Director*
EMP: 6 **EST:** 2014
SALES (est): 508.3K **Privately Held**
WEB: www.biofusemedical.com
SIC: 3845 Electromedical equipment

(G-8379)
BLUE SIREN INC
3030 Venture Ln Ste 103 (32934-8172)
PHONE...................................321 242-0300
Janet Stile, *President*
EMP: 50 **EST:** 2010
SALES (est): 3.1MM **Privately Held**
WEB: www.blue-siren.com
SIC: 3823 Industrial process control instruments

(G-8380)
BONITA BOATS INC
2900 Dusa Dr (32934-8102)
PHONE...................................321 978-1376
Mitchel Larson, *President*
EMP: 12 **EST:** 2018
SALES (est): 688.1K **Privately Held**
WEB: www.bonitaboats.com
SIC: 3732 Boats, fiberglass: building & repairing

(G-8381)
BRADY BUILT TECHNOLOGIES INC
Also Called: Brady Builders
3661 Waynesboro Way (32934-8396)
PHONE...................................270 692-6866
Joseph Brady, *President*
EMP: 6 **EST:** 1989
SALES (est): 574.2K **Privately Held**
SIC: 3499 Machine bases, metal

(G-8382)
BRAID SALES AND MARKETING INC (PA)
Also Called: Full House
320 North Dr (32934-9206)
PHONE...................................321 752-8180
Fred Braid, *CEO*
Todd W Braid, *President*
Beau Braid, *Vice Pres*
Chad Braid, *Vice Pres*
Jeff Paine, *Purchasing*
◆ **EMP:** 20 **EST:** 1982
SQ FT: 40,000
SALES (est): 5MM **Privately Held**
WEB: www.full-house.com
SIC: 3553 Woodworking machinery

(G-8383)
BREVARD BUSINESS NEWS
4300 Fortune Pl Ste D (32904-1527)
PHONE...................................321 951-7777
Adrienne Roth, *President*
EMP: 10 **EST:** 1988

SALES (est): 935.7K **Privately Held**
WEB: www.brevardbusinessnews.com
SIC: 2711 Newspapers, publishing & printing

(G-8384)
CEM LTD
Also Called: Candleworks
7331 Office Park Pl (32940-8239)
PHONE...................................321 253-1160
Mark Samji, *President*
EMP: 30
SALES (corp-wide): 12.2MM **Privately Held**
WEB: www.cemltd.com
SIC: 3672 Printed circuit boards
PA: Cem Ltd.
700 Blue Point Rd
Holtsville NY 11742
631 758-8100

(G-8385)
CENTRAL FLA PRTG GRAPHICS LLC
772 Washburn Rd Ste A (32934-7329)
PHONE...................................321 752-8753
Mark Liles, *Owner*
EMP: 6 **EST:** 2011
SALES (est): 433.8K **Privately Held**
WEB: www.centralflprinting.com
SIC: 2752 Commercial printing, offset

(G-8386)
CHEM-TEK METAL FINISHING CORP
Also Called: Chem-Tek Plating Industries
636 Atlantis Rd (32904-2315)
PHONE...................................321 722-2227
Robert G Galligan Jr, *President*
EMP: 10 **EST:** 2006
SALES (est): 400.1K **Privately Held**
WEB: www.chem-tekplating.com
SIC: 3471 Finishing, metals or formed products; electroplating of metals or formed products

(G-8387)
CHRISTIAN WORKSHOP LLC
405 West Dr Ste C (32904-1084)
PHONE...................................321 676-2396
Esther Kennedy, *Office Mgr*
Timothy Kennedy, *Mng Member*
Tim Kennedy,
EMP: 8 **EST:** 1971
SQ FT: 3,000
SALES (est): 125K **Privately Held**
WEB: www.caseworksoft.com
SIC: 3172 Personal leather goods

(G-8388)
CLARIOS LLC
Also Called: Johnson Controls
1060 Aurora Rd (32935-5911)
PHONE...................................321 253-4000
EMP: 59
SALES (corp-wide): 47.9B **Privately Held**
WEB: www.clarios.com
SIC: 2531 Seats, automobile
HQ: Clarios, Llc
5757 N Green Bay Ave
Milwaukee WI 53209

(G-8389)
CLASSIC KITCHENS BREVARD INC
670 S Wickham Rd (32904-1645)
PHONE...................................321 327-5972
Christopher L Hampson, *President*
EMP: 7 **EST:** 2008
SALES (est): 869.3K **Privately Held**
WEB: www.classickitchensofbrevard.com
SIC: 2434 Wood kitchen cabinets

(G-8390)
CNC CABINET COMPONENTS INC
560 Distribution Dr (32904-1183)
PHONE...................................321 956-3470
Earl Matthews, *President*
▲ **EMP:** 14 **EST:** 1998
SALES (est): 1.8MM **Privately Held**
WEB: www.cnccabinetcomponents.com
SIC: 2434 Wood kitchen cabinets

(G-8391)
COASTAL DIRECTORY COMPANY
1900 S Hbr Cy Blvd Ste 30 (32901)
P.O. Box 33665, Indialantic (32903-0665)
PHONE...................................321 777-7076
Wilson Sims, *President*
Dave Fishburne, *Principal*
David K Fishburne, *Director*
Walter W Sims, *Director*
EMP: 10 **EST:** 2003
SALES (est): 941.3K **Privately Held**
WEB: www.coastaldirectoryco.com
SIC: 2741 Telephone & other directory publishing

(G-8392)
COMMUNICATIONS LABS INC
Also Called: Comlabs
4005 Opportunity Dr (32934-9296)
PHONE...................................321 701-9000
Roland Lussier, *President*
Avis Lussier, *Vice Pres*
Scott Hawksley, *Purchasing*
Tom Restivo, *Engineer*
Gary R Gorthe, *CFO*
EMP: 16 **EST:** 1985
SQ FT: 9,800
SALES (est): 3.6MM **Privately Held**
WEB: www.comlabs.com
SIC: 3661 Telephone & telegraph apparatus

(G-8393)
COMPSYS INC
4255 Dow Rd (32934-9218)
PHONE...................................321 255-0399
Scott M Lewit, *President*
Ronnal P Reichard, *Chairman*
Crystal Jacoby, *Vice Pres*
EMP: 56 **EST:** 1992
SQ FT: 40,000
SALES (est): 7.2MM **Privately Held**
WEB: www.preforms.com
SIC: 3086 Insulation or cushioning material, foamed plastic

(G-8394)
CONTEC AMERICAS INC
3991 Sarno Rd (32934-7239)
PHONE...................................321 728-0172
Alex Blochtein, *CEO*
Daniel Butler, *General Mgr*
Randall Poliner, *Chairman*
Ryan Legg, *Vice Pres*
Ishikawa Hideki, *Project Dir*
▲ **EMP:** 95 **EST:** 1991
SQ FT: 31,000
SALES: 66.6MM **Privately Held**
WEB: www.eshop.contecamericas.com
SIC: 3571 7373 Electronic computers; computer integrated systems design
HQ: Contec Co., Ltd.
3-9-31, Himesato, Nishiyodogawa-Ku
Osaka OSK 555-0

(G-8395)
CRUCIAL CLLSION PRDUCTIONS LLC
3334 Henry St (32901-8041)
P.O. Box 120071 (32912-0071)
PHONE...................................321 501-1722
Terry Lynn Howard II, *Mng Member*
EMP: 10 **EST:** 2020
SALES (est): 460K **Privately Held**
SIC: 3577 Data conversion equipment, media-to-media: computer

(G-8396)
D R S OPTRONICS INC
100 N Babcock St (32935-6715)
PHONE...................................321 309-1500
EMP: 11 **EST:** 2019
SALES (est): 1.6MM **Privately Held**
WEB: www.leonardodrs.com
SIC: 3827 Optical instruments & lenses

(G-8397)
DATA FLOW SYSTEMS INC
Also Called: D F S
605 N John Rodes Blvd (32934-9105)
PHONE...................................321 259-5009
Thomas F Smaidris, *President*
Colleen Reilly, *General Mgr*
Roger B Saunders, *Vice Pres*

Steve Whitlock, *Vice Pres*
Kim Donovan, *Project Mgr*
EMP: 80 **EST:** 1981
SQ FT: 18,100
SALES (est): 17.6MM **Privately Held**
WEB: www.dataflowsys.com
SIC: 3825 Electrical energy measuring equipment

(G-8398)
DEEP PLANET RESEARCH LLC
2412 Irwin St (32901-7316)
PHONE...................................517 740-1526
Scott Hasbrouck, *President*
EMP: 6 **EST:** 2020
SALES (est): 562.3K **Privately Held**
WEB: www.deepplanet.co
SIC: 3812 7371 8711 Aircraft/aerospace flight instruments & guidance systems; software programming applications; engineering services

(G-8399)
DEFRANCISCI MACHINE CO LLC
Also Called: Demaco
2681 Aurora Rd (32935-2854)
PHONE...................................321 952-6600
Joseph Defrancisci, *Mng Member*
Leonard J Defrancisci,
EMP: 15 **EST:** 1914
SQ FT: 30,000
SALES (est): 2.9MM **Privately Held**
WEB: www.demaco.com
SIC: 3556 Pasta machinery

(G-8400)
DFA DAIRY BRANDS FLUID LLC
650 S Wickham Rd (32904-1645)
PHONE...................................386 775-6700
Randy Vick, *Branch Mgr*
EMP: 9
SALES (corp-wide): 19.3B **Privately Held**
SIC: 2026 Fluid milk
HQ: Dfa Dairy Brands Fluid, Llc
1405 N 98th St
Kansas City KS 66111
816 801-6455

(G-8401)
DIAMOND MT INC
Also Called: Diamond-Mt
4200 Dow Rd Ste Cd (32934-9295)
PHONE...................................321 339-3377
EMP: 10 **Privately Held**
SIC: 3672 Printed Circuit Boards

(G-8402)
DICTAPHONE CORPORATION
3984 Pepsi Cola Dr (32934-9299)
P.O. Box 36814 (32934)
PHONE...................................321 255-8668
Janice Evans, *Sales Staff*
Laine E Howell, *Architect*
Joe Delaney, *Manager*
EMP: 153
SALES (corp-wide): 198.2B **Publicly Held**
WEB: www.dictaphone.com
SIC: 3579 Dictating machines
HQ: Dictaphone Corporation
3191 Broadbridge Ave
Stratford CT 06614
203 381-7000

(G-8403)
DRS ADVANCED ISR LLC
100 N Babcock St (32935-6715)
PHONE...................................321 622-1202
Aaron Hankins, *Mng Member*
EMP: 13
SALES (corp-wide): 16B **Privately Held**
WEB: www.leonardodrs.com
SIC: 3812 Cabin environment indicators
HQ: Drs Icas, Llc
2601 Mssion Pt Blvd Ste 2
Beavercreek OH 45431

(G-8404)
DRS CENGEN LLC (DH)
100 Babcock St Melbourne (32935)
PHONE...................................321 622-1500
Terry Murphy, *VP Admin*
EMP: 268 **EST:** 2011
SALES (est): 39.3MM
SALES (corp-wide): 16B **Privately Held**
SIC: 3812 Search & navigation equipment

HQ: Leonardo Drs, Inc.
2345 Crystal Dr Ste 1000
Arlington VA 22202
703 416-8000

(G-8405)
DRS LAND ELECTRONICS
100 N Babcock St (32935-6715)
PHONE..................................321 622-1435
EMP: 8 **EST:** 2017
SALES (est): 189.8K **Privately Held**
WEB: www.leonardodrs.com
SIC: 3812 Search & navigation equipment

(G-8406)
DRS NTWORK IMAGING SYSTEMS LLC (DH)
100 N Babcock St (32935-6715)
PHONE..................................321 309-1500
Michael Sarrica, *President*
Toby Mannheimer, *Vice Pres*
Thomas P Crimmins, *Treasurer*
▲ **EMP:** 500 **EST:** 1995
SQ FT: 225,000
SALES (est): 343.3MM
SALES (corp-wide): 10.2B **Privately Held**
WEB: www.leonardodrs.com
SIC: 3812 Search & navigation equipment
HQ: Leonardo Drs, Inc.
2345 Crystal Dr Ste 1000
Arlington VA 22202
703 416-8000

(G-8407)
DRS S AND T OPTRONICS DIV
100 N Babcock St (32935-6715)
PHONE..................................321 309-1500
EMP: 12
SALES (est): 1.8MM **Privately Held**
SIC: 3812 Mfg Search/Navigation Equipment

(G-8408)
DRS SENSORS TARGETING SYSTEMS
100 N Babcock St (32935-6715)
PHONE..................................321 309-1500
Sally Wallace, *Principal*
EMP: 27 **EST:** 2009
SALES (est): 4.8MM **Privately Held**
SIC: 3812 Search & navigation equipment

(G-8409)
DRS SONETICOM INC
Also Called: Drs Technology
100 N Babcock St (32935-6715)
PHONE..................................321 733-0400
Timothy Reynolds, *CEO*
James Kingsley, *Vice Pres*
Wendi-Lynn Reeves, *Vice Pres*
Melissa Zimak, *Opers Staff*
Leo Torres, *Engineer*
▲ **EMP:** 30 **EST:** 1998
SQ FT: 26,600
SALES (est): 16.1MM
SALES (corp-wide): 16B **Privately Held**
WEB: www.leonardodrs.com
SIC: 3812 Search & navigation equipment
HQ: Drs Signal Solutions, Inc.
1 Milestone Center Ct
Germantown MD 20876
301 948-7550

(G-8410)
DRS SYSTEMS INC
100 N Babcock St (32935-6715)
PHONE..................................973 451-3525
Terence Murphy, *President*
EMP: 4 **EST:** 2001
SQ FT: 400
SALES (est): 4.6MM
SALES (corp-wide): 16B **Privately Held**
WEB: www.leonardodrs.com
SIC: 3812 Search & navigation equipment
HQ: Leonardo Drs, Inc.
2345 Crystal Dr Ste 1000
Arlington VA 22202
703 416-8000

(G-8411)
DRS TACTICAL SYSTEMS INC
100 N Babcock St (32935-6715)
PHONE..................................321 727-3672
Sally Wallace, *President*
Jason I Rinsky II, *Vice Pres*
Russ Marsh, *Vice Pres*

Wayne Grimes, *Engineer*
W Christopher Durborow, *Treasurer*
EMP: 98 **EST:** 1998
SALES (est): 27.1MM
SALES (corp-wide): 16B **Privately Held**
SIC: 3812 Search & navigation equipment
HQ: Leonardo Drs, Inc.
2345 Crystal Dr Ste 1000
Arlington VA 22202
703 416-8000

(G-8412)
DYNASYSTEMS LLC
3445 Spring Branch Trl # 360
(32935-0001)
PHONE..................................410 343-7759
EMP: 7
SQ FT: 1,800
SALES (est): 507.7K **Privately Held**
SIC: 3669 Mfg Communications Equipment

(G-8413)
E&T HORIZONS LTD LIABILITY CO
2623 Chapel Bridge Ln (32940-7992)
PHONE..................................321 704-1244
Terri Gelman, *Principal*
Eric Gelman, *Principal*
Jeff Moore, *Principal*
▲ **EMP:** 11 **EST:** 2012
SALES (est): 1MM **Privately Held**
SIC: 2599 Stools, factory

(G-8414)
EASYLIFT N BANSBACH AMER INC
50 West Dr (32904-1074)
PHONE..................................321 253-1999
Robert Rose, *CEO*
Thomas Weiss, *President*
Cristina Rose, *Exec VP*
John Blackledge, *Vice Pres*
Vickery David, *Vice Pres*
▲ **EMP:** 40 **EST:** 2007
SALES (est): 5.3MM **Privately Held**
WEB: www.bansbach.com
SIC: 3593 Fluid power cylinders & actuators

(G-8415)
EDAK INC (DH)
630 Distribution Dr (32904-1179)
PHONE..................................321 674-6804
Gregg T Benoit, *President*
Susan M Denyer, *President*
Hans F Kaeser, *Admin Sec*
▲ **EMP:** 8 **EST:** 1986
SQ FT: 25,000
SALES (est): 13.9MM
SALES (corp-wide): 440.6MM **Privately Held**
SIC: 3499 Boxes for packing & shipping, metal
HQ: Edak Ag
Rheinauerweg 17
Dachsen ZH 8447
526 472-200

(G-8416)
EDGE POWER SOLUTIONS INC
Also Called: Manufacturer
5131 Industry Dr Ste 107 (32940-7198)
PHONE..................................321 499-1919
Jeromy Kendall, *CEO*
EMP: 10 **EST:** 2016
SALES (est): 995.8K **Privately Held**
WEB: www.edgepowersolutions.net
SIC: 3679 Electronic loads & power supplies

(G-8417)
ELECTRIC PCTURE DSPLAY SYSTEMS
6425 Anderson Way (32940-7467)
PHONE..................................321 757-8484
Robert Higgins, *President*
Pam Higgins, *Vice Pres*
EMP: 5 **EST:** 2003
SQ FT: 2,500
SALES (est): 2MM **Privately Held**
WEB: www.electricpicture.com
SIC: 3823 Digital displays of process variables

(G-8418)
ELECTRNIC SHTMTAL CRFTSMEN FLA
3675 W New Haven Ave (32904-3556)
PHONE..................................321 727-0633
Ricky W Miller, *President*
Chris Miller, *Purch Mgr*
EMP: 30 **EST:** 1973
SQ FT: 25,000
SALES (est): 4.8MM **Privately Held**
WEB: www.esc-of-fl.com
SIC: 3444 Sheet metal specialties, not stamped

(G-8419)
EMBRAER EXECUTIVE AIRCRAFT INC (DH)
Also Called: Embraer Executive Jets
1111 General Aviation Dr (32935-6316)
PHONE..................................321 751-5050
Ernie Edwards, *President*
Philip Krull, *COO*
Phillip Krull, *COO*
Christian Zinn, *Counsel*
Peter Griffith, *Vice Pres*
EMP: 172 **EST:** 2012
SALES (est): 30.6MM **Privately Held**
SIC: 3721 Aircraft

(G-8420)
ENDURIS EXTRUSIONS INC
605 Distribution Dr Ste 1 (32904-1185)
PHONE..................................321 914-0897
Dan Whitson, *Principal*
EMP: 61
SALES (corp-wide): 9.1MM **Privately Held**
WEB: www.enduris.com
SIC: 3999 Atomizers, toiletry
PA: Enduris Extrusions, Inc.
7167 Old Kings Rd
Jacksonville FL 32219
904 421-3304

(G-8421)
ENVIRNMENTAL MFG SOLUTIONS LLC (PA)
Also Called: E M S
7705 Progress Cir (32904-1657)
PHONE..................................321 837-0050
Tim Otto, *Vice Pres*
John Macdonald, *Executive*
Charlene Macdonald,
EMP: 12 **EST:** 2001
SQ FT: 25,000
SALES (est): 9.9MM **Privately Held**
WEB: www.enviromfg.com
SIC: 2869 Industrial organic chemicals

(G-8422)
ERCHONIA CORPORATION LLC
650 Atlantis Rd (32904-2315)
PHONE..................................321 473-1251
Steven C Shanks, *President*
Mark Shanks, *COO*
Charlie Shanks, *Vice Pres*
Kevin Tycek, *Chief Engr*
Jeremy Tucek, *Engineer*
▲ **EMP:** 38 **EST:** 1996
SQ FT: 18,000
SALES (est): 10MM **Privately Held**
WEB: www.erchonia.com
SIC: 3845 5047 Laser systems & equipment, medical; medical equipment & supplies

(G-8423)
EXTANT CMPNNTS GROUP HLDNGS IN
Also Called: Extant Aerospace
1615 W Nasa Blvd (32901-2613)
PHONE..................................321 254-1500
Jim Gerwien, *CEO*
Gary Boekenkamp, *Exec VP*
Michael Donlan, *Vice Pres*
Charles Mitchell, *VP Opers*
Edward Dietze, *CFO*
EMP: 5 **EST:** 2010
SALES (est): 2.6MM
SALES (corp-wide): 4.8B **Publicly Held**
WEB: www.extantaerospace.com
SIC: 3324 Aerospace investment castings, ferrous

PA: Transdigm Group Incorporated
1301 E 9th St Ste 3000
Cleveland OH 44114
216 706-2960

(G-8424)
FASTSIGNS 176101
Also Called: McCord Holding
7640 N Wickham Rd (32940-8146)
PHONE..................................321 307-2400
EMP: 12 **EST:** 2017
SALES (est): 941K **Privately Held**
WEB: www.fastsigns.com
SIC: 3993 Signs & advertising specialties

(G-8425)
FIBERTRONICS INC
2900 Dusa Dr (32934-8102)
PHONE..................................321 473-8933
Barbara A Larson, *President*
Mitchel Larson, *QC Mgr*
EMP: 33 **EST:** 2009
SALES (est): 3.9MM **Privately Held**
WEB: www.fibertronics.com
SIC: 3357 Communication wire

(G-8426)
FLAMINGO PRINTING BREVARD INC
1785 Waverly Pl (32901-4641)
PHONE..................................321 723-2771
Stacey Norman, *President*
Lisa Norman, *Admin Sec*
EMP: 8 **EST:** 1969
SQ FT: 2,000
SALES (est): 646.3K **Privately Held**
WEB: www.flamingoprinting.com
SIC: 2752 Commercial printing, offset

(G-8427)
FLORIDA SPCIALTY COATINGS CORP
3270 Suntree Blvd Ste 214 (32940-7505)
PHONE..................................727 224-6883
Jessica Walker, *Principal*
EMP: 8 **EST:** 2016
SALES (est): 69.9K **Privately Held**
SIC: 3479 Coating of metals & formed products

(G-8428)
GEODETIC SERVICES INC
1511 Riverview Dr (32901-4694)
PHONE..................................321 724-6831
John Brown, *President*
Gary Johanning, *General Mgr*
Theresa Brown, *Treasurer*
John Vehec, *Manager*
Christos Stamatopoulos, *CTO*
EMP: 16 **EST:** 1977
SQ FT: 4,600
SALES (est): 2.3MM **Privately Held**
WEB: www.geodetic.com
SIC: 3829 Photogrammetrical instruments

(G-8429)
GIVR PACKAGING LLC
2428 Irwin St (32901-7316)
PHONE..................................321 345-6875
Jeremy Bower, *CEO*
EMP: 5 **EST:** 2018
SALES (est): 582.1K **Privately Held**
WEB: www.givrpack.com
SIC: 2653 Corrugated boxes, partitions, display items, sheets & pad

(G-8430)
GOLDFIELD CNSLD MINES CO (DH)
100 Rialto Pl Ste 500 (32901-3015)
PHONE..................................321 724-1700
Patrick Freeman, *President*
John Sottile, *Vice Pres*
Stephen Wherry, *Treasurer*
John Starling, *Admin Sec*
EMP: 100 **EST:** 1971
SALES (est): 6.8MM
SALES (corp-wide): 188.9MM **Privately Held**
SIC: 1021 1041 1044 Copper ores; gold ores; silver ores
HQ: The Goldfield Corporation Del
1688 W Hibiscus Blvd
Melbourne FL 32901
321 724-1700

▲ = Import ▼=Export
◆ =Import/Export

(G-8431)
HALLIDAY INDUSTRIES LLC
7715 Ellis Rd Ste A (32904-1159)
PHONE...................................321 288-3979
David J Halliday, *Principal*
EMP: 7 **EST:** 2018
SALES (est): 425.7K **Privately Held**
SIC: 3999 Manufacturing industries

(G-8432)
HAMANT AIRBOATS LLC
1705 Southland Ave (32935-6141)
PHONE...................................321 259-6998
Kevin Murphy, *Principal*
EMP: 8 **EST:** 2013
SALES (est): 696.9K **Privately Held**
WEB: www.hamantboats.com
SIC: 3732 Boat building & repairing

(G-8433)
HAMMOND KITCHENS & BATH LLC
7618 Silver Sands Rd (32904-1128)
PHONE...................................321 768-9549
Nathan A Hammond, *President*
EMP: 15 **EST:** 1983
SQ FT: 10,000
SALES (est): 5MM **Privately Held**
WEB: www.hammondkitchens.com
SIC: 2434 Wood kitchen cabinets

(G-8434)
HELICOPTER HELMET LLC (PA)
Also Called: Helicopter Helmets.com
274 West Dr (32904-1042)
PHONE...................................843 556-0405
Ron Abbott, *Owner*
Gloria Abbott,
▲ **EMP:** 4 **EST:** 2000
SQ FT: 2,000
SALES (est): 3.1MM **Privately Held**
WEB: www.helicopterhelmet.com
SIC: 3469 7363 Helmets, steel; pilot service, aviation

(G-8435)
HELLER CABINETRY INC
415 Stan Dr (32904-1046)
PHONE...................................321 729-9690
Kristen S Heller, *President*
Stephen M Heller, *Vice Pres*
EMP: 11 **EST:** 2002
SALES (est): 1.7MM **Privately Held**
WEB: www.hellercabinetry.com
SIC: 2434 1799 Wood kitchen cabinets; counter top installation

(G-8436)
HIGH TECH HOIST CORP
3682 N Wickham Rd 225 (32935-2334)
PHONE...................................321 733-3387
Henry M Powers Jr, *President*
EMP: 10 **EST:** 1987
SQ FT: 11,000
SALES (est): 1MM **Privately Held**
WEB: www.betamaxhoist.com
SIC: 3536 Hoists

(G-8437)
HILLS INC
7785 Ellis Rd (32904-1105)
PHONE...................................321 723-5560
Arnold Wilkie, *President*
Penny Wilkie, *Corp Secy*
Shirley Hill, *Shareholder*
Bill Hills, *Shareholder*
Michelle Dawson, *Admin Asst*
◆ **EMP:** 53 **EST:** 1971
SALES (est): 14MM **Privately Held**
WEB: www.hillsinc.net
SIC: 3552 Fabric forming machinery & equipment

(G-8438)
HOUSMANS ALUM & SCREENING INC
2911 Dusa Dr Ste E (32934-8100)
PHONE...................................321 255-2778
Mark J Housman, *President*
EMP: 14 **EST:** 2009
SALES (est): 1.7MM **Privately Held**
WEB: www.housmansaluminum.com
SIC: 3448 Screen enclosures

(G-8439)
HY-TECH THERMAL SOLUTIONS LLC
159 Park Hill Blvd (32904-5115)
P.O. Box 216 (32902-0216)
PHONE...................................321 984-9777
Tony Abruzzese, *Manager*
Anthony Abruzzese,
EMP: 9 **EST:** 1996
SALES (est): 1.6MM **Privately Held**
WEB: www.hytechsales.com
SIC: 2851 5231 5198 Paints & paint additives; paint; paints

(G-8440)
ILS MANAGEMENT LLC
Also Called: Interactive Legal
930 S Hbr Cy Blvd Ste 505 (32901)
PHONE...................................321 252-0100
Deanne McDougall, *Opers Staff*
James McLelland, *Controller*
Steve Palumbo, *Sales Staff*
Michael L Graham, *Mng Member*
Linda Moses, *Manager*
EMP: 21 **EST:** 2003
SQ FT: 2,600
SALES (est): 6.4MM **Privately Held**
WEB: www.interactivelegal.com
SIC: 7372 Business oriented computer software

(G-8441)
IMPRINT PROMOTIONS LLC
Also Called: Custom Engraving Company
405 N Wickham Rd Ste A (32935-8628)
PHONE...................................321 622-8946
▲ **EMP:** 8
SQ FT: 1,800
SALES (est): 1.1MM **Privately Held**
SIC: 2759 2399 3993 Commercial Printing Mfg Fabricated Textile Products Mfg Signs/Advertising Specialties

(G-8442)
IQ VALVES CO
425 West Dr (32904-1035)
PHONE...................................321 729-9634
V Sampath Kumar, *Principal*
John Lee, *Purchasing*
Brad Mohr, *QC Mgr*
Hung Ho, *Engineer*
EMP: 29 **EST:** 2007
SALES (est): 4.4MM **Privately Held**
WEB: www.iqvalves.com
SIC: 3491 Industrial valves

(G-8443)
JOSEPH J TAYLOR TRUSS
2599 Larry Ct (32935-2835)
PHONE...................................321 482-4039
Joseph J Taylor, *Principal*
EMP: 8 **EST:** 2010
SALES (est): 102.2K **Privately Held**
SIC: 2439 Structural wood members

(G-8444)
JOYS INTERNATIONAL FOODS INC
Also Called: Joy's Gourmet
2600 Aurora Rd Ste Q (32935-2884)
PHONE...................................321 242-6520
Jean F Najjar, *President*
Eugenie K Najjar, *Vice Pres*
Jean Najjar, *Opers Staff*
EMP: 6 **EST:** 2004
SQ FT: 3,000
SALES (est): 622.1K **Privately Held**
WEB: www.joyofgarlic.com
SIC: 2035 5149 Spreads, garlic; sauces

(G-8445)
JUNIORS BAIT AND SEAFOOD INC
1500 Maple Ave (32935-5962)
PHONE...................................321 480-5492
Mark B Maynard Jr, *President*
EMP: 20 **EST:** 2010
SQ FT: 22,000
SALES (est): 2MM **Privately Held**
WEB: www.sinisterballyhoo.com
SIC: 2092 Shellfish, fresh: shucked & packed in nonsealed containers

(G-8446)
JUST-IN-TIME MFG CORP
3153 Skyway Cir Ste 101 (32934-7369)
PHONE...................................321 752-7552
Patricia Scardino, *President*
George Scardino, *Vice Pres*
EMP: 15 **EST:** 1995
SALES (est): 2MM **Privately Held**
WEB: www.justintimemanufacturing.com
SIC: 3679 3441 Electronic circuits; fabricated structural metal

(G-8447)
JW AUSTIN INDUSTRIES INC
7713 Ellis Rd (32904-1119)
P.O. Box 511058, Melbourne Beach (32951-1058)
PHONE...................................321 723-2422
James W Austin, *CEO*
Lucy A Murphy, *President*
Steve Austin, *Admin Sec*
EMP: 7 **EST:** 1975
SQ FT: 10,000
SALES (est): 963.2K **Privately Held**
WEB: www.jwaustin.com
SIC: 3089 Plastic processing

(G-8448)
KATIONX CORP (PA)
2412 Irwin St Ste 61 (32901-7316)
PHONE...................................321 338-5050
William Cox, *President*
Thomas Tempske, *Principal*
William White, *Principal*
Jimmie White, *Regional Mgr*
Sondee Lima, *COO*
EMP: 6 **EST:** 2019
SALES (est): 1MM **Privately Held**
WEB: www.kationx.com
SIC: 3589 Commercial cleaning equipment

(G-8449)
KIINDE LLC
6300 N Wickham Rd Ste 130 (32940-2029)
PHONE...................................914 303-6308
Vijay Brihmadesam, *Mng Member*
Kailas Narendran,
Barbara Roth,
▼ **EMP:** 6 **EST:** 2011
SQ FT: 300
SALES (est): 2.6MM **Privately Held**
WEB: www.kiinde.com
SIC: 3221 3565 Milk bottles, glass; bottle washing & sterilizing machines
PA: Kiinde Holdings, Llc
2060 Highway A1a Ste 303
Indian Harbour Beach FL 32937
617 216-7719

(G-8450)
KITCHEN DSGNS BY JOAN E RBBINS
7690 Industrial Rd (32904-1629)
PHONE...................................321 727-0012
Joan E Robbins, *Owner*
Lee Hochadel, *Human Resources*
Jeff Hochadel, *Sales Staff*
EMP: 6 **EST:** 1983
SQ FT: 6,000
SALES (est): 453K **Privately Held**
SIC: 2541 Cabinets, except refrigerated: show, display, etc.: wood

(G-8451)
KONA GOLD LLC
746 North Dr Ste A (32934-9252)
PHONE...................................844 714-2224
Robert Clark, *CEO*
Lori Radcliffe, *CFO*
Jazmin Gonzalez, *Office Mgr*
EMP: 10 **EST:** 2015
SALES (est): 1.1MM **Privately Held**
WEB: www.konagoldhemp.com
SIC: 2086 Bottled & canned soft drinks

(G-8452)
L & L AUTOMOTIVE ELECTRIC INC
4575 Carolwood Dr (32934-7182)
PHONE...................................631 471-5230
Lawrence Holmes, *President*
Linda Holmes, *Vice Pres*
EMP: 9 **EST:** 1987
SQ FT: 3,000

SALES (est): 488.1K **Privately Held**
SIC: 3694 7539 Engine electrical equipment; electrical services

(G-8453)
L-3 CMMNCTONS NTRONIX HOLDINGS
1025 W Nasa Blvd (32919-0001)
PHONE...................................212 697-1111
Michael T Strianese, *President*
Steven M Post, *Senior VP*
Curtis Brunson, *Vice Pres*
Gary Haag, *Project Engr*
Ralph G D'Ambrosio, *CFO*
EMP: 65 **EST:** 2003
SALES (est): 28.3MM
SALES (corp-wide): 17.8B **Publicly Held**
SIC: 3625 3699 8711 Marine & navy auxiliary controls; underwater sound equipment; marine engineering
HQ: L3 Technologies, Inc.
600 3rd Ave Fl 34
New York NY 10016
321 727-9100

(G-8454)
L3 TECHNOLOGIES INC
Communction Systms-Wst/Lnkabit
1200 Woody Burke Rd (32901-2757)
PHONE...................................321 409-6122
Marla Bartel, *General Mgr*
Mace Lund, *General Mgr*
Allison Carberry, *Finance*
David Lynn, *Finance*
Amy Scheerens, *Finance*
EMP: 137
SALES (corp-wide): 17.8B **Publicly Held**
WEB: www.l3harris.com
SIC: 3812 3577 Search & navigation equipment; computer peripheral equipment
HQ: L3 Technologies, Inc.
600 3rd Ave Fl 34
New York NY 10016
321 727-9100

(G-8455)
L3HARRIS TECHNOLOGIES INC (PA)
1025 W Nasa Blvd (32919-0001)
PHONE...................................321 727-9100
Christopher E Kubasik, *CEO*
William M Brown, *Ch of Bd*
Dana A Mehnert, *President*
Sean J Stackley, *President*
Edward J Zoiss, *President*
▲ **EMP:** 269 **EST:** 1890
SALES (est): 17.8B **Publicly Held**
WEB: www.l3harris.com
SIC: 3812 3663 3699 3661 Search & navigation equipment; radio & TV communications equipment; satellites, communications; microwave communication equipment; receiver-transmitter units (transceiver); security control equipment & systems; telephones & telephone apparatus; switching equipment, telephone; PBX equipment, manual or automatic; integrated circuits, semiconductor networks, etc.

(G-8456)
L3HARRIS TECHNOLOGIES INC
407 N John Rodes Blvd (32934-8059)
P.O. Box 37 (32902-0037)
PHONE...................................321 309-7848
Stephen Bolze, *Owner*
David Allen, *Engineer*
Barbara Widerman, *Marketing Staff*
Nicole Walther, *Manager*
Tracy Dash, *Software Engr*
EMP: 671
SALES (corp-wide): 17.8B **Publicly Held**
WEB: www.l3harris.com
SIC: 3663 3699 Radio & TV communications equipment; electrical equipment & supplies
PA: L3harris Technologies, Inc.
1025 W Nasa Blvd
Melbourne FL 32919
321 727-9100

(G-8457)
L3HARRIS TECHNOLOGIES INC
Harris Corporation
150 S Wickham Rd (32904-1132)
P.O. Box 37 (32902-0037)
PHONE..................................321 984-0782
John Yates, *Project Mgr*
Ronda R Henning, *Engineer*
James A Proctor, *Branch Mgr*
Keith Hayes, *Sr Project Mgr*
Kenneth Luan, *Manager*
EMP: 20
SALES (corp-wide): 17.8B **Publicly Held**
WEB: www.l3harris.com
SIC: 3661 Telephone & telegraph apparatus
PA: L3harris Technologies, Inc.
　　1025 W Nasa Blvd
　　Melbourne FL 32919
　　321 727-9100

(G-8458)
L3HARRIS TECHNOLOGIES INC
Also Called: Harris Corporation, Gcsd
1025 W Nasa Blvd (32902)
P.O. Box 9002 (32902-9002)
PHONE..................................321 727-4000
Pete Olavarria, *Manager*
EMP: 90
SALES (corp-wide): 17.8B **Publicly Held**
WEB: www.l3harris.com
SIC: 3812 5088 Search & navigation equipment; navigation equipment & supplies
PA: L3harris Technologies, Inc.
　　1025 W Nasa Blvd
　　Melbourne FL 32919
　　321 727-9100

(G-8459)
L3HARRIS TECHNOLOGIES INC
Rf Communications
1025 W Nasa Blvd (32919-0001)
P.O. Box 9001 (32902-9001)
PHONE..................................321 727-9100
Allen Greathouse, *Vice Pres*
Leon Shivamber, *Vice Pres*
Steve Wallick, *Branch Mgr*
Thomas Dattilo, *Bd of Directors*
EMP: 105
SALES (corp-wide): 17.8B **Publicly Held**
WEB: www.l3harris.com
SIC: 3661 3671 Telephone & telegraph apparatus; electron tubes
PA: L3harris Technologies, Inc.
　　1025 W Nasa Blvd
　　Melbourne FL 32919
　　321 727-9100

(G-8460)
LIFETIME WELLNESS CENTERS INC
618 Washburn Rd Ste A (32934-7320)
PHONE..................................321 693-8698
Kathy Pihlaja Lacina, *President*
EMP: 10 **EST:** 2003
SALES (est): 647.2K **Privately Held**
WEB: www.lifetimewellnesscenters.com
SIC: 3949 Exercise equipment

(G-8461)
LIGHTING SCIENCE GROUP CORP (HQ)
3905 W Eau Gallie Blvd # 101 (32934-7232)
PHONE..................................321 779-5520
Khim Lee, *President*
David Friedman, *President*
Jonathan Pale, *VP Engrg*
David Quigley, *CFO*
Fredric Maxik, *CTO*
▲ **EMP:** 1 **EST:** 1988
SALES (est): 52.7MM **Privately Held**
SIC: 3646 3648 Commercial indusl & institutional electric lighting fixtures; street lighting fixtures

(G-8462)
LIVETV
1333 Gateway Dr Ste 1007 (32901-2646)
PHONE..................................321 722-0783
Bill Parker, *Purch Mgr*
David Walker, *Engineer*
Karen Hawkins, *Finance*
Jim Bowe, *Manager*

Mareeswari Lakshmanan, *Software Dev*
EMP: 16 **EST:** 1938
SALES (est): 288.5K **Privately Held**
SIC: 3769 Guided missile & space vehicle parts & auxiliary equipment

(G-8463)
LOCUS DIAGNOSTICS LLC
Also Called: Locususa
1055 S John Rodes Blvd (32904-2005)
PHONE..................................321 727-3077
Joseph Rey,
Susan Jaramillo,
EMP: 15 **EST:** 2009
SQ FT: 6,000
SALES (est): 2.1MM **Privately Held**
WEB: www.locususa.com
SIC: 3825 Radio frequency measuring equipment

(G-8464)
LOCUS LOCATION SYSTEMS LLC
1055 S John Rodes Blvd (32904-2005)
PHONE..................................321 727-3077
Susan Jaramillo, *President*
Joe Rey, *Managing Prtnr*
Joseph Rey, *Managing Prtnr*
Stephen Perrone, *CFO*
Heather Weightman, *Administration*
EMP: 24 **EST:** 2001
SALES (est): 5.7MM **Privately Held**
WEB: www.locususa.com
SIC: 3441 Tower sections, radio & television transmission

(G-8465)
LX LIMITED LLC
1756 Pontiac Cir N (32935-4970)
PHONE..................................888 610-0642
Lamar Johnson,
EMP: 8
SALES (est): 409.5K **Privately Held**
SIC: 2519 Household furniture

(G-8466)
M C TEST SERVICE INC (DH)
Also Called: M C Assembly
425 North Dr (32934-9209)
PHONE..................................321 253-0541
Edward Smith, *President*
Tim Jameson, *Vice Pres*
Mark McReynolds, *Vice Pres*
Raul Irizarry, *Opers Staff*
Donna Meurett, *Mfg Staff*
▲ **EMP:** 146 **EST:** 1984
SQ FT: 135,000
SALES (est): 313.6MM **Privately Held**
SIC: 3663 3672 Radio & TV communications equipment; printed circuit boards

(G-8467)
MACK TECHNOLOGIES FLORIDA INC
7505 Technology Dr (32904-1574)
PHONE..................................321 725-6993
John Kovach, *President*
Larry Walk, *President*
Randy Boduch, *Treasurer*
Will Kendall, *Executive*
▲ **EMP:** 103 **EST:** 2000
SQ FT: 141,000
SALES (est): 46.5MM
SALES (corp-wide): 856.4MM **Privately Held**
WEB: www.macktech.com
SIC: 3672 Printed circuit boards
HQ: Mack Technologies, Inc.
　　27 Carlisle Rd
　　Westford MA 01886

(G-8468)
MAGNUS HITECH INDUSTRIES INC
1605 Lake St (32901-4697)
PHONE..................................321 724-9731
Frank Bonarrigo, *General Mgr*
David Farris, *Opers Mgr*
Kathy Montagnino, *Purch Mgr*
Melanie Sechrist, *Purch Agent*
Bonarrigo Angelo, *Engineer*
EMP: 48 **EST:** 1984
SQ FT: 50,000

SALES (est): 11.1MM
SALES (corp-wide): 34.6MM **Privately Held**
WEB: www.micorind.com
SIC: 3599 3444 Machine shop, jobbing & repair; sheet metal specialties, not stamped
HQ: Micor Industries, Llc
　　1314 State Docks Rd
　　Decatur AL 35601
　　256 560-0770

(G-8469)
MARK HOUSMAN SCREEN RPS INC
2911 Dusa Dr Ste E (32934-8100)
PHONE..................................321 255-2778
Mark J Housman, *President*
▲ **EMP:** 45 **EST:** 1995
SALES (est): 3.6MM **Privately Held**
SIC: 3448 Screen enclosures

(G-8470)
MC ASSEMBLY HOLDINGS INC (DH)
425 North Dr (32934-9209)
PHONE..................................321 253-0541
George W Moore, *President*
David Burns, *General Mgr*
Jorge Benedito, *Vice Pres*
Vicki Cooke, *Vice Pres*
Thomas Hansen, *Vice Pres*
▲ **EMP:** 5 **EST:** 1984
SALES (est): 366.7MM **Privately Held**
SIC: 3672 8734 Printed circuit boards; testing laboratories
HQ: Smtc Manufacturing Corporation Of Canada
　　7050 Woodbine Ave
　　Markham ON L3R 4
　　905 479-1810

(G-8471)
MC ASSEMBLY INTERNATIONAL LLC (DH)
425 North Dr (32934-9209)
PHONE..................................321 253-0541
George Moore,
EMP: 10 **EST:** 2004
SALES (est): 57.2MM **Privately Held**
SIC: 3825 1389 Test equipment for electronic & electrical circuits; testing, measuring, surveying & analysis services
HQ: M C Test Service, Inc.
　　425 North Dr
　　Melbourne FL 32934
　　321 253-0541

(G-8472)
MC ASSEMBLY LLC
425 North Dr (32934-9209)
PHONE..................................321 253-0541
George Moore, *CEO*
Luis Ramirez, *COO*
Jake Kulp, *Vice Pres*
Mark McReynolds, *CFO*
EMP: 355 **EST:** 2010
SALES (est): 8MM **Privately Held**
SIC: 3672 Printed circuit boards
HQ: Mc Assembly Holdings, Inc.
　　425 North Dr
　　Melbourne FL 32934

(G-8473)
MEDICOMP INC (PA)
600 Atlantis Rd (32904-2315)
PHONE..................................321 676-0010
Tony Balda, *CEO*
Michael Thomas, *President*
Daniel Balda, *Principal*
David Gibson, *Vice Pres*
Michael McLean, *Opers Mgr*
EMP: 84 **EST:** 1981
SQ FT: 25,000
SALES (est): 24.6MM **Privately Held**
WEB: www.medicompinc.com
SIC: 3845 Cardiographs

(G-8474)
MELBOURNE ARCHITECTURAL MLLWK
Also Called: Zahbuilt
325 East Dr (32904-1030)
PHONE..................................321 308-3297
Thomas W Soyk, *President*

Fran Walker, *Manager*
Donna D Soyk, *Admin Sec*
EMP: 11 **EST:** 1998
SQ FT: 6,900
SALES (est): 2.8MM **Privately Held**
WEB: www.mamillwork.com
SIC: 2431 1751 Millwork; carpentry work

(G-8475)
MGI USA INC
Also Called: M G I USA Inc Mastercarte
3143 Skyway Cir (32934-7334)
P.O. Box 372520, Satellite Beach (32937-0520)
PHONE..................................321 751-6755
Kevin Abergel, *Vice Pres*
Michael Abergel, *Vice Pres*
Steve Bruno, *Natl Sales Mgr*
Peter Lim, *Sales Staff*
Raymond Pena, *Sales Staff*
▲ **EMP:** 14 **EST:** 1995
SQ FT: 10,000
SALES (est): 3.2MM **Privately Held**
WEB: www.mgi-fr.com
SIC: 3555 Printing trades machinery
PA: M.G.I
　　19 A Rue De Chatillon
　　Rennes

(G-8476)
MICRO TECHNOLOGY OF BREVARD
255 West Dr (32904-1043)
PHONE..................................321 733-1766
Fred Rech, *President*
Charlotte Rech, *Vice Pres*
EMP: 8 **EST:** 1978
SQ FT: 4,000
SALES (est): 848.2K **Privately Held**
SIC: 3679 Electronic circuits

(G-8477)
MONSTA PERFORMANCE INC
691 Washburn Rd (32934-7318)
PHONE..................................321 848-7256
Lee Yearwood, *Principal*
EMP: 6 **EST:** 2018
SALES (est): 304.4K **Privately Held**
WEB: www.monstaperformanceinc.com
SIC: 3993 Signs & advertising specialties

(G-8478)
NCH (FL) FUNDING LLC
525 N Harbor City Blvd (32935-6837)
PHONE..................................321 777-7777
James H Nance, *Manager*
EMP: 7 **EST:** 2001
SALES (est): 139.7K **Privately Held**
SIC: 2842 Specialty cleaning, polishes & sanitation goods

(G-8479)
NEOS TECHNOLOGIES INC (PA)
4300 Fortune Pl Ste C (32904-1527)
PHONE..................................321 242-7818
William P Shannonhouse, *President*
Huey-Chin Ho, *Vice Pres*
EMP: 5 **EST:** 2010
SALES (est): 917.9K **Privately Held**
SIC: 3674 Semiconductors & related devices

(G-8480)
NIDA CORPORATION (PA)
300 S John Rodes Blvd (32904-1052)
PHONE..................................321 727-2265
Joseph Beauseigneur, *CEO*
Lydia Beauseigneur, *President*
Katie Beauseigneur, *Business Mgr*
Jay Buckman, *Vice Pres*
Robin Asplund, *Sales Mgr*
◆ **EMP:** 45 **EST:** 1972
SQ FT: 22,000
SALES (est): 9.2MM **Privately Held**
WEB: www.nida.com
SIC: 3699 Electronic training devices

(G-8481)
NORTHROP GRMMAN TCHNCAL SVCS I
1235 Evans Rd (32904-2314)
PHONE..................................321 837-7000
Craig Donnelly, *President*
EMP: 8 **Publicly Held**
SIC: 3812 Search & navigation equipment

▲ = Import ▼ =Export
◆ =Import/Export

HQ: Northrop Grumman Technical Services, Inc.
7575 Colshire Dr
Mc Lean VA 22102
703 556-1144

(G-8482)
NORTHROP GRUMMAN CORPORATION
2000 W Nasa Blvd (32904-2322)
PHONE..................................321 951-5000
Thomas Boyle, *Counsel*
Victor Carrion, *Project Mgr*
Anthony Calabro, *Opers Staff*
Dave Huddleston, *Technical Mgr*
Roy Schering, *Chief Engr*
EMP: 2000 **Publicly Held**
WEB: www.northropgrumman.com
SIC: 3812 Search & detection systems & instruments
PA: Northrop Grumman Corporation
2980 Fairview Park Dr
Falls Church VA 22042

(G-8483)
NORTHROP GRUMMAN ISS INTL INC
2000 W Nasa Blvd (32904-2322)
PHONE..................................321 951-5695
EMP: 12 **EST:** 1991
SALES (est): 271.3K **Privately Held**
SIC: 3812 Search & navigation equipment

(G-8484)
NORTHROP GRUMMAN SYSTEMS CORP
Also Called: Northrop Grumman Corporation
2000 W Nasa Blvd (32904-2322)
P.O. Box 9650 (32902-9650)
PHONE..................................321 951-5000
John Saunders, *Engineer*
Dianne Farrar, *Accountant*
Allen Doshier, *Manager*
Carol Hansen, *Manager*
Antonio Wright, *Planning*
EMP: 1719 **Publicly Held**
WEB: www.northropgrumman.com
SIC: 3812 Radar systems & equipment
HQ: Northrop Grumman Systems Corporation
2980 Fairview Park Dr
Falls Church VA 22042
703 280-2900

(G-8485)
NORTHSTAR AVIATION USA LLC
1431 General Aviation Dr (32935-6332)
PHONE..................................321 600-4557
Lyle Becka, *Vice Pres*
Amy Styers, *Officer*
EMP: 23 **EST:** 2012
SQ FT: 8,000
SALES (est): 2.1MM **Privately Held**
WEB: www.usanstar.com
SIC: 3721 3728 Aircraft; aircraft parts & equipment

(G-8486)
O I INC
Also Called: Inter Ordnance
295 North Dr Ste A (32934-9261)
PHONE..................................321 212-7801
Ulrich Wiegand, *President*
Richard Wade, *Manager*
◆ **EMP:** 20 **EST:** 2005
SQ FT: 60,000
SALES (est): 7.4MM **Privately Held**
SIC: 3484 5091 Small arms; guns (firearms) or gun parts, 30 mm. & below; ammunition, sporting; firearms, sporting

(G-8487)
OGRE CUSTOM FABRICATIONS LLC
2495 Jen Dr Ste 10 (32940-7495)
PHONE..................................321 544-2142
Paul M Stewart, *Principal*
▼ **EMP:** 5 **EST:** 2011
SALES (est): 491.4K **Privately Held**
WEB: www.ogrecustomfab.com
SIC: 3399 Primary metal products

(G-8488)
OMEGA GARAGE DOORS INC
7751 Industrial Rd (32904-1630)
PHONE..................................352 620-8830
Darrell Wright, *Sales Mgr*
Duane Wright, *Manager*
EMP: 10
SALES (corp-wide): 4.7MM **Privately Held**
WEB: www.omegadoorsflorida.com
SIC: 2431 3442 3231 Door screens, metal covered wood; fire doors, metal; insulating glass; made from purchased glass
PA: Omega Garage Doors, Inc.
328 Seaboard Ave
Venice FL 34285
941 627-0150

(G-8489)
OSTRICH MARKET INC
381 Dayton Blvd (32904-3715)
PHONE..................................954 873-1957
Henry G Slaughter, *President*
EMP: 5 **EST:** 2005
SALES (est): 373.4K **Privately Held**
WEB: www.ostrichmarket.com
SIC: 3172 Personal leather goods

(G-8490)
PALMAS PRINTING INC (PA)
200 East Dr (32904-1027)
PHONE..................................321 984-4451
Bruce Budney, *General Mgr*
Diamela Hernandez, *General Mgr*
J Robert Gunther, *Principal*
James Love, *Vice Pres*
Jean Chapman, *CFO*
◆ **EMP:** 20 **EST:** 1998
SQ FT: 30,000
SALES (est): 7.6MM **Privately Held**
WEB: www.palmasprinting.com
SIC: 2759 2679 Screen printing; labels, paper: made from purchased material

(G-8491)
PARABEL INC
Also Called: (A DEVELOPMENT STAGE COMPANY)
1901 S Hbr Cy Blvd Ste 60 (32901)
PHONE..................................321 409-7415
Anthony John Phipps Tiarks, *Ch of Bd*
Carlos Morales, *Production*
Lucille Forbes, *Purchasing*
Syed Naqvi, *CFO*
Nelson Ciriaco, *Accountant*
EMP: 38 **EST:** 2006
SALES (est): 650K **Privately Held**
WEB: www.lemnatureusa.com
SIC: 2869 6794 Industrial organic chemicals; patent buying, licensing, leasing

(G-8492)
PATRIOT FIRE DEFENSE INC
4451 Enterprise Ct (32934-9202)
PHONE..................................321 313-2265
EMP: 7 **EST:** 2018
SALES (est): 505.5K **Privately Held**
WEB: www.patriotfiredefense.com
SIC: 2899 Fire extinguisher charges

(G-8493)
PEPSI-COLA METRO BTLG CO INC
3951 Sarno Rd (32934-7275)
PHONE..................................321 242-2984
Jim Harrington, *Sales/Mktg Mgr*
Anthony Munroe, *Manager*
EMP: 29
SALES (corp-wide): 70.3B **Publicly Held**
WEB: www.pepsico.com
SIC: 2086 Carbonated soft drinks, bottled & canned
HQ: Pepsi-Cola Metropolitan Bottling Company, Inc.
700 Anderson Hill Rd
Purchase NY 10577
914 767-6000

(G-8494)
PHLEXAPEEL LLC
100 Rialto Pl Ste 743 (32901-3072)
P.O. Box 410250 (32941-0250)
PHONE..................................407 990-1854
George D Sergio, *Owner*
EMP: 5 **EST:** 2014

SALES (est): 534K **Privately Held**
WEB: www.phlexapeel.com
SIC: 2869 Industrial organic chemicals

(G-8495)
PHOTOTELESIS LP
1615 W Nasa Blvd (32901-2613)
PHONE..................................321 254-1500
Deon Harkey, *Partner*
Judi Padilla, *Partner*
▲ **EMP:** 18 **EST:** 2005
SALES (est): 613.5K **Privately Held**
WEB: www.extantaerospace.com
SIC: 3663 5065 Radio & TV communications equipment; electronic parts & equipment

(G-8496)
PLANET INHOUSE INC
3000 N Wickham Rd (32935-2303)
P.O. Box 411306 (32941-1306)
PHONE..................................321 216-2189
Todd Hillhouse, *CEO*
Brandon Riley, *Vice Pres*
EMP: 9 **EST:** 2013
SALES (est): 932.1K **Privately Held**
WEB: www.planetinhouse.com
SIC: 3861 Motion picture film

(G-8497)
PRECIOUS METAL EXCHANGE
2610 Ranch Rd (32904-9067)
PHONE..................................321 727-2278
Ronald Beolet, *Principal*
EMP: 7 **EST:** 2009
SALES (est): 202.4K **Privately Held**
SIC: 3339 Precious metals

(G-8498)
PRECISION TECH MACHINING LLC
1421 Albert Dr (32935-2807)
PHONE..................................321 693-3469
Kevin S Walker, *Mng Member*
Wanda G Walker,
EMP: 8 **EST:** 2007
SALES (est): 537.9K **Privately Held**
SIC: 3599 Machine shop, jobbing & repair

(G-8499)
PRESTIGE/AB READY MIX LLC
Also Called: Prestige Concrete
2585 Avocado Ave (32935-5586)
PHONE..................................321 751-2566
Bryan Moffit, *Branch Mgr*
EMP: 63
SALES (corp-wide): 11.2MM **Privately Held**
SIC: 3273 Ready-mixed concrete
PA: Prestige/Ab Ready Mix, Llc
7228 Westport Pl Ste C
West Palm Beach FL 33413
561 478-9980

(G-8500)
PRINT PRODUCTION SERVICES INC
2435 Michigan St (32904-6134)
PHONE..................................321 557-4414
Ralph J Zito, *Principal*
EMP: 7 **EST:** 2008
SALES (est): 11.3K **Privately Held**
WEB: www.areyoupaidwhatyourworth.com
SIC: 2752 Commercial printing, lithographic

(G-8501)
PROMO DADDY LLC
812 N Apollo Blvd (32935-5068)
PHONE..................................877 557-2336
Bill Stevens, *Branch Mgr*
EMP: 11
SALES (corp-wide): 3.7MM **Privately Held**
WEB: www.promodaddy.com
SIC: 3993 2396 2399 3999 Advertising novelties; screen printing on fabric articles; emblems, badges & insignia; coins & tokens, non-currency; buttons
PA: Promo Daddy Llc
800 N Apollo Blvd
Melbourne FL 32935
352 390-3081

(G-8502)
PROMO DADDY LLC (PA)
Also Called: Custom Button Company
800 N Apollo Blvd (32935-5068)
PHONE..................................352 390-3081
Ian McRoberts, *CEO*
▲ **EMP:** 20 **EST:** 2001
SALES (est): 3.7MM **Privately Held**
WEB: www.promodaddy.com
SIC: 3993 Advertising novelties

(G-8503)
PUBLIFY PRESS INC (PA)
2412 Irwin St Ste 53 (32901-7316)
PHONE..................................774 248-4056
Peter Lopez, *CEO*
EMP: 12 **EST:** 2020
SALES (est): 350K **Privately Held**
WEB: www.publifypress.com
SIC: 2741 Miscellaneous publishing

(G-8504)
PURE WAVE ORGANICS INC
Also Called: Laughing Mermaid The
2861 Saint James Ln (32935-3602)
PHONE..................................321 368-7002
John McElhinny, *President*
EMP: 7 **EST:** 2013
SALES (est): 86.3K **Privately Held**
SIC: 2834 7389 5169 Dermatologicals; ; organic chemicals, synthetic

(G-8505)
PUSH DESIGNS PRINTING INC
1101 W Hibiscus Blvd # 204 (32901-2718)
PHONE..................................321 591-1645
Timothy Jackson, *Principal*
EMP: 7 **EST:** 2016
SALES (est): 111.6K **Privately Held**
SIC: 2752 Commercial printing, lithographic

(G-8506)
QP CONSULTING INC
Also Called: Paragon Printers
2110 Dairy Rd Ste 102 (32904-5200)
PHONE..................................321 727-2442
John Stewart, *President*
Mary Stewart, *Vice Pres*
EMP: 6 **EST:** 1983
SQ FT: 8,000
SALES (est): 763.7K **Privately Held**
SIC: 2752 Commercial printing, offset

(G-8507)
QUALITY CUSTOM CABINETS LLC
1155 Sanddune Ln Apt 206 (32935-5235)
PHONE..................................201 873-6607
Nick Noreika, *Branch Mgr*
EMP: 22
SALES (corp-wide): 57.2K **Privately Held**
SIC: 2434 Wood kitchen cabinets
PA: Quality Custom Cabinets Llc
914 Saint Clair St
Melbourne FL

(G-8508)
QUEST ENVIRONMENTAL PDTS INC
6928 Sonny Dale Dr Ste A (32904-2200)
PHONE..................................321 984-4423
Fred K Ungerer, *President*
Lynda Ungerer, *Admin Sec*
EMP: 9 **EST:** 1994
SQ FT: 8,500
SALES (est): 1.7MM **Privately Held**
WEB:
www.questenvironmentalproducts.com
SIC: 2819 Industrial inorganic chemicals

(G-8509)
RELIABLE FINISHES
7730 Industrial Rd (32904-1631)
PHONE..................................321 723-3334
Greg Becker, *Owner*
EMP: 8 **EST:** 2007
SALES (est): 551.2K **Privately Held**
WEB: www.reliablefinishes.com
SIC: 3479 Painting of metal products

(G-8510)
RELM COMMUNICATIONS INC
Also Called: Bk Technologies
7100 Technology Dr (32904-1521)
PHONE.................................321 953-7800
D Kyle Cerminara, *Ch of Bd*
Timothy A Vitou, *President*
Lewis Johnson, *Chairman*
Henry R Willis, *COO*
Tina Boucher, *Vice Pres*
▲ EMP: 114 EST: 1945
SQ FT: 54,000
SALES (est): 22.9MM
SALES (corp-wide): 45.3MM **Publicly
Held**
WEB: www.bktechnologies.com
SIC: 3825 3663 Power measuring equip-
ment, electrical; mobile communication
equipment; cellular radio telephone; re-
ceiver-transmitter units (transceiver)
HQ: Bk Technologies, Inc.
7100 Technology Dr
West Melbourne FL 32904

(G-8511)
ROCKWELL COLLINS INC
1100 W Hibiscus Blvd (32901-2704)
P.O. Box 1060 (32902-1060)
PHONE.................................321 768-7303
Jeff Moore, *Principal*
Frank Joslin, *Prdtn Mgr*
Clara Centeno, *Mfg Staff*
Shelby Armstrong, *Engineer*
Eldredge Don, *Engineer*
EMP: 100
SALES (corp-wide): 64.3B **Publicly Held**
WEB: www.rockwellcollins.com
SIC: 3663 3812 Radio & TV communica-
tions equipment; search & navigation
equipment
HQ: Rockwell Collins, Inc.
400 Collins Rd Ne
Cedar Rapids IA 52498

(G-8512)
RTI DONOR SERVICES INC
401 N Wickham Rd Ste 143 (32935-8667)
PHONE.................................321 431-2464
Tom Cannan, *Manager*
EMP: 245
SALES (corp-wide): 90.5MM **Publicly
Held**
WEB: www.rtix.com
SIC: 3841 Surgical & medical instruments
HQ: Rti Donor Services, Inc.
11621 Research Cir
Alachua FL 32615

(G-8513)
SAGRAD INC
202 West Dr (32904-1042)
PHONE.................................321 726-9400
Adam K Harriman, *President*
Martha J Harriman, *Vice Pres*
Tony Crosthwaite, *Opers Mgr*
Dawn Harris, *QC Mgr*
James Brown, *Engineer*
◆ EMP: 15 EST: 2004
SQ FT: 1,200
SALES (est): 4.4MM **Privately Held**
WEB: www.sagrad.com
SIC: 3629 5065 Electronic generation
equipment; electronic parts & equipment

(G-8514)
SALTY INDUSTRIES LLC
729 Columbus Ave Unit 102 (32901-4603)
PHONE.................................321 626-6331
George D Hirst, *CEO*
EMP: 5 EST: 2016
SALES (est): 395.3K **Privately Held**
WEB: www.saltyindustriesllc.com
SIC: 3999 Manufacturing industries

(G-8515)
**SATCOM DIRECT GOVERNMENT
INC (PA)**
Also Called: SD Government
1050 Satcom Ln (32940-7010)
P.O. Box 372667, Satellite Beach (32937-
0667)
PHONE.................................321 777-3000
James W Jensen, *CEO*
David Greenhill, *President*
James Jensen, *President*
Darlene Ciarcia, *Vice Pres*

Zachary Cotner, *CFO*
EMP: 10 EST: 2003
SQ FT: 3,500
SALES (est): 96.3MM **Privately Held**
WEB: www.satcomdirect.com
SIC: 3663 Satellites, communications

(G-8516)
SBS PRECISION SHTMTL INC
Also Called: SBS
615 Distribution Dr (32904-1178)
PHONE.................................321 951-7411
Don Morse, *President*
Debi Johnson, *Human Res Mgr*
EMP: 20 EST: 1985
SQ FT: 11,000
SALES (est): 4.3MM **Privately Held**
WEB: www.sbspre.net
SIC: 3441 3429 3444 3469 Fabricated
structural metal; manufactured hardware
(general); sheet metal specialties, not
stamped; machine parts, stamped or
pressed metal

(G-8517)
SDI INDUSTRIES INC
1216 Prospect Ave 101 (32901-7330)
PHONE.................................321 733-1128
Cristian Ahumada, *COO*
Jim Suggs, *VP Engrg*
Dave Bodenheimer, *Engng Exec*
Alejandro Deluca, *CFO*
Carol Soltys, *Branch Mgr*
EMP: 25
SALES (corp-wide): 56.5MM **Privately
Held**
WEB: www.sdi.systems
SIC: 3535 3537 8748 8711 Conveyors &
conveying equipment; industrial trucks &
tractors; business consulting; engineering
services; machinery installation
PA: Sdi Industries, Inc.
13000 Pierce St
Pacoima CA 91331
818 890-6002

(G-8518)
SEA GEAR CORPORATION
700 S John Rodes Blvd B1 (32904-1508)
PHONE.................................321 728-9116
Bobbie Lee Seigler, *President*
EMP: 5 EST: 1975
SQ FT: 3,500
SALES (est): 664.9K **Privately Held**
WEB: www.sea-gear.net
SIC: 3826 8731 Water testing apparatus;
biological research

(G-8519)
SENIOR LIFE OF FLORIDA
7350 Shoppes Dr Ste 102 (32940-6076)
PHONE.................................321 242-1235
Jill Gaines, *President*
EMP: 10 EST: 2010
SALES (est): 348.6K **Privately Held**
WEB: www.vieravoice.com
SIC: 2711 Newspapers, publishing & print-
ing

(G-8520)
SHELTON GROUP LLC
Also Called: Homes & Land Magazine
1333 Gateway Dr Ste 1013 (32901-2647)
PHONE.................................321 676-8981
Tom Shelton, *Manager*
EMP: 7 EST: 1999
SALES (est): 545.8K **Privately Held**
SIC: 2721 Magazines: publishing & printing

(G-8521)
SIGN MAN INC
4580 N Us Highway 1 (32935-7202)
PHONE.................................321 259-1703
Patrick L Neve, *President*
Colleen Jones, *Corp Secy*
Anna Neve, *Vice Pres*
EMP: 8 EST: 1979
SQ FT: 2,600
SALES (est): 400K **Privately Held**
WEB: www.signmaninc.com
SIC: 3993 Signs & advertising specialties

(G-8522)
SILVERHORSE RACING LLC
700 S John Rodes Blvd (32904-1507)
PHONE.................................321 722-2813

Joseph Marcello Canitano, *Principal*
▼ EMP: 7 EST: 2004
SQ FT: 3,000
SALES (est): 1.3MM **Privately Held**
WEB: www.silverhorseracing.com
SIC: 3714 Motor vehicle parts & acces-
sories

(G-8523)
SINGER HOLDINGS INC
Also Called: Florida Sheet Metal
3160 Skyway Cir (32934-7333)
PHONE.................................321 724-0900
Deeon Singer, *President*
Henry L Singer II, *Vice Pres*
EMP: 12 EST: 2003
SALES (est): 2.1MM **Privately Held**
WEB: www.floridasheetmetal.com
SIC: 3444 Sheet metal specialties, not
stamped

(G-8524)
SMITTYS WELDING SHOP
2526 S Harbor City Blvd (32901-7206)
PHONE.................................321 723-4533
Jonathon David Bauer, *Owner*
EMP: 6 EST: 1978
SQ FT: 2,400
SALES (est): 448K **Privately Held**
SIC: 7692 Welding repair

(G-8525)
**SPACE CAST INTLLGENT
SLTONS IN**
770 North Dr Ste B (32934-9270)
PHONE.................................321 622-6858
Brian J Jaskiewicz, *President*
Bill Anderson, *General Mgr*
James A Ralph, *Vice Pres*
Seth McLeod, *Engineer*
Jeff White, *Engineer*
EMP: 11 EST: 2008
SALES (est): 1.6MM **Privately Held**
WEB: www.goscis.com
SIC: 3812 Defense systems & equipment

(G-8526)
SPACE COAST MAP LLC
1359 Richmond Dr (32935-5325)
P.O. Box 361893 (32936-1893)
PHONE.................................321 242-4538
Julia Perian, *Principal*
EMP: 7 EST: 2012
SALES (est): 229.6K **Privately Held**
SIC: 3471 Plating of metals or formed
products

(G-8527)
**SPACECAST PLTG MET
RFNSHING IN**
975 Aurora Rd (32935-5968)
PHONE.................................321 254-2880
David P Pratt, *President*
Sandra Pratt, *Vice Pres*
EMP: 15 EST: 1996
SQ FT: 15,000
SALES (est): 1.1MM **Privately Held**
WEB: www.spacecoast-plating.com
SIC: 3471 Plating of metals or formed
products

(G-8528)
**SPECIALTY PHARMACY SVCS
INC**
1555 W Nasa Blvd Ste B (32901-2640)
PHONE.................................321 953-2004
Barbara Switzler, *President*
Thomas Switzler, *Vice Pres*
Joy Leffler, *Manager*
EMP: 7 EST: 1996
SALES (est): 400K **Privately Held**
WEB: www.specialty-pharmacy.com
SIC: 2834 5122 Pharmaceutical prepara-
tions; pharmaceuticals

(G-8529)
SPOONS CHILLY
4980 N Wickham Rd Ste 106 (32940-7320)
PHONE.................................321 610-8966
EMP: 6
SALES (est): 417K **Privately Held**
SIC: 2026 Mfg Fluid Milk

(G-8530)
SS & S INDUSTRIES INC
620 Di Lido St Ne (32907-2029)
PHONE.................................321 327-2500
EMP: 13 EST: 2017
SALES (est): 548.6K **Privately Held**
SIC: 3999 Manufacturing industries

(G-8531)
STERN BRANDS INC
Also Called: Trinetics Group
3153 Skyway Cir (32934-7386)
PHONE.................................321 622-8584
Sara Stern, *CEO*
Sara T Stern, *Admin Sec*
EMP: 14 EST: 2017
SALES (est): 1.3MM **Privately Held**
SIC: 3679 Harness assemblies for elec-
tronic use: wire or cable

(G-8532)
STRATEGIC PRODUCTS INC
5100 Laguna Vista Dr (32934-7837)
PHONE.................................321 752-0441
Art Markuson, *President*
Jeff Markuson, *Vice Pres*
Joe Giusti, *Manager*
EMP: 12 EST: 1984
SQ FT: 9,000
SALES (est): 229.8K **Privately Held**
WEB: www.accuheat2.com
SIC: 3631 Convection ovens, including
portable: household

(G-8533)
STRATOS LIGHT WAVE INC
Also Called: Stratos Optical
1333 Gateway Dr Ste 1007 (32901-2646)
PHONE.................................321 308-4100
Brian Mason, *President*
Dale Reed, *VP Sales*
Mike Nipper, *Regl Sales Mgr*
EMP: 1 EST: 2000
SQ FT: 13,000
SALES (est): 10.4MM
SALES (corp-wide): 543.4MM **Publicly
Held**
SIC: 3678 Electronic connectors
HQ: Stratos International, Inc.
299 Johnson Ave Sw
Waseca MN 56093
507 833-8822

(G-8534)
**STRUCTURAL COMPOSITES
INC**
360 East Dr (32904-1029)
PHONE.................................321 951-9464
Ronnal P Reichard, *Ch of Bd*
Scott M Lewit, *President*
Peter Hedger, *Vice Pres*
Michael Nichols, *Vice Pres*
Crystal Newberry, *Opers Staff*
EMP: 14 EST: 1987
SQ FT: 13,000
SALES (est): 2.5MM **Privately Held**
WEB: www.structuralcomposites.com
SIC: 3089 8711 Plastic boats & other ma-
rine equipment; marine engineering

(G-8535)
**STRUCTURAL STEEL OF
BREVARD**
6951 Vickie Cir Ste A (32904-2203)
PHONE.................................321 726-0271
EMP: 10 EST: 2017
SALES (est): 885.7K **Privately Held**
SIC: 3441 Fabricated structural metal

(G-8536)
SUMMATION RESEARCH INC
305 East Dr Ste D (32904-1033)
PHONE.................................321 254-2580
Todd Gross, *President*
Tracy Daneau, *General Mgr*
Tom Drago, *Vice Pres*
EMP: 11 EST: 1989
SQ FT: 14,700
SALES (est): 1.7MM **Privately Held**
WEB: www.summationresearch.com
SIC: 3663 7371 Receivers, radio commu-
nications; computer software develop-
ment

▲ = Import ▼=Export
◆ =Import/Export

(G-8537)
SUN NUCLEAR CORP
425 Pineda Ct Ste A (32940-7537)
PHONE..................................321 259-6862
Zakaryan Konstantin, *Manager*
EMP: 44
SALES (corp-wide): 154.1MM **Publicly Held**
WEB: www.sunnuclear.com
SIC: 3829 Nuclear radiation & testing apparatus
HQ: Sun Nuclear Corp.
3275 Suntree Blvd
Melbourne FL 32940
321 259-6862

(G-8538)
SUN NUCLEAR CORP (DH)
3275 Suntree Blvd (32940-7514)
PHONE..................................321 259-6862
Jeffery A Simon, *CEO*
William E Simon, *President*
EMP: 126 **EST:** 1984
SQ FT: 13,000
SALES (corp-wide): 154.1MM **Publicly Held**
WEB: www.sunnuclear.com
SIC: 3829 8734 7699 Nuclear radiation & testing apparatus; testing laboratories; professional instrument repair services

(G-8539)
SUNSET PUBLICATIONS INC
630 S Wickham Rd Ste 107 (32904-1429)
PHONE..................................321 727-8500
Michael McIntyre, *Principal*
EMP: 7 **EST:** 2010
SALES (est): 110K **Privately Held**
SIC: 2741 Miscellaneous publishing

(G-8540)
SUNTREE DIAGNOSTIC CENTER
7970 N Wickham Rd Ste 102 (32940-8299)
PHONE..................................321 259-8800
Thomas Foster, *Director*
EMP: 7 **EST:** 1991
SQ FT: 4,800
SALES (est): 757.2K **Privately Held**
SIC: 2835 In vitro & in vivo diagnostic substances

(G-8541)
SUPPORT SYSTEMS ASSOCIATES INC
700 S John Rodes Blvd (32904-1507)
PHONE..................................321 724-5566
John P Zoltak, *Branch Mgr*
EMP: 30
SALES (corp-wide): 24MM **Privately Held**
WEB: www.ssai.org
SIC: 3728 Aircraft parts & equipment
PA: Support Systems Associates, Inc.
304 S Hbr Cy Blvd Ste 100
Melbourne FL 32901
321 724-5566

(G-8542)
SWISS COMPONENTS INC
405 West Dr Ste A (32904-1084)
PHONE..................................321 723-6729
Abner Telebrico, *President*
Bernice O Morris, *Treasurer*
Bernice Morris, *Treasurer*
Angela Carter, *Manager*
Matthew Cordeau, *Prgrmr*
EMP: 12 **EST:** 2000
SQ FT: 6,000
SALES (est): 2.7MM **Privately Held**
WEB: www.swisscomponents.com
SIC: 3599 3443 Machine shop, jobbing & repair; fabricated plate work (boiler shop)

(G-8543)
SYMETRICS INDUSTRIES LLC
Also Called: Extant Aerospace
1615 W Nasa Blvd (32901-2613)
PHONE..................................321 254-1500
James Gerwien-Moreta, *CEO*
Eric Hilliard, *President*
David Minton, *General Mgr*
Bill White, *Business Mgr*
Thomas Deasy, *Vice Pres*
▲ **EMP:** 150 **EST:** 1998
SQ FT: 40,000

SALES (est): 76.6MM
SALES (corp-wide): 4.8B **Publicly Held**
WEB: www.extantaerospace.com
SIC: 3699 Electrical equipment & supplies
PA: Transdigm Group Incorporated
1301 E 9th St Ste 3000
Cleveland OH 44114
216 706-2960

(G-8544)
SYMETRICS TECHNOLOGY GROUP LLC
1615 W Nasa Blvd (32901-2613)
PHONE..................................321 254-1500
James Gerwien, *CEO*
D Mitchell Garner, *Principal*
Dudley Garner, *Principal*
EMP: 16 **EST:** 2013
SALES (est): 4.2MM
SALES (corp-wide): 4.8B **Publicly Held**
WEB: www.extantaerospace.com
SIC: 3699 Security devices
PA: Transdigm Group Incorporated
1301 E 9th St Ste 3000
Cleveland OH 44114
216 706-2960

(G-8545)
TECORE GOVERNMENT SERVICES LLC
295 North Dr Ste G (32934-9261)
PHONE..................................410 872-6000
Joseph F Gerrity, *CFO*
Joseph Gerrity, *Manager*
Deniz Hardy, *General Counsel*
EMP: 7 **EST:** 2015
SQ FT: 48,000
SALES (est): 128.5K **Privately Held**
SIC: 3663 Radio broadcasting & communications equipment

(G-8546)
TEK-LITE INC
1279 Tipperary Dr (32940-6029)
PHONE..................................410 775-7123
Kevin F McDermott, *President*
EMP: 8 **EST:** 1978
SQ FT: 9,000
SALES (est): 829.7K **Privately Held**
WEB: www.teklite.com
SIC: 3646 Commercial indusl & institutional electric lighting fixtures

(G-8547)
TEKNIFAB INDUSTRIES INC
179 Park Hill Blvd (32904-5115)
PHONE..................................321 722-1922
Sean Makowsky, *President*
Rebecca Makowsky, *Vice Pres*
EMP: 6 **EST:** 1995
SALES (est): 770K **Privately Held**
WEB: www.teknifab.com
SIC: 3441 Fabricated structural metal

(G-8548)
TEKNOCRAFT INC
425 West Dr (32904-1035)
PHONE..................................321 729-9634
Sampath V Kumar, *President*
EMP: 21 **EST:** 1983
SQ FT: 52,000
SALES (est): 1.4MM **Privately Held**
WEB: www.teknocraft.com
SIC: 3599 5084 3494 3492 Machine shop, jobbing & repair; industrial machinery & equipment; valves & pipe fittings; fluid power valves & hose fittings

(G-8549)
TERRY LABORATORIES LLC
7005 Technology Dr (32904-1512)
PHONE..................................321 259-1630
Jim Gambino, *General Mgr*
Chris Dougall, *Marketing Staff*
Rex Maughan, *Mng Member*
James A Gambino, *Manager*
◆ **EMP:** 13 **EST:** 1973
SQ FT: 19,000
SALES (est): 3.2MM **Privately Held**
WEB: www.terrylabs.com
SIC: 2833 2844 2869 Medicinals & botanicals; toilet preparations; industrial organic chemicals

(G-8550)
TIME INDUSTRIES INC
709 Silver Palm Ave Ste J (32901-4803)
PHONE..................................321 676-2080
Fred Zeit, *President*
EMP: 5 **EST:** 2002
SQ FT: 1,600
SALES (est): 461.4K **Privately Held**
WEB: www.timeind.com
SIC: 3545 Precision measuring tools

(G-8551)
TITAN AMERICA LLC
2575 Avocado Ave (32935-5586)
PHONE..................................321 259-0490
Jim Armstrong, *Manager*
Jeff Sharp, *Products*
EMP: 31
SALES (corp-wide): 177.9K **Privately Held**
WEB: www.titanamerica.com
SIC: 3273 Ready-mixed concrete
HQ: Titan America Llc
5700 Lake Wright Dr # 300
Norfolk VA 23502
757 858-6500

(G-8552)
TK TIRES & WHEELS INC
2400 S Harbor City Blvd (32901-5531)
PHONE..................................321 473-8945
Timothy Fitzwater, *Director*
EMP: 9 **EST:** 2011
SALES (est): 109.5K **Privately Held**
SIC: 3312 Wheels

(G-8553)
TRIPLE PLAY CMMUNICATIONS CORP
250 East Dr Ste F (32904-1031)
PHONE..................................321 327-8997
Keith Riffee, *President*
Jim Wernlund, *VP Engrg*
EMP: 6 **EST:** 2006
SQ FT: 3,050
SALES (est): 840.3K **Privately Held**
WEB: www.tripleplaycomm.com
SIC: 3674 Semiconductors & related devices

(G-8554)
TRU MENSION MFG SOLUTIONS
3900 Dow Rd Ste C (32934-9255)
PHONE..................................321 255-4665
Kenneth J Sheehan, *President*
Kenneth Sheehan, *Vice Pres*
EMP: 8 **EST:** 1986
SALES (est): 827.6K **Privately Held**
SIC: 3499 3334 Machine bases, metal; pigs, aluminum

(G-8555)
UROSHAPE LLC
Also Called: Sola Therapy
1130 S Harbor City Blvd (32901-1947)
PHONE..................................321 960-2484
Ralph Zipper, *CEO*
Steve Bowers, *Vice Pres*
EMP: 10 **EST:** 2010
SALES (est): 1.2MM **Privately Held**
WEB: www.solapelvictherapy.com
SIC: 3841 5047 Surgical & medical instruments; medical instruments & equipment, blood & bone work; instruments, surgical & medical

(G-8556)
US BLANKS LLC
282 N Wickham Rd (32935-8650)
PHONE..................................321 253-3626
EMP: 48
SALES (corp-wide): 7.8MM **Privately Held**
WEB: www.usblanks.com
SIC: 2821 Plastics materials & resins
PA: Us Blanks, Llc
14700 S San Pedro St
Gardena CA 90248
310 225-6774

(G-8557)
VERTICAL FLIGHT TECHNOLOGY INC
3385 Shady Run Rd (32934-8567)
PHONE..................................407 687-3126

Laura Rvtd Melnik, *Principal*
EMP: 12 **EST:** 2012
SALES (est): 604.5K **Privately Held**
WEB: www.demonheli.com
SIC: 2591 Blinds vertical

(G-8558)
VIATECH OF DELAWARE INC
Also Called: Skycross
7341 Office Park Pl # 102 (32940-8280)
PHONE..................................321 308-6600
EMP: 24
SQ FT: 10,000
SALES (est): 1.9MM **Privately Held**
SIC: 3663 Design/Mfg Wireless Antennas

(G-8559)
VISION BLOCKS INC
1634 Cypress Ave (32935-5931)
PHONE..................................321 254-7478
Judy Pollard, *President*
Allan Pollard, *General Mgr*
EMP: 10 **EST:** 1979
SQ FT: 6,000
SALES (est): 500K **Privately Held**
WEB: www.visionblocks.com
SIC: 3231 Safety glass: made from purchased glass

(G-8560)
VISION SYSTEMS NORTH AMER INC
1801 Penn St Ste 104 (32901-2693)
PHONE..................................321 265-5110
Carl Putman, *President*
Catherine Robin, *President*
Robin Bokilo, *COO*
EMP: 14 **EST:** 2013
SALES (est): 3.5MM **Privately Held**
WEB: www.vision-systems.fr
SIC: 3728 Aircraft parts & equipment
HQ: Vision Systems Corporate
Zone Industrielle
Brignais 69530
472 319-810

(G-8561)
WHITTINGTON ENERGY CO
730 E Strwbrdge Ave Ste 2 (32901)
PHONE..................................321 984-2128
Richard A Whittington, *President*
Barbara C Whittington, *Vice Pres*
EMP: 7 **EST:** 1996
SALES (est): 452.4K **Privately Held**
SIC: 1382 Oil & gas exploration services

(G-8562)
WINCHSTER INTERCONNECT RF CORP
3950 Dow Rd (32934-8902)
PHONE..................................800 881-9689
Donald Neuterman, *Design Engr*
Irene Roth, *Sales Staff*
EMP: 30
SALES (corp-wide): 14.3B **Privately Held**
SIC: 3678 Electronic connectors
HQ: Winchester Interconnect Rf Corporation
245 Lynnfield St
Peabody MA 01960
978 532-0775

(G-8563)
WINCHSTER INTRCNNECT HRMTICS L (DH)
3950 Dow Rd (32934-8902)
PHONE..................................321 254-4067
Kevin Perhamus, *CEO*
Tom Drago, *Vice Pres*
Vincent Garrett, *Vice Pres*
▲ **EMP:** 65 **EST:** 2003
SQ FT: 25,000
SALES (est): 25.7MM
SALES (corp-wide): 14.3B **Privately Held**
SIC: 3679 Hermetic seals for electronic equipment

(G-8564)
WIND RIVER SYSTEMS INC
100 Rialto Pl Ste 525 (32901-3007)
PHONE..................................321 726-9463
Brian Donaldson, *Manager*
EMP: 9

SALES (corp-wide): 2.3B **Publicly Held**
WEB: www.windriver.com
SIC: 7372 Application computer software
HQ: Wind River Systems, Inc.
 500 Wind River Way
 Alameda CA 94501
 510 748-4100

(G-8565)
YP ADVRTISING PUBG LLC NOT LLC
Also Called: BellSouth
 100 Rialto Pl Ste 300 (32901-3073)
 PHONE.....................321 956-5400
 Jim Watkins, *Director*
 EMP: 266
 SALES (corp-wide): 1.4B **Publicly Held**
 SIC: 2741 Directories: publishing only, not printed on site
 HQ: Yp Advertising & Publishing Llc (Not Llc)
 2247 Northlake Pkwy
 Tucker GA 30084

Melbourne Beach
Brevard County

(G-8566)
INFINITY GENOME SCIENCES INC
 301 Riverside Dr (32951-2141)
 PHONE.....................321 327-7365
 John Detter, *Principal*
 EMP: 7 EST: 2017
 SALES (est): 195.8K **Privately Held**
 SIC: 2835 Microbiology & virology diagnostic products

(G-8567)
INSPIRED THERAPEUTICS LLC
 7309 S Highway A1a (32951-3514)
 PHONE.....................339 222-0847
 Kurt Dasse, *CEO*
 Priscilla Petit, *Principal*
 Barry Gellman, *COO*
 John Whiting, *CFO*
 EMP: 7 EST: 2017
 SALES (est): 104.8K **Privately Held**
 SIC: 3841 Surgical & medical instruments

(G-8568)
PINNACLE FOODS INC
 5905 S Highway A1a (32951-3704)
 PHONE.....................321 952-7926
 Mohammed Elguindy, *President*
 Alice Elguindy, *Vice Pres*
 EMP: 5 EST: 1991
 SQ FT: 8,000
 SALES (est): 495.5K **Privately Held**
 SIC: 2066 Chocolate & cocoa products

(G-8569)
QUANTUM PHARMACEUTICALS LLC
 429 Riverview Ln (32951-2716)
 PHONE.....................321 724-0625
 Steven Strauss,
 Mark Steele,
 Valerie Strauss,
 EMP: 5 EST: 2004
 SALES (est): 446.5K **Privately Held**
 SIC: 2834 Proprietary drug products

(G-8570)
RAPID REPRODUCTIONS LLC
 108 Seagrape Rd (32951-4029)
 PHONE.....................607 843-2221
 Bryant Latourette, *Mng Member*
 EMP: 8 EST: 1977
 SALES (est): 480K **Privately Held**
 WEB: www.rapidreproductions.net
 SIC: 2752 Commercial printing, offset

Melrose
Putnam County

(G-8571)
LAKE AREA WATERSPORTS LLC
Also Called: Pro Water Sports
 829 N State Road 21 (32666-4162)
 PHONE.....................352 475-3434
 Scott Diley, *Manager*
 Chad Hovsepian,
 EMP: 8 EST: 2004
 SQ FT: 2,000
 SALES (est): 1MM **Privately Held**
 WEB: www.lakeareawatersports.com
 SIC: 3949 5091 Water sports equipment; boats, canoes, watercrafts & equipment

Merritt Island
Brevard County

(G-8572)
AIR LIQUIDE LARGE INDS US LP
 7007 N Courtenay Pkwy (32953-7112)
 PHONE.....................321 452-2214
 Rudy Strickland, *Manager*
 EMP: 7
 SQ FT: 7,320
 SALES (corp-wide): 109.4MM **Privately Held**
 WEB: www.airliquide.com
 SIC: 2813 Industrial gases
 HQ: Air Liquide Large Industries U.S. Lp
 9811 Katy Fwy Ste 100
 Houston TX 77024
 713 624-8000

(G-8573)
AIRBUS ONEWEB SATELLITES LLC (PA)
 8301 Newspace Dr (32953-6700)
 PHONE.....................321 522-6645
 James Hinds, *CEO*
 Anthony Gingiss, *CEO*
 Roman Winzelle, *CFO*
 Kai Schmidt, *Persnl Dir*
 Laura Kraus, *Director*
 EMP: 29 EST: 2016
 SALES (est): 182.5MM **Privately Held**
 WEB: www.airbusonewebsatellites.com
 SIC: 3663 Satellites, communications

(G-8574)
AIRBUS ONWEB STLLTES N AMER LL (HQ)
 8301 Newspace Dr (32953-6700)
 PHONE.....................321 522-6645
 James Hinds, *CEO*
 Anthony Gingiss, *CEO*
 Roman Winzelle, *CFO*
 Kai Schmidt, *Persnl Dir*
 Laura Kraus, *Director*
 EMP: 31 EST: 2015
 SALES (est): 170.1MM
 SALES (corp-wide): 182.5MM **Privately Held**
 SIC: 3663 Space satellite communications equipment
 PA: Airbus Oneweb Satellites Llc
 8301 Newspace Dr
 Merritt Island FL 32953
 321 522-6645

(G-8575)
AIRBUS ONWEB STLLTES N AMER LL
 8301 Newspace Dr (32953-6700)
 PHONE.....................321 522-6645
 John Timmermann, *Principal*
 EMP: 100
 SALES (corp-wide): 182.5MM **Privately Held**
 SIC: 3663 Space satellite communications equipment
 HQ: Airbus Oneweb Satellites North America Llc
 8301 Newspace Dr
 Merritt Island FL 32953
 321 522-6645

(G-8576)
ATLANTIC COAST ROOFING & METAL
 350 Myrtice Ave Ste 201 (32953-4720)
 PHONE.....................321 449-9494
 David R Lightholder Jr, *Principal*
 EMP: 7 EST: 2009
 SALES (est): 508.8K **Privately Held**
 SIC: 3499 Fabricated metal products

(G-8577)
AUTOCRAFT MANUFACTURING CO
 810 Kemp St (32952-3768)
 P.O. Box 540475 (32954-0475)
 PHONE.....................321 453-1850
 Martha Mc Leod, *President*
 ▲ EMP: 30 EST: 1964
 SQ FT: 65,000
 SALES (est): 2MM **Privately Held**
 WEB: www.autocraftmfg.com
 SIC: 3714 3732 3647 Motor vehicle parts & accessories; boat building & repairing; vehicular lighting equipment

(G-8578)
BILL & RENEE ENTERPRISES INC
Also Called: PIP Printing
 275 Magnolia Ave Ste 2 (32952-4839)
 PHONE.....................321 452-2800
 Renee Frederick, *President*
 Bill Frederick, *Vice Pres*
 EMP: 9 EST: 1996
 SQ FT: 1,300
 SALES (est): 1MM **Privately Held**
 SIC: 2789 2752 Bookbinding & related work; commercial printing, lithographic

(G-8579)
BLUE ORIGIN FLORIDA LLC (HQ)
 8082 Space Commerce Way (32953-8703)
 PHONE.....................253 437-9300
 Bob Smith, *President*
 EMP: 1 EST: 2015
 SALES (est): 10.2MM **Privately Held**
 WEB: www.blueorigin.com
 SIC: 3761 Guided missiles & space vehicles

(G-8580)
BREVARD SOFTBALL MAGAZINE INC
 400 Nora Ave (32952-5123)
 PHONE.....................321 453-3711
 Gene Smith, *President*
 Bill Ballew, *Manager*
 EMP: 10 EST: 1996
 SALES (est): 845.9K **Privately Held**
 WEB: www.softballmag.com
 SIC: 2721 8641 Magazines: publishing & printing; civic social & fraternal associations

(G-8581)
CENTRAL FLORIDA PLATING INC
 675 Cypress Dr (32952-3719)
 PHONE.....................321 452-7234
 Tibor Menyhart, *President*
 Barbara Menyhart, *Vice Pres*
 Cal Dixon, *Human Res Dir*
 Davis Joan, *Admin Sec*
 EMP: 5 EST: 1986
 SQ FT: 4,000
 SALES (est): 500K **Privately Held**
 SIC: 3471 Electroplating of metals or formed products

(G-8582)
COUNTRKRAFT SOLID SURFACES INC
 3390 N Courtenay Pkwy P (32953-8310)
 PHONE.....................321 456-5928
 Larry Griffin, *President*
 Tracy Griffin, *Vice Pres*
 Bill Conley, *Purch Mgr*
 Frank Cocco, *Manager*
 EMP: 10 EST: 2001
 SQ FT: 6,000
 SALES (est): 1.5MM **Privately Held**
 WEB: www.counterkraft.com
 SIC: 2541 Counter & sink tops

(G-8583)
DARK STORM MANUFACTURING LLC ✪
 3390 N Courtenay Pkwy (32953-8310)
 PHONE.....................516 983-3473
 Edward Newman, *Mng Member*
 EMP: 5 EST: 2021
 SALES (est): 535.7K **Privately Held**
 SIC: 3484 Small arms

(G-8584)
EMF INC
Also Called: Engineering & Met Fabrication
 124 Imperial St (32952-3630)
 PHONE.....................321 453-3670
 David W Clark, *President*
 Jeff Flick, *Vice Pres*
 Tim Kaiser, *Vice Pres*
 James Hoskins, *Project Mgr*
 William Shaw, *Project Mgr*
 EMP: 117 EST: 1971
 SQ FT: 25,000
 SALES (est): 22.2MM **Privately Held**
 WEB: www.emfinc.net
 SIC: 3441 7692 Fabricated structural metal; welding repair

(G-8585)
FAMILY VISION CENTER
 228 S Courtenay Pkwy # 5 (32952-4857)
 PHONE.....................321 454-3002
 EMP: 5 EST: 2019
 SALES (est): 321.2K **Privately Held**
 WEB: www.familyvisioncenter.com
 SIC: 3827 Optical instruments & lenses

(G-8586)
HEALTH STAR INC
 625 E Merritt Ave Ste I (32953-3483)
 PHONE.....................321 914-6012
 Bryan Sylver, *President*
 Bryan B Sylver, *Principal*
 EMP: 8 EST: 2015
 SALES (est): 398.4K **Privately Held**
 SIC: 3841 Surgical & medical instruments

(G-8587)
MERRITT PRECISION TECH INC
 3425 N Courtenay Pkwy (32953-8315)
 PHONE.....................321 453-2334
 Douglas Keehn, *President*
 Ben Ousley, *Vice Pres*
 Joshua Brown, *Engineer*
 EMP: 7 EST: 2002
 SQ FT: 7,500
 SALES (est): 643.4K **Privately Held**
 WEB: www.merrittprecision.com
 SIC: 3229 2221 Glass fiber products; fiberglass fabrics

(G-8588)
MIGRANDY CORP
 675 Cypress Dr (32952-3719)
 PHONE.....................321 459-0044
 Tibor Menyhart, *President*
 Barbara Menyhart, *Vice Pres*
 Mike Menyhart, *Plant Mgr*
 Greg Menyhart, *Purchasing*
 EMP: 33 EST: 1981
 SQ FT: 15,000
 SALES (est): 2.2MM **Privately Held**
 WEB: www.migrandy.com
 SIC: 3452 3412 Screws, metal; barrels, shipping: metal

(G-8589)
ORBITAL SCIENCES LLC
 5335 N Courtenay Pkwy (32953-7327)
 PHONE.....................703 406-5474
 Blake Larson, *Principal*
 EMP: 233 **Publicly Held**
 WEB: www.northropgrumman.com
 SIC: 3812 Defense systems & equipment
 HQ: Orbital Sciences Llc
 2980 Fairview Park Dr
 Falls Church VA 22042

(G-8590)
PERII INC
Also Called: Perii Software
 2755 N Bnana Rver Dr Ste (32952)
 PHONE.....................321 253-2269
 James E Witcher, *President*
 EMP: 7 EST: 2003

SALES (est): 200K **Privately Held**
SIC: 7372 Prepackaged software

(G-8591)
REDSTONE CORPORATION
606 Gladiola St Hngr 255 (32952-3728)
PHONE...............................321 213-2135
Michael Kruse, *President*
Thorwald Eide, *Vice Pres*
Dominic Gilbert, *CFO*
EMP: 7 EST: 2008
SQ FT: 10,000
SALES (est): 463.2K **Privately Held**
SIC: 3728 8711 8742 Aircraft parts &
equipment; engineering services; aviation
&/or aeronautical engineering; manage-
ment consulting services

(G-8592)
SCREEN TECH
1501 Bermuda Ave (32952-5740)
PHONE...............................321 536-6091
Douglas Buford, *Principal*
EMP: 6 EST: 2005
SALES (est): 427.4K **Privately Held**
SIC: 2759 Screen printing

(G-8593)
SEA RAY BOATS INC
Also Called: Merritt Island Plant
350 Sea Ray Dr (32953-4194)
PHONE...............................321 459-9463
Jim Barclay, *Manager*
Jonathan Paul, *Technician*
EMP: 219
SALES (corp-wide): 5.8B **Publicly Held**
WEB: www.searay.com
SIC: 3732 Boats, fiberglass: building & re-
pairing
HQ: Sea Ray Boats, Inc.
800 S Gay St Ste 1200
Knoxville TN 37929
865 522-4181

(G-8594)
SEA RAY BOATS INC
Sykes Creek Division
350 Sea Ray Dr (32953-4194)
PHONE...............................321 459-2930
Steve Fielder, *Manager*
EMP: 115
SALES (corp-wide): 5.8B **Publicly Held**
WEB: www.searay.com
SIC: 3732 Boats, fiberglass: building & re-
pairing
HQ: Sea Ray Boats, Inc.
800 S Gay St Ste 1200
Knoxville TN 37929
865 522-4181

(G-8595)
SEA RAY BOATS INC
Also Called: Sea Ray PD&e
200 Sea Ray Dr (32953-4195)
PHONE...............................321 452-9876
Terry McNew, *Manager*
EMP: 117
SALES (corp-wide): 5.8B **Publicly Held**
WEB: www.searay.com
SIC: 3732 Boats, fiberglass: building & re-
pairing
HQ: Sea Ray Boats, Inc.
800 S Gay St Ste 1200
Knoxville TN 37929
865 522-4181

(G-8596)
SEALIFT LLC
3390 N Courtenay Pkwy A (32953-8341)
PHONE...............................321 638-0301
Stephen Johns, *Owner*
▼ EMP: 10 EST: 2005
SALES (est): 285K **Privately Held**
WEB: www.sealiftusa.com
SIC: 3569 Jacks, hydraulic

(G-8597)
STAMP CONCRETE & PAVERS
INC
230 Cherry Ave (32953-4310)
PHONE...............................561 880-1527
Denise A Spiva, *Principal*
EMP: 8 EST: 2012
SALES (est): 231.9K **Privately Held**
SIC: 3531 Pavers

(G-8598)
SUNDOG SOFTWARE LLC
Also Called: Sundog Education
4022 Tradewinds Trl (32953-8077)
PHONE...............................425 635-8683
Frank Kane,
Frank J Kane,
EMP: 5 EST: 2009
SALES (est): 414K **Privately Held**
WEB: www.sundog-soft.com
SIC: 7372 Business oriented computer
software

(G-8599)
TOM HAGGETTS PRESSURE
CLEANING
3781 Sierra Dr (32953-8035)
PHONE...............................407 932-0140
Tom Haggett, *Owner*
EMP: 5 EST: 2013
SALES (est): 605.5K **Privately Held**
SIC: 3399 Primary metal products

(G-8600)
TRASPORT JOHN
Also Called: American Cabinet Mill & Supply
645 S Plumosa St Ste 5 (32952-3108)
PHONE...............................321 452-6789
John Trasport, *Owner*
EMP: 7 EST: 1992
SALES (est): 573.1K **Privately Held**
SIC: 2541 Cabinets, except refrigerated:
show, display, etc.: wood

(G-8601)
TROPICAL SIGNS & GRAPHICS
425 Deb Ln (32952-4915)
PHONE...............................321 458-7742
Maria G Christel, *Principal*
EMP: 8 EST: 2016
SALES (est): 254.6K **Privately Held**
WEB: www.tropicalsignsmerrittisland.com
SIC: 3993 Signs & advertising specialties

(G-8602)
TUA SYSTEMS INC
Also Called: AMS
3645 N Courtenay Pkwy (32953-8104)
PHONE...............................321 453-3200
Ted Unkel Jr, *President*
EMP: 9 EST: 1988
SQ FT: 7,500
SALES (est): 945.5K **Privately Held**
WEB: www.tua-systems.com
SIC: 3479 Coating of metals & formed
products

(G-8603)
TUA SYSTEMS OF FLORIDA INC
3645 N Courtenay Pkwy (32953-8104)
PHONE...............................321 341-4944
Theodore Lawrence Unkel, *Principal*
EMP: 10 EST: 1989
SALES (est): 523.1K **Privately Held**
WEB: www.tua-systems.com
SIC: 3479 Coating of metals & formed
products

(G-8604)
TWINOXIDE-USA INC
3700 N Courtenay Pkwy (32953-8193)
PHONE...............................321 207-8524
Donald Lenci, *CEO*
Johannes G Verwater, *President*
EMP: 7 EST: 2015
SALES (est): 248K **Privately Held**
WEB: www.aarondotjpeg.com
SIC: 3589 Water treatment equipment, in-
dustrial

Miami
Miami-Dade County

(G-8605)
123 DOLLAR PLUS INC
7181 Sw 8th St (33144-4659)
PHONE...............................305 456-4561
Jazmin G Martinez, *Principal*
EMP: 7 EST: 2010
SALES (est): 122K **Privately Held**
SIC: 3643 Outlets, electric: convenience

(G-8606)
1600 LENOX LLC
7350 Biscayne Blvd (33138-5151)
PHONE...............................786 360-2553
EMP: 6 EST: 2018
SALES (est): 437.9K **Privately Held**
SIC: 3585 Refrigeration & heating equip-
ment

(G-8607)
1SOURCE BIOTECHNOLOGY
LLC
4300 Sw 73rd Ave (33155-4512)
PHONE...............................305 668-5888
Robert Dicrisci, *Principal*
EMP: 8 EST: 2011
SALES (est): 312.6K **Privately Held**
SIC: 2834 Pharmaceutical preparations

(G-8608)
2 GUYS COMPANY
9315 Sw 77th Ave Apt 228 (33156-7922)
PHONE...............................786 970-9275
Daniel Avalos, *Vice Pres*
EMP: 8 EST: 2016
SALES (est): 280.2K **Privately Held**
SIC: 3999 Candles

(G-8609)
360 ENERGY SOLUTIONS LLC
7650 Nw 50th St (33166-4700)
PHONE...............................786 348-2156
Antonio Noa, *President*
Bryan Garcia, *Principal*
EMP: 23 EST: 2013
SALES (est): 6MM **Privately Held**
WEB: www.360energysolutions.net
SIC: 3519 3621 Gas engine rebuilding;
motors & generators; power generators

(G-8610)
3LMETALS INC
12987 Sw 19th Ter (33175-1309)
PHONE...............................305 497-4038
Erick Arce Zubizarreta, *Principal*
EMP: 10 EST: 2018
SALES (est): 592.4K **Privately Held**
SIC: 3441 Fabricated structural metal

(G-8611)
4ELEMENTUM LLC
9149 Sw 157th Ct (33196-1167)
PHONE...............................305 989-1106
Jennifer Pinillos, *Chairman*
EMP: 7 EST: 2013
SALES (est): 233.3K **Privately Held**
WEB: www.4elementum.com
SIC: 2844 Toilet preparations

(G-8612)
A & A ORTHOPEDICS MFG
12250 Sw 129th Ct Ste 101 (33186-6492)
PHONE...............................305 256-8119
Migdalia Ugarte, *President*
EMP: 6 EST: 2016
SQ FT: 1,500
SALES (est): 387.9K **Privately Held**
WEB: www.aaorthopedics.com
SIC: 3842 Abdominal supporters, braces &
trusses; cervical collars; braces, orthope-
dic; braces, elastic

(G-8613)
A & C CONCRETE PRODUCTS
INC
9741 Sw 168th Ter (33157-4325)
P.O. Box 561094 (33256-1094)
PHONE...............................305 232-1631
David E Cunningham, *President*
EMP: 5 EST: 2001
SQ FT: 1,566
SALES (est): 345K **Privately Held**
SIC: 3272 Concrete products

(G-8614)
A & J AEROSPACE CORP
8356 Nw 66th St (33166-2674)
PHONE...............................786 564-9986
Mayra Martin, *Principal*
EMP: 9 EST: 2018
SALES (est): 270.4K **Privately Held**
SIC: 3599 Machine shop, jobbing & repair

(G-8615)
A & S ENTERTAINMENT LLC
Also Called: Office, The
250 Ne 183rd St (33179-4507)
PHONE...............................305 627-3456
Alix Beaubrun, *Mng Member*
Claudette M Pierre,
▼ EMP: 10 EST: 2010
SALES (est): 958.9K **Privately Held**
SIC: 2253 Lounge, bed & leisurewear

(G-8616)
A 1 A SIGNS & SERVICE INC
Also Called: A 1a Displays
8965 Ne 10th Ave (33138-3337)
PHONE...............................305 757-6950
Ira Knigin, *President*
Paula Knigin, *Vice Pres*
EMP: 9 EST: 1968
SQ FT: 8,000
SALES (est): 410.4K **Privately Held**
WEB: www.a1asigns.com
SIC: 3993 Electric signs

(G-8617)
A AND A CONCRETE BLOCK INC
4410 Sw 115th Ave (33165-5526)
PHONE...............................305 986-5128
Jose Atanay, *Principal*
EMP: 9 EST: 2006
SALES (est): 130.6K **Privately Held**
SIC: 3271 Blocks, concrete or cinder: stan-
dard

(G-8618)
A AND A ORTHOPEDICS INC
12250 Sw 129th Ct Ste 101 (33186-6492)
P.O. Box 441645 (33144-1645)
PHONE...............................305 256-8119
Migdalia Ugarte, *President*
EMP: 7 EST: 2000
SALES (est): 496.5K **Privately Held**
WEB: www.aaorthopedics.com
SIC: 3842 Prosthetic appliances

(G-8619)
A D COACHES CORNER INC
13365 Sw 135th Ave # 102 (33186-6220)
PHONE...............................786 242-2229
Alexander Diaz, *President*
EMP: 7 EST: 2005
SQ FT: 2,340
SALES (est): 597.7K **Privately Held**
SIC: 2759 Screen printing

(G-8620)
A FINE PRINT OF MIAMI LLC
Also Called: Lucy Print
2420 Sw 27th Ave (33145-3655)
PHONE...............................305 441-5263
Lucia Landsberg, *Mng Member*
EMP: 5 EST: 2008
SALES (est): 305.4K **Privately Held**
WEB: www.lucyprint.com
SIC: 2752 Commercial printing, offset

(G-8621)
A G A ELECTRONICS CORP
Also Called: AGA
7209 Nw 41st St (33166-6711)
PHONE...............................305 592-1860
Andre M Apaid, *President*
Renaldo Perez, *General Mgr*
Gerald Apaid, *Vice Pres*
Carlos Perez, *Treasurer*
◆ EMP: 12 EST: 1977
SQ FT: 13,000
SALES (est): 2.8MM **Privately Held**
WEB: www.agacorp.com
SIC: 2321 2361 2311 Men's & boys'
sports & polo shirts; t-shirts & tops: girls',
children's & infants'; men's & boys' uni-
forms

(G-8622)
A H WOODCRAFTER
7313 Nw 56th St (33166-4203)
PHONE...............................305 885-2136
Alcides Hernandez, *Principal*
EMP: 5 EST: 2008
SALES (est): 445.8K **Privately Held**
SIC: 3553 Bandsaws, woodworking

(G-8623)
A PLUS LAMINATION & FINSHG INC
5559 Nw 36th Ave (33142-2709)
PHONE..............................305 636-9888
Nubia Marcela Perez, *Owner*
EMP: 10 **EST:** 2006
SALES (est): 3MM **Privately Held**
WEB: www.apluslam.com
SIC: 2671 Paper coated or laminated for packaging

(G-8624)
A R COMPONENTS CORP
8544 Nw 66th St (33166-2635)
PHONE..............................786 703-8456
Ana Maria Soto Quintana, *President*
EMP: 13 **EST:** 2016
SALES (est): 873.3K **Privately Held**
WEB: www.aarcorp.com
SIC: 3728 Aircraft parts & equipment

(G-8625)
A SOTOLONGO POLISHING MARBLE C
5435 Sw 99th Ct (33165-7138)
PHONE..............................305 271-7957
Adolfo Sotolongo, *Principal*
EMP: 5 **EST:** 2002
SALES (est): 326K **Privately Held**
SIC: 3471 Polishing, metals or formed products

(G-8626)
A-MARI-MIX LLC
9700 Sw 24th St (33165-7500)
PHONE..............................305 603-9134
Mariela Reyes, *Principal*
EMP: 9 **EST:** 2014
SALES (est): 1.2MM **Privately Held**
WEB: www.amarimix.com
SIC: 3273 Ready-mixed concrete

(G-8627)
A-N-L HOME SOLUTIONS LLC
1000 Ne 196th St (33179-3514)
PHONE..............................954 648-2623
Nahum Gabriel,
EMP: 10 **EST:** 2020
SALES (est): 419K **Privately Held**
SIC: 3651 Home entertainment equipment, electronic

(G-8628)
A1CM SHADES AND BLIND INC
5521 Nw 7th Ave (33127-1401)
PHONE..............................305 726-3139
Juan Jose Castellanos, *President*
EMP: 10 **EST:** 2015
SALES (est): 575.6K **Privately Held**
WEB: www.a1-cm.com
SIC: 2591 Window blinds

(G-8629)
A2F LLC
Also Called: COMPOUND MIAMI THE
2010 Nw Miami Ct Unit A (33127-4920)
PHONE..............................305 984-9205
Bewille Datelma, *CEO*
EMP: 9 **EST:** 2016
SALES (est): 516.9K **Privately Held**
WEB: www.a2fstudios.com
SIC: 2741 7999 7922 Miscellaneous publishing; night club, not serving alcoholic beverages; entertainment promotion

(G-8630)
AAW PRODUCTS INC
Also Called: Mdg Tools
825 Brckhllday Dr Ste 246 (33130)
PHONE..............................305 330-6863
Andre Woolery, *President*
▲ **EMP:** 5 **EST:** 2005
SALES (est): 512.3K **Privately Held**
SIC: 3545 Tool holders

(G-8631)
AB USED PALLETS INC
6350 Nw 72nd Ave (33166-3626)
P.O. Box 667930 (33166-9408)
PHONE..............................305 594-2776
Anna Lesteiro, *Owner*
EMP: 12 **EST:** 2001
SQ FT: 1,080

SALES (est): 198K **Privately Held**
WEB: www.premier-pallets.com
SIC: 2448 3999 Pallets, wood; manufacturing industries

(G-8632)
AB WOOD WORK INC
13365 Sw 135th Ave Ste 10 (33186-8116)
PHONE..............................786 701-3611
Alexander Briceno, *Principal*
EMP: 7 **EST:** 2016
SALES (est): 302K **Privately Held**
SIC: 2431 Millwork

(G-8633)
ABAKAN INC (PA)
2665 S Byshr Dr Ste 450 (33133-5410)
PHONE..............................786 206-5368
Robert H Miller, *President*
Stephen Goss, *COO*
EMP: 9 **EST:** 2009
SQ FT: 800
SALES (est): 4.8MM **Privately Held**
WEB: www.abakaninc.com
SIC: 3479 Coating of metals & formed products

(G-8634)
ABB INC
Also Called: A B B Power Technolgies Div
8785 Sw 165th Ave Ste 302 (33193-5828)
PHONE..............................305 471-0844
Richard Lindo, *General Mgr*
Jukka Varis, *Vice Pres*
Lloyd Parsons, *VP Opers*
Adriana Andino, *Engineer*
Everett Jones, *Engineer*
EMP: 88
SALES (corp-wide): 28.9B **Privately Held**
WEB: www.abb.com
SIC: 3613 3625 3675 3612 Switchgear & switchboard apparatus; distribution boards, electric; generator control & metering panels; relays & industrial controls; electronic capacitors; power & distribution transformers
HQ: Abb Inc.
　305 Gregson Dr
　Cary NC 27511

(G-8635)
ABC SHUTTERS PROTECTION CORP
7420 Sw 38th St (33155-6612)
PHONE..............................785 547-9527
Alberto Quile, *Principal*
EMP: 7 **EST:** 2018
SALES (est): 280.7K **Privately Held**
SIC: 3442 Shutters, door or window: metal

(G-8636)
ABCO PRODUCTS INC
6800 Nw 36th Ave (33147-6504)
PHONE..............................888 694-2226
Carlos Albir Jr, *President*
Isacio Albir, *Vice Pres*
Christopher Meaney, *Vice Pres*
Luis Janania, *Officer*
Yanay Valladares, *Clerk*
◆ **EMP:** 27 **EST:** 1979
SQ FT: 5,000
SALES (est): 34.2MM **Privately Held**
WEB: www.abcoproducts.com
SIC: 3069 5199 Floor coverings, rubber; broom, mop & paint handles

(G-8637)
ABOVE GROUND LEVEL AEROSPACE
Also Called: Agl Aerospace
13420 Sw 131st St (33186-5817)
PHONE..............................305 713-2629
Francisco A Aracena, *President*
Dorys Acena, *General Mgr*
EMP: 12 **EST:** 2018
SALES (est): 1MM **Privately Held**
WEB: www.aglaerospace.com
SIC: 3721 Aircraft

(G-8638)
ABRACOL NORTH AMERICA CORP
5220 Nw 72nd Ave Ste 22 (33166-4858)
PHONE..............................305 431-5596
Peter Chirdaris, *President*

EMP: 5 **EST:** 2015
SALES (est): 462.8K **Privately Held**
SIC: 3291 Aluminum oxide (fused) abrasives

(G-8639)
AC INDUSTRIAL SERVICE INC
Also Called: A C Master Motors & Controls
14291 Sw 120th St (33186-7286)
PHONE..............................305 887-5541
Oscar Zelezniak, *President*
◆ **EMP:** 10 **EST:** 1979
SALES (est): 889.1K **Privately Held**
WEB: www.acindustrialservice.com
SIC: 7694 5084 Electric motor repair; engines & parts, air-cooled

(G-8640)
ACASI MACHINERY INC
7085 Nw 46th St (33166-5605)
PHONE..............................305 805-8533
Isaac Possin, *President*
Maria Brenes, *Office Mgr*
◆ **EMP:** 15 **EST:** 2002
SQ FT: 8,000
SALES (est): 4.3MM **Privately Held**
WEB: www.acasi.com
SIC: 3565 Packaging machinery

(G-8641)
ACCAR LTD INC
Also Called: Bezels For Watches
56 Ne 1st St (33132-2412)
PHONE..............................305 375-0620
Joseph Akar, *President*
EMP: 5 **EST:** 1993
SQ FT: 3,400
SALES (est): 659.1K **Privately Held**
WEB: www.watchstox.com
SIC: 3911 5094 Jewelry, precious metal; jewelry & precious stones

(G-8642)
ACCENDO TOBACCO LLC
7575 Nw 70th St (33166-2815)
PHONE..............................305 407-2222
William Hill, *Mng Member*
EMP: 5 **EST:** 2013
SALES (est): 1.1MM **Privately Held**
SIC: 2131 Smoking tobacco
PA: Ignis Group Inc.
　7575 Nw 70th St
　Miami FL 33166
　305 407-2222

(G-8643)
ACE PRINTING INC
Also Called: Ace Industries
2846 Nw 79th Ave (33122-1033)
PHONE..............................305 358-2572
Mario Cerratto, *President*
Andrea Ferreti, *Sales Staff*
▼ **EMP:** 18 **EST:** 1958
SQ FT: 12,000
SALES (est): 548.2K **Privately Held**
WEB: www.ace-printing.net
SIC: 2752 2796 3953 Commercial printing, offset; platemaking services; marking devices

(G-8644)
ACE RESTORATION SERVICES LLC
11921 Sw 130th St Ste 402 (33186-5256)
PHONE..............................786 487-1870
Juan Cabrera,
EMP: 15 **EST:** 2010
SALES (est): 1.6MM **Privately Held**
WEB: www.ace2restore.com
SIC: 3842 Cosmetic restorations

(G-8645)
ACE SALES CORP
Also Called: Sanacare
8085 Nw 68th St (33166-2794)
P.O. Box 561126 (33256-1126)
PHONE..............................305 835-0310
Frank A Maresma, *President*
Michelle Maresma, *Accounts Exec*
Lisbet Gonzalez, *Med Doctor*
Tony Falcon, *Director*
▼ **EMP:** 10 **EST:** 1957
SALES (est): 2.3MM **Privately Held**
WEB: www.sanacare.com
SIC: 3842 Linemen's safety belts

(G-8646)
ACM SCREEN PRINTING INC
2106 Nw 22nd Ct (33142-7346)
PHONE..............................305 547-1552
Luis Gutierrez, *President*
▼ **EMP:** 8 **EST:** 1996
SALES (est): 656.6K **Privately Held**
WEB: www.acmscreenprinting.com
SIC: 2759 7389 Screen printing; embroidering of advertising on shirts, etc.

(G-8647)
ACME SERVICE CORP
Also Called: Acme Miami
1290 Nw 74th St (33147-6428)
P.O. Box 380876 (33238-0876)
PHONE..............................305 836-4800
Chuck Levine, *President*
Gloria Levine, *Advt Staff*
▼ **EMP:** 10 **EST:** 1965
SQ FT: 14,400
SALES (est): 1.7MM **Privately Held**
WEB: www.acmemiami.com
SIC: 3585 3632 3621 7539 Refrigeration equipment, complete; household refrigerators & freezers; motors & generators; powertrain components repair services; pumps & pumping equipment

(G-8648)
ACRYPLEX INC
2380 Nw 21st Ter Unit A (33142-7206)
PHONE..............................305 633-7636
Aileen Lastra, *President*
Tomas Lastra, *President*
Mayra E Lastra, *Corp Secy*
Aileen I Lastra, *Vice Pres*
EMP: 6 **EST:** 1987
SQ FT: 3,500
SALES (est): 886.3K **Privately Held**
WEB: www.acryplexmiami.com
SIC: 3083 3732 1751 2542 Plastic finished products, laminated; boats, rigid: plastics; cabinet & finish carpentry; office & store showcases & display fixtures; marine hardware; doors, glass: made from purchased glass

(G-8649)
ACTION PRINTING INC
612 Nw 134th Ave (33182-1669)
PHONE..............................305 592-4646
William Tamayo, *President*
EMP: 5 **EST:** 1998
SALES (est): 344.8K **Privately Held**
WEB: www.actionprintinginc.com
SIC: 2752 Commercial printing, offset

(G-8650)
ADELMAN STEEL CORP
12040 Sw 113th Ave (33176-4402)
PHONE..............................305 691-7740
Marty Adelman, *President*
▼ **EMP:** 19 **EST:** 1927
SQ FT: 6,500
SALES (est): 1.4MM **Privately Held**
SIC: 3441 Fabricated structural metal

(G-8651)
ADMIRAL
1690 Ne 205th Ter (33179-2117)
PHONE..............................305 493-4355
Warren Copper, *Owner*
EMP: 9 **EST:** 2006
SALES (est): 570.7K **Privately Held**
SIC: 3732 Yachts, building & repairing

(G-8652)
ADONEL BLOCK MFG CORP
2101 Nw 110th Ave (33172-1904)
PHONE..............................561 615-9500
EMP: 11 **EST:** 2019
SALES (est): 159.9K **Privately Held**
WEB: www.adonelconcrete.com
SIC: 3999 Manufacturing industries

(G-8653)
ADONEL CON PMPG FNSHG S FLA IN (PA)
2101 Nw 110th Ave (33172-1904)
P.O. Box 226950 (33222-6950)
PHONE..............................305 392-5416
Gerardo L Garcia, *President*
Irvyn Rivas, *Purch Agent*
Alan Silverman, *Controller*

▲ = Import ▼ =Export
◆ =Import/Export

Alexander Sarite, *Bookkeeper*
Fatima Dominguez, *Credit Staff*
▼ EMP: 82 EST: 1993
SALES (est): 52MM Privately Held
WEB: www.adonelconcrete.com
SIC: 3273 1771 Ready-mixed concrete;
concrete pumping

(G-8654)
ADORGRAF CORP
7770 Nw 64th St (33166-2705)
PHONE..................................786 752-1680
Ruben Valladares, *President*
EMP: 8 EST: 2019
SALES (est): 409.3K Privately Held
WEB: www.adorgrafus.com
SIC: 2752 Commercial printing, litho-
graphic

(G-8655)
ADRENALINE PRODUCTIONS
LLC
Also Called: Jacu Coffee
1200 Brickell Ave # 1950 (33131-3214)
PHONE..................................305 697-6445
EMP: 7 EST: 2019
SALES (est): 299.9K Privately Held
WEB: www.adrenalinefilms.com
SIC: 2095 Roasted coffee

(G-8656)
ADVANCE ONE WHEELS INC
Also Called: Adv1
14397 Sw 143rd Ct Ste 105 (33186-6730)
PHONE..................................305 238-5833
Jordan Swerdloff, *President*
Mike Burroughs, *CFO*
Michael Espinel, *Admin Sec*
▲ EMP: 15 EST: 2010
SQ FT: 15,000
SALES (est): 2.8MM Privately Held
SIC: 3312 Wheels

(G-8657)
ADVANCED BIOPROCESS LLC
3200 Nw 67th Ave Bldg 3 (33166-2239)
PHONE..................................305 927-3661
EMP: 7 EST: 2017
SALES (est): 125.4K Privately Held
SIC: 2835 Microbiology & virology diagnos-
tic products

(G-8658)
ADVERTISERS PRESS
4135 Sw 108th Ct (33165-4826)
PHONE..................................305 879-3227
EMP: 7 EST: 2019
SALES (est): 89.3K Privately Held
WEB: www.adpress.com
SIC: 2741 Miscellaneous publishing

(G-8659)
AE TENT LLC
Also Called: Economy Tent International
2995 Nw 75th St (33147-5943)
PHONE..................................305 691-0191
Helen Bage, *Sales Staff*
Hal Paul Lapping, *Manager*
EMP: 40 EST: 2011
SALES (est): 8.3MM
SALES (corp-wide): 45.7MM Privately
Held
WEB: www.economytent.com
SIC: 2394 Tents: made from purchased
materials
PA: Anchor Industries Inc.
1100 Burch Dr
Evansville IN 47725
812 867-2421

(G-8660)
AENOVA NORTH AMERICA INC
14193 Sw 119th Ave (33186-6013)
PHONE..................................786 345-5505
Markus Nussbaumer, *President*
Brad Carlson, *Vice Pres*
EMP: 32 EST: 1994
SALES (est): 5.5MM Privately Held
SIC: 2834 Pharmaceutical preparations

(G-8661)
AERCAP LEASING USA I LLC
801 Brickell Ave Ste 1500 (33131-4901)
PHONE..................................425 237-4000
EMP: 11 EST: 1989

SALES (est): 327.6K Privately Held
WEB: www.aercap.com
SIC: 3721 7359 8711 Aircraft; aircraft
rental; aviation &/or aeronautical engineering

(G-8662)
AERO TECHNOLOGY MFG INC
7735 Nw 64th St Ste 1 (33166-3501)
PHONE..................................305 345-7747
Bruno Diaz, *General Mgr*
Claudia Diaz, *Principal*
EMP: 10 EST: 2016
SQ FT: 5,550
SALES (est): 1.3MM Privately Held
WEB: www.atmcorp.net
SIC: 3469 7539 3599 Machine parts,
stamped or pressed metal; machine shop,
automotive; machine & other job shop
work

(G-8663)
AEROTOOLS CONNECTION LLC
12625 Sw 134th Ct Ste 208 (33186-6423)
PHONE..................................305 234-3034
Dino Armetta, *President*
EMP: 7 EST: 2015
SALES (est): 598.2K Privately Held
WEB: www.aerotoolsconnection.com
SIC: 3728 5599 5088 Aircraft parts &
equipment; aircraft instruments, equip-
ment or parts; aircraft equipment & sup-
plies

(G-8664)
AFFORDABLE AT HOME HAS
INC
8870 Sw 40th St Ste 7 (33165-5465)
PHONE..................................786 200-0484
Diaz Jesus, *Principal*
EMP: 6 EST: 2016
SALES (est): 374.6K Privately Held
SIC: 3842 Hearing aids

(G-8665)
AFFORDABLE MED SCRUBS
LLC (PA)
Also Called: AMS Uniforms
888 Brickell Ave Ste 100 (33131-2913)
PHONE..................................419 222-1088
Ted Ralston, *President*
▲ EMP: 17 EST: 2003
SQ FT: 15,000
SALES (est): 9.7MM Privately Held
SIC: 2326 Medical & hospital uniforms,
men's

(G-8666)
AGAPE GRAPHICS & PRINTING
INC
14255 Sw 119th Ave (33186-6008)
PHONE..................................305 252-9147
Robert Winant Jr, *President*
Barbara B Winant, *Director*
EMP: 6 EST: 1989
SQ FT: 3,200
SALES (est): 490.9K Privately Held
WEB: www.agapegraphicsandprinting.com
SIC: 2752 Commercial printing, offset

(G-8667)
AGROTEK SERVICES
INCORPORATED
Also Called: Industrias De Aslntes Y Acero
6414 Nw 82nd Ave (33166-2734)
PHONE..................................305 599-3818
Yuri J Fernandez Camacho, *President*
Lisbeth 4 Cols De Fernandez, *Vice Pres*
▲ EMP: 8 EST: 2009
SALES (est): 942.5K Privately Held
WEB: www.agrotekservices.com
SIC: 2999 Coke

(G-8668)
AIOLOS GROUP INC
2529 Nw 74th Ave (33122-1417)
PHONE..................................305 496-7674
Alejandro Nasio, *Principal*
EMP: 5 EST: 2010
SALES (est): 941.5K Privately Held
WEB: www.aiolos-group.com
SIC: 3841 Surgical & medical instruments

(G-8669)
AIR ESSCENTIALS INC
Also Called: Air Essentials
7055 Sw 47th St (33155-4651)
PHONE..................................305 446-1670
Spence Levy, *President*
Marc Levy, *Exec VP*
John Cejka, *Vice Pres*
Walter Nunez, *Controller*
EMP: 32 EST: 2007
SQ FT: 8,500
SALES (est): 5.5MM Privately Held
WEB: www.airesscentials.com
SIC: 2869 Perfume materials, synthetic

(G-8670)
AIR OPERATIONS
4000 Nw 28th St (33142-5612)
PHONE..................................305 871-5449
Mario La Torre, *Principal*
EMP: 9 EST: 2010
SALES (est): 260K Privately Held
SIC: 3728 Aircraft parts & equipment

(G-8671)
AIR PURIFYING SYSTEMS INC
3750 Nw 28th St Unit 206 (33142-6204)
PHONE..................................954 962-0450
Carlos Jimenez, *President*
EMP: 6 EST: 1999
SQ FT: 1,500
SALES (est): 459.4K Privately Held
WEB: www.pure-air.com
SIC: 3564 Air purification equipment

(G-8672)
AIRAM STONE DESIGNS INC
8900 Sw 104th St (33176-3714)
PHONE..................................305 477-8009
Maria Garcia, *President*
Freddy Castillo, *Vice Pres*
▼ EMP: 7 EST: 2001
SALES (est): 777.5K Privately Held
WEB: www.airamstonedesigns.com
SIC: 3281 Curbing, granite or stone; mar-
ble, building: cut & shaped

(G-8673)
AIRCO PLATING COMPANY INC
3650 Nw 46th St (33142-3944)
PHONE..................................305 633-2476
Michael King, *President*
George L King, *President*
I Stanley Levine, *Treasurer*
Cynthia Randall, *Office Mgr*
Sherry Morris, *Director*
EMP: 42 EST: 1955
SQ FT: 30,000
SALES (est): 4.9MM Privately Held
WEB: www.aircoplating.com
SIC: 3471 Electroplating of metals or
formed products

(G-8674)
AIRCON FLEET MANAGEMENT
CORP
12334 Sw 131st Ave (33186-6484)
PHONE..................................305 234-8174
Noel Caballero, *President*
EMP: 26 EST: 2012
SALES (est): 1.8MM Privately Held
WEB: www.airconfleetmanagement.com
SIC: 3728 8741 8734 Research & dev by
manuf., aircraft parts & auxiliary equip;
management services; calibration & certi-
fication

(G-8675)
AIRE-TECH ROTORCRAFT SVCS
LLC
6270 Nw 37th Ave (33147-7522)
PHONE..................................305 696-8001
EMP: 12
SALES (est): 734.6K Privately Held
SIC: 3728 Mfg Aircraft Parts/Equipment

(G-8676)
AIRFREE USA LLC
25 Se 2nd Ave Ste 1235 (33131-1606)
PHONE..................................305 772-6577
Carlos Matias, *Manager*
EMP: 8 EST: 2017
SALES (est): 982.6K Privately Held
WEB: www.airfree.com
SIC: 3634 Air purifiers, portable

PA: Airfree - Produtos ElectrOnicos, S.A.
Rua Julieta FerrAo, Torre 10 9o
Lisboa 1600-

(G-8677)
AIT USA CORP
Also Called: Atlantic Island Trading
8485 Nw 74th St (33166-2325)
PHONE..................................786 953-5918
Jose A Paradiso, *CEO*
Jose C De Faria, *Director*
Alexander Fernandes, *Director*
EMP: 6 EST: 2015
SQ FT: 6,500
SALES (est): 967.3K Privately Held
SIC: 2032 5141 Italian foods: packaged in
cans, jars, etc.; food brokers

(G-8678)
AJ CHEM ENTERPRISES LLC
14261 Sw 120th St (33186-7270)
PHONE..................................754 203-6714
Riyaz Nasir,
EMP: 10
SALES (est): 409.5K Privately Held
SIC: 2833 Botanical products, medicinal:
ground, graded or milled

(G-8679)
AL-RITE FRUITS AND SYRUPS
INC
Also Called: Master Syrup Makers
18524 Ne 2nd Ave (33179-4427)
PHONE..................................305 652-2540
Steve Bragg, *President*
William M S Bragg, *President*
Clifford Spring, *Controller*
Anne Efros, *Admin Sec*
▲ EMP: 9 EST: 1964
SQ FT: 8,500
SALES (est): 1.1MM Privately Held
WEB: www.al-rite.com
SIC: 2087 2099 2086 Beverage bases;
concentrates, drink; syrups, drink; cocktail
mixes, nonalcoholic; food preparations;
bottled & canned soft drinks

(G-8680)
ALBASOL LLC
325 S Biscayne Blvd (33131-2306)
PHONE..................................830 334-3280
Alejandro Solis, *Principal*
EMP: 7 EST: 2012
SALES (est): 345.9K Privately Held
WEB: www.harvest-pipeline.com
SIC: 1382 Oil & gas exploration services

(G-8681)
ALBERT J ANGEL
1895 Ne 214th Ter (33179-1532)
PHONE..................................954 718-3000
Barry Leeper, *Founder*
EMP: 7 EST: 2017
SALES (est): 131.5K Privately Held
SIC: 3578 Calculating & accounting equip-
ment

(G-8682)
ALDANAS PAVERS INC
3281 Nw 18th St (33125-1837)
PHONE..................................305 970-5339
Ingrid M Aldana, *President*
EMP: 9 EST: 2005
SALES (est): 109.9K Privately Held
SIC: 2951 Asphalt paving mixtures &
blocks

(G-8683)
ALDORA ALUMINUM & GL PDTS
INC (PA)
Also Called: Smith Mountain
7350 Nw 37th Ave (33147-5814)
PHONE..................................954 441-5057
Leon Silverstein, *President*
Joel Fletcher, *CFO*
Carin Novellom, *Treasurer*
Andrew Wiegand, *Admin Sec*
◆ EMP: 40 EST: 2013
SALES (est): 19.8MM Privately Held
WEB: www.aldoraglass.com
SIC: 3354 3211 5039 Aluminum extruded
products; structural glass; structural as-
semblies, prefabricated: non-wood; glass
construction materials

(G-8684)
ALFA MANUFACTURING LLC
4701 Nw 77th Ave (33166-5521)
PHONE...................................305 436-8150
Alejandro Valdes Mana, *Principal*
▲ EMP: 12 EST: 2013
SALES (est): 1.7MM **Privately Held**
SIC: 2833 Vitamins, natural or synthetic:
bulk, uncompounded

(G-8685)
ALFRESCO AIR
690 Sw 1st Ct Unit Cui (33130-2991)
PHONE...................................786 275-5111
Fabricio Cordoba, *President*
EMP: 14 EST: 2017
SALES (est): 975.4K **Privately Held**
SIC: 1389 Oil & gas field services

(G-8686)
ALGY TRIMMINGS CO INC
Also Called: Algy Dance Costumes
7478 Nw 54th St (33166-4811)
PHONE...................................954 457-8100
Herbert Lieberman, *Ch of Bd*
Susan Gordon, *President*
Laurie Godbout, *Corp Secy*
Shannon Berkstresser, *Marketing Staff*
Karen Clough, *Executive*
EMP: 60 EST: 1926
SALES (est): 12.6MM **Privately Held**
WEB: www.algyperforms.com
SIC: 2389 2339 Theatrical costumes;
women's & misses' outerwear

(G-8687)
ALIENWARE CORP
13462 Sw 131st St (33186-5891)
PHONE...................................786 260-9625
John Beekley, *VP Mktg*
Claudina Lopez, *Marketing Mgr*
Patrick Theodore, *Manager*
Christophe Maire, *Director*
Frank Azor, *Officer*
EMP: 7 EST: 2018
SALES (est): 447.7K **Privately Held**
WEB: www.alienware.com
SIC: 3571 Electronic computers

(G-8688)
ALL AMERICAN SEALCOATING LLC
1200 Brickell Ave # 1950 (33131-3214)
PHONE...................................305 961-1655
EMP: 7 EST: 2019
SALES (est): 768.4K **Privately Held**
WEB: allasco.business.site
SIC: 2952 Asphalt felts & coatings

(G-8689)
ALL IN ONE MAIL SHOP INC
Also Called: All In One Drect Mktg Slutions
11950 Sw 128th St (33186-5207)
PHONE...................................305 233-6100
Shelley Jacoby, *President*
▲ EMP: 10 EST: 1989
SQ FT: 16,000
SALES (est): 1MM **Privately Held**
WEB: www.allinonedirectms.com
SIC: 2752 Commercial printing, offset

(G-8690)
ALL MIAMI SIGNS INC
7508 Nw 55th St (33166-4220)
PHONE...................................305 406-2420
Gregory Perdomo, *Principal*
EMP: 12 EST: 2010
SALES (est): 401.4K **Privately Held**
SIC: 3993 Signs & advertising specialties

(G-8691)
ALL THINGS DIGITAL INC
Also Called: Atdsat
7213 Nw 54th St (33166-4807)
PHONE...................................305 887-9464
▼ EMP: 20
SQ FT: 10,000
SALES (est): 2.5MM **Privately Held**
SIC: 3679 Mfg Electronic Components

(G-8692)
ALL-JER CONSTRUCTION USA INC
12225 Sw 217th St (33170-2830)
PHONE...................................305 257-0225

EMP: 6 EST: 2008
SALES (est): 400K **Privately Held**
SIC: 1389 Oil/Gas Field Services

(G-8693)
ALLAPATTAH ELECTRIC MOTOR REPR
1746 Nw 21st Ter (33142-7438)
PHONE...................................305 325-0330
David Galdona, *President*
Miguel Betancourt, *President*
Gregory Gonzales, *President*
EMP: 7 EST: 1973
SQ FT: 4,000
SALES (est): 458.5K **Privately Held**
WEB: www.allapattahelectric.com
SIC: 7694 Electric motor repair

(G-8694)
ALLAPATTAH INDUSTRIES INC
Also Called: Lakewood Juices
1035 Nw 21st Ter (33127-4517)
P.O. Box 12311, Gainesville (32604-0311)
PHONE...................................305 324-5900
Thomas R Fuhrman, *CEO*
Vivian Calzadilla, *President*
Scott P Fuhrman, *COO*
Carmen Delgado, *Purch Agent*
Cathy Garcia, *Controller*
◆ EMP: 50 EST: 1956
SQ FT: 105,000
SALES (est): 15.3MM **Privately Held**
WEB: www.lakewoodorganic.com
SIC: 2037 5142 2033 Fruit juices; pack-
aged frozen goods; canned fruits & spe-
cialties

(G-8695)
ALLIED USA INCORPORATED
2824 Sw 138th Path (33175-6663)
PHONE...................................305 235-3950
Rodolfo Martinez, *President*
Ernesto Vila, *Vice Pres*
◆ EMP: 7 EST: 2000
SQ FT: 6,000
SALES (est): 1.6MM **Privately Held**
WEB: www.alliedusainc.com
SIC: 2865 5169 Food dyes or colors, syn-
thetic; chemicals & allied products
PA: Allied Industrial Corp., Ltd.
12f, No. 76, Dunhua S. Rd., Sec. 2
Taipei City TAP 10683

(G-8696)
ALM GLOBAL LLC
Also Called: Daily Business Review
1 Se 3rd Ave Ste 1750 (33131-1704)
PHONE...................................305 347-6650
Daniel Casey, *Partner*
Sherry Costello, *General Mgr*
Carley Beckum, *Editor*
Raychel Lean, *Editor*
Danielle Ling, *Editor*
EMP: 80
SALES (corp-wide): 202.2MM **Privately Held**
WEB: www.alm.com
SIC: 2759 2711 Commercial printing;
newspapers
HQ: Alm Global, Llc
150 E 42nd St
New York NY 10017
212 457-9400

(G-8697)
ALMANAC LLC
2223 Sw 22nd Ter (33145-3512)
PHONE...................................305 570-4311
Estibaliz N Brooks, *Branch Mgr*
EMP: 24
SALES (corp-wide): 129.6K **Privately Held**
WEB: www.almanac.com
SIC: 2711 Newspapers
PA: Almanac Llc
1457 Sw 14th Ter
Miami FL 33145
415 310-5143

(G-8698)
ALMAR INDUSTRIES INC
6301 Sw 157th Pl (33193-3684)
PHONE...................................305 385-8284
Alberto Gonzalez Jr, *Vice Pres*
EMP: 7 EST: 2012

SALES (est): 158.8K **Privately Held**
WEB: www.almarindustries.com
SIC: 3999 Manufacturing industries

(G-8699)
ALONSO DEFENSE GROUP LLC
5076 Nw 74th Ave (33166-5550)
PHONE...................................305 989-0927
Alonso F Juan, *Principal*
EMP: 7 EST: 2013
SALES (est): 339.4K **Privately Held**
WEB: www.ciguera.com
SIC: 3812 Defense systems & equipment

(G-8700)
ALOQUA GMS INC
400 Sw 107th Ave Fl 5 (33174-1434)
PHONE...................................786 673-6838
Alexander Calderon, *CEO*
EMP: 78 EST: 2010
SALES (est): 3.2MM **Privately Held**
WEB: www.aloquagmsinc.com
SIC: 2599 Furniture & fixtures

(G-8701)
ALTANET CORPORATION
7950 Nw 53rd St Ste 337 (33166-4791)
PHONE...................................786 228-5758
Lorena Altamirano, *Vice Pres*
EMP: 8 EST: 2012
SALES (est): 2.7MM **Privately Held**
WEB: www.altanet-corp.com
SIC: 3661 Telephone station equipment &
parts, wire
PA: Altielectronica Cia. Ltda.
Republica 89125 Amazonas
Quito

(G-8702)
ALTIRA INC
3225 Nw 112th St (33167-3330)
PHONE...................................305 687-8074
Ramon E Poo, *CEO*
Tino Poo, *General Mgr*
Ramon E Poo Jr, *Senior VP*
Anthony L Poo, *Vice Pres*
Cristina M Poo, *Vice Pres*
▲ EMP: 85 EST: 1984
SQ FT: 50,000
SALES (est): 25.1MM **Privately Held**
WEB: www.altira.com
SIC: 3085 2759 Plastics bottles; commer-
cial printing

(G-8703)
ALTIS AJU KINGWOOD LLC
175 Sw 7th St Ste 1106 (33130-2941)
PHONE...................................305 338-5232
Frank Guerra, *Principal*
EMP: 6 EST: 2012
SALES (est): 380K **Privately Held**
SIC: 3369 Nonferrous foundries

(G-8704)
ALTON MANUFACTURING INC
9511 Fontnbleau Blvd # 402 (33172-6824)
PHONE...................................305 821-0701
Moshe Engel, *President*
◆ EMP: 7 EST: 1980
SALES (est): 578.2K **Privately Held**
SIC: 3634 Personal electrical appliances

(G-8705)
ALUTECH CORPORATION
8548 Nw 64th St (33166-2627)
PHONE...................................305 593-2080
▼ EMP: 9
SQ FT: 6,000
SALES (est): 1.3MM **Privately Held**
SIC: 3442 Mfg Metal Doors/Sash/Trim

(G-8706)
ALWAYS FLOWERS INC
6955 Nw 52nd St (33166-4844)
PHONE...................................305 572-1122
Karen J Cohen, *President*
Elaine Chehebar, *Vice Pres*
Raquel Pena, *Manager*
Irma Hernandez, *Director*
▲ EMP: 12 EST: 1996
SALES (est): 1.1MM **Privately Held**
SIC: 3999 5992 Flowers, artificial & pre-
served; florists

(G-8707)
AMA WATERS LLC
Also Called: Amazonia Beverages
6701 Nw 7th St Ste 175 (33126-6033)
PHONE...................................786 400-1630
Gabriel Filassi, *CEO*
▲ EMP: 9 EST: 2010
SQ FT: 1,000
SALES (est): 955.4K **Privately Held**
SIC: 2086 Pasteurized & mineral waters,
bottled & canned

(G-8708)
AMADO WHEEL FINISHING
15050 Sw 137th St (33196-5747)
PHONE...................................786 732-6249
Amado A Fernandez, *President*
EMP: 7 EST: 2017
SALES (est): 230.1K **Privately Held**
SIC: 3471 Polishing, metals or formed
products

(G-8709)
AMAZON SERVICES INC
Also Called: Amazon Printers
7186 Sw 47th St (33155-4656)
PHONE...................................305 663-0585
Cristina Serralta, *President*
Linda Uriarte, *Marketing Staff*
Hector Medina, *Technician*
▼ EMP: 19 EST: 1987
SQ FT: 2,800
SALES (est): 1MM **Privately Held**
WEB: www.amazonprinters.com
SIC: 2752 Commercial printing, offset

(G-8710)
AMBA HAM COMPANY INC
6863 Ne 3rd Ave (33138-5510)
PHONE...................................305 754-0001
Ricardo Navarro, *President*
EMP: 6 EST: 1981
SALES (est): 691.6K **Privately Held**
WEB: www.ambaham.com
SIC: 2013 Ham, boiled: from purchased
meat; ham, boneless: from purchased
meat; ham, roasted: from purchased
meat; ham, smoked: from purchased
meat

(G-8711)
AMBER JEWELERS CORP
Also Called: Rafael Moreaun
36 Ne 1st St Ste 1002 (33132-2492)
PHONE...................................305 373-8089
Walter Suarez, *President*
EMP: 8 EST: 1968
SQ FT: 2,000
SALES (est): 450K **Privately Held**
SIC: 3911 7631 Jewel settings & mount-
ings, precious metal; jewelry repair serv-
ices

(G-8712)
AMBIANCE INTERIORS MFG CORP
7456 Sw 48th St (33155-4469)
PHONE...................................305 668-4995
Enrique Beltran, *Manager*
Jhonatan Rivera, *Manager*
EMP: 9 EST: 2012
SALES (est): 1MM **Privately Held**
WEB: www.ambinter.net
SIC: 3446 Architectural metalwork

(G-8713)
AMERICA TRADING INC
9355 Sw 144th St (33176-6820)
PHONE...................................305 256-0101
Fabio Chazyn, *President*
◆ EMP: 13 EST: 2001
SALES (est): 490.9K **Privately Held**
SIC: 2451 Mobile homes

(G-8714)
AMERICAN BLIND CORPORATION
4232 Sw 75th Ave (33155-4425)
PHONE...................................305 262-2009
Rolando Rodriguiz, *President*
Jesus Sanchez, *Vice Pres*
Regino Rodriguez, *Director*
▼ EMP: 20 EST: 1982
SQ FT: 10,000

SALES (est): 1MM **Privately Held**
SIC: 2591 Blinds vertical

(G-8715)
AMERICAN CHIROPRACTOR
8619 Nw 68th St Ste C0138 (33166-2685)
P.O. Box 527948 (33152-7948)
PHONE..............................305 434-8865
Richard Busch Jr, *Ch of Bd*
Tracy Pate, *Publisher*
Heidi Garcia, *Sales Mgr*
James Busch, *Director*
Joseph Busch, *Director*
EMP: 10 EST: 2009
SALES (est): 717.5K **Privately Held**
WEB: www.theamericanchiropractor.com
SIC: 2721 Magazines: publishing & printing

(G-8716)
AMERICAN FRAME FURNITURE INC
1857 Nw 21st Ter (33142-7439)
PHONE..............................305 548-3018
Zoila Diaz, *President*
EMP: 6 EST: 1999
SQ FT: 10,000
SALES (est): 350K **Privately Held**
SIC: 2511 Wood household furniture

(G-8717)
AMERICAN HYGENIC LABORATORIES
Also Called: D' Lanerg
1800 Ne 114th St Ste J (33181-3415)
PHONE..............................305 891-9518
EMP: 10 EST: 1946
SQ FT: 5,000
SALES: 250K **Privately Held**
SIC: 2844 Mfg Toilet Preparations

(G-8718)
AMERICAN LED DISPLAY SOLUTIONS
8060 Nw 71st St (33166-2350)
PHONE..............................561 227-8048
Orlando Pavon, *President*
Guillermo Hanger, *Vice Pres*
EMP: 7 EST: 2015
SALES (est): 928.7K **Privately Held**
WEB: www.americanleddisplays.com
SIC: 3674 Light emitting diodes

(G-8719)
AMERICAN NATURAL PDTS LAB INC
7350 Nw 7th St Ste 101 (33126-2976)
PHONE..............................305 261-5152
Rodolfo Cruz, *President*
▲ EMP: 8 EST: 2000
SQ FT: 7,000
SALES (est): 1.5MM **Privately Held**
SIC: 2833 Vitamins, natural or synthetic: bulk, uncompounded

(G-8720)
AMERICAN STAINLESS MFRS (PA)
8390 Nw 68th St (33166-2655)
PHONE..............................786 275-4458
Jorge A Sanders, *President*
EMP: 7 EST: 2016
SALES (est): 436.4K **Privately Held**
SIC: 3312 Stainless steel

(G-8721)
AMERICAN WLDG & INSTALLATION
4851 Nw 36th Ave (33142-3909)
PHONE..............................786 391-4800
Jose M Carballo, *President*
EMP: 8 EST: 2011
SALES (est): 259.8K **Privately Held**
SIC: 7692 Welding repair

(G-8722)
AMERIFOOD CORP
1717 Nw 22nd St 6 (33142-7441)
P.O. Box 421852 (33242-1852)
PHONE..............................305 305-5951
Victor Angulo, *President*
EMP: 5 EST: 2015
SALES (est): 509.4K **Privately Held**
SIC: 2075 Soybean oil mills

(G-8723)
AMETS WOODWORKS CORP
1312 Nw 29th Ter (33142-6628)
PHONE..............................786 537-5982
Yorbi M Sequera, *President*
EMP: 7 EST: 2017
SALES (est): 85.2K **Privately Held**
SIC: 2431 Millwork

(G-8724)
AMG PRINTING SOLUTIONS CORP
2454 Nw 78th St (33147-5540)
PHONE..............................954 235-8007
Maurice D Gadson, *Principal*
EMP: 9 EST: 2016
SALES (est): 109.5K **Privately Held**
WEB: www.amgprinting.com
SIC: 2752 Commercial printing, offset

(G-8725)
AMIGO PALLETS INC
10251 Sw 109th St (33176-3464)
PHONE..............................305 302-9751
Olga L Alfonso, *Principal*
EMP: 10 EST: 2010
SALES (est): 265.2K **Privately Held**
WEB: www.amigopallets.com
SIC: 2448 Pallets, wood & wood with metal

(G-8726)
AMK PLASTICS LLC
7120 Nw 51st St (33166-5630)
PHONE..............................305 470-9088
Madelyn Hernandez, *President*
EMP: 9 EST: 2018
SALES (est): 620.8K **Privately Held**
WEB: www.amk-plastics.com
SIC: 3089 Bottle caps, molded plastic

(G-8727)
AMP AERO SERVICES LLC
12901 Sw 122nd Ave # 105 (33186-6279)
PHONE..............................833 267-2376
Natasha Marie Pinder, *Manager*
EMP: 11 EST: 2019
SALES (est): 3.3MM **Privately Held**
WEB: www.amp-aero.com
SIC: 3728 Aircraft body & wing assemblies & parts

(G-8728)
AMS GLOBAL SUPPLIERS GROUP LLC
200 S Biscayne Blvd (33131-2310)
PHONE..............................305 714-9441
Jose D Lacayo Vindas, *Mng Member*
EMP: 5 EST: 2015
SALES (est): 307.2K **Privately Held**
WEB: www.amscompostable.com
SIC: 3641 Electric light bulbs, complete

(G-8729)
AMTEC SALES INC
Also Called: Print Media
1594 Nw 159th St (33169-5635)
PHONE..............................800 994-3318
Robert Gonzalez, *President*
Mary Comas, *CFO*
Arturo Comas, *Controller*
Adrian Mandreanu, *Sales Mgr*
Mario Grandela, *Manager*
▲ EMP: 17 EST: 1993
SALES (est): 3.6MM **Privately Held**
SIC: 2754 2752 2759 2679 Business form & card printing, gravure; business form & card printing, lithographic; tag, ticket & schedule printing: lithographic; schedule, ticket & tag printing & engraving; pin tickets, paper: made from purchased paper

(G-8730)
ANDIRALI CORPORATION
Also Called: Andriali
1221 Brickell Ave Ste 900 (33131-3800)
PHONE..............................305 542-5374
Andrie Iglesias, *President*
Esra Andriali, *Founder*
▲ EMP: 5 EST: 2016
SQ FT: 1,200

SALES (est): 744.7K **Privately Held**
WEB: www.andrialicontract.com
SIC: 2299 2391 2392 2259 Batting, wadding, padding & fillings; curtains & draperies; cushions & pillows; curtains & bedding, knit; upholstery fabrics, woven

(G-8731)
ANMAPEC CORPORATION
5210 Nw 5th St (33126-5034)
PHONE..............................786 897-5389
Maria Clemente, *President*
Tito Clemente, *Vice Pres*
Angel Clemente, *Treasurer*
EMP: 11 EST: 1978
SQ FT: 5,000
SALES (est): 264K **Privately Held**
SIC: 2329 2339 2326 Men's & boys' sportswear & athletic clothing; sportswear, women's; men's & boys' work clothing

(G-8732)
ANTIFAZ WOODWORK INC
13365 Sw 135th Ave (33186-8116)
PHONE..............................786 306-7740
Alexander Briceno, *Principal*
EMP: 8 EST: 2012
SALES (est): 149.1K **Privately Held**
SIC: 2431 Millwork

(G-8733)
ANUE LIGNE INC
Also Called: A' Nue Miami
3300 Nw 41st St (33142-4306)
P.O. Box 520549 (33152-0549)
PHONE..............................305 638-7979
Lois Varat, *President*
EMP: 5 EST: 1990
SALES (est): 677.8K **Privately Held**
WEB: www.anuemiami.com
SIC: 2339 Women's & misses' outerwear

(G-8734)
APEX AVIATION GROUP LLC
801 Brickell Ave Ste 900 (33131-2979)
PHONE..............................305 789-6695
Eduardo Palma, *President*
EMP: 7 EST: 2016
SALES (est): 2.1MM **Privately Held**
WEB: www.apexaviationlv.com
SIC: 3728 Aircraft parts & equipment

(G-8735)
APPAREL IMPORTS INC
Also Called: Formal Wear International
10893 Nw 17th St Unit 126 (33172-2059)
PHONE..............................800 428-6849
Esperanza Campo, *President*
Arturo Alcantara, *Vice Pres*
Sandra P Vallejo, *Treasurer*
◆ EMP: 30 EST: 1989
SQ FT: 15,000
SALES (est): 4.9MM **Privately Held**
SIC: 2311 5137 5136 Formal jackets, men's & youths': from purchased materials; tuxedos: made from purchased materials; women's & children's clothing; men's & boys' clothing

(G-8736)
APPROVED PERFORMANCE TOOLING
Also Called: APT
8405 Nw 66th St (33166-2630)
PHONE..............................305 592-7775
Hyman Ash, *President*
Peter Field, *Corp Secy*
Richard Kandarian, *Vice Pres*
◆ EMP: 35 EST: 1971
SQ FT: 38,000
SALES (est): 1.2MM **Privately Held**
SIC: 3545 Drill bits, metalworking

(G-8737)
APURE DISTRIBUTION LLC
5555 Biscayne Blvd Fl 3 (33137-2656)
PHONE..............................305 351-1025
Uli Petzold, *CEO*
EMP: 15 EST: 2010
SQ FT: 6,000
SALES (est): 1.3MM **Privately Held**
WEB: www.apure-system.com
SIC: 3674 7349 Light emitting diodes; lighting maintenance service

(G-8738)
ARA FOOD CORPORATION
8001 Nw 60th St (33166-3412)
PHONE..............................305 592-5558
Alberto R Abrante, *Vice Pres*
Rick Samudio, *Plant Mgr*
Marta Devarona, *Purch Dir*
Marta E De Varona, *Treasurer*
Julia Leal, *Asst Controller*
◆ EMP: 60 EST: 1975
SQ FT: 7,000
SALES (est): 14.4MM **Privately Held**
WEB: www.arafood.com
SIC: 2099 Food preparations

(G-8739)
ARAYA INC
9582 Sw 40th St Ste 5 (33165-4064)
PHONE..............................305 229-6868
Adelys C Marquez, *Principal*
EMP: 8 EST: 2012
SALES (est): 256.4K **Privately Held**
SIC: 2066 Chocolate

(G-8740)
ARCA LLC
1220 Nw 7th St (33125-3702)
PHONE..............................305 470-1430
John Irvin, *Manager*
EMP: 13 EST: 2006
SALES (est): 410.1K **Privately Held**
WEB: www.arca.com
SIC: 3423 Jewelers' hand tools

(G-8741)
ARCHITCTRAL MLDING MLLWRKS INC
3545 Nw 50th St (33142-3931)
PHONE..............................305 638-8900
Shanon Siegfried, *President*
Scott Gumora, *Vice Pres*
Eric Siegfried, *Vice Pres*
Shanon Smith, *Info Tech Mgr*
▼ EMP: 17 EST: 1996
SQ FT: 42,000
SALES (est): 2.3MM **Privately Held**
WEB: www.millworks.biz
SIC: 2431 2439 Moldings, wood: unfinished & prefinished; structural wood members

(G-8742)
ARCHITECTURAL MOULDING CORP
3545 Nw 50th St (33142-3931)
PHONE..............................305 638-8900
Manuel Espinosa, *Principal*
EMP: 8 EST: 2010
SALES (est): 251K **Privately Held**
WEB: www.mouldings.cc
SIC: 2431 Millwork

(G-8743)
ARD PRINTING SOLUTIONS LL
14016 Sw 140th St (33186-5547)
PHONE..............................305 785-7200
EMP: 8 EST: 2018
SALES (est): 723.1K **Privately Held**
SIC: 2752 Commercial printing, lithographic

(G-8744)
ARDE APPAREL INC
Also Called: Denise Marie
1852 Nw 21st St (33142-7436)
PHONE..............................305 326-0861
Arturo A Dopazo, *President*
Hilda Dopazo, *Vice Pres*
EMP: 25 EST: 1981
SALES (est): 1.9MM **Privately Held**
SIC: 2335 Women's, juniors' & misses' dresses

(G-8745)
ARES DISTRIBUTORS INC
2601 S Bayshore Dr # 1150 (33133-5431)
PHONE..............................305 858-0163
Eduardo Rodriguez, *President*
Olga Michel, *Partner*
Giancarlo Orlando, *Vice Pres*
Jackelyne Rodriguez, *Vice Pres*
Felix Menendez, *Credit Staff*
EMP: 8 EST: 2009

SALES (est): 1.1MM **Privately Held**
WEB: www.aresdistributors.com
SIC: **2911** Gasoline blending plants

(G-8746)
ARGOS
12201 Nw 25th St (33182-1504)
PHONE..............................305 592-3501
EMP: 7 EST: 2015
SALES (est): 965.9K **Privately Held**
WEB: www.argos-us.com
SIC: **1422** Crushed & broken limestone

(G-8747)
ARGOS NAUTIC MANUFACTURING LLC (PA)
2600 Sw 3rd Ave Ste 800 (33129-2301)
PHONE..............................305 856-7586
EMP: 9 EST: 2015
SALES (est): 177.2K **Privately Held**
WEB: www.argosnautic.com
SIC: **3999** Manufacturing industries

(G-8748)
ARMADILLO SOUNDS INC
Also Called: Apara Productions
4246 Nw 37th Ave (33142-4224)
PHONE..............................305 801-7906
Enrique O Vega, *President*
Jeany Oliva, *Vice Pres*
EMP: 8 EST: 2001
SALES (est): 889.2K **Privately Held**
WEB: www.armadillosoundandstaging.net
SIC: **3648** 5099 Stage lighting equipment; video & audio equipment

(G-8749)
ARMANDO GRCIA CSTM CBINETS INC
220 Sw 30th Rd (33129-2726)
PHONE..............................305 775-5674
Armando R Garcia Jr, *Principal*
EMP: 7 EST: 2010
SALES (est): 283.8K **Privately Held**
WEB: www.agcustomcabinets.com
SIC: **2434** Wood kitchen cabinets

(G-8750)
ARMSTRONG POWER SYSTEMS LLC (PA)
5100 Nw 72nd Ave (33166-5607)
PHONE..............................305 470-0058
Enrique Villacrez,
◆ EMP: 7 EST: 1990
SQ FT: 13,000
SALES (est): 2.3MM **Privately Held**
WEB: www.armstrongpower.com
SIC: **3621** 5063 Generators & sets, electric; generators

(G-8751)
AROMA CHIMIE INC
1001 Brickell Bay Dr (33131-4900)
PHONE..............................305 930-5667
Saman Moradi, *President*
EMP: 50
SALES (est): 1.4MM **Privately Held**
SIC: **2048** Livestock feeds

(G-8752)
ARPI INTERNATIONAL CORPORATION
16275 Sw 208th Ter (33187-4421)
PHONE..............................305 984-9056
Marco A Prieto Puga, *President*
EMP: 14 EST: 2014
SALES (est): 1.2MM **Privately Held**
SIC: **3442** Metal doors, sash & trim

(G-8753)
ARTCO GROUP INC
5851 Nw 35th Ave (33142-2001)
PHONE..............................305 638-1785
Dan Romeu, *President*
Luis Victoria, *Exec VP*
Manuel Romero, *Vice Pres*
Martha Robles, *Buyer*
Mariela Corte, *Administration*
◆ EMP: 90 EST: 2001
SQ FT: 65,000
SALES (est): 12.1MM **Privately Held**
WEB: www.artcogroup.com
SIC: **2541** Store fixtures, wood; cabinets, lockers & shelving

(G-8754)
ARTEX COMPUTER LLC
4737 Nw 72nd Ave (33166-5616)
PHONE..............................407 844-2253
Angel Ramirez, *Mng Member*
Iriana Urdaneta,
EMP: 5 EST: 2015
SQ FT: 2,800
SALES (est): 449.5K **Privately Held**
WEB: english.artexcomputer.com
SIC: **3571** 3663 Minicomputers; mobile communication equipment

(G-8755)
ARTISTIC PAVER MFG INC
120 Ne 179th St Ste 1 (33162-1002)
PHONE..............................305 653-7283
Daniel Essig, *President*
Sandy Llorenty, *Accounting Mgr*
Sal Franco, *Sales Executive*
Eduardo Sznajderman, *Manager*
Rubens Defaria, *Officer*
◆ EMP: 50 EST: 2000
SQ FT: 60,000
SALES (est): 9.7MM **Privately Held**
WEB: www.artisticpavers.com
SIC: **2951** 3271 3251 Asphalt paving mixtures & blocks; concrete block & brick; brick & structural clay tile

(G-8756)
ARTS WORK UNLIMITED INC
22150 Sw 154th Ave (33170-4002)
P.O. Box 700513 (33170-0513)
PHONE..............................305 247-9257
Arthur Ballard, *President*
Phil Heermance, *Vice Pres*
Mary Peterson, *Manager*
Kathleen Ballard, *Admin Sec*
▼ EMP: 7 EST: 1972
SALES (est): 991.5K **Privately Held**
WEB: www.artsworkunlimited.com
SIC: **3446** 1799 Ornamental metalwork; gates, ornamental metal; fences or posts, ornamental iron or steel; fence construction

(G-8757)
ASB SPORTS GROUP LLC
Also Called: Storngerrx
801 Brickell Bay Dr (33131-2952)
PHONE..............................305 775-4689
Omar Cordero, *Mng Member*
EMP: 9 EST: 2005
SQ FT: 5,000
SALES (est): 385.4K **Privately Held**
WEB: www.game-one.com
SIC: **3949** Sporting & athletic goods

(G-8758)
ASG AEROSPACE LLC
12906 Sw 139th Ave (33186-5348)
PHONE..............................305 253-0802
Arthur Thompson, *Principal*
Art Thompson, *Maintence Staff*
Mariana Thompson, *Maintence Staff*
EMP: 7 EST: 2013
SALES (est): 1MM **Privately Held**
WEB: www.asgaerospace.com
SIC: **3721** Aircraft

(G-8759)
ASKA COMMUNICATION CORP
2020 Nw 129th Ave Ste 205 (33182-2438)
PHONE..............................954 708-2387
Toshi Nigorikawa, *President*
Debbie Okamoto, *Admin Sec*
◆ EMP: 7 EST: 1992
SALES (est): 988.1K **Privately Held**
WEB: www.askacom.com
SIC: **3663** Radio & TV communications equipment

(G-8760)
ASPEN ELECTRONICS INC
7288 Nw 54th St (33166-4808)
PHONE..............................305 863-2151
Edwardo A Trelles, *President*
EMP: 19 EST: 1985
SALES (est): 1.5MM **Privately Held**
WEB: www.aspenelectronics.us
SIC: **3679** Electronic circuits

(G-8761)
ASSOCIATED CARBONIC INDS LLC
8610 Sw 109th St (33156-3589)
PHONE..............................786 464-1260
EMP: 7 EST: 2008
SALES (est): 110.8K **Privately Held**
WEB: www.acidryice.com
SIC: **3999** Manufacturing industries

(G-8762)
ASSOCIATED MACHINE COMPANY INC
6540 Nw 35th Ave (33147-7563)
PHONE..............................305 836-6163
Jesse A Jones, *President*
Ellen M Smith, *Admin Sec*
EMP: 90 EST: 1963
SQ FT: 13,000
SALES (est): 15MM **Privately Held**
WEB: www.assocmachine.com
SIC: **3599** Machine shop, jobbing & repair

(G-8763)
ATLANTIC DRY ICE CORPORTION
6950 Nw 12th St (33126-1336)
PHONE..............................305 592-7000
Kenia Montejo, *President*
▼ EMP: 18 EST: 1988
SALES (est): 2.8MM **Privately Held**
SIC: **2813** 5169 2097 Dry ice, carbon dioxide (solid); dry ice; manufactured ice

(G-8764)
ATLANTIC SAILS MAKERS
Also Called: Uk Sails Makers
2801 Sw 31st Ave Ste 2a (33133-3540)
PHONE..............................305 567-1773
Mark Wood, *President*
EMP: 5 EST: 1977
SQ FT: 3,200
SALES (est): 383.4K **Privately Held**
SIC: **2394** Sails: made from purchased materials

(G-8765)
ATLANTIC STEEL CNSTR LLC
18851 Ne 29th Ave Ste 700 (33180-2845)
PHONE..............................419 236-2200
Brooke A Emrick, *Principal*
EMP: 5 EST: 2011
SALES (est): 515.5K **Privately Held**
WEB: www.atlantic-steel.com
SIC: **3449** Bars, concrete reinforcing: fabricated steel

(G-8766)
ATLANTIS PORCELAIN ART CORP
4241 Sw 154th Ct (33185-4259)
PHONE..............................305 582-8663
Jorge Martinez, *Principal*
Roberto Lodeiro, *Sales Mgr*
▲ EMP: 6 EST: 2008
SALES (est): 600.6K **Privately Held**
WEB: www.atlantisporcelainsink.com
SIC: **3431** Bathroom fixtures, including sinks

(G-8767)
ATLAS METAL INDUSTRIES INC
1135 Nw 159th Dr (33169-5882)
PHONE..............................305 625-2451
Joseph F Meade, *Ch of Bd*
David C Meade, *President*
Joseph F Meade III, *Vice Pres*
Mark Siegfriedt, *Vice Pres*
Tito Orozco, *Plant Mgr*
EMP: 120 EST: 1948
SQ FT: 52,253
SALES: 11.7MM
SALES (corp-wide): 94.5MM **Privately Held**
WEB: www.atlasfoodserv.com
SIC: **3589** 3523 3535 Commercial cooking & foodwarming equipment; driers (farm); grain, hay & seed; conveyors & conveying equipment
PA: Mercury Aircraft Inc.
8126 Cty Rd Rte 88
Hammondsport NY 14840
607 569-4200

(G-8768)
ATLAS PAPER MILLS LLC (DH)
3301 Nw 107th St (33167-3714)
PHONE..............................800 562-2860
Jim Brown, *President*
Reda Filali, *Vice Pres*
Scott Robey, *Vice Pres*
Greg Englert, *Sales Staff*
◆ EMP: 16 EST: 1979
SQ FT: 240,000
SALES (est): 49.7MM
SALES (corp-wide): 2.8B **Privately Held**
WEB: www.atlaspapermills.com
SIC: **2621** Toilet tissue stock; absorbent paper
HQ: Resolute Fp Florida Inc.
3301 Nw 107th St
Miami FL 33167
800 562-2860

(G-8769)
ATLAS POLYMERS CORP
1809 Micanopy Ave (33133-3329)
PHONE..............................786 312-2131
Adolfo S Rosendo R, *Vice Pres*
EMP: 11 EST: 2013
SALES (est): 940.7K **Privately Held**
WEB: www.atlas-polymers.com
SIC: **2821** Plastics materials & resins

(G-8770)
ATLAS RENEWABLE ENERGY USA LLC
1221 Brickell Ave # 1200 (33131-3224)
PHONE..............................786 358-5614
Carlos Barrera, *CEO*
Alfredo Solar, *General Mgr*
Javier Barajas, *CFO*
Diana Castellanos, *Marketing Staff*
Renato Valdivia, *Director*
EMP: 11 EST: 2016
SALES (est): 2.5MM **Privately Held**
WEB: www.atlasrenewableenergy.com
SIC: **3674** Solar cells

(G-8771)
ATTESA HOLDINGS GROUP LLC
2949 Coconut Ave Unit 20 (33133-3795)
P.O. Box 972330 (33197-2330)
PHONE..............................305 777-3567
Salvador J Juncadella III, *Principal*
Angel R Kerkado,
◆ EMP: 3 EST: 2012
SQ FT: 1,200
SALES (est): 5MM **Privately Held**
SIC: **2671** Plastic film, coated or laminated for packaging

(G-8772)
AURUM CHEMICALS CORP
9485 Sw 72nd St Ste A190 (33173-5417)
PHONE..............................305 412-4141
Rodrigo A Castellanos, *President*
▲ EMP: 5 EST: 1997
SALES (est): 401.3K **Privately Held**
WEB: www.aurum-chemicals.co
SIC: **2899** Chemical preparations

(G-8773)
AVAYA INC
1000 Nw 57th Ct Ste 100 (33126-3284)
PHONE..............................305 264-7021
Fax: 813 655-2088
EMP: 111
SALES (corp-wide): 4.3B **Privately Held**
SIC: **3661** Mfg Telephone/Telegraph Apparatus
HQ: Avaya Inc.
4655 Great America Pkwy
Santa Clara CA 27713
908 953-6000

(G-8774)
AVBORNE ACCESORY GROUP LLC (HQ)
Also Called: Sargent Aerospace and Defense
7500 Nw 26th St (33122-1404)
PHONE..............................305 593-6038
Scott Wargo, *General Mgr*
Gary Johnson, *Director*
EMP: 21 EST: 2015
SQ FT: 150,000

SALES (est): 40MM
SALES (corp-wide): 942.9MM **Publicly
Held**
SIC: 3728 Aircraft parts & equipment
PA: Rbc Bearings Incorporated
102 Willenbrock Rd Bldg B
Oxford CT 06478
203 267-7001

(G-8775)
**AVBORNE ACCESSORY GROUP
INC (DH)**
Also Called: Aersale Component Solutions
7600 Nw 26th St (33122-1416)
P.O. Box 522537 (33152-2537)
PHONE..................................305 593-6038
Nicolas Finazzo, *CEO*
Scott Wargo, *General Mgr*
Daniel Bergeron, *COO*
Harold Labbe, *Opers Staff*
Pedro Cabezas, *Buyer*
▲ EMP: 38 EST: 2004
SQ FT: 150,000
SALES (est): 43.7MM
SALES (corp-wide): 208.9MM **Publicly
Held**
WEB: www.aersale.com
SIC: 3728 Aircraft parts & equipment

(G-8776)
**AVERY DENNISON
CORPORATION**
5200 Blue Lagoon Dr # 130 (33126-7006)
PHONE..................................305 228-8740
EMP: 115
SALES (corp-wide): 6.3B **Publicly Held**
SIC: 2672 Mfg Coated/Laminated Paper
PA: Avery Dennison Corporation
207 N Goode Ave Fl 6
Glendale CA 44060
626 304-2000

(G-8777)
AVIACOL USA CORP
2299 Nw 108th Ave (33172-2022)
PHONE..................................786 701-2152
Hugo Francisco Fajardo, *President*
Harold Giovanny Bocanegra, *Vice Pres*
Antanas Jurksaitis, *Admin Sec*
EMP: 9 EST: 2014
SALES (est): 442.9K **Privately Held**
WEB: www.aviacolusacorp.com
SIC: 3728 Aircraft parts & equipment

(G-8778)
**AVIONICS SUPPORT GROUP
INC**
13155 Sw 132nd Ave # 200 (33186-6148)
PHONE..................................305 378-9786
Armand Wong, *President*
Hugo Fortes, *General Mgr*
Hugo L Fortes, *Vice Pres*
Alex Rodrigo, *Vice Pres*
Alex J Rodrigo, *Opers Mgr*
EMP: 20 EST: 1996
SQ FT: 2,400
SALES (est): 6.2MM **Privately Held**
WEB: www.asginc.net
SIC: 3728 Aircraft parts & equipment

(G-8779)
**AVON CORRUGATED/FLORIDA
CORP**
15600 Nw 15th Ave (33169-5604)
PHONE..................................305 770-3439
Selwyn Cain, *President*
Robert Farbish, *Vice Pres*
▼ EMP: 16 EST: 1989
SQ FT: 60,000
SALES (est): 432.6K **Privately Held**
SIC: 2653 Boxes, corrugated: made from
purchased materials

(G-8780)
AW PUBLISHING
3135 Sw 3rd Ave (33129-2711)
PHONE..................................305 856-7000
Anthony G Aguirre, *President*
Veronica Wolman, *Vice Pres*
EMP: 10 EST: 1995
SQ FT: 1,200
SALES (est): 911.5K **Privately Held**
SIC: 2759 2711 Schedules, transportation:
printing; newspapers

(G-8781)
AW-TRONICS LLC
100 Biscayne Blvd # 1315 (33132-2309)
PHONE..................................786 228-7835
Arash Caby, *Mng Member*
Catherine Caby, *Mng Member*
Marco Gutierrez, *Manager*
EMP: 20 EST: 2010
SALES (est): 2.2MM **Privately Held**
WEB: www.awtronics.com
SIC: 3672 Circuit boards, television & radio
printed

(G-8782)
AWE DIAGNOSTICS LLC
3401 N Miami Ave Ste 230 (33127-3546)
PHONE..................................786 285-0755
Luis A Urrea, *Principal*
Dr Pablo Guzman, *Principal*
Leon Levy, *Principal*
Joaquin Sabaris, *Principal*
EMP: 25 EST: 2020
SALES (est): 1.2MM **Privately Held**
SIC: 3829 Measuring & controlling devices

(G-8783)
AXXIUM ENGINEERING LLC
14032 Sw 140th St 16 (33186-5548)
PHONE..................................786 573-9808
Paul H Lopez, *Principal*
EMP: 5 EST: 2006
SALES (est): 365.8K **Privately Held**
WEB: www.axxiumengineering.com
SIC: 3715 Truck trailers

(G-8784)
**AYURDEVAS NATURAL
PRODUCTS LLC**
2076 Nw 21st St (33142-7316)
PHONE..................................786 322-0909
Jordi Verite, *Managing Prtnr*
Leonardo Gutter, *Managing Prtnr*
EMP: 9 EST: 2011
SQ FT: 3,000
SALES (est): 371.2K **Privately Held**
SIC: 2844 Toilet preparations

(G-8785)
**AZEX FLOW TECHNOLOGIES
INC**
Also Called: A F T
13431 Nw 19th Ln (33182-1909)
PHONE..................................305 393-8037
Carlos Matani, *President*
Alvaro P Diaz, *Vice Pres*
▼ EMP: 8 EST: 2003
SQ FT: 800
SALES (est): 1MM **Privately Held**
SIC: 3494 3491 7363 5085 Pipe fittings;
automatic regulating & control valves; in-
dustrial help service; valves & fittings

(G-8786)
**B & C SHEET METAL DUCT
CORP**
Also Called: Little Steps Daycare
1025 Sw 82nd Ave (33144-4241)
PHONE..................................305 316-9212
Arleny Barruelo, *Principal*
EMP: 9 EST: 2008
SALES (est): 996.3K **Privately Held**
SIC: 3444 Sheet metalwork

(G-8787)
B & G INSTRUMENTS INC
5000 Nw 36th St Bldg 875 (33166-2763)
P.O. Box 661073, Miami Springs (33266-
1073)
PHONE..................................305 871-4445
Robert L Brown, *President*
Robert Serra, *General Mgr*
Pablo Gonzalez, *Vice Pres*
Ady Lebrija, *Purch Mgr*
EMP: 12 EST: 1982
SQ FT: 3,600
SALES (est): 1.3MM **Privately Held**
WEB: www.bginstruments.net
SIC: 3829 Measuring & controlling devices

(G-8788)
**B AND M SUGAR PRODUCTS
LLC**
Also Called: B&M
936 Sw 1st Ave 345 (33130-4520)
PHONE..................................305 897-8427

Jurgen Murrle, *Mng Member*
Ana Maria Borrero, *Director*
▲ EMP: 2 EST: 2010
SALES (est): 16.7MM **Privately Held**
SIC: 2062 Cane sugar refining

(G-8789)
B&C PUBLISHING INC
13010 N Calusa Club Dr (33186-1704)
PHONE..................................305 385-8216
Maria Christina, *President*
EMP: 9 EST: 2000
SALES (est): 130K **Privately Held**
SIC: 2741 Miscellaneous publishing

(G-8790)
B/E AEROSPACE INC
6303 Blue Lagoon Dr (33126-6002)
PHONE..................................786 337-8144
Amin J Khoury, *Ch of Bd*
Kiran Chand, *Manager*
Aimee Elmquist, *Manager*
Bob Durk, *Director*
Thomas Ward, *Director*
EMP: 7
SALES (corp-wide): 64.3B **Publicly Held**
WEB: www.beaerospace.com
SIC: 2531 3728 3647 Seats, aircraft; air-
craft parts & equipment; aircraft lighting
fixtures
HQ: B/E Aerospace, Inc.
1400 Corporate Center Way
Wellington FL 33414
410 266-2048

(G-8791)
**BABY ABUELITA PRODUCTIONS
LLC**
6619 S Dixie Hwy Ste 139 (33143-7919)
PHONE..................................305 662-7320
Carol Fenster, *CEO*
EMP: 6 EST: 2007
SQ FT: 1,250
SALES (est): 303.4K **Privately Held**
SIC: 3942 Dolls & stuffed toys

(G-8792)
BACHILLER IRON WORKS INC
Also Called: BIW
295 Ne 71st St (33138-5527)
PHONE..................................305 751-7773
Felix Bachiller, *President*
Gypsy Bachiller, *Vice Pres*
EMP: 20 EST: 1993
SQ FT: 9,000
SALES (est): 2.6MM **Privately Held**
WEB: www.biwiron.com
SIC: 3446 Architectural metalwork

(G-8793)
BAG LADY DOLLS INC
4392 Sw 74th Ave (33155-4406)
PHONE..................................305 265-0081
EMP: 10 EST: 1994
SQ FT: 3,000
SALES (est): 886.4K **Privately Held**
SIC: 2499 Kitchen, bathroom & household
ware: wood

(G-8794)
**BAHAMAS UPHL & MAR
CANVAS INC**
4548 Sw 75th Ave (33155-4431)
PHONE..................................305 992-4346
Marina Fernandez, *President*
EMP: 14 EST: 2018
SALES (est): 1.3MM **Privately Held**
WEB: www.bahamasupholsterymiami.com
SIC: 2211 Canvas

(G-8795)
BAKER NORTON US INC
74 Nw 176th St (33169-5043)
PHONE..................................305 575-6000
Thomas Beier, *President*
RAO Uppaluri, *Treasurer*
Steven D Rubin, *Admin Sec*
Marianne Hurd-Nation, *Asst Sec*
EMP: 62 EST: 1986
SALES (est): 4.7MM **Privately Held**
SIC: 2834 Pharmaceutical preparations
HQ: Ivax Corporation
4400 Biscayne Blvd
Miami FL 33137
305 329-3795

(G-8796)
BARBECUE SUPERSTORE
Also Called: Weeks Gas Hme of The Brbc
Sprs
3800 Nw 59th St (33142-2032)
PHONE..................................305 635-4427
Jeffrey Miller, *President*
Freddy Royero, *Vice Pres*
Steve Kenorr, *CFO*
EMP: 7 EST: 2001
SQ FT: 30,000
SALES (est): 736K **Privately Held**
WEB: www.thebbqsuperstore.com
SIC: 2033 Barbecue sauce: packaged in
cans, jars, etc.

(G-8797)
BARCO LLC
475 Brickell Ave (33131-2498)
PHONE..................................305 677-9600
Victor Barroso, *Principal*
▼ EMP: 7 EST: 2010
SALES (est): 234.6K **Privately Held**
SIC: 3663 Radio & TV communications
equipment

(G-8798)
BARD SPORTS CORP (PA)
Also Called: Gold Eagle
14516 Sw 119th Ave (33186-6100)
PHONE..................................305 233-2200
Mitchel M Lombard, *President*
EMP: 9 EST: 1986
SALES (est): 750.3K **Privately Held**
WEB: www.bard.edu
SIC: 3949 Rackets & frames: tennis, bad-
minton, squash, lacrosse, etc; tennis
equipment & supplies; golf equipment

(G-8799)
BARNARD NUT COMPANY INC
Also Called: Nuts About Florida
2801 Nw 125th St (33167-2514)
P.O. Box 453636 (33245-3636)
PHONE..................................305 836-9999
Julio J Rosa, *President*
Jennifer Rosa, *Vice Pres*
Dinora Rosa, *Admin Sec*
▼ EMP: 60 EST: 1942
SQ FT: 30,500
SALES (est): 7.5MM **Privately Held**
WEB: www.nutsaboutflorida.com
SIC: 2099 2064 5145 Popcorn, pack-
aged: except already popped; nuts, candy
covered; popcorn & supplies; nuts, salted
or roasted

(G-8800)
BARON PAVERS CORP
3281 Nw 18th St (33125-1837)
PHONE..................................786 389-2894
Jorge Aldana, *Principal*
EMP: 8 EST: 2009
SALES (est): 453.4K **Privately Held**
SIC: 3531 Pavers

(G-8801)
BARRAU & COIRIN INC
Also Called: Sign-A-Rama
6214 Ne 4th Ct (33138-6106)
PHONE..................................305 571-5051
Lucien Barrau, *President*
Christine Barrau, *Vice Pres*
▼ EMP: 5 EST: 2005
SALES (est): 527.6K **Privately Held**
WEB: www.signarama.com
SIC: 3993 Signs & advertising specialties

(G-8802)
BARTON & GUESTIER USA INC
4700 Biscayne Blvd # 503 (33137-3200)
PHONE..................................305 895-9757
Phillippe T Marion, *CEO*
Jean-Luc G Noel, *CEO*
Hubert D Surville, *COO*
Laurent P Prada, *Vice Pres*
▲ EMP: 7 EST: 2011
SALES (est): 1.4MM
SALES (corp-wide): 80.7K **Privately Held**
WEB: www.barton-guestier.com
SIC: 2084 Wines
HQ: Barton & Guestier
Chateau Magnol
Blanquefort 33290
556 954-800

(G-8803)
BAUDUCCO MANUFACTURING INC
1705 Nw 133rd Ave Ste 101 (33182-2293)
PHONE....................................305 477-9270
Stefano L Mozzi, *President*
Leonardo T Dib, *Treasurer*
Ricardo Yuki, *Admin Sec*
Magdalena Lopez, *Asst Sec*
EMP: 12 EST: 2019
SALES (est): 3MM Privately Held
SIC: 2051 Bread, cake & related products; breads, rolls & buns
HQ: Bauducco Usa Holding Company
1705 Nw 133rd Ave Ste 101
Miami FL 33182
305 477-9270

(G-8804)
BAUDUCCO USA HOLDING COMPANY (DH)
1705 Nw 133rd Ave Ste 101 (33182-2293)
PHONE....................................305 477-9270
Stefano L Mozzi, *President*
Leonardo T Dib, *Treasurer*
Ricardo Yuki, *Admin Sec*
Magdalena A Lopez, *Asst Sec*
EMP: 4 EST: 2018
SALES (est): 3.7MM Privately Held
SIC: 2051 5149 Bread, cake & related products; crackers, cookies & bakery products

(G-8805)
BAYSIDE SMALL CAP SENIOR LOAN
1450 Brickell Ave Fl 31 (33131-3460)
PHONE....................................305 381-4100
EMP: 8 EST: 2016
SALES (est): 4.4MM Privately Held
SIC: 3313 Electrometallurgical products
HQ: H.I.G. Capital, L.L.C.
1450 Brickell Ave Fl 31
Miami FL 33131
305 379-2322

(G-8806)
BCC-BGLE CMMNCTONS CRP-CLRIN L
Also Called: El Clarin
8900 Sw 107th Ave Ste 30 (33176-1451)
PHONE....................................305 270-3333
Jose Noboa, *President*
▼ EMP: 11 EST: 1979
SALES (est): 951.5K Privately Held
WEB: www.elclarin.com
SIC: 2711 Newspapers, publishing & printing

(G-8807)
BCDIRECT CORP
Also Called: Robotray
15625 Nw 15th Ave (33169-5601)
PHONE....................................305 623-3838
Luis A Lacal, *President*
Juan Lacal, *Vice Pres*
EMP: 12 EST: 2000
SALES (est): 2.7MM Privately Held
SIC: 3569 Robots, assembly line: industrial & commercial

(G-8808)
BDD INTERNATIONAL CORP
Also Called: Sir Speedy
203 Nw 36th St Ste 2 (33127-3128)
PHONE....................................305 573-2416
Julio Bielich, *President*
Logo Bielich, *Vice Pres*
Martha Bielich, *Director*
Miguel Bielich, *Director*
Luis Bielich, *Admin Sec*
EMP: 8 EST: 1980
SQ FT: 2,100
SALES (est): 1.6MM Privately Held
WEB: www.sirspeedy.com
SIC: 2752 Commercial printing, lithographic

(G-8809)
BDNZ ASSOCIATES INC
Also Called: Fastsigns
9481 Sw 134th St (33176-5749)
PHONE....................................305 379-7993
Susan Chai-Onn, *President*
Roger D Chai-Onn, *Vice Pres*
EMP: 7 EST: 2004
SQ FT: 1,800
SALES (est): 934.8K Privately Held
WEB: www.fastsigns.com
SIC: 3993 Signs & advertising specialties

(G-8810)
BECKMAN COULTER INC
Also Called: Iris Diagnostics
11800 Sw 147th Ave (33196-2500)
PHONE....................................305 380-2175
Jorge Fernandez, *Engineer*
Luis Gamarra, *Engineer*
Juan Perdomo, *Engineer*
Jose Rabade, *Engineer*
Victor Rodriguez, *Engineer*
EMP: 15
SALES (corp-wide): 29.4B Publicly Held
WEB: www.beckmancoulter.com
SIC: 3826 Analytical instruments
HQ: Beckman Coulter, Inc.
250 S Kraemer Blvd
Brea CA 92821
714 993-5321

(G-8811)
BECKMAN COULTER INC
11800 Sw 147th Ave (33196-2500)
PHONE....................................305 380-3800
Jorge Fernandez, *Engineer*
Cruz Manderico, *Engineer*
Loti Marc, *Engineer*
Sergio Sanchez, *Engineer*
Carlos Centurion, *Human Res Mgr*
EMP: 191
SALES (corp-wide): 29.4B Publicly Held
WEB: www.beckmancoulter.com
SIC: 3826 Analytical instruments
HQ: Beckman Coulter, Inc.
250 S Kraemer Blvd
Brea CA 92821
714 993-5321

(G-8812)
BELLATRIX TRADE LLC
Also Called: International Trader Company
20225 Ne 16th Pl Fl 2 (33179-2719)
PHONE....................................786 536-2905
Marilyn Nozaki, *President*
Andre Nozaki, *Principal*
Tatiana Pellgrini, *Principal*
Jose Romero, *Principal*
EMP: 12 EST: 2020
SALES (est): 782.3K Privately Held
SIC: 3069 5047 6221 Fabricated rubber products; medical & hospital equipment; commodity traders, contracts

(G-8813)
BENFRESH LLC
7337 Nw 37th Ave Unit 3/4 (33147-5803)
PHONE....................................786 403-5046
Christian P Benazzi Lemme,
EMP: 6 EST: 2019
SALES (est): 305.1K Privately Held
SIC: 2033 Vegetable juices: fresh

(G-8814)
BERKANT CORP
6370 Nw 82nd Ave (33166-3427)
PHONE....................................305 771-5578
Rapahel Diaz, *Vice Pres*
EMP: 10 EST: 2017
SALES (est): 449.5K Privately Held
WEB: www.hilmiberkanttunc.com
SIC: 2844 Toilet preparations

(G-8815)
BERKSHIRE MANAGMENT ASSOCIATES
Also Called: Techcrete Archtectural Precast
12841 Sw 117th St (33186-4653)
PHONE....................................305 883-3277
Tom Ban, *Owner*
Gerry Mihalick, *Portfolio Mgr*
EMP: 11 EST: 2002
SALES (est): 105.3K Privately Held
SIC: 3273 Ready-mixed concrete

(G-8816)
BEST FINISHER
2780 Nw 122nd St (33167-2508)
PHONE....................................305 688-8174
Casimiro Saboya, *Owner*
EMP: 13 EST: 1978
SQ FT: 20,000
SALES (est): 750.9K Privately Held
WEB: www.bestfinishers.com
SIC: 3479 Coating of metals & formed products

(G-8817)
BEST TRUSS COMPANY (PA)
7035 Sw 44th St (33155-4643)
PHONE....................................305 667-6797
Antonio Sierra, *President*
Carlos Blume, *Vice Pres*
▼ EMP: 35 EST: 1987
SQ FT: 52,000
SALES (est): 8MM Privately Held
WEB: www.fortdallastruss.com
SIC: 2439 Trusses, wooden roof; trusses, except roof: laminated lumber

(G-8818)
BESTCANVAS INC
3343 Nw 107th St (33167-3714)
PHONE....................................305 759-7800
Daniel Muehlbauer, *President*
Philipp Muehlbauer, *Vice Pres*
▲ EMP: 11 EST: 2010
SQ FT: 5,000
SALES (est): 1.4MM Privately Held
WEB: www.canvasdiscount.com
SIC: 2211 Canvas

(G-8819)
BETABLOCKS COMPANY
54 Bay Heights Dr (33133-2606)
PHONE....................................424 353-1978
Roberto Machado, *CEO*
EMP: 7 EST: 2018
SALES (est): 330.9K Privately Held
WEB: www.betablocks.com
SIC: 7372 Prepackaged software

(G-8820)
BETTY ENGINES MACHINE SHOP INC
7120 Sw 44th St Ste A (33155-4638)
PHONE....................................305 458-1467
Marco Valcarcel, *Principal*
EMP: 8 EST: 2015
SALES (est): 155.7K Privately Held
WEB: www.birdroadmachine.com
SIC: 3599 Machine shop, jobbing & repair

(G-8821)
BEV-CO ENTERPRISES INC (PA)
2761 Nw 82nd Ave (33122-1041)
PHONE....................................786 362-6368
Enoc Martinez, *Principal*
EMP: 6 EST: 2009
SALES (est): 320.1K Privately Held
SIC: 2087 Beverage bases

(G-8822)
BEVERAGE CANNERS INTERNATIONAL
Also Called: BCI
3505 Nw 107th St (33167-3794)
PHONE....................................305 714-7000
Nick Cabrella, *President*
▼ EMP: 16 EST: 2002
SALES (est): 422K Privately Held
SIC: 2086 Soft drinks: packaged in cans, bottles, etc.

(G-8823)
BEVERAGE CORP INTL INC
3505 Nw 107th St (33167-3716)
PHONE....................................305 714-7000
Joseph Caporella, *President*
Nick Caporella, *Chairman*
George Bracken, *Vice Pres*
Alan Domzalski, *Vice Pres*
Dean McCoy, *Vice Pres*
◆ EMP: 100 EST: 1985
SALES (est): 13.4MM
SALES (corp-wide): 1.1B Publicly Held
WEB: www.nationalbeverage.com
SIC: 2086 Soft drinks: packaged in cans, bottles, etc.; water, pasteurized: packaged in cans, bottles, etc.; fruit drinks (less than 100% juice): packaged in cans, etc.
PA: National Beverage Corp.
8100 Sw 10th St Ste 4000
Plantation FL 33324
954 581-0922

(G-8824)
BEYOND WHITE SPA LLC
Also Called: Ezywipe of America
6725 Nw 36th St Unit 600 (33166-6807)
PHONE....................................866 399-8867
Alex Munoz, *Mng Member*
Carmelina Natale,
Cesar Sordo,
◆ EMP: 28 EST: 2014
SQ FT: 2,014
SALES (est): 1.9MM Privately Held
WEB: www.ezywipe.info
SIC: 2392 Towels, fabric & nonwoven: made from purchased materials

(G-8825)
BIG CYPRESS DISTILLERY LLC
13995 Sw 144th Ave # 207 (33186-8656)
PHONE....................................786 228-9740
Fernando Plata, *Mng Member*
Danny Garo,
Mark A Graham,
▼ EMP: 6 EST: 2015
SQ FT: 1,900
SALES (est): 499.3K Privately Held
WEB: www.bigcypressdistillery.com
SIC: 2085 Distilled & blended liquors

(G-8826)
BIJOL AND SPICES INC
Also Called: Bijol & Spices
2154 Nw 22nd Ct (33142-7346)
P.O. Box 420189 (33242-0189)
PHONE....................................305 634-9030
Ida M Borges, *President*
Iliat M Llamozas, *COO*
Diego Borges, *Vice Pres*
Ivette V Borges, *Admin Sec*
▲ EMP: 8 EST: 1962
SQ FT: 4,000
SALES (est): 879.1K Privately Held
WEB: www.bijol.com
SIC: 2099 5499 Spices, including grinding; spices & herbs

(G-8827)
BINGO BAKERY INC
2125 Nw 8th Ave (33127-4609)
PHONE....................................305 545-9993
Joel Gali, *President*
Ann Gali, *Corp Secy*
▲ EMP: 16 EST: 1975
SQ FT: 8,000
SALES (est): 303.6K Privately Held
WEB: www.bingobakery.com
SIC: 2052 Bakery products, dry

(G-8828)
BINICK DIGITAL IMAGING LLC
Also Called: Binickimaging
6220 Nw 37th Ave (33147-7522)
PHONE....................................786 420-2067
Nicholas Castillo, *President*
Bianca Castillo,
EMP: 10 EST: 2013
SALES (est): 1MM Privately Held
WEB: www.binickimaging.com
SIC: 3993 Signs & advertising specialties

(G-8829)
BIO-NUCLEONICS PHARMA INC
Also Called: Bio Nucleonics
1 Ne 19th St (33132-1030)
PHONE....................................305 576-0996
Stanley Satz, *President*
Rosanne Satz, *Vice Pres*
EMP: 18 EST: 2002
SALES (est): 301.2K Privately Held
SIC: 2834 Pharmaceutical preparations

(G-8830)
BIOCHEM MANUFACTURING INC
7300 N Kendall Dr Ste 640 (33156-7840)
PHONE....................................786 210-1290
EMP: 7 EST: 2019
SALES (est): 153.6K Privately Held
WEB: www.bmichem.com
SIC: 3999 Manufacturing industries

(G-8831)
BIOENERSOURCE INC
2951 Nw 21st Ter (33142-7019)
PHONE....................................786 797-0496
EMP: 7 EST: 2010
SALES (est): 195.2K Privately Held
SIC: 3533 Mfg Oil/Gas Field Machinery

▲ = Import ▼=Export
◆ =Import/Export

(G-8832)
BIRDIEBOX LLC
2129 Nw 86th Ave (33122-1527)
PHONE......................786 762-2975
Pat Depirro, *CEO*
Kristine Reeder, *Vice Pres*
Sharita McNealy, *Accounts Exec*
Caitlin Huiting, *Sales Staff*
Frances Gulick, *Marketing Staff*
EMP: 27 **EST:** 2014
SQ FT: 1,500
SALES (est): 9.6MM **Privately Held**
WEB: www.birdiebox.com
SIC: 2653 5199 7389 Boxes, corrugated:
made from purchased materials; gifts &
novelties; packaging & labeling services

(G-8833)
**BISCAYNE AWNING & SHADE
CO**
2333 Nw 8th Ave (33127-4216)
PHONE......................305 638-7933
Conrado Perez, *President*
Alicia Perez, *Corp Secy*
▼ **EMP:** 24 **EST:** 1924
SQ FT: 8,000
SALES (est): 933.9K **Privately Held**
WEB: www.biscayneawning.com
SIC: 2394 2591 Awnings, fabric: made
from purchased materials; canvas covers
& drop cloths; drapery hardware & blinds
& shades

(G-8834)
**BISCAYNE ELECTRIC MOTOR &
PUMP**
830 Nw 144th St (33168-3024)
PHONE......................305 681-8171
Peter Ross, *President*
John Birri, *President*
Sheila Birri, *Vice Pres*
▼ **EMP:** 5 **EST:** 1963
SQ FT: 1,500
SALES (est): 919.2K **Privately Held**
WEB: www.biscayneelectricmotor.com
SIC: 7694 5063 5999 Electric motor re-
pair; motors, electric; motors, electric

(G-8835)
BISCAYNE TENNIS LLC
19021 Biscayne Blvd (33180-2819)
PHONE......................786 231-8372
Alexander Pinto, *Mng Member*
Alberto Acosta, *Mng Member*
Horacio Pinto, *Mng Member*
EMP: 6 **EST:** 2012
SALES (est): 336.9K **Privately Held**
SIC: 3949 Tennis equipment & supplies;
fencing equipment (sporting goods)

(G-8836)
BLACKFIST MAGAZINE LLC (PA)
382 Ne 191st St Ste 73388 (33179-3899)
PHONE......................904 864-8695
Nicole Teamer,
EMP: 7 **EST:** 2018
SALES (est): 957.8K **Privately Held**
SIC: 2721 Magazines: publishing only, not
printed on site

(G-8837)
**BLANCO GOMEZ MALDONADO
LLC**
15588 Sw 72nd St (33193-1922)
PHONE......................305 380-1114
Jose T Gomez, *Owner*
EMP: 7 **EST:** 2010
SALES (est): 213.9K **Privately Held**
SIC: 2051 Cakes, bakery: except frozen

(G-8838)
BLINDS 321 INC
12335 Nw 7th St (33182-2048)
PHONE......................305 336-9221
EMP: 7 **EST:** 2019
SALES (est): 108.2K **Privately Held**
WEB: www.myblinds321.com
SIC: 2591 Window blinds

(G-8839)
BLINDS R US CORP
5946 Sw 162nd Path (33193-5666)
PHONE......................305 303-2072
Jorge Perez, *President*
EMP: 8 **EST:** 2010

SALES (est): 59.6K **Privately Held**
WEB: www.blindsr-us.com
SIC: 2591 Venetian blinds

(G-8840)
BLUES DESIGN GROUP LLC
Also Called: Green Surfaces
3724 Nw 43rd St (33142-4238)
PHONE......................305 586-3630
Ricardo Mucenic, *Mng Member*
▲ **EMP:** 9 **EST:** 2010
SQ FT: 8,000
SALES (est): 636.6K **Privately Held**
WEB: www.greensurfacesgroup.com
SIC: 2541 Counter & sink tops

(G-8841)
BMG AEROSPACE
245 Ne 14th St Apt 3701 (33132-1639)
P.O. Box 371558 (33137-1558)
PHONE......................786 725-4959
Brian Gordillo, *Principal*
EMP: 9 **EST:** 2016
SALES (est): 181K **Privately Held**
SIC: 3721 Aircraft

(G-8842)
BOATRAX CORP ✪
1901 Brickell Ave B201 (33129-1701)
PHONE......................855 727-5647
Arturo E Malave, *CEO*
EMP: 8 **EST:** 2021
SALES (est): 509.2K **Privately Held**
WEB: www.boatrax.com
SIC: 3429 Marine hardware

(G-8843)
**BOHNERT SHEET METAL &
ROOFG CO**
2225 Nw 76th St (33147-6092)
PHONE......................305 696-6851
William Marvel Jr, *President*
Christopher Marvel, *Corp Secy*
▼ **EMP:** 12 **EST:** 1912
SQ FT: 17,400
SALES (est): 2.5MM **Privately Held**
WEB: www.bohnertsheetmetal.com
SIC: 3444 Sheet metal specialties, not
stamped

(G-8844)
BOLD LOOK INC
6721 Nw 36th Ave (33147-6501)
PHONE......................305 687-8725
Kenneth Bold, *President*
Madelin Castillo, *General Mgr*
Janet Bold, *Principal*
Ericka Rodriguez, *Business Mgr*
Michelle Padilla, *Sales Staff*
▲ **EMP:** 32 **EST:** 1989
SALES (est): 6MM **Privately Held**
WEB: www.boldlook.net
SIC: 2389 Uniforms & vestments

(G-8845)
**BOLLOU TRANSPORTATION
LLC** ✪
11626 Ne 2nd Ave (33161-6104)
PHONE......................800 548-1768
Kevin Lecsaint, *Mng Member*
EMP: 10 **EST:** 2021
SALES (est): 360.4K **Privately Held**
SIC: 3799 Transportation equipment

(G-8846)
BOOSTAN INC
Also Called: Minuteman Press
8300 W Flagler St Ste 155 (33144-2098)
PHONE......................305 223-5981
Ray Dehbozorgi, *President*
Hamid Zolfaghari, *Vice Pres*
EMP: 5 **EST:** 1989
SQ FT: 1,200
SALES (est): 500K **Privately Held**
WEB: www.minutemanpress.com
SIC: 2752 2759 Commercial printing, litho-
graphic; thermography

(G-8847)
BORGESFS INC
14920 Sw 137th St Unit 2 (33196-5623)
PHONE......................786 210-0327
Amaury Borges, *Principal*
EMP: 7 **EST:** 2014

SALES (est): 117.7K **Privately Held**
WEB: www.aerospaceconnectionsinc.com
SIC: 3728 Aircraft parts & equipment

(G-8848)
BORIS SKATEBOARDS MFG INC
695 Ne 77th St (33138-5105)
PHONE......................305 519-3544
Matthew McNertney, *Principal*
EMP: 7 **EST:** 2010
SALES (est): 157K **Privately Held**
WEB: www.centurycarecherryville.com
SIC: 3949 Skateboards

(G-8849)
**BOSTON NTRCEUTICAL
SCIENCE LLC**
801 Brickell Ave (33131-2951)
PHONE......................617 848-4560
Daniel Shina, *Mng Member*
EMP: 10 **EST:** 2015
SALES (est): 1.1MM **Privately Held**
SIC: 2833 5122 Vitamins, natural or syn-
thetic: bulk, uncompounded; vitamins &
minerals

(G-8850)
**BOULDER BLIMP COMPANY
INC**
13350 Sw 131st St # 106 (33186-6187)
PHONE......................303 664-1122
Loni Gilfedder, *CEO*
Frank Rider, *President*
Ben Azadi, *Accounts Exec*
Dan Pagano, *Sales Staff*
Jessica Lila, *Office Mgr*
◆ **EMP:** 13 **EST:** 1980
SALES (est): 573.9K **Privately Held**
WEB: www.boulderblimp.com
SIC: 3069 2399 Balloons, advertising &
toy: rubber; banners, made from fabric

(G-8851)
BRAIN POWER INCORPORATED
Also Called: B P I
4470 Sw 74th Ave (33155-4495)
P.O. Box 559501 (33255-9501)
PHONE......................305 264-4465
Herbert A Wertheim MD, *President*
William Moore, *COO*
Yelena Marrero, *Design Engr*
Jean Brill, *CFO*
Philip Boyce, *Accountant*
▲ **EMP:** 46 **EST:** 1971
SQ FT: 85,000
SALES (est): 10.6MM **Privately Held**
WEB: www.callbpi.com
SIC: 3827 3841 Optical instruments &
lenses; ophthalmic instruments & appara-
tus

(G-8852)
BRICKMED LLC
1800 Sw 27th Ave Ste 505 (33145-2400)
PHONE......................305 774-0081
Jewel D Lambert, *Vice Pres*
Peter Legor, *Vice Pres*
Roland J Millas, *Treasurer*
Peter Legorburu, *Mng Member*
EMP: 5 **EST:** 1991
SQ FT: 2,200
SALES (est): 700.7K **Privately Held**
WEB: www.brickmed.com
SIC: 3695 5045 5734 8741 Computer
software tape & disks: blank, rigid &
floppy; computer software; computer &
software stores; management services

(G-8853)
BRITISH BOYS & ASSOCIATES
14480 Sw 151st Ter (33186-5666)
PHONE......................305 278-1790
Stuart Hinde, *President*
Mohannad Iqbal, *Corp Secy*
EMP: 5 **EST:** 1991
SALES (est): 383.2K **Privately Held**
WEB: www.britishboysmiami.com
SIC: 3448 1799 1521 Screen enclosures;
screening contractor: window, door, etc.;
general remodeling, single-family houses

(G-8854)
BRITVIC NORTH AMERICA LLC
360 Nw 27th St (33127-4158)
PHONE......................786 641-5041
Susi Casey, *CEO*

Olivier Mercier, *Managing Dir*
John Daly, *Principal*
Paramjeet Pahdi, *Opers Dir*
Edward Barnett, *Opers Staff*
EMP: 40 **EST:** 2011
SALES (est): 23.1MM
SALES (corp-wide): 1.9B **Privately Held**
SIC: 2834 Pharmaceutical preparations
PA: Britvic Plc
Breakspear Park
Hemel Hempstead HERTS HP2 4
121 711-1102

(G-8855)
BROMMA CONQUIP
6161 Blue Lagoon Dr (33126-2057)
PHONE......................786 501-7130
Per-Anders Holmstrom, *Principal*
EMP: 7 **EST:** 2015
SALES (est): 90.7K **Privately Held**
WEB: www.bromma.com
SIC: 3531 Construction machinery

(G-8856)
BROOKLYN STITCH INC
20213 Ne 16th Pl (33179-2719)
PHONE......................786 280-1730
David Douenias, *Ch of Bd*
EMP: 5 **EST:** 2017
SALES (est): 676.5K **Privately Held**
WEB: www.brooklynstitch.com
SIC: 2395 Embroidery & art needlework

(G-8857)
BROWN (USA) INC
2245 Nw 72nd Ave (33122-1825)
PHONE......................305 593-9228
Peter Browne, *CEO*
Michael Browne, *President*
Stephano Annicchiarico, *Regional Mgr*
Peter Braley, *COO*
Dawn Johnson, *Vice Pres*
◆ **EMP:** 11 **EST:** 2012
SALES (est): 1.9MM **Privately Held**
WEB: www.brown-usa.com
SIC: 3429 3272 5961 Manufactured hard-
ware (general); building materials, except
block or brick: concrete; tools & hardware,
mail order

(G-8858)
BRUNSTEEL CORP
14065 Sw 142nd St (33186-5565)
PHONE......................305 251-7607
EMP: 6
SQ FT: 8,000
SALES (est): 1.3MM **Privately Held**
SIC: 3449 Mfg Fabricated Steel Concrete
Reinforcing Bars

(G-8859)
BUILT STORY LLC
1581 Brickell Ave # 2207 (33129-1215)
PHONE......................305 671-3890
Brian Alonso,
EMP: 10 **EST:** 2018
SALES (est): 452.5K **Privately Held**
WEB: www.builtstory.com
SIC: 3679 3999 8322 Electronic circuits;
education aids, devices & supplies; travel-
ers' aid

(G-8860)
**BULLDOG NEON SIGN
COMPANY INC**
5728 Ne 4th Ave (33137-2528)
PHONE......................786 277-6366
EMP: 7 **EST:** 2019
SALES (est): 240.3K **Privately Held**
WEB: www.bulldogneon.com
SIC: 3993 Neon signs

(G-8861)
BURKE BRANDS LLC
Also Called: Cafe Don Pablo
521 Ne 189th St (33179-3909)
PHONE......................305 249-5628
Darron J Burke, *CEO*
Jonson LI, *Managing Prtnr*
Hernan Cabrera, *General Mgr*
Tracy Walsh, *COO*
Eliana Burke, *Vice Pres*
▲ **EMP:** 30 **EST:** 2004
SQ FT: 12,000

SALES (est): 20MM **Privately Held**
WEB: www.donpablocoffee.com
SIC: **2095** Coffee roasting (except by
wholesale grocers)

(G-8862)
BURN PROOF GEAR LLC
7121 N Miami Ave (33150-3717)
PHONE..............................786 634-7406
Alceu R Aragao Jr, *CEO*
EMP: 6 EST: 2015
SALES (est): 513.5K **Privately Held**
WEB: www.burnproofgear.com
SIC: **3949** 2311 Sporting & athletic goods;
men's & boys' uniforms

(G-8863)
BUSINESS CENTER &
PRINTSHOP
815 Nw 119th St (33168-2336)
PHONE..............................786 547-6681
Susana Sanchez, *Principal*
EMP: 7 EST: 2015
SALES (est): 111.2K **Privately Held**
SIC: **2752** Commercial printing, offset

(G-8864)
BUSINESS WORLD TRADING
INC
Also Called: Best Buy Awnings
13275 Sw 136th St Unit 22 (33186-5832)
PHONE..............................305 238-0724
EMP: 16
SQ FT: 3,000
SALES (est): 117.4K **Privately Held**
SIC: **2211** 5039 5999 Mfg Whol And Ret
Awnings

(G-8865)
BUTLER GRAPHICS INC
Also Called: Alta Graphics
5055 Nw 74th Ave Unit 5 (33166-5505)
PHONE..............................305 477-1344
Kathy Butler, *President*
John Butler, *Corp Secy*
▼ EMP: 6 EST: 1991
SALES (est): 943.6K **Privately Held**
WEB: www.alta-graphics.com
SIC: **2752** Commercial printing, offset

(G-8866)
BUVIN JEWELRY FLORIDA INC
36 Ne 1st St Ste 217 (33132-2474)
PHONE..............................305 358-0170
Stanislas Sowinski, *President*
Anna Maria De Sowinski, *Principal*
EMP: 10 EST: 1980
SQ FT: 800
SALES (est): 772.3K **Privately Held**
WEB: www.buvinjewelry.com
SIC: **3911** 5094 Jewelry, precious metal;
jewelry & precious stones

(G-8867)
BYBLOS GROUP INC
7175 Sw 47th St Ste 210 (33155-4637)
PHONE..............................305 662-6666
Kamal T Farah, *President*
Leila Farah, *Vice Pres*
▲ EMP: 8 EST: 2000
SQ FT: 1,300
SALES (est): 645.5K **Privately Held**
WEB: www.byblosgroup.com
SIC: **2599** 2541 Cabinets, factory; counter
& sink tops

(G-8868)
C & C MULTISERVICES CORP
2849 Nw 7th St (33125-4303)
PHONE..............................305 200-5851
Milagros Campos, *President*
EMP: 12 EST: 2000
SALES (est): 462.7K **Privately Held**
SIC: **3661** Communication headgear, tele-
phone

(G-8869)
C C 1 LIMITED PARTNERSHIP
Also Called: Coca-Cola
3201 Nw 72nd Ave (33122-1317)
PHONE..............................305 599-2337
Carlos M Delacruz, *Partner*
Manuel Kadre, *Partner*
Aberto De La Cruz, *Partner*
Miriam Carballes, *Sales Staff*

▲ EMP: 1000 EST: 1995
SQ FT: 80,000
SALES (est): 240.3MM **Privately Held**
SIC: **2086** Bottled & canned soft drinks

(G-8870)
C L F ENTERPRISES
Also Called: General Sign
111 Sw 17th Ave (33135-2126)
PHONE..............................305 643-3222
Eddy Lopez, *President*
EMP: 8 EST: 1973
SQ FT: 3,000
SALES (est): 481.2K **Privately Held**
SIC: **3993** Electric signs

(G-8871)
C&D PURVEYORS INC
8242 Nw 70th St (33166-2742)
PHONE..............................305 562-8541
Horacio Zapata, *President*
EMP: 11 EST: 2014
SALES (est): 584.6K **Privately Held**
WEB: www.lasmercedes.com.co
SIC: **2095** Roasted coffee

(G-8872)
C1 AEROSPACE LLC
14519 Sw 138th Pl (33186-7215)
PHONE..............................786 712-9949
Chris J Annoual, *President*
EMP: 6 EST: 2017
SALES (est): 406.4K **Privately Held**
SIC: **3721** Aircraft

(G-8873)
CA INC
15298 Sw 17th Ter (33185-5873)
PHONE..............................305 559-4640
EMP: 142
SALES (corp-wide): 4.6B **Publicly Held**
SIC: **7372** Prepackaged Software Svcs
PA: Ca, Inc.
    1 Ca Plz Ste 100
    Islandia NY 10022
    800 225-5224

(G-8874)
CA INC
1221 Brickell Ave 907 (33131-3224)
PHONE..............................305 347-5140
Margaret Herstedt, *Branch Mgr*
EMP: 30
SALES (corp-wide): 27.4B **Publicly Held**
WEB: www.broadcom.com
SIC: **7372** Prepackaged software; busi-
ness oriented computer software
HQ: Ca, Inc.
    520 Madison Ave
    New York NY 10022
    800 225-5224

(G-8875)
CA PIPELINE INC
15621 Sw 209th Ave (33187-5677)
PHONE..............................305 969-4655
EMP: 7 EST: 2019
SALES (est): 1.9MM **Privately Held**
SIC: **1389** Oil field services

(G-8876)
CABALLERO METALS CORP
7315 Sw 45th St (33155-4534)
PHONE..............................305 266-9085
Jose A Caballero, *President*
Pedro Caballero, *Vice Pres*
EMP: 7 EST: 2012
SALES (est): 140.4K **Privately Held**
SIC: **3446** Architectural metalwork

(G-8877)
CABALLERO METALS CORP
7315 Sw 45th St Ste 4 (33155-4534)
PHONE..............................305 266-9085
Pedro J Caballero, *President*
Jose Caballero, *Vice Pres*
EMP: 10 EST: 1982
SQ FT: 3,000
SALES (est): 1MM **Privately Held**
SIC: **3446** Architectural metalwork

(G-8878)
CAF USA INC
9400 Nw 37th Ave (33147-2703)
PHONE..............................305 753-5371
EMP: 8 EST: 2017

SALES (est): 552.4K **Privately Held**
WEB: www.cafusa.com
SIC: **3743** Railroad equipment

(G-8879)
CAFCO LLC
Also Called: Pawtitas
3370 Ne 190th St Apt 2206 (33180-2418)
PHONE..............................240 848-5574
Francisco Hoheb, *Mng Member*
Ingrid Randolf, *Mng Member*
EMP: 6 EST: 2017
SALES (est): 1.6MM **Privately Held**
SIC: **3999** Pet supplies

(G-8880)
CAL AIR FORWARDING
3000 Nw 74th Ave (33122-1428)
PHONE..............................305 871-4552
Jeff Cac, *General Mgr*
Brandon Rounds, *Marketing Staff*
Jeff Higdon, *Branch Mgr*
M Tracking, *Director*
EMP: 7 **Privately Held**
WEB: www.calaircargo.com
SIC: **2448** Cargo containers, wood & wood
with metal
PA: Cal Air Forwarding
    6830 Via Del Oro Ste 210
    San Jose CA 95119

(G-8881)
CAMEL ENTERPRISES CORP
Also Called: Camel Power Drinks
2120 Ne 203rd Ter (33179-2217)
P.O. Box 3691, Hallandale (33008-3691)
PHONE..............................954 234-2559
Tarek Hamandi, *Principal*
EMP: 10 EST: 2010
SALES (est): 273.9K **Privately Held**
SIC: **2086** 0781 5047 Soft drinks: pack-
aged in cans, bottles, etc.; landscape
services; instruments, surgical & medical

(G-8882)
CAMILO OFFICE FURNITURE
INC (PA)
Also Called: Camilo Muebles
7344 Sw 48th St Ste 202 (33155-5521)
P.O. Box 560147 (33256-0147)
PHONE..............................305 261-5366
Camilo Lopez Jr, *President*
Camilo Lopez III, *Vice Pres*
Luis Lopez, *Treasurer*
Ricardo Lopez, *Treasurer*
Jose Lopez, *Admin Sec*
▲ EMP: 84 EST: 1963
SQ FT: 74,000
SALES (est): 7.5MM **Privately Held**
SIC: **2521** Chairs, office: padded, uphol-
stered or plain: wood

(G-8883)
CAMILO OFFICE FURNITURE
INC
18360 Sw 224th St (33170-3507)
PHONE..............................305 261-5366
Jose Lopez, *Admin Sec*
EMP: 7 EST: 2010
SALES (est): 90.4K **Privately Held**
WEB: www.camilo.com
SIC: **2521** Wood office furniture

(G-8884)
CAMPEONES MARINA CORP
600 Nw 7th Ave (33136-3104)
PHONE..............................305 491-5738
Mario Hernandez Sr, *President*
EMP: 10 EST: 2007
SALES (est): 317K **Privately Held**
WEB: www.campeonesmarina.com
SIC: **3732** Yachts, building & repairing

(G-8885)
CANSORTIUM CHARITIES INC
82 Ne 26th St (33137-4428)
PHONE..............................305 902-2720
Jose Hidalgo, *CEO*
EMP: 25 EST: 2017
SALES (est): 748K **Privately Held**
WEB: investors.getfluent.com
SIC: **2833** Medicinals & botanicals

(G-8886)
CAPE BRITT CORP INC
2960 Nw 72nd Ave (33122-1312)
PHONE..............................305 593-5027
Jorge Jimenez, *Principal*
◆ EMP: 7 EST: 2010
SALES (est): 157.3K **Privately Held**
SIC: **2087** Beverage bases

(G-8887)
CAPITOL RENTAL BLDG EQP
INC
Also Called: Capital Steel Structures
2188 Nw 25th Ave (33142-7121)
PHONE..............................305 633-5008
Ruben Diaz, *President*
Alicia Diaz, *Vice Pres*
Pablo Garcia, *Project Mgr*
Yolanda Garcia, *Assistant*
EMP: 15 EST: 1973
SQ FT: 8,700
SALES (est): 4.2MM **Privately Held**
WEB: www.capitolsteelstructures.com
SIC: **3441** Fabricated structural metal

(G-8888)
CAPTIVA CONTAINERS LLC
75 95 Ne 179th St (33162)
PHONE..............................800 861-3868
Adriana Aponte, *Supervisor*
Alan Katz, *Exec Dir*
Daniela Morgenstern, *Exec Dir*
Freddy Morgenstern.
Luisa Vethencourt, *Analyst*
▲ EMP: 70 EST: 2013
SQ FT: 35,000
SALES (est): 10.5MM **Privately Held**
WEB: www.captivaco.com
SIC: **3085** Plastics bottles

(G-8889)
CAQ INTERNATIONAL LLC
900 Biscayne Blvd # 4906 (33132-1574)
PHONE..............................305 744-1472
Victor Samama Jr, *Mng Member*
EMP: 5 EST: 2011
SQ FT: 260
SALES (est): 587.2K **Privately Held**
SIC: **2834** Adrenal pharmaceutical prepa-
rations

(G-8890)
CARDENAS ROBERTO BLINDS
OF FLA
13301 Sw 132nd Ave Unit 2 (33186-6188)
PHONE..............................315 807-6878
Roberto Rodriguez Guerra, *Principal*
EMP: 7 EST: 2020
SALES (est): 170.7K **Privately Held**
SIC: **2591** Window blinds

(G-8891)
CARIBBEAN BOX COMPANY
3123 Nw 73rd St (33147-5947)
PHONE..............................305 667-4900
Miguel Garcia Armengol, *President*
EMP: 24 EST: 1987
SQ FT: 45,000
SALES (est): 250.3K **Privately Held**
SIC: **2657** Folding paperboard boxes

(G-8892)
CARIBBEAN CANVAS AND MARI
7296 Sw 42nd Ter (33155-4532)
PHONE..............................786 972-6377
EMP: 7 EST: 2018
SALES (est): 407.4K **Privately Held**
SIC: **2211** Canvas

(G-8893)
CARIBBEAN FIBERGLASS
PRODUCTS
5445 Nw 72nd Ave (33166-4246)
PHONE..............................305 888-0774
Cirilo F Padron, *President*
Elvis Padron, *Owner*
Everardo E Padron, *Treasurer*
▼ EMP: 10 EST: 1977
SQ FT: 30,000
SALES (est): 586.4K **Privately Held**
SIC: **2519** Furniture, household: glass,
fiberglass & plastic

(G-8894)
CARIBBEAN FUELS INC
15001 Sw 141st Ter (33196-4691)
PHONE..................................305 233-3016
Bernando Sanchez, *Vice Pres*
EMP: 10 **EST:** 2005
SALES (est): 272.3K **Privately Held**
WEB: www.caribbeanfuels.com
SIC: 2869 Fuels

(G-8895)
CARIBBEAN TRAILERS CORP
12240 Sw 130th St (33186-6217)
PHONE..................................305 256-1505
Carlos Colunga, *President*
▼ **EMP:** 5 **EST:** 2004
SALES (est): 496.2K **Privately Held**
WEB: www.caribbeantrailer.com
SIC: 3799 Boat trailers

(G-8896)
CARIBE EXPRESS ASSOCIATES INC
7320 Nw 12th St Ste 111 (33126-1913)
PHONE..................................305 222-9057
Rosario Dieguez, *President*
Alberto Dieguez, *Vice Pres*
EMP: 10
SALES (corp-wide): 523.3K **Privately Held**
WEB: www.caribeexpress.com
SIC: 2819 Carbides
PA: Caribe Express Associates, Inc.
6710 Bergenline Ave
Guttenberg NJ 07093
201 869-2822

(G-8897)
CARLEES CREATIONS INC
Also Called: I Wed Today
12275 Sw 129th Ct (33186-6435)
P.O. Box 836673 (33283-6673)
PHONE..................................786 232-0050
Ka'sandra Bryant-Jones, *CEO*
EMP: 8 **EST:** 2007
SQ FT: 1,500
SALES (est): 420K **Privately Held**
WEB: www.carleescreations.com
SIC: 2051 5461 7371 5999 Cakes, pies & pastries; cakes; computer software development & applications; cake decorating supplies; notary publics; wedding chapel, privately operated

(G-8898)
CARNE ASADA TORTILLERIA NICA
10404 W Flagler St Ste 5 (33174-1669)
PHONE..................................305 221-7001
Jacqueline Garcia, *Principal*
EMP: 8 **EST:** 2007
SALES (est): 488.3K **Privately Held**
SIC: 2099 Tortillas, fresh or refrigerated

(G-8899)
CASA DEL MARINERO CORP
288 Ne 2nd St (33132-2213)
PHONE..................................305 374-5386
Wilson Ramirez, *President*
▼ **EMP:** 8 **EST:** 1993
SALES (est): 953.5K **Privately Held**
SIC: 3676 5731 Electronic resistors; radio, television & electronic stores

(G-8900)
CASTILLOS FARMS INC
Also Called: Castillo's Farm Equipment
19744 Sw 177th Ave (33187-2600)
PHONE..................................305 232-0771
Manuel Del Castillo, *President*
EMP: 8 **EST:** 1999
SALES (est): 636.9K **Privately Held**
SIC: 3523 Sprayers & spraying machines, agricultural

(G-8901)
CATAPULT 13 CRTIVE STUDIOS LLC
5 Nw 39th St Street1 (33127-2944)
PHONE..................................305 788-6948
Rodrigo Londono, *Principal*
EMP: 6 **EST:** 2010
SALES (est): 1.2MM **Privately Held**
WEB: www.catapult13.com
SIC: 3599 Catapults

(G-8902)
CAVO DEVELOPMENT INC
16380 Sw 137th Ave (33177-1904)
PHONE..................................305 255-7465
James C Cavo, *President*
Martin O Stelling, *CFO*
Volker Meldner, *Admin Sec*
EMP: 11 **EST:** 1989
SQ FT: 1,800
SALES (est): 238.1K **Privately Held**
SIC: 3531 Dredging machinery

(G-8903)
CAWY BOTTLING CO INC
2440 Nw 21st Ter (33142-7182)
PHONE..................................305 634-8669
Vincent Cossio, *President*
Frank Garcia, *Vice Pres*
Ramon Rodriguez, *Purchasing*
Alex Garcia, *Treasurer*
Domingo Villalba, *Treasurer*
▼ **EMP:** 27 **EST:** 1964
SQ FT: 50,000
SALES (est): 6.7MM **Privately Held**
WEB: www.cawy.net
SIC: 2086 Soft drinks: packaged in cans, bottles, etc.

(G-8904)
CBI INDUSTRIES INC
Also Called: Seagear Performance Apparel
13225 Sw 95th Ave (33176-5732)
PHONE..................................305 796-9346
Robert Francis, *President*
▲ **EMP:** 9 **EST:** 1998
SALES (est): 800K **Privately Held**
SIC: 2221 5699 5136 Shirting fabrics, manmade fiber & silk; shirts, custom made; shirts, men's & boys'

(G-8905)
CCP OF MIAMI INC
13601 Sw 143rd Ct (33186-5604)
PHONE..................................305 233-6534
Seudial Paul Ramsingh, *Principal*
EMP: 10 **EST:** 2005
SALES (est): 237.6K **Privately Held**
SIC: 2542 Partitions & fixtures, except wood

(G-8906)
CEDAR FRESH HOME PRODUCTS LLC (PA)
4207 University Dr (33146-1140)
PHONE..................................305 975-8524
Howard J Goldman, *Mng Member*
Kanas Fisher,
Steven Gerson,
William Grossman,
AVI Weinpraub,
▲ **EMP:** 4 **EST:** 2003
SQ FT: 2,000
SALES (est): 3MM **Privately Held**
SIC: 2511 Cedar chests

(G-8907)
CELLULAR MASTERS INC
Also Called: Fifo Wireless
10900 Nw 21st Ste 210 (33172-2006)
PHONE..................................305 592-7906
Abderrahim McHatet, *President*
Hamid McHatet, *Vice Pres*
Abraham Mekki, *Sales Associate*
▲ **EMP:** 25 **EST:** 2000
SQ FT: 10,000
SALES (est): 4.8MM **Privately Held**
SIC: 3661 Telephone cords, jacks, adapters, etc.

(G-8908)
CEMENT MIAMI TERMINAL
1200 Nw 137th Ave (33182-1803)
PHONE..................................305 221-2502
▲ **EMP:** 6 **EST:** 2005
SALES (est): 960.5K **Privately Held**
SIC: 3273 Ready-mixed concrete

(G-8909)
CEMEX MATERIALS LLC
Also Called: Rinker Portland Cement
1200 Nw 137th Ave (33182-1803)
PHONE..................................305 223-6934
EMP: 147 **Privately Held**
SIC: 3273 Ready-mixed concrete

HQ: Cemex Materials Llc
1720 Centrepark Dr E # 100
West Palm Beach FL 33401
561 833-5555

(G-8910)
CEMEX MATERIALS LLC
2201 Nw 38th Ct (33142-6749)
PHONE..................................305 558-0315
Robert Suarez, *Branch Mgr*
EMP: 167 **Privately Held**
SIC: 3271 3273 3272 1422 Blocks, concrete or cinder: standard; ready-mixed concrete; pipe, concrete or lined with concrete; crushed & broken limestone
HQ: Cemex Materials Llc
1720 Centrepark Dr E # 100
West Palm Beach FL 33401
561 833-5555

(G-8911)
CENTRAL METAL FABRICATORS INC
900 Sw 70th Ave (33144-4614)
PHONE..................................305 261-6262
Harold Baskin, *President*
Raul J Cossio, *Vice Pres*
Richard Estevez, *Engineer*
Beth Colacurto, *Office Mgr*
Joshua Baskin, *Technology*
EMP: 45 **EST:** 1948
SQ FT: 32,000
SALES (est): 5.6MM **Privately Held**
WEB: www.cmf-co.com
SIC: 3443 3444 3441 Fabricated plate work (boiler shop); sheet metalwork; fabricated structural metal

(G-8912)
CEPERO REMODELING INC
6972 Sw 4th St (33144-3642)
PHONE..................................305 265-1888
Maria Cepero, *President*
EMP: 6 **EST:** 1998
SQ FT: 2,500
SALES (est): 919.4K **Privately Held**
SIC: 2434 Wood kitchen cabinets

(G-8913)
CERAMICA VEREA USA CORP ✪
7035 Sw 44th St (33155-4643)
PHONE..................................305 665-3923
Manuel Menendez, *Principal*
▼ **EMP:** 12 **EST:** 2022
SALES (est): 333.1K **Privately Held**
WEB: www.comacastcorp.com
SIC: 3259 Roofing tile, clay

(G-8914)
CERENOVAS INC (HQ)
6303 Blue Lagoon Dr # 21 (33126-6002)
PHONE..................................800 255-2500
Mark Dickinson, *President*
Gavin Kirkpatrick, *Sales Staff*
EMP: 46 **EST:** 1969
SALES: 212MM
SALES (corp-wide): 93.7B **Publicly Held**
SIC: 3841 Surgical & medical instruments
PA: Johnson & Johnson
1 Johnson And Johnson Plz
New Brunswick NJ 08933
732 524-0400

(G-8915)
CERNO PHARMACEUTICALS LLC
6714 Nw 72nd Ave (33166-3045)
PHONE..................................786 763-2766
Pedro Paz, *Principal*
Juan J Hernandez, *Mng Member*
EMP: 7 **EST:** 2013
SALES (est): 196.1K **Privately Held**
WEB: www.cernopharma.com
SIC: 2023 2834 Dietary supplements, dairy & non-dairy based; pharmaceutical preparations

(G-8916)
CEW LLC
14008 Sw 140th St (33186-5547)
PHONE..................................305 232-8892
Christopher Wilson, *President*
John Hawk, *Mng Member*
▼ **EMP:** 5 **EST:** 2006

SALES (est): 504K **Privately Held**
WEB: www.miamiwaterjet.com
SIC: 3599 Machine shop, jobbing & repair

(G-8917)
CEW TECHNOLOGIES INC
14008 Sw 140th St (33186-5547)
PHONE..................................305 232-8892
Christopher Wilson, *President*
EMP: 6 **EST:** 2016
SQ FT: 7,000
SALES (est): 897.6K **Privately Held**
WEB: www.cewtechnologies.com
SIC: 3599 Machine shop, jobbing & repair

(G-8918)
CHAE DUPONT PA
7765 Sw 87th Ave Ste 102 (33173-2535)
PHONE..................................305 697-7771
Chae A Dupont, *Principal*
EMP: 8 **EST:** 2016
SALES (est): 74.4K **Privately Held**
WEB: www.chaedupont.com
SIC: 2879 Agricultural chemicals

(G-8919)
CHANNEL LETTER NETWORK CORP
7204 Nw 31st St (33122-1216)
PHONE..................................305 594-3360
Alvaro Brito, *President*
Rafael Valenzuela, *General Mgr*
▼ **EMP:** 16 **EST:** 2009
SALES (est): 888.9K **Privately Held**
WEB: www.dcsigns.com
SIC: 3993 Electric signs

(G-8920)
CHANNEL LOGISTICS LLC
Also Called: Space-Eyes
888 Biscayne Blvd Ste 505 (33132-1509)
PHONE..................................856 614-5441
Brian Breck, *Architect*
Jatin S Bains, *Mng Member*
Christine Atherholt, *Administration*
EMP: 18 **EST:** 2001
SQ FT: 2,500
SALES (est): 1.2MM **Privately Held**
WEB: www.space-eyes.com
SIC: 7372 7371 Business oriented computer software; software programming applications

(G-8921)
CHARCOAL CHEF USA LLC
Also Called: Josper Chef USA
554 Nw 41st St (33127-2834)
PHONE..................................786 273-6511
Agusti Comabella, *Mng Member*
EMP: 8 **EST:** 2016
SALES (est): 1.4MM **Privately Held**
SIC: 3634 Broilers, electric

(G-8922)
CHELLY COSMETICS MANUFACTURING
7172 Sw 30th Rd (33155-2844)
P.O. Box 559062 (33255-9062)
PHONE..................................305 471-9608
Juan C Granado, *President*
Carlos V Granado, *Vice Pres*
◆ **EMP:** 11 **EST:** 1993
SQ FT: 6,000
SALES (est): 1MM **Privately Held**
SIC: 3999 5122 2844 Fingernails, artificial; cosmetics; toilet preparations

(G-8923)
CHRISTIAN L INTERNATIONAL INC
2297 Ne 164th St (33160-3703)
PHONE..................................305 947-1722
▲ **EMP:** 7
SALES (est): 990.5K **Privately Held**
SIC: 2844 Mfg Toilet Preparations

(G-8924)
CHUCULU LLC
9455 Sw 78th St (33173-3395)
PHONE..................................305 595-4577
Daniel Agruelles, *Mng Member*
Linda Arguelles,
▲ **EMP:** 10 **EST:** 2003

SALES (est): 250K Privately Held
SIC: 2952 1761 1521 Roofing materials;
roofing contractor; single-family housing
construction

(G-8925)
CIELO ENTERPRISE SOLUTIONS LLC
12457 Sw 130th St (33186-6238)
PHONE..................................786 292-4111
Guillermo Younger,
Carolina Younger,
EMP: 11 EST: 2018
SALES (est): 676.8K Privately Held
SIC: 7372 Prepackaged software

(G-8926)
CITILUBE INC
3300 Nw 112th St (33167-3313)
PHONE..................................305 681-6064
Gregory Bass, President
Alexander Bass, Vice Pres
▼ EMP: 17 EST: 2004
SQ FT: 45,000
SALES (est): 4.7MM Privately Held
WEB: www.citilube.com
SIC: 2911 Oils, lubricating

(G-8927)
CITY ELEVATOR SERVICE CORP
15107 Sw 138th Pl (33186-5795)
PHONE..................................305 345-1951
Elsie Mercado Sanchez, Director
EMP: 6 EST: 2005
SALES (est): 412.2K Privately Held
WEB: www.southfloridaelevatorservice.com
SIC: 3534 Elevators & moving stairways

(G-8928)
CJ LABS INC
12245 Sw 128th St Unit 30 (33186-5999)
PHONE..................................305 234-9644
Carlos Alvarez, President
Odalys Gonzalez, Vice Pres
Andy Alvarez, Manager
EMP: 13 EST: 2004
SQ FT: 1,000
SALES (est): 4MM Privately Held
WEB: www.cjlabs.com
SIC: 2833 Vitamins, natural or synthetic:
bulk, uncompounded

(G-8929)
CJL BRICKS & PAVERS INC
9301 Nw 33rd Ct (33147-2945)
PHONE..................................305 527-4240
Jose L Torres, Director
EMP: 9 EST: 2001
SALES (est): 251.1K Privately Held
SIC: 2951 Asphalt paving mixtures &
blocks

(G-8930)
CLASSIC STARS INC
2355 Nw 35th Ave (33142-6825)
PHONE..................................305 871-6767
Carlos Padrino, Principal
EMP: 7 EST: 2010
SALES (est): 91.5K Privately Held
SIC: 2335 Wedding gowns & dresses

(G-8931)
CLOUD VENEER LLC
1001 Brickell Bay Dr # 2700 (33131-4900)
PHONE..................................305 230-7379
Anthony Richardson,
EMP: 7 EST: 2019
SQ FT: 8,000
SALES (est): 475.4K Privately Held
SIC: 7372 4813 7379 Business oriented
computer software; ; ; computer related
consulting services

(G-8932)
CLR ROASTERS LLC
2131 Nw 72nd Ave (33122-1823)
PHONE..................................305 591-0040
Sonia Aguila, Vice Pres
Lidier Reyes, Production
Kathleen Ruiz, Controller
David Briskie, Mng Member
▲ EMP: 21 EST: 2007
SQ FT: 34,000

SALES (est): 8.2MM
SALES (corp-wide): 147.4MM Publicly Held
WEB: www.clrroasters.com
SIC: 2095 Roasted coffee
HQ: Al Global Corporation
2400 Boswell Rd
Chula Vista CA 91914

(G-8933)
CME ARMA INC
4500 Nw 36th Ave (33142-4220)
PHONE..................................305 633-1524
Katherine Yasgar, President
Howard Yasgar, Vice Pres
Vannessa Jimenez, Sales Staff
◆ EMP: 22 EST: 1991
SQ FT: 14,500
SALES (est): 5.6MM Privately Held
WEB: www.cmearma.com
SIC: 3531 5088 Construction machinery;
transportation equipment & supplies

(G-8934)
CMN STEEL FABRICATORS INC
7993 Nw 60th St (33166-3410)
PHONE..................................305 592-5466
Timothy P Kressly, President
Carlos Perez, Engineer
Marisa M Nunez, Admin Sec
EMP: 58 EST: 2016
SALES (est): 7MM Privately Held
WEB: www.cmnsteel.com
SIC: 3317 3448 Steel pipe & tubes;
trusses & framing: prefabricated metal

(G-8935)
COCA-COLA BEVERAGES FLA LLC
16569 Sw 117th Ave (33177-2183)
PHONE..................................305 378-1073
David Cross, Vice Pres
Joe Gentry, Vice Pres
Felix Hernandez, Branch Mgr
EMP: 9
SALES (corp-wide): 366.5MM Privately Held
WEB: www.cocacolaflorida.com
SIC: 2086 5149 Bottled & canned soft
drinks; soft drinks
PA: Coca-Cola Beverages Florida, Llc
10117 Princess Palm Ave
Tampa FL 33610
800 438-2653

(G-8936)
COCA-COLA BOTTLING CO
16569 Sw 117th Ave (33177-2183)
PHONE..................................305 378-1073
Scott Turner, Manager
Brian Powers, Director
EMP: 10 EST: 2010
SALES (est): 344.1K Privately Held
WEB: www.coca-cola.com
SIC: 2086 Bottled & canned soft drinks

(G-8937)
COCO COSMETICS INC
20325 Ne 15th Ct (33179-2709)
PHONE..................................305 622-3488
Anna P Hua, President
Tien Lowe, Vice Pres
▼ EMP: 10 EST: 2009
SALES (est): 622.7K Privately Held
WEB: www.coco-cosmetics.com
SIC: 2844 Cosmetic preparations

(G-8938)
COCO GELATO CORP (PA)
3514 Nw 36th St (33142-5040)
PHONE..................................786 621-2444
Gustavo Sidelnik, President
EMP: 23 EST: 1994
SQ FT: 1,000
SALES (est): 4.4MM Privately Held
WEB: www.cocogelato.com
SIC: 2024 5812 Ice cream & ice milk; ice
cream stands or dairy bars

(G-8939)
COCRYSTAL DISCOVERY INC
4400 Biscayne Blvd # 101 (33137-3212)
PHONE..................................425 750-7208
EMP: 7 EST: 2018

SALES (est): 187.9K Privately Held
WEB: www.cocrystalpharma.com
SIC: 2834 Pharmaceutical preparations

(G-8940)
COCRYSTAL PHARMA INC
4400 Biscayne Blvd (33137-3212)
PHONE..................................877 262-7123
EMP: 5 EST: 2020
SALES (est): 428.7K Privately Held
SIC: 2834 Pharmaceutical preparations

(G-8941)
COFFEE CLLLOID PRODUCTIONS LLC
12240 Sw 132nd Ct (33186-6476)
PHONE..................................305 424-8900
Joseph A Daoud, CEO
EMP: 9 EST: 2010
SALES (est): 155.9K Privately Held
WEB: www.newterritory.media
SIC: 3089 Celluloid products

(G-8942)
COIN-O-MATIC INC
3950 Nw 31st Ave (33142-5123)
PHONE..................................305 635-4141
Stephen Cohen, President
▼ EMP: 25 EST: 1984
SQ FT: 20,500
SALES (est): 2.4MM Privately Held
WEB: www.coinomaticinc.com
SIC: 3582 Washing machines, laundry:
commercial, incl. coin-operated; commer-
cial laundry equipment

(G-8943)
COLD STORAGE ENGINEERING CO (PA)
703 Nw 62nd Ave Ste 650 (33126-4680)
PHONE..................................305 448-0099
Fred Garcia, President
▼ EMP: 9 EST: 1981
SALES (est): 941.6K Privately Held
SIC: 3585 Refrigeration equipment, com-
plete

(G-8944)
COLDFLO INC
Also Called: J & J Refregrator
1050 Nw 21st St (33127-4514)
PHONE..................................305 324-8555
Elan Feldman, President
Nancy Feldman, Treasurer
◆ EMP: 8 EST: 1987
SQ FT: 16,000
SALES (est): 995.2K Privately Held
WEB: www.coldflow.com
SIC: 3585 Parts for heating, cooling & re-
frigerating equipment

(G-8945)
COLONIAL PRESS INTL INC
3690 Nw 50th St (33142-3987)
PHONE..................................305 633-1581
Jorge Gomez, President
Jose A Gomez, Corp Secy
Henry Hernandez, Exec VP
Jeff Statler, Exec VP
Darryl Wiggins, Exec VP
◆ EMP: 200 EST: 1952
SQ FT: 120,000
SALES (est): 25.8MM Privately Held
WEB: www.colonialpressintl.com
SIC: 2752 2789 Commercial printing, off-
set; lithography on metal; bookbinding &
related work

(G-8946)
COLOR PRESS CORP
1835 Nw 112th Ave Ste 184 (33172-1839)
PHONE..................................786 621-8491
EMP: 8 EST: 2008
SALES (est): 797.9K Privately Held
SIC: 2741 Misc Publishing

(G-8947)
COLORAMAX PRINTING INC
3215 Nw 7th St (33125-4101)
PHONE..................................305 541-0322
Xiomara Romero, President
EMP: 10 EST: 1963
SQ FT: 6,945

SALES (est): 688K Privately Held
WEB: www.coloramaxprinting.com
SIC: 2752 2791 2789 Commercial printing, offset; typesetting; bookbinding & related work

(G-8948)
COLORMET FOODS LLC
3610 Ne 1st Ave (33137-3602)
P.O. Box 613114 (33261-3114)
PHONE..................................888 775-3966
Eva Colmenares, Principal
EMP: 11 EST: 2015
SQ FT: 1,200
SALES (est): 2.1MM Privately Held
WEB: www.seriouscow.com
SIC: 2026 5143 Yogurt; yogurt

(G-8949)
COLORPRINT DESIGN
1220 Sw 78th Ct (33144-4310)
PHONE..................................305 229-8880
Mathew Jordan, CEO
EMP: 7 EST: 2008
SALES (est): 237.3K Privately Held
SIC: 2752 Color lithography

(G-8950)
COMA CAST CORP
4383 Sw 70th Ct (33155-4622)
P.O. Box 557044 (33255-7044)
PHONE..................................305 667-6797
Carlos Blume, President
◆ EMP: 18 EST: 1971
SALES (est): 2.4MM Privately Held
WEB: www.comacastcorp.com
SIC: 3272 5032 2952 Roofing tile & slabs,
concrete; tile & clay products; asphalt
felts & coatings

(G-8951)
COMM DOTS LLC CONNECTING
3890 Coco Grove Ave (33133-6120)
PHONE..................................305 505-6009
Emilia Burbano, President
Margarita Gomez, Vice Pres
Maria Clara Burbano, Manager
EMP: 12 EST: 2013
SALES (est): 80K Privately Held
SIC: 2741 8742 7389 ; marketing con-
sulting services;

(G-8952)
COMPLIANCE MEDS TECH LLC
20855 Ne 16th Ave Ste C13 (33179-2140)
PHONE..................................786 319-9826
Moses Zonana, CEO
Daniel E Dosoretz, Principal
Moses A Zonana, Controller
EMP: 10 EST: 2010
SALES (est): 1.4MM Privately Held
WEB: www.cmtcares.com
SIC: 3845 7389 3085 7352 Patient moni-
toring apparatus; packaging & labeling
services; design services; plastics bottles;
medical equipment rental

(G-8953)
COMPUTECH LLC
1840 Coral Way Ste 306 (33145-2748)
PHONE..................................786 605-0012
Tamara Aravind, Mng Member
EMP: 150 EST: 2007
SALES (est): 13.7MM Privately Held
SIC: 3571 Computers, digital, analog or
hybrid

(G-8954)
CONCEPT ELEVATOR GROUP LLC (PA)
8027 Nw 71st Ct (33166-2303)
PHONE..................................786 845-8955
Rolando M Nieves, CEO
Daniel Nieves, Opers Mgr
Gabriel Garcia, Engineer
Adrian Rodriguez, Controller
Randy Jimenez, Mktg Coord
◆ EMP: 30 EST: 2003
SQ FT: 60,000
SALES (est): 8.3MM Privately Held
WEB: www.conceptelevator.com
SIC: 3534 Elevators & equipment

(G-8955)
CONCORDIA PHARMACEUTICALS INC
2600 Sw 3rd Ave Ste 950 (33129-2355)
PHONE.................................786 304-2083
Reginald Hardy, *President*
Andrew Sklawer, *Opers Staff*
EMP: 5 EST: 2005
SALES (est): 378.3K Privately Held
WEB: www.concordiapharma.com
SIC: 2834 Pharmaceutical preparations

(G-8956)
CONCRETE STRUCTURES INC
12100 Nw 58th St (33010)
PHONE.................................305 597-9393
Dick Salonia, *President*
EMP: 13 EST: 1991
SQ FT: 230
SALES (est): 344.2K Privately Held
SIC: 3272 Precast terrazo or concrete products

(G-8957)
CONQUEST FINANCIAL MANAGEMENT
Also Called: Source Outdoor
11451 Nw 36th Ave (33167-2910)
PHONE.................................305 630-8950
Gerald Shvartsman, *CEO*
Michael Greenberg, *Sales Staff*
Jeniffer Bello, *Marketing Mgr*
Daniel Stevens, *Marketing Mgr*
Melissa Harrington, *Manager*
◆ **EMP: 75 EST: 2009**
SQ FT: 70,000
SALES (est): 8.6MM Privately Held
WEB: www.sourcefurniture.com
SIC: 2519 Wicker & rattan furniture

(G-8958)
CONSULTCANVAS LLC
Also Called: Board Certified Media
1951 Nw S Rver Dr Apt 170 (33125)
PHONE.................................863 214-3115
Marcos Rivera, *Principal*
EMP: 7 EST: 2015
SALES (est): 55.9K Privately Held
SIC: 2211 Canvas

(G-8959)
CONTACT CENTER SOLUTIONS INC
66 W Flagler St (33130-1807)
PHONE.................................305 499-0163
Jeff Entel, *President*
EMP: 20 EST: 2014
SALES (est): 1.2MM Privately Held
WEB: www.genesys.com
SIC: 7372 Business oriented computer software

(G-8960)
CONTECH ENGNERED SOLUTIONS LLC
7765 Sw 75th Ave (33143-4143)
PHONE.................................561 582-2558
Dale Church, *Manager*
Brian Musser, *Manager*
EMP: 15 Privately Held
WEB: www.conteches.com
SIC: 3443 3444 3354 Fabricated plate work (boiler shop); sheet metalwork; aluminum extruded products
HQ: Contech Engineered Solutions Llc
9025 Centre Pointe Dr # 400
West Chester OH 45069
513 645-7000

(G-8961)
CONTEMPORARY DESIGN CONCEPTS
12491 Sw 130th St Ste C (33186-6209)
PHONE.................................305 253-2044
Ali Farzamipour, *President*
Lisa McIntosh, *Manager*
EMP: 10 EST: 1985
SQ FT: 7,000
SALES (est): 618.1K Privately Held
SIC: 2511 Wood household furniture

(G-8962)
CONTINENTAL BELT CORP
Also Called: Continental Belt & Tie
2267 Nw 20th St (33142-7371)
PHONE.................................305 573-8871
Eli Bick, *President*
Linda Bick, *Treasurer*
▲ **EMP: 6 EST: 1974**
SQ FT: 5,000
SALES (est): 383.3K Privately Held
WEB: www.continentalbelt.com
SIC: 3172 5136 Personal leather goods; apparel belts, men's & boys'

(G-8963)
CONTINENTAL SERVICES GROUP INC (PA)
Also Called: Continental Blood Bank
1300 Nw 36th St (33142-5556)
P.O. Box 420950 (33242-0950)
PHONE.................................305 633-7700
Cherry D Wheeler-Capik, *CEO*
Richard W Capik, *President*
Christopher Stroup, *Opers Mgr*
Paul Wilson, *Administration*
◆ **EMP: 30 EST: 1970**
SQ FT: 15,500
SALES (est): 6.4MM Privately Held
WEB: www.continentalbloodbank.com
SIC: 2835 In vitro & in vivo diagnostic substances

(G-8964)
CONVIVIUM PRESS INC
7661 Nw 68th St Unit 108 (33166-2840)
PHONE.................................305 889-0489
Rafael F Luciani Rivero, *President*
Maria Rosa Malave Carrasco, *CFO*
Manuel Polanco, *Admin Sec*
EMP: 5 EST: 2007
SALES (est): 352.6K Privately Held
WEB: www.conviumpress.com
SIC: 2741 Miscellaneous publishing

(G-8965)
COOKIE APP LLC
2 S Biscayne Blvd # 2680 (33131-1806)
PHONE.................................305 330-5099
Alex Pereira,
EMP: 5 EST: 2017
SALES (est): 309.3K Privately Held
SIC: 7372 Educational computer software

(G-8966)
COOLHEAD HELMET LLC
999 Brickell Bay Dr (33131-2934)
PHONE.................................786 292-4829
Sergejs Zelinskis,
EMP: 7 EST: 2018
SALES (est): 286.7K Privately Held
WEB: www.coolheadhelmet.com
SIC: 2353 Helmets, jungle cloth: wool lined

(G-8967)
CORAL CABINET INC
14378 Sw 98th Ter (33186-1146)
PHONE.................................305 484-8702
Eduardo Ricci, *Vice Pres*
EMP: 6 EST: 2018
SALES (est): 324.2K Privately Held
SIC: 2434 Wood kitchen cabinets

(G-8968)
CORAL GABLES CUSTOM DESIGN INC
4038 Nw 32nd Ave (33142-5002)
PHONE.................................305 591-7575
Leandro Morris, *President*
EMP: 13 EST: 2008
SALES (est): 785.1K Privately Held
SIC: 2499 Decorative wood & woodwork

(G-8969)
CORALDOM USA LLC
4434 Nw 74th Ave (33166-6443)
PHONE.................................305 716-0200
G Gomez, *Sales Staff*
Gustavo G Cruz,
◆ **EMP: 5 EST: 2010**
SALES (est): 1MM Privately Held
WEB: www.coraldom.com
SIC: 1499 Asphalt mining & bituminous stone quarrying

(G-8970)
CORE ONCOLOGY INC (PA)
1101 Brickell Ave 503s (33131-3105)
PHONE.................................206 236-2100
Travis Gay, *President*
Christopher Nicholson, *CFO*
Bruce Church, *VP Sales*
EMP: 4 EST: 2007
SQ FT: 3,000
SALES (est): 6.5MM Privately Held
SIC: 3842 Surgical appliances & supplies

(G-8971)
CORESYSTEMS SOFTWARE USA INC
Also Called: Coresystems USA
801 Brickell Ave Ste 1400 (33131-2945)
PHONE.................................786 497-4477
Manuel Grenacher, *CEO*
Arti Sahgal, *Executive*
EMP: 8 EST: 2014
SALES (est): 111.2K Privately Held
SIC: 7372 Business oriented computer software

(G-8972)
CORPDESIGN
6695 Nw 36th Ave (33147-7519)
PHONE.................................866 323-6055
Steve Baricko, *Sales Staff*
EMP: 8 EST: 2015
SALES (est): 169.3K Privately Held
WEB: www.corpdesign.com
SIC: 2521 Wood office furniture

(G-8973)
CORPORATE PRINTING & ADVG INC
13515 Sw 99th St (33186-2805)
PHONE.................................305 273-6000
Robert Distillator, *President*
Susana Araya, *Vice Pres*
EMP: 10 EST: 2000
SQ FT: 3,700
SALES (est): 739.5K Privately Held
SIC: 2759 Advertising literature: printing

(G-8974)
CORPORATE PRINTING SVCS INC
13288 Sw 114th Ter (33186-7918)
P.O. Box 526900 (33152-6900)
PHONE.................................305 273-6000
Robert Distillator, *President*
EMP: 6 EST: 1989
SQ FT: 2,500
SALES (est): 606.3K Privately Held
SIC: 2752 Commercial printing, offset

(G-8975)
COSTEX CORPORATION (PA)
Also Called: Costex Tractor Parts
5800 Nw 74th Ave (33166-3740)
PHONE.................................305 592-9769
Gilberto C Uribe, *President*
Teresa Uribe, *Corp Secy*
Melissa Uribe Gil, *Vice Pres*
Melissa Gil, *Vice Pres*
Gonzalo Gonzalez, *Purch Mgr*
◆ **EMP: 130 EST: 1980**
SALES (est): 62.4MM Privately Held
WEB: www.costex.com
SIC: 3531 5084 Construction machinery; industrial machinery & equipment

(G-8976)
COUNTRY FRITS JUICES NURS CORP
12100 Sw 177th Ave (33196-3046)
PHONE.................................786 302-8487
Felix Calle, *Principal*
EMP: 8 EST: 2016
SALES (est): 68.6K Privately Held
SIC: 2037 Fruit juices

(G-8977)
CRAMCO INC
5600 Nw 36th Ave (33142-2712)
PHONE.................................305 634-7500
Paul Cramer, *Owner*
Beth Wiegand, *Sales Staff*
Zuelma Calle, *Manager*
EMP: 8
SALES (corp-wide): 25.1MM Privately Held
WEB: www.cramco.net
SIC: 2514 2511 Metal household furniture; wood household furniture
PA: Cramco Inc
2200 E Ann St
Philadelphia PA 19134
215 427-9500

(G-8978)
CREATIVE WOODWORK MIAMI INC
6001 Nw 37th Ave (33142-2013)
PHONE.................................305 634-3100
Luis Sanchez, *President*
EMP: 18 EST: 1993
SQ FT: 23,000
SALES (est): 2.3MM Privately Held
SIC: 2511 Wood household furniture

(G-8979)
CRESPO DOORS DISTRIBUTION ✪
2513 Nw 74th Ave (33122-1417)
PHONE.................................305 244-9130
EMP: 30 EST: 2022
SALES (est): 2.5MM Privately Held
WEB: www.crespodoors.com
SIC: 2431 Doors & door parts & trim, wood

(G-8980)
CRUSELLAS & CO INC
7014 Sw 4th St (33144-2707)
P.O. Box 440814 (33144-0814)
PHONE.................................305 261-9580
Luis R Santeiro, *President*
Juan Santalla, *Vice Pres*
Maria Santeiro, *Treasurer*
Maria Santalla, *Asst Treas*
▲ **EMP: 10 EST: 1967**
SQ FT: 3,500
SALES (est): 948.1K Privately Held
WEB: www.crusellasandcompany.com
SIC: 2844 Perfumes, natural or synthetic

(G-8981)
CST USA INC
20533 Biscayne Blvd # 565 (33180-1529)
PHONE.................................404 695-2249
Peter Kesper, *President*
Toni Sims, *Acting CEO*
EMP: 16 EST: 2014
SALES (est): 1.4MM
SALES (corp-wide): 192.6MM Privately Held
SIC: 3555 Printing trades machinery
HQ: Cst Colour Scanner Technology Gmbh
Konigsberger Str. 117
Krefeld NW 47809
215 115-9226

(G-8982)
CTM BIOMEDICAL LLC
78 Sw 7th St Ste 500 (33130-3782)
P.O. Box 231, Lake Worth (33460-0231)
PHONE.................................561 650-4027
Bryan Banman, *Manager*
EMP: 16 EST: 2018
SALES (est): 797.8K Privately Held
WEB: www.ctmbiomedical.com
SIC: 3842 Implants, surgical

(G-8983)
CUBOS LLC
13832 Sw 142nd Ave (33186-6772)
PHONE.................................786 299-2671
Juan Carlos Gonzalez,
EMP: 6 EST: 2013
SALES (est): 350K Privately Held
WEB: www.cubosllc.com
SIC: 2499 2431 Decorative wood & woodwork; woodwork, interior & ornamental

(G-8984)
CUSTOM STAINLESS STL EQP INC
16215 Nw 15th Ave (33169-5613)
P.O. Box 884, Labelle (33975-0884)
PHONE.................................305 627-6049
Antonio Carnero, *CEO*
Robin Carnero, *Office Mgr*
Craig Dubov, *Manager*
Jordan Morales, *Data Proc Exec*
▼ **EMP: 40 EST: 1991**

SQ FT: 64,000
SALES (est): 8MM **Privately Held**
WEB: www.customstainless.com
SIC: 3312 Stainless steel

(G-8985)
CUSTOM WD ARCHITECTURAL MLLWK
13119 Sw 122nd Ave (33186-6231)
PHONE.....................786 290-5412
EMP: 7 EST: 2019
SALES (est): 65.1K **Privately Held**
WEB: www.millworks.biz
SIC: 2431 Millwork

(G-8986)
CVG AEROSPACE LLC
13500 Sw 134th Ave Ste 6 (33186-4553)
PHONE.....................786 293-9923
EMP: 8 EST: 2019
SALES (est): 388.5K **Privately Held**
WEB: www.cvgaerospace.com
SIC: 3728 Aircraft parts & equipment

(G-8987)
CYBER MANUFACTURING INC
14440 Sw 110th St (33186-6624)
PHONE.....................786 457-1973
Chin-Sheng Chen, *Principal*
EMP: 7 EST: 2000
SALES (est): 105K **Privately Held**
SIC: 7372 Prepackaged software

(G-8988)
CZARNIKOW GROUP LTD
333 Se 2nd Ave Ste 3410 (33131-2182)
PHONE.....................786 476-0000
Mario Bolival, *Partner*
Debra Proenza, *Office Mgr*
Carolina Marques, *Manager*
Luis Felipe Trindade, *Associate Dir*
Samuel Mejia, *Analyst*
EMP: 6 EST: 2013
SALES (est): 411.2K **Privately Held**
WEB: www.czarnikow.com
SIC: 3556 Sugar plant machinery

(G-8989)
D & G MILLWORK & CABINETRY LLC
2618 Ne 191st St (33180-2632)
PHONE.....................305 830-3000
Eli Ran, *Mng Member*
Carpenter Grushka, *Master*
EMP: 5 EST: 2008
SALES (est): 611.9K **Privately Held**
WEB: www.dgmillwork.com
SIC: 2434 Wood kitchen cabinets

(G-8990)
D AND I TRUCKING EXPRESS INC
21009 Nw 14th Pl Apt 353 (33169-2887)
PHONE.....................786 443-3320
Nadine Andrews, *Vice Pres*
EMP: 7 EST: 2012
SALES (est): 76.9K **Privately Held**
SIC: 3479 Metal coating & allied service

(G-8991)
D D B CORPORATION
Also Called: Sundrinks
7340 Nw 35th Ave (33147-5808)
PHONE.....................305 721-9506
Carlo Darbouze, *President*
Maryse Bateau, *Vice Pres*
▼ EMP: 5 EST: 1999
SQ FT: 6,000
SALES (est): 379.9K **Privately Held**
SIC: 2086 Carbonated beverages, nonalcoholic: bottled & canned

(G-8992)
D1 LOCKER LLC
4880 Nw 4th St (33126-2168)
PHONE.....................305 446-9041
EMP: 6
SALES (est): 376.4K **Privately Held**
SIC: 2741 Internet Publishing And Broadcasting

(G-8993)
DACCORD SHIRTS & GUAYABERAS
7320 Nw 12th St (33126-1912)
PHONE.....................305 576-0926
Contreras Rafael, *Principal*
EMP: 7 EST: 2015
SALES (est): 285.9K **Privately Held**
WEB: www.daccordshirts.com
SIC: 2759 Screen printing

(G-8994)
DADE ENGINEERING GROUP LLC
7700 Nw 37th Ave (33147-4423)
PHONE.....................305 885-2766
Donald M Pittsley, *Mng Member*
EMP: 12 EST: 2014
SQ FT: 30,000
SALES (est): 2.6MM **Privately Held**
WEB: www.dadecoolers.com
SIC: 3441 3585 Building components, structural steel; refrigeration & heating equipment

(G-8995)
DADE EQUIPMENT
8260 Nw 70th St (33166-2778)
PHONE.....................305 717-9901
Gerardo Paz, *Principal*
EMP: 7 EST: 2016
SALES (est): 351.9K **Privately Held**
WEB: www.dadeequipment.com
SIC: 3531 Construction machinery

(G-8996)
DADE PUMP & SUPPLY CO
Also Called: De Ruiter Electric Motor
14261 S Dixie Hwy (33176-7224)
PHONE.....................305 235-5000
John K Delaney, *President*
Mary Hernandez, *General Mgr*
Marilyn Delaney, *Corp Secy*
◆ EMP: 9 EST: 1960
SQ FT: 4,000
SALES (est): 2.4MM **Privately Held**
WEB: www.dadepump.com
SIC: 7694 7699 5063 5084 Electric motor repair; pumps & pumping equipment repair; motors, electric; pumps & pumping equipment

(G-8997)
DADE TRUSS COMPANY INC
Also Called: Dtc Stairs
6401 Nw 74th Ave (33166-3634)
PHONE.....................305 592-8245
Salvador A Jurado, *President*
Mike Toyota, *General Mgr*
Jose Alonso Jurado Jr, *Corp Secy*
Alex Jurado, *Vice Pres*
Manuel Alegre, *Sales Staff*
▼ EMP: 130 EST: 1978
SQ FT: 900
SALES (est): 19.3MM **Privately Held**
WEB: www.dadetruss.com
SIC: 2439 2431 Trusses, wooden roof; millwork

(G-8998)
DAILY MELT
3401 N Miami Ave (33127-3525)
PHONE.....................305 519-2585
Gregg Lurie, *Principal*
EMP: 7 EST: 2011
SALES (est): 387.1K **Privately Held**
SIC: 2711 Newspapers, publishing & printing

(G-8999)
DANLY CORPORATION (PA)
3121 Commodore Plz Ph 5 (33133-5846)
PHONE.....................305 285-0111
James C Danly Jr, *President*
Michael D Danly, *Corp Secy*
EMP: 2 EST: 1992
SALES (est): 13MM **Privately Held**
SIC: 3544 Industrial molds

(G-9000)
DANNYS PRTG SVC SUPS & EQP INC
7233 Biscayne Blvd (33138-5118)
PHONE.....................305 757-2282
Elvia Alvarenga, *President*
Jose D Alvarenga, *Vice Pres*
EMP: 5 EST: 1991
SQ FT: 1,200
SALES (est): 457.4K **Privately Held**
WEB: www.dannysprinting.com
SIC: 2752 5112 2791 2789 Commercial printing, offset; business forms; typesetting; bookbinding & related work; commercial printing

(G-9001)
DANNYS WELDING SERVICES INC
702 Sw 32nd Ave (33135-2624)
PHONE.....................786 436-8087
Danny Diaz, *Principal*
EMP: 7 EST: 2018
SALES (est): 25K **Privately Held**
WEB: dannys-welding-services-inc.business.site
SIC: 7692 Welding repair

(G-9002)
DASAN ZHONE SOLUTIONS INC
801 Brickell Ave Fl 9 (33131-2945)
PHONE.....................305 789-6680
Antonio Jonusas, *Branch Mgr*
EMP: 10
SALES (corp-wide): 350.2MM **Publicly Held**
WEB: www.dzsi.com
SIC: 3661 Telephone & telegraph apparatus
PA: Dzs Inc.
5700 Tennyson Pkwy # 400
Plano TX 75024
469 327-1531

(G-9003)
DAT SOFTWARE INC
560 Nw 59th Ave (33126-3134)
PHONE.....................305 266-5150
Paulo F Dattoli, *Principal*
EMP: 8 EST: 2011
SALES (est): 106.9K **Privately Held**
WEB: www.dat.com
SIC: 7372 Prepackaged software

(G-9004)
DATA ACCESS INTERNATIONAL INC
14000 Sw 119th Ave (33186-6017)
P.O. Box 770970 (33177-0017)
PHONE.....................305 238-0012
Charles L Casanave III, *President*
Stephen W Meely, *Vice Pres*
Charles L Casanave Jr, *CFO*
EMP: 55 EST: 1993
SQ FT: 25,000
SALES (est): 1.1MM
SALES (corp-wide): 7.6MM **Privately Held**
WEB: www.dataaccess.com
SIC: 7372 Prepackaged software
PA: Data Access Corporation
18001 Old Cutier Rd # 43
Palmetto Bay FL 33157
305 238-0012

(G-9005)
DEAKO COATING & CHEMICAL INC
2540 Nw 29th Ave Ste 105 (33142-6438)
PHONE.....................305 634-5162
Rocio Fernandez, *President*
▼ EMP: 8 EST: 1973
SQ FT: 5,000
SALES (est): 651.1K **Privately Held**
SIC: 2851 Paints: oil or alkyd vehicle or water thinned

(G-9006)
DECOY INC
Also Called: Decoy Next Level In Apparel
2480 Nw 20th St Unit D (33142-7116)
PHONE.....................305 633-6384
Yaron Gilboa, *Principal*
▲ EMP: 9 EST: 2007
SALES (est): 1.1MM **Privately Held**
WEB: www.etzo.com
SIC: 2331 2341 5137 Women's & misses' blouses & shirts; women's & children's underwear; women's & children's clothing

(G-9007)
DEEPSTREAM DESIGNS INC
2699 Tigertail Ave Apt 54 (33133-4662)
PHONE.....................305 857-0466
Sheila K Boyce, *President*
Thomas H Boyce, *Vice Pres*
EMP: 5 EST: 2009
SQ FT: 9,400
SALES (est): 795.2K **Privately Held**
WEB: www.deepstreamdesign.com
SIC: 2599 Hotel furniture

(G-9008)
DELET DOORS INC
9250 Sw 117th Ter (33176-4234)
PHONE.....................786 250-4506
Marlene Harris, *President*
E M Harris, *President*
Ronit Moll, *Vice Pres*
Ana Y Santos, *Vice Pres*
Jeronimo Pineda, *Director*
▼ EMP: 10 EST: 2006
SQ FT: 3,500
SALES (est): 1MM **Privately Held**
WEB: www.nationaltradersinc.com
SIC: 2431 2499 Windows, wood; woodenware, kitchen & household

(G-9009)
DELI FRESH FOODS INC
Also Called: Mak Food Service
18630 Ne 2nd Ave (33179-4452)
PHONE.....................305 652-2848
Charles Chmelir, *President*
EMP: 10 EST: 2008
SALES (est): 1.2MM **Privately Held**
SIC: 2099 Sandwiches, assembled & packaged: for wholesale market

(G-9010)
DELICATE DESIGNS EVENT PLG INC
12080 Ne 16th Ave Apt 201 (33161-6514)
PHONE.....................305 833-8725
Regina Bryant, *CEO*
EMP: 5 EST: 2020
SALES (est): 300K **Privately Held**
SIC: 2752 Business form & card printing, lithographic

(G-9011)
DELICIOSA FOOD GROUP INC
1177 Nw 81st St (33150-2739)
PHONE.....................954 492-6131
Jorge A Bravo, *CEO*
EMP: 10 EST: 2018
SALES (est): 2.8MM **Privately Held**
WEB: www.deliciosafoodgroup.com
SIC: 2024 Ice cream & frozen desserts

(G-9012)
DELL USA LP
14591 Sw 120th St (33186-8638)
PHONE.....................512 728-8391
Steve Leboeuf, *Accounts Exec*
Rich Rothberg, *General Counsel*
EMP: 12 EST: 2015
SALES (est): 1.4MM **Privately Held**
WEB: www.dell.com
SIC: 3571 Personal computers (microcomputers)

(G-9013)
DELTA INTERNATIONAL INC
4856 Sw 72nd Ave (33155-5526)
PHONE.....................305 665-6573
Elena De La Torre, *President*
Claudia De La Torre, *QC Mgr*
Michelle Lomeli, *Sales Executive*
◆ EMP: 10 EST: 1976
SQ FT: 4,000
SALES (est): 2.9MM **Privately Held**
WEB: www.deltaintl.com
SIC: 3545 3546 3444 Machine tool accessories; drills & drilling tools; sheet metalwork

(G-9014)
DELUXE CLSETS CABINETS STN LLC
15290 Sw 36th Ter (33185-4795)
PHONE.....................786 879-3371
Rigoberto Arias Sala, *Manager*
EMP: 8 EST: 2018

▲ = Import ▼ =Export
◆ =Import/Export

SALES (est): 351.8K **Privately Held**
SIC: **2434** Wood kitchen cabinets

(G-9015)
DEMACO LLC
121 Sw 109th Ave Apt M2 (33174-1230)
PHONE..............................321 952-6600
Roberth E Gomez, *Principal*
EMP: 7 EST: 2010
SALES (est): 125.9K **Privately Held**
WEB: www.demaco.com
SIC: **3559** Special industry machinery

(G-9016)
DEMERX INC
1951 Nw 7th Ave Ste 300 (33136-1112)
PHONE..............................954 607-3670
Holger Weis, *President*
Steve Gorlin, *Principal*
Michael Karukin, *COO*
Elizabeth Yager, *Admin Asst*
EMP: 11 EST: 2010
SALES (est): 3.2MM **Privately Held**
WEB: www.demerx.com
SIC: **2836** Biological products, except diagnostic

(G-9017)
DEPUY INC
6303 Blue Lagoon Dr (33126-6002)
PHONE..............................305 412-8010
EMP: 42
SALES (corp-wide): 71.3B **Publicly Held**
SIC: **3842** Mfg Surgical Appliances/Supplies
HQ: Depuy Synthes Inc.
1 Johnson And Johnson Plz
New Brunswick NJ 08901
732 524-0400

(G-9018)
DEPUY SYNTHES PRODUCTS INC
Also Called: Cerenovus
6303 Blue Lagoon Dr (33126-6002)
PHONE..............................305 265-6842
EMP: 19
SALES (corp-wide): 93.7B **Publicly Held**
SIC: **3841** Surgical & medical instruments
HQ: Depuy Synthes Products, Inc.
325 Paramount Dr
Raynham MA 02767
508 880-8100

(G-9019)
DESCO INDUSTRIES
13937 Sw 119th Ave (33186-6202)
PHONE..............................305 255-7744
▼ EMP: 8
SALES (est): 612.3K **Privately Held**
SIC: **3999** Mfg Misc Products

(G-9020)
DESCO INDUSTRIES INC
13937 Sw 119th Ave (33186-6202)
PHONE..............................305 255-7744
Rob Darosa, *Regl Sales Mgr*
Odalys Olazabal, *Branch Mgr*
EMP: 20
SQ FT: 63
SALES (corp-wide): 66.3MM **Privately Held**
WEB: www.descoindustries.com
SIC: **3629** Static elimination equipment, industrial
PA: Desco Industries, Inc.
3651 Walnut Ave
Chino CA 91710
909 627-8178

(G-9021)
DESIGN YOUR KIT CLSET MORE INC
13400 Sw 134th Ave Ste 5 (33186-4523)
PHONE..............................786 227-6412
Shaukat Ali, *President*
Monica Ali-Gordon, *CFO*
EMP: 7 EST: 2017
SALES (est): 364.6K **Privately Held**
SIC: **2434** 5031 Wood kitchen cabinets; kitchen cabinets

(G-9022)
DESIGNERS SPECIALTY CAB CO INC
Also Called: Designer Speciality Millwork
1730 Biscayne Blvd 201g (33132-1124)
PHONE..............................954 776-4500
EMP: 23 **Privately Held**
SIC: **2431** Mfg Millwork
PA: Designer's Specialty Cabinet Company, Inc.
1320 Nw 65th Pl
Fort Lauderdale FL 33309

(G-9023)
DESIGNERS TOPS INC
4725 Nw 36th Ave (33142-3907)
PHONE..............................305 599-9973
Tony Pino, *CEO*
Erlinda Pino, *President*
Pablo Pino, *Vice Pres*
Roberto Pino, *Treasurer*
◆ EMP: 23 EST: 1984
SALES (est): 3MM **Privately Held**
WEB: www.designerstops.com
SIC: **2541** 3281 2821 Counter & sink tops; cut stone & stone products; plastics materials & resins

(G-9024)
DESIRE FRAGRANCES INC
Also Called: Petite Beaute
848 Brickell Ave Ste 1225 (33131-2947)
PHONE..............................646 832-3051
Antonio Lemma, *CEO*
Nathalia Rusanova, *General Mgr*
EMP: 4 EST: 2019
SALES (est): 9.6MM **Privately Held**
WEB: www.desirefragrances.net
SIC: **2844** Perfumes & colognes

(G-9025)
DEXTRUM LABORATORIES INC
Also Called: Agnus Distributors
6993 Nw 82nd Ave Ste 20 (33166-2782)
PHONE..............................305 594-4020
Rabames Riesgo, *President*
▲ EMP: 8 EST: 2000
SALES (est): 1.1MM **Privately Held**
WEB: www.dextrumlabs.com
SIC: **2834** Vitamin preparations

(G-9026)
DHL EXPRESS (USA) INC
5945 Nw 18th St (33126-7330)
PHONE..............................305 526-1112
Michael Schmitt, *Vice Pres*
Idalys Martinez, *Buyer*
Eugenio Arce, *Purchasing*
Jon Koch, *Sales Staff*
David Hart, *Program Mgr*
EMP: 34
SALES (corp-wide): 92.5B **Privately Held**
WEB: locations.us.express.dhl.com
SIC: **3444** Mail (post office) collection or storage boxes, sheet metal
HQ: Dhl Express (Usa), Inc.
16592 Collections Ctr Dr
Chicago IL 60693
954 888-7000

(G-9027)
DHS POWER CORP
8061 Nw 67th St (33166-2750)
PHONE..............................305 599-1022
Danny Hernandez, *President*
◆ EMP: 6 EST: 2010
SALES (est): 897.6K **Privately Held**
WEB: www.dhspower.com
SIC: **3537** 5531 Industrial trucks & tractors; automotive parts

(G-9028)
DIANTHUS MIAMI INC (PA)
7635 Nw 27th Ave (33147-5503)
PHONE..............................786 800-8365
Johannes Kornman, *President*
Dianthus Miami, *Creative Dir*
Jan Korman, *Master*
EMP: 10 EST: 2010
SALES (est): 354.6K **Privately Held**
WEB: www.dianthusmiami.com
SIC: **3999** Artificial flower arrangements

(G-9029)
DIATOMITE CORP OF AMERICA
19925 Ne 39th Pl (33180-3088)
PHONE..............................305 466-0075
Allan Applestein, *President*
EMP: 9 EST: 1956
SQ FT: 2,500
SALES (est): 285K **Privately Held**
SIC: **1481** 0811 6552 3295 Mine development, nonmetallic minerals; timber tracts; subdividers & developers; minerals, ground or treated

(G-9030)
DIESEL MACHINERY INTL USA
4121 Sw 90th Ct (33165-5367)
PHONE..............................305 551-4424
Franco Giangradi, *President*
Charles Matuszak, *Vice Pres*
▼ EMP: 5 EST: 1991
SALES (est): 497.1K **Privately Held**
WEB: www.dmi-usa.com
SIC: **3519** Diesel engine rebuilding

(G-9031)
DIESEL PRO POWER INC
Also Called: Diesel Pro Power USA
760 Nw 4th St Ste 100 (33128-1464)
PHONE..............................305 545-5588
Luis Uva, *President*
◆ EMP: 15 EST: 2003
SQ FT: 11,000
SALES (est): 5MM **Privately Held**
WEB: www.dieselpro.com
SIC: **3519** 5084 Parts & accessories, internal combustion engines; engines & parts, diesel

(G-9032)
DIGITAL LIGHTING SYSTEMS INC
Also Called: D L S Electronics
7588 Nw 8th St Fl 2 (33126-2915)
PHONE..............................305 264-8391
Alif Khawand, *President*
Elias Khawand, *Vice Pres*
EMP: 7 EST: 1978
SQ FT: 6,000
SALES (est): 800K **Privately Held**
WEB: www.digitallighting.com
SIC: **3648** 8711 Lighting equipment; electrical or electronic engineering

(G-9033)
DISCOS Y EMPANADAS ARGENTINA
2181 Nw 10th Ave (33127-4635)
PHONE..............................305 326-9300
Albert Muniz, *President*
Jesus Guerra, *Corp Secy*
▼ EMP: 10 EST: 1986
SQ FT: 3,000
SALES (est): 1.1MM **Privately Held**
WEB: www.empanadawholesale.com
SIC: **2038** 2013 Frozen specialties; sausages & other prepared meats

(G-9034)
DISCOUNT WELDS LLC
2745 Nw 21st St (33142-7015)
PHONE..............................305 637-3939
Silvio Fernandez, *Principal*
EMP: 7 EST: 2017
SALES (est): 899.4K **Privately Held**
WEB: www.discountwelds.com
SIC: **7692** Welding repair

(G-9035)
DISCOVERY CANVAS EAST COAST CO
1386 Nw 54th St (33142-3859)
PHONE..............................786 487-8897
Mercedes Abreut, *Principal*
Juan C Sarmento, *Principal*
EMP: 9 EST: 2010
SALES (est): 10.5K **Privately Held**
SIC: **2211** Canvas

(G-9036)
DITAS CORP
10322 Sw 27th St (33165-2804)
PHONE..............................305 558-5766
Rick Ditas, *President*
EMP: 8 EST: 2005

SALES (est): 65.9K **Privately Held**
WEB: www.dita.com
SIC: **3851** Ophthalmic goods

(G-9037)
DIVAS FASHION
8382 Bird Rd (33155-3355)
PHONE..............................786 717-7039
Sirlhey Guerrero Nunez, *Principal*
EMP: 7 EST: 2016
SALES (est): 121.3K **Privately Held**
SIC: **2299** Jute & flax textile products

(G-9038)
DOCUPRINT CORPORATION
7950 Nw 53rd St Ste 337 (33166-4791)
PHONE..............................305 639-8618
Antonio Analia, *Principal*
EMP: 11 EST: 2000
SALES (est): 813.5K **Privately Held**
WEB: www.docuprint.com
SIC: **2752** Commercial printing, offset

(G-9039)
DOLCI PECCATI LLC
1900 N Bayshore Dr (33132-3001)
PHONE..............................954 632-8551
Natalie Yepes Lasprilla, *Principal*
EMP: 5 EST: 2010
SALES (est): 393.4K **Privately Held**
WEB: www.dolcipeccatigelato.com
SIC: **2024** Ice cream & frozen desserts

(G-9040)
DOLPHIN KITCHEN & BATH
2051 Nw 112th Ave Ste 123 (33172-1835)
PHONE..............................305 482-9486
Roberto Colatosti, *President*
EMP: 9 EST: 2007
SALES (est): 120K **Privately Held**
SIC: **2499** Kitchen, bathroom & household ware: wood

(G-9041)
DONICA INTERNATIONAL INC
7500 Nw 52nd St (33166-5511)
PHONE..............................954 217-7616
Guanglu Wang, *President*
Guy Kennett, *Principal*
EMP: 10 EST: 2011
SALES (est): 299.6K **Privately Held**
WEB: www.donica.com
SIC: **3728** Aircraft assemblies, subassemblies & parts

(G-9042)
DONNELLEY FINANCIAL LLC
200 S Biscayne Blvd # 1750 (33131-2310)
PHONE..............................305 371-3900
Paul Nuttaol, *Manager*
EMP: 10
SQ FT: 3,500
SALES (corp-wide): 993.3MM **Publicly Held**
WEB: www.dfinsolutions.com
SIC: **2752** 7373 Commercial printing, offset; computer integrated systems design
HQ: Donnelley Financial, Llc
35 W Wacker Dr
Chicago IL 60601
844 866-4337

(G-9043)
DOOR STYLES INC
1178 Nw 163rd Dr (33169-5816)
PHONE..............................305 653-4447
Eduardo Zegarra, *President*
▼ EMP: 21 EST: 1995
SQ FT: 5,000
SALES (est): 835.8K **Privately Held**
SIC: **2431** Door frames, wood; window frames, wood

(G-9044)
DORAL IMAGING INSTITUTE LLC
2760 Sw 97th Ave Apt 101 (33165-2685)
PHONE..............................305 594-2881
Amy Dusee, *Mktg Dir*
Viana Vivar,
EMP: 9 EST: 2007
SALES (est): 825.1K **Privately Held**
SIC: **3841** Diagnostic apparatus, medical

(G-9045)
DOT BLUE TRADING INC
3100 Nw 72nd Ave Ste 126 (33122-1336)
PHONE......................................954 646-0448
Pedro E Quinteros, *Principal*
EMP: 9 **EST:** 2016
SALES (est): 1MM **Privately Held**
WEB: www.bluedot-trading.com
SIC: 3564 Filters, air: furnaces, air conditioning equipment, etc.

(G-9046)
DOTCHI LLC
Also Called: Crescent Garden
6807 Biscayne Blvd (33138-6214)
PHONE......................................305 477-0024
Harry Tchira, *President*
Paula Douer, *Vice Pres*
Andrea Cepero, *Controller*
Barbara Wise, *Marketing Staff*
Dito Loret, *Office Mgr*
EMP: 22 **EST:** 2014
SALES (est): 7.3MM **Privately Held**
SIC: 3089 Air mattresses, plastic

(G-9047)
DOUBLE DOWN BOAT WORKS INC
8204 Sw 103rd Ave (33173-3906)
PHONE......................................305 984-3000
Brill Arielle, *Principal*
EMP: 8 **EST:** 2015
SALES (est): 249.9K **Privately Held**
SIC: 3732 Boat building & repairing

(G-9048)
DRAZCANNA INC (PA)
Also Called: Sibling Group Holdings, Inc.
6340 Sunset Dr (33143-4836)
PHONE......................................786 618-1472
Julie E Young, *CEO*
Angelle Judice, *CFO*
EMP: 33 **EST:** 1988
SALES (est): 5.2MM **Privately Held**
WEB: www.gpaed.com
SIC: 7372 8299 Educational computer software; educational services

(G-9049)
DREW ESTATE LLC (PA)
12415 Sw 136th Ave Ste 7 (33186-6488)
PHONE......................................786 581-1800
John Hazard, *Partner*
Richard Neuwirth, *Senior VP*
David Lazarus, *Vice Pres*
William Gentry, *Opers Mgr*
Michael Garcia, *Purchasing*
◆ **EMP:** 24 **EST:** 1996
SALES (est): 14MM **Privately Held**
WEB: www.drewestate.com
SIC: 2131 Chewing & smoking tobacco

(G-9050)
DRINKS ON ME 305 LLC
6118 Nw 7th Ave (33127-1112)
PHONE......................................786 488-2356
Chazemon Fenderson,
EMP: 10 **EST:** 2018
SALES (est): 160K **Privately Held**
SIC: 2599 Food wagons, restaurant

(G-9051)
DRONE PICS AND VIDS CORP
13237 Sw 45th Ln (33175-3932)
PHONE......................................786 558-4027
Christian Mirabal, *Principal*
EMP: 7 **EST:** 2016
SALES (est): 80K **Privately Held**
SIC: 3721 Motorized aircraft

(G-9052)
DS HEALTHCARE GROUP INC
Also Called: Ds Laboratories
1395 Brickell Ave Ste 800 (33131-3302)
PHONE......................................888 404-7770
EMP: 102
SALES (corp-wide): 37.3MM **Privately Held**
WEB: www.dslaboratories.com
SIC: 2844 Hair preparations, including shampoos
HQ: Ds Healthcare Group, Inc.
1850 Nw 84th Ave Ste 108
Doral FL 33126
888 829-4212

(G-9053)
DSIGN SOLUTIONS INC
1173 Nw 123rd Pl (33182-2475)
PHONE......................................786 447-4165
Iran Barroso, *General Mgr*
EMP: 7 **EST:** 2010
SALES (est): 248.4K **Privately Held**
SIC: 3993 Advertising artwork

(G-9054)
DUTCH PACKING CO INC
74 Sw Coral Ter Ste 101 (33155)
P.O. Box 143518, Coral Gables (33114-3518)
PHONE......................................305 871-3640
Victor Rodriguez, *President*
Raul Rodriguez, *President*
William Rodriguez, *Vice Pres*
EMP: 6 **EST:** 1961
SQ FT: 10,000
SALES (est): 7MM **Privately Held**
WEB: www.garciasausagebrand.com
SIC: 2013 2011 Sausages & other prepared meats; meat packing plants

(G-9055)
DYNASTIC INVESTMENTS INC
808 Ne 214th Ln (33179-1278)
PHONE......................................513 570-7153
Abraham Yisrael, *CEO*
EMP: 30 **EST:** 1987
SALES (est): 1.2MM **Privately Held**
WEB: www.uspatriot.biz
SIC: 2752 Commercial printing, offset

(G-9056)
E & P PRINTING CORP
7882 Nw 64th St (33166-2706)
PHONE......................................305 715-9545
Cesar Casamayor, *President*
▼ **EMP:** 7 **EST:** 1977
SQ FT: 1,300
SALES (est): 798.1K **Privately Held**
WEB: www.carrillocigars.com
SIC: 2752 Commercial printing, offset

(G-9057)
E T C R INC
3181 Nw 36th Ave (33142-4921)
PHONE......................................305 637-0999
Milagros Espinosa, *President*
◆ **EMP:** 26 **EST:** 2005
SALES (est): 4.3MM **Privately Held**
SIC: 3272 Floor slabs & tiles, precast concrete

(G-9058)
E&P SOLUTIONS AND SERVICES INC
7884 Nw 64th St (33166-2706)
PHONE......................................305 715-9545
Cesar Casamayor, *President*
EMP: 6 **EST:** 2009
SALES (est): 359.5K **Privately Held**
SIC: 2759 8742 Commercial printing; transportation consultant

(G-9059)
E-STONE USA CORPORATION (HQ)
1565 Nw 36th St (33142-5559)
PHONE......................................863 214-8281
Andrea Di Giuseppe, *President*
Giuseppe Bisazza, *Vice Pres*
James A Gorsuch, *Vice Pres*
Cristiano Tonini, *CFO*
Tino Biszza, *Treasurer*
▲ **EMP:** 9 **EST:** 2005
SQ FT: 150,000
SALES (est): 41.8MM
SALES (corp-wide): 46.8MM **Privately Held**
SIC: 3272 Floor slabs & tiles, precast concrete
PA: Trend Usa Ltd.
10306 Usa Today Way
Miramar FL 33025
954 435-5538

(G-9060)
EAGLE ATHLETICA LLC ✪
1000 Brickell Ave Ste 715 (33131-3047)
PHONE......................................305 209-7002
Oguzhan Avcioglu, *Mng Member*
EMP: 9 **EST:** 2021

SALES (est): 900K **Privately Held**
SIC: 3949 Sporting & athletic goods

(G-9061)
EASTERN AERO MARINE INC
Also Called: Eam Worldwide
5502 Nw 37th Ave (33142-2718)
P.O. Box 660067, Miami Springs (33266-0067)
PHONE......................................305 871-4050
Miriam Oroshnik, *President*
Sandra Leguina, *Export Mgr*
Judith Gallo, *QC Mgr*
George Quirk, *Engineer*
Ana Reyes, *Engineer*
◆ **EMP:** 185 **EST:** 1953
SQ FT: 62,000
SALES (est): 24.1MM **Privately Held**
WEB: www.eamworldwide.com
SIC: 3069 7699 Life rafts, rubber; life saving & survival equipment, non-medical: repair

(G-9062)
EASTMAN CHEMICAL COMPANY
Eastman Chemical Latin America
9155 S Ddland Blvd 1116 (33156)
PHONE......................................305 671-2800
Dennis Cooper, *Opers Staff*
Sedric Love, *Opers Staff*
Carlos Panozzo, *Human Res Dir*
Juan Carlos Parodi, *Branch Mgr*
Juan Moncada, *Director*
EMP: 19 **Publicly Held**
WEB: www.eastman.com
SIC: 2869 2821 2282 2865 Industrial organic chemicals; plastics materials & resins; manmade & synthetic fiber yarns: twisting, winding, etc.; cyclic crudes & intermediates; cellulosic manmade fibers
PA: Eastman Chemical Company
200 S Wilcox Dr
Kingsport TN 37660

(G-9063)
EASY DIGITAL CORP
16585 Nw 2nd Ave Ste 100 (33169-6002)
PHONE......................................305 940-1001
Nervys E Lopez, *Principal*
EMP: 9 **EST:** 2006
SALES (est): 347.8K **Privately Held**
SIC: 2759 Commercial printing

(G-9064)
EASY FOODS INC (PA)
1728 Coral Way Ste 900 (33145-2795)
PHONE......................................305 599-0357
William Isaias, *President*
Juan Viejo, *COO*
Andres Isaias, *Vice Pres*
Luis N Isaias, *Vice Pres*
Mariadelcarmen Morla, *Vice Pres*
◆ **EMP:** 23 **EST:** 2005
SALES (est): 30.7MM **Privately Held**
WEB: www.easyfoodsinc.com
SIC: 2099 Tortillas, fresh or refrigerated

(G-9065)
EATON & WOLK
2665 S Byshr Dr Ste 609 (33133-5401)
PHONE......................................305 249-1640
EMP: 6 **EST:** 2019
SALES (est): 431.8K **Privately Held**
WEB: www.eatonwolk.com
SIC: 3625 Motor controls & accessories

(G-9066)
EBERJEY INTIMATES
7400 Nw 7th St Ste 102 (33126-2943)
PHONE......................................305 260-0030
Mariela Rovito, *President*
EMP: 7 **EST:** 2018
SALES (est): 128.3K **Privately Held**
WEB: www.eberjey.com
SIC: 2341 Women's & children's underwear

(G-9067)
EBS QUALITY SERVICE INC
Also Called: Kings Creek Flowers
13210 Sw 132nd Ave Ste 1 (33186-6136)
PHONE......................................305 595-4048
Aristides Borrell, *CEO*
Aristides H Borrell, *CEO*
Emma Borrell, *Vice Pres*
EMP: 12 **EST:** 2000

SQ FT: 1,400
SALES (est): 1.3MM **Privately Held**
WEB: www.ebsqualityserviceinc.com
SIC: 2051 5193 5992 7379 Bakery: wholesale or wholesale/retail combined; flowers & florists' supplies; florists' supplies; florists;

(G-9068)
ECLIPSE SCREEN AND SHUTTERS
3120 Nw 114th Ave (33165-2116)
PHONE......................................305 216-4716
Carlos Fernando Saavedra, *Principal*
EMP: 7 **EST:** 2016
SALES (est): 159.1K **Privately Held**
SIC: 3442 Shutters, door or window: metal

(G-9069)
ECO INFORMATIVO
1901 Brickell Ave B201 (33129-1724)
PHONE......................................786 362-6789
Jose A Aybar, *Principal*
EMP: 7 **EST:** 2012
SALES (est): 109.3K **Privately Held**
SIC: 2711 Newspapers

(G-9070)
ECONOMY TENT INTERNATIONAL INC
2995 Nw 75th St (33147-5943)
PHONE......................................305 691-0191
Hal Paul Lapping, *President*
H Steven Mishket, *Vice Pres*
H Mishket, *Vice Pres*
Rebecca C Mishket, *Treasurer*
Rebecca Mishket, *Treasurer*
◆ **EMP:** 45 **EST:** 1948
SQ FT: 25,000
SALES (est): 837.9K **Privately Held**
WEB: www.economytent.com
SIC: 2394 Tents: made from purchased materials

(G-9071)
EDIGITALPRINTINGCOM INC
11950 Sw 128th St (33186-5207)
PHONE......................................305 378-2325
Michael Stoyanovich, *President*
EMP: 8 **EST:** 2000
SQ FT: 2,000
SALES (est): 1MM **Privately Held**
WEB: www.theprintingcrew.com
SIC: 2752 Commercial printing, offset

(G-9072)
EDITCAR PRINTING CORP
1929 Nw 22nd St (33142-7331)
PHONE......................................305 324-5252
EMP: 8 **EST:** 2009
SALES (est): 83.9K **Privately Held**
WEB: www.editcarprinting.com
SIC: 2752 Commercial printing, lithographic

(G-9073)
EFFEARREDI USA INC
123 Nw 23rd St (33127-4409)
PHONE......................................786 725-4948
Fabio Giovanni Allievi, *Principal*
▲ **EMP:** 6 **EST:** 2012
SALES (est): 748.1K
SALES (corp-wide): 6.2MM **Privately Held**
WEB: www.effearredi.it
SIC: 2431 Millwork
PA: Effearredi Srl
Viale Industria 37
Castelli Calepio BG
035 442-5460

(G-9074)
EGEA FOOD LLC
4313 Sw 75th Ave (33155-4474)
PHONE......................................833 353-6637
Tufan Aycicek, *Principal*
EMP: 13 **EST:** 2017
SALES (est): 3MM **Privately Held**
WEB: www.egeafood.com
SIC: 2011 Meat packing plants

▲ = Import ▼ =Export
◆ =Import/Export

(G-9075)
EL COLUSA NEWS
2550 Nw 72nd Ave Ste 308 (33122-1348)
P.O. Box 165739 (33116-5739)
PHONE...................786 845-6868
Gabrael Martinez, *Owner*
Claudia Villarraga, *Marketing Mgr*
EMP: 7 **EST:** 2001
SALES (est): 399K **Privately Held**
WEB: en.elcolusa.com
SIC: 2711 Newspapers, publishing & printing

(G-9076)
EL SABOR SPICES INC
3501 Nw 67th St (33147-7554)
PHONE...................305 691-2300
Ercida Echemendia, *President*
EMP: 15 **EST:** 2012
SALES (est): 750.7K **Privately Held**
WEB: www.elsaborspices.com
SIC: 2099 5149 5499 Spices, including grinding; spices & seasonings; spices & herbs

(G-9077)
EL TEIDE NORTH INDUSTRIES
7763 Nw 64th St Ste 4 (33166-3503)
PHONE...................786 830-7506
Nicolas Mesa, *Principal*
EMP: 7 **EST:** 2016
SALES (est): 276.6K **Privately Held**
WEB: www.elteidenorth.com
SIC: 3999 Manufacturing industries

(G-9078)
EL TORO MEAT PACKING CORP
Also Called: Morrison Meat Packers
738 Nw 72nd St (33150-3613)
PHONE...................305 836-4461
Claudio Rodriguez, *President*
Gilda M Rodriguez, *Admin Sec*
▲ **EMP:** 47 **EST:** 1966
SQ FT: 14,000
SALES (est): 5.6MM **Privately Held**
WEB: www.morrisonmeat.com
SIC: 2011 Meat packing plants

(G-9079)
ELECTROLYTIC TECHNOLOGIES CORP
19597 Ne 10th Ave Ste G (33179-3578)
PHONE...................305 655-2755
Edmund M Cudworth, *CEO*
Derek B Lubie, *President*
Derick Oubie, *President*
Manuel EE, *Engrg Dir*
Manuel Gonzalez, *Engrg Dir*
▲ **EMP:** 17 **EST:** 2001
SQ FT: 13,179
SALES (est): 3.9MM **Privately Held**
WEB: www.electrolytictech.com
SIC: 3589 Water treatment equipment, industrial

(G-9080)
ELECTROSTATIC INDUSTRIAL PNTG
6801 Nw 25th Ave (33147-6803)
PHONE...................305 696-4556
Guillermo Lugo, *President*
Jose Lugo, *Vice Pres*
▲ **EMP:** 8 **EST:** 1979
SQ FT: 10,000
SALES (est): 568.9K **Privately Held**
SIC: 3479 Painting of metal products

(G-9081)
ELEMENT INC CO
6606 Sw 52nd Ter (33155-6406)
PHONE...................786 208-5693
Christian Ortiz, *Principal*
EMP: 8 **EST:** 2012
SALES (est): 152.7K **Privately Held**
WEB: investors.mullenusa.com
SIC: 2819 Industrial inorganic chemicals

(G-9082)
ELEMENTS ACCOUNTING INC
7344 Sw 48th St Ste 301 (33155-5521)
P.O. Box 347875 (33234-7875)
PHONE...................305 662-4448
Eillen Aguirre, *President*
EMP: 7 **EST:** 2005

SALES (est): 255.4K **Privately Held**
WEB: www.elementsaccounting.com
SIC: 2819 8721 Industrial inorganic chemicals; billing & bookkeeping service; auditing services

(G-9083)
ELI LILLY AND COMPANY
Also Called: Elanco Animal Health
8251 Sw 92nd Ave (33173-4156)
PHONE...................305 987-7000
Cassandre Arnold, *Sales Staff*
Jessica McLemore, *Sales Staff*
EMP: 10
SALES (corp-wide): 28.3B **Publicly Held**
WEB: www.lilly.com
SIC: 2834 Pharmaceutical preparations
PA: Eli Lilly And Company
Lilly Corporate Ctr
Indianapolis IN 46285
317 276-2000

(G-9084)
ELICAR PRINTING
1929 Nw 22nd St (33142-7331)
PHONE...................305 324-5252
Roberto Valverde, *Principal*
EMP: 7 **EST:** 2001
SALES (est): 145.3K **Privately Held**
SIC: 2796 Lithographic plates, positives or negatives

(G-9085)
ELITE FLOWER SERVICES INC
6755 Nw 36th St Unit 180 (33166-6813)
PHONE...................305 436-7400
Lorena Amaya, *Sales Staff*
Pamela Duperly, *Sales Staff*
Angela Fajardo, *Sales Staff*
Claudia Guevara, *Sales Staff*
Andres Pinto, *Sales Staff*
EMP: 30
SALES (corp-wide): 77.8MM **Privately Held**
WEB: www.eliteflower.com
SIC: 3999 Barber & beauty shop equipment
PA: Elite Flower Services, Inc.
6745 Nw 36th St Unit 290
Miami FL 33166
305 436-7400

(G-9086)
ELITE INTL GROUP LLC
Also Called: E L I T E Intergroup
7950 Nw 53rd St Ste 337 (33166-4791)
PHONE...................305 901-5005
Alvin Zacarias, *CEO*
EMP: 15 **EST:** 2014
SALES (est): 1.7MM **Privately Held**
SIC: 3728 7363 8249 3721 Aircraft training equipment; pilot service, aviation; aviation school; aircraft; aircraft engines & engine parts

(G-9087)
ELITE POWDER COATING
8298 Nw 64th St (33166-2740)
PHONE...................786 616-8084
Isidro F Suarez, *Principal*
EMP: 8 **EST:** 2016
SALES (est): 407.4K **Privately Held**
WEB: www.elitecoating.com
SIC: 3479 Coating of metals & formed products

(G-9088)
ELITE POWER PRTG SOLUTIONS INC
10103 Sw 166th Ct (33196-1043)
PHONE...................786 387-7164
Markus Kahlig, *Director*
EMP: 9 **EST:** 2014
SALES (est): 340.1K **Privately Held**
SIC: 2752 Commercial printing, lithographic

(G-9089)
ELLIOT TECHNOLOGIES INC
Also Called: Lunchclub
4100 Ne 2nd Ave Ste 302 (33137-3525)
PHONE...................203 548-0069
Vladimir Novakovski, *CEO*
EMP: 20 **EST:** 2017
SALES (est): 1.5MM **Privately Held**
SIC: 7372 Application computer software

(G-9090)
ELORE ENTERPRISES LLC
1055 Nw 159th Dr (33169-5805)
PHONE...................305 477-1650
Maylin Fojo, *CFO*
Sergio Pires, *Sales Dir*
Philippe Pinel,
Jesus Elejabarrieta,
Juan A Elejabarrieta,
◆ **EMP:** 32 **EST:** 2007
SALES (est): 11.5MM
SALES (corp-wide): 297.6K **Privately Held**
WEB: www.palacios.us
SIC: 2013 Sausages from purchased meat
HQ: Elore Holdings, Inc.
1055 Nw 159th Dr
Miami FL 33169
305 477-1650

(G-9091)
ELORE HOLDINGS INC (DH)
Also Called: El Quijote
1055 Nw 159th Dr (33169-5805)
PHONE...................305 477-1650
Francisco J Palacios, *President*
Angel P Palacios, *Vice Pres*
Maylin Fojo, *CFO*
Teresa Perez, *Director*
▲ **EMP:** 8 **EST:** 1986
SQ FT: 12,000
SALES (est): 19.3MM
SALES (corp-wide): 297.6K **Privately Held**
WEB: www.palacios.us
SIC: 2013 Sausages from purchased meat

(G-9092)
EMBROIDERY USA INC
6900 Nw 50th St (33166-5632)
PHONE...................305 477-9973
Jorge Murcia, *President*
Carol Yidi, *Admin Sec*
EMP: 6 **EST:** 1992
SQ FT: 5,000
SALES (est): 436.9K **Privately Held**
WEB: www.embrousa.com
SIC: 2395 Embroidery & art needlework

(G-9093)
EMBROSERVICE LLC
7003 N Waterway Dr # 222 (33155-2897)
PHONE...................305 267-2323
Miguel Marmol, *Partner*
EMP: 15 **EST:** 1999
SALES (est): 545.9K **Privately Held**
WEB: www.embroservice.com
SIC: 2395 Embroidery products, except schiffli machine

(G-9094)
EMC2 IMPROVEMENT CORPORATION
1720 Sw 99th Ct (33165-7545)
PHONE...................786 564-9683
Hans C Eskelsen, *Principal*
EMP: 7 **EST:** 2014
SALES (est): 186.6K **Privately Held**
SIC: 3572 Computer storage devices

(G-9095)
EMD SERONO RESEARCH & DEV INST
801 Brickell Ave (33131-2951)
PHONE...................978 715-1804
EMP: 8 **EST:** 2018
SALES (est): 1.2MM **Privately Held**
SIC: 2834 Pharmaceutical preparations

(G-9096)
EMMANUEL HOLDINGS INC
Also Called: USA Plastic Industry
2190 Nw 46th St (33142-4017)
PHONE...................305 558-3088
Miguel Ruiz, *President*
Albert Marryschow, *General Mgr*
Maria Ruiz, *Admin Sec*
▼ **EMP:** 21 **EST:** 2005
SQ FT: 41,171
SALES (est): 788.6K **Privately Held**
SIC: 3089 Extruded finished plastic products

(G-9097)
EMPANADA LADY CO
6732 Ne 4th Ave (33138-5515)
PHONE...................786 271-6460
Boris Marinovic, *President*
EMP: 8 **EST:** 2015
SALES (est): 245K **Privately Held**
WEB: www.artpieusa.com
SIC: 2051 Pies, bakery: except frozen

(G-9098)
ENDO-GEAR LLC
Also Called: Zag Medical
4390 Sw 74th Ave (33155-4406)
PHONE...................305 710-6662
John Zabalo, *Mng Member*
Alvaro Angulo, *Mng Member*
Carlos Gonzalez, *Mng Member*
EMP: 10 **EST:** 2013
SQ FT: 3,500
SALES (est): 663.5K **Privately Held**
WEB: www.endogear.com
SIC: 3845 3841 Endoscopic equipment, electromedical; gastroscopes, except electromedical

(G-9099)
ENERGY SVING SOLUTIONS USA LLC
1031 Ives Dairy Rd # 228 (33179-2521)
PHONE...................305 735-2878
Peter J Stein, *Managing Dir*
Peter Stein,
▲ **EMP:** 11 **EST:** 2010
SALES (est): 2MM **Privately Held**
WEB: www.energysavingindustry.com
SIC: 3646 Commercial indusl & institutional electric lighting fixtures

(G-9100)
ENTECH CONTROLS CORP
1031 Ives Dairy Rd Bldg 4 (33179-2521)
PHONE...................954 613-2971
Alan D Jorczak, *President*
Cecelia L Jorczak, *Corp Secy*
EMP: 7 **EST:** 1980
SQ FT: 10,000
SALES (est): 1.2MM **Privately Held**
WEB: www.entechcontrolscorp.com
SIC: 3613 5065 3625 Switches, electric power except snap, push button, etc.; electronic parts & equipment; relays & industrial controls

(G-9101)
ENVIRALUM INDUSTRIES INC
5100 Nw 72nd Ave Unit C (33166-5608)
PHONE...................305 752-4411
Frank Messa, *President*
EMP: 11 **EST:** 2010
SALES (est): 2MM **Privately Held**
WEB: www.enviralum.net
SIC: 3231 Doors, glass: made from purchased glass

(G-9102)
ENVISION GRAPHICS INC
7335 Nw 35th St (33122-1268)
PHONE...................305 470-0083
Janoy Fuentes, *President*
Edilberto Fuentes, *Vice Pres*
EMP: 27 **EST:** 1999
SQ FT: 3,700
SALES (est): 2.5MM **Privately Held**
SIC: 2759 2752 Commercial printing; commercial printing, lithographic

(G-9103)
EP CLOTHING LLC
13275 Sw 136th St (33186-5824)
PHONE...................786 827-9187
Malik Dandridge,
EMP: 9
SALES (est): 557.3K **Privately Held**
SIC: 2326 Men's & boys' work clothing

(G-9104)
EPARE LLC
117 Ne 1st Ave (33132-2125)
PHONE...................347 682-5121
Yevgeniy Khayman, *President*
Eugene Khayman, *Vice Pres*
EMP: 7 **EST:** 2012

SALES (est): 874K **Privately Held**
WEB: www.epare.com
SIC: **3469** Household cooking & kitchen
　utensils, metal

(G-9105)
EPITOMI INC
12201 Sw 128th Ct Ste 108 (33186-6425)
P.O. Box 561564 (33256-1564)
PHONE...................................305 971-5370
▼ EMP: 20
SALES (est): 3.3MM **Privately Held**
SIC: **2844** Mfg Toiletry Preparations

(G-9106)
EPOWER 360 LLC (PA)
7780 Sw 71st Ave (33143-4313)
PHONE...................................305 330-6684
Saied Hussaini, *CEO*
Iliana Hussaini, *Office Mgr*
▲ EMP: 6 EST: 2014
SQ FT: 1,500
SALES (est): 1.1MM **Privately Held**
WEB: www.epower360.com
SIC: **3714** Booster (jump-start) cables, au-
tomotive

(G-9107)
EQUIGRAPH TRADING CORP
13331 Sw 132nd Ave (33186-6197)
PHONE...................................786 237-5665
Natalia E Polla, *President*
Joan M Zuniga, *Vice Pres*
Pablo M Zuniga, *Vice Pres*
EMP: 8 EST: 2016
SALES (est): 995.2K **Privately Held**
WEB: www.equigraf.com
SIC: **3555** Printing trade parts & attach-
ments

(G-9108)
EQUISERVISA USA CORP
13544 Sw 124th Avenue Rd (33186-6556)
PHONE...................................773 530-6964
Marco Trujillo, *President*
EMP: 10
SALES (est): 216.3K **Privately Held**
SIC: **1389** 7389 Construction, repair & dis-
mantling services;

(G-9109)
ES TUDIOS CORP
5483 Nw 72nd Ave (33166-4223)
PHONE...................................305 300-9262
Enrique A Sarubbi, *Principal*
EMP: 7 EST: 2012
SALES (est): 117.1K **Privately Held**
SIC: **3691** Storage batteries

(G-9110)
ESE & ASSOC INC
11939 Sw 75th St (33183-3768)
PHONE...................................718 767-2367
Susan Alvarez, *Treasurer*
EMP: 7 EST: 2000
SALES (est): 91.2K **Privately Held**
SIC: **3625** Relays & industrial controls

(G-9111)
**ESPRESSO DISPOSITION CORP
1 (HQ)**
6262 Bird Rd Ste 2i (33155-4882)
PHONE...................................305 594-9062
Angel L Souto, *CEO*
Jose Enrique Souto, *CEO*
Jose A Souto Jr, *President*
◆ EMP: 84 EST: 1961
SQ FT: 53,000
SALES (est): 34.8MM
SALES (corp-wide): 8B **Publicly Held**
SIC: **2095** Coffee roasting (except by
wholesale grocers)
PA: The J M Smucker Company
　1 Strawberry Ln
　Orrville OH 44667
　330 682-3000

(G-9112)
ESTAL USA INC
150 Se 2nd Ave (33131-1518)
PHONE...................................305 728-3272
Frederic Alberti, *Director*
EMP: 17 EST: 2013

SALES (est): 1.3MM
SALES (corp-wide): 33.6MM **Privately
Held**
WEB: www.estal.com
SIC: **2656** 2671 Sanitary food containers;
packaging paper & plastics film, coated &
laminated
PA: Estal Packaging Sa
　Calle Taper (Pol Industrial Bujonis) 23
　Sant Feliu De Guixols 17220
　972 821-676

(G-9113)
ETI-LABEL INC
Also Called: Aetiquetas Araragua
6961 Nw 82nd Ave (33166-2774)
PHONE...................................305 716-0094
Carlo Damas, *President*
Carlo Lina Damas, *Manager*
EMP: 5 EST: 2006
SALES (est): 450.3K **Privately Held**
WEB: www.etilabels.net
SIC: **2754** Commercial printing, gravure

(G-9114)
EURO GEAR (USA) INC (PA)
1395 Brickell Ave Ste 800 (33131-3302)
PHONE...................................518 578-1775
Greg Gohrt, *President*
Eloise Gohrt, *Vice Pres*
EMP: 22 EST: 2001
SQ FT: 15,000
SALES (est): 5.4MM **Privately Held**
WEB: www.eurogearinc.com
SIC: **3241** 3599 Natural cement; machine
& other job shop work

(G-9115)
EVERGREEN SWEETENERS INC
3601 Nw 62nd St (33147-7539)
PHONE...................................305 835-6907
EMP: 13
SALES (corp-wide): 10.3MM **Privately
Held**
WEB: www.esweeteners.com
SIC: **2099** Food preparations
PA: Evergreen Sweeteners, Inc.
　1936 Hollywood Blvd # 20
　Hollywood FL 33020
　954 381-7776

(G-9116)
EVERYBODYWINCO ❂
66 W Flagler St Ste 900 (33130-1807)
PHONE...................................954 214-4172
Wilfonda Nicholson, *CEO*
EMP: 7 EST: 2022
SALES (est): 311.5K **Privately Held**
SIC: **3612** Distribution transformers, elec-
tric

(G-9117)
EXCEL CONVERTING INC
6950 Nw 37th Ct (33147-6533)
P.O. Box 668826 (33166-9423)
PHONE...................................786 318-2222
Rafael A Marin, *President*
▼ EMP: 10 EST: 2000
SALES (est): 1.5MM **Privately Held**
SIC: **2621** Paper mills

(G-9118)
EXCEL HANDBAGS CO INC
3651 Nw 81st St (33147-4444)
PHONE...................................305 836-8800
Brian D Fink, *President*
▲ EMP: 10 EST: 1941
SQ FT: 30,000
SALES (est): 720.6K **Privately Held**
WEB: www.excelhandbags.com
SIC: **3171** 5137 Handbags, women's;
handbags

(G-9119)
EXCELAG CORP (PA)
7300 N Kendall Dr Ste 640 (33156-7840)
PHONE...................................305 670-0145
Jorge Cepeda, *President*
Daniel Cepeda, *Vice Pres*
Nely V Cepeda, *Vice Pres*
Violeta Cepeda, *Vice Pres*
David L Miles, *Treasurer*
◆ EMP: 5 EST: 2001
SQ FT: 1,500

SALES (est): 4.2MM **Privately Held**
WEB: www.excelag.com
SIC: **2879** Agricultural chemicals

(G-9120)
EXEC TECHNOLOGY CORP
7224 Nw 56th St (33166-4247)
PHONE...................................305 394-8132
Hamilton Costa, *Director*
Luciane Soares, *Assistant*
EMP: 7 EST: 2003
SALES (est): 124.1K **Privately Held**
SIC: **7372** Prepackaged software

(G-9121)
EXOTICS CAR WRAPS
245 Ne 183rd St Ste 3a (33179-4500)
PHONE...................................786 768-6798
EMP: 6 EST: 2018
SALES (est): 484.6K **Privately Held**
SIC: **3993** Signs & advertising specialties

(G-9122)
EXPORT DIESEL LLC (PA)
1835 Nw 112th Ave Ste 173 (33172-1819)
PHONE...................................305 396-1943
Miguel A Figueroa, *Principal*
Catalina Figueroa, *Principal*
German A Figueroa Jr, *Principal*
Carlos Figueroa, *Manager*
▲ EMP: 4 EST: 2009
SALES (est): 23.5MM **Privately Held**
WEB: www.exportdiesel.com
SIC: **2911** Diesel fuels

(G-9123)
EXPRESS IRONING INC
Also Called: Express Ironing of Miami
4707 Sw 75th Ave (33155-4436)
PHONE...................................305 261-1072
Alina Perez, *Principal*
EMP: 9 EST: 2005
SALES (est): 861.5K **Privately Held**
WEB: www.expressironing.co.uk
SIC: **2741** Miscellaneous publishing

(G-9124)
EYEDOSE INC
Also Called: Leisurelay365
66 W Flagler St Ste 900 (33130-1807)
PHONE...................................786 853-6194
Zettie Jones, *President*
EMP: 6 EST: 2010
SALES (est): 358.7K **Privately Held**
SIC: **2254** Shirts & t-shirts (underwear),
knit

(G-9125)
**EYESON DGTAL SRVLLNCE
MGT SYST**
64 Ne 1st St (33132-2412)
PHONE...................................305 808-3344
Raphael Adouth, *Principal*
EMP: 5 EST: 2004
SALES (est): 1MM **Privately Held**
SIC: **3861** 7382 Cameras & related equip-
ment; security systems services

(G-9126)
FABIS GROUP CORPORATION
8025 Nw 68th St (33166-2794)
PHONE...................................305 718-3638
Jose Latella, *President*
Juana Pelosi, *Vice Pres*
▲ EMP: 7 EST: 2011
SALES (est): 153.4K **Privately Held**
WEB: www.fabis.us
SIC: **2394** Canvas awnings & canopies

(G-9127)
FABRIC INNOVATIONS INC
7318 Sw 48th St (33155-5523)
PHONE...................................305 860-5757
Deborah Herman, *President*
Alison Goldman, *Vice Pres*
Gonzalo Leon, *Vice Pres*
Leonardo Chica, *Controller*
Mayling Jaramillo, *Finance Dir*
▲ EMP: 24 EST: 1997
SALES (est): 19MM **Privately Held**
WEB: www.fabricinnovations.com
SIC: **2391** 5023 5719 Curtains &
draperies; pillowcases; beddings & linens

(G-9128)
**FACELOVE COSMETICS INC
(PA)**
18202 Homestead Ave (33157-5532)
PHONE...................................786 346-7357
Alona Naylor, *President*
EMP: 8 EST: 2015
SQ FT: 4,500
SALES (est): 1.6MM **Privately Held**
SIC: **2844** Toilet preparations; face creams
or lotions; cosmetic preparations

(G-9129)
FACTORFOX SOFTWARE LLC
14221 Sw 120th St (33186-7236)
PHONE...................................305 671-9526
Arlen Tejada, *Opers Staff*
Qian Hu, *Accounting Mgr*
Kayla Miller, *Cust Mgr*
Atul Kumar, *CTO*
Atul K Yadav, *CTO*
EMP: 5 EST: 2014
SALES (est): 634.2K **Privately Held**
WEB: www.factorfox.com
SIC: **7372** Prepackaged software

(G-9130)
**FALCON COMMERCIAL
AVIATION LLC**
13500 Sw 134th Ave Ste 3 (33186-4553)
PHONE...................................786 340-9464
Civa Civarajah, *CEO*
Thanushan Sivothayan, *President*
EMP: 12 EST: 2007
SALES (est): 1.2MM **Privately Held**
SIC: **3724** Aircraft engines & engine parts

(G-9131)
FALKEN DESIGN CORPORATION
1200 Brickell Bay Dr # 2715 (33131-3266)
PHONE...................................765 688-0809
Hung Anh Nguyen, *CEO*
EMP: 8 EST: 2017
SALES (est): 1.3MM **Privately Held**
WEB: www.falkenacrylic.com
SIC: **2821** 3081 Acrylic resins; plastic film
& sheet

(G-9132)
**FAMOUS MBL CAR WASH
PRSSURE CL**
8255 Nw 22nd Ave (33147)
PHONE...................................786 720-1326
Eddie Young,
EMP: 10 EST: 2016
SALES (est): 655.7K **Privately Held**
SIC: **3589** Car washing machinery

(G-9133)
FARARTIS LLC
Also Called: Pagnifique
12050 Nw 28th Ave (33167-2518)
PHONE...................................305 594-5704
Pablo De Leon, *Opers Staff*
Julia Palacio, *Sales Staff*
Marcelo Picasso, *Sales Staff*
Luis Abella, *Mng Member*
Heidy Noda, *Administration*
EMP: 4 EST: 2010
SQ FT: 29,965
SALES (est): 7.6MM **Privately Held**
SIC: **2051** Bakery: wholesale or whole-
sale/retail combined

(G-9134)
FARMA INTERNATIONAL INC
9400 S Ddland Blvd Ste 60 (33156)
PHONE...................................305 670-4416
Maria E Medina, *President*
Michael Milgrom, *Vice Pres*
Victor Medellin, *Opers Staff*
◆ EMP: 13 EST: 1966
SALES (est): 7.5MM **Privately Held**
WEB: www.farmainternational.com
SIC: **2834** Pharmaceutical preparations

(G-9135)
FAVER INC
3430 Main Hwy (33133-5916)
PHONE...................................305 448-6060
George Farge, *Principal*
EMP: 7 EST: 2008
SALES (est): 144.3K **Privately Held**
WEB: www.faverinc.com
SIC: **3531** Construction machinery

▲ = Import ▼=Export
◆ =Import/Export

(G-9136)
FEICK CORPORATION
8869 Sw 131st St (33176-5944)
PHONE....................................305 271-8550
EMP: 65
SQ FT: 800
SALES (est): 3.4MM Privately Held
SIC: 7372 6531 Prepackaged Software Services

(G-9137)
FENIX WESTER CORP
2006 Nw 20th St (33142-7308)
PHONE....................................305 324-9105
Noria Cordova, President
EMP: 7 EST: 2007
SALES (est): 136.1K Privately Held
SIC: 2341 Women's & children's underwear

(G-9138)
FERRARI EXPRESS INC
36 Ne 1st St Ste 1049 (33132-2494)
PHONE....................................305 374-5003
Andrea Deldotto, Branch Mgr
EMP: 27 Privately Held
WEB: www.ferrarigroup.net
SIC: 2741 Miscellaneous publishing
PA: Ferrari Express Inc.
215 Mill St
Lawrence NY 11559

(G-9139)
FI AEROSPACE SOLUTIONS INC
7938 Nw 66th St (33166-2726)
PHONE....................................786 395-3289
Francisco Ramirez, President
EMP: 8 EST: 2018
SALES (est): 222K Privately Held
WEB: www.fiaerospace.com
SIC: 3728 Aircraft parts & equipment

(G-9140)
FIBERFLON USA INC
1835 Nw 112th Ave (33172-1817)
PHONE....................................786 953-7329
EMP: 8 EST: 2017
SALES (est): 1.1MM Privately Held
WEB: www.fiberflon.de
SIC: 2821 Plastics materials & resins

(G-9141)
FILTER KING LLC
Also Called: Myfilterking.com
200 Se 1st St Ste 502 (33131-1903)
PHONE....................................877 570-9755
Richard Hoskins, CEO
Tassia Hoskins,
Robert Thorell,
EMP: 15 EST: 2018
SALES (est): 1.2MM Privately Held
WEB: www.filterking.com
SIC: 3585 3564 Heating & air conditioning combination units; filters, air: furnaces, air conditioning equipment, etc.

(G-9142)
FILTHY FOOD LLC
16500 Nw 15th Ave (33169-5620)
PHONE....................................786 916-5556
Daniel Singer, CEO
Charlie Hart, COO
Jennifer Hughes, Senior VP
Robert Shell, Vice Pres
Andrea Pinto, Purch Mgr
EMP: 60 EST: 2009
SQ FT: 50,000
SALES (est): 7.8MM Privately Held
WEB: www.filthyfood.com
SIC: 2035 Olives, brined: bulk

(G-9143)
FINESTA INC
12650 Nw 25th St Ste 112 (33182-1512)
PHONE....................................786 439-1647
Henry Waissmann, President
Hugo Beltran, Finance Dir
▲ EMP: 6 EST: 2009
SQ FT: 3,000
SALES (est): 1MM Privately Held
SIC: 2339 Women's & misses' accessories

(G-9144)
FINOTEX USA CORP (PA)
6942 Nw 50th St (33166-5632)
PHONE....................................305 593-1102

Carlos Yidi, President
Carlos Yidi Jr, Vice Pres
William Yidi, Vice Pres
Andres Yidi, Treasurer
Caridad Hernandez, Accountant
◆ EMP: 40 EST: 1989
SQ FT: 18,500
SALES (est): 11.3MM Privately Held
WEB: www.finotex.com
SIC: 2269 Labels, cotton: printed

(G-9145)
FIRST AMERICA PRODUCTS LLC
9710 E Indigo St Ste 203 (33157-5613)
PHONE....................................904 215-8075
Arjun Saluja,
Suraj Saluja,
EMP: 5 EST: 2010
SALES (est): 384.9K Privately Held
WEB: www.firstamericaproducts.com
SIC: 3585 Air conditioning units, complete: domestic or industrial

(G-9146)
FIRST TEE MIAMI DAGA
1802 Nw 37th Ave (33125-1052)
PHONE....................................305 633-4583
Lucca Charles III, Principal
Carlos Rodriguez, Adv Board Mem
John Reed, Vice Pres
John Moscoso, Director
Mike Golf, Program Dir
EMP: 13 EST: 2011
SALES (est): 968.7K Privately Held
WEB: www.thefirstteemiami.org
SIC: 3949 Shafts, golf club

(G-9147)
FIRSTCUT
3030 Virginia St (33133-4524)
PHONE....................................786 740-3683
Jorge Soto, Principal
EMP: 7 EST: 2017
SALES (est): 100.4K Privately Held
SIC: 3089 Molding primary plastic

(G-9148)
FLASH ROOFING AND SHTMTL LLC
17425 Sw 109th Ct (33157-4046)
PHONE....................................786 237-9440
EMP: 8 EST: 2019
SALES (est): 1MM Privately Held
WEB: www.flashroofingmiami.com
SIC: 3444 Sheet metalwork

(G-9149)
FLEURISSIMA INC (PA)
Also Called: Robba, Emilio
4242 Ne 2nd Ave (33137-3520)
PHONE....................................305 572-0203
Emilio Robba, President
Antoine G Lamarche, General Mgr
Michel Robba, Vice Pres
Jean-Pierre De Regaini, Treasurer
Iris Cheng, Consultant
◆ EMP: 13 EST: 1999
SQ FT: 5,000
SALES (est): 2.8MM Privately Held
SIC: 3299 5023 5999 7389 Non-metallic mineral statuary & other decorative products; decorating supplies; art, picture frames & decorations; interior decorating

(G-9150)
FLEXO CONCEPTS MANUFACTURING
13552 Sw 129th St (33186-6276)
PHONE....................................305 233-7075
Raul Ford, President
Jorge Ford, Principal
Luis Rodriguez, Vice Pres
EMP: 5 EST: 2002
SALES (est): 508.2K Privately Held
WEB: www.flexoconcepts.com
SIC: 3565 Labeling machines, industrial

(G-9151)
FLEXOFFERSCOM INC
990 Biscayne Blvd (33132-1557)
P.O. Box 7520, Fort Lauderdale (33338-7520)
PHONE....................................305 999-9940
Alexander Daskaloff, President

Vanessa Cardona, Finance
Louise Forbes, Marketing Staff
Stephen Martin, Marketing Staff
Fillipe Oliveira, Marketing Staff
EMP: 5 EST: 2010
SALES (est): 2.7MM Privately Held
WEB: www.flexoffers.com
SIC: 3993 7311 Signs & advertising specialties; advertising agencies

(G-9152)
FLIGHT AEROTECH LLC
7241 Nw 54th St (33166-4807)
PHONE....................................305 901-6001
Luis F Rodriguez Sr, Principal
EMP: 9 EST: 2015
SALES (est): 1.5MM Privately Held
WEB: www.flightaerotech.com
SIC: 3728 Aircraft parts & equipment

(G-9153)
FLORIBBEAN INC
6800 Bird Rd (33155-3708)
PHONE....................................844 282-8459
Mary Jo Mellinger, Principal
EMP: 8 EST: 2010
SALES (est): 111.4K Privately Held
WEB: www.floribbeansea.com
SIC: 2099 Food preparations

(G-9154)
FLORIDA ELC MTR CO MIAMI INC
6350 Ne 4th Ct (33138-6108)
PHONE....................................305 759-3835
Vicky Assalone, President
John Assalone, Vice Pres
Lisa Assalone, Admin Sec
▲ EMP: 21 EST: 1951
SQ FT: 23,000
SALES (est): 1.6MM Privately Held
SIC: 7694 5063 7349 Electric motor repair; motors, electric; cleaning service, industrial or commercial

(G-9155)
FLORIDA ENGINE REBUILDERS CORP
12500 Sw 130th St Ste 13 (33186-6206)
PHONE....................................305 232-8784
Miguel D Gonzalez, President
Teresita Gonzalez, Vice Pres
EMP: 5 EST: 1990
SQ FT: 900
SALES (est): 481.6K Privately Held
WEB: www.miamiferco.com
SIC: 3599 Machine shop, jobbing & repair

(G-9156)
FLORIDA FRESH SEAFOOD CORP
7337 Nw 37th Ave Unit 7 (33147-5806)
PHONE....................................305 694-1733
Carlos E Tabora, President
Leuis Alonso, Vice Pres
◆ EMP: 11 EST: 1985
SQ FT: 10,000
SALES (est): 1MM Privately Held
WEB: www.flafreshseafood.com
SIC: 2092 5146 Seafoods, fresh: prepared; seafoods

(G-9157)
FLORIDA HOSE & HYDRAULICS INC
7128 Nw 72nd Ave Ste 336 (33166-2932)
PHONE....................................305 887-9577
E F Mendia, President
Gloria Mendia, Corp Secy
▼ EMP: 5 EST: 1981
SQ FT: 5,000
SALES (est): 477.5K Privately Held
WEB: www.floridahose.com
SIC: 3492 Hose & tube couplings, hydraulic/pneumatic

(G-9158)
FLORIDA MOTORS INC
1515 Nw 167th St Ste 300 (33169-5106)
PHONE....................................786 524-9001
EMP: 6 EST: 2018
SALES (est): 469.1K Privately Held
WEB: www.myfloridamotors.com
SIC: 3714 Motor vehicle parts & accessories

(G-9159)
FLORIDA PRSTHTICS ORTHTICS INC
9981 Sw 12th St (33174-2808)
PHONE....................................305 553-1217
Rolando Torres, Principal
EMP: 8 EST: 2008
SALES (est): 151.6K Privately Held
SIC: 3842 Prosthetic appliances

(G-9160)
FLORIDIAN BLINDS LLC
10735 Sw 216th St Unit 40 (33170-3151)
PHONE....................................786 250-4697
EMP: 9 EST: 2019
SALES (est): 536.2K Privately Held
WEB: www.floridianblinds.com
SIC: 2591 Window blinds

(G-9161)
FLORIDIAN TITLE GROUP INC
20801 Biscayne Blvd # 306 (33180-1430)
PHONE....................................305 792-4911
Oscar Grisales Racini, Principal
EMP: 5 EST: 2005
SALES (est): 460.5K Privately Held
SIC: 3469 Tile, floor or wall: stamped metal

(G-9162)
FLOWERS BAKING CO MIAMI LLC (DH)
17800 Nw Miami Ct (33169-5092)
P.O. Box 693483 (33269-0483)
PHONE....................................305 652-3416
Stephanie B Tillman, Counsel
Ken Redd, Opers Staff
Andrew Herrin, Engineer
Danna Jones, Treasurer
Kenneth Reeves, Controller
◆ EMP: 98 EST: 1977
SQ FT: 40,000
SALES (est): 12.2MM
SALES (corp-wide): 4.3B Publicly Held
SIC: 2051 5461 Breads, rolls & buns; bakeries
HQ: Flowers Baking Co. Of Thomasville, Inc.
1919 Flowers Cir
Thomasville GA 31757
229 226-9110

(G-9163)
FLOWHANCE INC
1951 Nw 7th Ave (33136-1104)
PHONE....................................305 690-0784
Davis Nunez, CEO
EMP: 11 EST: 2018
SALES (est): 586.8K Privately Held
WEB: www.flowhance.com
SIC: 2741

(G-9164)
FOAM DECORATION INC
13800 Sw 142nd Ave (33186-7309)
PHONE....................................786 293-8813
Noel Garcia, President
EMP: 5 EST: 2002
SALES (est): 515.3K Privately Held
SIC: 3086 Plastics foam products

(G-9165)
FOH INC
Also Called: Front of House Rm 360 By Foh
7630 Biscayne Blvd (33138-5136)
PHONE....................................305 757-7940
Simone Mayer, President
Mayda Perez, Treasurer
◆ EMP: 146 EST: 2013
SALES (est): 13.7MM Privately Held
WEB: www.frontofthehouse.com
SIC: 3229 Barware

(G-9166)
FOR-A LATIN AMERICA INC
5200 Blue Lagoon Dr # 130 (33126-7006)
PHONE....................................305 261-2345
EMP: 6
SALES (est): 683K Privately Held
SIC: 3823 Mfg Process Control Instruments

(G-9167)
FORIS INC
1111 Brickell Ave (33131-3112)
PHONE....................................904 394-2618

Kris Marszalek, *President*
EMP: 31 **EST:** 2019
SALES (est): 879.4K **Privately Held**
SIC: 7372 Application computer software

(G-9168)
FORWARD EXPRESS ONE LLC
Also Called: Aerotools Connection
12625 Sw 134th Ct Ste 208 (33186-6423)
PHONE.................................305 234-3034
Lorenzo Locurcio,
EMP: 10 **EST:** 2011
SQ FT: 4,500
SALES (est): 645.1K **Privately Held**
SIC: 3728 Aircraft parts & equipment

(G-9169)
FORWARD INERTIA LLC ✪
1010 Brickell Ave # 4004 (33131-3788)
PHONE.................................617 794-8877
Colin King,
EMP: 7 **EST:** 2022
SALES (est): 226.8K **Privately Held**
SIC: 3161 7389 Clothing & apparel carrying cases;

(G-9170)
FRAGRANCE EXPRESSCOM LLC
Also Called: Fragrance Health and Buty Aids
1221 Nw 165th St (33169-5809)
PHONE.................................800 372-4726
Jose M Norona, *Mng Member*
John Alexander, *Mng Member*
Ernesto Erdmann, *Mng Member*
Mary Barnes,
Bob Bartlett,
EMP: 9 **EST:** 2007
SQ FT: 50,000
SALES (est): 421.5K **Privately Held**
WEB: www.fragranceexpress.com
SIC: 2844 Toilet preparations

(G-9171)
FRAKO CONCRETE SERVICES INC
10312 Sw 3rd St (33174-1709)
P.O. Box 440541 (33144-0541)
PHONE.................................305 551-8196
EMP: 5
SALES (est): 348.3K **Privately Held**
SIC: 3273 Mfg Ready-Mixed Concrete

(G-9172)
FRAMORS TRADING INC
14951 Sw 70th St (33193-1054)
PHONE.................................305 382-8782
Franklin Morales, *President*
Frankcarlo Morales, *Vice Pres*
▲ **EMP:** 7 **EST:** 1998
SALES (est): 231.1K **Privately Held**
SIC: 2092 Seafoods, frozen: prepared

(G-9173)
FREEMAN S MAGIC LLC ✪
12420 Sw 18th Ter (33175-7715)
PHONE.................................786 286-8197
Carlos Freeman,
EMP: 5 **EST:** 2021
SALES (est): 330.8K **Privately Held**
SIC: 1389 Construction, repair & dismantling services

(G-9174)
FRITANGA Y TORTILLA MODRA
1885 W Flagler St (33135-1939)
PHONE.................................305 649-9377
Teofilo C Mondragon, *Principal*
EMP: 7 **EST:** 2009
SALES (est): 320.1K **Privately Held**
SIC: 2099 Tortillas, fresh or refrigerated

(G-9175)
FRONT OF HOUSE INC
7630 Biscayne Blvd # 105 (33138-5136)
PHONE.................................305 757-7940
Simone Mayer, *President*
◆ **EMP:** 20 **EST:** 2002
SALES (est): 3.6MM **Privately Held**
WEB: www.frontofthehouse.com
SIC: 2541 Table or counter tops, plastic laminated

(G-9176)
FROSTBITE NITROGEN ICE CREAM
2305 Ne 197th St (33180-2150)
PHONE.................................305 933-5482
Jeffrey Saunders, *Principal*
EMP: 8 **EST:** 2016
SALES (est): 398.7K **Privately Held**
SIC: 2813 Nitrogen

(G-9177)
FROZEN WHEELS LLC
Also Called: B H Med Supplies
16565 Nw 15th Ave (33169-5619)
PHONE.................................305 799-2258
Isaac Halwani,
EMP: 18 **EST:** 2010
SALES (est): 8.1MM **Privately Held**
SIC: 3312 Wheels

(G-9178)
FRUSELVA USA LLC
801 Brickell Ave Ste 800 (33131-2978)
PHONE.................................949 798-0061
Javier Hernandez, *CEO*
◆ **EMP:** 10 **EST:** 2017
SALES (est): 1.2MM **Privately Held**
WEB: www.globalfruselva.com
SIC: 2033 Fruits: packaged in cans, jars, etc.

(G-9179)
FUN ELECTRONICS INC
2999 Ne 191st St Ph 2 (33180-3117)
PHONE.................................305 933-4646
David Levy, *CEO*
Eyal Levy, *Vice Pres*
Yizhak Toledano, *CFO*
▲ **EMP:** 12 **EST:** 2009
SQ FT: 20,000
SALES (est): 492.1K **Privately Held**
SIC: 3571 3651 5731 Personal computers (microcomputers); audio electronic systems; consumer electronic equipment

(G-9180)
FUTURE MODES INC
1910 Ne 206th St (33179-2254)
PHONE.................................305 654-9995
Michael Fischer, *President*
Mindy Fischer, *Treasurer*
▼ **EMP:** 7 **EST:** 1984
SQ FT: 5,000
SALES (est): 766.4K **Privately Held**
WEB: www.futuremodes.com
SIC: 2431 3089 3442 Door shutters, wood; window shutters, wood; shutters, plastic; shutters, door or window: metal

(G-9181)
FWS DISTRIBUTORS LLC (PA)
Also Called: Progress Wine Group
14501 Nw 57th Ave Ste 113 (33014)
PHONE.................................407 543-6291
Hunter Seidel, *Sales Staff*
Jeff Seidel, *Mng Member*
Proal Perry, *Consultant*
Robert Camacho,
Jono Carlon,
EMP: 8 **EST:** 2017
SALES (est): 2.3MM **Privately Held**
SIC: 2084 Wines

(G-9182)
G METAL INDUSTRIES INC
3670 Nw 49th St (33142-3928)
PHONE.................................305 633-0300
Omar Valdez, *President*
EMP: 12 **EST:** 2000
SALES (est): 1MM **Privately Held**
WEB: www.gmetalcorporation.com
SIC: 3443 Metal parts

(G-9183)
GABRIELAS MEMOIRS INC
5750 Sw 45th Ter (33155-6002)
PHONE.................................305 666-9991
Diana M De Los Reyes, *President*
EMP: 7 **EST:** 2004
SALES (est): 72.5K **Privately Held**
SIC: 2759 Commercial printing

(G-9184)
GADAL LABORATORIES INC
12178 Sw 128th St (33186-5230)
PHONE.................................786 732-2571
Giodardo Del Campo, *President*
EMP: 6 **EST:** 2010
SQ FT: 5,000
SALES (est): 700K **Privately Held**
WEB: www.gadallaboratories.com
SIC: 2834 Pharmaceutical preparations

(G-9185)
GALAN EXPRESS INC
1150 Sw 154th Ave (33194-2676)
PHONE.................................305 438-8738
Maikel Galan, *President*
EMP: 10 **EST:** 2005
SALES (est): 267.5K **Privately Held**
SIC: 2741 Miscellaneous publishing

(G-9186)
GALEA CORPORATION
Also Called: Instant Signs of South Florida
4679 Sw 72nd Ave (33155-4540)
PHONE.................................305 663-0244
Alejandro A Handal, *Vice Pres*
Louis Latorre, *Vice Pres*
Giancarla Latorre, *Treasurer*
Lissette Handal, *Admin Sec*
▼ **EMP:** 9 **EST:** 1984
SQ FT: 1,800
SALES (est): 879K **Privately Held**
WEB: www.galeadrinks.com
SIC: 3993 Signs & advertising specialties

(G-9187)
GARBO SPORT INTERNATIONAL INC
11231 Nw 20th St Unit 122 (33172-1857)
PHONE.................................305 599-8797
▲ **EMP:** 6
SALES (est): 650.1K **Privately Held**
SIC: 3949 Mfg Sporting/Athletic Goods

(G-9188)
GARCIA CUSTOM CABINETRY
1000 Nw 1st Ave (33136-3629)
PHONE.................................864 420-3882
Johan Garcia Lopera, *President*
EMP: 7 **EST:** 2015
SALES (est): 85.9K **Privately Held**
SIC: 2434 Wood kitchen cabinets

(G-9189)
GARCIA DOOR & WINDOW INC
2787 Nw 34th St (33142-5216)
PHONE.................................305 635-0644
Leonardo Garcia, *President*
◆ **EMP:** 6 **EST:** 1974
SQ FT: 5,000
SALES (est): 971.8K **Privately Held**
WEB: www.garciadoorandwindow.com
SIC: 3442 Window & door frames

(G-9190)
GARWARE FULFLEX USA INC (PA) ✪
1695 Nw 110th Ave Ste 301 (33172-1929)
PHONE.................................305 436-8915
Maria Teresa Santiago, *President*
EMP: 1 **EST:** 2021
SALES (est): 75MM **Privately Held**
WEB: www.fulflex.com
SIC: 2241 Rubber & elastic yarns & fabrics

(G-9191)
GAS TURBINE SUPPORT INC
13901 Sw 119th Ave (33186-6202)
PHONE.................................786 242-4513
Orlando Martinez, *Owner*
EMP: 7 **EST:** 2019
SALES (est): 206.9K **Privately Held**
WEB: www.gtsiparts.com
SIC: 3724 Aircraft engines & engine parts

(G-9192)
GAUMARD SCIENTIFIC COMPANY INC
14700 Sw 136th St (33196-5691)
P.O. Box 140098 (33114-0098)
PHONE.................................305 971-3790
Daphne Eggert, *President*
Eddy Bermudez, *Editor*
John Eggert, *Exec VP*
James Archetto, *Vice Pres*

David Cohen, *Vice Pres*
EMP: 40 **EST:** 1961
SQ FT: 15,000
SALES (est): 11.1MM **Privately Held**
WEB: www.gaumard.com
SIC: 3841 Surgical & medical instruments

(G-9193)
GB ENERGY MANAGEMENT LLC
2875 Ne 191st St Ste 901 (33180-2842)
PHONE.................................305 792-4650
Edwin Marcano, *CFO*
Reuven Bigio, *Mng Member*
EMP: 7 **EST:** 2013
SALES (est): 4.4MM **Privately Held**
SIC: 2992 Lubricating oils & greases
PA: Gulfstream Petroleum Dominicana S. De R.L.
Calle 50 Y Aquilino De La Guardia
Plaza Banco General
Panama City

(G-9194)
GBIG CORPORATION
Also Called: Continental Marketing Group
8744 Sw 133rd St (33176-5929)
PHONE.................................866 998-8466
Sandra L Gordon, *President*
EMP: 8 **EST:** 1978
SQ FT: 3,800
SALES (est): 660.4K **Privately Held**
SIC: 3953 Marking devices

(G-9195)
GE GLASS INC
4455 Nw 73rd Ave (33166-6436)
PHONE.................................305 599-7725
Eugenio M Benitez, *President*
EMP: 10 **EST:** 2005
SALES (est): 336.5K **Privately Held**
SIC: 3231 Products of purchased glass

(G-9196)
GEAR DYNAMICS INC
Also Called: Southern Gear
3685 Nw 106th St (33147-1030)
PHONE.................................305 691-0151
Alex Perdomo, *President*
Patricia Nader, *Purch Agent*
Lou Torchetti, *Shareholder*
Chris Turnau, *Shareholder*
Allan S Arch, *Admin Sec*
EMP: 5 **EST:** 1988
SALES (est): 796.4K **Privately Held**
SIC: 3714 5531 Gears, motor vehicle; automotive parts

(G-9197)
GEEKSHIVE INC
9100 S Ddland Blvd Ste 15 (33156)
PHONE.................................888 797-4335
Borras J Sebastian, *Principal*
Borras Sebastian, *Principal*
Claudio S Martinez, *Vice Pres*
Martinez Corina Gabriela, *Plant Mgr*
Claudio Martinez, *Plant Mgr*
EMP: 16 **EST:** 2010
SALES (est): 4.7MM **Privately Held**
WEB: www.geekshive.com
SIC: 2389 3571 Apparel for handicapped; electronic computers

(G-9198)
GEMINI GROUP USA INC
16371 Sw 56th Ter (33193-5634)
PHONE.................................305 338-1066
William Barros, *Principal*
EMP: 10 **EST:** 2018
SALES (est): 64.4K **Privately Held**
WEB: www.geminigroup.net
SIC: 3089 Injection molding of plastics

(G-9199)
GENERAL ASPHALT CO INC
4850 Nw 72nd Ave (33166-5642)
P.O. Box 522306 (33152-2306)
PHONE.................................305 592-6005
Robert A Lopez, *President*
Albert J Lopez, *Vice Pres*
Royal Webster Jr, *Vice Pres*
Gabriel Martinez, *Project Mgr*
Emilio Zamora, *Project Mgr*
EMP: 150 **EST:** 1966
SQ FT: 10,000

▲ = Import ▼=Export
◆ =Import/Export

SALES (est): 22.5MM **Privately Held**
WEB: www.generalasphalt.com
SIC: 2951 Asphalt paving mixtures &
blocks

(G-9200)
GENERAL OCEANICS INC
Also Called: Geo Environmental
1295 Nw 163rd St (33169-5830)
PHONE.....................305 621-2882
Regis Cook, *CEO*
Sylvia Martin, *Vice Pres*
▲ EMP: 17 EST: 1966
SQ FT: 12,000
SALES (est): 2.4MM **Privately Held**
WEB: www.generaloceanics.com
SIC: 3829 8731 Measuring & controlling
devices; commercial research laboratory

(G-9201)
GENERAL SCREEN SERVICE CO
5033 Sw 151st Pl (33185-4002)
PHONE.....................305 226-0741
Zoe Alberto Rodiguez, *Owner*
EMP: 5 EST: 1972
SALES (est): 347.3K **Privately Held**
SIC: 3861 Screens, projection

(G-9202)
GENIE SHELF
10935 Sw 138th Ct (33186-3231)
PHONE.....................305 213-4382
Pauline Hamian, *President*
EMP: 7 EST: 2011
SALES (est): 141.7K **Privately Held**
WEB: www.shelfgenie.com
SIC: 2511 Wood household furniture

(G-9203)
GENZYME CORPORATION
Also Called: Genzyme Genetics
1031 Ives Dairy Rd # 228 (33179-2538)
PHONE.....................800 245-4363
EMP: 93
SALES (corp-wide): 400.4MM **Privately Held**
SIC: 2835 Mfg Diagnostic Substances
HQ: Genzyme Corporation
500 Kendall St
Cambridge MA 02141
617 252-7500

(G-9204)
GEORGIAN AMERICAN ALLOYS INC (PA)
200 Suth Bscyne Blvd Ste (33131)
PHONE.....................305 375-7560
Mordechai Korf, *President*
Barry Nuss, *CFO*
Zakaria Zalikashvili, *Pub Rel Dir*
EKA Kiria, *Manager*
Oleg Yakovlev, *Manager*
▲ EMP: 40 EST: 2012
SALES (est): 110.7MM **Privately Held**
WEB: www.delivery-plan-fact.com
SIC: 1061 Manganese ores mining

(G-9205)
GERBER COBURN OPTICAL INC
Coburn Technologies
2585 Nw 74th Ave (33122-1417)
PHONE.....................305 592-4705
Pedro Parra, *Sales/Mktg Mgr*
Jesus Rodriguez, *Sales Staff*
Ram Narayanan, *Exec Dir*
EMP: 30 **Privately Held**
WEB: www.coburntechnologies.com
SIC: 3851 Ophthalmic goods
HQ: Coburn Gerber Optical Inc
55 Gerber Rd E
South Windsor CT 06074

(G-9206)
GERMAIN CANVAS & AWNING CO
Also Called: Germain Awning Center
921 Belle Meade Island Dr (33138-5249)
PHONE.....................305 751-4963
Milton Hughs, *President*
Rita Hughs, *Corp Secy*
EMP: 6 EST: 1977
SQ FT: 3,300

SALES (est): 310.1K **Privately Held**
SIC: 2394 1799 Canvas & related products; awning installation

(G-9207)
GEROGARI DSPLAY MNFACTURE CORP
5517 Nw 72nd Ave (33166-4205)
PHONE.....................305 888-0993
German Galvin, *President*
Jeshica Miedda, *Vice Pres*
EMP: 7 EST: 1992
SALES (est): 512.9K **Privately Held**
SIC: 3089 Injection molding of plastics

(G-9208)
GETABSTRACT INC
20900 Ne 30th Ave Ste 315 (33180-2163)
PHONE.....................305 936-2626
Carey Halpern, *President*
Manuela Nieth, *President*
Danielle Goodrum, *Vice Pres*
Arnhild Walz-Rasilier, *Vice Pres*
Michael Albert, *CFO*
EMP: 33 EST: 1999
SALES (est): 7.1MM **Privately Held**
WEB: www.getabstract.com
SIC: 2731 Book publishing

(G-9209)
GFX INC (PA)
4810 Nw 74th Ave (33166-5512)
P.O. Box 668440 (33166-9416)
PHONE.....................305 499-9789
George Feldenkreis, *President*
Fanny Hanono, *President*
Gabriela Hanono, *Treasurer*
Diego Garcia, *Accounts Exec*
Evan Hanono, *Accounts Exec*
▲ EMP: 36 EST: 1961
SQ FT: 32,000
SALES (est): 5MM **Privately Held**
WEB: www.gfxcorp.com
SIC: 3568 3714 5063 5023 Power transmission equipment; transmission housings or parts, motor vehicle; electrical apparatus & equipment; home furnishings

(G-9210)
GG PROFESSIONAL PAINTING CORP
2001 Ludlam Rd Apt 317 (33155-1897)
PHONE.....................786 716-8972
Ronnie Saldana, *President*
EMP: 10 EST: 2019
SALES (est): 280K **Privately Held**
SIC: 3479 Painting, coating & hot dipping

(G-9211)
GGB1 LLC
9828 Sw 146th Pl (33186-8404)
PHONE.....................305 387-5334
Edgard R Kamel, *Principal*
EMP: 8 EST: 2007
SALES (est): 138.9K **Privately Held**
SIC: 3568 Power transmission equipment

(G-9212)
GHX INDUSTRIAL LLC
Also Called: Amazon Hose & Rubber
1001 Nw 159th Dr (33169-5805)
PHONE.....................305 620-4313
Rich Potero, *Principal*
Jim Donlan, *Principal*
George Malgoza, *Principal*
EMP: 10 EST: 2007
SALES (est): 252.9K **Privately Held**
WEB: www.ghxinc.com
SIC: 3052 Rubber & plastics hose & beltings

(G-9213)
GILD CORPORATION
15411 Sw 160th St (33187-1410)
PHONE.....................305 378-6982
Monique Gilles, *Principal*
EMP: 9 EST: 2009
SALES (est): 179.6K **Privately Held**
SIC: 2834 Pharmaceutical preparations

(G-9214)
GIZ STUDIO INC
601 Nw 11th St (33136-2414)
PHONE.....................305 416-5001
Fax: 305 663-0975

▼ EMP: 16
SQ FT: 22,000
SALES (est): 1.3MM **Privately Held**
SIC: 3211 Mfg Flat Glass

(G-9215)
GLASS TECH CORP
3103 Nw 20th St (33142-6935)
PHONE.....................305 633-6491
Nelson Fernandez Jr, *President*
◆ EMP: 35 EST: 1984
SQ FT: 90,000
SALES (est): 4.8MM **Privately Held**
WEB: www.glass-tech.com
SIC: 3732 Yachts, building & repairing

(G-9216)
GLASSARIUM LLC
444 Ne 30th St Unit 804 (33137-4312)
PHONE.....................786 631-7080
Sergij Zelinsky, *Partner*
EMP: 50
SALES (est): 2.1MM **Privately Held**
WEB: www.glassarium.com
SIC: 3334 3259 3446 Primary aluminum; architectural clay products; architectural metalwork

(G-9217)
GLOBAL EQUIPMENT & MFG LLC
7650 Nw 50th St (33166-4700)
PHONE.....................800 436-1932
Michael Mathon,
EMP: 25 EST: 2018
SALES (est): 3MM **Privately Held**
WEB: www.gem360.net
SIC: 3585 Air conditioning equipment, complete

(G-9218)
GLOBAL MIND USA LLC
250 Nw 23rd St Unit 212 (33127-4308)
PHONE.....................305 402-2190
Scott Hughes, *Director*
David Mark Wein, *Director*
EMP: 56 EST: 2009
SALES (est): 3.2MM **Privately Held**
SIC: 3577 Data conversion equipment, media-to-media: computer
HQ: Iprospect.Com Inc.
85 Devonshire St
Boston MA 02109
617 449-4300

(G-9219)
GLOBAL PORTE
601 Nw 11th St (33136-2414)
PHONE.....................305 416-5001
Rolando Serra, *Principal*
EMP: 9 EST: 2008
SALES (est): 6.7K **Privately Held**
SIC: 3231 Ornamental glass: cut, engraved or otherwise decorated

(G-9220)
GLOBAL TRADING INC (PA)
7500 Nw 25th St Unit 12 (33122-1700)
PHONE.....................305 471-4455
Viraj S Wikramanayake, *President*
◆ EMP: 10 EST: 1991
SQ FT: 11,000
SALES (est): 2.7MM **Privately Held**
WEB: www.gtim.com
SIC: 3021 2311 2326 Protective footwear, rubber or plastic; men's & boys' uniforms; policemen's uniforms: made from purchased materials; work uniforms

(G-9221)
GLOBE BOYZ INTERNATIONAL LLC ✪
1365 Nw 84th Ter (33147-4337)
PHONE.....................305 308-8160
Bremond Harris,
EMP: 10 EST: 2021
SALES (est): 331.3K **Privately Held**
SIC: 2741 Music books: publishing & printing

(G-9222)
GLOBE SPECIALTY METALS INC (HQ)
600 Brickell Ave Ste 3100 (33131-3089)
P.O. Box 157, Beverly OH (45715-0157)
PHONE.....................786 509-6900
Alan Kestenbaum, *Chairman*
Jeff Watson, *Vice Pres*
J M Perkins, *VP Sales*
Kevin Shoemaker, *Manager*
Lee Payssa, *Director*
EMP: 16 EST: 2006
SQ FT: 10,566
SALES (est): 608.1MM
SALES (corp-wide): 1.7B **Privately Held**
SIC: 3313 3339 Ferrosilicon, not made in blast furnaces; silicon refining (primary, over 99% pure)
PA: Ferroglobe Plc
5 Fleet Place
London EC4M
203 129-2420

(G-9223)
GLOVES USA CORP ✪
Also Called: Luvix Group
6842 Nw 77th Ct Ste W301 (33166-2713)
PHONE.....................786 536-2905
Marilyn Nozaki, *CEO*
EMP: 12 EST: 2021
SALES (est): 439.8K **Privately Held**
WEB: www.luvixgroup.com
SIC: 3999 Manufacturing industries

(G-9224)
GOLD BANNER USA INC
2660 Nw 3rd Ave (33127-4103)
PHONE.....................305 576-2215
▲ EMP: 11
SQ FT: 6,000
SALES (est): 1MM **Privately Held**
SIC: 3021 Mfg Rubber/Plastic Footwear

(G-9225)
GOLDEN BOAR PRODUCT CORP
Also Called: Lucky Pig
7224 Nw 25th St (33122-1701)
P.O. Box 521094 (33152-1094)
PHONE.....................305 500-9392
Felix Martinez, *President*
Oscar Martinez, *Vice Pres*
EMP: 6 EST: 2012
SQ FT: 4,000
SALES (est): 1.5MM **Privately Held**
SIC: 2013 Ham, boiled: from purchased meat

(G-9226)
GONTECH CUSTOM WOOD CORP
2005 Sw 129th Ct (33175-1327)
PHONE.....................305 323-0765
Gilfredo Gonzalez, *President*
EMP: 7 EST: 2005
SALES (est): 200.2K **Privately Held**
SIC: 2434 Wood kitchen cabinets

(G-9227)
GOOD CATCH INC
6713 Ne 3rd Ave (33138-5509)
P.O. Box 370366 (33137-0366)
PHONE.....................305 757-7700
David Bloom, *President*
Travis Macdonald, *Sales Staff*
EMP: 5 EST: 1992
SQ FT: 2,400
SALES (est): 500K **Privately Held**
WEB: www.goodcatch.com
SIC: 2395 2759 Embroidery products, except schiffli machine; screen printing

(G-9228)
GOPI GLASS SALES & SVCS CORP
7450 Nw 41st St (33166-6716)
PHONE.....................305 592-2089
Marlen De Varona, *President*
Rafael De Varona, *Vice Pres*
◆ EMP: 22 EST: 1971
SQ FT: 20,000

SALES (est): 2.2MM **Privately Held**
WEB: www.gopiglass.com
SIC: 3442 5039 Store fronts, prefabricated, metal; window & door frames; exterior flat glass: plate or window

(G-9229)
GOVPAY NETWORK LLC
12855 Sw 132nd St Ste 204 (33186-7221)
PHONE..................................866 893-9678
Anthony J Garay,
EMP: 6 EST: 2010
SALES (est): 797.4K **Privately Held**
WEB: www.govpaynetwork.com
SIC: 7372 Business oriented computer
software

(G-9230)
GRADUATE PLASTICS INC (PA)
Also Called: Quantum Storage Systems
15800 Nw 15th Ave (33169-5606)
PHONE..................................305 687-0405
Laurent Groll, President
Anthony Cohen, Vice Pres
Tony Cohen, Vice Pres
Scott Frobese, Sales Staff
Rick Diaz, Manager
◆ EMP: 200 EST: 1986
SQ FT: 30,000
SALES (est): 53.6MM **Privately Held**
WEB: www.quantumstorage.com
SIC: 3089 Injection molding of plastics

(G-9231)
GRAFTON FURNITURE COMPANY
3401 Nw 71st St (33147-6652)
PHONE..................................305 696-3811
Steve Grafton Jr, President
Melissa Grafton, Marketing Staff
Grafton Steve,
EMP: 25 EST: 1963
SQ FT: 20,000
SALES (est): 2.7MM **Privately Held**
WEB: www.graftonfurniture.com
SIC: 2512 7641 Upholstered household
furniture; reupholstery

(G-9232)
GRAIN MACHINERY MFG CORP
Also Called: Grainman
1130 Nw 163rd Dr (33169-5816)
PHONE..................................305 620-2525
Octavio Castellanos, President
Clemente Dieguez, Vice Pres
◆ EMP: 14 EST: 1975
SQ FT: 13,000
SALES (est): 2.4MM **Privately Held**
WEB: www.grainman.com
SIC: 3523 3565 Driers (farm): grain, hay &
seed; bag opening, filling & closing ma-
chines

(G-9233)
GRANADA PRTG & GRAPHICS CORP
Also Called: Granada Art Service
8693 Nw 66th St (33166-2670)
P.O. Box 668106 (33166-9411)
PHONE..................................305 593-5266
EMP: 13
SQ FT: 10,000
SALES (est): 1.4MM **Privately Held**
SIC: 2759 Graphic Designer

(G-9234)
GRAPHIC MASTERS INC
801 Brickell Ave Ste 300 (33131-2900)
Drawer 2600 S, League City TX (77573)
PHONE..................................800 230-3873
EMP: 60
SALES (est): 6.5MM **Privately Held**
SIC: 2752 8742 7336 Lithographic Com-
mercial Printing Management Consulting
Services Commercial Art/Graphic Design

(G-9235)
GRAPHICA SERVICES INC
12943 Sw 133rd Ct (33186-5853)
P.O. Box 160322 (33116-0322)
PHONE..................................305 232-5333
Eloy Delvalle, President
Eloy Valle, Sales Staff
EMP: 6 EST: 1990
SQ FT: 15,000

SALES (est): 793.6K **Privately Held**
WEB: www.graphicaservices.com
SIC: 2752 Commercial printing, offset

(G-9236)
GRAPHICS TYPE COLOR ENTPS INC
Also Called: GTC Media
2300 Nw 7th Ave (33127-4204)
PHONE..................................305 591-7600
Manuel Perez, President
Mark Quetgles, COO
Carlos M Perez, Vice Pres
Ralph Matos, Prdtn Mgr
Steve Freixas, Sales Mgr
▼ EMP: 45 EST: 1990
SQ FT: 15,563
SALES (est): 7.1MM **Privately Held**
SIC: 2759 7336 2791 2752 Commercial
printing; commercial art & graphic design;
typesetting; commercial printing, litho-
graphic

(G-9237)
GRASS CHOPPERS
11861 Sw 180th St (33177-2412)
PHONE..................................305 253-1217
Reinaldo Fernandez, Principal
EMP: 7 EST: 2006
SALES (est): 146.9K **Privately Held**
SIC: 3751 Motorcycles & related parts

(G-9238)
GREAT AMERICAN IMPORTS LLC
3758 Nw 54th St (33142-3215)
PHONE..................................786 524-4120
Paul Groll, Mng Member
Theresa Grace, Manager
EMP: 6 EST: 2020
SALES (est): 1.4MM **Privately Held**
SIC: 2434 Wood kitchen cabinets

(G-9239)
GREATER 7TH DIGITAL PRESS INC
14627 Nw 7th Ave (33168-3029)
PHONE..................................305 681-2412
Lefevre Wisly, Principal
Wisly Lefevre, Principal
EMP: 8 EST: 2011
SALES (est): 855K **Privately Held**
SIC: 2759 Commercial printing

(G-9240)
GREATER MIAMI ELKS LODGE INC
5150 Nw 2nd Ave (33127-2127)
PHONE..................................305 754-5899
EMP: 14
SQ FT: 3,869
SALES (est): 967.7K **Privately Held**
SIC: 2389 Mfg Apparel/Accessories

(G-9241)
GREEN BIOFUELS LLC
3123 Nw 73rd St (33147-5947)
PHONE..................................305 639-3030
Jose Bergonsi, Mng Member
Sara Sanchez, Admin Sec
▲ EMP: 16 EST: 2009
SALES (est): 2.5MM **Privately Held**
WEB: www.gbcorp.biz
SIC: 2869 Fuels

(G-9242)
GREEN BIOFUELS MIAMI LLC
3123 Nw 73rd St Ste A-C (33147-5947)
PHONE..................................305 639-3030
Fabio Santos, CEO
Edilson Bianconi, Principal
Guilherme Cirino, Principal
Sandra Daza, Principal
EMP: 13 EST: 2013
SQ FT: 26,500
SALES (est): 2.2MM **Privately Held**
WEB: www.gbcorp.biz
SIC: 2869 Industrial organic chemicals;
fuels

(G-9243)
GREEN ESSENTIALS LLC
7480 Bird Rd Ste 810 (33155-6660)
PHONE..................................786 584-4377
Gerardo Mujica,

EMP: 20 EST: 2020
SALES (est): 860K **Privately Held**
SIC: 2023 Dietary supplements, dairy &
non-dairy based

(G-9244)
GREEN LIGHT PRINTING INC
151 Nw 36th St (33127-3107)
PHONE..................................305 576-5858
Mercedes Quanch, President
Andro Mateu, Vice Pres
EMP: 7 EST: 1994
SALES (est): 69.5K **Privately Held**
WEB: www.leonarts.com
SIC: 2752 Commercial printing, offset

(G-9245)
GREEN MARINE FUELS INC
3220 S Dixie Hwy (33133-3631)
PHONE..................................305 775-3546
James Doddo, Principal
EMP: 8 EST: 2010
SALES (est): 161.8K **Privately Held**
SIC: 2869 Fuels

(G-9246)
GREEN PLANT LLC
3600 Nw 59th St (33142-2030)
PHONE..................................305 397-9394
Federico Intriago, CEO
EMP: 35 EST: 2015
SALES (est): 3.2MM **Privately Held**
WEB: www.bevnet.com
SIC: 2037 Frozen fruits & vegetables

(G-9247)
GREGOMARC LLC
Also Called: La Sin Rival
9772 Sw 8th St (33174-2902)
PHONE..................................305 559-9777
Rodrigues Pereira Jose G, Mng Member
Cafe Metro Plaza CA, Mng Member
EMP: 8 EST: 2010
SALES (est): 561.8K **Privately Held**
SIC: 2051 Cakes, bakery: except frozen

(G-9248)
GRESSO LLC
495 Brickell Ave Apt 3902 (33131-2859)
PHONE..................................305 515-8677
Andrey Kalashnikov, Mng Member
EMP: 7 EST: 2011
SALES (est): 1.6MM
SALES (corp-wide): 4.9MM **Privately
Held**
WEB: www.gresso.com
SIC: 3669 Intercommunication systems,
electric
PA: Alan-Abris, Ooo
　22 Ul. Bogdanova
　Penza 44005
　841 245-2380

(G-9249)
GRILLE TECH INC
5101 Nw 36th Ave (33142-3226)
PHONE..................................305 537-0053
Isidro Gonzalez, President
◆ EMP: 25 EST: 2002
SALES (est): 4.4MM **Privately Held**
WEB: www.grilletechinc.com
SIC: 3496 Grilles & grillework, woven wire

(G-9250)
GRILLE TECH INC
3611 Nw 74th St (33147-5827)
PHONE..................................305 537-0053
EMP: 12 EST: 2002
SALES (est): 72.1K **Privately Held**
WEB: www.grilletechinc.com
SIC: 3496 Grilles & grillework, woven wire

(G-9251)
GRIZZLY PRINTING PARLOUR LLC
14244 Sw 90th Ter (33186-7800)
PHONE..................................786 416-2494
Christopher Algaze, Principal
EMP: 8 EST: 2012
SALES (est): 156.3K **Privately Held**
SIC: 2752 Commercial printing, litho-
graphic

(G-9252)
GROUP HEROS INC
Also Called: Victores Machine Shop
5720 Nw 35th Ave (33142-2708)
PHONE..................................305 635-0219
Jesus Victores, President
EMP: 5 EST: 1990
SQ FT: 35,000
SALES (est): 539.2K **Privately Held**
SIC: 3599 Machine shop, jobbing & repair

(G-9253)
GROUP STEEL INC
2437 Sw 138th Ave (33175-6367)
PHONE..................................305 965-0614
Erick Gonzalez, President
EMP: 7
SALES (corp-wide): 1.5MM **Privately
Held**
SIC: 3441 Fabricated structural metal
PA: Group Steel Inc.
　3492 W 84th St
　Hialeah FL 33018
　786 319-1222

(G-9254)
GROVE MEDICAL LLC
11926 Sw 8th St (33184-1671)
PHONE..................................305 903-6402
Art Miller, Mng Member
Robert Beau,
Josh Glick,
EMP: 5 EST: 2005
SQ FT: 1,500
SALES (est): 375.9K **Privately Held**
SIC: 3069 Birth control devices, rubber

(G-9255)
GRUNENTHAL SERVICES INC
1005 Sw 87th Ave (33174-3208)
PHONE..................................786 364-6308
Jan Van Ruymbeke, CEO
Victor Barbosa, Vice Pres
Karina Salazar, Vice Pres
Joao Simoes, Treasurer
Megan Renze, Legal Staff
EMP: 19 EST: 2011
SALES (est): 9MM
SALES (corp-wide): 1.6B **Privately Held**
WEB: www.grunenthal.com
SIC: 2834 Analgesics
HQ: Grunenthal Gmbh
　Zieglerstr. 6
　Aachen NW 52078
　241 569-0

(G-9256)
GRUPO DE DIARIOS AMERICA LLC
848 Brickell Ave Ste 600 (33131-2946)
PHONE..................................305 577-0094
Jose Romano, Director
EMP: 6 EST: 1991
SALES (est): 873.4K **Privately Held**
WEB: www.gda.com
SIC: 2711 Newspapers: publishing only,
not printed on site

(G-9257)
GRUPO PHOENIX CORP SVCS LLC (HQ)
2980 Ne 207th St Ste 705 (33180-1465)
PHONE..................................954 241-0023
Brenda Chamulak, President
Jarrett Barnett, Business Mgr
Ed Kopetman, Vice Pres
Humberto Melo, Vice Pres
Jesus Villaverde, Plant Mgr
◆ EMP: 30 EST: 2003
SALES (est): 215.2MM
SALES (corp-wide): 996.3MM **Privately
Held**
WEB: www.grupophoenix.com
SIC: 3089 Cups, plastic, except foam
PA: Tekni-Plex, Inc.
　460 E Swedesford Rd # 3000
　Wayne PA 19087
　484 690-1520

(G-9258)
GT PALLETS LLC
958 Nw 73rd St (33150-3627)
PHONE..................................786 541-6532
EMP: 6

▲ = Import ▼=Export
◆ =Import/Export

SALES (est): 363.3K **Privately Held**
SIC: 2448 Mfg Wood Pallets/Skids

(G-9259)
GVJ CORP
15120 Sw 159th Ct (33196-5765)
PHONE....................786 224-2808
Johnson P Charuvila, *President*
EMP: 7 **EST:** 2012
SALES (est): 53.5K **Privately Held**
WEB: www.gvjcorp.com
SIC: 2299 Batting, wadding, padding & fillings

(G-9260)
H & J ASPHALT INC
Also Called: H&J Asphalt Plant
4310 Nw 35th Ave (33142-4323)
PHONE....................305 635-8110
Lorenzo J Humberto, *President*
Jorge Lorenzo, *Vice Pres*
EMP: 8 **EST:** 1987
SQ FT: 1,000
SALES (est): 4.3MM **Privately Held**
WEB: www.hjasphaltinc.com
SIC: 2951 Asphalt paving mixtures & blocks

(G-9261)
HAPPY ENDINGS OF MIAMI INC
651 Nw 106th St (33150-1124)
PHONE....................305 759-4467
Martin F Marotta, *President*
Maria Walker, *Vice Pres*
▼ **EMP:** 9 **EST:** 1976
SQ FT: 1,350
SALES (est): 931.2K **Privately Held**
WEB: www.happyendingstshirts.com
SIC: 2261 2759 Screen printing of cotton broadwoven fabrics; screen printing

(G-9262)
HARDWARE CONCEPTS INC
3758 Nw 54th St (33142-3215)
PHONE....................305 685-1337
Paul Groll, *President*
Phil Rodriguez, *General Mgr*
Henry Sanchez, *Vice Pres*
◆ **EMP:** 9 **EST:** 1988
SALES (est): 1.1MM **Privately Held**
WEB: www.hardwareconcepts.com
SIC: 3089 3429 Injection molded finished plastic products; manufactured hardware (general)

(G-9263)
HASBRO LATIN AMERICA INC (DH)
5200 Blue Lagoon Dr Fl 10 (33126-2089)
PHONE....................305 931-3180
Augusto Brambilla, *General Mgr*
◆ **EMP:** 6 **EST:** 1998
SQ FT: 9,000
SALES (est): 890.9K
SALES (corp-wide): 6.4B **Publicly Held**
SIC: 3944 5092 Board games, children's & adults'; toys & hobby goods & supplies

(G-9264)
HAUTE LIVING INC
999 Brickell Ave Ste 520 (33131-3041)
PHONE....................305 798-1373
Seth Semilof, *President*
Betty Krause, *Opers Mgr*
Nathaniel Ross, *Comms Mgr*
Deyvanshi Masrani, *Director*
▼ **EMP:** 31 **EST:** 2005
SALES (est): 3.5MM **Privately Held**
WEB: www.hauteliving.com
SIC: 2721 Magazines: publishing only, not printed on site

(G-9265)
HAVANA DREAMS LLC
Also Called: Havana Dream Cigars
2621 Sw 132nd Ave (33175-1110)
PHONE....................305 322-7599
Ivette Carreno, *Mng Member*
EMP: 9 **EST:** 2009
SALES (est): 111.5K **Privately Held**
SIC: 2121 Cigars

(G-9266)
HEALTH & MUSCLES
14144 Sw 8th St (33184-3105)
PHONE....................305 225-2929

EMP: 6
SALES (est): 438K **Privately Held**
SIC: 2023 Mfg Dry/Evaporated Dairy Products

(G-9267)
HEALTH ROBOTICS CANADA LLC
6303 Blue Lagoon Dr # 310 (33126-6068)
PHONE....................786 388-5339
EMP: 10
SALES (est): 1.1MM **Privately Held**
SIC: 3569 Mfg General Industrial Machinery

(G-9268)
HEALTHEINTENTIONS INC (PA)
Also Called: Juicera
500 Ne 185th St Unit 8 (33179-4541)
PHONE....................954 394-8867
Stephanie C De Filippo, *President*
Natalie Alazrathi, *Principal*
Richard Epstein, *Principal*
Jennifer Rozman, *Principal*
Lori S Robinson, *Vice Pres*
EMP: 5 **EST:** 2011
SQ FT: 2,500
SALES (est): 760K **Privately Held**
SIC: 2037 5499 Fruit juices; juices, fruit or vegetable

(G-9269)
HEARA INC
19595 Ne 10th Ave Ste H (33179-3580)
PHONE....................305 651-5200
Yaeli Merenfeld, *President*
EMP: 8 **EST:** 2012
SALES (est): 738.7K **Privately Held**
SIC: 2051 Bread, cake & related products

(G-9270)
HECTOR & HECTOR INC
6790 Nw 84th Ave (33166-2615)
PHONE....................305 629-8864
Hector Sardinas Sr, *President*
Hector Sardinas Jr, *Vice Pres*
▼ **EMP:** 18 **EST:** 1985
SALES (est): 1.9MM **Privately Held**
WEB: www.hectorandhector.com
SIC: 2434 Wood kitchen cabinets

(G-9271)
HECTOR CORPORATION
2127 Nw 88th St (33147-4215)
PHONE....................786 308-5853
Hector Rodriguez, *Principal*
EMP: 5 **EST:** 2005
SALES (est): 387.9K **Privately Held**
WEB: hectorsalon.weebly.com
SIC: 1442 Construction sand & gravel

(G-9272)
HEICO AEROSPACE HOLDINGS CORP
7875 Nw 64th St (33166-2718)
PHONE....................305 463-0455
EMP: 12 **Publicly Held**
WEB: www.heico.com
SIC: 3724 Aircraft engines & engine parts
HQ: Heico Aerospace Holdings Corp.
3000 Taft St
Hollywood FL 33021
954 987-4000

(G-9273)
HEICO CORPORATION
825 Brickell Bay Dr # 1643 (33131-2920)
PHONE....................305 374-1745
Pedro Alvarez, *Engineer*
Patricia Camblor, *Accounts Mgr*
Isabel Fernandez, *Branch Mgr*
Mark Sorensen, *Director*
Vivian Machado, *Admin Asst*
EMP: 7 **Publicly Held**
WEB: www.heico.com
SIC: 3724 Aircraft engines & engine parts
PA: Heico Corporation
3000 Taft St
Hollywood FL 33021

(G-9274)
HEICO CORPORATION
7900 Nw 64th St (33166-2722)
PHONE....................305 463-0455
Laurans A Mendelson, *Ch of Bd*

Paul Belisle, *General Mgr*
Bill Fenne, *General Mgr*
Barbara N Williams, *Principal*
Vickie Brint, *Vice Pres*
EMP: 20 **Publicly Held**
WEB: www.heico.com
SIC: 3724 Aircraft engines & engine parts
PA: Heico Corporation
3000 Taft St
Hollywood FL 33021

(G-9275)
HEPBURN INDUSTRIES INC
300 Ne 59th St (33137-2114)
PHONE....................305 757-6688
Timothy Klink, *President*
◆ **EMP:** 7 **EST:** 1995
SQ FT: 13,210
SALES (est): 990.2K **Privately Held**
WEB: www.hepburnsuperior.com
SIC: 2869 Embalming fluids

(G-9276)
HERNANDEZ METAL FABRICATORS
15062 Sw 9th Way (33194-2770)
PHONE....................305 970-4145
Andre Hernandez, *President*
EMP: 7 **EST:** 2008
SALES (est): 910K **Privately Held**
WEB: www.hernandezmetalfab.net
SIC: 3441 Fabricated structural metal

(G-9277)
HERNANDEZ PRINTING SERVICE INC
Also Called: Hps
1771 W Flagler St (33135-2015)
PHONE....................305 642-0483
Modesto Hernandez, *President*
Maria Hernandez, *Admin Sec*
EMP: 10 **EST:** 1976
SQ FT: 8,000
SALES (est): 1.1MM **Privately Held**
SIC: 2752 2789 2759 Commercial printing, offset; bookbinding & related work; commercial printing

(G-9278)
HI TECH AVIATION WELDING LLC
Also Called: HI Tech Welding
8060 Nw 67th St (33166-2730)
PHONE....................305 591-3393
Wayne Amodie,
EMP: 7 **EST:** 1988
SALES (est): 600K **Privately Held**
WEB: www.hitechweldingfl.com
SIC: 7692 Welding repair

(G-9279)
HIDALGO CORP
Also Called: Hidalgo Jewelry
14 Ne 1st Ave Ste 805 (33132-2411)
PHONE....................305 379-0110
Silvio Hidalgo, *Ch of Bd*
◆ **EMP:** 6 **EST:** 1975
SQ FT: 4,000
SALES (est): 457.7K **Privately Held**
WEB: www.hidalgocg.com
SIC: 3911 5094 Jewelry, precious metal; jewelry

(G-9280)
HIGGINS GROUP CORP
3198 Nw 125th St (33167-2516)
PHONE....................305 681-4444
Andres D Perea, *President*
Andres Perea, *Owner*
Suzanne Perea, *Vice Pres*
Magaly Bustamante, *Administration*
◆ **EMP:** 40 **EST:** 1972
SQ FT: 15,000
SALES (est): 15.1MM
SALES (corp-wide): 3.1MM **Privately Held**
WEB: www.higginspremium.com
SIC: 3999 2048 Pet supplies; prepared feeds
HQ: Versele-Laga
Kapellestraat 70
Deinze 9800
938 132-00

(G-9281)
HIGH TOP PRODUCTS CORP
8187 Nw 8th St Apt 108 (33126-2894)
PHONE....................305 633-3287
Mariano Vazquez, *President*
Charles Vazquez, *Owner*
Marilyn Vazquez, *Corp Secy*
Eloy Vazquez, *Vice Pres*
EMP: 100 **EST:** 1965
SQ FT: 31,000
SALES (est): 5MM **Privately Held**
WEB: www.hightop-products.com
SIC: 2013 2011 Ham, boneless: from purchased meat; sausages from purchased meat; variety meats, fresh edible organs

(G-9282)
HILCRAFT ENGRAVING INC
3960 Nw 26th St (33142-6728)
P.O. Box 110687, Hialeah (33011-0687)
PHONE....................305 871-6100
Edel Lopez, *President*
Frances Morales, *Vice Pres*
EMP: 9 **EST:** 1945
SQ FT: 10,000
SALES (est): 747.3K **Privately Held**
WEB: www.hilcraft.com
SIC: 2796 2752 2791 2759 Engraving platemaking services; commercial printing, offset; typesetting; commercial printing

(G-9283)
HIRE AUTHORITY
8445 Miller Dr (33155-5426)
PHONE....................561 477-6663
Peter Brown, *Principal*
EMP: 10 **EST:** 2007
SALES (est): 517K **Privately Held**
WEB: www.hireauthoritygaragedoors.com
SIC: 2431 Garage doors, overhead: wood

(G-9284)
HISPANIC AMERCN PUBG GROUP INC
1200 Brickell Ave # 1950 (33131-3214)
PHONE....................305 961-1132
Trino Adolfo Ramos, *CEO*
EMP: 7 **EST:** 2007
SALES (est): 307.6K **Privately Held**
WEB: www.digohispanicmedia.com
SIC: 2721 Periodicals

(G-9285)
HITEX MARKETING GROUP INC
1566 Nw 108th Ave (33172-2052)
PHONE....................305 406-1150
Enrique Perez, *President*
Peter Perez, *Vice Pres*
Catalina Gonzalez, *Sales Executive*
Richely Lopez, *Marketing Staff*
Marlo Byrne, *Consultant*
◆ **EMP:** 5 **EST:** 1996
SQ FT: 12,000
SALES (est): 2.4MM **Privately Held**
WEB: www.hitexmarketingsolutions.com
SIC: 2653 5099 Display items, corrugated: made from purchased materials; video & audio equipment

(G-9286)
HM FACTORY LLC
2952 Nw 72nd Ave (33122-1312)
PHONE....................305 897-0004
Adolfo Heller, *Mng Member*
Alejandro Carboni,
EMP: 11 **EST:** 2017
SALES (est): 830K **Privately Held**
SIC: 2024 Ice cream & frozen desserts

(G-9287)
HNC MACHINE SHOP CORP
13900 Sw 139th Ct (33186-5555)
PHONE....................305 299-4023
Caballero Noe, *Principal*
EMP: 8 **EST:** 2015
SALES (est): 109K **Privately Held**
SIC: 3599 Machine shop, jobbing & repair

(G-9288)
HNM MEDICAL LLC
20855 Ne 16th Ave Ste C15 (33179-2140)
PHONE....................866 291-8498
Noe Roitman, *Partner*
Noah Ritman, *Vice Pres*

Dominique Camacho, *Sales Staff*
Todd Sapp, *Sales Staff*
Mike Massana, *Manager*
▲ **EMP:** 20 **EST:** 2004
SALES (est): 2.6MM **Privately Held**
WEB: www.hnmmedical.com
SIC: 3841 Surgical & medical instruments

(G-9289)
HOME & GARDEN INDUSTRIES INC
5700 Nw 32nd Ave (33142-2193)
PHONE..........................305 634-0681
Theodore F Moczik, *President*
EMP: 15 **EST:** 1967
SQ FT: 10,000
SALES (est): 2.4MM **Privately Held**
WEB: www.homeandgardenind.com
SIC: 3444 3432 3088 3523 Irrigation
   pipe, sheet metal; plumbing fixture fittings
   & trim; plastics plumbing fixtures; farm
   machinery & equipment; blast furnaces &
   steel mills

(G-9290)
HOMYN ENTERPRISES CORP
Also Called: Secure Wrap
4050 Nw 29th St (33142-5616)
PHONE..........................305 870-9720
Radames Villalon, *President*
Minet Villalon, *Vice Pres*
Anthony Vega, *Financial Analy*
Christian Alonso, *Legal Staff*
▲ **EMP:** 100 **EST:** 1996
SQ FT: 10,000
SALES (est): 16.1MM **Privately Held**
WEB: www.wrap-link.com
SIC: 3089 4581 4783 Cases, plastic; air-
   ports, flying fields & services; packing &
   crating

(G-9291)
HOUSE OF LLULL ATELIER LLC
13850 Sw 143rd Ct Ste 19 (33186-6123)
PHONE..........................305 964-7921
Carla Llull, *Owner*
EMP: 7 **EST:** 2015
SALES (est): 470.1K **Privately Held**
WEB: www.houseofllull.com
SIC: 2253 Bathing suits & swimwear, knit

(G-9292)
HUNTSMAN PROPERTIES LLC
951 Nw 200th Ter (33169-2816)
PHONE..........................305 653-2288
David Huntsman, *Branch Mgr*
EMP: 48
SALES (corp-wide): 286.5K **Privately
Held**
WEB: www.huntsman.com
SIC: 2821 Plastics materials & resins
PA: Huntsman Properties Llc
   2145 Davie Blvd Ste 101
   Fort Lauderdale FL 33312
   954 282-1797

(G-9293)
HURRICANE SHUTTER & PLUS INC
8004 Sw 149th Ave (33193-3145)
PHONE..........................786 287-0007
Rodolfo Rizo, *President*
EMP: 10 **EST:** 2005
SALES (est): 128K **Privately Held**
WEB: www.hurricaneshuttersflorida.com
SIC: 3442 Shutters, door or window: metal

(G-9294)
HYGENATOR PILLOW SERVICE INC
10100 E Calusa Club Dr (33186-2344)
PHONE..........................305 325-0250
Tomiko Erickson, *President*
Young Soong, *Vice Pres*
Ellen Erickson, *Admin Sec*
EMP: 5 **EST:** 1955
SQ FT: 27,000
SALES (est): 470.5K **Privately Held**
SIC: 2392 7389 Pillows, bed: made from
   purchased materials; interior design serv-
   ices

(G-9295)
I J PRECIOUS METALS INC
22 Ne 1st St (33132-2459)
PHONE..........................305 371-3009
Igor Alishayev, *Principal*
EMP: 8 **EST:** 2012
SALES (est): 140.3K **Privately Held**
SIC: 3339 Precious metals

(G-9296)
I2K DIGITAL SOLUTIONS LLC
7884 Nw 64th St (33166-2706)
PHONE..........................305 507-0707
Humberto Santana,
Cesar Casamayor,
EMP: 12 **EST:** 2017
SALES (est): 1MM **Privately Held**
WEB: www.i2kdigital.com
SIC: 3993 Signs & advertising specialties

(G-9297)
IAG ENGINE CENTER LLC
6929 Nw 46th St (33166-5603)
PHONE..........................305 591-0643
Mauricio Luna, *CEO*
Alex Alonso, *Controller*
EMP: 65 **EST:** 2012
SALES (est): 25.5MM **Privately Held**
WEB: www.iagaerogroup.com
SIC: 3724 Aircraft engines & engine parts

(G-9298)
ICHOSEN1 INC
1441 Brickell Ave Ste 17 (33131-3362)
PHONE..........................844 403-4055
Christopher Rogers, *President*
Genevieve Bassett, *Principal*
EMP: 10 **EST:** 2018
SALES (est): 269.2K **Privately Held**
SIC: 7372 Prepackaged software

(G-9299)
ICM PRECIOUS METALS INC
36 Ne 1st St (33132-2403)
PHONE..........................917 327-8171
Huseyin E Saygili, *Principal*
EMP: 8 **EST:** 2016
SALES (est): 445.9K **Privately Held**
SIC: 3339 Precious metals

(G-9300)
ICOME2FIX LLC
400 Nw 26th St (33127-4120)
PHONE..........................954 789-4102
Juvonal Allen,
EMP: 11 **EST:** 2019
SALES (est): 325K **Privately Held**
SIC: 2741

(G-9301)
IDEAL FASTENER CORPORATION
10800 Biscayne Blvd # 810 (33161-7402)
PHONE..........................201 207-6722
EMP: 61
SALES (corp-wide): 40.3MM **Privately
Held**
WEB: www.idealfastener.com
SIC: 3965 Zipper
PA: Ideal Fastener Corporation
   603 W Industry Dr
   Oxford NC 27565
   919 693-3115

(G-9302)
IES SALES AND SERVICE LLC
5050 Nw 36th Ave (33142-3225)
PHONE..........................305 687-9400
Osniel Sanchez,
Janet Sanchez,
▼ **EMP:** 8 **EST:** 2009
SALES (est): 1.6MM **Privately Held**
WEB: www.refusewastequip.com
SIC: 2631 Container, packaging &
   boxboard

(G-9303)
IES SALES AND SERVICE LLC
2233 Nw 77th Ter (33147-5531)
PHONE..........................305 525-6079
Janet Sanchez, *Mng Member*
EMP: 7 **EST:** 2016
SALES (est): 950K **Privately Held**
SIC: 2611 Pulp mills, mechanical & recy-
   cling processing

(G-9304)
IL NUTS INC
19098 W Dixie Hwy (33180-2638)
PHONE..........................786 366-4536
Joseph Hagby, *President*
EMP: 5 **EST:** 2013
SALES (est): 620K **Privately Held**
WEB: www.yossef-roasting.com
SIC: 2068 Nuts: dried, dehydrated, salted
   or roasted

(G-9305)
IMC LIGHTING INC
Also Called: Space Lighting
2915 Biscayne Blvd # 301 (33137-4155)
PHONE..........................305 373-4422
Jean L Raphael, *President*
▲ **EMP:** 7 **EST:** 2010
SQ FT: 10,000
SALES (est): 834.3K **Privately Held**
WEB: www.spacelighting.com
SIC: 3648 Lighting equipment

(G-9306)
IMPACT KINGS LLC
7141 N Waterway Dr (33155-2809)
PHONE..........................786 842-3166
Johnny Nassar, *CEO*
EMP: 20
SALES (est): 799.3K **Privately Held**
SIC: 3442 Metal doors, sash & trim

(G-9307)
IMPRESSIONS OF MIAMI INC
6960 Sw 47th St (33155-4645)
PHONE..........................305 666-0277
Jose Segrera, *President*
Dannaliz Segrera, *Vice Pres*
EMP: 5 **EST:** 1985
SQ FT: 4,700
SALES (est): 411.9K **Privately Held**
SIC: 2759 Commercial printing

(G-9308)
INCLAN MACHINE SHOP INC
4401 Sw 75th Ave (33155-4445)
PHONE..........................305 846-9675
Raul Aroix, *Principal*
EMP: 7 **EST:** 2016
SALES (est): 165.4K **Privately Held**
SIC: 3599 Machine shop, jobbing & repair

(G-9309)
INDUSTRIAL GALVANIZERS MIAMI
3350 Nw 119th St (33167-2902)
PHONE..........................305 681-8844
Sandy Robertson, *President*
◆ **EMP:** 22 **EST:** 1999
SALES (est): 944.8K **Privately Held**
WEB: www.valmontcoatings.com
SIC: 3547 3312 Galvanizing lines (rolling
   mill equipment); blast furnaces & steel
   mills

(G-9310)
INDUSTRIAL GLVANIZERS AMER INC
Also Called: Industrial Galvanizers Miami
3350 Nw 119th St (33167-2902)
PHONE..........................305 681-8844
Javier Dela Vega, *Branch Mgr*
EMP: 43
SQ FT: 25,496 **Privately Held**
WEB: www.valmontcoatings.com
SIC: 3479 Galvanizing of iron, steel or end-
   formed products
HQ: Industrial Galvanizers America, Inc.
   3535 Halifax Rd Ste A
   Petersburg VA 23805

(G-9311)
INDUSTRIAL GLVNZERS STHEASTERN
Also Called: Valmont Stheastern Galvanizing
3350 Nw 119th St (33167-2902)
PHONE..........................813 621-8990
Todd G Atkinson, *President*
Mark Mellon, *Marketing Staff*
Maria Elena Albo, *Manager*
Shaun G Sheppard, *Admin Sec*
▲ **EMP:** 70 **EST:** 1995

SALES (est): 10.2MM
SALES (corp-wide): 3.5B **Publicly Held**
WEB: www.valmontmiami.com
SIC: 3479 Galvanizing of iron, steel or end-
   formed products
PA: Valmont Industries, Inc.
   15000 Valmont Plz
   Omaha NE 68154
   402 963-1000

(G-9312)
INFINITE RET DESIGN & MFG CORP
7320 Nw 36th Ave (33147-5810)
PHONE..........................305 967-8339
Hector Gonzalez, *President*
▼ **EMP:** 12 **EST:** 2013
SALES (est): 427.9K **Privately Held**
WEB: www.faceless.marketing
SIC: 2511 2431 2491 1751 Wood house-
   hold furniture; millwork; millwork, treated
   wood; cabinet & finish carpentry; finish &
   trim carpentry; wood kitchen cabinets

(G-9313)
INFLATABLE DESIGN WORKS CORP
13350 Sw 131st St Unit 10 (33186-6186)
PHONE..........................786 242-1049
Alejandro S Handal, *Owner*
Lissette R Caras, *CFO*
Richard Desaulniers, *VP Sales*
▼ **EMP:** 17 **EST:** 2002
SALES (est): 2.1MM **Privately Held**
WEB: www.idwcorp.com
SIC: 2759 3993 Promotional printing; ad-
   vertising novelties

(G-9314)
INKLAB SIGNS INC
12324 Sw 117th Ct (33186-3919)
PHONE..........................786 430-8100
Carlos J Parets, *President*
EMP: 8 **EST:** 2013
SALES (est): 166.4K **Privately Held**
SIC: 3993 Signs & advertising specialties

(G-9315)
INNFOCUS INC
12415 Sw 136th Ave Ste 3 (33186-6488)
PHONE..........................305 378-2651
Randy Lindholm, *Ch of Bd*
Russ Trenary, *President*
Leonard Pinchuk, *Founder*
Yasushi Kato, *Vice Pres*
Yasushi P Kato, *Vice Pres*
EMP: 12 **EST:** 2006
SQ FT: 10,000
SALES (est): 6.4MM **Privately Held**
WEB: www.innfocusinc.com
SIC: 3841 Surgical & medical instruments
PA: Santen Pharmaceutical Co., Ltd.
   4-20, Ofukacho. Kita-Ku
   Osaka OSK 530-0

(G-9316)
INNOCOR FOAM TECH - ACP INC
3225 Nw 107th St (33167-3713)
PHONE..........................305 685-6341
Michele Boyd, *Office Mgr*
Hermann Leopold, *Branch Mgr*
EMP: 100 **Privately Held**
SIC: 3086 Plastics foam products
HQ: Innocor Foam Technologies - Acp, Inc.
   200 Schulz Dr Ste 2
   Red Bank NJ 07701
   732 945-6222

(G-9317)
INNOVA ECO BLDG SYSTEMS LLC
Also Called: Mgo America
3300 Nw 110th St (33167-3720)
PHONE..........................305 455-7707
Jerry Gillman, *CEO*
◆ **EMP:** 41 **EST:** 2012
SALES (est): 7.1MM **Privately Held**
SIC: 2452 Panels & sections, prefabri-
   cated, wood

(G-9318)
INNOVA SOFTGEL LLC
Also Called: Innova Gel
14193 Sw 119th Ave (33186-6013)
PHONE..................................855 536-8872
Scott Woodruff, *CEO*
Freddie Rangel, *Facilities Mgr*
Francisco Tafoya, *Warehouse Mgr*
Ramesh Kumar, *Mfg Staff*
Adriana Martinez, *Purch Agent*
◆ **EMP:** 153 **EST:** 2015
SALES (est): 57.2MM
SALES (corp-wide): 2.6MM **Privately
Held**
SIC: 2834 Pharmaceutical preparations
HQ: Marine Ingredients, Llc
794 Sunrise Blvd
Mount Bethel PA 18343
570 260-6900

(G-9319)
INOVINOX USA LLC
7875 Sw 104th St (33156-2677)
PHONE..................................800 780-1017
EMP: 5 **EST:** 2017
SALES (est): 390.6K **Privately Held**
WEB: www.inovinox.com
SIC: 3491 Industrial valves

(G-9320)
INSIGHTEC INC (HQ)
801 Brickell Ave Ste 1600 (33131-4901)
PHONE..................................786 534-3849
Maurice Ferre, *President*
Debra Luckey, *General Mgr*
Oded Tamir, *COO*
Catherine Macomber, *Counsel*
Xen M Aderka, *Vice Pres*
EMP: 3 **EST:** 2010
SQ FT: 8,400
SALES (est): 8.8MM **Privately Held**
WEB: www.insightec.com
SIC: 3845 Medical cleaning equipment, ul-
trasonic

(G-9321)
**INTELLGENT HARING SYSTEMS
CORP (PA)**
6860 Sw 81st St (33143-7708)
PHONE..................................305 668-6102
Edward Miskiel, *President*
Rafael Delgato, *Exec VP*
Rafael E Delgado, *Vice Pres*
Ozdamar Ozcan, *Vice Pres*
Jonathon Toft Nielsen, *Engineer*
EMP: 15 **EST:** 1983
SQ FT: 3,000
SALES (est): 6MM **Privately Held**
WEB: www.ihsys.info
SIC: 3841 5734 5045 8731 Diagnostic
apparatus, medical; computer & software
stores; computer software; commercial
physical research

(G-9322)
**INTELLICLEAN SOLUTIONS LLC
(PA)**
444 Brickell Ave Ste 800 (33131-2442)
PHONE..................................615 293-2299
Amanda Harrington, *Marketing Mgr*
Larry York, *Mng Member*
Tim Harrington, *Mng Member*
Randy Spencer, *Mng Member*
EMP: 5 **EST:** 2016
SQ FT: 2,000
SALES (est): 2.2MM **Privately Held**
SIC: 3635 Household vacuum cleaners

(G-9323)
INTERBEVERAGE LLC
3100 Nw 74th Ave (33122-1226)
PHONE..................................305 961-1110
Juan Vaamonde Gomez, *Mng Member*
Andrea R Taddei Dennett,
Claudio P Taddei Dennett,
Luis E Osorio Pedauga,
▲ **EMP:** 6 **EST:** 2011
SALES (est): 455.2K **Privately Held**
WEB: www.rwbmd.com
SIC: 2086 Carbonated beverages, nonal-
coholic: bottled & canned

(G-9324)
INTERFRIES INC (PA)
18800 Ne 29th Ave Apt 426 (33180-2863)
PHONE..................................786 427-1427
David Winiarz, *President*
▲ **EMP:** 3 **EST:** 2010
SALES (est): 3.5MM **Privately Held**
WEB: www.interfries.com
SIC: 2037 Potato products, quick frozen &
cold pack

(G-9325)
**INTERNATIONAL CLOTHIERS
INC**
Also Called: Uniform Authority, The
4000 Twrside Ter Ste 2412 (33138)
PHONE..................................914 715-5600
Steven M Singer, *President*
Elizabeth M Singer, *Vice Pres*
Matthew Singer, *Vice Pres*
▲ **EMP:** 14 **EST:** 2015
SQ FT: 2,000
SALES (est): 8MM **Privately Held**
WEB: www.inclothiers.com
SIC: 2326 2337 Work uniforms; uniforms,
except athletic: women's, misses' & jun-
iors'

(G-9326)
INTERNATIONAL CNSTR PUBG
Also Called: Construccion-Pan Americana
4913 Sw 75th Ave (33155-4440)
PHONE..................................305 668-4999
Luis Suao, *President*
Adriana Suao, *Corp Secy*
EMP: 8 **EST:** 1972
SQ FT: 3,800
SALES (est): 735.4K **Privately Held**
SIC: 2721 Magazines: publishing & printing

(G-9327)
**INTERNATIONAL
GREENSCAPES LLC**
Also Called: International Treescapes
20855 Ne 16th Ave Ste C4 (33179-2125)
PHONE..................................760 631-6789
Juan Ascencio, *Branch Mgr*
EMP: 75
SALES (corp-wide): 596.1K **Privately
Held**
SIC: 3999 Artificial trees & flowers; flowers,
artificial & preserved; foliage, artificial &
preserved; plants, artificial & preserved
PA: International Greenscapes, Llc
180 Vallecitos De Oro
San Marcos CA 92069
760 631-6789

(G-9328)
**INTERNATIONAL MCH WORKS
INC**
Also Called: International Machine Shop
3631 Nw 48th Ter (33142-3923)
PHONE..................................305 635-3585
James Patterson, *President*
Marie Patterson, *Vice Pres*
▼ **EMP:** 11 **EST:** 1981
SQ FT: 30,000
SALES (est): 2.4MM **Privately Held**
SIC: 3534 7699 Elevators & equipment;
elevators: inspection, service & repair

(G-9329)
**INTERNATIONAL POWER USA
LLC**
2091 Nw 139th St (33015)
PHONE..................................305 534-7993
Chain Carlos, *Mng Member*
EMP: 7 **EST:** 2008
SALES (est): 942.3K **Privately Held**
WEB: www.internationalpower.com
SIC: 3089 Automotive parts, plastic
PA: Industria De Servicios Tecnicos In-
seteca, Ca
Ave. Michelena, C.C.Arpe, Local 15
Nave B
Valencia

(G-9330)
**INTERNTNAL EXPORT
UNIFORMS INC**
Also Called: International Uniform
4000 Nw 29th St (33142-5616)
PHONE..................................305 869-9900

Roger Gorwitz, *President*
Maria T Garcia, *Vice Pres*
Richard Barnes, *CIO*
Yumis Rodriguez, *Administration*
◆ **EMP:** 18 **EST:** 1981
SQ FT: 5,500
SALES (est): 2.8MM **Privately Held**
WEB: www.intluniforms.com
SIC: 2337 5136 Uniforms, except athletic:
women's, misses' & juniors'; uniforms,
men's & boys'

(G-9331)
INTERTECH SUPPLY INC
13334 Sw 9th Ter (33184-1934)
PHONE..................................786 200-0561
Carlos Hierro, *Vice Pres*
◆ **EMP:** 7 **EST:** 2009
SALES (est): 485.8K **Privately Held**
WEB: www.intertechus.com
SIC: 3674 Semiconductors & related de-
vices

(G-9332)
INTERTEX MIAMI LLC
50 Ne 179th St Bay 1-2 (33162-1014)
PHONE..................................305 627-3536
David Ojalvo, *Mng Member*
Jessica Gonzales,
Sonia Klainbaum,
Jose Mugrabi,
EMP: 6 **EST:** 2012
SALES (est): 380.7K **Privately Held**
WEB: www.intertexmiami.com
SIC: 2211 Denims

(G-9333)
**INVERSNES WLLDEL
ASOCIADOS INC (PA)**
4700 Nw 72nd Ave (33166-5617)
PHONE..................................305 591-0118
William A Delgado Sr, *President*
William Delgado, *Owner*
Rafael Palomino, *Sales Staff*
▼ **EMP:** 5 **EST:** 2006
SALES (est): 1.1MM **Privately Held**
SIC: 3441 Railroad car racks, for transport-
ing vehicles: steel

(G-9334)
INVOINET INC (HQ)
1111 Brickell Ave # 1860 (33131-3112)
PHONE..................................305 432-5366
Pablo Sanucci, *CEO*
Martin Almirall, *Vice Pres*
EMP: 12 **EST:** 2004
SQ FT: 10,752
SALES (est): 262.9K
SALES (corp-wide): 3MM **Privately Held**
SIC: 2782 Receipt, invoice & memoran-
dum books
PA: Invoinet Holdings, Llc
1111 Brickell Ave # 1100
Miami FL 33131
305 913-7149

(G-9335)
IPG NETWORK CORP
3155 Nw 40th St (33142-5109)
PHONE..................................305 681-4001
Adeniyi Oyegunle, *President*
EMP: 14 **EST:** 2005
SALES (est): 556.6K **Privately Held**
WEB: www.ipgnetwork.net
SIC: 3299 Gravel painting

(G-9336)
IPLINE LLC
18152 Sw 144th Ct (33177-3308)
PHONE..................................305 675-4235
Joaquin Cabada, *Principal*
EMP: 10 **EST:** 2015
SALES (est): 395.9K **Privately Held**
SIC: 3429 Manufactured hardware (gen-
eral)

(G-9337)
IPQ TRADE CORP
488 Ne 18th St Ste Cu1 (33132-1120)
PHONE..................................786 522-2310
Paolo Fontanot, *Owner*
EMP: 12 **EST:** 2016
SALES (est): 540K **Privately Held**
SIC: 2051 Bakery: wholesale or whole-
sale/retail combined

(G-9338)
IRIS INTERNATIONAL INC (DH)
11800 Sw 147th Ave (33196-2500)
PHONE..................................818 709-1244
Cesar M Garcia, *Ch of Bd*
Bernard M Alfano, *President*
Robert A Mello, *President*
Lawrence J Blecka, *Vice Pres*
David W Gates, *Vice Pres*
◆ **EMP:** 77 **EST:** 1979
SQ FT: 98,446
SALES (est): 130.7MM
SALES (corp-wide): 29.4B **Publicly Held**
SIC: 3841 3845 Surgical & medical instru-
ments; electromedical equipment
HQ: Beckman Coulter, Inc.
250 S Kraemer Blvd
Brea CA 92821
714 993-5321

(G-9339)
IRON CONTAINER LLC (PA)
8505 Nw 74th St (33166-2327)
PHONE..................................305 726-2150
Julian Charles, *Sales Dir*
Stephanie L Irons, *Mng Member*
Jonathan S Leoniff, *Mng Member*
Rick Rubio, *Executive*
▼ **EMP:** 20 **EST:** 2009
SALES (est): 26.5MM **Privately Held**
WEB: www.ironcontainer.com
SIC: 3469 Metal stampings

(G-9340)
IRON STRENGTH CORP
Also Called: Jr Electronics
9568 Sw 40th St (33165-4036)
PHONE..................................305 226-6866
Espinel Guadarrama, *President*
Francisco Espinel, *Vice Pres*
Ricardo Rodriguez, *Vice Pres*
EMP: 11 **EST:** 2016
SALES (est): 426.9K **Privately Held**
SIC: 3714 Automotive wiring harness sets

(G-9341)
ISA GROUP CORP
2665 S Byshr Dr Ste 710 (33133-5406)
PHONE..................................305 748-1578
Veruska Chalbaud, *Vice Pres*
EMP: 9 **EST:** 2013
SALES (est): 257.5K **Privately Held**
WEB: www.isagroupca.com
SIC: 3552 3565 3535 Textile machinery;
packaging machinery; conveyors & con-
veying equipment

(G-9342)
ISOFRUT COMPANY INC
380 Nw 24th St (33127-4326)
PHONE..................................305 961-1681
Faquiry Diaz Cala, *Principal*
EMP: 7 **EST:** 2015
SALES (est): 106.8K **Privately Held**
SIC: 2034 Dehydrated fruits, vegetables,
soups

(G-9343)
ITALIAN CABINETRY INC
Also Called: Mirrors 2 Go
3250 Ne 1st Ave Ste 305 (33137-4295)
PHONE..................................786 534-2742
Rodrigo Mattevi, *CEO*
EMP: 13 **EST:** 2014
SQ FT: 15,000
SALES (est): 1.1MM **Privately Held**
WEB: www.italiancabinetry-usa.com
SIC: 2434 2599 Wood kitchen cabinets;
hotel furniture

(G-9344)
IVAX CORPORATION (HQ)
4400 Biscayne Blvd (33137-3212)
PHONE..................................305 329-3795
Phillip Frost MD, *Ch of Bd*
Jane Hsiao PHD, *Vice Ch Bd*
Neil W Flanzraich, *President*
William Marth, *President*
Austin Theis, *Business Mgr*
◆ **EMP:** 175 **EST:** 1985
SALES (est): 407.5MM **Privately Held**
WEB: www.tevapharm.com
SIC: 2834 Drugs acting on the cardiovas-
cular system, except diagnostic

(G-9345)
IVAX PHARMACEUTICALS LLC (DH)
74 Nw 176th St　(33169-5043)
PHONE..................................305 575-6000
Rafick Henein,
▲ EMP: 200 EST: 1995
SALES (est): 107.9MM Privately Held
SIC: 2834 Pharmaceutical preparations
HQ: Ivax Corporation
　　4400 Biscayne Blvd
　　Miami FL 33137
　　305 329-3795

(G-9346)
IVAX RESEARCH INC (DH)
4400 Biscayne Blvd　(33137-3212)
PHONE..................................305 668-7688
Neil Flanzraich, President
Jane Hsiao, Vice Pres
EMP: 70 EST: 1986
SQ FT: 74,200
SALES (est): 60MM Privately Held
SIC: 2834 Pharmaceutical preparations
HQ: Ivax Corporation
　　4400 Biscayne Blvd
　　Miami FL 33137
　　305 329-3795

(G-9347)
IVM USA INC
800 Brickell Ave Ste 550　(33131-2970)
PHONE..................................786 693-2755
Pietro Iemmolo, President
▲ EMP: 22 EST: 2009
SALES (est): 678.8K Privately Held
SIC: 3732 Yachts, building & repairing
PA: Ivm Spa
　　Via Toscana 2/A
　　Padova PD 35127

(G-9348)
IZABELLAS CREATIONS INC
Also Called: Mega Stitch Embroidery
14252 Sw 140th St Ste 111　(33186-7367)
PHONE..................................786 429-3441
Andrew D Melogy II, President
Silvia A Melogy, Vice Pres
EMP: 7 EST: 2012
SALES (est): 124.6K Privately Held
SIC: 2395 2759 5199 Art needlework:
　　made from purchased materials; screen
　　printing; advertising specialties

(G-9349)
J & V PAVERSCORP
2614 Sw 36th Ave　(33133-2722)
PHONE..................................786 510-4389
Jorge Cardoza, Principal
EMP: 6 EST: 2012
SALES (est): 414.9K Privately Held
WEB: www.jvpaverscorporation.com
SIC: 2951 Asphalt paving mixtures &
　　blocks

(G-9350)
J A BLNDS DECORATIONS MORE LLC
12540 Sw 37th St　(33175-2959)
PHONE..................................754 422-4778
Javier A Andino, Principal
EMP: 7 EST: 2017
SALES (est): 84.5K Privately Held
SIC: 2591 Window blinds

(G-9351)
J J CABINETS APPLIANCES
8833 Sw 129th St　(33176-5918)
PHONE..................................786 573-0300
John Villoria, Principal
EMP: 8 EST: 2010
SALES (est): 469K Privately Held
WEB: www.jandjcabinets.com
SIC: 2434 Wood kitchen cabinets

(G-9352)
J W DAWSON CO INC
3739 Nw 43rd St　(33142-4237)
P.O. Box 554, Eaton Park　(33840-0554)
PHONE..................................305 634-8618
Earl S Heatherdale, President
Beverly Heatherdale, Corp Secy
EMP: 25 EST: 1971
SQ FT: 2,000

SALES (est): 709.1K Privately Held
SIC: 2421 Sawdust & shavings

(G-9353)
JA UNIFORMS INC
12333 Sw 132nd Ct　(33186-6477)
PHONE..................................305 234-1231
Alexander Arencibia, President
Menchu Dominicis, Vice Pres
Mario Nunez, Manager
Morningstar Stewart, Manager
▲ EMP: 12 EST: 1997
SQ FT: 6,000
SALES (est): 2.3MM Privately Held
WEB: www.jauniforms.com
SIC: 2326 5137 Work uniforms; uniforms,
　　women's & children's

(G-9354)
JABBERWOCKY LLC
2 S Biscayne Blvd # 2680　(33131-1806)
PHONE..................................310 717-3343
Alex Pereira,
EMP: 5 EST: 2016
SALES (est): 324.1K Privately Held
WEB: www.jabberwockyetc.com
SIC: 2731 Book publishing

(G-9355)
JANUSZ ART STONE INC
7025 Ne 2nd Ave　(33138-5507)
PHONE..................................305 754-7171
Janusz Niedbala, Principal
EMP: 7 EST: 2016
SALES (est): 223.5K Privately Held
WEB: www.urbanstoneworks.com
SIC: 3272 Concrete products

(G-9356)
JAY MORE CORPORATION
Also Called: Ann More
540 Nw 26th St　(33127-4334)
PHONE..................................786 384-1299
Morela Rojas, Principal
EMP: 12 EST: 2017
SALES (est): 390.3K Privately Held
WEB: www.annmoreshoes.com
SIC: 3999 Manufacturing industries

(G-9357)
JC & A OF SOUTH FLORIDA INC
3109 Grand Ave　(33133-5103)
PHONE..................................305 445-6665
Jeff Capanach, President
EMP: 5 EST: 1984
SALES (est): 561.8K Privately Held
SIC: 3086 Packaging & shipping materials,
　　foamed plastic

(G-9358)
JC BEST FINISH CABINET INC
2150 Nw 35th St　(33142-5428)
PHONE..................................786 216-5571
Julio C Letran, President
EMP: 8 EST: 2010
SALES (est): 161.9K Privately Held
SIC: 2434 Wood kitchen cabinets

(G-9359)
JC INDUSTRIAL MFG CORP
Also Called: J C Machine Shop
5700 Nw 32nd Ct　(33142-2141)
PHONE..................................305 634-5280
Pedro L Amador, President
Francis Chester, Business Mgr
Jorge Amador, Vice Pres
Annabelle Amador, Treasurer
Richard Nardone, Sales Staff
◆ EMP: 36 EST: 1980
SQ FT: 40,000
SALES (est): 3.1MM Privately Held
SIC: 3599 7692 3444 Machine shop, job-
　　bing & repair; welding repair; sheet metal-
　　work

(G-9360)
JC MACHINE WORKS CORP
Also Called: J. C. Mch Sp & Met Fabrication
5700 Nw 32nd Ct　(33142-2141)
PHONE..................................305 634-5280
Pedro L Amador, President
Jorge L Amador, Vice Pres
▲ EMP: 30 EST: 2010
SQ FT: 27,575

SALES (est): 5.4MM Privately Held
WEB: www.jcmachineshop.com
SIC: 3599 Machine shop, jobbing & repair

(G-9361)
JCP SIGNS INC
20483 Sw 127th Pl　(33177-5102)
PHONE..................................305 790-5336
Jon Pineiro, President
EMP: 8 EST: 2007
SALES (est): 224.8K Privately Held
SIC: 3993 Signs & advertising specialties

(G-9362)
JDM OF MIAMI LLC
14195 Sw 139th Ct　(33186-5599)
PHONE..................................305 253-4650
Carlos Montealegre, Principal
▼ EMP: 8 EST: 2005
SALES (est): 942.5K Privately Held
WEB: www.jdmofmiami.com
SIC: 3621 Motors & generators

(G-9363)
JEFFERSON SLNOID VLVES USA INC
20225 Ne 15th Ct　(33179-2710)
PHONE..................................305 249-8120
Jose Dadin, Principal
Maria Castro, Opers Mgr
▲ EMP: 100 EST: 1999
SALES (est): 8.1MM Privately Held
WEB: www.jeffersonvalves.com
SIC: 3491 Solenoid valves

(G-9364)
JESSICA PAVERS INC
555 Ne 160th Ter　(33162-4340)
PHONE..................................305 970-4879
Carlos H Hernandez, Principal
EMP: 7 EST: 2008
SALES (est): 98.3K Privately Held
SIC: 3531 Pavers

(G-9365)
JET GRAPHICS INC
4101 Sw 73rd Ave　(33155-4520)
PHONE..................................305 264-4333
Teresita Garcia Calvo, President
Isabel M Garcia, Vice Pres
EMP: 21 EST: 1994
SQ FT: 8,000
SALES (est): 2.1MM Privately Held
WEB: www.jetgraphics.com
SIC: 2752 2791 2789 Commercial print-
　　ing, offset; typesetting; bookbinding & re-
　　lated work

(G-9366)
JF AEROSPACE INC
12242 Sw 132nd Ct　(33186-6476)
PHONE..................................786 242-6686
Joe Balleste, President
EMP: 8 EST: 1998
SALES (est): 755.4K Privately Held
WEB: www.amcohenlaw.com
SIC: 3728 Aircraft parts & equipment

(G-9367)
JHK LLC
7950 Nw 53rd St Ste 215　(33166-4638)
PHONE..................................786 871-0150
▲ EMP: 5
SALES: 950K Privately Held
SIC: 3499 Mfg Misc Fabricated Metal
　　Products

(G-9368)
JIREH AC & RFRGN INC
5001 Sw 142nd Pl　(33175-5027)
PHONE..................................305 216-2774
Jose Acosta, President
Jorge Pinto, Vice Pres
Jose Luis Rodriguez, Treasurer
EMP: 13 EST: 1984
SALES (est): 2.3MM Privately Held
WEB: www.miamihvac.org
SIC: 3822 Air conditioning & refrigeration
　　controls

(G-9369)
JMP FASHION INC (PA)
2199 Nw 20th St Unit 2　(33142-7399)
PHONE..................................305 633-9920
Jorge Perez, President

Maritza Perez, Corp Secy
Telmo Perez, Vice Pres
◆ EMP: 9 EST: 1985
SALES (est): 2.5MM Privately Held
WEB: www.jmpwarehouse.com
SIC: 2339 2329 5621 Sportswear,
　　women's; men's & boys' sportswear &
　　athletic clothing; women's sportswear

(G-9370)
JOHNNY DEVIL INC
Also Called: Johnny Heaven
7301 Nw 36th Ct　(33147-5811)
PHONE..................................305 634-0700
Mario Frati, President
EMP: 8 EST: 1993
SALES (est): 258.7K Privately Held
SIC: 2331 2339 Blouses, women's & jun-
　　iors': made from purchased material;
　　shirts, women's & juniors': made from
　　purchased materials; slacks: women's,
　　misses' & juniors'

(G-9371)
JOHNSON & JOHNSON
6303 Blue Lagoon Dr # 450　(33126-6029)
P.O. Box 25323　(33102-5323)
PHONE..................................305 261-3500
Hannah Foley, General Mgr
Randy Godard, Counsel
Judy Jimenez, Project Mgr
Pei-Yu Chung, Engineer
Jessica Pierre, Credit Staff
EMP: 36
SALES (corp-wide): 93.7B Publicly Held
WEB: www.jnj.com
SIC: 3842 Surgical appliances & supplies
PA: Johnson & Johnson
　　1 Johnson And Johnson Plz
　　New Brunswick NJ 08933
　　732 524-0400

(G-9372)
JOSE MORALES HURRICANE SHUTTER
13271 Sw 17th Ln　(33175-7650)
PHONE..................................786 315-1835
Jose Morales, Principal
EMP: 9 EST: 2008
SALES (est): 255.3K Privately Held
SIC: 3442 Shutters, door or window: metal

(G-9373)
JOSE POLANCO
Also Called: T-Shirt Florida
614 Sw 22nd Ave　(33135-3119)
PHONE..................................305 631-1784
Jose Polanco, Owner
EMP: 5 EST: 2013
SALES (est): 348.1K Privately Held
WEB: www.tshirtsflorida.com
SIC: 2759 Screen printing

(G-9374)
JOSE RODRIGUEZ MET FABRICATION
2451 Brickell Ave　(33129-2436)
PHONE..................................305 305-6110
Jose Rodriguez, Principal
▼ EMP: 7 EST: 2012
SALES (est): 182.5K Privately Held
SIC: 3499 Fabricated metal products

(G-9375)
JP CUSTOM METALS INC
7200 Nw 29th Ct　(33147-5960)
PHONE..................................786 318-2855
George Peron, President
Stephanie Peron, Office Mgr
◆ EMP: 10 EST: 1998
SALES (est): 1.2MM Privately Held
WEB: www.jpcustommetals.net
SIC: 3444 Sheet metalwork

(G-9376)
JR EMBROIDERY INC
12321 Sw 133rd Ct　(33186-6434)
PHONE..................................305 253-6968
Fax: 305 251-7353
EMP: 5
SQ FT: 2,000
SALES (est): 432.1K Privately Held
SIC: 2395 Embroidery Work

(G-9377)
JR WOOD WORKS INC
7954 Ne 4th Ave (33138-4408)
PHONE..................................305 401-6056
Jose A Rodriguez, *President*
EMP: 7 **EST:** 2005
SALES (est): 124.5K **Privately Held**
SIC: 2431 Millwork

(G-9378)
JSN BLUE THUNDER LLC
1876 Nw 7th St (33125-3504)
PHONE..................................786 398-5222
Jeffrey S Nunberg, *Principal*
EMP: 9 **EST:** 2011
SALES (est): 252K **Privately Held**
SIC: 3482 Small arms ammunition

(G-9379)
JTI DUTY-FREE USA INC
501 Brickell Dr Ste 402 (33131)
PHONE..................................305 377-3922
Ignacio Luthessa, *CEO*
EMP: 5 **EST:** 2000
SALES (est): 2.5MM **Privately Held**
SIC: 2131 Chewing & smoking tobacco
HQ: Japan Tobacco International U.S.A.,
Inc.
Glenpnte Ctr E 300 Frank
Teaneck NJ 07666
201 871-1210

(G-9380)
JUAN F MONTANO
7895 Sw 57th Ter (33143-1622)
PHONE..................................305 274-0512
Juan Montano, *President*
Juan F Montano, *Owner*
Olga Montana, *Vice Pres*
EMP: 8 **EST:** 2004
SALES (est): 267.1K **Privately Held**
SIC: 2051 Cakes, bakery: except frozen

(G-9381)
JUAN PAMPANAS DESIGNS INC
32 Nw 20th St (33127-4908)
PHONE..................................305 573-7550
Juan Pampanas, *President*
EMP: 7 **EST:** 1984
SQ FT: 10,000
SALES (est): 300K **Privately Held**
WEB: www.pampanas.com
SIC: 2426 1751 Carvings, furniture: wood;
cabinet & finish carpentry

(G-9382)
K COLOR CORP
Also Called: Color K Graphics
7255 Nw 68th St Ste 1 (33166-3015)
PHONE..................................305 579-2290
Fax: 305 882-8353
▼ **EMP:** 14
SALES (est): 1.7MM **Privately Held**
SIC: 2752 Lithographic Commercial Print-
ing

(G-9383)
KALUZ LLC
Also Called: Decocandles
7105 Nw 41st St (33166-6818)
PHONE..................................786 991-2260
Karen Lawrence, *Mng Member*
▼ **EMP:** 49 **EST:** 2001
SALES (est): 4.5MM **Privately Held**
WEB: www.kaluzrestaurant.com
SIC: 3999 5199 Candles; candles

(G-9384)
KARIGAM ENTERPRISES INC
1110 Brickell Ave Ste 702 (33131-3136)
PHONE..................................305 358-7755
EMP: 9
SALES (est): 1MM **Privately Held**
SIC: 2339 Mfg Women's/Misses' Outer-
wear

(G-9385)
KASEYA US LLC (PA)
701 Brickell Ave Ste 400 (33131-2833)
PHONE..................................415 694-5700
Fred Voccola, *CEO*
Tara Newman, *Partner*
Joe Smolarski, *COO*
Alexandra Letts, *Exec VP*
Tim Blaszak, *Vice Pres*
EMP: 25 **EST:** 2009

SALES (est): 10MM **Privately Held**
WEB: www.kaseya.com
SIC: 7372 Prepackaged software

(G-9386)
KD-PHARMA USA INC
14193 Sw 119th Ave Ste 10 (33186-6013)
PHONE..................................786 345-5500
Peter Lembke, *President*
EMP: 7 **EST:** 2018
SALES (est): 378.6K **Privately Held**
WEB: www.kdpharmagroup.com
SIC: 2834 Pharmaceutical preparations

(G-9387)
KEL GLO CORP
54 Ne 73rd St (33138-5350)
PHONE..................................305 751-5641
Ron Smalzer, *President*
▼ **EMP:** 7 **EST:** 1952
SQ FT: 10,000
SALES (est): 989.2K **Privately Held**
WEB: www.kel-glo.com
SIC: 2851 Paints: oil or alkyd vehicle or
water thinned; plastics base paints & var-
nishes

(G-9388)
KENDALL FUEL INC
9949 N Kendall Dr (33176-1720)
PHONE..................................305 270-7735
Ehsan U Haq, *President*
EMP: 5 **EST:** 2009
SALES (est): 10MM **Privately Held**
SIC: 2869 5541 Fuels;

(G-9389)
KENDALL SIGN AND DESIGN INC
Also Called: Sign-A-Rama
14271 Sw 120th St Ste 103 (33186-7375)
PHONE..................................305 595-2000
Paul Klugerman, *President*
EMP: 5 **EST:** 1995
SALES (est): 496.1K **Privately Held**
WEB: www.signarama.com
SIC: 3993 Signs & advertising specialties

(G-9390)
KING TECH PRINT LLC
7205 Nw 44th St (33166-6418)
PHONE..................................786 362-6249
Pablo E Fernandez, *Principal*
EMP: 7 **EST:** 2014
SALES (est): 305.9K **Privately Held**
SIC: 2752 Commercial printing, litho-
graphic

(G-9391)
KISKEYA MINERALS USA LLC
Also Called: White Cliff
8249 Nw 70th St (33166-2743)
PHONE..................................305 328-5082
Douglas Lofland,
James Cole,
EMP: 9 **EST:** 2009
SQ FT: 5,500
SALES (est): 648.1K **Privately Held**
SIC: 1481 Mine & quarry services, non-
metallic minerals

(G-9392)
KLAAVENTURA LLC
600 Sw 1st Ave (33130-3002)
PHONE..................................305 931-2322
Roberto X Ortega, *Principal*
EMP: 8 **EST:** 2010
SALES (est): 167.1K **Privately Held**
SIC: 3825 Instruments to measure electric-
ity

(G-9393)
KLINCO INC ✪
2164 Nw 22nd Ct (33142-7346)
PHONE..................................734 949-4999
Janeth Bayona Quinonez, *President*
EMP: 5 **EST:** 2021
SALES (est): 441.5K **Privately Held**
SIC: 3582 Ironers, commercial laundry &
drycleaning

(G-9394)
KMS MEDICAL LLC
13755 Sw 119th Ave (33186-6265)
PHONE..................................305 266-3388

Sean McBrayer,
Matt Palmer,
Kevin W Smith,
EMP: 10 **EST:** 2004
SALES (est): 954.7K **Privately Held**
WEB: www.kms-medical.com
SIC: 3841 8731 Surgical & medical instru-
ments; medical research, commercial

(G-9395)
KNIGHT-RDDR/MIAMI HERALD CR UN
1 Herald Plz Fl 2 (33132-1609)
PHONE..................................305 376-2181
Debra Touhey, *Manager*
▲ **EMP:** 9 **EST:** 1966
SQ FT: 745
SALES (est): 304.7K **Privately Held**
SIC: 2711 Newspapers, publishing & print-
ing

(G-9396)
KORANGY PUBLISHING INC
6318 Biscayne Blvd (33138-6226)
PHONE..................................786 334-5052
EMP: 60
SALES (corp-wide): 25.6MM **Privately
Held**
WEB: www.therealdeal.com
SIC: 2741 Miscellaneous publishing
PA: Korangy Publishing Inc.
450 W 31st St Fl 4
New York NY 10001
212 260-1332

(G-9397)
KRAMER PHARMACAL INC
8900 Sw 24th St (33165-2075)
PHONE..................................305 226-0641
Juan Ruiz, *President*
EMP: 13 **EST:** 2000
SALES (est): 198.1K **Privately Held**
SIC: 2834 Pharmaceutical preparations

(G-9398)
KREATE PRINTING INC
Also Called: Kreatech
3440 Ne 192nd St Apt 1c (33180-2422)
PHONE..................................305 542-1336
Florinda M Saul, *President*
EMP: 7 **EST:** 2018
SALES (est): 118.5K **Privately Held**
WEB: www.kreateprinting.com
SIC: 2752 Commercial printing, offset

(G-9399)
KREYOL ESSENCE LLC
8325 Ne 2nd Ave Ste 117 (33138-3815)
PHONE..................................786 453-8287
Stephane Jean-Baptiste, *COO*
EMP: 14 **EST:** 2013
SALES (est): 1.1MM **Privately Held**
WEB: www.kreyolessence.com
SIC: 2844 Toilet preparations

(G-9400)
KROME BREWING COMPANY LLC
17480 Sw 232nd St (33170-5504)
PHONE..................................786 601-9337
Gustavo Fernandez, *Manager*
EMP: 11 **EST:** 2016
SALES (est): 503.8K **Privately Held**
SIC: 2082 Beer (alcoholic beverage)

(G-9401)
KUANDO TRADING CORP
1001 Brickell Bay Dr (33131-4900)
PHONE..................................786 603-3772
Reddy Stehlin, *President*
◆ **EMP:** 10 **EST:** 2017
SALES (est): 632.3K **Privately Held**
SIC: 2013 Frozen meats from purchased
meat

(G-9402)
L & A QUALITY PRODUCTS INC
2181 Nw 10th Ave (33127-4635)
PHONE..................................305 326-9300
Albert Muniz, *President*
Olga Gaugrra, *Owner*
Jesus Guerra, *Admin Sec*
EMP: 9 **EST:** 1999

SALES (est): 550.9K **Privately Held**
WEB: www.laqualityproducts.com
SIC: 2099 Food preparations

(G-9403)
L A ORNAMENTAL & RACK CORP
3708 Nw 82nd St (33147-4457)
PHONE..................................305 696-0419
Jesus Velunza, *President*
Aleida Velunza, *Vice Pres*
▼ **EMP:** 5 **EST:** 1978
SQ FT: 17,500
SALES (est): 1.2MM **Privately Held**
WEB: www.laornamental.com
SIC: 3315 1731 3446 2411 Fence gates
posts & fittings: steel; access control sys-
tems specialization; fences or posts, or-
namental iron or steel; gates, ornamental
metal; rails, fence: round or split

(G-9404)
LA CORONELLA MEAT PROCESSING
9566 Nw 7th Ave (33150-1844)
PHONE..................................305 691-2630
Isidoro Fernandez, *President*
Ramona Fernandez, *Vice Pres*
Margarita Garcia, *Admin Sec*
EMP: 10 **EST:** 1973
SQ FT: 2,400
SALES (est): 1.1MM **Privately Held**
SIC: 2013 Prepared pork products from
purchased pork; sausages from pur-
chased meat

(G-9405)
LA CUISINE INTL DISTRS INC
Also Called: LCI DISTRIBUTORS
2005 Nw 115th Ave (33172-4919)
PHONE..................................305 418-0010
Josu Gaubeka, *President*
Rafael Guerrero, *COO*
Lissett Lopez, *Opers Mgr*
Cynthia Carneiro, *Purchasing*
Jaime Miranda, *Technical Mgr*
◆ **EMP:** 24 **EST:** 2004
SALES (est): 11.4MM **Privately Held**
WEB: www.lacuisineinternational.com
SIC: 3639 5023 5064 Major kitchen appli-
ances, except refrigerators & stoves;
kitchenware; electrical appliances, televi-
sion & radio

(G-9406)
LA FABRIKA RETAIL SERVICES LLC
6303 Blue Lagoon Dr Ste 4 (33126-6002)
PHONE..................................786 525-4491
Salomon Amador,
EMP: 5 **EST:** 2015
SQ FT: 700
SALES (est): 413.4K **Privately Held**
SIC: 2542 7319 Stands, merchandise dis-
play: except wood; display advertising
service

(G-9407)
LA LECHONERA PRODUCTS INC
Also Called: La Lechonera Media
2161 Nw 22nd Ct (33142-7301)
PHONE..................................305 635-2303
Luis Mejuto, *President*
Ernesto Sobalvarro, *General Mgr*
Sonia Matos, *Office Mgr*
EMP: 17 **EST:** 1974
SALES (est): 924.6K **Privately Held**
WEB: www.lalechoneraproducts.com
SIC: 2035 Seasonings, meat sauces (ex-
cept tomato & dry)

(G-9408)
LA LUNA LTD
1638 Sw 8th St (33135-5220)
PHONE..................................305 644-0444
Gael Decourtivron, *President*
EMP: 5 **EST:** 1997
SALES (est): 493K **Privately Held**
WEB: www.lalunacigars.com
SIC: 2121 Cigars

(G-9409)
LA MANSION LATINA LLC
Also Called: Biscotti Gourmet Bakery
9183 Sw 152nd Path (33196-1262)
PHONE....................................305 406-1606
EMP: 6
SALES (est): 390K Privately Held
SIC: 2051 Mfg Bread/Related Products

(G-9410)
LA MONTINA INC
Also Called: Tiger Meat & Provisions
1445 Nw 22nd St (33142-7741)
P.O. Box 14260 (33101-4260)
PHONE....................................305 324-0083
Manuel Alonso, President
Luis Requejo, Vice Pres
EMP: 21 EST: 1975
SQ FT: 6,000
SALES (est): 2.8MM Privately Held
SIC: 2013 2011 Ham, canned: from pur-
chased meat; sausages from purchased
meat; meat packing plants

(G-9411)
LA MOTI ROOF & TILE INC
1360 Nw 29th St (33142-6620)
PHONE....................................305 635-2641
Ruben Bernal, President
Elizabeth Bernal, Corp Secy
▼ EMP: 7 EST: 1977
SQ FT: 1,200
SALES (est): 906K Privately Held
WEB: www.lamotirooftile.com
SIC: 3272 Roofing tile & slabs, concrete;
tile, precast terrazzo or concrete

(G-9412)
LA PROVIDENCIA EXPRESS CO
Also Called: Anavini
4728 Sw 74th Ave (33155-4417)
P.O. Box 559048 (33255-9048)
PHONE....................................305 409-9894
Ana Del Velasquez, President
Jose Velasquez, Vice Pres
EMP: 7 EST: 1990
SQ FT: 1,200
SALES (est): 811.4K Privately Held
SIC: 2361 2321 2325 5137 Dresses:
girls', children's & infants'; men's & boys'
furnishings; shorts (outerwear): men's,
youths' & boys'; women's & children's
clothing

(G-9413)
LA PROVINCE INC
2106 Nw 13th Ave (33142-7704)
PHONE....................................305 538-2406
EMP: 18
SQ FT: 8,485
SALES (est): 1.5MM Privately Held
SIC: 2051 5149 Mfg Bread/Related Prod-
ucts Whol Groceries

(G-9414)
LA REAL FOODS INC
Also Called: La Real Tortillas
13013 Sw 122nd Ave (33186-6240)
PHONE....................................305 232-6449
Yair Rosemberg, CEO
▼ EMP: 25 EST: 1991
SQ FT: 6,500
SALES (est): 2.9MM Privately Held
WEB: www.larealfoods.com
SIC: 2099 Tortillas, fresh or refrigerated

(G-9415)
**LA VILLARENA MEAT & PORK
INC (PA)**
6455 Ne 3rd Ave (33138-6096)
PHONE....................................305 759-0555
Osvaldo Castillo, President
Candelario Rodriguez, Vice Pres
Teresa Garcia, Admin Sec
EMP: 11 EST: 1968
SQ FT: 8,898
SALES (est): 5.4MM Privately Held
WEB: www.lavillarena.com
SIC: 2013 5144 5147 Frozen meats from
purchased meat; smoked meats from pur-
chased meat; poultry & poultry products;
meats, cured or smoked; meats, fresh

(G-9416)
LAAL MANUFACTURING INC
55 Ne 1st St Ste 55 # 55 (33132-2484)
PHONE....................................786 859-3613
Otero Garcia, Principal
EMP: 9 EST: 2013
SALES (est): 251.3K Privately Held
SIC: 3999 Manufacturing industries

(G-9417)
LAHIA AMERICA CORP
12401 Sw 134th Ct (33186-6413)
PHONE....................................305 254-6212
George Vithayathil, President
▲ EMP: 10 EST: 2009
SALES (est): 810K Privately Held
SIC: 2299 Textile goods

(G-9418)
LAKEWOOD ORGANICS LLC
2125 Nw 10th Ct (33127-4501)
PHONE....................................305 324-5900
Aaron L Peterson, Branch Mgr
EMP: 76
SALES (corp-wide): 9.4MM Privately
Held
SIC: 2033 Fruit juices: fresh
PA: Lakewood Organics, Llc
3104 W Baseline Rd
Shelby MI 49455
231 861-6333

(G-9419)
LAN DESIGNS INC
Also Called: By Dancers For Dancers
7169 Sw 44th St (33155-4636)
PHONE....................................305 661-7878
Liz Nieves, President
EMP: 6 EST: 2004
SALES (est): 499.3K Privately Held
SIC: 2339 5621 Athletic clothing:
women's, misses' & juniors'; women's
sportswear

(G-9420)
LAN INDUSTRIES LLC
Also Called: Life All Natural
5413 Nw 74th Ave (33166-4225)
PHONE....................................305 889-2087
Alejandro Meneses, CEO
Matthew Guccione, Accountant
EMP: 16 EST: 2019
SALES (est): 1.4MM Privately Held
SIC: 2833 Vitamins, natural or synthetic:
bulk, uncompounded

(G-9421)
LAN MUSIC CORP
13611 S Dixie Hwy (33176-7258)
PHONE....................................305 722-5842
Ricardo Boevri, President
▼ EMP: 3 EST: 2005
SALES (est): 30MM Privately Held
SIC: 3931 Musical instruments

(G-9422)
LAND LEATHER INC
1927 Nw 135th Ave (33182-1925)
PHONE....................................305 594-2260
Susie Iszler, CEO
Karl Iszler, Admin Sec
EMP: 5 EST: 1969
SALES (est): 2.5MM Privately Held
WEB: www.landleather.com
SIC: 3199 5199 5948 Leather goods;
leather goods, except footwear, gloves,
luggage, belting; leather goods, except
luggage & shoes

(G-9423)
LANZAS DISTRIBUTOR INC
Also Called: Lanzas Foods
7251 Nw 54th St (33166-4807)
PHONE....................................305 885-5966
Antonio M Lanzas, President
Maria S Lanzas, Vice Pres
▲ EMP: 5 EST: 1992
SQ FT: 25,000
SALES (est): 626.3K Privately Held
WEB: www.lanzasfoods.com
SIC: 2022 Natural cheese

(G-9424)
LARAS
3841 Ne 2nd Ave Ste 301 (33137-3639)
PHONE....................................305 576-0036

Nores Alvaro, Principal
EMP: 8 EST: 2006
SALES (est): 197K Privately Held
SIC: 2741 Music book & sheet music pub-
lishing

(G-9425)
LARGENT FUELS USA LLC
1200 Brickell Ave Ste 240 (33131-3893)
PHONE....................................786 431-5981
Jennifer Ahumada, Sales Mgr
Pablo Condeza,
Raul Condeza,
Luisa Solorzano,
EMP: 6 EST: 2015
SALES (est): 1MM Privately Held
WEB: www.largentfuels.com
SIC: 2869 Fuels

(G-9426)
LARSEN CABINETMAKER CO
14374 Sw 142nd Ave (33186-6769)
PHONE....................................305 252-1212
Ivan Larsen, Owner
EMP: 7 EST: 1981
SALES (est): 293.4K Privately Held
SIC: 2599 2541 2434 Bar, restaurant &
cafeteria furniture; wood partitions & fix-
tures; wood kitchen cabinets

(G-9427)
**LAS AMRCAS MLTIMEDIA
GROUP LLC**
Also Called: Diario Las Americas
888 Brickell Ave Ste 500 (33131-2913)
PHONE....................................305 633-3341
Ricardo Ballesteros, Editor
Tulio Casal, Editor
Beatriz Mendoza, Editor
Aquiles Presilla, COO
Diario Enriques, Natl Sales Mgr
EMP: 18 EST: 2012
SALES (est): 3.2MM Privately Held
WEB: www.diariolasamericas.com
SIC: 2711 8999 Newspapers: publishing
only, not printed on site; advertising copy
writing

(G-9428)
LAS ZIRH AMERICAS INC
2792 Nw 24th St (33142-7006)
PHONE....................................305 942-7597
Burak P Yolga, President
EMP: 8 EST: 2017
SALES (est): 148.6K Privately Held
WEB: www.laszirhusa.com
SIC: 3496 Tire chains

(G-9429)
LASER SURGICAL FLORIDA INC
900 Biscayne Blvd # 2001 (33132-1561)
PHONE....................................954 609-7639
Russell Wright, CEO
Gerald Wright, President
EMP: 6 EST: 2009
SALES (est): 531.3K Privately Held
WEB: www.lasersurgicaloflorida.com
SIC: 3841 Surgical & medical instruments

(G-9430)
LASH MAKERS LLC
65 Ne 16th St (33132)
PHONE....................................800 989-6912
Maria Jaime, CEO
Elena Meluk, Founder
EMP: 6 EST: 2015
SALES (est): 367.1K Privately Held
WEB: www.lashmakers.com
SIC: 3999 Eyelashes, artificial

(G-9431)
LATAM GROUP CORP
12453 Sw 124th Ter (33186-5497)
PHONE....................................305 793-8961
Gabriel Sebastian, President
Angel Mendez, Vice Pres
EMP: 7 EST: 2012
SALES (est): 91K Privately Held
SIC: 2822 5113 5169 Synthetic rubber; in-
dustrial & personal service paper; chemi-
cals & allied products

(G-9432)
LATAM OPTICAL LLC
2585 Nw 74th Ave (33122-1417)
PHONE....................................786 275-3284

Nestor A Descarso, Principal
Mauricio Paez, Opers Mgr
◆ EMP: 6 EST: 2014
SALES (est): 842.1K Privately Held
WEB: www.latamoptical.com
SIC: 3089 Lenses, except optical: plastic

(G-9433)
**LATELIER PRIS HUTE DESIGN
LLC**
6151 Biscayne Blvd (33137-2226)
PHONE....................................800 792-3550
Victoria Lane, VP Sales
Elisa Waysenson, VP Sales
Ricardo Moraes,
Maria Moraes,
EMP: 12 EST: 2019
SALES (est): 2MM Privately Held
WEB: www.leatelierparis.com
SIC: 3469 Kitchen fixtures & equipment:
metal, except cast aluminum

(G-9434)
**LATIN AMERCN MEATS &
FOODS USA (PA)**
Also Called: Baby Beef USA
6939 Nw 82nd Ave (33166-2766)
PHONE....................................305 477-2700
Jose Azuaje, President
Juan J Tamayo, Director
EMP: 8 EST: 2015
SALES (est): 893.3K Privately Held
SIC: 2013 5147 5142 5143 Sausages &
other prepared meats; meats, fresh;
meat, frozen: packaged; cheese

(G-9435)
**LATIN AMRCN FNCL PBLCTIONS
INC (HQ)**
Also Called: Latinfinance
1101 Brickell Ave # 1200 (33131-3105)
PHONE....................................305 416-5261
Stuart Allen, CEO
Robert Chandler, Partner
Mick Bowen, Editor
Richard Ensor, Chairman
Karah Niemann, Regional Mgr
▲ EMP: 14 EST: 1988
SQ FT: 3,441
SALES (est): 7.9MM
SALES (corp-wide): 461MM Privately
Held
WEB: www.latinfinance.com
SIC: 2721 Magazines: publishing only, not
printed on site
PA: Euromoney Institutional Investor Plc
6-8 Bouverie Street
London EC4Y
207 779-8888

(G-9436)
LATIN DAIRY FOODS LLC
Also Called: Jls Dairy Holdings
2175 Nw 24th Ave (33142-7279)
PHONE....................................305 888-1788
Jose Salazar, CEO
EMP: 19 EST: 2010
SQ FT: 5,000
SALES (est): 554.9K Privately Held
SIC: 2024 5143 Dairy based frozen
desserts; frozen dairy desserts

(G-9437)
LATIN PRESS INC
600 Sw 22nd Ave (33135-3119)
PHONE....................................305 285-3133
Max Jaramillo, CEO
Duvan Chaverra, Editor
Sandra Camacho, Project Mgr
Jaramillo Max, Opers Mgr
Manuela Jaramillo, CFO
EMP: 15 EST: 1993
SALES (est): 2.2MM Privately Held
WEB: www.latinpressinc.com
SIC: 2721 Magazines: publishing only, not
printed on site

(G-9438)
LAU INTERNATIONAL INC
Also Called: Ojm
36 Ne 1st St Ste 438 (33132-2493)
PHONE....................................305 381-9855
Fax: 305 539-0794
▲ EMP: 8
SQ FT: 1,500

▲ = Import ▼=Export
◆ =Import/Export

SALES (est): 954.7K **Privately Held**
SIC: 3911 Mfg Precious Jewelry

(G-9439)
LAZA IRON WORKS INC
7251 N Miami Ave (33150-3719)
PHONE................................305 754-8200
Israel Laza, *President*
Estrella Moussawel, *Vice Pres*
▼ EMP: 12 EST: 1980
SQ FT: 4,500
SALES (est): 1.9MM **Privately Held**
WEB: www.lazairon.com
SIC: 3446 Architectural metalwork

(G-9440)
LCN INCORPORATED
Also Called: Consolidated Parking Equipment
6949 Nw 82nd Ave (33166-2766)
PHONE................................305 461-2770
Alexandre Oliva, *CEO*
Iris Del, *Vice Pres*
Anthony D'Ambrosio, *Treasurer*
Jerry Acosta, *Sales Staff*
Robbie Mancl, *Technician*
EMP: 25 EST: 2006
SALES (est): 3.3MM **Privately Held**
WEB: www.consolidatedparking.com
SIC: 3559 Parking facility equipment &
supplies

(G-9441)
LDM INDUSTRIES INC
12904 Sw 132nd Ct (33186-5819)
PHONE................................305 216-1545
Elizabeth Murialdo, *Principal*
EMP: 8 EST: 2008
SALES (est): 361.9K **Privately Held**
WEB: www.ldmindustries.com
SIC: 3999 Manufacturing industries

(G-9442)
LE LABO
2621 Nw 2nd Ave (33127-4155)
PHONE................................786 636-6928
Monica Carvajal, *Store Mgr*
EMP: 9 EST: 2017
SALES (est): 311K **Privately Held**
WEB: www.lelabofragrances.com
SIC: 2844 Perfumes & colognes

(G-9443)
LE MUNDO VINO LLC
12323 Sw 130th St (33186-6208)
PHONE................................786 369-5232
Lazara Villalobos,
Juan Cabrales,
▲ EMP: 10 EST: 2010
SALES (est): 769.2K **Privately Held**
WEB: www.lemundovino.com
SIC: 2082 Beer (alcoholic beverage)

(G-9444)
LE WOOD WORK INC
3325 Nw 80th St (33147-4627)
PHONE................................786 269-4275
Luis F Hernandez, *Principal*
EMP: 7 EST: 2008
SALES (est): 146.3K **Privately Held**
SIC: 2431 Millwork

(G-9445)
LEAD ENTERPRISES INC
3300 Nw 29th St (33142-6310)
PHONE................................305 635-8644
Thomas Taylor, *CEO*
Juan Betancourt, *Controller*
Joaquin Velazquez, *Sales Staff*
◆ EMP: 15 EST: 1961
SQ FT: 6,600
SALES (est): 1.7MM **Privately Held**
WEB: www.leadenterprises.com
SIC: 3949 3844 Fishing tackle, general; X-
ray apparatus & tubes

(G-9446)
LEADEX
4731 Sw 75th Ave (33155-4436)
PHONE................................305 266-2028
Cary Rogirguez, *Manager*
EMP: 10 EST: 1977
SALES (est): 399.3K **Privately Held**
WEB: www.leadexcorp.com
SIC: 3356 Nonferrous rolling & drawing

(G-9447)
LEANDRO MORA STUDIO LLC
4038 Nw 32nd Ave (33142-5002)
PHONE................................786 376-9166
EMP: 7 EST: 2016
SALES (est): 261.6K **Privately Held**
WEB: www.leandromorastudio.com
SIC: 2431 5712 Millwork; custom made
furniture, except cabinets

(G-9448)
LEBLON LLC
Also Called: Leblon Cachaca
2701 S Le Jeune Rd (33134-5809)
PHONE................................954 649-0148
Eric Goldman, *President*
▲ EMP: 7 EST: 2005
SALES (est): 149K **Privately Held**
SIC: 2085 Distilled & blended liquors

(G-9449)
LEEDER GROUP INC
8508 Nw 66th St (33166-2635)
PHONE................................305 436-5030
Mark Webster, *President*
◆ EMP: 30 EST: 1996
SQ FT: 13,000
SALES (est): 2.3MM **Privately Held**
WEB: www.leedergroup.com
SIC: 3842 Orthopedic appliances

(G-9450)
LEITON DECOR & DESIGN
4237 Nw 37th Ct (33142-4233)
PHONE................................786 286-4776
Dennis Leiton, *President*
EMP: 6 EST: 2008
SALES (est): 564.3K **Privately Held**
WEB: www.leitondecor.com
SIC: 2434 Wood kitchen cabinets

(G-9451)
LENNOX NATIONAL ACCOUNT S
4418 Sw 74th Ave (33155-4408)
PHONE................................954 745-3482
EMP: 7 EST: 2018
SALES (est): 270.7K **Privately Held**
WEB: www.lennoxnas.com
SIC: 3585 Refrigeration & heating equip-
ment

(G-9452)
LERNESS SHOE CORP
2155 Sw 8th St (33135-3319)
Rural Route 2155 Sw 8t (33135)
PHONE................................305 643-6525
Mark Saracino, *Manager*
EMP: 8 EST: 1967
SQ FT: 2,700
SALES (est): 745.6K **Privately Held**
WEB: www.lernessshoes.com
SIC: 3144 3143 5661 Women's footwear,
except athletic; men's footwear, except
athletic; women's shoes; men's shoes

(G-9453)
LESTER MANUFACTURING LLC
2131 Nw 23rd Ct (33142-7251)
PHONE................................305 898-0306
Lester I Rivera, *Branch Mgr*
EMP: 7
SALES (corp-wide): 244K **Privately Held**
SIC: 3999 Barber & beauty shop equip-
ment
PA: Lester Manufacturing, Llc
1250 Sw 12th Ct
Miami FL

(G-9454)
LEXMARK INTERNATIONAL INC
5201 Blue Lagoon Dr # 87 (33126-2064)
PHONE................................305 467-2200
Carlota Blom, *Managing Dir*
Jose Cantor, *Manager*
EMP: 15 **Privately Held**
WEB: www.lexmark.com
SIC: 3577 5065 Printers, computer; elec-
tronic parts & equipment
HQ: Lexmark International, Inc.
740 W New Circle Rd
Lexington KY 40511

(G-9455)
LEXPRINT LLC
4255 Sw 72nd Ave (33155-4527)
PHONE................................305 661-2424

Ernesto Rodriguez, *Principal*
EMP: 6 EST: 2007
SALES (est): 503.4K **Privately Held**
WEB: www.lexprintusa.com
SIC: 2752 Commercial printing, offset

(G-9456)
LG SMART BLINDS CORP
8752 Sw 2nd Ter (33174-3937)
PHONE................................305 704-0696
EMP: 9 EST: 2020
SALES (est): 281.1K **Privately Held**
SIC: 2591 Window blinds

(G-9457)
LIFT AEROSPACE CORP
6960 Nw 50th St (33166-5632)
PHONE................................305 851-5237
Reinaldo Barroso, *Partner*
Michael Jaramillo, *Business Mgr*
William Lagos, *Prdtn Mgr*
Jonathan Cruz, *Sales Mgr*
Maria Rojas, *Director*
EMP: 21 EST: 2013
SALES (est): 4.7MM **Privately Held**
WEB: www.liftaerospace.com
SIC: 3721 5088 5046 5065 Aircraft;
transportation equipment & supplies;
commercial equipment; electronic parts &
equipment; airports, flying fields & serv-
ices; freight transportation arrangement

(G-9458)
LIGHTNET USA INC
123 Nw 23rd St (33127-4409)
PHONE................................305 260-6444
Christoph Rosslenbroich, *President*
EMP: 11 EST: 2013
SALES (est): 270K **Privately Held**
SIC: 3648 8748 8712 Area & sports lumi-
naries; lighting consultant; architectural
services

(G-9459)
LIGHTWORKS INC
7035 Sw 47th St Ste A (33155-4625)
PHONE................................305 456-3520
Mainnor Pino, *President*
Solange P Boiangin, *Principal*
Fabrice Pellegrino, *Vice Pres*
Manfred Koberg, *Project Mgr*
EMP: 6 EST: 2017
SQ FT: 35,000
SALES (est): 506.6K **Privately Held**
WEB: www.lightworksflorida.com
SIC: 3699 Electrical equipment & supplies

(G-9460)
LILAS DESSERTS INC
12309 Sw 130th St (33186-6208)
PHONE................................305 252-1441
Reinaldo Navarro Jr, *President*
EMP: 17 EST: 1989
SQ FT: 10,000
SALES (est): 5MM **Privately Held**
WEB: www.lilasdesserts.com
SIC: 2024 Custard, frozen

(G-9461)
LIMITED DESIGNS LLC
382 Ne 191st St 87394 (33179-3899)
PHONE................................305 547-9909
Elizabeta Dimkova,
EMP: 8 EST: 2018
SALES (est): 314.2K **Privately Held**
SIC: 2759 Commercial printing

(G-9462)
LINCOLN-MARTI CMNTY AGCY
INC (PA)
2700 Sw 8th St (33135-4619)
PHONE................................305 643-4888
Martin Anorga, *President*
Dominica Alcantara, *Vice Pres*
EMP: 70 EST: 1990
SQ FT: 13,009
SALES: 32.8MM **Privately Held**
SIC: 2732 8211 5812 8351 Book printing;
specialty education; private elementary &
secondary schools; contract food serv-
ices; child day care services; preschool
center; nursery school; head start center,
except in conjunction with school

(G-9463)
LINCOLN-MARTI CMNTY AGCY
INC
Also Called: Marti Lincoln Community Agency
450 Sw 16th Ave (33135-3625)
PHONE................................646 463-6120
EMP: 247
SALES (corp-wide): 32.8MM **Privately
Held**
SIC: 2732 Book printing
PA: Lincoln-Marti Community Agency, Inc.
2700 Sw 8th St
Miami FL 33135
305 643-4888

(G-9464)
LISA TODD INTERNATIONAL
LLC
1441 Nw N River Dr 3a (33125-2601)
PHONE................................305 445-2632
Lisa A Shapiro, *Mng Member*
Coralia J Rodriguez,
EMP: 6 EST: 2013
SALES (est): 317.3K **Privately Held**
SIC: 2339 Women's & misses' outerwear

(G-9465)
LIST + BEISLER CORP
200 South Bscyne Blvd Lvl Level (33131)
PHONE................................646 866-6960
Robert Heuveldop, *Managing Prtnr*
Jan Walter, *Managing Prtnr*
Philip Von Der Goltz, *Principal*
EMP: 30 EST: 2018
SALES (est): 1.9MM **Privately Held**
WEB: www.list-beisler.coffee
SIC: 2095 Roasted coffee

(G-9466)
LITECRETE INC
Also Called: Lite Crete Insulated Concrete
8095 Nw 64th St (33166-2747)
PHONE................................305 500-9373
Bernardo Duran, *President*
Yunior Afonso, *Superintendent*
Eugenio Fernandez, *Vice Pres*
Jay Sanchez, *Project Mgr*
Lina Vidales, *Manager*
▼ EMP: 35 EST: 1997
SALES (est): 8.4MM **Privately Held**
WEB: www.litecrete.com
SIC: 3273 3446 Ready-mixed concrete;
architectural metalwork

(G-9467)
LITHO ART INC
Also Called: Lithographing Art
12190 Sw 131st Ave (33186-6446)
PHONE................................305 232-7098
Edwardo Valdes, *President*
Berta Huerta, *Director*
Isidro Huerta, *Director*
Ada E Valdes, *Director*
EMP: 7 EST: 1990
SALES (est): 837.2K **Privately Held**
WEB: www.printnmore.com
SIC: 2752 Commercial printing, offset

(G-9468)
LIVE AEROSPACE INC
7205 Nw 68th St Ste 11 (33166-3016)
PHONE................................305 910-0091
Janet Ayo, *President*
EMP: 8 EST: 2010
SALES (est): 914.2K **Privately Held**
WEB: www.liveaerospace.com
SIC: 3728 Aircraft parts & equipment

(G-9469)
LLORENS PHRM INTL DIV INC
7080 Nw 37th Ct (33147-6531)
P.O. Box 720008 (33172-0001)
PHONE................................305 716-0595
Jose Llorens, *President*
Jose Hernadez, *Director*
EMP: 12 EST: 2001
SQ FT: 18,000
SALES (est): 3.5MM **Privately Held**
WEB: www.llorenspharm.com
SIC: 2834 Pharmaceutical preparations

(G-9470)
LOFTON ENTERPRISES TRCKG LLC ✪
1065 Sw 8th St (33130-3601)
PHONE..786 220-6053
Jacques Lofton, *Mng Member*
EMP: 10 EST: 2022
SALES (est): 413.1K **Privately Held**
SIC: 3537 Trucks: freight, baggage, etc.: industrial, except mining

(G-9471)
LOGISCENTER LLC
Also Called: Barcode Distributor
5201 Blue Lagoon Dr Fl 8 (33126-7050)
PHONE..800 729-0236
Manuel Campos Galvan, *Manager*
Juan L Manaute Lopez, *Manager*
EMP: 6 EST: 2015
SALES (est): 409.4K **Privately Held**
WEB: www.logiscenter.us
SIC: 3577 Bar code (magnetic ink) printers

(G-9472)
LOGISTIC SYSTEMS INC (PA)
Also Called: L S I
2175 Nw 115th Ave (33172-4920)
PHONE..305 477-4999
Francisco Casanova, *President*
Carlos R Villarreal, *Treasurer*
▼ EMP: 5 EST: 1994
SQ FT: 2,325
SALES (est): 1.6MM **Privately Held**
WEB: www.lsi-logistics.com
SIC: 3533 3559 Oil & gas drilling rigs & equipment; oil field machinery & equipment; petroleum refinery equipment

(G-9473)
LOGOI INC
12900 Sw 128th St Ste 204 (33186-6274)
P.O. Box 770128 (33177-0003)
PHONE..305 232-5880
Joseph Linn, *Ch of Bd*
Leslie Thompson, *President*
Angie Moure, *Editor*
Edward Thompson, *Vice Pres*
Oscar Oglieve, *Treasurer*
EMP: 7 EST: 1959
SQ FT: 5,000
SALES (est): 331.7K **Privately Held**
WEB: www.logoi.org
SIC: 2731 Textbooks: publishing only, not printed on site

(G-9474)
LONGCHAMP USA INC
1450 Brickell Ave # 2140 (33131-3455)
PHONE..305 372-1628
Olivier Cassegrain, *Managing Dir*
Sandrine Bigratnewton, *Store Mgr*
Sean Tweedale, *Store Mgr*
Anita Wingerter, *Store Mgr*
Donald Rose, *Train & Dev Mgr*
EMP: 54 **Privately Held**
WEB: www.longchamp.com
SIC: 3199 Equestrian related leather articles
PA: Longchamp Usa, Inc.
4 Applegate Dr B
Robbinsville NJ 08691

(G-9475)
LONGEVERON INC
1951 Nw 7th Ave Ste 520 (33136-1121)
PHONE..305 909-0840
Joshua M Hare, *Ch of Bd*
Geoff Green, *President*
Anthony Oliva, *Senior VP*
Lisa McClainmoss, *Vice Pres*
Aaron Fils, *Research*
EMP: 12 EST: 2014
SQ FT: 15,000
SALES (est): 1.3MM **Privately Held**
WEB: www.longeveron.com
SIC: 2834 8731 Pharmaceutical preparations; biotechnical research, commercial

(G-9476)
LOOK WORLDWIDE INC
6851 Sw 31st St (33155-3823)
PHONE..305 662-1287
William Sancho, *President*
Vincent Sancho, *Vice Pres*
EMP: 6 EST: 1996
SQ FT: 1,500

SALES (est): 389.6K **Privately Held**
SIC: 3999 Advertising display products

(G-9477)
LOPEZ & COMPANY INC (PA)
Also Called: Lopco Aviation
2221 Ne 164th St (33160-3703)
PHONE..305 302-3045
Jose E Lopez, *President*
EMP: 5 EST: 2008
SALES (est): 737.4K **Privately Held**
SIC: 3728 Military aircraft equipment & armament

(G-9478)
LOREFICE STEEL CORP
3510 Nw 31st St (33142-5718)
PHONE..786 609-1593
Miguel Lorefice, *President*
EMP: 9 EST: 2016
SALES (est): 318.7K **Privately Held**
SIC: 3291 Abrasive metal & steel products

(G-9479)
LOS PRIMOS EXPRESS SVCS LLC
Also Called: LP Express Services
12039 Sw 132nd Ct (33186-4783)
PHONE..786 701-3297
Judith Cruz, *President*
EMP: 6 EST: 2016
SALES (est): 615.9K **Privately Held**
WEB: www.losprimosexpress.com
SIC: 1389 1799 7299 1522 Construction, repair & dismantling services; cleaning new buildings after construction; home/office interiors finishing, furnishing & remodeling; handyman service; remodeling, multi-family dwellings; moving services

(G-9480)
LOTUS CONTAINERS INC
1000 Brickell Ave Ste 640 (33131-3033)
PHONE..786 590-1056
Willem-Alexander Dous, *CEO*
Marcus Rocha, *President*
Eva Partsch, *Opers Dir*
Joanna Alruzzi, *Opers Mgr*
Marcin Chruszcz, *Opers Mgr*
EMP: 9 EST: 2018
SALES (est): 2.9MM **Privately Held**
WEB: www.lotus-containers.com
SIC: 3499 7359 3799 Boxes for packing & shipping, metal; rental store, general; transportation equipment

(G-9481)
LRVS BARRICADES LLC
8461 Nw 61st St (33166-3307)
PHONE..305 343-6101
Jack Lurvey, *Principal*
EMP: 6 EST: 2016
SALES (est): 339.9K **Privately Held**
WEB: www.ssbarricades.com
SIC: 3499 Barricades, metal

(G-9482)
LUGLOC LLC
550 Nw 29th St (33127-3918)
PHONE..305 961-1765
EMP: 10
SQ FT: 6,000
SALES: 700K **Privately Held**
SIC: 3669 8748 Mfg Communications Equipment Business Consulting Services

(G-9483)
LUMENIS LTD
6800 Sw 40th St Ste 102 (33155-3708)
PHONE..305 508-5052
EMP: 15
SALES (est): 920K **Privately Held**
SIC: 3841 Business Services

(G-9484)
LUMILUM LLC
12400 Sw 134th Ct Ste 1 (33186-6499)
PHONE..305 233-2844
Michael Meiser, *President*
Steven Ditusa, *Consultant*
▲ EMP: 12 EST: 2012
SQ FT: 2,500

SALES (est): 1.2MM **Privately Held**
WEB: www.lumilum.com
SIC: 3646 5063 5719 Commercial indusl & institutional electric lighting fixtures; lighting fixtures, commercial & industrial; lighting fixtures

(G-9485)
LUMIRON INC
20725 Ne 16th Ave Ste A33 (33179-2126)
PHONE..305 652-2599
Shai Dinari, *President*
Laura Dinari, *Vice Pres*
EMP: 5 EST: 2002
SALES (est): 1MM **Privately Held**
WEB: www.lumiron.com
SIC: 3674 Light emitting diodes

(G-9486)
LUNA NEGRA PRODUCTIONS INC
3110 Sw 129th Ave (33175-2508)
PHONE..786 247-1215
EMP: 8 EST: 1999
SALES (est): 258.1K **Privately Held**
WEB: www.reyruiz.com
SIC: 2741 Music book & sheet music publishing

(G-9487)
LUSA SUPPLIER LLC
7339 Nw 66th St (33166-3009)
PHONE..305 885-7634
Carlos Sousa,
◆ EMP: 9 EST: 2009
SALES (est): 1.1MM **Privately Held**
WEB: www.lusasupplier.com
SIC: 3714 Water pump, motor vehicle

(G-9488)
LUX UNLIMITED INC
Also Called: Future Designs By Lahijani
4121 Nw 27th St (33142-5605)
P.O. Box 144979, Coral Gables (33114-4979)
PHONE..305 871-8774
Mike Lahijani, *President*
Elsa Lahijani, *Admin Sec*
◆ EMP: 5 EST: 1979
SQ FT: 15,000
SALES (est): 834.3K **Privately Held**
WEB: www.luxunlimited.com
SIC: 3648 Lighting equipment

(G-9489)
M & M PLASTICS INC
15800 Nw 15th Ave (33169-5606)
PHONE..305 688-4335
Anthony Cohen, *President*
▲ EMP: 26 EST: 2009
SALES (est): 1.7MM **Privately Held**
SIC: 3089 Injection molding of plastics

(G-9490)
M F B INTERNATIONAL INC
Also Called: Magic Faucet Bidet
8323 Nw 64th St (33166-2601)
PHONE..305 436-6601
Roger Mora, *President*
Jose Romeu, *Sales Mgr*
▲ EMP: 5 EST: 1981
SALES (est): 394.3K **Privately Held**
SIC: 3261 3432 Bidets, vitreous china; plumbing fixture fittings & trim

(G-9491)
M L SOLUTIONS INC
1395 Brckell Ave Ste 800 (33132)
PHONE..305 506-5113
Michelle Lynn Adderley, *President*
Vicki Drane, *Admin Sec*
EMP: 5 EST: 2010
SQ FT: 1,000
SALES (est): 305.7K **Privately Held**
SIC: 2752 Commercial printing, lithographic

(G-9492)
M R M S INC
Also Called: Priority Manufacturing
571 Nw 29th St (33127-3917)
PHONE..305 576-3000
Fax: 305 576-2672
▼ EMP: 6
SQ FT: 3,800

SALES (est): 500K **Privately Held**
SIC: 2326 Mfg Men's/Boy's Suits/Coats Mfg Women's/Misses' Suits/Coats Mfg Men's/Boy's Work Clothing

(G-9493)
MA GLASS & MIRROR LLC
Also Called: La Glass
6550 Nw 82nd Ave (33166-2736)
PHONE..305 593-8555
Nelson Morelo,
Roger Abdo.
EMP: 11 EST: 2014
SALES (est): 1MM **Privately Held**
WEB: www.la-glass.com
SIC: 3231 1793 Products of purchased glass; glass & glazing work

(G-9494)
MA METAL FABRICATORS INC
937 Nw 97th Ave Apt 104 (33172-2383)
PHONE..786 343-0268
Marco A Perez, *President*
EMP: 7 EST: 2012
SALES (est): 495.7K **Privately Held**
WEB: www.metal-fabricators.org
SIC: 3499 Furniture parts, metal

(G-9495)
MACHIN SIGNS INC
2530 Nw 77th St (33147-5506)
PHONE..305 694-0464
Jose Machin, *President*
EMP: 8 EST: 2007
SALES (est): 996.1K **Privately Held**
WEB: www.machinsigns.com
SIC: 3993 Electric signs

(G-9496)
MAGNATRADE INTERNATIONAL CORP
745 Sw 35th Ave Ste 204 (33135-4141)
PHONE..305 696-5694
Raul Bellatin Galdos, *President*
Maria B Arias, *Admin Sec*
EMP: 8 EST: 2007
SALES (est): 108.2K **Privately Held**
SIC: 2899 Carbon removing solvent

(G-9497)
MAGNETO SPORTS LLC
360 Nw 27th St (33127-4158)
PHONE..760 593-4589
Andrew Curtis, *President*
EMP: 6 EST: 2017
SALES (est): 383.3K **Privately Held**
SIC: 3949 Skateboards

(G-9498)
MAGNUM MARINE CORPORATION
2900 Ne 188th St (33180-2998)
PHONE..305 931-4292
Katrin Theodoli, *President*
▼ EMP: 18 EST: 1975
SQ FT: 10,000
SALES (est): 1.1MM **Privately Held**
WEB: www.magnummarine.com
SIC: 3732 Boats, fiberglass: building & repairing

(G-9499)
MAHNKES ORTHTICS PRSTHTICS OF (PA)
Also Called: Sun Coast Orthotics Assn
4990 Sw 72nd Ave Ste 107 (33155-5524)
PHONE..954 772-1299
Silvio Martinez, *President*
EMP: 8 EST: 1975
SQ FT: 3,000
SALES (est): 1.1MM **Privately Held**
WEB: www.mahnkesop.com
SIC: 3842 5047 Prosthetic appliances; medical & hospital equipment

(G-9500)
MAIN PACKAGING SUPPLY
7317 Nw 61st St (33166-3703)
P.O. Box 1148, Coshocton OH (43812-6148)
PHONE..305 863-7176
Adianes Piloto, *President*
Betty Rodriguez, *Vice Pres*
Ramon Perez, *Treasurer*
▼ EMP: 20 EST: 2001

SQ FT: 7,000
SALES (est): 2.8MM **Privately Held**
WEB: www.mainpackagingsupply.net
SIC: **2621** 5131 Wrapping & packaging
papers; labels

(G-9501)
MAIN USA CORP
Also Called: Voda USA
8549 Nw 68th St (33166-2664)
PHONE..................................305 499-4994
Dario Boyortnik, *President*
Albert Serge, *Vice Pres*
▲ EMP: 6 EST: 2002
SQ FT: 5,000
SALES (est): 752.1K **Privately Held**
WEB: www.watermainusa.com
SIC: **3589** Water purification equipment,
household type

(G-9502)
MALETA IMPORT
6928 Nw 12th St (33126-1336)
PHONE..................................305 592-2410
Hsiu-MEI Chang, *President*
Chih-Cheng Chen, *Vice Pres*
Lisa Chen, *Treasurer*
Anna Vasquez, *Manager*
▲ EMP: 6 EST: 1999
SQ FT: 10,000
SALES (est): 494.6K **Privately Held**
WEB: www.cyluggageinc.com
SIC: **3161** Luggage

(G-9503)
MAMALU WOOD LLC
7003 N Waterway Dr # 207 (33155-2842)
PHONE..................................305 261-6332
EMP: 8
SALES (est): 44K **Privately Held**
SIC: **2499** Mfg Wood Products

(G-9504)
MAMBI CHEESE COMPANY INC
Also Called: Sanchelima Dairy Products
2151 Nw 10th Ave (33127-4635)
PHONE..................................305 324-5282
Juan A Sanchelima, *President*
Victoria Wedmeyer, *Treasurer*
Maximo Cuesta, *Controller*
Sabrina Prendes, *Supervisor*
Jenny Romney, *Director*
▲ EMP: 22 EST: 1975
SQ FT: 1,824
SALES (est): 843.2K **Privately Held**
SIC: **2022** Natural cheese

(G-9505)
MANDALA TOOL COMPANY INC
18588 Ne 2nd Ave (33179-4427)
PHONE..................................305 652-4575
James Power, *President*
Karen Power, *Vice Pres*
EMP: 5 EST: 1979
SQ FT: 2,500
SALES (est): 474.6K **Privately Held**
WEB: www.mandalatool.com
SIC: **3599** Machine shop, jobbing & repair

(G-9506)
MANUTECH ASSEMBLY INC (PA)
7901 Nw 67th St (33166-2632)
PHONE..................................305 888-2800
Lance P Durban, *President*
Nadia Durban, *Chairman*
Sam Seyfi, *Vice Pres*
Laila Durban, *Opers Mgr*
Bernadette Villagracia, *Engineer*
◆ EMP: 3 EST: 2010
SQ FT: 25,000
SALES (est): 55MM **Privately Held**
WEB: www.manutech.us
SIC: **3612** 3677 Power transformers, elec-
tric; inductors, electronic

(G-9507)
MAR COMPANY DISTRIBUTORS LLC
Also Called: AROMAR
6750 Nw 79th Ave (33166-2779)
PHONE..................................786 477-4174
Marcelo Moreno, *Sales Mgr*
Mauricio Garcia, *Products*
EMP: 48 EST: 2013

SALES (est): 12.3MM **Privately Held**
SIC: **2844** Concentrates, perfume

(G-9508)
MARES SERVICES CORP
14758 Sw 56th St (33185-4067)
PHONE..................................305 752-0093
Jany De La Nuez, *Principal*
EMP: 10 EST: 2013
SALES (est): 288.6K **Privately Held**
SIC: **3441** Fabricated structural metal

(G-9509)
MAREY INTERNATIONAL LLC
8113 Nw 68th St (33166-2757)
P.O. Box 6281, San Juan PR (00914-6281)
PHONE..................................787 727-0277
Victor Yanguas, *Mng Member*
Lourdes Yanguas,
EMP: 7 EST: 2014
SALES (est): 733.1K **Privately Held**
WEB: www.marey.com
SIC: **3639** 5074 Hot water heaters, house-
hold; water heaters, except electric

(G-9510)
MARGARITA INTERNL TRADING INC
Also Called: Margarita International
5601 Nw 72nd Ave (33166-4207)
PHONE..................................305 688-1300
▲ EMP: 12
SQ FT: 20,000
SALES (est): 1.5MM **Privately Held**
SIC: **3142** Mfg House Slippers

(G-9511)
MARIA FUENTES LLC
10130 Sw 32nd St (33165-2915)
PHONE..................................305 717-3404
Maria Fuentes,
EMP: 7 EST: 2013
SALES (est): 292.5K **Privately Held**
SIC: **2339** 7389 Women's & misses' ac-
cessories;

(G-9512)
MARIO KENNY
Also Called: Cosmo Leather Co
789 Ne 83rd St (33138-4119)
PHONE..................................786 274-0527
Mario Kenny, *Partner*
EMP: 5 EST: 1999
SALES (est): 348.1K **Privately Held**
SIC: **2326** 4725 2311 2299 Men's &
boys' work clothing; arrangement of travel
tour packages, wholesale; men's & boys'
suits & coats; batting, wadding, padding &
fillings

(G-9513)
MARIOS CASTING JEWELRY INC
36 Ne 1st St Ste 851 (33132-2467)
PHONE..................................305 374-2894
Martha Camero, *President*
Elsa Martinez, *Corp Secy*
▼ EMP: 9 EST: 1968
SQ FT: 420
SALES (est): 910.4K **Privately Held**
WEB: www.marioscasting.com
SIC: **3915** 5944 3911 Jewelers' materials
& lapidary work; jewelry, precious stones
& precious metals; jewelry, precious metal

(G-9514)
MARTELL GLASS
7246 Nw 25th St (33122-1701)
PHONE..................................786 336-0142
Luis Miduel, *Principal*
▼ EMP: 8 EST: 2007
SALES (est): 164.5K **Privately Held**
WEB: www.martellgallery.com
SIC: **3088** 3231 3431 Shower stalls, fiber-
glass & plastic; doors, glass: made from
purchased glass; shower stalls, metal

(G-9515)
MARTINEZ DISTRIBUTORS CORP
3081 Nw 74th Ave (33122-1427)
P.O. Box 526368 (33152-6368)
PHONE..................................305 882-8282
Fabian J Martinez, *Branch Mgr*
EMP: 14

SALES (corp-wide): 49MM **Privately Held**
WEB: www.mdist.us
SIC: **2011** Meat packing plants
PA: Martinez Distributors Corp.
7379 Nw 31st St
Miami FL 33122
305 882-8282

(G-9516)
MASSIMO ROMA LLC
1395 Brickell Ave Ste 900 (33131-3302)
PHONE..................................561 302-5998
Massimiliano Mattetti, *Mng Member*
EMP: 5 EST: 2014
SALES (est): 443.8K **Privately Held**
WEB: www.massimoroma.com
SIC: **3999** Atomizers, toiletry

(G-9517)
MASTER FABRICATORS INC
12101 Sw 114th Pl (33176-4492)
PHONE..................................786 537-7440
Heriberto Rosales, *President*
Mayra Sixto, *Partner*
Myra Rosales, *Vice Pres*
▲ EMP: 10 EST: 1997
SQ FT: 5,000
SALES (est): 858.6K **Privately Held**
WEB: www.masterfabricatorsinc.com
SIC: **3441** Fabricated structural metal

(G-9518)
MASTER PAINTING & SEALANTS LLC
480 Ne 112th St (33161-7160)
PHONE..................................305 910-5104
Manuel Turcios, *Principal*
EMP: 9 EST: 2008
SALES (est): 254K **Privately Held**
SIC: **2891** Sealants

(G-9519)
MASTER UNIVERSE LLC ✪
1410 Ne 200th St (33179-5136)
PHONE..................................786 246-3190
Carolina Lugo, *CEO*
EMP: 10 EST: 2021
SALES (est): 552.9K **Privately Held**
SIC: **2051** Bakery: wholesale or whole-
sale/retail combined

(G-9520)
MATRIX PACKAGING OF FLORIDA (DH)
1001 Brickell Bay Dr (33131-4900)
PHONE..................................305 358-9696
Joseph Artiga, *President*
Joaquin Vinas, *Corp Secy*
◆ EMP: 8 EST: 1989
SQ FT: 2,300
SALES (est): 55.4MM **Privately Held**
SIC: **2655** 2631 6794 5087 Fiber cans,
drums & similar products; paperboard
mills; franchises, selling or licensing;
beauty parlor equipment & supplies; cos-
metics
HQ: Conitex Sonoco Holding B.V.
Prinses Margrietplnts 88 Wtc Toren E,
's-Gravenhage
850 700-300

(G-9521)
MAXAM GROUP LLC
Also Called: Brainchild Nutritionals
20725 Ne 16th Ave Ste A1 (33179-2123)
PHONE..................................305 952-3227
Samuel Swerdlow, *President*
EMP: 10 EST: 1998
SALES (est): 973.7K **Privately Held**
SIC: **2023** Dietary supplements, dairy &
non-dairy based

(G-9522)
MAZI GROUP INC
333 Se 2nd Ave (33131-2176)
PHONE..................................786 800-2425
Robin Rouquart, *CEO*
EMP: 34 EST: 2019
SALES (est): 2.3MM **Privately Held**
WEB: www.mazi.store
SIC: **2844** 5122 5963 5999 Cosmetic
preparations; cosmetics; cosmetic sales,
house-to-house; toiletries, cosmetics &
perfumes

(G-9523)
MC INTL TRANSPORTATION
8321 Nw 68th St (33166-2662)
P.O. Box 526661 (33152-6661)
PHONE..................................305 805-8228
Franceseo Monetti, *Principal*
Fulvio Monetti, *Manager*
EMP: 17 EST: 2007
SALES (est): 869.9K **Privately Held**
WEB: www.mcitransport.com
SIC: **3537** Trucks: freight, baggage, etc.:
industrial, except mining

(G-9524)
MD AUDIO ENGINEERING INC
6941 Nw 42nd St (33166-6800)
PHONE..................................305 593-8361
Jose L Telle, *President*
Maryelin Cedeno, *President*
▲ EMP: 8 EST: 2011
SQ FT: 27,000
SALES (est): 1MM **Privately Held**
WEB: www.orioncaraudio.com
SIC: **3651** Audio electronic systems

(G-9525)
MDINTOUCH US INC
11735 Sw 103rd Ave (33176-4000)
P.O. Box 562916 (33256-2916)
PHONE..................................786 268-1161
Kent Wreder, *President*
Ashley Xivir, *Manager*
Karen Wreder, *Admin Sec*
EMP: 8 EST: 1999
SALES (est): 1.4MM **Privately Held**
WEB: www.mdintouch.com
SIC: **7372** 7338 Business oriented com-
puter software; secretarial & typing serv-
ice

(G-9526)
MECOL OIL TOOLS CORP
1741 Nw 21st St (33142-7433)
PHONE..................................305 638-7686
Claudio Pietrobelli, *Principal*
Alejandro Pietrobelli, *Principal*
Fausto Pietrobelli, *Principal*
EMP: 12 EST: 2009
SALES (est): 1.9MM **Privately Held**
WEB: www.mecol.com
SIC: **1389** Running, cutting & pulling cas-
ings, tubes & rods
PA: Mecol Americas Colombia S A
Calle 88 30 74
Bogota 820

(G-9527)
MED DENTAL EQUIPMENT (IMPORT)
7795 Sw 161st Ave (33193-3405)
PHONE..................................786 417-8486
Victor Bernal, *Principal*
EMP: 7 EST: 2008
SALES (est): 85.8K **Privately Held**
SIC: **3843** Dental equipment

(G-9528)
MEDALLION LEISURE FURNITURE
800 Nw 166th St (33169-5820)
PHONE..................................305 626-0000
Robert L Gass Jr, *President*
Albert Careaga, *Sales Staff*
▼ EMP: 18 EST: 1972
SQ FT: 20,000
SALES (est): 513.2K **Privately Held**
WEB: www.medallionfurniture.com
SIC: **2514** Lawn furniture: metal

(G-9529)
MEDICAL OUTFITTERS INC (PA)
8062 Nw 66th St (33166-2728)
PHONE..................................305 885-4045
Miguel Machuca, *President*
Susan Traino, *Exec VP*
Viviana Machuca, *Vice Pres*
Victor Chaviano, *Engineer*
Zelinsky Mark, *Engineer*
EMP: 3 EST: 2010
SALES (est): 6.9MM **Privately Held**
WEB: www.medicaloutfitter.net
SIC: **3826** 5047 Magnetic resonance im-
aging apparatus; medical & hospital
equipment

(G-9530)
MEDTEK MEDICAL SOLUTIONS LLC
6961 Nw 82nd Ave (33166-2774)
PHONE....................................786 458-8080
Felix M Zuniga, *President*
Arnie Appell, *COO*
Jeffrey S Appell, *Vice Pres*
Roxanne Zuniga, *Opers Staff*
EMP: 13 EST: 2007
SALES (est): 1MM Privately Held
WEB: www.medtek-ms.com
SIC: 2599 7363 Hospital beds; medical help service

(G-9531)
MEGATRON EQUITY PARTNERS INC
801 Brickell Ave Ste 900 (33131-2979)
PHONE....................................305 789-6688
John B Schmidt, *President*
EMP: 14 EST: 2007
SQ FT: 10,000
SALES (est): 311.3K Privately Held
SIC: 2052 Bakery products, dry

(G-9532)
MENU MEN INC
1301 Nw 27th Ave (33125-2509)
PHONE....................................305 633-7925
Walter Baker Sr, *President*
Donald Baker, *Vice Pres*
Michele Benesch, *Vice Pres*
Aracelys Pena, *Office Mgr*
Don Baker, *CIO*
▼ EMP: 19 EST: 1968
SQ FT: 13,000
SALES (est): 2.4MM Privately Held
WEB: www.menumen.com
SIC: 2752 2791 Commercial printing, offset; typesetting

(G-9533)
MERCED INDUSTRIAL CORP
230 Nw 107th Ave Apt 106 (33172-3887)
PHONE....................................908 309-0170
Oscar Merced, *President*
Nancy M Eman, *Vice Pres*
EMP: 6 EST: 2007
SQ FT: 3,000
SALES (est): 313K Privately Held
SIC: 3731 Landing ships, building & repairing

(G-9534)
MERCOFRAMES OPTICAL CORP
Also Called: Merco Frame
5555 Nw 74th Ave (33166-4200)
PHONE....................................305 882-0120
Alejandro Gutman, *President*
Marina Gonzalez Ugarte, *Vice Pres*
◆ EMP: 5 EST: 1999
SQ FT: 3,500
SALES (est): 952K Privately Held
WEB: www.mercoframes.com
SIC: 3827 Optical instruments & lenses

(G-9535)
MERIT INTERNATIONAL ENTPS INC
Also Called: Access Tools
1628 Nw 28th St (33142-6668)
PHONE....................................305 635-1011
Aurelio A Vigil, *President*
◆ EMP: 20 EST: 1984
SQ FT: 26,000
SALES (est): 3MM Privately Held
WEB: www.accesstoolsusa.com
SIC: 3423 Hand & edge tools

(G-9536)
MERKAVAH INTERNATIONAL INC
201 S Biscayne Blvd (33131-4332)
PHONE....................................305 909-6798
Barry Schneer, *CEO*
Claudia Mesa, *President*
Oscar Gonzalez, *Corp Secy*
Chad Altieri, *COO*
Leo Snari, *Vice Pres*
EMP: 7 EST: 2008

SALES (est): 115.7K Privately Held
WEB: www.merkavahsugar.com
SIC: 2062 Cane sugar refining

(G-9537)
MERLOLA INDUSTRIES LLC
7950 Nw 53rd St Ste 341 (33166-4791)
PHONE....................................888 418-0408
Cery Perle,
EMP: 7 EST: 2020
SALES (est): 771.2K Privately Held
WEB: www.merlolaindustries.com
SIC: 3841 Surgical & medical instruments

(G-9538)
MERRILL-STEVENS DRY DOCK CO (PA)
Also Called: Merrill-Stevens Yachts
1270 Nw 11th St (33125-1680)
PHONE....................................305 640-5676
Fred W Kirtland, *CEO*
Hugh Westbrook, *Ch of Bd*
Ron Baker, *President*
Carole Shields Westbrook, *Chairman*
Aaron Leatherwood, *Consultant*
▲ EMP: 90 EST: 1923
SQ FT: 60,000
SALES (est): 9MM Privately Held
WEB: www.msyachts.com
SIC: 3732 7389 Boat building & repairing; yacht brokers

(G-9539)
METAL EXPRESS LLC
7216 Nw 25th St (33122-1701)
PHONE....................................786 391-0093
EMP: 5 EST: 2019
SALES (est): 460.3K Privately Held
SIC: 3499 Fabricated metal products

(G-9540)
METAL IMPROVEMENT COMPANY LLC
1940 Nw 70th Ave (33126-1326)
PHONE....................................305 592-5960
Jose Lapuerta, *Manager*
Jose Puerta, *Manager*
Yvonne Engle, *Administration*
EMP: 7
SQ FT: 8,000
SALES (corp-wide): 2.5B Publicly Held
WEB: www.cwst.com
SIC: 3398 Shot peening (treating steel to reduce fatigue)
HQ: Metal Improvement Company, Llc
80 E Rte 4 Ste 310
Paramus NJ 07652
201 843-7800

(G-9541)
METRO DOOR BRICKELL LLC
2660 Ne 189th St (33180-2628)
PHONE....................................786 326-4748
Jose Alter, *Principal*
EMP: 8 EST: 2014
SALES (est): 928.3K Privately Held
WEB: www.metrodooraventura.com
SIC: 2434 Wood kitchen cabinets

(G-9542)
MIA CONSULTING & TRADING INC (PA)
Also Called: Fine Things
7806 Nw 71st St Ste 209 (33166-2345)
PHONE....................................305 640-3077
Fermin B Gonzalez, *President*
EMP: 6 EST: 2017
SQ FT: 4,500
SALES (est): 686.9K Privately Held
SIC: 3625 Truck controls, industrial battery

(G-9543)
MIACUCINA LLC
3650 N Miami Ave (33127-3114)
PHONE....................................305 792-9494
Maika Dongellini, *Opers Staff*
Sandhya Murphy, *Office Mgr*
Reynaldo Rouco,
Mark Murphy,
Ariel Wainer,
◆ EMP: 7 EST: 2001
SALES (est): 1.2MM Privately Held
WEB: www.miacucina.com
SIC: 2434 Wood kitchen cabinets

(G-9544)
MIAMI
3661 S Miami Ave Ste 407 (33133-4230)
PHONE....................................954 874-7707
Julie Nida, *Owner*
EMP: 31 EST: 2011
SALES (est): 598.7K Privately Held
WEB: www.greatermiamiaudiology.com
SIC: 3842 5999 5047 Hearing aids; hearing aids; hearing aids

(G-9545)
MIAMI BANNERS & SIGNS INC
Also Called: Miami Balloons & Signs
6335 Nw 74th Ave (33166-3632)
PHONE....................................305 262-4460
Edwin Pagan, *CEO*
EMP: 9 EST: 2011
SALES (est): 1MM Privately Held
WEB: www.mbssigns.com
SIC: 3993 Signs & advertising specialties

(G-9546)
MIAMI BEACH AWNING CO
Also Called: Miami Awning
3905 Nw 31st Ave (33142-5122)
PHONE....................................305 576-2029
Michael Reilly, *CEO*
Joseph Riley, *General Mgr*
Joan R Garvey, *Corp Secy*
William Garvey, *Vice Pres*
Federico Bordignon, *Project Mgr*
◆ EMP: 45 EST: 1929
SQ FT: 12,000
SALES (est): 9MM Privately Held
WEB: www.miamiawning.com
SIC: 2394 1799 Awnings, fabric: made from purchased materials; awning installation

(G-9547)
MIAMI COCKTAIL COMPANY INC (PA)
2750 Nw 3rd Ave Ste 14 (33127-4143)
PHONE....................................305 482-1974
Ross Graham, *CEO*
Michael Brandes, *Marketing Staff*
EMP: 9 EST: 2016
SALES (est): 564K Privately Held
WEB: www.miamicocktail.com
SIC: 2085 Cocktails, alcoholic

(G-9548)
MIAMI COMPRESSOR RBLDRS INC
Also Called: Usacompressors.com
3230 Nw 38th St (33142-5032)
PHONE....................................305 303-2251
Robert G Gonzalez, *President*
Alex Fernandez, *Controller*
▼ EMP: 10 EST: 1975
SQ FT: 5,500
SALES (est): 659.3K Privately Held
WEB:
www.miamicompressorrebuilders.com
SIC: 7694 Rebuilding motors, except automotive

(G-9549)
MIAMI CORDAGE LLC
Also Called: Florida Wire and Rigging Works
2475 Nw 38th St (33142-5369)
PHONE....................................305 636-3000
Fran Hoffman, *CEO*
Audrey Stirman, *President*
Jason Hoffman, *Vice Pres*
John Easton, *Engineer*
Hermi Recio, *CFO*
◆ EMP: 37 EST: 1960
SQ FT: 40,000
SALES (est): 8MM Privately Held
WEB: www.miamicordage.com
SIC: 2298 5088 3496 Cable, fiber; rope, except asbestos & wire; slings, rope; wire rope centers; marine crafts & supplies; miscellaneous fabricated wire products

(G-9550)
MIAMI DECOR INC
7351 Nw 61st St (33166-3703)
PHONE....................................800 235-2197
Faber Aristizabal, *President*
Piedad Aristizabal, *Vice Pres*
Melida Aristizabal, *Shareholder*
▼ EMP: 9 EST: 1979

SQ FT: 12,000
SALES (est): 721.4K Privately Held
WEB: www.miamidecormoulding.com
SIC: 2499 Picture & mirror frames, wood

(G-9551)
MIAMI ENGRV CO-OXFORD PRTG CO
Also Called: Oxford Acquisition
54 Nw 11th St (33136-2803)
PHONE....................................305 371-9595
Mario Cerratto, *President*
Richard Freeman, *President*
EMP: 8 EST: 1957
SQ FT: 10,250
SALES (est): 501.6K Privately Held
SIC: 2759 2754 Invitation & stationery printing & engraving; commercial printing, gravure

(G-9552)
MIAMI HERALD
4302 Sw 73rd Ave (33155-4550)
PHONE....................................305 269-7768
EMP: 23 EST: 2009
SALES (est): 700K Privately Held
SIC: 2711 Newspapers, publishing & printing

(G-9553)
MIAMI LEASING INC
14532 Sw 129th St (33186-5305)
PHONE....................................786 431-1215
Maria Mikluscak, *Vice Pres*
EMP: 7 EST: 2004
SALES (est): 673.7K Privately Held
SIC: 3724 Aircraft engines & engine parts

(G-9554)
MIAMI POWER WHEELS
9500 Sw 40th St Ste 305 (33165-4036)
PHONE....................................305 553-1888
Manuel Acosta, *Owner*
▼ EMP: 8 EST: 2004
SALES (est): 624.1K Privately Held
WEB: www.miamipowerwheels.com
SIC: 3312 Wheels

(G-9555)
MIAMI PRESTIGE INTERIORS INC
3000 Nw 125th St Unit C (33167-2515)
PHONE....................................305 685-3343
Reinier Lopez, *CEO*
Rogelio Delarosa, *President*
Richard Delarosa, *Vice Pres*
Kathy De La Rosa, *Admin Sec*
Cathy Dela Rosa, *Admin Sec*
◆ EMP: 45 EST: 1971
SALES (est): 4.2MM Privately Held
WEB: www.miamiprestige.com
SIC: 2392 2221 Boat cushions; upholstery fabrics, manmade fiber & silk

(G-9556)
MIAMI QUALITY GRAPHICS INC
Also Called: Miami Quality Packg & Finshg
3701 Nw 51st St (33142-3240)
PHONE....................................305 634-9506
Rafael Farah, *President*
Lesley Acosta, *VP Opers*
Carlos Hernandez, *Plant Mgr*
EMP: 50 EST: 1999
SQ FT: 37,000
SALES (est): 7.5MM Privately Held
WEB: www.miamiquality.com
SIC: 2752 2759 3544 Trading stamps, lithographed; embossing on paper; die sets for metal stamping (presses)

(G-9557)
MIAMI QUALITY PAVERS CORP
5800 Sw 177th Ave Ste 101 (33193-5302)
PHONE....................................305 408-3444
Jorge A Rinaldi, *President*
EMP: 6 EST: 2006
SALES (est): 537.6K Privately Held
WEB: www.mqpavers.com
SIC: 3271 Concrete block & brick

(G-9558)
MIAMI RAILING DESIGN CORP
4401 Sw 75th Ave Ste 10 (33155-4445)
PHONE....................................305 926-0062
Kalet Suarez, *Principal*

▲ = Import ▼=Export
◆ =Import/Export

EMP: 6 EST: 2017
SALES (est): 456.3K **Privately Held**
WEB: www.miamirailingdesign.com
SIC: 3446 Architectural metalwork

(G-9559)
MIAMI SWITCHGEAR COMPANY
7060 Nw 52nd St (33166-4845)
PHONE..................................786 336-5783
Federico Anselmetti, *President*
◆ EMP: 7 EST: 2012
SALES (est): 880.2K **Privately Held**
WEB: www.miamiswitchgear.com
SIC: 3613 Time switches, electrical
switchgear apparatus; switchgear &
switchgear accessories

(G-9560)
MIAMI TECH INC (PA)
3611 Nw 74th St (33147-5827)
PHONE..................................305 693-7054
Isidro J Gonzalez, *President*
Chris Gonzalez, *Manager*
Maria Ventriere, *Admin Sec*
◆ EMP: 20 EST: 1981
SQ FT: 1,000
SALES (est): 14.9MM **Privately Held**
WEB: www.miamitech.com
SIC: 3444 Sheet metal specialties, not
stamped

(G-9561)
MIAMI TIMES
900 Nw 54th St (33127-1897)
PHONE..................................305 694-6210
Rachel R Reeves, *President*
Karen Franklin, *Opers Mgr*
EMP: 38 EST: 1921
SALES (est): 4.6MM **Privately Held**
WEB: www.miamitimesonline.com
SIC: 2711 Newspapers, publishing & print-
ing

(G-9562)
**MIAMI-DADE TRUCK & EQP SVC
INC**
3294 Nw 69th St (33147-6640)
PHONE..................................305 691-2932
Onelio Cruz Sr, *President*
▼ EMP: 11 EST: 1980
SQ FT: 12,000
SALES (est): 456.7K **Privately Held**
SIC: 3713 5521 Truck beds; trucks, trac-
tors & trailers: used

(G-9563)
MICHEL 1 TRUCKING LLC ✪
66 W Flagler St Ste 900 (33130-1807)
PHONE..................................786 297-9681
Yoan Martinez, *CEO*
Yoan M Martinez Sin,
EMP: 10 EST: 2021
SALES (est): 100K **Privately Held**
SIC: 3537 Truck trailers, used in plants,
docks, terminals, etc.

(G-9564)
**MICHELLE LYNN SOLUTIONS
INC**
1395 Brickell Ave Ste 800 (33131-3302)
PHONE..................................786 413-0455
Michelle Adderley, *President*
Dwight Drane, *Vice Pres*
EMP: 6 EST: 2003
SALES (est): 593.8K **Privately Held**
WEB: www.naacp100store.com
SIC: 2261 Screen printing of cotton broad-
woven fabrics

(G-9565)
MICHELSONS TROPHIES INC
14730 Nw 7th Ave (33168-3104)
PHONE..................................305 687-9898
Keith Stunson, *President*
James L Michelson, *Corp Secy*
Bruno Valle, *Asst Mgr*
▼ EMP: 8 EST: 1958
SQ FT: 6,000
SALES (est): 850K **Privately Held**
WEB: www.michelsonstrophies.com
SIC: 3914 5947 Trophies; gift, novelty &
souvenir shop

(G-9566)
**MIDNIGHT EXPRESS PWR
BOATS INC**
351 Ne 185th St (33179-4510)
PHONE..................................954 745-8284
Bert M Glaser, *President*
Eric Glaser, *Vice Pres*
Harris Glaser, *Vice Pres*
Jimmie Simpson, *Technician*
▼ EMP: 41 EST: 1998
SALES (est): 6.6MM **Privately Held**
WEB: www.midnightboats.com
SIC: 3732 5551 Boats, fiberglass: building
& repairing; boat dealers

(G-9567)
**MIKES TRCK PRTS MCH SP
PLUS I**
7337 Nw 54th St (33166-4831)
PHONE..................................786 534-9608
Miguel Morejon, *Principal*
EMP: 8 EST: 2015
SALES (est): 104.7K **Privately Held**
SIC: 3599 Machine shop, jobbing & repair

(G-9568)
MILENIUM PUBLISHING LLC
12742 Sw 103rd Ct (33176-4769)
PHONE..................................786 573-9974
Juan J Wong, *Manager*
EMP: 7 EST: 2010
SALES (est): 4.2K **Privately Held**
WEB: www.milenium.group
SIC: 2741 Miscellaneous publishing

(G-9569)
MILES OF WOOD INC
5951 Sw 44th Ter (33155-5216)
PHONE..................................305 300-6370
Miles Black, *Principal*
EMP: 5 EST: 2001
SALES (est): 414.6K **Privately Held**
WEB: www.milesofwood.com
SIC: 2431 Millwork

(G-9570)
**MILLENIUM OIL & GAS DISTRS
INC**
Also Called: Food Spot 59
12801 Sw 42nd St (33175-3424)
PHONE..................................305 220-3669
Elena G Hasan, *President*
Allan Hasan, *Owner*
EMP: 12 EST: 2001
SALES (est): 998.7K **Privately Held**
SIC: 1389 Testing, measuring, surveying &
analysis services

(G-9571)
MILLENIUM WOOD BOXES INC
13139 Sw 122nd Ave (33186-6232)
PHONE..................................305 969-5510
Miguel Cabrera, *Manager*
EMP: 5 EST: 2001
SALES (est): 456.8K **Privately Held**
WEB: www.mwoodboxes.com
SIC: 2449 Rectangular boxes & crates,
wood

(G-9572)
MILLENNIUM GLASS INC
5851 Nw 35th Ave (33142-2001)
PHONE..................................305 638-1785
Luis Victoria, *Principal*
Mickey Minagorri, *Exec VP*
EMP: 7 EST: 2007
SALES (est): 231.7K **Privately Held**
SIC: 2431 Millwork

(G-9573)
MILLERKNOLL INC
4141 Ne 2nd Ave (33137-3527)
PHONE..................................305 572-2909
EMP: 24
SALES (corp-wide): 3.9B **Publicly Held**
WEB: www.hermanmiller.com
SIC: 2521 Wood office furniture
PA: Millerknoll, Inc.
855 E Main Ave
Zeeland MI 49464
616 654-3000

(G-9574)
MINERAL LIFE INTL INC
6732 Sw 71st Ct (33143-3022)
PHONE..................................305 661-9854
David L Shankman, *President*
Marlon J Garcia, *COO*
◆ EMP: 9 EST: 1976
SQ FT: 1,200
SALES (est): 655.3K **Privately Held**
WEB: www.minerallife.com
SIC: 3274 3479 Lime; coating of metals &
formed products

(G-9575)
MIROCOS LLC
8450 Nw 68th St (33166-2645)
PHONE..................................305 674-6921
Osmany Vazquez, *Mng Member*
Lucas Raul Isola,
Nicolas Sattler,
EMP: 7 EST: 2016
SALES (est): 145.9K **Privately Held**
WEB: mirocoswines.business.site
SIC: 2084 Wines

(G-9576)
**MISHAAL AEROSPACE
CORPORATION**
31 Se 5th St Apt 3415 (33131-2526)
PHONE..................................786 353-2685
Mishaal Ashemimry, *President*
EMP: 7 EST: 2010
SALES (est): 204.1K **Privately Held**
WEB: www.mishaalaerospace.com
SIC: 3761 Guided missiles & space vehi-
cles

(G-9577)
MISHAS CUPCAKES INC (PA)
5616 Sunset Dr (33143-5611)
PHONE..................................786 200-6153
Misha Kuryla, *President*
Michelle Gomez, *Principal*
EMP: 14 EST: 2007
SALES (est): 4.2MM **Privately Held**
WEB: www.mishascupcakes.com
SIC: 2051 5812 Bakery: wholesale or
wholesale/retail combined; snack bar

(G-9578)
MK MONOMERS LLC
905 Brickell Bay Dr # 23 (33131-2935)
PHONE..................................732 928-5800
James Kronenthal, *President*
Edward Kronenthal, *Vice Pres*
Ted Maceda, *Vice Pres*
Mirela Fabreti, *Manager*
EMP: 8 EST: 2013
SALES (est): 151.8K **Privately Held**
SIC: 2899 Chemical preparations

(G-9579)
MMX MANUFACTURING LLC
6508 Nw 77th Ct (33166-2710)
PHONE..................................786 456-5072
Jaime Gomez,
EMP: 10 EST: 2020
SALES (est): 556.3K **Privately Held**
SIC: 3999 5047 Manufacturing industries;
medical equipment & supplies

(G-9580)
**MO STEEL FBRICATOR
ERECTOR INC**
353 Ne 185th St (33179-4510)
PHONE..................................305 945-4855
Maurice Sutton, *Owner*
Miguel Gutierrez, *Opers Staff*
◆ EMP: 8 EST: 2004
SALES (est): 2.5MM **Privately Held**
WEB: www.mosteel.com
SIC: 3441 Fabricated structural metal

(G-9581)
MOBVIOUS CORP
2100 Coral Way Ste 200 (33145-2657)
PHONE..................................786 497-6620
Giuliano Stiglitz, *Principal*
EMP: 8 EST: 2016
SALES (est): 164.8K **Privately Held**
WEB: www.prisabrandsolutions.us
SIC: 7372 Prepackaged software

(G-9582)
MODEL SHIPWAYS INC
Also Called: Model Expo
2613 Nw 20th St (33142-7105)
PHONE..................................800 222-3876
Marc Mosko, *President*
Eva Mosko, *Treasurer*
▲ EMP: 20 EST: 1976
SALES (est): 2.4MM **Privately Held**
WEB: www.modelexpo-online.com
SIC: 3731 5551 3999 Shipbuilding & re-
pairing; boat dealers; barber & beauty
shop equipment

(G-9583)
MODERN GARDEN MIAMI LLC
422 Nw North River Dr (33128-1628)
PHONE..................................305 440-4200
Carlos Miranda, *President*
EMP: 7 EST: 2014
SALES (est): 114.8K **Privately Held**
WEB: www.seaspice.com
SIC: 2092 Fresh or frozen packaged fish

(G-9584)
MODULEX MIAMI LLC
14 Ne 1st Ave Ste 707 (33132-2411)
PHONE..................................786 424-0857
Ketil M Staalesen, *General Mgr*
James Gaydos, *Managing Dir*
Ketil Molbach, *Principal*
Andres Becerra, *Project Mgr*
Nathan Brenneman, *Project Mgr*
EMP: 11 EST: 2013
SALES (est): 2.1MM **Privately Held**
WEB: www.modulex.com
SIC: 3993 Electric signs; neon signs; let-
ters for signs, metal

(G-9585)
MOLD BUSTERS LLC
12900 Sw 80th St (33183-4213)
PHONE..................................786 360-6464
Yvette C Blanco, *Manager*
EMP: 8 EST: 2018
SALES (est): 428K **Privately Held**
SIC: 3544 Industrial molds

(G-9586)
**MOMENTUM COMFORT GEAR
INC**
470 Ne 185th St (33179-4511)
PHONE..................................305 653-5050
Yariv Shaked, *President*
EMP: 11 EST: 2017
SALES (est): 454.5K **Privately Held**
WEB: www.momentumcomfortgear.com
SIC: 2339 Service apparel, washable:
women's

(G-9587)
MONISON PALLETS INC (PA)
5420 Nw 37th Ave (33142-2716)
PHONE..................................305 637-1600
Victor Carrascal, *President*
Gem Vasquez, *Vice Pres*
Mavila Vasquez, *Vice Pres*
EMP: 10 EST: 1986
SQ FT: 115,000
SALES (est): 4.6MM **Privately Held**
WEB: www.monisonpallets.net
SIC: 2448 Pallets, wood

(G-9588)
MORLEE LAMPSHADE CO INC
6915 Nw 43rd St (33166-6844)
PHONE..................................305 500-9310
EMP: 26
SQ FT: 6,500
SALES: 820K **Privately Held**
SIC: 3645 Manufactures Lamp Shades

(G-9589)
**MORSE ENTERPRISES LIMITED
INC**
Also Called: Keyplex
400 N Ny Ave Ste 200 (33129)
PHONE..................................407 682-6500
Gerald C O'Connor, *President*
Steven Bessette, *President*
Gerald O'Connor, *Vice Pres*
Shannon Newman, *Sales Staff*
EMP: 6 EST: 1980

SALES (est): 603.3K **Privately Held**
SIC: 2879 5191 Agricultural chemicals; farm supplies

(G-9590)
MOSCH INTERNATIONAL CORP
6400 Nw 72nd Ave (33166-3627)
PHONE.....................................786 616-9108
Socors E Perez- Rodriguez, *President*
Juan Pablo Vergara, *Vice Pres*
EMP: 7 **EST:** 2014
SALES (est): 123.2K **Privately Held**
SIC: 3253 5032 Ceramic wall & floor tile; ceramic wall & floor tile

(G-9591)
MOTOR SERVICE GROUP LLC
6600 Nw 77th Ct (33166-2795)
PHONE.....................................305 592-2440
Robert Valdes, *Mng Member*
EMP: 8 **EST:** 2015
SQ FT: 10,000
SALES (est): 1MM **Privately Held**
WEB: www.motorservicegroup.com
SIC: 3599 5013 Machine shop, jobbing & repair; automotive supplies & parts

(G-9592)
MOTOR SERVICE INC
6600 Nw 77th Ct (33166-2795)
PHONE.....................................305 592-2440
Fax: 305 592-2443
EMP: 8
SQ FT: 12,000
SALES: 1MM **Privately Held**
SIC: 3599 5013 Mfg Industrial Machinery Whol Auto Parts/Supplies

(G-9593)
MOTORSPORT GAMES INC (HQ)
5972 Ne 4th Ave (33137-2134)
PHONE.....................................305 507-8799
Dmitry Kozko, *Ch of Bd*
Stephen Hood, *President*
Jonathan New, *CFO*
EMP: 11 **EST:** 2018
SQ FT: 2,000
SALES: 15MM
SALES (corp-wide): 35MM **Publicly Held**
WEB: www.motorsportgames.com
SIC: 7372 Prepackaged software
PA: Motorsport Network, Llc
5972 Ne 4th Ave
Miami FL 33137
305 507-8799

(G-9594)
MP&TR CORP
Also Called: Impex
1717 N Byshore Dr Apt 345 (33132)
PHONE.....................................305 456-9292
Patricio Martinelli, *President*
EMP: 5 **EST:** 2011
SALES (est): 304.5K **Privately Held**
WEB: www.mptrcorp.com
SIC: 3825 Energy measuring equipment, electrical

(G-9595)
MPR AUDIO SYSTEM LLC
3465 Nw 71st Ter (33147-6667)
PHONE.....................................305 988-8524
Rebeca Lange, *Mng Member*
EMP: 8 **EST:** 2015
SALES (est): 477.6K **Privately Held**
SIC: 3651 Audio electronic systems

(G-9596)
MR COOL WATERS INC (PA)
12009 Sw 129th Ct Unit 5 (33186-6918)
PHONE.....................................305 234-6311
EMP: 16
SALES (est): 2.2MM **Privately Held**
SIC: 2671 Mfg Packaging Paper/Film

(G-9597)
MTNG USA CORP
11334 Sw 157th Pl (33196-3129)
P.O. Box 560668 (33256-0668)
PHONE.....................................305 670-0979
Pascual Ros, *President*
Santiago Ros, *Vice Pres*
Sergio Ros, *Director*
▲ **EMP:** 7 **EST:** 2010
SALES (est): 105.6K **Privately Held**
SIC: 3089 Molding primary plastic

(G-9598)
MULLER FIRE PROTECTION INC
2311 Sw 98th Pl (33165-7526)
P.O. Box 162226 (33116-2226)
PHONE.....................................305 636-9780
Carlos S Muller, *President*
Carlos A Muller, *President*
EMP: 23 **EST:** 1995
SALES (est): 5.1MM **Privately Held**
WEB: www.mullerfireprotection.com
SIC: 3569 Sprinkler systems, fire: automatic

(G-9599)
MULTI SOFT II INC
4400 Biscayne Blvd Fl 10 (33137-3212)
PHONE.....................................305 579-8000
Charles J Lombardo, *Ch of Bd*
Miriam G Jarney, *Exec VP*
EMP: 12 **EST:** 1985
SQ FT: 4,200 **Privately Held**
SIC: 7372 Application computer software

(G-9600)
MULTI-COMMERCIAL SERVICES CORP
Also Called: Turbo Rotating Spare US
15420 Sw 136th St Unit 26 (33196-2673)
PHONE.....................................305 235-1373
Enrique D Rasch, *CEO*
Freddy E Barcena, *President*
▼ **EMP:** 5 **EST:** 2008
SQ FT: 2,800
SALES (est): 1MM **Privately Held**
WEB: www.turborots.com
SIC: 3621 Inverters, rotating: electrical

(G-9601)
MUNICIPAL LIGHTING SYSTEMS INC (PA)
Also Called: Florida Coast Lighting Systems
7035 Sw 47th St Ste A (33155-4625)
P.O. Box 140134, Coral Gables (33114-0134)
PHONE.....................................305 666-4210
Roy Bustillo, *President*
Scott Stefan, *Treasurer*
Rosa Zampieri, *Accountant*
EMP: 5 **EST:** 1995
SQ FT: 4,000
SALES (est): 1.5MM **Privately Held**
SIC: 3646 Commercial indusl & institutional electric lighting fixtures

(G-9602)
N V TEXPACK GROUP
3225 Aviation Ave Ste 303 (33133-4741)
PHONE.....................................305 358-9696
Joseph Artiga, *President*
Joaquin Vinas, *Treasurer*
Miguel Domingo, *Director*
EMP: 20 **EST:** 2004
SALES (est): 248.9K **Privately Held**
SIC: 2621 Paper mills

(G-9603)
NAC USA CORPORATION
Also Called: Dermaccina Dossier
9000 Sw 137th Ave (33186-1411)
PHONE.....................................800 396-0149
Diego Ariza, *Principal*
EMP: 8 **EST:** 2015
SALES (est): 298.9K **Privately Held**
WEB: www.cremadermanac.com
SIC: 2844 Face creams or lotions

(G-9604)
NAHUEL TRADING CORP
17838 State Road 9 (33162-1008)
PHONE.....................................305 999-9944
Oscar A Mouras, *President*
Natalia C Mouras, *Treasurer*
Hugo D Mouras, *Director*
Elisa B De Mouras, *Admin Sec*
EMP: 14 **EST:** 1993
SQ FT: 3,800
SALES (est): 503.7K **Privately Held**
SIC: 3663 Television broadcasting & communications equipment

(G-9605)
NAKED WHEY INC
382 Ne 191st St (33179-3899)
P.O. Box 348634, Coral Gables (33234-8634)
PHONE.....................................352 246-7294
Stephen E Zieminski, *President*
EMP: 8 **EST:** 2014
SALES (est): 849.3K **Privately Held**
WEB: www.nakednutrition.com
SIC: 2023 Powdered whey

(G-9606)
NANOCANN RESEARCH LABS LLC ○
7328 Sw 48th St (33155-5523)
PHONE.....................................850 630-4676
Brandon Moreau,
EMP: 5 **EST:** 2022
SALES (est): 360.8K **Privately Held**
SIC: 2834 Emulsions, pharmaceutical

(G-9607)
NATIONAL PALLETS
2160 Nw 8th Ave (33127-4638)
PHONE.....................................305 324-1021
Norma R Garcia, *President*
Raul N Garcia Jr, *Vice Pres*
EMP: 25 **EST:** 1973
SQ FT: 30,000
SALES (est): 1.2MM **Privately Held**
WEB: www.nationalpallets.net
SIC: 2448 Pallets, wood

(G-9608)
NAVATECH USA LLC
20200 Nw 2nd Ave Ste 106 (33169-2560)
PHONE.....................................305 600-4458
Richard Luce, *General Mgr*
Eliezer Navarsky, *Mng Member*
EMP: 5 **EST:** 2008
SQ FT: 1,000
SALES (est): 2MM **Privately Held**
WEB: www.navatech-usa.com
SIC: 3291 Grit, steel

(G-9609)
NEGLEX INC
300 Sw 107th Ave Ste 114 (33174-3601)
PHONE.....................................305 551-4177
Jose M Negrin, *President*
EMP: 15 **EST:** 1999
SALES (est): 410.1K **Privately Held**
SIC: 2834 Pharmaceutical preparations

(G-9610)
NELVER AIRPARTS INC
12360 Sw 132nd Ct Ste 205 (33186-6461)
PHONE.....................................305 378-0072
Nelson Pacheco, *Manager*
EMP: 5 **EST:** 2006
SALES (est): 375.4K **Privately Held**
WEB: www.nelver.com
SIC: 3812 Aircraft/aerospace flight instruments & guidance systems

(G-9611)
NEOCIS INC
2800 Biscayne Blvd # 600 (33137-4523)
PHONE.....................................855 963-6247
Alon Mozes, *CEO*
Andres Carrillo, *Vice Pres*
Christopher Sells, *Vice Pres*
Darshini Balamurugan, *Engineer*
Omar Blandon, *Engineer*
EMP: 75 **EST:** 2012
SALES (est): 12.5MM **Privately Held**
WEB: www.neocis.com
SIC: 3841 Surgical & medical instruments

(G-9612)
NEW CENTURY
7950 Sunset Dr (33143-3944)
PHONE.....................................305 670-3510
Alex De La Cruz, *Principal*
EMP: 9 **EST:** 2010
SALES (est): 476.1K **Privately Held**
WEB: www.newcenturydancecompany.com
SIC: 2121 Cigars

(G-9613)
NEW ERA MUSIC GROUP LLC ○
Also Called: New Era, The
66 W Flagler St Ste 900 (33130-1807)
PHONE.....................................800 454-9751

Darnell Butler, *Mng Member*
EMP: 10 **EST:** 2022
SALES (est): 521.6K **Privately Held**
SIC: 3695 5961 Magnetic & optical recording media; general merchandise, mail order

(G-9614)
NEW VISION SIGNS CORP
15446 Sw 25th Ter (33185-5761)
PHONE.....................................786 514-6822
Juan Carlos Garcia, *President*
EMP: 7 **EST:** 2014
SALES (est): 294.9K **Privately Held**
SIC: 3993 Signs & advertising specialties

(G-9615)
NEW WORLD WELDING INC
3714 Nw 50th St (33142-3936)
PHONE.....................................786 423-1575
Noel Cutino, *Principal*
EMP: 8 **EST:** 2017
SALES (est): 64.7K **Privately Held**
WEB: www.ddwelding.com
SIC: 7692 Welding repair

(G-9616)
NEXT STEP ADVERTISING INC
1444 Biscayne Blvd # 208 (33132-1430)
PHONE.....................................305 371-4428
Jaime J De Toro Lopez Pazo, *President*
EMP: 5 **EST:** 2012
SALES (est): 379.9K **Privately Held**
WEB: www.nextstepadvertisingdm.com
SIC: 2711 Newspapers

(G-9617)
NEXTSOURCE BIOTECHNOLOGY LLC
80 Sw 8th St (33130-3003)
PHONE.....................................305 753-6360
Mohamed Osman, *Mng Member*
Steve Schafer,
Christopher Yankana,
EMP: 5 **EST:** 2011
SQ FT: 2,000
SALES (est): 1.2MM
SALES (corp-wide): 2.3MM **Privately Held**
WEB: www.nextsourcepharmaceuticals.com
SIC: 2834 Pharmaceutical preparations
PA: Tri-Source Pharma, Llc
80 Sw 8th St Ste 2660
Miami FL 33130
844 696-4667

(G-9618)
NFK CORPORATION (PA)
8158 Sw 118th Pl (33183-3832)
PHONE.....................................305 378-2116
Farissa Khan, *President*
EMP: 12 **EST:** 2001
SALES (est): 1.5MM **Privately Held**
SIC: 3089 Boxes, plastic

(G-9619)
NIAGARA INDUSTRIES INC
2540 Nw 38th Ct (33142-6746)
PHONE.....................................305 876-9010
Alejandro Bolivar, *President*
Israel Laitano, *Accounts Exec*
Carlos Linchenat, *Manager*
◆ **EMP:** 10 **EST:** 1985
SQ FT: 10,000
SALES (est): 1.6MM **Privately Held**
WEB: www.tanklesswaterheater.com
SIC: 3822 5064 Auto controls regulating residntl & coml environmt & applncs; water heaters, electric

(G-9620)
NIAGRATECH INDUSTRIES INC
2540 Nw 38th Ct (33142-6746)
PHONE.....................................305 876-9010
Alejandro Bolivar, *Principal*
Rene Vassaux, *Prdtn Mgr*
▼ **EMP:** 7 **EST:** 2009
SALES (est): 224.6K **Privately Held**
SIC: 3999 Manufacturing industries

(G-9621)
NIFTYS INC ○
78 Sw 7th St (33130-3402)
PHONE.....................................786 878-4725
Jeff Marsilio, *CEO*

EMP: 15 **EST:** 2021
SALES (est): 1MM **Privately Held**
WEB: www.niftys.com
SIC: 7372 3679 Application computer software; antennas, receiving

(G-9622)
NIOBIUM TECHNOLOGY GROUP LLC
3100 Nw 72nd Ave Ste 108 (33122-1336)
PHONE....................786 292-2613
Enoc Martinez, *Mng Member*
Ali Bohorquez,
Rafael Conde,
Ricardo Conde,
Antonio Perez,
EMP: 5 **EST:** 2014
SALES (est): 526.7K **Privately Held**
WEB: www.niobium.tech
SIC: 3663 Mobile communication equipment

(G-9623)
NO EQUAL DESIGN INC
6995 Nw 46th St A (33166-5603)
PHONE....................305 971-5177
Casparus D Otto, *President*
EMP: 5 **EST:** 2008
SALES (est): 495.4K **Privately Held**
WEB: www.shadeports.com
SIC: 3444 Awnings & canopies

(G-9624)
NOMI RUBINSTEIN INC
267 Ne 166th St (33162-3555)
PHONE....................305 467-7888
Nomi Rubinstein, *President*
Moshe Rubinstein, *Vice Pres*
EMP: 7 **EST:** 1978
SQ FT: 2,000
SALES (est): 157.6K **Privately Held**
SIC: 2335 2337 Women's, juniors' & misses' dresses; women's & misses' suits & coats

(G-9625)
NOODLE TIME INC
8685 Nw 53rd Ter (33166)
PHONE....................305 593-0770
Joel Schwartz, *President*
EMP: 33 **EST:** 2005
SALES (est): 1MM
SALES (corp-wide): 2.1B **Privately Held**
SIC: 2098 Noodles (e.g. egg, plain & water), dry
HQ: Benihana Inc.
21500 Biscayne Blvd # 100
Miami FL 33180
305 593-0770

(G-9626)
NORSEMAN SHIPBUILDING CORP
437 Nw South River Dr (33128-1496)
PHONE....................305 545-6815
Richard A Herron, *President*
Jane J Herron, *Vice Pres*
Carlos Narajo, *Info Tech Mgr*
Warren M Salomon, *Admin Sec*
▼ **EMP:** 30 **EST:** 1969
SQ FT: 50,000
SALES (est): 4.3MM **Privately Held**
WEB: www.norsemanshipbuilding.com
SIC: 3731 Shipbuilding & repairing

(G-9627)
NORTEK GLOBAL HVAC LLC
12250 Nw 25th St Ste 100 (33182-1507)
PHONE....................305 592-6154
Antoine Alincourt, *Manager*
EMP: 69
SALES (corp-wide): 2.9B **Privately Held**
WEB: www.nortekhvac.com
SIC: 3585 Refrigeration & heating equipment
HQ: Nortek Global Hvac, Llc
8000 Phoenix Pkwy
O Fallon MO 63368
636 561-7300

(G-9628)
NORTH AMERICAN COAL CORP
Also Called: Florida Dragline Operations
18300 Sw 122nd St (33196-1954)
PHONE....................305 824-9018
Ted Duna, *General Mgr*

EMP: 8
SALES (corp-wide): 191.8MM **Publicly Held**
WEB: www.nacoal.com
SIC: 1221 Bituminous coal & lignite-surface mining
HQ: The North American Coal Corporation
5340 Legacy Dr Ste 300
Plano TX 75024
972 448-5400

(G-9629)
NORTHWINGS ACCESSORIES CORP (DH)
Also Called: Heico Component Repair Group
7875 Nw 64th St (33166-2718)
PHONE....................305 463-0455
Luis J Morell, *President*
Javier Diaz, *Vice Pres*
Laurans Mendelson, *Vice Pres*
Regieleime Albea, *Engineer*
Alexa Merrifield, *Accounts Mgr*
EMP: 67 **EST:** 1991
SQ FT: 1,000
SALES (est): 43.3MM **Publicly Held**
SIC: 3724 Aircraft engines & engine parts
HQ: Heico Aerospace Corporation
3000 Taft St
Hollywood FL 33021
954 987-6101

(G-9630)
NOSTA INC
Also Called: Nosta Carpenter Shop
1235 Nw 29th St (33142-6617)
PHONE....................305 634-1435
Emilio Nosta, *President*
Jorge Noste, *Vice Pres*
Emilio Noste Jr, *Treasurer*
▼ **EMP:** 8 **EST:** 1970
SQ FT: 5,000
SALES (est): 500K **Privately Held**
WEB: www.nostainc.com
SIC: 2434 2511 Wood kitchen cabinets; wood household furniture

(G-9631)
NOVEN PHARMACEUTICALS INC (HQ)
11960 Sw 144th St (33186-6109)
PHONE....................305 964-3393
Naruhito Higo, *CEO*
Jay Kolman, *Counsel*
Joel Lippman, *Exec VP*
Peter Amanatides, *Vice Pres*
Brian J Board, *Vice Pres*
▲ **EMP:** 150 **EST:** 1987
SQ FT: 20,000
SALES (est): 127.7MM **Privately Held**
WEB: www.noven.com
SIC: 2834 Pharmaceutical preparations

(G-9632)
NOVEN THERAPEUTICS LLC
11960 Sw 144th St (33186-6109)
PHONE....................212 682-4420
Naruhito Higo, *Director*
Arthur Besteman, *Director*
EMP: 418 **EST:** 2004
SQ FT: 31,000
SALES (est): 10.5MM **Privately Held**
WEB: www.noven.com
SIC: 2834 Pharmaceutical preparations
HQ: Noven Pharmaceuticals, Inc.
11960 Sw 144th St
Miami FL 33186
305 964-3393

(G-9633)
NSK LATIN AMERICA INC (DH)
11601 Nw 107th St Ste 200 (33178-3386)
PHONE....................305 477-0605
Marco Rodriguez, *President*
Angel Salgado, *Sales Executive*
◆ **EMP:** 8 **EST:** 1995
SALES (est): 3.9MM **Privately Held**
SIC: 3562 5085 3568 Ball & roller bearings; industrial supplies; power transmission equipment

(G-9634)
NU-ART SIGNS INC
3343 Nw 7th Ave (33127-3303)
PHONE....................305 531-9850
David Burnard, *President*
Maria Burnard, *Treasurer*

Wayne Grabein, *Office Mgr*
EMP: 5 **EST:** 1956
SQ FT: 1,200
SALES (est): 551.5K **Privately Held**
WEB: www.nuartsigns.net
SIC: 3993 Signs & advertising specialties

(G-9635)
NUEVO MUNDO COMPANY
9702 Sw 40th St (33165-4075)
PHONE....................305 207-8155
Pedro López, *Principal*
EMP: 10 **EST:** 2007
SALES (est): 362.8K **Privately Held**
WEB: nuevo-mundo-miami.edan.io
SIC: 7372 Home entertainment computer software

(G-9636)
NUTRASOURCE LLC (PA)
1395 Brickell Ave Ste 800 (33131-3302)
PHONE....................786 427-4305
Luis Gonzalez, *Manager*
EMP: 5 **EST:** 2010
SALES (est): 679.6K **Privately Held**
WEB: www.nutravive.org
SIC: 2834 Vitamin, nutrient & hematinic preparations for human use

(G-9637)
OCEAN DYNAMICS USA INC
18377 Ne 4th Ct (33179-4531)
PHONE....................305 770-1800
Ron Kaplan, *President*
Ron Kappy, *Director*
◆ **EMP:** 6 **EST:** 1993
SQ FT: 5,000
SALES (est): 991.6K **Privately Held**
WEB: www.oceandynamics.com
SIC: 3429 3231 Furniture builders' & other household hardware; products of purchased glass

(G-9638)
OFFICE EXPRESS CORP
1835 Nw 112th Ave Ste 174 (33172-1819)
PHONE....................786 503-6800
Noslen A Anaya, *Principal*
◆ **EMP:** 13 **EST:** 2015
SALES (est): 1.5MM **Privately Held**
WEB: www.officexpress-us.com
SIC: 2522 Office furniture, except wood

(G-9639)
OFFICINE GULLO USA LLC
Also Called: Le Atelier Paris Haute Design
6151 Biscayne Blvd (33137-2226)
PHONE....................800 781-7125
Ricardo Moraes,
▲ **EMP:** 9 **EST:** 2012
SALES (est): 506.5K **Privately Held**
WEB: www.officinegullo.com
SIC: 3469 Kitchen fixtures & equipment: metal, except cast aluminum

(G-9640)
OH CATERING INC
3006 Sw 155th Ave (33185-5908)
PHONE....................305 903-9271
EMP: 6
SALES (est): 421.4K **Privately Held**
SIC: 2099 Mfg Food Preparations

(G-9641)
OILS R US 1 800
3300 Nw 112th St (33167-3313)
PHONE....................305 681-0909
Gregory Bass, *Owner*
EMP: 7 **EST:** 2015
SALES (est): 707.8K **Privately Held**
WEB: www.1800oilsrus.com
SIC: 1389 Oil field services

(G-9642)
OLDCASTLE BUILDINGENVELOPE INC
17851 Nw Miami Ct (33169-5016)
PHONE....................305 651-6630
Ashlie Lee, *Project Mgr*
Mike Sanford, *Sales Mgr*
Ed Diaz, *Manager*
Daniel Daluz,
EMP: 121

SALES (corp-wide): 1.5B **Privately Held**
WEB: www.obe.com
SIC: 3231 5039 Reflector glass beads, for highway signs or reflectors; exterior flat glass: plate or window
PA: Oldcastle Buildingenvelope, Inc.
5005 Lyndon B Johnson Fwy
Dallas TX 75244
214 273-3400

(G-9643)
OLIAN INC
Also Called: Analili Analili
13011 Sw 132nd St (33186-7197)
PHONE....................305 233-9116
Liliana A Delcueto, *President*
Adriana Gonzalez, *General Mgr*
Ricardo A Delcueto, *Vice Pres*
Conchita N Alentado, *Treasurer*
Conchita Alentado, *Treasurer*
◆ **EMP:** 30 **EST:** 1984
SQ FT: 44,000
SALES (est): 3MM **Privately Held**
WEB: www.olianmaternity.com
SIC: 2339 Maternity clothing

(G-9644)
OLMEDO PRINTING CORP
710 Sw 73rd Ct (33144-2642)
PHONE....................305 262-4666
Manuel Olmedo Jr, *President*
Carlos Olmedo, *Vice Pres*
EMP: 5 **EST:** 1973
SQ FT: 2,800
SALES (est): 519.5K **Privately Held**
WEB: www.olmedoprinting.com
SIC: 2752 Commercial printing, offset

(G-9645)
OLY CUSTOM CABINETS MIAMI INC
13285 Sw 39th St (33175-3223)
PHONE....................305 216-3947
Leon Eduardo, *President*
EMP: 8 **EST:** 2001
SALES (est): 189.7K **Privately Held**
SIC: 2434 Wood kitchen cabinets

(G-9646)
OMEGA ENERGY USA LLC
600 Brickell Ave Ste 1530 (33131-3068)
PHONE....................786 245-0642
Omar Leal, *CEO*
Sofia Santo Domingo, *Vice Pres*
Brandon Banks, *Mng Member*
EMP: 7 **EST:** 2010
SQ FT: 5,000
SALES (est): 2.5MM **Privately Held**
WEB: www.omegaenergyusa.com
SIC: 2869 Ethyl alcohol, ethanol
PA: Omega Energy Colombia
Calle 113 7 45 Torre B Oficina 918 Edificio Teleport
Bogota

(G-9647)
OMEGA GAS INC
18401 Sw 115th Ave (33157-6513)
PHONE....................786 277-2176
Pablo Moncada, *Principal*
EMP: 9 **EST:** 2006
SALES (est): 213.1K **Privately Held**
SIC: 2911 Gases & liquefied petroleum gases

(G-9648)
OMNISPHERE CORPORATION (PA)
9950 Sw 107th Ave Ste 100 (33176-2767)
PHONE....................305 388-4075
Alexander F Valdes, *President*
Maria Limccarthy, *Controller*
Magdalia Alfonso, *Accounting Dir*
Yolanda Hernandez, *Director*
Jerry Jakob, *Director*
◆ **EMP:** 11 **EST:** 1973
SQ FT: 4,000
SALES (est): 67.8MM **Privately Held**
WEB: www.omnisphere.net
SIC: 2679 5093 5162 Paper products, converted; waste paper; plastics materials

(G-9649)
ON-Q SOFTWARE INC
13764 Sw 11th St (33184-2771)
PHONE....................305 553-6566

Terry Cajigas, *President*
EMP: 5 **EST:** 2001
SALES (est): 443.6K **Privately Held**
WEB: www.on-qsoftware.com
SIC: 7372 Application computer software

(G-9650)
ONARIS
14 Ne 1st Ave Ste 607 (33132-2431)
PHONE..................................305 579-0056
Michael Pezua, *President*
Edgar Pezua, *Vice Pres*
▼ **EMP:** 10 **EST:** 2008
SQ FT: 3,500
SALES (est): 525.5K **Privately Held**
SIC: 3714 Acceleration equipment, motor vehicle

(G-9651)
ONE MILO INC
1010 Brickell Ave # 2709 (33131-3757)
PHONE..................................305 804-0266
Russell Leigh,
EMP: 10 **EST:** 2018
SQ FT: 4,000
SALES (est): 1.2MM **Privately Held**
WEB: www.onemilo.com
SIC: 3841 7371 Surgical & medical instruments; computer software development & applications

(G-9652)
ONE STEP PAPERS LLC (PA)
12105 Sw 130th St Ste 202 (33186-5260)
PHONE..................................305 238-2296
Arturo Ortiz, *Comptroller*
Carey Kummelman, *Mng Member*
Rodney Croes,
Rick Hess,
◆ **EMP:** 5 **EST:** 1996
SQ FT: 10,000
SALES (est): 1.7MM **Privately Held**
WEB: www.onesteppapers.com
SIC: 2672 2893 Transfer paper, gold or silver: from purchased materials; printing ink

(G-9653)
ONE WORLD RESOURCE LLC
Also Called: Coast To Coast Designs
4608 Sw 74th Ave (33155-4422)
PHONE..................................305 445-9199
Claudia Parra, *Project Mgr*
Nick Hammond, *Sales Staff*
Vanessa Garcia, *Manager*
Douglas H Olson,
▲ **EMP:** 20 **EST:** 2003
SQ FT: 4,000
SALES (est): 1.2MM **Privately Held**
WEB: www.c2cdesigns.com
SIC: 2599 Hotel furniture

(G-9654)
ONETOWN BOARDS
580 Nw 120th St (33168-3529)
P.O. Box 680940 (33168-0940)
PHONE..................................786 704-5921
Felix Ernesto Puello, *Owner*
Socrates Elie, *Principal*
EMP: 7 **EST:** 2015
SALES (est): 185.7K **Privately Held**
SIC: 3949 5961 Skateboards; fitness & sporting goods, mail order

(G-9655)
ONLINEWALL
169 Nw 36th St (33127-3107)
PHONE..................................800 210-0194
Taner Ziya, *Principal*
EMP: 8 **EST:** 2008
SALES (est): 126.1K **Privately Held**
SIC: 3999 Framed artwork

(G-9656)
ONPOINT GLOBAL
8325 Ne 2nd Ave Ste 100 (33138-3815)
PHONE..................................651 788-1274
EMP: 20 **EST:** 2018
SALES (est): 7MM **Privately Held**
WEB: www.onpointglobal.com
SIC: 2782 Ledger, inventory & account books

(G-9657)
ONYX PROTECTIVE GROUP INC
Also Called: Onyx Armor
7359 Nw 34th St (33122-1272)
PHONE..................................305 282-4455
Ana Maria Cuartas, *President*
Juan Gutierrez, *Principal*
Javier Rocha, *Director*
▼ **EMP:** 10 **EST:** 2012
SQ FT: 20,000
SALES (est): 1.8MM **Privately Held**
WEB: www.onyxarmor.com
SIC: 3842 2311 Bulletproof vests; policemen's uniforms: made from purchased materials

(G-9658)
OPEN HOUSE MAGAZINE INC
505 Ne 30th St Apt 405 (33137-4303)
PHONE..................................305 576-6011
Patricia G Ernst, *President*
EMP: 7 **EST:** 1989
SQ FT: 1,500
SALES (est): 271K **Privately Held**
WEB: www.openhousemagazineinc.com
SIC: 2721 Magazines: publishing only, not printed on site

(G-9659)
OPKO CURNA LLC
4400 Biscayne Blvd (33137-3212)
PHONE..................................305 575-4100
Allyson Parker, *Vice Pres*
EMP: 9 **EST:** 2011
SALES (est): 595.6K **Privately Held**
WEB: www.opko.com
SIC: 3841 Surgical & medical instruments

(G-9660)
OPKO HEALTH INC (PA)
4400 Biscayne Blvd (33137-3212)
PHONE..................................305 575-4100
Phillip Frost, *Ch of Bd*
Jane H Hsiao, *Vice Ch Bd*
Steve Rubin, *Exec VP*
Steven D Rubin, *Exec VP*
Rishard Weitz, *Exec VP*
EMP: 144 **EST:** 2007
SQ FT: 29,500
SALES (est): 1.7B **Publicly Held**
WEB: www.opko.com
SIC: 2834 2835 8731 Pharmaceutical preparations; in vitro & in vivo diagnostic substances; biotechnical research, commercial

(G-9661)
ORACLE AMERICA INC
6505 Blue Lagoon Dr # 40 (33126-6009)
PHONE..................................305 260-7200
Loveen Koshy, *Consultant*
EMP: 7 **EST:** 2019
SALES (est): 1MM
SALES (corp-wide): 42.4B **Publicly Held**
SIC: 7372 Prepackaged software
PA: Oracle Corporation
2300 Oracle Way
Austin TX 78741
737 867-1000

(G-9662)
ORELLANA COATINGS INC
9447 Fontainebleau Blvd (33172-7520)
PHONE..................................305 389-4610
Rafael A Orellana, *Principal*
EMP: 10 **EST:** 2010
SALES (est): 112.7K **Privately Held**
SIC: 3479 Metal coating & allied service

(G-9663)
ORELLANA INVESTMENTS INC
Also Called: Minuteman Press
2818 Nw 79th Ave (33122-1033)
PHONE..................................305 477-2817
Luz M Orellana, *President*
Daniel Orellana, *CFO*
▼ **EMP:** 8 **EST:** 2007
SALES (est): 996.9K **Privately Held**
SIC: 2752 Commercial printing, lithographic

(G-9664)
ORIA LAB LLC
13140 Sw 134th St Ste 12 (33186-4467)
PHONE..................................786 302-8142
Michael Oria, *Mng Member*

EMP: 20 **EST:** 2019
SALES (est): 1.2MM **Privately Held**
SIC: 3999

(G-9665)
ORIENTAL PACKING COMPANY INC (PA)
12221 Sw 104th Ter (33186-3612)
PHONE..................................305 235-1829
Herman D Lue, *President*
Lillas Lue, *Principal*
Deborah L Lue, *Vice Pres*
Natalie A Lue, *Vice Pres*
▼ **EMP:** 10 **EST:** 1981
SALES (est): 1MM **Privately Held**
WEB: www.orientalpacking.com
SIC: 2099 Spices, including grinding

(G-9666)
ORIENTAL RED APPLE LLC
255 Park Blvd (33126-8009)
PHONE..................................646 853-1468
Liya Liu, *Principal*
EMP: 8 **EST:** 2016
SALES (est): 408.7K **Privately Held**
SIC: 3571 Electronic computers

(G-9667)
ORIGIN PC LLC
12400 Sw 134th Ct Ste 8 (33186-6499)
PHONE..................................305 971-1000
Maria Inirio, *Purch Mgr*
Naveen Kumar, *Engineer*
Francisco Lujan, *Accounts Mgr*
Diego Castillo, *Sales Staff*
Arturo Hernandez, *Sales Staff*
▲ **EMP:** 30 **EST:** 2009
SQ FT: 2,000
SALES (est): 10.4MM **Publicly Held**
WEB: www.originpc.com
SIC: 3571 5734 Computers, digital, analog or hybrid; software, computer games; personal computers
HQ: Corsair Gaming, Inc.
115 N Mccarthy Blvd
Milpitas CA 95035
510 657-8747

(G-9668)
ORLANDO FLORES
3841 Sw 92nd Ave (33165-4154)
PHONE..................................305 898-2111
Orlando Flores, *Principal*
EMP: 7 **EST:** 2010
SALES (est): 111.2K **Privately Held**
SIC: 3844 X-ray apparatus & tubes

(G-9669)
OSCAR E PEREZ
13901 Sw 26th Ter (33175-6503)
PHONE..................................786 442-6889
Oscar Perez, *President*
EMP: 7 **EST:** 2011
SALES (est): 275.1K **Privately Held**
SIC: 3444 Sheet metalwork

(G-9670)
OTUS CORP INTL LLC
8306 Mills Dr 222 (33183-4838)
PHONE..................................305 833-6078
Joel Mateu, *Mng Member*
Yolanda Fischer,
EMP: 8 **EST:** 2010
SALES (est): 284.7K **Privately Held**
WEB: us100548355.trustpass.alibaba.com
SIC: 2911 2992 Oils, fuel; lubricating oils & greases

(G-9671)
OUTFORM INC (PA)
82 Ne 26th St Unit 103 (33137-4442)
PHONE..................................800 204-0524
Ariel Haroush, *President*
Ashley Alejandro, *Project Mgr*
Sergio Oliva, *Project Mgr*
Kelsea Hemings, *Opers Staff*
Lorraine McNicholas, *Opers Staff*
▲ **EMP:** 9 **EST:** 2008
SALES (est): 4.9MM **Privately Held**
WEB: www.outform.com
SIC: 3823 Digital displays of process variables

(G-9672)
OXLEY CABINET WAREHOUSE INC
1031 Ives Dairy Rd (33179-2521)
PHONE..................................786 377-4281
Bill Oxley, *President*
Helene Stang, *Corp Secy*
Joey Connell, *Vice Pres*
Laurie Oxley-Connell, *Vice Pres*
Rob Higginbotham, *Sales Staff*
EMP: 7 **EST:** 2004
SQ FT: 15,184
SALES (est): 1.8MM **Privately Held**
WEB: www.oxleycabinets.com
SIC: 2434 Wood kitchen cabinets

(G-9673)
OXPECKER ENTERPRISE INC
Also Called: Hunting Report The
12182 Sw 128th St (33186-5230)
P.O. Box 972682 (33197-2682)
PHONE..................................305 253-5301
Donald Causey, *President*
EMP: 6 **EST:** 1991
SQ FT: 961
SALES (est): 452.8K **Privately Held**
SIC: 2721 Magazines: publishing only, not printed on site

(G-9674)
PACHECO CREATIVE GROUP INC
Also Called: Evolutions - Graphics Designs-
2164 Nw 19th Ave (33142-7452)
PHONE..................................305 541-1400
Manriquel Pacheco, *President*
EMP: 9 **EST:** 2010
SALES (est): 387.8K **Privately Held**
WEB: www.evolutionsgraphics.com
SIC: 3993 Signs & advertising specialties

(G-9675)
PACIFIC
8526 Nw 70th St (33166-2652)
PHONE..................................305 785-9068
Victor Sales, *CEO*
EMP: 5 **EST:** 2015
SALES (est): 321.8K **Privately Held**
WEB: www.pacific-ltd.com
SIC: 3531 Scrapers, graders, rollers & similar equipment

(G-9676)
PACIFIC LIMITED INTERNATIONAL
825 Brickell Bay Dr # 17 (33131-2936)
PHONE..................................305 358-1900
Jose Massuh, *President*
EMP: 5 **EST:** 2019
SALES (est): 11.1MM **Privately Held**
SIC: 2821 5162 Plastics materials & resins; resins

(G-9677)
PACIFIC LTD CORP
Also Called: Pacific Limited
825 Brickell Bay Dr # 17 (33131-2936)
PHONE..................................305 358-1900
Jose Massuh, *President*
Virginia Bolona, *Credit Mgr*
▼ **EMP:** 7 **EST:** 1982
SQ FT: 3,000
SALES (est): 1.9MM **Privately Held**
WEB: www.pacific-ltd.com
SIC: 2821 Plastics materials & resins

(G-9678)
PACKAGING CORPORATION AMERICA
Also Called: PCA/Miami Gardens 350
15600 Nw 15th Ave Ste A (33169-5609)
PHONE..................................305 770-3439
Luis Perez, *Sales Staff*
Bob Farbish, *Branch Mgr*
Ivette Garay, *Associate*
EMP: 65
SALES (corp-wide): 7.7B **Publicly Held**
WEB: www.packagingcorp.com
SIC: 2653 Boxes, corrugated: made from purchased materials
PA: Packaging Corporation Of America
1 N Field Ct
Lake Forest IL 60045
847 482-3000

(G-9679)
PACKAGING CORPORATION AMERICA
Timbar Packaging & Display
3500 Nw 110th St (33167-3724)
PHONE..................305 685-8956
Gilbert Becker, *General Mgr*
Anthony Veliz, *Mfg Staff*
Keith Shipley, *Sales Staff*
Nikole Bianco, *Program Mgr*
Brian Amentini, *Manager*
EMP: 104
SQ FT: 44,000
SALES (corp-wide): 7.7B **Publicly Held**
WEB: www.packagingcorp.com
SIC: 2653 Boxes, corrugated: made from purchased materials
PA: Packaging Corporation Of America
1 N Field Ct
Lake Forest IL 60045
847 482-3000

(G-9680)
PAINTS N COCKTAILS INC
14710 Ne 2nd Ct (33161-2013)
PHONE..................954 514-7383
Lynn Smith Clyne, *CEO*
EMP: 14 EST: 2011
SALES (est): 985.1K **Privately Held**
WEB: www.paintsncocktails.com
SIC: 3993 5199 Signs & advertising specialties; advertising specialties

(G-9681)
PALEO BAKEHOUSE INC ✪
12581 Sw 134th Ct Ste 101 (33186-6490)
PHONE..................786 253-1051
Joselyne Peralta, *Principal*
EMP: 8 EST: 2022
SALES (est): 582.9K **Privately Held**
WEB: www.pbhfoods.com
SIC: 2052 Cookies & crackers

(G-9682)
PALLET ENTERPRISES OF FLORIDA
7525 Nw 37th Ave Unit D (33147-5802)
PHONE..................305 836-3204
Pepe Lopez, *President*
▲ EMP: 9 EST: 2004
SALES (est): 286.7K **Privately Held**
SIC: 2448 Pallets, wood

(G-9683)
PALLET SOLUTIONS INC
7525 Nw 37th Ave Unit D (33147-5802)
P.O. Box 138717, Hialeah (33013-8717)
PHONE..................305 801-8314
Rene Mendoza, *Principal*
EMP: 7 EST: 2012
SALES (est): 243.6K **Privately Held**
SIC: 2448 Pallets, wood

(G-9684)
PALLETS TO GO INC
1691 Nw 23rd St (33142-7625)
PHONE..................305 654-0303
Rigoberto Lesceiro, *President*
Susie Ayerdis, *Admin Sec*
EMP: 10 EST: 1997
SALES (est): 848.4K **Privately Held**
WEB: www.sfpallets.com
SIC: 2448 Pallets, wood

(G-9685)
PALMETTO PRINTING INC
3065 Ohio St (33133-4418)
PHONE..................305 253-2444
Eduardo Rivas, *President*
Joaquin Rivas, *Production*
Wendy Miranda, *Finance*
Linda Salisbury, *Admin Sec*
▼ EMP: 10 EST: 1974
SALES (est): 762.8K **Privately Held**
WEB: www.palmettoprinting.com
SIC: 2752 7334 Commercial printing, offset; photocopying & duplicating services

(G-9686)
PAMPLONA FOODS INC
9600 Sw 122nd Ct (33186-2538)
PHONE..................305 970-4120
Carlos M Garcia, *President*
Juan G Guerra, *Vice Pres*
Jesus Garcia, *Admin Sec*

EMP: 8 EST: 1995
SALES (est): 131.9K **Privately Held**
SIC: 2013 Canned meats (except baby food) from purchased meat

(G-9687)
PANAMCO LLC
701 Nw 62nd Ave Ste 800 (33126-4684)
PHONE..................305 856-7100
Francisco Sanchez,
EMP: 10 EST: 2000
SALES (est): 220.3K **Privately Held**
SIC: 2086 Bottled & canned soft drinks

(G-9688)
PANELFOLD INC
10700 Nw 36th Ave (33167-3785)
P.O. Box 680130 (33168-0130)
PHONE..................305 688-3501
Guy E Dixon III, *President*
Dale Gurley, *Vice Pres*
Marsha A Kallstrom, *Vice Pres*
Marsha Kallstroms, *Vice Pres*
James Lyons, *Vice Pres*
◆ EMP: 165 EST: 1953
SQ FT: 140,000
SALES (est): 22.9MM **Privately Held**
WEB: www.panelfold.com
SIC: 2679 3442 Wallboard, decorated: made from purchased material; sash, door or window: metal; window & door frames; storm doors or windows, metal

(G-9689)
PANTALEON COMMODITIES CORP
601 Brickell Key Dr # 60 (33131-2662)
PHONE..................786 542-6333
Diego Herrera, *President*
EMP: 16 EST: 2018
SALES (est): 1MM **Privately Held**
SIC: 2099 Sugar

(G-9690)
PANTHER SOFTWARE INC
Also Called: Practicepanther
10800 Biscayne Blvd # 201 (33161-7482)
PHONE..................800 856-8729
Kristin Neill, *Vice Pres*
Shawn Clark, *Engineer*
Michael Crocker, *Senior Engr*
Soumya Nettimi, *CFO*
Eytan Haddad, *Manager*
EMP: 12 EST: 2015
SALES (est): 1MM **Privately Held**
WEB: www.practicepanther.com
SIC: 7372 Prepackaged software

(G-9691)
PARA TODO MAL MEZCAL LLC
2100 Coral Way Ste 703 (33145-2600)
PHONE..................786 837-3119
Adriana S Estrada Vazquez, *Principal*
EMP: 7 EST: 2011
SALES (est): 142.9K **Privately Held**
SIC: 2085 Distilled & blended liquors

(G-9692)
PARADISE AWNINGS CORPORATION
Also Called: Paradise Archtctral Panels Stl
4310 Nw 36th Ave (33142-4220)
PHONE..................305 597-5714
Juan Chaviano, *President*
Iris Hernandez, *Counsel*
Manny Alcibar, *Vice Pres*
▼ EMP: 23 EST: 1998
SQ FT: 18,000
SALES (est): 4MM **Privately Held**
WEB: www.panelsandsteel.com
SIC: 2394 1799 Awnings, fabric: made from purchased materials; awning installation

(G-9693)
PARADISE EMB & SILKSCREEN INC
8801 Sw 129th St (33176-5918)
PHONE..................305 595-6441
Cheryl Vihlen, *President*
EMP: 6 EST: 1998
SALES (est): 386.8K **Privately Held**
WEB: www.logofactory.com
SIC: 2395 Embroidery products, except schiffli machine

(G-9694)
PARKER-HANNIFIN CORPORATION
7400 Nw 19th St Ste A (33126-1217)
PHONE..................305 470-8800
Patricia Fonseca, *Export Mgr*
Miguel Marchand, *Engineer*
Eric Schisler, *Engineer*
Marcos Barros, *Branch Mgr*
Felice Ferri, *Technical Staff*
EMP: 34
SALES (corp-wide): 14.3B **Publicly Held**
WEB: www.parker.com
SIC: 3561 3494 3599 5084 Pumps & pumping equipment; valves & pipe fittings; custom machinery; industrial machinery & equipment
PA: Parker-Hannifin Corporation
6035 Parkland Blvd
Cleveland OH 44124
216 896-3000

(G-9695)
PARRAS PLASTIC INC
13894 Sw 139th Ct (33186-5512)
PHONE..................305 972-9537
EMP: 5
SALES (est): 569.3K **Privately Held**
SIC: 3089 Mfg Plastic Products

(G-9696)
PATLON INDUSTRIES INC
13913 Sw 119th Ave (33186-6202)
PHONE..................305 255-7744
Michael J Mann, *President*
Stephen Mann, *Exec VP*
Mike Little, *Vice Pres*
Lisa Mann, *Vice Pres*
Walter F Pettit, *Vice Pres*
EMP: 5 EST: 1985
SQ FT: 7,500
SALES (est): 1MM **Privately Held**
WEB: www.patlon.com
SIC: 3629 Static elimination equipment, industrial

(G-9697)
PAVERS & BRICKS SERVICES CORP
749 Ne 81st St (33138-4616)
PHONE..................305 986-2544
Paulo Ramos, *Principal*
EMP: 8 EST: 2010
SALES (est): 231.7K **Privately Held**
SIC: 2951 Asphalt paving mixtures & blocks

(G-9698)
PAX CTHOLIC COMMUNICATIONS INC
Also Called: Radio Paz
1779 Nw 28th St (33142-6016)
PHONE..................305 638-9729
Father Federico Capdebon, *Principal*
Jorge Diazdiaz, *Corp Comm Staff*
EMP: 22 EST: 1994
SALES (est): 5.2MM **Privately Held**
WEB: www.paxcc.org
SIC: 3663 Radio broadcasting & communications equipment

(G-9699)
PEACE MILLWORK CO INC
3535 Nw 50th St (33142-3931)
PHONE..................305 573-6222
George W Peace, *President*
Tomi Peace, *Admin Sec*
EMP: 23 EST: 1990
SQ FT: 20,000
SALES (est): 1.2MM **Privately Held**
WEB: www.peacemillwork.com
SIC: 2431 2434 Interior & ornamental woodwork & trim; panel work, wood; wood kitchen cabinets

(G-9700)
PEAK ELECTRONICS INC
7255 Nw 68th St Ste 8 (33166-3015)
PHONE..................305 888-1588
Jose Alvarez, *President*
EMP: 8 EST: 1993
SQ FT: 2,500

SALES (est): 696.1K **Privately Held**
WEB: www.peakelectronics.com
SIC: 3825 Test equipment for electronic & electric measurement

(G-9701)
PENA GENERAL WELDING INC
4788 Sw 75th Ave (33155-4435)
PHONE..................786 255-2153
Medardo Pena, *President*
EMP: 9 EST: 2004
SALES (est): 233.4K **Privately Held**
SIC: 7692 Welding repair

(G-9702)
PENGUIN RANDOM HOUSE LLC
8950 Sw 74th Ct Ste 2010 (33156-3179)
PHONE..................305 206-8715
Silvia Matute, *Principal*
EMP: 16
SALES (corp-wide): 147.7MM **Privately Held**
WEB: www.prhspeakers.com
SIC: 2731 Books: publishing only
HQ: Penguin Random House Llc
1745 Broadway Frnt 1
New York NY 10019
212 782-9000

(G-9703)
PENINSULA TISSUE CORPORATION
2630 Nw 72nd Ave (33122-1306)
PHONE..................305 863-0704
Hermelice Tineo, *Principal*
◆ EMP: 5 EST: 2011
SALES (est): 847.2K **Privately Held**
WEB: www.peninsulatissue.com
SIC: 2621 Paper mills

(G-9704)
PEPSICO BEVERAGE DISTRIBUTORS
1000 Nw 57th Ct (33126-3274)
PHONE..................305 537-4477
EMP: 14 EST: 2014
SALES (est): 1.2MM **Privately Held**
WEB: www.pepsico.com
SIC: 2086 Carbonated soft drinks, bottled & canned

(G-9705)
PEPSICO LATIN AMERICA BEVERAGE
1000 Nw 57th Ct Ste 800 (33126-3288)
PHONE..................305 537-4477
EMP: 8 EST: 2015
SALES (est): 346K **Privately Held**
WEB: www.pepsico.com
SIC: 2086 Carbonated soft drinks, bottled & canned

(G-9706)
PERFORMNCE GLZING SLUTIONS LLC
7239 Nw 54th St (33166-4807)
PHONE..................305 975-3717
Victor F Rosado, *Managing Prtnr*
Eduardo A Recio, *Managing Prtnr*
EMP: 7 EST: 2016
SALES (est): 298.3K **Privately Held**
WEB: www.performanceglazing.com
SIC: 2431 3442 Windows & window parts & trim, wood; metal doors, sash & trim

(G-9707)
PERMASTEELISA NORTH AMER CORP
703 Nw 62nd Ave Ste 950 (33126-4678)
PHONE..................305 265-4405
Robert Picarrelli, *Manager*
Arelis Abreu, *Manager*
EMP: 22 **Privately Held**
SIC: 3443 Fabricated plate work (boiler shop)
HQ: Permasteelisa North America Corp.
1300 Hall Blvd Ste 1a
Bloomfield CT 06002

(G-9708)
PETROSOL PROCESSING & REFINING
2655 S Le Jeune Rd # 1003 (33134-5803)
PHONE..................305 442-7400

EMP: 10
SALES (est): 1.2MM **Privately Held**
SIC: 2911 Petroleum Refining

(G-9709)
PHARMACY HN LLC ✪
3501 Nw 67th St Ste B (33147-7554)
PHONE........................786 307-0509
Alejandra Lucia Villar Ruiz,
Marco Antonio Villar Mondragon,
EMP: 10 **EST:** 2021
SALES (est): 513.8K **Privately Held**
SIC: 2834 Pharmaceutical preparations

(G-9710)
PHILIAS SUPREME LLC
1362 Nw 100th Ter (33147-1866)
PHONE........................786 865-1335
Charite Philias, *CEO*
EMP: 7 **EST:** 2018
SALES (est): 365.6K **Privately Held**
SIC: 2396 Automotive & apparel trimmings

(G-9711)
PHILIPS NORTH AMERICA LLC
13305 Sw 106th Ave (33176-6053)
PHONE........................305 969-7447
Sinforiano Echeverria, *Director*
EMP: 63
SALES (corp-wide): 133.6MM **Privately
Held**
WEB: usa.philips.com
SIC: 3651 Household audio & video equip-
ment
HQ: Philips North America Llc
222 Jacobs St Fl 3
Cambridge MA 02141
978 659-3000

(G-9712)
**PHOENIX MEDICAL RESEARCH
LLC**
8900 Sw 24th St Ste 210 (33165-2075)
PHONE........................786 762-2040
EMP: 8 **EST:** 2012
SALES (est): 122.4K **Privately Held**
SIC: 2834 Pharmaceutical preparations

(G-9713)
PHOTO OFFSET INC
4824 Sw 72nd Ave (33155-5526)
PHONE........................305 666-1067
John Knowles, *President*
Anne Knowles, *Admin Sec*
EMP: 12 **EST:** 1952
SQ FT: 2,000
SALES (est): 736.7K **Privately Held**
WEB: www.photooffset.com
SIC: 2752 Commercial printing, offset

(G-9714)
PHOTON TOWERS INC
17290 Sw 192nd St (33187-5101)
PHONE........................305 235-7337
Sergio Cabrera, *Principal*
EMP: 7 **EST:** 2016
SALES (est): 77.5K **Privately Held**
SIC: 3661 Fiber optics communications
equipment

(G-9715)
PHY-MED
8905 Sw 87th Ave Ste 200 (33176-2214)
PHONE........................305 925-0141
Diego Cordova, *Administration*
EMP: 7 **EST:** 2018
SALES (est): 255.7K **Privately Held**
SIC: 3821 Laboratory apparatus & furniture

(G-9716)
PICANOVA INC
3443 Nw 107th St (33167-3715)
PHONE........................786 705-2120
Frederik Huhn, *President*
EMP: 16 **EST:** 2010
SALES (est): 565.9K **Privately Held**
SIC: 2394 Canvas & related products

(G-9717)
**PILLOW PLUS
MANUFACTURING INC**
515 Ne 189th St (33179-3909)
PHONE........................305 652-2218
Raymond Alemany, *President*
EMP: 7 **EST:** 2001

SQ FT: 4,000
SALES (est): 558K **Privately Held**
WEB: www.pillowplusmfrs.com
SIC: 2392 Mattress pads; pillows, bed:
made from purchased materials

(G-9718)
PINZON CARAMEL SYRUP
6937 Nw 52nd St (33166-4844)
PHONE........................305 591-2472
Florentino Fernandez, *President*
Carlo Fernandez, *Senior VP*
▲ **EMP:** 5 **EST:** 2006
SALES (est): 404.1K **Privately Held**
WEB: www.pinzoncaramel.com
SIC: 2087 Syrups, flavoring (except drink)

(G-9719)
PKOLINO LLC
Also Called: P'Kolino Studio
7300 Nw 35th Ave (33147-5808)
PHONE........................888 403-8992
Antonio Turco-Rivas, *Mng Member*
JB Schneider,
▲ **EMP:** 8 **EST:** 2004
SQ FT: 2,500
SALES (est): 1.6MM **Privately Held**
WEB: www.pkolino.com
SIC: 2511 Wood household furniture

(G-9720)
**PLANTAIN PRODUCTS
COMPANY**
2440 Nw 116th St Ste 100 (33167-0005)
PHONE........................800 477-2447
Antonio Rivas, *President*
Maria Aguilar, *Accounts Mgr*
Liam Clarke, *Manager*
Margarita Guillen, *Admin Mgr*
◆ **EMP:** 30 **EST:** 1963
SQ FT: 22,000
SALES (est): 5.4MM **Privately Held**
WEB: www.chifleschips.com
SIC: 2099 Food preparations

(G-9721)
**PLAYBILL SOUTHERN
PUBLISHING**
Also Called: Playbill Magazine
10001 Sw 54th St (33165-7117)
PHONE........................305 595-1984
Leslie Feldman, *President*
EMP: 10 **EST:** 1975
SALES (est): 352.7K **Privately Held**
SIC: 2721 Magazines: publishing & printing

(G-9722)
PLD ACQUISITIONS LLC
Also Called: Avema Pharma Solutions
10400 Nw 29th Ter Miami (33172)
PHONE........................305 463-2270
Mitchel Singer, *CEO*
EMP: 99 **EST:** 2007
SQ FT: 63,000
SALES (est): 19.8MM **Privately Held**
SIC: 2834 Pharmaceutical preparations
PA: P & L Development, Llc
609 Cantiague Rock Rd 2a
Westbury NY 11590

(G-9723)
PM ENGRAVING CORP
18425 Sw 200th St (33187-2506)
PHONE........................786 573-5292
Mary Castellanos, *President*
EMP: 10 **EST:** 2000
SALES (est): 856.6K **Privately Held**
WEB: www.pmengraving.net
SIC: 3271 7389 Blocks, concrete or cin-
der: standard; engraving service

(G-9724)
POD ALL SOLUTIONS CORP
5203 Sw 159th Ct (33185-5056)
PHONE........................805 291-2675
Olga Orrino, *Principal*
EMP: 7 **EST:** 2019
SALES (est): 73.2K **Privately Held**
SIC: 2759 Commercial printing

(G-9725)
POGI BEAUTY LLC
3800 Ne 1st Ave (33137-3604)
PHONE........................305 600-1305
Erica Han,

EMP: 7 **EST:** 2018
SALES (est): 309.8K **Privately Held**
SIC: 7372 Educational computer software

(G-9726)
POLI GROUP INTL INC
Also Called: Poli Sign Supplies
1574 Nw 108th Ave (33172-2052)
PHONE........................305 468-8986
CHI Ting Cheung, *CEO*
◆ **EMP:** 10 **EST:** 2001
SQ FT: 1,100
SALES (est): 1.4MM **Privately Held**
WEB: www.polisigns.com
SIC: 3993 5085 Signs & advertising spe-
cialties; signmaker equipment & supplies

(G-9727)
POLICRETE LLC
3399 Nw 72nd Ave Ste 108 (33122-1339)
PHONE........................305 552-7026
Romel Pana, *Mng Member*
EMP: 7 **EST:** 2011
SALES (est): 139.8K **Privately Held**
WEB: www.policrete.com
SIC: 3471 Cleaning, polishing & finishing

(G-9728)
POLY-CHEM CORP
3039 Ne Quayside Ln (33138-2258)
PHONE........................305 593-1928
Carlos Diaz, *Owner*
EMP: 9 **EST:** 1989
SALES (est): 139.3K **Privately Held**
WEB: www.pcipcc.com
SIC: 2821 Plastics materials & resins

(G-9729)
**PONCE DE LEON
CONSTRUCTION**
440 Nw 132nd Ave (33182-1152)
PHONE........................786 554-3685
Maria J Ponce De Leon, *Vice Pres*
EMP: 8 **EST:** 1997
SALES (est): 215.9K **Privately Held**
WEB:
www.newportpropertyconstruction.com
SIC: 3272 Concrete products

(G-9730)
POSEIDON SERVICES INC
12685 Nw 11th Ln (33182-2453)
PHONE........................786 294-8529
Alexei Diaz, *Principal*
EMP: 7 **EST:** 2018
SALES (est): 200.7K **Privately Held**
SIC: 3589 Water treatment equipment, in-
dustrial

(G-9731)
POSITIVE ENERGY INC
Also Called: Positivenergy
1221 Brickell Ave Ste 900 (33131-3800)
PHONE........................929 220-5880
Edward Wise, *CEO*
David Gould, *COO*
EMP: 11 **EST:** 2019
SALES (est): 452.4K **Privately Held**
WEB: www.positivenergy.us
SIC: 3621 Storage battery chargers, motor
& engine generator type

(G-9732)
POTENZA SERVICES INC
Also Called: Potenza Hrc
10711 Sw 216th St (33170-3139)
PHONE........................305 400-4938
Cesar Giraldo, *President*
EMP: 6 **EST:** 2016
SALES (est): 507.8K **Privately Held**
WEB: www.potenzahrc.com
SIC: 3829 3842 Thermometers, including
digital; clinical; orthopedic appliances

(G-9733)
PPA MIAMI CORP
8620 Nw 64th St Ste 10 (33166-2672)
PHONE........................305 436-0460
Sebastian R Barbosa, *President*
▲ **EMP:** 7 **EST:** 2000
SALES (est): 518.2K **Privately Held**
SIC: 3441 Dam gates, metal plate

(G-9734)
PREMIUM LATIN MUSIC INC
1545 Sw 14th Ter (33145-1544)
PHONE........................212 873-1472
Franklin Jr Romero, *Branch Mgr*
EMP: 14
SALES (corp-wide): 73K **Privately Held**
SIC: 2741 Miscellaneous publishing
PA: Premium Latin Music Inc.
601 Ne 36th St Apt 2802
Miami FL

(G-9735)
PREMIUM MARINE INC
777 Brickell Ave Ste 500 (33131-2803)
PHONE........................786 903-0851
Charles Lee, *President*
Chip Hampton, *Vice Pres*
Dick Bramer, *Engineer*
EMP: 17 **EST:** 2000
SQ FT: 10,000
SALES (est): 761.2K **Privately Held**
WEB: www.premiummarine.com
SIC: 3732 Boat building & repairing

(G-9736)
PREMIUM RUBBER BANDS INC
9430 Sw 136th St (33176-6802)
PHONE........................305 321-0333
Christian Chamizo, *Principal*
EMP: 8 **EST:** 2016
SALES (est): 83.5K **Privately Held**
SIC: 3069 Rubber bands

(G-9737)
PREPAID SOLUTIONS LLC
601 Brickell Key Dr # 70 (33131-2662)
PHONE........................305 834-7422
Edward Madera, *CEO*
EMP: 15 **EST:** 2010
SQ FT: 5,000
SALES (est): 1.6MM **Privately Held**
WEB: www.prepaid.solutions
SIC: 3661 8748 Telephone sets, all types
except cellular radio; telecommunications
consultant

(G-9738)
PRESSNET CORP
Also Called: Calle Ocho News
321 Nw 63rd Ct (33126-4542)
P.O. Box 260011 (33126-0002)
PHONE........................786 728-1369
Marta Rosell, *Principal*
EMP: 8 **EST:** 1998
SALES (est): 250K **Privately Held**
WEB: www.pressnetcorp.com
SIC: 2711 Newspapers, publishing & print-
ing

(G-9739)
PRESYS INSTRUMENTS INC
14453 Sw 84th St (33183-3906)
PHONE........................305 495-3335
William F Charles, *Principal*
Marc Vantournhoudt, *Sales Mgr*
EMP: 7 **EST:** 2016
SALES (est): 1MM **Privately Held**
WEB: www.presyscorp.com
SIC: 3823 Industrial instrmnts msrmnt dis-
play/control process variable

(G-9740)
PRINT BOLD CORP
Also Called: Orion Press
13995 Sw 144th Ave Ste 20 (33186-8655)
PHONE........................305 517-1281
Hernandez Sandra, *Principal*
EMP: 22 **EST:** 2010
SALES (est): 756.4K **Privately Held**
SIC: 2752 Commercial printing, offset

(G-9741)
PRINT FARM INC (PA)
Also Called: Printfarm
3511 Nw 74th Ave (33122-1233)
PHONE........................305 592-2895
Albert Alvarez, *President*
Floyd Jackson, *Sales Executive*
EMP: 22 **EST:** 2000
SQ FT: 3,500
SALES (est): 3.2MM **Privately Held**
WEB: www.pf-solutions.com
SIC: 2752 Commercial printing, offset

▲ = Import ▼=Export
◆ =Import/Export

(G-9742)
PRINT PRO SHOP INC
Also Called: Orion Visual Group
660 Nw 85th St (33150-2560)
PHONE....................................305 859-8282
Alex Peysakhovich, *President*
Mike Peysakhovich, *Vice Pres*
Alejandro Salcedo, *Production*
EMP: 13 EST: 2012
SALES (est): 2.3MM Privately Held
WEB: pps.printproshop.com
SIC: 2752 Commercial printing, litho-
graphic

(G-9743)
PRINT RITE CO
748 Ne 79th St (33138-4752)
PHONE....................................305 757-0611
Benjamin Kram, *Owner*
EMP: 6 EST: 1953
SQ FT: 2,500
SALES (est): 520.8K Privately Held
SIC: 2752 Letters, circular or form: litho-
graphed; lithographing on metal

(G-9744)
PRINT SIGNS & BANNERS
4244 Sw 73rd Ave (33155-4545)
PHONE....................................305 600-1349
EMP: 7 EST: 2016
SALES (est): 220K Privately Held
WEB: www.psbmiami.com
SIC: 3993 Signs & advertising specialties

(G-9745)
**PRINTING GRPHICS CNNECTION
INC**
823 Nw 133rd Ct (33182-2205)
PHONE....................................305 222-6144
Octavio J Del Castillo, *President*
Catherine Del Castillo, *Vice Pres*
EMP: 5 EST: 1985
SQ FT: 3,300
SALES (est): 482.6K Privately Held
WEB: www.pgcprinting.com
SIC: 2752 Commercial printing, offset

(G-9746)
PRISNA LATINO
7455 Nw 50th St (33166-5538)
PHONE....................................305 525-9292
Victor M Fernandez Jr, *President*
Victor M Fernandez Sr, *Vice Pres*
Sofia Fernandez, *Admin Sec*
EMP: 5 EST: 2009
SQ FT: 1,700
SALES (est): 800K Privately Held
SIC: 2732 Book printing

(G-9747)
PRO FUSE
11231 Nw 20th St (33172-1856)
PHONE....................................305 982-8457
Jonathan Borges, *Principal*
EMP: 8 EST: 2016
SALES (est): 158.8K Privately Held
SIC: 3679 Electronic components

(G-9748)
**PROANDRE HYGIENE SYSTEMS
INC**
1200 Brickell Ave # 1950 (33131-3214)
PHONE....................................305 433-3493
Enrique Cerezalez, *President*
▲ EMP: 17 EST: 2007
SALES (est): 721.3K
SALES (corp-wide): 1.2MM Privately
Held
SIC: 3089 Tops: dispenser, shaker, etc.:
plastic
PA: Proandre Sl
Calle Conestable De Portugal, 43 - 45
3
Granollers 08402
938 600-341

(G-9749)
PRODUCTIV ELEMENTS LLC
8815 Sw 96th St (33176-2927)
PHONE....................................305 283-4790
Carmen Algeciras, *Principal*
EMP: 7 EST: 2014
SALES (est): 229.9K Privately Held
SIC: 2819 Industrial inorganic chemicals

(G-9750)
PROFESSIONAL BINDERY INC
3668 Nw 48th Ter (33142-3924)
PHONE....................................305 633-3761
Fax: 305 633-3762
EMP: 12
SQ FT: 4,500
SALES (est): 670K Privately Held
SIC: 2789 Bookbinding And Related Work

(G-9751)
PROFESSIONAL SIGNS
6460 Sw 35th St (33155-3960)
PHONE....................................305 662-5957
Maria J Bertot, *Principal*
EMP: 5 EST: 1997
SALES (est): 391.5K Privately Held
WEB: www.kingsignsmiami.com
SIC: 3993 Signs & advertising specialties

(G-9752)
PROMOITALIA LLC
1221 Brickell Ave (33131-3224)
PHONE....................................305 347-5178
Valerio Matano,
EMP: 10 EST: 2018
SALES (est): 388.8K Privately Held
WEB: us.webpromoitalia.com
SIC: 2844 Cosmetic preparations

(G-9753)
PROPGLIDE USA CORP
4769 Nw 72nd Ave (33166-5616)
PHONE....................................305 520-0150
Rola Zaki, *Vice Pres*
Jason Revie, *Director*
EMP: 5 EST: 2017
SALES (est): 378.8K Privately Held
WEB: www.propglide.com
SIC: 3714 Motor vehicle parts & acces-
sories

(G-9754)
PROSOLUS INC (HQ)
6701 Nw 7th St Ste 165 (33126-6032)
PHONE....................................305 514-0270
Alex Moreno, *CEO*
Juan Mantelle, *COO*
Rod L Hartwig, *Vice Pres*
David Houze, *Research*
Arturo Serrano-Batista, *Senior Mgr*
EMP: 9 EST: 2015
SALES (est): 4.9MM Privately Held
WEB: www.prosoluspharma.com
SIC: 2834 Pharmaceutical preparations

(G-9755)
PSB MIAMI CORP
Also Called: Print Signs and Banners
7406 Sw 48th St (33155-4415)
PHONE....................................786 870-4880
Norlan Rojas, *Principal*
Joel Rivera, *Production*
EMP: 7 EST: 2016
SALES (est): 297.6K Privately Held
WEB: www.psbmiami.com
SIC: 2752 Commercial printing, offset

(G-9756)
**PUBLISHERS DIRECT CHOICE
LLC**
1440 Sw 78th Ave (33144-5210)
PHONE....................................305 264-5998
Alvvaro Uribe, *Principal*
EMP: 7 EST: 2010
SALES (est): 244.2K Privately Held
WEB: www.publishersdirectchoice.com
SIC: 2741 Miscellaneous publishing

(G-9757)
PUMA MARBLE CO INC
5445 Nw 2nd Ave (33127-1794)
PHONE....................................305 758-6461
Theresa Puma, *President*
Robert Seitz, *Vice Pres*
Mary Seitz, *Vice Pres*
Maryellen Seitz, *Treasurer*
Melissa B Mestre, *Admin Sec*
◆ EMP: 15 EST: 1969
SQ FT: 1,500
SALES (est): 1.6MM Privately Held
WEB: www.pumamarble.com
SIC: 3281 1743 Marble, building: cut &
shaped; marble installation, interior

(G-9758)
PUPPET WORKSHOP INC
7040 Sw 47th St Fl 2 (33155-4647)
PHONE....................................305 666-2655
EMP: 30
SALES (corp-wide): 21.7MM Privately
Held
SIC: 3999 Mfg Puppets
PA: The Puppet Workshop Inc
295 E 10th Ct
Hialeah FL 33010
305 666-2655

(G-9759)
PUROVITE INC
7347 Sw 45th St (33155-4509)
PHONE....................................305 364-5727
Momin Dowlah, *President*
Tarif Gaffar, *Vice Pres*
EMP: 10 EST: 2016
SALES (est): 575.3K Privately Held
SIC: 2833 Medicinals & botanicals

(G-9760)
Q2 AEROSPACE LLC
1751 Nw 129th Ave Ste 115 (33182-2512)
PHONE....................................305 591-9469
Frank Chirino, *Manager*
Jewel Marshall, *Manager*
◆ EMP: 5 EST: 2007
SALES (est): 556.9K Privately Held
SIC: 3449 Miscellaneous metalwork

(G-9761)
QUALITY WOOD MACHINE INC
8410 Sw 33rd Ter (33155-3248)
PHONE....................................305 221-0218
Rogerio Pereira, *Director*
EMP: 7 EST: 2001
SALES (est): 175.3K Privately Held
SIC: 3599 Machine shop, jobbing & repair

(G-9762)
QUALITYSAT CORP
13355 Sw 135th Ave (33186-6268)
PHONE....................................305 232-4211
Ana M Obregon, *Principal*
EMP: 7 EST: 2008
SALES (est): 179K Privately Held
SIC: 3663 Satellites, communications

(G-9763)
QUANTUM ASSETS LLC
638 Nw 11th St (33136-2404)
PHONE....................................786 484-1187
Adam A Avhad, *Principal*
EMP: 7 EST: 2010
SALES (est): 144.8K Privately Held
SIC: 3572 Computer storage devices

(G-9764)
QUANTUM GROUP LLC (PA)
12769 Sw 146th Ln (33186-6356)
PHONE....................................305 926-1036
Carlos Ortega,
EMP: 7 EST: 2019
SALES (est): 446.6K Privately Held
SIC: 3572 Computer storage devices

(G-9765)
**QUANTUM SAFETY SERVICES
INC**
20280 Sw 190th St (33187-1871)
PHONE....................................786 420-0735
Javier Duran, *Principal*
EMP: 7 EST: 2016
SALES (est): 85.9K Privately Held
SIC: 3572 Computer storage devices

(G-9766)
**QUANTUM SERVICING
CORPORATION**
790 Nw 107th Ave Ste 400 (33172-3159)
PHONE....................................305 229-6675
EMP: 8 EST: 2019
SALES (est): 454K Privately Held
SIC: 3572 Computer storage devices

(G-9767)
QUANTURO PUBLISHING INC
Also Called: Quantoro Publishing
4141 Ne 2nd Ave Ste 202 (33137-3539)
PHONE....................................305 373-3700
EMP: 23

SALES: 300K Privately Held
SIC: 2721 Magazine Publisher

(G-9768)
**QUEEN B HAIR COLLECTION
LLC**
17111 Nw 10th Ct (33169-5240)
PHONE....................................954 393-2791
Reigna Booker, *President*
EMP: 10 EST: 2019
SALES (est): 565.4K Privately Held
SIC: 3999 Hair, dressing of, for the trade

(G-9769)
QUIRANTES ORTHOPEDICS INC
5840 W Flagler St (33144-3399)
PHONE....................................305 261-1382
Tulio Quirantes, *President*
EMP: 6 EST: 1983
SQ FT: 1,500
SALES (est): 663.5K Privately Held
WEB: www.quirantesortho.com
SIC: 3842 5999 Orthopedic appliances;
orthopedic & prosthesis applications

(G-9770)
R & R STONE INDUSTRIES INC
7941 Nw 67th St (33166-2694)
PHONE....................................888 999-4921
Ramos A Diego, *Principal*
▲ EMP: 5 EST: 2015
SALES (est): 461.9K Privately Held
WEB: www.rrstoneind.com
SIC: 3589 Shredders, industrial & commer-
cial

(G-9771)
R C R MANUFACTURING INC
9279 Sw 38th St (33165-4143)
PHONE....................................786 499-9245
Raidy Concepcion Gomez, *Principal*
EMP: 8 EST: 2016
SALES (est): 292.2K Privately Held
SIC: 3999 Manufacturing industries

(G-9772)
R M EQUIPMENT INC
6975 Nw 43rd St (33166-6844)
PHONE....................................305 477-9312
Ronald Martin, *President*
Todd Griffin, *Vice Pres*
EMP: 17 EST: 1972
SQ FT: 6,000
SALES (est): 1.2MM Privately Held
WEB: www.rm-equipment.com
SIC: 3484 Guns (firearms) or gun parts, 30
mm. & below

(G-9773)
R Y D ENTERPRISES INC
Also Called: Ryd Enterprises
20815 Ne 16th Ave Ste B7 (33179-2124)
PHONE....................................305 655-1045
Ronen Dagan, *President*
◆ EMP: 24 EST: 1991
SQ FT: 6,000
SALES (est): 425.4K Privately Held
WEB: www.rydembroidery.com
SIC: 2395 Embroidery products, except
schiffli machine

(G-9774)
**R&S INTRNATIONAL INV GROUP
LLC**
571 Nw 29th St (33127-3917)
PHONE....................................305 576-3000
Leonardo Roa, *President*
EMP: 10 EST: 2014
SALES (est): 375.6K Privately Held
SIC: 2326 2331 Work uniforms; medical &
hospital uniforms, men's; aprons, work,
except rubberized & plastic: men's; jack-
ets, overall & work; women's & misses'
blouses & shirts

(G-9775)
RACING SPIRIT LLC
241 Ne 61st St (33137-2126)
PHONE....................................305 373-6671
Gabriele Pedone,
EMP: 8 EST: 2012
SALES (est): 453.6K Privately Held
WEB: www.racingspirit.com
SIC: 3949 Sporting & athletic goods

GEOGRAPHIC

(G-9776)
RAINBOW EB BUENAVISTA
8554 Sw 8th St (33144-4053)
PHONE...............................305 982-8153
Ernesto Borges, *President*
EMP: 8 EST: 2010
SALES (est): 225.8K Privately Held
SIC: 3564 Air cleaning systems

(G-9777)
RALLY MANUFACTURING INC
7200 Corp Ctr Dr Ste 308 (33126)
PHONE...............................305 628-2886
Christian Iacovelli, *President*
David Kraus, *CFO*
Acacia Lopez, *Manager*
◆ EMP: 150 EST: 1980
SQ FT: 17,000
SALES (est): 22MM Privately Held
WEB: www.rallymfg.com
SIC: 3714 Motor vehicle parts & accessories

(G-9778)
RAM SALES LLC
Also Called: Ram Steel Framing
7400 Nw 37th Ave (33147-5816)
PHONE...............................844 726-6382
Andy Redmond, *CEO*
Ryan Smith, *Exec VP*
Roberto Colina, *Vice Pres*
Eduardo Gracia, *Mng Member*
Michael Barker,
◆ EMP: 80 EST: 2001
SQ FT: 105,000
SALES (est): 24MM Privately Held
WEB: www.ramsalellc.com
SIC: 3442 Window & door frames

(G-9779)
RAMPMASTER INC
11098 Biscayne Blvd # 401 (33161-7429)
P.O. Box 530176 (33153-0176)
PHONE...............................305 691-9090
Robert Davis, *President*
Ron Bowser, *Mfg Staff*
Hunt Davis, *Manager*
EMP: 14 EST: 1968
SQ FT: 35,000
SALES (est): 1.1MM Privately Held
WEB: www.rampsonline.com
SIC: 3448 3446 3537 3429 Ramps: prefabricated metal; ladders, for permanent installation: metal; industrial trucks & tractors; manufactured hardware (general)

(G-9780)
RAP SNACKS INC
150 Se 2nd Ave Ph 6 (33131-1516)
PHONE...............................305 926-9594
James Lindsay, *CEO*
Taylor McCain, *COO*
EMP: 8 EST: 2018
SALES (est): 25MM Privately Held
WEB: www.rapsnacks.net
SIC: 2096 Potato chips & similar snacks

(G-9781)
RAPTOR WEAR PRODUCTS USA INC
7842 Nw 71st St (33166-2344)
PHONE...............................786 972-0326
Robin Miller, *General Mgr*
EMP: 12 EST: 2013
SALES (est): 705.9K Privately Held
WEB: www.raptormining.com
SIC: 3599 Machine shop, jobbing & repair

(G-9782)
RASS FAST PALLET INC
4214 Nw 11th Pl (33127-2711)
PHONE...............................786 877-2854
Raquel Sebastian, *President*
EMP: 8 EST: 2006
SALES (est): 501.6K Privately Held
SIC: 2448 Pallets, wood

(G-9783)
RATIONAL EDISCOVERY LLC
35 Ne 40th St Fl 3 (33137-3502)
PHONE...............................518 489-3000
Marissa A Jorgensen, *Principal*
Bill Duker, *Marketing Staff*
Brent Popp, *Software Dev*
Robert Conley, *Director*

Stephanie Forman, *Director*
EMP: 8
SALES (est): 807.4K
SALES (corp-wide): 10MM Privately Held
WEB: www.rationalenterprise.com
SIC: 7372 Prepackaged software
PA: Rational Retention, Llc
2 Tower Pl Ste 13
Albany NY 12203
518 489-3000

(G-9784)
RAZIENT LLC
990 Biscayne Blvd Ste 503 (33132-1556)
PHONE...............................855 747-5911
EMP: 7
SALES (est): 430K Privately Held
SIC: 7372 Prepackaged Software Services

(G-9785)
RB HOME GOODS LLC
218 Nw 12th Ave Apt 801 (33128-2203)
PHONE...............................786 690-3008
Roberto Basso, *President*
EMP: 10 EST: 2020
SALES (est): 297.9K Privately Held
SIC: 2051 Bakery: wholesale or wholesale/retail combined

(G-9786)
RECON GROUP LLP
Also Called: Gotrg
20200 W Dixie Hwy # 1005 (33180-1926)
PHONE...............................855 874-8741
EMP: 16 EST: 2014
SALES (est): 1MM Privately Held
SIC: 7372 Prepackaged software

(G-9787)
REFLY OF MIAMI INC
7360 Nw 35th St (33122-1267)
PHONE...............................786 762-2748
Oscar Molina Jr, *President*
EMP: 10 EST: 1995
SQ FT: 11,000
SALES (est): 1.6MM Privately Held
SIC: 3572 3571 Computer storage devices; electronic computers

(G-9788)
REFRIGERATION PANELS INC
7215 Nw 36th Ave (33147-5876)
PHONE...............................305 836-6900
Juan Hernandez, *President*
Mercedes Hernandez, *Corp Secy*
▼ EMP: 18 EST: 1969
SQ FT: 30,000
SALES (est): 1.8MM Privately Held
WEB: www.refrigerationpanels.com
SIC: 3585 Refrigeration equipment, complete

(G-9789)
REFRIGRTION ENGNRED SYSTEMS IN
Also Called: Refrigeration Panels
7215 Nw 36th Ave (33147-5835)
PHONE...............................305 836-6900
Juan J Hernandez, *President*
Aurea Rodriguez, *Corp Secy*
Maria E Gestido, *Vice Pres*
Maggie Suarez, *Admin Asst*
◆ EMP: 45 EST: 1969
SQ FT: 30,000
SALES (est): 3.9MM Privately Held
SIC: 3585 Refrigeration equipment, complete

(G-9790)
RELA USA LLC
Also Called: Best Custom Tape
8398 Nw 70th St (33166-2623)
PHONE...............................786 656-5069
EMP: 8 EST: 2018
SALES (est): 1MM Privately Held
WEB: www.relabrand.com
SIC: 3572 Computer storage devices

(G-9791)
REMIOR INDUSTRIES INC
9165 Nw 96th St (33178-1407)
PHONE...............................305 883-8722
Lazaro Rolando Remior, *President*
Marta Remior, *Vice Pres*
Silvia Remior, *Vice Pres*

Epifeania Remior, *Treasurer*
Rolando Remior, *Shareholder*
EMP: 21 EST: 1975
SQ FT: 21,000
SALES (est): 4.7MM Privately Held
WEB: www.remiorindustries.com
SIC: 2431 3446 Staircases & stairs, wood; stair railings, wood; railings, bannisters, guards, etc.: made from metal pipe

(G-9792)
RENACER BROS LLC
18839 Biscayne Blvd # 150 (33180-3397)
PHONE...............................305 935-6777
Leonardo Ring, *Owner*
EMP: 6 EST: 2016
SALES (est): 403.5K Privately Held
SIC: 2024 Ice cream & frozen desserts

(G-9793)
RENCO USA INC
5959 Blue Lagoon Dr (33126-2039)
PHONE...............................321 637-1000
Kenneth A Smuts, *President*
Vedat Kalkuz, *CFO*
EMP: 12 EST: 2011
SALES (est): 261.6K Privately Held
WEB: www.rencousa.com
SIC: 3677 5065 Electronic transformers; transformers power supply, electronic type; coil windings, electronic; inductors, electronic; electronic tubes: receiving & transmitting or industrial; electronic parts; coils, electronic

(G-9794)
RENEWABLE FUELS GROUP LLC
15184 Sw 111th St (33196-2502)
PHONE...............................305 388-3028
Octavio B Castillo, *Principal*
EMP: 9 EST: 2008
SALES (est): 331.6K Privately Held
WEB: www.regi.com
SIC: 2869 Fuels

(G-9795)
REPLENISH INK INC
701 Brickell Ave Key Blvd (33131-2813)
P.O. Box 310070 (33231-0070)
PHONE...............................818 206-2424
Hector Erquiaga, *President*
▼ EMP: 5 EST: 2006
SQ FT: 1,300
SALES (est): 769.9K Privately Held
WEB: www.replenishink.com
SIC: 3955 5112 Print cartridges for laser & other computer printers; office supplies

(G-9796)
REPROGRAPHIC SERVICES INC
1036 Sw 8th St (33130-3602)
PHONE...............................305 859-8282
Alex Poysakhovich, *President*
Joe Pulik, *Vice Pres*
EMP: 10 EST: 2002
SQ FT: 3,000
SALES (est): 611.9K Privately Held
SIC: 2754 Job printing, gravure

(G-9797)
REPUBLIC DRILL/APT CORP (PA)
Also Called: Michigan Drill
7840 Nw 62nd St (33166-3539)
PHONE...............................305 592-7777
Cloys Arnett, *General Mgr*
Mark Linari, *General Mgr*
Marc Zeitlin, *Vice Pres*
Andrea Flores, *Purchasing*
Irene Garcia, *Purchasing*
▲ EMP: 80 EST: 1974
SQ FT: 40,000
SALES (est): 26MM Privately Held
WEB: www.michigandrill.com
SIC: 3541 Machine tools, metal cutting type

(G-9798)
RESOLUTE FP FLORIDA INC (HQ)
3301 Nw 107th St (33167-3714)
PHONE...............................800 562-2860
Jim Brown, *CEO*
Lester Martino, *Research*

Kim Orozco, *Manager*
EMP: 212 EST: 2014
SALES: 72.2MM
SALES (corp-wide): 2.8B Privately Held
SIC: 2621 Toilet tissue stock; absorbent paper
PA: Resolute Forest Products Inc
1010 Rue De La Gauchetiere O Bureau 400
Montreal QC H3B 2
514 875-2160

(G-9799)
RESOLUTE TISSUE LLC
Also Called: Atlas Tissue A Resolute Bus
3301 Nw 107th St (33167-3714)
PHONE...............................305 636-5741
Tim Loughrey, *Sales Staff*
Enrique Llorente, *Manager*
EMP: 14 EST: 2017
SALES (est): 1.6MM Privately Held
WEB: www.resolutetissue.com
SIC: 2621 Paper mills

(G-9800)
REYES CABINETS INSTALLATION
10311 Sw 45th St (33165-5611)
PHONE...............................305 216-1683
Angel Reyes, *President*
EMP: 7 EST: 2005
SALES (est): 145.7K Privately Held
SIC: 2434 Wood kitchen cabinets

(G-9801)
REYES GRANITE & MARBLE CORP
7905 Nw 60th St (33166-3410)
PHONE...............................305 599-7330
Pedro Reyes, *President*
EMP: 10 EST: 1994
SALES (est): 1.4MM Privately Held
WEB: www.reyesgranitemarble.com
SIC: 3281 1411 Granite, cut & shaped; statuary, marble; dimension stone

(G-9802)
REYES JEWELERS CORP
36 Ne 1st St Ste 734 (33132-2481)
PHONE...............................305 431-8303
Jonathan Reyes, *Principal*
EMP: 7 EST: 2014
SALES (est): 516K Privately Held
WEB: reyes-jewelers-corp.business.site
SIC: 3911 Jewelry, precious metal

(G-9803)
RFG CONSULTING SERVICES INC
801 Brickell Ave Ste 900 (33131-2979)
PHONE...............................786 498-2177
Jose G Guevara, *President*
EMP: 5 EST: 2011
SALES (est): 417.7K Privately Held
WEB: www.rfgconsultingservices.com
SIC: 3599 Machine & other job shop work

(G-9804)
RIBBON WHOLESALE CORP
219 Sw 21st Ct (33135-1712)
PHONE...............................786 457-0555
Luis Bravo, *Manager*
EMP: 7 EST: 2001
SALES (est): 201.9K Privately Held
WEB: www.jkmribbon.com
SIC: 3955 Ribbons, inked: typewriter, adding machine, register, etc.

(G-9805)
RICE MACHINERY SUPPLY CO INC
1130 Nw 163rd Dr (33169-5816)
PHONE...............................305 620-2274
Maria Dieguez, *President*
▲ EMP: 10 EST: 1990
SALES (est): 739.2K Privately Held
WEB: www.rimacusa.com
SIC: 3556 Food products machinery

(G-9806)
RIMA CARGO LLC
8375 Nw 68th St (33166-2663)
PHONE...............................305 477-8002
Ricardo Gutierrez, *Mng Member*
Maryori Berrueta, *Mng Member*

▼ EMP: 8 EST: 2009
SALES (est): 798.4K Privately Held
WEB: www.rimacargo.com
SIC: 2448 Cargo containers, wood & metal combination

(G-9807)
RINKER MATERIALS CORP
8800 Sw 177th Ave (33196-2904)
P.O. Box 960700 (33296-0700)
PHONE...................305 386-0078
Haim Pillosof, *Manager*
EMP: 12 EST: 2014
SALES (est): 325.6K Privately Held
WEB: www.rinkerpipe.com
SIC: 3273 Ready-mixed concrete

(G-9808)
RISING STONERS INC
3533 Jefferson St (33133-5632)
PHONE...................305 300-7851
Colin Brown, *Principal*
EMP: 8 EST: 2010
SALES (est): 137.8K Privately Held
SIC: 3281 Building stone products

(G-9809)
RIVAL ROOF TILE DELIVERY CORP
103 Sw 18th Ave Apt 7 (33135-2021)
PHONE...................786 251-2631
Maritza A Rivera, *President*
EMP: 7 EST: 2005
SALES (est): 189K Privately Held
SIC: 3272 Roofing tile & slabs, concrete

(G-9810)
RJ FORKLIFT SERVICES INC
8567 Coral Way (33155-2335)
PHONE...................786 539-6613
Jabier Alfonso Alba, *President*
EMP: 7 EST: 2012
SALES (est): 301.8K Privately Held
WEB: www.rjforkliftservices.com
SIC: 3537 Forklift trucks

(G-9811)
RM CUSTOM WOODCRAFT INC
10400 Nw 36th Ct (33147-1034)
PHONE...................786 355-7387
Ricardo Malaver, *President*
EMP: 8 EST: 2013
SALES (est): 178.6K Privately Held
SIC: 2511 Wood household furniture

(G-9812)
RME STUDIO INC
Also Called: Peixoto
7245 Ne 4th Ave Ste 102 (33138-5371)
PHONE...................305 409-0856
Rafael M Esquenazi, *Principal*
EMP: 7 EST: 2010
SALES (est): 230.2K Privately Held
SIC: 2369 Bathing suits & swimwear: girls', children's & infants'

(G-9813)
RMK MERRILL STEVENS PRPTS LLC
Also Called: Rmk Merrill-Stevens
881 Nw 13th Ave (33125-3713)
PHONE...................305 324-5211
John Spencer, *CEO*
Michael Rhyne, *Project Mgr*
Brent Allsop, *Opers Mgr*
Ibrahim Guldiken, *CFO*
Ybrahim Lopez, *Accounting Mgr*
EMP: 2 EST: 2013
SALES (est): 3.1MM Privately Held
WEB: www.rmkmerrill-stevens.com
SIC: 3731 3732 Shipbuilding & repairing; yachts, building & repairing

(G-9814)
ROBERTO VALVERDE
1929 Nw 22nd St (33142-7331)
PHONE...................305 324-5252
Roberto Valverde, *Principal*
EMP: 8 EST: 2006
SALES (est): 101.9K Privately Held
SIC: 3577 Printers & plotters

(G-9815)
ROCK INTL DISTRIBUTORS INC
8279 Nw 66th St (33166-2721)
PHONE...................305 513-3314
Maria C Ortiz, *President*
Amado L Ortiz, *Treasurer*
EMP: 35 EST: 2006
SALES (est): 2.4MM Privately Held
SIC: 3264 Porcelain electrical supplies

(G-9816)
ROCKERS STONE INC
3615 Plaza St (33133-6222)
PHONE...................305 447-1231
Josh Billig, *President*
Michelle McGonigal, *Admin Sec*
EMP: 6 EST: 1978
SALES (est): 481.8K Privately Held
WEB: www.rockersstone.com
SIC: 1411 Dimension stone

(G-9817)
RODES PRINTING CORP
8369 Bird Rd (33155-3353)
PHONE...................305 559-5263
Roberto Escobar, *President*
◆ EMP: 5 EST: 1984
SQ FT: 1,800
SALES (est): 492.8K Privately Held
SIC: 2752 Commercial printing, offset

(G-9818)
RODRIGUEZ WELDING
220 Nw 6th St (33130-2911)
PHONE...................305 856-3749
Gilberto Rodriguez, *Owner*
▲ EMP: 5 EST: 1975
SQ FT: 2,000
SALES (est): 321.6K Privately Held
SIC: 3599 7692 Machine & other job shop work; welding repair

(G-9819)
ROJA MED INC
168 Se 1st St Ste 403 (33131-1446)
PHONE...................305 381-5803
Rodney O Orton, *President*
Peter Wilcox,
EMP: 40 EST: 1984
SQ FT: 2,500
SALES (est): 12MM Privately Held
SIC: 2834 Vitamin preparations

(G-9820)
ROLLING DOOR PARTS INC
8187 Nw 71st St (33166-2341)
PHONE...................305 888-5020
Vincent Giatonia, *President*
◆ EMP: 5 EST: 1997
SALES (est): 837K Privately Held
WEB: www.rollingdoorparts.com
SIC: 3442 Rolling doors for industrial buildings or warehouses, metal

(G-9821)
ROMA CASTING INC
14 Ne 1st Ave Ste 306 (33132-2404)
PHONE...................305 577-0289
Luis Reyes, *President*
EMP: 7 EST: 1983
SQ FT: 1,700
SALES (est): 750K Privately Held
WEB: roma-casting-inc-fl.hub.biz
SIC: 3915 3911 Jewelers' castings; jewelry, precious metal

(G-9822)
ROMANO GROUP LLC
12253 Sw 130th St (33186-6218)
PHONE...................305 255-4242
Ricardo Romano, *Principal*
Ricardo Robaina, *Manager*
▲ EMP: 18 EST: 2011
SALES (est): 1.3MM Privately Held
WEB: www.romanogrp.com
SIC: 2844 Cosmetic preparations

(G-9823)
RON MATUSALEM & MATUSA FLA INC
Also Called: Matusalem & Company
1205 Sw 37th Ave Ste 300 (33135-4226)
PHONE...................305 448-8255
Claudio Alvarez MD, *President*
EMP: 13 EST: 1961

SALES (est): 880.9K Privately Held
SIC: 2085 Rum (alcoholic beverage)

(G-9824)
RONNIE & MOES ITALIAN ICE LLC
7900 Nw 27th Ave Ste 602a (33147-4911)
P.O. Box 813124, Hollywood (33081-3124)
PHONE...................786 970-1805
Ronnie Melton, *Principal*
EMP: 6 EST: 2016
SALES (est): 328.9K Privately Held
SIC: 2024 5812 Ice cream & frozen desserts; eating places

(G-9825)
ROQUE BROTHERS CORP
5646 Nw 35th Ct (33142-2730)
PHONE...................305 885-6995
Roberto F Roque Sr, *President*
Marina Roque, *Corp Secy*
Raul Roque, *Vice Pres*
Roberto A Roque Jr, *Vice Pres*
EMP: 25 EST: 1972
SQ FT: 30,000
SALES (est): 526.4K Privately Held
SIC: 2521 Wood office furniture

(G-9826)
RQ WELDING INC
6011 Sw 109th Ave (33173-1246)
PHONE...................786 609-3384
Roger Quesada, *President*
EMP: 7 EST: 2015
SALES (est): 155.6K Privately Held
WEB: www.rqweldinginc.com
SIC: 3315 3312 Fence gates posts & fittings: steel; rails, steel or iron

(G-9827)
RUBBER 2 GO LLC
Also Called: Leader Mulch
3551 Nw 116th St (33167-2923)
PHONE...................305 688-8566
Alfredo Reviati, *Mng Member*
EMP: 8 EST: 2013
SALES (est): 1.6MM Privately Held
SIC: 3069 Medical & laboratory rubber sundries & related products

(G-9828)
RUDYS READY MIX
5800 Sw 122nd Ave (33183-1510)
PHONE...................305 382-9283
Rudy Delamora, *Owner*
EMP: 5 EST: 1994
SALES (est): 523.3K Privately Held
WEB: www.concrete-readymix.com
SIC: 3273 Ready-mixed concrete

(G-9829)
RUNN-IT LLC ✪
66 W Flagler St Ste 900 (33130-1807)
PHONE...................800 932-8052
John Dieurestil,
EMP: 9 EST: 2021
SALES (est): 250K Privately Held
SIC: 3537 Trucks: freight, baggage, etc.: industrial, except mining

(G-9830)
RXGENESYS LLC
175 Nw 7th St Ste 2417 (33130-2966)
PHONE...................786 220-8366
Kirsty Barany, *Mng Member*
EMP: 5 EST: 2015
SALES (est): 500K Privately Held
WEB: www.rxgenesys.com
SIC: 2844 Cosmetic preparations

(G-9831)
S & B INDUSTRIES INC
11052 Sw 162nd Ter (33157-2845)
PHONE...................305 367-1068
Scott Lyn, *Principal*
EMP: 7 EST: 2010
SALES (est): 81.8K Privately Held
SIC: 3999 Manufacturing industries

(G-9832)
S PRINTING INC
2207 Nw 23rd Ave (33142-7355)
PHONE...................305 633-3343
Ofelia Fern, *President*
▼ EMP: 5 EST: 1970

SQ FT: 12,000
SALES (est): 703.8K Privately Held
WEB: s-printing-miami.business.site
SIC: 2752 2791 Commercial printing, offset; typesetting

(G-9833)
S3 INDUSTRIES INC
4160 Sw 99th Ave (33165-5139)
PHONE...................305 498-8364
Joseph Sankows, *Principal*
EMP: 7 EST: 2018
SALES (est): 91.1K Privately Held
WEB: www.s3industriesinc.com
SIC: 3999 Manufacturing industries

(G-9834)
SACYR ENVIRONMENT USA LLC
3191 Coral Way Ste 510 (33145-3227)
PHONE...................202 361-4568
Brian Kirby, *General Mgr*
Laurenia Augustin, *Director*
EMP: 13 EST: 2014
SALES (est): 2.2MM
SALES (corp-wide): 90MM Privately Held
SIC: 3822 Auto controls regulating residntl & coml environmt & applncs
HQ: Valoriza Servicios Medioambientales Sa
Calle Condesa De Venadito 7
Madrid 28027
915 455-000

(G-9835)
SAFEGUARD AMERICA INC (PA)
3935 Nw 26th St (33142-6727)
PHONE...................305 859-9000
Steven Masdeu, *President*
EMP: 11 EST: 1998
SALES (est): 3.1MM Privately Held
WEB: www.americastransportation.com
SIC: 3699 Security devices; security control equipment & systems

(G-9836)
SAFEPRINTS LLC
9155 S Dadeland Blvd # 1504 (33156-2737)
PHONE...................305 960-7391
Luis A Rojas, *President*
EMP: 6 EST: 2012
SALES (est): 426.7K Privately Held
WEB: www.safeprints.com
SIC: 2759 Flexographic printing

(G-9837)
SAFILO USA INC
703 Nw 62nd Ave Ste 100 (33126-4686)
PHONE...................305 262-5727
Ana Crola, *Manager*
Loredana Galli, *Manager*
Ana Fleitas,
Lidia Autuori, *Regional*
EMP: 91
SALES (corp-wide): 1.2MM Privately Held
WEB: www.safilogroup.com
SIC: 3229 Optical glass
HQ: Safilo Usa, Inc.
300 Lighting Way Fl 4
Secaucus NJ 07094
973 952-2800

(G-9838)
SAINT GEORGE INDUSTRIES LLC
9130 S Dadelnd Blvd 180 (33156)
PHONE...................786 212-1176
Patrick Stallings,
Karan Cerutti,
EMP: 25 EST: 2012
SQ FT: 7,988
SALES (est): 2.2MM Privately Held
WEB: www.stgeorgeindustries.com
SIC: 2326 2339 2396 Work apparel, except uniforms; service apparel, washable: women's; linings, apparel: made from purchased materials

(G-9839)
SAL AEROSPACE ENGINEERING LLC
11990 Sw 128th St (33186-5207)
PHONE...................305 791-0593
Michael Salomon, *President*

GEOGRAPHIC

Jonathan Martinez, *Purchasing*
Joel Navarro, *Engineer*
EMP: 10 **EST:** 2010
SQ FT: 4,500
SALES (est): 2MM **Privately Held**
WEB: www.salaerospace.com
SIC: 3728 Aircraft parts & equipment

(G-9840)
SALSA TROPICAL LLC
15110 Sw 56th St (33185-4182)
PHONE................................786 362-9034
Meikel M Betancourt, *Principal*
EMP: 7 **EST:** 2013
SALES (est): 338.7K **Privately Held**
SIC: 2099 Dips, except cheese & sour
  cream based

(G-9841)
SALTEX GROUP CORP
7509 Nw 36th St (33166-6708)
PHONE................................305 477-3187
Mauricio Salmon, *President*
Nicholas Salmon, *Project Mgr*
Liliam De Armas, *Accounts Mgr*
Gladys Yera, *Sales Staff*
Giovanny Vanegas, *Marketing Staff*
EMP: 8 **EST:** 1997
SALES (est): 2.4MM **Privately Held**
WEB: www.saltexgroup.com
SIC: 3699 Security control equipment &
  systems

(G-9842)
SAMEDAY PRINTING INC
6815 Biscayne Blvd (33138-6292)
PHONE................................800 411-3106
Kevin Henao, *President*
▼ **EMP:** 6 **EST:** 2011
SALES (est): 619.7K **Privately Held**
WEB: www.samedayprinting.com
SIC: 2752 Commercial printing, offset

(G-9843)
SAMSON & SURREY LLC
8950 Sw 74th Ct Ste 1909 (33156-3178)
PHONE................................305 902-3336
Robert Furniss Roe, *CEO*
Juan Rovira, *COO*
EMP: 12 **EST:** 2014
SALES (est): 515.5K
SALES (corp-wide): 195.5MM **Privately
Held**
WEB: www.samsonandsurrey.com
SIC: 2085 Bourbon whiskey
PA: Heaven Hill Distilleries, Inc.
  1064 Loretto Rd
  Bardstown KY 40004
  502 348-3921

(G-9844)
SANIFLOW CORPORATION
3325 Nw 70th Ave (33122-1332)
PHONE................................305 424-2433
Luis Sau, *President*
David Ruiz, *Vice Pres*
Anais Blanco, *Marketing Staff*
▲ **EMP:** 5 **EST:** 2004
SQ FT: 3,000
SALES (est): 704K **Privately Held**
WEB: www.saniflowcorp.com
SIC: 3634 Dryers, electric: hand & face

(G-9845)
**SANTILLANA USA PUBG CO INC
(DH)**
8333 Nw 53rd St Ste 402 (33166-4787)
PHONE................................305 591-9522
Miguel Tapia, *CEO*
Marta Moldes, *COO*
Stephen Marban, *Vice Pres*
Hector Miralles, *CFO*
Efrain Santa, *CFO*
▲ **EMP:** 28 **EST:** 1972
SALES (est): 16.2MM
SALES (corp-wide): 120.1MM **Privately
Held**
WEB: www.santillanausa.com
SIC: 2731 Books: publishing only
HQ: Grupo Santillana Educacion Global Slu
  Calle Gran Via 32
  Madrid 28013
  917 449-060

(G-9846)
SANZAY CORPORATION
Also Called: Integrated Diagnostics Group
1080 Nw 163rd Dr (33169-5818)
PHONE................................305 826-9886
Maria R Sanchez, *President*
Franciso J Perez, *COO*
▲ **EMP:** 15 **EST:** 2005
SALES (est): 2.1MM **Privately Held**
WEB: www.idgone.com
SIC: 2835 8071 In vitro & in vivo diagnos-
  tic substances; medical laboratories; test-
  ing laboratories

(G-9847)
SAPORE DI VINO INC
6905 Nw 51st St (33166-5627)
PHONE................................561 818-8411
Medici Francesco, *President*
EMP: 9 **EST:** 2018
SALES (est): 450.2K **Privately Held**
WEB: www.saporedicasamiami.com
SIC: 2084 Wines

(G-9848)
SAS USA INC
6801 Nw 77th Ave Ste 302 (33166-2848)
PHONE................................305 428-0200
Adria Gimeno, *Principal*
◆ **EMP:** 8 **EST:** 2014
SALES (est): 97.4K **Privately Held**
SIC: 7372 Application computer software

(G-9849)
SATHYAM PUBLICATIONS INC
400 Sw 107th Ave (33174-1434)
PHONE................................562 667-6622
Issac Vadavana, *President*
EMP: 10
SALES (est): 546.9K **Privately Held**
SIC: 2711 Newspapers, publishing & print-
  ing

(G-9850)
SATIN SENSATION CO
16657 Sw 79th Ter (33193-5776)
PHONE................................786 290-4114
Di Paolo Juan, *Principal*
EMP: 8 **EST:** 2013
SALES (est): 91.5K **Privately Held**
WEB: www.satinsensationpr.com
SIC: 2221 Satins

(G-9851)
SAVING FOR COLLEGE LLC
444 Brickell Ave Ste 820 (33131-2407)
PHONE................................954 770-5136
Marcos Cordero, *CEO*
Marc Suhr, *Manager*
EMP: 12 **EST:** 2012
SQ FT: 1,700
SALES (est): 1MM **Privately Held**
WEB: www.savingforcollege.com
SIC: 2741

(G-9852)
SC PARENT CORPORATION
1450 Brickell Ave Fl 31 (33131-3460)
PHONE................................703 351-0200
Matthew Small, *CEO*
Keval Patel, *Ch of Bd*
Justin Tan, *COO*
Ryan Geary, *Vice Pres*
Ryan Kaplan, *Vice Pres*
EMP: 99
SQ FT: 15,000
SALES (est): 2.2MM **Privately Held**
SIC: 7372 7371 Application computer soft-
  ware; computer software development &
  applications

(G-9853)
SC PURCHASER CORPORATION
1450 Brickell Ave Fl 31 (33131-3460)
PHONE................................703 351-0200
Matthew Small, *CEO*
Keval Patel, *Ch of Bd*
Justin Tan, *COO*
Ryan Geary, *Vice Pres*
Ryan Kaplan, *Vice Pres*
EMP: 99
SQ FT: 15,000
SALES (est): 2.4MM **Privately Held**
SIC: 7372 7371 Application computer soft-
  ware; computer software development &
  applications

(G-9854)
SCANID INC
444 Brickell Ave (33131-2403)
PHONE................................305 607-3523
Nicolas Nicolaou, *CEO*
EMP: 5 **EST:** 2017
SALES (est): 500K **Privately Held**
SIC: 7372 Prepackaged software

(G-9855)
SCHICK LLC
20417 Ne 15th Ct (33179-2708)
PHONE................................718 810-3804
EMP: 9 **EST:** 2011
SALES (est): 183.1K **Privately Held**
WEB: www.schick.com
SIC: 3944 Games, toys & children's vehi-
  cles

(G-9856)
**SCHNUPP MANUFACTURING CO
INC**
2113 Nw 17th Ave (33142-7477)
PHONE................................305 325-0520
Leo E Schnupp Jr, *President*
◆ **EMP:** 6 **EST:** 1948
SQ FT: 5,000
SALES (est): 560.1K **Privately Held**
WEB: www.schnuppumbrellas.com
SIC: 3999 2394 Garden umbrellas; can-
  vas & related products

(G-9857)
SCOPE WORKER LLC
2121 Nw 2nd Ave Ste 203 (33127-4830)
PHONE................................917 855-5379
Justin Duval, *CEO*
Michael Freid, *Manager*
Joshua Mangerson,
John Rafferty,
Sean Yazbeck,
EMP: 20 **EST:** 2017
SALES (est): 1.4MM **Privately Held**
WEB: www.scopeworker.com
SIC: 7372 Prepackaged software

(G-9858)
SCOTT SLIDE FASTENERS INC
Also Called: Notions
545 Nw 26th St (33127-4367)
PHONE................................305 576-3328
Maria Srebnick, *President*
Ben Horstein, *Vice Pres*
Rene Gutierrez, *Controller*
Ivette Barros, *Technology*
EMP: 8 **EST:** 1966
SQ FT: 10,000
SALES (est): 163.6K **Privately Held**
SIC: 3965 5072 Fasteners, buttons, nee-
  dles & pins; miscellaneous fasteners

(G-9859)
SEA SITE INC
1180 Nw 163rd Dr (33169-5816)
PHONE................................305 403-3002
Murray Ginsberg, *Principal*
EMP: 9 **EST:** 2010
SALES (est): 102.9K **Privately Held**
SIC: 3479 Etching & engraving

(G-9860)
**SEAL-TITE PLASTIC PACKG CO
INC**
4655 Sw 74th Ave (33155-4411)
P.O. Box 558748 (33255-8748)
PHONE................................305 264-9015
James B Black Jr, *President*
Sheri Jude, *Controller*
▼ **EMP:** 90 **EST:** 1962
SQ FT: 20,000
SALES (est): 20.4MM **Privately Held**
WEB: www.seal-tite.us
SIC: 2673 3083 3081 Food storage &
  frozen food bags, plastic; laminated plas-
  tics plate & sheet; unsupported plastics
  film & sheet

(G-9861)
SEAQUEST MARINE LLC
777 Brickell Ave (33131-2809)
PHONE................................781 888-8850
Antonios Sikolas,
EMP: 4 **EST:** 2018

SALES (est): 3.5MM **Privately Held**
WEB: www.seaquest.co
SIC: 3731 Shipbuilding & repairing

(G-9862)
SEAT SAVERS PLUS INC
Also Called: Supreme Seat Covers
12105 Sw 129th Ct Bay 10 (33186-6845)
PHONE................................305 256-7863
Juan Alfonso, *President*
Carmen Alfonso, *Vice Pres*
EMP: 6 **EST:** 1994
SALES (est): 704.5K **Privately Held**
WEB: www.seatsavers.com
SIC: 2399 Seat covers, automobile

(G-9863)
SECURITY TECH GROUP INC
Also Called: Home Protection Team
9425 Sw 72nd St Ste 100 (33173-3295)
P.O. Box 560243 (33256-0243)
PHONE................................305 631-2228
Sandra Di Mara, *President*
EMP: 7 **EST:** 2011
SALES (est): 833.9K **Privately Held**
WEB: www.securitytechfl.com
SIC: 3669 Burglar alarm apparatus, elec-
  tric

(G-9864)
**SELLINK AVIATION FUEL DIV
LLC**
Also Called: Sellinkafs
4019 Nw 28th St (33142-5611)
PHONE................................305 336-6627
EMP: 8
SALES (est): 783.9K **Privately Held**
SIC: 2911 Petroleum Refiner

(G-9865)
**SEMINOLE PAPER & PRINTING
CO**
60 Nw 3rd St (33128)
PHONE................................305 379-8481
Sidney Goldston, *President*
EMP: 8 **EST:** 1953
SQ FT: 10,000
SALES (est): 113.1K **Privately Held**
SIC: 2752 Commercial printing, offset

(G-9866)
SENDA DE VIDA PUBLISHERS
14320 Sw 143rd Ct # 705 (33186-7612)
P.O. Box 559055 (33255-9055)
PHONE................................305 262-2627
Marco Calderon, *President*
▼ **EMP:** 31 **EST:** 1997
SALES (est): 3.7MM **Privately Held**
WEB: www.sendadevida.us
SIC: 2731 Books: publishing only

(G-9867)
SENIORS VENT MGMT INC
6100 Blue Lagoon Dr # 110 (33126-7036)
PHONE................................305 266-0988
Felix Martin, *Principal*
EMP: 5 **EST:** 2010
SALES (est): 365.1K **Privately Held**
SIC: 7372 Prepackaged software

(G-9868)
SEPAC CORP
5201 Blue Lagoon Dr (33126-2064)
PHONE................................305 718-3379
Louis Lechevalier, *President*
Silvia Lechevalier, *Vice Pres*
Fernando Barilari, *VP Sales*
EMP: 14 **EST:** 2010
SALES (est): 503.7K **Privately Held**
WEB: www.sepaccorp.com
SIC: 3674 3625 4911 3629 Semiconduc-
  tors & related devices; relays & industrial
  controls; ; electronic generation equip-
  ment; measuring & controlling devices; in-
  dustrial process control instruments

(G-9869)
SERGIOS PRINTING INC
14265 Sw 140th St (33186-6760)
PHONE................................305 971-4112
Sergio Fernandez, *President*
Miriam Fernandez, *Vice Pres*
EMP: 10 **EST:** 1998

SALES (est): 1.5MM **Privately Held**
WEB: www.sergiosprinting.com
SIC: **2791** 2752 Typesetting; commercial
printing, lithographic

(G-9870)
SERIES USA LLC
20900 Ne 30th Ave Ste 901 (33180-2166)
PHONE...................................305 932-4626
Maria Breton, *Accounting Mgr*
Roberto Gomez, *Manager*
EMP: 9 EST: 2008
SALES (est): 661.4K **Privately Held**
WEB: www.seriesusa.net
SIC: **2531** School furniture

(G-9871)
SET MACHINE INC
6630 Sw 45th St (33155-5927)
PHONE...................................786 488-9788
Gabriela Soto, *Principal*
EMP: 8 EST: 2018
SALES (est): 254.4K **Privately Held**
WEB: www.miamimachine.com
SIC: **3599** Machine shop, jobbing & repair

(G-9872)
SEYER - TECH INDUSTRIES INC
1420 Sw 152nd Pl (33194-2663)
PHONE...................................305 233-2672
Adrian Reyes, *Principal*
▲ EMP: 9 EST: 2010
SALES (est): 157.1K **Privately Held**
WEB: www.seyer-tech.com
SIC: **3999** Manufacturing industries

(G-9873)
SG GLOBAL LLC (PA)
Also Called: Velgen Wheels
12120 Sw 105th Ter (33186-3808)
PHONE...................................305 726-3439
Scott Gibson, *Mng Member*
EMP: 2 EST: 2013
SQ FT: 4,000
SALES (est): 3MM **Privately Held**
SIC: **3312** Wheels

(G-9874)
SGS US EAST COAST LLC
Also Called: Miami Diver
12062 Nw 27th Ave (33167-2651)
PHONE...................................305 571-9700
Thomas Zels, *CEO*
Paul Peters, *President*
◆ EMP: 35 EST: 1981
SALES (est): 5MM **Privately Held**
SIC: **3731** Shipbuilding & repairing

(G-9875)
**SH SHOWER & TUB
ENCLOSURES LLC**
4101 Sw 74th Ct (33155-4423)
PHONE...................................786 229-2529
Manuel Monteagudo, *Manager*
EMP: 7 EST: 2017
SALES (est): 150K **Privately Held**
SIC: **3088** Plastics plumbing fixtures

(G-9876)
SHADES BY ANA INC
12240 Sw 128th St (33186-5419)
PHONE...................................305 238-4858
Ana Lerin, *President*
EMP: 6
SALES (est): 495.8K **Privately Held**
WEB: www.shadesbyana.com
SIC: **2391** Draperies, plastic & textile: from
purchased materials

(G-9877)
SHANTUI AMERICA CORP
5201 Nw 77th Ave Ste 600 (33166-4838)
PHONE...................................786 491-9114
Zhi Zhu, *President*
WEI Cheng, *Vice Pres*
EMP: 18 EST: 2015
SALES (est): 4.6MM
SALES (corp-wide): 52.3B **Privately Held**
WEB: en.shantui.com
SIC: **3531** Construction machinery
HQ: Shandong Shantui Machinery Co., Ltd.
No.6, Jiejia Road, High-Tech Zone
Jining 27210

(G-9878)
SHEILA SHINE INC
Also Called: Pan American Chemical Co.
1201 Nw 1st Pl (33136-2609)
P.O. Box 4784, Hialeah (33014-0784)
PHONE...................................305 557-1729
William Wallach, *President*
James G Wallach, *Principal*
David J Wallach, *Principal*
Rita Wallach, *Vice Pres*
▼ EMP: 29 EST: 1961
SQ FT: 26,000
SALES (est): 6.8MM **Privately Held**
WEB: www.sheilashineinc.com
SIC: **2842** 3291 Cleaning or polishing
preparations; abrasive products

(G-9879)
SHELL AEROSPACE LLC
7500 Nw 25th St Unit 1a (33122-1729)
PHONE...................................786 400-2660
Carlos A Suito, *Mng Member*
EMP: 8 EST: 2017
SALES (est): 703K **Privately Held**
SIC: **3369** Aerospace castings, nonferrous:
except aluminum

(G-9880)
SHELLEYS CUSHIONS MFG INC
Also Called: Shelleys Cshions Umbrellas Mfg
3640 Nw 52nd St (33142-3245)
PHONE...................................305 633-1790
Raul M Mollera, *President*
Aracelia Mollera, *Vice Pres*
EMP: 33 EST: 1973
SALES (est): 1MM **Privately Held**
SIC: **3999** 2393 Garden umbrellas; cush-
ions, except spring & carpet: purchased
materials

(G-9881)
**SHERRY MANUFACTURING CO
INC**
3287 Nw 65th St (33147-7590)
PHONE...................................305 693-7000
Quentin H Sandler, *Ch of Bd*
Scott Coltune, *President*
Sherry Zimand, *Vice Pres*
Jayne Walker, *Executive*
◆ EMP: 150 EST: 1948
SQ FT: 220,000
SALES (est): 25.4MM **Privately Held**
WEB: www.sherrymfg.com
SIC: **2261** Screen printing of cotton broad-
woven fabrics

(G-9882)
**SHISEIDO AMERICAS
CORPORATION**
1221 Brickell Ave Fl 26 (33131-3224)
PHONE...................................305 416-6021
Michael Gebrael, *Manager*
EMP: 10 **Privately Held**
WEB: jobs.shiseidoamericas.com
SIC: **2844** 5122 Cosmetic preparations;
toilet preparations; cosmetics; toilet
preparations
HQ: Shiseido Americas Corporation
390 Madison Ave
New York NY 10017
212 805-2300

(G-9883)
SHORES GLOBAL LLC
2440 Nw 116th St Ste 600 (33167-0009)
PHONE...................................305 716-0848
Justin King, *Vice Pres*
Antonia Eggers, *Project Mgr*
Karina Baban, *Purch Mgr*
Jose Cordero, *Manager*
William Schuitema, *Manager*
EMP: 9 EST: 2016
SALES (est): 3.3MM **Privately Held**
WEB: www.shoresglobal.co
SIC: **2512** 5021 Upholstered household
furniture; furniture

(G-9884)
**SIGN DEVELOPMENT
CORPORATION**
Also Called: Fastsigns
8240 W Flagler St (33144-2028)
PHONE...................................305 227-6250
Burt Poppeliers, *President*
Arthur Zalduondo, *Corp Secy*

EMP: 8 EST: 1990
SQ FT: 900
SALES (est): 780.9K **Privately Held**
WEB: www.fastsigns.com
SIC: **3993** Signs & advertising specialties

(G-9885)
SIGN ROCKERS LLC
12485 Sw 137th Ave # 206 (33186-4216)
PHONE...................................866 212-9697
Carlos Bethencourt,
EMP: 20 EST: 2017
SALES (est): 116K **Privately Held**
WEB: www.signrockers.com
SIC: **3993** Signs & advertising specialties

(G-9886)
SIGN SAVERS CORP (PA)
12385 Sw 129th Ct Ste 1 (33186-6407)
PHONE...................................305 909-9967
Gabriel Barker, *President*
Roberto Arreaza, *Prdtn Mgr*
EMP: 7 EST: 2012
SALES (est): 761.4K **Privately Held**
WEB: www.thesignsavers.com
SIC: **3993** Signs & advertising specialties

(G-9887)
SIGN SPACE
2365 Nw 70th Ave (33122-1819)
PHONE...................................786 360-2670
Adrian Gonzalez, *President*
EMP: 8 EST: 2017
SALES (est): 471.6K **Privately Held**
WEB: www.thesignspace.com
SIC: **3993** Signs & advertising specialties

(G-9888)
SIGNS 2 U INC
Also Called: Fastsigns
8240 W Flagler St (33144-2028)
PHONE...................................305 227-6250
Walter Prio, *President*
EMP: 8 EST: 2013
SALES (est): 766.2K **Privately Held**
WEB: www.signs2uboise.com
SIC: **3993** Signs & advertising specialties

(G-9889)
SIGNS CONNECTION INC
600 Ne 36th St Apt 807 (33137-3933)
PHONE...................................305 978-5777
Armando Santacruz, *Principal*
EMP: 7 EST: 2008
SALES (est): 307.4K **Privately Held**
WEB: www.signsconnection.com
SIC: **3993** Signs & advertising specialties

(G-9890)
SIGNS FOR YOU INC
7495 Nw 48th St (33166-5501)
PHONE...................................305 635-6662
Anthony Yazbek, *President*
Constantine Stavro, *Vice Pres*
Haroutiun Jlinkrian, *Prdtn Mgr*
▼ EMP: 22 EST: 1997
SALES (est): 2.3MM **Privately Held**
WEB: www.signsforyou.com
SIC: **3993** Electric signs

(G-9891)
**SIGNS INTERNATIONAL DISTR
CORP**
Also Called: Sid Signs
8461 Nw 61st St (33166-3307)
PHONE...................................305 715-0017
Antonio De Fonseca Nadais, *President*
Sidney T Dos Santos, *Director*
◆ EMP: 5 EST: 2006
SALES (est): 986.3K **Privately Held**
WEB: www.signsfy.com
SIC: **3993** Signs & advertising specialties

(G-9892)
SILENT GIANT PUBLISHING CO
20009 Ne 6th Court Cir (33179-2408)
PHONE...................................305 725-7911
Leroy Hutson, *Owner*
G Eubanks, *Vice Pres*
EMP: 7 EST: 2015
SALES (est): 88.9K **Privately Held**
SIC: **2741** Miscellaneous publishing

(G-9893)
SILVERLINE FURNITURE CORP
15940 Sw 60th St (33193-5810)
PHONE...................................305 663-9560
Roger Silverio, *President*
Regina Morais, *Controller*
▲ EMP: 8 EST: 2000
SQ FT: 7,500
SALES (est): 569.9K **Privately Held**
SIC: **2511** Wood household furniture

(G-9894)
SIMKINS INDUSTRIES INC
5080 Biscayne Blvd Ste A (33137-3218)
PHONE...................................305 899-8184
David Simkins, *CEO*
Barbara P Camera, *Corp Secy*
Anthony Battaglia, *CFO*
Tony Battaglia, *CFO*
Ronald Simkins, *Director*
▲ EMP: 50 EST: 1901
SALES (est): 5.5MM **Privately Held**
WEB: www.simkinsindustries.com
SIC: **2652** Setup paperboard boxes

(G-9895)
SIMONS HALLANDALE INC
850 Ives Dairy Rd Ste T9 (33179-2412)
PHONE...................................561 468-1174
Dani Shimon, *President*
Ilan Shimon, *Vice Pres*
EMP: 50 EST: 2013
SALES (est): 4.3MM **Privately Held**
SIC: **3949** 5651 Sporting & athletic goods;
family clothing stores

(G-9896)
SIMPLESHOW USA CORP
7300 Biscayne Blvd # 100 (33138-5135)
PHONE...................................844 468-5447
Susanne Schmidt, *President*
Daniel Pichardo, *Project Mgr*
Monica Pimienta, *Project Mgr*
Elizabeth Yanez, *Opers Mgr*
Rachel Barash, *Sales Mgr*
EMP: 22 EST: 2014
SALES (est): 2.5MM **Privately Held**
WEB: www.simpleshow.com
SIC: **2741** 7373 ; computer integrated
systems design

(G-9897)
SINDONI NORTH AMERICA LLC
2665 S Bayshore Dr (33133-5448)
PHONE...................................786 536-9171
Jorge Arias,
EMP: 5 EST: 2020
SALES (est): 310K **Privately Held**
SIC: **2051** Bakery: wholesale or whole-
sale/retail combined

(G-9898)
SINERGIE PRINTING INC
1717 N Bayshore Dr (33132-1180)
PHONE...................................786 493-6167
Paul Sainz, *President*
EMP: 7 EST: 2013
SQ FT: 1,000
SALES (est): 254.1K **Privately Held**
SIC: **2621** 2741 Book, bond & printing pa-
pers; art copy & poster publishing

(G-9899)
SIPPERS BY DESIGN
555 Ne 15th St (33132-1451)
PHONE...................................305 371-5087
Lisa Dominique, *Principal*
Edgard Lequerique, *Vice Pres*
Andriene Johnson, *Sales Staff*
Diego Villarreal, *Sales Associate*
Jordan Alfonso, *Marketing Staff*
EMP: 6 EST: 2011
SALES (est): 2.5MM **Privately Held**
WEB: www.sippersbydesign.com
SIC: **3089** Plastic processing

(G-9900)
SIR WINSTON GARMENTS INC
Also Called: Sea Suns
13428 Sw 131st St (33186-5817)
PHONE...................................305 499-3144
Valentina Lozada, *President*
Jacqueline Chaleff, *President*
Marguerite Domville, *Treasurer*
EMP: 12 EST: 1979
SQ FT: 5,000

SALES (est): 282.3K **Privately Held**
WEB: www.seasuns.net
SIC: 2339 Sportswear, women's

(G-9901)
SKIDE LLC
6303 Blue Lagoon Dr (33126-6002)
PHONE...................................305 537-4275
Jorge Abuim,
Edgar Bermudez,
Ricardo Nunez,
EMP: 10 **EST:** 2007
SALES (est): 885.1K **Privately Held**
WEB: www.skidenet.com
SIC: 3533 8742 Oil & gas field machinery;
industry specialist consultants

(G-9902)
SKINMETICS INC
Also Called: Wilma Schumann Skin Care
Pdts
4850 Sw 72nd Ave (33155-5526)
PHONE...................................305 663-5750
Pedro Ortega, *President*
Barbara Ortega, *Vice Pres*
▲ **EMP:** 15 **EST:** 1997
SALES (est): 2.1MM **Privately Held**
WEB: www.wilmaschumann.com
SIC: 2844 5122 Cosmetic preparations;
cosmetics, perfumes & hair products

(G-9903)
SLATE GROUP LLC
9357 Sw 77th Ave (33156-7900)
PHONE...................................786 484-9408
Robert Inguanzo, *Principal*
EMP: 9 **EST:** 2012
SALES (est): 274.3K
SALES (corp-wide): 3.1B **Publicly Held**
WEB: www.slate.com
SIC: 2741
PA: Graham Holdings Company
1300 17th St N Fl 17
Arlington VA 22209
703 345-6300

(G-9904)
SLG SOLUTIONS INC
12000 Sw 210th Ter (33177-5368)
PHONE...................................786 379-4676
Mirta S Denis, *Mng Member*
EMP: 6 **EST:** 2016
SALES (est): 388.4K **Privately Held**
SIC: 1389 7349 Construction, repair & dis-
mantling services; janitorial service, con-
tract basis

(G-9905)
SLTONS ENVIRNMNTAL GROUP
ASSOC
Also Called: Ecopod
2950 Sw 27th Ave Ste 2 (33133-3765)
PHONE...................................305 665-5594
Henry Pino, *President*
Gabriela Pino, *Co-Founder*
Matt Gawne, *COO*
EMP: 15 **EST:** 2016
SALES (est): 940.7K **Privately Held**
WEB: www.ecopod.us
SIC: 2842 Specialty cleaning, polishes &
sanitation goods; laundry cleaning prepa-
rations

(G-9906)
SMART FOR LIFE INC (PA)
Also Called: Bonne Sante Group
990 Biscayne Blvd # 1203 (33132-1559)
PHONE...................................786 749-1221
Darren C Minton, *President*
Alfonso J Cervantes, *Chairman*
Alan Bergman, *CFO*
EMP: 10 **EST:** 2017
SALES (est): 9MM **Publicly Held**
WEB: www.smartforlifecorp.com
SIC: 2834 Vitamin, nutrient & hematinic
preparations for human use

(G-9907)
SMART SHUTTERS INC
3070 Nw 72nd Ave (33122-1314)
PHONE...................................786 391-1100
Anwar Ladhani, *President*
EMP: 8 **EST:** 2017
SALES (est): 149.1K **Privately Held**
SIC: 3442 Shutters, door or window: metal

(G-9908)
SMOOTHIE CORP
10211 Sw 137th Ct (33186-6896)
PHONE...................................305 588-0867
Antonio De La Maza, *Branch Mgr*
EMP: 65
SALES (corp-wide): 459.1K **Privately**
Held
WEB: www.smoothiespotmiami.com
SIC: 2037 Frozen fruits & vegetables
PA: Smoothie, Corp
12520 Sw 88th St
Miami FL 33186
305 598-7004

(G-9909)
SMX-US INC
Also Called: Socialmetrix
80 Sw 8th St Ste 2000 (33130-3038)
PHONE...................................914 840-5631
Martin Enriquez, *CEO*
Walter Ciffer, *CFO*
EMP: 30 **EST:** 2014
SQ FT: 3,300
SALES (est): 2MM **Privately Held**
WEB: www.smxusa.com
SIC: 7372 8732 Application computer soft-
ware; business oriented computer soft-
ware; business research service

(G-9910)
SNIF-SNAX LTD
540 Brickell Key Dr C2 (33131-3827)
PHONE...................................786 613-7007
Jonathan Brown, *CEO*
Hannah Brown, *Vice Pres*
Aaron Brown, *Production*
Hunter Barnes, *Sales Staff*
Karen Gumpel, *Director*
EMP: 10 **EST:** 2016
SALES (est): 1.5MM **Privately Held**
WEB: www.snifsnax.com
SIC: 2047 Dog food

(G-9911)
SOFTECH INTERNATIONAL INC
1421 Sw 107th Ave (33174-2526)
PHONE...................................305 233-4813
EMP: 14
SQ FT: 3,500
SALES (est): 1.9MM **Privately Held**
SIC: 7372 Prepackaged Software Services

(G-9912)
SOLAR TURBINES
INCORPORATED
701 Nw 62nd Ave Ste 600 (33126-4683)
PHONE...................................305 476-6855
Jamie Saldarriago, *Director*
Nishul Arora, *Representative*
EMP: 10
SALES (corp-wide): 50.9B **Publicly Held**
WEB: www.solarturbines.com
SIC: 3511 Gas turbine generator set units,
complete
HQ: Solar Turbines Incorporated
2200 Pacific Hwy
San Diego CA 92101
619 544-5000

(G-9913)
SOLAR VENETIAN BLINDS INC
3639 Nw 47th St (33142-3947)
PHONE...................................305 634-4553
Kenneth Gordon, *President*
Betty Gordon, *Treasurer*
▼ **EMP:** 5 **EST:** 1947
SQ FT: 5,000
SALES (est): 480.8K **Privately Held**
SIC: 2591 Window shade rollers & fittings;
blinds vertical; venetian blinds

(G-9914)
SOLO PRINTING LLC
7860 Nw 66th St (33166-2708)
PHONE...................................305 594-8699
Manuel Hernandez, *President*
Luis Fiallos, *General Mgr*
Robert Hernandez, *Principal*
Jorge Hernandez, *Vice Pres*
Liz Valdez, *Accounts Mgr*
◆ **EMP:** 152 **EST:** 1985
SQ FT: 100,000
SALES (est): 41.2MM **Privately Held**
WEB: www.soloprinting.com
SIC: 2752 Commercial printing, offset

(G-9915)
SOLUCNES ELCTRCAS
INTGRLES LLC
2609 Ne 189th St (33180-2627)
PHONE...................................305 804-4201
Juan Araujo, *Principal*
▲ **EMP:** 11 **EST:** 2009
SQ FT: 2,000
SALES (est): 161.2K **Privately Held**
SIC: 3612 Electric furnace transformers;
electronic meter transformers

(G-9916)
SOMAY MANUFACTURING INC
(PA)
4301 Nw 35th Ave (33142-4382)
PHONE...................................305 637-4757
Dario Echeverry, *President*
Josephine Garcia, *General Mgr*
Russell Lewis, *Treasurer*
Francisco J Guerra, *Admin Sec*
EMP: 5 **EST:** 2015
SALES (est): 5.4MM **Privately Held**
WEB: www.somay.com
SIC: 2851 Paints & allied products

(G-9917)
SOMETHING IN A TIN INC
2401 Ne 199th St (33180-1829)
PHONE...................................305 785-6891
Linda S Pierre, *Principal*
Linda Pierre, *Principal*
▼ **EMP:** 9 **EST:** 2009
SALES (est): 152.4K **Privately Held**
SIC: 3356 Tin

(G-9918)
SONOBRANDS LLC (PA)
Also Called: Chiptronics
1970 Nw 129th Ave Ste 108 (33182-2399)
PHONE...................................305 418-9367
Melissa C Cuartero,
Angelica Paranzino-Cedeno,
EMP: 8 **EST:** 2015
SALES (est): 465.5K **Privately Held**
SIC: 3651 Audio electronic systems

(G-9919)
SONY DISCOS
3390 Mary St Ste 220 (33133-5282)
PHONE...................................305 420-4540
Luis Rodriguez, *President*
EMP: 9 **EST:** 2009
SALES (est): 1MM **Privately Held**
SIC: 2741 Miscellaneous publishing
PA: Sony Group Corporation
1-7-1, Konan
Minato-Ku TKY 108-0

(G-9920)
SOS SOFTWARE CORP
950 Brickell Bay Dr # 53 (33131-3931)
PHONE...................................786 237-4903
Juan Basanez, *Principal*
EMP: 8 **EST:** 2015
SALES (est): 678.7K **Privately Held**
SIC: 7372 Prepackaged software

(G-9921)
SOTO METAL FABRICATION INC
(PA)
7025 Sw 16th Ter (33155-1668)
PHONE...................................786 486-7125
Angel Soto, *Principal*
EMP: 7 **EST:** 2018
SALES (est): 551.9K **Privately Held**
SIC: 3499 Fabricated metal products

(G-9922)
SOURCE CONTRACT LLC
11451 Nw 36th Ave (33167-2910)
PHONE...................................305 630-8950
Candice McCarthy, *Opers Dir*
Iveta Dunn, *Sales Staff*
Golan Rabin, *Mng Member*
EMP: 15 **EST:** 2010
SALES (est): 2.8MM **Privately Held**
WEB: www.sourcefurniture.com
SIC: 2519 Wicker & rattan furniture

(G-9923)
SOUTH AMERCN LBR & TIMBER
LLC
78 Sw 7th St Ste 500 (33130-3782)
PHONE...................................786 280-8326
Mario Auvert,
EMP: 8 **EST:** 2019
SALES (est): 505.6K **Privately Held**
SIC: 2411 Wooden logs

(G-9924)
SOUTH FLORIDA CON BLOCK
LLC
5800 Sw 177th Ave Ste 101 (33193-5302)
PHONE...................................305 408-3444
Jorge Rinaldi, *Mng Member*
Sergio Rinaldi,
EMP: 6 **EST:** 2007
SALES (est): 992.5K **Privately Held**
WEB: www.sfcblocks.com
SIC: 3273 Ready-mixed concrete

(G-9925)
SOUTH FLORIDA PALLET INC
224 Nw 136th Pl (33182-1942)
PHONE...................................305 330-7663
Joel Gil, *Sales Mgr*
EMP: 7 **EST:** 2011
SALES (est): 95.3K **Privately Held**
WEB: www.sfpallets.com
SIC: 2448 Pallets, wood

(G-9926)
SOUTHEAST ATLANTIC BEVERA
5900 Nw 72nd Ave (33166-3736)
PHONE...................................904 739-1000
Bob Vargos, *CEO*
▼ **EMP:** 7 **EST:** 2009
SALES (est): 147.4K **Privately Held**
SIC: 2086 Bottled & canned soft drinks

(G-9927)
SOUTHERN DIE CASTING CORP
3560 Nw 59th St (33142-2022)
PHONE...................................305 635-6571
Allan F Hippler, *President*
◆ **EMP:** 51 **EST:** 1962
SQ FT: 40,000
SALES (est): 1.3MM **Privately Held**
WEB: www.thesdccorp.com
SIC: 3364 3089 3363 3429 Zinc & zinc-
base alloy die-castings; window frames &
sash, plastic; aluminum die-castings;
manufactured hardware (general); nonfer-
rous foundries; aluminum foundries

(G-9928)
SOUTHERN GEAR & MACHINE
INC
3685 Nw 106th St (33147-1099)
PHONE...................................305 691-6300
Allan Arch, *President*
Susan Arch, *Corp Secy*
Alex Perdomo, *Vice Pres*
Lihn Tran, *Plant Mgr*
Raphael Rivera, *Production*
EMP: 82 **EST:** 1957
SQ FT: 30,000
SALES (est): 15.1MM **Privately Held**
WEB: www.southerngear.com
SIC: 3728 3568 Gears, aircraft power
transmission; sprockets (power transmis-
sion equipment)

(G-9929)
SOUTHERN INTERNATIONAL
SVCS
18970 Ne 4th Ct (33179-3902)
PHONE...................................954 349-7321
Robert Mercado, *President*
Anahi Mercado, *Vice Pres*
◆ **EMP:** 15 **EST:** 1993
SQ FT: 2,000
SALES (est): 300.6K **Privately Held**
SIC: 2395 7219 2396 Embroidery prod-
ucts, except schiffli machine; laundry, ex-
cept power & coin-operated; automotive &
apparel trimmings

(G-9930)
SOUTHERN MANUFACTURING
INC
7064 Sw 10th St (33144-4608)
PHONE...................................305 267-1943

Isaac Canteli, *President*
Bernardo Yepes, *Vice Pres*
Hermes Rivas, *Opers Mgr*
Gabriel Cabrera, *Engineer*
Jerome Gibson, *Prgrmr*
EMP: 15 **EST:** 1992
SQ FT: 50,000
SALES (est): 2.5MM **Privately Held**
WEB: www.southernmanufacturing.com
SIC: 3599 Machine shop, jobbing & repair

(G-9931)
SPA WORLD CORPORATION
(PA)
Also Called: SW
5701 Nw 35th Ave (33142-2707)
PHONE................................866 588-8008
Joseph Schwartz, *President*
Kris Tatur, *Vice Pres*
Kristoff Tatur, *Vice Pres*
Eduardo Perez, *Plant Mgr*
Michelle Ceglarek, *Controller*
▲ **EMP:** 38 **EST:** 1996
SALES (est): 19.4MM **Privately Held**
WEB: www.swcorp.com
SIC: 3088 Bathroom fixtures, plastic

(G-9932)
SPACIOS DESIGN GROUP INC
7370 Nw 36th Ave (33147-5810)
PHONE................................305 696-1766
Carlos Lopez, *President*
Luiz Gonzales, *President*
EMP: 18 **EST:** 2001
SALES (est): 879.4K **Privately Held**
SIC: 2511 Wood household furniture

(G-9933)
SPANCRETE INC
7907 Nw 53rd St 347 (33166-4603)
PHONE................................305 599-8885
Gary Schmidt, *President*
EMP: 35 **EST:** 1986
SQ FT: 3,000
SALES (est): 3.4MM **Privately Held**
SIC: 3272 Prestressed concrete products

(G-9934)
SPANGLISH ADVERTISING COR
6857 Ne 3rd Ave (33138-5510)
PHONE................................305 244-0918
EMP: 6 **EST:** 2018
SALES (est): 310K **Privately Held**
SIC: 2752 Commercial printing, litho-
graphic

(G-9935)
SPANISH PUBLISHERS LLC
8871 Sw 129th St (33176-5918)
PHONE................................305 233-3365
Lucia Laratelli, *Principal*
Lucialaratell Ucia, *Manager*
▲ **EMP:** 9 **EST:** 2009
SALES (est): 1.1MM **Privately Held**
WEB: www.spanishpublishers.net
SIC: 2741 Miscellaneous publishing

(G-9936)
SPECIAL AMERICAS BBQ INC
Also Called: Mr Tango Sausages
11411 Nw 107th St Ste 1 (33178-4063)
P.O. Box 960458 (33296-0458)
PHONE................................305 637-7377
Maria Ruiz, *President*
Carlos Rincon, *Plant Mgr*
EMP: 36 **EST:** 1995
SQ FT: 10,000
SALES (est): 5.6MM **Privately Held**
WEB: www.mrtangosausages.com
SIC: 2011 2013 Meat packing plants;
sausages & other prepared meats

(G-9937)
SPECIALTY FORGED WHEELS
INC
12146 Sw 114th Pl (33176-4473)
PHONE................................786 332-5925
Carlos Gonzalez, *President*
EMP: 6 **EST:** 2014
SALES (est): 790.7K **Privately Held**
WEB: www.specialtyforged.com
SIC: 3312 Wheels

(G-9938)
SPECIALTY PRODUCTIONS INC
2476 Sw 25th Ter (33133-2217)
PHONE................................786 399-1393
Henry Benavides, *President*
EMP: 6 **EST:** 2010
SALES (est): 390.8K **Privately Held**
SIC: 2771 Greeting cards

(G-9939)
SPECIALTY STEEL HOLDCO INC
200 Biscayne Blvd (33132-2219)
PHONE................................305 375-7560
EMP: 9 **EST:** 2020
SALES (est): 480.7K **Privately Held**
SIC: 3317 Steel pipe & tubes

(G-9940)
SPECTRA POWDER COATING
INC
7242 Nw 33rd St (33122-1204)
PHONE................................786 351-7448
Heidi Hernandez, *Mng Member*
EMP: 10 **EST:** 2020
SALES (est): 1MM **Privately Held**
SIC: 3479 7389 Aluminum coating of
metal products;

(G-9941)
SPEED MOBILE OIL CHANGE
INC
5580 Sw 88th Pl (33165-6766)
PHONE................................305 763-4352
Lazaro Diaz, *Principal*
EMP: 7 **EST:** 2016
SALES (est): 171.2K **Privately Held**
SIC: 1311 Crude petroleum & natural gas

(G-9942)
SPEED PRINT ONE INC
8840 Sw 86th St (33173-4539)
PHONE................................305 374-5936
Guillermo Bru, *President*
Maria Bru, *Vice Pres*
EMP: 8 **EST:** 1971
SALES (est): 692.2K **Privately Held**
WEB: www.speedprintone.com
SIC: 2752 Commercial printing, offset

(G-9943)
SPI LLC
11200 Nw 107th St Ste 8 (33178-3298)
PHONE................................786 907-4022
EMP: 182
SALES (corp-wide): 144.6MM **Privately**
Held
WEB: www.spi-ok.com
SIC: 3339 Precious metals
PA: Spi Llc
2101 Rexford Rd Ste 300e
Charlotte NC 28211
704 336-9555

(G-9944)
SPORTAILOR INC
6501 Ne 2nd Ct (33138-6093)
PHONE................................305 754-3255
Frank Rudman, *President*
Albert Rudman, *Vice Pres*
Terry Alfonso, *Comptroller*
Miriam Rudman, *Admin Sec*
Marisela Collazo, *Admin Asst*
◆ **EMP:** 52 **EST:** 1962
SQ FT: 50,000
SALES (est): 6.6MM **Privately Held**
WEB: www.sportailor.com
SIC: 2329 5136 5137 Men's & boys'
sportswear & athletic clothing; men's &
boys' sportswear & work clothing;
women's & children's sportswear & swim-
suits

(G-9945)
SQUARE ONE ARMORING SVCS
CO
12370 Sw 130th St (33186-6229)
PHONE................................305 477-1109
Maria Elena Cardenal, *President*
Julio C Cardenal, *Vice Pres*
Julio Cardenal, *Prdtn Mgr*
Margarita Gonzalez, *CFO*
Laura Fernandez, *Manager*
◆ **EMP:** 70 **EST:** 1991
SQ FT: 10,800

SALES (est): 13.1MM **Privately Held**
WEB: www.sq1armor.com
SIC: 3711 3714 3231 Cars, armored, assembly of; motor vehicle parts & accessories; products of purchased glass

(G-9946)
STAR BAKERY INC
Also Called: Galletas La Unica
3914 Nw 32nd Ave (33142-5010)
PHONE................................305 633-4284
Manuel Sendina, *President*
Ana Gloria Sendina, *Vice Pres*
Jose Castillo, *Plant Mgr*
Gabriel Sandino, *Analyst*
▲ **EMP:** 18 **EST:** 1966
SQ FT: 10,000
SALES (est): 3.4MM **Privately Held**
WEB: www.sbmia.com
SIC: 2052 2051 Bakery products, dry;
bread, cake & related products

(G-9947)
STAYFILM INC
2234 Sw 8th St (33135-4914)
PHONE................................786 961-1007
Douglas Almeida, *CEO*
Daniel Almeida, *Security Dir*
EMP: 7 **EST:** 2017
SALES (est): 3.1MM **Privately Held**
WEB: www.stayfilm.com
SIC: 7372 Application computer software

(G-9948)
STEERING & SUSPENSION
PARTS
Also Called: SSP
2740 Nw 35th St (33142-5238)
PHONE................................786 523-3726
Laura Torres, *Principal*
EMP: 8 **EST:** 2016
SALES (est): 348.2K **Privately Held**
WEB: www.sspparts.net
SIC: 3714 Motor vehicle parts & acces-
sories

(G-9949)
STEEVIE STASH LLC
1733 Nw 112th Ter (33167-3536)
PHONE................................954 860-3138
Stevonne Frederick, *Principal*
EMP: 10 **EST:** 2018
SALES (est): 619.3K **Privately Held**
SIC: 2676 7389 Feminine hygiene paper
products; business services

(G-9950)
STEPINCORP AUTO SOLUTIONS
LLC
12480 Nw 25th St Ste 115 (33182-1535)
PHONE................................786 864-3222
Igor Borisov, *Mng Member*
EMP: 8 **EST:** 2019
SALES (est): 50K **Privately Held**
SIC: 3069 Bushings, rubber

(G-9951)
STERN BLOOM MEDIA INC
Also Called: Aventura Magazine
20454 Ne 34th Ct (33180-1650)
PHONE................................954 454-8522
Michael Stern, *President*
Amit Bloom, *Vice Pres*
Mike Pariso, *Prdtn Dir*
David Bloom, *Treasurer*
EMP: 22 **EST:** 1998
SALES (est): 3.8MM **Privately Held**
WEB: www.sternbloom.com
SIC: 2721 Magazines: publishing only, not
printed on site

(G-9952)
STITCHED NATIONAL HARBOR
LLC
701 S Miami Ave Unit 177c (33130-1953)
PHONE................................786 483-8740
Eamon M Springall, *Principal*
EMP: 7 **EST:** 2017
SALES (est): 47.9K **Privately Held**
SIC: 2395 Embroidery & art needlework

(G-9953)
STITCHING AROUND INC
4862 Sw 72nd Ave (33155-5526)
PHONE................................305 665-1600

Claudia C Kitchens, *President*
▼ **EMP:** 5 **EST:** 2005
SALES (est): 416.6K **Privately Held**
WEB: www.stitchingaround.com
SIC: 2395 Embroidery products, except
schiffli machine

(G-9954)
STONE AND EQUIPMENT INC
4681 Sw 72nd Ave Ste 104 (33155-4540)
PHONE................................305 665-0002
Lissette Rodriguez, *CEO*
Daniel Tormo, *CFO*
EMP: 20 **EST:** 1999
SALES (est): 1.2MM **Privately Held**
WEB: www.stoneandequipment.com
SIC: 3281 5032 Table tops, marble; mar-
ble building stone

(G-9955)
STONEWORKS INC
Also Called: Stoneworks of Art
6840 Sw 81st Ter (33143-7712)
PHONE................................305 666-6676
Clement Zanzuri, *President*
Kelly Young, *Sales Staff*
Victor Colon,
◆ **EMP:** 16 **EST:** 1984
SQ FT: 27,000
SALES (est): 2.9MM **Privately Held**
WEB: www.trimstonepanels.com
SIC: 3281 Marble, building: cut & shaped;
granite, cut & shaped

(G-9956)
STRANDS INC (PA)
3390 Mary St Ste 116 (33133-5255)
PHONE................................415 398-4333
Erik Brieva, *CEO*
Cesar Richardson, *General Mgr*
Jordi Teixido, *COO*
Pablo De La Concepcion, *Manager*
Mark Torrens, *CIO*
EMP: 7 **EST:** 2005
SALES (est): 2.8MM **Privately Held**
WEB: www.strands.com
SIC: 7372 Business oriented computer
software

(G-9957)
STRASSE FORGED LLC
13979 Sw 140th St (33186-5528)
PHONE................................786 701-3649
Christian Carrillo, *Mng Member*
Eriana Blanco, *Manager*
EMP: 9 **EST:** 2009
SALES (est): 468.4K **Privately Held**
WEB: www.strassewheels.com
SIC: 3714 Motor vehicle parts & acces-
sories

(G-9958)
STRATUS PHARMACEUTICALS
INC
12379 Sw 130th St (33186-6208)
PHONE................................305 254-6793
Alberto Hoyo, *President*
John Billoch, *Treasurer*
Carlos Hoyo, *Admin Sec*
EMP: 36 **EST:** 1988
SQ FT: 26,000
SALES (est): 8.8MM **Privately Held**
WEB: www.stratuspharmaceuticals.com
SIC: 2834 Pharmaceutical preparations

(G-9959)
STRUMBA MEDIA LLC (PA)
Also Called: Miracle Noodle
382 Ne 191st St Ste 6920 (33179-3899)
PHONE................................800 948-4205
Jonathan Carp, *CEO*
Susan Carp, *Vice Pres*
Jill Goldstein, *Vice Pres*
◆ **EMP:** 5 **EST:** 2006
SALES (est): 4.5MM **Privately Held**
SIC: 2099 Noodles, uncooked: packaged
with other ingredients

(G-9960)
STUART COMPOSITES LLC
6900 Nw 77th Ct (33166-2714)
PHONE................................772 266-4285
Moises Rodriguez,
EMP: 40 **EST:** 2014

SALES (est): 4.6MM **Privately Held**
WEB: www.stuartcomposites.com
SIC: 3732 Boat building & repairing

(G-9961)
STUART INDUSTRIES INC
526 Ne 190th St (33179-3919)
PHONE................................305 651-3474
Stuart Collins, *President*
Marsha Collins, *Corp Secy*
Sheldon Collins, *Vice Pres*
EMP: 11 EST: 1982
SQ FT: 20,000
SALES (est): 1.3MM **Privately Held**
WEB: www.stuartfishingtackle.com
SIC: 3949 3429 3769 Lures, fishing: artificial; fishing tackle, general; marine hardware; guided missile & space vehicle parts & auxiliary equipment

(G-9962)
STYLE-VIEW PRODUCTS INC
Also Called: Aluma Craft Products
1800 N Byshore Dr Apt 400 (33132)
PHONE................................305 634-9688
Mark A Caplan, *President*
Albert M Caplan, *Vice Pres*
▼ EMP: 30 EST: 1964
SQ FT: 80,000
SALES (est): 1MM **Privately Held**
WEB: www.aluma-craft.com
SIC: 3442 3444 3443 3354 Storm doors or windows, metal; awnings, sheet metal; canopies, sheet metal; fabricated plate work (boiler shop); aluminum extruded products

(G-9963)
SUGAR FANCIES LLC
1091 Sw 134th Ct (33184-3318)
PHONE................................786 558-9087
Sandra Rios Monsante, *Principal*
EMP: 8 EST: 2011
SALES (est): 477.5K **Privately Held**
SIC: 2053 Cakes, bakery: frozen

(G-9964)
SUMMIT AEROSPACE INC
4000 Nw 28th St (33142-5612)
PHONE................................305 871-5449
EMP: 7
SALES (corp-wide): 16.7MM **Privately Held**
WEB: www.summitmro.com
SIC: 3728 Aircraft parts & equipment
PA: Summit Aerospace, Inc.
　　8130 Nw 74th Ave
　　Medley FL 33166
　　305 267-6400

(G-9965)
SUNCO PLASTICS INC
8501 Nw 90th St (33166-2187)
PHONE................................305 238-2864
Harold Bailey, *President*
Kurt Maree, *Manager*
▼ EMP: 13 EST: 1966
SQ FT: 35,000
SALES (est): 209.1K **Privately Held**
WEB: www.suncoplastics.com
SIC: 3089 3544 Injection molding of plastics; special dies, tools, jigs & fixtures

(G-9966)
SUNCOAST POST-TENSION LTD
7223 Nw 46th St 29 (33166-6422)
PHONE................................305 592-5075
Phil Arana, *Manager*
EMP: 25 **Privately Held**
WEB: www.suncoast-pt.com
SIC: 3315 3316 5072 Cable, steel: insulated or armored; cold finishing of steel shapes; builders' hardware
HQ: Suncoast Post-Tension, Ltd.
　　509 N Sam Houston Pkwy E # 300
　　Houston TX 77060
　　281 445-8886

(G-9967)
SUNILAND PRESS INC
7379 Nw 31st St (33122-1240)
P.O. Box 561108 (33256-1108)
PHONE................................305 235-8811
Peter Rood, *President*
Florence Rood, *Corp Secy*
▲ EMP: 42 EST: 1972

SQ FT: 65,000
SALES (est): 1.1MM **Privately Held**
WEB: www.sunilandpress.com
SIC: 2752 Commercial printing, offset

(G-9968)
SUNSHINE CORDAGE CORPORATION
7190 Nw 12th St (33126-1304)
PHONE................................305 592-3750
Joel Ellison, *President*
Guillermo Carranza, *Vice Pres*
Ellison Joel, *CFO*
◆ EMP: 6 EST: 1969
SALES (est): 983.9K **Privately Held**
WEB: www.sunshinecordage.com
SIC: 2298 Rope, except asbestos & wire; twine

(G-9969)
SUNSHINE OIL AND GAS INC (PA)
Also Called: Sunshine Oil and Gas Fla Inc
13230 Sw 132nd Ave Ste 22 (33186-6144)
PHONE................................305 367-3100
Rishi Burke, *President*
EMP: 5 EST: 2013
SALES (est): 666.3K **Privately Held**
SIC: 1389 Oil & gas wells: building, repairing & dismantling

(G-9970)
SUPER BRITE SCREW CORP
16 Sw 1st Ave (33130-1606)
PHONE................................305 822-6560
Carlos Hernandez, *Vice Pres*
EMP: 12 EST: 1977
SALES (est): 245.7K **Privately Held**
SIC: 3452 Bolts, nuts, rivets & washers

(G-9971)
SUPERIOR OIL 2016 INC
5477 Nw 72nd Ave (33166-4223)
PHONE................................305 851-5140
Ronald Brio, *Principal*
EMP: 8 EST: 2016
SALES (est): 402.1K **Privately Held**
SIC: 1382 Oil & gas exploration services

(G-9972)
SUPERIOR STORM SOLUTIONS
1501 Nw 79th St (33147-5343)
PHONE................................305 638-8420
Jorg Rios, *Owner*
EMP: 6 EST: 2020
SALES (est): 410.6K **Privately Held**
SIC: 3442 Metal doors, sash & trim

(G-9973)
SUPERMIX CONCRETE (PA)
Also Called: Continental Concrete
4300 Sw 74th Ave (33155-4406)
P.O. Box 13128, Fort Lauderdale (33316-0100)
PHONE................................954 858-0780
Frank Anderson, *President*
Robert Cordone, *Exec VP*
Martin Bodg, *Vice Pres*
▲ EMP: 25 EST: 1975
SQ FT: 13,500
SALES (est): 12.3MM **Privately Held**
SIC: 3273 5032 Ready-mixed concrete; concrete & cinder block

(G-9974)
SUPPER ON WHEELS INC
2423 Sw 147th Ave (33185-4082)
PHONE................................305 205-8999
Eunice Gibson, *Exec Dir*
EMP: 5 EST: 2019
SALES (est): 500K **Privately Held**
SIC: 2099 Ready-to-eat meals, salads & sandwiches

(G-9975)
SUPPORT AIRCRAFT PARTS INC
13058 Sw 133rd Ct (33186-5855)
PHONE................................305 975-3767
Ricardo L Cerioni, *Principal*
EMP: 16 EST: 2007
SALES (est): 1.7MM **Privately Held**
SIC: 3728 Aircraft parts & equipment

(G-9976)
SUREFIRE STRGC SOLUTIONS LLC
9611 Sw 130th St (33176-5741)
PHONE................................305 720-7118
Robert E Schurr, *Principal*
EMP: 7 EST: 2011
SALES (est): 154.8K **Privately Held**
SIC: 3842 Surgical appliances & supplies

(G-9977)
SUTTON DRAPERIES INC
1762 Ne 205th Ter (33179-2112)
PHONE................................305 653-7738
Steven Barg, *President*
Vicki Colenzo, *Vice Pres*
EMP: 10 EST: 1971
SQ FT: 7,000
SALES (est): 605.7K **Privately Held**
WEB: www.suttondraperies.com
SIC: 2391 2591 5023 Draperies, plastic & textile: from purchased materials; window blinds; window shades; vertical blinds

(G-9978)
SUVICHE INTERNATIONAL LLC
2175 Nw 24th Ave (33142-7279)
PHONE................................305 777-3530
Andrei Stern, *President*
Aliosha Stern, *President*
EMP: 12 EST: 2013
SALES (est): 1MM **Privately Held**
WEB: www.suviche.com
SIC: 2099 Food preparations

(G-9979)
SUVILLAGA CONSTRUCTION MGT LLC
11411 Nw 7th St Apt 206 (33172-3566)
PHONE................................305 323-8380
Juan Carlos Gonzalez, *Principal*
EMP: 10 EST: 2019
SALES (est): 276.1K **Privately Held**
SIC: 1389 Construction, repair & dismantling services

(G-9980)
SWATCH GROUP CARIBBEAN
5301 Blue Lagoon Dr # 620 (33126-2098)
PHONE................................877 839-5224
Nick Hayek, *President*
Dibra Lucius, *Manager*
EMP: 13 EST: 2015
SALES (est): 472.5K **Privately Held**
WEB: www.swatchgroup.com
SIC: 3961 Costume jewelry

(G-9981)
SWEET AND VICIOUS LLC (PA)
Also Called: Bubbles Body Wear
111 Ne 21st St (33137-4820)
PHONE................................305 576-0012
Karen E Jones, *Principal*
EMP: 6 EST: 2003
SALES (est): 1.2MM **Privately Held**
WEB: www.sweet-vicious.com
SIC: 2341 Women's & children's underwear

(G-9982)
SWEETWATER TODAY INC
35 Sw 114th Ave (33174-1002)
PHONE................................305 456-4724
Doug Mayorga, *Principal*
EMP: 8 EST: 2013
SALES (est): 92.9K **Privately Held**
SIC: 2711 Newspapers

(G-9983)
SWIRE PACIFIC HOLDINGS INC
Coca-Cola
98 Se 7th St Ste 610 (33131-3530)
PHONE................................305 371-3877
J Megan Kelly, *Senior VP*
Pinky Yu, *Human Res Mgr*
Tina Chan, *Marketing Mgr*
Stephen L Owens, *Branch Mgr*
Fora Leung, *Exec Sec*
EMP: 89
SALES (corp-wide): 16.1B **Privately Held**
WEB: www.swirecc.com
SIC: 2086 Bottled & canned soft drinks

HQ: Swire Pacific Holdings Inc.
　　12634 S 265 W Bldg A
　　Draper UT 84020
　　801 816-5300

(G-9984)
SYANA ENTERPRISES INC
1880 Sw 24th St (33145-3834)
PHONE................................305 582-4708
Yohana Rodriguez, *President*
EMP: 5 EST: 2005
SALES (est): 336.5K **Privately Held**
SIC: 2891 Adhesives & sealants

(G-9985)
SYNKT GAMES INC
1820 Micanopy Ave (33133-3330)
PHONE................................305 779-5611
Bryan Abboud, *CEO*
David Depaulis, *Marketing Staff*
EMP: 14 EST: 2013
SALES (est): 152.4K **Privately Held**
WEB: www.synktgames.miami
SIC: 7372 Prepackaged software

(G-9986)
SYNOLD LLC
Also Called: Syntheon
13755 Sw 119th Ave (33186-6265)
PHONE................................305 266-3388
Derek Deville, *Vice Pres*
Matt Palmer, *Vice Pres*
Carlos Rivera, *Vice Pres*
Jeff Meeker, *Research*
Michael Kirk, *Engineer*
EMP: 5 EST: 2008
SALES (est): 2.6MM **Privately Held**
WEB: www.syntheon.com
SIC: 3841 Surgical & medical instruments

(G-9987)
T & M ATLANTIC INC
436 Sw 8th St (33130-2814)
PHONE................................786 332-4773
Alexander Afonskiy, *President*
▲ EMP: 7 EST: 2010
SALES (est): 606.8K **Privately Held**
WEB: www.tmatlantic.com
SIC: 3825 Instruments to measure electricity

(G-9988)
T & R STORE FIXTURES INC
2700 N Miami Ave (33127-4466)
PHONE................................305 751-0377
Reynaldo Hechavarria, *President*
Antonio Hechevarria Sr, *Treasurer*
▼ EMP: 24 EST: 1972
SQ FT: 16,000
SALES (est): 824.8K **Privately Held**
SIC: 2541 2542 Store fixtures, wood; partitions & fixtures, except wood

(G-9989)
T A C ARMATURES & PUMPS CORP
800 Nw 73rd St (33150-3625)
PHONE................................305 835-8845
Jorge F Martinez, *President*
▲ EMP: 15 EST: 1973
SQ FT: 3,000
SALES (est): 977.4K **Privately Held**
WEB: www.tacarmature.com
SIC: 7694 5551 Electric motor repair; boat dealers

(G-9990)
T SHIRT CENTER INC
Also Called: Vivid Sportwear
19900 Ne 15th Ct (33179-2715)
PHONE................................305 655-1955
Sasson Jacoby, *President*
▲ EMP: 8 EST: 2015
SALES (est): 989.3K **Privately Held**
SIC: 2339 2329 5136 5137 Sportswear, women's; men's & boys' sportswear & athletic clothing; sportswear, men's & boys'; sportswear, women's & children's

(G-9991)
T-SHIRTS PLUS COLOR INC
4156 Sw 74th Ct (33155-4414)
PHONE................................305 267-7664
Susana Grossen, *President*
▲ EMP: 7 EST: 1991
SQ FT: 4,500

SALES (est): 880.4K **Privately Held**
WEB: www.tshirtspluscolor.com
SIC: 2759 Screen printing

(G-9992)
TAG & LABEL OF FLORIDA INC
Also Called: Printing Online
13375 Sw 128th St Ste 106 (33186-6288)
PHONE..............................305 255-1050
Ralph Perez, *Manager*
EMP: 5 EST: 1981
SQ FT: 2,500
SALES (est): 531.5K **Privately Held**
WEB: www.tagsandlabelsofflorida.com
SIC: 2752 Commercial printing, offset

(G-9993)
TAGUA LEATHER CORPORATION
2047 Nw 24th Ave (33142-7237)
PHONE..............................305 637-3014
Luis Kellemen, *Principal*
Miguel Coronel, *Opers Mgr*
Juan Valdez, *Sales Staff*
EMP: 10 EST: 2015
SALES (est): 250.5K **Privately Held**
WEB: www.taguagunleather.com
SIC: 2386 2387 Coats & jackets, leather & sheep-lined; garments, leather; apparel belts

(G-9994)
TARGET MANUFACTURING INC
Also Called: Guardian Fire Equipment
3430 Nw 38th St (33142-5034)
PHONE..............................305 633-0361
Richard H Childress, *President*
Lisa C Petersen, *Treasurer*
▲ EMP: 7 EST: 1984
SQ FT: 13,500
SALES (est): 495K **Privately Held**
WEB: www.guardianfire.com
SIC: 3569 3494 3491 3432 Firefighting apparatus & related equipment; valves & pipe fittings; industrial valves; plumbing fixture fittings & trim; nonferrous die-castings except aluminum

(G-9995)
TAVAREZ SPORTING GOODS INC
1840 Coral Way (33145-2748)
PHONE..............................347 441-9690
Manuel Tavarez, *CEO*
EMP: 5 EST: 2014
SALES (est): 309.2K **Privately Held**
SIC: 3949 Helmets, athletic; balls: baseball, football, basketball, etc.; polo equipment & supplies, general; gloves, sport & athletic: boxing, handball, etc.

(G-9996)
TECHNICAL INTERNATIONAL CORP
1000 Brickell Ave Ste 625 (33131-3047)
PHONE..............................305 374-1054
Albertina Genghini, *President*
Donald A McGregor Jr, *Vice Pres*
Anita M Wong, *Treasurer*
Albertina McGregor, *Sales Staff*
Kattia Goldstein, *Shareholder*
◆ EMP: 8 EST: 1984
SQ FT: 1,028
SALES (est): 4.5MM **Privately Held**
WEB: www.tic-usa.com
SIC: 3589 3825 3532 Water treatment equipment, industrial; electrical energy measuring equipment; mining machinery

(G-9997)
TECHNISYS LLC
701 Brickell Ave Ste 1550 (33131-2824)
PHONE..............................305 728-5372
Miguel Santos, *CEO*
EMP: 500 EST: 2003
SALES (est): 44.7MM **Privately Held**
WEB: www.technisys.com
SIC: 7372 Prepackaged software

(G-9998)
TECHNOMARINE USA INC
7600 Corp Ctr Dr Ste 4 (33126)
PHONE..............................305 438-0880
Jacques P Auriol, *CEO*
Pedro Fernandez, *Manager*

▲ EMP: 18 EST: 1998
SALES (est): 1.3MM **Privately Held**
SIC: 3873 Watches, clocks, watchcases & parts

(G-9999)
TEES BY BO INC
13220 Sw 66th St (33183-2361)
PHONE..............................305 382-8551
Dan Bowersox, *President*
EMP: 9 EST: 1989
SQ FT: 1,500
SALES (est): 737.5K **Privately Held**
SIC: 2326 Men's & boys' work clothing

(G-10000)
TEKMATIC CORP
7522 Sw 143rd Ave (33183-2920)
PHONE..............................305 972-1300
Gregg Tekerman, *Principal*
EMP: 9 EST: 2012
SALES (est): 335.1K **Privately Held**
WEB: www.tekmatic.com
SIC: 3552 Textile machinery

(G-10001)
TENTECH CORPORATION
7330 Nw 66th St (33166-3010)
PHONE..............................305 938-0389
Andres Hernandez, *President*
▲ EMP: 16 EST: 2009
SALES (est): 2.1MM **Privately Held**
WEB: www.tentech.com
SIC: 3625 Control equipment, electric

(G-10002)
TERRACASSA LLC
950 Nw 72nd St Unit 102 (33150-3618)
PHONE..............................786 581-7741
Jordi Trulla, *Mng Member*
EMP: 7 EST: 2017
SALES (est): 159.2K **Privately Held**
WEB: www.terracassa.com
SIC: 2299 3643 3261 Batting, wadding, padding & fillings; power outlets & sockets; bathroom accessories/fittings, vitreous china or earthenware

(G-10003)
TERRASTONE INC
8747 Sw 134th St (33176-5930)
PHONE..............................305 234-8384
Rolando Cabezas, *President*
◆ EMP: 5 EST: 1984
SALES (est): 608.1K **Privately Held**
WEB: www.terrastonepr.com
SIC: 3281 Curbing, granite or stone

(G-10004)
TEVA PHARMACEUTICALS USA INC
74 Nw 176th St (33169-5043)
PHONE..............................305 575-6000
William M Marth, *President*
Brendan O 'grady, *Exec VP*
David Stark, *Exec VP*
Lori Queisser, *Senior VP*
Gary Cockroft, *Opers Mgr*
EMP: 25 EST: 2008
SALES (est): 2.4MM **Privately Held**
WEB: www.tevapharm.com
SIC: 2834 Pharmaceutical preparations

(G-10005)
THIDA THAI JEWELRY
47 E Flagler St (33131-1003)
PHONE..............................561 455-4249
Salvatore S Esposito, *Principal*
EMP: 8 EST: 2008
SALES (est): 182.7K **Privately Held**
SIC: 3423 Jewelers' hand tools

(G-10006)
THINKING FOODS INC
123 Nw 23rd St (33127-4409)
PHONE..............................305 433-8287
Roberto Brisciani, *President*
Julia G De La Morena, *Admin Sec*
◆ EMP: 15 EST: 2011
SALES (est): 756.8K **Privately Held**
SIC: 3556 Food products machinery

(G-10007)
TI-PAGOS USA INC
20200 W Dixie Hwy Ste 603 (33180-1925)
PHONE..............................786 310-7423
Anderson Cicotoste, *Principal*
EMP: 9 EST: 2017
SALES (est): 705.5K **Privately Held**
SIC: 3111 Leather tanning & finishing
HQ: Pinbank Brasil Instituicao De Pagamento S/A
Al. Araguaia 750
Barueri SP 06455

(G-10008)
TIC LIGHT ELECTRICAL CORP
11519 Sw 172nd Ter (33157-3976)
PHONE..............................305 712-3499
Sameh Tadros, *President*
EMP: 8 EST: 2014
SALES (est): 681.6K **Privately Held**
SIC: 3625 5063 Industrial electrical relays & switches; boxes & fittings, electrical; hanging & fastening devices, electrical; receptacles, electrical; service entrance equipment, electrical

(G-10009)
TICKET DROP TRAFFIC DEFENSE
20137 Ne 16th Pl (33179-2720)
PHONE..............................305 332-3186
Carlos Saltz, *Principal*
EMP: 7 EST: 2016
SALES (est): 241.7K **Privately Held**
WEB: www.trafficticketoffice.com
SIC: 3812 Defense systems & equipment

(G-10010)
TIKORE INDUSTRIES LLC
14397 Sw 143rd Ct Ste 106 (33186-6730)
PHONE..............................954 616-5902
Joshua A Montagna, *Principal*
Elliot Evelyn, *Engineer*
EMP: 8 EST: 2010
SALES (est): 340.5K **Privately Held**
SIC: 3999 Manufacturing industries

(G-10011)
TINFOIL HATS LLC
11858 Sw 100th Ter (33186-2744)
PHONE..............................407 844-0578
Don Montes, *Principal*
EMP: 6 EST: 2018
SALES (est): 463.9K **Privately Held**
SIC: 2353 Hats, caps & millinery

(G-10012)
TITA ITLN IMPORT & EXPORT LLC
1408 Nw 23rd St (33142-7624)
PHONE..............................305 608-4258
Gianluca Vietti, *Opers Staff*
Nicolo Tita,
◆ EMP: 5 EST: 2009
SALES (est): 583.1K **Privately Held**
WEB: www.titaitalia.com
SIC: 2084 Wines

(G-10013)
TITAN AMERICA LLC
7355 Sw 48th St (33155-5519)
PHONE..............................305 667-2522
Paul Colman, *Branch Mgr*
EMP: 10
SALES (corp-wide): 177.9K **Privately Held**
WEB: www.titanamerica.com
SIC: 3273 Ready-mixed concrete
HQ: Titan America Llc
5700 Lake Wright Dr # 300
Norfolk VA 23502
757 858-6500

(G-10014)
TLC FOOD TRUCK LLC
8602 Nw 22nd Ave (33147-4108)
PHONE..............................305 879-2488
Katrina Toles,
EMP: 17 EST: 2015
SALES (est): 580K **Privately Held**
SIC: 2599 Food wagons, restaurant

(G-10015)
TNT CUSTOM MARINE INC (PA)
3030 Ne 188th St (33180-2856)
PHONE..............................305 931-3157
John Tomlinson, *President*
Mike Thomas, *Vice Pres*
▼ EMP: 6 EST: 1986
SQ FT: 30,000
SALES (est): 1.2MM **Privately Held**
WEB: www.tntcustommarine.com
SIC: 3731 Marine rigging

(G-10016)
TNT PACKAGING INC
Also Called: Coale Industries
17375 Ne 7th Ave (33162-2037)
P.O. Box 402883, Miami Beach (33140-0883)
PHONE..............................305 769-0616
Harold Tokayer, *CEO*
Barry J Tokayer, *President*
Jeffrey Tokayer, *Vice Pres*
Marilyn Tokayer, *Treasurer*
EMP: 10 EST: 1981
SALES (est): 1.5MM **Privately Held**
SIC: 2653 Boxes, corrugated: made from purchased materials

(G-10017)
TOBRUK INTERNATIONAL CORP
Also Called: Tic Logistics
6970 Nw 50th St (33166-5632)
PHONE..............................305 406-0263
Silvia Gutierrez, *President*
Manuel Polo, *Vice Pres*
Andres Torres, *Vice Pres*
▼ EMP: 7 EST: 1991
SQ FT: 3,532
SALES (est): 921.8K **Privately Held**
SIC: 3728 5088 Aircraft parts & equipment; aircraft equipment & supplies

(G-10018)
TODAYS FROZEN DESSERTS INC
7156 Nw 50th St (33166-5636)
PHONE..............................305 994-9940
Ely Cukierman, *President*
▼ EMP: 10 EST: 1987
SQ FT: 5,000
SALES (est): 1.2MM **Privately Held**
WEB: ice-cream-wholesalers.cmac.ws
SIC: 2024 Dairy based frozen desserts

(G-10019)
TODO EN UNO
6601 W Flagler St (33144-2921)
PHONE..............................305 263-6934
Carlos R Fernandez, *Principal*
EMP: 8 EST: 2009
SALES (est): 287.5K **Privately Held**
WEB: todo-en-uno-cuban-restaurant.business.site
SIC: 2051 Cakes, bakery: except frozen

(G-10020)
TOLEDO DOORS INC
Also Called: Toledo Iron Works
4710 Nw 37th Ave (33142-3914)
PHONE..............................305 633-4352
Bill Suarez, *President*
Guillermo Suarez, *Shareholder*
▲ EMP: 10 EST: 1969
SALES (est): 1.9MM **Privately Held**
WEB: www.toledoironworks.com
SIC: 3446 3442 Architectural metalwork; metal doors, sash & trim

(G-10021)
TOLEDO SALES INC
835 Nw 7th Street Rd (33136-3024)
PHONE..............................305 389-3441
Manuel Toledo, *President*
Silvio J Toledo, *Vice Pres*
◆ EMP: 5 EST: 2004
SALES (est): 419.4K **Privately Held**
WEB: www.toledosalesinc.com
SIC: 3732 5941 Boat building & repairing; fishing equipment

(G-10022)
TONE PRINTING LLC (PA)
1221 Brickell Ave Fl 9 (33131-3800)
PHONE..............................855 505-8663
Steven Thompson,

EMP: 5 **EST:** 2005
SQ FT: 4,000
SALES (est): 1.1MM **Privately Held**
SIC: 3993 2752 2732 2759 Signs & advertising specialties; offset & photolithographic printing; pamphlets: printing & binding, not published on site; advertising literature: printing; stationery: printing; commercial printing, gravure

(G-10023)
TOP CHOICE CABINETS AND TOPS
785 Nw 126th Ct (33182-2090)
PHONE......................786 389-4590
Arencibia Michel, *Principal*
EMP: 8 **EST:** 2014
SALES (est): 59.9K **Privately Held**
SIC: 2434 Wood kitchen cabinets

(G-10024)
TOP DRINKS USA CORP
3550 Biscayne Blvd # 507 (33137-3841)
PHONE......................305 407-3514
Antonio Regojo, *Principal*
EMP: 7 **EST:** 2016
SALES (est): 68.6K **Privately Held**
SIC: 2087 Beverage bases

(G-10025)
TOP FLITE MANUFACTURING INC
Also Called: Topflite Components
14262 Sw 140th St Ste 108 (33186-7365)
PHONE......................800 219-2601
Bruce Price, *President*
Jonathan Falco, *Vice Pres*
Brenda Lola, *Purchasing*
Marcos Molinares, *Sales Staff*
EMP: 16 **EST:** 2008
SALES (est): 2.4MM **Privately Held**
WEB: www.topflitecomponents.com
SIC: 3643 Connectors & terminals for electrical devices

(G-10026)
TOP NOTCH WOOD WORKS INC
526 Nw 43rd Pl (33126-5412)
PHONE......................954 445-7861
Yunia Dieguez Jomarron, *Principal*
EMP: 7 **EST:** 2015
SALES (est): 244.5K **Privately Held**
SIC: 2431 Millwork

(G-10027)
TOP OPTICAL LAB
4444 Sw 71st Ave Ste 111 (33155-4658)
PHONE......................305 662-2893
Angel Pardinas, *President*
Carlos Pardinas, *Vice Pres*
EMP: 10 **EST:** 1975
SQ FT: 1,313
SALES (est): 606.6K **Privately Held**
SIC: 3851 Ophthalmic goods

(G-10028)
TOP WINES IMPORT LLC (PA)
80 Sw 8th St Ste 2000 (33130-3038)
PHONE......................305 917-3600
Antonino Nigrelli, *Mng Member*
▲ **EMP:** 10 **EST:** 2012
SALES (est): 1.5MM **Privately Held**
WEB: www.topwinesimport.com
SIC: 2084 Wines

(G-10029)
TOUCHE SOFTWARE LLC
15616 Sw 62nd St (33193-2572)
PHONE......................786 241-9907
Ruben Dorrego, *President*
Zaskia Montesino, *Mktg Dir*
EMP: 7 **EST:** 2010
SALES (est): 361.4K **Privately Held**
WEB: www.touchesoftware.com
SIC: 7372 Prepackaged software

(G-10030)
TOYS FOR BOYS MIAMI LLC
1924 N Miami Ave (33136-1314)
PHONE......................786 464-0160
Rafael E Gill, *Principal*
Jilian Sanz, *Chief*
EMP: 9 **EST:** 2013

SALES (est): 270.9K **Privately Held**
WEB: www.toysforboysmagazine.com
SIC: 2741 Miscellaneous publishing

(G-10031)
TRA PUBLISHING LLP
245 Ne 37th St (33137-3710)
PHONE......................305 424-6468
Andrea Gollin, *Manager*
Ilona Oppenheim, *Director*
Raul Lira, *Director*
Rita Delcarmen Martin, *Director*
Rita Martin, *Account Dir*
EMP: 10 **EST:** 2016
SALES (est): 473.7K **Privately Held**
WEB: www.trapublishing.com
SIC: 2731 Books: publishing & printing

(G-10032)
TRACTO PARTS CORP
7401 Nw 68th St Ste 122 (33166-2807)
PHONE......................305 972-1357
Hernan Alvarez, *President*
◆ **EMP:** 9 **EST:** 2000
SALES (est): 190.6K **Privately Held**
WEB: www.tractopartscorp.com
SIC: 3523 Farm machinery & equipment

(G-10033)
TRADEPAK INC
4041 Nw 25th St A (33142-6723)
PHONE......................305 871-2247
Peter A Hoffmann Jr, *President*
Erika Hoffmann, *Shareholder*
Paul E Hoffmann, *Shareholder*
◆ **EMP:** 6 **EST:** 2003
SALES (est): 1MM **Privately Held**
WEB: www.tradepak.net
SIC: 2821 Plastics materials & resins

(G-10034)
TRADINGFLEX INC
Also Called: Labelflex
1395 Brickell Ave Ste 800 (33131-3302)
PHONE......................877 522-3535
Kevin Blanco-Uribe, *President*
EMP: 10 **EST:** 2014
SQ FT: 2,400
SALES (est): 956.5K **Privately Held**
WEB: www.tradingflex.com
SIC: 2759 Labels & seals: printing

(G-10035)
TRANE CENTRAL AMERICA INC
7650 Nw 19th St Ste 270 (33126-1220)
PHONE......................305 592-8646
William Sekkel, *CEO*
◆ **EMP:** 50 **EST:** 2008
SALES (est): 13.6MM **Privately Held**
SIC: 3585 Air conditioning equipment, complete
HQ: The Trane Company
3600 Pammel Creek Rd
La Crosse WI 54601
608 787-2000

(G-10036)
TRANE US INC
7600 Nw 19th St Ste 105 (33126-1219)
PHONE......................305 592-8646
Karin Smith, *Accountant*
Elias Carmo, *Branch Mgr*
Sean Bencsik, *Senior Mgr*
EMP: 8 **Privately Held**
WEB: www.trane.com
SIC: 3585 Refrigeration & heating equipment
HQ: Trane U.S. Inc.
800 Beaty St Ste E
Davidson NC 28036
704 655-4000

(G-10037)
TRANSAMERICA INTL BRDCSTG INC
Also Called: Omb America
3100 Nw 72nd Ave Ste 112 (33122-1336)
PHONE......................305 477-0973
Antonia Ormab, *President*
Julian Muro, *President*
Rafael Arreaz, *Principal*
◆ **EMP:** 6 **EST:** 1991
SQ FT: 2,500
SALES (est): 830.4K **Privately Held**
SIC: 3663 Radio & TV communications equipment

(G-10038)
TRAP WORLD LLC
2125 Biscayne Blvd # 400 (33137-5031)
PHONE......................305 517-5676
Mike Upton, *Principal*
EMP: 76 **EST:** 2014
SQ FT: 7,000
SALES (est): 6MM **Privately Held**
SIC: 3861 Motion picture film

(G-10039)
TREND AT LLC
2627 S Bayshore Dr (33133-5438)
PHONE......................786 300-2550
John H Schulte, *Principal*
Juan Valencia, *CFO*
Andres E Toro, *Mng Member*
EMP: 20 **EST:** 2018
SALES (est): 73.9MM **Privately Held**
WEB: www.trendatcorp.com
SIC: 2759 5111 5999 2671 Commercial printing; printing paper; packaging materials: boxes, padding, etc.; packaging paper & plastics film, coated & laminated; bags: uncoated paper & multiwall

(G-10040)
TRIDOR GROUP INC
Also Called: TGI
10118 W Flagler St (33174-1897)
PHONE......................786 707-2241
Joseph Rosa, *President*
EMP: 8 **EST:** 2015
SALES (est): 230.3K **Privately Held**
SIC: 3663 2451 7629 Mobile communication equipment; mobile homes, industrial or commercial use; telecommunication equipment repair (except telephones)

(G-10041)
TROPICAL PRINTS INC A CORP
4401 Sw 75th Ave Ste 2 (33155-4445)
PHONE......................305 261-9926
George Sanchez, *Principal*
EMP: 8 **EST:** 2008
SALES (est): 172K **Privately Held**
SIC: 2752 Commercial printing, lithographic

(G-10042)
TROPICAL SANDS
16000 Sw 200th St (33187-2902)
PHONE......................786 573-3094
Anna Vidal, *Manager*
EMP: 6 **EST:** 2018
SALES (est): 569.6K **Privately Held**
SIC: 1442 Construction sand & gravel

(G-10043)
TRUJILLO OIL PLANT INC
3325 Nw 62nd St (33147-7533)
PHONE......................305 696-8701
Lucas Trujillo Jr, *President*
Alberto Trujillo, *Vice Pres*
Joseph Murphy, *Plant Engr Mgr*
◆ **EMP:** 15 **EST:** 1996
SQ FT: 5,000
SALES (est): 2.4MM **Privately Held**
WEB: www.trujilloandsons.com
SIC: 2076 Vegetable oil mills

(G-10044)
TUKA IMPORTS LLC
3729 Nw 71st St (33147-6521)
PHONE......................305 640-8336
Michael Kuper, *Mng Member*
▲ **EMP:** 10 **EST:** 2011
SALES (est): 444.9K **Privately Held**
WEB: www.tukaimports.com
SIC: 2392 Blankets, comforters & beddings

(G-10045)
TULY CORPORATION
Also Called: Galletas Yeya
3820 Nw 32nd Ave (33142-5008)
PHONE......................305 633-0710
EMP: 16 **EST:** 1974
SQ FT: 5,000
SALES (est): 1.1MM **Privately Held**
SIC: 2052 2051 Mfg Cookies/Crackers Mfg Bread/Related Products

(G-10046)
TUTTI HOGAR INTERNATIONAL LLC
19472 Diplomat Dr (33179-6434)
PHONE......................305 705-4735
Johnny Dejman,
EMP: 8 **EST:** 2017
SALES (est): 400.9K **Privately Held**
SIC: 2671 Packaging paper & plastics film, coated & laminated

(G-10047)
TUUCI WORLDWIDE LLC (PA)
2900 Nw 35th St (33142-5240)
PHONE......................305 634-5116
Tammy Lenham, *Sales Staff*
Chintu Stanley, *Info Tech Dir*
Dougan H Clarke,
◆ **EMP:** 181 **EST:** 2008
SALES (est): 65.9MM **Privately Held**
WEB: www.tuuci.com
SIC: 2514 Metal household furniture

(G-10048)
TV FILM INTERNATIONAL INC
2600 Sw 3rd Ave Ste 850 (33129-2329)
PHONE......................305 671-3265
Pamela D Argandona, *Director*
EMP: 6 **EST:** 2000
SALES (est): 800K **Privately Held**
WEB: www.tvfilminternational.com
SIC: 3663 Radio & TV communications equipment

(G-10049)
TWINS & MARTIN EQUIPMENT CORP
80 Sw 8th St Ste 2056 (33130-3003)
PHONE......................954 802-0345
Mauro Levinton, *President*
Tomas Levinton, *COO*
Alejandro Levinton, *CFO*
Martin Levinton, *Marketing Staff*
EMP: 5 **EST:** 2008
SALES (est): 477.8K **Privately Held**
WEB: www.twinsandmartin.com
SIC: 3841 Diagnostic apparatus, medical

(G-10050)
TWO LITTLE FISHIES INC
Also Called: Ricordea Publishing
15801 Nw 15th Ave (33169-5605)
PHONE......................305 623-7695
Julian Sprung, *President*
Ines Betancourt, *Office Mgr*
▲ **EMP:** 9 **EST:** 1991
SALES (est): 1.3MM **Privately Held**
WEB: www.twolittlefishies.com
SIC: 2731 2899 3677 Books: publishing only; chemical preparations; filtration devices, electronic

(G-10051)
TX TRADING INC
20355 Ne 34th Ct Apt 427 (33180-3311)
PHONE......................786 303-9950
Beny Ichilevici, *President*
EMP: 5 **EST:** 2013
SALES (est): 5.2MM **Privately Held**
WEB: www.txtradings.com
SIC: 3663 Mobile communication equipment

(G-10052)
TYCOON TUTTI INC
1361 Nw 155th Dr (33169-5723)
P.O. Box 546375, Miami Beach (33154-0375)
PHONE......................305 624-7811
▼ **EMP:** 45
SQ FT: 16,000
SALES (est): 2.5MM **Privately Held**
SIC: 2321 2311 Mfg Children' Apparel

(G-10053)
TYREX ORE & MINERALS COMPANY
8950 Sw 74th Ct Fl 22 (33156-3171)
PHONE......................305 333-5288
Maurice Hoo, *Principal*
EMP: 7 **EST:** 2018
SALES (est): 75MM **Privately Held**
SIC: 1011 3291 Iron ore mining; abrasive metal & steel products

(G-10054)
U M P
6262 Bird Rd (33155-4882)
PHONE...................................305 740-4996
Carmen Ferrida, *Principal*
EMP: 8 **EST:** 2008
SALES (est): 124.6K **Privately Held**
SIC: 3568 Bearings, bushings & blocks

(G-10055)
UFP PALM BCH LLC DBA UFP MAMI
11400 Nw 32nd Ave (33167-2905)
PHONE...................................786 837-0552
Michael Nuclo, *Principal*
EMP: 26 **EST:** 2020
SALES (est): 2.7MM
SALES (corp-wide): 8.6B **Publicly Held**
SIC: 2421 Outdoor wood structural products
PA: Ufp Industries, Inc.
2801 E Beltline Ave Ne
Grand Rapids MI 49525
616 364-6161

(G-10056)
ULTRA AEROSPACE INC
12235 Sw 128th St (33186-5993)
PHONE...................................305 728-6361
Michael Naranjo, *President*
EMP: 13 **EST:** 2015
SALES (est): 1.2MM **Privately Held**
WEB: www.ultra-aero.com
SIC: 3728 Aircraft parts & equipment

(G-10057)
ULTRA GRAPHICS CORP
132 Sw 96th Ave (33174-2009)
PHONE...................................305 593-0202
Humberto Luis Sr, *President*
Ceneira Luis, *Corp Secy*
Bertha Luis, *Vice Pres*
Humberto Luis Jr, *Vice Pres*
◆ **EMP:** 5 **EST:** 1972
SQ FT: 4,000
SALES (est): 328.8K **Privately Held**
WEB: ultragraphics.homestead.com
SIC: 2752 Commercial printing, offset

(G-10058)
ULTRAPANEL MARINE INC
2665 S Byshr Dr Ste 220 (33133-5402)
PHONE...................................772 285-4258
Ivo Gomis, *President*
Amarilis Gomis, *Vice Pres*
◆ **EMP:** 30 **EST:** 1987
SALES (est): 6.2MM **Privately Held**
WEB: www.ultrapanel.net
SIC: 3613 3732 3625 Panelboards & distribution boards, electric; boat building & repairing; relays & industrial controls

(G-10059)
UNICRAFT CORP
3640 Nw 52nd St (33142-3245)
PHONE...................................305 633-4945
Martin Gopman, *President*
◆ **EMP:** 10 **EST:** 1983
SQ FT: 10,000
SALES (est): 1.9MM **Privately Held**
WEB: www.unicraftcorp.com
SIC: 3552 Cloth spreading machines

(G-10060)
UNIDAD EDITORIAL
1444 Biscayne Blvd (33132-1430)
PHONE...................................305 371-4428
Bensin Joseph, *Branch Mgr*
EMP: 14
SALES (corp-wide): 224.6K **Privately Held**
SIC: 2711 Newspapers
PA: Wwrt Llc
4640 Medina Rd
Copley OH

(G-10061)
UNIMAT INDUSTRIES LLC
6980 Nw 43rd St (33166-6826)
PHONE...................................305 716-0358
Masaru Ceja, *Principal*
◆ **EMP:** 6 **EST:** 2010
SALES (est): 1MM **Privately Held**
WEB: www.unimatindustries.com
SIC: 2512 Upholstered household furniture

HQ: Unimat De Mexico, S.A. De C.V.
Calle 4 No. 25-D
Naucalpan EDOMEX. 53370

(G-10062)
UNIQUE CUSTOM CABINET INC
6900 Nw 77th Ct (33166-2714)
PHONE...................................786 247-4196
Jonathan Faieta, *Owner*
EMP: 12 **EST:** 1991
SALES (est): 1.1MM **Privately Held**
WEB: www.uniquecustomcabinet.com
SIC: 2434 Wood kitchen cabinets

(G-10063)
UNIQUE CUSTOM TRUCK & TRLR LLC
Also Called: Uct2
7248 Sw 42nd Ter (33155-4531)
PHONE...................................305 403-7042
Michael Frank,
Ana Frank,
EMP: 10 **EST:** 2004
SQ FT: 20,000
SALES (est): 1MM **Privately Held**
SIC: 3715 Truck trailers

(G-10064)
UNIQUE MARBLE POLISHING INC
18093 Sw 135th Ave (33177-7117)
PHONE...................................305 969-1554
Pablo Perez, *President*
Johanni Ravel, *Vice Pres*
EMP: 5 **EST:** 2000
SALES (est): 437.1K **Privately Held**
SIC: 3471 Polishing, metals or formed products

(G-10065)
UNITED ELECTRONICS CORPORATION
1 Se 3rd Ave Ste 158 (33131-1714)
PHONE...................................954 888-1024
Shane Scanlon, *CEO*
Dave York, *President*
Mario Alvarez, *Vice Pres*
Gavriel Meidar, *Director*
Hanna Meidar, *Director*
▲ **EMP:** 78 **EST:** 2003
SQ FT: 20,000
SALES (est): 12.8MM **Privately Held**
WEB: www.uecus.com
SIC: 3643 Current-carrying wiring devices

(G-10066)
UNITED EXPRESS INTL CORP
7302 Nw 34th St (33122-1262)
PHONE...................................305 591-3292
Sharon Asrillion, *President*
EMP: 7
SALES (corp-wide): 2.3MM **Privately Held**
WEB: www.unitedexpressintl.com
SIC: 3444 Mail (post office) collection or storage boxes, sheet metal
PA: United Express International, Corp.
7300 Nw 34th St
Miami FL 33122
305 591-3292

(G-10067)
UNITED OIL PACKERS INC
Also Called: United Oil Company
3200 Nw 125th St Stop 4 (33167-2403)
PHONE...................................305 687-6457
Henry Hamersmith, *President*
Minda Hamersmith, *Admin Sec*
Maria Redondo, *Admin Asst*
◆ **EMP:** 28 **EST:** 1981
SQ FT: 280,000
SALES (est): 17.6MM
SALES (corp-wide): 22MM **Privately Held**
WEB: www.unitedoilcompany.com
SIC: 2079 Olive oil
PA: Hamersmith, Inc.
3200 Nw 125th St Stop 4
Miami FL 33167
305 685-7451

(G-10068)
UNITED PILLOW MFG INC
5646 Nw 35th Ct (33142-2730)
PHONE...................................305 636-9747

Miguel Angel Rodriguez, *President*
Juan Roddriguez, *Vice Pres*
▼ **EMP:** 17 **EST:** 2004
SQ FT: 11,000
SALES (est): 2MM **Privately Held**
WEB: www.unitedpillow.com
SIC: 2392 Pillows, bed: made from purchased materials

(G-10069)
UNITED VERTICAL BLINDS LLC
1261 Nw 175th St (33169-4656)
PHONE...................................786 348-8000
Desmond Patten, *Principal*
EMP: 7 **EST:** 2019
SALES (est): 381.3K **Privately Held**
SIC: 2591 Blinds vertical

(G-10070)
UNIVERSAL CRGO DOORS & SVC LLC
8490 Nw 68th St (33166-2661)
P.O. Box 660460, Miami Springs (33266-0460)
PHONE...................................305 594-9175
David Sandri, *President*
Roy Sandri, *COO*
Marli Sandri, *Treasurer*
EMP: 35 **EST:** 1988
SQ FT: 22,000
SALES (est): 5MM **Privately Held**
WEB: www.universalcargodoors.com
SIC: 3728 Aircraft parts & equipment

(G-10071)
UNIVERSAL PRINTING COMPANY
3100 Nw 74th Ave (33122-1226)
PHONE...................................305 592-5387
Jack Nicol, *President*
Gloria Bechtel, *Corp Secy*
▼ **EMP:** 36 **EST:** 1961
SQ FT: 57,000
SALES (est): 1.1MM **Privately Held**
WEB: www.universalprintingco.com
SIC: 2752 Commercial printing, offset

(G-10072)
UNIVERSAL RIBBON CORPORATION
8111 Nw 68th St (33166-2757)
PHONE...................................305 471-0828
Juan Rios, *President*
Irene Rios, *Vice Pres*
David Rios, *Vice Pres*
◆ **EMP:** 18 **EST:** 1988
SQ FT: 6,000
SALES (est): 748.7K **Privately Held**
WEB: www.universalribbon.com
SIC: 3955 Print cartridges for laser & other computer printers

(G-10073)
UNIVERSAL SEAT CVERS AUTO ACC (PA)
2370 Ludlam Rd (33155-1846)
PHONE...................................305 262-3955
Isora Del Cristo, *President*
▼ **EMP:** 5 **EST:** 1986
SQ FT: 5,000
SALES (est): 1.3MM **Privately Held**
SIC: 2399 Seat covers, automobile

(G-10074)
UNIVERSAL SURGICAL APPLIANCE
400 Ne 191st St (33179-3986)
P.O. Box 693099 (33269-0099)
PHONE...................................305 652-0810
Ira S Lehman, *President*
Shirley Lehman, *Corp Secy*
David Lehman, *Vice Pres*
Lisa Lehman, *Vice Pres*
EMP: 9 **EST:** 1962
SQ FT: 8,000
SALES (est): 259.3K **Privately Held**
SIC: 3842 3841 Surgical appliances & supplies; abdominal supporters, braces & trusses; belts: surgical, sanitary & corrective; braces, orthopedic; surgical & medical instruments

(G-10075)
UNIVERSAL TECH INC
3042 Nw 72nd Ave (33122-1314)
PHONE...................................786 220-8032
Ling Chen, *President*
EMP: 8 **EST:** 2013
SALES (est): 131.5K **Privately Held**
SIC: 2678 Stationery products

(G-10076)
UPTON HOUSE COOLER CORPORATION
2490 Nw 7th Ave (33127-4206)
PHONE...................................305 633-2531
Dimas Beret, *President*
EMP: 5 **EST:** 1952
SQ FT: 15,000
SALES (est): 467.9K **Privately Held**
SIC: 3564 3444 Ventilating fans: industrial or commercial; blowing fans: industrial or commercial; exhaust fans: industrial or commercial; sheet metalwork

(G-10077)
URANO PUBLISHING INC
8871 Sw 129th Ter (33176-5905)
PHONE...................................305 233-3365
Lucia Laratelli, *President*
◆ **EMP:** 12 **EST:** 2000
SALES (est): 372.3K **Privately Held**
WEB: www.edicionesurano.com
SIC: 2741 Miscellaneous publishing

(G-10078)
URBAN STONE WORKS
7025 Ne 2nd Ave (33138-5507)
PHONE...................................305 754-7171
Janusz Niedbala, *President*
◆ **EMP:** 10 **EST:** 1988
SQ FT: 5,000
SALES (est): 1.6MM **Privately Held**
WEB: www.urbanstoneworks.com
SIC: 3272 Concrete products, precast

(G-10079)
US AMERICAN PLASTIC CORP
2164 Nw 22nd Ct (33142-7346)
PHONE...................................305 200-3683
Hector Pino, *President*
Adrian Alfonso, *Vice Pres*
Ulises Cruz, *Vice Pres*
EMP: 10 **EST:** 2016
SALES (est): 760.7K **Privately Held**
SIC: 2673 Bags: plastic, laminated & coated

(G-10080)
US GLOBAL GLASS LLC
Also Called: Florida Laminated Tempered GL
220 Ne 187th St (33179-4516)
PHONE...................................305 651-6630
Frank Wilson, *President*
John Parell, *Chairman*
Patrick Tschrin, *COO*
J Randy Beard, *Finance*
EMP: 18 **EST:** 2001
SQ FT: 75,000
SALES (est): 289.6K **Privately Held**
SIC: 3211 Window glass, clear & colored

(G-10081)
US SHEET METAL INC
7333 Nw 66th St (33166-3009)
PHONE...................................305 884-7705
Francisco M Valdes, *President*
Barbara Valdes, *Vice Pres*
◆ **EMP:** 18 **EST:** 1997
SQ FT: 5,798
SALES (est): 2.4MM **Privately Held**
SIC: 3444 Ducts, sheet metal

(G-10082)
USA EXPRESS PALLETS CORP
4655 Nw 36th Ave (33142-3938)
PHONE...................................786 251-9543
Raul Gomez, *Principal*
EMP: 8 **EST:** 2005
SALES (est): 502.6K **Privately Held**
SIC: 2448 Pallets, wood

(G-10083)
USA RECMAR CORP
918 Nw 106th Avenue Cir (33172-3123)
PHONE...................................786 554-3505
Amadeo N Roig, *President*

Martiza Gonzalez, *General Mgr*
EMP: 9 **EST:** 2018
SALES (est): 120.2K **Privately Held**
SIC: 2591 Drapery hardware & blinds & shades

(G-10084)
USA SIGNS INC
7230 Nw 46th St (33166-6423)
PHONE..................305 470-2333
Jose Pacheco, *President*
Katya Caceres, *Sales Staff*
EMP: 8 **EST:** 2001
SALES (est): 500K **Privately Held**
WEB: www.usasigns.us
SIC: 3993 Electric signs

(G-10085)
USG INTERNATIONAL LTD
3001 Nw 125th St (33167-2524)
PHONE..................305 688-8744
EMP: 10 **EST:** 2014
SALES (est): 1.5MM **Privately Held**
SIC: 3272 Wall & ceiling squares, concrete

(G-10086)
V & C SUPPLY ORNAMENTAL CORP
6400 Nw 72nd Ave (33166-3627)
PHONE..................305 634-9040
Maria V Solano, *President*
Ronald Solano, *Vice Pres*
Jose Solano, *Director*
◆ **EMP:** 6 **EST:** 2002
SALES (est): 832K **Privately Held**
WEB: www.vcmetalsupply.com
SIC: 3548 3089 Welding apparatus; fences, gates & accessories: plastic

(G-10087)
V & F AIR CONDITIONING SUP LLC
7320 Nw 12th St Ste 107 (33126-1913)
PHONE..................305 477-1040
Dainel D Fuentes, *Mng Member*
Rolando Vento,
EMP: 11 **EST:** 2014
SALES (est): 5MM **Privately Held**
WEB: www.vfacsupply.com
SIC: 3585 Air conditioning equipment, complete

(G-10088)
V M VISUAL MDSG DCTR GROUP INC
600 Nw 62nd St (33150-4330)
PHONE..................305 759-9910
Rafael Velazquez, *President*
EMP: 10 **EST:** 2001
SALES (est): 636.6K **Privately Held**
SIC: 2392 Cushions & pillows; blankets, comforters & beddings; tablecloths & table settings; sheets, fabric: made from purchased materials

(G-10089)
V2 CIGS
3050 Biscayne Blvd # 700 (33137-4184)
PHONE..................305 240-6387
David Turner, *Branch Mgr*
EMP: 38
SALES (corp-wide): 789.6K **Privately Held**
WEB: www.v2.com
SIC: 2111 Cigarettes
PA: V2 Cigs
1521 Alton Rd Ste 275
Miami Beach FL 33139
305 517-1149

(G-10090)
VALENTINA SIGNA INC
Also Called: G & B Trading Imports
7343 Nw 56th St (33166-4203)
PHONE..................305 264-0673
Gun Gilgim, *President*
EMP: 5 **EST:** 1991
SALES (est): 309K **Privately Held**
WEB: www.valentinagb.com
SIC: 2339 Neckwear & ties: women's, misses' & juniors'

(G-10091)
VALENTINI ITALIAN SPC CO
4290 Nw 37th Ct (33142-4234)
PHONE..................305 638-0822
Lislei Gamarra, *Branch Mgr*
EMP: 7
SALES (corp-wide): 3.6MM **Privately Held**
WEB: www.valentiniicecream.com
SIC: 2024 Ice cream, bulk
PA: Valentini Italian Specialties, Co.
4071 W 108th St Unit 1
Hialeah FL
305 638-3177

(G-10092)
VAMPA TIRES SUPPLIES INC
7243 Nw 54th St (33166-4807)
PHONE..................305 888-1001
Emilio Perez, *President*
Lazaro Perez, *Vice Pres*
◆ **EMP:** 5 **EST:** 1999
SQ FT: 600
SALES (est): 939.2K **Privately Held**
WEB: www.vampa.net
SIC: 3559 Tire retreading machinery & equipment

(G-10093)
VAN TEAL INC
Also Called: Bb & T
7240 Ne 4th Ave (33138-5316)
PHONE..................305 751-6767
Hivo Gonzalez, *CEO*
Estella Van Teal, *President*
Eddy Van Teal, *Exec VP*
Eduardo Vanteal, *Exec VP*
Eddie Gonzalez, *Vice Pres*
▲ **EMP:** 30 **EST:** 1974
SQ FT: 50,000
SALES (est): 4.7MM **Privately Held**
WEB: www.vanteal.com
SIC: 3645 3221 3648 Residential lighting fixtures; glass containers; lighting equipment

(G-10094)
VANDALIZE BOAT WORKS
3480 Nw 21st St (33142-6911)
PHONE..................305 450-2014
EMP: 6 **EST:** 2018
SALES (est): 455.3K **Privately Held**
SIC: 3731 Shipbuilding & repairing

(G-10095)
VAPOR GROUP INC (PA)
20725 Ne 16th Ave Ste A4 (33179-2123)
PHONE..................954 792-8450
David Zinger, *President*
Yaniv Nahon, *COO*
Jorge Schcolnik, *CFO*
Dror Svorai, *Treasurer*
EMP: 8 **EST:** 1990
SQ FT: 500
SALES (est): 1.9MM **Publicly Held**
WEB: www.vaporgroup.com
SIC: 2111 5571 Cigarettes; motor scooters

(G-10096)
VAPOR GROUP INC (PA)
20200 W Dixie Hwy Ste 906 (33180-1926)
PHONE..................954 792-8450
Yaniv Nahon, *President*
Jorge Schcolnik, *CFO*
EMP: 5 **EST:** 2012
SALES (est): 1.1MM **Privately Held**
SIC: 3634 Cigarette lighters, electric

(G-10097)
VARIBELT INCORPORATED
13216 Sw 45th Ln (33175-3931)
PHONE..................305 775-1568
Davut Ozdemir, *President*
Nazlican Ozdemir Serin, *Vice Pres*
EMP: 5 **EST:** 2020
SALES (est): 304.7K **Privately Held**
WEB: www.myvbelt.com
SIC: 3052 Rubber & plastics hose & beltings

(G-10098)
VC ATLANTIC WOODWORK
14322 Sw 117th Ter (33186-8633)
PHONE..................305 219-9411
Claudio Barrueto, *Principal*
EMP: 7 **EST:** 2009

SALES (est): 120K **Privately Held**
SIC: 2431 Millwork

(G-10099)
VECTOR GROUP LTD (PA)
4400 Biscayne Blvd (33137-3212)
PHONE..................305 579-8000
Howard M Lorber, *President*
Nicholas P Anson, *President*
Richard J Lampen, *COO*
J David Ballard, *Senior VP*
Marc N Bell, *Senior VP*
EMP: 53 **EST:** 1873
SQ FT: 12,390
SALES (est): 1.2B **Publicly Held**
WEB: www.vectorgroupltd.com
SIC: 2111 6552 Cigarettes; subdividers & developers

(G-10100)
VENCHI US INC
1111 Brickell Ave # 2650 (33131-3112)
PHONE..................646 448-8663
Davide Cravero, *CEO*
EMP: 8 **EST:** 2015
SALES (est): 245.1K **Privately Held**
WEB: us.venchi.com
SIC: 2066 Chocolate

(G-10101)
VENSOFT CORP
2530 Ne 208th Ter (33180-1316)
PHONE..................786 991-2080
Moises Romero, *President*
◆ **EMP:** 12 **EST:** 1999
SALES (est): 139.4K **Privately Held**
WEB: www.vensoft.com
SIC: 7372 5734 Prepackaged software; computer & software stores

(G-10102)
VERU INC (PA)
Also Called: Veru Healthcare
2916 N Miami Ave Ste 1000 (33127-3965)
PHONE..................305 509-6897
Mitchell S Steiner, *Ch of Bd*
Harry Fisch, *Vice Ch Bd*
Rachel Steiner, *General Mgr*
Jason Davies, *Exec VP*
Phillip Kuhn, *Exec VP*
EMP: 66 **EST:** 1971
SQ FT: 12,000
SALES (est): 61.2MM **Publicly Held**
WEB: www.verupharma.com
SIC: 2834 3069 Pharmaceutical preparations; birth control devices, rubber

(G-10103)
VERY TASTY LLC
2177 Nw 24th Ct (33142-7114)
PHONE..................305 636-4140
Pedro A Cardenas, *Principal*
EMP: 10 **EST:** 2011
SQ FT: 4,500
SALES (est): 978.4K **Privately Held**
WEB: www.very-tasty.com
SIC: 2038 Ethnic foods, frozen

(G-10104)
VGR HOLDING LLC (HQ)
4400 S Biscayne Blvd # 10 (33131-2303)
PHONE..................305 579-8000
Richard J Lampen, *Manager*
Marc N Bell, *Manager*
EMP: 14 **EST:** 1999
SALES (est): 162.9MM **Publicly Held**
SIC: 2111 6552 Cigarettes; subdividers & developers

(G-10105)
VICBAG LLC
80 Sw 8th St Ste 2000 (33130-3038)
PHONE..................305 423-7042
Djamal Bellechilli, *Mng Member*
◆ **EMP:** 5 **EST:** 2005
SQ FT: 371
SALES (est): 1.1MM
SALES (corp-wide): 401.6K **Privately Held**
WEB: www.vicbag.com
SIC: 2759 Bags, plastic: printing
HQ: Vicbag
23 Rue Du Depart
Paris 75014
141 029-040

(G-10106)
VICCARBE INC
8950 Sw 74th Ct Ste 1406 (33156-3173)
PHONE..................305 670-0979
Rodrigo Roche Silvia, *QC Dir*
Benedito Gonzalez Daniel, *Comms Dir*
Carrasco Berlanga Victor Manue, *Manager*
EMP: 28 **EST:** 2013
SALES (est): 17.3MM
SALES (corp-wide): 2.7B **Publicly Held**
WEB: www.viccarbe.com
SIC: 2521 2522 Wood office furniture; wood office chairs, benches & stools; benches, office: wood; chairs, office: padded, upholstered or plain: wood; office chairs, benches & stools, except wood
HQ: Viccarbe Habitat Sl
Camino Raco (Pg Ind Norte) 23
Beniparrell 46469
961 201-010

(G-10107)
VICENTE GANDIA PLA
Also Called: Vicente Gandia USA
7300 N Kendall Dr Ste 470 (33156-7854)
P.O. Box 560668 (33256-0668)
PHONE..................310 699-8559
▲ **EMP:** 120
SALES: 44.5MM **Privately Held**
SIC: 2084 5182 Mfg Wines/Brandy/Spirits Whol Wine/Distilled Beverages

(G-10108)
VICENTE GANDIA USA INC
7300 N Kendall Dr Ste 470 (33156-7854)
PHONE..................310 699-8559
Jose Maria Gandia, *President*
Laura Gordon, *Vice Pres*
EMP: 9 **EST:** 2011
SALES (est): 102.8K **Privately Held**
WEB: www.vicentegandiausa.com
SIC: 2084 Wines

(G-10109)
VICTUS LLC (PA)
4918 Sw 74th Ct (33155-4400)
PHONE..................305 663-2129
Ivonne Perez, *Business Mgr*
Victor Garcia, *Vice Pres*
Dallal Hammoud, *Purchasing*
Carlos Fernandez, *CFO*
Arturo Celis, *Finance*
◆ **EMP:** 30 **EST:** 1999
SQ FT: 14,000
SALES (est): 3.7MM **Privately Held**
WEB: www.victus.com
SIC: 2834 3069 Vitamin, nutrient & hematinic preparations for human use; medical & laboratory rubber sundries & related products

(G-10110)
VIDREPUR OF AMERICA LLC
2301 Nw 84th Ave (33122-1531)
PHONE..................305 468-9008
June Rodgers, *Comptroller*
Darren Caraway, *Manager*
Eduardo Sanchez,
Jose Santapou,
◆ **EMP:** 15 **EST:** 2001
SQ FT: 45,000
SALES (est): 2.1MM **Privately Held**
WEB: www.vidrepur.us
SIC: 3253 Mosaic tile, glazed & unglazed: ceramic

(G-10111)
VILLAGRAN PRINTING CORP
765 Nw 34th St (33127-3343)
PHONE..................786 230-6638
Silvia Villagran, *Vice Pres*
EMP: 7 **EST:** 2011
SALES (est): 82K **Privately Held**
SIC: 2752 Commercial printing, offset

(G-10112)
VINYL CORP (DH)
8000 Nw 79th Pl Ste 4 (33166-2181)
PHONE..................305 477-6464
Garden W Smith, *President*
Ernie Reyes, *General Mgr*
Arthur L Whitman, *Vice Pres*
Nick Apan, *VP Sales*
▼ **EMP:** 2 **EST:** 1987
SQ FT: 84,000

▲ = Import ▼=Export
◆ =Import/Export

SALES (est): 5.5MM **Privately Held**
WEB: www.clarkdietrich.com
SIC: 3089 Plastic hardware & building
products

(G-10113)
VIP 2000 TV INC
1200 Brickell Ave # 1575 (33131-4102)
PHONE......................305 373-2400
Roxana Rotundo, *President*
EMP: 13 EST: 2007
SALES (est): 528.1K **Privately Held**
SIC: 3861 Motion picture film

(G-10114)
VISION ANALYTICAL INC (PA)
4444 Sw 71st Ave Ste 112 (33155-4658)
PHONE......................305 801-7140
Pedro Bouza, *President*
Peter Bouza, *General Mgr*
EMP: 5 EST: 2005
SQ FT: 500
SALES (est): 541.6K **Privately Held**
WEB: www.particleshape.com
SIC: 3826 Analytical instruments

(G-10115)
VISION CANDLES INC
7363 Nw 36th Ave (33147-5809)
PHONE......................305 836-8650
Jose E Garcia, *President*
◆ EMP: 5 EST: 2004
SALES (est): 414.7K **Privately Held**
WEB: www.tuvisioncandles.com
SIC: 3999 Candles

(G-10116)
VISUAL ACOUSTICS LLC
591 Nw 35th St (33127-3436)
PHONE......................786 390-6128
Marc Lewin, *Mng Member*
EMP: 5 EST: 2003
SALES (est): 701K **Privately Held**
WEB: www.visualacoustics.net
SIC: 3651 7622 Home entertainment
equipment, electronic; home entertain-
ment repair services

(G-10117)
VITAL IMGING DIAGNSTC CTRS
LLC
7101 Sw 99th Ave Ste 109 (33173-4661)
PHONE......................305 569-9992
Dr Juan Puig, *Manager*
EMP: 12 EST: 2013
SALES (est): 2.5MM **Privately Held**
WEB: www.vitalimg.com
SIC: 3829 Medical diagnostic systems, nu-
clear

(G-10118)
VIVA LED LLC
2944 Nw 72nd Ave (33122-1312)
PHONE......................786 491-9290
EMP: 18
SALES (corp-wide): 2.7MM **Privately
Held**
WEB: www.viva-led.com
SIC: 3674 Light emitting diodes
PA: Viva Led Llc
2936 Nw 72nd Ave
Miami FL 33122
786 491-9290

(G-10119)
VLEX LLC
1200 Brickell Ave # 1800 (33131-3214)
PHONE......................800 335-6202
Lluis Faus, *Partner*
Guillermo Espindola, *Project Mgr*
Manuel Gonzales, *Manager*
Yuiskaly Galindez, *Consultant*
Giuseppe Guglielmi, *Administration*
EMP: 5 EST: 2013
SALES (est): 557.4K
SALES (corp-wide): 11.1MM **Privately
Held**
WEB: www.vlex.com.mx
SIC: 2741
PA: Vlex Networks Sl
Calle Tanger, 86 - Glories Oficina 07
107
Barcelona 08018
932 722-685

(G-10120)
VS CARBONICS INC
3491 Nw 79th St (33147-4532)
PHONE......................305 903-6501
Dios Vazquez,
EMP: 12 EST: 2009
SALES (est): 2.4MM **Privately Held**
WEB: www.vscarbonics.com
SIC: 2813 Industrial gases

(G-10121)
VS COATINGS LLC
3491 Nw 79th St (33147-4532)
PHONE......................305 677-6224
Carlos Alvarez, *Principal*
EMP: 9 EST: 2018
SALES (est): 619.1K **Privately Held**
WEB: www.vs-coatings.com
SIC: 3423 Hand & edge tools

(G-10122)
VTRONIX LLC
7900 Nw 68th St (33166-2796)
P.O. Box 267096, Weston (33326-7096)
PHONE......................305 471-7600
Nervyse Lugo, *Sales Staff*
Anil Gowda,
Nina Birnbach,
Jorge Cosio,
Chaiyasit Thampeera,
▲ EMP: 5 EST: 2001
SQ FT: 3,000
SALES (est): 708.4K **Privately Held**
WEB: www.vtronix.com
SIC: 3822 Thermostats, except built-in

(G-10123)
WAR CHEST RIVER LLC
675 Nw 97th St (33150-1652)
PHONE......................954 736-7704
Chapman Ducote, *Principal*
EMP: 6 EST: 2015
SALES (est): 398.1K **Privately Held**
SIC: 2741 Miscellaneous publishing

(G-10124)
WATCHFACTS INC
Also Called: Collective,
14 Ne 1st Ave Ste 1102 (33132-2409)
PHONE......................786 797-5705
John Cormier, *President*
Mufasa Holdings, *President*
Nawel Kiram, *Vice Pres*
EMP: 20 EST: 2010
SALES (est): 1.4MM **Privately Held**
WEB: www.watchfacts.com
SIC: 3873 Appliance timers

(G-10125)
WATERHUSE ARCHTCTRAL
WDWRK LLC
4261 Nw 36th Ave (33142-4217)
PHONE......................786 534-4943
Carlos E De Leon, *Mng Member*
EMP: 10 EST: 2018
SALES (est): 1MM **Privately Held**
WEB: www.waterhousewoodwork.com
SIC: 2431 Millwork

(G-10126)
WATSON STEEL PRODUCTS
8067 Nw 66th St (33166-2729)
PHONE......................716 853-2233
Jeff Watson, *President*
EMP: 8 EST: 2007
SALES (est): 613.5K **Privately Held**
WEB: www.watsonsteelandiron.com
SIC: 3599 Machine shop, jobbing & repair

(G-10127)
WD-40 COMPANY
2151 S Le Jeune Rd # 308 (33134-4200)
PHONE......................305 463-9158
Enrique Diaz, *Principal*
Charles Daniels, *Sales Staff*
Adrienne Tharp, *Sales Staff*
Craig Douglas, *Manager*
Bill Fantus, *Director*
EMP: 17
SALES (corp-wide): 488.1MM **Publicly
Held**
WEB: www.wd40.com
SIC: 2992 Lubricating oils

PA: Wd-40 Company
9715 Businesspark Ave
San Diego CA 92131
619 275-1400

(G-10128)
WHATEVER LO QUE SEA LLC
2087 Nw 135th Ave (33182-1926)
PHONE......................786 429-3462
Fede Annitto, *CEO*
EMP: 6 EST: 2018
SALES (est): 300K **Privately Held**
WEB: www.whateverloquesea.com
SIC: 2711 Commercial printing & newspa-
per publishing combined

(G-10129)
WHITE CARDBOARD CORP
3671 Nw 81st St (33147-4444)
PHONE......................786 260-4692
Oscar Fidalgo, *Principal*
▲ EMP: 11 EST: 2013
SALES (est): 308K **Privately Held**
SIC: 2631 Cardboard

(G-10130)
WHITEWATER BOAT CORP
280 Nw 73rd St (33150-3427)
PHONE......................305 756-9191
Norman Collins, *President*
Shane Collins, *Vice Pres*
EMP: 6 EST: 1980
SQ FT: 12,000
SALES (est): 490.1K **Privately Held**
WEB: www.whitewaterboat.com
SIC: 3732 1799 Boats, fiberglass: building
& repairing; rigging & scaffolding

(G-10131)
WHOLE COFFEE COMPANY LLC
Also Called: TN Cruz
1130 Nw 159th Dr (33169-5808)
PHONE......................786 364-4444
Thomas Ferguson, *CEO*
Wilmar Guasti, *Opers Mgr*
Liza Norona, *VP Sales*
Tony Farias, *Accounts Mgr*
▲ EMP: 80 EST: 2007
SQ FT: 42,000
SALES (est): 27.9MM **Privately Held**
SIC: 2066 2095 Chocolate; roasted coffee

(G-10132)
WILL & MIA CORP
1250 Ne 207th Ter (33179-2021)
PHONE......................617 943-6914
Mia Zabala, *Principal*
EMP: 8 EST: 2016
SALES (est): 78.8K **Privately Held**
SIC: 2711 Newspapers, publishing & print-
ing

(G-10133)
WINDSTAR EXPRESS INC
19499 Ne 10th Ave (33179-5732)
PHONE......................786 252-1569
Yoandy Navarro, *Principal*
EMP: 8 EST: 2012
SALES (est): 101.2K **Privately Held**
WEB: www.windstarexpress.com
SIC: 3537 Industrial trucks & tractors

(G-10134)
WINE WORLD INC
12650 Nw 25th St Ste 112 (33182-1512)
PHONE......................786 348-8780
Modesto Gil, *President*
Aldo Neyra, *Vice Pres*
EMP: 9 EST: 2014
SALES (est): 141.7K **Privately Held**
SIC: 2084 Wines

(G-10135)
WINSLOW MICROPLASTICS
CORP
20257 Ne 15th Ct (33179-2710)
PHONE......................305 493-3501
Adolfo Saul, *President*
Nora Saul, *President*
Jose Abadia, *Principal*
Gabriel E Saul, *Director*
Sebastian E Saul, *Director*
EMP: 6 EST: 1986
SALES (est): 551.3K **Privately Held**
SIC: 3089 Injection molding of plastics

(G-10136)
WINWOOD PRINT
591 Nw 29th St (33127-3917)
PHONE......................786 615-3188
EMP: 8 EST: 2017
SALES (est): 163K **Privately Held**
SIC: 2752 Commercial printing, litho-
graphic

(G-10137)
WIRELESS LATIN ENTRMT INC
Also Called: Wilaen
5301 Blue Lagoon Dr # 180 (33126-2093)
PHONE......................305 858-7740
Gabriel Abaroa, *CEO*
Luis Samra, *COO*
Gustavo Falkenhagen, *Opers Staff*
Ahmed Fernandez, *Opers Staff*
Alberto Espana, *CFO*
EMP: 5 EST: 2002
SALES (est): 782.7K **Privately Held**
SIC: 3357 Communication wire

(G-10138)
WONDER HOLDINGS
ACQUISITION
1450 Brickell Ave # 3100 (33131-3444)
PHONE......................305 379-2322
Anthony A Tamer, *CEO*
EMP: 12 EST: 2010
SALES (est): 159.8K **Privately Held**
SIC: 2834 Drugs acting on the respiratory
system

(G-10139)
WOOD SPLINTER CORP
15451 Sw 60th St (33193-2811)
PHONE......................305 721-7215
Armando Agustin, *Principal*
EMP: 8 EST: 2015
SALES (est): 45.6K **Privately Held**
SIC: 2499 Wood products

(G-10140)
WOOD ZONE INC
13751 Sw 147th Ave (33196-2884)
PHONE......................305 971-5550
Francisco Ormaza, *Owner*
▲ EMP: 6 EST: 1987
SALES (est): 427.3K **Privately Held**
WEB: www.woodzone.com
SIC: 2434 Wood kitchen cabinets

(G-10141)
WOODFIELD PHARMACEUTICAL
LLC
66 W Flagler St Ste 1000 (33130-1809)
PHONE......................281 530-3077
Adam Runsdorf, *President*
Willis Reed, *Opers Staff*
Harry Sun, *QC Mgr*
Jane Richmond, *Manager*
Amanda Kirkpatrick, *Director*
▲ EMP: 58 EST: 2014
SALES (est): 9MM **Privately Held**
SIC: 2834 Pharmaceutical preparations

(G-10142)
WOODIES INC
2041 Sw 82nd Pl (33155-1213)
PHONE......................305 266-9209
Augusto G Perez, *President*
Sandra C Figuerola, *Vice Pres*
EMP: 7 EST: 1996
SALES (est): 464.9K **Privately Held**
SIC: 3429 Cabinet hardware

(G-10143)
WORLD EVENT PROMOTIONS
LLC
Also Called: Wep Sourcing
4302 Sw 73rd Ave (33155-4550)
PHONE......................800 214-3408
Patrick Lowenthal, *CEO*
Giorgio Paredes, *Opers Mgr*
Edwin Guilcapi, *Accounts Mgr*
Yanet Texidor, *Associate*
EMP: 30 EST: 2015

SALES (est): 2.3MM **Privately Held**
WEB: www.activateswag.com
SIC: **2396** 2759 7389 8742 Apparel & other linings, except millinery; promotional printing; advertising, promotional & trade show services; embroidering of advertising on shirts, etc.; marketing consulting services

(G-10144)
WORLD FROST INC
14853 Sw 152nd Ter (33187-5544)
PHONE...................................786 439-4445
◆ EMP: 8
SQ FT: 4,000
SALES: 3.3MM **Privately Held**
SIC: **2085** Mfg Distilled/Blended Liquor

(G-10145)
WORLDBOX CORPORATION
Also Called: Bolbox
8333 Nw 66th St (33166-2626)
PHONE...................................305 253-8800
Patricia A Ortiz, *Principal*
EMP: 7 EST: 2012
SALES (est): 201.3K **Privately Held**
WEB: www.worldbox.net
SIC: **2711** Newspapers

(G-10146)
WORLDWIDE BUILDING INTL INC
1840 Coral Way (33145-2748)
PHONE...................................786 744-7076
Kevin Goldstein, *CEO*
EMP: 248 EST: 2008
SALES (est): 10.1MM **Privately Held**
WEB: www.wcrldbuildingprods.com
SIC: **3999** Manufacturing industries

(G-10147)
WPP GROUP USA INC
Also Called: Muv
601 Brickell Key Dr # 700 (33131-2649)
PHONE...................................305 341-8132
Spencer Aleman, *Accounts Mgr*
Taylor Devost, *Accounts Mgr*
Alexis Quintal, *Accounts Mgr*
Devin Zampaglione, *Accounts Mgr*
Sarah Bowyer, *Accounts Exec*
EMP: 13
SALES (corp-wide): 17B **Privately Held**
WEB: www.wpp.com
SIC: **3663** 7311 Mobile communication equipment; advertising agencies
HQ: Wpp Group Usa, Inc.
3 World Trade Ctr Grnwich
New York NY 10007
212 632-2200

(G-10148)
WYNOT INTERNATIONAL LLC
Also Called: Come Taste The Love Malaysia
230 Ne 4th St Apt 1012 (33132-2357)
PHONE...................................305 218-8794
Abel Sanchez, *CEO*
EMP: 10 EST: 2020
SALES (est): 349.1K **Privately Held**
WEB: www.wynotfitness.com
SIC: **2599** Food wagons, restaurant

(G-10149)
YAM MACHINE SHOP AND IRON WORK
3710 Nw 50th St (33142-3936)
PHONE...................................786 246-4174
Barbaro Y Abreu, *Manager*
EMP: 7 EST: 2011
SALES (est): 240.7K **Privately Held**
WEB: iron-work-services.cmac.ws
SIC: **3599** Machine shop, jobbing & repair

(G-10150)
YATFL INC
19425 Sw 188th St (33187-1948)
PHONE...................................786 643-8660
Yuliet Martinez, *President*
Yosvany Acosta, *Vice Pres*
EMP: 5 EST: 2009
SALES (est): 974.4K **Privately Held**
SIC: **1389** 8711 Construction, repair & dismantling services; consulting engineer

(G-10151)
YIPPY INC (PA)
999 Brickell Ave Ste 610 (33131-3043)
PHONE...................................877 947-7901
Richard Granville, *CEO*
John Macartney, *President*
John Routhier, *Exec VP*
EMP: 5 EST: 2006
SALES (est): 2.1MM **Privately Held**
WEB: www.yippyinc.com
SIC: **7372** Business oriented computer software

(G-10152)
YOLY MUNOZ CORP
102 Se 1st St (33131-1402)
PHONE...................................305 860-3839
Yolanda Munoz, *President*
Carlos Munoz, *Treasurer*
EMP: 6 EST: 1978
SQ FT: 2,500
SALES (est): 315.8K **Privately Held**
WEB: www.yolymunozcouture.com
SIC: **2335** 5621 Dresses, paper: cut & sewn; ready-to-wear apparel, women's

(G-10153)
YOUR PERFORMANCE SOLUTIONS
14417 Sw 143rd Ct (33186-5646)
PHONE...................................305 278-2762
Juan B De Pawlikowski, *President*
EMP: 8 EST: 2016
SALES (est): 124.5K **Privately Held**
SIC: **3949** Sporting & athletic goods

(G-10154)
YP GENERAL WORK & CABINETS
600 Nw 111th St (33168-3307)
PHONE...................................786 317-0973
Yusmar Pena, *Principal*
EMP: 7 EST: 2012
SALES (est): 146.8K **Privately Held**
SIC: **2434** Wood kitchen cabinets

(G-10155)
ZAP MOSQUITO SOLUTIONS INC
Also Called: Bask
13442 Sw 131st St (33186-5817)
PHONE...................................786 732-0772
Keith D Brookins, *President*
Raquel Brookins, *Vice Pres*
EMP: 5 EST: 2014
SALES (est): 596.6K **Privately Held**
SIC: **3569** 7342 Separators for steam, gas, vapor or air (machinery); pest control in structures

(G-10156)
ZEN DISTRIBUTORS GROUP II LLC
Also Called: Tagua Gun Leather
2047 Nw 24th Ave (33142-7237)
PHONE...................................305 637-3014
Jose Kellemen,
EMP: 10 EST: 2007
SALES (est): 1.1MM **Privately Held**
SIC: **3199** Holsters, leather

(G-10157)
ZETA KITCHEN & BATH INC
6905 Nw 82nd Ave (33166-2766)
PHONE...................................786 552-2322
Jorge F Zamora, *President*
Malena Mercedes Zamora, *Vice Pres*
Marilin Fuentes, *Admin Sec*
EMP: 8 EST: 2013
SALES (est): 279.3K **Privately Held**
WEB: www.zetakitchenandbath.com
SIC: **2499** Kitchen, bathroom & household ware: wood

(G-10158)
ZURIGO TRADING INC
5077 Nw 7th St Apt 1118 (33126-3465)
PHONE...................................305 244-4681
Alfredo Puglia, *President*
EMP: 8 EST: 2004
SALES (est): 89.1K **Privately Held**
SIC: **2851** Paints & allied products

Miami Beach
Miami-Dade County

(G-10159)
3 COOL CATS LLC
429 Lenox Ave (33139-6532)
PHONE...................................646 334-6229
Rocco Venneri, *CEO*
EMP: 9 EST: 2018
SALES (est): 626.7K **Privately Held**
WEB: www.drinkcoolcat.com
SIC: **2084** Wine coolers (beverages)

(G-10160)
ACCUWARE INC
235 Lincoln Rd Ste 306 (33139-3157)
PHONE...................................305 894-6874
Cyril Houri, *Principal*
EMP: 8 EST: 2015
SALES (est): 139.5K **Privately Held**
WEB: www.accuware.com
SIC: **7372** Prepackaged software

(G-10161)
ADIR SCOOTERS INC
Also Called: VIP Scooter Rental
739 5th St (33139-6517)
PHONE...................................305 532-0019
Gitai Levi, *Principal*
EMP: 6 EST: 2005
SALES (est): 375.5K **Privately Held**
SIC: **3751** Motor scooters & parts

(G-10162)
AICON YACHTS AMERICAS LLC
1801 West Ave (33139-1431)
PHONE...................................910 583-5299
Anton A Speciale, *President*
EMP: 7 EST: 2008
SALES (est): 141.2K **Privately Held**
SIC: **3732** Boat building & repairing

(G-10163)
AMAMI UNITED FLAVOURS OF WORLD
224 Espanola Way (33139-4106)
PHONE...................................305 397-8577
Cataldo Dell Anno, *Principal*
EMP: 8 EST: 2011
SALES (est): 436.9K **Privately Held**
WEB: www.amamius.com
SIC: **3421** Table & food cutlery, including butchers'

(G-10164)
AMERICAN COMPUTER & TECH CORP
Also Called: Mac Directory
1775 Washington Ave 3f (33139-7538)
PHONE...................................786 738-3220
Markin Abras, *President*
EMP: 5 EST: 1993
SQ FT: 750
SALES (est): 418.2K **Privately Held**
SIC: **2741** Directories: publishing & printing

(G-10165)
ANTI-GING ASTHTIC LSER CTR INC
4401 Collins Ave (33140-3227)
PHONE...................................786 539-4901
Oleg Rybak, *President*
Sergey Rybak, *Vice Pres*
EMP: 9 EST: 2007
SALES (est): 169.7K **Privately Held**
SIC: **3845** Laser systems & equipment, medical

(G-10166)
APPEL 26 CORP
4101 Pine Tree Dr Apt 111 (33140-3628)
PHONE...................................305 672-8645
Barry Appel, *President*
EMP: 8 EST: 2004
SALES (est): 165.8K **Privately Held**
SIC: **3571** Personal computers (microcomputers)

(G-10167)
ARKUP LLC
2100 Park Ave Apt 211s (33139-1757)
PHONE...................................786 448-8635
Nicolas Derouin,

Arnaud Luguet,
EMP: 6 EST: 2016
SALES (est): 309.9K **Privately Held**
WEB: www.arkup.com
SIC: **3732** 7011 4499 Yachts, building & repairing; resort hotel; boathouses, commercial

(G-10168)
ASG CORP
5235 N Bay Rd (33140-2010)
PHONE...................................718 641-4500
EMP: 7 EST: 2018
SALES (est): 67K **Privately Held**
WEB: www.asg.com
SIC: **3999** Manufacturing industries

(G-10169)
B-TOKEN USA INC
1111 Lincoln Rd Ste 400 (33139-2452)
PHONE...................................305 735-2065
EMP: 5 EST: 2012
SALES (est): 328K **Privately Held**
WEB: www.b-token.com
SIC: **3999** Mfg Misc Products

(G-10170)
BIGHILL CORPORATION
Also Called: Mangiamo
1111 Lincoln Rd Fl 4 (33139-2439)
PHONE...................................786 497-1875
EMP: 3
SALES: 5MM **Privately Held**
SIC: **2086** Mfg And Export Of Soft Drinks And Fruit Juices

(G-10171)
BKN INTERNATIONAL INC
Also Called: Izzycue
1610 Euclid Ave Apt B202 (33139-7776)
PHONE...................................301 518-7153
Kenneth Tan, *President*
Felecia Tan, *CFO*
EMP: 8 EST: 1997
SALES (est): 451K **Privately Held**
SIC: **2051** 0181 2023 Pastries, e.g. danish: except frozen; seeds, vegetable: growing of; dietary supplements, dairy & non-dairy based

(G-10172)
BROOKLANDS NEW MEDIA LLC
1000 5th St Ste 200 (33139-6510)
PHONE...................................305 370-3867
Vesta Lall, *Mng Member*
Davanand Lall, *Manager*
EMP: 20 EST: 2013
SALES (est): 1.2MM **Privately Held**
WEB: www.brooklandsnewmedia.com
SIC: **2721** Magazines: publishing only, not printed on site

(G-10173)
BUFALINDA USA LLC
2000 Bay Dr (33141-4554)
PHONE...................................305 979-9258
Alberto Enrique Duhau, *Manager*
EMP: 7 EST: 2017
SALES (est): 186.6K **Privately Held**
SIC: **2022** Natural cheese

(G-10174)
CANAM ELECTRIC
4835 Collins Ave (33140-2751)
PHONE...................................305 534-7903
EMP: 7 EST: 2007
SALES (est): 14.7K **Privately Held**
WEB: www.canamelectric.com
SIC: **3699** Electrical equipment & supplies

(G-10175)
CAREFREE GROUP INC (PA)
1029 5th St (33139-6504)
PHONE...................................866 800-1007
Anthony Marotta, *President*
Edgar Ward, *Vice Pres*
Ian Lamphere, *Admin Sec*
EMP: 3 EST: 2004
SALES (est): 4.1MM **Privately Held**
SIC: **2095** Roasted coffee

(G-10176)
CAXTON NEWSPAPERS INC
Also Called: Sunpost
1688 Meridian Ave Ste 404 (33139-2715)
P.O. Box 191870 (33119-1870)
PHONE..................................305 538-9700
Jeannette Stark, *President*
EMP: 25 **EST:** 1985
SALES (est): 1.5MM **Privately Held**
WEB: www.miamisunpost.com
SIC: 2711 2791 2752 Newspapers: publishing only, not printed on site; typesetting; commercial printing, lithographic

(G-10177)
CDA VENTURES INC
Also Called: Cda Group
270 N Shore Dr (33141-2426)
P.O. Box 414002 (33141-0002)
PHONE..................................305 428-2857
Ivan Alvarez, *Principal*
EMP: 10 **EST:** 2006
SALES (est): 334.9K **Privately Held**
WEB: www.cdaventures.com
SIC: 2741 Miscellaneous publishing

(G-10178)
CEPODS LLC
1348 Washington Ave # 257 (33139-4212)
PHONE..................................786 520-1412
Timothy Dunlap,
EMP: 5 **EST:** 2011
SALES (est): 489.3K **Privately Held**
WEB: www.cepods.com
SIC: 3715 Demountable cargo containers

(G-10179)
**CITY DEBATE PUBLISHING
COMPANY**
6538 Collins Ave (33141-4694)
PHONE..................................305 868-1161
J P Morgan, *Admin Sec*
EMP: 8 **EST:** 2001
SALES (est): 144.5K **Privately Held**
WEB: www.citydebate.com
SIC: 2741 Miscellaneous publishing

(G-10180)
CORVATSCH CORP
Also Called: True Loaf
1894 Bay Rd (33139-1416)
PHONE..................................305 775-2831
Tomas Strulovic, *President*
EMP: 14 **EST:** 2009
SALES (est): 661.2K **Privately Held**
SIC: 2051 Bread, cake & related products

(G-10181)
COZY BAR
500 S Pointe Dr (33139-7302)
PHONE..................................305 532-2699
Jean-Alexandre Maufroy, *Principal*
EMP: 7 **EST:** 2007
SALES (est): 270K **Privately Held**
WEB: www.thecozybar.com
SIC: 2064 Candy bars, including chocolate covered bars

(G-10182)
CRAIG ARMSTRONG
Also Called: Glu
1770 Normandy Dr Apt 2 (33141-4749)
PHONE..................................786 319-6514
Craig Armstrong, *Principal*
EMP: 10 **EST:** 2006
SALES (est): 588.7K **Privately Held**
SIC: 2891 Glue

(G-10183)
DION ATELIER INC
224 8th St (33139-5804)
PHONE..................................305 389-9711
Dion Atelier, *Principal*
EMP: 7 **EST:** 2017
SALES (est): 78.3K **Privately Held**
WEB: www.dionatelier-fl.com
SIC: 2381 Fabric dress & work gloves

(G-10184)
DO YOU REMEMBER INC
36 Island Ave Apt 45 (33139-1312)
PHONE..................................305 987-9111
Michael Gitter, *Principal*
EMP: 9 **EST:** 2018

SALES (est): 320.2K **Privately Held**
WEB: www.doyouremember.com
SIC: 2741

(G-10185)
DREZO MANUFACTURING INC
Also Called: Seal Tek
5956 Pine Tree Dr (33140-2125)
PHONE..................................305 864-9814
Sanford Goodman, *President*
EMP: 8 **EST:** 1953
SQ FT: 25,000
SALES (est): 113.5K **Privately Held**
SIC: 2295 Coated fabrics, not rubberized

(G-10186)
ELITE FITFOREVER LLC
4302 Alton Rd Ste 300 (33140-2818)
PHONE..................................305 902-2358
EMP: 7 **EST:** 2019
SALES (est): 572K **Privately Held**
WEB: www.elitefitforever.com
SIC: 2834 Pharmaceutical preparations

(G-10187)
ENHANCELL INC
910 West Ave Apt 824 (33139-5241)
PHONE..................................469 363-2038
Joni Pajala, *Principal*
EMP: 7 **EST:** 2015
SALES (est): 130.2K **Privately Held**
WEB: www.enhancell.com
SIC: 7372 Prepackaged software

(G-10188)
FILORGA AMERICAS INC
429 Lenox Ave (33139-6532)
PHONE..................................786 266-7429
Didier Tabary, *President*
Emmanuel Calvo, *Vice Pres*
EMP: 27 **EST:** 1999
SALES (est): 927.6K
SALES (corp-wide): 8.3MM **Privately Held**
SIC: 2844 Toilet preparations
PA: Laboratoires Fill-Med
2 4
Paris 75008
142 939-400

(G-10189)
FIRE BRANDS LLC ✪
1688 Meridian Ave Ste 600 (33139-2714)
PHONE..................................877 800-4398
Scott Lutz,
EMP: 10 **EST:** 2021
SALES (est): 328.1K **Privately Held**
SIC: 3411 Beverage cans, metal: except beer

(G-10190)
FLUENZ INC
1000 5th St Ste 200 (33139-6510)
PHONE..................................305 209-1695
Carlos Lizarralde, *Chairman*
Federica Silen, *Project Mgr*
Sonia Gil,
EMP: 7 **EST:** 2006
SQ FT: 1,100
SALES (est): 751.1K **Privately Held**
WEB: www.fluenz.com
SIC: 7372 Educational computer software

(G-10191)
FMC POWER INC
450 Alton Rd (33139-6713)
PHONE..................................786 353-2379
Fabio Mancini, *Principal*
EMP: 6 **EST:** 2015
SALES (est): 345.6K **Privately Held**
WEB: www.fmc.com
SIC: 2812 Alkalies & chlorine

(G-10192)
FRESH ON FIFTH
Also Called: Jafar On Fifth
448 Ocean Dr Ste 2 (33139-6614)
PHONE..................................305 234-5678
Safaaldin A Majeed, *Principal*
EMP: 8 **EST:** 2007
SALES (est): 326.2K **Privately Held**
WEB: www.freshonfifth.com
SIC: 2051 Bread, cake & related products

(G-10193)
GAND INC
1000 5th St Ste 200 (33139-6510)
PHONE..................................240 575-0622
George Sing, *CEO*
David Steed, *Vice Pres*
Douglas Tadaki, *Admin Sec*
EMP: 5 **EST:** 2017
SALES (est): 521K **Privately Held**
SIC: 2834 Solutions, pharmaceutical

(G-10194)
**GARMENT CORPORATION OF
AMERICA**
801 Arthur Godfrey Rd # 3 (33140-3323)
PHONE..................................305 531-4040
Joseph Shulevitz, *Ch of Bd*
David J Shulevitz, *President*
Catherine Marrero, *Credit Staff*
▲ **EMP:** 500 **EST:** 1967
SQ FT: 11,000
SALES (est): 13.1MM **Privately Held**
SIC: 2326 Industrial garments, men's & boys'

(G-10195)
GARMIN INTERNATIONAL INC
513 Lincoln Rd (33139-2913)
PHONE..................................305 674-7701
Ryan Drummond, *Sales Staff*
Darrell Rollins, *Manager*
Joey Serrano, *Manager*
David Story, *Technology*
Scott Clewell, *Software Engr*
EMP: 371
SALES (corp-wide): 3.7B **Privately Held**
WEB: www.garmin.com
SIC: 3812 Search & navigation equipment
HQ: Garmin International, Inc.
1200 E 151st St
Olathe KS 66062

(G-10196)
GELATERIA MILANI LLC
436 Espanola Way (33139-8123)
PHONE..................................305 532-8562
EMP: 10
SALES (est): 775.6K **Privately Held**
SIC: 2024 Mfg Ice Cream/Frozen Desert

(G-10197)
GRAND HAVANA INC
407 Lincoln Rd Ste 2a (33139-3018)
PHONE..................................305 297-2207
Robert Rico, *CEO*
Tanya Bredemeier, *Ch of Bd*
Louis Bustello, *COO*
Jorge Moreno, *Chief Mktg Ofcr*
EMP: 7 **EST:** 2009
SALES (est): 169.9K **Privately Held**
WEB: www.grandhavanacoffee.com
SIC: 2095 2099 5149 Roasted coffee; tea blending; coffee & tea

(G-10198)
**GULFSTREAM MSES
INVSTMNTS GROU**
1535 Biarritz Dr (33141-4721)
PHONE..................................305 975-6186
Jorge M Lopez, *Principal*
Ada O Lopez, *Principal*
EMP: 5 **EST:** 2001
SALES (est): 463.4K **Privately Held**
SIC: 3721 Aircraft

(G-10199)
HEY DAY
1825 West Ave (33139-1441)
PHONE..................................305 763-8660
Peter Hey, *Principal*
EMP: 8 **EST:** 2012
SALES (est): 195.4K **Privately Held**
SIC: 2759 Invitation & stationery printing & engraving

(G-10200)
**HILLIARD BRUCE VINEYARDS
LLC**
1521 Alton Rd Ste 842 (33139-3301)
PHONE..................................305 979-2601
John C Hilliard, *Principal*
EMP: 7 **EST:** 2015
SALES (est): 338.3K **Privately Held**
SIC: 2084 Wines, brandy & brandy spirits

(G-10201)
HUMMINGBIRDS AI INC
8140 Hawthorne Ave (33141-1009)
PHONE..................................305 432-2787
Nima Schei, *CEO*
EMP: 23 **EST:** 2020
SALES (est): 1.8MM **Privately Held**
WEB: www.hummingbirds.ai
SIC: 3699 7371 Security devices; software programming applications

(G-10202)
**HYDROGEN TECHNOLOGY
CORP**
900 West Ave Apt 501 (33139-5210)
PHONE..................................800 315-9554
Matthew Kane, *Vice Pres*
EMP: 27 **EST:** 2017
SALES (est): 3MM **Privately Held**
WEB: www.hydrogen.tech
SIC: 7372 Application computer software

(G-10203)
ILAY VENTURES LLC (PA) ✪
1688 Meridian Ave Ste 700 (33139-2713)
PHONE..................................786 503-5335
Zvi Benjamin Jarmon, *Mng Member*
Connie Guerrero,
EMP: 10 **EST:** 2021
SALES (est): 500K **Privately Held**
SIC: 7372 8742 Application computer software; management consulting services

(G-10204)
INDUSTRIAL OVIEDO LLC
7601 E Trsore Dr Unit 121 (33141)
PHONE..................................786 350-8153
Alam Oviedo, *Manager*
EMP: 7 **EST:** 2015
SALES (est): 348.1K **Privately Held**
SIC: 3599 Machine shop, jobbing & repair

(G-10205)
INPERIUM CORP
1111 Lincoln Rd Ste 760 (33139-2402)
PHONE..................................305 901-5650
Christian Ehrenthal, *CEO*
EMP: 37 **EST:** 2018
SALES (est): 1MM **Privately Held**
WEB: www.inperium.com
SIC: 7372 Business oriented computer software

(G-10206)
JEAN LA FRITE
1520 Washington Ave (33139-7801)
PHONE..................................305 397-8747
Jean La Frite, *Principal*
EMP: 8 **EST:** 2010
SALES (est): 59.3K **Privately Held**
SIC: 3421 Table & food cutlery, including butchers'

(G-10207)
JMG STRATEGIES LLC
300 S Pointe Dr Apt 907 (33139-7353)
PHONE..................................305 606-2117
J Mark Goode, *Manager*
EMP: 7 **EST:** 2018
SALES (est): 393.7K **Privately Held**
SIC: 3462 Horseshoes

(G-10208)
LENNOX MIAMI CORP
1900 Collins Ave (33139-1912)
PHONE..................................305 763-8655
Diego Agnelli, *Principal*
Eddie Rivera, *Chief Engr*
Jack Jernstrom, *Sales Mgr*
EMP: 24 **EST:** 2010
SALES (est): 5.1MM **Privately Held**
WEB: www.lennoxmiamibeach.com
SIC: 3585 Refrigeration & heating equipment

(G-10209)
**LOUIS DI RMNDO WRLDWIDE
INVSTM**
Also Called: All Amercian Hot Dog Cart Co
2410 N Shore Ter (33141-2448)
PHONE..................................786 536-7578
Louis D Raimondo, *President*
Louis Di Raimondo, *President*
▼ **EMP:** 10 **EST:** 1972
SQ FT: 5,500

SALES (est): 1MM **Privately Held**
SIC: 3589 Commercial cooking & food-warming equipment

(G-10210)
MASKCO TECHNOLOGIES INC
1348 Washington Ave (33139-4212)
PHONE....................877 261-6405
Scott Weissman, *CEO*
EMP: 10 EST: 2020
SALES (est): 283.1K **Privately Held**
WEB: www.maskcotech.com
SIC: 3999 Manufacturing industries

(G-10211)
MAU MAU CORPORATION
555 Jefferson Ave (33139-6302)
PHONE....................305 440-5203
Frank Amadeo, *President*
EMP: 25 EST: 2001
SALES (est): 518.5K **Privately Held**
WEB: www.mau.com
SIC: 7372 Prepackaged software

(G-10212)
MEGACOLOR PRINT LLC
221 Meridian Ave Apt 413 (33139-7071)
PHONE....................305 499-9395
Marcello Cabrier,
EMP: 10 EST: 2002
SALES (est): 740.5K **Privately Held**
WEB: www.megacolorprint.com
SIC: 2752 Commercial printing, offset

(G-10213)
MIRAMAR PUBLISHING INC
1030 14th St (33139-3816)
PHONE....................305 695-0639
Carolina G Hamshaw, *Principal*
EMP: 9 EST: 2010
SALES (est): 108.6K **Privately Held**
SIC: 2741 Miscellaneous publishing

(G-10214)
NATIONAL BIDET CORP
7150 Indian Creek Dr (33141-3083)
PHONE....................786 325-6593
Karel Giron-Milan, *Principal*
EMP: 7 EST: 2007
SALES (est): 146.2K **Privately Held**
SIC: 3261 Bathroom accessories/fittings, vitreous china or earthenware

(G-10215)
NEWS FEATURES USA INC
6301 Collins Ave (33141-4627)
PHONE....................305 298-5313
Christopher M Bott, *Director*
EMP: 9 EST: 2005
SALES (est): 143.2K **Privately Held**
SIC: 2711 Newspapers, publishing & printing

(G-10216)
NIKKI BEACH PUBLISHING LLC
1 Ocean Dr (33139-7321)
PHONE....................305 538-1111
Jack Penrod, *Manager*
EMP: 7 EST: 2003
SALES (est): 536.5K **Privately Held**
SIC: 2741 Miscellaneous publishing

(G-10217)
OCEANSTYLE LLC
Also Called: Oceanstyle By Burgess
390 Alton Rd Ste 2 (33139-8902)
PHONE....................305 672-9400
Alexander G Wheatley, *Mng Member*
EMP: 8 EST: 2005
SALES (est): 608.7K **Privately Held**
SIC: 2386 Garments, leather

(G-10218)
ORALBIOLIFE INC
1521 Alton Rd (33139-3301)
PHONE....................305 401-2622
Gordon Matz, *CEO*
EMP: 10
SALES (est): 413.1K **Privately Held**
SIC: 3843 Dental equipment & supplies

(G-10219)
PLAN AUTOMATION LLC
350 Lincoln Rd (33139-3154)
PHONE....................786 502-1812
Brendan Clery, *Mng Member*

EMP: 1 EST: 2019
SALES (est): 5MM **Privately Held**
SIC: 3565 Packaging machinery

(G-10220)
PLATINIUM ROSIS INC
1602 Alton Rd 602 (33139-2421)
PHONE....................786 617-9973
David Gardoqui, *President*
Silvia Romano, *Principal*
Greg Davis, *Principal*
Clara Romano De Feo, *Principal*
EMP: 7 EST: 2013
SALES (est): 83.9K **Privately Held**
SIC: 3443 2611 9511 1795 Dumpsters, garbage; pulp mills, mechanical & recycling processing; air, water & solid waste management; wrecking & demolition work; parking lot construction

(G-10221)
PREKCOM LLC
429 Lenox Ave (33139-6532)
PHONE....................877 773-5669
Ben Mayer, *Mng Member*
EMP: 9 EST: 2019
SALES (est): 637.9K **Privately Held**
SIC: 7372 Educational computer software

(G-10222)
PRESTIGE PUBLICATION GROUP
Also Called: Sunpost Newspaper Group
1688 Meridian Ave Ste 404 (33139-2715)
P.O. Box 191870 (33119-1870)
PHONE....................305 538-9700
Janet Stark, *President*
EMP: 25 EST: 1985
SALES (est): 1.2MM **Privately Held**
SIC: 2711 Newspapers, publishing & printing

(G-10223)
PRS IN VIVO HOLDINGS INC
1680 Michigan Ave Ste 722 (33139-2551)
PHONE....................305 420-5935
EMP: 7 EST: 2015
SALES (est): 72.6K **Privately Held**
SIC: 2741 Miscellaneous publishing

(G-10224)
RUBBER B LLC
605 Lincoln Rd Ste 210 (33139-2934)
PHONE....................305 771-2369
Arnaud B Tibi, *Mng Member*
Jean-Jacques G Sarkissian,
EMP: 5 EST: 2010
SALES (est): 443K **Privately Held**
WEB: www.rubberb.com
SIC: 3172 Watch straps, except metal

(G-10225)
SCRIPT CENTRAL LLC
1680 Michigan Ave Ste 800 (33139-2519)
PHONE....................954 805-8581
EMP: 8 EST: 2015
SALES (est): 151.5K **Privately Held**
WEB: www.scriptcentral.com
SIC: 2834 Pharmaceutical preparations

(G-10226)
SELECT WINES LLC ✪
6039 Collins Ave Apt 901 (33140-2251)
PHONE....................786 642-7445
EMP: 7 EST: 2022
SALES (est): 357.9K **Privately Held**
SIC: 2084 Wines

(G-10227)
SIMPLIFIED SYSTEMS INC
4014 Chase Ave Ph (33140-3490)
PHONE....................305 672-7676
Paula Turk, *President*
Bernardo Cano, *President*
EMP: 10 EST: 1971
SQ FT: 3,000
SALES (est): 625.9K **Privately Held**
WEB: www.thecommunicatorfl.com
SIC: 3843 3841 Ultrasonic dental equipment; surgical & medical instruments

(G-10228)
SKY PHONE LLC (PA)
Also Called: Sky Device
1348 Washington Ave # 350 (33139-4212)
PHONE....................305 531-5218
Enrique Quimper, *Mng Member*
Raffael Attar,
▲ EMP: 10 EST: 2013
SQ FT: 4,000
SALES (est): 42MM **Privately Held**
SIC: 3663 5065 5999 Cellular radio telephone; mobile telephone equipment; mobile telephones & equipment

(G-10229)
SOBE EXPRESS
1205 Lincoln Rd Ste 209 (33139-2365)
PHONE....................305 674-4454
Wilfredo Lugo, *President*
EMP: 5 EST: 2016
SALES (est): 335.3K **Privately Held**
WEB: www.sobeexpress.com
SIC: 2752 Commercial printing, offset

(G-10230)
SOCIETEES INC
3200 Collins Ave Apt 114 (33140-4031)
PHONE....................786 208-9880
Simon A Shenker, *Principal*
EMP: 7 EST: 2018
SALES (est): 244.3K **Privately Held**
WEB: www.thesocietees.com
SIC: 2759 Screen printing

(G-10231)
SONY MUSIC PUBLISHING (US) LLC
1111 Lincoln Rd Ste 803 (33139-2451)
PHONE....................305 532-9064
Jorge Mejia, *Manager*
EMP: 7 **Privately Held**
WEB: www.sonymusic.com
SIC: 2741 Catalogs: publishing & printing
HQ: Sony Music Publishing (Us) Llc
25 Madison Ave Fl 24
New York NY 10010
212 833-7730

(G-10232)
SOPHIST RESEARCH LLC
110 Wshngton Ave Apt 1524 (33139)
PHONE....................305 763-8184
EMP: 7 EST: 2018
SALES (est): 392.2K **Privately Held**
SIC: 2741 Miscellaneous publishing

(G-10233)
SOUTH BEACH CIGAR FACTORY LLC
1059 Collins Ave Ste 108 (33139-5036)
PHONE....................786 216-7475
Mireya Mayor, *Principal*
EMP: 8 EST: 2012
SALES (est): 406K **Privately Held**
SIC: 2121 Cigars

(G-10234)
SPORTS STRUCTURE INTL LLC
Also Called: Kiddidoo USA
1680 Michigan Ave Ste 700 (33139-2551)
PHONE....................305 777-2225
Johan Bos, *Managing Dir*
EMP: 5 EST: 2012
SQ FT: 1,000
SALES (est): 474.5K **Privately Held**
SIC: 2329 Men's & boys' sportswear & athletic clothing

(G-10235)
STADIUM 1 SOFTWARE LLC
7115 Rue Notre Dame (33141-3618)
PHONE....................561 498-8356
Ed Mullen, *Vice Pres*
Kathy Shea, *Sales Staff*
Lewis Gordon,
EMP: 23 EST: 2011
SALES (est): 2.3MM **Privately Held**
WEB: www.stadium1.com
SIC: 7372 Prepackaged software

(G-10236)
STRIPPING ALPACA LLC
Also Called: Food Supply & Wine
2301 Collins Ave Apt 1143 (33139-1606)
PHONE....................207 208-9687

Bruno Corvalan, *Owner*
Corvalan Bruno,
EMP: 15 EST: 2019
SALES (est): 553.3K **Privately Held**
SIC: 2099 5182 2035 0161 Vegetables, peeled for the trade; wine; spreads, garlic; onion farm; insurance agents, brokers & service; meditation therapy

(G-10237)
STUNTWEAR LLC
Also Called: Cold Fire Direct
6538 Collins Ave Unit 414 (33141-4694)
PHONE....................305 842-2115
Lars Mohlin, *Owner*
EMP: 8 EST: 2010
SQ FT: 2,000
SALES (est): 250K **Privately Held**
SIC: 2389 Apparel for handicapped

(G-10238)
SUPERFLOW INC
1400 Lincoln Rd Apt 604 (33139-2166)
PHONE....................786 238-8253
EMP: 7 EST: 2018
SALES (est): 496.6K **Privately Held**
WEB: www.superflow.com
SIC: 3829 Measuring & controlling devices

(G-10239)
TROPICOLOR PHOTO SERVICE INC
Also Called: Tropicolor Display Graphics
1442 Alton Rd (33139-3828)
PHONE....................305 672-3720
Tom Chien, *President*
John Chien, *Vice Pres*
TSE-Dao Chien, *Vice Pres*
EMP: 8 EST: 1986
SQ FT: 4,000
SALES (est): 1.3MM **Privately Held**
WEB: www.tropicolor.com
SIC: 2759 Posters, including billboards: printing; security certificates: engraved

(G-10240)
UMG RECORDINGS INC
Also Called: Universal Recording
404 Wshington Ave Ste 800 (33139)
PHONE....................305 532-4754
Jesus Lopez, *Chairman*
EMP: 316 **Privately Held**
SIC: 2782 Record albums
HQ: Umg Recordings, Inc.
5822 Haverford Ave
Philadelphia PA

(G-10241)
UPROXX MEDIA INC
1602 Alton Rd Ste 447 (33139-2421)
PHONE....................917 603-2374
Jarret Myer, *CEO*
Brian Brater, *President*
EMP: 10 EST: 2008
SALES (est): 2.8MM **Publicly Held**
WEB: www.uproxx.com
SIC: 2721 Trade journals: publishing only, not printed on site
HQ: Wovexx Holdings, Inc.
10381 Jefferson Blvd
Culver City CA 90232

(G-10242)
URBAN CHARGE LLC
1330 West Ave Apt 1411 (33139-0906)
PHONE....................305 809-6625
EMP: 5
SALES: 1,000K **Privately Held**
SIC: 3714 Mfg Motor Vehicle Parts/Accessories

(G-10243)
V2 CIGS (PA)
1521 Alton Rd Ste 275 (33139-3301)
PHONE....................305 517-1149
David Turner, *Manager*
EMP: 5 EST: 2011
SALES (est): 789.6K **Privately Held**
WEB: www.v2.com
SIC: 2111 Cigarettes

(G-10244)
VENTI GROUP LLC
1521 Alton Rd Ste 697 (33139-3301)
PHONE....................949 264-3185
Henry Adamany, *Managing Dir*

▲ = Import ▼ =Export
◆ =Import/Export

Dow A Eichenlaub, *Managing Dir*
Ludovic Bainvel, *Principal*
Robert Mark, *Vice Pres*
Dow Eichenlaub, *Director*
EMP: 7 **EST:** 2009
SALES (est): 121.6K **Privately Held**
WEB: www.ventigroup.com
SIC: 3663 Antennas, transmitting & communications

(G-10245)
VENTUM LLC
1100 14th St (33139-3818)
P.O. Box 460, Heber City UT (84032-0460)
PHONE.................................786 838-1113
Diaa Nour, *Mng Member*
EMP: 8 **EST:** 2015
SALES (est): 466.4K **Privately Held**
WEB: www.ventumracing.com
SIC: 3751 5961 Bicycles & related parts; fitness & sporting goods, mail order

(G-10246)
VISTA PUBLISHING CORPORATION
Also Called: Vista Magazine
6538 Collins Ave (33141-4694)
PHONE.................................305 416-4644
EMP: 10
SQ FT: 2,850
SALES (est): 710K **Privately Held**
SIC: 2721 Periodicals-Publishing/Printing

(G-10247)
WORLDS GREATEST ICE CREAM INC
Also Called: Frieze, The
1626 Michigan Ave (33139-2504)
P.O. Box 190646, Miami (33119-0646)
PHONE.................................305 538-0207
Lisa Warren, *President*
Robert Warren, *Vice Pres*
EMP: 10 **EST:** 1987
SQ FT: 1,200
SALES (est): 949.1K **Privately Held**
WEB: www.thefrieze.com
SIC: 2024 5451 Ice cream, bulk; ice cream (packaged)

Miami Gardens
Miami-Dade County

(G-10248)
ADNAN ENTERPRISES
4699 Nw 183rd St (33055-3051)
PHONE.................................305 430-9752
Kishwar Khan, *Principal*
EMP: 5 **EST:** 2008
SALES (est): 353.2K **Privately Held**
SIC: 3578 Automatic teller machines (ATM)

(G-10249)
AHUS INC
Also Called: Adriana Hoyos
3361 Nw 168th St (33056-4229)
PHONE.................................305 572-9052
Eduardo Perez, *President*
Diana Mejia, *Chairman*
Eduardo Perez Darquea, *Vice Pres*
Adriana Hoyos, *Vice Pres*
Angela Hoyos, *Vice Pres*
▲ **EMP:** 25 **EST:** 2001
SALES (est): 3.9MM **Privately Held**
SIC: 2511 Wood household furniture

(G-10250)
ALFA MANUFACTURING GROUP LLC
17401 Nw 2nd Ave Ste 7 (33169-5039)
PHONE.................................305 979-7344
Alexandros Kyritsis,
EMP: 5 **EST:** 2020
SALES (est): 358.2K **Privately Held**
SIC: 2844 Cosmetic preparations

(G-10251)
ALSE INDUSTRIES LLC
Also Called: American Architectural Mtls GL
16201 Nw 49th Ave (33014-6314)
PHONE.................................305 688-8778
Francisco A Serrano, *Mng Member*
EMP: 19 **EST:** 2020

SALES (est): 1.8MM **Privately Held**
WEB: www.aamg.us
SIC: 3441 3446 Fabricated structural metal; architectural metalwork

(G-10252)
BLINDS BY RANDY LLC
3274 Nw 181st St (33056-3432)
PHONE.................................305 300-1147
Randolph White, *Principal*
EMP: 7 **EST:** 2013
SALES (est): 158.1K **Privately Held**
SIC: 2591 7389 Window blinds;

(G-10253)
BLUEGATE INC
16409 Nw 8th Ave (33169-5812)
PHONE.................................305 628-8391
Alizera Haghayegh, *President*
▲ **EMP:** 12 **EST:** 1998
SQ FT: 75,000
SALES (est): 600K **Privately Held**
WEB: www.glowbackledstore.com
SIC: 3648 Decorative area lighting fixtures

(G-10254)
CHEN TECHNOLOGY INC
1000 Park Centre Blvd # 100 (33169-5373)
PHONE.................................305 621-0023
Mary Chen, *President*
Christopher Chen, *Vice Pres*
EMP: 11 **EST:** 2011
SALES (est): 383K
SALES (corp-wide): 25.2MM **Privately Held**
WEB: www.chenmed.com
SIC: 7372 Application computer software
PA: Chen Medical Associates, P.A.
  1395 Nw 167th St Ste 122
  Miami FL 33169
  305 621-0023

(G-10255)
DOUGLAS FUEL II INC
3701 Nw 167th St (33055-4510)
PHONE.................................305 620-0707
Eden Herrera, *Principal*
EMP: 7 **EST:** 2013
SALES (est): 274.5K **Privately Held**
SIC: 2869 Fuels

(G-10256)
DUNCAN AND SONS CNSTR EQP INC
2750 Nw 209th Ter (33056-1443)
PHONE.................................305 216-3115
Adrian M Duncan, *President*
EMP: 10 **EST:** 2020
SALES (est): 528.5K **Privately Held**
SIC: 3531 Graders, road (construction machinery)

(G-10257)
FLASH PRINTS LLC
19401 Nw 23rd Ave (33056-2638)
PHONE.................................786 422-3195
Antoinette Payne, *CEO*
Lamott Croom,
EMP: 5 **EST:** 2019
SALES (est): 516.2K **Privately Held**
SIC: 2752 Commercial printing, lithographic

(G-10258)
FLASH SALES INC
4401 Nw 167th St (33055-4311)
PHONE.................................954 914-2689
Jacob Levy, *President*
Barry Rub, *Vice Pres*
◆ **EMP:** 5 **EST:** 2003
SQ FT: 10,000
SALES (est): 1.1MM **Privately Held**
WEB: www.flashsales.com
SIC: 3634 5064 Electric housewares & fans; electrical appliances, television & radio

(G-10259)
GLOVAL DISPLAYS INC
1100 Nw 159th Dr (33169-5808)
PHONE.................................800 972-0353
Joan Barrientos, *President*
Bernardo Botero, *Engineer*
EMP: 20 **EST:** 2008

SALES (est): 2.3MM **Privately Held**
WEB: www.glovaldisplays.com
SIC: 2431 2541 2789 3999 Millwork; store & office display cases & fixtures; display fixtures, wood; counters or counter display cases, wood; display mounting; preparation of slides & exhibits

(G-10260)
GOLDEN GLADES RACEWAY LLC
17021 Nw 27th Ave (33056-4407)
P.O. Box 560962, Miami (33256-0962)
PHONE.................................305 321-9627
Jorge Almirall, *Principal*
EMP: 7 **EST:** 2015
SALES (est): 117.6K **Privately Held**
SIC: 3644 Raceways

(G-10261)
GOODRICH CORPORATION
Also Called: UTC Aerospace Systems
3201 Nw 167th St (33056-4253)
PHONE.................................305 622-4500
Greg Watson, *President*
Donald Dass, *Materials Mgr*
Karen Corpuz, *Manager*
EMP: 8
SALES (corp-wide): 64.3B **Publicly Held**
WEB: www.collinsaerospace.com
SIC: 3724 3728 7372 Aircraft engines & engine parts; aircraft parts & equipment; prepackaged software
HQ: Goodrich Corporation
  2730 W Tyvola Rd
  Charlotte NC 28217
  704 423-7000

(G-10262)
GROWTH LOGISTICS INC
67 Nw 183rd St (33169-4516)
PHONE.................................800 846-2363
Jean Vincent, *Principal*
EMP: 10
SALES (est): 413.1K **Privately Held**
SIC: 2519 Household furniture

(G-10263)
HURRICANE GRAPHICS INC
Also Called: Printing Sensations
3331 Nw 168th St (33056-4229)
PHONE.................................305 760-9154
Michael Gherman, *President*
Denise Dunleavymcpartl, *Office Mgr*
EMP: 20 **EST:** 1989
SQ FT: 7,500
SALES (est): 3.9MM **Privately Held**
WEB: www.printingsensations.com
SIC: 2752 Commercial printing, offset

(G-10264)
IN GEAR FASHIONS INC (PA)
Also Called: Ingear
4401 Nw 167th St (33055-4311)
PHONE.................................305 830-2900
Kevin N Frija, *President*
Jacob D Levy, *Vice Pres*
Jacob Levy, *Vice Pres*
Alyx Fisten, *Sales Staff*
Christine Vitale, *Sales Executive*
◆ **EMP:** 75 **EST:** 1990
SQ FT: 30,000
SALES (est): 20.4MM **Privately Held**
SIC: 2339 2329 Sportswear, women's; beachwear: women's, misses' & juniors'; men's & boys' sportswear & athletic clothing

(G-10265)
ISCAR GSE CORP
1182 Nw 159th Dr (33169-5808)
PHONE.................................305 364-8886
EMP: 30
SALES (est): 1.7MM **Privately Held**
SIC: 3537 Mfg Industrial Trucks/Tractors

(G-10266)
ISCAR GSE CORP
Also Called: Iscar Ground Services Eqp
1180 Nw 159th Dr (33169-5808)
PHONE.................................305 364-8886
Israel S Carruyo, *President*
Victor M Carruyo, *Vice Pres*
Victor Carruyo, *Mng Member*
Israel J Carruyo, *Admin Sec*
EMP: 30 **EST:** 2010

SQ FT: 70,000
SALES (est): 2.7MM **Privately Held**
WEB: www.iscar-gse.com
SIC: 3537 Trucks: freight, baggage, etc.: industrial, except mining

(G-10267)
LEADING EDGE AEROSPACE LLC
16115 Nw 52nd Ave (33014-6205)
PHONE.................................305 608-6826
Daniel Flores, *General Mgr*
Jorge Reyes, *Sales Staff*
Steven A Server,
Anthony Flores, *Technician*
Marbel Izquierdo,
EMP: 7 **EST:** 2014
SALES (est): 990.2K **Privately Held**
WEB: www.leadingedgeaero.com
SIC: 3594 Pumps, hydraulic, aircraft

(G-10268)
NEW GENERATION PACKAGING LLC
16542 Nw 54th Ave (33014-6113)
P.O. Box 5705, Hialeah (33014-1705)
PHONE.................................786 259-6670
Tam Muk Chan,
Sze Y Chan,
Szeon Chan,
EMP: 8 **EST:** 2016
SALES (est): 715.3K **Privately Held**
WEB: www.newgenpack.com
SIC: 3089 Boxes, plastic

(G-10269)
QUANTUM CREATIONS LLC
15705 Nw 13th Ave (33169-5703)
PHONE.................................786 233-6769
Arthur V Rodriguez,
EMP: 12 **EST:** 2013
SALES (est): 3.3MM **Privately Held**
SIC: 3572 Computer storage devices

(G-10270)
REALTI HUB LLC
18801 Nw 42nd Ave (33055-2733)
PHONE.................................754 242-4759
Junior Pierre, *Mng Member*
EMP: 5 **EST:** 2016
SALES (est): 493.2K **Privately Held**
SIC: 1389 1521 Construction, repair & dismantling services; single-family housing construction

(G-10271)
RESTORATION ARTS
15301 Nw 34th Ave (33054-2459)
P.O. Box 541601, Opa Locka (33054-1601)
PHONE.................................305 953-9755
Micheal Minor, *President*
EMP: 8 **EST:** 1992
SALES (est): 953.5K **Privately Held**
WEB: www.restorationartsandlighting.com
SIC: 3646 Commercial indusl & institutional electric lighting fixtures

(G-10272)
RIDER KITCHEN CABINETS INC
5320 Nw 180th Ter (33055-3160)
PHONE.................................786 502-6663
Rider Ricardo, *Branch Mgr*
EMP: 35
SALES (corp-wide): 295.7K **Privately Held**
WEB: www.vicarismarketgourmet.com
SIC: 2434 Wood kitchen cabinets
PA: Rider Kitchen Cabinets Inc
  13467 Nw 47th Ave
  Opa Locka FL

(G-10273)
SECURITY WORLD ELECTRONICS
19704 Nw 48th Ct (33055-1720)
PHONE.................................786 285-5303
Raul Fernandez, *President*
Maria E Fernandez, *Admin Sec*
EMP: 6 **EST:** 1985
SQ FT: 3,000
SALES (est): 588.4K **Privately Held**
SIC: 2431 Millwork

(G-10274)
SPIRIT LLC
Also Called: Ds18
1400 Nw 159th St Ste 101 (33169-5704)
PHONE..............................954 592-0227
Robert Chin, *Sales Staff*
Alberto Susterman, *Mng Member*
Etti Susterman, *Graphic Designe*
Sasha Daniel Susterman,
◆ **EMP:** 45 **EST:** 2007
SQ FT: 15,000
SALES (est): 5.5MM **Privately Held**
SIC: 3651 Audio electronic systems

(G-10275)
STEINER-ATLANTIC LLC
1714 Nw 215th St (33056-1153)
PHONE..............................305 754-4551
Zachary Mangones, *Principal*
Diane Nino, *Principal*
Richard O'Connell Jr, *Principal*
Robert Lazar, *Mng Member*
EMP: 33 **EST:** 2020
SALES (est): 3.1MM **Privately Held**
SIC: 3582 Drycleaning equipment & machinery, commercial

(G-10276)
TG EXPRESS SERVICES LLC
160 Nw 176th St (33169-5021)
PHONE..............................862 218-7752
Nixon Valcin, *Mng Member*
EMP: 7 **EST:** 2018
SALES (est): 282.8K **Privately Held**
SIC: 2448 Wood pallets & skids

(G-10277)
ULTIMATE CONTAINERS PRO LLC
355 Nw 171st St (33169-5908)
PHONE..............................786 241-4306
Bladimir Parra, *Mng Member*
EMP: 10 **EST:** 2019
SALES (est): 1.1MM **Privately Held**
WEB: www.ultimatecontainerspro.com
SIC: 3089 Garbage containers, plastic

(G-10278)
VENAIR INC
16713 Park Centre Blvd (33169-5300)
PHONE..............................305 362-8920
Miguel Fernandez, *CEO*
Nicholas Bechtel, *Vice Pres*
Bill Matlock, *Sales Staff*
Joseph Vattimo, *Sales Executive*
◆ **EMP:** 7 **EST:** 2005
SQ FT: 20,000
SALES (est): 4.5MM
SALES (corp-wide): 310.6K **Privately Held**
WEB: www.venair.com
SIC: 2822 Silicone rubbers
HQ: Venair Iberica Sa
Calle Cerdanya 26
Terrassa 08226
937 364-860

Miami Lakes
Miami-Dade County

(G-10279)
ADVENTRY CORP
Also Called: Goodyear Belts
8190 Commerce Way (33016-1645)
PHONE..............................305 582-2977
Tara Cevallos, *CEO*
Jorge Gomariz, *Ch of Bd*
EMP: 12 **EST:** 2018
SALES (est): 1MM **Privately Held**
SIC: 3052 Rubber belting

(G-10280)
AIRCRAFT ELECTRIC MOTORS INC
5800 Nw 163rd St (33014-5600)
PHONE..............................305 885-9476
William A Clot, *Ch of Bd*
Stephen J Clot, *President*
Lester R Johnson, *Vice Pres*
Lester Solorzano, *Prdtn Mgr*
Rodger Reynolds, *QC Mgr*
EMP: 100 **EST:** 1972
SQ FT: 30,000

SALES (est): 15.8MM **Privately Held**
WEB: www.aem.us
SIC: 7694 Rewinding services

(G-10281)
AMERICAN AUTOMTN SYSTEMS INC
Also Called: Aas
5471 Nw 159th St (33014-6723)
PHONE..............................305 620-0077
Fax: 305 558-9082
EMP: 5
SQ FT: 4,000
SALES (est): 922.3K **Privately Held**
SIC: 3535 Mfg Conveyors/Equipment

(G-10282)
ASSOCATED PRTG PRODUCTIONS INC
Also Called: Appi
13925 Nw 60th Ave (33014-3126)
PHONE..............................305 623-7600
Jjohn P Beadel, *President*
John P Beadel, *President*
Marni Bauman, *General Mgr*
Linda Beadel, *Vice Pres*
Jimmie Davis, *Production*
▼ **EMP:** 50 **EST:** 1991
SQ FT: 20,000
SALES (est): 9.4MM **Privately Held**
WEB: www.appi1.com
SIC: 2796 2791 2789 Platemaking services; typesetting; bookbinding & related work

(G-10283)
AVANTI NUTRITIONAL LABS LLC (PA)
14101 Commerce Way (33016-1513)
PHONE..............................305 822-3880
Adolfo Gomez, *Mng Member*
Leydilian Carrera, *Manager*
EMP: 35 **EST:** 2014
SALES (est): 85MM **Privately Held**
SIC: 2834 Vitamin preparations

(G-10284)
BEST CLOSURES INC
9780 Nw 79th Ave (33016-2514)
PHONE..............................305 821-6607
Santiago A Suarez, *President*
Brian E Santore, *Vice Pres*
EMP: 7 **EST:** 2013
SALES (est): 133.2K **Privately Held**
SIC: 3549 Coilers (metalworking machines); coiling machinery

(G-10285)
BETANCOURT SPORTS NTRTN LLC (HQ)
14700 Nw 60th Ave (33014-2813)
PHONE..............................305 593-9296
Colin Watts, *CEO*
Michael Beardall, *President*
Jason Reiser, *COO*
Brenda Galgano, *CFO*
EMP: 5 **EST:** 2009
SALES (est): 2.1MM
SALES (corp-wide): 3.2B **Publicly Held**
SIC: 2023 Dietary supplements, dairy & non-dairy based
PA: Franchise Group, Inc.
109 Innovation Ct Ste J
Delaware OH 43015
740 363-2222

(G-10286)
BIOREP TECHNOLOGIES INC
15804 Nw 57th Ave (33014-6702)
PHONE..............................305 330-4449
Ramon E Poo, *President*
Felipe Echeverri, *Managing Dir*
Alexander Orozco, *Business Dir*
EMP: 18 **EST:** 1994
SQ FT: 6,000
SALES (est): 4MM **Privately Held**
WEB: www.biorep.com
SIC: 3841 8733 Anesthesia apparatus; medical research

(G-10287)
BREFAROS NOBILE FOOD LLC
Also Called: Fiori Bruna Pasta Products
5340 Nw 163rd St (33014-6228)
PHONE..............................305 621-0074

Jose Yamin, *CEO*
Mayid Yamin,
◆ **EMP:** 30 **EST:** 1985
SQ FT: 8,000
SALES (est): 5.4MM **Privately Held**
SIC: 2099 Pasta, uncooked: packaged with other ingredients

(G-10288)
CALIFORNIA SHUTTERS INC
16350 Nw 48th Ave (33014-6417)
PHONE..............................305 827-9333
Ana Salomon, *Ch of Bd*
Edmond Salomon, *Vice Pres*
Marlise Cummings, *Treasurer*
George Cummings, *Admin Sec*
▼ **EMP:** 5 **EST:** 1987
SALES (est): 700K **Privately Held**
WEB: www.californiashutters.com
SIC: 3442 Shutters, door or window: metal

(G-10289)
CAME AMERICAS AUTOMATION LLC
5863 Nw 159th St (33014-6717)
PHONE..............................305 433-3307
Winslow Wise, *Managing Dir*
Gustavo Beltran, *Managing Dir*
H Gonzalez, *Business Mgr*
◆ **EMP:** 13 **EST:** 2007
SALES (est): 2.6MM **Privately Held**
WEB: www.came.com
SIC: 3699 Security devices

(G-10290)
CANDIES AND BEYOND INC
Also Called: Coffee Candy Store, The
14100 Nw 60th Ave (33014-3131)
PHONE..............................954 828-2255
Carlos Simao, *President*
EMP: 7 **EST:** 2014
SALES (est): 107.8K **Privately Held**
SIC: 2064 5149 Lollipops & other hard candy; beverages, except coffee & tea

(G-10291)
CHAMPION WELDING SERVICES LLC
5608 Nw 161st St (33014-6129)
PHONE..............................786 262-5727
Victor Tuckler,
EMP: 5 **EST:** 2008
SALES (est): 509.9K **Privately Held**
WEB: www.championweldingservices.com
SIC: 7692 Welding repair

(G-10292)
CHEMCO CORP
4920 Nw 165th St (33014-6323)
PHONE..............................305 623-4445
Eitelberg G Montarroyos, *CEO*
Natalia Urquiza, *Project Mgr*
Andrew Jenks, *Purch Mgr*
Jack Wang, *Purch Agent*
Amy S Montarroyos, *CFO*
◆ **EMP:** 50 **EST:** 1957
SQ FT: 60,000
SALES (est): 22.2MM **Privately Held**
WEB: www.echemco.com
SIC: 2844 2842 Shampoos, rinses, conditioners: hair; manicure preparations; cleaning or polishing preparations

(G-10293)
CORDIS CORPORATION (HQ)
14201 Nw 60th Ave (33014-2894)
PHONE..............................786 313-2000
Shar Matin, *CEO*
George Adams MD, *Chief*
John M Adams, *Vice Pres*
Christian M Spaulding, *Vice Pres*
Jose Barroso, *Materials Mgr*
◆ **EMP:** 191 **EST:** 1959
SQ FT: 480,000
SALES (est): 597.3MM
SALES (corp-wide): 181.3B **Publicly Held**
SIC: 3841 3842 Surgical & medical instruments; catheters; surgical appliances & supplies; implants, surgical
PA: Cardinal Health, Inc.
7000 Cardinal Pl
Dublin OH 43017
614 757-5000

(G-10294)
DARMAR CABINETS INC
5273 Nw 161st St (33014-6221)
PHONE..............................786 556-5784
Norberto Ricardo, *President*
EMP: 9 **EST:** 2010
SALES (est): 256.1K **Privately Held**
SIC: 2434 Wood kitchen cabinets

(G-10295)
DEGGY CORP
15485 Eagle Nest Ln # 100 (33014-2221)
PHONE..............................305 377-2233
▼ **EMP:** 6
SALES (est): 610K **Privately Held**
SIC: 3699 Mfg Electrical Equipment/Supplies

(G-10296)
DEMETECH CORPORATION (PA)
5980 Miami Lakes Dr (33014-2404)
PHONE..............................305 824-1048
Luis M Arguello Sr, *CEO*
Maria E Arguello, *President*
Christopher A Arguello, *Vice Pres*
Karla V Arguello, *Vice Pres*
Jorge Perez, *Plant Mgr*
◆ **EMP:** 48 **EST:** 2000
SALES (est): 29MM **Privately Held**
WEB: shop.demetech.us
SIC: 3842 Sutures, absorbable & non-absorbable

(G-10297)
DREW SCIENTIFIC INC (DH)
Also Called: Danam Electronics
14050 Nw 57th Ct (33014-3105)
PHONE..............................305 418-2320
Richard J Depiano Jr, *CEO*
Douglas P Nickols, *President*
Jim Acock, *Principal*
Dr Andrew Kinney, *Senior VP*
Francis Matuszak Jr, *Vice Pres*
◆ **EMP:** 34 **EST:** 1999
SALES (est): 15.9MM **Publicly Held**
SIC: 3829 3841 Geophysical or meteorological electronic equipment; medical instruments & equipment, blood & bone work; blood transfusion equipment
HQ: Erba Diagnostics, Inc.
14100 Nw 57th Ct
Miami Lakes FL 33014
305 324-2300

(G-10298)
ECOPRINTQ INC
14261 Commerce Way # 101 (33016-1646)
PHONE..............................305 681-7445
Alfredo Milanes, *President*
Ever Milanes, *Vice Pres*
Rebeca Estevez, *Sales Staff*
Jodi Lindner, *Sales Staff*
Diana Ochoa, *Sales Staff*
EMP: 10 **EST:** 2011
SQ FT: 3,500
SALES (est): 4MM **Privately Held**
WEB: www.ecoprintq.com
SIC: 7372 Operating systems computer software

(G-10299)
EMC QUALITY GROUP CORP
6625 Mami Lkes Dr E Ste 2 (33014)
PHONE..............................786 501-5891
Elder Maldonado, *President*
EMP: 8 **EST:** 2017
SALES (est): 203.6K **Privately Held**
SIC: 3572 Computer storage devices

(G-10300)
ERBA DIAGNOSTICS INC (DH)
14100 Nw 57th Ct (33014-3107)
PHONE..............................305 324-2300
Hayden Jeffreys, *CEO*
Suresh Vazirani, *Ch of Bd*
Mohan Gopalkrishnan, *VP Opers*
Aidan Rivero, *Production*
Russell Cooper, *Purch Agent*
▲ **EMP:** 34 **EST:** 1980
SALES (est): 32.5MM **Publicly Held**
SIC: 2834 3841 Pharmaceutical preparations; diagnostic apparatus, medical

▲ = Import ▼=Export
◆ =Import/Export

(G-10301)
EXPRESS PAPER COMPANY INC
Also Called: South Florida Tissue Paper Co
5590 Nw 163rd St (33014-6132)
PHONE...................................305 685-4929
Juan E Corzo, *President*
Alfredo Cortes, *CFO*
Clara V Crocker-Morales, *Treasurer*
◆ **EMP:** 15 **EST:** 1998
SQ FT: 40,000
SALES (est): 4.5MM **Privately Held**
WEB: www.southfloridatissuepaper.com
SIC: 2679 Paper products, converted

(G-10302)
FASTSIGNS
15925 Nw 57th Ave (33014-6703)
PHONE...................................305 628-3278
Sergio Smith, *Owner*
EMP: 12 **EST:** 2009
SALES (est): 978.9K **Privately Held**
WEB: www.fastsigns.com
SIC: 3993 Signs & advertising specialties

(G-10303)
FLA PROPERTY HOLDINGS INC
13980 Nw 58th Ct (33014-3115)
PHONE...................................813 888-8796
Jennifer Bly, *President*
Mitch Rotberg, *CFO*
EMP: 22 **EST:** 1936
SQ FT: 22,000
SALES (est): 1MM **Privately Held**
SIC: 2759 Screen printing

(G-10304)
FLORIDA KOLMIAMI CORPORATION
6491 Cow Pen Rd Apt H102 (33014-6641)
PHONE...................................305 582-0114
Julian Orozco, *President*
EMP: 9 **EST:** 2001
SQ FT: 500
SALES (est): 507.4K **Privately Held**
SIC: 2899 Oils & essential oils

(G-10305)
GLOBAL CABINET DISTRIBUTORS
16355 Nw 48th Ave (33014-6416)
PHONE...................................305 625-9814
Terri Reeves, *Principal*
▲ **EMP:** 7 **EST:** 2009
SALES (est): 346K **Privately Held**
SIC: 2434 Wood kitchen cabinets

(G-10306)
GUARDIAN HURRICANE PROTECTION
5729 Nw 159th St (33014-6750)
PHONE...................................305 805-7050
Pablo J Ramos, *CEO*
Andrea Ramos, *President*
▼ **EMP:** 13 **EST:** 2000
SALES (est): 2.8MM **Privately Held**
WEB: www.guardian-shutters.com
SIC: 3442 2431 Shutters, door or window: metal; door shutters, wood; window shutters, wood

(G-10307)
INDUSTRIAL PLASTIC PDTS INC
14025 Nw 58th Ct (33014-3116)
PHONE...................................305 822-3223
Veronika Thorne, *President*
George Thorne, *Exec VP*
Tania Ortiz, *Vice Pres*
▲ **EMP:** 50 **EST:** 1975
SQ FT: 35,000
SALES (est): 4.9MM **Privately Held**
WEB: www.industrialplasticproducts.com
SIC: 3089 2821 Injection molding of plastics; plastics materials & resins

(G-10308)
INTERNATIONAL CASTING CORP
Also Called: ICC
6187 Miami Lakes Dr E (33014-2407)
PHONE...................................305 558-3515
Walter Alvarez, *Owner*
Jesus Marrero, *Manager*
EMP: 30 **EST:** 1998

SALES (est): 2.6MM **Privately Held**
SIC: 3272 Concrete products, precast

(G-10309)
INTERNATIONAL VAPOR GROUP LLC (DH)
14300 Commerce Way (33016-1501)
PHONE...................................305 824-4027
Marc Waxman, *COO*
Ditmar Berberich, *Vice Pres*
Nichele Thompson, *Mktg Coord*
Nick Rucci, *IT/INT Sup*
EMP: 17 **EST:** 2009
SALES (est): 50MM
SALES (corp-wide): 445.4MM **Publicly Held**
WEB: www.turningpointbrands.com
SIC: 3999 5194 5993 Cigarette & cigar products & accessories; cigarettes;
HQ: Turning Point Brands, Llc
5201 Interchange Way
Louisville KY 40229
502 778-4421

(G-10310)
KELLSTROM COML AROSPC INC
14400 Nw 77th Ct Ste 306 (33016-1592)
PHONE...................................305 818-5400
Vincia McClainsalter, *Vice Pres*
Kevin Bravo, *Sales Staff*
Jeff Lund, *Manager*
EMP: 47
SALES (corp-wide): 1B **Privately Held**
SIC: 3728 Aircraft parts & equipment
HQ: Kellstrom Commercial Aerospace, Inc.
450 Medinah Rd
Roselle IL 60172
847 233-5800

(G-10311)
LADOVE INC
Also Called: Headwear International
5701 Miami Lakes Dr E (33014-2417)
P.O. Box 5169, Hialeah (33014-1169)
PHONE...................................305 823-8051
Sheree Kent, *President*
Michael Bass, *Exec VP*
Catalina Vz, *Opers Staff*
Jeanette Reneau, *Purch Mgr*
Penelope Santana, *Purch Mgr*
▲ **EMP:** 55 **EST:** 1977
SQ FT: 20,000
SALES (est): 16.3MM **Privately Held**
WEB: www.ladove.com
SIC: 2844 Shampoos, rinses, conditioners: hair

(G-10312)
LADOVE INDUSTRIES INC
5701 Miami Lakes Dr E (33014-2417)
P.O. Box 5169, Hialeah (33014-1169)
PHONE...................................305 624-2456
Sheree Lacove, *President*
EMP: 9 **EST:** 1977
SALES (est): 250.3K **Privately Held**
WEB: www.ladove.com
SIC: 2844 Hair preparations, including shampoos

(G-10313)
LAWRENCE FACTOR INC
4790 Nw 157th St (33014-6421)
PHONE...................................305 430-9152
Lawrence Kaplan, *President*
Judy Cummings, *Corp Secy*
Michael Casey, *Vice Pres*
John S Kostick, *Vice Pres*
Robert Laughlin, *Vice Pres*
▼ **EMP:** 30 **EST:** 1981
SQ FT: 23,000
SALES (est): 5.9MM **Privately Held**
WEB: www.lawrence-factor.com
SIC: 3599 Air intake filters, internal combustion engine, except auto

(G-10314)
LIOHER ENTERPRISE CORP
13939 Nw 60th Ave (33014-3126)
PHONE...................................305 685-0005
Armando R Gonzalez-Diaz, *President*
Raul Gonzalez Lio, *Vice Pres*
Reynaldo Ruiz, *Treasurer*
Matias Cobo, *Director*
▲ **EMP:** 5 **EST:** 2010

SALES (est): 1MM **Privately Held**
WEB: www.lioher.com
SIC: 3553 5712 Woodworking machinery; customized furniture & cabinets

(G-10315)
LPS PRODUCTION LLC
Also Called: Lps Lighting Sound Video Prod
15901 Nw 59th Ave (33014-6718)
PHONE...................................786 208-6217
Jose Laria, *President*
EMP: 10 **EST:** 2015
SALES (est): 847.6K **Privately Held**
WEB: www.lpsproduction.com
SIC: 3648 Lighting equipment

(G-10316)
MAQ INVESTMENTS GROUP INC
Also Called: D G Steel Rule Die Mfg
14312 Commerce Way (33016-1501)
PHONE...................................305 691-1468
Daniel Ziadi, *President*
▲ **EMP:** 25 **EST:** 1937
SALES (est): 2.5MM **Privately Held**
SIC: 2675 Die-cut paper & board

(G-10317)
MASON VITAMINS INC
15750 Nw 59th Ave (33014-6716)
PHONE...................................800 327-6005
Yosuke Honjo, *CEO*
Ofelia Perez, *President*
Garcia Richard, *Vice Pres*
Freddy De Cordova, *Purch Mgr*
Manuel Albelo, *Purchasing*
▼ **EMP:** 100 **EST:** 1967
SQ FT: 40,000
SALES (est): 20.7MM **Privately Held**
WEB: www.masonvitamins.com
SIC: 2834 Vitamin, nutrient & hematinic preparations for human use; vitamin preparations

(G-10318)
MASTER TOOL CO INC
6115 Nw 153rd St (33014-2480)
PHONE...................................305 557-1020
Paul Roos, *President*
Paul Kevin Roos, *President*
Julie Estock, *Vice Pres*
EMP: 35 **EST:** 1957
SALES (est): 5MM **Privately Held**
WEB: www.mastertoolusa.com
SIC: 3089 Injection molding of plastics

(G-10319)
MEDTRONIC
14420 Nw 60th Ave (33014-2807)
PHONE...................................305 458-7260
Sacha Hall, *Engineer*
Arismely Duverge, *Auditor*
Randy Krueger, *Branch Mgr*
Ventura Martha, *Technician*
EMP: 23 **Privately Held**
WEB: www.heartware.com
SIC: 3841 Medical instruments & equipment, blood & bone work
HQ: Medtronic
14400 Nw 60th Ave
Miami Lakes FL 33014
305 818-4100

(G-10320)
MEDTRONIC (DH)
14400 Nw 60th Ave (33014-2807)
PHONE...................................305 818-4100
Douglas Godshall, *President*
Larry Knopf, *Senior VP*
Peter McAree, *Senior VP*
Jim Schuermann, *Senior VP*
Lauren Farrell, *Vice Pres*
EMP: 70 **EST:** 1998
SQ FT: 59,000
SALES (est): 45.9MM **Privately Held**
WEB: www.heartware.com
SIC: 3841 Surgical & medical instruments

(G-10321)
MERCK SHARP & DOHME CORP
14240 Plmetto Frontage Rd (33016-1533)
PHONE...................................305 512-6062
EMP: 78
SALES (corp-wide): 39.8B **Publicly Held**
SIC: 2834 Mfg Pharmaceuticals

HQ: Merck Sharp & Dohme Corp.
2000 Galloping Hill Rd
Kenilworth NJ 07065
908 740-4000

(G-10322)
MERCK SHARP & DOHME LLC
13900 Nw 57th Ct (33014-3103)
PHONE...................................305 698-4600
Max Rodriguez, *Engineer*
Caryn Rooth, *Finance*
Jennifer Dodge, *Sales Staff*
Esteban Reyes, *Sales Staff*
Vanessa Juon, *Marketing Staff*
EMP: 216
SQ FT: 183,405
SALES (corp-wide): 48.7B **Publicly Held**
WEB: www.merck.com
SIC: 2834 Pharmaceutical preparations
HQ: Merck Sharp & Dohme Llc
126 E Lincoln Ave
Rahway NJ 07065
908 740-4000

(G-10323)
MFR EMPIRE CORP
5729 Nw 151st St (33014-2481)
PHONE...................................786 558-7122
Landy Munoz, *Vice Pres*
EMP: 7 **EST:** 2019
SALES (est): 337.7K **Privately Held**
SIC: 3999 Manufacturing industries

(G-10324)
MIAMI SCREENPRINT SUPPLY INC
5566 Nw 161st St (33014-6127)
PHONE...................................305 622-7532
Kevin Flury, *President*
Maureen Alvarez, *Vice Pres*
▼ **EMP:** 6 **EST:** 2006
SALES (est): 826.8K **Privately Held**
WEB: www.miamiscreenprintsupply.com
SIC: 2759 Screen printing

(G-10325)
MIAMI TEES INC
5120 Nw 165th St Ste 101 (33014-6340)
PHONE...................................305 623-3908
Michael Chavez, *President*
▲ **EMP:** 65 **EST:** 1988
SALES (est): 4.7MM **Privately Held**
WEB: www.miamitees.us
SIC: 2759 Screen printing

(G-10326)
MILTECHNOLOGIES INC
13980 Nw 58th Ct (33014-3115)
PHONE...................................305 817-4244
Jorge Mejia, *President*
▼ **EMP:** 5 **EST:** 2004
SQ FT: 5,500
SALES (est): 596.2K **Privately Held**
SIC: 3724 Aircraft engines & engine parts

(G-10327)
MJM MANUFACTURING INC
5205 Nw 161st St (33014-6221)
P.O. Box 5427, Miami (33101-5427)
PHONE...................................305 620-2020
Michael J Mijares, *President*
Alex Mijares, *General Mgr*
Michael Mijares, *General Mgr*
Renard Amaro, *Vice Pres*
Aida Mijares, *Vice Pres*
EMP: 60 **EST:** 1979
SQ FT: 57,000
SALES (est): 10.7MM **Privately Held**
WEB: www.mjmmfg.com
SIC: 3444 Sheet metal specialties, not stamped

(G-10328)
MTSERVICER LLC
8140 Nw 155th St (33016-5999)
PHONE...................................305 200-1254
Jorge Barreto, *Principal*
EMP: 7 **EST:** 2011
SALES (est): 259.1K **Privately Held**
SIC: 3621 Generators & sets, electric

(G-10329)
NATIONAL MOLDING LLC (PA)
Also Called: Security Plastics
14427 Nw 60th Ave (33014-2806)
PHONE...................................305 823-5440

Paul Frascoia, *President*
Mike Curran, *General Mgr*
Tony Wong, *Vice Pres*
Gerardo Palmer, *Engineer*
Evan Steinman, *Engineer*
◆ **EMP:** 140 **EST:** 1965
SQ FT: 7,700
SALES (est): 50.9MM **Privately Held**
WEB: www.nationalmolding.com
SIC: 3089 Injection molding of plastics

(G-10330)
NEW GENERATION COMPUTING INC (HQ)
14900 Nw 79th Ct Ste 100 (33016-5791)
PHONE....................................800 690-0642
Alan Brooks, *Chairman*
Ramon Nunez, *Production*
Clinton Dye, *Engineer*
Lilly Sabin, *Controller*
Maria Saavedra, *Mktg Dir*
EMP: 60 **EST:** 1982
SQ FT: 5,000
SALES (est): 21MM
SALES (corp-wide): 127.5MM **Publicly Held**
WEB: www.ngcsoftware.com
SIC: 7372 Business oriented computer software
PA: American Software, Inc.
　　470 E Paces Ferry Rd Ne
　　Atlanta GA 30305
　　404 261-4381

(G-10331)
NEW LASER TECH INC
7003 Greentree Ln (33014-2077)
PHONE....................................305 450-0456
Mark Chariff, *Principal*
EMP: 8 **EST:** 2007
SALES (est): 90.6K **Privately Held**
SIC: 3699 Laser systems & equipment

(G-10332)
NEW UNDERGROUND RR PUBG CO
14411 Commerce Way # 320 (33016-1596)
PHONE....................................305 825-1444
EMP: 15
SALES (est): 1.1MM **Privately Held**
SIC: 2731 4011 Books-Publishing/Printing
　　Railroad Line-Haul Operator

(G-10333)
ONE INNOVATION LABS LLC
Also Called: Innovation Laboratories
14520 Nw 60th Ave (33014-2809)
PHONE....................................305 985-3950
Guillermo Salazar, *President*
Anthony Armas, *Executive*
EMP: 35 **EST:** 2019
SALES (est): 3.7MM **Privately Held**
WEB: www.oneinnovationlabs.com
SIC: 2833 Medicinals & botanicals

(G-10334)
OUTDOOR AMERICA IMAGES INC
Also Called: Rose Poster Printing
13982 Nw 58th Ct (33014-3115)
PHONE....................................813 888-8796
Mick Taylor, *General Mgr*
John Wurster, *General Mgr*
Eric Blanc, *Business Mgr*
Whitney Jude, *Accounts Mgr*
Kristina Lausier, *Manager*
EMP: 31 **Privately Held**
SIC: 2759 Screen printing
PA: Outdoor America Images, Inc.
　　4545 W Hillsborough Ave
　　Tampa FL 33614

(G-10335)
PC MASTERS CORP
5951 Nw 151st St Ste 35 (33014-2423)
PHONE....................................305 582-5595
Will Angel, *General Mgr*
EMP: 6
SALES (est): 370K **Privately Held**
SIC: 3571 Electronic computers

(G-10336)
PERFORMANCE CNC CORP
5535 Nw 161st St (33014-6101)
PHONE....................................786 334-6445

Rafael E Fuentes, *Principal*
EMP: 7 **EST:** 2020
SALES (est): 87.9K **Privately Held**
WEB: performance-cnc-corp.negocio.site
SIC: 3599 Machine shop, jobbing & repair

(G-10337)
PFAFFCO INC
Also Called: Pfaff Engraving
14329 Commerce Way (33016-1502)
PHONE....................................305 635-0986
Daniel Pfaff, *President*
Kimberly E Pfaff, *Vice Pres*
Kathleen N Pfaff, *Admin Sec*
◆ **EMP:** 10 **EST:** 1970
SQ FT: 2,500
SALES (est): 447.9K **Privately Held**
SIC: 2759 2752 2796 Stationery: printing;
thermography; commercial printing, litho-
graphic; platemaking services

(G-10338)
PHARMALAB ENTERPRISES INC (PA)
14501 Nw 60th Ave (33014-2808)
PHONE....................................305 821-4002
Alberto J Perez, *President*
Ramona Perez, *Admin Sec*
EMP: 13 **EST:** 2004
SALES (est): 8.4MM **Privately Held**
WEB: www.pharmalabenterprises.com
SIC: 2834 Vitamin preparations

(G-10339)
PIONEER LED LIGHTING CORP
Also Called: Zollan
4980 Nw 165th St Unit A1 (33014-6304)
P.O. Box 823691, Pembroke Pines (33082-
3691)
PHONE....................................305 620-5300
Robert Behnejad, *President*
Mitra K Behnejad, *Vice Pres*
EMP: 8 **EST:** 2009
SALES (est): 491.8K **Privately Held**
WEB: www.zollan.com
SIC: 3646 Commercial indusl & institu-
tional electric lighting fixtures

(G-10340)
POINT BLANK ENTERPRISES INC
Also Called: Protective Group A Pt Blank Co
14100 Nw 58th Ct (33014-3119)
PHONE....................................305 820-4270
Jorge Bernal, *Engineer*
Denise Garib, *IT/INT Sup*
Elizabeth Serrania, *Director*
Ashley Reynolds,
EMP: 67 **Privately Held**
WEB: www.pointblankenterprises.com
SIC: 3699 3842 Security devices; bullet-
proof vests
HQ: Point Blank Enterprises, Inc.
　　2102 Sw 2nd St
　　Pompano Beach FL 33069
　　954 630-0900

(G-10341)
PRECISION TECH AERO INC
6051 Nw 153rd St (33014-2413)
PHONE....................................305 603-8347
Luiz Taves, *General Mgr*
Luiz M Taves, *Principal*
Taves Luiz M, *Principal*
Maickel Vazquez, *Supervisor*
Anibal Corona, *Maintence Staff*
EMP: 12 **EST:** 2013
SALES (est): 2.3MM **Privately Held**
WEB: www.ptaero.com
SIC: 3728 Aircraft parts & equipment

(G-10342)
PRIKO CORP
16500 Nw 86th Ct (33016-6144)
PHONE....................................305 556-3558
Humberto Gomez, *Principal*
Julia A Gomez, *Principal*
EMP: 15 **EST:** 2007
SALES (est): 232K **Privately Held**
SIC: 3465 Body parts, automobile:
stamped metal

(G-10343)
PROFAST CORPORATION
5854 Miami Lakes Dr E (33014-2402)
PHONE....................................305 827-7801

Joel Asseraf, *President*
Laurence Asseraf, *Vice Pres*
◆ **EMP:** 27 **EST:** 1983
SQ FT: 12,000
SALES (est): 3.3MM **Privately Held**
WEB: www.profastusa.com
SIC: 3089 Boxes, plastic; plastic hardware
& building products

(G-10344)
PROFAST USA INC
5854 Miami Lakes Dr E (33014-2402)
PHONE....................................305 827-7801
Marcos M Drobiner, *President*
Beatrice R Drobiner, *Vice Pres*
Byron Castro, *Accounts Exec*
Oscar Gutierrez, *Sales Staff*
◆ **EMP:** 16 **EST:** 2006
SALES (est): 2.2MM **Privately Held**
WEB: www.profastusa.com
SIC: 3462 Anchors, forged

(G-10345)
PROTECTIVE GROUP INC
14100 Nw 58th Ct (33014-3119)
PHONE....................................305 820-4266
EMP: 30 **Privately Held**
SIC: 3699 3842 Electrical Equipment And
Supplies, Nec, N
PA: The Protective Group Inc
　　14100 Nw 58th Ct
　　Miami Lakes FL 33014
　　305 820-4270

(G-10346)
R & R MICA WORKS INC
6541 Lake Blue Dr (33014-3003)
PHONE....................................305 231-1887
Rigo Malpica, *President*
EMP: 6 **EST:** 1988
SQ FT: 5,000
SALES (est): 482.3K **Privately Held**
SIC: 2511 Tables, household: wood

(G-10347)
RECOMMEND TRAVEL PUBLICATIONS
5979 Nw 151st St Ste 120 (33014-2448)
P.O. Box 171070, Hialeah (33017-1070)
PHONE....................................305 826-4763
EMP: 17
SQ FT: 7,000
SALES (est): 1.5MM
SALES (corp-wide): 7.9MM **Privately Held**
SIC: 2721 Periodicals-Publishing/Printing
PA: Worth International Media Group
　　5979 Nw 151st St Ste 120
　　Miami Lakes FL 33014
　　305 826-4763

(G-10348)
RENNAK INC
Also Called: Sir Speedy
6161 Miami Lakes Dr E (33014-2408)
PHONE....................................305 558-0144
Reuven Kanner, *President*
Susanne Kanner, *Corp Secy*
Manny Pose, *Sales Staff*
▼ **EMP:** 6 **EST:** 1979
SQ FT: 3,000
SALES (est): 1MM **Privately Held**
WEB: www.sirspeedy.com
SIC: 2752 Commercial printing, litho-
graphic

(G-10349)
RICH WOODTURNING INC
5626 Nw 161st St (33014-6129)
PHONE....................................305 573-9142
Richard Rocard, *President*
▼ **EMP:** 10 **EST:** 1952
SQ FT: 8,000
SALES (est): 677.9K **Privately Held**
WEB: www.richwoodturning.com
SIC: 2499 2431 Carved & turned wood;
millwork

(G-10350)
SCENTS NATURE ENTERPRISES CORP
Also Called: Botanical Scents Nature Entps
7850 Nw 98th St (33016-2429)
PHONE....................................305 547-2334
◆ **EMP:** 15
SQ FT: 20,000

SALES: 2.5MM **Privately Held**
SIC: 2899 Mfg Chemical Preparations

(G-10351)
SCENTS OF NATURE ENTERPRISES
Also Called: Sonec
7850 Nw 98th St (33016-2429)
PHONE....................................305 547-2334
EMP: 20
SALES: 5MM **Privately Held**
SIC: 3999 Mfg Misc Products

(G-10352)
SIGNATURE PRINTING INC
5725 Nw 151st St (33014-2481)
P.O. Box 820021, Pembroke Pines (33082-
0021)
PHONE....................................305 828-9992
Jaime Prada, *President*
Maria Prada, *Corp Secy*
Jose Prada, *Vice Pres*
Maria Watson, *Admin Sec*
EMP: 10 **EST:** 1982
SQ FT: 2,000
SALES (est): 843.1K **Privately Held**
WEB: www.signature-printing.com
SIC: 2752 Commercial printing, offset

(G-10353)
SKY TECHNICS AVIATION SLS INC
15915 Nw 59th Ave (33014-6718)
PHONE....................................305 885-7499
Manuel Castaneda, *President*
Milton Aguilera, *Vice Pres*
EMP: 9 **EST:** 2014
SALES (est): 525.5K **Privately Held**
WEB: www.sta-repairs.com
SIC: 3728 5088 Aircraft parts & equip-
ment; aeronautical equipment & supplies

(G-10354)
SOLAR PACKAGING CORP
4920 Nw 165th St (33014-6323)
PHONE....................................305 621-5551
John Carson, *President*
EMP: 8 **EST:** 2008
SALES (est): 136.5K **Privately Held**
SIC: 2844 Toilet preparations

(G-10355)
SOLARA INC
Also Called: Solara Labs
5105 Nw 159th St (33014-6336)
PHONE....................................305 592-4748
Jose Rocca, *CEO*
Jeff Powlowsky, *President*
Maria Bolivar, *Project Mgr*
Oscar Reyes, *Opers Staff*
Kristena Shaw, *Marketing Staff*
▼ **EMP:** 18 **EST:** 2007
SQ FT: 7,200
SALES (est): 4.9MM **Privately Held**
WEB: www.solaralabs.com
SIC: 2834 Vitamin, nutrient & hematinic
preparations for human use

(G-10356)
SOUTHEAST ID LLC
5830 Nw 163rd St (33014-5600)
PHONE....................................954 571-6665
Alan Mendelson, *CEO*
Jacob Brafman, *CFO*
Albert Villacampa, *Info Tech Mgr*
EMP: 16 **EST:** 2015
SALES (est): 999.4K **Privately Held**
WEB: www.southeastid.com
SIC: 3089 2672 Identification cards, plas-
tic; coated & laminated paper

(G-10357)
SOUTHEAST OFFSET INC
4880 Nw 157th St (33014-6434)
PHONE....................................305 623-7788
Troy Clowdus, *President*
▼ **EMP:** 17 **EST:** 1995
SQ FT: 36,000
SALES (est): 1.2MM **Privately Held**
WEB: www.southeastoffset.com
SIC: 2711 Commercial printing & newspa-
per publishing combined

▲ = Import ▼ =Export
◆ =Import/Export

(G-10358)
SOUTHERN FIBER INC
4715 Nw 157th St Ste 104 (33014-6433)
PHONE.................................786 916-3052
Robert Ruberti, *Branch Mgr*
EMP: 8
SQ FT: 22,900
SALES (corp-wide): 8.5MM **Privately Held**
WEB: www.southernfiberinc.com
SIC: 2281 Manmade & synthetic fiber yarns, spun
PA: Southern Fiber, Inc.
1041 S Grove Ext
Lincolnton NC 28093
704 736-0011

(G-10359)
SOUTHERN UNDERGROUND INDS
5979 Nw 151st St Ste 223 (33014-2467)
PHONE.................................954 226-3865
John Brady, *Principal*
EMP: 7 EST: 2017
SALES (est): 984.3K **Privately Held**
SIC: 1389 Oil field services

(G-10360)
SOUTHWINGS AVIONICS AND ACC
5429 Nw 161st St (33014-6124)
PHONE.................................305 825-6755
Manuel Lopez, *Principal*
EMP: 8 EST: 2010
SALES (est): 810.8K **Privately Held**
SIC: 3721 Aircraft

(G-10361)
SUN CATALINA HOLDINGS LLC
16200 Nw 59th Ave Ste 101 (33014-7541)
PHONE.................................305 558-4777
Dorothy Ardito, *Vice Pres*
Dennis Poppe, *Vice Pres*
Sandra Roy, *Controller*
David Garcia, *Sales Staff*
Joe Kitchel, *Director*
EMP: 46 EST: 2001
SALES (est): 1.9MM
SALES (corp-wide): 3.4B **Privately Held**
SIC: 3645 3646 3648 3641 Residential lighting fixtures; commercial indusl & institutional electric lighting fixtures; lighting equipment; electric lamps
PA: Sun Capital Partners, Inc.
5200 Town Center Cir # 450
Boca Raton FL 33486
561 394-0550

(G-10362)
SUNCREST SHEDS OF SOUTH FLA
9600 Nw 77th Ave (33016-2501)
PHONE.................................305 231-1990
Juan Carlos Zamora, *President*
Javier Parra, *Sales Mgr*
EMP: 10 EST: 2006
SALES (est): 954.4K **Privately Held**
WEB: www.sheddepotsheds.com
SIC: 3448 1542 Buildings, portable: prefabricated metal; commercial & office building contractors

(G-10363)
SWEEPY GROUP PRODUCTS LLC
14501 Nw 60th Ave Unit 37 (33014-2808)
PHONE.................................305 556-3450
EMP: 5
SALES (est): 4.5MM **Privately Held**
SIC: 3565 Mfg Packaging Machinery

(G-10364)
TEXENE LLC
Also Called: Manufacturer
5860 Miami Lakes Dr E (33014-2402)
PHONE.................................305 200-5001
Carlos Echeverria, *CEO*
Dee Glowa, *Accountant*
▼ EMP: 12 EST: 2007
SALES (est): 961.5K **Privately Held**
WEB: www.texene.com
SIC: 2394 2869 5131 Tarpaulins, fabric: made from purchased materials; olefins; synthetic fabrics

(G-10365)
TONER CARTRIDGE RECHARGE INC
7923 Nw 163rd Ter (33016-6105)
PHONE.................................305 968-1045
Nino Clares-Prieto, *President*
Marcia Clares, *Admin Sec*
EMP: 5 EST: 1997
SALES (est): 623.9K **Privately Held**
SIC: 3955 Print cartridges for laser & other computer printers

(G-10366)
TOP DRAWER INC
5190 Nw 165th St (33014-6303)
PHONE.................................305 620-1102
Richard Herman, *President*
Adam Herman, *COO*
Craig Herman, *Vice Pres*
Catalina Bermudez, *Office Mgr*
EMP: 10 EST: 1974
SQ FT: 10,000
SALES (est): 1MM **Privately Held**
SIC: 2752 Commercial printing, offset

(G-10367)
TOP DRAWER PRINTERS INC
5190 Nw 165th St (33014-6303)
PHONE.................................305 620-1102
Richard E Herman, *President*
Adam Herman, *COO*
Craig F Herman, *Vice Pres*
Marilyn Herman, *Treasurer*
Catalina Bermudez, *Office Mgr*
EMP: 21 EST: 1974
SQ FT: 10,000
SALES (est): 421K **Privately Held**
SIC: 2752 Commercial printing, offset

(G-10368)
TORRO FOODS LLC
6725 Main St (33014-2071)
PHONE.................................305 558-3212
Hector F Rodriguez, *Principal*
EMP: 6 EST: 2009
SALES (est): 512.7K **Privately Held**
SIC: 2099 Food preparations

(G-10369)
UNITED SIERRA GROUP CORP (PA)
8218 Commerce Way (33016-1536)
PHONE.................................305 297-5835
David Khan, *CEO*
Bernadett Csillag, *President*
Asif Khan, *CFO*
Nasir M Khan, *Director*
Alicia Anderson, *Creative Dir*
EMP: 73 EST: 2018
SALES (est): 8.2MM **Privately Held**
SIC: 2842 Bleaches, household: dry or liquid

(G-10370)
UNITED SIERRA GROUP CORP
8200 Commerce Way (33016-1536)
PHONE.................................305 297-5835
EMP: 22
SALES (corp-wide): 8.2MM **Privately Held**
SIC: 2842 Bleaches, household: dry or liquid
PA: United Sierra Group Corp
8218 Commerce Way
Miami Lakes FL 33016
305 297-5835

(G-10371)
UNITED TOOL CORPORATION
16258 Nw 78th Pl (33016-6178)
PHONE.................................305 884-3068
Rogelio F Fagundo, *Principal*
EMP: 7 EST: 2010
SALES (est): 248.7K **Privately Held**
WEB: www.unitedtoolcompany.com
SIC: 3599 Machine shop, jobbing & repair

(G-10372)
UNIWARE HOUSEWARE CORP
5275 Nw 163rd St (33014-6225)
PHONE.................................305 952-4958
Lily Dong, *President*
EMP: 33 **Privately Held**
WEB: www.uniwarehouseware.com
SIC: 3634 Electric housewares & fans

PA: Uniware Houseware Corp.
1 Newport Plz
Freeport NY 11520

(G-10373)
US BINDERY INC
5330 Nw 161st St (33014-6224)
PHONE.................................305 622-7070
Celestino Carballo Sr, *President*
Celestino A Carballo Jr, *Vice Pres*
Nayza Hernandez, *Vice Pres*
Ron Dearing, *Executive*
EMP: 28 EST: 1977
SQ FT: 18,000
SALES (est): 2.3MM **Privately Held**
SIC: 2789 Binding only: books, pamphlets, magazines, etc.

(G-10374)
USPHARMA LTD
13900 Nw 57th Ct (33014-3103)
PHONE.................................954 817-4418
Dr Manesh A Dixit, *CEO*
Greg Rocklin, *Vice Pres*
Manoharan Govindaraj, *CFO*
Kevin Nunez, *Business Anlyst*
William Franco, *Manager*
EMP: 78 EST: 2017
SQ FT: 150,000
SALES (est): 18.2MM **Privately Held**
WEB: www.uspharmaltd.com
SIC: 2834 5122 Pharmaceutical preparations; pharmaceuticals

(G-10375)
VANLEX CLOTHING INC
5850 Miami Lakes Dr E (33014-2402)
PHONE.................................305 431-4669
Ish Gonzalez, *President*
EMP: 20 EST: 2009
SALES (est): 1.1MM **Privately Held**
WEB: www.vanlexclothing.com
SIC: 2396 2759 3953 Screen printing on fabric articles; screen printing; screens, textile printing

(G-10376)
VISION WEB OFFSET LLC
13930 Nw 60th Ave (33014-3127)
PHONE.................................305 433-6188
Mohamed Sadik, *President*
EMP: 10 EST: 2013
SALES (est): 475.5K **Privately Held**
SIC: 2759 Magazines: printing

(G-10377)
VITAMIN SHOPPE FLORIDA LLC (DH)
Also Called: Fdc Vitamins, LLC
14620 Nw 60th Ave (33014-2811)
PHONE.................................305 468-1600
Colin Watts, *CEO*
Dan Alhadeff, *COO*
◆ EMP: 31 EST: 2001
SQ FT: 120,000
SALES (est): 57.7MM
SALES (corp-wide): 3.2B **Publicly Held**
SIC: 2833 Vitamins, natural or synthetic: bulk, uncompounded

(G-10378)
WHEELER TRADING INC
5851 Nw 159th St (33014-6717)
PHONE.................................305 430-7100
Emanuel Daskos, *President*
▲ EMP: 12 EST: 2001
SALES (est): 363.8K **Privately Held**
SIC: 2395 Tucking, for the trade

(G-10379)
WORTH INTL MEDIA GROUP (PA)
Also Called: Recommend Magazine
5979 Nw 151st St Ste 120 (33014-2448)
P.O. Box 171070, Hialeah (33017-1070)
PHONE.................................305 826-4763
Harold Herman, *President*
Hal Herman, *Editor*
Paloma V De Rico, *Chief*
Laurel A Herman, *Exec VP*
Geraldine Ellis, *Vice Pres*
◆ EMP: 40 EST: 1970
SQ FT: 6,500

SALES (est): 12.7MM **Privately Held**
WEB: www.recommend.com
SIC: 2721 Magazines: publishing only, not printed on site

(G-10380)
XCESSIVE INC
Also Called: Xcessive Engines
8714 Nw 153rd Ter (33018-1353)
PHONE.................................866 919-9527
Rick Malaga, *President*
◆ EMP: 5 EST: 2007
SQ FT: 3,000
SALES (est): 568.6K **Privately Held**
SIC: 3462 3519 Automotive & internal combustion engine forgings; marine engines

(G-10381)
YFAN LLC
5340 Nw 163rd St (33014-6228)
PHONE.................................786 453-3724
Jose A Yamin, *Principal*
EMP: 8 EST: 2015
SALES (est): 94.1K **Privately Held**
SIC: 2099 Food preparations

Miami Shores
Miami-Dade County

(G-10382)
ENCHANTING CREATIONS
210 Ne 98th St (33138-2408)
PHONE.................................305 978-2828
Alex Darnel Matamoros, *Owner*
EMP: 8 EST: 2011
SALES (est): 492.9K **Privately Held**
WEB: www.midisparate.design
SIC: 2051 Bakery: wholesale or wholesale/retail combined

(G-10383)
HERITAGE SKIN CARE INC
180 Ne 99th St (33138-2341)
PHONE.................................305 757-9264
Fax: 305 757-9267
▲ EMP: 11
SALES (est): 1.4MM **Privately Held**
SIC: 2834 Mfg Pharmaceutical Preparations

(G-10384)
UNITED STATES GYPSUM COMPANY
3301 Nw 125th St (33167-2409)
PHONE.................................305 688-8744
Mike Falcon, *Branch Mgr*
EMP: 12
SALES (corp-wide): 12.4B **Privately Held**
WEB: www.usg.com
SIC: 3275 Gypsum board
HQ: United States Gypsum Company
550 W Adams St Ste 1300
Chicago IL 60661
312 606-4000

Miami Springs
Miami-Dade County

(G-10385)
A PLUS LUMBER CORP
356 Palmetto Dr A (33166-5824)
PHONE.................................786 899-0535
EMP: 8 EST: 2020
SALES (est): 449.3K **Privately Held**
SIC: 2448 Pallets, wood

(G-10386)
AIRLOCK USA LLC
145 Curtiss Pkwy (33166-5220)
PHONE.................................305 888-6454
Linda Carlson, *Principal*
EMP: 10 EST: 2007
SQ FT: 1,933
SALES (est): 378.1K **Privately Held**
SIC: 3443 Airlocks

(G-10387)
CALEV SYSTEMS INC (PA)
5575 Nw 36th St (33166-5812)
PHONE.................................305 672-2900

Mark Calev, *CEO*
Christine Palermo, *Chief*
Dave Tanis, *COO*
Loyd Walker, *Exec VP*
Carlos Cueto, *Vice Pres*
◆ **EMP:** 30 **EST:** 2000
SQ FT: 4,600
SALES (est): 25.6MM **Privately Held**
WEB: www.calevsystems.com
SIC: 2752 8748 Commercial printing, off-set; promotional printing, lithographic; business consulting

(G-10388)
DOLPHIN/CURTIS PUBLISHING CO (PA)
Also Called: Dolphin Publishing
53 Curtiss Pkwy (33166-5218)
P.O. Box 526600, Miami (33152-6600)
PHONE............................305 594-0508
Thomas Curtis, *President*
Debrah Curtis, *Vice Pres*
Tammi Curtis, *Treasurer*
Andrew Cohen, *Admin Sec*
EMP: 8 **EST:** 1974
SQ FT: 2,000
SALES (est): 1.1MM **Privately Held**
SIC: 2721 Magazines: publishing only, not printed on site

(G-10389)
INTERNATIONAL FOOD EQP INC
1280 Partridge Ave (33166-3128)
PHONE............................305 785-5100
Robert Klopfenstein, *President*
Bruce D Barrington, *Director*
Richard L Owens, *Director*
Charles E Verkler, *Admin Sec*
EMP: 9 **EST:** 1980
SALES (est): 239.7K **Privately Held**
SIC: 3589 Food warming equipment, commercial

(G-10390)
LINDORM INC
601 Plover Ave (33166-3928)
PHONE............................305 888-0762
Ulf Erlingsson, *CEO*
EMP: 10 **EST:** 2006
SALES (est): 711.6K **Privately Held**
WEB: www.lindorm.com
SIC: 3826 Environmental testing equipment

(G-10391)
LOMBARDIS WOODWORKING
1000 Oriole Ave (33166-3847)
PHONE............................305 439-7208
Paul Christopher Lombardi, *President*
Lizette Martinez, *CIO*
EMP: 7 **EST:** 2009
SALES (est): 86.5K **Privately Held**
WEB: www.lombardiswoodworking.net
SIC: 2431 Millwork

(G-10392)
OBEM FOODS INC
Also Called: Cheesecake Etc Desserts
400 Swallow Dr (33166-4432)
PHONE............................305 887-0258
Orlando Irsula, *President*
Belinda Irsula, *Vice Pres*
EMP: 5 **EST:** 2011
SALES (est): 474.9K **Privately Held**
SIC: 2051 Bread, cake & related products

(G-10393)
RHODES BROTHERS MIAMI INC
37 Deer Run (33166-5785)
PHONE............................305 456-9682
John Rhodes, *Principal*
EMP: 7 **EST:** 2010
SALES (est): 104.3K **Privately Held**
SIC: 2869 Fuels

(G-10394)
T & W INC
Also Called: Cheesecake, Etc
400 Swallow Dr (33166-4432)
PHONE............................305 887-0258
William J Wolar, *President*
Suzanne Conlon Wolar, *Vice Pres*
Terry Wolar, *Director*
William Wolar Sr, *Director*
EMP: 7 **EST:** 1974
SQ FT: 10,000

SALES (est): 690.6K **Privately Held**
SIC: 2051 Bread, cake & related products

Micanopy
Alachua County

(G-10395)
ANALYTICAL RESEARCH SYSTEMS
Also Called: ARS
12109 Highway 441 S (32667-5310)
P.O. Box 140218, Gainesville (32614-0218)
PHONE............................352 466-0051
ARA Manukian, *President*
Lloyde Manukian, *Principal*
Rudy Strohschein, *Vice Pres*
EMP: 10 **EST:** 1994
SQ FT: 7,000
SALES (est): 902.4K **Privately Held**
WEB: www.ars-fla.com
SIC: 3826 8732 8711 8748 Analytical instruments; business research service; engineering services; business consulting; scientific instruments

(G-10396)
FRONTIER ELECTRONICS
Also Called: Frontier Communications
255 W Smith Ave (32667-4025)
PHONE............................954 255-0911
Robert Mance, *President*
Jesse Falto, *Education*
EMP: 8 **EST:** 1998
SALES (est): 148K **Privately Held**
SIC: 3812 Antennas, radar or communications

(G-10397)
GOODWIN LUMBER COMPANY INC
Also Called: Goodwin Heart Pine Company
106 Sw 109th Pl (32667-3441)
PHONE............................352 466-0339
George Goodwin, *President*
Carol Goodwin, *President*
Andrew Stjames, *General Mgr*
Jeffrey L Forbes, *Marketing Mgr*
Jeffrey Forbes, *Mktg Coord*
EMP: 13 **EST:** 1984
SQ FT: 35,000
SALES (est): 3.1MM **Privately Held**
WEB: www.tantumandhumphrey.com
SIC: 2426 2435 2431 Flooring, hardwood; hardwood veneer & plywood; millwork

(G-10398)
JER-AIR MANUFACTURING INC
22750 Highway 441 N (32667-7529)
P.O. Box 656, Mc Intosh (32664-0656)
PHONE............................352 591-2674
C Jerry Philman, *President*
Janice Philman, *Vice Pres*
EMP: 23 **EST:** 1974
SQ FT: 10,000
SALES (est): 3.5MM **Privately Held**
WEB: www.jerair.com
SIC: 3444 3585 3433 Ducts, sheet metal; refrigeration & heating equipment; heating equipment, except electric

(G-10399)
JPT-TECH LLC
11094 Nw 188th Street Rd (32667-8030)
PHONE............................352 219-7860
Jacques Thimote, *General Mgr*
Jacques Patrick Thimote,
EMP: 7 **EST:** 2012
SALES (est): 240K **Privately Held**
WEB: www.jpttech.com
SIC: 3571 Computers, digital, analog or hybrid

Middleburg
Clay County

(G-10400)
BLACK CREEK LOGGING
4159 County Road 218 (32068-4846)
P.O. Box 520 (32050-0520)
PHONE............................904 591-9681
EMP: 6 **EST:** 2010

SALES (est): 508.2K **Privately Held**
SIC: 2411 Logging

(G-10401)
CALIBRATED CONTROLS LLC
1931 Choctaw Trl (32068-4222)
PHONE............................904 718-0541
Joseph A Barbieri III, *Principal*
EMP: 9 **EST:** 2018
SALES (est): 285K **Privately Held**
WEB: www.calibrated-controls.com
SIC: 3823 Industrial instrmnts msrmnt display/control process variable

(G-10402)
HUNTLEY STEMWOOD INC
2785 Black Creek Dr (32068-5713)
PHONE............................904 237-4005
John Huntley Jr, *President*
EMP: 7 **EST:** 1978
SALES (est): 928K **Privately Held**
SIC: 2411 Pulpwood contractors engaged in cutting

(G-10403)
IRONWORKS INC OF ORANGE PARK
1701 Blanding Blvd (32068-4095)
P.O. Box 65849, Orange Park (32065-0015)
PHONE............................904 291-9330
Michael A Vallencourt, *President*
EMP: 18 **EST:** 1998
SALES (est): 492.4K **Privately Held**
SIC: 3446 Architectural metalwork

(G-10404)
KINGDOM COATINGS INC
2779 Indigo Cir (32068-6083)
PHONE............................904 600-1424
Nicholas C Oliver, *President*
EMP: 7 **EST:** 2016
SALES (est): 71.8K **Privately Held**
SIC: 3479 Metal coating & allied service

(G-10405)
N & H CONSTRUCTION INC
1708 Nolan Rd (32068-3054)
PHONE............................904 282-2224
EMP: 15
SALES (est): 2.1MM **Privately Held**
SIC: 3669 Mfg Communications Equipment

(G-10406)
NEIGHBOR TO NEIGHBOR NEWSPAPER
1906 Farm Way (32068-6734)
P.O. Box 1988 (32050-1988)
PHONE............................904 278-7256
Debra H Brown, *Owner*
EMP: 7 **EST:** 2010
SALES (est): 76.9K **Privately Held**
WEB: www.neighbortoneighbor.info
SIC: 2711 Newspapers, publishing & printing

(G-10407)
NORTHEAST FLORIDA COATINGS
299 N Mimosa Ave (32068-4693)
PHONE............................904 383-0749
Hunter Wiest, *Principal*
EMP: 7 **EST:** 2016
SALES (est): 227.4K **Privately Held**
SIC: 3479 Coating of metals & formed products

(G-10408)
PADGETTS PULPWOOD INC
3745 Old Jennings Rd (32068-3733)
PHONE............................904 282-5112
Jerry A Padgett, *President*
Anita Paggett, *Admin Sec*
EMP: 7 **EST:** 1959
SALES (est): 845.6K **Privately Held**
SIC: 2411 Pulpwood contractors engaged in cutting

(G-10409)
REILEY TOOL COMPANY LLC
3950 Equestrian Ct (32068-3296)
PHONE............................360 929-0350
Jonathon Reiley, *Manager*
EMP: 7 **EST:** 2018

SALES (est): 248.9K **Privately Held**
SIC: 3541 Machine tools, metal cutting type

(G-10410)
UNIVERSAL PROF COATINGS INC
2125 Candlewood Ct (32068-3618)
PHONE............................954 294-5236
Brian Wherry, *Principal*
EMP: 7 **EST:** 2011
SALES (est): 98.9K **Privately Held**
SIC: 3479 Metal coating & allied service

(G-10411)
WHITLEY WELDING COMPANY L
4280 Chokeberry Rd (32068-7003)
PHONE............................904 576-3410
EMP: 7 **EST:** 2018
SALES (est): 520.8K **Privately Held**
SIC: 7692 Welding repair

Midway
Gadsden County

(G-10412)
EXCEL MILLWORK & MOULDING INC
7001 Fortune Blvd (32343-6520)
P.O. Box 1086, Leavenworth WA (98826-1586)
PHONE............................850 576-7228
Scott Campbell, *President*
Jerry W Ruis, *President*
Donald Ray Ruis, *Vice Pres*
EMP: 28 **EST:** 1989
SQ FT: 35,000
SALES (est): 1.2MM **Privately Held**
SIC: 2431 5031 2499 Moldings, wood: unfinished & prefinished; woodwork, interior & ornamental; molding, all materials; decorative wood & woodwork

(G-10413)
SUPERIOR REDI-MIX
61 Commerce Ln (32343-6608)
PHONE............................850 575-1532
Danny Colins, *Owner*
EMP: 15 **EST:** 2004
SALES (est): 940.2K **Privately Held**
SIC: 3273 Ready-mixed concrete

(G-10414)
T-FORMATION INC TALLAHASSEE
864 Commerce Blvd (32343-6618)
PHONE............................850 574-0122
Alan H Gentry, *President*
Edwin D Mitchell, *Assistant VP*
Barton R Mitchell, *Vice Pres*
Philip Brown, *CFO*
Melanie D Mitchell, *Controller*
EMP: 100 **EST:** 1987
SQ FT: 42,000
SALES (est): 19.6MM **Privately Held**
SIC: 2399 Emblems, badges & insignia

Milton
Santa Rosa County

(G-10415)
5 STAR BLINDS AND SHADES LLC
4306 Seventh Ave (32571-1818)
PHONE............................850 463-4155
Gary S Cooley, *Manager*
EMP: 7 **EST:** 2020
SALES (est): 68.5K **Privately Held**
WEB: www.5starblindsandshades.com
SIC: 2591 Window blinds

(G-10416)
AEROSYNC ENGRG CONSULTING INC
Also Called: Aerosync Support
5848 Moors Oaks Dr (32583-2807)
PHONE............................316 208-3367
Greg F Bartlett, *President*
Diana Bartlett, *Vice Pres*
Greg Bartlett, *Vice Pres*

▲ = Import ▼ =Export
◆ =Import/Export

Jim McCall, *Supervisor*
EMP: 6 **EST:** 2012
SQ FT: 2,500
SALES (est): 900.9K **Privately Held**
WEB: www.aerosyncsupport.com
SIC: 3724 Aircraft engines & engine parts

(G-10417)
ANDREWS CABINETS INC
4025 Bell Ln (32571-2755)
PHONE..................850 994-0836
Dearl Andrews Jr, *President*
Paul S Andrews, *Principal*
Oliver Scott, *Principal*
Donald W Andrews, *Vice Pres*
EMP: 10 **EST:** 1982
SQ FT: 4,000
SALES (est): 966.6K **Privately Held**
SIC: 2434 Wood kitchen cabinets

(G-10418)
ARROW EMBROIDERY
6434 Open Rose Dr (32570-6864)
PHONE..................850 626-1796
Denise McDonald, *Owner*
EMP: 10 **EST:** 1997
SALES (est): 308.5K **Privately Held**
WEB: www.arrowemb.com
SIC: 2759 Commercial printing

(G-10419)
BLACKWATER FOLK ART INC
4917 Glover Ln (32570-4528)
P.O. Box 488, Bagdad (32530-0488)
PHONE..................850 623-3470
Pam Mitchell, *President*
EMP: 6 **EST:** 1990
SALES (est): 513.7K **Privately Held**
WEB: www.blackwaterfolkart.com
SIC: 2499 3469 3444 Kitchen, bathroom & household ware: wood; metal stampings; sheet metalwork

(G-10420)
BLACKWATER TRUSS SYSTEMS LLC
6603 Old Bagdad Hwy (32583-7603)
P.O. Box 186, Bagdad (32530-0186)
PHONE..................850 623-1414
Kenneth J Smith, *Mng Member*
Faye E Smith,
K David Smith,
Meredith J Smith,
EMP: 6 **EST:** 2009
SQ FT: 3,000
SALES (est): 600K **Privately Held**
WEB: www.blackwatertruss.com
SIC: 3443 Truss plates, metal

(G-10421)
C & S SIGNS INC
8895 S Lynn Rd (32583-2581)
PHONE..................850 983-9540
Jessica Wilbourn, *President*
Stanley Wilbourn, *President*
Jessica Wilbourm, *Office Admin*
EMP: 7 **EST:** 1987
SQ FT: 38,000
SALES (est): 681.2K **Privately Held**
WEB: www.cssigns.com
SIC: 3993 Electric signs

(G-10422)
CENTRAL WIRE INDUSTRIES LLC
Also Called: Strand Core
5881 Commerce Rd (32583-2318)
PHONE..................850 983-9926
Paul From, *President*
Tommy Leonard, *Maint Spvr*
Chris Charron, *CFO*
▲ **EMP:** 35 **EST:** 2014
SALES (est): 4.6MM **Privately Held**
WEB: www.strandcore.com
SIC: 3496 Miscellaneous fabricated wire products

(G-10423)
EMERALD COAST TRUSS LLC
Also Called: Milton Truss Company
5817 Commerce Rd (32583-2318)
P.O. Box 888 (32572-0888)
PHONE..................850 623-1967
Charles Smith, *Mng Member*
Deanna D Smith,
Tony Kelley, *Representative*

EMP: 49 **EST:** 1980
SQ FT: 9,000
SALES (est): 1MM **Privately Held**
WEB: www.miltontruss.com
SIC: 2439 Trusses, wooden roof

(G-10424)
FORMWELD FITTING INC
8118 Progress Dr (32583-7700)
PHONE..................850 626-4888
Charles Hartwig, *President*
Clint Dinwiddie, *Sales Staff*
EMP: 27 **EST:** 1989
SQ FT: 30,000
SALES (est): 4.1MM **Privately Held**
WEB: www.formweldfitting.us
SIC: 3498 3443 3494 Fabricated pipe & fittings; fabricated plate work (boiler shop); valves & pipe fittings

(G-10425)
FOSSCO INC
3948 Garcon Point Rd (32583-9035)
PHONE..................850 983-1330
Scott Foss, *President*
EMP: 7 **EST:** 2005
SQ FT: 12,500
SALES (est): 1.4MM **Privately Held**
WEB: www.fosscoinc.com
SIC: 3724 Aircraft engines & engine parts

(G-10426)
GRACE BIBLE CHURCH
6331 Chestnut St (32570-8794)
P.O. Box 643 (32572-0643)
PHONE..................850 623-4671
Tod Brainard, *Pastor*
EMP: 12 **EST:** 1999
SALES (est): 354.3K **Privately Held**
SIC: 2759 8661 Commercial printing; miscellaneous denomination church

(G-10427)
GROUP III ASPHALT INC
6108 Wastle Rd (32583-8941)
P.O. Box 3687, Pensacola (32516-3687)
PHONE..................850 983-0611
Johnnie Long, *President*
Jerry Long, *Vice Pres*
Donald Long, *Treasurer*
EMP: 10 **EST:** 1995
SALES (est): 1.7MM **Privately Held**
WEB:
www.panhandlegradingandpaving.com
SIC: 2951 5032 Asphalt & asphaltic paving mixtures (not from refineries); paving materials

(G-10428)
GULF CABLE LLC
5700 Industrial Blvd (32583-8736)
PHONE..................201 720-2417
Orin Singh, *Branch Mgr*
EMP: 150
SALES (corp-wide): 81.8MM **Privately Held**
SIC: 2298 Cable, fiber
PA: Gulf Cable, Llc
777 Terrace Ave Ste 101
Hasbrouck Heights NJ 07604
201 242-9906

(G-10429)
JOINERS ENTERPRISES INC
4973 Joiner Cir (32583-2781)
PHONE..................850 623-5593
William Joiner, *President*
Kimberly Jerenigan, *Corp Secy*
EMP: 13 **EST:** 1973
SALES (est): 667.3K **Privately Held**
SIC: 2411 Logging

(G-10430)
MARTIN MARIETTA MATERIALS INC
Also Called: Milton Yard
6134 Wastle Rd (32583-8941)
PHONE..................850 981-9020
Todd Weller, *Branch Mgr*
EMP: 10 **Publicly Held**
WEB: www.martinmarietta.com
SIC: 1422 Crushed & broken limestone
PA: Martin Marietta Materials Inc
4123 Parklake Ave
Raleigh NC 27612

(G-10431)
MILTON NEWSPAPERS INC
Also Called: The Press Gazette
6576 Caroline St (32570-4778)
PHONE..................850 623-2120
Jim Fletcher, *Principal*
EMP: 926 **EST:** 1907
SQ FT: 10,000
SALES (est): 4.1MM
SALES (corp-wide): 3.2B **Publicly Held**
WEB: www.srpressgazette.com
SIC: 2711 2752 Newspapers, publishing & printing; commercial printing, lithographic
HQ: Panama City News Herald
501 W 11th St
Panama City FL 32401
850 747-5000

(G-10432)
PIONEER AEROSPACE CORPORATION
Airlift Technologies Intl
8101 Opportunity Dr (32583-8728)
PHONE..................850 623-3330
Bryon Woram, *President*
EMP: 11
SQ FT: 11,907
SALES (corp-wide): 650.7MM **Privately Held**
WEB: www.perfectdomain.com
SIC: 3728 Aircraft assemblies, subassemblies & parts
HQ: Pioneer Aerospace Corporation
131 Phoenix Xing
Bloomfield CT 06002
860 528-0092

(G-10433)
PRODAIR CORPORATION (HQ)
4575 Highway 90 (32571-2043)
PHONE..................850 994-5511
Jessica J Holliday, *CEO*
James T Christy, *President*
Richard L Sutton, *Vice Pres*
Tom Van Dorp, *Vice Pres*
Margaret Pulgini, *Treasurer*
EMP: 5 **EST:** 1972
SALES (est): 110.1MM
SALES (corp-wide): 10.3B **Publicly Held**
SIC: 2813 Industrial gases
PA: Air Products And Chemicals, Inc.
1940 Air Products Blvd
Allentown PA 18106
610 481-4911

(G-10434)
PRODUCTION METAL STAMPINGS INC
8133 Opportunity Dr (32583-8728)
PHONE..................850 981-8240
T Barry Fulford, *President*
Meriel C Fulford, *Vice Pres*
EMP: 10 **EST:** 1988
SQ FT: 8,000
SALES (est): 983.1K **Privately Held**
WEB: www.productionmetal.net
SIC: 3599 3469 7692 3542 Machine & other job shop work; custom machinery; metal stampings; welding repair; machine tools, metal forming type; sheet metalwork

(G-10435)
QUIKRETE COMPANIES LLC
Also Called: Quikrete of Pensacola
7101 Windwood Ln (32583-3216)
P.O. Box 510, Bagdad (32530-0510)
PHONE..................850 623-0559
Emory Peacock, *Financial Analy*
Shane Scoggins, *Manager*
EMP: 21 **Privately Held**
WEB: www.quikrete.com
SIC: 3272 1442 5032 3241 Concrete products; construction sand mining; sand, construction; cement, hydraulic; masonry materials & supplies
HQ: The Quikrete Companies Llc
5 Concourse Pkwy Ste 1900
Atlanta GA 30328
404 634-9100

(G-10436)
R & K BUILDINGS INC
Also Called: R & K Portable Builders
4213 Avalon Blvd (32583-2810)
PHONE..................850 995-9525
Glennon Russell, *President*
Toby Russell, *Vice Pres*
Ashley Russell, *Admin Sec*
EMP: 30 **EST:** 1981
SQ FT: 1,408
SALES (est): 2.6MM **Privately Held**
WEB: rnkmilton.wixsite.com
SIC: 3448 Prefabricated metal buildings

(G-10437)
STEP ZONE LLC
6674 Elva St (32570-4723)
PHONE..................850 983-3758
Fax: 850 983-3358
EMP: 5
SALES (est): 705.4K **Privately Held**
SIC: 2451 Mfg Mobile Homes

(G-10438)
STERLING FIBERS INC
5005 Sterling Way (32571-2799)
PHONE..................850 994-5311
James Hagerott, *President*
Susan Allender, *Vice Pres*
Brian Hagerott, *Production*
◆ **EMP:** 70 **EST:** 1996
SALES (est): 13.6MM **Privately Held**
WEB: www.sterlingfibers.com
SIC: 2824 Acrylic fibers

(G-10439)
SYSTEMATIX INC
5953 Commerce Rd (32583-2320)
PHONE..................850 983-2213
James S Hogan, *President*
Guy Verville, *General Mgr*
Chris Hogan, *Vice Pres*
Linda B Hogan, *Treasurer*
EMP: 25 **EST:** 1989
SQ FT: 11,000
SALES (est): 3MM **Privately Held**
WEB: www.systematix.org
SIC: 3646 2522 Desk lamps, commercial; chairs, office: padded or plain, except wood

(G-10440)
TITAN SPECIALTY CNSTR INC
Also Called: Titan Sunrooms
8188 Armstrong Rd (32583-8738)
PHONE..................850 916-7660
Fred D Genkin, *President*
▲ **EMP:** 45 **EST:** 2002
SALES (est): 5.3MM **Privately Held**
WEB: www.titansunrooms.com
SIC: 3448 1761 3471 3354 Sunrooms, prefabricated metal; gutter & downspout contractor; coloring & finishing of aluminum or formed products; aluminum extruded products

(G-10441)
TPR SYSTEMS INC
8100 Armstrong Rd (32583-8738)
PHONE..................850 983-8600
Richard Todd, *Principal*
EMP: 11 **EST:** 2014
SALES (est): 764.8K **Privately Held**
WEB: www.tpr-systems.com
SIC: 3599 Machine shop, jobbing & repair

(G-10442)
TURBINE PARTS REPAIR INC
8100 Armstrong Rd (32583-8738)
PHONE..................850 983-8600
Chuck Pyritz, *Principal*
EMP: 6 **EST:** 2006
SALES (est): 513.3K **Privately Held**
WEB: www.turbinepartsrepair.com
SIC: 3599 Machine shop, jobbing & repair

(G-10443)
WHEEL WRIGHT
6899 Deception Rd (32583-8187)
PHONE..................850 626-2662
George Pilling, *Principal*
EMP: 7 **EST:** 2008
SALES (est): 91.7K **Privately Held**
SIC: 3312 Blast furnaces & steel mills

(G-10444)
WHIP-IT INVENTIONS INC (PA)
5946 Commerce Rd (32583-2319)
PHONE..................................850 626-6300
John Alessi, *CEO*
Joann Watson, *COO*
Mark Kreisler, *CFO*
EMP: 20 **EST:** 2010
SQ FT: 12,000
SALES (est): 3MM **Privately Held**
WEB: www.amazingwhipit.com
SIC: 2841 Soap & other detergents

(G-10445)
WPR INC
4175 Briarglen Rd (32583-2884)
PHONE..................................850 626-7713
D Pete Russell, *President*
Lauren Coogle, *Controller*
Lauren C Coogle, *Controller*
EMP: 35 **EST:** 1973
SQ FT: 22,784
SALES (est): 5.1MM **Privately Held**
WEB: www.wprincfl.com
SIC: 3272 3273 Septic tanks, concrete;
ready-mixed concrete

Mims
Brevard County

(G-10446)
ARI SPECIALTIES LLC
3660 Us Highway 1 (32754-5505)
P.O. Box 765 (32754-0765)
PHONE..................................321 269-2244
Eric A Anderson,
EMP: 6 **EST:** 2008
SALES (est): 337.9K **Privately Held**
SIC: 3999 Manufacturing industries

(G-10447)
CTR INDUSTRIES
3980 Hammock Rd (32754-5693)
P.O. Box 171 (32754-0171)
PHONE..................................321 264-1458
George L Newman, *Principal*
EMP: 8 **EST:** 2007
SALES (est): 565.3K **Privately Held**
SIC: 3999 Manufacturing industries

(G-10448)
INDUSTRIAL FILTER PUMP MFG CO
2680 Us Highway 1 (32754-3804)
P.O. Box 1079 (32754-1079)
PHONE..................................708 656-7800
John Keegan, *CEO*
Zubin Mehta, *Director*
Gregory Shalov, *Director*
▲ **EMP:** 7 **EST:** 2004
SALES (est): 862.9K **Privately Held**
WEB: www.industrialfilter.com
SIC: 3569 Filters, general line: industrial;
filters

(G-10449)
LINDE INC
Praxair
2801 Hammock Rd (32754-5688)
PHONE..................................321 267-2311
Dennis Reilley, *CEO*
EMP: 23 **Privately Held**
WEB: www.lindeus.com
SIC: 2813 Nitrogen
HQ: Linde Inc.
10 Riverview Dr
Danbury CT 06810
203 837-2000

(G-10450)
STAT BIOMEDICAL LLC
2865 Night Heron Dr (32754-6508)
PHONE..................................210 365-1495
Troy Richie, *Principal*
EMP: 6 **EST:** 2016
SALES (est): 506.5K **Privately Held**
WEB: www.stat-biomedical.com
SIC: 2836 Biological products, except diagnostic

Minneola
Lake County

(G-10451)
GUERRILLA PRTG SOLUTIONS LLC
Also Called: Minuteman Press
304 Mohawk Rd (34715-7434)
PHONE..................................352 394-7770
Kenneth S Rose, *Principal*
EMP: 6 **EST:** 2005
SALES (est): 551.8K **Privately Held**
WEB: www.minutemanpress.com
SIC: 2752 Commercial printing, lithographic

(G-10452)
SYNERGISTIC OFFICE SOLUTIONS
Also Called: SOS Software
11350 Tuscarora Ln (34715-7914)
PHONE..................................352 242-9100
Seth Krieger, *President*
Katherine Peres, *Vice Pres*
Seth Kreiger, *Consultant*
Stephane Tessier, *Prgrmr*
EMP: 10 **EST:** 1985
SALES (est): 1MM **Privately Held**
WEB: www.sosoft.com
SIC: 7372 Application computer software

(G-10453)
TREADWAY INDUSTRIES LLC
Also Called: Elega Fam FL More Drect Axic
410 Virginia St (34715-7496)
PHONE..................................352 326-3313
Steve Vanderwall, *Project Mgr*
Ben Whitehouse, *Project Mgr*
Lyonel Nichols, *Opers Staff*
Chip Robart, *Engineer*
Coral Nolan, *Marketing Staff*
▼ **EMP:** 20 **EST:** 1983
SALES (est): 2.6MM **Privately Held**
WEB: www.treadwayindustries.com
SIC: 3069 Foam rubber

Miramar
Broward County

(G-10454)
20-100 DELICIOUS SEASONING LLC
6438a Pembroke Rd (33023-2138)
PHONE..................................954 687-5124
Mario Vincent, *Manager*
EMP: 6 **EST:** 2020
SALES (est): 304.5K **Privately Held**
SIC: 2099 Food preparations

(G-10455)
3A PRODUCTS LLC
2737 N Commerce Pkwy (33025-3955)
PHONE..................................754 263-2968
Preeti Singh, *President*
EMP: 5 **EST:** 2014
SQ FT: 1,500
SALES (est): 800K **Privately Held**
WEB: www.3aproducts.com
SIC: 3086 Packaging & shipping materials,
foamed plastic

(G-10456)
AARA INDUSTRIES
13165 Sw 24th St (33027-2632)
PHONE..................................954 342-9526
Alfonso A Relano, *Principal*
EMP: 8 **EST:** 2007
SALES (est): 70K **Privately Held**
SIC: 3999 Manufacturing industries

(G-10457)
ABB INC
A B B Marine &TUrbo Charger
10004 Premier Pkwy (33025-3210)
PHONE..................................954 450-9544
EMP: 50
SALES (corp-wide): 34.3B **Privately Held**
SIC: 3519 Mfg Internal Combustion Engines

HQ: Abb Inc.
305 Gregson Dr
Cary NC 27511

(G-10458)
AD INVESTMENT GROUP LLC
11500 Miramar Pkwy # 300 (33025-5813)
PHONE..................................954 784-6900
Leon Silverstein, *CEO*
▼ **EMP:** 160 **EST:** 2012
SALES (est): 15.3MM **Privately Held**
SIC: 3334 1793 Primary aluminum; glass
& glazing work

(G-10459)
ADVANCED SERVICES INTL INC
3600 Caldwell Rd Ste 406 (33027)
PHONE..................................954 889-1366
Glory Manolo, *Office Mgr*
EMP: 6 **EST:** 2011
SALES (est): 836.7K **Privately Held**
WEB: www.adsintl.net
SIC: 7372 Prepackaged software

(G-10460)
AERO PRECISION HOLDINGS LP (PA)
15501 Sw 29th St Ste 101 (33027-5257)
PHONE..................................925 455-9900
Frank Cowle, *Partner*
Dick Drinkward, *Exec VP*
Gregory Friedman, *Buyer*
Donna Kleinwaks, *Credit Mgr*
Tahmina Saberi, *Sales Mgr*
EMP: 29 **EST:** 2016
SALES (est): 278MM **Privately Held**
WEB: www.goallclear.com
SIC: 3728 Aircraft parts & equipment

(G-10461)
AFINA SYSTEMS INC (DH)
3350 Sw 148th Ave Ste 401 (33027-3259)
PHONE..................................305 261-1433
Pedro Galatas, *President*
Fernando Rivera, *Treasurer*
Javier San Juan, *Executive*
◆ **EMP:** 9 **EST:** 2000
SALES (est): 2.5MM
SALES (corp-wide): 31.6B **Publicly Held**
SIC: 7372 Prepackaged software
HQ: Westcon Group, Inc.
520 White Plains Rd # 200
Tarrytown NY 10591
914 829-7000

(G-10462)
ALCO SERVICES INC
15501 Sw 29th St (33027-5255)
PHONE..................................954 538-2189
Christopher R Celtruda, *President*
Nathan A Skop, *Exec VP*
Jikun Kim, *CFO*
EMP: 20 **EST:** 2013
SQ FT: 35,000
SALES (est): 764.8K
SALES (corp-wide): 63.2MM **Privately Held**
SIC: 3728 Aircraft parts & equipment
PA: Kellstrom Holding Corporation
100 N Pcf Cast Hwy Ste 19
El Segundo CA 90245
561 222-7455

(G-10463)
ALFA LAVAL AALBORG INC (DH)
3118 Commerce Pkwy (33025-3943)
PHONE..................................954 435-5999
Holger Nielsen, *President*
Kristen Langkj, *Vice Pres*
Olga Uresti, *Admin Sec*
▲ **EMP:** 105 **EST:** 1999
SQ FT: 3,000
SALES (est): 10.4MM **Privately Held**
WEB: www.alfalaval.us
SIC: 3443 Boilers: industrial, power, or marine

(G-10464)
ALL POLISHING SOLUTIONS
3056 S State Road 7 (33023-5285)
PHONE..................................954 505-4041
Antonio Rios, *Principal*
▼ **EMP:** 5 **EST:** 2012
SALES (est): 449.8K **Privately Held**
SIC: 3291 Abrasive products

(G-10465)
ALLCLEAR AEROSPACE & DEF INC (DH)
Also Called: Kellstrom Defense
15501 Sw 29th St Ste 101 (33027-5257)
PHONE..................................954 239-7844
Greg Beason, *CEO*
Juan Forero, *Vice Pres*
Diamy Dunton, *Opers Staff*
Jose Rivera, *Opers Staff*
Richard Drinkward, *CFO*
▲ **EMP:** 10 **EST:** 2002
SQ FT: 75,860
SALES (est): 50.2MM
SALES (corp-wide): 278MM **Privately Held**
WEB: www.goallclear.com
SIC: 3728 Aircraft parts & equipment

(G-10466)
ALLURING GROUP INC
Also Called: Belladonna Hair Bar
7451 Riviera Blvd Ste 112 (33023-6567)
PHONE..................................800 731-2280
Utonia Lloyd, *CEO*
EMP: 12 **EST:** 2017
SALES (est): 657.1K **Privately Held**
SIC: 2389 Apparel & accessories

(G-10467)
ALUMICENTER INC
3160 Sw 176th Way (33029-5610)
PHONE..................................954 674-2631
Juan Cohen, *President*
Ivonne Cohen, *Vice Pres*
EMP: 5 **EST:** 2009
SQ FT: 2,200
SALES (est): 648.5K **Privately Held**
WEB: www.alumcenter.net
SIC: 3448 Screen enclosures

(G-10468)
AMCOR FLEXIBLES LLC
Also Called: Amcor Rigid Packg Latin Amer
2801 Sw 149th Ave Fl 3 (33027-4146)
PHONE..................................954 499-4800
Marlene Berrio, *Branch Mgr*
EMP: 21
SALES (corp-wide): 12.8B **Privately Held**
SIC: 2671 2621 2821 3466 Plastic film,
coated or laminated for packaging; paper
mills; plastics materials & resins; crowns
& closures
HQ: Amcor Flexibles Llc
2150 E Lake Cook Rd
Buffalo Grove IL 60089
224 313-7000

(G-10469)
ARTECHE USA INC
3401 Sw 160th Ave Ste 430 (33027-6306)
PHONE..................................954 438-9499
Juan Pablo Estrada, *Chairman*
Ligia Cobos, *Credit Staff*
Enrique Hurtado Aguado, *Finance*
Nadia Contreras, *Finance*
James Levine, *Sales Staff*
EMP: 10 **EST:** 2010
SALES (est): 5.5MM
SALES (corp-wide): 260.3K **Privately Held**
WEB: www.arteche.com
SIC: 3612 Instrument transformers (except portable)
HQ: Arteche Lantegi Elkartea, Sa
Camino Derio 28
Mungia 48100

(G-10470)
AVEVA DRUG DLVRY SYSTEMS INC
3280 Executive Way (33025-3930)
PHONE..................................954 430-3340
EMP: 59
SALES (corp-wide): 1.1B **Privately Held**
SIC: 2834 Pharmaceutical preparations
HQ: Aveva Drug Delivery Systems, Inc.
3250 Commerce Pkwy
Miramar FL 33025

(G-10471)
AVEVA DRUG DLVRY SYSTEMS INC (DH)
3250 Commerce Pkwy (33025-3907)
PHONE..................................954 430-3340

▲ = Import ▼=Export
◆ =Import/Export

Jeremy B Desai, *President*
Pere Paton, *President*
Jeff Watson, *President*
Steven Liberty, *Exec VP*
Juan Troncoso, *Mfg Staff*
▲ **EMP:** 21 **EST:** 1991
SQ FT: 74,000
SALES (est): 61MM
SALES (corp-wide): 1.1B **Privately Held**
SIC: 2834 Pharmaceutical preparations

(G-10472)
AZOPHARMA INC
6137 Sw 19th St (33023-2914)
PHONE..................................954 536-4738
Ed Kuper, *Principal*
EMP: 7 **EST:** 2010
SALES (est): 109.5K **Privately Held**
SIC: 2834 Pharmaceutical preparations

(G-10473)
BAA LLC
16482 Sw 18th St (33027-4470)
PHONE..................................954 292-9449
Barbara M Sharief, *Principal*
EMP: 11 **EST:** 2009
SALES (est): 1MM **Privately Held**
SIC: 2869 Fuels

(G-10474)
BECKER AVIONICS INC
Also Called: Becker USA
10376 Usa Today Way (33025-3901)
PHONE..................................954 450-3137
Roland Becker, *CEO*
Arturo Garcia, *Sales Mgr*
Kenneth Oliver, *Cust Mgr*
Brett Gardner, *Marketing Staff*
Virginia Gomez, *Manager*
EMP: 13 **EST:** 1975
SQ FT: 7,000
SALES (est): 5.7MM **Privately Held**
WEB: www.becker-avionics.com
SIC: 3663 3812 Airborne radio communications equipment; aircraft flight instruments

(G-10475)
BLUESTAR LATIN AMERICA INC
3561 Enterprise Way (33025-6545)
PHONE..................................954 485-1931
Albert B Vivet, *President*
Stephen G Cuntz, *President*
Luis Fernando Proano, *Vice Pres*
Javier Ramirez, *Finance*
Doug J Bivins, *Admin Sec*
◆ **EMP:** 50 **EST:** 1994
SQ FT: 50,000
SALES (est): 30.3MM
SALES (corp-wide): 253.9MM **Privately Held**
SIC: 3578 5045 Point-of-sale devices; printers, computer
PA: United Radio Incorporated
3345 Point Pleasant Rd
Hebron KY 41048
800 354-9776

(G-10476)
BRUNSWICK CORPORATION
Also Called: Mercury Marine
15351 Sw 29th St Ste 800 (33027-5254)
PHONE..................................954 744-3500
Diego Effio, *Branch Mgr*
EMP: 24
SALES (corp-wide): 5.8B **Publicly Held**
WEB: www.brunswick.com
SIC: 3519 Marine engines
PA: Brunswick Corporation
26125 N Riverwoods Blvd # 500
Mettawa IL 60045
847 735-4700

(G-10477)
C Q MOLDING INC
2081 Bahama Dr (33023-2640)
PHONE..................................786 314-1312
Julio Guanche, *Principal*
EMP: 7 **EST:** 2010
SALES (est): 172.7K **Privately Held**
SIC: 3089 Molding primary plastic

(G-10478)
CASA DE RPRSNTCONES JMW CA LLC
12486 Sw 54th St (33027-5481)
PHONE..................................754 707-1689
Jad Waked, *Mng Member*
EMP: 13
SALES (est): 496.7K **Privately Held**
SIC: 2834 Pharmaceutical preparations

(G-10479)
CASTLE DISTRIBUTING INDS INC
6506 Sw 19th St (33023-2119)
PHONE..................................305 336-0855
James V Colbert, *President*
EMP: 8 **EST:** 2001
SALES (est): 469.1K **Privately Held**
SIC: 3999 Manufacturing industries

(G-10480)
CITEL AMERICA INC
10108 Usa Today Way (33025-3903)
PHONE..................................954 430-6310
Patrick Coyle, *CEO*
Vincent Crevenat, *Engineer*
David McClellan, *Engineer*
Christophe Cussac, *CFO*
Daniel Cardoso, *Regl Sales Mgr*
▲ **EMP:** 10 **EST:** 1983
SQ FT: 4,000
SALES (est): 4.7MM
SALES (corp-wide): 61.7MM **Privately Held**
WEB: www.citel.us
SIC: 3671 5063 Electron tubes; electrical fittings & construction materials
HQ: Citel 2 C P
2 Rue Troyon
Sevres 92310
141 235-033

(G-10481)
COCO LOPEZ INC (PA)
3401 Sw 160th Ave Ste 350 (33027-6306)
PHONE..................................954 450-3100
Leonardo Vargas, *President*
Jake Jacobsen, *Regional Mgr*
Gisela Alexander, *Vice Pres*
Luis Martinez, *Controller*
Jose L Suarez, *Sales Mgr*
◆ **EMP:** 7 **EST:** 1994
SQ FT: 2,500
SALES (est): 2.5MM **Privately Held**
WEB: www.cocolopez.com
SIC: 2033 2099 Fruit juices: packaged in cans, jars, etc.; food preparations

(G-10482)
CPS PRODUCTS INC (HQ)
3600 Enterprise Way (33025-6616)
PHONE..................................305 687-4121
James Williamson, *CEO*
Edward Jeffers, *President*
John D Jeffers, *Vice Pres*
Trina King, *Vice Pres*
Scott Krampitz, *Vice Pres*
◆ **EMP:** 71 **EST:** 1989
SALES (est): 36.9MM
SALES (corp-wide): 1.2B **Privately Held**
WEB: www.cpsproducts.com
SIC: 3585 3825 3823 3812 Refrigeration & heating equipment; instruments to measure electricity; industrial instrmnts msrmnt display/control process variable; search & navigation equipment
PA: Harbour Group Ltd.
7733 Forsyth Blvd Fl 23
Saint Louis MO 63105
314 727-5550

(G-10483)
DERMATONUS
5262 Sw 158th Ave (33027-4989)
PHONE..................................305 229-3923
Patricia Erazo, *Treasurer*
EMP: 8 **EST:** 2008
SALES (est): 344.1K **Privately Held**
WEB: www.dermatonusglobal.com
SIC: 2834 Pharmaceutical preparations

(G-10484)
DIGITAL COMPOSITING SYSTEMS
Also Called: Moore Computer Consultants
3309 Onyx Rd (33025-2820)
P.O. Box 245746, Pembroke Pines (33024-0112)
PHONE..................................954 432-4988
John L Moore, *President*
EMP: 5 **EST:** 1992
SALES (est): 300.8K **Privately Held**
SIC: 3695 Computer software tape & disks: blank, rigid & floppy

(G-10485)
DIVATTI & CO LLC
1050 E 17th St (33027)
PHONE..................................786 354-1888
Henry Orellana, *Mng Member*
EMP: 6 **EST:** 2015
SQ FT: 8,000
SALES (est): 600K **Privately Held**
SIC: 2531 Public building & related furniture

(G-10486)
DURABODY USA LLC
11800 Miramar Pkwy (33025-5800)
PHONE..................................954 357-2333
Teddy Teixeira, *Sales Mgr*
Teodoro Teixeira, *Manager*
EMP: 8 **EST:** 2015
SALES (est): 302.5K **Privately Held**
WEB: www.durabodysports.com
SIC: 3949 Sporting & athletic goods

(G-10487)
ELEMENT ELIQUID LLC
Also Called: Element E-Liquid
11411 Interchange Cir S (33025-6009)
PHONE..................................754 260-5500
David Botton,
▲ **EMP:** 8 **EST:** 2014
SALES (est): 996.5K **Privately Held**
WEB: www.elementeliquids.com
SIC: 2046 Liquid starch

(G-10488)
ENERGY SERVICES PROVIDERS INC (DH)
3700 Lakeside Dr 6 (33027-3264)
PHONE..................................305 947-7880
Douglas W Marcille, *CEO*
Brian Rose, *Vice Pres*
David Weinberg, *Treasurer*
EMP: 5 **EST:** 2006
SQ FT: 7,500
SALES (est): 14.1MM
SALES (corp-wide): 12B **Publicly Held**
SIC: 2211 Broadwoven fabric mills, cotton
HQ: U.S. Gas & Electric, Inc.
6555 Sierra Dr
Irving TX 75039
954 947-7880

(G-10489)
ESTEEMED BRANDS INC
3450 Lakeside Dr Ste 120 (33027-3262)
PHONE..................................954 442-3923
Leslie Almond, *President*
Craig Mansfield, *CFO*
◆ **EMP:** 15 **EST:** 2012
SQ FT: 2,000
SALES (est): 3MM **Privately Held**
WEB: www.esteemed-brands.com
SIC: 2676 2844 Feminine hygiene paper products; toilet preparations

(G-10490)
FAMILY SYSTEM SOLUTION WHL INC
8409 Sheraton Dr (33025-2824)
PHONE..................................954 431-5254
Maud B Pasquet, *President*
EMP: 7 **EST:** 2011
SALES (est): 199.8K **Privately Held**
SIC: 3312 Wheels

(G-10491)
FIVE STAR BAKERY
6847 Miramar Pkwy (33023-6023)
PHONE..................................954 983-6133
Bernard Brown, *President*
EMP: 8 **EST:** 2003

SALES (est): 258.6K **Privately Held**
SIC: 2051 Bread, cake & related products

(G-10492)
FOOD MARKETING CONSULTANTS INC
Also Called: San Bernardo Ice Cream
2805 N Commerce Pkwy (33025-3956)
PHONE..................................954 322-2668
Robert Tammara, *CEO*
Jonathan Tammara, *President*
Robyn Bofshever, *Marketing Staff*
▼ **EMP:** 12 **EST:** 1979
SQ FT: 13,500
SALES (est): 10MM **Privately Held**
WEB: www.sanbernardofoods.com
SIC: 2024 Ice cream, bulk; sorbets, non-dairy based; ice cream, packaged: molded, on sticks, etc.; sherbets, dairy based

(G-10493)
FOR EYES OPTCAL CCNUT GROVE IN (DH)
3601 Sw 160th Ave Ste 400 (33027-6312)
PHONE..................................305 557-9004
Phillip Wolman, *President*
Robert Messa, *Vice Pres*
Johnny Ampuero, *Software Dev*
EMP: 200 **EST:** 1975
SALES (est): 119.7MM
SALES (corp-wide): 1.7MM **Privately Held**
WEB: www.foreyes.com
SIC: 3851 5995 Eyeglasses, lenses & frames; opticians

(G-10494)
FRED INTERNATIONAL LLC
3350 Sw 148th Ave Ste 120 (33027-3258)
PHONE..................................786 539-1600
Moises Gonto, *Sales Staff*
Francisco Diaz, *Mng Member*
Flor Brito, *Manager*
Rodolfo Martnez,
▼ **EMP:** 12 **EST:** 2003
SQ FT: 2,900
SALES (est): 2.5MM **Privately Held**
WEB: www.fredcorporation.com
SIC: 3533 Oil & gas field machinery

(G-10495)
GAR INTERNATIONAL
3315 Commerce Pkwy (33025-3954)
PHONE..................................954 704-9590
Peter Voigt, *Manager*
EMP: 7 **EST:** 2017
SALES (est): 270.5K **Privately Held**
SIC: 3531 Construction machinery

(G-10496)
GENERAL METAL INTL INC
Also Called: Sun Light Products
13580 Sw 51st St (33027-5937)
PHONE..................................305 628-2052
Zhihua Deng, *President*
Albert Deng, *Manager*
EMP: 8 **EST:** 1995
SALES (est): 201.3K **Privately Held**
SIC: 3645 Lamp & light shades

(G-10497)
GLOBAL FORCE ENTERPRISES LLC
2331 W Lake Miramar Cir (33025-4807)
PHONE..................................786 317-8197
Kim Griffith, *President*
EMP: 5 **EST:** 2010
SALES (est): 351.8K **Privately Held**
WEB: www.mandingocondoms.com
SIC: 3069 Fabricated rubber products

(G-10498)
GLOBAL GALAN LOGISTICS INC
3132 Sw 173rd Ter (33029-5581)
PHONE..................................754 263-2708
George Galan, *President*
Carmen Caino, *Vice Pres*
Carmen Galan, *Vice Pres*
▼ **EMP:** 6 **EST:** 2005
SALES (est): 696.6K **Privately Held**
WEB: www.gglusa.com
SIC: 2448 Cargo containers, wood & metal combination

(G-10499)
GREEN LEAF FOODS LLC
4050 Sw 145th Ter (33027-3775)
Rural Route 4050 Sw 145 Ter (33027)
PHONE..............................305 308-9167
Brandy Chappell, *CEO*
Fernando Siman,
EMP: 6 **EST:** 2013
SALES (est): 495.5K **Privately Held**
WEB: www.greenleaffood.com
SIC: 2034 2676 Dehydrated fruits, vegetables, soups; towels, napkins & tissue paper products

(G-10500)
HCW BIOLOGICS INC
Also Called: HCW THERAPEUTICS
2929 N Commerce Pkwy (33025-3957)
PHONE..............................954 842-2024
Hing C Wong, *CEO*
Lee Flowers, *Senior VP*
Jin-An Jiao, *Vice Pres*
Peter Rhode, *Vice Pres*
Rebecca Byam, *CFO*
EMP: 40 **EST:** 2018
SQ FT: 12,250
SALES: 4.1MM **Privately Held**
WEB: www.hcwbiologics.com
SIC: 2836 Biological products, except diagnostic

(G-10501)
HOME IMPRV & DEVELOPERS LLC
11070 Sw 25th Ct Apt 1030 (33025-7662)
PHONE..............................305 902-3015
Pest Ferrada,
EMP: 10 **EST:** 2020
SALES (est): 168K **Privately Held**
SIC: 1389 Construction, repair & dismantling services

(G-10502)
I T MANAGEMENT EXPRESS INC
16140 Sw 51st St Ste 1 (33027-4963)
PHONE..............................954 237-6999
Tanios Chamoun, *Principal*
Blanca Flores, *Vice Pres*
EMP: 7 **EST:** 2009
SALES (est): 68.5K **Privately Held**
SIC: 3577 5112 Printers & plotters; computer & photocopying supplies

(G-10503)
IN FOCUS INTERACTIVE MAGAZINE
3001 Sw 64th Ter (33023-3847)
P.O. Box 4492, Hollywood (33083-4492)
PHONE..............................954 966-1233
Fax: 954 989-2993
EMP: 6
SALES (est): 410K **Privately Held**
SIC: 2721 Periodicals-Publishing/Printing

(G-10504)
INGERSOLL RAND
2884 Corporate Way (33025-6546)
PHONE..............................954 391-4500
Thaddeus Riesbeck, *Business Mgr*
Shawn Chambers, *Vice Pres*
Tammy Daniels, *Project Mgr*
Mark Tillinghast, *Opers Mgr*
Michael Heidemann, *Opers Staff*
EMP: 17 **EST:** 2009
SALES (est): 585K **Privately Held**
SIC: 3131 Rands

(G-10505)
INSIGHT OPTICAL MFG CO FLA INC
3601 Sw 160th Ave Ste 400 (33027-6312)
PHONE..............................787 758-9096
Jorge Gervasi, *Principal*
EMP: 7 **EST:** 2017
SALES (est): 39.6K **Privately Held**
SIC: 3999 Manufacturing industries

(G-10506)
IVA PARTS BROKER LLC
2708 Sw 165th Ave (33027-5241)
PHONE..............................239 222-2604
Igor Villalobos, *Principal*
◆ **EMP:** 8 **EST:** 2010

SALES (est): 773.6K **Privately Held**
WEB: www.ivapartsbroker.com
SIC: 3469 Machine parts, stamped or pressed metal

(G-10507)
J J M SERVICES INC
Also Called: Minuteman Press
12004 Miramar Pkwy (33025-7000)
PHONE..............................954 437-1880
Joanne Miner, *President*
EMP: 5 **EST:** 1988
SQ FT: 2,500
SALES (est): 481.9K **Privately Held**
WEB: www.minuteman.com
SIC: 2752 2791 2789 2759 Commercial printing, lithographic; typesetting; bookbinding & related work; commercial printing

(G-10508)
LENZ GROUP LLC
4925 Sw 185th Ter (33029-6297)
PHONE..............................305 467-5351
Karlenz Lacroix, *President*
EMP: 7 **EST:** 2014
SALES (est): 112.4K **Privately Held**
WEB: www.mywebsitebiz.com
SIC: 7372 Prepackaged software

(G-10509)
LODEX ENTERPRISES CORP
17048 Sw 38th Dr (33027-4601)
PHONE..............................954 442-3843
Luis I Gutierrez, *President*
EMP: 7 **EST:** 2008
SQ FT: 10,000
SALES (est): 900.7K **Privately Held**
SIC: 3569 3561 3589 5085 Separators for steam, gas, vapor or air (machinery); pumps & pumping equipment; water treatment equipment, industrial; industrial supplies

(G-10510)
LUJOTEX LLC
Also Called: UPS Store 4332, The
14359 Miramar Pkwy # 290 (33027-4134)
PHONE..............................954 322-1001
Luis J Delgado Pda,
EMP: 7 **EST:** 2011
SALES (est): 466.3K **Privately Held**
SIC: 2759 Commercial printing

(G-10511)
LUTIMI NR CORP
3190 S State Road 7 # 18 (33023-5280)
PHONE..............................954 245-7986
Miguel Angel S Noriega R, *President*
EMP: 9 **EST:** 2015
SALES (est): 443.6K **Privately Held**
SIC: 2752 Photolithographic printing

(G-10512)
MACTECH POWER LINE AND CABLE
15120 Sw 49th St (33027-3644)
PHONE..............................954 895-9966
Dale A Dunkley, *Principal*
EMP: 8 **EST:** 2019
SALES (est): 256.3K **Privately Held**
SIC: 3643 Power line cable

(G-10513)
MDY SERVICES INC
19418 Sw 27th St (33029-2484)
PHONE..............................954 392-1542
Manuel Codecido, *President*
EMP: 7 **EST:** 2013
SALES (est): 89.4K **Privately Held**
SIC: 3651 7389 Home entertainment equipment, electronic;

(G-10514)
MIAMI MIX CORP
15014 Sw 21st St (33027-4366)
PHONE..............................954 704-9682
Hector Neciosup, *Principal*
EMP: 9 **EST:** 2008
SALES (est): 114.2K **Privately Held**
SIC: 3273 Ready-mixed concrete

(G-10515)
MIRAMAR MRMIDS SYNCHRO TEAM LL
16801 Miramar Pkwy (33027-4588)
PHONE..............................786 520-6678
Grasy Noriega, *President*
EMP: 6 **EST:** 2013
SALES (est): 312.2K **Privately Held**
WEB: www.miramarmermaids.com
SIC: 3621 Synchros

(G-10516)
MOUNTED MEMORIES INC
15701 Sw 29th St (33027-5260)
PHONE..............................866 236-2541
Mitch Adelstein, *President*
Scott Widelitz, *Vice Pres*
Ross Tannenbaum, *CFO*
EMP: 19 **EST:** 1993
SQ FT: 22,000
SALES (est): 508.8K **Privately Held**
SIC: 2499 5199 Novelties, wood fiber; gifts & novelties

(G-10517)
MTN GOVERNMENT SERVICES INC
3044 N Commerce Pkwy (33025-3969)
PHONE..............................954 538-4000
Errol Olivier, *Principal*
EMP: 10 **EST:** 2014
SALES (est): 441.1K **Privately Held**
SIC: 3679 Quartz crystals, for electronic application

(G-10518)
NEXPUB INC
3820 Executive Way (33025-3947)
PHONE..............................954 392-5889
Robert Edgman, *Acting CFO*
EMP: 14 **EST:** 1999
SQ FT: 18,000
SALES (est): 375.6K **Privately Held**
WEB: www.nexpub.com
SIC: 2752 Commercial printing, offset

(G-10519)
NISSI & JIREH INC
2413 Main St 232 (33025-7809)
PHONE..............................866 897-7657
Byongchul Kim, *President*
EMP: 21
SALES (corp-wide): 618.1K **Privately Held**
WEB: www.nissiandjireh.com
SIC: 3069 5999 5137 Baby pacifiers, rubber; infant furnishings & equipment; baby goods
PA: Nissi & Jireh, Inc.
  5356 Desmond Ln
  Orlando FL 32821
  866 897-7657

(G-10520)
NO LIVE BAIT NEEDED LLC
12078 Miramar Pkwy (33025-7003)
PHONE..............................305 479-8719
Brandon S Ramos R, *Mng Member*
EMP: 8 **EST:** 2020
SALES (est): 357.1K **Privately Held**
WEB: www.nolivebaitneeded.com
SIC: 3949 Fishing tackle, general

(G-10521)
NUWAS DEVA LLC
2240 N Sherman Cir # 507 (33025-5157)
PHONE..............................786 859-2819
Valentino Charlemagne, *CEO*
EMP: 6 **EST:** 2018
SALES (est): 410.3K **Privately Held**
SIC: 3537 Trucks: freight, baggage, etc.: industrial, except mining

(G-10522)
OLEVIN COMPOUNDS LLC
12758 Sw 47th St (33027-6031)
PHONE..............................954 993-5148
Farhat Syed, *Mng Member*
EMP: 6 **EST:** 2017
SALES (est): 478K **Privately Held**
WEB: www.olevincompounds.com
SIC: 2821 Plastics materials & resins

(G-10523)
ONE NURSING CARE LLC
3351 Executive Way (33025-3935)
PHONE..............................954 441-6644
Guillermo Salazar, *CEO*
EMP: 142 **EST:** 2013
SALES (est): 2.4MM
SALES (corp-wide): 83B **Publicly Held**
WEB: www.onehome.health
SIC: 2834 Pharmaceutical preparations
PA: Humana Inc.
  500 W Main St Ste 300
  Louisville KY 40202
  502 580-1000

(G-10524)
PANAMERICAN FOOD LLC (PA)
Also Called: Pagnifique USA
10491 N Commerce Pkwy (33025-3971)
PHONE..............................305 594-5704
Fernando Abella, *Managing Dir*
Pablo De Leon, *Opers Staff*
Erika Perez-Espinosa, *Controller*
Juan Funes, *Sales Staff*
Julia Palacio, *Sales Staff*
◆ **EMP:** 25 **EST:** 2002
SQ FT: 29,397
SALES (est): 7.4MM **Privately Held**
WEB: www.pagnifique.com
SIC: 2051 Bread, all types (white, wheat, rye, etc): fresh or frozen

(G-10525)
PATTERN GRADING & MARKER SVCS
Also Called: Pgms
3650 Sw 141st Ave (33027-3240)
PHONE..............................305 495-9963
Regina Gottlieb, *Vice Pres*
Saul Gottlieb, *Director*
EMP: 6 **EST:** 2001
SALES (est): 487K **Privately Held**
WEB: www.pattern-maker.com
SIC: 3543 5136 5137 Industrial patterns; men's & boys' clothing; women's & children's clothing

(G-10526)
PENIEL INC
11844 Sw 27th St (33025-0783)
PHONE..............................305 594-2739
Sergio D Daldi, *President*
EMP: 11 **EST:** 2000
SALES (est): 352.5K **Privately Held**
WEB: www.camppeniel.org
SIC: 2741 Miscellaneous publishing

(G-10527)
PICASSO EMBROIDERY SYSTEMS
11952 Miramar Pkwy (33025-7005)
PHONE..............................305 827-9666
Emeric Silberman, *President*
EMP: 10 **EST:** 1996
SALES (est): 958.6K **Privately Held**
WEB: www.picassoindustries.com
SIC: 2759 Screen printing

(G-10528)
PREMIUM QUALITY MEATS INC
7979 Riviera Blvd (33023-6440)
PHONE..............................239 309-4418
Timothy Mooti Persad, *President*
Ivan Mooti Persad, *Vice Pres*
EMP: 13 **EST:** 2019
SALES (est): 506.6K **Privately Held**
WEB: www.pqmfl.com
SIC: 2015 5142 Poultry sausage, luncheon meats & other poultry products; frozen fish, meat & poultry

(G-10529)
PRESS-RITE INC
Also Called: Dlp Industries
2125 Sw 60th Way (33023-2941)
PHONE..............................954 963-7373
Dave Phipps, *President*
EMP: 9
SALES (corp-wide): 1.2MM **Privately Held**
WEB: www.pressritehardware.com
SIC: 3469 3429 Metal stampings; manufactured hardware (general)

PA: Press-Rite, Inc.
2125 Sw 60th Way
Miramar FL 33023
954 963-7373

(G-10530)
PRINT FACTORY LLC
Also Called: Nexpub
3820 Executive Way (33025-3947)
PHONE.................954 392-5889
Laurie Edgman, *Mng Member*
Robert Edgman,
Neal Polan,
EMP: 7 **EST:** 2002
SQ FT: 9,800
SALES (est): 989.3K **Privately Held**
WEB: www.nexpub.com
SIC: 2752 Commercial printing, offset

(G-10531)
PRISMA DIRECT
17773 Sw 24th Ct (33029-5121)
PHONE.................954 638-4753
Marta B Salgado, *Principal*
EMP: 7 **EST:** 2006
SALES (est): 184.9K **Privately Held**
WEB: www.prismastyles.com
SIC: 3423 Jewelers' hand tools

(G-10532)
**PRO LAB SUPPLY
CORPORATION**
Also Called: Biochrom
12086 Miramar Pkwy (33025-7003)
PHONE.................305 600-0444
Paolo Paparcuri, *President*
Beverley C Paparcuri, *Corp Secy*
Luis Urich, *Vice Pres*
▲ **EMP:** 6 **EST:** 1998
SALES (est): 1.3MM **Privately Held**
WEB: www.biochromcorp.com
SIC: 3821 Laboratory equipment: fume
hoods, distillation racks, etc.

(G-10533)
**PROFESSNAL KIT INSTLLER
GROUP**
Also Called: Pki Group
1892 Sw 152nd Ter (33027-4312)
PHONE.................954 436-1513
Benjamin Colon, *President*
EMP: 12 **EST:** 2004
SQ FT: 3,400
SALES (est): 2.3MM **Privately Held**
WEB: www.thepkigroup.com
SIC: 3469 1799 Kitchen fixtures & equip-
ment: metal, except cast aluminum;
kitchen cabinet installation

(G-10534)
PROPULSION TECH INTL LLC
Also Called: P T I
15301 Sw 29th St Ste 100 (33027-5248)
PHONE.................954 874-0274
Michael Mitchell, *CEO*
Tom Gowen, *Engineer*
Jeronimo Gracian, *Engineer*
Michelle Knoll, *Engineer*
Gregory Miller, *Engineer*
EMP: 300 **EST:** 2001
SQ FT: 40,000
SALES (est): 37.7MM **Privately Held**
WEB: www.ptechi.com
SIC: 3724 Engine mount parts, aircraft

(G-10535)
**REGINA BEHAR ENTERPRISES
INC**
Also Called: Ike Behar
11440 Interchange Cir N (33025-6005)
PHONE.................305 557-5212
Ike Behar, *CEO*
Regina Behar, *President*
Lawrence Behar, *Vice Pres*
Steve Behar, *Admin Sec*
▲ **EMP:** 27 **EST:** 1957
SALES (est): 2.7MM **Privately Held**
SIC: 2321 Men's & boys' dress shirts;
men's & boys' sports & polo shirts

(G-10536)
RENOVA LAND AND SEA LLC
4954 Sw 128th Ave (33027-5828)
PHONE.................786 916-2695
Dennis Rodriguez, *Mng Member*

EMP: 5 **EST:** 2015
SALES (est): 322.6K **Privately Held**
SIC: 3441 Fabricated structural metal

(G-10537)
ROLO GANG LLC
11503 Sw 26th Pl (33025-7543)
PHONE.................561 538-8173
Brian L Gamble, *Manager*
EMP: 13 **EST:** 2018
SALES (est): 438.3K **Privately Held**
SIC: 2782 Record albums

(G-10538)
RUSSELL HOBBS INC (DH)
3633 S Flamingo Rd (33027-2936)
PHONE.................954 883-1000
Terry L Polistina, *President*
Ivan R Habibe, *CFO*
▲ **EMP:** 100 **EST:** 1991
SQ FT: 110,000
SALES (est): 109.7MM
SALES (corp-wide): 3B **Publicly Held**
SIC: 3634 3873 3648 2499 Electric
household cooking appliances; watches,
clocks, watchcases & parts; lighting
equipment; picture & mirror frames, wood;
picture frames, metal
HQ: Spectrum Brands, Inc.
3001 Deming Way
Middleton WI 53562
608 275-3340

(G-10539)
**SAFETY COMPLIANCE PUBL
INC**
3600 S State Road 7 # 204 (33023-5200)
PHONE.................844 556-3149
Valle Patricia, *Principal*
EMP: 8 **EST:** 2017
SALES (est): 89.2K **Privately Held**
WEB: www.safetypub.net
SIC: 2741 Miscellaneous publishing

(G-10540)
SAS R & D SERVICES INC
2371 Sw 195th Ave (33029-5917)
PHONE.................954 432-2345
Ted Sas, *CEO*
▼ **EMP:** 19 **EST:** 1988
SQ FT: 7,000
SALES (est): 5MM **Privately Held**
WEB: www.sasrad.com
SIC: 3812 Defense systems & equipment

(G-10541)
SDMO GENERATING SETS INC
Also Called: Kohler Sdmo
3801 Commerce Pkwy (33025-3940)
PHONE.................305 863-0012
Jacky Pluchon, *President*
Roberto Piccolo, *Regl Sales Mgr*
Lucile Bonal, *Marketing Mgr*
Nicolas Lahera, *Director*
Jackie Pluchon, *Director*
◆ **EMP:** 26 **EST:** 2000
SQ FT: 14,000
SALES (est): 4.5MM
SALES (corp-wide): 1.4B **Privately Held**
WEB: us.sdmo.com
SIC: 3621 Generator sets: gasoline, diesel
or dual-fuel
HQ: S.D.M.O. Industries
270 Rue De Kereryern
Guipavas 29490
298 411-388

(G-10542)
SECURUS BROT LLC
2400 Sw 132nd Ter (33027-2684)
PHONE.................954 532-8065
Gregory St Fort,
EMP: 9 **EST:** 2011
SALES (est): 751.4K **Privately Held**
SIC: 2752 Commercial printing, litho-
graphic

(G-10543)
SIMTEC SILICONE PARTS LLC
9658 Premier Pkwy (33025-3203)
PHONE.................954 656-4212
Frank Dilly, *Managing Dir*
Franz Dilly, *Managing Dir*
Zeno Weidenthaler, *Vice Pres*
Luis Angel Marrero, *Engineer*
Kirsten Palma, *Project Engr*

▼ **EMP:** 22 **EST:** 2002
SQ FT: 10,000
SALES (est): 14.9MM
SALES (corp-wide): 355.8K **Privately
Held**
WEB: www.simtec-silicone.com
SIC: 3089 Injection molding of plastics
PA: Rico Group Gmbh
Am Thalbach 8
Thalheim Bei Wels
724 276-460

(G-10544)
SINCERE FUEL INC
16100 Sw 51st St (33027-4963)
PHONE.................954 433-3577
Ward George, *Principal*
EMP: 7 **EST:** 2010
SALES (est): 138.2K **Privately Held**
SIC: 2869 Fuels

(G-10545)
SPEED PRO MIAMI
11341 Interchange Cir S (33025-6008)
PHONE.................954 534-9503
EMP: 5 **EST:** 2014
SALES (est): 319.9K **Privately Held**
WEB: www.speedpro.com
SIC: 3993 Signs & advertising specialties

(G-10546)
**STATESIDE INDUS SOLUTIONS
LLC**
14900 Sw 30th St # 278663 (33027-7329)
PHONE.................305 301-4052
Rochy J Rodriguez,
EMP: 8 **EST:** 2017
SALES (est): 1MM **Privately Held**
WEB: www.statesideindustrial.com
SIC: 3645 Lamp & light shades

(G-10547)
**STEMTECH HEALTHSCIENCES
CORP** ✪
10370 Usa Today Way (33025-3901)
PHONE.................954 715-6000
Ray C Carter Jr, *Principal*
John Meyer, *Vice Pres*
Debbie Anders, *Accountant*
Juan Horta, *Manager*
Brianne Rogers, *Manager*
EMP: 27 **EST:** 2021
SALES (est): 10.1MM **Privately Held**
WEB: www.stemtech.com
SIC: 2834 Pharmaceutical preparations

(G-10548)
**STS DISTRIBUTION SOLUTIONS
LLC**
Also Called: STS Air-Pro
11650 Miramar Pkwy # 500 (33025-5823)
PHONE.................844 359-4673
Thomas Covella, *President*
EMP: 15 **EST:** 2015
SALES (est): 7MM **Privately Held**
SIC: 3492 Hose & tube couplings, hy-
draulic/pneumatic; hose & tube fittings &
assemblies, hydraulic/pneumatic

(G-10549)
**SUN SHELL BLINDS & SHADES
CORP**
17649 Sw 54th St (33029-5085)
PHONE.................678 975-1082
Huanyu Ren, *Principal*
EMP: 7 **EST:** 2020
SALES (est): 95.3K **Privately Held**
SIC: 2591 Window blinds

(G-10550)
SUNTYX LLC
Also Called: Poggesi USA
11550 Interchange Cir N (33025-6006)
PHONE.................786 558-2233
Gabriela Tuaty, *Accounts Exec*
Danny Tuaty, *Mng Member*
David Bensadon, *Senior Mgr*
Marianne Luis, *Director*
EMP: 30 **EST:** 2016
SALES (est): 8.3MM **Privately Held**
SIC: 3999 Garden umbrellas

(G-10551)
**SURVITEC SURVIVOR CFT MAR
INC**
9640 Premier Pkwy (33025-3203)
PHONE.................954 374-4276
Issac Ancona, *General Mgr*
Mike Glover, *Fire Chief*
Steve Blair, *Manager*
▲ **EMP:** 7 **EST:** 2012
SQ FT: 1,500
SALES (est): 661.6K **Privately Held**
SIC: 3732 5091 Lifeboats, building & re-
pairing; boats, canoes, watercrafts &
equipment

(G-10552)
TACO METALS LLC (HQ)
Also Called: Taco Marine
3020 N Commerce Pkwy (33025-3969)
PHONE.................305 652-8566
Lenny Ogle, *Purch Mgr*
Hendrik Amirkhanian, *QC Mgr*
Kevin Cunningham, *Engineer*
Christopher Smith, *Engineer*
Hana Nash, *Human Res Mgr*
◆ **EMP:** 12 **EST:** 1959
SALES (est): 45.6MM
SALES (corp-wide): 4B **Publicly Held**
WEB: www.tacometals.com
SIC: 3531 5999 Marine related equipment;
architectural supplies
PA: Patrick Industries, Inc.
107 W Franklin St
Elkhart IN 46516
574 294-7511

(G-10553)
THREE60PRINTING LLC
3350 Sw 148th Ave Ste 110 (33027-3237)
P.O. Box 8142, Fort Lauderdale (33310-
8142)
PHONE.................954 271-2701
Omar R Turral, *CEO*
EMP: 10 **EST:** 2012
SALES (est): 716.9K **Privately Held**
WEB: www.three60printing.com
SIC: 2752 7389 3499 5199 Commercial
printing, lithographic; advertising, promo-
tional & trade show services; embroider-
ing of advertising on shirts, etc.; novelties
& giftware, including trophies; advertising
specialties

(G-10554)
TRANE US INC
Also Called: South Florida Trane
2884 Corporate Way (33025-6546)
PHONE.................954 499-6900
Pascal Sprimont, *Project Mgr*
Roberto Masson, *Accounts Mgr*
Lou Zaccone, *Branch Mgr*
Harry Torres, *Technician*
EMP: 85 **Privately Held**
WEB: www.trane.com
SIC: 3585 Refrigeration & heating equip-
ment
HQ: Trane U.S. Inc.
800 Beaty St Ste E
Davidson NC 28036
704 655-4000

(G-10555)
TROPICAL SKOOPS LLC
11635 Red Rd (33025-7810)
PHONE.................954 440-8736
Shanillia Forbes, *CEO*
EMP: 10 **EST:** 2013
SALES (est): 340.2K **Privately Held**
WEB: tropical-skoops.weebly.com
SIC: 2024 Ice cream & frozen desserts

(G-10556)
TURBINE CONTROLS LLC
3501 Enterprise Way (33025-6545)
PHONE.................954 517-1706
Glen Greenberg, *President*
Eric Fraher, *Vice Pres*
EMP: 97 **EST:** 2012
SALES (est): 17.6MM
SALES (corp-wide): 24.1MM **Privately
Held**
WEB: www.tcimro.com
SIC: 3728 Aircraft parts & equipment

PA: Turbine Controls, Inc.
5 Old Windsor Rd
Bloomfield CT 06002
860 242-0448

(G-10557)
UNITED AEROSPACE CORPORATION
9800 Premier Pkwy (33025-3211)
PHONE.....................954 364-0085
Manuel Martinez, *President*
Martin Cantillo, *General Mgr*
Abelardo Cantillo, *Vice Pres*
Ana Munoz, *VP Sales*
Marlene Cardenas, *Sales Staff*
EMP: 26 EST: 1972
SQ FT: 35,000
SALES (est): 5.8MM **Privately Held**
WEB: www.unitedaerospace.com
SIC: 3728 Aircraft parts & equipment

(G-10558)
UNIVERSAL 3D INNOVATION INC
3891 Commerce Pkwy (33025-3940)
PHONE.....................516 837-9423
Tomer Yariz, *President*
Adam Gansky, *Officer*
EMP: 10 EST: 2013
SALES (est): 2.2MM **Privately Held**
WEB: www.3d-innovation.com
SIC: 3993 Signs, not made in custom sign painting shops

(G-10559)
UPPER KEYS SNACKS LLC
2841 Sw 175th Ave (33029-5553)
PHONE.....................305 298-6109
Carlos M Gutierrez, *Manager*
EMP: 7 EST: 2014
SALES (est): 266.7K **Privately Held**
SIC: 3131 Footwear cut stock

(G-10560)
UTC AEROSPACE SYSTEMS
3601 S Flamingo Rd (33027-2936)
PHONE.....................954 538-8971
EMP: 8 EST: 2020
SALES (est): 1.3MM **Privately Held**
SIC: 3728 Aircraft parts & equipment

(G-10561)
VINYLIZE CREATION LLC
2201 Sw 84th Ter (33025-5131)
PHONE.....................954 478-3172
EMP: 6 EST: 2018
SALES (est): 513.2K **Privately Held**
WEB: www.vinylizecreationllc.com
SIC: 3993 Signs & advertising specialties

(G-10562)
VSI & PARTNERS INC
Also Called: Lake Aerospace Services
14501 Sw 39th St (33027-3794)
PHONE.....................954 205-8653
Antonio Valdes, *CEO*
EMP: 10 EST: 2000
SALES (est): 689.1K **Privately Held**
SIC: 3721 Aircraft

(G-10563)
WATSON THERAPEUTICS INC
3400 Enterprise Way (33025-3941)
PHONE.....................954 266-1000
Andrew Boyer, *President*
Brian Shanahan, *Vice Pres*
EMP: 24 EST: 2013
SALES (est): 6.7MM **Privately Held**
SIC: 2834 Pharmaceutical preparations
HQ: Actavis Laboratories Fl, Inc.
5 Giralda Farms
Madison NJ 07940
862 261-7000

(G-10564)
WETHERILL ASSOCIATES INC (PA)
Also Called: Wai Corporate - USA
3300 Corporate Way (33025-3945)
PHONE.....................800 877-3340
Jeffery W Sween, *CEO*
Earl Proud, *President*
Richard Welland, *Managing Dir*
Douglas Moul, *COO*
Jordan Siegel, *COO*

◆ EMP: 200 EST: 1978
SQ FT: 100,000
SALES (est): 92.2MM **Privately Held**
SIC: 3714 5013 4731 Motor vehicle parts & accessories; automotive supplies & parts; freight forwarding

(G-10565)
WINRISE ENTERPRISES LLC
15701 Sw 29th St 100 (33027-5260)
PHONE.....................786 621-6705
Peter Loucks, *Mng Member*
▲ EMP: 8 EST: 2008
SQ FT: 4,000
SALES (est): 832.4K **Privately Held**
WEB: www.winrise.com
SIC: 3355 Aluminum rod & bar

(G-10566)
ZEBRA TECHNOLOGIES CORPORATION
3100 Sw 145th Ave Ste 350 (33027-6611)
PHONE.....................305 716-2200
James Sojka, *Partner*
Edward Caplin, *Branch Mgr*
Arnie Martinez, *Manager*
Maria Ochoa, *Analyst*
Sarah Salpeter, *Education*
EMP: 9
SALES (corp-wide): 5.6B **Publicly Held**
WEB: www.zebra.com
SIC: 3577 Computer peripheral equipment
PA: Zebra Technologies Corporation
3 Overlook Pt
Lincolnshire IL 60069
847 634-6700

(G-10567)
ZSNO FT LAUDERDALE
3801 Commerce Pkwy (33025-3940)
PHONE.....................954 792-2223
Ginger Dairsaw, *Owner*
EMP: 7 EST: 2010
SALES (est): 116.8K **Privately Held**
SIC: 3577 Printers & plotters

Miramar Beach
Walton County

(G-10568)
BOTE LLC
Also Called: Bote Boards
12598 Emerald Coast Pkwy (32550-2101)
PHONE.....................888 855-4450
Josh Flenniken, *Business Mgr*
Sondra Moffit, *Controller*
Willie Vernon, *Marketing Staff*
Corey M Cooper, *Mng Member*
Magdalena Cooper, *Mng Member*
EMP: 12 EST: 2010
SQ FT: 800
SALES (est): 1.3MM **Privately Held**
WEB: www.boteboard.com
SIC: 3949 5941 5551 5091 Surfboards; surfing equipment & supplies; canoe & kayak dealers; sporting & recreation goods

(G-10569)
COASTAL CABINETS & COUNTERTOPS
12889 Us Highway 98 W 109a (32550-3241)
PHONE.....................850 424-3940
Wayne Martin, *Owner*
Sharon Martin, *Co-Owner*
EMP: 7 EST: 2008
SALES (est): 457.2K **Privately Held**
WEB: www.coastalcabinetsandcounters.com
SIC: 2434 Wood kitchen cabinets

(G-10570)
PAVERSCAPE SOLUTIONS LLC
21 Professional Ct (32550-6821)
PHONE.....................850 497-5557
Joshua Fleming, *Principal*
EMP: 8 EST: 2015
SALES (est): 193.4K **Privately Held**
WEB: www.uspaverscape.com
SIC: 2951 Asphalt paving mixtures & blocks

(G-10571)
PVH CORP
Also Called: Van Heusen
10746 Us Highway 98 W # 158 (32550-7119)
PHONE.....................850 269-0482
Harlen Ozoria, *Branch Mgr*
Polina Bess, *Technology*
EMP: 10
SALES (corp-wide): 9.1B **Publicly Held**
WEB: www.pvh.com
SIC: 2321 Men's & boys' dress shirts
PA: Pvh Corp.
200 Madison Ave
New York NY 10016
212 381-3500

(G-10572)
RENOVATION FLOORING LLC
Also Called: Payfin Enterprises
11714 Us Highway 98 W (32550-6969)
PHONE.....................850 460-7295
Mike Anderson, *CEO*
Chris Turner, *Project Mgr*
Colby Cannon, *Opers Mgr*
Amy Flagstad, *Office Mgr*
Crissie C Anderson,
EMP: 31 EST: 2015
SQ FT: 2,500
SALES (est): 4.5MM **Privately Held**
WEB: www.renovationflooring.com
SIC: 2426 5211 1771 1743 Flooring, hardwood; flooring, wood; tile, ceramic; flooring contractor; tile installation, ceramic; wood floor installation & refinishing

(G-10573)
SP PUBLICATIONS LLC
495 Grand Blvd Ste 206 (32550-1897)
PHONE.....................239 595-9040
Stephane Perrin,
EMP: 7 EST: 2009
SALES (est): 362.6K **Privately Held**
WEB: www.patriciacupcakes.com
SIC: 2741 Miscellaneous publishing

(G-10574)
US IRON LLC
755 Grand Blvd Ste 105b (32550-1839)
PHONE.....................765 210-4111
Mark Miller, *President*
Cathy Howard, *Executive Asst*
EMP: 15 EST: 2005
SALES (est): 1.4MM **Privately Held**
WEB: www.usmagnetite.com
SIC: 1011 Iron ore mining

Miromar Lakes
Lee County

(G-10575)
POWERCASES INC
18281 Via Caprini Dr (33913-7611)
PHONE.....................239 415-3846
Jeff Mason, *Director*
EMP: 6 EST: 2014
SALES (est): 375.1K **Privately Held**
WEB: usa.powercases.com
SIC: 3523 Farm machinery & equipment

(G-10576)
WIZTEL USA INC
18281 Via Caprini Dr (33913-7611)
PHONE.....................416 457-5513
Jeff Mason, *CEO*
EMP: 7 EST: 2005
SALES (est): 549.9K **Privately Held**
WEB: www.wiztelusainc.com
SIC: 3663 7389 Citizens' band (CB) radio;

Molino
Escambia County

(G-10577)
CLASSIC HARDWOOD DESIGN
3895 Highway 97 (32577-5062)
PHONE.....................850 232-6473
Van Deese, *Owner*
EMP: 7 EST: 2002
SALES (est): 354K **Privately Held**
SIC: 3999 Furniture, barber & beauty shop

(G-10578)
EDS ALUMINUM BUILDINGS INC
Hwy 29 (32577)
PHONE.....................850 476-2169
Tim Vignolo, *Manager*
EMP: 8
SALES (corp-wide): 733K **Privately Held**
WEB: www.edsaluminumbuildings.com
SIC: 3448 5211 Prefabricated metal buildings; prefabricated buildings
PA: Ed's Aluminum Buildings, Inc.
9555 Pensacola Blvd
Pensacola FL 32534
850 476-2169

(G-10579)
SOUL KASS BOUTIQUE LLC
1218 Bet Raines Rd (32577-7125)
PHONE.....................682 429-4323
Angel Ross, *Branch Mgr*
EMP: 10
SALES (corp-wide): 20K **Privately Held**
SIC: 3172 Personal leather goods
PA: Soul Kass Boutique Llc
212 S Chickasaw St
Webb MS 38966
682 429-4323

Monticello
Jefferson County

(G-10580)
BBTS LOGGING LLC
2182 S Jefferson Hwy (32344-5136)
P.O. Box 15 (32345-0015)
PHONE.....................850 997-2436
Benjamin D Walton, *Principal*
EMP: 8 EST: 2014
SALES (est): 454K **Privately Held**
SIC: 2411 Logging camps & contractors

(G-10581)
HEALTHQUEST TECHNOLOGIES LLC
1817 W Capps Hwy (32344-7109)
PHONE.....................850 997-6300
Tim Kerr, *Partner*
EMP: 7
SALES (corp-wide): 1.8MM **Privately Held**
WEB: www.pionair.net
SIC: 3634 Air purifiers, portable
PA: Healthquest Technologies, L.L.C.
1819 Meredith Park Dr
Mcdonough GA 30253
770 320-9900

(G-10582)
JOINER LAND CLEARING LLC
1417 Government Farm Rd (32344-5163)
PHONE.....................850 997-5729
Donald F Joiner, *Principal*
Linda Joiner, *Co-Owner*
EMP: 11 EST: 1972
SALES (est): 535K **Privately Held**
SIC: 2411 Pulpwood contractors engaged in cutting

(G-10583)
MONTICELLO MILLING CO INC
500 S Jefferson St (32344-1822)
PHONE.....................850 997-5521
Gerald Miller, *President*
Sara L Mc Call, *Treasurer*
EMP: 7 EST: 1964
SQ FT: 900
SALES (est): 665.8K **Privately Held**
SIC: 2048 Livestock feeds

(G-10584)
MONTICELLO NEWS
Also Called: ECB Publishing
180 W Washington St (32344-1954)
P.O. Box 428 (32345-0428)
PHONE.....................850 997-3568
Emerald Greene, *Owner*
Ron Cichon, *Owner*
EMP: 10 EST: 1971
SQ FT: 2,500
SALES (est): 954.9K **Privately Held**
WEB: www.ecbpublishing.com
SIC: 2711 Newspapers, publishing & printing

2022 Harris Florida
Manufacturers Directory

▲ = Import ▼=Export
◆ =Import/Export

(G-10585)
RANDY WHEELER
Also Called: Georgia-Florida Bark and Mulch
1560 Spring Hollow Dr (32344-1662)
PHONE................................850 997-1248
Randy Wheeler, *Owner*
EMP: 8 **EST:** 1971
SQ FT: 10,000
SALES (est): 934.5K **Privately Held**
SIC: 2499 0783 Mulch, wood & bark; ornamental shrub & tree services

(G-10586)
WESTERN GRAPHITE INC (PA)
1045 E Washington St (32344-3022)
PHONE................................850 270-2808
David Wimberly, *CEO*
EMP: 5 **EST:** 2006
SQ FT: 2,000
SALES (est): 2.2MM **Privately Held**
WEB: www.westerngraphite.com
SIC: 1499 Graphite mining

(G-10587)
WHARTON PEPPER CO
2873a St Augustine Rd (32344-6945)
PHONE................................850 997-4359
William Wharton, *President*
EMP: 6 **EST:** 1987
SALES (est): 373.8K **Privately Held**
SIC: 2033 2035 Chili sauce, tomato: packaged in cans, jars, etc.; pickles, sauces & salad dressings

Montverde
Lake County

(G-10588)
EMILIO CRAIG FOOTWEAR LLC
16637 Magnolia Ter (34756-3514)
PHONE................................954 999-8302
Emil Torres,
EMP: 7 **EST:** 2014
SALES (est): 100K **Privately Held**
SIC: 2211 Apparel & outerwear fabrics, cotton

Moore Haven
Glades County

(G-10589)
CEMEX CNSTR MTLS FLA LLC
Also Called: Readymix - Moore Haven Rm
1290 Foxmoor St (33471-9201)
PHONE................................800 992-3639
Paul Alt, *Branch Mgr*
EMP: 12 **Privately Held**
SIC: 1442 Construction sand & gravel
HQ: Cemex Construction Materials Florida, Llc
1501 Belvedere Rd
West Palm Beach FL 33406

(G-10590)
LEGEND MOTO LLC
1100 Us Highway 27 (33471-5517)
PHONE................................863 946-2002
Odalis Remedios, *Principal*
EMP: 5 **EST:** 2017
SALES (est): 375.9K **Privately Held**
WEB: www.legendmoto.net
SIC: 2221 Broadwoven fabric mills, manmade

(G-10591)
MAXANT BUTTONS LLC
213 Florida Ave Nw (33471-2723)
PHONE................................770 460-2227
Stephen Reed,
EMP: 5 **EST:** 2015
SALES (est): 521.6K **Privately Held**
WEB: www.coverbuttons.com
SIC: 3965 Fasteners, buttons, needles & pins

(G-10592)
SCOTT SAFETY LLC
13999 W Sr 78 (33471)
PHONE................................239 340-8695
John Scott,
EMP: 32 **EST:** 2018

SALES (est): 1.5MM **Privately Held**
WEB: www.scottsafetyfl.com
SIC: 3444 1611 Guard rails, highway: sheet metal; highway signs & guardrails; highway & street sign installation; highway reflector installation

Morriston
Levy County

(G-10593)
A&H LOGGING INC
2752 Se 174th Ct (32668)
P.O. Box 277 (32668-0277)
PHONE................................352 528-3868
Art Nussel, *Owner*
EMP: 7 **EST:** 1988
SALES (est): 396.7K **Privately Held**
SIC: 2411 Logging camps & contractors

(G-10594)
NORTON MANUFACTURING & SVC INC
11590 Se 30th St (32668-3296)
PHONE................................352 225-1225
Norton Scott R, *Principal*
EMP: 8 **EST:** 2014
SALES (est): 116.1K **Privately Held**
SIC: 3999 Manufacturing industries

Mossy Head
Walton County

(G-10595)
TRANN TECHNOLOGIES INC
12526 Us Hwy 90 (32434)
PHONE................................888 668-6700
Charity Prescott, *General Mgr*
Bryan E Kilbey, *Director*
EMP: 9 **EST:** 2002
SALES (est): 138.7K **Privately Held**
WEB: www.tranntech.com
SIC: 2295 Laminating of fabrics

Mount Dora
Lake County

(G-10596)
AMERICRAFT COOKWARE LLC
152 E 3rd Ave (32757-5503)
P.O. Box 347 (32756-0347)
PHONE................................352 483-7600
Bryan D Hurley, *Principal*
EMP: 24 **EST:** 2008
SALES (est): 4.2MM **Privately Held**
WEB: americraft.myshopify.com
SIC: 3269 Vases, pottery

(G-10597)
ATA GROUP OF COMPANIES INC
Also Called: Aishwarya Tari Apparels
8020 Arcadian Ct (32757-9122)
PHONE................................352 735-1588
Rajesh S Tari, *President*
EMP: 9 **EST:** 2000
SQ FT: 2,100
SALES (est): 196.9K **Privately Held**
WEB: www.mimiseafood.com
SIC: 2211 2411 2037 0751 Apparel & outerwear fabrics, cotton; timber, cut at logging camp; frozen fruits & vegetables; frozen fruits & vegetables; fruit juices; cattle services; timber tracts, hardwood

(G-10598)
C P ENTERPRISES OF APOPKA INC
Also Called: V J Pro Fabrics
3351 Laughlin Rd (32757-7322)
PHONE................................407 886-3321
Charles Poillion, *President*
EMP: 7 **EST:** 1980
SQ FT: 15,000
SALES (est): 954.2K **Privately Held**
SIC: 3448 3523 Greenhouses: prefabricated metal; trailers & wagons, farm

(G-10599)
CASMIN INC
2255 Crescent Dr (32757-4708)
P.O. Box 895250, Leesburg (34789-5250)
PHONE................................352 253-5000
Valerie Burleigh, *Manager*
EMP: 9
SALES (corp-wide): 10MM **Privately Held**
SIC: 2439 Trusses, wooden roof
PA: Casmin, Inc.
32506 County Road 473
Leesburg FL
352 343-0680

(G-10600)
DATA GRAPHICS INC
Also Called: Dg Promotions
3800 Progress Blvd (32757-2214)
PHONE................................352 589-1312
Brad Butterstein, *President*
Tim Shephard, *President*
Robert K Welter III, *Owner*
Buffy Carroll, *Vice Pres*
Liz Minson, *Mfg Staff*
EMP: 54 **EST:** 1984
SQ FT: 22,000
SALES (est): 11MM **Privately Held**
WEB: www.datagraphicsinc.com
SIC: 3993 Signs & advertising specialties

(G-10601)
EMERGE NUTRACEUTICALS INC
721 S Rossiter St (32757-6140)
PHONE................................888 352-1683
Taniqua Medina, *President*
EMP: 12 **EST:** 2018
SALES (est): 1.2MM **Privately Held**
SIC: 2834 Pharmaceutical preparations

(G-10602)
HALLMARK NAMEPLATE INC
1717 Lincoln Ave (32757-4108)
PHONE................................352 383-8142
Daniel Fortuna, *CEO*
Gary A Stura, *President*
John Santiago, *Vice Pres*
EMP: 100 **EST:** 1958
SQ FT: 32,000
SALES (est): 23.1MM **Privately Held**
WEB: www.hallmarknameplate.com
SIC: 3613 3993 Panel & distribution boards & other related apparatus; name plates: except engraved, etched, etc.: metal

(G-10603)
HEDRICK WALKER & ASSOC INC
3425 Lake Center Dr Ste 2 (32757-2345)
PHONE................................352 735-2600
Edgar J Hedrick, *President*
Scott Coffield, *Managing Prtnr*
Robert S Walker, *Vice Pres*
Joe Luttrell, *Sales Staff*
EMP: 5 **EST:** 1970
SALES (est): 418.2K **Privately Held**
WEB: www.hedrick-walker.com
SIC: 3824 Mechanical & electromechanical counters & devices

(G-10604)
INTERNATIONAL OZONE SVCS LLC
320924 Sunnygo Dr Ste 210 (32757)
PHONE................................352 978-9785
John Gaudaur, *Mng Member*
EMP: 5 **EST:** 2014
SALES (est): 469.1K **Privately Held**
WEB: www.io3services.com
SIC: 3559 7629 Ozone machines; electrical measuring instrument repair & calibration

(G-10605)
MID-FLORIDA PUBLICATIONS INC (PA)
Also Called: Triangle Shopping Guide
4645 N Highway 19a (32757-2039)
PHONE................................352 589-8811
Ann Yager, *Adv Dir*
Donna Covert, *Manager*
EMP: 6
SQ FT: 20,000

SALES (est): 1.9MM **Privately Held**
SIC: 2711 Newspapers, publishing & printing

(G-10606)
MOUNT DORA OLIVE OIL COMPANY
351b N Donnelly St (32757-5524)
PHONE................................352 735-8481
EMP: 6 **EST:** 2019
SALES (est): 567.6K **Privately Held**
WEB: www.mountdoraoliveoil.com
SIC: 2079 Olive oil

(G-10607)
NATURAL ORGANIC PRODUCTS INTL
Also Called: Nopi
710 S Rossiter St (32757-6139)
PHONE................................352 383-8252
Fax: 352 383-7307
EMP: 5
SQ FT: 60,000
SALES (est): 510K **Privately Held**
SIC: 2899 2873 2869 Mfg Chemical Preparations Mfg Nitrogenous Fertilizers Mfg Industrial Organic Chemicals

(G-10608)
NILLIUM HOLDINGS LLC
6751 Jones Ave (32757)
P.O. Box 220, Zellwood (32798-0220)
PHONE................................352 720-7070
Amy Yoder, *Mng Member*
Gary Dahms,
Ed Zughaft,
EMP: 12 **EST:** 2009
SALES (est): 12.2MM **Privately Held**
SIC: 2873 Fertilizers: natural (organic), except compost

(G-10609)
PANDIA PRESS INC
312 Forest Rd (32757-9503)
PHONE................................352 789-8156
Blair Lee, *Author*
EMP: 9 **EST:** 2019
SALES (est): 282.4K **Privately Held**
WEB: www.pandiapress.com
SIC: 2741 Miscellaneous publishing

(G-10610)
PHYSICIANS IMAGING LLC (PA)
3615 Lake Center Dr (32757-2364)
P.O. Box 8723, Coral Springs (33075-8723)
PHONE................................352 383-3716
Elias J Gerth, *Principal*
EMP: 6 **EST:** 2007
SALES (est): 2MM **Privately Held**
WEB: www.physiciansimagingllc.com
SIC: 2835 In vitro & in vivo diagnostic substances

(G-10611)
PRINCE MINERALS INC
710 S Rossiter St (32757-6139)
PHONE................................832 241-2169
EMP: 7 **EST:** 2015
SALES (est): 2.2MM **Privately Held**
WEB: www.princecorp.com
SIC: 2819 Industrial inorganic chemicals

(G-10612)
SERONIX CORPORATION
27109 Oak Shadow Ln (32757-7142)
PHONE................................352 406-1698
Scott Morrell, *CEO*
Scott Russell, *President*
Kerrie Russell, *CFO*
Christopher Straut, *Shareholder*
Marie Straut, *Shareholder*
EMP: 7 **EST:** 2003
SALES (est): 675.1K **Privately Held**
WEB: www.seronix.com
SIC: 7372 Application computer software

(G-10613)
SIMPLEX INC
4085 N Highway 19a (32757-2005)
PHONE................................352 357-2828
Tom Burkett, *President*
Beau Burkett, *Project Mgr*
David Pfister, *Sales Staff*
Dustin Williams, *Manager*

EMP: 20 **EST:** 1982
SQ FT: 8,000
SALES (est): 4.2MM **Privately Held**
WEB: www.simplexglass.net
SIC: 3442 5231 Screen doors, metal; screens, window, metal; glass

(G-10614)
SPECIALIZED OFF ROAD VEHICLES
2183 Croat St (32757-6802)
PHONE..........................352 735-1385
Mark Hyland, *Owner*
EMP: 7 **EST:** 2002
SALES (est): 72.8K **Privately Held**
SIC: 3799 Off-road automobiles, except recreational vehicles

(G-10615)
TCT MANUFACTURING
21911 Us Highway 441 (32757-9737)
P.O. Box 1659, Sorrento (32776-1659)
PHONE..........................352 735-5070
James Urmson, *President*
Jim Urmson, *Vice Pres*
Shirley Urmson, *Vice Pres*
Ian Nicholson, *Sr Software Eng*
EMP: 15 **EST:** 1997
SQ FT: 20,000
SALES (est): 1.5MM **Privately Held**
SIC: 3546 Saws & sawing equipment

(G-10616)
TRIANGLE SHOPPING GUIDE INC
Also Called: Lake News
4645 N Highway 19a (32757-2039)
PHONE..........................352 589-8811
William Matthews, *Chairman*
EMP: 5 **EST:** 1964
SQ FT: 2,300
SALES (est): 708.3K
SALES (corp-wide): 1.9MM **Privately Held**
WEB: www.midfloridanewspapers.com
SIC: 2711 Newspapers, publishing & printing
PA: Mid-Florida Publications Inc
4645 N Highway 19a
Mount Dora FL 32757
352 589-8811

(G-10617)
TRUEAR INC
18997 Us Highway 441 (32757-6735)
PHONE..........................352 314-8805
Adam Woodard, *CEO*
Catherine B Rathbun, *CPA*
EMP: 14 **EST:** 2017
SALES (est): 2.1MM **Privately Held**
WEB: www.truearhearing.com
SIC: 3842 Hearing aids

Mulberry
Polk County

(G-10618)
ACC HOLDCO INC
4800 State Road 60 E (33860-7905)
PHONE..........................863 578-1206
Glen Varnadoe, *President*
Robert Brinkman, *CFO*
EMP: 129 **EST:** 1998
SALES (est): 11.2MM **Privately Held**
SIC: 2899 Acid resist for etching

(G-10619)
ARRMAZ PRODUCTS INC (HQ)
Also Called: Arr-Maz Custom Chemicals
4800 State Road 60 E (33860-7905)
PHONE..........................863 578-1206
Hank Waters, *President*
Martin Poveda, *Partner*
William Cook, *Vice Pres*
Patrick Lavin, *Vice Pres*
Ronald S Lueptow, *Vice Pres*
▲ **EMP:** 100 **EST:** 1994
SQ FT: 125,000

SALES (est): 51.9MM
SALES (corp-wide): 129MM **Privately Held**
WEB: www.arrmaz.com
SIC: 2899 2869 Chemical preparations; industrial organic chemicals
PA: Arkema
420 Rue D Estienne D Orves
Colombes 92700
149 008-080

(G-10620)
BBH GENERAL PARTNERSHIP
610 N Industrial Park Rd (33860)
P.O. Box 826 (33860-0826)
PHONE..........................863 425-5626
Stan Hobby, *Partner*
Ronnie Bashlor, *Partner*
EMP: 11 **EST:** 2002
SQ FT: 10,142
SALES (est): 282.5K **Privately Held**
SIC: 3559 Rubber working machinery, including tires

(G-10621)
DANIELLE FENCE MFG CO INC
4855 State Road 60 W (33860-7820)
P.O. Box 1019 (33860-1019)
PHONE..........................863 425-3182
Marc Jeffrey Glogower, *President*
Paul Robert Glogower, *Vice Pres*
Celeste Thornton, *Comptroller*
▼ **EMP:** 75 **EST:** 1976
SALES (est): 16MM **Privately Held**
WEB: www.daniellefence.com
SIC: 2499 3699 1799 1521 Fencing, wood; security devices; fence construction; patio & deck construction & repair

(G-10622)
DEL MONTE FRESH PRODUCTION INC
5050 State Rte 60w (33860)
PHONE..........................863 844-5836
Bruce A Jordan, *Senior VP*
EMP: 10 **EST:** 2015
SALES (est): 140.5K **Privately Held**
WEB: www.freshdelmonte.com
SIC: 3824 Production counters

(G-10623)
DIVERSE CO
Also Called: Diverse Transport Systems
1950 Industrial Park Rd (33860-6610)
P.O. Box 975 (33860-0975)
PHONE..........................863 425-4251
C A Williams, *President*
Adele Williams, *Admin Sec*
EMP: 40 **EST:** 1985
SQ FT: 13,000
SALES (est): 3MM **Privately Held**
WEB: www.ihcus.com
SIC: 3312 1796 7699 Blast furnaces & steel mills; millwright; industrial machinery & equipment repair

(G-10624)
DSE INC
Also Called: Balimoy Manufacturing
2701 State Rd 37 S (33860)
PHONE..........................863 425-1745
Chuck Holbrook, *Manager*
EMP: 35
SQ FT: 8,574 **Privately Held**
WEB: www.dse.net
SIC: 3679 3482 Harness assemblies for electronic use: wire or cable; small arms ammunition
PA: Dse, Inc.
10401 Frog Pond Dr
Riverview FL 33569

(G-10625)
FLORIDA METALLIZING SVC INC
1810 State Road 37 S (33860-6915)
P.O. Box 585 (33860-0585)
PHONE..........................863 425-1143
Thomas Crews, *President*
Ismael Garcia, *Foreman/Supr*
Becky Kerber, *Office Mgr*
EMP: 32 **EST:** 1955
SQ FT: 26,562
SALES (est): 3.4MM **Privately Held**
WEB: www.fmsmulberry.com
SIC: 3599 Machine shop, jobbing & repair

(G-10626)
FUSE FABRICATION LLC
1935 Industrial Park Rd (33860-6605)
P.O. Box 6441, Lakeland (33807-6441)
PHONE..........................863 225-5698
Chad Marshall, *CEO*
EMP: 28 **EST:** 2010
SALES (est): 4MM **Privately Held**
WEB: www.fusefab.com
SIC: 3443 3441 3449 3599 Boiler & boiler shop work; fabricated structural metal; miscellaneous metalwork; machine shop, jobbing & repair; machine parts, stamped or pressed metal; iron work, structural

(G-10627)
HICKS INDUSTRIES INC (PA)
Also Called: Carlton Funeral Service
2005 Industrial Park Rd (33860-9619)
P.O. Box 1303 (33860-1303)
PHONE..........................863 425-4155
Daniel Hicks, *President*
Stephen Hatfield, *Exec VP*
Linda Lake, *Human Res Dir*
EMP: 41 **EST:** 1998
SALES (est): 9.2MM **Privately Held**
WEB: www.hicksindustries.com
SIC: 3273 Ready-mixed concrete

(G-10628)
JKS INDUSTRIES INC
2701 Cozart Rd (33860-8966)
PHONE..........................863 425-1745
Ken Shin, *Branch Mgr*
EMP: 50 **Privately Held**
WEB: www.jksindustries.net
SIC: 3499 Strapping, metal
PA: Jks Industries, Inc.
4644 W Gandy Blvd
Tampa FL 33611

(G-10629)
K C INDUSTRIES LLC
2420 Old Highway 60 (33860-7212)
P.O. Box 646 (33860-0646)
PHONE..........................863 425-1195
Steve McCarter, *Vice Pres*
Steven McCarter, *Mng Member*
◆ **EMP:** 8 **EST:** 1999
SQ FT: 1,600
SALES (est): 3MM **Privately Held**
WEB: www.kcindustries.com
SIC: 2819 Industrial inorganic chemicals

(G-10630)
LANGSTONS UTILITY BUILDINGS
4298 State Road 60 W (33860-6663)
PHONE..........................813 659-0141
Lloyd Langston, *Owner*
Brent McKinney, *Manager*
EMP: 5 **EST:** 1982
SALES (est): 382.5K **Privately Held**
WEB: www.langstonsutilitybuildings.com
SIC: 3448 5039 Buildings, portable: prefabricated metal; prefabricated structures

(G-10631)
MASTER MACHINE & TOOL CO II
2010 Moores Ln (33860-6666)
P.O. Box 495 (33860-0495)
PHONE..........................863 425-4902
Joseph Nemechek, *President*
▼ **EMP:** 19 **EST:** 1965
SQ FT: 15,000
SALES (est): 2.2MM **Privately Held**
WEB: www.mmt-llc.com
SIC: 3599 Machine shop, jobbing & repair

(G-10632)
METPRO SUPPLY INC
5070 State Road 60 E (33860-7907)
PHONE..........................863 425-7155
Jay Hazen, *President*
James Hazen, *Vice Pres*
Julian Hazen, *Vice Pres*
Julie Wells, *Vice Pres*
Chuck Bromley, *Sales Staff*
EMP: 24 **EST:** 1985
SQ FT: 13,000
SALES (est): 4MM **Privately Held**
WEB:
www.aggregateminingequipment.com
SIC: 3441 Fabricated structural metal

(G-10633)
MINERAL DEVELOPMENT LLC
4000 Sr 60 E (33860)
PHONE..........................863 354-3113
Lance McNeill, *CEO*
Chris Berg,
EMP: 10 **EST:** 2014
SALES (est): 1MM **Privately Held**
WEB: www.mineraldevelopment.us
SIC: 1475 Phosphate rock

(G-10634)
MOS HOLDINGS INC
Also Called: IMC Agrico
5000 Old Highway 37 (33860-8863)
P.O. Box 2000 (33860-1100)
PHONE..........................763 577-2700
Mr Willie Timms, *Safety Mgr*
Levi Buzzell, *Engineer*
Steven Garcia, *Branch Mgr*
EMP: 58 **Publicly Held**
SIC: 2874 Phosphatic fertilizers
HQ: Mos Holdings Inc.
3033 Campus Dr Ste E490
Plymouth MN 55441
763 577-2700

(G-10635)
QUALITY BLOCK & SUPPLY INC
Also Called: Ouality Precast
1590 Industrial Park Rd (33860-9504)
P.O. Box 247, Seffner (33583-0247)
PHONE..........................863 425-3070
Richard Phelps, *Vice Pres*
Preston Sparkman, *VP Sales*
Jake Rayos, *Manager*
EMP: 6 **EST:** 1987
SALES (est): 1MM **Privately Held**
WEB: www.qualityblocksupply.com
SIC: 3273 Ready-mixed concrete

(G-10636)
RJ FOODS
104 N Church Ave (33860-2497)
PHONE..........................863 425-3282
Ricky Joe Jackson, *Principal*
EMP: 6 **EST:** 2013
SALES (est): 345.3K **Privately Held**
WEB: www.rjfoods.us
SIC: 2099 Food preparations

(G-10637)
SAINT-GOBAIN CORPORATION
Also Called: Phoenix Coating Resources
2377 State Road 37 S (33860-6920)
PHONE..........................863 425-3299
EMP: 1221
SALES (corp-wide): 340.6MM **Privately Held**
WEB: www.saint-gobain-northamerica.com
SIC: 3728 Aircraft parts & equipment
HQ: Saint-Gobain Corporation
20 Moores Rd
Malvern PA 19355

(G-10638)
SHAWS FIBERGLASS INC
6925b State Road 60 W (33860-7803)
PHONE..........................863 425-9176
Charles Shaw, *President*
Conchita Shaw, *Admin Sec*
EMP: 6 **EST:** 1998
SALES (est): 512K **Privately Held**
SIC: 3441 3312 Fabricated structural metal; stainless steel

(G-10639)
SOUTHERN AIR COMPRSR SVC INC
2260 Peerless Rd (33860-4448)
P.O. Box 468 (33860-0468)
PHONE..........................863 425-9111
Charles T Caveney Sr, *President*
Charles T Caveney Jr, *Vice Pres*
Edna Caveney, *Admin Sec*
EMP: 5 **EST:** 1992
SQ FT: 1,800
SALES (est): 998.2K **Privately Held**
WEB: www.sacs-fla.com
SIC: 3563 Air & gas compressors

(G-10640)
SOUTHSTERN RAIL SVCS MLBRRY FL
Also Called: Mulberry Railcar
1200 Prairie Mine Rd (33860-8168)
P.O. Box 1038 (33860-1038)
PHONE.....................863 425-4986
Stephen Howell, *President*
Josh Conley, *Accounting Mgr*
David Howell,
EMP: 12 **EST:** 2014
SQ FT: 4,000
SALES (est): 3.1MM **Privately Held**
WEB: www.mulberryrailcar.com
SIC: 3743 Railroad car rebuilding

(G-10641)
SPX CORPORATION
399 N Prairie Indus Pkwy (33860-9076)
PHONE.....................863 602-9061
EMP: 10
SALES (corp-wide): 1.5B **Publicly Held**
WEB: www.spx.com
SIC: 3443 Heat exchangers, condensers & components
PA: Spx Corporation
6325 Ardrey Kell Rd # 400
Charlotte NC 28277
980 474-3700

(G-10642)
TIDAL WAVE TANKS FABRICATIONS
3275 Mulford Rd (33860-8667)
P.O. Box 252 (33860-0252)
PHONE.....................863 425-7795
Martha E Jennings, *President*
EMP: 6 **EST:** 2016
SALES (est): 855.2K **Privately Held**
WEB: www.tidalwavetanks.com
SIC: 3441 Fabricated structural metal

(G-10643)
VALLEY PROTEINS (DE) INC
465 Caboose Pl (33860-9165)
PHONE.....................910 282-7900
Duane Royal, *Branch Mgr*
EMP: 39
SALES (corp-wide): 473.5MM **Privately Held**
WEB: www.valleyproteins.com
SIC: 2077 Animal & marine fats & oils
PA: Valley Proteins (De), Inc.
151 Valpro Dr
Winchester VA 22603
540 877-2533

Myakka City
Manatee County

(G-10644)
COASTAL MARINE POWER INC
30710 Saddlebag Trl (34251-8415)
PHONE.....................941 322-8182
Richard B Stem, *President*
EMP: 8 **EST:** 2005
SALES (est): 288.8K **Privately Held**
WEB: www.coastalmarinecenterinc.com
SIC: 3443 Boilers: industrial, power, or marine

(G-10645)
CROWN WELDING & FABG INC
6030 Wauchula Rd (34251-9027)
P.O. Box 293 (34251-0293)
PHONE.....................941 737-6844
Travis L Barfield, *Principal*
EMP: 8 **EST:** 2016
SALES (est): 247K **Privately Held**
SIC: 7692 Welding repair

(G-10646)
RESOURCE GROUP US LLC ✪
Also Called: Resource Myakka
1510 Logue Rd (34251-5863)
PHONE.....................833 223-3266
Anthony M Cialone,
EMP: 7 **EST:** 2021
SALES (est): 382.4K **Privately Held**
SIC: 3523 Soil preparation machinery, except turf & grounds

(G-10647)
STONY CORAL INVESTMENTS LLC
Also Called: Nextreef Systems
23410 78th Ave E (34251-6064)
PHONE.....................941 704-5391
EMP: 11
SQ FT: 5,500
SALES (est): 1.3MM **Privately Held**
SIC: 3231 Products Of Purchased Glass

Naples
Collier County

(G-10648)
ABBOT HILL LLC
5880 Shirley St Ste 201 (34109-2308)
PHONE.....................239 260-5246
Petru Sacacian, *Mng Member*
EMP: 7 **EST:** 2016
SALES (est): 296.9K **Privately Held**
SIC: 2434 Wood kitchen cabinets

(G-10649)
ABC RECYCLERS COLLIER CNTY INC
Also Called: Wholesale Trade
4930 21st Pl Sw (34116-5726)
PHONE.....................239 643-2302
Don Dunmire, *President*
Viola Dunmire, *Vice Pres*
EMP: 5 **EST:** 1999
SQ FT: 14,000
SALES (est): 565.8K **Privately Held**
SIC: 2611 Pulp manufactured from waste or recycled paper

(G-10650)
ABOVE PROPERTY LLC
3555 Kraft Rd Unit 400 (34105-5079)
PHONE.....................239 263-7406
Aaron Shepherd, *CEO*
Steve Lapekas, *COO*
Pete Elhke, *Vice Pres*
Karen Shepherd, *Vice Pres*
Judy Lenart, *Senior Engr*
EMP: 23 **EST:** 2012
SQ FT: 15,310
SALES (est): 2.7MM **Privately Held**
WEB: www.aboveproperty.com
SIC: 7372 5045 Prepackaged software; computer software

(G-10651)
ACTUAL WOODWORKING INC
668 104th Ave N (34108-3227)
PHONE.....................305 606-7849
Duvan E Pineda, *President*
EMP: 8 **EST:** 2013
SALES (est): 155.7K **Privately Held**
SIC: 2431 Millwork

(G-10652)
ADELHEIDIS COMMERCIAL INC
3847 Tamiami Trl E (34112-6201)
PHONE.....................239 384-8642
David Hoffman, *President*
Marion Scheuppenhauer, *Vice Pres*
Jens C Schuppenhauer, *Vice Pres*
EMP: 5 **EST:** 2018
SALES (est): 800K **Privately Held**
SIC: 2099 Food preparations

(G-10653)
ADVANCED SHEET METAL & WELDING
4443 Arnold Ave (34104-3339)
PHONE.....................239 430-1155
Steven Trapasso, *Principal*
EMP: 8 **EST:** 2001
SALES (est): 931.7K **Privately Held**
WEB: advanced-sheet-metal-welding.business.site
SIC: 3444 Sheet metalwork

(G-10654)
AEROESSENTIALS LLC
2335 Tamiami Trl N # 407 (34103-4456)
PHONE.....................239 263-9915
Kenneth W Wingate, *Manager*
EMP: 8 **EST:** 2009
SALES (est): 114.3K **Privately Held**
SIC: 3999 Airplane models, except toy

(G-10655)
AGM KITCHEN & BATH LLC
4384 Progress Ave (34104-7045)
PHONE.....................239 300-4739
Raybert Hernandez Ortis,
EMP: 7 **EST:** 2020
SALES (est): 295.9K **Privately Held**
WEB: www.agmkitchenandbath.com
SIC: 3131 Counters

(G-10656)
AIRCEL LLC
3033 Riviera Dr Ste 101 (34103-2746)
PHONE.....................865 681-7066
Steven E Moellers, *CEO*
▲ **EMP:** 35 **EST:** 1994
SQ FT: 30,000
SALES (est): 4.3MM **Privately Held**
WEB: www.airceldryers.com
SIC: 3563 5084 Air & gas compressors; processing & packaging equipment

(G-10657)
ALBERTOS ON FIFTH
868 5th Ave S (34102-6630)
PHONE.....................239 430-1060
Alberto Varetto, *Principal*
EMP: 8 **EST:** 2011
SALES (est): 533.2K **Privately Held**
WEB: www.albertosonfifth.com
SIC: 3421 Table & food cutlery, including butchers'

(G-10658)
ALL WELD INC
4416 18th Pl Sw (34116-5920)
PHONE.....................239 348-9550
Javier Betancourt, *Principal*
EMP: 7 **EST:** 2015
SALES (est): 54.2K **Privately Held**
SIC: 7692 Welding repair

(G-10659)
ALLIED CIRCUITS LLC
18018 Royal Tree Pkwy (34114-8941)
PHONE.....................239 970-2299
Ralph Bayer, *Principal*
EMP: 7 **EST:** 2015
SALES (est): 129.6K **Privately Held**
WEB: www.alliedcircuits.com
SIC: 3679 Electronic circuits

(G-10660)
ALTERNATIVE COATINGS OF SW FLA
3411 1st Ave Nw (34120-2705)
PHONE.....................239 537-6153
Clint R Cox, *Principal*
EMP: 8 **EST:** 2012
SALES (est): 97.3K **Privately Held**
WEB: www.lawtondentalandimplants.com
SIC: 3479 Metal coating & allied service

(G-10661)
ALTERNATIVE LABORATORIES LLC
Also Called: Shipping Dept
2190 Kirkwood Ave (34112-4702)
PHONE.....................239 732-5337
EMP: 67
SALES (corp-wide): 18.1MM **Privately Held**
WEB: www.alternativelabs.com
SIC: 2834 Vitamin, nutrient & hematinic preparations for human use
PA: Alternative Laboratories, Llc
4740 S Cleveland Ave
Fort Myers FL 33907
239 692-9160

(G-10662)
ALUMINUM DESIGNS LLC
3573 Entp Ave Ste 75 (34104)
PHONE.....................239 289-3388
Vernon Hanks,
Nancy Hanks,
EMP: 6 **EST:** 1999
SALES (est): 484.8K **Privately Held**
WEB: www.aluminiumdesign.net
SIC: 3441 Fabricated structural metal

(G-10663)
AMAZON CLEANING & MORE INC
2015 Morning Sun Ln (34119-3326)
PHONE.....................239 594-1733
Deborah Ward, *Manager*
EMP: 9 **EST:** 2007
SALES (est): 371.1K **Privately Held**
SIC: 2842 Specialty cleaning preparations

(G-10664)
AMAZON ORIGINS INC
5911 Livermore Ln (34119-4626)
PHONE.....................239 404-1818
Jeffrey A Moats, *Principal*
▲ **EMP:** 6 **EST:** 1998
SALES (est): 422.7K **Privately Held**
WEB: www.amazonorigins.com
SIC: 2064 Candy & other confectionery products

(G-10665)
AMERICA MARINE & FUEL INC
895 10th St S Ste 100 (34102-6956)
PHONE.....................239 261-3715
EMP: 7 **EST:** 2008
SALES (est): 650K **Privately Held**
SIC: 2869 Mfg Industrial Organic Chemicals

(G-10666)
AMERICAN BUSINESS CARDS INC
Also Called: Print Avenue
16475 Seneca Way (34110-3280)
P.O. Box 1378, Maryland Heights MO (63043-0378)
PHONE.....................314 739-0800
Mark B Zimmer, *President*
Shane Styker, *Manager*
Janice Zimmer, *Admin Sec*
EMP: 40 **EST:** 1981
SALES (est): 5MM **Privately Held**
SIC: 2759 2796 2791 2789 Thermography; embossing on paper; engraving; platemaking services; typesetting; bookbinding & related work; commercial printing, lithographic

(G-10667)
AMERICAN LED TECHNOLOGY INC
1210 Wildwood Lakes Blvd # 202 (34104-5807)
PHONE.....................850 863-8777
EMP: 12
SALES (est): 1.8MM **Privately Held**
SIC: 3993 1799 Mfg Signs/Advertising Specialties Trade Contractor

(G-10668)
ANARCHY OFFROAD LLC (PA)
2430 Vanderbilt Beach Rd (34109-2654)
PHONE.....................239 919-6681
Brian Collins, *Principal*
EMP: 8 **EST:** 2018
SALES (est): 188.5K **Privately Held**
WEB: www.anarchyoffroad.com
SIC: 3646 Commercial indusl & institutional electric lighting fixtures

(G-10669)
ANNAT INC
Also Called: Municipal Supply & Sign
6203 Janes Ln Ste D (34109-6208)
P.O. Box 1765 (34106-1765)
PHONE.....................239 262-4639
Leonard Ciarrocchi, *President*
Sandy Steinkopf, *Controller*
◆ **EMP:** 11 **EST:** 1962
SALES (est): 1.6MM **Privately Held**
SIC: 3993 Signs, not made in custom sign painting shops

(G-10670)
AP RICHTER HOLDING CO LLC
1617 Gulfstar Dr S (34112-6407)
PHONE.....................239 732-9440
August P Richter, *Principal*
EMP: 12 **EST:** 2009
SALES (est): 804.9K **Privately Held**
SIC: 3399 Primary metal products

(G-10671)
APOLLO METRO SOLUTIONS INC
2975 Horseshoe Dr S # 500 (34104-6103)
PHONE...................................239 444-6934
Ulrich Altvater, *CEO*
Michael Shoaff, *COO*
▲ **EMP:** 10 **EST:** 2012
SALES (est): 739.2K **Privately Held**
WEB: www.apollometro.com
SIC: 3646 3648 3674 Commercial,indust
& institutional electric lighting fixtures;
lighting equipment; street lighting fixtures;
light emitting diodes

(G-10672)
ARCHITCTRAL WDWKG CONCEPTS INC
3863 Entp Ave Unit 2 (34104)
PHONE...................................239 434-0549
Nelson Badilio, *President*
Eulalia Badilio, *Corp Secy*
EMP: 5 **EST:** 1998
SQ FT: 3,000
SALES (est): 400K **Privately Held**
WEB: www.awci.company
SIC: 2512 Upholstered household furniture

(G-10673)
ARCHITCTURAL WD PDTS OF NAPLES
Also Called: Architecture Wood Products
2154 J And C Blvd (34109-2052)
PHONE...................................239 260-7156
Aaron Johnson, *President*
EMP: 5 **EST:** 1978
SQ FT: 4,000
SALES (est): 760.8K **Privately Held**
WEB: www.archwoodproducts.com
SIC: 2431 5211 Millwork; millwork & lumber

(G-10674)
ARTHREX INC (PA)
1370 Creekside Blvd (34108-1945)
PHONE...................................239 643-5553
Reinhold D Schmieding, *President*
Luc Peeters, *General Mgr*
Christopher Corwin, *Counsel*
Lauren Frame, *Counsel*
Tricia Couto, *Vice Pres*
◆ **EMP:** 150 **EST:** 1991
SQ FT: 90,000
SALES (est): 616MM **Privately Held**
WEB: www.arthrex.com
SIC: 3841 Surgical & medical instruments

(G-10675)
ARTHREX CALIFORNIA INC
1370 Creekside Blvd (34108-1945)
PHONE...................................239 643-5553
EMP: 10 **EST:** 1991
SALES (est): 86.6K **Privately Held**
WEB: www.arthrex.com
SIC: 3841 Surgical & medical instruments

(G-10676)
ARTHREX MANUFACTURING INC
1370 Creekside Blvd (34108-1945)
PHONE...................................239 643-5553
Reinhold Schmieding, *CEO*
Bryan King, *Opers Staff*
Kyle Armstrong, *Engineer*
Jon W Cheek, *Treasurer*
John Taylor, *Director*
EMP: 115 **EST:** 2002
SALES (est): 34.6MM
SALES (corp-wide): 616MM **Privately Held**
WEB: www.arthrex.com
SIC: 3841 Surgical instruments & apparatus
PA: Arthrex, Inc.
1370 Creekside Blvd
Naples FL 34108
239 643-5553

(G-10677)
ARTHREX TRAUMA INC
1370 Creekside Blvd (34108-1945)
PHONE...................................239 643-5553
Reinhold D Schmieding, *President*
EMP: 13 **EST:** 2020

SALES (est): 1MM
SALES (corp-wide): 616MM **Privately Held**
WEB: www.arthrex.com
SIC: 3841 Surgical & medical instruments
PA: Arthrex, Inc.
1370 Creekside Blvd
Naples FL 34108
239 643-5553

(G-10678)
ARTISAN WOOD WORKS INC
701 Grove Dr (34120-1420)
PHONE...................................239 321-9122
Yorky Rodriguez, *Branch Mgr*
EMP: 24
SALES (corp-wide): 81.5K **Privately Held**
SIC: 2431 Millwork
PA: Artisan Wood Works Inc
10501 Regent Cir
Naples FL

(G-10679)
ARTISANIS GUILD
1510 Rail Head Blvd (34110-8402)
PHONE...................................239 591-3203
Doug Poe, *General Mgr*
John Pomeroy, *Principal*
Les Faircloth, *Vice Pres*
Mark Bolton, *Project Mgr*
Anthony Sorrell, *Design Engr*
EMP: 9 **EST:** 2013
SALES (est): 404.6K **Privately Held**
WEB: www.thomasriley.net
SIC: 2431 Millwork

(G-10680)
ASG FEDERAL INC
708 Goodlette-Frank Rd N (34102-5644)
PHONE...................................239 435-2200
Arthur L Allen, *President*
EMP: 25
SALES (est): 5.4MM **Privately Held**
SIC: 7372 Prepackaged software

(G-10681)
ATLANTIC WEST MOLDING & MLLWK
4530 Arnold Ave Ste 3 (34104-3344)
PHONE...................................239 261-2874
Kevin Sperry, *Principal*
EMP: 10 **EST:** 2008
SALES (est): 481.9K **Privately Held**
WEB: www.atlanticwestmoldingandmill-work.com
SIC: 2431 Millwork

(G-10682)
ATOMIC MACHINE & EDM INC
1236 Industrial Blvd (34104-3616)
PHONE...................................239 353-9100
Clyde Colburn, *President*
John Neader, *President*
Max Lowther, *Engineer*
Bill Colburn, *CFO*
Jay Minarcin, *CFO*
EMP: 9 **EST:** 1994
SQ FT: 3,575
SALES (est): 2.6MM
SALES (corp-wide): 4.7MM **Privately Held**
WEB: www.atomicmachine.com
SIC: 3451 3429 3484 1623 Screw machine products; aircraft hardware; small arms; oil & gas pipeline construction; aircraft engines & engine parts
PA: Technical Ordnance Solutions, Llc
9495 Puckett Rd
Perry FL 32348
850 223-2393

(G-10683)
AV BYTE
4520 Tamiami Trl N (34103-3001)
PHONE...................................239 262-1290
George Burt, *Principal*
EMP: 7 **EST:** 2010
SALES (est): 167.5K **Privately Held**
SIC: 3651 Electronic kits for home assembly: radio, TV, phonograph

(G-10684)
AVSTAR SYSTEMS LLC
4025 Skyway Dr (34112-2926)
PHONE...................................239 793-5511
Dale Mohrbacher, *Principal*

EMP: 8 **EST:** 2004
SALES (est): 422.8K **Privately Held**
WEB: www.avstardirect.com
SIC: 3634 Electric housewares & fans

(G-10685)
AWL MANUFACTURING INC
4406 Exchange Ave Ste 109 (34104-7024)
PHONE...................................239 643-5780
Ralph Shaw, *President*
Dan Shaw, *Vice Pres*
EMP: 7 **EST:** 1983
SQ FT: 3,500
SALES (est): 642.5K **Privately Held**
SIC: 3561 3825 Pumps, domestic: water or sump; spark plug testing equipment, electric

(G-10686)
AXOP INDUSTRIES INC
5091 Cherry Wood Dr (34119-1445)
PHONE...................................239 273-0911
Christopher Davies, *Principal*
EMP: 7 **EST:** 2008
SALES (est): 106K **Privately Held**
SIC: 3999 Manufacturing industries

(G-10687)
AZT TECHNOLOGY LLC
10130 Market St Ste 7 (34112-3444)
PHONE...................................239 352-0600
Len Zaiser IV, *CEO*
Emeric Robert, *CFO*
EMP: 120 **EST:** 2017
SQ FT: 45,000
SALES (est): 51MM **Privately Held**
SIC: 3541 Machine tools, metal cutting type
PA: Azt Holdings, Llc
10130 Market St Ste 7
Naples FL 34112
239 352-0600

(G-10688)
BALISTIC 2400 LLC
2338 Immokalee Rd Ste 177 (34110-1445)
PHONE...................................407 955-0065
Charles Hager,
EMP: 10 **EST:** 2017
SALES (est): 348.9K **Privately Held**
SIC: 3999 Manufacturing industries

(G-10689)
BALZARANO JOHN
781 14th St Se (34117-3698)
PHONE...................................239 455-1231
Balzarano John, *Principal*
EMP: 11 **EST:** 2005
SALES (est): 352K **Privately Held**
SIC: 2253 T-shirts & tops, knit

(G-10690)
BAR BEVERAGE CTRL SYSTEMS FLA
3427 Exchange Ave Ste 7 (34104-3731)
PHONE...................................239 213-3301
Daniel Richman, *Owner*
EMP: 6 **EST:** 1999
SALES (est): 422.1K **Privately Held**
SIC: 3823 Fluidic devices, circuits & systems for process control

(G-10691)
BAY DESIGN MARINE GROUP INC
2319 J And C Blvd Ste 1 (34109-2009)
PHONE...................................239 825-8094
Joel Arvilla, *Director*
EMP: 8 **EST:** 2005
SALES (est): 172.3K **Privately Held**
SIC: 3669 Sirens, electric: vehicle, marine, industrial & air raid

(G-10692)
BELATRIX SOFTWARE INC
9128 Strada Pl Ste 10115 (34108-2937)
PHONE...................................801 673-8331
Silvana Gaia, *Vice Pres*
Pablo Lecea, *Vice Pres*
Ariel Seoane, *Vice Pres*
Horacio Cappa, *Human Res Dir*
Mart N Alfieri, *Manager*
EMP: 31 **EST:** 2014

SALES (est): 3.6MM **Privately Held**
WEB: www.globant.com
SIC: 7372 Prepackaged software

(G-10693)
BESTPRINTINGONLINECOM LLC
4408 Corporate Sq (34104-4755)
PHONE...................................239 263-2106
EMP: 30
SALES (est): 2.2MM **Privately Held**
SIC: 2752 Lithographic Commercial Printing

(G-10694)
BGT HOLDINGS LLC
200 Aviation Dr N Ste 5 (34104-3501)
PHONE...................................239 643-9949
Bill Bond, *CEO*
EMP: 6 **EST:** 2011
SALES (est): 379.1K **Privately Held**
WEB: www.bgtholdings.com
SIC: 3621 Generators & sets, electric

(G-10695)
BIO FUEL PROFESSIONALS
25 Mentor Dr (34110-1353)
PHONE...................................239 591-3835
Jesse T Goges, *Principal*
EMP: 10 **EST:** 2008
SALES (est): 253.3K **Privately Held**
SIC: 2869 Fuels

(G-10696)
BIOMECH GOLF EQUIPMENT LLC
711 5th Ave S Ste 212 (34102-6628)
PHONE...................................401 932-0479
Frank Fornari, *Principal*
EMP: 10 **EST:** 2014
SQ FT: 2,000
SALES (est): 353.1K **Privately Held**
SIC: 3949 Golf equipment

(G-10697)
BODMAN OIL & GAS LLC
3007 Rum Row (34102-7851)
PHONE...................................239 430-8545
Richard S Bodman, *Manager*
EMP: 9 **EST:** 2005
SALES (est): 904.2K **Privately Held**
SIC: 1389 Oil & gas field services

(G-10698)
BRAINCHILD CORP
3050 Horseshoe Dr N # 210 (34104-7909)
PHONE...................................239 263-0100
Jeffrey Cameron, *President*
Joey Gamble, *COO*
Steven Anderson, *Manager*
Robert Winslow, *Database Admin*
EMP: 16 **EST:** 1991
SQ FT: 5,000
SALES (est): 2.9MM **Privately Held**
WEB: www.brainchild.com
SIC: 7372 3999 5734 Educational computer software; publishers' computer software; education aids, devices & supplies; computer & software stores

(G-10699)
BRIGHTSKY LLC
Also Called: Simplify
1004 Collier Center Way # 2 (34110-8468)
PHONE...................................239 919-8551
Matthew Miller, *Exec VP*
Tod Williams, *Chief Mktg Ofcr*
John Shevillo, *Mng Member*
Mark Hedstrom, *CTO*
EMP: 15 **EST:** 2004
SALES (est): 2MM **Privately Held**
SIC: 3663 Mobile communication equipment

(G-10700)
BROIT BUILDERS INC
Also Called: Broit Lifting
1588 Vizcaya Ln (34113-8638)
PHONE...................................239 300-6900
Troy Broitzman, *President*
Quenby A Broitzman, *President*
EMP: 20 **EST:** 2015
SALES (est): 2.8MM **Privately Held**
WEB: www.broit.com
SIC: 1389 Construction, repair & dismantling services

▲ = Import ▼=Export
◆ =Import/Export

(G-10701)
BURN BY ROCKY PATEL
9110 Strada Pl Ste 6160 (34108-2396)
PHONE..................................239 653-9013
Rocky Patel, *President*
Christina Knight, *General Mgr*
Richie Constancia, *Principal*
Emily Metzger, *Manager*
Kenneth Staudt, *Manager*
EMP: 9 EST: 2012
SALES (est): 847.1K Privately Held
WEB: www.burnbyrockypatel.com
SIC: 3911 5813 Cigar & cigarette accessories; bars & lounges

(G-10702)
CAGE WORKS
1801 Commercial Dr (34112-4751)
PHONE..................................239 707-0847
Salvatore John Iandimarino, *Principal*
EMP: 8 EST: 2005
SALES (est): 144.7K Privately Held
WEB: www.aluminummasterllc.com
SIC: 3448 Screen enclosures

(G-10703)
CANNON T4 INC
188 Price St (34113-8435)
PHONE..................................347 583-0477
Matthew Goulding, *Principal*
EMP: 7 EST: 2011
SALES (est): 199.1K Privately Held
SIC: 3559 Electronic component making machinery

(G-10704)
CARTER DAY HOLDING INC (PA)
27 Casa Mar Ln (34103-3685)
PHONE..................................239 280-0361
Paul W Ernst, *President*
Tim Ryan, *Treasurer*
◆ EMP: 80 EST: 1992
SALES (est): 22.9MM Privately Held
SIC: 3569 3556 Assembly machines, non-metalworking; dairy & milk machinery

(G-10705)
CATALYST ORTHOSCIENCE INC (PA)
14710 Tamiami Trl N # 102 (34110-6208)
PHONE..................................239 325-9976
Carl Oconnell, *President*
Steven Goldberg, *Founder*
Logan Morton, *Design Engr*
Denise Holt, *CFO*
Ryan Bosco, *Controller*
EMP: 9 EST: 2014
SQ FT: 2,400
SALES (est): 1.7MM Privately Held
WEB: www.catalystortho.com
SIC: 3842 Implants, surgical

(G-10706)
CATALYST ORTHOSCIENCE INC
14700 Tamiami Trl N # 26 (34110-6220)
PHONE..................................317 625-7548
EMP: 7
SALES (corp-wide): 1.7MM Privately Held
WEB: www.catalystortho.com
SIC: 3842 Implants, surgical
PA: Catalyst Orthoscience Inc.
14710 Tamiami Trl N # 102
Naples FL 34110
239 325-9976

(G-10707)
CBG BIOTECH LTD CO (PA)
100 Glenview Pl Apt 1003 (34108-3132)
PHONE..................................239 514-1148
Camiener Gerald W, *Mng Member*
Gerald W Camiener, *Mng Member*
EMP: 1 EST: 1995
SQ FT: 4,000
SALES (est): 7.3MM Privately Held
WEB: www.cbgbiotech.com
SIC: 3821 Laboratory apparatus, except heating & measuring

(G-10708)
CEMEX CNSTR MTLS FLA LLC
Also Called: Prospect Avenue Rm
3728 Prospect Ave (34104-3712)
PHONE..................................855 292-8453
Warren Anderson, *Branch Mgr*

EMP: 18 Privately Held
SIC: 1422 Crushed & broken limestone
HQ: Cemex Construction Materials Florida, Llc
1501 Belvedere Rd
West Palm Beach FL 33406

(G-10709)
CENTER FOR BUSINESS OWNERSHIP
956 Glen Lake Cir (34119-2313)
PHONE..................................239 455-9393
Paul Willax, *Owner*
EMP: 5 EST: 2004
SALES (est): 900K Privately Held
SIC: 2731 Books: publishing only

(G-10710)
CENTER FOR VITAL LIVING DBA
2132 Tamiami Trl N (34102-4807)
PHONE..................................239 213-2222
Francis A Oakes, *Principal*
EMP: 10 EST: 2010
SALES (est): 571.9K Privately Held
SIC: 2082 Malt beverage products

(G-10711)
CESIBON
8807 Tamiami Trl N (34108-2525)
PHONE..................................239 682-5028
Mohammad Rahman, *Owner*
EMP: 7 EST: 2008
SALES (est): 260.1K Privately Held
WEB: www.cesibongelato.com
SIC: 2024 Ice cream, bulk

(G-10712)
CHARLES GABLE INC
18511 Royal Hammock Blvd (34114-8947)
PHONE..................................239 300-0220
Charles Gable, *President*
EMP: 6 EST: 2008
SALES (est): 381.7K Privately Held
WEB: charles-gable-inc.business.site
SIC: 3589 High pressure cleaning equipment

(G-10713)
CINCINNATI PRINTING SERVICE
174 Via Perignon (34119-4733)
PHONE..................................239 455-0960
James C Tosti, *President*
EMP: 7 EST: 1997
SALES (est): 87.2K Privately Held
SIC: 2752 Commercial printing, offset

(G-10714)
CL WATERSIDE NAPLES LLC
5455 Tamiami Trl N (34108-2870)
PHONE..................................239 734-8534
Edward W Beiner,
EMP: 10 EST: 2006
SALES (est): 261.7K Privately Held
SIC: 3851 Ophthalmic goods

(G-10715)
CLARIOS LLC
Also Called: Johnson Controls
2900 Horseshoe Dr S # 130 (34104-6127)
PHONE..................................866 866-0886
EMP: 48
SALES (corp-wide): 47.9B Privately Held
WEB: www.clarios.com
SIC: 2531 Seats, automobile
HQ: Clarios, Llc
5757 N Green Bay Ave
Milwaukee WI 53209

(G-10716)
CLASSICA & TELECARD CORP
Also Called: Classica Tlcard Comm Srevices
12355 Collier Blvd Ste C (34116-6027)
PHONE..................................239 354-3727
Inirida Sandoval, *President*
Orlando E Primera, *Vice Pres*
EMP: 7 EST: 2001
SALES (est): 468.9K Privately Held
WEB: www.classicatelecard.com
SIC: 3089 5023 5499 Kitchenware, plastic; kitchen tools & utensils; gourmet food stores

(G-10717)
CLEAN & SHINE AUTO MARINE
4451 Gulf Shore Blvd N (34103-2690)
PHONE..................................239 261-6563
James Williams, *Owner*
EMP: 7 EST: 2006
SALES (est): 145.2K Privately Held
SIC: 2842 Automobile polish

(G-10718)
COLE MACHINE LLC
Also Called: Cole Machine Naples
5740 Shirley St (34109-1814)
PHONE..................................239 571-4364
Lawrence W Cole, *Mng Member*
EMP: 7 EST: 2015
SALES (est): 513.2K Privately Held
WEB: www.colemachinenaples.com
SIC: 3599 Custom machinery

(G-10719)
COLLIER BUSINESS SYSTEMS
2280 Linwood Ave (34112-4738)
PHONE..................................239 649-5554
EMP: 7 EST: 2011
SALES (est): 111.7K Privately Held
WEB: www.colliertaxcollector.com
SIC: 2754 Business form & card printing, gravure

(G-10720)
COUNTER
9110 Strada Pl Ste 6130 (34108-2396)
PHONE..................................239 566-0644
EMP: 13 Privately Held
WEB: www.thecounter.com
SIC: 3131 Counters
PA: The Counter
2901 Ocean Park Blvd # 102
Santa Monica CA 90405

(G-10721)
COUNTERTOP SOLUTIONS INC
3930 Domestic Ave Ste B (34104-3674)
PHONE..................................239 961-0663
Blanca Sauceda, *Principal*
EMP: 5 EST: 2010
SALES (est): 497.5K Privately Held
WEB: www.countertopsolutionsfl.com
SIC: 2541 Counter & sink tops

(G-10722)
CRONUS LITHO LLC
9010 Strada Stell Ct # 103 (34109-4424)
PHONE..................................239 325-4846
Kathleen Conley, *Principal*
EMP: 7 EST: 2015
SALES (est): 213.6K Privately Held
SIC: 2752 Commercial printing, lithographic

(G-10723)
DANS CUSTOM SHEET METAL INC
Also Called: Dcsm
5700 Washington St (34109-1930)
PHONE..................................239 594-0530
Dan Osborne, *President*
Amy Beall, *Manager*
▼ EMP: 25 EST: 1993
SQ FT: 15,000
SALES (est): 4.8MM Privately Held
WEB: www.dcsm.net
SIC: 3444 Metal roofing & roof drainage equipment

(G-10724)
DAVE SILER TRANSPORT
111 14th St Se (34117-3686)
PHONE..................................239 348-3283
David Siler, *Principal*
EMP: 8 EST: 2004
SALES (est): 619.1K Privately Held
SIC: 3531 Construction machinery

(G-10725)
DC KERCKHOFF COMPANY
1901 Elsa St (34109-6219)
P.O. Box 9053 (34101-9053)
PHONE..................................239 597-7218
Daniel C Kerckhoff, *President*
Laura Kerckhoff, *Vice Pres*
Laura H Kerckhoff, *VP Sales*
▼ EMP: 18 EST: 1975
SQ FT: 5,000

SALES (est): 2.7MM Privately Held
WEB: www.kerckhoffstone.com
SIC: 3272 Concrete products, precast

(G-10726)
DEBANIE INC
Also Called: Marble Designs
6631 Sable Ridge Ln (34109-0525)
PHONE..................................239 254-1222
Enrico Piccaluga, *President*
Cathy Piccaluga, *Vice Pres*
▲ EMP: 29 EST: 1984
SALES (est): 2.5MM Privately Held
SIC: 3281 Marble, building: cut & shaped

(G-10727)
DECORATIVE PRECAST LLC
420 Sharwood Dr (34110-5726)
PHONE..................................239 566-9503
EMP: 10
SALES (est): 1.1MM Privately Held
SIC: 3272 Mfg Concrete Products

(G-10728)
DESIGNERS WHL WORKROOM INC
1035 Industrial Blvd (34104-3613)
PHONE..................................239 434-7633
Joe Pla, *President*
Norma Pla, *Vice Pres*
Tammi Chaffee, *Bookkeeper*
Angela Pla, *Executive*
EMP: 10 EST: 1997
SALES (est): 1.1MM Privately Held
WEB: www.dwworkroom.com
SIC: 2211 2591 Draperies & drapery fabrics, cotton; drapery hardware & blinds & shades

(G-10729)
DION MONEY MANAGEMENT LLC
3101 Green Dolphin Ln (34102-7915)
PHONE..................................413 458-4700
Donald R Dion Jr, *Chairman*
EMP: 16 EST: 1995
SQ FT: 12,000
SALES (est): 754.2K Privately Held
SIC: 2741 8742 Miscellaneous publishing; financial consultant

(G-10730)
DISTINCTIVE CABINET DESIGNS
5556 Yahl St Ste A (34109-1944)
PHONE..................................239 641-5165
Renee K Boyce, *President*
EMP: 7 EST: 1993
SQ FT: 4,020
SALES (est): 545.3K Privately Held
WEB: www.distinctivecabinet.com
SIC: 2434 Wood kitchen cabinets

(G-10731)
DIVERSIFIED PUBG & DESIGN
975 Imperl Golf Cours Bld (34110)
PHONE..................................239 598-4826
Anthony Spano, *Owner*
EMP: 9 EST: 2004
SALES (est): 758.3K Privately Held
SIC: 2741 Miscellaneous publishing

(G-10732)
DOLL MAKER LLC
Also Called: Doll Maker, The
11330 Tamiami Trl E (34113-8614)
PHONE..................................800 851-5183
Craig Schoenhals, *Engineer*
Whitney Sties, *Manager*
Linda Rick,
▲ EMP: 6 EST: 1992
SQ FT: 11,000
SALES (est): 609.2K Privately Held
WEB: www.thedollmakerdolls.com
SIC: 3942 Dolls, except stuffed toy animals

(G-10733)
DOMESTIC CUSTOM METALS COMPANY
Also Called: Domestic Metals
4275 Progress Ave (34104-7044)
PHONE..................................239 643-2422
Thomas H Grandy, *President*
EMP: 6 EST: 1985
SQ FT: 7,410

SALES (est): 977.1K **Privately Held**
SIC: 3441 Fabricated structural metal

(G-10734)
EAGLE READY MIX
9210 Collier Blvd (34114-2541)
PHONE..................................239 732-9333
EMP: 7 **EST:** 2015
SALES (est): 133.7K **Privately Held**
SIC: 3273 Ready-mixed concrete

(G-10735)
EBELLA MAGAZINE
5647 Naples Blvd (34109-2023)
PHONE..................................239 431-7231
Sharon L Hood, *Principal*
EMP: 7 **EST:** 2015
SALES (est): 205.5K **Privately Held**
WEB: www.ebellamag.com
SIC: 2721 Magazines: publishing only, not printed on site

(G-10736)
ELITE CABINETRY INC
5435 Jaeger Rd Ste 100 (34109-5802)
PHONE..................................239 262-1144
Amy Rogers, *Owner*
EMP: 8 **EST:** 2006
SALES (est): 1MM **Privately Held**
WEB: www.elitecabinetrynaples.com
SIC: 2434 Wood kitchen cabinets

(G-10737)
ENDURANCE LASERS LLC
8285 Ibis Club Dr 81 (34104-2420)
PHONE..................................239 302-0053
George Fomitichev,
EMP: 12 **EST:** 2019
SALES (est): 417.8K **Privately Held**
WEB: www.endurancelasers.com
SIC: 2759 7389 Laser printing;

(G-10738)
ENERGENICS CORPORATION
1470 Don St (34104-3366)
PHONE..................................239 643-1711
John T Hutterly, *President*
Ingrid Naranjo, *Purch Mgr*
Maryann Hawk, *Controller*
Tim Dunigan, *Executive*
EMP: 25 **EST:** 1974
SQ FT: 12,000
SALES (est): 6.7MM **Privately Held**
WEB: www.energenics.com
SIC: 3564 Filters, air: furnaces, air conditioning equipment, etc.; air purification equipment

(G-10739)
ENGITORK INDUSTRIES LLC
222 Industrial Blvd # 13 (34104-3704)
PHONE..................................239 877-8499
Jasmin Beslija, *Principal*
EMP: 7 **EST:** 2012
SALES (est): 494.9K **Privately Held**
SIC: 3999 Manufacturing industries

(G-10740)
ENTREE MAGAZINE FLORIDA LLC
15275 Collier Blvd # 201 (34119-6750)
PHONE..................................239 354-1245
EMP: 7 **EST:** 2002
SALES (est): 110.7K **Privately Held**
WEB: www.entreemagazine.com
SIC: 2721 Magazines: publishing only, not printed on site

(G-10741)
EVAMPED LLC
13751 Luna Dr (34109-0571)
PHONE..................................614 205-4467
Scott Klabunde, *Principal*
EMP: 7 **EST:** 2017
SALES (est): 246K **Privately Held**
WEB: www.evamped.com
SIC: 3714 Motor vehicle parts & accessories

(G-10742)
EVERAXIS USA INC (DH)
3030 Horseshoe Dr S (34104-6143)
PHONE..................................239 263-3102
Todd Marshke, *President*
Gary Bucholtz, *Treasurer*

Shane Boggs, *Controller*
Miguel Torres, *Info Tech Mgr*
EMP: 13 **EST:** 2015
SALES (est): 16.5MM
SALES (corp-wide): 167.1K **Privately Held**
WEB: www.everaxis.com
SIC: 3674 Semiconductors & related devices

(G-10743)
EVERAXIS USA INC
3030 Horseshoe Dr S (34104-6143)
PHONE..................................239 263-3102
Shane Boggs, *Controller*
Gary Bucholz, *Director*
Todd Marshke, *Admin Sec*
EMP: 77
SQ FT: 44,000
SALES (corp-wide): 167.1K **Privately Held**
WEB: www.everaxis.com
SIC: 3621 3643 3625 Sliprings, for motors or generators; electric switches; relays & industrial controls
HQ: Everaxis Usa, Inc.
    3030 Horseshoe Dr S
    Naples FL 34104
    239 263-3102

(G-10744)
F I B US CORP
3966 Arnold Ave (34104-3302)
PHONE..................................239 262-6070
Ricardo Arias, *President*
EMP: 5 **EST:** 1999
SALES (est): 430.1K **Privately Held**
SIC: 3711 Cars, armored, assembly of

(G-10745)
FANTASY BREWMASTERS LLC
Also Called: FB Beer Company
950 Commercial Blvd (34104-7096)
PHONE..................................239 206-3247
Christopher Guerra, *Manager*
Chris D Guerra, *Manager*
EMP: 7 **EST:** 2009
SALES (est): 108.2K **Privately Held**
WEB: fantasy-brewmasters.myshopify.com
SIC: 2082 Malt beverages

(G-10746)
FEKEL STUCCO PLASTERING INC
3780 29th Ave Sw (34117-8428)
PHONE..................................239 571-5464
Fekel Altimeaux, *President*
EMP: 8 **EST:** 2003
SALES (est): 79.3K **Privately Held**
SIC: 3299 Stucco

(G-10747)
FIVE STAR GURMET FOODS FLA INC
3600 Shaw Blvd (34117-8408)
PHONE..................................239 280-0336
Tal Shoshan, *CEO*
Michelle Eoff, *Exec VP*
Wendy Lemons, *Senior Buyer*
Masha Simonian, *CFO*
EMP: 125 **EST:** 2015
SALES (est): 10.3MM **Privately Held**
SIC: 2099 Ready-to-eat meals, salads & sandwiches

(G-10748)
FLEXIINTERNATIONAL SFTWR INC
856 3rd Ave S Ste 200 (34102-6336)
PHONE..................................239 298-5700
Stefan R Bothe, *Manager*
Spencer Kuo, *Manager*
EMP: 8 **Publicly Held**
WEB: www.flexi.com
SIC: 7372 Application computer software
PA: Flexiinternational Software, Inc.
    2 Trap Falls Rd Ste 501
    Shelton CT 06484

(G-10749)
FOAM MASTERS INC
4506 Mercantile Ave (34104-3361)
PHONE..................................239 403-0755
David Ashenbrener, *President*
Cheryl Ashenbrener, *Vice Pres*

EMP: 28 **EST:** 1996
SQ FT: 23,000
SALES (est): 1.7MM **Privately Held**
WEB: www.foammastersinc.com
SIC: 3086 Insulation or cushioning material, foamed plastic

(G-10750)
FOX INDUSTRIES OF SWFL INC
Also Called: Gutters Unlimited Plus
5701 Houchin St Ste 7 (34109-1901)
PHONE..................................239 732-6199
Brent Fox, *President*
EMP: 18 **EST:** 2011
SALES (est): 701.1K **Privately Held**
SIC: 3999 Manufacturing industries

(G-10751)
FREDERIC THOMAS USA INC
5621 Strand Blvd Ste 301 (34110-7307)
PHONE..................................239 593-8000
Frederic Reimer, *President*
Brian Michalowski, *Vice Pres*
Todd Reimer, *Vice Pres*
Carl Greene, *Engineer*
▲ **EMP:** 10 **EST:** 1998
SALES (est): 1.1MM **Privately Held**
WEB: www.fredericthomasusa.com
SIC: 2731 Books: publishing only

(G-10752)
FRUIT DYNAMICS LLC
4206 Mercantile Ave (34104-3346)
PHONE..................................239 643-7373
Robert Eddy,
EMP: 136 **EST:** 2000
SQ FT: 2,200
SALES (est): 11MM **Privately Held**
WEB: www.incrediblefresh.com
SIC: 2033 Vegetables & vegetable products in cans, jars, etc.

(G-10753)
FUEL AIR SPARK TECHNOLOGY
160 10th St N (34102-6219)
PHONE..................................901 260-3278
Chris Hoffmann, *Controller*
EMP: 10 **EST:** 2005
SALES (est): 537.7K **Privately Held**
WEB: www.fuelairspark.com
SIC: 3089 Automotive parts, plastic

(G-10754)
FUNDAMENTAL MICRO LP
9130 Galleria Ct Fl 3 (34109-4380)
PHONE..................................239 434-7434
Daniel Cerminara, *President*
EMP: 7 **EST:** 2017
SALES (est): 134.6K **Privately Held**
SIC: 2591 Micro blinds

(G-10755)
FUSION INDUSTRIES
1998 Trade Center Way (34109-6260)
PHONE..................................239 592-7070
Trevor Johnson, *Project Mgr*
Scotta Ens, *Engineer*
EMP: 8 **EST:** 2011
SALES (est): 149.6K **Privately Held**
WEB: www.fusionindustriesllc.com
SIC: 3999 Manufacturing industries

(G-10756)
FYI SOFTWARE INC
4850 Tamiami Trl N # 301 (34103-3029)
PHONE..................................239 272-6016
Stefan Bothe, *President*
Nicholas Fusaro, *Sales Dir*
Daniel Lyons, *Sales Staff*
Marc Meyer, *Marketing Staff*
Mina Farag, *Consultant*
EMP: 20 **EST:** 2016
SALES (est): 5MM **Privately Held**
WEB: www.fyisoft.com
SIC: 7372 Prepackaged software

(G-10757)
G AND W CRAFTSMAN LLC
2249 Kirkwood Ave (34112-4713)
PHONE..................................440 453-2770
Warren Hunsicker, *Mng Member*
EMP: 7 **EST:** 2014
SALES (est): 469.9K **Privately Held**
WEB: www.gandwcraftsman.com
SIC: 2499 Decorative wood & woodwork

(G-10758)
GALACTIC NEWS SERVICE
6809 Wellington Dr (34109-7207)
PHONE..................................239 431-7470
Jeffrey Bruce, *Principal*
EMP: 7 **EST:** 2010
SALES (est): 123.3K **Privately Held**
SIC: 2711 Newspapers

(G-10759)
GEM REMOTES INC
Also Called: Gem Inc of Capri
3527 Plover Ave Unit 2 (34117-8439)
PHONE..................................239 642-0873
Jim Muth, *General Mgr*
Richard Shanahan, *Principal*
EMP: 10 **EST:** 1985
SQ FT: 3,000
SALES (est): 2.2MM **Privately Held**
WEB: www.gemremotes.com
SIC: 3519 5084 Controls, remote, for boats; industrial machinery & equipment

(G-10760)
GENEREX LABORATORIES LLC
Also Called: Generex Labs
1915 Trade Center Way (34109-6220)
PHONE..................................239 592-7255
Robert Riess, *CEO*
EMP: 5 **EST:** 2007
SALES (est): 789.3K **Privately Held**
WEB: www.generexlabs.com
SIC: 2833 Medicinals & botanicals

(G-10761)
GETITCLEANED
3520 6th Ave Ne (34120-4983)
PHONE..................................239 331-2891
Christopher Felts, *Principal*
EMP: 10 **EST:** 2010
SALES (est): 1.2MM **Privately Held**
SIC: 3589 High pressure cleaning equipment

(G-10762)
GLOBAL INTRCNNECT SLUTIONS LLC
4522 Executive Dr Ste 103 (34119-9013)
PHONE..................................239 254-0326
Alfredo Ronca,
EMP: 2 **EST:** 2009
SQ FT: 1,500
SALES (est): 5MM **Privately Held**
WEB:
www.globalinterconnectsolutions.com
SIC: 3672 Printed circuit boards

(G-10763)
GLOBALINK MFG SOLUTIONS
3893 Mannix Dr Ste 514 (34114-5417)
PHONE..................................239 455-5166
Jorge Barreto, *Principal*
Byron Chestnut, *Production*
Timothy O 'meara, *Marketing Staff*
▲ **EMP:** 16 **EST:** 2006
SALES (est): 1.4MM **Privately Held**
WEB: www.globalinkmfg.com
SIC: 3841 Surgical & medical instruments

(G-10764)
GOODCAT LLC
1440 Rail Head Blvd Ste 5 (34110-8442)
PHONE..................................239 254-8288
Shawn Hall, *General Mgr*
Brandy Irons, *Production*
Raymond M Keller, *Mng Member*
▲ **EMP:** 37 **EST:** 2009
SQ FT: 34,000
SALES (est): 5MM **Privately Held**
WEB: www.goodcatlabs.com
SIC: 3999 Cigarette & cigar products & accessories

(G-10765)
GRAND WOODWORKING LLC
663 Hickory Rd (34108-2638)
PHONE..................................239 594-9663
EMP: 10
SALES (est): 1.6MM **Privately Held**
SIC: 2431 Mfg Millwork

▲ = Import ▼ =Export
◆ =Import/Export

(G-10766)
GREAT LAKES WTR TRTMNT SYSTEMS
Also Called: Geat Lakes Water Cond Systems
1000 Wiggins Pass Rd (34110-6300)
PHONE...................................269 381-0210
Glenn Rockafellow, *Owner*
EMP: 6 **EST:** 1970
SALES (est): 530.8K **Privately Held**
SIC: 3589 Water purification equipment, household type

(G-10767)
GUARD DOG VALVES INC
14500 Tamiami Trl E (34114-8428)
PHONE...................................239 793-6886
Jerome Guidish, *President*
EMP: 6 **EST:** 2015
SALES (est): 484K **Privately Held**
WEB: www.guarddogvalves.com
SIC: 3491 Automatic regulating & control valves

(G-10768)
GULF COAST AIRWAYS INC
526 Terminal Dr (34104-3570)
PHONE...................................239 403-3020
Joel Johnson, *President*
EMP: 5 **EST:** 1998
SQ FT: 1,000
SALES (est): 419.8K **Privately Held**
WEB: www.gulfcoastairways.com
SIC: 3721 Aircraft

(G-10769)
H H TERRY CO INC
4445 Dunlin Ct (34119-8905)
PHONE...................................239 593-0132
John Bobela, *President*
Thomas G Settineri, *Vice Pres*
EMP: 10 **EST:** 1968
SQ FT: 10,000
SALES (est): 135.8K **Privately Held**
SIC: 3724 3769 Aircraft engines & engine parts; guided missile & space vehicle parts & aux eqpt, rsch & dev

(G-10770)
HALEX CORPORATION
2059 Trade Center Way (34109-6244)
PHONE...................................239 216-4444
Lauren Maxwell, *Principal*
EMP: 9 **EST:** 2008
SALES (est): 258.5K **Privately Held**
WEB: www.halexco.com
SIC: 3423 Hand & edge tools

(G-10771)
HARTMAN ENTERPRISES
14960 Collier Blvd (34119-7713)
PHONE...................................239 200-8998
EMP: 7 **EST:** 2018
SALES (est): 116.7K **Privately Held**
WEB: www.hartmanenterprises.com
SIC: 3599 Machine shop, jobbing & repair

(G-10772)
HEALTHME TECHNOLOGY INC
1250 Pine Ridge Rd (34108-8913)
PHONE...................................888 994-3627
Michael Havig, *CEO*
EMP: 7
SALES (est): 281.3K **Privately Held**
SIC: 7372 Application computer software

(G-10773)
HINCKLEY
535 5th Ave S (34102-6613)
PHONE...................................239 919-8142
Whitney Brackin, *Admin Asst*
EMP: 8 **EST:** 2012
SALES (est): 114.9K **Privately Held**
WEB: www.hinckleyyachts.com
SIC: 3732 Boat building & repairing

(G-10774)
HIPAAT INTERNATIONAL INC
340 9th St N (34102-5803)
PHONE...................................905 405-6299
Terry Callahan, *Managing Dir*
Christine Callahan, *Principal*
Kelly Callahan, *Vice Pres*
EMP: 11 **EST:** 2010
SALES (est): 113.4K **Privately Held**
WEB: www.hipaat.com
SIC: 7372 Application computer software

(G-10775)
HOERNDLER INC
4165 Corporate Sq (34104-4754)
PHONE...................................239 643-2008
Georg Hoerndler, *Principal*
EMP: 9 **EST:** 2007
SALES (est): 403K **Privately Held**
SIC: 2035 Seasonings, meat sauces (except tomato & dry)

(G-10776)
HOME AND DESIGN MAGAZINE
809 Walkerbilt Rd Ste 4 (34110-1511)
PHONE...................................239 598-4826
Tony Spano, *Principal*
EMP: 5 **EST:** 2008
SALES (est): 607.7K **Privately Held**
WEB: www.homeanddesign.net
SIC: 2721 Magazines: publishing only, not printed on site

(G-10777)
HOUSE OF MARBLE & GRANITE INC (PA)
440 Tamiami Trl N (34102-5805)
PHONE...................................239 261-0099
Lewis G Soriero, *President*
Raisa Soriero, *Vice Pres*
EMP: 6 **EST:** 1964
SQ FT: 4,500
SALES (est): 678.5K **Privately Held**
SIC: 3281 Cut stone & stone products

(G-10778)
I M I PUBLISHING INC
425 Cove Twr Dr Apt 1204 (34110)
PHONE...................................615 957-9288
Annie Stivers, *Principal*
EMP: 7 **EST:** 2012
SALES (est): 286.4K **Privately Held**
SIC: 2741 Miscellaneous publishing

(G-10779)
IMI PUBLISHING INC
640 21st St Nw (34120-1812)
PHONE...................................239 529-5081
Angel Jarvis, *Director*
EMP: 8 **EST:** 2012
SALES (est): 418.2K **Privately Held**
SIC: 2741 Miscellaneous publishing

(G-10780)
INDIGO MOUNTAIN INC
4280 Mourning Dove Dr (34119-8867)
PHONE...................................239 947-0023
Yatin Shelar, *President*
Alanna Shelar, *Vice Pres*
◆ **EMP:** 5 **EST:** 1996
SALES (est): 405.8K **Privately Held**
SIC: 2211 5136 Apparel & outerwear fabrics, cotton; men's & boys' clothing

(G-10781)
INDUSTRIAL NANOTECH INC
1415 Panther Ln (34109-7874)
PHONE...................................800 767-3998
George S Burchill, *President*
Francesca Crolley, *President*
Laurie Burchill, *Vice Pres*
EMP: 8 **EST:** 2005
SQ FT: 2,000
SALES (est): 1.3MM **Privately Held**
WEB: www.industrial-nanotech.com
SIC: 3479 Coating of metals with silicon

(G-10782)
INSTORESCREEN LLC
2338 Immokalee Rd (34110-1445)
PHONE...................................646 301-4690
EMP: 7 **EST:** 2012
SALES (est): 612.7K **Privately Held**
WEB: www.instorescreen.com
SIC: 2893 Screen process ink

(G-10783)
INTELLGENT INSTRUMENTATION INC (PA)
Also Called: I3
1421 Pine Ridge Rd # 120 (34109-2116)
PHONE...................................520 573-0887
Richard Daniel, *President*

Robert M Auman, *President*
Paul Liska, *Vice Pres*
Darshan Phillips, *Director*
EMP: 10 **EST:** 1984
SALES (est): 2.1MM **Privately Held**
WEB: www.lanpoint.com
SIC: 3823 Computer interface equipment for industrial process control

(G-10784)
INTERNATIONAL MDSE SOURCES INC (PA)
4551 Gulf Shore Blvd N (34103-2219)
PHONE...................................239 430-9993
John Brooking, *President*
Dennis R Back, *Vice Pres*
▲ **EMP:** 29 **EST:** 2006
SALES (est): 10.9MM **Privately Held**
SIC: 2273 Carpets & rugs

(G-10785)
INTERNATIONAL PACKAGING MCHS
Also Called: I P M
3963 Enterprise Ave (34104-3640)
PHONE...................................239 643-2020
J R Humphrey, *President*
Eileen Curran Lagan, *Vice Pres*
Douglas Arthur, *Project Mgr*
EMP: 8 **EST:** 1962
SQ FT: 21,000
SALES (est): 697.2K **Privately Held**
SIC: 3565 3523 Wrapping machines; farm machinery & equipment

(G-10786)
IPEG CORPORATION
5400 Jaeger Rd Ste 2 (34109-5807)
PHONE...................................239 963-1470
Alan Haddy, *Owner*
Annie Burns, *Manager*
EMP: 11 **EST:** 2012
SALES (est): 1.7MM **Privately Held**
WEB: www.utto.com
SIC: 3823 Temperature measurement instruments, industrial

(G-10787)
IRECO INC
853 Palm View Dr (34110-1242)
PHONE...................................239 593-3749
Peter F Fagan Ptd, *Principal*
EMP: 11 **EST:** 2010
SALES (est): 104.1K **Privately Held**
WEB: www.ireco.com
SIC: 2892 Explosives

(G-10788)
ISLAND PRINT SHOP
3888 Mannix Dr Ste 301 (34114-5408)
P.O. Box 1363, Marco Island (34146-1363)
PHONE...................................239 642-0077
Jeffrey J Biden, *CEO*
EMP: 5 **EST:** 1988
SALES (est): 465.5K **Privately Held**
SIC: 2752 Commercial printing, offset

(G-10789)
JBT LLC
2875 Citrus Lake Dr # 205 (34109-7640)
PHONE...................................513 238-4218
Joseph R Nugent, *Branch Mgr*
EMP: 100
SALES (corp-wide): 2.5MM **Privately Held**
WEB: www.jbtc.com
SIC: 3556 Food products machinery
PA: Jbt Llc
528 W Yale St
Orlando FL 32804
407 463-2045

(G-10790)
JFAURE LLC
Also Called: Coastal Kitchen Interiors
22758 J&C Blvd (34109)
PHONE...................................239 631-5324
Shelly Benfield, *Office Mgr*
Stephen Kilchenstein, *Manager*
EMP: 10 **EST:** 2014
SALES (est): 473.8K **Privately Held**
SIC: 2434 Wood kitchen cabinets

(G-10791)
JOHN S WILSON INC
6222 Parkers Hammock Rd (34112-2992)
PHONE...................................410 442-2400
John S Wilson, *President*
Sue O 'donnell, *Sales Staff*
EMP: 10 **EST:** 2002
SALES (est): 803K **Privately Held**
WEB: www.johnswilson.com
SIC: 2431 Millwork

(G-10792)
JOHNSON & JOHNSON SERVICES INC
5811 Pelican Bay Blvd (34108-2733)
PHONE...................................239 598-4444
John Sarrett, *Branch Mgr*
EMP: 129
SALES (corp-wide): 93.7B **Publicly Held**
WEB: www.jnj.com
SIC: 3842 Surgical appliances & supplies
HQ: Johnson & Johnson Services, Inc.
One Johnson/Johnson Plaza
New Brunswick NJ 08933

(G-10793)
JSI SCIENTIFIC INC
862 105th Ave N Ste 18 (34108-1844)
PHONE...................................732 845-1925
Kathleen V Kuchinski, *President*
EMP: 6 **EST:** 2013
SALES (est): 373.3K **Privately Held**
WEB: www.jsiscientific.com
SIC: 3823 7389 Chromatographs, industrial process type;

(G-10794)
JUST NOW JENNINGS LLC
Also Called: Minuteman Press
6542 Chestnut Cir (34109-7810)
PHONE...................................239 331-0315
Anthony Jennings, *Manager*
EMP: 9 **EST:** 2016
SALES (est): 722.6K **Privately Held**
WEB: www.minutemanpress.com
SIC: 2024 Ice cream & frozen desserts

(G-10795)
K R O ENTERPRISES LTD
Also Called: Printing Unlimited
7950 Preserve Cir Apt 816 (34119-6743)
PHONE...................................309 797-2213
Karen Osterhaus, *President*
EMP: 6 **EST:** 1984
SQ FT: 1,500
SALES (est): 936.6K **Privately Held**
SIC: 2752 3993 2791 2789 Commercial printing, offset; signs & advertising specialties; typesetting; bookbinding & related work; manifold business forms

(G-10796)
KEITH DENNIS MARKHAM
Also Called: Aqua Pure of SW Florida Lc
220 24th Ave Ne (34120-2386)
PHONE...................................239 353-4122
Keith Markham, *Owner*
EMP: 9 **EST:** 2006
SALES (est): 1.3MM **Privately Held**
SIC: 7372 Application computer software

(G-10797)
KENNEDY CRAFT CABINETS INC
5790 Washington St (34109-1930)
PHONE...................................239 598-1566
Mike Kennedy, *President*
EMP: 6 **EST:** 1985
SQ FT: 3,300
SALES (est): 497.5K **Privately Held**
SIC: 2439 5712 Timbers, structural: laminated lumber; customized furniture & cabinets

(G-10798)
KENNETH E KELLER
4110 Entp Ave Ste 116 (34116)
PHONE...................................239 649-7579
Kenneth E Keller, *President*
EMP: 7 **EST:** 2010
SALES (est): 407.2K **Privately Held**
SIC: 2431 Awnings, blinds & shutters, wood

(G-10799)
KM PRECAST INC
7701 Gardner Dr Unit 101 (34109-0639)
PHONE..................................239 438-2146
Kelly R Montgomery, *President*
EMP: 12 EST: 2005
SALES (est): 352.3K **Privately Held**
SIC: 3272 Precast terrazo or concrete products

(G-10800)
LAKE & BAY BOATS LLC
5770 Shirley St (34109-1814)
PHONE..................................813 949-7300
Michael A Del Duca, *Principal*
EMP: 7 EST: 2008
SALES (est): 449.5K **Privately Held**
WEB: www.lakeandbay.com
SIC: 3732 Boat building & repairing

(G-10801)
LED SURF LIGHTING INC
3425 Radio Rd Ste 202 (34104-3758)
PHONE..................................239 687-4458
Leonard Felliciano, *Principal*
▲ EMP: 5 EST: 2013
SALES (est): 477.5K **Privately Held**
WEB: www.ledsurf.com
SIC: 3648 Lighting equipment

(G-10802)
LEISURE FURNITURE POWDER CT
1076 Business Ln Ste 7 (34110-8466)
PHONE..................................239 597-4343
EMP: 7 EST: 2019
SALES (est): 944.2K **Privately Held**
WEB: www.leisurefurniture.net
SIC: 3479 Metal coating & allied service

(G-10803)
LENKBAR LLC
2705 Corporate Flight Dr (34104-3524)
PHONE..................................239 732-5915
Louis Lauch, *Principal*
James Magee, *Prdtn Mgr*
Lauren Schmelzle, *Marketing Staff*
Erik Papenfuss, *Mng Member*
Vicki Dedio, *Manager*
EMP: 60 EST: 2011
SALES (est): 7.8MM **Privately Held**
WEB: www.lenkbar.com
SIC: 3841 Surgical & medical instruments

(G-10804)
LIGHTNING PRTCTION SYSTEMS INC
38818 Exchange Ave (34104)
PHONE..................................239 643-4323
Lance Fleming, *President*
Sandy Langley, *Corp Secy*
EMP: 10 EST: 1974
SQ FT: 1,500
SALES (est): 1.9MM **Privately Held**
WEB:
www.lightningprotectionsystemsinc.com
SIC: 3643 Lightning protection equipment

(G-10805)
LINGA POS LLC (PA)
4501 Tamiami Trl N # 400 (34103-3023)
PHONE..................................800 619-5931
Onur Haytac, *President*
Oscar Fandino, *Manager*
Bob Frazier, *Officer*
EMP: 6 EST: 2004
SALES (est): 2.2MM **Privately Held**
WEB: www.lingaros.com
SIC: 7372 Prepackaged software

(G-10806)
LOKSAK INC
6507 Marbella Dr (34105-5045)
P.O. Box 7127 (34101-7127)
PHONE..................................239 331-5550
Ottavio Cinelli, *Sales Staff*
Ryan Zvibleman, *Executive*
EMP: 7 EST: 1992
SALES (est): 908.2K **Privately Held**
WEB: www.loksak.com
SIC: 2385 Waterproof outerwear

(G-10807)
LOOS & CO INC
Also Called: Cableware Technology Division
901 Industrial Blvd (34104-3715)
PHONE..................................239 643-5667
Tony Carminati, *Materials Mgr*
Chris Albury, *Purch Mgr*
Charlie Hill, *Engineer*
Curtis Schopfer, *Engineer*
Charles Hill, *Plant Engr*
EMP: 80
SQ FT: 100,000
SALES (corp-wide): 97.8MM **Privately Held**
WEB: www.loosco.com
SIC: 3728 3812 3429 Aircraft parts & equipment; search & navigation equipment; manufactured hardware (general)
PA: Loos & Co., Inc.
　16b Mashamoquet Rd
　Pomfret CT 06258
　860 928-7981

(G-10808)
LUPIN ONCOLOGY INC ✪
5801 Pelican Bay Blvd # 5 (34108-2755)
PHONE..................................239 316-1900
Vinita Gupta, *Director*
EMP: 10 EST: 2021
SALES (est): 166.2K **Privately Held**
SIC: 2834 Pharmaceutical preparations
PA: Lupin Limited
　Kalpataru Inspire, 3rd Floor,
　Mumbai MH 40005

(G-10809)
M-BIOLABS INC
Also Called: MBL
1415 Panther Ln (34109-7874)
PHONE..................................239 571-0435
Corey Sandmann, *Principal*
Bria Thamarus, *Exec VP*
EMP: 6 EST: 2016
SALES (est): 330.4K **Privately Held**
WEB: www.mbiolabs.com
SIC: 2836 Biological products, except diagnostic

(G-10810)
MANLEY FARMS INC (PA)
Also Called: Manley Farms North
1040 Collier Center Way # 12 (34110-8480)
PHONE..................................239 597-6416
Kent Manley, *President*
Judy Manley, *Treasurer*
▲ EMP: 5 EST: 1972
SQ FT: 20,000
SALES (est): 4.9MM **Privately Held**
SIC: 3523 Soil preparation machinery, except turf & grounds

(G-10811)
MARBLE BRIDGE INC
3827 Arnold Ave (34104-3301)
PHONE..................................239 213-1411
Onelio Caballero, *Owner*
EMP: 13 EST: 2004
SALES (est): 1.1MM **Privately Held**
SIC: 3499 Fabricated metal products

(G-10812)
MARCH INC
Also Called: March Performance
16160 Performance Way (34110-2224)
PHONE..................................239 593-4074
Kim March, *President*
Craig J March, *Vice Pres*
▲ EMP: 40 EST: 1973
SQ FT: 27,000
SALES (est): 4.9MM **Privately Held**
WEB: www.marchperformance.com
SIC: 3714 Motor vehicle parts & accessories

(G-10813)
MARIOS METALCRAFT
Also Called: Marios Mtalcraft Powdr Coating
4227 Mercantile Ave Ste A (34104-3389)
PHONE..................................239 649-0085
David Heinemann, *Owner*
EMP: 5 EST: 1985
SQ FT: 14,000
SALES (est): 805.8K **Privately Held**
WEB: www.mariosmetalcraft.com
SIC: 3645 3471 Table lamps; chandeliers; residential; plating & polishing

(G-10814)
MARMON AEROSPACE & DEFENSE LLC
Also Called: Cable USA
2584 Horseshoe Dr S (34104-6131)
PHONE..................................239 643-6400
Tim Grass, *President*
EMP: 70
SALES (corp-wide): 354.6B **Publicly Held**
WEB: www.marmon-ad.com
SIC: 3496 Miscellaneous fabricated wire products
HQ: Marmon Aerospace & Defense Llc
　680 Hayward St
　Manchester NH 03103
　603 622-3500

(G-10815)
MC JOHNSON CO
2037 J And C Blvd (34109-6213)
PHONE..................................239 293-0901
Richard Ballo, *Principal*
EMP: 10 EST: 2010
SALES (est): 212.3K **Privately Held**
WEB: www.mcjohnson.com
SIC: 3841 Surgical & medical instruments

(G-10816)
MC OIL AND GAS LLC
4301 Gulf Shore Blvd N (34103-3485)
PHONE..................................239 649-7013
Mitchell Cybulski, *Principal*
EMP: 5 EST: 2017
SALES (est): 447.4K **Privately Held**
SIC: 1389 Oil field services

(G-10817)
MEADOWBROOK INC
Also Called: Meadowbrook Press
970 Egrets Run Apt 102 (34108-2480)
PHONE..................................800 338-2232
▲ EMP: 22
SQ FT: 16,000
SALES (est): 2.3MM **Privately Held**
SIC: 2731 Books-Publishing/Printing

(G-10818)
MEG SYSTEMS INC
2030 River Reach Dr # 138 (34104-5257)
PHONE..................................239 263-5833
Elena Gracia, *President*
Charles Harris, *Vice Pres*
EMP: 5 EST: 1998
SALES (est): 454.1K **Privately Held**
WEB: www.pcmakers.org
SIC: 3825 Network analyzers

(G-10819)
MHKAP LLC
2059 Tamiami Trl E (34112-4636)
PHONE..................................239 919-0786
Matthew Kragh, *Owner*
Gary Blessing, *Director*
EMP: 8 EST: 2018
SALES (est): 1.5MM **Privately Held**
WEB: www.mhkarchitecture.com
SIC: 2599 Hospital beds

(G-10820)
MICRO CMPT SYSTEMS STHWEST FLA (PA)
2553 Longboat Dr (34104-3327)
PHONE..................................239 643-6672
Stephen Meek, *President*
Mary Meek, *Corp Secy*
EMP: 1 EST: 1984
SQ FT: 2,000
SALES (est): 24.5MM **Privately Held**
SIC: 3679 Electronic circuits

(G-10821)
MOLD PROS FRANCHISING INC
3428 Runaway Ln Ste 106 (34114-8440)
PHONE..................................239 262-6653
John Bohde, *President*
EMP: 15 EST: 2016
SALES (est): 1.2MM **Privately Held**
SIC: 3544 Industrial molds

(G-10822)
MOLLYS MARINE SERVICE LLC
895 10th St S (34102-6949)
PHONE..................................239 262-2628
Danny Commers, *Principal*
EMP: 6 EST: 2009
SALES (est): 896.1K **Privately Held**
WEB: www.mollysmarineservice.com
SIC: 2211 Canvas

(G-10823)
MONTAGUE ENTERPRISES INC
Also Called: Activedata
1004 Collier Center Way # 206 (34110-8484)
PHONE..................................239 631-5292
James Montague, *President*
Valerie Montague, *Vice Pres*
EMP: 5 EST: 2010
SALES (est): 407.4K **Privately Held**
SIC: 7372 7371 Prepackaged software; custom computer programming services

(G-10824)
MONTALVOS RACEWAY LLC
280 35th Ave Ne (34120-1874)
PHONE..................................239 289-6931
Oscar Montalvo, *Principal*
EMP: 8 EST: 2013
SALES (est): 404.1K **Privately Held**
SIC: 3644 Raceways

(G-10825)
MONTY SANITATION INC
5545 Shirley St (34109-1809)
PHONE..................................239 597-2486
Robert M Montgomery, *President*
EMP: 5 EST: 1974
SALES (est): 704K **Privately Held**
WEB: www.montysanitationsws.com
SIC: 3272 7699 7359 Septic tanks, concrete; septic tank cleaning service; portable toilet rental

(G-10826)
N MEDIA GROUP LLC (PA)
4500 Executive Dr Ste 320 (34119-8908)
PHONE..................................239 594-1322
Thomas Brown, *Mng Member*
EMP: 25 EST: 1999
SQ FT: 4,000
SALES (est): 3.6MM **Privately Held**
SIC: 2721 Periodicals: publishing & printing

(G-10827)
NAPLES HOTRODS & PRFMCE LLC
6122 Janes Ln (34109-6224)
PHONE..................................239 653-9076
James Hurd, *Principal*
EMP: 7 EST: 2011
SALES (est): 126.9K **Privately Held**
SIC: 3711 Motor vehicles & car bodies

(G-10828)
NAPLES ILLUSTRATED
3066 Tamiami Trl Mre 10 Moore Ste 102 (34102)
PHONE..................................239 434-6966
Fax: 239 435-0409
EMP: 7
SALES (est): 590.6K **Privately Held**
SIC: 2721 Periodicals-Publishing/Printing

(G-10829)
NAPLES IRON WORKS INC
4551 Arnold Ave (34104-3339)
PHONE..................................239 649-7265
James W Sauerwald, *President*
EMP: 20 EST: 1997
SALES (est): 4.9MM **Privately Held**
WEB: www.naplesironworks.com
SIC: 3441 3446 3444 3354 Fabricated structural metal; architectural metalwork; sheet metalwork; aluminum extruded products

(G-10830)
NAPLES POWDER COATING LLC
1141 19th St Sw (34117-4435)
PHONE..................................239 352-3500
Terry L Kelly, *Manager*
EMP: 6 EST: 2019

▲ = Import ▼=Export
◆ =Import/Export

SALES (est): 840.4K **Privately Held**
WEB: www.naplespowdercoating.com
SIC: 3479 Coating of metals & formed products

(G-10831)
NAPLES PRINTING INC
1100 Coml Blvd Ste 114 (34104)
PHONE....................239 643-2442
Michael Couture, *Principal*
EMP: 7 **EST:** 2009
SALES (est): 161.3K **Privately Held**
WEB: www.intechprinting.com
SIC: 2752 Commercial printing, offset

(G-10832)
NAPLES STONE CONSULTING LLC
1881 Trade Center Way (34109-1863)
PHONE....................239 325-8653
Michael Gonzales, *President*
EMP: 11 **EST:** 2016
SALES (est): 1MM **Privately Held**
SIC: 3281 Granite, cut & shaped

(G-10833)
NAPLES WOODWORKS INC
6080 Golden Oaks Ln (34119-1214)
PHONE....................239 287-1632
Theresa M Martin, *Principal*
EMP: 7 **EST:** 2016
SALES (est): 67.1K **Privately Held**
SIC: 2431 Millwork

(G-10834)
NATIONAL CUSTOM TABLE PADS
6030 English Oaks Ln (34119-1328)
PHONE....................239 596-6805
Jerry Goldberg, *Principal*
EMP: 7 **EST:** 2001
SALES (est): 160K **Privately Held**
SIC: 2392 Pads & padding, table: except asbestos, felt or rattan

(G-10835)
NAUTILUS CABINETRY INC
1826 Trade Center Way I (34109-1808)
PHONE....................239 598-1011
Matthew Chadwick, *President*
EMP: 7 **EST:** 2015
SALES (est): 80.7K **Privately Held**
WEB: www.nautiluscabs.com
SIC: 2434 Wood kitchen cabinets

(G-10836)
NGP CORPORATE SQUARE INC
Also Called: Intech Graphics
4408 Corporate Sq (34104-4755)
PHONE....................239 643-3430
David Wacker, *President*
Bob Greenhalgh, *Accounts Exec*
Steve Bello, *Manager*
EMP: 26 **EST:** 1991
SQ FT: 10,000
SALES (est): 3.9MM **Privately Held**
WEB: www.intechprinting.com
SIC: 2752 2791 2789 Commercial printing, offset; typesetting; bookbinding & related work

(G-10837)
NUTRIFUSION LLC
10641 Airport Rd N Ste 31 (34109-7330)
PHONE....................404 240-0030
Myra Grand,
EMP: 9 **EST:** 2017
SALES (est): 1.1MM **Privately Held**
WEB: www.nutrifusion.com
SIC: 2099 Food preparations

(G-10838)
NVIP LLC
2231 Linwood Ave (34112-4737)
PHONE....................469 955-4427
Tony Gaines,
EMP: 8 **EST:** 2020
SALES (est): 574.7K **Privately Held**
WEB: www.nvipllc.com
SIC: 2842 Sanitation preparations, disinfectants & deodorants

(G-10839)
NVS COATING SYSTEMS INC
250 Stanhope Cir (34104-0810)
PHONE....................239 784-3972
Andres Bel, *Principal*
EMP: 9 **EST:** 2015
SALES (est): 113K **Privately Held**
SIC: 3479 Metal coating & allied service

(G-10840)
OBSERVER GROUP AND GULF COAST
2960 Immokalee Rd (34110-1439)
PHONE....................239 263-0122
EMP: 7 **EST:** 2017
SALES (est): 106.5K **Privately Held**
SIC: 2711 Job printing & newspaper publishing combined

(G-10841)
OLD WORLD MARBLE AND GRAN INC
1998 Trade Center Way # 1 (34109-6260)
PHONE....................239 596-4777
Marc Beaudet, *President*
▲ **EMP:** 9 **EST:** 1998
SALES (est): 527.6K **Privately Held**
SIC: 1411 3281 Dimension stone; marble, building: cut & shaped

(G-10842)
OLIVE NAPLES OIL COMPANY (PA)
2368 Immokalee Rd (34110-1446)
PHONE....................239 596-3000
Marilyn J McGinty, *Principal*
EMP: 7 **EST:** 2005
SALES (est): 533.1K **Privately Held**
WEB: www.naplesoliveoilcompany.com
SIC: 2079 Olive oil

(G-10843)
ORACLE SYSTEMS CORPORATION
2640 Golden Gate Pkwy (34105-3220)
PHONE....................650 506-7000
Henry Ong, *General Mgr*
William Cohrs, *Principal*
Jason McKee, *Regional Mgr*
Luis Meisler, *Vice Pres*
Usha Arora, *Vice Pres*
EMP: 23
SALES (corp-wide): 42.4B **Publicly Held**
SIC: 7372 Business oriented computer software; application computer software
HQ: Oracle Systems Corporation
500 Oracle Pkwy
Redwood City CA 94065

(G-10844)
PALLET CREATIONS INC
421 18th St Ne (34120-3642)
PHONE....................239 601-0606
Noel Perodin, *President*
EMP: 7 **EST:** 2018
SALES (est): 102.7K **Privately Held**
SIC: 2448 Pallets, wood

(G-10845)
PALLET DIRECT INC
5660 Cypress Hollow Way (34109-5907)
PHONE....................888 433-1727
Ann Stillwell, *President*
EMP: 5 **EST:** 1997
SALES (est): 368.3K **Privately Held**
WEB: palletdirect34.ueniweb.com
SIC: 2448 7389 Pallets, wood;

(G-10846)
PALM BEACH MEDIA GROUP INC
Also Called: Naples Illustrated
3066 Tamiami Trl N # 102 (34103-2757)
PHONE....................239 434-6966
Cathy Chestnut, *Editor*
Loretta Grantham, *Chief*
Todd Schmidt, *Opers Dir*
Kathy Beuttel, *Sales Executive*
Linda Sciuto, *Mktg Dir*
EMP: 8 **Privately Held**
WEB: www.palmbeachmedia.com
SIC: 2721 Magazines: publishing only, not printed on site

PA: Palm Beach Liquidation Company
1000 N Dixie Hwy Ste C
West Palm Beach FL 33401

(G-10847)
PANDA PRINTING LLC
16010 Old 41 N Unit 102 (34110-8496)
PHONE....................239 970-9727
Patrick B Breen, *Principal*
Douglas Clarke, *Vice Pres*
EMP: 14 **EST:** 2019
SALES (est): 1MM **Privately Held**
WEB: www.panda-printing.com
SIC: 2752 Commercial printing, lithographic

(G-10848)
PAPENFUSS HOLDINGS INC
11430 Tamiami Trl E (34113-7915)
PHONE....................239 775-9090
Hans Papenfuss, *President*
Erik Papan, *Vice Pres*
EMP: 6 **EST:** 1984
SQ FT: 3,000
SALES (est): 775.9K **Privately Held**
SIC: 3544 Industrial molds; special dies & tools

(G-10849)
PARADISE WLDG CSTM FABRICATION
3888 Mannix Dr Ste 310 (34114-5408)
PHONE....................239 961-8864
Kenneth J Marino, *Principal*
EMP: 5 **EST:** 2009
SALES (est): 465.8K **Privately Held**
WEB: www.paradiseweldinginc.com
SIC: 7692 Welding repair

(G-10850)
PARKER-HANNIFIN CORPORATION
Fluid Systems Division
3580 Shaw Blvd (34117-8408)
PHONE....................239 304-1000
John Juliano, *Engineer*
Michael Dill, *Branch Mgr*
Lawrence Tinner, *Technician*
EMP: 24
SALES (corp-wide): 14.3B **Publicly Held**
WEB: www.parker.com
SIC: 3728 3724 Aircraft assemblies, subassemblies & parts; aircraft engines & engine parts
PA: Parker-Hannifin Corporation
6035 Parkland Blvd
Cleveland OH 44124
216 896-3000

(G-10851)
PARTSVU LLC
829 Airport Pulling Rd N (34104-6106)
PHONE....................239 643-2292
Philip Osborne, *Principal*
EMP: 117 **EST:** 2015
SALES (est): 4.2MM
SALES (corp-wide): 1.2B **Publicly Held**
SIC: 3714 5571 Motor vehicle parts & accessories; all terrain vehicle parts and accessories
PA: Onewater Marine Inc.
6275 Lanier Islands Pkwy
Buford GA 30518
678 541-6300

(G-10852)
PEPSI-COLA BOTTLING CO TAMPA
Also Called: Pepsico
1171 Industrial Blvd (34104-3630)
PHONE....................239 643-4642
Matt Edwards, *Branch Mgr*
EMP: 161
SALES (corp-wide): 70.3B **Publicly Held**
WEB: www.pepsico.com
SIC: 2086 Carbonated soft drinks, bottled & canned
HQ: Pepsi-Cola Bottling Company Of Tampa
11315 N 30th St
Tampa FL 33612
813 971-2550

(G-10853)
PFCI LLC
Also Called: Precast Keystone
4610 Enterprise Ave (34104-7014)
PHONE....................239 435-3575
Elio Jacome, *Project Mgr*
Jason Stubell, *Opers Staff*
William Towers, *Mng Member*
Ed Towers,
Gretchen Towers,
EMP: 25 **EST:** 2010
SALES (est): 2.9MM **Privately Held**
SIC: 3272 Concrete products

(G-10854)
PHELPS MOTORSPORTS LLC
2255 Linwood Ave (34112-4737)
PHONE....................239 417-2042
Robert J Phelps,
EMP: 8 **EST:** 2001
SALES (est): 124.3K **Privately Held**
WEB: www.phelps-motorsports.com
SIC: 3711 Automobile assembly, including specialty automobiles

(G-10855)
PHOENIX MOUNTAIN INDS LLC
351 Burnt Pine Dr (34119-9775)
PHONE....................239 348-9895
Frank D Teets Jr, *Principal*
EMP: 7 **EST:** 2010
SALES (est): 123.8K **Privately Held**
WEB: www.phoenixmountain.com
SIC: 3999 Manufacturing industries

(G-10856)
PHOTO FINISHING NEWS INC
Also Called: Photofinishing News
11618 Quail Village Way (34119-8872)
PHONE....................239 992-4421
Don Franz, *President*
George Gamaz, *Vice Pres*
EMP: 6 **EST:** 1983
SQ FT: 1,000
SALES (est): 475.2K **Privately Held**
SIC: 2711 Newspapers: publishing only, not printed on site

(G-10857)
PHYSICIAN HEARING CARE
11121 Health Park Blvd # 700 (34110-5739)
PHONE....................239 261-7722
William Laswski, *Owner*
Taite Seals, *Owner*
EMP: 10 **EST:** 2002
SALES (est): 538.2K **Privately Held**
WEB: www.phctennessee.com
SIC: 3842 Hearing aids

(G-10858)
PICKLE PRO LLC
3527 Plover Ave Unit 2 (34117-8439)
PHONE....................844 332-7069
Todd Pree,
EMP: 7 **EST:** 2013
SQ FT: 4,500
SALES (est): 352K **Privately Held**
SIC: 3949 Rackets & frames: tennis, badminton, squash, lacrosse, etc

(G-10859)
PIONEER DEVELOPMENT ENTPS INC
5901 Shirley St (34109-1817)
PHONE....................239 592-0001
Robert Hunter, *President*
Matthew Hunter, *Principal*
Bryan Hunter, *Vice Pres*
EMP: 16 **EST:** 1999
SQ FT: 7,500
SALES (est): 625.6K **Privately Held**
SIC: 3448 3444 1761 Screen enclosures; sheet metalwork; roofing, siding & sheet metal work

(G-10860)
PK GROUP INC
Also Called: Allegra Naples
3930 Domestic Ave Ste A (34104-3674)
PHONE....................239 643-2442
Paul J Kessen, *President*
Pamela L Kessen, *Vice Pres*
Doug McGilvra, *Prdtn Mgr*
Randy Baily, *Accounts Mgr*

Brenda Devaney, *Manager*
EMP: 18 **EST:** 2009
SALES (est): 2.7MM **Privately Held**
SIC: 2752 8742 3993 Commercial printing, offset; marketing consulting services; signs & advertising specialties

(G-10861)
PLASTIC SPECIALTIES INC
3573 Arnold Ave Ste B (34104-3372)
PHONE..................239 643-0933
Steven Gnerre, *President*
EMP: 18 **EST:** 2004
SALES (est): 3.3MM **Privately Held**
WEB: www.plasticspecialtiesofflorida.com
SIC: 3089 Plastic containers, except foam

(G-10862)
PLC CABINETS INSTALLED LTD
1408 Rail Head Blvd (34110-8421)
PHONE..................239 641-7565
EMP: 8 **EST:** 2018
SALES (est): 714.6K **Privately Held**
WEB: www.plcclosets.com
SIC: 2434 Wood kitchen cabinets

(G-10863)
PMC ENTERPRISES MGMT DIVISION
11216 Tamiami Trl N (34110-1640)
PHONE..................239 949-6566
Patrick F McHugh Jr, *President*
EMP: 15 **EST:** 2004
SALES (est): 2.4MM **Privately Held**
SIC: 3544 Industrial molds

(G-10864)
POHL CUSTOM CABINETRY INC
3601 Arnold Ave (34104-3379)
PHONE..................239 643-5661
Daniel Brister, *Principal*
Dan Brister, *Principal*
EMP: 6 **EST:** 2012
SALES (est): 709.3K **Privately Held**
WEB: www.pohlcustomcabinets.com
SIC: 2434 Wood kitchen cabinets

(G-10865)
PORTALP USA INC
1030 Collier Center Way # 10
(34110-8477)
PHONE..................800 474-3667
◆ **EMP:** 17
SALES (est): 3.1MM **Privately Held**
SIC: 3699 3822 Mfg Electrical Equipment/Supplies Mfg Environmental Controls

(G-10866)
PRO EDGE CUTLERY LLC
Also Called: Pro Edge Paper
4484 Arnold Ave (34104-3340)
PHONE..................239 304-8000
Rudy Ambrosi, *Mng Member*
▲ **EMP:** 8 **EST:** 2005
SALES (est): 1.5MM **Privately Held**
WEB: www.proedgepaper.com
SIC: 2621 Art paper

(G-10867)
PRO-TRIM MILLWORK INC
3995 Upolo Ln (34119-7510)
PHONE..................239 592-5454
Michael Cannivet, *Director*
EMP: 9 **EST:** 2005
SALES (est): 499.7K **Privately Held**
WEB: www.protrimmillwork.com
SIC: 2431 Millwork

(G-10868)
PROGRESS RAIL SERVICES CORP
3581 Mercantile Ave (34104-3309)
PHONE..................239 643-3013
Stephen Hunt, *General Mgr*
Marty Haycraft, *Senior VP*
EMP: 75
SALES (corp-wide): 50.9B **Publicly Held**
WEB: www.progressrail.com
SIC: 3519 5084 3714 Internal combustion engines; fuel injection systems; fuel pumps, motor vehicle

HQ: Progress Rail Services Corporation
1600 Progress Dr
Albertville AL 35950
256 505-6421

(G-10869)
PROLINK SOFTWARE CORPORATION
999 Vanderbilt Beach Rd (34108-3508)
PHONE..................860 659-5928
Bruce Brigham, *Vice Pres*
Charles Marks, *Sales Staff*
Jeff Clews, *Analyst*
EMP: 9 **EST:** 2013
SALES (est): 1.1MM **Privately Held**
WEB: www.prolinksoftware.com
SIC: 7372 Prepackaged software

(G-10870)
Q PLASTERING AND STUCCO INC
5422 Texas Ave (34113-7859)
PHONE..................239 530-1712
Gerard Pierre, *Principal*
EMP: 7 **EST:** 2011
SALES (est): 68.4K **Privately Held**
SIC: 3299 Stucco

(G-10871)
QUALITY LIFE PUBLISHING CO
6210 Shirley St Ste 112 (34109-0268)
PHONE..................239 513-9907
Karla Wheeler, *President*
Anthony Perez, *Production*
Candice Webb, *Administration*
Katie Jensen, *Assistant*
EMP: 9 **EST:** 1999
SALES (est): 1.2MM **Privately Held**
WEB: www.qolpublishing.com
SIC: 2741 8743 8322 Miscellaneous publishing; public relations services; outreach program

(G-10872)
RACING SHELL COVERS LLC
3899 Mannix Dr Ste 409 (34114-5414)
PHONE..................732 236-0435
Alex Grigoriev, *Principal*
EMP: 5 **EST:** 2018
SALES (est): 376.8K **Privately Held**
WEB: www.racingshellcovers.com
SIC: 3069 Fabricated rubber products

(G-10873)
RAS CONCRETE CONSTRUCTION INC
5501 Cynthia Ln (34112-5455)
PHONE..................239 775-3709
Susan G Smith, *President*
Roger Smith, *Vice Pres*
EMP: 23 **EST:** 1976
SQ FT: 7,000
SALES (est): 3.4MM **Privately Held**
SIC: 3272 Concrete products

(G-10874)
RECORDSONE LLC
10641 Airport Rd N Pullingr (34109-7334)
PHONE..................301 440-8119
Steven Bonney, *Exec VP*
Charles Neuenberger, *Mng Member*
Kean Kaufmann, *Software Dev*
Tara Conklin, *Director*
Brent Smith, *Director*
EMP: 16 **EST:** 2014
SALES (est): 1.4MM **Privately Held**
WEB: www.recordsone.com
SIC: 7372 Business oriented computer software

(G-10875)
RICHARD WAGNER LLC
9601 Campbell Cir (34109-4506)
PHONE..................239 450-1721
Richard L Wagner, *Principal*
Richard Wagner, *Principal*
EMP: 5 **EST:** 2010
SALES (est): 320.7K **Privately Held**
SIC: 2679 Wallpaper

(G-10876)
RICHTER INDUSTRIES INC
1617 Gulfstar Dr S (34112-6407)
PHONE..................239 732-9440
August Richter, *Principal*

EMP: 8
SALES (corp-wide): 3.9MM **Privately Held**
WEB: www.richterindustries.net
SIC: 3999 Atomizers, toiletry
PA: Richter Industries, Inc.
4910 70th Ave
Kenosha WI 53144
262 656-0097

(G-10877)
RITTER KIT BATH & CLOSET LLC
4870 Tallowood Way (34116-5002)
PHONE..................239 272-4551
Chuck Ritter,
EMP: 9 **EST:** 2007
SALES (est): 343.5K **Privately Held**
WEB: www.kbcnaples.com
SIC: 2434 Wood kitchen cabinets

(G-10878)
RMMJ INC
Also Called: Monty Sanitation
5545 Shirley St (34109-1809)
PHONE..................239 597-2486
Robert M Montgomery Jr, *Principal*
EMP: 23 **EST:** 2002
SALES (est): 844.6K **Privately Held**
SIC: 3272 Precast terrazo or concrete products

(G-10879)
ROBERT E WEISSENBORN SR (PA)
Also Called: Naples Armature Works
1101 5th Ave S (34102-6415)
PHONE..................239 262-1771
R E Weissenborn Jr, *Co-Owner*
Janet Blumert, *Co-Owner*
Irene Weissenborn, *Co-Owner*
Robert E Weissenborn Jr, *Co-Owner*
EMP: 6 **EST:** 1948
SQ FT: 11,400
SALES (est): 912.9K **Privately Held**
WEB: www.naplesarmature.com
SIC: 7694 5083 5063 7699 Electric motor repair; irrigation equipment; motors, electric; pumps & pumping equipment repair; power transmission equipment & apparatus

(G-10880)
SAFEBOOT CORP
2640 Golden Gate Pkwy # 1 (34105-3220)
PHONE..................239 298-7000
Gerhard Watzinger, *CEO*
Frank Jorissen, *Vice Pres*
Eric Sommerton, *Vice Pres*
Piet Weijers, *CFO*
Simon Hunt, *CTO*
EMP: 55 **EST:** 1991
SQ FT: 100,000
SALES (est): 7.3MM
SALES (corp-wide): 1.9B **Privately Held**
SIC: 7372 Prepackaged software
HQ: Mcafee, Llc
6220 America Center Dr
San Jose CA 95002

(G-10881)
SALVIA TILE & STONE INC
303 Airport Pulling Rd N (34104-3507)
PHONE..................239 643-7770
Gerardo Salvia, *President*
David Wood, *Vice Pres*
Steve Cushing, *Treasurer*
Joann Salvia, *Admin Sec*
◆ **EMP:** 12 **EST:** 2005
SQ FT: 16,000
SALES (est): 558K **Privately Held**
WEB: www.salviastone.com
SIC: 2541 5032 Counter & sink tops; ceramic wall & floor tile

(G-10882)
SAMARIAN PRODUCTS LLC
780 Fifth Ave S Ste 200 (34102-6632)
PHONE..................212 781-2121
Alfred Zaccagnino, *Mng Member*
Mark Schneider, *Mng Member*
EMP: 20 **EST:** 2020
SALES (est): 40MM **Privately Held**
SIC: 2842 2326 Sanitation preparations, disinfectants & deodorants; medical & hospital uniforms, men's

(G-10883)
SANO ASSOCIATES INC
Also Called: High Velocity
3827 Progress Ave (34104-3647)
PHONE..................239 403-2650
Steven Camposano, *President*
Jean Camposano, *Treasurer*
Matt Poinsett, *Sales Staff*
EMP: 34 **EST:** 1994
SQ FT: 30,000
SALES (est): 6.2MM **Privately Held**
WEB: www.category5.com
SIC: 3442 Shutters, door or window: metal

(G-10884)
SARA GLOVE COMPANY INC
7935 Airprt Pulling N Ste (34109)
PHONE..................866 664-7272
Sara Delio, *President*
Joseph Delio, *COO*
EMP: 8 **EST:** 2018
SQ FT: 1,500
SALES (est): 6.4MM **Privately Held**
WEB: www.saraglove.com
SIC: 2385 3151 5099 Waterproof outerwear; gloves, leather: work; safety equipment & supplies

(G-10885)
SAW PALMETTO BERRIES COOPERATI
7440 Friendship Ln (34120-2459)
PHONE..................239 775-4286
EMP: 7 **EST:** 2015
SALES (est): 565.5K **Privately Held**
WEB: www.sawpalmettoflorida.com
SIC: 2834 Vitamin, nutrient & hematinic preparations for human use

(G-10886)
SAW PALMETTO FLORIDA LLC
7440 Friendship Ln (34120-2459)
PHONE..................239 775-4286
Zlatko Altiparmakov,
EMP: 13 **EST:** 2017
SALES (est): 1MM **Privately Held**
WEB: www.sawpalmettoflorida.com
SIC: 2834 Vitamin, nutrient & hematinic preparations for human use

(G-10887)
SCALABLE SOFTWARE INC
2060 Painted Palm Dr (34119-3372)
PHONE..................239 603-7090
Ryan Rafaloff, *Principal*
EMP: 12 **EST:** 2010
SALES (est): 120K **Privately Held**
WEB: www.scalable.com
SIC: 7372 Prepackaged software

(G-10888)
SCHOOL-ON-WHEELS
13520 Tamiami Trl E (34114-8703)
PHONE..................239 530-8522
Patricia Brennan, *Manager*
EMP: 10 **EST:** 2011
SALES (est): 150K **Privately Held**
WEB: www.schoolonwheels.org
SIC: 3312 Wheels

(G-10889)
SENTINEL INC
Also Called: Sentinel Storm Protection
3673 Exchange Ave Ste 1 (34104-3743)
PHONE..................239 263-9888
Mike Marczak, *President*
EMP: 17 **EST:** 2002
SALES (est): 2.7MM **Privately Held**
WEB: www.sentinelstormprotection.com
SIC: 3442 Shutters, door or window: metal

(G-10890)
SHELFGENIE
16422 Carrara Way # 102 (34110-3286)
PHONE..................877 814-3643
EMP: 7 **EST:** 2013
SALES (est): 109.6K **Privately Held**
WEB: www.shelfgenie.com
SIC: 2511 Wood household furniture

(G-10891)
SHUTTERMAN STORM & SECURITY
751 4th St Ne (34120-2024)
PHONE..................239 455-9166

Curt Barnicle, *President*
Carol Barnicle, *Office Mgr*
Dennis Barnicle, *Admin Sec*
EMP: 22 **EST:** 1998
SALES (est): 1.1MM **Privately Held**
WEB: www.myshutterman.com
SIC: 2431 7699 Door shutters, wood; door
& window repair

(G-10892)
SIC PRODUCTS LLC
5130 Kristin Ct (34105-2113)
PHONE..............................904 374-2639
Erik D Howe, *Mng Member*
Robert Harrington,
EMP: 7 **EST:** 2015
SALES (est): 490.8K **Privately Held**
SIC: 2656 Paper cups, plates, dishes &
utensils

(G-10893)
SIGNARAMA NAPLES
Also Called: Sign-A-Rama
1095 5th Ave N (34102-5818)
PHONE..............................239 330-3737
Marc Estes, *Principal*
EMP: 7 **EST:** 2015
SALES (est): 139.1K **Privately Held**
WEB: www.signarama.com
SIC: 3993 Signs & advertising specialties

(G-10894)
SIMPLY CUPCAKES
2490 Outrigger Ln (34104-6905)
PHONE..............................239 262-5184
Kenneth Glasgow, *Principal*
EMP: 7 **EST:** 2007
SALES (est): 164.3K **Privately Held**
SIC: 2051 Bread, cake & related products

(G-10895)
SMDK CORP
4802 Kittiwake Ct (34119-8864)
PHONE..............................239 444-1736
Addison M Fischer, *Ch of Bd*
Michael S Battaglia, *President*
Steve Armfield, *Vice Pres*
Charles Klinker, *Vice Pres*
Anderw Warner, *CFO*
▲ **EMP:** 20 **EST:** 1997
SQ FT: 27,000
SALES (est): 1.3MM **Privately Held**
WEB: www.smdkcorp.com
SIC: 3577 7372 Computer peripheral
equipment; prepackaged software

(G-10896)
SOSUMI HOLDINGS INC
Also Called: Intech Printing & Direct Mail
4408 Corporate Sq (34104-4755)
PHONE..............................239 634-3430
Rodney Held, *CEO*
Dale Haddad, *CFO*
EMP: 23 **EST:** 2015
SQ FT: 15,000
SALES (est): 2.5MM **Privately Held**
WEB: www.intechprinting.com
SIC: 2732 2752 Books: printing & binding;
commercial printing, offset

(G-10897)
**SOUTHEAST PUBLISHING CO
INC (PA)**
Also Called: Southeast Food Service News
2539 Avila Ln (34105-3059)
PHONE..............................239 213-1277
Dal Rasmussen, *President*
Elliott Fischer, *Admin Sec*
EMP: 6 **EST:** 1976
SALES (est): 683.5K **Privately Held**
WEB: www.sfsn.com
SIC: 2711 Newspapers

(G-10898)
SOUTHERN LITHO II LLC
9010 Strada Stell Ct # 103 (34109-4425)
PHONE..............................724 394-3693
Daniel J Conley, *Principal*
EMP: 21 **EST:** 2012
SALES (est): 4.3MM **Privately Held**
WEB: www.northernlitho.com
SIC: 2752 Commercial printing, litho-
graphic

(G-10899)
**SOUTHWEST CUSTOM
COATINGS INC**
4498 22nd Ave Se (34117-9277)
PHONE..............................239 682-9462
Stone Vance H, *Principal*
EMP: 7 **EST:** 2014
SALES (est): 223.1K **Privately Held**
SIC: 3479 Metal coating & allied service

(G-10900)
SOUTHWEST WOODWORK INC
429 Production Blvd (34104-4724)
PHONE..............................239 213-0126
Sherrad Reites, *President*
Sherrad J Reites, *President*
EMP: 14 **EST:** 1980
SQ FT: 10,000
SALES (est): 966.4K **Privately Held**
WEB: www.southwestwoodwork.com
SIC: 2431 1751 5712 8712 Millwork;
cabinet building & installation; custom
made furniture, except cabinets; architec-
tural services

(G-10901)
**SPACEMAKERS CLOSETS SW
FLA INC**
2044 J And C Blvd (34109-6214)
PHONE..............................239 598-0222
Mark A Delashmet, *Vice Pres*
EMP: 14 **EST:** 2011
SALES (est): 279.6K **Privately Held**
SIC: 2434 Wood kitchen cabinets

(G-10902)
SPECIAL COATINGS INC
6210 Shirley St Ste 105 (34109-6258)
PHONE..............................239 301-2714
Douglas A Treadwell, *President*
EMP: 7 **EST:** 2015
SALES (est): 152.5K **Privately Held**
WEB: www.special-coatings.com
SIC: 3479 Coating of metals & formed
products

(G-10903)
SPECTRUM SIGNWORKS LLC
2920 Leonardo Ave (34119-7723)
PHONE..............................239 908-0505
Scott Levy, *CEO*
EMP: 6 **EST:** 2014
SALES (est): 504.1K **Privately Held**
WEB: www.signarama.com
SIC: 3993 Signs & advertising specialties

(G-10904)
**SPOT-ON WLDG MET
FBRCATION LLC**
2365 14th Ave Ne (34120-4015)
PHONE..............................239 825-7452
Helvaci Armahan, *Principal*
EMP: 7 **EST:** 2016
SALES (est): 484.5K **Privately Held**
SIC: 3499 Fabricated metal products

(G-10905)
ST MARYS CABINETRY INC
4660 22nd Ave Se (34117-9439)
PHONE..............................239 331-1030
Trevor A Chambers, *Principal*
EMP: 8 **EST:** 2011
SALES (est): 147.8K **Privately Held**
SIC: 2434 Wood kitchen cabinets

(G-10906)
STEVE UNSER CABINETRY INC
5550 Shirley St (34109-1869)
PHONE..............................239 631-2951
Steve M Unser, *Principal*
EMP: 10 **EST:** 2015
SALES (est): 341.5K **Privately Held**
WEB: www.steveunsercabinetry.com
SIC: 2434 Wood kitchen cabinets

(G-10907)
STONELIGHT LLC
4775 Aston Gardens Way # 205
(34109-3573)
PHONE..............................239 514-3272
Dick Metchear, *CEO*
Betsy Piper, *CFO*
Elizabeth Piper, *CFO*
EMP: 7 **EST:** 2009

SALES (est): 628.3K **Privately Held**
WEB: www.stonelight.com
SIC: 3648 Lighting equipment

(G-10908)
**STRUCTURE MEDICAL LLC
(HQ)**
9935 Business Cir (34112-3317)
PHONE..............................239 262-5551
Paul Goldman, *Vice Pres*
Dean McCann, *Vice Pres*
Edison Tungpalan, *Vice Pres*
Daniel Dipalma, *Prdtn Mgr*
Mark Gilbert, *Prdtn Mgr*
▼ **EMP:** 70 **EST:** 2008
SQ FT: 30,000
SALES (est): 50MM **Privately Held**
WEB: www.structuremedical.com
SIC: 3842 Orthopedic appliances

(G-10909)
**SUMMIT ORTHOPEDIC TECH
INC**
2975 Horseshoe Dr S # 100 (34104-6153)
PHONE..............................239 919-8081
Adam Ferrell, *President*
Jason Blake, *COO*
Ron Dunn, *Vice Pres*
EMP: 45 **EST:** 2014
SALES (est): 2.5MM **Privately Held**
WEB: www.summit.tech
SIC: 3841 Surgical & medical instruments

(G-10910)
SUNBELT USA INC
132 Vista Ln (34119-4666)
PHONE..............................239 353-5519
S John Conti, *President*
Ryan J Conti, *Director*
Randi C Ordetx, *Director*
EMP: 13 **EST:** 2007
SALES (est): 1.8MM **Privately Held**
WEB: www.sunbeltusa.net
SIC: 2752 Commercial printing, offset

(G-10911)
SUNCOAST FABRICS INC
Also Called: Suncoast Window Fashion
5400 Yahl St Ste A (34109-1910)
PHONE..............................239 566-3313
Barbara M Minkler, *President*
Allen M Minkler, *Vice Pres*
EMP: 8 **EST:** 1981
SALES (est): 238.6K **Privately Held**
SIC: 2391 Draperies, plastic & textile: from
purchased materials

(G-10912)
SUNFLEX WALL SYSTEMS LP
1494 Pacaya Cv (34119-3367)
PHONE..............................239 220-1570
▲ **EMP:** 9 **EST:** 2008
SALES (est): 537.9K **Privately Held**
WEB: www.sunflex-aluminiumsystems.com
SIC: 3089 Fiberglass doors

(G-10913)
SUNLUVER SMOOTHIES INC
160 12th Ave Nw (34120-2305)
PHONE..............................239 331-5431
Krista Lefchak, *Principal*
EMP: 7 **EST:** 2007
SALES (est): 94.9K **Privately Held**
SIC: 2037 Frozen fruits & vegetables

(G-10914)
SUNMASTER OF NAPLES INC
900 Industrial Blvd (34104-3612)
PHONE..............................239 261-3581
John H Wilkinson, *President*
William Mitchell, *General Mgr*
David J Rinker, *Vice Pres*
David Rinker, *Vice Pres*
Tom Napierkowski, *Purch Mgr*
EMP: 40 **EST:** 1969
SQ FT: 23,000
SALES (est): 6.4MM **Privately Held**
WEB: www.sunmasterinc.com
SIC: 3357 5999 5031 Aircraft wire &
cable, nonferrous; awnings; doors, combi-
nation, screen-storm

(G-10915)
**SUPERIOR CHROME PLATING
INC**
861 101st Ave N (34108-3208)
PHONE..............................832 659-0873
Robert L Baker, *President*
EMP: 10 **EST:** 2002
SALES (est): 622.9K **Privately Held**
WEB: www.justchromeit.com
SIC: 3471 Plating of metals or formed
products

(G-10916)
SWEET TREATS
7935 Airprt Plng Rd N 1 Ste 11 (34109)
PHONE..............................239 598-3311
EMP: 7
SALES (est): 458.9K **Privately Held**
SIC: 2024 Mfg Ice Cream/Frozen Desert

(G-10917)
SWEETREATS OF NAPLES INC
7935 Airport Pulling Rd N (34109-1732)
PHONE..............................239 598-3311
EMP: 8
SALES (est): 310K **Privately Held**
SIC: 2024 Mfg Ice Cream/Frozen Desert

(G-10918)
SYNERGY SPORTS LLC
Also Called: Naples Team Sports Center
6300 Taylor Rd (34109-1841)
PHONE..............................239 593-9374
Kurt Swiderski,
Beth Swiderski,
EMP: 7 **EST:** 1984
SQ FT: 10,200
SALES (est): 744.5K **Privately Held**
WEB: www.synergysports.com
SIC: 2396 5941 Screen printing on fabric
articles; sporting goods & bicycle shops

(G-10919)
TACO MIX CORP
1740 Wilson Blvd N (34120-2339)
PHONE..............................239 498-9448
Yadil Caceres, *Principal*
EMP: 7 **EST:** 2007
SALES (est): 84.5K **Privately Held**
SIC: 3273 Ready-mixed concrete

(G-10920)
TALARIA COMPANY LLC
3450 Westview Dr Unit 11 (34104-4293)
PHONE..............................239 261-2870
Don Brophy, *Sales Staff*
Jack Erbes, *Branch Mgr*
EMP: 90
SALES (corp-wide): 110.7MM **Privately
Held**
WEB: www.hinckleyyachts.com
SIC: 3732 Yachts, building & repairing
PA: The Talaria Company Llc
1 Little Harbor Lndg
Portsmouth RI 02871
401 683-7100

(G-10921)
**TE OLDE FOUNDRY SHOPPE
INC**
4573 Exchange Ave Ste 7 (34104-7027)
PHONE..............................239 261-3911
Doug Howard, *President*
EMP: 7 **EST:** 2004
SALES (est): 120.9K **Privately Held**
WEB: www.yeoldefoundryshoppeoffla.com
SIC: 3354 Aluminum extruded products

(G-10922)
TECHTRON CORPORATION
1400 Rail Head Blvd (34110-8421)
PHONE..............................239 513-0800
Samuel Freedland, *President*
EMP: 14 **EST:** 1989
SALES (est): 1.4MM **Privately Held**
WEB: www.techtroncorporation.com
SIC: 3825 Instruments to measure electric-
ity

(G-10923)
TESCO OF SWFL INC
Also Called: American Led Technology
3992 Prospect Ave Ste C (34104-3725)
PHONE..............................239 234-6490
Steven Pursley, *President*

EMP: 9 **EST:** 2017
SALES (est): 720.8K **Privately Held**
WEB: www.swfinc.com
SIC: 3674 Light emitting diodes

(G-10924)
THOMAS A GLASSMAN LLC
3840 7th Ave Nw (34120-1614)
PHONE..................................239 822-2219
Thomas A Glassman, *Manager*
EMP: 7 **EST:** 2010
SALES (est): 206.8K **Privately Held**
SIC: 3423 Carpenters' hand tools, except
saws: levels, chisels, etc.

(G-10925)
THOMAS RLEY ARTISANS GUILD INC (PA)
Also Called: Hyland Custom Cabinetry
1510 Rail Head Blvd (34110-8402)
PHONE..................................239 591-3203
Matthew Riley, *CEO*
Thomas S Riley III, *CEO*
Benjamin T Riley, *President*
Ben Riley, *COO*
Richard Schalk, *VP Opers*
EMP: 49 **EST:** 1991
SQ FT: 21,000
SALES (est): 12.7MM **Privately Held**
WEB: www.thomasriley.net
SIC: 2434 2435 2436 2511 Wood kitchen
cabinets; hardwood veneer & plywood;
softwood veneer & plywood; wood house-
hold furniture; millwork; doors, wood; resi-
dential construction

(G-10926)
THOMPSONS ARPRT HNGER SVCS LLC
11622 Laertes Ln (34114-7525)
PHONE..................................239 825-7466
Deborah L Thompson, *Principal*
EMP: 6 **EST:** 2015
SALES (est): 409.8K **Privately Held**
SIC: 1389 Oil & gas field services

(G-10927)
TIMBERCRAFT OF NAPLES INC
802 Tallow Tree Ct (34108-8207)
PHONE..................................239 566-2559
Richard Daniel, *President*
EMP: 9 **EST:** 1991
SALES (est): 880.1K **Privately Held**
SIC: 2431 1799 Blinds (shutters), wood;
window treatment installation

(G-10928)
TOPHET-BLYTH LLC
1415 Panther Ln Ste 402 (34109-7874)
PHONE..................................239 594-5477
Kenneth D Mac Alpine, *Principal*
▲ **EMP:** 11 **EST:** 2008
SALES (est): 481.5K **Privately Held**
WEB: www.tophet.com
SIC: 3549 Marking machines, metalwork-
ing

(G-10929)
UNITED ABRASIVES INC
3551 Westview Dr (34104-4045)
PHONE..................................239 300-0033
Eric Marcialli, *President*
EMP: 16
SALES (corp-wide): 32.5MM **Privately
Held**
WEB: www.unitedabrasives.com
SIC: 3291 Abrasive products
PA: United Abrasives, Inc.
185 Boston Post Rd
North Windham CT 06256
860 456-7131

(G-10930)
UNITED DRONES LLC
9146 Quartz Ln (34120-4368)
PHONE..................................305 978-1480
Harrison Hubschman, *Principal*
Gary Brecka, *Principal*
Chris Knott, *Principal*
Curt Winter, *Principal*
EMP: 8 **EST:** 2012
SALES (est): 200.4K **Privately Held**
WEB: www.uniteddrones.com
SIC: 3761 Rockets, space & military, com-
plete

(G-10931)
UPTOWN CSTM CABINETS OF NAPLES
6260 Shirley St Ste 603 (34109-6257)
PHONE..................................239 825-8432
Aaron Elbe, *President*
EMP: 9 **EST:** 2007
SALES (est): 575.7K **Privately Held**
WEB: www.uptowncustomcabinets.com
SIC: 2434 Wood kitchen cabinets

(G-10932)
VET-EQUIP LLC
999 Vanderbilt Beach Rd # 200
(34108-3508)
PHONE..................................239 537-3402
Robert Gibbs,
Courtney McCoy, *Administration*
EMP: 5 **EST:** 2013
SQ FT: 400
SALES (est): 420K **Privately Held**
WEB: www.vetequip.com
SIC: 3751 7352 Bicycles & related parts;
medical equipment rental

(G-10933)
VFINITY INC
837 5th Ave S Ste 200 (34102-6660)
P.O. Box 1949 (34106-1949)
PHONE..................................239 244-2555
Murray Polischuk, *Principal*
EMP: 12 **EST:** 2014
SALES (est): 2.7MM **Privately Held**
WEB: www.vfinity.com
SIC: 7372 Prepackaged software

(G-10934)
VIENNA BEAUTY PRODUCTS CO (PA)
Also Called: White Cross Supply Co
222 Harbour Dr Apt 100 (34103-4071)
PHONE..................................937 228-7109
Timothy K Miller, *President*
Robert H Miller Sr, *Treasurer*
EMP: 13 **EST:** 1956
SQ FT: 20,000
SALES (est): 1MM **Privately Held**
SIC: 2844 Face creams or lotions

(G-10935)
VINYL LETTERING AND SIGNS
1315 Wildwood Lakes Blvd # 8
(34104-6421)
PHONE..................................239 537-7355
Jorge Casas, *Principal*
EMP: 7 **EST:** 2017
SALES (est): 46K **Privately Held**
SIC: 3993 Signs & advertising specialties

(G-10936)
VOGUE AEROSPACE & DEFENSE INC
1712 Commercial Dr (34112-4752)
PHONE..................................321 289-0872
Michael Ressa, *Principal*
Travis Matthew, *Principal*
Giuseppe Ressa, *Principal*
EMP: 5 **EST:** 2019
SALES (est): 337K **Privately Held**
WEB: www.vogueaerospace.com
SIC: 3721 Aircraft

(G-10937)
WESTVIEW CORP INC
Also Called: Screen Printing Unlimited
3419 Westview Dr (34104-4042)
PHONE..................................239 643-5699
John D Dick, *President*
Nancy J Dick, *Vice Pres*
Nancy Dick, *Vice Pres*
Jason Marshall, *Graphic Designe*
EMP: 6 **EST:** 1994
SQ FT: 3,200
SALES (est): 1.1MM **Privately Held**
WEB: www.screenprintingunlimited.com
SIC: 2759 Screen printing

(G-10938)
WHOLESALE SCREEN PRTG NPLES IN
3584 Mercantile Ave Ste B (34104-3381)
PHONE..................................239 263-7061
Dustin Goeggle, *President*
Perrin Kelley, *Tech Recruiter*
EMP: 5 **EST:** 1989

SQ FT: 2,000
SALES (est): 994.1K **Privately Held**
WEB: www.wholescreenprinting.com
SIC: 2759 3953 Screen printing; screens,
textile printing

(G-10939)
WILLS PRESTRESS INC
680 31st St Sw (34117-3112)
PHONE..................................239 417-9117
David V Will, *President*
EMP: 13 **EST:** 1999
SALES (est): 2.3MM **Privately Held**
SIC: 3272 Piling, prefabricated concrete

(G-10940)
WIRE EXPERTS GROUP INC (PA)
Also Called: Pelican Wire
3650 Shaw Blvd (34117-8408)
PHONE..................................239 597-8555
Theodore Bill, *President*
John Niggle, *Business Mgr*
Robert Ferris, *Vice Pres*
Paul Snapp, *Mfg Mgr*
Andrew Schultz, *Production*
EMP: 80 **EST:** 1977
SQ FT: 35,000
SALES (est): 38.8MM **Privately Held**
WEB: www.wireexperts.com
SIC: 3496 Miscellaneous fabricated wire
products

(G-10941)
WISHBONE WOODWORKING INC
121 Pinehurst Cir (34113-8330)
PHONE..................................239 262-7230
Gregory Beall, *Director*
EMP: 7 **EST:** 2005
SALES (est): 129.3K **Privately Held**
WEB: www.wishbonewoodworking.com
SIC: 2431 Millwork

(G-10942)
WOODWORKERS CABINET INC
6189 Taylor Rd Ste 2 (34109-2301)
PHONE..................................239 593-1718
Gary Fusco, *President*
EMP: 11 **EST:** 2006
SALES (est): 505.9K **Privately Held**
WEB: www.woodworkersnaples.com
SIC: 2431 Millwork

(G-10943)
WOODWORKERS CABINET NAPLES INC
6189 Taylor Rd (34109-2301)
PHONE..................................239 593-1718
Daniel Fusco, *Principal*
EMP: 8 **EST:** 2012
SALES (est): 53.7K **Privately Held**
WEB: woodworkersnaples.blogspot.com
SIC: 2434 Wood kitchen cabinets

(G-10944)
WORLDWIDE PALLET LLC
686 Polar Bear Rd (34113-8580)
PHONE..................................205 671-5210
Thomas R Dritlein, *Principal*
EMP: 8 **EST:** 2011
SALES (est): 392.9K **Privately Held**
WEB: www.markcsmith.com
SIC: 2448 Pallets, wood

(G-10945)
YAHL MULCHING & RECYCLING INC
Also Called: Naples C&D Recycling Facility
2250 Washburn Ave (34117-4032)
PHONE..................................239 352-7888
Theresa Filmore, *President*
John Filmore, *Vice Pres*
EMP: 15 **EST:** 1997
SQ FT: 2,000
SALES (est): 2.5MM **Privately Held**
WEB: www.collierrecycling.com
SIC: 2499 4953 4212 Mulch, wood &
bark; recycling, waste materials; local
trucking, without storage

(G-10946)
YOUTHFUL INNOVATIONS LLC
Also Called: Original Seat Sack Company.
3066 Tamiami Trl N # 101 (34103-2758)
PHONE..................................239 596-2200
Timothy Mullins, *Principal*
EMP: 7 **EST:** 2018
SALES (est): 457.1K **Privately Held**
SIC: 2393 Textile bags

Navarre
Santa Rosa County

(G-10947)
CONSOLIDATED ACE HDWR SUP INC
Also Called: Benjamin Moore Authorized Ret
8188 Navarre Pkwy (32566-6906)
P.O. Box 1449, Defuniak Springs (32435-
7449)
PHONE..................................850 939-9800
EMP: 10 **EST:** 2018
SALES (est): 599K **Privately Held**
WEB: www.benjaminmoore.com
SIC: 3429 5231 Manufactured hardware
(general); paint, glass & wallpaper

(G-10948)
FISHGUM (PA)
2040 Jamaica Dr (32566-7648)
PHONE..................................256 394-2761
Francis A Faggioni III, *Manager*
Francis Faggioni, *Manager*
EMP: 7 **EST:** 2019
SALES (est): 83.7K **Privately Held**
SIC: 3949 Bait, artificial: fishing

(G-10949)
INTEGRITRUST SOLUTIONS LLC
2078 Bahama Dr (32566-7696)
PHONE..................................850 685-9801
Greg Britton, *President*
EMP: 7 **EST:** 2016
SALES (est): 459.8K **Privately Held**
WEB: www.integritrustsolutions.com
SIC: 3728 3599 8742 Aircraft body & wing
assemblies & parts; machine & other job
shop work; management consulting serv-
ices; manufacturing management consult-
ant

(G-10950)
K & N INDUSTRIES INC
9218 Navarre Pkwy (32566-2936)
PHONE..................................850 939-7722
Isaac T Newlin, *Principal*
EMP: 5 **EST:** 2013
SALES (est): 342.9K **Privately Held**
SIC: 3999 Manufacturing industries

(G-10951)
KOBETRON LLC
1778 Sea Lark Ln (32566-7472)
PHONE..................................850 939-5222
Greg Kobe, *President*
Grant Stousland, *Engineer*
Paul Magno,
James Maida,
EMP: 15 **EST:** 1984
SALES (est): 250K **Privately Held**
WEB: www.kobetron.com
SIC: 3825 Test equipment for electronic &
electrical circuits

(G-10952)
LASER ASSAULT
9863 Creet Cir (32566-3347)
PHONE..................................801 374-3400
Jim Degroot, *Mng Member*
Jim De Groot, *Mng Member*
EMP: 6 **EST:** 2004
SALES (est): 336.5K **Privately Held**
WEB: www.laserassault.net
SIC: 3699 Laser systems & equipment

(G-10953)
NAVARRE 3D PRINTING LLC
8131 Country Bay Blvd (32566-7978)
PHONE..................................850 281-6780
Trevor McIntosh, *Branch Mgr*
EMP: 17

▲ = Import ▼ =Export
◆ =Import/Export

SALES (corp-wide): 119.1K **Privately Held**
WEB: www.navarre3dprinting.com
SIC: 2752 Commercial printing, lithographic
PA: Navarre 3d Printing Llc
300 Mary Esther Blvd # 66
Mary Esther FL 32569
850 281-6780

(G-10954)
REAL PRO WELDING INC
Also Called: R P Welding
8285 East Bay Blvd (32566-9388)
PHONE.................................850 939-3469
Randal L Patton, *President*
Randall Patton, *President*
EMP: 7 EST: 2004
SALES (est): 385.6K **Privately Held**
WEB: www.rpwelding.net
SIC: 7692 Welding repair

(G-10955)
SALMI AND COMPANY INC
8328 Randall Dr (32566-9419)
PHONE.................................443 243-8537
Steven Salmi, *President*
Kimberly Adams, *Corp Secy*
Marva Salmi, *Vice Pres*
EMP: 6 EST: 1997
SALES (est): 478.5K **Privately Held**
SIC: 3731 Shipbuilding & repairing

(G-10956)
SANDPAPER MARKETING INC
Also Called: Navarre Fishing Rodeo
7502 Harvest Village Ct (32566-7319)
PHONE.................................850 939-8040
Sandra F Kemp, *Principal*
Melisa Monno, *Graphic Designe*
EMP: 8 EST: 2016
SALES (est): 275.8K **Privately Held**
WEB: www.sandpapermarketing.com
SIC: 3291 Sandpaper

(G-10957)
WOODCRAFT LLC
2218 Avenida De Sol (32566-9206)
PHONE.................................850 217-7757
Harold J Comalander, *Manager*
EMP: 8 EST: 2011
SALES (est): 237.1K **Privately Held**
WEB: www.woodcraft.com
SIC: 2511 Wood household furniture

Neptune Beach
Duval County

(G-10958)
EUROSPA
1487 Atlantic Blvd (32266-1715)
PHONE.................................904 242-8200
EMP: 7 EST: 2010
SALES (est): 88.3K **Privately Held**
SIC: 3845 Colonascopes, electromedical

(G-10959)
TSB EMULSIONS LLC
1306 Big Tree Rd (32266-3197)
PHONE.................................904 249-5115
Thomas S Bloodworth, *Manager*
EMP: 7 EST: 2015
SALES (est): 101.6K **Privately Held**
SIC: 2951 Asphalt paving mixtures & blocks

(G-10960)
VITALLEO LLC
Also Called: Vitalleo Health
2300 Marsh Point Rd 302c (32266-1646)
PHONE.................................904 474-5330
John M McGuire, *Mng Member*
EMP: 8 EST: 2017
SALES (est): 558.5K **Privately Held**
WEB: www.vitalleohealth.com
SIC: 2833 Vitamins, natural or synthetic: bulk, uncompounded

New Port Richey
Pasco County

(G-10961)
AQUINAS INC
Also Called: Printing Place, The
4936 Us Highway 19 (34652-4251)
PHONE.................................727 842-2254
Angie Burke, *President*
Thomas A Burke, *Vice Pres*
Kimberly M Burke, *Admin Sec*
▼ EMP: 5 EST: 1988
SQ FT: 2,400
SALES (est): 1.2MM **Privately Held**
WEB: www.printnowdigital.com
SIC: 2752 Commercial printing, offset

(G-10962)
AUTO GARD QMI INC
5318 Lemon St (34652-3731)
PHONE.................................727 847-5441
John H Nicholson, *President*
Shane Willis, *Vice Pres*
EMP: 10 EST: 1996
SQ FT: 1,000
SALES (est): 291.3K **Privately Held**
SIC: 2819 5169 Industrial inorganic chemicals; chemicals & allied products

(G-10963)
BROTHERS POWDER COATING INC
7721 Rutillio Ct Ste D (34653-1134)
PHONE.................................727 846-0717
Steve Burton, *President*
Michael Burton, *Treasurer*
EMP: 5 EST: 2006
SALES (est): 507.2K **Privately Held**
WEB: www.brotherspowdercoating.com
SIC: 3479 Coating of metals & formed products

(G-10964)
CANNON INDUSTRIES INC
5349 Seafoam Dr (34652-6040)
PHONE.................................727 320-5040
Diana L Perez, *Principal*
EMP: 8 EST: 2016
SALES (est): 50.5K **Privately Held**
WEB: www.cannonind.com
SIC: 3999 Manufacturing industries

(G-10965)
CLASSICS REBORN PUBLISHING LLC
9954 Sweet Bay Ct (34654-5702)
PHONE.................................727 232-6739
Stanley Singer, *Principal*
EMP: 7 EST: 2012
SALES (est): 235.7K **Privately Held**
SIC: 2741 Miscellaneous publishing

(G-10966)
DANIFER PRINTING INC
Also Called: Minuteman Press
7117 Us Highway 19 (34652-1638)
PHONE.................................727 849-5883
James Curtin, *President*
Dorothy Curtin, *Corp Secy*
Bonnie J Howard, *Director*
EMP: 5 EST: 2002
SALES (est): 871.7K **Privately Held**
WEB: www.minutemanpress.com
SIC: 2752 Commercial printing, lithographic

(G-10967)
GRACE PRSTHTIC FABRICATION INC
7928 Rutillio Ct (34653-1103)
PHONE.................................727 842-2265
Anthony Culver, *President*
William Edward Grace, *President*
Tony Culver, *Vice Pres*
▲ EMP: 8 EST: 1990
SQ FT: 5,000
SALES (est): 1.2MM **Privately Held**
WEB: www.gpfinc.com
SIC: 3842 Limbs, artificial; prosthetic appliances

(G-10968)
HOLIDAY CLEANERS INC
3640 Calera Dr (34652-6416)
PHONE.................................727 842-6989
Joseph J Cinquemano, *President*
Catherine Cinquemano, *Corp Secy*
EMP: 6 EST: 1992
SQ FT: 1,500
SALES (est): 864.2K **Privately Held**
WEB: www.holidaycleaners.biz
SIC: 2842 7212 Drycleaning preparations; polishing preparations & related products; laundry & drycleaner agents

(G-10969)
ICEBLOX INC
7436 Evesborough Ln (34655-4209)
PHONE.................................717 697-1900
Brion P McMullen, *CEO*
Dawn McMullen, *CFO*
EMP: 6 EST: 2010
SALES (est): 442.1K **Privately Held**
SIC: 3524 Lawn & garden equipment

(G-10970)
JEFFREY BOWDEN CABINETS LLC
12437 Banbury Ave (34654-4156)
PHONE.................................727 992-9187
Jeffrey D Bowden, *Principal*
EMP: 7 EST: 2008
SALES (est): 164.5K **Privately Held**
SIC: 2434 Wood kitchen cabinets

(G-10971)
KRS MSA LLC
1324 Seven Springs Blvd (34655-5635)
PHONE.................................727 264-7605
Aaron Hunziker, *Exec VP*
Karen Cofield,
EMP: 6 EST: 2005
SALES (est): 493.1K **Privately Held**
SIC: 2834 Pharmaceutical preparations

(G-10972)
LORIS 1 INC
3544 Grand Blvd (34652-6407)
PHONE.................................727 847-4499
Eleftheria Mougros, *President*
EMP: 7 EST: 2014
SALES (est): 204.7K **Privately Held**
SIC: 2841 Soap & other detergents

(G-10973)
MAC ENTPS TAMPA BAY INC
4928 Ladyfish Ct (34652-1015)
PHONE.................................813 363-2601
Joseph M Doyne, *Principal*
EMP: 7 EST: 2008
SALES (est): 174.9K **Privately Held**
SIC: 2434 Wood kitchen cabinets

(G-10974)
MILLWORK MASTERS LLC
7013 Us Highway 19 (34652-1636)
PHONE.................................727 807-6221
Joseph Gatto, *Principal*
Crystal Marcoux, *Principal*
EMP: 15 EST: 2007
SALES (est): 1.3MM **Privately Held**
SIC: 2431 Millwork

(G-10975)
MORGANNAS ALCHEMY LLC
10347 Palladio Dr (34655-2196)
PHONE.................................727 505-8376
Maya Williams,
EMP: 5 EST: 2006
SALES (est): 491.3K **Privately Held**
WEB: www.morgannasalchemy.com
SIC: 2833 7389 Medicinals & botanicals;

(G-10976)
OCEAN GLOBAL INC
Also Called: Alta Labs
4925 Southshore Dr (34652-3029)
P.O. Box 901, Victor ID (83455-0901)
PHONE.................................727 842-7544
Jamie Petersen, *President*
EMP: 5 EST: 2004
SQ FT: 10,000
SALES (est): 514.8K **Privately Held**
WEB: www.motioneaze.com
SIC: 2833 Drugs & herbs: grading, grinding & milling

(G-10977)
OMEGA PUBLISHING
6014 Us Highway 19 # 305 (34652-2505)
PHONE.................................727 815-0402
Carolyn Greenwood, *President*
EMP: 6 EST: 1996
SALES (est): 400K **Privately Held**
SIC: 2741 Miscellaneous publishing

(G-10978)
OMEGA SIGN SERVICE CORPORATION
11301 Biddeford Pl (34654-4496)
PHONE.................................727 505-7833
Anthony Garcia, *President*
EMP: 9 EST: 2009
SALES (est): 486.9K **Privately Held**
WEB: www.omegasignservice.com
SIC: 3993 Signs & advertising specialties

(G-10979)
ON THE GO FOOD & FUEL INC
6444 Massachusetts Ave (34653-2532)
PHONE.................................727 815-0823
Masood Sial, *President*
EMP: 8 EST: 2010
SALES (est): 870.2K **Privately Held**
SIC: 2869 Fuels

(G-10980)
PALL AEROPOWER CORPORATION (DH)
10540 Ridge Rd Ste 100 (34654-5111)
PHONE.................................727 849-9999
Lawrence Mr Kingsley, *President*
Gregory Daddazio, *Vice Pres*
Mark Morris, *Vice Pres*
David Childs, *Engineer*
Matt May, *Engineer*
◆ EMP: 500 EST: 1981
SALES: 170.8MM
SALES (corp-wide): 29.4B **Publicly Held**
SIC: 3569 Filters, general line: industrial
HQ: Pall Corporation
25 Harbor Park Dr
Port Washington NY 11050
516 484-5400

(G-10981)
POINT DISTILLERY LLC
11807 Little Rd (34654-1012)
PHONE.................................727 269-5588
Spencer Wolf, *Mng Member*
EMP: 12 EST: 2018
SALES (est): 1.2MM **Privately Held**
WEB: www.thepointdistillery.com
SIC: 3556 Distillery machinery

(G-10982)
RUSSELL ASSOCIATES INC (DH)
10540 Ridge Rd Ste 300 (34654-5111)
PHONE.................................727 815-3100
Don Stevens, *President*
Godwin Abele, *Senior VP*
Gregory Horne, *Vice Pres*
EMP: 6 EST: 1942
SQ FT: 1,800
SALES: 13.9MM
SALES (corp-wide): 29.4B **Publicly Held**
WEB: www.russellassociatesinc.com
SIC: 3812 Acceleration indicators & systems components, aerospace
HQ: Pall Corporation
25 Harbor Park Dr
Port Washington NY 11050
516 484-5400

(G-10983)
SHALOM ADVENTURE
5160 Spike Horn Dr (34653-7008)
PHONE.................................727 375-7502
Jeff Zaremsky, *Editor*
Barbara Zaremsky, *Editor*
EMP: 8 EST: 2013
SALES (est): 253.2K **Privately Held**
SIC: 2721 8661 Magazines: publishing & printing; religious organizations

(G-10984)
SOUTHERN LIGHTS
3822 Grayton Dr (34652-5711)
PHONE.................................727 849-4442
EMP: 7
SALES (est): 160K **Privately Held**
SIC: 3229 Fiber Optics/Assembly

G E O G R A P H I C

(G-10985)
STATEWIDE BLNDS SHTTERS MORE I
3030 Starkey Blvd (34655-2175)
PHONE..............................813 480-8638
Larry M Vanderhoof, *President*
EMP: 8 **EST:** 2017
SALES (est): 378.3K **Privately Held**
SIC: 2591 Window blinds

(G-10986)
SUNYBELL LLC
4344 Cold Harbor Dr (34653-6117)
PHONE..............................727 301-2832
Eyal Gamili Holtzeker,
EMP: 10 **EST:** 2020
SALES (est): 334.8K **Privately Held**
SIC: 2759 Imprinting

(G-10987)
SWISSCOSMET CORP
5540 Rowan Rd (34653-4551)
PHONE..............................727 842-9419
Roland C Pfister, *President*
Gene Galianese, *Vice Pres*
▲ **EMP:** 7 **EST:** 2008
SALES (est): 658.4K **Privately Held**
WEB: www.cellcosmet-cellmen.us
SIC: 2844 5122 Cosmetic preparations;
cosmetics

(G-10988)
SYRAC ORDNANCE INC
6626 Osteen Rd Ste 331 (34653-3665)
PHONE..............................727 612-6090
Jason M Adams, *President*
EMP: 5 **EST:** 2011
SALES (est): 461.5K **Privately Held**
WEB: www.syracordnance.com
SIC: 3489 3483 Guns or gun parts, over
30 mm.; ammunition components

(G-10989)
TRI TECH METAL INC
6925 Daubon Ct (34655-5605)
PHONE..............................727 946-1229
Carlo Parente, *President*
Thomas Parente, *Vice Pres*
EMP: 5 **EST:** 2005
SALES (est): 450.9K **Privately Held**
SIC: 3449 Miscellaneous metalwork

(G-10990)
TRINITY MOBILITY INC
8343 Royal Hart Dr (34653-7004)
PHONE..............................727 389-1438
Gerald Gluck, *President*
EMP: 8 **EST:** 2010
SALES (est): 233.7K **Privately Held**
WEB: www.trinitymobility.com
SIC: 3842 Wheelchairs

(G-10991)
UTOPIA GRILLING LLC
3511 Cockatoo Dr (34652-6415)
PHONE..............................727 488-1355
Derek Joseph, *Mng Member*
EMP: 7 **EST:** 2019
SALES (est): 1MM **Privately Held**
SIC: 2511 Kitchen & dining room furniture

New Smyrna
Volusia County

(G-10992)
GREEN BULL PRODUCTS INC
310 Washington St (32168-7070)
PHONE..............................386 402-0409
Michael McNerney, *CEO*
▲ **EMP:** 5 **EST:** 2008
SALES (est): 354.8K **Privately Held**
WEB: www.greenbull.us
SIC: 2842 Specialty cleaning preparations

New Smyrna Beach
Volusia County

(G-10993)
ADVANCED MACHINING INC
1500 Airway Cir (32168-5929)
PHONE..............................386 424-7333
Robert E Kayat, *President*
EMP: 9 **EST:** 1995
SQ FT: 7,000
SALES (est): 1.1MM **Privately Held**
WEB: www.advmach.com
SIC: 3599 Machine shop, jobbing & repair

(G-10994)
ATLANTIC GAS SERVICES LLC
2948 Meleto Blvd (32168-6479)
P.O. Box 2301 (32170-2301)
PHONE..............................386 957-3668
Donald Fitzgerald Jr, *Principal*
EMP: 5 **EST:** 2012
SALES (est): 407.4K **Privately Held**
WEB: www.atlanticgasservices.com
SIC: 1382 Aerial geophysical exploration
oil & gas

(G-10995)
BAILEY-SIGLER INC
1050 Fremont St (32168-6239)
P.O. Box 393 (32170-0393)
PHONE..............................386 428-5566
Dean Sigler, *President*
Jack Schafer, *Vice Pres*
Charlie Sigler, *Vice Pres*
Caroline Sigler, *Treasurer*
Hugh Sigler, *Shareholder*
EMP: 7 **EST:** 1962
SQ FT: 1,500
SALES (est): 796K **Privately Held**
WEB: www.baileysigler.com
SIC: 3272 Concrete products, precast

(G-10996)
BAJIO INC
1674 Tionia Rd (32168-9208)
PHONE..............................630 461-0915
Alvin P Perkinson III, *CEO*
EMP: 8 **EST:** 2020
SALES (est): 2.5MM **Privately Held**
SIC: 3851 Eyeglasses, lenses & frames

(G-10997)
BEACH EMBROIDERY & SCREEN PTG
806 E 3rd Ave (32169-3136)
PHONE..............................386 478-3931
Laura Wooley, *Owner*
EMP: 7 **EST:** 2014
SALES (est): 173.2K **Privately Held**
WEB: www.beachembroidery.com
SIC: 2759 Screen printing; card printing &
engraving, except greeting

(G-10998)
CAPTAIN FOODS INC
207 Sapphire Rd (32169-2325)
PHONE..............................386 428-5833
Douglas Feindt, *President*
Kathryn Feindt, *Vice Pres*
Chris Feindt, *VP Sales*
Bryan Forand, *Sales Staff*
▼ **EMP:** 7 **EST:** 1994
SALES (est): 1MM **Privately Held**
WEB: www.house-autry.com
SIC: 2099 Food preparations

(G-10999)
DAVIS KWIK KERB LLC
656 S State Road 415 (32168-9175)
PHONE..............................386 690-0058
EMP: 6 **EST:** 2009
SALES (est): 340K **Privately Held**
SIC: 3281 Mfg Cut Stone/Products

(G-11000)
DAYTONA PARTS COMPANY
1191 Turnbull Bay Rd (32168-6001)
P.O. Box 247 (32170-0247)
PHONE..............................386 427-7108
Ron Hewitt, *Owner*
▲ **EMP:** 8 **EST:** 1972
SQ FT: 6,000
SALES (est): 867.9K **Privately Held**
WEB: www.daytonaparts.com
SIC: 3592 3714 Carburetors; motor vehi-
cle electrical equipment

(G-11001)
GOSS INC
1419 Industrial Dr (32168-5957)
PHONE..............................386 423-0311
Sharon Krepp, *Office Mgr*
Herb Schubert, *Manager*
EMP: 20
SQ FT: 20,292
SALES (corp-wide): 10MM **Privately
Held**
WEB: www.gossonline.com
SIC: 3545 3548 Precision tools, machin-
ists'; welding apparatus
PA: Goss Inc.
1511 Route 8
Glenshaw PA 15116
412 486-6100

(G-11002)
HORIZON PUBLICATIONS INC
Also Called: Observer, The
508 Tanal St (32168)
PHONE..............................386 427-1000
EMP: 9
SQ FT: 2,400
SALES (corp-wide): 72.1MM **Privately
Held**
SIC: 2711 Mfg Newspapers
PA: Horizon Publications Inc.
1120 N Carbon St Ste 100
Marion IL 62959
618 993-1711

(G-11003)
JL OPTICAL INC
Also Called: Jl Optical Microscopes
2908 Palma Ln (32168-6362)
PHONE..............................386 428-6928
George Walker, *President*
EMP: 5 **EST:** 1992
SALES (est): 647.9K **Privately Held**
WEB: secure28.securewebsession.com
SIC: 3826 5999 Microscopes, electron &
proton; binoculars & telescopes

(G-11004)
LIFESTYLE MAGAZINE
1210 S Riverside Dr (32168-7768)
P.O. Box 1251 (32170-1251)
PHONE..............................386 423-2772
W Reed, *Owner*
EMP: 5 **EST:** 1985
SALES (est): 334.7K **Privately Held**
WEB: www.lifestylemagazineflorida.com
SIC: 2721 Periodicals

(G-11005)
MEDICAL WASTE INDUSTRIES INC
612 Downing St (32168-6909)
PHONE..............................407 325-4832
Ron Kroll, *Principal*
EMP: 9 **EST:** 2016
SALES (est): 95.7K **Privately Held**
WEB: www.medicalwasteindustries.com
SIC: 3999 Manufacturing industries

(G-11006)
MGM BLINDS AND SHUTTERS INC
145 Canal St (32168-7067)
Nicole Earl, *Principal*
EMP: 8 **EST:** 2019
SALES (est): 197.4K **Privately Held**
WEB: www.mgmblindsandshutters.com
SIC: 2591 Mfg Drapery Hardware/Blinds

(G-11007)
OHANA LIQUIDS LLC
900 N Atlantic Ave (32169-2312)
PHONE..............................888 642-6244
Joseph Savas, *CEO*
Joseph N Savas, *Manager*
EMP: 7 **EST:** 2018
SQ FT: 37,000
SALES (est): 648.4K **Privately Held**
WEB: www.ohanaliquids.com
SIC: 2023 Dietary supplements, dairy &
non-dairy based

(G-11008)
SABIC INNOVATIVE PLASTICS
703 South St (32168-5867)
PHONE..............................386 409-5540
Richard Moeller, *Principal*
Ralph Buoniconti, *Engineer*
EMP: 10 **EST:** 2010
SALES (est): 728.3K **Privately Held**
SIC: 2295 Resin or plastic coated fabrics

(G-11009)
SAND DOLLAR CHARTERS LLC
147 Middle Way (32169-5212)
PHONE..............................903 734-5376
Donald Owens,
EMP: 5 **EST:** 2019
SALES (est): 580.8K **Privately Held**
WEB: www.sanddollarboatrentals.com
SIC: 2541 Wood partitions & fixtures

(G-11010)
SEN-PACK INC
820 Rasley Rd (32168-5219)
PHONE..............................386 763-3312
Adam Vinoskey, *President*
Gert Gast, *Buyer*
Pete Connor, *Electrical Engi*
Tamyra Cook, *Sales Staff*
Will Watson, *Technician*
EMP: 22 **EST:** 2007
SALES (est): 5.8MM **Privately Held**
WEB: www.sentryequipment.com
SIC: 3556 Food products machinery

(G-11011)
SONAPA LLC
3406 S Atlantic Ave (32169-3626)
PHONE..............................407 782-0459
Adam R Barringer, *Principal*
EMP: 7 **EST:** 2010
SALES (est): 241.4K **Privately Held**
SIC: 2084 Wines

(G-11012)
SONOCO PRODUCTS COMPANY
Also Called: New Smyrna Beach Plas Plant
1601 Tionia Rd (32168-9290)
PHONE..............................386 424-0970
Cathy Cottle, *Manager*
EMP: 30
SALES (corp-wide): 5.5B **Publicly Held**
WEB: www.sonoco.com
SIC: 2631 Paperboard mills
PA: Sonoco Products Company
1 N 2nd St
Hartsville SC 29550
843 383-7000

(G-11013)
SUGAR WORKS DISTILLERY LLC
1714 State Road 44 (32168-8339)
P.O. Box 1261 (32170-1261)
PHONE..............................386 463-0120
Thomas McPeek, *Mng Member*
Danay McPeek, *Mng Member*
EMP: 8 **EST:** 2017
SALES (est): 279.6K **Privately Held**
WEB: www.sugarworksdistillery.com
SIC: 2085 Distilled & blended liquors

(G-11014)
TIGER COMPOSITES INC
1531 Airway Cir (32168-5929)
P.O. Box 730125, Ormond Beach (32173-
0125)
PHONE..............................386 334-0941
Aaron Duncan, *President*
Colleen Duncan, *Shareholder*
EMP: 11 **EST:** 2014
SQ FT: 32,000
SALES (est): 506.5K **Privately Held**
WEB: www.tigercomposites.com
SIC: 3721 3732 Motorized aircraft; gliders
(aircraft); boats, fiberglass; building & re-
pairing

Newberry
Alachua County

(G-11015)
AAA EVENT SERVICES LLC
Also Called: AAA Porta Serve
25370 Nw 8th Ln (32669-2538)
P.O. Box 907, High Springs (32655-0907)
PHONE..............................386 454-0929
Ross Ambrose, *Managing Prtnr*
Steven Carson,
Thomas Hewlett,
James Wood,
EMP: 12 **EST:** 2014

SALES (est): 2.2MM **Privately Held**
WEB: www.aaaportaserve.com
SIC: **3431 7342 7359** Portable chemical toilets, metal; washroom sanitation service (industrial locations); portable toilet rental

(G-11016)
AGNET MEDIA INC
Also Called: Citrus Industry Magazine
27206 Sw 22nd Pl (32669-4302)
PHONE.................................352 671-1909
Robin Loftin, *President*
Tacy Callies, *Editor*
Ernie Neff, *Editor*
Ron Linkous, *Business Mgr*
Taylor Hillman, *Opers Staff*
EMP: 17 EST: 1984
SQ FT: 5,414
SALES (est): 1.3MM **Privately Held**
WEB: www.agnetmedia.com
SIC: **2721** Magazines: publishing only, not printed on site

(G-11017)
ARGOS USA LLC
Also Called: Cement Plant
4000 Nw County Road 235 Th (32669-2380)
PHONE.................................352 472-4722
EMP: 57 **Privately Held**
WEB: www.argos-us.com
SIC: **3272** Concrete products
HQ: Argos Usa Llc
3015 Windward Plz Ste 300
Alpharetta GA 30005
678 368-4300

(G-11018)
EASTERN IRRIGATION SUPPLY
5328 Nw State Road 45 (32669-2523)
P.O. Box 1089 (32669-1089)
PHONE.................................352 472-3323
Cliff Brown, *President*
Nona H Brown, *Treasurer*
Bob Jocens, *Shareholder*
Clifton A Brown, *Admin Sec*
▲ EMP: 7 EST: 1999
SQ FT: 13,000
SALES (est): 1MM **Privately Held**
WEB: www.irrigationdistributors.com
SIC: **3523** Irrigation equipment, self-propelled

(G-11019)
ENDOSCOPY RPLACEMENT PARTS INC
25430 Nw 8th Ln (32669-3518)
PHONE.................................352 472-5120
David Bello, *President*
John Hartnett, *Vice Pres*
EMP: 6 EST: 1997
SALES (est): 1MM **Privately Held**
WEB: www.endoscopeparts.com
SIC: **3599** Machine shop, jobbing & repair

(G-11020)
EVREN TECHNOLOGIES INC
404 Sw 140th Ter Ste 50 (32669-3655)
PHONE.................................352 494-0950
Weaver Gaines, *CEO*
EMP: 5 EST: 2018
SALES (est): 612.3K **Privately Held**
WEB: www.evrenvns.com
SIC: **3845 3841** Electromedical equipment; surgical & medical instruments

(G-11021)
FLORIDA ROCK
4000 Nw County Road 235 (32669-2380)
PHONE.................................352 472-4722
Fred Cohrs, *Principal*
Kip Rouse, *Consultant*
Lisa Penney, *Cashier*
Mike Waldrep, *Cashier*
◆ EMP: 17 EST: 2010
SALES (est): 1MM **Privately Held**
SIC: **3273** Ready-mixed concrete

(G-11022)
GULF ATL PUMP & DREDGE LLC (PA)
954 Nw 244th Dr (32669-2676)
PHONE.................................386 362-2761
Randy P Carter, *Mng Member*
EMP: 3 EST: 2000

SQ FT: 9,000
SALES (est): 6.1MM **Privately Held**
WEB: www.gapdllc.com
SIC: **3561** Pumps & pumping equipment

(G-11023)
INSPIRED ENERGY INC
25440 Nw 8th Pl (32669-2539)
PHONE.................................352 472-4855
Alexander Jacobs, *Principal*
Dave Baggley, *Principal*
Daniel Kane, *Mfg Staff*
Daniel Rodriguez, *Engineer*
Lisa Baggaley, *Finance Mgr*
EMP: 24 EST: 2001
SALES (est): 5.9MM **Privately Held**
WEB: www.inspired-energy.com
SIC: **3691** Storage batteries

(G-11024)
INSPIRED ENERGY LLC
25440 Nw 8th Pl (32669-2539)
PHONE.................................352 472-4855
Alisha Redding, *General Mgr*
Kato Pinder, *Engineer*
Alexander Jacobs, *Mng Member*
Alexander I Jacobs, *Mng Member*
Samantha Smith, *Manager*
◆ EMP: 101 EST: 2001
SQ FT: 29,855
SALES (est): 26.8MM **Privately Held**
WEB: www.inspired-energy.com
SIC: **3691** Alkaline cell storage batteries

(G-11025)
PRECON CORPORATION
115 Sw 140th Ter (32669-3026)
PHONE.................................352 332-1200
Richard G Moore, *President*
Colin Tenney, *Superintendent*
Patrick J Wheeler, *Vice Pres*
Kurt Linebarger, *Project Mgr*
Vineyard Mort, *Project Mgr*
EMP: 150 EST: 1980
SQ FT: 3,200
SALES (est): 34.1MM **Privately Held**
WEB: www.precontanks.com
SIC: **3272** Tanks, concrete; prestressed concrete products

(G-11026)
RG GROUNDWORKS LLC
5915 Nw 210th St (32669-2342)
PHONE.................................352 474-7949
Renato S Gomez Gonzalez R, *Principal*
EMP: 7 EST: 2020
SALES (est): 530.5K **Privately Held**
WEB: www.rggroundworksfl.com
SIC: **3561 2951 1771** Pumps & pumping equipment; asphalt paving mixtures & blocks; concrete work

(G-11027)
SOUTHERN FUELWOOD INC
28826 W Newberry Rd (32669-2674)
P.O. Box 1319 (32669-1319)
PHONE.................................352 472-4324
Patrick M Post, *Owner*
Rudy Davis, *Principal*
Keith Oliver, *Principal*
Joan Feuston, *Manager*
EMP: 40 EST: 1985
SQ FT: 1,000
SALES (est): 4.4MM **Privately Held**
WEB: www.southernfuelwood.com
SIC: **2421 5211 5031** Sawdust, shavings & wood chips; lumber & other building materials; lumber, plywood & millwork

Niceville
Okaloosa County

(G-11028)
CLJP INC
Also Called: Legacy Cabinet Company, The
200 Hart St (32578-1037)
P.O. Box 191 (32588-0191)
PHONE.................................850 678-8819
Charles R Agnew, *President*
Chris Shaw, *General Mgr*
John Agnew, *Vice Pres*
Bill Gronenthal, *Opers Staff*
Jenna Sheely, *Controller*
EMP: 30 EST: 2004

SALES (est): 16.3MM **Privately Held**
WEB: www.thelegacycabinetcompany.com
SIC: **2434** Wood kitchen cabinets

(G-11029)
EMERALD PRINTS LLC
1169 John Sims Pkwy E (32578-2752)
PHONE.................................850 460-5532
Kent Nguyen, *President*
EMP: 5 EST: 2017
SALES (est): 464.8K **Privately Held**
WEB: www.emeraldprints.com
SIC: **2752** Commercial printing, lithographic

(G-11030)
GENERAL DYNAMICS CORPORATION
115 Hart St (32578-1040)
PHONE.................................850 897-9700
Edward Lawrence, *Engineer*
Rosemary Hillyer, *Branch Mgr*
Cecile Bonum, *Manager*
Doug King, *Technician*
Philip Soto, *Government*
EMP: 35
SALES (corp-wide): 38.4B **Publicly Held**
WEB: www.gd.com
SIC: **3721** Aircraft
PA: General Dynamics Corporation
11011 Sunset Hills Rd
Reston VA 20190
703 876-3000

(G-11031)
GR DYNAMICS LLC
115 Hart St (32578-1040)
PHONE.................................850 897-9700
Ken Morgan, *Principal*
EMP: 14 EST: 2008
SALES (est): 2.1MM
SALES (corp-wide): 38.4B **Publicly Held**
WEB: www.gd-ots.com
SIC: **3489** Ordnance & accessories
PA: General Dynamics Corporation
11011 Sunset Hills Rd
Reston VA 20190
703 876-3000

(G-11032)
HELMS HAULING & MATERIALS LLC
Also Called: Helms Hauling and Materials
1423 Pine St (32578-9780)
PHONE.................................850 218-6895
Scott Michael Helms,
Lauren Helms,
EMP: 10 EST: 2012
SQ FT: 600
SALES (est): 1.8MM **Privately Held**
WEB: www.helmshauling.com
SIC: **1442 1422 5211 5032** Construction sand & gravel; crushed & broken limestone; sand & gravel; limestone; mulching services, lawn

(G-11033)
NORTH METRO MEDIA
Also Called: Homes & Land of Emerald Coast
160 Baywind Dr (32578-4800)
P.O. Box 1854, Destin (32540-1854)
PHONE.................................850 650-1014
Kate Kelley, *Prdtn Mgr*
Joe Nacchia, *Office Mgr*
EMP: 10 EST: 1993
SALES (est): 923.6K **Privately Held**
SIC: **2741** Telephone & other directory publishing

(G-11034)
POLLY CONCRETE PRODUCTS CO
1495 Cedar St (32578-9748)
PHONE.................................850 897-3314
Sherrie Venghaus, *Owner*
EMP: 10 EST: 1963
SQ FT: 3,850
SALES (est): 793.4K **Privately Held**
SIC: **3272** Concrete products, precast

(G-11035)
POPE ENTERPRISES INC
Also Called: Accent Signs
516 John Sims Pkwy E (32578-2028)
PHONE.................................850 729-7446

James G Pope, *CEO*
Greg Pope, *President*
Victoria Pope, *Corp Secy*
Patti Checkler, *Bookkeeper*
Michael Depoorter, *Information Mgr*
EMP: 10 EST: 1984
SQ FT: 5,000
SALES (est): 1.1MM **Privately Held**
SIC: **3993** Signs, not made in custom sign painting shops

(G-11036)
RMC EWELL INC
16040 State Highway 20 (32578-8215)
PHONE.................................850 879-0959
EMP: 21
SALES (corp-wide): 13.3B **Privately Held**
SIC: **3273 3272** Manufactures Ready Mix Concrete And Concrete Pipe
HQ: Ewell Rmc Inc
801 Mccue Rd
Lakeland FL
863 688-5787

(G-11037)
S&S CONSULTING PARTNERS LLC
139 Bayside Dr (32578-8257)
PHONE.................................850 803-8379
Benjamin Schladenhauffen, *Manager*
EMP: 6 EST: 2016
SALES (est): 323.1K **Privately Held**
WEB: www.ssconsultingllc.net
SIC: **3629** Series capacitors

(G-11038)
TELEDYNE FLIR LLC
701 John Sims Pkwy E (32578-2059)
PHONE.................................850 678-4503
Charlotte Clark, *Manager*
EMP: 7
SALES (corp-wide): 4.6B **Publicly Held**
WEB: www.flir.com
SIC: **3826** Analytical instruments
HQ: Teledyne Flir, Llc
27700 Sw Parkway Ave
Wilsonville OR 97070
503 498-3547

(G-11039)
VINTAGE ART AND SIGN LLC
1419 29th St 3 (32578-2724)
PHONE.................................770 815-7887
Kim M Sutton, *Principal*
EMP: 9 EST: 2013
SALES (est): 572.4K **Privately Held**
WEB: www.vintagesignandlight.com
SIC: **3993** Signs & advertising specialties

(G-11040)
ZITEC INC
1031 Partin Dr N (32578-1419)
PHONE.................................850 678-9747
Daniel T Mank, *President*
EMP: 5 EST: 2000
SALES (est): 668K **Privately Held**
WEB: www.zitecusa.com
SIC: **3728** Military aircraft equipment & armament

Nokomis
Sarasota County

(G-11041)
365 SUN LLC
Also Called: Natalia Likhacheva
225 Nippino Trl E (34275-3122)
PHONE.................................208 357-8062
Lance I Thompson, *Manager*
EMP: 9 EST: 2017
SALES (est): 685K **Privately Held**
SIC: **2844** Hair preparations, including shampoos

(G-11042)
BUDDY BRIDGE INC (PA)
350 Sorrento Ranches Dr (34275-2468)
PHONE.................................941 488-0799
James F Gordon, *President*
EMP: 5 EST: 2010
SALES (est): 350.9K **Privately Held**
WEB: www.bridgebuddy.net
SIC: **2759** Playing cards: printing

(G-11043)
CARIBBEAN BASIN INDUSTRIES INC
2407 Casey Key Rd (34275-3384)
PHONE..............................941 726-7272
Diane K McNeer, *Principal*
EMP: 8 **EST:** 2012
SALES (est): 184.3K **Privately Held**
SIC: 3999 Manufacturing industries

(G-11044)
CLOVER INTERIOR SYSTEMS INC
505 Lyons Bay Rd (34275-3074)
P.O. Box 508 (34274-0508)
PHONE..............................941 484-1300
Joseph De Falco, *President*
Mary Ann De Falco, *Vice Pres*
EMP: 12 **EST:** 1971
SQ FT: 15,000
SALES (est): 1MM **Privately Held**
SIC: 2434 Vanities, bathroom: wood

(G-11045)
EDWARDS CO
188 Camelot Dr (34275-1867)
PHONE..............................215 343-2133
Pam Edwards, *Owner*
David Wheeler, *Engineer*
EMP: 8 **EST:** 2000
SALES (est): 808.8K **Privately Held**
WEB: www.edwards.com
SIC: 3499 Metal household articles

(G-11046)
IMPRINT
3449 Tech Dr Unit 212 (34275)
PHONE..............................941 484-5151
Walter Rossmann, *Owner*
Brad Murray, *Director*
Brad Prepress, *Director*
EMP: 5 **EST:** 2006
SALES (est): 670.2K **Privately Held**
WEB: www.iloveimprint.com
SIC: 2752 Commercial printing, offset

(G-11047)
INNOVATIVE FABRICATORS FLA INC
Also Called: Innovative Contractors
104 Palmetto Rd W (34275-2035)
P.O. Box 1545, Osprey (34229-1545)
PHONE..............................941 375-8668
Jason Tison, *President*
EMP: 6 **EST:** 2002
SALES (est): 1.1MM **Privately Held**
WEB: www.innovative-contractors.com
SIC: 3441 Fabricated structural metal

(G-11048)
JAZZY DOGS PUBLISHING LLC
204 Millet Pl (34275-1332)
PHONE..............................941 726-0343
Jeffrey Johnson, *Principal*
EMP: 8 **EST:** 2016
SALES (est): 270K **Privately Held**
WEB: www.swflplacemats.com
SIC: 2741 Miscellaneous publishing

(G-11049)
KENT MANUFACTURING VENICE INC
155 Toscavilla Blvd (34275-1013)
PHONE..............................941 485-8871
Kent Drobisch, *President*
Chad Drobisch, *Vice Pres*
EMP: 15 **EST:** 1973
SALES (est): 2.4MM **Privately Held**
WEB: www.kentmfg.com
SIC: 3949 Golf equipment

(G-11050)
LIME GROUP
416 Lime Dr (34275-3742)
PHONE..............................941 485-0272
Raymond F Daiuto, *Principal*
EMP: 7 **EST:** 2010
SALES (est): 131.3K **Privately Held**
SIC: 3274 Lime

(G-11051)
METALEX LLC
3816 Cutlass Byu (34275-3343)
PHONE..............................941 918-4431

Robert Metzger, *President*
EMP: 100 **EST:** 2017
SALES (est): 5.8MM **Privately Held**
WEB: www.metlx.com
SIC: 2295 Metallizing of fabrics

(G-11052)
PRECISION FABRICATION CORP
510 Church St (34275-2723)
P.O. Box 666 (34274-0666)
PHONE..............................941 488-2474
Christopher Van Pelt, *President*
Deborah Van Pelt, *Vice Pres*
EMP: 19 **EST:** 1983
SQ FT: 10,500
SALES (est): 4MM **Privately Held**
WEB: www.precisionfabricationfl.com
SIC: 3444 Sheet metal specialties, not stamped

(G-11053)
TEN4 SOLUTIONS LLC
2342 Laurel Rd E # 7308 (34275-3594)
PHONE..............................302 544-1120
Barry McMonigle,
EMP: 8 **EST:** 2020
SALES (est): 260.5K **Privately Held**
WEB: www.ten4.us
SIC: 1389 Construction, repair & dismantling services

(G-11054)
TITAN AMERICA LLC
515 Gene Green Rd (34275-3604)
PHONE..............................941 486-2220
EMP: 15
SALES (corp-wide): 177.9K **Privately Held**
WEB: www.titanamerica.com
SIC: 3273 Ready-mixed concrete
HQ: Titan America Llc
　5700 Lake Wright Dr # 300
　Norfolk VA 23502
　757 858-6500

(G-11055)
TITAN AMERICA TARMAC
500 Gene Green Rd (34275-3624)
PHONE..............................941 484-2276
James Brown, *Principal*
EMP: 7 **EST:** 2007
SALES (est): 188.8K **Privately Held**
SIC: 3273 Ready-mixed concrete

(G-11056)
VENICE CUSTOM CABINETS INC
510 Colonia Ln E (34275-2607)
PHONE..............................941 488-5000
Paul R Willhite, *Owner*
EMP: 8 **EST:** 1983
SQ FT: 5,000
SALES (est): 600K **Privately Held**
SIC: 2434 Wood kitchen cabinets

North Bay Village
Miami-Dade County

(G-11057)
ADVANCED CABINETRY INVENTIONS
7601 E Treasure Dr # 2120 (33141-4391)
PHONE..............................305 866-1160
Francisco Irace, *Principal*
EMP: 8 **EST:** 2013
SALES (est): 180.4K **Privately Held**
WEB: www.kitchencabinetscorp.com
SIC: 2434 Wood kitchen cabinets

(G-11058)
MEDICAL OUTFITTERS INC
1666 J F Kennedy Cswy # 409
(33141-4169)
PHONE..............................305 332-9103
Mark Zelinsky, *President*
Carlos Naya, *Vice Pres*
EMP: 22
SALES (corp-wide): 6.9MM **Privately Held**
WEB: www.medicaloutfitter.net
SIC: 3826 Magnetic resonance imaging apparatus

PA: Medical Outfitters Inc.
　8062 Nw 66th St
　Miami FL 33166
　305 885-4045

(G-11059)
OMNIAELECTRONICS LLC
Also Called: Syxa Enterprise
7945 East Dr Apt 204 (33141-3304)
PHONE..............................631 742-5719
Gianluca Aprea, *CEO*
EMP: 8 **EST:** 2016
SALES (est): 470.2K **Privately Held**
SIC: 3629 Electronic generation equipment

(G-11060)
STAINLESS STEEL KITCHENS CORP
7601 E Treasure Dr # 2120 (33141-4391)
PHONE..............................305 999-1543
Klische Mirta, *Principal*
EMP: 9 **EST:** 2010
SALES (est): 268.1K **Privately Held**
WEB: www.steelkitchenweb.com
SIC: 3312 Stainless steel

North Fort Myers
Lee County

(G-11061)
GOLDEN MANUFACTURING INC
Also Called: Golden Boatlifts
17611 East St Unit B (33917-2138)
PHONE..............................239 337-4141
William Golden, *CEO*
Ken Felty, *Vice Pres*
Tom Flynn, *Sales Staff*
Tommy Fryer, *Manager*
Liz Travis, *Manager*
◆ **EMP:** 23 **EST:** 1997
SQ FT: 29,000
SALES (est): 6.9MM **Privately Held**
WEB: www.goldenboatlifts.com
SIC: 3536 Boat lifts

(G-11062)
MIDWEST MTAL FBRCTION CSTM RLL
13331 Seaside Harbour Dr (33903-7119)
PHONE..............................317 769-6489
Thomas Riddle, *President*
Mike Nickels, *Vice Pres*
EMP: 17 **EST:** 1989
SQ FT: 35,000
SALES (est): 964.3K **Privately Held**
SIC: 3443 3449 Fuel tanks (oil, gas, etc.): metal plate; miscellaneous metalwork

(G-11063)
NORTH FORT MYERS PRESCR SP
16251 N Cleveland Ave # 13 (33903-2176)
PHONE..............................239 599-4120
Lisa Lawrence, *President*
Lawrence Lisa, *President*
EMP: 8 **EST:** 2011
SALES (est): 248.2K **Privately Held**
WEB: www.therxshops.com
SIC: 2834 Dermatologicals; hormone preparations; medicines, capsuled or ampuled

(G-11064)
ON-SPOT PORTABLE MACHINE CO
20612 Dennisport Ln (33917-8710)
PHONE..............................734 525-0880
James Burnett, *President*
EMP: 5 **EST:** 1974
SALES (est): 414K **Privately Held**
SIC: 3599 Machine shop, jobbing & repair

(G-11065)
PAINTS & COATINGS INC
17660 East St (33917-2120)
PHONE..............................239 997-6645
Carl Laguidara, *President*
Jeff Yingling, *Vice Pres*
Melissa Giustina, *Office Mgr*
EMP: 30 **EST:** 1995
SALES (est): 3.8MM **Privately Held**
WEB: www.paintsandcoatings.net
SIC: 2851 Undercoatings, paint

(G-11066)
PELLICCIONE BUILDERS SUP INC
17056 Wayzata Ct (33917-3816)
PHONE..............................941 334-3014
Larry Pelliccione, *President*
EMP: 16 **EST:** 1973
SQ FT: 3,200
SALES (est): 664.6K **Privately Held**
SIC: 2439 Trusses, wooden roof

(G-11067)
PRECISION ECONOWIND LLC
8940 N Fork Dr (33903-1421)
PHONE..............................239 997-3860
Loyal Tingley III, *President*
Jeremy Krenzelak, *Accounting Mgr*
EMP: 12 **EST:** 2007
SALES (est): 7MM **Privately Held**
WEB: www.precisioneconowind.com
SIC: 3677 Coil windings, electronic

(G-11068)
SCOTTIES CANVAS & MAR SUP LLC
2211 N Tamiami Trl (33903-2806)
PHONE..............................239 995-7479
Mike Lueneburg, *General Mgr*
Patricia A Givens, *Principal*
EMP: 7 **EST:** 2016
SALES (est): 251.2K **Privately Held**
WEB: www.scottiescanvas.com
SIC: 2394 Canvas & related products

(G-11069)
SIGN AND DESIGN DEPOT LLC
960 Pondella Rd Ste C (33903-3514)
PHONE..............................239 995-7446
Greg Bullock, *Mng Member*
Margaret Wolter, *Graphic Designe*
Mary Bullock,
EMP: 9 **EST:** 2010
SQ FT: 1,800
SALES (est): 666.5K **Privately Held**
WEB: www.signanddesigndepot.com
SIC: 3993 Signs & advertising specialties

(G-11070)
SIGNARAMA
Also Called: Sign-A-Rama
4621 Bayshore Rd (33917-3986)
PHONE..............................239 997-1644
EMP: 7 **EST:** 2014
SALES (est): 171.6K **Privately Held**
WEB: www.signarama.com
SIC: 3993 5999 2759 Signs & advertising specialties; banners, flags, decals & posters; commercial printing

(G-11071)
TELEMATIC SYSTEMS INC
2029 Club House Rd (33917-2519)
PHONE..............................239 217-0629
William P Tassic, *President*
Don Tassic, *Manager*
EMP: 9 **EST:** 1978
SALES (est): 646.9K **Privately Held**
SIC: 3679 Electronic circuits

(G-11072)
UPRIGHT ALUMINUM INC
7908 Interstate Ct (33917-2112)
PHONE..............................239 731-6644
Randy Dull, *General Mgr*
EMP: 8 **EST:** 2013
SALES (est): 2.1MM **Privately Held**
WEB: www.uprightaluminum.com
SIC: 3442 Metal doors, sash & trim

(G-11073)
WANTED DEAD OR ALIVE INC
1011 April Ln (33903-5206)
PHONE..............................239 633-5080
Christopher Oncken, *Principal*
EMP: 8 **EST:** 2007
SALES (est): 295.1K **Privately Held**
SIC: 3531 Automobile wrecker hoists

North Lauderdale
Broward County

(G-11074)
A1 ELEVATORS LLC
8185 S Coral Cir (33068-4119)
PHONE..............................954 773-4443
Tracy Louis, *Co-Owner*
Ebony Louis, *Co-Owner*
EMP: 7 EST: 2014
SALES (est): 513.3K Privately Held
SIC: 3534 Stair elevators, motor,powered

(G-11075)
AMERICAN PAYMENT SYSTEMS
1655 S State Road 7 (33068-4694)
PHONE..............................954 968-6920
EMP: 9 EST: 2006
SALES (est): 88.5K Privately Held
WEB: www.americanpaymentsystems.com
SIC: 3812 Defense systems & equipment

(G-11076)
BURNHAM WOODS UNTD CIVIC GROUP
8211 Sw 19th St (33068-4702)
PHONE..............................954 532-2675
Hallam Batson, *Principal*
EMP: 7 EST: 2015
SALES (est): 99.7K Privately Held
SIC: 2499 Wood products

(G-11077)
CERTIFIED CLEAN CUTS - LLC
7210 Southgate Blvd (33068-1426)
PHONE..............................954 903-1733
Guerdine Belizaire, *President*
Guerdine Delidaire, *Mng Member*
EMP: 12 EST: 2018
SALES (est): 1MM Privately Held
SIC: 3999 Barber & beauty shop equipment

(G-11078)
DMONEY365 LOGISTIC LLC ✪
1331 S State Road 7 (33068-4023)
PHONE..............................954 529-8202
Davens Deville,
EMP: 10 EST: 2021
SALES (est): 571.8K Privately Held
SIC: 3537 Trucks: freight, baggage, etc.: industrial, except mining

(G-11079)
EVM WOODWORK CORP
971 Sw 70th Way (33068-2557)
PHONE..............................954 970-4352
EMP: 7 EST: 2019
SALES (est): 165.5K Privately Held
SIC: 2431 Millwork

(G-11080)
EVM WOODWORKS CORP
7542 W Mcnab Rd (33068-5487)
PHONE..............................954 655-6414
EMP: 8 EST: 2017
SALES (est): 553.9K Privately Held
SIC: 2431 Millwork

(G-11081)
JADUS JUSTICE APPERAL LLC
1478 Avon Ln (33068-5583)
PHONE..............................954 394-6259
Jadus Burgess,
EMP: 10
SALES (est): 331.8K Privately Held
SIC: 2326 7389 Men's & boys' work clothing;

(G-11082)
KDAVID WOODWORK + DESIGN INC
7546 W Mcnab Rd (33068-5484)
PHONE..............................754 205-2433
Diego A Cadavid, *Principal*
EMP: 14 EST: 2013
SALES (est): 491.8K Privately Held
SIC: 2431 Millwork

(G-11083)
LADIESFITCAMP LLC
6876 Sw 15th St (33068-4310)
PHONE..............................954 226-7034

Savalas Williams, *President*
EMP: 22 EST: 2019
SALES (est): 1.2MM Privately Held
SIC: 1389 Construction, repair & dismantling services

(G-11084)
MY PASSION ON A PLATE LLC
7901 Southgate Blvd C3 (33068-1161)
PHONE..............................954 857-6382
EMP: 10 EST: 2020
SALES (est): 105K Privately Held
SIC: 2599 Food wagons, restaurant

(G-11085)
RICHARD LYN
7944 Forest Blvd (33068-1115)
PHONE..............................954 326-1017
Richard Lyn, *Principal*
EMP: 6 EST: 2007
SALES (est): 497.4K Privately Held
SIC: 3589 High pressure cleaning equipment

(G-11086)
SAP ENTERPRISES INC
309 Sw 77th Ave (33068-1220)
PHONE..............................954 871-8688
Shaun Allaham, *President*
EMP: 10 EST: 2008
SALES (est): 595.9K Privately Held
SIC: 3581 Automatic vending machines

North Miami
Miami-Dade County

(G-11087)
ADVANCED PHARMACEUTICAL INC
1065 Ne 125th St Ste 211 (33161-5832)
PHONE..............................866 259-7122
Ronel L Pierre, *President*
EMP: 8 EST: 2004
SALES (est): 164.3K Privately Held
SIC: 2834 Pharmaceutical preparations

(G-11088)
AJF SHEET METALS INC
7495 Nw 7th St Ste 10 (33181)
PHONE..............................305 970-6359
Alejo Fernandez, *President*
EMP: 7 EST: 2010
SALES (est): 653.8K Privately Held
SIC: 3444 Sheet metalwork

(G-11089)
AMERICAN SPECIALTY SALES CORP
Also Called: K & C The Printer
14286 Biscayne Blvd (33181-1204)
PHONE..............................305 947-9700
Robert K Minick, *President*
EMP: 8 EST: 1987
SQ FT: 4,000
SALES (est): 642.3K Privately Held
SIC: 2752 Commercial printing, offset

(G-11090)
ARTNEXUS ONLINE INC
12500 Ne 8th Ave (33161-4963)
PHONE..............................305 891-7270
Celia S Birbragher, *President*
Zulema Roca, *Sales Mgr*
Mercedes Guerrero, *Sales Staff*
EMP: 24 EST: 2001
SALES (est): 1.7MM Privately Held
WEB: www.artnexus.com
SIC: 2721 Magazines: publishing & printing

(G-11091)
AVENTURA CUSTOM WOODWORK
1450 Ne 130th St (33161-4411)
PHONE..............................305 891-9093
Isaiah Frometa, *Principal*
EMP: 7 EST: 2010
SALES (est): 71K Privately Held
SIC: 2431 Millwork

(G-11092)
BANKINGLY INC
1942 Ne 148th St (33181-1161)
PHONE..............................734 201-0007

Martin Naor, *CEO*
EMP: 20 EST: 2015
SQ FT: 1,000
SALES (est): 1MM Privately Held
SIC: 7372 Prepackaged software

(G-11093)
BOBBIE WEINER ENTERPRISES LLC
12355 Ne 13th Ave Unit 40 (33161-5972)
PHONE..............................817 615-8610
Bobbie Weiner, *Owner*
▲ EMP: 6 EST: 1997
SALES (est): 465.7K Privately Held
SIC: 2844 5122 Cosmetic preparations; cosmetics

(G-11094)
BORDERS & ACCENTS INC
1890 Ne 144th St (33181-1420)
PHONE..............................305 947-6200
Ignacio Paz, *President*
EMP: 10 EST: 1995
SQ FT: 16,000
SALES (est): 893.2K Privately Held
SIC: 3281 Building stone products

(G-11095)
BYOMED LLC
1555 Ne 123rd St (33161-6029)
PHONE..............................305 634-6763
Tarek Hamandi, *Mng Member*
EMP: 10 EST: 2016
SALES (est): 510.2K Privately Held
SIC: 3841 Medical instruments & equipment, blood & bone work

(G-11096)
CABUS USA INC
Also Called: Professional Engrv & Trophy
12300 Nw 7th Ave (33168-2604)
PHONE..............................305 681-0872
Pierre Dubose, *President*
Roselis Dubose, *Vice Pres*
◆ EMP: 5 EST: 1964
SQ FT: 1,500
SALES (est): 440.2K Privately Held
SIC: 3499 5944 Trophies, metal, except silver; jewelry, precious stones & precious metals; watches; silverware

(G-11097)
CCT SOFTWARE LLC
1801 Ne 123rd St Ste 314 (33181-2883)
PHONE..............................305 747-5682
Andrea Kreuter,
Uwe Kreuter,
EMP: 6 EST: 2012
SALES (est): 747.6K Privately Held
WEB: www.cct-solutions.com
SIC: 7372 Prepackaged software

(G-11098)
CINEMA CRAFTERS INC
Also Called: First Impression Design MGT
12564 Ne 14th Ave (33161-4439)
PHONE..............................305 891-6121
Jeffrey Smith, *CEO*
Mohni Kundnani, *Exec VP*
EMP: 8 EST: 1999
SQ FT: 15,000
SALES (est): 299.3K Privately Held
WEB: www.cineloungers.com
SIC: 2531 5049 Theater furniture; theatrical equipment & supplies

(G-11099)
COBRA POWER CORPORATION
13353 Ne 17th Ave (33181-1714)
PHONE..............................305 893-5018
Randy Garciga, *President*
Albert Levey, *Technical Staff*
◆ EMP: 5 EST: 1981
SQ FT: 11,000
SALES (est): 915.5K Privately Held
WEB: www.cobrapower.com
SIC: 3519 7699 Marine engines; marine engine repair

(G-11100)
CODSWORTH INDUSTRIES INC
Also Called: Prestige Entertainment
12864 Biscayne Blvd Ste 3 (33181-2007)
PHONE..............................203 622-5151
Steven Lichtman, *President*
EMP: 8 EST: 2016

SALES (est): 179.5K Privately Held
SIC: 3999 Manufacturing industries

(G-11101)
CSR ENTERPRISE LTD
370 Nw 123rd St (33168-3543)
PHONE..............................954 624-2284
Cranston Rolle, *CEO*
EMP: 8 EST: 2018
SALES (est): 129K Privately Held
SIC: 2673 Plastic bags: made from purchased materials

(G-11102)
DELAB CARE USA LLC
Also Called: Balm Tattoo
2321 Laguna Cir (33181-1067)
PHONE..............................754 317-5678
Alberto Martin Charlo,
EMP: 7 EST: 2015
SALES (est): 74.4K Privately Held
SIC: 2844 Toilet preparations

(G-11103)
ENERGETICO INC
2260 Ne 123rd St (33181-2904)
PHONE..............................213 550-5211
Abe Sher, *CEO*
EMP: 4 EST: 2019
SALES (est): 10MM Privately Held
WEB: www.energetico.com
SIC: 3585 Air conditioning equipment, complete

(G-11104)
EXOTIC MARBLE POLISHING INC
12325 Ne 9th Ave Apt 4 (33161-5733)
PHONE..............................786 318-6568
Jose R Hidalgo, *Principal*
EMP: 7 EST: 2009
SALES (est): 50.6K Privately Held
SIC: 3471 Polishing, metals or formed products

(G-11105)
FUEL CONNECTION
14290 W Dixie Hwy (33161-2533)
PHONE..............................305 354-8115
EMP: 5 EST: 2008
SALES (est): 733.4K Privately Held
SIC: 2869 Mfg Industrial Organic Chemicals

(G-11106)
HEMCO INDUSTRIES INC (PA)
2500 Ne 135th St Ph 5 (33181-3616)
PHONE..............................305 769-0606
Aurelio F Hernandez Jr, *President*
Aida Hernandez, *Treasurer*
EMP: 19 EST: 1965
SALES (est): 1.5MM Privately Held
SIC: 3661 3699 Telephone & telegraph apparatus; security devices

(G-11107)
J M INTERIORS INC
Also Called: First Impressions Industries
12564 Ne 14th Ave (33161-4439)
PHONE..............................305 891-6121
Jeffrey W Smith, *President*
EMP: 8 EST: 1990
SQ FT: 9,000
SALES (est): 411.9K Privately Held
SIC: 2434 2511 2514 2541 Wood kitchen cabinets; wood household furniture; metal household furniture; wood partitions & fixtures

(G-11108)
LASER LIGHT LITHO CORP
1440 Ne 131st St (33161-4424)
PHONE..............................305 899-0713
Clifford Warren, *President*
Armando Bacigalupi, *Treasurer*
Doug Bressler, *Sales Mgr*
Hal Lieberman, *Technology*
Brian Pringle, *Technology*
EMP: 10 EST: 1980
SQ FT: 4,000
SALES (est): 978K Privately Held
WEB: www.laserlightlitho.com
SIC: 2752 Commercial printing, offset

(G-11109)
LATAMREADY LLC
12550 Biscayne Blvd (33181-2541)
PHONE.............................786 600-2641
Carlos A Zumaeta Aurazo, *Manager*
EMP: 8 **EST:** 2014
SALES (est): 197.6K **Privately Held**
WEB: www.latamready.com
SIC: 3652 Pre-recorded records & tapes

(G-11110)
M D R INTERNATIONAL INC
14861 Ne 20th Ave (33181-1143)
PHONE.............................305 944-5335
Bernard Ghelbendorf, *President*
Jeana Ghelbendorf, *Treasurer*
EMP: 14 **EST:** 1973
SQ FT: 20,000
SALES (est): 885.8K **Privately Held**
WEB: www.mdrinternational.com
SIC: 3089 3965 3914 Injection molding of
plastics; buttons & parts; trophies

(G-11111)
MG COATING AND SEALANTS LLC
1280 Ne 137th Ter (33161-3421)
PHONE.............................305 409-0915
Miguel Reyes, *Principal*
EMP: 9 **EST:** 2014
SALES (est): 586.1K **Privately Held**
SIC: 2891 Sealants

(G-11112)
MICHAEL GIORDANO INTL INC (PA)
14851 Ne 20th Ave (33181-1143)
PHONE.............................305 948-6673
Debra L Beilman, *President*
Michael Giardina, *Chairman*
Vito Giardina, *Corp Secy*
◆ **EMP:** 17 **EST:** 1987
SQ FT: 15,000
SALES (est): 14.2MM **Privately Held**
WEB: www.giordanocolors.com
SIC: 2844 Cosmetic preparations

(G-11113)
MOLDS AND PLASTIC MCHY INC
13180 N Bayshore Dr (33181-2149)
PHONE.............................305 828-3456
Bruce Miller, *President*
Guillermo Sanchez, *Corp Secy*
Jose Anton, *Vice Pres*
◆ **EMP:** 8 **EST:** 1996
SALES (est): 882.3K **Privately Held**
WEB: www.moldsplastic.us
SIC: 3089 Injection molding of plastics

(G-11114)
NEMAL ELECTRONICS INTL INC (PA)
12240 Ne 14th Ave (33161-6521)
PHONE.............................305 899-0900
Benjamin L Nemser, *President*
Valber Mascarenhas, *VP Sales*
Madelene Torres, *Sales Mgr*
Robert Larish, *Sales Executive*
Ketty Inguanzo, *Supervisor*
▼ **EMP:** 20 **EST:** 1975
SQ FT: 40,000
SALES (est): 6.5MM **Privately Held**
WEB: www.nemal.com
SIC: 3577 5065 Computer peripheral
equipment; electronic parts & equipment

(G-11115)
PARKER PROTECTIVE PRODUCTS LLC
1965 Ne 148th St (33181-1136)
PHONE.............................800 879-0329
Ian Parker,
EMP: 10 **EST:** 2020
SALES (est): 525.4K **Privately Held**
SIC: 2381 Fabric dress & work gloves

(G-11116)
PROUD TSHIRTS CORP
1801 Ne 123rd St Ste 314 (33181-2883)
PHONE.............................888 233-3426
Gueveny Stgeorges, *President*
EMP: 11 **EST:** 2017
SALES (est): 776.9K **Privately Held**
WEB: www.proudtshirts.com
SIC: 2759 Screen printing

(G-11117)
PUBLISHING RESEARCH INC
1313 Ne 125th St (33161-5975)
PHONE.............................954 921-4026
Benjamin R Jacobi, *President*
EMP: 8 **EST:** 2011
SALES (est): 171.4K **Privately Held**
SIC: 2741 Miscellaneous publishing

(G-11118)
PVC WINDOORS INC
1815 Ne 144th St (33181-1419)
PHONE.............................305 940-3608
Gaston Boudreau, *President*
▼ **EMP:** 15 **EST:** 1996
SQ FT: 33,000
SALES (est): 1.4MM **Privately Held**
WEB: www.pvcwindoors.com
SIC: 3089 Window frames & sash, plastic

(G-11119)
SABROSOL LABORATORIES LLC
12585 Ne 7th Ave (33161-4811)
PHONE.............................305 290-4038
EMP: 8 **EST:** 2014
SALES (est): 181.8K **Privately Held**
SIC: 2844 Hair preparations, including
shampoos; cosmetic preparations

(G-11120)
SEAVEE BOATS
1950 Ne 135th St (33181-2127)
PHONE.............................305 705-3158
EMP: 7 **EST:** 2018
SALES (est): 297.6K **Privately Held**
WEB: www.seaveeboats.com
SIC: 3732 Boat building & repairing

(G-11121)
SFADA TAG AGENCY INC
625 Ne 124th St (33161-5522)
PHONE.............................305 981-1077
Richard A Baker, *President*
EMP: 17 **EST:** 1962
SALES (est): 982.3K **Privately Held**
SIC: 2631 5511 Tagboard; new & used car
dealers

(G-11122)
SKYWAYS TECHNICS AMERICAS LLC
13447 Ne 17th Ave (33181-1716)
PHONE.............................786 615-2443
Lucas Ansinelli, *Sales Staff*
Hernan Morales, *Sales Staff*
Juan Pablo Dorrejo, *Manager*
EMP: 9 **EST:** 2019
SALES (est): 1MM **Privately Held**
WEB: www.skywaystechnics.com
SIC: 3728 Aircraft parts & equipment

(G-11123)
SLIM AND SOFT BREAD LLC
15051 Royal Oaks Ln # 2105
(33181-2457)
PHONE.............................305 759-2126
Robert D Retondaro,
Eduardo E Jimenez,
▲ **EMP:** 10 **EST:** 2002
SQ FT: 15,000
SALES (est): 566K **Privately Held**
WEB: www.slimandsoft.com
SIC: 2051 Breads, rolls & buns

(G-11124)
TD COATING INC
12420 Nw 5th Ave (33168-3608)
PHONE.............................786 325-4211
Tamara Diaz, *President*
EMP: 8 **EST:** 2015
SALES (est): 150.8K **Privately Held**
SIC: 3479 Coating of metals & formed
products

(G-11125)
TECHNO-COATINGS INC
Also Called: Techno Aerospace
1865 Ne 144th St (33181-1419)
PHONE.............................305 945-2220
Juan P Camargo, *CEO*
Saul Camargo, *Chairman*
Rosario Camargo, *Corp Secy*
Carlos Camargo, *Engineer*
Paola Suarez, *CFO*

EMP: 250 **EST:** 1978
SQ FT: 25,000
SALES (est): 23.6MM **Privately Held**
WEB: www.techno-coatings.com
SIC: 3471 Plating of metals or formed
products

(G-11126)
UNITED METAL FABRICATIONS INC
1635 Ne 133rd St (33181-1704)
P.O. Box 611844, Miami (33261-1844)
PHONE.............................305 962-1608
Tomas Casal, *Principal*
Tomas M Casal, *Principal*
▲ **EMP:** 8 **EST:** 2009
SALES (est): 356.1K **Privately Held**
SIC: 3499 Fabricated metal products

(G-11127)
WBT APPAREL INC
1175 Ne 125th St Ste 102 (33161-5009)
PHONE.............................305 891-1107
Kenneth J Tate, *President*
Howard Posner, *COO*
James D Tate, *Vice Pres*
Steven Lieberman, *CFO*
EMP: 8 **EST:** 2007
SALES (est): 261.7K **Privately Held**
SIC: 2331 Women's & misses' blouses &
shirts

(G-11128)
WILD DIAMOND VINEYARDS LLC
1680 Ne 135th St (33181-1725)
PHONE.............................305 892-8699
Robert C Bowling, *Principal*
EMP: 7 **EST:** 2014
SALES (est): 326.8K **Privately Held**
SIC: 2084 Wines, brandy & brandy spirits

(G-11129)
WORKEP INC
11930 N Bayshore Dr (33181-2900)
PHONE.............................787 634-1115
EMP: 7 **EST:** 2018
SALES (est): 198.7K **Privately Held**
SIC: 3652 Pre-recorded records & tapes

North Miami Beach
Miami-Dade County

(G-11130)
AMERICAN INDUSTRIAL GROUP INC
3363 Ne 163rd St Ste 611 (33160-4436)
PHONE.............................703 757-7683
Yan Aronov, *CEO*
EMP: 10 **EST:** 2020
SALES (est): 500K **Privately Held**
SIC: 2869 Alcohols, non-beverage

(G-11131)
BELOVED INC
14040 Biscayne Blvd # 516 (33181-1536)
PHONE.............................404 643-5177
Danie Spikes, *CEO*
EMP: 10 **EST:** 2016
SALES (est): 503.6K **Privately Held**
WEB: www.beloved-press.com
SIC: 2844 Perfumes & colognes

(G-11132)
CHROME CONNECTION CORP
15405 W Dixie Hwy (33162-6093)
PHONE.............................305 947-9191
Natalio Zaglul, *President*
Newlove Tone, *Vice Pres*
▲ **EMP:** 13 **EST:** 2002
SALES (est): 133.1K **Privately Held**
SIC: 2211 5137 Apparel & outerwear fab-
rics, cotton; women's & children's clothing

(G-11133)
DHSS LLC
Also Called: Sleep Group Solutions
16830 Ne 19th Ave (33162-3108)
PHONE.............................305 405-4001
Ran Ben-David, *Principal*
John Nadeau, *Vice Pres*
Donna Davidovitch, *Manager*
Raymond Champ, *Representative*

EMP: 20 **EST:** 2007
SALES (est): 3.4MM **Privately Held**
SIC: 3841 5047 Surgical & medical instru-
ments; medical & hospital equipment

(G-11134)
DIY BLINDS INC
19515 Presidential Way (33179-6406)
PHONE.............................305 692-8877
Arnold S Goldin, *Principal*
EMP: 7 **EST:** 2018
SALES (est): 207.7K **Privately Held**
SIC: 2591 Window blinds

(G-11135)
EDS DELIGHT LLC
2080 Ne 186th Dr (33179-4387)
PHONE.............................305 632-3051
Edward Sthilaire,
EMP: 8 **EST:** 2019
SALES (est): 567.3K **Privately Held**
SIC: 2024 Ice cream & frozen desserts

(G-11136)
ELECTROLYTIC TECH SVCS LLC
19501 Ne 10th Ave Ste 203 (33179-3576)
PHONE.............................305 655-2755
Derek Lubie, *Mng Member*
EMP: 9 **EST:** 2019
SALES (est): 486.3K **Privately Held**
WEB: www.electrolytictech.com
SIC: 3589 Water treatment equipment, in-
dustrial

(G-11137)
EMC AEROSPACE INC
570 Ne 185th St (33179-4513)
PHONE.............................954 316-6015
Edward Monserrat, *CEO*
Christine Monserrat, *CFO*
EMP: 20
SALES (est): 1MM **Privately Held**
WEB: www.emcaerospace.com
SIC: 3721 Aircraft

(G-11138)
FASTSIGNS
15405 W Dixie Hwy (33162-6093)
PHONE.............................305 945-4700
Rudolf Bauer, *Principal*
EMP: 12 **EST:** 2010
SALES (est): 477.3K **Privately Held**
WEB: www.fastsigns.com
SIC: 3993 Signs & advertising specialties

(G-11139)
FBR 1804 INC
18320 Ne 21st Ct (33179-5022)
PHONE.............................305 340-3114
Irvin Pean, *CEO*
EMP: 11 **EST:** 2018
SALES (est): 250K **Privately Held**
SIC: 2741

(G-11140)
FRESH PRESS
15334 W Dixie Hwy (33162-6030)
PHONE.............................305 942-8571
Jovanni Garofolo, *Administration*
EMP: 9 **EST:** 2014
SALES (est): 407.6K **Privately Held**
WEB: www.freshpressmiami.com
SIC: 2741 Miscellaneous publishing

(G-11141)
FUEL SOLUTIONS DISTRS LLC
Also Called: Fuel Medics
3777 Ne 163rd St Pmb 148 (33160-4104)
PHONE.............................305 528-3758
David E Suaya, *Mng Member*
David Suaya, *Mng Member*
Samantha Suaya,
◆ **EMP:** 6 **EST:** 2008
SALES (est): 466.3K **Privately Held**
SIC: 2911 5169 Fuel additives; oil addi-
tives

(G-11142)
GENUINE DENIM
851 Ne 182nd Ter (33162-1156)
PHONE.............................305 491-1326
Ovadia Tamir, *Principal*
EMP: 7 **EST:** 2016
SALES (est): 83.9K **Privately Held**
SIC: 2211 Denims

▲ = Import ▼=Export
◆ =Import/Export

(G-11143)
GREEN PAPERS INC
Also Called: Green Toad Printers
15660 W Dixie Hwy (33162-6036)
PHONE.....................305 956-3535
Carlos A Girlando, *President*
EMP: 5 EST: 2009
SALES (est): 647.1K **Privately Held**
SIC: 2752 Publication printing, lithographic

(G-11144)
INTERNATIONAL H20 INC
18387 Ne 4th Ct (33179-4531)
PHONE.....................954 854-1638
Juhani C Defazio, *President*
EMP: 7 EST: 2013
SQ FT: 6,000
SALES (est): 933.4K **Privately Held**
WEB: www.internationalh2o.com
SIC: 3585 Coolers, milk & water: electric

(G-11145)
IVER SERVICES
2381 Ne 135th Ter (33181-1847)
PHONE.....................786 329-3018
EMP: 12
SALES (est): 329.6K **Privately Held**
SIC: 3999 Mfg Misc Products

(G-11146)
J&S INKS LLC
1212 Ne 176th Ter (33162-1208)
PHONE.....................305 999-0304
Shlomo Friedman, *Principal*
EMP: 9 EST: 2006
SALES (est): 319.1K **Privately Held**
SIC: 2893 Printing ink

(G-11147)
KOLLSUT INTERNATIONAL INC
1763 Ne 162nd St (33162-4757)
PHONE.....................305 438-6877
Arkady Teplitsky, *President*
Enrique Berrios, *President*
Mingze Chen,
Binoy Joese,
Jing Wang,
EMP: 9 EST: 2006
SALES (est): 317.2K **Privately Held**
WEB: www.kollsut.com
SIC: 3841 5047 Surgical & medical instruments; surgical equipment & supplies

(G-11148)
LAURA KNIT COLLECTION INC (PA)
3224 Ne 167th St (33160-3848)
PHONE.....................305 945-8222
Joseph Feuer, *President*
Linda Feuer, *Corp Secy*
▲ EMP: 152 EST: 1979
SQ FT: 40,000
SALES (est): 8MM **Privately Held**
SIC: 2337 2335 Suits: women's, misses & juniors'; women's, juniors' & misses' dresses

(G-11149)
MC MONUMENTAL GROUP INC
281 Ne 168th Ter (33162-2323)
PHONE.....................305 651-9113
Jean Casimir, *President*
EMP: 8 EST: 2017
SALES (est): 285.5K **Privately Held**
SIC: 3272 Monuments & grave markers, except terrazo

(G-11150)
MIAMI SIGN SHOP INC
13899 Biscayne Blvd # 155 (33181-1600)
PHONE.....................305 431-2455
David Dibenedetto, *President*
EMP: 5 EST: 2018
SALES (est): 334.9K **Privately Held**
WEB: www.miamisignshop.com
SIC: 3993 Signs & advertising specialties

(G-11151)
MISS BS INC
13899 Biscayne Blvd # 309 (33181-1600)
PHONE.....................305 981-9900
Brenda Bontarii, *President*
Emmanouil Alevropoulos, *Manager*
EMP: 6 EST: 1991

SALES (est): 892.8K **Privately Held**
WEB: www.missbs.com
SIC: 2389 Costumes

(G-11152)
MUSCLE FX LLC
2221 Ne 164th St Ste 1267 (33160-3703)
PHONE.....................305 514-0061
Akshat Bhatia, *CEO*
EMP: 5 EST: 2008
SALES (est): 760K **Privately Held**
WEB: www.getmusclefx.com
SIC: 2834 Vitamin, nutrient & hematinic preparations for human use

(G-11153)
NEW DAIRY OPCO LLC
501 Ne 181st St (33162-1006)
PHONE.....................305 652-3720
EMP: 36
SALES (corp-wide): 577.7MM **Privately Held**
SIC: 2023 Dry, condensed, evaporated dairy products
PA: New Dairy Opco, Llc
12400 Coit Rd Ste 200
Dallas TX 75251
214 258-1200

(G-11154)
PALM PHEON MUSIC PUBG LLC
Also Called: Bay Eight Studios
15421 W Dixie Hwy (33162-6059)
PHONE.....................305 705-2405
Matthew P Defreitas, *President*
EMP: 10 EST: 2016
SALES (est): 2.2MM **Privately Held**
WEB: www.bayeight.com
SIC: 2741 Miscellaneous publishing

(G-11155)
PERFORMANCE BOATS INC
2050 Ne 153rd St (33162-6020)
PHONE.....................305 956-9549
Bob Cetrealt, *President*
Debbie Divich, *Vice Pres*
◆ EMP: 10 EST: 2001
SQ FT: 7,889
SALES (est): 655.5K **Privately Held**
WEB: www.performancepowerboats.com
SIC: 3732 Motorized boat, building & repairing

(G-11156)
PRIVE INTERNATIONAL INC
19597 Ne 10th Ave Ste F (33179-3578)
PHONE.....................888 750-5850
Valentina Cohen, *President*
EMP: 20 EST: 2013
SALES (est): 1.1MM **Privately Held**
WEB: www.prive-international.com
SIC: 2844 Cosmetic preparations

(G-11157)
PROFBOX OF AMERICA INC
17071 W Dixie Hwy Ste 116 (33160-3773)
PHONE.....................786 454-8148
Tatiana Sokolova, *Vice Pres*
EMP: 7 EST: 2012
SALES (est): 948.5K **Privately Held**
WEB: www.amprofbox.com
SIC: 3089 Plastics products

(G-11158)
R & Y AUTOMOTIVE AC CMPSR
15315 Ne 21st Ave (33162-6005)
PHONE.....................305 919-9232
Jacob Shaked, *Exec VP*
Prosper Mamane, *Manager*
EMP: 20 **Privately Held**
WEB: www.rycompressors.com
SIC: 3585 Compressors for refrigeration & air conditioning equipment
PA: R & Y Automotive Air Conditioning Compressors, Inc
15315 Ne 21st Ave
North Miami Beach FL 33162

(G-11159)
R & Y AUTOMOTIVE AC CMPSR (PA)
15315 Ne 21st Ave (33162-6005)
PHONE.....................305 947-1173
Prosper Mamane, *President*
▼ EMP: 17 EST: 1988
SQ FT: 19,495

SALES (est): 3.4MM **Privately Held**
WEB: www.rycompressors.com
SIC: 3585 Compressors for refrigeration & air conditioning equipment

(G-11160)
RADWAG USA LLC
19599 Ne 10th Ave Ste E (33179-3579)
PHONE.....................305 651-3522
Pawel Gorzalczynski, *Export Mgr*
Adrian Casanova, *Sales Mgr*
Alfonso Romero, *Sales Executive*
Maciej Lewandowski, *Mng Member*
Ernesto Garcia, *Manager*
▲ EMP: 9 EST: 2006
SALES (est): 1.2MM **Privately Held**
WEB: www.radwagusa.com
SIC: 3596 Weighing machines & apparatus

(G-11161)
SCALE MODELS ARTS & TECH
Also Called: Smartt
15455 W Dixie Hwy Ste G (33162-6067)
P.O. Box 600505 (33160-0505)
PHONE.....................305 949-1706
Michael Hart, *President*
Mark Rothman, *Engineer*
Tom Kapatelis, *Manager*
EMP: 12 EST: 1995
SALES (est): 1MM **Privately Held**
WEB: www.smarttinc.com
SIC: 3999 3944 Models, general, except toy; games, toys & children's vehicles

(G-11162)
STITCH COUNT INC
Also Called: Bid Uniforms.com
20404 Ne 16th Pl (33179-2704)
PHONE.....................609 929-9019
Michael Ryba, *President*
EMP: 7 EST: 2011
SQ FT: 2,000
SALES (est): 325.8K **Privately Held**
WEB: bid-excellence-co-llc.business.site
SIC: 2326 5136 2311 Work apparel, except uniforms; men's & boys' sportswear & work clothing; men's & boys' uniforms

(G-11163)
SUNNY SKIES ENTERPRISES INC
570 Ne 185th St (33179-4513)
PHONE.....................954 316-6015
Edward J Monserrat, *CEO*
Jenny Alonzo, *Manager*
Mike Lopez, *Manager*
Leo Matamoros, *Manager*
Edward Lee Morgan, *Manager*
EMP: 30 EST: 1997
SQ FT: 10,000
SALES (est): 10.9MM
SALES (corp-wide): 168.6MM **Privately Held**
SIC: 3728 Aircraft parts & equipment
HQ: Velocity Aerospace Group, Inc.
7460 Warren Pkwy Ste 180
Frisco TX 75034
214 988-9898

(G-11164)
SWEET TOOTH INC
18435 Ne 19th Ave (33179-5033)
PHONE.....................305 682-1400
Leigh Kersh, *President*
Johnny Berman, *Principal*
▼ EMP: 6 EST: 1983
SALES (est): 1MM **Privately Held**
WEB: www.thesweettooth.com
SIC: 2064 5812 5441 2066 Chocolate candy, except solid chocolate; caterers; candy; chocolate & cocoa products

(G-11165)
SWIM BY CHUCK HANDY INC
15415 Ne 21st Ave (33162-6007)
PHONE.....................305 519-4946
Charles J Handy, *President*
Mary Lou Handy, *Vice Pres*
◆ EMP: 6 EST: 2010
SALES (est): 342.3K **Privately Held**
WEB: www.buychuckhandy.com
SIC: 2253 5137 Bathing suits & swimwear, knit; swimsuits: women's, children's & infants'

(G-11166)
VELOCITY AEROSPACE - NMB INC
570 Ne 185th St (33179-4513)
PHONE.....................214 396-9030
Dale Gabel, *CEO*
Dennis Lainez, *General Mgr*
Vilma Figueroa, *Accountant*
EMP: 40 EST: 2015
SQ FT: 39,000
SALES (est): 8MM
SALES (corp-wide): 168.6MM **Privately Held**
SIC: 3728 Aircraft parts & equipment
HQ: Velocity Aerospace Group, Inc.
7460 Warren Pkwy Ste 180
Frisco TX 75034
214 988-9898

(G-11167)
VENETA CUCINE INC
2020 Ne 163rd St Ste 100 (33162-4927)
PHONE.....................305 949-5223
Corrado Bonanno, *Manager*
EMP: 7 EST: 2007
SALES (est): 269K **Privately Held**
WEB: www.venetacucine.us
SIC: 2434 Wood kitchen cabinets

(G-11168)
VONN LLC
Also Called: Vonn Lighting
3323 Ne 163rd St Ph 706 (33160-5599)
PHONE.....................888 604-8666
Sergio Magarik, *CEO*
Lenny Valdberg, *President*
EMP: 18 EST: 2015
SQ FT: 7,000
SALES (est): 10MM **Privately Held**
WEB: www.vonn.com
SIC: 3646 3645 Commercial indusl & institutional electric lighting fixtures; residential lighting fixtures

(G-11169)
WE LOVE TEC LLC
2032 Ne 155th St (33162-6058)
PHONE.....................305 433-4453
Nicolas Massri, *Mng Member*
EMP: 5 EST: 2016
SALES (est): 805.3K **Privately Held**
WEB: www.welovetec.com
SIC: 3812 Electronic field detection apparatus (aeronautical)

(G-11170)
WHITE SANDS DMG INC
Also Called: Sign-A-Rama
1798 Ne 163rd St (33162-4733)
PHONE.....................305 947-7731
Roger Maxfield, *President*
Marisol Maxfield, *Vice Pres*
EMP: 5 EST: 1988
SQ FT: 1,550
SALES (est): 487.4K **Privately Held**
WEB: www.signarama.com
SIC: 3993 Signs & advertising specialties

(G-11171)
WISH INC
33 Nw 168th St (33169-6027)
PHONE.....................305 653-9474
Allan Moiseyev, *President*
▲ EMP: 10 EST: 2010
SALES (est): 1.2MM **Privately Held**
SIC: 3465 Body parts, automobile: stamped metal

(G-11172)
Y F LEUNG INC (PA)
1155 Ne 177th Ter (33162-1211)
PHONE.....................305 651-6851
Man Chung Leung, *President*
Yuen Cheung Leung, *Vice Pres*
EMP: 8 EST: 1978
SQ FT: 15,000
SALES (est): 568.2K **Privately Held**
SIC: 2431 1799 2541 2517 Millwork; home/office interiors finishing, furnishing & remodeling; wood partitions & fixtures; wood television & radio cabinets; wood household furniture; wood kitchen cabinets

North Palm Beach
Palm Beach County

(G-11173)
ALPHA COMMERCIAL PRINTING
838 Northlake Blvd (33408-5210)
PHONE...................................561 841-1415
Panos Antonio, *Owner*
Catherine Antonio, *Co-Owner*
EMP: 5 EST: 1997
SALES (est): 328.3K **Privately Held**
WEB: www.alphacommercialcards.com
SIC: 2752 Commercial printing, offset

(G-11174)
ASD SURFACES LLC
531 Us Highway 1 (33408-4900)
PHONE...................................561 845-5009
Naiomy Vasquez, *Sales Staff*
Nina Wasserman, *Mng Member*
EMP: 6 EST: 2012
SQ FT: 6,000
SALES (est): 3MM **Privately Held**
WEB: www.asdsurfaces.com
SIC: 3253 1411 5023 5211 Floor tile, ceramic; limestone & marble dimension stone; wood flooring; tile, ceramic

(G-11175)
ATTITUDE DRINKS INCORPORATED (PA)
712 Us Highway 1 Ste 200 (33408-4521)
PHONE...................................561 227-2727
Roy Warren, *Ch of Bd*
Tommy Kee, *CFO*
EMP: 4 EST: 2007
SALES (est): 4.3MM **Publicly Held**
WEB: www.attitudedrinks.com
SIC: 2026 Milk drinks, flavored

(G-11176)
BEACON PUBLISHING INC
631 Us Highway 1 Ste 201 (33408-4614)
PHONE...................................888 618-5253
Matthew Kelly, *President*
EMP: 8 EST: 2003
SALES (est): 212.4K **Privately Held**
WEB: www.bluesparrowbooks.org
SIC: 2731 Books: publishing & printing

(G-11177)
BEST PUBLISHING COMPANY
631 Us Highway 1 Ste 307 (33408-4618)
PHONE...................................561 776-6066
John S Peters, *Owner*
John Peters, *Sales Mgr*
Eric Vanbok, *Director*
EMP: 11 EST: 2009
SALES (est): 1MM **Privately Held**
WEB: www.bestpub.com
SIC: 2741 Miscellaneous publishing

(G-11178)
BF WESTON LLC (PA)
105 Us Highway 1 (33408-5401)
PHONE...................................561 844-5528
John Rosatti, *Mng Member*
EMP: 6 EST: 2014
SALES (est): 1.6MM **Privately Held**
SIC: 3011 Tires & inner tubes

(G-11179)
CHERVO USA INC
1201 Us Highway 1 Ste 435 (33408-8509)
PHONE...................................561 510-2458
Marianne Strelec, *Principal*
EMP: 8 EST: 2017
SALES (est): 301K **Privately Held**
WEB: www.chervo.com
SIC: 2323 Men's & boys' neckwear

(G-11180)
MUELBY CONSTRUCTION SERVICES
378 Northlake Blvd (33408-5421)
PHONE...................................561 376-7614
Michael Moss, *President*
EMP: 50 EST: 2020
SALES (est): 3.3MM **Privately Held**
SIC: 1389 Construction, repair & dismantling services

(G-11181)
PATIENT PORTAL TECH INC (PA)
2000 Pga Blvd Ste 4440 (33408-2738)
PHONE...................................877 779-6627
Brian Kelly, *CEO*
John O'Mara, *President*
Thomas Hagan, *CFO*
EMP: 18 EST: 2003
SALES (est): 4MM **Publicly Held**
WEB: www.patientportal.com
SIC: 7372 Prepackaged software

(G-11182)
PURAGEN LLC
11300 Us Highway 1 # 203 (33408-3217)
PHONE...................................760 630-5724
Mark McCormick, *Vice Pres*
EMP: 50
SALES (corp-wide): 859.6MM **Privately Held**
WEB: www.puragen.com
SIC: 2819 Charcoal (carbon), activated
HQ: Puragen Llc
1601 Forum Pl Ste 1400
West Palm Beach FL 33401
561 907-5400

(G-11183)
TRANSDERMAL TECHNOLOGIES INC
521 Northlake Blvd Ste B (33408-5418)
PHONE...................................561 848-2345
Kenneth B Kirby, *President*
Bruce Crawford, *Exec VP*
EMP: 7 EST: 1990
SQ FT: 9,000
SALES (est): 929.8K **Privately Held**
SIC: 2834 Ointments

(G-11184)
UNIVERSAL GRAPHICS & PRTG INC
Also Called: Minuteman Press
120 Us Highway 1 Ste 1 (33408-5404)
PHONE...................................561 845-6404
Dennis Beck, *President*
Phyllis Beck, *Vice Pres*
EMP: 5 EST: 1991
SQ FT: 1,300
SALES (est): 749.8K **Privately Held**
WEB: www.minuteman.com
SIC: 2752 2791 2789 Commercial printing, offset; typesetting; bookbinding & related work

(G-11185)
WOOD STILE INC
644 Marbella Ln (33403-1239)
PHONE...................................561 329-4671
Andrew Hanbury, *President*
EMP: 5 EST: 2013
SALES (est): 358.6K **Privately Held**
SIC: 2599 Cabinets, factory

North Port
Sarasota County

(G-11186)
ADAMS BROS CABINETRY INC
Also Called: Adams Group
2221 Murphy Ct (34289-9314)
PHONE...................................941 639-7188
Ethan M Adams, *President*
Maria Adams, *Vice Pres*
Kevin Stanley, *Project Mgr*
Josh Underdown, *Project Mgr*
Steve Walker, *Project Mgr*
EMP: 89 EST: 1978
SQ FT: 50,000
SALES (est): 17MM **Privately Held**
SIC: 2431 8071 Millwork; medical laboratories

(G-11187)
AIR INFINITY INC
2616 Tusket Ave (34286-4909)
PHONE...................................941 423-1355
Michael P Martin, *President*
EMP: 8 EST: 1999
SALES (est): 248.7K **Privately Held**
SIC: 3585 Heating & air conditioning combination units

(G-11188)
BIMBO BAKERIES USA
2625 Commerce Pkwy # 112 (34289-9347)
PHONE...................................941 875-5945
EMP: 8 EST: 2011
SALES (est): 116.5K **Privately Held**
SIC: 2051 Bakery: wholesale or wholesale/retail combined

(G-11189)
BUSY BEE CABINETS INC
2845 Commerce Pkwy (34289-9303)
PHONE...................................941 628-2025
Matthew M Uebelacker, *President*
Diana R Uebelacker, *Vice Pres*
Kenny Midgett, *Sales Mgr*
Linda Simmons, *Sales Staff*
Nancy Dietzman, *Sales Executive*
EMP: 80 EST: 1982
SQ FT: 27,000
SALES (est): 9.7MM **Privately Held**
WEB: www.busybeecabinets.com
SIC: 2434 Wood kitchen cabinets

(G-11190)
BUTLER PAVERS INC
6862 Van Camp St (34291-4026)
PHONE...................................941 423-3977
EMP: 9 EST: 2004
SALES (est): 114.1K **Privately Held**
WEB: www.butlerpavers.com
SIC: 2951 Asphalt paving mixtures & blocks

(G-11191)
C&S OSTOMY POUCH COVERS INC
2214 Cloras St (34287-5174)
PHONE...................................941 423-8542
Bonnie Coker, *President*
EMP: 5 EST: 2010
SALES (est): 327.8K **Privately Held**
WEB: www.cspouchcovers.com
SIC: 2258 Covers, lace: chair, dresser, piano & table

(G-11192)
CUSTOMER 1ST LLC
6413 Taneytown St (34291-4715)
PHONE...................................941 585-5123
John McKee, *Principal*
EMP: 8 EST: 2011
SALES (est): 340.6K **Privately Held**
SIC: 3499 Fabricated metal products

(G-11193)
EURO-WALL SYSTEMS LLC
2200 Murphy Ct (34289-9302)
PHONE...................................941 979-5316
Michael Zurbrigen, *Mng Member*
Carolina Zurbrigen,
◆ EMP: 32 EST: 2012
SALES (est): 15.9MM **Privately Held**
WEB: www.euro-wall.com
SIC: 3442 Metal doors, sash & trim

(G-11194)
GEMSTONE CABINETRY LLC
2845 Commerce Pkwy (34289-9303)
PHONE...................................941 426-5656
Matt Uebelacker, *Principal*
EMP: 8 EST: 2016
SALES (est): 115.7K **Privately Held**
WEB: www.gemstonecabinetry.com
SIC: 2434 Wood kitchen cabinets

(G-11195)
HOT SAUCE HARRYS INC
1077 Innovation Ave # 10 (34289-9345)
PHONE...................................941 423-7092
Dianne P Harris, *President*
Bob Harris, *Vice Pres*
EMP: 6 EST: 1994
SALES (est): 770K **Privately Held**
WEB: www.hotsauceharrys.com
SIC: 2033 5149 Barbecue sauce: packaged in cans, jars, etc.; groceries & related products

(G-11196)
INNOVATIVE OPTICS LLC
8520 Bessemer Ave (34287-3700)
PHONE...................................239 994-0695
Matthew H Potratz, *Principal*
EMP: 7 EST: 2017

SALES (est): 120.1K **Privately Held**
WEB: www.innovativeoptics.com
SIC: 3827 Optical instruments & lenses

(G-11197)
KING PLASTIC CORPORATION
1100 N Toledo Blade Blvd (34288-8694)
PHONE...................................941 423-8666
Jeff King, *CEO*
Thomas M King, *Chairman*
Diane Charest, *Buyer*
Nathan Martin, *Engineer*
Craig Calhoun, *CFO*
EMP: 120 EST: 1968
SQ FT: 150,000
SALES (est): 79.8MM **Privately Held**
WEB: www.kingplastic.com
SIC: 3081 3082 Plastic film & sheet; rods, unsupported plastic

(G-11198)
MARINER PUBLICATIONS LLC (PA)
2250 Firebrand Rd (34288-8474)
PHONE...................................941 426-9645
Michael Jones, *Principal*
EMP: 6 EST: 2011
SALES (est): 699.3K **Privately Held**
SIC: 2741 Miscellaneous publishing

(G-11199)
MCR COMPRESSION SERVICES LLC (PA)
1261 S Haberland Blvd (34288-8164)
P.O. Box 13180, Odessa TX (79768-3180)
PHONE...................................432 552-8720
Pamela Trout,
EMP: 8 EST: 2012
SALES (est): 4MM **Privately Held**
SIC: 1389 Gas field services; oil field services

(G-11200)
MCR COMPRESSION SERVICES LLC
1158 S Haberland Blvd (34288-8173)
PHONE...................................210 760-7650
Pamela Trout,
EMP: 10
SALES (corp-wide): 4MM **Privately Held**
WEB: www.mcroilandgas.com
SIC: 1389 Gas field services; oil field services
PA: Mcr Compression Services Llc
1261 S Haberland Blvd
North Port FL 34288
432 552-8720

(G-11201)
MONROE CABLE LLC
Also Called: ATI
2529 Commerce Pkwy (34289-9355)
PHONE...................................941 429-8484
Richard Samuels, *General Mgr*
Robin Nichols, *Finance*
EMP: 70 EST: 1989
SQ FT: 17,000
SALES (est): 20.6MM
SALES (corp-wide): 66.1MM **Privately Held**
SIC: 3679 3661 3663 3357 Electronic circuits; telephone & telegraph apparatus; television monitors; nonferrous wiredrawing & insulating
PA: Monroe Engineering, Llc
2990 Technology Dr
Rochester Hills MI 48309
877 740-1077

(G-11202)
NORTH PORT PAVERS INC
6099 Estates Dr (34291-4600)
PHONE...................................941 391-7557
Adeleimar Figueiredo, *Principal*
EMP: 8 EST: 2010
SALES (est): 198.4K **Privately Held**
SIC: 3531 Pavers

(G-11203)
PICKLES PLUS
6196 Tidwell St (34291-2003)
PHONE...................................941 661-6139
Denise Proper, *Owner*
EMP: 8 EST: 2006

SALES (est): 129K **Privately Held**
WEB: www.picklesplus.com
SIC: 2035 Pickled fruits & vegetables

(G-11204)
ROTARY MANUFACTURING LLC
3276 Commerce Pkwy (34289-9339)
PHONE.................................941 564-8038
McAloon Scott, *Mng Member*
EMP: 8 **EST:** 2012
SALES (est): 259.8K **Privately Held**
WEB: www.rotarymfg.com
SIC: 2679 Pipes & fittings, fiber: made
from purchased material

(G-11205)
UNIQUE LED PRODUCTS LLC
408 Madonna (34287-2536)
PHONE.................................440 520-4959
Linda Frycz, *General Mgr*
Darrell Frycz, *Mng Member*
EMP: 6 **EST:** 2012
SALES (est): 345.2K **Privately Held**
WEB: www.uniqueledproducts.com
SIC: 3993 Signs & advertising specialties

(G-11206)
XYZ MANUFACTURING INC
3455 Bobcat Vlg Ctr Rd (34288-8976)
PHONE.................................941 426-5656
EMP: 7 **EST:** 2016
SALES (est): 63.5K **Privately Held**
SIC: 3999 Atomizers, toiletry

North Venice
Sarasota County

(G-11207)
B G INSTRUMENT CORP
112 Morse Ct (34275-3635)
PHONE.................................941 485-7700
Robert Gredick, *President*
EMP: 14 **EST:** 1946
SQ FT: 5,000
SALES (est): 217.9K **Privately Held**
SIC: 3599 Machine shop, jobbing & repair

(G-11208)
**BOAT STEERING SOLUTIONS
LLC**
1070 Endeavor Ct (34275-3623)
PHONE.................................727 400-4746
EMP: 5 **EST:** 2019
SALES (est): 927.6K **Privately Held**
WEB: www.boatsteer.com
SIC: 3714 Motor vehicle parts & accessories

(G-11209)
COYOTE ACQUISITION CO (HQ)
1070 Technology Dr (34275-3617)
PHONE.................................941 480-1600
Rodney Hershberger, *Principal*
EMP: 31 **EST:** 2018
SALES (est): 55.6MM
SALES (corp-wide): 1.1B **Publicly Held**
SIC: 3442 Window & door frames
PA: Pgt Innovations, Inc.
1070 Technology Dr
North Venice FL 34275
941 480-1600

(G-11210)
DENNYS ELECTRONICS INC
1044 Endeavor Ct (34275-3623)
PHONE.................................941 485-5400
Dennis Bartosik, *President*
EMP: 21 **EST:** 1977
SQ FT: 16,000
SALES (est): 1.6MM **Privately Held**
WEB: www.dennyselectronics.com
SIC: 3944 Games, toys & children's vehicles

(G-11211)
**DIVERSFIED MTL SPECIALISTS
INC**
Also Called: D M S I
105 Triple Dmd Blvd Ste 1 (34275-3646)
PHONE.................................941 244-0935
Jeff Dalonzo, *President*
Jeneth Dalonzo, *Vice Pres*
Brandon Woodward, *Vice Pres*

Dustin Hall, *Regl Sales Mgr*
Nick Berg, *Director*
▲ **EMP:** 5 **EST:** 1996
SALES (est): 1.2MM **Privately Held**
WEB: www.dmsimfg.com
SIC: 3678 8742 7373 3357 Electronic
connectors; management consulting services; systems integration services; communication wire; engineering services;
computer (hardware) development

(G-11212)
GAUTIER FABRICATION INC
1049 Endeavor Ct (34275-3622)
PHONE.................................941 485-2464
Michael Gautier, *President*
Sonya Murphy, *Office Admin*
EMP: 19 **EST:** 1994
SALES (est): 5.1MM **Privately Held**
WEB: www.gautierfabrication.com
SIC: 3444 Sheet metalwork

(G-11213)
JANSEN SHUTTERS & SPC LTD
115 Morse Ct (34275-3636)
PHONE.................................941 484-4700
Phillip Jansen, *Executive*
Susan Jansen,
Travis Jansen,
Ashley Jansen, *Assistant*
EMP: 8 **EST:** 2002
SALES (est): 2.4MM **Privately Held**
WEB: www.jansenshutters.com
SIC: 3442 Shutters, door or window: metal

(G-11214)
MASTER MOLD CORP
123 Morse Ct (34275-3636)
PHONE.................................941 486-0000
Danny Davis, *President*
EMP: 7 **EST:** 2000
SQ FT: 2,000
SALES (est): 755.7K **Privately Held**
WEB: www.master-mold.net
SIC: 3089 3944 Injection molding of plastics; dice & dice cups

(G-11215)
PGT ESCROW ISSUER INC
1070 Technology Dr (34275-3617)
PHONE.................................941 480-1600
Tonda Brickey, *Controller*
EMP: 12 **EST:** 2018
SALES (est): 195.5K **Privately Held**
WEB: www.pgtinnovations.com
SIC: 3442 Metal doors, sash & trim

(G-11216)
PGT INDUSTRIES INC (HQ)
Also Called: PGT Custom Windows Doors
1070 Technology Dr (34275-3617)
P.O. Box 1529, Nokomis (34274-1529)
PHONE.................................941 480-1600
Rodney Hershberger, *President*
Rachel Evans, *Vice Pres*
Benji Hershberger, *Vice Pres*
Debbie Raho, *Buyer*
Brad West, *CFO*
◆ **EMP:** 900 **EST:** 1980
SQ FT: 420,000
SALES (est): 493.9MM
SALES (corp-wide): 1.1B **Publicly Held**
WEB: www.pgtwindows.com
SIC: 3442 2431 3231 Window & door
frames; windows & window parts & trim,
wood; doors & door parts & trim, wood;
products of purchased glass
PA: Pgt Innovations, Inc.
1070 Technology Dr
North Venice FL 34275
941 480-1600

(G-11217)
PGT INNOVATIONS INC
Also Called: Ilab By PGT Innovations
3440 Technology Dr (34275-3618)
PHONE.................................941 480-1600
EMP: 54
SALES (corp-wide): 1.1B **Publicly Held**
WEB: www.pgtwindows.com
SIC: 3442 Window & door frames
PA: Pgt Innovations, Inc.
1070 Technology Dr
North Venice FL 34275
941 480-1600

(G-11218)
PGT INNOVATIONS INC (PA)
1070 Technology Dr (34275-3617)
PHONE.................................941 480-1600
Jeffrey T Jackson, *President*
▼ **EMP:** 131 **EST:** 1980
SQ FT: 363,000
SALES: 1.1B **Publicly Held**
WEB: www.pgtinnovations.com
SIC: 3442 2431 3211 Window & door
frames; windows & window parts & trim,
wood; doors & door parts & trim, wood;
laminated glass

(G-11219)
SRQ WELDING INC
Also Called: Sarasota Welding
121 Triple Dmd Blvd (34275-3600)
PHONE.................................941 484-5947
Robert Angelo, *Principal*
EMP: 7 **EST:** 2017
SALES (est): 162.1K **Privately Held**
SIC: 7692 Welding repair

(G-11220)
**TERVIS TUMBLER COMPANY
(PA)**
201 Triple Diamond Blvd (34275-3634)
PHONE.................................941 966-2114
John P Redmond Jr, *CEO*
Dorothy Lierman, *President*
Joshua Quillen, *General Mgr*
Norbert Donnelly, *Chairman*
Chad Blankenship, *Vice Pres*
◆ **EMP:** 200 **EST:** 1946
SQ FT: 55,830
SALES (est): 80.5MM **Privately Held**
WEB: www.tervis.com
SIC: 3089 Cups, plastic, except foam

(G-11221)
WEBER MFG & SUPPLIES INC
Also Called: Weber Manufacturing
3430 Technology Dr (34275-3618)
PHONE.................................941 488-5185
Pamela J Prost, *CEO*
Louis Samuel Prost, *President*
Patrick C Smith, *Vice Pres*
Aaron Prost, *Sales Staff*
Lynda Hayes, *Office Admin*
EMP: 17 **EST:** 1963
SQ FT: 15,000
SALES (est): 2.9MM **Privately Held**
WEB: www.webermfg.com
SIC: 3451 3599 Screw machine products;
machine & other job shop work

(G-11222)
WINDOOR INCORPORATED
1070 Technology Dr (34275-3617)
PHONE.................................407 481-8400
Frank R Lukens Jr, *President*
Lizmarie Torres, *Production*
Catherine Terry, *Human Res Mgr*
George Hanus, *Marketing Mgr*
Bradley Ringstrom, *IT/INT Sup*
◆ **EMP:** 105 **EST:** 2001
SALES (est): 24.3MM
SALES (corp-wide): 1.1B **Publicly Held**
WEB: www.windoorinc.com
SIC: 3231 3211 Doors, glass: made from
purchased glass; window glass, clear &
colored
HQ: Pgt Industries, Inc.
1070 Technology Dr
North Venice FL 34275

O Brien
Suwannee County

(G-11223)
ASTELLAS PHARMA US INC
9159 220th St (32071-3233)
PHONE.................................386 935-1220
Curtis Humphreys, *Owner*
EMP: 24 **Privately Held**
WEB: www.astellas.us
SIC: 2834 Vitamin, nutrient & hematinic
preparations for human use
HQ: Astellas Pharma Us, Inc.
1 Astellas Way
Northbrook IL 60062

(G-11224)
HOUGH INDUSTRIES INC
21612 N County Road 349 (32071-1902)
PHONE.................................863 634-1664
Jonica K Hough, *President*
EMP: 7 **EST:** 2017
SALES (est): 251.1K **Privately Held**
WEB: www.electricsaver1200.info
SIC: 3999 Manufacturing industries

(G-11225)
STRAW LIFE INC
25434 87th Dr (32071-3911)
PHONE.................................386 935-2850
Verlin R Sherrell, *President*
Millicent Perry, *Vice Pres*
EMP: 8 **EST:** 2015
SALES (est): 232K **Privately Held**
SIC: 3999 Straw goods

Oakland
Orange County

(G-11226)
ABC ENTERPRISES
16274 Lake Johns Cir (34787-9426)
P.O. Box 218 (34760-0218)
PHONE.................................407 656-6503
Andrew Arsenio, *Owner*
Tammy Steen, *Vice Pres*
EMP: 7 **EST:** 1987
SQ FT: 1,008
SALES (est): 330.3K **Privately Held**
SIC: 3841 Surgical & medical instruments

(G-11227)
**CREATIVE AUTO BOUTIQUE
LLC**
17949 W Colonial Dr (34787-9768)
PHONE.................................407 654-7300
Omar I Alli, *Mng Member*
Brian Jankuhn,
EMP: 8 **EST:** 2009
SALES (est): 946.1K **Privately Held**
WEB: www.creativeautoboutique.com
SIC: 3714 Acceleration equipment, motor
vehicle

(G-11228)
CUSTOM METAL DESIGNS INC
921 W Oakland Ave (34760-8855)
P.O. Box 783037, Winter Garden (34778-
3037)
PHONE.................................407 656-7771
Saul Grimes, *Ch of Bd*
Steven Grimes, *President*
Ann Grimes, *Corp Secy*
H T Lucas Jr, *Vice Pres*
Dale Williams, *Project Mgr*
EMP: 55 **EST:** 1972
SQ FT: 25,000
SALES (est): 13.4MM **Privately Held**
WEB: www.custommetaldesigns.com
SIC: 3535 Conveyors & conveying equipment

(G-11229)
MPACT SALES SOLUTIONS
622 Largovista Dr (34787-8973)
PHONE.................................630 669-5937
EMP: 9
SALES (est): 50K **Privately Held**
SIC: 2834 Mfg Pharmaceutical Preparations

(G-11230)
**SOUTHWIND AVIATION SUPPLY
LLC**
752 Strihal Loop (34787-8957)
P.O. Box 1256 (34760-1256)
PHONE.................................405 491-0500
Gary P Henricksen, *Vice Pres*
Sandi Chuck, *Controller*
George S Andrews,
Justin Nalley,
Ronald O Shrum,
EMP: 12 **EST:** 2004
SALES (est): 2.2MM **Privately Held**
WEB: www.southwindaviation.com
SIC: 3728 Aircraft parts & equipment

Oakland Park
Broward County

(G-11231)
300 TECHNOLOGIES INC
4905 Ne 12th Ave (33334-4805)
PHONE....................954 234-0018
EMP: 11 EST: 2016
SALES (est): 329.1K Privately Held
SIC: 3714 Mfg Motor Vehicle Parts/Accessories

(G-11232)
A MEANS TO A VEND INC
4700 N Dixie Hwy (33334-3915)
PHONE....................954 533-8330
Bary J Bass, President
EMP: 12 EST: 2012
SALES (est): 870.7K Privately Held
WEB: www.ameanstoavend.com
SIC: 2024 Ice cream, bulk

(G-11233)
ACRYLIC IMAGES INC
2011 Nw 29th St (33311-2128)
PHONE....................954 484-6633
Donald V Potter Jr, President
Jackie Potter, Admin Sec
EMP: 10 EST: 1992
SQ FT: 5,000
SALES (est): 978.8K Privately Held
SIC: 3089 Injection molding of plastics

(G-11234)
AIGEAN NETWORKS
3496 Ne 12th Ter (33334-4565)
PHONE....................754 223-2240
Richard McLaughlin, Principal
EMP: 7 EST: 2015
SALES (est): 644.5K Privately Held
WEB: www.aigean.com
SIC: 3861 Photographic equipment & supplies

(G-11235)
ALL STAR GRAPHIX INC
5055 Ne 12th Ave (33334-4916)
PHONE....................954 772-1972
Joshua Gorelick, President
EMP: 6 EST: 2019
SALES (est): 348.8K Privately Held
WEB: www.allstargraphix.com
SIC: 2759 Screen printing

(G-11236)
AMS FABRICATIONS INC
2816 Nw 30th Ave (33311-2003)
PHONE....................813 420-0784
EMP: 8 EST: 2017
SALES (est): 522.8K Privately Held
WEB: www.amsfabrications.com
SIC: 3444 Sheet metalwork

(G-11237)
APA WIRELESS TECHNOLOGIES INC
4066 Ne 5th Ave (33334-2202)
PHONE....................954 563-8833
Eliot Fenton, President
Eliot D Fenton, President
William W Dietz, Vice Pres
Stefan Babulal, Engineer
Kim London, Manager
EMP: 10 EST: 1993
SALES (est): 1.8MM Privately Held
WEB: www.apawireless.com
SIC: 3679 Oscillators

(G-11238)
APEX MACHINE COMPANY (PA)
3000 Ne 12th Ter (33334-4497)
PHONE....................954 563-0209
A Robert Coningsby III, Ch of Bd
Todd D Coningsby, President
Raghav Podar, Managing Dir
Russell W Coningsby, Corp Secy
Gregg O Coningsby, Vice Pres
◆ EMP: 71 EST: 1906
SQ FT: 25,000
SALES (est): 24.7MM Privately Held
WEB: www.apexmachine.com
SIC: 3555 Printing trades machinery

(G-11239)
ARCCO INC
Also Called: Sealites
939 Nw 35th Ct (33309-5906)
PHONE....................954 564-0827
Fax: 954 564-0827
EMP: 9
SALES: 400K Privately Held
SIC: 3679 Mfg Electronic Components

(G-11240)
ARTISTIC COLUMNS INC
533 Ne 33rd St (33334-2139)
PHONE....................954 530-5537
Arthur C Harold, President
Joanne B Harold, Treasurer
EMP: 6 EST: 1970
SALES (est): 839.6K Privately Held
WEB: www.artisticcolumnsfl.com
SIC: 3272 3281 Columns, concrete; cut stone & stone products

(G-11241)
ARTISTIC GATE RAILING
5100 Ne 12th Ave (33334-4919)
PHONE....................954 348-9752
Carlton A Dwyer Sr, Principal
EMP: 11 EST: 2011
SALES (est): 513.3K Privately Held
SIC: 3441 Fabricated structural metal

(G-11242)
ARTISTIC WELDING INC
802 Ne 40th Ct (33334-3018)
PHONE....................954 563-3098
Joseph Uskert IV, President
EMP: 6 EST: 1979
SQ FT: 2,500
SALES (est): 774.8K Privately Held
SIC: 3446 Ornamental metalwork

(G-11243)
ATLANTIC CAST PRCAST S FLA LLC
533 Ne 33rd St (33334-2139)
PHONE....................954 564-6245
James A Rushton,
Anthony M Rushton,
Anthony Rushton,
EMP: 20 EST: 1965
SALES (est): 3.2MM Privately Held
WEB: www.atlanticcoastprecast.com
SIC: 3272 Concrete products, precast

(G-11244)
AXION SIGNS INC
1027 Ne 44th St (33334-3821)
PHONE....................954 274-1146
Freddy F Fernadez Sr, President
EMP: 7 EST: 2002
SALES (est): 72.8K Privately Held
SIC: 3993 Signs & advertising specialties

(G-11245)
BARCO SALES & MFG INC
4201 Ne 6th Ave (33334-3107)
PHONE....................954 563-3922
Richard L Kellogg, President
Bob Behrendt, Corp Secy
Toni Kellogg, Vice Pres
Chris Kellogg, Prdtn Dir
EMP: 10 EST: 1995
SQ FT: 10,000
SALES (est): 1.5MM Privately Held
WEB: www.ebarco.com
SIC: 3081 3086 2653 Packing materials, plastic sheet; plastics foam products; corrugated & solid fiber boxes

(G-11246)
BATHROOM WORLD MANUFACTURING
4160 Ne 6th Ave (33334-2211)
PHONE....................954 566-0451
Wesley G Masterson, President
Michael Masterson, Vice Pres
Carol Masterson, Admin Sec
▼ EMP: 6 EST: 1966
SQ FT: 10,000
SALES (est): 710.2K Privately Held
WEB: www.bathroomworld.com
SIC: 3842 3431 3281 3088 Whirlpool baths, hydrotherapy equipment; metal sanitary ware; cut stone & stone products; plastics plumbing fixtures

(G-11247)
BRANDON CROOKES
Also Called: Signature Cabinets
1034 Ne 44th Ct (33334-3824)
PHONE....................954 563-8584
Brandon Crookes, Owner
EMP: 6 EST: 2017
SALES (est): 410.1K Privately Held
WEB: www.signaturecontractingpm.com
SIC: 2434 Wood kitchen cabinets

(G-11248)
BRIGHTWATTS INC
1967 Nw 22nd St (33311-2938)
PHONE....................954 513-3352
Shih Tza Wu, President
Tsai Hui Wu, Admin Sec
▲ EMP: 13 EST: 2006
SALES (est): 208.1K Privately Held
WEB: www.brightwatts.com
SIC: 3674 Solar cells

(G-11249)
CADILLAC GRAPHICS INC
Also Called: Classic Architecutal
4521 Ne 5th Ter (33334-2307)
PHONE....................954 772-2440
David Braden, President
Larry Braden, Treasurer
EMP: 9 EST: 1959
SQ FT: 50,000
SALES (est): 857.4K Privately Held
WEB: www.cadillacgraphics.com
SIC: 3993 Electric signs

(G-11250)
CAREGIVERCOM INC
1871e W Oakland Park Blvd (33311-1517)
PHONE....................954 893-0550
Gary E Barg, CEO
Steven C Barg, COO
EMP: 8 EST: 2011
SALES (est): 1.3MM Privately Held
WEB: www.caregiver.com
SIC: 2836 Culture media

(G-11251)
CHAINBRIDGE DISTILLERY LLC
3500 Ne 11th Ave (33334-2838)
PHONE....................440 212-4992
EMP: 6 EST: 2019
SALES (est): 304.2K Privately Held
WEB: www.chainbridgedistillery.com
SIC: 2085 Distilled & blended liquors

(G-11252)
COASTAL WLDG FABRICATIONS INC
740 Ne 45th St (33334-3250)
PHONE....................954 938-7933
Scott Thompson, President
Mark Thompson, Vice Pres
Rj Forsythe, Project Mgr
EMP: 14 EST: 1988
SQ FT: 35,000
SALES (est): 3.1MM Privately Held
WEB: www.coastalweldfab.com
SIC: 7692 Welding repair

(G-11253)
CREATIVE SHIRTS INTL INC
5214 Ne 12th Ave (33334-4921)
PHONE....................954 351-0909
Joel McCall, President
EMP: 14 EST: 1990
SQ FT: 7,000
SALES (est): 1.4MM Privately Held
WEB: www.creativeshirts.com
SIC: 2395 2262 Embroidery & art needlework; screen printing: manmade fiber & silk broadwoven fabrics

(G-11254)
CUSTOM MARINE JOINERY INC
4032 Ne 5th Ter (33334-2213)
PHONE....................954 822-6057
Jose Almiron, Principal
EMP: 8 EST: 2015
SALES (est): 65.4K Privately Held
SIC: 2431 Millwork

(G-11255)
CYIPCOM INC
300 E Oakland Park Blvd # 358 (33334-2148)
PHONE....................954 727-2500
Nolan Fleishman, CEO
EMP: 6 EST: 1992
SALES (est): 714.7K Privately Held
WEB: www.cyipcom.com
SIC: 3661 3577 5065 5999 Telephones & telephone apparatus; data conversion equipment, media-to-media: computer; telephone equipment; telephone & communication equipment; telephone services; computer related consulting services

(G-11256)
DEAL TO WIN INC
Also Called: Monogram Online
4050 Ne 9th Ave (33334-3006)
PHONE....................718 609-1165
Shlomi Matalon, President
EMP: 30 EST: 2015
SALES (est): 2.4MM Privately Held
WEB: www.monogramonline.com
SIC: 3999 Barber & beauty shop equipment

(G-11257)
DENNIS BOATWORKS INC
2207 Nw 29th St (33311-2145)
PHONE....................954 260-6855
Denis F Page, Principal
EMP: 6 EST: 2006
SALES (est): 576.5K Privately Held
WEB: www.dennisboatworks.com
SIC: 3732 Boat building & repairing

(G-11258)
DESCO MACHINE COMPANY LLC
3000 Ne 12th Ter (33334-4403)
PHONE....................954 565-2739
A Robert I Coningsby II,
Gregg O Coningsby,
Russell W Coningsby III,
EMP: 8 EST: 2015
SALES (est): 2.7MM
SALES (corp-wide): 24.7MM Privately Held
WEB: www.apexmachine.com
SIC: 3714 Motor vehicle parts & accessories
PA: Apex Machine Company
3000 Ne 12th Ter
Oakland Park FL 33334
954 563-0209

(G-11259)
DESIGNERS MFG CTR INC
Also Called: DMC
4131 Ne 6th Ave (33334-2210)
PHONE....................954 530-7622
Robert A Lutz, Owner
EMP: 6 EST: 2013
SALES (est): 462.7K Privately Held
WEB: dmcinc.comcastbiz.net
SIC: 3553 7641 Furniture makers' machinery, woodworking; reupholstery

(G-11260)
DOLPH MAP COMPANY INC
1600 E Commercial Blvd (33334-5719)
P.O. Box 11207, Fort Lauderdale (33339-1207)
PHONE....................954 763-4732
Ryan H Dolph, President
Patrick O Loughlin, Treasurer
Maggie Davis, Manager
EMP: 19 EST: 1959
SQ FT: 5,000
SALES (est): 599.5K Privately Held
WEB: www.dolphmap.com
SIC: 2741 Miscellaneous publishing

(G-11261)
DON SCHICK LLC
4741 Ne 13th Ave (33334-4811)
PHONE....................954 491-9042
Don Schick, Owner
EMP: 8 EST: 2005
SALES (est): 919.9K Privately Held
SIC: 1446 Blast sand mining

▲ = Import ▼=Export
◆ =Import/Export

(G-11262)
EASY SIGNS INC
4860 N Dixie Hwy (33334-3929)
PHONE...............................954 673-0118
Isreal Mike Gedj, *President*
▲ EMP: 9 EST: 2006
SQ FT: 1,700
SALES (est): 474.5K Privately Held
WEB: www.easysignsinc.com
SIC: 3993 Signs & advertising specialties

(G-11263)
ECO WOODWORK AND DESIGN INC
3761 Ne 4th Ave (33334-2230)
PHONE...............................954 326-8806
Gustavo Mendez, *President*
EMP: 5 EST: 2010
SQ FT: 3,000
SALES (est): 350K Privately Held
SIC: 2434 Wood kitchen cabinets

(G-11264)
ESSE SALES INC
2725 Nw 30th Ave (33311-2030)
PHONE...............................954 368-3900
Shalom Edelkopf, *President*
▲ EMP: 8 EST: 2013
SALES (est): 469.2K Privately Held
SIC: 3589 Swimming pool filter & water
conditioning systems

(G-11265)
FABSOUTH LLC (HQ)
721 Ne 44th St (33334-3150)
PHONE...............................954 938-5800
Craig Cape, *Project Mgr*
Marshall Cayll, *Project Mgr*
Timothy Burns, *CFO*
Aaron McKee, *Controller*
Kurt Langsenkamp,
EMP: 12 EST: 2004
SALES (est): 410.5MM
SALES (corp-wide): 586.3MM Privately
Held
WEB: www.fabsouthllc.com
SIC: 3441 Fabricated structural metal
PA: Canam Steel Corporation
4010 Clay St
Point Of Rocks MD 21777
301 874-5141

(G-11266)
FELIX REYNOSO
Also Called: R & H Platting
3062 Nw 23rd Ter (33311-1403)
PHONE...............................954 497-2330
Felix Reynoso, *Owner*
EMP: 7 EST: 1995
SQ FT: 17,000
SALES (est): 670.7K Privately Held
SIC: 2899 Bluing

(G-11267)
FLORIDAS HOTSPOTS PUBLISHING
5090 Ne 12th Ave (33334-4917)
PHONE...............................954 928-1862
Jason Bell, *President*
EMP: 10 EST: 1986
SQ FT: 8,000
SALES (est): 1.5MM Privately Held
WEB: www.hotspotsmagazine.com
SIC: 2721 Magazines: publishing only, not
printed on site

(G-11268)
GARCIA WOODWORK ENTPS INC
1961 Nw 29th St (33311-2126)
PHONE...............................954 226-3906
EMP: 7 EST: 2017
SALES (est): 458.1K Privately Held
SIC: 2431 Millwork

(G-11269)
GRAPHIC BANNER LLP
1330 E Commercial Blvd (33334-5723)
PHONE...............................954 491-9441
Wayne Shim, *Managing Prtnr*
Richard Vilissov, *Managing Prtnr*
EMP: 6 EST: 2003
SQ FT: 1,400

SALES (est): 576.5K Privately Held
WEB: www.graphicbanner.com
SIC: 3993 Signs & advertising specialties

(G-11270)
H LAMM INDUSTRIES INC
4425 Ne 6th Ter (33334-3253)
PHONE...............................954 491-8929
Helmut Lamm, *President*
Julie Lamm, *Corp Secy*
Jefery Hawk, *Vice Pres*
Robert A Tolleson, *Vice Pres*
Don Curtis, *Sales Mgr*
▲ EMP: 120 EST: 1974
SQ FT: 7,000
SALES (est): 23.8MM Privately Held
WEB: www.hlamm.com
SIC: 3444 Sheet metalwork

(G-11271)
ILLUMINATED LIGHTPANELS INC
2011 Nw 29th St (33311-2128)
PHONE...............................954 484-6633
Donald V Potter Jr, *President*
▲ EMP: 7 EST: 2012
SALES (est): 364.6K Privately Held
WEB: www.lightpanelsled.com
SIC: 3648 Lighting equipment

(G-11272)
INNOVATIVE POWDER COATING INC
550 Ne 33rd St (33334-2140)
PHONE...............................954 537-2558
Tom Bates, *Owner*
EMP: 11 EST: 2009
SALES (est): 646K Privately Held
WEB: www.innovativepowdercoating.com
SIC: 3479 Coating of metals & formed
products

(G-11273)
INTERNATIONAL JWLY DESIGNS INC
Also Called: Diwi Jewelry
4750 N Dixie Hwy Ste 3 (33334-3948)
PHONE...............................954 577-9099
Larry Goldberg, *President*
Claudia Zambrano, *Purch Agent*
Robert Goldberg, *Treasurer*
Marilyn Pagni, *Accounting Mgr*
Johanna Buenos, *Sales Associate*
◆ EMP: 9 EST: 1984
SALES (est): 1.5MM Privately Held
WEB: www.ijdi.net
SIC: 3961 5094 Costume jewelry; jewelry

(G-11274)
JAY ROBINSON CABINET SALES INC
683 Ne 42nd St (33334-3140)
PHONE...............................954 298-3009
Jay Robinson, *Principal*
Jay S Robinson, *Principal*
EMP: 7 EST: 2008
SALES (est): 140.7K Privately Held
SIC: 2434 Wood kitchen cabinets

(G-11275)
LAKES METAL FABRICATION INC
2350 Nw 30th Ct (33311-1416)
PHONE...............................954 731-2010
Reddy Thiagarajan, *Principal*
EMP: 7 EST: 2007
SQ FT: 3,566
SALES (est): 615.4K Privately Held
SIC: 3499 Fabricated metal products

(G-11276)
MAGNAPRINT CORP
1522 E Commercial Blvd (33334-5751)
PHONE...............................954 376-8416
EMP: 7 EST: 2019
SALES (est): 327.3K Privately Held
SIC: 2752 Commercial printing, offset

(G-11277)
MAJESTIC ULTIMATE DESIGN INC
4431 Ne 6th Ave (33334-2309)
PHONE...............................954 533-8677
Dora Russo, *Office Mgr*

EMP: 10 EST: 2010
SALES (est): 755.3K Privately Held
SIC: 3442 Window & door frames

(G-11278)
MARK V PRINTING LLC
140 Ne 32nd Ct (33334-1136)
PHONE...............................954 563-2505
Gustavo Baner,
EMP: 8 EST: 1972
SQ FT: 1,600
SALES (est): 1MM Privately Held
WEB: www.m5p.net
SIC: 2752 Commercial printing, offset

(G-11279)
MIAMI SHIP REPAIR & WLDG SVCS
Also Called: Msr Welding
4460 Ne 16th Ave (33334-5534)
PHONE...............................305 491-4161
Winston Bernardino Felix, *Principal*
EMP: 7 EST: 2018
SALES (est): 263.9K Privately Held
SIC: 7692 Welding repair

(G-11280)
NE MEDIA GROUP INC
2880 W Okland Prk Blvd # 207
(33311-1354)
PHONE...............................954 733-8393
Jack O'Neill, *Principal*
EMP: 8
SALES (corp-wide): 453.3MM Privately
Held
SIC: 2711 Newspapers, publishing & print-
ing
PA: Ne Media Group Inc.
1 Exchange Pl Ste 201
Boston MA 02109
617 929-2000

(G-11281)
NO 1 BEAUTY SALON FURNITURE
Also Called: No. 1 Bsf
4712 Ne 12th Ave (33334-4802)
P.O. Box 190706, Fort Lauderdale (33319-
0706)
PHONE...............................954 981-0403
Hripsime Carocatsanis, *President*
◆ EMP: 5 EST: 1988
SQ FT: 6,000
SALES (est): 389.7K Privately Held
WEB: www.bsfi.com
SIC: 3999 5087 Barber & beauty shop
equipment; beauty parlor equipment &
supplies

(G-11282)
OPEN MAGNETIC SCANNING LTD
Also Called: Windsor Imaging
4805 N Dixie Hwy (33334-3928)
PHONE...............................954 202-5097
Raymond M Windsor, *Partner*
Scott Windsor, *Mktg Dir*
EMP: 9 EST: 2002
SQ FT: 4,000
SALES (est): 1.9MM Privately Held
SIC: 3826 Magnetic resonance imaging
apparatus

(G-11283)
ORBE INC
2310 Nw 30th Ct (33311-1416)
PHONE...............................954 534-2264
Orlando Ortiz, *Principal*
EMP: 8 EST: 2009
SALES (est): 369.6K Privately Held
WEB: www.orbeinc.com
SIC: 3429 Marine hardware

(G-11284)
PLASTICS DYNAMICS INC
4301 Ne 11th Ave (33334-3801)
PHONE...............................954 565-7122
▲ EMP: 6
SQ FT: 10,000
SALES (est): 500K Privately Held
SIC: 3089 Plastics Products, Nec, Nsk

(G-11285)
POMPER SHEET METAL INC
4444 Ne 11th Ave (33334-3883)
PHONE...............................954 492-9717
Keith Pomper, *President*
Kenneth Pomper, *Vice Pres*
EMP: 5 EST: 1977
SQ FT: 6,000
SALES (est): 772.3K Privately Held
SIC: 3444 Sheet metal specialties, not
stamped

(G-11286)
POWER VAC CORPORATION
4811 Ne 12th Ave (33334-4803)
PHONE...............................954 491-0188
Daniel Boeckler, *President*
▲ EMP: 5 EST: 1995
SQ FT: 1,600
SALES (est): 650.8K Privately Held
WEB: www.powervac.com
SIC: 3699 Cleaning equipment, ultrasonic,
except medical & dental

(G-11287)
POWLESS DRAPERY SERVICE INC
Also Called: P D Services
4029 Ne 10th Ave (33334-3009)
PHONE...............................954 566-7863
Joseph Materdomini, *President*
Richard Materdomini, *Vice Pres*
▼ EMP: 15 EST: 1962
SALES (est): 1.9MM Privately Held
WEB: www.powless.net
SIC: 2391 Draperies, plastic & textile: from
purchased materials

(G-11288)
PRINTMASTER INC
5220 Ne 12th Ave (33334-4921)
PHONE...............................954 771-6104
John W Snyder Jr, *President*
Matthew Snyder, *Vice Pres*
EMP: 6 EST: 1971
SQ FT: 4,000
SALES (est): 671.9K Privately Held
WEB: www.printbasics.com
SIC: 2752 Commercial printing, offset

(G-11289)
PROSPECT PLASTICS INC
Also Called: Prospects Plastics
836 Ne 44th St (33334-3131)
PHONE...............................954 564-7282
Lawrence Million Jr, *President*
Robert Jennings, *Vice Pres*
Marci Million, *Vice Pres*
Misty Sammons, *Vice Pres*
EMP: 8 EST: 1974
SQ FT: 6,000
SALES (est): 1MM Privately Held
WEB: www.prospectplastics.com
SIC: 3089 Injection molding of plastics

(G-11290)
R & R DESIGNER CABINETS INC
3063 Nw 23rd Way (33311-1404)
PHONE...............................954 735-6435
Reynaldo Miranda, *President*
EMP: 6 EST: 1976
SALES (est): 637.7K Privately Held
WEB: www.randrdesignercabinets.com
SIC: 2434 5712 Wood kitchen cabinets;
cabinets, except custom made: kitchen

(G-11291)
RACEWAY TOWING LLC
Also Called: Junk Cars Broward County
480 Ne 35th Ct Unit 4 (33334-2170)
PHONE...............................754 244-9597
Nisan Tamir, *President*
EMP: 7 EST: 2016
SALES (est): 448.5K Privately Held
SIC: 3644 Raceways

(G-11292)
SEBCO INDUSTRIES INC
Also Called: Fastsigns
211 E Oakland Park Blvd (33334-1155)
PHONE...............................954 566-8500
Sebastian Spada, *President*
EMP: 8 EST: 1993
SQ FT: 2,400

SALES (est): 1.2MM **Privately Held**
WEB: www.fastsigns.com
SIC: 3993 Signs & advertising specialties

(G-11293)
SHARP MARKETING LLC
655 W Prospect Rd (33309-3948)
PHONE.....................954 565-2711
Nestor Villalobos,
◆ **EMP:** 9 **EST:** 1989
SALES (est): 1.1MM **Privately Held**
WEB: www.sharppromo.com
SIC: 2395 5199 3951 5137 Embroidery
products, except schiffli machine; carnival
supplies; pens & mechanical pencils;
women's & children's clothing; uniforms

(G-11294)
**SHORELINE PRINTING
COMPANY**
5100 Ne 12th Ave A (33334-4919)
PHONE.....................954 491-0311
Carlos Pasos, *President*
EMP: 6 **EST:** 1985
SQ FT: 5,000
SALES (est): 481.1K **Privately Held**
WEB: www.tfaccounting.com
SIC: 2752 Commercial printing, offset

(G-11295)
SOTA MANUFACTURING LLC
124 Ne 32nd Ct (33334-1136)
PHONE.....................561 251-3389
Brian Burke, *Branch Mgr*
EMP: 28
SALES (corp-wide): 3MM **Privately Held**
WEB: www.sotamfg.com
SIC: 3999 Barber & beauty shop equip-
ment
PA: Sota Manufacturing, Inc.
1561 Sw 6th Ave
Boca Raton FL 33486
561 368-8007

(G-11296)
SPACE MASTERS
3700 Ne 3rd Ave (33334-1226)
PHONE.....................954 561-8800
Ronald Annechiarico V, *Principal*
EMP: 11 **EST:** 2002
SALES (est): 257.6K **Privately Held**
SIC: 2673 Wardrobe bags (closet acces-
sories): from purchased materials

(G-11297)
SPYDER GRAPHICS INC
3601 Ne 5th Ave (33334-2214)
PHONE.....................954 561-9725
Michael Gorelick,
EMP: 8 **EST:** 2002
SALES (est): 724.5K **Privately Held**
WEB: www.spydergraphicsinc.com
SIC: 2752 Commercial printing, offset

(G-11298)
STEEL FABRICATORS LLC (DH)
721 Ne 44th St (33334-3150)
PHONE.....................954 772-0440
David Cericola, *Superintendent*
Sidney Blaauw, *Vice Pres*
Marshall Cayll, *Project Mgr*
Eduardo Dominguez, *Project Mgr*
Steven Potts, *Project Mgr*
◆ **EMP:** 200 **EST:** 1962
SQ FT: 14,000
SALES (est): 50.2MM
SALES (corp-wide): 586.3MM **Privately
Held**
WEB: www.sfab.com
SIC: 3441 Fabricated structural metal
HQ: Fabsouth Llc
721 Ne 44th St
Oakland Park FL 33334
954 938-5800

(G-11299)
STEVEN R DURANTE
Also Called: Acrylic Fabrication
1056 Ne 44th Pl (33334-3827)
PHONE.....................954 564-9913
Steven R Durante, *Owner*
EMP: 6 **EST:** 2015
SALES (est): 508.8K **Privately Held**
WEB: www.acrylicparts.com
SIC: 3089 Injection molding of plastics

(G-11300)
TAURUS CHUTES INC
3030 Nw 23rd Ave (33311-1428)
P.O. Box 221907, Hollywood (33022-1907)
PHONE.....................954 445-0146
Jose S Calderon, *Principal*
EMP: 7 **EST:** 2017
SALES (est): 2.2MM **Privately Held**
WEB: www.tauruschutesinc.com
SIC: 3444 Sheet metalwork

(G-11301)
TRITECH INDUSTRIES LLC
5204 Ne 12th Ave (33334-4921)
PHONE.....................954 383-3545
Donna Carey, *Engineer*
Dan Hosley, *Natl Sales Mgr*
Don Applegate, *Regl Sales Mgr*
Barry Barrett, *Manager*
Anis Buonpensiere,
EMP: 9 **EST:** 2004
SQ FT: 6,000
SALES (est): 353.6K **Privately Held**
SIC: 3728 Aircraft parts & equipment

(G-11302)
TROPICAL ASSEMBLIES INC
4066 Ne 5th Ave (33334-2202)
PHONE.....................954 396-9999
Randall A Dietz, *President*
Fred Manfrdonia, *VP Opers*
Sofia Contoral, *Purchasing*
Fred Manfredonia, *Treasurer*
Mark Goddard, *Info Tech Mgr*
EMP: 55 **EST:** 1994
SALES (est): 14.1MM **Privately Held**
WEB: www.tropicalassemblies.com
SIC: 3672 Printed circuit boards

(G-11303)
TURBOUSA INC
1867 Ne 33rd St (33306-1003)
PHONE.....................954 767-8631
Willem Franken, *President*
EMP: 13 **EST:** 1994
SALES (est): 2.1MM **Privately Held**
WEB: www.turbo-usa.com
SIC: 3519 Diesel, semi-diesel or duel-fuel
engines, including marine

(G-11304)
TWO B PRINTING INC
625 Ne 42nd St (33334-3140)
PHONE.....................954 566-4886
William T Schenden, *Principal*
EMP: 6 **EST:** 1996
SQ FT: 2,000
SALES (est): 1.5MM **Privately Held**
SIC: 2752 7336 Commercial printing, off-
set; commercial art & graphic design

(G-11305)
ULTIMATE TOOL INC
5105 Ne 12th Ave (33334-4918)
PHONE.....................954 489-9996
Maxine Moore, *Owner*
EMP: 13 **EST:** 1995
SALES (est): 172.5K **Privately Held**
SIC: 3599 Machine shop, jobbing & repair

(G-11306)
UNI-BOX INC
Also Called: Unifab Co
1700 Nw 27th St (33311-2106)
P.O. Box 8083, Fort Lauderdale (33310-
8083)
PHONE.....................954 733-3550
David S Pearl, *President*
▲ **EMP:** 21 **EST:** 1979
SQ FT: 24,000
SALES (est): 885.9K **Privately Held**
WEB: www.unibox-inc.com
SIC: 2653 Boxes, corrugated: made from
purchased materials

(G-11307)
US BULLNOSING
216 Ne 33rd St (33334-1144)
PHONE.....................954 567-0404
Ozgur Avsar, *Principal*
Yara Monteiro, *Admin Asst*
▲ **EMP:** 12 **EST:** 2007
SALES (est): 4.7MM **Privately Held**
WEB: www.usbullnosing.com
SIC: 3272 Floor slabs & tiles, precast con-
crete

(G-11308)
VAN CHARLES INC
4794 Ne 11th Ave (33334-3908)
PHONE.....................954 394-3242
Peter Whittington, *CEO*
Vanessa Whittington, *President*
Paul Skyers, *CFO*
Vincent Brown, *Director*
Marguerite Deal, *Admin Sec*
EMP: 8 **EST:** 2015
SALES (est): 246.7K **Privately Held**
WEB: migration.vancharles.com
SIC: 2752 Commercial printing, litho-
graphic

(G-11309)
VERSACOMP INC
4021 Ne 5th Ter (33334-2228)
PHONE.....................954 561-8778
Richard Ulrich, *Principal*
EMP: 9 **EST:** 2005
SALES (est): 351.5K **Privately Held**
SIC: 3544 5571 Special dies & tools; mo-
torcycle dealers

(G-11310)
**VERSATILE MANUFACTURING
INC (PA)**
Also Called: Versatile Water Jet
4021 Ne 5th Ter (33334-2228)
PHONE.....................954 561-8083
Dick Ulrich, *President*
EMP: 20 **EST:** 1971
SQ FT: 18,000
SALES (est): 2.7MM **Privately Held**
SIC: 3444 3544 Sheet metalwork; die sets
for metal stamping (presses)

(G-11311)
**VERSATILE MANUFACTURING
INC**
4020 Ne 5th Ter (33334-2213)
PHONE.....................954 561-8083
Dick Ulrich, *President*
EMP: 10
SALES (corp-wide): 2.7MM **Privately
Held**
SIC: 3444 3544 Sheet metalwork; die sets
for metal stamping (presses)
PA: Versatile Manufacturing, Inc.
4021 Ne 5th Ter
Oakland Park FL 33334
954 561-8083

(G-11312)
WILSON MANIFOLDS INC
4700 Ne 11th Ave (33334-3952)
PHONE.....................954 771-6216
Keith D Wilson, *President*
Keith Wilson, *President*
Frederick Chapman, *Sales Associate*
David Secunda, *Marketing Staff*
EMP: 20 **EST:** 1985
SQ FT: 3,400
SALES (est): 4.5MM **Privately Held**
WEB: www.wilsonmanifolds.com
SIC: 3714 Manifolds, motor vehicle

Ocala
Marion County

(G-11313)
A & F PAVING LLC
4802 Sw 44th Cir (34474-9652)
P.O. Box 357413, Gainesville (32635-7413)
PHONE.....................352 359-2282
◆ **EMP:** 6
SALES (est): 426.7K **Privately Held**
SIC: 2951 Mfg Asphalt Mixtures/Blocks

(G-11314)
**ADVANCED MANUFACTURING &
ENGRG**
Also Called: AME
3220 Ne 24th St (34470-3926)
PHONE.....................352 629-1494
Michael Dyess, *CEO*
Lisa Dyess, *Manager*
EMP: 7 **EST:** 2007
SALES (est): 1MM **Privately Held**
WEB: www.advancedamecorp.com
SIC: 3441 Fabricated structural metal

(G-11315)
ADVTRAVL INC
Also Called: Ocoos
116 S Magnolia Ave Ste 2 (34471-1178)
P.O. Box 6078 (34478-6078)
PHONE.....................978 549-5013
Rahul Razdan, *CEO*
Robert Powers, *Business Mgr*
WEI Song, *Marketing Staff*
EMP: 8 **EST:** 2012
SQ FT: 1,200
SALES (est): 1.1MM **Privately Held**
SIC: 7372 Application computer software

(G-11316)
AGRI - SOURCE INC
4001 Ne 35th St (34479-3128)
P.O. Box 879, Fruitland Park (34731-0879)
PHONE.....................352 351-2700
Ralph T Spencer, *President*
Mark Browne, *Executive*
EMP: 30 **EST:** 1994
SALES (est): 5.4MM **Privately Held**
SIC: 2499 Mulch or sawdust products,
wood

(G-11317)
AIM IMMUNOTECH INC (PA)
2117 Sw Highway 484 (34473-7949)
PHONE.....................352 448-7797
Thomas K Equels, *CEO*
William M Mitchell, *Ch of Bd*
Peter W Rodino III, *COO*
Robert Dickey IV, *CFO*
Carol Smith, *Chief Mktg Ofcr*
EMP: 10 **EST:** 1966
SALES (est): 135K **Publicly Held**
WEB: www.aimimmuno.com
SIC: 2834 Pharmaceutical preparations

(G-11318)
ALL STAR MATERIALS LLC
6760 Nw 27th Avenue Rd (34475-7417)
PHONE.....................352 598-7590
Scott Ritchey,
EMP: 9 **EST:** 2018
SALES (est): 224.4K **Privately Held**
WEB: www.allstarmaterialsfl.com
SIC: 3273 Ready-mixed concrete

(G-11319)
ALUMA TEC ALUMINUN
4412 Ne 2nd St (34470-1491)
PHONE.....................352 732-7362
Rick Mixson, *President*
Emelio Canganelli, *Partner*
EMP: 8 **EST:** 1995
SQ FT: 1,500
SALES (est): 479.3K **Privately Held**
WEB: www.aluma-tec.com
SIC: 3448 5211 Screen enclosures; lum-
ber & other building materials

(G-11320)
**AMERICAN PANEL
CORPORATION**
5800 Se 78th St (34472-3412)
PHONE.....................352 245-7055
Danny E Duncan, *President*
Laura G Duncan, *Corp Secy*
Juho Chong. *Vice Pres*
R Kevin Graham, *Vice Pres*
Harmon S Lewis, *Vice Pres*
▲ **EMP:** 135 **EST:** 1963
SQ FT: 100,000
SALES (est): 39.7MM **Privately Held**
WEB: www.americanpanel.com
SIC: 3585 Refrigeration equipment, com-
plete

(G-11321)
AMERICAN POLYLACTIDE INDS
3666 Ne 25th St (34470-3143)
PHONE.....................352 653-5963
Adel Arami, *President*
EMP: 7 **EST:** 2000
SALES (est): 124.4K **Privately Held**
WEB: www.americanpolylactide.com
SIC: 3999 Barber & beauty shop equip-
ment

(G-11322)
AMI GRAPHICS INC
Also Called: Quality Banner Company
1302 Sw 42nd Ave (34474-8592)
PHONE..................352 629-4455
Peter Wensberg, *President*
Isaiah Tamblingson, *Prdtn Mgr*
Lee Weedman, *Opers Staff*
Claire Trepanier, *Purchasing*
Cindy Coker, *Controller*
EMP: 45 **Privately Held**
WEB: www.amigraphics.com
SIC: 2399 Banners, made from fabric; pennants; flags, fabric
PA: Ami Graphics, Inc.
223 Drake Hill Rd
Strafford NH 03884

(G-11323)
AMINO CELL INC
5640 Sw 6th Pl Ste 500 (34474-8591)
PHONE..................352 291-0200
Analissa Benedetti, *President*
Cesar Nieves, *Principal*
EMP: 10 **EST:** 2001
SQ FT: 3,000
SALES (est): 600K **Privately Held**
SIC: 2834 2836 2023 Veterinary pharmaceutical preparations; veterinary biological products; dietary supplements, dairy & non-dairy based

(G-11324)
ANTEBELLUM MANUFACTURING LLC
1120 N Magnolia Ave (34475-5106)
PHONE..................352 877-3888
Chris Boyd, *Mng Member*
Robby Bray,
EMP: 35 **EST:** 2014
SALES (est): 5MM **Privately Held**
WEB:
www.antebellumdecorativefences.com
SIC: 3315 Fence gates posts & fittings: steel

(G-11325)
ANTENNAS FOR CMMNCTONS OCALA F
2499 Sw 60th Ave (34474-4324)
PHONE..................352 687-4121
Ronald S Posner, *President*
Jill Posner, *Admin Sec*
▲ **EMP:** 44 **EST:** 1972
SQ FT: 40,000
SALES (est): 7.4MM **Privately Held**
WEB: www.afcsat.com
SIC: 3661 3663 5731 Telephone & telegraph apparatus; satellites, communications; radio, television & electronic stores

(G-11326)
APOLLO RENAL THERAPEUTICS LLC
Also Called: Artemis Plastics
2811 Ne 14th St (34470-4819)
PHONE..................202 413-0963
Gary Mishki, *President*
EMP: 21 **EST:** 2011
SQ FT: 31,500
SALES (est): 4.9MM **Privately Held**
WEB: www.artemisplastics.com
SIC: 3841 3089 Surgical & medical instruments; injection molded finished plastic products

(G-11327)
ARNOLD INDUSTRIES SOUTH INC
1601 Ne 6th Ave (34470-3642)
PHONE..................352 867-0190
George Arnold, *President*
Kathie Arnold, *Vice Pres*
EMP: 6 **EST:** 1987
SQ FT: 6,700
SALES (est): 653.6K **Privately Held**
SIC: 7692 3599 Welding repair; machine & other job shop work

(G-11328)
ASHTIN INC
Also Called: Tin Cup Catering
1800 Sw College Rd (34471-1622)
PHONE..................352 867-1900

Teresa Vadney, *Principal*
Ramy Tarawneh, *Sales Mgr*
Rosemary Shell, *Assistant*
EMP: 8 **EST:** 2010
SALES (est): 231.8K **Privately Held**
SIC: 3356 Tin

(G-11329)
ATLANTIC PUBLISHING GROUP INC (PA)
1396 Ne 20th Ave Ste 300 (34470-7737)
PHONE..................352 622-6220
Bob Montgomery, *CEO*
Douglas R Brown, *President*
Sherry Frazier, *Vice Pres*
Crystal Edwards, *Office Mgr*
Jack Bussell, *Consultant*
▲ **EMP:** 38 **EST:** 1981
SQ FT: 40,000
SALES (est): 8.8MM **Privately Held**
WEB: www.atlantic-pub.com
SIC: 2741 Miscellaneous publishing

(G-11330)
AVL SYSTEMS INC
5540 Sw 6th Pl (34474-9372)
PHONE..................352 854-1170
Philip Hale, *President*
Karen Sturgeon, *Opers Mgr*
Michelle Weeks, *Opers Staff*
Charles Carrender, *Natl Sales Mgr*
Megan Ford, *Sr Project Mgr*
▼ **EMP:** 50 **EST:** 1983
SQ FT: 36,000
SALES (est): 5.3MM **Privately Held**
WEB: www.avlonline.com
SIC: 2522 Panel systems & partitions, office: except wood

(G-11331)
B & E RV SERVICE & REPAIR LLC
6028 Ne 26th Ave (34479-1840)
PHONE..................352 401-7930
Bobby Sumter, *Principal*
EMP: 7 **EST:** 2006
SALES (est): 491.5K **Privately Held**
WEB: www.bandervservicerepair.com
SIC: 3799 Recreational vehicles

(G-11332)
B & T METALWORKS INC
4630 Ne 35th St (34479-3230)
PHONE..................352 236-6000
Wade G Tackett, *President*
Jeffrey E Tackett, *Vice Pres*
EMP: 27 **EST:** 1987
SQ FT: 4,800
SALES (est): 4.3MM **Privately Held**
WEB: www.btmetalworksocala.com
SIC: 3444 Sheet metal specialties, not stamped

(G-11333)
BEDROCK RESOURCES LLC
Also Called: Ocala Bedrock
2441 E Fort King St 202 (34471-2558)
PHONE..................352 369-8600
Darryl C Lanker, *President*
Lee Madsen, *Administration*
EMP: 30 **EST:** 1984
SQ FT: 2,700
SALES (est): 6.1MM **Privately Held**
WEB: www.bedrockresources.com
SIC: 1422 Limestones, ground

(G-11334)
BIG SUN EQUINE PRODUCTS INC (PA)
Also Called: Big Sun Products
1883 Nw 58th Ln (34475-3047)
PHONE..................352 629-9645
Marilyn Kenworthy, *President*
Steve Kenworthy, *Corp Secy*
Ken Aldrich, *Vice Pres*
▼ **EMP:** 5 **EST:** 1989
SALES (est): 1.3MM **Privately Held**
WEB: www.bigsunfencing.com
SIC: 3363 Aluminum die-castings

(G-11335)
BIG SUN PLASTICS INC
2615 Nw Old Blitchton Rd (34475-5256)
PHONE..................352 671-1844
William Boothby, *President*

EMP: 16 **EST:** 1999
SQ FT: 10,000
SALES (est): 750K **Privately Held**
SIC: 3089 Injection molding of plastics

(G-11336)
BMW & ASSOCIATES INC
Also Called: BMW Window Coverings
4380 Se 53rd Ave (34480-7404)
P.O. Box 291 (34478-0291)
PHONE..................352 694-2300
Katherine Mullis, *President*
EMP: 7 **EST:** 1992
SQ FT: 5,000
SALES (est): 691.5K **Privately Held**
SIC: 2211 5023 2591 Upholstery, tapestry & wall coverings: cotton; window furnishings; window blinds

(G-11337)
BOYD WELDING LLC
802 Nw 27th Ave (34475-5620)
PHONE..................352 447-2405
David E Boyd III,
EMP: 9 **EST:** 1998
SQ FT: 6,500
SALES (est): 1.3MM **Privately Held**
WEB: www.boydwelding.com
SIC: 3443 7692 Boiler shop products: boilers, smokestacks, steel tanks; welding repair

(G-11338)
BRANCH PROPERTIES INC (PA)
Also Called: Seminole Marico Fertilizer Div
335 Ne Watula Ave (34470-5806)
P.O. Box 940 (34478-0940)
PHONE..................352 732-4143
Greg Branch, *President*
Greg Allen, *Vice Pres*
Gregory S Allen, *Vice Pres*
Richard De Simone, *Vice Pres*
Richard Simone, *Vice Pres*
EMP: 71 **EST:** 1934
SQ FT: 120,000
SALES (est): 15.8MM **Privately Held**
WEB: www.seminolefeed.com
SIC: 2048 5999 5191 Livestock feeds; feed & farm supply; farm supplies

(G-11339)
BRAY WELDING INC
1120 N Magnolia Ave (34475-5106)
PHONE..................352 622-7780
W Steven Bray, *President*
Karen Bray, *Corp Secy*
EMP: 9 **EST:** 1938
SQ FT: 20,000
SALES (est): 980.4K **Privately Held**
SIC: 7692 Welding repair

(G-11340)
BURLAKOFF MANUFACTURING CO
826 Se 9th Ter (34471-3969)
PHONE..................972 889-2502
Jim Burlakoff, *Vice Pres*
EMP: 7 **EST:** 2018
SALES (est): 506.5K **Privately Held**
SIC: 3629 Electrical industrial apparatus

(G-11341)
C W MACHINING INC
2820 Nw 8th Pl (34475-5660)
PHONE..................352 732-5824
Paul Cox, *President*
Emily Cox, *Vice Pres*
EMP: 6 **EST:** 1988
SQ FT: 8,000
SALES (est): 682.3K **Privately Held**
SIC: 3599 Machine shop, jobbing & repair

(G-11342)
CAPRIS FURNITURE INDS INC
1401 Nw 27th Ave (34475-4723)
PHONE..................352 629-8889
Pedro R Interian, *President*
C A Stubbs, *Vice Pres*
Donald R Beaudet, *CFO*
Chris Brady, *Sales Staff*
William Ingram, *Director*
◆ **EMP:** 140 **EST:** 1986
SQ FT: 180,000

SALES (est): 22.9MM **Privately Held**
WEB: www.beachcraftrattan.com
SIC: 2512 2519 Wood upholstered chairs & couches; rattan furniture: padded or plain; wicker furniture: padded or plain

(G-11343)
CAR WASH SOLUTIONS FLORIDA INC
3310 Sw 7th St Unit 2 (34474-1911)
P.O. Box 15285, Sarasota (34277-1285)
PHONE..................941 323-8817
John Hamill, *CEO*
EMP: 32 **EST:** 2015
SALES (est): 2.8MM **Privately Held**
SIC: 3589 Car washing machinery

(G-11344)
CARDINAL LG COMPANY
1300 Sw 44th Ave (34474-8747)
PHONE..................352 237-4410
Kyle Petersen, *Plant Mgr*
Yvonne Roach, *Human Resources*
Ted Paget, *Sales Mgr*
Michelle Arredondo, *Sales Staff*
Dustin Jones, *Manager*
EMP: 81
SALES (corp-wide): 1B **Privately Held**
WEB: www.cardinalcorp.com
SIC: 3231 Products of purchased glass
HQ: Cardinal Lg Company
250 Griffin St E
Amery WI 54001

(G-11345)
CARPORT SOLUTION LLC
8975 Sw Highway 200 (34481-7704)
PHONE..................352 789-1149
William C Simmons, *Mng Member*
Javier Urdaneta, *Mng Member*
EMP: 10 **EST:** 2010
SQ FT: 700
SALES (est): 384.3K **Privately Held**
WEB: www.carportsolution.com
SIC: 3448 1541 Prefabricated metal buildings; steel building construction; truck & automobile assembly plant construction

(G-11346)
CEMEX CEMENT INC
619 Sw 17th Loop (34471-3610)
PHONE..................352 867-5794
EMP: 118 **Privately Held**
WEB: www.cemexusa.com
SIC: 3273 Ready-mixed concrete
HQ: Cemex Cement, Inc.
10100 Katy Fwy Ste 300
Houston TX 77043
713 650-6200

(G-11347)
CENTRAL FLA KIT BATH SRFCES IN
2800 Se 62nd St (34480-8038)
P.O. Box 137, Summerfield (34492-0137)
PHONE..................352 307-2333
Decnis Villeda, *President*
EMP: 16 **EST:** 2007
SQ FT: 5,280
SALES (est): 1.7MM **Privately Held**
WEB: www.centralfloridakitchenbath.com
SIC: 3088 2541 Shower stalls, fiberglass & plastic; wood partitions & fixtures

(G-11348)
CENTRAL FLA STL BLDG & SUP LLC
4750 S Pine Ave (34480-9104)
PHONE..................352 266-6795
William White, *Mng Member*
Mike Martin,
Bruce Pritchet,
EMP: 7 **EST:** 2016
SALES (est): 1.5MM **Privately Held**
WEB: www.cfsteelbuildings.com
SIC: 3441 5051 Building components, structural steel; steel

(G-11349)
CFU PLATING
7575 S Us Highway 441 # 118
(34480-8079)
PHONE..................386 795-5198
David Hellmuth, *Principal*
EMP: 7 **EST:** 2010

SALES (est): 212.8K **Privately Held**
SIC: 3471 Plating of metals or formed products

(G-11350)
CHARIOT EAGLE INC (PA)
931 Nw 37th Ave (34475-5683)
PHONE..............................623 936-7545
Robert Holliday, *President*
Elaine Morris, *Human Res Dir*
Heather Sims, *Sales Staff*
Dale Frisbie, *Director*
▼ **EMP:** 100 **EST:** 1984
SQ FT: 31,000
SALES (est): 13.7MM **Privately Held**
WEB: www.charioteagle.com
SIC: 3792 2452 2451 House trailers, except as permanent dwellings; prefabricated wood buildings; mobile homes

(G-11351)
CHARITY HOMES LLC
12830 Sw 58th Cir (34473-5255)
PHONE..............................352 274-0306
Paul Charity, *Principal*
EMP: 7 **EST:** 2015
SALES (est): 207.1K **Privately Held**
SIC: 2439 Trusses, wooden roof

(G-11352)
CITY OF OCALA
Also Called: Ocala Engineering-Traffic Div
1307 Nw 4th Ave (34475-5142)
PHONE..............................352 622-6803
Wayne Little, *Director*
EMP: 48
SQ FT: 9,755
SALES (corp-wide): 91.8MM **Privately Held**
WEB: www.ocalafl.org
SIC: 3669 9111 Traffic signals, electric; mayors' offices
PA: City Of Ocala
110 Se Watula Ave
Ocala FL 34471
352 401-3914

(G-11353)
CLARKWESTERN DIETRICH BUILDING
331 Sw 57th Ave (34474-9346)
PHONE..............................800 693-3018
EMP: 52
SALES (est): 20.2B **Privately Held**
SIC: 3441 Structural Metal Fabrication
HQ: Clarkwestern Dietrich Building Systems Llc
9050 Centre Pointe Dr
West Chester OH 45069

(G-11354)
CLOSETMAID LLC
720 Sw 17th Pl (34471-1233)
PHONE..............................352 351-6100
Dale Debruycker, *Vice Pres*
Mike Williams, *Purch Agent*
Michle Mosher, *Personnel Exec*
Rob Clements, *Manager*
EMP: 97
SQ FT: 100,000
SALES (corp-wide): 2.2B **Publicly Held**
WEB: www.homebyames.com
SIC: 3496 Shelving, made from purchased wire
HQ: Closetmaid Llc
13485 Veterans Way
Orlando FL 32827
352 401-6000

(G-11355)
COLE-PARMER INSTRUMENT CO LLC
Also Called: Zefon International
5350 Sw 1st Ln (34474-9303)
PHONE..............................352 854-8080
Jeffrey Mantz, *General Mgr*
Luc Belec, *Engineer*
Martin Harper, *Director*
EMP: 95
SALES (corp-wide): 679.1MM **Privately Held**
WEB: www.coleparmer.com
SIC: 3826 Analytical instruments

HQ: Cole-Parmer Instrument Company Llc
625 Bunker Ct
Vernon Hills IL 60061
847 549-7600

(G-11356)
COMPACT CONTRACT INC
1822 Sw 34th Ct (34474-2834)
PHONE..............................352 817-8058
Ronnie Jones, *Owner*
EMP: 5 **EST:** 2008
SALES (est): 380.6K **Privately Held**
SIC: 1389 Construction, repair & dismantling services

(G-11357)
CONTEMPORARY INTERIORS INC
2626 Nw 35th St (34475-3342)
PHONE..............................352 620-8686
David Silk, *President*
Ryan Anderson, *Vice Pres*
EMP: 15 **EST:** 1989
SALES (est): 2.1MM **Privately Held**
WEB: www.contemporaryinteriors.com
SIC: 2512 2521 5712 5021 Upholstered household furniture; wood office furniture; furniture stores; furniture; public building & related furniture; wood household furniture

(G-11358)
CORDELL INTERNATIONAL INC
1056 Ne 16th St (34470-4204)
PHONE..............................352 694-1800
Kyle P Cordell, *President*
Brad Cordell, *Vice Pres*
Mary Lynne Cordell, *Admin Sec*
▲ **EMP:** 10 **EST:** 2007
SQ FT: 33,000
SALES (est): 2MM **Privately Held**
WEB: www.cordellinternational.com
SIC: 3442 Metal doors, sash & trim

(G-11359)
CRANDON ENTERPRISES INC
Also Called: Crandon Electric Co
255 Sw 96th Ln (34476-7615)
PHONE..............................352 873-8400
Gary Crandon, *President*
Greg Artliaff, *Vice Pres*
Paulet Crandon, *Admin Sec*
EMP: 6 **EST:** 1965
SALES (est): 919.4K **Privately Held**
SIC: 3699 1731 Electrical welding equipment; banking machine installation & service
PA: Crandon Enterprises Inc
1731 Se 83rd St
Ocala FL

(G-11360)
CREATIVE ENERGIES INC
1805 Ne 19th Ave (34470-4775)
PHONE..............................352 351-9448
Roxanne Free, *Vice Pres*
EMP: 8 **EST:** 2010
SALES (est): 448.1K **Privately Held**
WEB: www.lightdomecanopies.com
SIC: 2394 Canvas & related products

(G-11361)
CUSTOM WINDOW SYSTEMS INC
1900 Sw 44th Ave (34474-8743)
PHONE..............................352 368-6922
Greg Schorr, *CEO*
Matthew Shaw, *CFO*
◆ **EMP:** 600 **EST:** 1986
SQ FT: 200,000
SALES (est): 130.4MM
SALES (corp-wide): 2B **Privately Held**
WEB: www.cws.cc
SIC: 3442 Window & door frames
PA: Pella Corporation
102 Main St
Pella IA 50219
641 621-1000

(G-11362)
CWS HOLDING COMPANY LLC
Also Called: Custom Window Systems
1900 Sw 44th Ave (34474-8743)
PHONE..............................352 368-6922
Greg Schorr, *CEO*
EMP: 28 **EST:** 2014

SALES (est): 6.9MM **Privately Held**
WEB: www.cws.cc
SIC: 2431 3211 Window frames, wood; window glass, clear & colored
PA: Nautic Partners, Llc
100 Westminster St # 1220
Providence RI 02903

(G-11363)
D & S PALLET RECYCLE CENTER
2640 Nw 35th St (34475-3342)
PHONE..............................352 351-0070
Steve Wojtaszak, *Owner*
EMP: 8 **EST:** 1982
SQ FT: 5,000
SALES (est): 936.7K **Privately Held**
SIC: 2448 Pallets, wood

(G-11364)
DAVID R NASSIVERA INC
2250 Ne 70th St (34479-1414)
PHONE..............................352 351-1176
David Nassivera, *President*
Susan Nassivera, *Admin Sec*
EMP: 23 **EST:** 1974
SQ FT: 10,500
SALES (est): 959.3K **Privately Held**
SIC: 2426 Furniture stock & parts, hardwood

(G-11365)
DELZOTTO PRODUCTS FLORIDA INC
4575 W Highway 40 (34482-4042)
PHONE..............................352 351-3834
Laura Del Zotto, *President*
Steve Rutkowski, *Opers Mgr*
EMP: 100 **EST:** 1999
SQ FT: 4,000
SALES (est): 23.2MM **Privately Held**
WEB: www.delzottoproducts.com
SIC: 3272 Concrete products, precast

(G-11366)
DFA DAIRY BRANDS FLUID LLC
2205 N Pine Ave (34475-9256)
PHONE..............................352 622-4666
Darrin Spence, *Manager*
EMP: 13
SALES (corp-wide): 19.3B **Privately Held**
SIC: 2026 Fluid milk
HQ: Dfa Dairy Brands Fluid, Llc
1405 N 98th St
Kansas City KS 66111
816 801-6455

(G-11367)
DIXIE LIME ANDSTONE CO
2441 E Fort King St (34471-2558)
PHONE..............................352 512-0180
Darrel Lanker, *President*
William Moore, *Sales Staff*
EMP: 8 **EST:** 2013
SALES (est): 580K **Privately Held**
WEB: www.dixielime.com
SIC: 1422 Crushed & broken limestone

(G-11368)
DIXIE METAL PRODUCTS INC (PA)
Also Called: D M P
442 Sw 54th Ct (34474-1893)
PHONE..............................352 873-2554
J Philip Schnorr, *Ch of Bd*
Christine Galvez, *Principal*
Dave Carroll, *COO*
John Schnorr, *COO*
Keith Holman, *Vice Pres*
EMP: 95 **EST:** 1968
SQ FT: 75,000
SALES (est): 25.5MM **Privately Held**
WEB: www.dixiemetals.com
SIC: 3441 Fabricated structural metal

(G-11369)
DIXIE WORKSHOP INC
2350 Nw 42nd St (34475-3121)
PHONE..............................352 629-4699
Michael Miller, *President*
EMP: 12 **EST:** 1994
SQ FT: 4,000

SALES (est): 1.1MM **Privately Held**
WEB: www.dixieworkshop.net
SIC: 2499 2511 2434 Decorative wood & woodwork; wood household furniture; wood kitchen cabinets

(G-11370)
DONARRA EXTRUSIONS LLC
Also Called: Bluegator Ground Protection
1811 Sw 42nd Ave (34475-9814)
P.O. Box 770599 (34477-0599)
PHONE..............................352 369-5552
John K Donohue, *Mng Member*
Kevin Donahue,
Maryann G Donohue,
▲ **EMP:** 12 **EST:** 2010
SALES (est): 2.6MM **Privately Held**
WEB: www.donarraextrusions.com
SIC: 3089 Injection molding of plastics; plastic processing

(G-11371)
DOUBLE R MFG OCALA INC
5529 Sw 1st Ln (34474-9308)
PHONE..............................352 873-1441
Richard Moore, *President*
Thomas Moore, *President*
Julia Moore, *Treasurer*
David Anderson, *Consultant*
▲ **EMP:** 19 **EST:** 1992
SQ FT: 7,800
SALES (est): 3.8MM **Privately Held**
WEB: www.doubler mfg.com
SIC: 7692 Welding repair

(G-11372)
DR PEPPER/SEVEN UP INC
3337 Sw 7th St (34474-1956)
PHONE..............................352 732-9777
John Scullin, *Branch Mgr*
EMP: 40
SQ FT: 2,400 **Publicly Held**
WEB: www.drpepper.com
SIC: 2086 Soft drinks: packaged in cans, bottles, etc.
HQ: Dr Pepper/Seven Up, Inc.
6425 Hall Of Fame Ln
Frisco TX 75034
972 673-7000

(G-11373)
DR XIES JING-TANG HERBAL INC
4815 Nw 8th St (34482-8773)
PHONE..............................352 591-2141
Zhen Zhao, *CEO*
EMP: 11 **EST:** 2003
SALES (est): 388.8K **Privately Held**
WEB: www.tcvmherbal.com
SIC: 2834 Veterinary pharmaceutical preparations

(G-11374)
DRAGGIN TRAILERS INC
3100 Se 50th Pl (34480-5795)
PHONE..............................352 351-8790
Dorothy A Griffin, *President*
Dorothy Driffin, *President*
Kenneth Griffin Jr III, *Vice Pres*
EMP: 6 **EST:** 1997
SQ FT: 1,200
SALES (est): 500K **Privately Held**
WEB: www.draggintrailers.com
SIC: 3715 Truck trailers

(G-11375)
E-ONE INC (HQ)
Also Called: E-One Parts Central
1601 Sw 37th Ave (34474-2829)
PHONE..............................352 237-1122
Rod Rushing, *CEO*
Kent Tyler, *President*
James Meyer, *COO*
Dino Cusumano, *Vice Pres*
Davis Neal, *Vice Pres*
◆ **EMP:** 483 **EST:** 1967
SQ FT: 391,750
SALES (est): 184.5MM **Publicly Held**
WEB: www.e-one.com
SIC: 3711 Fire department vehicles (motor vehicles), assembly of

▲ = Import ▼ =Export
◆ =Import/Export

(G-11376)
E-ONE INC
1701 Sw 37th Ave (34474-2827)
P.O. Box 2710 (34478-2710)
PHONE................................352 237-1122
Frank Carmody, *President*
Steve Savage, *Opers Mgr*
Michael Campbell, *Production*
Scott Flinn, *Production*
Jason Lemstrom, *Production*
EMP: 74 **Publicly Held**
WEB: www.e-one.com
SIC: 3711 Fire department vehicles (motor vehicles), assembly of
HQ: E-One, Inc.
1601 Sw 37th Ave
Ocala FL 34474
352 237-1122

(G-11377)
ELSTER AMCO WATER LLC
Also Called: Elster Amco Wtr Mtring Systems
10 Sw 49th Ave Ste 101 (34474-1825)
PHONE................................352 369-6500
Alex Watson,
◆ **EMP:** 19 **EST:** 1962
SQ FT: 90,000
SALES (est): 20MM
SALES (corp-wide): 34.3B **Publicly Held**
WEB: smartenergy.honeywell.com
SIC: 3824 Water meters
PA: Honeywell International Inc.
855 S Mint St
Charlotte NC 28202
704 627-6200

(G-11378)
ENDEAVOR PUBLICATIONS INC
Also Called: Canine Chronicle, The
4727 Nw 80th Ave (34482-2031)
PHONE................................352 369-1104
Thomas Grabe, *President*
Amy Grabe, *Admin Sec*
EMP: 7 **EST:** 1997
SQ FT: 1,500
SALES (est): 1.5MM **Privately Held**
WEB: www.caninechronicle.com
SIC: 2721 Magazines: publishing & printing

(G-11379)
ESD WASTE2WATER INC
495 Oak Rd (34472-3005)
PHONE................................800 277-3279
Jon E Houchens, *President*
Kevin Hawkins, *General Mgr*
Cody Lasley, *Regional Mgr*
Charles Hunt, *Vice Pres*
Alan Pierce, *Vice Pres*
▼ **EMP:** 85 **EST:** 1993
SQ FT: 170,000
SALES (est): 115.3MM **Privately Held**
WEB: www.waste2water.com
SIC: 3589 Water treatment equipment, industrial

(G-11380)
EVORA ENTERPRISES INC
Also Called: Tarps and Beyond
2608 Nw 6th St (34475-5794)
P.O. Box 520397, Miami (33152-0397)
PHONE................................305 261-4522
Brenda Evora, *President*
▲ **EMP:** 10 **EST:** 1974
SQ FT: 8,000
SALES (est): 926K **Privately Held**
WEB: www.evora.biz
SIC: 2394 Canvas covers & drop cloths

(G-11381)
EXPRESS BRAKE INTERNATIONAL
4376 Ne 35th St (34479-3236)
PHONE................................352 304-6263
Drew Larsen, *President*
Branchard Tucker, *CFO*
Pat McLaughlin, *Director*
EMP: 10 **EST:** 1994
SALES (est): 920K **Privately Held**
WEB: www.extremebrake.com
SIC: 3714 Motor vehicle brake systems & parts

(G-11382)
EXTREME BRAKE INTEGRATION INC
5817 Nw 44th Ave (34482-7891)
P.O. Box 216 (34478-0216)
PHONE................................352 342-9596
Kevin Reed, *President*
EMP: 8 **EST:** 2013
SALES (est): 1.4MM **Privately Held**
WEB: www.extremebrake.com
SIC: 3714 Motor vehicle brake systems & parts

(G-11383)
EXTREME BRAKE INTEGRATION INC
1909 Ne 25th Ave (34470-4848)
PHONE................................888 844-7734
J Schatt, *Agent*
EMP: 7 **EST:** 2017
SALES (est): 96.8K **Privately Held**
WEB: www.extremebrake.com
SIC: 3714 Motor vehicle parts & accessories

(G-11384)
EXTREME MANUFACTURING LLC
1909 Ne 25th Ave (34470-4848)
PHONE................................888 844-7734
Valerie Reed, *Mng Member*
Kevin Reed,
EMP: 12 **EST:** 2018
SALES (est): 2.3MM **Privately Held**
WEB: www.extremebrake.com
SIC: 3714 Motor vehicle parts & accessories

(G-11385)
F & J SPECIALTY PRODUCTS INC
404 Cypress Rd (34472-3106)
P.O. Box 2888 (34478-2888)
PHONE................................352 680-1177
Frank Gavila, *President*
Paul Cheries, *Vice Pres*
Lisa Brault, *QC Mgr*
Tonda King, *Marketing Staff*
Kenneth King, *IT/INT Sup*
EMP: 15 **EST:** 1979
SQ FT: 17,000
SALES (est): 3.7MM
SALES (corp-wide): 3.9MM **Privately Held**
WEB: www.fjspecialty.com
SIC: 3826 3822 3829 Environmental testing equipment; auto controls regulating residntl & coml environmt & applncs; measuring & controlling devices
PA: Ga-Ma & Associates, Inc.
404 Cypress Rd
Ocala FL 34472
352 687-8840

(G-11386)
FIDELITY MANUFACTURING LLC
1900 Ne 25th Ave (34470-4849)
PHONE................................352 414-4700
Randy Landry, *QC Mgr*
Steve Parsons, *Engineer*
Donathan Sweat, *Engineer*
Loretta Jackson, *Human Res Mgr*
Todd Bowman, *Sales Engr*
EMP: 38 **EST:** 2014
SQ FT: 70,000
SALES (est): 6.6MM **Privately Held**
WEB: www.fidelitymfg.com
SIC: 3795 7538 Tanks & tank components; general automotive repair shops

(G-11387)
FINGER LAKES CUSTOM MFG LLC
1211 Ne 17th Rd (34470-4611)
PHONE................................315 283-4849
Neal P Purdy, *Principal*
EMP: 6 **EST:** 2019
SALES (est): 328.3K **Privately Held**
SIC: 3999 Manufacturing industries

(G-11388)
FINYL PRODUCTS INC
8657 Nw 80th Ave (34482-1105)
P.O. Box 6241 (34478-6241)
PHONE................................352 351-4033
Ted L Hagemeyer, *President*
Marilyn Kenworthy, *Owner*
EMP: 8 **EST:** 1997
SALES (est): 118.9K **Privately Held**
WEB: www.finylsales.com
SIC: 2851 5211 5162 Vinyl coatings, strippable; lumber & other building materials; plastics materials & basic shapes

(G-11389)
FIRST IMPRESSIONS PRINTING
1847 Sw 27th Ave (34471-2037)
PHONE................................352 237-6141
Joshua Dinesen, *Principal*
Dennis Dimatteo, *Vice Pres*
Daniel Opitz, *Vice Pres*
Gail Haile, *Sales Staff*
Terry Steele, *Sales Staff*
EMP: 17 **EST:** 1965
SQ FT: 10,000
SALES (est): 2.1MM **Privately Held**
WEB: www.fipprinting.com
SIC: 2752 Commercial printing, offset

(G-11390)
FLAIRE CORPORATION
Also Called: Kemp
4647 Sw 40th Ave (34474-5799)
PHONE................................352 237-1220
James Doherty, *President*
James Daugherty, *President*
Richard Porri, *Vice Pres*
Keith Miller, *CFO*
Cor Stokenborg, *Sales Staff*
▲ **EMP:** 169 **EST:** 1986
SQ FT: 120,000
SALES (est): 10.5MM
SALES (corp-wide): 1.5B **Privately Held**
SIC: 3564 3594 Blowers & fans; fluid power pumps & motors
HQ: Spx Flow Technology Usa, Inc.
4647 Se 40th Ave
Ocala FL 34474

(G-11391)
FLORIDA EQINE PUBLICATIONS INC
Also Called: Floridahorse, The
801 Sw 60th Ave (34474-8593)
PHONE................................352 732-8686
J Michael, *General Mgr*
J Michael O'Farrell Jr, *Chairman*
Robert A Cromartie, *Vice Pres*
Richard E Hancock, *Treasurer*
K Behrens, *Manager*
EMP: 13 **EST:** 1957
SQ FT: 3,139
SALES (est): 837.3K **Privately Held**
WEB: www.wiretowire.net
SIC: 2721 0752 Magazines: publishing only, not printed on site; animal specialty services

(G-11392)
FLORIDA GENERAL TRADING INC (PA)
6195 N Us Highway 441 (34475-1519)
P.O. Box 89189, Tampa (33689-0403)
PHONE................................813 391-2149
Aosama Alatabi, *Principal*
▼ **EMP:** 5 **EST:** 2005
SALES (est): 1MM **Privately Held**
WEB: www.floridageneraltrading.com
SIC: 3531 Construction machinery

(G-11393)
FLUID ROUTING SOLUTIONS LLC
3100 Se Maricamp Rd (34471-6250)
PHONE................................352 732-0222
Gary Franks, *Principal*
Laura Cole, *Engineer*
Tony Stamour, *Engineer*
Brent Scott, *Supervisor*
EMP: 304
SALES (corp-wide): 1.4B **Publicly Held**
WEB: www.pkoh.com
SIC: 3052 3714 Rubber hose; motor vehicle parts & accessories

HQ: Fluid Routing Solutions, Llc
30000 Stephenson Hwy B
Madison Heights MI 48071
248 228-8900

(G-11394)
FLYRITE BANNER MAKERS INC
3459 Sw 74th Ave Ste 100 (34474-7235)
PHONE................................352 873-7501
Fred Nonnemacher, *CEO*
EMP: 10 **EST:** 1983
SQ FT: 5,500
SALES (est): 995.9K **Privately Held**
WEB: www.flyritebanners.com
SIC: 2399 Banners, made from fabric; banners, pennants & flags

(G-11395)
FUEL TANKS TO GO LLC
13 Cypress Road Pass (34472-3535)
PHONE................................865 604-4726
Mark Green, *General Mgr*
Tim Shively, *Production*
EMP: 6 **EST:** 2013
SALES (est): 480K **Privately Held**
WEB: www.fueltankstogo.com
SIC: 3443 Fuel tanks (oil, gas, etc.): metal plate

(G-11396)
FULLER AMUSEMENTS
2250 Se 52nd St (34480-7554)
PHONE................................352 629-2792
Kurt Folson, *President*
EMP: 5 **EST:** 1960
SQ FT: 7,800
SALES (est): 431.5K **Privately Held**
WEB: www.fulleramusement.com
SIC: 3999 Coin-operated amusement machines

(G-11397)
FUQUA SAWMILL INC
1751 Nw 33rd Ave (34475-4617)
PHONE................................352 236-3456
Larry Fuqua, *President*
John Fuqua, *Admin Sec*
EMP: 5 **EST:** 1950
SQ FT: 1,000
SALES (est): 494.4K **Privately Held**
WEB: www.warfauction.com
SIC: 2421 Custom sawmill

(G-11398)
GA-MA & ASSOCIATES INC (PA)
404 Cypress Rd (34472-3106)
P.O. Box 2918 (34478-2918)
PHONE................................352 687-8840
Frank M Gavila, *President*
Paul Cheries, *Sales Dir*
Sharon Rodriguez, *Sales Mgr*
Carl Rahbein, *Info Tech Mgr*
David Albury, *Director*
EMP: 7 **EST:** 1975
SQ FT: 8,000
SALES (est): 3.9MM **Privately Held**
WEB: www.ga-maassociates.com
SIC: 3069 3821 Medical & laboratory rubber sundries & related products; laboratory apparatus & furniture

(G-11399)
GLOBAL BAMBOO TECHNOLOGIES INC
Also Called: Bamcore
310 Cypress Rd (34472-3102)
PHONE................................707 730-0288
Hal Hinkle, *CEO*
Zack Zimmerman, *Risk Mgmt Dir*
EMP: 26 **EST:** 2020
SALES (est): 2.5MM **Privately Held**
SIC: 2448 Wood pallets & skids

(G-11400)
GML INDUSTRIES LLC
5542 Sw 6th Pl (34474-9317)
PHONE................................352 671-7619
Del Lukens, *Managing Prtnr*
Del McGighan Lukens, *Mng Member*
Melinda Freeman,
Gerri McGighan-Lukens,
EMP: 40 **EST:** 2011
SALES (est): 5.4MM **Privately Held**
WEB: www.gmlindustries.com
SIC: 3999 Barber & beauty shop equipment

(G-11401)
GOOD TIME OUTDOORS INC
Also Called: Gto Performance Air Boats
4600 W Highway 326　(34482-1257)
PHONE 352 401-9070
Norman P Clifton, *President*
Brad McCullough, *Vice Pres*
▼ EMP: 20 EST: 1992
SALES (est): 3.5MM **Privately Held**
WEB: www.goodtimeoutdoors.com
SIC: 3732 5551 Boat building & repairing;
　boat dealers

(G-11402)
GOODTIME PRINTING INC
1522 E Silver Sprng Blvd　(34470-6818)
PHONE 352 629-8838
Butch White, *President*
Marie Green, *Vice Pres*
Robert White, *Admin Sec*
EMP: 7 EST: 1984
SQ FT: 3,400
SALES (est): 776.7K **Privately Held**
WEB: www.goodtimeprinting.com
SIC: 2752 Commercial printing, offset

(G-11403)
GREAT NORTHERN REHAB PC (PA)
Also Called: Gnr Orthopedic Designs
2620 Se Merrycamp Rd　(34471)
PHONE 352 732-8868
Richard W Shutes, *President*
Raymond Brown, *Corp Secy*
Donald Riley, *Training Spec*
Natalie Ozella, *Assistant*
EMP: 9 EST: 1970
SQ FT: 1,000
SALES (est): 1.9MM **Privately Held**
WEB: www.greatnorthernrehab.com
SIC: 3842 8049 5047 Orthopedic appli-
　ances; physical therapist; medical & hos-
　pital equipment

(G-11404)
GREAT NORTHERN REHAB PC
2620 Se Maricamp Rd　(34471-5582)
PHONE 352 732-8868
Rick Shutes, *Branch Mgr*
EMP: 10
SALES (corp-wide): 1.9MM **Privately
Held**
WEB: www.greatnorthernrehab.com
SIC: 3842 8049 5047 Orthopedic appli-
　ances; physical therapist; medical & hos-
　pital equipment
PA: Great Northern Rehab Pc
　2620 Se Merrycamp Rd
　Ocala FL 34471
　352 732-8868

(G-11405)
GREENES RESERVE INC
3373 Nw 10th St Bldg 200　(34475-4547)
PHONE 954 304-0791
Jeff Greene, *CEO*
EMP: 19 EST: 2020
SALES (est): 1MM **Privately Held**
WEB: www.greenesreserve.com
SIC: 2099 Food preparations

(G-11406)
HA MORTON CORP
Also Called: Qualtec Solutions
2930 Ne 24th St　(34470-3932)
P.O. Box 527, Headland AL　(36345-0527)
PHONE 352 220-9790
Harold Morton, *President*
EMP: 20 EST: 2016
SALES (est): 1.5MM **Privately Held**
WEB: www.m3powergroup.com
SIC: 7692 Welding repair

(G-11407)
HALE PRODUCTS INC
Also Called: Class 1
607 Nw 27th Ave　(34475-5623)
PHONE 352 629-5020
Bill Simmons, *CEO*
Bruce Lear, *Vice Pres*
Palmer Pendleton, *Mfg Staff*
Paula Flinn, *Buyer*
Donna Sharlow, *Buyer*
▲ EMP: 240 EST: 1991
SQ FT: 70,000
SALES (est): 51.4MM
SALES (corp-wide): 2.7B **Publicly Held**
WEB: www.haleproducts.com
SIC: 3625 3088 3714 3699 Electric con-
　trols & control accessories, industrial;
　plastics plumbing fixtures; motor vehicle
　parts & accessories; electrical equipment
　& supplies
PA: Idex Corporation
　3100 Sanders Rd Ste 301
　Northbrook IL 60062
　847 498-7070

(G-11408)
HANKISON
4647 Sw 40th Ave　(34474-5730)
PHONE 352 273-1220
Bill Jenkins, *Plant Mgr*
EMP: 7 EST: 2009
SALES (est): 129.9K **Privately Held**
SIC: 3563 Air & gas compressors

(G-11409)
HICKORY SPRINGS MFG CO
5407 Nw 44th Ave　(34482-2814)
P.O. Box 4679　(34478-4679)
PHONE 352 622-7583
Jonathan Clark, *Sales Staff*
Peter Kussmin, *Manager*
EMP: 51
SALES (corp-wide): 430.3MM **Privately
Held**
WEB: www.hickorysprings.com
SIC: 3086 Insulation or cushioning mate-
　rial, foamed plastic
PA: Hickory Springs Manufacturing Com-
　pany
　235 2nd Ave Nw
　Hickory NC 28601
　828 328-2201

(G-11410)
HOSELINE INC
701 Nw 37th Ave　(34475-5682)
PHONE 541 258-8984
EMP: 16 EST: 2019
SALES (est): 2.8MM **Privately Held**
WEB: www.hoseline.com
SIC: 3585 Refrigeration & heating equip-
　ment

(G-11411)
IBS MANUFACTURING LLC
18 Ne 16th St　(34470-4109)
PHONE 352 629-9752
Ivedent Lloyd Sr, *Principal*
EMP: 7 EST: 2013
SALES (est): 144.4K **Privately Held**
SIC: 3999 Barber & beauty shop equip-
　ment

(G-11412)
ISLAND MILLWORK INC
3621 Ne 36th Ave　(34479-2253)
PHONE 352 694-5565
Andrew D Slagel, *President*
EMP: 11 EST: 2017
SALES (est): 907K **Privately Held**
WEB: www.islandmillworkinc.com
SIC: 2431 Millwork

(G-11413)
J & V CABINETS & MORE INC
2321 Ne 43rd St　(34479-2519)
PHONE 352 390-6378
James L Wolcott III, *Principal*
EMP: 7 EST: 2010
SALES (est): 176.8K **Privately Held**
SIC: 2434 Wood kitchen cabinets

(G-11414)
JR PLASTICS CORPORATION
5111 S Pine Ave Ste G　(34480-7176)
PHONE 352 401-0880
Rick Diamond, *President*
Robert Ruwitch, *Chairman*
James Wear, *Vice Pres*
◆ EMP: 100 EST: 1997
SQ FT: 100,000
SALES (est): 21.9MM **Privately Held**
WEB: www.jrplastics.com
SIC: 2671 2673 Plastic film, coated or
　laminated for packaging; plastic & pliofilm
　bags

(G-11415)
JUST IN TIME CNC MACHININ
4551 Nw 44th Ave　(34482-2889)
PHONE 585 247-3850
Jim Alexander, *Principal*
EMP: 5 EST: 2006
SALES (est): 453.2K **Privately Held**
WEB: www.jitmachine.com
SIC: 3599 Machine shop, jobbing & repair

(G-11416)
KAROB INSTRUMENT INC
1644 Ne 22nd Ave　(34470-7748)
PHONE 352 732-2414
Karl Windischmann, *President*
Robert Windischmann, *Vice Pres*
Andrea Wright, *Manager*
EMP: 8 EST: 1984
SALES (est): 1.2MM **Privately Held**
WEB: www.karobinstrument.com
SIC: 3728 Aircraft parts & equipment

(G-11417)
KAROB MANUFACTURING INC
1644 Ne 22nd Ave Bldg Ste　(34470-7748)
PHONE 352 732-2414
Karl C Windischmann Jr, *President*
Andrea Wright, *Corp Secy*
Robert Windischmann, *Vice Pres*
EMP: 27 EST: 1963
SQ FT: 7,500
SALES (est): 498K **Privately Held**
WEB: www.karobinstrument.com
SIC: 3599 Machine shop, jobbing & repair

(G-11418)
KAY ENTERPRISES
2026 Se 3rd Pl　(34471-2516)
PHONE 352 732-5770
Mary Kay, *Owner*
▲ EMP: 6 EST: 1991
SALES (est): 340.9K **Privately Held**
SIC: 3993 Signs & advertising specialties

(G-11419)
KEITHCO INC
Also Called: Budget Print Center
1519 S Pine Ave　(34471-6547)
PHONE 352 351-4741
Stephen M Chancas, *President*
Barbara Chancas, *Owner*
EMP: 9 EST: 1982
SQ FT: 6,200
SALES (est): 998.7K **Privately Held**
SIC: 2752 2796 2791 2789 Commercial
　printing, offset; platemaking services;
　typesetting; bookbinding & related work;
　commercial printing; coated & laminated
　paper

(G-11420)
KOVATCH MOBILE EQUIPMENT CORP
Also Called: Kme
1703 Sw 42nd Ave　(34474-8742)
PHONE 800 235-3928
Rodney N Rushing, *Principal*
Stephen Boettinger, *Principal*
EMP: 7 EST: 2007
SALES (est): 82.5K **Privately Held**
SIC: 3711 Motor vehicles & car bodies

(G-11421)
KPA LLC
1720 Sw 27th Pl　(34471-7801)
PHONE 352 671-9249
Katica Pavicic, *Principal*
EMP: 13 EST: 2015
SALES (est): 636.3K **Privately Held**
WEB: www.kpa.io
SIC: 3822 Auto controls regulating residntl
　& coml environmt & applncs

(G-11422)
KRAUSZ USA INC
331 Sw 57th Ave　(34474-9346)
P.O. Box 770207　(34477-0207)
PHONE 352 509-3600
Dan Krausz, *CEO*
Mary Edwards, *Business Mgr*
Cindy Kransler, *Vice Pres*
Alistair M Vaughan-Edwards, *Vice Pres*
Keith Jones, *Sales Staff*
◆ EMP: 16 EST: 2013
SQ FT: 50,000
SALES (est): 4.7MM **Privately Held**
WEB: www.hymaxusa.com
SIC: 3443 3533 Water tanks, metal plate;
　water well drilling equipment

(G-11423)
L C SOUTHWIND MANUFACTURING
415 Cypress Rd　(34472-3107)
PHONE 352 687-1999
Charles Perry, *Owner*
Colleen Winchester, *Purchasing*
Denise Tinline, *Bookkeeper*
Charles A Perry, *Mng Member*
▲ EMP: 18 EST: 1996
SQ FT: 20,000
SALES (est): 2.7MM **Privately Held**
WEB: www.southwindmfg.com
SIC: 3089 Injection molding of plastics

(G-11424)
L M COMPRESSOR LLC
5800 Sw 25th St Ste 100　(34474-9747)
PHONE 352 484-0850
EMP: 5 EST: 2018
SALES (est): 1.1MM **Privately Held**
WEB: www.lmcompressor.com
SIC: 3563 Air & gas compressors

(G-11425)
LASALLE BRISTOL CORPORATION
Also Called: Imperial Fabric and Decorators
9798 Se Maricamp Rd　(34472-2407)
PHONE 352 687-2151
John Borowski, *Manager*
EMP: 10
SALES (corp-wide): 4B **Publicly Held**
WEB: www.lasallebristol.com
SIC: 2391 2392 Draperies, plastic & tex-
　tile: from purchased materials; household
　furnishings
HQ: Lasalle Bristol Corporation
　601 County Road 17
　Elkhart IN 46516
　574 295-8400

(G-11426)
LEWIS VAULT & PRECAST INC
1731 Sw 7th Ave　(34471-1315)
P.O. Box 3275　(34478-3275)
PHONE 352 351-2992
David Lewis, *President*
John Lewis, *Vice Pres*
Cheryl Cochran, *Treasurer*
EMP: 8 EST: 1982
SQ FT: 624
SALES (est): 338.8K **Privately Held**
SIC: 3272 Burial vaults, concrete or pre-
　cast terrazzo

(G-11427)
LHOIST NORTH AMERICA TENN INC
Also Called: Lowell Plant Usf5
11661 Nw Gainesville Rd　(34482-1486)
P.O. Box 10, Lowell　(32663-0010)
PHONE 352 629-7990
Phillip Curtin, *Plant Mgr*
Stephen Hedrick, *QC Mgr*
EMP: 17
SALES (corp-wide): 2.6MM **Privately
Held**
WEB: www.lhoist.com
SIC: 1422 5032 Crushed & broken lime-
　stone; brick, except refractory
HQ: Lhoist North America Of Tennessee,
　Inc.
　750 Old Hickry Blvd 200-2
　Brentwood TN 37027
　615 259-4222

(G-11428)
LIFETIME ENVIRONMENTAL DESIGNS
3550 Sw 74th Ave　(34474-6451)
P.O. Box 770891　(34477-0891)
PHONE 352 237-7177
John K Van Fleet, *President*
Kim Van Fleet, *Vice Pres*
EMP: 6 EST: 1997
SQ FT: 5,200
SALES (est): 443K **Privately Held**
SIC: 2511 Lawn furniture: wood

(G-11429)
LILES CUSTOM TRAILERS
Also Called: ACR Custom Trailer Products
4940 N Us Highway 441 (34475-1522)
PHONE..................352 368-2652
Arthur C Richardson, *Owner*
A C Richardson, *Owner*
EMP: 7 EST: 1985
SALES (est): 749K **Privately Held**
SIC: 3799 Trailers & trailer equipment

(G-11430)
LIQUID METAL PRODUCTS INC
901 Sw 73rd Street Rd (34476-6877)
PHONE..................402 895-4436
Eugene T Harmel, *President*
Janis Silverberg, *Treasurer*
EMP: 6 EST: 1984
SALES (est): 628.7K **Privately Held**
SIC: 3291 Abrasive metal & steel products

(G-11431)
LOCKHEED MARTIN CORPORATION
Lockheed Martin Mis Fire Ctrl
498 Oak Rd (34472-3099)
PHONE..................352 687-2163
Mike Sarpu, *General Mgr*
Brian O 'connor, *General Mgr*
Gary Cochran, *Maint Spvr*
Maurice Hill, *Mfg Staff*
Frank Boria, *Engineer*
EMP: 72 **Publicly Held**
WEB: www.gyrocamsystems.com
SIC: 3812 3769 Search & navigation
equipment; guided missile & space vehi-
cle parts & auxiliary equipment
PA: Lockheed Martin Corporation
6801 Rockledge Dr
Bethesda MD 20817

(G-11432)
LOW VISION AIDS INC (PA)
Also Called: Magnifying America
2125 Sw Highway 484 (34473-7949)
PHONE..................954 722-1580
John Palmer, *President*
Peggy Palmer, *Vice Pres*
EMP: 9 EST: 1991
SALES (est): 3.2MM **Privately Held**
WEB: www.magnifyingamerica.com
SIC: 3827 5049 Optical instruments & ap-
paratus; magnifying instruments, optical;
optical goods

(G-11433)
LUV ENTERPRISES INC
Also Called: Adrian Lucas Aluminum
141 Sw 71st Pl (34476-6887)
PHONE..................352 867-8440
Brian Lucas, *President*
EMP: 12 EST: 1989
SQ FT: 15,000
SALES (est): 904.3K **Privately Held**
SIC: 3365 3231 5211 Aluminum
foundries; products of purchased glass;
fencing

(G-11434)
M BILT ENTERPRISES INC
Also Called: Well Bilt Industries
1821 Sw 28th St (34471-7732)
PHONE..................352 528-5566
Carol Bilt, *President*
EMP: 14 EST: 1969
SQ FT: 23,500
SALES (est): 1.7MM **Privately Held**
SIC: 3442 5088 Hangar doors, metal; air-
craft equipment & supplies

(G-11435)
MAGNOLIAS GURMET BKY ITLN DELI
Also Called: Magnolia Bakery
1412 N Magnolia Ave (34475-9077)
PHONE..................352 207-2667
Salvatore Castello, *President*
Landa Castello, *Vice Pres*
EMP: 6 EST: 1974
SQ FT: 15,000
SALES (est): 426.5K **Privately Held**
WEB: www.magnoliabakery.com
SIC: 2051 5812 2052 Bakery: wholesale
or wholesale/retail combined; eating
places; cookies & crackers

(G-11436)
MAJIC STAIRS INC (PA)
120 Cypress Rd (34472-5169)
PHONE..................352 446-6295
John K Liles, *Principal*
EMP: 6 EST: 2016
SALES (est): 1MM **Privately Held**
WEB: www.majicstairsinc.com
SIC: 3446 Stairs, staircases, stair treads:
prefabricated metal

(G-11437)
MARION METAL WORKS INC
4750 S Pine Ave (34480-9104)
P.O. Box 830307 (34483-0307)
PHONE..................352 351-4221
Linda L Bourne, *Manager*
EMP: 20 EST: 1986
SQ FT: 18,000
SALES (est): 2.2MM **Privately Held**
WEB: www.mmwcfl.com
SIC: 3444 Sheet metalwork

(G-11438)
MARION PRECISION TOOL INC
1800 Nw 10th St (34475-5331)
PHONE..................352 867-0080
Barbara Luider, *President*
Edward Luider, *Vice Pres*
EMP: 12 EST: 1997
SALES (est): 1.1MM **Privately Held**
WEB: www.marionprecisiontoolinc.com
SIC: 3599 Machine shop, jobbing & repair

(G-11439)
MARION ROCK INC
5979 Se Maricamp Rd (34472-2003)
PHONE..................352 687-2023
James Boutwell, *President*
John F Boutwell, *Vice Pres*
EMP: 35 EST: 1996
SALES (est): 11.4MM **Privately Held**
WEB: www.marionrock.com
SIC: 1499 Mineral abrasives mining

(G-11440)
MAXIMILIAN ZENHO & CO INC
2775 Nw 49th Ave Unit 205 (34482-6213)
PHONE..................352 875-1190
Pablo Fernandez, *CEO*
EMP: 7 EST: 2012
SQ FT: 1,500
SALES (est): 572K **Privately Held**
WEB: www.tattoocyn.net
SIC: 2834 Pharmaceutical preparations

(G-11441)
MEDX CORPORATION
839 Nw 25th Ave (34475-5789)
PHONE..................352 351-2005
Micheal Dettmers, *President*
David Fleming, *CFO*
◆ EMP: 30 EST: 1988
SQ FT: 100,000
SALES (est): 2.9MM **Privately Held**
WEB: www.medxonline.net
SIC: 3949 Exercise equipment

(G-11442)
MESTIZO FOODS LLC
3031 W Silver Sprng Blvd (34475-5647)
PHONE..................352 414-4900
Mariellen Cabral, *Manager*
Andy Westervelt,
Lydia Karschner,
Daniel Villanueva,
EMP: 104 EST: 2017
SALES (est): 10.5MM **Privately Held**
SIC: 2099 Food preparations

(G-11443)
METALCRAFT INDUSTRIES INC
120 Cypress Rd (34472-5169)
PHONE..................352 680-3555
Kevin Liles, *President*
EMP: 16 EST: 1997
SQ FT: 10,000
SALES (est): 4.9MM **Privately Held**
WEB: www.metalcraftindustries.net
SIC: 3444 Sheet metalwork

(G-11444)
MICHIGAN AVENUE BRIDGE INC
Also Called: Rainbow Cabinets
4690 Ne 35th St (34479-3230)
PHONE..................352 236-4044
Marilyn J Busse, *President*
Mark S Allin, *Vice Pres*
EMP: 15 EST: 2005
SALES (est): 1.2MM **Privately Held**
WEB: www.rainbowcabinets.com
SIC: 2434 Wood kitchen cabinets

(G-11445)
MICKEY TRUCK BODIES INC
601 Nw 24th Ct (34475-5718)
PHONE..................352 620-0015
Sid Merrill, *Principal*
Kevin Turpin, *Plant Mgr*
Scott Whittmier, *Executive*
EMP: 10
SALES (corp-wide): 108.1MM **Privately Held**
WEB: www.mickeybody.com
SIC: 3713 Truck & bus bodies
PA: Mickey Truck Bodies Inc.
1305 Trinity Ave
High Point NC 27260
336 882-6806

(G-11446)
MOR EZ CLIPS
4151 Ne 22nd Ct (34479-2546)
PHONE..................352 867-1879
Denise Collett, *Manager*
Maury Collett, *Manager*
EMP: 5 EST: 2002
SALES (est): 361.9K **Privately Held**
WEB: www.morezclips.com
SIC: 3496 Clips & fasteners, made from
purchased wire

(G-11447)
MOYO
6027 Sw 54th St Ste 201 (34474-5547)
PHONE..................352 208-2770
Christina Harper, *Principal*
EMP: 7 EST: 2012
SALES (est): 127.6K **Privately Held**
SIC: 3421 Table & food cutlery, including
butchers'

(G-11448)
MULCH & STONE EMPORIUM INC
7699 Sw Highway 200 (34476-7051)
PHONE..................352 237-7870
Chris Winn, *President*
Lisa Winn, *Office Mgr*
EMP: 5 EST: 2008
SALES (est): 327K **Privately Held**
WEB: www.mulchandstonesuperstore.com
SIC: 3524 Lawn & garden equipment

(G-11449)
NANOTECHNOVATION CORPORATION
Also Called: Clairson Plastics
2811 Ne 14th St (34470-4819)
PHONE..................352 732-3244
Don Sauey, *CEO*
Troy Carswell, *President*
Kelly Jemison, *Controller*
Marcelle West, *Administration*
EMP: 25 EST: 2007
SALES (est): 679.5K **Privately Held**
SIC: 3089 Injection molded finished plastic
products

(G-11450)
NELSONS TRUCK AND TRLR SLS LLC
4131 Nw Blitchton Rd (34482-4058)
PHONE..................352 732-8908
EMP: 9 EST: 2010
SALES (est): 506.4K **Privately Held**
WEB: www.nelsonstrailers.com
SIC: 3715 Truck trailers

(G-11451)
NOBILITY HOMES INC (PA)
3741 Sw 7th St (34474-1945)
PHONE..................352 732-5157
Terry E Trexler, *Ch of Bd*
Steve Cary, *Vice Pres*
Thomas W Trexler, *CFO*
Lynn J Cramer Jr, *Treasurer*
Lj Anderson, *Manager*
EMP: 28 EST: 1967
SQ FT: 72,000
SALES (est): 45MM **Publicly Held**
WEB: www.nobilityhomes.com
SIC: 2451 5271 Mobile homes; mobile
homes

(G-11452)
OCALA BREEDERS SALES CO INC (PA)
Also Called: Ocala Breeders' Feed & Supply
1701 Sw 60th Ave (34474-1800)
P.O. Box 99 (34478-0099)
PHONE..................352 237-4667
Thomas Ventura, *President*
EMP: 50 EST: 1977
SQ FT: 20,000
SALES (est): 13.2MM **Privately Held**
WEB: www.obssales.com
SIC: 2048 7389 7999 Livestock feeds;
auctioneers, fee basis; gambling & lottery
services

(G-11453)
OCALA CONCRETE SERVICES LLC
3498 W Highway 326 (34475-2464)
PHONE..................352 694-4300
Gonzalo Pozo Sr, *Mng Member*
EMP: 7 EST: 2009
SALES (est): 925.6K **Privately Held**
WEB: www.ocalaconcrete.com
SIC: 3273 Ready-mixed concrete

(G-11454)
OCALA MAGAZINE
Also Called: Gainesville/Ocala Business
743 E Fort King St (34471-2233)
P.O. Box 4649 (34478-4649)
PHONE..................352 622-2995
Linda Marks, *President*
Philip Glassman, *Publisher*
Dr William Eyerly, *Vice Pres*
Jean Mc Connell, *Vice Pres*
Randy Woodruff, *CFO*
EMP: 24 EST: 1984
SALES (est): 1MM **Privately Held**
WEB: www.ocalamagazine.com
SIC: 2721 Magazines: publishing only, not
printed on site; magazines: publishing &
printing

(G-11455)
OCALA MANUFACTURING
10245 N Us Highway 27 (34482-1848)
PHONE..................352 433-6643
Richard Estes, *Principal*
EMP: 7 EST: 2010
SALES (est): 179.8K **Privately Held**
WEB: web.ocalacep.com
SIC: 3999 Manufacturing industries

(G-11456)
OCALA METAL PRODUCTS INC
800 N Pine Ave (34475-8879)
PHONE..................352 861-4500
Bob E Hatcher, *President*
EMP: 7 EST: 2008
SALES (est): 550.8K **Privately Held**
SIC: 3448 Prefabricated metal buildings

(G-11457)
OCALA PHARMACY LLC
8290 Sw Highway 200 (34481-9677)
PHONE..................352 509-7890
Rameshbhai S Patel, *Principal*
EMP: 7 EST: 2015
SALES (est): 1MM **Privately Held**
WEB: www.ocalapharmacy.com
SIC: 2834 Pharmaceutical preparations

(G-11458)
OCALA PRINT QUICK INC
Also Called: Concord Print Shops
600 S Magnolia Ave (34471-0976)
PHONE..................352 629-0736
William Marren, *President*
EMP: 9 EST: 1973
SQ FT: 3,575
SALES (est): 992.7K **Privately Held**
WEB: www.concordprintocala.com
SIC: 2752 7334 2791 2789 Commercial
printing, offset; photocopying & duplicat-
ing services; typesetting; bookbinding &
related work

(G-11459)
OCALA PUBLICATION INCORPORATED
Also Called: Ocala Style Magazine
908 Se 16th St (34471-3904)
PHONE..................................352 732-0073
Kathy Johnson, *President*
Evelyn Anderson, *Marketing Staff*
EMP: 20 **EST:** 2006
SALES (est): 1.2MM **Privately Held**
WEB: www.ocalastyle.com
SIC: 2721 Magazines: publishing only, not printed on site

(G-11460)
OFAB INC
1909 Ne 25th Ave (34470-4848)
PHONE..................................352 629-0040
Larry Amyotte, *President*
Gary Ringo, *Vice Pres*
Melissa Vachon, *Executive*
Ben Davis, *Shareholder*
Marissa Davis, *Shareholder*
EMP: 65 **EST:** 1984
SQ FT: 18,000
SALES (est): 15.2MM **Privately Held**
WEB: www.ofab.net
SIC: 3443 3599 4214 Fabricated plate work (boiler shop); machine shop, jobbing & repair; local trucking with storage

(G-11461)
PACIFIC ARCHES CORPORATION
1740 Se 18th St Ste 1302 (34471-5454)
PHONE..................................352 236-7787
Lori Findlay, *Principal*
EMP: 19 **EST:** 2008
SALES (est): 4.9MM **Privately Held**
WEB: www.pacarches.com
SIC: 2439 Structural wood members

(G-11462)
PACKAGING ALTERNATIVES CORP (PA)
4130 Sw 13th St (34474-8589)
P.O. Box 770907 (34477-0907)
PHONE..................................352 867-5050
James F Byrne, *President*
Sandra E Byrne, *Vice Pres*
EMP: 11 **EST:** 1994
SQ FT: 20,000
SALES (est): 4.5MM **Privately Held**
WEB: www.packagingalternatives.com
SIC: 2653 2675 Corrugated & solid fiber boxes; die-cut paper & board

(G-11463)
PARAMOUNT MARKETING INC
138 Juniper Loop Cir (34480-5211)
PHONE..................................352 608-8801
Johnny Mansfield, *General Mgr*
Hronec Sharon D, *Principal*
Keren Guerrido, *Sales Staff*
Michelle Coulter, *Marketing Staff*
EMP: 9 **EST:** 2014
SALES (est): 152.8K **Privately Held**
WEB: www.paramountmarketing.net
SIC: 2741 Miscellaneous publishing

(G-11464)
PEPSI-COLA METRO BTLG CO INC
525 Sw 16th St (34471-0601)
PHONE..................................352 629-8911
Mike McCullough, *Manager*
EMP: 32
SQ FT: 19,400
SALES (corp-wide): 70.3B **Publicly Held**
WEB: www.pepsico.com
SIC: 2086 Carbonated soft drinks, bottled & canned
HQ: Pepsi-Cola Metropolitan Bottling Company, Inc.
700 Anderson Hill Rd
Purchase NY 10577
914 767-6000

(G-11465)
PHILLIPS GRAPHICS INC
1711 Sw 17th St (34471-1200)
PHONE..................................352 622-1776
Joseph G Phillips Jr, *President*
Jolea S Phillips, *Treasurer*
Jolea Womble, *Finance*

Stacie C Phillips, *Admin Sec*
EMP: 6 **EST:** 1985
SALES (est): 661.6K **Privately Held**
WEB: www.phillipsgraphics.com
SIC: 2752 Commercial printing, offset

(G-11466)
PHOENIX WOOD PRODUCTS INC (PA)
3761 Ne 36th Ave (34479-2251)
PHONE..................................888 304-1131
Brian Knight, *President*
Glenn Ryan, *General Mgr*
Stan Redrick, *Vice Pres*
Dakota Campbell, *Production*
Steve Redrick, *Treasurer*
EMP: 40 **EST:** 1993
SQ FT: 2,500
SALES (est): 13.3MM **Privately Held**
WEB: www.phoenixwood.com
SIC: 2448 Pallets, wood

(G-11467)
PIP PRINTING
11 Sw 1st Ave (34471-1101)
PHONE..................................352 622-3224
Rich Bierema, *President*
Nancy Bierema, *Treasurer*
EMP: 8 **EST:** 1979
SQ FT: 2,500
SALES (est): 600K **Privately Held**
WEB: www.pip.com
SIC: 2752 2791 2789 Commercial printing, offset; typesetting; bookbinding & related work

(G-11468)
PLASTIC AND PRODUCTS MKTG LLC
3445 Sw 6th St (34474-1916)
PHONE..................................352 867-8078
Eileen Eyelea Keeler, *General Mgr*
Jeffrey Stein, *Mng Member*
Eileen Keeler, *Manager*
Liz Troutman, *Manager*
EMP: 14 **EST:** 1986
SALES (est): 2MM **Privately Held**
WEB: www.plasticpm.com
SIC: 2821 3354 2434 3469 Thermoplastic materials; shapes, extruded aluminum; wood kitchen cabinets; metal stampings; plastics sheets & rods

(G-11469)
PNEUMATIC PRODUCTS CORPORATION
Also Called: SPX Flow Technology
4647 Sw 40th Ave (34474-5730)
PHONE..................................352 873-5793
Carl Ruder, *General Mgr*
Keith Lassiter, *Purch Mgr*
George Rogers, *Research*
Harry Derkay, *Sales Mgr*
EMP: 7 **EST:** 2010
SALES (est): 1.7MM **Privately Held**
SIC: 3569 General industrial machinery

(G-11470)
POWDER SYSTEMS INC
120 Cypress Rd (34472-5169)
PHONE..................................352 680-3558
Michael Murdock, *President*
John Kevin Liles, *Vice Pres*
EMP: 5 **EST:** 1994
SQ FT: 9,600
SALES (est): 505K **Privately Held**
SIC: 3599 Chemical milling job shop

(G-11471)
PRIMA FOODS INTERNATIONAL INC
2140 Ne 36th Ave (34470-3183)
P.O. Box 2208, Silver Springs (34489-2208)
PHONE..................................352 732-9148
Hector Viale, *President*
Celeste Viale, *Vice Pres*
EMP: 8 **EST:** 1985
SQ FT: 4,000
SALES (est): 992.6K **Privately Held**
WEB: www.primafoodsinc.com
SIC: 2087 Concentrates, drink

(G-11472)
PRO POLY OF AMERICA INC
230 Ne 25th Ave Ste 300 (34470-7075)
PHONE..................................352 629-1414
Tim Dean, *President*
Nick Dean, *Vice Pres*
Tyson Hammer, *Opers Staff*
Missy Allen, *Comptroller*
Mollie Miranda, *Marketing Staff*
EMP: 9
SALES (corp-wide): 10MM **Privately Held**
WEB: www.propolyamerica.com
SIC: 2821 Thermosetting materials
PA: Pro Poly Of America, Inc.
1821 Nw 57th St
Ocala FL 34475
352 629-1414

(G-11473)
PRO POLY OF AMERICA INC (PA)
1821 Nw 57th St (34475-3031)
PHONE..................................352 629-1414
Tim Dean, *President*
Branden Sharbono, *Design Engr*
EMP: 40 **EST:** 1996
SQ FT: 12,500
SALES (est): 10MM **Privately Held**
WEB: www.propolyamerica.com
SIC: 2821 Plastics materials & resins

(G-11474)
PROFAB CORPORATION
1056 Ne 16th St (34470-4204)
PHONE..................................352 369-5010
Keith Hoffmann, *Branch Mgr*
EMP: 8 **Privately Held**
WEB: www.profabplastics.net
SIC: 2821 Plastics materials & resins
PA: Profab Corporation
4901 Nw 5th St
Ocala FL 34482

(G-11475)
PROFAB CORPORATION (PA)
Also Called: Profab Plastics
4901 Nw 5th St (34482-3287)
PHONE..................................352 369-5515
Keith Hoffmann, *CEO*
Ralph Milykovic, *CEO*
Jim Gischia, *Vice Pres*
Alexis Monigal Leitzki, *Vice Pres*
EMP: 17 **EST:** 1996
SQ FT: 10,000
SALES (est): 4.8MM **Privately Held**
WEB: www.profabplastics.net
SIC: 2821 Plastics materials & resins

(G-11476)
R&D MANUFACTURING INDS INC
1031 Ne 16th St (34470-4203)
PHONE..................................352 351-8800
Ronald L Malone, *Principal*
EMP: 8 **EST:** 2011
SALES (est): 202.8K **Privately Held**
SIC: 3999 Manufacturing industries

(G-11477)
RAINBOW CABINETS INC
4690 Ne 35th St (34479-3230)
PHONE..................................352 236-4044
Marilyn Busse, *President*
Mark Allin, *Officer*
EMP: 10 **EST:** 1987
SALES (est): 497.6K **Privately Held**
SIC: 2434 Wood kitchen cabinets

(G-11478)
REALPURE BOTTLING INC
2445 Nw 42nd St (34475-3144)
P.O. Box 1059, Silver Springs (34489-1059)
PHONE..................................601 849-9910
Keith Richmond, *President*
Cheryl McPhillips, *Director*
Kane Richmond, *Director*
Kirk Richmond, *Director*
EMP: 16 **EST:** 2016
SALES (est): 621.7K **Privately Held**
SIC: 3221 Bottles for packing, bottling & canning: glass

(G-11479)
RELIABLE BUSINESS TECHNOLOGIES
8497 Sw 136th Loop (34473-6811)
PHONE..................................386 561-9944
Chris Mitchell, *Principal*
EMP: 7 **EST:** 2016
SALES (est): 266.1K **Privately Held**
WEB: www.rbtsupport.com
SIC: 7372 Application computer software

(G-11480)
RELIANCE PETRO HOLDINGS LLC
1820 Se 18th Ave Ste 3 (34471-8303)
PHONE..................................352 390-8039
Neil Patel, *Vice Pres*
Bharat P Patel,
Neel Patel, *Maintence Staff*
Mulka J Patel,
Trupti B Patel,
EMP: 10 **EST:** 2004
SQ FT: 4,000
SALES (est): 1.5MM **Privately Held**
WEB: reliancepetroleumllc.wordpress.com
SIC: 1382 5541 Oil & gas exploration services; gasoline service stations

(G-11481)
RESHARP INDUSTRIES
5101 Se 11th Ave (34480-6666)
PHONE..................................352 362-1730
Timothy A Staub, *Principal*
EMP: 9 **EST:** 2002
SALES (est): 245.7K **Privately Held**
WEB: www.resharpindustries.com
SIC: 3999 Manufacturing industries

(G-11482)
ROLLING GREENS MOBILE HOME PK
1899 Se 58th Ave (34480-5847)
PHONE..................................352 624-0022
Jim Ford, *Senior VP*
EMP: 8 **EST:** 1995
SALES (est): 170.6K **Privately Held**
WEB: www.covecommunities.com
SIC: 2451 Mobile homes, except recreational

(G-11483)
RUBBER DESIGNS LLC
500 Sw 6th Ter (34471)
PHONE..................................706 383-7528
EMP: 34 **Privately Held**
WEB: www.rubberdesigns.com
SIC: 3069 Rubber floor coverings, mats & wallcoverings
HQ: Rubber Designs, Llc
100 Rus Dr Se
Calhoun GA 30701
706 383-7528

(G-11484)
SCORPION EQUITY LLC
Also Called: Scorpion Racing Products
5817 Nw 44th Ave (34482-7891)
PHONE..................................352 512-0800
Kyle Weaver, *Prdtn Mgr*
Zac Collins, *Design Engr*
Kate Weaver, *Director*
Kenneth Kirkpatrick,
Parker Eiland,
EMP: 33 **EST:** 2016
SALES (est): 3.8MM **Privately Held**
WEB: www.scorpionracingproducts.com
SIC: 3462 Automotive & internal combustion engine forgings

(G-11485)
SEMINOLE STORES INC
Also Called: Seminole Feed Division
335 Ne Watula Ave (34470-5806)
P.O. Box 940 (34478-0940)
PHONE..................................352 732-4143
O C Branch Jr, *Ch of Bd*
Greg Branch, *President*
◆ **EMP:** 13 **EST:** 1987
SQ FT: 120,000
SALES (est): 12.6MM
SALES (corp-wide): 15.8MM **Privately Held**
WEB: www.seminolefeed.com
SIC: 2048 5999 Frozen pet food (except dog & cat); feed & farm supply

▲ = Import ▼=Export
◆ =Import/Export

PA: Branch Properties, Inc.
335 Ne Watula Ave
Ocala FL 34470
352 732-4143

(G-11486)
SHADE SAVER INC
3330 Nw 95th Avenue Rd (34482-3895)
PHONE..................................850 650-0884
Bryan K Myers, *Director*
EMP: 5 **EST:** 2012
SALES (est): 471.7K **Privately Held**
SIC: 3578 Accounting machines & cash registers

(G-11487)
SHADE SYSTEMS INC
4150 Sw 19th St (34474-2860)
PHONE..................................352 237-0135
Alan A Bayman, *President*
Eric Kinoti, *Managing Dir*
Brad Buzard, *Natl Sales Mgr*
Margo Ross, *Cust Mgr*
Margo Talbot, *Cust Mgr*
▲ **EMP:** 30 **EST:** 2003
SQ FT: 50,000
SALES (est): 5.1MM **Privately Held**
WEB: www.shadesystemsinc.com
SIC: 2421 Outdoor wood structural products

(G-11488)
SHASHY ENTERPRISES INC
Also Called: Southern Blade & Supply
1824 N Magnolia Ave (34475-9112)
P.O. Box 2063 (34478-2063)
PHONE..................................352 732-3904
Shashy Marion, *Vice Pres*
EMP: 6 **EST:** 1984
SQ FT: 2,400
SALES (est): 874.3K **Privately Held**
SIC: 3399 5072 Metal fasteners; hardware

(G-11489)
SHEALY REVEL B INC
606 Ne 35th St (34479-2714)
P.O. Box 634 (34478-0634)
PHONE..................................352 629-1552
Preston Shealy, *President*
EMP: 6 **EST:** 1990
SALES (est): 413.8K **Privately Held**
SIC: 3271 Concrete block & brick

(G-11490)
SIBE AUTOMATION LLC
1521 Sw 12th Ave Ste 700 (34471-0541)
PHONE..................................352 690-1741
Rehan Lalani, *Supervisor*
Simon Gaysinsky,
EMP: 15 **EST:** 2012
SALES (est): 2.3MM **Privately Held**
WEB: www.sibeautomation.com
SIC: 3089 Thermoformed finished plastic products

(G-11491)
SIGNATURE BRANDS LLC (PA)
Also Called: Paas
808 Sw 12th St (34471-0540)
PHONE..................................352 622-3134
Jared Konstanty, *CEO*
Jennifer Ellis, *Business Mgr*
Mike Tomasetti, *Vice Pres*
Michael Garritano, *Safety Mgr*
Patrick Riffel, *Warehouse Mgr*
◆ **EMP:** 104 **EST:** 1951
SQ FT: 240,000
SALES (est): 104.7MM **Privately Held**
WEB: www.signaturebrands.com
SIC: 2064 Cake ornaments, confectionery

(G-11492)
SIGNATURE BRANDS LLC
1930 Sw 38th Ave Ste 300 (34474-4903)
PHONE..................................352 622-3134
Jerry Reardon, *CEO*
Hannah Baderschneider, *Vice Pres*
Michael Garritano, *Safety Mgr*
Ashley Kelty, *Warehouse Mgr*
Sean Green, *Maint Spvr*
EMP: 357
SALES (corp-wide): 104.7MM **Privately Held**
WEB: www.signaturebrands.com
SIC: 2064 Candy & other confectionery products

PA: Signature Brands, Llc
808 Sw 12th St
Ocala FL 34471
352 622-3134

(G-11493)
SIGNATURE BRANDS LLC
1921 Sw 44th Ave (34474-8744)
PHONE..................................352 622-3134
Jared Konstanty, *Mng Member*
EMP: 17
SALES (corp-wide): 104.7MM **Privately Held**
WEB: www.signaturebrands.com
SIC: 2064 Cake ornaments, confectionery
PA: Signature Brands, Llc
808 Sw 12th St
Ocala FL 34471
352 622-3134

(G-11494)
SIGNS UNLIMITED - SEA INC
618 S Magnolia Ave (34471-0976)
PHONE..................................352 732-7341
Victor Buttermore, *President*
Irma P Buttermore, *Treasurer*
EMP: 14 **EST:** 1991
SQ FT: 4,224
SALES (est): 574.7K **Privately Held**
SIC: 3993 7336 7389 Signs & advertising specialties; silk screen design; embroidering of advertising on shirts, etc.

(G-11495)
SIMAR INDUSTRIES INC
805 Nw 25th Ave (34475-5784)
PHONE..................................352 622-2287
Derek T Evans, *President*
Marlene Evans, *Corp Secy*
Vince Troisi, *Opers Staff*
Robin Phillips, *Purch Mgr*
Peggy White, *VP Sls/Mktg*
EMP: 20 **EST:** 1992
SQ FT: 18,000
SALES (est): 4.7MM **Privately Held**
WEB: www.simarindustries.com
SIC: 3444 Sheet metal specialties, not stamped

(G-11496)
SPECIAL PUBLICATIONS INC
Also Called: Today Magazines Group
743 Se Fort King Rd (34471)
P.O. Box 4649 (34478-4649)
PHONE..................................352 622-2995
Linda Marks, *President*
EMP: 10 **EST:** 1976
SALES (est): 1.2MM **Privately Held**
SIC: 2721 7311 Magazines: publishing & printing; advertising agencies

(G-11497)
SPICER INDUSTRIES INC
840 Nw 24th Ct (34475-5768)
PHONE..................................352 732-5300
Paul J Spicer, *President*
EMP: 10 **EST:** 1953
SQ FT: 9,000
SALES (est): 920K **Privately Held**
SIC: 3465 3469 3499 Body parts, automobile: stamped metal; metal stampings; furniture parts, metal

(G-11498)
SPX FLOW TECHNOLOGY USA INC (HQ)
Also Called: Kemp
4647 Se 40th Ave (34474)
PHONE..................................352 237-1220
Marc Michael, *President*
Dwight Gibson, *President*
David Kowalski, *President*
Tony Renzi, *President*
David J Wilson, *President*
◆ **EMP:** 108 **EST:** 1992
SALES (est): 10.5MM
SALES (corp-wide): 1.5B **Privately Held**
SIC: 3443 Fabricated plate work (boiler shop)
PA: Spx Flow, Inc.
13320 Balntyn Corp Pl
Charlotte NC 28277
704 752-4400

(G-11499)
STEVEN CHANCAS
Also Called: Keithco Enterprises
1519 S Pine Ave (34471-6547)
PHONE..................................352 629-5016
Steven Chancas, *Owner*
EMP: 9 **EST:** 1973
SQ FT: 7,500
SALES (est): 215.7K **Privately Held**
SIC: 2759 3993 2752 2396 Letterpress printing; screen printing; signs & advertising specialties; commercial printing, lithographic; automotive & apparel trimmings

(G-11500)
THERMO KING OF OCALA INC
6015 Nw 44th Ave (34482-2221)
PHONE..................................352 867-7700
Kent Wilson, *President*
Chris Murphy, *Principal*
EMP: 9 **EST:** 2009
SALES (est): 971.6K **Privately Held**
WEB: www.ingersollrand.com
SIC: 3561 Pumps & pumping equipment

(G-11501)
THI E-COMMERCE LLC
Also Called: Running Board Warehouse
4414 Sw College Rd # 14 (34474-4790)
PHONE..................................352 327-4058
William Reminder, *President*
Kelly Kneifl, *COO*
Jim Bresingham, *CFO*
Jeff Adkinson, *Sales Staff*
Kristin Lloyd, *Supervisor*
▲ **EMP:** 98 **EST:** 1997
SQ FT: 18,000
SALES (est): 27.1MM
SALES (corp-wide): 820.3MM **Privately Held**
WEB: www.thiecommerce.com
SIC: 3714 Motor vehicle parts & accessories
HQ: Tectum Holdings, Inc.
5400 Data Ct
Ann Arbor MI 48108
734 205-9093

(G-11502)
TRANE INC
4500 Sw 40th Ave (34474-5731)
PHONE..................................352 237-0136
Jim Gamble, *Manager*
EMP: 15 **Privately Held**
WEB: www.trane.com
SIC: 3585 Refrigeration & heating equipment
HQ: Trane Inc.
1 Centennial Ave Ste 101
Piscataway NJ 08854
732 652-7100

(G-11503)
TRUSCO MANUFACTURING COMPANY
545 Nw 68th Ave (34482-8255)
PHONE..................................352 237-0311
Brad Harris, *Vice Pres*
Brandon Harris, *Vice Pres*
Bruce Harris, *Vice Pres*
Daniel Harris, *Vice Pres*
EMP: 6 **EST:** 1965
SQ FT: 9,000
SALES (est): 994K **Privately Held**
WEB: www.truscomfg.com
SIC: 3563 Dusting outfits for metals, paints & chemicals

(G-11504)
TURBO PARTS LLC
810 Nw 25th Ave Ste 102 (34475-5781)
PHONE..................................352 351-4510
EMP: 12
SALES (est): 1.9MM **Privately Held**
SIC: 3599 Mfg Industrial Machinery

(G-11505)
U-DUMP TRAILERS LLC
Also Called: Trailer Source, The
2610 Nw 10th St (34475-5709)
PHONE..................................352 351-8510
Betty Duffy, *General Mgr*
Ken Lenox, *Sales Staff*
Anthony Manna, *Mng Member*
Ken Krismanth, *Mng Member*
◆ **EMP:** 52 **EST:** 1979

SQ FT: 16,000
SALES (est): 8.1MM **Privately Held**
WEB: www.udumptrailers.com
SIC: 3715 Truck trailers

(G-11506)
UNITED PLASTIC FABRICATING INC
5000 Nw 5th St (34482-3286)
PHONE..................................352 291-2477
Robert Farnell, *Production*
Lisa Schrader, *Production*
Jeffrey Jacklin, *Engineer*
Nelson Lateer, *Manager*
Marcia Anderson, *Manager*
EMP: 51
SALES (corp-wide): 41.6MM **Privately Held**
WEB: www.unitedplastic.com
SIC: 3089 Injection molding of plastics; plastic processing
PA: United Plastic Fabricating, Inc.
165 Flagship Dr
North Andover MA 01845
978 975-4520

(G-11507)
US HEMP AND OIL LLC
1010 Ne 16th St (34470-4204)
PHONE..................................352 817-2455
Robert Ergle, *Mng Member*
EMP: 8 **EST:** 2019
SALES (est): 541.4K **Privately Held**
WEB: www.ushempandoil.com
SIC: 3999

(G-11508)
USA SCIENTIFIC INC (DH)
346 Sw 57th Ave (34474-9345)
P.O. Box 3565 (34478-3565)
PHONE..................................352 237-6288
Robert Declerk, *President*
Richard Olson, *Partner*
Linda Anastos, *Regional Mgr*
Howard Epstein, *Vice Pres*
Cheri Kreutchic, *Vice Pres*
▲ **EMP:** 33 **EST:** 1982
SALES (est): 26.9MM
SALES (corp-wide): 177.9K **Privately Held**
WEB: www.usascientific.com
SIC: 3826 Analytical instruments
HQ: Eppendorf Se
Barkhausenweg 1
Hamburg HH 22339
405 380-10

(G-11509)
VIKING WOODWORKING
13401 W Highway 328 (34482-7056)
PHONE..................................352 237-5050
Bert Eriksen, *Owner*
EMP: 6 **EST:** 1977
SQ FT: 3,350
SALES (est): 397.2K **Privately Held**
SIC: 2434 Wood kitchen cabinets

(G-11510)
VIPER COMMUNICATION SYSTEMS (HQ)
4211 Sw 13th St (34474-8595)
PHONE..................................352 694-7030
Jimmy Comont, *President*
Don Jones, *Principal*
James Conant, *Principal*
Preston Spurlin, *Principal*
EMP: 25 **EST:** 1997
SQ FT: 5,000
SALES (est): 16.4MM
SALES (corp-wide): 63.5MM **Privately Held**
WEB: www.mtsi.com
SIC: 3669 3441 1791 Visual communication systems; fabricated structural metal; structural steel erection
PA: Microwave Transmission Systems, Inc
1751 Jay Ell Dr
Richardson TX 75081
972 669-0591

(G-11511)
VISTA-PRO AUTOMOTIVE LLC
2410 Nw 8th Pl (34475-5774)
PHONE..................................352 867-7272
EMP: 16

GEOGRAPHIC

SALES (corp-wide): 81.4MM **Privately Held**
SIC: 3714 Mfg Motor Vehicle Parts/Accessories
HQ: Vista-Pro Automotive, Llc
　15 Century Blvd Ste 600
　Nashville TN 37214
　888 250-2676

(G-11512)
WELL BILT INDUSTRIES USA LLC
3001 Sw 67th Avenue Rd # 100 (34474-1708)
PHONE.................................352 528-5566
Tim Schendel, *Vice Pres*
Virginia Macdonald, *Marketing Mgr*
Mark Macdonald,
EMP: 19 **EST:** 2009
SQ FT: 25,000
SALES (est): 3MM **Privately Held**
WEB: www.wellbiltdoors.com
SIC: 3442 Hangar doors, metal

(G-11513)
WINCO MFG LLC (PA)
Also Called: Transmotion Medical
5516 Sw 1st Ln (34474-9366)
PHONE.................................352 854-2929
Jim Ankoviak, *CEO*
David Martin, *Buyer*
Richard Burchett, *Engineer*
Jessica Cuebas, *Sales Staff*
Mark Lazzeri, *Marketing Staff*
▲ **EMP:** 90 **EST:** 2010
SALES (est): 30.9MM **Privately Held**
WEB: www.wincomfg.com
SIC: 2599 Hospital furniture, except beds

(G-11514)
WOODS PRINTING OCALA INC
1740 Ne 23rd Ter (34470-4790)
PHONE.................................352 629-1665
James Wood, *President*
EMP: 6 **EST:** 1976
SQ FT: 3,000
SALES (est): 872.5K **Privately Held**
WEB: www.woodspfa.com
SIC: 2752 2759 Commercial printing, offset; letterpress printing

(G-11515)
YANDLES QUALITY ROOF TRUSSES
834 N Magnolia Ave (34475-8874)
PHONE.................................352 732-3000
Lanas C Yandle, *President*
EMP: 6 **EST:** 1985
SQ FT: 20,300
SALES (est): 659.3K **Privately Held**
SIC: 2439 5211 Trusses, wooden roof; roofing material

(G-11516)
YES SOLUTIONS GALLERY LLC
Also Called: Yes Ink Solutions
4901 E Slver Sprng Blvd (34470-3228)
PHONE.................................352 622-7937
Ron Corbett,
Sydney B Corbett,
EMP: 7 **EST:** 2007
SQ FT: 3,000
SALES (est): 235.8K **Privately Held**
SIC: 2893 Printing ink

Ocean Ridge
Palm Beach County

(G-11517)
FUZION PRFMCE COATINGS LLC
6790 N Ocean Blvd (33435-3350)
PHONE.................................561 364-2474
Edward Sivri, *Principal*
EMP: 7 **EST:** 2010
SALES (est): 202K **Privately Held**
SIC: 3479 Metal coating & allied service

(G-11518)
TDK ELECTRONICS INC
6530 N Ocean Blvd (33435-5249)
PHONE.................................561 509-7771
EMP: 10 **Privately Held**

WEB: tdk-electronics.tdk.com
SIC: 3679 5065 3546 Electronic crystals; diskettes, computer; power-driven hand-tools; grinders, portable: electric or pneumatic
HQ: Tdk Electronics Inc.
　485b Us Highway 1 S # 200
　Iselin NJ 08830
　732 906-4300

Ocklawaha
Marion County

(G-11519)
GRUENEWALD MFG CO INC
9800 Se 176th Court Rd (32179-4526)
PHONE.................................978 777-0200
Thomas Muldoon, *President*
Rickey Schwed, *Sales Staff*
▼ **EMP:** 10 **EST:** 1939
SALES (est): 1MM **Privately Held**
WEB: www.whipcream.com
SIC: 3556 Food products machinery

Ocoee
Orange County

(G-11520)
AMERICAN SANI PARTITION CORP
300 Enterprise St (34761-3002)
P.O. Box 99 (34761-0099)
PHONE.................................407 656-0611
Ronald Birkenmaier, *President*
Gerald Birkenmaier, *Shareholder*
◆ **EMP:** 45 **EST:** 1934
SQ FT: 75,000
SALES (est): 7.5MM **Privately Held**
WEB: www.am-sanitary-partition.com
SIC: 2542 Partitions for floor attachment, prefabricated: except wood

(G-11521)
FCS INDUSTRIES CORP
406 Anessa Rose Loop (34761-4623)
PHONE.................................407 947-3127
Willie D Fisher, *President*
EMP: 7 **EST:** 2014
SALES (est): 159.6K **Privately Held**
SIC: 3999 Manufacturing industries

(G-11522)
KREATIVE CERAMICS INC
2165 Twisted Pine Rd (34761-7671)
PHONE.................................321 278-9889
Christopher Taylor, *Director*
EMP: 7 **EST:** 2005
SALES (est): 60.5K **Privately Held**
SIC: 3269 Pottery products

(G-11523)
LIMITLESS MOBILE WHOLESALE INC (PA)
885 Sedalia St (34761-3164)
PHONE.................................321 710-6936
Jim Croal, *CTO*
EMP: 11 **EST:** 2013
SALES (est): 5.8MM **Privately Held**
SIC: 3663 Mobile communication equipment

(G-11524)
PHYSIORX LLC
2706 Rew Cir (34761-4215)
PHONE.................................407 718-5549
Denise Masson, *Principal*
EMP: 8 **EST:** 2001
SALES (est): 357.3K **Privately Held**
WEB: www.physiorx.com
SIC: 3842 Implants, surgical

(G-11525)
QUALITY VAULTS INC (PA)
751 S Bluford Ave (34761-2942)
PHONE.................................407 656-8781
James Tramonte, *President*
Donna G Bryce, *Corp Secy*
Donna G Butler, *Corp Secy*
Boettcher Joyce, *Vice Pres*
EMP: 13 **EST:** 1970

SALES (est): 2.4MM **Privately Held**
WEB: www.qualityvaults.com
SIC: 3272 5032 Burial vaults, concrete or precast terrazzo; brick, stone & related material

(G-11526)
STONE BRICK PAVERS INC
1699 Cambridge Village Ct (34761-6986)
PHONE.................................407 844-1455
Domingos Oliveira, *Principal*
EMP: 8 **EST:** 2010
SALES (est): 516.5K **Privately Held**
WEB: www.rusticbrickpavers.com
SIC: 3531 Pavers

(G-11527)
TEAK ISLE INC
Also Called: Teak Isle Manufacturing
401 Capitol Ct (34761-3024)
P.O. Box 417 (34761-0417)
PHONE.................................407 656-8885
Patrick H Brown, *President*
David R Brown, *Vice Pres*
Brian Oleary, *Project Mgr*
Rick Bailey, *Mfg Mgr*
Bill Burrows, *Production*
◆ **EMP:** 225 **EST:** 1980
SALES (est): 45.8MM **Privately Held**
WEB: www.teakisle.com
SIC: 2821 2542 2431 Plastics materials & resins; partitions & fixtures, except wood; millwork

(G-11528)
TMMR HOLDINGS LLC (PA)
Also Called: Verticals Unlimited
301 Enterprise St Unit A (34761-3030)
PHONE.................................407 295-5200
Thomas Mostardi, *General Mgr*
Lois Janofsky, *Bookkeeper*
Ahren Nevins, *Sales Staff*
Tracy Davis, *Office Mgr*
Michelle Mostardi, *Mng Member*
EMP: 22 **EST:** 2010
SALES (est): 3.1MM **Privately Held**
SIC: 2591 1799 Drapery hardware & blinds & shades; window treatment installation

(G-11529)
U C FAB OF FLORIDA LLC
301 Enterprise St Unit C (34761-3030)
PHONE.................................407 614-4210
Rosa Dalbow, *Mng Member*
EMP: 9 **EST:** 2009
SALES (est): 517.2K **Privately Held**
SIC: 3448 Prefabricated metal components

Odessa
Hills County

(G-11530)
ICOSI MANUFACTURING LLC
11134 Challenger Ave (33556-3436)
PHONE.................................813 854-1333
EMP: 10 **EST:** 2007
SALES (est): 1.1MM **Privately Held**
SIC: 3469 3541 Mfg Metal Stampings Mfg Machine Tools-Cutting

Odessa
Hillsborough County

(G-11531)
3M RESIDENT MONITORING INC
1838 Gunn Hwy (33556-3524)
PHONE.................................813 749-5453
▲ **EMP:** 25
SALES (est): 3.4MM **Privately Held**
SIC: 3845 Mfg Electromedical Equipment

(G-11532)
A M TOOL & ENGINEERING COMPANY
2343 Destiny Way (33556-3411)
PHONE.................................727 375-5002
Jerry Mendik, *President*
EMP: 9 **EST:** 1997
SQ FT: 10,000

SALES (est): 601K **Privately Held**
SIC: 3599 Machine shop, jobbing & repair

(G-11533)
ADVANCED CNC MANUFACTURING INC
2313 Destiny Way (33556-3411)
P.O. Box 991 (33556-0991)
PHONE.................................727 372-8222
Miguel Carrosso, *President*
Maggie Carrosso, *Vice Pres*
Maria Carrosso, *Director*
EMP: 14 **EST:** 2002
SQ FT: 11,000
SALES (est): 2MM **Privately Held**
WEB: www.advanced-cnc.com
SIC: 3599 Machine shop, jobbing & repair

(G-11534)
AERONAUTICAL SYSTEMS ENGRG INC
2448 Destiny Way (33556-3412)
PHONE.................................727 375-2520
Faiek Zora, *President*
Jeffrey Kuliga, *Exec VP*
Alejandro Monroy, *Software Engr*
Matt Carullo, *Administration*
Joseph Caulfield, *Graphic Designe*
▲ **EMP:** 8 **EST:** 1994
SQ FT: 7,200
SALES (est): 2.4MM **Privately Held**
WEB: www.aerosyseng.com
SIC: 3699 Electrical equipment & supplies

(G-11535)
AIRCRAFT SYSTEMS GROUP INC
11528 Perpetual Dr (33556-3464)
PHONE.................................727 376-9292
Audrey Gallagher, *President*
Robert Gallagher, *Vice Pres*
EMP: 5 **EST:** 2004
SALES (est): 658.7K **Privately Held**
WEB: www.aircraftsystemsgroup.com
SIC: 3721 Aircraft

(G-11536)
ANVIL IRON WORKS INC
11607 Perpetual Dr (33556-3467)
PHONE.................................727 375-2884
Dennis Moulton, *President*
William Cheatley, *Vice Pres*
EMP: 21 **EST:** 1991
SQ FT: 14,000
SALES (est): 3.4MM **Privately Held**
SIC: 3444 3449 Sheet metalwork; miscellaneous metalwork

(G-11537)
ATLANTIC CUSTOM WOODCRAFT CORP
11146 Challenger Ave # 101 (33556-3425)
PHONE.................................727 645-6905
Trevor Haughey, *President*
Nichole Haughey, *Corp Secy*
Peter Atkins, *Vice Pres*
James R Haughey, *Vice Pres*
Donald Spence, *Vice Pres*
EMP: 20 **EST:** 1993
SQ FT: 15,000
SALES (est): 2.5MM **Privately Held**
WEB: www.atlanticcustomwoodcraft.com
SIC: 2431 Millwork

(G-11538)
ATTENTI US INC (PA)
Also Called: Electronic Monitoring
1838 Gunn Hwy (33556-3524)
PHONE.................................813 749-5454
Yoaz Reisman, *CEO*
Rachel Semago, *General Mgr*
Chris Violante, *Regional Mgr*
Arnold Roese, *Vice Pres*
Randy Buffington, *Research*
▲ **EMP:** 99 **EST:** 1999
SQ FT: 10,000
SALES (est): 28.5MM **Privately Held**
WEB: www.attentigroup.com
SIC: 3669 Intercommunication systems, electric

(G-11539)
BAY TECH INDUSTRIES INC
13275 Byrd Dr (33556-5307)
PHONE.................................813 854-1774

▲ = Import ▼=Export
◆ =Import/Export

Robert P Bourassa, *President*
Rick Seal, *Vice Pres*
EMP: 48 **EST:** 1986
SQ FT: 11,800
SALES (est): 5.4MM **Privately Held**
WEB: www.baytechindustries.com
SIC: 3599 Machine shop, jobbing & repair

(G-11540)
BINNEY FAMILY OF FLORIDA INC
Also Called: Environmental Graphics
11232 Challenger Ave (33556-3420)
PHONE...................727 376-5596
Keith Binney, *President*
Ray Binney, *Vice Pres*
Laura Binney, *Treasurer*
Charisse Clouse, *Manager*
Jan Jansen, *Manager*
EMP: 10 **EST:** 1993
SQ FT: 3,000
SALES (est): 1.6MM **Privately Held**
WEB: www.egisigns.com
SIC: 3993 Signs & advertising specialties

(G-11541)
BK PLASTICS INDUSTRY INC
13414 Byrd Dr (33556-5310)
PHONE...................813 920-3628
Bruce Knecht, *President*
Robin Knecht, *Vice Pres*
▲ **EMP:** 16 **EST:** 1997
SQ FT: 22,000
SALES (est): 2.6MM **Privately Held**
WEB: www.bkplastics.com
SIC: 3089 Thermoformed finished plastic products; plastic processing

(G-11542)
CAN CAN CONCEALMENT LLC
2521b Success Dr (33556-3401)
PHONE...................727 841-6930
Darlene Cahill, *Partner*
Douglas Erickson, *Partner*
EMP: 6 **EST:** 2013
SALES (est): 494.5K **Privately Held**
WEB: www.cancanconcealment.com
SIC: 2389 2339 Men's miscellaneous accessories; garter belts; garters; women's & misses' accessories

(G-11543)
COAST WCP
Also Called: Bengal Industries
1806 Gunn Hwy (33556-3524)
PHONE...................727 572-4249
John Guthrie, *President*
▲ **EMP:** 32 **EST:** 1981
SQ FT: 20,000
SALES (est): 546.6K **Privately Held**
SIC: 3714 3728 Gears, motor vehicle; gears, aircraft power transmission

(G-11544)
COMPONENT GENERAL INC
2445 Success Dr (33556-3429)
PHONE...................727 376-6655
James A Cook, *President*
▲ **EMP:** 22 **EST:** 1973
SQ FT: 16,000
SALES (est): 4.4MM **Privately Held**
WEB: www.componentgeneral.com
SIC: 3676 5065 3663 3577 Electronic resistors; electronic parts & equipment; radio & TV communications equipment; computer peripheral equipment

(G-11545)
CONVEYOR CONSULTING & RBR CORP
2511 Destiny Way (33556-3473)
PHONE...................813 385-1254
Ronald D Fernandes, *President*
George Gano, *Sales Staff*
Colette Stanley, *Administration*
◆ **EMP:** 7 **EST:** 1997
SQ FT: 12,500
SALES (est): 4MM **Privately Held**
WEB: www.ccrconveyor.com
SIC: 3535 Conveyors & conveying equipment

(G-11546)
D G MORRISON INC (PA)
Also Called: Arete Industries
13209 Byrd Dr (33556-5307)
PHONE...................813 865-0208
Donald Morrison, *CEO*
Dan Morrison, *Vice Pres*
James Slanina, *Opers Staff*
Tom Johnson, *QC Mgr*
▲ **EMP:** 19 **EST:** 2000
SQ FT: 15,000
SALES (est): 2.9MM **Privately Held**
WEB: www.siteessentialscompany.com
SIC: 3281 3993 3949 2759 Granite, cut & shaped; signs & advertising specialties; sporting & athletic goods; commercial printing; bar, restaurant & cafeteria furniture; architectural metalwork

(G-11547)
DAIS CORP
11552 Prosperous Dr (33556-3452)
PHONE...................727 375-8484
Timothy N Tangredi, *Ch of Bd*
Megan Bartig, *General Mgr*
Tracie Rusch, *Accountant*
Brian C Johnson, *CTO*
EMP: 10 **EST:** 1993
SQ FT: 7,200
SALES (est): 422.5K **Privately Held**
WEB: www.daisanalytic.com
SIC: 3822 3589 Air conditioning & refrigeration controls; air flow controllers, air conditioning & refrigeration; temperature controls, automatic; electric heat controls; sewage & water treatment equipment

(G-11548)
EASTERN RIBBON & ROLL CORP (PA)
Also Called: Paper Converter
1920 Gunn Hwy (33556-3524)
PHONE...................813 676-8600
▲ **EMP:** 22
SQ FT: 100,000
SALES (est): 5.6MM **Privately Held**
SIC: 3955 5044 5131 Carbon Paper And Inked Ribbons

(G-11549)
ELECTRO MECH SOLUTIONS INC
Also Called: E M S
1555 Gunn Hwy (33556-5308)
PHONE...................813 792-0400
Venkata Boyanapalli, *President*
Venkat Boyanapalli, *President*
RAO Jupalli, *Finance Mgr*
EMP: 25 **EST:** 2001
SQ FT: 45,000
SALES (est): 3.8MM **Privately Held**
WEB: www.emsinc.net
SIC: 3444 3542 8711 Sheet metalwork; sheet metalworking machines; mechanical engineering

(G-11550)
EUCLID CHEMICAL COMPANY
Also Called: Increte Systems
19215 Redwood Rd (33556)
P.O. Box 196 (33556-0196)
PHONE...................813 886-8811
Richard Nagler, *Sales Staff*
Nathan Blackburn, *Technical Staff*
▼ **EMP:** 12 **EST:** 2007
SALES (est): 1.2MM **Privately Held**
WEB: www.euclidchemical.com
SIC: 2899 Chemical preparations

(G-11551)
FLEDA PHARMACEUTICALS CORP
13231 Byrd Legg Dr (33556-5325)
PHONE...................813 920-9882
Yang Wang, *CEO*
EMP: 5 **EST:** 2018
SALES (est): 512K **Privately Held**
WEB: www.fledausa.com
SIC: 2023 Dietary supplements, dairy & non-dairy based

(G-11552)
FLORIDA CUSTOM MOLD INC (PA)
Also Called: Fcm
1806 Gunn Hwy (33556-3524)
PHONE...................813 343-5080
Michael A Cave, *President*
Joe Duren, *General Mgr*
Gary Krivan, *Plant Mgr*
Austin Cave, *Engineer*
Cynthia Park, *Controller*
◆ **EMP:** 89 **EST:** 1988
SQ FT: 54,000
SALES (est): 10.1MM **Privately Held**
WEB: www.fla-mold.com
SIC: 3089 Injection molding of plastics

(G-11553)
GATECRAFTERSCOM
13100 State Road 54 (33556-3419)
PHONE...................800 537-4283
Anthony Gaeto, *President*
EMP: 16 **EST:** 2000
SALES (est): 811.5K **Privately Held**
WEB: www.gatecrafters.com
SIC: 3699 Security devices

(G-11554)
GFSF INC
Also Called: Power Quality International
2404 Merchant Ave (33556-3460)
P.O. Box 190437, Boise ID (83719-0437)
PHONE...................727 478-7284
Gregory NC Ferguson, *Ch of Bd*
Shaun D Ferguson, *President*
EMP: 6 **EST:** 1994
SQ FT: 7,500
SALES (est): 875.1K **Privately Held**
WEB: www.powerqualityinternational.com
SIC: 3612 Transformers, except electric

(G-11555)
GREAT AMERICAN WOODWORKS INC
Also Called: Tables Designs
11445 Pyramid Dr (33556-3455)
PHONE...................727 375-1212
Jennifer Bilthouse, *President*
Bob Bilthouse, *Corp Secy*
Jakea Cates, *Sales Associate*
Kevin Bilthouse, *Agent*
EMP: 35 **EST:** 1979
SQ FT: 15,000
SALES (est): 4.3MM **Privately Held**
WEB: www.tabledesigns.com
SIC: 2599 Factory furniture & fixtures

(G-11556)
H&M PHILLIPS INC
Also Called: Liberty Printing
12772 Burns Dr (33556-4071)
PHONE...................727 797-4600
Mitch Phillips, *President*
EMP: 9 **EST:** 1986
SALES (est): 232.1K **Privately Held**
SIC: 2752 Commercial printing, offset

(G-11557)
INCRETE SYSTEMS
1725 Gunn Hwy (33556-5305)
PHONE...................813 886-8811
D Richey, *Sales Staff*
EMP: 13 **EST:** 2015
SALES (est): 1.9MM **Privately Held**
WEB: www.euclidchemical.com
SIC: 2899 Chemical preparations

(G-11558)
INTERCULTURAL COMMUNICATIONS
18411 Keystone Grove Blvd (33556-4813)
PHONE...................813 926-2617
Tammy Johnson, *Vice Pres*
EMP: 7 **EST:** 2017
SALES (est): 67K **Privately Held**
SIC: 2711 1731 3663 Newspapers; communications specialization; radio broadcasting & communications equipment; television broadcasting & communications equipment

(G-11559)
INTERNATIONAL GRAN & STONE LLC
Also Called: Granite Tampa Bay
1842 Gunn Hwy (33556-3524)
PHONE...................813 920-6500
Lisa Banks, *Project Mgr*
Melody Haasl, *Project Mgr*
Nate Faiella, *Production*
Ryan Hulsey, *Production*
Bill Stivali, *Controller*
▲ **EMP:** 45 **EST:** 2002
SQ FT: 20,000
SALES (est): 9.9MM **Privately Held**
WEB: www.igscountertops.com
SIC: 3281 1799 Cut stone & stone products; counter top installation

(G-11560)
INTERNATIONAL IMAGING MTLS INC
Also Called: Talon Industries
2300 Destiny Way (33556-3403)
PHONE...................727 834-8200
EMP: 12
SALES (corp-wide): 133.8MM **Privately Held**
SIC: 2899 Mfg Chemical Preparations
PA: International Imaging Materials, Inc.
310 Commerce Dr
Amherst NY 14228
716 691-6333

(G-11561)
JACORE TECHNOLOGIES
1346 Osceola Hollow Rd (33556-3823)
PHONE...................813 860-7465
Corman D Jennifer, *Vice Pres*
EMP: 9 **EST:** 2018
SALES (est): 301K **Privately Held**
SIC: 3599 Machine shop, jobbing & repair

(G-11562)
JENASIS STRUCTURES INC
6514 Grazing Ln (33556-1809)
P.O. Box 9223, Tampa (33674-9223)
PHONE...................813 238-7620
Tom Jones, *President*
EMP: 17 **EST:** 1995
SQ FT: 1,100
SALES (est): 1.3MM **Privately Held**
SIC: 3272 Wall & ceiling squares, concrete

(G-11563)
KMG MARKETING LLC
Also Called: Abco Graphics & Printing
11515 Pyramid Dr (33556-3457)
PHONE...................727 376-7200
Kelly McKnight Goelz, *CEO*
Kelly McKnightgoelz, *General Mgr*
Deb Smith, *Production*
Cathy Lange, *Manager*
EMP: 9 **EST:** 2016
SALES (est): 1.1MM **Privately Held**
WEB: www.abcotogo.com
SIC: 2752 Commercial printing, offset

(G-11564)
LIGHTNING SPECIALISTS INC
11498 Prosperous Dr (33556-3519)
PHONE...................727 938-3560
Charles O Wilson, *President*
EMP: 5 **EST:** 2001
SALES (est): 759.8K **Privately Held**
WEB: www.lsi-fl.com
SIC: 3643 Current-carrying wiring devices

(G-11565)
LINDSEY MACKE BINDERY PRINTING
11626 Prosperous Dr (33556-3458)
PHONE...................727 514-3570
Edgar Lee Lindsey Jr, *Principal*
EMP: 7 **EST:** 2008
SALES (est): 133.9K **Privately Held**
SIC: 2752 Commercial printing, offset

(G-11566)
MASKING SYSTEMS OF AMERICA
13221 Byrd Dr (33556-5307)
PHONE...................813 920-2271
EMP: 18
SALES (est): 2MM **Privately Held**
SIC: 2891 Mfg Adhesives/Sealants

GEOGRAPHIC

(G-11567)
NICRAF SOFTWARE & CREAT INC
17413 Equestrian Trl (33556-1847)
PHONE..........................813 842-9648
Nicholas M Gordon, *Principal*
EMP: 9 EST: 2007
SALES (est): 372.6K Privately Held
WEB: www.nicraf.com
SIC: 7372 Prepackaged software

(G-11568)
NU TREK INC
Also Called: Everett-Morrison Motorcars
16708 Hutchison Rd (33556-2321)
PHONE..........................813 920-4348
Buford R Everett, *President*
Brett Everett, *Vice Pres*
Bruce Everett, *Treasurer*
EMP: 13 EST: 1983
SQ FT: 15,000
SALES (est): 146.5K Privately Held
SIC: 3711 Cars, armored, assembly of

(G-11569)
PHARMAWORKS LLC
Also Called: Micron Pharmaworks, LLC
2346 Success Dr (33556-3430)
PHONE..........................727 232-8200
Peter Buczynsky, *CEO*
Ben Brower, *Vice Pres*
Ingo Federle, *Vice Pres*
Jesse Hitt, *Engineer*
Frank Lovetere, *CFO*
▲ EMP: 105 EST: 2002
SQ FT: 35,926
SALES (est): 28.3MM Privately Held
WEB: www.pharmaworks.com
SIC: 3565 Packaging machinery
HQ: Pro Mach, Inc.
　50 E Rvrcnter Blvd Ste 18
　Covington KY 41011
　513 831-8778

(G-11570)
PLASMA ENERGY GROUP LLC
17402 Isbell Ln (33556-1962)
PHONE..........................813 760-6385
Stacy Y Patrick, *Principal*
EMP: 11 EST: 2015
SALES (est): 456.2K Privately Held
WEB: www.plasmaenergy-group.com
SIC: 2836 Plasmas

(G-11571)
POLARIS SALES CO INC
Also Called: Polaris Electrical Connectors
11625 Prosperous Dr (33556-3459)
PHONE..........................727 372-1703
Janeen Patten, *President*
Lisaann Armes, *President*
Luke Hill, *Vice Pres*
Troje Zibilich, *Opers Mgr*
Rich Fish, *Engineer*
▲ EMP: 112 EST: 1973
SQ FT: 48,334
SALES (est): 21.3MM Privately Held
WEB: www.polarisconnectors.com
SIC: 3643 Connectors & terminals for electrical devices

(G-11572)
POWER QUALITY INTL LLC
2404 Merchant Ave (33556-3460)
P.O. Box 190437, Boise ID (83719-0437)
PHONE..........................727 478-7284
Jarrod Dobbs, *Vice Pres*
Jane Wilhite, *Controller*
Gregory Ferguson,
Shaun Ferguson,
Jeff Turner,
EMP: 8 EST: 2013
SALES (est): 1.4MM Privately Held
WEB: www.powerqualityinternational.com
SIC: 3612 Power & distribution transformers

(G-11573)
PRECAST SOLUTION SYSTEM INC
2045 Chesapeake Dr Ste 2 (33556-3669)
PHONE..........................813 949-7929
EMP: 10
SALES (est): 1.2MM Privately Held
SIC: 3272 Mfg Concrete Products

(G-11574)
PREMIER ARCHTCTURAL SHTMTL INC
8501 Northton Groves Blvd (33556-1402)
PHONE..........................727 373-8937
Angel L Torres Jr, *Vice Pres*
EMP: 12 EST: 2019
SALES (est): 321.8K Privately Held
SIC: 3444 Sheet metalwork

(G-11575)
ROORDA BUIDERS INC
15115 Race Track Rd (33556-2913)
PHONE..........................727 410-7776
Milt Roorda, *President*
EMP: 6 EST: 1994
SALES (est): 317.7K Privately Held
WEB: www.roordabuilders.com
SIC: 2426 Frames for upholstered furniture, wood

(G-11576)
SEQUOIA BRANDS INC
13100 State Road 54 (33556-3419)
PHONE..........................813 969-2000
Anthony Gaeto, *President*
EMP: 25 EST: 2010
SALES (est): 1.1MM Privately Held
WEB: www.sequoiabrands.com
SIC: 3953 Irons, marking or branding

(G-11577)
SHUTTERREFLECTIONS
19111 Larchmont Dr (33556-2269)
PHONE..........................813 351-9979
Jorge Alatorre, *Principal*
EMP: 7 EST: 2005
SALES (est): 83.1K Privately Held
SIC: 3442 Shutters, door or window: metal

(G-11578)
SILCO SOFTWARE TECHNOLOGY INC
16223 Ivy Lake Dr (33556-6047)
PHONE..........................813 475-4591
Rama Juturu, *President*
Chandra Juturu, *Vice Pres*
EMP: 10 EST: 1995
SALES (est): 805K Privately Held
WEB: www.ramaonhealthcare.com
SIC: 7372 Prepackaged software

(G-11579)
SOUTHERN CLOSET SYSTEMS INC
13211 Byrd Dr (33556-5307)
PHONE..........................813 926-9348
Wayne Smith, *President*
Joanne Smith, *Treasurer*
EMP: 6 EST: 1983
SQ FT: 4,000
SALES (est): 521.8K Privately Held
WEB: www.southerncloset.com
SIC: 2449 5211 Wood containers; closets, interiors & accessories

(G-11580)
SPECTRUM ENGINEERING & MFG INC
11609 Pyramid Dr (33556-3450)
PHONE..........................727 376-5510
Nicholas Juranko, *President*
Dan Juranko, *Treasurer*
Anthony Juranko, *Admin Sec*
EMP: 5 EST: 1991
SQ FT: 4,200
SALES (est): 814.7K Privately Held
SIC: 3444 8711 Sheet metalwork; engineering services

(G-11581)
STAINLESS FABRICATORS INC
11107 Challenger Ave (33556-3439)
PHONE..........................813 926-7113
Keith B Binney, *President*
Diana Binney, *Vice Pres*
Scott J Binney, *Vice Pres*
Brian Binney, *Project Mgr*
Djordje Miokovic, *Prdtn Mgr*
▼ EMP: 47 EST: 1986
SQ FT: 25,000

SALES (est): 10.1MM Privately Held
WEB: www.stainlessfabinc.com
SIC: 3446 3444 3429 3312 Railings, bannisters, guards, etc.: made from metal pipe; fences or posts, ornamental iron or steel; sheet metalwork; manufactured hardware (general); blast furnaces & steel mills

(G-11582)
STRATCO PHARMACEUTICALS LLC
2600 Lakepointe Pkwy (33556-4375)
PHONE..........................813 403-5060
Brian Nugent, *President*
Alex Sierra, *Manager*
Alexander Sierra, *Manager*
EMP: 12 EST: 2011
SALES (est): 5.3MM
SALES (corp-wide): 84.1MM Privately Held
WEB: www.stratfordrx.com
SIC: 2834 Pharmaceutical preparations
HQ: Stratford Care Usa, Inc.
　2600 Lakepointe Pkwy
　Odessa FL 33556
　877 498-2002

(G-11583)
STRATFORD CARE USA INC (HQ)
2600 Lakepointe Pkwy (33556-4375)
PHONE..........................877 498-2002
Brian Nugent, *CEO*
Nicole Ladue, *Vice Pres*
Jenny Graflind, *Director*
Hakan Lagerberg, *Director*
EMP: 10 EST: 2020
SALES (est): 5.3MM
SALES (corp-wide): 84.1MM Privately Held
WEB: www.stratfordrx.com
SIC: 2048 Mineral feed supplements
PA: Swedencare Ab (Publ)
　Per Albin Hanssons Vag 41
　MalmO　214 3
　408 593-3

(G-11584)
TOCKWOGH LLC
15406 Patterson Rd (33556-2721)
PHONE..........................813 920-3413
William H Horwitz, *Principal*
EMP: 7 EST: 2010
SALES (est): 171.4K Privately Held
WEB: www.ymcacamptockwogh.org
SIC: 2521 Chairs, office: padded, upholstered or plain: wood

(G-11585)
TOUCHPOINT MEDICAL INC (PA)
2200 Touchpoint Dr (33556-4435)
PHONE..........................813 854-1905
Brian McNeill, *CEO*
Pascal Testeil, *President*
Michael McCluhan, *Area Mgr*
Greg Wendel, *Prdtn Mgr*
Kevin Webb, *Mfg Staff*
EMP: 43 EST: 2016
SALES (est): 69.5MM Privately Held
WEB: www.touchpointmed.com
SIC: 3845 Laser systems & equipment, medical

(G-11586)
TRINITY CREAMERY INC
14167 Wadsworth Dr (33556-4303)
PHONE..........................813 926-2023
Robert J Byrne, *Principal*
EMP: 8 EST: 2009
SALES (est): 120.9K Privately Held
SIC: 2021 Creamery butter

(G-11587)
TRU SIMULATION + TRAINING INC
1551 Gunn Hwy (33556-5308)
PHONE..........................813 792-9300
Justin Bourdon, *Vice Pres*
Troy Fey, *Vice Pres*
John Hayward, *Vice Pres*
Gerald Messaris, *Vice Pres*
Kristen Samson, *Vice Pres*
EMP: 100

SALES (corp-wide): 12.3MM Publicly Held
WEB: www.trusimulation.com
SIC: 3443 3699 Space simulation chambers, metal plate; flight simulators (training aids), electronic
HQ: Tru Simulation + Training Inc.
　5 Alliance Dr
　Goose Creek SC 29445
　843 574-5469

(G-11588)
UNITED CHAIR INDUSTRIES LLC
16442 Ivy Lake Dr (33556-6049)
PHONE..........................386 333-0800
Jalal Chowdhury, *CEO*
Victor Yan, *Managing Dir*
EMP: 6 EST: 2015
SQ FT: 60,000
SALES (est): 328K Privately Held
WEB: www.unitedofficechair.com
SIC: 2522 5021 Office chairs, benches & stools, except wood; chairs

(G-11589)
USB PLASTICS
11805 State Road 54 (33556-3469)
PHONE..........................727 375-8840
James Bylone, *Principal*
EMP: 7 EST: 2013
SALES (est): 238.4K Privately Held
WEB: www.usbplastics.com
SIC: 3089 Injection molding of plastics

(G-11590)
USBEV PRODUCTS INC
11805 State Road 54 (33556-3469)
PHONE..........................727 375-8840
Charles Williams, *President*
▼ EMP: 10 EST: 2011
SALES (est): 337.1K Privately Held
WEB: www.usbplastics.com
SIC: 3089 Injection molding of plastics

(G-11591)
VUESSENCE INC
17633 Gunn Hwy Ste 107 (33556-1912)
PHONE..........................813 792-7123
Maha Sallam, *President*
EMP: 5 EST: 2010
SALES (est): 318.3K Privately Held
WEB: www.vuessence.com
SIC: 3841 Surgical & medical instruments

(G-11592)
WOODWORKS KIT & BATH DESIGNS
8717 Gunn Hwy (33556-3210)
PHONE..........................813 926-0570
Eva D Nesbitt, *Owner*
EMP: 13 EST: 2014
SALES (est): 2MM Privately Held
WEB: www.woodworksdesigns.com
SIC: 2434 Wood kitchen cabinets

(G-11593)
ZEL CUSTOM MANUFACTURING LLC
11419 Challenger Ave (33556-3446)
PHONE..........................303 880-8701
Michael Brendzel, *Principal*
EMP: 8 EST: 2010
SALES (est): 415.9K Privately Held
SIC: 3999 Manufacturing industries

Okahumpka
Lake County

(G-11594)
AMERICAN MFG & MCH INC
Also Called: Vac-Tron Equipment
27137 County Road 33 (34762-3207)
PHONE..........................352 728-2222
Don M Buckner Sr, *President*
Gene M Buckner, *Vice Pres*
EMP: 69 EST: 1999
SQ FT: 70,000
SALES (est): 6.2MM Privately Held
SIC: 3443 3544 3563 3531 Industrial vessels, tanks & containers; industrial molds; air & gas compressors; construction machinery

▲ = Import ▼ =Export
◆ =Import/Export

(G-11595)
CEMEX MATERIALS LLC
27111 County Road 33 (34762-3209)
PHONE................................352 435-0783
Rick Rhodes, *Branch Mgr*
EMP: 108
SQ FT: 17,463 **Privately Held**
SIC: 3271 3273 3272 1422 Blocks, concrete or cinder: standard; ready-mixed concrete; pipe, concrete or lined with concrete; crushed & broken limestone
HQ: Cemex Materials Llc
1720 Centrepark Dr E # 100
West Palm Beach FL 33401
561 833-5555

(G-11596)
CORESLAB STRCTURES ORLANDO INC
2720 County Road 470 (34762-3117)
PHONE................................407 855-3191
Luigi Franciosa, *President*
Matthew Metz, *President*
Mario Franciosa, *Exec VP*
Dominic Franciosa, *Vice Pres*
Michael Harrison, *Vice Pres*
◆ **EMP:** 42 **EST:** 1993
SQ FT: 17,000
SALES (est): 15.1MM **Privately Held**
WEB: www.coreslab.com
SIC: 3272 Concrete products
PA: Arge Umweltzentrum Lauingen
Kastellstr.
Lauingen (Donau) BY

(G-11597)
FLORIDA WILBERT INC
27439 Hayward Worm Frm Rd (34762)
PHONE................................352 728-3531
Sam Smart, *Manager*
EMP: 9
SQ FT: 9,600
SALES (corp-wide): 3MM **Privately Held**
WEB: www.floridawilbert.com
SIC: 3272 Burial vaults, concrete or precast terrazzo
PA: Florida Wilbert Inc
5050 New Kings Rd
Jacksonville FL 32209
904 765-2641

Okeechobee
Okeechobee County

(G-11598)
AWNIT CORPORATION
820 S Parrott Ave (34974-5140)
Austin Harvey, *Principal*
EMP: 7 **EST:** 2020
SALES (est): 110K **Privately Held**
SIC: 2591 Mfg Drapery Hardware/Blinds

(G-11599)
CHAMPION COATINGS INC
102 Ne 60th Ave (34974-7901)
PHONE................................561 512-5985
Roland A O Neal, *Principal*
EMP: 7 **EST:** 2010
SALES (est): 212.2K **Privately Held**
WEB: www.championcoatings.net
SIC: 3479 Coating of metals & formed products

(G-11600)
CHARLES COMPOSITES LLC
Also Called: Charles Industries
1252 Ne 12th St (34972-3073)
PHONE................................863 357-2500
Joseph T Charles, *Mng Member*
EMP: 10 **EST:** 2012
SQ FT: 40,000
SALES (est): 1.2MM **Privately Held**
SIC: 3229 Tubing, glass

(G-11601)
COMMUNICATION EQP & ENGRG CO
Also Called: Ceeco
519 Sw Park St (34972-4166)
PHONE................................863 357-0798
Nancy M Haist, *Chairman*
Mike Freeman, *Administration*
EMP: 15 **EST:** 1930

SALES (est): 2.4MM **Privately Held**
WEB: www.ceeco.net
SIC: 3661 Telephone & telegraph apparatus

(G-11602)
DAIRY FEEDS INC (PA)
1901 Nw 9th St (34972-2074)
P.O. Box 1365 (34973-1365)
PHONE................................863 763-0258
Louis E Larson Jr, *President*
John Brooks, *Vice Pres*
EMP: 5 **EST:** 1978
SQ FT: 6,000
SALES (est): 2.6MM **Privately Held**
SIC: 2048 Feed premixes

(G-11603)
DIAMOND R FERTILIZER CO INC
Ranch Fertilizer Div
710 Ne 5th Ave (34972-2601)
PHONE................................863 763-2158
Preston Green, *Plant Mgr*
Wayne Prevatt, *Prdtn Mgr*
Tim McKenna, *Sales Staff*
Pat Hood, *Manager*
Matthew Wilkins, *Manager*
EMP: 30
SALES (corp-wide): 109.3MM **Privately Held**
WEB: www.diamond-r.com
SIC: 2875 2879 Fertilizers, mixing only; agricultural chemicals
HQ: Diamond R Fertilizer Co., Inc.
4100 Glades Cut Off Rd
Fort Pierce FL 34981
772 464-9300

(G-11604)
ECOTEC MANUFACTURING INC
312 Sw 7th Ave (34974-4279)
P.O. Box 5501, Fort Lauderdale (33310-5501)
PHONE................................863 357-4500
Neal Markus, *President*
Neil Markus, *President*
Michael D Fishman, *Vice Pres*
◆ **EMP:** 22 **EST:** 2001
SALES (est): 3.2MM **Privately Held**
WEB: www.ecotecsolar.com
SIC: 3999 Barber & beauty shop equipment

(G-11605)
GALLEY MAID MARINE PDTS INC
60 Ne 110th St (34972-7507)
PHONE................................863 467-6070
Laura Tumoszwicz, *President*
Ernie Tumoszwicz, *Vice Pres*
Ronald Tumoszwicz, *Vice Pres*
◆ **EMP:** 10 **EST:** 1967
SQ FT: 75,000
SALES (est): 1.2MM **Privately Held**
WEB: www.galleymaid.com
SIC: 3429 Marine hardware

(G-11606)
GATOR FEED CO INC
1205 Us Highway 98 N (34972-8766)
P.O. Box 756 (34973-0756)
PHONE................................863 763-3337
Patricia Ziglar, *President*
Tom Ziglar, *Vice Pres*
Larry Davis, *Treasurer*
Jeannie Tindall, *Office Mgr*
Linda Davis, *Admin Sec*
EMP: 15 **EST:** 1958
SQ FT: 8,000
SALES (est): 2.4MM **Privately Held**
WEB: www.gatorfeedco.com
SIC: 2048 Livestock feeds

(G-11607)
GRANNYS CHEESECAKE & MORE INC
17003 Nw 32nd Ave (34972-8430)
PHONE................................561 847-6599
EMP: 7
SALES (est): 279.6K **Privately Held**
SIC: 2591 Window blinds

(G-11608)
HERNANDEZ MOBILE WELDING INC
20320 Nw 258th St (34972-6993)
PHONE................................954 347-4071
Estuardo Hernandez, *Principal*
EMP: 7 **EST:** 2002
SALES (est): 58.6K **Privately Held**
WEB: www.hmweld.com
SIC: 7692 Welding repair

(G-11609)
INDEPENDENT NEWSMEDIA INC USA
Also Called: Clewiston News
107 Sw 17th St Ste D (34974-6110)
PHONE................................863 983-9148
EMP: 8 **Privately Held**
SIC: 2711 Newspapers-Publishing/Printing
HQ: Independent Newsmedia Usa, Inc.
110 Galaxy Dr
Dover DE 19901
302 674-3600

(G-11610)
JFE COMPOST
11000 Red Barn Rd Ne (34974)
PHONE................................863 532-9629
Gene Lewis, *Principal*
EMP: 9 **EST:** 2015
SALES (est): 879K **Privately Held**
SIC: 2875 Compost

(G-11611)
LAKESIDE RECREATIONAL INC
4074 Us Highway 441 Se (34974-7213)
PHONE................................863 467-1530
Gary Ruppert, *Principal*
EMP: 7 **EST:** 2008
SALES (est): 115.5K **Privately Held**
SIC: 3799 Recreational vehicles

(G-11612)
OKEECHBEE ASP RADY MXED CON IN
503 Nw 9th St (34972-2123)
P.O. Box 1994 (34973-1994)
PHONE................................863 763-7373
Christopher M Lynch, *President*
Robert P Gent, *Vice Pres*
Jim Haywood, *Manager*
Raquel M Rodriguez, *Director*
EMP: 9 **EST:** 2007
SALES (est): 1.4MM **Privately Held**
SIC: 3273 Ready-mixed concrete

(G-11613)
OUR VILLAGE OKEECHOBEE INC
205 Ne 2nd St (34972-2974)
PHONE................................863 467-0158
Leah Suarez, *CEO*
Lonnie Kirsch, *Vice Pres*
Kris Schwartz, *Production*
EMP: 10 **EST:** 2015
SALES (est): 43.9K **Privately Held**
SIC: 2711 Newspapers, publishing & printing

(G-11614)
ROOF TILE ADMINISTRATION INC
1289 Ne 9th Ave (34972-3501)
PHONE................................863 467-0042
Reinaldo Padron, *Principal*
EMP: 15 **EST:** 2007
SQ FT: 54,976
SALES (est): 1.6MM **Privately Held**
SIC: 3272 Roofing tile & slabs, concrete

(G-11615)
ROOF TILE INC
Also Called: Entegra Roof Tile
1289 Ne 9th Ave (34972-3501)
PHONE................................863 467-0042
Michael Johnson, *President*
Lionel Lujan, *Production*
Kimberly Azevedo, *Manager*
EMP: 51 **EST:** 1997
SALES (est): 13.2MM **Privately Held**
SIC: 3272 3271 Concrete products; concrete block & brick

HQ: Headwaters Incorporated
10701 S River Front Pkwy # 300
South Jordan UT 84095

(G-11616)
SAND HILL ROCK LLC
7660 Ne 304th St (34972-0329)
P.O. Box 13896, Fort Pierce (34979-3896)
PHONE................................772 216-4852
J Andrew Murphy, *Mng Member*
EMP: 7 **EST:** 2013
SALES (est): 841.5K **Privately Held**
SIC: 1446 Silica sand mining

(G-11617)
SEMINOLE SIGN COMPANY LLC
16900 Reservation Rd Ne (34974-2803)
PHONE................................863 623-6600
Laverne D Thomas, *Manager*
EMP: 8 **EST:** 2011
SALES (est): 659.2K **Privately Held**
SIC: 3993 Signs & advertising specialties

(G-11618)
SUPERIOR CAST STONE LLC
6344 Se 30th Pkwy (34974-1171)
PHONE................................863 634-4771
Jose Nunez, *Principal*
▲ **EMP:** 12 **EST:** 2010
SALES (est): 3.5MM **Privately Held**
SIC: 3272 Concrete products

(G-11619)
WHERRELL MACHINE LLC
107 Sw 2nd St (34974-4301)
PHONE................................863 357-0900
M Chad Wherrell, *Manager*
EMP: 7 **EST:** 2011
SALES (est): 101.4K **Privately Held**
WEB: www.wherrellmachine.com
SIC: 3599 Machine shop, jobbing & repair

(G-11620)
WORLD BOAT MANUFACTURING INC
8040 Nw 144th Trl (34972-9678)
PHONE................................863 824-0015
Stanley White, *President*
EMP: 9 **EST:** 1995
SQ FT: 11,152
SALES (est): 420.2K **Privately Held**
SIC: 3732 Boats, fiberglass: building & repairing

Old Town
Dixie County

(G-11621)
ANDERSON MINING CORPORATION (HQ)
624 Ne Highway 349 (32680-5031)
P.O. Box 38 (32680-0038)
PHONE................................352 542-7942
Rolfe Wall, *President*
Joe Anderson Jr, *Corp Secy*
Joe Anderson III, *Vice Pres*
EMP: 3 **EST:** 1980
SQ FT: 4,000
SALES (est): 9.4MM
SALES (corp-wide): 168.7MM **Privately Held**
SIC: 1422 Lime rock, ground
PA: Anderson Columbia Co., Inc.
871 Nw Guerdon St
Lake City FL 32055
386 752-7585

(G-11622)
HENRY W LONG
Also Called: Long, H W Logging
264 Se 752nd Ave (32680-4520)
PHONE................................352 542-7068
Henry W Long, *Owner*
EMP: 5 **EST:** 1969
SALES (est): 328.3K **Privately Held**
SIC: 2411 Logging camps & contractors

(G-11623)
RPM CO
27908 Se Hwy 19 (32680-4842)
PHONE................................352 542-3110
Dave Jarnigan, *Principal*
EMP: 5 **EST:** 2010

SALES (est): 351.9K **Privately Held**
WEB: www.rpm-co.com
SIC: 3715 Trailers or vans for transporting horses

Oldsmar
Pinellas County

(G-11624)
ALLCASES REEKSTIN & ASSOC INC
300 Mears Blvd (34677-3047)
PHONE...................................813 891-1313
Deborah A Reekstin, *President*
Amanda Terry, *General Mgr*
Karl R Reekstin, *Vice Pres*
Karl Reekstin, *Vice Pres*
Pearlman Ginny, *Engineer*
▼ EMP: 12 EST: 1985
SQ FT: 7,500
SALES (est): 2.8MM **Privately Held**
WEB: www.allcases.com
SIC: 2449 2441 3199 Shipping cases, wood; wirebound; shipping cases, wood: nailed or lock corner; boxes, leather

(G-11625)
AMERX HEALTH CARE CORP
164 Douglas Rd E (34677-2939)
PHONE...................................727 443-0530
James B Anderson, *CFO*
Sheri Kempinski, *Sales Mgr*
Stephanie Miron, *Accounts Mgr*
Jennifer Creel, *Manager*
Jennifer Lachtara, *Supervisor*
EMP: 15 EST: 1993
SALES (est): 3.2MM **Publicly Held**
WEB: www.amerxhc.com
SIC: 2834 Ointments
PA: Procyon Corporation
1300 S Highland Ave
Clearwater FL 33756

(G-11626)
ANDRITZ IGGESUND TOOLS INC (HQ)
220 Scarlet Blvd (34677-3016)
PHONE...................................813 855-6902
John Tillte, *President*
Dawn Fernandez, *Vice Pres*
Dan Asher, *Engineer*
Jeffrey Herron, *Engineer*
Matias Macias, *Engineer*
▲ EMP: 20 EST: 1983
SQ FT: 16,500
SALES (est): 18.9MM **Privately Held**
SIC: 3423 3545 3541 3421 Knives, agricultural or industrial; machine tool accessories; machine tools, metal cutting type; cutlery
PA: Ramab Iggesund Ab
Villagatan 19, Tr 1tr
Stockholm
650 291-01

(G-11627)
ARJ MEDICAL INC
209 State St E (34677-3654)
PHONE...................................813 855-1557
Morris Behar, *Principal*
EMP: 10 EST: 1996
SALES (est): 265.2K **Privately Held**
SIC: 2819 3821 Chemicals, reagent grade: refined from technical grade; laboratory apparatus, except heating & measuring

(G-11628)
ARJAY PRINTING COMPANY INC
131 Burbank Rd (34677-4900)
PHONE...................................904 764-6070
Andrew Fraser, *President*
Andy Fraser, *Vice Pres*
EMP: 6 EST: 1986
SQ FT: 5,000
SALES (est): 508.7K **Privately Held**
SIC: 2752 Commercial printing, offset

(G-11629)
AROMAVALUE INC
Also Called: Scent Fill
720 Brooker Creek Blvd # 210 (34677-2937)
PHONE...................................866 223-7561
Mark Callison, *President*
EMP: 5 EST: 2016
SQ FT: 6,450
SALES (est): 600K **Privately Held**
WEB: www.scentfill.com
SIC: 2844 Toilet preparations

(G-11630)
ASTRA PRODUCTS CO INC TAMPA
3675 Tampa Rd (34677-6311)
P.O. Box 711 (34677-0711)
PHONE...................................813 855-3021
Steve Ladoniczki, *President*
Steven Ladoniczki, *General Mgr*
Bill Ladoniczki, *Treasurer*
Clara Ladoniczki, *Admin Sec*
EMP: 32 EST: 1967
SQ FT: 40,000
SALES (est): 5.7MM **Privately Held**
WEB: www.astraprodco.com
SIC: 3651 Amplifiers: radio, public address or musical instrument

(G-11631)
BAY CNC MACHINE LLC
305 Scarlet Blvd (34677-3019)
PHONE...................................813 362-9626
EMP: 6 EST: 2019
SALES (est): 350.9K **Privately Held**
WEB: www.baycncmachine.com
SIC: 3599 Machine shop, jobbing & repair

(G-11632)
BBULL USA INC
260 Scarlet Blvd (34677-3016)
PHONE...................................813 855-1400
Guido Luis Riveros, *President*
Michael John L Lawn, *Vice Pres*
Georg Krauss, *Senior Mgr*
Berhard Bull, *Director*
Richard J Riveros, *Admin Sec*
EMP: 8 EST: 2010
SALES (est): 351.9K **Privately Held**
WEB: www.bbull.com
SIC: 3565 Packaging machinery

(G-11633)
BEAM ASSOCIATES LLC (PA)
301 Commerce Blvd Ste 2 (34677-2806)
PHONE...................................813 855-5695
Brook Massey, *Mng Member*
EMP: 9 EST: 2012
SALES (est): 85.2MM **Privately Held**
SIC: 3585 Refrigeration & heating equipment

(G-11634)
BELAC LLC
420 Commerce Blvd (34677-2808)
PHONE...................................813 749-3200
Chong Yi, *President*
Dennis Piotrowski, *Vice Pres*
Pete Cirak, *QC Mgr*
Kevin Tuttle, *QC Mgr*
Thomas Eckert, *Engineer*
EMP: 60 EST: 1998
SQ FT: 30,000
SALES (est): 17.1MM **Privately Held**
WEB: www.belac.com
SIC: 3511 Turbines & turbine generator sets

(G-11635)
BELL HEARING INSTRUMENTS INC (PA)
Also Called: Sonus-USA
700 Stevens Ave Ste B (34677-2987)
P.O. Box 1888 (34677-1888)
PHONE...................................813 814-2355
William Bell, *President*
EMP: 14 EST: 1988
SQ FT: 15,000
SALES (est): 2.3MM **Privately Held**
WEB: www.bellhearingaids.com
SIC: 3842 5999 Hearing aids; hearing aids

(G-11636)
BRYCOAT INC
207 Vollmer Ave (34677-2938)
P.O. Box 1976 (34677-6976)
PHONE...................................727 490-1000
Robert A Smith, *CEO*
Michael Smith, *President*
Mark McDonough, *Vice Pres*
Clinton Thoma, *Production*
Damon Phelps, *Purch Agent*
EMP: 45 EST: 1990
SQ FT: 22,000
SALES (est): 9.9MM **Privately Held**
WEB: www.brycoat.com
SIC: 3479 Coating of metals & formed products

(G-11637)
CEMEX CNSTR MTLS FLA LLC
Also Called: Oldsmar Ready Mix Con Plant
501 Douglas Rd E (34677-4923)
PHONE...................................800 992-3639
Robert Snook, *Branch Mgr*
EMP: 8
SQ FT: 1,131 **Privately Held**
SIC: 3272 3273 Pipe, concrete or lined with concrete; ready-mixed concrete
HQ: Cemex Construction Materials Florida, Llc
1501 Belvedere Rd
West Palm Beach FL 33406

(G-11638)
CLEARWATER MANUFACTURING CO
203 Tower Dr (34677-2964)
PHONE...................................813 818-0959
Frank Wenglasz Jr, *President*
Anna Wenglasz, *Corp Secy*
Charles Wenglasz, *Vice Pres*
EMP: 5 EST: 1976
SQ FT: 6,000
SALES (est): 391K **Privately Held**
WEB: www.clrwtr.net
SIC: 3599 Machine shop, jobbing & repair

(G-11639)
COATING TECHNOLOGY INC
360 Scarlet Blvd (34677-3018)
PHONE...................................813 854-3674
Steve Pantle, *President*
EMP: 33 EST: 1995
SQ FT: 7,800
SALES (est): 3.3MM **Privately Held**
WEB: www.coatingtechinc.com
SIC: 3471 Electroplating of metals or formed products

(G-11640)
COFFMAN SYSTEMS INC
300 Stevens Ave (34677-2919)
PHONE...................................813 891-1300
Dale D Windsor, *President*
Richard Peck, *Vice Pres*
EMP: 13 EST: 1995
SQ FT: 22,000
SALES (est): 1.2MM **Privately Held**
WEB: www.coffmansystems.com
SIC: 3823 Water quality monitoring & control systems

(G-11641)
COUNTRYSIDE PUBLISHING CO INC
Also Called: Federal Suppliers Guide
477 Commerce Blvd (34677-2809)
P.O. Box 1735 (34677-1735)
PHONE...................................813 925-0195
Yvonne Shawn, *President*
EMP: 26 EST: 2001
SQ FT: 20,000
SALES (est): 1.1MM **Privately Held**
WEB: www.gsaapplicationservices.info
SIC: 2741 Miscellaneous publishing

(G-11642)
DIGITAL DIRECT CORPORATION
Also Called: Bay Diecutting
131 Burbank Rd (34677-4900)
PHONE...................................813 448-9071
Kenneth Fraser, *President*
EMP: 6 EST: 2002
SQ FT: 10,443

SALES (est): 823.7K **Privately Held**
WEB: www.digitalpubfl.com
SIC: 2732 2741 Book printing; technical manual & paper publishing

(G-11643)
DIGITAL PUBLISHING LLC
131 Burbank Rd (34677-4900)
PHONE...................................813 749-8640
EMP: 7 EST: 2019
SALES (est): 500.6K **Privately Held**
WEB: www.digitaldata-corp.com
SIC: 2741 Miscellaneous publishing

(G-11644)
DSC SALES OF SC INC (PA)
Also Called: Diversified Sales Company
455 Commerce Blvd (34677-2809)
P.O. Box 2123 (34677-7123)
PHONE...................................813 854-3131
Leslie L Lipsey, *President*
L Richard Lipsey, *President*
Lauren Wanzie, *Corp Secy*
Gregory L Shattuck, *Vice Pres*
Dana Z Lipsey, *Director*
▲ EMP: 10 EST: 1985
SALES (est): 12MM **Privately Held**
SIC: 2369 Beachwear: girls', children's & infants'

(G-11645)
DYNAMIC CABINETS INC
304 Marlborough St (34677-3108)
PHONE...................................813 891-0667
Michael Dalhburg, *President*
EMP: 5 EST: 1990
SALES (est): 377.4K **Privately Held**
SIC: 2434 Wood kitchen cabinets

(G-11646)
E-Z FASTENING SOLUTIONS INC
640 Brooker Creek Blvd # 425 (34677-2931)
PHONE...................................813 854-3937
Edgard Zayas, *President*
▲ EMP: 5 EST: 2010
SALES (est): 1MM **Privately Held**
WEB: www.ez-fastening.com
SIC: 3429 3545 3965 5072 Manufactured hardware (general); precision tools, machinists'; fasteners; hardware

(G-11647)
EDMUND OPTICS INC
Also Called: Edmund Optics Florida
141 Burbank Rd (34677-4900)
PHONE...................................813 855-1900
Sean Cleary, *CFO*
EMP: 40
SALES (corp-wide): 439.7MM **Privately Held**
WEB: www.edmundoptics.com
SIC: 3699 Laser systems & equipment
PA: Edmund Optics, Inc.
101 E Gloucester Pike
Barrington NJ 08007
856 547-3488

(G-11648)
ELECTRO LAB INC
369 Douglas Rd E (34677-2922)
P.O. Box 1135 (34677-1135)
PHONE...................................813 818-7605
William Grady Harder Jr, *President*
Gradey Harder, *COO*
Lonnie Harder, *Mfg Staff*
V J Houston, *Manager*
Patricia Anne Harder, *Shareholder*
EMP: 15 EST: 1956
SQ FT: 12,000
SALES (est): 2.3MM **Privately Held**
WEB: www.electrolab2.com
SIC: 3471 Electroplating of metals or formed products

(G-11649)
ENFORCEMENT ONE INC
Also Called: Fleet Spc An Enforcement One
381 Roberts Rd (34677-4914)
PHONE...................................727 816-9833
Aaron S Watkins, *Principal*
EMP: 13 EST: 2011

▲ = Import ▼=Export
◆ =Import/Export

SALES (est): 637.7K **Privately Held**
WEB: www.johnsonsecurityservices.com
SIC: **3714** Motor vehicle parts & accessories

(G-11650)
GARDNER-WATSON DECKING INC
305 Scarlet Blvd Ste A (34677-3019)
PHONE.................................813 891-9849
Bruce Nichols, *President*
Geoff Kress, *Vice Pres*
Geoffrey G Kress, *Vice Pres*
Andrew Boothe, *Project Mgr*
Carla Williams, *Office Admin*
EMP: 43 EST: 2005
SALES (est): 9MM **Privately Held**
WEB: www.gwdeck.com
SIC: **3441** Fabricated structural metal

(G-11651)
GEOTECHNICAL & MATERIALS INC
530 Lafayette Blvd (34677-3723)
PHONE.................................813 814-0671
Cynthia R Jean, *Principal*
EMP: 7 EST: 2010
SALES (est): 66K **Privately Held**
SIC: **1442** Gravel mining

(G-11652)
GILCO SPRING OF FLORIDA INC
3991 Tampa Rd (34677-3233)
PHONE.................................813 855-4631
Patrick Gillum, *CEO*
Todd Gaito, *General Mgr*
▲ EMP: 20 EST: 1987
SQ FT: 3,000
SALES (est): 4.7MM **Privately Held**
WEB: www.gilco.com
SIC: **3495** Wire springs

(G-11653)
GOODRICH LIGHTING SYSTEMS INC
129 Fairfield St (34677-3618)
PHONE.................................813 891-7100
Henry F Brooks, *Principal*
EMP: 49 EST: 1983
SALES (est): 26.3MM
SALES (corp-wide): 64.3B **Publicly Held**
SIC: **3728** Aircraft parts & equipment
HQ: Goodrich Corporation
2730 W Tyvola Rd
Charlotte NC 28217
704 423-7000

(G-11654)
GULF FIBEROPTICS INC
448 Commerce Blvd (34677-2808)
PHONE.................................813 891-1993
Christopher Kerns, *President*
Craig Vogeley, *Vice Pres*
Nick Malure, *QC Mgr*
Chris Bailey, *Design Engr*
Paige Redditt, *Human Resources*
EMP: 45 EST: 1997
SALES (est): 4.5MM **Privately Held**
WEB: www.gulffiberoptics.com
SIC: **3229** Fiber optics strands

(G-11655)
GULF MEDICAL FIBEROPTICS INC
448 Commerce Blvd (34677-2808)
PHONE.................................813 855-6618
Patrick Bennetts, *CEO*
Christophe Kerns, *President*
Vogeley Craig, *VP Opers*
Nick Malure, *QC Mgr*
Kim Pilkenton, *Accounts Mgr*
EMP: 8 EST: 2002
SQ FT: 15,000
SALES (est): 1.4MM **Privately Held**
SIC: **3841** Surgical instruments & apparatus

(G-11656)
GULF PHOTONICS INC
448 Commerce Blvd (34677-2808)
PHONE.................................813 855-6618
Patrick Bennetts, *President*
Craig Vogeley, *Vice Pres*
Christopher Kerns, *Treasurer*

EMP: 9 EST: 2010
SQ FT: 13,600
SALES (est): 771.6K **Privately Held**
WEB: www.gulfphotonics.com
SIC: **3357** Fiber optic cable (insulated)

(G-11657)
HUNT RDS INC
Also Called: Fastsigns
3898 Tampa Rd (34677-3137)
PHONE.................................813 249-7551
Robert G Hunt, *Principal*
EMP: 13 EST: 2016
SALES (est): 281.3K **Privately Held**
WEB: www.fastsigns.com
SIC: **3993** Signs & advertising specialties

(G-11658)
HYDRO-DYNE ENGINEERING INC
4750 118th Ave N (34677)
PHONE.................................727 532-0777
Jay R Conroy, *President*
Timothy L Pe Hunt, *Vice Pres*
Christy Walsh, *Vice Pres*
James Ranno, *Project Mgr*
Randall Dow, *Sales Dir*
EMP: 38 EST: 1978
SALES (est): 4.1MM **Privately Held**
WEB: www.hydro-dyne.com
SIC: **3589** Water purification equipment, household type

(G-11659)
IN STOCK PRINTERS INC
725 Stevens Ave (34677-2917)
PHONE.................................727 447-2515
Frank Gonzalez, *President*
Morgan Schmid, *Vice Pres*
EMP: 8 EST: 2010
SALES (est): 92.1K **Privately Held**
SIC: **2752** Commercial printing, lithographic

(G-11660)
INDUSTRY WEAPON INC
4033 Tampa Rd Ste 103 (34677-3224)
PHONE.................................877 344-8450
David Wible, *CEO*
Brian Pullman, *Business Mgr*
Brian Harris, *Vice Pres*
Dani Shirer, *Project Mgr*
Matthew Polaski, *Production*
EMP: 41 EST: 2007
SALES (est): 4.5MM **Privately Held**
WEB: www.spectrio.com
SIC: **7372** Application computer software

(G-11661)
INTEGRATED DEALER SYSTEMS INC
640 Brooker Creek Blvd (34677-2929)
PHONE.................................800 962-7872
Dawn Tillotson, *Branch Mgr*
Lindsey Manders, *Analyst*
EMP: 10
SALES (corp-wide): 5.1B **Privately Held**
WEB: www.ids-astra.com
SIC: **3571 3577** Personal computers (microcomputers); computer peripheral equipment
HQ: Integrated Dealer Systems Inc.
12339 Wake Union Church R
Wake Forest NC 27587
919 790-5442

(G-11662)
J & D MANUFACTURING INC
375 Mears Blvd (34677-3048)
P.O. Box 1945 (34677-6945)
PHONE.................................813 854-1700
James L Villa, *President*
David M Kaercher, *Vice Pres*
EMP: 11 EST: 1959
SQ FT: 84,000
SALES (est): 1MM **Privately Held**
SIC: **3081** Packing materials, plastic sheet

(G-11663)
JUSTI GROUP INC
Also Called: Specialty Glass
305 Marlborough St (34677-3107)
PHONE.................................813 855-5779
Colleen Morrisette, *President*
Pam Zurbrick, *Office Mgr*
EMP: 20 EST: 1977

SQ FT: 20,000
SALES (est): 2.5MM **Privately Held**
WEB: www.thespecialtyglass.com
SIC: **3231** Products of purchased glass
PA: Justi Group, Inc.
804 Old Lancaster Rd
Berwyn PA 19312

(G-11664)
KEN R AVERY PAINTING INC
3704 State Road 580 W (34677-5618)
PHONE.................................813 855-5037
Ken R Avery, *President*
EMP: 26
SALES (corp-wide): 2.4MM **Privately Held**
SIC: **2851 1721** Paints & allied products; painting & paper hanging
PA: Ken R Avery Painting Inc
3650 Old Keystone Rd
Tarpon Springs FL 34688
813 855-5037

(G-11665)
KESIN PHARMA CORPORATION
3874 Tampa Rd Ste 100 (34677-3126)
PHONE.................................833 537-4679
Peter Sullivan, *Principal*
Cheryl Esposito, *Principal*
Steven Esposito, *Principal*
EMP: 5 EST: 2019
SALES (est): 532.3K **Privately Held**
SIC: **2834** Pills, pharmaceutical

(G-11666)
KLOPP INTERNATIONAL INC
Also Called: Klopp Coin Counters
237 Dunbar Ct (34677-2956)
P.O. Box 985 (34677-0985)
PHONE.................................813 855-6789
Rick Nelson, *President*
Brian Bump, *Technical Staff*
▲ EMP: 17 EST: 1930
SQ FT: 12,000
SALES (est): 1MM **Privately Held**
WEB: www.kloppcoin.com
SIC: **3578 3579** Coin counters; coin wrapping machines

(G-11667)
KLOPP OF FLORIDA INC
251 Dunbar Ave (34677-2900)
P.O. Box 1109 (34677-1109)
PHONE.................................813 855-6789
Daniel Nelson, *President*
▲ EMP: 8 EST: 2006
SALES (est): 137K **Privately Held**
WEB: www.kloppcoin.com
SIC: **3578** Coin counters

(G-11668)
KW PRODUCTS INC
305 Mears Blvd (34677-3048)
PHONE.................................813 855-7817
Carlos Sevillano, *President*
EMP: 13 EST: 1986
SALES (est): 1.9MM **Privately Held**
WEB: www.kwproducts.org
SIC: **3599** Machine shop, jobbing & repair

(G-11669)
LABELCLICK INC
630 Brooker Creek Blvd # 340 (34677-2927)
PHONE.................................727 548-8345
EMP: 8 EST: 2004
SALES (est): 116.7K **Privately Held**
WEB: www.vitalityvet.com
SIC: **2834** Pharmaceutical preparations

(G-11670)
LIQUID TECHNOLGY CORP
340 Scarlet Blvd (34677-3018)
PHONE.................................832 804-8650
Dave Cagrise, *President*
Tim Hoeksema,
EMP: 9 EST: 2015
SALES (est): 420.9K **Privately Held**
SIC: **2813 5085** Industrial gases; gas equipment, parts & supplies

(G-11671)
LOCKHEED MARTIN CORPORATION
3655 Tampa Rd (34677-6308)
PHONE.................................813 855-5711

Drew Putzel, *Mfg Staff*
Lamont Gooding, *Engineer*
Barbara Julian, *Finance Mgr*
Courtney Dupree, *Manager*
Lisa Williams, *Manager*
EMP: 450
SQ FT: 198,678 **Publicly Held**
WEB: www.lockheedmartin.com
SIC: **3812 7371 3571** Defense systems & equipment; custom computer programming services; electronic computers
PA: Lockheed Martin Corporation
6801 Rockledge Dr
Bethesda MD 20817

(G-11672)
MARINE SPC CSTM FABRICATOR
360 Mears Blvd (34677-3047)
PHONE.................................813 855-0554
Thomas S Foley, *President*
EMP: 7 EST: 1986
SQ FT: 10,000
SALES (est): 350K **Privately Held**
WEB: www.marinespecialties.com
SIC: **3531 5551** Marine related equipment; boat dealers

(G-11673)
MEDFAB CORPORATION
210 Douglas Rd E (34677-2912)
P.O. Box 2366 (34677-2193)
PHONE.................................813 854-2646
Brad Hugus, *President*
Mike Sullivan, *General Mgr*
Mike Curtis, *Vice Pres*
Brad P Hugus, *Vice Pres*
EMP: 7 EST: 1994
SALES (est): 1.4MM **Privately Held**
WEB: www.medfabusa.com
SIC: **3086 3069** Plastics foam products; molded rubber products

(G-11674)
METAL INDUSTRIES INC
Also Called: X Metal Industrie
301 Commerce Blvd Bldg 4 (34677-2806)
P.O. Box 1128 (34677-1128)
PHONE.................................813 855-5695
Sam Gregory, *Manager*
EMP: 46
SALES (corp-wide): 1.2B **Privately Held**
WEB: www.mihvac.com
SIC: **3585** Parts for heating, cooling & refrigerating equipment
HQ: Metal Industries, Inc.
1985 Carroll St
Clearwater FL 33765
727 441-2651

(G-11675)
METAL INDUSTRIES INC
Also Called: Micon Packaging Products
301 Commerce Blvd (34677-2806)
P.O. Box 789 (34677-0789)
PHONE.................................813 855-4651
Peter Tracey, *Principal*
David Hawkins, *Officer*
EMP: 44
SALES (corp-wide): 1.2B **Privately Held**
WEB: www.mihvac.com
SIC: **2653** Boxes, corrugated: made from purchased materials
HQ: Metal Industries, Inc.
1985 Carroll St
Clearwater FL 33765
727 441-2651

(G-11676)
MI METALS INC (HQ)
301 Commerce Blvd (34677-2806)
PHONE.................................813 855-5695
Brook Massey, *President*
Dakota Fuller, *President*
Sarah Guthrie, *Vice Pres*
Kevin Sponsler, *Vice Pres*
Scott Evans, *Plant Mgr*
EMP: 1 EST: 1997
SQ FT: 200,000
SALES (est): 85.2MM **Privately Held**
WEB: www.mimetals.com
SIC: **3585** Refrigeration & heating equipment

PA: Beam Associates, Llc
301 Commerce Blvd Ste 2
Oldsmar FL 34677
813 855-5695

(G-11677)
MICON PACKAGING INC
301 Commerce Blvd Bldg 1 (34677-2806)
P.O. Box 789 (34677-0789)
PHONE..............................813 855-4651
Peter Tracey, *President*
▲ **EMP:** 115 **EST:** 1998
SQ FT: 283,000
SALES (est): 22.9MM **Privately Held**
WEB: www.miconpackaging.com
SIC: 2653 Boxes, corrugated: made from
purchased materials
HQ: Stronghaven, Incorporated
2727 Paces Ferry Rd Se 1-1850
Atlanta GA 30339
678 235-2713

(G-11678)
MICROLUMEN INC
1 Microlumen Way (34677-2983)
PHONE..............................813 886-1200
Roger O Roberds, *CEO*
M Scott Roberds, *President*
Rod Peifer, *Vice Pres*
Brandon Day, *Project Mgr*
Donald Burke, *Warehouse Mgr*
EMP: 80 **EST:** 1987
SQ FT: 59,000
SALES (est): 30.1MM **Privately Held**
WEB: www.microlumen.com
SIC: 3082 3644 Tubes, unsupported plas-
tic; noncurrent-carrying wiring services

(G-11679)
NOVICON INDUSTRIES
400 Roberts Rd (34677-4915)
P.O. Box 2366 (34677-2193)
PHONE..............................813 854-3235
EMP: 7 **EST:** 2018
SALES (est): 85.1K **Privately Held**
WEB: www.noviconusa.com
SIC: 3086 Plastics foam products

(G-11680)
NU TECH COATING SYSTEMS
525 Lafayette Blvd (34677-3724)
PHONE..............................813 448-9381
David Gray, *Principal*
EMP: 7 **EST:** 2005
SALES (est): 70.3K **Privately Held**
SIC: 3479 Metal coating & allied service

(G-11681)
OL PRODUCTS INC
100 Mount Vernon St (34677-3009)
PHONE..............................813 854-3575
George Carollo, *Branch Mgr*
EMP: 90 **Privately Held**
WEB: www.olproducts.com
SIC: 2844 Toilet preparations
PA: O.L. Products, Inc.
3874 Tampa Rd Ste 200
Oldsmar FL 34677

(G-11682)
ONE SOURCE INDUSTRIES INC
200 Pine Ave N Ste A (34677-4646)
PHONE..............................813 855-3440
Gary Woodward, *President*
Robert King, *Vice Pres*
Philip Gozo, *Accounts Exec*
Anton Yalch, *Accounts Exec*
Joanie Gentile, *Manager*
EMP: 9 **EST:** 1998
SQ FT: 2,000
SALES (est): 1.3MM **Privately Held**
WEB: www.alphacard.com
SIC: 3999 Identification badges & insignia

(G-11683)
OSGOOD INDUSTRIES LLC
601 Burbank Rd (34677-4903)
PHONE..............................813 448-9041
Rich Mueller, *Exec VP*
Ed Cichon, *Purch Mgr*
Ed Chicon, *Purch Agent*
Dalibor Bodruzic, *Engineer*
Dan Brentnall, *Engineer*
▲ **EMP:** 120 **EST:** 1976
SQ FT: 40,043

SALES (est): 35.8MM
SALES (corp-wide): 355.8K **Privately Held**
SIC: 3444 3561 3565 8711 Sheet metal-
work; pumps & pumping equipment;
packaging machinery; bag opening, filling
& closing machines; engineering services
HQ: Syntegon Technology Gmbh
Stuttgarter Str. 130
Waiblingen BW 71332
715 114-0

(G-11684)
PA C PUBLISHING INC
Also Called: Nightmoves Magazine
850 Dunbar Ave (34677-2901)
P.O. Box 492, Palm Harbor (34682-0492)
PHONE..............................813 814-1505
Paul A Cianci, *President*
Paul Allen,
EMP: 5 **EST:** 1990
SQ FT: 8,000
SALES (est): 646.6K **Privately Held**
WEB: www.pacpublishing.com
SIC: 2721 Magazines: publishing only, not
printed on site

(G-11685)
PERIPHERAL SERVICES INC
Also Called: PSI
103 Pine Ave S (34677-3026)
P.O. Box 1086 (34677-1086)
PHONE..............................813 854-1181
Bill Small, *President*
James Harrington, *General Mgr*
Jim Harrington, *Vice Pres*
William Small, *Executive*
EMP: 26 **EST:** 1987
SQ FT: 6,200
SALES (est): 969.3K **Privately Held**
WEB: www.periph.com
SIC: 3577 7699 Printers, computer; print-
ing trades machinery & equipment repair

(G-11686)
PLATESMART TECHNOLOGIES
640 Brooker Creek Blvd # 465
(34677-2934)
PHONE..............................813 749-0892
John Chigos, *Owner*
Randall Raszick, *Engineer*
Richard Shapiro, *Engineer*
Kenn Campbell, *CFO*
Tricia Parzuchowski, *Sales Staff*
EMP: 10 **EST:** 2012
SALES (est): 1.4MM **Privately Held**
WEB: www.platesmart.com
SIC: 7372 Prepackaged software

(G-11687)
POWER KLEEN CORPORATION
101 S Bayview Blvd (34677-3101)
PHONE..............................813 854-2648
John Sanders, *President*
Joyce M Sanders, *Corp Secy*
David Huddleston, *Purch Agent*
Nancy Harris, *Office Mgr*
▼ **EMP:** 30 **EST:** 1973
SQ FT: 6,000
SALES (est): 5.5MM **Privately Held**
WEB: www.powerkleen.com
SIC: 2842 7699 5087 Cleaning or polish-
ing preparations; industrial machinery &
equipment repair; dry cleaning plant
equipment & supplies

(G-11688)
PRECISION COATING RODS INC
600 Mount Vernon St (34677-3024)
P.O. Box 10594, Tampa (33679-0594)
PHONE..............................813 855-5054
Fax: 813 891-9904
EMP: 10
SQ FT: 3,000
SALES (est): 890K **Privately Held**
SIC: 3821 Mfg Lab Apparatus/Furniture

(G-11689)
PREMIER FABRICATING LLC
232 Dunbar Ct (34677-2956)
P.O. Box 1767, Derry NH (03038-6767)
PHONE..............................813 855-4633
Keith Laggett, *Mng Member*
Sandra Usling,
EMP: 19 **EST:** 2008
SQ FT: 19,000

SALES (est): 2.3MM **Privately Held**
WEB: www.premierfabricating.com
SIC: 3444 3469 Sheet metalwork; metal
stampings

(G-11690)
PREMIUM DYNAMIC LENS
640 Brooker Creek Blvd # 435
(34677-2929)
PHONE..............................813 891-9912
Cheryl Swartz, *Principal*
Carlos Perez, *Program Mgr*
Jason McLachlan, *Manager*
Ian Peterson, *Manager*
John Kivlen, *Network Enginr*
EMP: 8 **EST:** 2007
SALES (est): 191.1K **Privately Held**
SIC: 3851 5049 5995 Ophthalmic goods;
optical goods; optical goods stores

(G-11691)
PRINT ONE INC
Also Called: Unlimited Printing & Copying
3898 Tampa Rd Ste B (34677-3137)
PHONE..............................813 273-0240
William Wilkerson, *President*
Sally Williams, *Vice Pres*
EMP: 6 **EST:** 1986
SALES (est): 704.9K **Privately Held**
WEB: www.unlimitedprinting.com
SIC: 2752 2791 7334 Commercial print-
ing, offset; typesetting; photocopying &
duplicating services

(G-11692)
PRINTEC INC
241 Douglas Rd E Ste 1 (34677-2913)
PHONE..............................813 854-1075
EMP: 7 **EST:** 2019
SALES (est): 238.3K **Privately Held**
WEB: www.printec-ht.com
SIC: 2759 Screen printing

(G-11693)
PRINTING DEPOT INC
3898 Tampa Rd Ste B (34677-3137)
PHONE..............................813 855-6758
Robert Hunt, *President*
Becky Harness, *Creative Dir*
EMP: 7 **EST:** 1984
SQ FT: 6,000
SALES (est): 946.9K **Privately Held**
WEB: www.goprintingdepot.com
SIC: 2752 Commercial printing, offset

(G-11694)
PROMEDICA INC
114 Douglas Rd E (34677-2933)
PHONE..............................813 854-1905
Edward C Padinske, *CEO*
Ronald J Padinske, *President*
Robert E Wade, *CFO*
EMP: 370 **EST:** 1987
SQ FT: 62,000
SALES (est): 9MM
SALES (corp-wide): 69.5MM **Privately Held**
WEB: www.touchpointmed.com
SIC: 3841 Surgical & medical instruments
PA: Touchpoint Medical, Inc.
2200 Touchpoint Dr
Odessa FL 33556
813 854-1905

(G-11695)
QTM INC
300 Stevens Ave (34677-2919)
PHONE..............................813 891-1300
Richard K Peck, *CEO*
Richard Barnes, *CIO*
EMP: 26 **EST:** 1989
SQ FT: 21,000
SALES (est): 4.8MM **Privately Held**
WEB: www.qtminc.com
SIC: 3599 Machine shop, jobbing & repair

(G-11696)
R&D MACHINE LLC ✪
130 Scarlet Blvd (34677-3002)
PHONE..............................813 891-9109
Gary Holcomb, *President*
Justin Kovscek, *Vice Pres*
EMP: 36 **EST:** 2022

SALES (est): 3MM
SALES (corp-wide): 3.6MM **Privately Held**
WEB: www.rdmachine.com
SIC: 3599 Machine shop, jobbing & repair
PA: Compass Precision, Llc
4600 Westinghouse Blvd
Charlotte NC 28273
704 790-6764

(G-11697)
RONECKER HOLDINGS LLC
Also Called: On Demand Printing
303 Mears Blvd (34677-3048)
PHONE..............................813 855-5559
EMP: 9
SQ FT: 1,800
SALES (est): 1.4MM **Privately Held**
SIC: 2711 6719 Commercial-
Publishing/Printing

(G-11698)
**STRUCTALL BUILDING
SYSTEMS INC (PA)**
Also Called: Oldsmar Service Center
350 Burbank Rd (34677-4906)
PHONE..............................813 855-2627
Steve Meyerson, *President*
Mark Van Dame, *COO*
Jim Forsberg, *Vice Pres*
Ken Matuza, *Project Mgr*
Dan O 'keefe, *Prdtn Mgr*
◆ **EMP:** 30 **EST:** 1987
SQ FT: 54,000
SALES (est): 25.2MM **Privately Held**
WEB: www.structall.com
SIC: 3449 Miscellaneous metalwork

(G-11699)
**TAMPA MACHINE PRODUCTS
INC**
151 Vollmer Ave (34677-2936)
PHONE..............................813 854-3332
James Lyngholm, *President*
EMP: 27 **EST:** 1974
SQ FT: 20,000
SALES (est): 507.5K **Privately Held**
SIC: 3599 Machine shop, jobbing & repair

(G-11700)
ULTRA CLEAN SYSTEMS INC
110 Douglas Rd E (34677-2910)
PHONE..............................813 925-1003
Billy O Cale, *President*
Rebecca Cale, *Corp Secy*
Michael Cale, *Vice Pres*
Norman Cale, *Vice Pres*
Becky Cale, *VP Opers*
EMP: 18 **EST:** 1999
SALES (est): 7.3MM **Privately Held**
WEB: www.ultracleansystems.com
SIC: 3841 Surgical & medical instruments

(G-11701)
UNITED ADVANTAGE SIGNS INC
Also Called: United Signs Systems
206 Tower Dr (34677-2964)
PHONE..............................813 855-3300
Steven Higger, *President*
Bob Bennett, *Project Mgr*
Forrest Massa, *Project Mgr*
Andy Noethen, *Project Mgr*
John Scott, *Purchasing*
EMP: 66 **EST:** 1984
SQ FT: 40,000
SALES (est): 7.8MM **Privately Held**
SIC: 3993 Electric signs

(G-11702)
UNITED VISUAL BRANDING LLC
206 Tower Dr (34677-2964)
PHONE..............................813 855-3300
Bill Thiele, *Vice Pres*
Lisa Gerstner, *Production*
Tim Kramer, *Purchasing*
Cayla Duckworth, *Human Resources*
Kylee Chlopecki, *Sales Staff*
EMP: 95 **EST:** 2018
SALES (est): 6.2MM **Privately Held**
WEB: www.uvbrand.com
SIC: 3993 Signs & advertising specialties

(G-11703)
USBEV PLASTICS LLC
3874 Tampa Rd (34677-3126)
PHONE..............................813 855-0700

▲ = Import ▼=Export
◆ =Import/Export

Santo Carollo, *Mng Member*
EMP: 16 **EST:** 2012
SQ FT: 22,500
SALES (est): 1.1MM **Privately Held**
SIC: 3089 Molding primary plastic

(G-11704)
UVLRX THERAPEUTICS INC
640 Brooker Creek Blvd (34677-2929)
PHONE................................813 309-1976
Michael Harter, *CEO*
EMP: 11 **EST:** 2016
SALES (est): 1.3MM **Privately Held**
SIC: 2834 Pharmaceutical preparations

(G-11705)
VANGUARD PRODUCTS GROUP INC
Also Called: Vanguard Protex Global
720 Brooker Creek Blvd (34677-2935)
PHONE................................813 855-9639
Christopher Kelsch, *President*
Rodney Surratt, *COO*
John O 'bryan, *Vice Pres*
John Obryan, *Vice Pres*
Stephen Wood, *Vice Pres*
▲ **EMP:** 70 **EST:** 2000
SQ FT: 8,000
SALES (est): 23.8MM **Privately Held**
WEB: www.vanguardprotexglobal.com
SIC: 3669 3699 7382 Burglar alarm apparatus, electric; security devices; burglar alarm maintenance & monitoring

(G-11706)
VETBIOTEK INC
640 Douglas Rd E Ste A (34677-4925)
PHONE................................727 308-2030
Thomas Bell, *President*
Brian Bell, *Vice Pres*
Kyle Kerley, *Regl Sales Mgr*
Julie Russel, *Sales Staff*
Nicholas Hargrave, *Manager*
EMP: 10 **EST:** 2014
SQ FT: 6,800
SALES (est): 1.5MM **Privately Held**
WEB: www.vetbiotek.com
SIC: 2834 Veterinary pharmaceutical preparations

(G-11707)
WORLDWIDE TECHNOLOGY INC (PA)
141 Stevens Ave Ste 10 (34677-2954)
P.O. Box 1693 (34677-1693)
PHONE................................813 855-2443
Edward M Contreras, *President*
Doris A Contreras, *Corp Secy*
Tom Gain, *Vice Pres*
Sara Goellner, *Vice Pres*
Mike Taylor, *CTO*
EMP: 26 **EST:** 1986
SALES (est): 3.1MM **Privately Held**
SIC: 3564 3589 3559 Air cleaning systems; water purification systems, household type; ozone machines

(G-11708)
YOUNG GUNS EMBROIDERY INC
143 Scarlet Blvd (34677-3015)
PHONE................................813 814-9172
Michael Schumacher, *President*
EMP: 8 **EST:** 2002
SALES (est): 580.4K **Privately Held**
WEB: www.ygapparel.com
SIC: 2395 Embroidery products, except schiffli machine

Ona
Hardee County

(G-11709)
FLORIDA FENCE POST CO INC (PA)
5251 State Road 64 W (33865-8704)
P.O. Box 645 (33865-0645)
PHONE................................863 735-1361
F L Revell Jr, *President*
Alice Salas, *Corp Secy*
Oneita Revell, *Vice Pres*
▼ **EMP:** 9 **EST:** 1946
SQ FT: 20,000

SALES (est): 2.5MM **Privately Held**
WEB: www.flfencepost.com
SIC: 2411 5211 5999 Posts, wood: hewn, round or split; fencing; alarm & safety equipment stores

Opa Locka
Miami-Dade County

(G-11710)
AAA SECURITY DEPOT CORP
12815 Nw 45th Ave Ste 2 (33054-5100)
PHONE................................305 652-8567
Shirley Jacobowitz, *President*
Ron Jacobowitz, *Vice Pres*
▲ **EMP:** 20 **EST:** 2007
SALES (est): 2MM **Privately Held**
WEB: www.aaasecuritydepot.com
SIC: 3699 Security control equipment & systems

(G-11711)
ACTION PLATING CORP
1220 Ali Baba Ave (33054-3613)
PHONE................................305 685-6313
William J Bain, *President*
EMP: 14 **EST:** 1977
SQ FT: 38,465
SALES (est): 2.2MM **Privately Held**
WEB: www.actionplatingcorp.com
SIC: 3471 Plating of metals or formed products; electroplating of metals or formed products

(G-11712)
AERO PRECISION PRODUCTS INC
Also Called: Appi
14000 Nw 19th Ave (33054-4190)
PHONE................................305 688-2565
Paul R Fournier, *President*
Robert Fout, *COO*
Vanessa Sao, *Sales Staff*
Sal Rodriguez, *CIO*
▼ **EMP:** 85 **EST:** 1966
SQ FT: 50,000
SALES (est): 15.5MM **Privately Held**
WEB: www.appiusa.com
SIC: 3599 3469 Machine shop, jobbing & repair; stamping metal for the trade

(G-11713)
ALEXIS WELDING EXPRESS CORP
12900 Nw 30th Ave (33054-5011)
PHONE................................786 626-4090
Alexis Cepero, *Principal*
EMP: 7 **EST:** 2018
SALES (est): 232.2K **Privately Held**
SIC: 7692 Welding repair

(G-11714)
ALLCOFFEE LLC
12815 Nw 45th Ave Ste 6b (33054-5100)
PHONE................................305 685-6856
Benedetto Mazzucco, *CEO*
Giuseppe Cecinato, *Mktg Dir*
Alexandro Centofanti, *Officer*
EMP: 5 **EST:** 2006
SALES (est): 592.9K **Privately Held**
WEB: www.allcoffee.com
SIC: 2095 Roasted coffee

(G-11715)
ALLIED GENERAL ENGRV & PLAS
3485 Nw 167th St (33056-4118)
PHONE................................305 626-6585
Bedros Kazazian, *President*
Berge Kazazian, *Vice Pres*
▲ **EMP:** 10 **EST:** 1978
SALES (est): 789.3K **Privately Held**
SIC: 3089 2759 3544 2789 Injection molding of plastics; engraving; special dies, tools, jigs & fixtures; bookbinding & related work

(G-11716)
AMERICAN THRMPLASTIC EXTRUSION
Also Called: Ateco
4851 Nw 128th Street Rd (33054-5134)
PHONE................................305 769-9566

Donald P Miller, *Ch of Bd*
Don Gellett, *President*
Mark J Baker, *Treasurer*
Jeff Trattner, *VP Mktg*
Angela K Gillett, *Admin Sec*
EMP: 150 **EST:** 1959
SQ FT: 61,000
SALES (est): 52MM
SALES (corp-wide): 220.7MM **Privately Held**
SIC: 3089 3083 Extruded finished plastic products; laminated plastics plate & sheet
PA: Roppe Holding Company
1602 N Union St
Fostoria OH 44830
419 435-8546

(G-11717)
ANDRE T JEAN
Also Called: Bubble Bath Detailing Car Wash
2306 Ali Baba Ave (33054-3134)
PHONE................................305 647-8744
Andre T Jean, *Owner*
EMP: 7 **EST:** 2020
SALES (est): 57.6K **Privately Held**
SIC: 3589 Car washing machinery

(G-11718)
AQUARIUS PRESS INC
13795 Nw 19th Ave (33054-4215)
PHONE................................305 688-0066
Valerie Doten, *President*
James A Williams, *Vice Pres*
▼ **EMP:** 10 **EST:** 1976
SQ FT: 3,600
SALES (est): 763.2K **Privately Held**
WEB: www.aquariuspress.com
SIC: 2752 Commercial printing, offset

(G-11719)
ARSO ENTERPRISES INC
Also Called: Sol-A-Trol Aluminum Products
4101 Nw 132nd St (33054-4510)
PHONE................................305 681-2020
Antonio L Soler, *President*
Marie Soler, *Corp Secy*
Anthony M Soler, *Vice Pres*
Anthony Soler, *Vice Pres*
◆ **EMP:** 37 **EST:** 1976
SALES (est): 4.7MM **Privately Held**
WEB: arsoenterprises.openfos.com
SIC: 3442 1751 5031 1793 Window & door frames; window & door (prefabricated) installation; building materials, exterior; building materials, interior; glass & glazing work; products of purchased glass

(G-11720)
B & P MOTOR HEADS INC
1815 Opa Locka Blvd (33054-4223)
PHONE................................305 769-3183
Pedro Finales, *President*
EMP: 7 **EST:** 1990
SQ FT: 25,000
SALES (est): 200K **Privately Held**
SIC: 3599 5015 Machine shop, jobbing & repair; automotive parts & supplies, used

(G-11721)
B & P MOTORS INC
1815 Opa Locka Blvd (33054-4223)
PHONE................................305 687-7337
Pedro Finales, *President*
Pedro Finalen, *President*
EMP: 8 **EST:** 2001
SALES (est): 535.6K **Privately Held**
SIC: 3545 Machine tool accessories

(G-11722)
BEAUTY COSMETICA
Also Called: Keratin Cure
3406 Nw 151st Ter (33054-2450)
PHONE................................305 406-1022
EMP: 15
SALES (est): 799.6K **Privately Held**
SIC: 3999 Mfg Misc Products

(G-11723)
BEAUTY LAB INC
2360 Nw 150th St (33054-2706)
PHONE................................305 687-0071
▼ **EMP:** 20
SQ FT: 56,000
SALES (est): 1.5MM **Privately Held**
SIC: 2844 Mfg Toilet Preparations

(G-11724)
BOLIDT CRUISE CONTROL CORP
14501 Nw 57th Ave Ste 111 (33054-2375)
PHONE................................305 607-4172
Antoine M Dons Mr, *General Mgr*
Overbeek Jacco, *Principal*
Jacco Van Overbeek Mr, *Vice Pres*
Peter Plaisier Mr, *Director*
▲ **EMP:** 11 **EST:** 1999
SALES (est): 2.4MM **Privately Held**
WEB: www.bolidt.com
SIC: 3069 Flooring, rubber: tile or sheet

(G-11725)
BON VIVANT INTERIORS INC
Also Called: Bon Vivant Custom Woodworking
4400 Nw 135th St (33054-4420)
PHONE................................305 576-8066
Ricardo Rammos, *President*
EMP: 35 **EST:** 1982
SQ FT: 30,000
SALES (est): 4.5MM **Privately Held**
WEB: www.bvmiami.com
SIC: 2512 2517 2511 Upholstered household furniture; wood television & radio cabinets; wood household furniture

(G-11726)
C M I ENTERPRISES INC (PA)
Also Called: CMI
13145 Nw 45th Ave (33054-4305)
P.O. Box 941150, Miami (33194-1150)
PHONE................................305 622-6410
Michael Novick, *President*
Jorge Canamero, *Vice Pres*
Ricardo Porras, *CFO*
◆ **EMP:** 40 **EST:** 1984
SQ FT: 25,000
SALES (est): 28.7MM **Privately Held**
WEB: www.cmi-enterprises.com
SIC: 3999 2295 Boat models, except toy; resin or plastic coated fabrics

(G-11727)
CAIRO JM CAR PARTS INC
12780 Cairo Ln (33054-4611)
PHONE................................305 688-4044
Jose Djabbour, *President*
Misak Kalbakdjian, *Vice Pres*
EMP: 9 **EST:** 2015
SALES (est): 105.5K **Privately Held**
SIC: 3714 Universal joints, motor vehicle

(G-11728)
CHICK N PORTIONS INC
12725 Nw 38th Ave (33054-4524)
PHONE................................305 687-0000
Tom Higgobotham, *Principal*
EMP: 75 **EST:** 1981
SQ FT: 3,000
SALES (est): 3.1MM **Privately Held**
SIC: 2015 Poultry, processed: fresh

(G-11729)
CIGARETTE RACING TEAM LLC
4355 Nw 128th St (33054-5123)
PHONE................................305 769-4350
Chad Braver, *Engineer*
Mark Belisle, *Sales Staff*
Skip Braver, *Mng Member*
Bud Lorow, *Manager*
▲ **EMP:** 99 **EST:** 2002
SALES (est): 16.1MM **Privately Held**
WEB: www.cigaretteracing.com
SIC: 3732 Motorized boat, building & repairing

(G-11730)
CLERO ENTERPRISES INC
3881 Nw 125th St (33054-4515)
PHONE................................305 681-4877
Jorge Clero, *President*
Mary Martinez, *Purchasing*
William G Clero, *Admin Sec*
EMP: 6 **EST:** 1998
SALES (est): 832.8K **Privately Held**
WEB: www.cleroaviation.com
SIC: 3728 Aircraft parts & equipment

(G-11731)
CM2 INDUSTRIES INC
Also Called: SBC Laser
1769 Opa Locka Blvd (33054-4221)
PHONE..................................305 685-4812
Nicholas Caito, *President*
EMP: 8 EST: 2018
SALES (est): 50K **Privately Held**
SIC: 3479 Etching on metals

(G-11732)
COFFEE UNLIMITED LLC
Also Called: Allcoffee
12815 Nw 45th Ave Ste 6b (33054-5100)
PHONE..................................305 685-6366
Juan Mendes,
EMP: 10 **EST:** 2019
SALES (est): 632.8K **Privately Held**
WEB: www.coffeeunlimited.com
SIC: 2095 Coffee roasting (except by
wholesale grocers)

(G-11733)
CONCEPT BOATS INC
2410 Nw 147th St (33054-3130)
PHONE..................................305 635-8712
Luis Avila, *President*
Susan Patterson, *Vice Pres*
Chris Box, *Sales Dir*
Anay Santos, *Admin Mgr*
▼ **EMP:** 25 **EST:** 1986
SQ FT: 10,000
SALES (est): 5MM **Privately Held**
WEB: www.conceptboats.com
SIC: 3732 5551 Boat building & repairing;
boat dealers

(G-11734)
**CUPCAKES FRSTING
SPRINKLES LLC**
2301 Nw 155th St (33054-2750)
PHONE..................................305 769-3393
Minerva B Hector, *Manager*
EMP: 7 EST: 2013
SALES (est): 146.9K **Privately Held**
SIC: 2051 Bread, cake & related products

(G-11735)
D N L PERFORMANCE INC
1797 Opa Locka Blvd (33054-4221)
PHONE..................................786 295-8831
David Rivera, *Principal*
EMP: 7 EST: 2012
SALES (est): 191.9K **Privately Held**
SIC: 2992 Lubricating oils

(G-11736)
DIDI DESIGNS INC
Also Called: Elana Kattan
13376 Nw 42nd Ave (33054-4526)
PHONE..................................305 836-0266
Elana Henry, *President*
Richard Henry, *Vice Pres*
Rami Kattan, *Vice Pres*
Abraham Kattan, *Admin Sec*
◆ **EMP:** 19 **EST:** 1982
SALES (est): 1.8MM **Privately Held**
WEB: www.elanakattan.com
SIC: 2339 Leotards: women's, misses' &
juniors'; athletic clothing: women's,
misses' & juniors'

(G-11737)
**DISTRIBUIDORA GIORGIO USA
LLC**
12815 Nw 45th Ave (33054-5116)
PHONE..................................305 685-6366
Mazzucco Benedetto,
Centofanti Alexandro,
Cecinato Giuseppe,
Taurchini Stefano,
◆ **EMP:** 16 **EST:** 2007
SALES (est): 681.6K **Privately Held**
SIC: 2095 Roasted coffee

(G-11738)
DONE RITE PUMPS
Also Called: Repair Electrical Motors Ac/DC
4240 Nw 133rd St (33054-4400)
PHONE..................................305 953-3380
Luis Navarro, *President*
EMP: 8 EST: 2012

SALES (est): 1MM **Privately Held**
WEB: www.doneritepumps.com
SIC: 7694 7699 Electric motor repair; in-
dustrial equipment services

(G-11739)
**DOSAL TOBACCO
CORPORATION (PA)**
4775 Nw 132nd St (33054-4313)
PHONE..................................305 685-2949
Margarita Dosal, *President*
Margarita D Owen, *Exec VP*
George Dosal, *Vice Pres*
Yolanda Snader, *CFO*
Ted Rathbun, *Sales Staff*
▲ **EMP:** 22 **EST:** 1962
SALES (est): 31.2MM **Privately Held**
SIC: 2111 2121 Cigarettes; cigars

(G-11740)
DYNASTY APPAREL CORP (PA)
13000 Nw 42nd Ave (33054-4500)
PHONE..................................305 685-3490
Ignacio Mendez, *President*
Caridad Mendez, *Admin Sec*
Ovidio Mendez, *Admin Sec*
◆ **EMP:** 90 **EST:** 1978
SQ FT: 72,000
SALES (est): 24.9MM **Privately Held**
WEB: www.dynastyapparel.com
SIC: 2325 2321 Shorts (outerwear):
men's, youths' & boys'; trousers, dress
(separate): men's, youths' & boys'; men's
& boys' sports & polo shirts; sport shirts,
men's & boys': from purchased materials

(G-11741)
**EASTERN SHORES PRINTING
(PA)**
Also Called: Eastern Shres Prtg Woven Label
4476 Nw 128th St (33054-5126)
PHONE..................................305 685-8976
Gladys Marcus, *President*
Laurie Marcus, *Corp Secy*
Steven Marcus, *Vice Pres*
◆ **EMP:** 30 **EST:** 1974
SQ FT: 12,000
SALES (est): 5.6MM **Privately Held**
WEB: www.easternshoresprint.com
SIC: 2752 2396 2241 Lithographing on
metal; tags, lithographed; automotive &
apparel trimmings; narrow fabric mills

(G-11742)
ENDFLEX LLC
4760 Nw 128th St (33054-5132)
PHONE..................................305 622-4070
Louis Taraborelli, *President*
Frank Milone, *President*
Jorge Perez, *Vice Pres*
Nicholas Taraborelli, *Vice Pres*
Jazmin Aguirrre, *Office Mgr*
▲ **EMP:** 35 **EST:** 2008
SQ FT: 14,475
SALES (est): 2.6MM **Privately Held**
WEB: www.endflex.com
SIC: 3565 Carton packing machines

(G-11743)
**ERIMARK ELECTRIC SIGN CO
INC**
14851 Nw 27th Ave (33054-3352)
PHONE..................................954 423-1364
John Annis, *President*
EMP: 7 EST: 2001
SALES (est): 153.5K **Privately Held**
SIC: 3993 Electric signs

(G-11744)
EVERGLADES CREATIONS INC
Also Called: Winston Manufacturing
2335 Nw 149th St (33054-3131)
PHONE..................................305 822-3344
William Di Scipio, *President*
EMP: 26 **EST:** 2007
SALES (est): 2.4MM **Privately Held**
SIC: 3172 Personal leather goods

(G-11745)
**EVOLUTION WLDNGS
FBRCATION LLC**
2095 Nw 141st St (33054-4136)
PHONE..................................786 702-4703
Cristian Aguilar,
Vladimir Madan Marrero,

EMP: 7 EST: 2019
SALES (est): 258.7K **Privately Held**
SIC: 7692 Welding repair

(G-11746)
FIS GROUP INC
3820 Nw 125th St (33054-4541)
PHONE..................................786 622-3308
EMP: 8 EST: 2017
SALES (est): 733.7K **Privately Held**
WEB: www.fisgroupwelding.com
SIC: 3441 Fabricated structural metal

(G-11747)
FLORIDA ICE CORPORATION
13401 Nw 38th Ct (33054-4512)
PHONE..................................305 685-9377
Miguel Angel Guerra, *President*
Maria Rodriguez, *Corp Secy*
EMP: 10 **EST:** 1999
SQ FT: 13,600
SALES (est): 1MM **Privately Held**
WEB: www.floridaice.net
SIC: 2097 Manufactured ice

(G-11748)
**FLORIDA POLSG &
RESTORATION**
2163 Opa Locka Blvd (33054-4229)
PHONE..................................305 688-2988
Evelyn Venerio, *Principal*
EMP: 5 **EST:** 2010
SALES (est): 353.5K **Privately Held**
SIC: 3471 Polishing, metals or formed
products

(G-11749)
FLORIDA STORM PANELS INC
14475 Nw 26th Ave (33054-3121)
PHONE..................................305 685-9000
Victor Cruz, *President*
▲ **EMP:** 10 **EST:** 1993
SQ FT: 26,000
SALES (est): 991.2K **Privately Held**
SIC: 3444 Sheet metal specialties, not
stamped

(G-11751)
GABOL SCREEN PRINTING CO
12815 Nw 45th Ave (33054-5116)
PHONE..................................305 681-3882
Ken Curley, *Owner*
EMP: 7 EST: 2001
SALES (est): 132.6K **Privately Held**
SIC: 2752 Commercial printing, litho-
graphic

(G-11751)
GSE JETALL INC
4821 Nw 128th St (33054-5134)
PHONE..................................305 688-2111
Marisol G Alvarez, *Administration*
EMP: 9 **EST:** 2014
SALES (est): 943.9K **Privately Held**
WEB: www.jetall.com
SIC: 3728 3511 Aircraft parts & equip-
ment; turbines & turbine generator sets

(G-11752)
H SIXTO DISTRIBUTORS INC
Also Called: Sixto Packaging
13301 Nw 38th Ct (33054-4517)
PHONE..................................305 688-5242
Carmen Sixto, *President*
Andres Sixto, *Vice Pres*
Alan Raines, *Production*
Felipe Humberto Sixto, *Treasurer*
Emilio Sixto, *Admin Sec*
◆ **EMP:** 12 **EST:** 1978
SALES (est): 3.5MM **Privately Held**
WEB: www.sixtopack.com
SIC: 2673 2396 Cellophane bags, un-
printed: made from purchased materials;
automotive & apparel trimmings

(G-11753)
HIGHLANDER STONE CORP
14105 Nw 19th Ave (33054-4141)
PHONE..................................786 333-1151
Miguel A Garutti, *Principal*
EMP: 10 **EST:** 2012
SALES (est): 654.3K **Privately Held**
SIC: 3281 Cut stone & stone products

(G-11754)
INEN USA CORP
12750 Cairo Ln (33054-4611)
PHONE..................................305 343-6666
Jesus A Berrio Ramirez, *Principal*
Lina Arenas, *Manager*
EMP: 6 **EST:** 2008
SALES (est): 367.1K **Privately Held**
SIC: 3549 Metalworking machinery

(G-11755)
INTERNATIONAL PAINT LLC
3489 Nw 167th St (33056-4118)
PHONE..................................305 620-9220
Robert Hall, *Manager*
EMP: 8
SQ FT: 5,013
SALES (corp-wide): 10.8B **Privately Held**
WEB: www.akzonobel.com
SIC: 2851 Paints & allied products
HQ: International Paint Llc
535 Marriott Dr Ste 500
Nashville TN 37214
713 684-5839

(G-11756)
**INVINCIBLE BOAT COMPANY
LLC**
4700 Nw 132nd St (33054-4314)
PHONE..................................305 685-2704
John Dorton, *CEO*
Ian Birdsall, *Vice Pres*
Ben Dorton, *Vice Pres*
Oliver Huntsman, *Export Mgr*
Anthony Porben, *Purchasing*
▼ **EMP:** 30 **EST:** 2005
SALES (est): 14.1MM
SALES (corp-wide): 40MM **Privately
Held**
WEB: www.invincibleboats.com
SIC: 3732 Boat building & repairing
PA: Warbird Marine Holdings, Llc
4700 Nw 132nd St
Opa Locka FL 33054
844 341-2504

(G-11757)
J & J STONE TOPS INC
13760 Nw 19th Ave (33054-4233)
PHONE..................................305 305-8993
Julio Rodriguez, *President*
Jackie Alva, *Vice Pres*
▲ **EMP:** 5 **EST:** 2000
SQ FT: 4,500
SALES (est): 600K **Privately Held**
SIC: 3281 Table tops, marble

(G-11758)
**JOHN M CALDWELL DISTRG CO
INC**
Also Called: Custom Screen Printing Florida
1150 Ali Baba Ave (33054-3611)
PHONE..................................305 685-9822
John M Caldwell, *President*
EMP: 10 **EST:** 1972
SQ FT: 14,000
SALES (est): 363.3K **Privately Held**
SIC: 2339 2329 Sportswear, women's;
men's & boys' sportswear & athletic cloth-
ing

(G-11759)
KELLYS BAKERY CORP
Also Called: Atlantic Coastal Bakery
3990 Nw 132nd St Unit A (33054-4535)
PHONE..................................305 685-4622
Elango Ellappan, *President*
Brian Hersch, *Principal*
EMP: 11 **EST:** 1998
SALES (est): 1MM **Privately Held**
SIC: 2051 Bakery: wholesale or whole-
sale/retail combined

(G-11760)
KINGSPAN INSULATION LLC
Dyplast Products
12501 Nw 38th Ave (33054-4543)
PHONE..................................305 921-0100
Vincent Fuster, *General Mgr*
EMP: 57 **Privately Held**
WEB: www.dyplastproducts.com
SIC: 3086 5033 Insulation or cushioning
material, foamed plastic; roofing & siding
materials

▲ = Import ▼=Export
◆ =Import/Export

HQ: Kingspan Insulation Llc
2100 Riveredge Pkwy # 175
Atlanta GA 30328
678 589-7331

(G-11761)
KOHTLER ELEVATOR INDS INC (PA)
4115 Nw 132nd St Unit B (33054-4539)
PHONE....................305 687-7037
Olga V Diaz, *President*
EMP: 5 **EST:** 2008
SALES (est): 2.9MM **Privately Held**
WEB: www.kohtler.com
SIC: 3534 1761 Elevators & equipment; sheet metalwork

(G-11762)
LANDING AEROSPACE INC
4604 Nw 133rd St (33054-4406)
PHONE....................305 687-0100
Mery L Ramirez, *Principal*
▲ **EMP:** 8 **EST:** 2013
SALES (est): 374.4K **Privately Held**
WEB: www.landingaerospace.net
SIC: 3728 Aircraft parts & equipment

(G-11763)
LEAR INVESTORS INC (PA)
Also Called: International Trading Company
4154 Nw 132nd St (33054-4511)
PHONE....................305 681-8582
Leon Bekerman, *President*
Freny Bekerman, *Vice Pres*
▲ **EMP:** 7 **EST:** 1985
SQ FT: 4,200
SALES (est): 802.2K **Privately Held**
WEB: www.lear.com
SIC: 2339 5137 Sportswear, women's; sportswear, women's & children's

(G-11764)
LUDLOW FIBC CORP
13260 Nw 45th Ave (33054-4308)
PHONE....................305 702-5000
Carol Barber, *Manager*
▲ **EMP:** 5 **EST:** 2008
SALES (est): 372.8K **Privately Held**
SIC: 3496 Miscellaneous fabricated wire products

(G-11765)
MARTINSON MICA WOOD PDTS INC
13740 Nw 19th Ave (33054-4211)
PHONE....................305 688-4445
Martin Del Ray, *President*
EMP: 6 **EST:** 1994
SQ FT: 5,000
SALES (est): 754.3K **Privately Held**
SIC: 2512 Upholstered household furniture

(G-11766)
MASTER NUTRITION LABS INC
13165 Nw 47th Ave (33054-4309)
PHONE....................786 847-2000
Solomon Brander, *Principal*
EMP: 9 **EST:** 2016
SALES (est): 90K **Privately Held**
WEB: www.masternutritionlabs.com
SIC: 2834 Vitamin preparations

(G-11767)
MEELKO CO
3890 Nw 132nd St Unit F (33054-4537)
PHONE....................845 600-3379
Edu Y Cristian Moreno, *CEO*
EMP: 7 **EST:** 2013
SALES (est): 462.5K **Privately Held**
WEB: www.meelko.com
SIC: 1011 Iron ore pelletizing

(G-11768)
MENDEZ BROTHERS LLC
13000 Nw 42nd Ave (33054-4405)
PHONE....................305 685-3490
Armando Mendez, *Manager*
EMP: 11 **EST:** 2005
SALES (est): 509.4K **Privately Held**
SIC: 2759 Commercial printing

(G-11769)
MIAMI METALS II INC
Also Called: RMC
12900 Nw 38th Ave (33054-4527)
PHONE....................305 685-8505
Jason Rubin, *CEO*
Scott Avila, *Principal*
Rose Rubin, *Vice Pres*
James Snyder, *Vice Pres*
Emre Karalar, *Engineer*
◆ **EMP:** 150 **EST:** 1980
SALES (est): 39.3MM **Privately Held**
WEB: www.republicmetalscorp.com
SIC: 3339 Precious metals

(G-11770)
MOBILE MINI INC
12905 Nw 32nd Ave (33054-4913)
PHONE....................954 745-0026
Mark Graham, *Administration*
EMP: 7 **EST:** 2016
SALES (est): 105.7K **Privately Held**
WEB: www.mobilemini.com
SIC: 3448 Prefabricated metal buildings

(G-11771)
MR GUMMY VITAMINS LLC
12845 Nw 45th Ave (33054-5119)
PHONE....................855 674-8669
Monica G Suarez, *Mng Member*
EMP: 6 **EST:** 2013
SALES (est): 449.9K **Privately Held**
WEB: www.mrgummyvitamins.com
SIC: 2048 5122 Feed supplements; vitamins & minerals

(G-11772)
MTI AVIATION INC
13150 Nw 45th Ave (33054-4306)
PHONE....................305 817-4244
Jorge Mejia, *CEO*
Milagros Mejia, *President*
Millie Mejia, *Vice Pres*
Oscar Ramudo, *Cust Mgr*
EMP: 30 **EST:** 2013
SALES (est): 3.8MM **Privately Held**
WEB: www.mtiaviation.com
SIC: 3724 Aircraft engines & engine parts

(G-11773)
NATURAL VITAMINS LAB CORP
12845 Nw 45th Ave (33054-5119)
PHONE....................305 265-1660
EMP: 136 **Privately Held**
SIC: 2834 Mfg Pharmaceutical Preparations
PA: Natural Vitamins Laboratory Corporation
12845 Nw 45th Ave
Opa Locka FL 33054

(G-11774)
NATURAL VITAMINS LAB CORP
Also Called: Natural Vitamins Labs
4400 Nw 133rd St (33054-4402)
PHONE....................305 265-1660
Karan Arora, *President*
Tejas Choksi, *Vice Pres*
Tejus Choski, *Treasurer*
Shruti Shah, *Manager*
◆ **EMP:** 200 **EST:** 1995
SALES (est): 40.6MM **Privately Held**
WEB: www.nvlabs.net
SIC: 2834 Vitamin preparations

(G-11775)
NELSON MCH SP WLDG & ENGRG INC
13990 Nw 22nd Ave (33054-4127)
PHONE....................305 710-5029
Mariuxi Salazar, *Principal*
EMP: 10 **EST:** 2012
SALES (est): 260.3K **Privately Held**
SIC: 3599 Machine shop, jobbing & repair

(G-11776)
NEW VISION FURNITURE INC
4115 Nw 132nd St Unit I (33054-4539)
PHONE....................305 562-9428
Juan Benavente, *President*
EMP: 7 **EST:** 2013
SQ FT: 5,000
SALES (est): 631.5K **Privately Held**
SIC: 2522 5712 Office furniture, except wood; office furniture

(G-11777)
OPA-LOCKA PALLETS INC
3180 Nw 131st St (33054-4921)
PHONE....................305 681-8212
Jose Almendares, *President*
Maria Almendares, *Vice Pres*
▲ **EMP:** 16 **EST:** 1985
SQ FT: 800
SALES (est): 2MM **Privately Held**
WEB: www.opalockapallets.com
SIC: 2448 Pallets, wood

(G-11778)
ORTEGA INDUSTRIES AND MFG
13281 Nw 43rd Ave (33054-4436)
PHONE....................305 688-0090
Omar Dube, *President*
Magdalena Dube, *Vice Pres*
Alex Pea, *Accounts Mgr*
◆ **EMP:** 100 **EST:** 1971
SQ FT: 65,000
SALES (est): 8.3MM **Privately Held**
WEB: www.ortegaindustries.com
SIC: 2591 5023 Blinds vertical; window covering parts & accessories

(G-11779)
PAPER BAG MANUFACTURERS INC
4131 Nw 132nd St (33054-4510)
PHONE....................305 685-1100
Joseph Greenspan, *President*
Susan Hernandez, *Vice Pres*
▲ **EMP:** 17 **EST:** 1994
SALES (est): 1.8MM **Privately Held**
WEB: www.paperbag.com
SIC: 2393 2674 Bags & containers, except sleeping bags: textile; bags: uncoated paper & multiwall

(G-11780)
PASA SERVICES INC
Also Called: Flamingo Graphics
13015 Nw 38th Ave (33054-4501)
PHONE....................305 594-8662
Blanca Bichara, *CEO*
Tatiana Bautista, *President*
Edwin Mora, *General Mgr*
EMP: 41 **EST:** 1988
SQ FT: 17,000
SALES (est): 9.5MM **Privately Held**
SIC: 2752 2759 Commercial printing, lithographic; security certificates: engraved

(G-11781)
PAVEMENT MARKING & SIGNS INC
2039 Opa Locka Blvd (33054-4227)
PHONE....................786 431-6788
Patrick Coakley, *Principal*
EMP: 9 **EST:** 2018
SALES (est): 259.4K **Privately Held**
SIC: 3993 Signs & advertising specialties

(G-11782)
PEARSON GROUP LLC
3115 Nw 135th St (33054-4829)
PHONE....................786 498-3532
Stanley Pearson, *Mng Member*
EMP: 7 **EST:** 2019
SALES (est): 284.4K **Privately Held**
SIC: 1389 Construction, repair & dismantling services

(G-11783)
PLASTICS FOR MANKIND INC (PA)
Also Called: Plastiform
13050 Nw 47th Ave (33054-4326)
PHONE....................305 687-5917
Jorge G Blodek, *President*
George G Blodek, *President*
EMP: 9 **EST:** 1984
SQ FT: 24,000
SALES (est): 1.2MM **Privately Held**
SIC: 3827 3089 Optical instruments & lenses; molding primary plastic

(G-11784)
REMCRAFT LIGHTING PRODUCTS INC
Also Called: Baci By Remcraft
12870 Nw 45th Ave (33054-5120)
P.O. Box 541487 (33054-1487)
PHONE....................305 687-9031

Mitchell J Robboy, *CEO*
Jeffrey Robboy, *President*
David Crossley, *Natl Sales Mgr*
◆ **EMP:** 20 **EST:** 1920
SQ FT: 40,000
SALES (est): 2.4MM **Privately Held**
WEB: www.bacihospitality.com
SIC: 3645 3646 Residential lighting fixtures; commercial indusl & institutional electric lighting fixtures

(G-11785)
REPUBLIC PACKAGING FLORIDA INC
4570 Nw 128th St (33054-5128)
PHONE....................305 685-5175
Charles Wood, *President*
Tommy Briggs, *Business Mgr*
EMP: 43 **EST:** 1961
SQ FT: 45,000
SALES (est): 9.2MM
SALES (corp-wide): 19.9MM **Privately Held**
WEB: www.repco.com
SIC: 3086 2653 Packaging & shipping materials, foamed plastic; corrugated & solid fiber boxes
PA: Republic Packaging Corp.
9160 S Green St Ste 1
Chicago IL 60620
773 233-6530

(G-11786)
ROYAL PRECISION PRODUCTS INC
13171 Nw 43rd Ave (33054-4424)
PHONE....................305 685-5490
Scott Lettiere, *CEO*
Albert Stoyanov, *President*
Rick Deleon, *Finance Mgr*
Tatiana Viena, *Comptroller*
Laura Alvarado, *Office Mgr*
EMP: 29 **EST:** 1975
SQ FT: 12,000
SALES (est): 4.7MM **Privately Held**
WEB: www.royalprecisionproducts.com
SIC: 3451 Screw machine products

(G-11787)
RYDER WELDING SERVICE INC
350 Ali Baba Ave (33054-3815)
P.O. Box 540796 (33054-0796)
PHONE....................305 685-6630
Joel Gaus, *President*
EMP: 12 **EST:** 1971
SQ FT: 10,000
SALES (est): 1.7MM **Privately Held**
SIC: 3599 7692 3441 Machine shop, jobbing & repair; welding repair; fabricated structural metal

(G-11788)
SOL-A-TROL ALUMINUM PDTS INC
4101 Nw 132nd St (33054-4510)
PHONE....................305 681-2020
Anthony M Soler, *President*
Sammy Delahoz, *CFO*
EMP: 20 **EST:** 2006
SALES (est): 1.3MM **Privately Held**
WEB: www.solatrol.com
SIC: 2431 Windows & window parts & trim, wood; louver windows, glass, wood frame

(G-11789)
ST IVES BURRUPS
13449 Nw 42nd Ave (33054-4513)
PHONE....................305 685-7381
Wayne Angstrom, *CEO*
EMP: 8 **EST:** 2014
SALES (est): 160.1K **Privately Held**
SIC: 2759 Commercial printing

(G-11790)
STAINLESS MARINE INC
13800 Nw 19th Ave (33054-4220)
PHONE....................305 681-7893
Jerry Schmid, *President*
Leticia Romero, *Principal*
Norris Perez, *Admin Sec*
◆ **EMP:** 20 **EST:** 1978
SQ FT: 24,000
SALES (est): 2.9MM **Privately Held**
WEB: www.stainlessmarine.com
SIC: 3429 Marine hardware

(G-11791)
SUPER STONE INC (PA)
1251 Burlington St (33054-3618)
PHONE.....................................305 681-3561
Janine Lutz, *CEO*
◆ **EMP:** 22 **EST:** 1978
SQ FT: 25,500
SALES (est): 5.1MM **Privately Held**
WEB: www.superstone.com
SIC: 2952 Asphalt felts & coatings

(G-11792)
SWIM BUOY
2596 Ali Baba Ave (33054-3138)
PHONE.....................................305 953-4101
Decantillon S Brasington, *Principal*
EMP: 6 **EST:** 2010
SALES (est): 470.4K **Privately Held**
WEB: www.swimbuoy.com
SIC: 3949 Sporting & athletic goods

(G-11793)
TEX Z-E CORP
12815 Nw 45th Ave (33054-5116)
PHONE.....................................305 769-0202
Jorge Zarur, *President*
Edwardo Elias, *Vice Pres*
▲ **EMP:** 5 **EST:** 2002
SQ FT: 42,000
SALES (est): 526.1K **Privately Held**
SIC: 2211 Broadwoven fabric mills, cotton

(G-11794)
TOMMY & GIORDY BUY/SELL
15060 Nw 22nd Ave (33054-2827)
PHONE.....................................786 797-6973
Shananya C Santana, *Principal*
EMP: 7 **EST:** 2013
SALES (est): 113.9K **Privately Held**
SIC: 2631 Cardboard

(G-11795)
TSA REWINDS FLORIDA INC
13050 Nw 47th Ave (33054-4326)
PHONE.....................................305 681-2030
Mike Cean, *President*
EMP: 9 **EST:** 2010
SALES (est): 329.3K **Privately Held**
SIC: 7694 Rewinding services

(G-11796)
TWO SCENTS LLC DBA
VINEVIDA
14935 Nw 27th Ave (33054-3354)
PHONE.....................................888 527-6805
Jake Myara, *President*
EMP: 20 **EST:** 2017
SALES (est): 539.3K **Privately Held**
SIC: 2899 2911 5149 5122 Oils & essential oils; essential oils; aromatic chemical products; flavourings & fragrances; cosmetics, perfumes & hair products

(G-11797)
UNIVERSAL BAKERY LLC
Also Called: Aaron Best Pita
1050 Ali Baba Ave (33054-3610)
PHONE.....................................786 566-3303
Francisco R Lin, *Owner*
EMP: 9 **EST:** 2011
SALES (est): 226.7K **Privately Held**
SIC: 2051 Bakery: wholesale or wholesale/retail combined

(G-11798)
V-LUMBER LLC
15201 Nw 34th Ave (33054-2449)
PHONE.....................................305 510-4458
Antonio P Mannella,
EMP: 15 **EST:** 2017
SALES (est): 1.4MM **Privately Held**
WEB: www.vlumber.com
SIC: 2448 Pallets, wood

(G-11799)
WARBIRD MARINE HOLDINGS
LLC (PA)
4700 Nw 132nd St (33054-4314)
PHONE.....................................844 341-2504
John Dorton, *CEO*
Thomas Wieners, *COO*
Jeff Needles, *CFO*
EMP: 16 **EST:** 2019
SALES (est): 40MM **Privately Held**
SIC: 3732 Boat building & repairing

(G-11800)
WORLD PERFUMES INC
Also Called: Pharmachem
2360 Nw 150th St (33054-2706)
PHONE.....................................305 822-0004
Rios Saul, *President*
Saul Rios, *President*
▲ **EMP:** 15 **EST:** 2001
SQ FT: 8,000
SALES (est): 2.1MM **Privately Held**
WEB: www.worldperfumesus.com
SIC: 2844 2833 Toilet preparations; medicinals & botanicals

(G-11801)
XTREME TOOLS
INTERNATIONAL INC
Also Called: Okay Pure Naturals
15400 Nw 34th Ave (33054-2461)
PHONE.....................................305 622-7474
Ali Mithavayani, *CEO*
Osmani Mithavayan, *Vice Pres*
Mira Mithavayani, *Vice Pres*
◆ **EMP:** 46 **EST:** 2003
SQ FT: 50,000
SALES (est): 5.3MM **Privately Held**
WEB: www.okaypurenaturals.com
SIC: 2844 5961 Hair coloring preparations; cosmetics & perfumes, mail order

(G-11802)
YALE OGRON MFG CO INC (PA)
Also Called: Florida Screen Enterprise
15201 Nw 34th Ave (33054-2449)
PHONE.....................................305 687-0424
Jeffrey Ogron, *President*
Jeffrey D Ogron, *Exec VP*
Sharry Ogron, *Shareholder*
▼ **EMP:** 38 **EST:** 1958
SQ FT: 53,000
SALES (est): 8MM **Privately Held**
SIC: 3442 Screen doors, metal; screens, window, metal; shutters, door or window: metal

(G-11803)
YALE OGRON MFG CO INC
Florida Screen Enterprises
15201 Nw 34th Ave (33054-2449)
PHONE.....................................305 687-0424
Jeffrey Ogron, *General Mgr*
EMP: 25
SQ FT: 45,000
SALES (corp-wide): 8MM **Privately Held**
SIC: 3496 3442 3312 3231 Screening, woven wire: made from purchased wire; metal doors, sash & trim; blast furnaces & steel mills; products of purchased glass; lumber, plywood & millwork
PA: Yale Ogron Manufacturing Company, Inc.
15201 Nw 34th Ave
Opa Locka FL 33054
305 687-0424

Orange City
Volusia County

(G-11804)
COPACO INC
366 E Graves Ave Ste B (32763-5266)
PHONE.....................................407 333-3041
J Stephen Dowd, *President*
Micheal Dowd, *Vice Pres*
EMP: 16 **EST:** 1986
SQ FT: 750
SALES (est): 520.4K **Privately Held**
SIC: 1499 4449 Gypsum & calcite mining; calcite mining; canal & intracoastal freight transportation

(G-11805)
DIXIE SPTIC TANK ORANGE CY
LLC
1200 S Leavitt Ave (32763-7114)
PHONE.....................................386 775-3051
Eugene M Evans, *President*
EMP: 25 **EST:** 1969
SQ FT: 1,200
SALES (est): 1MM **Privately Held**
SIC: 3272 1711 4953 3084 Septic tanks, concrete; septic system construction; refuse systems; plastics pipe

(G-11806)
LR PRINTING LLC
1060 E Industrial Dr L (32763-7112)
PHONE.....................................407 558-0543
Stan Rohr, *Mng Member*
EMP: 6 **EST:** 2014
SALES (est): 387.4K **Privately Held**
WEB: www.lr-printing.com
SIC: 2759 Screen printing

(G-11807)
MRM CREATIVE LLC
Also Called: Bizcard Xpress
1209 Saxon Blvd Ste 4 (32763-8402)
PHONE.....................................386 218-5940
Michael W Weber, *Principal*
EMP: 8 **EST:** 2014
SALES (est): 374.6K **Privately Held**
WEB: www.mrm.com
SIC: 2752 Commercial printing, lithographic

(G-11808)
PALLET EXCHANGE INC
1219 Doris St (32763-8813)
PHONE.....................................386 734-0133
EMP: 10
SQ FT: 1,900
SALES (est): 1.1MM **Privately Held**
SIC: 2448 Mfg Wood Pallets/Skids

(G-11809)
SHENK ENTERPRISES LLC
985 Harley Strcklnd Blvd (32763-7980)
PHONE.....................................386 753-1959
EMP: 12
SQ FT: 2,100
SALES (est): 1.3MM **Privately Held**
SIC: 3845 Mfg Electromedical Equipment

(G-11810)
SUPERIOR SHEDS INC (PA)
Also Called: Sheds Plus Miami
2323 S Volusia Ave (32763-7615)
PHONE.....................................386 774-9861
Alex Martens, *President*
David N Sexton, *Vice Pres*
Bill Zile, *Transptn Dir*
Jorge Gaitan, *Manager*
Raquel Gibson, *Administration*
EMP: 27 **EST:** 1994
SQ FT: 10,000
SALES (est): 13.4MM **Privately Held**
WEB: www.superiorsheds.com
SIC: 3448 Buildings, portable: prefabricated metal

Orange Park
Clay County

(G-11811)
ADVANCED PROSTHETICS
AMER INC
Also Called: Hanger Clinic
4611 Us Highway 17 Ste 4 (32003-8248)
PHONE.....................................904 269-4993
Sam Liang, *President*
Vinit Asar, *Principal*
Thomas Kirk PHD, *Branch Mgr*
EMP: 18
SALES (corp-wide): 1.1B **Publicly Held**
SIC: 3841 8011 Surgical & medical instruments; specialized medical practitioners, except internal
HQ: Advanced Prosthetics Of America, Inc.
601 Mount Homer Rd
Eustis FL 32726
352 383-0396

(G-11812)
AERO-HOSE CORP
1845 Town Center Blvd # 140
(32003-4300)
PHONE.....................................904 215-9638
Joseph Lemieux, *President*
Lin Dixson, *Sales Staff*
Tom Carmody, *Marketing Staff*
EMP: 15 **EST:** 2004
SQ FT: 5,500
SALES (est): 12MM
SALES (corp-wide): 354.6B **Publicly**
Held
WEB: www.aero-hose.com
SIC: 3728 Aircraft parts & equipment
HQ: Marmon Distribution Services, Inc.
225 E Cunningham St
Butler PA 16001

(G-11813)
AERO-NEWS NETWORK INC
1335 Kingsley Ave # 831 (32067-7819)
PHONE.....................................863 299-8680
James Campbell, *CEO*
EMP: 9 **EST:** 2002
SALES (est): 253.2K **Privately Held**
WEB: www.aero-news.net
SIC: 2741

(G-11814)
AMERICAN VLY AVNICS
CLBRTION L ✪
Also Called: Avacs
137 Industrial Loop W (32073-2859)
PHONE.....................................904 644-8630
Stephen Carlo, *Mng Member*
EMP: 10 **EST:** 2021
SALES (est): 707K **Privately Held**
SIC: 3728 Aircraft parts & equipment

(G-11815)
BANNERS-N-SIGNS ETC INC
Also Called: Banners & Signs
1970 Solomon St (32073-4735)
PHONE.....................................904 272-3395
Bobby Hartley, *President*
Louis Hartley, *Vice Pres*
EMP: 6 **EST:** 1994
SALES (est): 963.9K **Privately Held**
WEB: www.bnsigns.com
SIC: 3993 Signs, not made in custom sign painting shops

(G-11816)
BRIDGESTONE HOSEPOWER
LLC (HQ)
50 Industrial Loop N (32073-6258)
PHONE.....................................904 264-1267
J Palmer Clarkson, *CEO*
Pat Terranova, *General Mgr*
Troy Osborne, *Regional Mgr*
Larry Sparkman, *District Mgr*
Todd Jorgensen, *Vice Pres*
◆ **EMP:** 100 **EST:** 1990
SQ FT: 135,000
SALES (est): 170.1MM **Privately Held**
WEB: www.hosepower.com
SIC: 3542 5085 Crimping machinery, metal; pistons & valves

(G-11817)
CEMEX CEMENT INC
340 Corporate Way Ste 100 (32073-2851)
PHONE.....................................904 296-2400
Charlie Buotman, *Branch Mgr*
EMP: 162 **Privately Held**
WEB: www.cemexusa.com
SIC: 3273 Ready-mixed concrete
HQ: Cemex Cement, Inc.
10100 Katy Fwy Ste 300
Houston TX 77043
713 650-6200

(G-11818)
CEMEX CNSTR MTLS FLA LLC
Also Called: Jacksnvlle Ornge Pk Rdymx Con
4807 Collins Rd (32073)
PHONE.....................................800 992-3639
Calvin Tucker, *Mfg Staff*
Martin Steele, *Branch Mgr*
Brian Leslie, *Manager*
EMP: 14
SQ FT: 8,800 **Privately Held**
SIC: 3273 Ready-mixed concrete
HQ: Cemex Construction Materials Florida, Llc
1501 Belvedere Rd
West Palm Beach FL 33406

(G-11819)
CEMEX CNSTR MTLS FLA LLC
Also Called: Materials Div-Jacksonville ADM
340 Corporate Way Ste 100 (32073-2851)
PHONE.....................................904 213-8860
Ryan Chandley, *Branch Mgr*
EMP: 10 **Privately Held**

▲ = Import ▼=Export
◆ =Import/Export

SIC: 3273 Ready-mixed concrete
HQ: Cemex Construction Materials Florida, Llc
1501 Belvedere Rd
West Palm Beach FL 33406

(G-11820)
CINEGA CSTM FRMNG & DESIGN INC
3513 Pebble Stone Ct (32065-4227)
PHONE....................904 686-5654
Juan Cienega, *Principal*
EMP: 26
SALES (corp-wide): 222.5K Privately Held
SIC: 2499 Picture frame molding, finished
PA: Cinega Custom Framing And Design, Inc.
490 Hillside Dr
Orange Park FL 32073
904 495-1846

(G-11821)
CROWS NEST INDUSTRIES INC
2708 Lexington Dr (32073-7237)
PHONE....................740 466-2926
Glenn Minney, *Principal*
EMP: 9 EST: 2017
SALES (est): 58.6K Privately Held
WEB: www.crowsnest-venice.com
SIC: 3999 Manufacturing industries

(G-11822)
CUSTOM GRAPHICS & SIGN DESIGN
99 Industrial Loop N (32073-2849)
PHONE....................904 264-7667
Marvin Thole, *President*
Pat Thole, *Vice Pres*
EMP: 8 EST: 1988
SALES (est): 1.3MM Privately Held
WEB: www.cgsigns.net
SIC: 3993 Electric signs; neon signs

(G-11823)
DOCTOR EASY MEDICAL PDTS LLC
1029 Blanding Blvd # 701 (32065-7753)
P.O. Box 1717 (32067-1717)
PHONE....................904 276-7200
Marsha Garcia, *President*
Sterling E Price, *Vice Pres*
Charlene Reilly, *Sales Mgr*
Emily Garcia, *Director*
EMP: 8 EST: 1993
SQ FT: 1,500
SALES (est): 5MM Privately Held
WEB: www.doctor-easy.com
SIC: 3841 Surgical & medical instruments

(G-11824)
DOVER CYLINDER HEAD OF JACKSON
80 Industrial Loop N A (32073-6263)
EMP: 10
SQ FT: 5,000
SALES: 610.2K Privately Held
SIC: 3714 Rebuilds Cylinder Heads For Engines

(G-11825)
DUVAL BAKERY PRODUCTS INC
985 Cobblestone Dr (32065-5807)
PHONE....................904 354-7878
Robert Gorsuch, *President*
Richard Mc Cullough, *Corp Secy*
EMP: 5 EST: 1972
SALES (est): 415K Privately Held
SIC: 2051 Bread, cake & related products

(G-11826)
EYES MED BILLING & CONSULTING
785 Oaklf Plntn Pkwy (32065-3533)
PHONE....................618 308-7016
Evelyn Rivera, *Principal*
EMP: 6 EST: 2014
SALES (est): 336.9K Privately Held
SIC: 3999 Candles

(G-11827)
FAIRING XCHANGE LLC
144 Industrial Loop E (32073-6281)
PHONE....................904 589-5253
EMP: 7 EST: 2016
SALES (est): 223.4K Privately Held
WEB: www.thefairingxchange.com
SIC: 2821 Plastics materials & resins

(G-11828)
FIREBIRD SCRUBS AND MORE LLC
805 Glendale Ln (32065-5631)
PHONE....................904 258-7514
Judith Phoenix, *CEO*
EMP: 9 EST: 2020
SALES (est): 505.6K Privately Held
WEB: www.firebirdscrubs.com
SIC: 2211 Scrub cloths

(G-11829)
FIRST AMERICA PRODUCTS
153 Industrial Loop S (32073-6259)
PHONE....................904 683-1253
Garfield West, *Principal*
EMP: 10 EST: 2015
SALES (est): 999.2K Privately Held
WEB: www.firstamericaproducts.com
SIC: 3585 Air conditioning units, complete: domestic or industrial

(G-11830)
FIRST COAST PAVERS CORP
204 Blairmore Blvd (32073-4319)
PHONE....................904 410-0278
Jason Dugger, *President*
EMP: 15 EST: 2010
SALES (est): 973.6K Privately Held
SIC: 3531 Pavers

(G-11831)
HAWKHEAD INTERNATIONAL INC
90 Industrial Loop N (32073-6258)
PHONE....................904 264-4295
Russell Ross, *President*
Cheryll Ross, *Vice Pres*
EMP: 8 EST: 1983
SQ FT: 10,000
SALES (est): 942K Privately Held
WEB: www.hatcheryequipment.com
SIC: 3523 5083 Incubators & brooders, farm; poultry equipment

(G-11832)
L3 TECHNOLOGIES INC
208 Industrial Loop S (32073-2858)
PHONE....................904 269-5026
EMP: 7
SALES (corp-wide): 17.8B Publicly Held
WEB: www.l3harris.com
SIC: 3663 4899 3812 3721 Telemetering equipment, electronic; data communication services; aircraft/aerospace flight instruments & guidance systems; aircraft
HQ: L3 Technologies, Inc.
600 3rd Ave Fl 34
New York NY 10016
321 727-9100

(G-11833)
LLOYD INDUSTRIES INC
138 Industrial Loop W (32073-6221)
PHONE....................904 541-1655
William Lloyd, *President*
EMP: 66 EST: 2004
SQ FT: 55,000
SALES (est): 3.7MM
SALES (corp-wide): 13.5MM Privately Held
SIC: 3444 5084 5051 Sheet metalwork; metalworking machinery; metals service centers & offices
PA: Lloyd Industries, Inc.
231 Commerce Dr
Montgomeryville PA 18936
215 367-5863

(G-11834)
MOBILE MINI INC
2850 Country Club Blvd (32073-5728)
PHONE....................866 344-4092
EMP: 7 EST: 2016
SALES (est): 90.8K Privately Held
WEB: www.mobilemini.com
SIC: 3448 Buildings, portable: prefabricated metal

(G-11835)
OLD KENTUCKY LEATHER WORKS INC
Also Called: Kentucky Leatherworks
1532 Arena Rd (32003-7728)
PHONE....................904 269-1369
Edward W Walker, *President*
Amparo S Walker, *Vice Pres*
EMP: 5 EST: 1992
SQ FT: 1,200
SALES (est): 324.4K Privately Held
SIC: 3199 Dog furnishings: collars, leashes, muzzles, etc.: leather

(G-11836)
ORANGE PARK MACHINE INC
84 Industrial Loop N (32073-6258)
PHONE....................904 269-1935
Keith F Stoudenmire, *President*
J Palmer Clarkson, *Owner*
Eben Barnes, *Opers Mgr*
▲ EMP: 29 EST: 1994
SALES (est): 3MM Privately Held
WEB: www.orangeparkmachine.com
SIC: 3599 Machine shop, jobbing & repair

(G-11837)
PIN-N-WIN WRESTLING CLUB INC
117 Suzanne Ave (32073-6425)
PHONE....................904 276-8038
Christopher L McNealy, *President*
EMP: 7 EST: 2011
SALES (est): 138.7K Privately Held
WEB: www.pin-n-winwrestling.com
SIC: 3452 Pins

(G-11838)
POWDERTECH PLUS INC
98 Industrial Loop N (32073-6279)
PHONE....................904 269-1719
Richard Pittman, *President*
Dawn Pittman, *Vice Pres*
EMP: 6 EST: 2007
SALES (est): 558.6K Privately Held
WEB: www.powdertechplus.com
SIC: 3479 Coating of metals & formed products

(G-11839)
SCIENCE OF WATER LLC
1177 Park Ave Ste 5 (32073-4150)
PHONE....................904 654-0778
Jack Stoudenmire, *Manager*
EMP: 6 EST: 2018
SALES (est): 647.2K Privately Held
WEB: www.thescienceofwater.com
SIC: 3589 Sewage & water treatment equipment

(G-11840)
SIGMA PRESS INC
Also Called: Sigma Marketing
1543 Kingsley Ave Ste 7 (32073-4583)
PHONE....................904 264-6006
Michael J Sapit, *President*
Deena Lauderdale-Berry, *Vice Pres*
Sherry Dehner, *Marketing Staff*
Donald Sapit, *Shareholder*
EMP: 15 EST: 1963
SQ FT: 5,500
SALES: 3MM Privately Held
WEB: www.sigmacalendars.com
SIC: 2741 Miscellaneous publishing

(G-11841)
SIGNINGORDERCOM LLC
410-10 Blnding Blvd Ste 1 (32073)
PHONE....................904 300-0104
Kristofer C Killinger, *Mng Member*
EMP: 50 EST: 2010
SALES (est): 1MM Privately Held
WEB: www.directclosers.com
SIC: 7372 Business oriented computer software

(G-11842)
STRONGBRIDGE INTERNATIONAL LLC
154 Industrial Loop S (32073-2858)
P.O. Box 58177, Jacksonville (32241-8177)
PHONE....................904 278-7499
Sandra P Cote, *President*
Andre B Cote, *Vice Pres*
▲ EMP: 50 EST: 2006
SALES (est): 5.3MM Privately Held
WEB: www.strongbridge.us
SIC: 3498 Fabricated pipe & fittings

(G-11843)
SUN STATE SYSTEMS INC
140 Industrial Loop W (32073-6221)
PHONE....................904 269-2544
Gary Armbruster, *President*
Michael Anthony Rhodes, *Vice Pres*
Harry Golob, *Engineer*
Sami Aji, *Enginr/R&D Asst*
Julie Rhodes, *Human Resources*
EMP: 11 EST: 1991
SQ FT: 8,000
SALES (est): 2.4MM Privately Held
WEB: www.sunstatesystems.com
SIC: 3625 Control equipment, electric

(G-11844)
TUCKER LITHOGRAPHIC CO
661 Blanding Blvd Ste 103 (32073-5066)
PHONE....................904 276-0568
Eliot P Tucker, *Principal*
EMP: 8 EST: 2008
SALES (est): 95.7K Privately Held
WEB: www.tuckerlithographic.com
SIC: 2752 Commercial printing, lithographic

(G-11845)
VISION MANUFACTURING TECH INC
Also Called: Vision Mt
137 Industrial Loop W (32073-2859)
PHONE....................904 579-5272
Stephen J Carlo, *President*
Lisa Machel, *President*
EMP: 30 EST: 2018
SALES (est): 4.1MM Privately Held
SIC: 3728 Aircraft parts & equipment

(G-11846)
VOLPINO CORP
1551 Pine Hammock Trl (32003-7214)
PHONE....................904 264-8808
Fabrizio Volpino, *President*
▲ EMP: 11 EST: 2005
SALES (est): 220.2K Privately Held
WEB: www.volpino.com
SIC: 3423 Jewelers' hand tools

(G-11847)
ZILLA INC
Also Called: First Coast Continuous Forms
4265 Eldridge Loop (32073-3023)
PHONE....................904 610-1436
Charles Zilla, *President*
EMP: 10 EST: 1984
SQ FT: 10,000
SALES (est): 912.5K Privately Held
SIC: 2761 Continuous forms, office & business

Orlando
Orange County

(G-11848)
0ENERGY LIGHTING INC
1110 Sligh Blvd (32806-1031)
PHONE....................855 955-1055
EMP: 15
SALES (est): 1.7MM
SALES (corp-wide): 29.8MM Privately Held
SIC: 3648 Mfg Lighting Equipment
PA: Bulbtronics Inc.
45 Banfi Plz N
Farmingdale NY 11735
631 249-2272

(G-11849)
3 MIRACLES CORPORATION
Also Called: 3miracles
6843 Conway Rd Ste 120　(32812-3605)
PHONE....................................407 796-9292
Daniela Schiming Silva, *CEO*
John Schiming, *Principal*
EMP: 9 **EST:** 2018
SALES (est): 1.6MM　**Privately Held**
SIC: 2821　Plastics materials & resins
PA: Schiming Promocao De Vendas E
　　Transportes Eireli
　　Av. Rudolf Dafferner 400
　　Sorocaba SP

(G-11850)
3D PERCEPTION　INC
12605 Challenger Pkwy # 1　(32826-2711)
PHONE....................................321 235-7999
Anders Fagerhaug, *COO*
Adam McCard, *Vice Pres*
Brianna Boswell, *Project Mgr*
Jason Harmon, *Project Mgr*
Ahmed Mubaraka, *Project Mgr*
▲ **EMP:** 10 **EST:** 2002
SQ FT: 5,500
SALES (est): 3.1MM　**Privately Held**
WEB: www.3d-perception.com
SIC: 3861　8711　7629　8249　Projectors,
　still or motion picture, silent or sound; en-
　gineering services; electrical equipment
　repair services; aviation school; visual ef-
　fects production
PA: 3d Perception As
　　Nye Vakas Vei 14
　　Hvalstad　1395

(G-11851)
3DFX INC
279 N Texas Ave　(32805-1231)
PHONE....................................407 237-6249
Wayne Sargeant, *President*
Mark Lamm, *President*
▲ **EMP:** 10 **EST:** 2000
SQ FT: 40,000
SALES (est): 1MM　**Privately Held**
SIC: 3599　3993　3441　5199　Amusement
　park equipment; signs & advertising spe-
　cialties; fabricated structural metal; statu-
　ary; theme park, amusement; tourist
　attractions, amusement park concessions
　& rides

(G-11852)
4 POWER INTERNATIONAL
STONES
2704 Hazelhurst Ave　(32804-2718)
PHONE....................................407 286-4677
Sharif Abu Snaineh, *President*
EMP: 7 **EST:** 2016
SQ FT: 25,000
SALES (est): 660.2K　**Privately Held**
SIC: 1499　Gem stones (natural) mining

(G-11853)
4EVER MUSIC LLC
8201 Holmstrom Way　(32827-7874)
PHONE....................................407 490-0977
Jamar West, *Manager*
EMP: 27 **EST:** 2019
SALES (est): 1MM　**Privately Held**
SIC: 2731　Book music: publishing & print-
　ing

(G-11854)
5DT INC
12249 Science Dr Ste 135　(32826-2905)
PHONE....................................407 734-5377
Paul Olckers, *CEO*
Dennis Mayo, *General Mgr*
Jared Baer, *COO*
Ana Vela, *Research*
Frikkie Klopper, *Manager*
EMP: 25 **EST:** 1998
SQ FT: 3,000
SALES (est): 1.2MM　**Privately Held**
WEB: www.5dt.com
SIC: 3699　7373　Flight simulators (training
　aids); electronic; automotive driving simu-
　lators (training aids), electronic; systems
　software development services; value-
　added resellers, computer systems

(G-11855)
7 UP SNAPPLE SOUTHEAST
1181 Tradeport Dr　(32824-6823)
PHONE....................................407 839-1706
EMP: 8 **EST:** 2009
SALES (est): 145.9K　**Privately Held**
SIC: 2086　Soft drinks: packaged in cans,
　bottles, etc.

(G-11856)
A & A ELECTRIC MTRS & PUMP
SVC
1320 W Central Blvd　(32805-1708)
PHONE....................................407 843-5005
Andy K Maraj, *President*
▲ **EMP:** 6 **EST:** 1999
SQ FT: 2,500
SALES (est): 817.3K　**Privately Held**
WEB: www.aaelectricmotors.com
SIC: 7694　Electric motor repair

(G-11857)
A & L SEPTIC TANK PRODUCTS
INC
9304 E Colonial Dr　(32817-4130)
P.O. Box 677878　(32867-7878)
PHONE....................................407 273-2149
Roger Anderson, *President*
Patricia Anderson, *Corp Secy*
EMP: 6 **EST:** 1984
SQ FT: 5,000
SALES (est): 896.5K　**Privately Held**
WEB: www.alsepticfl.com
SIC: 3272　7699　Septic tanks, concrete;
　septic tank cleaning service

(G-11858)
A-1 BLOCK CORPORATION
1617 S Division Ave　(32805-4797)
PHONE....................................407 422-3768
Adam Freeman, *President*
Gail Freeman, *Corp Secy*
John Freeman, *Vice Pres*
Gary Seremet, *Sales Staff*
EMP: 44 **EST:** 1952
SQ FT: 1,600
SALES (est): 18MM　**Privately Held**
WEB: www.a1block.com
SIC: 3271　5032　Blocks, concrete or cin-
　der: standard; brick, stone & related ma-
　terial

(G-11859)
ABBOTT LABS US SBSDRIES
ALERE (HQ)
Also Called: Abbott Rapid Dx North Amer LLC
30 S Keller Rd Ste 100　(32810-6297)
PHONE....................................877 441-7440
John Yonkin, *President*
Jon Russell, *Corp Secy*
Cory Courtney, *Exec VP*
▲ **EMP:** 93 **EST:** 2007
SALES (est): 48.1MM
SALES (corp-wide): 43B　**Publicly Held**
SIC: 3841　Surgical & medical instruments
PA: Abbott Laboratories
　　100 Abbott Park Rd
　　Abbott Park IL 60064
　　224 667-6100

(G-11860)
ABBOTT RAPID DIAGNOSTICS
30 S Keller Rd Ste 100　(32810-6297)
PHONE....................................877 441-7440
EMP: 6
SALES (est): 335.1K　**Privately Held**
SIC: 3841　Diagnostic apparatus, medical

(G-11861)
ABBOTT RAPID DX NORTH
AMER LLC
Also Called: Abbott Rapid Diagnostics
30 S Keller Rd Ste 100　(32810-6297)
PHONE....................................877 441-7440
EMP: 12 **EST:** 2007
SALES (est): 86.6K　**Privately Held**
SIC: 3841　Diagnostic apparatus, medical

(G-11862)
ABSEN INC (HQ)
7120 Lake Ellenor Dr　(32809-5721)
PHONE....................................407 203-8870
Yonghong Ren, *CEO*
Chunlin Liu, *President*
Steven Tian, *Engineer*

Shengkai Hsu, *Finance Mgr*
Scott Hsu, *Finance*
▲ **EMP:** 14 **EST:** 2012
SQ FT: 6,000
SALES (est): 13.2MM　**Privately Held**
WEB: www.usabsen.com
SIC: 3674　Light emitting diodes

(G-11863)
AC SIGNS　LLC
Also Called: Decamil
11100 Astronaut Blvd　(32837-9202)
PHONE....................................407 857-5565
Angela Martinez, *Project Mgr*
Alvaro Chica,
Armando Chica,
EMP: 25 **EST:** 2005
SALES (est): 3.9MM　**Privately Held**
WEB: www.acsigns.com
SIC: 3993　Signs, not made in custom sign
　painting shops

(G-11864)
ACADEMY PUBLISHING　INC
Also Called: School New Letter Program
210 S Semoran Blvd　(32807-3802)
PHONE....................................407 736-0100
Christopher Kircher, *CEO*
Rebecca Rivera, *Technology*
Chris Dodgion, *Graphic Designe*
Amanda Horta, *Graphic Designe*
Sylvia Oberlin, *Graphic Designe*
EMP: 20 **EST:** 1992
SQ FT: 3,000
SALES (est): 2.6MM　**Privately Held**
WEB: www.academypublishing.com
SIC: 2759　2721　Commercial printing; peri-
　odicals

(G-11865)
ACCOUNTING & COMPUTER
SYSTEMS
810 Alameda St　(32804-7203)
PHONE....................................407 353-1570
Jackelyn Smith, *Principal*
EMP: 5 **EST:** 1988
SALES (est): 366.9K　**Privately Held**
SIC: 7372　Prepackaged software

(G-11866)
ACE
CONSTRUCTION
MANAGEMENT
801 N Pine Hills Rd　(32808-7209)
PHONE....................................407 704-7803
Jaja Wade, *CEO*
EMP: 7 **EST:** 2019
SALES (est): 256.9K　**Privately Held**
WEB:
www.aceconstructionmanagement.com
SIC: 3449　Miscellaneous metalwork

(G-11867)
ADDISON HVAC LLC
7050 Overland Rd　(32810-3404)
PHONE....................................407 292-4400
Bill Young, *Buyer*
Bryan Armocida, *Engineer*
Gus Olivera, *Engineer*
Charles Brown, *Mng Member*
Leon Folts, *Technician*
▼ **EMP:** 120 **EST:** 2008
SALES (est): 29.3MM
SALES (corp-wide): 2.9B　**Privately Held**
WEB: www.addison-hvac.com
SIC: 3585　Heating & air conditioning com-
　bination units
HQ: Roberts-Gordon Llc
　　1250 William St
　　Buffalo NY 14206
　　716 852-4400

(G-11868)
ADIDAS NORTH AMERICA　INC
Also Called: Adidas Outlet Store Orlando
8200 Vineland Ave Ste 350　(32821-6824)
PHONE....................................321 677-0078
Fred GM, *Branch Mgr*
EMP: 19
SALES (corp-wide): 24B　**Privately Held**
SIC: 2329　Athletic (warmup, sweat & jog-
　ging) suits: men's & boys'; men's & boys'
　athletic uniforms; knickers, dress (sepa-
　rate): men's & boys'

HQ: Adidas North America, Inc.
　　3449 N Anchor St Ste 500
　　Portland OR 97217
　　971 234-2300

(G-11869)
ADRIANO GB BRICK PAVERS
LLC
9851 Cypress Park Dr　(32824-8405)
PHONE....................................407 497-1517
Adriano F De Oliveira, *Principal*
EMP: 8 **EST:** 2012
SALES (est): 485.5K　**Privately Held**
SIC: 3531　Pavers

(G-11870)
ADVANCED MICRO DEVICES
INC
3501 Quadrangle Blvd # 375　(32817-8330)
PHONE....................................407 541-6800
Trenton Tuggle, *Engineer*
Dave Erskine, *Branch Mgr*
Mike Mantor, *Fellow*
EMP: 15
SALES (corp-wide): 16.4B　**Publicly Held**
WEB: ir.amd.com
SIC: 3674　Integrated circuits, semiconduc-
　tor networks, etc.
PA: Advanced Micro Devices, Inc.
　　2485 Augustine Dr
　　Santa Clara CA 95054
　　408 749-4000

(G-11871)
ADVANCED MILLWORK　INC
2645 Regent Ave　(32804-3337)
PHONE....................................407 294-1927
Garry Filger, *President*
Justin Olivier, *Superintendent*
JP Jeanpaul Negron, *COO*
Shea L Figler, *Vice Pres*
Camilo Saravia, *Project Mgr*
▲ **EMP:** 35 **EST:** 1992
SQ FT: 32,862
SALES (est): 7.4MM　**Privately Held**
WEB: www.advancedmillwork.net
SIC: 2431　Millwork

(G-11872)
ADVANCED XRGRPHICS IMGING
SYST
Also Called: Axis
6851 Tpc Dr Ofc Ofc　(32822-5141)
PHONE....................................407 351-0232
David R Salazar, *President*
Teresa Salazar, *Corp Secy*
Claudia Alexander, *Controller*
EMP: 48 **EST:** 1991
SQ FT: 45,840
SALES (est): 5.4MM　**Privately Held**
SIC: 2759　7331　7374　Laser printing; mail-
　ing service: data processing service

(G-11873)
ADVANTAGECARE　INC
Also Called: Consultant - Med Rview Offcer
7081 Grand National Dr # 113
(32819-8385)
PHONE....................................407 345-8877
William Brooks, *President*
Kimberly Rivera, *Office Mgr*
EMP: 5 **EST:** 1990
SALES (est): 865.4K　**Privately Held**
WEB: www.advcare.com
SIC: 2899　8099　8742　; medical services
　organization; management consulting
　services

(G-11874)
ADVANTOR SYSTEMS
CORPORATION
12612 Challenger Pkwy # 3　(32826-2759)
PHONE....................................407 859-3350
Richard Clifton, *CEO*
Jeffrey Whirley, *President*
Grant Herring, *Vice Pres*
Mike Ollivier, *Vice Pres*
Kurt Kuenn, *Project Mgr*
EMP: 150 **EST:** 1997
SALES (est): 33.5MM
SALES (corp-wide): 1.7B　**Publicly Held**
WEB: www.advantor.com
SIC: 3669　Emergency alarms

▲ = Import　▼=Export
◆ =Import/Export

PA: V2x, Inc.
2424 Grdn Of The Gods Rd
Colorado Springs CO 80919
719 591-3600

(G-11875)
ADVENTUROUS
ENTERTAINMENT LLC
6424 Milner Blvd 4 (32809-6670)
PHONE..................................407 483-4057
Victor Romero, *Mng Member*
EMP: 13 EST: 2016
SQ FT: 7,013
SALES (est): 100K Privately Held
WEB: www.adenter.io
SIC: 7372 Prepackaged software

(G-11876)
AERO-TEL WIRE HARNESS
CORP
Also Called: Arvin's Engineered Solutions
4650 Old Winter Garden Rd (32811-1760)
PHONE..................................407 445-1722
Antoine J Donatto, *President*
Nikki Ray, *Admin Asst*
EMP: 20 EST: 1999
SALES (est): 5.8MM Privately Held
WEB: www.aerotelwireharness.com
SIC: 3699 Electrical equipment & supplies

(G-11877)
AEROJET RCKTDYNE CLMAN
ARSPC I
7675 Municipal Dr (32819-8930)
PHONE..................................407 354-0047
Tyler Evans, *President*
Brendan King, *Principal*
James S Simpson, *Principal*
Arjun L Kampani, *Vice Pres*
Julie Beechy, *Production*
EMP: 99 EST: 2017
SQ FT: 80,000
SALES (est): 12.8MM
SALES (corp-wide): 2.1B Publicly Held
WEB: www.rocket.com
SIC: 3812 Defense systems & equipment
PA: Aerojet Rocketdyne Holdings, Inc.
222 N Pcf Cast Hwy Ste 50
El Segundo CA 90245
310 252-8100

(G-11878)
AGRI MACHINERY & PARTS INC
Also Called: A M P
3489 All American Blvd (32810-4722)
PHONE..................................407 299-1592
Gillian Dobes, *President*
Mark S Dobes, *Vice Pres*
▼ EMP: 18 EST: 1976
SQ FT: 25,000
SALES (est): 5.5MM Privately Held
WEB: www.ouramp.com
SIC: 3523 3535 Farm machinery & equipment; conveyors & conveying equipment

(G-11879)
AIR DUCT SYSTEMS INC
2106 W Central Blvd (32805-2131)
P.O. Box 770038 (32877-0038)
PHONE..................................407 839-3313
EMP: 12 EST: 2018
SALES (est): 1MM Privately Held
WEB: www.airductsystemsinc.com
SIC: 3441 Fabricated structural metal

(G-11880)
AIR LIQUIDE AMERICA LP
6675 W Wood Blvd Ste 330 (32821-6015)
PHONE..................................407 855-8286
Dan Pund, *Manager*
EMP: 22
SQ FT: 25,090
SALES (corp-wide): 109.4MM Privately
Held
WEB: industry.airliquide.us
SIC: 2813 Industrial gases
HQ: Air Liquide America L.P.
9811 Katy Fwy Ste 100
Houston TX 77024
713 624-8000

(G-11881)
AIR PRODUCTS AND
CHEMICALS INC
8300 Exchange Dr (32809-7652)
PHONE..................................407 859-5141
Mark Evans, *Plant Mgr*
Christopher Barly, *Manager*
EMP: 15
SQ FT: 13,690
SALES (corp-wide): 10.3B Publicly Held
WEB: www.airproducts.com
SIC: 2813 5169 Industrial gases; industrial gases
PA: Air Products And Chemicals, Inc.
1940 Air Products Blvd
Allentown PA 18106
610 481-4911

(G-11882)
AIR-FLITE CONTAINERS INC
2699 N Forsyth Rd Ste 101 (32807-6497)
PHONE..................................407 679-1200
Kevin E McDonald, *President*
Mark Prince, *General Mgr*
▼ EMP: 7 EST: 1973
SQ FT: 16,000
SALES (est): 746K Privately Held
WEB: www.air-flite.com
SIC: 2441 2653 Nailed wood boxes & shook; boxes, corrugated: made from purchased materials

(G-11883)
AIRCRAFT ENGRG INSTLLTION
SVCS
101 W Landstreet Rd (32824-7820)
PHONE..................................407 438-4436
John R Corthell, *President*
Maria Burgos, *General Mgr*
Amber Cenci, *Purchasing*
Rafael Rivera, *Supervisor*
EMP: 20 EST: 1993
SQ FT: 28,000
SALES (est): 5.3MM Privately Held
WEB: www.aei.aero
SIC: 3728 Aircraft parts & equipment

(G-11884)
AIRGAS USA LLC
Also Called: Airgas Puritan Medical
3100 Silver Star Rd (32808-4616)
PHONE..................................407 293-6630
Daniel Murray, *Branch Mgr*
EMP: 9
SALES (corp-wide): 109.4MM Privately
Held
WEB: www.airgas.com
SIC: 2813 5984 5169 Oxygen, compressed or liquefied; propane gas, bottled; industrial gases
HQ: Airgas Usa, Llc
259 N Radnor Chester Rd
Radnor PA 19087
216 642-6600

(G-11885)
AIRSTAR AMERICA INC (HQ)
Also Called: Airstar Orlando
9603 Satellite Blvd # 150 (32837-8476)
PHONE..................................407 851-7830
Pierre Chabert, *President*
Michael Cross, *Opers Mgr*
Yan Rigoulot, *Prdtn Mgr*
Dean Pritchard, *Treasurer*
Kristine Maguire, *Accounting Mgr*
▲ EMP: 15 EST: 1998
SQ FT: 20,000
SALES (est): 9.3MM Privately Held
WEB: www.airstar-light.us
SIC: 3648 7359 Outdoor lighting equipment; sound & lighting equipment rental

(G-11886)
ALCEE INDUSTRIES INC
Also Called: Beach King
1701 Acme St 32805 (32805-3603)
PHONE..................................407 468-4573
Ashwin A Mehta, *Director*
J A Mehta, *Director*
▲ EMP: 11 EST: 1999
SQ FT: 48,000
SALES (est): 277.9K Privately Held
SIC: 2211 Towels & toweling, cotton

(G-11887)
ALCOHOL CNTRMASURE
SYSTEMS INC
Also Called: Alcolock USA
5776 Hoffner Ave Ste 303 (32822-4810)
PHONE..................................407 207-3337
Felix Comeau, *President*
Adam Comeau, *Exec VP*
Felix Adam Comeau, *Vice Pres*
Abe Verghis, *Engineer*
Wendy Wilburn, *Comms Mgr*
EMP: 110 EST: 1976
SALES (est): 7.1MM Privately Held
WEB: www.alcolock.net
SIC: 3829 Breathalyzers

(G-11888)
ALCOLOCK FL INC
5776 Hoffner Ave Ste 303 (32822-4810)
PHONE..................................407 207-3337
Felix J E Comeau, *President*
Adam Comeau, *Exec VP*
▲ EMP: 8 EST: 2003
SALES (est): 651.9K Privately Held
SIC: 3694 Ignition apparatus & distributors

(G-11889)
ALEAVIA BRANDS LLC
3025 Middlesex Rd (32803-1128)
PHONE..................................407 289-2632
Douglas J Graham, *President*
EMP: 6 EST: 2016
SALES (est): 310.6K Privately Held
WEB: www.aleavia.com
SIC: 2844 Toilet preparations

(G-11890)
ALGOMA HARDWOODS INC
7630 Currency Dr (32809-6925)
PHONE..................................865 471-6300
Libby Trivett, *Manager*
EMP: 40
SALES (corp-wide): 2.6B Publicly Held
WEB: architectural.masonite.com
SIC: 2431 Doors, wood
HQ: Algoma Hardwoods, Inc.
1001 Perry St
Algoma WI 54201
920 487-5221

(G-11891)
ALL STATE PALLETS COMPANY
LLC
9801 Recycle Center Rd (32824-8151)
PHONE..................................407 855-8087
Kyle Zuchowski,
EMP: 14 EST: 1998
SALES (est): 520.6K Privately Held
WEB: www.allstatepallets.com
SIC: 2448 Pallets, wood

(G-11892)
ALLAN INDUSTRIES
1901 Summit Tower Blvd (32810-5904)
PHONE..................................407 875-0897
Louis Bracero, *Payroll Mgr*
EMP: 9 EST: 2016
SALES (est): 42.8K Privately Held
WEB: www.allanindustries.com
SIC: 3999 Manufacturing industries

(G-11893)
ALLEGRA DIRECT - SOUTH INC
2420 Lakemont Ave (32814-6164)
PHONE..................................586 226-1400
Joanne Crispignani, *President*
EMP: 7 EST: 2012
SALES (est): 318.4K Privately Held
SIC: 2752 Commercial printing, offset

(G-11894)
ALLIANCE RSRVATIONS
NETWRK LLC (DH)
7380 W Sand Lake Rd # 360 (32819-5248)
PHONE..................................602 889-5505
Pete Bertenshaw, *CEO*
Peter Strank, *President*
Kim Andreello, *Vice Pres*
David Friend, *CFO*
Carlyle Rood, *Software Dev*
EMP: 11 EST: 1995
SQ FT: 3,500
SALES (est): 5.6MM Publicly Held
WEB: www.alliancereservations.com
SIC: 7372 Business oriented computer software
HQ: Rci, Llc
9998 N Michigan Rd
Carmel IN 46032
317 805-9000

(G-11895)
ALLIED PRECAST PRODUCTS
CO INC
5640 Carder Rd (32810-4704)
P.O. Box 607460 (32860-7460)
PHONE..................................407 745-5605
William P Thomas Sr, *CEO*
Banner Lee Thomas, *President*
Thomas Ellen D, *Corp Secy*
EMP: 31 EST: 1957
SQ FT: 40,000
SALES (est): 2.6MM Privately Held
WEB: www.alliedprecastinc.net
SIC: 3272 Concrete products, precast; septic tanks, concrete; lintels, concrete; sills, concrete

(G-11896)
ALPHA PRESS INC
4333 Silver Star Rd # 19 (32808-5100)
PHONE..................................407 299-2121
Alex Latorre, *President*
Madeline I Latorre, *Admin Sec*
◆ EMP: 10 EST: 1998
SQ FT: 2,000
SALES (est): 2MM Privately Held
WEB: www.apiprint.net
SIC: 2752 Commercial printing, offset

(G-11897)
ALTERNA POWER INC
390 N Orange Ave (32801-1640)
PHONE..................................407 287-9148
Raushan A Murshid, *President*
Claudia L Harris, *Vice Pres*
EMP: 11 EST: 2017
SALES (est): 982K Privately Held
SIC: 3674 1711 8748 8742 Solar cells; solar energy contractor; systems analysis & engineering consulting services; management consulting services

(G-11898)
ALUMI TECH INC
5104 S Orange Ave (32809-3020)
PHONE..................................407 826-5373
Ramon Reel, *President*
EMP: 18 EST: 1986
SQ FT: 10,000
SALES (est): 2.2MM Privately Held
WEB: www.alumitech.net
SIC: 3732 3354 Hydrofoil boats; aluminum extruded products

(G-11899)
AMCOR RIGID PACKAGING USA
LLC
10260 Ringhaver Dr (32824-7066)
PHONE..................................407 859-7560
Hector Ordonez, *Production*
Melissa Coolich, *Engineer*
Rainer Elskamp, *Engineer*
Thomas Halewicz, *Engineer*
Scott Kelly, *Engineer*
EMP: 8
SALES (corp-wide): 12.8B Privately Held
SIC: 3089 Plastic containers, except foam
HQ: Amcor Rigid Packaging Usa, Llc
10521 S M 52
Manchester MI 48158

(G-11900)
AMERICAN ALL SCURE GTES
FNCE L
1316 29th St (32805-6116)
PHONE..................................407 423-4962
John Mills,
EMP: 10 EST: 2010
SALES (est): 975.3K Privately Held
WEB: www.securitygate.com
SIC: 3446 5039 Fences, gates, posts & flagpoles; wire fence, gates & accessories

(G-11901)
AMERICAN GIRL BRANDS LLC
8001 S Orange Blossom Trl # 1460
(32809-9169)
PHONE..............................407 852-9771
EMP: 41
SALES (corp-wide): 5.4B **Publicly Held**
WEB: www.americangirl.com
SIC: 3942 Dolls & doll clothing
HQ: American Girl Brands, Llc
8400 Fairway Pl
Middleton WI 53562
608 836-4848

(G-11902)
AMERICAN INCINERATORS CORP
Also Called: US Cremation Equipment
2814 Silver Star Rd 201d (32808-3940)
PHONE..............................321 282-7357
Luis Llorens, *President*
Randy Bryant, *Production*
Brian Gamage, *Marketing Staff*
EMP: 35 EST: 2004
SALES (est): 10.2MM **Privately Held**
WEB: www.uscremationequipment.com
SIC: 3561 Pumps & pumping equipment

(G-11903)
AMERICAN METAL PRODUCTS INC
4026 Silver Star Rd Ste A (32808-4657)
PHONE..............................407 293-0090
Jeanell Pritchett, *President*
Robert Headberg, *Vice Pres*
EMP: 6 EST: 1982
SQ FT: 25,000
SALES (est): 997.1K **Privately Held**
WEB: www.americanmp.com
SIC: 2599 5046 Carts, restaurant equipment; restaurant equipment & supplies

(G-11904)
AMERICAN PAYMENT SYSTEMS
11500 S Ornge Blossom Trl (32837-9418)
PHONE..............................407 856-8524
Maria P Castano, *Principal*
EMP: 10 EST: 2007
SALES (est): 197.3K **Privately Held**
WEB: www.americanpaymentsystems.com
SIC: 3629 Electronic generation equipment

(G-11905)
AMERICAN PHARMACEUTICAL SVCS
6001 Silver Star Rd Ste 2 (32808-8219)
PHONE..............................407 704-5937
Bamidele D Obaitan, *Principal*
EMP: 11 EST: 2009
SALES (est): 331.4K **Privately Held**
SIC: 2834 Pharmaceutical preparations

(G-11906)
AMERICANS GBC CORP
2484 San Tecla St # 205 (32835-3233)
PHONE..............................407 371-9584
Dos Anjos Fabio Jose, *Principal*
EMP: 7 EST: 2015
SALES (est): 109.8K **Privately Held**
SIC: 2653 Corrugated & solid fiber boxes

(G-11907)
AMERISIGNS
1718 Acme St (32805-3604)
PHONE..............................407 492-5644
Michael Kunda, *Owner*
EMP: 11 EST: 2018
SALES (est): 1MM **Privately Held**
SIC: 3993 Electric signs

(G-11908)
AMES COMPANIES INC
13485 Veterans Way # 200 (32827-7718)
PHONE..............................352 401-6370
EMP: 55
SALES (corp-wide): 2.2B **Publicly Held**
WEB: global.ames.com
SIC: 3423 Garden & farm tools, including shovels; shovels, spades (hand tools)
HQ: The Ames Companies Inc
465 Railroad Ave
Camp Hill PA 17011

(G-11909)
AMPHENOL CUSTOM CABLE INC
7461 Currency Dr (32809)
PHONE..............................407 393-3886
Jack Freed, *Branch Mgr*
EMP: 20
SALES (corp-wide): 10.8B **Publicly Held**
WEB: www.customcable.com
SIC: 3827 3357 Optical instruments & lenses; fiber optic cable (insulated)
HQ: Amphenol Custom Cable, Inc.
3221 Cherry Palm Dr
Tampa FL 33619
813 623-2232

(G-11910)
ANDERSEN CUSTOM CABINETRY LLC
3071 N Orange Blossom Trl (32804-3468)
PHONE..............................407 702-4891
John Andersen, *Administration*
EMP: 6 EST: 2015
SALES (est): 410.4K **Privately Held**
WEB: www.orlandoclosetdesigns.com
SIC: 2434 Wood kitchen cabinets

(G-11911)
ANDREW PRATT STUCCO & PLST INC
8048 Bridgestone Dr (32835-8016)
PHONE..............................407 501-2609
Andrew M Pratt, *Principal*
EMP: 12 EST: 2012
SALES (est): 346.5K **Privately Held**
WEB: www.andrewprattstucco.com
SIC: 3299 5032 Stucco; stucco

(G-11912)
ANDREWS FILTER AND SUPPLY CORP (PA)
2309 Coolidge Ave (32804-4897)
PHONE..............................407 423-3310
Wallace W Andrews, *President*
Mark D Andrews, *Vice Pres*
W Lee Andrews, *Vice Pres*
Shirley W Andrews, *Treasurer*
Mark Andrews, *Sales Executive*
▼ EMP: 30 EST: 1971
SQ FT: 34,000
SALES (est): 4.9MM **Privately Held**
WEB: www.andrewsfilter.com
SIC: 3564 5075 3585 Filters, air: furnaces, air conditioning equipment, etc.; air filters; refrigeration & heating equipment

(G-11913)
AP BUCK INC
7101 Presidents Dr # 110 (32809-5649)
PHONE..............................407 851-8602
Broir Nguyen, *President*
Probir Gayen, *Manager*
EMP: 15 EST: 1981
SQ FT: 6,600
SALES (est): 1.9MM **Privately Held**
WEB: www.apbuck.com
SIC: 3823 Primary elements for process flow measurement

(G-11914)
APRU LLC
3125 Lake George Cove Dr (32812-6822)
PHONE..............................888 741-3777
David Anthony Torgerud, *CEO*
EMP: 8 EST: 2016
SALES (est): 1.3MM
SALES (corp-wide): 2.8MM **Privately Held**
WEB: www.applerush.com
SIC: 2086 Carbonated soft drinks, bottled & canned; iced tea & fruit drinks, bottled & canned
PA: Apple Rush Company, Inc.
1419 Chaffee Dr Ste 4
Titusville FL 32780
888 741-3777

(G-11915)
AQUA PURE LLC
Also Called: Livie Water
6541 N Orange Blossom Trl (32810-4101)
P.O. Box 965, Gotha (34734-0965)
PHONE..............................407 521-3055
Eric Morris,
EMP: 5 EST: 1998
SQ FT: 8,500
SALES (est): 602.9K **Privately Held**
WEB: www.liviewater.com
SIC: 2086 5149 Mineral water, carbonated: packaged in cans, bottles, etc.; mineral or spring water bottling

(G-11916)
ARCHITECTURAL METAL SYSTEMS
4881 Distribution Ct (32822-4918)
PHONE..............................407 277-1364
Terry Davis, *President*
EMP: 19 EST: 1979
SALES (est): 1.4MM **Privately Held**
SIC: 3446 3444 3442 Architectural metalwork; sheet metalwork; store fronts, prefabricated, metal

(G-11917)
ARGOS USA LLC
2858 Sidney Ave (32810-5134)
PHONE..............................407 299-9924
Reuben Ginorio, *Credit Staff*
EMP: 40 **Privately Held**
WEB: www.argos-us.com
SIC: 3273 Ready-mixed concrete
HQ: Argos Usa Llc
3015 Windward Plz Ste 300
Alpharetta GA 30005
678 368-4300

(G-11918)
ARGOS-US LLC
5109 Carder Rd (32810-5111)
PHONE..............................407 298-1900
EMP: 10 EST: 2014
SALES (est): 893.2K **Privately Held**
WEB: www.argos-us.com
SIC: 3271 Concrete block & brick

(G-11919)
ARGOSY GROUP INTERNATIONAL LLC
2405 W Princeton St Ste 9 (32804-4725)
PHONE..............................888 350-7643
Henry Wang, *CEO*
Raphael Doromal, *COO*
EMP: 7 EST: 2013
SALES (est): 477.5K **Privately Held**
WEB: www.argosygroupintl.com
SIC: 3589 Commercial cooking & food-warming equipment

(G-11920)
ARIZONA BEVERAGE COMPANY LLC
8350 Parkline Blvd Ste 14 (32809-8122)
PHONE..............................516 812-0303
Ron Gallagher, *Manager*
EMP: 10
SALES (corp-wide): 284.6MM **Privately Held**
SIC: 2086 Iced tea & fruit drinks, bottled & canned
HQ: Arizona Beverage Company Llc
60 Crossways Park Dr W # 400
Woodbury NY 11797
516 812-0300

(G-11921)
AROMATECH FLAVORINGS INC
7001 Mccoy Rd Ste 200 (32822-4717)
PHONE..............................407 277-5727
Jaques Martel, *CEO*
Yvan Grattarola, *Director*
David Pujol, *Director*
Regis Baudot, *Administration*
▲ EMP: 5 EST: 2007
SALES (est): 1.2MM
SALES (corp-wide): 498.9K **Privately Held**
WEB: www.aromatech.fr
SIC: 2087 Extracts, flavoring
HQ: Aromatech
Parc D Activites
Saint Cezaire Sur Siagne 06530
493 608-444

(G-11922)
ARRIVE ALIVE TRAFFIC CTRL LLC
3165 N John Young Pkwy (32804-4128)
PHONE..............................407 578-5431
EMP: 14 EST: 2018
SALES (est): 4MM **Privately Held**
WEB: www.arrivealivetrafficcontrol.com
SIC: 3993 Signs & advertising specialties

(G-11923)
ART & FRAME DIRECT INC (PA)
Also Called: Timeless Reflections
11423 Satellite Blvd (32837-9225)
PHONE..............................407 857-6000
George Eouse, *President*
Corey Craftsman, *Exec VP*
Dorothy A Eouse, *Vice Pres*
John H Esguera, *Vice Pres*
Lexy Bell, *Purch Dir*
◆ EMP: 150 EST: 1991
SQ FT: 500,000
SALES (est): 40.7MM **Privately Held**
WEB: www.afdhome.com
SIC: 2499 5999 3231 3999 Picture & mirror frames, wood; artists' supplies & materials; mirrored glass; plaques, picture, laminated; frames for artists' canvases

(G-11924)
ART & FRAME DRCT/TIMELESS INDS
11423 Satellite Blvd (32837-9225)
PHONE..............................407 857-6000
▲ EMP: 10 EST: 2013
SALES (est): 255.3K **Privately Held**
SIC: 2499 Cork & cork products

(G-11925)
ARTISTIC ADVENTURES INC
2517 Shader Rd Unit 2 (32804-2771)
PHONE..............................407 297-0557
Michael Grenell, *President*
EMP: 6 EST: 1998
SQ FT: 12,000
SALES (est): 478.5K **Privately Held**
WEB: www.artisticadventuresinc.com
SIC: 3993 Displays & cutouts, window & lobby

(G-11926)
ASOTTU INC ●
1317 Edgewater Dr # 3455 (32804-6350)
PHONE..............................626 627-6021
Shangguan Jiao, *CEO*
EMP: 15 EST: 2021
SALES (est): 591.4K **Privately Held**
SIC: 2542 Office & store showcases & display fixtures

(G-11927)
ASSISTRX INC (PA)
4700 Millenia Blvd # 500 (32839-6013)
PHONE..............................855 421-4607
Jeff Spafford, *President*
Jan Nielsen, *President*
Richard Prest, *Exec VP*
Gary Steier, *Senior VP*
Dustin Fergesen, *Vice Pres*
EMP: 100 EST: 2009
SALES (est): 54.7MM **Privately Held**
WEB: www.assistrx.com
SIC: 2834 Medicines, capsuled or ampuled

(G-11928)
ASSISTRX INC
2400 Sand Lake Rd Ste 200 (32809-9100)
PHONE..............................855 382-2533
EMP: 60
SALES (corp-wide): 54.7MM **Privately Held**
WEB: www.assistrx.com
SIC: 2834 Medicines, capsuled or ampuled
PA: Assistrx, Inc.
4700 Millenia Blvd # 500
Orlando FL 32839
855 421-4607

(G-11929)
ASTRONICS TEST SYSTEMS INC
12889 Ingenuity Dr (32826-3001)
PHONE..............................407 381-6062
Kotyk John, *Engineer*
Butch Thornburg, *Engineer*
Quentin Avery, *Sales Staff*
Lou Salzano, *Manager*
EMP: 130
SQ FT: 50,800

▲ = Import ▼ = Export
◆ = Import/Export

SALES (corp-wide): 444.9MM **Publicly Held**
WEB: www.astronics.com
SIC: **3812** 3699 Search & navigation equipment; electrical equipment & supplies
HQ: Astronics Test Systems Inc.
4 Goodyear
Irvine CA 92618
800 722-2528

(G-11930)
ATLAS CONCRETE PRODUCTS INC
6452 E Colonial Dr (32807-3651)
PHONE.................................407 277-0841
Michael C Payment, *President*
Adair Payment, *Corp Secy*
Chris C Payment, *Vice Pres*
Joseph C Payment, *Vice Pres*
EMP: 7 **EST:** 1949
SQ FT: 2,000
SALES (est): 1MM **Privately Held**
SIC: **3272** 3271 Burial vaults, concrete or precast terrazzo; concrete products, precast; furniture, garden: concrete; brick, concrete

(G-11931)
ATLAS WALLS LLC
10500 Rocket Ct (32824-8567)
P.O. Box 540316 (32854-0316)
PHONE.................................800 951-9201
Michael Madden,
▼ **EMP:** 8 **EST:** 2013
SQ FT: 2,000
SALES (est): 766.1K **Privately Held**
WEB: www.atlaswalls.com
SIC: **3272** Floor slabs & tiles, precast concrete

(G-11932)
ATMFLA INC (PA)
4601 Sw 34th St Ste 100 (32811-6415)
P.O. Box 618346 (32861-8346)
PHONE.................................407 425-7708
Glen Lyon, *President*
Mac Cochran, *Vice Pres*
EMP: 6 **EST:** 1989
SQ FT: 8,000
SALES (est): 2.8MM **Privately Held**
WEB: www.atmfla.com
SIC: **3578** Automatic teller machines (ATM)

(G-11933)
AUDIO EXCELLENCE (PA)
477 N Semoran Blvd (32807-3323)
PHONE.................................407 277-8790
Halah Abed, *President*
EMP: 5 **EST:** 2002
SALES (est): 945.7K **Privately Held**
WEB: www.beyond-comparison.com
SIC: **3999** Atomizers, toiletry

(G-11934)
AUTOMATED BUILDINGS INC
5520 Hansel Ave (32809-3464)
PHONE.................................407 857-0140
Mark Zeitler, *President*
Megan Finch-Bates, *Administration*
EMP: 10 **EST:** 1999
SALES (est): 1.7MM **Privately Held**
WEB: www.abi-fla.com
SIC: **3822** 1711 Building services monitoring controls, automatic; plumbing, heating, air-conditioning contractors

(G-11935)
AUTOMTED LGIC CORP KENNESAW GA
Also Called: ALC Controls of Florida
7305 Greenbriar Pkwy (32819-8935)
PHONE.................................877 866-1226
William Hirschi, *Technician*
EMP: 10
SALES (corp-wide): 20.6B **Publicly Held**
WEB: www.automatedlogic.com
SIC: **3625** 5084 7629 Electric controls & control accessories, industrial; instruments & control equipment; electrical equipment repair services
HQ: Automated Logic Corporation, Kennesaw, Ga
1150 Roberts Blvd Nw
Kennesaw GA

(G-11936)
AVIAN INVENTORY MANAGEMENT LLC ✪
8649 Transport Dr Ste 100 (32832-7102)
PHONE.................................407 787-9100
Kian Gurekian, *Manager*
EMP: 7 **EST:** 2021
SALES (est): 253.2K **Privately Held**
WEB: www.avianparts.com
SIC: **3429** Aircraft hardware

(G-11937)
AVRA MEDICAL ROBOTICS INC
3259 Progress Dr Ste 112a (32826-3230)
PHONE.................................407 956-2250
Barry F Cohen, *CEO*
Ray Powers, *COO*
Farhan Taghizadeh, *Chief Mktg Ofcr*
EMP: 10 **EST:** 2015
WEB: www.avramedicalrobotics.com
SIC: **3841** Surgical & medical instruments

(G-11938)
B-N-J POWDER COATINGS LLC
111 W Pineloch Ave Ste 2 (32806-8563)
PHONE.................................407 999-8448
Steve Bronovitsky, *Principal*
EMP: 7 **EST:** 2007
SALES (est): 1.3MM **Privately Held**
WEB: www.b-n-jpowdercoating.com
SIC: **3399** Silver powder

(G-11939)
BADGER WELDING ORLANDO LLC
806 W Landstreet Rd (32824-8023)
P.O. Box 593982 (32859-3982)
PHONE.................................407 648-1100
Jennifer Heidenreich,
EMP: 6 **EST:** 2006
SQ FT: 20,000
SALES (est): 564.3K **Privately Held**
WEB: www.badgerwelding.net
SIC: **7692** Welding repair

(G-11940)
BANKER STEEL SOUTH LLC
6635 Edgewater Dr (32810-4205)
P.O. Box 10875, Lynchburg VA (24506-0875)
PHONE.................................407 293-0120
Gregory R Nichols, *Mng Member*
EMP: 10 **EST:** 2012
SALES (est): 1MM **Privately Held**
WEB: www.bankersteel.com
SIC: **3441** Building components, structural steel

(G-11941)
BARRS EQUIPMENT SERVICE INC
2506 Taylor Ave (32806-4428)
PHONE.................................407 999-5214
George D Barr, *President*
Patsy Barr, *Admin Sec*
EMP: 10 **EST:** 1960
SQ FT: 5,340
SALES (est): 951.6K **Privately Held**
WEB: www.welderfix.com
SIC: **7692** Welding repair

(G-11942)
BARRY RESNICK
480 27th St (32806-4451)
PHONE.................................407 296-9999
Barry Resnick, *Principal*
EMP: 8 **EST:** 2012
SALES (est): 314.7K **Privately Held**
SIC: **3569** Generators: steam, liquid oxygen or nitrogen

(G-11943)
BEDROCK INDUSTRIES INC
10500 Rocket Ct (32824-8567)
PHONE.................................407 859-1300
Lou Deberandinis, *President*
Linda Owens, *Accounts Mgr*
EMP: 19 **EST:** 1998
SQ FT: 9,290
SALES (est): 3.9MM **Privately Held**
WEB: www.bedrockindustries.com
SIC: **3271** Blocks, concrete or cinder: standard

(G-11944)
BEHRS CHOCOLATES BY DESIGN
3450 Vineland Rd Ste B (32811-6421)
PHONE.................................407 648-2020
Glenn Behr, *President*
Debra Behr, *Vice Pres*
Shannon Everhart, *Creative Dir*
▲ **EMP:** 5 **EST:** 1983
SQ FT: 2,500
SALES (est): 1.2MM **Privately Held**
WEB: www.behrschocolates.com
SIC: **2066** 2064 Chocolate candy, solid; candy & other confectionery products

(G-11945)
BESPOKE STITCHERY LLC
2437 E Landstreet Rd (32824-7945)
PHONE.................................407 412-9937
Scott Sims, *Managing Prtnr*
EMP: 7 **EST:** 2014
SALES (est): 351.1K **Privately Held**
SIC: **3172** 5131 Personal leather goods; piece goods & notions

(G-11946)
BEST PAVERS LLC
8730 Hastings Beach Blvd (32829-8818)
PHONE.................................407 259-9020
Ivonne I Irizarry, *Principal*
EMP: 7 **EST:** 2014
SALES (est): 136K **Privately Held**
SIC: **2951** Asphalt paving mixtures & blocks

(G-11947)
BETTER PLASTICS INC
780 Central Florida Pkwy (32824-8502)
PHONE.................................407 480-2909
W A Messina, *Principal*
EMP: 8 **EST:** 2012
SALES (est): 150.5K **Privately Held**
SIC: **3089** Injection molding of plastics

(G-11948)
BIG BOY INC
Also Called: Big Boy Restaurant
5972 Bent Pine Dr 1710 (32822-3342)
PHONE.................................407 434-9251
Alexis Brown, *President*
EMP: 9 **EST:** 2019
SALES (est): 571.9K **Privately Held**
WEB: www.bigboy.com
SIC: **1389** 5999 Construction, repair & dismantling services; miscellaneous retail stores

(G-11949)
BIG CAT HUMN PWRED VHICLES LLC
Also Called: Big Cat H P V
2016 Stanhome Way (32804-5114)
PHONE.................................407 999-0200
Mark Egeland, *General Mgr*
Paulo Camasmie, *Mng Member*
▲ **EMP:** 13 **EST:** 2000
SQ FT: 22,000
SALES (est): 4MM **Privately Held**
SIC: **3751** Bicycles & related parts

(G-11950)
BIG IRON INTL INC
3936 S Semoran Blvd Ste 2 (32822-4015)
PHONE.................................407 222-2573
M Vilayath Ali, *President*
EMP: 8 **EST:** 2017
SALES (est): 976.9K **Privately Held**
WEB: www.bigironintl.com
SIC: **3441** 7353 Fabricated structural metal; cranes & aerial lift equipment, rental or leasing

(G-11951)
BIO-LOGIC SYSTEMS CORP
12301 Lake Underhill Rd # 201 (32828-4511)
PHONE.................................847 949-0456
James B Hawkins, *President*
Frank Mancuso, *Research*
Michael J Hanley, *Controller*
EMP: 58 **EST:** 1979

SALES (est): 11.3MM
SALES (corp-wide): 28.4MM **Privately Held**
WEB: www.biologic.net
SIC: **3845** 3571 3841 Electromedical equipment; electronic computers; surgical & medical instruments
HQ: Natus Medical Incorporated
6701 Koll Center Pkwy # 12
Pleasanton CA 94566
925 223-6700

(G-11952)
BIOSAFE SUPPLIES LLC
9436 Southridge Park Ct # 400 (32819-8639)
PHONE.................................407 281-6658
David Pittman, *Prdtn Mgr*
Evelyne Cook, *Sales Staff*
Nadine Monico, *Mng Member*
Kenneth Ford, *Director*
EMP: 15 **EST:** 1999
SQ FT: 6,000
SALES (est): 2.2MM **Privately Held**
WEB: www.biosafesupplies.com
SIC: **3841** Medical instruments & equipment, blood & bone work

(G-11953)
BIOZONE SCIENTIFIC INTL INC (PA)
7616 Southland Blvd # 114 (32809-8513)
PHONE.................................407 876-2000
ARI Ahola, *President*
McKay Howell, *Project Mgr*
John Phillips, *Engineer*
Paul Morris, *Sales Staff*
Matti Ahola, *Manager*
▲ **EMP:** 8 **EST:** 1999
SQ FT: 25,000
SALES (est): 4.2MM **Privately Held**
WEB: www.biozonescientific.com
SIC: **3564** 3589 Air purification equipment; water purification equipment, household type

(G-11954)
BLA SOFTWARE INC
10424 Sparkle Ct (32836-6000)
P.O. Box 692005 (32869-2005)
PHONE.................................407 355-0800
Rozalia Deborde, *CFO*
EMP: 5 **EST:** 2006
SALES (est): 346.4K **Privately Held**
WEB: www.blasoftware.com
SIC: **7372** Business oriented computer software

(G-11955)
BLACK BEE AROMATHERAPY LLC ✪
7726 Winegard Rd (32809-7147)
PHONE.................................866 399-4233
Lareese Robinson, *CEO*
EMP: 5 **EST:** 2021
SALES (est): 301.6K **Privately Held**
SIC: **3999** 8742 Candles; retail trade consultant

(G-11956)
BLACKTON FLOORING INC
1714 Alden Rd (32803-1480)
PHONE.................................407 898-2661
Sean Monett, *President*
Pam Blanchard, *Accounting Mgr*
Danny Keefer, *Supervisor*
EMP: 9 **EST:** 2010
SALES (est): 482.2K **Privately Held**
WEB: www.blacktoninc.com
SIC: **3253** Ceramic wall & floor tile

(G-11957)
BLAZER BOATS INC
12001 Res Pkwy Ste 236 (32826)
PHONE.................................321 307-4761
Keith E Craft, *President*
Lonnie G Craft, *Corp Secy*
Kelly Dougherty, *Office Mgr*
Lonnie N Craft, *Shareholder*
Scott Scarboro, *Admin Sec*
◆ **EMP:** 45 **EST:** 1977
SQ FT: 70,000
SALES (est): 8.6MM **Privately Held**
WEB: www.blazerboats.com
SIC: **3732** Boats, fiberglass: building & repairing

(G-11958)
BLP RACING PRODUCTS LLC
1015 W Church St (32805-2215)
PHONE..............................407 422-0394
Joe Hilerio, *Mng Member*
EMP: 19 **EST:** 2016
SALES (est): 2.9MM **Privately Held**
WEB: www.blp.com
SIC: 3714 Motor vehicle parts & accessories

(G-11959)
BLUE DIAMOND ORTHOPEDIC LLC
6439 Milner Blvd Ste 4 (32809-6692)
PHONE..............................407 613-2001
David J Hendricks, *Principal*
EMP: 8 **EST:** 2015
SALES (est): 366.8K **Privately Held**
WEB: www.bluediamondorthopedic.com
SIC: 3842 Surgical appliances & supplies

(G-11960)
BLUE HIPPO LLC
1090 Gills Dr Ste 100 (32824-8040)
PHONE..............................407 325-4090
EMP: 13 **EST:** 2019
SALES (est): 811.7K **Privately Held**
WEB: www.bluehippo.com
SIC: 2519 Household furniture

(G-11961)
BLUEDROP USA INC
3275 Progress Dr Ste D (32826-2932)
PHONE..............................800 563-3638
Belinda Lewis, *CEO*
Brett Ulander, *President*
Brad Driscoll, *CFO*
EMP: 8 **EST:** 2020
SALES (est): 1.1MM **Privately Held**
WEB: www.bluedropusa.com
SIC: 3699 8331 Flight simulators (training aids), electronic; job training services

(G-11962)
BLUWORLD INNOVATIONS LLC
635 W Michigan St (32805-6203)
PHONE..............................888 499-5433
Betty Cunnigham, *Vice Pres*
Clint Siddens, *Vice Pres*
Darin Effron, *Foreman/Supr*
Lewen Rosario, *Engineer*
Betty Cunningham, *Controller*
▲ **EMP:** 100 **EST:** 1999
SQ FT: 7,800
SALES (est): 17.6MM **Privately Held**
WEB: www.bluworldusa.com
SIC: 2899 Water treating compounds

(G-11963)
BLUWORLD OF WATER LLC
3093 Caruso Ct Ste 40-A (32806-8556)
PHONE..............................407 426-7674
Asa Peacock, *Prdtn Mgr*
Daniel Gunn, *Engineer*
Marty Effron, *CFO*
Janet Dorsey, *Controller*
Michelle Effron, *Marketing Staff*
▲ **EMP:** 55 **EST:** 2010
SALES (est): 10.9MM **Privately Held**
WEB: www.bluworldusa.com
SIC: 3648 Fountain lighting fixtures

(G-11964)
BOEING COMPANY
13501 Ingenuity Dr # 204 (32826-3018)
PHONE..............................407 306-8782
EMP: 196
SALES (corp-wide): 58.1B **Publicly Held**
SIC: 3721 Mfg Aircraft
PA: The Boeing Company
100 N Riverside Plz
Chicago IL 22202
312 544-2000

(G-11965)
BOHEMIA INTRCTIVE SMLTIONS INC
3050 Tech Pkwy Ste 110 (32826)
PHONE..............................407 608-7000
John F Givens, *President*
Gregg Owens, *President*
Rusmat Ahmed, *Vice Pres*
Oliver Arup, *Vice Pres*
Scott Hooper, *Vice Pres*
EMP: 10 **EST:** 2010
SALES (est): 4MM **Privately Held**
WEB: www.bisimulations.com
SIC: 7372 Prepackaged software
PA: Bohemia Interactive Simulations K.S.
Pernerova 691/42
Praha 8 - Karlin 186 0

(G-11966)
BOLT SYSTEMS INC
1700 Silver Star Rd (32804-3444)
PHONE..............................407 425-0012
Wallace C Beitl Sr, *President*
Margaret M Beitl, *Vice Pres*
EMP: 9 **EST:** 1992
SALES (est): 368.3K **Privately Held**
WEB: www.boltsystems.com
SIC: 3842 5999 Braces, orthopedic; orthopedic & prosthesis applications

(G-11967)
BPC PLASMA INC
2501 Discovery Dr (32826-3718)
PHONE..............................407 207-1932
Gregor Schulz, *Branch Mgr*
EMP: 13
SALES (corp-wide): 480.7MM **Privately Held**
WEB: www.biotestplasma.com
SIC: 2834 Pharmaceutical preparations
HQ: Bpc Plasma, Inc.
901 W Yamato Rd Ste 101
Boca Raton FL 33431

(G-11968)
BRICK PVERS DRVEWAY BIG PAVERS
6111 Metrowest Blvd (32835-2958)
PHONE..............................407 928-1217
Edelson Silva, *Administration*
EMP: 5 **EST:** 2015
SALES (est): 976.2K **Privately Held**
WEB: www.bigpavers.com
SIC: 2951 Asphalt paving mixtures & blocks

(G-11969)
BRISTOL VENTURE SERVICE LLC
16121 Bristol Lake Cir (32828-6963)
PHONE..............................407 844-8629
Feng Fu, *Principal*
EMP: 8 **EST:** 2013
SALES (est): 168.6K **Privately Held**
SIC: 2621 Paper mills

(G-11970)
BROWNLEE LIGHTING INC
4600 Dardanelle Dr (32808-3832)
PHONE..............................407 297-3677
Curtis M Brownlee, *President*
Thomas M Brownlee, *Chairman*
Thomas J Brownlee, *Vice Pres*
Stephanie Galbraith, *Mfg Staff*
Charlotte McCree, *Purchasing*
◆ **EMP:** 40 **EST:** 1977
SQ FT: 30,000
SALES (est): 7.5MM **Privately Held**
WEB: www.brownlee.com
SIC: 3646 3645 Commercial indusl & institutional electric lighting fixtures; residential lighting fixtures

(G-11971)
C & H SIGN ENTERPRISES INC
Also Called: Fastsigns
9900 Universal Blvd # 114 (32819-8716)
PHONE..............................407 826-0155
EMP: 7
SQ FT: 2,800
SALES (est): 1MM **Privately Held**
SIC: 3993 Signsadv Specs

(G-11972)
C & S PRESS INC
405 27th St (32806-4452)
PHONE..............................407 841-3000
Frank J Tantillo, *President*
Daniel B Ellis, *Principal*
Raymond G Cody, *Corp Secy*
Sheryl Nuzzo, *Vice Pres*
Jeff Lambert, *Purch Agent*
EMP: 60 **EST:** 1985
SQ FT: 18,500

(G-11973)
C L INDUSTRIES INC
Also Called: LCI
8188 S Orange Ave (32809-6731)
P.O. Box 490180, Leesburg (34749-0180)
PHONE..............................800 333-2660
Fred Horton Jr, *CEO*
Horton Fred Jr, *Principal*
Jones Gary L, *Principal*
Jeff Cherry, *Vice Pres*
Paskiet Sherrie L, *Vice Pres*
◆ **EMP:** 40 **EST:** 1971
SQ FT: 40,000
SALES (est): 13.5MM
SALES (corp-wide): 51.2MM **Privately Held**
WEB: www.clindustries.com
SIC: 3281 5032 Pedestals, marble; marble building stone
PA: Consolidated Minerals, Inc.
8500 Us Highway 441
Leesburg FL 34788
352 365-6522

(G-11974)
C4 ADVNCED TCTICAL SYSTEMS LLC
Also Called: C4ats
243 Wetherbee Rd (32824-8623)
PHONE..............................407 206-3886
Theresa Smith, *Exec VP*
David Garcia, *Warehouse Mgr*
Niki Tyburczy, *Senior Buyer*
Carla Dennard, *Buyer*
Ruben Esquilin, *Buyer*
◆ **EMP:** 99 **EST:** 2005
SALES (est): 31.4MM **Privately Held**
WEB: www.c4ats.com
SIC: 3489 3795 3769 Ordnance & accessories; specialized tank components, military; casings, missiles & missile components: storage
HQ: Rafael U.S.A., Inc.
6903 Rockledge Dr Ste 850
Bethesda MD 20817

(G-11975)
CABINETS ONE LLC
4502 Old Winter Garden Rd (32811-1747)
PHONE..............................407 227-1147
Enrique Batista, *Principal*
EMP: 5 **EST:** 2018
SALES (est): 443.6K **Privately Held**
WEB: www.cabinetsone.com
SIC: 2434 Wood kitchen cabinets

(G-11976)
CABLES AND SENSORS LLC (PA)
5874 S Semoran Blvd (32822-4817)
PHONE..............................866 373-6767
Kevin Allen, *Vice Pres*
Jill Walker, *Human Res Mgr*
Steve Carpio, *Sales Staff*
Jenna Chatillon, *Sales Staff*
Michelle Pignaloso, *Sales Staff*
EMP: 6 **EST:** 2010
SALES (est): 5.8MM **Privately Held**
WEB: www.cablesandsensors.com
SIC: 3061 5999 Oil & gas field machinery rubber goods (mechanical); medical apparatus & supplies

(G-11977)
CAMARA INDUSTRIES LLC
9927 Dean Cove Ln (32825-6570)
PHONE..............................407 879-2549
Israel Camara,
EMP: 11 **EST:** 2014
SALES (est): 669.3K **Privately Held**
WEB: www.camaraindustries.com
SIC: 2448 Wood pallets & skids

(G-11978)
CANTOR DESIGN ON GRANITE
Also Called: Cantor Granite & Marble
4180 Player Cir (32808-2245)
PHONE..............................407 230-1568
Gerson Cevallos, *Owner*
Oswaldo Cevallos, *General Mgr*
EMP: 8 **EST:** 1998

SQ FT: 4,600
SALES (est): 494.2K **Privately Held**
SIC: 3281 Granite, cut & shaped

(G-11979)
CANVAS FREAKS LLC
11300 Space Blvd Ste 4 (32837-9209)
PHONE..............................407 978-6224
Atikur Motiwala, *Principal*
EMP: 10 **EST:** 2017
SALES (est): 7.9MM **Privately Held**
WEB: www.canvasfreaks.com
SIC: 2211 Canvas

(G-11980)
CANVAS SHOP INC
635 Wilmer Ave (32808-7635)
PHONE..............................407 898-6001
Boris Roitman, *Principal*
ABI Roitman, *Assistant*
EMP: 10 **EST:** 2010
SALES (est): 364.5K **Privately Held**
WEB: www.horizonenvironmental.com
SIC: 2394 Awnings, fabric: made from purchased materials

(G-11981)
CAPTEL INC
2602 Challenger Tech Ct (32826-2741)
PHONE..............................407 730-3397
Reina Soto, *Owner*
Anna Perez, *Opers Staff*
Victor Allison, *Agent*
Destani Anderson, *Supervisor*
Madison Bower, *Supervisor*
EMP: 296
SALES (corp-wide): 87.6MM **Privately Held**
WEB: www.captel.com
SIC: 3842 Hearing aids
PA: Captel, Inc.
450 Science Dr
Madison WI 53711
608 238-5400

(G-11982)
CARLOS VELEZ CABINETS & INSTAL
5314 Ira St (32807-1717)
PHONE..............................407 929-3402
Carlos Velez Jr, *Principal*
EMP: 9 **EST:** 2005
SALES (est): 141.1K **Privately Held**
SIC: 2434 Wood kitchen cabinets

(G-11983)
CARPE DIEM SALES & MKTG INC (PA)
4560 36th St (32811-6526)
PHONE..............................407 682-1400
Mike Giordano, *President*
Philip Fry, *Vice Pres*
Amanda Bini, *Purch Mgr*
Rondi Boudreau, *Accounts Mgr*
Kathryn C Mathews, *Accounts Exec*
◆ **EMP:** 22 **EST:** 1993
SQ FT: 22,000
SALES (est): 8.2MM **Privately Held**
WEB: www.thesourcinggroup.com
SIC: 2759 5136 5137 Screen printing; men's & boys' clothing; women's & children's clothing

(G-11984)
CARTER-HEALTH DISPOSABLES LLC
4201 Vinelnd Rd I-13 (32811)
PHONE..............................407 296-6689
Roda Carter, *Mng Member*
▲ **EMP:** 5 **EST:** 2009
SALES (est): 471.3K **Privately Held**
WEB: www.carter-health.com
SIC: 2389 Hospital gowns

(G-11985)
CASTE CRETE
515 Ferguson Dr Ste A (32805-1040)
PHONE..............................407 295-1959
EMP: 8 **EST:** 2012
SALES (est): 245.6K **Privately Held**
WEB: www.castcrete.com
SIC: 3272 Concrete products

2022 Harris Florida
Manufacturers Directory

▲ = Import ▼=Export
◆ =Import/Export

(G-11986)
CATAPULT PRINT AND PACKG LLC (HQ)
5945 Hazeltine Nat Dr (32822-5019)
PHONE..................................407 717-4323
Lewis Cook, *Managing Prtnr*
James Christie, *Sales Mgr*
Mark Cook, *Mng Member*
Chris Mountain, *Manager*
Quincy Riviere, *Manager*
EMP: 10 EST: 2017
SALES (est): 3.1MM
SALES (corp-wide): 17.4MM **Privately Held**
WEB: www.catapultprint.com
SIC: 2752 Commercial printing, offset
PA: Catapult Holdco, Llc
5945 Hazeltine Nat Dr
Orlando FL 32822
407 890-6400

(G-11987)
CAUSEY MACHINE WORKS INC
Also Called: Victoriano Pantoja
12131 Science Dr (32826-3232)
PHONE..................................407 277-7570
Maria Pantoja, *President*
Victoriano Pantoja Sr, *Vice Pres*
EMP: 10 EST: 1980
SQ FT: 15,000
SALES (est): 1.6MM **Privately Held**
WEB: www.causeymachine.com
SIC: 3599 Machine shop, jobbing & repair

(G-11988)
CAVADAS RUBEN & TRISHA WAGNER
3125 Crystal Creek Blvd (32837-5072)
PHONE..................................407 248-2659
Eliane Cavadas, *Principal*
EMP: 7 EST: 2003
SALES (est): 82.9K **Privately Held**
SIC: 2673 Cellophane bags, unprinted:
made from purchased materials

(G-11989)
CEDARS BAKERY GROUP INC
4704 L B Mcleod Rd (32811-6408)
PHONE..................................407 476-6593
Imad Nasnas, *President*
Issam Sleiman, *Vice Pres*
EMP: 16 EST: 2013
SQ FT: 6,800
SALES (est): 2MM **Privately Held**
WEB: www.cedarsbread.com
SIC: 2051 Bread, cake & related products

(G-11990)
CELLOFOAM NORTH AMERICA INC
11237 Astronaut Blvd (32837-9203)
PHONE..................................407 888-4667
Mike Grunnet, *Exec VP*
Alejandro Guevara, *Vice Pres*
Sergio Acuna, *Plant Mgr*
Ryan J Rutledge, *Sales Staff*
Erika Davila, *Office Mgr*
EMP: 78
SALES (corp-wide): 143.4MM **Privately Held**
WEB: www.cellofoam.com
SIC: 2821 Plastics materials & resins
PA: Cellofoam North America Inc.
1977 Weaver Ct
Conyers GA 30013
770 929-3688

(G-11991)
CELLTRONIX
2305 S Orange Ave (32806-3046)
PHONE..................................407 610-7852
EMP: 18
SALES (corp-wide): 4.9MM **Privately Held**
WEB: www.mycelltronix.com
SIC: 2451 Mobile homes
PA: Celltronix
1718 S Orange Blossom Trl
Apopka FL 32703
407 880-2355

(G-11992)
CEMI INTERNATIONAL INC
Also Called: Celmark International
2600 Titan Row (32809-5659)
PHONE..................................407 859-7701
Keith Frankel, *President*
EMP: 150 EST: 2007
SQ FT: 80,000
SALES (est): 25.7MM **Privately Held**
WEB: www.celmarkint.com
SIC: 2844 Cosmetic preparations

(G-11993)
CENTRAL FLA REMANUFACTURING
Also Called: Central Florida Remanufactory
2526 W Washington St (32805-1257)
PHONE..................................407 299-9011
Ray Osorio, *President*
Leandra Osorio, *Vice Pres*
Nelson Madruga, *Manager*
EMP: 7 EST: 1979
SQ FT: 800
SALES (est): 948.2K **Privately Held**
WEB:
www.centralfloridaremanufactory.com
SIC: 3621 3694 Starters, for motors; alter-
nators, automotive

(G-11994)
CENTRAL FLORIDA CENTRAL FLA
4157 Seaboard Rd (32808-3849)
PHONE..................................407 674-2626
Evan John, *Principal*
Kris Keprios, *Sales Staff*
Jack Cormier, *Corp Comm Staff*
Kelly Rote, *Corp Comm Staff*
Lisa Rizer, *Manager*
EMP: 18 EST: 2016
SALES (est): 8.9MM **Privately Held**
WEB: centralfl.ashe.pro
SIC: 3564 Blowers & fans

(G-11995)
CENTRAL FLORIDA CNSTR WALLS
5923 Bamboo Dr (32807-4405)
PHONE..................................407 448-2350
Manuel Quilli, *President*
EMP: 10 EST: 2010
SALES (est): 1.1MM **Privately Held**
WEB: www.cflconstructionwalls.com
SIC: 3271 1742 Concrete block & brick;
stucco work, interior

(G-11996)
CENTRAL FLORIDA CSTM TRLRS INC (PA)
Also Called: Ram-Lin
2136 4th St (32824-7709)
PHONE..................................407 851-1144
David McCorkle, *President*
EMP: 47 EST: 1993
SQ FT: 30,000
SALES (est): 13.1MM **Privately Held**
WEB: www.ramlin.com
SIC: 3799 Trailers & trailer equipment;
boat trailers

(G-11997)
CENTRAL FLORIDA DRIVESHAFT
Also Called: Advance Driveline
5512 Carder Rd (32810-4729)
PHONE..................................407 299-1100
David Crutch, *Manager*
EMP: 8
SQ FT: 5,059
SALES (corp-wide): 1.8MM **Privately Held**
WEB: www.centralfloridadriveshaft.com
SIC: 3714 Drive shafts, motor vehicle
PA: Central Florida Driveshaft
307 S Combee Rd
Lakeland FL 33801
863 666-3874

(G-11998)
CENTRAL FLORIDA ICE SERVICES
410 27th St (32806-4451)
PHONE..................................407 779-0161
Julio Zaldivar, *President*
EMP: 12 EST: 2020
SALES (est): 553.5K **Privately Held**
WEB: www.leesicf.com
SIC: 2097 Manufactured ice

(G-11999)
CENTRAL FLORIDA LBR & SUP CO
Also Called: Mills & Nebraska
2721 Regent Ave (32804-3337)
P.O. Box 536548 (32853-6548)
PHONE..................................407 298-5600
Thomas Pulsifer, *President*
Bridget A Pulsifer, *Vice Pres*
John Harter, *Project Mgr*
Susan T Pulsifer, *Treasurer*
Zondria Jones, *Human Res Mgr*
▼ EMP: 65 EST: 1933
SALES (est): 16.2MM **Privately Held**
WEB: www.millsnebraska.com
SIC: 3442 5211 Metal doors; lumber &
other building materials

(G-12000)
CENTURY METAL PRODUCTS INC
3108 Friendly Ave (32808-3907)
PHONE..................................407 293-8871
Tim Dewald, *President*
EMP: 27 EST: 1947
SQ FT: 4,980
SALES (est): 2.1MM **Privately Held**
SIC: 3444 Sheet metalwork

(G-12001)
CG ROXANE LLC
Also Called: Crystal Geyser
2224 Hazelhurst Ave (32804-2714)
PHONE..................................407 241-1640
EMP: 22 **Privately Held**
WEB: www.crystalgeyserplease.com
SIC: 2086 Water, pasteurized: packaged in
cans, bottles, etc.
PA: Cg Roxane Llc
1400 Marys Dr
Weed CA 96094

(G-12002)
CHANCE ALUMINUM CORP ✪
11616 Landstar Blvd (32824-9025)
PHONE..................................407 789-1606
Xiangming Cheng, *President*
EMP: 18 EST: 2021
SALES (est): 6.3MM
SALES (corp-wide): 400.5MM **Privately Held**
WEB: www.chancealuminum.com
SIC: 3313 Electrometallurgical products
PA: Chance Corporation
11616 Landstar Blvd
Orlando FL 32824
407 377-0246

(G-12003)
CHANGE THIS WORLD
6790 Edgwter Cmmerce Pkwy
(32810-4278)
PHONE..................................407 900-8840
Steven Hooper, *Principal*
Loren Cusati, *Human Res Mgr*
EMP: 7 EST: 2010
SALES (est): 433.2K **Privately Held**
WEB: www.ushunger.org
SIC: 2041 Flour & other grain mill products

(G-12004)
CHARGERS AND CASES LLC
Also Called: Distinct.ink
5310 Alpha Dr (32810-4422)
PHONE..................................352 587-2539
Daren Ellington, *Principal*
Daren M Ellington, *Manager*
EMP: 11 EST: 2011
SALES (est): 1MM **Privately Held**
SIC: 3523 Farm machinery & equipment

(G-12005)
CHARLES K SEWELL
Also Called: C K S
333 W Michigan St (32806-4422)
PHONE..................................407 423-1870
Charles K Sewell, *Owner*
EMP: 8 EST: 2006
SALES (est): 881.1K **Privately Held**
WEB: www.ckspackaging.com
SIC: 2821 Plastics materials & resins

(G-12006)
CHASE AEROSPACE INC
5342 Greenside Ct (32819-3829)
PHONE..................................407 812-4545
Nick Thomas, *President*
Brenda Thomas, *Admin Sec*
▲ EMP: 10 EST: 1997
SQ FT: 11,250
SALES (est): 2.1MM **Privately Held**
WEB: www.chaseaerospace.com
SIC: 3728 Aircraft parts & equipment

(G-12007)
CHEFS COMMISSARY LLC
6929 Narcoossee Rd # 509 (32822-5567)
PHONE..................................321 303-2947
Michael J Birnbaum, *Mng Member*
John Brauner,
Warren G Dietel,
Raul Matias,
Daniel E Robinson,
EMP: 65 EST: 2013
SQ FT: 15,000
SALES (est): 3MM **Privately Held**
WEB: www.chefscommissary.com
SIC: 2038 Frozen specialties

(G-12008)
CHENEY OFS INC
Also Called: Grand Western
3875 Bengert St (32808-4603)
PHONE..................................407 292-3223
Bill Folwy, *President*
Sean Stout, *Sales Staff*
David Pinna, *Representative*
EMP: 719 EST: 2010
SALES (est): 20.7MM
SALES (corp-wide): 1.8B **Privately Held**
SIC: 2013 5149 Sausages & other pre-
pared meats; spaghetti
PA: Cheney Bros., Inc.
1 Cheney Way
Riviera Beach FL 33404
561 845-4700

(G-12009)
CHOICE CABINETS & COUNTERS
11139 Sunup Ln (32825-7424)
PHONE..................................407 670-8944
Ricardo Lorenzo, *Principal*
EMP: 7 EST: 2008
SALES (est): 214.3K **Privately Held**
SIC: 3131 Counters

(G-12010)
CHRISTIE LITES ENTPS USA LLC (PA)
6990 Lake Ellenor Dr (32809-4604)
PHONE..................................407 856-0016
Karina Mendoza, *Vice Pres*
Jeni Ofarril, *Purch Agent*
Jennifer George, *VP Finance*
Jenn Bodshaug, *Manager*
Terry Crain, *Manager*
EMP: 125 EST: 2013
SALES (est): 20.2MM **Privately Held**
SIC: 3648 Lighting equipment

(G-12011)
CHRISTIE LITES ORLANDO LLC (HQ)
2479 Eunice Ave (32808-4609)
PHONE..................................206 223-7200
Huntly Christie, *CEO*
Justin Oakland, *Top Exec*
Pete P Hulin, *VP Opers*
Katy Marx, *Project Mgr*
Rohan Wallace, *Project Mgr*
▲ EMP: 1 EST: 1998
SQ FT: 19,200
SALES (est): 4.6MM
SALES (corp-wide): 20.2MM **Privately Held**
SIC: 3648 Lighting equipment
PA: Christie Lites Enterprises Usa, Llc
6990 Lake Ellenor Dr
Orlando FL 32809
407 856-0016

(G-12012)
CHUNKY PLATES LLC
2550 W Colonial Dr (32804-8017)
PHONE..................................321 746-3346
Latisha Nicole Boykin, *Owner*

G
E
O
G
R
A
P
H
I
C

Pastorq Hepburn, *Director*
Phuong Hepburn, *Administration*
EMP: 6 **EST:** 2016
SALES (est): 497.8K **Privately Held**
SIC: 2037 Frozen fruits & vegetables

(G-12013)
CITORY SOLUTIONS LLC
10524 Moss Park Rd # 204 (32832-5898)
PHONE................................407 766-6533
Gerald J Leo Connet, *Manager*
Eddie Hurn, *Director*
Mark Riggin, *Director*
EMP: 15 **EST:** 2011
SALES (est): 3.9MM **Privately Held**
WEB: www.citory.com
SIC: 3446 Architectural metalwork

(G-12014)
CITY PRINTS LLC
200 E Colonial Dr (32801-1204)
PHONE................................407 409-0509
Rodney Thompson, *Manager*
Katie Rodono, *Consultant*
EMP: 6 **EST:** 2016
SALES (est): 513.6K **Privately Held**
SIC: 2752 Commercial printing, lithographic

(G-12015)
CKS PACKAGING INC
333 W Michigan St (32806-4422)
PHONE................................407 423-0333
Melvin Brown, *Opers Mgr*
Brian McClarty Proj, *Engineer*
Brian Walsh, *Engineer*
Tom Heller, *Sales Executive*
Jim Stuhr, *Branch Mgr*
EMP: 109
SALES (corp-wide): 539.6MM **Privately Held**
WEB: www.ckspackaging.com
SIC: 3089 3085 5085 Plastic containers, except foam; plastics bottles; commercial containers
PA: C.K.S. Packaging, Inc.
350 Great Sw Pkwy
Atlanta GA 30336
404 691-8900

(G-12016)
CKS PACKAGING INC
7400 S Orange Ave (32809-6057)
PHONE................................407 420-9529
Lloyd Martin, *Mfg Staff*
EMP: 52
SALES (corp-wide): 539.6MM **Privately Held**
WEB: www.ckspackaging.com
SIC: 3089 Plastic containers, except foam
PA: C.K.S. Packaging, Inc.
350 Great Sw Pkwy
Atlanta GA 30336
404 691-8900

(G-12017)
CLARIOS LLC
Also Called: Johnson Controls
4127 Seaboard Rd (32808-3848)
PHONE................................407 850-0147
Anthony Pascucci, *Branch Mgr*
EMP: 50
SALES (corp-wide): 47.9B **Privately Held**
WEB: www.clarios.com
SIC: 2531 3714 3691 Seats, automobile; motor vehicle body components & frame; lead acid batteries (storage batteries)
HQ: Clarios, Llc
5757 N Green Bay Ave
Milwaukee WI 53209

(G-12018)
CLASSIC SCREEN PRTG DESIGN INC
1353 Pine Ave (32824-7939)
PHONE................................407 850-0112
John W Nanstiel, *President*
EMP: 7 **EST:** 1999
SQ FT: 6,000
SALES (est): 618.3K **Privately Held**
WEB: www.classicscreenprinting.com
SIC: 2759 Screen printing

(G-12019)
CLEARANT INC (PA)
6001 Lexington Park (32819-4433)
PHONE................................407 876-3134
Jon M Garfield, *CEO*
Michael Bartlett, *Ch of Bd*
Susan E Etzel, *...*
◆ **EMP:** 8 **EST:** 1999
SQ FT: 2,500
SALES (est): 5.2MM **Privately Held**
SIC: 2836 7389 Blood derivatives; product sterilization service

(G-12020)
CLEVER COVERS INC
524 W Winter Park St (32804-4435)
PHONE................................407 423-5959
John Smith, *President*
EMP: 6 **EST:** 1996
SALES (est): 543.5K **Privately Held**
SIC: 3465 Hub caps, automobile: stamped metal

(G-12021)
CLOSETMAID LLC (DH)
13485 Veterans Way (32827-7718)
PHONE................................352 401-6000
Robert J Clements Jr, *President*
Michael Peterson, *Manager*
◆ **EMP:** 165 **EST:** 1965
SALES (est): 350.6MM
SALES (corp-wide): 2.2B **Publicly Held**
WEB: www.homebyames.com
SIC: 2511 5712 Storage chests, household: wood; furniture stores

(G-12022)
CLOUDFACTORS LLC
7380 W Sand Lake Rd # 500 (32819-5248)
PHONE................................407 768-3160
James Keefner, *President*
EMP: 5 **EST:** 2011
SALES (est): 468.5K **Privately Held**
WEB: education.cloudfactors.com
SIC: 7372 7373 7371 5734 Application computer software; value-added resellers; computer systems; computer software development & applications; computer software development; personal computers

(G-12023)
COASTAL AWNGS HRRCANE PRTCTION
14438 Avalon Reserve Blvd (32828-5196)
PHONE................................407 923-9482
Gracie I Whittaker, *President*
EMP: 5
SALES (est): 417.2K **Privately Held**
WEB: www.crystalcoastawnings.com
SIC: 2394 3444 3089 3442 Canvas awnings & canopies; canvas covers & drop cloths; awnings & canopies; awnings, fiberglass & plastic combination; storm doors or windows, metal; roofing, siding & sheet metal work; millwork

(G-12024)
COBALT LASER
965 W Taft Vineland Rd # 107 (32824-8024)
PHONE................................407 855-2833
Marvin J Sweers, *Principal*
EMP: 6 **EST:** 2008
SALES (est): 384.5K **Privately Held**
WEB: www.cobaltlaser.com
SIC: 2752 Commercial printing, lithographic

(G-12025)
COCA-COLA BEVERAGES FLA LLC
2900 Mercy Dr (32808-3897)
PHONE................................407 295-9290
Fax: 407 294-2320
EMP: 150
SALES (corp-wide): 481.3MM **Privately Held**
SIC: 2086 5149 Mfg Bottled/Canned Soft Drinks Whol Groceries
PA: Coca-Cola Beverages Florida, Llc
10117 Princess Palm Ave # 100
Tampa FL 33610
813 327-7294

(G-12026)
COCA-COLA COMPANY
2900 Mercy Dr (32808-3897)
PHONE................................407 295-9290
Fax: 407 294-2322
EMP: 112
SALES (corp-wide): 35.4B **Publicly Held**
SIC: 2086 Mfg Bottled/Canned Soft Drinks
PA: The Coca-Cola Company
1 Coca Cola Plz Nw
Atlanta GA 30313
404 676-2121

(G-12027)
CODA OCTOPUS GROUP INC (PA)
3300 S Hiawassee Rd # 104 (32835-6350)
PHONE................................407 735-2402
Annmarie Gayle, *Ch of Bd*
Blair Cunningham, *President*
Charlie Pearson, *Engineer*
Michael Midgley, *CFO*
EMP: 12 **EST:** 1994
SQ FT: 3,000
SALES (est): 21.3MM **Publicly Held**
WEB: www.codaoctopusgroup.com
SIC: 3812 Search & navigation equipment; sonar systems & equipment

(G-12028)
COLEMAN AEROSPACE
5950 Lakehurst Dr (32819-8345)
PHONE................................407 354-0047
Mark Stephen, *Vice Pres*
Julie Beechy, *Engineer*
EMP: 15 **EST:** 2005
SALES (est): 2.8MM **Privately Held**
WEB: www.rocket.com
SIC: 3721 Aircraft

(G-12029)
COLL BUILDERS SUPPLY INC
6663 Narcoossee Rd # 178 (32822-5549)
PHONE................................407 745-4641
Humberto Collazo, *President*
Collazo Adrian, *President*
Adrian Collazo, *General Mgr*
EMP: 12 **EST:** 2012
SQ FT: 6,300
SALES (est): 946.2K **Privately Held**
WEB: www.pr1mo.net
SIC: 3965 Fasteners

(G-12030)
COLLIDECOM LLC
4700 Mllnia Blvdn Ste 400 (32839)
PHONE................................407 903-5626
Dan Thresher, *...*
EMP: 10 **EST:** 2015
SALES (est): 347.4K **Privately Held**
SIC: 2741

(G-12031)
COLLINS RESEARCH INC
Also Called: Flame Boss
6790 Edgwter Cmmerce Pkwy (32810-4278)
PHONE................................321 401-6060
Micheal Collins, *CEO*
Roger Collins, *President*
Bob Hack, *General Mgr*
Robert Hack, *Vice Pres*
Janet Collins, *Manager*
EMP: 16 **EST:** 2007
SQ FT: 190,000
SALES (est): 800K **Privately Held**
SIC: 3829 Measuring & controlling devices

(G-12032)
COMMERCIAL CABINETRY LLC
6135 Cyril Ave (32809-5045)
PHONE................................407 440-4601
Warren A Skipper, *...*
EMP: 5 **EST:** 2010
SALES (est): 693.7K **Privately Held**
SIC: 3553 Cabinet makers' machinery

(G-12033)
COMMERCIAL METAL PHOTOGRAPHY
Also Called: C M P G
1934a Silver Star Rd (32804-3302)
P.O. Box 547155 (32854-7155)
PHONE................................407 295-8182
Lawrence Albrecht, *President*

EMP: 6 **EST:** 1983
SQ FT: 3,000
SALES (est): 591.5K **Privately Held**
SIC: 3999 7336 Identification plates; silk screen design

(G-12034)
COMMERCIAL MILLWORKS INC
1120 S Hughey Ave Ste A (32806-1011)
PHONE................................407 648-2787
Robert Coursey, *President*
Gayle King, *Vice Pres*
EMP: 14 **EST:** 1992
SQ FT: 15,000
SALES (est): 2MM **Privately Held**
WEB: www.commercialmillworksinc.com
SIC: 2431 Millwork

(G-12035)
COMMSCOPE TECHNOLOGIES LLC
11310 Satellite Blvd (32837-9224)
PHONE................................407 944-9116
Jim Watkins, *Manager*
EMP: 10 **Publicly Held**
WEB: www.commscope.com
SIC: 3663 Radio & TV communications equipment
HQ: Commscope Technologies Llc
4 Westbrook Corp Ctr
Westchester IL 60154
800 366-3891

(G-12036)
COMPLEMENTARY COATINGS CORP
Also Called: Insl-X Coronado Lenmar
9592 Parksouth Ct (32837-8383)
PHONE................................386 428-6461
EMP: 200
SALES (corp-wide): 242.1B **Publicly Held**
SIC: 2851 Mfg Paints & Industrial Coatings
HQ: Complementary Coatings Corp.
101 Paragon Dr
Montvale NJ 07645

(G-12037)
COMTECH ANTENNA SYSTEMS INC
212 Outlook Point Dr # 100 (32809-7200)
PHONE................................407 854-1950
Tom Christi, *President*
Justin O'Neill, *Marketing Staff*
Bill Parke, *Director*
▼ **EMP:** 129 **EST:** 1984
SQ FT: 35,000
SALES (est): 30.8MM
SALES (corp-wide): 486.2MM **Publicly Held**
WEB: www.comtech.com
SIC: 3663 Satellites, communications; antennas, transmitting & communications
PA: Comtech Telecommunications Corp.
68 S Service Rd Ste 230
Melville NY 11747
631 962-7000

(G-12038)
COMTECH SYSTEMS INC
212 Outlook Point Dr # 100 (32809-7200)
PHONE................................407 854-1950
Fred Kornberg, *Ch of Bd*
Richard Luhrs, *President*
Rich Luhrs, *President*
Joe Smith, *Engineer*
Tom Sheehan, *Senior Engr*
▼ **EMP:** 72 **EST:** 1974
SALES (est): 17.2MM
SALES (corp-wide): 486.2MM **Publicly Held**
WEB: www.comtech.com
SIC: 3663 Satellites, communications; microwave communication equipment
PA: Comtech Telecommunications Corp.
68 S Service Rd Ste 230
Melville NY 11747
631 962-7000

(G-12039)
CON-AIR INDUSTRIES INC
4157 Seaboard Rd (32808-3849)
PHONE................................407 298-5733
Jack Lefort, *CEO*
Robert N Hering Jr, *CEO*

▲ = Import ▼ =Export
◆ =Import/Export

Charles Adkinson, *Regional Mgr*
William Hohns, *Corp Secy*
Crissy Adkinson, *COO*
EMP: 100 **EST:** 1980
SQ FT: 100,000
SALES (est): 25MM **Privately Held**
WEB: www.conairindustries.com
SIC: 3585 5075 7623 Refrigeration &
heating equipment; air filters; air condi-
tioning repair
HQ: Filtration Group Llc
912 E Washington St Ste 1
Joliet IL 60433
803 628-2410

(G-12040)
CONCRETE EDGE COMPANY
1952 Saturn Blvd (32837-9417)
PHONE..............................407 658-2788
Robert Matthias, *President*
Colleen McKay, *Sales Mgr*
▼ **EMP:** 8 **EST:** 1993
SALES (est): 1.2MM **Privately Held**
WEB: www.lilbubbacurb.com
SIC: 3559 5211 5083 0782 Concrete
products machinery; masonry materials &
supplies; landscaping equipment; land-
scape contractors; landscape planning
services

(G-12041)
**CONDUENT IMAGE SOLUTIONS
INC**
Also Called: ACS
4209 Vineland Rd Ste J2 (32811-6630)
PHONE..............................407 849-0279
Amanda Mas, *Controller*
Marty Martinez, *Manager*
EMP: 227
SALES (corp-wide): 4.1B **Publicly Held**
WEB: www.conduent.com
SIC: 3577 Computer peripheral equipment
HQ: Conduent Image Solutions, Inc.
100 Campus Dr Ste 200e
Florham Park NJ 07932

(G-12042)
**CONKLIN METAL INDUSTRIES
INC**
3060 Pennington Dr (32804-3334)
PHONE..............................407 688-0900
Ron Wigginton, *VP Bus Dvlpt*
Brian Campbell, *Sales Mgr*
Samantha Kirkland, *Marketing Staff*
Dave Hills, *Branch Mgr*
Angel Sante, *Manager*
EMP: 18
SALES (corp-wide): 106.3MM **Privately
Held**
WEB: www.conklinmetal.com
SIC: 3444 Sheet metalwork
PA: Conklin Metal Industries, Inc.
684 Antone St Nw Ste 100
Atlanta GA 30318
404 688-4510

(G-12043)
CONQUEST ENGINEERING LLC
7901 Kingspointe Pkwy # 17 (32819-6520)
PHONE..............................407 731-0519
Joao Vianna, *CEO*
EMP: 20 **EST:** 2018
SALES (est): 1.1MM **Privately Held**
SIC: 1389 Construction, repair & disman-
tling services

(G-12044)
CONSUMER SOURCE INC
Also Called: Apartment Guide
8026 Sunport Dr Ste 304 (32809-8108)
PHONE..............................407 888-0745
EMP: 9 **Privately Held**
SIC: 2741 Publisher
HQ: Consumer Source Inc.
3585 Engrg Dr Ste 100
Norcross GA 30092
678 421-3000

(G-12045)
**CONTROL LASER
CORPORATION**
Also Called: CLC
8251 Presidents Dr # 1688 (32809-7653)
PHONE..............................407 926-3500
Renjie Liu, *President*

Fred Nielsen, *Vice Pres*
Nikki Rice, *Purchasing*
Sumedha Hewagama, *Engineer*
Nengda Jiang, *Engineer*
▲ **EMP:** 40 **EST:** 1965
SQ FT: 80,000
SALES (est): 10.8MM **Privately Held**
WEB: www.controllaser.com
SIC: 3699 Laser systems & equipment
PA: Han's Laser Technology Industry Group
Co., Ltd.
No.9988, Shennan Avenue, Nanshan
District
Shenzhen GD 51800

(G-12046)
CONVERGENT TECHNOLOGIES
14764 Sapodilla Dr (32828-7321)
PHONE..............................407 482-4381
Scott C Barry, *Principal*
EMP: 10 **EST:** 2008
SALES (est): 992.9K **Privately Held**
SIC: 3674 Semiconductors & related de-
vices

(G-12047)
COOL TREAT
7001 International Dr (32819-8221)
PHONE..............................407 248-0743
Roger Patel, *Principal*
EMP: 9 **EST:** 2007
SALES (est): 389.2K **Privately Held**
SIC: 2024 Ice cream, bulk

(G-12048)
CORKCICLE LLC
1300 Brookhaven Dr Ste 2 (32803-2547)
P.O. Box 547965 (32854-7965)
PHONE..............................866 780-0007
Dylon York, *Partner*
Sharrie Booker, *Vice Pres*
Scott Newman, *Prdtn Mgr*
Jay Langford, *Production*
Brandon Blahnik, *Cust Mgr*
◆ **EMP:** 28 **EST:** 2010
SALES (est): 6.2MM **Privately Held**
WEB: www.corkcicle.com
SIC: 3089 Plastic kitchenware, tableware &
houseware

(G-12049)
CORONADO PAINT CO INC
9592 Parksouth Ct (32837-8383)
P.O. Box 308, Edgewater (32132-0308)
PHONE..............................386 428-6461
James Weil, *President*
▼ **EMP:** 154 **EST:** 1957
SQ FT: 193,000
SALES (est): 30MM
SALES (corp-wide): 354.6B **Publicly
Held**
SIC: 2851 Paints & allied products
HQ: Benjamin Moore & Co.
101 Paragon Dr
Montvale NJ 07645
201 573-9600

(G-12050)
COSTECH LAB LLC
2100 Consulate Dr Ste 100 (32837-8397)
PHONE..............................407 476-3488
Tianxiang Wang,
EMP: 7 **EST:** 2020
SALES (est): 477.9K **Privately Held**
SIC: 3999 Manufacturing industries

(G-12051)
COUNTY OF ORANGE
400 E South St (32801-2816)
PHONE..............................407 649-0076
Laury Edwards, *Sheriff*
Eric Perez, *Sheriff*
Scott Hall, *Vice Pres*
John Davis, *Project Mgr*
Carlos Cuevas, *Opers Staff*
EMP: 62
SALES (corp-wide): 2.5B **Privately Held**
WEB: www.occompt.com
SIC: 2741 Miscellaneous publishing
PA: County Of Orange
201 S Rosalind Ave Fl 5
Orlando FL 32801
407 836-7350

(G-12052)
**CRAIG CATAMARAN
CORPORATION**
4333 Silver Star Rd # 1 (32808-5100)
PHONE..............................407 290-8778
Robert Craig, *President*
Erik Craig, *Vice Pres*
Evana Craig, *Vice Pres*
▼ **EMP:** 7 **EST:** 1970
SQ FT: 5,000
SALES (est): 1MM **Privately Held**
WEB: www.craigcat.com
SIC: 3732 Boat building & repairing

(G-12053)
**CREATIVE EVENTS AND
EXHIBITS (PA)**
Also Called: Zweifel International
405 Fairlane Ave (32809-4104)
PHONE..............................407 851-4754
John Zweifel, *President*
▲ **EMP:** 8 **EST:** 1955
SQ FT: 50,000
SALES (est): 375.1K **Privately Held**
SIC: 3999 Advertising display products

(G-12054)
**CREATIVE PROMOTIONAL
PRODUCTS**
1325 E Harding St (32806-4115)
PHONE..............................407 383-7114
Annie McRae, *Principal*
Judy Elowe, *Vice Pres*
Rich Block, *Sales Staff*
Jerry Gleicher, *Sales Staff*
Loni Vaccaro, *Marketing Staff*
EMP: 7 **EST:** 2008
SALES (est): 135.8K **Privately Held**
SIC: 2759 Promotional printing

(G-12055)
**CREATIVE PRTG GRPHIC DSIGN
INC**
1009 Pine St (32824-8342)
PHONE..............................407 855-0202
Rick Pearce, *President*
Randy Pearce, *Vice Pres*
Sheila Shell, *Sales Mgr*
Jim Rowland, *Cust Mgr*
Brandy Bennett, *Sales Staff*
EMP: 27 **EST:** 1982
SQ FT: 16,000
SALES (est): 5.7MM **Privately Held**
WEB: www.creativepgm.com
SIC: 2752 2796 2791 2789 Commercial
printing, offset; platemaking services;
typesetting; bookbinding & related work;
commercial printing

(G-12056)
**CRESS CHEMICAL & EQP CO
INC**
519 19th St (32805-4747)
P.O. Box 555649 (32855-5649)
PHONE..............................407 425-2846
Stephen E Cressman, *President*
Stephen Cressman, *Vice Pres*
EMP: 5 **EST:** 1970
SQ FT: 4,000
SALES (est): 592.9K **Privately Held**
SIC: 2851 5084 Removers & cleaners;
cleaning equipment, high pressure, sand
or steam

(G-12057)
**CROWN EQUIPMENT
CORPORATION**
Also Called: Crown Lift Trucks
404 Sunport Ln Ste 150 (32809-8131)
PHONE..............................407 438-5401
Steve Scholz, *Manager*
Andrew Barrera, *Technician*
EMP: 51
SALES (corp-wide): 5.2B **Privately Held**
WEB: www.crown.com
SIC: 3537 Lift trucks, industrial: fork, plat-
form, straddle, etc.
PA: Crown Equipment Corporation
44 S Washington St
New Bremen OH 45869
419 629-2311

(G-12058)
**CROWN INDUSTRIES OF
FLORIDA**
827 W Yale St (32804-5254)
PHONE..............................321 432-0014
Thomas Cuff, *Principal*
EMP: 9 **EST:** 2018
SALES (est): 54.4K **Privately Held**
SIC: 3999 Manufacturing industries

(G-12059)
CSL OF AMERICA INC
1900 S Orange Blossom Trl (32805-4652)
PHONE..............................407 849-7070
Cesar S Leirias, *President*
EMP: 9 **EST:** 2005
SALES (est): 192.2K **Privately Held**
SIC: 2298 Nets, rope

(G-12060)
CSMC INC
Also Called: Allegra Print & Imaging
4498 Vineland Rd (32811-7334)
PHONE..............................407 246-1567
Don Snyder, *President*
EMP: 36 **EST:** 1982
SALES (est): 6.6MM **Privately Held**
WEB: www.allegramarketingprint.com
SIC: 2752 2791 2789 2759 Commercial
printing, offset; typesetting; bookbinding &
related work; commercial printing

(G-12061)
**CUBIC ADVNCED LRNG
SLTIONS INC**
2001 W Oak Ridge Rd (32809-3813)
PHONE..............................407 859-7410
Theresa W Kohl, *President*
Thomas D Echols, *Vice Pres*
Angela L Hartley, *Admin Sec*
EMP: 22 **EST:** 2013
SALES (est): 6.8MM
SALES (corp-wide): 1.4B **Privately Held**
SIC: 3699 3812 7372 Flight simulators
(training aids), electronic; defense sys-
tems & equipment; application computer
software
HQ: Cubic Corporation
9233 Balboa Ave
San Diego CA 92123
858 277-6780

(G-12062)
CUBIC CORPORATION
3862 Quadrangle Blvd # 100 (32817-8368)
PHONE..............................407 859-7410
Penny Romano, *Buyer*
Ray Boyles, *Engineer*
Ed Campbell, *Engineer*
Jason Schwartz, *Engineer*
Sonia Scott, *Senior Engr*
EMP: 114
SALES (corp-wide): 1.4B **Privately Held**
WEB: www.cubic.com
SIC: 3812 Defense systems & equipment
HQ: Cubic Corporation
9233 Balboa Ave
San Diego CA 92123
858 277-6780

(G-12063)
**CUBIC SIMULATION SYSTEMS
INC**
Also Called: Cubic Transportation Systems
2001 W Oak Ridge Rd # 100 (32809-3813)
PHONE..............................407 641-2037
Robert L Collins, *CEO*
William W Boyle, *CEO*
Bradley H Feldmann, *President*
Walter C Zable, *Chairman*
Glenn C Andrew, *COO*
◆ **EMP:** 140 **EST:** 1951
SQ FT: 398,086
SALES (est): 20.3MM
SALES (corp-wide): 1.4B **Privately Held**
SIC: 3699 Electronic training devices
HQ: Cubic Corporation
9233 Balboa Ave
San Diego CA 92123
858 277-6780

(G-12064)
CULINARY CONCEPTS INC
2215 Tradeport Dr (32824-7005)
P.O. Box 2066, Winter Park (32790-2066)
PHONE...................................407 228-0069
Moorefield Margaret D, *Principal*
Hal Valdes, *Vice Pres*
Manny Garcia, *Vice Pres*
Anthony Pace, *Vice Pres*
Thomas F Gilbertson, *Director*
EMP: 34 **EST:** 1998
SALES (est): 2MM **Privately Held**
SIC: 2099 5812 2035 2034 Food preparations; eating places; pickles, sauces & salad dressings; dehydrated fruits, vegetables, soups

(G-12065)
CUSANOS ITALIAN BAKERY INC
Also Called: Cusano's Baking Co.
1904 Premier Row (32809-6206)
PHONE...................................786 506-4281
EMP: 36
SALES (corp-wide): 28.2MM **Privately Held**
WEB: www.cusanos.com
SIC: 2051 Bakery: wholesale or wholesale/retail combined
PA: Cusano's Italian Bakery, Inc.
5480 W Hillsboro Blvd
Coconut Creek FL 33073
954 458-1010

(G-12066)
CUSTOM CORNHOLE BOARDS INC
Also Called: Wholesale Cornhole Bags
6169 Cyril Ave (32809-5045)
PHONE...................................407 203-6886
Daniel A Jones Sr, *President*
Laurence Ragan, *President*
EMP: 20 **EST:** 2014
SQ FT: 9,000
SALES (est): 2.3MM **Privately Held**
WEB: www.cornholeboards.us
SIC: 2493 Hardboard, tempered

(G-12067)
CUSTOM FAB INC (DH)
109 5th St (32824-8258)
PHONE...................................407 859-3954
Christopher M Comins, *President*
Holly Porter, *General Mgr*
Kevin Larrabee, *Project Mgr*
Henry Herrera, *CFO*
Robin Mitchem, *Asst Controller*
▲ **EMP:** 86 **EST:** 2005
SQ FT: 2,400
SALES (est): 28.6MM **Privately Held**
WEB: www.uspipe.com
SIC: 3317 3498 Steel pipe & tubes; coils, pipe: fabricated from purchased pipe
HQ: United States Pipe And Foundry Company Llc
2 Chase Corporate Dr # 200
Hoover AL 35244
205 263-8540

(G-12068)
CUSTOM METAL FABRICATORS INC
1415 Long St (32805-2410)
PHONE...................................407 841-8551
Earl Potts, *President*
Kevin Potts, *Vice Pres*
EMP: 7 **EST:** 1973
SQ FT: 8,162
SALES (est): 997.9K **Privately Held**
WEB: www.custommetalfabricators.com
SIC: 3444 Sheet metal specialties, not stamped

(G-12069)
D & A MACHINE INC
7220 Old Cheney Hwy (32807-6222)
PHONE...................................407 275-5770
EMP: 8 **EST:** 2019
SALES (est): 245.4K **Privately Held**
WEB: www.damachine.com
SIC: 3469 Stamping metal for the trade

(G-12070)
D&D WOOD WORKING INC
8622 Brackenwood Dr (32829-8628)
PHONE...................................407 427-0106
David A Batista, *President*
EMP: 7 **EST:** 2004
SALES (est): 79.8K **Privately Held**
SIC: 2431 Millwork

(G-12071)
DAHLQUIST ENTERPRISES INC
Also Called: Dahlquists Printing & Graphics
1315 N Mills Ave (32803-2542)
PHONE...................................407 896-2294
George Dahlquist, *President*
EMP: 9 **EST:** 1978
SQ FT: 4,200
SALES (est): 741.1K **Privately Held**
WEB: www.dahlquistprinting.com
SIC: 2752 2791 2789 2759 Commercial printing, offset; typesetting; bookbinding & related work; commercial printing

(G-12072)
DANIELS MANUFACTURING CORP
526 Thorpe Rd (32824-8133)
P.O. Box 593872 (32859-3872)
PHONE...................................407 855-6161
George G Daniels, *CEO*
Erik Francoforte, *General Mgr*
James D Vargo, *Corp Secy*
Andre Hulsbosch, *Purch Agent*
John Kokat, *Purchasing*
▲ **EMP:** 170 **EST:** 1949
SQ FT: 60,000
SALES (est): 38.3MM **Privately Held**
WEB: www.dmctools.com
SIC: 3546 3423 Power-driven handtools; hand & edge tools

(G-12073)
DARLAND BAKERY INC
42 Cardamon Dr (32825-3658)
PHONE...................................407 894-1061
EMP: 15
SQ FT: 8,000
SALES (est): 155.1K **Privately Held**
SIC: 2051 Mfg Pies Cakes & Muffins

(G-12074)
DART INDUSTRIES INC (HQ)
14901 S Ornge Blssom Trl (32837-6600)
P.O. Box 2353 (32802-2353)
PHONE...................................407 826-5050
E V Goings, *President*
Richard A Lisec, *Vice Pres*
Shirley Bush, *Purch Agent*
Thomas M Roehlk, *Admin Sec*
▲ **EMP:** 350 **EST:** 1928
SALES (est): 467.5MM **Publicly Held**
SIC: 3089 Plastic containers, except foam

(G-12075)
DATAMAX INTERNATIONAL CORP (DH)
4501 Pkwy Commerce Blvd (32808-1013)
PHONE...................................407 578-8007
William Bouverie, *President*
David Winder, *Vice Pres*
▲ **EMP:** 121 **EST:** 1991
SQ FT: 90,000
SALES (est): 69.9MM
SALES (corp-wide): 34.3B **Publicly Held**
SIC: 3577 2754 Input/output equipment, computer; labels: gravure printing

(G-12076)
DATAMAX-ONEIL CORPORATION (HQ)
4501 Pkwy Commerce Blvd (32808-1013)
PHONE...................................800 816-9649
Michael Savignac, *President*
John Yuncza, *CFO*
Phillip Pastore, *Controller*
Karl Tao, *Asst Sec*
◆ **EMP:** 160 **EST:** 1984
SQ FT: 70,000
SALES (est): 103.3MM
SALES (corp-wide): 34.3B **Publicly Held**
SIC: 3577 2754 Input/output equipment, computer; labels: gravure printing

PA: Honeywell International Inc.
855 S Mint St
Charlotte NC 28202
704 627-6200

(G-12077)
DAVID DELIGHTS LLC
4677 L B Mcleod Rd Ste J (32811-5609)
PHONE...................................407 648-2020
Walter David,
EMP: 5 **EST:** 2004
SALES (est): 488.1K **Privately Held**
SIC: 2066 Chocolate & cocoa products

(G-12078)
DAYTON SUPERIOR CORPORATION
7415 Emerald Dunes Dr # 1200 (32822-4710)
PHONE...................................407 859-4541
Scot Perry, *Regional Mgr*
Corey Garrison, *Vice Pres*
Judy Williams, *Manager*
EMP: 7
SALES (corp-wide): 47.9B **Privately Held**
WEB: www.daytonsuperior.com
SIC: 3429 3444 Builders' hardware; concrete forms, sheet metal
HQ: Dayton Superior Corporation
1125 Byers Rd
Miamisburg OH 45342
937 866-0711

(G-12079)
DBN INVESTMENT LLC
3300 S Hiawassee Rd # 107 (32835-6350)
PHONE...................................407 917-2525
Shahabadeen Khan,
EMP: 14 **EST:** 2013
SALES (est): 478.1K **Privately Held**
SIC: 1389 Construction, repair & dismantling services

(G-12080)
DDCI INC
Also Called: Csg
995 W Kennedy Blvd Ste 35 (32810-6139)
PHONE...................................407 814-0225
Dino Derose, *President*
Howard Sullivan, *General Mgr*
Christopher E Inman, *Vice Pres*
Shane Bowen, *Project Mgr*
Chris Schronski, *Project Mgr*
EMP: 80 **EST:** 1987
SQ FT: 12,000
SALES (est): 8.4MM
SALES (corp-wide): 3.3B **Privately Held**
WEB: www.ddci.com
SIC: 3669 5063 Burglar alarm apparatus, electric; alarm systems
HQ: Convergint Technologies Llc
1 Commerce Dr
Schaumburg IL 60173
847 620-5000

(G-12081)
DEFENSE FLIGHT AEROSPACE LLC
5448 Hoffner Ave Ste 105 (32812-2506)
PHONE...................................321 442-7255
Stephen Pratt,
EMP: 13 **EST:** 2018
SALES (est): 545.9K **Privately Held**
SIC: 3589 Service industry machinery

(G-12082)
DELIVERY SIGNS LLC
Also Called: Art Signs The
40 W Crystal Lake St # 100 (32806-4404)
PHONE...................................407 362-7896
D A Quiroz Zaiter, *Mng Member*
Daniel A Quiroz Zaiter, *Mng Member*
EMP: 5 **EST:** 2010
SALES (est): 502.8K **Privately Held**
WEB: www.deliverysigns.com
SIC: 3993 Signs, not made in custom sign painting shops

(G-12083)
DELURE PUBLISHING LLC
1021 Santa Barbara Rd (32808-7133)
P.O. Box 608781 (32860-8781)
PHONE...................................407 866-5448
Michael Brandon Ashford, *Principal*
EMP: 7 **EST:** 2016

SALES (est): 50K **Privately Held**
SIC: 2741 Miscellaneous publishing

(G-12084)
DELUXE CARS LLC
Also Called: Girgis Auto Brothers
6302 Old Cheney Hwy (32807-3669)
PHONE...................................407 982-7978
R G Girgis,
EMP: 7 **EST:** 2016
SALES (est): 279.5K **Privately Held**
SIC: 2782 Checkbooks

(G-12085)
DESIGN COMMUNICATIONS LTD
10611 Satellite Blvd (32837-8429)
PHONE...................................407 856-9661
Dana Lanasa, *Project Mgr*
Jason Abbatoy, *Prdtn Mgr*
Craig Kutner, *Branch Mgr*
Scott Saccullo, *Manager*
Roger Stone, *Executive*
EMP: 13
SALES (corp-wide): 29.2MM **Privately Held**
WEB: www.designcommunicationsltd.com
SIC: 3993 Signs & advertising specialties
PA: Design Communications, Ltd.
85 Bodwell St Ste 1
Avon MA 02322
617 542-9620

(G-12086)
DESIGN FURNISHINGS INC
3647 All American Blvd (32810-4726)
PHONE...................................407 294-0507
John Follo, *President*
EMP: 28 **EST:** 1986
SQ FT: 30,000
SALES (est): 4.8MM **Privately Held**
WEB: www.designfurnishings.net
SIC: 2599 2512 Bar furniture; restaurant furniture, wood or metal; chairs: upholstered on wood frames; couches, sofas & davenports: upholstered on wood frames

(G-12087)
DESIGNERS PRESS INC
6305 Chancellor Dr (32809-5609)
PHONE...................................407 843-3141
David R Simons, *CEO*
Tina Bean, *Production*
Ellen Benton, *Consultant*
Daniel B Wolfe, *Director*
Karen Caufield,
EMP: 64 **EST:** 1990
SQ FT: 36,000
SALES (est): 15.1MM
SALES (corp-wide): 121.9MM **Privately Held**
WEB: www.sandyinc.com
SIC: 2759 2752 Commercial printing; commercial printing, lithographic
PA: Sandy Alexander, Inc.
200 Entin Rd
Clifton NJ 07014
973 470-8100

(G-12088)
DESIND INDUSTRIES CORP
150 E Robinson St # 1009 (32801-1695)
PHONE...................................212 729-0192
Brian Desind, *Principal*
EMP: 9 **EST:** 2014
SALES (est): 240.9K **Privately Held**
SIC: 3999 Barber & beauty shop equipment

(G-12089)
DEVON CHASE & COMPANY
2814 Silver Star Rd # 5 (32808-3938)
P.O. Box 593730 (32859-3730)
PHONE...................................407 438-6466
Thomas M Tedesco, *President*
Sue Tedesco, *Admin Sec*
EMP: 7 **EST:** 1989
SQ FT: 20,000
SALES (est): 484.7K **Privately Held**
WEB: www.devonchase.com
SIC: 2512 2515 Wood upholstered chairs & couches; mattresses & foundations

(G-12090)
DF MULTI SERVICES LLC
845 N Garland Ave (32801-1095)
PHONE...................................407 683-2223

Paulo Fabiano Carneiro, *President*
EMP: 5 **EST:** 2017
SALES (est): 667.5K **Privately Held**
SIC: 3448 1799 1741 Screen enclosures; fence construction; unit paver installation

(G-12091)
DIAMOND CABINETS & SERVICE
1411 Edgewater Dr Ste 200 (32804-6361)
PHONE......................321 689-8289
EMP: 7 **EST:** 2012
SALES (est): 168.2K **Privately Held**
WEB: www.diamondcabinets.com
SIC: 2434 Wood kitchen cabinets

(G-12092)
DIAZ GO GREEN INC
413 Brailiff Ct (32824-5970)
PHONE......................407 501-2724
Maribel Diaz, *Vice Pres*
EMP: 7 **EST:** 2012
SALES (est): 132.8K **Privately Held**
SIC: 3714 Motor vehicle parts & accessories

(G-12093)
DIDNA INC
206 Hillcrest St (32801-1212)
PHONE......................239 851-0966
Deke Hooper, *CEO*
Dwight Hooper, *Ch of Bd*
Troy Bubley, *President*
William Lutzen, *CFO*
Chris Cazabon, *Software Dev*
EMP: 7 **EST:** 2016
SALES (est): 527.1K **Privately Held**
WEB: www.didna.io
SIC: 7372 8742 Publishers' computer software; management consulting services

(G-12094)
DIGITAL ANTOMY SMLTONS FOR HLT
1720 S Orange Ave Ste 300 (32806-2967)
PHONE......................937 623-7377
Jack Stubbs,
EMP: 6 **EST:** 2020
SALES (est): 500K **Privately Held**
SIC: 3842 Models, anatomical

(G-12095)
DIGITAL MONARCH INC ✪
1317 Edgewater Dr # 2032 (32804-6350)
PHONE......................407 259-2901
Peter Brosky, *President*
EMP: 5 **EST:** 2021
SALES (est): 311K **Privately Held**
SIC: 3571 Computers, digital, analog or hybrid

(G-12096)
DIGITAL PIXEL DISPLAYS LLC (PA)
111 N Orange Ave (32801-2316)
PHONE......................321 948-3751
Khaled Khuda, *Mng Member*
EMP: 5 **EST:** 2019
SALES (est): 377.4K **Privately Held**
WEB: www.digitalpixeldisplays.com
SIC: 3679 Liquid crystal displays (LCD)

(G-12097)
DIGITAL PROPAGANDA INC
997 W Kennedy Blvd A12 (32810-6140)
PHONE......................407 644-8444
EMP: 14
SALES (est): 1.7MM **Privately Held**
SIC: 2731 Publishing And Printing

(G-12098)
DISTINGSHED GNTLMAN MBL DTLING
7512 Dr Phillips Blvd 50-1 (32819-5131)
PHONE......................321 200-4331
Jonathan Brown,
EMP: 6 **EST:** 2020
SALES (est): 300K **Privately Held**
WEB: www.thedgmd.com
SIC: 2842 Automobile polish

(G-12099)
DIVERSIFIED GRAPHICS INC
720 Franklin Ln (32801-3624)
PHONE......................407 425-9443
Edwin T Stephens, *President*

Norma Stephens, *Treasurer*
Carolyn Sasser, *Office Mgr*
Dean Leatherbarrow, *Analyst*
EMP: 10 **EST:** 1976
SQ FT: 16,000
SALES (est): 715.4K **Privately Held**
WEB: www.diversified-graphics.com
SIC: 2796 2752 Color separations for printing; commercial printing, lithographic

(G-12100)
DIVINITAS DISPLAYS LLC
7598 Currency Dr (32809-6923)
PHONE......................407 660-6625
Kitt Hancock, *Vice Pres*
Bronson Lam, *Marketing Staff*
Perry J Degregorio,
EMP: 9 **EST:** 2013
SALES (est): 1.3MM **Privately Held**
WEB: www.divinitasnow.com
SIC: 3993 Signs & advertising specialties

(G-12101)
DL CABINETRY ORLANDO LLC
7025 W Colonial Dr (32818-6705)
PHONE......................504 669-7847
Junxiu Ren, *Mng Member*
EMP: 9 **EST:** 2017
SALES (est): 569K **Privately Held**
WEB: www.dlcabinetryorlando.com
SIC: 2434 Wood kitchen cabinets

(G-12102)
DOUGLAS ABBOTT
3708 S John Young Pkwy (32839-9204)
PHONE......................407 422-3597
Douglas Abbott, *Owner*
EMP: 8 **EST:** 2001
SALES (est): 132.7K **Privately Held**
SIC: 3643 Rail bonds, electric: for propulsion & signal circuits

(G-12103)
DP PET PRODUCTS INC
Also Called: Pro Pet Distributors
5340 Young Pine Rd 8 (32829-7415)
PHONE......................407 888-4627
David Canning, *President*
▲ **EMP:** 10 **EST:** 1991
SALES (est): 953.7K **Privately Held**
SIC: 3199 Dog furnishings: collars, leashes, muzzles, etc.: leather

(G-12104)
DR PEPPER BOTTLING CO
1700 Directors Row (32809-6226)
PHONE......................407 354-5800
Don Dignan, *CFO*
EMP: 10 **EST:** 2007
SALES (est): 140.8K **Privately Held**
SIC: 2086 Soft drinks: packaged in cans, bottles, etc.

(G-12105)
DRAGONFIRE INDUSTRIES INC
4065 L B Mcleod Rd Ste G1 (32811-5663)
PHONE......................407 999-2215
Tim Titus, *President*
Tammy Titus, *Vice Pres*
Doris Titus, *Treasurer*
EMP: 5 **EST:** 1994
SALES (est): 562.6K **Privately Held**
WEB: www.dragonfireindustries.com
SIC: 3993 Signs, not made in custom sign painting shops

(G-12106)
DRAKE TOOL CO INC
10211 General Dr (32824-8529)
PHONE......................407 859-4221
Lenville G Drake, *President*
Mary Drake, *Corp Secy*
EMP: 8 **EST:** 1985
SQ FT: 5,100
SALES (est): 943.2K **Privately Held**
WEB: www.draketoolco.com
SIC: 3599 Machine shop, jobbing & repair

(G-12107)
DRIP COMMUNICATION LLC
6831 Edgwter Cmmerce Pkwy (32810-4224)
PHONE......................407 730-5519
Ricardo Rosa,
EMP: 11 **EST:** 2016

SALES (est): 435.6K **Privately Held**
WEB: www.dripcommunications.com
SIC: 2759 Promotional printing

(G-12108)
DRONE IMAGING SERVICES LLC
8540 Summerville Pl (32819-3928)
PHONE......................407 620-5258
William Woodard, *Principal*
EMP: 8 **EST:** 2017
SALES (est): 637.2K **Privately Held**
SIC: 3721 Motorized aircraft

(G-12109)
DRY COLOR USA LLC
8701 S Ct Skinner (32824)
PHONE......................407 856-7788
Clovis Filipov, *President*
Eliezer Filipov, *Director*
Silas Filipov, *Director*
Priscila F Silva, *Director*
▲ **EMP:** 5 **EST:** 2012
SQ FT: 39,000
SALES (est): 2.2MM **Privately Held**
WEB: www.drycolor.com
SIC: 2816 Color pigments
PA: Dry Color Especialidades Quimicas Ltda
Rua Pedro Suzan 170
Cosmopolis SP 13157

(G-12110)
DRYWALL ELEMENTS
1700 35th St Ste 110 (32839-8950)
PHONE......................407 454-7293
Ronald Sisson, *Project Mgr*
EMP: 16 **EST:** 2019
SALES (est): 6.6MM **Privately Held**
SIC: 2819 Elements

(G-12111)
DUSOBOX CORPORATION
Also Called: Dusobox Creative Packg Group
2501 Investors Row # 500 (32837-8387)
PHONE......................407 855-5120
John L Kelley, *President*
Richard J Kelley Sr, *Chairman*
Greg Cetera, *Business Mgr*
Richard J Kelley Jr, *Vice Pres*
Kyle Yerdon, *Engineer*
▼ **EMP:** 83 **EST:** 1955
SQ FT: 65,000
SALES (est): 20MM **Privately Held**
WEB: www.dusobox.com
SIC: 2653 Boxes, corrugated: made from purchased materials

(G-12112)
EAGLE METAL DISTRIBUTORS INC
603 W Landstreet Rd Ste B (32824-7856)
PHONE......................407 367-0688
Von Plourde, *President*
▲ **EMP:** 9 **EST:** 2003
SQ FT: 36,000
SALES (est): 4.5MM **Privately Held**
WEB: www.eaglemetalsinc.com
SIC: 3354 Aluminum extruded products

(G-12113)
EAST COAST FLOATS LLC
4832 New Broad St (32814-6628)
PHONE......................407 203-5628
Mark Bowers,
Laurie J Samulonis-Bowers,
EMP: 8 **EST:** 2013
SALES (est): 280.4K **Privately Held**
WEB: www.eastcoastfloats.com
SIC: 2452 Sauna rooms, prefabricated, wood

(G-12114)
ECHODOG INDUSTRIES INC
9350 Bentley Park Cir (32819-5345)
P.O. Box 2568, Windermere (34786-2568)
PHONE......................407 909-1636
Bobby L Moore, *Principal*
EMP: 7 **EST:** 2007
SALES (est): 128K **Privately Held**
SIC: 3999 Manufacturing industries

(G-12115)
ECO CUPS INTERNATIONAL CORP
2814 Silver Star Rd Apt 4 (32808-3938)
PHONE......................407 308-1764
Karel P Hartinger, *President*
Stella M Hartinger, *Principal*
Abriela C Granes Alvarez, *Director*
Armando P Valdes Garrido-Lecca, *Director*
Adele E Gobelli, *Director*
EMP: 11 **EST:** 2017
SALES (est): 2.3MM **Privately Held**
WEB: www.ecocups.us
SIC: 2656 3229 Paper cups, plates, dishes & utensils; bowls, glass

(G-12116)
EDUMATICS INC
7649 W Clnl Dr Ste 120 (32818)
PHONE......................407 656-0661
Kietta Mayweather Gamble, *President*
Soraya Smith, *Admin Asst*
EMP: 15 **EST:** 2012
SALES (est): 907K **Privately Held**
WEB: www.edumaticsprogram.com
SIC: 3999 7812 7373 Education aids, devices & supplies; educational motion picture production, television; motion picture production & distribution; computer-aided manufacturing (CAM) systems service

(G-12117)
EI INTERACTIVE LLC
121 S Orange Ave Ste 1400 (32801-3240)
PHONE......................407 579-0993
Fabio Cardoso, *Mng Member*
EMP: 9 **EST:** 2012
SQ FT: 1,630
SALES (est): 584.4K **Privately Held**
SIC: 7372 Business oriented computer software

(G-12118)
EJM COPPER INC
Also Called: E J M Gutter
1911 Ellman St (32804-4201)
PHONE......................407 447-0074
Edward J Majewski, *CEO*
Angie Majewski, *Vice Pres*
EMP: 14 **EST:** 1999
SQ FT: 5,000
SALES (est): 2.4MM **Privately Held**
WEB: www.ejmcopper.com
SIC: 3331 Primary copper

(G-12119)
ELECTRONIC ARTS INC
515 W Amelia St (32801-1196)
PHONE......................407 838-8000
Jeff Aho, *Editor*
Jason Jones, *Editor*
Scott Forrest, *Senior VP*
Roy Harvey, *Vice Pres*
Daryl Holt, *Vice Pres*
EMP: 10
SALES (corp-wide): 6.9B **Publicly Held**
WEB: www.ea.com
SIC: 7372 Home entertainment computer software
PA: Electronic Arts Inc.
209 Redwood Shores Pkwy
Redwood City CA 94065
650 628-1500

(G-12120)
ELEMENTS OF SPACE LLC
10142 Pink Carnation Ct (32825-8814)
PHONE......................407 718-9690
Wendy J Hilton, *Principal*
EMP: 8 **EST:** 2015
SALES (est): 224.5K **Privately Held**
WEB: www.elementsofspace.com
SIC: 3555 Engraving machinery & equipment, except plates; blocks, wood: engravers'

(G-12121)
ELITE DISTRIBUTORS LLC
1716 Premier Row A (32809-6202)
PHONE......................407 601-6665
Naushad Manjani, *Manager*
EMP: 12 **EST:** 2017
SALES (est): 1.1MM **Privately Held**
SIC: 3489 Smoke generators (ordnance)

(G-12122)
ELITE METAL FINISHING EAST LLC ✪
Also Called: A.M. Metal Finishing
7594 Chancellor Dr (32809-6919)
PHONE................................407 843-0182
Joel Clemons, CEO
Gregory Hansen, CFO
EMP: 15 EST: 2021
SQ FT: 20,000
SALES (est): 2.8MM
SALES (corp-wide): 20.1MM Privately Held
SIC: 3471 Anodizing (plating) of metals or formed products; chromium plating of metals or formed products
PA: Elite Metal Finishing, L.L.C.
540 Spectrum Cir
Oxnard CA 93030
805 983-4320

(G-12123)
ELLIPSIS BREWING
7500 Tpc Blvd Ste 8 (32822-5181)
PHONE................................407 556-3241
Robert McKee, Principal
EMP: 7 EST: 2016
SQ FT: 7,500
SALES (est): 220.4K Privately Held
WEB: www.ellipsisbrewing.com
SIC: 2082 Beer (alcoholic beverage)

(G-12124)
EMBROIDERY SOLUTIONS INC
6001 S Orange Ave (32809-4237)
PHONE................................407 438-8188
Leo Ambrose, President
Andrew Nazareth, Vice Pres
EMP: 6 EST: 1998
SALES (est): 716.4K Privately Held
WEB: www.embroiderysolutions.com
SIC: 2759 Screen printing

(G-12125)
EMINEL CORPORATION INC
Also Called: Tiregraficx
8600 Com Cir Unit 148 (32819)
PHONE................................407 900-0190
Steven M Mandala, President
EMP: 10 EST: 2014
SQ FT: 3,000
SALES (est): 3MM Privately Held
SIC: 3011 Tire & inner tube materials & related products

(G-12126)
EMPOWER SOFTWARE SOLUTIONS INC
Also Called: Empower Sftwr Sltions A Kronos
315 E Robinson St Ste 350 (32801-1668)
PHONE................................407 233-2000
Jim Hoefflin, President
Chad A Hensley, Exec VP
Carrie Norden, Exec VP
John Whisner, Exec VP
EMP: 255 EST: 2007
SQ FT: 1,000
SALES (est): 25.1MM
SALES (corp-wide): 1.1B Privately Held
SIC: 7372 Prepackaged software
HQ: Kronos Incorporated
900 Chelmsford St
Lowell MA 01851
978 250-9800

(G-12127)
EMS TECHNOLOGIES NA LLC
121 S Orange Ave Ste 1500 (32801-3241)
P.O. Box 162797, Altamonte Springs (32716-2797)
PHONE................................321 259-5979
Chris Moats, Mng Member
EMP: 10 EST: 2006
SALES (est): 3MM Privately Held
WEB: www.ems-technologies.com
SIC: 3541 Machine tools, metal cutting type

(G-12128)
ENABLESOFT INC
11825 High Tech Ave # 100 (32817-8474)
PHONE................................407 233-2626
Richard L Milam, CEO
Scott Heureux, President
Karen Reichle, Exec VP

Aaron Bultman, Vice Pres
Craig Petersen, CFO
EMP: 16 EST: 1995
SQ FT: 4,510
SALES (est): 2.5MM
SALES (corp-wide): 153.1MM Privately Held
WEB: www.nintex.com
SIC: 7372 8748 Business oriented computer software; systems engineering consultant, ex. computer or professional
HQ: Nintex Usa, Inc.
10800 Ne 8th St Ste 400
Bellevue WA 98004

(G-12129)
ENGAGE UNI LLC
Also Called: Engage Surgical
3505 Lake Lynda Dr (32817-8324)
PHONE................................833 364-2432
Daniel Justin, CEO
EMP: 13 EST: 2017
SALES (est): 3.3MM
SALES (corp-wide): 5.2B Privately Held
SIC: 3842 Implants, surgical
PA: Smith & Nephew Plc
Building 5, Croxley Park
Watford HERTS WD18
800 015-7573

(G-12130)
ENTERPRISE SYSTEM ASSOC INC (PA)
Also Called: E S A I
3259 Progress Dr (32826-3230)
PHONE................................407 275-0220
Robert Barbour, President
Santiago Tula, Principal
EMP: 10 EST: 2000
SALES (est): 1.7MM Privately Held
WEB: www.esaigroup.com
SIC: 7372 Business oriented computer software

(G-12131)
ENTERPRISE TECH PARTNERS LLC
37 N Orange Ave Ste 616 (32801-2449)
PHONE................................918 851-3285
Sandra Dennard, Manager
EMP: 10 EST: 2000
SALES (est): 376.4K Privately Held
WEB: www.etpco.com
SIC: 3571 Electronic computers

(G-12132)
ENVIRONMENTAL TECTONICS CORP
Etc
2100 N Alafaya Trl # 900 (32826-4747)
PHONE................................407 282-3378
Chad Minor, Project Mgr
Bob Rubeo, Project Mgr
Phil Driscoll, Maint Spvr
Katarzyna Wrzesinski, Opers Staff
Paul Biocic, QC Mgr
EMP: 10
SALES (corp-wide): 73.8MM Publicly Held
WEB: www.etcusa.com
SIC: 3699 Electronic training devices
PA: Environmental Tectonics Corporation
125 James Way
Southampton PA 18966
215 355-9100

(G-12133)
ERICSSON INC
360 S Lake Destiny Dr (32810-6226)
PHONE................................856 230-6268
EMP: 11
SALES (corp-wide): 25.3B Privately Held
SIC: 3663 Radio & TV communications equipment
HQ: Ericsson Inc
6300 Legacy Dr
Plano TX 75024
972 583-0000

(G-12134)
ESTEREL TECHNOLOGIES INC
Also Called: North American Operations
1082 N Alsaya Trl Ste 124 (32826)
PHONE................................724 746-3304
Chip Downing, CEO

Tony Karam, General Mgr
Antoine Karam, Sr Consultant
EMP: 10 EST: 2001
SQ FT: 500
SALES (est): 571.5K Privately Held
SIC: 7372 Prepackaged software

(G-12135)
ETERNAL SMOKE INC
1321 Edgewater Dr Ste 1 (32804-6387)
PHONE................................407 984-5090
Angela Denise Smith, President
EMP: 7 EST: 2018
SALES (est): 705.8K Privately Held
WEB: www.eternalsmoke.com
SIC: 2131 Smoking tobacco

(G-12136)
EUROASIA PRODUCTS INC
3956 W Town Center Blvd # 166 (32837-6103)
PHONE................................321 221-9398
John Bowers, President
▲ EMP: 5 EST: 1998
SQ FT: 2,000
SALES (est): 708.3K Privately Held
WEB: www.euroasiaproducts.com
SIC: 3589 5023 Cooking equipment, commercial; home furnishings

(G-12137)
EUROGAN-USA INC
502 Sunport Ln Ste 350 (32809-8135)
PHONE................................321 356-5248
Luis Hernandez, President
Raul Hernandez, COO
▲ EMP: 10 EST: 2014
SQ FT: 10,000
SALES (est): 2MM Privately Held
SIC: 3089 Injection molded finished plastic products

(G-12138)
EVANIOS LLC
2875 S Orange Ave 500-8 (32806-5451)
PHONE................................617 233-4986
Marc Jarjour, General Mgr
Andy Ray, Mng Member
Sherard Pulmano, Practice Mgr
EMP: 12 EST: 2012
SALES (est): 484.1K Privately Held
WEB: www.hp.com
SIC: 3571 Personal computers (microcomputers)

(G-12139)
EVEREST CABINETS INC
6100 Hanging Moss Rd # 5 (32807-3790)
PHONE................................407 790-7819
Ming Shu Lu, Principal
EMP: 8 EST: 2018
SALES (est): 252.3K Privately Held
WEB: www.everestcabinetorlando.com
SIC: 2434 Wood kitchen cabinets

(G-12140)
EVOLUTION LINERS INC
40 W Illiana St (32806-4455)
PHONE................................407 839-6213
Stan Patterson, CEO
EMP: 9 EST: 2004
SALES (est): 845.1K Privately Held
WEB: www.evoii.com
SIC: 3842 Prosthetic appliances

(G-12141)
EVOLUTION VOICE INC
5728 Major Blvd Ste 720 (32819-7973)
PHONE................................407 204-1614
Neil Tolley, President
EMP: 10 EST: 2019
SALES (est): 434.2K Privately Held
WEB: www.fourteenip.com
SIC: 7372 Business oriented computer software

(G-12142)
EXCELOR LLC
7380 W Sand Lake Rd # 500 (32819-5248)
PHONE................................321 300-3315
Joseph S Vangala, President
EMP: 10 EST: 2001

SALES (est): 813.5K Privately Held
WEB: www.excelor.com
SIC: 7372 8721 Business oriented computer software; accounting services, except auditing

(G-12143)
FABBRO MARINE GROUP INC
Also Called: Cape Horn Boats
100 E Pine St Ste 110 (32801-2759)
PHONE................................321 701-8141
Christopher R Fabbro, President
Franklin Davis, Corp Secy
Tyler Cesar, Vice Pres
EMP: 28 EST: 1988
SQ FT: 25,000
SALES (est): 5.9MM Privately Held
WEB: www.capehornboats.com
SIC: 3732 Boats, fiberglass: building & repairing

(G-12144)
FANTASY CHOCOLATES INC
Also Called: Williams & Bennett
1815 Cypress Lake Dr (32837-8457)
PHONE................................561 276-9007
Becky Gardner, President
William Gardner, Vice Pres
EMP: 50 EST: 1994
SQ FT: 30,000
SALES (est): 21.1MM
SALES (corp-wide): 757.1MM Publicly Held
WEB: www.williamsandbennett.com
SIC: 2066 Chocolate
HQ: Bbx Capital, Inc.
401 E Las Olas Blvd Fl 8
Fort Lauderdale FL 33301

(G-12145)
FANTO GROUP LLC (PA)
9550 Satellite Blvd # 170 (32837-8471)
PHONE................................407 857-5101
William Eickenberg, General Mgr
Tom Sublette, Vice Pres
Cheryl Henning, Project Mgr
Christopher O 'steen, Project Mgr
Fanto F J, Mng Member
◆ EMP: 6 EST: 2004
SALES (est): 2.4MM Privately Held
WEB: www.fantogroup.com
SIC: 3648 Lighting equipment

(G-12146)
FCA NORTH AMERICA HOLDINGS LLC
Also Called: Southeast Business Center
10300 Boggy Creek Rd # 1 (32824-7033)
PHONE................................407 826-7021
Carlos Jimenez, Branch Mgr
EMP: 30 Privately Held
WEB: www.chrysler.com
SIC: 3711 3714 Motor vehicles & car bodies; automobile assembly, including specialty automobiles; truck & tractor truck assembly; bus & other large specialty vehicle assembly; motor vehicle parts & accessories; motor vehicle engines & parts
HQ: Fca Us Llc
1000 Chrysler Dr
Auburn Hills MI 48326

(G-12147)
FCS INDUSTRIES CORP
6996 Piazza Grande Ave # 314 (32835-8756)
PHONE................................407 412-5642
Willie Daniel Fisher, Owner
EMP: 10 EST: 2015
SALES (est): 481.1K Privately Held
WEB: www.palhumanesociety.org
SIC: 3999 Manufacturing industries

(G-12148)
FERMATEX ENTERPRISES INC
Also Called: Royal Press
685 S Rnald Reagan Blvd (32808)
PHONE................................407 332-8320
Luis Quiroz, President
EMP: 7 EST: 1983
SQ FT: 2,300
SALES (est): 1.1MM Privately Held
WEB: fermatex.openfos.com
SIC: 2752 Commercial printing, offset

G E O G R A P H I C

(G-12149)
FGT CABINETRY LLC
1031 Crews Comm Dr Ste 13 (32837)
PHONE...............................321 800-2036
Jinming Fang,
Xin Jiang,
EMP: 7 EST: 2018
SALES (est): 740.8K Privately Held
WEB: www.fgtshop.com
SIC: 2434 Wood kitchen cabinets

(G-12150)
FILTA GROUP INC (PA)
7075 Kingspointe Pkwy # 1 (32819-6541)
PHONE...............................407 996-5550
Tom Dunn, CEO
Victor Clewes, President
Colin Hecht, General Mgr
Rob Totten, COO
Adam Blake, Vice Pres
◆ EMP: 17 EST: 2003
SQ FT: 12,000
SALES (est): 6.5MM Privately Held
WEB: www.gofilta.com
SIC: 3677 Filtration devices, electronic

(G-12151)
FINASTRA USA CORPORATION
8010 Sunport Dr Ste 101 (32809-7897)
PHONE...............................800 394-8778
Michelle Willis, Branch Mgr
EMP: 68
SALES (corp-wide): 1.6B Privately Held
WEB: www.finastra.com
SIC: 7372 Prepackaged software
HQ: Finastra Usa Corporation
    555 Sw Morrison St # 300
    Portland OR 97204
    407 804-6600

(G-12152)
FIRETAINMENT INC
2415 N John Young Pkwy (32804-4105)
PHONE...............................888 552-7897
Shawn Clark, CEO
EMP: 9 EST: 2010
SALES (est): 1.1MM Privately Held
WEB: www.firetainment.com
SIC: 3631 Barbecues, grills & braziers
(outdoor cooking)

(G-12153)
FIRST CHECK DIAGNOSTICS LLC
30 S Keller Rd Ste 100 (32810-6297)
PHONE...............................858 805-2425
EMP: 22 EST: 2007
SALES: 817.7K
SALES (corp-wide): 43B Publicly Held
SIC: 3841 Diagnostic apparatus, medical
PA: Abbott Laboratories
    100 Abbott Park Rd
    Abbott Park IL 60064
    224 667-6100

(G-12154)
FL PRECAST LLC
12679 Maribou Cir (32828-7120)
PHONE...............................321 356-9673
Victor S Vallejo R, President
Victor Vallejo,
EMP: 8 EST: 2016
SALES (est): 411.8K Privately Held
SIC: 3272 Window sills, cast stone

(G-12155)
FLEX BEAUTY LABS LLC
7512 Dr Phillips Blvd (32819-5131)
PHONE...............................646 302-8542
George Mandras,
Christopher Mandras,
Lauren Mandras,
EMP: 13 EST: 2017
SALES (est): 3MM Privately Held
WEB: www.flexbeautylabs.com
SIC: 3999 Hair & hair-based products

(G-12156)
FLEX PACK USA LLC
1205 Pine Ave (32824-7937)
PHONE...............................407 704-0800
Intaaf Ali, Mng Member
EMP: 5 EST: 2015

SALES (est): 511.4K Privately Held
WEB: www.flexpackusallc.com
SIC: 2631 Container, packaging &
boxboard

(G-12157)
FLOOR TECH LLC
Also Called: All State Pallets
9801 Recycle Center Rd (32824-8151)
PHONE...............................407 855-8087
Robert Zuchowski, COO
Kyle Zuchowski, Mng Member
Mark Hayes,
EMP: 15 EST: 1983
SQ FT: 7,110
SALES (est): 2.4MM Privately Held
SIC: 2448 Pallets, wood; pallets, wood &
wood with metal

(G-12158)
FLORIDA BUS UNLIMITED INC
1925 W Princeton St (32804-4705)
PHONE...............................407 656-1175
James Bay, President
Jeffrey Slack, Vice Pres
Michael Stotler, Vice Pres
Tod Chapman, Admin Sec
EMP: 29 EST: 1981
SQ FT: 38,000
SALES (est): 511.1K Privately Held
SIC: 3711 5561 Buses, all types, assem-
bly of; recreational vehicle dealers

(G-12159)
FLORIDA CATHOLIC MEDIA INC
50 E Robinson St (32801-1619)
P.O. Box 4993 (32802-4993)
PHONE...............................407 373-0075
Ann B Slade Publisher, Principal
Diana Garcia, Manager
Shana Coulthurst, Director
Susan Diaz, Executive Asst
EMP: 6 EST: 1939
SALES (est): 991K Privately Held
WEB: www.thefloridacatholic.org
SIC: 2711 8661 Newspapers: publishing
only, not printed on site; religious organi-
zations

(G-12160)
FLORIDA COPIER CONNECTIONS
Also Called: Green Holness
8022 Office Ct Ste 100 (32809-6768)
PHONE...............................407 844-9690
Green Holness, President
EMP: 9 EST: 2009
SQ FT: 13,000
SALES (est): 245.6K Privately Held
WEB: www.copiersflorida.com
SIC: 3861 Photocopy machines

(G-12161)
FLORIDA HOSPITAL ASSN MGT CORP
Also Called: Park Lake Printers
827 Highland Ave (32803-3919)
PHONE...............................407 841-6230
Frances Owens, Principal
John Mines, Vice Pres
Rebecca Ryan, Admin Asst
EMP: 6 EST: 2008
SALES (est): 584.9K Privately Held
WEB: www.fha.org
SIC: 2752 Commercial printing, litho-
graphic

(G-12162)
FLORIDA NONWOVENS INC
1111 Central Florida Pkwy (32837-9258)
PHONE...............................407 241-2701
Dan Dobbins, CEO
Mike Wood, Vice Pres
◆ EMP: 25 EST: 1998
SALES (est): 744.4K Privately Held
SIC: 3299 Ceramic fiber

(G-12163)
FLORIDA PILLOW COMPANY
1012 Sligh Blvd (32806-1029)
PHONE...............................407 648-9121
Chris A Allard, President
Christopher Allard, Owner
▼ EMP: 5 EST: 1982
SQ FT: 4,700

SALES (est): 590K Privately Held
WEB: www.floridapillow.com
SIC: 2392 Cushions & pillows; pillows,
bed: made from purchased materials

(G-12164)
FLORIDA Q-RAILING CO
3734 Mercy Star Ct # 130 (32808-4615)
PHONE...............................407 450-1808
Ronald Guliker, Principal
EMP: 7 EST: 2020
SALES (est): 319.2K Privately Held
WEB: www.q-railing.com
SIC: 2431 Staircases, stairs & railings

(G-12165)
FLORIDA ROCK INDUSTRIES
2858 Sidney Ave (32810-5134)
PHONE...............................407 299-7494
Chris Thorne, President
EMP: 8 Publicly Held
WEB: www.flarock.com
SIC: 3999 Barber & beauty shop equip-
ment
HQ: Florida Rock Industries
    4707 Gordon St
    Jacksonville FL 32216
    904 355-1781

(G-12166)
FLORIDA SCREEN SERVICES INC
805 W Central Blvd (32805-1808)
PHONE...............................407 316-0466
Gil Adkins, President
Linda Adkins, Corp Secy
Steven Adkins, Vice Pres
Smith Lawrence W, Vice Pres
Heather Adkins, Manager
EMP: 10 EST: 1980
SQ FT: 6,000
SALES (est): 647.2K Privately Held
SIC: 2759 2396 Screen printing; automo-
tive & apparel trimmings

(G-12167)
FLORIDA SIGN SOURCE
505 W Robinson St (32801-1721)
P.O. Box 521135, Longwood (32752-1135)
PHONE...............................407 316-0466
Stephen Adkins, Principal
EMP: 5 EST: 2011
SALES (est): 407.4K Privately Held
WEB: www.floridasignsource.com
SIC: 3993 Signs & advertising specialties

(G-12168)
FLORIDA SUNSHINE STUCCO LLC
9484 Boggy Creek Rd (32824-8720)
PHONE...............................407 947-2088
Milena C Neal, Principal
EMP: 8 EST: 2008
SALES (est): 85K Privately Held
SIC: 3299 Stucco

(G-12169)
FLORIDA TRUSS CORPORATION
1302 Abberton Dr (32837-6520)
PHONE...............................407 438-2553
Carlos A Mendez, Principal
Carlos Mendez, Officer
EMP: 8 EST: 2012
SALES (est): 363.6K Privately Held
WEB: www.floridatrusscorp.com
SIC: 2439 Structural wood members

(G-12170)
FLORIDA WIRE & RIGGING SUP INC
4524 36th St (32811-6526)
P.O. Box 180127, Casselberry (32718-
0127)
PHONE...............................407 422-6218
Ronald J Worswick, President
Scott Battaglia, General Mgr
Dennis E Worswick, Senior VP
Douglas Worswick, Senior VP
Connie Gahnz, CFO
▼ EMP: 7 EST: 1968
SQ FT: 6,180
SALES (est): 910.8K Privately Held
WEB: www.floridawire.com
SIC: 3496 Miscellaneous fabricated wire
products

(G-12171)
FLOWERS BKG CO BRADENTON LLC
Also Called: Flowers Baking Company
4301 N Pine Hills Rd (32808-2546)
PHONE...............................941 758-5656
Chris Peer, Manager
EMP: 25
SALES (corp-wide): 4.3B Publicly Held
WEB: www.flobradconf.com
SIC: 2051 Bread, cake & related products
HQ: Flowers Baking Co. Of Bradenton, Llc
    6490 Parkland Dr
    Sarasota FL 34243

(G-12172)
FONON TECHNOLOGIES INC (PA)
1101 N Keller Rd Ste G (32810-5917)
PHONE...............................407 477-5618
Dmitri Nikitin, Vice Pres
Wayne Tupuola, Vice Pres
Arnold Bykov, Director
EMP: 24 EST: 2013
SQ FT: 45,000
SALES (est): 3.2MM Publicly Held
SIC: 3699 Laser welding, drilling & cutting
equipment; laser systems & equipment

(G-12173)
FORM-CO INC
2487 Tradeport Dr Ste 200 (32824-7067)
PHONE...............................800 745-3700
Jeffrey D Church, Principal
EMP: 7 EST: 2010
SALES (est): 123.4K Privately Held
WEB: www.formrx.com
SIC: 3531 Construction machinery

(G-12174)
FRESH CHOICE MA RKET
10249 S John Young Pkwy (32837-4022)
PHONE...............................407 448-8956
Amine Harb, Principal
EMP: 10 EST: 2011
SALES (est): 473.3K Privately Held
SIC: 3421 Table & food cutlery, including
butchers'

(G-12175)
FRESH INK PRINT LLC
Also Called: Fresh Ink Signs & Graphics
4729 Patch Rd Ste 200 (32822-3579)
PHONE...............................407 412-5905
Gabriel Boy, Managing Prtnr
Carlos A Rivero, Manager
Deann Kroeplin, Manager
Christian Stanley, Manager
EMP: 6 EST: 2012
SQ FT: 3,800
SALES (est): 773.2K Privately Held
WEB: www.freshinkorlando.com
SIC: 3993 7336 Electric signs; signs, not
made in custom sign painting shops;
graphic arts & related design

(G-12176)
FRESHETECH LLC
1211 Pine Ave (32824-7937)
PHONE...............................516 519-3453
Chase Mills, Sales Staff
Adam Schwartz, Mng Member
Robinson Rob, Manager
EMP: 13 EST: 2013
SALES (est): 5MM Privately Held
WEB: www.freshe.tech
SIC: 3651 Home entertainment equipment,
electronic

(G-12177)
FRITO-LAY NORTH AMERICA INC
2800 Silver Star Rd (32808-3941)
PHONE...............................407 295-1810
Tamara Kimball, Sales Staff
Leslie Starr, Branch Mgr
Kristina Casanova, Manager
Bob Zak, Manager
Angela Jerry, Technical Staff
EMP: 228
SQ FT: 175,562
SALES (corp-wide): 70.3B Publicly Held
WEB: www.fritolay.com
SIC: 2096 2099 Potato chips & similar
snacks; food preparations

HQ: Frito-Lay North America, Inc.
7701 Legacy Dr
Plano TX 75024

(G-12178)
FUTURE FOAM INC
1351 Gemini Blvd (32837-9276)
PHONE..................................407 857-2510
Jeffrey Hosko, *Opers Mgr*
Rafael Rodriguez, *Mfg Staff*
EMP: 71
SALES (corp-wide): 494.9MM **Privately Held**
WEB: www.futurefoam.com
SIC: 3086 Insulation or cushioning material, foamed plastic
PA: Future Foam, Inc.
1610 Avenue N
Council Bluffs IA 51501
712 323-9122

(G-12179)
FW SHORING COMPANY
Also Called: Professional Shoring & Supply
11128 Boggy Creek Rd (32824-7415)
PHONE..................................517 676-8800
Wayne Agamie, *Branch Mgr*
EMP: 9
SALES (corp-wide): 9.9MM **Privately Held**
WEB: www.efficiencyproduction.com
SIC: 3531 Construction machinery
PA: Fw Shoring Company
685 Hull Rd
Mason MI 48854
517 676-8800

(G-12180)
G J EMBROIDERY INC
6839 Narcoossee Rd Ste 33 (32822-5581)
PHONE..................................407 284-8036
Basem E Farag, *Principal*
EMP: 6 EST: 2015
SALES (est): 486.7K **Privately Held**
WEB: www.gjembroidery.com
SIC: 2395 Embroidery products, except schiffli machine

(G-12181)
GAM LASER INC (PA)
7100 Tpc Dr Ste 200 (32822-5125)
PHONE..................................407 851-8999
Gordon A Murray, *President*
Ray Lambert, *Manager*
EMP: 10 EST: 1986
SQ FT: 8,000
SALES (est): 1.1MM **Privately Held**
WEB: www.gamlaser.com
SIC: 3826 Laser scientific & engineering instruments

(G-12182)
GAS TURBINE EFFICIENCY INC
Also Called: GTE
300 Sunport Ln Ste 100 (32809-8121)
PHONE..................................407 304-5200
Steven Zwolinski, *Principal*
Chris Watson, *Principal*
EMP: 50 EST: 2005
SQ FT: 60,000
SALES (est): 26MM
SALES (corp-wide): 6.4B **Privately Held**
WEB: www.gtefficiency.com
SIC: 3511 Steam turbines
PA: John Wood Group Plc
15 Justice Mill Lane
Aberdeen AB11
122 485-1000

(G-12183)
GAS TURBINE EFFICIENCY LLC
Also Called: GTE
300 Sunport Ln Ste 100 (32809-8121)
PHONE..................................407 304-5200
Steven Zwolinski, *CEO*
Bob Knott, *Vice Pres*
Dan Rashy, *Vice Pres*
Roger Seaver, *Vice Pres*
James Corrigan, *Project Mgr*
EMP: 50 EST: 1999
SQ FT: 60,000

SALES (est): 27.6MM
SALES (corp-wide): 6.4B **Privately Held**
WEB: www.gtefficiency.com
SIC: 3823 8711 5084 3613 Industrial process measurement equipment; petroleum engineering; industrial machinery & equipment; switchgear & switchboard apparatus; steam turbines
PA: John Wood Group Plc
15 Justice Mill Lane
Aberdeen AB11
122 485-1000

(G-12184)
GB BRICK PAVERS INC
4409 S Kirkman Rd Apt 303 (32811-2827)
PHONE..................................407 453-5505
Eraldo J Benedito, *Principal*
EMP: 7 EST: 2006
SALES (est): 131.7K **Privately Held**
WEB: www.totalbrickpavers.com
SIC: 2951 Asphalt paving mixtures & blocks

(G-12185)
GELTECH INC
2603 Challenger Tech Ct # 100 (32826-2716)
PHONE..................................407 382-4003
Dr Jean-Luz Nogues, *Vice Pres*
EMP: 177 EST: 1985
SQ FT: 22,000
SALES (est): 4.6MM
SALES (corp-wide): 35.5MM **Publicly Held**
WEB: www.lightpath.com
SIC: 3231 Products of purchased glass
PA: Lightpath Technologies, Inc.
2603 Challenger Tech Ct
Orlando FL 32826
407 382-4003

(G-12186)
GEM ASSET ACQUISITION LLC
Also Called: Gemseal Pvments Pdts - Orlando
6441 Pinecastle Blvd (32809-6673)
PHONE..................................407 888-2080
EMP: 28
SALES (corp-wide): 19.3MM **Privately Held**
SIC: 2951 Asphalt paving mixtures & blocks
PA: Gem Asset Acquisition Llc
1855 Lindbergh St Ste 500
Charlotte NC 28208
704 225-3321

(G-12187)
GENCOR INDUSTRIES INC (PA)
5201 N Orange Blossom Trl (32810-1038)
PHONE..................................407 290-6000
John E Elliott, *CEO*
E J Elliott, *Ch of Bd*
Marc G Elliott, *President*
Dennis B Hunt, *Senior VP*
Eric E Mellen, *CFO*
EMP: 200 EST: 1968
SQ FT: 215,000
SALES (est): 85.2MM **Publicly Held**
WEB: www.gencor.com
SIC: 3531 3823 3443 Asphalt plant, including gravel-mix type; combustion control instruments; heat exchangers, condensers & components

(G-12188)
GENERAL CLAMP INDUSTRIES INC
Also Called: United States Crene
1155 Central Florida Pkwy (32837-9258)
P.O. Box 593290 (32859-3290)
PHONE..................................407 859-6000
Rick Ridley, *CEO*
Linda Ames, *President*
EMP: 11 EST: 1994
SALES (est): 558.4K **Privately Held**
WEB: www.superclamp.com
SIC: 3531 3429 Ladder ditchers, vertical boom or wheel; manufactured hardware (general)

(G-12189)
GENERAL DYNAMICS CORPORATION
3275 Progress Dr (32826-2932)
PHONE..................................407 380-9384
EMP: 44
SALES (corp-wide): 31.3B **Publicly Held**
SIC: 3731 Shipbuilding And Repairing
PA: General Dynamics Corporation
2941 Frview Pk Dr Ste 100
Falls Church VA 20190
703 876-3000

(G-12190)
GENERAL DYNMICS MSSION SYSTEMS
12001 Res Pkwy Ste 500 (32826)
PHONE..................................407 823-7000
Robert Parrish, *Chief Engr*
Tom Bates, *Engineer*
Michael Burman, *Engineer*
Paul Cailleteau, *Engineer*
Judd Cheatwood, *Engineer*
EMP: 25
SALES (corp-wide): 38.4B **Publicly Held**
WEB: www.gdmissionsystems.com
SIC: 3571 Electronic computers
HQ: General Dynamics Mission Systems, Inc.
12450 Fair Lakes Cir
Fairfax VA 22033
877 449-0600

(G-12191)
GENESIS REFERENCE LABORATORIES
7924 Forest Cy Rd Ste 210 (32810)
PHONE..................................407 232-7130
Ernest Traynham, *CEO*
Ernest Fisher, *CEO*
Chris Hansen, *Managing Prtnr*
Britt Traynham, *COO*
Kayla Hall, *Marketing Staff*
EMP: 100 EST: 2015
SALES (est): 10.2MM **Privately Held**
WEB: www.genesisreferencelabs.com
SIC: 3821 8734 Clinical laboratory instruments, except medical & dental; testing laboratories

(G-12192)
GENESYS BAND
2036 Torrey Dr (32818-5779)
PHONE..................................347 701-5670
Jonathan Singh, *Principal*
EMP: 7 EST: 2010
SALES (est): 41.7K **Privately Held**
SIC: 7372 Business oriented computer software

(G-12193)
GENICON INC
2455 Ridgemoor Dr (32828-7513)
PHONE..................................407 657-4851
Jim Kirchberg, *Vice Pres*
Ken Roger, *Prdtn Mgr*
Nathan Baker, *Production*
Dario N Vitali, *Engineer*
Daniel Doerr, *Design Engr*
EMP: 45 EST: 2013
SALES (est): 5.5MM **Privately Held**
SIC: 3841 Surgical & medical instruments

(G-12194)
GEORGE BIRNEY JR
6714 Bouganvillea Cres Dr (32809-6615)
PHONE..................................407 851-5604
George Birney, *Principal*
EMP: 8 EST: 2007
SALES (est): 172.4K **Privately Held**
SIC: 3423 Jewelers' hand tools

(G-12195)
GHX INDUSTRIAL LLC
Also Called: Amazon Hose & Rubber
4105 Seaboard Rd (32808-3848)
PHONE..................................407 843-8190
Rich Potero, *Principal*
Jim Donlan, *Principal*
George Malgoza, *Principal*
EMP: 7 EST: 2007
SALES (est): 77.4K **Privately Held**
WEB: www.ghxinc.com
SIC: 3052 Rubber & plastics hose & beltings

(G-12196)
GLORY SANDBLASTING INC
Also Called: Glory Company
2922 38th St (32839-8631)
PHONE..................................407 422-0078
Linda Marjama, *CEO*
James Marjama, *Vice Pres*
Fernando Ortiz, *Manager*
EMP: 11 EST: 1982
SQ FT: 12,000
SALES (est): 1.1MM **Privately Held**
WEB: www.glorysandblasting.com
SIC: 3479 1721 Coating of metals & formed products; exterior commercial painting contractor

(G-12197)
GOEN3 CORPORATION (PA)
Also Called: Invel
6555 Sanger Rd Ste 100 (32827-7585)
PHONE..................................407 601-6000
Carla H Taba, *CEO*
EMP: 9 EST: 2015
SALES (est): 654K **Privately Held**
WEB: www.goen3.com
SIC: 2325 2331 Men's & boys' trousers & slacks; blouses, women's & juniors': made from purchased material

(G-12198)
GOLOSO FOOD LLC
Also Called: Gran Savana USA
1700 35th St Ste 107 (32839-8950)
PHONE..................................321 277-2055
Leo Calligaro,
Johanna Bracho,
▼ EMP: 9 EST: 2012
SALES (est): 767.4K **Privately Held**
SIC: 2022 5143 Cheese, natural & processed; cheese

(G-12199)
GRANDSTAND PUBLISHING LLC
Also Called: Baseball Digest
390 N Orange Ave Ste 2300 (32801-1684)
PHONE..................................847 491-6440
Norman Jacobs, *Publisher*
EMP: 7 EST: 2012
SALES (est): 629.9K **Privately Held**
WEB: www.baseballdigest.com
SIC: 2721 Magazines: publishing only, not printed on site

(G-12200)
GREAT HSE MDIA GROUP OF PBLS I
Also Called: Media Publishing
4449 Riverton St (32817-1451)
P.O. Box 780172 (32878-0172)
PHONE..................................407 779-3846
Michael O Lattiboudeaire, *CEO*
EMP: 10 EST: 2016
SALES (est): 397.3K **Privately Held**
SIC: 2741 7929 8661 5963 Miscellaneous publishing; ; entertainment group; Pentecostal Church; encyclopedias & publications, direct sales; book publishing

(G-12201)
GRIFFIN INDUSTRIES LLC
408 W Landstreet Rd (32824-7805)
PHONE..................................407 857-5474
Dennis Griffin, *Chairman*
Betty Woods, *Assistant*
EMP: 40
SQ FT: 8,728
SALES (corp-wide): 4.7B **Publicly Held**
SIC: 2077 Animal & marine fats & oils
HQ: Griffin Industries Llc
4221 Alexandria Pike
Cold Spring KY 41076
859 781-2010

(G-12202)
GRIFFITHS CORPORATION
Also Called: Wrico Stamping Co of Florida
10659 Rocket Blvd (32824-8517)
PHONE..................................407 851-8342
Richard Albright, *Principal*
Jerry Wilson, *Executive*
EMP: 87
SQ FT: 34,500

SALES (corp-wide): 147.9MM **Privately Held**
WEB: www.griffithscorp.com
SIC: 3469 7692 Stamping metal for the trade; welding repair
HQ: Griffiths Corporation
2717 Niagara Ln N
Minneapolis MN 55447
763 557-8935

(G-12203)
GWB COATINGS LLC
3612 Danby Ct (32812-6018)
PHONE................407 271-7732
Gary Baxter, *Principal*
EMP: 7 **EST:** 2016
SALES (est): 108.8K **Privately Held**
WEB: www.gwbcoatings.com
SIC: 3479 Metal coating & allied service

(G-12204)
H & H PRINTING INC
1406 W Washington St (32805-1738)
P.O. Box 560176 (32856-0176)
PHONE................407 422-2932
Ronald Hoevenaar, *CEO*
Chris Hoevenaar, *Vice Pres*
Lucille Hoevenaar, *Vice Pres*
Yvonne Hoevenaar, *Admin Sec*
EMP: 7 **EST:** 1963
SQ FT: 5,400
SALES (est): 431.1K **Privately Held**
WEB: www.hhprintinginc.com
SIC: 2752 2759 2789 Commercial printing, offset; commercial printing; bookbinding & related work

(G-12205)
H & H PRODUCTS COMPANY
6600 Magnolia Homes Rd (32810-4285)
PHONE................407 299-5410
Morris L Hartley, *President*
Richard Wissenbach, *Exec VP*
Morris L Hartley Jr, *Vice Pres*
Emily Hauptvogel, *Vice Pres*
Casey Stokes, *Plant Mgr*
EMP: 26 **EST:** 1964
SQ FT: 40,500
SALES (est): 6.3MM **Privately Held**
WEB: www.hhproductscompany.com
SIC: 2086 2087 Fruit drinks (less than 100% juice): packaged in cans, etc.; syrups, flavoring (except drink); concentrates, drink

(G-12206)
H D QUICKPRINT & DISC OFF SUPS
Also Called: H D Quikprint & Disc Off Sups
7820 Wendell Rd (32807-8542)
PHONE................407 678-1355
J K Berthold, *CEO*
Mark Berthold, *President*
Cristine Schilling, *Vice Pres*
EMP: 5 **EST:** 1977
SALES (est): 450K **Privately Held**
SIC: 2752 5943 Commercial printing, offset; office forms & supplies

(G-12207)
H PARK SERVICES LLC ✪
200 E Robinson St (32801-1945)
PHONE................844 607-2142
Ashley McKenzie, *CEO*
EMP: 5 **EST:** 2022
SALES (est): 345.1K **Privately Held**
SIC: 7372 Business oriented computer software

(G-12208)
HALLIDAY PRODUCTS INC
6401 Edgewater Dr (32810-4293)
PHONE................407 298-4470
Don Ahlberg, *President*
Chris Halliday, *Vice Pres*
Bill Lovejoy, *Vice Pres*
Earl Sande, *Marketing Staff*
Donna Willis, *Manager*
▼ **EMP:** 55 **EST:** 1966
SQ FT: 60,000

SALES (est): 10MM **Privately Held**
WEB: www.hallidayproducts.com
SIC: 3442 3321 3446 3444 Metal doors, sash & trim; manhole covers, metal; architectural metalwork; sheet metalwork; fabricated plate work (boiler shop); manufactured hardware (general)

(G-12209)
HARRISON CONCRETE INC
2021 E Grant Ave (32806-3260)
PHONE................321 276-0562
Scott V Riddle P, *Vice Pres*
EMP: 7 **EST:** 2019
SALES (est): 110.8K **Privately Held**
WEB: www.harrisonconcreteinc.com
SIC: 3273 Ready-mixed concrete

(G-12210)
HARVEST MOON DISTRIBUTORS LLC
3450 Parkway Center Ct (32808-1012)
PHONE................321 297-7942
Cherie L Rivett, *Principal*
Gloria Richards, *Principal*
Cherie Rivett, *Principal*
▲ **EMP:** 5 **EST:** 2012
SALES (est): 938.8K **Privately Held**
SIC: 2084 Wines, brandy & brandy spirits

(G-12211)
HATALOM CORPORATION
11315 Corp Blvd Ste 210 (32817)
PHONE................407 567-2556
John Hinnant, *CEO*
Michelle Neeld, *Opers Staff*
Jeff Bentz, *Manager*
Patrick Price, *Manager*
Shawn Kyler, *Software Engr*
EMP: 30 **EST:** 2017
SALES (est): 4.8MM **Privately Held**
WEB: www.hatalom.com
SIC: 3571 3572 7379 8742 Computers, digital, analog or hybrid; computer storage devices; computer related maintenance services; materials mgmt. (purchasing, handling, inventory) consultant; computer software development; systems engineering consultant, ex. computer or professional

(G-12212)
HEADWATERS INCORPORATED
5100 S Alafaya Trl (32831-2005)
PHONE................407 273-9221
Nick Murrow, *Branch Mgr*
EMP: 23 **Privately Held**
WEB: www.ecomaterial.com
SIC: 3272 Siding, precast stone
HQ: Headwaters Incorporated
10701 S River Front Pkwy # 300
South Jordan UT 84095

(G-12213)
HELPING ADLSCNTS LIVE OPTMSTCL
Also Called: H.A.L.o
4844 Cason Cove Dr # 204 (32811-6309)
PHONE................407 257-8221
Amanda Jenkins, *President*
▲ **EMP:** 7 **EST:** 2012
SALES (est): 72K **Privately Held**
SIC: 3272 Furniture, church: concrete

(G-12214)
HEROAL USA INC
7022 Tpc Dr Ste 100 (32822-5139)
PHONE................888 437-6257
Sarah Koring, *Vice Pres*
Adam Schott, *Officer*
EMP: 800 **EST:** 2016
SALES (est): 33.5MM **Privately Held**
WEB: www.heroal.de
SIC: 3365 Machinery castings, aluminum

(G-12215)
HG BROKERAGE SERVICES INC
2813 S Hiawassee Rd # 301 (32835-6690)
PHONE................407 294-3507
Enrique I Gonzalez, *President*
Migdalia S Gonzalez, *Vice Pres*
EMP: 6 **EST:** 2010

SALES (est): 983.2K **Privately Held**
SIC: 2656 Frozen food containers: made from purchased material

(G-12216)
HG2 EMERGENCY LIGHTING LLC
477 N Semoran Blvd (32807-3323)
PHONE................407 426-7700
Monsour Baker, *Principal*
Malek Baker, *Opers Staff*
Helen Rosario, *Controller*
Susan Tatum, *Accounts Exec*
Bhojani Ali, *Sales Staff*
EMP: 10 **EST:** 2010
SALES (est): 1.6MM **Privately Held**
WEB: www.hg2lighting.com
SIC: 3647 Vehicular lighting equipment

(G-12217)
HI TECH GRANITE AND MARBLE
11362 Space Blvd (32837-9265)
PHONE................407 230-4363
Keith Damario, *Manager*
EMP: 5 **EST:** 2011
SALES (est): 413.1K **Privately Held**
WEB: www.hitechgranite.com
SIC: 3281 Granite, cut & shaped

(G-12218)
HIGHVAC CO LLC
Also Called: Amazonia Marine Products
3842 Commerce Loop (32808-3818)
PHONE................407 969-0399
Richard Ghamandi, *Project Mgr*
Bob Ghamandi, *Manager*
EMP: 12 **EST:** 2002
SALES (est): 861.4K **Privately Held**
WEB: www.highvacco.com
SIC: 3541 Machine tools, metal cutting type

(G-12219)
HITACHI VANTARA CORPORATION
5950 Hazeltine Nat Dr (32822-5028)
PHONE................407 517-4532
Divaldo Suzuki, *Opers Staff*
Rich Vining, *Marketing Mgr*
James Daly, *Manager*
Antonio Catale, *Director*
EMP: 20 **Privately Held**
WEB: www.hitachivantara.com
SIC: 3572 Computer storage devices
HQ: Hitachi Vantara Corporation
2535 Augustine Dr
Santa Clara CA 95054
858 225-2095

(G-12220)
HM FROYOS LLC
8204 Firenze Blvd (32836-8767)
PHONE................561 339-0603
Omar Vaid, *Principal*
EMP: 7 **EST:** 2014
SALES (est): 127.5K **Privately Held**
SIC: 2024 Yogurt desserts, frozen

(G-12221)
HOFFMAN COMMERCIAL GROUP INC (HQ)
Also Called: Hoffman's Chocolates
1815 Cypress Lake Dr (32837-8457)
PHONE................561 967-2213
Fredrick Meltzer, *CEO*
Jarett Levan, *President*
Chuck Mohr, *President*
Sandra Hoffman, *Exec VP*
Randall Vitale, *Vice Pres*
▲ **EMP:** 30 **EST:** 1975
SQ FT: 15,000
SALES (est): 8MM
SALES (corp-wide): 313.6MM **Publicly Held**
WEB: www.hoffmans.com
SIC: 2064 5145 5441 2066 Candy & other confectionery products; candy; confectionery produced for direct sale on the premises; candy; chocolate candy, solid
PA: Bbx Capital, Inc.
201 E Las Olas Blvd # 1900
Fort Lauderdale FL 33301
954 940-4900

(G-12222)
HOLLYWOOD CLLCTIBLES GROUP LLC
11491 Rocket Blvd (32824-8514)
PHONE................407 985-4613
Mark Hilliard, *President*
Linda Hiltonv, *Vice Pres*
▲ **EMP:** 6 **EST:** 2005
SALES (est): 537.7K **Privately Held**
WEB: www.hollywood-collectibles.com
SIC: 3999 5961 7389 Models, general, except toy; miniatures; collectibles & antiques, mail order;

(G-12223)
HOOSIER LIGHTENING INC
2415 N John Young Pkwy (32804-4105)
PHONE................407 290-3323
David Elkins, *Principal*
EMP: 7 **EST:** 2000
SALES (est): 125.7K **Privately Held**
SIC: 3648 Lighting equipment

(G-12224)
HOTSPRAY INDUSTRIAL COATINGS
1932 N Goldenrod Rd (32807-8406)
PHONE................407 658-5700
Lyle Cummings, *President*
EMP: 10 **EST:** 1997
SQ FT: 3,000
SALES (est): 1.4MM **Privately Held**
WEB: www.hotspray.com
SIC: 2851 Lacquers, varnishes, enamels & other coatings

(G-12225)
HOUGHTON MIFFLIN HARCOURT
9400 S Park Loop (32819)
PHONE................407 345-2000
Diane Lampitt, *President*
Javan Walker, *Financial Analy*
Rudi Ali, *Webmaster*
Stephanie Vretenarski, *Analyst*
EMP: 50 **EST:** 2001
SALES (est): 7.4MM **Privately Held**
SIC: 2731 Book publishing

(G-12226)
HOUGHTON MIFFLIN HARCOURT PUBG
Also Called: Harcourt Education
9400 S Park Center Loop (32819-8647)
PHONE................407 345-2000
Margaret Creed, *Editor*
Susan Watkins, *Editor*
Karen Winklewright, *District Mgr*
Michelle Armstrong, *Business Mgr*
Jim Diamond, *Senior VP*
EMP: 131
SALES (corp-wide): 1B **Privately Held**
WEB: www.hmhco.com
SIC: 2731 Book publishing
HQ: Houghton Mifflin Harcourt Publishing Company
125 High St Ste 900
Boston MA 02110
617 351-5000

(G-12227)
HOUSE PLASTICS UNLIMITED INC
2580 S Orange Blossom Trl (32805-5455)
PHONE................407 843-3290
John J Davis, *CEO*
Todd Davis, *President*
Jeanne Davis, *Corp Secy*
Victor Velez, *Sales Executive*
EMP: 20 **EST:** 1969
SQ FT: 14,000
SALES (est): 4.8MM **Privately Held**
WEB: www.hopu.com
SIC: 3089 Injection molding of plastics

(G-12228)
HOVERFLY TECHNOLOGIES INC
12151 Res Pkwy Ste 100 (32826)
PHONE................407 985-4500
Robert Topping, *CEO*
Stephen Walters, *President*
Gerri Dundi, *General Mgr*
Daniel Burroughs, *Vice Pres*

Kevin Cochie, *Vice Pres*
EMP: 65 **EST:** 2010
SALES (est): 9MM **Privately Held**
WEB: www.hoverflytech.com
SIC: 3663 Radio & TV communications equipment

(G-12229)
HP PREFERRED LTD PARTNERS
Also Called: Halliday Product
6401 Edgewater Dr (32810-4203)
PHONE..........................407 298-4470
Doug Halliday, *Partner*
Tre Freeland, *Vice Pres*
Marc Semones, *Sales Staff*
Earl Sande, *Marketing Staff*
Donna Willis, *Marketing Staff*
EMP: 12 **EST:** 1970
SALES (est): 628.5K **Privately Held**
WEB: www.hallidayproducts.com
SIC: 3365 Aluminum foundries

(G-12230)
HT MEDICAL LLC
Also Called: Xenix Medical
111 W Jefferson St # 100 (32801-1820)
PHONE..........................888 594-8633
Ryan Phillips, *Mng Member*
EMP: 8 **EST:** 2014
SALES (est): 643.2K **Privately Held**
WEB: www.htmedicalusa.com
SIC: 3842 Implants, surgical

(G-12231)
HUGHES TRIM LLC
7613 Currency Dr (32809-6924)
PHONE..........................863 206-6048
Don Pool, *VP Opers*
Benjamin Worth, *Mng Member*
EMP: 75 **EST:** 2008
SALES (est): 4.3MM **Privately Held**
WEB: www.hughestrim.com
SIC: 2431 1751 Moldings, wood: unfinished & prefinished; staircases, stairs & railings; carpentry work

(G-12232)
HYLTON & ASSOC
1449 Sackett Cir (32818-9066)
PHONE..........................321 303-2862
Rohan Hylton, *President*
EMP: 6 **EST:** 1989
SALES (est): 396.1K **Privately Held**
SIC: 3581 Automatic vending machines

(G-12233)
IAIRE LLC
2100 Consulate Dr Ste 102 (32837-8397)
PHONE..........................407 873-2538
Chuck Eno, *Vice Pres*
Ady Alhamra, *Engineer*
EMP: 7
SALES (corp-wide): 4.6MM **Privately Held**
WEB: www.myiaire.com
SIC: 3564 Air purification equipment
PA: Iaire, Llc
6805 Hillsdale Ct
Indianapolis IN 46250
317 806-2750

(G-12234)
ICE MAGIC-ORLANDO INC (PA)
Also Called: Ice Magic Holdings
9468 American Eagle Way # 100 (32837-8380)
PHONE..........................407 816-1905
William Whidden, *President*
◆ **EMP:** 6 **EST:** 1996
SALES (est): 621.2K **Privately Held**
WEB: www.icemagic.com
SIC: 2097 Manufactured ice

(G-12235)
ILSC HOLDINGS LC
Also Called: Katmai Electronic Systems
12001 Science Dr Ste 160 (32826-2916)
PHONE..........................480 935-4230
Melinda Popwell, *Asst Controller*
Don Becker, *Manager*
Lena Delgado, *Administration*
EMP: 8

SALES (corp-wide): 161.4MM **Privately Held**
WEB: www.katmaicorp.com
SIC: 3812 Search & navigation equipment; acceleration indicators & systems components, aerospace
HQ: Ilsc Holdings Lc
11001 Omalley Centre Dr # 204
Anchorage AK 99515

(G-12236)
IMAGINATION ENTERPRISES LLC
Also Called: Magic Candle
7616 Southland Blvd # 102 (32809-6993)
PHONE..........................504 289-9691
Keith Mahne,
EMP: 19 **EST:** 2017
SALES (est): 7MM **Privately Held**
SIC: 3999 5961 Candles; general merchandise, mail order

(G-12237)
IMAGING DIAGNOSTIC SYSTEMS INC
Also Called: (A DEVELOPMENT STAGE COMPANY)
1221 E Robinson St (32801-2115)
PHONE..........................954 581-9800
Linda B Grable, *CEO*
Michael Addley, *COO*
Deborah O'Brien, *Senior VP*
Jose Cisneros, *Research*
David Fong, *CFO*
EMP: 10 **EST:** 1993 **Privately Held**
WEB: www.imds.com
SIC: 3841 Surgical & medical instruments

(G-12238)
IMPRESS INK LLC (PA)
Also Called: Impress Ink Screen Prtg & EMB
540 N Goldenrod Rd Ste A (32807-8295)
PHONE..........................407 982-5646
Michael Cho, *Mng Member*
Xi Guo,
EMP: 8 **EST:** 2009
SALES (est): 2.3MM **Privately Held**
WEB: www.impressink.com
SIC: 2759 Screen printing

(G-12239)
IMPRESS INK LLC
1462 Bella Coola Dr (32828-5267)
PHONE..........................561 635-6442
Michael Cho, *Principal*
EMP: 8
SALES (corp-wide): 2.3MM **Privately Held**
WEB: www.impressink.com
SIC: 2759 Screen printing
PA: Impress Ink Llc
540 N Goldenrod Rd Ste A
Orlando FL 32807
407 982-5646

(G-12240)
IMPROVED RACING PRODUCTS LLC
4855 Dist Ct Ste 1 (32822)
PHONE..........................407 705-3054
Richard M Ihns,
EMP: 5 **EST:** 2008
SQ FT: 5,500
SALES (est): 779.4K **Privately Held**
WEB: www.improvedracing.com
SIC: 3714 Lubrication systems & parts, motor vehicle

(G-12241)
INDRA SYSTEMS INC
3505 Lake Lynda Dr # 200 (32817-8324)
PHONE..........................407 567-1977
Carlos Acosta, *CEO*
Oznur Vural, *General Mgr*
Alex Pagan, *Mfg Staff*
Eduardo Viaggio, *Senior Engr*
Pio Cabanillas Alonso, *Director*
▲ **EMP:** 28 **EST:** 2002
SQ FT: 20,000
SALES (est): 18.6MM
SALES (corp-wide): 1.1B **Privately Held**
SIC: 3825 3699 Test equipment for electronic & electric measurement; flight simulators (training aids), electronic

PA: Indra Sistemas, Sociedad Anonima
Avenida De Bruselas 35
Alcobendas 28108
914 805-000

(G-12242)
INDUSTRIAL SMOKE & MIRRORS INC
Also Called: I S M
3024 Shader Rd (32808-3922)
PHONE..........................407 299-9400
Andrew W Garvis, *President*
Joseph Barnicki, *Opers Staff*
Matthew Bower, *Production*
Yohana Pina, *QC Mgr*
Brian Lynn, *Engineer*
EMP: 42 **EST:** 1995
SQ FT: 35,000
SALES (est): 10.1MM **Privately Held**
WEB: www.industrialsmokeandmirrors.com
SIC: 3699 Security control equipment & systems

(G-12243)
INFINITY SIGNS & GRAPHIX LLC
1887 Central Florida Pkwy (32837-9287)
PHONE..........................407 270-6733
Sal Kalai, *Vice Pres*
EMP: 10 **EST:** 2016
SALES (est): 635.4K **Privately Held**
WEB: www.infinitysignindustries.com
SIC: 3993 Signs & advertising specialties

(G-12244)
INGENRIA PRCURA Y CNSTRCCION C
Also Called: IPC Company USA
12250 Menta St Ste 202 (32837-7539)
PHONE..........................407 639-4288
Albino Pineiro, *President*
EMP: 6 **EST:** 2012
SALES (est): 498.3K **Privately Held**
SIC: 1389 8711 Construction, repair & dismantling services; construction & civil engineering

(G-12245)
INGENUS PHARMACEUTICALS LLC (PA)
4901 Vineland Rd Ste 260 (32811-7193)
PHONE..........................407 354-5365
Raju Mantena, *CEO*
Andrew Gellman, *President*
Matthew Baumgartner, *CFO*
Brahmaji Valiveti, *Officer*
▲ **EMP:** 10 **EST:** 2009
SALES (est): 18.3MM **Privately Held**
WEB: www.ingenus.com
SIC: 2834 Cough medicines

(G-12246)
INNOVATIVE SVC SOLUTIONS LLC
Also Called: Honeywell Authorized Dealer
3144 N John Young Pkwy (32804-4127)
PHONE..........................407 296-5211
Grant Wood, *General Mgr*
Joe Terry, *Engineer*
Richard A Bodwell, *Mng Member*
Gregory Suarez, *Manager*
Stacie Martucci, *Info Tech Mgr*
EMP: 23 **EST:** 2002
SQ FT: 5,000
SALES (est): 5.1MM **Privately Held**
WEB: www.issmechanical.com
SIC: 3585 7623 Air conditioning equipment, complete; air conditioning repair

(G-12247)
INPRO CORP IKE
9025 Boggy Creek Rd (32824-7716)
PHONE..........................407 342-9912
EMP: 8 **EST:** 2018
SALES (est): 263.4K **Privately Held**
SIC: 3081 Unsupported plastics film & sheet

(G-12248)
INSTANATURAL LLC
12001 Res Pkwy Ste 244 (32826)
PHONE..........................800 290-6932
Patel Atit, *CEO*
Hannah Balatbat, *Opers Staff*
Sue Taraboulous, *CFO*
Ethelbert Williams, *Chief Mktg Ofcr*

Aditya Patel,
EMP: 40 **EST:** 2013
SALES (est): 2.5MM **Privately Held**
WEB: www.instanatural.com
SIC: 2844 5122 Cosmetic preparations; cosmetics

(G-12249)
INTEPLAST ENGINEERED FILMS INC
7549 Brokerage Dr (32809-5625)
PHONE..........................407 851-6620
Lee Seidel, *Controller*
Ryan Smith, *Regl Sales Mgr*
C Bowman, *Maintence Staff*
EMP: 100 **Privately Held**
WEB: www.inteplastef.com
SIC: 2673 Food storage & trash bags (plastic); trash bags (plastic film): made from purchased materials; plastic bags: made from purchased materials
HQ: Inteplast Engineered Films Inc.
2875 Market St Ste 100
Garland TX 75041
800 373-9410

(G-12250)
INTERLINK SOFTWARE INC
8946 Leeland Archer Blvd (32836-8836)
PHONE..........................407 927-0898
Lloyd Hopkins, *President*
Collin Griffiths, *Vice Pres*
Barry Hopkins, *Vice Pres*
David Arrowsmith, *Sales Staff*
Matthew Sweeney, *Consultant*
EMP: 7 **EST:** 2003
SALES (est): 3MM **Privately Held**
WEB: www.interlinksoftware.com
SIC: 3695 Computer software tape & disks: blank, rigid & floppy

(G-12251)
INTERNATIONAL KEG RENTAL LLC
10450 Trkey Lk Rd Unit 69 (32819)
PHONE..........................407 900-9992
Thadeus Avvampato, *Mng Member*
EMP: 10 **EST:** 2020
SALES (est): 518.7K **Privately Held**
WEB: www.intlkeg.com
SIC: 2082 7359 Beer (alcoholic beverage); business machine & electronic equipment rental services

(G-12252)
INTERNATIONAL PAPER COMPANY
711 E Lancaster Rd (32809-6638)
PHONE..........................407 855-2121
Mark Crowson, *Principal*
John Kilroy, *Mfg Mgr*
John Thrist, *Branch Mgr*
Timothy Judkins,
EMP: 49
SALES (corp-wide): 19.3B **Publicly Held**
WEB: www.internationalpaper.com
SIC: 2653 Boxes, corrugated: made from purchased materials
PA: International Paper Company
6400 Poplar Ave
Memphis TN 38197
901 419-7000

(G-12253)
INTERNTNAL SYNRGY FOR TCHNCAL
Also Called: Is4ts
12001 Res Pkwy Ste 236 (32826)
PHONE..........................321 305-0863
Abdelhamid Elkheir, *CEO*
EMP: 6 **EST:** 2016
SALES (est): 456.6K **Privately Held**
WEB: www.is4ts.com
SIC: 3724 3728 7699 5999 Aircraft engines & engine parts; research & dev by manuf., aircraft parts & auxiliary equip; aircraft & heavy equipment repair services; electronic parts & equipment; corporate objectives & policies consultant

(G-12254)
INTERSTATE RECYCLING WASTE INC
5232 Laval Dr (32839-6902)
PHONE..........................407 812-5555

Wanda Santiago, *President*
Saul Ortega, *Vice Pres*
EMP: 14 **EST:** 2004
SALES (est): 2MM **Privately Held**
WEB: interstate-recycling-waste-inc.business.site
SIC: 3443 Dumpsters, garbage

(G-12255)
INTOUCH INC
5036 Dr Phillips Blvd (32819-3310)
PHONE....................702 572-4786
John Jackson, *Principal*
EMP: 14 **EST:** 2010
SALES (est): 594.6K **Privately Held**
WEB: www.24-7intouch.com
SIC: 3999 Manufacturing industries

(G-12256)
INVIRO TEK INC
11334 Boggy Creek Rd # 1 (32824-7416)
PHONE....................215 499-1209
EMP: 8 **EST:** 2015
SALES (est): 505.5K **Privately Held**
SIC: 3699 Electrical equipment & supplies

(G-12257)
INVISION AUTO SYSTEMS INC
3001 Directors Row (32809-5675)
PHONE....................407 956-5161
Phillip Prince, *Sales Mgr*
Robert Hughes, *Accounts Mgr*
Leigh Long, *Accounts Mgr*
Lisa Swanson, *Branch Mgr*
EMP: 100
SALES (corp-wide): 635.9MM **Publicly Held**
SIC: 3699 Automotive driving simulators (training aids), electronic
HQ: Invision Automotive Systems Inc.
 2351 J Lawson Blvd
 Orlando FL 32824

(G-12258)
INVISION AUTO SYSTEMS INC (HQ)
2351 J Lawson Blvd (32824-4386)
PHONE....................407 956-5161
Thomas C Malone, *President*
Loriann Shelton, *Vice Pres*
Charles M Stoehr, *Vice Pres*
Philip Prince, *Sales Mgr*
Ryan Savage, *Sales Staff*
EMP: 99 **EST:** 2010
SALES (est): 64.3MM
SALES (corp-wide): 635.9MM **Publicly Held**
SIC: 3699 Automotive driving simulators (training aids), electronic
PA: Voxx International Corporation
 2351 J Lawson Blvd
 Orlando FL 32824
 800 645-7750

(G-12259)
INVISION INDUSTRIES INC
2351 J Lawson Blvd (32824-4386)
PHONE....................407 451-8353
EMP: 8 **EST:** 2017
SALES (est): 57.3K **Privately Held**
WEB: www.invisiondirect.com
SIC: 3699 Electrical equipment & supplies

(G-12260)
IRONWIFI LLC
3071 N Orange Blossom Trl C (32824-3455)
PHONE....................800 963-6221
Martin Benuska, *Principal*
EMP: 10 **EST:** 2014
SALES (est): 665.6K **Privately Held**
WEB: www.ironwifi.com
SIC: 7372 Business oriented computer software

(G-12261)
ISP OPTICS CORPORATION (HQ)
2603 Challenger Tech Ct # 100 (32826-2716)
PHONE....................914 591-3070
Mark Lifshotz, *CEO*
Joseph Menaker, *President*
Iryna Kutsiaba, *Accountant*
▲ **EMP:** 19 **EST:** 1993

SALES (est): 11.4MM
SALES (corp-wide): 35.5MM **Publicly Held**
WEB: www.ispoptics.com
SIC: 3827 Optical instruments & apparatus
PA: Lightpath Technologies, Inc.
 2603 Challenger Tech Ct
 Orlando FL 32826
 407 382-4003

(G-12262)
ITYX SOLUTIONS INC
2915 Musselwhite Ave (32804-4549)
P.O. Box 2448 (32802-2448)
PHONE....................407 474-4383
Joe Radomsky, *General Mgr*
EMP: 11 **EST:** 2014
SALES (est): 172K **Privately Held**
WEB: www.ityxsolutions.com
SIC: 7372 Prepackaged software

(G-12263)
J & A BIG PAVERS LLC
6214 W Robinson St (32835-1362)
PHONE....................321 948-0019
Jenny Avila, *Principal*
EMP: 7 **EST:** 2014
SALES (est): 179.1K **Privately Held**
SIC: 2951 Asphalt paving mixtures & blocks

(G-12264)
JACQULNES LVELY DRPES BLNDS LL
11407 Bentry St (32824-4419)
PHONE....................407 826-1566
Jacqueline Campbell,
EMP: 7 **EST:** 2020
SALES (est): 191.1K **Privately Held**
WEB: www.jacquelineslovelydrapes.com
SIC: 2591 Window blinds

(G-12265)
JAMES A DE FLIPPO CO
4665 Gatlin Oaks Ln (32806-7249)
P.O. Box 560067 (32856-0067)
PHONE....................407 851-2765
James A Deflippo, *President*
Joyce Deflippo, *Vice Pres*
EMP: 7 **EST:** 1974
SQ FT: 1,000
SALES (est): 474.8K **Privately Held**
SIC: 3961 5094 5099 Costume jewelry, ex. precious metal & semiprecious stones; jewelry; brass goods

(G-12266)
JAMES SIMMONS CABINETS INC
4835 Berrywood Dr (32812-7327)
PHONE....................407 468-1802
James Simmons, *Principal*
EMP: 8 **EST:** 2008
SALES (est): 409.5K **Privately Held**
SIC: 2434 Wood kitchen cabinets

(G-12267)
JANUS INTERNATIONAL GROUP LLC
10407 Rocket Blvd (32824-8512)
PHONE....................407 859-6770
Joe Burkhalter, *Opers Mgr*
David B Curtis, *Branch Mgr*
EMP: 10
SALES (corp-wide): 750.1MM **Publicly Held**
WEB: www.janusintl.com
SIC: 3442 Metal doors
PA: Janus International Group, Llc
 135 Janus Intl Blvd
 Temple GA 30179
 770 562-2850

(G-12268)
JAYCO INTERNATIONAL LLC
7451 Brokerage Dr (32809-5623)
PHONE....................407 855-8880
James Rutledge, *General Mgr*
Larry Tulchinsky, *Sales Staff*
James R Rutledge Jr,
EMP: 53 **EST:** 2005
SQ FT: 24,900

SALES (est): 3MM **Privately Held**
WEB: www.jaycointernational.net
SIC: 2258 Bedspreads, lace: made on lace machines

(G-12269)
JBT LLC (PA)
528 W Yale St (32804-5338)
PHONE....................407 463-2045
Jamieson Thomas, *Principal*
Gary Vance, *Vice Pres*
Carlos Saavedra, *Marketing Mgr*
Crystal Morris, *Manager*
EMP: 5 **EST:** 2012
SALES (est): 2.5MM **Privately Held**
WEB: www.jbtc.com
SIC: 3556 Food products machinery

(G-12270)
JD WINE CONCEPTS LLC
Also Called: Quantum Leap Winery
1312 Wilfred Dr (32803-2537)
PHONE....................407 730-3082
Trey Wheeler, *Manager*
Jill Ramsier,
▲ **EMP:** 6 **EST:** 2013
SALES (est): 538.4K **Privately Held**
WEB: www.quantumleapwinery.com
SIC: 2084 Wines

(G-12271)
JEFFREY B GOULD
1711 Cotswold Dr (32825-8406)
PHONE....................410 463-0796
Jeffrey B Gould, *Principal*
EMP: 7 **EST:** 2010
SALES (est): 134.9K **Privately Held**
WEB: www.kidsstuffsuperstore.com
SIC: 2791 Typesetting

(G-12272)
JENARD FRESH INCORPORATED
Also Called: Spice World
1144 Mid Florida Dr (32824-7064)
PHONE....................407 240-4545
John Kalal, *COO*
Maria Valentin, *Supervisor*
Kevin Smith, *CIO*
▲ **EMP:** 62 **EST:** 1991
SALES (est): 10MM **Privately Held**
SIC: 2099 Food preparations

(G-12273)
JEWELS HANDMADE LLC
2648 Renegade Dr Apt 101 (32818-2622)
PHONE....................407 283-9951
Emmanuel Hampton,
EMP: 10 **EST:** 2020
SALES (est): 258.5K **Privately Held**
SIC: 2389 Apparel & accessories

(G-12274)
JF FLAKES AND POWERS INC
2313 Windcrest Lake Cir (32824-5667)
PHONE....................407 414-6467
Jose Figueroa, *Principal*
EMP: 7 **EST:** 2012
SALES (est): 137.5K **Privately Held**
SIC: 3531 Pavers

(G-12275)
JOHN BEAN TECHNOLOGIES CORP
Also Called: Jbt Aerotech-Military Programs
7300 Presidents Dr (32809-5620)
PHONE....................407 851-3377
Roy Fulcher, *General Mgr*
Bryant Lowery, *Exec VP*
Rich Cainan, *Senior VP*
Josh Parkin, *Plant Mgr*
Terry Brecht, *Project Mgr*
EMP: 25 **Publicly Held**
WEB: www.jbtc.com
SIC: 3556 3585 3537 Food products machinery; refrigeration & heating equipment; containers (metal), air cargo
PA: John Bean Technologies Corporation
 70 W Madison St Ste 4400
 Chicago IL 60602

(G-12276)
JOHNSON CONTROLS INC
4433 Parkbreeze Ct (32808-1021)
PHONE....................407 291-1971

Bobby Pickney, *General Mgr*
Steve Muzzy, *Manager*
EMP: 38 **Privately Held**
WEB: www.johnsoncontrols.com
SIC: 2531 7699 1731 Seats, automobile; thermostat repair; electrical work
HQ: Johnson Controls, Inc.
 5757 N Green Bay Ave
 Glendale WI 53209
 414 524-1200

(G-12277)
JOMAR METAL FABRICATION INC
1239 Spruce Ave (32824-7935)
PHONE....................407 857-1259
Marvin Sweers, *President*
John Edmondson, *Vice Pres*
Frances Sweers, *Admin Sec*
EMP: 7 **EST:** 1996
SQ FT: 10,000
SALES (est): 835.9K **Privately Held**
WEB: www.jomarmetal.com
SIC: 3441 Fabricated structural metal

(G-12278)
JORDAN NORRIS INC
997 W Kennedy Blvd Ste A1 (32810-6100)
P.O. Box 421922, Kissimmee (34742-1922)
PHONE....................407 846-1400
Kathy Groover, *President*
William Groover, *Vice Pres*
EMP: 8 **EST:** 1976
SQ FT: 6,000
SALES (est): 825.1K **Privately Held**
WEB: www.jordannorris.com
SIC: 2752 Commercial printing, offset

(G-12279)
JTA INDUSTRIES LLC (PA)
9165 Phillips Grove Ter (32836-5058)
PHONE....................407 352-4255
Peter Anthony Jr, *Principal*
EMP: 9 **EST:** 2018
SALES (est): 44.7K **Privately Held**
SIC: 3999 Manufacturing industries

(G-12280)
JTA INDUSTRIES LLC
3391 S Kirkman Rd # 1223 (32811-1943)
PHONE....................321 663-4395
Joshua T Anthony, *Branch Mgr*
EMP: 13
SALES (corp-wide): 44.7K **Privately Held**
SIC: 3999 Atomizers, toiletry
PA: Jta Industries Llc
 9165 Phillips Grove Ter
 Orlando FL 32836
 407 352-4255

(G-12281)
JV INSTALLATIONS CORP
1310 W Central Blvd (32805-1708)
PHONE....................407 849-0262
James Vargas, *President*
Liliana Vargas, *Prdtn Mgr*
Alicia Vargas, *Manager*
Stewart Vargas, *Manager*
Jennifer Diaz, *Officer*
EMP: 30 **EST:** 2000
SQ FT: 13,500
SALES (est): 5.3MM **Privately Held**
WEB: www.jvinstallationscorp.com
SIC: 3281 2434 Granite, cut & shaped; wood kitchen cabinets

(G-12282)
KAMAN PRECISION PRODUCTS INC (DH)
6655 E Colonial Dr (32807-5200)
PHONE....................407 282-1000
Gerald C Ricketts, *President*
Clarence Close, *Vice Pres*
Jeffrey Leeper, *Vice Pres*
Robert Renz, *Vice Pres*
Robert D Starr, *Treasurer*
▼ **EMP:** 217 **EST:** 2002
SQ FT: 90,000
SALES (est): 38.4MM
SALES (corp-wide): 708.9MM **Publicly Held**
WEB: www.kamansensors.com
SIC: 3483 3489 Ammunition, except for small arms; ordnance & accessories

(G-12283)
KAWNEER COMPANY INC
Also Called: Kawneer Architectural Products
4645 L B Mcleod Rd (32811-6405)
PHONE......................................407 648-4511
Brian Norberg, *Manager*
EMP: 130
SALES (corp-wide): 7.5B **Publicly Held**
WEB: www.kawneer.com
SIC: 3446 Architectural metalwork
HQ: Kawneer Company, Inc.
    555 Guthridge Ct
    Norcross GA 30092
    770 449-5555

(G-12284)
KEMET VENTURES LLC
10524 Moss Park Rd (32832-5898)
PHONE......................................407 403-2958
Magued S Sherif, *Principal*
EMP: 6 EST: 2015
SALES (est): 400.7K **Privately Held**
WEB: www.kemet.com
SIC: 3675 Electronic capacitors

(G-12285)
KENNEY COMMUNICATIONS INC (PA)
1215 Spruce Ave (32824-7935)
PHONE......................................407 859-3113
Barbara A Kenney, *President*
Holly McBride, *Vice Pres*
EMP: 19 EST: 1984
SQ FT: 23,600
SALES (est): 2.9MM **Privately Held**
WEB: www.kenneycom.com
SIC: 2721 2741 7319 Magazines: pub-
lishing only, not printed on site; miscella-
neous publishing; guides: publishing only,
not printed on site; distribution of advertis-
ing material or sample services

(G-12286)
KENS STUMP GRINDING LLC
3848 Beachman Dr (32810-3649)
PHONE......................................407 948-5031
Kenneth E Faulkner, *Branch Mgr*
EMP: 12
SALES (corp-wide): 25.6K **Privately Held**
SIC: 3599 Grinding castings for the trade
PA: Kens Stump Grinding Llc
    6662 82nd Avenue Ct N
    Pinellas Park FL 33781
    727 289-9968

(G-12287)
KINDORF ENTERPRISES INC
Also Called: AlphaGraphics
1650 Sand Lake Rd Ste 115 (32809-7671)
PHONE......................................407 858-0331
EMP: 9 EST: 1998
SQ FT: 3,000
SALES (est): 750K **Privately Held**
WEB: www.alphagraphics.com
SIC: 2752 Commercial printing, litho-
graphic

(G-12288)
KIRCHMAN CORPORATION (PA)
Also Called: Metavante Banking Solutions
2001 Summit Park Dr # 100 (32810-5906)
PHONE......................................877 384-0936
Rachel Landrum, *President*
Paul T Danola, *Chairman*
Michael D Hayford, *Exec VP*
Mark Viselli, *Exec VP*
Jerry White, *Vice Pres*
EMP: 48 EST: 2004
SALES (est): 5.8MM **Privately Held**
SIC: 7372 Application computer software

(G-12289)
KITCHENS BY US
4201 L B Mcleod Rd (32811-5616)
PHONE......................................407 745-4923
Calvin Chew, *Vice Pres*
EMP: 8 EST: 2018
SALES (est): 879.3K **Privately Held**
WEB: www.kitchensbyus.com
SIC: 2434 Wood kitchen cabinets

(G-12290)
KITCHENS RTA LLC
2467 N John Young Pkwy (32804-4123)
PHONE......................................407 969-0902

Madison Pruitt, *President*
EMP: 7 EST: 2017
SALES (est): 159.7K **Privately Held**
WEB: www.kitchensrta.com
SIC: 2434 Wood kitchen cabinets

(G-12291)
KITEMAN PRODUCTIONS INC
5200 Ridgeway Dr (32819-7431)
PHONE......................................407 943-8480
Bruce Flora, *President*
EMP: 7 EST: 1991
SQ FT: 6,000
SALES (est): 401.5K **Privately Held**
WEB: www.kiteman.net
SIC: 2399 Banners, made from fabric

(G-12292)
KNB MANUFACTURERS
1817 Barksdale Dr (32822-4607)
PHONE......................................407 733-0364
Klever Nieves, *Principal*
EMP: 7 EST: 2015
SALES (est): 131.1K **Privately Held**
SIC: 3999 Manufacturing industries

(G-12293)
KOLLSMAN INC
12600 Challenger Pkwy (32826-2754)
PHONE......................................407 312-1384
Jeff Crystal, *Branch Mgr*
EMP: 7 **Privately Held**
SIC: 3812 3629 Search & navigation
equipment; electrochemical generators
(fuel cells)
HQ: Kollsman, Inc.
    220 Daniel Webster Hwy
    Merrimack NH 03054

(G-12294)
KONNECTED INC
5718 Old Cheney Hwy (32807-3525)
PHONE......................................407 286-3138
EMP: 7 EST: 2019
SALES (est): 865.8K **Privately Held**
WEB: www.konnected.io
SIC: 3571 7371 Electronic computers;
computer software development & appli-
cations

(G-12295)
KONY INC
7380 W Sand Lake Rd # 390 (32819-5290)
PHONE......................................407 730-5669
Andrew Timblin, *Vice Pres*
Paul Mansky, *Vice Pres*
Xina Seaton, *Vice Pres*
Amy Kaufman, *VP Finance*
Sean Julien, *Sales Dir*
EMP: 34
SALES (corp-wide): 18.6MM **Privately Held**
WEB: www.temenos.com
SIC: 7372 Application computer software
HQ: Kony, Inc.
    9225 Bee Cave Rd Bldg As
    Austin TX 78733

(G-12296)
KRATOS DEF & SEC SOLUTIONS INC
8601 Transport Dr (32832-7102)
PHONE......................................866 606-5867
David Laird, *Vice Pres*
Tom Parker, *Mfg Staff*
Rich Baker, *Engineer*
Richard Owen, *Engineer*
Marcus Laster, *Electrical Engi*
EMP: 21 **Publicly Held**
WEB: www.kratosdefense.com
SIC: 3761 8744 7382 Guided missiles &
space vehicles; facilities support services;
security systems services
PA: Kratos Defense & Security Solutions,
    Inc.
    10680 Treena St Ste 600
    San Diego CA 92131

(G-12297)
L & C METALS LLC
711 Central Florida Pkwy (32824-8501)
PHONE......................................407 859-2600
Michael Steadman, *Mng Member*
Luard Steadman,
Melanie Wright,
EMP: 6 EST: 2004

SALES (est): 486.7K **Privately Held**
WEB: www.landcmetals.com
SIC: 7692 Welding repair

(G-12298)
L R GATOR CORPORATION
4380 L B Mcleod Rd (32811-5619)
PHONE......................................407 578-6616
EMP: 7 EST: 2014
SALES (est): 505.8K **Privately Held**
WEB: www.signaramaorlando.com
SIC: 3993 Signs & advertising specialties

(G-12299)
L-3 CMMNCTONS ADVNCED LSER SYS
Also Called: Advanced Lser Systems Tech
Div
2500 N Orange Blossom Trl (32804-4807)
PHONE......................................407 295-5878
Lawrence Van Blerkom, *Vice Pres*
Steve Post, *Admin Sec*
EMP: 74 EST: 1987
SQ FT: 40,000
SALES (est): 12.1MM
SALES (corp-wide): 17.8B **Publicly Held**
SIC: 3699 Laser systems & equipment
HQ: L3 Technologies, Inc.
    600 3rd Ave Fl 34
    New York NY 10016
    321 727-9100

(G-12300)
L3 TECHNOLOGIES INC
Also Called: Advanced Laser Systems
2500 N Orange Blossom Trl (32804-4807)
PHONE......................................407 295-5878
EMP: 89
SALES (corp-wide): 17.8B **Publicly Held**
WEB: www.l3harris.com
SIC: 3699 Laser systems & equipment
HQ: L3 Technologies, Inc.
    600 3rd Ave Fl 34
    New York NY 10016
    321 727-9100

(G-12301)
L3 TECHNOLOGIES INC
7675 Municipal Dr (32819-8930)
PHONE......................................407 354-0047
Chris Anzalone, *President*
EMP: 61
SALES (corp-wide): 17.8B **Publicly Held**
WEB: www.l3harris.com
SIC: 3663 Telemetering equipment, elec-
tronic
HQ: L3 Technologies, Inc.
    600 3rd Ave Fl 34
    New York NY 10016
    321 727-9100

(G-12302)
L3HARRIS TECHNOLOGIES INC
7022 Tpc Dr Ste 500 (32822-5140)
PHONE......................................407 581-3782
Dan Keppel, *Project Mgr*
Curt Jones, *Manager*
Andrew R Brown, *Director*
EMP: 21
SALES (corp-wide): 17.8B **Publicly Held**
WEB: www.l3harris.com
SIC: 3812 Search & navigation equipment
PA: L3harris Technologies, Inc.-
    1025 W Nasa Blvd
    Melbourne FL 32919
    321 727-9100

(G-12303)
LA CHIQUITA TORTILLA MFR
6918 Presidents Dr (32809-5668)
PHONE......................................407 251-8290
EMP: 12 EST: 2016
SALES (est): 651.7K **Privately Held**
WEB: www.lachiquitatortilla.com
SIC: 2099 Tortillas, fresh or refrigerated

(G-12304)
LA MAR ORLANDO LLC
Also Called: Sir Speedy
621 Commonwealth Ave (32803-5223)
PHONE......................................407 423-2051
Michael Levangie, *Partner*
Laurence Nye, *Partner*
Belinda Danals, *COO*
Etta Lazarus, *Vice Pres*
Matthew Diehl, *Opers Mgr*

EMP: 28 EST: 2008
SALES (est): 9.7MM **Privately Held**
WEB: www.sirspeedy.com
SIC: 2752 Commercial printing, litho-
graphic

(G-12305)
LA PAVERS INC
2349 Lake Debra Dr (32835-6625)
PHONE......................................407 209-9163
Lourival Aguiar, *Principal*
EMP: 9 EST: 2005
SALES (est): 203.8K **Privately Held**
WEB: www.lapavers.com
SIC: 2951 Asphalt paving mixtures &
blocks

(G-12306)
LAKE NEWS LLC
9836 Sweetleaf St (32827-6812)
PHONE......................................407 251-1314
Allyn Maycumber, *Principal*
EMP: 8 EST: 2010
SALES (est): 362.3K **Privately Held**
SIC: 2711 Newspapers, publishing & print-
ing

(G-12307)
LAMBERT CORPORATION FLORIDA
20 Coburn Ave (32805-2198)
PHONE......................................407 841-2940
Matthew L Ledlow, *CEO*
Patrick Enelus, *Production*
Armand Hamilton, *Production*
Tyron Peter, *Production*
Damarcus Johnson, *Research*
◆ EMP: 21 EST: 1978
SQ FT: 26,000
SALES (est): 22.4MM **Privately Held**
WEB: www.lambertusa.net
SIC: 2819 2851 2891 3272 Industrial in-
organic chemicals; paints & allied prod-
ucts; adhesives & sealants; concrete
products; gypsum products
PA: Meyer Ledlow, Llc
    20 Coburn Ave
    Orlando FL 32805
    407 481-2940

(G-12308)
LANCO & HARRIS CORP
600 Mid Florida Dr (32824-7008)
PHONE......................................407 240-4000
Sergio Blanco, *President*
Inrique Blanco, *Vice Pres*
Guillermo Blanco, *Treasurer*
◆ EMP: 60 EST: 2003
SQ FT: 100,000
SALES (est): 11.1MM **Privately Held**
WEB: www.lancopro.com
SIC: 2851 Paints & allied products

(G-12309)
LAPEL PIN & BUTTON COMPANY INC (PA)
10151 University Blvd (32817-1904)
PHONE......................................407 677-6144
Carey P Stewart, *President*
EMP: 14 EST: 1999
SQ FT: 4,800
SALES (est): 1.3MM **Privately Held**
WEB: www.signaturepatches.com
SIC: 3965 Fasteners, buttons, needles &
pins

(G-12310)
LAPIN SHEET METAL COMPANY
3825 Gardenia Ave (32839-9201)
PHONE......................................407 423-9897
Ronald Lapin, *President*
Janet Lapin, *President*
Daniel Lapin, *Vice Pres*
Mary Davis, *Purch Mgr*
Ernest Agustin, *CFO*
EMP: 75 EST: 1973
SQ FT: 50,000
SALES (est): 12.6MM **Privately Held**
WEB: www.lapinsm.com
SIC: 3444 Ducts, sheet metal

2022 Harris Florida
Manufacturers Directory

▲ = Import ▼=Export
◆ =Import/Export

(G-12311)
LASERSIGHT INCORPORATED (PA)
10244 E Clnl Dr Ste 201 (32817)
PHONE....................407 678-9900
Xian Ding Weng, *Ch of Bd*
Danghui Liu, *President*
Dorothy M Cipolla, *CFO*
Zhaokai Tang, *Treasurer*
Jeanette Williams, *Accounting Mgr*
EMP: 7 EST: 1987
SQ FT: 156,000
SALES (est): 4.1MM Privately Held
SIC: 3845 3699 6794 Electromedical equipment; laser systems & equipment; patent owners & lessors

(G-12312)
LASERSIGHT TECHNOLOGIES INC
10244 E Clnl Dr Ste 201 (32817)
PHONE....................407 678-9900
Michael R Farris, *President*
D Michael Litscher, *COO*
Gregory Wilson, *CFO*
EMP: 13 EST: 1991
SALES (est): 4.1MM Privately Held
WEB: www.lase.com
SIC: 3845 5049 Electromedical equipment; optical goods
PA: Lasersight Incorporated
10244 E Clnl Dr Ste 201
Orlando FL 32817

(G-12313)
LASERSTAR TECHNOLOGIES CORP
2461 Orlando Central Pkwy (32809-5619)
PHONE....................401 438-1500
David Braman, *Vice Pres*
Diane Voorhees, *Buyer*
Robert Fairhurst, *Engineer*
Raphael Dos Santos, *Engineer*
David Montoya, *Electrical Engi*
EMP: 15 EST: 2019
SALES (est): 5MM Privately Held
WEB: www.laserstar.net
SIC: 3599 Machine shop, jobbing & repair

(G-12314)
LASERSTAR TECHNOLOGIES CORP
2453 Orlando Central Pkwy (32809-5619)
PHONE....................407 248-1142
Orlando Sarmientos, *Sales Staff*
Albert Smith, *Executive*
Richard Hacker, *Planning*
EMP: 7
SALES (corp-wide): 5.6MM Privately Held
WEB: www.laserstar.net
SIC: 3559 3699 Jewelers' machines; electrical equipment & supplies
PA: Laserstar Technologies Corporation
1 Industrial Ct
Riverside RI 02915
401 438-1500

(G-12315)
LATINO ENTPS LA CHQITA TRTILLA
6918 Presidents Dr (32809-5668)
PHONE....................407 251-8290
EMP: 10 EST: 2015
SALES (est): 496.1K Privately Held
WEB: www.lachiquitatortilla.com
SIC: 2099 Tortillas, fresh or refrigerated

(G-12316)
LAWTON PRINTERS INC
Also Called: Lawton Connect
649 Triumph Ct (32805-1276)
PHONE....................407 260-0400
Kimberly Lawton Koon, *President*
Ty Koon, *Vice Pres*
Tyler Koon, *Vice Pres*
Jim Bissonnette, *Plant Mgr*
Dave Dragan, *Plant Mgr*
▼ EMP: 30 EST: 1900
SQ FT: 21,000
SALES (est): 7.1MM Privately Held
WEB: www.lawtonconnect.com
SIC: 2752 Commercial printing, offset

(G-12317)
LEEDS MACHINING CO
4025 Bibb Ln (32817-1635)
PHONE....................407 671-3688
William Leeds, *Principal*
EMP: 7 EST: 1996
SALES (est): 134.4K Privately Held
SIC: 3544 Special dies, tools, jigs & fixtures

(G-12318)
LEGACY DELIGHTS LLC
1317 Edgewater Dr # 5119 (32804-6350)
PHONE....................321 222-9330
Deidre Stovall, *CEO*
EMP: 7 EST: 2020
SALES (est): 319.8K Privately Held
WEB: www.legacydelights.com
SIC: 2599 7929 Food wagons, restaurant; entertainers

(G-12319)
LEGACY VULCAN LLC
8500 Florida Rock Rd (32824-7841)
PHONE....................407 855-9902
Brad Bushur, *Manager*
EMP: 8
SQ FT: 1,798 Publicly Held
SIC: 3273 Ready-mixed concrete
HQ: Legacy Vulcan, Llc
1200 Urban Center Dr
Vestavia AL 35242
205 298-3000

(G-12320)
LEGACY VULCAN LLC
2858 Sidney Ave (32810-5134)
PHONE....................407 299-7494
Patton A Wasson, *President*
EMP: 12 Publicly Held
SIC: 3271 3273 8741 Blocks, concrete or cinder: standard; ready-mixed concrete; management services
HQ: Legacy Vulcan, Llc
1200 Urban Center Dr
Vestavia AL 35242
205 298-3000

(G-12321)
LEIDOS SEC DTCTION AUTOMTN INC
7558 Southland Blvd # 130 (32809-6974)
PHONE....................407 926-1900
Glenn Anderson, *Director*
EMP: 14 Publicly Held
SIC: 3663 Telemetering equipment, electronic
HQ: Leidos Security Detection & Automation, Inc.
1 Radcliff Rd
Tewksbury MA 01876
781 970-1563

(G-12322)
LENSAR INC
2800 Discovery Dr Ste 100 (32826-3010)
PHONE....................888 536-7271
Nicholas T Curtis, *CEO*
William J Link, *Ch of Bd*
Alan B Connaughton, *COO*
Edward Palmer, *Production*
Brenda Davis, *Buyer*
▼ EMP: 30 EST: 2004
SQ FT: 35,000
SALES (est): 34.4MM Privately Held
WEB: www.lensar.com
SIC: 3841 Surgical & medical instruments; surgical lasers

(G-12323)
LEWIS-RIGGS CUSTOM GUITARS INC
1001 Lake Sherwood Dr (32818-6612)
PHONE....................407 538-3710
Barry Lewis, *President*
Leland Riggs, *Vice Pres*
EMP: 6 EST: 2006
SQ FT: 2,800
SALES (est): 348K Privately Held
SIC: 3931 5099 Guitars & parts, electric & nonelectric; musical instruments

(G-12324)
LEXINGTON DSIGN + FBRCTION E L
Also Called: Caylex
613 Triumph Ct Ste 1 (32805-1248)
PHONE....................407 578-4720
Tom Hughes, *Mng Member*
▲ EMP: 14 EST: 1994
SQ FT: 15,000
SALES: 6.8MM
SALES (corp-wide): 42.6MM Privately Held
SIC: 3441 Fabricated structural metal
PA: Nassal Company
415 W Kaley St
Orlando FL 32806
407 648-0400

(G-12325)
LGL GROUP INC (PA)
2525 Shader Rd (32804-2721)
PHONE....................407 298-2000
Marc J Gabelli, *Ch of Bd*
Michael J Ferrantino, *President*
James W Tivy, *CFO*
Ivan Arteaga, *Director*
Timothy Foufas, *Director*
EMP: 2 EST: 1928
SQ FT: 71,000
SALES (est): 28.1MM Publicly Held
WEB: www.lglgroup.com
SIC: 3679 3559 Electronic circuits; electronic component making machinery

(G-12326)
LIDARIT INC
7208 W Sand Lake Rd (32819-5200)
PHONE....................407 632-2622
Andres Valencia Vidarte, *President*
Carlos Juri Feghali, *Vice Pres*
EMP: 20 EST: 2020
SALES (est): 968.2K Privately Held
WEB: www.lidarit.com
SIC: 7372 Utility computer software

(G-12327)
LIFELINK FOUNDATION INC
1739 S Orange Ave (32806-2935)
PHONE....................407 218-8783
Dennis Heinricks, *Branch Mgr*
EMP: 35
SALES (corp-wide): 128.9MM Privately Held
WEB: www.lifelinkfoundation.org
SIC: 2676 Towels, napkins & tissue paper products
PA: Lifelink Foundation, Inc.
9661 Delaney Creek Blvd
Tampa FL 33619
813 253-2640

(G-12328)
LIFT SPECTRUM TECHNOLOGIES LLC
Also Called: Lst
4700 Millenia Blvd # 175 (32839-6013)
PHONE....................407 228-8343
Jim Hukill,
EMP: 5 EST: 2008
SALES (est): 399.3K Privately Held
SIC: 3577 Computer peripheral equipment

(G-12329)
LIGHTPATH TECHNOLOGIES INC (PA)
2603 Challenger Tech Ct (32826-2716)
PHONE....................407 382-4003
Louis Leeburg, *Ch of Bd*
Shmuel Rubin, *President*
Al Symmons, *COO*
Peter Greif, *Vice Pres*
Mark Palvino, *Vice Pres*
EMP: 67 EST: 1985
SQ FT: 38,000
SALES: 35.5MM Publicly Held
WEB: www.lightpath.com
SIC: 3827 Optical instruments & lenses

(G-12330)
LIMBITLESS SOLUTIONS INC (PA)
4217 E Plaza Dr (32816-8013)
PHONE....................407 494-3661
Albert Manero, *CEO*
Albert Francis, *Assistant VP*
Dominique Courbin, *Production*
Anne Smallwood, *Bd of Directors*
Angie Carloss, *Admin Sec*
EMP: 6 EST: 2014
SALES (est): 618.2K Privately Held
WEB: www.limbitless-solutions.org
SIC: 3842 Limbs, artificial

(G-12331)
LINOGRAPHICS INC
Also Called: Digital Graphics
617 N Magnolia Ave (32801-1258)
PHONE....................407 422-8700
Gary Michael, *President*
EMP: 18 EST: 1979
SALES (est): 304.1K Privately Held
SIC: 2791 7336 2796 2752 Typesetting; commercial art & graphic design; platemaking services; commercial printing, lithographic

(G-12332)
LINPHARMA INC
5401 S Kirkman Rd Ste 310 (32819-7937)
PHONE....................888 989-3237
EMP: 9 EST: 2011
SALES (est): 154.9K Privately Held
SIC: 2834 Pharmaceutical preparations

(G-12333)
LION LOCS LLC
1002 Lucerne Ter (32806-1015)
PHONE....................704 802-2752
Nathan Watson,
EMP: 10 EST: 2019
SALES (est): 324.2K Privately Held
WEB: www.lionlocs.com
SIC: 3999 Hair & hair-based products

(G-12334)
LIQUID SOUL DGTAL GRAPHICS LLC
Also Called: Specialty Stamp & Sign
3628 E Esther St (32812-5117)
P.O. Box 568444 (32856-8444)
PHONE....................407 948-6973
Sean McLaughlin,
Melanie Lexner,
EMP: 8 EST: 2005
SALES (est): 219.4K Privately Held
SIC: 3993 Signs & advertising specialties

(G-12335)
LITEWORKS LIGHTING PRODUCTIONS
752 Palm Dr (32803-4221)
PHONE....................407 888-8677
Dave Eveson, *President*
Andrew Douglas, *Vice Pres*
Robin Eveson, *Manager*
EMP: 11 EST: 2000
SALES (est): 232.9K Privately Held
SIC: 3648 7336 Stage lighting equipment; art design services

(G-12336)
LLC BEST BLOCK (PA)
2858 Sidney Ave (32810-5134)
PHONE....................239 789-3531
Thilo D Best,
EMP: 7 EST: 2015
SALES (est): 2.2MM Privately Held
SIC: 3251 Paving brick, clay

(G-12337)
LM INDUSTRIAL INC
1429 Central Florida Pkwy (32837-9405)
PHONE....................407 240-8911
Lois McGinnis, *President*
Tim McGinnis, *Vice Pres*
EMP: 7 EST: 1994
SQ FT: 2,500
SALES (est): 898K Privately Held
SIC: 3441 1799 Fabricated structural metal; welding on site

(G-12338)
LOBO INDUSTRIES LLC
14179 Amelia Island Way (32828-4811)
PHONE....................407 310-3219
Samuel Meyers, *President*
EMP: 8 EST: 2014
SALES (est): 280.5K Privately Held
SIC: 3999 Manufacturing industries

(G-12339)
LOCKHEED MARTIN CORPORATION
100 Global Innovation Cir (32825-5003)
PHONE.............................407 306-6405
David Tatro, *Opers Staff*
Courtney Netzer, *Mfg Staff*
Jacob Barkley, *Engineer*
Adam Breed, *Engineer*
Matt Byrne, *Engineer*
EMP: 1332 **Publicly Held**
WEB: www.lockheedmartin.com
SIC: 3812 Search & navigation equipment
PA: Lockheed Martin Corporation
6801 Rockledge Dr
Bethesda MD 20817

(G-12340)
LOCKHEED MARTIN CORPORATION
12506 Lake Underhill Rd (32825-5002)
PHONE.............................407 306-1000
Bob Hunt, *Principal*
Dan Norton, *Vice Pres*
Frank St John, *Vice Pres*
Patricia D Armond, *Senior Buyer*
Dave Keeran, *Buyer*
EMP: 584 **Publicly Held**
WEB: www.lockheedmartin.com
SIC: 3761 3699 Ballistic missiles, complete; electrical equipment & supplies
PA: Lockheed Martin Corporation
6801 Rockledge Dr
Bethesda MD 20817

(G-12341)
LOCKHEED MARTIN CORPORATION
1700 Tradeport Dr (32824-7018)
PHONE.............................407 517-6627
Monica McManus, *Vice Pres*
Shauna M Ferguson, *Mfg Staff*
Cindy Hampton, *Financial Analy*
Glen Ives, *Manager*
Kenny King, *Software Engr*
EMP: 25 **Publicly Held**
WEB: www.gyrocamsystems.com
SIC: 3812 5072 Search & navigation equipment; hardware
PA: Lockheed Martin Corporation
6801 Rockledge Dr
Bethesda MD 20817

(G-12342)
LOCKHEED MARTIN CORPORATION
4504 Bridgeton Ln (32817-3827)
PHONE.............................407 306-4803
Jennifer Sayles, *Analyst*
EMP: 134 **Publicly Held**
WEB: www.gyrocamsystems.com
SIC: 3812 Search & navigation equipment
PA: Lockheed Martin Corporation
6801 Rockledge Dr
Bethesda MD 20817

(G-12343)
LOCKHEED MARTIN CORPORATION
Also Called: Lockheed Martin Mis Fire Ctrl
5600 W Sand Lake Rd (32819-8907)
PHONE.............................407 356-2000
Lauren Douglass, *General Mgr*
Jennifer Kuss, *Business Mgr*
Jed Clear, *Vice Pres*
Mary Sturtevant, *Vice Pres*
Adam Koffler, *Opers Staff*
EMP: 10 **Publicly Held**
WEB: www.lockheedmartin.com
SIC: 3812 Search & navigation equipment
PA: Lockheed Martin Corporation
6801 Rockledge Dr
Bethesda MD 20817

(G-12344)
LOCKHEED MARTIN CORPORATION
Also Called: Lockheed Martin Mis Fire Ctrl
8751 Lockheed Martin Blvd (32819-8913)
PHONE.............................407 356-1034
Alexander Shuster, *IT/INT Sup*
EMP: 29 **Publicly Held**
WEB: www.gyrocamsystems.com
SIC: 3812 Search & navigation equipment

PA: Lockheed Martin Corporation
6801 Rockledge Dr
Bethesda MD 20817

(G-12345)
LOCKHEED MARTIN CORPORATION
5600 W Sand Lake Rd Mp-26
(32819-8907)
PHONE.............................407 356-2000
Stanley Arthur, *President*
Sorina Terrell, *Planning*
EMP: 49 **Publicly Held**
WEB: www.lockheedmartin.com
SIC: 3483 3829 3812 3761 Ammunition, except for small arms; measuring & controlling devices; search & navigation equipment; guided missiles & space vehicles; motor vehicle parts & accessories
PA: Lockheed Martin Corporation
6801 Rockledge Dr
Bethesda MD 20817

(G-12346)
LOCKHEED MRTIN GYRCAM SYSTEMS
5600 W Sand Lake Rd Mp-265
(32819-8907)
PHONE.............................407 356-6500
Jay Pitman, *CEO*
Dan Kiehl, *Opers Mgr*
Al Bryan, *Manager*
Rita Flaherty, *Manager*
David J Huber, *Manager*
EMP: 102 EST: 2003
SALES (est): 9.9MM **Publicly Held**
SIC: 3812 Search & navigation equipment
PA: Lockheed Martin Corporation
6801 Rockledge Dr
Bethesda MD 20817

(G-12347)
LOCKHEED MRTIN INTGRTED SYSTEM
5600 W Sand Lake Rd (32819-8907)
PHONE.............................407 356-2000
William Boysen, *Manager*
EMP: 133 **Publicly Held**
SIC: 3812 Search & navigation equipment
HQ: Lockheed Martin Integrated Systems, Llc
6801 Rockledge Dr
Bethesda MD 20817

(G-12348)
LOCKHEED MRTIN MLLMTER TECH IN
5600 W Sand Lake Rd (32819-8907)
PHONE.............................407 356-4186
James Sharp, *Principal*
EMP: 19 EST: 2007
SALES (est): 3.3MM **Publicly Held**
SIC: 3721 Aircraft
PA: Lockheed Martin Corporation
6801 Rockledge Dr
Bethesda MD 20817

(G-12349)
LOCKHEED MRTIN TRNING SLTONS I (HQ)
Also Called: Lockheed Mrtin Rtary Mssion Sy
100 Global Innovation Cir (32825-5003)
PHONE.............................856 722-3317
Marillyn A Hewson, *CEO*
Nick Ali, *President*
Harold Browning, *Vice Pres*
Robert Lyle, *Engineer*
Bruce L Tanner, *CFO*
◆ EMP: 86 EST: 1984
SQ FT: 1,200
SALES (est): 165.2MM **Publicly Held**
SIC: 3812 Search & navigation equipment

(G-12350)
LOGIC CONTROLS INC
Also Called: Bematech
404 Sunport Ln Ste 550 (32809-8115)
PHONE.............................800 576-9647
Fabio Roman, *President*
Jeffrey Gugick, *Treasurer*
Marc Schuster, *Admin Sec*
▲ EMP: 33 EST: 1982

SALES (est): 14.5MM **Privately Held**
WEB: www.logiccontrols.com
SIC: 3578 Accounting machines & cash registers; cash registers; point-of-sale devices; registers, credit account
HQ: Totvs Large Enterprise Tecnologia Sa
Av. Braz Leme 1000
Sao Paulo SP 02511

(G-12351)
LOGOS PROMOTE INC
3804 N John Young Pkwy (32804-3201)
PHONE.............................407 447-5646
Gerald Hynes, *Principal*
Leslie Hynes, *Principal*
EMP: 8 EST: 2005
SALES (est): 1.1MM **Privately Held**
WEB: www.logospromote.com
SIC: 2759 Screen printing

(G-12352)
LOS ATNTCOS SNDWICH CUBAN CAFE
7339 E Colonial Dr Ste 1 (32807-6380)
PHONE.............................407 282-2322
Robert Y Cruz, *Owner*
EMP: 9 EST: 2008
SALES (est): 154.8K **Privately Held**
SIC: 2035 2099 5149 Spreads, sandwich: salad dressing base; ready-to-eat meals, salads & sandwiches; sandwiches

(G-12353)
LUFTCAR LLC ✪
12001 Res Pkwy Ste 236 (32826)
PHONE.............................408 905-0036
Santh Sathya, *Mng Member*
EMP: 18 EST: 2021
SALES (est): 1.2MM **Privately Held**
WEB: www.luftcar.com
SIC: 3721 Aircraft

(G-12354)
LUG USA LLC
8546 Palm Pkwy Ste 305 (32836-6415)
P.O. Box 91239, Austin TX (78709-1239)
PHONE.............................855 584-5433
Jason Richter, *Partner*
▲ EMP: 14 EST: 2006
SALES (est): 1MM **Privately Held**
SIC: 3161 Luggage

(G-12355)
LUMINAR LLC
Also Called: Luminar Holdco, LLC
2603 Discovery Dr Ste 100 (32826-3006)
PHONE.............................407 900-5259
Austin Russell, *President*
Tom Fennimore, *CFO*
Alan Prescott, *Officer*
Traci Tobolik, *Analyst*
EMP: 372 EST: 2020
SALES (est): 31.9MM **Publicly Held**
SIC: 3647 3519 3812 7372 Vehicular lighting equipment; radiators, stationary engine; search & navigation equipment; prepackaged software
PA: Luminar Technologies, Inc.
2603 Discovery Dr Ste 100
Orlando FL 32826
407 900-5259

(G-12356)
LUMINAR TECHNOLOGIES INC (PA)
2603 Discovery Dr Ste 100 (32826-3006)
PHONE.............................407 900-5259
Austin Russell, *Ch of Bd*
Lonnie Bernardoni, *Vice Pres*
Leo Chan, *Engineer*
Mark Eremeev, *Engineer*
Ahmed Fouda, *Engineer*
EMP: 37 EST: 2018
SQ FT: 120,716
SALES (est): 31.9MM **Publicly Held**
WEB: www.luminartech.com
SIC: 3714 Motor vehicle parts & accessories

(G-12357)
LUMINAR TECHNOLOGIES INC
12601 Research Pkwy (32826-3226)
PHONE.............................407 900-5259
EMP: 20

SALES (corp-wide): 31.9MM **Publicly Held**
WEB: www.luminartech.com
SIC: 3714 Motor vehicle parts & accessories
PA: Luminar Technologies, Inc.
2603 Discovery Dr Ste 100
Orlando FL 32826
407 900-5259

(G-12358)
LUXURY MOTOR CARS LLC
420 S Orange Ave Ste 220 (32801-4910)
PHONE.............................407 398-6933
Steve Parmee, *Mng Member*
EMP: 10 EST: 2018
SALES (est): 583.8K **Privately Held**
SIC: 3714 Motor vehicle parts & accessories

(G-12359)
M&B STEEL FABRICATORS INC
2536 Hansrob Rd (32804-3318)
PHONE.............................407 486-1774
Jose D Mansilla, *President*
Gregory G Baker, *Vice Pres*
Tyler Pelleymounter, *Admin Sec*
EMP: 18 EST: 2010
SQ FT: 14,000
SALES (est): 1.2MM **Privately Held**
SIC: 3446 Ornamental metalwork

(G-12360)
MAC GREGOR SMITH BLUEPRINTERS
1500 S Division Ave (32805-4724)
PHONE.............................407 423-5944
Brenda M Smith, *President*
Alexander Smith, *President*
Thomas M Gregorsmith, *Vice Pres*
Thomas Mac Gregor-Smith Jr, *Vice Pres*
Greg Smith, *Vice Pres*
EMP: 18 EST: 1958
SQ FT: 7,500
SALES (est): 2.5MM **Privately Held**
WEB: www.macgregorsmith.com
SIC: 3861 Reproduction machines & equipment

(G-12361)
MAHER INDUSTRIES INC
5434 Osprey Isle Ln (32819-4015)
PHONE.............................407 928-5288
Blake A Maher, *Principal*
EMP: 7 EST: 2016
SALES (est): 108.4K **Privately Held**
WEB: www.maher.com
SIC: 3999 Manufacturing industries

(G-12362)
MANATEE BAY ENTERPRISES INC
2234 W Taft Vnlnd Rd A (32837-7800)
PHONE.............................407 245-3600
Robert W Palmiero, *Ch of Bd*
Steve Horne, *Vice Pres*
Larrie McCleary, *Vice Pres*
EMP: 11 EST: 1990
SQ FT: 10,000
SALES (est): 376.9K **Privately Held**
SIC: 2396 2339 2369 Screen printing on fabric articles; women's & misses' outerwear; girls' & children's outerwear

(G-12363)
MANSCI INC
6925 Lake Ellenor Dr # 136 (32809-4648)
PHONE.............................866 763-2122
Ed Godman, *CEO*
Michael Cauley, *President*
EMP: 9 EST: 2005
SALES (est): 580K **Privately Held**
WEB: www.mansci.com
SIC: 3821 Laboratory equipment: fume hoods, distillation racks, etc.

(G-12364)
MARUTI TECHNOLOGY INC
Also Called: Maruti Fence
1775 Colton Dr (32822-5909)
PHONE.............................407 704-4775
Ketankumar S Dave, *President*
EMP: 8 EST: 2010
SALES (est): 149.3K **Privately Held**
WEB: www.fence4sale.com
SIC: 3084 Plastics pipe

(G-12365)
MASTER CONSTRUCTION PDTS INC (PA)
Also Called: MCP
501 Thorpe Rd (32824-8134)
P.O. Box 593918 (32859-3918)
PHONE..............................407 857-1221
Kevin Decker, *President*
Josh Antrobus, *Opers Mgr*
Adriana Arone, *Purchasing*
Brandon Brown, *Branch Mgr*
Jim Senecal, *Manager*
EMP: 24 **EST:** 2002
SQ FT: 5,000
SALES (est): 8.1MM **Privately Held**
WEB:
www.masterconstructionproducts.com
SIC: 3272 Precast terrazo or concrete products

(G-12366)
MASTER SCREEN PRINTING
6782 N Orng Blflm Trl D (32810)
PHONE..............................407 625-8902
Thanh Tran, *Branch Mgr*
EMP: 8 **Privately Held**
WEB: www.masterprintwear.com
SIC: 2752 Commercial printing, offset
PA: Master Screen Printing
N171w20999 Industrial Dr
Jackson WI 53037

(G-12367)
MEADS INTERNATIONAL INC (HQ)
5600 W Sand Lake Rd (32819-8907)
PHONE..............................407 356-8400
Jim Cravens, *President*
Volker Weidemann, *Engineer*
James Hanbbery, *Treasurer*
Robert Grubbs, *Director*
▲ **EMP:** 60 **EST:** 1996
SALES (est): 28.5MM **Publicly Held**
WEB: www.meads-amd.com
SIC: 3812 Search & navigation equipment

(G-12368)
MECHANICAL SVCS CENTL FLA INC (HQ)
Also Called: Honeywell Authorized Dealer
9820 Satellite Blvd (32837-8447)
PHONE..............................407 857-3510
Bernard B Horne, *CEO*
David Goerke, *President*
Tim Miles, *Vice Pres*
Steve Patiry, *Vice Pres*
Debbie Alazraki, *CFO*
EMP: 201 **EST:** 1974
SQ FT: 50,000
SALES (est): 37.8MM
SALES (corp-wide): 9.9B **Publicly Held**
WEB: www.msifla.com
SIC: 3444 1761 1711 7623 Pipe, sheet metal; sheet metalwork; mechanical contractor; refrigeration repair service
PA: Emcor Group, Inc.
301 Merritt 7 Fl 6
Norwalk CT 06851
203 849-7800

(G-12369)
MED ALERT RESPONSE INC
6239 Edgewater Dr Ste N1 (32810-4735)
PHONE..............................407 730-3571
Dorothy King, *President*
EMP: 5 **EST:** 1987
SALES (est): 489.4K **Privately Held**
WEB: www.getmedalert.com
SIC: 3669 5999 Emergency alarms; hospital equipment & supplies

(G-12370)
MEI MICRO INC
4767 New Broad St Ste 337 (32814-6405)
PHONE..............................407 514-2619
Louis Ross, *CEO*
EMP: 50 **EST:** 2017
SQ FT: 54,150
SALES (est): 2.2MM **Privately Held**
SIC: 3674 7371 Microcircuits, integrated (semiconductor); monolithic integrated circuits (solid state); computer software development

(G-12371)
MELODON SOFTWARE INC
2813 S Hiawassee Rd # 302 (32835-6690)
PHONE..............................407 654-1234
Faramarz Saberian, *President*
EMP: 8 **EST:** 2010
SALES (est): 208.4K **Privately Held**
WEB: www.melodon.healthcare
SIC: 7372 Prepackaged software

(G-12372)
MERCHSPIN INC
Also Called: Akt Enterprises
6424 Forest City Rd (32810-4322)
PHONE..............................877 306-3651
Alex Tchekmeian, *President*
Robert Pfeffer, *Opers Mgr*
Maria Johnson, *Controller*
Erin Broxton, *Representative*
Luigi Caiazzo, *Representative*
▼ **EMP:** 50 **EST:** 2005
SALES (est): 10.9MM **Privately Held**
WEB: www.aktenterprises.com
SIC: 2759 8741 Screen printing; management services

(G-12373)
METALHOUSE LLC
4705 S Apk Vnlnd Rd # 140 (32819-3105)
PHONE..............................407 270-3000
John Unsalan, *Mng Member*
John C Unsalan, *Mng Member*
EMP: 6 **EST:** 2014
SALES (est): 1.1MM **Privately Held**
WEB: www.metalhouse.us
SIC: 3547 5051 8742 3315 Rolling mill machinery; reinforcement mesh, wire; marketing consulting services; steel wire & related products

(G-12374)
METALMASTER MACHINE SHOP INC
Also Called: Metalmaster Manufacturing Svcs
4549 L B Mcleod Rd (32811-6405)
PHONE..............................407 423-9049
Joe Skawinski, *President*
▼ **EMP:** 12 **EST:** 1981
SQ FT: 7,000
SALES (est): 1.7MM **Privately Held**
WEB: www.metalmaster.biz
SIC: 3599 Machine shop, jobbing & repair

(G-12375)
METTLER-TOLEDO INC
45 N Magnolia Ave (32801-2427)
PHONE..............................407 423-3856
Floyd Haenson, *Branch Mgr*
EMP: 12
SALES (corp-wide): 3.7B **Publicly Held**
WEB: www.mt.com
SIC: 3596 Industrial scales
HQ: Mettler-Toledo, Llc
1900 Polaris Pkwy Fl 6
Columbus OH 43240
614 438-4511

(G-12376)
MFX CORP
7065 Westpointe Blvd # 205 (32835-8758)
PHONE..............................407 429-4051
Flavio Boghossian, *President*
Martha Norena, *Principal*
Marcus A El Huaick, *Treasurer*
Adriana B El Huaick, *Admin Sec*
EMP: 10 **EST:** 2013
SALES (est): 4MM **Privately Held**
WEB: www.mfxcorp.com
SIC: 3085 8742 Plastics bottles; marketing consulting services
HQ: Riopet Embalagens Sa
Rua Professor Eduardo Vianna 175
Nova Iguacu RJ 26012

(G-12377)
MGM CARGO LLC
Also Called: Fastsigns
7154 W Colonial Dr (32818-6751)
PHONE..............................407 770-1500
Frank Adam, *Mng Member*
Jose Marin,
EMP: 6 **EST:** 2015

SALES (est): 740.8K **Privately Held**
WEB: www.fastsigns.com
SIC: 3993 7313 7336 Signs & advertising specialties; printed media advertising representatives; commercial art & graphic design

(G-12378)
MICHIGAN PMPS ELC MTRS REPR CO
Also Called: Michigan St Pump & Electric
1210 W Michigan St (32805-5451)
PHONE..............................407 841-6800
Jeff Ramsammy, *President*
Sharmilee Ramsammy, *Vice Pres*
EMP: 8 **EST:** 2002
SQ FT: 5,000
SALES (est): 917.4K **Privately Held**
WEB: www.michstpump.com
SIC: 7694 3599 Electric motor repair; machine shop, jobbing & repair

(G-12379)
MID-FLORIDA PLASTICS INC
Also Called: Engineered Plastic Specialists
780 Central Florida Pkwy (32824-8502)
PHONE..............................407 856-1805
James Z Golembiski, *President*
Gary Golembeski, *Vice Pres*
EMP: 25 **EST:** 1992
SQ FT: 17,000
SALES (est): 2.5MM **Privately Held**
WEB: www.engineeredplastics.net
SIC: 3089 Injection molded finished plastic products; injection molding of plastics

(G-12380)
MILLENNIUM PHARMACEUTICALS INC
6509 Hazeltine Nat Dr (32822-5203)
PHONE..............................866 466-7779
Ron McKillip, *Principal*
EMP: 66 **Privately Held**
WEB: www.takedaoncology.com
SIC: 2834 Pharmaceutical preparations
HQ: Millennium Pharmaceuticals, Inc.
40 Landsdowne St
Cambridge MA 02139

(G-12381)
MILLS & NEBRASKA DOOR & TRIM
2721 Regent Ave (32804-3358)
P.O. Box 536548 (32853-6548)
PHONE..............................407 472-2742
John M Pulsifer, *President*
Roy Pulsifer, *Treasurer*
Thomas S Pulsifer, *Admin Sec*
EMP: 14 **EST:** 1973
SQ FT: 800
SALES (est): 381.2K **Privately Held**
SIC: 2431 5031 3442 Door frames, wood; doors; metal doors, sash & trim

(G-12382)
MILSAV LLC
Also Called: Metronow
10542 Wittenberg Way (32832-7024)
PHONE..............................407 556-5055
Jorge Bravo,
EMP: 17 **EST:** 2007
SALES (est): 165.9K **Privately Held**
SIC: 3661 Telephone sets, all types except cellular radio

(G-12383)
MIX IT LOOP INC
12517 Greco Dr (32824-5823)
PHONE..............................407 902-9334
Rodney Harter, *Principal*
EMP: 9 **EST:** 2010
SALES (est): 91.9K **Privately Held**
SIC: 3273 Ready-mixed concrete

(G-12384)
MOBILE RUGGED TECH CORP
4767 New Broad St (32814-6405)
PHONE..............................781 771-6743
Robinson B Nunez, *President*
EMP: 5 **EST:** 2008
SALES (est): 489.4K **Privately Held**
SIC: 3429 Manufactured hardware (general)

(G-12385)
MOBILITY FREEDOM INC
7260 Narcoossee Rd (32822-5534)
PHONE..............................407 495-1333
EMP: 15
SALES (corp-wide): 218.5MM **Privately Held**
WEB: www.mobilityworks.com
SIC: 3842 7699 Wheelchairs; hospital equipment repair services
HQ: Mobility Freedom, Inc.
20354 Us Highway 27
Clermont FL 34715
352 322-2256

(G-12386)
MODERN WELDING COMPANY FLA INC
1801 Atlanta Ave (32806-3924)
P.O. Box 568678 (32856-8678)
PHONE..............................407 843-1270
James E Jones, *President*
Vince Pedigo, *Warehouse Mgr*
Karen Bleddyn, *Accounting Dir*
Lee Alexander, *Sales Staff*
Jeff Herter, *Sales Staff*
▼ **EMP:** 54 **EST:** 1948
SQ FT: 2,500
SALES (est): 18.5MM
SALES (corp-wide): 154.3MM **Privately Held**
WEB: www.modweldco.com
SIC: 3443 5051 Tanks, standard or custom fabricated: metal plate; steel
PA: Modern Welding Company, Inc.
2880 New Hartford Rd
Owensboro KY 42303
270 685-4400

(G-12387)
MODEST LOGISTICS LLC ✿
2295 S Hiawassee Rd (32835-8746)
PHONE..............................321 314-2825
David Modeste, *Mng Member*
EMP: 11 **EST:** 2021
SALES (est): 120K **Privately Held**
SIC: 3537 Trucks: freight, baggage, etc.: industrial, except mining

(G-12388)
MONARCH SAFETY PRODUCTS INC
121 S Orange Ave Ste 1500 (32801-3241)
PHONE..............................407 442-0269
Nigel Graham, *President*
EMP: 10 **EST:** 2000
SQ FT: 2,500
SALES (est): 247.3K **Privately Held**
SIC: 2385 Waterproof outerwear

(G-12389)
MOOG INC
Also Called: Electro-Optical Imaging
7455 Emerald Dunes Dr # 2200 (32822-5266)
PHONE..............................321 435-8722
Chris Fedele, *Principal*
EMP: 10
SALES (corp-wide): 2.8B **Publicly Held**
WEB: www.moog.com
SIC: 3812 3769 3861 Electronic detection systems (aeronautical); defense systems & equipment; missile guidance systems & equipment; pictorial deviation indicators; guided missile & space vehicle parts & aux eqpt, rsch & dev; photo reconnaissance systems
PA: Moog Inc.
400 Jamison Rd
Elma NY 14059
716 652-2000

(G-12390)
MOOG INC
Also Called: Moog IDS
7455 Emerald Dunes Dr # 2200 (32822-5266)
PHONE..............................407 451-9534
John Scannel, *CEO*
James Riedel, *President*
Maureen Athoe, *Vice Pres*
Timothy Balkin, *Treasurer*
John Drenning, *Admin Sec*
EMP: 8 **EST:** 2006
SQ FT: 6,640

SALES (est): 2.5MM
SALES (corp-wide): 2.8B **Publicly Held**
SIC: 3812 Search & navigation equipment
PA: Moog Inc.
400 Jamison Rd
Elma NY 14059
716 652-2000

(G-12391)
MOOSE TRACTS INC
2325 Ohio Dr (32803-2027)
PHONE.............................407 491-1412
Eric Moose, *Owner*
EMP: 7 EST: 2018
SALES (est): 199.2K **Privately Held**
SIC: 2434 Wood kitchen cabinets

(G-12392)
MORNING GLORY LAWN MAINT INC
4750 Nantucket Ln (32808-2622)
PHONE.............................407 376-5833
Kelvin Rumph, *CEO*
EMP: 5 EST: 2008
SALES (est): 385.4K **Privately Held**
SIC: 3524 Lawn & garden equipment

(G-12393)
MORRIS VISITOR PUBLICATIONS
801 N Magnolia Ave # 201 (32803-3842)
PHONE.............................407 423-0618
John Byrne, *Principal*
EMP: 13 EST: 2005
SALES (est): 445.8K **Privately Held**
WEB: www.morris.com
SIC: 2759 Publication printing

(G-12394)
MP 93 SCREEN PRINT AND EMB LLC
3330 Vineland Rd Ste C (32811-6453)
PHONE.............................407 592-3657
Philip Fry, *Administration*
EMP: 10 EST: 2017
SALES (est): 482.7K **Privately Held**
SIC: 2752 Commercial printing, lithographic

(G-12395)
MPS NORTH AMERICA LLC (DH)
5728 Major Blvd Ste 528 (32819-7962)
PHONE.............................407 472-1280
Robin Blakely, *COO*
Marie McNamara, *Vice Pres*
Yamini Tandon, *Mng Member*
EMP: 1 EST: 2013
SALES (est): 4.6MM **Privately Held**
WEB: www.mpslimited.com
SIC: 2731 Book publishing

(G-12396)
MR AMERICAS 2 LLC
15771 State Road 535 K (32821-5605)
PHONE.............................407 217-2282
Matheus Cabral,
EMP: 7 EST: 2020
SALES (est): 600K **Privately Held**
SIC: 2099 Ready-to-eat meals, salads & sandwiches

(G-12397)
MTC SEAL COATING SERVICES INC
4221 Drexel Ave (32808-2129)
PHONE.............................313 759-9423
Alejandro Gonzalez Campos, *Principal*
EMP: 8 EST: 2017
SALES (est): 101.9K **Privately Held**
SIC: 3479 Metal coating & allied service

(G-12398)
MULTICORE PHOTONICS INC
5832 N Dean Rd (32817-3249)
PHONE.............................407 325-7800
Darren Engle, *CEO*
Jody Wilson, *COO*
Chris Adams, *Vice Pres*
Son Ho, *Vice Pres*
Umar Piracha, *Vice Pres*
EMP: 6 EST: 2015

SALES (est): 409.2K **Privately Held**
WEB: www.multicore-photonics.com
SIC: 3826 3674 3827 Analytical instruments; semiconductors & related devices; optical instruments & apparatus

(G-12399)
MULTICORE PHOTONICS INC
319 N Crystal Lake Dr (32803-5831)
PHONE.............................407 325-7800
EMP: 9 EST: 2016
SALES (est): 414.5K **Privately Held**
SIC: 3661 Fiber optics communications equipment

(G-12400)
MULTICORE TECHNOLOGIES LLC
319 N Crystal Lake Dr (32803-5831)
PHONE.............................407 325-7800
Jody Wilson, *COO*
EMP: 5 EST: 2019
SALES (est): 302.2K **Privately Held**
WEB: www.disruptfiber.tech
SIC: 3674 Semiconductors & related devices

(G-12401)
MUSCLE MIXES INC
1617 Hillcrest St (32803-4809)
P.O. Box 533967 (32853-3967)
PHONE.............................407 872-7576
Denise Imbesi, *President*
Randi Solomon, *Vice Pres*
EMP: 10 EST: 1988
SQ FT: 3,070
SALES (est): 915K **Privately Held**
WEB: www.musclemixes.com
SIC: 3652 5735 Pre-recorded records & tapes; audio tapes, prerecorded

(G-12402)
MUSE GELATO INC
Also Called: Orlando Ice Cream Company
7362 Futures Dr Ste 20 (32819-9088)
PHONE.............................407 363-1443
Andrea N Moss Davidoff, *President*
Richard Gandara, *Prdtn Mgr*
EMP: 10 EST: 2010
SALES (est): 1.2MM **Privately Held**
WEB: www.musegelato.com
SIC: 2024 5143 Ice cream, bulk; ice cream & ices

(G-12403)
NANA FOODS INC
5219 Timberview Ter (32819-3924)
PHONE.............................407 363-7183
Awad Mubarak, *Principal*
EMP: 7 EST: 2012
SALES (est): 212.6K **Privately Held**
SIC: 2099 Food preparations

(G-12404)
NATIONAL CYLINDER SERVICES LLC (PA)
4601 Dardanelle Dr (32808-3833)
PHONE.............................407 299-8454
Harold Berg III, *Partner*
Harold William Berg Jr,
EMP: 21 EST: 2006
SALES (est): 2.8MM **Privately Held**
WEB: www.natcyl.com
SIC: 3714 Cylinder heads, motor vehicle

(G-12405)
NATIONAL WOODWORKS INC
4122 Mercy Industrial Ct (32808-3811)
PHONE.............................407 489-3572
John R Gardner, *Director*
Richard D Reimann, *Director*
EMP: 8 EST: 2013
SALES (est): 256.1K **Privately Held**
WEB: www.nationalwoodworks.com
SIC: 2431 Millwork

(G-12406)
NATURES FUEL INC
2254 Saw Palmetto Ln (32828-4650)
PHONE.............................407 808-4272
Kleinberg Alan J Sr, *Principal*
EMP: 6 EST: 2014
SALES (est): 473.2K **Privately Held**
WEB: www.naturesfuelorlando.com
SIC: 2869 Fuels

(G-12407)
NATUS MEDICAL INCORPORATED
12301 Lake Underhill Rd # 201 (32828-4511)
PHONE.............................321 235-8213
Dana Bienvenu, *Business Mgr*
Ross Peterson, *Engineer*
Beth Spinda, *Controller*
Josh Cheuvront, *Accountant*
Jose Leon, *Manager*
EMP: 30
SALES (corp-wide): 28.4MM **Privately Held**
WEB: www.natus.com
SIC: 3845 Electromedical equipment
HQ: Natus Medical Incorporated
6701 Koll Center Pkwy # 12
Pleasanton CA 94566
925 223-6700

(G-12408)
NATUS MEDICAL INCORPORATED
Also Called: Bio-Logic Systems
12301 Lake Underhill Rd # 201 (32828-4511)
PHONE.............................847 949-5200
EMP: 14
SALES (corp-wide): 530.8MM **Publicly Held**
SIC: 3845 Mfg Electromedical Equipment
PA: Natus Medical Incorporated
6701 Koll Center Pkwy # 12
Pleasanton CA 94566
925 223-6700

(G-12409)
NCG MEDICAL SYSTEMS INC (PA)
Also Called: Perfect Care
1402 Edgewater Dr Ste 101 (32804-6396)
PHONE.............................407 788-1906
Tony Arias, *President*
Bill Monroe, *Vice Pres*
Riaz Latib, *Engineer*
Jackie Huasupoma, *Mktg Coord*
John Giddings, *Manager*
EMP: 28 EST: 1978
SALES (est): 6MM **Privately Held**
WEB: www.ncgmedical.com
SIC: 7372 7371 Business oriented computer software; custom computer programming services

(G-12410)
NEJAT ARSLANER
Also Called: Coating Heaven
2555 N Forsyth Rd Ste E (32807-6463)
PHONE.............................321 300-5464
Nejat Arslaner, *Owner*
EMP: 7 EST: 2017
SALES (est): 93K **Privately Held**
SIC: 3479 Coating of metals & formed products

(G-12411)
NEPHRON PHARMACEUTICALS
1162 Bella Vida Blvd (32828-6758)
PHONE.............................407 913-3142
Hieu Pham, *Principal*
Justin Austin, *Opers Staff*
Emily Phillippi, *Research*
Alexander Santulli, *Research*
Jon Burgess, *Engineer*
EMP: 16 EST: 2010
SALES (est): 3.4MM **Privately Held**
WEB: www.nephronpharm.com
SIC: 2834 Pharmaceutical preparations

(G-12412)
NEPHRON PHARMACEUTICALS CORP
4121 Sw 34th St (32811-6475)
PHONE.............................407 999-2225
Susan Rucker, *Chief*
Brad Reddick, *Vice Pres*
Coley Beavers, *Research*
Zachary Bowyer, *Research*
Brittany Heiser, *Research*
EMP: 19 EST: 2019
SALES (est): 10MM **Privately Held**
WEB: www.nephronpharm.com
SIC: 2834 Pharmaceutical preparations

(G-12413)
NEW VISION DISPLAY INC
Also Called: Osd Display
135 W Central Blvd # 330 (32801-2430)
PHONE.............................407 480-5800
Khaled R Khuda, *Branch Mgr*
EMP: 7 **Privately Held**
WEB: www.newvisiondisplay.com
SIC: 3679 Liquid crystal displays (LCD)
HQ: New Vision Display, Inc.
1430 Blue Oaks Blvd # 100
Roseville CA 95747
916 786-8111

(G-12414)
NEW YORK INTL BREAD CO
1500 W Church St (32805-2408)
PHONE.............................407 843-9744
Vincent Masella Jr, *President*
Laura Masella, *Vice Pres*
Craig Amster, *Opers Staff*
Sandy Mobley, *CFO*
Abigail Parks, *Asst Mgr*
EMP: 90 EST: 1985
SQ FT: 30,000
SALES (est): 18MM **Privately Held**
WEB: www.nyibco.com
SIC: 2051 Bakery: wholesale or wholesale/retail combined; bread, all types (white, wheat, rye, etc): fresh or frozen; rolls, bread type: fresh or frozen

(G-12415)
NEXT STEP PRODUCTS LLC
9400 Southridge Park Ct # 200 (32819-8643)
PHONE.............................407 857-9900
Mark Masterman, *President*
Kathy Cregan,
Rosa Rodriguez,
EMP: 9 EST: 2008
SALES (est): 714.2K **Privately Held**
WEB: www.jandy.com
SIC: 3648 Lighting equipment

(G-12416)
NIGHTHAWK RUNNING LLC
Also Called: Nighthawk Safety
1623 Wycliff Dr (32803-1929)
PHONE.............................407 443-8404
Douglas R Storer, *Manager*
EMP: 11 EST: 2013
SALES (est): 295.5K **Privately Held**
WEB: www.nighttechgear.com
SIC: 3949 Sporting & athletic goods

(G-12417)
NINA PLASTIC BAGS INC (PA)
Also Called: Nina Plastics
1903 Cypress Lake Dr (32837-8459)
P.O. Box 2758, Windermere (34786-2758)
PHONE.............................407 802-6828
Satish Sharma, *President*
James Snell, *Vice Pres*
◆ EMP: 60 EST: 1979
SQ FT: 75,000
SALES (est): 11.2MM **Privately Held**
SIC: 3081 Unsupported plastics film & sheet

(G-12418)
NIS PRINT INC
Also Called: National Indexing Systems
1809 S Division Ave (32805-4729)
PHONE.............................407 423-7575
Sheryl A Batchelder, *President*
EMP: 44 EST: 1986
SQ FT: 30,000
SALES (est): 4.3MM **Privately Held**
WEB: www.nisprint.com
SIC: 2759 Commercial printing

(G-12419)
NITESOL INC
1831 Tallokas Ave (32805-4735)
PHONE.............................407 557-4042
EMP: 6
SALES (est): 440K **Privately Held**
SIC: 3993 Mfg Signs/Advertising Specialties

(G-12420)
NORMAN ENGINEERING CORPORATION
2579 N Orange Blossom Trl (32804-4808)
PHONE 407 425-6433
Anne Belderes, *President*
John Belderes, *Vice Pres*
Bill Newsom, *Treasurer*
EMP: 7 EST: 1972
SQ FT: 2,400
SALES (est): 589.7K Privately Held
SIC: 3599 Machine shop, jobbing & repair

(G-12421)
NORTH ORANGE AVENUE PROPERTIES
633 N Orange Ave (32801-1325)
PHONE 407 420-5000
Kathleen Waltz, *President*
Michael D Slason, *Vice Pres*
Crane H Kenney, *Admin Sec*
EMP: 2 EST: 2008
SALES (est): 3.2MM
SALES (corp-wide): 4.6B Publicly Held
WEB: www.ustler.net
SIC: 2711 Newspapers, publishing & printing
HQ: Tribune Media Company
515 N State St Ste 2400
Chicago IL 60654
312 222-3394

(G-12422)
NORTHROP GRUMMAN SYSTEMS CORP
Also Called: Combat Systems Mssion Radiness
2300 Discovery Dr Ste 150 (32826-3712)
PHONE 321 235-3800
Alice Reed, *Principal*
Charles Kristofek, *Engineer*
Jackie Smith, *Business Dir*
Debi Johnson, *Executive*
Frank Desanto, *Technician*
EMP: 45 Publicly Held
WEB: www.northropgrumman.com
SIC: 3812 Search & navigation equipment
HQ: Northrop Grumman Systems Corporation
2980 Fairview Park Dr
Falls Church VA 22042
703 280-2900

(G-12423)
NORTHROP GRUMMAN SYSTEMS CORP
Also Called: Northrop Grmman Mssion Systems
11474 Corp Blvd Ste 120 (32817)
PHONE 407 737-4900
James Harvey, *Division Mgr*
Frank Demauro, *Vice Pres*
Marty Amen, *Branch Mgr*
Derek Batts, *Administration*
EMP: 218 Publicly Held
WEB: www.northropgrumman.com
SIC: 3812 Search & navigation equipment
HQ: Northrop Grumman Systems Corporation
2980 Fairview Park Dr
Falls Church VA 22042
703 280-2900

(G-12424)
NOUVEAU COSMETIQUE USA INC
189 S Orange Ave Ste 1110 (32801-3257)
PHONE 321 332-6976
Armand Hoes, *President*
Robert Waters, *Vice Pres*
Joeren Kluge, *Director*
EMP: 6 EST: 2009
SQ FT: 2,000
SALES (est): 501.4K Privately Held
WEB: www.nouveaucontourusa.com
SIC: 3841 Surgical & medical instruments

(G-12425)
NOVA LASERLIGHT LLC
7600 Dr Phillips Blvd (32819-7231)
PHONE 407 226-0609
Jan V Karlin, *Mng Member*
EMP: 12 EST: 2011

SALES (est): 631K Privately Held
SIC: 3845 Laser systems & equipment, medical

(G-12426)
NOVELTY CRYSTAL CORP
9326 Bentley Park Cir (32819-5345)
PHONE 352 429-9036
Rivka Michaeli, *President*
Ed Coslett, *COO*
Sara Coslett, *Exec VP*
Asher Michaeli, *Exec VP*
Joseph Michaeli, *Senior VP*
▲ **EMP: 100 EST: 1961**
SALES (est): 9.6MM Privately Held
WEB: www.noveltycrystal.com
SIC: 3421 3089 Cutlery; plastic kitchenware, tableware & houseware; kitchenware, plastic

(G-12427)
NOVENA TEC LLC (PA)
4767 New Broad St (32814-6405)
PHONE 407 392-1868
Robby Thirun, *Mng Member*
Thanuja Thevan,
EMP: 9 EST: 2014
SQ FT: 4,000
SALES (est): 2.1MM Privately Held
WEB: www.novenatec.com
SIC: 3559 3699 Semiconductor manufacturing machinery; high-energy particle physics equipment

(G-12428)
NSCRYPT INC
12151 Res Pkwy Ste 150 (32826)
PHONE 407 275-4720
Kenneth H Church, *President*
Beth Dickerson, *General Mgr*
Debra Brownell, *Vice Pres*
Xudong Chen, *Vice Pres*
Mike Newton, *Vice Pres*
EMP: 35 EST: 2002
SQ FT: 125,000
SALES (est): 9.8MM Privately Held
WEB: www.nscrypt.com
SIC: 3577 Printers, computer
PA: Sciperio, Inc.
12151 Res Pkwy Ste 150
Orlando FL 32826
407 275-4755

(G-12429)
NTS INDUSTRIES INC
1218 W New Hampshire St (32804-5759)
P.O. Box 540602 (32854-0602)
PHONE 317 847-6675
Nathan Shanabruch, *Principal*
EMP: 11 EST: 2009
SALES (est): 70.7K Privately Held
WEB: www.nts.com
SIC: 3999 Manufacturing industries

(G-12430)
OBERON INDUSTRIES INC
1900 Stanley St (32803-5531)
PHONE 321 245-7338
Randall Krull, *President*
EMP: 7 EST: 2017
SALES (est): 62K Privately Held
WEB: www.oberonwireless.com
SIC: 3999 Manufacturing industries

(G-12431)
OCEAN OPTICS INC
3500 Quadrangle Blvd (32817-8326)
PHONE 407 673-0041
Steven Frey, *Vice Pres*
Martha Gomez, *Vice Pres*
Colin Vanexel, *Vice Pres*
Keith Lorenz, *Project Mgr*
Angelina Roblin, *Project Mgr*
EMP: 38
SALES (corp-wide): 2B Privately Held
WEB: www.oceaninsight.com
SIC: 3826 Analytical instruments
HQ: Ocean Optics, Inc.
3500 Quadrangle Blvd
Orlando FL 32817

(G-12432)
OCEAN OPTICS INC (HQ)
Also Called: Ocean Insight
3500 Quadrangle Blvd (32817-8326)
P.O. Box 2249, Dunedin (34697-2249)
PHONE 407 673-0041
Michael Edwards, *President*
WEI Tang, *Business Mgr*
Martha Gomez, *Vice Pres*
Mary Judah, *Vice Pres*
Ron Shah, *Vice Pres*
▲ **EMP: 50 EST: 1989**
SQ FT: 20,000
SALES (est): 72.1MM
SALES (corp-wide): 2B Privately Held
WEB: www.oceaninsight.com
SIC: 3826 3827 Analytical instruments; optical instruments & lenses
PA: Halma Public Limited Company
Misbourne Court Rectory Way
Amersham BUCKS HP7 0
149 472-1111

(G-12433)
OCEAN OPTICS INC
Ocean Thin Films
3500 Quadrangle Blvd (32817-8326)
PHONE 727 545-0741
Phillip Buchsbaum, *General Mgr*
EMP: 38
SALES (corp-wide): 2B Privately Held
WEB: www.oceaninsight.com
SIC: 3826 3827 Analytical instruments; optical instruments & lenses
HQ: Ocean Optics, Inc.
3500 Quadrangle Blvd
Orlando FL 32817

(G-12434)
OCEAN WAY TRANSPORT LLC
4529 Piedmont St (32811-4528)
PHONE 407 669-3822
Kervens Ocean, *Mng Member*
EMP: 5 EST: 2020
SALES (est): 316.5K Privately Held
SIC: 3537 Trucks, tractors, loaders, carriers & similar equipment

(G-12435)
OCOA LLC
800 N Magnolia Ave # 1400 (32803-3248)
PHONE 407 898-1961
Dagmar Moore, *Mng Member*
EMP: 20 EST: 2015
SALES (est): 859.8K Privately Held
WEB: www.ocoa.com
SIC: 3652 Pre-recorded records & tapes

(G-12436)
ODYSSEY MANUFACTURING CO
250 Central Florida Pkwy (32824-7601)
PHONE 407 582-9051
Randy Hancock, *Plant Supt*
EMP: 7 EST: 2016
SALES (est): 82.3K Privately Held
WEB: www.odysseymanufacturing.com
SIC: 3999 Manufacturing industries

(G-12437)
OLD & NEW BRICK PAVERS LLC
5221 Alligator Flag Ln (32811-6409)
PHONE 908 249-6130
Andre H Desouza, *Principal*
EMP: 7 EST: 2014
SALES (est): 105.7K Privately Held
WEB: www.oldeworldbrickpavers.com
SIC: 2951 Asphalt paving mixtures & blocks

(G-12438)
OLDCASTLE INFRASTRUCTURE INC
690 W Taft Vineland Rd (32824-8007)
PHONE 407 855-7580
John Blanchard, *Manager*
EMP: 44
SALES (corp-wide): 30.9B Privately Held
WEB: www.oldcastleinfrastructure.com
SIC: 3272 Concrete products
HQ: Oldcastle Infrastructure, Inc.
7000 Central Pkwy Ste 800
Atlanta GA 30328
770 270-5000

(G-12439)
OMNIMARK ENTERPRISES LLC
6843 Narcoossee Rd (32822-5512)
PHONE 516 351-9075
Jason Kilner, *Principal*
EMP: 7 EST: 2015
SALES (est): 159.7K Privately Held
SIC: 2023 Dietary supplements, dairy & non-dairy based

(G-12440)
OPEN MARKET ENTERPRISES LLC
Also Called: Communicate 360
3461 Parkway Center Ct (32808-1047)
PHONE 407 322-5434
Ana Torres, *President*
EMP: 9 EST: 2017
SALES (est): 826.5K Privately Held
SIC: 2396 2752 Fabric printing & stamping; commercial printing, lithographic; commercial printing, offset; promotional printing, lithographic; business form & card printing, lithographic

(G-12441)
OPENKM USA LLC
1715 Branchwater Trl (32825-8508)
PHONE 407 257-2640
Mario Zules,
EMP: 7 EST: 2017
SALES (est): 395.7K Privately Held
WEB: www.openkm.us
SIC: 7372 Prepackaged software

(G-12442)
OPENWATER SEAFOOD LLC
13435 S Orange Ave (32824-6012)
PHONE 407 440-0656
Patrick Nierle, *CEO*
EMP: 4 EST: 2017
SALES (est): 4MM Privately Held
SIC: 2077 Marine fats, oils & meals

(G-12443)
OPTIMUS FLEET LLC
7550 Futures Dr (32819-9095)
PHONE 407 590-5060
Juan Martinez, *COO*
Sergio Barcellos, *Mng Member*
Richard Barcellos, *Director*
Patricia Martinez, *Director*
EMP: 10 EST: 2018
SALES (est): 100K Privately Held
SIC: 7372 Operating systems computer software

(G-12444)
OPTRONIC LABORATORIES LLC
4632 36th St (32811-6532)
PHONE 407 422-3171
Jay Silverman, *President*
EMP: 16 EST: 2018
SQ FT: 25,000
SALES (est): 2.5MM Privately Held
WEB: www.optroniclabs.com
SIC: 3825 Instruments to measure electricity

(G-12445)
ORACLE AMERICA INC
Also Called: Sun Microsystems
3501 Quadrangle Blvd # 151 (32817-8330)
PHONE 407 380-0058
Melanie Wargo, *Manager*
EMP: 15
SALES (corp-wide): 42.4B Publicly Held
WEB: www.oracle.com
SIC: 3571 Minicomputers
HQ: Oracle America, Inc.
500 Oracle Pkwy
Redwood City CA 94065
650 506-7000

(G-12446)
ORACLE AMERICA INC
7453 T G Lee Blvd (32822-4416)
PHONE 407 458-1200
EMP: 25
SALES (corp-wide): 42.4B Publicly Held
WEB: www.oracle.com
SIC: 3571 Minicomputers

HQ: Oracle America, Inc.
　　500 Oracle Pkwy
　　Redwood City CA 94065
　　650 506-7000

(G-12447)
ORACLE AMERICA INC
7453 T G Lee Blvd (32822-4416)
PHONE.........................813 287-1700
Dennis Baldwin, *Project Dir*
Leon Soares, *Engineer*
Beth Wade, *Engineer*
Sean Donahue, *Sales Staff*
David Enoch, *Sales Staff*
EMP: 15
SALES (corp-wide): 42.4B **Publicly Held**
WEB: www.oracle.com
SIC: 3571 7373 8748 7374 Minicomputers; computer integrated systems design; business consulting; data processing & preparation
HQ: Oracle America, Inc.
　　500 Oracle Pkwy
　　Redwood City CA 94065
　　650 506-7000

(G-12448)
ORACLE SYSTEMS
CORPORATION
7453 T G Lee Blvd (32822-4416)
PHONE.........................407 458-1200
Carissa Bergeron, *Engineer*
Marion Guatimozim, *Engineer*
Maricarmen Saldivar, *Engineer*
Jennifer Richards, *Manager*
Michele Casalgrandi, *Manager*
EMP: 48
SALES (corp-wide): 42.4B **Publicly Held**
SIC: 7372 Prepackaged software
HQ: Oracle Systems Corporation
　　500 Oracle Pkwy
　　Redwood City CA 94065

(G-12449)
ORION TECHNOLOGIES LLC
12605 Challenger Pkwy # 130
(32826-2711)
PHONE.........................407 476-2120
Nirav Pandya, *CEO*
Larry Ford, *Vice Pres*
Richard Miller, *Vice Pres*
Jeffrey Van Anda, *Vice Pres*
Daniel Hawkins, *Project Mgr*
EMP: 28 **EST:** 2011
SQ FT: 12,000
SALES (est): 7MM
SALES (corp-wide): 916.2MM **Privately Held**
WEB: www.oriontechnologies.com
SIC: 3571 Electronic computers
PA: Phoenix Mecano Ag
　　Hofwisenstrasse 6
　　Stein Am Rhein SH 8260
　　432 554-255

(G-12450)
ORLANDO BLINDS FACTORY
210 N Goldenrod Rd Ste 1 (32807-8222)
PHONE.........................407 697-0521
EMP: 7 **EST:** 2019
SALES (est): 387.8K **Privately Held**
WEB: www.orlandoblindsfactory.com
SIC: 2591 Window blinds

(G-12451)
ORLANDO BREWING
PARTNERS
1401 W Gore St Ste 3 (32805-3778)
PHONE.........................407 843-6783
John Cheek, *President*
EMP: 7 **EST:** 2002
SALES (est): 156.2K **Privately Held**
WEB: www.orlandobrewing.com
SIC: 2082 Malt beverages

(G-12452)
ORLANDO ICE SERVIVE CORP
410 27th St (32806-4451)
PHONE.........................407 999-4940
Alex Zaldibar, *President*
Carlos Herrera, *Principal*
Eddie Roque, *Vice Pres*
EMP: 6 **EST:** 2007
SALES (est): 777.5K **Privately Held**
SIC: 2097 Manufactured ice

(G-12453)
ORLANDO METAL FABRICATION
INC
11516 Satellite Blvd (32837-9228)
PHONE.........................407 850-4313
Robert Matthias, *General Mgr*
Jack Scales, *Vice Pres*
EMP: 13 **EST:** 2005
SALES (est): 1.3MM **Privately Held**
WEB: www.orlandometalfab.net
SIC: 3441 Fabricated structural metal

(G-12454)
ORLANDO NOVELTY LLC (PA)
Also Called: Orlando Novelty Wholesale
1624 Premier Row (32809-5712)
PHONE.........................407 858-9499
Almi Athraf, *Mng Member*
EMP: 5 **EST:** 2014
SALES (est): 596.1K **Privately Held**
WEB: www.orlandonovelty.com
SIC: 3911 Cigar & cigarette accessories

(G-12455)
ORLANDO PLATING CO
601 N Orange Blossom Trl (32805-1491)
P.O. Box 2609 (32802-2609)
PHONE.........................407 843-1140
Servet Aral, *President*
Gary Hall, *Corp Secy*
Cynthia Scott, *Vice Pres*
Norleen Hilliard, *Bookkeeper*
EMP: 8 **EST:** 1940
SQ FT: 20,000
SALES (est): 720.2K **Privately Held**
WEB: www.orlandoplating.com
SIC: 3471 Finishing, metals or formed products

(G-12456)
ORLANDO TIMES INC
4403 Vineland Rd Ste B5 (32811-7362)
P.O. Box 555339 (32855-5339)
PHONE.........................407 841-3052
Calvin Collins Jr, *President*
Lottie Collins, *Admin Sec*
EMP: 5 **EST:** 1976
SALES (est): 473.3K **Privately Held**
WEB: www.orlando-times.com
SIC: 2711 8661 Newspapers: publishing only, not printed on site; religious organizations

(G-12457)
ORLANDOS FORKLIFT SERVICE
LLC
3138 Natoma Way (32825-7183)
PHONE.........................407 761-9104
Orlando Rodriguez, *Principal,*
EMP: 6 **EST:** 2016
SALES (est): 354.5K **Privately Held**
SIC: 3537 Forklift trucks

(G-12458)
ORTHOMERICA PRODUCTS INC
6333 N Orange Blossom Trl (32810-4223)
P.O. Box 607129 (32860-7129)
PHONE.........................407 290-6592
David C Kerr, *President*
Shannon Schwenn, *Exec VP*
Felix Ortiz, *Plant Mgr*
Nancy Cobb, *Senior Buyer*
Vicki Lewis, *Purch Agent*
▲ **EMP:** 180 **EST:** 1989
SQ FT: 80,000
SALES (est): 31.3MM **Privately Held**
WEB: www.orthomerica.com
SIC: 3842 Orthopedic appliances

(G-12459)
OUTDOOR IMAGES CENTRAL
FLA INC
4061 Forrestal Ave Unit 2 (32806-6151)
PHONE.........................407 825-9944
Ken D Luzadder, *President*
David Wood, *Vice Pres*
EMP: 5 **EST:** 1990
SQ FT: 2,400
SALES (est): 441.1K **Privately Held**
WEB: www.outdoorimagesinc.net
SIC: 3993 5046 Signs & advertising specialties; neon signs; signs, electrical

(G-12460)
P B C CENTRAL
Also Called: Behrs
3450 Vineland Rd Ste B (32811-6421)
PHONE.........................407 648-2020
Douglass Davis, *Principal*
EMP: 6 **EST:** 1998
SALES (est): 301.6K **Privately Held**
SIC: 2066 2064 Chocolate candy, solid; candy & other confectionery products

(G-12461)
P&A MACHINE
7220 Old Cheney Hwy (32807-6222)
PHONE.........................407 275-5770
Edward Ditges, *Principal*
EMP: 9 **EST:** 2006
SALES (est): 363.8K **Privately Held**
SIC: 3469 3599 Stamping metal for the trade; machine shop, jobbing & repair

(G-12462)
PACK4U LLC
7531 Currency Dr (32809-6922)
PHONE.........................407 857-2871
Jane Garrison, *General Mgr*
Brent Herman, *Director*
Shane Bishop, *Director*
Barry Hart, *Director*
EMP: 17 **EST:** 2011
SALES (est): 4.7MM **Privately Held**
WEB: www.pack4u.com
SIC: 2834 Druggists' preparations (pharmaceuticals)

(G-12463)
PACKAGING CORPORATION
AMERICA
Also Called: PCA/Supply Services 302c
3785 Bryn Mawr St (32808-4605)
PHONE.........................407 299-1300
Jim Delk, *Manager*
EMP: 7
SALES (corp-wide): 7.7B **Publicly Held**
WEB: www.packagingcorp.com
SIC: 2653 Boxes, corrugated: made from purchased materials
PA: Packaging Corporation Of America
　　1 N Field Ct
　　Lake Forest IL 60045
　　847 482-3000

(G-12464)
PAMATIAN GROUP INC (PA)
Also Called: Minuteman Press
997 W Kennedy Blvd Ste A1 (32810-6100)
PHONE.........................407 291-8387
Mark Peeples, *President*
Ken Windsor, *Principal*
Jayson Kraus, *Area Mgr*
Neil Macleod, *Vice Pres*
Tim Yousef, *Treasurer*
EMP: 4 **EST:** 1970
SALES (est): 5.4MM **Privately Held**
WEB: www.minutemanpress.com
SIC: 2752 Commercial printing, lithographic

(G-12465)
PANAMA JACK INC
230 Ernestine St (32801-3622)
PHONE.........................407 843-8110
Jack Katz, *Ch of Bd*
Kimberly Mana, *President*
Larry Green, *Vice Pres*
Beau Katz, *Project Mgr*
Jeffrey Bowma, *CFO*
▼ **EMP:** 10 **EST:** 1974
SQ FT: 27,000
SALES (est): 2.5MM **Privately Held**
WEB: www.panamajack.com
SIC: 2844 Suntan lotions & oils

(G-12466)
PANOPTEX TECHNOLOGIES INC
6555 Sanger Rd Ste 100 (32827-7585)
PHONE.........................407 412-0222
EMP: 21 **EST:** 2017
SALES (est): 551.9K **Privately Held**
SIC: 3652 Pre-recorded records & tapes

(G-12467)
PAPER PALM LLC
Also Called: Sir Speedy
621 Commonwealth Ave (32803-5223)
PHONE.........................407 647-3328
EMP: 6
SALES (est): 908.5K **Privately Held**
SIC: 2752 Comm Prtg Litho

(G-12468)
PAPILA DESIGN INC
701 W Landstreet Rd (32824-8022)
PHONE.........................407 240-2992
Ayhan Papila, *President*
◆ **EMP:** 9 **EST:** 1992
SQ FT: 20,000
SALES (est): 1MM **Privately Held**
WEB: www.papiladesign.com
SIC: 3645 Table lamps

(G-12469)
PASSUR AEROSPACE INC (PA)
3452 Lake Lynda Dr # 190 (32817-1429)
PHONE.........................203 622-4086
G S Beckwith Gilbert, *Ch of Bd*
Brian G Cook, *President*
Allison O'Neill, *Exec VP*
Evee Burgard, *Vice Pres*
Andy Washbum, *Engineer*
EMP: 17 **EST:** 1967
SQ FT: 1,793
SALES (est): 6.1MM **Publicly Held**
WEB: www.passur.com
SIC: 3812 Search & navigation equipment

(G-12470)
PASSUR AEROSPACE INC
5750 Major Blvd Ste 530 (32819-7965)
PHONE.........................631 589-6800
G S Beckwith Gilbert, *Ch of Bd*
James T Barry, *President*
Renee Alter, *Vice Pres*
John Keller, *Vice Pres*
Bill Leber, *Vice Pres*
EMP: 6 **EST:** 1978
SALES (est): 2.1MM
SALES (corp-wide): 6.1MM **Publicly Held**
WEB: www.passur.com
SIC: 3671 Cathode ray tubes, including rebuilt
PA: Passur Aerospace, Inc.
　　3452 Lake Lynda Dr # 190
　　Orlando FL 32817
　　203 622-4086

(G-12471)
PASTRANA PRIME LLC ✪
524 Madrigal Ct (32825-3367)
PHONE.........................407 470-9339
Danny Pastrana, *Owner*
EMP: 10 **EST:** 2021
SALES (est): 322.9K **Privately Held**
SIC: 2511 5023 5719 Kitchen & dining room furniture; decorative home furnishings & supplies; kitchen tools & utensils; lighting, lamps & accessories

(G-12472)
PATRIOT PRESS INC
14141 Lake Price Dr (32826-3504)
PHONE.........................407 625-7516
Arnie B Eastlick, *President*
EMP: 10 **EST:** 2000
SALES (est): 382.5K **Privately Held**
WEB: www.patriotpress.net
SIC: 2752 Commercial printing, offset

(G-12473)
PATTISON SIGN LEASE (US)
LLC
7576 Kingspointe Pkwy # 18 (32819-8590)
PHONE.........................407 345-8010
Jim Pattison, *Principal*
Sean Flynn, *Vice Pres*
EMP: 7 **EST:** 2006
SALES (est): 95.2K **Privately Held**
SIC: 3993 Signs & advertising specialties

(G-12474)
PAVER SYSTEMS LLC
Also Called: Tarmac America
39 E Landstreet Rd (32824-7814)
PHONE.........................407 859-9117
Rod Ross, *Engrg Mgr*
Nancy Murphy, *Office Mgr*

EMP: 47
SALES (corp-wide): 137.2MM **Privately Held**
WEB: www.oldcastlecoastal.com
SIC: 3281 3272 3271 2816 Paving blocks, cut stone; concrete products; concrete block & brick; inorganic pigments; masonry materials & supplies; paving materials
HQ: Paver Systems, Llc
7167 Interpace Rd
Riviera Beach FL 33407
561 844-5202

(G-12475)
PAVERSCAPE INC
2914 Dean Ridge Rd (32825-8701)
PHONE....................................407 381-1022
Charles Paul Miller, *President*
EMP: 19 **EST:** 1989
SALES (est): 2.8MM **Privately Held**
WEB: www.paverscapeinc.net
SIC: 3531 Pavers

(G-12476)
PBC PAVERS BORBA CO
1841 S Kirkman Rd # 1311 (32811-2378)
PHONE....................................407 296-7727
Sidney S Borba, *President*
EMP: 7 **EST:** 2004
SALES (est): 72.1K **Privately Held**
SIC: 2951 Asphalt paving mixtures & blocks

(G-12477)
PEI SHORES INC
4100 Silver Star Rd Ste C (32808-4618)
PHONE....................................407 523-2899
Jack Law, *President*
EMP: 7 **EST:** 2012
SALES (est): 228.1K **Privately Held**
WEB: www.embroideryworksplus.com
SIC: 2395 Embroidery & art needlework

(G-12478)
PELLICONI FLORIDA LLC (HQ)
2501 Principal Row (32837-8357)
PHONE....................................407 855-6984
Pier Nigito, *Opers Mgr*
Cristina Casalboni, *Human Resources*
Massimo Sabattini, *Sales Staff*
Anthony Chaplet, *Mng Member*
Marco Checchi,
◆ **EMP:** 20 **EST:** 2009
SALES (est): 15.2MM
SALES (corp-wide): 206.4MM **Privately Held**
WEB: www.pelliconi.com
SIC: 3565 Packaging machinery
PA: Pelliconi & C. Spa
Via Emilia 314
Ozzano Dell'emilia BO 40064
051 651-2611

(G-12479)
PENINSULA METAL FINISHING INC
2550 Dinneen Ave (32804-4204)
P.O. Box 540899 (32854-0899)
PHONE....................................407 291-1023
C David Roach, *President*
F Smith Coachman, *Corp Secy*
EMP: 35 **EST:** 1985
SQ FT: 22,000
SALES (est): 1.3MM **Privately Held**
WEB: www.pmforlando.com
SIC: 3471 Anodizing (plating) of metals or formed products; plating of metals or formed products

(G-12480)
PEPSI BEVERAGES COMPANY
7701 Southland Blvd (32809-6948)
PHONE....................................407 241-4110
Bruce Matzner, *Vice Pres*
EMP: 23 **EST:** 2019
SALES (est): 1.5MM
SALES (corp-wide): 70.3B **Publicly Held**
WEB: www.pepsico.com
SIC: 2086 Carbonated soft drinks, bottled & canned
PA: Pepsico, Inc.
700 Anderson Hill Rd
Purchase NY 10577
914 253-2000

(G-12481)
PEPSI-COLA BOTTLING CO TAMPA
1700 Directors Row (32809-6299)
P.O. Box 593889 (32859-3889)
PHONE....................................407 857-3301
Laurence Roethel, *Opers Mgr*
Emmanuel Ige, *Production*
Argenis Mora, *Sales Staff*
John Williams, *Marketing Staff*
John Nichols, *Manager*
EMP: 10
SQ FT: 33,000
SALES (corp-wide): 70.3B **Publicly Held**
WEB: www.pepsico.com
SIC: 2086 Carbonated soft drinks, bottled & canned
HQ: Pepsi-Cola Bottling Company Of Tampa
11315 N 30th St
Tampa FL 33612
813 971-2550

(G-12482)
PEPSI-COLA BOTTLING CO TAMPA
7501 Monetary Dr (32809-5730)
PHONE....................................407 826-5929
EMP: 161
SALES (corp-wide): 70.3B **Publicly Held**
WEB: www.pepsico.com
SIC: 2086 Carbonated soft drinks, bottled & canned
HQ: Pepsi-Cola Bottling Company Of Tampa
11315 N 30th St
Tampa FL 33612
813 971-2550

(G-12483)
PEPSI-COLA METRO BTLG CO INC
7380 W Sand Lake Rd # 230 (32819-5248)
PHONE....................................407 354-5800
Rebecca Ross, *Marketing Staff*
Rich Panner, *Manager*
Greg Merthie, *Manager*
Pam Jennings, *Info Tech Mgr*
EMP: 71
SALES (corp-wide): 70.3B **Publicly Held**
WEB: www.pepsico.com
SIC: 2086 Carbonated soft drinks, bottled & canned
HQ: Pepsi-Cola Metropolitan Bottling Company, Inc.
700 Anderson Hill Rd
Purchase NY 10577
914 767-6000

(G-12484)
PERFUMELAND
5216 Vanguard St (32819-8527)
PHONE....................................407 354-3342
EMP: 13
SALES (est): 3.4MM **Privately Held**
SIC: 2844 Mfg Toilet Preparations

(G-12485)
PHINTEC LLC
618 E South St Ste 500 (32801-2986)
PHONE....................................321 214-2500
Todd Ludington,
EMP: 5 **EST:** 1996
SALES (est): 525.9K **Privately Held**
WEB: www.phintec.com
SIC: 3571 7373 Electronic computers; value-added resellers, computer systems

(G-12486)
PIEZO TECHNOLOGY INC (HQ)
Also Called: Mtronpti
2525 Shader Rd (32804-2721)
PHONE....................................407 298-2000
William Drafts, *President*
Luis Romaguera, *General Mgr*
Paul A Dechen, *Vice Pres*
Mike Howard, *Vice Pres*
Ed Vargas, *Prdtn Mgr*
EMP: 100 **EST:** 1967
SQ FT: 75,000

SALES (est): 9.6MM
SALES (corp-wide): 28.1MM **Publicly Held**
WEB: www.mtronpti.com
SIC: 3679 3677 3825 Oscillators; resonant reed devices, electronic; piezoelectric crystals; filtration devices, electronic; instruments to measure electricity
PA: Lgl Group, Inc.
2525 Shader Rd
Orlando FL 32804
407 298-2000

(G-12487)
PILKINGTON NORTH AMERICA INC
4500 Seaboard Rd Ste A (32808-3846)
PHONE....................................407 295-8560
Kevin Howel, *Manager*
EMP: 10 **Privately Held**
WEB: www.pilkington.com
SIC: 3211 Flat glass
HQ: Pilkington North America, Inc.
811 Madison Ave Fl 3
Toledo OH 43604
419 247-3731

(G-12488)
PINE FUEL LLC
5004 Old Winter Garden Rd (32811-1636)
PHONE....................................407 345-7960
Premji Sapna, *Principal*
EMP: 7 **EST:** 2011
SALES (est): 133.3K **Privately Held**
SIC: 2869 Fuels

(G-12489)
PIXELTEQ INC (DH)
3500 Quadrangle Blvd (32817-8326)
PHONE....................................727 545-0741
Phil Buchsbaum, *CEO*
Mark Lavelee, *President*
Gordon McPhee, *Vice Pres*
Richard Eichholtz, *Mfg Dir*
Brad Bishop, *Mfg Staff*
▲ **EMP:** 9 **EST:** 2009
SALES (est): 9.3MM
SALES (corp-wide): 2B **Privately Held**
WEB: www.oceaninsight.com
SIC: 3827 Optical instruments & lenses
HQ: Halma Holdings Inc.
535 Sprngfeld Ave Ste 110
Summit NJ 07901
513 772-5501

(G-12490)
PLANAR ENERGY DEVICES INC
653 W Michigan St (32805-6203)
PHONE....................................407 459-1440
EMP: 10
SALES (est): 1.5MM **Privately Held**
SIC: 3674 Semiconductors And Related Devices, Nsk

(G-12491)
PLAYLIST LIVE INC
Also Called: Akt
6424 Forest City Rd (32810-4322)
PHONE....................................877 306-3651
Jared Mendelewicz, *Vice Pres*
Matthew Apostol, *Production*
EMP: 37 **EST:** 2010
SALES (est): 2.9MM **Privately Held**
WEB: www.playlist-live.com
SIC: 2752 Offset & photolithographic printing

(G-12492)
PNC SOLUTIONS INC
Also Called: Appiskey
219 N Brown Ave (32801-2103)
PHONE....................................407 401-8275
Naveed Chinoy, *Owner*
Jose Rodriguez, *Project Mgr*
EMP: 8 **EST:** 2014
SQ FT: 1,200
SALES (est): 862.8K **Privately Held**
WEB: www.pncdigital.com
SIC: 2752 7371 Commercial printing, lithographic; computer software development & applications; software programming applications

(G-12493)
POBLOCKI SIGN CO SOUTHEAST LLC
3851 Center Loop (32808-3147)
PHONE....................................407 660-3174
EMP: 14
SALES (est): 536.5K **Privately Held**
WEB: www.poblocki.com
SIC: 3993 Signs & advertising specialties

(G-12494)
POPCORN JUNKIE LLC
4649 Parkbreeze Ct (32808-1044)
PHONE....................................407 634-0042
Neal Crosier, *Mng Member*
EMP: 6 **EST:** 2016
SALES (est): 510.5K **Privately Held**
WEB: www.mypopcornjunkie.com
SIC: 2099 5441 Popcorn, packaged: except already popped; popcorn, including caramel corn

(G-12495)
POWDER COATING FACTORY LLC
635 Wilmer Ave (32808-7635)
PHONE....................................407 286-4550
Boris Roitman, *Branch Mgr*
EMP: 7
SALES (corp-wide): 696.8K **Privately Held**
WEB: www.thepowdercoatingfactory.com
SIC: 3479 Coating of metals & formed products
PA: The Powder Coating Factory Llc
1453 Valley Pine Cir
Apopka FL

(G-12496)
POWER EVOLUTION INC
14163 Sapphire Bay Cir (32828-7482)
PHONE....................................305 318-8476
Omar Masri, *President*
EMP: 8 **EST:** 2016
SALES (est): 163.7K **Privately Held**
SIC: 3651 Audio electronic systems

(G-12497)
POWERDMS INC
Also Called: Innovative Data Solutions
101 S Garland Ave Ste 300 (32801-3277)
P.O. Box 2468 (32802-2468)
PHONE....................................407 992-6000
David Digiacomo, *CEO*
Joshua J Brown, *President*
Jared Goldberg, *Partner*
Christine Goracke, *Partner*
Ryan Robinson, *Partner*
EMP: 75 **EST:** 2000
SQ FT: 15,506
SALES (est): 11.5MM **Privately Held**
WEB: www.powerdms.com
SIC: 7372 Prepackaged software

(G-12498)
PRAESTO ENTERPRISES LLC
Also Called: JW Machine
2525 Industrial Blvd (32804-4209)
PHONE....................................407 298-9171
Mark Chen, *CEO*
Phyllis Chen, *Mng Member*
EMP: 8 **EST:** 1986
SQ FT: 4,000
SALES (est): 1.2MM **Privately Held**
WEB: www.jwmachinecorp.com
SIC: 3599 8711 3451 3452 Machine shop, jobbing & repair; mechanical engineering; screw machine products; bolts, nuts, rivets & washers; acceleration indicators & systems components, aerospace

(G-12499)
PRAXIS SOFTWARE INC
7575 Kingspointe Pkwy # 9 (32819-8593)
PHONE....................................407 226-5691
Rhonda Copley, *President*
Amin Ismail, *Vice Pres*
EMP: 10 **EST:** 1998
SALES (est): 727.8K **Privately Held**
SIC: 7372 7371 Prepackaged software; custom computer programming services

(G-12500)
PRECAST DESIGNS INC
Also Called: T & T Concrete Specialties
10305 Rocket Ct (32824-8559)
PHONE.............................407 856-5444
David E Ford, *President*
EMP: 15 EST: 1975
SALES (est): 3.3MM **Privately Held**
WEB: www.precastdesigns.net
SIC: 3272 Concrete products, precast

(G-12501)
PRECISION INFINITY SYSTEMS INC
14569 Jamaica Dogwood Dr (32828-4833)
P.O. Box 781005 (32878-1005)
PHONE.............................407 490-2320
Michael Adamission, *President*
EMP: 5 EST: 2006
SALES (est): 348.6K **Privately Held**
SIC: 7372 7389 Application computer software;

(G-12502)
PREFERRED METAL PRODUCTS INC
3614 Princeton Oaks St (32808-5636)
PHONE.............................407 296-4449
Lawrence Bechtold, *President*
Angela Bechtold, *Vice Pres*
Ryan Bechtold, *Treasurer*
EMP: 13 EST: 1988
SQ FT: 14,000
SALES (est): 2.2MM **Privately Held**
WEB: www.preferredmetal.com
SIC: 3444 Sheet metalwork

(G-12503)
PRESTIGE FLRG INSTLLATIONS INC
Also Called: Prestige Granite & Marble
3065 Pennington Dr (32804-3333)
PHONE.............................407 291-0609
Mark D'Agostino, *President*
Karen D'Agostino, *Vice Pres*
▲ EMP: 15 EST: 1989
SQ FT: 8,000
SALES (est): 839.6K **Privately Held**
WEB: www.prestigegranite.net
SIC: 3281 1752 Granite, cut & shaped; floor laying & floor work

(G-12504)
PRICE CHOPPER INC
Also Called: Price Chopper Wristbands
6325 Mccoy Rd (32822-5167)
PHONE.............................407 679-1600
Shara Sooknarine, *President*
Jefferson Sooknarine, *Chairman*
Jennifer Collins, *Vice Pres*
Deven Pathak, *Vice Pres*
Nyla Sooknarine, *CFO*
◆ EMP: 40 EST: 1997
SQ FT: 43,000
SALES (est): 9.1MM **Privately Held**
WEB: www.pchopper.com
SIC: 2389 Arm bands, elastic

(G-12505)
PRICE CHPPER MED WRSTBANDS INC
Also Called: Medical ID Solutions
6325 Mccoy Rd (32822-5167)
PHONE.............................407 505-5809
Tory Jacobson, *Sales Staff*
Leslie Gray, *Manager*
Ricardo Rivera, *Manager*
Shara Sooknarine, *Director*
Deven Pathak, *Director*
EMP: 5 EST: 2006
SALES (est): 746.5K **Privately Held**
WEB: www.medicalbands.com
SIC: 3089 Bands, plastic

(G-12506)
PRIMUS STERILIZER COMPANY LLC (HQ)
7936 Forest City Rd (32810-2907)
PHONE.............................402 344-4200
Michael Douglas, *President*
David Counley, *Vice Pres*
Dave Schall, *Vice Pres*
Dan Schenk, *Plant Mgr*
Gary Molacek, *Materials Mgr*

EMP: 15 EST: 1990
SALES: 14.8MM
SALES (corp-wide): 73.1MM **Privately Held**
WEB: www.spire-is.com
SIC: 3842 Sterilizers, hospital & surgical
PA: K S T Industries Inc
6400 Northam Dr
Mississauga ON
905 362-6400

(G-12507)
PRINTERS EDGE LLC
6229 Edgewater Dr Ste 400 (32810-4773)
P.O. Box 160602, Altamonte Springs
(32716-0602)
PHONE.............................407 294-8542
EMP: 13
SALES (est): 1.5MM **Privately Held**
SIC: 2752 Lithographic Commercial Printing

(G-12508)
PRINTING USA INC
4732 S Orange Blossom Trl (32839-1708)
PHONE.............................407 857-7468
Robert Hill, *President*
Susan Hill, *Sales Staff*
Tierney Stecher, *Sales Staff*
Rick Hill, *Manager*
EMP: 14 EST: 1982
SQ FT: 8,821
SALES (est): 3.4MM **Privately Held**
WEB: www.printingusa.org
SIC: 2752 Commercial printing, offset

(G-12509)
PRO CHEM PRODUCTS INC
1340 W Central Blvd (32805-1754)
PHONE.............................407 425-5533
EMP: 6
SQ FT: 7,500
SALES: 1MM **Privately Held**
SIC: 2842 5064 5013 2841 Mfg Polish/Sanitation Gd Whol Appliances/Tv/Radio Whol Auto Parts/Supplies Mfg Soap/Other Detergent

(G-12510)
PRO DUFFERS ORLANDO
1144 Ballyshannon Pkwy (32828-8682)
PHONE.............................407 641-7626
Otis Windham, *Principal*
EMP: 8 EST: 2010
SALES (est): 245.7K **Privately Held**
WEB: www.produffersorlando.com
SIC: 3949 Shafts, golf club

(G-12511)
PRO-CRETE MATERIAL CORPORATION
1617 S Division Ave (32805-4725)
PHONE.............................352 748-1505
Adam Freeman, *President*
EMP: 17 EST: 2011
SALES (est): 806.7K **Privately Held**
SIC: 3272 Concrete products, precast

(G-12512)
PRO-MACHINE INC
6150 Edgewater Dr Ste H (32810-4861)
PHONE.............................407 296-5031
Roger Bolen, *President*
EMP: 5 EST: 1994
SQ FT: 4,000
SALES (est): 400.4K **Privately Held**
WEB: www.promachineinc.com
SIC: 3599 Machine shop, jobbing & repair

(G-12513)
PROFITSWORD LLC
7512 Dr Phillips Blvd (32819-5131)
PHONE.............................407 909-8822
Keenan Banks, *Engineer*
April Hepburn, *Human Res Dir*
Jenn Schram, *Train & Dev Mgr*
Michele Beardsley, *Accounts Mgr*
Dana Ertler, *Accounts Mgr*
EMP: 50 EST: 2001
SALES (est): 6.7MM **Privately Held**
WEB: www.profitsword.com
SIC: 7372 Business oriented computer software

(G-12514)
PROFORM FINISHING PRODUCTS LLC
Also Called: National Gypsum Company
1650 Central Florida Pkwy (32837-9411)
PHONE.............................407 438-3450
Rex Gulick, *Prdtn Mgr*
Eric Anderson, *Plant Engr*
Sam Beard, *Manager*
EMP: 39
SALES (corp-wide): 795.8MM **Privately Held**
WEB: www.nationalgypsum.com
SIC: 3275 Gypsum products
HQ: Proform Finishing Products, Llc
2001 Rexford Rd
Charlotte NC 28211

(G-12515)
PROFOUNDA HEALTH & BEAUTY
10501 S Orange Ave # 124 (32824-7749)
PHONE.............................407 270-7792
Todd Maclaughlan, *Principal*
EMP: 10 EST: 2019
SALES (est): 957.6K **Privately Held**
WEB: www.profounda.com
SIC: 2834 Pharmaceutical preparations

(G-12516)
PUCH MANUFACTURING CORPORATION
3701 Saint Valentine Way (32811-6515)
PHONE.............................407 650-9926
Carl Puch, *President*
Dale Puch, *Vice Pres*
Neil Perkins, *Purch Agent*
EMP: 30 EST: 1966
SQ FT: 27,000
SALES (est): 3.1MM **Privately Held**
WEB: www.puch.com
SIC: 3599 Machine shop, jobbing & repair

(G-12517)
PULAU INTERNATIONAL CORP (PA)
12633 Challenger Pkwy # 2 (32826-2713)
PHONE.............................407 380-9191
Lou Harding, *Ch of Bd*
Michael Armstrong, *President*
Sarina Stogel, *Principal*
Charles Wendland, *Exec VP*
Todd Hancock, *CFO*
EMP: 15 EST: 1995
SQ FT: 15,960
SALES (est): 96MM **Privately Held**
SIC: 3699 6512 7379 Electronic training devices; flight simulators (training aids), electronic; commercial & industrial building operation; computer related maintenance services

(G-12518)
PURECYCLE TECHNOLOGIES INC (PA)
5950 Hazeltine National D (32822-5035)
PHONE.............................877 648-3565
Michael Otworth, *Ch of Bd*
Michael Dee, *CFO*
David Brenner, *Ch Credit Ofcr*
Dustin Olson, *Chief Mktg Ofcr*
Brad Kalter, *Admin Sec*
EMP: 15 EST: 2015
SQ FT: 2,870 **Publicly Held**
WEB: www.purecycle.com
SIC: 2821 4953 Polypropylene resins; recycling, waste materials

(G-12519)
QUALCOMM ATHEROS INC
5955 T G Lee Blvd Ste 600 (32822-4431)
PHONE.............................407 284-7314
Shu Zhang, *Engineer*
Bob Guarnieri, *Branch Mgr*
EMP: 10
SALES (corp-wide): 33.5B **Publicly Held**
SIC: 3674 Semiconductors & related devices
HQ: Qualcomm Atheros, Inc.
1700 Technology Dr
San Jose CA 95110
408 773-5200

(G-12520)
QUALITY CABLE CONTRACTORS INC
Also Called: Quality Cable & Communications
1936 Premier Row (32809-6206)
PHONE.............................407 246-0606
Gabriel Del Rio, *CEO*
Jorge Del Rio, *President*
Milagros Del Rio, *Vice Pres*
Milagros Rio, *Vice Pres*
Justin Carter, *Technician*
EMP: 46 EST: 1986
SQ FT: 2,100
SALES (est): 5.7MM **Privately Held**
WEB: www.qcciflorida.com
SIC: 3663 1799 1623 5063 Cable television equipment; cable splicing service; cable laying construction; cable conduit; fiber optic cable installation; access control systems specialization; burglar alarm maintenance & monitoring

(G-12521)
QUEST DRAPE
10003 Satellite Blvd # 210 (32837-8473)
PHONE.............................407 888-8164
Nicole Peters, *Sales Mgr*
Megan Burge, *Office Mgr*
Shannen Stewart, *Director*
EMP: 8 EST: 2015
SALES (est): 149.9K **Privately Held**
WEB: www.questevents.com
SIC: 2391 Curtains & draperies

(G-12522)
QWIKPIK GOLF LLC
10096 Tavistock Rd (32827-7053)
PHONE.............................407 505-5546
Mary T Spacone,
EMP: 5 EST: 2010
SALES (est): 347.9K **Privately Held**
SIC: 3949 Golf equipment

(G-12523)
R & A POWER GRAPHICS INC
Also Called: Fastsigns
5000 E Colonial Dr (32803-4312)
PHONE.............................407 898-5770
Renee Friedman, *President*
Samir Martinez, *Opers Mgr*
Jill Gordon, *Accounts Mgr*
Renee Friedman Codron, *Admin Sec*
EMP: 11 EST: 2001
SALES (est): 2.9MM **Privately Held**
WEB: www.fastsigns.com
SIC: 3993 Signs & advertising specialties

(G-12524)
R B CASTING INC
637 22nd St (32805-5311)
PHONE.............................407 648-2005
Randy Beasley, *Principal*
EMP: 8 EST: 2004
SALES (est): 72.8K **Privately Held**
SIC: 3324 Steel investment foundries

(G-12525)
R G MANAGEMENT INC
Also Called: Spectrum Packaging
3640 Princeton Oaks St (32808-5636)
PHONE.............................407 889-3100
Michael F Rogers, *President*
Mark Mills, *Vice Pres*
Hannah Pepper, *Engineer*
Missy Todd, *Manager*
Elizabeth L Cassese, *Representative*
EMP: 47 EST: 1996
SQ FT: 26,400
SALES (est): 17MM **Privately Held**
WEB: www.thinkspc.com
SIC: 2657 Folding paperboard boxes

(G-12526)
R HUNTER HOLDINGS INC
7594 Chancellor Dr (32809-6919)
PHONE.............................407 843-0182
Toll Free:.............................888 -
Richard Hunter, *President*
EMP: 25 EST: 1984
SQ FT: 21,000
SALES (est): 2.4MM **Privately Held**
SIC: 3471 Anodizing (plating) of metals or formed products; chromium plating of metals or formed products

(G-12527)
R K CONSTRUCTORS OF CENTL FLA
4630 S Kirkman Rd Ste 221 (32811-2833)
PHONE....................................407 222-5376
Stanton Reich, *President*
EMP: 7 **EST:** 1992
SQ FT: 3,500
SALES (est): 181K **Privately Held**
SIC: 2431 Millwork

(G-12528)
R R DONNELLEY & SONS COMPANY
Also Called: Rrd Commercial Print - Orlando
9125 Bachman Rd (32824-8020)
PHONE....................................407 859-2030
Mike Marhee, *President*
EMP: 31
SALES (corp-wide): 4.9B **Privately Held**
WEB: www.rrd.com
SIC: 2759 Commercial printing
HQ: R. R. Donnelley & Sons Company
35 W Wacker Dr
Chicago IL 60601
312 326-8000

(G-12529)
RADIXX SOLUTIONS INTL INC (HQ)
20 N Orange Ave Ste 150 (32801-4604)
PHONE....................................407 856-9009
John Elieson, *President*
Jamie Schulze, *COO*
Ludvik Olason, *Vice Pres*
Blair Morgan, *Sales Staff*
Jamie O'Coin, *Marketing Staff*
EMP: 50 **EST:** 1993
SQ FT: 15,000
SALES (est): 11.4MM **Publicly Held**
WEB: www.radixx.com
SIC: 7372 Prepackaged software

(G-12530)
RAFAB SPCIALTY FABRICATION INC
2116 W Central Blvd (32805-2131)
P.O. Box 585665 (32858-5665)
PHONE....................................407 422-3750
Rick Arnold, *President*
EMP: 18 **EST:** 1987
SQ FT: 12,000
SALES (est): 2.4MM **Privately Held**
WEB: www.rafab.com
SIC: 3441 3444 Fabricated structural metal; sheet metalwork

(G-12531)
RAVAGO AMERICAS LLC (HQ)
Also Called: Amco Polymers
1900 Smmit Twr Blvd Ste 9 (32810)
PHONE....................................407 773-7777
James Duffy, *President*
Carl Hill, *General Mgr*
Anthony Segale, *General Mgr*
Melissa Pineda, *Counsel*
Oscar Novo, *Senior VP*
◆ **EMP:** 520 **EST:** 2003
SALES (est): 814.6MM **Privately Held**
WEB: www.amcopolymers.com
SIC: 2821 5162 Plastics materials & resins; plastics resins

(G-12532)
RAVAGO HOLDINGS AMERICA INC (PA)
1900 Smmit Twr Blvd Ste 9 (32810)
PHONE....................................407 875-9595
James Duffy, *President*
Joe Moran, *Vice Pres*
John Provost Jr, *Vice Pres*
Hector Rodriguez, *Vice Pres*
Jason Vaughn, *Plant Mgr*
▲ **EMP:** 75 **EST:** 2006
SALES (est): 1.7B **Privately Held**
SIC: 2821 Plastics materials & resins

(G-12533)
RAYTHEON COMPANY
12792 Research Pkwy # 100 (32826-3245)
PHONE....................................407 207-9223
Donna McCullough, *Accounts Mgr*
Lisa Nguyen, *Branch Mgr*
Diane Bryant, *Program Mgr*

EMP: 55
SALES (corp-wide): 64.3B **Publicly Held**
WEB: www.rtx.com
SIC: 3812 Search & navigation equipment
HQ: Raytheon Company
870 Winter St
Waltham MA 02451
781 522-3000

(G-12534)
RAYTHEON COMPANY
2603 Challenger Tech Ct (32826-2716)
PHONE....................................321 235-1700
Bishi Das, *Finance*
Mike Edwards, *Branch Mgr*
Douglas Dayton, *Software Engr*
EMP: 11
SALES (corp-wide): 64.3B **Publicly Held**
WEB: www.rtx.com
SIC: 3812 Defense systems & equipment
HQ: Raytheon Company
870 Winter St
Waltham MA 02451
781 522-3000

(G-12535)
RE-THINK IT INC
6770 Curtis St (32807-5111)
PHONE....................................407 671-6000
Amy M Shumway, *President*
Craig Shumway, *Vice Pres*
▲ **EMP:** 15 **EST:** 1987
SQ FT: 2,500
SALES (est): 3.1MM **Privately Held**
WEB: www.re-play.com
SIC: 3069 Sponge rubber & sponge rubber products

(G-12536)
REAL THREAD INC
1101 N Keller Rd Ste A (32810-5944)
PHONE....................................407 679-3895
Dru A Dalton, *President*
Brandon Baker, *Finance*
Sarah Brody, *Accounts Mgr*
Rob Cochran, *Accounts Mgr*
Tiffany Kitts, *Accounts Exec*
EMP: 20 **EST:** 2011
SALES (est): 4.9MM **Privately Held**
WEB: www.realthread.com
SIC: 2759 Screen printing

(G-12537)
REBAH FABRICATION INC
12081 Stone Bark Trl (32824-7394)
PHONE....................................407 857-3232
Pamela L Haber, *President*
Lauren Haber, *Vice Pres*
EMP: 18 **EST:** 1977
SALES (est): 2.4MM **Privately Held**
SIC: 3365 3441 Aluminum foundries; fabricated structural metal

(G-12538)
RED METERS LLC
Also Called: Manufctring Prcess Ctrl Instrs
6520 Pinecastle Blvd (32809-6675)
PHONE....................................407 337-0110
Ken Baker, *Business Mgr*
Marion Moth, *COO*
Rosie Moth, *Mktg Dir*
David Moth,
EMP: 13 **EST:** 2016
SALES (est): 3.5MM **Privately Held**
WEB: www.redmeters.com
SIC: 3823 Industrial instrmnts msrmnt display/control process variable

(G-12539)
REDAT OF NORTH AMERICA INC
120 Bonnie Loch Ct (32806-2910)
PHONE....................................407 246-1600
Atillio Cortella, *President*
Raymond Roach, *Vice Pres*
▲ **EMP:** 5 **EST:** 1980
SQ FT: 8,500
SALES (est): 910K **Privately Held**
WEB: www.redatnorthamerica.com
SIC: 3714 Motor vehicle parts & accessories

(G-12540)
REDDY ICE INC
1920 Commerce Oak Ave (32808-5640)
PHONE....................................407 296-8300
Gil Cassagne, *CEO*

Don Plante, *Principal*
Debi Griffin, *Director*
Jane Plante, *Admin Sec*
Eileen Paul, *Asst Sec*
EMP: 1 **EST:** 1946
SQ FT: 56,000
SALES (est): 11.7MM **Privately Held**
WEB: www.reddyice.com
SIC: 2097 Manufactured ice
HQ: Reddy Ice Holdings, Inc.
5720 Lbj Fwy Ste 200
Dallas TX 75240
214 526-6740

(G-12541)
REED BRENNAN MEDIA ASSOCIATES
Also Called: Reed Brenan
628 Virginia Dr (32803-1858)
PHONE....................................407 894-7300
Tim Brennan, *President*
Tony Decarlo, *Prdtn Mgr*
EMP: 47 **EST:** 1993
SALES (est): 12MM
SALES (corp-wide): 4.2B **Privately Held**
WEB: www.rbma.com
SIC: 2711 7311 Newspapers: publishing only, not printed on site; advertising consultant
PA: The Hearst Corporation
300 W 57th St Fl 42
New York NY 10019
212 649-2000

(G-12542)
REFLECTION MANUFACTURING
10336 Pointview Ct (32836-3736)
PHONE....................................407 297-5727
◆ **EMP:** 53
SALES (est): 2.7MM **Privately Held**
SIC: 3999 Mfg Misc Products

(G-12543)
REGAL MARINE INDUSTRIES INC (PA)
Also Called: Regal Boats
2300 Jetport Dr (32809-7895)
PHONE....................................407 851-4360
Duane Kuck, *President*
Paul Kuck, *Vice Pres*
Timothy Kuck, *Vice Pres*
Kristin Lutzke, *Vice Pres*
Don Smith, *Vice Pres*
◆ **EMP:** 350 **EST:** 1969
SQ FT: 300,000
SALES (est): 87.4MM **Privately Held**
WEB: www.regalboats.com
SIC: 3732 Boats, fiberglass: building & repairing

(G-12544)
REHRIG PACIFIC COMPANY
7452 Presidents Dr (32809-5608)
PHONE....................................407 857-3888
Livan Torres, *Foreman/Supr*
Philana Haumiller, *Purchasing*
Eric Wilson, *Controller*
Susan Wilburn, *Regl Sales Mgr*
Andres Guttierrez, *Branch Mgr*
EMP: 10 **Privately Held**
WEB: www.rehrigpacific.com
SIC: 3089 2821 Cases, plastic; garbage containers, plastic; molding primary plastic; plasticizer/additive based plastic materials
HQ: Rehrig Pacific Company
4010 E 26th St
Vernon CA 90058
323 262-5145

(G-12545)
RELIABLE POOL ENCLSRES SCRENS
Also Called: Reliable Pool Enclsres Screens
5558 Force Four Pkwy (32839-2968)
PHONE....................................407 731-3408
EMP: 9 **EST:** 2017
SALES (est): 1.8MM **Privately Held**
WEB: www.rpesfl.com
SIC: 3442 Screens, window, metal

(G-12546)
RELION ENTERPRISES LLC
Also Called: Minuteman Press
13526 Village Park Dr # 202 (32837-7685)
PHONE....................................321 287-4225
Javier Santos,
EMP: 9 **EST:** 2017
SALES (est): 609.8K **Privately Held**
WEB: www.theinstallersgroup.com
SIC: 2752 Commercial printing, lithographic

(G-12547)
REPRO PLUS INC
Also Called: Triangle Reprogressives
850 S Hughey Ave (32801-3630)
PHONE....................................407 843-1492
Roger Garner, *President*
Joanne F Garner, *President*
Thomas Jennie F, *Vice Pres*
J F Thomas, *Vice Pres*
EMP: 16 **EST:** 1975
SQ FT: 1,000
SALES (est): 539.2K **Privately Held**
SIC: 2752 Commercial printing, offset

(G-12548)
RESIDUAL INNOVATIONS LLC
7253 Pleasant Dr (32818-5867)
PHONE....................................407 459-5497
Michael Bridgett, *Principal*
EMP: 8 **EST:** 2015
SALES (est): 140.9K **Privately Held**
SIC: 2911 Residues

(G-12549)
REVOLOGY CARS LLC
6756 Edgwter Cmmrce Pkwy (32810-4200)
PHONE....................................800 974-4463
Thomas Scarpello, *Mng Member*
EMP: 12 **EST:** 2017
SALES (est): 310.4K **Privately Held**
WEB: www.revologycars.com
SIC: 3711 7549 5511 Automobile assembly, including specialty automobiles; high performance auto repair & service; new & used car dealers

(G-12550)
RHINESTNTRANSFERSDIRECTCOM INC
1821 Verde Way (32835-8174)
PHONE....................................484 254-6410
Christina Demuth, *Principal*
EMP: 8 **EST:** 2013
SALES (est): 177.5K **Privately Held**
WEB: www.rhinestonetransfersdirect.com
SIC: 2395 Embroidery & art needlework

(G-12551)
RHINO TIRE USA LLC
11423 Satelite Blvd (32837-9225)
PHONE....................................407 777-5598
William Yi, *General Mgr*
Yi Langang, *Mng Member*
EMP: 5 **EST:** 2016
SALES (est): 864.9K **Privately Held**
WEB: www.rhinotireusa.com
SIC: 3011 3714 5014 Motorcycle tires, pneumatic; wheels, motor vehicle; tires & tubes

(G-12552)
RIBEIRO STONES LLC
2207 Silver Star Rd (32804-3307)
PHONE....................................407 723-8802
Linholene Ribeiro, *President*
Gabriel V Ribeiro,
Rafael V Ribeiro,
EMP: 7 **EST:** 2015
SALES (est): 734.8K **Privately Held**
WEB: www.ribeirostones.com
SIC: 3281 Granite, cut & shaped

(G-12553)
RICHARD BRYAN INGRAM LLC
Also Called: Artios
2454 N Forsyth Rd (32807-6430)
PHONE....................................407 677-7779
Bryan Ingram, *Mng Member*
EMP: 7 **EST:** 2004
SQ FT: 9,000

SALES (est): 923.3K **Privately Held**
WEB: www.artioscabinetry.com
SIC: **2434** 5031 Wood kitchen cabinets;
kitchen cabinets

(G-12554)
RIEKER LLC
5337 Foxshire Ct (32819-3824)
PHONE......................407 496-1555
Kathleen M Rieker, *Principal*
Peter Hanchette, *Manager*
EMP: 8 EST: 2007
SALES (est): 214.1K **Privately Held**
WEB: www.rieker.us
SIC: **3829** Measuring & controlling devices

(G-12555)
RIO PAVERS INC
7297 Mardell Ct (32835-2672)
PHONE......................321 388-6757
Paulo Monteiro, *Officer*
EMP: 6 EST: 2007
SALES (est): 420.1K **Privately Held**
WEB: www.riopavers.com
SIC: **3531** Pavers

(G-12556)
RIVER CRAFT LLC
2148 Orinoco Dr Ste 356 (32837-8933)
PHONE......................407 867-0584
Luis D Rivera,
EMP: 12 EST: 2017
SALES (est): 474.3K **Privately Held**
WEB: www.rivercraftllc.com
SIC: **2431** Millwork

(G-12557)
RLCJC INC
Also Called: Good Feet
4684 Millenia Plaza Way (32839-2434)
P.O. Box 568392 (32856-8392)
PHONE......................407 370-3338
Rebecca Conner, *President*
EMP: 5 EST: 2008
SALES (est): 303.1K **Privately Held**
SIC: **3842** Foot appliances, orthopedic

(G-12558)
RMC EWELL INC
7400 Narcoossee Rd (32822-5586)
PHONE......................407 282-0984
EMP: 18
SALES (corp-wide): 15.4B **Privately Held**
SIC: **3273** 3272 Manufactures Ready Mix
Concrete And Concrete Pipes
HQ: Ewell Rmc Inc
801 Mccue Rd
Lakeland FL
863 688-5787

(G-12559)
ROCK BRICK PAVERS INC
344 S Hart Blvd (32835-1948)
PHONE......................407 692-6816
Maria Lopez, *Principal*
EMP: 7 EST: 2014
SALES (est): 110.9K **Privately Held**
SIC: **2951** Asphalt paving mixtures &
blocks

(G-12560)
ROYAL BATHS
MANUFACTURING CO
1920 Premier Row (32809-6206)
PHONE......................407 854-1740
Kevin Sommerio, *General Mgr*
Elvin Santana, *Office Mgr*
EMP: 62
SALES (corp-wide): 91.4MM **Privately
Held**
WEB: www.royal-mfg.com
SIC: **3842** Whirlpool baths, hydrotherapy
equipment
PA: Royal Baths Manufacturing Company
14635 Chrisman Rd
Houston TX 77039
281 442-3400

(G-12561)
ROYALTEA
714 N Mills Ave (32803-4039)
PHONE......................407 401-9969
EMP: 6 EST: 2019
SALES (est): 307.3K **Privately Held**
WEB: www.royalteaus.com
SIC: **2024** Ice cream & frozen desserts

(G-12562)
RUSTWERKS
5519 Commerce Dr (32839-2989)
PHONE......................407 399-2262
Sandra R Patercsak, *Manager*
EMP: 7 EST: 2017
SALES (est): 331.7K **Privately Held**
WEB: rustwerkscom.wordpress.com
SIC: **3446** Architectural metalwork

(G-12563)
RXPRINTING AND GRAPHICS
LLC
4909 S Orange Ave (32806-6932)
PHONE......................407 965-3039
Raymon Diaz, *Principal*
EMP: 7 EST: 2009
SALES (est): 123K **Privately Held**
SIC: **2752** Commercial printing, offset

(G-12564)
S E INC
Also Called: Strong Enterprises
6448 Pinecastle Blvd # 104 (32809-6682)
PHONE......................407 859-9317
Marcia Lavanway, *President*
Mike Rinaldi, *Vice Pres*
Jessica Hanson, *Admin Sec*
◆ EMP: 43 EST: 1961
SALES (est): 3.6MM **Privately Held**
WEB: www.seincwy.com
SIC: **2399** 8611 Parachutes; business as-
sociations

(G-12565)
S M I CABINETRY INC
Also Called: SMI Cabinetry Stone Millwork
2525 N Orange Blossom Trl (32804-4808)
PHONE......................407 841-0292
Michelle Hull, *CEO*
William Bergin, *President*
Eileen Bergin, *Corp Secy*
Russell Bergin, *Vice Pres*
EMP: 40 EST: 1985
SQ FT: 22,000
SALES (est): 4.5MM **Privately Held**
WEB: www.smi-cabinetry.com
SIC: **2541** 2521 2434 2431 Cabinets, ex-
cept refrigerated: show, display, etc.:
wood; counters or counter display cases,
wood; desks, office: wood; wood kitchen
cabinets; millwork; cabinet & finish car-
pentry

(G-12566)
S&L CNSTRCTION SPECIALISTS
INC
13412 Heswall Run (32832-6156)
PHONE......................407 300-5080
Saulo M Laceda, *President*
EMP: 5 EST: 2013
SALES (est): 395.8K **Privately Held**
SIC: **2952** 3444 3299 Siding materials;
gutters, sheet metal; stucco

(G-12567)
SAGE IMPLEMENTATIONS LLC
Also Called: Flexfield Express
7648 San Remo Pl (32835-2674)
PHONE......................407 290-6952
Helene Abrams, *CEO*
Chris Busbee,
EMP: 8 EST: 2005
SALES (est): 517K **Privately Held**
WEB: www.flex-field.com
SIC: **7372** Application computer software

(G-12568)
SAI SUPER SOFTWARE
SOLUTIONS
5230 Cona Reef Ct (32810-4075)
PHONE......................407 445-2520
Sridhar Rangaswamy, *Principal*
EMP: 5 EST: 2012
SALES (est): 350.7K **Privately Held**
WEB: www.saisupersol.com
SIC: **7372** Application computer software;
educational computer software

(G-12569)
SAIKOU OPTICS
INCORPORATED
3259 Progress Dr Ste 128 (32826-3230)
PHONE......................407 986-4200
Eric Sanford, *CEO*

EMP: 5 EST: 2015
SQ FT: 400
SALES (est): 448.8K **Privately Held**
WEB: www.saikouoptics.com
SIC: **3827** 3823 3812 Optical instruments
& lenses; industrial instrmnts msrmnt dis-
play/control process variable; search &
navigation equipment

(G-12570)
SALON TECHNOLOGIES INTL
8810 Com Cir Ste 20-22 (32819)
P.O. Box 2320, Windermere (34786-2320)
PHONE......................407 301-3726
Ted A Khoury, *Principal*
Gaston A Khoury, *Principal*
Pascal N Khoury, *Principal*
Henriette Khoury, *Vice Pres*
EMP: 8 EST: 1998
SALES (est): 300.9K **Privately Held**
WEB: www.salontechnologiesint.com
SIC: **2844** Suntan lotions & oils

(G-12571)
SALT 1 TO 1
11221 John Wycliffe Blvd (32832-7013)
PHONE......................407 538-2134
Brenda Metcalf, *Vice Pres*
EMP: 6 EST: 2018
SALES (est): 431.8K **Privately Held**
WEB: www.salt1to1.com
SIC: **2752** Commercial printing, offset

(G-12572)
SALT 1TO1 INC
214 N Goldenrod Rd Ste 8 (32807-8220)
PHONE......................407 721-8107
Anthony W Metcalf, *Principal*
Brenda P Metcalf, *Principal*
Brenda Metcalf, *Vice Pres*
EMP: 10 EST: 2007
SALES (est): 347.8K **Privately Held**
SIC: **2899** Salt

(G-12573)
SANOFI US SERVICES INC
2501 Discovery Dr (32826-3718)
PHONE......................407 736-0226
Janice Moser, *Director*
EMP: 43 **Privately Held**
WEB: www.sanofi.us
SIC: **2834** Pharmaceutical preparations
HQ: Sanofi Us Services Inc.
55 Corporate Dr
Bridgewater NJ 08807
336 407-4994

(G-12574)
SATCOM SCIENTIFIC INC
5644 Commerce Dr Ste G (32839-2962)
PHONE......................407 856-1050
Angelo J Miceli, *President*
James Abbott, *CFO*
◆ EMP: 10 EST: 2007
SQ FT: 7,500
SALES (est): 947.1K **Privately Held**
WEB: www.satcomscientific.com
SIC: **3663** 4899 Radio & TV communica-
tions equipment; data communication
services

(G-12575)
SAWSTREET LLC
6450 Kingspointe Pkwy # 6 (32819-6508)
PHONE......................407 601-4907
Aaron Lopez, *Production*
Darren Bradley, *Accounts Mgr*
James L Young, *Manager*
Kevin Gagne, *Supervisor*
Jennifer S Young, *Admin Sec*
EMP: 28 EST: 2008
SALES (est): 3.2MM **Privately Held**
WEB: www.sawstreet.com
SIC: **3674** Semiconductors & related de-
vices

(G-12576)
SBR CUSTOM CABINETS INC
4093 Floralwood Ct (32812-7912)
PHONE......................407 765-8134
Steven B Rumplik Sr, *Principal*
EMP: 7 EST: 2010
SALES (est): 70.1K **Privately Held**
SIC: **2434** Wood kitchen cabinets

(G-12577)
SBT RIVER PIP PROJECT
4400 N Alafaya Trl (32826-2301)
PHONE......................919 469-5095
EMP: 19 EST: 2011
SALES (est): 1.1MM **Privately Held**
SIC: **2752** Commercial printing, offset

(G-12578)
SCHWARTZ ELECTRO-OPTICS
INC
8337 Southpark Cir (32819-9049)
PHONE......................407 297-8988
Jeffrey A Saunders, *President*
EMP: 20 EST: 1984
SALES (est): 1MM **Privately Held**
SIC: **3699** Laser systems & equipment

(G-12579)
SCOTT WASHER INC
1513 Regan Ave (32807-8316)
PHONE......................407 432-2648
Scott V Washer, *Principal*
EMP: 8 EST: 2008
SALES (est): 61.7K **Privately Held**
SIC: **3452** Washers

(G-12580)
SCREENWORKS USA INC
2234 W Taft Vineland Rd (32837-7800)
PHONE......................407 426-9999
Sharad Mehta, *President*
Brian Dezavala, *Exec VP*
Kelsey Martin, *Software Dev*
Carlos Dezavala, *Shareholder*
Ernie Dezavala, *Shareholder*
◆ EMP: 130 EST: 1999
SQ FT: 65,000
SALES (est): 22MM **Privately Held**
WEB: www.screenworksusa.com
SIC: **2261** Screen printing of cotton broad-
woven fabrics

(G-12581)
SEA CREATIONS INC
408 Bif Ct (32809-6668)
PHONE......................407 857-2000
Diane Dinger, *President*
Robert Dinger, *Vice Pres*
◆ EMP: 5 EST: 1981
SQ FT: 12,000
SALES (est): 408.7K **Privately Held**
WEB: www.sea-creations.com
SIC: **3999** Novelties: bone, beaded or shell

(G-12582)
SEAL SHIELD LLC (PA)
111 N Magnolia Ave # 1025 (32801-2372)
PHONE......................877 325-7443
Andrew McCarthy, *President*
J Andrew McCarthy, *Vice Pres*
Russell Verhovec, *Vice Pres*
Leo Bauer, *Warehouse Mgr*
Vincent Schreber, *CFO*
◆ EMP: 22 EST: 2007
SALES (est): 24MM **Privately Held**
WEB: www.sealshield.com
SIC: **3575** 2842 3641 Keyboards, com-
puter, office machine; disinfectants,
household or industrial plant; ultraviolet
lamps

(G-12583)
SEALY MATTRESS MFG CO LLC
11220 Space Blvd (32837-9244)
PHONE......................407 855-8523
JD Barksdale, *Sales Staff*
John Fowler, *Branch Mgr*
Herb Quiller, *Supervisor*
EMP: 79
SQ FT: 97,600
SALES (corp-wide): 4.9B **Publicly Held**
SIC: **2515** Mattresses & bedsprings
HQ: Sealy Mattress Manufacturing Com-
pany, Llc
1000 Tempur Way
Lexington KY 40511
859 455-1000

▲ = Import ▼=Export
◆ =Import/Export

(G-12584)
SENTINEL CMMNCTONS NEWS VNTRES (DH)
Also Called: Orlando Sentinel Media Group
633 N Orange Ave (32801-1325)
P.O. Box 2833 (32802-2833)
PHONE 407 420-5000
Howard Greenberg, *CEO*
Chris Hays, *Editor*
Glenn McCarthy, *District Mgr*
Avido Khahaifa, *Senior VP*
Bert Ortiz, *Vice Pres*
EMP: 577 **EST:** 1885
SQ FT: 50,000
SALES (est): 138MM
SALES (corp-wide): 4.6B **Publicly Held**
SIC: 2711 Commercial printing & newspaper publishing combined
HQ: Tribune Media Company
515 N State St Ste 2400
Chicago IL 60654
312 222-3394

(G-12585)
SENTINEL CMMNCTONS NEWS VNTRES
Also Called: Sentinel Direct
75 E Amelia St (32801-1320)
P.O. Box 2833 (32802-2833)
PHONE 407 420-5291
Ashley Allen, *CEO*
EMP: 9
SALES (corp-wide): 4.6B **Publicly Held**
SIC: 2711 2741 Newspapers, publishing & printing; miscellaneous publishing
HQ: Sentinel Communications News Ventures Inc.
633 N Orange Ave
Orlando FL 32801
407 420-5000

(G-12586)
SFI INC
1730 N Forsyth Rd (32807-5274)
PHONE 407 834-2258
Anthony J Sano Jr, *President*
Mandy D Fuller, *Vice Pres*
EMP: 45 **EST:** 1978
SQ FT: 27,000
SALES (est): 5.9MM **Privately Held**
WEB: www.sfiinc.com
SIC: 3444 3499 Sheet metalwork; coal chutes, prefabricated sheet metal; aerosol valves, metal

(G-12587)
SGM LIGHTING INC
7806 Kingspointe Pkwy (32819-8520)
PHONE 407 440-3601
Filippo Frigeri, *Principal*
▲ **EMP:** 6 **EST:** 2015
SALES (est): 875.5K **Privately Held**
SIC: 3648 Lighting equipment

(G-12588)
SHELBIE PRESS INC
1203 N Mills Ave (32803-2540)
PHONE 407 896-4600
Debbie Simmons, *President*
Michelle Murray, *Vice Pres*
EMP: 5 **EST:** 1993
SQ FT: 1,300
SALES (est): 372.5K **Privately Held**
WEB: www.shelbiepress.com
SIC: 2752 Commercial printing, offset

(G-12589)
SHELFGENIE-ORLANDO
Also Called: Shelf Genie
10603 Arbor View Blvd (32825-4479)
PHONE 407 808-5925
EMP: 7 **EST:** 2011
SALES (est): 129K **Privately Held**
WEB: www.shelfgenie.com
SIC: 2511 Wood household furniture

(G-12590)
SHERRY J BERTUCELLI INC
3827 E Kaley Ave (32812-9148)
PHONE 407 760-7585
Sherry J Bertucelli, *Owner*
EMP: 7 **EST:** 2006
SALES (est): 76.4K **Privately Held**
SIC: 1389 Construction, repair & dismantling services

(G-12591)
SHGAR KANE COUTURE INC
4900 Silver Oaks Village (32808-2092)
PHONE 407 205-8038
Charmaine P Allwood, *Principal*
EMP: 6 **EST:** 2012
SALES (est): 418.4K **Privately Held**
SIC: 2339 7389 Women's & misses' athletic clothing & sportswear; apparel designers, commercial

(G-12592)
SIEMENS CORPORATION
4041 Forest Island Dr (32826-2621)
PHONE 407 736-5629
William R Weir, *Principal*
Julia Lopez, *Regional Mgr*
Kevin Schmidt, *Project Mgr*
Elvira Anoshkina, *Engineer*
Charmaine Davignon Sphr, *Human Resources*
EMP: 25
SALES (corp-wide): 73B **Privately Held**
WEB: new.siemens.com
SIC: 3661 Telephones & telephone apparatus
HQ: Siemens Corporation
300 New Jersey Ave Nw # 100
Washington DC 20001
202 434-4800

(G-12593)
SIEMENS ENERGY INC
3850 Quadrangle Blvd (32817-8368)
PHONE 407 736-1400
Mick McCormic, *Principal*
Steve Auman, *Project Mgr*
Ron Shires, *Project Mgr*
Gregor Braunschweig, *Engineer*
Hunter Buck, *Engineer*
EMP: 1811
SALES (corp-wide): 33.4B **Privately Held**
WEB: new.siemens.com
SIC: 3511 Turbines & turbine generator sets
HQ: Siemens Energy, Inc.
4400 N Alafaya Trl
Orlando FL 32826
407 736-2000

(G-12594)
SIEMENS ENERGY INC
11842 Corporate (32817)
PHONE 407 206-5008
Randy Zwirn, *President*
Leon Armstrong, *Project Mgr*
Dilshan Canagasaby, *Engineer*
Bernd Fuetterer, *Engineer*
George Haas, *Engineer*
EMP: 191
SALES (corp-wide): 33.4B **Privately Held**
WEB: new.siemens.com
SIC: 3511 Turbines & turbine generator sets
HQ: Siemens Energy, Inc.
4400 N Alafaya Trl
Orlando FL 32826
407 736-2000

(G-12595)
SIEMENS ENERGY INC
11950 Corporate Blvd (32817)
PHONE 407 736-7957
Sundar Raghavan, *Project Mgr*
Christopher Deconda, *Engineer*
David Fortna, *Engineer*
Reinhard Schilp, *Engineer*
Angelique Falkenberg, *Project Engr*
EMP: 66
SALES (corp-wide): 33.4B **Privately Held**
WEB: new.siemens.com
SIC: 3511 Steam turbines
HQ: Siemens Energy, Inc.
4400 N Alafaya Trl
Orlando FL 32826
407 736-2000

(G-12596)
SIEMENS GMESA RNWBLE ENRGY INC (DH)
11950 Corporate Blvd (32817)
PHONE 407 736-2000
Shannon Sturgil, *CEO*
Kirk Johnson, *Vice Pres*
Karl Armond, *Project Mgr*
Ron Mixon, *Project Mgr*

George Barkulis, *Opers Staff*
EMP: 36 **EST:** 2016
SALES (est): 477.8MM
SALES (corp-wide): 33.4B **Privately Held**
WEB: www.siemensgamesa.com
SIC: 3511 Turbines & turbine generator sets

(G-12597)
SIEMENS GMESA RNWBLE ENRGY INC
4400 N Alafaya Trl Q2 (32826-2301)
PHONE 407 721-3273
EMP: 522
SALES (corp-wide): 33.4B **Privately Held**
WEB: www.siemensgamesa.com
SIC: 3511 Turbines & turbine generator sets
HQ: Siemens Gamesa Renewable Energy, Inc.
11950 Corporate Blvd
Orlando FL 32817
407 736-2000

(G-12598)
SIEMENS INDUSTRY INC
4506 L B Mcleod Rd Ste C (32811-5665)
PHONE 407 650-3570
Jason Voelker, *Project Mgr*
Miriam Arnold, *Engineer*
Craig Cortes, *Engineer*
John Gates, *Engineer*
Thomas Harpel, *Engineer*
EMP: 9
SALES (corp-wide): 73B **Privately Held**
WEB: new.siemens.com
SIC: 3569 5999 5074 Filters; water purification equipment; water purification equipment
HQ: Siemens Industry, Inc.
1000 Deerfield Pkwy
Buffalo Grove IL 60089
847 215-1000

(G-12599)
SIEMENS INDUSTRY SOFTWARE INC
2101 Park Center Dr # 290 (32835-7626)
PHONE 407 517-5919
Tiago Leite, *Project Mgr*
Antonio Fernandez, *Engineer*
Michael McClure, *Project Engr*
Ray Prevallet, *Project Engr*
Alice Curtis, *Marketing Staff*
EMP: 9
SALES (corp-wide): 73B **Privately Held**
WEB: www.siemens.com
SIC: 7372 Business oriented computer software
HQ: Siemens Industry Software Inc.
5800 Granite Pkwy Ste 600
Plano TX 75024
972 987-3000

(G-12600)
SIGN & VEHICLE WRAPS INC
1011 W Lancaster Rd Ste 7 (32809-5888)
PHONE 407 859-8631
Marcos A Diaz Diaz, *Principal*
EMP: 5 **EST:** 2010
SALES (est): 508.7K **Privately Held**
WEB: www.signsvw.com
SIC: 3993 Signs & advertising specialties

(G-12601)
SIGN DEPOT CO
1100 W Colonial Dr Unit 1 (32804-7334)
PHONE 407 894-0090
Tuan T MAI, *President*
◆ **EMP:** 12 **EST:** 2006
SALES (est): 1.1MM **Privately Held**
WEB: www.yardsignwholesale.com
SIC: 2759 5099 5999 Screen printing; signs, except electric; banners, flags, decals & posters

(G-12602)
SIGN PRODUCERS INC
Also Called: SPI
555 W Landstreet Rd (32824-7808)
PHONE 407 855-8864
Deborah Scime, *President*
▼ **EMP:** 24 **EST:** 1986
SQ FT: 2,500

SALES (est): 3.3MM **Privately Held**
WEB: www.signproducers.com
SIC: 3993 7336 Signs, not made in custom sign painting shops; commercial art & graphic design

(G-12603)
SIGN STAPLER
1969 S Alafaya Trl (32828-8732)
PHONE 800 775-3971
EMP: 7 **EST:** 2017
SALES (est): 223.3K **Privately Held**
WEB: www.signstapler.com
SIC: 3993 Signs & advertising specialties

(G-12604)
SIGNATURE AVI US HOLDINGS INC (DH)
Also Called: BBA Aviation Group
13485 Veterans Way # 600 (32827-7719)
PHONE 407 648-7230
Joseph I Goldstein, *President*
Steve Bongiorno, *General Mgr*
Lori Golda, *Area Mgr*
Sandy Montalbano, *Area Mgr*
Daniel Marcinik, *Treasurer*
EMP: 14 **EST:** 1994
SALES (est): 146.5MM
SALES (corp-wide): 687.1K **Privately Held**
WEB: www.signatureflight.com
SIC: 3728 2399 3052 Aircraft parts & equipment; belting; fabric: made from purchased materials; rubber belting

(G-12605)
SINGLETONS AV SOLUTIONS INC
8907 Southern Breeze Dr (32836-5044)
PHONE 407 404-1506
Tyler Singleton, *Principal*
EMP: 8 **EST:** 2009
SALES (est): 240K **Privately Held**
WEB: www.singletonsavsolutions.com
SIC: 3578 Calculating & accounting equipment

(G-12606)
SINGULAR GRAPE INC
7380 W Sand Lake Rd (32819-5248)
PHONE 305 508-4000
Victor Friedman, *CEO*
Einav Raff, *President*
EMP: 8 **EST:** 2007
SALES (est): 1.2MM **Privately Held**
WEB: www.singulargrape.com
SIC: 7372 Business oriented computer software

(G-12607)
SKY AEROSPACE ENGINEERING
4219 Lindy Cir (32827-5309)
PHONE 407 251-7111
EMP: 7 **EST:** 2020
SALES (est): 1.1MM **Privately Held**
WEB: www.jetsae.com
SIC: 3728 Aircraft parts & equipment

(G-12608)
SKY AEROSPACE ENGINEERING INC (PA)
Also Called: SAE
9419 Tradeport Dr (32827-5345)
PHONE 407 251-7111
Joseph Fernandez, *President*
Monica Fernandez, *Treasurer*
EMP: 6 **EST:** 2008
SALES (est): 1.6MM **Privately Held**
WEB: www.jetsae.com
SIC: 3728 Aircraft parts & equipment

(G-12609)
SKYLINE ATTRACTIONS LLC
5233 Alleman Dr (32809-3026)
PHONE 407 587-0080
Jeffrey Pike, *Partner*
Christopher M Gray, *Partner*
Anya Lehrner, *Design Engr*
Anya Tyler, *Design Engr*
Evan Souliere, *Treasurer*
EMP: 10 **EST:** 2014
SALES (est): 962K **Privately Held**
WEB: www.skylineattractions.com
SIC: 3599 Amusement park equipment

(G-12610)
SMARTE CARTE INC
9251 Jeff Fuqua Blvd # 1596 (32827-4450)
PHONE.............................407 857-5841
EMP: 7 **EST:** 2019
SALES (est): 152.8K **Privately Held**
WEB: www.smartecarte.com
SIC: 2599 Furniture & fixtures

(G-12611)
SNA SOFTWARE LLC (PA)
1730 Santa Maria Pl (32806-1446)
P.O. Box 531146 (32853-1146)
PHONE.............................866 389-6750
Nicholas Pisano, *Mng Member*
EMP: 7 **EST:** 2007
SALES (est): 1.4MM **Privately Held**
WEB: www.sna-software.com
SIC: 7372 Publishers' computer software

(G-12612)
SOUTH EAST FUEL LLC
5600 Butler National Dr (32812-3000)
PHONE.............................407 392-4668
EMP: 8
SALES (est): 884.4K **Privately Held**
SIC: 2869 Mfg Industrial Organic Chemi-
cals

(G-12613)
**SOUTHEAST FINISHING GROUP
INC (PA)**
2807 Mercy Dr (32808-3807)
PHONE.............................407 299-4620
Robert S Clark Jr, *President*
James R Clark, *Owner*
Julian Malkiewicz, *Plant Mgr*
Dianne Clark, *Admin Sec*
EMP: 50 **EST:** 1970
SQ FT: 24,800
SALES (est): 6.5MM **Privately Held**
WEB: www.southeastfinishing.com
SIC: 2759 2657 2796 2789 Commercial
printing; folding paperboard boxes;
platemaking services; bookbinding & re-
lated work; die-cut paper & board

(G-12614)
**SOUTHERN EXHIBITS
GRAPHICS INC**
4360 36th St Unit 1 (32811-6506)
PHONE.............................407 423-2860
Gary Churchill, *President*
EMP: 9 **EST:** 2017
SALES (est): 382.8K **Privately Held**
WEB: www.southernexhibits.com
SIC: 3993 Signs & advertising specialties

(G-12615)
SOVITA RETAIL INC
1317 Edgewater Dr # 1943 (32804-6350)
PHONE.............................888 871-2408
Talika Moore, *President*
Charlika Stubbs, *Vice Pres*
EMP: 35 **EST:** 2002
SQ FT: 6,500
SALES (est): 1.2MM **Privately Held**
SIC: 2339 Athletic clothing: women's,
misses' & juniors'

(G-12616)
**SPEED CUSTOM CABINET
CORP**
6923 Narcoossee Rd (32822-5572)
PHONE.............................407 953-1479
Dani Garcia, *President*
EMP: 8 **EST:** 2006
SALES (est): 157.9K **Privately Held**
WEB: www.speedcustomcabinet.co
SIC: 2434 Wood kitchen cabinets

(G-12617)
SPICE WORLD LLC (PA)
8101 Presidents Dr (32809-9113)
PHONE.............................407 851-9432
Andrew P Caneza, *CEO*
Gary Caneza, *President*
Susan Whitson, *Corp Secy*
Mitch Dimarco, *Vice Pres*
Keith Schafer, *Vice Pres*
◆ **EMP:** 197 **EST:** 1949
SQ FT: 68,000
SALES (est): 30.8MM **Privately Held**
WEB: www.spiceworldinc.com
SIC: 2099 Food preparations

(G-12618)
**SPORTS N STUFF SCREEN
PRINTING**
3975 Forrestal Ave # 600 (32806-8545)
PHONE.............................407 859-0437
Charles R Maxwell,
EMP: 5 **EST:** 1993
SALES (est): 492.3K **Privately Held**
SIC: 2759 Screen printing

(G-12619)
**SRM WATERPROOFING
SEALANTS INC**
2899 Burwood Ave (32837-8557)
PHONE.............................407 963-3619
Falero Alexis, *Principal*
EMP: 7 **EST:** 2014
SALES (est): 81.3K **Privately Held**
SIC: 2891 Sealants

(G-12620)
STAN WEAVER AND COMPANY
3663 All American Blvd (32810-4726)
PHONE.............................407 581-6940
Gary Walther, *Warehouse Mgr*
Mark Streicher, *Sales Staff*
Brian White, *Branch Mgr*
EMP: 20 **Privately Held**
WEB: www.stanweaver.com
SIC: 3585 Refrigeration & heating equip-
ment
PA: Stan Weaver And Company
4607 N Cortez Ave
Tampa FL 33614

(G-12621)
STAND VERTICAL INC
983 Bennett Rd Apt 103 (32814-6092)
PHONE.............................407 474-0456
Micheal Morgan, *Principal*
EMP: 8 **EST:** 2008
SALES (est): 62.2K **Privately Held**
SIC: 2591 Blinds vertical

(G-12622)
STAR PRODUCTS
1632 Brook Hollow Dr (32824-6366)
PHONE.............................407 929-6969
Isaiah Walker, *Principal*
EMP: 7 **EST:** 2018
SALES (est): 96.6K **Privately Held**
WEB: www.starpipeproducts.com
SIC: 3498 Fabricated pipe & fittings

(G-12623)
**STEEL CNSTR SYSTEMS
HOLDG CO**
11250 Astronaut Blvd (32837-9204)
P.O. Box 3949, Spokane WA (99220-3949)
PHONE.............................407 438-1664
Dan Dry, *General Mgr*
Gerald Hockenberry, *Controller*
EMP: 25 **EST:** 2016
SQ FT: 30,000
SALES (est): 14MM **Privately Held**
SIC: 3444 Studs & joists, sheet metal

(G-12624)
**STELLAR SIGN AND DESIGN
LLC**
3851 Center Loop (32808-3147)
PHONE.............................407 660-3174
Kenneth Soday, *President*
Steven Hauck, *Managing Prtnr*
Wanda Erickson, *General Mgr*
Tom Hughes, *General Mgr*
EMP: 18 **EST:** 2014
SALES (est): 2.5MM **Privately Held**
WEB: www.stellarsignanddesign.com
SIC: 3993 Electric signs

(G-12625)
STEMWORKS LLC
12301 Lake Underhill Rd (32828-4508)
PHONE.............................407 595-8451
Jennifer A Englert, *Mng Member*
Jace Hovey, *Mng Member*
Alexander L Timmerman, *Mng Member*
EMP: 8 **EST:** 2020
SALES (est): 860.9K **Privately Held**
WEB: www.stemworksllc.com
SIC: 3599 Machine & other job shop work

(G-12626)
**STEWARTS ELC MTR WORKS
INC**
8951 Trussway Blvd (32824-7812)
PHONE.............................407 859-1837
Michael Joe Stewart, *President*
Helon G Stewart, *Exec VP*
Paul E Stewart, *Vice Pres*
Billy Johns, *Treasurer*
Myra L Williams, *Treasurer*
EMP: 25 **EST:** 1982
SQ FT: 15,400
SALES (est): 4.2MM **Privately Held**
WEB: www.semw.net
SIC: 7694 5999 Electric motor repair;
rewinding services; motors, electric

(G-12627)
STONE PALACE
1901 N Orange Ave (32804-5530)
PHONE.............................407 896-0872
EMP: 10
SALES (est): 650K **Privately Held**
SIC: 3281 Mfg Cut Stone/Products

(G-12628)
SUBLIMATION STATION INC
1656 N Goldenrod Rd (32807-8454)
PHONE.............................407 605-5300
Khrystine Roman, *President*
EMP: 8 **EST:** 2015
SALES (est): 593.4K **Privately Held**
WEB: www.thesublimationstation.com
SIC: 2759 Screen printing

(G-12629)
SULZER EMS INC
7200 Lake Ellenor Dr (32809-5700)
PHONE.............................407 858-9447
EMP: 32 **Privately Held**
SIC: 3599 Mfg Industrial Machinery
HQ: Sulzer Ems Inc.
2412 W Durango St
Phoenix AZ 85009
602 258-8545

(G-12630)
**SUMMIT ATL PRODUCTIONS
LLC**
Also Called: Unconventional Marine
3320 Vineland Rd Ste A (32811-6452)
PHONE.............................407 930-5488
Justin P Massicotte,
EMP: 8 **EST:** 2016
SALES (est): 261.3K **Privately Held**
WEB: www.summitatlantic.com
SIC: 2499 Decorative wood & woodwork

(G-12631)
**SUN GRO HORTICULTURE DIST
INC**
6021 Beggs Rd (32810-2600)
PHONE.............................407 291-1676
EMP: 20 **Privately Held**
SIC: 1499 2875 Peat grinding; peat min-
ing; fertilizers, mixing only
PA: Sun Gro Horticulture Distribution Inc.
770 Silver St
Agawam MA 01001

(G-12632)
SUN-TEK MANUFACTURING INC
Also Called: Sun-Tek Skylights
10303 General Dr (32824-8555)
PHONE.............................407 859-2117
Glen R Sincic, *Director*
▲ **EMP:** 50 **EST:** 1979
SQ FT: 64,400
SALES (est): 6.7MM **Privately Held**
WEB: www.sun-tek.com
SIC: 3089 3211 Windows, plastic; skylight
glass

(G-12633)
SUNNYPICS LLC
618 E South St Ste 500 (32801-2986)
PHONE.............................407 992-6210
Dmitriy Toroptsev, *CEO*
EMP: 5 **EST:** 2017
SALES (est): 510.8K **Privately Held**
WEB: www.sunny-pics.com
SIC: 3581 5946 5087 Automatic vending
machines; camera & photographic supply
stores; vending machines & supplies

(G-12634)
**SUNRISE FINANCIAL ASSOC
INC**
Also Called: Realstargps
14004 Chcora Crssing Blvd (32828-7744)
PHONE.............................321 439-9797
Nadir Dalal, *President*
EMP: 5 **EST:** 2008
SALES (est): 314.4K **Privately Held**
SIC: 3699 Security control equipment &
systems

(G-12635)
**SUNSHINE SUPPLEMENTS INC
(PA)**
Also Called: What To Drink B4 You Drink
120 E Marks St Ste 250 (32803-3829)
PHONE.............................407 751-4299
John Mansour, *Principal*
David Larue, *Principal*
EMP: 6 **EST:** 2017
SALES (est): 2.7MM **Privately Held**
WEB: www.drinkb4.com
SIC: 2023 Dietary supplements, dairy &
non-dairy based

(G-12636)
SUPER COLOR DIGITAL LLC
3450 Vineland Rd Ste 200 (32811-6421)
PHONE.............................407 240-1660
Pat Pidgeon, *Manager*
EMP: 10 **Privately Held**
WEB: www.supercolor.com
SIC: 2759 Commercial printing
PA: Super Color Digital, Llc
16761 Hale Ave
Irvine CA 92606

(G-12637)
SUPERIOR METAL
Also Called: Laser
2409 N John Young Pkwy (32804-4105)
PHONE.............................407 522-8100
Lyndell N Freeman II, *President*
EMP: 10 **EST:** 1987
SQ FT: 10,000
SALES (est): 906.5K **Privately Held**
WEB: www.superiormetalfab.com
SIC: 3444 Sheet metalwork

(G-12638)
**SUPERIOR METAL
FABRICATORS INC**
Also Called: Superiorlaser
2411 N John Young Pkwy (32804-4105)
PHONE.............................407 295-5772
Lyndell N Freeman II, *President*
Charles T Gross, *Vice Pres*
▼ **EMP:** 23 **EST:** 1987
SQ FT: 10,000
SALES (est): 4.5MM **Privately Held**
WEB: www.superiormetalfab.com
SIC: 3444 3699 Sheet metalwork; electri-
cal equipment & supplies

(G-12639)
SUPERIOR SIGNS INC
3975 Forrestal Ave # 600 (32806-6198)
PHONE.............................407 601-7964
Daniel Eric Shiman, *Principal*
EMP: 13 **EST:** 2004
SALES (est): 475.1K **Privately Held**
WEB: www.asuperiorsign.com
SIC: 3993 5099 1799 Signs & advertising
specialties; signs, except electric; sign in-
stallation & maintenance

(G-12640)
SUREPODS LLC
2300 Principal Row # 101 (32837-8810)
PHONE.............................407 859-7034
Bill Seery, *Vice Pres*
Marcus Rodriguez, *Plant Supt*
Lauren Foertsch, *Project Mgr*
Shaun Jacobs, *Controller*
Rosa Rodriguez, *Controller*
▲ **EMP:** 70 **EST:** 2016
SALES (est): 11MM **Privately Held**
WEB: www.surepods.com
SIC: 2452 Prefabricated buildings, wood

(G-12641)
SWISSTECH MACHINERY LLC
8815 Conroy Windermere Rd
(32835-3129)
PHONE...................................407 416-2383
Page Spinetti, *Mng Member*
EMP: 5 EST: 2007
SALES (est): 512.2K Privately Held
WEB: www.swisstechmachinery.com
SIC: 3545 Machine tool accessories

(G-12642)
SYMME3D LLC
1 S Orange Ave Ste 502 (32801-2626)
PHONE...................................321 220-1584
Calin Brandabur, *CEO*
Kennan Clark, *Chairman*
EMP: 12
SQ FT: 1,200
SALES (est): 1.4MM Privately Held
SIC: 3549 Metalworking machinery
PA: Symme3d Manufacturing Srl
Calea Sagului Nr. 85 Bl. 11 Sc. G Ap.
30
Timisoara

(G-12643)
SYNTHES3D USA INC
1800 Pembrook Dr (32810-6928)
PHONE...................................321 946-1303
Vivien Poujade, *Principal*
EMP: 7 EST: 2016
SALES (est): 128.7K Privately Held
WEB: www.synthes3d.com
SIC: 3577 Computer peripheral equipment

(G-12644)
T R S
Also Called: Trs
6330 Silver Star Rd (32818-3119)
PHONE...................................407 298-5490
Carl Summers, *President*
Randy Summers, *Exec VP*
Ardis Summers, *Admin Sec*
Scott Malloch, *Planning*
EMP: 51 EST: 1973
SQ FT: 26,000
SALES (est): 3MM Privately Held
WEB: www.trselectric.com
SIC: 3694 3625 5063 5013 Alternators,
automotive; starter, electric motor; motor
controls, starters & relays: electric; alter-
nators; automotive parts

(G-12645)
TAR BUILDING LLC
1155 N Orange Ave (32804-6407)
PHONE...................................407 896-7252
Thomas Rensenhouse, *Principal*
EMP: 7 EST: 2011
SALES (est): 160.3K Privately Held
SIC: 2865 Tar

(G-12646)
TAYLOR FARMS FLORIDA INC
7492 Chancellor Dr (32809-6242)
PHONE...................................407 859-3373
Bruce Taylor, *Ch of Bd*
Tim Unick, *President*
Esteban Arreguin, *Vice Pres*
Lewis Swarts, *Opers Mgr*
Terry Kitts, *Purch Mgr*
▲ EMP: 480 EST: 1983
SQ FT: 66,000
SALES (est): 210.5MM Privately Held
WEB: www.taylorfarms.com
SIC: 2099 Ready-to-eat meals, salads &
sandwiches
PA: Taylor Fresh Foods, Inc.
150 Main St Ste 400
Salinas CA 93901

(G-12647)
TECHTRADE LLC
6900 Tvstock Lkes Blvd St (32827)
PHONE...................................201 706-8130
Harvey T Bart, *President*
Tim Stark, *Warehouse Mgr*
▲ EMP: 7 EST: 2003
SALES (est): 1.1MM Privately Held
WEB: www.techtradellc.com
SIC: 3841 Surgical & medical instruments

(G-12648)
TECPORT OPTICS INC
6457 Hazeltine National D (32822-5162)
PHONE...................................407 855-1212
Tam V Le, *President*
Joseph Kim, *Exec VP*
Oleg Shkraba, *Engineer*
Jong Woo, *Engineer*
Dale Flowers, *CFO*
▲ EMP: 15 EST: 1997
SQ FT: 3,300
SALES (est): 4.3MM Privately Held
WEB: www.tecportoptics.com
SIC: 3827 Optical instruments & lenses

(G-12649)
TELEDYNE FLIR LLC
8210 Presidents Dr (32809-7623)
PHONE...................................407 816-0091
June N Diaz, *Business Mgr*
June De Arce, *Draft/Design*
Jon Gionta, *Engineer*
Robert Pollard, *Engineer*
Jon Van Anda, *Engineer*
EMP: 72
SQ FT: 78,407
SALES (corp-wide): 4.6B Publicly Held
WEB: www.flir.com
SIC: 3861 7372 3812 8731 Photographic
equipment & supplies; prepackaged soft-
ware; detection apparatus:
electronic/magnetic field, light/heat; in-
frared object detection equipment; com-
mercial physical research; industrial
instrmnts msrmnt display/control process
variable
HQ: Teledyne Flir, Llc
27700 Sw Parkway Ave
Wilsonville OR 97070
503 498-3547

(G-12650)
TEMSA NORTH AMERICA INC
404 Zell Dr (32824-7625)
PHONE...................................407 807-6950
Fatih Kozan, *Director*
EMP: 21 EST: 2018
SALES (est): 3.7MM Privately Held
SIC: 3713 Bus bodies (motor vehicles)

(G-12651)
TEN IN MOTION LLC
8544 Commodity Cir (32819-9001)
PHONE...................................407 226-0204
Marc A Plogstedt, *President*
Itec Entertainment Corp,
EMP: 10 EST: 2000
SALES (est): 1.1MM Privately Held
SIC: 3577 Data conversion equipment,
media-to-media: computer

(G-12652)
TERANEX SYSTEMS INC
2602 Challenger Tech Ct # 240
(32826-2782)
PHONE...................................407 888-4300
Fax: 407 858-6001
EMP: 30
SALES (est): 4MM
SALES (corp-wide): 30MM Privately
Held
SIC: 3651 Mfg Home Audio/Video Equip-
ment
PA: Jupiter Systems
31015 Huntwood Ave
Hayward CA 94544
510 675-1000

(G-12653)
TEXTRON AVIATION INC
Also Called: Cessna Orlndo Citation Svc Ctr
4134 Bear Rd (32827-5002)
PHONE...................................407 859-1245
Matthew Greene, *General Mgr*
Gary B Wilson, *Chief*
David Chant, *Counsel*
William Martin, *Export Mgr*
Brendan Compton, *Production*
EMP: 116
SALES (corp-wide): 12.3MM Publicly
Held
WEB: www.txtav.com
SIC: 3721 Aircraft

HQ: Textron Aviation Inc.
1 Cessna Blvd
Wichita KS 67215
316 517-6000

(G-12654)
TFL OF ORLANDO
2586 N Orange Blossom Trl (32804-4865)
PHONE...................................407 936-1553
Frank Gulfroy, *Owner*
EMP: 7 EST: 2011
SALES (est): 147.6K Privately Held
SIC: 3537 Industrial trucks & tractors

(G-12655)
THE SCRANTON TIMES L P
Also Called: Orlando Weekly
16 W Pine St (32801-2612)
PHONE...................................407 377-0400
Danielle Lebron, *Accounts Mgr*
Rich Schreiber, *Manager*
Hollie Mahadeo, *Director*
Zackary Rowe, *Director*
Michael Wagner, *Creative Dir*
EMP: 52
SALES (corp-wide): 63.5MM Privately
Held
WEB: www.thetimes-tribune.com
SIC: 2711 Commercial printing & newspa-
per publishing combined
PA: The Scranton Times L P
149 Penn Ave Ste 1
Scranton PA 18503
570 348-9100

(G-12656)
THERMAL SCANNING INC
5121 Contoura Dr (32810-1807)
PHONE...................................407 617-2927
William I Murphy, *Principal*
EMP: 8 EST: 2006
SALES (est): 111.9K Privately Held
SIC: 3577 Computer peripheral equipment

(G-12657)
THREADBIRD LLC
7550 Brokerage Dr (32809-5650)
PHONE...................................407 545-6506
Brian Seay, *Opers Staff*
Ilene Appel, *Production*
Martha Christine, *Production*
Joshua Metts, *Production*
Kristen Koran, *Purch Mgr*
EMP: 7 EST: 2008
SALES (est): 1MM Privately Held
WEB: www.threadbird.com
SIC: 2759 Screen printing

(G-12658)
TICKS-N-ALL LLC
4503 Winderwood Cir (32835-2639)
PHONE...................................321 445-9497
Kevin Newell, *CEO*
EMP: 6 EST: 2014
SALES (est): 442.4K Privately Held
WEB: www.ticks-n-all.com
SIC: 2879 Insecticides & pesticides

(G-12659)
TITAN AMERICA LLC
339 Thorpe Rd Ofc (32824-8152)
PHONE...................................407 240-9824
Tony Szynaka, *Sales Staff*
Don Claxton, *Branch Mgr*
EMP: 15
SALES (corp-wide): 177.9K Privately
Held
WEB: www.titanamerica.com
SIC: 3273 Ready-mixed concrete
HQ: Titan America Llc
5700 Lake Wright Dr # 300
Norfolk VA 23502
757 858-6500

(G-12660)
TITANIUM DEVELOPMENT LLC
Also Called: Titanium Pavers
3209 Prkchster Sq Blvd Ap (32835-7551)
PHONE...................................407 844-8664
Andreia B Piroupo, *Principal*
EMP: 6 EST: 2017
SALES (est): 848.1K Privately Held
WEB: www.titaniumpavers.com
SIC: 3356 Titanium

(G-12661)
TJ CABINETRY INC
4333 Silver Star Rd # 14 (32808-5100)
PHONE...................................407 886-8294
David Sabuncu, *President*
EMP: 11 EST: 1992
SQ FT: 3,000
SALES (est): 363.1K Privately Held
WEB: www.tjcustomcabinets.com
SIC: 2434 Wood kitchen cabinets

(G-12662)
TOP OF THE LINE COATING INC
13209 Briar Forest Ct (32828-4610)
PHONE...................................407 485-8546
Jose Rivera, *Principal*
EMP: 8 EST: 2008
SALES (est): 103.5K Privately Held
SIC: 3479 Metal coating & allied service

(G-12663)
TOTAL VISION DESIGN GROUP
Also Called: Pictures and Mirrors
7552 10th Chancellor Dr (32809)
PHONE...................................407 438-6933
Arno Heyder, *President*
EMP: 10 EST: 2012
SALES (est): 502.7K Privately Held
WEB: www.totalvisiondesigngroup.com
SIC: 2499 Picture & mirror frames, wood

(G-12664)
**TOTEUM ALL TRCKG
TRNSPRTING L**
5401 S Kirkman Rd Ste 310 (32819-7937)
PHONE...................................888 506-5890
Eddie McIntosh III, *CEO*
EMP: 50 EST: 2020
SALES (est): 2MM Privately Held
SIC: 3537 Trucks: freight, baggage, etc.:
industrial, except mining

(G-12665)
TOUCHLESS COVER LLC
10150 Central Port Dr (32824-7059)
PHONE...................................407 679-2217
Slate Kirk, *President*
Carlos Cardenas, *Plant Mgr*
Holly Engilis, *Accounting Mgr*
◆ EMP: 21 EST: 1998
SQ FT: 3,000
SALES (est): 4.4MM Privately Held
WEB: www.touchlesscover.com
SIC: 3536 Boat lifts

(G-12666)
**TP AEROSPACE TECHNICS LLC
(DH)**
6470 Narcoossee Rd Ste A (32822-5594)
PHONE...................................407 730-9988
Peter Lyager, *CEO*
Thomas Ibs, *President*
Nikolaj Lei Jacobsen, *COO*
Maia Jensen, *Supervisor*
EMP: 2 EST: 2014
SALES (est): 4.4MM
SALES (corp-wide): 430.8K Privately
Held
WEB: www.tpaerospace.com
SIC: 3721 Aircraft

(G-12667)
**TRAFFIC CONTROL PDTS FLA
INC**
249 N Ivey Ln Ste A (32811-4253)
PHONE...................................407 521-6777
Mike Bartlett, *Manager*
EMP: 10
SALES (corp-wide): 15.5MM Privately
Held
WEB: www.trafficcontrolproducts.org
SIC: 3499 Barricades, metal
PA: Traffic Control Products Of Florida, Inc.
5514 Carmack Rd
Tampa FL 33610
813 621-8484

(G-12668)
TRANSTAT EQUIPMENT INC
510 Thorpe Rd (32824-8133)
P.O. Box 593865 (32859-3865)
PHONE...................................407 857-2040
Otto L Schodorf Jr, *Ch of Bd*
John Reetz, *President*
Paul Schodorf, *Corp Secy*

Leroy Peterson, *Exec VP*
EMP: 11 **EST:** 1900
SQ FT: 17,000
SALES (est): 640.8K **Privately Held**
SIC: 3713 7532 7538 Truck bodies (motor vehicles); body shop, trucks; general automotive repair shops

(G-12669)
TRI-TECH ELECTRONICS INC
9480 E Colonial Dr (32817-4198)
P.O. Box 678028 (32867-8028)
PHONE.............................407 277-2131
Joseph Gurvich, *President*
Stanton A J Jr, *Corp Secy*
EMP: 60 **EST:** 1957
SQ FT: 27,000
SALES (est): 9.3MM **Privately Held**
WEB: www.tri-techelectronics.com
SIC: 3728 3845 3679 7629 Aircraft body & wing assemblies & parts; electromedical apparatus; electronic circuits; harness assemblies for electronic use: wire or cable; electrical personal use appliance repair; electronic equipment repair; sanitary engineers; electrical or electronic engineering

(G-12670)
TRIAD ISOTOPES INC (PA)
4205 Vineland Rd Ste L13 (32811-6601)
PHONE.............................407 455-6700
Dom Meffe, *President*
William McCormick, *Vice Pres*
Brian Schumer, *Vice Pres*
Shane Scott, *Vice Pres*
Debbie Vanerka, *VP Bus Dvlpt*
◆ **EMP:** 30 **EST:** 2006
SALES (est): 97.8MM **Privately Held**
WEB: www.jdiri.com
SIC: 2834 Pharmaceutical preparations

(G-12671)
TRIBUNE MEDIA SERVICES INC
Also Called: T V Log
64 E Concord St (32801-1331)
PHONE.............................407 420-6200
Patty Hinson, *Manager*
EMP: 62
SALES (corp-wide): 4.6B **Publicly Held**
WEB: www.tribunemedia.com
SIC: 3993 7383 Advertising artwork; news syndicates
HQ: Tribune Media Services, Inc.
435 N Michigan Ave # 1500
Chicago IL 60611
312 222-4444

(G-12672)
TRIKAROO
5525 Commerce Dr Ste 1 (32839-2988)
PHONE.............................800 679-3415
Gina Garcia, *President*
▲ **EMP:** 5 **EST:** 2013
SALES (est): 443K **Privately Held**
WEB: www.trikaroo.com
SIC: 3711 Motor vehicles & car bodies

(G-12673)
TRIM-PAK CORPORATION (PA)
8700 S Orange Ave (32824-7901)
PHONE.............................407 851-8900
David L Smith, *President*
Tony Wingerter, *Sales Associate*
EMP: 20 **EST:** 1977
SQ FT: 125,000
SALES (est): 10.5MM **Privately Held**
WEB: www.trim-pak.com
SIC: 2434 5031 5072 5211 Wood kitchen cabinets; doors; kitchen cabinets; builders' hardware; doors, storm: wood or metal; builders' hardware

(G-12674)
TRIUMVIRATE ENVIRONMENTAL
10100 Rocket Blvd (32824-8565)
PHONE.............................407 859-4441
Kaitlyn Weindorfer, *Technical Mgr*
John McQuillan Jr, *Mng Member*
EMP: 49
SALES (corp-wide): 113MM **Privately Held**
WEB: www.triumvirate.com
SIC: 3822 Auto controls regulating residntl & coml environmt & applncs

PA: Triumvirate Environmental, Inc.
200 Innerbelt Rd 4
Somerville MA 02143
617 628-8098

(G-12675)
TRS WIRELESS INC
1711 S Division Ave (32805-4727)
PHONE.............................407 447-7333
John Raga, *CEO*
Moreno Evelyn, *Sales Staff*
April Bennett, *Office Mgr*
Tim Bennett, *Info Tech Mgr*
Charlie Weddle, *Executive*
EMP: 21 **EST:** 1969
SALES (est): 1.4MM **Privately Held**
WEB: www.trswireless.com
SIC: 3663 5999 Transmitter-receivers, radio; telephone & communication equipment

(G-12676)
TRUSSWAY MANUFACTURING INC
8850 Trussway Blvd (32824-7897)
PHONE.............................407 857-2777
Daniel Durski, *Vice Pres*
Dan Eberle, *Plant Mgr*
Jose Ramirez, *Plant Mgr*
Kirk Crowe, *Project Mgr*
Travis Anderson, *Opers Staff*
EMP: 22
SALES (corp-wide): 19.8B **Publicly Held**
WEB: www.trussway.com
SIC: 2439 Trusses, wooden roof
HQ: Trussway Manufacturing, Llc
9411 Alcorn St
Houston TX 77093

(G-12677)
TUPPERWARE BRANDS CORPORATION (PA)
14901 S Ornge Blossom Trl (32837-6600)
P.O. Box 2353 (32802-2353)
PHONE.............................407 826-5050
Susan M Cameron, *Ch of Bd*
Miguel Fernandez, *President*
Hector Lezama, *President*
Lucy Orlando, *President*
Deepak Chhabra, *Managing Dir*
▲ **EMP:** 406 **EST:** 1996
SALES (est): 1.6B **Publicly Held**
WEB: www.tupperwarebrands.com
SIC: 3089 2844 Kitchenware, plastic; toilet preparations; toilet preparations

(G-12678)
TUPPERWARE INTL HOLDINGS CORP (HQ)
14901 S Ornge Blossom Trl (32837-6600)
PHONE.............................407 826-5050
E V Goings, *Ch of Bd*
EMP: 10 **EST:** 1999
SALES (est): 4.3MM **Publicly Held**
SIC: 3089 2844 Plastic kitchenware, tableware & houseware; plastic containers, except foam; toilet preparations; toilet preparations

(G-12679)
TUPPERWARE PRODUCTS INC
14901 S Ornge Blossom Trl (32837-6600)
PHONE.............................407 826-5050
Miguel Fernandez, *President*
Randy Griswold, *Manager*
EMP: 18 **EST:** 1996
SALES (est): 10MM **Publicly Held**
WEB: www.tupperware.com
SIC: 2821 Molding compounds, plastics
PA: Tupperware Brands Corporation
14901 S Ornge Blossom Trl
Orlando FL 32837

(G-12680)
TUPPERWARE TURKEY INC
14901 S Orange Blossom Tr (32837-6600)
PHONE.............................407 826-5050
EMP: 16 **EST:** 1996
SALES (est): 152.3K **Privately Held**
WEB: www.tupperwarebrands.com
SIC: 3089 Plastic kitchenware, tableware & houseware

(G-12681)
TUPPERWARE US INC (HQ)
14901 S Ornge Blossom Trl (32837-6600)
P.O. Box 2353 (32802-2353)
PHONE.............................407 826-5050
Thomas M Roehlk, *CEO*
Ev Goings, *Ch of Bd*
Pablo Munoz, *President*
Christian Skr Der, *Vice Pres*
Jos Timmerman, *Vice Pres*
▲ **EMP:** 66 **EST:** 1989
SQ FT: 10,000
SALES (est): 87.4MM **Publicly Held**
WEB: www.tupperware.com
SIC: 3089 Jars, plastic

(G-12682)
TURNSTILE PUBLISHING COMPANY (DH)
Also Called: Golfweek
1500 Park Center Dr (32835-5704)
P.O. Box 783908, Winter Garden (34778-3908)
PHONE.............................407 563-7000
Francis Farrell, *President*
Cindy Crain, *Corp Secy*
Patti Green, *Vice Pres*
Eric Beckson, *CFO*
EMP: 60 **EST:** 1975
SQ FT: 9,740
SALES (est): 32.6MM
SALES (corp-wide): 3.2B **Publicly Held**
SIC: 2721 Magazines: publishing only, not printed on site; periodicals: publishing only
HQ: Usa Today Sports Media Group, Llc
7950 Jones Branch Dr
Mc Lean VA 22102
703 854-6000

(G-12683)
UFP ORLANDO LLC
7205 Rose Ave (32810-3414)
PHONE.............................407 982-3312
Gabe High, *Manager*
EMP: 14 **EST:** 2016
SALES (est): 2.5MM
SALES (corp-wide): 8.6B **Publicly Held**
SIC: 2491 Millwork, treated wood
PA: Ufp Industries, Inc.
2801 E Beltline Ave Ne
Grand Rapids MI 49525
616 364-6161

(G-12684)
ULTIMATE MARINE CENTL FLA LLC
3419 Wd Judge Dr Ste 150 (32808-7443)
PHONE.............................407 849-1100
Melanie Labon,
EMP: 10 **EST:** 2020
SALES (est): 860.4K **Privately Held**
WEB: www.ultimatemarine.com
SIC: 3732 Boat building & repairing

(G-12685)
ULTIMATE OVERSTOCK LLC
Also Called: VIP Sports Idrive
4967 Intl Dr Ste 3a27 (32819-6213)
PHONE.............................407 851-1017
Javed Iqbal, *Mng Member*
EMP: 20 **EST:** 2018
SALES (est): 1.1MM **Privately Held**
SIC: 2329 Men's & boys' sportswear & athletic clothing

(G-12686)
UNFOLDINGWORD CORPORATION
Also Called: Distant Shores Media
10524 Moss Park Rd # 204 (32832-5898)
PHONE.............................407 900-3005
David Reeves, *CEO*
Christopher Klapp, *Research*
Jan Perry, *CFO*
Lincoln Brunner, *Marketing Staff*
EMP: 18 **EST:** 2003
SALES (est): 4.2MM **Privately Held**
WEB: www.unfoldingword.org
SIC: 7372 Educational computer software

(G-12687)
UNIQUE ELECTRONICS INC (PA)
1320 26th St (32805-5297)
PHONE.............................407 422-3051
George Singleton, *CEO*
Michael M Klinger, *President*
Jay Cooper, *Engineer*
James T Giuliano, *CFO*
Thuy Nguyen, *Bookkeeper*
EMP: 129 **EST:** 1980
SQ FT: 25,145
SALES (est): 19.4MM **Privately Held**
WEB: www.uniqueelectronics.com
SIC: 3679 Harness assemblies for electronic use: wire or cable

(G-12688)
UNITED MACHINING SERVICE INC
2410 Coolidge Ave (32804-4812)
PHONE.............................407 422-7710
Samuel D Reynolds, *President*
EMP: 5 **EST:** 1995
SALES (est): 962.7K **Privately Held**
SIC: 3549 Metalworking machinery

(G-12689)
UNITED SPACE ALLIANCE
5530 Gross Ct (32810-4506)
PHONE.............................321 853-3417
George Kirk, *Master*
EMP: 7 **EST:** 2018
SALES (est): 113K **Privately Held**
WEB: www.ulalaunch.com
SIC: 3761 Guided missiles & space vehicles

(G-12690)
UNITED TROPHY MANUFACTURING (PA)
Also Called: Fleaworld Div
610 N Orange Ave (32801-1398)
PHONE.............................407 841-2525
Sydney Allen Levy, *President*
Marianne Levy, *Corp Secy*
▲ **EMP:** 50 **EST:** 1952
SQ FT: 17,000
SALES (est): 14MM **Privately Held**
WEB: www.unitedtrophy.com
SIC: 3914 7389 7996 Trophies, plated (all metals); flea market; amusement parks

(G-12691)
UNIVERSAL PC ORGANIZATION INC
8082 Wellsmere Cir (32835-5360)
PHONE.............................321 285-9206
Mark Wascher, *President*
Joseph Machado, *Director*
EMP: 6 **EST:** 2013
SALES (est): 466.6K **Privately Held**
SIC: 2611 Pulp mills, mechanical & recycling processing

(G-12692)
UNIVERSAL POLISHING SYSTEMS
4333 Silver Star Rd # 175 (32808-5170)
PHONE.............................407 227-9516
Abrasive Xiaoyu, *Principal*
Andrew Knopp, *Sales Mgr*
▲ **EMP:** 5 **EST:** 2010
SALES (est): 335.8K **Privately Held**
WEB: www.universalpolishingsystems.com
SIC: 3471 Polishing, metals or formed products

(G-12693)
US GOLF LIQUIDATORS INC
6955 Hanging Moss Rd (32807-5372)
PHONE.............................407 677-1118
EMP: 30 **EST:** 1995
SQ FT: 2,750
SALES (est): 1.6MM **Privately Held**
SIC: 3949 Golf equipment

(G-12694)
US PIPE FABRICATION LLC
109 5th St (32824-8258)
PHONE.............................860 769-6097
Rob Morris, *Branch Mgr*
EMP: 55 **Privately Held**
WEB: www.uspipe.com

▲ = Import ▼ =Export
◆ =Import/Export

SIC: **3498** 3312 Fabricated pipe & fittings; pipes, iron & steel
HQ: Us Pipe Fabrication, Llc
2 Chase Corporate Dr # 200
Hoover AL 35244

(G-12695)
VESTAGEN TCHNICAL TEXTILES INC
Also Called: Vestex
1301 W Colonial Dr (32804-7133)
PHONE....................................407 781-2570
Bill Bold, *CEO*
Dale Pfost, *Ch of Bd*
Uncas B Favret III, *President*
Stewart B Davis, *Vice Pres*
Stewart Davis, *Vice Pres*
◆ **EMP:** 5 **EST:** 2009
SALES (est): 1.4MM **Privately Held**
SIC: **2819** 2843 5023 8731 Fluorine, elemental; textile finishing agents; sheets, textile; commercial physical research

(G-12696)
VIA CABINETS CORP
3113 Willie Mays Pkwy (32811-5523)
PHONE....................................407 633-1915
Bernardo Das Chagas Viana, *President*
Monica Cristina Viana, *Vice Pres*
EMP: 7 **EST:** 2018
SALES (est): 392.9K **Privately Held**
SIC: **2511** Wood household furniture

(G-12697)
VIA OPTRONICS LLC
6220 Hzltine Nat Dr Ste 1 (32822-5145)
PHONE....................................407 745-5031
Jurgen Eichner, *CEO*
Gilena Fuentes, *Sales Staff*
Ed Illingworth, *Manager*
◆ **EMP:** 20 **EST:** 2009
SQ FT: 52,000
SALES (est): 12MM **Privately Held**
WEB: www.via-optronics.com
SIC: **3679** Liquid crystal displays (LCD)
HQ: Via Optronics Gmbh
Sieboldstr. 18
Nurnberg BY 90411

(G-12698)
VICTORY TAILGATE LLC
8673 Transport Dr (32832-7102)
PHONE....................................407 704-8775
Scott D Sims, *CEO*
Marcos Olivares, *Production*
Monica Acevedo, *Accountant*
Pranil Patel, *Accounts Mgr*
Jessica Brand, *Cust Mgr*
◆ **EMP:** 160 **EST:** 2009
SALES (est): 35.2MM
SALES (corp-wide): 313.6MM **Publicly Held**
WEB: www.victorytailgate.com
SIC: **3944** Board games, children's & adults'
HQ: Indian Industries Inc
817 Maxwell Ave
Evansville IN 47711
812 467-1200

(G-12699)
VIOLET DEFENSE LLC
189 S Orange Ave Ste 1400 (32801-3258)
PHONE....................................407 433-1104
Terrance Berland, *CEO*
Jessica Jones, *Vice Pres*
Mike Halter, *Engineer*
Mark Nathan, *Mng Member*
Richard Barnes, *CIO*
EMP: 25 **EST:** 2015
SALES (est): 4.6MM **Privately Held**
WEB: www.violetdefense.com
SIC: **3646** Commercial indusl & institutional electric lighting fixtures

(G-12700)
VISIONS SKY CORP
18154 Cadence St (32820-2728)
PHONE....................................888 788-8609
David Barefoot, *Principal*
EMP: 7 **EST:** 2012
SALES (est): 125.6K **Privately Held**
WEB: www.visionssky.com
SIC: **7372** Prepackaged software

(G-12701)
VISUAL SIGNS LLC
7041 Grand National Dr (32819-8381)
PHONE....................................407 693-0200
EMP: 8 **EST:** 2019
SALES (est): 960.7K **Privately Held**
WEB: www.visualsignsandgraphics.com
SIC: **3993** Signs & advertising specialties

(G-12702)
VITAL HEALTH CORPORATION (HQ)
Also Called: Inprovit Vital Health
6000 Metrowest Blvd # 200 (32835-7629)
PHONE....................................407 522-1125
Julio Correa, *President*
Sergio Correa, *Admin Sec*
EMP: 8 **EST:** 2000
SQ FT: 6,000
SALES (est): 14.2MM **Privately Held**
WEB: www.vitalhealthus.com
SIC: **2023** Dietary supplements, dairy & non-dairy based

(G-12703)
VITAL SIGNS OF ORLANDO INC
Also Called: Vso
2111 S Division Ave Ste A (32805-6206)
PHONE....................................407 297-0680
David New, *President*
Gary Stephens, *Research*
Kenneth Mulenga, *Marketing Staff*
EMP: 6 **EST:** 1987
SALES (est): 953.8K **Privately Held**
WEB: www.vitalsignsorlando.com
SIC: **3993** Signs, not made in custom sign painting shops

(G-12704)
VOXX AUTOMOTIVE CORP (HQ)
2351 J Lawson Blvd (32824-4386)
PHONE....................................631 231-7750
Patrick M Lavelle, *President*
Patrick Lavelle, *Director*
EMP: 40 **EST:** 2018
SALES (est): 11.3MM
SALES (corp-wide): 635.9MM **Publicly Held**
WEB: www.voxxautomotive.com
SIC: **3699** Automotive driving simulators (training aids), electronic
PA: Voxx International Corporation
2351 J Lawson Blvd
Orlando FL 32824
800 645-7750

(G-12705)
VOXX AUTOMOTIVE CORPORATION
2351 J Lawson Blvd (32824-4386)
PHONE....................................407 842-7000
EMP: 8 **EST:** 2019
SALES (est): 3.1MM
SALES (corp-wide): 635.9MM **Publicly Held**
WEB: www.voxxautomotive.com
SIC: **3711** Motor vehicles & car bodies
PA: Voxx International Corporation
2351 J Lawson Blvd
Orlando FL 32824
800 645-7750

(G-12706)
VOXX INTERNATIONAL CORPORATION (PA)
2351 J Lawson Blvd (32824-4386)
PHONE....................................800 645-7750
Patrick M Lavelle, *President*
◆ **EMP:** 330 **EST:** 1960
SALES: 635.9MM **Publicly Held**
WEB: www.voxxintl.com
SIC: **3711** 3651 3663 5013 Motor vehicles & car bodies; household audio & video equipment; audio electronic systems; video camera-audio recorders, household use; radio & TV communications equipment; automotive supplies & parts; electronic parts & equipment

(G-12707)
VOXXHIRSCHMANN CORPORATION
Also Called: Voxx Electronics
2351 J Lawson Blvd (32824-4386)
PHONE....................................866 869-7888

Ludwig Geis, *President*
EMP: 250 **EST:** 2014
SALES (est): 17.9MM **Privately Held**
WEB: www.voxxautomotive.com
SIC: **3714** Motor vehicle parts & accessories

(G-12708)
VPR 4X4
1870 Saturn Blvd (32837-9416)
PHONE....................................305 468-9818
EMP: 6 **EST:** 2019
SALES (est): 363.1K **Privately Held**
WEB: www.vpr4x4.com
SIC: **3714** Motor vehicle parts & accessories

(G-12709)
VUAANT INC (PA)
Also Called: Care.ai
7300 Sandlake Commons Blv (32819-8008)
PHONE....................................407 701-6975
Chakravarthy Toleti, *CEO*
EMP: 8 **EST:** 2018
SALES (est): 2.5MM **Privately Held**
SIC: **7372** 7389 Application computer software;

(G-12710)
WALDEN CONSULTING LLC
Also Called: Turbo Vacuum
1021 E Robinson St Ste A (32801-2004)
PHONE....................................407 563-3620
Scott E Walden, *Mng Member*
EMP: 5 **EST:** 2004
SQ FT: 1,500
SALES (est): 509.7K **Privately Held**
WEB: www.turbovacuum.com
SIC: **3821** Vacuum pumps, laboratory

(G-12711)
WASHINGTON SHORES ELEMENT
944 W Lake Mann Dr (32805-3435)
PHONE....................................407 250-6260
EMP: 8 **EST:** 2014
SALES (est): 1.1MM **Privately Held**
WEB: washingtonshores.ocps.net
SIC: **2819** Elements

(G-12712)
WESTROCK CP LLC
4364 Sw 34th St (32811-6414)
PHONE....................................407 843-1300
Tom Grahan, *Manager*
John Cole, *Manager*
John Conley, *Manager*
EMP: 50
SALES (corp-wide): 18.7B **Publicly Held**
WEB: www.westrock.com
SIC: **2631** Paperboard mills
HQ: Westrock Cp, Llc
1000 Abernathy Rd Ste 125
Atlanta GA 30328

(G-12713)
WESTROCK CP LLC
375 W 7th St (32824-8145)
PHONE....................................407 859-9701
EMP: 20
SALES (corp-wide): 14.1B **Publicly Held**
SIC: **2653** Mfg Corrugated/Solid Fiber Boxes
HQ: Westrock Cp, Llc
504 Thrasher St
Norcross GA 30328

(G-12714)
WHIRLPOOL CORPORATION
13201 S Orange Ave (32824-6104)
PHONE....................................407 438-5899
Darlan Lima, *Manager*
EMP: 22
SALES (corp-wide): 21.9B **Publicly Held**
WEB: www.whirlpoolcorp.com
SIC: **3633** Household laundry machines, including coin-operated
PA: Whirlpool Corporation
2000 N M 63
Benton Harbor MI 49022
269 923-5000

(G-12715)
WJ BERGIN CABINETRY LLC
1228 28th St (32805-6103)
PHONE....................................407 271-8982
William Bergin, *President*
EMP: 46 **EST:** 2009
SALES (est): 5.5MM **Privately Held**
WEB: www.wjbergin.com
SIC: **2599** Cabinets, factory

(G-12716)
WOLF AMERICAS LLC
Also Called: Wolf Rock Drills
3113 Willie Mays Pkwy (32811-5523)
PHONE....................................407 704-2051
Tiago Wolf, *Mng Member*
EMP: 5 **EST:** 2014
SALES (est): 1.7MM **Privately Held**
SIC: **3532** Drills & drilling equipment, mining (except oil & gas)
PA: Wolf Equipamentos De Perfuracao Ltda
Rod. Engenheiro Ermenio De Oliveira Penteado(Sp-075) 54,5
Indaiatuba SP 13340

(G-12717)
WONDER EMPORIUM MILLWORK FAB
10779 Satellite Blvd (32837-8422)
PHONE....................................407 850-3131
Winnie Abram, *Principal*
James Conner, *Senior VP*
Peter Abram, *Vice Pres*
EMP: 10 **EST:** 2016
SALES (est): 268.9K **Privately Held**
SIC: **2431** 2521 2541 Millwork; wood office furniture; wood partitions & fixtures

(G-12718)
WONDERWORLD 100 LLC
2209 S Fern Creek Ave (32806-4185)
PHONE....................................407 618-3207
Keshia Almonor, *CEO*
EMP: 10 **EST:** 2020
SALES (est): 300K **Privately Held**
SIC: **2676** 7389 Infant & baby paper products;

(G-12719)
WOOD MACHINE CORP
491 Thorpe Rd (32824-8132)
PHONE....................................407 851-8714
Daniel Thomas Wood, *President*
EMP: 8 **EST:** 1982
SQ FT: 10,000
SALES (est): 665.5K **Privately Held**
WEB: www.woodmachineinc.com
SIC: **3599** Machine shop, jobbing & repair

(G-12720)
WORLDWIDE CHALLENGE MAGAZINE
100 Lake Hart Dr Ste 1600 (32832-0100)
PHONE....................................407 826-2390
Steve Douglas, *President*
Judy Nelson, *Principal*
Farai Katsande, *Vice Pres*
Dan Willmann, *Vice Pres*
Mike Adamson, *Comms Dir*
EMP: 24 **EST:** 2002
SALES (est): 572K **Privately Held**
WEB: www.cru.org
SIC: **2721** Magazines: publishing only, not printed on site

(G-12721)
XEROX BUSINESS SERVICES LLC
2290 Premier Row (32809-6212)
PHONE....................................407 926-4228
EMP: 7 **EST:** 2015
SALES (est): 155.3K **Privately Held**
SIC: **3861** Photographic equipment & supplies

(G-12722)
XTREME DUMPSTER SERVICES CORP
6142 Buford St (32835-2942)
PHONE....................................407 272-8899
Ricardo M Cabo, *President*
EMP: 7 **EST:** 2017
SALES (est): 217.2K **Privately Held**
SIC: **3443** Dumpsters, garbage

(G-12723)
XTREME SIGNS & PRINTING INC
4401 Vineland Rd Ste A9 (32811-7361)
PHONE..............................321 438-3954
Lina M Orozco, *Principal*
EMP: 8 EST: 2016
SALES (est): 370.8K Privately Held
WEB: www.xtremeprinting.net
SIC: 3993 Signs & advertising specialties

(G-12724)
XX PRESS ONE INC
3257 S Chickasaw Trl (32829-8517)
PHONE..............................407 287-2673
Prakash Ramlochan, *President*
EMP: 7 EST: 2015
SALES (est): 136.6K Privately Held
SIC: 2741 Miscellaneous publishing

(G-12725)
XYMOGEN INC (PA)
Also Called: Atlantic Pro-Nutrients
6900 Kingspointe Pkwy (32819-6544)
PHONE..............................407 445-0203
Brian Blackburn, *President*
Kamran Asgharzadeh, *General Mgr*
Stephanie Blackburn, *Vice Pres*
Mike Mahoney, *Vice Pres*
Darrell Parkhill, *Project Mgr*
▲ EMP: 249 EST: 1979
SQ FT: 3,500
SALES (est): 94.4MM Privately Held
WEB: www.xymogen.com
SIC: 2833 Adrenal derivatives

(G-12726)
XYMOGEN MANUFACTURING LLC
6900 Kingspointe Pkwy (32819-6544)
PHONE..............................800 647-6100
EMP: 9 EST: 2020
SALES (est): 529.1K Privately Held
WEB: www.xymogen.com
SIC: 3841 Surgical & medical instruments

(G-12727)
XYMOPRINT LLC
6900 Kingspointe Pkwy (32819-6544)
PHONE..............................407 504-2170
David Perlmutte, *CEO*
EMP: 122 EST: 2012
SALES (est): 963.1K Privately Held
WEB: www.xymoprint.com
SIC: 2752 Commercial printing, lithographic
PA: Xymogen, Inc.
6900 Kingspointe Pkwy
Orlando FL 32819

(G-12728)
YKK AP AMERICA INC
7608 Currency Dr (32809-6925)
PHONE..............................407 856-0660
Barry Wampler, *Manager*
EMP: 18 Privately Held
WEB: www.ykkap.com
SIC: 3442 Sash, door or window: metal
HQ: Ykk Ap America Inc.
270 Rverside Pkwy Ste 100
Austell GA 30168

(G-12729)
YOGURT BREEZE LLC
10727 Narcoossee Rd B4 (32832-6943)
PHONE..............................407 412-5939
Daphny Feria, *Mng Member*
EMP: 7 EST: 2012
SALES (est): 563K Privately Held
WEB: www.yogurtbreeze.com
SIC: 2026 2024 Yogurt; ice cream & frozen desserts

(G-12730)
YORK INTERNATIONAL CORPORATION
10003 Satellite Blvd (32837-8473)
PHONE..............................407 850-0147
EMP: 11 Privately Held
WEB: www.shumakerwilliams.com
SIC: 3585 Refrigeration & heating equipment

HQ: York International Corporation
631 S Richland Ave
York PA 17403
800 481-9738

(G-12731)
ZAHO GLOBAL ENTERPRISES LLC
2275 Hillshire Dr (32828-7505)
PHONE..............................321 239-0653
Edmond Zaho, *Mng Member*
EMP: 5 EST: 2020
SALES (est): 563K Privately Held
WEB: www.zahoglobal.com
SIC: 2431 Millwork

(G-12732)
ZESTY BRANDS LLC
2160 Premier Row (32809-6210)
PHONE..............................954 348-2827
Evgenii Ianchik, *Mng Member*
Mikhail Kogegoe,
Oxana Makarenko,
EMP: 12 EST: 2016
SQ FT: 13,000
SALES (est): 0 Privately Held
SIC: 2038 Snacks, including onion rings, cheese sticks, etc.

(G-12733)
ZESTY PAWS LLC
12124 High Tech Ave Ste 2 (32817-8373)
PHONE..............................407 358-6601
Chris Jaromin, *Senior VP*
Tad Godsil, *CFO*
Steven Ball,
EMP: 45 EST: 2019
SALES (est): 5MM Privately Held
WEB: www.zestypaws.com
SIC: 2047 Dog & cat food

(G-12734)
ZIEHM IMAGING INC
6280 Hzltine Nat Dr 100 (32822-5114)
PHONE..............................407 615-8560
Nelson Mendes, *CEO*
Dr Jorg Strobel, *President*
Dmitry Makovkin, *Business Mgr*
Bert Parlevliet, *Business Mgr*
Christian Eras, *Vice Pres*
▲ EMP: 50 EST: 2005
SQ FT: 30,000
SALES (est): 26.3MM
SALES (corp-wide): 2.6MM Privately Held
WEB: www.ziehm.com
SIC: 3844 X-ray apparatus & tubes
HQ: Ziehm Imaging Gmbh
Lina-Ammon-Str. 10
Nurnberg BY 90471
911 660-670

(G-12735)
ZK CABINETS INC
5509 Commerce Dr (32839-2987)
PHONE..............................407 421-7307
Zein Khater, *President*
EMP: 9 EST: 2004
SALES (est): 145.8K Privately Held
SIC: 2434 Wood kitchen cabinets

(G-12736)
ZOE EXPRESS LOGISTICS LLC ✪
4530 S Orange Blossom Trl U (32839-1704)
PHONE..............................407 967-8762
Simpson St Louis,
EMP: 5 EST: 2021
SALES (est): 395.3K
SALES (corp-wide): 510.4K Privately Held
SIC: 3537 Trucks, tractors, loaders, carriers & similar equipment
PA: D Moli Holdings Llc
4530 S Orange Blossom Trl
Orlando FL 32839
407 967-8762

(G-12737)
ZOM MONTERRA LP
2001 Summit Park Dr # 300 (32810-5945)
PHONE..............................407 644-6300
Steven K Buck, *Manager*
EMP: 10 EST: 2011

SALES (est): 568K Privately Held
SIC: 3669 Emergency alarms

Ormond Beach
Volusia County

(G-12738)
A CERTIFIED SCREEN SERVICE
560 S Yonge St (32174-7540)
PHONE..............................386 673-0054
Todd Orie, *President*
EMP: 17 EST: 2003
SALES (est): 5.2MM Privately Held
WEB: www.acertifiedscreen.com
SIC: 3444 Metal housings, enclosures, casings & other containers

(G-12739)
ABA ENGINEERING & MFG INC
5 Aviator Way (32174-2982)
PHONE..............................386 672-9665
Winston Tomlinson, *President*
Thomas Bonarrigo, *Vice Pres*
EMP: 17 EST: 1992
SQ FT: 8,500
SALES (est): 383.6K Privately Held
SIC: 3444 3599 Sheet metalwork; machine & other job shop work; machine shop, jobbing & repair

(G-12740)
ABB INSTALLATION PRODUCTS INC
Also Called: Homac Manufacturing
12 Southland Rd (32174-3002)
PHONE..............................386 677-9110
Dominic Pileggi, *President*
Janie Barberio, *Human Resources*
Matt Cawood, *Sales Staff*
EMP: 95
SALES (corp-wide): 28.9B Privately Held
WEB: www-public.tnb.com
SIC: 3643 Connectors & terminals for electrical devices
HQ: Abb Installation Products Inc.
860 Ridge Lake Blvd
Memphis TN 38120
901 252-5000

(G-12741)
AKER DATA LLC
124 N Nova Rd (32174-5122)
PHONE..............................385 394-2537
Frank Nickens, *CEO*
EMP: 18 EST: 2020
SALES (est): 1.5MM Privately Held
SIC: 2869 8711 Alcohols, industrial: denatured (non-beverage); engineering services

(G-12742)
AMERITECH DIE & MOLD SOUTH INC
Also Called: Ameritech Die & Mold & South
1 E Tower Cir (32174-8760)
PHONE..............................386 677-1770
Rusty Rotman, *Manager*
EMP: 9
SQ FT: 9,152
SALES (corp-wide): 4MM Privately Held
WEB: www.amdiemold.com
SIC: 3544 Industrial molds; dies, plastics forming; dies, steel rule
PA: Ameritech Die & Mold South, Inc.
107 Knob Hill Rd
Mooresville NC 28117
704 664-0801

(G-12743)
ARISTCRETE COATING EXPERTS LLC
1264 Riverbreeze Blvd (32176-4154)
PHONE..............................386 882-3660
Matthew Carolin, *Principal*
EMP: 9 EST: 2016
SALES (est): 653.9K Privately Held
SIC: 2952 Asphalt felts & coatings

(G-12744)
ATLANTIC MBL IMAGING SVCS INC
1400 Hand Ave Ste A (32174-8195)
PHONE..............................386 239-8271

Vernon Thurman, *President*
EMP: 15 EST: 2001
SQ FT: 768
SALES (est): 2MM Privately Held
WEB: www.atlanticmobileimaging.com
SIC: 3844 X-ray apparatus & tubes

(G-12745)
BELLOWSTECH LLC
115 Business Center Dr (32174-6620)
PHONE..............................386 615-7530
Jeff Heywood, *Materials Mgr*
Jason Loukes, *Engineer*
Glenn Weinrich,
Jessica Kempfer, *Admin Asst*
Tammy Nowacki, *Technician*
EMP: 28 EST: 1999
SQ FT: 6,000
SALES (est): 5.4MM
SALES (corp-wide): 1B Privately Held
WEB: www.mwcomponents.com
SIC: 3599 Bellows, industrial: metal
HQ: Precision Manufacturing Group Llc
501 Little Falls Rd
Cedar Grove NJ 07009
973 785-4630

(G-12746)
BLANE E TAYLOR WELDING INC
1760 N Us Highway 1 (32174-2540)
PHONE..............................386 931-1240
EMP: 8 EST: 2013
SALES (est): 377.5K Privately Held
SIC: 7692 Welding repair

(G-12747)
BLUE COAST BAKERS LLC
1899 N Us Highway 1 (32174-2579)
PHONE..............................386 944-0800
Amber Caballero, *Human Res Mgr*
David Z Lu, *Mng Member*
Ardeshir Asassan,
▲ EMP: 25 EST: 2013
SQ FT: 195,000
SALES (est): 2.6MM Privately Held
WEB: www.bluecoastbakers.com
SIC: 2053 Frozen bakery products, except bread

(G-12748)
C & J INDUSTRIES INC
105 John Anderson Dr (32176-5703)
PHONE..............................386 589-4907
Corina Nesbit, *Principal*
Barry Stainbrook, *Regl Sales Mgr*
Melissa White, *Regl Sales Mgr*
EMP: 10 EST: 2011
SALES (est): 221.8K Privately Held
SIC: 3089 Injection molding of plastics

(G-12749)
CARTERS CABINETRY INC
4 Aviator Way (32174-2982)
PHONE..............................386 677-4192
Fred A Carter, *President*
EMP: 18 EST: 1989
SALES (est): 2MM Privately Held
WEB: www.carterscabinetry.com
SIC: 2434 Wood kitchen cabinets

(G-12750)
CLOSET RODZ LLC (PA)
215 Greenwood Ave (32174-5239)
PHONE..............................386 212-8188
Rodney D Lane, *Principal*
EMP: 7 EST: 2013
SALES (est): 256K Privately Held
WEB: www.closetrodz.com
SIC: 2434 Wood kitchen cabinets

(G-12751)
CO2METER INC
Also Called: Co2meter.com
131 Business Center Dr A3 (32174-6625)
PHONE..............................386 310-4933
Travis Lenander, *CEO*
Joshua Pringle, *Vice Pres*
Ayaris Rivera, *Mfg Staff*
Ray Hicks, *Engineer*
John Houck, *Engineer*
EMP: 18 EST: 2010
SALES (est): 2.7MM Privately Held
WEB: www.co2meter.com
SIC: 3829 Thermometers & temperature sensors; gas detectors

(G-12752)
COMMAND MEDICAL PRODUCTS INC
15 Signal Ave (32174-2984)
PHONE.................................386 677-7775
David T Slick, *Ch of Bd*
Jim Carnall, *President*
Brian Earley, *Project Mgr*
Chad Tremaroli, *Opers Staff*
Ken Grocke, *Production*
◆ EMP: 135 EST: 1982
SQ FT: 56,000
SALES (est): 29MM Privately Held
WEB: www.commandmedical.com
SIC: 3841 Surgical & medical instruments

(G-12753)
CONCENTRATED ALOE CORP
20 W Tower Cir (32174-8761)
PHONE.................................386 673-7566
Brian Meadows, *Sales Staff*
EMP: 7 EST: 2019
SALES (est): 1MM Privately Held
WEB: www.conaloe.com
SIC: 2833 Medicinals & botanicals

(G-12754)
CUSTOM DESIGN GOLF LLC
38 Sand Dollar Dr (32176-2187)
PHONE.................................770 926-4653
John B Carilli, *President*
Melody Carilli
EMP: 5 EST: 1992
SALES (est): 356.1K Privately Held
WEB: www.customdesigngolf.com
SIC: 3949 5941 Golf equipment; golf
goods & equipment

(G-12755)
DELTA P SYSTEMS INC
3 E Tower Cir (32174-8760)
PHONE.................................386 236-0950
Mark D Blais, *President*
Julia S Blais, *Vice Pres*
Michael Moyer, *Engineer*
EMP: 10 EST: 1994
SQ FT: 10,000
SALES (est): 2MM Privately Held
WEB: www.deltapcarver.com
SIC: 3561 Pumps & pumping equipment

(G-12756)
DENTERPRISE INTERNATIONAL INC
100 E Granada Blvd # 219 (32176-6660)
P.O. Box 36 (32175-0036)
PHONE.................................386 672-0450
Claude Berthoin, *President*
Jason Lomoriello, *Sales Associate*
Ivan Mihajlovik, *Marketing Staff*
Michaelle Berthoin Todd, *Manager*
Triston Hughes, *Technical Staff*
EMP: 10 EST: 1996
SQ FT: 3,200
SALES (est): 953.2K Privately Held
WEB: www.denterpriseintl.com
SIC: 3843 Dental materials

(G-12757)
DIVA STUFF
1368 N Us Highway 1 # 406 (32174-8909)
PHONE.................................386 256-2521
James P Nadeau Jr,
EMP: 7 EST: 2014
SALES (est): 1.5MM Privately Held
WEB: www.divastuff.com
SIC: 2834 Dermatologicals

(G-12758)
DOUBLE H ENTERPRISES INC
170 Bear Foot Trl (32174-3201)
PHONE.................................972 562-8588
Beth Hobensack, *President*
Yvonne Hensley, *Vice Pres*
EMP: 9 EST: 2002
SALES (est): 796.6K Privately Held
SIC: 2759 Screen printing

(G-12759)
EAST COAST STEEL INC
1084 Landers St (32174-3311)
PHONE.................................386 233-1385
Daryl W Novack, *Principal*
EMP: 7 EST: 2017

SALES (est): 115.2K Privately Held
WEB: www.eastcoaststeel.net
SIC: 3441 Fabricated structural metal

(G-12760)
EDGEWELL PER CARE BRANDS LLC
1190 N Rte 1 (32174)
PHONE.................................386 677-9559
Sue Craggs, *Administration*
EMP: 10
SALES (corp-wide): 2B Publicly Held
WEB: www.eveready.com
SIC: 3421 Cutlery
HQ: Edgewell Personal Care Brands, Llc
6 Research Dr
Shelton CT 06484
203 944-5500

(G-12761)
EDGEWELL PERSONAL CARE COMPANY
Also Called: Alpha To Omega
1190 N Us Highway 1 (32174-2997)
P.O. Box 265111, Daytona Beach (32126-5111)
PHONE.................................386 673-2024
Barbara Ciaramella, *Vice Pres*
Daniel Oswalt, *Engineer*
John Sousa, *Senior Engr*
Dan Mirchandani, *Finance*
Jessica Palladino, *Human Res Mgr*
EMP: 400
SALES (corp-wide): 2B Publicly Held
WEB: www.schick.com
SIC: 2844 Suntan lotions & oils
PA: Edgewell Personal Care Company
6 Research Dr Ste 400
Shelton CT 06484
203 944-5500

(G-12762)
ESSENTIALS
150a W Granada Blvd (32174-6304)
PHONE.................................386 677-7444
Donna Bushara, *Owner*
EMP: 7 EST: 2006
SALES (est): 206.7K Privately Held
SIC: 3571 5045 Electronic computers;
computers, peripherals & software

(G-12763)
FAB DEFENSE INC
873 Hull Rd Unit 5 (32174-0738)
PHONE.................................386 263-3054
Ido Solomon, *President*
EMP: 7 EST: 2018
SALES (est): 573.7K Privately Held
WEB: www.fab-defenseus.com
SIC: 3812 Defense systems & equipment

(G-12764)
FABROX LLC
Also Called: Fitusa Manufacturing
2 Sunshine Blvd (32174-8754)
PHONE.................................904 342-4048
Troy Olson,
EMP: 48 EST: 2016
SALES (est): 2.5MM Privately Held
SIC: 2329 2326 Men's & boys' sportswear
& athletic clothing; men's & boys' athletic
uniforms; medical & hospital uniforms,
men's

(G-12765)
FLORIDA PRODUCTION ENGRG INC (HQ)
Also Called: Automotive Mfg & Indus PDT
2 E Tower Cir (32174-8759)
PHONE.................................386 677-2566
Larry Jutte, *President*
Brad Gotts, *Principal*
Derrick Redding, *COO*
Vinc E Ellerbrock, *Vice Pres*
Joe Hasson, *Opers Mgr*
▲ EMP: 250 EST: 1987
SQ FT: 110,000
SALES (est): 122.7MM
SALES (corp-wide): 338.9MM Privately
Held
WEB: www.fpe-inc.com
SIC: 3465 3089 Moldings or trim, automo-
bile: stamped metal; injection molded fin-
ished plastic products; injection molding
of plastics; automotive parts, plastic

PA: Ernie Green Industries, Inc.
1785 Big Hill Rd
Dayton OH 45439
614 219-1423

(G-12766)
GERMFREE LABORATORIES INC
4 Sunshine Blvd (32174-8754)
PHONE.................................386 265-4300
Keith Landy, *CEO*
Kevin Kyle, *President*
Jeff Serle, *Senior VP*
Brennen Kozlowski, *Vice Pres*
Andrew D 'anna, *Buyer*
◆ EMP: 185 EST: 1962
SQ FT: 170,000
SALES (est): 36MM Privately Held
WEB: www.germfree.com
SIC: 3821 Laboratory equipment: fume
hoods, distillation racks, etc.

(G-12767)
GRUB COMPANY
6 Fernwood Trl (32174-4955)
PHONE.................................347 464-9770
Motty Hershkowitz, *CEO*
Shmuel Albukerk, *Director*
Chaya Hershkowit, *Director*
Yehuda Lewis, *Director*
EMP: 12 EST: 2018
SALES (est): 45K Privately Held
SIC: 2013 Snack sticks, including jerky:
from purchased meat

(G-12768)
HAROLD BRLEY FOR ORMOND BCH CY
902 Village Dr (32174-6142)
PHONE.................................386 853-9000
Harold Briley, *Principal*
EMP: 7 EST: 2017
SALES (est): 124K Privately Held
WEB: www.ormondbeachobserver.com
SIC: 2711 Newspapers, publishing & print-
ing

(G-12769)
HES PRODUCTS INC
Also Called: Research II
87 Old Wiggins Ln (32174-2616)
PHONE.................................407 834-0741
Ronald E Sarzier, *President*
Ann T Sarzier, *Corp Secy*
EMP: 6 EST: 1976
SALES (est): 507.2K Privately Held
SIC: 2759 7389 2396 2395 Screen print-
ing; embroidering of advertising on shirts,
etc.; automotive & apparel trimmings;
pleating & stitching

(G-12770)
HOT ACTION SPORTSWEAR INC
307 Division Ave (32174-6249)
PHONE.................................386 677-5680
Melissa Penland, *President*
Robert Pomerenke, *Vice Pres*
Kim Jarvis, *Production*
Cheryl Mannocchi, *Buyer*
Irene Lipsey, *Treasurer*
EMP: 45 EST: 1990
SQ FT: 13,500
SALES (est): 7.3MM Privately Held
WEB: www.hotactionsportswear.com
SIC: 2759 Screen printing

(G-12771)
HUDSON TOOL & DIE COMPANY INC
Also Called: Hudson Technologies
1327 N Us Highway 1 (32174-2900)
PHONE.................................386 672-2000
Bret Schmitz, *President*
Mark Andrews, *President*
EMP: 220 EST: 1940
SALES (est): 34.3MM
SALES (corp-wide): 1B Privately Held
WEB: www.hudson-technologies.com
SIC: 3469 Stamping metal for the trade
PA: Jsj Corporation
700 Robbins Rd
Grand Haven MI 49417
616 842-6350

(G-12772)
IMPERIAL FOAM & INSUL MFG CO
2360 Old Tomoka Rd W (32174-2529)
PHONE.................................386 673-4177
Robert W Ahrens, *President*
Harry Merryday, *President*
Aileen Ahrens, *Vice Pres*
▲ EMP: 55 EST: 1973
SQ FT: 45,000
SALES (est): 7.3MM Privately Held
SIC: 3086 Insulation or cushioning mate-
rial, foamed plastic

(G-12773)
INFORMATION MGT SVCS INC
Also Called: I M S
107 Sundance Trl (32176-5743)
P.O. Box 1918 (32175-1918)
PHONE.................................386 677-5073
C William Phillips, *President*
EMP: 11 EST: 1979
SALES (est): 1MM Privately Held
WEB: www.imsutility.com
SIC: 7372 5734 Business oriented com-
puter software; computer & software
stores

(G-12774)
ITA INC
9 W Tower Cir Ste C (32174-0740)
PHONE.................................386 301-5172
Adam Potter, *Principal*
EMP: 15 EST: 2013
SALES (est): 929.5K Privately Held
SIC: 2431 Window shutters, wood

(G-12775)
KITCHEN COUNTER CONNECTIONS
123 N Orchard St Ste 3e (32174-9513)
PHONE.................................386 677-9471
John Pehr, *Partner*
Cong MAI, *Partner*
EMP: 17 EST: 1991
SALES (est): 4.7MM Privately Held
SIC: 2542 2541 Counters or counter dis-
play cases: except wood; wood partitions
& fixtures

(G-12776)
KOPY KATS CLUB ORMOND BCH INC
74 Bridgewater Ln (32174-9266)
PHONE.................................386 437-3281
EMP: 7 EST: 2010
SALES (est): 140K Privately Held
WEB: www.ormondbeach.org
SIC: 2752 Lithographic Commercial Print-
ing

(G-12777)
LUCAS CONSTRUCTION INC
5 Echo Woods Way (32174-6754)
P.O. Box 730908 (32173-0908)
PHONE.................................386 623-0088
Doug Lucas, *President*
Janet Lucas, *Corp Secy*
EMP: 5 EST: 1978
SALES (est): 536.8K Privately Held
WEB: www.lucascg.com
SIC: 1389 1531 Construction, repair & dis-
mantling services; speculative builder,
single-family houses

(G-12778)
MAJOR PRODUCTS COMPANY
841 Buena Vista Ave (32174-7616)
PHONE.................................386 673-8381
EMP: 25
SALES (corp-wide): 25.7MM Privately
Held
WEB: www.majorproducts.com
SIC: 2034 Soup mixes
PA: Major Products Co. Inc.
66 Industrial Ave
Little Ferry NJ 07643
201 641-5555

(G-12779)
MAYHEW/BESTWAY LLC
2a Sunshine Blvd (32174-8754)
PHONE.................................631 586-4702
John Lawless,
EMP: 24 EST: 2019

SALES (est): 1.3MM **Privately Held**
SIC: 3423 Mechanics' hand tools

(G-12780)
MICROFLEX INC
Also Called: Microflex Automotive
1810 N Us Highway 1 (32174-2578)
P.O. Box 730068 (32173-0068)
PHONE..........................386 672-1945
John Atanasoski, *General Mgr*
Matt Russell, *Materials Mgr*
Graydon Parsons, *Opers Staff*
James Lalanne, *Buyer*
Jim Darling, *Sales Staff*
EMP: 22
SALES (corp-wide): 23.4MM **Privately Held**
WEB: www.microflexinc.com
SIC: 3599 3494 Hose, flexible metallic; expansion joints pipe
PA: Microflex, Inc.
1800 N Us Highway 1
Ormond Beach FL 32174
386 677-8100

(G-12781)
MOSSBERG GROUP INC
14 Broadriver Rd (32174-8743)
PHONE..........................386 274-5882
Johnathan Mossberg, *President*
EMP: 12 **EST:** 2000
SQ FT: 33,000
SALES (est): 770.8K **Privately Held**
WEB: www.iguntechnology.com
SIC: 3484 Small arms

(G-12782)
OFFICIAL GEAR COMPANY INC
106 Deer Run Lake Dr (32174-8142)
PHONE..........................407 721-9110
Brian Holt, *President*
EMP: 5 **EST:** 2005
SQ FT: 3,000
SALES (est): 392.4K **Privately Held**
WEB: www.officialgearpromotions.com
SIC: 2211 5136 5699 Apparel & outerwear fabrics, cotton; men's & boys' clothing; uniforms & work clothing

(G-12783)
ORMOND BEACH CLINICAL RES LLC
1400 Hand Ave Ste L (32174-8196)
PHONE..........................386 310-7462
Nicole Morris, *President*
EMP: 10 **EST:** 2016
SALES (est): 544.3K **Privately Held**
WEB: www.ormondbeachobserver.com
SIC: 3821 Clinical laboratory instruments, except medical & dental

(G-12784)
ORMOND BEACH OBSERVER
310 Wilmette Ave Ste 3 (32174-5276)
P.O. Box 353850, Palm Coast (32135-3850)
PHONE..........................386 492-2784
Richard Dichiera, *Principal*
Simmons Jonathan, *Manager*
EMP: 8 **EST:** 2016
SALES (est): 136.4K **Privately Held**
WEB: www.ormondbeachobserver.com
SIC: 2711 Newspapers, publishing & printing

(G-12785)
PLAYTEX MANUFACTURING INC
1190 N Us Highway 1 (32174-2997)
PHONE..........................386 677-9559
Karen Jesse, *Vice Pres*
Jack Surrette, *Vice Pres*
Dennis Lott, *VP Engrg*
Stephanie Mellenberndt, *Marketing Staff*
Mischelle Romesberg, *Branch Mgr*
EMP: 29
SALES (corp-wide): 2B **Publicly Held**
SIC: 2676 Sanitary paper products
HQ: Playtex Manufacturing, Inc.
50 N Dupont Hwy
Dover DE 19901
302 678-6000

(G-12786)
POWELL STEEL LLC
603 S Center St (32174-7310)
PHONE..........................386 406-1017
Heidi Powell, *Manager*
EMP: 9 **EST:** 2019
SALES (est): 2.4MM **Privately Held**
SIC: 3441 Fabricated structural metal

(G-12787)
POWER PLUS INC
550 Parque Dr (32174-7703)
PHONE..........................386 672-7579
David Tanges, *President*
Anita Tanges, *Manager*
EMP: 8 **EST:** 1994
SQ FT: 6,200
SALES (est): 1MM **Privately Held**
WEB: www.power-plus.net
SIC: 3824 Mechanical & electromechanical counters & devices

(G-12788)
PRIME GLOBAL GROUP INC
3 E Tower Cir (32174-8760)
P.O. Box 730957 (32173-0957)
PHONE..........................386 676-2200
Stephen Honczarenko, *CEO*
Maryann Honczarenko, *President*
Stephen J Honczarenko, *Vice Pres*
Stephen Mandarano, *Production*
Jose Colon, *Engineer*
EMP: 23 **EST:** 2015
SALES (est): 2.4MM **Privately Held**
SIC: 3552 3549 Winders, textile machinery; coiling machinery

(G-12789)
PROFESSIONAL HOLIDAY LIGHTING
Also Called: Phl Pool Services
181 Royal Dunes Cir (32176-4744)
PHONE..........................208 709-2968
Scott A Brown, *Principal*
EMP: 7 **EST:** 2010
SALES (est): 180.2K **Privately Held**
WEB: www.proholidaylighting.com
SIC: 3648 Lighting equipment

(G-12790)
PROGRESSIVE MACHINE CO INC
3 E Tower Cir (32174-8760)
PHONE..........................386 333-6850
Stephen Honczarenko, *Principal*
EMP: 15 **EST:** 2019
SALES (est): 1.2MM **Privately Held**
WEB: www.progressivewinders.com
SIC: 3552 Winders, textile machinery

(G-12791)
REZOLIN LLC
131 Business Center Dr A7 (32174-6624)
PHONE..........................386 677-8238
Carl Dellinger,
Dave Morton,
Jeff Scherer,
EMP: 8 **EST:** 2002
SQ FT: 7,000
SALES (est): 773.6K **Privately Held**
WEB: www.rezolin.com
SIC: 2851 Putty

(G-12792)
SKYO INDUSTRIES INC
2 Sunshine Blvd (32174-8754)
PHONE..........................631 586-4702
Warren Anderson, *President*
Wayne Anderson, *President*
Arleen Anderson Cassutti, *Admin Sec*
◆ **EMP:** 40 **EST:** 1961
SQ FT: 26,000
SALES (est): 3.8MM **Privately Held**
SIC: 3423 3714 Hand & edge tools; motor vehicle parts & accessories

(G-12793)
SOLAR X
Also Called: Solar-X of Daytona
630 S Yonge St Us1 (32174-7654)
PHONE..........................386 673-2111
Howard Smith, *President*
EMP: 2 **EST:** 1973
SQ FT: 2,070

SALES (est): 12MM **Privately Held**
WEB: www.solarxglasstinting.com
SIC: 3081 5211 1799 Unsupported plastics film & sheet; door & window products; glass tinting, architectural or automotive

(G-12794)
SOUTHERN PLASTICS & RUBBER CO
565 Parque Dr (32174-7529)
PHONE..........................386 672-1167
Frank Noce Jr, *President*
Sandra Noce, *Admin Sec*
EMP: 21 **EST:** 1958
SQ FT: 14,000
SALES (est): 3MM **Privately Held**
WEB: www.southernplasticandrubber.com
SIC: 3061 2821 Mechanical rubber goods; molding compounds, plastics

(G-12795)
STANDARD TECHNOLOGY INC
1230 N Us Highway 1 # 18 (32174-6637)
PHONE..........................386 671-7406
Anthony J Bilello, *President*
Lisa Beasor, *Admin Mgr*
EMP: 15 **EST:** 2005
SALES (est): 1MM **Privately Held**
WEB: www.standardtechinc.com
SIC: 3699 3677 3625 Automotive driving simulators (training aids); electronic; electronic coils, transformers & other inductors; solenoid switches (industrial controls)

(G-12796)
SUN KRAFTS OF VOLUSIA COUNTY
217 Royal Dunes Cir (32176-4746)
PHONE..........................386 441-1961
Bob Marcinko, *President*
Hariklia Marcinko, *Vice Pres*
Paula L Estridge, *Manager*
EMP: 6 **EST:** 1979
SQ FT: 9,000
SALES (est): 467.5K **Privately Held**
SIC: 3999 5199 Novelties: bone, beaded or shell; seashells

(G-12797)
TANNING RESEARCH LABS LLC (HQ)
1190 N Us Highway 1 (32174-2997)
PHONE..........................386 677-9559
Amy Williams, *Controller*
EMP: 22 **EST:** 2009
SALES (est): 42.9MM
SALES (corp-wide): 2B **Publicly Held**
SIC: 2844 Cosmetic preparations
PA: Edgewell Personal Care Company
6 Research Dr Ste 400
Shelton CT 06484
203 944-5500

(G-12798)
VANGUARDISTAS LLC
564 S Yonge St (32174-7540)
PHONE..........................386 868-2919
Mark Pratt, *Principal*
EMP: 7 **EST:** 2007
SALES (est): 275.1K **Privately Held**
WEB: www.vanguardistas.net
SIC: 7372 Prepackaged software

(G-12799)
WILTCHER INDUSTRIES INC
1034 Sudbury Ln (32174-2207)
PHONE..........................704 907-9838
EMP: 5 **EST:** 2019
SALES (est): 403.2K **Privately Held**
WEB: www.wiltcherindustries.com
SIC: 3999 Manufacturing industries

(G-12800)
WR KERSHAW INC
12 Aviator Way (32174-2983)
PHONE..........................386 673-0602
Richard Kershaw, *President*
Richard D Kershaw, *President*
EMP: 7 **EST:** 1982
SQ FT: 4,500
SALES (est): 732K **Privately Held**
WEB: www.kershawinc.com
SIC: 3089 3085 Injection molding of plastics; plastics bottles

Osprey
Sarasota County

(G-12801)
CHICKASHA MANUFACTURING CO INC
277 Saratoga Ct (34229-9386)
PHONE..........................405 224-0229
Larry Lewis, *President*
Glenn McNatt, *Vice Pres*
Jennifer Jones, *QC Mgr*
Linda Freeman, *Info Tech Mgr*
EMP: 36 **EST:** 1946
SALES (est): 2.4MM **Privately Held**
WEB: www.chickashamfg.com
SIC: 3599 Machine shop, jobbing & repair

(G-12802)
MEDICA360 LLC ✪
1109 Millpond Ct (34229-8863)
PHONE..........................941 500-2890
Edward Lin, *Principal*
EMP: 8 **EST:** 2021
SALES (est): 293.5K **Privately Held**
SIC: 3841 Surgical & medical instruments

Oviedo
Seminole County

(G-12803)
AMERIBUILT STL STRUCTURES LLC
1016 Moccasin Run Rd (32765-5646)
P.O. Box 623001 (32762-3001)
PHONE..........................407 340-9401
James D Horgan,
Renee' M Horgan,
EMP: 8 **EST:** 2004
SALES (est): 599.2K **Privately Held**
WEB: www.ameribuiltsteel.com
SIC: 3441 Building components, structural steel

(G-12804)
ARCA PRO RETRACTABLES LLC
366 Loyd Ln (32765-6774)
PHONE..........................407 844-5013
Joseph M Arcamone, *Manager*
EMP: 6 **EST:** 2015
SALES (est): 429.9K **Privately Held**
WEB: www.proretractable.com
SIC: 3069 Fabricated rubber products

(G-12805)
ART EDIBLES INC
428 Wilmington Cir (32765-6186)
PHONE..........................407 603-4043
Paul B Joachim, *President*
EMP: 7 **EST:** 2013
SALES (est): 39.5K **Privately Held**
SIC: 2066 Chocolate

(G-12806)
ASIAN FOOD SOLUTIONS INC
5600 Elmhurst Cir (32765-4100)
PHONE..........................888 499-6888
Lincoln Yee, *President*
Allan Lam, *CFO*
EMP: 22 **EST:** 2008
SQ FT: 1,500
SALES (est): 4.8MM **Privately Held**
WEB: www.internationalfoodsolutions.com
SIC: 2015 2038 Poultry, processed: frozen; ethnic foods, frozen
PA: International Food Solutions, Inc.
5600 Elmhurst Cir
Oviedo FL 32765

(G-12807)
ATTICUS SCREEN PRINTING T
159 N Central Ave Ste I (32765-6334)
PHONE..........................407 365-9911
Donna Rohr, *Manager*
EMP: 6 **EST:** 2005
SALES (est): 476.1K **Privately Held**
WEB: www.atticusprinting.com
SIC: 2759 2395 Screen printing; emblems, embroidered

(G-12808)
AZURE COMPUTING INC
Also Called: Elite Simulation Solutions
5700 Dot Com Ct Ste 1010 (32765-3400)
PHONE..........................407 359-8787
John Dixion, *President*
EMP: 7 **EST:** 1995
SQ FT: 5,000
SALES (est): 2MM **Privately Held**
SIC: 7372 Publishers' computer software

(G-12809)
B & B INDUSTRIES ORLANDO INC
3008 Kananwood Ct Ste 124 (32765-2200)
PHONE..........................407 366-1800
William S Clark, *President*
Michael A Clark, *Corp Secy*
EMP: 9 **EST:** 1980
SQ FT: 15,000
SALES (est): 778.1K **Privately Held**
SIC: 2339 2329 Women's & misses' athletic clothing & sportswear; men's & boys' sportswear & athletic clothing

(G-12810)
BEST QUALITY WATER SYS OF FLA (PA)
2200 Winter Springs Blvd # 106 (32765-9358)
PHONE..........................407 971-2537
Mark Smith, *President*
Monica Smith, *Vice Pres*
Delta Tooney, *Treasurer*
EMP: 33 **EST:** 1985
SALES (est): 5.3MM **Privately Held**
SIC: 3221 Water bottles, glass

(G-12811)
BOT INTERNATIONAL INC
1320 Tall Maple Loop (32765-7785)
PHONE..........................407 366-6547
Mark P Perry, *President*
EMP: 9 **EST:** 1999
SALES (est): 840.9K **Privately Held**
WEB: www.botinternational.com
SIC: 2741 Technical manual & paper publishing

(G-12812)
CENTRAL FLA ATTRNSFSONISTS INC
1005 Hart Branch Dr (32765-6024)
PHONE..........................321 299-6019
James M Frank, *Vice Pres*
EMP: 7 **EST:** 2008
SALES (est): 192.8K **Privately Held**
SIC: 3841 Surgical & medical instruments

(G-12813)
CLONTS GROVES INC
285 Howard Ave (32765-6840)
PHONE..........................407 359-4103
W Rex Clonts Jr, *President*
EMP: 10 **EST:** 2001
SALES (est): 660.7K **Privately Held**
SIC: 2037 Frozen fruits & vegetables

(G-12814)
COMIDA VIDA INC
5600 Elmhurst Cir (32765-4100)
PHONE..........................855 720-7663
Lincoln Yee, *President*
EMP: 5 **EST:** 2016
SALES (est): 346K **Privately Held**
SIC: 2038 Ethnic foods, frozen

(G-12815)
CONTINUITY UNLIMITED INC
1750 W Broadway St # 112 (32765-9618)
PHONE..........................561 358-8171
David Bateman, *President*
Bob Becker, *Vice Pres*
James Walker, *VP Sales*
EMP: 15 **EST:** 1986
SQ FT: 5,000
SALES (est): 1.4MM **Privately Held**
SIC: 3679 3672 Electronic circuits; printed circuit boards

(G-12816)
COPY VAN OF FLORIDA INC
Also Called: Copy Van Printing
2224 Andrew Ln (32765-9494)
PHONE..........................407 366-7126
Carol Goad, *President*
EMP: 5 **EST:** 1967
SQ FT: 2,500
SALES (est): 346.4K **Privately Held**
WEB: www.copyvanofflorida.com
SIC: 2752 8721 Commercial printing, offset; accounting services, except auditing

(G-12817)
DAN BOUDREAU INC
3325 Red Ash Cir (32766-8105)
PHONE..........................407 491-7611
Dan Boudreau, *Principal*
EMP: 7 **EST:** 2008
SALES (est): 72.2K **Privately Held**
SIC: 2439 Trusses, wooden roof

(G-12818)
DYNAMIC MATERIAL SYSTEMS LLC
269 Aulin Ave Ste 1003 (32765-4806)
PHONE..........................407 353-6885
William Easter, *CEO*
Arnold Hill, *Principal*
EMP: 6 **EST:** 2013
SALES (est): 416.5K **Privately Held**
SIC: 2821 Plastics materials & resins

(G-12819)
ENGINEERICA SYSTEMS INC
7250 Red Bug Lake Rd # 1036 (32765-9290)
PHONE..........................407 542-4982
Maan Nassereddeen, *Principal*
Jenelle Conner, *Office Mgr*
Laura Alvarez, *Manager*
Krissi Clapper, *Admin Asst*
EMP: 18 **EST:** 1994
SALES (est): 2MM **Privately Held**
WEB: www.engineerica.com
SIC: 7372 7371 Prepackaged software; custom computer programming services

(G-12820)
EXCESS LIQUIDATOR LLC
Also Called: Shop Munki
3012 Kananwood Ct Ste 132 (32765-2204)
PHONE..........................407 247-9105
Paul SMR Bergeron, *Mng Member*
Paul Bergeron, *Mng Member*
Yvette Bergeron,
EMP: 7 **EST:** 2014
SALES (est): 552.2K **Privately Held**
WEB: www.shopmunki.com
SIC: 2339 5621 2329 Women's & misses' athletic clothing & sportswear; women's clothing stores; athletic (warmup, sweat & jogging) suits: men's & boys'

(G-12821)
FASTSIGNS
2200 Winter Springs Blvd # 118 (32765-9358)
PHONE..........................407 542-1234
Liz Allen, *Principal*
EMP: 7 **EST:** 2017
SALES (est): 46K **Privately Held**
WEB: www.fastsigns.com
SIC: 3993 Signs & advertising specialties

(G-12822)
FSF MANUFACTURING INC
575 Econ River Pl (32765-7343)
PHONE..........................407 971-8280
Jacqueline M Amrhein, *President*
James A Amrhein, *Vice Pres*
James Amrhein, *Vice Pres*
Jim Amrhein Jt, *Vice Pres*
Nick Shepherd, *Project Mgr*
▼ **EMP:** 112 **EST:** 1984
SQ FT: 53,000
SALES (est): 20.1MM **Privately Held**
WEB: www.fsfmfg.com
SIC: 3441 Fabricated structural metal

(G-12823)
GENENSYS LLC
7269 Winding Lake Cir (32765-5664)
PHONE..........................407 701-4158
Murthy Bondada, *Vice Pres*
Francis Cabrera, *Project Mgr*
Farhan Shamsi, *Manager*
Julee Clark, *Manager*
Naveen Dua, *Manager*
EMP: 7 **EST:** 2012

SALES (est): 244K **Privately Held**
WEB: www.genensys.com
SIC: 7372 Business oriented computer software

(G-12824)
HAYMAN SAFE CO INC
1291 N County Road 426 (32765-7102)
PHONE..........................407 365-5434
William Hayman, *CEO*
Gary Hayman, *President*
Carolyn Hayman, *Corp Secy*
Dick Divittorio, *Vice Pres*
◆ **EMP:** 15 **EST:** 1970
SQ FT: 7,500
SALES (est): 2.1MM **Privately Held**
WEB: www.haymansafe.com
SIC: 3499 Safes & vaults, metal

(G-12825)
HOLESHOT RACEWAY INC
434 Terrace Dr (32765-7741)
PHONE..........................407 864-1095
Kristopher B James, *Principal*
EMP: 9 **EST:** 2012
SALES (est): 242.4K **Privately Held**
WEB: www.hsraceway.com
SIC: 3644 Raceways

(G-12826)
HOPSCOTCH TECHNOLOGY GROUP INC ✪
1288 Sanctuary Dr (32766-6604)
PHONE..........................305 846-0942
Oliver Von Trapp, *CEO*
EMP: 10 **EST:** 2021
SALES (est): 474.4K **Privately Held**
SIC: 7372 Educational computer software

(G-12827)
I-CON SYSTEMS INC
3100 Camp Rd (32765-7532)
PHONE..........................407 365-6241
Shawn Bush, *President*
Ray Elliott, *Vice Pres*
Heather Booth, *Accountant*
Dane Bouchie, *Software Engr*
Colton Kelly, *IT/INT Sup*
▲ **EMP:** 56 **EST:** 1994
SQ FT: 55,000
SALES (est): 17.4MM
SALES (corp-wide): 47.7MM **Privately Held**
WEB: www.i-con.com
SIC: 3679 8711 Electronic circuits; professional engineer
PA: I-Con Systems Holdings, Llc
3100 Camp Rd
Oviedo FL 32765
407 365-6241

(G-12828)
INFORMULATE LLC
7437 Winding Lake Cir (32765-5666)
PHONE..........................866 222-2307
Annie Menon, *Managing Prtnr*
Madelina Figueroa, *Marketing Staff*
EMP: 9 **EST:** 2010
SALES (est): 926.9K **Privately Held**
WEB: www.informulate.com
SIC: 7372 7371 Application computer software; computer software systems analysis & design, custom

(G-12829)
INTERNATIONAL FD SOLUTIONS INC (PA)
Also Called: Asian Food Solutions
5600 Elmhurst Cir (32765-4100)
PHONE..........................888 499-6888
Allan Lam, *President*
Lincoln Yee, *President*
Gary Vix, *Controller*
Jeff Millard, *Regl Sales Mgr*
John Eberts, *Sales Staff*
EMP: 21 **EST:** 2008
SQ FT: 1,500
SALES (est): 7.1MM **Privately Held**
WEB: www.internationalfoodsolutions.com
SIC: 2015 2038 Poultry, processed: frozen; ethnic foods, frozen

(G-12830)
JAPAN FABRICARE INC
Also Called: Motherkin Cleaners
9 Alafaya Woods Blvd (32765-6232)
PHONE..........................407 366-9986
Ung J Park, *President*
Ung Park, *Owner*
EMP: 8 **EST:** 2002
SALES (est): 142.8K **Privately Held**
SIC: 3633 Drycleaning machines, household: including coin-operated

(G-12831)
K C SCREEN
1705 Evans St (32765-9371)
PHONE..........................407 977-9636
Carl Anderson, *President*
Kimberly M Anderson, *Vice Pres*
EMP: 5 **EST:** 2003
SQ FT: 1,300
SALES (est): 674.7K **Privately Held**
WEB: www.kcscreen.com
SIC: 3448 1521 Screen enclosures; patio & deck construction & repair

(G-12832)
KALITEC DIRECT LLC
Also Called: Kalitec Medical
865 Oviedo Blvd Ste 1017 (32765-3523)
PHONE..........................407 545-2063
Scott J Winn, *Manager*
EMP: 9 **EST:** 2011
SALES (est): 347.2K **Privately Held**
WEB: www.kalitecmed.com
SIC: 3841 Surgical & medical instruments

(G-12833)
KAMEL SOFTWARE INC
1809 E Broadway St # 134 (32765-8597)
PHONE..........................407 672-0202
Keith Linn, *President*
Michael Linn, *Vice Pres*
Patti Linn, *Vice Pres*
EMP: 8 **EST:** 1988
SQ FT: 3,000
SALES (est): 952.8K **Privately Held**
WEB: www.kamelsoftware.com
SIC: 7372 7371 Prepackaged software; custom computer programming services

(G-12834)
KELSIES BLINDS
Also Called: KELSIES BLINDS
2464 W State Rd Ste 1028 (32765)
PHONE..........................407 977-0827
David Wright, *President*
Nicole Compton, *Admin Sec*
▼ **EMP:** 9 **EST:** 1994
SALES (est): 2.1MM **Privately Held**
WEB: www.orlandoblinds.com
SIC: 2591 5719 Window blinds; window shades

(G-12835)
LASERPATH TECHNOLOGIES LLC
2789 Wrights Rd Ste 1021 (32765-8528)
PHONE..........................407 247-3930
Robert J Hopkins,
▼ **EMP:** 5 **EST:** 2001
SQ FT: 3,000
SALES (est): 737.7K **Privately Held**
SIC: 3699 Laser systems & equipment

(G-12836)
LEVIL TECHNOLOGY CORP
1704 Kennedy Pt Ste 1124 (32765-5188)
PHONE..........................407 542-3971
Carmen C Diaz, *President*
Ruben D Leon, *Principal*
Larry Rivera, *Marketing Staff*
EMP: 8 **EST:** 2009
SQ FT: 3,500
SALES (est): 2.4MM **Privately Held**
WEB: www.levil.com
SIC: 3552 3541 Spindles, textile; drilling machine tools (metal cutting)

(G-12837)
LIFETIME SHUTTERS INC
3005 Juneberry Ter (32766-6632)
PHONE..........................407 402-3365
Michelle M Pasciak, *President*
EMP: 7 **EST:** 2017

SALES (est): 90K **Privately Held**
WEB: www.lifetimeshuttersinc.com
SIC: 3442 Shutters, door or window: metal

(G-12838)
NGF DISTRIBUTORS INC
3035 Turkey Ave (32765-7925)
P.O. Box 622062 (32762-2062)
PHONE...........................407 816-7554
Josue Moncata, *President*
EMP: 10 EST: 2005
SALES (est): 1MM **Privately Held**
WEB: www.ngfdistributors.com
SIC: 3999 Framed artwork

(G-12839)
OBD GENIE LLC
Also Called: Obdgenie
500 Geneva Dr (32765-9117)
PHONE...........................321 250-3650
Tom Indrunas, *CEO*
EMP: 6 EST: 2016
SALES (est): 860.3K **Privately Held**
WEB: www.obdgenie.com
SIC: 7372 5511 Prepackaged software;
  new & used car dealers

(G-12840)
OPTIGRATE CORPORATION
562 S Econ Cir (32765-4303)
PHONE...........................407 542-7704
Alexei Glebov, *President*
Brian Domian, *Managing Dir*
Vadim Smirnov, *Vice Pres*
Joshua Beharry, *Engineer*
Valeri Koulechov, *Engineer*
EMP: 34 EST: 1999
SALES (est): 8.4MM
SALES (corp-wide): 1.4B **Publicly Held**
WEB: www.optigrate.com
SIC: 3827 Optical elements & assemblies,
  except ophthalmic
PA: Ipg Photonics Corporation
  50 Old Webster Rd
  Oxford MA 01540
  508 373-1100

(G-12841)
ORLANDO BRANDING AGENCY LLC
Also Called: Real Producers
1035 Covington St (32765-7037)
PHONE...........................407 692-8868
Aaron Ludin,
EMP: 10 EST: 2013
SALES (est): 552.1K **Privately Held**
WEB: www.orlandobranding.com
SIC: 2741 Miscellaneous publishing

(G-12842)
PALM TREE COMPUTER SYSTEMS INC (PA)
19 E Broadway St (32765-7529)
PHONE...........................407 359-3356
Paul Rosarius, *Vice Pres*
EMP: 7 EST: 1996
SQ FT: 4,200
SALES (est): 1.5MM **Privately Held**
WEB: www.palmtreetechcenter.com
SIC: 3571 5045 Electronic computers;
  computers, peripherals & software

(G-12843)
PET DOC FL LLC
1630 Sand Key Cir (32765-6968)
PHONE...........................407 437-6614
Margaret A Martinez, *Principal*
EMP: 5 EST: 2009
SALES (est): 811.4K **Privately Held**
WEB: www.petvetcarefl.com
SIC: 2836 Vaccines

(G-12844)
PREMIER CABINETS LLC
3036 Kananwood Ct # 1024 (32765-8830)
PHONE...........................407 760-9060
David Arocho, *Administration*
EMP: 7 EST: 2018
SALES (est): 403.1K **Privately Held**
WEB: www.premiercabinets.net
SIC: 2434 Wood kitchen cabinets

(G-12845)
R & A INDUSTRIES INC
306 Aulin Ave (32765-9314)
PHONE...........................352 307-6655
EMP: 9 EST: 2013
SALES (est): 1.1MM **Privately Held**
WEB: www.randaindustries.com
SIC: 3999 Manufacturing industries

(G-12846)
RANDAL R YOUNG
Also Called: Scratchoffstore
876 Geneva Dr (32765-9605)
PHONE...........................800 584-9937
EMP: 7 EST: 2011
SALES (est): 80.1K **Privately Held**
SIC: 2621 Paper mills

(G-12847)
SEMPLASTICS
269 Aulin Ave Ste 1003 (32765-4806)
PHONE...........................407 353-6885
Wiliam Easter, *Principal*
Arnold Hill, *CTO*
Sue Easter, *Director*
EMP: 11 EST: 2012
SALES (est): 2.5MM **Privately Held**
WEB: www.semplastics.com
SIC: 3089 Plastics products

(G-12848)
STRUCTURAL CNSTR ORLANDO INC
2200 Winter Springs Blvd (32765-9358)
PHONE...........................407 383-9719
James Courtney, *President*
EMP: 30 EST: 2001
SQ FT: 1,800
SALES (est): 3.6MM **Privately Held**
SIC: 3272 Concrete products

(G-12849)
T&T SONS INC
1999 N County Road 426 (32765-8150)
PHONE...........................859 576-3316
Maryanne F Taylor, *Principal*
EMP: 7 EST: 2017
SALES (est): 129.2K **Privately Held**
SIC: 3312 Blast furnaces & steel mills

(G-12850)
TACTICAL PHASER CORP
2993 Moore Dr (32765-7632)
PHONE...........................321 262-4140
Lucian Randolph, *CEO*
EMP: 5 EST: 2015
SALES (est): 331.4K **Privately Held**
SIC: 3571 Electronic computers

(G-12851)
TAYLOR MADE SYSTEMS BRDNTON IN (PA)
2750 Kansas St (32765-7726)
PHONE...........................941 747-1900
James W Taylor, *Ch of Bd*
Dennis Flint, *President*
John Martin, *General Mgr*
Tom Smethers, *QC Mgr*
Bradley Atchison, *Engineer*
▲ EMP: 114 EST: 1998
SQ FT: 120,000
SALES (est): 10.9MM **Privately Held**
WEB: www.tmsbradenton.com
SIC: 3429 8742 2394 3732 Manufac-
  tured hardware (general); management
  consulting services; canvas & related
  products; boat building & repairing

(G-12852)
XILINX INC
3518 Buckingham Ct (32765-5123)
PHONE...........................407 365-8644
EMP: 10
SALES (corp-wide): 3B **Publicly Held**
SIC: 3674 Mfg Semiconductors/Related
  Devices
PA: Xilinx, Inc.
  2100 All Programable
  San Jose CA 95124
  408 559-7778

Oxford
Sumter County

(G-12853)
AMERICAN CONTAINER CONC
5274 Bowline Ct (34484-3704)
PHONE...........................631 737-6300
Charles Blor, *President*
EMP: 8 EST: 2018
SALES (est): 122.2K **Privately Held**
SIC: 2653 Boxes, corrugated: made from
  purchased materials

(G-12854)
WHISPERING OAKS WINERY
10934 County Road 475 (34484-3126)
PHONE...........................352 748-0449
Brent Trela, *Principal*
EMP: 7 EST: 2014
SALES (est): 368.9K **Privately Held**
WEB: www.winesofflorida.com
SIC: 2084 Wines

(G-12855)
WOODWORK UNLIMITED INC
4075 County Road 106 (34484-3525)
PHONE...........................352 267-4051
Carlos Balsinde, *President*
Martha A Balsinde, *Manager*
EMP: 8 EST: 2010
SALES (est): 139.6K **Privately Held**
SIC: 2431 1771 1611 Millwork; concrete
  work; general contractor, highway & street
  construction

Ozona
Pinellas County

(G-12856)
DORADO MARINE INC
270 Hedden Ct (34660)
PHONE...........................727 786-3800
Bob Lickert, *President*
EMP: 9 EST: 1987
SQ FT: 22,000
SALES (est): 326.6K **Privately Held**
WEB: www.doradocustomboats.com
SIC: 3732 Boat building & repairing

Pace
Santa Rosa County

(G-12857)
ELEMENT OUTDOORS LLC
5412 Covered Bridge Ln (32571-6420)
PHONE...........................888 589-9589
Christopher Nallick, *Vice Pres*
Christopher R Nallick, *Manager*
EMP: 7 EST: 2015
SALES (est): 146.3K **Privately Held**
WEB: www.elementoutdoors.com
SIC: 2323 Men's & boys' neckwear

(G-12858)
HARDY LOGGING COMPANY INC
3901 Willard Norris Rd (32571-9463)
PHONE...........................850 994-1955
Theresa K Hardy, *Principal*
EMP: 9 EST: 2018
SALES (est): 556.1K **Privately Held**
SIC: 2411 Logging

(G-12859)
VOLAC INC
4132 Castle Gate Dr (32571-7347)
P.O. Box 593, Byron IL (61010-0593)
PHONE...........................800 759-7569
David Neville, *President*
Tomas O 'reilly, *Business Mgr*
Kate Oleszko, *Business Mgr*
Ken Stroud, *Business Mgr*
Laura St George, *Treasurer*
EMP: 5 EST: 1996
SALES (est): 1.2MM **Privately Held**
WEB: usa.ecosyl.com
SIC: 2879 Agricultural chemicals

Pahokee
Palm Beach County

(G-12860)
OSCEOLA FARMS CO
Us Highway 98 Hatton Hwy (33476)
P.O. Box 679 (33476-0679)
PHONE...........................561 924-7156
Carlos Rionda, *Manager*
EMP: 1545
SALES (corp-wide): 2.1B **Privately Held**
SIC: 2099 2062 Sugar grinding; cane
  sugar refining
HQ: Osceola Farms Co
  340 Royal Poinciana Way # 315
  Palm Beach FL 33480
  561 655-6303

Palatka
Putnam County

(G-12861)
4 C TIMBER INC
130 Odom Rd (32177-8212)
PHONE...........................386 937-0806
EMP: 8
SQ FT: 2,000
SALES (est): 1MM **Privately Held**
SIC: 2411 Logging & Pulpwood Contractor
  And Siteprep Work And Road Work

(G-12862)
A J GIAMMANCO & ASSOCIATES
Also Called: Lion Pool Products
115 Rachel Rd (32177-9598)
PHONE...........................386 328-1254
EMP: 19
SQ FT: 25,000
SALES (est): 2.5MM **Privately Held**
SIC: 3648 3991 Mfg Lighting Equipment
  Mfg Brooms/Brushes

(G-12863)
CARAUSTAR INDUS CNSMR PDTS GRO
Also Called: Palatka Tube Plant
188 Comfort Rd (32177-8636)
PHONE...........................386 328-8335
Stacy Robinson, *Opers-Prdtn-Mfg*
EMP: 70
SALES (corp-wide): 5.5B **Publicly Held**
SIC: 2655 Tubes, for chemical or electrical
  uses: paper or fiber; cones, fiber: made
  from purchased material
HQ: Caraustar Industrial And Consumer
  Products Group Inc
  5000 Austell Powder Ste
  Austell GA 30106
  803 548-5100

(G-12864)
CONTINENTAL PALATKA LLC
886 N Highway 17 (32177-8647)
PHONE...........................703 480-3800
Ike Preston, *President*
Dennis Romps, *CFO*
EMP: 100 EST: 2013
SALES (est): 11.1MM
SALES (corp-wide): 528MM **Privately Held**
SIC: 2493 3275 2891 Building board &
  wallboard, except gypsum; building
  board, gypsum; sealing compounds for
  pipe threads or joints
HQ: Certainteed Gypsum Products, Inc.
  12950 Worldgate Dr # 700
  Herndon VA 20170
  703 480-3800

(G-12865)
DAILY NEWS INC
Also Called: Palatka Daily News
1825 Saint Johns Ave (32177-4442)
P.O. Box 777 (32178-0777)
PHONE...........................386 312-5200
Wayne Anucales, *President*
Wayne Anucles, *President*
Michael Leonard, *Publisher*
Anthony Clarke, *Principal*
Rusty Starr, *Principal*
EMP: 1 EST: 1885

GEOGRAPHIC

SQ FT: 10,000
SALES (est): 5.2MM
SALES (corp-wide): 53.1MM **Privately Held**
WEB: www.palatkadailynews.com
SIC: 2711 Commercial printing & newspaper publishing combined; newspapers, publishing & printing
PA: Community Newspapers, Inc.
2365 Prince Ave A
Athens GA 30606
706 548-0010

(G-12866)
FLORIDA HYDRO POWER & LIGHT CO
171 Comfort Rd (32177-8637)
PHONE....................386 328-2470
Herbert L Williams, *President*
EMP: 7 EST: 1998
SALES (est): 724.1K **Privately Held**
SIC: 3511 Turbines & turbine generator sets

(G-12867)
FLORIDA NORTH EMULSIONS INC
701 N Moody Rd Ste 151 (32177-2343)
PHONE....................386 328-1733
Jeffrey King, *President*
EMP: 9 EST: 2003
SALES (est): 1.5MM **Privately Held**
WEB: www.northfloridaemulsions.com
SIC: 2951 Asphalt paving mixtures & blocks

(G-12868)
FORTERRA PRESSURE PIPE INC
245 Comfort Rd (32177-8634)
PHONE....................386 328-8841
Steven M Braxton, *Branch Mgr*
EMP: 192
SQ FT: 10,000
SALES (corp-wide): 42.1MM **Privately Held**
SIC: 3321 3272 Pressure pipe & fittings, cast iron; concrete products
PA: Forterra Pressure Pipe, Inc.
4416 Prairie Hill Rd
South Beloit IL 61080
815 389-4800

(G-12869)
GEORGIA-PACIFIC LLC
155 Country Ct (32177-8695)
P.O. Box 1458 (32178-1458)
PHONE....................386 328-8826
Nickolas Anders, *Engineer*
Marion House, *Manager*
Justin Collier, *Manager*
Caroline Parker, *Analyst*
Richard Price, *Analyst*
EMP: 96
SALES (corp-wide): 36.9B **Privately Held**
WEB: www.gp.com
SIC: 2621 Paper mills
HQ: Georgia-Pacific Llc
133 Peachtree St Nw
Atlanta GA 30303
404 652-4000

(G-12870)
GEORGIA-PACIFIC LLC
County Rd 216 E (32177)
P.O. Box 1040 (32178-1040)
PHONE....................386 328-8826
Gorman Edison, *Manager*
EMP: 25
SALES (corp-wide): 36.9B **Privately Held**
WEB: www.gp.com
SIC: 2621 Paper mills
HQ: Georgia-Pacific Llc
133 Peachtree St Nw
Atlanta GA 30303
404 652-4000

(G-12871)
H JONES TIMBER LLC
546 W Peniel Rd (32177-8941)
P.O. Box 2246 (32178-2246)
PHONE....................386 312-0603
EMP: 6
SALES (est): 826.5K **Privately Held**
SIC: 2411 Logging

(G-12872)
HOLBROOK METAL FABRICATION LLC
341 N Highway 17 (32177-8616)
PHONE....................386 937-5441
EMP: 12 EST: 2019
SALES (est): 1.1MM **Privately Held**
WEB: www.holbrookmetalfabrication.com
SIC: 3441 Fabricated structural metal

(G-12873)
LIFES A STITCH
2510 Crill Ave (32177-4272)
PHONE....................386 385-3079
Laurie Cannon, *Owner*
EMP: 7 EST: 2014
SALES (est): 104.5K **Privately Held**
SIC: 2395 Embroidery & art needlework

(G-12874)
LJ&J LATHING INC
402 N 16th St B6 (32177-3143)
P.O. Box 277, Bostwick (32007-0277)
PHONE....................386 325-5040
Sindy Hunt, *Principal*
EMP: 7 EST: 2009
SALES (est): 59.4K **Privately Held**
SIC: 3541 Lathes

(G-12875)
NEW BEST PACKERS INC
1122 Bronson St (32177-3362)
PHONE....................386 328-5127
Michael K Drew, *President*
EMP: 30 EST: 1966
SQ FT: 35,000
SALES (est): 2.2MM **Privately Held**
WEB: www.newbestpackers.com
SIC: 2013 Sausages from purchased meat; smoked meats from purchased meat; frankfurters from purchased meat; roast beef from purchased meat

(G-12876)
PALATKA WELDING SHOP INC
1301 Madison St (32177-3298)
PHONE....................386 328-1507
John W Buckles, *President*
Ginger Buckles De Loach, *Corp Secy*
Clifford Buckles Jr, *Vice Pres*
Ginger Buckles De Loac, *Treasurer*
EMP: 22 EST: 1948
SQ FT: 10,000
SALES (est): 2.1MM **Privately Held**
SIC: 7692 7538 7549 3441 Welding repair; general automotive repair shops; towing services; fabricated structural metal

(G-12877)
PORT PALM COLD STORAGE INC
1122 Bronson St (32177-3362)
PHONE....................386 328-5127
Michael Drew, *Manager*
EMP: 26
SALES (corp-wide): 2.3MM **Privately Held**
WEB: www.portofpalmcoldstorage.com
SIC: 2013 Sausages & other prepared meats
PA: Port Of Palm Cold Storage, Inc.
1800 Dr Mrtn Lther King J
Riviera Beach FL 33404
561 743-8001

(G-12878)
PRICE BROTHERS COMPANY
245 Comfort Rd (32177-8634)
P.O. Box 1770 (32178-1770)
PHONE....................386 328-8841
Steven M Braxton, *Executive*
EMP: 9 EST: 2010
SALES (est): 132.3K **Privately Held**
WEB: www.pricebrotherskc.com
SIC: 3498 Fabricated pipe & fittings

(G-12879)
PUTNAM PAPER & PACKAGING INC
109 Jax Ln (32177)
P.O. Box 2068 (32178-2068)
PHONE....................904 328-5101
John Robinson, *President*
Kay Hood, *Controller*

EMP: 10 EST: 1985
SQ FT: 15,000
SALES (est): 979.7K **Privately Held**
SIC: 2679 Paper products, converted

(G-12880)
SMITH PRODUCTS CO INC (PA)
Also Called: Smith Products Kitchens
1005 Kirby St (32177-5157)
P.O. Box 114 (32178-0114)
PHONE....................386 325-4534
Richard Loosemore, *President*
Steven Rodrigue, *Vice Pres*
EMP: 14 EST: 1951
SQ FT: 15,000
SALES (est): 2.6MM **Privately Held**
WEB: www.smith-products.com
SIC: 2511 Wood household furniture; vanities, bathroom: wood

(G-12881)
SMOKEY MOUNTAIN CABINETS INC
103 E Lake St (32177-9198)
PHONE....................386 325-1677
David Smith, *President*
EMP: 10 EST: 2004
SALES (est): 1MM **Privately Held**
WEB: www.smokeymountaincabinets.com
SIC: 2434 Wood kitchen cabinets

(G-12882)
SOFTEX PAPER INC (PA)
1400 Reid St (32177-3240)
PHONE....................386 328-8488
Paul Lucien Lieuw, *President*
Kari Smith, *Editor*
Robin Wilkinson, *Human Res Mgr*
Robb Burgie, *Manager*
Glenize Nazario, *Manager*
◆ EMP: 65 EST: 2001
SQ FT: 80,000
SALES (est): 16.2MM **Privately Held**
SIC: 2676 Towels, napkins & tissue paper products

(G-12883)
ST JOHNS SHIP BUILDING INC
560 Stokes Landing Rd (32177-8485)
PHONE....................386 328-6054
Jeffery Bukoski, *President*
Steve Ganoe, *General Mgr*
Glen Steiger, *Corp Secy*
Marcia Ganoe, *Prdtn Mgr*
Karen Revels, *Warehouse Mgr*
◆ EMP: 145 EST: 2006
SALES (est): 18MM **Privately Held**
WEB: www.stjohnsshipbuilding.com
SIC: 3731 Shipbuilding & repairing

(G-12884)
TK CABINETS
500 N Pine St (32177-2732)
PHONE....................386 325-6906
Hoyt Knowles, *CEO*
Glenn Thomas, *Vice Pres*
EMP: 7 EST: 2004
SALES (est): 792.6K **Privately Held**
WEB: www.tkcabinets.net
SIC: 2434 Wood kitchen cabinets

Palm Bay
Brevard County

(G-12885)
AAR AIRLIFT GROUP INC (HQ)
2301 Commerce Park Dr Ne # 11 (32905-2611)
PHONE....................321 837-2345
David P Storch, *CEO*
Randy Martinez, *President*
Timothy J Romenesko, *President*
Michael K Carr, *Vice Pres*
Peter K Chapman, *Vice Pres*
EMP: 37 EST: 1998
SALES (est): 35.6MM
SALES (corp-wide): 1.8B **Publicly Held**
SIC: 3728 Aircraft parts & equipment
PA: Aar Corp.
1100 N Wood Dale Rd
Wood Dale IL 60191
630 227-2000

(G-12886)
AIR BALANCE CORP
1789 Canova St Se Ste B (32909-4207)
PHONE....................305 401-8780
Bernard S Moltz, *Principal*
EMP: 7 EST: 2010
SALES (est): 94.5K **Privately Held**
WEB: www.airbalance.com
SIC: 3444 Sheet metalwork

(G-12887)
ART-KRAFT SIGN CO INC
2675 Kirby Cir Ne (32905-3403)
PHONE....................321 727-7324
Donald H Reilly, *President*
Steve Hart, *Vice Pres*
Katie Hart, *Finance*
Don Riley, *Human Res Mgr*
Eveline England, *Sales Staff*
EMP: 30 EST: 1968
SQ FT: 17,500
SALES (est): 3.9MM **Privately Held**
WEB: www.art-kraft.com
SIC: 3993 1799 Electric signs; sign installation & maintenance

(G-12888)
AVIATION WORLDWIDE SVCS LLC (HQ)
Also Called: AAR Airlift Group
2301 Commerce Park Dr Ne (32905-2611)
PHONE....................321 837-2345
Jeff Schloesser, *Mng Member*
Timothy Childrey,
EMP: 18 EST: 2003
SQ FT: 6,000
SALES (est): 15.5MM
SALES (corp-wide): 1.8B **Publicly Held**
SIC: 3728 Aircraft parts & equipment
PA: Aar Corp.
1100 N Wood Dale Rd
Wood Dale IL 60191
630 227-2000

(G-12889)
B & D MACHINE AND TOOL INC
1720 Main St Ne Ste 3 (32905-3427)
PHONE....................321 727-0098
Duard Anzengruber, *President*
EMP: 12 EST: 1978
SQ FT: 5,000
SALES (est): 952.7K **Privately Held**
WEB: www.bndmt.com
SIC: 3599 Machine shop, jobbing & repair

(G-12890)
BETA MAX INC
Also Called: Beta Max Hoist
1895 Rbert J Cnlan Blvd N (32905-3409)
P.O. Box 2750, Melbourne (32902-2750)
PHONE....................321 727-3737
Tony D Rowell, *President*
◆ EMP: 30 EST: 1993
SQ FT: 30,000
SALES (est): 7.7MM **Privately Held**
WEB: www.betamaxhoist.com
SIC: 3536 Hoists

(G-12891)
BETA MAX INC
2750 Hudson Ave Ne (32905-3422)
PHONE....................321 914-0918
EMP: 7 EST: 2019
SALES (est): 284.7K **Privately Held**
WEB: www.betamaxhoist.com
SIC: 3536 Hoists, cranes & monorails

(G-12892)
BLACK WIDOW CUSTOM CASES
1720 Main St Ne (32905-3427)
PHONE....................321 327-8058
EMP: 5 EST: 2019
SALES (est): 465.8K **Privately Held**
SIC: 3523 Farm machinery & equipment

(G-12893)
BLUE PLANET ENVMTL SYSTEMS INC
2600 Kingswood Dr Ne (32905-2508)
P.O. Box 60790 (32906-0790)
PHONE....................321 255-1931
Craig Allen Smith, *President*
EMP: 6 EST: 1997

SALES (est): 1.2MM **Privately Held**
WEB: www.blueplanetenv.com
SIC: 2899 Chemical preparations

(G-12894)
C-HORSE SOFTWARE INC
1510 Charles Blvd Ne (32907-2403)
PHONE.....................321 952-0692
Alfredo Padilla, *President*
EMP: 5 EST: 2005
SALES (est): 353.1K **Privately Held**
SIC: 7372 Prepackaged software

(G-12895)
CONSUMER ENGINEERING INC
1240 Clearmont St Ne # 1 (32905-4048)
PHONE.....................321 984-8550
Jerrell P Hollaway, *President*
Sharon Hollaway, *Vice Pres*
Charlotte Parker, *Treasurer*
EMP: 18 EST: 1986
SQ FT: 16,000
SALES (est): 3.4MM **Privately Held**
WEB: www.consumerengineering.com
SIC: 3613 3589 8711 Control panels,
   electric; commercial cleaning equipment;
   water treatment equipment, industrial;
   professional engineer

(G-12896)
DIAMOND PRECISION MACHINE INC
2300 Commerce Park Dr Ne (32905-2619)
PHONE.....................321 729-8453
Robin Squillante, *CEO*
Michael Squillante, *President*
EMP: 10 EST: 1990
SQ FT: 6,450
SALES (est): 1MM **Privately Held**
WEB: www.diamondprecision.net
SIC: 3599 3089 Machine shop, jobbing &
   repair; injection molded finished plastic
   products

(G-12897)
DRS NTWORK IMAGING SYSTEMS LLC
3520 Dixie Hwy Ne (32905-2700)
PHONE.....................321 309-1500
Joseph Danielle, *Engineer*
Lou Demore, *Engineer*
Steve Marteney, *Engineer*
Dennis Wills, *Engineer*
Terry Neuhart, *Project Engr*
EMP: 132
SALES (corp-wide): 16B **Privately Held**
WEB: www.leonardodrs.com
SIC: 3674 Infrared sensors, solid state
HQ: Drs Network & Imaging Systems, Llc
   100 N Babcock St
   Melbourne FL 32935

(G-12898)
DRT SERVICES
861 Young Ave Nw (32907-7728)
PHONE.....................321 549-1431
Derek Austin, *Principal*
EMP: 7 EST: 2010
SALES (est): 633.2K **Privately Held**
SIC: 3674 Semiconductors & related de-
   vices

(G-12899)
FAR RESEARCH INC
Also Called: Far Chemical
2210 Wilhelmina Ct Ne (32905-2548)
PHONE.....................321 723-6160
Joeph Beatty, *CEO*
Joe Beatty, *Vice Pres*
Geoffrey Crook, *Production*
Patricia Wichmann, *Purch Agent*
Alan Cramer, *Research*
▲ EMP: 25 EST: 1982
SALES (est): 11.2MM
SALES (corp-wide): 404.6MM **Privately Held**
WEB: www.far-chemical.com
SIC: 2899 Chemical preparations
HQ: Cyalume Technologies, Inc.
   96 Windsor St
   West Springfield MA 01089
   888 858-7881

(G-12900)
FILTER RESEARCH CORPORATION
1270 Clearmont St Ne # 15 (32905-4016)
P.O. Box 60898 (32906-0898)
PHONE.....................321 802-3444
Ahmed El-Mahdawy, *President*
EMP: 20 EST: 1977
SQ FT: 12,000
SALES (est): 2MM **Privately Held**
WEB: www.frccorp.com
SIC: 3677 Electronic transformers

(G-12901)
FLORIDA ENGINEERED CONSTRU
Also Called: Cast-Crete
2590 Kirby Cir Ne (32905-3416)
PHONE.....................321 953-5161
Dustin Hirsch, *Purchasing*
Jeff Roble, *Sales Associate*
Carl Eschmann, *Manager*
Daniel Grajeda, *Manager*
EMP: 7
SALES (corp-wide): 28.5MM **Privately Held**
WEB: www.castcrete.com
SIC: 3272 Precast terrazo or concrete
   products
PA: Florida Engineered Construction Prod-
   ucts Corporation
   6324 County Road 579
   Seffner FL 33584
   813 621-4641

(G-12902)
FRC ELECTRICAL INDUSTRIES INC (PA)
1260 Clearmont St Ne (32905-4030)
P.O. Box 60898 (32906-0898)
PHONE.....................321 676-3300
Ahmed El-Mahdawy, *President*
EMP: 1 EST: 1994
SALES (est): 4.4MM **Privately Held**
SIC: 3679 3444 Hermetic seals for elec-
   tronic equipment; sheet metalwork

(G-12903)
GROUP E HOLDINGS INC
Also Called: Custom Aerospace Machine
2144 Franklin Dr Ne (32905-4021)
PHONE.....................321 724-0127
Evan Cramer, *CEO*
Michael Huber, *Engineer*
Chris Hoffman,
James McCandless,
EMP: 53 EST: 2011
SQ FT: 12,500
SALES (est): 6.1MM **Privately Held**
WEB: www.custommoldandtool.com
SIC: 3599 Machine shop, jobbing & repair

(G-12904)
INNOVATIVE TECH BY DESIGN INC
Also Called: Itd Food Safety
2469 Palm Bay Rd Ne 9 (32905-3353)
PHONE.....................321 676-3194
Jason Mobley, *President*
Kelly Mobley, *Vice Pres*
Karen Hennessey, *Opers Staff*
EMP: 10 EST: 2005
SALES (est): 1.5MM **Privately Held**
WEB: www.itdfoodsafety.com
SIC: 3829 Measuring & controlling devices

(G-12905)
KBN CORPORATION
4670 Lipscomb St Ne Ste 6 (32905-2927)
PHONE.....................321 327-9792
Kelly B Nesmith, *CEO*
EMP: 5 EST: 2020
SALES (est): 502K **Privately Held**
WEB: www.kbncorporation.com
SIC: 3612 3613 3621 3629 Transform-
   ers, except electric; switchgear & switch-
   board apparatus; motors & generators;
   electrical industrial apparatus; current-
   carrying wiring devices

(G-12906)
L3HARRIS TECHNOLOGIES INC
Also Called: Mdso Security Office
   Plant 16 Troutman Blvd (32905)
P.O. Box 37, Melbourne (32902-0037)
PHONE.....................321 727-4255
Sheldon J Fox, *Vice Pres*
Joyce Williams, *Manager*
Dayne Barrow, *Manager*
EMP: 20
SALES (corp-wide): 17.8B **Publicly Held**
WEB: www.l3harris.com
SIC: 3661 Telephone & telegraph appara-
   tus
PA: L3harris Technologies, Inc.
   1025 W Nasa Blvd
   Melbourne FL 32919
   321 727-9100

(G-12907)
L3HARRIS TECHNOLOGIES INC
Harris Corporation
1000 Charles J Herbert Dr (32905)
PHONE.....................321 727-4660
K Alaskiewicz, *Branch Mgr*
EMP: 31
SALES (corp-wide): 17.8B **Publicly Held**
WEB: www.l3harris.com
SIC: 3728 Aircraft parts & equipment
PA: L3harris Technologies, Inc.
   1025 W Nasa Blvd
   Melbourne FL 32919
   321 727-9100

(G-12908)
MELBOURNE-TILLMAN WTR CTRL DST
5990 Minton Rd Nw (32907-1977)
PHONE.....................321 723-7233
John Devivo, *President*
Daniel Anderson, *Agent*
EMP: 23 EST: 1922
SQ FT: 3,984
SALES (est): 2.2MM **Privately Held**
WEB: www.melbournetillman.org
SIC: 3822 Auto controls regulating residntl
   & coml environmt & applncs

(G-12909)
NEXGEN FRAMING SYSTEM LLC
2288 Wilhelmina Ct Ne (32905-2536)
PHONE.....................321 508-6763
EMP: 10 EST: 2019
SALES (est): 1.4MM **Privately Held**
SIC: 2439 Trusses, wooden roof

(G-12910)
NOHBO LABS LLC
1581 Robert J Conlan Blvd (32905-3563)
PHONE.....................321 345-5319
Melinda Warren, *Mng Member*
Carrie Warren,
EMP: 7 EST: 2017
SALES (est): 809K **Privately Held**
WEB: www.nohbo.com
SIC: 2844 Cosmetic preparations

(G-12911)
OAKRIDGE GLOBL ENRGY SLTONS IN
3520 Dixie Hwy Ne (32905-2700)
PHONE.....................321 610-7959
Stephen J Barber, *Ch of Bd*
EMP: 42 EST: 1986
SALES (est): 3.6MM **Privately Held**
WEB: www.pregunteme.wiki
SIC: 3692 Primary batteries, dry & wet

(G-12912)
PREMIER CABINETS & TRIM LLC
1240 Clearmont St Ne # 10 (32905-4048)
PHONE.....................321 345-4923
Julius Thompson, *Principal*
Michelle Sicard, *Office Mgr*
EMP: 11 EST: 2017
SALES (est): 2.4MM **Privately Held**
WEB: www.premiercabinetsfl.com
SIC: 2434 Wood kitchen cabinets

(G-12913)
RECALL TECHNOLOGIES INC
1651 Seabury Point Rd Nw (32907-6335)
P.O. Box 100546 (32910-0546)
PHONE.....................321 952-4422

Susan Voelkel, *President*
John Voelkel, *Vice Pres*
EMP: 5 EST: 1994
SQ FT: 2,000
SALES (est): 501.3K **Privately Held**
WEB: www.recall3.com
SIC: 3661 Telephone & telegraph appara-
   tus

(G-12914)
RENESAS ELECTRONICS AMER INC
1650 Rbert J Cnlan Blvd N (32905-3406)
P.O. Box 65004 (32906-5004)
PHONE.....................321 724-7000
Vern Kelley, *Vice Pres*
Wayman Aldridge Jr, *Branch Mgr*
Brannon Harris, *Senior Mgr*
Joey Jenne, *Technology*
Robin Nursey, *Director*
EMP: 600 **Privately Held**
WEB: www.renesas.com
SIC: 3674 Semiconductors & related de-
   vices
HQ: Renesas Electronics America Inc.
   6024 Silver Creek Vly Rd
   San Jose CA 95138
   408 284-8200

(G-12915)
RONCO AIRCRAFT AND MARINE INC (PA)
1774 Plantation Cir Se (32909-7111)
PHONE.....................321 220-0209
Ronald A Waddell, *Principal*
EMP: 5 EST: 2012
SALES (est): 882.1K **Privately Held**
WEB: www.sgjacobiphd.com
SIC: 3721 Aircraft

(G-12916)
SAILOR MADE CSTM WOODWORKS LLC
190 Wading Bird Cir Sw (32908-6410)
PHONE.....................805 587-1197
William Vega,
EMP: 7 EST: 2017
SALES (est): 165.2K **Privately Held**
WEB: www.sailormadecww.com
SIC: 2431 Millwork

(G-12917)
SHAPES GROUP LTD CO
Also Called: Shapes Precision Manufacturing
1415 Fundation Pk Blvd Se (32909-2104)
PHONE.....................321 837-0500
Kyle Benusa, *President*
T Kyle Benusa, *President*
Carman Cicarella, *Purch Agent*
Debbie Delp, *Engineer*
Roberta Westenbarger, *Engineer*
▲ EMP: 83 EST: 2002
SQ FT: 65,000
SALES (est): 12.5MM **Privately Held**
WEB: www.shapesmfg.com
SIC: 3441 Fabricated structural metal

(G-12918)
SOD DEPOT & GRAVEL INC
1378 Malabar Rd Se (32907-2553)
PHONE.....................321 728-2766
Saul Ventura, *Principal*
EMP: 8 EST: 2015
SALES (est): 66K **Privately Held**
WEB: www.soddepotgravel.com
SIC: 1442 Construction sand & gravel

(G-12919)
SOLUNET
1571 Robert J Conlan Blvd (32905-3562)
PHONE.....................321 369-9719
Dan Kinnick, *Sales Executive*
EMP: 7 EST: 2015
SALES (est): 138.4K **Privately Held**
SIC: 3579 Office machines

(G-12920)
SOUND ANCHORS INC
2835 Kirby Cir Ne Ste 110 (32905-3411)
PHONE.....................321 724-1237
Robert Worzalla, *President*
Debbie Worzalla, *Vice Pres*
▲ EMP: 7 EST: 1986
SQ FT: 5,600

▲ = Import ▼ =Export
◆ =Import/Export

SALES (est): 500K **Privately Held**
WEB: www.soundanchors.com
SIC: 3651 5731 Household audio equipment; radio, television & electronic stores

(G-12921)
SOUTHEASTERN ENGINEERING INC
1340 Clearmont St Ne # 304 (32905-4049)
P.O. Box 61442 (32906-1442)
PHONE....................321 984-2521
Harry Zeek, *President*
EMP: 28 EST: 1978
SQ FT: 12,000
SALES (est): 1.2MM **Privately Held**
SIC: 3663 3728 3714 Satellites, communications; aircraft parts & equipment; motor vehicle parts & accessories

(G-12922)
STEEN AERO LAB LLC
1451 Clearmont St Ne (32905-4017)
PHONE....................321 725-4160
Cheryl Everette, *Office Mgr*
Mike Whaley, *Webmaster*
Paul Goetsch,
Jeri Larson,
EMP: 9 EST: 2000
SALES (est): 1.1MM **Privately Held**
WEB: www.steenaero.com
SIC: 3728 Aircraft assemblies, subassemblies & parts

(G-12923)
STONE MOSAICS
1735 Biltz Ave Ne (32905-3413)
PHONE....................321 773-3635
Roger Sinigoi, *President*
EMP: 8 EST: 2015
SALES (est): 1.2MM **Privately Held**
WEB: www.stonemosaics.net
SIC: 1411 Dimension stone

(G-12924)
SYNCRON EMS LLC
2330 Commerce Park Dr Ne # 6 (32905-7721)
PHONE....................321 409-0025
John Sjolander, *CEO*
Dave Glionna, *Engineer*
Cheri Bia, *Program Mgr*
EMP: 85 EST: 2008
SQ FT: 25,000
SALES (est): 21.6MM **Privately Held**
WEB: www.syncron-ems.com
SIC: 3679 Electronic circuits

(G-12925)
TECHNOLOGY PRODUCTS DESIGN INC
3806 Hield Rd Nw (32907-6303)
PHONE....................321 432-3537
Charles Burr, *Principal*
EMP: 11 EST: 2001
SALES (est): 168.3K **Privately Held**
SIC: 3674 Semiconductors & related devices

(G-12926)
ULTRA PRCSION MCHNING GRNDING
2870 Kirby Cir Ne Ste 6 (32905-3438)
PHONE....................321 725-9655
Mike Higley, *President*
Paul Hill, *QC Mgr*
EMP: 17 EST: 1995
SQ FT: 2,200
SALES (est): 1.7MM **Privately Held**
WEB: www.ultramachining.com
SIC: 3599 Machine shop, jobbing & repair

(G-12927)
WALTERS TOOLS LLC
Also Called: Cornwell
2998 Hester Ave Se (32909-7600)
PHONE....................321 537-4788
EMP: 6 EST: 2018
SALES (est): 843.3K **Privately Held**
SIC: 1389 Oil field services

Palm Beach
Palm Beach County

(G-12928)
ABB PARTNERS LLC
340 Royal Poinciana Way # 3 (33480-4048)
PHONE....................917 843-4430
Matti C Anttila, *CEO*
EMP: 15 EST: 2006
SALES (est): 1.1MM
SALES (corp-wide): 28.9B **Privately Held**
SIC: 3612 Transformers, except electric
PA: Abb Ltd
  Affolternstrasse 44
  ZUrich ZH 8050
  433 177-111

(G-12929)
BENCHMARK OF PALM BEACH (PA)
205 Worth Ave Ste 315 (33480-4618)
PHONE....................706 258-3553
Ken Burns, *President*
EMP: 7 EST: 2006
SALES (est): 282.4K **Privately Held**
WEB: www.benchmarkofpalmbeach.com
SIC: 3423 Jewelers' hand tools

(G-12930)
CAMPER & NICHOLSONS USA INC (PA)
450 Royal Palm Way # 100 (33480-4144)
PHONE....................561 655-2121
Russell Preston III, *President*
Paolo Casani, *Managing Dir*
Fabrizio Scerch, *Managing Dir*
Jillian Montgomery, *COO*
Elodie Arnaud, *Opers Staff*
◆ EMP: 23 EST: 1992
SALES (est): 12.6MM **Privately Held**
WEB: www.camperandnicholsons.com
SIC: 3732 5551 Yachts, building & repairing; boat dealers

(G-12931)
CONNECTRONICS US INC
101 Bradley Pl Ste 202 (33480-3828)
PHONE....................954 534-3335
Lee Hauradou, *President*
EMP: 5 EST: 2011
SQ FT: 1,500
SALES (est): 300K **Privately Held**
WEB: www.customrfconnectors.com
SIC: 3559 Electronic component making machinery

(G-12932)
DIVERSITYINC MEDIA LLC
111 Reef Rd (33480-3058)
P.O. Box 348, Princeton NJ (08542-0348)
PHONE....................973 494-0539
Carolynn Johnson, *COO*
Evan Tarte, *COO*
Lucas J Visconti, *Mng Member*
EMP: 19 EST: 2001
SQ FT: 5,500
SALES (est): 2.5MM **Privately Held**
WEB: www.diversityinc.com
SIC: 2721 Magazines: publishing only, not printed on site

(G-12933)
EXOSIS INC
Also Called: Biotech
109 Everglade Ave (33480-3717)
P.O. Box 509 (33480-0509)
PHONE....................240 417-4477
Stephen Trevisan, *CEO*
John Holaday, *President*
Mathew Lo, *Exec VP*
EMP: 5 EST: 2018
SALES (est): 380K **Privately Held**
WEB: www.exosis.com
SIC: 2836 Vaccines & other immunizing products

(G-12934)
FLO SUN LAND CORPORATION
Also Called: Florida Crystals
340 Royal Poinciana Way # 316 (33480-4048)
PHONE....................561 655-6303

Alfonso Fanjul Jr, *Ch of Bd*
Jose Fanjul, *President*
Rolando Anillo, *Counsel*
Donald W Carson, *Exec VP*
Oscar R Hernandez, *Vice Pres*
◆ EMP: 52 EST: 1950
SQ FT: 9,000
SALES (est): 690.8K **Privately Held**
SIC: 2099 0133 6552 Sugar grinding; sugarcane farm; subdividers & developers

(G-12935)
GARRISON LICKLE AIRCRAFT
400 S Ocean Blvd Ofc (33480-6715)
PHONE....................561 833-7111
Garrison Lickle, *Principal*
EMP: 7 EST: 2005
SALES (est): 160.5K **Privately Held**
SIC: 3721 Aircraft

(G-12936)
HRF EXPLORATION & PROD LLC (PA)
250 El Dorado Ln (33480-3302)
P.O. Box 160, Gaylord MI (49734-0160)
PHONE....................561 847-4743
H R Fruehauf III, *President*
EMP: 18 EST: 1994
SALES (est): 6.5MM **Privately Held**
SIC: 1382 Oil & gas exploration services

(G-12937)
LIFE SPICE AND INGREDIENTS LLC (PA)
300 Cherry Ln (33480-3419)
PHONE....................708 301-0447
Dawn Pavela, *VP Finance*
Peter Garvy, *Mng Member*
EMP: 9 EST: 2009
SQ FT: 5,000
SALES (est): 1.7MM **Privately Held**
WEB: www.lifespiceingredients.com
SIC: 2099 Spices, including grinding

(G-12938)
MAUI HOLDINGS LLC
250 Royal Palm Way # 201 (33480-4319)
PHONE....................904 741-5400
Nicholas Sokolow, *Manager*
EMP: 2533 EST: 2012
SALES (est): 37.4MM **Privately Held**
SIC: 2311 Policemen's uniforms: made from purchased materials

(G-12939)
OSCEOLA FARMS CO (HQ)
340 Royal Poinciana Way # 315 (33480-4048)
P.O. Box 1059 (33480-1059)
PHONE....................561 655-6303
Alfonso Fanjul Jr, *Ch of Bd*
Jose Fanjul, *President*
Donald W Carson, *Vice Pres*
Oscar R Hernandez, *VP Finance*
Roland Gonzalez, *Manager*
▲ EMP: 35 EST: 1960
SQ FT: 9,000
SALES (est): 205.3MM
SALES (corp-wide): 2.1B **Privately Held**
SIC: 2099 Sugar grinding
PA: Fanjul Corp.
  1 N Clematis St Ste 200
  West Palm Beach FL 33401
  561 655-6303

(G-12940)
RAMPELL SOFTWARE
122 N County Rd (33480-3917)
PHONE....................561 628-5102
Alex Rampell, *Principal*
EMP: 8 EST: 2016
SALES (est): 101.7K **Privately Held**
SIC: 2273 Carpets & rugs

(G-12941)
UAS DRONE CORP (PA)
420 Royal Palm Way # 100 (33480-4133)
PHONE....................561 693-1424
Yossi Balucka, *President*
Chris Leith, *Corp Secy*
Sagiv Aharon, *CTO*
EMP: 8 EST: 2015
SALES (est): 833.3K **Privately Held**
WEB: www.airborneresponse.com
SIC: 3721 Aircraft

(G-12942)
VECELLIO MANAGEMENT SVCS INC
450 Royal Palm Way Fl 2 (33480-4180)
P.O. Box 15065, West Palm Beach (33416-5065)
PHONE....................561 793-2102
Leo A Vecellio Jr, *President*
Robert D Smith, *Corp Secy*
Christopher Vecellio, *Vice Pres*
Kathryn C Vecellio, *Vice Pres*
Michael A Vecellio, *Vice Pres*
EMP: 19 EST: 1961
SALES (est): 15MM **Privately Held**
WEB: www.vecelliogroup.com
SIC: 1241 Mining services: lignite

(G-12943)
Y3K LLC
44 Cocoanut Row Ste T1 (33480-4069)
PHONE....................561 835-0404
Peter Lester,
EMP: 7 EST: 2005
SALES (est): 119.9K **Privately Held**
WEB: www.y3kfoods.com
SIC: 2024 Ice cream & frozen desserts

Palm Beach Gardens
Palm Beach County

(G-12944)
ACE-PIPE WELDING LLC
305 Camellia St (33410-4812)
PHONE....................561 727-6345
Ronald C Miles, *Principal*
EMP: 6 EST: 2013
SALES (est): 497.8K **Privately Held**
SIC: 7692 Welding repair

(G-12945)
ALL AMERICAN PET COMPANY INC
3801 Pga Blvd Ste 600 (33410-2756)
PHONE....................561 337-5340
Barry Schwartz, *CEO*
EMP: 11 EST: 2003
SQ FT: 1,000
SALES (est): 585.8K **Privately Held**
SIC: 2047 Dog & cat food

(G-12946)
ALLIANT TCHSYSTEMS OPRTONS LLC
348 Hiatt Dr Ste 100 (33418-7234)
PHONE....................561 776-9876
John Hayes, *Principal*
Alice Reed, *Principal*
EMP: 22 **Publicly Held**
SIC: 3812 Search & navigation equipment
HQ: Alliant Techsystems Operations Llc
  2980 Fairview Park Dr
  Falls Church VA 22042

(G-12947)
ANNONA BIOSCIENCES INC
2401 Pga Blvd Ste 196 (33410-3500)
PHONE....................888 204-4980
Donna Douglas, *Principal*
EMP: 5 EST: 2009
SALES (est): 388.9K **Privately Held**
SIC: 2834 Pharmaceutical preparations

(G-12948)
AQUALOGIX INC (PA)
4440 Pga Blvd Ste 600 (33410-6542)
PHONE....................858 442-4550
Donald Hofmann, *President*
William Richardson, *Manager*
David Sevelovitz, *Manager*
EMP: 12 EST: 2013
SQ FT: 5,000
SALES (est): 95.5K **Privately Held**
WEB: www.aqualogix.com
SIC: 3823 7389 7371 Water quality monitoring & control systems; water softener service; computer software development & applications

(G-12949)
ARCHITCTRAL WDWRKS CBNETRY INC
219 Coral Cay Ter (33418-4003)
PHONE....................................561 848-8595
Chris Williams, *President*
Jose Montero, *President*
Jason Long, *Vice Pres*
▼ EMP: 18 EST: 1989
SALES (est): 1.6MM **Privately Held**
SIC: 2434 2431 Wood kitchen cabinets; woodwork, interior & ornamental

(G-12950)
BIOMET INC
4555 Riverside Dr (33410-4200)
PHONE....................................561 385-8405
Lars Ganson, *Vice Pres*
Mike Haligowski, *Sales Staff*
Heath Gomez, *Manager*
Erin Moore, *Manager*
Zach Suttin, *Director*
EMP: 13
SALES (corp-wide): 7.8B **Publicly Held**
WEB: www.zimmerbiomet.com
SIC: 3842 Orthopedic appliances
HQ: Biomet, Inc.
345 E Main St
Warsaw IN 46580
574 267-6639

(G-12951)
BIOMET 3I LLC
Also Called: 3i Implant Innovations
4555 Riverside Dr (33410-4200)
PHONE....................................561 775-9928
Alex Garcia, *Purch Mgr*
Andrew Hood, *Manager*
Richard Lazzara,
Keith Beaty,
Jeffrey R Binder,
▼ EMP: 600 EST: 1987
SQ FT: 67,000
SALES (est): 138.6MM
SALES (corp-wide): 148.1MM **Publicly Held**
WEB: www.zimvie.com
SIC: 3843 Dental materials
PA: Zimvie Inc.
10225 Westmoor Dr
Westminster CO 80021
303 443-7500

(G-12952)
BLUE BIOFUELS INC
3710 Buckeye St Ste 120 (33410-4290)
PHONE....................................561 693-1943
Benjamin Slager, *CEO*
Anthony Santelli, *COO*
Eric Libra, *Lab Dir*
George Bolton,
EMP: 8 EST: 2012 **Privately Held**
WEB: www.bluebiofuels.com
SIC: 2869 Fuels

(G-12953)
BRIEMAD INC
Also Called: Nutrition World Health Market
2401 Pga Blvd Ste 136 (33410-3515)
PHONE....................................561 626-4377
Bruce S Cohen, *President*
Bruce Cohen, *Manager*
EMP: 9 EST: 2011
SALES (est): 483K **Privately Held**
WEB: www.nutritionworld.com
SIC: 2834 Pharmaceutical preparations

(G-12954)
CANVAS CLINICAL RESEARCH
8227 Kelso Dr (33418-6017)
PHONE....................................561 229-0002
Perez Robert, *Branch Mgr*
EMP: 12
SALES (corp-wide): 306.1K **Privately Held**
WEB: www.canvascr.com
SIC: 2211 Canvas
PA: Canvas Clinical Research
3898 Via Poinciana
Lake Worth FL 33467
561 229-0002

(G-12955)
CARRIER CORPORATION (HQ)
Also Called: Carrier Transicold
13995 Pasteur Blvd (33418-7231)
P.O. Box 4808, Syracuse NY (13221-4808)
PHONE....................................800 379-6484
David Appel, *CEO*
Michael Cenci, *Vice Pres*
Cindy Cox, *Vice Pres*
Kyle Crockett, *Vice Pres*
Rishi Grover, *Vice Pres*
◆ EMP: 170 EST: 1978
SALES (est): 12.3B
SALES (corp-wide): 20.6B **Publicly Held**
WEB: www.rtx.com
SIC: 3585 Air conditioning equipment, complete; heating equipment, complete; room coolers, portable; heat pumps, electric
PA: Carrier Global Corporation
13995 Pasteur Blvd
Palm Beach Gardens FL 33418
561 365-2000

(G-12956)
CARRIER GLOBAL CORPORATION (PA)
13995 Pasteur Blvd (33418-7231)
PHONE....................................561 365-2000
David Gitlin, *Ch of Bd*
Christopher Nelson, *President*
Jurgen Timperman, *President*
Timothy White, *President*
Ajay Agrawal, *Senior VP*
◆ EMP: 108 EST: 1902
SALES (est): 20.6B **Publicly Held**
WEB: corporate.carrier.com
SIC: 3585 Refrigeration & heating equipment

(G-12957)
CAST-STONE INTERNATIONAL CORP
11555 Us Highway 1 (33408-3025)
PHONE....................................561 625-0333
Albert Barrera, *President*
◆ EMP: 10 EST: 1988
SALES (est): 503.3K **Privately Held**
WEB: www.pbcaststone.com
SIC: 3272 Concrete products

(G-12958)
CHROMALLOY CASTINGS TAMPA CORP (DH)
3999 Rca Blvd (33410-4219)
PHONE....................................561 935-3571
Armand F Lauzon, *President*
Mike Beffel, *Vice Pres*
Tom Trotter, *Vice Pres*
Walt Dorman, *Opers Staff*
Michele Tomasello, *Senior Buyer*
▲ EMP: 110 EST: 1970
SQ FT: 105,000
SALES (est): 63.3MM
SALES (corp-wide): 8.7B **Publicly Held**
WEB: www.chromalloy.com
SIC: 3369 3714 3511 Machinery castings, nonferrous: ex. alum., copper, die, etc.; motor vehicle parts & accessories; turbines & turbine generator sets
HQ: Chromalloy Gas Turbine Llc
4100 Rca Blvd
Palm Beach Gardens FL 33410
561 935-3571

(G-12959)
CHROMALLOY GAS TURBINE LLC (DH)
Also Called: Gemoco Division
4100 Rca Blvd (33410-4251)
PHONE....................................561 935-3571
Mike Harris, *General Mgr*
Jim Adkins, *Vice Pres*
Dan Albert, *Vice Pres*
Michael Boehm, *Vice Pres*
Costa Brian, *Vice Pres*
▲ EMP: 1234 EST: 1951
SQ FT: 15,000

SALES (est): 1B
SALES (corp-wide): 8.7B **Publicly Held**
WEB: www.chromalloy.com
SIC: 3724 7699 4581 3764 Aircraft engines & engine parts; engine repair & replacement, non-automotive; aircraft servicing & repairing; guided missile & space vehicle propulsion unit parts; guided missile & space vehicle parts & auxiliary equipment; oil & gas field machinery
HQ: Sequa Corporation
3999 Rca Blvd
Palm Beach Gardens FL 33410
561 935-3571

(G-12960)
CL GARDENS LLC
3101 Pga Blvd (33410-2820)
PHONE....................................561 567-0504
Edward W Beiner,
EMP: 8 EST: 2006
SALES (est): 395.5K **Privately Held**
SIC: 3851 Ophthalmic goods

(G-12961)
CLINE RESOURCE AND DEV CO (PA)
Also Called: Cline Group
3825 Pga Blvd Ste 1101 (33410-2991)
PHONE....................................561 626-4999
Christopher Cline, *President*
EMP: 5 EST: 2006
SALES (est): 2.3MM **Privately Held**
SIC: 1241 Coal mining services

(G-12962)
CONCEPT GROUP LLC
350 Hiatt Dr Ste 120 (33418-7197)
PHONE....................................856 767-5506
Maryann Tucker, *Owner*
Daniel Prall, *Opers Staff*
Jake Bruns, *Engineer*
Ricard Riabko, *Manager*
EMP: 11
SALES (corp-wide): 10.1MM **Privately Held**
WEB: www.conceptgroupllc.com
SIC: 3679 3599 Antennas, receiving; machine shop, jobbing & repair
HQ: Concept Group, Llc
380 Cooper Rd
West Berlin NJ 08091
856 767-5506

(G-12963)
CROSS MATCH TECHNOLOGIES INC (DH)
3950 Rca Blvd Ste 5001 (33410-4227)
PHONE....................................561 622-1650
Richard Agostinelli, *CEO*
Donald E Nickelson, *Ch of Bd*
David Buckley, *President*
George McClurg, *Principal*
Don Sutton, *Regional Mgr*
◆ EMP: 205 EST: 1996
SQ FT: 71,000
SALES (est): 47.5MM
SALES (corp-wide): 10.3B **Privately Held**
SIC: 3999 Fingerprint equipment

(G-12964)
CYBER FUELS INC
2401 Pga Blvd Ste 196 (33410-3500)
PHONE....................................866 771-3580
Ronald W Mills, *President*
Brian Pybus, *CFO*
EMP: 2 EST: 2012
SALES (est): 4.1MM **Publicly Held**
WEB: www.cyberfuelsinc.com
SIC: 2911 Light distillates
PA: Nutex Health Inc.
6030 S Rice Ave Ste C
Houston TX 77081

(G-12965)
DISTILLERY DEERFIELD LLC ✪
7277 Oxford Ct (33418-3426)
PHONE....................................954 531-6813
EMP: 5 EST: 2021
SALES (est): 354.3K **Privately Held**
SIC: 2085 Distilled & blended liquors

(G-12966)
DONNA LYNN ENTERPRISES INC
Also Called: PIP Printing
10358 Rverside Dr Ste 130 (33410)
PHONE....................................772 286-2812
Lloyd Blank, *President*
Donna Blank, *Office Mgr*
EMP: 7 EST: 1984
SQ FT: 2,000
SALES (est): 973.7K **Privately Held**
WEB: www.pip.com
SIC: 2789 2752 Bookbinding & related work; commercial printing, lithographic

(G-12967)
EMBROIDERY CHIMP LLC
3954 Northlake Blvd (33403-1501)
P.O. Box 212426, Royal Palm Beach (33421-2426)
PHONE....................................561 775-9195
EMP: 11
SALES (corp-wide): 230.4K **Privately Held**
SIC: 2395 Embroidery & art needlework
PA: Embroidery Chimp Llc
107 Sycamore Dr
Royal Palm Beach FL

(G-12968)
EMJ PHARMA INC
133 Playa Rienta Way (33418-6210)
PHONE....................................973 600-9087
Elizabeth B Marchese, *Principal*
EMP: 8 EST: 2009
SALES (est): 144.8K **Privately Held**
SIC: 2834 Pharmaceutical preparations

(G-12969)
FITTEAM GLOBAL LLC
4440 Pga Blvd Ste 600 (33410-6542)
PHONE....................................586 260-1487
Christine Madrazo, *Partner*
Racheal Hustad, *Opers Mgr*
Christopher S Hummel, *Manager*
Brent Niblo, *Manager*
Linda Pesonen, *Executive*
EMP: 7 EST: 2014
SQ FT: 1,200
SALES (est): 2.4MM **Privately Held**
WEB: www.fitteam.com
SIC: 2834 Pharmaceutical preparations

(G-12970)
FLORIDA FLVORS CNCENTRATES INC
205 Sedona Way (33418-1718)
PHONE....................................561 775-5714
Didier Hardy, *President*
Gina M Cieri, *Treasurer*
EMP: 9 EST: 2010
SALES (est): 115.9K **Privately Held**
SIC: 2087 5148 Flavoring extracts & syrups; fresh fruits & vegetables

(G-12971)
FORESIGHT RESERVES LP
3801 Pga Blvd Ste 903 (33410-2761)
PHONE....................................561 626-4999
Christopher Cline, *Partner*
Insight Resource, *General Ptnr*
EMP: 7 EST: 2004
SALES (est): 247.7K **Privately Held**
SIC: 1241 Coal mining services

(G-12972)
HARRIS WOODWORKS LLC
4078 Jonquil Cir S (33410-5531)
PHONE....................................561 543-3265
James C Harris II, *Principal*
EMP: 7 EST: 2019
SALES (est): 288.7K **Privately Held**
SIC: 2431 Millwork

(G-12973)
HID GLOBAL CORP
3950 Rca Blvd Ste 5001 (33410-4227)
PHONE....................................561 622-9013
EMP: 13 EST: 1991
SALES (est): 1.2MM **Privately Held**
WEB: www.hidglobal.com
SIC: 3825 Instruments to measure electricity

▲ = Import ▼=Export
◆ =Import/Export

(G-12974)
HORIZON PHARMACEUTICALS INC
10180 Riverside Dr Ste 8 (33410)
PHONE..................................561 844-7227
Adam Ibrahim, *CEO*
Ali Kutom, *President*
Julio Abreu, *Managing Dir*
Mary Ann Brody, *Controller*
EMP: 55 EST: 2008
SQ FT: 65,000
SALES (est): 10.5MM **Privately Held**
WEB: www.horizonph.com
SIC: 2834 Pharmaceutical preparations

(G-12975)
INDUSTRIAL MARKING EQP CO INC
4152 Lazy Hammock Rd (33410-6114)
PHONE..................................561 626-8520
Gary Samwick, *President*
Marilyn Samwick, *Corp Secy*
EMP: 9 EST: 1941
SQ FT: 15,000
SALES (est): 222.7K **Privately Held**
SIC: 3565 Labeling machines, industrial

(G-12976)
INFINITE HANDLING SERVICES LLC
Also Called: Forklifts
4440 Pga Blvd Ste 600 (33410-6542)
PHONE..................................561 939-6336
Craig Schreiber, *Mng Member*
EMP: 7 EST: 2020
SALES (est): 546.7K **Privately Held**
SIC: 3537 Lift trucks, industrial: fork, platform, straddle, etc.

(G-12977)
INTEGRATED SENSORS LLC
201 Thornton Dr (33418-8036)
PHONE..................................419 536-3212
Peter Friedman, *Mng Member*
EMP: 6 EST: 2004
SALES (est): 750K **Privately Held**
WEB: www.isensors.net
SIC: 3674 Radiation sensors

(G-12978)
INTEGRITY IMPLANTS INC
Also Called: Accelus
354 Hiatt Dr Ste 100 (33418-7241)
PHONE..................................561 529-3861
Christopher Walsh, *CEO*
Wyatt Geist, *President*
Lynn Wiley, *General Mgr*
Michele Wilyey, *General Mgr*
Rachelle Yusufbekov, *Research*
EMP: 50 EST: 2016
SQ FT: 15,000
SALES (est): 5MM **Privately Held**
WEB: www.accelusinc.com
SIC: 3841 Surgical & medical instruments

(G-12979)
IT LABS LLC
1810 Flower Dr (33410-1700)
PHONE..................................310 490-6142
Branislav Gjorcevski, *CEO*
Ilija Misov, *Technical Dir*
EMP: 15 EST: 2013
SALES (est): 1.7MM **Privately Held**
WEB: www.it-labs.com
SIC: 7372 7371 7373 Application computer software; computer software development; systems software development services

(G-12980)
JUPITER COMPASS LLC
600 S Entrada Way Apt 204 (33410-5320)
PHONE..................................561 444-6740
Paul O'Meara, *Principal*
EMP: 7 EST: 2016
SALES (est): 304.6K **Privately Held**
WEB: www.jupitercompass.com
SIC: 7372 Prepackaged software

(G-12981)
JWDI REALTY LLC
8830 Lyndall Ln (33403-1640)
PHONE..................................561 331-2481
Abraline Louis, *Mng Member*
EMP: 7 EST: 2015

SALES (est): 120K **Privately Held**
SIC: 2519 6531 7389 Furniture, household: glass, fiberglass & plastic; real estate brokers & agents;

(G-12982)
L C CLARK PUBLISHING INC
Also Called: World of Window Coverings
600 Sandtree Dr Ste 107 (33403-1538)
P.O. Box 13079, North Palm Beach (33408-7079)
PHONE..................................561 627-3393
John Clark, *President*
Valerie Cohen, *Vice Pres*
Kelley C Whitt, *Vice Pres*
EMP: 15 EST: 1983
SQ FT: 4,800
SALES (est): 901.3K **Privately Held**
WEB: www.dwcdesignet.com
SIC: 2721 Magazines: publishing only, not printed on site

(G-12983)
LAKESIDE PUBLISHING CO LLC
3180 Burgundy Dr N (33410-1485)
PHONE..................................847 491-6440
Barry Jacobs, *Principal*
Dale Jacobs, *Prdtn Mgr*
EMP: 5 EST: 2008
SALES (est): 431.4K **Privately Held**
SIC: 2721 Magazines: publishing only, not printed on site

(G-12984)
LESTER A DINE INC
351 Hiatt Dr (33418-7198)
PHONE..................................561 624-3009
William Glassgold, *President*
Selda Dine, *Corp Secy*
Enid Glassgold, *Vice Pres*
Matt Glassgold, *Vice Pres*
Colleen Glassgold, *Opers Staff*
EMP: 8 EST: 1949
SQ FT: 8,000
SALES (est): 1.1MM **Privately Held**
WEB: www.dinecorp.com
SIC: 3861 5946 Photographic equipment & supplies; cameras; photographic supplies

(G-12985)
LOCUS SOLUTIONS LLC
Also Called: Locus Traxx Worlwide
7121 Fairway Dr Ste 400 (33418-3776)
PHONE..................................561 575-7600
EMP: 65 EST: 2006
SQ FT: 60,000
SALES (est): 15MM
SALES (corp-wide): 18.2B **Publicly Held**
SIC: 3663 7374 ; data processing service
PA: Emerson Electric Co.
8000 West Florissant Ave
Saint Louis MO 63136
314 553-2000

(G-12986)
LOGICAL DATA SOLUTIONS INC
31 Windward Isle (33418-8046)
PHONE..................................561 694-9229
Valerie King, *President*
William King, *Vice Pres*
Chuck Partridge, *Technical Staff*
EMP: 10 EST: 1983
SQ FT: 1,200
SALES (est): 923.9K **Privately Held**
WEB: www.logicaldata.net
SIC: 7372 8748 Prepackaged software; business consulting

(G-12987)
LRP CONFERENCES LLC (HQ)
360 Hiatt Dr (33418-7106)
PHONE..................................215 784-0860
Ken Kahn, *President*
Emanuel Cotronakis, *Exec VP*
EMP: 33 EST: 2006
SALES (est): 9.8MM
SALES (corp-wide): 77.6MM **Privately Held**
WEB: www.lrp.com
SIC: 2759 Commercial printing
PA: Lrp Publications, Inc.
360 Hiatt Dr
Palm Beach Gardens FL 33418
215 784-0860

(G-12988)
LRP PUBLICATIONS INC (PA)
Also Called: L R P
360 Hiatt Dr (33418-7106)
PHONE..................................215 784-0860
Kenneth Kahn, *President*
Jennifer Herseim, *Editor*
Jim Sarmiento, *Editor*
Florence Simmons, *Editor*
Lee Tiemann, *COO*
EMP: 150 EST: 1975
SQ FT: 60,000
SALES (est): 77.6MM **Privately Held**
WEB: www.lrp.com
SIC: 2721 Magazines: publishing only, not printed on site

(G-12989)
MICHAEL RYBVICH SONS BOAT WRKS
2175 Idlewild Rd (33410-2583)
PHONE..................................561 627-9168
Blake Gill, *Purch Mgr*
Ben Brownlee, *Broker*
David Parchesco, *Broker*
Josee Olsen, *Office Mgr*
Michael Rybovich,
EMP: 17 EST: 2010
SALES (est): 6.8MM **Privately Held**
WEB: www.michaelrybovichandsons.com
SIC: 3732 Boat building & repairing

(G-12990)
MOLD CONTROL SYSTEMS INC
2000 Pga Blvd Ste 4440 (33408-2738)
PHONE..................................561 316-5412
Shashrul Khan, *President*
Raymon Jabar, *Vice Pres*
Jeff Clark, *Creative Dir*
▲ EMP: 8 EST: 1991
SQ FT: 10,000
SALES (est): 2.4MM **Privately Held**
SIC: 3822 3559 Thermostats, except built-in; plastics working machinery

(G-12991)
NEXUS MINT LLC
4440 Pga Blvd Ste 600 (33410-6542)
PHONE..................................561 306-9898
Lonelle Davis, *Mng Member*
EMP: 5 EST: 2020
SALES (est): 1MM **Privately Held**
SIC: 3356 Nonferrous rolling & drawing

(G-12992)
NIGHTINGALE CORP
11380 Prosperity Farms Rd (33410-3474)
PHONE..................................800 363-8954
William R Breen, *CEO*
Edward Breen, *President*
EMP: 7 EST: 2017
SQ FT: 2,795
SALES (est): 1MM
SALES (corp-wide): 1.9MM **Privately Held**
WEB: www.nightingalechairs.com
SIC: 2522 Office chairs, benches & stools, except wood
PA: Nightingale Corp
2301 Dixie Rd
Mississauga ON L4Y 1
905 896-3434

(G-12993)
NORTH PALM PRINTING CENTER
4588 Juniper Ln (33418-4521)
PHONE..................................561 622-2839
John Amann, *President*
Cathy Amann, *Corp Secy*
EMP: 6 EST: 1985
SALES (est): 444.4K **Privately Held**
SIC: 2752 Commercial printing, offset

(G-12994)
NORTHROP GRUMMAN SYSTEMS CORP
Also Called: Weapons Systems
348 Hiatt Dr Ste 100 (33418-7234)
PHONE..................................561 515-3651
Scott Longshore, *Engineer*
Alicia Howard, *Senior Engr*
Chris Gettinger, *Branch Mgr*
Beth Byrne, *Program Mgr*
Alice Reed, *Analyst*

EMP: 50 **Publicly Held**
WEB: www.northropgrumman.com
SIC: 3812 Search & navigation equipment
HQ: Northrop Grumman Systems Corporation
2980 Fairview Park Dr
Falls Church VA 22042
703 280-2900

(G-12995)
OLDCASTLE APG SOUTH INC
Also Called: Coastal
3801 Pga Blvd Ste 806 (33410-2757)
PHONE..................................813 367-9780
Ian Crabtree, *Ch of Bd*
Tim Ortman, *President*
Jim Coldwell, *Finance*
Keith A Haas, *Director*
Paul R Valentine, *Director*
▲ EMP: 1500 EST: 1986
SALES (est): 213.1MM
SALES (corp-wide): 30.9B **Privately Held**
WEB: www.oldcastlecoastal.com
SIC: 3272 Concrete products
HQ: Crh Americas, Inc.
900 Ashwood Pkwy Ste 600
Atlanta GA 30338
770 804-3363

(G-12996)
OTIS ELEVATOR COMPANY
11760 Us Highway 1 # 600 (33408-3029)
PHONE..................................561 623-4594
EMP: 619
SALES (corp-wide): 14.3B **Publicly Held**
WEB: www.otis.com
SIC: 3534 Elevators & equipment
HQ: Otis Elevator Company
1 Carrier Pl
Farmington CT 06032
860 676-6000

(G-12997)
PAPERS UNLIMITED PLUS INC (PA) ✪
161 Remo Pl (33418-1740)
PHONE..................................215 947-1155
Dustin Seidman, *President*
EMP: 3 EST: 2021
SALES (est): 20MM **Privately Held**
WEB: www.papersunlim.com
SIC: 2676 2621 Towels, napkins & tissue paper products; packaging paper

(G-12998)
PHARMASEAL LLC
3330 Fairchild Grdns Ave (33420-5001)
PHONE..................................561 840-0050
Howard Rosenkranz, *Mng Member*
EMP: 10 EST: 2010
SALES (est): 442.2K **Privately Held**
SIC: 2673 Plastic bags: made from purchased materials

(G-12999)
PIN KING LLC
11562 Winchester Dr (33410-2663)
PHONE..................................561 622-6367
John Umbarila, *Principal*
EMP: 7 EST: 2009
SALES (est): 86.3K **Privately Held**
SIC: 3452 Pins

(G-13000)
PREMIER GLOBAL ENTERPRISES
Also Called: Sir Speedy
261 Isle Way (33418-4596)
PHONE..................................561 747-7303
Richard Goldberg, *Owner*
Rick Goldberg, *Finance*
EMP: 8 EST: 1983
SALES (est): 1MM **Privately Held**
WEB: www.sirspeedy.com
SIC: 2752 2791 Commercial printing, lithographic; typesetting

(G-13001)
PRET-EE LLC
Also Called: Heet
4440 Pga Blvd Ste 600 (33410-6542)
PHONE..................................561 839-4338
Meredith Devore,
EMP: 5 EST: 2009

GEOGRAPHIC

SALES (est): 466.3K **Privately Held**
WEB: www.shopheet.com
SIC: **3961** Jewelry apparel, non-precious metals

(G-13002)
PRINT HEADQUARTERS
10358 Rverside Dr Ste 130 (33410)
PHONE............................772 286-2812
Donna Blank, *President*
Lloyd Blank, *Principal*
EMP: 10 EST: 2000
SALES (est): 610.9K **Privately Held**
WEB: www.printheadquarters.com
SIC: **2752** Commercial printing, offset

(G-13003)
PROVICTUS INC
4440 Pga Blvd Ste 635 (33410-6539)
PHONE............................561 437-0232
David Park, *CEO*
EMP: 20 EST: 2011
SALES (est): 738.1K **Privately Held**
SIC: **7372** Application computer software

(G-13004)
RA CO AMO INC
4100 Burns Rd (33410-4695)
PHONE............................561 626-7232
Carl Volk, *Ch of Bd*
Margaret Volk, *President*
EMP: 12 EST: 1976
SQ FT: 32,656
SALES (est): 557.8K **Privately Held**
WEB: www.racoamo.com
SIC: **3672 1761 3825 7629** Circuit boards, television & radio printed; sheet metalwork; test equipment for electronic & electrical circuits; electronic equipment repair; electronic computers

(G-13005)
RAINBOW PRECISION MFG CORP
4371 Northlake Blvd (33410-6253)
PHONE............................561 691-1658
Richard Thew, *President*
EMP: 9 EST: 2002
SALES (est): 170.9K **Privately Held**
SIC: **3089 3444** Injection molded finished plastic products; injection molding of plastics; metal housings, enclosures, casings & other containers

(G-13006)
RESPECT FOODS
4731 Cadiz Cir (33418-8981)
PHONE............................561 557-2832
EMP: 6
SALES (est): 300K **Privately Held**
SIC: **2099** Mfg Food Preparations

(G-13007)
SCREENCO NORTH INC
11211 81st Ct N (33412-1520)
PHONE............................561 840-3300
Richard Prince, *President*
▲ EMP: 22 EST: 1960
SQ FT: 30,000
SALES (est): 2.3MM **Privately Held**
WEB: www.princedevelopmentgroup.com
SIC: **3446 3448** Architectural metalwork; screen enclosures

(G-13008)
SEQUA CORPORATION (HQ)
Also Called: Kollsman Instrument Division
3999 Rca Blvd (33410-4219)
PHONE............................561 935-3571
Armand F Lauzon, *CEO*
Martin Weinstein, *CEO*
Gerard M Dombek, *President*
Carlo Luzzatto, *President*
Kathleen Peskens, *President*
◆ EMP: 1234 EST: 1929
SQ FT: 45,000
SALES (est): 6.4B
SALES (corp-wide): 8.7B **Publicly Held**
WEB: www.sequa.com
SIC: **3764 3812 3699 3845** Guided missile & space vehicle propulsion unit parts; search & navigation equipment; flight simulators (training aids); electronic; electromedical apparatus; metal container making machines: cans, etc.; airfoils, aircraft engine

PA: The Carlyle Group Inc
1001 Pennsylvania Ave Nw 220s
Washington DC 20004
202 729-5626

(G-13009)
SHUTTER2THINK INC
1014 Raintree Ln (33410-5200)
PHONE............................850 291-8301
Chester I Miller, *Principal*
EMP: 8 EST: 2007
SALES (est): 85.3K **Privately Held**
SIC: **3442** Shutters, door or window: metal

(G-13010)
SPIN FREE LLC
11316 Avery Rd (33410-3402)
PHONE............................561 775-2534
Robert Saunders, *Owner*
EMP: 10 EST: 2012
SALES (est): 217.3K **Privately Held**
SIC: **3531** Construction machinery

(G-13011)
SUNGARD ASSET MGT SYSTEMS INC
100 Village Square Xing (33410-4545)
PHONE............................561 656-2007
Jim Simmons, *President*
EMP: 11
SALES (corp-wide): 13.8B **Publicly Held**
SIC: **7372** Prepackaged software
HQ: Sungard Asset Management Systems Inc.
200 Campus Dr
Collegeville PA 19426
610 251-6500

(G-13012)
SWEET ADDITIONS LLC (PA)
4440 Pga Blvd Ste 600 (33410-6542)
PHONE............................561 472-0178
Crystal Blankenship, *Opers Staff*
Carla Davis, *Marketing Mgr*
Kenneth Valdivia, *Mng Member*
EMP: 10 EST: 2012
SALES (est): 8.4MM **Privately Held**
WEB: www.sweetadditions.com
SIC: **2099** Food preparations

(G-13013)
TITANIUM INTEGRATION LLC
11211 Prosperity Farms Rd (33410-3446)
PHONE............................561 775-1898
Robert C Vogel, *Manager*
EMP: 5 EST: 2010
SALES (est): 1.1MM **Privately Held**
SIC: **3356** Titanium

(G-13014)
UNITED ASSOCIATES GROUP INC
Also Called: Process Solutions
3330 Frchild Gdns Ave (33410-3236)
PHONE............................561 840-0050
Howard Rosenkranz, *President*
◆ EMP: 21 EST: 1991
SQ FT: 20,000
SALES (est): 1.3MM **Privately Held**
SIC: **3552** Textile machinery

(G-13015)
UNIVERSAL BRASS FABRICATION
109 Palm Point Cir (33418-4636)
PHONE............................561 691-5445
EMP: 10
SALES (est): 989K **Privately Held**
SIC: **2342** Mfg Bras/Girdles

(G-13016)
WATERJET ROBOTICS USA LLC
86 Cayman Pl (33418-8096)
PHONE............................772 403-2192
Linda Bisbee, *Manager*
Stephen R Johnson,
EMP: 8 EST: 2015
SALES (est): 783.5K **Privately Held**
WEB: www.waterjetroboticsusa.com
SIC: **3549** Assembly machines, including robotic

(G-13017)
WELDING ANYTHING ANYWHERE LLC
6231 Pga Blvd (33418-4033)
PHONE............................561 762-1404
Dalton Wiita, *Principal*
EMP: 5 EST: 2014
SALES (est): 491.8K **Privately Held**
WEB: www.palmbeachmobilewelding.com
SIC: **7692** Welding repair

(G-13018)
YARD HOUSE HALLANDALE BCH LLC
11701 Lk Vctr Grdn Ave (33410-2706)
PHONE............................561 691-6901
Harold Herrmann, *Owner*
EMP: 9 EST: 2011
SALES (est): 273.8K **Privately Held**
SIC: **2599** Bar, restaurant & cafeteria furniture

(G-13019)
ZIMMER DENTAL INC
4555 Riverside Dr (33410-4200)
PHONE............................561 776-6700
Rachel Ellingson, *Vice Pres*
David Kunz, *Vice Pres*
Pamela Puryear, *Vice Pres*
Ivor Reid, *Engineer*
Jonathan Gold, *Finance Dir*
EMP: 79 EST: 1990
SALES (est): 13.2MM
SALES (corp-wide): 7.8B **Publicly Held**
WEB: www.zimmerbiomet.com
SIC: **3842** Orthopedic appliances
PA: Zimmer Biomet Holdings, Inc.
345 E Main St
Warsaw IN 46580
574 267-6131

(G-13020)
ZOAG LLC
102 Alegria Way (33418-1722)
PHONE............................862 591-2969
Zoltan Hetzer, *Mng Member*
▲ EMP: 8 EST: 2013
SALES (est): 547.9K **Privately Held**
SIC: **3965** Fasteners

Palm City
Martin County

(G-13021)
ADDITIVE TECHNOLOGIES LLC
Also Called: Additec
4413 Sw Cargo Way (34990-5523)
PHONE............................702 686-5190
Brian Matthews, *CEO*
EMP: 5 EST: 2015
SALES (est): 1.7MM **Privately Held**
WEB: www.additec.net
SIC: **3313** Alloys, additive, except copper: not made in blast furnaces

(G-13022)
AIR BURNERS INC
4390 Sw Cargo Way (34990-5577)
PHONE............................772 220-7303
Brian O'Connor, *President*
EMP: 12 EST: 2011
SALES (est): 1.9MM **Privately Held**
WEB: www.airburners.com
SIC: **3567** Industrial furnaces & ovens

(G-13023)
AWARENESS TECHNOLOGY INC (PA)
2325 Sw Martin Hwy (34990-3222)
P.O. Box 1679 (34991-6679)
PHONE............................772 283-6540
Mary Freeman, *CEO*
Gary S Freeman, *Admin Sec*
EMP: 74 EST: 1982
SQ FT: 50,000
SALES (est): 13.8MM **Privately Held**
WEB: www.awaretech.com
SIC: **3826 2869** Analytical instruments; laboratory chemicals, organic

(G-13024)
AWARENESS TECHNOLOGY INC
1935 Sw Martin Hwy (34990-3228)
PHONE............................772 283-6540
EMP: 31
SALES (corp-wide): 13.8MM **Privately Held**
WEB: www.awaretech.com
SIC: **3826 2869** Analytical instruments; laboratory chemicals, organic
PA: Awareness Technology Inc
2325 Sw Martin Hwy
Palm City FL 34990
772 283-6540

(G-13025)
B4C TECHNOLOGIES INC
4306 Sw Cargo Way (34990-5577)
PHONE............................772 463-1557
Kenneth Hoffman, *CEO*
Ed McComas, *Chairman*
EMP: 6 EST: 2010
SQ FT: 10,000
SALES (est): 1.1MM **Privately Held**
WEB: www.b4ctechnologies.com
SIC: **3471** Electroplating of metals or formed products

(G-13026)
CAMERON TEXTILES INC
Also Called: Aresco Manufacturing & Safety
2740 Sw Martin Downs Blvd (34990-6046)
PHONE............................954 454-6482
Darby Cameron, *President*
Michael Cameron, *Vice Pres*
▲ EMP: 9 EST: 1982
SQ FT: 6,000
SALES (est): 688.8K **Privately Held**
SIC: **2393 2326 2392** Canvas bags; aprons, work, except rubberized & plastic: men's; vests: made from purchased materials; bags, laundry: made from purchased materials; personal safety equipment; industrial safety devices: first aid kits & masks

(G-13027)
CERAMLOCK COATINGS INC
3912 Sw Bruner Ter (34990-5549)
PHONE............................772 781-2141
Doug Byron, *Principal*
▼ EMP: 9 EST: 2010
SALES (est): 731.4K **Privately Held**
SIC: **3479** Coating of metals & formed products

(G-13028)
CHEMPLEX INDUSTRIES INC
2820 Sw 42nd Ave (34990-5573)
PHONE............................772 283-2700
Monte J Solazzi, *President*
Dillon Voss, *Supervisor*
EMP: 12 EST: 1971
SQ FT: 22,000
SALES (est): 2MM **Privately Held**
WEB: www.chemplex.com
SIC: **3826** Spectroscopic & other optical properties measuring equipment

(G-13029)
CHITTUM YACHTS LLC (PA)
4577 Sw Cargo Way (34990-5521)
PHONE............................386 589-7224
Harold Thomas Chittum III,
George Sawley,
EMP: 15 EST: 2010
SALES (est): 2.6MM **Privately Held**
SIC: **3732** Yachts, building & repairing

(G-13030)
COASTAL POWDER COATINGS INC
2049 Sw Poma Dr (34990-6602)
PHONE............................772 283-5311
Frank Poma, *President*
Jason Poma, *Vice Pres*
EMP: 9 EST: 2008
SALES (est): 1.1MM **Privately Held**
WEB: www.coastalpowder.com
SIC: **3479** Coating of metals & formed products

▲ = Import ▼=Export
◆ =Import/Export

(G-13031)
CORE LABEL LLC
4313 Sw Port Way (34990-5584)
PHONE..................................772 287-2141
EMP: 15
SALES (corp-wide): 3.9B **Privately Held**
SIC: 2759 Commercial printing
HQ: Core Label, Llc
13985 S Eagle Valley Rd
Tyrone PA 16686
814 684-0934

(G-13032)
CUSTOM AGRONOMICS INC
2300 Sw Poma Dr (34990-6611)
PHONE..................................772 223-0775
Michael F Ciferri Sr, *President*
Mike Ciferri, *President*
Brian Scott, *Vice Pres*
Michael Williams, *Vice Pres*
Bryan Scott, *Purchasing*
◆ **EMP:** 10 **EST:** 2009
SQ FT: 20,000
SALES (est): 4.3MM **Privately Held**
WEB: www.customagronomics.com
SIC: 2879 Agricultural chemicals

(G-13033)
EAGLE I TECH INC
Also Called: Florida Rs Technology
4529 Sw Cargo Way (34990-5521)
PHONE..................................772 221-8188
Al Ragl, *President*
Mike Trivison, *Business Mgr*
Tim Spacek, *Vice Pres*
Don Kerens, *Prdtn Mgr*
Ken Peters, *Opers Staff*
◆ **EMP:** 47 **EST:** 1993
SALES (est): 9.7MM **Privately Held**
WEB: www.flrst.com
SIC: 3678 Electronic connectors

(G-13034)
**ELECTRON BEAM
DEVELOPMENT**
3591 Sw Deggeller Ct (34990-5548)
PHONE..................................772 219-4600
James S Bickel, *President*
Edward L Bancroft, *Corp Secy*
EMP: 20 **EST:** 1976
SQ FT: 10,000
SALES (est): 525.9K **Privately Held**
WEB: www.ebairfoils.com
SIC: 7692 Welding repair

(G-13035)
EZ BOATWORKS INC
10602 Sw Corey Pl (34990-7801)
PHONE..................................772 475-8721
Garcia Ester, *Principal*
EMP: 8 **EST:** 2014
SALES (est): 155.6K **Privately Held**
SIC: 3732 Boat building & repairing

(G-13036)
FATOVICH TECHNOLOGIES LLC
2159 Sw Cameron Ln (34990-6225)
PHONE..................................772 597-1326
Bronco Fatovich, *Mng Member*
Kathleen M Fatovich, *Mng Member*
EMP: 7 **EST:** 2008
SALES (est): 466.1K **Privately Held**
WEB: www.fatovichtechnologies.com
SIC: 2822 Ethylene-propylene rubbers,
EPDM polymers

(G-13037)
FIVE OCEANS FLORIDA INC
Also Called: Florida Rs Technology
4529 Sw Cargo Way (34990-5521)
PHONE..................................772 221-8188
Chester Claudon, *President*
Carol Claudon, *Human Resources*
EMP: 34 **EST:** 2016
SALES (est): 3.1MM **Privately Held**
WEB: www.flrst.com
SIC: 3643 Current-carrying wiring devices

(G-13038)
**FLORIDA CYPRESS & FENCE
CO**
3922 Sw Saint Lucie Ln (34990-3826)
PHONE..................................561 392-3011
▼ **EMP:** 8
SQ FT: 8,000

SALES (est): 944.3K **Privately Held**
SIC: 2499 5031 Mfg Wood Products Whol
Lumber/Plywood/Millwork

(G-13039)
**FLORIDA POLE SETTLERS &
CRANE**
4157 Sw Moore St (34990-5650)
PHONE..................................772 283-6820
Kenneth A Wieser, *President*
EMP: 11 **EST:** 2006
SQ FT: 3,322
SALES (est): 446.3K **Privately Held**
WEB: www.floridapolesetters.com
SIC: 2411 Pole cutting contractors

(G-13040)
FORT DEARBORN COMPANY
Roll-Fed Labels Division
4313 Sw Port Way (34990-5584)
PHONE..................................772 600-2756
Jeff Ganswindt, *Manager*
EMP: 73
SALES (corp-wide): 3.9B **Privately Held**
WEB: www.mcclabel.com
SIC: 2759 2752 Flexographic printing;
commercial printing, offset
HQ: Fort Dearborn Company
1530 Morse Ave
Elk Grove Village IL 60007
847 357-9500

(G-13041)
GEN-PRODICS INC
2029 Sw Oak Ridge Rd (34990-2156)
PHONE..................................772 221-8464
EMP: 5
SALES (est): 515.9K **Privately Held**
SIC: 3674 Mfg Semiconductors/Related
Devices

(G-13042)
GMS SHEET METAL & AC INC
3377 Sw 42nd Ave Ste D (34990-5595)
PHONE..................................772 221-0585
Michael Mazzilli, *Principal*
EMP: 15 **EST:** 2012
SALES (est): 2.5MM **Privately Held**
SIC: 3444 Sheet metalwork

(G-13043)
GUERILLA TECHNOLOGIES INC
4203 Sw High Meadows Ave (34990-3726)
PHONE..................................772 283-0500
Camille M Parrott, *CEO*
Robert A Parrott IV, *President*
Bill Bradshaw, *VP Sales*
Sal Terranova, *Sales Staff*
Erin Haithcox, *Sales Executive*
EMP: 10 **EST:** 2004
SQ FT: 2,600
SALES (est): 764.5K **Privately Held**
WEB: www.guerillatechnologies.com
SIC: 3699 Electrical equipment & supplies

(G-13044)
H I T LIGHTING CORP
3399 Sw 42nd Ave (34990-5554)
P.O. Box 1199 (34991-1199)
PHONE..................................772 221-1155
Donald Cantor, *President*
EMP: 8 **EST:** 1992
SALES (est): 1MM **Privately Held**
SIC: 3646 Commercial indusl & institu-
tional electric lighting fixtures

(G-13045)
**INTELLIGENT OPERATING TECH
INC**
Also Called: Gex
4437 Sw Cargo Way (34990-5523)
PHONE..................................303 400-9640
Gary Pageau, *CEO*
Mike Pageau, *President*
John Crotty, *Treasurer*
Michelle Cowan, *Marketing Staff*
William Schimdt, *Admin Sec*
EMP: 20 **EST:** 1991
SQ FT: 9,000
SALES (est): 3.2MM **Privately Held**
WEB: www.gexcorp.com
SIC: 3829 8734 Measuring & controlling
devices; testing laboratories

(G-13046)
INTERNATIONAL WHL TILE LLC
3500 Sw 42nd Ave (34990-5613)
PHONE..................................772 223-5151
Paul Boushar, *President*
Michael Dagostino, *CFO*
Lori Veal, *Cust Mgr*
Nelson Lopez, *Department Mgr*
Ray Getty, *Manager*
▲ **EMP:** 60 **EST:** 2008
SQ FT: 1,750
SALES (est): 19.7MM
SALES (corp-wide): 24.8MM **Privately
Held**
WEB: www.internationalwholesaletile.com
SIC: 3251 Brick & structural clay tile
PA: Iwt Holdings Llc
3500 Sw 42nd Ave
Palm City FL 34990
772 223-5151

(G-13047)
KAZDIN INDUSTRIES INC
5258 Sw Anhinga Ave (34990-4043)
P.O. Box 2472 (34991-2472)
PHONE..................................772 223-5511
Richard H Kazdin, *President*
Sharon J Kazdin, *Vice Pres*
EMP: 8 **EST:** 2007
SALES (est): 99.5K **Privately Held**
SIC: 3554 Paper industries machinery

(G-13048)
KRUNCHY KRISPS LLC
2740 Sw Martin Downs Blvd (34990-6046)
PHONE..................................561 309-7049
EMP: 5
SALES (est): 500K **Privately Held**
SIC: 2038 Mfg Frozen Specialties

(G-13049)
**L & S DESIGN &
CONSTRUCTION**
3561 Sw Corporate Pkwy (34990-8152)
PHONE..................................772 220-1745
Jeff Seyler, *President*
EMP: 6 **EST:** 1996
SALES (est): 456.7K **Privately Held**
SIC: 3732 Boat building & repairing

(G-13050)
MATAWAN TOOL & MFG CO INC
2861 Sw Brighton Way (34990-6075)
PHONE..................................772 221-3706
EMP: 5 **EST:** 1946
SQ FT: 5,000
SALES (est): 350K **Privately Held**
SIC: 3599 Jobbing Machine Shop

(G-13051)
OUTSTANDING EVENTS INC
5380 Sw Landing Creek Dr (34990-4125)
PHONE..................................772 463-5406
Eve M Thompson, *Director*
EMP: 12 **EST:** 2001
SALES (est): 853.8K **Privately Held**
WEB: www.outstandingevents.com
SIC: 3411 Food & beverage containers

(G-13052)
PAC SEATING SYSTEMS INC
3370 Sw 42nd Ave (34990-5541)
PHONE..................................772 286-6670
Charles Tufano, *President*
Jad Azzi, *Vice Pres*
Jonathan Neale, *QC Mgr*
Madhan Kallem, *Engineer*
Sree Reddy, *Engineer*
EMP: 35 **EST:** 2002
SALES (est): 9.4MM **Privately Held**
WEB: www.pac-fl.com
SIC: 2531 Seats, aircraft

(G-13053)
PARADISE AIR FRESH LLC
3029 Sw 42nd Ave (34990-5556)
PHONE..................................561 972-0375
Bradley Simons, *Vice Pres*
Ryan Simon, *Mng Member*
EMP: 13 **EST:** 2017
SALES (est): 1.9MM **Privately Held**
WEB: www.paradiseairfresh.com
SIC: 2842 Sanitation preparations, disin-
fectants & deodorants

(G-13054)
**PEAK SHEET METAL
SOLUTIONS INC**
5283 Sw Leeward Ln (34990-1203)
PHONE..................................954 775-6393
Donald Peak Jr, *President*
EMP: 5 **EST:** 2019
SALES (est): 366.2K **Privately Held**
SIC: 3444 Sheet metalwork

(G-13055)
PIONEER SCREEN INC
2740 Sw Martin Downs Blvd (34990-6046)
PHONE..................................772 260-3068
Craig Davis Rice, *Principal*
EMP: 8 **EST:** 2009
SALES (est): 136.1K **Privately Held**
SIC: 3442 Screen & storm doors & win-
dows

(G-13056)
PLAZADOOR CORP
4425 Sw Cargo Way (34990-5523)
PHONE..................................561 578-5450
Michael Fry, *CEO*
EMP: 25 **EST:** 2018
SALES (est): 1.3MM **Privately Held**
WEB: www.plazadoorcompany.com
SIC: 3089 1793 Fiberglass doors; glass &
glazing work

(G-13057)
RUSSANOS EXPRESS LLC
2946 Sw Mapp Rd (34990-2724)
PHONE..................................772 220-3329
Frank Romano, *Principal*
EMP: 9 **EST:** 2006
SALES (est): 528.9K **Privately Held**
SIC: 2741 Miscellaneous publishing

(G-13058)
**SHURHOLD PRODUCTS
COMPANY**
3119 Sw 42nd Ave (34990-5558)
PHONE..................................772 287-1313
Barry Burhoff, *President*
Brett Berhoff, *Vice Pres*
Lioyd Berhoff, *Vice Pres*
Nicole Veldhius, *Relations*
▲ **EMP:** 9 **EST:** 1972
SQ FT: 9,660
SALES (est): 1.5MM **Privately Held**
WEB: www.shurhold.com
SIC: 3991 3732 2298 Brushes, household
or industrial; boat building & repairing;
cordage & twine

(G-13059)
**SOUTHEASTERN PRINTING CO
INC**
4313 Sw Port Way (34990-5584)
PHONE..................................772 287-2141
Richard Buchalter, *Production*
John Egan, *Production*
Eric Ellison, *Sales Staff*
Chuck Gerardi, *Sales Staff*
Lawrence Reger, *Branch Mgr*
EMP: 8
SALES (corp-wide): 50.7MM **Privately
Held**
WEB: www.seprint.com
SIC: 2732 2752 2759 2789 Book print-
ing; commercial printing, lithographic;
commercial printing; bookbinding & re-
lated work
PA: Southeastern Printing Co Inc
950 Se 8th St
Hialeah FL 33010
772 287-2141

(G-13060)
**SPECTOR MANUFACTURING
INC**
22 Sw Riverway Blvd (34990-4238)
PHONE..................................860 559-6068
EMP: 7 **EST:** 2017
SALES (est): 96K **Privately Held**
WEB: www.spectec.biz
SIC: 3999 Manufacturing industries

(G-13061)
TENDONEASE LLC
1738 Sw Foxpoint Trl (34990-5726)
PHONE..................................888 224-0319
EMP: 5 **EST:** 2007

SALES (est): 340K **Privately Held**
SIC: 3842 3949 Mfg Surgical Appliances/Supplies Mfg Sporting/Athletic Goods

(G-13062)
TREASURE CST CURB & THERM PLAS
2580 Sw Hidden Pond Way (34990-2053)
PHONE..................................772 287-0391
Mary Bailey, *President*
EMP: 6 **EST:** 1996
SALES (est): 453.3K **Privately Held**
SIC: 3272 Concrete products, precast

(G-13063)
UCT COATINGS INC (PA)
Also Called: Uct Defense
3300 Sw 42nd Ave (34990-5539)
PHONE..................................772 872-7110
Don Weeks, *CEO*
Tim Donahue, *Chairman*
John S Bourret, *Vice Pres*
Scott Bourret, *Vice Pres*
Lou D'Ambrosio, *Vice Pres*
▲ **EMP:** 18 **EST:** 2000
SQ FT: 24,000
SALES (est): 13.1MM **Privately Held**
WEB: www.uctcoatings.com
SIC: 3479 Coating of metals & formed products

(G-13064)
W KOST INC
4175 Sw Martin Hwy (34990-5524)
PHONE..................................772 286-3700
Walter G Kost, *CEO*
Chris Kost, *President*
Christopher J Kost, *Principal*
▼ **EMP:** 50 **EST:** 1980
SQ FT: 16,000
SALES (est): 2.7MM **Privately Held**
SIC: 2439 Trusses, wooden roof

(G-13065)
WELDING AROUND
5205b Sw 69th St (34990-5176)
PHONE..................................772 342-3233
Brice Atkinson, *Principal*
EMP: 7 **EST:** 2016
SALES (est): 469.1K **Privately Held**
SIC: 7692 Welding repair

Palm Coast
Flagler County

(G-13066)
5THELEMENT INDIAN CUISINE LLC
101 Palm Harbor Pkwy (32137-8004)
PHONE..................................386 302-0202
Jerry Martinho Fernandes,
EMP: 5 **EST:** 2017
SALES (est): 2.4MM **Privately Held**
WEB: www.flaglerrestaurants.com
SIC: 2819 Elements

(G-13067)
ACE TOOLS
17 Lee Dr (32137-9700)
PHONE..................................386 302-5152
Mark Grillo, *Principal*
EMP: 8 **EST:** 2016
SALES (est): 479.7K **Privately Held**
WEB: www.acetools.com
SIC: 3599 Industrial machinery

(G-13068)
AIR SUPPORT TECKS
14 Bird Haven Pl (32137-9318)
PHONE..................................386 986-5301
Jillian S Burns, *Principal*
EMP: 8 **EST:** 2009
SALES (est): 75.3K **Privately Held**
SIC: 3721 Aircraft

(G-13069)
ALTIUM PACKAGING LLC
71 Hargrove Grade (32137-5114)
PHONE..................................386 246-4000
Danny Lafferman, *Branch Mgr*
EMP: 17

SALES (corp-wide): 14.6B **Publicly Held**
WEB: www.altiumpkg.com
SIC: 3089 Plastic containers, except foam
HQ: Altium Packaging Llc
2500 Windy Ridge Pkwy Se # 1400
Atlanta GA 30339
678 742-4600

(G-13070)
AVEOENGINEERING LLC
Also Called: Aveotech International
1200 Cinnamon Beach Way # 1122 (32137-5328)
PHONE..................................631 747-6671
Christian Nielsen, *CEO*
Jana Nielsen, *General Mgr*
Michal Gregor, *Supervisor*
EMP: 7 **EST:** 2010
SALES (est): 970.9K **Privately Held**
WEB: www.aveoengineering.com
SIC: 3728 Research & dev by manuf., aircraft parts & auxiliary equip

(G-13071)
AVRORA INC
7 Richfield Pl (32164-6518)
PHONE..................................386 246-9112
Andrei Zborovsky, *President*
EMP: 6 **EST:** 2005
SALES (est): 406.3K **Privately Held**
WEB: www.avrorainc.com
SIC: 2511 Wood household furniture

(G-13072)
CANE PROOF LLC
Also Called: Cane Proof Window and Doors
5 Ethel Ln (32164-6227)
PHONE..................................386 445-2290
Brain Wieskoph,
EMP: 5 **EST:** 2004
SALES (est): 476.6K **Privately Held**
SIC: 3442 Metal doors, sash & trim

(G-13073)
CLASS A PRINTING LLC
11 Industry Dr (32137-5104)
PHONE..................................386 447-0520
Christina Rice, *President*
EMP: 5 **EST:** 1997
SQ FT: 1,258
SALES (est): 520.9K **Privately Held**
WEB: www.classaprinting.com
SIC: 2752 Commercial printing, offset

(G-13074)
CONC-STEEL INC
250 Palm Coast Pkwy Ne (32137-8224)
PHONE..................................516 882-5551
John S Koszalkowski, *Principal*
EMP: 6 **EST:** 2018
SALES (est): 386.2K **Privately Held**
WEB: www.conc-steel.com
SIC: 3312 Blast furnaces & steel mills

(G-13075)
CREATIONS IN CABINETRY INC
2 Market Pl (32137-5107)
PHONE..................................386 237-3082
Robert Baez, *Principal*
EMP: 7 **EST:** 2008
SALES (est): 138.1K **Privately Held**
SIC: 2434 Wood kitchen cabinets

(G-13076)
DYNAMIC ENGRG INNOVATIONS INC
32 Hargrove Grade (32137-5101)
P.O. Box 352919 (32135-2919)
PHONE..................................386 445-6000
Robert Stockman, *President*
Richard Stockman, *Vice Pres*
Erica Zevallos, *Marketing Staff*
▲ **EMP:** 211 **EST:** 1939
SQ FT: 48,000
SALES (est): 23.1MM **Privately Held**
WEB: www.amradmanufacturing.com
SIC: 3675 Electronic capacitors

(G-13077)
FLIGHT VELOCITY
279 Old Moody Blvd (32164-2470)
PHONE..................................866 937-9371
EMP: 8 **EST:** 2017
SALES (est): 1MM **Privately Held**
WEB: www.flightvelocity.com
SIC: 3728 Aircraft parts & equipment

(G-13078)
GALTRONICS TELEMETRY INC
1 Hargrove Grade Ste 5 (32137-5159)
P.O. Box 803338, Chicago IL (60680-3338)
PHONE..................................386 202-2055
Graydon Parsons, *President*
Michael Lafferty, *Vice Pres*
Sean Lafferty, *Vice Pres*
Terry Pugh, *Sales Staff*
Patrick Ward, *Director*
EMP: 10 **EST:** 2009
SQ FT: 4,000
SALES (est): 1MM **Privately Held**
SIC: 3822 Auto controls regulating residntl & coml environmt & applncs

(G-13079)
GIOIA SAILS SOUTH LLC
14 Commerce Blvd (32164-3126)
P.O. Box 352918 (32135-2918)
PHONE..................................386 597-2876
Donald T Gioia, *Mng Member*
EMP: 55 **EST:** 2007
SALES (est): 14.8MM **Privately Held**
WEB: www.gioiasailssouth.com
SIC: 2394 Canvas & related products
PA: Gioia Sails, Inc.
1951 Rutgers Blvd
Lakewood NJ 08701
732 901-6770

(G-13080)
INTERNATIONAL TOOL MCHS OF FLA
Also Called: ITM
5 Industry Dr (32137-5104)
P.O. Box 351641 (32135-1641)
PHONE..................................386 446-0500
Karl H Giebmanns, *President*
Karl Giebmanns, *Chief Engr*
Jennifr Sager, *Med Doctor*
Peter Chenson, *Director*
Karola Giebmanns, *Admin Sec*
▲ **EMP:** 32 **EST:** 1981
SQ FT: 25,000
SALES (est): 4.4MM **Privately Held**
WEB: www.floridagrincing.com
SIC: 3541 Machine tool replacement & repair parts, metal cutting types

(G-13081)
KEITH EICKERT POWER PDTS LLC
11 Industry Dr (32137-5108)
PHONE..................................386 446-0660
Julian Sullivan, *President*
Juliana L Sullivan,
EMP: 10 **EST:** 1990
SQ FT: 10,000
SALES (est): 2MM **Privately Held**
SIC: 3519 5088 Marine engines; marine crafts & supplies

(G-13082)
MANAGED DATA ASSOC INC
Also Called: Custom Cable Crafters
80 Beechwood Ln (32137-8677)
PHONE..................................386 449-8419
Donna Shadron, *President*
EMP: 6 **EST:** 2017
SALES (est): 362.1K **Privately Held**
WEB: www.mdacables.com
SIC: 3357 5063 Fiber optic cable (insulated); telephone & telegraph wire & cable

(G-13083)
NEWS-JOURNAL CORPORATION
4984 Palm Coast Pkwy Nw # 5 (32137-3620)
PHONE..................................386 283-5664
EMP: 15
SALES (corp-wide): 68.8MM **Privately Held**
WEB: www.news-journalonline.com
SIC: 2711 Newspapers, publishing & printing
PA: News-Journal Corporation
901 6th St
Daytona Beach FL 32117
386 252-1511

(G-13084)
PALM COAST OBSERVER LLC
1 Florida Park Dr N # 103 (32137-3843)
P.O. Box 353850 (32135-3850)
PHONE..................................386 447-9723
Jonathan Simmons, *Editor*
Susan Moore, *Accounts Mgr*
Jessica Godwin, *Advt Staff*
Bonnie Hamilton, *Office Mgr*
Matthew G Walsh,
EMP: 20 **EST:** 2010
SALES (est): 2.9MM **Privately Held**
WEB: www.palmcoastobserver.com
SIC: 2711 Newspapers, publishing & printing

(G-13085)
R & C SALES & MFG INC
18 Hargrove Grade Ste 101 (32137-5161)
PHONE..................................904 824-2223
Robert Atkins, *President*
Carol Atkins, *Corp Secy*
EMP: 13 **EST:** 1978
SALES (est): 1MM **Privately Held**
SIC: 3523 Farm machinery & equipment

(G-13086)
SDM INDUSTRIES INC
13 Hargrove Grade (32137-5114)
PHONE..................................904 814-2814
Shawn D Moksnes, *Principal*
EMP: 9 **EST:** 2012
SALES (est): 401.3K **Privately Held**
SIC: 3999 Manufacturing industries

(G-13087)
SMART GUARD SHUTTERS LLC
79 Pritchard Dr (32164-7184)
PHONE..................................386 227-6295
EMP: 5 **EST:** 2018
SALES (est): 472.8K **Privately Held**
WEB: www.smartguardshutters.com
SIC: 3442 Shutters, door or window: metal

(G-13088)
SUNRISE
26 N Village Dr (32137-1603)
PHONE..................................386 627-5029
Sonya Romero, *Principal*
EMP: 7 **EST:** 2015
SALES (est): 72.4K **Privately Held**
SIC: 2591 Window blinds

(G-13089)
SWEETSIES
26 Ullman Pl (32164-5906)
P.O. Box 731764, Ormond Beach (32173-1764)
PHONE..................................386 566-6762
Amber Hadley, *Principal*
EMP: 8 **EST:** 2010
SALES (est): 421.2K **Privately Held**
SIC: 2051 Cakes, bakery: except frozen

(G-13090)
THOSE CABINET GUYS INC
8 Market Place Ct (32137-5105)
PHONE..................................703 927-2460
EMP: 5 **EST:** 2019
SALES (est): 310.5K **Privately Held**
WEB: www.thosecabinetguys.com
SIC: 2434 Wood kitchen cabinets

(G-13091)
TOTAL PERFORMANCE INC
Also Called: Cool Flex
75 N Lakewalk Dr (32137-1302)
PHONE..................................203 265-5667
Michael V Lauria, *President*
Brian Mc Allister, *Sales Mgr*
EMP: 15 **EST:** 1971
SQ FT: 7,500
SALES (est): 269.3K **Privately Held**
WEB: www.totalperformanceinc.com
SIC: 3711 3714 3592 5531 Motor vehicles & car bodies; motor vehicle parts & accessories; carburetors; automotive parts; automotive supplies & parts

(G-13092)
VLADMIR LTD
Also Called: Amrad
32 Hargrove Grade (32137-5101)
PHONE..................................386 445-6000
EMP: 25

▲ = Import ▼=Export
◆ =Import/Export

SALES (corp-wide): 28.2MM **Privately Held**
WEB: www.globalthesource.com
SIC: 3675 Electronic capacitors
PA: Vladmir, Ltd.
1648 N Lake Pass
Universal City TX 78148
800 531-5967

(G-13093)
WATTCORE INC
4 Commerce Blvd (32164-3119)
PHONE...................................571 482-6777
Chanty Khek, *President*
◆ **EMP: 8 EST:** 2009
SALES (est): 708.6K **Privately Held**
WEB: www.wattcore.com
SIC: 3677 Electronic coils, transformers &
other inductors

(G-13094)
WILWOODMAN INC
3 Market Pl Ste C (32137-5140)
PHONE...................................386 334-7929
Negroa Wilfredd, *President*
EMP: 6 EST: 2005
SALES (est): 356.1K **Privately Held**
WEB: www.wilwoodman.com
SIC: 2541 Wood partitions & fixtures

Palm Harbor
Pinellas County

(G-13095)
ACCENT NEON & SIGN
COMPANY (PA)
1179 Ridgecrest Ct (34683-2732)
PHONE...................................727 784-8414
Todd Ritchey, *Owner*
EMP: 5 EST: 1984
SALES (est): 411K **Privately Held**
WEB: www.accentneon.com
SIC: 3993 1799 5046 Neon signs; sign in-
stallation & maintenance; neon signs

(G-13096)
ALH SYSTEMS INC
1862 Eagle Ridge Blvd (34685-3302)
PHONE...................................727 787-6306
EMP: 9
SQ FT: 3,750
SALES: 1.4MM **Privately Held**
SIC: 3549 Assembly Of Machines Special-
izing In Flight Training Equipment And
Flight Simulators

(G-13097)
AMERCN CABINETS GRANITE
FLOORS
32140 Us Highway 19 N (34684-3709)
PHONE...................................727 303-0678
EMP: 9 **EST:** 2018
SALES (est): 474.1K **Privately Held**
WEB: www.americancgf.com
SIC: 2541 2434 3996 Counter & sink
tops; wood kitchen cabinets; hard surface
floor coverings

(G-13098)
ANTIQUE AUTOMOBILE RADIO
INC
700 Tampa Rd (34683-5454)
PHONE...................................727 785-8733
Daniel Schulz, *President*
Daisy Schulz, *General Mgr*
Matt Simanteris, *Production*
EMP: 6 EST: 1993
SQ FT: 5,604
SALES (est): 505.7K **Privately Held**
WEB: www.radiosforoldcars.com
SIC: 3663 Radio receiver networks

(G-13099)
ASSET GUARDIAN INC
2706 Alt 19 Ste 254 (34683-2655)
PHONE...................................727 942-2246
Wade B Moss, *Principal*
Iain Rennie, *Manager*
EMP: 6 EST: 2010
SALES (est): 320.3K **Privately Held**
WEB: www.polygraphtampabay.com
SIC: 3829 Polygraph devices

(G-13100)
AVERY DENNISON
CORPORATION
720 Sandy Hook Rd (34683-3734)
PHONE...................................727 787-1651
EMP: 118
SALES (corp-wide): 6.9B **Publicly Held**
SIC: 2672 Paper; Coated And Laminated,
Nec
PA: Avery Dennison Corporation
207 N Goode Ave
Glendale CA 44060
626 304-2000

(G-13101)
AVERY DENNISON
CORPORATION
2706 Altmate 19 N Ste 314 (34683)
PHONE...................................727 785-6995
EMP: 115
SALES (corp-wide): 6.3B **Publicly Held**
SIC: 2672 Mfg Coated/Laminated Paper
PA: Avery Dennison Corporation
207 N Goode Ave Fl 6
Glendale CA 44060
626 304-2000

(G-13102)
BAY AREA SECURITY SHRED
Also Called: Secure On-Site Shredding
301 Bear Ridge Cir (34683-5483)
P.O. Box 357, Dunedin (34697-0357)
PHONE...................................877 974-7337
Gloria Schmeider, *President*
John D Schmeider, *Vice Pres*
John Schmeider, *Vice Pres*
EMP: 10 EST: 1994
SQ FT: 2,000
SALES (est): 1MM **Privately Held**
SIC: 3589 7389 Shredders, industrial &
commercial; document & office record de-
struction

(G-13103)
BEAST ROW INC
Also Called: Mixers Bar & Grille
3430 E Lake Rd Ste 1 (34685-2414)
PHONE...................................727 787-2710
Nancy A Dattilo, *Principal*
EMP: 7 EST: 2009
SALES (est): 160.1K **Privately Held**
SIC: 2599 Bar, restaurant & cafeteria furni-
ture

(G-13104)
BECK GRAPHICS INC
1114 Florida Ave Ste B (34683-4331)
PHONE...................................727 443-3803
John D Beck, *President*
Paul Beck, *Treasurer*
EMP: 19 EST: 1985
SQ FT: 3,000
SALES (est): 920.7K **Privately Held**
SIC: 2752 Commercial printing, offset

(G-13105)
CAVOK CAPITAL LLC
855 Virginia Ave (34683-5227)
PHONE...................................727 789-0951
Todd Dolphin, *Mng Member*
EMP: 16 EST: 2019
SALES (est): 1MM **Privately Held**
SIC: 3999 1731 Manufacturing industries;
electric power systems contractors

(G-13106)
CELLMIC LLC
34266 Us Highway 19 N (34684-2147)
PHONE...................................310 443-2070
Neven Karlovac, *CEO*
EMP: 6 EST: 2011
SALES (est): 407.1K **Privately Held**
SIC: 3826 Analytical instruments

(G-13107)
CORINTHIAN CATAMARANS
LLC
4338 Auston Way (34685-4017)
PHONE...................................813 334-1029
Robert Muhlhan,
Paula J Muhlhan,
EMP: 10 EST: 2002
SQ FT: 2,000

SALES (est): 980.3K **Privately Held**
WEB: www.corinthiancatamarans.com
SIC: 3732 Boat building & repairing

(G-13108)
CRAEMER US CORPORATION
2927 Pinewood Run (34684-4920)
PHONE...................................727 312-8859
Axel Breitkreuz, *President*
EMP: 7 EST: 2018
SALES (est): 234.5K **Privately Held**
WEB: www.craemer.com
SIC: 3089 Pallets, plastic

(G-13109)
DOWNES TRADING CO
5730 Stag Thicket Ln (34685-2536)
PHONE...................................813 855-7122
James Downes, *President*
Mary Downes, *Vice Pres*
EMP: 8 EST: 2003
SALES (est): 638.2K **Privately Held**
SIC: 1389 5199 Construction, repair & dis-
mantling services; nondurable goods

(G-13110)
DREAM CUIZINE
4952 Ridgemoor Blvd (34685-1744)
PHONE...................................727 943-8289
Gayle Kufro, *President*
Jolene Essex, *Vice Pres*
Frank Essex, *Director*
Joseph Kufro, *Director*
EMP: 6 EST: 2005
SALES (est): 340K **Privately Held**
WEB: www.oregonrvdealers.com
SIC: 2099 Ready-to-eat meals, salads &
sandwiches

(G-13111)
GOFORIT INC
Also Called: Sir Speedy
34034 Us Highway 19 N (34684-2645)
PHONE...................................727 785-7616
Eugene M Goldman, *President*
Ronnie Goldman, *Treasurer*
EMP: 5 EST: 1982
SQ FT: 1,600
SALES (est): 470.1K **Privately Held**
WEB: www.goforitapp.com
SIC: 2752 7334 Commercial printing, litho-
graphic; photocopying & duplicating serv-
ices

(G-13112)
GULF COAST PROGRAM
3515 Alt 19 Ste B (34683-1413)
PHONE...................................727 945-1402
Phillip Nathanson, *President*
EMP: 5 EST: 1997
SALES (est): 395.3K **Privately Held**
SIC: 7372 Prepackaged software

(G-13113)
HARBOR MACHINE INC
374 Foxcroft Dr E (34683-5613)
PHONE...................................727 772-9515
Garry J Czipri, *President*
EMP: 7 EST: 2008
SALES (est): 292.1K **Privately Held**
WEB: www.harbormachine.com
SIC: 3599 Machine shop, jobbing & repair

(G-13114)
INSPECS USA LC
30798 Us Highway 19 N (34684-4411)
PHONE...................................727 771-7710
Vincent Wright, *President*
Annalisa De, *Sales Staff*
Brookelyn Sager, *Sales Staff*
▲ **EMP: 16 EST:** 1999
SQ FT: 5,679
SALES (est): 5.2MM
SALES (corp-wide): 246.4MM **Privately**
Held
WEB: www.inspecs.com
SIC: 3851 Protective eyewear
HQ: Inspecs Limited
7-10 Kelso Place Upper Bristol Road
Bath BA1 3
122 571-7060

(G-13115)
J P POLY BAG COMPANY
1783 Marsh Wren Way (34683-6144)
PHONE...................................727 804-5866

Olga Pochodaj, *Principal*
EMP: 7 EST: 2008
SALES (est): 135K **Privately Held**
SIC: 2673 Bags: plastic, laminated &
coated

(G-13116)
JDB DENSE FLOW INC
1004 Bee Pond Rd (34683-1407)
P.O. Box 38 (34682-0038)
PHONE...................................727 785-8500
Cameron Boothe, *President*
EMP: 10 EST: 1985
SQ FT: 1,300
SALES (est): 1MM **Privately Held**
WEB: www.jdbdenseflow.com
SIC: 3535 5084 Pneumatic tube conveyor
systems; industrial machinery & equip-
ment

(G-13117)
KEVINS CUSTOM
WOODWORKING
Also Called: Kcw Cnc and Laser Engraving
246 Arbor Dr E (34683-5705)
PHONE...................................727 804-8422
Terrie Leadbeater, *Principal*
Kevin Leadbeater, *Mng Member*
EMP: 6 EST: 2009
SALES (est): 384.5K **Privately Held**
WEB: www.kevinscustomwoodworking.com
SIC: 2431 Millwork

(G-13118)
LANE CARE LLC
3241 Fox Chase Cir N (34683-2359)
PHONE...................................727 316-3708
Matthew Lane, *CEO*
Jamie Jackson,
EMP: 10 EST: 2020
SALES (est): 573.7K **Privately Held**
SIC: 3841 5047 Surgical & medical instru-
ments; medical equipment & supplies

(G-13119)
MATRIX MEDIA LLC
989 Georgia Ave (34683-4255)
PHONE...................................435 313-2877
Robert Pulsipher,
EMP: 7 EST: 2019
SALES (est): 163.2K **Privately Held**
SIC: 3571 Computers, digital, analog or
hybrid

(G-13120)
NEW ENGLAND CRFTSMEN
BSTON IRN
4177 Corporate Ct (34683-1481)
PHONE...................................727 789-1618
Michael Fabiano, *Principal*
EMP: 7 EST: 2016
SALES (est): 149.5K **Privately Held**
SIC: 3446 Architectural metalwork

(G-13121)
NEW MARKET ENTERPRISES
LTD
Also Called: Dynamo Shredder Company
392 Harbor Ridge Dr (34683-1426)
PHONE...................................484 341-8004
James Mokhiber, *CEO*
Johanna E Mokhiber, *President*
Christopher J Mokhiber, *Vice Pres*
Elizabeth Ficca, *Treasurer*
▲ **EMP: 10 EST:** 1997
SALES (est): 754.7K **Privately Held**
WEB: www.newmarketent.com
SIC: 3579 5044 Forms handling equip-
ment; office equipment

(G-13122)
OSCOR INC (HQ)
3816 Desoto Blvd (34683)
PHONE...................................727 937-2511
Thomas Osypka, *President*
Miguel Rodriguez, *COO*
Doug Myers, *Vice Pres*
Bethania Tavarez, *Vice Pres*
David Henderson, *Facilities Mgr*
◆ **EMP: 123 EST:** 1982
SQ FT: 25,000
SALES (est): 21.1MM
SALES (corp-wide): 1.2B **Publicly Held**
SIC: 3841 5047 Surgical & medical instru-
ments; medical equipment & supplies

PA: Integer Holdings Corporation
5830 Gran Pkwy Ste 1150
Plano TX 75024
214 618-5243

(G-13123)
PITMAN ALLEN BOAT REPR & MAINT
970 Cortland Way (34683-6011)
PHONE..................................727 772-9848
Allen Pitman, *President*
EMP: 9 **EST:** 1998
SALES (est): 588K **Privately Held**
SIC: 3732 Boat building & repairing

(G-13124)
PRINT STORE LLC
4722 Kylemore Ct (34685-2648)
PHONE..................................727 656-1376
Joseph Sineno Jr, *President*
EMP: 7 **EST:** 2011
SALES (est): 222.4K **Privately Held**
SIC: 2752 Commercial printing, offset

(G-13125)
PROSERV TECHNOLOGIES INC
2148 Tamarron Ter (34683-4937)
PHONE..................................727 265-3190
Dean R Zasadny, *Principal*
EMP: 11 **EST:** 2012
SALES (est): 272.4K **Privately Held**
WEB: www.proserv.com
SIC: 1389 Oil & gas field services

(G-13126)
R&K MEHALL INC
211 Whisper Lake Rd (34683-5547)
P.O. Box 342, Crystal Beach (34681-0342)
PHONE..................................727 781-8780
Richard J Mehall, *Principal*
EMP: 8 **EST:** 2007
SALES (est): 378.9K **Privately Held**
SIC: 3582 Washing machines, laundry: commercial, incl. coin-operated

(G-13127)
RADIANCE RADIOLOGY INC
37566 Us Highway 19 N (34684-1019)
PHONE..................................727 934-5500
Andrey Salamakha, *President*
EMP: 5 **EST:** 2009
SALES (est): 476.8K **Privately Held**
WEB: www.radianceradiology.com
SIC: 3826 Magnetic resonance imaging apparatus

(G-13128)
RAINBOWS END
Also Called: Rainbows End Quilt Shoppe
1450 Wetherington Way (34683-6446)
PHONE..................................727 733-8572
Mary Ellen Facsina, *Partner*
Eileen Roski, *Partner*
Michelle Facsina, *Co-Owner*
EMP: 14 **EST:** 1984
SALES (est): 1MM **Privately Held**
WEB:
rainbowsendquiltshoppe.blogspot.com
SIC: 2395 5949 Quilting & quilting supplies; sewing, needlework & piece goods

(G-13129)
REAL PRINT & SHIP INC
4047 Carlyle Lakes Blvd (34685-1040)
PHONE..................................727 787-1949
Alan Goniwich, *Principal*
EMP: 10 **EST:** 2017
SALES (est): 391.7K **Privately Held**
SIC: 2752 Commercial printing, lithographic

(G-13130)
REGENERATIVE PROC PLANT LLC
34176 Us Highway 19 N (34684-2144)
PHONE..................................727 781-0818
C Randall Harrell, *CEO*
Paulo Carreiro, *Senior VP*
Marissa Morris, *Vice Pres*
Ramune Stankeviciute, *QC Dir*
Pam Perko, *Comptroller*
EMP: 20 **EST:** 2013
SALES (est): 1.9MM **Privately Held**
WEB: www.regenerativeplant.org
SIC: 2834 Pharmaceutical preparations

(G-13131)
SARNIYA ENTERPRISES INC
3620 Arbor Chase Dr (34683-3717)
PHONE..................................352 347-6030
Nizar N Dhamani, *Principal*
EMP: 8 **EST:** 2009
SALES (est): 278.8K **Privately Held**
SIC: 3578 Automatic teller machines (ATM)

(G-13132)
SKY-HIGH SIGN & LIGHTING INC
30 Citrus Dr (34684-1207)
PHONE..................................813 994-3954
Don Stapleton, *Principal*
EMP: 8 **EST:** 2009
SALES (est): 357.8K **Privately Held**
WEB: www.skyhigh-signs.com
SIC: 3993 Electric signs

(G-13133)
SOUTHERN SWITCH & CONTACTS
855 Virginia Ave (34683-5227)
PHONE..................................727 789-0951
Mahendra Doshi, *President*
AMI Shah, *Vice Pres*
EMP: 10 **EST:** 1993
SQ FT: 6,000
SALES (est): 2MM **Privately Held**
WEB: www.southernswitch.com
SIC: 3643 3625 Contacts, electrical; industrial electrical relays & switches

(G-13134)
SUNCOAST LED DISPLAYS LLC
2366 Knoll Ave S (34683-3115)
PHONE..................................727 683-2777
John Kinsel, *Sales Mgr*
Jordan Kinsel, *Mng Member*
EMP: 14 **EST:** 2011
SALES (est): 1MM **Privately Held**
WEB: www.suncoastleddisplays.com
SIC: 3674 3577 Light emitting diodes; graphic displays, except graphic terminals

(G-13135)
TARVIN MOBILE HOME SERVICE
329 Archimedes St (34683)
PHONE..................................727 734-3400
Melvin B Tarvin, *Principal*
EMP: 9 **EST:** 2001
SALES (est): 89.5K **Privately Held**
SIC: 3365 Aluminum foundries

(G-13136)
TK - AUTEK INC
Also Called: Autek Spray Booths
270 Foxcroft Dr E (34683-5611)
PHONE..................................727 572-7473
Jack Kimball, *President*
Cheri Kimball, *Corp Secy*
Thomas Kimball, *Vice Pres*
EMP: 8 **EST:** 1999
SALES (est): 629.1K **Privately Held**
SIC: 3444 Booths, spray: prefabricated sheet metal

(G-13137)
VODA TECHNOLOGIES LLC
3909 Mimosa Pl (34685-3675)
PHONE..................................727 645-6030
Elzina Singh, *Manager*
EMP: 5 **EST:** 2019
SALES (est): 328.5K **Privately Held**
SIC: 3589 Water filters & softeners, household type

(G-13138)
VREELAND WOODWORKING LLC
1407 Tampa Rd (34683-5649)
PHONE..................................727 365-0241
Benjamin Vreeland, *Principal*
EMP: 7 **EST:** 2010
SALES (est): 221.1K **Privately Held**
SIC: 2431 Millwork

(G-13139)
WESTLUND ENGINEERING INC
Also Called: W&W Engineering Company
3116 Roxmere Dr (34685-1733)
PHONE..................................727 572-4343
Paul O Wright, *President*
Rory L Westlund, *Vice Pres*

Ryan Vernick, *Technician*
EMP: 8 **EST:** 1993
SQ FT: 16,000
SALES (est): 702.6K **Privately Held**
WEB: www.westlundeng.com
SIC: 3549 3565 Assembly machines, including robotic; packaging machinery

(G-13140)
ZOHO STONE LLC
34318 Us Highway 19 N (34684-2149)
PHONE..................................727 230-6956
Michel Zohouri, *Mng Member*
▲ **EMP:** 5 **EST:** 2008
SALES (est): 390K **Privately Held**
WEB: www.zohostone.com
SIC: 3272 Concrete products

Palm Springs
Palm Beach County

(G-13141)
ALENAC METALS CORP
Also Called: Alenac & Associates
2180 S Congress Ave Ste 1 (33406-7631)
PHONE..................................561 877-4109
Nathalia Pabon, *President*
Guillermo Pabon, *Vice Pres*
Alejandro Pabon, *CFO*
Carmenza Chahin, *Admin Sec*
EMP: 24 **EST:** 2013
SALES (est): 3.4MM **Privately Held**
WEB: www.alenacmetals.com
SIC: 3446 Architectural metalwork

(G-13142)
ALL AMRCAN TRLR CONNECTION INC
3531 Lake Worth Rd (33461-4030)
PHONE..................................561 582-1800
Shawn Lago, *CEO*
Theresa Lago, *President*
John M Lago, *Vice Pres*
Linda Combast, *Office Mgr*
Frank Dipento, *Agent*
▼ **EMP:** 8 **EST:** 1980
SALES (est): 1.9MM **Privately Held**
WEB: www.allamericantrailer.com
SIC: 3715 5511 5599 Truck trailers; trucks, tractors & trailers: new & used; utility trailers

(G-13143)
AMERICAN MBL RESTORATION INC
43 Barbados Dr (33461-2829)
PHONE..................................561 502-0764
Roberto Reyes, *President*
EMP: 9 **EST:** 2013
SALES (est): 205.1K **Privately Held**
SIC: 3281 Cut stone & stone products

(G-13144)
DESIGNSTOGO INC
4317 10th Ave N (33461-2312)
PHONE..................................561 432-1313
Cesar Sanchez, *President*
EMP: 7 **EST:** 1988
SALES (est): 940.9K **Privately Held**
SIC: 3993 Signs & advertising specialties

(G-13145)
M WEGENER INC
24 Springdale Cir (33461-6323)
PHONE..................................561 848-2408
M Wegener, *President*
EMP: 5 **EST:** 1997
SALES (est): 310K **Privately Held**
WEB: www.mwegenercabinets.com
SIC: 2434 Wood kitchen cabinets

(G-13146)
MARKO GARAGE DOORS & GATES INC
248 Davis Rd (33461-1903)
PHONE..................................561 547-4001
Timothy W Coorough, *Principal*
Crystal Marko, *Sales Staff*
EMP: 7 **EST:** 2008

SALES (est): 270.4K **Privately Held**
WEB: www.markogaragedoors.com
SIC: 2431 3429 Garage doors, overhead: wood; door opening & closing devices, except electrical

(G-13147)
MG CABINET INSTALLERS LLC
3860 Miller Rd Apt B (33461-3697)
PHONE..................................561 530-7961
Manuel Garcia Garcia, *Principal*
EMP: 7 **EST:** 2018
SALES (est): 534K **Privately Held**
SIC: 2434 Wood kitchen cabinets

(G-13148)
OXYGEN DEVELOPMENT LLC (PA)
1525 S Congress Ave (33406-5916)
PHONE..................................954 480-2675
Alex Venot, *General Mgr*
Zach McElroy, *Business Mgr*
Anna Yapor, *Business Mgr*
Karen Cera, *Prdtn Mgr*
Nelson Gandhi, *Production*
◆ **EMP:** 97 **EST:** 2002
SQ FT: 200,000
SALES (est): 57.4MM **Privately Held**
WEB: www.oxygendevelopment.com
SIC: 2844 Toilet preparations

(G-13149)
PALM BEACH PRECIOUS METALS
3200 Frost Rd (33406-7928)
PHONE..................................561 662-6025
Joseph H Trebbe, *Principal*
EMP: 8 **EST:** 2008
SALES (est): 105.4K **Privately Held**
SIC: 3339 Precious metals

(G-13150)
SOUTH FLORIDA LABORATORY LLC
3395 Lake Worth Rd (33461-6902)
P.O. Box 904107, Charlotte NC (28290-0001)
PHONE..................................954 889-0335
Flavia Tanner, *Mng Member*
Marc Tanner,
EMP: 10 **EST:** 2011
SALES (est): 642.5K **Privately Held**
SIC: 3821 Clinical laboratory instruments, except medical & dental

---

Palmetto
Manatee County

(G-13151)
AAA ARCHITECTURAL ELEMENTS
Also Called: A A A Architectural Materials
1751 12th St E (34221-6461)
P.O. Box 282 (34220-0282)
PHONE..................................941 722-1910
Richard Cary, *President*
Steven Kosoff, *Vice Pres*
EMP: 18 **EST:** 1988
SQ FT: 22,940
SALES (est): 2.1MM **Privately Held**
WEB: www.buildingshapes.com
SIC: 3086 2851 Plastics foam products; lacquers, varnishes, enamels & other coatings

(G-13152)
AAA CAST STONE INC
1470 12th St E (34221-4176)
PHONE..................................941 721-8092
Larry Haveman, *President*
Bryan Haveman, *Sales Executive*
Sandra Eichmuller, *Office Mgr*
Erika Thereau, *Office Mgr*
EMP: 20 **EST:** 2002
SALES (est): 3.7MM **Privately Held**
WEB: www.aaacaststone.com
SIC: 3272 Cast stone, concrete

(G-13153)
ALLEGRO NUTRITION INC
Also Called: Gaspari Nutrition
6111 Horse Mill Pl (34221-7398)
PHONE..................................732 364-3777

▲ = Import ▼=Export
◆ =Import/Export

Richard Gaspari, *President*
Oscar Iturralde, *Treasurer*
Troy Johnson, *Sales Staff*
Jeff Rougeaux, *Sales Staff*
Michael Maling, *Manager*
▼ **EMP:** 25 **EST:** 2014
SALES (est): 4.6MM **Privately Held**
SIC: 2023 Dietary supplements, dairy &
non-dairy based
HQ: Allegro Limited
Jamestown House
Dublin D11 P
185 806-00

(G-13154)
**ALLIED MOLDED PRODUCTS
LLC**
1145 13th Ave E (34221-4167)
P.O. Box 186 (34220-0186)
PHONE..................................941 723-3072
Bill Harvey, *CEO*
Greg Miller, *President*
Larry Fox, *Chairman*
EMP: 50 **EST:** 1990
SQ FT: 40,000
SALES (est): 8.5MM **Privately Held**
WEB: www.allied-molded.com
SIC: 3229 Glass fiber products

(G-13155)
ATI ACCURATE TECHNOLOGY
1180 8th Ave W (34221-3810)
PHONE..................................239 206-1240
EMP: 8 **EST:** 2019
SALES (est): 1.1MM **Privately Held**
WEB: www.igbts.us
SIC: 3312 Stainless steel

(G-13156)
AUTOMOTIVE ARMOR MFG INC
1150 13th Ave E (34221-4166)
PHONE..................................941 721-3335
Stephen A Rodhouse, *President*
Gloria Rodhouse, *Treasurer*
Jeffrey M Rodhouse, *Manager*
Paul Rodhouse, *Admin Sec*
▲ **EMP:** 11 **EST:** 1998
SQ FT: 6,500
SALES (est): 2.6MM **Privately Held**
WEB: www.auto-armor.com
SIC: 3312 Armor plate

(G-13157)
BJM ENTERPRISES INC
Also Called: Johnson Printing
1500 15th Avenue Dr E # 104
(34221-2823)
PHONE..................................941 746-4171
John Johnson, *President*
Sherman Kirkpatrick, *Accounts Exec*
EMP: 13 **EST:** 1977
SALES (est): 2.5MM **Privately Held**
WEB: www.johnsonprint.com
SIC: 2752 2796 2791 2789 Commercial
printing, offset; platemaking services;
typesetting; bookbinding & related work

(G-13158)
CASUAL TONE INC
Also Called: Casualcraft
509 9th St W (34221-4713)
PHONE..................................941 722-5643
Craig Libkie, *President*
James Stewart, *General Mgr*
Tony Zulino, *CFO*
EMP: 13 **EST:** 2001
SALES (est): 107.1K **Privately Held**
WEB: www.floridapatio.net
SIC: 2514 Metal lawn & garden furniture

(G-13159)
CEMEX MATERIALS LLC
600 9th St W (34221-4716)
PHONE..................................941 722-4578
Mark McHayle, *Branch Mgr*
EMP: 147
SQ FT: 28,888 **Privately Held**
SIC: 3273 5032 5211 3441 Ready-mixed
concrete; concrete mixtures; concrete &
cinder block; fabricated structural metal;
concrete block & brick; brick & structural
clay tile
HQ: Cemex Materials Llc
1720 Centrepark Dr E # 100
West Palm Beach FL 33401
561 833-5555

(G-13160)
CHRIS INDUSTRIES CORP
Also Called: CIC Conveyors
1118 8th Ave W (34221-3810)
PHONE..................................941 729-7600
Jeff Van Hoose, *President*
Eric Jackson, *Principal*
EMP: 9 **EST:** 2010
SALES (est): 121.5K **Privately Held**
SIC: 3535 Conveyors & conveying equip-
ment

(G-13161)
COASTAL FUELS MKTG INC
804 N Dock St (34221-6612)
PHONE..................................941 722-7753
Greg Pound, *President*
▲ **EMP:** 8 **EST:** 1989
SALES (est): 573.1K **Privately Held**
SIC: 2869 Fuels

(G-13162)
COMPUTER TECHNICIAN INC
829 8th Ave W (34221-4709)
P.O. Box 21378, Bradenton (34204-1378)
PHONE..................................941 479-0242
Cedrick Lane, *Principal*
Tayon Wynn, *Manager*
EMP: 7 **EST:** 2016
SALES (est): 103.1K **Privately Held**
SIC: 3571 3572 7378 Electronic comput-
ers; computer storage devices; computer
& data processing equipment repair/main-
tenance

(G-13163)
**CUSTOM MEDICAL SYSTEMS
INC**
404 10th Ave W (34221-5032)
PHONE..................................941 722-3434
Allan A Lovesky, *President*
EMP: 7 **EST:** 1991
SQ FT: 2,000
SALES (est): 900.6K **Privately Held**
WEB: www.custommedicalsystemsinc.com
SIC: 3842 Wheelchairs

(G-13164)
DENKE LABORATORIES INC
Also Called: Hascall-Denke
12285 Us Highway 41 N (34221-8607)
P.O. Box 909 (34220-0909)
PHONE..................................941 721-0568
Michael Hascall, *President*
Tim Delille, *Project Mgr*
Roy Schneider, *Research*
Bill Armstrong, *Engineer*
Mary Hascall, *Admin Sec*
EMP: 25 **EST:** 1986
SQ FT: 28,000
SALES (est): 3.7MM **Privately Held**
WEB: www.hascall-denke.com
SIC: 3663 Antennas, transmitting & com-
munications

(G-13165)
EN-VISION AMERICA INC
825 4th St W (34221-5013)
PHONE..................................309 452-3088
David Raistrick, *President*
Phillip C Raistrick, *President*
Tom Morr, *Opers Staff*
Lindsay Haley, *Sales Staff*
Amanda Tolson, *Sales Staff*
▲ **EMP:** 28 **EST:** 1996
SQ FT: 3,000
SALES (est): 2.6MM **Privately Held**
WEB: www.envisionamerica.com
SIC: 2679 5999 Labels, paper: made from
purchased material; medical apparatus &
supplies

(G-13166)
FATHYM INC
2303 14th St W (34221-2957)
P.O. Box 3007, Boulder CO (80307-3007)
PHONE..................................303 905-4402
Matthew Smith, *President*
Carly Howard, *Opers Staff*
George Hatch, *Engineer*
Gerard Verbeck, *CFO*
Christina Szoke, *Chief Mktg Ofcr*
EMP: 12 **EST:** 2014

SALES (est): 18K **Privately Held**
WEB: www.fathym.com
SIC: 2721 7371 8711 Periodicals; custom
computer programming services; engineering services

(G-13167)
FLORIDA FINISHER INC
509 9th St W (34221-4713)
PHONE..................................941 722-5643
James Stewart, *President*
Blair Squire, *Vice Pres*
Greg Stewart, *Vice Pres*
EMP: 6 **EST:** 1996
SALES (est): 448.2K **Privately Held**
SIC: 2514 5712 Metal lawn & garden fur-
niture; furniture stores

(G-13168)
**GAEMMERLER (US)
CORPORATION**
2906 Corporate Way (34221-8488)
PHONE..................................941 465-4400
Gunter Gammerler, *Principal*
▲ **EMP:** 7 **EST:** 2008
SALES (est): 138.3K **Privately Held**
SIC: 3535 Conveyors & conveying equip-
ment

(G-13169)
**GREEN FOREST INDUSTRIES
INC**
1365 12th St E (34221-4169)
PHONE..................................941 721-0504
Brian Vance, *President*
EMP: 20 **EST:** 1994
SQ FT: 10,000
SALES (est): 2MM **Privately Held**
WEB: www.greenforestindustries.com
SIC: 3299 2431 Ornamental & architec-
tural plaster work; millwork

(G-13170)
**GULF COAST GROWERS
FLORIDA LLC**
2105 S Dock St (34221-8667)
PHONE..................................941 981-3888
James Grainer, *Mng Member*
EMP: 100 **EST:** 2020
SALES (est): 6MM **Privately Held**
SIC: 2033 Tomato purees: packaged in
cans, jars, etc.

(G-13171)
**GULFSTREAM NATURAL GAS
SYS LLC**
4610 Buckeye Rd (34221-9502)
PHONE..................................941 723-7000
Al Taylor, *Manager*
EMP: 8 **Privately Held**
WEB: www.gulfstreamgas.com
SIC: 1382 Oil & gas exploration services
PA: Gulfstream Natural Gas System, L.L.C.
2701 N Rocky Point Dr # 1050
Tampa FL 33607

(G-13172)
H Q INC
210 9th Street Dr W (34221-4802)
PHONE..................................941 721-7588
William S Hicks, *President*
Lee Carbonelli, *General Mgr*
Steven Cook, *Engineer*
EMP: 14 **EST:** 1986
SQ FT: 2,000
SALES (est): 681.2K **Privately Held**
WEB: www.hqinc.net
SIC: 3845 3823 Electromedical apparatus;
industrial instrmnts msrmnt display/control
process variable

(G-13173)
**HASCALL ENGINEERING AND
MFG CO**
Also Called: Denke Labratories
1608 20th Ave E (34221-6504)
P.O. Box 909 (34220-0909)
PHONE..................................941 723-2833
Michael Hascall, *President*
Roy Schneider, *Research*
Daniel Pakosz, *Director*
EMP: 10 **EST:** 1988
SQ FT: 5,000

SALES (est): 859.8K **Privately Held**
SIC: 3679 Antennas, receiving; electronic
circuits

(G-13174)
HTI
210 9th Street Dr W (34221-4802)
PHONE..................................941 723-4570
Vaughn Y Haight, *CEO*
Lee Carbonell, *General Mgr*
Lee Carbonelli, *Marketing Staff*
EMP: 7 **EST:** 2008
SALES (est): 119K **Privately Held**
SIC: 3841 Surgical & medical instruments

(G-13175)
HYDROPLUS INC
615 Riviera Dunes Way # 207
(34221-7146)
PHONE..................................941 479-7473
Hasan Kocahan, *President*
EMP: 10 **EST:** 1992
SALES (est): 3.1MM
SALES (corp-wide): 16.9MM **Privately
Held**
SIC: 3511 1629 Hydraulic turbine genera-
tor set units, complete; dams, waterways,
docks & other marine construction
HQ: Hydroplus
1973 Boulevard De La Defense
Nanterre 92000

(G-13176)
ILLINOIS TOOL WORKS INC
ITW Hobart Ground Power
11001 Us Highway 41 N (34221-7700)
PHONE..................................941 721-1000
William Bamford, *General Mgr*
EMP: 38
SALES (corp-wide): 14.4B **Publicly Held**
WEB: www.itw.com
SIC: 3537 3621 Industrial trucks & trac-
tors; generating apparatus & parts, elec-
trical
PA: Illinois Tool Works Inc.
155 Harlem Ave
Glenview IL 60025
847 724-7500

(G-13177)
JSB ENTERPRISES INC
Also Called: Die Verse Tool & Manufacturing
1650 12th St E (34221-6437)
PHONE..................................941 723-2288
Jeffrey S Bauman, *President*
EMP: 20 **EST:** 1985
SQ FT: 20,000
SALES (est): 2MM **Privately Held**
SIC: 3544 Dies & die holders for metal cut-
ting, forming, die casting

(G-13178)
**JUPITER MAR INTL HOLDINGS
INC (PA)**
1103 12th Ave E (34221-4146)
PHONE..................................941 729-5000
Carl M Herndon Sr, *President*
Carisa Albrecht, *Principal*
Lawrence S Tierney, *COO*
Craig Herndon, *Vice Pres*
Jack Aguero, *Warehouse Mgr*
▼ **EMP:** 43 **EST:** 1989
SQ FT: 4,800
SALES (est): 13.2MM **Privately Held**
WEB: www.jupitermarine.com
SIC: 3732 Boat building & repairing

(G-13179)
MANOR STEEL FABRICATORS
1507 18th Avenue Dr E (34221-6503)
PHONE..................................941 722-8077
Deborah Shuck, *Owner*
EMP: 8 **EST:** 2010
SALES (est): 178.5K **Privately Held**
SIC: 3441 Fabricated structural metal

(G-13180)
MASTER CABINET MAKER INC
5004 Us Highway 41 N A (34221-2031)
PHONE..................................941 723-0278
Christina Schipper, *Principal*
EMP: 8 **EST:** 2005
SALES (est): 866.9K **Privately Held**
WEB: www.themastercabinetmaker.com
SIC: 2434 Wood kitchen cabinets

(G-13181)
MEDTEL SERVICES LLC (PA)
2511 Corporate Way (34221-8478)
PHONE..................................941 753-5000
Timothy Callahan, *Exec VP*
Duncan Anderson, *Vice Pres*
Robert Ramey, *Vice Pres*
David Rourke, *Vice Pres*
German Godoy, *Traffic Mgr*
▲ EMP: 22 EST: 2012
SQ FT: 5,000
SALES (est): 7.5MM **Privately Held**
WEB: www.medtelservices.com
SIC: 3661 Telephones & telephone apparatus

(G-13182)
MITTEN MANUFACTURING
1614 20th St E Unit 102 (34221-3291)
PHONE..................................941 722-1818
Chad Seyer, *President*
Gene Waggoner, *Manager*
EMP: 7 EST: 2011
SALES (est): 171.3K **Privately Held**
WEB: www.mitten-manufacturing.com
SIC: 3999 Manufacturing industries

(G-13183)
PALMETTO CANNING COMPANY
3601 Us Highway 41 N (34221-8801)
P.O. Box 155 (34220-0155)
PHONE..................................941 722-1100
Jonathan Greenlaw, *President*
Heather Baggs, *Corp Secy*
Stephanie G Gardner, *Vice Pres*
◆ EMP: 15 EST: 1927
SQ FT: 32,000
SALES (est): 3.3MM **Privately Held**
WEB: www.palmettocanning.com
SIC: 2033 Jellies, edible, including imitation: in cans, jars, etc.; preserves, including imitation: in cans, jars, etc.; marmalade: packaged in cans, jars, etc.; fruit juices: packaged in cans, jars, etc.

(G-13184)
PATHWAY HOLDINGS LLC
5002 Us Highway 41 N (34221-2025)
PHONE..................................813 514-7899
Stephen Gans, *Mng Member*
EMP: 7 EST: 2008
SALES (est): 246.3K **Privately Held**
SIC: 2873 Fertilizers: natural (organic), except compost

(G-13185)
PICKHARDT PROFESSIONAL SR
4329 14th Street Cir (34221-5702)
P.O. Box 415, Parrish (34219-0415)
PHONE..................................941 737-7262
Vernon Pickhardt, *President*
EMP: 5 EST: 2010
SALES (est): 461.8K **Privately Held**
WEB: www.purcorpest.com
SIC: 3524 Lawn & garden equipment

(G-13186)
PORT MANATEE SHIP REPAIR
2114 Piney Point Rd (34221-9551)
P.O. Box 2547, Oldsmar (34677-0048)
PHONE..................................941 417-2613
Carlos Buqueras, *CFO*
Frank Kerney,
EMP: 48 EST: 2015
SQ FT: 12,000
SALES (est): 5MM **Privately Held**
WEB: www.manateeshiprepair.com
SIC: 3731 Shipbuilding & repairing

(G-13187)
PROGRESSIVE INDUSTRIAL INC
1412 18th Avenue Dr E (34221-6500)
PHONE..................................941 723-0201
Michael McCormick, *President*
Brian Degulis, *Vice Pres*
EMP: 12 EST: 1994
SQ FT: 7,500
SALES (est): 1.8MM **Privately Held**
WEB: www.pushboats-barges.com
SIC: 3731 3732 Tugboats, building & repairing; barges, building & repairing; boat building & repairing

(G-13188)
PROVEN INDUSTRIES INC
2310 S Dock St Ste 111 (34221-8892)
PHONE..................................813 895-4385
Ronald I Lee, *President*
EMP: 10 EST: 2011
SALES (est): 958.5K **Privately Held**
WEB: www.provenlocks.com
SIC: 3429 Keys, locks & related hardware

(G-13189)
QUEST CONTROLS INC (PA)
208 9th Street Dr W (34221-4802)
PHONE..................................941 729-4799
Edward Goggin, *President*
Kenneth Nickel, *Exec VP*
Todd Carlin, *Project Mgr*
Michael Mills, *Project Mgr*
Diane Griebe, *QC Mgr*
EMP: 11 EST: 1989
SQ FT: 10,000
SALES (est): 9MM **Privately Held**
WEB: www.questcontrols.com
SIC: 3829 3625 Measuring & controlling devices; relays & industrial controls

(G-13190)
READY CONTAINMENT LLC
2300 S Dock St Ste 101 (34221-8890)
PHONE..................................941 739-9486
Scott Sagalow,
Dianne McQuillen, *Admin Asst*
Lisa Eisenberg,
Rich Eisenberg,
Doreen Salow,
EMP: 17 EST: 2003
SQ FT: 21,000
SALES (est): 4.4MM **Privately Held**
WEB: www.readycontainment.com
SIC: 3069 Rubber automotive products

(G-13191)
SEA FORCE CENTER CONSOLE LLC (PA)
12277 Us Highway 41 N (34221-8607)
PHONE..................................941 417-7017
Mark Calzaretta,
EMP: 7 EST: 2020
SALES (est): 251.9K **Privately Held**
SIC: 3732 Boat building & repairing

(G-13192)
ST PETE PAPER COMPANY
2324 20th St E (34221-3288)
PHONE..................................727 572-9868
EMP: 7
SALES (est): 1.5MM **Privately Held**
SIC: 2653 Mfg Corrugated/Solid Fiber Boxes

(G-13193)
STORAGE BUILDING COMPANY LLC
429 10th Ave W Ste B (34221-5048)
P.O. Box 7805, Lakeland (33807-7805)
PHONE..................................863 738-1319
Thomas Massarella, *Mng Member*
EMP: 15 EST: 2019
SALES (est): 5.5MM **Privately Held**
WEB: www.storagebuildingcompany.com
SIC: 3441 1791 Building components, structural steel; structural steel erection

(G-13194)
SUNCOAST INVESTMENS OF PA
1511 20th Ave E (34221-6524)
PHONE..................................941 722-5391
Robert Knapp, *Owner*
Knapp Robert, *Owner*
Lawhun Jed, *Exec VP*
EMP: 8 EST: 2014
SALES (est): 310.3K **Privately Held**
SIC: 3993 Signs & advertising specialties

(G-13195)
T C B PRODUCTS INC
1507 17th St E (34221-2854)
PHONE..................................941 723-9820
Lindsay Rolfe, *President*
◆ EMP: 23 EST: 1998
SQ FT: 22,000
SALES (est): 1.1MM **Privately Held**
WEB: www.tcbproducts.com
SIC: 3694 Ignition coils, automotive

(G-13196)
TAYLOR CONCRETE INC
503 10th St E (34221)
P.O. Box 740, Parrish (34219-0740)
PHONE..................................941 737-7225
Nathan Taylor Jr, *President*
Spencer Taylor, *Vice Pres*
Rachael Perez, *Treasurer*
EMP: 5 EST: 1954
SQ FT: 3,000
SALES (est): 440.5K **Privately Held**
SIC: 3272 1711 Septic tanks, concrete; septic system construction

(G-13197)
TELESIS TECHNOLOGY CORPORATION
1611 12th St E (34221-6473)
PHONE..................................941 795-7441
Hasit Vibhakar, *Ch of Bd*
Shefali Gandhi, *Exec VP*
▲ EMP: 14 EST: 2002
SQ FT: 6,700
SALES (est): 1.6MM **Privately Held**
SIC: 3812 7699 Defense systems & equipment; aircraft & heavy equipment repair services; aircraft flight instrument repair

(G-13198)
TRILECTRON
11001 Us Highway 41 N (34221-7700)
PHONE..................................941 721-1000
Cheryl Morton, *Principal*
Doug Garner, *Project Mgr*
Shelley Liddy, *Controller*
Kathleen Burns, *Sales Staff*
▲ EMP: 5 EST: 2007
SALES (est): 601.9K **Privately Held**
WEB: www.itwgse.com
SIC: 3812 Aircraft flight instruments

(G-13199)
TROPIC ISLES CO-OP INC
1503 28th Ave W (34221-3519)
PHONE..................................941 721-8888
Clyde Martin, *President*
Mark Kreuger, *Admin Sec*
EMP: 12 EST: 2002
SALES (est): 1.1MM **Privately Held**
WEB: www.tropicisles.net
SIC: 2451 Mobile homes

(G-13200)
VERA CUSTOM WOODWORKING I
1468 12th St E (34221-4176)
PHONE..................................941 726-8831
EMP: 7 EST: 2019
SALES (est): 260.7K **Privately Held**
WEB: www.veracustomwoodworking.com
SIC: 2431 Millwork

(G-13201)
VERA CUSTOM WOODWORKING INC
9113 49th Ave E (34221-8967)
PHONE..................................321 355-0161
Mauro Vera, *Principal*
EMP: 7 EST: 2017
SALES (est): 54.1K **Privately Held**
WEB: www.veracustomwoodworking.com
SIC: 2431 Millwork

(G-13202)
VERDE GSE INC
12291 Us Highway 41 N (34221-8607)
P.O. Box 601, Ellenton (34222-0601)
PHONE..................................888 837-5221
Richard Hansen, *CEO*
Alex Long, *Principal*
Ben Newell, *Principal*
Ty Newell, *Principal*
Christina Hansen, *COO*
EMP: 23 EST: 2013
SALES (est): 4.9MM **Privately Held**
WEB: www.verdegse.com
SIC: 3585 Refrigeration & heating equipment

(G-13203)
VIENNA BEEF LTD
Also Called: Chipico South
2650 Corporate Way (34221-8480)
PHONE..................................941 723-7234

Fran Ohhhhhhh, *Controller*
Callie Sullivan, *Human Resources*
Cindy Bogusz, *Manager*
EMP: 273
SQ FT: 24,530
SALES (corp-wide): 86.5MM **Privately Held**
WEB: www.viennabeef.com
SIC: 2013 2035 Prepared beef products from purchased beef; pickles, sauces & salad dressings
PA: Vienna Beef Ltd.
2501 W Fulton St
Chicago IL 60612
773 278-7800

(G-13204)
WALKER PRODUCTS
1507 17th St E (34221-2854)
PHONE..................................941 723-9820
EMP: 77
SALES (corp-wide): 48.3MM **Privately Held**
WEB: www.walkerproducts.com
SIC: 3714 Motor vehicle parts & accessories
PA: Walker Products, Inc.
525 W Congress St
Pacific MO 63069
636 257-2400

(G-13205)
WESTCOAST METALWORKS INC
Also Called: Stainless Stl Fbrction Svcs Fl
3308 39th St E (34221-6330)
PHONE..................................941 920-3201
Sheldon K Clements, *Principal*
EMP: 9 EST: 2005
SALES (est): 531.9K **Privately Held**
WEB: www.westcoastmetalworks.com
SIC: 7692 Welding repair

(G-13206)
WIRETEC IGNITION INC
1901 4th St W (34221-4305)
PHONE..................................407 578-4569
Brian Moore, *President*
David Dirkse, *Principal*
Brenda Obrien, *CFO*
◆ EMP: 12 EST: 1995
SQ FT: 40,000
SALES (est): 613.1K **Privately Held**
SIC: 3694 3357 Spark plugs for internal combustion engines; automotive wire & cable, except ignition sets: nonferrous

Palmetto Bay
Miami-Dade County

(G-13207)
AMER-CON CORP
18001 Old Cutler Rd # 401 (33157-6434)
P.O. Box 566359, Miami (33256-6359)
PHONE..................................786 293-8004
Carlos Rapaport, *President*
Guillermo Rapaport, *Vice Pres*
Richard Rapaport, *Vice Pres*
Robert Rapaport, *Vice Pres*
Henry Rapaport, *CFO*
◆ EMP: 25 EST: 1988
SQ FT: 4,500
SALES (est): 3.4MM **Privately Held**
WEB: www.amer-con.com
SIC: 3537 3711 3713 4131 Industrial trucks & tractors; bus & other large specialty vehicle assembly; truck & bus bodies; intercity & rural bus transportation; school buses; construction machinery

(G-13208)
CARIBBEAN TODAY NEWS MAGAZINE
Also Called: Caribbean Publishing Service
9020 Sw 152nd St (33157-1928)
PHONE..................................305 238-2868
Peter Webley, *Publisher*
Gordon Williams, *Editor*
EMP: 10 EST: 1989
SALES (est): 1.1MM **Privately Held**
WEB: www.caribbeantoday.com
SIC: 2711 Newspapers, publishing & printing

▲ = Import ▼=Export
◆ =Import/Export

(G-13209)
FUELMATICS CORP
17641 Sw 87th Ave (33157-6024)
PHONE...............................305 807-4923
Sten Corfitsen, *Principal*
EMP: 7 **EST:** 2010
SALES (est): 161.9K **Privately Held**
WEB: www.fuelmatics.com
SIC: 3714 8742 Motor vehicle parts & accessories; automation & robotics consultant

(G-13210)
GOLDEN HANDS WELDING INC
9161 Sw 181st Ter (33157-5941)
PHONE...............................786 728-6838
Jorge L Pena, *Branch Mgr*
EMP: 14
SALES (corp-wide): 98.2K **Privately Held**
SIC: 7692 Welding repair
PA: Golden Hands Welding, Inc.
13166 Sw 10th St
Miami FL 33184
786 328-6838

(G-13211)
HOLYLAND TAPESTRIES INC
14565 Sw 75th Ave (33158-1620)
PHONE...............................305 255-7955
Micki Lewis, *President*
EMP: 7 **EST:** 2001
SALES (est): 121.3K **Privately Held**
WEB: www.holylandtapestries.com
SIC: 2211 Tapestry fabrics, cotton

(G-13212)
ICO USA CORP
15815 Sw 89th Ave (33157-1910)
PHONE...............................305 253-0871
Yolanda Padilla, *President*
Andres G Padilla, *Vice Pres*
Manuel De Quintana, *Manager*
EMP: 5 **EST:** 2005
SALES (est): 364K **Privately Held**
SIC: 3699 Security control equipment & systems

(G-13213)
INKPRESSIONS INC
Also Called: Expert Printing and Graphics
13804 Sw 83rd Ct (33158-1028)
PHONE...............................305 261-0872
Alberto Silveira, *President*
Enrique Barrios, *Vice Pres*
EMP: 14 **EST:** 1988
SALES (est): 640K **Privately Held**
SIC: 2752 Commercial printing, offset

(G-13214)
METAL 2 METAL INC
Also Called: Manufacturing
17040 Sw 87th Ct (33157-4639)
PHONE...............................954 253-9450
Alejandro Selva, *President*
EMP: 5 **EST:** 2009
SALES (est): 410.5K **Privately Held**
SIC: 3443 3444 7381 3711 Weldments; pipe, sheet metal; sheet metal specialties, not stamped; detective & armored car services; cars, armored, assembly of

(G-13215)
MICROTOOL AND INSTRUMENT INC
15203 Sw 87th Ave (33157-2047)
PHONE...............................786 242-8780
Jennifer Leach, *President*
Neil Leach, *Vice Pres*
EMP: 36 **EST:** 1954
SQ FT: 4,500
SALES (est): 528.6K
SALES (corp-wide): 5.7MM **Privately Held**
SIC: 3545 3532 3425 3291 Diamond cutting tools for turning, boring, burnishing, etc.; mining machinery; saw blades & handsaws; abrasive products
PA: Diamonds Unlimited
1401 Brickell Ave
Miami FL
305 358-7770

(G-13216)
PAGE GOLFS YELLOW DIRECTORY
7251 Sw 152nd St (33157-2513)
PHONE...............................305 378-8038
David M Burnham, *President*
EMP: 10 **EST:** 1994
SALES (est): 543.5K **Privately Held**
WEB: www.golfyellowpages.com
SIC: 2741 Telephone & other directory publishing

(G-13217)
PG5 INDUSTRIES LLC
15604 Sw 78th Pl (33157-2371)
PHONE...............................786 256-0896
Rosa M Pernas, *Manager*
EMP: 7 **EST:** 2013
SALES (est): 122.8K **Privately Held**
WEB: www.plaster-craft.com
SIC: 3999 Manufacturing industries

(G-13218)
SERVDATA INC
7401 Sw 163rd St (33157-3825)
PHONE...............................305 269-7374
Yadira Chavez, *Financial Analy*
Kenneth L Burkhart, *Director*
EMP: 6 **EST:** 1999
SALES (est): 735.8K **Privately Held**
WEB: www.servdata.us
SIC: 7372 Prepackaged software

(G-13219)
SUNRISE FIBERGLASS INC
15750 Sw 92nd Ave Unit 32 (33157-1991)
PHONE...............................305 636-4111
Gervacia Minerva Tapanes, *President*
Jesus Mesa, *Vice Pres*
EMP: 6 **EST:** 1983
SALES (est): 467K **Privately Held**
WEB: www.registrar-transfers.com
SIC: 3089 Injection molding of plastics

(G-13220)
SYNNOVA HEALTH INC
18001 Old Cutler Rd # 42 (33157-6422)
PHONE...............................305 253-5433
Norberto Menendez, *CEO*
EMP: 5 **EST:** 2019
SALES (est): 1MM **Privately Held**
SIC: 7372 Publishers' computer software

(G-13221)
TRAVELING CANVAS CORPORATION
15400 Sw 67th Ct (33157-2612)
PHONE...............................305 259-2001
Claudette B Davis, *Principal*
EMP: 7 **EST:** 2010
SALES (est): 68.9K **Privately Held**
SIC: 2211 Canvas

(G-13222)
VERTICAL REALITY INC
17511 Sw 99th Rd (33157-5313)
PHONE...............................305 238-4522
Anthony Kay, *CEO*
Kenneth Sharkey, *President*
◆ **EMP:** 8 **EST:** 1995
SQ FT: 5,000
SALES (est): 658.9K **Privately Held**
WEB: www.verticalreality.com
SIC: 3599 3949 Amusement park equipment; sporting & athletic goods

(G-13223)
VERTICAL REALITY MFG INC
17511 Sw 99th Rd (33157-5313)
PHONE...............................305 238-4522
Kenneth Sharkey, *CEO*
▲ **EMP:** 3 **EST:** 2008
SALES (est): 6.5MM **Privately Held**
SIC: 3599 Amusement park equipment

Panacea
Wakulla County

(G-13224)
BROOKS WELDING & CONCRETE SHOP
Also Called: Brooks Concrete Service
1532 Coastal Hwy (32346-2154)
P.O. Box 82 (32346-0082)
PHONE...............................850 984-5279
James Brooks II, *President*
EMP: 10 **EST:** 1974
SQ FT: 2,000
SALES (est): 903.2K **Privately Held**
SIC: 3273 Ready-mixed concrete

Panama City
Bay County

(G-13225)
AIR TEMP OF AMERICA INC
423 E 16th St (32405-5456)
PHONE...............................850 340-3017
Ricardo Herrera, *Manager*
EMP: 1 **EST:** 2018
SQ FT: 10,000
SALES (est): 7MM **Privately Held**
SIC: 3714 3629 Motor vehicle parts & accessories; radiators & radiator shells & cores, motor vehicle; condensers, for motors or generators
HQ: Air Temp De Mexico, S.A. De C.V.
Km. 10 Carr. Merida - Uman Tablaje
Rustico No. 419
Uman YUC 97390

(G-13226)
AMERICAN BOTTLING COMPANY
3333 Highway 77 (32405-5008)
PHONE...............................850 763-9069
EMP: 70 **Publicly Held**
WEB: www.keurigdrpepper.com
SIC: 2086 Soft drinks: packaged in cans, bottles, etc.
HQ: The American Bottling Company
6425 Hall Of Fame Ln
Frisco TX 75034

(G-13227)
AMERICAN CLASSIFIEDS
Also Called: Thrifty Nickle Want ADS
1522 Chestnut Ave (32405-2576)
P.O. Box 35115 (32412-5115)
PHONE...............................850 747-1155
Frank Kerr, *President*
EMP: 17 **EST:** 2006
SALES (est): 808.9K **Privately Held**
SIC: 2711 2741 Job printing & newspaper publishing combined; miscellaneous publishing

(G-13228)
ARGOS USA LLC
1601 Maple Ave (32405-6044)
PHONE...............................850 872-1209
Dave Gober, *Transportation*
Romelda Porter, *Purch Mgr*
Rocky Dillard, *Credit Staff*
Patrick Passmore, *Human Res Mgr*
Tom Slosser, *Sales Staff*
EMP: 32 **Privately Held**
WEB: www.argos-us.com
SIC: 3273 Ready-mixed concrete
HQ: Argos Usa Llc
3015 Windward Plz Ste 300
Alpharetta GA 30005
678 368-4300

(G-13229)
ART OF IRON INC
311 W 35th Ct (32405-3358)
P.O. Box 32 (32402-0032)
PHONE...............................850 819-1500
Debra S Sanders, *Principal*
EMP: 7 **EST:** 2006
SALES (est): 306.7K **Privately Held**
WEB: www.artofironpanamacity.com
SIC: 7692 Welding repair

(G-13230)
ASAP BRICK PAVERS AND MORE
2320 N East Ave (32405-6218)
PHONE...............................850 522-7123
Daniel Brooks, *Principal*
EMP: 8 **EST:** 2015
SALES (est): 113.3K **Privately Held**
WEB: www.asapbrickpavers.com
SIC: 2951 Asphalt paving mixtures & blocks

(G-13231)
BERG EUROPIPE HOLDING CORP (HQ)
5315 W 19th St (32401-1090)
P.O. Box 59209 (32412-0209)
PHONE...............................850 769-2273
Michael Graef, *Ch of Bd*
Dave Delie, *President*
Koichi Konuma, *VP Bus Dvlpt*
Angela Cherry, *Human Res Dir*
Corey Haisten, *Technician*
EMP: 210 **EST:** 1983
SALES (est): 78.7MM
SALES (corp-wide): 743.8MM **Privately Held**
WEB: www.bergpipe.com
SIC: 3312 Pipes, iron & steel
PA: Europipe Gmbh
Pilgerstr. 2
Mulheim An Der Ruhr NW 45473
208 976-0

(G-13232)
BERG PIPE PANAMA CITY CORP (DH)
5315 W 19th St (32401-1090)
P.O. Box 59209 (32412-0209)
PHONE...............................850 769-2273
Ingo Riemer, *President*
George Price, *General Mgr*
Michael Berg, *Principal*
Vincent N Berg, *Principal*
John Burton, *COO*
◆ **EMP:** 210 **EST:** 1979
SQ FT: 20,000
SALES (est): 78.7MM
SALES (corp-wide): 743.8MM **Privately Held**
WEB: www.bergpipe.com
SIC: 3317 Pipes, seamless steel

(G-13233)
BESTWAY PORTABLE BUILDING INC
2919 N Highway 231 (32405-6801)
PHONE...............................850 747-1984
Ricky Smith, *Manager*
EMP: 10
SQ FT: 7,600 **Privately Held**
WEB: www.bestwayportablebuildings.com
SIC: 3448 Prefabricated metal buildings
PA: Bestway Portable Building Inc
2815 E 15th St
Panama City FL 32405

(G-13234)
BIG COUNTRY SMALL ENGINE
5412 E Highway 22 (32404-6324)
PHONE...............................850 348-9022
David Lagrange, *General Mgr*
EMP: 7 **EST:** 2012
SALES (est): 149.4K **Privately Held**
SIC: 3599 Machine shop, jobbing & repair

(G-13235)
BISI FASTENERS LLC
2009 Poplar Pl 302 (32405-8213)
PHONE...............................850 913-0101
EMP: 7 **EST:** 2018
SALES (est): 304.1K **Privately Held**
WEB: www.bisifasteners.com
SIC: 3965 Fasteners

(G-13236)
BRUNSWICK CORPORATION
Also Called: Mercury Marine Power Division
11 College Ave (32401-4847)
PHONE...............................850 769-1011
Bill Harris, *Branch Mgr*
EMP: 9
SALES (corp-wide): 5.8B **Publicly Held**
WEB: www.brunswick.com
SIC: 3519 Outboard motors

PA: Brunswick Corporation
26125 N Riverwoods Blvd # 500
Mettawa IL 60045
847 735-4700

(G-13237)
C4 GROUP LLC
7551 Holley Cir (32408-4953)
PHONE..........................850 230-4541
Kent Henry, *Buyer*
Scott E Therriault, *Mng Member*
Karen Therriault,
EMP: 14 **EST:** 2005
SALES (est): 1.3MM **Privately Held**
WEB: www.c4group.biz
SIC: 3599 Machine & other job shop work

(G-13238)
CCBCC OPERATIONS LLC
Also Called: Coca-Cola
300 W 5th St (32401-2608)
PHONE..........................850 785-6171
Grey Brewington, *Branch Mgr*
EMP: 57
SQ FT: 10,000
SALES (corp-wide): 5.5B **Publicly Held**
WEB: www.coca-cola.com
SIC: 2086 Bottled & canned soft drinks
HQ: Ccbcc Operations, Llc
4100 Coca Cola Plz
Charlotte NC 28211
704 364-8728

(G-13239)
CEDAR CREEK LOGGING INC
4138 Harry Wells Rd (32409-2472)
PHONE..........................850 832-0133
Shane Messick, *Principal*
EMP: 14 **EST:** 2013
SALES (est): 987K **Privately Held**
SIC: 2411 Logging camps & contractors

(G-13240)
CEMEX MATERIALS LLC
714 Transmitter Rd (32401-5365)
PHONE..........................850 769-2243
Eric Werning, *Principal*
EMP: 69 **Privately Held**
SIC: 3273 Ready-mixed concrete
HQ: Cemex Materials Llc
1720 Centrepark Dr E # 100
West Palm Beach FL 33401
561 833-5555

(G-13241)
CHARLES BRYANT ENTERPRISES
Also Called: Mrs Traylors Plntn Style Foods
2700 Whisperwood Ln (32405-4485)
PHONE..........................850 785-3604
Charles Bryant, *President*
Steve Schnackenberg, *Vice Pres*
Carolyn Bryant, *Admin Sec*
EMP: 7 **EST:** 1982
SQ FT: 1,600
SALES (est): 535.1K **Privately Held**
SIC: 2041 2099 2038 Doughs, frozen or refrigerated; food preparations; frozen specialties

(G-13242)
CHENEGA MANUFACTURING SVCS LLC
1509 Saint Andrews Blvd (32405-2835)
P.O. Box 240988, Anchorage AK (99524-0988)
PHONE..........................850 763-6013
Paul Edwards, *General Mgr*
Robert Kelly, *Buyer*
Ken Ogden,
Lori Schneider, *Administration*
EMP: 35
SALES (est): 620.9K **Privately Held**
WEB: www.chenegaehf.com
SIC: 3629 Electronic generation equipment
PA: Chenega Corporation
3000 C St Ste 301
Anchorage AK 99503

(G-13243)
COASTAL ACQUISITIONS FLA LLC (PA)
2120 E Business 98 (32401-4383)
PHONE..........................850 769-9423
William Carr,

Jerry Carr,
Phillip Santora,
EMP: 7 **EST:** 2017
SALES (est): 2.1MM **Privately Held**
WEB: www.allmetalbuildingsystems.com
SIC: 3441 Fabricated structural metal

(G-13244)
COASTAL ACQUISITIONS FLA LLC
Also Called: All Metal Roofing
2120 E 5th St (32401-4383)
PHONE..........................850 769-9423
Jim Armour, *Branch Mgr*
EMP: 10
SALES (corp-wide): 2.1MM **Privately Held**
WEB: www.allmetalbuildingsystems.com
SIC: 2952 1761 Roofing materials; roofing contractor
PA: Coastal Acquisitions Of Florida, Llc
2120 E Business 98
Panama City FL 32401
850 769-9423

(G-13245)
COASTAL LOGGING INC
4138 Harry Wells Rd (32409-2472)
PHONE..........................850 832-0133
Russell Scott, *Principal*
EMP: 13 **EST:** 2009
SALES (est): 717.3K **Privately Held**
SIC: 2411 Logging

(G-13246)
COASTAL MACHINE LLC
7424 Coastal Dr (32404-4015)
PHONE..........................850 769-6117
Gregory Clubbs,
EMP: 7 **EST:** 2016
SALES (est): 532.4K **Privately Held**
SIC: 3451 3728 3443 3541 Screw machine products; aircraft parts & equipment; fabricated plate work (boiler shop); machine tools, metal cutting type; machine tools, metal forming type

(G-13247)
COASTAL MILLWORX LLC
1714 Wolfrun Ln (32405-8804)
PHONE..........................850 250-6672
Derik Hall, *Manager*
EMP: 7 **EST:** 2017
SALES (est): 152.8K **Privately Held**
SIC: 2431 Millwork

(G-13248)
COCA-COLA BOTTLING CO UNTD INC
2825 Forester Trl (32405-8218)
PHONE..........................850 785-0697
Steve Cox, *Human Res Dir*
Matt Hallman, *Sales Mgr*
EMP: 70
SALES (corp-wide): 2B **Privately Held**
WEB: www.coca-cola.com
SIC: 2086 Bottled & canned soft drinks
PA: Coca-Cola Bottling Company United, Inc.
4600 E Lake Blvd
Birmingham AL 35217
205 841-2653

(G-13249)
COLOR PRESS PRINT INC
3430 Highway 77 Ste D (32405-5011)
PHONE..........................850 763-9884
Lorayne J Evans, *President*
Henry H Evans III, *Vice Pres*
EMP: 5 **EST:** 1985
SQ FT: 5,000
SALES (est): 559.2K **Privately Held**
WEB: www.colorpressprinting.com
SIC: 2752 Commercial printing, offset

(G-13250)
CREAMER CORP
338 W Highway 388 (32409-1108)
P.O. Box 8566 (32409-8566)
PHONE..........................850 265-2700
EMP: 7
SALES (est): 885K **Privately Held**
SIC: 2411 2421 Logging Sawmill/Planing Mill

(G-13251)
CREATIVE PRINTING BAY CNTY INC
Also Called: Creative Prtg & Screen Designs
1328 Harrison Ave (32401-2435)
PHONE..........................850 784-1645
Stephen J Ruff, *President*
Sheila Ruff, *Vice Pres*
EMP: 10 **EST:** 1982
SQ FT: 5,000
SALES (est): 1.2MM **Privately Held**
WEB: www.getcreativepc.com
SIC: 3993 2752 Signs & advertising specialties; commercial printing, offset

(G-13252)
DESTINATION PAVERS LLC
2827 Cynthia Ct (32405-7210)
PHONE..........................850 319-6551
Filho Osvaldino A Santos, *Principal*
EMP: 9 **EST:** 2012
SALES (est): 1.7MM **Privately Held**
SIC: 3531 Pavers

(G-13253)
DETECT INC (HQ)
2817 Highway 77 (32405-4409)
PHONE..........................850 763-7200
Gary W Andrews, *Ch of Bd*
Ronald L Merritt, *Chairman*
Edward Zakrajsek, *Exec VP*
Adam Kelly, *Vice Pres*
Larry Hayes, *Prdtn Mgr*
EMP: 19 **EST:** 2003
SQ FT: 7,000
SALES (est): 28.8MM
SALES (corp-wide): 734K **Privately Held**
WEB: www.detect-inc.com
SIC: 3812 Radar systems & equipment

(G-13254)
DIGITRAX INC
2443 Transmitter Rd (32404-3157)
PHONE..........................850 872-9890
Zana Ireland, *President*
Anthony Ireland, *Chairman*
Stan Miller, *Purch Mgr*
▲ **EMP:** 45 **EST:** 1993
SQ FT: 12,000
SALES (est): 7.2MM **Privately Held**
WEB: www.digitrax.com
SIC: 3612 Power & distribution transformers; specialty transformers

(G-13255)
DOVER CYLINDER HEAD INC (PA)
2704 W 15th St 98 (32401-1360)
PHONE..........................850 785-6569
James Thomas Dover, *President*
Dianne Jones, *Corp Secy*
Dan Gardner, *Vice Pres*
EMP: 26 **EST:** 1979
SQ FT: 40,000
SALES (est): 2.4MM **Privately Held**
SIC: 3714 Motor vehicle parts & accessories

(G-13256)
EASTERN SHIPBUILDING GROUP INC (PA)
2200 Nelson Ave (32401-4969)
PHONE..........................850 763-1900
Brian D Isernia, *President*
Benny C Bramblette, *General Mgr*
Donnie Bowen, *Superintendent*
Henry Sapp, *Superintendent*
Ricky Schott, *Superintendent*
▲ **EMP:** 450 **EST:** 1996
SQ FT: 200,000
SALES (est): 147.8MM **Privately Held**
WEB: www.easternshipbuilding.com
SIC: 3731 Shipbuilding & repairing

(G-13257)
EASTERN SHIPBUILDING GROUP INC
13300 Allanton Rd (32404-2816)
PHONE..........................850 522-7400
Matt Disernia, *Project Mgr*
Kenneth Winpigler, *Project Mgr*
Joe Murphy, *Purch Mgr*
Carol Decker, *Buyer*
Cindy Jorde, *Buyer*
EMP: 525

SALES (corp-wide): 147.8MM **Privately Held**
WEB: www.easternshipbuilding.com
SIC: 3441 Fabricated structural metal for ships; ship structural metal, prefabricated metal
PA: Eastern Shipbuilding Group, Inc.
2200 Nelson Ave
Panama City FL 32401
850 763-1900

(G-13258)
EASTERN SHIPYARDS INC
2200 Nelson Ave (32401-4969)
P.O. Box 960 (32402-0960)
PHONE..........................850 763-1900
Brian D'Isernia, *President*
Kenneth Monroe, *Vice Pres*
Marvin Serna, *VP Opers*
Joseph Murphy, *Purch Mgr*
EMP: 77 **EST:** 1987
SALES (est): 4.3MM **Privately Held**
SIC: 3731 Shipbuilding & repairing

(G-13259)
EL JALICIENSE INC
232 S Tyndall Pkwy (32404-6723)
PHONE..........................850 481-1232
Jesus Carranza, *President*
EMP: 15 **EST:** 2016
SALES (est): 603.3K **Privately Held**
WEB: www.jaliciense.com
SIC: 2099 Seasonings & spices

(G-13260)
FAT AND WEIRD COOKIE CO LLC
2540 Jenks Ave (32405-4310)
PHONE..........................850 832-9150
EMP: 14 **EST:** 2018
SALES (est): 4MM **Privately Held**
WEB: www.fatandweirdcookie.com
SIC: 2051 Bakery products, partially cooked (except frozen)

(G-13261)
FIBEROPTIC ENGINEERING CORP
6541 Bayline Dr (32404-4805)
PHONE..........................850 763-2289
Francis Pettis, *President*
Ken Pettis, *Vice Pres*
EMP: 11 **EST:** 1979
SQ FT: 8,900
SALES (est): 546.9K **Privately Held**
WEB: www.fiberopticengineeringcorp.com
SIC: 3827 Optical test & inspection equipment

(G-13262)
FINLAYSON ENTERPRISES INC
Also Called: CF Sign and Stamp Company
1802 Beck Ave (32405-2569)
PHONE..........................850 785-7953
Carolyn Finlayson, *President*
EMP: 8 **EST:** 1984
SQ FT: 2,000
SALES (est): 741.2K **Privately Held**
SIC: 3953 3993 3479 Embossing seals & hand stamps; signs, not made in custom sign painting shops; engraving jewelry silverware, or metal

(G-13263)
FLORIDA CUSTOM CABINETS INC
3536 E Orlando Rd (32404-2051)
PHONE..........................850 769-4781
William Lawrence, *President*
EMP: 6 **EST:** 2002
SQ FT: 4,000
SALES (est): 506.2K **Privately Held**
WEB: www.floridacustomcabinetsinc.com
SIC: 2434 Wood kitchen cabinets

(G-13264)
FLOWERS BAKING CO LLC
2133 Transmitter Rd (32404-3154)
PHONE..........................850 763-2541
Buddy Danley, *Manager*
EMP: 7
SALES (corp-wide): 4.3B **Publicly Held**
SIC: 2051 Bread, cake & related products

GEOGRAPHIC

HQ: Lynchburg Organic Baking Co., Llc
1905 Hollins Mill Rd
Lynchburg VA 24503
434 528-0441

(G-13265)
FREEMAN ELECTRIC CO INC
534 Oak Ave (32401-2648)
P.O. Box 2267 (32402-2267)
PHONE.................................850 785-7448
John T Duncan III, *President*
Michael A Duncan, *Vice Pres*
Margaret Duncan, *Treasurer*
Mike Conroy, *Manager*
EMP: 12 **EST:** 1936
SQ FT: 10,000
SALES (est): 1.5MM **Privately Held**
WEB:
www.freemanelectricsigncompany.com
SIC: 3993 1761 1731 Electric signs;
sheet metalwork; general electrical con-
tractor

(G-13266)
GARMENT GEAR INC
1522 Degama Ave (32405-3717)
PHONE.................................850 215-2121
Daniel Strickland, *President*
Kristin Alderman, *Opers Mgr*
Ann Brassellmills, *Bookkeeper*
EMP: 10 **EST:** 2000
SQ FT: 9,000
SALES (est): 2.4MM **Privately Held**
WEB: www.garmentgear.com
SIC: 2759 Screen printing

(G-13267)
GIGLI ENTERPRISES INC (PA)
Also Called: Divers Den
4833 E Business Hwy 98 (32404-7019)
PHONE.................................850 871-4777
Joann Moore, *President*
Stacie R Galbreath, *Vice Pres*
Lana Blood,
EMP: 6 **EST:** 1986
SQ FT: 8,000
SALES (est): 2.3MM **Privately Held**
WEB: www.giglienterprises.com
SIC: 3728 5941 Aircraft parts & equip-
ment; skin diving, scuba equipment &
supplies

(G-13268)
GKN AEROSPACE FLORIDA LLC
6051 Ventr Crossings Blvd (32409-1165)
P.O. Box 4009, Hazelwood MO (63042-
0609)
PHONE.................................314 412-8311
Clayton Fox, *Director*
Douglas Steinman,
EMP: 99 **EST:** 2016
SALES (est): 22.8MM
SALES (corp-wide): 11.6B **Privately Held**
SIC: 3721 3812 Aircraft; aircraft/aero-
space flight instruments & guidance sys-
tems
HQ: Gkn Limited
2nd Floor, One Central Boulevard
Solihull W MIDLANDS B90 8
121 210-9800

(G-13269)
GULF COAST HYPERBERIC INC
Also Called: Gulf Coast Hyperbarics
215 Forest Park Cir (32405-4916)
PHONE.................................850 271-1441
James W Mc Carthy, *President*
EMP: 5 **EST:** 1984
SALES (est): 432.7K **Privately Held**
WEB: www.gulfcoasthyperbarics.com
SIC: 3841 Medical instruments & equip-
ment, blood & bone work

(G-13270)
GULF COAST TIMBER COMPANY
8206 S Holland Rd (32409-2060)
PHONE.................................850 271-8818
EMP: 8
SALES (est): 952K **Privately Held**
SIC: 2411 Logging

(G-13271)
GULF GLO BANNERS AND SIGNS LLC
8808 Front Beach Rd (32407-4232)
P.O. Box 9591 (32417-9591)
PHONE.................................850 234-0952
John Anderson, *Mng Member*
Susan Anderson,
EMP: 7 **EST:** 1978
SQ FT: 1,200
SALES (est): 508.9K **Privately Held**
WEB: www.gulfglo.com
SIC: 2399 5961 Banners, made from fab-
ric; mail order house

(G-13272)
HELI-TECH INC
4405 De Len Dr (32404-4262)
PHONE.................................850 763-9000
Kennen Thrasher, *President*
Anna Thrasher, *Corp Secy*
James Gunner Thrasher, *Vice Pres*
EMP: 15 **EST:** 1988
SALES (est): 2.5MM **Privately Held**
WEB: www.helitechinc.com
SIC: 3721 3728 4581 5599 Helicopters;
aircraft parts & equipment; aircraft servic-
ing & repairing; aircraft instruments,
equipment or parts

(G-13273)
HOME WORKS BAY COUNTY INC
4902 E Highway 98 (32404-6831)
PHONE.................................850 215-7880
Gregory T Guidry, *President*
EMP: 5 **EST:** 2005
SALES (est): 329.4K **Privately Held**
WEB: www.homeworksofbaycounty.net
SIC: 2434 2499 Wood kitchen cabinets;
decorative wood & woodwork

(G-13274)
ICE SHEET METAL LLC
29 E 10th St (32401-2980)
PHONE.................................850 872-2129
Michael J Hobbs R,
Van Willoughby,
EMP: 8 **EST:** 2019
SALES (est): 572.2K **Privately Held**
SIC: 3444 Sheet metalwork

(G-13275)
INK-TRAX INC
238 W 5th St (32401-2643)
PHONE.................................850 235-4849
Jerry Walters, *President*
Josh Rich, *Art Dir*
Stephanie Tulacz, *Graphic Designe*
EMP: 10 **EST:** 1994
SQ FT: 7,500
SALES (est): 943.7K **Privately Held**
WEB: www.inktrax.com
SIC: 2759 Screen printing

(G-13276)
INSTITUTE FOR PROSTHETIC ADVAN
Also Called: IPA Prosthetics & Orthotics
2315 Ruth Hentz Ave (32405-2260)
P.O. Box 960, Lynn Haven (32444-0960)
PHONE.................................850 784-0320
John Fredrick, *Owner*
EMP: 8 **EST:** 1995
SQ FT: 3,180
SALES (est): 767.4K **Privately Held**
SIC: 3842 5999 Limbs, artificial; orthope-
dic & prosthesis applications

(G-13277)
J & J DOOR MANUFACTURING INC
2325 Transmitter Rd (32404-3156)
PHONE.................................850 769-2554
Jayson Gay, *President*
Jerry L Weeks Jr, *Vice Pres*
EMP: 29 **EST:** 1995
SQ FT: 16,000
SALES (est): 3.2MM **Privately Held**
WEB: www.jandjdoormfg.com
SIC: 2434 Wood kitchen cabinets

(G-13278)
JAYCO WOODWORKS INC
9338 Resota Beach Rd (32409-2184)
PHONE.................................850 814-3041
Michael J Parish, *Principal*
EMP: 7 **EST:** 2003
SALES (est): 213.9K **Privately Held**
SIC: 2431 Millwork

(G-13279)
JETBOATPILOT LLC
2743 Forester Trl (32405-8217)
PHONE.................................850 960-3236
Will Owen, *CEO*
EMP: 11 **EST:** 2010
SALES (est): 2.1MM **Privately Held**
WEB: www.jetboatpilot.com
SIC: 3531 5088 Marine related equipment;
marine supplies

(G-13280)
JOHNSON BROTHERS WHL MEATS INC
1640 Martin Luther King J (32405-5430)
P.O. Box 729 (32402-0729)
PHONE.................................850 763-2828
Paul Johnson, *President*
David Johnson, *General Mgr*
David M Johnson, *Corp Secy*
EMP: 27 **EST:** 1930
SQ FT: 2,115
SALES (est): 957.9K **Privately Held**
SIC: 2011 5141 2015 2013 Meat packing
plants; groceries, general line; poultry
slaughtering & processing; sausages &
other prepared meats

(G-13281)
K & K PRECISION MANUFACTURING
2307 Industrial Dr (32405-6039)
P.O. Box 839, Lynn Haven (32444-0839)
PHONE.................................850 769-9080
Ronald Kiefer, *President*
Glen Kiefer, *General Mgr*
Mary Kiefer, *Corp Secy*
EMP: 6 **EST:** 1978
SQ FT: 7,000
SALES (est): 479.5K **Privately Held**
SIC: 3599 Machine shop, jobbing & repair

(G-13282)
KRATON CHEMICAL LLC
2 S Everitt Ave (32401-4989)
PHONE.................................850 785-8521
Danielle Mason, *Engineer*
Callie Noble, *Sr Project Mgr*
EMP: 27 **EST:** 2017
SALES (est): 15MM **Privately Held**
WEB: www.kraton.com
SIC: 2819 2869 2899 5169 Industrial in-
organic chemicals; industrial organic
chemicals; chemical preparations; indus-
trial chemicals

(G-13283)
LISA MC CALL
1740 Sherman Ave (32405-6283)
PHONE.................................850 265-4241
Randell McCall, *Owner*
Lisa Mc Call, *Co-Owner*
EMP: 10 **EST:** 2005
SALES (est): 635.8K **Privately Held**
SIC: 3599 Machine shop, jobbing & repair

(G-13284)
MARITECH MACHINE INC
1740 Sherman Ave (32405-6283)
PHONE.................................850 872-0852
Randell McCall, *President*
Lisa McCall, *Vice Pres*
EMP: 20 **EST:** 1991
SQ FT: 7,000
SALES (est): 4.3MM **Privately Held**
WEB: www.maritechmachineinc.com
SIC: 3599 Machine shop, jobbing & repair

(G-13285)
MARTIN MARIETTA MATERIALS INC
Also Called: Panama City Yard
1602 B Ave (32401-1007)
PHONE.................................850 913-0083
Tom Turnage, *Manager*
EMP: 10 **Publicly Held**
WEB: www.martinmarietta.com
SIC: 1422 5032 Crushed & broken lime-
stone; stone, crushed or broken
PA: Martin Marietta Materials Inc
4123 Parklake Ave
Raleigh NC 27612

(G-13286)
MILLER MARINE YACHT SVC INC
7141 Grassy Point Rd (32409-1401)
P.O. Box 842, Lynn Haven (32444-0842)
PHONE.................................850 265-6768
William M Miller, *President*
EMP: 29 **EST:** 1998
SQ FT: 2,000
SALES (est): 1MM **Privately Held**
WEB: www.millermarineinc.net
SIC: 3731 3732 Shipbuilding & repairing;
boat building & repairing

(G-13287)
MONKEY SHACK
11840 Front Beach Rd A (32407-3684)
P.O. Box 9377 (32417-9377)
PHONE.................................850 234-0082
Danny Sedah, *Owner*
EMP: 6 **EST:** 2003
SALES (est): 362K **Privately Held**
SIC: 2254 Shirts & t-shirts (underwear),
knit

(G-13288)
MYERS CABINETRY LLC
3631 N Highway 231 (32404-5751)
PHONE.................................850 872-1794
Michael A Myers, *Manager*
EMP: 7 **EST:** 2011
SALES (est): 97.1K **Privately Held**
SIC: 2434 Wood kitchen cabinets

(G-13289)
NEWS HERALD
221 E 23rd St Ste B (32405-4557)
PHONE.................................850 785-6550
EMP: 9 **EST:** 2017
SALES (est): 345.6K **Privately Held**
WEB: www.newsherald.com
SIC: 2711 Newspapers, publishing & print-
ing

(G-13290)
NORTHSIDE SHEET METAL INC
2836 Transmitter Rd (32404-3031)
P.O. Box 934 (32402-0934)
PHONE.................................850 769-1461
Chris Crittendon, *President*
Annette Crinttendon, *Admin Sec*
EMP: 6 **EST:** 1971
SQ FT: 3,000
SALES (est): 925.4K **Privately Held**
WEB: www.scallionlaw.com
SIC: 3444 Sheet metalwork

(G-13291)
OCEANEERING INTERNATIONAL INC
Oceanering Umbilical Solutions
1700 C Ave (32401-1057)
PHONE.................................985 329-3282
Shaun Roedel, *Division Mgr*
Calvin Smith, *Project Mgr*
David Emery, *Project Engr*
Richard Squires, *Project Engr*
Shawn Middleton, *Prgrmr*
EMP: 150
SALES (corp-wide): 1.8B **Publicly Held**
WEB: www.oceaneering.com
SIC: 3357 3643 Fiber optic cable (insu-
lated); power line cable
PA: Oceaneering International Inc
11911 Fm 529 Rd
Houston TX 77041
713 329-4500

(G-13292)
PANAMA CITY CONCRETE INC
1119 Lindenwood Dr (32405-3623)
P.O. Box 15911 (32406-5911)
PHONE.................................850 851-3637
EMP: 8 **EST:** 2018
SALES (est): 192.9K **Privately Held**
WEB:
www.panamacityconcretecompany.com
SIC: 3273 Ready-mixed concrete

(G-13293)
PANAMA CITY NEWS HERALD (DH)
Also Called: Northwest Florida Daily News
501 W 11th St (32401-2330)
P.O. Box 1940 (32402-1940)
PHONE..................................850 747-5000
James Rosse, *Ch of Bd*
Ray Glenn, *Editor*
Will Glover, *Editor*
Dustin Kent, *Editor*
Jonathan Segal, *Vice Pres*
EMP: 68 **EST:** 1933
SQ FT: 46,000
SALES (est): 21.6MM
SALES (corp-wide): 3.2B **Publicly Held**
WEB: www.newsherald.com
SIC: 2711 Newspapers, publishing & printing
HQ: Gatehouse Media, Llc
　175 Sullys Trl Ste 203
　Pittsford NY 14534
　585 598-0030

(G-13294)
PANAMA CITY PALLET INC
1706 Maple Ave (32405-6022)
PHONE..................................850 769-1040
EMP: 20 **EST:** 2019
SALES (est): 2.4MM **Privately Held**
SIC: 2448 Pallets, wood

(G-13295)
PANAMA CITY TINT CENTER
526 E 6th St (32401-3025)
PHONE..................................850 640-0167
Isaiah Dewan Gardner, *Owner*
EMP: 7 **EST:** 2012
SALES (est): 110K **Privately Held**
WEB: www.panamacitytoyota.com
SIC: 3211 Window glass, clear & colored

(G-13296)
PANAMA PALLETS CO INC
1706 Maple Ave (32405-6022)
PHONE..................................850 769-1040
Douglas H Lindsey, *President*
Tim Newitt, *Vice Pres*
EMP: 9 **EST:** 1995
SALES (est): 880K **Privately Held**
WEB: www.panamapallet.com
SIC: 2448 Pallets, wood

(G-13297)
PARTHENON PRINTS INC
909 W 39th St (32405-4841)
P.O. Box 2505 (32402-2505)
PHONE..................................850 769-8321
Gus Harris Jr, *CEO*
Theonne Harris, *President*
Gus Ajr Harris, *Vice Pres*
Paul O 'connor, *Opers Mgr*
Chris Harris, *Safety Mgr*
▲ **EMP:** 35 **EST:** 1979
SQ FT: 112,000
SALES (est): 6.8MM **Privately Held**
WEB: www.parthenonprints.com
SIC: 2679 2396 Wallpaper; fabric printing & stamping

(G-13298)
POINT BLANK SCRNPRNTING DESIGN
116 Rusty Gans Dr (32408-4510)
PHONE..................................850 234-9745
Richard Hernandez, *Principal*
EMP: 7 **EST:** 2001
SALES (est): 146.1K **Privately Held**
SIC: 2759 Screen printing

(G-13299)
PREMIER BRUSH INC
2230 Industrial Dr (32405-6036)
P.O. Box 15695 (32406-5695)
PHONE..................................850 271-5736
Brian Stopka, *President*
EMP: 8 **EST:** 1989
SQ FT: 10,000
SALES (est): 775.7K **Privately Held**
WEB: www.premierbrush.com
SIC: 3991 Brushes, except paint & varnish

(G-13300)
RAY MACHINE INC
3711 N Highway 231 (32404-9745)
PHONE..................................850 784-1116
Anthony Ray, *President*
Deborah Ray, *Controller*
EMP: 10 **EST:** 1989
SQ FT: 8,000
SALES (est): 1.6MM **Privately Held**
WEB: www.raymachine.us
SIC: 3599 Machine shop, jobbing & repair

(G-13301)
REDDY ICE CORPORATION
1225 Moylan Rd (32407-4065)
P.O. Box 9083 (32417-9083)
PHONE..................................850 233-0128
David Ciatk, *Manager*
EMP: 9 **Privately Held**
WEB: www.reddyice.com
SIC: 2097 Manufactured ice
HQ: Reddy Ice Llc
　5710 Lbj Fwy Ste 300
　Dallas TX 75240
　214 526-6740

(G-13302)
RICHARDSONS CABINET WORKS
3724 Chandler Fenn Dr (32404-2246)
PHONE..................................850 832-8298
Charles T Richardson, *Principal*
EMP: 8 **EST:** 2008
SALES (est): 130.5K **Privately Held**
WEB: www.richardsoncabinetworks.com
SIC: 2434 Wood kitchen cabinets

(G-13303)
ROBOTIC SECURITY SYSTEMS INC
6530 E Highway 22 (32404-9521)
PHONE..................................850 871-9300
Joey Blair, *CEO*
Beth Barn, *Bookkeeper*
Michael Suesens, *Manager*
Justin Jacobs, *Prgrmr*
EMP: 37 **EST:** 2003
SALES (est): 2.6MM **Privately Held**
WEB: www.rssi.com
SIC: 3441 Fabricated structural metal

(G-13304)
ROBOTICS FABRICATION INC
5835 Bay Line Dr (32404-5492)
PHONE..................................850 896-4987
William Lewis, *President*
Larry Eod, *Opers Staff*
Lawrence Johns, *Opers Staff*
Keith Stallter Cfcm, *Contract Mgr*
Keith Stallter, *Contract Mgr*
EMP: 21 **EST:** 2011
SALES (est): 4MM **Privately Held**
WEB: www.roboticsfabrication.com
SIC: 3549 8744 1794 Assembly machines, including robotic; ; excavation & grading, building construction

(G-13305)
RSSI BARRIERS LLC
6530 E Highway 22 (32404-9521)
PHONE..................................850 871-9300
JD Dunn, *Parts Mgr*
Amanda B Blair, *Mng Member*
George Douglas, *Sr Project Mgr*
Michael Suesens, *Senior Mgr*
Joey W Blair,
EMP: 20 **EST:** 2010
SQ FT: 10,000
SALES (est): 5.6MM **Privately Held**
WEB: www.rssi.com
SIC: 3499 Barricades, metal

(G-13306)
SIGNS 2 SELL LLC
6804 Highway 77 (32409-1568)
PHONE..................................850 277-0518
Marianne N Varnes, *Mng Member*
EMP: 7 **EST:** 2005
SALES (est): 46K **Privately Held**
WEB: www.signs2sell.com
SIC: 3993 Signs & advertising specialties

(G-13307)
SIGNS UNLIMITED BAY COUNTY INC
507 E 7th St (32401-3036)
P.O. Box 1664 (32402-1664)
PHONE..................................850 785-1061
Martin E Bell, *President*
Matin Bell II, *Vice Pres*
EMP: 5 **EST:** 1980
SQ FT: 5,000
SALES (est): 643.1K **Privately Held**
WEB: www.signsunlimitedpc.com
SIC: 3993 1799 Electric signs; neon signs; sign installation & maintenance

(G-13308)
SILVER SHEET-FLORIDA INC
17742 Ashley Dr (32413-5119)
PHONE..................................850 230-9711
Tollie Potgieter, *President*
Annaliz Potgieter, *Vice Pres*
Paul Theiss, *Sales Staff*
Mark Walden, *Manager*
EMP: 16 **EST:** 2003
SALES (est): 1.5MM **Privately Held**
WEB: www.silversheetenterprises.com
SIC: 3444 Sheet metalwork

(G-13309)
SISCO MARINE LLC
Also Called: Marine Inland Fabricators
1725 Buchanan St (32409-1482)
PHONE..................................850 265-1383
Rudy Sistrunk, *Mng Member*
▼ **EMP:** 20 **EST:** 1980
SQ FT: 5,472
SALES (est): 2.3MM **Privately Held**
SIC: 3731 Shipbuilding & repairing

(G-13310)
SRM CONCRETE
17803 Ashley Dr (32413-5003)
PHONE..................................850 588-7677
EMP: 7 **EST:** 2019
SALES (est): 130.8K **Privately Held**
WEB: www.smyrnareadymix.com
SIC: 3273 Ready-mixed concrete

(G-13311)
STEEL CITY INC
749 E 15th St (32405-5416)
P.O. Box 35036 (32412-5036)
PHONE..................................850 785-9596
Randall Coatney Jr, *CEO*
Steve Barnett, *President*
Rhonda C Williams, *Principal*
Rhonda Williams, *Treasurer*
EMP: 12 **EST:** 1983
SQ FT: 45,000
SALES (est): 2.6MM **Privately Held**
WEB: www.steelcitypc.com
SIC: 3441 5051 3444 1791 Fabricated structural metal; steel; sheet metalwork; structural steel erection; cranes & aerial lift equipment, rental or leasing

(G-13312)
SUNSHINE PIPING INC
6513 Bayline Dr (32404)
P.O. Box 270, Youngstown (32466-0270)
PHONE..................................850 763-4834
Shirley P Scott, *President*
EMP: 25 **EST:** 1990
SQ FT: 60,000
SALES (est): 3.6MM **Privately Held**
WEB: hstrial-sunshinepipingin.homestead.com
SIC: 3498 Fabricated pipe & fittings

(G-13313)
TEX-COTE LLC (HQ)
2422 E 15th St (32405-6348)
PHONE..................................800 454-0340
Chase Bean, *President*
Daniel Curry, *Vice Pres*
EMP: 22 **EST:** 2019
SALES (est): 5.9MM
SALES (corp-wide): 129.5MM **Privately Held**
WEB: www.texcote.com
SIC: 2851 Paints & paint additives; lacquers, varnishes, enamels & other coatings
PA: Tnemec Company, Inc.
　123 W 23rd Ave
　Kansas City MO 64116
　816 483-3400

(G-13314)
TRANE TECHNOLOGIES COMPANY LLC
Also Called: Ingersoll-Rand
200 Aberdeen Loop (32405-6413)
P.O. Box 1410, Lynn Haven (32444-6210)
PHONE..................................850 873-8200
Julie Smith, *Branch Mgr*
EMP: 700 **Privately Held**
WEB: www.trane.com
SIC: 3585 Air conditioning units, complete: domestic or industrial
HQ: Trane Technologies Company Llc
　800 Beaty St Ste E
　Davidson NC 28036
　704 655-4000

(G-13315)
U D T INC
2304 Grant Ave (32405-1359)
PHONE..................................850 784-0537
Troy Balsters, *President*
Cassie Osborn, *General Mgr*
John Balsters, *Vice Pres*
Ken Clammer, *Program Mgr*
Robert Anglen, *IT/INT Sup*
EMP: 8 **EST:** 1971
SQ FT: 15,000
SALES (est): 1.5MM **Privately Held**
WEB: www.udtmachine.com
SIC: 3599 Machine shop, jobbing & repair

(G-13316)
US IRONWORKS COMPANY
328 Wahoo Rd (32408-7264)
P.O. Box 9220, Panama City Beach (32417-9220)
PHONE..................................850 588-5995
Michael R Owen, *President*
Joseph Fanell, *Vice Pres*
Ji H Bushell, *Admin Sec*
EMP: 15 **EST:** 2010
SALES (est): 1.3MM **Privately Held**
SIC: 3446 Architectural metalwork

(G-13317)
VERTICAL LAND INC (PA)
7950 Front Beach Rd (32407-4817)
PHONE..................................850 819-2535
Cynthia M Carter, *President*
EMP: 13 **EST:** 1977
SQ FT: 6,000
SALES (est): 2.4MM **Privately Held**
SIC: 2231 5714 5719 Felts, blanketing & upholstery fabrics: wool; draperies; window shades

(G-13318)
VERTICAL LAND INC
621 Mckenzie Ave (32401-3061)
PHONE..................................850 244-5263
Peggy Unknw, *President*
EMP: 12
SALES (corp-wide): 2.4MM **Privately Held**
SIC: 2591 2391 Blinds vertical; curtains & draperies
PA: Vertical Land, Inc.
　7950 Front Beach Rd
　Panama City FL 32407
　850 819-2535

(G-13319)
WANT ADS OF HOT SPRINGS INC (PA)
Also Called: Thrifty Nickle, The
713 E 12th St (32401-3343)
PHONE..................................501 623-4404
Danny Enlow, *General Mgr*
EMP: 6 **EST:** 1988
SALES (est): 1MM **Privately Held**
SIC: 2711 2741 Newspapers: publishing only, not printed on site; miscellaneous publishing

(G-13320)
WELLSTREAM INTERNATIONAL LTD
6521 Bayline Dr (32404-4805)
PHONE..................................850 636-4800

Jeff Jordan, *Manager*
EMP: 250
SALES (corp-wide): 20.5B **Publicly Held**
SIC: 3317 3084 Steel pipe & tubes; plastics pipe
HQ: Wellstream International Limited
Wellstream House
Newcastle-Upon-Tyne NE6 3

(G-13321)
WESTROCK CP LLC
1 S Everitt Ave (32401-6900)
PHONE.....................850 785-4311
Joy Jones, *Branch Mgr*
EMP: 86
SALES (corp-wide): 18.7B **Publicly Held**
WEB: www.westrock.com
SIC: 2653 Boxes, corrugated: made from purchased materials
HQ: Westrock Cp, Llc
1000 Abernathy Rd Ste 125
Atlanta GA 30328

(G-13322)
WORLD STONE AND DESIGN LLC
19709 Panama Cy Bch Pkwy (32413-3924)
PHONE.....................850 235-0399
Rodrigo Mancilla, *Mng Member*
Girley Leiti,
EMP: 9 **EST:** 2004
SALES (est): 763.2K **Privately Held**
WEB: www.worldstonedesign.com
SIC: 3443 Fabricated plate work (boiler shop)

Panama City
Walton County

(G-13323)
ARRIAGA ORIGINALS
10343 E County Highway 30 # 112 (32461-6943)
PHONE.....................850 231-0084
EMP: 12
SALES (est): 1.2MM **Privately Held**
SIC: 3911 Mfg Precious Metal Jewelry

Panama City Beach
Bay County

(G-13324)
5 STAR COATINGS LLC
126 Escanaba Ave (32413-2205)
PHONE.....................850 628-3743
James Paravalos, *Principal*
EMP: 8 **EST:** 2011
SALES (est): 64.4K **Privately Held**
SIC: 3479 Metal coating & allied service

(G-13325)
ARGOS USA LLC
17800 Ashley Dr (32413-5001)
PHONE.....................850 235-9600
Ross Adolph, *Regl Sales Mgr*
Jeremy Swinyer, *Sales Executive*
Andy Workman, *Branch Mgr*
Darrel Sibley, *Manager*
EMP: 32 **Privately Held**
WEB: www.argos-us.com
SIC: 3273 Ready-mixed concrete
HQ: Argos Usa Llc
3015 Windward Plz Ste 300
Alpharetta GA 30005
678 368-4300

(G-13326)
BAY CABINETS AND MILLWORKS
20679 Panama Cy Bch Pkwy (32413-3722)
PHONE.....................850 215-1485
EMP: 7 **EST:** 2018
SALES (est): 470K **Privately Held**
WEB: www.baycabinetspc.com
SIC: 2434 Wood kitchen cabinets

(G-13327)
BOBCAT OF WIREGRASS INC (PA)
127 Griffin Blvd (32413-5123)
PHONE.....................334 792-5121
Ricky Ball, *President*
Heather Willis, *Office Mgr*
EMP: 10 **EST:** 2003
SALES (est): 1.2MM **Privately Held**
SIC: 3694 Engine electrical equipment

(G-13328)
COAST PRODUCTS LLC
169 Griffin Blvd Unit 106 (32413-5239)
PHONE.....................850 235-2090
Robert Easter, *Mng Member*
EMP: 13 **EST:** 2009
SQ FT: 2,000
SALES (est): 2.1MM **Privately Held**
WEB: www.coastproductsusa.com
SIC: 3088 Plastics plumbing fixtures

(G-13329)
DAVID PERKINS ENTERPRISES INC
Also Called: Dp Enterprises
7538 Mcelvey Rd (32408-4919)
PHONE.....................850 234-0002
David Perkins, *President*
EMP: 8 **EST:** 1998
SALES (est): 926.8K **Privately Held**
SIC: 3841 8732 Medical instruments & equipment, blood & bone work; research services, except laboratory

(G-13330)
EDGE AERODYNAMIX INC
8317 Front Beach Rd # 21 (32407-4893)
PHONE.....................850 238-8610
EMP: 13 **EST:** 2011
SALES (est): 579.6K **Privately Held**
WEB: www.edgeaerodynamix.com
SIC: 3728 Aircraft parts & equipment

(G-13331)
GNS EMBROIDERY
1713 Moylan Rd (32407-4016)
PHONE.....................850 775-1147
Steve Owens, *Owner*
EMP: 6 **EST:** 2015
SALES (est): 310.3K **Privately Held**
WEB: www.gnsembroideryshop.com
SIC: 2395 Embroidery products, except schiffli machine; embroidery & art needlework

(G-13332)
GULF COAST CABINETRY INC
22200 Panama Cy Bch Pkwy (32413-3226)
PHONE.....................850 769-3799
Roger Clark, *President*
EMP: 6 **EST:** 2016
SQ FT: 1,800
SALES (est): 1.3MM **Privately Held**
WEB: www.gulfcoastcabinetry.com
SIC: 2434 Wood kitchen cabinets

(G-13333)
JOYNER INC
9740 Steel Field Rd (32413-9462)
PHONE.....................850 832-6326
Jeff B Joyner, *President*
EMP: 7 **EST:** 2007
SALES (est): 1.4MM **Privately Held**
SIC: 2411 5031 Logging; lumber, plywood & millwork

(G-13334)
MINE SURVIVAL INC
9210 Pnama Cy Bch Pkwy St (32407)
PHONE.....................850 774-0025
Robert N Moran, *President*
David Cowgill, *Vice Pres*
▼ **EMP:** 5 **EST:** 2014
SQ FT: 5,000
SALES (est): 5MM **Privately Held**
WEB: www.minesurvival.com
SIC: 3949 Skin diving equipment, scuba type

(G-13335)
PANHANDLE PAINT & DCTG LLC
Also Called: Benjamin Moore Authorized Ret
8103 Panama City Bch Pkwy (32407-4860)
P.O. Box 1810, Lynn Haven (32444-5810)
PHONE.....................850 596-9248
George Bass, *Mng Member*
EMP: 7 **EST:** 2013
SALES (est): 1.8MM **Privately Held**
WEB: www.panhandlepaints.com
SIC: 2851 5251 5231 Paints & allied products; hardware; paint, glass & wallpaper

(G-13336)
PARADIGM LEADERS LLC
Also Called: Paradigm Plastics
7946 Front Beach Rd (32407-4817)
PHONE.....................850 441-3289
Jamiel Vadell, *CEO*
Michelle Darko, *Office Mgr*
Richard Barnes, *CIO*
EMP: 5 **EST:** 2015
SALES (est): 458.5K **Privately Held**
WEB: www.paradigmleaders.com
SIC: 3089 8331 8249 5999 Injection molding of plastics; job training & vocational rehabilitation services; job training services; manpower training; business training services; educational aids & electronic training materials

(G-13337)
PRESS PRINT GRAPHICS LLC
106 N Gulf Blvd Ste C (32413-2884)
PHONE.....................850 249-3700
Jeff Weeks, *Manager*
Jeffrey Weeks,
Christopher Weeks,
EMP: 12 **EST:** 2008
SALES (est): 928.9K **Privately Held**
WEB: www.pressprintgraphics.com
SIC: 2752 Commercial printing, offset

(G-13338)
SEA BREEZE SMALL ENGINE
415 Fernwood St (32407-2929)
PHONE.....................205 329-0759
Crystal Chaillou, *Principal*
EMP: 7 **EST:** 2018
SALES (est): 173.5K **Privately Held**
WEB: sea-breeze-small-engine.business.site
SIC: 3599 Machine shop, jobbing & repair

(G-13339)
SIMPLY CABINETS LLC
630 Malaga Pl (32413-3934)
PHONE.....................850 541-3712
Zebulon T Taft, *Branch Mgr*
EMP: 18
SALES (corp-wide): 77.1K **Privately Held**
WEB: www.simplycabinetspcb.com
SIC: 2434 Wood kitchen cabinets
PA: Simply Cabinets, Llc
9527 Clarence St
Panama City Beach FL

(G-13340)
TEXTURED COATINGS
169 Griffin Blvd (32413-5238)
P.O. Box 35008, Panama City (32412-5008)
PHONE.....................850 360-1451
EMP: 5 **EST:** 2019
SALES (est): 351.9K **Privately Held**
WEB: www.texcote.com
SIC: 2851 Paints & allied products

(G-13341)
WORTHINGTON MILLWORK LLC
17842 Ashley Dr C (32413-5001)
PHONE.....................800 872-1608
Jay Kyle Boatwright, *Principal*
Lindsay Haisten, *Office Mgr*
Kyle Boatwright, *Analyst*
Sunshine Menefee, *Commercial*
EMP: 8 **EST:** 2004
SQ FT: 30,000
SALES (est): 945K **Privately Held**
SIC: 2431 Millwork

Parkland
Broward County

(G-13342)
ABSOLUTE TECHNOLOGIES INC
6320 Nw 61st Ave (33067-4400)
PHONE.....................954 868-9045
John E Dagostino, *Principal*
EMP: 11 **EST:** 2012
SALES (est): 78K **Privately Held**
WEB: www.absolutetechnologies.com
SIC: 3599 Machine shop, jobbing & repair

(G-13343)
ATLANTIC MULTI FAMILY I LLC
9045 Vista Way (33076-2865)
PHONE.....................301 233-1261
James W Theobald, *Administration*
EMP: 21 **EST:** 2010
SALES (est): 1.8MM **Privately Held**
SIC: 3571 Personal computers (microcomputers)

(G-13344)
BECKER MICROBIAL PRODUCTS INC
11146 Nw 69th Pl (33076-3846)
PHONE.....................954 345-9321
Terry L Couch, *President*
▼ **EMP:** 8 **EST:** 1980
SALES (est): 670.6K **Privately Held**
WEB:
www.beckermicrobialproductsinc.com
SIC: 2836 8733 Bacteriological media; bacteriological research

(G-13345)
CK DOCKSIDE SERVICES INC
6141 Nw 80th Ter (33067-1132)
PHONE.....................954 254-0263
Craig Koblitz, *Principal*
EMP: 8 **EST:** 2008
SALES (est): 270.4K **Privately Held**
SIC: 3732 Boat building & repairing

(G-13346)
HESS LOGISTICS INC
7508 Appalachian Ln (33067-2367)
PHONE.....................954 668-7101
David Hess, *Principal*
Jessica Hess, *Principal*
EMP: 6 **EST:** 2019
SALES (est): 372.5K **Privately Held**
WEB: www.hess.com
SIC: 1382 Oil & gas exploration services

(G-13347)
HYDRODYNAMIC COATINGS LLC
12149 Nw 77th Mnr (33076-4515)
PHONE.....................954 344-8830
Ledford Parnell, *Principal*
EMP: 7 **EST:** 2016
SALES (est): 140.4K **Privately Held**
SIC: 3479 Metal coating & allied service

(G-13348)
JIMENEZ ENTERPRISES GROUP
5851 Holmberg Rd Apt 3723 (33067-4527)
PHONE.....................561 391-6800
Eduardo Jimenez, *Principal*
EMP: 39
SALES (corp-wide): 290.5K **Privately Held**
SIC: 3841 Surgical & medical instruments
PA: Jimenez Enterprises Group, Corp
10855 Nw 50th St Apt 204
Doral FL 33178
561 542-7709

(G-13349)
LEMON GRASS INDUSTRIES INC
5920 Nw 59th Ave (33067-4427)
PHONE.....................954 418-6110
Suzette Cascio, *President*
Frances Cascio, *Vice Pres*
▼ **EMP:** 5
SALES (est): 443.4K **Privately Held**
WEB: www.lemongrasscandles.com
SIC: 3999 Candles

(G-13350)
PROMOWEAR
9547 Cinnamon Ct (33076-4419)
PHONE................................561 372-0505
Andrea Bomwell, *President*
EMP: 6 EST: 2006
SALES (est): 429.1K **Privately Held**
WEB: www.promowearusa.com
SIC: 2395 Embroidery products, except
schiffli machine; embroidery & art needle-
work

(G-13351)
R&M ORTHOTICS INC
10939 Nw 62nd Ct (33076-3726)
PHONE................................954 547-6722
Mindy Brietman, *Manager*
EMP: 8 EST: 2017
SALES (est): 135.5K **Privately Held**
SIC: 3842 Orthopedic appliances

(G-13352)
REESE CORPORATION
Also Called: Wedding Bells
12140 Porto Way (33076-4824)
PHONE................................305 653-1000
Samuel Reese, *President*
Miriam Reese, *Corp Secy*
Jonathan Reese, *Vice Pres*
EMP: 9 EST: 1947
SALES (est): 580K **Privately Held**
SIC: 3911 Jewelry, precious metal

(G-13353)
**SAFETOGETHER LTD LIABILITY
CO** ✪
5917 Nw 63rd Way (33067-1525)
PHONE................................954 227-2236
Todd Darling, *CEO*
Scott Racy, *CEO*
Mehron Talebi, *Principal*
Robert King, *Exec VP*
Christopher Mackie, *Director*
EMP: 8 EST: 2021
SALES (est): 319.7K **Privately Held**
SIC: 3646 Commercial indusl & institu-
tional electric lighting fixtures

(G-13354)
SIPRADIUS LLC (PA)
5814 Nw 74th Ter (33067-1243)
PHONE................................954 290-2434
Sergio Ammirata, *Mng Member*
EMP: 5 EST: 2006
SALES (est): 304.4K **Privately Held**
WEB: www.sipradius.com
SIC: 7372 2741 4813 Operating systems
computer software; ; ;

(G-13355)
SUPERIOR FABRICS INC
7901 S Woodridge Dr (33067-2392)
PHONE................................954 975-8122
Alex Fryburg, *Ch of Bd*
Robert Fryburg, *President*
David Fryburg, *Vice Pres*
EMP: 25 EST: 1895
SALES (est): 750.2K **Privately Held**
WEB: www.superiorfabrics.com
SIC: 2211 2297 2221 Broadwoven fabric
mills, cotton; nonwoven fabrics; broadwo-
ven fabric mills, manmade

Parrish
Manatee County

(G-13356)
ANGLO SILVER LINER CO
7019 Indus Valley Cir (34219-2861)
PHONE................................508 943-1440
Dilip Mehta, *President*
Paul Fitzpatrick, *Editor*
EMP: 10 EST: 1998
SALES (est): 242.5K **Privately Held**
SIC: 2221 Broadwoven fabric mills, man-
made

(G-13357)
CARRIERS DIRECT INC
2623 Little Country Rd (34219-9262)
PHONE................................941 776-2979
Neil Bradley, *CEO*
EMP: 14 EST: 2011

SQ FT: 27,000
SALES (est): 1.7MM **Privately Held**
WEB: www.carriersdirect.us
SIC: 3537 Trucks: freight, baggage, etc.:
industrial, except mining

(G-13358)
**E-Z ANCHOR PULLER MFG CO
LLC**
8955 Us Highway 301 N (34219-8701)
PHONE................................800 800-1640
Christy Funk, *Principal*
EMP: 6
SALES (est): 349.3K **Privately Held**
WEB: www.ezanchorpuller.com
SIC: 3999 Manufacturing industries

(G-13359)
**GRAPHIX SOLUTIONS OF
AMERICA**
12015 Major Turner Run (34219-1263)
PHONE................................727 898-6744
Lee F Romig, *President*
EMP: 16 EST: 1938
SQ FT: 6,000
SALES (est): 546.6K **Privately Held**
SIC: 2752 2759 Commercial printing, off-
set; commercial printing

(G-13360)
**NAVIGTOR KITCHENS
CABINETS INC**
Also Called: Navigator Kitchens & Cnstr
12726 24th Street Cir E (34219-6941)
PHONE................................941 776-9482
Neil McGowan, *Principal*
EMP: 6 EST: 2017
SALES (est): 358.3K **Privately Held**
WEB: www.navigatorkitchenscabinets.com
SIC: 2434 Wood kitchen cabinets

(G-13361)
**PHOENIX DEFENSE GROUP
LLC**
3013 Old Orchard Ln (34219-9352)
PHONE................................941 776-8714
L Michael Swingley, *Principal*
▲ EMP: 8 EST: 2010
SALES (est): 356.4K **Privately Held**
SIC: 3812 Defense systems & equipment

Pembroke Park
Broward County

(G-13362)
CLASSIC INSTALLATIONS LLC
2401 Sw 32nd Ave (33023-7708)
PHONE................................954 966-1148
Jose Garcia, *Principal*
Joseph Garcia Jr, *Principal*
John Jovonovich, *Principal*
Geoff Monsalvatge, *Principal*
EMP: 9 EST: 2006
SALES (est): 343.9K **Privately Held**
SIC: 3442 Metal doors, sash & trim

(G-13363)
INUSA MANUFACTURING LLC
2500 Sw 32nd Ave (33023-7703)
PHONE................................786 451-5227
Moises Sterental, *Principal*
EMP: 9 EST: 2014
SALES (est): 464.4K **Privately Held**
SIC: 3999 Framed artwork

(G-13364)
PSTEIN INC
Also Called: Philip Stein
4350 W Hllandale Bch Blvd (33023-4479)
PHONE................................305 373-0037
Wilhelm Stein, *President*
Miguel Martinez, *President*
Ruthie Assouline, *Vice Pres*
Ruthie Mink, *Vice Pres*
Letty Gebrehiwet, *Opers Staff*
◆ EMP: 40 EST: 2002
SQ FT: 9,662
SALES (est): 5.4MM **Privately Held**
WEB: www.philipstein.com
SIC: 3873 Watches, clocks, watchcases &
parts

(G-13365)
ROWE INDUSTRIES INC
2525 Sw 32nd Ave (33023-7706)
P.O. Box 189, Annapolis MD (21404-0189)
PHONE................................302 855-0585
Brooke Kinney, *President*
Doug Kinney, *Principal*
Betty J Adkins, *Vice Pres*
EMP: 16 EST: 1985
SALES (est): 2.7MM **Privately Held**
WEB: www.roweindustries.com
SIC: 2822 3496 Silicone rubbers; miscel-
laneous fabricated wire products
PA: Anr Partners, Inc.
626 Main St
Ceredo WV 25507

(G-13366)
SALT INTERNATIONAL CORP
2798 Sw 32nd Ave (33023-7702)
PHONE................................305 698-8889
Salvatore Tizzoni, *President*
▲ EMP: 7 EST: 2008
SALES (est): 2.2MM **Privately Held**
WEB: www.saltintl.com
SIC: 3429 Furniture builders' & other
household hardware

Pembroke Pines
Broward County

(G-13367)
**A CROWN MOLDING
SPECIALIST**
9714 Nw 24th Ct (33024-1436)
PHONE................................954 665-5640
Shawn Kelker, *Principal*
EMP: 8 EST: 2010
SALES (est): 509.7K **Privately Held**
WEB: www.crownmaxmolding.com
SIC: 3089 Molding primary plastic

(G-13368)
**ADHESIVE MANUFACTURERS
INC**
1572 Nw 182nd Way (33029-3091)
PHONE................................305 495-8018
Alan Klein, *President*
EMP: 8 EST: 2001
SALES (est): 87.2K **Privately Held**
SIC: 2891 Adhesives

(G-13369)
**ADVANCED LIVING QUARTERS
INC**
Also Called: Alq Business Development
426 Sw 191st Ter (33029-5463)
PHONE................................954 684-9392
Julio Juarbe, *Principal*
EMP: 8 EST: 2016
SALES (est): 248.7K **Privately Held**
SIC: 3131 Quarters

(G-13370)
AERIAL BANNERS INC
601 Sw 77th Way (33023-2591)
PHONE................................954 893-0099
Bob Benyo, *President*
Luis De Varona, *Business Mgr*
Dana Benyo, *Vice Pres*
Dan Banners, *Maintence Staff*
EMP: 15 EST: 1994
SALES (est): 2.3MM **Privately Held**
WEB: www.aerialbanners.com
SIC: 3993 Signs & advertising specialties

(G-13371)
AERONATE INC
20851 Johnson St Ste 109 (33029-1924)
PHONE................................954 358-7145
Roberto Carcano, *President*
Juan Pablo Carcano, *Vice Pres*
EMP: 7 EST: 2010
SALES (est): 798.3K **Privately Held**
WEB: www.aeronate.com
SIC: 3728 Aircraft parts & equipment

(G-13372)
AEROSPACE AUTOMATION LLC
830 Sw 174th Ter (33029-4213)
PHONE................................954 260-2844
Shane M Link, *Mng Member*
David Krebs, *Mng Member*

Terence Link, *Mng Member*
EMP: 8 EST: 2008
SALES (est): 270.2K **Privately Held**
SIC: 3812 Aircraft/aerospace flight instru-
ments & guidance systems

(G-13373)
ALL GOLF
Also Called: Allgolf
950 N Flamingo Rd (33028-1002)
PHONE................................954 441-1333
Jeff Osenkowski, *General Mgr*
EMP: 9 EST: 2001
SALES (est): 428.6K **Privately Held**
SIC: 3949 Sporting & athletic goods

(G-13374)
AMERICA ENERGY INC
20861 Johnson St Ste 116 (33029-1927)
PHONE................................954 762-7763
Alberto Aure, *President*
Claudia Pl, *Finance*
▲ EMP: 9 EST: 2007
SALES (est): 1MM **Privately Held**
WEB: www.america-energy.com
SIC: 3563 3613 Air & gas compressors in-
cluding vacuum pumps; vacuum pumps,
except laboratory; control panels, electric

(G-13375)
AVENTURA COOKIES INC
1868 Nw 140th Ter (33028-2845)
PHONE................................954 447-4525
Mohammed Alamgir, *Principal*
EMP: 7 EST: 2005
SALES (est): 81.4K **Privately Held**
SIC: 2052 Cookies

(G-13376)
AVPRINTING SOLUTIONS LLC
6100 Hollywood Blvd (33024-7900)
PHONE................................866 207-6295
Avraham Ayashe, *Mng Member*
▲ EMP: 7 EST: 2008
SALES (est): 262.5K **Privately Held**
WEB: www.avel-print.com
SIC: 2741 Business service newsletters:
publishing & printing

(G-13377)
BECKMAN COULTER INC
1 Sw 129th Ave Ste 201 (33027-1716)
PHONE................................954 432-4336
Dean Beckman, *Principal*
Ernie Thomas, *Manager*
EMP: 11 EST: 2012
SALES (est): 680.8K **Privately Held**
WEB: www.beckmancoulter.com
SIC: 3826 Analytical instruments

(G-13378)
BEDESCHI AMERICA INC
20170 Pines Blvd Ste 301 (33029-1262)
PHONE................................954 602-2175
Kyle Campbell, *Branch Mgr*
EMP: 96
SALES (corp-wide): 173.5MM **Privately
Held**
WEB: www.bedeschi.com
SIC: 3542 High energy rate metal forming
machines
HQ: Bedeschi America, Inc.
2600 N Military Trl # 245
Boca Raton FL 33431
954 602-2175

(G-13379)
**BIGBYTE SOFTWARE SYSTEMS
INC**
2214 Nw 171st Ter (33028-2050)
PHONE................................917 370-1733
David Ging, *CFO*
EMP: 8 EST: 2016
SALES (est): 30.7K **Privately Held**
WEB: www.bigbytesoftware.com
SIC: 7372 Prepackaged software

(G-13380)
CEMEX MATERIALS LLC
Also Called: Pembroke Pines FL Readymix
17301 Pines Blvd (33029-1508)
PHONE................................954 431-7655
David Packerd, *Branch Mgr*
EMP: 128
SQ FT: 17,263 **Privately Held**

SIC: 3273 5032 5211 Ready-mixed concrete; concrete mixtures; concrete & cinder block
HQ: Cemex Materials Llc
1720 Centrepark Dr E # 100
West Palm Beach FL 33401
561 833-5555

(G-13381)
CHRISALEN CABINETS INC
8701 Johnson St (33024-6501)
PHONE.....................................954 682-9390
Rene A Bedoya, *Principal*
EMP: 8 **EST:** 2006
SALES (est): 116.8K **Privately Held**
SIC: 2434 Wood kitchen cabinets

(G-13382)
CITADINOS CORP
18483 Sw 7th St (33029-6001)
PHONE.....................................954 435-7529
Ana Maria Citadino, *Principal*
EMP: 7 **EST:** 2011
SALES (est): 103.9K **Privately Held**
SIC: 7372 Prepackaged software

(G-13383)
COOPPA NEWS REPORTER
13550 Sw 10th St (33027-6445)
PHONE.....................................954 437-8864
Maritza Bulnes, *Principal*
EMP: 11 **EST:** 1997
SALES (est): 296.9K **Privately Held**
SIC: 2711 Newspapers, publishing & print-
ing

(G-13384)
DESIROUS CANDLES INC
10240 Nw 3rd St (33026-3972)
PHONE.....................................347 622-6987
Carmela Martinez, *CEO*
EMP: 5 **EST:** 2015
SALES (est): 312.4K **Privately Held**
SIC: 3999 1541 2051 Candles; food prod-
ucts manufacturing or packing plant con-
struction; cakes, bakery: except frozen

(G-13385)
DREAMLINE AEROSPACE
7649 Pines Blvd (33024-6912)
PHONE.....................................954 544-2365
Rafaela Martinez, *Principal*
EMP: 7 **EST:** 2013
SALES (est): 134.2K **Privately Held**
SIC: 3721 Aircraft

(G-13386)
EMPHASYS CMPT SOLUTIONS INC
Also Called: Emphasys Software
1200 Sw 145th Ave Ste 310 (33027-6240)
PHONE.....................................305 599-2531
Michael Byrne, *CEO*
Andrew Seminari, *Business Mgr*
Steve Thomas, *Opers Staff*
Madhu Varma, *Engineer*
Frankie Valle, *Accounts Mgr*
EMP: 50 **EST:** 1983
SALES (est): 12.3MM
SALES (corp-wide): 5.1B **Privately Held**
WEB: www.emphasys-software.com
SIC: 7372 Prepackaged software
PA: Constellation Software Inc
20 Adelaide St E Suite 1200
Toronto ON M5C 2

(G-13387)
ETHNERGY INTERNATIONAL INC
1524 Sw 59 Ln (33027)
PHONE.....................................954 499-1582
EMP: 40
SALES (est): 6.8MM **Privately Held**
SIC: 2869 Industrial Organic Chemicals,
Nec

(G-13388)
EVOLUTION LIGHTING LLC (PA)
880 Sw 145th Ave Ste 100 (33027-6171)
P.O. Box 398299, Miami Beach (33239-
8299)
PHONE.....................................305 558-4777
A Corydon Meyer, *CEO*
Richard Giron, *Exec VP*
Wilfredo Figueras, *Vice Pres*

Adam Herman, *Vice Pres*
Marc J Leder, *Vice Pres*
◆ **EMP:** 30 **EST:** 2009
SALES (est): 22.6MM **Privately Held**
WEB: www.luciditylights.com
SIC: 3645 3648 3646 Residential lighting
fixtures; lighting equipment; desk lamps,
commercial

(G-13389)
FIZGIG LLC ✪
1174 Sw 121st Ave (33025-5776)
PHONE.....................................754 423-0349
Tana Dejean, *Mng Member*
EMP: 10 **EST:** 2021
SALES (est): 534.4K **Privately Held**
SIC: 7372 Application computer software

(G-13390)
GGS SNACKS & THINGS INC
10010 Sw 11th St (33025-3612)
PHONE.....................................954 297-9375
Leicester B Green, *Principal*
EMP: 7 **EST:** 2020
SALES (est): 67.3K **Privately Held**
SIC: 2096 Potato chips & similar snacks

(G-13391)
GLAMER MEDSPA LLC
2114 N Flamingo Rd (33028-3501)
PHONE.....................................305 744-6908
Danique Campbell,
EMP: 10 **EST:** 2018
SALES (est): 409.5K **Privately Held**
SIC: 2844 Cosmetic preparations

(G-13392)
GOOD CHANCE INC
20851 Johnson St Ste 107 (33029-1924)
PHONE.....................................754 263-2792
Thomas Tong, *Principal*
▲ **EMP:** 7 **EST:** 2008
SALES (est): 109.9K **Privately Held**
SIC: 2299 Textile goods

(G-13393)
GOOD CHANCE TEXTILE INC
20851 Johnson St Ste 107 (33029-1924)
PHONE.....................................754 263-2792
Chuen F Chan, *President*
◆ **EMP:** 17 **EST:** 2005
SALES (est): 903.5K **Privately Held**
WEB: www.goodchancetextile.com
SIC: 2329 Men's & boys' sportswear & ath-
letic clothing

(G-13394)
GYPSUM BD SPECIALISTS USA CORP
Also Called: GBS
241 Nw 217th Way (33029-1019)
PHONE.....................................954 348-8869
Jeannie Juri, *President*
EMP: 5 **EST:** 2016
SALES (est): 416.1K **Privately Held**
SIC: 3275 Gypsum board

(G-13395)
HAWK PROTECTION INCORPORATED
1020 Sw 98th Ave (33025-3698)
PHONE.....................................954 980-9631
Eugene Greene, *CEO*
EMP: 6 **EST:** 2003
SALES (est): 741.4K
SALES (corp-wide): 87.2MM **Privately Held**
SIC: 3842 Personal safety equipment
PA: Cooneen By Design Limited
23 Cooneen Road
Fivemiletown BT75
288 952-1401

(G-13396)
HOIPONG CUSTOMS INC
18331 Pines Blvd (33029-1421)
PHONE.....................................954 684-9232
Pong Craig Hoi, *President*
EMP: 8 **EST:** 2012
SALES (est): 308.7K **Privately Held**
SIC: 2752 Commercial printing, litho-
graphic

(G-13397)
INPRODELCA INC
702 Nw 170th Ter (33028-2119)
PHONE.....................................865 687-7921
Jesus Caballero, *Principal*
EMP: 8 **EST:** 2010
SALES (est): 86.5K **Privately Held**
SIC: 3441 Fabricated structural metal

(G-13398)
JET FUEL CATERING LLC
1920 Nw 137th Way (33028-2608)
PHONE.....................................954 804-1146
Robert A Del Castillo Jr, *Manager*
EMP: 9 **EST:** 2017
SALES (est): 666.7K **Privately Held**
WEB: www.jetfuelmeals.com
SIC: 2911 Jet fuels

(G-13399)
JMF DGITAL PRINT SOLUTIONS INC
19150 Sw 16th St (33029-6137)
PHONE.....................................954 362-4929
Maria D Ochoa, *Principal*
EMP: 7 **EST:** 2009
SALES (est): 128.7K **Privately Held**
WEB: www.jmf-digital.com
SIC: 2752 Commercial printing, litho-
graphic

(G-13400)
LW ROZZO INC
17200 Pines Blvd (33029-1505)
PHONE.....................................954 435-8501
John C Sessa, *President*
EMP: 47 **EST:** 1955
SALES (est): 12.8MM **Privately Held**
SIC: 1411 Dimension stone

(G-13401)
M X CORPORATION
Also Called: Kitchens By US
1531 Nw 180th Way (33029-3040)
PHONE.....................................305 597-9881
Simon Chew, *President*
EMP: 5 **EST:** 1990
SALES (est): 852.9K **Privately Held**
SIC: 2434 Wood kitchen cabinets

(G-13402)
MERCAWORLD AND CIA LLC
20871 Johnson St Ste 115 (33029-1918)
PHONE.....................................786 212-5905
Marianne Caesar, *Editor*
Chris Shearer, *Manager*
Karin Gould, *Senior Mgr*
Fabio Lozano, *Director*
Colleen Moore, *Assistant*
EMP: 7 **EST:** 2013
SALES (est): 684.1K **Privately Held**
SIC: 2721 Periodicals
PA: Mercaworld Y Compania Sas
Avenida 19 118 95 Ofc 602
Bogota

(G-13403)
MIAMI EYEWORKS INC
Also Called: Optical Whl Opt Frmes Opt Sngl
2114 N Flamingo Rd # 115 (33028-3501)
PHONE.....................................954 316-6757
Johann Kolassa, *President*
EMP: 7 **EST:** 1991
SALES (est): 96.6K **Privately Held**
SIC: 3851 5099 Frames, lenses & parts,
eyeglass & spectacle; sunglasses

(G-13404)
MINK BAR LLC
10231 Sw 4th Ct Unit 202 (33025-1643)
PHONE.....................................954 758-2085
Porsha Pelissier, *Mng Member*
EMP: 5 **EST:** 2017
SALES (est): 76.5K **Privately Held**
SIC: 3999 Eyelashes, artificial

(G-13405)
MITO CORP ✪
1488 Nw 158th Ln (33028-1669)
PHONE.....................................786 208-3114
Alberto Bassotti, *Principal*
EMP: 11 **EST:** 2021

SALES (est): 1.2MM **Privately Held**
WEB: www.mitocorp.io
SIC: 3585 7389 Air conditioning equip-
ment, complete;

(G-13406)
MONUMENTAL ENTERPRISES INC
7958 Pines Blvd Ste 242 (33024-6918)
PHONE.....................................305 803-8493
Jessica Serrano, *Principal*
EMP: 5 **EST:** 2016
SALES (est): 341.6K **Privately Held**
SIC: 3272 8742 Monuments & grave
markers, except terrazo; marketing con-
sulting services

(G-13407)
MWR SIGN ENTERPRISES INC
Also Called: Fastsigns
9909 Pines Blvd (33024-6174)
PHONE.....................................954 914-2709
Mike Ruckdefchel, *Owner*
EMP: 7 **EST:** 2001
SALES (est): 981.1K **Privately Held**
WEB: www.fastsigns.com
SIC: 3993 Signs & advertising specialties

(G-13408)
NOXTAK CORP
21011 Johnson St Ste 110 (33029-1914)
PHONE.....................................786 586-7927
Jose Joaquin Machado Luengas, *CEO*
Marianella Romero Fernandez,
Development
Carlos Emilio Aguilar, *CFO*
Jeremias Martorell, *Accountant*
Carlos Augusto Aguilar Silva, *Director*
EMP: 6 **EST:** 2016
SQ FT: 1,690
SALES (est): 629.5K **Privately Held**
WEB: www.noxtak.com
SIC: 3822 3823 Auto controls regulating
residntl & coml environmt & applncs;
computer interface equipment for indus-
trial process control

(G-13409)
PRESS ROOM INC
619 Sw 159th Ter (33027-1140)
PHONE.....................................954 792-6729
Joseph Digiaimo, *President*
EMP: 5 **EST:** 1989
SALES (est): 538.6K **Privately Held**
SIC: 2752 Commercial printing, offset

(G-13410)
R & A PERFORMANCE FUEL INC
12951 Nw 1st St (33028-2286)
PHONE.....................................954 237-9824
Roberto Dominguez, *Principal*
EMP: 8 **EST:** 2010
SALES (est): 128.1K **Privately Held**
SIC: 2869 Fuels

(G-13411)
RICHARDS BRAZILIAN SAUSAGE LLC
18503 Pines Blvd Ste 310 (33029-1406)
PHONE.....................................786 609-3554
Richard Santos,
EMP: 8 **EST:** 2013
SALES (est): 560.7K **Privately Held**
WEB: www.richardsbraziliansausage.com
SIC: 2013 Sausages & other prepared
meats

(G-13412)
SALSA PEMBROKE PINES INC
601 Sw 145th Ter (33027-1449)
PHONE.....................................954 461-0532
David Pettit, *Principal*
EMP: 30 **EST:** 2006
SALES (est): 1.4MM **Privately Held**
SIC: 2099 Dips, except cheese & sour
cream based

(G-13413)
SCHOTT SOLUTIONS INC
201 Sw 97th Ter (33025-1055)
PHONE.....................................786 340-5116
Priscilla Schott, *Vice Pres*
EMP: 7 **EST:** 2018

SALES (est): 65.4K **Privately Held**
WEB: www.schott.com
SIC: **3211** Flat glass

(G-13414)
SIEMENS INDUSTRY INC .
2270 Nw 185th Way (33029-3864)
PHONE................................954 436-8848
EMP: 71
SALES (corp-wide): **89.6B Privately Held**
SIC: **3613** Mfg Switchboards
HQ: Siemens Industry, Inc.
1000 Deerfield Pkwy
Buffalo Grove IL 60089
847 215-1000

(G-13415)
SOUTH FLORIDA SHEET METAL
(PA)
2038 Nw 141st Ave (33028-2853)
PHONE................................954 647-6457
Wayne Boser, *President*
Harold Woods, *Vice Pres*
EMP: 5 EST: 1998
SALES (est): **1.2MM Privately Held**
SIC: **3444** Ducts, sheet metal

(G-13416)
SUPPLY EXPEDITERS INTL INC
911 Nw 209th Ave Ste 103 (33029-2112)
PHONE................................305 805-4255
▼ EMP: 12
SQ FT: 2,400
SALES (est): **2.2MM Privately Held**
SIC: **3443** Mfg Fabricated Plate Work

(G-13417)
SYNDESIS INC
392 Sw 159th Dr (33027-1141)
PHONE................................954 483-9548
Kleanthis Goozis, *Principal*
EMP: 8 EST: 2008
SALES (est): **220K Privately Held**
SIC: **2819** Industrial inorganic chemicals

(G-13418)
TAPIOCA FIT
156 N University Dr (33024-6714)
PHONE................................954 842-3924
Luiz A Da Silva Machado, *Principal*
EMP: 8 EST: 2016
SALES (est): **305K Privately Held**
SIC: **2046** Tapioca

(G-13419)
TECNOMETALES ONIS CNC LLC
21011 Johnson St Ste 110 (33029-1914)
PHONE................................786 637-8316
Jose L Suarez, *Mng Member*
EMP: 6 EST: 2017
SALES (est): **458.2K Privately Held**
SIC: **3315** Staples, steel: wire or cut

(G-13420)
TRUSS WILLIAM
17800 Nw 14th St (33029-3133)
PHONE................................954 438-4710
William Truss, *Principal*
EMP: 8 EST: 2005
SALES (est): **212.2K Privately Held**
SIC: **2439** Structural wood members

(G-13421)
TWS FABRICATORS
2001 N Us Highway 27 (33029-2109)
PHONE................................954 983-9749
EMP: 8 EST: 2020
SALES (est): **2MM Privately Held**
WEB: www.twsfab.com
SIC: **3599** Industrial machinery

(G-13422)
ULTIMATE COMPRESSOR LLC
400 S Hollybrook Dr Apt 1 (33025-1290)
PHONE................................305 720-3079
Steven Orozco, *Principal*
EMP: 5 EST: 2017
SALES (est): **499.9K Privately Held**
SIC: **3563** Air & gas compressors

(G-13423)
VENTILEX INC
Also Called: Motors For Less
20871 Jhnson St Units 103 (33029)
PHONE................................954 433-1321

Jacques Urrutia, *President*
Iise Murillo, *Bookkeeper*
Morita Casoetto, *Sales Staff*
Evlyn Amador, *Admin Sec*
EMP: 8 EST: 2005
SALES (est): **923K Privately Held**
WEB: www.motorsnation.net
SIC: **3564** Ventilating fans: industrial or
commercial

(G-13424)
VINLAND MARKETING INC
1152 N University Dr # 304 (33024-5000)
PHONE................................954 602-2177
Glauber Granero, *President*
EMP: 9 EST: 1998
SALES (est): **156.7K Privately Held**
WEB: www.vinlandpaper.com
SIC: **2621** 2679 Paper mills; paper prod-
ucts, converted

(G-13425)
YMG IRON WORK & METAL
DESIGN
21650 Nw 3rd Pl (33029-1043)
PHONE................................305 343-2537
Munoz Garcia Yovannys A, *Principal*
EMP: 7 EST: 2014
SALES (est): **486.4K Privately Held**
WEB: www.ymgironworks.com
SIC: **3446** Architectural metalwork

(G-13426)
YOLO CONSULTING LLC
Also Called: Citypavers
2364 Nw 159th Ave (33028-2439)
PHONE................................954 993-4517
Roger Jung,
EMP: 7 EST: 2012
SALES (est): **127.2K Privately Held**
SIC: **2951** Asphalt paving mixtures &
blocks

Pensacola
Escambia County

(G-13427)
850 SCREEN PRINTING LLC
698 E Heinberg St Ste 101 (32502-4154)
PHONE................................850 549-7861
Chris Phillips, *Principal*
EMP: 7 EST: 2017
SALES (est): **485.3K Privately Held**
WEB: www.850screenprinting.com
SIC: **2759** Screen printing

(G-13428)
A A A CABINETS
Also Called: AAA Custom Cabinets
6435 Ard Rd (32526-9406)
P.O. Box 19012 (32523-9012)
PHONE................................850 438-8337
Donnie Brusso, *Owner*
EMP: 6 EST: 1979
SQ FT: 3,200
SALES (est): **372.6K Privately Held**
SIC: **2434** 5712 2511 Wood kitchen cabi-
nets; cabinet work, custom; wood house-
hold furniture

(G-13429)
A BEKA BOOK INC (PA)
240 Waveland St Ste B (32503-7989)
P.O. Box 19100 (32523-9100)
PHONE................................850 478-8933
Price Jeff, *Project Mgr*
Jeff Price, *Traffic Mgr*
Wade Gerard, *Engineer*
Emily Horak, *Cust Svc Dir*
Brooks Stoodt, *Cust Svc Dir*
◆ EMP: 11 EST: 1996
SALES (est): **11.9MM Privately Held**
WEB: www.abeka.com
SIC: **2741** Miscellaneous publishing

(G-13430)
ABEKA PRINT SHOP INC
Also Called: PCC Print Shop, Inc.
118 Saint John St (32503-7644)
PHONE................................850 478-8496
Bill Rice III, *Ch of Bd*
Arlin Horton, *Vice Ch Bd*
Ben M East, *Treasurer*
Brent Phillips, *Manager*

Beverly M Crawford, *Director*
EMP: 40 EST: 1996
SALES (est): **12.4MM**
SALES (corp-wide): **124.3MM Privately**
Held
SIC: **2759** Commercial printing
PA: Pensacola Christian College, Inc.
250 Brent Ln
Pensacola FL 32503
850 478-8496

(G-13431)
ABOVE LLC
Also Called: Big Rhino Screen Printing
140 Industrial Blvd (32505-2202)
PHONE................................850 469-9028
Carol Mackey, *Sales Executive*
Lifford Van Gestel,
Joseph Kowalski,
EMP: 17 EST: 2015
SALES (est): **5.3MM Privately Held**
WEB: www.bigrhino.com
SIC: **2759** 2395 5199 5699 Screen print-
ing; embroidery products, except schiffli
machine; advertising specialties; T-shirts,
custom printed

(G-13432)
ACCU METAL
3987 N W St Ste 13 (32505-4063)
PHONE................................850 912-4855
Daniel Widmer, *Owner*
EMP: 5 EST: 1985
SQ FT: 6,917
SALES (est): **926.2K Privately Held**
SIC: **3544** 3089 Special dies & tools; jigs
& fixtures; injection molding of plastics

(G-13433)
ACTIGRAPH LLC
102 E Garden St (32502-5624)
PHONE................................850 332-7900
Doug Cross, *Engineer*
Leslie Broadus, *Manager*
EMP: 9 EST: 2017
SALES (est): **379.6K Privately Held**
WEB: www.actigraphcorp.com
SIC: **3845** Electromedical equipment

(G-13434)
ACTIGRAPH LLC
49 E Chase St (32502-5619)
PHONE................................850 332-7900
Keith Biggs, *CEO*
Jeff Arnett, *President*
Jeff Miller, *President*
Cyntech Trust, *Principal*
Matt Biggs, *Vice Pres*
EMP: 17 EST: 2004
SQ FT: 3,500
SALES (est): **3.6MM Privately Held**
WEB: www.theactigraph.com
SIC: **3845** 7371 Patient monitoring appa-
ratus; custom computer programming
services

(G-13435)
ADAMS HURRICANE
PROTECTION INC
Also Called: Rolltech Hurricanes Shutters
2302 Whaley Ave (32503-4972)
PHONE................................850 434-2336
John Adams, *President*
EMP: 10 EST: 2000
SALES (est): **850.5K Privately Held**
WEB: www.rolltechhurricaneshutters.com
SIC: **3442** Shutters, door or window: metal

(G-13436)
ADVANCED BIOSERVICES LLC
5401 Corp Wds Dr Ste 500 (32504-5912)
PHONE................................850 476-7999
EMP: 115 **Privately Held**
SIC: **2836** Mfg Biological Products
PA: Advanced Bioservices Llc
19255 Vanowen St
Reseda CA 91335

(G-13437)
ADVANCED DSIGN TECH
SYSTEMS IN
1300 E Olive Rd (32514-4820)
PHONE................................850 462-2868
Kevin W Stephens, *President*
Rodger Stephens, *Vice Pres*
EMP: 36 EST: 2008

SALES (est): **1.1MM Privately Held**
SIC: **3699** Security control equipment &
systems

(G-13438)
ADVANCED FURNITURE SVCS
INC
8631 Match St (32514-3488)
PHONE................................850 390-3442
Tirell Wilson, *President*
EMP: 11 EST: 2004
SALES (est): **567.6K Privately Held**
SIC: **2522** Office furniture, except wood

(G-13439)
AGRI-SOURCE FUELS LLC
120 E Main St Ste A (32502-6096)
PHONE................................352 521-3460
EMP: 42
SQ FT: 60,000
SALES (est): **4.7MM Privately Held**
SIC: **2869** Mfg Industrial Organic Chemi-
cals

(G-13440)
AGS ELECTRONICS INC
4400 Bayou Blvd Ste 53b (32503-1909)
PHONE................................850 471-1551
Giulio Simonelli, *President*
Patricia Simonelli, *Vice Pres*
◆ EMP: 5 EST: 1996
SQ FT: 3,400
SALES (est): **1.5MM Privately Held**
WEB: www.agselectronics.com
SIC: **3674** Semiconductors & related de-
vices

(G-13441)
AIR-TECH OF PENSACOLA INC
2317 Town St (32505-5121)
P.O. Box 18180 (32523-8180)
PHONE:...............................850 433-6443
Samuel T Brubaker, *President*
Todd Brubaker, *Vice Pres*
Joe Hoggle, *Engineer*
Jim Kemp, *Engineer*
Paul Atkins, *Sales Staff*
EMP: 15 EST: 2005
SALES (est): **5.1MM Privately Held**
WEB: www.airtechfl.com
SIC: **3634** Fans, exhaust & ventilating,
electric: household

(G-13442)
APW
911 N 63rd Ave (32506-4523)
PHONE................................850 332-7023
Carl Crenshaw, *Principal*
EMP: 9 EST: 2011
SALES (est): **203.9K Privately Held**
WEB: www.apwks.com
SIC: **3644** Raceways

(G-13443)
ARCHITECTURAL SPC TRDG CO
310 Hickory St (32505-4406)
PHONE................................850 435-2507
Jeffrey S Taggart, *CEO*
Jeff Taggart, *CEO*
Thomas J Stevens, *President*
Edna Howard, *Corp Secy*
Mathew S Stevens, *Vice Pres*
EMP: 59 EST: 1990
SQ FT: 55,000
SALES (est): **6.8MM Privately Held**
WEB: www.astcinc.com
SIC: **2431** Millwork

(G-13444)
ARCO MARINE INC
Also Called: Arco Automotive Products
3921 W Navy Blvd (32507-1221)
P.O. Box 16547 (32507-6547)
PHONE................................850 455-5476
Jason Crawford, *President*
Jenni Auxier, *Accountant*
Richard Martin, *VP Sales*
▲ EMP: 30 EST: 1960
SQ FT: 10,000
SALES (est): **4.5MM Privately Held**
WEB: www.arcomarine.com
SIC: **3694** 5063 Engine electrical equip-
ment; electrical apparatus & equipment

▲ = Import ▼=Export
◆ =Import/Export

(G-13445)
ARMORED FROG INC
12 E Belmont St (32501-4839)
PHONE.............................850 418-2048
Joe Sinkovich, *President*
Janet Wayman, *Manager*
EMP: 7 **EST:** 2012
SALES (est): 649.3K **Privately Held**
WEB: www.thearmoredfrog.com
SIC: 2519 Lawn & garden furniture, except
wood & metal

(G-13446)
ARMSTRONG WORLD INDUSTRIES INC
300 Myrick St (32505-8064)
P.O. Box 1991 (32591-1991)
PHONE.............................850 433-8321
Gregg Hunter, *Opers Staff*
Shane Player, *Sales Staff*
Russell E Johnson, *Manager*
Dietmar Laenger, *Manager*
Donita Edwards, *Supervisor*
EMP: 62
SALES (corp-wide): 1.1B **Publicly Held**
WEB: www.armstrong.com
SIC: 3272 Wall & ceiling squares, concrete
PA: Armstrong World Industries, Inc.
2500 Columbia Ave
Lancaster PA 17603
717 397-0611

(G-13447)
ARNOLD MANUFACTURING INC
Also Called: Arnold Mnfacturing-A M C Trlrs
2300 Town St (32505-5122)
PHONE.............................850 470-9200
Fax: 850 470-1040
EMP: 8
SQ FT: 15,000
SALES: 1MM **Privately Held**
SIC: 3715 Builds Truck Trailers

(G-13448)
AUTOMATED ACCOUNTING ASSOC INC
1665 Governors Dr (32514-8497)
PHONE.............................512 669-1000
G Talburt, *President*
Talburt Greg, *Principal*
EMP: 5 **EST:** 1996
SALES (est): 362.6K **Privately Held**
SIC: 7372 8721 8621 Prepackaged soft-
ware; accounting, auditing & bookkeep-
ing; accounting association

(G-13449)
AUTOMATION CONSULTING INC
Also Called: Porche Systems
7100 Plantation Rd Ste 17 (32504-6234)
PHONE.............................850 477-6477
Charles M Sanders, *President*
Lorna Gay Sanders, *Corp Secy*
John Abrams, *Vice Pres*
Kary Louden, *Analyst*
EMP: 14 **EST:** 1983
SQ FT: 4,050
SALES (est): 338.8K **Privately Held**
WEB: www.autocon.net
SIC: 3669 7371 3429 Intercommunication
systems, electric; custom computer pro-
gramming services; manufactured hard-
ware (general)

(G-13450)
B H C P INC
4109 N Davis Hwy (32503-2749)
PHONE.............................850 444-9300
Clarence O Conner, *President*
EMP: 7 **EST:** 2002
SQ FT: 3,000
SALES (est): 93.5K **Privately Held**
SIC: 2434 Wood kitchen cabinets

(G-13451)
BAM ENTERPRISES INC
Also Called: Eye-Dye
2906 N Davis Hwy (32503-3532)
P.O. Box 2280 (32513-2280)
PHONE.............................850 469-8872
Robert Bizzell, *President*
Sara Jiron, *COO*
Scott Martin, *Vice Pres*
Michael Hays, *Accountant*
EMP: 19 **EST:** 1987

SQ FT: 10,000
SALES (est): 2.6MM **Privately Held**
WEB: www.eye-dye.com
SIC: 2261 2759 Dyeing cotton broadwo-
ven fabrics; screen printing

(G-13452)
BAUER SMALL ARMS TRNING CTR IN
5615 Bauer Rd (32507-9077)
PHONE.............................850 862-1811
Theodore Johnson, *Principal*
EMP: 7 **EST:** 2017
SALES (est): 73.4K **Privately Held**
WEB: www.bauersmallarms.com
SIC: 3484 Small arms

(G-13453)
BELL STEEL COMPANY (PA)
530 S C St (32502-5426)
P.O. Box 12109 (32591-2109)
PHONE.............................850 432-1545
Randall R Bell III, *President*
Britney B Thompson, *Project Mgr*
James Herbert, *Warehouse Mgr*
Carl Trahan, *Purch Mgr*
Curtis Smith, *QC Mgr*
EMP: 72 **EST:** 1957
SQ FT: 361,000
SALES (est): 18MM **Privately Held**
WEB: www.bellsteel.com
SIC: 3441 5051 Building components,
structural steel; steel

(G-13454)
BELL STEEL COMPANY
Also Called: Steel Systems
8788 Paul Starr Dr (32514-7047)
P.O. Box 9579 (32513-9579)
PHONE.............................850 479-2980
Randall R Bell III, *Branch Mgr*
Randall Bell, *Branch Mgr*
EMP: 14
SALES (corp-wide): 18MM **Privately Held**
WEB: www.bellsteel.com
SIC: 3441 Building components, structural
steel
PA: Bell Steel Company
530 S C St
Pensacola FL 32502
850 432-1545

(G-13455)
BEST PRICE DIGITAL LENSES INC
2013 W Yonge St (32501-1560)
PHONE.............................850 361-4401
EMP: 8 **EST:** 2014
SALES (est): 874.7K **Privately Held**
WEB: www.bpdigitallab.com
SIC: 3851 Ophthalmic goods

(G-13456)
BLACKLIDGE EMULSIONS INC
4375 Mccoy Dr (32503-2224)
PHONE.............................850 432-3496
EMP: 7
SALES (corp-wide): 44.4MM **Privately Held**
SIC: 2951 Mfg Asphalt Mixtures/Blocks
PA: Blacklidge Emulsions, Inc.
12251 Bernard Pkwy # 200
Gulfport MS 39503
228 863-3878

(G-13457)
BLUE TARPON CONSTRUCTION LLC
119 W Garden St (32502-5617)
PHONE.............................251 223-3630
Sydney Cody, *CEO*
EMP: 7 **EST:** 2019
SALES (est): 78.8K **Privately Held**
SIC: 1389 Construction, repair & disman-
tling services

(G-13458)
BLUMS WOODWORKING LLC
6708 Chelsea St (32506-4552)
PHONE.............................850 449-7729
Nicholas E Blum, *Branch Mgr*
EMP: 12
SALES (corp-wide): 54.1K **Privately Held**
SIC: 2431 Millwork

PA: Blums Woodworking Llc
5331 Pleateau Rd
Pensacola FL

(G-13459)
BODREE PRINTING COMPANY INC
3310 N W St (32505-3953)
P.O. Box 3005 (32516-3005)
PHONE.............................850 455-8511
Gay Bodree, *President*
EMP: 13 **EST:** 1963
SALES (est): 574.8K **Privately Held**
WEB: www.bodree.com
SIC: 2752 2789 Commercial printing, off-
set; bookbinding & related work

(G-13460)
BONSAL AMERICAN INC
Also Called: Bonsai American
150 E Olive Rd (32514-4529)
PHONE.............................850 476-4223
Chris Cox, *President*
EMP: 9
SQ FT: 14,824
SALES (corp-wide): 30.9B **Privately Held**
SIC: 3272 Dry mixture concrete
HQ: Bonsal American, Inc.
625 Griffith Rd Ste 100
Charlotte NC 28217
704 525-1621

(G-13461)
BRASWELL CUSTOM CABINETS
9 Clarinda Ln (32505-4309)
PHONE.............................850 436-2645
Jerry Braswell, *Owner*
EMP: 7 **EST:** 1999
SQ FT: 17,000
SALES (est): 718.1K **Privately Held**
WEB: www.braswellcabinets.com
SIC: 2434 Wood kitchen cabinets

(G-13462)
BREATHING SYSTEMS INC
8800 Grow Dr (32514-7050)
PHONE.............................850 477-2324
Peter Thew, *President*
David Marrie, *General Mgr*
Gordon Bradley Alidor, *Treasurer*
EMP: 6 **EST:** 1986
SQ FT: 3,600
SALES (est): 1.1MM
SALES (corp-wide): 92MM **Privately Held**
WEB: www.breathingsystems.us
SIC: 3841 Surgical & medical instruments
HQ: Hydroprocessing Associates, Llc
6016 Highway 63
Moss Point MS 39563

(G-13463)
BROWNSVILLE ORNA IR WORKS INC
Also Called: Brownsville Welding
3520 Mobile Hwy (32505-6540)
PHONE.............................850 433-0521
Paul Stinson, *President*
Kay Stinson, *Corp Secy*
Anthony Alex Stinson, *Vice Pres*
EMP: 21 **EST:** 1989
SQ FT: 5,000
SALES (est): 4.3MM **Privately Held**
WEB: www.brownsvillewelding.com
SIC: 3446 Architectural metalwork

(G-13464)
BRUNKEN MANUFACTURING CO INC
4205 W Jackson St (32505-7233)
PHONE.............................850 438-2478
Curtis Boone, *President*
Cornelia Boone, *Corp Secy*
Lavona Boone, *Vice Pres*
EMP: 6 **EST:** 1968
SQ FT: 4,500
SALES (est): 403.3K **Privately Held**
WEB: www.brunkenmfg.com
SIC: 2399 Fishing nets

(G-13465)
BUFFALO ROCK COMPANY
Pepsico
8801 Grow Dr (32514-7051)
PHONE.............................850 857-3774

Rickey Linton, *General Mgr*
Warren Austin, *Vice Pres*
Kathy Dufrene, *Hum Res Coord*
Lester Stevens, *Sales Staff*
John Isbell, *Branch Mgr*
EMP: 124
SALES (corp-wide): 390.8MM **Privately Held**
WEB: www.buffalorock.com
SIC: 2086 Carbonated soft drinks, bottled
& canned
PA: Buffalo Rock Company
111 Oxmoor Rd
Birmingham AL 35209
205 942-3435

(G-13466)
BUMPER DOCTOR
95 Airport Blvd (32503-7623)
PHONE.............................850 341-1771
Dave Lee, *Principal*
EMP: 8 **EST:** 2007
SALES (est): 107.2K **Privately Held**
SIC: 3479 Painting of metal products

(G-13467)
BURRIS INVESTMENT GROUP INC
10648 Mac Gregor Dr (32514-8309)
PHONE.............................850 623-3845
Howard Burris, *Ch of Bd*
Greg Lowery, *President*
William Burris, *Vice Pres*
EMP: 35 **EST:** 1983
SALES (est): 5.1MM
SALES (corp-wide): 1.1B **Publicly Held**
SIC: 2045 Doughs, frozen or refrigerated:
from purchased flour
PA: J & J Snack Foods Corp.
6000 Central Hwy
Pennsauken NJ 08109
856 665-9533

(G-13468)
CABINET DESIGN AND CNSTR LLC
Also Called: Cdc Woodworking
101 S Pace Blvd (32502-5003)
PHONE.............................850 393-9724
William A Hinson,
Matthew Hinson,
EMP: 8 **EST:** 2004
SALES (est): 820.7K **Privately Held**
WEB: www.cdcwoodworking.com
SIC: 2434 2431 Wood kitchen cabinets;
millwork

(G-13469)
CANTWELL MISC FABRICATORS INC
100 E Roberts Rd (32534-9535)
PHONE.............................850 438-2912
Brian K Cantwell, *President*
EMP: 50 **EST:** 2004
SALES (est): 2.6MM **Privately Held**
SIC: 3446 Stairs, fire escapes, balconies,
railings & ladders

(G-13470)
CARPET CLINIC LLC
6927 Kelvin Ter (32503-7351)
P.O. Box 11544 (32524-1544)
PHONE.............................850 232-1170
Brian Ross,
EMP: 8 **EST:** 2009
SALES (est): 225.7K **Privately Held**
WEB: www.thecarpetclinic.com
SIC: 2273 Carpets & rugs

(G-13471)
CLASSIC DESIGN AND MFG
Also Called: Classic Sign & Mirror
909 N Tarragona St (32501-3178)
PHONE.............................850 433-4981
Michael Sheehan, *President*
Suzanne Zukoski, *Vice Pres*
EMP: 6 **EST:** 1981
SQ FT: 6,000
SALES (est): 861.4K **Privately Held**
WEB: www.durabrac.com
SIC: 3993 Signs, not made in custom sign
painting shops

(G-13472)
COASTAL FOAM SYSTEMS LLC
3276 W Scott St (32505-5427)
PHONE...................................850 470-9827
Randy Marshal, *Mng Member*
Eric Alford,
Curtis Bolton,
Danny Marshal,
EMP: 5 EST: 2005
SALES (est): 480.4K **Privately Held**
SIC: 3086 Insulation or cushioning material, foamed plastic

(G-13473)
COCA-COLA BOTTLING CO UNTD INC
7330 N Davis Hwy (32504-6389)
PHONE...................................850 478-4800
Steve Langham, *Manager*
EMP: 226
SALES (corp-wide): 2B **Privately Held**
WEB: www.coca-cola.com
SIC: 2086 5149 Bottled & canned soft drinks; groceries & related products
PA: Coca-Cola Bottling Company United, Inc.
4600 E Lake Blvd
Birmingham AL 35217
205 841-2653

(G-13474)
COLLEGEFROG INC
418 W Garden St (32502-4752)
PHONE...................................850 696-1500
Jeff Phillips, *President*
James Hosman, *Treasurer*
Joshua Sams, *Admin Sec*
EMP: 7 EST: 2012
SALES (est): 655K **Privately Held**
WEB: www.accountingfly.com
SIC: 7372 Business oriented computer software

(G-13475)
COMMERCIAL DOOR SYSTEMS FLA LL
612 W Romana St (32502-5549)
PHONE...................................850 466-5906
Deborah Volentine, *Project Mgr*
Steve Ball, *Sales Staff*
Kent Simmons, *Mng Member*
Travis Miller, *Maintence Staff*
EMP: 18 EST: 2017
SALES (est): 3.3MM **Privately Held**
WEB: www.commdoorsystems.com
SIC: 2431 Doors & door parts & trim, wood

(G-13476)
COMMSTRUCTURES INC
101 E Roberts Rd (32534-9535)
PHONE...................................850 968-9293
James B Hobbs, *President*
James Y Harpole, *Vice Pres*
James Harpole, *Vice Pres*
Kevin Wilkes, *Plant Mgr*
Charles Sumlin, *Project Mgr*
◆ EMP: 53 EST: 1997
SQ FT: 56,300
SALES (est): 16.8MM **Privately Held**
WEB: www.commstructures.com
SIC: 3663 Antennas, transmitting & communications

(G-13477)
COPY CAT PRINTING LLC
3636 N L St Ste D-A (32505-5663)
PHONE...................................850 438-5566
Janet McDonald, *Mng Member*
EMP: 7 EST: 2012
SALES (est): 482.7K **Privately Held**
WEB: www.copycatpensacola.com
SIC: 2752 Commercial printing, offset

(G-13478)
COTTON PICKIN SHIRTS PLUS
2211 N Pace Blvd (32505-5837)
PHONE...................................850 435-3133
Charles Campbell, *Ch of Bd*
EMP: 7 EST: 1991
SQ FT: 1,500
SALES (est): 343.4K **Privately Held**
WEB: cotton-pickin-shirts.hub.biz
SIC: 2395 2759 5699 Embroidery products, except schiffli machine; screen printing; customized clothing & apparel

(G-13479)
CURRENT PRODUCTS COMPANY LLC
1995 Hollywood Ave (32505-5369)
PHONE...................................850 435-4994
Willis J Mullet, *President*
Mike Fox, *Mfg Staff*
Phil Gurvitz, *Engineer*
Curtis Scott, *Electrical Engi*
Bette Denniston, *CFO*
EMP: 24 EST: 2010
SQ FT: 40,000
SALES (est): 2MM **Privately Held**
WEB: nka.kvs.mybluehost.me
SIC: 2591 Shade, curtain & drapery hardware

(G-13480)
CURRIN GRAPHICS
2821 Copter Rd Ste 700 (32514-7666)
PHONE...................................850 505-0955
David Currin, *President*
EMP: 8 EST: 2004
SALES (est): 575.1K **Privately Held**
WEB: www.curringraphics.com
SIC: 2759 Screen printing

(G-13481)
CUSTOM WD DESIGNS OF PENSACOLA
3335 Addison Dr (32514-7065)
P.O. Box 537, Bagdad (32530-0537)
PHONE...................................850 476-9663
EMP: 10
SQ FT: 7,500
SALES: 600K **Privately Held**
SIC: 2434 2431 Mfg Wood Kitchen Cabinets Mfg Millwork

(G-13482)
CYPRESS PENSACOLA LLC
1124 W Garden St (32502-4502)
PHONE...................................850 724-1124
Sarah M Lovelace, *Principal*
EMP: 6 EST: 2018
SALES (est): 414.1K **Privately Held**
SIC: 2092 Fresh or frozen packaged fish

(G-13483)
D & D WELDING INC
2715 N W St (32505-4937)
PHONE...................................850 438-9011
David Siefert, *President*
Sharen Siefert, *Admin Sec*
EMP: 5 EST: 1973
SQ FT: 5,000
SALES (est): 622.2K **Privately Held**
SIC: 7692 Welding repair

(G-13484)
D & M TRUSS CO
2620 W Michigan Ave (32526-2213)
PHONE...................................850 944-4864
F O Dickerson, *President*
John Williams, *Bookkeeper*
Jeromey Smith, *Technician*
EMP: 18 EST: 1965
SQ FT: 10,000
SALES (est): 4MM **Privately Held**
WEB: www.dmtruss.com
SIC: 2439 Trusses, wooden roof

(G-13485)
D-LUX PRINTING INC
Also Called: Dlux Printing & Publishing
3320 N W St (32505-3953)
PHONE...................................850 457-8494
Gerald Mandel, *President*
Michelle Mandel, *CFO*
Jimmy Robinson, *Sales Staff*
Tiffany Carmichael, *Sales Associate*
Janet Carter, *Technician*
EMP: 16 EST: 1991
SALES (est): 4.8MM **Privately Held**
SIC: 2752 Commercial printing, offset

(G-13486)
DE LUNA COFFEE INTL INC
Also Called: Twisted Coffee Canyon Roasters
1014 Underwood Ave Ste D (32504-8929)
PHONE...................................850 478-6371
Edward F Lemox III, *President*
Brett Lemox, *COO*
EMP: 9 EST: 2014
SQ FT: 6,500

SALES (est): 900K **Privately Held**
WEB: www.delunacoffee.com
SIC: 2095 5149 Roasted coffee; coffee & tea

(G-13487)
DEFENSE STAMPINGS & ENGRG INC
3911 Mobile Hwy (32505-6126)
PHONE...................................850 438-6105
Anita Nordendale, *CEO*
Mark Strader, *President*
Kelly Nordendale, *Vice Pres*
EMP: 35 EST: 1989
SQ FT: 33,000
SALES (est): 2.5MM **Privately Held**
WEB: defense-stamping-engineering.sb-contract.com
SIC: 3599 3469 3312 Machine shop, jobbing & repair; metal stampings; tool & die steel

(G-13488)
DEMING DESIGNS INC
1090 Cobblestone Dr (32514-7159)
PHONE...................................850 478-5765
Micheal S Deming, *President*
EMP: 15 EST: 1994
SALES (est): 1MM **Privately Held**
WEB: www.beachwheelchair.com
SIC: 3842 7389 Wheelchairs;

(G-13489)
DIGECON PLASTICS INTERNATIONAL
Also Called: Address-O-Lite
3255 Potter St (32514-3518)
PHONE...................................850 477-5483
Ronald R Smith, *President*
EMP: 13 EST: 1990
SQ FT: 41,000
SALES (est): 483.5K **Privately Held**
SIC: 3645 3641 3646 5063 Garden, patio, walkway & yard lighting fixtures; electric; electric lamps; commercial indusl & institutional electric lighting fixtures; lighting fixtures

(G-13490)
DIXON SCREEN PRINTING LLC
Also Called: Jack W Dixon
312 W Detroit Blvd (32534-3771)
PHONE...................................850 476-3924
Jack Dixon, *President*
Jack W Dixon, *Owner*
EMP: 9 EST: 1973
SQ FT: 11,800
SALES (est): 928.5K **Privately Held**
WEB: www.dixontshirts.com
SIC: 2396 5941 Screen printing on fabric articles; team sports equipment

(G-13491)
E M CHADBOURNE INDS LLC
192 Hewitt St (32503-2265)
P.O. Box 6480 (32503-0480)
PHONE...................................850 429-1797
Caroline C Demaria, *Manager*
EMP: 8 EST: 2006
SALES (est): 159.9K **Privately Held**
SIC: 3999 Manufacturing industries

(G-13492)
EASTBURN WOODWORKS INC
2620 Hollywood Ave (32505-4845)
PHONE...................................850 456-8090
Kenneth Eastburn, *President*
Iris Eastburn, *Vice Pres*
EMP: 14 EST: 1997
SQ FT: 8,000
SALES (est): 1MM **Privately Held**
WEB: www.eastburnwoodworks.com
SIC: 2434 Wood kitchen cabinets

(G-13493)
EDS ALUMINUM BUILDINGS INC (PA)
9555 Pensacola Blvd (32534-1239)
PHONE...................................850 476-2169
Ed Vignolo, *President*
EMP: 7 EST: 1972
SQ FT: 3,000

SALES (est): 733K **Privately Held**
WEB: www.edsaluminumbuildings.com
SIC: 3448 5211 5599 Buildings, portable: prefabricated metal; prefabricated buildings; utility trailers

(G-13494)
ELITE PRINTING & MARKETING INC
3636 N L St Ste D-A (32505-5248)
PHONE...................................850 474-0894
Andrew Dennis III, *Owner*
EMP: 5 EST: 1982
SQ FT: 10,000
SALES (est): 577.5K **Privately Held**
WEB: printingbyelite.espwebsite.com
SIC: 2752 2759 3993 Commercial printing, offset; letterpress & screen printing; letterpress printing; signs & advertising specialties

(G-13495)
ELLIS TRAP AND CAGE MFG INC
9601 N Palafox St Ste 6b (32534-1273)
PHONE...................................850 969-1302
Sean Ellis, *President*
EMP: 5 EST: 1995
SQ FT: 3,000
SALES (est): 514.1K **Privately Held**
WEB: www.drpalu.com
SIC: 3429 3496 Animal traps, iron or steel; crab traps, steel; traps, animal & fish

(G-13496)
EMERALD COAST FABRICATORS
2120 W Wright St (32505-7941)
PHONE...................................850 554-6172
David Scallan, *Manager*
EMP: 6 EST: 2017
SALES (est): 403.1K **Privately Held**
WEB: www.frmpeo.com
SIC: 3441 Fabricated structural metal

(G-13497)
EMERALD COAST MFG LLC
4121 Warehouse Ln (32505-4061)
PHONE...................................850 469-1133
Sharon C Yarbrough,
Ronnie E Jones,
EMP: 9 EST: 2019
SALES (est): 773.1K **Privately Held**
WEB: www.emeraldcoastmfg.com
SIC: 3519 Marine engines

(G-13498)
ESCAMBIA WELDING AND FAB INC
2474 W Nine Mile Rd B (32534-9419)
PHONE...................................850 477-3901
Phyllis Keller, *President*
EMP: 5 EST: 2005
SALES (est): 457.6K **Privately Held**
SIC: 7692 Welding repair

(G-13499)
EYE WALL INDUSTRIES INC
3920 W Navy Blvd (32507-1200)
PHONE...................................850 607-2288
Kristian R Fernandez, *Principal*
EMP: 7 EST: 2018
SALES (est): 284.6K **Privately Held**
WEB: www.wallindustries.com
SIC: 3999 Manufacturing industries

(G-13500)
FAIRBANKS AND FAIRBANKS INC
405 S K St (32502-5206)
PHONE...................................850 293-1184
William R Fairbanks, *Principal*
EMP: 7 EST: 2013
SALES (est): 112.8K **Privately Held**
SIC: 3489 Ordnance & accessories

(G-13501)
FASTSIGNS
6060 Tippin Ave (32504-8218)
PHONE...................................850 477-9744
Scott Thomas, *President*
Mary Thomas, *Vice Pres*
Jason Lamb, *Graphic Designe*
EMP: 6 EST: 1991
SQ FT: 1,500

SALES (est): 708.8K Privately Held
WEB: www.fastsigns.com
SIC: 3993 7319 5999 Signs & advertising
specialties; display advertising service;
banners

(G-13502)
FERTEC INC
141 Terry Dr (32503-7066)
PHONE..................................850 478-6480
Ronald Bray, *President*
John R Bray, *Chairman*
EMP: 13 EST: 1976
SALES (est): 219K Privately Held
SIC: 3448 Prefabricated metal components

(G-13503)
**FISHER CABINET COMPANY
LLC**
3900 N Palafox St (32505-4418)
PHONE..................................850 944-4171
Scott Fisher, *President*
Scott A Fisher, *President*
EMP: 24 EST: 1987
SQ FT: 14,000
SALES: 2.8MM Privately Held
SIC: 2541 2434 3083 Cabinets, except
refrigerated: show, display, etc.: wood;
wood kitchen cabinets; plastic finished
products, laminated

(G-13504)
FLAT ISLAND BOATWORKS LLC
700 Myrick St (32505-8051)
PHONE..................................850 434-8295
Michael Bredesen, *Owner*
EMP: 7 EST: 2009
SALES (est): 631.7K Privately Held
WEB: www.flatislandboatworks.com
SIC: 3732 Boat building & repairing

(G-13505)
FLUID METALWORKS INC
55 S A St (32502-5551)
PHONE..................................850 332-0103
EMP: 17 EST: 2011
SALES (est): 1.2MM Privately Held
SIC: 3441 Fabricated structural metal

(G-13506)
FLUID METALWORKS INC -105
55 S A St (32502-5551)
PHONE..................................850 332-0103
Brandon Godwin, *Principal*
EMP: 6 EST: 2012
SALES (est): 858.7K Privately Held
WEB: www.fluidmetalworks.com
SIC: 3446 Architectural metalwork

(G-13507)
FOIL INC
201 E Wright St (32501-4917)
PHONE..................................442 233-3645
EMP: 7 EST: 1989
SALES (est): 112.7K Privately Held
WEB: www.getfoil.com
SIC: 3949 Water sports equipment

(G-13508)
FOOT-IN-YOUR-MOUTH INC
Also Called: Thermodyne Powder Coating
9721 Fowler Ave (32534-1007)
PHONE..................................850 438-0876
Jeffrey Hoskins, *President*
Julie Taylor, *Accountant*
EMP: 10 EST: 1989
SQ FT: 60,000
SALES (est): 1MM Privately Held
WEB: www.thermodynepowdercoating.com
SIC: 3479 Coating of metals & formed
products

(G-13509)
FORMSYSTEMS INC
Also Called: FSI Group
3700 Creighton Rd Ste 3 (32504-4600)
P.O. Box 11187 (32524-1187)
PHONE..................................850 479-0800
Karen Webb, *President*
Joe Webb, *Vice Pres*
Justin Goss, *Accounts Mgr*
EMP: 8 EST: 1995
SALES (est): 1.2MM Privately Held
WEB: www.formsystems.net
SIC: 2759 5943 Commercial printing; of-
fice forms & supplies

(G-13510)
FORTIFIED BUILDING PDTS INC
Also Called: Fortified Shutters
2001 W Government St (32502-5151)
P.O. Box 4905 (32507-0905)
PHONE..................................850 432-2485
John Roche, *President*
EMP: 14 EST: 2014
SALES (est): 2.7MM Privately Held
WEB: www.fortifiedshutters.com
SIC: 3442 Louvers, shutters, jalousies &
similar items

(G-13511)
**FRANKLIN BAKING COMPANY
LLC**
Also Called: Flowers Baking
9201 N Davis Hwy (32514-5846)
PHONE..................................850 478-8360
Tim Watson, *Branch Mgr*
EMP: 9
SALES (corp-wide): 4.3B Publicly Held
WEB: franklin-co4goldsboro.edan.io
SIC: 2051 Bread, cake & related products
HQ: Franklin Baking Company, Llc
500 W Grantham St
Goldsboro NC 27530
919 735-0344

(G-13512)
**GE RENEWABLES NORTH AMER
LLC (HQ)**
Also Called: G E Generators
8301 Scenic Hwy (32514-7810)
PHONE..................................850 474-4011
John C Rice, *CEO*
Lawrence Blystone, *Vice Pres*
Blair Simmons, *Mng Member*
John Kreniki, *Mng Member*
William Standera, *Mng Member*
◆ **EMP: 76 EST:** 2000
SALES (est): 73.2MM
SALES (corp-wide): 74.2B Publicly Held
SIC: 3621 Power generators
PA: General Electric Company
5 Necco St
Boston MA 02210
617 443-3000

(G-13513)
**GUARDFISH ENTERPRISES
LLC ✪**
Also Called: Plastic Arts Sign Co
3931 W Navy Blvd (32507-1256)
PHONE..................................850 455-4114
John Shipman, *Mng Member*
EMP: 7 EST: 2021
SALES (est): 321.8K Privately Held
SIC: 3993 1799 7389 Signs & advertising
specialties; sign installation & mainte-
nance; sign painting & lettering shop

(G-13514)
**GUIDED PARTICLE SYSTEMS
INC**
1000 College Blvd Bldg 11 (32504-8910)
P.O. Box 12621 (32591-2621)
PHONE..................................727 424-8790
Carolyn Fries, *President*
David Fries, *Vice Pres*
EMP: 6 EST: 2016
SQ FT: 448
SALES (est): 604.8K Privately Held
WEB: www.gparticle.com
SIC: 3559 3555 Semiconductor manufac-
turing machinery; photoengraving ma-
chines

(G-13515)
GULF COAST ELC MTR SVC INC
3810 Hopkins St (32505-5223)
P.O. Box 1322 (32591-1322)
PHONE..................................850 433-5134
Higinio Rodriguez, *President*
Higinio Rodriguez III, *Vice Pres*
Moises Rodriguez, *Vice Pres*
Victor Rodriguez, *Vice Pres*
Susana Rodriguez, *Treasurer*
EMP: 33 EST: 1978
SQ FT: 9,675
SALES (est): 12.3MM Privately Held
WEB: www.gcemsinc.com
SIC: 7694 7699 Rewinding stators; elec-
tric motor repair; pumps & pumping
equipment repair

(G-13516)
**GULF STATES AUTOMATION
INC**
245 W Airport Blvd Ste B (32505-2254)
PHONE..................................850 475-0724
Steve Gaidos, *President*
Lisa Cox, *Vice Pres*
Buzz Busby, *Vice Pres*
Henry Hiebert, *Project Mgr*
Phillip Brooker, *Sales Engr*
EMP: 21 EST: 1992
SQ FT: 2,000
SALES (est): 4.2MM Privately Held
WEB: www.gulfstatesautomation.com
SIC: 3822 Air conditioning & refrigeration
controls; temperature controls, automatic

(G-13517)
GULF TOOL CORPORATION
8470 Gulf Beach Hwy (32507-2636)
PHONE..................................850 456-0840
Paul Robinson, *President*
C Joe Robinson, *Chairman*
Joy Thomas, *CPA*
Barbara Robinson, *Admin Sec*
EMP: 19 EST: 1978
SQ FT: 11,000
SALES (est): 2.2MM Privately Held
WEB: www.gulftoolcorp.com
SIC: 3544 3545 Special dies & tools; ma-
chine tool accessories

(G-13518)
HEIGHTS TOWER SYSTEMS INC
1529 Gulf Beach Hwy (32507-3065)
PHONE..................................850 455-1210
Drake Dimitry, *President*
EMP: 6 EST: 1986
SQ FT: 12,000
SALES (est): 869.5K Privately Held
WEB: www.heightstowers.com
SIC: 3441 Tower sections, radio & televi-
sion transmission

(G-13519)
HILL ENTERPRISES LLC
125 Terry Dr (32503-7024)
PHONE..................................850 478-4455
Ned Jones, *Mng Member*
EMP: 8 EST: 2017
SALES (est): 501.5K Privately Held
WEB: www.hillenterprises.net
SIC: 2431 3442 Door sashes, wood; sash,
door or window: metal

(G-13520)
HITACHI CABLE AMERICA INC
Automotive Products Div
9101 Ely Rd (32514-7019)
PHONE..................................850 476-0907
Takao Otsuka, *Manager*
EMP: 118 Privately Held
WEB: hca.hitachi-cable.com
SIC: 3052 Automobile hose, rubber
HQ: Hitachi Cable America Inc.
2 Manhattanville Rd # 301
Purchase NY 10577
914 694-9200

(G-13521)
HRH DOOR CORP
Wayne- Dalton of Pensacola
3395 Addison Dr (32514-7066)
PHONE..................................850 474-9890
Robert Moore, *Maint Spvr*
George Krupp, *Mfg Staff*
Sid Wilson, *Research*
William Cid, *Engineer*
Kevin Holman, *Engineer*
EMP: 16
**SALES (corp-wide): 467.9MM Privately
Held**
WEB: www.wayne-dalton.com
SIC: 2431 3442 Garage doors, overhead:
wood; garage doors, overhead: metal
PA: Hrh Door Corp.
1 Door Dr
Mount Hope OH 44660
850 208-3400

(G-13522)
IAN-CONRAD BERGAN LLC (PA)
Also Called: Bergan Tank Control
1001 E Belmont St (32501-4100)
PHONE..................................850 434-1286
John Kyle Durden, *President*

Alex Hussmann, *Engineer*
Bob Toole, *Engineer*
Bridget McClendon, *CFO*
Knut Bergan, *Sales Staff*
◆ **EMP: 41 EST:** 1980
SQ FT: 40,000
SALES (est): 11.4MM Privately Held
SIC: 3823 Industrial instrmnts msrmnt dis-
play/control process variable

(G-13523)
IMMUDYNE NUTRITIONAL LLC
3930 Hollywood Ave (32505-3821)
PHONE..................................914 714-8901
Mark McLaughlin, *CEO*
Dr Arun Bahl, *CEO*
Anthony Bruzzese, *Ch of Bd*
James Wethington, *General Mgr*
Aaron Gruelle, *Vice Pres*
EMP: 6 EST: 1986
SALES (est): 915.1K Privately Held
SIC: 2833 Medicinals & botanicals

(G-13524)
INGRAM SIGNALIZATION INC
4522 N Davis Hwy (32503-2769)
PHONE..................................850 433-8267
Traci Ingram-Gay, *President*
William Wilson, *Vice Pres*
EMP: 32 EST: 1959
SQ FT: 6,500
SALES (est): 6.6MM Privately Held
WEB: www.ingramcorp.com
SIC: 3669 1731 Transportation signaling
devices; electrical work

(G-13525)
**INTERNATIONAL POLYMER
SVCS LLC**
3431 Mai Kai Dr (32526-2423)
PHONE..................................401 529-6855
Fred Sivell,
EMP: 7 EST: 2009
SALES (est): 591.1K Privately Held
SIC: 2822 Ethylene-propylene rubbers,
EPDM polymers

(G-13526)
**J R C CONCRETE PRODUCTS
INC**
994 S Fairfield Dr Lot 2 (32506-8926)
PHONE..................................850 456-9665
Jim Nicholson, *President*
Peggy Nicholson, *Vice Pres*
EMP: 7 EST: 2004
SQ FT: 2,172
SALES (est): 851.3K Privately Held
WEB: www.jrcconcreteproducts.com
SIC: 3272 Concrete products

(G-13527)
JAYCO SCREENS INC
9131 W Highway 98 (32506-6057)
P.O. Box 36214 (32516-6214)
PHONE..................................850 456-0673
Fax: 850 453-6949
EMP: 9
SQ FT: 14,000
SALES (est): 910K Privately Held
SIC: 3533 3496 5082 Mfg Oil/Gas Field
Machinery Mfg Misc Fabricated Wire
Products Whol Construction/Mining
Equipment

(G-13528)
**JOE HEARN INNOVATIVE TECH
LLC**
Also Called: Jhi Technology
600 Univ Ofc Blvd 17c (32504-6238)
P.O. Box 10562 (32524-0562)
PHONE..................................850 898-3744
Joseph Hearn Jr, *Principal*
Deena Hearn, *Principal*
EMP: 10 EST: 2013
SALES (est): 617.4K Privately Held
SIC: 3663 3812 1799 4959 ; search &
navigation equipment; office furniture in-
stallation; sanitary services; building
maintenance services; janitorial service,
contract basis

(G-13529)
JOHNNY UNDER PRESSURE LLC
7250 Frank Reeder Rd (32526-9117)
PHONE.................................850 530-8763
Regena Suchy, *Principal*
Johnny Stevison,
EMP: 8 **EST:** 2015
SALES (est): 882.1K **Privately Held**
WEB: www.pressurewashingboynton-beach.com
SIC: 2491 Wood preserving

(G-13530)
JOHNSON WELL EQUIPMENT INC
8480 Gulf Beach Hwy (32507-2636)
P.O. Box 3364 (32516-3364)
PHONE.................................850 453-3131
Julius W Davis, *President*
EMP: 8 **EST:** 1965
SQ FT: 15,000
SALES (est): 992.8K **Privately Held**
WEB: www.johnsonwellequipment.com
SIC: 3589 3496 Water filters & softeners, household type; miscellaneous fabricated wire products

(G-13531)
JONAS SOFTWARE USA INC
9295 Scenic Hwy (32514-8055)
PHONE.................................800 476-0094
EMP: 8 **EST:** 2015
SALES (est): 97.4K **Privately Held**
WEB: www.jonassoftware.com
SIC: 7372 Prepackaged software

(G-13532)
JUPITER BACH NORTH AMERICA INC
3301 Bill Metzger Ln (32514-7078)
PHONE.................................850 476-6304
Lars Steen Rasmussen, *CEO*
Winston Guidry, *Vice Pres*
Dan Henry, *Prdtn Mgr*
Henrick Nielsen, *CFO*
Edward Austin, *Human Resources*
▲ **EMP:** 180 **EST:** 2006
SALES (est): 58.2MM **Privately Held**
WEB: www.jupiterbach.com
SIC: 3511 Turbines & turbine generator set units, complete
HQ: Jupiter Bach A/S
　Theilgaards Alle 9, Sal 1tv
　Koge 4600
　558 933-33

(G-13533)
KELTON COMPANY LLC
220 W Garden St Ste 605 (32502-5744)
P.O. Box 230 (32591-0230)
PHONE.................................850 434-6830
Thom W Sylte, *Mng Member*
Edwina Burchardt,
Tom Sylte,
Edmund F Kelton Trust,
EMP: 8 **EST:** 1978
SQ FT: 1,600
SALES (est): 996.3K **Privately Held**
SIC: 1382 Oil & gas exploration services

(G-13534)
KENNETH S JARRELL INC
Also Called: David's Novelties
9859 N Palafox St (32534-1226)
PHONE.................................334 215-7774
Kenneth S Jarrell, *President*
John Sewell, *General Mgr*
▲ **EMP:** 10 **EST:** 1978
SALES (est): 1.3MM **Privately Held**
SIC: 2899 Incense

(G-13535)
LABEL COMPANY
680 E Heinberg St (32502-4146)
P.O. Box 1753 (32591-1753)
PHONE.................................850 438-7334
Roger Van Surksum, *President*
EMP: 25 **EST:** 1980
SQ FT: 12,000
SALES (est): 3.7MM **Privately Held**
WEB: www.thelabelco.com
SIC: 2752 Commercial printing, offset

(G-13536)
LIGHTING TECHNOLOGIES
1810 Barrancas Ave (32502-5215)
PHONE.................................850 462-1790
Greg Johnson, *Manager*
▲ **EMP:** 14 **EST:** 2014
SALES (est): 2MM **Privately Held**
WEB: www.lightingtechnologies.com
SIC: 3648 Outdoor lighting equipment

(G-13537)
LINENWOOD HOME LLC
24 E Brainerd St (32501-2619)
PHONE.................................850 607-7445
Natasha Williams, *Principal*
EMP: 5 **EST:** 2016
SALES (est): 332.3K **Privately Held**
WEB: www.linenwoodhome.com
SIC: 2499 Wood products

(G-13538)
LOCALTOOLBOX INC
Also Called: 100 Feet Deep
2720 Bayou Grande Blvd (32507-2882)
PHONE.................................415 250-3232
James Robbins, *Principal*
EMP: 7 **EST:** 2017
SALES (est): 341.9K **Privately Held**
WEB: www.localtoolbox.com
SIC: 2711 Newspapers, publishing & printing

(G-13539)
LOCKHEED MARTIN CORPORATION
5041 Bayou Blvd Ste 301 (32503-2558)
PHONE.................................850 475-0724
Tom Hestle, *Branch Mgr*
EMP: 9 **Publicly Held**
WEB: www.gyrocamsystems.com
SIC: 3721 Aircraft
PA: Lockheed Martin Corporation
　6801 Rockledge Dr
　Bethesda MD 20817

(G-13540)
LOSOBE LLC
943 Candlestick Ct (32514-1549)
PHONE.................................850 748-3162
Jeff Bere, *Principal*
EMP: 7 **EST:** 2016
SALES (est): 150.6K **Privately Held**
WEB: www.barehandcollective.com
SIC: 2431 Millwork

(G-13541)
M & W ELECTRIC MOTORS INC
1250 Barrancas Ave (32502-4513)
PHONE.................................850 433-0400
Thomas A Nichols Jr, *President*
Thomas Nichols Jr, *President*
Aaron Hall, *Vice Pres*
Bill Searcy, *Treasurer*
William F Searcy Jr, *Treasurer*
EMP: 8 **EST:** 1958
SQ FT: 6,160
SALES (est): 475.1K **Privately Held**
SIC: 7694 5063 5999 Electric motor repair; motors, electric; motors, electric

(G-13542)
MACHINE TOOL MASTERS INC
Also Called: Mtm
3947 Stoddard Rd (32526-8765)
P.O. Box 18369 (32523-8369)
PHONE.................................850 432-2829
EMP: 13
SQ FT: 6,000
SALES: 900K **Privately Held**
SIC: 3599 Mfg Industrial Machinery

(G-13543)
MARTIN LEONARD CORPORATION
Also Called: A & J Mugs
24 N Palafox St (32502-5626)
PHONE.................................850 434-2203
Daniel Lindemann, *President*
Dan Lindemann, *President*
EMP: 6 **EST:** 1981
SALES (est): 694.1K **Privately Held**
SIC: 2759 3269 5999 Decals: printing; business forms: printing; decalcomania work on china & glass; alcoholic beverage making equipment & supplies

(G-13544)
MC SQUARED GROUP INC
Also Called: Marketing Bar, The
260 S Tarragona St # 140 (32502-6061)
PHONE.................................850 435-4600
Michelle Sarra, *CEO*
Lollie Campbell, *Graphic Designe*
EMP: 6 **EST:** 2011
SQ FT: 1,400
SALES (est): 500.2K **Privately Held**
WEB: www.mc2printing.com
SIC: 2752 7311 8742 7389 Advertising posters, lithographed; advertising consultant; marketing consulting services; advertising, promotional & trade show services; graphic arts & related design; printed media advertising representatives

(G-13545)
MCDIRT INDUSTRIES INC
5570 Bellview Ave (32526-9415)
PHONE.................................850 944-0112
Phillip V McCoy, *President*
Linda McCoy, *Vice Pres*
EMP: 10 **EST:** 1992
SQ FT: 1,500
SALES (est): 850K **Privately Held**
WEB: www.mcdirt.net
SIC: 1442 Construction sand mining; gravel mining

(G-13546)
MCGRAIL SIGNS & GRAPHICS LLC
1011 N P St (32505-6837)
PHONE.................................850 435-1017
James McGrail, *Mng Member*
EMP: 6 **EST:** 1998
SALES (est): 401.6K **Privately Held**
SIC: 3993 Signs & advertising specialties

(G-13547)
MEDICAL ENERGY INC
8806 Paul Starr Dr (32514-7061)
P.O. Box 777818, Henderson NV (89077-7818)
PHONE.................................850 313-6277
David Lewing, *CEO*
Michelle Scottlewing, *Vice Pres*
Meghan Marchant, *Manager*
Jason Lewing, *Director*
EMP: 6 **EST:** 1987
SALES (est): 745.3K **Privately Held**
WEB: www.medicalenergy.com
SIC: 3841 Surgical & medical instruments

(G-13548)
MEDICAL SFTWR INTEGRATORS INC
5269 Springhill Dr (32503-2143)
PHONE.................................561 570-4680
EMP: 10 **EST:** 2003
SALES (est): 2.3MM **Privately Held**
WEB: www.msipcola.com
SIC: 7372 Prepackaged software

(G-13549)
MERCURY MACHINING CO INC (PA)
1085 W Gimble St (32502-5455)
PHONE.................................850 433-5017
Dale Macarthy, *President*
EMP: 39 **EST:** 1966
SQ FT: 7,000
SALES (est): 5.7MM **Privately Held**
WEB: www.mercurymachining.com
SIC: 3599 Machine shop, jobbing & repair

(G-13550)
METAL CRAFT OF PENSACOLA INC
Also Called: Metalcraft
4 E Hannah St (32534-3413)
PHONE.................................850 478-8333
Chris Stinson, *President*
EMP: 17 **EST:** 1994
SQ FT: 5,750
SALES (est): 623K **Privately Held**
WEB: www.metalcraftofpensacola.com
SIC: 2514 7692 Lawn furniture: metal; welding repair

(G-13551)
METALCRAFT OF PENSACOLA INC
4 E Hannah St (32534-3413)
PHONE.................................850 478-8333
EMP: 9 **EST:** 2009
SALES (est): 131.1K **Privately Held**
SIC: 3731 Shipbuilding & repairing

(G-13552)
METROTECH MEDIA & LIGHTING INC
38 S Blue Angel Pkwy # 108 (32506-6045)
PHONE.................................844 463-8761
David L Benavent, *COO*
EMP: 6 **EST:** 2015
SALES (est): 419.9K **Privately Held**
WEB: www.metrotechlight.com
SIC: 3646 Commercial indusl & institutional electric lighting fixtures

(G-13553)
MID WEST LETTERING COMPANY
Also Called: Sunbelt Lettering
7800 Sears Blvd (32514-4544)
PHONE.................................850 477-6522
Fax: 850 484-5390
EMP: 25
SQ FT: 8,880
SALES (est): 3.3MM
SALES (corp-wide): 5.6MM **Privately Held**
SIC: 3559 2399 2752 2395 Mfg Misc Industry Mach Mfg Fabrctd Textile Pdts Lithographic Coml Print Pleating/Stitching Svcs
PA: Mid West Lettering Company
　645 Bellefontaine Ave
　Marion OH
　740 382-1905

(G-13554)
NAI PRINT SOLUTIONS LLC
457 Strandview Dr (32534-1372)
PHONE.................................850 637-1260
Taris Wickizer, *Principal*
EMP: 6 **EST:** 2008
SALES (est): 407.4K **Privately Held**
WEB: www.naiprint.com
SIC: 2752 Commercial printing, offset

(G-13555)
NATIONAL STD PARTS ASSOC INC
Also Called: Nspa
1301 E Belmont St (32501-4135)
PHONE.................................850 456-5771
John E Endacott, *CEO*
J Brooks Endacott, *President*
▲ **EMP:** 52 **EST:** 1980
SQ FT: 15,000
SALES (est): 9MM **Privately Held**
WEB: www.nspa.com
SIC: 3643 3613 5085 Connectors & terminals for electrical devices; power connectors, electric; fasteners & fastening equipment

(G-13556)
NORTH AMERICAN SIGNAL LLC
1810 Barrancas Ave (32502-5215)
PHONE.................................850 462-1790
Greg Johnson, *Vice Pres*
Michael R Day, *Mng Member*
EMP: 8 **EST:** 2015
SALES (est): 176.9K **Privately Held**
WEB: www.northamericansignal.com
SIC: 3669 Traffic signals, electric

(G-13557)
NORTHROP GRUMMAN SYSTEMS CORP
130 West Ave Ste C (32508-5165)
PHONE.................................850 452-7970
EMP: 8 **EST:** 2018
SALES (est): 352.2K **Privately Held**
WEB: www.northropgrumman.com
SIC: 3812 Search & navigation equipment

▲ = Import ▼ =Export
◆ =Import/Export

(G-13558)
OASIS ALIGNMENT SERVICES INC
7501 Sears Blvd (32514-4539)
PHONE.....................850 484-2994
Myron Smith, *Principal*
Roger Cross, *Manager*
EMP: 10
SALES (corp-wide): 25.2MM **Privately Held**
WEB: www.oasisalignment.com
SIC: 3827 Aiming circles (fire control equipment)
HQ: Oasis Alignment Services, Llc
363 Pickering Rd
Rochester NH 03867
603 332-9641

(G-13559)
OFFSHORE INLAND MAR OLFLD SVCS
640 S Barracks St (32502-6053)
PHONE.....................251 443-5550
Robin D Roberts, *CEO*
Jesse Odom, *Superintendent*
Randy Hamblin, *Project Mgr*
Anna Smith, *Project Mgr*
Brian Hall, *Foreman/Supr*
▲ EMP: 125 EST: 2001
SALES (est): 43MM **Privately Held**
WEB: www.offshoreinland.com
SIC: 1389 Oil field services; oil consultants; gas field services
PA: Oimo Holdings, Inc
2735 Middle Rd
Mobile AL 36605

(G-13560)
OLD CITY BUILDING
201 E Government St (32502-6018)
PHONE.....................850 432-7723
W H F Wiltshire, *President*
Gordon E Welch
EMP: 8 EST: 1960
SALES (est): 1.1MM **Privately Held**
SIC: 1381 Drilling oil & gas wells

(G-13561)
ON-SITE LIGHTING & SIGN SVCS
5925 Flaxman St (32506-4029)
PHONE.....................256 693-1018
EMP: 7 EST: 2012
SALES (est): 98.3K **Privately Held**
SIC: 3993 Signs & advertising specialties

(G-13562)
ORDERCOUNTER INC
Also Called: Order Counter Com Point Svc S
9270 University Pkwy # 102 (32514-9447)
PHONE.....................850 332-5540
Thomas Barrineau IV, *CEO*
Crystal Barrineau, *Marketing Staff*
EMP: 12 EST: 2006
SQ FT: 500
SALES (est): 1.3MM **Privately Held**
WEB: home.ordercounter.com
SIC: 7372 Business oriented computer software

(G-13563)
OVERHEAD DOOR CORPORATION
3395 Addison Dr (32514-7066)
PHONE.....................850 474-9890
Jeff Hogue, *General Mgr*
Kevin Pang, *Mfg Staff*
Randolph Gardner, *Supervisor*
Boyd Selby, *Exec Dir*
EMP: 76 **Privately Held**
WEB: www.overheaddoor.com
SIC: 3442 3089 2431 Garage doors, overhead: metal; doors, folding: plastic or plastic coated fabric; doors, wood; garage doors, overhead: wood
HQ: Overhead Door Corporation
2501 S State Hwy 121 Ste
Lewisville TX 75067
469 549-7100

(G-13564)
P A VIVID PATHOLOGY (PA)
Also Called: Medical Examiners Office Dst 1
5149 N 9th Ave Ste 122 (32504-8779)
P.O. Box 10450 (32524-0450)
PHONE.....................850 416-7780
Thomas J Lawrence MD, *Principal*
John Bray, *Vice Pres*
Emily Arias, *Accountant*
Samantha Stevens, *Human Res Mgr*
Larry Seldenright, *Sales Staff*
EMP: 3 EST: 1969
SALES (est): 3.3MM **Privately Held**
WEB: www.vividpathology.com
SIC: 2711 Newspapers, publishing & printing

(G-13565)
PALAFOX MARINE INC
490 S L St (32502-5209)
PHONE.....................850 438-9354
Hunter Riddle, *Owner*
Suzanne Riddle, *Manager*
EMP: 10 EST: 1973
SQ FT: 5,900
SALES (est): 942.7K **Privately Held**
SIC: 2211 Sail cloth

(G-13566)
PARADIGM PARACHUTE AND DEFENSE
4040 Ashland Ave (32534-1050)
PHONE.....................928 580-9013
Aaron Nazaruk, *Principal*
Alexander Alvarado, *Principal*
Doris Cooper, *Principal*
EMP: 12 EST: 2019
SALES (est): 1MM **Privately Held**
WEB: www.paradigmparachute.com
SIC: 2399 Fabricated textile products

(G-13567)
PATTI MARINE ENTERPRISES INC
306 S Pinewood Ln (32507-1374)
P.O. Box 271 (32591-0271)
PHONE.....................850 453-1282
Frank M Patti, *President*
EMP: 12 EST: 2008
SALES (est): 4.2MM **Privately Held**
WEB: www.pattimarine.com
SIC: 3731 Shipbuilding & repairing

(G-13568)
PBI/GORDON CORP
8809 Ely Rd (32514-7064)
PHONE.....................850 478-2770
Cally Miller, *Analyst*
EMP: 7 EST: 2019
SALES (est): 340.1K **Privately Held**
WEB: www.pbigordon.com
SIC: 2879 Pesticides, agricultural or household

(G-13569)
PEGASUS LABORATORIES INC (HQ)
Also Called: Trophy Animal Health Care
8809 Ely Rd (32514-7064)
PHONE.....................850 478-2770
Richard E Martin, *President*
Scott Howard, *Vice Pres*
Andrew Hunt, *Vice Pres*
Donna Logan, *Vice Pres*
Keyli Whelan, *Project Mgr*
EMP: 38 EST: 1987
SQ FT: 46,000
SALES (est): 24.7MM
SALES (corp-wide): 154.3MM **Privately Held**
WEB: www.pegasuslabs.com
SIC: 2834 Veterinary pharmaceutical preparations
PA: Pbi-Gordon Corporation
22701 W 68th Ter
Shawnee KS 66226
816 421-4070

(G-13570)
PENSACOLA ORTHTC & PROSTETIC
5855 Creek Station Dr (32504-8626)
PHONE.....................850 478-7676
EMP: 8
SALES (est): 500K **Privately Held**
SIC: 3842 Mfg Surgical Appliances/Supplies

(G-13571)
PENSACOLA SIGN & GRAPHICS INC
Also Called: SIGNGEEK DBA PENSACOLA SIGN & GRAPHICS
3711 N Palafox St (32505-5236)
PHONE.....................850 433-7878
Steve Orlich, *President*
Adam Johnson, *Admin Asst*
EMP: 7 EST: 1994
SQ FT: 3,000
SALES (est): 849.7K **Privately Held**
WEB: www.pensacolasign.com
SIC: 3993 Signs, not made in custom sign painting shops

(G-13572)
PENSACOLA VOICE INC
213 E Yonge St (32503-3766)
PHONE.....................850 434-6963
Jacqueline Miles, *President*
EMP: 5 EST: 1970
SQ FT: 3,000
SALES (est): 616.5K **Privately Held**
WEB: www.pensacolavoice.com
SIC: 2711 8999 7338 Newspapers: publishing only, not printed on site; advertising copy writing; secretarial & court reporting

(G-13573)
PENSACOLA WOOD TREATING CO
1813 E Gadsden St (32501-3532)
PHONE.....................850 433-1300
Susan O McMillan, *President*
EMP: 10 EST: 2009
SALES (est): 220.2K **Privately Held**
SIC: 2491 Wood preserving

(G-13574)
PERFORMANCE MACHINING SVCS INC
4161 Warehouse Ln (32505-4061)
PHONE.....................850 469-9106
Jake Ziglioli, *President*
Carla Ziglioli, *Vice Pres*
Greg Mowry, *Manager*
EMP: 15 EST: 1995
SQ FT: 7,000
SALES (est): 2.2MM **Privately Held**
SIC: 3599 Machine shop, jobbing & repair

(G-13575)
PINNACLE CABINETS CLOSETS LLC ✪
9900b N Palafox St (32534-1227)
PHONE.....................850 477-5402
Sue Long,
EMP: 6 EST: 2022
SALES (est): 437.1K **Privately Held**
WEB: www.pinnaclecabinetsandclosets.com
SIC: 2434 Wood kitchen cabinets

(G-13576)
PLASMINE TECHNOLOGY INC (DH)
3298 Summit Blvd Ste 35 (32503-4350)
PHONE.....................850 438-8550
Steven J Violette, *President*
Lauren Amable, *Research*
Brandon Cook, *Research*
Scott Braun, *Sales Staff*
Brian Williquette, *Manager*
◆ EMP: 12 EST: 1990
SQ FT: 4,700
SALES (est): 14.2MM **Privately Held**
WEB: www.plasmine.com
SIC: 2819 Industrial inorganic chemicals
HQ: Harima Usa, Inc.
1965 Evergreen Blvd # 400
Duluth GA 30096
770 813-1720

(G-13577)
PLASTIC ART SIGN COMPANY INC
3931 W Navy Blvd (32507-1256)
PHONE.....................850 455-4114
John Navarro, *President*
Elizabeth Mae Navarro, *Corp Secy*
Scott Navarro, *Vice Pres*
EMP: 10 EST: 1969
SQ FT: 8,000
SALES (est): 981.4K **Privately Held**
WEB: www.plasticartssigns.com
SIC: 3993 Signs & advertising specialties

(G-13578)
PLASTIC COATED PAPERS INC
1701 E Kingsfield Rd (32534-9503)
PHONE.....................850 968-6100
David L Mayo, *President*
William O Helms, *Vice Pres*
James E McGahan, *Vice Pres*
David C Pitts, *Vice Pres*
Pinette M Steven, *Vice Pres*
EMP: 52 EST: 1952
SQ FT: 52,000
SALES (est): 16.2MM **Privately Held**
WEB: www.polycoated.com
SIC: 2671 Paper coated or laminated for packaging

(G-13579)
POLLAK INDUSTRIES
2313 Truman Ave (32505-4249)
PHONE.....................850 438-4651
Buffy Spurlock, *Director*
EMP: 7 EST: 2002
SQ FT: 6,480
SALES (est): 91K **Privately Held**
WEB: www.arc-gateway.org
SIC: 3272 Concrete products

(G-13580)
POTTERS COFFEE COMPANY
1727 Creighton Rd (32504-7145)
PHONE.....................850 525-1793
Kevin Webster, *President*
EMP: 8 EST: 2017
SQ FT: 360
SALES (est): 128.2K **Privately Held**
WEB: potters-coffee-company.business.site
SIC: 2095 7389 5149 Roasted coffee; coffee service; coffee, green or roasted

(G-13581)
PRECAST TECHNICAL ASSISTANCE
21 S Tarragona St Ste 101 (32502-6062)
PHONE.....................850 432-8446
William A Lovell Jr, *President*
EMP: 9 EST: 2015
SALES (est): 442.2K **Privately Held**
SIC: 3272 Precast terrazo or concrete products

(G-13582)
PRECISION LIFT INDUSTRIES LLC
3605 N Davis Hwy (32503-3021)
PHONE.....................877 770-5862
Scott Humbaugh, *Mng Member*
Brian Reeves, *Master*
EMP: 8 EST: 2010
SALES (est): 1.9MM **Privately Held**
WEB: www.precisionliftindustries.com
SIC: 3534 Elevators & equipment

(G-13583)
PRIME MANUFACTURING CANADA
9235 Roe St (32514-7034)
PHONE.....................850 332-7193
Michelle Jones, *Principal*
Brad Fisher, *VP Opers*
▲ EMP: 8 EST: 2009
SALES (est): 778.1K **Privately Held**
WEB: www.primerailroadproducts.com
SIC: 3999 Barber & beauty shop equipment

(G-13584)
PRIME PEDAL KARTS LLC
Also Called: Prime Karts
9235 Roe St (32514-7034)
PHONE.....................850 475-0450
Jeffrey L Fisher, *Exec VP*
Ronald Fisher, *Mng Member*
Jeff Fisher,
Derek Lother,
▲ EMP: 10 EST: 2004
SQ FT: 3,000
SALES (est): 962.1K **Privately Held**
WEB: www.primekarts.com
SIC: 3944 Automobiles, children's, pedal driven

GEOGRAPHIC

(G-13585)
PRINTERS OF PENSACOLA LLC
1207 W Garden St (32502-4556)
PHONE..................................850 434-2588
Ray Herring, *President*
Raymond Herring, *President*
Debra Herring, *Vice Pres*
EMP: 5 EST: 1975
SQ FT: 1,600
SALES (est): 495.9K Privately Held
WEB: www.printersofpensacola.com
SIC: 2752 7334 2791 Commercial printing, offset; photocopying & duplicating services; typesetting

(G-13586)
PRINTNOW INC
Also Called: Print Now-Business Cards Today
5555 N Davis Hwy Ste H (32503-2065)
P.O. Box 892, Gulf Breeze (32562-0892)
PHONE..................................850 435-1149
Kelley Chism, *President*
Robert A Chism, *Admin Sec*
EMP: 6 EST: 2000
SALES (est): 460K Privately Held
WEB: www.printnowinc.com
SIC: 2752 Commercial printing, offset

(G-13587)
PUBLISHERS CRCLTION FLFLLMENT
Also Called: PCF
3351b Mclemore Dr (32514-7074)
PHONE..................................877 723-6668
Elisabeth Harrison, *Manager*
EMP: 63
SALES (corp-wide): 58MM Privately Held
WEB: www.pcfcorp.com
SIC: 2741 Miscellaneous publishing
PA: Publishers Circulation Fulfillment, Inc.
502 Washington Ave Ste 500
Towson MD 21204
410 821-8614

(G-13588)
PWS INTERNATIONAL
5 Clarinda Ln (32505-4309)
PHONE..................................850 432-4222
EMP: 7 EST: 2010
SALES (est): 19.1K Privately Held
WEB: www.pwsintl.com
SIC: 3582 Commercial laundry equipment

(G-13589)
QLTY ALUMN BOAT LIFTS INC
2375 W Herman Ave (32505-4245)
PHONE..................................850 434-6446
Jayne Card, *Principal*
EMP: 6 EST: 2015
SALES (est): 456.7K Privately Held
SIC: 3536 Boat lifts

(G-13590)
QUALITY ALUM BOAT LIFTS INC
2375 W Herman Ave (32505-4245)
PHONE..................................850 434-6446
EMP: 8 EST: 2013
SALES (est): 452.8K Privately Held
SIC: 3536 Boat lifts

(G-13591)
R & K PORTABLE BUILDINGS
Also Called: R & K Builders
8120 Pensacola Blvd (32534-4352)
PHONE..................................850 857-7899
Glen Russell, *Partner*
EMP: 8 EST: 1981
SQ FT: 540
SALES (est): 129.1K Privately Held
WEB: rnkmilton.wixsite.com
SIC: 3448 1521 Prefabricated metal buildings; patio & deck construction & repair

(G-13592)
R K L ENTERPRISES OF PENSACOLA
Also Called: Speed-D-Print
3740 N Pace Blvd (32505-4352)
PHONE..................................850 432-2335
Rita K Loughridge, *President*
Jack Loughridge, *Corp Secy*
EMP: 10 EST: 1983
SQ FT: 3,600

SALES (est): 1.2MM Privately Held
WEB: www.speeddprint.com
SIC: 2752 Commercial printing, offset

(G-13593)
RACEWAY 6852
7910 Pine Forest Rd (32526-8722)
PHONE..................................850 944-8212
Mick Patel, *Principal*
EMP: 7 EST: 2010
SALES (est): 141K Privately Held
SIC: 3644 Raceways

(G-13594)
READY MACHINE CORP
6155 Drexel Rd (32504-7906)
PHONE..................................850 479-1722
Krzysztof Roszko, *Owner*
EMP: 7 EST: 2003
SALES (est): 490.4K Privately Held
WEB: ready-machine-corp.business.site
SIC: 3599 Machine shop, jobbing & repair

(G-13595)
REDDY ICE CORPORATION
1511 W Government St (32502-5318)
PHONE..................................850 433-2191
Kenneth Wilson, *Plant Engr*
Tim Brown, *Manager*
EMP: 13 Privately Held
WEB: www.reddyice.com
SIC: 2097 5999 Block ice; ice cubes; ice
HQ: Reddy Ice Llc
5710 Lbj Fwy Ste 300
Dallas TX 75240
214 526-6740

(G-13596)
RENAISSANCE MAN INCORPORATED
Also Called: Renaissance Fabrication
2203 N Pace Blvd (32505-5837)
PHONE..................................850 432-1177
Jon Kevin Marchetti, *President*
EMP: 6 EST: 1999
SALES (est): 750K Privately Held
WEB: www.renaissancefabrication.com
SIC: 3441 Fabricated structural metal

(G-13597)
RING OF FIRE RADIO LLC
316 S Baylen St (32502-5900)
PHONE..................................866 666-6114
J Michael Papantonio, *Manager*
EMP: 7 EST: 2005
SALES (est): 188.3K Privately Held
WEB: www.trofire.com
SIC: 2711 Newspapers, publishing & printing

(G-13598)
RUDD & SON WELDING INC
Also Called: Rudd Welding
81 E Ten Mile Rd (32534-9706)
P.O. Box 1087, Gonzalez (32560-1087)
PHONE..................................850 476-2110
Charles Edward Rudd, *President*
Patricia I Rudd, *Admin Sec*
EMP: 14 EST: 1953
SQ FT: 12,000
SALES (est): 1.6MM Privately Held
SIC: 7692 Welding repair

(G-13599)
S&J ALUMINUM WORKS INC
5623 Bauer Rd (32507-9077)
PHONE..................................850 492-5700
Scott Schlyer, *President*
EMP: 8 EST: 2002
SALES (est): 650K Privately Held
SIC: 3411 Aluminum cans

(G-13600)
SANTA ROSA AUTO PARTS INC
Also Called: Car City Engine and Machine
50 Industrial Blvd (32503-7602)
PHONE..................................850 477-7747
Kenneth A Schepper, *President*
Carl E Schepper, *Vice Pres*
David M Schepper, *Treasurer*
EMP: 20 EST: 1959
SQ FT: 13,000
SALES (est): 998.6K Privately Held
WEB: www.carcityengine.com
SIC: 3599 3714 Machine & other job shop work; motor vehicle parts & accessories

(G-13601)
SCHURR SAILS INC
490 S L St (32502-5267)
PHONE..................................850 438-9354
Hunter Riddle, *President*
Alfred L Schurr, *Principal*
Steve Bellows, *Corp Secy*
EMP: 10 EST: 1971
SQ FT: 5,000
SALES (est): 401K Privately Held
WEB: www.schurr-sails.com
SIC: 2394 3732 Sails: made from purchased materials; boat building & repairing

(G-13602)
SCHWARZ BROS MANUFACTURING CO
1455 Little Creek Dr (32506-8259)
PHONE..................................309 342-5814
Steven Gray, *President*
C Gray, *Treasurer*
EMP: 6 EST: 1940
SALES (est): 858.2K Privately Held
SIC: 3544 Special dies & tools; jigs & fixtures

(G-13603)
SILVER HORN JERKY INC
3715 Mobile Hwy (32505-6122)
PHONE..................................850 208-1433
Qua Dinh, *Principal*
EMP: 13 EST: 2018
SALES (est): 643.1K Privately Held
WEB: www.silverhornjerky.com
SIC: 2013 Snack sticks, including jerky: from purchased meat

(G-13604)
SMARTCOP INC
Also Called: Consolidated Tech Solutions
1765 E Nine Mile Rd (32514-5479)
PHONE..................................850 429-0082
George Kay Stephenson, *CEO*
George Stephenson, *President*
James Benson, *COO*
Steve Williams, *Vice Pres*
Steven Williams, *Vice Pres*
EMP: 50 EST: 1999
SALES (est): 10.8MM Privately Held
WEB: www.smartcop.com
SIC: 7372 Prepackaged software

(G-13605)
SOUTHERN ENVIRONMENTAL INC
Also Called: Florida Southern Environmental
6690 W Nine Mile Rd (32526-3211)
PHONE..................................850 944-4475
Michael W Hatsfelt, *President*
Andrew Lynch, *Regional Mgr*
John L Jernigan, *Vice Pres*
Johnny L Jernigan, *Vice Pres*
Johnny Jernigan, *Vice Pres*
EMP: 30 EST: 1973
SQ FT: 9,600
SALES (est): 6.1MM Privately Held
WEB: www.southernenvironmental.com
SIC: 3822 Thermostats & other environmental sensors

(G-13606)
SOUTHERN STATES GLUING SVCS
3865 N Palafox St (32505-5238)
PHONE..................................850 469-9667
EMP: 8
SQ FT: 8,000
SALES (est): 660K Privately Held
SIC: 2672 Adhesive Application

(G-13607)
SOUTHERN WOODWORKS FINE WDWKG
Also Called: Fine Wood Work
1170 Mahogany Mill Rd (32507-3902)
PHONE..................................850 456-0550
Rebecca Bennett, *President*
Becky Bennett, *President*
EMP: 10 EST: 1992
SQ FT: 5,000
SALES (est): 892.1K Privately Held
WEB: www.southernwoodworksinc.com
SIC: 2541 1751 Wood partitions & fixtures; cabinet & finish carpentry

(G-13608)
SPECIALTY PRODUCTS INC
Also Called: Ace Overhead Doors
2325 W Cervantes St (32505-7148)
PHONE..................................850 438-4264
Bud Segers, *President*
Scott McCandless, *Sales Staff*
EMP: 8 EST: 2002
SALES (est): 1.5MM Privately Held
SIC: 2431 3442 1799 1751 Garage doors, overhead: wood; garage doors, overhead: metal; dock equipment installation, industrial; window & door installation & erection; garage door, installation or erection; garage doors, sale & installation

(G-13609)
SPECTRUMIT INC
1101 N Palafox St (32501-2607)
PHONE..................................850 202-5263
Scott Pfeifer, *President*
Deborah Stuckey, *Opers Mgr*
Danielle Peiffer, *Manager*
Dan Lindley, *IT Specialist*
EMP: 14 EST: 2012
SALES (est): 4.8MM Privately Held
WEB: www.spectrumit.net
SIC: 3519 Internal combustion engines

(G-13610)
SPIKER USA CORPORATION
38 S Blue Angel Pkwy (32506-6045)
PHONE..................................850 710-3043
Karon P Butler, *President*
EMP: 8 EST: 2015
SALES (est): 323.7K Privately Held
SIC: 3221 Glass containers

(G-13611)
SPIKES PRESS & PRINTHOUSE LLC
1201 Barrancas Ave (32502-4512)
PHONE..................................850 438-2293
Luke T Keller, *Mng Member*
EMP: 7 EST: 2012
SALES (est): 258.7K Privately Held
WEB: www.spikesprinting.com
SIC: 2741 Miscellaneous publishing

(G-13612)
SUNPACK OF PENSACOLA INC
8500 Fowler Ave (32534-1801)
PHONE..................................850 476-9838
John M O Neil, *CEO*
John M Oneill, *President*
Jack Neill, *Sales Staff*
▲ EMP: 16 EST: 1998
SQ FT: 60,000
SALES (est): 4.8MM Privately Held
WEB: www.sunpackinc.com
SIC: 3452 5085 3462 Bolts, metal; gaskets; flange, valve & pipe fitting forgings, ferrous

(G-13613)
TECHNOLOGIES FOR TOMORROW INC
1106 N 9th Ave (32501-3236)
PHONE..................................850 478-5222
Elizabeth Doenlen, *President*
Pamela L Coco, *Vice Pres*
Daniel Coco, *CFO*
Angel Clark, *Manager*
Dale Collins, *Manager*
EMP: 16 EST: 1994
SQ FT: 4,100
SALES (est): 6.9MM Privately Held
WEB: www.tftcomputers.com
SIC: 3577 Computer peripheral equipment

(G-13614)
TRANSPORT A/C INC
91 S Madison Dr (32505-3615)
PHONE..................................954 254-4822
Jacob Baker, *CEO*
EMP: 6 EST: 2010
SALES (est): 421K Privately Held
SIC: 3585 Air conditioning, motor vehicle

(G-13615)
TRIOPS INC
Also Called: Toyops
3330 Mclemore Dr Ste B (32514-7077)
P.O. Box 11369 (32524-1369)
PHONE..................................850 479-4415

▲ = Import ▼ =Export
◆ =Import/Export

Eugene Hall, *President*
Christina Jones, *Manager*
Shannon Wix, *Manager*
▲ **EMP:** 6 **EST:** 1993
SALES (est): 621.5K **Privately Held**
WEB: www.triops.com
SIC: 3944 Science kits: microscopes, chemistry sets, etc.

(G-13616)
TURBINE RESOURCES INTL LLC
2595a Dog Track Rd (32506-7833)
PHONE.................................850 377-0449
James Patrick Meharg,
EMP: 8 **EST:** 2014
SALES (est): 195.7K **Privately Held**
SIC: 3511 Gas turbine generator set units, complete

(G-13617)
UNITED STATES GREEN ENRGY CORP
1074 Windchime Way (32503-2548)
PHONE.................................540 295-4843
▼ **EMP:** 30 **EST:** 2009
SQ FT: 300
SALES (est): 2.6MM **Privately Held**
SIC: 3433 Mfg Solar Equipment

(G-13618)
VERACITY TECH SOLUTIONS LLC
8245 Mccarty St (32534-1808)
PHONE.................................402 658-4113
Jim Wagner, *CEO*
Kevin McKinley, *President*
Curtis Evans, *COO*
Chris Chadwick, *Vice Pres*
Steven Estep, *Technician*
EMP: 18 **EST:** 2006
SALES (est): 1.3MM **Privately Held**
WEB: www.veracityts.com
SIC: 3829 8734 8331 Measuring & controlling devices; testing laboratories; job training services

(G-13619)
VERHI INC
824 Creighton Rd Ste A (32504-7082)
PHONE.................................850 477-4880
Steven L Gavin, *Principal*
Steve Gavin, *Principal*
EMP: 44 **EST:** 2005
SALES (est): 1.4MM
SALES (corp-wide): 1.1B **Publicly Held**
SIC: 3842 Wheelchairs
PA: Hanger, Inc.
10910 Domain Dr Ste 300
Austin TX 78758
512 777-3800

(G-13620)
VERTEC INC
141 Terry Dr (32503-7066)
PHONE.................................850 478-6480
Ronald R Bray, *President*
Quinlyn Bray, *Corp Secy*
John R Bray, *Vice Pres*
Kendall Bray, *Manager*
Valerie Bevis, *Admin Sec*
EMP: 11 **EST:** 1978
SQ FT: 22,000
SALES (est): 1.4MM **Privately Held**
WEB: www.vertec.net
SIC: 3823 3444 3845 Industrial process measurement equipment; sheet metal specialties, not stamped; electromedical apparatus

(G-13621)
VIEWPOINT SYSTEMS LLC
730 W Garden St Pensacola (32502)
PHONE.................................850 450-0681
David Conkle, *Partner*
John Kirkpatrick, *Opers Staff*
EMP: 12 **EST:** 2011
SALES (est): 1.7MM **Privately Held**
WEB: www.viewpointproducts.com
SIC: 3812 Search & navigation equipment

(G-13622)
VOWELLS DOWNTOWN INC
Also Called: Vowells Printing
1233 Barrancas Ave (32502-4512)
P.O. Box 12644 (32591-2644)
PHONE.................................850 432-5175
Mary Vowell, *President*
John Roberts, *Vice Pres*
Mike Vowell, *Vice Pres*
EMP: 9 **EST:** 1981
SQ FT: 5,000
SALES (est): 1MM **Privately Held**
WEB: www.vowells.com
SIC: 2752 2796 2791 2789 Commercial printing, offset; platemaking services; typesetting; bookbinding & related work

(G-13623)
WATER TECHNOLOGY PENSACOLA INC
Also Called: A T B Systems
3000 W Nine Mile Rd (32534-9473)
PHONE.................................850 477-4789
William Boesch, *President*
Elise Boesch, *Treasurer*
David Taylor, *Sales Mgr*
EMP: 30 **EST:** 1985
SQ FT: 9,200
SALES (est): 3.9MM **Privately Held**
WEB: www.atbsystems.com
SIC: 3599 Boiler tube cleaners

(G-13624)
WATERBOYZ-WBZ INC
Also Called: Wbz Boarding House
380 N 9th Ave (32502-4951)
PHONE.................................850 433-2929
Sean Fell, *President*
▲ **EMP:** 12 **EST:** 1989
SQ FT: 2,000
SALES (est): 792.2K **Privately Held**
WEB: www.waterboyz.com
SIC: 2759 5941 3993 5999 Screen printing; surfing equipment & supplies; signs & advertising specialties; sunglasses

(G-13625)
WIND BLUE TECHNOLOGY LLC
7502 Sears Blvd (32514-4538)
PHONE.................................850 218-9398
Henry A Kelley Jr,
EMP: 10 **EST:** 2019
SALES (est): 2.9MM **Privately Held**
WEB: www.bluewindtechnology.com
SIC: 3086 Plastics foam products

(G-13626)
WINGS THINGS MONOGRAMMING INC
3815 W Navy Blvd (32507-1219)
PHONE.................................850 455-3081
Larry Speed, *President*
EMP: 12 **EST:** 1987
SQ FT: 9,000
SALES (est): 554.4K **Privately Held**
WEB: www.wings-and-things.com
SIC: 2395 Emblems, embroidered; embroidery & art needlework

(G-13627)
WISE RECYCLING 1 LLC
Also Called: Reynolds Aluminum Recycl Div
601 W Hope Dr (32534-4215)
P.O. Box 28737, Baltimore MD (21240)
PHONE.................................850 477-5273
Harold Stone, *Manager*
Llori Freeman, *Manager*
EMP: 10
SALES (corp-wide): 30.2MM **Privately Held**
SIC: 3341 4953 Aluminum smelting & refining (secondary); refuse systems
PA: Wise Recycling 1, Llc
7600 Rolling Mill Rd
Baltimore MD 21224
410 285-6900

(G-13628)
WSA ENGINEERED SYSTEMS INC
3000 W Nine Mile Rd Ste A (32534-9473)
P.O. Box 619, Milwaukee WI (53201-0619)
PHONE.................................414 481-4120
Kaveh Someah, *President*
Mary Carabajal, *General Mgr*

Colleen Gottsacker, *Vice Pres*
▲ **EMP:** 15 **EST:** 1972
SALES (est): 1.6MM **Privately Held**
WEB: www.wsaes.com
SIC: 3589 3564 3494 Commercial cleaning equipment; blowers & fans; valves & pipe fittings

Perry
Taylor County

(G-13629)
AGNER TIMBER SERVICES INC
2450 W Fair Rd (32347-4900)
PHONE.................................850 251-6615
Chad Agner, *President*
EMP: 9 **EST:** 2005
SQ FT: 800
SALES (est): 2.5MM **Privately Held**
SIC: 2411 Logging

(G-13630)
AMERICAN ALUMINUM ACC INC
3291 S Us Highway 19 (32348-6402)
PHONE.................................850 277-0869
Tom Swain, *CEO*
Jennifer Arnold, *President*
Robert Swain, *President*
◆ **EMP:** 35 **EST:** 1989
SQ FT: 59,000
SALES (est): 8.1MM **Privately Held**
WEB: www.ezrideronline.com
SIC: 3443 Fabricated plate work (boiler shop)

(G-13631)
AMTEC LESS LETHAL SYSTEMS INC
Also Called: Pacem Defense
4700 Providence Rd (32347-1140)
PHONE.................................850 223-4066
Andrew Knaggs, *CEO*
Cory Mills, *Ch of Bd*
Michael Quesenberry, *President*
Jennifer Shoplak, *Principal*
Trystan Kasheta, *Finance Mgr*
▼ **EMP:** 75 **EST:** 2010
SALES (est): 11MM
SALES (corp-wide): 13.5MM **Privately Held**
WEB: www.lesslethal.com
SIC: 3559 Ammunition & explosives, loading machinery
PA: Pacem Solution International Llc
2941 Frview Pk Dr Ste 350
Falls Church VA 22042
703 309-1891

(G-13632)
BIG TOP MANUFACTURING INC
3255 Us Highway 19 N (32347-0894)
PHONE.................................850 584-7786
Jeffrey Merschman, *President*
Harishma Donthineni, *Project Mgr*
Marti Flowers, *Prdtn Mgr*
Sarah Johnson, *Engineer*
Joan Merschman, *Treasurer*
◆ **EMP:** 85 **EST:** 2014
SQ FT: 120,000
SALES (est): 12.6MM **Privately Held**
WEB: www.bigtopshelters.com
SIC: 2394 Canvas awnings & canopies

(G-13633)
BLUE ROCK INC (PA)
4010 Olan Davis Rd (32347-0366)
PHONE.................................850 584-4324
EMP: 4
SALES: 4.8MM **Privately Held**
SIC: 1422 Crushed/Broken Limestone

(G-13634)
BOLAND TIMBER COMPANY INC
3616 S Byron Butler Pkwy (32348-6434)
P.O. Box 337, Wacissa (32361-0337)
PHONE.................................850 997-5270
Jeffery Boland, *President*
James Boland Jr, *Vice Pres*
Bette Boland, *Treasurer*
Connie Boland, *Admin Sec*
EMP: 28 **EST:** 2000
SQ FT: 1,856
SALES (est): 5.5MM **Privately Held**
SIC: 2411 Logging camps & contractors

(G-13635)
CONSOLIDATED FOREST PDTS INC
320 Millinor Rd (32347-1254)
P.O. Box 520090, Longwood (32752-0090)
PHONE.................................407 830-7723
Art Gilpin, *Branch Mgr*
EMP: 7
SALES (corp-wide): 2.7MM **Privately Held**
WEB: www.consolidatedforestproducts.com
SIC: 2499 2869 Fencing, wood; fuels
PA: Consolidated Forest Products, Inc.
375 Commerce Way
Longwood FL 32750
407 830-7723

(G-13636)
DIVERSIFIED WELDING INC
20368 Ponce De Leon Rd (32348-8177)
P.O. Box 1273, Belle Glade (33430-6273)
PHONE.................................561 996-9398
EMP: 6 **EST:** 2009
SALES (est): 496.1K **Privately Held**
SIC: 7692 Welding repair

(G-13637)
FOLEY CELLULOSE LLC
3510 Contractors Rd (32348-7738)
PHONE.................................850 584-1121
James Hannan,
▲ **EMP:** 558 **EST:** 1992
SALES (est): 115.6MM
SALES (corp-wide): 36.9B **Privately Held**
SIC: 2611 Pulp mills
HQ: Georgia-Pacific Llc
133 Peachtree St Nw
Atlanta GA 30303
404 652-4000

(G-13638)
FRASER WEST
1509 S Byron Butler Pkwy (32348-5430)
P.O. Box 1727 (32348-7305)
PHONE.................................850 601-2560
Pete Massey, *Maintence Staff*
EMP: 7 **EST:** 2018
SALES (est): 1.2MM **Privately Held**
SIC: 2421 Sawmills & planing mills, general

(G-13639)
GEORGIA-PACIFIC LLC
1 Buckeye Dr (32348-7702)
PHONE.................................850 584-1121
Tim Kapperman, *Opers Mgr*
Richard Feagle, *Engineer*
Bob Lewis, *Engineer*
Vickie Brown, *Info Tech Dir*
Leo Dalton, *IT/INT Sup*
EMP: 8
SALES (corp-wide): 36.9B **Privately Held**
WEB: www.gp.com
SIC: 2676 Sanitary paper products
HQ: Georgia-Pacific Llc
133 Peachtree St Nw
Atlanta GA 30303
404 652-4000

(G-13640)
GULF COAST FABRICATORS INC
3480 S Byron Butler Pkwy (32348-6456)
P.O. Box 1421 (32348-7302)
PHONE.................................850 584-5979
Fred Morgan Jr, *President*
Yancie Brannen, *General Mgr*
EMP: 6 **EST:** 1993
SALES (est): 861K **Privately Held**
WEB: www.gcfab.com
SIC: 3441 Fabricated structural metal

(G-13641)
H B TUTUN JR LOGGING INC
2930 Old Foley Rd (32348-5862)
PHONE.................................850 584-9324
EMP: 5 **EST:** 2019
SALES (est): 400.1K **Privately Held**
SIC: 2411 Logging camps & contractors

(G-13642)
HB TUTEN JR LOGGING INC
3870 S Byron Butler Pkwy (32348-6448)
PHONE.................................850 584-9324
Harvey B Tuten Jr, *President*

Charlotte M Lanier, *Admin Sec*
EMP: 20 **EST:** 1996
SALES (est): 2.8MM **Privately Held**
SIC: 2411 Logging camps & contractors

(G-13643)
HBT FORESTRY SERVICES INC
2930 Old Foley Rd (32348-5862)
PHONE................................850 584-9324
Ben Tuten, *Vice Pres*
EMP: 15 **EST:** 2012
SALES (est): 492.2K **Privately Held**
SIC: 2411 Logging

(G-13644)
JOHN A CRUCE JR INC
311 Glenridge Rd (32348-2204)
P.O. Box 86 (32348-0086)
PHONE................................850 584-9755
John W Cruce, *President*
J Adam Cruce, *Vice Pres*
EMP: 31 **EST:** 1955
SQ FT: 400
SALES (est): 3.2MM **Privately Held**
SIC: 2411 2421 Logging camps & contractors; sawmills & planing mills, general

(G-13645)
KEENS PORTABLE BUILDINGS
2320 S Byron Butler Pkwy (32348-6106)
PHONE................................850 223-1939
Lyzza Keens, *Branch Mgr*
EMP: 11
SALES (corp-wide): 3.6MM **Privately Held**
WEB: www.keensbuildings.com
SIC: 3448 Buildings, portable: prefabricated metal
PA: Keens Portable Bu Idings
620 Howard St W
Live Oak FL 32064
386 364-7995

(G-13646)
LYNN INDUSTRIAL WELDING INC
182 E Park St (32348-5604)
PHONE................................850 584-4494
John Lynn, *President*
Nancy Lynn, *Corp Secy*
EMP: 7 **EST:** 1982
SALES (est): 778.4K **Privately Held**
WEB: www.rakemaster.net
SIC: 7692 Welding repair

(G-13647)
M&E TIMBER INC
2451 E Ellison Rd (32347-0637)
PHONE................................850 584-6650
Merritt Pruitt, *President*
EMP: 6 **EST:** 2002
SALES (est): 438.9K **Privately Held**
SIC: 2411 Timber, cut at logging camp

(G-13648)
PERRY COMPOSITES LLC
1290 Houck Rd (32348-7539)
PHONE................................850 584-8400
Albert Jarrell, *Mng Member*
Cynthia M Jarrell, *Mng Member*
EMP: 9 **EST:** 2009
SALES (est): 282.6K **Privately Held**
SIC: 3732 3229 Boat building & repairing; glass fiber products

(G-13649)
PERRY NEWSPAPERS INC
Also Called: Taco Time
123 S Jefferson St (32347-3232)
P.O. Box 888 (32348-0888)
PHONE................................850 584-5513
Frank Nixon, *Ch of Bd*
Donald Lincoln, *President*
Bruce E Ratliff, *Vice Pres*
EMP: 15 **EST:** 1964
SQ FT: 1,800
SALES (est): 511K **Privately Held**
WEB: www.perrynewspapers.com
SIC: 2711 Commercial printing & newspaper publishing combined

(G-13650)
RDS MANUFACTURING INC
300 Industrial Park Dr (32348-6323)
P.O. Box 1908 (32348-7306)
PHONE................................850 584-6898

Joseph R Roberts III, *President*
Dennis Davis, *Vice Pres*
Martha Sayers Davis, *Vice Pres*
Sandi Sparks, *Production*
Laurel Sturgeon, *Production*
▲ **EMP:** 115 **EST:** 1968
SQ FT: 3,800
SALES (est): 13MM **Privately Held**
WEB: www.rdsaluminum.com
SIC: 3443 3714 3469 3354 Fuel tanks (oil, gas, etc.): metal plate; motor vehicle parts & accessories; metal stampings; aluminum extruded products

(G-13651)
REAGAN H FOX III INC
Woods Creek Rd (32347)
PHONE................................850 584-9229
Reagan H Fox III, *President*
Carolyn T Fox, *Corp Secy*
EMP: 12 **EST:** 1984
SALES (est): 534.7K **Privately Held**
SIC: 2411 Logging camps & contractors

(G-13652)
ROBERTS LUMBER COMPANY INC
3655 E Us 27 Hwy (32347-4608)
P.O. Box 1601 (32348-7304)
PHONE................................850 584-4573
David Roberts, *President*
Jody Roberts, *Treasurer*
Joseph R Roberts, *Treasurer*
EMP: 12 **EST:** 1960
SQ FT: 3,400
SALES (est): 522.3K **Privately Held**
SIC: 2421 2426 Kiln drying of lumber; hardwood dimension & flooring mills

(G-13653)
SHAWS WELDING INC
Also Called: Shaw's Site Preparation
1530 S Dixie Hwy (32348-5702)
P.O. Box 1017 (32348-1017)
PHONE................................850 584-7197
John O Shaw, *President*
Irene Shaw, *Corp Secy*
Gilbert Shaw, *Vice Pres*
John E Shaw, *Vice Pres*
Martin Shaw, *Vice Pres*
EMP: 13 **EST:** 1961
SQ FT: 4,800
SALES (est): 1MM **Privately Held**
WEB: www.shawsweldinginc.com
SIC: 7692 Welding repair

(G-13654)
SUPER-PUFFT SNACKS USA INC
700 Super Pufft St (32348-4758)
PHONE................................905 564-1180
Mahmoud Mrouch, *President*
Walid Amrouch, *Vice Pres*
Lu Qin, *CFO*
Yousif Al-Ali, *Treasurer*
Debbie Cato, *Controller*
EMP: 24 **EST:** 2018
SQ FT: 100
SALES (est): 23.6MM
SALES (corp-wide): 712.7MM **Privately Held**
WEB: www.superpufft.com
SIC: 2096 Cheese curls & puffs
HQ: Super-Pufft Snacks Corp
880 Gana Crt
Mississauga ON L5S 1
905 564-1180

(G-13655)
T & R MARINE CORP
3309 E Us 27 Hwy (32347-0605)
PHONE................................850 584-4261
Troy Thompson III, *President*
Betty Ratliff, *Corp Secy*
Billy Thompson, *Vice Pres*
▼ **EMP:** 8 **EST:** 1970
SQ FT: 16,000
SALES (est): 1.3MM **Privately Held**
WEB: www.trmarine.com
SIC: 3429 Marine hardware

(G-13656)
TECHNICAL ORD SOLUTIONS LLC (PA)
9495 Puckett Rd (32348-8502)
PHONE................................850 223-2393
Clyde Colburn, *Mng Member*
EMP: 3 **EST:** 2015
SALES (est): 4.7MM **Privately Held**
WEB: www.techordnancesolutions.com
SIC: 3541 Drilling machine tools (metal cutting)

(G-13657)
THULE INC
Also Called: Thule North America
606 Industrial Park Dr (32348-6353)
PHONE................................850 584-3448
Mac McMullen, *Plant Mgr*
Jimmy Giddens, *Branch Mgr*
EMP: 61 **Privately Held**
WEB: www.thule.com
SIC: 3714 3799 Motor vehicle body components & frame; boat trailers
HQ: Thule, Inc.
42 Silvermine Rd
Seymour CT 06483

(G-13658)
WILLIAMS TIMBER INC
215 Sunset Ln (32348-6017)
PHONE................................850 584-2760
Bradley Williams, *President*
Velinda Williams, *Treasurer*
EMP: 29 **EST:** 2000
SQ FT: 3,737
SALES (est): 3.7MM **Privately Held**
SIC: 2411 Logging camps & contractors

(G-13659)
WOODS N WATER MAGAZINE INC
3427 Puckett Rd (32348-1801)
PHONE................................850 584-3824
Patricia Pillow, *President*
Billy Pillow, *Editor*
Billy D Pillow, *Vice Pres*
Jennifer Davis, *Advt Staff*
Declan Pillow, *Manager*
EMP: 7 **EST:** 1978
SQ FT: 4,750
SALES (est): 619.4K **Privately Held**
WEB: www.woodsnwater.net
SIC: 2721 Magazines: publishing only, not printed on site

(G-13660)
WW TIMBER LLC
8999 Us Highway 19 S (32348-5845)
P.O. Box 1167 (32348-1167)
PHONE................................352 584-4550
Kristopher D Ward, *Manager*
EMP: 7 **EST:** 2005
SALES (est): 314.5K **Privately Held**
SIC: 3999 Manufacturing industries

Pinecrest
Miami-Dade County

(G-13661)
ADVANCED ELECTRONICS LABS INC
7375 Sw 114th St (33156-4632)
PHONE................................305 255-6401
Alexander Aklepi, *CEO*
G Michele Ryslik, *Shareholder*
EMP: 5 **EST:** 2012
SALES (est): 511K **Privately Held**
WEB: www.advancedesys.com
SIC: 3571 7389 Electronic computers; business services

(G-13662)
ALL METAL FABRICATION
9621 S Dixie Hwy (33156-2804)
PHONE................................305 666-3312
David Zisman, *Principal*
▼ **EMP:** 8 **EST:** 2008
SALES (est): 135.5K **Privately Held**
WEB: www.allmetalfabinc.com
SIC: 3499 Fabricated metal products

(G-13663)
BRAZILIAN SMOOTHIE INC
13255 Sw 83rd Ave (33156-6605)
PHONE................................305 233-5543
Marcos Becari, *Principal*
EMP: 8 **EST:** 2012
SALES (est): 163K **Privately Held**
SIC: 2037 Frozen fruits & vegetables

(G-13664)
CASPER ENGINEERING CORP
7695 Sw 133rd St (33156-6839)
PHONE................................305 666-4046
Carlos Camps, *President*
Elena Camps, *Treasurer*
▼ **EMP:** 6 **EST:** 1976
SQ FT: 4,100
SALES (est): 995K **Privately Held**
WEB: www.casperengineering.com
SIC: 3569 3599 Gas producers, generators & other gas related equipment; machine shop, jobbing & repair

(G-13665)
CLS HOLDINGS USA INC (PA)
11767 S Dixie Hwy Ste 115 (33156-4438)
PHONE................................888 438-9132
Jeffrey Binder, *Ch of Bd*
Andrew Glashow, *President*
Gregg Carlson, *CFO*
Frank Koretsky, *Director*
EMP: 23 **EST:** 2011
SALES (est): 22.6MM **Publicly Held**
WEB: www.clsholdingsinc.com
SIC: 2833 Medicinals & botanicals

(G-13666)
JORO FASHIONS FLORIDA INC
6650 Sw 123rd St (33156-5557)
PHONE................................305 888-8110
Jonathan Rubenstein, *President*
◆ **EMP:** 13 **EST:** 1990
SQ FT: 12,500
SALES (est): 711.9K **Privately Held**
SIC: 2339 Women's & misses' outerwear

(G-13667)
NRZ INC
Also Called: Beach Access
12885 Sw 82nd Ave (33156-5916)
PHONE................................305 345-7303
Nir Tzanani, *CEO*
EMP: 8 **EST:** 2001
SALES (est): 198.5K **Privately Held**
SIC: 2253 Beachwear, knit

(G-13668)
POWERFUL FOODS LLC
Also Called: Powerful Yogurt
9171 S Dixie Hwy (33156-2907)
PHONE................................305 637-7300
Suzanne Nabavi, *Director*
Carlos Ramirez,
EMP: 5 **EST:** 2012
SALES (est): 3.2MM **Privately Held**
WEB: www.powerfulnutrition.com
SIC: 2026 5149 Yogurt; health foods

(G-13669)
PROFIRE INC
9621 S Dixie Hwy (33156-2804)
PHONE................................305 665-5313
David Zisman, *President*
Laura Zisman, *Corp Secy*
Jonathon Zisman, *Vice Pres*
EMP: 10 **EST:** 1994
SALES (est): 934.5K **Privately Held**
SIC: 3631 5046 Barbecues, grills & braziers (outdoor cooking); commercial equipment

(G-13670)
RSVP SKINNIES INC (PA)
11100 Sw 74th Ct (33156-4518)
PHONE................................786 853-8032
Mario Del Valle, *CEO*
EMP: 6 **EST:** 2015
SALES (est): 1.5MM **Privately Held**
WEB: www.rsvpskinnies.com
SIC: 2087 Powders, drink

▲ = Import ▼ =Export
◆ =Import/Export

Pinellas Park
Pinellas County

(G-13671)
ALL METALS CUSTOM INC
7200 59th St N (33781-4247)
PHONE...................................727 709-4297
Waylon Smith, *Principal*
EMP: 7 **EST:** 2010
SALES (est): 191.4K **Privately Held**
WEB: www.allmetalscustom.com
SIC: 3499 Fabricated metal products

(G-13672)
BAJU PROFESSIONAL BRICK PAVERS
5511 110th Ave N (33782-2234)
PHONE...................................727 234-5300
Daniele B Becil, *Director*
EMP: 8 **EST:** 2005
SALES (est): 153K **Privately Held**
SIC: 3531 Pavers

(G-13673)
BIGORRE AEROSPACE CORP
6295 42nd St N (33781-6041)
PHONE...................................727 525-8115
Fred Ladjimi, *President*
Eric Ladjimi, *Treasurer*
EMP: 11 **EST:** 1987
SQ FT: 2,475
SALES (est): 949.9K **Privately Held**
WEB: www.bigorreaerospace.com
SIC: 3728 Aircraft parts & equipment

(G-13674)
CARSON INNOVATION INC
46th St N (33781)
PHONE...................................727 348-0000
Kristopher N Nelson, *Director*
Justin T Carmack, *Director*
EMP: 8 **EST:** 2015
SALES (est): 84.4K **Privately Held**
SIC: 3324 Aerospace investment castings, ferrous

(G-13675)
CIRCUIT WORKS CO
6405 49th St N Ste B (33781-5764)
PHONE...................................727 544-5336
Jay Finehout, *Owner*
EMP: 6 **EST:** 1986
SQ FT: 2,500
SALES (est): 489.2K **Privately Held**
WEB: www.circuitworks1.com
SIC: 3672 Printed circuit boards

(G-13676)
CJ PUBLISHERS INC
4940 72nd Ave N Ste 200 (33781-4400)
PHONE...................................727 521-6277
Chuck Wray, *President*
EMP: 15 **EST:** 1989
SQ FT: 7,392
SALES (est): 2.6MM **Privately Held**
SIC: 2721 2741 Magazines: publishing only, not printed on site; miscellaneous publishing

(G-13677)
COMTEN INDUSTRIES INC
6405 49th St N Ste A (33781-5764)
PHONE...................................727 520-1200
EMP: 7 **EST:** 2019
SALES (est): 1MM **Privately Held**
SIC: 3829 Measuring & controlling devices

(G-13678)
CUSTOM GRAFIX INDUSTRIES INC
Also Called: Aerial Flags
5639 70th Ave N (33781-4237)
PHONE...................................727 530-7300
Stephen C Foster, *President*
EMP: 6 **EST:** 1972
SALES (est): 738.9K **Privately Held**
WEB: www.customgrafixindustries.com
SIC: 2396 Automotive & apparel trimmings

(G-13679)
CUSTOM METAL SPECIALTIES INC
3921 69th Ave N (33781-6146)
P.O. Box 2772 (33780-2772)
PHONE...................................727 522-3986
Curt Schlager, *President*
▲ **EMP:** 28 **EST:** 1989
SQ FT: 3,500
SALES (est): 1.4MM **Privately Held**
WEB: www.custommetalspecialtiesinc.com
SIC: 3446 3444 3441 Stairs, fire escapes, balconies, railings & ladders; ornamental metalwork; sheet metalwork; fabricated structural metal

(G-13680)
CUSTOM MFG & ENGRG INC
Also Called: C M E
3845 Gateway Centre Blvd # 360 (33782-6132)
PHONE...................................727 548-0522
Nancy P Crews, *President*
Edward Dembecki, *Mfg Staff*
Khoa Vu, *Engineer*
Silva Rick, *Senior Engr*
Patricia De Almeida, *Bookkeeper*
EMP: 65 **EST:** 1996
SQ FT: 40,000
SALES (est): 15.3MM **Privately Held**
WEB: www.custom-mfg-eng.com
SIC: 3699 8711 3679 3499 Electrical equipment & supplies; engineering services; electronic circuits; fire- or burglary-resistive products

(G-13681)
DALIMAR CORP
6295 42nd St N (33781-6041)
PHONE...................................727 525-8115
Eric Ladjimi, *President*
EMP: 8 **EST:** 2005
SQ FT: 9,750
SALES (est): 110.7K **Privately Held**
SIC: 3728 Aircraft parts & equipment

(G-13682)
DOMREY CIGAR LTD COMPANY
3001 Gateway Ctr Pkwy N (33782-6124)
PHONE...................................941 360-8200
Michael Chiusno, *President*
◆ **EMP:** 5 **EST:** 2000
SALES (est): 526.5K **Privately Held**
SIC: 2121 Cigars

(G-13683)
ELECTRIC MOTORS LIFT STN SVCS
4480 126th Ave N (33782)
PHONE...................................727 538-4778
EMP: 7 **EST:** 1988
SQ FT: 6,000
SALES (est): 802.5K **Privately Held**
SIC: 7694 Rebuilding motors, except automotive; hermetics repair

(G-13684)
ELSEVIER INC
8808 57th St N (33782-5069)
PHONE...................................813 579-3866
Olivier Dumon, *Research*
Corey Harper, *Research*
Kevin Moore, *Research*
Tom Reller, *Branch Mgr*
Christopher Tancock, *Author*
EMP: 17
SALES (corp-wide): 9.6B **Privately Held**
WEB: www.elsevier.com
SIC: 2741 Miscellaneous publishing
HQ: Elsevier Inc.
230 Park Ave Fl 8
New York NY 10169
212 989-5800

(G-13685)
ENERSYS ADVANCED SYSTEMS INC
5430 70th Ave N (33781-4228)
PHONE...................................610 208-1934
Mike Kulesky, *General Mgr*
Nicole Buchan, *Associate*
EMP: 87
SQ FT: 72,500
SALES (corp-wide): 3.3B **Publicly Held**
SIC: 3691 Storage batteries

HQ: Enersys Advanced Systems Inc.
104 Rock Rd
Horsham PA 19044

(G-13686)
ES MANUFACTURING INC
4590 62nd Ave N (33781-5906)
P.O. Box 11692, Saint Petersburg (33733-1692)
PHONE...................................727 323-4040
Thomas D Elder, *CEO*
▲ **EMP:** 16 **EST:** 1973
SQ FT: 10,000
SALES (est): 1.8MM **Privately Held**
WEB: www.esmfg.com
SIC: 3423 3546 Hand & edge tools; power-driven handtools

(G-13687)
FORCELEADER INC
Also Called: Bioseb
6405 49th St N Ste A (33781-5764)
PHONE...................................727 521-1808
Mary Desevre, *President*
Mireille Desevre, *President*
▼ **EMP:** 9 **EST:** 2008
SQ FT: 30,000
SALES (est): 836.4K **Privately Held**
SIC: 3829 3495 Measuring & controlling devices; clock springs, precision

(G-13688)
FOREMOST CHEMICALS INC
6543 46th St N Ste 1102 (33781-5957)
P.O. Box 21306, Saint Petersburg (33742-1306)
PHONE...................................727 522-8518
EMP: 5 **EST:** 1964
SALES (est): 410K **Privately Held**
SIC: 2841 Detergents, synthetic organic or inorganic alkaline

(G-13689)
FRONTIER READY MIX INC
8311 63rd Way N (33781-1235)
PHONE...................................727 544-1000
Edwin L Shearer Jr, *Principal*
EMP: 14 **EST:** 2006
SALES (est): 1MM **Privately Held**
WEB: www.frontierreadymix.com
SIC: 3273 Ready-mixed concrete

(G-13690)
GLOBAL DIVERSIFIED PRODUCTS
Also Called: Hook International
5195 102nd Ave N (33782-3502)
P.O. Box 17822, Clearwater (33762-0822)
PHONE...................................727 209-0854
Kamal S Juneja, *President*
Dwight Moody, *Finance*
▲ **EMP:** 36 **EST:** 1993
SQ FT: 30,000
SALES (est): 3.4MM **Privately Held**
WEB: www.globaldiversifiedproducts.com
SIC: 3291 2992 2899 3425 Wheels, grinding: artificial; lubricating oils & greases; antifreeze compounds; saw blades & handsaws; business consulting

(G-13691)
H&S SWANSON FMLY HOLDINGS INC (HQ)
9000 68th St N (33782-4401)
PHONE...................................727 541-3575
James H Swanson, *President*
Ronald Hiley, *Vice Pres*
Dave Weaver, *Plant Mgr*
Joe Minarik, *Mfg Staff*
Edmund Bajorek, *Engineer*
EMP: 80 **EST:** 1951
SQ FT: 58,000
SALES (est): 14.1MM
SALES (corp-wide): 99.4MM **Privately Held**
WEB: www.hsswansons.com
SIC: 3599 Machine shop, jobbing & repair

(G-13692)
H2R CORP (PA)
3921 76th Ave N (33781-3610)
PHONE...................................727 541-3444
Daniel Hart, *CEO*
Jeremiah Curry, *Engineer*
Thai Nguyen, *Engineer*
Ricardo Ruiz, *Department Mgr*

Tom Carney, *Manager*
EMP: 13 **EST:** 2016
SQ FT: 9,800
SALES (est): 3.1MM **Privately Held**
WEB: www.h2rcorp.com
SIC: 1481 1781 1794 8711 Mine exploration, nonmetallic minerals; water well drilling; excavation work; engineering services; testing laboratories

(G-13693)
HIS CABINETRY INC
Also Called: His
6200 49th St N (33781-5718)
PHONE...................................727 527-7262
Quynh Tran, *President*
Skip Fritz, *General Mgr*
Randy Harrison, *Design Engr*
Kathie Hill, *Bookkeeper*
Jeffrey Macdonald, *Director*
EMP: 80 **EST:** 1995
SQ FT: 1,700
SALES (est): 18MM **Privately Held**
WEB: www.hiscabinetry.com
SIC: 2434 Wood kitchen cabinets

(G-13694)
INTERIOR VIEWS INC
5625 70th Ave N (33781-4237)
PHONE...................................727 527-8899
Cat Donovan, *President*
EMP: 5 **EST:** 1981
SQ FT: 2,000
SALES (est): 348.3K **Privately Held**
SIC: 2211 Draperies & drapery fabrics, cotton

(G-13695)
INVACARE CORPORATION
Also Called: Top End
4457 63rd Cir N (33781-5981)
PHONE...................................800 532-8677
Jeremy Petty, *Sales Staff*
EMP: 8
SALES (corp-wide): 872.4MM **Publicly Held**
WEB: global.invacare.com
SIC: 3842 Surgical appliances & supplies
PA: Invacare Corporation
1 Invacare Way
Elyria OH 44035
440 329-6000

(G-13696)
INVACARE CORPORATION
Also Called: Top End Wheelchair Sports
4501 63rd Cir N (33781-5914)
PHONE...................................727 522-8677
Jeremy Petty, *Sales Staff*
Al Crisp, *Branch Mgr*
EMP: 11
SALES (corp-wide): 872.4MM **Publicly Held**
WEB: global.invacare.com
SIC: 3842 Wheelchairs
PA: Invacare Corporation
1 Invacare Way
Elyria OH 44035
440 329-6000

(G-13697)
JACE FABRICATION INC
9930 62nd St N (33782-3125)
PHONE...................................727 547-6873
John S Wallace Jr, *Principal*
EMP: 8 **EST:** 2008
SALES (est): 122K **Privately Held**
SIC: 3446 Architectural metalwork

(G-13698)
JSP MANUFACTURING HOLDINGS LLC
6203 80th Ave N (33781-2204)
PHONE...................................727 488-5353
Rocco Braccio, *President*
EMP: 8 **EST:** 2018
SALES (est): 975K **Privately Held**
WEB: www.jspmanufacturing.com
SIC: 3999 Manufacturing industries

(G-13699)
KLING FABRICATION INC
6563 46th St N Ste 705 (33781-5926)
PHONE...................................727 321-7233
Laura L Klingensmith, *Principal*
EMP: 8 **EST:** 2019

SALES (est): 845.7K **Privately Held**
WEB: www.klingfabrication.com
SIC: 3444 Sheet metalwork

(G-13700)
KORAL MANUFACTURING INC
8720 66th Ct N (33782-4557)
PHONE.....................727 548-5040
Marla Barkoviak, *President*
EMP: 6 **EST:** 1995
SQ FT: 7,200
SALES (est): 778.8K **Privately Held**
WEB: www.koralmfg.com
SIC: 3599 Machine shop, jobbing & repair

(G-13701)
KORAL PRECISION LLC
8720 66th Ct N (33782-4557)
PHONE.....................727 548-5040
Kimberly Nagulpelli, *Exec Dir*
EMP: 10 **EST:** 2020
SALES (est): 703.4K **Privately Held**
SIC: 3599 Machine & other job shop work

(G-13702)
KWIKIE DUP CTR PINELLAS PK INC
Also Called: Kwikie Printing
8520 49th St N (33781-1554)
PHONE.....................727 544-7788
Charles Kemp, *President*
Patty Hall, *Vice Pres*
Jackie Kemp, *Treasurer*
EMP: 5 **EST:** 1973
SQ FT: 3,000
SALES (est): 486.2K **Privately Held**
SIC: 2752 7389 Commercial printing, off-set; printing broker

(G-13703)
LA ZERO INC
8100 Park Blvd N Ste 41 (33781-3778)
PHONE.....................727 545-1175
Lee Aust, *President*
Ann Aust, *Vice Pres*
EMP: 5 **EST:** 1996
SALES (est): 998.1K **Privately Held**
WEB: www.lazero.org
SIC: 3599 Custom machinery

(G-13704)
LAPURE WATER PRODUCTS INC
6330 46th St N Ste 112 (33781-5970)
P.O. Box 8773, Madeira Beach (33738-8773)
PHONE.....................727 521-3993
Robert Papolos, *President*
Linda Papolos, *Corp Secy*
EMP: 7 **EST:** 1992
SQ FT: 3,500
SALES (est): 303.8K **Privately Held**
SIC: 3589 4941 Water purification equipment, household type; water supply

(G-13705)
LIBERTY WOODWORKING INC
6563 46th St N Ste 702 (33781-5926)
PHONE.....................727 642-9652
William Francis Dunn, *Principal*
William Dunn, *Sales Staff*
EMP: 9 **EST:** 2008
SALES (est): 523.9K **Privately Held**
WEB: www.libertywoodworking.com
SIC: 2431 Millwork

(G-13706)
LOCKHEED MARTIN CORPORATION
Also Called: Lockheed Martin Aeronautics
9300 28th St N Ste A (33782-6122)
PHONE.....................727 578-6940
Nancy King, *Engineer*
Steve Cobb, *Manager*
Lindsay Muth, *Director*
Beth Ferguson, *Director*
EMP: 150 **Publicly Held**
WEB: www.lockheedmartin.com
SIC: 3812 Search & navigation equipment
PA: Lockheed Martin Corporation
6801 Rockledge Dr
Bethesda MD 20817

(G-13707)
MADICO INC (DH)
9251 Belcher Rd N Ste A (33782-4203)
PHONE.....................727 327-2544
Shawn Kitchell, *CEO*
Melanie Kuklis, *Vice Pres*
Lisa Castellana, *Purchasing*
Michael Vegas, *Engineer*
Loren Rideout, *Project Engr*
◆ **EMP:** 100 **EST:** 1903
SQ FT: 122,000
SALES (est): 54.6MM **Privately Held**
WEB: www.madico.com
SIC: 3081 2295 Unsupported plastics film & sheet; laminating of fabrics; metallizing of fabrics

(G-13708)
MILL-RITE WOODWORKING CO INC
6401 47th St N (33781-5917)
PHONE.....................727 527-7808
Jennifer Clark, *President*
Robert Clark, *Vice Pres*
EMP: 54 **EST:** 1966
SQ FT: 54,000
SALES (est): 8.5MM **Privately Held**
WEB: www.mill-rite.com
SIC: 2431 Doors, wood

(G-13709)
MINUTEMAN PRESS
9600 66th St N Ste A (33782-4540)
PHONE.....................727 214-2275
EMP: 7 **EST:** 2017
SALES (est): 83.9K **Privately Held**
WEB: www.minutemanpress.com
SIC: 2752 Commercial printing, litho-graphic

(G-13710)
MODERN SILICONE TECH INC
10601 Us Highway 19 N (33782-3426)
PHONE.....................727 873-1805
Paul Capek, *Warehouse Mgr*
Jerry Robinson, *Purch Mgr*
Michelle Wasielewski, *Controller*
Rachel Grunfeld, *Branch Mgr*
David Singer, *Director*
EMP: 130 **Privately Held**
WEB: www.modernsilicone.com
SIC: 3053 3061 2822 Gaskets, packing & sealing devices; mechanical rubber goods; synthetic rubber
PA: Modern Silicone Technologies, Inc.
101 Schelter Rd Ste 102b
Lincolnshire IL 60069

(G-13711)
MOLEX LLC
Also Called: Molex Tampa Bay Operations
4650 62nd Ave N (33781-5944)
PHONE.....................727 521-2700
John Rochford, *Plt & Fclts Mgr*
Chip Walsh, *Manager*
EMP: 14
SALES (corp-wide): 36.9B **Privately Held**
WEB: www.molex.com
SIC: 3678 3679 3643 3357 Electronic connectors; electronic switches; elec-tronic circuits; connectors & terminals for electrical devices; communication wire; fiber optic cable (insulated)
HQ: Molex, Llc
2222 Wellington Ct
Lisle IL 60532
630 969-4550

(G-13712)
NAIA BRICK PAVERS INC
8216 43rd Way N (33781-1631)
PHONE.....................727 638-4734
Weslley Dasilva, *Principal*
EMP: 8 **EST:** 2010
SALES (est): 151.4K **Privately Held**
SIC: 3531 Pavers

(G-13713)
NBS PRFORMANCE FABRICATION INC
5649 70th Ave N (33781-4237)
PHONE.....................727 541-1833
David A Stephens, *President*
EMP: 7 **EST:** 2001

SALES (est): 15K **Privately Held**
SIC: 3999 Manufacturing industries

(G-13714)
NOVAK MACHINING INC
3921 69th Ave N (33781-6146)
PHONE.....................727 527-5473
Mark Novak, *President*
EMP: 5 **EST:** 1990
SQ FT: 3,500
SALES (est): 503K **Privately Held**
WEB: www.novakmachininginc.com
SIC: 3535 3599 Conveyors & conveying equipment; machine & other job shop work

(G-13715)
OCTAL VENTURES INC
Also Called: Sunrise Yacht Products
6544 44th St N Ste 1205 (33781-5936)
PHONE.....................727 526-9288
Matthew Brunnig, *President*
◆ **EMP:** 11 **EST:** 2018
SQ FT: 7,500
SALES (est): 950K **Privately Held**
SIC: 3496 3089 Netting, woven wire; made from purchased wire; synthetic resin finished products

(G-13716)
ORANGE STATE STEEL CNSTR INC
6201 80th Ave N (33781-2204)
PHONE.....................727 544-3398
Rex Joyner, *President*
Chris Powell, *Vice Pres*
Joel Powell, *Vice Pres*
Pam McGeorge, *Admin Sec*
EMP: 21 **EST:** 1965
SQ FT: 18,000
SALES (est): 2.5MM **Privately Held**
WEB: www.orangestatesteel.com
SIC: 3441 1791 Fabricated structural metal; precast concrete structural framing or panels, placing of

(G-13717)
PERFECT COPY & PRINT INC
6541 44th St N Ste 6002 (33781-5937)
PHONE.....................727 743-0913
Jane L Byers, *President*
EMP: 8 **EST:** 2014
SALES (est): 258.6K **Privately Held**
WEB: www.pcpstpete.com
SIC: 2752 Commercial printing, offset

(G-13718)
PHARMACY AUTOMTN SYSTEMS LLC
8790 66th Ct N (33782-4557)
PHONE.....................727 544-6522
Norm Knoth, *Managing Dir*
EMP: 7 **EST:** 2010
SALES (est): 141.8K **Privately Held**
WEB:
www.pharmacyautomationsystems.com
SIC: 3559 Pharmaceutical machinery

(G-13719)
PLATINUM MFG INTL INC
10166 66th St N (33782-3015)
PHONE.....................727 544-4555
Steve Miller, *Principal*
Alex Lashchou, *Opers Staff*
EMP: 11 **EST:** 2010
SALES (est): 266.2K **Privately Held**
SIC: 3999 Manufacturing industries

(G-13720)
POLYPACK INC (PA)
3301 Gateway Ctr Blvd N (33782-6108)
PHONE.....................727 578-5000
Alain A Cerf, *President*
Jacqueline Cerf, *Corp Secy*
Emmanuel Cerf, *Vice Pres*
Olivier Cerf, *Vice Pres*
Cindy Herbeck, *Opers Mgr*
◆ **EMP:** 90 **EST:** 1973
SQ FT: 43,000
SALES (est): 16.4MM **Privately Held**
WEB: www.polypack.com
SIC: 3565 Wrapping machines

(G-13721)
POLYPACK LIMITED PARTNERSHIP
3301 Gateway Ctr Blvd N (33782-6108)
PHONE.....................727 578-5000
Alain A Cerf, *Managing Prtnr*
Stefan Cerf, *Partner*
Olivier Cerf, *VP Opers*
Arturo Davila, *Prdtn Mgr*
Kurt Spears, *Engineer*
EMP: 26 **EST:** 1994
SQ FT: 43,000
SALES (est): 1.7MM **Privately Held**
WEB: www.polypack.com
SIC: 3565 Packaging machinery

(G-13722)
PRESTIGE SPAS INC
Also Called: Prestige Spa Covers
2875 Mci Dr N (33781-6105)
PHONE.....................727 576-8600
Wesley J Wiley, *President*
David Duszynski, *Production*
◆ **EMP:** 75 **EST:** 1989
SQ FT: 50,000
SALES (est): 15.7MM **Privately Held**
WEB: www.prestigespacovers.com
SIC: 3999 Hot tub & spa covers

(G-13723)
PRISTINE ENVIRONMENT LLC
6575 80th Ave N (33781-2136)
PHONE.....................727 541-5748
Kevin Pawlowski, *Mng Member*
EMP: 15 **EST:** 2006
SALES (est): 1.4MM **Privately Held**
SIC: 3589 Water purification equipment, household type

(G-13724)
PROCESS AUTOMATION CORPORATION
Also Called: Pac Printing
5260 87th Ave N (33782-5138)
PHONE.....................727 541-6280
Robert Trope, *President*
John Trope, *Vice Pres*
EMP: 7 **EST:** 1983
SQ FT: 3,200
SALES (est): 950K **Privately Held**
WEB: www.magpac.com
SIC: 3993 Advertising novelties

(G-13725)
PROMED BIOSCIENCES INC
9375 Us Highway 19 N A (33782-5420)
PHONE.....................888 655-9155
Olga Krynina, *Ch of Bd*
EMP: 10 **EST:** 2019
SALES (est): 1,000K **Privately Held**
SIC: 3999

(G-13726)
R S DESIGN INC
6351 46th St N (33781-5921)
PHONE.....................727 525-8292
Richard Smith, *President*
Amy Mensch, *CIO*
EMP: 10 **EST:** 1992
SQ FT: 3,200
SALES (est): 1.9MM **Privately Held**
WEB: www.rsdesigninc.com
SIC: 3089 Injection molding of plastics

(G-13727)
ROCK N ROLL CUSTOM SCREENED S
Also Called: Native Sun Sports
4590 62nd Ave N (33781-5906)
P.O. Box 40085, Saint Petersburg (33743-0085)
PHONE.....................727 528-2111
George A Mitcheson, *President*
George Mitcheson, *Administration*
▲ **EMP:** 5 **EST:** 1973
SQ FT: 25,000
SALES (est): 484.9K **Privately Held**
SIC: 2261 5136 5699 Screen printing of cotton broadwoven fabrics; sportswear, men's & boys'; sports apparel

(G-13728)
S N S AUTO SPORTS LLC
7061 49th St N (33781-4402)
PHONE.....................727 546-2700

Brian Grondin, *Principal*
EMP: 7 **EST:** 2012
SALES (est): 263.5K **Privately Held**
WEB: www.snsautosports.com
SIC: 3011 3493 3651 Tires & inner tubes;
automobile springs; household audio &
video equipment

(G-13729)
SHEET METAL SYSTEMS INC
6482 Park Blvd N Ste A (33781-3141)
PHONE................................727 548-1711
Raul Perera, *President*
Christine Perera, *Vice Pres*
EMP: 10 **EST:** 2001
SQ FT: 250
SALES (est): 607.6K **Privately Held**
WEB: www.superiormechanical.net
SIC: 3441 Fabricated structural metal

(G-13730)
**SUNRISE TRAMPOLINES AND
NETS**
Also Called: Sunrise Yacht Products
6544 44th St N Ste 1205 (33781-5936)
PHONE................................727 526-9288
Richard Leng, *President*
Eliose Leng, *Admin Sec*
◆ **EMP:** 8 **EST:** 1987
SQ FT: 5,000
SALES (est): 585K **Privately Held**
WEB: www.multihullnets.com
SIC: 3949 Trampolines & equipment

(G-13731)
TOM SWEET
6310 103rd Ave N (33782-2437)
PHONE................................727 515-9015
Tom Sweet, *Principal*
EMP: 6 **EST:** 2010
SALES (est): 323.8K **Privately Held**
WEB: www.tomsdigitalelectronics.com
SIC: 3545 Gauges (machine tool acces-
sories)

(G-13732)
TRANSITIONS OPTICAL INC
Also Called: Transitions Lenses
9251 Belcher Rd N Ste B (33782-4201)
P.O. Box 700 (33780-0700)
PHONE................................727 545-0400
Paddy McDermott, *President*
Miriam Bermudo, *Editor*
Noel Gotangogan, *Editor*
Isabelle Dekker, *Business Mgr*
Blesila Telebangco, *Vice Pres*
▲ **EMP:** 500 **EST:** 1990
SQ FT: 150,000
SALES (est): 89.3MM
SALES (corp-wide): 1.7MM **Privately
Held**
SIC: 3229 3851 Ophthalmic glass, except
flat; lenses, ophthalmic
PA: Essilorluxottica
147 Rue De Paris
Charenton Le Pont 94220
149 774-224

(G-13733)
VIN-DOTCO INC
2875 Mci Dr N Unit B (33782-6105)
PHONE................................727 217-9200
John Dotolo, *President*
EMP: 10 **EST:** 1975
SQ FT: 30,000
SALES (est): 1.4MM **Privately Held**
SIC: 2842 Cleaning or polishing prepara-
tions

Placida
Charlotte County

(G-13734)
COLONIAL READY MIX LLC
5250 Linwood Rd (33946-5137)
PHONE................................941 698-4022
Victor G Mellor, *Mng Member*
▲ **EMP:** 7 **EST:** 2007
SALES (est): 133.6K **Privately Held**
SIC: 3273 Ready-mixed concrete

(G-13735)
**LEMON BAY TRUSS & SUPPLY
CO**
5300 Linwood Rd (33946-5138)
PHONE................................941 698-0800
Mike Vermeulen, *President*
Allen Triebe, *Vice Pres*
Jane Keim, *Admin Sec*
EMP: 9 **EST:** 1992
SQ FT: 1,200
SALES (est): 140.1K **Privately Held**
SIC: 2439 Trusses, wooden roof

Plant City
Hillsborough County

(G-13736)
AMAYA SOLUTIONS INC (PA)
Also Called: American Water Chemicals
1802 Corporate Center Ln (33563-7162)
PHONE................................813 246-5448
Mohannad Almalki, *President*
Rudy Canezo, *Treasurer*
EMP: 29 **EST:** 2019
SALES (est): 2.5MM **Privately Held**
SIC: 2899 Chemical preparations

(G-13737)
**AMERICAN ENGINEERING SVCS
INC (PA)**
Also Called: AES
1802 Corporate Center Ln (33563-7162)
PHONE................................813 621-3932
MO Malki, *President*
Rudy Zaneco, *Controller*
Ana Padgett, *Sales Engr*
▲ **EMP:** 7 **EST:** 1985
SQ FT: 23,800
SALES (est): 6.7MM **Privately Held**
WEB: www.aesh2o.com
SIC: 3589 1629 Sewage treatment equip-
ment; water treatment equipment, indus-
trial; waste water & sewage treatment
plant construction

(G-13738)
**AMERICAN WATER CHEMICALS
INC**
Also Called: A W C
1802 Corporate Center Ln (33563-7162)
PHONE................................813 246-5448
Mohannad Malki, *CEO*
Mohannad Almalki, *President*
Tarek Elshafie, *Vice Pres*
Irvin Veras, *Engineer*
Rudy Canezo, *Treasurer*
◆ **EMP:** 14 **EST:** 1993
SQ FT: 5,000
SALES (est): 6.7MM **Privately Held**
WEB: www.membranechemicals.com
SIC: 2899 Water treating compounds
PA: American Engineering Services, Incor-
porated
1802 Corporate Center Ln
Plant City FL 33563
813 621-3932

(G-13739)
ANUVIA PLANT CITY LLC
660 E County Line Rd (33565)
PHONE................................407 719-7798
Amy Yoder, *Mng Member*
EMP: 18 **EST:** 2019
SALES (est): 10.2MM **Privately Held**
WEB: www.anuviaplantnutrients.com
SIC: 2873 Fertilizers: natural (organic), ex-
cept compost

(G-13740)
ARMOR PRODUCTS MFG INC
2610 Airport Rd (33563-1143)
PHONE................................813 764-8844
David Carmichael, *President*
Jackie Carmichael, *Corp Secy*
◆ **EMP:** 10 **EST:** 2007
SQ FT: 10,000
SALES (est): 737.7K **Privately Held**
WEB: www.armorbags.com
SIC: 2392 2393 Laundry, garment & stor-
age bags; canvas bags; duffle bags, can-
vas: made from purchased materials;
bags & containers, except sleeping bags:
textile

(G-13741)
ATCO RUBBER PRODUCTS INC
2407 Police Center Dr (33566-7173)
PHONE................................813 754-6678
William Garrow, *Branch Mgr*
EMP: 57 **Publicly Held**
WEB: www.atcoflex.com
SIC: 3564 Air cleaning systems
HQ: Atco Rubber Products, Inc.
7101 Atco Dr
Fort Worth TX 76118
817 595-2894

(G-13742)
B & M INDUSTRIES INC
Also Called: Bodolay Packaging Machine Div
2401 Airport Rd Unit C (33563-1113)
PHONE................................813 754-9960
Mostafa Farid, *President*
Bill Jeffery, *Sales Mgr*
Gretchen Farid, *Office Mgr*
Farid Bijan, *Officer*
EMP: 7 **EST:** 1988
SQ FT: 7,500
SALES (est): 1.2MM **Privately Held**
WEB: www.bodolaypackaging.com
SIC: 3565 Packaging machinery

(G-13743)
**B & N WLDG & FABRICATION
INC**
4200 National Guard Dr (33563-1156)
P.O. Box 4767 (33563-0031)
PHONE................................813 719-3956
Amanda L Bell, *President*
Jamie Bell, *Vice Pres*
Amanda Bell, *Director*
EMP: 30 **EST:** 1999
SQ FT: 1,600
SALES (est): 4.3MM **Privately Held**
WEB: www.bnwelding.com
SIC: 7692 Welding repair

(G-13744)
**BANKS AIRCONDITIONING &
RFRGN**
5001 Miley Rd (33565-3805)
PHONE................................813 917-8685
Jeff Banks, *President*
Jeannie Banks, *Vice Pres*
EMP: 5 **EST:** 2001
SALES (est): 361.8K **Privately Held**
SIC: 3585 Refrigeration equipment, com-
plete

(G-13745)
BAY AREA SIGNS INC
3858 E Knights Griffin Rd (33565-2206)
PHONE................................813 677-0237
Ed M Martin, *President*
Pat Martin, *Vice Pres*
EMP: 10 **EST:** 2003
SQ FT: 5,000
SALES (est): 852.6K **Privately Held**
SIC: 3993 Displays & cutouts, window &
lobby; electric signs

(G-13746)
BE WHOLE NUTRITION LLC
5840 Highway 60 E (33567-1759)
PHONE................................813 420-3057
Sean Gill, *Mng Member*
John Gill,
EMP: 8 **EST:** 2014
SALES (est): 340K **Privately Held**
SIC: 2834 5122 Vitamin preparations; vita-
mins & minerals

(G-13747)
**BULK MANUFACTURING
FLORIDA INC**
3106 Central Dr (33566-1159)
PHONE................................813 757-2313
Thomas Wawrzyniakowski, *President*
Michael Warczytowa, *Vice Pres*
▼ **EMP:** 15 **EST:** 2000
SQ FT: 32,000
SALES (est): 3.3MM **Privately Held**
WEB: www.bmfla.com
SIC: 3713 Tank truck bodies

(G-13748)
BULK RESOURCES INC (PA)
1507 S Alexander St # 102 (33563-8413)
P.O. Box 3296 (33563-0005)
PHONE................................813 764-8420
Terry Taylor, *President*
Sherri Alexander, *Admin Sec*
▼ **EMP:** 4 **EST:** 2002
SALES (est): 4.5MM **Privately Held**
WEB: www.bulkresources.biz
SIC: 3523 6159 Trailers & wagons, farm;
finance leasing, vehicles: except automo-
biles & trucks

(G-13749)
C & C SERVICES OF TAMPA INC
Also Called: Honeywell Authorized Dealer
1007 Robinson Rd (33563-1150)
P.O. Box 47988, Tampa (33646-0117)
PHONE................................813 477-8559
John F Carlucci, *President*
Alan Carter, *Vice Pres*
EMP: 6 **EST:** 2004
SQ FT: 1,300
SALES (est): 1.7MM **Privately Held**
WEB: www.ccservicesoftampainc.com
SIC: 3822 Air conditioning & refrigeration
controls

(G-13750)
CANOPY SPECIALIST LLC
3301 State Road 574 (33563-4522)
P.O. Box 5224 (33563-0040)
PHONE................................813 703-6844
Jerry A Jaeger, *Mng Member*
EMP: 10 **EST:** 2012
SALES (est): 548.3K **Privately Held**
WEB: www.canopyspecialist.com
SIC: 2394 Canvas awnings & canopies

(G-13751)
CAS INDUSTRIES LLC
2914 Appling Woods Pl (33565-5647)
PHONE................................813 986-2694
Curtis Devane, *Principal*
EMP: 7 **EST:** 2017
SALES (est): 261.6K **Privately Held**
SIC: 3999 Manufacturing industries

(G-13752)
**CATAMOUNT MACHINE WORKS
LLC**
2804 Sydney Rd (33566-1173)
PHONE................................813 659-0505
Chris Basgall, *Mng Member*
EMP: 12 **EST:** 2020
SALES (est): 574K **Privately Held**
SIC: 3599 Machine shop, jobbing & repair

(G-13753)
CF INDUSTRIES INC
10608 Paul Buchman Hwy (33565)
P.O. Box L (33564)
PHONE................................813 782-1591
Herschelle E Morris, *General Mgr*
EMP: 59 **Publicly Held**
WEB: www.cfindustries.com
SIC: 2874 2875 Phosphatic fertilizers; fer-
tilizers, mixing only
HQ: Cf Industries, Inc.
4 Parkway North Blvd # 400
Deerfield IL 60015
847 405-2400

(G-13754)
**CHARLES MACHINE WORKS
INC**
Also Called: Ditch Central & South Florida
506 E Park Rd (33563-6998)
PHONE................................813 704-4865
Kent Stevenson, *General Mgr*
EMP: 15
SALES (corp-wide): 3.9B **Publicly Held**
WEB: www.ditchwitch.com
SIC: 3531 Construction machinery
HQ: The Charles Machine Works Inc
1959 W Fir St
Perry OK 73077
580 572-2693

(G-13755)
CHEMICAL DYNAMICS INC
4206 Business Ln (33566-1163)
P.O. Box 486 (33564-0486)
PHONE................................813 752-4950

Webster Carson, *Ch of Bd*
David Carson, *President*
Hayley Pena, *Buyer*
Betty Carson, *Treasurer*
Jason Britt, *Controller*
◆ **EMP:** 31 **EST:** 1973
SQ FT: 18,000
SALES (est): 7.8MM **Privately Held**
WEB: www.chemicaldynamics.com
SIC: 2875 5191 Fertilizers, mixing only; chemicals, agricultural

(G-13756)
COMMERCIAL CONCRETE PDTS INC
2705 Sammonds Rd (33563-4556)
PHONE....................813 659-3707
James L Byrd Jr, *President*
Mark Baker, *Vice Pres*
Kevin Houston, *Foreman/Supr*
Jimmy Byrd, *CFO*
Terri Linton, *Accountant*
EMP: 45 **EST:** 1983
SQ FT: 7,585
SALES (est): 8.9MM **Privately Held**
WEB:
www.commercialconcreteproducts.com
SIC: 3272 5211 Concrete products, pre-cast; concrete & cinder block

(G-13757)
CORONET INDUSTRIES INC
4082 Coronet Rd (33566-4004)
PHONE....................813 752-1161
David K Denner, *CEO*
Chris T Burgess, *Vice Pres*
Sudo Hideo, *Admin Sec*
EMP: 37 **EST:** 1993
SQ FT: 2,000
SALES (est): 9.5MM **Privately Held**
WEB: www.coronetindustries.com
SIC: 2048 Feed supplements
HQ: Onoda Chemical Industry Co., Ltd.
1-15-1, Kaigan
Minato-Ku TKY 105-0

(G-13758)
CUSTOM FABRICATION INC
2604 E Us Highway 92 (33566-7531)
PHONE....................813 754-7571
Jeffrey J Cook, *Director*
Melanie Curtis, *Assistant*
EMP: 30 **EST:** 1994
SQ FT: 33,000
SALES (est): 6.1MM **Privately Held**
WEB: www.customfabsteel.com
SIC: 3441 Fabricated structural metal

(G-13759)
CW21 INC
3404 E Us Highway 92 (33566-7432)
P.O. Box 3748 (33563-0013)
PHONE....................813 754-1760
EMP: 23
SALES (est): 2.4MM **Privately Held**
SIC: 3089 Plastic And Metal Fabrication

(G-13760)
DART CONTAINER COMPANY FLA LLC
4610 Airport Rd (33563-1114)
PHONE....................813 752-1990
Robert C Dart, *CEO*
EMP: 200 **EST:** 2005
SALES (est): 19MM **Privately Held**
SIC: 3086 3089 Cups & plates, foamed plastic; plastic containers, except foam

(G-13761)
DUKES BREWHOUSE INC
1808 James L Redman Pkwy
(33563-6914)
PHONE....................813 758-9309
Louis Mendel, *Principal*
EMP: 13 **EST:** 2015
SALES (est): 379.4K **Privately Held**
WEB: www.dukesbrewhouse.com
SIC: 2082 Malt beverages

(G-13762)
DUNCO ROCK & GRAVEL INC
Also Called: Dunco Materials
3115 Sammonds Rd (33563-7314)
PHONE....................813 752-5622
Monteen Dunn, *President*
Dan Secor, *Vice Pres*

EMP: 5 **EST:** 1983
SALES (est): 1MM **Privately Held**
WEB: www.duncomaterials.com
SIC: 3273 Ready-mixed concrete

(G-13763)
EL JEFE STUCCO LATH INC
8903 Franklin Rd (33565-3015)
PHONE....................352 399-4837
Jessica M Romero, *Principal*
EMP: 7 **EST:** 2018
SALES (est): 54.1K **Privately Held**
SIC: 3541 Lathes

(G-13764)
EL MIRA SOL INC (PA)
4008 Airport Rd (33563-1108)
PHONE....................813 754-5857
Guillermo Gama, *President*
Raoul Garcia, *General Mgr*
Patircia L Gama, *Vice Pres*
Marisa Cano, *Sales Staff*
Veronica Salinas, *Sales Staff*
EMP: 60 **EST:** 1987
SQ FT: 20,000
SALES (est): 10.4MM **Privately Held**
WEB: www.elmirasolinc.com
SIC: 2096 5141 5411 Tortilla chips; groceries, general line; grocery stores, independent

(G-13765)
FARM CUT LLC
Also Called: Marjon Specialty Foods
3508 Sydney Rd (33566-1185)
PHONE....................813 754-3321
Anthony High, *President*
Lisa Minnes, *Exec VP*
Josh Brittenham, *Office Mgr*
EMP: 180 **EST:** 1972
SQ FT: 21,000
SALES (est): 9MM **Privately Held**
SIC: 2099 2032 2035 5148 Food preparations; canned specialties; seasonings & sauces, except tomato & dry; vegetables, fresh

(G-13766)
FLORIDA BRICK AND CLAY CO INC
1708 Turkey Creek Rd (33566-0056)
P.O. Box 3341 (33563-0006)
PHONE....................813 754-1521
Remy Hermida, *CEO*
Antonio Azorin, *President*
William Dodson, *President*
Tony Azorin, *Safety Dir*
Fay Savage, *Mktg Dir*
◆ **EMP:** 13 **EST:** 1963
SQ FT: 2,000
SALES (est): 908.4K **Privately Held**
WEB: www.floridabrickandclay.com
SIC: 3253 3251 Quarry tile, clay; paving brick, clay

(G-13767)
FLOYD PUBLICATIONS INC
702 W Dr Mrtn Lther King (33563-5119)
PHONE....................813 707-8783
Michael Floyd, *President*
Mike Floyd, *Publisher*
Cierra Craft, *Editor*
Dede Floyd, *Office Mgr*
EMP: 6 **EST:** 2000
SALES (est): 689.1K **Privately Held**
WEB: www.focusplantcity.com
SIC: 2741 Miscellaneous publishing

(G-13768)
FREEWING FLIGHT TECH INC
607 S Alexander St Ste (33563-5053)
PHONE....................813 752-8552
Tom Sash, *President*
EMP: 5 **EST:** 2002
SALES (est): 312.8K **Privately Held**
WEB: www.freewing.net
SIC: 3728 Aircraft parts & equipment

(G-13769)
FRIO DISTRIBUTORS INC
Also Called: Ice Pop Factory
1406 Mercantile Ct (33563-1151)
P.O. Box 3514 (33563-0010)
PHONE....................813 567-1493
Margarita Sanchez, *President*
Ray Sanchez, *General Mgr*

▲ **EMP:** 11 **EST:** 2005
SQ FT: 8,000
SALES (est): 1MM **Privately Held**
WEB: www.icepopfactory.com
SIC: 2024 Juice pops, frozen

(G-13770)
GATSBY SPAS INC
4408 Airport Rd (33563-1112)
PHONE....................813 754-4122
Don Divine, *President*
Roy Jacuzzi, *Chairman*
Brian Mills, *Opers Mgr*
Curtis Falany, *Finance Dir*
Luis Espin, *Data Proc Dir*
EMP: 150 **EST:** 1984
SQ FT: 100,000
SALES (est): 26.1MM
SALES (corp-wide): 362.2K **Privately Held**
SIC: 3088 Hot tubs, plastic or fiberglass
HQ: Jacuzzi Inc.
14525 Monte Vista Ave
Chino CA 91710
909 606-7733

(G-13771)
GERDAU AMERISTEEL US INC
Ameristeel Tmapa Fab Rnfrcing
4006 Paul Buchman Hwy (33565)
P.O. Box 3009 (33563-0001)
PHONE....................813 752-7550
Paul Morin, *Branch Mgr*
Angela Jackson, *Analyst*
EMP: 62
SQ FT: 53,587 **Privately Held**
WEB: www.gerdau.com
SIC: 3449 3441 Miscellaneous metalwork; fabricated structural metal
HQ: Gerdau Ameristeel Us Inc.
4221 W Boy Scout Blvd # 600
Tampa FL 33607
813 286-8383

(G-13772)
GERDAU AMERISTEEL US INC
2100 Joe Mcintosh Rd (33565-7413)
PHONE....................813 752-7550
S Nakamura, *Vice Pres*
EMP: 13 **EST:** 2003
SALES (est): 89.4K **Privately Held**
SIC: 3312 Blast furnaces & steel mills

(G-13773)
GOLDEN ALUMINUM EXTRUSION LLC
1650 Alumax Cir (33566-8461)
PHONE....................330 372-2300
Tom Ploughe, *President*
EMP: 23 **EST:** 1987
SQ FT: 300,000
SALES (est): 1.2MM **Privately Held**
SIC: 3354 Shapes, extruded aluminum

(G-13774)
GREAT WESTERN MALTING CO
Also Called: Country Malt Group
225 S County Line Rd (33566-7301)
PHONE....................360 991-0888
Mike O'Toole, *President*
EMP: 99 **Privately Held**
WEB: www.greatwesternmalting.com
SIC: 2083 Malt
HQ: Great Western Malting Co.
1705 Nw Harborside Dr
Vancouver WA 98660
360 693-3661

(G-13775)
GT GRANDSTANDS INC
2810 Sydney Rd (33566-1173)
PHONE....................813 305-1415
John Oconley, *CEO*
Tom Ennis, *President*
Greg Bucknermgr, *Principal*
Brian Wilson, *Business Mgr*
Ross Rob, *Project Mgr*
EMP: 31 **EST:** 2001
SQ FT: 2,000
SALES (est): 8MM **Privately Held**
WEB: www.gtgrandstands.com
SIC: 2531 Public building & related furniture

(G-13776)
INTERNATIONAL PAPER COMPANY
2402 Police Center Dr (33566-7173)
PHONE....................813 717-9100
Rob Bordeau, *General Mgr*
William G Black, *Sales Mgr*
Linda White, *Manager*
EMP: 70
SALES (corp-wide): 19.3B **Publicly Held**
WEB: www.internationalpaper.com
SIC: 2653 Boxes, corrugated: made from purchased materials
PA: International Paper Company
6400 Poplar Ave
Memphis TN 38197
901 419-7000

(G-13777)
JAMES CALDWELL STUMP GRINDING
1310 Whitehurst Rd (33563-1350)
PHONE....................813 843-1262
James Caldwell, *Principal*
EMP: 7 **EST:** 2005
SALES (est): 134.1K **Privately Held**
SIC: 3599 Grinding castings for the trade

(G-13778)
JAMES HARDIE BUILDING PDTS INC
Also Called: Hardie Pipe
809 S Woodrow Wilson St (33563-4945)
PHONE....................813 478-1758
Wendy Kowalski, *Vice Pres*
Shawn Stevens, *Mfg Staff*
Joe Haslwanter, *Electrical Engi*
Mike Schulte, *Manager*
EMP: 85 **Privately Held**
WEB: www.jameshardie.com
SIC: 3259 Clay sewer & drainage pipe & tile
HQ: James Hardie Building Products Inc.
231 S La Salle St # 2000
Chicago IL 60604
312 291-5072

(G-13779)
JTAC INDUSTRIES LLC
2509 Trkey Creek Rd Ste 1 (33566)
PHONE....................813 928-0628
Joel Jaeb, *CEO*
Joseph Jaeb, *COO*
Stephen Jaeb, *Manager*
EMP: 8 **EST:** 2014
SALES (est): 794.6K **Privately Held**
WEB: www.jtacindustries.com
SIC: 3999 Barber & beauty shop equipment

(G-13780)
KEEL & CURLEY WINERY LLC
5210 Thonotosassa Rd (33565-5700)
PHONE....................813 752-9100
C Joseph I Keel,
EMP: 18 **EST:** 2008
SALES (est): 3.4MM **Privately Held**
WEB: www.keelfarms.com
SIC: 2084 Wines

(G-13781)
KERRY I&F CONTRACTING COMPANY
1111 W Dr Mrtn Lther King (33563-5106)
PHONE....................813 359-5182
EMP: 13 **EST:** 2003
SALES (est): 129.1K **Privately Held**
SIC: 2099 Food preparations

(G-13782)
KERRY INC
Also Called: Kerry Ingredients & Flavours
1111 W Dr Mrtn Lther King (33563-5106)
PHONE....................813 359-5181
Susie Brown, *Branch Mgr*
EMP: 54
SQ FT: 21,270 **Privately Held**
WEB: www.kerry.com
SIC: 2034 2037 Dehydrated fruits, vegetables, soups; frozen fruits & vegetables
HQ: Kerry Inc.
3400 Millington Rd
Beloit WI 53511
608 363-1200

▲ = Import ▼ = Export
◆ = Import/Export

(G-13783)
KONE CRANE MAINTENANCE SVCS
Also Called: K C I Kone Crane
2007 Wood Ct Ste 5 (33563-6343)
PHONE...................................813 707-0086
Dayle Smith, *Vice Pres*
EMP: 22 EST: 1980
SALES (est): 605K **Privately Held**
WEB: www.konecranes.com
SIC: 3536 Hoists, cranes & monorails

(G-13784)
MCCAIN MILLS INC
5605 Paul Buchman Hwy (33565-7305)
PHONE...................................813 752-6478
Joshua D McCain, *Principal*
Trisha Howard, *Manager*
EMP: 9 EST: 2018
SALES (est): 1.5MM **Privately Held**
WEB: www.mccainmills.com
SIC: 2421 Sawmills & planing mills, general

(G-13785)
METAL SYSTEMS INC
Also Called: Discount Metal Mart
3301 Paul Buchman Hwy (33565-5051)
PHONE...................................813 752-7088
Ferris Waller, *President*
▼ EMP: 6 EST: 1993
SQ FT: 1,560
SALES (est): 978.3K **Privately Held**
WEB: jam-sessions.meetup.com
SIC: 3441 Building components, structural steel

(G-13786)
MTEC TRAILER SUPPLY
3804 Sydney Rd (33566-1191)
PHONE...................................813 659-1647
Dan Wilson, *Chairman*
EMP: 18 EST: 1994
SQ FT: 10,000
SALES (est): 267.4K **Privately Held**
SIC: 3451 Screw machine products

(G-13787)
NUCYCLE ENERGY OF TAMPA LLC
2067 S County Line Rd (33566-4545)
PHONE...................................813 848-0509
Amy Radke, *Opers Staff*
Brandon Hagerman, *Engineer*
Zach Schonberger, *CFO*
Rachel Leone, *Finance*
Zachary Schonberger, *Administration*
EMP: 25 EST: 2017
SALES (est): 3.2MM **Privately Held**
WEB: www.nucycleenergy.com
SIC: 2097 Block ice

(G-13788)
PAJ INNOVATIVE CONCEPTS INC
Also Called: Catamont Machine Works
2804 Sydney Rd (33566-1173)
PHONE...................................813 659-0505
Allen Jenkins, *CEO*
Peggy Jenkins, *President*
EMP: 14 EST: 2002
SALES (est): 973.3K **Privately Held**
SIC: 3599 Machine shop, jobbing & repair; gasoline filters, internal combustion engine, except auto

(G-13789)
PALLET EXPRESS INC
1503 Turkey Creek Rd (33566-0054)
PHONE...................................813 752-1600
Michael Oliveira, *President*
Claire Glunt, *Manager*
EMP: 18 EST: 2002
SALES (est): 2MM **Privately Held**
WEB: www.palletexpressinc.com
SIC: 2448 Pallets, wood

(G-13790)
PALLET SERVICES INC (PA)
Also Called: Pallet Services of Plant City
1705 Turkey Creek Rd (33566-0057)
P.O. Box 1804, Valrico (33595-1804)
PHONE...................................813 754-7719
George Bernico, *President*
Sarah Bernico, *General Mgr*

Diane Bernico,
EMP: 8 EST: 1985
SQ FT: 1,500
SALES (est): 901.7K **Privately Held**
WEB: www.palletservicesofpc.com
SIC: 2448 Pallets, wood

(G-13791)
PALLET SERVICES PLANT CITY LLC
1705 Turkey Creek Rd (33566-0057)
PHONE...................................813 752-1600
Ryan Antuono, *Principal*
EMP: 11 EST: 2012
SALES (est): 142.2K **Privately Held**
WEB: www.palletservicesofpc.com
SIC: 2448 Pallets, wood

(G-13792)
PALLETS PLUS INC
2606 N Airport Rd (33563-1147)
PHONE...................................813 759-6355
Jeffrey Phillips, *President*
Rhonda Phillips, *Vice Pres*
EMP: 9 EST: 1993
SALES (est): 987.8K **Privately Held**
SIC: 2448 Pallets, wood

(G-13793)
PARADISE LABEL INC
4021 S Frontage Rd (33566-7504)
PHONE...................................863 860-8779
Darold Stagner, *President*
▼ EMP: 16 EST: 2003
SQ FT: 100,000
SALES (est): 341K **Privately Held**
SIC: 2679 Labels, paper: made from purchased material

(G-13794)
PENINSULA STEEL INC
4504 Sydney Rd (33566-1195)
PHONE...................................813 473-8133
EMP: 20
SALES (corp-wide): 16.5MM **Privately Held**
SIC: 3315 Mfg Steel Wire/Related Products
PA: Peninsula Steel, Inc.
4119 Free Trade St
Laredo TX 33566
956 795-1966

(G-13795)
PENINSULA STEEL INC (HQ)
4504 Sydney Rd (33566-1195)
PHONE...................................956 795-1966
David Villarreal Valle, *President*
Pablo Villarreal, *President*
Sylvia C Miranda, *Vice Pres*
Aylen Gonzalez, *Manager*
Joe Kuykendall, *Manager*
EMP: 24 EST: 2015
SQ FT: 37,131
SALES (est): 10.8MM **Privately Held**
WEB: www.peninsulasteel.com
SIC: 3315 Steel wire & related products

(G-13796)
PLANT CITY OBSERVER LLC
110 E Reynolds St 100b (33563-3361)
PHONE...................................813 704-6850
Sarah Holt, *Manager*
EMP: 7 EST: 2019
SALES (est): 281.5K **Privately Held**
WEB: www.plantcityobserver.com
SIC: 2711 Newspapers, publishing & printing

(G-13797)
PRO HORIZONS INC
2610 Airport Rd (33563-1143)
PHONE...................................813 764-8844
David Carmichael, *President*
Jackie Carmichael, *Vice Pres*
▲ EMP: 9 EST: 1999
SALES (est): 143.6K **Privately Held**
WEB: www.paddleboardinglock.com
SIC: 2299 Batting, wadding, padding & fillings

(G-13798)
QUIKRETE COMPANIES LLC
1902 Wood Ct (33563-6303)
PHONE...................................813 719-6612
Bob Carlberg, *Branch Mgr*

EMP: 28 **Privately Held**
WEB: www.quikrete.com
SIC: 3272 3251 Dry mixture concrete; brick & structural clay tile
HQ: The Quikrete Companies Llc
5 Concourse Pkwy Ste 1900
Atlanta GA 30328
404 634-9100

(G-13799)
RESA PWR SLUTIONS PLANT CY LLC
Also Called: Switchgear Unlimited
1401 Mercantile Ct (33563-1152)
PHONE...................................813 752-6550
Larry Loucks, *President*
Al Vila, *General Mgr*
Arsen Shagoian, *Technician*
EMP: 15 EST: 1986
SQ FT: 70,000
SALES (est): 5.4MM **Privately Held**
WEB: www.resapower.com
SIC: 3625 5063 Switches, electric power; switchgear
HQ: Resa Power, Llc
8300 Cypress Creek Pkwy # 225
Houston TX 77070
832 900-8340

(G-13800)
REYES INTERLOCKING PAVERS INC
1317 E Calhoun St (33563-3809)
PHONE...................................863 698-9179
Angel Picon Jacinto, *Principal*
EMP: 8 EST: 2008
SALES (est): 1MM **Privately Held**
WEB: www.reyesinterlockingpavers.com
SIC: 3531 Pavers

(G-13801)
ROLLS AXLE LC
702 Hitchcock St (33563-5608)
PHONE...................................813 764-0242
Daniel M Gallagher Jr, *Partner*
Dniel Glger III, *Mng Member*
EMP: 8 EST: 1998
SQ FT: 8,000
SALES (est): 225.8K **Privately Held**
WEB: www.rollsaxle.com
SIC: 3799 3841 3792 Boat trailers; surgical & medical instruments; travel trailers & campers

(G-13802)
SENSENICH TECHNOLOGIES INC
2008 Wood Ct (33563-6305)
PHONE...................................813 703-8446
Steve Boser, *President*
John Hozik, *Principal*
EMP: 7 EST: 2013
SALES (est): 511.4K **Privately Held**
WEB: www.sensenich.com
SIC: 3728 Aircraft parts & equipment

(G-13803)
SHUTTER DOWN STORM PROTECTION
3940 E Knights Griffin Rd (33565-2208)
PHONE...................................813 957-8936
Richard C Bliss, *President*
EMP: 10 EST: 2005
SALES (est): 116.3K **Privately Held**
SIC: 3442 Shutters, door or window: metal

(G-13804)
SOUTHAST CLKING SLANT SVCS LLC
2426 Branchwood Rd (33567-3800)
PHONE...................................813 731-8778
Robert G Woods, *Manager*
Robert Woods, *Manager*
EMP: 7 EST: 2015
SALES (est): 346.6K **Privately Held**
WEB: www.southeastcaulking.com
SIC: 2891 Sealants

(G-13805)
SQUIRE INDUSTRIES INC
1118 Sparkman Rd (33566-4714)
PHONE...................................813 523-1505
James Tothill, *Principal*
EMP: 8 EST: 2011

SALES (est): 92.9K **Privately Held**
SIC: 3999 Manufacturing industries

(G-13806)
STONE METALS LLC
4021 S Frontage Rd (33566-7504)
PHONE...................................813 605-7363
Brian Wedding,
EMP: 7 EST: 2019
SALES (est): 2.1MM **Privately Held**
SIC: 1411 Limestone & marble dimension stone

(G-13807)
TATA TEA EXTRACTIONS INC
1001 W Dr Mlk Jr Blvd Martin Luther (33563)
PHONE...................................813 754-2602
Ravi Sankararaman, *President*
Raji Thankappan, *Principal*
◆ EMP: 30 EST: 1979
SQ FT: 45,000
SALES (est): 8.8MM **Privately Held**
SIC: 2099 Tea blending
PA: Tata Consumer Products Limited
11/13, Botawala Building, 1st Floor,
Mumbai MH 40000

(G-13808)
TELESE INC
Also Called: Quality Metal Works
1207 Wood Ct (33563-6302)
PHONE...................................813 752-6015
Anthony Telese, *President*
Mark Telese, *Vice Pres*
EMP: 42 EST: 1983
SQ FT: 22,000
SALES (est): 9.9MM **Privately Held**
SIC: 3444 2542 Sheet metal specialties, not stamped; partitions & fixtures, except wood

(G-13809)
TELESE PROPERTIES INC
Also Called: Quality Metal Works
1207 Wood Ct (33563-6302)
PHONE...................................813 752-6015
Anthony G Telese, *President*
Mark Telese, *Vice Pres*
Bob Youngblood, *Opers Mgr*
Amiee Spivey, *Human Res Mgr*
Carrie Ponce,
EMP: 60 EST: 2001
SALES (est): 8.3MM **Privately Held**
SIC: 3499 Fire- or burglary-resistive products

(G-13810)
TEMPLE TERRACE INDUSTRIES INC
4208 Business Ln (33566-1163)
PHONE...................................813 752-7546
W C Hammontree, *President*
Joseph P Hammontree, *Vice Pres*
David Hammontree, *Treasurer*
Doris J Hammontree, *Admin Sec*
EMP: 21 EST: 1952
SQ FT: 50,000
SALES (est): 1.1MM **Privately Held**
WEB: www.reelco.us
SIC: 2499 Reels, plywood

(G-13811)
THOMAS WHITE LLC
1302 N Orange St (33563-2348)
PHONE...................................813 704-4406
Thomas White, *Principal*
EMP: 8 EST: 2007
SALES (est): 77.6K **Privately Held**
SIC: 2952 Roofing materials

(G-13812)
USMI PALLETS INC
3301 Sam Allen Oaks Cir (33565-5597)
PHONE...................................813 765-4309
Grover D Garrett, *President*
EMP: 9 EST: 2009
SALES (est): 278.4K **Privately Held**
WEB: www.usmipallets.com
SIC: 2448 Pallets, wood

(G-13813)
VANAVAC INC
1309 Joe Mcintosh Rd (33565-7454)
PHONE...................................813 752-1391
EMP: 7

SQ FT: 1,500
SALES (est): 1.2MM **Privately Held**
SIC: 2819 Mfg Industrial Inorganic Chemicals

(G-13814)
WARREN EQUIPMENT INC
2299 Us Highway 92 E (33563-2145)
PHONE..................................813 752-5126
Russell Warren, *President*
Robert Flavin, *General Mgr*
Duane Chambers, *Vice Pres*
William Gordon, *Plant Mgr*
Alexander Silfa, *Engineer*
EMP: 45 EST: 2001
SQ FT: 80,000
SALES (est): 11.6MM **Privately Held**
WEB: www.warrentrailers.com
SIC: 3715 5013 3713 Truck trailers; truck parts & accessories; dump truck bodies

(G-13815)
WEDGWORTH FARMS INC
2607 Sammonds Rd (33563-4554)
PHONE..................................561 996-2076
EMP: 8
SALES (corp-wide): 67.8MM **Privately Held**
WEB: www.wedgworth.com
SIC: 2875 Fertilizers, mixing only
PA: Wedgworth Farms Inc
    32260 State Rd 80
    Belle Glade FL 33430
    561 996-2076

Plantation
Broward County

(G-13816)
2LEAF PRESS INC
1200 S Pine Island Rd (33324-4413)
PHONE..................................646 801-4227
Gabrielle David, *Principal*
EMP: 7 EST: 2019
SALES (est): 338.1K **Privately Held**
WEB: www.2leafpress.org
SIC: 2731 Book publishing

(G-13817)
A-PLUS PRTG & GRAPHIC CTR INC
6561 Nw 18th Ct (33313-4520)
PHONE..................................954 327-7315
Richard Erens, *President*
Andrew Moreau, *Manager*
EMP: 40 EST: 1991
SALES (est): 9.2MM **Privately Held**
SIC: 2752 2754 7336 Commercial printing, offset; commercial printing, gravure; graphic arts & related design

(G-13818)
AB ENZYMES INC
150 S Pine Island Rd # 270 (33324-2677)
PHONE..................................954 278-3975
Martin Nielsen, *President*
Karen Lewis, *CFO*
Kelly Lamanna, *Treasurer*
Mauricio Quiros, *Manager*
Jessica Sonnenfeld, *Manager*
▼ EMP: 8 EST: 2017
SQ FT: 3,000
SALES (est): 4.4MM
SALES (corp-wide): 19B **Privately Held**
WEB: www.abenzymes.com
SIC: 2869 Enzymes
HQ: Ab Enzymes Gmbh
    Feldbergstr. 78
    Darmstadt HE 64293
    615 136-8010

(G-13819)
AB VISTA INC (HQ)
150 S Pine Island Rd (33324-2669)
PHONE..................................954 278-3965
Richard Cooper, *President*
Kelly Lamanna, *Vice Pres*
Dieter Suida, *Vice Pres*
Ian Vincent, *CFO*
Jaarg Kaahler, *Sales Staff*
▲ EMP: 9 EST: 2002

SALES (est): 8.7MM
SALES (corp-wide): 19B **Privately Held**
WEB: www.abvista.com
SIC: 2048 Prepared feeds
PA: Associated British Foods Plc
    10 Grosvenor Street
    London W1K 4
    207 399-6500

(G-13820)
ABDIVERSIFIED LLC
6825 W Sunrise Blvd (33313-4512)
PHONE..................................954 791-6050
EMP: 62 EST: 2016
SALES (est): 964.9K
SALES (corp-wide): 11.9MM **Privately Held**
SIC: 2844 Hair preparations, including shampoos
PA: Fekkai Retail, Llc
    6825 W Sunrise Blvd
    Plantation FL 33313
    866 514-8048

(G-13821)
ADMASK INC
Also Called: Superior Printers
6531 Nw 13th Ct (33313-4550)
PHONE..................................954 962-2040
Adib K Skaf, *President*
Maria I Skaf, *Treasurer*
EMP: 6 EST: 1994
SALES (est): 743.5K **Privately Held**
SIC: 2752 Commercial printing, offset

(G-13822)
ALASKA INC
317 S State Road 7 (33317-3736)
PHONE..................................954 792-0545
Nilo Berra, *General Mgr*
EMP: 8
SALES (corp-wide): 14.6MM **Privately Held**
WEB: www.alaskamiami.com
SIC: 3695 Computer software tape & disks: blank, rigid & floppy
PA: Alaska, Inc.
    3008 Nw 72nd Ave
    Miami FL 33122
    305 591-1444

(G-13823)
ALLEZ LLC
5171 Sw 17th Ct (33317-5405)
PHONE..................................205 216-6330
Jovan Conde, *CEO*
Jerry Baptiste, *Principal*
EMP: 14 EST: 2016
SALES (est): 1MM **Privately Held**
WEB: www.groupe-allez.com
SIC: 2821 8742 4212 Plastics materials & resins; manufacturing management consultant; hazardous waste transport

(G-13824)
ALLIED TELECOMMUNICATIONS LTD
1500 Nw 65th Ave (33313-4507)
PHONE..................................954 370-9900
Frank D Reynolds, *CEO*
EMP: 15 EST: 1989
SQ FT: 3,700
SALES (est): 272K **Privately Held**
SIC: 3661 5065 Carrier equipment, telephone or telegraph; telephone equipment

(G-13825)
ALNOOR IMPORT INC
6851 W Sunrise Blvd (33313-4572)
PHONE..................................954 683-9897
Maher Almasri, *President*
◆ EMP: 5 EST: 2007
SALES (est): 504.9K **Privately Held**
WEB: www.alnourimports.com
SIC: 2099 Food preparations

(G-13826)
AMERICAS ATM LLC
8751 W Broward Blvd # 30 (33324-2668)
PHONE..................................954 414-0341
Brad Daniel, *Mng Member*
EMP: 12 EST: 2014
SALES (est): 699.1K **Privately Held**
WEB: www.americanatm.com
SIC: 3578 Automatic teller machines (ATM)

(G-13827)
ARMEN CO INC
12140 Nw 12th St (33323-2436)
PHONE..................................305 206-1601
George Davitian, *President*
▼ EMP: 70 EST: 1984
SQ FT: 20,000
SALES (est): 4.3MM **Privately Held**
SIC: 2339 2329 2369 2269 Sportswear, women's; men's & boys' sportswear & athletic clothing; girls' & children's outerwear; finishing plants; finishing plants, manmade fiber & silk fabrics; finishing plants, cotton

(G-13828)
AROUND AND ABOUT INC
450 N State Road 7 (33317-2834)
PHONE..................................954 584-1954
Richard Conrey, *President*
Carmelo Guerrero, *Research*
Adam Friedman, *CFO*
Amy Rivero, *Accounts Exec*
Shani Villalba, *Graphic Designe*
EMP: 10 EST: 2004
SQ FT: 4,696
SALES (est): 1.6MM **Privately Held**
WEB: www.upnwalk.com
SIC: 3842 Limbs, artificial; prosthetic appliances

(G-13829)
AUTOMATIC MFG SYSTEMS INC
Also Called: Accuplace
1800 Nw 69th Ave Ste 102 (33313-4583)
PHONE..................................954 791-1500
Jamie P Schlinkmann, *President*
Tony Haubrich, *Engineer*
Reshma Papali, *Engineer*
Mike Terry, *Sales Staff*
Laura Bellamy, *Manager*
▲ EMP: 30 EST: 1997
SQ FT: 75,000
SALES (est): 8.9MM **Privately Held**
WEB: www.accuplace.com
SIC: 3549 3569 Metalworking machinery; assembly machines, non-metalworking

(G-13830)
AVIATION PARTS & TRADE CORP
12331 Nw 7th St (33325-1729)
P.O. Box 15431 (33318-5431)
PHONE..................................954 944-2828
Carlos E Ulloa, *President*
EMP: 6 EST: 2012
SALES (est): 681.4K **Privately Held**
WEB: www.aptc.aero
SIC: 3429 3721 Aircraft hardware; aircraft

(G-13831)
BETTER AIR NORTH AMERICA LLC
691 Carrotwood Ter (33324-8223)
PHONE..................................844 447-7624
Taly Dery, *CEO*
Dery Taly, *Supervisor*
EMP: 8 EST: 2015
SALES (est): 1.2MM **Privately Held**
SIC: 3564 Air purification equipment

(G-13832)
BIO THERAPEUTICS INC
Also Called: Phylomed
1850 Nw 69th Ave Ste 1 (33313-4569)
PHONE..................................954 321-5553
Suzanne Mundschenk, *President*
EMP: 8 EST: 1984
SALES (est): 824.7K **Privately Held**
SIC: 2834 8733 Pharmaceutical preparations; medical research

(G-13833)
BIOIVT LLC
7500 Nw 5th St (33317-1612)
PHONE..................................516 876-7902
Jorge Bichara, *Site Mgr*
EMP: 7 EST: 2013
SALES (est): 107.3K **Privately Held**
WEB: www.bioivt.com
SIC: 2836 Veterinary biological products

(G-13834)
BLACK-TIE PUBLISHING INC
10131 Nw 14th St (33322-6531)
PHONE..................................954 472-6003
Ron Feller, *Publisher*
Ronald Feller, *Principal*
EMP: 8 EST: 2001
SALES (est): 282.8K **Privately Held**
WEB: www.blacktiepublishing.com
SIC: 2741 Miscellaneous publishing

(G-13835)
CLASSIC PIZZA CRUSTS INC
841 Mockingbird Ln (33324-3405)
PHONE..................................954 570-8383
Rosalind Fimiano, *President*
▼ EMP: 8 EST: 1998
SALES (est): 966.3K **Privately Held**
WEB: www.classicpizza.com
SIC: 2038 2041 5812 Pizza, frozen; pizza dough, prepared; pizza restaurants

(G-13836)
CLINICAL DAGNSTC SOLUTIONS INC
1800 Nw 65th Ave (33313-4544)
PHONE..................................954 791-1773
Andrew C Swanson, *President*
Dr Harold R Crews, *Senior VP*
Donald Grantham, *Senior VP*
Karen Bornstein, *Vice Pres*
James Carter, *Vice Pres*
◆ EMP: 38 EST: 1997
SQ FT: 47,000
SALES (est): 20.4MM **Privately Held**
WEB: www.cdsolinc.com
SIC: 2835 2899 2834 Hemotology diagnostic agents; chemical preparations; pharmaceutical preparations
PA: Boule Diagnostics Ab
    Domnarvsgatan 4
    SpAnga 163 5

(G-13837)
COLORTONE INC
6531 Nw 18th Ct (33313-4520)
PHONE..................................954 455-0200
Mike Hasson, *President*
Shlomo Hasson, *Vice Pres*
Andrew Weitz, *Director*
▲ EMP: 38 EST: 1994
SALES (est): 8.3MM **Privately Held**
WEB: www.tiedyeusa.com
SIC: 2261 2269 Finishing plants, cotton; chemical coating or treating of narrow fabrics

(G-13838)
COOL OCEAN LLC
9810 Sw 4th St (33324-2826)
PHONE..................................954 848-4060
Avraham Zeitoune,
EMP: 7 EST: 2013
SALES (est): 509.7K **Privately Held**
WEB: www.coolocean123.com
SIC: 2231 Weaving mill, broadwoven fabrics: wool or similar fabric

(G-13839)
COUNTRY PRIME MEATS USA INC
9695 W Broward Blvd (33324-2321)
PHONE..................................250 396-4111
Peter Springmann, *President*
Markus Springmann, *Director*
EMP: 5 EST: 2016
SALES (est): 412K **Privately Held**
WEB: www.countryprime.com
SIC: 2013 Snack sticks, including jerky: from purchased meat

(G-13840)
CROMPCO INC
Also Called: Park Row Printing
6531 Nw 13th Ct (33313-4550)
PHONE..................................954 584-8488
George V Crompton, *President*
Howard Crompton, *Vice Pres*
Judith Crompton, *Admin Sec*
EMP: 10 EST: 1976
SQ FT: 3,500
SALES (est): 2MM **Privately Held**
WEB: www.crompco.com
SIC: 2752 Commercial printing, offset

▲ = Import ▼=Export
◆ =Import/Export

(G-13841)
CUG LLC
950 S Pine Island Rd (33324-3926)
PHONE......................................786 858-0499
Sahily Sanchez,
Edgar Banks,
Isabel Cardoza,
Luis La Verde,
EMP: 15 **EST:** 2018
SALES (est): 5.2MM **Privately Held**
WEB: www.chinausagranites.com
SIC: 3281 3272 5032 Granite, cut &
shaped; floor slabs & tiles, precast con-
crete; ceramic construction materials, ex-
cluding refractory

(G-13842)
DAILY ROOM
1000 S Pine Island Rd # 160 (33324-3904)
PHONE......................................754 200-5153
Sebastien Tribout, *Principal*
EMP: 8 **EST:** 2012
SALES (est): 472.5K **Privately Held**
WEB: www.thedailyroom.com
SIC: 2711 Newspapers, publishing & print-
ing

(G-13843)
**DAX COPYING AND PRINTING
INC**
1868 N University Dr # 106 (33322-4129)
PHONE......................................954 236-3000
Bruce Batchelder, *President*
EMP: 6 **EST:** 2009
SQ FT: 3,000
SALES (est): 647.3K **Privately Held**
WEB: www.nationalcolorcopy.com
SIC: 2752 Commercial printing, offset

(G-13844)
DEFEND COATINGS LLC
9200 Nw 14th Ct (33322-4308)
PHONE......................................954 612-5593
Gary Kabot, *Principal*
EMP: 7 **EST:** 2017
SALES (est): 69.9K **Privately Held**
SIC: 3479 Metal coating & allied service

(G-13845)
**E-LIQUIDS INVESTMENT GROUP
LLC**
Also Called: Humo E-Liquids
6500 Nw 16th St Ste 1 (33313-4522)
PHONE......................................954 507-6060
Steven Sosa,
EMP: 20 **EST:** 2016
SALES (est): 1.9MM **Privately Held**
WEB: www.eliquidsgroup.com
SIC: 2899 Chemical preparations

(G-13846)
ELECTROSOURCE INC
11785 Nw 5th St (33325-1909)
PHONE......................................954 723-0840
Carmen Di Mase, *Principal*
EMP: 10 **EST:** 2010
SALES (est): 150.6K **Privately Held**
SIC: 3679 Microwave components

(G-13847)
ELEMENT-M LLC
9835 Nw 5th Pl (33324-7041)
PHONE......................................954 288-8683
David Kustin, *Principal*
Kristin Murphy, *Editor*
EMP: 8 **EST:** 2010
SALES (est): 1MM **Privately Held**
WEB: www.element-m.com
SIC: 2819 Industrial inorganic chemicals

(G-13848)
**EURAMERICA GAS AND OIL
CORP**
1333 S University Dr # 202 (33324-4087)
PHONE......................................954 858-5714
EMP: 5 **EST:** 2018
SALES (est): 308.9K **Privately Held**
WEB: www.euramericagasoil.com
SIC: 1389 Oil & gas field services

(G-13849)
EVERFRESH JUICE CO INC
8100 Sw 10th St Ste 4000 (33324-3224)
PHONE......................................954 581-0922
Marty Rose, *General Mgr*

Albert Allen, *Principal*
Joe Jarrett, *Manager*
EMP: 22 **EST:** 2010
SALES (est): 2.2MM
SALES (corp-wide): 1.1B **Publicly Held**
WEB: www.everfreshjuice.com
SIC: 2086 Carbonated beverages, nonal-
coholic: bottled & canned; water, pasteur-
ized: packaged in cans, bottles, etc.; fruit
drinks (less than 100% juice): packaged
in cans, etc.
PA: National Beverage Corp.
8100 Sw 10th St Ste 4000
Plantation FL 33324
954 581-0922

(G-13850)
FEKKAI BRANDS LLC
6825 W Sunrise Blvd (33313-4512)
PHONE......................................954 791-6050
Joel B Ronkin, *Mng Member*
EMP: 7 **EST:** 2015
SALES (est): 389.9K **Privately Held**
SIC: 2844 Shampoos, rinses, conditioners:
hair

(G-13851)
FEKKAI RETAIL LLC (PA)
6825 W Sunrise Blvd (33313-4512)
PHONE......................................866 514-8048
Joel Ronkin, *Principal*
EMP: 18 **EST:** 2015
SQ FT: 65,000
SALES (est): 11.9MM **Privately Held**
WEB: www.fekkai.com
SIC: 2844 7231 Hair preparations, includ-
ing shampoos; unisex hair salons

(G-13852)
**FIREFLY AIRCRAFT PARTS
INC ✪**
150 S Pine Island Rd (33324-2669)
PHONE......................................954 870-7833
Anna Bascle, *CEO*
Anna Karina Da Luz, *CEO*
EMP: 6 **EST:** 2021
SALES (est): 664.4K **Privately Held**
WEB: www.fireflyaircraftparts.com
SIC: 3728 8742 7389 Aircraft body as-
semblies & parts; retail trade consultant;
brokers' services

(G-13853)
FIRST MATE INC
11950 Nw 27th St (33323-1760)
PHONE......................................954 475-2750
Ron Adams, *President*
Cheryl Adams, *Vice Pres*
EMP: 7 **EST:** 1996
SALES (est): 646.9K **Privately Held**
WEB: www.matesfirst.com
SIC: 3699 Door opening & closing devices,
electrical

(G-13854)
FRIEDMAN & GREENBERG PA
8181 W Broward Blvd # 300 (33324-2049)
PHONE......................................954 370-4774
Robert Friedman, *President*
EMP: 8 **EST:** 1990
SALES (est): 749.6K **Privately Held**
WEB: www.friedmangreenberg.com
SIC: 3312 Fence posts, iron & steel

(G-13855)
GLC 3 & RENTAL CORP
Also Called: GLC 3 Concrete
11490 Nw 20th Ct (33323-2006)
PHONE......................................954 916-1551
George J Lacker, *President*
▼ **EMP:** 5 **EST:** 2001
SALES (est): 654.2K **Privately Held**
SIC: 3271 Concrete block & brick

(G-13856)
GREENIE TOTS INC
772 Nw 132nd Ave (33325-6173)
PHONE......................................888 316-6126
Jilea Hemmings, *CEO*
EMP: 6 **EST:** 2004
SALES (est): 379.4K **Privately Held**
WEB: www.greenietots.com
SIC: 2038 Frozen specialties

(G-13857)
IBS PARTNERS LTD (PA)
1 N University Dr Ut400a (33324-2038)
PHONE......................................954 581-0922
Nick A Caporella, *General Ptnr*
Nick Caporella, *General Ptnr*
Dean McCoy, *Controller*
◆ **EMP:** 40 **EST:** 1985
SALES (est): 57.1MM **Privately Held**
SIC: 2086 Soft drinks: packaged in cans,
bottles, etc.

(G-13858)
ID PRINT INC
6561 Nw 18th Ct (33313-4520)
P.O. Box 16486, Fort Lauderdale (33318-
6486)
PHONE......................................954 923-8374
Steve Machusko, *President*
▼ **EMP:** 5 **EST:** 2008
SALES (est): 521.4K **Privately Held**
SIC: 3861 Printing equipment, photo-
graphic

(G-13859)
J ROSS PUBLISHING INC
300 S Pine Island Rd # 305 (33324-2621)
PHONE......................................954 727-9333
Dennis Buda, *President*
Stephen Buda, *Vice Pres*
▲ **EMP:** 7 **EST:** 2002
SQ FT: 1,500
SALES (est): 1.1MM **Privately Held**
WEB: www.jrosspub.com
SIC: 2741 Miscellaneous publishing

(G-13860)
J S TRADING INC
6524 Nw 13th Ct (33313-4549)
PHONE......................................954 791-9035
Surjit Singh, *CEO*
Raj Singh, *Vice Pres*
◆ **EMP:** 6 **EST:** 1984
SQ FT: 15,000
SALES (est): 1MM **Privately Held**
WEB: www.jstrading.com
SIC: 2673 2674 Plastic bags: made from
purchased materials; paper bags: made
from purchased materials

(G-13861)
J SCHOR R INC
Also Called: Sign Solutions
1776 N Pine Island Rd (33322-5233)
PHONE......................................954 621-5279
Robert J Schor, *President*
EMP: 11 **EST:** 2002
SALES (est): 237.2K **Privately Held**
SIC: 3083 Laminated plastics plate & sheet

(G-13862)
**KENNETH A JEFFUS FINE ART
LLC**
9355 Nw 18th Pl (33322-5655)
PHONE......................................954 849-0553
Kenneth Jeffus, *Principal*
EMP: 8 **EST:** 2009
SALES (est): 79.9K **Privately Held**
WEB: www.dailychew.com
SIC: 2711 Newspapers, publishing & print-
ing

(G-13863)
KING KANINE LLC
150 S Pine Island Rd # 115 (33324-2669)
PHONE......................................833 546-4738
Jeffrey M Riman, *CEO*
Lynnette San Miguel,
EMP: 5 **EST:** 2016
SQ FT: 1,500
SALES (est): 3.2MM **Privately Held**
WEB: www.kingkanine.com
SIC: 3999 5999 Pet supplies; pet supplies

(G-13864)
LUXE BRANDS INC (PA)
6825 W Sunrise Blvd (33313-4512)
PHONE......................................954 791-6050
Arvinder S Bajaj, *President*
Jogindar S Bajaj, *Vice Pres*
James Allen Fantau, *Human Res Mgr*
Patricia Buttacavoli, *Accounts Exec*
Kimberley Kladis, *Marketing Staff*
▲ **EMP:** 30 **EST:** 1999

SALES (est): 11.8MM **Privately Held**
WEB: www.luxebrands.com
SIC: 2844 Toilet preparations

(G-13865)
LUXEBRANDS LLC
6825 W Sunrise Blvd (33313-4512)
PHONE......................................866 514-8048
Arvinder S Bajaj, *President*
EMP: 53 **EST:** 2016
SALES (est): 301K
SALES (corp-wide): 11.9MM **Privately
Held**
SIC: 2844 Hair preparations, including
shampoos
PA: Fekkai Retail, Llc
6825 W Sunrise Blvd
Plantation FL 33313
866 514-8048

(G-13866)
MARITIME EXECUTIVE LLC
Also Called: Marex
7473 Nw 4th St (33317-2216)
PHONE......................................954 848-9955
Brett Keil, *Vice Pres*
Thomas Cox, *Regl Sales Mgr*
Charlie Helms, *Regl Sales Mgr*
Ben Lennon, *Marketing Mgr*
Zamaslie Corraliza, *Mktg Coord*
EMP: 8 **EST:** 2006
SALES (est): 1.1MM **Privately Held**
WEB: www.maritime-executive.com
SIC: 2721 Magazines: publishing only, not
printed on site

(G-13867)
**MAXANT BUTTON & SUPPLY
INC**
5901 Plantation Rd (33317-1345)
PHONE......................................770 460-2227
Lorna Marden, *President*
Jim Marden, *Admin Sec*
EMP: 5 **EST:** 2002
SQ FT: 5,000
SALES (est): 325K **Privately Held**
SIC: 3965 Buttons & parts

(G-13868)
METHOD MERCHANT INC
Also Called: Godatafeed
150 S Pine Island Rd # 530 (33324-2676)
PHONE......................................954 745-7998
Karen Meany, *Vice Pres*
Lorraine Carcamo, *Accounts Mgr*
Erick Martinez, *Accounts Mgr*
Amber McCalla, *Accounts Mgr*
Sean Dailey, *Sales Staff*
EMP: 17 **EST:** 2008
SALES (est): 625.9K **Privately Held**
SIC: 7372 Business oriented computer
software

(G-13869)
MOR PRINTING INC
Also Called: Mor Printing & Envelopes
6561 Nw 18th Ct (33313-4520)
PHONE......................................954 377-1197
Owen Luttinger, *President*
Dave Groth, *Purch Mgr*
Richard Luttinger, *Treasurer*
Rick Bell, *Accounts Mgr*
Valerie Giliberti, *Manager*
▼ **EMP:** 13 **EST:** 1988
SALES (est): 4.8MM **Privately Held**
WEB: www.morprinting.com
SIC: 2752 Commercial printing, offset

(G-13870)
MOTOROLA SOLUTIONS INC
8000 W Sunrise Blvd (33322-4170)
PHONE......................................954 723-5000
Kent Martin, *Regional Mgr*
Andrew Crawford, *Business Mgr*
Avishai Yavetz, *Business Mgr*
John Kedzierski, *Senior VP*
Patty Holtschneider, *Vice Pres*
EMP: 2000
SALES (corp-wide): 8.1B **Publicly Held**
WEB: www.motorolasolutions.com
SIC: 3663 Radio broadcasting & communi-
cations equipment
PA: Motorola Solutions, Inc.
500 W Monroe St Ste 4400
Chicago IL 60661
847 576-5000

(G-13871)
MULTIMEDIA EFFECTS INC
Also Called: Storage Heaven
9715 W Broward Blvd Ste 3 (33324-2351)
PHONE..............................800 367-3054
Oral Gordon, *Director*
EMP: 10 **EST:** 2010
SQ FT: 5,000
SALES (est): 2MM **Privately Held**
SIC: 3577 Data conversion equipment,
media-to-media: computer

(G-13872)
**NATIONAL BEVERAGE CORP
(PA)**
8100 Sw 10th St Ste 4000 (33324-3224)
P.O. Box 16720, Fort Lauderdale (33318-
6720)
PHONE..............................954 581-0922
Nick A Caporella, *Ch of Bd*
Joseph G Caporella, *President*
Michael M King, *Counsel*
James Bolton, *Exec VP*
Charles Maier, *Exec VP*
EMP: 64 **EST:** 1985
SALES: 1.1B **Publicly Held**
WEB: www.nationalbeverage.com
SIC: 2086 Soft drinks: packaged in cans,
bottles, etc.; carbonated beverages, non-
alcoholic: bottled & canned; water, pas-
teurized: packaged in cans, bottles, etc.;
fruit drinks (less than 100% juice): pack-
aged in cans, etc.

(G-13873)
**NATIONAL CHEMICAL SUPPLY
INC**
6930 Sw 16th St (33317-5084)
P.O. Box 16785, Fort Lauderdale (33318-
6785)
PHONE..............................954 683-1645
Phillip Shaffer, *President*
EMP: 8 **EST:** 1991
SQ FT: 4,700
SALES (est): 975K **Privately Held**
WEB: www.nationalchemicalsupply.com
SIC: 2819 Industrial inorganic chemicals

(G-13874)
NEWBEVCO INC (HQ)
8100 Sw 10th St (33324-3279)
PHONE..............................954 581-0922
Nick A Caporella, *President*
Joseph G Caporella, *President*
EMP: 40 **EST:** 1991
SALES (est): 437.3MM
SALES (corp-wide): 1.1B **Publicly Held**
SIC: 2086 Soft drinks: packaged in cans,
bottles, etc.
PA: National Beverage Corp.
8100 Sw 10th St Ste 4000
Plantation FL 33324
954 581-0922

(G-13875)
NXGEN BRANDS LLC
Also Called: LEAFYWELL
8032 Lakepointe Dr (33322-5789)
PHONE..............................888 315-6339
Angel Burgos, *CEO*
Tom Reeves, *President*
Nick Brana, *Managing Dir*
Nicholas Brana,
EMP: 30 **EST:** 2017
SALES (est): 230K
SALES (corp-wide): 2.1MM **Privately
Held**
WEB: www.leafywell.com
SIC: 2834 3999 5159 3663 Pharmaceuti-
cal preparations; ; ;
PA: Nxgen Brands, Inc.
2322 Se 8th St
Cape Coral FL 33990
954 329-2205

(G-13876)
PANAMTECH INC (PA)
700 Nw 70th Ter (33317-1100)
PHONE..............................954 587-3769
Gloria Carreras, *President*
Rick Carreras, *President*
EMP: 9 **EST:** 1981
SALES (est): 763.2K **Privately Held**
SIC: 3643 Current-carrying wiring devices

(G-13877)
**PLANTATION JOURNAL
CORPORATION**
7860 Peters Rd Ste F110 (33324-4027)
PHONE..............................954 226-6170
Kevin D Bingham, *President*
EMP: 8 **EST:** 2009
SALES (est): 92K **Privately Held**
SIC: 2711 Newspapers, publishing & print-
ing

(G-13878)
**PRECISION ANALOG SYSTEMS
CO**
1021 Sw 75th Ave (33317-3234)
P.O. Box 15576 (33318-5576)
PHONE..............................954 587-0668
Lawrence N Arbuckle, *President*
Barbara L Arbuckle, *Vice Pres*
EMP: 5 **EST:** 1990
SQ FT: 1,200
SALES (est): 756.4K **Privately Held**
WEB: www.precisionanalog.com
SIC: 3823 7389 Controllers for process
variables, all types; design, commercial &
industrial

(G-13879)
**QUALITY PAVERS SOUTH FLA
LLC**
11200 Nw 18th St (33323-2214)
PHONE..............................954 881-1919
Dean Ferrerio, *Principal*
EMP: 7 **EST:** 2014
SALES (est): 224.2K **Privately Held**
SIC: 2951 Asphalt paving mixtures &
blocks

(G-13880)
QUICK PRINTS LLC
8201 Peters Rd Ste 1000 (33324-3266)
PHONE..............................954 594-9415
EMP: 6 **EST:** 2016
SALES (est): 474.1K **Privately Held**
SIC: 2752 Commercial printing, offset

(G-13881)
ROBS BAGELAND INC
8201 W Sunrise Blvd (33322-5403)
PHONE..............................954 640-5470
Robert Elbaum, *Principal*
EMP: 8 **EST:** 2012
SALES (est): 951.6K **Privately Held**
WEB: www.robsbageland.net
SIC: 3421 Table & food cutlery, including
butchers'

(G-13882)
ROV RAILWAY INDUSTRY LLC
10135 W Sunrise Blvd # 101 (33322-5664)
PHONE..............................305 299-8264
Joris Briand, *Branch Mgr*
EMP: 10
SALES (corp-wide): 248.4K **Privately
Held**
WEB: www.rovrailwayindustry.com
SIC: 3743 Railroad equipment
PA: Rov Railway Industry, Llc
10242 Nw 47th St Ste 35
Sunrise FL

(G-13883)
RUSH FLYERS
6561 Nw 18th Ct (33313-4520)
PHONE..............................954 332-0509
Richard B Erens, *Principal*
EMP: 9 **EST:** 2009
SALES (est): 295.2K **Privately Held**
WEB: www.rushflyers.com
SIC: 2752 Commercial printing, offset

(G-13884)
**S & K PRFMCE MACHINING &
FAB**
11911 Nw 27th Ct (33323-1713)
PHONE..............................954 306-2214
David Krivak, *Owner*
EMP: 7 **EST:** 2015
SALES (est): 125.8K **Privately Held**
SIC: 3599 Machine shop, jobbing & repair

(G-13885)
SALSA THREE INC
10167 W Sunrise Blvd (33322-7619)
PHONE..............................954 990-2223
Jay N Boros, *Principal*
EMP: 8 **EST:** 2014
SALES (est): 227.9K **Privately Held**
SIC: 2099 Dips, except cheese & sour
cream based

(G-13886)
SHASTA BEVERAGES INTL INC
Also Called: Add Some Pop
8100 Sw 10th St Ste 4000 (33324-3224)
PHONE..............................954 581-0922
Nick A Caporella, *President*
Caporella Joseph G, *Vice Pres*
Nin Elsie, *Admin Sec*
EMP: 50 **EST:** 1990
SALES (est): 37.5MM
SALES (corp-wide): 1.1B **Publicly Held**
SIC: 2086 5149 Carbonated beverages,
nonalcoholic: bottled & canned; bever-
ages, except coffee & tea
HQ: Newbevco, Inc.
8100 Sw 10th St
Plantation FL 33324

(G-13887)
SHORE TRENDZ LLC
560 Nw 118th Ave (33325-1828)
PHONE..............................954 608-7375
Mark Deift, *Principal*
Erica Deift, *Principal*
EMP: 8 **EST:** 2013
SALES (est): 412.7K **Privately Held**
WEB: www.shoretrendz.com
SIC: 2389 2369 Disposable garments &
accessories; bathing suits & swimwear:
girls', children's & infants'

(G-13888)
SKYHIGH ACCESSORIES INC
4344 Peters Rd (33317-4543)
PHONE..............................954 316-3936
Kirk Drellich, *President*
Christy Benson, *Sales Staff*
Scott Ferris, *Sales Staff*
EMP: 5 **EST:** 2001
SQ FT: 4,000
SALES (est): 1MM **Privately Held**
WEB: www.skyhighaccessories.com
SIC: 3728 Aircraft parts & equipment

(G-13889)
SMART GLASS SYSTEMS INC
8201 Peters Rd (33324-3265)
PHONE..............................954 801-5349
Alex Martinez, *President*
◆ **EMP:** 5 **EST:** 2009
SALES (est): 522.2K **Privately Held**
WEB: www.smartglass-systems.com
SIC: 3231 Products of purchased glass

(G-13890)
SOCATI CORP
1776 N Pine Island Rd # 309 (33322-5235)
PHONE..............................503 634-2378
EMP: 19
SALES (corp-wide): 11MM **Privately Held**
WEB: www.socati.com
SIC: 2833 Medicinals & botanicals
PA: Socati Corp.
1250 S Capital Of Texas H
West Lake Hills TX 78746
503 634-2378

(G-13891)
**SOLAR SHADES DRAPERIES &
MORE**
1081 Nw 101st Way (33322-6505)
PHONE..............................954 600-3419
Marisol Hernandez, *Principal*
EMP: 8 **EST:** 2005
SALES (est): 82.5K **Privately Held**
SIC: 2391 Curtains & draperies

(G-13892)
SOREN TECHNOLOGIES INC
817 S University Dr # 106 (33324-3309)
PHONE..............................954 236-9998
Faiz Satteh, *President*
Shahnaz Satteh, *Vice Pres*
EMP: 10 **EST:** 1997

SALES (est): 589.5K **Privately Held**
SIC: 7372 7374 Prepackaged software;
computer graphics service

(G-13893)
SOUTH FLORIDA JAZZ INC
7860 Peters Rd Ste F110 (33324-4027)
PHONE..............................954 474-8889
Joel A Schneider, *Branch Mgr*
EMP: 23
SALES (corp-wide): 490.6K **Privately
Held**
WEB: www.southfloridajazz.org
SIC: 2741 Music book & sheet music pub-
lishing
PA: South Florida Jazz, Inc
10460 Kestrel St
Plantation FL 33324
954 424-4440

(G-13894)
THALES DIS CPL USA INC
900 S Pine Island Rd (33324-3920)
PHONE..............................954 888-6200
EMP: 17
SALES (corp-wide): 279.3MM **Privately
Held**
SIC: 7372 Prepackaged software
HQ: Thales Dis Cpl Usa, Inc.
9442 Cpitl Of Txas Hwy Pl
Austin TX 78759
410 931-7500

(G-13895)
THALES ESECURITY INC
900 S Pine Island Rd (33324-3920)
PHONE..............................954 888-6200
EMP: 116
SALES (corp-wide): 279.3MM **Privately
Held**
WEB: cpl.thalesgroup.com
SIC: 7372 Prepackaged software
HQ: Thales Esecurity, Inc.
2125 Zanker Rd
San Jose CA 95131
408 433-6000

(G-13896)
TIP TOP CANVAS AND UPHL INC
Also Called: Will Garrett Towers
6501 E Tropical Way (33317-3310)
PHONE..............................954 524-6214
David Crosby, *President*
Jeroen Candel, *General Mgr*
Laurence Simone, *Manager*
▼ **EMP:** 14 **EST:** 1989
SALES (est): 738.2K **Privately Held**
SIC: 2394 Canvas & related products

(G-13897)
**TRADESTATION
TECHNOLOGIES INC (DH)**
8050 Sw 10th St Ste 2000 (33324-3205)
PHONE..............................954 652-7000
William R Cruz, *Ch of Bd*
Ralph Cruz, *Ch of Bd*
Salomon Sredni, *President*
Michael Cavanaugh, *Vice Pres*
Benjamin Davis, *Opers Staff*
EMP: 145 **EST:** 1982
SQ FT: 70,000
SALES (est): 49.2MM **Privately Held**
WEB: www.tradestation.com
SIC: 7372 Prepackaged software
HQ: Tradestation Group, Inc.
8050 Sw 10th St Ste 4000
Plantation FL 33324
954 652-7000

(G-13898)
US DIAGNOSTICS INC
Also Called: Vertaloc
6600 Nw 16th St Ste 1 (33313-4554)
PHONE..............................866 216-5308
Edward Letko, *President*
▲ **EMP:** 20 **EST:** 2005
SALES (est): 1.8MM **Privately Held**
WEB: www.usdiagnostics.net
SIC: 2835 In vitro & in vivo diagnostic sub-
stances

(G-13899)
**VERTICAL SYSTEMS
INSPCTONS INC**
899 E Country Club Cir (33317-4505)
PHONE..............................954 775-6023

Hector Jiminez, *Principal*
EMP: 8 **EST:** 2008
SALES (est): 203.9K **Privately Held**
SIC: 2591 Blinds vertical

(G-13900)
VINLAND CORPORATION
11600 Nw 20th St (33323-2060)
PHONE...................................954 475-9093
Bertho Boman, *President*
▲ **EMP:** 27 **EST:** 1977
SQ FT: 3,000
SALES (est): 2.8MM **Privately Held**
WEB: www.vinland.com
SIC: 3699 8748 Electrical equipment &
supplies; systems analysis or design

(G-13901)
VINLAND INTERNATIONAL INC
1700 Nw 65th Ave Ste 12 (33313-4558)
PHONE...................................954 316-2007
Bertho Boman, *President*
Teresita Boman, *Vice Pres*
Eric Olaes, *Executive*
▲ **EMP:** 27 **EST:** 1994
SQ FT: 3,000
SALES (est): 3.2MM **Privately Held**
WEB: www.vinland.com
SIC: 3571 Electronic computers

(G-13902)
WEPLENISH LLC
150 S Pine Island Rd (33324-2669)
PHONE...................................954 909-4183
Rotem Grosman, *Principal*
Bill Deme, *Opers Staff*
Michael Medwin, *Officer*
EMP: 5 **EST:** 2015
SALES (est): 1.4MM **Privately Held**
WEB: www.weplenish.com
SIC: 3411 Food & beverage containers

Polk City
Polk County

(G-13903)
T BOWER ENTERPRISES INC
1824 Pearce Rd (33868-9751)
PHONE...................................863 984-3050
Todd Bower, *President*
Cathie Bower, *Vice Pres*
EMP: 8 **EST:** 1993
SALES (est): 702.1K **Privately Held**
SIC: 3273 Ready-mixed concrete

Pompano Beach
Broward County

(G-13904)
10X VEGAN LLC
1612 S Cypress Rd (33060-9137)
PHONE...................................954 256-4094
Jermaine Palmer, *CEO*
EMP: 11 **EST:** 2020
SALES (est): 541.7K **Privately Held**
WEB: www.10xvegan.com
SIC: 2099 Food preparations

(G-13905)
AB FIRE SPRINKLERS LLC
2759 Nw 19th St (33069-5232)
PHONE...................................954 973-8054
Linda Kanter,
EMP: 7 **EST:** 2018
SALES (est): 333.6K **Privately Held**
WEB: www.abfire.com
SIC: 3432 5063 Lawn hose nozzles &
sprinklers; fire alarm systems

(G-13906)
ABRASIVE DYNAMICS INC
1531 Se 24th Ter (33062-7511)
PHONE...................................860 291-0664
Joseph Jakab, *President*
Carol Jakab, *Shareholder*
EMP: 14 **EST:** 1986
SQ FT: 6,000
SALES (est): 515.7K **Privately Held**
SIC: 3291 Abrasive products

(G-13907)
ABSOLUTE POWDER COATING INC
1254 Nw 21st St (33069-1400)
PHONE...................................954 917-2715
Robert Marks, *President*
Daniel H Harcavi, *Technical Staff*
Charles Camacho, *Director*
EMP: 17 **EST:** 2003
SALES (est): 1.3MM **Privately Held**
WEB: www.absolutepowdercoat.com
SIC: 3479 Coating of metals & formed
products

(G-13908)
ACROCRETE INC (DH)
1259 Nw 21st St (33069-1428)
PHONE...................................954 917-4114
Gary Hasbach, *President*
Howard L Ehler Jr, *Vice Pres*
▼ **EMP:** 7 **EST:** 1988
SALES (est): 4.9MM
SALES (corp-wide): 387.6MM **Privately
Held**
SIC: 2821 Acrylic resins
HQ: Imperial Industries, Inc.
1259 Nw 21st St
Pompano Beach FL 33069
954 917-4114

(G-13909)
ADF INTERNATIONAL INC
Also Called: Adf Group
1925 Nw 15th St Ste A (33069-1641)
PHONE...................................954 931-5150
EMP: 12
SALES (corp-wide): 135.8MM **Privately
Held**
SIC: 3448 Mfg Prefabricated Metal Build-
ings
HQ: Adf International, Inc.
1900 Great Bear Ave
Great Falls MT 59404
800 895-4425

(G-13910)
ADHESIVES TECHNOLOGY CORP
Also Called: A T C
450 E Copans Rd (33064-5509)
PHONE...................................754 399-1684
Daniel Pelton, *CEO*
Tj Bland, *President*
Tom Richardson, *Vice Pres*
Roy Seroussi, *Vice Pres*
Steve Shade, *Vice Pres*
◆ **EMP:** 67 **EST:** 1988
SALES (est): 26.3MM **Privately Held**
WEB: www.atcepoxy.com
SIC: 2891 Adhesives; epoxy adhesives

(G-13911)
ADVANCED MDULAR STRUCTURES INC
Also Called: Advanced Modular Systems
1911 Nw 15th St (33069-1601)
PHONE...................................954 960-1550
Gary Willis, *CEO*
Patti Willis, *Vice Pres*
Marty Madura, *Project Mgr*
▼ **EMP:** 7 **EST:** 1988
SQ FT: 2,500
SALES (est): 955.9K **Privately Held**
WEB: www.advancedmodular.com
SIC: 2452 1541 Prefabricated wood build-
ings; steel building construction

(G-13912)
AFFORDABLE SCREE ENCLOSURE LLC
1425 Sw 1st Ct Ste 25 (33069-3247)
PHONE...................................800 900-8586
EMP: 10 **EST:** 2014
SALES (est): 1.8MM **Privately Held**
WEB: www.affordablepoolenclosure.com
SIC: 3448 3442 3355 Prefabricated metal
buildings; metal doors, sash & trim; alu-
minum rolling & drawing

(G-13913)
AIR SHELTERS USA LLC (PA)
650 Sw 16th Ter (33069-4533)
P.O. Box 667227 (33066-7227)
PHONE...................................215 957-6128
Christine Gagliardi, *Office Mgr*

Newton B Park, *Mng Member*
EMP: 21 **EST:** 2016
SALES (est): 5.1MM **Privately Held**
WEB: www.zumro.com
SIC: 2394 8322 Canvas awnings &
canopies; emergency shelters

(G-13914)
AIR SUPPLY OF FUTURE INC
1950 Nw 15th St Ste A (33069-1614)
PHONE...................................954 977-0877
Paul Bedard, *President*
Liza Muschett, *Principal*
▲ **EMP:** 13 **EST:** 1983
SALES (est): 4.1MM **Privately Held**
WEB: www.airsupplyflorida.com
SIC: 3561 Pumps & pumping equipment

(G-13915)
ALARIS AEROSPACE SYSTEMS LLC
1721 Blount Rd Ste 1 (33069-5104)
PHONE...................................954 596-8736
Bikramjit Jaswal, *President*
Dennis Anderon, *General Mgr*
Ramnik Soni, *COO*
Josef Kazes, *Exec VP*
Ian Coke, *QC Mgr*
▼ **EMP:** 19 **EST:** 2009
SQ FT: 13,033
SALES (est): 6.2MM **Privately Held**
WEB: www.alarisaero.com
SIC: 3728 Aircraft parts & equipment

(G-13916)
ALL GLASS & MIRROR LLC
Also Called: Superior Frameless Showers
4100 N Powerline Rd Ste A (33073-3083)
PHONE...................................561 914-5277
Paul Kuenzle, *Mng Member*
Amanda Kuenzle,
EMP: 10 **EST:** 2020
SALES (est): 915.1K **Privately Held**
SIC: 3231 Mirrored glass

(G-13917)
ALL PRO PAVERS HARDSCAPES INC
430 S Dixie Hwy E (33060-6910)
PHONE...................................954 300-6281
Batista Bianca, *Principal*
EMP: 7 **EST:** 2015
SALES (est): 195.4K **Privately Held**
SIC: 2951 Asphalt paving mixtures &
blocks

(G-13918)
ALL TANK SERVICES LLC
1903 W Mcnab Rd B (33069-4301)
PHONE...................................954 260-9443
Andrew Driessen, *General Mgr*
EMP: 8 **EST:** 2017
SALES (est): 764.5K **Privately Held**
WEB: www.alltankservicesfl.com
SIC: 2851 3732 Marine paints; boat build-
ing & repairing

(G-13919)
ALL VENUE GRAPHICS AND SIGNS
1700 Nw 15th Ave Ste 360 (33069-1717)
PHONE...................................954 399-7446
Randy Risley, *Principal*
EMP: 9 **EST:** 2017
SALES (est): 628.6K **Privately Held**
WEB: www.pompanosigncompany.com
SIC: 3993 Signs & advertising specialties

(G-13920)
ALLIANCE COMMERCIAL EQP INC
2460 Nw 17th Ln Ste 1 (33064-1537)
PHONE...................................772 232-8149
John Bartell, *CEO*
EMP: 15 **EST:** 2012
SQ FT: 9,000
SALES (est): 264.6K **Privately Held**
SIC: 3537 Industrial trucks & tractors

(G-13921)
ALPHA WOODWORK INC
2840 Ne 9th Ter (33064-5326)
PHONE...................................954 347-6251
Daniella Gomes, *Principal*
EMP: 9 **EST:** 2010

SALES (est): 182.2K **Privately Held**
WEB: www.alphawoodwork.com
SIC: 2431 Millwork

(G-13922)
ALPINE ENGINEREED PRODUCTS
1200 Park Central Blvd S (33064-2215)
PHONE...................................954 781-3333
Chris Cronje, *President*
EMP: 18 **EST:** 2000
SALES (est): 586.7K **Privately Held**
SIC: 3429 Manufactured hardware (gen-
eral)

(G-13923)
AMERICAN AUTO / MAR WIRG INC
1414 Sw 13th Ct (33069-4709)
PHONE...................................954 782-0193
Phil Schultz, *President*
EMP: 5 **EST:** 1978
SQ FT: 2,500
SALES (est): 706.5K **Privately Held**
WEB: www.customwiring.com
SIC: 3672 7539 3694 Wiring boards; au-
tomotive repair shops; engine electrical
equipment

(G-13924)
AMERICAN LW & PROMO PRODS LLC
100 Sw 5th St (33060-7904)
PHONE...................................954 946-5252
Annette Catania, *Marketing Staff*
Keith Treiber,
Salvatore Catania,
EMP: 6 **EST:** 2012
SALES (est): 339.2K **Privately Held**
WEB: www.americanlogowear.com
SIC: 2353 3993 5136 Uniform hats &
caps; signs & advertising specialties; ad-
vertising novelties; men's & boys' outer-
wear; men's & boys' sportswear & work
clothing

(G-13925)
AMERICAN PAVERS CONSULTANTS
Also Called: American Pavers Manufacturing
1251 Ne 48th St (33064-4910)
PHONE...................................954 418-0000
Joseph S Brito, *President*
EMP: 37 **EST:** 1988
SQ FT: 80,000
SALES (est): 1.5MM **Privately Held**
WEB: www.tremron.com
SIC: 3251 Brick & structural clay tile

(G-13926)
AMERICAN PAVERS MANUFACTURING (PA)
1251 Ne 48th St (33064-4910)
PHONE...................................954 418-0000
Joseph Brito, *President*
◆ **EMP:** 5 **EST:** 1985
SALES (est): 1.4MM **Privately Held**
SIC: 3271 Paving blocks, concrete

(G-13927)
AMERICAN POLYMER COMPANY
2201 Nw 16th St (33069-1550)
PHONE...................................786 877-4690
Scott M Genovesi, *Principal*
EMP: 17 **EST:** 2019
SALES (est): 2.5MM **Privately Held**
SIC: 2821 Plastics materials & resins

(G-13928)
AMERICAN TROPHY CO
Also Called: American Name Plate
831 W Mcnab Rd (33060-8937)
PHONE...................................954 782-2250
Steve Trodick, *President*
Harvey Flomenhoft, *Principal*
EMP: 7 **EST:** 1972
SQ FT: 2,500
SALES (est): 658K **Privately Held**
WEB: www.americantrophy.net
SIC: 3914 3999 Trophies; plaques, pic-
ture, laminated

(G-13929)
AMWARE LOGISTICS SERVICES INC
2203 Sw 3rd St (33069-3118)
PHONE.............................970 337-7000
Dave Robinson, *Branch Mgr*
Carlos Hernandez, *Manager*
EMP: 15
SALES (corp-wide): 91.9MM **Privately Held**
WEB: www.amwarelogistics.com
SIC: 2448 4731 Pallets, wood; truck transportation brokers
PA: Amware Logistics Services, Inc.
4050 Newpoint Pl
Lawrenceville GA 30043
678 377-8585

(G-13930)
APOLLO ENERGY SYSTEMS INC (PA)
4100 N Powerline Rd D3 (33073-3038)
PHONE.............................954 969-7755
Robert Aronsson, *CEO*
Raymond Douglas, *President*
Barry Iseard, *Vice Pres*
Nejat Veziroglu, *Vice Pres*
Sonny Spoden, *CFO*
▲ EMP: 7 EST: 1994
SQ FT: 7,000
SALES (est): 1.6MM **Privately Held**
WEB: www.apolloenergysystems.com
SIC: 3629 Electronic generation equipment

(G-13931)
AQUATHIN CORP
950 S Andrews Ave (33069-4604)
PHONE.............................800 462-7634
Alfred J Lipshultz, *President*
Debra L Lipshultz, *Corp Secy*
▼ EMP: 20 EST: 1980
SQ FT: 60,000
SALES (est): 3.9MM **Privately Held**
WEB: www.aquathin.com
SIC: 3589 Water purification equipment, household type; water treatment equipment, industrial

(G-13932)
ARCHITCTRAL DESIGNS METALWORKS
1773 Blount Rd Ste 307 (33069-5124)
PHONE.............................954 532-1331
Richard Gray, *President*
EMP: 7 EST: 2000
SALES (est): 98.9K **Privately Held**
SIC: 3446 Stairs, staircases, stair treads: prefabricated metal

(G-13933)
ARCHITECTURAL FOAM SUPPLY INC
100 Sw 12th Ave (33069-3222)
PHONE.............................954 943-6949
John Belcher, *President*
EMP: 19 EST: 2001
SQ FT: 65,000
SALES (est): 1.4MM **Privately Held**
WEB: www.foamsupply.com
SIC: 3086 Packaging & shipping materials, foamed plastic

(G-13934)
ARMALASER INC
4699 N Federal Hwy # 110 (33064-6510)
PHONE.............................954 937-6054
Richard Hovsepian, *President*
Pat Thompson, *Principal*
EMP: 7 EST: 2005
SALES (est): 629K **Privately Held**
WEB: www.armalaser.com
SIC: 3699 Laser systems & equipment

(G-13935)
ART CONNECTION USA LLC
2860 Center Port Cir (33064-2136)
PHONE.............................954 781-0125
David Harari, *President*
Ofer Sadik, *Vice Pres*
◆ EMP: 20 EST: 1985
SQ FT: 15,000

SALES (est): 3.9MM **Privately Held**
WEB: www.artconnectionusa.com
SIC: 2499 5023 Picture & mirror frames, wood; mirrors & pictures, framed & unframed

(G-13936)
ART CRAFT METALS INC
1630 Sw 13th Ct (33069-4713)
PHONE.............................954 946-4620
Russell L Davis, *President*
Mark C Davis, *Vice Pres*
Shirley R Davis, *Vice Pres*
Bret R Davis, *Treasurer*
EMP: 24 EST: 1958
SALES (est): 8.2MM **Privately Held**
SIC: 3446 Railings, bannisters, guards, etc.: made from metal pipe

(G-13937)
ARTISTIC STATUARY INC
1490 N Powerline Rd (33069-1917)
PHONE.............................954 975-9533
Steve Harrold, *President*
Joanne B Harrold, *Corp Secy*
Arthur C Harrold Sr, *Vice Pres*
Lisa Harrold, *Vice Pres*
◆ EMP: 21 EST: 1960
SQ FT: 8,400
SALES (est): 1.5MM **Privately Held**
WEB: www.artisticstatuary.com
SIC: 3272 Fountains, concrete; concrete products, precast

(G-13938)
ASSOCIATED STEEL & ALUM CO INC
3017 Nw 25th Ave (33069-1028)
PHONE.............................954 974-7890
Tim Mather, *President*
Nick Anton, *President*
Carmen Anton, *Vice Pres*
Roxana Reich, *Accounts Mgr*
▼ EMP: 18 EST: 2004
SALES (est): 4.5MM **Privately Held**
WEB: www.asaltdinc.com
SIC: 3312 3354 Blast furnaces & steel mills; aluminum extruded products

(G-13939)
ASSOCIATED STEEL & ALUM LTD
3017 Nw 25th Ave (33069-1028)
PHONE.............................954 974-7890
EMP: 9 EST: 2017
SALES (est): 142.9K **Privately Held**
WEB: www.asaltdinc.com
SIC: 3312 Blast furnaces & steel mills

(G-13940)
ASSURA WINDOWS AND DOORS LLC (PA)
1543 N Powerline Rd (33069-1620)
PHONE.............................954 781-4430
Edward Pooley, *President*
EMP: 2 EST: 2016
SALES (est): 21.6MM **Privately Held**
WEB: www.assurawindows.com
SIC: 3211 Window glass, clear & colored

(G-13941)
ATLANTIC MOLDING INC (PA)
2750 Ne 4th Ave (33064-5408)
PHONE.............................954 781-9340
Glen K Jones, *President*
Robert E Gunn, *Vice Pres*
▼ EMP: 12 EST: 1993
SQ FT: 8,000
SALES (est): 1MM **Privately Held**
SIC: 3089 Injection molding of plastics; plastic processing

(G-13942)
AXIS GROUP
4701 N Federal Hwy # 440 (33064-6562)
PHONE.............................954 580-6000
Tom Pughe, *President*
Tom Edwards, *Vice Pres*
EMP: 10 EST: 2006
SALES (est): 509.5K **Privately Held**
WEB: www.axisgroup.com
SIC: 3629 Electronic generation equipment

(G-13943)
B R Q GROSSMANS INC
Also Called: Copans Marketing and Advg
2087 N Powerline Rd Ste 1 (33069-1279)
PHONE.............................954 971-1077
Gary Grossman, *President*
Sheila Grossman, *Corp Secy*
Bob Meadows, *Accounts Exec*
EMP: 11 EST: 1982
SQ FT: 3,000
SALES (est): 1.6MM **Privately Held**
WEB: www.copansprinting.com
SIC: 2752 2791 2789 2759 Commercial printing, offset; typesetting; bookbinding & related work; commercial printing

(G-13944)
B R SIGNS INC
1301 W Copans Rd Ste B6 (33064-2227)
PHONE.............................954 973-7700
Bill Reicherter, *Manager*
EMP: 7 EST: 2018
SALES (est): 374.4K **Privately Held**
SIC: 3993 Signs & advertising specialties

(G-13945)
BADGER CORPORATION
3450 Ne 6th Ter (33064-5218)
PHONE.............................954 942-5277
William B Buerosse Jr, *President*
Diana S Buerosse, *Vice Pres*
EMP: 9 EST: 1993
SQ FT: 4,000
SALES (est): 1.5MM **Privately Held**
WEB: www.badgermetalcorp.com
SIC: 3444 Ducts, sheet metal

(G-13946)
BALLISTIC RECOVERY SYSTEMS INC
1543 N Powerline Rd # 3 (33069-1620)
PHONE.............................651 457-7491
Gary Moore, *Vice Pres*
David Blanchard, *Branch Mgr*
EMP: 100
SALES (corp-wide): 28.3MM **Privately Held**
SIC: 3728 Aircraft parts & equipment
PA: Ballistic Recovery Systems, Inc.
41383 Us 1 Hwy
Pinebluff NC 28373
651 457-7491

(G-13947)
BANKS SIGN SYSTEMS INC
Also Called: Banks, Roy Sign Systems
1791 Blount Rd Ste 1001 (33069-5137)
PHONE.............................954 979-0055
Roy Banks, *President*
Catherine Trinboli, *Vice Pres*
Maria Banks, *Treasurer*
EMP: 7 EST: 1983
SQ FT: 2,000
SALES (est): 474.6K **Privately Held**
WEB: www.roybanks.com
SIC: 3993 2752 Signs, not made in custom sign painting shops; commercial printing, lithographic

(G-13948)
BAR MAID CORPORATION (PA)
2950 Nw 22nd Ter (33069-1045)
PHONE.............................954 960-1468
George E Shepherd, *President*
Diane Michaud, *Vice Pres*
Lisa Grimes, *Admin Asst*
▲ EMP: 10 EST: 1946
SQ FT: 8,000
SALES (est): 2.6MM **Privately Held**
WEB: www.bestinthebar.com
SIC: 3589 2841 Dishwashing machines, commercial; soap & other detergents

(G-13949)
BARI MILLWORK & SUPPLY LLC
Also Called: Rome Supply
1975 Nw 18th St Ste C (33069-1650)
PHONE.............................954 969-9440
Darlene Baldino, *Vice Pres*
John Lewis, *Purch Mgr*
Wayne Baldino,
EMP: 28 EST: 2007
SALES (est): 5.3MM **Privately Held**
WEB: www.barimillworksupply.com
SIC: 2431 Millwork

(G-13950)
BIOSTEM TECHNOLOGIES INC
2836 Center Port Cir (33064-2136)
PHONE.............................954 380-8342
Jason Matuszewski, *CEO*
Andrew Vanvurst, *COO*
Michael Fortunato, *Controller*
EMP: 25 EST: 2014
SALES (est): 4.2MM **Privately Held**
WEB: www.biostemtechnologies.com
SIC: 2836 Biological products, except diagnostic

(G-13951)
BLACKLIDGE EMULSIONS INC
2501 Wiles Rd (33073-3017)
PHONE.............................954 275-7225
James Russo, *Manager*
EMP: 17 **Privately Held**
WEB: www.blacklidge.com
SIC: 2951 Asphalt & asphaltic paving mixtures (not from refineries)
PA: Blacklidge Emulsions, Inc.
12251 Bernard Pkwy # 200
Gulfport MS 39503

(G-13952)
BRAND LABS USA
325 Sw 15th Ave (33069-3246)
PHONE.............................954 532-5390
David Pollock, *CEO*
Austin Pollock, *Project Mgr*
EMP: 31 EST: 2015
SALES (est): 2.6MM **Privately Held**
WEB: www.brandlabsusa.com
SIC: 2844 5999 Cosmetic preparations; hair care products

(G-13953)
BRAND YOU WATERS LLC
2402 Bay Dr (33062-2917)
PHONE.............................786 312-0840
Robert V Plath, *Managing Prtnr*
R V Plath, *Partner*
Michael McBride, *Partner*
EMP: 6 EST: 2008
SALES (est): 356.7K **Privately Held**
SIC: 3221 Water bottles, glass

(G-13954)
BRIDGE CHEMICALS INC
2455 Se 7th Dr (33062-6410)
PHONE.............................954 545-9459
Christopher Liuzzo, *Director*
EMP: 8 EST: 2001
SALES (est): 133.5K **Privately Held**
SIC: 2813 Industrial gases

(G-13955)
BROSKI CIDERWORKS LLC
1465 Sw 6th Ct (33069-4532)
PHONE.............................954 657-8947
Cesar D Verdugo,
Daniel Verdugo,
EMP: 8 EST: 2015
SALES (est): 368.1K **Privately Held**
WEB: www.broskiciderworks.com
SIC: 2099 Cider, nonalcoholic

(G-13956)
BROWNIES MARINE GROUP INC (PA)
3001 Nw 25th Ave Ste 1 (33069-1028)
PHONE.............................954 462-5570
Christopher Constable, *CEO*
Robert Carmichael, *President*
▲ EMP: 8 EST: 1981
SQ FT: 16,566
SALES (est): 6.2MM **Publicly Held**
WEB: www.browniesmarinegroup.com
SIC: 3949 3563 Sporting & athletic goods; skin diving equipment, scuba type; air & gas compressors

(G-13957)
BUDGET SIGNS INC
1820 Sw 7th Ave (33060-9028)
PHONE.............................954 941-5710
Bill Simmons, *President*
April Simmons, *Vice Pres*
EMP: 10 EST: 1989
SQ FT: 3,000
SALES (est): 627.4K **Privately Held**
SIC: 3993 1799 Electric signs; sign installation & maintenance

▲ = Import ▼ =Export
◆ =Import/Export

(G-13958)
BUST OUT PROMOTIONS LLC
1375 Sw 12th Ave (33069-4630)
PHONE..............................561 305-8313
Michael Meier, *Exec Dir*
EMP: 7 Privately Held
WEB: www.mugrugs.net
SIC: 2392 Tablecloths & table settings;
tablecloths: made from purchased materi-
als; placemats, plastic or textile
PA: Bust Out Promotions Llc
1050 Hillsboro Mile
Hillsboro Beach FL 33062

(G-13959)
BYRD TECHNOLOGIES INC
Also Called: Mar-Quipt
3100 Sw 10th St (33069-4815)
PHONE..............................954 957-8333
Robert L Byrd, *President*
Garnett Byrd, *President*
Natasha Sabater, *Project Mgr*
Ronda Hood, *Manager*
Tim Schrader, *Manager*
◆ **EMP: 50 EST: 1992**
SQ FT: 56,776
SALES (est): 9.3MM Privately Held
WEB: www.marquipt.com
SIC: 3429 Marine hardware

(G-13960)
C&A BOATWORKS INC
1711 N Powerline Rd (33069-1698)
PHONE..............................754 366-5549
EMP: 7 EST: 2019
SALES (est): 138.6K Privately Held
WEB: www.jessiboats.com
SIC: 3732 Boat building & repairing

(G-13961)
C-WORTHY CORP
Also Called: C-Worthy Custom Yacht Canvas
241 Sw 5th Ct (33060-7911)
PHONE..............................954 784-7370
Carol Dykes, *President*
EMP: 14 EST: 1995
SALES (est): 3.5MM Privately Held
WEB: www.cworthycorp.com
SIC: 2394 3732 2392 Canvas covers &
drop cloths; boat building & repairing;
household furnishings

(G-13962)
CABINET WHOLESALE LLC
1301 W Copans Rd E1-4 (33064-2221)
PHONE..............................954 751-7200
EMP: 12
**SALES (corp-wide): 972.7K Privately
Held**
WEB: www.cabinetwholesale.com
SIC: 2434 Wood kitchen cabinets
PA: Cabinet Wholesale Llc
4100 N 29th Ave
Hollywood FL 33020
954 204-0123

(G-13963)
CABINETS BY MARYLIN INC
696 Sw 15th St (33060-8637)
PHONE..............................954 729-3995
Lincon Borda, *Director*
EMP: 8 EST: 2001
SALES (est): 100.3K Privately Held
WEB: www.tribecashoes.com
SIC: 2434 Wood kitchen cabinets

(G-13964)
**CALIFORNIA GREENS
CORPORATION**
301 N Ocean Blvd (33062-5113)
PHONE..............................630 423-5760
Mohammed Kotb Gobara, *Vice Pres*
EMP: 9 EST: 2016
SALES (est): 74.4K Privately Held
SIC: 2834 Pharmaceutical preparations

(G-13965)
CATSKILL EXPRESS LLC
1249 Hammondville Rd (33069-2927)
PHONE..............................954 784-5151
Andrew Brooks, *Principal*
▼ **EMP: 9 EST: 2006**
SALES (est): 633.2K Privately Held
SIC: 2741 Miscellaneous publishing

(G-13966)
CEMEX CNSTR MTLS FLA LLC
Also Called: Mat Div-Ft Lauder Maint Shop
1150 Nw 24th St (33064-2202)
PHONE..............................954 977-9222
Tim Coughlin, *Branch Mgr*
EMP: 7
SQ FT: 39,156 Privately Held
SIC: 3273 Ready-mixed concrete
HQ: Cemex Construction Materials Florida,
Llc
1501 Belvedere Rd
West Palm Beach FL 33406

(G-13967)
CENTERED MEMORIES LLC
2001 N Federal Hwy G209 (33062-1030)
PHONE..............................915 308-3224
Lashonda Joseph, *Principal*
EMP: 7 EST: 2020
SALES (est): 253K Privately Held
SIC: 2392 Tablecloths & table settings

(G-13968)
**CERTIFIED METAL FINISHING
INC**
Also Called: CMF
1420 Sw 28th Ave (33069-4817)
PHONE..............................954 979-0707
David W Sexton Jr, *President*
Fred Binda, *General Mgr*
Antonia Sexton, *Vice Pres*
Fred Lafond, *Manager*
EMP: 30 EST: 1982
SQ FT: 5,510
SALES (est): 4.9MM Privately Held
WEB: www.certifiedmetalfinishing.com
SIC: 3471 Anodizing (plating) of metals or
formed products; electroplating of metals
or formed products

(G-13969)
**CHEMKO TECHNICAL SERVICES
INC**
1000 E Atl Blvd Ste 115 (33060-7471)
PHONE..............................954 783-7673
EMP: 30
SQ FT: 5,000
SALES: 1MM Privately Held
SIC: 3823 7699 3312 Mfg Process Con-
trol Instruments Repair Services Blast
Furnace-Steel Works

(G-13970)
CMC BAKERY LLC
4100 N Powerline Rd M2 (33073-3042)
PHONE..............................978 682-2382
David Cafua,
EMP: 40 EST: 2015
SALES (est): 1.2MM Privately Held
SIC: 2051 Bakery: wholesale or whole-
sale/retail combined

(G-13971)
COASTAL WOODWORK INC
380 Sw 12th Ave (33069-3502)
PHONE..............................561 218-3353
Lori Nelson, *President*
EMP: 8 EST: 2013
SALES (est): 374.1K Privately Held
SIC: 2431 Millwork

(G-13972)
COLUMBIA FILMS INC
43 S Pompano Pkwy Ste 461
(33069-3001)
PHONE..............................800 531-3238
Sharond Ragin, *President*
EMP: 9 EST: 2013
SQ FT: 3,000
SALES (est): 730.9K Privately Held
SIC: 3861 7335 7384 Motion picture film;
color separation, photographic & movie
film; home movies, developing & process-
ing

(G-13973)
COMODERM CORP
2175 N Andrews Ave Ste 4 (33069-1431)
P.O. Box 122, Dania (33004-0122)
PHONE..............................561 756-2929
Sandra Mento, *President*
Elizabeth Mento, *Corp Secy*
Frank Mento, *Vice Pres*
EMP: 5 EST: 1994

SALES (est): 497K **Privately Held**
SIC: 2911 Petroleum refining

(G-13974)
CONCEPT 2 MARKET INC
3000 Nw 25th Ave Ste 11 (33069-1048)
PHONE..............................954 974-0022
Maria Kirkeeng, *CEO*
Todd Kirkeeng, *President*
Stephen Ballard, *Vice Pres*
Barbara Mahoney, *Purch Mgr*
EMP: 15 EST: 1994
SALES (est): 5MM Privately Held
WEB: www.c2mfl.com
SIC: 3679 3672 Loads, electronic; printed
circuit boards

(G-13975)
**CONQUEST MANUFACTURING
FLA LLC**
1121 Nw 31st Ave (33069-1109)
PHONE..............................954 655-0139
EMP: 10 EST: 2015
SALES (est): 493.7K Privately Held
SIC: 3999 Manufacturing industries

(G-13976)
**CONSTRUCTION AND ELEC
PDTS INC**
1800 Nw 15th Ave Ste 155 (33069-1410)
PHONE..............................954 972-9787
Michael L Brody, *President*
▲ **EMP: 11 EST: 2007**
SALES (est): 867.6K Privately Held
WEB: www.constructionandelectrical.com
SIC: 3545 5085 2673 3053 Machine tool
accessories; gaskets; gaskets & seals;
plastic & pliofilm bags; gaskets & sealing
devices; screw machine products; bolts,
nuts, rivets & washers

(G-13977)
**CONSUMER INFORMATION BUR
INC**
2301 W Sample Rd Ste 4-2a (33073-3010)
PHONE..............................954 971-5079
Jason Bowen, *Owner*
Ashley Christman, *Sales Staff*
EMP: 5 EST: 2002
SALES (est): 488.6K Privately Held
WEB:
www.consumerinformationbureau.com
SIC: 7372 Business oriented computer
software

(G-13978)
CONTACT ENTERPRISES INC
3170 N Federal Hwy # 100 (33064-6881)
PHONE..............................561 900-5134
Francisco Franca, *Principal*
EMP: 9 EST: 2015
SALES (est): 164.8K Privately Held
WEB: www.labels123.com
SIC: 2679 Converted paper products

(G-13979)
COOLCRAFT INC
1700 Nw 15th Ave Ste 330 (33069-1716)
PHONE..............................954 946-0070
Glen Ayers, *President*
▲ **EMP: 8 EST: 2000**
SQ FT: 5,000
SALES (est): 801.5K Privately Held
SIC: 3432 Plumbing fixture fittings & trim

(G-13980)
COUNTY PLASTICS CORP
1801 Nw 22nd St (33069-1317)
PHONE..............................954 971-9205
Alfred Bohnomme, *Manager*
EMP: 10
**SALES (corp-wide): 46.9MM Privately
Held**
WEB: www.chemtainer.com
SIC: 3089 Synthetic resin finished prod-
ucts; plastic containers, except foam
PA: County Plastics Corp.
361 Neptune Ave
West Babylon NY 11704
631 422-8300

(G-13981)
**CRETA GRANITE & MARBLE
INC**
1900 Nw 33rd St Ste 10 (33064-1340)
PHONE..............................954 956-9993
Sara O Gloria, *President*
Christiano Gloria, *Vice Pres*
EMP: 6 EST: 1999
SALES (est): 643K Privately Held
WEB: www.comefromtheheart.com
SIC: 3281 5032 1743 Granite, cut &
shaped; marble, building: cut & shaped;
granite building stone; terrazzo, tile, mar-
ble, mosaic work

(G-13982)
CRF GROUP INC
Also Called: Sign-A-Rama
4716 N Powerline Rd (33073-3076)
PHONE..............................954 428-7446
Gary Bogen, *CEO*
Randy Bogen, *Vice Pres*
EMP: 17 EST: 2002
SALES (est): 2.4MM Privately Held
WEB: www.signarama.com
SIC: 3993 Signs & advertising specialties

(G-13983)
**CROWN EQUIPMENT
CORPORATION**
Also Called: Crown Lift Trucks
2971 Center Port Cir (33064-2134)
PHONE..............................954 786-8889
Luisa Sierra, *Sales Staff*
Erick Suarez, *Sales Staff*
Andre Lauber, *Manager*
EMP: 65
SQ FT: 16,000
SALES (corp-wide): 5.2B Privately Held
WEB: www.crown.com
SIC: 3537 5084 Lift trucks, industrial: fork,
platform, straddle, etc.; industrial machin-
ery & equipment
PA: Crown Equipment Corporation
44 S Washington St
New Bremen OH 45869
419 629-2311

(G-13984)
CROWN PRODUCTS LLC (PA)
935 Nw 31st Ave Ste 4 (33069-1190)
PHONE..............................954 917-1118
Fredrick Levine, *CFO*
Jane Trunsky,
▲ **EMP: 5 EST: 2002**
SALES (est): 3.8MM Privately Held
WEB: www.crownproductsonline.com
SIC: 2673 2842 3999 Plastic bags: made
from purchased materials; cleaning or
polishing preparations; pet supplies

(G-13985)
CUSTOM CRAFTERS
170 Sw 5th St (33060-7904)
PHONE..............................954 792-6119
Nancy Hebert, *President*
Dan Hebert, *Vice Pres*
EMP: 5 EST: 1973
SALES (est): 483.1K Privately Held
SIC: 2434 Wood kitchen cabinets

(G-13986)
**CUSTOM MARINE CONCEPTS
INC (PA)**
Also Called: Active Thunderboats
2500 Ne 5th Ave (33064-5414)
PHONE..............................954 782-1111
Patrick Haughey, *President*
EMP: 10 EST: 1992
SQ FT: 200
SALES (est): 1.1MM Privately Held
SIC: 3732 Boat building & repairing

(G-13987)
CYBER GROUP USA LLC
Also Called: Cushybeds
3770 Park Central Blvd N (33064-2225)
PHONE..............................888 574-9555
Gus Novaes, *Mng Member*
EMP: 15 EST: 2015
SALES (est): 1MM Privately Held
SIC: 2023 Dietary supplements, dairy &
non-dairy based

(G-13988)
CYCLONE POWER TECHNOLOGIES INC (PA)
601 Ne 26th Ct (33064-5429)
P.O. Box 10916 (33061-6916)
PHONE..................954 943-8721
Harry Schoell, *Ch of Bd*
Christopher Nelson, *President*
Frankie Fruge, *COO*
Jacob Smitter, *Engineer*
Bruce Schames, *CFO*
EMP: 11 **EST:** 2004
SALES (est): 175K **Publicly Held**
WEB: www.cyclonepower.com
SIC: 3519 Internal combustion engines

(G-13989)
D R C INDUSTRIES INC
4100 N Powerline Rd Z1 (33073-3077)
PHONE..................954 971-0699
Roy H Cadogan, *President*
Diana R Cadogan, *Vice Pres*
EMP: 5 **EST:** 1989
SQ FT: 3,200
SALES (est): 474.3K **Privately Held**
SIC: 3471 Finishing, metals or formed products

(G-13990)
DAHER INC (PA)
601 Ne 10th St (33060-5749)
PHONE..................954 893-1400
Nicolas Chabbert, *Senior VP*
Philippe Santoro, *Network Mgr*
EMP: 6 **EST:** 2018
SALES (est): 5.5MM **Privately Held**
WEB: www.tbm.aero
SIC: 3728 Aircraft parts & equipment

(G-13991)
DENIM LILY LLC
2785 Se 11th St (33062-7034)
PHONE..................754 264-9331
Kim Spatz, *Owner*
EMP: 7 **EST:** 2011
SALES (est): 132.9K **Privately Held**
SIC: 2211 Denims

(G-13992)
DENTATE PORCELAIN INC
2722 Ne 1st St Ste 1 (33062-4934)
PHONE..................917 359-7696
Jaime Aponte, *Principal*
EMP: 8 **EST:** 2007
SALES (est): 237.5K **Privately Held**
SIC: 3843 Enamels, dentists'

(G-13993)
DEVCON SECURITY SERVICES CORP
Also Called: Gator Telecom
2801 Gateway Dr (33069-4324)
PHONE..................813 386-3849
EMP: 20
SALES (corp-wide): 98.4MM **Privately Held**
SIC: 3699 Mfg Electrical Equipment/Supplies
HQ: Devcon Security Services Corp.
2801 Gateway Dr
Pompano Beach FL 33069

(G-13994)
DHB ARMOR GROUP INC (PA)
2102 Sw 2nd St (33069-3116)
PHONE..................800 413-5155
David Brooks, *Ch of Bd*
EMP: 2 **EST:** 1995
SALES (est): 28.5MM **Privately Held**
WEB: www.pointblankenterprises.com
SIC: 3842 Bulletproof vests

(G-13995)
DHS UNLIMITED INC
Also Called: Dhs Equiptment
4100 N Powerline Rd G3 (33073-3040)
P.O. Box 770776, Coral Springs (33077-0776)
PHONE..................954 532-2142
David Schatz, *President*
Carrie Schatz, *Vice Pres*
EMP: 5 **EST:** 2003
SQ FT: 4,000

SALES (est): 928.8K **Privately Held**
SIC: 3531 5082 Construction machinery; general construction machinery & equipment

(G-13996)
DIABETIC CARE RX LLC (PA)
Also Called: Patient Care America
3890 Park Central Blvd N (33064-2264)
PHONE..................866 348-0441
Patrick Smith, *CEO*
Carlos Fonseca, *Warehouse Mgr*
Ana Andujar, *Accounting Mgr*
Kim Pollack, *Human Res Dir*
Jessica Thomas, *Sales Dir*
EMP: 30 **EST:** 2005
SQ FT: 8,000
SALES (est): 27.2MM **Privately Held**
WEB: www.pcacorp.com
SIC: 2834 Pharmaceutical preparations

(G-13997)
DIADEM SPORTS LLC (PA)
200 Park Central Blvd S (33064-2197)
PHONE..................844 434-2336
Michael Manglardi, *VP Opers*
Evan Specht, *Opers Staff*
Joel Evan Specht, *Mng Member*
Corbin Gapski, *Manager*
Alex J Bartlett, *Manager*
EMP: 5 **EST:** 2012
SALES (est): 1MM **Privately Held**
WEB: www.diademsports.com
SIC: 3949 Racket sports equipment

(G-13998)
DISTRICT 95 WOOD WORKING INC
Also Called: Prime Custom Cabinets & Design
1040 Sw 10th Ave Ste 4 (33069-4628)
PHONE..................888 400-3136
Franklin Herrera, *President*
Mel O'Keeffe, *Vice Pres*
EMP: 7 **EST:** 2017
SALES (est): 1.2MM **Privately Held**
WEB: www.district95woodwork.com
SIC: 2434 2521 Wood kitchen cabinets; cabinets, office: wood

(G-13999)
DOLL MARINE METAL FABRICATION
250 S Dixie Hwy E (33060-6935)
PHONE..................954 941-5093
James Doll, *President*
EMP: 5 **EST:** 1991
SALES (est): 528.7K **Privately Held**
SIC: 7692 Welding repair

(G-14000)
DOWNEY GROUP LLC
1100 Nw 15th Ave (33069-1943)
PHONE..................954 972-0026
Dan Downey, *Mng Member*
Laura Battye, *Manager*
Hugh Higgins,
Joshua Shapiro,
Angela D Soto,
◆ **EMP:** 50 **EST:** 1993
SQ FT: 60,000
SALES (est): 9.8MM **Privately Held**
WEB: www.downeyglass.com
SIC: 3231 Products of purchased glass

(G-14001)
DYNAMIC COLOR INC
200 Park Central Blvd S (33064-2197)
PHONE..................954 462-0261
Jeffrey Roschman, *President*
EMP: 13 **EST:** 2000
SALES (est): 4.5MM **Privately Held**
WEB: www.dynamiccolor.com
SIC: 2816 Color pigments

(G-14002)
DYNO LLC (PA)
Also Called: Dyno Merchandise
1571 W Copans Rd Ste 105 (33064-1527)
PHONE..................954 971-2910
David Gold, *CEO*
Jorge Suarez, *Warehouse Mgr*
Pattie Jackson, *Purchasing*
Marty Weinbaum, *CFO*
Karen Edwards, *Controller*
◆ **EMP:** 28 **EST:** 2005

SQ FT: 55,000
SALES (est): 18.7MM **Privately Held**
WEB: www.dynollc.com
SIC: 3999 Sewing kits, novelty

(G-14003)
EARTH GROUP INC
2200 N Andrews Ave (33064-1423)
PHONE..................954 979-8444
Gerald Bieber, *President*
▲ **EMP:** 10 **EST:** 1991
SQ FT: 15,860
SALES (est): 1.6MM **Privately Held**
SIC: 2841 Detergents, synthetic organic or inorganic alkaline

(G-14004)
EAST COAST DOOR INC
1297 Se 5th Ave (33060-9304)
PHONE..................954 868-4700
Lisa Clark, *Manager*
EMP: 8 **EST:** 2000
SALES (est): 209.9K **Privately Held**
WEB: www.eastcoastwindows.com
SIC: 2431 1799 Door frames, wood; special trade contractors

(G-14005)
EDAFA INDUSTRIES INC
1460 Sw 3rd St Ste 6 (33069-3216)
PHONE..................954 946-0830
Dario Perez, *President*
EMP: 7 **EST:** 1983
SALES (est): 602K **Privately Held**
WEB: www.edafaindustries.com
SIC: 3599 Machine shop, jobbing & repair

(G-14006)
EDWIN B STIMPSON COMPANY INC (PA)
1515 Sw 13th Ct (33069-4710)
PHONE..................954 946-3500
Howard C Rau, *CEO*
Ralph E Rau Jr, *President*
Charles Tarling, *President*
Scott H Thomas, *President*
James E Cuenin, *Vice Pres*
▲ **EMP:** 228 **EST:** 1852
SALES (est): 54.9MM **Privately Held**
WEB: www.stimpson.com
SIC: 3452 3469 Washers, metal; rivets, metal; electronic enclosures, stamped or pressed metal

(G-14007)
ELECTRIDUCT INC
1650 Nw 18th St Unit 801 (33069-1634)
PHONE..................954 867-9100
Joseph R Proto, *President*
Tiffani Taylor, *Director*
▲ **EMP:** 30 **EST:** 1955
SQ FT: 10,000
SALES (est): 4.1MM **Privately Held**
WEB: www.electriduct.com
SIC: 3679 5063 5961 Power supplies, all types: static; cable conduit; tools & hardware, mail order

(G-14008)
ELECTRO-OPTIX INC
2181 N Powerline Rd Ste 1 (33069-1261)
PHONE..................954 973-2800
Chris Schoenjohn, *President*
Jim Stevens, *Vice Pres*
Freda Zalman, *Vice Pres*
▲ **EMP:** 12 **EST:** 1964
SQ FT: 10,000
SALES (est): 1MM **Privately Held**
WEB: www.electro-optix.com
SIC: 3827 3829 3851 Magnifying instruments, optical; thermometers & temperature sensors; ophthalmic goods

(G-14009)
EMERGENCY VEHICLE SUP CO LLC
2251 Hammondville Rd (33069-1505)
P.O. Box 667392 (33066-7392)
PHONE..................954 428-5201
Robert G Windesheim,
EMP: 30 **EST:** 2005
SQ FT: 10,000

SALES (est): 4.7MM **Privately Held**
SIC: 3711 5531 3647 5063 Patrol wagons (motor vehicles), assembly of; automobile & truck equipment & parts; automotive parts; dome lights, automotive; flasher lights, automotive; flashlights

(G-14010)
EMPOWERED DIAGNOSTICS LLC
3341 W Mcnab Rd (33069-4808)
PHONE..................206 228-5990
Rick Hennessey,
EMP: 7 **EST:** 2020
SALES (est): 1.1MM **Privately Held**
WEB: www.empowereddiagnostics.com
SIC: 2836 Biological products, except diagnostic

(G-14011)
ENGEAD GB DESIGN & PRTG INC
414 E Sample Rd (33064-4424)
PHONE..................954 783-5161
EMP: 7
SALES (est): 880.6K **Privately Held**
SIC: 2759 Commercial Printing

(G-14012)
ENOLGAS USA INC
2530 N Powerline Rd # 401 (33069-1056)
PHONE..................754 205-7902
Vittorio Bonomi, *President*
Juan Ramirez, *Graphic Designe*
▲ **EMP:** 5 **EST:** 2008
SQ FT: 3,200
SALES (est): 2.5MM
SALES (corp-wide): 55.5MM **Privately Held**
WEB: www.enolgas.it
SIC: 3494 1711 3432 Valves & pipe fittings; plumbing, heating, air-conditioning contractors; plumbing fixture fittings & trim
PA: Enolgas Bonomi Spa
Via Europa 227/229
Concesio BS 25062
030 218-4311

(G-14013)
EPS METAL FINISHING
640 Ne 26th Ct (33064-5430)
PHONE..................954 782-3073
Campbell Errol, *Principal*
EMP: 8 **EST:** 2011
SALES (est): 109.8K **Privately Held**
SIC: 3471 Finishing, metals or formed products

(G-14014)
ESSEX PLASTICS MIDWEST LLC LC
1531 Nw 12th Ave (33069-1796)
PHONE..................954 956-1100
Brian Stevenson, *CEO*
▲ **EMP:** 600 **EST:** 1967
SQ FT: 117,000
SALES (est): 51.8MM
SALES (corp-wide): 105.1MM **Privately Held**
SIC: 3081 Polyethylene film
HQ: Flexsol Packaging Corp. Of Pompano Beach
1531 Nw 12th Ave
Pompano Beach FL 33069
800 325-7740

(G-14015)
EXOTIC COUNTERTOP INC
2160 Nw 22nd St (33069-1341)
PHONE..................954 979-8188
Ellyson Medeiros, *President*
Milton Freitas, *Vice Pres*
EMP: 6 **EST:** 2009
SALES (est): 600.4K **Privately Held**
WEB: www.exoticcountertops.com
SIC: 3281 5032 Granite, cut & shaped; marble building stone

(G-14016)
EXPRESSIONS IN WOOD
4270 Nw 19th Ave Ste A (33064-8717)
PHONE..................954 956-0005
EMP: 8

▲ = Import ▼ =Export
◆ =Import/Export

SALES (est): 811.7K **Privately Held**
SIC: 2512 Mfg Upholstered Household Furniture

(G-14017)
FANTASY MARBLE & GRANITE INC
400 Sw 12th Ave Ste 4/5 (33069-3514)
PHONE...............................954 788-0433
Dominic Mathiot, *President*
Anthony Ventura, *Vice Pres*
Haakon Hodge, *Treasurer*
▲ **EMP:** 8 **EST:** 2000
SQ FT: 7,000
SALES (est): 593.5K **Privately Held**
WEB: www.fantasymarbleandgranite.com
SIC: 3281 5032 Granite, cut & shaped; marble building stone

(G-14018)
FCBN LLC
2637 E Atl Blvd 22868 (33062-4939)
PHONE...............................408 505-1324
Heather Obrien,
Kent Clothier,
EMP: 6 **EST:** 2009
SALES (est): 309.6K **Privately Held**
SIC: 7372 Prepackaged software

(G-14019)
FGA PRINTING
Also Called: Creative Printing
2550 N Powerline Rd # 105 (33069-5901)
PHONE...............................954 763-1122
Jim Mautner, *President*
EMP: 5 **EST:** 1990
SALES (est): 450.3K **Privately Held**
SIC: 2752 2791 2759 Commercial printing, offset; typesetting; commercial printing

(G-14020)
FIBERBUILT UMBRELLAS INC
2201 W Atlantic Blvd (33069-2792)
P.O. Box 667110 (33066-7110)
PHONE...............................954 484-9139
Paul Knapp, *President*
Jordan Beckner, *Vice Pres*
Diane Repole, *Purch Mgr*
Jonel Neda, *CFO*
Jessica B Rosenfeld, *Sales Mgr*
◆ **EMP:** 25 **EST:** 2000
SQ FT: 17,500
SALES (est): 6.9MM **Privately Held**
WEB: www.fiberbuiltumbrellas.com
SIC: 2211 Umbrella cloth, cotton

(G-14021)
FIRST MARKETING COMPANY (PA)
3300 Gateway Dr (33069-4883)
PHONE...............................954 979-0700
Ronald Drenning II, *President*
Ronald Grening, *President*
Harold Hale, *CFO*
David Goldstone, *Director*
Sandra Olivieri, *Director*
EMP: 160 **EST:** 1999
SALES (est): 29.2MM **Privately Held**
WEB: www.first-marketing.com
SIC: 2721 8742 Trade journals: publishing only, not printed on site; management consulting services

(G-14022)
FIRST SIGN CORP
2085 N Powerline Rd Ste 1 (33069-1283)
PHONE...............................954 972-7222
Marilyn Young, *President*
Greg Young, *Treasurer*
Julene Beddow, *Sales Staff*
Jon Calder, *Sales Staff*
Sandy Haradon, *Admin Sec*
▼ **EMP:** 10 **EST:** 1980
SQ FT: 6,000
SALES (est): 1.1MM **Privately Held**
WEB: www.firstsign.com
SIC: 3993 Signs, not made in custom sign painting shops

(G-14023)
FIRSTPATH LABORATORY SVCS LLC
Also Called: Ritetest
3141 W Mcnab Rd (33069-4806)
PHONE...............................954 977-6977
Ronald M Giffler, *Principal*
EMP: 9 **EST:** 2011
SALES (est): 5.1MM **Privately Held**
WEB: www.firstpathlab.com
SIC: 2869 Laboratory chemicals, organic

(G-14024)
FISCHER PANDA GENERATORS INC
351 S Andrews Ave (33069-3501)
PHONE...............................954 462-2800
Anthony Rushton, *President*
James Ashly Rushton, *COO*
James Rushton, *COO*
Tony Rushton, *Vice Pres*
Kyle Riebel, *Project Engr*
◆ **EMP:** 17 **EST:** 1995
SQ FT: 8,344
SALES (est): 3MM **Privately Held**
WEB: www.fischerpanda.com
SIC: 3621 Motors & generators

(G-14025)
FISCHER PANDA GENERATORS LLC
351 S Andrews Ave (33069-3501)
PHONE...............................954 462-2800
Antoine Miller, *Project Mgr*
Anthony Rushton, *Mng Member*
Alan Cowen, *Manager*
EMP: 30 **EST:** 2010
SALES (est): 3.7MM **Privately Held**
WEB: www.fischerpanda.com
SIC: 3621 Motors & generators

(G-14026)
FIVE STAR MILLWORK INC
4100 N Powerline Rd Y4 (33073-3077)
PHONE...............................954 956-7665
William Santana, *President*
Susan Santana, *Treasurer*
EMP: 13 **EST:** 2001
SALES (est): 2.4MM **Privately Held**
WEB: www.fivestarmillwork.net
SIC: 2431 Millwork

(G-14027)
FL INDUSTRIES INC
2930 Ne 8th Ave (33064-5330)
PHONE...............................954 422-3766
Ricardo Fernandez, *President*
EMP: 7 **EST:** 2016
SALES (est): 102.8K **Privately Held**
SIC: 3999 Manufacturing industries

(G-14028)
FLAGSTONE PAVERS SOUTH
1251 Ne 48th St (33064-4910)
PHONE...............................239 225-5646
EMP: 7 **EST:** 2016
SALES (est): 195.6K **Privately Held**
WEB: www.flagstonepavers.com
SIC: 3281 Flagstones

(G-14029)
FLAVANA LLC
1480 S Dixie Hwy E (33060-8517)
P.O. Box 669270 (33066-9270)
PHONE...............................561 285-7034
William Riddick, *Mng Member*
Kenneth Christian, *Mng Member*
David Vogel, *Mng Member*
EMP: 5 **EST:** 2013
SQ FT: 5,100
SALES (est): 400.3K **Privately Held**
SIC: 2111 Cigarettes

(G-14030)
FLEXITEEK AMERICAS INC
3109 Nw 25th Ave (33069-1030)
PHONE...............................954 973-4335
Edward Hoch, *CEO*
◆ **EMP:** 8 **EST:** 2002
SQ FT: 14,000
SALES (est): 3.4MM **Privately Held**
WEB: www.flexiteek.com
SIC: 3732 Boat building & repairing

HQ: Flexiteek International As
Tjuvholmen Kanalen 5
Oslo 0252

(G-14031)
FLEXSOL HOLDING CORP (PA)
1531 Nw 12th Ave (33069-1730)
PHONE...............................954 941-6333
Dave Clarke, *President*
Brian Stevenson, *President*
Ed Stranberg, *COO*
Ros Poplak, *CIO*
◆ **EMP:** 20 **EST:** 1999
SALES (est): 105.1MM **Privately Held**
WEB: www.isoflexpackaging.com
SIC: 2673 3082 3081 Plastic & pliofilm bags; plastic bags: made from purchased materials; tubes, unsupported plastic; plastic film & sheet; polyethylene film; packing materials, plastic sheet

(G-14032)
FLORIDA PRINTING GROUP INC
1850 S Ocean Blvd Apt 904 (33062-7914)
PHONE...............................954 956-8570
Philip Lomenzo, *President*
EMP: 8 **EST:** 1993
SQ FT: 5,000
SALES (est): 298.5K **Privately Held**
WEB: www.thefloridaprintinggroup.com
SIC: 2752 Commercial printing, offset

(G-14033)
FLORIDA QUALITY TRUSS INC
3635 Park Central Blvd N (33064-2262)
PHONE...............................954 975-3384
Tolga Adak, *Principal*
EMP: 7 **EST:** 2016
SALES (est): 1.6MM **Privately Held**
WEB: www.floridaqualitytruss.com
SIC: 2439 Trusses, wooden roof

(G-14034)
FLORIDA QUALITY TRUSS INDS INC (PA)
3635 Park Central Blvd N (33064-2262)
PHONE...............................954 971-3167
Rasmin Adak, *President*
Rasim Guney Adak, *President*
Tolga Adak, *Vice Pres*
◆ **EMP:** 10 **EST:** 1987
SQ FT: 3,000
SALES (est): 5.3MM **Privately Held**
WEB: www.floridaqualitytruss.com
SIC: 2439 Trusses, wooden roof

(G-14035)
FORT LAUDERDALE WDWKG INC
3001 Sw 10th St (33069-4814)
PHONE...............................954 935-0366
Charles R Watts, *President*
Sandra L Watts, *Corp Secy*
EMP: 40 **EST:** 1979
SQ FT: 40,000
SALES (est): 3.2MM **Privately Held**
WEB: www.fortlauderdalewoodworking.com
SIC: 2431 Millwork

(G-14036)
FURNITURE CONCEPTS 2000 INC
454 Ne 28th St (33064-5438)
PHONE...............................954 946-0310
Dan Kelly, *President*
EMP: 6 **EST:** 1982
SQ FT: 6,000
SALES (est): 512.1K **Privately Held**
SIC: 2434 2511 Wood kitchen cabinets; wood household furniture

(G-14037)
GB PRINTING
Also Called: Need Printing
414 E Sample Rd (33064-4424)
PHONE...............................954 941-3778
Lewis Rovero, *President*
EMP: 10 **EST:** 2004
SALES (est): 608.9K **Privately Held**
WEB: www.gbprinting.net
SIC: 2752 Commercial printing, offset

(G-14038)
GCATO 1959 ENTERPRISES LLC
2750 Nw 11th St (33069-1831)
PHONE...............................954 937-6282
Te Andre Gomion, *Mng Member*
EMP: 8 **EST:** 2020
SALES (est): 285.5K **Privately Held**
SIC: 2599 Food wagons, restaurant

(G-14039)
GCN PUBLISHING INC
Also Called: Gcn Media Services
49 N Federal Hwy 338 (33062-4304)
PHONE...............................203 665-6211
Joanne Persico, *President*
Elaine Goncalves, *Accounts Exec*
EMP: 7 **EST:** 2002
SALES (est): 168.6K **Privately Held**
WEB: www.gcnpublishing.com
SIC: 2741

(G-14040)
GK WINDOW TREATMENTS INC
231 Sw 5th St (33060-7905)
PHONE...............................954 786-2927
Garo Kalpakjian, *President*
EMP: 11 **EST:** 1988
SQ FT: 6,375
SALES (est): 1.7MM **Privately Held**
WEB: www.gkwindowtreatments.com
SIC: 2591 2391 Blinds vertical; curtains & draperies

(G-14041)
GLOBAL HOLDINGS AND DEV LLC
3850 Oaks Clubhouse Dr (33069-3668)
PHONE...............................949 500-4997
Barbara Kaufman, *CEO*
Mark Parsons, *COO*
EMP: 7 **EST:** 2010
SALES (est): 24.6MM **Privately Held**
SIC: 2821 4953 Plastics materials & resins; recycling, waste materials

(G-14042)
GLOBAL PERFORMANCE WINDOWS INC
Also Called: Global Windows
1881 Sw 3rd St (33069-3105)
PHONE...............................954 942-3322
Jean Lefrancois, *President*
Gabriel Matteau, *Corp Secy*
Alain Lefrancois, *Vice Pres*
▲ **EMP:** 15 **EST:** 2006
SALES (est): 3.8MM
SALES (corp-wide): 12.4MM **Privately Held**
WEB: www.epsylon.ca
SIC: 3211 1751 3231 Window glass, clear & colored; window & door (prefabricated) installation; insulating units, multiple-glazed: made from purchased glass
PA: Epsylon Concept Inc.
1010 Av Nordique
Quebec QC G1C 0
418 661-6262

(G-14043)
GPT MEDIA GROUP CORPORATION
Also Called: Thinkprint
140 Park Central Blvd S (33064-2138)
PHONE...............................954 315-0990
Brian Boyd, *President*
Cetta Boyd, *Vice Pres*
EMP: 29 **EST:** 1998
SALES (est): 3.4MM **Privately Held**
WEB: www.lithoprint.net
SIC: 2752 Commercial printing, offset

(G-14044)
GRAPHIC IMAGES INC
2301 Nw 33rd Ct Ste 105 (33069-1000)
PHONE...............................954 984-0015
Gerald J Goudreau, *President*
Ryan Goudreau, *Sales Staff*
Pam Goudreau, *Representative*
EMP: 10 **EST:** 1972
SQ FT: 10,000
SALES (est): 1.9MM **Privately Held**
WEB: www.giprint.com
SIC: 3993 Signs & advertising specialties

(G-14045)
GREAT LOCATIONS INC (PA)
2745 E Atl Blvd Ste 305 (33062-4976)
PHONE....................................954 943-1188
Charles Russell, *President*
EMP: 8 EST: 1991
SALES (est): 1.5MM **Privately Held**
WEB: www.yourguidesoflo.com
SIC: 2731 Books: publishing only

(G-14046)
GROUP III INTERNATIONAL INC
2981 W Mcnab Rd Ste 1 (33069-4804)
PHONE....................................954 984-1607
John Pulichino, *CEO*
Robert Arbelo, *Opers Staff*
Ana Hernandez, *Accountant*
Ed Whitty, *Marketing Staff*
Michael Benharroch, *Manager*
▲ EMP: 78 EST: 1984
SQ FT: 48,700
SALES (est): 18.8MM **Privately Held**
WEB: www.groupiiico.com
SIC: 3172 5099 Personal leather goods;
luggage

(G-14047)
GURTAN DESIGNS
Also Called: Wall Sculpture By Grutan
1048 Sw 4th Ter (33060-8604)
P.O. Box 1708 (33061-1708)
PHONE....................................954 972-6100
Vedat Gurtan, *Partner*
Huat Gurtan, *Partner*
EMP: 8 EST: 1978
SQ FT: 4,000
SALES (est): 350K **Privately Held**
WEB: www.gurtan.com
SIC: 3446 Ornamental metalwork

(G-14048)
HAMILTON SUNDSTRAND CORP
Also Called: UTC Aerospace Systems
2901 Nw 27th Ave (33069-1010)
PHONE....................................860 654-6252
EMP: 87
SALES (corp-wide): 64.3B **Publicly Held**
WEB: www.collinsaerospace.com
SIC: 3724 Aircraft engines & engine parts
HQ: Hamilton Sundstrand Corporation
1 Hamilton Rd
Windsor Locks CT 06096
860 654-6000

(G-14049)
HI TECH PRINTING SYSTEMS INC
3411 Ne 6th Ter (33064-5217)
P.O. Box 50556, Lighthouse Point (33074-0556)
PHONE....................................954 933-9155
David L Trudeau Sr, *President*
Priscilla Trudea, *Vice Pres*
David Trudeau, *Vice Pres*
EMP: 24 EST: 1988
SQ FT: 6,400
SALES (est): 4.1MM **Privately Held**
WEB: www.hi-techprinting.com
SIC: 2752 Commercial printing, offset

(G-14050)
HISPANIC CERTIFIED FOODS INC
1741 Nw 33rd St (33064-1327)
PHONE....................................305 772-6815
Perry Burke, *President*
◆ EMP: 5 EST: 2006
SQ FT: 800,000
SALES (est): 442.1K **Privately Held**
SIC: 2099 5141 Food preparations; food
brokers

(G-14051)
HOERBGER CMPRSSION TECH AMER H (DH)
3350 Gateway Dr (33069-4841)
PHONE....................................954 974-5700
Franz Gruber, *President*
Peter Laube, *Treasurer*
▲ EMP: 350 EST: 1999
SQ FT: 25,000

SALES (est): 118.5MM
SALES (corp-wide): 278MM **Privately Held**
SIC: 3494 7699 Valves & pipe fittings;
valve repair, industrial
HQ: Hoerbiger Holding Ag
Baarerstrasse 18
Zug ZG 6302
415 601-000

(G-14052)
HOERBIGER CORP AMERICA INC (DH)
Also Called: Hoerbiger Compression Techno
lo
3350 Gateway Dr (33069-4841)
PHONE....................................954 974-5700
Don York, *President*
Thomas Rabil, *Corp Secy*
Hannes Hunschosky, *Exec VP*
Bruce Driggett, *Vice Pres*
Christean Kapp, *Vice Pres*
▲ EMP: 260 EST: 1963
SQ FT: 185,000
SALES (est): 79.6MM
SALES (corp-wide): 278MM **Privately Held**
SIC: 3491 Industrial valves
HQ: Hoerbiger Compression Technology
America Holding, Inc.
3350 Gateway Dr
Pompano Beach FL 33069
954 974-5700

(G-14053)
HOME HEALTHCARE 2000 INC
1290 Sw 30th Ave (33069-4825)
P.O. Box 668864 (33066-8864)
PHONE....................................954 977-4450
Joseph Chang, *President*
Barry Cleveland, *Sales Mgr*
EMP: 6 EST: 2011
SQ FT: 49,000
SALES (est): 341.8K **Privately Held**
SIC: 3845 Laser systems & equipment,
medical

(G-14054)
HOOVER PUMPING SYSTEMS CORP
2801 N Powerline Rd (33069-1009)
PHONE....................................954 971-7350
Brent Hoover, *President*
Kevin Cavaioli, *Vice Pres*
Lori Douvris, *Opers Staff*
Matt Eggerman, *Opers Staff*
Kevin Nowacki, *CFO*
▼ EMP: 30 EST: 1984
SQ FT: 21,000
SALES (est): 8.3MM **Privately Held**
WEB: www.hooverpumping.com
SIC: 3561 1623 Industrial pumps & parts;
water main construction

(G-14055)
HOUGHTON MIFFLIN HARCOURT PUBG
1840 Nw 16th St (33069-1627)
PHONE....................................954 975-0508
Mike Mc Tiernan, *Controller*
EMP: 19
SALES (corp-wide): 1B **Privately Held**
WEB: www.hmhco.com
SIC: 2731 Textbooks: publishing only, not
printed on site
HQ: Houghton Mifflin Harcourt Publishing
Company
125 High St Ste 900
Boston MA 02110
617 351-5000

(G-14056)
HYBRID ENGINES CORP
1001 S Riverside Dr (33062-6583)
PHONE....................................954 591-5303
William Wiens, *Principal*
EMP: 7 EST: 2008
SALES (est): 92.3K **Privately Held**
SIC: 3519 Internal combustion engines

(G-14057)
I BE CAKIN LLC
720 Nw 17th St (33060-5146)
PHONE....................................954 707-3865
Nikitress Cleveland, *CEO*

EMP: 7 EST: 2020
SALES (est): 368.1K **Privately Held**
SIC: 2051 5963 Bakery products, partially
cooked (except frozen); bakery goods,
house-to-house

(G-14058)
IBIZ INC
Also Called: Ibiz Wrld Class Detailing Pdts
1700 Nw 15th Ave (33069-1711)
PHONE....................................954 781-4714
Robert Nathans, *President*
Ibi Nathans, *Vice Pres*
EMP: 10 EST: 1992
SALES (est): 828.5K **Privately Held**
WEB: www.waxdirect.com
SIC: 2842 Polishing preparations & related
products; automobile polish

(G-14059)
IMAGE GRAPHICS 2000 INC
2450 W Sample Rd Ste 20 (33073-3074)
P.O. Box 670276 (33067-0005)
PHONE....................................954 332-3380
Wade Davis, *President*
Chris Burns, *Manager*
Maria Gomez, *Manager*
EMP: 11 EST: 2001
SQ FT: 3,500
SALES (est): 823.4K **Privately Held**
WEB: www.igxboatwraps.com
SIC: 2759 Commercial printing

(G-14060)
IMPERIAL INDUSTRIES INC (HQ)
1259 Nw 21st St (33069-1428)
PHONE....................................954 917-4114
Howard L Ehler Jr, *CEO*
Steven M Healy, *CFO*
◆ EMP: 9 EST: 1968
SQ FT: 19,600
SALES (est): 15.6MM
SALES (corp-wide): 387.6MM **Privately Held**
SIC: 3441 3272 Building components,
structural steel; concrete products
PA: Q.E.P. Co., Inc.
1001 Broken Sound Pkwy Nw A
Boca Raton FL 33487
561 994-5550

(G-14061)
IMPERIAL PRIVACY SYSTEMS LLC
1400 Sw 8th St (33069-4512)
P.O. Box 578 (33061-0578)
PHONE....................................954 782-7130
Brandon Bernardo, *CEO*
Patricia Zane, *President*
Gerald F Shea, *Corp Secy*
Robert J Shea, *Vice Pres*
Gerald Shea, *Treasurer*
▼ EMP: 40 EST: 1967
SQ FT: 18,000
SALES (est): 3.2MM **Privately Held**
WEB: www.imperialprivacy.com
SIC: 2591 Curtain & drapery rods, poles &
fixtures

(G-14062)
INOX STAINLESS SPECIALIST LLC
1336 Sw 8th St (33069-4510)
PHONE....................................407 764-2456
Jorge H Rodriguez, *CEO*
EMP: 5 EST: 2014
SALES (est): 432.8K **Privately Held**
WEB: www.quickmetalshop.com
SIC: 3441 Fabricated structural metal

(G-14063)
INTERNATIONAL MEDICAL INDS INC
Also Called: IMI
2981 Gateway Dr (33069-4326)
PHONE....................................954 917-9570
Jonathan Vitello, *President*
Gene Streicher, *Vice Pres*
Susan Vitello, *Vice Pres*
Mohammed Alshehri, *Engineer*
Blaise Barone, *Engineer*
◆ EMP: 30 EST: 1969
SQ FT: 16,000

SALES (est): 9.5MM **Privately Held**
WEB: www.imiweb.com
SIC: 3841 Surgical & medical instruments

(G-14064)
J & K 8 INC
Also Called: J&K Kitchen, Bath and Stone
1591 N Powerline Rd (33069-1604)
PHONE....................................954 984-8585
Chuen K Cheng, *President*
Ken Yeung, *Vice Pres*
EMP: 18 EST: 2005
SALES (est): 1MM **Privately Held**
SIC: 2499 Kitchen, bathroom & household
ware: wood

(G-14065)
JAS BUSINESS SOLUTIONS INC
Also Called: JAS Interconnect Solutions
200 Park Central Blvd S (33064-2197)
PHONE....................................954 975-0025
Ronald Scoppettone, *President*
John Scerbo, *President*
EMP: 33 EST: 2006
SALES (est): 2MM **Privately Held**
SIC: 3674 Solid state electronic devices

(G-14066)
JET FACTORY LLC (PA)
1900 Nw 33rd Ct Ste 5 (33064-1332)
PHONE....................................786 387-6865
EMP: 7 EST: 2017
SALES (est): 116.6K **Privately Held**
SIC: 3999 Manufacturing industries

(G-14067)
JMH MARINE INC
Also Called: Accudock
1790 Sw 13th Ct (33069-4715)
P.O. Box 1200, Charlestown NH (03603-1200)
PHONE....................................954 785-7557
John Harrison, *President*
Jason Harrison, *General Mgr*
Aj Barcz, *Principal*
Christine Catalano, *Principal*
Kim Holt, *Principal*
▼ EMP: 10 EST: 1992
SALES (est): 4.8MM **Privately Held**
WEB: www.accudock.com
SIC: 3089 3731 5091 Extruded finished
plastic products; drydocks, floating; sport-
ing & recreation goods; watersports
equipment & supplies; boats, canoes, wa-
tercrafts & equipment

(G-14068)
JONES AWNINGS & CANVAS INC
127 Nw 16th St (33060-5250)
PHONE....................................954 784-6966
Brad Jones, *President*
Scott Riolino, *General Mgr*
Barbara Jones, *Vice Pres*
EMP: 37 EST: 1999
SALES (est): 4.8MM **Privately Held**
WEB: www.jonesawnings.com
SIC: 2394 Awnings, fabric: made from pur-
chased materials

(G-14069)
JS2 AEROSPACE CORP
1888 Nw 21st St (33069-1334)
PHONE....................................954 840-3620
Jeffrey Smith, *Principal*
Austin Smith, *Technician*
EMP: 9 EST: 2018
SALES (est): 1MM **Privately Held**
WEB: www.js2aero.aero
SIC: 3728 Aircraft parts & equipment

(G-14070)
KIDSTANCE LLC
Also Called: Modified Kids Ride On Toys
2441 Nw 16th Ln (33064-1579)
PHONE....................................954 245-9916
Denver Pettigrew, *President*
EMP: 5 EST: 2014
SALES (est): 357.8K **Privately Held**
WEB: www.kidstancebuilt.com
SIC: 3944 Banks, toy

(G-14071)
KIRA LABS INC
3400 Gateway Dr Ste 100 (33069-4866)
PHONE....................................954 978-4549

▲ = Import ▼=Export
◆ =Import/Export

David H Rosen, *President*
Lindi Rosen, *Vice Pres*
Ruben Martinez, *Maint Spvr*
Jean Saintal, *Mfg Staff*
Jose Zayas, *Mfg Staff*
▲ **EMP:** 10 **EST:** 2003
SQ FT: 28,000
SALES (est): 4.9MM **Privately Held**
WEB: www.kiralabs.com
SIC: 2844 Cosmetic preparations

(G-14072)
KOLICH ELECTRIC MOTOR CO INC
3420 Nw 25th Ave (33069-1063)
PHONE................................954 969-8605
EMP: 6 **EST:** 2019
SALES (est): 323.1K **Privately Held**
WEB: www.klimekelectricmotor.com
SIC: 7694 Electric motor repair

(G-14073)
KPC SOUTHERN INDUSTRIES INC
600 Ne 28th St (33064-5451)
P.O. Box 1210 (33061-1210)
PHONE................................954 943-0254
Steve Gladfelter, *President*
Kim Gladfelter, *Vice Pres*
Peg Stockfelth, *Vice Pres*
EMP: 15 **EST:** 1972
SQ FT: 13,000
SALES (est): 2.5MM **Privately Held**
WEB: www.kpcsouthern.com
SIC: 3471 Plating of metals or formed products

(G-14074)
L&R IMAGING
2450 W Sample Rd Ste 8 (33073-3034)
PHONE................................678 691-3204
EMP: 5 **EST:** 2010
SALES (est): 596.3K **Privately Held**
SIC: 3845 Mfg Electromedical Equipment

(G-14075)
LAIRD INTERNATIONAL CORP
2300 Nw 30th Pl Bldg 9 (33069-1025)
PHONE................................954 532-3794
Cliff Harding, *Principal*
▲ **EMP:** 8 **EST:** 2007
SALES (est): 789.9K
SALES (corp-wide): 2MM **Privately Held**
WEB: www.lairdinternational.com
SIC: 3949 Golf equipment
PA: Cutler Sports Corp
4140a Sladeview Cres Unit 5
Mississauga ON L5L 6
905 271-6555

(G-14076)
LEILA K MOAVERO
Also Called: Executive Prtg & Mailing Svcs
1800 Nw 15th Ave Ste 140 (33069-1410)
PHONE................................954 978-0018
Leila Moavero, *Owner*
EMP: 5 **EST:** 2011
SQ FT: 2,500
SALES (est): 501.5K **Privately Held**
SIC: 2741 2752 2791 Business service newsletters: publishing & printing; commercial printing, lithographic; typesetting

(G-14077)
LHOIST NORTH AMERICA ALA LLC
Also Called: Matco Transload Us06
1263 Hammondville Rd (33069-2927)
PHONE................................817 732-8164
EMP: 25
SALES (corp-wide): 99.4MM **Privately Held**
SIC: 3274 Manufacture Of Lime Products
HQ: Lhoist North America Of Alabama, Llc
3700 Hulen St
Fort Worth TX 76109
817 732-8164

(G-14078)
LION PRESS INC
Also Called: Destination Athlete Broward FL
1913 W Copans Rd (33064-1517)
PHONE................................954 971-6193
Cynthia Martin, *President*
Jodi Thompson, *General Mgr*

EMP: 5 **EST:** 1975
SQ FT: 2,000
SALES (est): 1MM **Privately Held**
WEB: www.thelionpressprinting.com
SIC: 2752 Commercial printing, offset

(G-14079)
LIVING WITH ART KITCHENS AND
1041 Se 7th Ave (33060-9415)
PHONE................................954 561-4030
Alfredo Masso, *Principal*
EMP: 7 **EST:** 2012
SALES (est): 128.7K **Privately Held**
SIC: 2499 Kitchen, bathroom & household ware: wood

(G-14080)
LMB CONSULTANTS INC
Also Called: American Speedy Printing
1280 S Powerline Rd # 17 (33069-4339)
PHONE................................954 537-9590
Leroy M Borofsky, *President*
Sandra Borofsky, *Admin Sec*
EMP: 9 **EST:** 1985
SQ FT: 1,325
SALES (est): 350K **Privately Held**
WEB: www.lmbconsultants.com
SIC: 2752 Commercial printing, offset

(G-14081)
LOGOXPRESS INC
Also Called: Sew Right
2520 N Powerline Rd # 303 (33069-1055)
P.O. Box 290640, Port Orange (32129-0640)
PHONE................................954 973-4994
Naresh Manek, *President*
EMP: 7 **EST:** 2015
SALES (est): 397K **Privately Held**
WEB: www.mylogoxpress.com
SIC: 2395 Embroidery products, except schiffli machine

(G-14082)
LUBREXX SPECIALTY PRODUCTS LLC
Also Called: Fluxxer
4100 N Powerline Rd O1 (33073-3083)
PHONE................................561 988-7500
Michael A Jimenez,
EMP: 7 **EST:** 2016
SQ FT: 7,000
SALES (est): 1.8MM **Privately Held**
SIC: 2992 Lubricating oils

(G-14083)
M MICRO TECHNOLOGIES INC
Also Called: Microtechnologies
2901 Gateway Dr (33069-4326)
PHONE................................954 973-6166
Michele Hamilton, *Principal*
Mario Zuchovicki, *Vice Pres*
Antonio Bossiello, *Treasurer*
Tony Bossiello, *Administration*
EMP: 500 **EST:** 2003
SALES (est): 34.3MM **Privately Held**
SIC: 3629 3699 Electronic generation equipment; electrical equipment & supplies; high-energy particle physics equipment

(G-14084)
MAGNETIC JEWELLRY INC
2900 W Sample Rd (33073-3024)
PHONE................................954 975-5868
Michael Goldstein, *Principal*
EMP: 5 **EST:** 2010
SALES (est): 361.1K **Privately Held**
SIC: 3961 Costume jewelry

(G-14085)
MAN CAPITAL CORPORATION (PA)
591 Sw 13th Ter (33069-3519)
PHONE................................954 946-9092
Siejberd Rottach, *President*
Vin Ritraj, *Treasurer*
◆ **EMP:** 35 **EST:** 1980
SQ FT: 1,500
SALES (est): 28.8MM **Privately Held**
SIC: 3519 Diesel, semi-diesel or duel-fuel engines, including marine

(G-14086)
MANCINI INC
Also Called: United States Concrete Pipe
1878 Nw 21st St (33069-1334)
PHONE................................954 583-7220
Albert P Mancini, *President*
Harry Hargrave, *Vice Pres*
Harold Hendrix, *Vice Pres*
Nicholas D Mancini II, *Vice Pres*
David W Mancini, *Treasurer*
EMP: 27 **EST:** 1983
SQ FT: 48,000
SALES (est): 4.8MM **Privately Held**
WEB: www.unitedstatesconcrete.com
SIC: 3272 Pipe, concrete or lined with concrete

(G-14087)
MARKER INDUSTRIES LLC
3980 Oaks Clubhouse Dr (33069-3684)
PHONE................................954 907-2647
Mark D Kerr, *Principal*
EMP: 8 **EST:** 2018
SALES (est): 255.4K **Privately Held**
WEB: www.milemarker.com
SIC: 3999 Manufacturing industries

(G-14088)
MARLIN YACHT MANUFACTURING
1350 Hammondville Rd A (33069-2907)
PHONE................................305 586-3586
Giuseppe Gismondi, *President*
▼ **EMP:** 5 **EST:** 2012
SQ FT: 5,000
SALES (est): 465.1K **Privately Held**
SIC: 3732 Yachts, building & repairing

(G-14089)
MASA TRADING LLC
1454 Sw 11th Ter (33069-4701)
PHONE................................561 729-3293
Sun Xian, *Mng Member*
▲ **EMP:** 10 **EST:** 2011
SALES (est): 1.2MM **Privately Held**
SIC: 2092 Fish, frozen: prepared

(G-14090)
MAXIGRAPHICS INC
2201 W Sample Rd Ste 8-2a (33073-3096)
PHONE................................954 978-0740
Patricia Silverts, *President*
Douglas Rodibaugh, *Manager*
EMP: 10 **EST:** 1988
SQ FT: 2,500
SALES (est): 744.5K **Privately Held**
WEB: www.maxigraphics.com
SIC: 2759 2752 Commercial printing; commercial printing, lithographic

(G-14091)
MCILPACK INC
1750 Nw 15th Ave Ste 535 (33069-1710)
PHONE................................561 988-8545
Susana Arango, *President*
Juan Pinto, *Purchasing*
▲ **EMP:** 13 **EST:** 2002
SALES (est): 2.4MM **Privately Held**
WEB: www.mcilpack.com
SIC: 2844 Cosmetic preparations

(G-14092)
MCNEILL SIGNS INC (PA)
555 S Dixie Hwy E (33060-6911)
P.O. Box 1093, Bunnell (32110-1093)
PHONE................................561 737-6304
Jay R McNeill, *President*
Daniel G Scroggins, *Principal*
Tiffany D Scroggins, *Principal*
Martia S McNeill, *Vice Pres*
EMP: 13 **EST:** 1956
SQ FT: 10,000
SALES (est): 3.2MM **Privately Held**
WEB: www.mcneillsigns.com
SIC: 3993 Neon signs; electric signs; advertising artwork

(G-14093)
MCNEILUS TRUCK AND MFG INC
1700 Nw 33rd St (33064-1307)
PHONE................................954 366-4769
EMP: 23

SALES (corp-wide): 7.7B **Publicly Held**
WEB: www.mcneiluscompanies.com
SIC: 3713 Cement mixer bodies
HQ: Mcneilus Truck And Manufacturing, Inc.
524 E Highway St
Dodge Center MN 55927
507 374-6321

(G-14094)
MEDISCOPE MANUFACTURING INC
401 Briny Ave Apt 405 (33062-5819)
PHONE................................954 975-9997
Ralph Martinez, *Branch Mgr*
EMP: 21 **Privately Held**
WEB: www.mediscope-mfg.com
SIC: 3599 Machine shop, jobbing & repair
PA: Mediscope Manufacturing Inc
744 Mountain Blvd Fl 2w
Watchung NJ 07069

(G-14095)
MERRY MAILMAN INC
3907 N Federal Hwy (33064-6042)
PHONE................................954 786-1146
Carla Felini, *Principal*
EMP: 8 **EST:** 2011
SALES (est): 407.9K **Privately Held**
WEB: www.themerrymailman.com
SIC: 3086 Packaging & shipping materials, foamed plastic

(G-14096)
METAL MAGIX INC
3711 Ne 11th Ave Ste 4 (33064-5164)
PHONE................................754 235-9996
Frank W Jones, *Principal*
EMP: 7 **EST:** 2010
SALES (est): 911.7K **Privately Held**
WEB: www.metalmagix.com
SIC: 3441 Fabricated structural metal

(G-14097)
MG WOODWORK INC
5540 Nw 76th Pl Ste A (33073-3824)
PHONE................................561 459-7552
Marcio Gama, *Principal*
EMP: 12 **EST:** 2010
SALES (est): 307.2K **Privately Held**
SIC: 2431 Millwork

(G-14098)
MICRO CONTACTS INC
2901 Gateway Dr (33069-4326)
PHONE................................954 973-6166
Gerald F Tucci, *Branch Mgr*
EMP: 10
SALES (corp-wide): 9MM **Privately Held**
WEB: www.microcontacts.com
SIC: 3643 Contacts, electrical
PA: Micro Contacts, Inc.
1 Enterprise Pl Unit E
Hicksville NY 11801
516 433-4830

(G-14099)
MICRO PNEUMATIC LOGIC INC
Also Called: Microtechnologies
2901 Gateway Dr (33069-4326)
PHONE................................954 935-6821
G F Tucci, *President*
Michael F Tucci, *President*
Dennis Semet, *Engineer*
Antonio Bossiello, *Treasurer*
Daniel Bracewell, *Sales Dir*
◆ **EMP:** 145 **EST:** 1973
SQ FT: 40,000
SALES (est): 29.5MM **Privately Held**
SIC: 3492 Control valves, aircraft: hydraulic & pneumatic

(G-14100)
MICRO TYPING SYSTEMS INC
1295 Sw 29th Ave (33069-4359)
PHONE................................954 970-9500
Charles J Sobolewski, *President*
Harry Malyska, *VP Mfg*
▲ **EMP:** 50 **EST:** 1988
SQ FT: 21,000
SALES (est): 14.7MM
SALES (corp-wide): 3.7B **Publicly Held**
SIC: 3829 Measuring & controlling devices

HQ: Ortho Clinical Diagnostics Holdings Plc
1001 Route 202
Raritan NJ 08869
908 218-8000

(G-14101)
MIRART INC
Also Called: Innovations By Mirart
2707 Gateway Dr (33069-4323)
PHONE................................954 974-5230
Jeff Oster, *President*
Dale Oster, *Corp Secy*
◆ **EMP:** 25 **EST:** 1976
SQ FT: 36,000
SALES (est): 4.3MM **Privately Held**
WEB: www.mirart.com
SIC: 2824 Acrylic fibers

(G-14102)
MIRRORS & MORE INC
3390 Ne 6th Ter (33064-5216)
PHONE................................954 782-7272
Paul Menditto Jr, *President*
John F Heinle, *Vice Pres*
Jacqueline F Menditto, *Admin Sec*
EMP: 5 **EST:** 1985
SQ FT: 3,000
SALES (est): 444K **Privately Held**
WEB: www.mirrorsandmoreinc.com
SIC: 3231 Mirrored glass

(G-14103)
MJK INDUSTRIES INC
201 Se 3rd Ct (33060-7126)
PHONE................................954 788-7494
Michael J Kuhl, *President*
EMP: 8 **EST:** 2001
SALES (est): 548.8K **Privately Held**
WEB: www.mjk.com
SIC: 3999 Manufacturing industries

(G-14104)
MODULAR THERMAL TECH LLC (PA)
Also Called: Life Wear Technologies
1520 Sw 5th Ct (33069-3523)
PHONE................................954 785-1055
Bradley Waugh, *CEO*
Colin Hall, *Exec VP*
Gil Harmon, *Vice Pres*
Mark Lovley, *Vice Pres*
Zachary Wunsch, *CFO*
EMP: 20 **EST:** 1974
SALES (est): 9.9MM **Privately Held**
WEB: www.lifeweartechnologies.com
SIC: 2833 Vitamins, natural or synthetic:
bulk, uncompounded

(G-14105)
MORRIS MICA CABINETS INC
1920 Nw 22nd Ct (33069-1340)
PHONE................................954 979-6838
Wesley Wong, *President*
Tyrone Wong, *Vice Pres*
Carlisle Wong, *Director*
EMP: 7 **EST:** 1978
SQ FT: 5,600
SALES (est): 886K **Privately Held**
SIC: 2434 2599 Wood kitchen cabinets;
cabinets, factory

(G-14106)
N & N INVESTMENT CORPORATION
Also Called: Baron Manufacturing
3001 Nw 16th Ter (33064-1407)
PHONE................................954 590-3800
Hasu Gavan, *President*
Juan Leal, *Prdtn Mgr*
Karina Lozada, *Purch Mgr*
Ramila Gavan, *Admin Sec*
▼ **EMP:** 50 **EST:** 1961
SQ FT: 100,000
SALES (est): 7.9MM **Privately Held**
SIC: 2431 2521 2511 3993 Millwork;
wood office furniture; wood household fur-
niture; signs & advertising specialties;
wood partitions & fixtures; partitions & fix-
tures, except wood

(G-14107)
NEBULA GLASS INTERNATIONAL INC
Also Called: Glasslam
1601 Blount Rd (33069-5102)
PHONE................................954 975-3233
Stephen E Howes, *CEO*
Violet Howes, *Vice Pres*
◆ **EMP:** 39 **EST:** 1984
SQ FT: 17,000
SALES (est): 2.6MM **Privately Held**
WEB: www.world-spacer.com
SIC: 3229 5169 Art, decorative & novelty
glassware; adhesives & sealants

(G-14108)
NOBLE WOOD WORKS
225 Nw 16th St (33060-5252)
PHONE................................561 702-2889
Luis Fernando Prudente, *Principal*
EMP: 9 **EST:** 2010
SALES (est): 537.9K **Privately Held**
SIC: 2431 Millwork

(G-14109)
NUFORM CABINETRY
1745 N Powerline Rd (33069-1624)
PHONE................................954 532-2746
Shu Cai, *Principal*
EMP: 7 **EST:** 2016
SALES (est): 115.3K **Privately Held**
WEB: www.nuformkitchen.com
SIC: 2434 Wood kitchen cabinets

(G-14110)
OLDCASTLE RETAIL INC
Also Called: Bonsal American
1200 Nw 18th St (33069-1722)
PHONE................................954 971-1200
John Holloway, *Branch Mgr*
EMP: 267
SALES (corp-wide): 30.9B **Privately Held**
WEB: www.oldcastlecoastal.com
SIC: 3272 3255 Concrete products, pre-
cast; tile & brick refractories, except plas-
tic
HQ: Oldcastle Retail, Inc.
625 Griffith Rd Ste 100
Charlotte NC 28217
704 525-1621

(G-14111)
OPELLE ENTERPRISES INC
Also Called: Bageland
1471 Sw 5th Ct (33069-3524)
PHONE................................954 942-7338
Jorge Fidel, *CEO*
Iris Fidel, *Vice Pres*
Natalia Fidel, *Sales Staff*
EMP: 28 **EST:** 1989
SQ FT: 20,000
SALES (est): 2.6MM **Privately Held**
WEB: www.opelle.com
SIC: 2051 Bread, cake & related
products; bagels, fresh or frozen; frozen
bakery products, except bread

(G-14112)
OPERATONS PRCRMENT SUP CHAIN S
2501 Nw 34th Pl Ste B21b (33069-5928)
PHONE................................954 960-5890
Luca Pastore, *President*
Anthony Bruzzone, *Vice Pres*
John Leung, *Treasurer*
Federico Bruzzone, *Admin Sec*
EMP: 5 **EST:** 2015
SALES (est): 568K **Privately Held**
WEB: www.ops-corp.com
SIC: 3724 Aircraft engines & engine parts

(G-14113)
OUR WAREHOUSE INC
Also Called: Stonehenge Gems
2749 E Atlantic Blvd (33062-4941)
PHONE................................954 786-1234
Frances Wilson, *President*
Suzette Waldron, *Corp Secy*
EMP: 9 **EST:** 1973
SQ FT: 3,000
SALES (est): 517.3K **Privately Held**
WEB: www.jewelryandcoinbuyer.com
SIC: 3915 5094 Jewelers' findings & mate-
rials; jewelry

(G-14114)
P&S INDUSTRIES LLC
3635 Park Central Blvd N (33064-2262)
PHONE................................954 975-3384
Tolga Adak,
EMP: 8 **EST:** 2010
SALES (est): 101.8K **Privately Held**
SIC: 2952 Roofing materials

(G-14115)
PALLET CONSULTANTS LLC (HQ)
810 Nw 13th Ave (33069-2029)
P.O. Box 1692 (33061-1692)
PHONE................................954 946-2212
Gustavo Gutierrez, *CEO*
Brian L Groene, *President*
Tony Buroker, *General Mgr*
John Gamez, *General Mgr*
Nathan Schuster, *Opers Mgr*
◆ **EMP:** 22 **EST:** 1992
SQ FT: 400,000
SALES (est): 15MM
SALES (corp-wide): 604.7MM **Privately
Held**
WEB: www.palletconsultants.com
SIC: 2448 7699 8742 Pallets, wood; pal-
let repair; management consulting serv-
ices
PA: 48forty Solutions, Llc
3650 Mansell Rd Ste 100
Alpharetta GA 30022
678 722-3984

(G-14116)
PANTHER PRINTING LLC (PA)
5101 N Federal Hwy (33064-7001)
PHONE................................239 936-5050
Michael Yolich, *Manager*
EMP: 8 **EST:** 2019
SALES (est): 218.7K **Privately Held**
WEB: www.pantherprinting.net
SIC: 2752 Commercial printing, offset

(G-14117)
PANTHER PRINTING LLC
551 Fairway Dr (33069-1176)
PHONE................................954 651-7766
Michael Yolich, *Branch Mgr*
EMP: 12
SALES (corp-wide): 218.7K **Privately
Held**
WEB: www.pantherprinting.net
SIC: 2752 Commercial printing, offset
PA: Panther Printing Llc
5101 N Federal Hwy
Pompano Beach FL 33064
239 936-5050

(G-14118)
PARAMOUNT INDUSTRIES INC (PA)
Also Called: Paramount Sales & Consulting
1020 Sw 10th Ave Ste 6 (33069-4632)
P.O. Box 1030, Boca Raton (33429-1030)
PHONE................................954 781-3755
Mike Degrandchamp, *President*
Michael De Grandchamp, *Human Res Mgr*
EMP: 25 **EST:** 1982
SQ FT: 12,600
SALES (est): 4.1MM **Privately Held**
WEB: www.paradisecableind.com
SIC: 3679 3672 3643 Harness assem-
blies for electronic use: wire or cable;
printed circuit boards; current-carrying
wiring devices

(G-14119)
PATRIOT WELDING INC
151 Sw 5th St W (33060-7903)
P.O. Box 651022, Vero Beach (32965-
1022)
PHONE................................954 798-8819
Carrie W Llano, *Principal*
EMP: 7 **EST:** 2015
SALES (est): 256.8K **Privately Held**
SIC: 7692 Welding repair

(G-14120)
PAVER ACTION INC
3741 Ne 18th Ave (33064-6638)
PHONE................................954 868-1468
Evair Hottz, *President*
EMP: 8 **EST:** 2005

SALES (est): 172.8K **Privately Held**
SIC: 2951 Asphalt paving mixtures &
blocks

(G-14121)
PENEK CHEMICAL INDUSTRIES INC
4100 N Powerline Rd Z5 (33073-3083)
PHONE................................954 978-6501
Kevin Ressler, *President*
EMP: 6 **EST:** 2006
SALES (est): 382.2K **Privately Held**
SIC: 2899 Fuel tank or engine cleaning
chemicals

(G-14122)
PERFECT OIL INC
2900 W Sample Rd (33073-3024)
PHONE................................954 984-8944
Jociane L Landolfa, *Branch Mgr*
EMP: 9 **Privately Held**
WEB: www.perfectoil.com
SIC: 1381 Drilling oil & gas wells
PA: Perfect Oil, Inc.
51 Atwell Dr
West Palm Beach FL 33411

(G-14123)
PETES SEAL COATING
2300 Ne 15th Ter (33064-5535)
PHONE................................857 251-1912
Pete Smith, *Owner*
EMP: 7 **EST:** 2017
SALES (est): 119.8K **Privately Held**
SIC: 3479 Metal coating & allied service

(G-14124)
PETTIT TOOLS & SUPPLIES INC
4391 Ne 11th Ave (33064-5951)
PHONE................................954 781-2640
Uzi Jacoby, *President*
William T Pettit Jr, *Vice Pres*
▲ **EMP:** 10 **EST:** 1992
SQ FT: 5,000
SALES (est): 500K **Privately Held**
SIC: 3423 Hand & edge tools

(G-14125)
PHOENIX PUBLICATIONS
777 S Federal Hwy (33062-5968)
PHONE................................954 609-7586
Patti Gottesman, *Principal*
Wendy Weber, *Vice Pres*
EMP: 7 **EST:** 2010
SALES (est): 138.4K **Privately Held**
WEB:
www.hometowncouponmagazines.com
SIC: 2741 Miscellaneous publishing

(G-14126)
PHOSCRETE CORPORATION (PA)
1800 Nw 15th Ave Ste 130 (33069-1435)
PHONE................................561 420-0595
Jean Tremblay, *Exec VP*
Brian Mintz, *Vice Pres*
Marlen La Paz, *Project Dir*
Kyle Bartfay, *Sales Mgr*
Erica Gerhart, *Admin Sec*
EMP: 7 **EST:** 2011
SALES (est): 3.5MM **Privately Held**
WEB: www.phoscrete.com
SIC: 3272 3273 Concrete products, pre-
cast; ready-mixed concrete

(G-14127)
PILOT STEEL INC
1950 W Copans Rd (33064-1518)
PHONE................................954 978-3615
Stuart Andrew Disbury, *President*
◆ **EMP:** 38 **EST:** 1987
SQ FT: 10,000
SALES (est): 6.1MM **Privately Held**
WEB: www.pilotsteel.com
SIC: 3441 Fabricated structural metal

(G-14128)
PK GRAPHICZ
1000 W Mcnab Rd (33069-4719)
PHONE................................305 534-2184
Joyce Paredes, *Principal*
EMP: 5 **EST:** 2010
SALES (est): 348.8K **Privately Held**
WEB: www.pkgraphics.com
SIC: 2752 Commercial printing, offset

(G-14129)
PLASTIC PARTS INC
4100 N Powerline Rd Z5 (33073-3077)
PHONE.....................................954 974-3051
Todd Pores, *President*
EMP: 21 **EST:** 2004
SQ FT: 15,000
SALES (est): 1.1MM **Privately Held**
WEB: www.plasticpartsinc.com
SIC: 3089 Injection molding of plastics

(G-14130)
PLASTIC SEALING COMPANY INC
1940 Nw 18th St Ste 1 (33069-1724)
PHONE.....................................954 956-9797
Mark Macbride, *Principal*
EMP: 5 **EST:** 1998
SALES (est): 800K **Privately Held**
WEB: www.plasticsealing.com
SIC: 2752 7389 Menus, lithographed; laminating service

(G-14131)
PLASTIC SOLUTIONS OF POMPANO
4100 N Powerline Rd Z5 (33073-3083)
PHONE.....................................800 331-7081
Gilbert Gomez, *President*
EMP: 6 **EST:** 2004
SALES (est): 582.5K **Privately Held**
SIC: 3089 Injection molding of plastics

(G-14132)
PLYWOOD EXPRESS INC
2601 Gateway Dr Ste B (33069-4321)
PHONE.....................................954 956-7576
Giovana Rodrigues, *President*
Angel Ruiz, *President*
Tuiane Kuratomi, *Purchasing*
Roberta Pereira, *Finance Mgr*
Danny Silva, *Sales Staff*
▲ **EMP:** 25 **EST:** 2011
SALES (est): 3.9MM **Privately Held**
WEB: www.plywoodexpress.com
SIC: 2435 Hardwood veneer & plywood

(G-14133)
POINT BLANK ENTERPRISES INC
Also Called: Protective Products Entps
2102 Sw 2nd St (33069-3116)
PHONE.....................................954 846-8222
Tom Steffen, *CEO*
Shelby Carpenter, *Senior VP*
Susan Carrasco, *Buyer*
Cory Provenzano, *Director*
David Kiefer, *Admin Sec*
EMP: 824 **Privately Held**
WEB: www.pointblankenterprises.com
SIC: 2389 2221 Uniforms & vestments; broadwoven fabric mills, manmade
HQ: Point Blank Enterprises, Inc.
    2102 Sw 2nd St
    Pompano Beach FL 33069
    954 630-0900

(G-14134)
POINT BLANK ENTERPRISES INC (HQ)
Also Called: Protective Group A Point Blank
2102 Sw 2nd St (33069-3116)
PHONE.....................................954 630-0900
Daniel Gaston, *CEO*
Paulo Motoki, *COO*
Mark Edwards, *Exec VP*
Michael Foreman, *Exec VP*
Clarence Hutton, *Exec VP*
◆ **EMP:** 824 **EST:** 2011
SALES (est): 216.9MM **Privately Held**
WEB: www.pointblankenterprises.com
SIC: 3842 3462 Bulletproof vests; armor plate, forged iron or steel

(G-14135)
POINT BLANK INTRMDATE HLDG LLC
2102 Sw 2nd St (33069-3116)
PHONE.....................................954 630-0900
Daniel Gaston, *CEO*
Samuel White, *President*
Michael Anderson, *Vice Pres*
Shelby Carpenter, *Vice Pres*
Michael Foreman, *Vice Pres*

EMP: 23 **EST:** 2011
SALES (est): 1.8MM **Privately Held**
WEB: www.pointblankenterprises.com
SIC: 2399 Hand woven apparel

(G-14136)
POINT BLANK PROTECTIVE APPRL (PA)
2102 Sw 2nd St (33069-3116)
PHONE.....................................954 630-0900
Daniel Gaston, *CEO*
EMP: 41 **EST:** 2017
SALES (est): 58.8MM **Privately Held**
WEB: www.pointblankenterprises.com
SIC: 2311 Military uniforms, men's & youths; purchased materials

(G-14137)
POMPANO PRECISION PRODUCTS INC
141 Sw 5th St (33060-7903)
PHONE.....................................954 942-5900
Daniel G Bozin, *Branch Mgr*
EMP: 8
SALES (corp-wide): 5.2MM **Privately Held**
WEB: www.pompanoprecision.com
SIC: 3599 Machine shop, jobbing & repair
PA: Pompano Precision Products, Inc.
    1100 Sw 12th Ave
    Pompano Beach FL 33069
    954 946-6059

(G-14138)
POMPANO PRECISION PRODUCTS INC (PA)
1100 Sw 12th Ave (33069-4615)
PHONE.....................................954 946-6059
George J Spirio, *President*
Anthony Botticello, *General Mgr*
Debra A Spirio, *Corp Secy*
Debbie Spirio,
EMP: 23 **EST:** 1971
SQ FT: 14,000
SALES (est): 5.2MM **Privately Held**
WEB: www.pompanoprecision.com
SIC: 3599 Machine shop, jobbing & repair

(G-14139)
PRE-MIX MARBLE TITE INC
1259 Nw 21st St (33069-1428)
PHONE.....................................954 917-7665
Howard Ehler, *President*
Steve Brown, *Vice Pres*
◆ **EMP:** 50 **EST:** 1995
SALES (est): 5.2MM **Privately Held**
WEB: www.pmmproducts.com
SIC: 3299 Stucco

(G-14140)
PRECISION BRAZING INC
471 Ne 28th St (33064-5437)
PHONE.....................................954 942-8971
Joan Bonneau, *President*
EMP: 9 **EST:** 1995
SALES (est): 491.3K **Privately Held**
WEB: www.precisionbrazing.com
SIC: 7692 Brazing

(G-14141)
PRECISION METAL INDUSTRIES INC
1408 Sw 8th St (33069-4512)
PHONE.....................................954 942-6303
Gregory S Wilson, *President*
Gerald E Flint, *Vice Pres*
Flint Jerry, *Vice Pres*
Greg Wilson, *Vice Pres*
Susan Rosen, *Marketing Staff*
▲ **EMP:** 81 **EST:** 1986
SQ FT: 140,000
SALES (est): 23.9MM **Privately Held**
WEB: www.pmiquality.com
SIC: 3444 Sheet metal specialties, not stamped

(G-14142)
PRECISION SMALL ENGINE COMPANY
2510 Nw 16th Ln (33064-1562)
PHONE.....................................954 974-1960
Andrew Masciarella, *President*
▼ **EMP:** 22 **EST:** 1979
SQ FT: 15,000

SALES (est): 4.1MM **Privately Held**
WEB: www.precisionusa.com
SIC: 3524 Lawn & garden equipment

(G-14143)
PREMIX-MARBLETITE MFG CO (DH)
1259 Nw 21st St (33069-1428)
PHONE.....................................954 970-6540
Howard L Ehler Jr, *President*
Betty J Murchison, *Principal*
Lisa M Brock, *Director*
◆ **EMP:** 10 **EST:** 1950
SQ FT: 20,000
SALES (est): 5.7MM
SALES (corp-wide): 387.6MM **Privately Held**
WEB: www.pmmproducts.com
SIC: 3299 3531 Stucco; mixers: ore, plaster, slag, sand, mortar, etc.
HQ: Imperial Industries, Inc.
    1259 Nw 21st St
    Pompano Beach FL 33069
    954 917-4114

(G-14144)
PRESTIGE SERVICE GROUP
2520 Nw 16th Ln (33064-1529)
PHONE.....................................954 532-9014
Joseph Richelieu, *Principal*
EMP: 7 **EST:** 2012
SALES (est): 144K **Privately Held**
SIC: 3559 Metal finishing equipment for plating, etc.

(G-14145)
PRIMA FOOD CORP
Also Called: Diana Food Group
4020 Ne 10th Way (33064-5169)
PHONE.....................................954 788-0411
Richard Wodnicki, *President*
Diana Berenson, *VP Admin*
Lidia Lopez, *Controller*
Susan Cameron, *VP Sales*
EMP: 40 **EST:** 2002
SQ FT: 15,000
SALES (est): 5.3MM **Privately Held**
WEB: www.dianafoodgroup.com
SIC: 2099 Food preparations

(G-14146)
PRINTERS PRINTER INC
2681 W Mcnab Rd (33069-4801)
PHONE.....................................954 917-2773
Lou Yovino, *President*
Joey Pompa, *Opers Mgr*
Robert Zelinka, *Controller*
Pamela Laine, *Assistant*
▼ **EMP:** 13 **EST:** 1994
SQ FT: 5,000
SALES (est): 3.4MM **Privately Held**
WEB: www.theprintersprinter.com
SIC: 2731 2759 Book publishing; commercial printing

(G-14147)
PRINTING CORP OF AMERICAS INC
Also Called: PCA
620 Sw 12th Ave (33069-4526)
PHONE.....................................954 943-6087
Jan D Tuchman, *President*
Gus Gonzalez, *Plant Mgr*
Steve Konecky, *Sales Mgr*
▼ **EMP:** 30 **EST:** 1979
SQ FT: 16,000
SALES (est): 4.3MM **Privately Held**
WEB: www.pcaprinting.com
SIC: 2752 Color lithography

(G-14148)
PRINTING MART INC
1951 W Copans Rd Ste 2 (33064-1549)
PHONE.....................................954 753-0323
Veronica Massimino, *President*
John Massimino, *Vice Pres*
Nick Massimino, *Manager*
EMP: 8 **EST:** 1975
SQ FT: 5,000
SALES (est): 601.6K **Privately Held**
WEB: www.theprintingmart.com
SIC: 2752 Commercial printing, offset

(G-14149)
PRINTING MART INC SOUTH FLA
1951 W Copans Rd Ste 2 (33064-1549)
PHONE.....................................954 753-0323
John Massimino, *CEO*
Veronica Massimino, *Vice Pres*
EMP: 10 **EST:** 2000
SALES (est): 533K **Privately Held**
SIC: 2759 Commercial printing

(G-14150)
PROFAB ELECTRONICS INC
2855 W Mcnab Rd (33069-4803)
PHONE.....................................954 917-1998
Debra Levy, *President*
Mark Levy, *President*
Ryan Levy, *General Mgr*
Yoram Rozenberg, *General Mgr*
Gregory Page, *Business Mgr*
▲ **EMP:** 42 **EST:** 1993
SQ FT: 13,000
SALES (est): 16MM **Privately Held**
WEB: www.profabelectronics.com
SIC: 3672 Circuit boards, television & radio printed

(G-14151)
PROTECTIVE PRODUCTS ENTPS INC
2102 Sw 2nd St (33069-3116)
PHONE.....................................954 630-0900
Pat Stallings, *VP Opers*
Ivan Habibe, *CFO*
Denise Clark, *Sales Staff*
Tom Steffen,
◆ **EMP:** 41 **EST:** 2010
SQ FT: 20,000
SALES (est): 10MM **Privately Held**
WEB: www.pointblankenterprises.com
SIC: 3842 Bulletproof vests
HQ: Point Blank Enterprises, Inc.
    2102 Sw 2nd St
    Pompano Beach FL 33069
    954 630-0900

(G-14152)
PSP INDUSTRIAL LAUNDRY EQP LLC
2700 Gateway Dr (33069-4322)
PHONE.....................................305 517-1421
Eric Zamora, *Executive*
EMP: 11 **EST:** 2008
SALES (est): 532.4K **Privately Held**
WEB: www.pspindustrial.com
SIC: 3582 Commercial laundry equipment

(G-14153)
QUALITY FINISHERS INC
640 Ne 26th Ct (33064-5430)
PHONE.....................................954 782-3073
EMP: 8
SQ FT: 8,200
SALES (est): 540K **Privately Held**
SIC: 3471 Plating/Polishing Service

(G-14154)
R & Z VENTURES INC
Also Called: Kennesaw Fruit & Juice
1300 Sw 1st Ct (33069-3204)
PHONE.....................................954 532-7938
Len Roseberg, *President*
Matthew G Roseberg, *Vice Pres*
William T Zukerman, *Vice Pres*
Ed Zukerman, *CFO*
▲ **EMP:** 72 **EST:** 1960
SQ FT: 38,000
SALES (est): 15.7MM **Privately Held**
WEB: www.kennesawjuice.com
SIC: 2033 Fruits & fruit products in cans, jars, etc.

(G-14155)
RAW ENERGY MATERIALS CORP
170 Se 13th St (33060-9226)
PHONE.....................................954 270-9000
Don Smith, *President*
Bill Flores, *Sales Dir*
▲ **EMP:** 9 **EST:** 2008
SALES (est): 430.2K **Privately Held**
WEB: www.newrebar.com
SIC: 3449 Bars, concrete reinforcing: fabricated steel

(G-14156)
REDITEK CORPORATION
2826 Center Port Cir (33064-2136)
PHONE...................................954 781-1069
Bernardo P Laverde Sr, *President*
Bernardo Laverde, *Vice Pres*
Felipe Laverde, *Mfg Staff*
Bernardo R Laverde Jr, *Director*
Anna Lucena, *Admin Sec*
◆ EMP: 16 EST: 2001
SALES (est): 1MM **Privately Held**
WEB: www.reditek.net
SIC: 3644 Electric conduits & fittings

(G-14157)
REINECKER GRINDERS CORP
1700 Nw 15th Ave Ste 310 (33069-1707)
PHONE...................................954 974-6190
Frank Holubeck, *President*
▲ EMP: 7 EST: 2005
SALES (est): 86.4K **Privately Held**
SIC: 3541 Jig boring & grinding machines

(G-14158)
RELIANCE SUPPLY CO USA LLC
1880 Nw 18th St (33069-1616)
PHONE...................................954 971-9111
Paul E Daly, *President*
Nancy Daly, *Corp Secy*
John C Daly, *Vice Pres*
George Chubeck, *Mfg Mgr*
▼ EMP: 6 EST: 1950
SQ FT: 5,000
SALES (est): 1MM **Privately Held**
WEB: www.surfacelogix.net
SIC: 2851 Paints & allied products

(G-14159)
REVOLUTION AIR CRAFT SERVICES
2511 Nw 16th Ln Ste 3 (33064-1538)
PHONE...................................954 747-4773
Rich Brown, *Principal*
Michael Mannise, *Sales Staff*
EMP: 12 EST: 2011
SALES (est): 1MM **Privately Held**
WEB: www.revolutionfyi.com
SIC: 3812 Aircraft/aerospace flight instruments & guidance systems

(G-14160)
RINSEWORKS INC
1700 Nw 15th Ave Ste 330 (33069-1716)
PHONE...................................954 946-0070
Glenn Ayers, *President*
▲ EMP: 10 EST: 2012
SQ FT: 6,000
SALES (est): 721.3K **Privately Held**
WEB: www.rinseworks.com
SIC: 3261 Bidets, vitreous china

(G-14161)
ROLLS SHADING SYSTEMS LLC
1301 W Copans Rd (33064-2903)
PHONE...................................561 955-0557
Merlin Hafida, *Manager*
EMP: 6 EST: 2016
SALES (est): 656.2K **Privately Held**
WEB: www.rollsshadingsystems.com
SIC: 3442 Louvers, shutters, jalousies & similar items

(G-14162)
ROSS INDUSTRIES INC
Also Called: Nu-Pac Industries
11440 W Sample Rd (33065-7053)
P.O. Box 8528 (33075-8528)
PHONE...................................954 752-2800
EMP: 80
SALES (corp-wide): 18.7MM **Privately Held**
SIC: 3993 3951 Mfg Signs/Advertising Specialties Mfg Pens/Mechanical Pencils
PA: Ross Industries, Inc.
11440 W Sample Rd
Coral Springs FL
845 292-7677

(G-14163)
RTP CORP
2832 Center Port Cir (33064-2136)
P.O. Box 106030, Atlanta GA (30348-6030)
PHONE...................................954 597-5333
Salvatore Provanzano, *President*
Salvatore R Provanzano, *President*

Warren Bitter, *Mfg Dir*
Andrew Haber, *Design Engr*
Eric Wagoner, *Sales Staff*
EMP: 8 EST: 1994
SQ FT: 25,000
SALES (est): 4.8MM **Privately Held**
WEB: www.rtpcorp.com
SIC: 3672 Printed circuit boards

(G-14164)
RWC GROUP LLC
Also Called: Kalashnikov USA
3901 Ne 12th Ave Ste 400 (33064-5196)
PHONE...................................754 222-1407
Peter Viskovatykh, *President*
Christopher Maugham, *Engineer*
Everold Henry, *CFO*
▲ EMP: 35 EST: 2011
SQ FT: 21,000
SALES (est): 5.4MM **Privately Held**
SIC: 3484 Guns (firearms) or gun parts, 30 mm. & below; pistols or pistol parts, 30 mm. & below; shotguns or shotgun parts, 30 mm. & below

(G-14165)
S & S PROPELLER CO INC
3040 Sw 10th St (33069-4813)
PHONE...................................718 359-3393
John Georgil, *President*
EMP: 9
SALES (corp-wide): 5.4MM **Privately Held**
WEB: www.sspropeller.com
SIC: 3366 Propellers, ship
PA: S & S Propeller Co Inc
2615 123rd St
Flushing NY 11354
718 359-3393

(G-14166)
S A MICROTECHNOLOGIES LLC
2901 Gateway Dr (33069-4326)
PHONE...................................954 973-6166
Michael Tucci, *CEO*
Mario Zuchovicki, *COO*
Arturo Araya, *Engineer*
Robert Schaeffer, *Sales Dir*
Godfrey Ponteur, *Admin Mgr*
EMP: 15 EST: 2015
SQ FT: 8,000
SALES (est): 6MM **Privately Held**
WEB: www.microtechnologiessa.com
SIC: 3643 3491 Electric switches; compressed gas cylinder valves
PA: Micro Technologies, S.A.
Condominios Logisticos Rc,
Alajuela

(G-14167)
SAVVY ASSOCIATE INC
Also Called: Tromtech
1480 Sw 3rd St Ste 5 (33069-3225)
PHONE...................................954 941-6986
Derrick Miller, *President*
EMP: 10 EST: 1983
SQ FT: 3,000
SALES (est): 560K **Privately Held**
SIC: 3599 3841 3769 3728 Electrical discharge machining (EDM); surgical & medical instruments; guided missile & space vehicle parts & auxiliary equipment; aircraft parts & equipment; manufactured hardware (general)

(G-14168)
SC CAPITAL VENTURES INC
Also Called: Next Level
3025 Nw 25th Ave (33069-1028)
PHONE...................................954 657-8563
EMP: 59
SALES (corp-wide): 2.9MM **Privately Held**
WEB: www.nextlevelstorage.com
SIC: 2542 Pallet racks: except wood
PA: Sc Capital Ventures, Inc.
401 Ryland St Ste 200a
Reno NV 89502
800 230-8846

(G-14169)
SCREEN GRAPHICS FLORIDA INC (PA)
1801 N Andrews Ave (33069-1422)
PHONE...................................800 346-4420
Nick Glaros, *President*

Lynn Opperman, *VP Opers*
Natasha Bumbeck, *Production*
Mayelin Crespo, *Production*
Elena Borrell, *Purch Agent*
◆ EMP: 45 EST: 1973
SQ FT: 47,800
SALES (est): 13.9MM **Privately Held**
WEB: www.screen-graphics.com
SIC: 2759 2754 Screen printing; commercial printing, gravure

(G-14170)
SDS DENTAL INC
Also Called: Summit Dental Systems
1280 Sw 27th Ave (33069-4320)
PHONE...................................954 730-3636
Cesar Coral, *President*
Shaun Taylor, *Vice Pres*
Larry Brady, *Sales Staff*
Michael Goss, *Clerk*
▲ EMP: 28 EST: 1986
SQ FT: 50,000
SALES (est): 8.6MM **Privately Held**
WEB: www.summitdental.com
SIC: 3843 Dental equipment

(G-14171)
SE CUSTOM LIFT SYSTEMS INC
1801 Sw 7th Ave (33060-9027)
P.O. Box 1715 (33061-1715)
PHONE...................................954 941-8090
Mitchell Scavone, *President*
Denise Scavone, *Treasurer*
EMP: 8 EST: 1996
SQ FT: 5,000
SALES (est): 872.7K **Privately Held**
WEB: www.secboatlifts.com
SIC: 3536 Boat lifts

(G-14172)
SEA 21-21 LLC
2211 Nw 30th Pl (33069-1026)
PHONE...................................954 366-4677
Jorge Fernandez,
EMP: 8 EST: 2015
SALES (est): 842.9K **Privately Held**
SIC: 2023 Dietary supplements, dairy & non-dairy based

(G-14173)
SEALMASTER OF WISCONSIN
1831 Nw 33rd St (33064-1308)
PHONE...................................954 979-5458
Pedro Rosi, *Owner*
EMP: 30 **Privately Held**
WEB: www.sealmaster.net
SIC: 2759 Letterpress & screen printing
PA: Sealmaster Of Wisconsin
W140n5985 Lilly Rd
Menomonee Falls WI 53051

(G-14174)
SEASIDE GRAPHICS INC
100 Sw 5th St (33060-7904)
PHONE...................................954 782-7151
Stephen Blake, *President*
▼ EMP: 7 EST: 1975
SQ FT: 3,600
SALES (est): 650K **Privately Held**
SIC: 2759 Screen printing

(G-14175)
SER-MAT INTERNATIONAL LLC
3200 Nw 27th Ave Ste 106 (33069-6001)
PHONE...................................954 525-1417
Mark Kreisel, *President*
Gregory R Hartenhoff, *General Mgr*
Carlos Camacho, *Opers Staff*
▲ EMP: 33 EST: 1953
SQ FT: 5,700
SALES (est): 3.3MM **Privately Held**
WEB: www.sermat.aero
SIC: 2273 Carpets & rugs

(G-14176)
SEVEN KEYS CO OF FLORIDA
450 Sw 12th Ave (33069-3504)
PHONE...................................954 946-5010
Henry Stevens, *President*
Sophia Sanso, *Admin Sec*
EMP: 8 EST: 1956
SQ FT: 15,000
SALES (est): 951.6K **Privately Held**
SIC: 2033 Jellies, edible, including imitation: in cans, jars, etc.; preserves, including imitation: in cans, jars, etc.

(G-14177)
SIGN UP NOW SIGN COMPANY LLC
3993 Cypress Reach Ct # 205 (33069-4923)
PHONE...................................754 224-9091
Kimberly A Purinton, *Principal*
EMP: 8 EST: 2011
SALES (est): 270.1K **Privately Held**
WEB: www.signupnowsigncompany.com
SIC: 3993 Signs & advertising specialties

(G-14178)
SIGNS OF REILLY
1121 W Mcnab Rd (33069-4720)
PHONE...................................954 263-7829
Michael Reilly, *President*
EMP: 7 EST: 2007
SALES (est): 256.5K **Privately Held**
WEB: www.signsofreilly.com
SIC: 3993 Signs & advertising specialties

(G-14179)
SILVER HAWK AEROSPACE INC
1041 Nw 31st Ave (33069-1107)
PHONE...................................954 301-1453
Paulo R Soares, *President*
Carlos A Mandari, *Vice Pres*
EMP: 14 EST: 2007
SALES (est): 2.9MM **Privately Held**
WEB: www.silverhawkaero.com
SIC: 3728 Aircraft parts & equipment

(G-14180)
SINCERUS PHARMACEUTICALS INC (PA)
3265 W Mcnab Rd (33069-4807)
PHONE...................................800 604-5032
Spencer J Malkin, *CEO*
Jonathan Fenster, *COO*
Doris Scabo, *Vice Pres*
EMP: 13 EST: 2015
SALES (est): 15MM **Privately Held**
WEB: www.sknv.com
SIC: 2844 2834 5122 Cosmetic preparations; dermatologicals; cosmetics

(G-14181)
SMART KID USA INC ✪
2701 Ne 23rd St (33062-1119)
PHONE...................................754 366-6666
Jerry Dabrowski, *CEO*
EMP: 5 EST: 2022
SALES (est): 309.7K **Privately Held**
SIC: 3944 Child restraint seats, automotive

(G-14182)
SMITH BOAT DESIGNS INC
Also Called: Smith Power Boats
1200 S Dixie Hwy W (33060-8519)
PHONE...................................954 782-1000
Don Smith, *President*
Dawn Dovner, *Manager*
EMP: 15 EST: 1984
SQ FT: 16,000
SALES (est): 482.3K **Privately Held**
SIC: 3732 Motorized boat, building & repairing

(G-14183)
SMITH SURFACE PREP SYSTEMS INC
Also Called: Smith Surface-Prep Solutions
2504 Nw 19th St (33069-5229)
PHONE...................................954 941-9744
Mark William Sheahan, *CEO*
EMP: 23 EST: 2019
SALES (est): 4.2MM
SALES (corp-wide): 1.9B **Publicly Held**
SIC: 3561 Industrial pumps & parts
PA: Graco Inc.
88 11th Ave Ne
Minneapolis MN 55413
612 623-6000

(G-14184)
SOBEL WESTEX
750 Nw 33rd St Ste B (33064-2005)
PHONE...................................954 942-5777
Steve Findlay, *Owner*
Edgar Aldana, *Sales Staff*
Javier Ashlyn, *Sales Staff*
Ignacio Cerruto, *Sales Staff*
Eric Romanchuk, *Sales Executive*
EMP: 69

▲ = Import ▼ =Export
◆ =Import/Export

SALES (corp-wide): 126.4MM **Privately Held**
WEB: www.sobelathome.com
SIC: 2392 5023 Blankets, comforters & beddings; linens, table
PA: Sobel Westex
2670 Western Ave
Las Vegas NV 89109
702 735-4973

(G-14185)
SOLAR MANUFACTURING INC (PA)
1888 Nw 22nd Ct (33069-1312)
PHONE.....................954 973-8488
David Stiles, *President*
Phyllis Stiles, *Corp Secy*
Richard Stiles, *Vice Pres*
EMP: 19 **EST:** 1982
SALES (est): 2.8MM **Privately Held**
SIC: 3272 Concrete products, precast

(G-14186)
SOLAR MANUFACTURING INC
2195 N Andrews Ave Ste 11 (33069-1430)
PHONE.....................954 973-8488
David Stiles, *President*
EMP: 36
SQ FT: 15,500
SALES (corp-wide): 2.8MM **Privately Held**
SIC: 3272 Concrete products, precast
PA: Solar Manufacturing, Inc.
1888 Nw 22nd Ct
Pompano Beach FL 33069
954 973-8488

(G-14187)
SONG-CHUAN USA INC
2841 Center Port Cir (33064-2135)
PHONE.....................954 788-5889
Roger Biddle, *CEO*
Robert Foster, *Corp Secy*
Sean McCarthy, *Vice Pres*
Bill Simon, *Warehouse Mgr*
Rogerio Pereira, *Controller*
◆ **EMP:** 14 **EST:** 1996
SQ FT: 10,000
SALES (est): 6.4MM **Privately Held**
WEB: www.songchuanusa.com
SIC: 3625 Relays & industrial controls
PA: Song Chuan Precision Co., Ltd.
No. 377, Zhonghua Rd.
New Taipei City TAP 23858

(G-14188)
SOUTH FLA PAVEMENT COATINGS
1831 Nw 33rd St (33064-1308)
PHONE.....................954 979-5997
Gregory Scott Polk, *President*
EMP: 10 **EST:** 2015
SALES (est): 925K **Privately Held**
SIC: 2851 Lacquers, varnishes, enamels & other coatings

(G-14189)
SOUTH FLORIDA STRIP-TEES INC
1740 Nw 22nd Ct Ste 10 (33069-1327)
PHONE.....................954 972-4899
Robert Freeman, *President*
EMP: 13 **EST:** 1997
SQ FT: 2,000
SALES (est): 969K **Privately Held**
WEB: www.sportswearcollection.com
SIC: 2261 Screen printing of cotton broad-woven fabrics

(G-14190)
SOUTH FLORIDA TEXTILE INC
1301 W Copans Rd Ste E7 (33064-2228)
PHONE.....................954 973-5677
Joseph Lanzaro, *President*
EMP: 15 **EST:** 1987
SQ FT: 4,500
SALES (est): 454.9K **Privately Held**
SIC: 2339 Women's & misses' outerwear

(G-14191)
SOUTHEAST SECURITY PRODUCTS
1387 Sw 12th Ave (33069-4630)
PHONE.....................954 786-5900
Roy Nilsen, *President*

Margaret Debonis, *Opers Mgr*
John Sprague, *Sales Mgr*
Margaret Lananowitz, *Office Mgr*
Erik Nilsen, *Manager*
EMP: 8 **EST:** 1993
SALES (est): 1MM **Privately Held**
WEB: www.sesproducts.com
SIC: 3699 Security control equipment & systems

(G-14192)
SOUTHERN BOATING & YACHTING
Also Called: Southern Boating Magazine
1591 E Atl Blvd Ste 200 (33060-6765)
PHONE.....................954 522-5515
George A Allen Jr, *Chairman*
Steve Davis, *Chief*
Jenilee Pharo, *Sales Associate*
Vincent Scutellaro, *Adv Dir*
Clayton Therrien, *Manager*
▼ **EMP:** 43 **EST:** 1972
SALES (est): 5MM **Privately Held**
WEB: www.southernboating.com
SIC: 2721 Magazines: publishing only, not printed on site

(G-14193)
SOUTHERN GROUTS & MORTARS INC (PA)
Also Called: S G M
1502 Sw 2nd Pl (33069-3291)
PHONE.....................954 943-2288
Ron Picou, *President*
Elizabeth Picou-Mckee, *Exec VP*
Scott Maguire, *Opers Staff*
Jason Eckenrod, *Sales Staff*
Tonya Grogg,
◆ **EMP:** 70 **EST:** 1978
SQ FT: 50,000
SALES (est): 18.9MM **Privately Held**
WEB: www.sgm.cc
SIC: 2891 Adhesives

(G-14194)
SOUTHERN MICRO ETCH INC
610 Ne 29th St (33064-5447)
P.O. Box 1089 (33061-1089)
PHONE.....................954 781-5999
Fax: 954 781-8188
EMP: 12
SALES (est): 1.5MM **Privately Held**
SIC: 3479 Coating/Engraving Service

(G-14195)
SOUTHSTERN ARSPC SVCS LTD LBLT
1816 Sw 7th Ave (33060-9028)
PHONE.....................305 992-8257
Nicolas S Smith, *President*
EMP: 7 **EST:** 2015
SALES (est): 801.4K **Privately Held**
SIC: 3721 Aircraft

(G-14196)
SPIEGEL PAVERS INC
3400 Blue Lake Dr Apt 102 (33064-2028)
PHONE.....................954 687-5797
Marcio E Vieira, *President*
EMP: 7 **EST:** 2012
SALES (est): 155.2K **Privately Held**
SIC: 2951 Asphalt paving mixtures & blocks

(G-14197)
SSE AND ASSOCIATES INC
Also Called: SSE AND ASSOCIATES, INC.
1500 W Copans Rd Ste A9 (33064-1521)
PHONE.....................954 973-7144
EMP: 33 **EST:** 2014
WEB: www.sseteam.com
SIC: 3949 Sporting & athletic goods
PA: Sse And Associates, Inc
569 Canal St
New Smyrna Beach FL 32168

(G-14198)
STEEDA ENGINEERING AND MFG LLC
1351 Nw Steeda Way (33069-1521)
PHONE.....................954 960-0774
Dario Orlando, *Manager*
EMP: 7 **EST:** 2004
SALES (est): 39.6K **Privately Held**
SIC: 3999 Manufacturing industries

(G-14199)
STIMWAVE LLC
1310 Park Central Blvd S (33064-2217)
PHONE.....................800 965-5134
Aure Bruneau, *CEO*
Viktor Eckel, *General Mgr*
Denis Cue, *Engineer*
Oscar Steven Gil, *Engineer*
Mario Rosales, *Engineer*
EMP: 10 **EST:** 2015
SALES (est): 5.2MM **Privately Held**
WEB: www.stimwavefreedom.com
SIC: 3845 Electromedical equipment
PA: Stimwave Technologies Incorporated
1310 Park Central Blvd S
Pompano Beach FL 33064
800 965-5134

(G-14200)
STIMWAVE TECHNOLOGIES INC (PA)
1310 Park Central Blvd S (33064-2217)
PHONE.....................800 965-5134
Laura Perryman, *President*
James M Rallo, *CFO*
Martin West, *Controller*
Erin Valin, *Mktg Coord*
Kimberly Letourneau, *Marketing Staff*
EMP: 5 **EST:** 2010
SALES (est): 5.2MM **Privately Held**
WEB: www.stimwavefreedom.com
SIC: 3845 Laser systems & equipment, medical

(G-14201)
STONE DESIGN BY SANTOS LLC
1440 Nw 14th Ave (33069-1913)
PHONE.....................954 366-1919
Marcela P Santos, *Mng Member*
Farley Dos Santos, *Mng Member*
EMP: 8 **EST:** 2018
SALES (est): 610.1K **Privately Held**
WEB: www.stonedesignbysantos.com
SIC: 3281 Building stone products

(G-14202)
STONY CREEK SAND & GRAVEL LLC (PA)
2103 N Riverside Dr (33062-1225)
PHONE.....................804 229-0015
Brian C Purcell,
EMP: 5 **EST:** 2011
SALES (est): 447.4K **Privately Held**
WEB: www.stonycreeksand.com
SIC: 1442 Construction sand & gravel

(G-14203)
STRATEGIC BRANDS INC
Also Called: Laurey Co
2810 Center Port Cir (33064-2136)
PHONE.....................516 745-6100
Steven Friedel, *Chairman*
Sansford Steiger, *Vice Pres*
Jeremy Friedel, *Natl Sales Mgr*
◆ **EMP:** 10 **EST:** 1994
SQ FT: 1,600
SALES (est): 1.3MM **Privately Held**
WEB:
www.strategicbrandsincorporated.com
SIC: 3429 Cabinet hardware; door locks, bolts & checks

(G-14204)
SUN 3D CORPORATION
1951 W Copans Rd Ste 8 (33064-1549)
PHONE.....................954 210-6010
Gustavo Lopez, *President*
Janice Atherton, *Admin Sec*
EMP: 9 **EST:** 2014
SALES (est): 605.2K **Privately Held**
WEB: www.sun3dcorporation.com
SIC: 2752 Commercial printing, offset

(G-14205)
SUN NATION CORP
2861 Nw 22nd Ter (33069-1045)
PHONE.....................954 822-5460
Cary Chen, *CEO*
▲ **EMP:** 11 **EST:** 2018
SALES (est): 551.5K **Privately Held**
WEB: www.sunnationcorp.com
SIC: 3559 Automotive maintenance equipment

(G-14206)
SUNBELT TRANSFORMER LTD
2063 Blount Rd (33069-5110)
PHONE.....................305 517-3657
Eric Johnson, *Branch Mgr*
EMP: 9
SALES (corp-wide): 22.7MM **Privately Held**
WEB: www.sunbeltsolomon.com
SIC: 3612 Power & distribution transformers
PA: Sunbelt Transformer, Ltd.
1922 S Mrtn Lther King Jr
Temple TX 76504
800 433-3128

(G-14207)
SUPERIOR SIGNS AND PRINTS
1800 Nw 15th Ave (33069-1403)
PHONE.....................954 780-6351
Kris Lim, *Principal*
EMP: 7 **EST:** 2014
SALES (est): 227.8K **Privately Held**
WEB: www.superiorsignsandprints.com
SIC: 2752 Commercial printing, lithographic

(G-14208)
SYMMETRICAL STAIR INC
2115 Sw 2nd St (33069-3100)
PHONE.....................561 228-4800
Alphonso J Cheponis III, *President*
Mindy Discala, *Vice Pres*
EMP: 15 **EST:** 1995
SQ FT: 55,000
SALES (est): 802.3K **Privately Held**
WEB: www.symmetricalstair.com
SIC: 2431 Staircases & stairs, wood; stair railings, wood

(G-14209)
T M BUILDING PRODUCTS LTD
601 Nw 12th Ave (33069-2003)
PHONE.....................954 781-4430
Thomas J Metzger, *President*
T M Acquisition Corp, *General Ptnr*
EMP: 5 **EST:** 1989
SQ FT: 85,000
SALES (est): 1.5MM
SALES (corp-wide): 9.8MM **Privately Held**
SIC: 3442 Sash, door or window: metal
PA: Andlinger & Company, Inc.
520 White Plins Rd Ste 50
Tarrytown NY 10591
914 332-4900

(G-14210)
TANNOUS INNOVATIONS LLC
2157 Nw 22nd St (33069-1344)
PHONE.....................754 220-6645
▲ **EMP:** 5
SALES (est): 561.9K **Privately Held**
SIC: 3631 Mfg Household Cooking Equipment

(G-14211)
TEKK SUPPLY INC
290 Sw 14th Ave (33069-3232)
PHONE.....................954 444-5782
Robert Reiner, *President*
EMP: 6 **EST:** 2012
SALES (est): 1.8MM **Privately Held**
WEB: www.tekkpirates.com
SIC: 3965 5251 5085 Fasteners; tools; industrial supplies

(G-14212)
TILES OF POMPANO INC
119 S Federal Hwy (33062-5320)
PHONE.....................954 642-1993
Jill Uhl, *President*
EMP: 10 **EST:** 2009
SALES (est): 514.6K **Privately Held**
WEB: www.tilesofpompano.com
SIC: 3253 Ceramic wall & floor tile

(G-14213)
TK CUSTOM CANVAS & UPHOLSTERY
1849 S Dixie Hwy (33060-8946)
PHONE.....................954 609-3477
EMP: 7 **EST:** 2010

SALES (est): 120.4K **Privately Held**
WEB: www.tkcustomcanvas.com
SIC: 2211 Canvas

(G-14214)
TKO PRINT SOLUTIONS INC
Also Called: Think Print
140 Park Central Blvd S (33064-2138)
PHONE................................954 315-0990
John Laudadio, *President*
EMP: 25 EST: 2014
SALES (est): 3.8MM **Privately Held**
WEB: www.thinkprint.com
SIC: 2752 Commercial printing, offset

(G-14215)
TOPS KITCHEN CABINET LLC
1900 Nw 18th St (33069-1618)
PHONE................................954 933-9988
Ping Lin, *President*
◆ EMP: 10 EST: 2006
SALES (est): 786.6K **Privately Held**
WEB: www.topscabinet.net
SIC: 2434 Wood kitchen cabinets

(G-14216)
TOUCAN INDUSTRIES INC
1857 Sw 3rd St (33069-3105)
PHONE................................954 590-2222
Allison Sattuar-Lopez, *President*
Robert Lopez, *Vice Pres*
EMP: 50 EST: 1993
SALES (est): 2.9MM **Privately Held**
WEB: www.toucanindustries.com
SIC: 3559 Sewing machines & hat & zipper making machinery

(G-14217)
TRANE INC
2103 Sw 3rd St (33069-3120)
PHONE................................954 421-7133
Dan Cromer, *Manager*
EMP: 41 **Privately Held**
WEB: www.trane.com
SIC: 3585 Refrigeration & heating equipment
HQ: Trane Inc.
1 Centennial Ave Ste 101
Piscataway NJ 08854
732 652-7100

(G-14218)
TRI-COUNTY WOODWORKING LLC ✪
3001 Sw 10th St (33069-4814)
PHONE................................954 850-2222
David R Morisette, *Manager*
EMP: 11 EST: 2022
SALES (est): 989.3K **Privately Held**
SIC: 2431 Millwork

(G-14219)
TRIFECTA PHRMCEUTICALS USA LLC (PA)
4100 N Powerline Rd J4 (33073-3083)
PHONE................................888 296-9067
Gregory Brondou, *Mng Member*
▲ EMP: 5 EST: 2013
SALES (est): 1.3MM **Privately Held**
WEB: www.trifecta-pharma.com
SIC: 2834 Pharmaceutical preparations

(G-14220)
TROPICAL SHOWERS INC
1433 Ne 28th St (33064-6817)
PHONE................................954 260-5196
Barry White, *Owner*
EMP: 7 EST: 2004
SALES (est): 84.1K **Privately Held**
SIC: 3444 Metal housings, enclosures, casings & other containers

(G-14221)
TRUGREEN PRODUCTS LLC
1010 S Ocean Blvd Apt 408 (33062-6625)
PHONE................................954 629-5794
Howard Serkin, *CEO*
EMP: 7 EST: 2017
SALES (est): 47.2K **Privately Held**
WEB: www.trugreen.com
SIC: 2841 7389 Soap & other detergents;

(G-14222)
UIP INTERNATIONAL INC (PA)
1350 S Dixie Hwy E (33060-8515)
P.O. Box 5088, Fort Lauderdale (33310-5088)
PHONE................................954 785-3539
Howard D White, *President*
Jeff Cronemiller, *Division Mgr*
Horace S White, *Vice Pres*
Howie White, *Vice Pres*
Nancy Bordan, *Controller*
◆ EMP: 4 EST: 1992
SQ FT: 100,000
SALES (est): 3MM **Privately Held**
WEB: www.uipintl.com
SIC: 3052 Plastic hose

(G-14223)
ULTRA PHARMA LLC
3131 W Mcnab Rd (33069)
PHONE................................954 532-7539
EMP: 5
SALES (est): 394K **Privately Held**
SIC: 2834 Mfg Pharmaceutical Preparations

(G-14224)
UNAFLEX LLC (PA)
1350 S Dixie Hwy E (33060-8515)
P.O. Box 1229, Anderson SC (29622-1229)
PHONE................................954 943-5002
Jimmy White, *Human Resources*
Tom Allen, *Accounts Mgr*
Howard D White, *Mng Member*
Horace Ted White II,
◆ EMP: 25 EST: 2010
SQ FT: 100,000
SALES (est): 20.7MM **Privately Held**
WEB: fluidhandling.kadant.com
SIC: 3052 3599 2822 Hose, pneumatic: rubber or rubberized fabric; hose, flexible metallic; neoprene, chloroprene

(G-14225)
UNIQUE RABBIT STUDIOS INC
1631 S Dixie Hwy Ste B1 (33060-8951)
PHONE................................954 691-1390
John W Belcher, *President*
Shane Mitchell, *General Mgr*
Jerry Seal, *Prdtn Mgr*
EMP: 9 EST: 2008
SALES (est): 757.6K **Privately Held**
WEB: www.uniquerabbitstudios.com
SIC: 3299 Architectural sculptures: gypsum, clay, papier mache, etc.

(G-14226)
UNITED CIRCUITS INC
1410 Sw 29th Ave Ste 300 (33069-4849)
PHONE................................954 971-6860
Javier C Ruiz, *President*
Bob Felder, *Vice Pres*
Cindy Ruiz, *Vice Pres*
Cynthia L Ruiz, *Vice Pres*
Jennifer Ruiz, *Director*
EMP: 12 EST: 1993
SQ FT: 5,000
SALES (est): 2.5MM **Privately Held**
WEB: www.united-circuits.com
SIC: 3672 Printed circuit boards

(G-14227)
UNITED PRINTING LLC
2323 Ne 26th Ave (33062-1147)
PHONE................................954 554-7969
John A Vanbrocklin, *Administration*
EMP: 9 EST: 2013
SALES (est): 525.1K **Privately Held**
WEB: www.united-processing.com
SIC: 2752 Commercial printing, lithographic

(G-14228)
UNITED PRINTING SALES INC
Also Called: Minutemen Printing
51 N Federal Hwy (33062-4304)
PHONE................................954 942-4300
Robert Johnson, *President*
Rosemary R Johnson, *Vice Pres*
EMP: 5 EST: 1996
SALES (est): 306.5K **Privately Held**
WEB: www.minutemanpress.com
SIC: 2752 Commercial printing, lithographic

(G-14229)
UNITED STATE FOAM & COATINGS
2303 W Mcnab Rd Ste 16 (33069-4360)
PHONE................................954 972-5005
Robert Kaplan, *Owner*
EMP: 7 EST: 2010
SALES (est): 68.6K **Privately Held**
SIC: 3479 Metal coating & allied service

(G-14230)
US CONCRETE PRODUCTS CORP
1878 Nw 21st St (33069-1334)
PHONE................................954 973-0368
Albert Mancini, *President*
Nicholas Mancini, *Treasurer*
▲ EMP: 70 EST: 1993
SQ FT: 3,600
SALES (est): 12.4MM **Privately Held**
WEB: www.unitedstatesconcrete.com
SIC: 3272 Concrete products, precast

(G-14231)
US CUSTOM FABRICATION INC
1858 Nw 21st St (33069-1306)
PHONE................................954 917-6161
Lynn Campbell, *President*
Lisa Edwards, *Treasurer*
EMP: 5 EST: 2002
SQ FT: 2,500
SALES (est): 726K **Privately Held**
WEB: www.uscustomfab.com
SIC: 3441 Fabricated structural metal

(G-14232)
US RECREATIONAL ALLIANCE INC
Also Called: Coastline Marine
820 Sw 14th Ct (33060-8526)
PHONE................................954 782-7279
James Strauss, *President*
EMP: 13 EST: 2016
SALES (est): 963.5K **Privately Held**
SIC: 3732 Motorboats, inboard or outboard: building & repairing

(G-14233)
VALLEY FORGE TEXTILES LLC
1390 Sw 30th Ave (33069-4823)
PHONE................................954 971-1776
Fax: 954 968-4111
▲ EMP: 8
SALES (est): 875.9K **Privately Held**
SIC: 2231 2299 2221 2241 Wool Brdwv Fabric Mill Mfg Textile Goods Manmad Brdwv Fabric Mill Narrow Fabric Mill Whol Piece Goods/Notions

(G-14234)
VALLEY SURGICAL INC
1000 W Mcnab Rd (33069-4719)
PHONE................................954 768-9886
Deran Maloumian, *President*
EMP: 8 EST: 2005
SALES (est): 1.5MM **Privately Held**
WEB: www.valleysurg.com
SIC: 3843 Dental equipment & supplies

(G-14235)
VEE ENTERPRISES INC
Also Called: Graves Company
4100 N Powerline Rd I5 (33073-3083)
P.O. Box 11269 (33061-7269)
PHONE................................954 960-0300
Peter Erdo, *President*
Deborah Vanzo, *Director*
EMP: 6 EST: 1946
SQ FT: 12,000
SALES (est): 480.2K **Privately Held**
WEB: www.gravescompany.com
SIC: 3915 Lapidary work, contract or other

(G-14236)
VENTILATION AIR INC
901 Ne 4th St (33060-6415)
PHONE................................954 975-9501
Konstantine Kokkoris, *Principal*
EMP: 9 EST: 2009
SALES (est): 126.6K **Privately Held**
SIC: 3444 Sheet metalwork

(G-14237)
VIVIDUS LLC
3265 W Mcnab Rd (33069-4807)
PHONE................................954 326-1954
Alex Chervinsky, *CEO*
Barry Reiter, *COO*
Marc Poirier, *CFO*
EMP: 7 EST: 2013
SALES (est): 486.3K **Privately Held**
WEB: www.vividus.com
SIC: 2834 Pharmaceutical preparations

(G-14238)
VURB LLC
2450 W Sample Rd Ste 14 (33073-3074)
PHONE................................561 441-8870
Anthony Mastrangelo, *Principal*
Jason Kelley, *Administration*
Carmelo Mastrangelo,
EMP: 8 EST: 2014
SALES (est): 296.6K **Privately Held**
WEB: www.popyourpup.com
SIC: 2759 Promotional printing

(G-14239)
W & B SCIENTIFIC INC
Also Called: Bioquem USA
1301 W Copans Rd Ste G1 (33064-2230)
PHONE................................954 607-1500
Carlos A S Barreto, *President*
EMP: 10 EST: 2015
SALES (est): 4.8MM **Privately Held**
WEB: www.wbscientific.com
SIC: 2869 3821 Laboratory chemicals, organic; chemical laboratory apparatus; clinical laboratory instruments, except medical & dental

(G-14240)
WATER WORKS TECH GROUP LLC
4100 N Powerline Rd Q3 (33073-3083)
PHONE................................954 979-2480
Kevin Doyle, *Mng Member*
EMP: 10 EST: 2014
SALES (est): 832.8K **Privately Held**
SIC: 3229 Bowls, glass

(G-14241)
WESTECH DEVELOPMENT GROUP INC
Also Called: Westech Industries
3010 N Andrews Avenue Ext (33064-2114)
PHONE................................954 505-5090
Ning Wang, *Treasurer*
Sam Pascucci, *Admin Sec*
EMP: 8 EST: 2011
SALES (est): 891.8K **Privately Held**
SIC: 3861 Cameras & related equipment

(G-14242)
WICKS UNLIMITED INC
1515 Sw 13th Ct (33069-4710)
PHONE................................631 472-2010
Edwin Stimpson, *Principal*
Bruce Campbell, *Director*
EMP: 8 EST: 2000
SQ FT: 300,000
SALES (est): 312.2K **Privately Held**
WEB: www.wicksunlimited.com
SIC: 3999 Candles

(G-14243)
WILLIAMS TENDERS USA INC
451 S Federal Hwy (33062-5901)
PHONE................................954 648-6560
Christopher Rimmer, *Principal*
◆ EMP: 12 EST: 2014
SALES (est): 1MM **Privately Held**
WEB: www.williamstendersusa.com
SIC: 3732 Boat building & repairing

(G-14244)
WILLIS AERONAUTICAL SVCS INC
3151 Nw 27th Ave Ste 101 (33069-1133)
PHONE................................561 272-5402
Don Nunemaker, *President*
Steve Destefano, *Vice Pres*
Al Landolfi, *Vice Pres*
Susan Leahy, *Vice Pres*
Sue Leahy, *VP Opers*
EMP: 15 EST: 2013

SALES (est): 5MM
SALES (corp-wide): 274.2MM **Publicly Held**
WEB: www.willisaero.com
SIC: 3728 3812 7699 Aircraft parts & equipment; aircraft/aerospace flight instruments & guidance systems; aviation propeller & blade repair
PA: Willis Lease Finance Corporation
4700 Lyons Tech Pkwy
Coconut Creek FL 33073
415 408-4700

(G-14245)
WYLDE WOODWORKING CO
4031 Ne 12th Ave (33064-6108)
PHONE...................................954 942-7630
Eric W Lachoff, *President*
EMP: 7 EST: 2005
SALES (est): 129.7K **Privately Held**
SIC: 2431 Millwork

(G-14246)
ZEPSA INDUSTRIES
41 Sw 6th St (33060-7915)
PHONE...................................754 307-2173
EMP: 7 EST: 2017
SALES (est): 70.5K **Privately Held**
WEB: www.zepsa.com
SIC: 3999 Manufacturing industries

(G-14247)
ZUMRO MANUFACTURING INC
650 Sw 16th Ter (33069-4533)
P.O. Box 667227 (33066-7227)
PHONE...................................954 782-7779
Win Vanbasten, *President*
Noelia Sanchez, *Prdtn Mgr*
▲ EMP: 23 EST: 2002
SQ FT: 10,000
SALES (est): 2.2MM **Privately Held**
WEB: www.zumro.com
SIC: 3669 Emergency alarms

Ponce De Leon
Walton County

(G-14248)
ARBAN & ASSOCIATES INC
1464 Line Rd (32455-6310)
PHONE...................................850 836-4362
Robert Arban, *President*
Sylvia J Arban, *Corp Secy*
Timothy Alford, *Vice Pres*
EMP: 17 EST: 1986
SQ FT: 1,400
SALES (est): 2.6MM **Privately Held**
SIC: 2439 Trusses, wooden roof

(G-14249)
S B LIGHTING LLC
2889 N Highway 81 (32455-6725)
PHONE...................................850 687-1166
Steven S Busby, *Manager*
EMP: 7 EST: 2010
SALES (est): 119.2K **Privately Held**
SIC: 3648 Lighting equipment

(G-14250)
U-LOAD DUMPSTERS LLC
Also Called: Brandon Brown Newsom
1450 Mitchell Rd (32455-6308)
PHONE...................................352 318-3045
Brandon Newsom, *Principal*
EMP: 7 EST: 2015
SALES (est): 205.1K **Privately Held**
SIC: 3443 Dumpsters, garbage

(G-14251)
UNITED NTONS SPACE CRPS MLTARY (PA)
Also Called: Majestic Unsc Spcial Intllgnce
10310 County Highway 3280 (32455-4305)
PHONE...................................702 373-2351
Aaron Taylor, *Exec Dir*
EMP: 5 EST: 2020
SALES (est): 522K **Privately Held**
SIC: 3443 8211 9221 9711 Nuclear reactors, military or industrial; military academy; bureau of criminal investigation, government; Air Force

Ponce Inlet
Volusia County

(G-14252)
SCOTT-CLARK LP
Also Called: Scott-Clark Medical
4670 Links Village Dr B10 (32127-3006)
PHONE...................................512 756-7300
Richard Flyn, *President*
Bill Bzdek, *COO*
William Bzdek, *COO*
Mike Ludwick, *Opers Mgr*
Owen Billingsley, *Prdtn Mgr*
EMP: 5 EST: 2013
SALES (est): 772.7K **Privately Held**
WEB: www.scott-clark.com
SIC: 3571 Electronic computers

Ponte Vedra
St. Johns County

(G-14253)
2JCP LLC
Also Called: Gt Ice LLC
101 Marketside Ave (32081-1541)
PHONE...................................904 834-3818
Trevor Richter, *VP Bus Dvlpt*
Paul Schuster, *Director*
Stephen Rippon,
Jan Paces,
Trevor Richer,
▲ EMP: 7 EST: 2012
SALES (est): 4.1MM **Privately Held**
WEB: www.2jcp.com
SIC: 3511 Gas turbine generator set units, complete
HQ: 2 Jcp A.S.
Racice 126
Racice 411 0
416 857-511

(G-14254)
3D PRINTING SOLUTIONS
243 Cross Branch Dr (32081-0843)
PHONE...................................850 443-4200
John Daly, *Principal*
EMP: 7 EST: 2018
SALES (est): 132.8K **Privately Held**
WEB: www.3dsystems.com
SIC: 2752 Commercial printing, lithographic

(G-14255)
COUNTER ACTIVE INC
Also Called: Silestone of Tampa
87 Sanchez Dr E (32082-2446)
PHONE...................................813 626-0022
Robert D Hutto, *President*
Pete Valentine, *Vice Pres*
▲ EMP: 11 EST: 1999
SQ FT: 20,000
SALES (est): 434.8K **Privately Held**
SIC: 2541 Counter & sink tops

(G-14256)
DAILYS 1113 SHELL
40 Settlement Dr (32081-0758)
PHONE...................................904 608-0219
EMP: 8 EST: 2015
SALES (est): 166.2K **Privately Held**
WEB: www.dailys.com
SIC: 2711 Newspapers

(G-14257)
FIVE STAR MARBLE AND STONE
117 Taylor Ridge Ave (32081-8453)
PHONE...................................904 887-4736
Bakir Mehmedinovic, *Principal*
EMP: 6 EST: 2019
SALES (est): 337.7K **Privately Held**
SIC: 3281 Cut stone & stone products

(G-14258)
OPTIMUM SPRING MFG INC
150 Hilden Rd Ste 316 (32081-8405)
P.O. Box 600070, Jacksonville (32260-0070)
PHONE...................................904 567-5999
Andrea De Palma, *Principal*
EMP: 7 EST: 2015

SALES (est): 266.8K **Privately Held**
WEB: www.optimumspring.com
SIC: 3495 Wire springs

(G-14259)
TREACE MEDICAL CONCEPTS INC
203 Fort Wade Rd Unit 150 (32081-5159)
PHONE...................................904 373-5940
John T Treace, *CEO*
James T Treace, *Ch of Bd*
Joe W Ferguson, *Senior VP*
Dipak A Rajhansa, *Senior VP*
Sean F Scanlan, *Senior VP*
EMP: 133 EST: 2014
SQ FT: 23,060
SALES (est): 94.4MM **Privately Held**
WEB: www.treace.com
SIC: 3841 Fixation appliances, internal

Ponte Vedra Beach
St. Johns County

(G-14260)
AI THOMAS LLC
Also Called: Ait Environmental Technology
220 Pnte Vdra Pk Dr Ste 1 (32082)
PHONE...................................904 553-6202
Dennis Holler, *General Mgr*
Angelo Passantino, *Regional Mgr*
Herman Everidge, *Vice Pres*
Michael Castranova, *Opers Staff*
Cameron Clements, *Manager*
EMP: 30 EST: 2006
SALES (est): 857.7K **Privately Held**
WEB: mailer.fsu.edu
SIC: 2879 Agricultural chemicals

(G-14261)
ALIVE BY NATURE INC
130 Corridor Rd Ste 3333 (32082-3225)
P.O. Box 3333 (32004-3333)
PHONE...................................800 810-1935
Bryan E Nettles, *President*
EMP: 10 EST: 2010
SALES (est): 610.9K **Privately Held**
WEB: www.alivebynature.com
SIC: 2833 Vitamins, natural or synthetic: bulk, uncompounded

(G-14262)
ALTA TECHNOLOGIES INC
285 Plantation Cir S (32082-3936)
PHONE...................................609 538-9500
Paul Snook, *President*
Percy F Leaper, *Chairman*
Laura Snook, *Vice Pres*
Mary Alice-Leaper, *Treasurer*
EMP: 9 EST: 1986
SQ FT: 12,000
SALES (est): 919.8K **Privately Held**
WEB: www.altatechnologies.com
SIC: 3644 2221 Noncurrent-carrying wiring services; fiberglass fabrics

(G-14263)
AMERICAN ATLAS CORP
2309 Sawgrass Village Dr (32082-5008)
PHONE...................................904 273-6090
W R Bornmiller, *President*
EMP: 5 EST: 1995
SALES (est): 309.6K **Privately Held**
SIC: 2741 Atlases: publishing & printing

(G-14264)
AQUATEKO INTERNATIONAL LLC
140 Deer Haven Dr (32082-2171)
PHONE...................................904 273-7200
Keith A Kessler, *Principal*
▲ EMP: 9 EST: 2009
SALES (est): 568.8K **Privately Held**
WEB: www.aquateko.com
SIC: 3496 Traps, animal & fish

(G-14265)
COLLOIDAL DYNAMICS LLC
5150 Palm Valley Rd # 303 (32082-4633)
PHONE...................................904 686-1536
Laurel Cannon, *Opers Mgr*
David W Cannon,
EMP: 5 EST: 2009
SQ FT: 3,000

SALES (est): 864.5K **Privately Held**
WEB: www.colloidal-dynamics.com
SIC: 3829 3821 Measuring & controlling devices; particle size reduction apparatus, laboratory

(G-14266)
COUNTRY CLUB CONCIERGE MAG INC
830-13 A1a N Ste 496 (32082)
PHONE...................................904 223-0204
Ava Electris Cannie, *CEO*
Matthew George Koob, *Admin Sec*
EMP: 6 EST: 2006
SALES (est): 448.1K **Privately Held**
WEB: www.countryclub-conciergemagazine.com
SIC: 2721 Magazines: publishing only, not printed on site

(G-14267)
EIGHTEEN DEGREES EIGHTEEN
3787 Palm Valley Rd # 101 (32082-4183)
PHONE...................................904 686-1892
David A San Juan, *Principal*
EMP: 7 EST: 2010
SALES (est): 93.5K **Privately Held**
SIC: 2024 Ice cream, bulk

(G-14268)
HANAYA LLC
543 Le Master Dr (32082-2313)
PHONE...................................904 285-7575
Jose R Cortes, *Partner*
George Tan, *Partner*
EMP: 17 EST: 2005
SQ FT: 3,000
SALES (est): 934K **Privately Held**
WEB: www.hanayainc.com
SIC: 3449 Miscellaneous metalwork

(G-14269)
INSURANCE PLUS
820 A1a N Ste W18 (32082-3326)
PHONE...................................904 567-1553
EMP: 8 EST: 2014
SALES (est): 198.6K **Privately Held**
WEB: www.insurefitness.com
SIC: 2721 Magazines: publishing & printing

(G-14270)
JT ENTERPRISES GROUP LLC (PA)
Also Called: J Turner & Co
280 Village Main St (32082-5087)
PHONE...................................904 803-9338
Jennifer A Turner,
EMP: 6 EST: 2014
SALES (est): 5.5MM **Privately Held**
WEB: www.jturner.com
SIC: 2519 Furniture, household: glass, fiberglass & plastic

(G-14271)
LYNN JACKSON KIMBERLY
Also Called: Kj Collections
12350 Arbor Dr (32082-2101)
PHONE...................................904 285-7745
Kimberly Jackson, *Principal*
EMP: 7 EST: 2007
SALES (est): 227.7K **Privately Held**
SIC: 3949 Sporting & athletic goods

(G-14272)
MACPAC INC
830-13 A1a N 477 (32082)
PHONE...................................904 315-6457
James E McDermott, *President*
EMP: 10 EST: 2008
SALES (est): 781K **Privately Held**
WEB: www.macpacpkg.com
SIC: 2653 Boxes, corrugated: made from purchased materials

(G-14273)
MAXIT CORPORATION
1102 A1a N Ste 206 (32082-4098)
PHONE...................................904 998-9520
Philip Baruch, *CFO*
EMP: 8 EST: 1995
SQ FT: 1,500

SALES (est): 1MM **Privately Held**
WEB: www.maxit.com
SIC: 7372 7371 Educational computer software; custom computer programming services

(G-14274)
METROPOLITAN MIX
3108 Sawgrass Village Cir (32082-5037)
PHONE................................904 242-0743
James Byrne, *Principal*
EMP: 8 EST: 2009
SALES (est): 143.3K **Privately Held**
SIC: 3273 Ready-mixed concrete

(G-14275)
MMI NORTH AMERICA INC
344 Ponte Vedra Blvd (32082-1812)
PHONE................................616 649-1912
EMP: 12
SALES (est): 473.7K **Privately Held**
SIC: 3841 7389 Instruments, microsurgical: except electromedical;

(G-14276)
PETERBROOKE CHOCLAT FCTRY LLC
880 State Rd A1a Ste 4 1 A (32082)
PHONE................................904 273-7878
Jackie Kolb, *Principal*
Beba Ramirez, *Sales Staff*
EMP: 9
SALES (corp-wide): 35.5MM **Privately Held**
WEB: www.peterbrooke.com
SIC: 2066 5145 Chocolate; candy
HQ: Copeland Chocolates, Llc
249 Copeland St
Jacksonville FL 32204
904 660-2300

(G-14277)
PONTE VEDRA WNS CIVIC ALIANCE
359 San Juan Dr (32082-2822)
PHONE................................904 834-3543
Barbara K Roberts, *Principal*
EMP: 9 EST: 2012
SALES (est): 148.4K **Privately Held**
SIC: 2711 Newspapers, publishing & printing

(G-14278)
PUBLISHERS GUILD INC
2309 Sawgrass Village Dr (32082-5008)
PHONE................................904 273-5394
W R Bornmiller, *President*
William Bornmille, *Vice Pres*
EMP: 4 EST: 1989
SQ FT: 1,700
SALES (est): 8.8MM **Privately Held**
WEB: www.fivestarpub.com
SIC: 2741 Posters: publishing only, not printed on site

(G-14279)
R RESIDUAL CORP
59 Ponte Vedra Blvd (32082-1311)
PHONE................................810 874-6727
Y E Hall, *Principal*
EMP: 9 EST: 2009
SALES (est): 193.9K **Privately Held**
WEB: www.exquisitefaceandbody.com
SIC: 2911 Residues

(G-14280)
RECOVER GEAR LLC
Also Called: One Hundred Ten Percent
822 A1a N (32082-3260)
PHONE................................904 280-9660
Jason Schoepfer, *Vice Pres*
David Green, *Mng Member*
Jim Philip,
EMP: 6 EST: 2009
SALES (est): 719.7K **Privately Held**
SIC: 2339 2329 Women's & misses' athletic clothing & sportswear; men's & boys' sportswear & athletic clothing

(G-14281)
TRUSSES UNLIMITED INC (PA)
Also Called: Lumber Unlimited
320 San Juan Dr (32082-1818)
P.O. Box 12267, Jacksonville (32209-0267)
PHONE................................904 355-6611

David Myers, *President*
Barbara Brown, *CFO*
Ken Kuester, *Director*
EMP: 46 EST: 1965
SQ FT: 6,000
SALES (est): 15.5MM **Privately Held**
WEB: www.djtrussesunlimited.com
SIC: 2439 5031 Trusses, wooden roof; millwork

(G-14282)
UNIVERSAL SCHOOL PRODUCTS INC
2309 Sawgrass Village Dr (32082-5008)
PHONE................................904 273-8590
Bill Bornmller, *CEO*
EMP: 7 EST: 2003
SALES (est): 595.9K **Privately Held**
SIC: 2678 Memorandum books, notebooks & looseleaf filler paper

(G-14283)
ZASSI HOLDINGS INC (PA)
Also Called: Ezassi
822 A1a N Ste 104 (32082-8208)
PHONE................................904 432-8315
Peter Von Dyck, *President*
Ray Brandstaetter, *CFO*
Victoria Lane, *Controller*
Eric Haulotte, *Manager*
Meri Tovmasyan, *Manager*
EMP: 7 EST: 1997
SQ FT: 5,000
SALES (est): 2.3MM **Privately Held**
WEB: www.ezassi.com
SIC: 3842 3845 Surgical appliances & supplies; electromedical apparatus

---

Port Charlotte
Charlotte County

(G-14284)
ALL PHASE CUSTOM MILL SHOP INC
7471 Sawyer Cir (33981-2654)
PHONE................................941 474-0903
William Woods, *President*
▼ EMP: 25 EST: 1998
SQ FT: 14,000
SALES (est): 3.3MM **Privately Held**
WEB: www.allphasecustommill.com
SIC: 2431 Millwork

(G-14285)
AMERICAN CNSTR ENTPS INC
Also Called: Ace Door Co
1232 Market Cir Unit 2b (33953-3829)
PHONE................................941 629-2070
Walter E Helm, *President*
Linda L Helm, *Vice Pres*
EMP: 5 EST: 1986
SQ FT: 14,000
SALES (est): 828.6K **Privately Held**
SIC: 2431 3442 Doors & door parts & trim, wood; metal doors

(G-14286)
ARGOS READY MIX
580 Prineville St (33954-1027)
PHONE................................941 629-7713
EMP: 7 EST: 2016
SALES (est): 110.5K **Privately Held**
SIC: 3273 Ready-mixed concrete

(G-14287)
ARMOURY PROPERTY & MOLD INSPEC
18682 Fort Smith Cir (33948-9686)
PHONE................................813 503-9765
Alex Oros, *President*
EMP: 10 EST: 2005
SALES (est): 91.8K **Privately Held**
SIC: 3544 Industrial molds

(G-14288)
BLADORN INVESTMENTS INC
Also Called: Monarch Printing & Design
1264 Market Cir Unit 6 (33953-3899)
PHONE................................941 627-0014
Michael D Bladorn, *President*
Beverly Jensen, *Graphic Designe*
EMP: 7 EST: 2006
SQ FT: 1,500

SALES (est): 927.8K **Privately Held**
SIC: 2752 Commercial printing, offset

(G-14289)
BOYLE PUBLICATIONS INC
1039 Tamiami Trl (33953-3805)
PHONE................................941 255-0187
EMP: 5 EST: 2019
SALES (est): 312.3K **Privately Held**
SIC: 2741 Miscellaneous publishing

(G-14290)
BRIDGESTONE AMERICAS INC
Also Called: Firestone Complete Auto Care
24040 Beatrix Blvd (33954-3869)
PHONE................................941 235-0445
EMP: 21 **Privately Held**
WEB: www.bridgestoneamericas.com
SIC: 3011 Tires & inner tubes
HQ: Bridgestone Americas, Inc.
200 4th Ave S Ste 100
Nashville TN 37201
615 937-1000

(G-14291)
CAST SYSTEMS LLC
19400 Peachland Blvd (33948-2146)
PHONE................................941 625-3474
Gary E Tschetter, *Mng Member*
EMP: 30 EST: 2001
SQ FT: 1,620
SALES (est): 6.1MM **Privately Held**
WEB: www.castsystemsllc.com
SIC: 3272 Concrete products, precast

(G-14292)
CHICAGO ELECTRONIC DISTRS INC
17097 Glenview Ave (33954-1564)
PHONE................................312 985-6175
Craig Lemoyne, *President*
EMP: 10 EST: 2013
SALES (est): 1.7MM **Privately Held**
WEB: www.chicagodist.com
SIC: 3491 3691 2493 3823 Automatic regulating & control valves; storage batteries; insulation board, cellular fiber; fluidic devices, circuits & systems for process control

(G-14293)
COASTAL HURRICANE FILM LLC
807 Thornton Ave Nw (33948-7755)
PHONE................................941 268-9693
Randy Stalnaker, *Principal*
EMP: 8 EST: 2008
SALES (est): 177.8K **Privately Held**
SIC: 3211 Window glass, clear & colored

(G-14294)
COMEX SYSTEMS INC
9380 Nastrand Cir (33981-4031)
P.O. Box 142, Placida (33946-0142)
PHONE................................908 881-6301
Doug Pryblowski, *President*
EMP: 5 EST: 1973
SQ FT: 2,400
SALES (est): 464K **Privately Held**
WEB: www.comexsystems.com
SIC: 2731 Books: publishing only

(G-14295)
DOMINION PRINTERS INC
5393 Kennel St (33981-1919)
PHONE................................757 340-1300
Stephan Pahno, *President*
Pete Pahno, *Treasurer*
Mike Pahno, *Admin Sec*
EMP: 9 EST: 1984
SQ FT: 4,125
SALES (est): 267.7K **Privately Held**
WEB: www.dominionprinters.com
SIC: 2752 Commercial printing, offset

(G-14296)
ED ALLEN INC
1312 Market Cir Unit 9 (33953-3831)
PHONE................................941 743-2646
Edward A Faiola, *Principal*
EMP: 9 EST: 2013
SALES (est): 207.7K **Privately Held**
SIC: 2591 Window blinds

(G-14297)
EDMUND C MIGA
Also Called: Rudolph & ME
23040 Bradford Ave (33952-1721)
PHONE................................941 628-5951
Edmund C Miga, *Owner*
EMP: 8 EST: 2007
SALES (est): 393K **Privately Held**
SIC: 3229 Christmas tree ornaments, from glass produced on-site

(G-14298)
FASTENER SPECIALTY CORP
24100 Tiseo Blvd Unit 14 (33980-5223)
PHONE................................631 903-4453
Steve Goodloe, *Sales Staff*
EMP: 7 EST: 2018
SALES (est): 181.6K **Privately Held**
WEB: www.fastenerspecialty.com
SIC: 3965 Fasteners

(G-14299)
FLORIDA ROCK
580 Prineville St (33954-1027)
PHONE................................941 625-1244
Edward Wickowski, *Owner*
EMP: 7 EST: 2010
SALES (est): 88.7K **Privately Held**
SIC: 3273 Ready-mixed concrete

(G-14300)
FLOWERS BKG CO BRADENTON LLC
23240 Bayshore Rd (33980-3213)
PHONE................................941 627-0752
EMP: 13
SQ FT: 6,480
SALES (corp-wide): 3.7B **Publicly Held**
SIC: 2051 Mfg Bread
HQ: Flowers Baking Co. Of Bradenton, Llc
6490 Parkland Dr
Sarasota FL 34243
941 758-5656

(G-14301)
FSHS INC
Also Called: Puromax
4210 Whidden Blvd (33980-8407)
PHONE................................941 625-5929
Kevin Greene, *President*
Jeremy Greene, *General Mgr*
Tracy Greene, *CFO*
Josh Greene, *Manager*
◆ EMP: 6 EST: 1996
SALES (est): 1MM **Privately Held**
WEB: www.puromax.com
SIC: 3589 5074 Water treatment equipment, industrial; water purification equipment, household type; water purification equipment

(G-14302)
GALAXY AMERICA INC
7431 Sawyer Cir (33981-2654)
PHONE................................941 697-0324
Robin Whincup, *President*
Carol Whincup, *Corp Secy*
Mike Whincup, *Senior Mgr*
◆ EMP: 16 EST: 2009
SALES (est): 4.7MM **Privately Held**
WEB: www.galaxymultirides.com
SIC: 3944 Hobby horses

(G-14303)
HARBOR IMAGING
3430 Tamiami Trl Ste B (33952-8148)
PHONE................................941 883-8383
James White, *President*
Laura Gaura, *Accountant*
James Renn, *Administration*
EMP: 23 EST: 2004
SALES (est): 1.8MM **Privately Held**
SIC: 3845 Ultrasonic scanning devices, medical

(G-14304)
JUST COUNTERS OTHER STUFF INC
1489 Market Cir Bldg 309 (33953-3807)
PHONE................................941 235-1300
Mark Kemeny, *President*
Kathy Kemeny, *Vice Pres*
EMP: 10 EST: 2002

SALES (est): 1MM **Privately Held**
WEB: www.justcountersandotherstuff.com
SIC: 2541 Counter & sink tops

(G-14305)
LARRYS EXTREME AUDIO TINT LLC
19360 Strathcona Ave (33954-2074)
PHONE...................................941 766-8468
Larry Sweeris, *Principal*
EMP: 5 EST: 2012
SALES (est): 472.8K **Privately Held**
SIC: 3356 Tin

(G-14306)
LERNER ENTERPRISES INC
19367 Abhenry Cir (33948-7725)
PHONE...................................440 323-5529
Arthur L Lerner, *Principal*
Janet Kurtz, *QC Mgr*
Paul Klug, *Administration*
▲ EMP: 30 EST: 1983
SQ FT: 30,000
SALES (est): 3.6MM **Privately Held**
SIC: 3452 Bolts, nuts, rivets & washers

(G-14307)
M D MOLD LLC
20439 Stardust Ave (33952-1320)
PHONE...................................941 214-0854
Mold MD, *Principal*
EMP: 7 EST: 2018
SALES (est): 221.7K **Privately Held**
SIC: 3544 Industrial molds

(G-14308)
MADOW GROUP
1409 Remington Trace Dr (33953-2250)
PHONE...................................410 526-4780
Madow Richard, *Vice Pres*
Sylvia Carlin, *Author*
EMP: 7 EST: 2012
SALES (est): 315.7K **Privately Held**
WEB: www.madow.com
SIC: 2741 Miscellaneous publishing

(G-14309)
NORTECH ENGINEERING INC
13001 Cedar Creek Dr (33953-7810)
PHONE...................................508 823-8520
EMP: 7
SQ FT: 10,125
SALES (est): 2.4MM **Privately Held**
SIC: 3571 Electronic Computers, Nsk

(G-14310)
ORACLE AMERICA INC
Also Called: Sun Microsystems
267 Harbor Blvd (33954-3257)
PHONE...................................888 595-6310
EMP: 8
SALES (corp-wide): 42.4B **Publicly Held**
WEB: www.oracle.com
SIC: 3571 Minicomputers
HQ: Oracle America, Inc.
    500 Oracle Pkwy
    Redwood City CA 94065
    650 506-7000

(G-14311)
PACE MACHINE TOOL INC
13564 Ingraham Blvd (33981-2823)
PHONE...................................248 960-9903
Linda Hobbel, *President*
Raymond Hobble, *Vice Pres*
EMP: 15 EST: 1989
SALES (est): 293.4K **Privately Held**
SIC: 3599 Machine shop, jobbing & repair

(G-14312)
PRO COLOR COATING LLC
244 Macarthur Dr (33954-2413)
PHONE...................................941 661-4769
Gordon C Frost, *Principal*
EMP: 7 EST: 2010
SALES (est): 101.9K **Privately Held**
SIC: 3479 Metal coating & allied service

(G-14313)
QUALITY MACHINE SERVICE INC
2199 Fernwood St (33948-1100)
PHONE...................................610 554-3917
Charles Rhoades, *President*
Debra Rhoades, *Treasurer*

EMP: 5 EST: 1988
SQ FT: 8,000
SALES (est): 419.9K **Privately Held**
WEB: www.qualitymachineserviceinc.net
SIC: 3599 Machine shop, jobbing & repair

(G-14314)
SIGNS BY AKOS LLC
3212 Elkcam Blvd (33952-6611)
PHONE...................................941 625-6845
EMP: 6 EST: 2019
SALES (est): 335.2K **Privately Held**
SIC: 3993 Signs & advertising specialties

(G-14315)
SOUTHERN CROSS SHUTTER SYSTEMS
21271 Dearborn Ave (33954-3135)
PHONE...................................941 585-2152
Brant J Smith, *Owner*
EMP: 7 EST: 2015
SALES (est): 514K **Privately Held**
SIC: 3442 Shutters, door or window: metal

(G-14316)
STEPHENS GROUP
20101 Peachland Blvd # 2 (33954-2180)
PHONE...................................941 623-9689
Craig Stephens, *Principal*
EMP: 7 EST: 2010
SALES (est): 102.1K **Privately Held**
SIC: 2731 Book publishing

(G-14317)
SUN COAST MEDIA GROUP INC (HQ)
Also Called: Punta Gorda Sun Herald
23170 Harborview Rd (33980-2100)
PHONE...................................941 206-1300
David Dunn-Rankin, *CEO*
Ronald Dupont, *Editor*
Robert Vedder, *Vice Pres*
Janelle Andou, *Marketing Staff*
Cynthia Acevedo, *Office Mgr*
EMP: 80 EST: 1977
SALES (est): 49.9MM
SALES (corp-wide): 333.5MM **Privately Held**
WEB: www.yoursun.com
SIC: 2711 2752 Newspapers, publishing & printing; commercial printing, lithographic
PA: Adams Publishing Group, Llc
    4095 Coon Rapids Blvd Nw
    Minneapolis MN 55433
    218 348-3391

(G-14318)
SUN COAST MEDIA GROUP INC
Also Called: Green Sheet, The
2726 Tamiami Trl Ste B (33952-5164)
PHONE...................................941 206-1900
Robert Knight, *General Mgr*
Garry Overbey, *Editor*
Omar Zucco, *Advt Staff*
Jeff Amero, *Director*
EMP: 10
SALES (corp-wide): 333.5MM **Privately Held**
WEB: www.yoursun.com
SIC: 2711 Newspapers, publishing & printing
HQ: Sun Coast Media Group, Inc.
    23170 Harborview Rd
    Port Charlotte FL 33980
    941 206-1300

(G-14319)
TROPICAL CUSTOM COATINGS
11354 Zola Ave (33981-7338)
PHONE...................................941 475-3663
Timothy Costello, *Principal*
EMP: 6 EST: 2012
SALES (est): 300.2K **Privately Held**
SIC: 3479 Metal coating & allied service

(G-14320)
UNDERWTER FISH LIGHT LTD LBLTY
20400 Veterans Blvd (33954-2241)
PHONE...................................941 391-5846
John Molle, *Mng Member*
Heidi L Molle,
EMP: 7 EST: 2008
SQ FT: 5,000

SALES (est): 932.4K **Privately Held**
WEB: www.underwaterfishlight.com
SIC: 3648 Underwater lighting fixtures

(G-14321)
UNITED SEAL & TAG LABEL CORP
19237 Pine Bluff Ct (33948-9672)
PHONE...................................941 625-6799
Robert Freda, *President*
EMP: 8 EST: 1919
SQ FT: 10,000
SALES (est): 766.8K **Privately Held**
SIC: 2759 2789 2671 Labels & seals: printing; tags: printing; bookbinding & related work; packaging paper & plastics film, coated & laminated

(G-14322)
VALUESAFES INC
24123 Peachland Blvd (33954-3774)
PHONE...................................877 629-6214
Jessica Gilmore, *Principal*
EMP: 5 EST: 2010
SALES (est): 394.6K **Privately Held**
WEB: www.valuesafesinc.com
SIC: 3499 Safes & vaults, metal

(G-14323)
VOYAGER OFFROAD LLC
1602 Market Cir Unit 8 (33953-3893)
PHONE...................................941 235-7225
Andrew J Nix,
EMP: 10 EST: 2011
SALES (est): 918.6K **Privately Held**
WEB: www.voyagerracks.com
SIC: 7692 Welding repair

(G-14324)
WESTCHSTER GOLD FBRICATORS INC
4200 Tamiami Trl Ste F (33952-9233)
PHONE...................................941 625-0666
Steven Duke, *President*
Jane Duke, *Vice Pres*
EMP: 8 EST: 1978
SQ FT: 5,000
SALES (est): 1MM **Privately Held**
WEB: www.westchestergold.com
SIC: 3911 5932 Jewelry, precious metal; pawnshop

(G-14325)
WOODS DISTINCTIVE DESIGNS INC
Also Called: Advanced Cabinetry Systems
7450 Sawyer Cir (33981-2653)
PHONE...................................941 698-7535
Frank Wood, *President*
Jeannette Woods, *Vice Pres*
EMP: 10 EST: 1997
SALES (est): 900K **Privately Held**
WEB: www.advancedcabinetrypc.com
SIC: 2434 Wood kitchen cabinets

Port Orange
Volusia County

(G-14326)
AUTOMATIC BUSINESS PRODUCTS CO
4480 Eastport Park Way (32127-6044)
PHONE...................................888 742-7639
EMP: 11 EST: 2011
SALES (est): 193.6K **Privately Held**
SIC: 2672 Adhesive papers, labels or tapes: from purchased material

(G-14327)
AVIATION TRNING FOUNDATION LLC
835 Brimfield Ct (32127-9214)
PHONE...................................844 746-4968
Steven Hawrylak, *Mng Member*
EMP: 8 EST: 2015
SALES (est): 416.2K **Privately Held**
WEB: www.aviationtrainingfoundation.com
SIC: 3699 Flight simulators (training aids), electronic

(G-14328)
BANAGHAN WOOD PRODUCTS INC
741 Tarry Town Trl (32127-4916)
P.O. Box 291922 (32129-1922)
PHONE...................................386 788-6114
EMP: 29 EST: 1993
SALES (est): 2.5MM **Privately Held**
SIC: 2499 Manufactures Wood Products Such As Posts And Poles

(G-14329)
BARROWS ALUMINUM INC
630 Oak Pl Ste H (32127-4372)
PHONE...................................386 767-3445
Raleigh Barrows, *President*
EMP: 10 EST: 2001
SALES (est): 910.2K **Privately Held**
WEB: www.tjslawnandgarden.com
SIC: 3355 Rails, rolled & drawn, aluminum

(G-14330)
BECKER DESIGNS INC
4188 Dairy Ct Ste C (32127-4473)
PHONE...................................386 760-2280
Susan Becker, *Owner*
EMP: 5 EST: 1994
SQ FT: 3,000
SALES (est): 399.7K **Privately Held**
WEB: www.abeckerdesign.com
SIC: 2339 Athletic clothing: women's, misses' & juniors'

(G-14331)
CUSTOMER SUCCESS LLC
1892 Clubhouse Dr (32128-7366)
PHONE...................................386 265-4882
Wanda Tarnoff, *Manager*
EMP: 16 EST: 2017
SALES (est): 624.6K **Privately Held**
WEB: www.totango.com
SIC: 7372 Prepackaged software

(G-14332)
DON BELL SIGNS LLC
365 Oak Pl (32127-4388)
PHONE...................................800 824-0080
Gary D Bell, *President*
Jim Wetherell, *Vice Pres*
Frank Boanno, *Sales Mgr*
Diana Grunderman, *Sales Staff*
Ron Hatcher, *Sales Staff*
EMP: 52 EST: 1947
SQ FT: 50,000
SALES (est): 12.5MM **Privately Held**
WEB: www.donbellsigns.com
SIC: 3993 Electric signs

(G-14333)
DRAPERY CONTROL SYSTEMS INC
Also Called: Brambier's Windows & Walls
3817 S Nova Rd Ste 104 (32127-4253)
PHONE...................................386 756-0101
Sean Malmo, *Project Mgr*
Dan Chandler, *Opers Mgr*
Jade Alvarez, *Sales Staff*
Jerry Fekete, *Sales Staff*
Lyle Brambier, *Branch Mgr*
EMP: 7
SALES (corp-wide): 2.5MM **Privately Held**
WEB: www.ver-tex.com
SIC: 2221 Upholstery, tapestry & wall covering fabrics
PA: Drapery Control Systems, Inc.
    5545 Nw 35th Ave D
    Fort Lauderdale FL 33309
    305 653-1712

(G-14334)
FUTURESCAPE INC
6119 Del Mar Dr (32127-6743)
PHONE...................................386 679-4120
Ira Wendorf, *President*
Alan Weininger, *Vice Pres*
EMP: 8 EST: 2005
SALES (est): 468.7K **Privately Held**
SIC: 2842 Sanitation preparations, disinfectants & deodorants

(G-14335)
GPS EDUCATION LLC
2463 Old Samsula Rd (32128-6538)
PHONE...................................386 756-7575

Gary Sedacca, *Manager*
EMP: 11 **EST:** 2008
SALES (est): 721.2K **Privately Held**
WEB: www.gps-edu.com
SIC: 3663 Radio & TV communications equipment

(G-14336)
JENZANO INCORPORATED
820 Oak St (32127-4332)
PHONE....................386 761-4474
John Douglas Jenzano, *President*
Joyce Aycock, *Corp Secy*
John J Jenzano, *Shareholder*
EMP: 10 **EST:** 1966
SALES (est): 1.9MM **Privately Held**
WEB: www.jenzano.com
SIC: 3569 3542 3625 Assembly machines, non-metalworking; machine tools, metal forming type; relays & industrial controls

(G-14337)
KWIK KERB LLC
844 Williams Ln (32127-5855)
PHONE....................386 453-1004
Mark Durkin, *Principal*
EMP: 8 **EST:** 2005
SALES (est): 159.1K **Privately Held**
WEB: www.kwikkerbbyadele.com
SIC: 3281 Curbing, paving & walkway stone

(G-14338)
LITHOCRAFT INC
4460 S Ridgewood Ave (32127-4516)
P.O. Box 10270, Daytona Beach (32120-0270)
PHONE....................386 761-3584
Ken Chrysler, *President*
Mary Chrysler, *Corp Secy*
EMP: 5 **EST:** 1976
SQ FT: 3,024
SALES (est): 429.3K **Privately Held**
WEB: www.lithocraftprinting.com
SIC: 2752 Commercial printing, offset

(G-14339)
MC MIETH MANUFACTURING INC
665 Herbert St (32129-3837)
P.O. Box 291129 (32129-1129)
PHONE....................386 767-3494
Greg Feldman, *President*
Elaine Feldman, *Corp Secy*
Angela Norris, *Vice Pres*
EMP: 11 **EST:** 1959
SQ FT: 4,500
SALES (est): 1.1MM **Privately Held**
WEB: www.holepunch.com
SIC: 3579 Ticket counting machines

(G-14340)
MIX MASTERS INC
523 Virginia Ave Unit B (32127-4450)
PHONE....................386 846-9239
EMP: 7 **EST:** 2001
SALES (est): 19.1K **Privately Held**
SIC: 3273 Ready-mixed concrete

(G-14341)
MPP COATINGS INC
3837 Long Grove Ln (32129-8629)
PHONE....................386 334-4484
Carrie L Erdelyan, *Principal*
Adam Erdelyan, *Vice Pres*
EMP: 5 **EST:** 2016
SALES (est): 366.8K **Privately Held**
WEB: www.mppcoatings.com
SIC: 3479 Coating of metals & formed products

(G-14342)
MYSKY AIRCRAFT INC
205 Cessna Blvd Ste 1 (32128-7538)
PHONE....................386 492-6908
Dieter Canje, *President*
▲ **EMP:** 7 **EST:** 2009
SQ FT: 5,000
SALES (est): 754.2K **Privately Held**
WEB: www.mysky.aero
SIC: 3721 Aircraft

(G-14343)
PDC
4480 Eastport Park Way (32127-6044)
PHONE....................386 322-2808
EMP: 10 **EST:** 2018
SALES (est): 983.5K **Privately Held**
WEB: www.pdcorp.com
SIC: 2834 Pharmaceutical preparations

(G-14344)
PLATINUM CBD INC
1709 Arash Cir (32128-7326)
PHONE....................386 756-1902
Christina L Kephart, *President*
EMP: 7 **EST:** 2017
SALES (est): 74.6K **Privately Held**
SIC: 3999

(G-14345)
PRIVACY WINDOW DESIGN INC
600 Oak St Ste 2b (32127-4364)
PHONE....................386 761-7306
Christine Hannah, *President*
John Hannah, *Vice Pres*
EMP: 6 **EST:** 1985
SQ FT: 4,000
SALES (est): 489.6K **Privately Held**
SIC: 2591 Venetian blinds

(G-14346)
SCREEN MACHINES LLC
2422 Old Samsula Rd (32128-6537)
P.O. Box 238083 (32123-8083)
PHONE....................386 527-1368
EMP: 9 **EST:** 2017
SALES (est): 252.4K **Privately Held**
WEB: www.screenmachine.com
SIC: 2752 Offset & photolithographic printing

(G-14347)
SHORELINE SHUTTER SYSTEMS INC
494 Nash Ln (32127-9527)
PHONE....................386 299-2219
David Vrondran, *Director*
EMP: 8 **EST:** 2001
SALES (est): 80.1K **Privately Held**
SIC: 3442 Shutters, door or window: metal

(G-14348)
SHUTTERS ON SALE INC
1307 Crepe Myrtle Ln (32128-7396)
PHONE....................386 756-0009
William G Burkett, *Principal*
EMP: 8 **EST:** 2005
SALES (est): 214K **Privately Held**
SIC: 3442 Shutters, door or window: metal

(G-14349)
SPRUCE CREEK CABINETRY INC
601 Lemon St Ste C (32127-4340)
P.O. Box 291597 (32129-1597)
PHONE....................386 756-0041
Ken Rose, *President*
Dean Rose, *CFO*
EMP: 20 **EST:** 1985
SQ FT: 7,000
SALES (est): 1.2MM **Privately Held**
WEB: www.sprucecreekcabinetry.com
SIC: 2541 2517 2434 5031 Cabinets, except refrigerated: show, display, etc.: wood; table or counter tops, plastic laminated; wood television & radio cabinets; wood kitchen cabinets; kitchen cabinets; cabinet & finish carpentry

(G-14350)
STOVER MANUFACTURING LLC
919 Alexander Ave (32129-3449)
PHONE....................386 235-7060
Robert Grooms, *Principal*
Jeff Harris, *Sales Mgr*
EMP: 14 **EST:** 2015
SALES (est): 1.6MM **Privately Held**
SIC: 3999 Manufacturing industries

(G-14351)
SUNSHINE LIGHTERS
730 Glades Ct (32127-4324)
PHONE....................386 322-1300
Sam Chebaro, *Principal*
▼ **EMP:** 6 **EST:** 2009

SALES (est): 454.8K **Privately Held**
WEB: www.sunshinewholesale.com
SIC: 3911 Cigarette lighters, precious metal

(G-14352)
TIME ADJUSTERS CONFERENCE INC
Also Called: Time Finance Adjusters
5807 Spruce Creek Wods Dr (32127-0904)
PHONE....................386 274-4210
Harvey Altes, *CEO*
Margaret Merthe, *President*
EMP: 5 **EST:** 1971
SALES (est): 478.5K **Privately Held**
WEB: www.timefinanceadjusters.com
SIC: 2721 8111 2741 Magazines: publishing only, not printed on site; legal services; telephone & other directory publishing

(G-14353)
WORLDWIDE EMBROIDERY INC
4471 Eastport Park Way (32127-6041)
PHONE....................386 761-2688
Manek Naresh, *President*
EMP: 12 **EST:** 1998
SQ FT: 10,000
SALES (est): 296.7K **Privately Held**
SIC: 2395 Embroidery products, except schiffli machine

(G-14354)
WORLDWIDE SPORTSWEAR INC
4471 Eastport Park Way (32127-6041)
P.O. Box 290640 (32129-0640)
PHONE....................386 761-2688
Naresh Manek, *President*
Perry Levine, *Vice Pres*
EMP: 25 **EST:** 1998
SALES (est): 2.6MM **Privately Held**
WEB: www.wwspwear.com
SIC: 2759 Screen printing

Port Richey
Pasco County

(G-14355)
BET-ER MIX HOLDING INC (PA)
9301 Denton Ave (34667-4340)
P.O. Box 5577, Hudson (34674-5577)
PHONE....................727 868-9226
Priscilla White, *Principal*
EMP: 8 **EST:** 2008
SALES (est): 22.5MM **Privately Held**
WEB: www.betermix.com
SIC: 3273 Ready-mixed concrete

(G-14356)
CARMACKS QUALITY ALUMINUM INC
8052 Leo Kidd Ave Ste 1 (34668-6620)
PHONE....................727 846-0305
Bob Carmack, *President*
EMP: 7 **EST:** 1990
SQ FT: 3,654
SALES (est): 875.1K **Privately Held**
WEB: www.carmacksqualityaluminum.net
SIC: 3355 Aluminum rolling & drawing

(G-14357)
CEMENT PRODUCTS INC
9301 Denton Ave (34667-4340)
P.O. Box 5577 (34674-5577)
PHONE....................727 868-9226
John Terry White, *President*
Priscila White, *Vice Pres*
Robert D Hatfield, *Admin Sec*
EMP: 28 **EST:** 1970
SQ FT: 800
SALES (est): 1.6MM **Privately Held**
SIC: 3272 3273 3271 3241 Concrete products; ready-mixed concrete; concrete block & brick; cement, hydraulic

(G-14358)
COASTAL RE-MANUFACTURING INC
7620 Valencia Ave (34668-2950)
PHONE....................727 869-4808
EMP: 7
SQ FT: 8,000

SALES (est): 545.7K **Privately Held**
SIC: 3714 Re-Mfg Brak Calipers Front Wheel Drive Axles Rack & Pinions

(G-14359)
COX DESIGNER WINDOWS INC
6810 Commerce Ave (34668-6816)
PHONE....................727 847-1046
Steven Roberts, *President*
Steven Jacobson, *Vice Pres*
Richard McDonald, *Vice Pres*
Domenic Prosperi, *Vice Pres*
EMP: 9 **EST:** 1996
SQ FT: 4,500
SALES (est): 840.1K **Privately Held**
SIC: 2431 Windows & window parts & trim, wood; window frames, wood

(G-14360)
D MAXWELL COMPANY INC
Also Called: Concrete Systems
8323 Arcola Ave (34667-3622)
PHONE....................727 868-9151
Dennis Maxwell, *President*
EMP: 5 **EST:** 1970
SQ FT: 9,600
SALES (est): 431.6K **Privately Held**
SIC: 3272 Concrete products, precast

(G-14361)
GENERAL CABINETS INC
15801 Archer St (34667-3817)
PHONE....................727 863-3404
Donald John Josephik, *President*
Dan Myrick, *Mfg Staff*
Ed Ellis, *Research*
Cindy Rainey, *Office Mgr*
EMP: 21 **EST:** 1978
SQ FT: 15,000
SALES (est): 1MM **Privately Held**
WEB: www.generalcabinets.com
SIC: 2434 Wood kitchen cabinets

(G-14362)
HUFF CARBIDE TOOL INC
6541 Industrial Ave (34668-6852)
PHONE....................727 848-4001
Craig Peterson, *President*
Craig W Peterson, *Vice Pres*
EMP: 14 **EST:** 1961
SQ FT: 6,200
SALES (est): 1.1MM **Privately Held**
SIC: 3541 3544 Machine tools, metal cutting type; special dies, tools, jigs & fixtures

(G-14363)
II-VI AEROSPACE & DEFENSE INC
6716 Industrial Ave (34668-6886)
PHONE....................727 375-8562
EMP: 120
SALES (corp-wide): 3.3B **Publicly Held**
WEB: www.iiviad.com
SIC: 3827 Optical elements & assemblies, except ophthalmic
HQ: Ii-Vi Aerospace & Defense Inc
36570 Briggs Rd
Murrieta CA 92563
951 926-2994

(G-14364)
ISOAID LLC
7824 Clark Moody Blvd (34668-6709)
P.O. Box 205, New Port Richey (34656-0205)
PHONE....................727 815-3262
Dennis Cappo, *Sales Staff*
John Cusack, *Director*
Max Taghizadeh,
Jean Hakim,
EMP: 20 **EST:** 2000
SQ FT: 4,000
SALES (est): 5.3MM **Privately Held**
WEB: www.isoaid.com
SIC: 2819 Iodine, elemental

(G-14365)
J & E CUSTOM CABINETS INC
9926 Denton Ave (34667-4388)
PHONE....................727 868-2820
Effie Mae Deskins, *President*
Johnny A Deskins, *Corp Secy*
EMP: 17 **EST:** 1983
SQ FT: 20,000

▲ = Import ▼ =Export
◆ =Import/Export

SALES (est): 999.9K **Privately Held**
SIC: 2434 Wood kitchen cabinets

(G-14366)
JAR-DEN LLC
7400 Castanea Dr (34668-3997)
PHONE..................................860 334-7539
EMP: 7 EST: 2015
SALES (est): 180.8K **Privately Held**
SIC: 3089 Plastics products

(G-14367)
L A R MANUFACTURING LLC
6828 Commerce Ave (34668-6816)
PHONE..................................727 846-7860
John W Birkel, *Mng Member*
Peter Reynolds, *Mng Member*
EMP: 5 EST: 1999
SQ FT: 2,400
SALES (est): 357K **Privately Held**
SIC: 3843 Dental metal

(G-14368)
MADEWELL KITCHENS INC
11619 State Road 52 (34669-3087)
PHONE..................................727 856-1014
James Madewell, *President*
Henry D Madewell Jr, *Vice Pres*
EMP: 27 EST: 1980
SQ FT: 9,000
SALES (est): 2.9MM **Privately Held**
WEB: www.madewellkitchens.com
SIC: 2434 Wood kitchen cabinets

(G-14369)
MARS PRECISION PRODUCTS
INC
8526 Leo Kidd Ave (34668-5313)
PHONE..................................727 846-0505
Christopher Tietz, *Manager*
EMP: 7 EST: 2014
SALES (est): 192.7K **Privately Held**
SIC: 3519 Internal combustion engines

(G-14370)
PERFECT BRICK PAVERS INC
5626 Quist Dr (34667-6336)
PHONE..................................727 534-2506
Christopher A Cherviok, *Principal*
EMP: 8 EST: 2014
SALES (est): 101.3K **Privately Held**
SIC: 2951 Asphalt paving mixtures &
blocks

(G-14371)
PREMIER PRINTING SIGNS
Also Called: PIP Printing
6520 Industrial Ave Ste 1 (34668-6856)
PHONE..................................727 849-2493
Theodore Cadwallader, *President*
EMP: 6 EST: 1981
SQ FT: 3,000
SALES (est): 919.9K **Privately Held**
WEB: www.digitalprintingportrichey.com
SIC: 2752 3993 Commercial printing, off-
set; signs & advertising specialties

(G-14372)
PRO TECH CUSTOM CABINET
9100 Bolton Ave (34667-3778)
P.O. Box 5962 (34674-5962)
PHONE..................................727 863-5143
EMP: 10
SQ FT: 7,000
SALES (est): 850K **Privately Held**
SIC: 2541 Mfg Cabinets

(G-14373)
PROLIFIC RESOURCE INC
Also Called: Siebers Graphic
12045 Cobble Stone Dr (34667-2414)
PHONE..................................727 868-9341
Dale Sieber, *President*
Rosemary Sieber, *Vice Pres*
EMP: 5 EST: 1974
SALES (est): 412.5K **Privately Held**
SIC: 2752 Commercial printing, offset

(G-14374)
SEAWAY PLASTICS ENGRG LLC
6041 Siesta Ln (34668-6754)
PHONE..................................727 777-6032
Henry Smitty, *Engineer*
Peter Komasinski, *Sales Engr*
Patrick Buttil, *Manager*

EMP: 37
SALES (corp-wide): 1.3B **Privately Held**
WEB: www.seawayplastics.com
SIC: 3089 Injection molding of plastics
HQ: Seaway Plastics Engineering Llc
6006 Siesta Ln
Port Richey FL 34668

(G-14375)
SEAWAY PLASTICS ENGRG LLC
(HQ)
6006 Siesta Ln (34668-6752)
P.O. Box 927 (34673-0927)
PHONE..................................727 845-3235
Tom Orr, *President*
Paul Bernard, *President*
Peter Poodiack, *Vice Pres*
Jeffrey Cox, *Opers Dir*
John Hanke, *Project Mgr*
▲ EMP: 58 EST: 1986
SQ FT: 67,000
SALES (est): 35MM
SALES (corp-wide): 1.3B **Privately Held**
WEB: www.seawayplastics.com
SIC: 3089 Injection molding of plastics
PA: Intermediate Capital Group Plc
Procession House
London EC4M
203 545-2000

(G-14376)
SUNCOAST NEWS
11321 Us Highway 19 (34668-1416)
PHONE..................................727 815-1023
Tim Wahl, *Sales Mgr*
EMP: 8 EST: 2019
SALES (est): 124.7K **Privately Held**
WEB: www.suncoastnews.com
SIC: 2711 Newspapers, publishing & print-
ing

(G-14377)
SUPERIOR SOLID SURFACE
INC
8609 Squib Dr (34668-5342)
PHONE..................................727 842-9947
Robert James, *President*
Brian James, *Corp Secy*
Harry James, *Vice Pres*
EMP: 12 EST: 1998
SQ FT: 1,500
SALES (est): 531.6K **Privately Held**
WEB: www.superiorsolidsurface.com
SIC: 2541 Counter & sink tops

(G-14378)
THUNDERFORCE INC
9920 Eagles Point Cir # 3 (34668-3613)
PHONE..................................315 403-8026
Erik Thorsteen, *CEO*
EMP: 11 EST: 2001
SALES (est): 1.2MM **Privately Held**
SIC: 3663 Radio & TV communications
equipment

(G-14379)
TIMES PUBLISHING COMPANY
Also Called: Saint Petersburg Times
11321 Us Highway 19 (34668-1416)
PHONE..................................727 849-6397
Bill Stevens, *Manager*
EMP: 23
SQ FT: 19,113
SALES (corp-wide): 14.9MM **Privately**
Held
WEB: www.tampabay.com
SIC: 2711 Newspapers, publishing & print-
ing
HQ: Times Publishing Company
490 1st Ave S
Saint Petersburg FL 33701
727 893-8111

(G-14380)
TRINU POWDER COATING LLC
7915 Congress St (34668-6763)
PHONE..................................727 316-6700
EMP: 5 EST: 2020
SALES (est): 328.9K **Privately Held**
WEB: www.trinupowdercoating.com
SIC: 3479 Coating of metals & formed
products

(G-14381)
TWINSTAR OPTICS & COATINGS
INC
Also Called: Twinstar Optics Ctngs Cyrstals
6741 Commerce Ave (34668-6815)
PHONE..................................727 847-2300
Mary Beth Toland, *President*
Robert Thomas, *Vice Pres*
Amanda Minier, *Purchasing*
Mary Beth Thomas-Toland, *CFO*
Corey Mercer, *Manager*
EMP: 18 EST: 1997
SQ FT: 16,600
SALES (est): 2.9MM **Privately Held**
WEB: www.twinstaroptics.com
SIC: 3827 3845 3695 3826 Lenses, opti-
cal: all types except ophthalmic; elec-
tromedical equipment; optical disks &
tape, blank; laser scientific & engineering
instruments

(G-14382)
US BARCODES INC
6740 Commerce Ave (34668-6814)
P.O. Box 1191, Elfers (34680-1191)
PHONE..................................727 849-1196
Junior A Matias, *CEO*
EMP: 7 EST: 2001
SALES (est): 467K **Privately Held**
WEB: www.usbarcodes.com
SIC: 3577 Bar code (magnetic ink) printers

(G-14383)
US SIGNS INC
16631 Scheer Blvd (34667-4237)
PHONE..................................727 862-7933
Sidney Cooper, *President*
Sussie Cooper, *Corp Secy*
Josh Cooper, *Vice Pres*
EMP: 22 EST: 1992
SQ FT: 4,000
SALES (est): 2.7MM **Privately Held**
WEB: www.ussignsandletters.com
SIC: 3993 Electric signs

(G-14384)
VINYL ETCHINGS INC
6641 Industrial Ave (34668-6864)
PHONE..................................727 845-5300
Thomas Walter, *President*
Stephen Lazorcak, *Vice Pres*
Jackie Gillespie, *Treasurer*
Vei Forbes, *Manager*
Nancy Forbes, *Admin Sec*
EMP: 9 EST: 2003
SALES (est): 447.9K **Privately Held**
WEB: www.vinyletchings.com
SIC: 3993 Signs & advertising specialties

(G-14385)
VLOC INCORPORATED
6716 Industrial Ave (34668-6886)
PHONE..................................727 375-8562
Steve Sacone, *President*
Francis Kramer, *Vice Pres*
Craig A Creaturo, *CFO*
EMP: 120 EST: 1996
SQ FT: 65,000
SALES (est): 33.4MM
SALES (corp-wide): 3.3B **Publicly Held**
SIC: 3827 Optical elements & assemblies,
except ophthalmic
PA: Coherent Corp.
375 Saxonburg Blvd
Saxonburg PA 16056
724 352-4455

(G-14386)
WHITES HOLDINGS INC CENTL
FLA
9301 Denton Ave (34667-4340)
P.O. Box 5577 (34674-5577)
PHONE..................................727 863-6072
Priscilla K White, *President*
John Terry White, *President*
EMP: 31 EST: 1981
SQ FT: 3,000
SALES (est): 2.5MM **Privately Held**
SIC: 3271 3273 Concrete block & brick;
ready-mixed concrete

(G-14387)
WIDELL INDUSTRIES INC (PA)
6622 Industrial Ave (34668-6897)
P.O. Box 580 (34673-0580)
PHONE..................................800 237-5963
Wayne A Widell, *President*
Chuck Lisowe, *Plant Mgr*
Wayne D Widell, *Admin Sec*
EMP: 65 EST: 1980
SQ FT: 70,000
SALES (est): 9.8MM **Privately Held**
WEB: www.widell.com
SIC: 3545 Taps, machine tool; thread cut-
ting dies; gauges (machine tool acces-
sories)

Port Saint Joe
Gulf County

(G-14388)
GULF COUNTY SHIP BUILDING
INC
1550 Old Dynamite Dock Rd (32456-6367)
PHONE..................................850 229-9300
John Dixon, *President*
Paul Duncan, *Superintendent*
EMP: 8 EST: 1998
SQ FT: 2,600
SALES (est): 154.5K **Privately Held**
WEB: www.gcship.com
SIC: 3731 Shipbuilding & repairing

(G-14389)
MONUMNTAL FABRICATION
AMER INC
Also Called: MFA
950 W Rutherford St (32456-5332)
PHONE..................................850 227-9500
Delilah Henderson, *Owner*
Alex Henderson, *Vice Pres*
EMP: 7 EST: 2005
SALES (est): 956.8K **Privately Held**
WEB: www.monumentalfabrication.com
SIC: 3446 Architectural metalwork

(G-14390)
RAMSEYS PRTG & OFF PDTS
INC
209 Reid Ave (32456-1823)
PHONE..................................850 227-7468
William Ramsey Jr, *President*
Eric Ramsey, *Vice Pres*
Shirley Ramsey, *Director*
EMP: 6 EST: 1995
SQ FT: 100,000
SALES (est): 639.5K **Privately Held**
WEB: www.ramseysprinting.com
SIC: 2752 5112 Commercial printing, litho-
graphic; stationery & office supplies

(G-14391)
READY MIX USA LLC
Also Called: Readymix - Port St Joe
1001 Ccil G Cstin Sr Blvd (32456-1655)
PHONE..................................850 227-7677
EMP: 17
SALES (corp-wide): 14.9B **Privately Held**
SIC: 3273 Mfg Ready-Mixed Concrete
HQ: Ready Mix Usa, Llc
2657 Ruffner Rd
Birmingham AL 35210
205 967-5211

(G-14392)
WALTER GREEN INC
252 Marina Dr (32456-1832)
PHONE..................................850 227-7946
George Duren, *Owner*
Karah Bradley, *Manager*
EMP: 7 EST: 2011
SALES (est): 491.4K **Privately Held**
WEB: www.waltergreenboutique.com
SIC: 2389 5632 Men's miscellaneous ac-
cessories; apparel accessories

GEOGRAPHIC

Port Saint Lucie
St. Lucie County

(G-14393)
3D NANO BATTERIES LLC
12544 Sw Gray Fox Ln (34987-6407)
PHONE..................................212 220-9300
Samuel R Hashim, *Principal*
EMP: 7 EST: 2018
SALES (est): 255.2K **Privately Held**
WEB: www.3dnanobatteries.com
SIC: 3691 Storage batteries

(G-14394)
ALCHEMIST HOLDINGS LLC
Rebar Alchemist
8283 S Us Highway 1 (34952-2859)
PHONE..................................772 340-7774
Andrew Cook, *Principal*
EMP: 34
SALES (corp-wide): 4.4MM **Privately Held**
SIC: 3441 Fabricated structural metal
PA: Alchemist Holdings, Llc
10482 Sw Tibre Ct
Port Saint Lucie FL 34987
772 343-1111

(G-14395)
ALCHEMIST HOLDINGS LLC (PA)
Also Called: Rebar Alchemist
10482 Sw Tibre Ct (34987-2347)
PHONE..................................772 343-1111
Magbis Riley, *Principal*
Asbel Viciedo, *Mng Member*
EMP: 16 EST: 2006
SQ FT: 5,500
SALES (est): 4.4MM **Privately Held**
SIC: 3441 Fabricated structural metal

(G-14396)
APPAREL MACHINERY SERVICES INC
1545 Se S Niemeyer Cir (34952-3507)
PHONE..................................772 335-5350
Ronald J Boser, *President*
Rosanna Boser, *Treasurer*
EMP: 5 EST: 1990
SQ FT: 9,000
SALES (est): 543.5K **Privately Held**
WEB: www.apparelmachinery.com
SIC: 2341 2299 Women's & children's underwear; batting, wadding, padding & fillings

(G-14397)
AQUABACK TECHNOLOGIES INC
9300 Scarborough Ct (34986-3360)
PHONE..................................978 863-1000
William H Zebuhr, *CEO*
Scott Newquist, *CEO*
David Dussault, *COO*
EMP: 10 EST: 2010
SALES (est): 1.8MM **Privately Held**
WEB: www.aquaback.com
SIC: 3556 Distillery machinery

(G-14398)
ARMSTRONG PRESS INC
2680 Sw Fair Isle Rd (34987-2094)
PHONE..................................561 247-1071
Ashley M Marino S, *Principal*
EMP: 9 EST: 2018
SALES (est): 521.3K **Privately Held**
SIC: 2741 Miscellaneous publishing

(G-14399)
ATLANTIC PRECISION INC
1461 Commerce Centre Dr A (34986-3355)
PHONE..................................772 466-1011
Tim Ritter, *President*
EMP: 30 EST: 1988
SQ FT: 34,000
SALES (est): 8.3MM
SALES (corp-wide): 354.6B **Publicly Held**
WEB: www.pccstructurals.com
SIC: 3728 Aircraft parts & equipment

HQ: Pcc Structurals, Inc.
4600 Se Harney Dr
Portland OR 97206
503 777-3881

(G-14400)
BLUEWATER FINISHING LLC
1913 Sw South Macedo Blvd (34984-4346)
PHONE..................................772 460-9457
Alan D Blandford, *Manager*
EMP: 5 EST: 2005
SALES (est): 397.2K **Privately Held**
SIC: 3299 Stucco

(G-14401)
BONGIOVI AVIATION LLC
649 Sw Whitmore Dr (34984-3567)
PHONE..................................772 879-0578
Brian Servis, *Business Mgr*
Lawrence Hamelink, *Manager*
Anthony Bongiovi, *Manager*
EMP: 10 EST: 2017
SALES (est): 917.3K **Privately Held**
WEB: www.bongiovacoustics.com
SIC: 3699 Electric sound equipment

(G-14402)
CABINET CNNCTION OF TRSURE CAS (PA)
740 Nw Enterprise Dr (34986-2228)
PHONE..................................772 621-4882
Gary Guterl, *President*
Kenneth Bianco, *Vice Pres*
EMP: 15 EST: 1994
SQ FT: 12,000
SALES (est): 4.6MM **Privately Held**
WEB: www.cabinetconnection.net
SIC: 2434 2541 Wood kitchen cabinets; table or counter tops, plastic laminated

(G-14403)
CATCH ONE COMM
Also Called: SC Edge
1850 Sw Fountainview Blvd # 103 (34986-3443)
PHONE..................................772 221-0225
Michael Visconte, *President*
Tina Luve, *Partner*
EMP: 7 EST: 1991
SALES (est): 445.5K **Privately Held**
SIC: 3993 Signs & advertising specialties

(G-14404)
CHARUVIL OIL INC DBA VALERO
815 E Prima Vista Blvd (34952-2331)
PHONE..................................772 871-9050
EMP: 5
SALES (est): 326.3K **Privately Held**
SIC: 1389 Oil/Gas Field Services

(G-14405)
CITY ELECTRIC SUPPLY COMPANY
Also Called: Tamilite Lighting
660 Nw Peacock Blvd (34986-2211)
PHONE..................................772 879-7440
EMP: 8
SALES (corp-wide): 782.2K **Privately Held**
SIC: 3641 Electric light bulbs, complete
HQ: City Electric Supply Company
400 S Record St Ste 1500
Dallas TX 75202
214 865-6801

(G-14406)
CORPORCION INTRNCNAL DE JYAS V
Also Called: Vm Jewelry
2868 Sw Port St Lcie Blvd (34953-2835)
PHONE..................................772 343-1721
Fernando Valbuena, *President*
Guerty Valbuena, *Principal*
EMP: 6 EST: 2013
SALES (est): 352.5K **Privately Held**
SIC: 3911 7631 Jewelry apparel; watch, clock & jewelry repair

(G-14407)
DISCOUNT DISTRIBUTORS INC
Also Called: Ball Busines Products
725 Se Port St Lucie Blvd # 106 (34984-5232)
PHONE..................................772 336-0092
Donald E Ball, *President*

Dana Ball, *Products*
EMP: 5 EST: 1990
SALES (est): 593.9K **Privately Held**
SIC: 3861 5112 Photographic equipment & supplies; photocopying supplies

(G-14408)
DRAGONFLY GRAPHICS
861 Sw Lakehurst Dr Ste B (34983-2462)
PHONE..................................772 879-9800
Richard G Coffey, *President*
Micheal Coffey, *Vice Pres*
Alan Coffey, *Treasurer*
EMP: 5 EST: 1999
SALES (est): 492.6K **Privately Held**
WEB: www.dragonflycentral.com
SIC: 2759 Screen printing

(G-14409)
EL HISPANO
102 Nw Airoso Blvd (34983-1652)
PHONE..................................772 878-6488
Adriana Maga, *Owner*
EMP: 7 EST: 2010
SALES (est): 219.5K **Privately Held**
WEB: www.elhispanoparatodos.com
SIC: 2711 Newspapers, publishing & printing

(G-14410)
ENVIROSEAL CORPORATION
1019 Se Hlbrook Ct 1021 (34952)
PHONE..................................772 335-8225
Thomas Stevens, *President*
William A Stevens, *Vice Pres*
▼ EMP: 5 EST: 1994
SQ FT: 10,000
SALES (est): 974.1K **Privately Held**
WEB: www.enviroseal.com
SIC: 2899 Chemical preparations

(G-14411)
EW SCRIPPS COMPANY
Also Called: Port St. Lucie News
1939 Se Federal Hwy (34986)
PHONE..................................772 408-5300
EMP: 200
SALES (corp-wide): 715.6MM **Publicly Held**
SIC: 2711 Newspapers
PA: The E W Scripps Company
312 Walnut St Ste 2800
Cincinnati OH 45202
513 977-3000

(G-14412)
EXPERT SHUTTER SERVICES INC
668 Sw Whitmore Dr (34984-3512)
PHONE..................................772 871-1915
Mike Heissenberg, *President*
Jamie Heissenberg, *Vice Pres*
EMP: 56 EST: 1983
SALES (est): 6.7MM **Privately Held**
WEB: www.expertshutters.com
SIC: 2431 3442 3354 Awnings, blinds & shutters, wood; metal doors, sash & trim; aluminum extruded products

(G-14413)
EZ LODER ADJSTBLE BOAT TRLRS S
1462 Commerce Centre Dr (34986-3208)
PHONE..................................800 323-8190
Randy Johnson, *President*
James Vassallo, *Vice Pres*
Christina Johnson, *Admin Sec*
▼ EMP: 5 EST: 2005
SALES (est): 862.4K
SALES (corp-wide): 98.2MM **Privately Held**
SIC: 3799 Boat trailers
PA: E Z Loader Boat Trailers, Inc.
717 N Hamilton St
Spokane WA 99202
574 266-0092

(G-14414)
FOUNTAIN YOUTH BATHROOMS INC
2559 Sw Kenilworth St (34953-2575)
PHONE..................................772 626-9626
Shane R Viens, *President*
Robert Viens, *Vice Pres*
EMP: 10 EST: 2007

SALES (est): 559.2K **Privately Held**
SIC: 3088 Tubs (bath, shower & laundry), plastic

(G-14415)
GROOVY TOYS LLC
Also Called: Grooyi
585 Nw Merc Pl Ste 108 (34986)
PHONE..................................772 878-0790
◆ EMP: 5
SQ FT: 2,400
SALES (est): 664K **Privately Held**
SIC: 3944 Mfg Games/Toys

(G-14416)
HESS EXPRESS
10453 S Us Highway 1 (34952-5645)
PHONE..................................772 335-9975
Johnson Hess, *President*
EMP: 6 EST: 1999
SALES (est): 385.8K **Privately Held**
WEB: www.hessexpress.com
SIC: 1389 Gas field services

(G-14417)
IDPRODUCTSOURCE LLC
651 Nw Enterprise Dr (34986-2262)
PHONE..................................772 336-4269
Karole A Aspinwall,
John P Aspinwall,
Gabrielle M Client, *Representative*
Kristen McGrath, *Representative*
EMP: 5 EST: 2001
SALES (est): 515.6K **Privately Held**
SIC: 3089 Identification cards, plastic

(G-14418)
JBR EXTERIORS INC
1201 Sw Biltmore St (34983-2486)
PHONE..................................772 873-0600
Brown Johnson, *President*
Jeremiah Johnson, *Vice Pres*
Rhonda Johnson, *Vice Pres*
John Williams, *Sales Mgr*
EMP: 5 EST: 1999
SQ FT: 5,824
SALES (est): 908.8K **Privately Held**
WEB: www.jbrexteriors.com
SIC: 3448 Screen enclosures

(G-14419)
JUST DOOR TOOLZ LLC
1552 Sw Abingdon Ave (34953-2550)
P.O. Box 7999 (34985-7999)
PHONE..................................954 448-6872
Glen McMorris, *Principal*
Sandra McMorris, *Principal*
EMP: 7 EST: 2011
SALES (est): 218.5K **Privately Held**
WEB: www.justdoortoolz.com
SIC: 3423 Carpenters' hand tools, except saws: levels, chisels, etc.

(G-14420)
KNIGHT INDUSTRIES
1001 Sw Cornelia Ave (34953-3238)
PHONE..................................772 344-2053
Allen Solomon, *Principal*
EMP: 7 EST: 2008
SALES (est): 66.9K **Privately Held**
SIC: 3999 Manufacturing industries

(G-14421)
LACTALOGICS INC
8883 S Us Highway 1 (34952-3401)
PHONE..................................772 202-0407
Glenn Snow, *CEO*
Laura Salter, *Exec Dir*
EMP: 5 EST: 2014
SALES (est): 502.1K **Privately Held**
WEB: www.lactalogics.com
SIC: 2836 Biological products, except diagnostic

(G-14422)
LCR SIGNS & SERVICES
2862 Se Buccaneer Cir (34952-6612)
PHONE..................................772 882-5276
Lawrence Riccard, *Principal*
EMP: 8 EST: 2014
SALES (est): 267.4K **Privately Held**
WEB: www.lcrsigns.com
SIC: 3993 Signs & advertising specialties

▲ = Import ▼=Export
◆ =Import/Export

(G-14423)
LIGHT SOURCE BUSINESS SYSTEMS
Also Called: Lightsource Imaging Solutions
582 Nw Mercantile Pl (34986-2252)
PHONE................................772 562-5046
Michael Stephens, *President*
Pam Stephens, *Vice Pres*
EMP: 19 EST: 1991
SALES (est): 1.9MM **Privately Held**
SIC: 2759 5734 7699 5943 Laser printing; printers & plotters: computers; printing trades machinery & equipment repair; stationery stores; photographic equipment & supplies

(G-14424)
LUXURY BOAT SERVICES INC
Also Called: Marine Electrical Engineer
1073 Sw Abingdon Ave (34953-2804)
PHONE................................360 451-2888
Joseph D'Alelio, *CEO*
EMP: 5 EST: 2018
SALES (est): 322.9K **Privately Held**
SIC: 3732 Yachts, building & repairing

(G-14425)
MEDMARD WIN TRTMNTS BLINDS INC
797 Sw Sail Ter (34953-2630)
PHONE................................772 344-5714
Michelle A Deslandes, *Principal*
EMP: 8 EST: 2009
SALES (est): 122K **Privately Held**
SIC: 2591 Window blinds

(G-14426)
MINUTEMAN PRESS
6967 Hancock Dr (34952-8207)
PHONE................................772 301-0222
EMP: 7 EST: 2018
SALES (est): 329.6K **Privately Held**
WEB: www.minutemanpress.com
SIC: 2752 Commercial printing, lithographic

(G-14427)
NEW GNRTION ABNDANT MSSION CH
Also Called: New Gnrtion Jews Abndant Mssio
2017 Sw Tropical Ter (34953-1337)
P.O. Box 324, Plattsburgh NY (12901-0324)
PHONE................................772 497-5871
Rikem Jean Philipp, *Principal*
EMP: 20 EST: 2005
SALES (est): 743.5K **Privately Held**
SIC: 2752 Commercial printing, lithographic

(G-14428)
NIDA-CORE CORPORATION (HQ)
541 Nw Interpark Pl (34986-2217)
PHONE................................772 343-7300
Damien Jacquinet, *President*
◆ EMP: 50 EST: 1987
SQ FT: 70,000
SALES (est): 13.3MM
SALES (corp-wide): 35.3B **Publicly Held**
SIC: 2679 3086 2821 2221 Honeycomb core & board: made from purchased material; plastics foam products; plastics materials & resins; fiberglass fabrics; flat panels, plastic; machine shop, jobbing & repair
PA: 3m Company
3m Center
Saint Paul MN 55144
651 733-1110

(G-14429)
NUBO BOTTLE COMPANY LLC
10241 Sw Visconti Way (34986-2863)
PHONE................................954 283-9057
Abraham K Kohl, *President*
Kirsten Kohl, *Treasurer*
EMP: 7 EST: 2010
SALES (est): 401.9K **Privately Held**
WEB: www.nubobottle.com
SIC: 2086 Water, pasteurized: packaged in cans, bottles, etc.

(G-14430)
OLIVEIRA SERVICES CORP
972 Sw Paar Dr (34953-5623)
PHONE................................772 834-4803
EMP: 5
SALES (est): 391.9K **Privately Held**
SIC: 2434 Mfg Wood Kitchen Cabinets

(G-14431)
ORACLE CORPORATION
1701 Se Hillmoor Dr D16 (34952-7541)
PHONE................................772 337-4141
Robin Roberts, *Manager*
Sandra Whitman, *Software Engr*
EMP: 191
SALES (corp-wide): 42.4B **Publicly Held**
WEB: www.oracle.com
SIC: 7372 Prepackaged software
PA: Oracle Corporation
2300 Oracle Way
Austin TX 78741
737 867-1000

(G-14432)
PLANTATION SHUTTERS INC
Also Called: Simply Shutters
1388 Commerce Ctr Dr (34986-1300)
P.O. Box 882096 (34988-2096)
PHONE................................772 208-8245
Timothy McBride, *President*
Jeri McBride, *Admin Sec*
EMP: 11 EST: 2017
SALES (est): 1MM **Privately Held**
WEB: www.plantationshuttersflorida.com
SIC: 3442 Shutters, door or window: metal

(G-14433)
PORT SAINT WICH LLC (PA)
3961 Sw Port St Lcie Blvd (34953-5631)
PHONE................................772 237-2000
EMP: 8 EST: 2018
SALES (est): 262.5K **Privately Held**
WEB: port-saint-wich.business.site
SIC: 2099 Food preparations

(G-14434)
PREMIER LAB SUPPLY INC
691 Nw Enterprise Dr (34986-2204)
PHONE................................772 873-1700
Daniel Pompa, *President*
Joseph Beckman, *Counsel*
Christina Pompa, *Vice Pres*
John Haugh, *Sales Mgr*
Rafaela Haramis, *Accounts Mgr*
◆ EMP: 9 EST: 1998
SQ FT: 8,500
SALES (est): 2.9MM **Privately Held**
WEB: www.premierlabsupply.com
SIC: 3089 3821 5023 Injection molding of plastics; sample preparation apparatus; glassware

(G-14435)
PROTEGE MEDIA LLC
5945 Nw Dowell Ct (34986-3832)
PHONE................................310 738-9567
Rodney Henry,
EMP: 5 EST: 2016
SALES (est): 1MM **Privately Held**
SIC: 3021 7812 Rubber & plastics footwear; educational motion picture production, television

(G-14436)
R & S METALWORKS & CO LLC
5690 Carlton Rd (34987-3201)
PHONE................................772 466-3303
Scott M Snowden, *Mng Member*
EMP: 17 EST: 2007
SQ FT: 500
SALES (est): 2.8MM **Privately Held**
SIC: 3548 3523 5084 Arc welders, transformer-rectifier; farm machinery & equipment; welding machinery & equipment

(G-14437)
R & S SNACKS LLC
1660 Sw Buttercup Ave (34953-4935)
PHONE................................954 839-5482
Beau Y Stager, *Manager*
EMP: 8 EST: 2017
SALES (est): 476.9K **Privately Held**
SIC: 2096 Potato chips & similar snacks

(G-14438)
R J REYNOLDS TOBACCO COMPANY
2687 Sw Domina Rd (34953-2778)
PHONE................................772 873-6955
John Wickline, *Manager*
EMP: 69 **Privately Held**
WEB: www.rjrt.com
SIC: 2111 Cigarettes
HQ: R. J. Reynolds Tobacco Company
401 N Main St
Winston Salem NC 27101
336 741-5000

(G-14439)
RACEWAY ELECTRIC LLC
208 Sw Aubudon Ave (34984-5030)
PHONE................................772 260-6530
Adam L Race, *Manager*
EMP: 7 EST: 2015
SALES (est): 467.9K **Privately Held**
WEB: www.racewayelectricfl.com
SIC: 3644 Raceways

(G-14440)
REPGAS INC
571 Nw Merc Pl Unit 102 (34986)
PHONE................................786 202-8434
Mainor A Reyes, *Director*
▼ EMP: 7 EST: 2005
SALES (est): 146.6K **Privately Held**
WEB: www.repgasinc.com
SIC: 1389 3824 2911 Gas field services; gasoline dispensing meters; oils, fuel

(G-14441)
REPROGRAPHIC SOLUTIONS INC (PA)
234 Sw Port Lucie Blvd (34984-5044)
PHONE................................772 340-3430
Bridget Demaio, *President*
EMP: 5 EST: 2001
SQ FT: 1,500
SALES (est): 957.5K **Privately Held**
WEB: www.repro718.com
SIC: 2759 5044 Maps: printing; blueprinting equipment

(G-14442)
ROGERS SEPTIC TANKS INC
10603 Sw Capraia Way (34986-2888)
PHONE................................203 259-9947
Roger Thoele, *President*
EMP: 9 EST: 1947
SALES (est): 196.1K **Privately Held**
SIC: 3272 Septic tanks, concrete

(G-14443)
RPP DEVICES
625 Nw Commodity Cv (34986-2250)
PHONE................................772 807-7098
Brian Smith, *Principal*
Alecia Ortiz, *Manager*
▲ EMP: 5 EST: 2008
SALES (est): 301.3K **Privately Held**
SIC: 3678 Electronic connectors

(G-14444)
SAVAGE VENTURES INC
Also Called: C&L Technologies
1702 Se Village Green Dr (34952-3456)
PHONE................................772 335-5655
Corey Nsavage, *President*
Miguel Campos, *Vice Pres*
Leo Ambrogi, *Vice Pres*
Ann K Savage, *Treasurer*
Sylvia Charton, *Controller*
EMP: 33 EST: 1957
SQ FT: 48,000
SALES (est): 4.7MM **Privately Held**
SIC: 3544 Special dies & tools

(G-14445)
SHUTTERTEK INC
566 Se Floresta Dr (34983-2241)
P.O. Box 881706 (34988-1706)
PHONE................................772 828-6149
Marco T Lopez Sr, *President*
EMP: 7 EST: 2012
SALES (est): 215.7K **Privately Held**
WEB: www.andrewmelcher.com
SIC: 3442 Shutters, door or window: metal

(G-14446)
SKIES LIMIT PRINTING
10504 S Us Highway 1 (34952-5603)
PHONE................................772 340-1090
Sande Kornblum, *Principal*
EMP: 6 EST: 2008
SALES (est): 521.8K **Privately Held**
WEB: www.skiesthelimitgraphics.com
SIC: 2759 Commercial printing

(G-14447)
SLATON & SONS ENTERPRISES INC
Also Called: Speedpro Imaging
7912 Plantation Lakes Dr (34986-3004)
PHONE................................561 308-7187
Michael Slaton, *Principal*
EMP: 7 EST: 2016
SALES (est): 243.4K **Privately Held**
WEB: www.speedpro.com
SIC: 3993 Signs & advertising specialties

(G-14448)
SLB1989 INC
Also Called: St Lucie Bakery
1066 Sw Bayshore Blvd (34983-2400)
PHONE................................772 344-3609
Kelley Arciprete, *President*
EMP: 7 EST: 2012
SALES (est): 115.4K **Privately Held**
SIC: 2051 Bread, cake & related products

(G-14449)
SOFTWARE TO SYSTEMS INC
2491 Se Gillette Ave (34952-7435)
PHONE................................513 893-4367
Vicki Humphreys, *President*
EMP: 8 EST: 2000
SALES (est): 681.7K **Privately Held**
WEB: www.software2sys.com
SIC: 7372 Prepackaged software

(G-14450)
STERLING FACILITY SERVICES LLC
Also Called: Trailer 1
523 Nw Peacock Blvd (34986-2210)
PHONE................................772 871-2161
Paul Taglieri, *Vice Pres*
EMP: 10 EST: 2004
SALES (est): 634.7K **Privately Held**
SIC: 3949 Team sports equipment

(G-14451)
SUN PIPE AND VALVES LLC
710 Nw Enterprise Dr (34986-2228)
PHONE................................772 408-5530
Rand Calender,
Albert Kocher,
EMP: 10 EST: 2005
SALES (est): 445.9K **Privately Held**
SIC: 3494 5074 Valves & pipe fittings; pipes & fittings, plastic

(G-14452)
SUPERIOR DENTAL & SURGICAL MFG
1501 Se Village Green Dr (34952-3494)
PHONE................................772 335-5200
Allan J Jochum, *President*
John H Schuldt, *Vice Pres*
EMP: 25 EST: 1935
SQ FT: 19,000
SALES (est): 2.8MM **Privately Held**
SIC: 3843 Dental equipment & supplies

(G-14453)
SYNERGY ANCILLARY SERVICES LLC
Also Called: Sas Group
11350 Sw Village Pkwy (34987-2352)
PHONE................................561 249-7238
Amy Naples, *Human Res Dir*
Matthew I Parra Sr,
EMP: 16 EST: 2014
SALES (est): 6.4MM **Privately Held**
SIC: 2869 Laboratory chemicals, organic

(G-14454)
SYSTEM DATA RESOURCE
Also Called: Software
11422 Sw Hillcrest Cir (34987-2706)
PHONE................................954 213-8008
Elva Kulinsky, *CEO*

Frederick Kulinsky, *Vice Pres*
EMP: 7 **EST:** 1989
SQ FT: 1,000
SALES (est): 129.5K **Privately Held**
WEB: www.systemdataresource.com
SIC: 7372 Prepackaged software

(G-14455)
TAMLITE LIGHTING - NEW WHSE
660 Nw Peacock Blvd (34986-2211)
PHONE..........................772 879-7440
Steven Hagadorn, *Regl Sales Mgr*
Melissa Leatherman, *Sales Staff*
Stephanie Norris, *Sales Staff*
EMP: 6 **EST:** 2017
SALES (est): 354.5K **Privately Held**
SIC: 3648 Lighting equipment

(G-14456)
TOTAL PAVERS CORP
2529 Sw Grotto Cir (34953-2927)
PHONE..........................561 902-7665
Wagner Santos, *Principal*
EMP: 13 **EST:** 2013
SALES (est): 553K **Privately Held**
SIC: 2951 Asphalt paving mixtures & blocks

(G-14457)
TRANE INC
400 Nw Enterprise Dr (34986-2201)
PHONE..........................772 621-3200
Kelli Easton, *Engineer*
Scott Nunn, *Accounts Mgr*
Bill Gholson, *Manager*
EMP: 40 **Privately Held**
WEB: www.trane.com
SIC: 3088 3585 Plastics plumbing fixtures; heating equipment, complete
HQ: Trane Inc.
    1 Centennial Ave Ste 101
    Piscataway NJ 08854
    732 652-7100

(G-14458)
TREASURE CAST PRENTING MAG INC
2162 Nw Reserve Park Trce (34986-3223)
P.O. Box 880894 (34988-0894)
PHONE..........................772 672-8588
Kara Ferraro, *President*
Don Ferraro, *COO*
EMP: 10 **EST:** 2008
SQ FT: 3,400
SALES (est): 715.3K **Privately Held**
WEB: www.indianrivermagazine.com
SIC: 2721 Magazines: publishing only, not printed on site

(G-14459)
TRUENORTH IQ INC
1193 Se Port St Lcie Blvd (34952-5332)
PHONE..........................678 849-5000
Scott Manderville, *CEO*
EMP: 9 **EST:** 2018
SALES (est): 380K **Privately Held**
WEB: www.truenorthiq.com
SIC: 3812 Defense systems & equipment

(G-14460)
UM KITCHEN CABINETS INC
965 Sw North Globe Ave (34953-3419)
PHONE..........................772 224-5445
Gonzalez Margaret, *Principal*
EMP: 7 **EST:** 2015
SALES (est): 77.3K **Privately Held**
SIC: 2434 Wood kitchen cabinets

(G-14461)
UNIQUE DESIGNS & FINISHES INC
1443 Se Huffman Rd (34952-3353)
PHONE..........................772 335-4884
Harry Sanka, *President*
EMP: 10 **EST:** 1997
SALES (est): 1MM **Privately Held**
WEB: www.uniquedesignsandfinishes.com
SIC: 3639 Major kitchen appliances, except refrigerators & stoves

(G-14462)
VELEZ CUSTOM CABINETRY CORP
5810 Nw Gillespie Ave (34986-3938)
PHONE..........................772 418-9565

Carlos A Velez, *Principal*
EMP: 8 **EST:** 2008
SALES (est): 237K **Privately Held**
WEB: www.velezcustomcabinetry.com
SIC: 2434 Wood kitchen cabinets

(G-14463)
VENTURA FOODS LLC
485 Nw Enterprise Dr (34986-2202)
PHONE..........................772 878-1400
Ventura Foods, *Branch Mgr*
EMP: 83 **Privately Held**
WEB: www.venturafoods.com
SIC: 2079 Edible fats & oils
PA: Ventura Foods, Llc
    40 Pointe Dr
    Brea CA 92821

(G-14464)
VERTICAL VILLAGE INC
10658 S Us Highway 1 (34952-6402)
PHONE..........................772 340-0400
James Daugaard, *President*
Chris Daugaard, *Owner*
Joseph Daugaard, *Vice Pres*
Christine Daugaard, *Admin Sec*
EMP: 5 **EST:** 1974
SQ FT: 1,800
SALES (est): 731.6K **Privately Held**
WEB: www.verticalvillage.net
SIC: 2591 2221 5714 5719 Drapery hardware & blinds & shades; window blinds; blinds vertical; draperies & drapery fabrics, manmade fiber & silk; draperies; vertical blinds

(G-14465)
WB MEDICAL TRANSPORT LLC
177 Sw Hawthorne Cir (34953-3531)
PHONE..........................561 827-8877
EMP: 6 **EST:** 2018
SALES (est): 424.1K **Privately Held**
SIC: 3089 Plastics products

(G-14466)
WE SIGN IT INC
17 Nuevo Leon (34952-3210)
PHONE..........................561 310-2542
Robert M Naklicki, *CEO*
EMP: 8 **EST:** 2010
SALES (est): 99K **Privately Held**
SIC: 3993 Signs & advertising specialties

(G-14467)
WE SIGN IT INC
889 E Prima Vista Blvd (34952-2342)
PHONE..........................772 800-7373
EMP: 19
SALES (corp-wide): 144.2K **Privately Held**
SIC: 3993 Signs & advertising specialties
PA: We Sign It Inc
    15838 Orange Ave
    Fort Pierce FL 34945
    772 577-4400

Port Salerno
Martin County

(G-14468)
REUSE SALVAGE INC
40668 Se Russell Way (34992)
P.O. Box 1509 (34992-1509)
PHONE..........................772 485-3248
Barbara Blodgett, *President*
EMP: 5 **EST:** 2012
SALES (est): 436.9K **Privately Held**
WEB: www.reusesalvage.com
SIC: 2611 Pulp manufactured from waste or recycled paper

Port St Lucie
St. Lucie County

(G-14469)
AIR SOURCE 1 LLC
585 Nw Merc Pl Ste 103 (34986)
PHONE..........................772 626-7604
Robert K Dumont, *Manager*
EMP: 7 **EST:** 2010

SALES (est): 793.9K **Privately Held**
WEB: www.airsource1llc.com
SIC: 3585 Air conditioning equipment, complete

(G-14470)
BROTHERS WHOLESALE INC
534 Nw Mercantile Pl (34986-2276)
PHONE..........................631 831-8484
Joseph Carfino, *President*
Jason Dippolito, *Shareholder*
EMP: 20 **EST:** 2014
SALES (est): 2.1MM **Privately Held**
SIC: 2051 Bagels, fresh or frozen

(G-14471)
CARIBBEAN GLOBAL GROUP CORP
5475 Nw Saint James Dr (34983-3444)
PHONE..........................786 449-2767
Francisca Bolton, *Principal*
James Bolton, *Principal*
Magen Bolton, *Principal*
EMP: 7 **EST:** 2016
SALES (est): 410.9K **Privately Held**
SIC: 2842 Specialty cleaning, polishes & sanitation goods

(G-14472)
CARVIZION INC
881 Sw Harvard Rd (34953-2310)
PHONE..........................772 807-0307
Hugh W Silvera, *President*
EMP: 7 **EST:** 2010
SALES (est): 71.3K **Privately Held**
SIC: 3714 Motor vehicle parts & accessories

(G-14473)
CASA CABINETS LLC (PA)
10770 S Us Highway 1 (34952-6418)
PHONE..........................850 459-3403
Sandra Wert-Ruiz,
Franklyn Ruiz,
EMP: 6 **EST:** 2005
SALES (est): 411.2K **Privately Held**
WEB: www.casacabinetsllc.com
SIC: 2521 Wood office filing cabinets & bookcases

(G-14474)
CITY ELECTRIC SUPPLY COMPANY
Also Called: Tamco Group
660 Nw Peacock Blvd (34986-2211)
PHONE..........................772 878-4944
Thomas Mackie, *CEO*
EMP: 235
SQ FT: 230,000
SALES (corp-wide): 782.2K **Privately Held**
SIC: 3646 3645 Commercial indusl & institutional electric lighting fixtures; residential lighting fixtures
HQ: City Electric Supply Company
    400 S Record St Ste 1500
    Dallas TX 75202
    214 865-6801

(G-14475)
COMPOSITE ESSENTIAL MTLS LLC
Also Called: C E M
315 Nw Peacock Blvd (34986-2206)
PHONE..........................772 344-0034
Maritsa Dan,
◆ **EMP:** 5 **EST:** 2013
SALES (est): 1.1MM **Privately Held**
WEB: www.compositeessentials.com
SIC: 2821 5162 3469 Polypropylene resins; resins; honeycombed metal

(G-14476)
HARTS MOBILITY LLC
5257 Nw Torino Lakes Cir (34986-3238)
PHONE..........................404 769-4234
Vanessa Freeman, *Principal*
EMP: 8 **EST:** 2017
SALES (est): 327K **Privately Held**
SIC: 3842 3841 Surgical appliances & supplies; surgical & medical instruments

(G-14477)
KING OF SOCKS
2085 Se N Blackwell Dr (34952-7000)
PHONE..........................772 204-3286
Jermaine Cooper, *Principal*
EMP: 7 **EST:** 2015
SALES (est): 95.2K **Privately Held**
SIC: 2252 Socks

(G-14478)
MOORE SOLUTIONS INC
1680 Se Lyngate Dr # 202 (34952-4300)
PHONE..........................772 337-4005
Terrance Moore, *CEO*
EMP: 7 **EST:** 1996
SALES (est): 579.1K **Privately Held**
WEB: www.mooresolutions.com
SIC: 7372 8748 Educational computer software; test development & evaluation service

(G-14479)
NATURES HEATHY GOURMET
1260 Sw Biltmore St (34983-2487)
PHONE..........................772 873-0180
Roland Joaquin, *Owner*
EMP: 30 **EST:** 2005
SALES (est): 2MM **Privately Held**
WEB: www.natureshealthygourmet.com
SIC: 2099 Food preparations

(G-14480)
OCULUS SURGICAL INC
562 Nw Merc Pl Ste 104 (34986)
PHONE..........................772 236-2622
Rainer Kirchhuebel, *Principal*
James Dodsworth, *Mfg Staff*
Mike Annen, *Engineer*
Tylor Richter, *Enginr/R&D Asst*
William Carpenter, *Sales Staff*
EMP: 35 **EST:** 2012
SALES (est): 4.3MM **Privately Held**
WEB: www.oculussurgical.us
SIC: 3841 5047 3829 3821 Surgical & medical instruments; medical & hospital equipment; thermometers, including digital: clinical; incubators, laboratory; optical instruments & lenses

(G-14481)
PAVER PARADISE LLC
2468 Sw Cameo Blvd (34953-2928)
PHONE..........................561 843-3031
Robert Malone, *Mng Member*
EMP: 7 **EST:** 2016
SALES (est): 579.2K **Privately Held**
SIC: 3531 Pavers

(G-14482)
REEF CLEANERS INC
2190 Nw Reserve Park Trce # 7 (34986-3328)
PHONE..........................772 905-7166
John Maloney, *President*
EMP: 7 **EST:** 2016
SALES (est): 326.9K **Privately Held**
WEB: www.reefcleaners.org
SIC: 3999 5199 Pet supplies; pets & pet supplies

(G-14483)
SOUTHEAST GEN CONTRS GROUP INC
10380 Sw Vlg Ctr Dr 232 (34987-1931)
PHONE..........................877 407-3535
Larry Mark McDonald, *Owner*
EMP: 8 **EST:** 2013
SQ FT: 1,500
SALES (est): 497.7K **Privately Held**
WEB: www.southeastcontracting.com
SIC: 3259 3069 1761 5033 Roofing tile, clay; roofing, membrane rubber; roofing contractor; roofing, asphalt & sheet metal

(G-14484)
TABER INCORPORATED
9624 Sw Nuova Way (34986-2831)
P.O. Box 881629, Port Saint Lucie (34988-1629)
PHONE..........................401 245-2800
Jeff D Taber, *President*
EMP: 7 **EST:** 2012
SALES (est): 626.5K **Privately Held**
SIC: 2861 Gum & wood chemicals

(G-14485)
TAMLITE
660 Nw Peacock Blvd (34986-2211)
PHONE....................................772 878-4944
Mike Fisher, *COO*
Johnathan Cole, *Sales Staff*
Keith Koratich, *Manager*
Jamie Nestic, *Office Admin*
EMP: 7 **EST:** 2017
SALES (est): 290K **Privately Held**
WEB: www.tamliteusa.com
SIC: 3645 Residential lighting fixtures

Princeton
Miami-Dade County

(G-14486)
BARREIRO CONCRETE MTLS INC
25440 Sw 140th Ave (33032-5433)
PHONE....................................305 805-0095
Americo Barreiro, *President*
Able Barreiro, *Vice Pres*
EMP: 48 **EST:** 2004
SQ FT: 25,000
SALES (est): 8.7MM **Privately Held**
SIC: 3272 Concrete products

(G-14487)
CLASSIC TRIM WTP INC
25400 Sw 141st Ave Ste B (33032-5431)
PHONE....................................305 258-3090
Frank Vasquez, *President*
Maria Vasquez, *Vice Pres*
EMP: 7 **EST:** 1999
SQ FT: 2,200
SALES (est): 413K **Privately Held**
WEB: www.classictrimwtp.com
SIC: 2396 Automotive & apparel trimmings

(G-14488)
KZ MANUFACTURING LLC
Also Called: Dolphin Boats
24601 Packinghouse Rd # 1 (33032-3807)
PHONE....................................305 257-2628
Karl Zimmermann,
▼ **EMP:** 8 **EST:** 1961
SQ FT: 7,500
SALES (est): 768.2K **Privately Held**
WEB: www.dolphinboats.com
SIC: 3732 5551 Boats, fiberglass: building & repairing; boat dealers

(G-14489)
SEA HUNTER INC
25545 Sw 140th Ave (33032-5402)
PHONE....................................305 257-3344
Jose R Montalvo, *President*
Eduardo Montalvo, *Treasurer*
Paul Myrtetus, *Sales Executive*
Isabel Rubiosambito, *Manager*
Charllie Schiffer, *Manager*
EMP: 59 **EST:** 2002
SQ FT: 9,000
SALES (est): 10.3MM **Privately Held**
WEB: www.seahunterboats.com
SIC: 3732 Boat building & repairing

Punta Gorda
Charlotte County

(G-14490)
ACCENT JEWELRY INC
Also Called: Accent Casting
2373 Talbrook Ter (33983-2732)
PHONE....................................941 391-6687
Robert Ricci, *President*
EMP: 10 **EST:** 1984
SALES (est): 638.7K **Privately Held**
SIC: 3961 3914 Costume jewelry, ex. precious metal & semiprecious stones; pewter ware

(G-14491)
APPLUS LABORATORIES USA INC (DH)
27256 Mooney Ave Bldg 10 (33982-2457)
PHONE....................................941 205-5700
Mark Pope, *Engineer*
Marcos Briseno, *Treasurer*
Lluis Martinez, *Director*

Gabriella Lombard, *Admin Asst*
EMP: 2 **EST:** 2014
SALES (est): 10.1MM
SALES (corp-wide): 60.8MM **Privately Held**
WEB: www.applus.com
SIC: 3829 Ultrasonic testing equipment

(G-14492)
ARCADIA AEROSPACE INDS LLC (DH)
27256 Mooney Ave Bldg 110 (33982-2457)
PHONE....................................941 205-5700
Charles Bushman, *CEO*
Gene Griffin, *General Mgr*
Jeff Phillips, *Opers Staff*
Ryan Herman, *Engineer*
Ben Lombard, *Engineer*
◆ **EMP:** 21 **EST:** 2008
SQ FT: 38,000
SALES (est): 4MM
SALES (corp-wide): 60.8MM **Privately Held**
WEB: www.arcadiaaerospace.com
SIC: 3728 Aircraft parts & equipment
HQ: Applus Laboratories Usa Inc.
27256 Mooney Ave Bldg 10
Punta Gorda FL 33982
941 205-5700

(G-14493)
ATLAS INNOVATIVE SERVICES INC
220 Shreve St (33950-3320)
P.O. Box 510422 (33951-0422)
PHONE....................................617 259-4529
Mark Ludwig, *Principal*
EMP: 9 **EST:** 2015
SALES (est): 473K **Privately Held**
WEB: www.atlasinnovative.com
SIC: 7692 Welding repair

(G-14494)
BAYSHORE PROFESSIONAL LLC
22655 Bayshore Rd Ste 110 (33980-2005)
PHONE....................................941 787-3023
Krishnamurty S Velamakanni, *Principal*
EMP: 7 **EST:** 2006
SALES (est): 225.5K **Privately Held**
SIC: 2752 Commercial printing, lithographic

(G-14495)
BDC SHELL & AGGREGATE LLC
2000 State Road 31 (33982-9725)
P.O. Box 511326 (33951-1326)
PHONE....................................941 875-6615
Jessica E Lehr,
EMP: 9 **EST:** 2013
SALES (est): 2.3MM **Privately Held**
SIC: 1442 5211 Gravel mining; sand & gravel

(G-14496)
BELLA BLSMIC PRESSED OLIVE INC (PA)
1200 W Retta Esplanade (33950-5325)
PHONE....................................941 249-3571
Rebecca Berlin, *CEO*
Jeremy Berlin, *CFO*
EMP: 10 **EST:** 2019
SALES (est): 941K **Privately Held**
WEB: www.bellabalsamic.net
SIC: 2079 Olive oil

(G-14497)
BERMONT EXCAVATING LLC
37390 Bermont Rd (33982-9525)
PHONE....................................866 367-9557
Joseph Boff, *President*
David Boff, *Vice Pres*
Joe Rice, *Opers Staff*
EMP: 15 **EST:** 2013
SALES (est): 1.8MM **Privately Held**
WEB: www.bermontexcavating.com
SIC: 1442 Construction sand & gravel

(G-14498)
BEST BINDERY CORP
3181 Aloe St (33982-1326)
PHONE....................................941 505-1779
Fernandez Victor, *Principal*
EMP: 7 **EST:** 2010

SALES (est): 76.5K **Privately Held**
SIC: 2789 Bookbinding & related work

(G-14499)
BLACKWELL FAMILY CORPORATION
Also Called: Quickprint Business Center
1869 Manzana Ave (33950-6048)
PHONE....................................941 639-0200
Steven Blackwell, *President*
EMP: 5 **EST:** 2001
SALES (est): 422K **Privately Held**
SIC: 2752 2261 2395 Commercial printing, offset; screen printing of cotton broadwoven fabrics; emblems, embroidered

(G-14500)
BUILT RIGHT POOL HEATERS LLC
28110 Challenger Blvd (33982-2423)
PHONE....................................941 505-1600
Bruce Brooks, *CEO*
Chris Wasdin, *Principal*
EMP: 5 **EST:** 2010
SALES (est): 2.7MM
SALES (corp-wide): 888.7MM **Privately Held**
WEB: www.builtrightpoolheaters.com
SIC: 3585 Heat pumps, electric
HQ: Zodiac Pool Systems Llc
2882 Whiptail Loop # 100
Carlsbad CA 92010
760 599-9600

(G-14501)
CHARLOTTE COUNTY MIN & MTL INC
Also Called: Southwest Aggregates
16070 Tamiami Trl (33955-7101)
PHONE....................................239 567-1800
Richard Neslund, *President*
EMP: 36 **EST:** 1996
SALES (est): 4MM **Privately Held**
SIC: 1442 1499 Construction sand mining; shell mining

(G-14502)
COUGHLAN PRODUCTS CORP
3043 Perdue Ter (33983-3314)
PHONE....................................973 904-1500
Randolph Reynolds, *President*
Patricia Campbell, *Vice Pres*
▲ **EMP:** 13 **EST:** 1990
SALES (est): 334.6K **Privately Held**
SIC: 2844 Toilet preparations

(G-14503)
CREATIVE CUSTOM STAIRS
3857 Acline Rd Unit 104 (33950-8403)
P.O. Box 510878 (33951-0878)
PHONE....................................941 505-0336
EMP: 7 **EST:** 2018
SALES (est): 533.8K **Privately Held**
WEB: www.creativecustomstairs.com
SIC: 2431 Millwork

(G-14504)
FLORIDA WOOD CREATIONS INC
42881 Lake Babcock Dr # 200 (33982-5042)
PHONE....................................239 561-5411
David Slabosz, *President*
Dorothy Slabosz, *Treasurer*
Jose Slabosz, *Director*
EMP: 5 **EST:** 1994
SALES (est): 465.5K **Privately Held**
WEB: www.floridawoodcreations.com
SIC: 2431 1799 Window shutters, wood; window treatment installation

(G-14505)
FUSION ENERGY SOLUTIONS LLC
5506 Independence Ct B (33982-7102)
PHONE....................................941 366-9936
Jacquelyn Johnson, *Partner*
▲ **EMP:** 5 **EST:** 2010
SALES (est): 507.5K **Privately Held**
WEB: www.fusionenergysolutions.net
SIC: 3648 Lighting equipment

(G-14506)
GULF CONTOURS INC
7500 Golf Course Blvd (33982-2424)
P.O. Box 511236 (33951-1236)
PHONE....................................941 639-3933
Jerry Goin, *President*
Janet Goin, *Vice Pres*
EMP: 7 **EST:** 1998
SQ FT: 3,600
SALES (est): 907.9K **Privately Held**
WEB: www.gulfcontours.com
SIC: 2434 Wood kitchen cabinets

(G-14507)
HARBOR VIEW BOAT TRAILERS
17 Callao St (33983-4258)
PHONE....................................941 916-3777
George Mazzo, *Principal*
EMP: 7 **EST:** 2010
SALES (est): 468.7K **Privately Held**
SIC: 3799 Boat trailers

(G-14508)
HARPERS MANUFACTURING SPC
24730 Sandhill Blvd # 902 (33983-5240)
PHONE....................................941 629-3490
Thomas J Trotter, *President*
Fay Trotter, *Corp Secy*
EMP: 6 **EST:** 1983
SALES (est): 576.7K **Privately Held**
SIC: 3496 Screening, woven wire: made from purchased wire

(G-14509)
INNERGY
315 E Olympia Ave # 251 (33950-3831)
PHONE....................................941 815-8655
Jonathan Adams, *Principal*
EMP: 7 **EST:** 2016
SALES (est): 111.1K **Privately Held**
WEB: www.innergy.com
SIC: 7372 Prepackaged software

(G-14510)
ISLAND FEVER LLC
1200 W Retta Esplanade # 19 (33950-5376)
PHONE....................................941 639-6400
John J Johnson, *Principal*
EMP: 6 **EST:** 2007
SALES (est): 353.3K **Privately Held**
WEB: www.islandfever.com
SIC: 3949 Water sports equipment

(G-14511)
KITCHEN CLASSICS LLC
4265 Tamiami Trl Unit K (33980-2149)
PHONE....................................941 629-6990
Brian Goetz, *President*
EMP: 7 **EST:** 2004
SALES (est): 527.5K **Privately Held**
WEB: www.kitchenclassicsonline.com
SIC: 2434 Wood kitchen cabinets

(G-14512)
LIVING WELL SPENDING LESS INC
307 Taylor St (33950-4829)
PHONE....................................941 209-1811
Chuck Soukup, *Principal*
EMP: 7 **EST:** 2018
SALES (est): 211.4K **Privately Held**
WEB: www.livingwellspendingless.com
SIC: 2741 Miscellaneous publishing

(G-14513)
MARDEN INDUSTRIES INC
26855 Airport Rd (33982-2408)
PHONE....................................863 682-7882
Thomas King, *President*
K David Julian, *Treasurer*
EMP: 18 **EST:** 1992
SQ FT: 27,000
SALES (est): 3.1MM **Privately Held**
WEB: www.mardenind.com
SIC: 3714 3523 3599 5084 Frames, motor vehicle; farm machinery & equipment; machine & other job shop work; industrial machinery & equipment; farm equipment & supplies

(G-14514)
MARQUIS MEDIA GROUP
26360 Trinilas Dr (33983-5333)
PHONE..941 255-0087
Shannon Black, *Principal*
EMP: 7 EST: 2004
SALES (est): 75.7K Privately Held
SIC: 2732 Books: printing only

(G-14515)
MERCERS FRESH ROASTED COFFEES
4678 Tamiami Trl Unit 109 (33980-2900)
PHONE..941 286-7054
David W Mercer, *Principal*
▲ EMP: 7 EST: 2011
SALES (est): 248.8K Privately Held
WEB:
www.mercersfreshroastedcoffeesfl.com
SIC: 2095 Roasted coffee

(G-14516)
METAL-TECH CONTROLS CORP
3441 Saint Croix Ct (33950-8142)
P.O. Box 512113 (33951-2113)
PHONE..941 575-7677
Glen F Koedding, *President*
Jayne S Koedding, *Vice Pres*
EMP: 7 EST: 1989
SQ FT: 3,200
SALES (est): 1MM Privately Held
WEB: www.metaltechcontrols.com
SIC: 3625 Control equipment, electric

(G-14517)
NEW WORLD TRADE INC
8249 Skylane Way Ste 111 (33982-2439)
PHONE..941 205-5873
Max Rodriguez, *President*
◆ EMP: 20 EST: 2002
SALES (est): 1.3MM Privately Held
SIC: 3949 Fishing tackle, general

(G-14518)
POSEIDON INDUSTRIES INC
5462 Williamsburg Dr (33982-1784)
PHONE..305 812-2582
Veronica Alva, *President*
EMP: 9 EST: 2010
SALES (est): 1.3MM Privately Held
WEB: www.poseidonmachinery.com
SIC: 3559 Stone working machinery

(G-14519)
PRO POWDER COATING INC
5474 Williamsburg Dr (33982-1716)
PHONE..941 505-8010
J Patrick Reagan, *President*
Jeremiah Reagan, *President*
EMP: 10 EST: 2001
SALES (est): 1.2MM Privately Held
WEB: www.propowdercoat.com
SIC: 3479 Coating of metals & formed products

(G-14520)
PROMOTIONAL MKTG ONLINE LLC
17377 Ophir Ln (33955-4530)
PHONE..941 347-8564
Peter Prins,
EMP: 6 EST: 2019
SALES (est): 301.7K Privately Held
WEB:
www.promotionalmarketingonline.com
SIC: 2759 Promotional printing

(G-14521)
PULSAFEEDER INC
27101 Airport Rd (33982-2411)
PHONE..941 575-2900
Paul Beldham, *Vice Pres*
EMP: 60
SQ FT: 13,255
SALES (corp-wide): 2.7B Publicly Held
WEB: www.pulsa.com
SIC: 3589 3561 Sewage & water treatment equipment; pumps & pumping equipment
HQ: Pulsafeeder, Inc.
2883 Brghton Hnrietta Twn
Rochester NY 14623
585 292-8000

(G-14522)
PULSAFEEDER SPO INC
27101 Airport Rd (33982-2411)
PHONE..941 575-3800
Sunil Samtani, *General Mgr*
EMP: 9 EST: 2015
SALES (est): 201.3K Privately Held
WEB: www.pulsatron.com
SIC: 3589 3561 Sewage & water treatment equipment; pumps & pumping equipment

(G-14523)
R AND R MACHINE SHOP
Also Called: R&R Racing Engines
6601 Taylor Rd (33950-8322)
PHONE..941 621-8143
Michael Riechers, *Principal*
EMP: 10 EST: 2015
SALES (est): 373.7K Privately Held
WEB: www.rrconnectingrods.com
SIC: 3599 Machine shop, jobbing & repair

(G-14524)
R TOWNSEND RESCREENS INC
30390 Cedar Rd (33982-3324)
P.O. Box 4150, North Fort Myers (33918-4150)
PHONE..239 244-4759
Rebecca Townsend, *President*
Rex Browning, *Vice Pres*
EMP: 6 EST: 2013
SALES (est): 574.9K Privately Held
WEB: www.rtownsendrescreens.com
SIC: 3448 3444 Screen enclosures; metal housings, enclosures, casings & other containers

(G-14525)
RAPID GRAPHIX INC
10251 Tamiami Trl (33950-8314)
PHONE..941 639-2043
Renee Bair, *President*
Duane Wright, *Production*
EMP: 5 EST: 2005
SALES (est): 507.4K Privately Held
WEB: www.rapidgraphix.net
SIC: 2752 Commercial printing, offset

(G-14526)
READY BUILDING PRODUCTS INC
7000 Progress Dr (33982-2433)
PHONE..941 639-6222
Pete Shoup, *CEO*
Merle E Bright, *Admin Sec*
Merle Bright, *Admin Sec*
EMP: 9 EST: 2010
SQ FT: 65,000
SALES (est): 284.6K Privately Held
SIC: 2674 Cement bags: made from purchased materials

(G-14527)
ROBERT GOMES PUBLISHING INC
8512 Alan Blvd (33982-2321)
PHONE..941 637-6080
Robert Gomes, *Principal*
EMP: 9 EST: 2010
SALES (est): 441.4K Privately Held
SIC: 2741 Miscellaneous publishing

(G-14528)
ROYAL PALM PRESS INC
25560 Technology Blvd (33950-4731)
PHONE..941 575-4299
Theodore D Dunn, *President*
EMP: 9 EST: 1997
SQ FT: 3,500
SALES (est): 865.1K Privately Held
WEB: www.royalpalmpress.com
SIC: 2732 Book printing

(G-14529)
RPM CRUSHERS AND SCREENS
24710 Sandhill Blvd # 8 (33983-5239)
PHONE..941 769-0420
Aisling Bumgardner, *Principal*
EMP: 11 EST: 2018
SALES (est): 975.9K Privately Held
WEB: www.rpmcrushersandscreens.com
SIC: 3599 Industrial machinery

(G-14530)
SHINELINE BUFFING & DETAIL
11338 1st Ave (33955-1321)
PHONE..941 268-1033
Diane Adams, *Principal*
EMP: 7 EST: 2005
SALES (est): 149.5K Privately Held
SIC: 3471 Buffing for the trade

(G-14531)
SIGN TECH INC
25191 Olympia Ave Ste 1 (33950-4066)
PHONE..941 575-1349
Mark Sturman, *Owner*
EMP: 5 EST: 2008
SALES (est): 530.1K Privately Held
WEB: www.signtechfl.com
SIC: 3993 Signs & advertising specialties

(G-14532)
SOTO INDUSTRIES LLC
3420 Bal Harbor Blvd (33950-8251)
PHONE..941 830-6000
Norman A Cardinale, *Principal*
EMP: 8 EST: 2018
SALES (est): 379.7K Privately Held
SIC: 3999 Manufacturing industries

(G-14533)
STANS SEPTIC SVC CON PDTS INC
5287 Duncan Rd (33982-1737)
P.O. Box 511049 (33951-1049)
PHONE..941 639-3976
Louie Pancic, *President*
EMP: 5 EST: 1966
SQ FT: 5,000
SALES (est): 496.9K Privately Held
WEB: www.stansseptic.com
SIC: 3272 1711 Septic tanks, concrete; septic system construction

(G-14534)
SUN COAST MEDIA GROUP INC
Also Called: Desoto Sun
23170 Harborview Rd (33980-2100)
PHONE..863 494-7600
Joe Gallimore, *General Mgr*
EMP: 7
SALES (corp-wide): 333.5MM Privately Held
WEB: www.yoursun.com
SIC: 2711 Newspapers, publishing & printing
HQ: Sun Coast Media Group, Inc.
23170 Harborview Rd
Port Charlotte FL 33980
941 206-1300

(G-14535)
SUPERIOR FABRICATION INC
5524 Independence Ct (33982-1700)
PHONE..941 639-2966
Andrew Giustina, *President*
Anna Giustina, *Corp Secy*
Lori Giustina, *Vice Pres*
EMP: 9 EST: 2009
SQ FT: 6,000
SALES (est): 929.1K Privately Held
WEB: www.superiorfabricationwelding.com
SIC: 7692 Welding repair

(G-14536)
SUPERTRAK INC
26855 Airport Rd (33982-2408)
PHONE..941 505-7800
Tom King, *President*
K David Julian, *Corp Secy*
Dave Sampson, *Vice Pres*
Ken Carter, *Purchasing*
Dan Platts, *Purchasing*
▲ EMP: 10 EST: 1986
SQ FT: 31,000
SALES (est): 2.5MM Privately Held
WEB: www.supertrak.com
SIC: 3531 Backhoes, tractors, cranes, plows & similar equipment

(G-14537)
SW PREMIER PRODUCTS LLC
28100 Challenger Blvd # 1 (33982-2403)
PHONE..941 275-6677
Shalon Wild,
Paul Wild,
EMP: 6 EST: 2018

SALES (est): 1.1MM Privately Held
WEB: www.swpremierproducts.com
SIC: 2676 Towels, napkins & tissue paper products

(G-14538)
T D R INC
Also Called: Tony Doukas Racing
30436 Holly Rd (33982-3336)
PHONE..941 505-0800
Tony Doukas, *President*
EMP: 5 EST: 1982
SQ FT: 4,500
SALES (est): 450.9K Privately Held
SIC: 3751 Motorcycles, bicycles & parts

(G-14539)
WATERPROOF CHARTERS INC
320 Cross St (33950-4802)
PHONE..941 639-7626
Shawn Bellestri, *President*
▼ EMP: 9 EST: 1993
SQ FT: 2,200
SALES (est): 956.1K Privately Held
WEB: www.waterproofcharts.com
SIC: 3812 Nautical instruments

(G-14540)
WEBER SOUTH FL LLC
40800 Cook Brown Rd (33982-7728)
PHONE..239 543-7240
Scott Webber,
Geraldine Weber,
Gregg Weber,
EMP: 8 EST: 2005
SALES (est): 1.8MM Privately Held
SIC: 1241 Coal mining services

Quincy
Gadsden County

(G-14541)
BASF CORPORATION
Also Called: Bc Quincy
1101 N Madison St (32352-0981)
PHONE..850 627-7688
William Galloway, *Opers Spvr*
Carlos Barrios, *Engineer*
Nathalie Legare, *Engineer*
Kenneth Tatum, *Sales Staff*
Mike Cunio, *Branch Mgr*
EMP: 185
SALES (corp-wide): 88.9B Privately Held
WEB: www.basf.com
SIC: 2869 Industrial organic chemicals
HQ: Basf Corporation
100 Park Ave
Florham Park NJ 07932
800 962-7831

(G-14542)
BIG BEND REBAR INC
1 Corporate Ct (32351-8002)
PHONE..850 875-8000
Patricia Bates Trotta, *President*
Joe Trotta, *Vice Pres*
EMP: 10 EST: 2002
SQ FT: 14,500
SALES (est): 1.3MM Privately Held
WEB: www.bigbendrebar.com
SIC: 3441 Fabricated structural metal

(G-14543)
CLASSIC SHIRTS INC
110 Zeta St (32351-2900)
PHONE..850 875-2200
Bill Sinn, *President*
William Steck, *Vice Pres*
◆ EMP: 16 EST: 1998
SALES (est): 1.9MM Privately Held
WEB: www.classicshirts.com
SIC: 2759 3993 Screen printing; signs & advertising specialties

(G-14544)
FLOWERS BAKERIES LLC
Also Called: Flowers Baking Company
321 W Jefferson St (32351-2325)
PHONE..850 875-4997
EMP: 47
SALES (corp-wide): 4.3B Publicly Held
SIC: 2051 Mfg Bread/Related Products

▲ = Import ▼ =Export
◆ =Import/Export

HQ: Flowers Bakeries, Llc
1919 Flowers Cir
Thomasville GA 31757

(G-14545)
GADSDEN COUNTY TIMES INC
Also Called: Gadsden County Shopping
Guide
9 W King St (32351-1701)
P.O. Box 790 (32353-0790)
PHONE............................850 627-7649
Alana Rich, *General Mgr*
Alice Dupont, *Editor*
Erin Hill, *Sheriff*
Leslie Robert, *Manager*
EMP: 10 EST: 1901
SALES (est): 905.1K Privately Held
WEB: www.gadsdencountytimes.com
SIC: 2711 2752 2759 Commercial printing
& newspaper publishing combined; com-
mercial printing, lithographic; commercial
printing

(G-14546)
IMERYS PERLITE USA INC
612 S Shelfer St (32351-3553)
P.O. Box 999 (32353-0999)
PHONE............................850 875-1282
Kenny Edwards, *Plant Mgr*
Kenneth Edwards, *Opers-Prdtn-Mfg*
Callie Warren, *Sales Mgr*
EMP: 20
SQ FT: 18,593
SALES (corp-wide): 3.2MM Privately
Held
SIC: 3295 Minerals, ground or treated
HQ: Imerys Perlite Usa, Inc.
1732 N 1st St Ste 450
San Jose CA 95112

(G-14547)
**JIMMY & TOONS ICECREAM SP
LLC**
104 E Washington St (32351-2458)
PHONE............................850 752-2291
Ebony Denson, *CEO*
EMP: 8
SALES (est): 563.6K Privately Held
SIC: 2024 Ice cream & frozen desserts

(G-14548)
SBM BEAUTY LLC ✪
831 Sikes St (32351-4403)
PHONE............................850 567-7338
Shonteesia McMillian,
EMP: 10 EST: 2021
SALES (est): 480K Privately Held
SIC: 3999 7389 Hair & hair-based prod-
ucts;

(G-14549)
SICAMU INC
1066 Strong Rd (32351-5241)
PHONE............................850 270-6283
Jose I Pons, *President*
Antonio J Pons, *Vice Pres*
Carmen M Siepermann, *Admin Sec*
EMP: 5 EST: 2007
SQ FT: 110,000
SALES (est): 677.8K Privately Held
WEB: www.sicamu.com
SIC: 2842 2841 Specialty cleaning, pol-
ishes & sanitation goods; soap & other
detergents

(G-14550)
**SOUTHERN BROTHERS RACING
LLC ✪**
443 Charlie Harris Loop (32352-6652)
PHONE............................850 509-2223
Larmarcus Haynes, *Mng Member*
EMP: 9 EST: 2021
SALES (est): 330.1K Privately Held
SIC: 3799 All terrain vehicles (ATV)

(G-14551)
**TRULIEVE CANNABIS CORP
(HQ)**
6749 Ben Bostic Rd (32351-9121)
PHONE............................844 878-5438
Kim Rivers, *CEO*
Steve White, *President*
Nicole Stanton, *Vice Pres*
EMP: 9 EST: 2018

SALES (est): 938.3MM
SALES (corp-wide): 944MM Privately
Held
SIC: 3999
PA: Trulieve, Inc.
3494 Martin Hurst Rd
Tallahassee FL 32312
844 878-5438

Reddick
Marion County

(G-14552)
DOUBLE R MANUFACTURING
15505 Nw 100th Avenue Rd (32686-3007)
PHONE............................352 878-4009
Thomas Moore, *Principal*
EMP: 7 EST: 2017
SALES (est): 147.7K Privately Held
WEB: www.doublermfg.com
SIC: 3999 Manufacturing industries

(G-14553)
SCI MATERIALS LLC
15251 N Highway 329 (32686-3038)
PHONE............................352 878-4979
Steven Counts, *Mng Member*
EMP: 32 EST: 2016
SALES (est): 5.3MM Privately Held
WEB: www.scirockit.com
SIC: 1422 Limestones, ground; agricultural
limestone, ground; lime rock, ground

Redington Shores
Pinellas County

(G-14554)
ROOT INTERNATIONAL INC
237 176th Terrace Dr E (33708-1203)
PHONE............................813 482-1732
David W Root, *Branch Mgr*
EMP: 7
SALES (corp-wide): 1.2MM Privately
Held
WEB: www.cases2go.com
SIC: 3086 Packaging & shipping materials,
foamed plastic
PA: Root International, Inc.
4910 Creekside Dr Ste B
Clearwater FL 33760
813 265-1808

Reunion
Osceola County

(G-14555)
VISIBLE RESULTS USA INC
1550 Corolla Ct 1 (34747-6741)
PHONE............................913 706-8248
Brandy Dixon, *Manager*
EMP: 10 Privately Held
WEB: www.globalred.com.au
SIC: 7372 Prepackaged software
PA: Lifecycle Digital Nz Limited
L 4, 152 Fanshawe Street
Auckland 1010

Riverview
Hillsborough County

(G-14556)
**AFFORDABLE BOAT CUSHIONS
INC**
6515 Riverview Dr (33578-4845)
PHONE............................877 350-2628
Angela Castillo, *President*
EMP: 7 EST: 2016
SALES (est): 216.3K Privately Held
WEB: www.affordableboatcushions.com
SIC: 2392 Boat cushions

(G-14557)
AIN PLASTICS OF FLORIDA INC
6317 Pelican Creek Cir (33578-8822)
PHONE............................813 242-6400
Richard J Greaves, *Principal*
EMP: 12 EST: 2008

SALES (est): 985.9K Privately Held
WEB: www.engineeredplasticsblog.info
SIC: 3089 Injection molding of plastics

(G-14558)
CECO & ASSOCIATES INC
Also Called: Ceco Coated Fasteners
6508 S 78th St (33578-8801)
PHONE............................727 528-0075
Gary Howard, *President*
Justin Howard, *Vice Pres*
Kathleen Howard, *Vice Pres*
▲ EMP: 8 EST: 2002
SQ FT: 30,000
SALES (est): 1.1MM Privately Held
SIC: 2819 5051 3965 Aluminum com-
pounds; aluminum bars, rods, ingots,
sheets, pipes, plates, etc.; fasteners

(G-14559)
CLEVER CABINETRY LLC ✪
10513 Anglecrest Dr (33569-8706)
PHONE............................813 992-0020
William J Faherty, *Manager*
EMP: 6 EST: 2021
SALES (est): 326.8K Privately Held
SIC: 2434 Wood kitchen cabinets

(G-14560)
CVISTA LLC
4333 Garden Vista Dr (33578-4613)
PHONE............................813 405-3000
Samuel Hicks, *Production*
Zaneta Munsie, *Buyer*
Chris Baker, *Technical Mgr*
Eddie Carley, *Manager*
Martin Paleske, *Director*
▲ EMP: 31 EST: 2005
SQ FT: 186,000
SALES (est): 11MM Privately Held
WEB: www.cvista.com
SIC: 2037 2087 Citrus pulp, dried; ex-
tracts, flavoring; bitters (flavoring concen-
trates)

(G-14561)
DSE INC (PA)
10401 Frog Pond Dr (33569-2715)
PHONE............................813 443-4809
Dae Y Shin, *President*
Joe D Bedore, *CFO*
Velton Thomas, *Manager*
Sue Shin, *Business Dir*
EMP: 18 EST: 1979
SALES (est): 9MM Privately Held
WEB: www.dse.net
SIC: 3489 3429 3545 3483 Artillery or ar-
tillery parts, over 30 mm.; motor vehicle
hardware; machine tool accessories; am-
munition, except for small arms

(G-14562)
EAGLE PROF FLRG REMOVAL
11548 Bay Gardens Loop (33569-2032)
PHONE............................813 520-3027
Jesus Ramos, *Principal*
EMP: 7 EST: 2014
SALES (est): 75.6K Privately Held
SIC: 2431 5023 1752 Floor baseboards,
wood; floor coverings; wood floor installa-
tion & refinishing

(G-14563)
GORILLA BATS LLC
11223 Saint Andrews Ct (33579-7045)
PHONE............................813 285-9409
Mike V Disalle, *Manager*
EMP: 7 EST: 2019
SALES (est): 261.7K Privately Held
WEB: www.gorillabaseballbats.com
SIC: 3949 Sporting & athletic goods

(G-14564)
**GRANNYS CHEESECAKE &
MORE INC**
13106 Barth Pl (33579-7133)
PHONE............................210 343-9610
Brenda Premont, *Principal*
EMP: 7 EST: 2015
SALES (est): 169.7K Privately Held
SIC: 2591 Window blinds

(G-14565)
**HARPER SCREEN
ENCLOSURES LLC**
11217 Rice Creek Rd (33569-5180)
PHONE............................813 417-5937
Daniel Harper, *Principal*
EMP: 7 EST: 2007
SALES (est): 252.8K Privately Held
WEB: www.harpersscreen.com
SIC: 3448 Screen enclosures

(G-14566)
**HOMERUN DERBY BATS ONLY
LLC**
6931 Potomac Cir (33578-8309)
PHONE............................813 545-3887
Jeffrey J Pendino, *Principal*
EMP: 8 EST: 2015
SALES (est): 224.3K Privately Held
WEB: www.homerunderbybatsonly.com
SIC: 3949 Sporting & athletic goods

(G-14567)
J&JH STUCCO INC
12713 Lovers Ln (33579-6840)
PHONE............................813 482-5282
Juan J Hernandez, *Principal*
EMP: 7 EST: 2012
SALES (est): 140.6K Privately Held
SIC: 3299 Stucco

(G-14568)
KELLER INDUSTRIAL INC
Also Called: Moretrench Enviromental Svcs
11001 Fern Hill Dr (33578-9370)
P.O. Box 70, Gibsonton (33534-0070)
PHONE............................813 831-1871
Al Schuman, *President*
Matthew Degregoris, *Division Mgr*
Steve Chapman, *Superintendent*
Scott Hamilton, *Superintendent*
Bradley Jones, *Superintendent*
EMP: 27 Privately Held
WEB: www.keller-na.com
SIC: 3561 5084 1794 1623 Pumps &
pumping equipment; pumps & pumping
equipment; excavation work; water, sewer
& utility lines
HQ: Keller Industrial, Inc.
100 Stickle Ave
Rockaway NJ 07866
262 652-4444

(G-14569)
LOYALTY MECHANICAL LLC
6619 S 78th St (33578-8841)
PHONE............................718 502-0632
Jeffrey Ramirez, *President*
Jeffrey A Ramirez, *Mng Member*
Jeffrey D Pogan, *Manager*
EMP: 12 EST: 2020
SALES (est): 632.2K Privately Held
WEB: www.loyaltymechanical.net
SIC: 1389 Construction, repair & disman-
tling services

(G-14570)
MOSAIC COMPANY
8817 S Us Highway 41 (33578)
PHONE............................813 775-2827
Sal Nsheiwat, *Manager*
Eric Gabel, *Supervisor*
EMP: 14 Publicly Held
WEB: www.mosaicco.com
SIC: 2874 Phosphatic fertilizers
PA: The Mosaic Company
101 E Kennedy Blvd # 2500
Tampa FL 33602

(G-14571)
NEWMILE PARTNERS LLC ✪
9030 Camden Field Pkwy (33578-0521)
PHONE............................800 674-3474
EMP: 8 EST: 2021
SALES (est): 325.2K Privately Held
SIC: 7372 Prepackaged software

(G-14572)
OSTARA USA LLC (PA)
2720 S Falkenburg Rd (33578-2561)
PHONE............................813 666-8123
Phillip Abrary, *President*
Jolie Lee, *Controller*
EMP: 5 EST: 2008

GEOGRAPHIC

SALES (est): 2.6MM **Privately Held**
WEB: www.ostara.com
SIC: 1479 Fertilizer mineral mining

(G-14573)
RANDAZZA ENTERPRISES INC
8824 Van Fleet Rd (33578-5042)
PHONE...................................813 677-0041
Nocif Espat, *President*
Kathleen Randazza, *Vice Pres*
▲ EMP: 10 EST: 1987
SALES (est): 664.6K **Privately Held**
WEB: www.randazzawastewater.com
SIC: 3589 Water treatment equipment, in-
    dustrial

(G-14574)
REFERRAL & RESIDUAL
EXCHANGE L
9376 Balm Riverview Rd (33569-5104)
PHONE...................................813 655-5000
EMP: 8 EST: 2015
SALES (est): 339.8K **Privately Held**
SIC: 2911 Residues

(G-14575)
RIVERVIEW DRONES INC
11326 Lake Lucaya Dr (33579-4103)
PHONE...................................813 451-4744
Michael Phillips, *Principal*
EMP: 7 EST: 2016
SALES (est): 82.9K **Privately Held**
SIC: 3721 Motorized aircraft

(G-14576)
SAVORY LIFE LLC
6766 Waterton Dr (33578-8388)
PHONE...................................813 981-2022
Lindsey Wherry, *President*
EMP: 8 EST: 2018
SALES (est): 229.3K **Privately Held**
SIC: 2099 Food preparations

(G-14577)
SIGNAGE PRO LLC
9624 Birnamwood St (33569-8201)
PHONE...................................813 671-4272
Cara L Diehl, *Principal*
EMP: 7 EST: 2011
SALES (est): 128.2K **Privately Held**
WEB: www.signageproonline.com
SIC: 3993 Signs & advertising specialties

(G-14578)
TAMPA BAY PRINT SHOP LLC
2904 S Falkenburg Rd (33578-2554)
PHONE...................................813 321-8790
Ryan Koenig,
EMP: 7 EST: 2018
SALES (est): 250K **Privately Held**
WEB: www.tampabayprintshop.co
SIC: 2759 Screen printing

(G-14579)
TAYLOR MADE SCRUB HATS
LLC ✪
10044 Creek Bluff Dr (33578-7559)
PHONE...................................615 348-7802
Chris Jordon,
EMP: 7 EST: 2021
SALES (est): 250K **Privately Held**
WEB: www.taylormadescrubhats.com
SIC: 2211 Scrub cloths

(G-14580)
ULTRAFLEX SYSTEMS FLORIDA
INC (PA)
6333 Pelican Creek Cir (33578-8822)
PHONE...................................973 664-6739
John Schleicher, *President*
Clint Green, *Managing Dir*
Ron Schleicher, *COO*
Tim Wilson, *Sales Staff*
EMP: 14 EST: 2016
SALES (est): 11.7MM **Privately Held**
WEB: www.ultraflexx.com
SIC: 2821 Polyvinyl chloride resins (PVC)

(G-14581)
UNIBEAST SPORTS LLC
14218 Poke Ridge Dr (33579-3522)
PHONE...................................813 255-2827
Daryl, *Principal*
EMP: 10

SALES (est): 413.1K **Privately Held**
SIC: 3949 7389 Football equipment &
    supplies, general;

(G-14582)
WEREVER PRODUCTS INC
Also Called: Werever Waterproof Cabinetry
6120 Pelican Creek Cir (33578-8978)
PHONE...................................813 241-9701
Matt Boettger, *President*
Jill Kliem, *Prdtn Mgr*
Jason Moore, *Manager*
EMP: 17 EST: 2001
SALES (est): 4.8MM **Privately Held**
WEB: www.werever.com
SIC: 2599 5719 5712 Cabinets, factory;
    barbeque grills; furniture stores

(G-14583)
WORKWEAR OUTFITTERS LLC
Also Called: Vf
8221 Eagle Palm Dr (33578-8893)
PHONE...................................813 671-2986
Laura Bear, *Manager*
EMP: 26
SALES (corp-wide): 2B **Privately Held**
WEB: www.redkap.com
SIC: 2395 5137 5136 Embroidery & art
    needlework; women's & children's cloth-
    ing; men's & boys' clothing
HQ: Workwear Outfitters, Llc
    545 Marriott Dr Ste 200
    Nashville TN 37214
    615 565-5000

Riviera Beach
Palm Beach County

(G-14584)
3D MEDICAL MANUFACTURING
INC
Also Called: 3d Machining
2001 N Congress Ave Ste F (33404-5101)
PHONE...................................561 842-7175
James E Davis Sr, *CEO*
James E Davis Jr, *President*
Joseph H Davis, *Exec VP*
Laura Thomas, *Warehouse Mgr*
Hector Artigas, *Engineer*
EMP: 203 EST: 1994
SALES (est): 39.1MM
SALES (corp-wide): 832.8MM **Privately**
Held
SIC: 3841 Surgical & medical instruments
HQ: Tecomet Inc.
    115 Eames St
    Wilmington MA 01887
    978 642-2400

(G-14585)
ABELE SHEETMETAL WORKS
INC
1964 W 9th St Ste 3 (33404-6426)
PHONE...................................561 471-1134
Fred Abele, *President*
EMP: 15 EST: 1995
SQ FT: 2,500
SALES (est): 2MM **Privately Held**
WEB: www.abelesheetmetal.com
SIC: 3444 Sheet metalwork

(G-14586)
ADATIF MEDICAL
INCORPORATED (HQ)
3660 Interstate Park Way (33404-5911)
PHONE...................................561 840-0395
Kerrigan Turner, *Ch of Bd*
Mike Richardson, *Vice Pres*
Jose Perezpozo, *QA Dir*
EMP: 1 EST: 1992
SQ FT: 24,000
SALES (est): 9.9MM
SALES (corp-wide): 2.5MM **Privately**
Held
WEB: www.perrybaromedical.com
SIC: 3841 Surgical & medical instruments
PA: Adatif International Ltd.
    211-4150 Rue Sainte-Catherine Ouest
    Westmount QC H3Z 2
    514 934-4966

(G-14587)
ADDCO MANUFACTURING
COMPANY
Also Called: Addco Industries
131 Riviera Dr (33404-2422)
PHONE...................................828 733-1560
Roland De Marcellus, *Ch of Bd*
Edmond G De Marcellus, *President*
Daniel W Osborne, *Vice Pres*
EMP: 35 EST: 1960
SQ FT: 60,000
SALES (est): 1MM **Privately Held**
WEB: www.addco.net
SIC: 3714 5521 Motor vehicle parts & ac-
    cessories; used car dealers

(G-14588)
ADVANCED AIR
INTERNATIONAL INC
6461 Garden Rd Ste 103 (33404-6315)
PHONE...................................561 845-8212
Dale L Bell, *President*
Steve Bell, *Vice Pres*
Steven M Bell, *Vice Pres*
Larry A Bell, *Treasurer*
EMP: 37 EST: 1989
SQ FT: 20,000
SALES (est): 4.9MM **Privately Held**
WEB: www.advancedair.net
SIC: 3089 Injection molding of plastics

(G-14589)
ADVANCED AIR WEST PALM
BCH INC
6461 Garden Rd Ste 102 (33404-6315)
PHONE...................................561 845-8289
Larry Bell, *President*
Larry A Bell, *President*
Steven M Bell, *Vice Pres*
EMP: 26 EST: 1989
SQ FT: 10,000
SALES (est): 4.5MM **Privately Held**
WEB: www.aabushings.net
SIC: 3599 5088 Machine shop, jobbing &
    repair; transportation equipment & sup-
    plies

(G-14590)
AFL INDUSTRIES INC
1101 W 13th St (33404-6701)
PHONE...................................561 848-1826
EMP: 8 EST: 2019
SALES (est): 177.5K **Privately Held**
WEB: www.rgf.com
SIC: 3589 Water treatment equipment, in-
    dustrial

(G-14591)
AKIKNAV INC
Also Called: Nemee
6667 42nd Ter N Ste 3 (33407-1241)
PHONE...................................561 842-8091
Nash Shah, *President*
Aarsh Shah, *Business Mgr*
Ashok Shah, *Shareholder*
Hetal Shah, *Shareholder*
Kamlesh Shah, *Shareholder*
EMP: 15 EST: 1986
SQ FT: 25,000
SALES (est): 2.6MM **Privately Held**
SIC: 2434 2541 2542 Wood kitchen cabi-
    nets; counters or counter display cases,
    wood; partitions & fixtures, except wood

(G-14592)
ALPHA HYDRAULICS LLC
999 W 17th St Ste 5 (33404-5402)
PHONE...................................561 355-0318
Sara Rodriguez, *CEO*
EMP: 5 EST: 2014
SALES (est): 304.5K **Privately Held**
WEB: www.alphahydraulicsllc.com
SIC: 3599 7699 3714 1799 Machine
    shop, jobbing & repair; hydraulic equip-
    ment repair; hydraulic fluid power pumps
    for auto steering mechanism; hydraulic
    equipment, installation & service; pistons
    & valves

(G-14593)
ALTEC INDUSTRIES INC
Also Called: West Palm Beach Service Cen-
ter
3755 Interstate Park Rd W (33404-5915)
PHONE...................................561 686-8550

Mark Thrash, *Business Mgr*
Omar Romero, *Accounts Mgr*
Winston Ramsaran, *Branch Mgr*
EMP: 14
SQ FT: 11,768
SALES (corp-wide): 1.2B **Privately Held**
WEB: www.altec.com
SIC: 3531 Construction machinery
HQ: Altec Industries, Inc.
    210 Inverness Center Dr
    Birmingham AL 35242
    205 991-7733

(G-14594)
AMY CABINETRY
6667 42nd Ter N (33407-1241)
PHONE...................................561 842-8091
Nash Shah, *Owner*
EMP: 25 EST: 1986
SALES (est): 1.1MM **Privately Held**
WEB: amycabinetry.business.site
SIC: 2434 Wood kitchen cabinets

(G-14595)
ATLAS SIGN INDUSTRIES FLA
LLC
1077 W Blue Heron Blvd (33404-4227)
PHONE...................................561 863-6659
Jim Adinolfe, *CEO*
Jeffrey Adinolfe, *CEO*
Mark Bragg, *Project Mgr*
Wanda Yarborough, *Project Mgr*
Kenny Melesky, *Asst Controller*
▼ EMP: 215 EST: 1992
SQ FT: 250,000
SALES (est): 44.3MM **Privately Held**
WEB: www.atlasbtw.com
SIC: 3993 Signs & advertising specialties
PA: Atlas Signs Holdings, Inc.
    1077 Blue Heron Blvd W
    Riviera Beach FL 33404

(G-14596)
B & A MANUFACTURING CO
3665 E Industrial Way (33404-3491)
PHONE...................................561 848-8648
Norman H Schmotzer, *President*
Carol Schmotzer, *Admin Sec*
◆ EMP: 45 EST: 1950
SQ FT: 25,000
SALES (est): 5.1MM **Privately Held**
WEB: www.bamanufacturing.com
SIC: 3545 3532 3423 Drill bits, metal-
    working; mining machinery; hand & edge
    tools

(G-14597)
BELL COMPOSITES INC
8376 Garden Rd (33404-1738)
PHONE...................................561 714-9045
EMP: 11
SALES (corp-wide): 200.2K **Privately**
Held
WEB: www.offshorecatamarans.com
SIC: 3732 Boat building & repairing
PA: Bell Composites Inc
    23 Oak Ridge Ln
    Jupiter FL 33469
    561 575-9175

(G-14598)
BLACK BART INTERNATIONAL
LLC
155 E Blue Heron Blvd R2 (33404-4546)
PHONE...................................561 842-4045
Bart Miller, *Ch of Bd*
John Tullis Jr, *President*
Gary Tillius, *Vice Pres*
Janck Tullius,
EMP: 8 EST: 2003
SQ FT: 3,500
SALES (est): 761.4K **Privately Held**
SIC: 3949 Fishing equipment

(G-14599)
BLACK CORAL RUM LLC (PA)
1231 W 13th St Bldg 15 (33404-6640)
PHONE...................................561 766-2493
Benjamin C Etheridge, *Manager*
EMP: 5 EST: 2012
SALES (est): 400.9K **Privately Held**
WEB: www.steeltiespirits.com
SIC: 2085 Distilled & blended liquors

▲ = Import ▼=Export
◆ =Import/Export

(G-14600)
BORGZINNER INC
1160 W 13th St Ste 10 (33404-6715)
PHONE...................................561 848-2538
Ken Stevens, *President*
EMP: 22 **EST:** 1891
SALES (est): 2.8MM **Privately Held**
WEB: www.borgzinner.com
SIC: 2599 Cabinets, factory; cafeteria furniture

(G-14601)
BRIGIZ INC ✪
7024 Hawks Nest Ter (33407-1124)
PHONE...................................404 400-5399
Vincent Barnett, *President*
EMP: 10 **EST:** 2021
SALES (est): 354.2K **Privately Held**
WEB: www.brigiz.com
SIC: 7372 7299 Prepackaged software; information services, consumer

(G-14602)
BUDGET PRINTING CENTER LLC
7241 Hvrhill Bus Pkwy # 110 (33407-1014)
PHONE...................................561 848-5700
Jay Goldfarb, *Mng Member*
EMP: 5 **EST:** 2000
SALES (est): 316.4K **Privately Held**
SIC: 2752 Commercial printing, offset

(G-14603)
BUSCH CANVAS
2428 Broadway (33404-4533)
PHONE...................................561 881-1605
Andrea Jarvis, *Principal*
EMP: 7 **EST:** 2010
SALES (est): 205.4K **Privately Held**
WEB: www.buschcanvas.com
SIC: 2394 Canvas & related products

(G-14604)
BUSCH CANVAS & INTERIORS INC
2428 Broadway (33404-4533)
PHONE...................................561 881-1605
Andrea Jarvis, *President*
Kim Crawford, *Admin Sec*
EMP: 5 **EST:** 1968
SALES (est): 515.1K **Privately Held**
WEB: www.buschcanvas.com
SIC: 2211 Canvas

(G-14605)
CANVAS DESIGNERS INC
Also Called: Nautical Flair
1500 Australian Ave Ste 1 (33404-5313)
PHONE...................................561 881-7663
Michael Erickson, *President*
Pamela Erickson, *Vice Pres*
Heidi Garrison, *Prdtn Mgr*
Diana Demarest, *Marketing Mgr*
Bob Renna, *Manager*
◆ **EMP:** 36 **EST:** 1985
SQ FT: 15,000
SALES (est): 5.5MM **Privately Held**
WEB: www.canvasdesigners.com
SIC: 2394 Canvas & related products

(G-14606)
CAREY-DUNN INC
Also Called: Florida Marine
2001 Broadway Ste 301 (33404-5612)
PHONE...................................561 840-1694
EMP: 15 **EST:** 1996
SQ FT: 25,000
SALES (est): 1.1MM **Privately Held**
SIC: 3732 Boatbuilding/Repairing

(G-14607)
CARPENTERS ROOFG & SHTMTL INC
1701 W 10th St (33404-6431)
PHONE...................................561 833-0341
James E Williams Jr, *President*
Joseph C Hart, *Vice Pres*
Jason Lovelady, *Vice Pres*
Mary Dodson, *Opers Staff*
Caleb Tuning, *Manager*
EMP: 39 **EST:** 1931
SQ FT: 10,000

SALES (est): 5MM **Privately Held**
WEB: www.carpentersroofing.com
SIC: 3444 2952 Sheet metalwork; asphalt felts & coatings

(G-14608)
CEMEX MATERIALS LLC
Also Called: Riviera Beach FL Warehouse Bm
501 Avenue S (33404-7109)
PHONE...................................561 881-4472
Arlene Larubbia, *Branch Mgr*
EMP: 128 **Privately Held**
SIC: 3273 Ready-mixed concrete
HQ: Cemex Materials Llc
1720 Centrepark Dr E # 100
West Palm Beach FL 33401
561 833-5555

(G-14609)
CHRISTOPHER R SHUMAN
Also Called: Custom Canvas and Cushions
176 E 21st St (33404-5608)
PHONE...................................561 800-8541
EMP: 6 **EST:** 2018
SALES (est): 518.9K **Privately Held**
WEB: www.customcanvas561.com
SIC: 2211 Canvas

(G-14610)
CLOCK SPRING COMPANY INC
3875 Fiscal Ct (33404-1795)
PHONE...................................561 683-6992
Matthew Boucher, *CEO*
Matt Green, *Vice Pres*
Ian Liess, *Vice Pres*
Ryan Schwarz, *Vice Pres*
Dariusz Chabuz, *Opers Staff*
EMP: 15
SALES (corp-wide): 49.2MM **Privately Held**
WEB: www.cs-nri.com
SIC: 2869 2295 5039 Silicones; chemically coated & treated fabrics; structural assemblies, prefabricated: non-wood
HQ: Clock Spring Company, Inc.
621 Lockhaven Dr
Houston TX 77073

(G-14611)
CONCRETE PDTS OF PALM BCHES IN
460 Avenue S (33404-7108)
PHONE...................................561 842-2743
Bernard Brunet, *Principal*
EMP: 36 **EST:** 2011
SALES (est): 9.9MM **Privately Held**
SIC: 3272 Concrete products, precast

(G-14612)
D & R DELIVERY SERVICES OF PB
312 Canterbury Dr W (33407-1321)
PHONE...................................561 602-6427
Morgan Rohan, *CEO*
EMP: 12 **EST:** 2013
SALES (est): 970K **Privately Held**
SIC: 3799 Transportation equipment

(G-14613)
D I H CORPORATION
Also Called: Cutoutz.com
1750 Australian Ave Ste 3 (33404-5328)
PHONE...................................561 881-8705
Henry Goldberg, *President*
Scott Goldberg, *Vice Pres*
EMP: 5 **EST:** 1954
SQ FT: 7,500
SALES (est): 608.3K **Privately Held**
WEB: www.cutoutz.com
SIC: 3993 Displays & cutouts, window & lobby

(G-14614)
DANA ANDREWS WOODWORKING
1748 Australian Ave (33404-5302)
PHONE...................................561 882-0444
Dana Andrews, *Principal*
EMP: 7 **EST:** 2006
SALES (est): 98.3K **Privately Held**
SIC: 2431 Millwork

(G-14615)
DAVID S STOYKA
Also Called: Battery Savers
8125 Monetary Dr Ste H6 (33404-1712)
PHONE...................................561 848-2599
David Stoyka, *Principal*
▲ **EMP:** 5 **EST:** 2005
SALES (est): 395.8K **Privately Held**
SIC: 3674 Computer logic modules

(G-14616)
DNA SURFACE CONCEPTS INC
1980 Avenue L (33404-5442)
PHONE...................................561 328-7302
Sean M Kelly, *President*
EMP: 10 **EST:** 2014
SALES (est): 793.9K **Privately Held**
WEB: www.dnasurfaceconcepts.com
SIC: 3479 Metal coating & allied service

(G-14617)
DOCTORS SCENTIFIC ORGANICA LLC (HQ)
Also Called: Smart For Life
1210 W 13th St (33404-6639)
PHONE...................................888 455-9031
Sasson Moulavi, *CEO*
Orlando Morales, *Technical Staff*
EMP: 10 **EST:** 2007
SALES (est): 6.8MM
SALES (corp-wide): 9MM **Publicly Held**
WEB: www.dsoprivatelabel.com
SIC: 2834 Pharmaceutical preparations
PA: Smart For Life, Inc.
990 Biscayne Blvd # 1203
Miami FL 33132
786 749-1221

(G-14618)
E-Z WELD INC
1661 Pres Barack Obama Hw (33404)
PHONE...................................561 844-0241
David Zerfoss, *President*
◆ **EMP:** 36 **EST:** 2006
SALES (est): 6.8MM **Privately Held**
WEB: www.e-zweld.com
SIC: 2952 Roof cement: asphalt, fibrous or plastic

(G-14619)
ELAINE SMITH INC
7740 Byron Dr (33404-3318)
PHONE...................................561 863-3333
Elaine Smith, *President*
EMP: 16 **EST:** 2005
SALES (est): 1.9MM **Privately Held**
WEB: www.elainesmith.com
SIC: 2392 5023 Cushions & pillows; pillowcases

(G-14620)
EXCELLENT PERFORMANCE INC
Also Called: Pettit Racing
4650 Dyer Blvd (33407-1027)
PHONE...................................561 296-0776
Cameron Worth, *President*
▲ **EMP:** 6 **EST:** 1992
SALES (est): 945K **Privately Held**
SIC: 3465 Body parts, automobile: stamped metal

(G-14621)
FAB RITE INC
4636 Dyer Blvd (33407-1027)
PHONE...................................561 848-8181
James Johnson, *CEO*
James Peters, *Vice Pres*
▼ **EMP:** 8 **EST:** 1987
SQ FT: 3,200
SALES (est): 1.4MM **Privately Held**
WEB: www.fabritesteel.com
SIC: 3441 3446 Fabricated structural metal; railings, prefabricated metal

(G-14622)
FISHERMANS CENTER INC
56 E Blue Heron Blvd (33404-4541)
PHONE...................................561 844-5150
William Buckland, *President*
EMP: 7 **EST:** 1955
SQ FT: 2,000

SALES (est): 837.3K **Privately Held**
WEB: www.fishermanscenter.com
SIC: 3949 5941 Fishing tackle, general; fishing equipment

(G-14623)
FLORIDA COCA-COLA BOTTLING CO
6553 Garden Rd (33404-6303)
PHONE...................................561 848-0055
Bernie Roy, *Manager*
EMP: 1046
SQ FT: 68,625
SALES (corp-wide): 33B **Publicly Held**
WEB: www.coca-cola.com
SIC: 2086 Bottled & canned soft drinks
HQ: Florida Coca-Cola Bottling Company
521 Lake Kathy Dr
Brandon FL 33510
813 569-2600

(G-14624)
FLORIDA MACHINE & CASTING CO
8011 Monetary Dr Ste A6 (33404-1702)
PHONE...................................561 655-3771
J Andrew Darien, *President*
EMP: 7 **EST:** 1946
SALES (est): 9.5MM
SALES (corp-wide): 22.8MM **Privately Held**
SIC: 3365 3366 Machinery castings, aluminum; copper foundries; brass foundry; bronze foundry
PA: Tri-State Cast Technologies Co, Inc
926 N Lake St
Boyne City MI 49712
231 582-0452

(G-14625)
GLOBAL MATERIALS COMPANY
2051 W Blue Heron Blvd (33404-5003)
PHONE...................................800 797-3736
Daniel Duke, *President*
EMP: 20 **EST:** 2010
SALES (est): 933.5K **Privately Held**
WEB: www.globalmaterialscompany.com
SIC: 2899 Chemical supplies for foundries

(G-14626)
HARMSCO INC (PA)
Also Called: Harmsco Filtration Products
7169 49th Ter N (33407-1003)
PHONE...................................561 848-9628
Harold H Harms, *President*
Greg Willis, *Principal*
Carl Vesperman, *Vice Pres*
Pascal Vanlindt, *Purchasing*
Lori Cooper, *Accounting Mgr*
◆ **EMP:** 75 **EST:** 1958
SQ FT: 120,000
SALES (est): 14.3MM **Privately Held**
WEB: www.harmsco.com
SIC: 3589 2674 Swimming pool filter & water conditioning systems; water treatment equipment, industrial; bags: uncoated paper & multiwall

(G-14627)
HARRY J HONAN
1051 Singer Dr (33404-2764)
PHONE...................................405 273-9315
EMP: 7 **EST:** 2018
SALES (est): 813.5K **Privately Held**
SIC: 3714 Motor vehicle parts & accessories

(G-14628)
HARTMAN WINDOWS AND DOORS LLC
2107 Blue Heron Blvd W (33404-5005)
PHONE...................................561 296-9600
Ashley Hartman, *Exec VP*
Eddie Bustamante, *Vice Pres*
Denise Beaton, *Office Mgr*
Dale McCallister, *Manager*
Clifford Hartman,
◆ **EMP:** 68 **EST:** 1996
SQ FT: 32,000
SALES (est): 10MM **Privately Held**
WEB: www.hartmanwindows.com
SIC: 2431 5031 Doors, wood; windows, wood; doors & windows

(G-14629)
ILLINOIS TOOL WORKS INC
Also Called: Versachem
2107 W Blue Heron Blvd (33404-5005)
PHONE....................................561 422-9241
Mike Underwood, *Manager*
EMP: 10
SALES (corp-wide): 14.4B **Publicly Held**
WEB: www.itw.com
SIC: 2891 5169 Adhesives & sealants;
chemicals & allied products
PA: Illinois Tool Works Inc.
155 Harlem Ave
Glenview IL 60025
847 724-7500

(G-14630)
INTERAMERICAS BEVERAGES INC
1726 Avenue L (33404-5438)
P.O. Box 1433, West Palm Beach (33402-1433)
PHONE....................................561 881-1340
Claudio Bruehmueller, *President*
Gina M Cieri, *Treasurer*
Gina Cieri, *Treasurer*
Lateef Khan, *Technical Staff*
Camilla Bruehmueller, *Admin Sec*
EMP: 6 **EST:** 2008
SALES (est): 2MM **Privately Held**
WEB: www.interamericasbeverages.com
SIC: 2087 Flavoring extracts & syrups

(G-14631)
IPTS INC
7221 Hvrhill Bus Pkwy # 103 (33407-1007)
PHONE....................................561 844-8216
Richard Diasio, *President*
John Signorino, *Sales Mgr*
Julia Diasio, *Admin Sec*
▲ **EMP:** 13 **EST:** 1980
SQ FT: 20,000
SALES (est): 3.1MM **Privately Held**
WEB: www.iptsinc.com
SIC: 3568 Power transmission equipment

(G-14632)
ITALIAN ROSE GARLIC PDTS LLC (HQ)
1380 W 15th St (33404-5310)
PHONE....................................561 863-5556
Angelo Fraggos, *CEO*
Byard Ebling, *Vice Pres*
John Lemay, *Vice Pres*
Jonathan Pressnell, *Vice Pres*
Stephen Sellier, *Prdtn Mgr*
EMP: 120 **EST:** 1979
SQ FT: 36,000
SALES (est): 45MM
SALES (corp-wide): 583MM **Privately Held**
WEB: www.italian-rose.com
SIC: 2099 2035 6282 Seasonings & spices; pickles, sauces & salad dressings; investment advisory service
PA: Blue Point Capital Partners Llc
127 Public Sq Ste 5100
Cleveland OH 44114
216 535-4700

(G-14633)
JADA TRANSITIONS LLC
Also Called: Your Vizion By Chance
1201 Abaco Ln (33404-6445)
P.O. Box 10972 (33419-0972)
PHONE....................................561 377-8194
La Chanta Thomas-Horne, *CEO*
EMP: 8 **EST:** 2018
SALES (est): 389K **Privately Held**
SIC: 2261 2389 Printing of cotton broadwoven fabrics; apparel & accessories

(G-14634)
K&M POWER SYSTEMS LLC
7641 Central Indus Dr (33404-3431)
PHONE....................................866 945-9100
Derrick E Hoskins, *Principal*
EMP: 5 **EST:** 2018
SALES (est): 475K **Privately Held**
WEB: www.kmpowersystems.com
SIC: 3621 Motors & generators

(G-14635)
K-RAIN MANUFACTURING CORP (PA)
Also Called: K Rain
1640 Australian Ave (33404-5306)
PHONE....................................561 844-1002
Carl Kah Jr, *CEO*
Carl L C Jr Kah, *President*
Deborah K Avis, *Vice Pres*
Gretchen W Kah, *Vice Pres*
Kah Chip, *Opers Mgr*
◆ **EMP:** 46 **EST:** 1971
SQ FT: 25,000
SALES (est): 10.4MM **Privately Held**
WEB: www.krain.com
SIC: 3494 3432 3523 3829 Sprinkler systems, field; lawn hose nozzles & sprinklers; irrigation equipment, self-propelled; rain gauges

(G-14636)
KADASSA INC
3541 Dr Martin Luther Kin (33404-6306)
PHONE....................................954 684-8361
Martin H Arias, *President*
Carmen Arias, *Vice Pres*
EMP: 17 **EST:** 2008
SALES (est): 1.1MM **Privately Held**
SIC: 3281 Curbing, granite or stone

(G-14637)
KENART HOLDINGS LLC
1380 W 15th St (33404-5310)
PHONE....................................561 863-5556
Ken Berger, *President*
Arthur Conlan, *Vice Pres*
Michael Colin, *Opers Mgr*
Beth Gibson, *Sales Staff*
Carlos Revollar, *Maintence Staff*
▲ **EMP:** 110 **EST:** 1979
SQ FT: 40,000
SALES (est): 12.6MM **Privately Held**
SIC: 2099 2035 Seasonings & spices; pickles, sauces & salad dressings

(G-14638)
KEVIN M LUKASIEWICZ
Also Called: Luke's Ice Cream
1025 W 17th St (33404-5407)
PHONE....................................561 588-5853
Kevin Lukasewicz, *President*
Jody Lukasewicz, *Vice Pres*
◆ **EMP:** 16 **EST:** 1984
SQ FT: 25,000
SALES (est): 2.5MM **Privately Held**
WEB: www.lukesicecream.com
SIC: 2024 Ice cream, bulk

(G-14639)
KNIGHT FIRE & SECURITY INC
7513 Central Indus Dr (33404-3429)
PHONE....................................561 471-8221
Jeffrey B Knight, *President*
EMP: 20 **EST:** 2006
SALES (est): 4.2MM **Privately Held**
SIC: 3699 Security devices

(G-14640)
L C ACME BARRICADES
3705 Interstate Park Way (33404-5912)
PHONE....................................561 657-8222
EMP: 9 **Privately Held**
WEB: www.acmebarricades.com
SIC: 3499 7389 Barricades, metal; flagging service (traffic control)
PA: Acme Barricades, L.C.
9800 Normandy Blvd
Jacksonville FL 32221

(G-14641)
LATICRETE INTERNATIONAL INC
6769 White Dr Ste A (33407-1235)
PHONE....................................561 844-4667
Morgan Ericksen, *Plant Mgr*
Luis Cintron, *Opers Staff*
Samuel Stivers, *Production*
Les Solecki, *Manager*
Arthur Mintie, *Technical Staff*
EMP: 25
SQ FT: 30,711

SALES (corp-wide): 135.7MM **Privately Held**
WEB: www.laticrete.com
SIC: 2891 Adhesives, paste; cement, except linoleum & tile; cement, linoleum & tile; epoxy adhesives
PA: Laticrete International, Inc.
1 Laticrete Park N
Bethany CT 06524
203 393-0010

(G-14642)
LAVI ENTERPRISES LLC
Also Called: Doctor Scientific Organica
1210 W 13th St (33404-6639)
PHONE....................................561 721-7170
Margot Hunte, *Principal*
EMP: 57 **EST:** 2012
SALES (est): 3.9MM **Privately Held**
SIC: 2052 Cookies

(G-14643)
LOCKHEED MARTIN CORPORATION
100 E 17th St (33404-5664)
PHONE....................................301 897-6000
John Pfeifler, *Mfg Dir*
Nicholas Asseff, *Engineer*
Ray Boettger, *Engineer*
Kevin Goble, *Engineer*
Joseph Hutchison, *Engineer*
EMP: 52 **Publicly Held**
WEB: www.lockheedmartin.com
SIC: 3812 Search & navigation equipment
PA: Lockheed Martin Corporation
6801 Rockledge Dr
Bethesda MD 20817

(G-14644)
M W M SERVICES INC
7655 Enterprise Dr Ste 4 (33404-3339)
PHONE....................................561 844-0955
Eva Carbone, *President*
Cliff Koziel, *General Mgr*
Koziel Waldek, *Mfg Staff*
EMP: 10 **EST:** 1983
SQ FT: 5,000
SALES (est): 1MM **Privately Held**
WEB: www.mwmservices.com
SIC: 3599 Machine shop, jobbing & repair

(G-14645)
MARINE EXHAUST SYSTEMS INC (PA)
3640 Fiscal Ct Ste D (33404-1781)
PHONE....................................561 848-1238
Woodrow E Woods, *Ch of Bd*
Angela Woods, *President*
Sheila Prieschl, *Vice Pres*
Darrin Woods, *Vice Pres*
Manuela Velasquez, *Human Res Dir*
◆ **EMP:** 78 **EST:** 1973
SQ FT: 52,000
SALES (est): 12MM **Privately Held**
WEB: www.marine-exhaust.com
SIC: 3732 7699 3498 3621 Tenders (small motor craft), building & repairing; professional instrument repair services; fabricated pipe & fittings; motors & generators; industrial machinery & equipment; transportation equipment & supplies

(G-14646)
MICRO TOOL & ENGINEERING INC
7575 Centl Indus Dr Ste A (33404-3422)
PHONE....................................561 842-7381
Fran Lacasse, *President*
Pierre La Casse, *Vice Pres*
Dinah Lacasse, *Vice Pres*
EMP: 15 **EST:** 1968
SQ FT: 10,000
SALES (est): 2MM **Privately Held**
WEB: www.mte-fl.com
SIC: 3599 3841 3769 3728 Machine shop, jobbing & repair; surgical & medical instruments; guided missile & space vehicle parts & auxiliary equipment; aircraft parts & equipment

(G-14647)
MOORES MAR OF PALM BEACHES INC
1410 Avenue E (33404-6199)
PHONE....................................561 841-2235

James P Moores, *President*
EMP: 6 **EST:** 1986
SQ FT: 5,190
SALES (est): 529.2K **Privately Held**
WEB: www.woodenboatrepair.com
SIC: 3732 Yachts, building & repairing

(G-14648)
MOSER AUTOMOTIVE
2391 President Barack Oba (33404-5456)
PHONE....................................561 881-5665
EMP: 40
SALES (est): 1.2MM **Privately Held**
SIC: 2396 3711 Mfg Auto/Apparel Trimming Mfg Motor Vehicle/Car Bodies

(G-14649)
NATIONAL BEDDING COMPANY LLC
3774 Interstate Park Rd N (33404-5908)
PHONE....................................561 840-8491
EMP: 207 **Privately Held**
WEB: jobs.serta.com
SIC: 2515 Mattresses, containing felt, foam rubber, urethane, etc.
HQ: National Bedding Company L.L.C.
2600 Forbs Ave
Hoffman Estates IL 60192

(G-14650)
NEPTUNE RESEARCH INC (PA)
Also Called: N R I
3875 Fiscal Ct Ste 100 (33404-1707)
PHONE....................................561 683-6992
Christopher Lazzar, *President*
Jason Lewis, *President*
Andrea Novak, *Human Res Mgr*
Tammy Bomia, *Regl Sales Mgr*
Tiffany Clark, *Technology*
▼ **EMP:** 38 **EST:** 1982
SQ FT: 27,500
SALES (est): 9.5MM **Privately Held**
WEB: www.cs-nri.com
SIC: 3317 Steel pipe & tubes

(G-14651)
NWL INC
Nwl Capacitors
8050 Monetary Dr (33404-1736)
P.O. Box 10416, West Palm Beach (33419-0416)
PHONE....................................561 848-9009
Robert Seitz, *President*
Arturo Fortuna, *Plant Engr Mgr*
EMP: 106
SALES (corp-wide): 103.4MM **Privately Held**
WEB: www.nwl.com
SIC: 3612 3675 Power transformers, electric; electronic capacitors
HQ: Nwl, Inc.
312 Rising Sun Rd
Bordentown NJ 08505
609 298-7300

(G-14652)
OASE NORTH AMERICA INC
7241 Hvrhill Bus Pkwy # 105 (33407-1014)
PHONE....................................800 365-3880
Andreas Szabados, *CEO*
Michael Selk, *Vice Pres*
Mary Szczecina, *Controller*
Shannon Wenzel, *Cust Mgr*
Birgit Kempe-Heeger, *Admin Sec*
◆ **EMP:** 6 **EST:** 1994
SALES (est): 2.5MM
SALES (corp-wide): 238.5MM **Privately Held**
WEB: us.oase-livingwater.com
SIC: 3594 3524 5251 Fluid power pumps; lawn & garden equipment; pumps & pumping equipment
HQ: Oase International Holding Gmbh
Tecklenburger Str. 161
Horstel NW
545 480-0

(G-14653)
OCEAN BLUE GRAPHICS INC
1841 W 10th St Ste 1 (33404-6415)
PHONE....................................561 881-2022
Alan Yansochak, *President*
EMP: 8 **EST:** 2015

▲ = Import ▼=Export
◆ =Import/Export

SALES (est): 377.2K Privately Held
WEB: www.oceanbluegraphics.com
SIC: 2759 2395 Screen printing; art goods for embroidering, stamped: purchased materials

(G-14654)
OCEAN BLUE GRAPHICS DESIGN INC
1841 W 10th St Ste 1 (33404-6415)
PHONE.................................561 881-2022
Alan Yanoschak, *Vice Pres*
▼ EMP: 6 EST: 2005
SALES (est): 428.2K Privately Held
WEB: www.oceanbluegraphics.com
SIC: 2759 Screen printing

(G-14655)
OCEAN MASTER MARINE INC
837 W 13th St Unit C (33404-6702)
PHONE.................................561 840-0448
Mark Hauptner, *President*
Bonnie Hauptner, *Treasurer*
EMP: 8 EST: 1975
SQ FT: 3,500
SALES (est): 552.3K Privately Held
WEB: www.oceanmasterboats.com
SIC: 3732 Fishing boats: lobster, crab, oyster, etc.: small

(G-14656)
OMEGA LIFT CORPORATION
6701 Garden Rd Ste 1 (33404-5900)
PHONE.................................561 840-0088
Howard Roenkranz, *President*
EMP: 13 EST: 1993
SQ FT: 15,000
SALES (est): 362.7K Privately Held
SIC: 3559 Rubber working machinery, including tires

(G-14657)
PAVER SYSTEMS LLC (HQ)
Also Called: Oldcastle Coastal
7167 Interpace Rd (33407-1023)
PHONE.................................561 844-5202
C Steven Berry, *Mng Member*
▼ EMP: 50 EST: 1974
SQ FT: 30,000
SALES (est): 11.2MM
SALES (corp-wide): 137.2MM Privately Held
WEB: www.oldcastlecoastal.com
SIC: 3272 Concrete products
PA: Eagle Corporation
1020 Harris St
Charlottesville VA 22903
434 971-2686

(G-14658)
PENDULUM ONE INC
Also Called: New Dimensions
6555 Garden Rd Ste 13 (33404-6318)
PHONE.................................561 844-8169
Ira D Smith Jr, *President*
Eleanor J Smith, *Corp Secy*
EMP: 6 EST: 1974
SQ FT: 5,000
SALES (est): 760.1K Privately Held
SIC: 2512 Chairs: upholstered on wood frames; couches, sofas & davenports: upholstered on wood frames; living room furniture: upholstered on wood frames

(G-14659)
PEPSI-COLA BTLG FT LDRDL-PALM
7305 Garden Rd (33404-3490)
PHONE.................................561 848-1000
Anna Davies, *Human Res Mgr*
Chris Morrissey, *Sales Staff*
Joel Condra, *Manager*
Conner Hale, *Manager*
Alejandra Negrin, *Manager*
EMP: 87 EST: 2019
SALES (est): 18.3MM
SALES (corp-wide): 70.3B Publicly Held
WEB: www.pepsico.com
SIC: 2086 Carbonated soft drinks, bottled & canned
PA: Pepsico, Inc.
700 Anderson Hill Rd
Purchase NY 10577
914 253-2000

(G-14660)
PERRY BAROMEDICAL CORPORATION (DH)
3750 Prospect Ave (33404-3443)
PHONE.................................561 840-0395
Kerrigan Turner, *Ch of Bd*
Wayne Mc Cullough, *President*
Michael Richardson, *Vice Pres*
Gregory Colonel, *Prdtn Mgr*
Tim Labuhn, *Electrical Engi*
◆ EMP: 24 EST: 1979
SQ FT: 24,000
SALES (est): 6.4MM
SALES (corp-wide): 2.5MM Privately Held
WEB: www.perrybaromedical.com
SIC: 3841 Surgical & medical instruments

(G-14661)
PILOT CORP OF PALM BEACHES
Also Called: Bradford Septic Tank Company
7117 49th Ter N (33407-1003)
PHONE.................................561 848-2928
Gary Pinkas, *President*
Janet Pinkas, *Vice Pres*
EMP: 14 EST: 1960
SALES (est): 3.3MM Privately Held
WEB: www.bradfordseptic.com
SIC: 3272 1711 Septic tanks, concrete; septic system construction

(G-14662)
PORT PRINTING CO
3532 Broadway (33404-2332)
P.O. Box 9162, West Palm Beach (33419-9162)
PHONE.................................561 848-1402
Ernie Garvey, *President*
Josie Studstille, *Vice Pres*
EMP: 8 EST: 1992
SQ FT: 2,100
SALES (est): 837.2K Privately Held
WEB: www.portprinting.net
SIC: 2752 Commercial printing, offset

(G-14663)
PRIME MOLDING TECHNOLOGIES INC
3765 Investment Ln Ste A (33404-1756)
PHONE.................................561 721-2799
Richard Volpe, *President*
Sergey Shulyak, *Vice Pres*
Dennis Terwilliger, *Vice Pres*
Karin Volpe, *Prdtn Mgr*
Bob Pfretzschner, *Design Engr*
▲ EMP: 25 EST: 2002
SQ FT: 15,000
SALES (est): 6.2MM Privately Held
WEB: www.primemolding.com
SIC: 3089 Injection molding of plastics

(G-14664)
RAMSAY MARINE SERVICES LLC
999 W 17th St Ste 1 (33404-5402)
PHONE.................................561 881-1234
Mark Ebanks, *Principal*
Patricia Humphries, *Principal*
EMP: 11 EST: 2009
SALES (est): 471.9K Privately Held
WEB: www.ramsaymarine.net
SIC: 7692 Welding repair

(G-14665)
REILLY FOAM CORP
3896 Westroads Dr (33407-1227)
PHONE.................................561 842-8090
Parker Rudd, *Sales Staff*
Matt Rider, *Branch Mgr*
Mark Burns, *Manager*
Robert Westerfer, *Manager*
EMP: 15
SQ FT: 67,184
SALES (corp-wide): 26.4MM Privately Held
WEB: www.reillyfoam.com
SIC: 3086 Plastics foam products
PA: Reilly Foam Corp.
751 5th Ave
King Of Prussia PA 19406
610 834-1900

(G-14666)
RELIABLE TOOL AND MACHINE INC
328 W 11th St (33404-7522)
PHONE.................................561 844-8848
Charles Goforth, *President*
EMP: 5 EST: 1988
SQ FT: 1,900
SALES (est): 485.8K Privately Held
WEB: www.reliablema.com
SIC: 3599 Machine shop, jobbing & repair

(G-14667)
RENICK ENTERPRISES INC
1211 W 13th St (33404-6640)
PHONE.................................561 863-4183
Mike Renick, *President*
Mary Ann Renick, *Corp Secy*
Jack Renick, *Vice Pres*
EMP: 8 EST: 1990
SQ FT: 6,300
SALES (est): 790.6K Privately Held
SIC: 3599 Machine shop, jobbing & repair

(G-14668)
RESO INC
1930 Avenue L (33404-5442)
PHONE.................................561 328-8539
Stanislav Kontanistov, *President*
EMP: 6 EST: 2019
SALES (est): 659.3K Privately Held
SIC: 2431 2434 2426 Doors, wood; wood kitchen cabinets; flooring, hardwood

(G-14669)
RGF ENVIRONMENTAL GROUP INC
1101 W 13th St (33404-6701)
PHONE.................................800 842-7771
Ronald G Fink, *CEO*
William Svec, *Vice Pres*
Brian Klaiber, *Purch Mgr*
Tony Julian, *VP Bus Dvlpt*
Lisa Bailey, *Sales Staff*
▲ EMP: 177 EST: 1992
SQ FT: 30,000
SALES (est): 31MM Privately Held
WEB: www.rgf.com
SIC: 3564 3589 Purification & dust collection equipment; water purification equipment, household type

(G-14670)
RGF MARINE ENVMTL TECH INC
Also Called: Rgf Environmental
1101 W 13th St (33404-6701)
PHONE.................................561 848-1826
Ronald G Fink, *President*
Sharon Rinehimer, *Vice Pres*
Bill Svec, *Vice Pres*
Lisa Bailey, *Sales Mgr*
Angela Solland, *Marketing Staff*
◆ EMP: 50 EST: 1992
SALES (est): 10.6MM Privately Held
WEB: www.rgf.com
SIC: 3589 Water treatment equipment, industrial

(G-14671)
RP HIGH PERFORMANCE INC
2391 President Barack Oba (33404-5456)
PHONE.................................561 863-2800
Ian Grunes, *President*
EMP: 12 EST: 2013
SALES (est): 434.1K Privately Held
SIC: 3711 Automobile assembly, including specialty automobiles

(G-14672)
SANCILIO & COMPANY INC
3874 Fiscal Ct Ste 200 (33404-1785)
PHONE.................................561 847-2302
Frederick Sancilio, *President*
EMP: 35
SQ FT: 15,000
SALES (corp-wide): 20MM Privately Held
WEB: www.sancilioandcompany.com
SIC: 2834 5122 8731 Pharmaceutical preparations; drugs & drug proprietaries; commercial physical research
PA: Sancilio & Company, Inc.
2129 N Congress Ave
Riviera Beach FL 33404
561 847-2302

(G-14673)
SC CABINET LLC
7655 Enterprise Dr (33404-3351)
PHONE.................................561 429-5369
EMP: 6 EST: 2018
SALES (est): 439K Privately Held
SIC: 2434 Wood kitchen cabinets

(G-14674)
SECURITY IMPACT GL HLDINGS LLC
Also Called: Safe Glass
6555 Garden Rd Ste 1 (33404-6318)
PHONE.................................561 844-3100
Arthur Marino, *Principal*
▲ EMP: 6 EST: 1998
SALES (est): 460.4K Privately Held
WEB: www.securityimpactglass.com
SIC: 2221 3231 Glass broadwoven fabrics; products of purchased glass

(G-14675)
SEMBCO STL ERECTION MET BLDG
3450 Dr Mrtn Lther King J (33404-6314)
PHONE.................................561 863-0606
Wallace C Sease, *President*
Christie Green, *Corp Secy*
Gloria C Sease, *Vice Pres*
EMP: 10 EST: 1974
SALES (est): 817.2K Privately Held
WEB: www.elbengel.de
SIC: 3441 Fabricated structural metal

(G-14676)
SOLARTECH UNIVERSAL LLC
Also Called: Solar Tech Universal
1800 President Barack Oba (33404-5451)
PHONE.................................561 440-8000
Amit Ramnarain, *Production*
Francisco Cestero, *CFO*
Jodilynn Brown, *Human Res Mgr*
Camille Eads, *Sales Staff*
Louis Koster, *Mng Member*
EMP: 46 EST: 2012
SQ FT: 30,000
SALES (est): 8.6MM Privately Held
WEB: www.solartechuniversal.com
SIC: 3674 Solar cells

(G-14677)
STERLING INDUSTRY LLC
834 W 13th Ct (33404-6727)
PHONE.................................561 845-2440
Arlene Brown, *General Mgr*
Thomas J Sterling Sr,
Aida Sterling,
EMP: 25 EST: 2017
SALES (est): 4MM Privately Held
SIC: 3444 Sheet metalwork

(G-14678)
STERLING STL CSTM ALUM FBRCTON
837 W 13th St (33404-6702)
PHONE.................................561 386-7166
Bryan S Bennett, *Principal*
EMP: 14 EST: 2014
SALES (est): 173.8K Privately Held
WEB: www.sscmetalfabrication.com
SIC: 3441 Fabricated structural metal

(G-14679)
STILLDRAGON NORTH AMERICA LLC
7788 Centl Indus Dr Ste 6 (33404-3450)
PHONE.................................561 845-8009
Brad Newell, *Sales Mgr*
Cory Hoang, *Marketing Staff*
Lawrence Taylor, *Manager*
Jeff Rasmussen, *Manager*
▲ EMP: 9 EST: 2012
SALES (est): 1MM Privately Held
WEB: www.stilldragon.com
SIC: 2085 Distilled & blended liquors

(G-14680)
SUPERIOR WATERWAY SERVICES INC
6701 Garden Rd Ste 1 (33404-5900)
PHONE.................................561 799-5852
Chris J York, *President*
Louis Palermo, *President*
EMP: 10 EST: 1999

SALES (est): 1.2MM **Privately Held**
WEB: www.superiorwaterway.com
SIC: **3589** Water treatment equipment, industrial

(G-14681)
TERA INDUSTRIES INC
Also Called: Industrial Technology
7634 Central Indus Dr (33404-3432)
PHONE...................................561 848-7272
Steven Malone, *President*
Edward Suh, *Vice Pres*
EMP: 30 EST: 1988
SQ FT: 25,000
SALES (est): 2.1MM **Privately Held**
SIC: **7692 3599** Welding repair; machine shop, jobbing & repair

(G-14682)
TITANIUM PROF HYRAULICS
1982 Avenue L Ste A (33404-5401)
PHONE...................................917 929-5044
Sheldon Greenbaum, *President*
EMP: 7 EST: 2017
SALES (est): 596.1K **Privately Held**
SIC: **3356** Titanium

(G-14683)
TOPLINE PRTG & GRAPHICS INC
Also Called: Print Pelican
1401 W 13th St Ste 104 (33404-6609)
PHONE...................................561 881-2267
Alan G Morris, *President*
Grant Morris, *President*
▼ EMP: 45 EST: 1998
SALES (est): 2.6MM **Privately Held**
SIC: **2752** Commercial printing, offset

(G-14684)
TOTAL SIGN SOLUTIONS
7655 Enterprise Dr Ste A8 (33404-3339)
PHONE...................................561 264-2551
EMP: 8 EST: 2018
SALES (est): 399.6K **Privately Held**
WEB: www.3ddynamicsolutions.com
SIC: **3993** Signs & advertising specialties

(G-14685)
US COMPOSITES
6670 White Dr (33407-1232)
PHONE...................................561 588-1001
Mark Ananos, *Principal*
▼ EMP: 5 EST: 2012
SALES (est): 785.8K **Privately Held**
WEB: www.uscomposites.com
SIC: **2821** Plastics materials & resins

(G-14686)
WEST PALM MACHINING & WELDING
4650 Dyer Blvd (33407-1027)
PHONE...................................561 841-2725
Magnolia Mendieta, *CEO*
Steven Mendieta, *General Mgr*
Jose H Mendieta, *Vice Pres*
EMP: 7 EST: 2004
SALES (est): 859.7K **Privately Held**
WEB: www.wpmachine.net
SIC: **3599 7692** Machine shop, jobbing & repair; welding repair

Rockledge
Brevard County

(G-14687)
AAR GOVERNMENT SERVICES INC
Also Called: AAR Wass
Aar Way Ste 101 (32955)
PHONE...................................321 361-3461
EMP: 11
SALES (corp-wide): 1.8B **Publicly Held**
WEB: www.aarcorp.com
SIC: **3728** Aircraft parts & equipment
HQ: Aar Government Services, Inc.
   1100 N Wood Dale Rd
   Wood Dale IL 60191
   630 227-2000

(G-14688)
ACCURATE METAL FINSHG FLA INC (PA)
Also Called: Accurate Metal Finishing Fla
500 Gus Hipp Blvd (32955-4803)
PHONE...................................321 636-4900
EMP: 11
SALES (est): 2.6MM **Privately Held**
SIC: **3399 3471** Primary Metal Products, Nsk

(G-14689)
ACCURATE METAL FINSHG FLA INC
500 Gus Hipp Blvd (32955-4803)
PHONE...................................321 636-4900
Norm Lindner, *President*
Norman Lindner, *President*
EMP: 10 EST: 1988
SALES (est): 1MM **Privately Held**
WEB: www.accuratemetalfl.com
SIC: **3471** Electroplating of metals or formed products

(G-14690)
ADVANCE SOLDER TECHNOLOGY INC
Also Called: Astec
315 Gus Hipp Blvd (32955-4806)
PHONE...................................321 633-4777
Mike Carey, *Principal*
EMP: 12 EST: 2015
SALES (est): 1.2MM **Privately Held**
SIC: **3699** Electrical equipment & supplies

(G-14691)
BERRY SIGNS INC
1740 Huntington Ln (32955-3140)
PHONE...................................321 631-6150
Dennis Berry, *President*
Kyle Berry, *Opers Mgr*
EMP: 5 EST: 1978
SQ FT: 10,000
SALES (est): 523.7K **Privately Held**
WEB: www.berrysigns.com
SIC: **3993** Electric signs; neon signs

(G-14692)
BLACKFIN MANUFACTURING LLC (PA)
1660 Barrett Dr Unit B (32955-3116)
PHONE...................................314 482-2766
Pablo J Gutierrez, *President*
EMP: 7 EST: 2017
SALES (est): 113.1K **Privately Held**
WEB: www.blackfinmfg.com
SIC: **3999** Manufacturing industries

(G-14693)
BREVARD ACHIEVEMENT CENTER INC
1845 Cogswell St (32955-3210)
PHONE...................................321 632-8610
Angie Hoffman, *COO*
Josephine Hughes, *Vice Pres*
Susan McGrath, *Vice Pres*
Andy Vega, *Vice Pres*
Ellen P Brown, *Project Mgr*
EMP: 470 EST: 1969
SQ FT: 35,000
SALES (est): 32.8MM **Privately Held**
WEB: www.bacemploy.com
SIC: **3999 8331 8211** Advertising display products; vocational rehabilitation agency; public elementary & secondary schools

(G-14694)
BRYSON OF BREVARD INC
Also Called: Kendal Signs
580 Gus Hipp Blvd (32955-4803)
PHONE...................................321 636-5116
Kendal Mullen, *President*
Sylvia Mulllen, *Vice Pres*
Anna Johnson, *Opers Staff*
Denise Berg, *Sales Staff*
David Clanton, *Manager*
EMP: 26 EST: 1996
SQ FT: 15,000
SALES (est): 4.3MM **Privately Held**
SIC: **3993** Electric signs

(G-14695)
CABINET DESIGNS OF CENTRAL FLA
596 International Pl (32955-4200)
PHONE...................................321 636-1101
Dan Scott, *President*
Derek Whitten, *Vice Pres*
Sherry Scott, *Treasurer*
EMP: 7 EST: 1982
SQ FT: 5,500
SALES (est): 783.9K **Privately Held**
WEB: www.cabinetdesignscfl.com
SIC: **2434** Wood kitchen cabinets

(G-14696)
CARLEY NIGEL HOLDINGS LLC ✪
1041 Cascade Cir Apt 103 (32955-8079)
PHONE...................................407 212-9341
Nigel Carley, *President*
EMP: 10 EST: 2021
SALES (est): 950K **Privately Held**
WEB: nigel-carley-holdings.business.site
SIC: **2599** Food wagons, restaurant

(G-14697)
CRANCO INDUSTRIES INC
Also Called: Bella Slata Spclty Drssngs Sce
1710 Baldwin St (32955-3205)
PHONE...................................321 690-2695
Ed Cranisky, *President*
Maryalice Kammerer, *Admin Asst*
EMP: 5 EST: 1992
SQ FT: 4,000
SALES (est): 478.2K **Privately Held**
WEB: www.crancofoods.com
SIC: **2099** Dressings, salad: dry mixes

(G-14698)
DELTA GROUP ELECTRONICS INC
Also Called: Delta Group Elec Inc Fla
395 Gus Hipp Blvd (32955-4806)
PHONE...................................321 631-0799
Ron Reef, *General Mgr*
Roland Baggay, *Project Mgr*
Lanny McCay, *Opers Staff*
Loy Hoskins, *Accounts Mgr*
Zoran Jecmenica, *Regl Sales Mgr*
EMP: 75
SQ FT: 34,778
SALES (corp-wide): 116.7MM **Privately Held**
WEB: www.deltagroupinc.com
SIC: **3679 3672** Electronic circuits; printed circuit boards
PA: Delta Group Electronics, Inc.
   4521a Osuna Rd Ne
   Albuquerque NM 87109
   505 883-7674

(G-14699)
DESAPRO INC
435 Gus Hipp Blvd (32955-4804)
PHONE...................................321 674-6804
Dominique E Schinabeck, *President*
Connie Kahler, *Controller*
Veronica Long, *Assistant*
EMP: 39 EST: 2015
SALES (est): 4.6MM **Privately Held**
WEB: www.desapro.com
SIC: **3499** Boxes for packing & shipping, metal

(G-14700)
DESIGNERS CHOICE CABINETRY
285 Barnes Blvd (32955-5325)
PHONE...................................321 632-0772
EMP: 15 EST: 2018
SALES (est): 1.4MM **Privately Held**
WEB: www.dccabinetry.com
SIC: **2434** Wood kitchen cabinets

(G-14701)
DESIGNERS CHOICE CABINETRY INC (DH)
Also Called: Designer's Choice Cabinetry
100 Tgk Cir (32955-3605)
PHONE...................................321 632-0772
James T Murfin, *CEO*
Celeste Zotto, *CFO*
Tammie Kovach, *Manager*
Jeff Duman, *Supervisor*

William Batten, *Technology*
◆ EMP: 2 EST: 1988
SQ FT: 91,000
SALES (est): 18.3MM
SALES (corp-wide): 103.7MM **Privately Held**
WEB: www.dccabinetry.com
SIC: **2434** Wood kitchen cabinets
HQ: Essential Cabinetry Holdings, Inc.
   2838 Grandview Dr
   Simpsonville SC 29680
   321 632-0772

(G-14702)
DG DESIGN AND PRINT CO LLC
4290 Us Highway 1 Ste A (32955-5317)
PHONE...................................321 446-6435
Daniel Rensing, *Principal*
EMP: 9 EST: 2013
SALES (est): 201.4K **Privately Held**
WEB: www.dgdesignandprint.com
SIC: **2752** Commercial printing, lithographic

(G-14703)
DRB PACKAGING LLC
386 Commerce Pkwy (32955-4208)
PHONE...................................321 877-2802
Aryeh Roberts, *CEO*
Craig Day, *President*
Glenn Merithew, *Sales Staff*
Melissa Driggers, *Office Mgr*
EMP: 7 EST: 2015
SQ FT: 18,000
SALES (est): 1.2MM **Privately Held**
WEB: www.drbpkg.com
SIC: **3086** Packaging & shipping materials, foamed plastic

(G-14704)
DRB PACKAGING LLC
386 Commerce Pkwy (32955-4208)
PHONE...................................321 877-2802
EMP: 7 EST: 2015
SQ FT: 18,490
SALES (est): 417.2K **Privately Held**
SIC: **3086** Mfg Plastic Foam Products

(G-14705)
EAST COAST CABINET CO
100 Eyster Blvd (32955-3606)
PHONE...................................321 392-4686
Billy Pentz, *Owner*
EMP: 8 EST: 2005
SALES (est): 1.1MM **Privately Held**
WEB: www.pullmanwest.com
SIC: **2434** Wood kitchen cabinets

(G-14706)
EAST COAST FOAM SUPPLY INC
392 Richard Rd (32955-3183)
PHONE...................................321 433-8231
Joe Lento, *President*
Wendy Zapata-Lento, *Vice Pres*
Wendy Lento, *Executive*
EMP: 9 EST: 2006
SALES (est): 979.3K **Privately Held**
WEB: www.eastcoastfoamsupply.com
SIC: **3086** Plastics foam products

(G-14707)
ENTECH ONSITE SERVICES LLC
280 Gus Hipp Blvd (32955-4801)
PHONE...................................407 956-8980
John P Marhoefer, *Mng Member*
Anne Herzog,
EMP: 5 EST: 2001
SQ FT: 50,000
SALES (est): 563.5K **Privately Held**
WEB: www.entechinnovative.com
SIC: **3599 8711** Carnival machines & equipment, amusement park; engineering services

(G-14708)
EXQUISITE WOOD WORKS BY AL
5565 Schenck Ave Ste 5 (32955-5812)
PHONE...................................321 634-5398
Alvaro Orozco, *Owner*
EMP: 8 EST: 2004

▲ = Import ▼=Export
◆ =Import/Export

SALES (est): 173.6K **Privately Held**
WEB: exquisitewoodworks.blogspot.com
SIC: 2431 Millwork

(G-14709)
FAAC INTERNATIONAL INC (DH)
3160 Murrell Rd (32955-4432)
PHONE...................................904 448-8952
Andrea Marcellan, *CEO*
Dan Ollar, *Corp Secy*
Dawn Joanne Kaiser, *Controller*
Kris Tate,
◆ EMP: 7 EST: 1986
SQ FT: 7,000
SALES (est): 10MM
SALES (corp-wide): 366.9K **Privately Held**
WEB: www.faacusa.com
SIC: 3625 Motor controls, electric
HQ: Faac Partecipazioni Industriali Srl
Via Monaldo Calari 10
Zola Predosa BO 40069
051 758-518

(G-14710)
GAR BUSINESS GROUP LLC
Also Called: Jr Boarts Packaging
386 Commerce Pkwy (32955-4208)
PHONE...................................321 632-5133
Yehuda Roberts,
EMP: 5 EST: 2009
SQ FT: 5,000
SALES (est): 468.3K **Privately Held**
SIC: 2653 Boxes, corrugated: made from
purchased materials

(G-14711)
GLASSER BOAT WORKS INC
1670 Barrett Dr (32955-3116)
PHONE...................................321 626-0061
Jonathan Glasser, *Principal*
EMP: 9 EST: 2016
SALES (est): 296.3K **Privately Held**
WEB: www.glasserboats.net
SIC: 3732 Boat building & repairing

(G-14712)
GOOD 4 TKLC INC
Also Called: Wwgso
5020 Nova Ave (32955-5515)
PHONE...................................321 632-4340
Christopher Brunais, *Vice Pres*
EMP: 7 EST: 2005
SQ FT: 1,829
SALES (est): 630.6K **Privately Held**
SIC: 2851 Paints, asphalt or bituminous

(G-14713)
**HELICAL COMMUNICATION
TECH INC**
634 Barnes Blvd Ste 206 (32955-5217)
PHONE...................................561 762-2823
Salvatore Bologna, *CEO*
EMP: 6 EST: 2013
SQ FT: 1,400
SALES (est): 686.5K **Privately Held**
WEB: www.helicomtech.com
SIC: 3663 Antennas, transmitting & com-
munications

(G-14714)
HMB STEEL CORPORATION
4080 Pines Industrial Ave (32955-5323)
PHONE...................................321 636-6511
Forrest F Brewton, *CEO*
Denise McCammon, *President*
Linda Verderame, *Business Mgr*
Grant McCammon, *COO*
Dina Brewton, *Vice Pres*
EMP: 17 EST: 1998
SQ FT: 29,150
SALES (est): 6MM **Privately Held**
WEB: www.hmbsteel.com
SIC: 3441 Building components, structural
steel

(G-14715)
**HURRICANE SHTTERS CNTL
FLA INC**
3460 Us Highway 1 (32955-4928)
PHONE...................................321 639-2622
Frank M Herrera, *Principal*
EMP: 9 EST: 2011
SALES (est): 266.7K **Privately Held**
SIC: 2431 Door shutters, wood

(G-14716)
**HYDRO PRECISION TUBING
USA LLC (DH)**
100 Gus Hipp Blvd (32955-4701)
PHONE...................................321 636-8147
Sergio Luiz Vendrasco, *President*
Chalonda Gilmore, *Production*
Lisa Douberly, *Treasurer*
Timothy Cordes, *Accounts Mgr*
Caroline Henrich, *Admin Sec*
◆ EMP: 184 EST: 1979
SQ FT: 165,000
SALES (est): 48.8MM **Privately Held**
SIC: 3354 3316 Shapes, extruded alu-
minum; tube, extruded or drawn, alu-
minum; cold finishing of steel shapes

(G-14717)
HYPERFORM INC (HQ)
Also Called: Seadek
5440 Schenck Ave (32955-5803)
PHONE...................................321 632-6503
Kurt D Wilson, *President*
Tiffany Chancey, *General Mgr*
Serenity Gardner, *COO*
Jason Gardner, *Vice Pres*
James C Wilson, *Vice Pres*
◆ EMP: 23 EST: 1982
SQ FT: 4,800
SALES (est): 10.9MM
SALES (corp-wide): 4B **Publicly Held**
WEB: www.hyperforminc.com
SIC: 3949 Surfboards; windsurfing boards
(sailboards) & equipment
PA: Patrick Industries, Inc.
107 W Franklin St
Elkhart IN 46516
574 294-7511

(G-14718)
**INTERFACE TECHNOLOGY
GROUP INC**
2107 Us Highway 1 (32955-3726)
PHONE...................................321 433-1165
Cathy Weber, *President*
Mark Weber, *Treasurer*
Mark J Weber, *Treasurer*
EMP: 6 EST: 1987
SQ FT: 5,000
SALES (est): 1.2MM **Privately Held**
WEB: www.interfacetechnologygroup.com
SIC: 3663 8711 Radio & TV communica-
tions equipment; engineering services

(G-14719)
IRMS INC
2191 Rockledge Dr (32955-5401)
PHONE...................................321 631-1161
Clairece M Knuutila, *President*
Alisa Smith, *Accountant*
Melissa Milito, *Client Mgr*
Yosdany Perez, *Sales Staff*
Charles Aikey, *Sales Executive*
EMP: 10 EST: 1997
SALES (est): 850K **Privately Held**
WEB: www.assuredpartners.com
SIC: 3523 3563 Spreaders, fertilizer;
spraying & dusting equipment

(G-14720)
**JP DONVAN PRCSION
MCHINING LLC**
201 Paint St (32955-5802)
PHONE...................................321 383-1171
John Donovan, *President*
EMP: 8 EST: 2017
SALES (est): 601.5K **Privately Held**
WEB: www.jpdonovan.com
SIC: 3499 Machine bases, metal

(G-14721)
**JW PERFORMANCE TRANSM
INC**
1826 Baldwin St (32955-3207)
PHONE...................................321 632-6205
John Winters Sr, *President*
Helen Winters, *Vice Pres*
John Winters Jr, *Treasurer*
Tracy Winters, *Admin Sec*
▲ EMP: 28 EST: 1976
SQ FT: 40,000

SALES (est): 4.5MM **Privately Held**
WEB: www.racewithjw.com
SIC: 3714 3568 3566 Transmissions,
motor vehicle; power transmission equipment; speed changers, drives & gears

(G-14722)
K-KRAFT CABINETS INC
1751 Cogswell St (32955-3208)
PHONE...................................321 632-8800
Robert Poloski, *President*
Susan Poloski, *Corp Secy*
EMP: 9 EST: 1990
SQ FT: 15,000
SALES (est): 862.9K **Privately Held**
WEB: www.kkraftcabinets.com
SIC: 2434 Wood kitchen cabinets

(G-14723)
K-KRAFT INDUSTRIES INC
1751 Cogswell St (32955-3208)
PHONE...................................321 632-8800
Robert Poloski Jr, *President*
Susan Poloski, *Corp Secy*
EMP: 10 EST: 1972
SQ FT: 3,500
SALES (est): 370.6K **Privately Held**
WEB: www.kkraftcabinets.com
SIC: 2434 Wood kitchen cabinets

(G-14724)
KENDAL SIGNS INC
580 Gus Hipp Blvd (32955-4803)
PHONE...................................321 636-5116
Kendal Mullen, *Principal*
EMP: 45 EST: 2016
SALES (est): 3.4MM **Privately Held**
WEB: www.kendalsigns.com
SIC: 3993 Electric signs

(G-14725)
**LOCKHEED MARTIN
CORPORATION**
2900 Murrell Rd (32955-4205)
PHONE...................................321 635-7621
Scott Higbie, *Opers Mgr*
Gary L Chung, *Systs Engr*
Richard Fjeldheim, *Engineer*
Cindy Schmidt, *Manager*
EMP: 435 **Publicly Held**
WEB: www.gyrocamsystems.com
SIC: 3812 Search & navigation equipment
PA: Lockheed Martin Corporation
6801 Rockledge Dr
Bethesda MD 20817

(G-14726)
LRG SOLUTIONS INC
1950 Murrell Rd Ste 3 (32955-3607)
PHONE...................................321 978-1050
Andrew M Lash, *Principal*
EMP: 9 EST: 2017
SALES (est): 442.2K **Privately Held**
WEB: www.lrgsolutions.com
SIC: 3272 Concrete products

(G-14727)
LRM INDUSTRIES INTL INC
Also Called: L R M
135 Gus Hipp Blvd (32955-4702)
PHONE...................................321 635-9797
E Gary Cook, *Ch of Bd*
Jim Callough, *President*
Christine Nowak, *CFO*
EMP: 20 EST: 2009
SALES (est): 4MM **Privately Held**
WEB: www.lrmind.com
SIC: 2821 8711 Polyesters; engineering
services

(G-14728)
MAGNETIC AUTOMATION CORP
3160 Murrell Rd (32955-4432)
PHONE...................................321 635-8585
Dieter Schwald, *CEO*
Thomas Braunwalder, *President*
Bruce Pate, *Vice Pres*
Hubert Giesbertz, *Treasurer*
Jean K Wortham, *Admin Sec*
◆ EMP: 31 **EST:** 1990
SQ FT: 31,004
SALES (est): 4.8MM **Privately Held**
WEB: www.macgolfcharity.com
SIC: 3829 7521 Measuring & controlling
devices; parking structure

(G-14729)
**MAINSTREAM ENGINEERING
CORP**
200 Yellow Pl (32955-5327)
PHONE...................................321 631-3550
Robert Scaringe, *President*
Kipp Koonce, *Plant Mgr*
Melissa Horstmann, *Production*
Lisa Rineholt, *Purch Dir*
Jim Chynoweth, *Purch Mgr*
EMP: 24 EST: 1986
SQ FT: 41,900
SALES (est): 13.6MM **Privately Held**
WEB: www.mainstream-engr.com
SIC: 3585 Refrigeration equipment, com-
plete

(G-14730)
MARCONI LINE INC
1870 Huntington Ln (32955-3156)
PHONE...................................321 639-1130
Francis Eades, *President*
Ernest Marconi, *Vice Pres*
Mark Marconi, *Vice Pres*
James Eades, *Treasurer*
Peter Raffaele, *Admin Sec*
EMP: 19 EST: 1988
SALES (est): 3.6MM **Privately Held**
WEB: www.marconiline.com
SIC: 3089 3949 Closures, plastic; bowl
covers, plastic; sporting & athletic goods

(G-14731)
MATRIX COMPOSITES INC
275 Barnes Blvd (32955-5325)
PHONE...................................321 633-4480
Farrokh Batliwala, *President*
Michael J Savinelli, *Vice Pres*
Tim Murphy, *QC Mgr*
Tami Green, *Engineer*
Jennifer Swain, *Engineer*
EMP: 106 EST: 1993
SQ FT: 30,000
SALES (est): 1.9MM
SALES (corp-wide): 2.7B **Publicly Held**
WEB: www.matrixcomp.com
SIC: 2821 Plastics materials & resins
PA: Itt Inc.
1133 Westchester Ave N-100
White Plains NY 10604
914 641-2000

(G-14732)
MERCY D LLC
Also Called: Cosmos Ice Cream
3320 Thurloe Dr (32955-6062)
PHONE...................................321 212-7712
Tanisha B Davis, *CEO*
EMP: 6 EST: 2018
SALES (est): 507.7K **Privately Held**
SIC: 2024 Ice cream & frozen desserts

(G-14733)
METAL ROOF FACTORY INC
599 Gus Hipp Blvd (32955-4810)
PHONE...................................321 632-8300
Thomas E Bruckner, *President*
EMP: 9 EST: 1983
SQ FT: 10,000
SALES (est): 1.7MM **Privately Held**
WEB: www.metalrooffactory.com
SIC: 3444 Metal roofing & roof drainage
equipment; roof deck, sheet metal

(G-14734)
NAROH MANUFACTURING LLC
185 Gus Hipp Blvd (32955-4702)
PHONE...................................321 806-4875
Robert Horan, *President*
EMP: 10 EST: 2012
SALES (est): 1MM **Privately Held**
SIC: 3484 Guns (firearms) or gun parts, 30
mm. & below

(G-14735)
NETWORKED SOLUTIONS INC
Also Called: Essentialnet Solutions
7145 Turner Rd Ste 102 (32955-5723)
PHONE...................................321 259-3242
John Redrup, *President*
EMP: 6 EST: 1997
SQ FT: 2,500
SALES (est): 1MM **Privately Held**
SIC: 7372 7374 Prepackaged software;
computer graphics service

(G-14736)
OATH CORPORATION
395 Richard Rd Ste D (32955-3182)
PHONE....................................407 221-7288
David Golloher, *President*
EMP: 5 **EST:** 2013
SQ FT: 2,000
SALES (est): 953.1K **Privately Held**
WEB: www.oathammo.com
SIC: 3482 3484 Small arms ammunition;
small arms

(G-14737)
PERRY FIBERGLAS PRODUCTS INC
5415 Village Dr (32955-6570)
PHONE....................................321 609-9036
Thomas E Pulliam, *President*
Richard G Chesrown, *Principal*
Drew H Severs, *Principal*
Michelle Hardway, *HR Admin*
▲ **EMP:** 20 **EST:** 1984
SQ FT: 34,000
SALES (est): 5.6MM **Privately Held**
WEB: www.perryfiberglass.com
SIC: 3089 Plastic containers, except foam

(G-14738)
PHANTOM PRODUCTS INC
474 Barnes Blvd (32955-5321)
PHONE....................................321 690-6729
Damien McDermott, *President*
EMP: 15 **EST:** 2004
SQ FT: 45,000
SALES (est): 4.6MM **Privately Held**
WEB: www.phantomlights.com
SIC: 3647 Vehicular lighting equipment

(G-14739)
PRECISION CIRCUITS INC
Also Called: PCI
550 Gus Hipp Blvd (32955-4821)
PHONE....................................321 632-8629
EMP: 20
SQ FT: 5,000
SALES (est): 3.4MM **Privately Held**
SIC: 3672 Mfg Printed Circuit Boards

(G-14740)
R & D SURF
488 Gus Hipp Blvd (32955-4800)
P.O. Box 372811, Satellite Beach (32937-0811)
PHONE....................................321 636-4456
Richard P Carroll, *President*
Marc Baker, *Manager*
▼ **EMP:** 10 **EST:** 1992
SQ FT: 4,800
SALES (est): 609.5K **Privately Held**
WEB: www.randdsurf.com
SIC: 3949 Surfboards

(G-14741)
RICHARDS PAINT MFG CO INC (PA)
200 Paint St (32955-5899)
PHONE....................................321 636-6200
Edward J Richard Sr, *President*
Eric S Richard, *President*
Tom Griffey, *Vice Pres*
Pati Lambert, *Vice Pres*
Debbie Richard, *Vice Pres*
▼ **EMP:** 60 **EST:** 1954
SQ FT: 40,000
SALES (est): 27MM **Privately Held**
WEB: www.richardspaint.com
SIC: 2851 5231 Paints & paint additives;
paint

(G-14742)
ROCKLEDGE PHRM MFG LLC
Also Called: RPM
417 Richard Rd (32955-3154)
PHONE....................................321 636-0717
Kl Spear, *Mng Member*
Lorri Renaud,
EMP: 17 **EST:** 1984
SQ FT: 30,000
SALES (est): 2.8MM **Privately Held**
WEB: www.rpmrx.com
SIC: 2834 Proprietary drug products
PA: Spear Pharmaceuticals, Inc.
1250 Sussex Tpke Ste G
Naples FL 34110

(G-14743)
SAFE INDUSTRIES INC
396 Gus Hipp Blvd Ste B (32955-4814)
PHONE....................................321 639-8646
Joanne Abernathy, *Principal*
Jesse Ayers, *Accounting Mgr*
Karen Alexander, *Sales Staff*
Tonya McCullough, *Manager*
Todd Hecker, *Director*
EMP: 10 **EST:** 2009
SALES (est): 2.1MM **Privately Held**
SIC: 2869 Fuels

(G-14744)
SAILOR MADE CUSTOM WOODWORKS L
571 Haverty Ct Ste H (32955-3610)
PHONE....................................805 587-1197
EMP: 5 **EST:** 2019
SALES (est): 303.5K **Privately Held**
SIC: 2431 Millwork

(G-14745)
SAPA PRCSION TUBING ADRIAN INC
100 Gus Hipp Blvd (32955-4701)
PHONE....................................321 636-8147
Greg Hall, *President*
Mike Hammer, *Plant Mgr*
Doug McCrary, *Plant Mgr*
Jim Vaughan, *Production*
Amanda Potts, *Purchasing*
▲ **EMP:** 82 **EST:** 1924
SQ FT: 180,000
SALES (est): 3.2MM **Privately Held**
SIC: 3354 3463 Aluminum extruded products; aluminum forgings

(G-14746)
SOLTEC ELECTRONICS LLC
1001 Pelican Ln (32955-6409)
PHONE....................................321 288-5689
Dawn Gluskin,
EMP: 5 **EST:** 2008
SALES (est): 376.2K **Privately Held**
WEB: www.consumershelper.com
SIC: 3679 Electronic circuits

(G-14747)
SOLUTIONS MANUFACTURING INC
570 Haverty Ct (32955-3600)
PHONE....................................321 848-0848
Patrick McDonough, *CEO*
Roger A Dixson, *President*
Luis Govantes, *General Mgr*
Tina Nash, *General Mgr*
Eric Coleman, *Engineer*
▲ **EMP:** 65 **EST:** 1997
SALES (est): 13.2MM **Privately Held**
WEB: www.solutionsmfg.com
SIC: 3672 Printed circuit boards

(G-14748)
SPACE COAST HYDRAULICS INC
1265 Us Highway 1 (32955-2711)
PHONE....................................321 504-6006
Daniel Ferretti, *President*
Karin Ferretti, *Vice Pres*
EMP: 13 **EST:** 2016
SALES (est): 1.1MM **Privately Held**
SIC: 3531 3492 3599 3052 Construction
machinery; hose & tube fittings & assemblies, hydraulic/pneumatic; hose, flexible metallic; hose, pneumatic: rubber or rubberized fabric; pistons & valves

(G-14749)
T AND C SALES INC
1950 Murrell Rd Ste 10 (32955-3607)
PHONE....................................321 632-0920
Robert C Cook, *President*
Sara Cook, *Treasurer*
EMP: 6 **EST:** 1978
SQ FT: 7,500
SALES (est): 3MM **Privately Held**
WEB: www.tcsalesinc.com
SIC: 3354 Aluminum extruded products

(G-14750)
TECVALCO USA INC
270 Barnes Blvd (32955-5319)
PHONE....................................866 427-3444
Michael Menger, *President*

EMP: 41 **EST:** 2015
SQ FT: 70,000
SALES (est): 6.4MM **Privately Held**
WEB: www.tecvalco.com
SIC: 3533 Oil & gas field machinery

(G-14751)
TEP MANUFACTURING CO
1950 Murrell Rd Ste 5 (32955-3607)
PHONE....................................321 632-1417
Ted Chrostowski, *Owner*
EMP: 5 **EST:** 1988
SALES (est): 372.7K **Privately Held**
SIC: 3599 Machine & other job shop work

(G-14752)
TRESE INC
Also Called: Trese Printing
2040 Murrell Rd (32955-3603)
PHONE....................................321 632-7272
Michael J F Trese, *President*
Rick Francis, *General Mgr*
EMP: 17 **EST:** 1978
SQ FT: 25,000
SALES (est): 1MM **Privately Held**
SIC: 2752 Commercial printing, offset

(G-14753)
V AND N ADVANCED AUTO SYS LLC
415 Gus Hipp Blvd (32955-4804)
PHONE....................................321 504-6440
Tito C Visi, *President*
Philip A Napolitano, *Vice Pres*
Jason Gass, *Engineer*
◆ **EMP:** 8 **EST:** 2004
SQ FT: 20,000
SALES (est): 3MM **Privately Held**
WEB: www.vnaas.com
SIC: 3479 5065 8742 3724 Coating of
metals & formed products; semiconductor devices; automation & robotics consultant; research & development on aircraft engines & parts

(G-14754)
WAGNER PAVERS CONTRACTOR
403 Hawk St Ste A (32955-3251)
PHONE....................................321 633-5131
Wagner Dutra, *President*
EMP: 6 **EST:** 2001
SQ FT: 3,424
SALES (est): 988.7K **Privately Held**
WEB: www.wagnerpavers.com
SIC: 3531 Pavers

(G-14755)
WHOLESALE SIGN SUPERSTORE INC
580 Gus Hipp Blvd (32955-4803)
PHONE....................................321 212-8458
EMP: 8 **EST:** 2019
SALES (est): 450.9K **Privately Held**
WEB: www.wholesalesignsuperstore.com
SIC: 3993 Signs & advertising specialties

Rocky Point
Hillsborough County

(G-14756)
ALL FLORIDA MARKETING
3001 N Rocky Point Dr E (33607-5810)
PHONE....................................813 281-4641
Jim Lee, *President*
EMP: 5 **EST:** 1998
SALES (est): 403.8K **Privately Held**
SIC: 2851 Paints & allied products

Roseland
Indian River County

(G-14757)
GYPSY MINING INC
Also Called: Cmk
12855 79th Ave (32957)
P.O. Box 144 (32957-0144)
PHONE....................................772 589-5547
Christopher M Kirrie, *President*
Robert C Kirrie, *Vice Pres*
EMP: 8 **EST:** 1982

SQ FT: 4,700
SALES (est): 750K **Privately Held**
SIC: 3369 3949 Lead castings, except die-castings; fishing tackle, general; skin diving equipment, scuba type

Rotonda West
Charlotte County

(G-14758)
US FUELS INC
928 Rotonda Cir (33947-1838)
PHONE....................................254 559-1212
David Jakobot, *Principal*
EMP: 10 **EST:** 2009
SALES (est): 618.3K **Privately Held**
SIC: 2869 Fuels

Royal Palm Beach
Palm Beach County

(G-14759)
ATELIER WOODWORKING
587 105th Ave N Unit 28 (33411-4333)
PHONE....................................561 386-0811
Alex Cosiuck, *President*
Simona Costiuc, *Officer*
EMP: 10 **EST:** 1992
SALES (est): 225.5K **Privately Held**
SIC: 2431 Millwork

(G-14760)
BON BRANDS INC
10299 Sthrn Blvd Unit 21 (33411-4337)
PHONE....................................800 590-7911
Jason Russo, *Owner*
EMP: 15 **EST:** 2020
SALES (est): 666.2K **Privately Held**
SIC: 2841 5122 5169 Soap & other detergents; drugs, proprietaries & sundries; chemicals & allied products

(G-14761)
BROOKLINK GREEN FUELS INC
7 Amherst Ct Apt B (33411-7913)
PHONE....................................561 514-1725
Florette Baldwin, *Principal*
EMP: 7 **EST:** 2008
SALES (est): 83.3K **Privately Held**
SIC: 2869 Fuels

(G-14762)
DAKIM INC
Also Called: Print It Plus
11420 Okeechobee Blvd D (33411-8703)
PHONE....................................561 790-0884
Kimberly Leland, *CEO*
David T Leland, *President*
Kimberly H Leland, *Vice Pres*
Sarah Cole, *Prdtn Mgr*
Mary Miller, *Manager*
EMP: 11 **EST:** 1988
SQ FT: 2,480
SALES (est): 1.8MM **Privately Held**
SIC: 3571 2752 1799 3993 Computers,
digital, analog or hybrid; commercial printing, offset; sign installation & maintenance; signs & advertising specialties; art copy: publishing & printing; posters: publishing & printing; banners, flags, decals & posters

(G-14763)
ESCUE ENERGY LLC
11903 Southern Blvd (33411-7644)
PHONE....................................561 762-1486
Sohail Quraeshi, *President*
EMP: 7 **EST:** 2015
SALES (est): 157.9K **Privately Held**
SIC: 3511 Turbines & turbine generator sets

(G-14764)
FUELTEC SYSTEMS LLC
11388 Okeechobee Blvd (33411-8705)
PHONE....................................828 212-1141
EMP: 6 **EST:** 2019
SALES (est): 976.3K **Privately Held**
WEB: www.fueltecsystems.com
SIC: 3559 Special industry machinery

▲ = Import ▼=Export
◆ =Import/Export

(G-14765)
HORIZON INDUSTRIES INC
180 Business Park Way B1 (33411-1726)
P.O. Box 212951 (33421-2951)
PHONE...............................561 315-5439
Julianna L Tristano, *President*
Josie Perez, *Manager*
Jason Rosenberg, *IT/INT Sup*
EMP: 10 **EST:** 2011
SALES (est): 853.3K **Privately Held**
WEB: www.horizonindustriesinc.com
SIC: 3999 Atomizers, toiletry

(G-14766)
HOUGHTON MIFFLIN HARCOURT PUBG
100 Gibraltar St (33411-1148)
PHONE...............................561 951-5518
Diane Fluty, *Mktg Dir*
Laura Fulton, *Consultant*
Mike Hiers, *Network Enginr*
Melissa Smith, *Associate*
EMP: 16
SALES (corp-wide): 1B **Privately Held**
WEB: www.hmhco.com
SIC: 2731 Textbooks: publishing only, not
printed on site
HQ: Houghton Mifflin Harcourt Publishing
Company
125 High St Ste 900
Boston MA 02110
617 351-5000

(G-14767)
IMPRINTS INTERNATIONAL INC
150 Businefl Pk Way Ste 2 (33411)
PHONE...............................561 202-0105
Amit Jain, *President*
EMP: 5 **EST:** 2004
SALES (est): 343.8K **Privately Held**
SIC: 3552 Silk screens for textile industry

(G-14768)
J-KO COMPANY
200 Business Park Way D (33411-1742)
PHONE...............................561 795-7377
Jon Kolquist, *Owner*
EMP: 7 **EST:** 2012
SALES (est): 1.1MM **Privately Held**
WEB: www.j-kocompany.com
SIC: 3589 Car washing machinery

(G-14769)
LANDTECH DATA CORPORATION
Also Called: Landtech Software Co.
1460 Royal Palm Bch Blvd (33411-1608)
PHONE...............................561 790-1265
Edward W Bell, *President*
Anna Flyam, *Software Dev*
EMP: 15 **EST:** 1979
SQ FT: 3,500
SALES (est): 2MM **Privately Held**
WEB: www.landtechdata.com
SIC: 7372 7371 Prepackaged software;
custom computer programming services

(G-14770)
MOLDED MOMENTS ART
1477 Running Oak Ln (33411-6153)
PHONE...............................954 913-0793
Molded Moments, *Principal*
EMP: 7 **EST:** 2012
SALES (est): 107.7K **Privately Held**
SIC: 3089 Molding primary plastic

(G-14771)
NILSSON NILS
Also Called: Advanced Elctronic Diagnostics
1128 Royal Palm Bch (33411-1607)
PHONE...............................561 790-2400
Nils Nilsson, *President*
EMP: 5 **EST:** 1989
SALES (est): 730.5K **Privately Held**
WEB: www.aedhealth.com
SIC: 2835 In vitro & in vivo diagnostic sub-
stances

(G-14772)
ROBERT OJEDA METALSMITH INC
10151 Yeoman Ln (33411-3142)
PHONE...............................561 507-5511
Robert J Ojeda, *Principal*
EMP: 7 **EST:** 2017

SALES (est): 430.1K **Privately Held**
WEB: www.rometalsmith.com
SIC: 3441 Fabricated structural metal

(G-14773)
WELLINGTON LEATHER LLC
Also Called: Arborossa Leather
320 Business Park Way (33411-1744)
PHONE...............................561 790-0034
Leonardo Mandelbaum, *Mng Member*
Alejandro Mandelbaum,
▲ **EMP:** 6 **EST:** 2013
SALES (est): 486K **Privately Held**
SIC: 3199 Boxes, leather

Ruskin
Hillsborough County

(G-14774)
B & M PRECISION INC
1225 4th St Sw (33570-5348)
PHONE...............................813 645-1188
Miroslav Mitusina, *CEO*
Fred Hopf, *General Mgr*
Wilfredo Malave, *COO*
Charlene Smith, *Vice Pres*
Steve Raith, *Mfg Dir*
▲ **EMP:** 275 **EST:** 1980
SQ FT: 50,000
SALES (est): 33.5MM **Privately Held**
WEB: www.bmprecision.com
SIC: 3841 Surgical & medical instruments

(G-14775)
BICENTRICS INC
Also Called: Slabs Plus
319 1st St Ne (33570-3629)
P.O. Box 729 (33575-0729)
PHONE...............................813 649-0225
John Haskins, *President*
EMP: 14 **EST:** 1998
SQ FT: 3,000
SALES (est): 764K **Privately Held**
WEB: www.slabsplus.com
SIC: 3851 Ophthalmic goods

(G-14776)
ENGINESAVER
123 Castillo Rd (33570-5613)
PHONE...............................813 493-3861
Travis Muse, *Principal*
EMP: 7 **EST:** 2011
SALES (est): 142.3K **Privately Held**
SIC: 3519 Internal combustion engines

(G-14777)
FARMCO MANUFACTURERS INC
1110 4th St Sw (33570-4534)
P.O. Box 1375 (33575-1375)
PHONE...............................813 645-0611
Harold Millis, *President*
Tina Millis, *Vice Pres*
▲ **EMP:** 18 **EST:** 1978
SQ FT: 16,600
SALES (est): 4.1MM **Privately Held**
SIC: 3523 Farm machinery & equipment

(G-14778)
FIVE STAR SCREENING LLC ✪
1615 Broad Winged Hawk Dr
(33570-4955)
PHONE...............................800 788-8315
Danielle Garrett,
EMP: 5 **EST:** 2021
SALES (est): 461.4K **Privately Held**
SIC: 2899

(G-14779)
JAN AND JEAN INC
Also Called: Mid State Plastics
1010 E Shell Point Rd (33570-5000)
P.O. Box 188 (33575-0188)
PHONE...............................813 645-0680
Richard L Donati, *President*
Jan Donati, *Treasurer*
◆ **EMP:** 6 **EST:** 1983
SQ FT: 5,000
SALES (est): 832.5K **Privately Held**
WEB: www.midstateplastics.com
SIC: 3089 2673 Plastic containers, except
foam; bags: plastic, laminated & coated

(G-14780)
KNOX ALUMINUM INC
720 4th St Sw Ste B (33570-4512)
PHONE...............................813 645-3529
Kenneth Knox, *President*
EMP: 15 **EST:** 1982
SALES (est): 4.6MM **Privately Held**
WEB: www.knoxaluminum.com
SIC: 3448 Screen enclosures

(G-14781)
WEIMER MECHANICAL SERVICES INC
Also Called: Weimer Services
1701 E Shell Point Rd (33570-5029)
PHONE...............................813 645-2258
Robert M Weimer, *CEO*
Susan Weimer, *Vice Pres*
Robert Ray Weimer, *Treasurer*
▼ **EMP:** 6 **EST:** 1981
SQ FT: 5,000
SALES (est): 744.9K **Privately Held**
WEB: www.weimerservices.com
SIC: 7692 7699 Welding repair; mechani-
cal instrument repair

Safety Harbor
Pinellas County

(G-14782)
ADVANCE TOOL COMPANY INC
940 Harbor Lake Ct (34695-2307)
PHONE...............................727 726-8907
James R Hill, *President*
Wesley Hill, *Corp Secy*
EMP: 10 **EST:** 1980
SQ FT: 7,200
SALES (est): 1MM **Privately Held**
WEB: www.advancetoolcompany.com
SIC: 3599 Machine shop, jobbing & repair

(G-14783)
BLITZ MICRO TURNING INC
945 Harbor Lake Ct (34695-2303)
P.O. Box 667 (34695-0667)
PHONE...............................727 725-5005
Mark Blitz, *President*
Herman Blitz, *Vice Pres*
Belinda Banister, *Admin Sec*
EMP: 9 **EST:** 1976
SQ FT: 5,000
SALES (est): 690K **Privately Held**
SIC: 3451 3843 Screw machine products;
dental equipment

(G-14784)
CLEAR-VUE INC (PA)
905 Delaware St (34695-3840)
P.O. Box 86 (34695-0086)
PHONE...............................727 726-5386
David Desaulniers, *President*
Carol A Desaulniers, *Corp Secy*
EMP: 20 **EST:** 1970
SQ FT: 1,200
SALES (est): 2.8MM **Privately Held**
WEB: www.clearvuewindows.net
SIC: 3083 1751 3496 3444 Window
sheeting, plastic; window & door (prefabri-
cated) installation; miscellaneous fabri-
cated wire products; sheet metalwork

(G-14785)
DECO POWER LIFT INC
Also Called: Deco Boat Lifts
1041 Harbor Lake Dr (34695-2311)
PHONE...............................727 736-4529
Richard Massell, *President*
Betty Massell, *Safety Mgr*
David Gilbo, *Foreman/Supr*
▼ **EMP:** 10 **EST:** 1994
SALES (est): 1.7MM **Privately Held**
WEB: www.decoboatlift.com
SIC: 3536 Boat lifts

(G-14786)
EMMETI USA LLC
202 10th Ave N Ste A (34695-3480)
PHONE...............................813 490-6252
Luis F Garcia, *Manager*
Fausto Savazzi,
EMP: 12 **EST:** 2005
SALES (est): 755.5K **Privately Held**
SIC: 3535 Robotic conveyors

(G-14787)
FELLOWSHIP ENTERPRISES INC
995 Harbor Lake Dr Ste 10 (34695-2309)
P.O. Box 276 (34695-0276)
PHONE...............................727 726-5997
Peter A Bragdon, *President*
Shirley A Bragdon, *Vice Pres*
EMP: 7 **EST:** 1988
SQ FT: 4,000
SALES (est): 627K **Privately Held**
WEB: www.countertopsflorida.com
SIC: 3089 1799 Synthetic resin finished
products; counter top installation

(G-14788)
JACOBSEN MANUFACTURING INC (PA)
Also Called: Jacobsen Homes
600 Packard Ct (34695-3001)
P.O. Box 368 (34695-0368)
PHONE...............................727 726-1138
William Robert Jacobsen, *CEO*
Dennis Schrader, *President*
Jon Pierce, *General Mgr*
Sidney Boughton, *Vice Pres*
Grace Lauer, *Consultant*
EMP: 205 **EST:** 1959
SQ FT: 2,000
SALES (est): 49.3MM **Privately Held**
WEB: www.jachomes.com
SIC: 2451 3448 2452 Mobile homes, ex-
cept recreational; prefabricated metal
buildings; prefabricated wood buildings

(G-14789)
K & M CUSTOM CABINETRY INC
977 Withlacoochee St A (34695-3466)
PHONE...............................727 791-3993
Michael Carr, *President*
Ronnie Wheelock, *Managing Dir*
Donna Carr, *Vice Pres*
Haleigh Wheelock, *Office Mgr*
EMP: 5 **EST:** 1990
SALES (est): 638.2K **Privately Held**
WEB: kmcabs.business.site
SIC: 2434 Wood kitchen cabinets

(G-14790)
MASTER ALUM & SEC SHUTTER CO
950 Harbor Lake Ct (34695-2307)
PHONE...............................727 725-1744
Mario E Calleja, *President*
Melinda Calleja, *Vice Pres*
EMP: 8 **EST:** 1987
SALES (est): 735.9K **Privately Held**
WEB: www.masteralum.com
SIC: 3442 1751 Shutters, door or window:
metal; window & door (prefabricated) in-
stallation

(G-14791)
MASTERCUT TOOL CORP
Also Called: McT
965 Harbor Lake Dr (34695-2309)
P.O. Box 902 (34695-0902)
PHONE...............................727 726-5336
Michael A Shaluly, *President*
Vito Ippolito, *Production*
Ylli Hysenlika, *Engineer*
Joel Lopez, *Engineer*
Donald Babinsky, *Technical Staff*
▲ **EMP:** 50 **EST:** 1985
SQ FT: 37,000
SALES (est): 12.4MM **Privately Held**
WEB: www.mastercuttool.com
SIC: 3545 Files, machine tool

(G-14792)
MIKE C LOHMEYER
Also Called: Harbor Woodworks
1010 Park Ct Bldg A (34695-3869)
PHONE...............................727 669-0808
Mike Lohmeyer, *Owner*
EMP: 7 **EST:** 1996
SALES (est): 490.7K **Privately Held**
WEB: www.harborwoodworks.com
SIC: 2431 Millwork

(G-14793)
PALEO SIMPLIFIED LLC
605 S Bayshore Blvd (34695-4003)
PHONE...............................813 446-5969
Tamie D Lange, *Vice Pres*

EMP: 7 EST: 2011
SALES (est): 104K **Privately Held**
WEB: www.paleosimplified.com
SIC: 2052 Cookies & crackers

(G-14794)
PARADIGM PLASTICS INC
912 3rd St N Ste D (34695-2222)
PHONE.................................727 797-3555
Tommy Edwards, *President*
William Luke Edwards, *Vice Pres*
EMP: 5 EST: 1986
SALES (est): 960K **Privately Held**
SIC: 2821 Plastics materials & resins

(G-14795)
SAWYER PRODUCTS INC
605 7th Ave N (34695-3027)
P.O. Box 188 (34695-0188)
PHONE.................................727 725-1177
Kurt Avery, *President*
Mary Bausum, *General Mgr*
John Smith, *General Mgr*
Cesar Santiago, *Purch Agent*
Susan Glick, *Office Admin*
▲ EMP: 20 EST: 1984
SQ FT: 16,000
SALES (est): 8MM **Privately Held**
WEB: www.sawyer.com
SIC: 3842 2879 3589 First aid, snake bite
& burn kits; agricultural chemicals; water
filters & softeners, household type

(G-14796)
SIGNATURE SIGNS INC
Also Called: Creative Wood Graphics
1450 10th St S Unit C (34695-4100)
PHONE.................................727 725-1044
Mark J Dinkel, *President*
Tom Bowers, *Vice Pres*
EMP: 10 EST: 1974
SQ FT: 7,500
SALES (est): 854.4K **Privately Held**
WEB: www.signaturesignsusa.com
SIC: 3993 Signs, not made in custom sign
painting shops

(G-14797)
SMARTCART EV LLC
245 10th Ave N (34695-3415)
PHONE.................................727 906-7001
Joshua Hooks, *CEO*
Jarrett Thorne, *Vice Pres*
EMP: 11
SALES (est): 670.2K **Privately Held**
SIC: 3694 Ignition apparatus & distributors

(G-14798)
SPAULDING CRAFT INC
Also Called: Florida Columns
1053 Harbor Lake Dr (34695-2311)
P.O. Box 357 (34695-0357)
PHONE.................................727 726-2316
Wayne C Spaulding, *President*
Wayne R Spaulding, *President*
Joan Spaulding, *Corp Secy*
▲ EMP: 18 EST: 1976
SQ FT: 18,900
SALES (est): 1.7MM **Privately Held**
WEB: www.spauldingcraft.com
SIC: 3544 3299 Industrial molds; columns,
papier mache or plaster of paris

(G-14799)
STREAMLINE EXTRUSION INC
3105 Ashwood Ln (34695-5002)
P.O. Box 1173 (34695-1173)
PHONE.................................727 796-4277
Paul Hendess, *President*
Susan Hendess, *Vice Pres*
EMP: 10 EST: 2006
SALES (est): 661.8K **Privately Held**
WEB: www.streamlineextrusion.com
SIC: 3083 Plastic finished products, lami-
nated

(G-14800)
VANLYMPIA INC
Also Called: Starmark
605 7th Ave N (34695-3027)
P.O. Box 908 (34695-0908)
PHONE.................................727 725-5055
Richard Lyke, *President*
EMP: 6 EST: 1985
SQ FT: 5,500

SALES (est): 477.5K **Privately Held**
SIC: 3842 First aid, snake bite & burn kits

(G-14801)
WATERFORD PRESS INC
1040 Harbor Lake Dr (34695-2310)
P.O. Box 1195, Dunedin (34697-1195)
PHONE.................................727 812-0140
James Kavanagh, *President*
Mary Carstensen, *Production*
Jenna Risano, *Accounts Mgr*
▲ EMP: 31 EST: 1994
SQ FT: 1,000
SALES (est): 2.6MM **Privately Held**
WEB: www.waterfordpress.com
SIC: 2741 Guides: publishing only, not
printed on site

(G-14802)
**WATERFORD PUBLISHING
GROUP LLC**
Also Called: Waterford Press
1040 Harbor Lake Dr (34695-2310)
PHONE.................................727 812-0140
Brad Hite, *Controller*
Heather Mann, *Manager*
Jill Kavanagh Smith,
James Kavanagh,
EMP: 15 EST: 2011
SALES (est): 947.8K **Privately Held**
WEB: www.waterfordpress.com
SIC: 2741 Guides: publishing only, not
printed on site

Saint Augustine
St. Johns County

(G-14803)
1565 WOODWORKS LLC
17 Linda Mar Dr (32080-6961)
PHONE.................................904 347-7664
Amber Halcrow, *Principal*
EMP: 8 EST: 2017
SALES (est): 493.3K **Privately Held**
WEB: www.1565woodworks.com
SIC: 2431 Millwork

(G-14804)
**2G CENRGY PWR SYSTEMS
TECH INC (HQ)**
Also Called: 2g - Cenergy
205 Commercial Dr (32092-0587)
PHONE.................................904 342-5988
Paul Glenister, *CEO*
Christian Grotholt, *Director*
Phillip Turwitt, *Director*
◆ EMP: 35 EST: 2009
SQ FT: 60,000
SALES (est): 12.1MM **Privately Held**
WEB: www.2g-energy.com
SIC: 3519 Internal combustion engines

(G-14805)
ABHAI LLC
194 Inlet Dr (32080-3813)
PHONE.................................215 579-1842
Frank Nekoranik, *CPA*
EMP: 7 EST: 2014
SALES (est): 168.4K **Privately Held**
SIC: 2834 Solutions, pharmaceutical

(G-14806)
**ADVANTAGE EARTH PRODUCTS
INC**
Also Called: AEP Group
317 Vicki Towers Dr (32092-1757)
PHONE.................................904 329-1430
Robert Randle, *President*
Georges Boyazis, *COO*
Marcela Randle, *CFO*
▲ EMP: 13 EST: 2009
SALES (est): 4.3MM **Privately Held**
SIC: 3084 Plastics pipe

(G-14807)
ALUMINUM PRODUCTS
1701 Lakeside Ave Unit 12 (32084-4116)
PHONE.................................904 829-9995
Laura Beckham, *Principal*
EMP: 7 EST: 2010
SALES (est): 134.6K **Privately Held**
SIC: 2952 Siding materials

(G-14808)
ALY FABRICATION INC
31 N Saint Augustine Blvd (32080-3780)
PHONE.................................724 898-2990
EMP: 6
SQ FT: 20,000
SALES (est): 996.7K **Privately Held**
SIC: 3443 Mfg Fabricated Plate Work

(G-14809)
**AML EXTREME
POWDERCOATING**
7750 Us Highway 1 S (32086-7919)
PHONE.................................904 794-4313
Maurice Brown, *Principal*
EMP: 8 EST: 2007
SALES (est): 358.8K **Privately Held**
SIC: 3479 Coating of metals & formed
products

(G-14810)
ANYWHERE GPS LLC
43 Sierras Loop (32086-9041)
PHONE.................................949 468-6842
Michael Shriner, *Manager*
EMP: 7 EST: 2017
SALES (est): 229.2K **Privately Held**
SIC: 3663

(G-14811)
ATLANTIC CANDY COMPANY
115 Whetstone Pl (32086-5772)
PHONE.................................904 429-7250
Henry M Whetstone Jr, *President*
Janice F Whetstone, *Vice Pres*
Philip Beale, *Technician*
EMP: 35 EST: 2015
SALES (est): 3.5MM **Privately Held**
WEB: www.atlanticcandy.com
SIC: 2066 Chocolate

(G-14812)
B & B OF SAINT AUGUSTINE INC
Also Called: B & B Trailers and Accessories
2875 Us Highway 1 S (32086-6303)
PHONE.................................904 829-6855
Thomas E Bennett Jr, *President*
T E Bennett Jr, *Vice Pres*
Debbie Bennett, *Admin Sec*
EMP: 7 EST: 1979
SQ FT: 3,375
SALES (est): 500K **Privately Held**
SIC: 7692 Welding repair

(G-14813)
**B & B TRAILERS AND
ACCESSORIES**
2875 Us Highway 1 S (32086-6303)
PHONE.................................904 829-6855
Thomas Bennett Jr, *President*
Deborah Bennett, *Admin Sec*
EMP: 15 EST: 2004
SALES (est): 1.1MM **Privately Held**
WEB: www.bbtrailersinc.com
SIC: 3714 5013 Trailer hitches, motor ve-
hicle; motor vehicle supplies & new parts;
truck parts & accessories; trailer parts &
accessories

(G-14814)
BACKYARD FEED LLC
6400 County Road 214 (32092-9301)
PHONE.................................813 846-5995
Sean J Hellein, *President*
EMP: 8 EST: 2020
SALES (est): 250.6K **Privately Held**
WEB: www.backyardfeedco.com
SIC: 2048 Chicken feeds, prepared

(G-14815)
BESTEST INTERNATIONAL INC
Also Called: Bestest Medical
701 Market St Ste 111-201 (32095-8800)
PHONE.................................714 974-8837
John Bogart, *President*
Jim Roberts, *Manager*
EMP: 16 EST: 1988
SQ FT: 9,200
SALES (est): 2.8MM **Privately Held**
SIC: 3823 3841 Industrial instrmnts
msrmnt display/control process variable;
surgical & medical instruments

(G-14816)
BODHI TREE WOODWORK INC
60 N Saint Augustine Blvd (32080-3753)
PHONE.................................904 540-2655
Thomas Boyle, *Principal*
EMP: 7 EST: 2016
SALES (est): 110K **Privately Held**
SIC: 2431 Millwork

(G-14817)
BROOKING INDUSTRIES INC
104 Liberty Center Pl (32092-0919)
PHONE.................................954 533-0765
Richard K Brooking, *President*
Spencer Brooking, *COO*
Edward Spencer Brooking, *Vice Pres*
Melissa Ratliff, *Sales Staff*
▲ EMP: 6 EST: 1997
SALES (est): 851.2K **Privately Held**
WEB: www.brookingindustries.com
SIC: 3999 Barber & beauty shop equip-
ment

(G-14818)
**BROWN JORDAN COMPANY
LLC (DH)**
475 W Town Pl Ste 200 (32092-3653)
PHONE.................................904 495-0717
Gene Moriarty, *CEO*
Jordan Brown, *Principal*
James B Hardy, *Division Pres*
Frank Taff, *Vice Pres*
Beth Lee, *Controller*
◆ EMP: 100 EST: 1995
SQ FT: 120,000
SALES (est): 59.4MM
SALES (corp-wide): 324MM **Privately
Held**
SIC: 2514 2511 Metal lawn & garden furni-
ture; wood lawn & garden furniture

(G-14819)
BUSHHOG N BLADE WORK
2846 Usina Road Ext (32084-0557)
PHONE.................................904 669-2764
George Smith, *Principal*
EMP: 7 EST: 2009
SALES (est): 476.6K **Privately Held**
SIC: 3523 Farm machinery & equipment

(G-14820)
CEMEX CNSTR MTLS FLA LLC
Also Called: Readymix
233 Industry Pl (32095-8601)
PHONE.................................904 827-0369
Brian Bussel, *Branch Mgr*
EMP: 7
SQ FT: 13,180 **Privately Held**
SIC: 3273 Ready-mixed concrete
HQ: Cemex Construction Materials Florida,
Llc
1501 Belvedere Rd
West Palm Beach FL 33406

(G-14821)
CENTERLINE STEEL LLC
Also Called: Centerline Brackets
208 W Davis Industrial Dr (32084-8413)
PHONE.................................904 217-4186
Tracy Smith, *CEO*
Bryan McCary, *Opers Dir*
Chris Smith,
EMP: 25 EST: 2013
SQ FT: 9,000
SALES (est): 2.7MM **Privately Held**
WEB: www.countertopbracket.com
SIC: 3499 Fire- or burglary-resistive prod-
ucts

(G-14822)
CORE OUTDOORS INC
134 Poole Blvd (32095-8402)
PHONE.................................904 215-6866
EMP: 10 EST: 2018
SALES (est): 577.8K **Privately Held**
SIC: 2499 Fencing, docks & other outdoor
wood structural products

(G-14823)
**DAVID DOBBS ENTERPRISES
INC (PA)**
Also Called: Menu Design
4600 Us 1 N (32095-5701)
PHONE.................................904 824-6171
David F Dobbs, *President*

▲ = Import ▼=Export
◆ =Import/Export

Peggy A Dobbs, *Senior VP*
John V Maguire, *Vice Pres*
Evelyn Torres, *Opers Staff*
Lindsay Lavercombe, *Sales Staff*
◆ **EMP:** 100 **EST:** 1980
SQ FT: 39,500
SALES (est): 20.3MM **Privately Held**
WEB: www.menudesigns.com
SIC: 2789 2679 2759 2389 Binding only:
books, pamphlets, magazines, etc.; book
covers, paper; menus: printing; apparel
for handicapped; signs & advertising spe-
cialties

(G-14824)
DAVID E ASHE SAWMILL
5440 State Road 13 N (32092-1531)
PHONE..............................904 377-4800
David Ashe, *Principal*
EMP: 12 **EST:** 2006
SALES (est): 239.7K **Privately Held**
WEB: www.ashesawmill.com
SIC: 2421 Sawmills & planing mills, gen-
eral

(G-14825)
DEFENSHIELD INC
7000 Us Highway 1 N # 401 (32095-8359)
PHONE..............................904 679-3942
William White, *President*
Robert Faille, *Vice Pres*
Jordan Settle, *Opers Staff*
Chris Pechtold, *Program Mgr*
EMP: 7 **EST:** 2002
SALES (est): 939.2K **Privately Held**
WEB: www.defenshield.com
SIC: 3231 3442 3448 7382 Products of
purchased glass; metal doors, sash &
trim; prefabricated metal buildings; secu-
rity systems services; engineering serv-
ices

(G-14826)
DENTZ DESIGN SCREEN PRTG
LLC
56 S Dixie Hwy Ste 3 (32084-0306)
PHONE..............................609 303-0827
Carolyn Dentz, *Principal*
EMP: 7 **EST:** 2011
SALES (est): 156.2K **Privately Held**
SIC: 2752 Commercial printing, litho-
graphic

(G-14827)
DESIGNATED SPORTS INC
Also Called: Designated Diver
3545 Us 1 S Ste A9 (32086-6330)
PHONE..............................904 797-9469
Lori Webb, *President*
Gary Webb, *Vice Pres*
▼ **EMP:** 10 **EST:** 1988
SQ FT: 25,000
SALES (est): 856K **Privately Held**
WEB: www.designatedsports.com
SIC: 2759 Screen printing

(G-14828)
DOERRS CSTM CABINETS TRIM
LLC
1300 Wildwood Dr (32086-9113)
PHONE..............................904 540-7024
Carl Doerr, *Owner*
EMP: 15 **EST:** 2014
SALES (est): 523.7K **Privately Held**
SIC: 2434 Wood kitchen cabinets

(G-14829)
DOERRS CUSTOM CABINETS &
TRIM
1761 Dobbs Rd (32084-6217)
PHONE..............................904 540-7024
EMP: 9 **EST:** 2018
SALES (est): 432.1K **Privately Held**
SIC: 2434 Wood kitchen cabinets

(G-14830)
ENDORPHIN FARMS INC
3255 Parker Dr (32084-0892)
PHONE..............................904 824-2006
Scott Martin, *President*
EMP: 12 **EST:** 1998
SALES (est): 1.6MM **Privately Held**
WEB: www.endorphinfarms.com
SIC: 3221 Bottles for packing, bottling &
canning: glass

(G-14831)
EVANS CUSTOM CABINETRY
LLC
3595 Fortner Rd (32084-0847)
PHONE..............................904 829-1973
Robert Evans, *Mng Member*
Candice Evans,
EMP: 8 **EST:** 1991
SALES (est): 653.7K **Privately Held**
WEB: www.evanscustomcabinetry.com
SIC: 2434 Wood kitchen cabinets

(G-14832)
FDA SIGNS LLC
Also Called: Fastsigns 176501
2303 N Ponce De Leon Blvd A
(32084-2606)
PHONE..............................904 800-1776
EMP: 12 **EST:** 2018
SALES (est): 911.9K **Privately Held**
WEB: www.fastsigns.com
SIC: 3993 Signs & advertising specialties

(G-14833)
FILTHY RICH OF JACKSONVILLE
41b King St (32084-4483)
PHONE..............................904 342-5092
Debra K Martin, *Principal*
EMP: 7 **EST:** 2007
SALES (est): 74.1K **Privately Held**
WEB: www.filthyrichofstaug.com
SIC: 3423 Jewelers' hand tools

(G-14834)
FUEL PRODUCTIONS LLC
1960 Us Highway 1 S 199 (32086-4233)
PHONE..............................904 342-7826
Jay S Ruditis, *Principal*
EMP: 7 **EST:** 2009
SALES (est): 521.7K **Privately Held**
WEB: www.fuelproductions.net
SIC: 2869 Fuels

(G-14835)
GATOR DOOR EAST INC
2150 Dobbs Rd (32086-5249)
PHONE..............................904 824-2827
Ron Platts, *President*
Barbara Platts, *Corp Secy*
Tim Callum, *Vice Pres*
Mike Ausili, *Sales Staff*
Chris Dupont, *Sales Staff*
EMP: 50 **EST:** 1990
SQ FT: 25,000
SALES (est): 9.8MM **Privately Held**
WEB: www.gatordooreast.com
SIC: 2431 3429 Doors & door parts & trim,
wood; moldings, wood: unfinished & pre-
finished; locks or lock sets

(G-14836)
GOLF AMERICA SOUTHWEST
FLA INC
Also Called: World Golf Collection
2049 Crown Dr (32092-3606)
PHONE..............................904 688-0280
Timothy J Constantine, *President*
▲ **EMP:** 5 **EST:** 1995
SALES (est): 411.3K **Privately Held**
SIC: 2329 Men's & boys' sportswear & ath-
letic clothing

(G-14837)
GREENWAY BRIDGE LLC
1340 Kings Estate Rd (32086-5358)
PHONE..............................631 901-4561
Timothy J Kris II, *Manager*
EMP: 8 **EST:** 2020
SALES (est): 491K **Privately Held**
SIC: 3429 Manufactured hardware (gen-
eral)

(G-14838)
H20LOGY INC
3233 County Road 208 (32092-0517)
PHONE..............................904 829-6098
Steve Brandvold, *Manager*
EMP: 5 **EST:** 1988
SQ FT: 3,500
SALES (est): 500K **Privately Held**
SIC: 2819 5074 Brine; water purification
equipment

(G-14839)
H2C BRANDS LLC (PA)
Also Called: Volt Resistance
110 Cumberland Park Dr # 205
(32095-8901)
PHONE..............................904 342-7485
Chris Haffly, *President*
▲ **EMP:** 5 **EST:** 2012
SALES (est): 321.6K **Privately Held**
WEB: www.voltheat.com
SIC: 2253 Warm weather knit outerwear,
including beachwear

(G-14840)
HYDRAULICNET LLC
Also Called: Hydraulic Net
6980 Us Highway 1 N # 107 (32095-8374)
PHONE..............................630 543-7630
Stephen L Smith,
▲ **EMP:** 14 **EST:** 1997
SQ FT: 10,000
SALES (est): 1.7MM **Privately Held**
WEB: www.hydraulic.net
SIC: 3566 Reduction gears & gear units for
turbines, except automotive

(G-14841)
HYDRO EXTRUSION USA LLC
200 Riviera Blvd (32086-7801)
PHONE..............................904 794-1500
Trond Gjellesvik, *Managing Dir*
Olaf Wigstol, *Managing Dir*
Erika Ahlqvist, *Exec VP*
Odd Ivar Biller, *Vice Pres*
Roland Kovacs, *Vice Pres*
EMP: 300
SQ FT: 250,000 **Privately Held**
SIC: 3354 3444 3316 Tube, extruded or
drawn, aluminum; pipe, extruded, alu-
minum; shapes, extruded aluminum;
sheet metalwork; cold finishing of steel
shapes
HQ: Hydro Extrusion Usa, Llc
6250 N River Rd Ste 5000
Rosemont IL 60018

(G-14842)
HYDRO REMELT
200 Riviera Blvd (32086-7801)
PHONE..............................904 794-1500
Peter Kukielski, *Director*
Marianne Wiinholt, *Director*
EMP: 10 **EST:** 2013
SALES (est): 1.9MM **Privately Held**
SIC: 3354 Aluminum extruded products

(G-14843)
ICEMULE COMPANY INC
601 S Ponce De Leon Blvd (32084-4227)
PHONE..............................904 325-9012
James Collie, *President*
▲ **EMP:** 19 **EST:** 2012
SALES (est): 3.3MM **Privately Held**
WEB: www.icemulecoolers.com
SIC: 3086 Ice chests or coolers (portable),
foamed plastic

(G-14844)
IDEAL DEALS LLC
Also Called: Ideal Aluminum
3200 Parker Dr (32084-0891)
PHONE..............................386 736-1700
Douglas J Brady, *Co-CEO*
Michael Siegel, *Co-CEO*
Lori Greaves, *COO*
Douglas Brady, *Marketing Mgr*
Chris Pavlik, *Manager*
◆ **EMP:** 107 **EST:** 2010
SQ FT: 170,000
SALES (est): 36.4MM **Privately Held**
WEB: www.ideal-ap.com
SIC: 3334 3479 Primary aluminum; alu-
minum coating of metal products

(G-14845)
IDEAL GAS LLC
3200 Parker Dr (32084-0891)
PHONE..............................904 417-6470
Bob Bell, *Area Mgr*
Leo Kirby, *COO*
Adrian Ibarra, *Sales Mgr*
Buddy Dingman, *Sales Staff*
Richard Poremba, *Sales Staff*
EMP: 5 **EST:** 2015

SALES (est): 2.2MM **Privately Held**
WEB: www.ideal-gas.com
SIC: 1321 Propane (natural) production

(G-14846)
INDUSTRIAL CNSTR SVCS
DSIGN IN (PA)
Also Called: Icon
4405 Sartillo Rd Ste A (32095-5240)
PHONE..............................904 827-9795
James Dewitt, *President*
Ronald Avery, *Chairman*
Jason Hoff, *Plant Mgr*
John Lamela, *Project Mgr*
Steve Jenkins, *Admin Sec*
EMP: 96 **EST:** 1981
SALES (est): 27.4MM **Privately Held**
WEB: www.icon-industrial.com
SIC: 3554 Paper mill machinery: plating,
slitting, waxing, etc.

(G-14847)
INSPIRED SURF BOARDS
2310 Dobbs Rd (32086-5218)
PHONE..............................904 347-8879
Philip A Baggett, *Owner*
EMP: 8 **EST:** 2000
SALES (est): 251.4K **Privately Held**
SIC: 3949 Surfboards

(G-14848)
INTELBASE SECURITY
CORPORATION
400 Night Hawk Ln (32080-7983)
PHONE..............................703 371-9181
Jose Rodriguez, *Principal*
EMP: 10 **EST:** 2016
SALES (est): 327.5K **Privately Held**
SIC: 3674 Microprocessors

(G-14849)
JLS OF ST AUGUSTINE INC
Also Called: Flamingo Travel
3161 Mac Rd (32086-5488)
PHONE..............................904 797-6098
Lynne S Stephenson, *Principal*
EMP: 7 **EST:** 2010
SALES (est): 94.3K **Privately Held**
WEB: www.staugustine.com
SIC: 2711 Newspapers, publishing & print-
ing

(G-14850)
JOHNSONS WOODWORK
INCORPORATED
175 Cumberland Park Dr (32095-8954)
PHONE..............................904 826-4100
EMP: 7
SQ FT: 800
SALES: 500K **Privately Held**
SIC: 2431 Mfg Millwork

(G-14851)
JORDAN BROWN INC (HQ)
Also Called: Winston Furniture Company Ala
475 W Town Pl Ste 200 (32092-3653)
PHONE..............................904 495-0717
Gene J Moriarty, *President*
Dave Biancofiore, *President*
Chris Carmicle, *President*
Bill Echols, *President*
David Kennedy, *President*
◆ **EMP:** 7 **EST:** 1945
SALES (est): 324MM **Privately Held**
WEB: www.brownjordaninc.com
SIC: 2512 2514 Chairs: upholstered on
wood frames; couches, sofas & daven-
ports: upholstered on wood frames; metal
household furniture; metal lawn & garden
furniture; metal kitchen & dining room fur-
niture
PA: Jordan Brown Acquisition Co Inc
475 W Town Pl Ste 200
Saint Augustine FL 32092
904 495-0717

(G-14852)
JRH SPORT INDUSTRIES INC
6550 State Road 16 (32092-2109)
PHONE..............................904 940-3381
EMP: 6
SQ FT: 1,600
SALES (est): 420K **Privately Held**
SIC: 3949 Mfg Sporting/Athletic Goods

(G-14853)
KJ REYNOLDS INC
Also Called: Standard Printing & Copy Ctr
3520 Ag Ctr Dr Ste 306 (32092)
PHONE..................................904 829-6488
Sandi Reynolds, *President*
EMP: 7 EST: 2003
SQ FT: 3,000
SALES (est): 902.2K **Privately Held**
WEB: www.kjreynoldsandassociates.com
SIC: 2759 Commercial printing

(G-14854)
LATITUDE 29 PUBLISHING
2104 Sandy Branch Pl (32092-4749)
PHONE..................................904 429-7889
Diane Thompson, *Principal*
EMP: 7 EST: 2011
SALES (est): 49K **Privately Held**
WEB: www.latitude29paddleboard.com
SIC: 2741 Miscellaneous publishing

(G-14855)
LYONS MACHINE TOOL CO INC
5115 Cres Technical Ct (32086-5625)
PHONE..................................904 797-1550
Kevin Lyons, *President*
Tim Dzioba, *General Mgr*
Christine Lyons, *Vice Pres*
Mike Haller, *Manager*
Kyle Lyons, *Manager*
EMP: 29 EST: 1965
SQ FT: 2,500
SALES (est): 3MM **Privately Held**
WEB: www.lyonsmachinetool.com
SIC: 3599 Machine shop, jobbing & repair

(G-14856)
MATSCHEL OF FLAGLER INC
239 Marshside Dr (32080-5836)
PHONE..................................386 446-4595
EMP: 7 EST: 2010
SALES (est): 71.5K **Privately Held**
SIC: 3312 Chemicals & other products de-
rived from coking

(G-14857)
MCKENZIE MARINE LLC
100 Douglas Park Dr (32084-8409)
PHONE..................................904 770-2488
Jourdan McKenzie Spires,
EMP: 6 EST: 2019
SALES (est): 567.7K **Privately Held**
WEB: www.mckenziemarine.com
SIC: 3732 Yachts, building & repairing

(G-14858)
MERIDIAN CABLE LLC
141 Senora Ct (32095-4838)
PHONE..................................904 770-4687
Karin Kinzalow, *Vice Pres*
Leslie Roland, *Warehouse Mgr*
Cyndi Zurek, *Manager*
Richard M Kinzalow,
▲ EMP: 14 EST: 2003
SALES (est): 2.4MM **Privately Held**
WEB: www.meridiancableassemblies.com
SIC: 2298 5051 7389 Cable, fiber; cable,
wire;

(G-14859)
METAL TECHNOLOGIES GROUP INC
1105 Registry Blvd (32092-3802)
PHONE..................................904 429-7727
Kimberly Sand, *Principal*
EMP: 12 EST: 2017
SALES (est): 65.4K **Privately Held**
SIC: 3599 Machine shop, jobbing & repair

(G-14860)
NEWCASTLE SHIPYARDS LLC
106 Dory Rd (32086-5714)
PHONE..................................386 312-0000
Nicholas Keith, *Opers Staff*
Whinter Leonesio, *Office Mgr*
Kevin Keith, *Mng Member*
Debbie Keith,
Deborah B Keith,
▲ EMP: 105 EST: 2002
SALES (est): 8.8MM **Privately Held**
WEB: www.newcastleyacht.com
SIC: 3731 Shipbuilding & repairing

(G-14861)
NORTHROP GRMMAN FELD SPPORT SV (DH)
5000 Us Highway 1 N B02-60
(32095-6200)
PHONE..................................904 810-4665
Ed Faye, *CEO*
▲ EMP: 60 EST: 1996
SALES (est): 51.3MM **Publicly Held**
SIC: 3721 3761 Aircraft; guided missiles &
space vehicles
HQ: Northrop Grumman Systems Corpora-
tion
2980 Fairview Park Dr
Falls Church VA 22042
703 280-2900

(G-14862)
NORTHROP GRMMAN TCHNCAL SVCS I
5000 Us Highway 1 N (32095-6200)
PHONE..................................904 825-3300
Steve Timmerman, *Manager*
EMP: 23 **Publicly Held**
SIC: 3812 Search & navigation equipment
HQ: Northrop Grumman Technical Serv-
ices, Inc.
7575 Colshire Dr
Mc Lean VA 22102
703 556-1144

(G-14863)
NORTHROP GRUMMAN SYSTEMS CORP
Also Called: Defense Systems Sector
5000 Us Highway 1 N (32095-6200)
PHONE..................................904 825-3300
Brian Mahoney, *Vice Pres*
Cecil Privett, *Materials Mgr*
Scott Burton, *Engineer*
Alexander Deloach, *Engineer*
Dan Edwards, *Engineer*
EMP: 680 **Publicly Held**
WEB: www.northropgrumman.com
SIC: 3721 Airplanes, fixed or rotary wing;
research & development on aircraft by the
manufacturer
HQ: Northrop Grumman Systems Corpora-
tion
2980 Fairview Park Dr
Falls Church VA 22042
703 280-2900

(G-14864)
NORTHROP GRUMMAN SYSTEMS CORP
125 International Golf (32095-8461)
PHONE..................................904 810-5957
Steve Congro, *General Mgr*
Sharlyn Anderson, *Purchasing*
Kyle Curtis, *Analyst*
EMP: 7 **Publicly Held**
WEB: www.northropgrumman.com
SIC: 3812 Search & navigation equipment
HQ: Northrop Grumman Systems Corpora-
tion
2980 Fairview Park Dr
Falls Church VA 22042
703 280-2900

(G-14865)
NORTHROP GRUMMAN SYSTEMS CORP
5000 Us Highway 1 N (32095-6200)
PHONE..................................904 825-3300
Robert Thomas, *Branch Mgr*
Alice Reed, *Analyst*
EMP: 231 **Publicly Held**
WEB: www.northropgrumman.com
SIC: 3721 3761 Airplanes, fixed or rotary
wing; guided missiles, complete
HQ: Northrop Grumman Systems Corpora-
tion
2980 Fairview Park Dr
Falls Church VA 22042
703 280-2900

(G-14866)
NWH PUBLISHING LLC
659 Los Caminos St (32095-7418)
PHONE..................................904 217-3911
Kevin B Carpenter, *Branch Mgr*
EMP: 9
SALES (corp-wide): 73.7K **Privately Held**
SIC: 2741 Miscellaneous publishing

PA: Nwh Publishing, Llc.
130 Corridor Rd Unit 577
Ponte Vedra Beach FL

(G-14867)
OLD CITY GATES
2008 W Lymington Way (32084-1103)
PHONE..................................904 669-7938
Joanna Sunderman, *Principal*
EMP: 7 EST: 2005
SALES (est): 187.5K **Privately Held**
WEB: www.oldcity.com
SIC: 2431 Garage doors, overhead: wood

(G-14868)
OLD CITY MARINE LLC
Also Called: Nbk Maintenance
76 Dockside Dr Ste 112 (32084-4229)
PHONE..................................904 252-6887
Sean Riley, *Mng Member*
Amy Riley,
EMP: 7 EST: 2019
SALES (est): 450.6K **Privately Held**
WEB: www.nbkmaintenance.com
SIC: 3731 Patrol boats, building & repair-
ing

(G-14869)
OLD PORT GROUP LLC
Also Called: Home Mag, The
1301 Plntn Is Dr S 206b (32080-3108)
PHONE..................................904 819-5812
Mark Matrazzo,
EMP: 10 EST: 2006
SQ FT: 2,500
SALES (est): 2.1MM **Privately Held**
SIC: 2721 Magazines: publishing & printing

(G-14870)
PARTS CAGE INC ✪
280 Business Park Cir # 412 (32095-8835)
PHONE..................................904 373-7800
Thomas Corrao, *President*
EMP: 10 EST: 2021
SALES (est): 515.8K **Privately Held**
WEB: www.mypartscage.com
SIC: 3728 Aircraft parts & equipment

(G-14871)
PELICAN WOODWORKS INC
4975 Moultrie Reserve Ct (32086-5658)
PHONE..................................904 687-5759
Carl M Rose, *Principal*
EMP: 7 EST: 2015
SALES (est): 64.9K **Privately Held**
SIC: 2431 Millwork

(G-14872)
PIGMENTS BLACK DIAMOND
1316 Barrington Cir (32092-3612)
PHONE..................................904 241-2533
Christopher Downer, *CEO*
EMP: 7 EST: 2017
SALES (est): 274.8K **Privately Held**
SIC: 2816 Black pigments

(G-14873)
PIP MARKETING SIGNS PRINT
248 State Road 312 (32086-4241)
PHONE..................................904 825-2372
EMP: 10 EST: 2020
SALES (est): 514K **Privately Held**
WEB: www.pip.com
SIC: 2752 Commercial printing, offset

(G-14874)
POWER TEK LLC
154 Cornell Rd (32086-6053)
PHONE..................................904 814-7007
Todd E Kelly, *CEO*
EMP: 9 EST: 2010
SALES (est): 256.5K **Privately Held**
SIC: 3479 Metal coating & allied service

(G-14875)
PRODUCTIVE PRODUCTS INC
321 Valverde Ln (32086-8885)
PHONE..................................904 570-5553
John Lawrence, *Manager*
EMP: 9
SALES (corp-wide): 863.9K **Privately Held**
WEB: www.productiveproducts.com
SIC: 2759 3993 7389 Screen printing;
signs, not made in custom sign painting
shops; lettering & sign painting services

PA: Productive Products Inc
1003 S Main St
Benton IL
618 439-6915

(G-14876)
RAIL SCALE INC
111 Nature Walk Pkwy # 105 (32092-3065)
PHONE..................................904 302-5154
James Myers, *CEO*
Jack Payne, *President*
Dennis Myers, *President*
Larry Croucher Sr, *Sales Mgr*
Linda Orlandi, *Office Mgr*
EMP: 20 EST: 1999
SQ FT: 1,200
SALES (est): 2.5MM **Privately Held**
WEB: www.railscale.com
SIC: 3825 Standards & calibration equip-
ment for electrical measuring

(G-14877)
RANKINE-HINMAN MFG CO
6980 Us Highway 1 N # 108 (32095-8374)
PHONE..................................904 808-0404
Robert Rankine, *CEO*
Brian Hinman, *President*
Ann Cummings, *General Mgr*
Fred Siemer, *General Mgr*
Dana Gould, *Admin Sec*
EMP: 10 EST: 1992
SQ FT: 4,000
SALES (est): 350K **Privately Held**
SIC: 3541 7692 3444 Machine tools,
metal cutting type; welding repair; sheet
metalwork

(G-14878)
RILEY GEAR CORPORATION (PA)
1 Precision Dr (32092-0593)
PHONE..................................904 829-5652
Donald Esarove, *CEO*
William Osborne III, *Ch of Bd*
Thomas Lowry, *President*
Ted Galeza, *Plant Mgr*
Brent Nicholson, *Plant Mgr*
▲ EMP: 70 EST: 1946
SQ FT: 48,400
SALES (est): 12.8MM **Privately Held**
WEB: www.rileygear.com
SIC: 3462 3566 Gears, forged steel;
speed changers, drives & gears; gears,
power transmission, except automotive

(G-14879)
RILEY RISK INC
1301 Plntn Is Dr S (32080-3108)
PHONE..................................202 601-0500
Jacob Allen, *CEO*
Jake Allen, *General Mgr*
Philip Dwyer, *Treasurer*
Rick Taylor, *Security Dir*
EMP: 7 EST: 2011
SALES (est): 718.6K **Privately Held**
WEB: www.rileyrisk.com
SIC: 7372 8742 Application computer soft-
ware; management consulting services

(G-14880)
ROBOT-COSTUMES TECHNOLOGIES
120 Cumberland Park Dr # 305
(32095-8922)
PHONE..................................904 535-0074
Jefferson Leininger, *Principal*
EMP: 7 EST: 2010
SALES (est): 202.8K
SALES (corp-wide): 1.2MM **Privately
Held**
WEB: www.robotcostumesusa.com
SIC: 2389 Costumes
PA: Creations Jean-Claude Tremblay Inc
3250 Rue Marconi Bureau 1
Mascouche QC J7K 3
450 474-0701

(G-14881)
ROX VOLLEYBALL
3520 Ag Ctr Dr Ste 310 (32092)
PHONE..................................877 769-2121
Danielle Olson, *President*
Troy Olson, *Vice Pres*
April Stapp, *Natl Sales Mgr*
EMP: 11 EST: 2009

528   2022 Harris Florida
Manufacturers Directory   ▲ = Import ▼=Export
◆ =Import/Export

SALES (est): 316.1K **Privately Held**
WEB: www.roxvolleyball.com
SIC: 2339 Uniforms, athletic: women's, misses' & juniors'

(G-14882)
RULON COMPANY OF GEORGIA
2000 Ring Way (32092-4745)
PHONE....................................904 584-1400
Wayne Robison, *President*
Emilio Khairallah, *Business Mgr*
Eleanor Robison, *Corp Secy*
Jared Atherton, *Project Mgr*
Caitlin Dunlop, *Project Mgr*
▼ **EMP:** 130 **EST:** 1973
SQ FT: 85,000
SALES (est): 36.9MM **Privately Held**
WEB: www.rulonco.com
SIC: 2421 Sawmills & planing mills, general

(G-14883)
RUSSELLS BINDERY INC
Also Called: Russell Bindery
90 Palmer St (32084-3454)
P.O. Box 860129 (32086-0129)
PHONE....................................904 829-3100
Tim McMandon, *President*
EMP: 8 **EST:** 1962
SQ FT: 5,000
SALES (est): 241.1K **Privately Held**
SIC: 2789 2782 Bookbinding & related work; blankbooks & looseleaf binders

(G-14884)
SAFETARP CORP
1950 State Road 16 (32084-0810)
PHONE....................................904 824-7277
Fred Payne, *President*
Barry Lawhorne, *Vice Pres*
Robert Moore, *Opers Staff*
Louis Krantz, *Admin Sec*
EMP: 60 **EST:** 1999
SQ FT: 5,000
SALES (est): 4.4MM **Privately Held**
WEB: www.tarpingsolllc.com
SIC: 3559 Foundry machinery & equipment

(G-14885)
SAINT AUGUSTINE CAST STONE
4960 Cres Technical Ct (32086-5615)
PHONE....................................904 794-2626
Steve Carcaba, *President*
Leslie Carcaba, *Mfg Staff*
EMP: 8 **EST:** 2003
SALES (est): 665.8K **Privately Held**
SIC: 3272 Stone, cast concrete

(G-14886)
SAPA EXTRSONS ST AUGUSTINE LLC
200 Riviera Blvd (32086-7801)
PHONE....................................904 794-1500
William Russell, *President*
EMP: 154 **EST:** 2014
SALES (est): 5.6MM **Privately Held**
WEB: www.americanconduit.com
SIC: 3365 3354 Aluminum foundries; tube, extruded or drawn, aluminum
HQ: Hydro Extrusion North America, Llc
6250 N River Rd
Rosemont IL 60018
877 710-7272

(G-14887)
SCHOENHUT LLC
Also Called: Schoenhut Piano Company
6480b Us Highway 1 N (32095-8263)
PHONE....................................904 810-1945
Renee Trinca, *Mng Member*
Leonard Trinca,
▲ **EMP:** 6 **EST:** 1996
SQ FT: 12,000
SALES (est): 1MM **Privately Held**
WEB: schoenhut-wholesale-store.myshopify.com
SIC: 3944 Toy musical instruments

(G-14888)
SEARAVEN GLAUBEN LLC
6429 Brevard St (32080-7649)
PHONE....................................727 230-8840
David Ting,
EMP: 10 **EST:** 2019

SALES (est): 513.9K **Privately Held**
SIC: 2911 Petroleum refining

(G-14889)
SEAVIN INC
Also Called: San Sebastian Winery
157 King St (32084-4379)
PHONE....................................904 826-1594
Rich Wojcik, *Prdtn Mgr*
Charles Cox, *Manager*
Ron Guzzetta, *Manager*
EMP: 25 **EST:** 1983
WEB: www.safeinc.com
PA: Seavin Inc
19239 Us Highway 27
Clermont FL 34715

(G-14890)
SECURITY AND FIRE ELEC INC (PA)
Also Called: Safe
2590 Dobbs Rd (32086-5244)
PHONE....................................904 844-0964
Donald S Grundy, *President*
Donald Grundy, *President*
Joseph Graham, *Vice Pres*
David H Grundy Jr, *Vice Pres*
Keith Randall, *Vice Pres*
EMP: 22 **EST:** 1983
SQ FT: 7,500
SALES (est): 3.2MM **Privately Held**
WEB: www.safeinc.com
SIC: 3699 1731 8711 Security devices; fire detection & burglar alarm systems specialization; designing: ship, boat, machine & product

(G-14891)
SHRI GURU KRUPA SMOOTHIES INC
112 Sea Grove Main St (32080-3310)
PHONE....................................904 461-9090
Amitbhai I Patel, *Principal*
EMP: 10 **EST:** 2009
SALES (est): 467.1K **Privately Held**
SIC: 2037 Frozen fruits & vegetables

(G-14892)
SIGNS NOW ST AUGUSTINE INC
1711 Lakeside Ave Ste 1 (32084-4102)
PHONE....................................904 810-5838
Alein Brown, *President*
Brad Brown, *Vice Pres*
EMP: 5 **EST:** 2000
SQ FT: 3,000
SALES (est): 618.7K **Privately Held**
WEB: www.signsnow.com
SIC: 3993 Signs & advertising specialties

(G-14893)
SIGNS UNLIMITED INC
331 A1a Beach Blvd (32080-5901)
PHONE....................................727 845-0330
Michael Rupp, *President*
Sandy Rupp, *Vice Pres*
EMP: 7 **EST:** 1996
SALES (est): 199.5K **Privately Held**
WEB: www.signsunlimitedinc.com
SIC: 3993 7349 Signs & advertising specialties; lighting maintenance service

(G-14894)
SOHACKI INDUSTRIES INC
185 Cumberland Park Dr (32095-8910)
PHONE....................................904 826-0130
Thomas Sohacki, *CEO*
Thomas J Sohacki, *President*
Joshua Sohacki, *Vice Pres*
Thomas Ferris, *Engineer*
David Kananen, *Engineer*
EMP: 35 **EST:** 1991
SQ FT: 20,000
SALES (est): 6MM **Privately Held**
WEB: www.sohackiindustries.com
SIC: 3545 3544 3599 3724 Gauges (machine tool accessories); die sets for metal stamping (presses); machine shop, jobbing & repair; aircraft engines & engine parts; machine parts, stamped or pressed metal; aircraft parts & equipment

(G-14895)
SOLAR STIK INC (PA)
13 N Leonardi St (32084-3425)
PHONE....................................800 793-4364

Brian Bosley, *CEO*
Albert Zaccor, *Principal*
Stephanie D Hollis, *COO*
Tim Ursery, *QC Mgr*
Brian Alano, *Engineer*
▼ **EMP:** 24 **EST:** 2006
SALES (est): 5.1MM **Privately Held**
WEB: www.solarstik.com
SIC: 3621 Generators for storage battery chargers

(G-14896)
SOUTHERN DRYDOCK INC
8153 Six Mile Way (32092-2237)
PHONE....................................904 355-9945
Edwin B Harwell, *President*
EMP: 18 **EST:** 2004
SQ FT: 4,000
SALES (est): 671.5K **Privately Held**
WEB: www.southerndrydock.com
SIC: 3731 Shipbuilding & repairing

(G-14897)
ST AGUSTINE ELC MTR WORKS INC
Also Called: Burnett Industrial Sales
14 Center St (32084-2758)
PHONE....................................904 829-8211
Paul W Burnett Jr, *President*
EMP: 10 **EST:** 1961
SQ FT: 7,800
SALES (est): 1.4MM **Privately Held**
WEB: www.staugustineelectricmotor-works.com
SIC: 7694 Electric motor repair

(G-14898)
ST AUGUSTINE DIST CO LLC
112 Riberia St (32084-4351)
P.O. Box 69 (32085-0069)
PHONE....................................904 825-4962
Matt Stevens, *General Mgr*
Lucas Smith, *Production*
Lucy Montecalvo, *Office Mgr*
Suzanne Flammi, *Manager*
Suzanne Flammia, *Manager*
EMP: 23 **EST:** 2011
SALES (est): 5.7MM **Privately Held**
WEB: www.staugustinedistillery.com
SIC: 2085 Distilled & blended liquors

(G-14899)
ST AUGUSTINE MARINA INC
404 Riberia St (32084-5108)
PHONE....................................904 824-4394
John H Luhrs, *President*
Shawn Bennett, *Manager*
Dave Bennett, *CIO*
Roger Yarborough, *Executive*
▼ **EMP:** 38 **EST:** 1993
SALES (est): 4.5MM **Privately Held**
WEB: www.mywindward.com
SIC: 3731 Shipbuilding & repairing

(G-14900)
ST AUGUSTINE RECORD
1 News Pl (32086-6520)
PHONE....................................904 829-6562
Fax: 904 819-3558
EMP: 48
SALES (est): 2.7MM **Privately Held**
SIC: 2711 Newspapers-Publishing/Printing

(G-14901)
ST AUGUSTINE TRAWLERS INC
Also Called: St Augustine Shipbuilding
404 Riberia St (32084-5108)
PHONE....................................904 824-4394
V J O'Neal, *President*
Virginia Weatherly, *Corp Secy*
Donald B Capo, *Vice Pres*
Roger Yarborough, *Executive*
EMP: 15 **EST:** 1971
SALES (est): 338.1K **Privately Held**
WEB: www.mywindward.com
SIC: 3731 Shipbuilding & repairing

(G-14902)
STA CABINET DEPOT
320 State Road 16 (32084-1943)
P.O. Box 840014 (32080-0014)
PHONE....................................719 502-5454
Dylan Jabs, *Principal*
EMP: 9 **EST:** 2018

SALES (est): 477.4K **Privately Held**
WEB: www.stacabinetdepot.com
SIC: 2434 Wood kitchen cabinets

(G-14903)
STATURE SOFTWARE LLC
620 Palencia Club Dr # 104 (32095-8840)
PHONE....................................888 782-8881
Joseph Patalano, *Manager*
EMP: 7 **EST:** 2012
SALES (est): 301.2K **Privately Held**
WEB: www.staturesoftware.com
SIC: 7372 Business oriented computer software

(G-14904)
SUNSTATE UAV LLC
1093 A1a Beach Blvd # 170 (32080-6733)
PHONE....................................904 580-4828
Christopher Stumpf,
EMP: 11 **EST:** 2017
SALES (est): 520.5K **Privately Held**
WEB: www.sunstateuav.com
SIC: 3728 Target drones

(G-14905)
TENSOLITE LLC
Also Called: Carlisle Interconnect Tech
100 Tensolite Dr (32092-0590)
PHONE....................................904 829-5600
Ray Tezack, *Plant Mgr*
Sara Cook, *Senior Buyer*
Shawn Jutte, *Engineer*
Peter Kulaga, *Sales Staff*
Jeanette Joya, *Manager*
▲ **EMP:** 1000 **EST:** 1941
SQ FT: 215,000
SALES (est): 192MM
SALES (corp-wide): 4.8B **Publicly Held**
WEB: www.carlisleit.com
SIC: 3357 3679 3643 Nonferrous wire-drawing & insulating; harness assemblies for electronic use: wire or cable; electric connectors
HQ: Carlisle Corporation
11605 N Community Hse Rd
Charlotte NC 28277

(G-14906)
TIL VALHALLA PROJECT LLC
Also Called: E-Commerce
3400 Agricultural Ctr Dr (32092-0890)
PHONE....................................904 579-3414
Korey Shaffer, *Owner*
EMP: 58 **EST:** 2017
SALES (est): 5.1MM **Privately Held**
WEB: www.tilvalhallaproject.com
SIC: 2389 2759 Apparel & accessories; screen printing

(G-14907)
TREETOP INDUSTRIES LLC
219 Marshside Dr (32080-5836)
PHONE....................................904 471-4412
EMP: 7 **EST:** 2018
SALES (est): 39.6K **Privately Held**
SIC: 3999 Manufacturing industries

(G-14908)
UPSTREAM INSTALLATION INC
1835 Us Highway 1 S # 119 (32084-4294)
PHONE....................................904 829-3507
Andrew Voss, *President*
EMP: 5 **EST:** 2006
SALES (est): 397.6K **Privately Held**
SIC: 2426 Flooring, hardwood

(G-14909)
VESTED METALS INTL LLC
7000 Us Highway 1 N # 503 (32095-8373)
PHONE....................................904 495-7278
Vivian Helwig, *CEO*
EMP: 8 **EST:** 2014
SALES (est): 4.3MM **Privately Held**
WEB: www.vestedmetals.net
SIC: 3499 5051 Machine bases, metal; metals service centers & offices

(G-14910)
VESTEN WOODWORKS LLC
200 Colorado Springs Way (32092-1926)
PHONE....................................407 780-9295
Steven D Williamson Jr, *Principal*
EMP: 7 **EST:** 2016

SALES (est): 198.8K **Privately Held**
WEB: www.vestenwoodworks.com
SIC: 2431 Millwork

(G-14911)
VILANO INTERIORS INC
112 Oak Ave (32084-2346)
PHONE..............................904 824-3439
Anthony Comeau, *President*
Rhoda Comeau, *Owner*
EMP: 8 EST: 1968
SALES (est): 599.1K **Privately Held**
WEB: www.vilanobeachfl.com
SIC: 3732 Boat building & repairing

(G-14912)
WEBIDCARD INC
Also Called: Swipe K12 School Solutions
89 Mitad Cir (32095-7445)
PHONE..............................443 280-1577
John Amatruda, *CEO*
EMP: 6 EST: 2005
SQ FT: 3,000
SALES (est): 400.6K **Privately Held**
WEB: www.swipesolutionsinc.com
SIC: 7372 Prepackaged software

(G-14913)
WHETSTONE INDUSTRIES INC
Also Called: Whetstone Chocolate Factory
100 Whetstone Pl Ste 100 # 100
(32086-5775)
PHONE..............................904 824-0888
Henry M Whetstone Jr, *President*
Greg Morris, *Prdtn Mgr*
EMP: 10 EST: 2009
SALES (est): 1.6MM **Privately Held**
SIC: 2026 Milk, chocolate
PA: Whetstone Industrial Holdings, Inc.
100 Whetstone Pl Ste 100 # 100
Saint Augustine FL 32086

(G-14914)
WILSON MCH & WLDG WORKS INC
5760 Us Highway 1 N (32095-8005)
PHONE..............................904 829-3737
Marvin Wilson, *President*
Janice Wilson, *Corp Secy*
EMP: 8 EST: 1957
SQ FT: 3,200
SALES (est): 1.1MM **Privately Held**
WEB: wilson-machine-welding-works-wilson.business.site
SIC: 3599 7692 Machine shop, jobbing & repair; welding repair

(G-14915)
WINDOWWARE PRO
2085 A1a S Ste 201 (32080-6506)
PHONE..............................904 584-9191
EMP: 7 EST: 2016
SALES (est): 338.1K **Privately Held**
WEB: www.windowwarepro.com
SIC: 7372 Prepackaged software

(G-14916)
WOODSHED WOODWORKS LLC
55 Florida Ave (32084-3163)
PHONE..............................904 540-0354
David S Hightower, *Principal*
EMP: 10 EST: 2015
SALES (est): 457.9K **Privately Held**
SIC: 2431 Woodwork, interior & ornamental

(G-14917)
YIELD DESIGN
Also Called: Yield - St. Augustine
25 Palmer St (32084-3445)
PHONE..............................402 321-2196
Rachel Grant, *COO*
Kelsey Heinze, *Director*
▲ EMP: 5 EST: 2014
SALES (est): 399.2K **Privately Held**
WEB: www.yielddesign.co
SIC: 2511 Novelty furniture: wood

Saint Cloud
Osceola County

(G-14918)
50 50 PARMLEY ENVMTL SVCS LLC
913 Robinson Ave (34769-2063)
PHONE..............................407 593-1165
Scott Brown, *Mng Member*
Rick Parmley, *Mng Member*
Rory Parmley, *Mng Member*
EMP: 7 EST: 2018
SALES (est): 300K **Privately Held**
SIC: 3523 7342 Spreaders, fertilizer; pest control in structures

(G-14919)
AADI INC
Also Called: St Cloud Door Company
190 E 12th St (34769-3937)
PHONE..............................407 957-4557
Kamlesh Shah, *President*
Ashok Shah, *Vice Pres*
Naresh Shah, *Vice Pres*
Vasant Shah, *Treasurer*
Kenny Shah, *Mktg Coord*
◆ EMP: 38 EST: 1992
SQ FT: 18,000
SALES (est): 5MM **Privately Held**
WEB: www.stclouddoors.com
SIC: 2434 Wood kitchen cabinets

(G-14920)
AMERA TRAIL INC
4840 E I Bronson Memrl (34771)
PHONE..............................407 892-1100
Scott Locke, *President*
Mark Ackerman, *General Mgr*
John Bonis, *Sales Mgr*
Don Moesch, *Sales Staff*
Arthur A Allison, *Manager*
▼ EMP: 40 EST: 1985
SQ FT: 24,000
SALES (est): 9.8MM **Privately Held**
WEB: www.ameratrail.com
SIC: 3799 3537 7539 5599 Boat trailers; trailers & trailer equipment; industrial trucks & tractors; trailer repair; utility trailers

(G-14921)
BELGIUM CO INC
1100 Grape Ave Ste 1 (34769-3914)
PHONE..............................407 957-1886
Ivan Mazzaro, *President*
Nino Mazzaro, *Vice Pres*
Gino Mazzaro, *Treasurer*
EMP: 14 EST: 1977
SALES (est): 2MM **Privately Held**
WEB: www.thebelgiumco.com
SIC: 2099 Butter, renovated & processed

(G-14922)
BEYERS WELDING INC
4950 Canoe Creek Rd (34772-9183)
PHONE..............................407 892-2834
Earl F Beyer, *Principal*
EMP: 7 EST: 1995
SALES (est): 25K **Privately Held**
SIC: 7692 Welding repair

(G-14923)
BIOTOXINS INC
Also Called: Reptile World
5705 E I Bronson Memrl (34771)
PHONE..............................407 892-6905
George Van Horne, *President*
Bonnie Watkins, *Treasurer*
EMP: 6 EST: 1972
SQ FT: 2,500
SALES (est): 463.4K **Privately Held**
WEB: www.reptileworldserpentarium.com
SIC: 2836 7999 Venoms; tourist attraction, commercial

(G-14924)
COMPLETE ACCESS CTRL CENTL FLA
2013 Jaffa Dr (34771-5835)
PHONE..............................407 498-0067
Karen P Mauro, *President*
Kandice Apy, *Vice Pres*
EMP: 7 EST: 2014

SALES (est): 909.4K **Privately Held**
WEB: www.cacocf.com
SIC: 3315 3699 Fence gates posts & fittings: steel; welding machines & equipment, ultrasonic

(G-14925)
FLORIDA CUSTOM FABRICATORS INC
2315 Tyson Rd (34771-7769)
P.O. Box 700668 (34770-0668)
PHONE..............................407 892-8538
Wesley Lassiter, *President*
Ronald Lasitter, *Principal*
Carol Lassiter, *Vice Pres*
EMP: 16 EST: 1967
SQ FT: 10,000
SALES (est): 1.5MM **Privately Held**
SIC: 2514 3431 3441 Metal kitchen & dining room furniture; sinks: enameled iron, cast iron or pressed metal; fabricated structural metal

(G-14926)
FOCUS COMMUNITY PUBLICATIONS
980 Orange Ave (34769-3923)
PHONE..............................407 892-0019
Betty Hawes, *President*
Dennis Hawes, *Vice Pres*
EMP: 6 EST: 1994
SALES (est): 510.7K **Privately Held**
WEB:
www.focuscommunitypublications.com
SIC: 2741 Miscellaneous publishing

(G-14927)
FREIGHT TRAIN TRUCKING CORP
2503 Bross Dr (34771-7809)
PHONE..............................407 509-0611
Elgin Jefferson, *President*
EMP: 7 EST: 1995
SALES (est): 611.5K **Privately Held**
SIC: 3715 Truck trailers

(G-14928)
HESS STATION 09307
Also Called: Amerada Stores
4500 13th St (34769-6706)
PHONE..............................407 891-7156
John Hess, *President*
EMP: 10 EST: 1999
SALES (est): 571.9K **Privately Held**
SIC: 1382 Oil & gas exploration services

(G-14929)
HOSELINE INC
1619 Park Commerce Ct (34769-4707)
PHONE..............................407 892-2599
Linda Grafton, *President*
William W Grafton, *Vice Pres*
Matt Grafton, *Sales Staff*
EMP: 13 EST: 1985
SQ FT: 15,000
SALES (est): 1.5MM **Privately Held**
WEB: www.hoseline.com
SIC: 3585 Air conditioning, motor vehicle

(G-14930)
KEMPFER SAWMILL INC
6254 Kempfer Rd (34773-9363)
PHONE..............................407 892-2955
William C Kempfer, *President*
EMP: 19 EST: 1984
SALES (est): 1MM **Privately Held**
WEB: www.kempfercattleco.com
SIC: 2421 Sawmills & planing mills, general

(G-14931)
LUCKY DOG PRINTING INC
1404 Hamlin Ave (34771-8585)
PHONE..............................407 346-1663
Don Rogers, *Principal*
▲ EMP: 8 EST: 2012
SALES (est): 334.5K **Privately Held**
WEB: www.luckydogprinting.com
SIC: 2752 Commercial printing, offset

(G-14932)
MASTERS BLOCK - NORTH LLC
1037 New York Ave (34769-3781)
PHONE..............................407 212-7704
Martha Hauser, *Manager*

EMP: 5 EST: 2016
SQ FT: 1,300
SALES (est): 308.7K **Privately Held**
SIC: 2951 3271 3251 5032 Paving blocks; paving blocks, concrete; structural brick & blocks; building blocks; industrial buildings, new construction

(G-14933)
MEGAMALLS INC
Also Called: St Cloud Prtg Signs & Cstm AP
2432 13th St (34769-4127)
P.O. Box 701215 (34770-1215)
PHONE..............................407 891-2111
Robert Caruso, *President*
Lynn Carptender, *CFO*
EMP: 11 EST: 1992
SQ FT: 3,750
SALES (est): 1.2MM **Privately Held**
WEB: www.stcloudprinting.net
SIC: 2752 Commercial printing, offset

(G-14934)
MIKES ALUMINUM PRODUCTS LLC
4445 Story Rd (34772-8918)
PHONE..............................407 855-1989
Michael Lebruno, *Mng Member*
EMP: 7 EST: 1984
SALES (est): 925.1K **Privately Held**
WEB: www.mikesalum.com
SIC: 3469 Metal stampings

(G-14935)
MIRAGE & CO INC
3826 Cedar Hammock Trl (34772-8732)
PHONE..............................407 301-5850
Luis Carlos Freites, *Vice Pres*
EMP: 11 EST: 2010
SALES (est): 144.1K **Privately Held**
WEB: www.mirage-mfg.com
SIC: 3732 Boats, fiberglass: building & repairing

(G-14936)
ORANGE PEEL GAZETTE INC
145 E 13th St (34769-4749)
P.O. Box 700792 (34770-0792)
PHONE..............................407 892-5556
Gregory Ke Tester, *Principal*
EMP: 6 EST: 2000
SALES (est): 317.4K **Privately Held**
WEB: www.orangepeelgazette.com
SIC: 2711 7313 Newspapers: publishing only, not printed on site; newspaper advertising representative

(G-14937)
RENOVATION TEAM SERVICES LLC
Also Called: Construction
5103 Caspian St (34771-7831)
P.O. Box 452694, Kissimmee (34745-2694)
PHONE..............................352 696-0215
Jose Cruz, *President*
EMP: 10 EST: 2020
SALES (est): 341.4K **Privately Held**
SIC: 1389 1799 Construction, repair & dismantling services; construction site cleanup

(G-14938)
SCHOEN INDUSTRIES INC
4831 Calasans Ave (34771-8269)
PHONE..............................305 491-5993
Marc A Schoen, *Principal*
EMP: 8 EST: 2017
SALES (est): 148.3K **Privately Held**
SIC: 3999 Manufacturing industries

(G-14939)
ST CLOUD WLDG FABRICATION INC
Also Called: St. Cloud Wldg & Fabrication
3724 Hickory Tree Rd (34772-7548)
P.O. Box 701475 (34770-1475)
PHONE..............................407 957-2344
Bobbie Jean Lollis, *President*
Quient O'Dell Lollis, *Vice Pres*
Dan Leblond, *Project Mgr*
Gene Lollis, *Director*
Jane Lollis, *Admin Sec*
EMP: 23 EST: 1976
SQ FT: 5,200

▲ = Import ▼ =Export
◆ =Import/Export

SALES (est): 5.8MM **Privately Held**
WEB: www.stcloudwelding.com
SIC: **7692** 7699 5074 1799 Welding repair; boiler repair shop; heating equipment (hydronic); welding on site

(G-14940)
SYNERGY REHAB TECHNOLOGIES INC
1404 Hamlin Ave Unit B (34771-8585)
PHONE................................407 943-7500
Paul A Barattiero, *President*
Laura Shantz, *Vice Pres*
Jacqueline M Barattiero, *Admin Sec*
EMP: 9 EST: 2005
SALES (est): 885.7K **Privately Held**
WEB: www.synergyrehab.net
SIC: **3842** Wheelchairs; canes, orthopedic; crutches & walkers

(G-14941)
WOODYS ENTERPRISES LLC
1110b Quotation Ct (34772-5432)
PHONE................................407 892-1900
Kent S Bowers, *Principal*
Bryan Hess, *Cashier*
EMP: 11 EST: 2007
SALES (est): 2.6MM **Privately Held**
WEB: www.woodysenterprises.com
SIC: **3088** Shower stalls, fiberglass & plastic

(G-14942)
ZEEEEES CORPORATION
Also Called: Fine D-Zign Signs
6164 Blue Pond Way (34771-9320)
PHONE................................407 624-3796
Curt Zielinski, *President*
EMP: 9 EST: 2016
SALES (est): 541.2K **Privately Held**
SIC: **3993** 7336 Signs, not made in custom sign painting shops; graphic arts & related design

Saint James City
Lee County

(G-14943)
1ST ENVIRO-SAFETY INC
10200 Betsy Pkwy (33956-3223)
PHONE................................239 283-1222
Julius Tidwell, *CEO*
Ted Tidwell, *CEO*
Leon Hesser, *President*
Ann P Tidwell, *President*
EMP: 7 EST: 1997
SQ FT: 4,000
SALES (est): 972.2K **Privately Held**
WEB: www.purelygreenclean.com
SIC: **2842** Specialty cleaning preparations

Saint Johns
St. Johns County

(G-14944)
AR2 PRODUCTS LLC
Also Called: Gopole
1820 State Road 13 Ste 11 (32259-8855)
PHONE................................800 667-1263
Russell Van Zile, *CEO*
Ryan Vosburg, *Vice Pres*
Anthony Anari, *Opers Staff*
▲ EMP: 6 EST: 2011
SALES (est): 649.3K **Privately Held**
WEB: shop.gopole.com
SIC: **3861** Cameras & related equipment; lens shades, camera; light meters, camera; shutters, camera

(G-14945)
CABINET OPTIONS INC
1170 Executive Cove Dr (32259-2801)
PHONE................................904 434-1564
Thomas Legg, *Principal*
EMP: 8 EST: 2007
SALES (est): 248.5K **Privately Held**
SIC: **2434** Wood kitchen cabinets

(G-14946)
HUMIC GROWTH SOLUTIONS INC
112 Badger Park Dr (32259-2179)
PHONE................................904 329-1012
Kevin Merritt, *President*
EMP: 9
SALES (corp-wide): 10MM **Privately Held**
WEB: www.humicgrowth.com
SIC: **2879** Soil conditioners
PA: Humic Growth Solutions, Inc.
709 Eastport Rd
Jacksonville FL 32218
904 392-7201

(G-14947)
VIDACANN LLC
4844 Race Track Rd (32259-2090)
PHONE................................772 672-1178
David Loop,
EMP: 11 EST: 2017
SALES (est): 1.4MM **Privately Held**
WEB: www.vidacann.com
SIC: **3999**

Saint Petersburg
Pinellas County

(G-14948)
3 DAUGHTERS BREWING LLC (PA)
Also Called: South Beach Brewing Company
222 22nd St S (33712-1240)
PHONE................................727 495-6002
Christian Harris, *General Mgr*
Ty Weaver, *Top Exec*
Brian Horne, *Vice Pres*
Jessica Bodkin, *Opers Staff*
Peter Lambie, *Sales Dir*
EMP: 10 EST: 2012
SALES (est): 10MM **Privately Held**
WEB: www.3dbrewing.com
SIC: **2082** Beer (alcoholic beverage)

(G-14949)
A CHEAPER SHOT LLC ✪
4604 49th St N (33709-3842)
PHONE................................727 221-3237
Anthony Thompson,
EMP: 10 EST: 2021
SALES (est): 150K **Privately Held**
SIC: **3799** Transportation equipment

(G-14950)
A TO Z CONCRETE PRODUCTS INC
Also Called: Stable Concrete Product
4451 8th Ave S (33711-1903)
PHONE................................727 321-6000
Graeme Malloch, *CEO*
William Majewski, *President*
Shaun Beesley, *Manager*
EMP: 18 EST: 1990
SQ FT: 20,000
SALES (est): 1.4MM **Privately Held**
SIC: **3272** 1542 Concrete stuctural support & building material; building materials, except block or brick: concrete; wall & ceiling squares, concrete; custom builders, non-residential

(G-14951)
AARON MEDICAL INDUSTRIES INC
7100 30th Ave N (33710-2902)
PHONE................................727 384-2323
Janis Dezso, *Director*
EMP: 10 EST: 1970
SALES (est): 123.9K **Privately Held**
SIC: **3841** Surgical & medical instruments

(G-14952)
ABSOLUTE HOME SVCS GROUP INC ✪
7830 38th Ave N Ste 9 (33710-1196)
PHONE................................727 275-0020
James Shipley, *CEO*
EMP: 10 EST: 2021
SALES (est): 1MM **Privately Held**
SIC: **1389** Construction, repair & dismantling services

(G-14953)
ACE HIGH PRINTING LLC
3801 16th St N Ste B (33703-5601)
PHONE................................727 542-3897
Richard A Herbert, *Manager*
EMP: 7 EST: 2010
SALES (est): 221.3K **Privately Held**
WEB: www.acehighprinting.com
SIC: **2752** Commercial printing, offset

(G-14954)
ADVANCED MANUFACTURING INC
12205 28th St N (33716-1823)
PHONE................................727 573-3300
Gary Kinley, *President*
Peter Dorflinger, *Corp Secy*
Amy Goodman, *Purchasing*
Leo Suchor, *Controller*
◆ EMP: 30 EST: 1998
SQ FT: 15,000
SALES (est): 4.7MM
SALES (corp-wide): 17.9MM **Privately Held**
WEB: www.amifla.com
SIC: **3679** 3829 3823 3672 Electronic circuits; measuring & controlling devices; industrial instrmnts msrmnt display/control process variable; printed circuit boards; electron tubes; motors & generators
PA: Advanced Medical Instruments, Inc.
5904 Chestnut Ct
Edmond OK 73025
918 250-0566

(G-14955)
AEROSMART ENTERPRISE LLC ✪
7901 4th St N Ste 300 (33702-4399)
PHONE................................310 499-8878
Eric Valdes, *Principal*
EMP: 31 EST: 2021
SALES (est): 1.9MM **Privately Held**
SIC: **3721** Aircraft

(G-14956)
AEROSPACE COMPONENTS INC
2625 75th St N (33710-2932)
PHONE................................727 347-9915
Alan Kussy, *President*
Kimberly Kussy, *Vice Pres*
EMP: 16 EST: 1986
SALES (est): 2.1MM **Privately Held**
WEB: www.aerospacecomponents.com
SIC: **3599** Machine shop, jobbing & repair
HQ: Hartzell Engine Technologies Llc
2900 Selma Hwy
Montgomery AL 36108

(G-14957)
AGORA SALES INC (PA)
Also Called: Agora Leather Products
2101 28th St N (33713-4246)
PHONE................................727 321-0707
Subhash Dave, *President*
Janie Dave, *Business Mgr*
Ragu Molleti, *Business Mgr*
Jagat Trivedi, *Vice Pres*
Jason Dave, *Project Mgr*
▲ EMP: 187 EST: 1985
SQ FT: 36,000
SALES (est): 30.6MM **Privately Held**
WEB: www.agoraedge.com
SIC: **3161** Cases, carrying

(G-14958)
AIR TECHNICAL LLC
7901 4th St N Ste 4612 (33702-4305)
PHONE................................305 837-3274
Ibrahim Sisic,
EMP: 10 EST: 2020
SALES (est): 283.1K **Privately Held**
SIC: **3999** Manufacturing industries

(G-14959)
ALPS SOUTH LLC
Also Called: Alps Orthotics
2895 42nd Ave N (33714-4547)
PHONE................................727 528-8566
Aldo Laghi, *President*
Kevin McLoone, *Vice Pres*
Jessica Plomatos, *Opers Mgr*
Tommy Hakvongsa, *Mfg Staff*
Nathaniel Vint, *Research*

▲ EMP: 85 EST: 1993
SQ FT: 20,000
SALES (est): 18.3MM **Privately Held**
WEB: www.easyliner.com
SIC: **3842** Prosthetic appliances

(G-14960)
ALUMFLO INC
2445 51st Ave N (33714-2601)
PHONE................................727 527-8494
Wanetta Rodriguez, *President*
Mark Daniel, *CEO*
Steve Rodriguez, *Vice Pres*
EMP: 8 EST: 1987
SQ FT: 10,000
SALES (est): 1.5MM **Privately Held**
WEB: www.alumflo.com
SIC: **3444** Awnings, sheet metal

(G-14961)
AMERICAN FIBERTEK INC
Also Called: Afi
745 43rd St S (33711-1920)
PHONE................................732 302-0660
Jack Fernandes, *President*
Edward Davis, *Vice Pres*
EMP: 50 EST: 1984
SALES (est): 9.5MM **Privately Held**
WEB: www.americanfibertek.com
SIC: **3679** 3577 Electronic circuits; input/output equipment, computer

(G-14962)
ANIMAL BUSINESS CONCEPTS LLC
Also Called: Cool Pet Holistics
2135 13th Ave N (33713-4001)
P.O. Box 76405 (33734-6405)
PHONE................................727 641-6176
Jennifer Guille Lewis, *Partner*
Jonathan Lewis,
EMP: 11 EST: 2004
SALES (est): 1.7MM **Privately Held**
WEB: www.animalbizconcepts.com
SIC: **2048** Feed supplements

(G-14963)
AOC TECHNOLOGIES INC
10560 Dr Martin L Kng Jr (33716-3718)
PHONE................................727 577-9749
EMP: 5 EST: 2016
SALES (est): 544.5K
SALES (corp-wide): 29.2B **Publicly Held**
SIC: **3672** Printed circuit boards
PA: Jabil Inc.
10800 Roosevelt Blvd N
Saint Petersburg FL 33716
727 577-9749

(G-14964)
AOG DETAILING SERVICES INC
6798 Crosswinds Dr N B203 (33710-5481)
PHONE................................727 742-7321
Permeseur Rampersaud, *President*
EMP: 7 EST: 2004
SALES (est): 522.9K **Privately Held**
WEB: www.aogsteel.com
SIC: **3441** 8711 1791 Fabricated structural metal; engineering services; structural steel erection

(G-14965)
AQUACAL (PA)
2730 24th St N (33713-4046)
PHONE................................727 898-2412
William Kent, *CEO*
Lynn Dean, *Manager*
Bari Fallon, *Manager*
Debbi Tawney, *Manager*
Jeff Harding, *Technology*
▼ EMP: 4 EST: 2010
SALES (est): 12MM **Privately Held**
WEB: www.aquacal.com
SIC: **3999** Hot tubs

(G-14966)
AQUACAL AUTOPILOT INC
2737 24th St N (33713-4037)
PHONE................................727 823-5642
William Kent, *President*
Kent William A, *Principal*
Jeff Tawney, *Vice Pres*
Timothy Brocklebank, *Production*
Jorge Arias, *Engineer*
◆ EMP: 150 EST: 1992
SQ FT: 35,000

SALES (est): 59.4MM **Privately Held**
WEB: www.aquacal.com
SIC: 3585 3569 Air conditioning units,
complete: domestic or industrial; heaters,
swimming pool: electric

(G-14967)
AQUAFLEX PRINTING LLC
3349 118th Ave N (33716-1852)
PHONE.................................727 914-4922
Tony D Mittelstaedt, *Administration*
EMP: 7 EST: 2014
SALES (est): 484K **Privately Held**
SIC: 2752 Commercial printing, offset

(G-14968)
**ARCHITCTRAL WD WKG
MLDING DIV**
3291 40th Ave N (33714-4512)
PHONE.................................727 527-7400
Alan Regel, *President*
Richard Regal, *Vice Pres*
EMP: 10 EST: 1994
SQ FT: 15,625
SALES (est): 908.8K **Privately Held**
WEB: www.architecturalwoodworking.com
SIC: 2431 Millwork

(G-14969)
**ARCHITECTURAL FOUNTAINS
INC**
2010 28th St N (33713-4223)
PHONE.................................727 323-6068
John Stack, *President*
Cathleen Stack, *Vice Pres*
EMP: 5 EST: 1983
SQ FT: 3,000
SALES (est): 726.4K **Privately Held**
WEB: www.architecturalfountaininc.com
SIC: 3272 3299 3499 Fountains, con-
crete; fountains, plaster of paris; fountains
(except drinking), metal

(G-14970)
ARJ ART INC
Also Called: Manatee Shirts and Graphics
517 35th Ave N (33704-1233)
PHONE.................................727 535-8633
Richard Groth, *Managing Prtnr*
Mary Kitchin, *Partner*
EMP: 8 EST: 2004
SALES (est): 552.7K **Privately Held**
WEB: www.livjaxdan.com
SIC: 2759 Screen printing

(G-14971)
**ART & FRAME SOURCE INC
(PA)**
4251 34th St N (33714-3707)
PHONE.................................727 329-6502
Steven Press, *President*
Mona Press, *Vice Pres*
Mona L Press, *Executive*
◆ EMP: 22 EST: 1978
SQ FT: 17,000
SALES (est): 3.5MM **Privately Held**
WEB: www.artandframesourceinc.com
SIC: 3952 5023 Frames for artists' can-
vases; home furnishings

(G-14972)
**ARTFUL ARNAUTIC
ASSEMBLIES LLC**
2877 47th Ave N (33714-3129)
PHONE.................................727 522-0055
Todd Freund, *General Mgr*
EMP: 6 EST: 2015
SALES (est): 652.1K **Privately Held**
WEB: www.artfulaeronautic.com
SIC: 3625 Marine & navy auxiliary controls

(G-14973)
ARTFUL CANVAS DESIGN INC
2877 47th Ave N (33714-3129)
PHONE.................................727 521-0212
Todd Freund, *President*
Casie Whitney, *Manager*
EMP: 10 EST: 1996
SALES (est): 2.3MM **Privately Held**
WEB: www.artfulcanvas.com
SIC: 2394 3441 Canvas boat seats; fabri-
cated structural metal for ships

(G-14974)
**ATLANTIC MEDICAL PRODUCTS
LLC**
Also Called: Scar Heal
9843 18th St N Ste 160 (33716-4208)
P.O. Box 1351, Tampa (33601-1351)
PHONE.................................727 535-0022
Thomas Christenberry, *CEO*
Darwin Salls, *General Mgr*
John Eshleman, *Sales Staff*
Emily Hudson, *Sales Staff*
Cameron Jones, *Marketing Mgr*
EMP: 10 EST: 1989
SALES (est): 1.6MM **Privately Held**
SIC: 2833 Medicinals & botanicals

(G-14975)
ATMCENTRAL
6468 5th Ave S (33707-2333)
PHONE.................................727 345-8460
Barbara Scian, *Principal*
John C Little, *VP Opers*
Jon Taylor, *Technician*
EMP: 5 EST: 2007
SALES (est): 407.2K **Privately Held**
WEB: www.atmcentral.com
SIC: 3578 6099 Automatic teller machines
(ATM); automated teller machine (ATM)
network

(G-14976)
**AURORA SEMICONDUCTOR
LLC**
9900 16th St N (33716-4230)
PHONE.................................727 235-6500
EMP: 30
SALES (est): 477.9K **Privately Held**
SIC: 3674 Semiconductors And Related
Devices, Nsk

(G-14977)
BARNETT & PUGLIANO INC
200 2nd Ave S (33701-4313)
PHONE.................................727 826-6075
Joseph M Pugliano, *CEO*
George D Sheets, *Vice Pres*
EMP: 8 EST: 1998
SALES (est): 197.7K **Privately Held**
SIC: 2752 Commercial printing, litho-
graphic

(G-14978)
BAY CITY WINDOW COMPANY
Also Called: Windows Doors Etc
3220 Bennett St N Ste A (33713-2645)
PHONE.................................727 323-5443
Devin Zimring, *President*
Gina Discianno, *General Mgr*
EMP: 14 EST: 1993
SALES (est): 3.6MM **Privately Held**
WEB: www.windowsdoorsetcflorida.com
SIC: 3089 2824 Window frames & sash,
plastic; vinyl fibers

(G-14979)
BAYFRONT PRINTING COMPANY
Also Called: Image360 St Petersburg Central
2235 16th Ave N (33713-5623)
PHONE.................................727 823-1965
Algimantas Karnavicius, *President*
Nancy Karnavicius, *Vice Pres*
EMP: 5 EST: 1981
SQ FT: 5,000
SALES (est): 712.2K **Privately Held**
WEB: www.bayprintonline.com
SIC: 3993 2752 Signs & advertising spe-
cialties; commercial printing, lithographic

(G-14980)
**BIDDISCOMBE INTERNATIONAL
LLC**
Also Called: Biddiscombe Labs Stylz Pdts
11961 31st Ct N (33716-1808)
PHONE.................................727 299-9287
John H Melville, *President*
Karen Swartz, *Office Mgr*
William Van Valzah, *Manager*
EMP: 10 EST: 1980
SQ FT: 8,500
SALES (est): 1.3MM **Privately Held**
WEB: www.biddiscombe.com
SIC: 2844 Cosmetic preparations

(G-14981)
**BIG FISH CO CUSTOM
CREATIONS**
3128 Dr M L K Jr St N Mlk (33704)
PHONE.................................727 525-5010
Carrie Amos Renner, *Principal*
EMP: 8 EST: 2008
SALES (est): 993.7K **Privately Held**
WEB: www.bigfishco.com
SIC: 2339 Women's & misses' outerwear

(G-14982)
BIG SLIDE ENTERPRISES INC
Also Called: Aquaworx, Inc.
10601 Oak St Ne (33716-3301)
PHONE.................................727 329-8845
Steve Hamilton, *President*
Patrick Powell, *Manager*
Alex Fletcher, *Representative*
EMP: 2 EST: 2009
SALES (est): 5.6MM **Privately Held**
WEB: www.aquaworxusa.com
SIC: 3089 Plastic & fiberglass tanks
HQ: Playcore Holdings, Inc.
544 Chestnut St
Chattanooga TN 37402
877 762-7563

(G-14983)
BIONEBICINE CORP
125 Estado Way Ne (33704-3619)
P.O. Box 7487 (33734-7487)
PHONE.................................401 648-0695
Donald Pell, *President*
Paul Messina, *Treasurer*
Erwin Vahlsing Jr, *Ch Credit Ofcr*
Nicholas Havercroft, *Director*
Dr Govindan Nair, *Director*
EMP: 7 EST: 2018
SALES (est): 333.3K **Privately Held**
WEB: www.bionebicine.com
SIC: 3841 Surgical & medical instruments

(G-14984)
BLUE GARDENIA LLC
661 Central Ave (33701-3633)
PHONE.................................727 560-0040
Richard T Alday, *Principal*
EMP: 6 EST: 2016
SALES (est): 301.6K **Privately Held**
SIC: 3949 Sporting & athletic goods

(G-14985)
**BLUEWATER MARINE SYSTEMS
INC**
360 Central Ave Ste 800 (33701-3984)
P.O. Box 14217 (33733-4217)
PHONE.................................619 499-7507
James C Booth, *President*
EMP: 6 EST: 2020
SALES (est): 797.5K **Privately Held**
SIC: 3448 Docks: prefabricated metal

(G-14986)
BODY LLC
Also Called: Body Nutrition
2950 47th Ave N (33714-3132)
PHONE.................................850 888-2639
Gregory W Simek,
▲ EMP: 18 EST: 2008
SQ FT: 63,000
SALES (est): 5.1MM **Privately Held**
WEB: www.bodynutrition.com
SIC: 2099 Dessert mixes & fillings

(G-14987)
BOYCE ENGINEERING INC
11861 31st Ct N (33716-1806)
PHONE.................................727 572-6318
Boyce D Crowe Sr, *President*
Jackie Crowe, *Marketing Staff*
EMP: 10 EST: 1972
SQ FT: 8,500
SALES (est): 936.9K **Privately Held**
SIC: 3089 Molding primary plastic

(G-14988)
BRAND BUILDERS RX LLC
9843 18th St N Ste 150 (33716-4208)
PHONE.................................727 576-4013
EMP: 9
SQ FT: 9,000
SALES (est): 730K **Privately Held**
SIC: 2844 5122 Cosmetic Mfg & Dist

(G-14989)
BREWFAB LLC
Also Called: Dimeg Process Solutions
2300 31st St N (33713-3703)
PHONE.................................727 823-8333
Rick Cureton, *Mng Member*
Kyle Cureton, *Mng Member*
Marie Demeza, *Manager*
EMP: 17 EST: 2013
SALES (est): 10.3MM **Privately Held**
WEB: www.brewfabusa.com
SIC: 3312 3443 5084 Stainless steel;
process vessels, industrial: metal plate;
tanks, standard or custom fabricated:
metal plate; brewery products manufac-
turing machinery, commercial

(G-14990)
BTU REPS LLC (PA)
185 23rd Ave N (33704-3431)
PHONE.................................727 235-3591
Joseph P Shukys, *Principal*
EMP: 6 EST: 2012
SALES (est): 448.7K **Privately Held**
WEB: www.btureps.com
SIC: 2097 Manufactured ice

(G-14991)
**BUFFALO MACHINE
MANUFACTURING**
3140 39th Ave N (33714-4530)
PHONE.................................727 321-1905
Matt Bryant, *President*
EMP: 6 EST: 1999
SQ FT: 2,580
SALES (est): 491.4K **Privately Held**
SIC: 3569 Assembly machines, non-metal-
working

(G-14992)
**BURKHART ROENTGEN INTL
INC**
Also Called: Usaxray
3232 Bennett St N (33713-2642)
PHONE.................................727 327-6950
George Burkhart, *President*
Ellen Burkhart, *Vice Pres*
EMP: 10 EST: 1996
SQ FT: 6,600
SALES (est): 952.9K **Privately Held**
WEB: www.usaxray.com
SIC: 3842 Radiation shielding aprons,
gloves, sheeting, etc.

(G-14993)
C & D PRINTING COMPANY
12150 28th St N (33716-1820)
PHONE.................................727 572-9999
William Serata, *President*
Darrin Blackburn, *Plant Mgr*
Todd Pemberton, *Opers Staff*
Denise Vilez, *Controller*
Jim Parker, *Accounts Exec*
EMP: 67 EST: 1974
SQ FT: 13,000
SALES (est): 10.8MM **Privately Held**
WEB:
SIC: 2752 Commercial printing, offset

(G-14994)
CAMP AIRCRAFT INC
5300 95th St N (33708-3795)
PHONE.................................727 397-6076
Don Camp, *President*
EMP: 10 EST: 1944
SQ FT: 40,000
SALES (est): 1.5MM **Privately Held**
SIC: 3644 3364 Electric conduits & fit-
tings: nonferrous die-castings except alu-
minum

(G-14995)
**CAMP COMPANY ST
PETERSBURG**
5300 95th St N (33708-3795)
PHONE.................................727 397-6076
Dominick Ciampolillo, *President*
EMP: 26 EST: 1977
SQ FT: 40,000
SALES (est): 4.4MM **Privately Held**
WEB: www.campcompany.com
SIC: 3369 Zinc & zinc-base alloy castings,
except die-castings

(G-14996)
CAMPOS CHEMICALS
3244 44th Ave N (33714-3810)
PHONE...................................727 412-2774
Roberto B Campos,
Michelle Lorenzo,
EMP: 8 **EST:** 2013
SALES (est): 407.2K **Privately Held**
WEB: campos-chemicals.business.site
SIC: 2842 5999 5169 2841 Specialty cleaning, polishes & sanitation goods; rug, upholstery, or dry cleaning detergents or spotters; cleaning equipment & supplies; detergents; soap: granulated, liquid, cake, flaked or chip

(G-14997)
CANVAS
1535 4th St N (33704-4411)
PHONE...................................727 317-5572
EMP: 7 **EST:** 2015
SALES (est): 56.3K **Privately Held**
WEB: www.shopcfg.com
SIC: 2211 Canvas

(G-14998)
CATALENT INC
Also Called: Catalent St Petersburg
2725 Scherer Dr N (33716-1016)
PHONE...................................727 803-2832
Greg Weibel, Production
Knight McGowan, Engineer
Leah Mejias, Engineer
Rob Naegely, Project Engr
Jorge Santiago, Project Engr
EMP: 15 **Publicly Held**
WEB: www.catalent.com
SIC: 2834 Pharmaceutical preparations
PA: Catalent, Inc.
14 Schoolhouse Rd
Somerset NJ 08873

(G-14999)
CATALENT PHARMA SOLUTIONS INC
2725 Scherer Dr N (33716-1016)
PHONE...................................727 572-4000
David Haines, President
Marcos Alaniz, Business Mgr
Timothy Doran, Vice Pres
Ricci Whitlow, Vice Pres
Laurie Goodings, Project Mgr
EMP: 554
SQ FT: 72,000 **Publicly Held**
WEB: www.catalent.com
SIC: 2899 2834 Gelatin capsules; pharmaceutical preparations
HQ: Catalent Pharma Solutions, Inc.
14 Schoolhouse Rd
Somerset NJ 08873

(G-15000)
CAVAFORM INC (PA)
2700 72nd St N (33710-2916)
PHONE...................................727 384-3676
Dave S Massie, President
Mark Kraf, Facilities Mgr
David Gunthrop, QC Mgr
Chris Outlaw, Engineer
Chuck Doerner, Project Engr
▲ **EMP:** 1 **EST:** 1978
SQ FT: 30,000
SALES (est): 33.7MM **Privately Held**
WEB: www.cavaform.com
SIC: 3089 Injection molding of plastics

(G-15001)
CAVAFORM INTERNATIONAL LLC
2700 72nd St N (33710-2916)
PHONE...................................727 384-3676
Nick Scalamogna, Partner
Ralph Acito, Production
Dave S Massie, Mng Member
Trent Shelby, Program Mgr
EMP: 75 **EST:** 1999
SQ FT: 30,000
SALES (est): 33.7MM **Privately Held**
WEB: www.cavaform.com
SIC: 3544 Industrial molds
PA: Cavaform, Inc.
2700 72nd St N
Saint Petersburg FL 33710
727 384-3676

(G-15002)
CB PARENT HOLDCO GP LLC
9620 Exec Ctr Dr N Ste 20 (33702-2429)
PHONE...................................727 827-0046
Sharon Love, Mng Member
Michael J Henricks,
EMP: 1800
SALES (est): 38.3MM **Privately Held**
WEB: www.communitybrands.com
SIC: 7372 Prepackaged software

(G-15003)
CEMEX CEMENT INC
601 24th St S (33712-1723)
PHONE...................................727 327-5730
Bill Poole, Branch Mgr
EMP: 118 **Privately Held**
WEB: www.cemexusa.com
SIC: 3273 Ready-mixed concrete
HQ: Cemex Cement, Inc.
10100 Katy Fwy Ste 300
Houston TX 77043
713 650-6200

(G-15004)
CENTRAL PRINTERS INC
4101 35th St N (33714-3798)
PHONE...................................727 527-5879
Steve Sanchez, President
Philip Sanchez, Vice Pres
EMP: 6 **EST:** 1935
SQ FT: 3,000
SALES (est): 601.9K **Privately Held**
WEB: www.centralprinters.com
SIC: 2752 Commercial printing, offset

(G-15005)
CHINA PUBLIC SECURITY TECH INC
4033 12th St Ne (33703-5221)
PHONE...................................866 821-9004
Jiang Huai Lin, Ch of Bd
John Maguire, President
Robin Huang, COO
Michael Lin, Vice Pres
Petie Parnell Maguire, Vice Pres
EMP: 26 **EST:** 1979
SALES (est): 30.3MM **Privately Held**
SIC: 2759 Commercial printing

(G-15006)
CHROMATECH DIGITAL INC
Also Called: Chromatech Printing
4301 31st St N (33714-4567)
PHONE...................................727 528-4711
George Emmanuel Sr, President
George Emmanuel Jr, Vice Pres
EMP: 22 **EST:** 1996
SQ FT: 20,000
SALES (est): 663K **Privately Held**
WEB: www.chromatechprinting.com
SIC: 2752 Commercial printing, offset

(G-15007)
CIEGA INC
4410 35th St N (33714-3720)
PHONE...................................727 526-9048
EMP: 8
SALES (est): 1.2MM **Privately Held**
SIC: 2842 5169 Whol & Mfg Environmental Supplies & Services

(G-15008)
CNC AIRCRAFT INC
7901 4th St N Ste 4616 (33702-4305)
PHONE...................................305 657-1230
Angelica Snyder, CEO
EMP: 9 **EST:** 2001
SALES (est): 221.2K **Privately Held**
SIC: 3728 Aircraft body assemblies & parts

(G-15009)
COLORGRAPHX INC
Also Called: Beck Graphics
1551 102nd Ave N Ste A (33716-5050)
PHONE...................................727 572-6364
George R Stulpin, President
George Stulpin, President
Lee Cox, Controller
EMP: 30 **EST:** 2004
SALES (est): 4.7MM **Privately Held**
WEB: www.colorgraphx.com
SIC: 2752 Commercial printing, offset

(G-15010)
COMMERCIAL INSTLLATION SYSTEMS
6175 Wdrow Wilson Blvd Ne (33703)
PHONE...................................727 525-2372
Fax: 727 526-7903
EMP: 8
SALES (est): 882.4K **Privately Held**
SIC: 2431 Mfg Millwork

(G-15011)
COMMERCIAL STONE CAB FBRCTORS
3120 46th Ave N (33714-3802)
PHONE...................................727 209-1141
Lisa Maddux, President
Danny Donegan, Principal
Steve Stutko, Sales Executive
EMP: 10 **EST:** 2012
SALES (est): 1.1MM **Privately Held**
WEB: www.cscfusa.com
SIC: 1411 1799 2541 1751 Granite dimension stone; kitchen cabinet installation; counter & sink tops; cabinet building & installation; composition stone, plastic

(G-15012)
COMMERCIAL STONE FBRCATORS INC
Also Called: Global Stone Project Entp
3120 46th Ave N (33714-3802)
PHONE...................................727 209-1141
Lisa Maddux, President
EMP: 10 **EST:** 2004
SALES (est): 1.6MM **Privately Held**
WEB: www.gspei.com
SIC: 1411 1799 2541 1751 Granite dimension stone; kitchen cabinet installation; counter top installation; counter & sink tops; cabinet building & installation; composition stone, plastic

(G-15013)
COMPASS BANNERS & PRINTING LLC
5502 Haines Rd N (33714-1999)
PHONE...................................727 522-7414
Alan Stanton, Administration
EMP: 5 **EST:** 2019
SALES (est): 338.1K **Privately Held**
WEB: www.compassbannersandsigns.com
SIC: 2752 Commercial printing, lithographic

(G-15014)
COMPULINK CORPORATION (HQ)
1205 Gandy Blvd N (33702-2428)
PHONE...................................727 579-1500
Stephen Shevlin, President
Robert T Wilkin, Vice Pres
Nick Kochey, Opers Staff
Edrick Chaney, Buyer
Debbie Wastney, Buyer
EMP: 500 **EST:** 1984
SQ FT: 30,000
SALES (est): 118.7MM **Privately Held**
WEB: www.compulink.com
SIC: 3643 5065 Current-carrying wiring devices; electronic parts

(G-15015)
CONTOURS RX LLC
200 2nd Ave S Ste 701 (33701-4313)
PHONE...................................727 827-7321
Britain Todd, Mng Member
EMP: 5 **EST:** 2014
SQ FT: 1,800
SALES (est): 342.7K **Privately Held**
WEB: www.contoursrx.com
SIC: 2844 Cosmetic preparations

(G-15016)
CRABIL MANUFACTURING INC
9600 18th St N (33716-4202)
PHONE...................................727 209-8368
Craig R Rennick, President
Stacie Rennick, Vice Pres
Michele Mathre, Engineer
EMP: 27 **EST:** 2001
SQ FT: 23,000
SALES (est): 4.8MM **Privately Held**
WEB: www.crabil.com
SIC: 3599 Machine shop, jobbing & repair

(G-15017)
CRYPTO CPITL PRECIOUS MTLS INC
10460 Roosevelt Blvd N (33716-3821)
PHONE...................................727 200-2108
Justin A Nichols, Principal
EMP: 7 **EST:** 2013
SALES (est): 65.1K **Privately Held**
SIC: 3339 Precious metals

(G-15018)
CUSTOM TEAK MARINE WOODWORK
4105 8th Ave S (33711-2005)
PHONE...................................727 768-6065
Dmitry Tsiorba, President
EMP: 5 **EST:** 2018
SALES (est): 301.2K **Privately Held**
WEB: www.teakmarinewoodwork.com
SIC: 2431 Millwork

(G-15019)
DARLY FILTRATION INC
4537 22nd St N (33714-4115)
PHONE...................................727 318-7064
EMP: 23
SALES (corp-wide): 4.1MM **Privately Held**
WEB: www.darllyfilter.com
SIC: 3569 Filters, general line: industrial
PA: Darly Filtration Inc
14225 Telephone Ave
Chino CA 91710
909 591-7999

(G-15020)
DAVID CHITTUM
Also Called: High Power Services
1800 Bonita Way S (33712-4212)
PHONE...................................386 754-6127
David Chittum, Owner
EMP: 6 **EST:** 2000
SALES (est): 503.8K **Privately Held**
SIC: 3699 Household electrical equipment

(G-15021)
DELPHI OF FLORIDA INC
12425 28th S N Ste 100 (33716)
PHONE...................................727 561-9553
Ed Dillabough, President
Karen Jones, Research
Laura Huckaby, Manager
Colleen Hekkanen, Director
Catherine Hall, Nurse
EMP: 13 **EST:** 2001
SALES (est): 289.8K **Privately Held**
SIC: 3714 Motor vehicle parts & accessories

(G-15022)
DERMAZONE SOLUTIONS INC
2440 30th Ave N (33713-2920)
PHONE...................................727 446-6882
Deborah Duffey, President
Karalyn Schuchert, Chairman
Zack Nalic, Plant Mgr
Jean Letellier, QC Mgr
Schuchart Joseph, Controller
EMP: 30 **EST:** 2001
SQ FT: 2,000
SALES (est): 7.8MM **Privately Held**
WEB: www.dermazone.com
SIC: 2844 5999 5122 8732 Cosmetic preparations; toiletries, cosmetics & perfumes; cosmetics; research services, except laboratory; commercial research laboratory

(G-15023)
DESIGNS TO SHINE INC
1033 34th St N (33713-6543)
PHONE...................................727 525-4297
Maria McGill, Owner
Summer Gray, Owner
Michelle Butler, Office Mgr
EMP: 38 **EST:** 1999
SALES (est): 3.4MM **Privately Held**
WEB: www.designstoshine.com
SIC: 2335 5699 Bridal & formal gowns; formal wear

(G-15024)
DGS RETAIL LLC
4400 34th St N Ste L (33714-3741)
PHONE...................................727 388-4975

Tom Ripley, *Branch Mgr*
EMP: 158
SALES (corp-wide): 200.5MM **Privately Held**
WEB: www.dgsretail.com
SIC: 3993 Signs, not made in custom sign painting shops
PA: Dgs Retail, Llc
60 Maple St Ste 100
Mansfield MA 02048
800 211-9646

(G-15025)
DGS RETAIL LLC
307044th Avenenue N (33714)
PHONE.................................727 388-4975
Tom Ripley, *Branch Mgr*
EMP: 10
SALES (corp-wide): 200.5MM **Privately Held**
WEB: www.dgsretail.com
SIC: 3993 Signs & advertising specialties
PA: Dgs Retail, Llc
60 Maple St Ste 100
Mansfield MA 02048
800 211-9646

(G-15026)
DJFS LLC
4604 49th St N Ste 1279 (33709-3842)
PHONE.................................727 551-1391
Derrick Freeman, *Mng Member*
EMP: 5 **EST:** 2020
SALES (est): 410K **Privately Held**
SIC: 3443 Housings, pressure

(G-15027)
DONOVAN HOME SERVICES LLC
Also Called: Kyaeto Systems
3390 Gandy Blvd N (33702-2058)
PHONE.................................813 644-9488
Michael Donovan, *CEO*
EMP: 14 **EST:** 2016
SALES (est): 999.9K **Privately Held**
SIC: 3577 8742 Computer peripheral equipment; management information systems consultant

(G-15028)
DONTECH INDUSTRIES INC
9 Jefferson Ct S (33711-5144)
PHONE.................................847 682-1776
D L Catton, *Principal*
EMP: 9 **EST:** 2010
SALES (est): 203.2K **Privately Held**
WEB: www.dontechindustriesinc.com
SIC: 3999 Manufacturing industries

(G-15029)
DOORS MOLDING AND MORE
2894 22nd Ave N (33713-4206)
PHONE.................................727 498-8552
Ngoc Huynh, *Principal*
EMP: 14 **EST:** 2012
SALES (est): 3.8MM **Privately Held**
WEB: www.dmmore.com
SIC: 3089 Molding primary plastic

(G-15030)
DORWARD ENERGY CORPORATION
447 3rd Ave N Ste 400 (33701-3255)
PHONE.................................727 490-1778
Dave Dorward Jr, *President*
EMP: 7 **EST:** 1955
SQ FT: 750
SALES (est): 1MM **Privately Held**
WEB: www.dorwardenergy.onlinerpts.com
SIC: 1311 Crude petroleum production

(G-15031)
DUJON INC
2480 25th St N (33713-4330)
PHONE.................................813 770-3179
Julius Brown, *CEO*
EMP: 12 **EST:** 2020
SALES (est): 225K **Privately Held**
SIC: 2321 2326 2331 Men's & boys' furnishings; men's & boys' work clothing; women's & misses' blouses & shirts

(G-15032)
E2G PARTNERS LLC
Also Called: Tampa Microwave
11200 Dr Mrtn Lther King (33716-2330)
PHONE.................................813 855-2251
Eric Guerrazzi, *President*
Scot Sherwood, *Consultant*
EMP: 28 **EST:** 1988
SALES (est): 1.9MM **Privately Held**
SIC: 3663 Microwave communication equipment

(G-15033)
EAGLE LABS INCORPORATED (PA)
5000 Park St N Ste 1202 (33709-2236)
PHONE.................................727 548-1816
Gary Dambach, *CEO*
Todd Dambach, *Vice Pres*
Janet Brambs, *Controller*
EMP: 24 **EST:** 2004
SALES (est): 5.7MM **Privately Held**
WEB: www.eaglelabsinc.com
SIC: 2834 2844 Vitamin, nutrient & hematinic preparations for human use; cosmetic preparations

(G-15034)
ELITE AERO LLC
4828 Queen Palm Ter Ne (33703-6300)
PHONE.................................727 244-3382
Mark Hansson,
EMP: 13 **EST:** 2009
SALES (est): 520.7K **Privately Held**
WEB: www.eliteaeroco.com
SIC: 3545 Precision tools, machinists'

(G-15035)
EMHART GLASS MANUFACTURING INC
Also Called: Emhart Inex
9875 18th St N (33716-4209)
PHONE.................................727 535-5502
Glen Long, *Director*
▲ **EMP:** 35 **EST:** 1993
SQ FT: 30,000
SALES (est): 21.8MM
SALES (corp-wide): 3.4B **Privately Held**
WEB: www.emhartglass.com
SIC: 3565 Bottling & canning machinery
HQ: Emhart Glass Sa
Hinterbergstrasse 22
Steinhausen ZG 6312
417 494-200

(G-15036)
ENSTAR HOLDINGS (US) LLC (HQ)
150 2nd Ave N Fl 3 (33701-3327)
PHONE.................................727 217-2900
Andrew Glasner, *VP Mfg*
Seth Wraight, *Engineer*
Fran Snavely, *Auditor*
Scott Wood, *Manager*
Cheryl D Davis, *Director*
EMP: 41 **EST:** 2014
SALES (est): 206.5MM **Privately Held**
SIC: 3714 3462 3568 Motor vehicle parts & accessories; iron & steel forgings; power transmission equipment

(G-15037)
ENVIRONMENTAL RECOVERY SYSTEMS
7001 Mango Ave S (33707-2023)
PHONE.................................727 344-3301
Karen Core, *Director*
EMP: 6 **EST:** 1990
SALES (est): 499.5K **Privately Held**
SIC: 3569 8731 3519 Separators for steam, gas, vapor or air (machinery); commercial physical research; internal combustion engines

(G-15038)
EVOLVEGENE LLC
12105 28th St N Ste A (33716-1817)
PHONE.................................727 623-4052
Mirela Pino, *President*
EMP: 9 **EST:** 2017
SALES (est): 351.5K **Privately Held**
SIC: 2835 Radioactive diagnostic substances

(G-15039)
EVOLVING COAL CORP
Also Called: Ecc
200 2nd Ave S Ste 733 (33701-4313)
PHONE.................................813 944-3100
Alan Petzold, *President*
Jose Bosch, *Vice Pres*
Terry Lin, *Vice Pres*
Roger Wertel, *Admin Sec*
▼ **EMP:** 5 **EST:** 2017
SQ FT: 750
SALES (est): 30MM **Privately Held**
SIC: 1221 1422 Coal preparation plant, bituminous or lignite; crushed & broken limestone

(G-15040)
EXCEL FUEL INC
6201 54th Ave N (33709-1701)
PHONE.................................727 547-5511
Mah'd Msawel, *Principal*
EMP: 9 **EST:** 2012
SALES (est): 365.9K **Privately Held**
SIC: 2869 Fuels

(G-15041)
EXTREME COATINGS
2895 46th Ave N (33714-3811)
PHONE.................................727 528-7998
Curt Kadau, *Principal*
Scott Caplan, *Vice Pres*
Steve Kelsay, *Sales Staff*
Kim Perez, *Sales Staff*
Kaitlyn Roy, *Sales Staff*
EMP: 7 **EST:** 2012
SALES (est): 282.7K **Privately Held**
WEB: www.extremecoatings.net
SIC: 3479 3089 3412 Chasing on metals; injection molding of plastics; barrels, shipping; metal

(G-15042)
FARMER MOLD AND MCH WORKS INC
2904 44th Ave N (33714-3804)
PHONE.................................727 522-0515
James O Gilmour, *President*
James Evers, *Principal*
Joseph Kniffin, *Engineer*
◆ **EMP:** 30 **EST:** 1938
SQ FT: 40,000
SALES (est): 5.8MM **Privately Held**
WEB: www.farmermold.com
SIC: 3599 Machine shop, jobbing & repair

(G-15043)
FASTSIGNS
4058 Park St N (33709-4034)
PHONE.................................727 341-0084
Michael Norris, *Principal*
EMP: 8 **EST:** 2012
SALES (est): 266.2K **Privately Held**
WEB: www.fastsigns.com
SIC: 3993 Signs & advertising specialties

(G-15044)
FIDELITY PRINTING CORPORATION
3662 Morris St N (33713-1697)
PHONE.................................727 522-9557
Robert Julian Hasson, *President*
Robert J Hasson Jr, *President*
James Allen Hasson, *Vice Pres*
William B Hasson, *Vice Pres*
Andy Belanger, *Sales Staff*
EMP: 60 **EST:** 1970
SQ FT: 9,000
SALES (est): 8.5MM **Privately Held**
WEB: www.fidelityprinting.com
SIC: 2752 2791 2789 2759 Commercial printing, offset; typesetting; bookbinding & related work; commercial printing

(G-15045)
FIELD FORENSICS INC
1601 3rd St S (33701-5542)
PHONE.................................727 490-3609
Craig Johnson, *President*
Christine Lekich, *Principal*
Jim Oneil, *Vice Pres*
Sean Meehan, *Research*
Katie Billi, *Accounts Mgr*
▼ **EMP:** 10 **EST:** 1999

SALES (est): 1.5MM **Privately Held**
WEB: www.fieldforensics.com
SIC: 3826 Analytical instruments

(G-15046)
FISHER ELECTRIC TECHNOLOGY INC
2801 72nd St N (33710-2903)
PHONE.................................727 345-9122
Richard Horbal MD, *Ch of Bd*
Nancy J Preis, *President*
Ned Schiff, *General Mgr*
EMP: 10 **EST:** 1987
SQ FT: 10,000
SALES (est): 895.8K **Privately Held**
WEB: www.motormagnetics.com
SIC: 3621 Motors & generators

(G-15047)
FIVE SPORTS INC
11880 28th St N Ste 100 (33716-1824)
PHONE.................................727 209-1750
Craig Baroncelli, *President*
EMP: 8 **EST:** 2007
SQ FT: 2,200
SALES (est): 717.7K **Privately Held**
SIC: 2721 Magazines: publishing & printing

(G-15048)
FLANDERS CORP
2399 26th Ave N (33713-4039)
PHONE.................................727 822-4411
Robert Amerson, *Chairman*
EMP: 17 **EST:** 2019
SALES (est): 412.7K **Privately Held**
SIC: 3564 Blowers & fans

(G-15049)
FLORIDA ELREHA CORPORATION
2510 Terminal Dr S (33712-1669)
PHONE.................................727 327-6236
Abdul Hamadeh, *President*
Rob Digiovanni, *Vice Pres*
Ahmad Hamadeh, *Vice Pres*
Junis Hamadeh, *Vice Pres*
▲ **EMP:** 47 **EST:** 1990
SQ FT: 100,000
SALES (est): 6.3MM **Privately Held**
WEB: www.elreha.de
SIC: 3672 Printed circuit boards

(G-15050)
FLORIDA FOREST PRODUCTS LLC
700 Beach Dr Ne Apt 803 (33701-2630)
P.O. Box 1345, Largo (33779-1345)
PHONE.................................727 585-2067
Diane Norton, *Controller*
Dona Skinner, *Controller*
Rafael Del, *Sales Mgr*
Ralph Valle, *Sales Mgr*
Dawn Ross, *Office Mgr*
EMP: 42 **EST:** 1994
SALES (est): 4.7MM **Privately Held**
WEB: www.ffptruss.com
SIC: 2439 Trusses, wooden roof

(G-15051)
FLORIDA PRINT SOLUTIONS INC (PA)
Also Called: Florida Laminating & Uv Svcs
432 31st St N (33713-7600)
PHONE.................................727 327-5500
Danielle Findley, *President*
Jessie Serrano, *President*
Jonathan Tallon, *Marketing Mgr*
Carol Thomas, *Manager*
EMP: 9 **EST:** 2012
SQ FT: 1,500
SALES (est): 2.2MM **Privately Held**
WEB: www.floridaprintsolutions.com
SIC: 2752 Commercial printing, offset

(G-15052)
FLORIDA SHED COMPANY INC (PA)
3865 Tyrone Blvd N (33709-4121)
PHONE.................................727 524-9191
Joseph H Campenella, *President*
Joseph Campenella, *President*
Robert Yankanich, *Admin Sec*
EMP: 28 **EST:** 1997

▲ = Import ▼ =Export
◆ =Import/Export

SALES (est): 4.4MM **Privately Held**
WEB: www.floridashed.com
SIC: 2452 Prefabricated buildings, wood

(G-15053)
FLORIDA STATE GRAPHICS INC
2828 20th Ave N (33713-4202)
PHONE......................727 328-0733
John Ruzecki, *President*
Richard Ruzecki, *Vice Pres*
EMP: 7 EST: 1989
SQ FT: 6,600
SALES (est): 800K **Privately Held**
WEB: www.vinylbinders.com
SIC: 2752 Commercial printing, lithographic

(G-15054)
FLORIDA VAULT SERVICE INC
3007 47th Ave N (33714-3133)
P.O. Box 3977, Bay Pines (33744-3977)
PHONE......................727 527-4992
Harry Sneadker, *Owner*
EMP: 7 EST: 2011
SALES (est): 218.9K **Privately Held**
SIC: 3272 Concrete products

(G-15055)
FORMULATED SOLUTIONS LLC
1776 11th Ave N (33713-5747)
PHONE......................727 456-0302
EMP: 9 EST: 2019
SALES (est): 408.6K **Privately Held**
WEB: www.formulatedsolutions.com
SIC: 2844 Cosmetic preparations

(G-15056)
G2 HARNESS LLC ✪
12000 28th St Nnull (33716)
PHONE......................915 892-2494
Chad London,
EMP: 5 EST: 2021
SALES (est): 652.9K **Privately Held**
WEB: www.g2harness.com
SIC: 3679 Harness assemblies for electronic use: wire or cable

(G-15057)
GA FD SVCS PINELLAS CNTY LLC (PA)
Also Called: G.A. Foods
12200 32nd Ct N (33716-1803)
PHONE......................727 573-2211
Glenn Davenport, *President*
Neil King, *General Mgr*
Shannon Linder, *Regional Mgr*
John D Hale, *COO*
John Hale, *COO*
▲ EMP: 300 EST: 1973
SQ FT: 180,000
SALES (est): 151.6MM **Privately Held**
WEB: www.sunmeadow.com
SIC: 2038 5812 Frozen specialties; contract food services

(G-15058)
GENERAL DYNAMICS-OTS INC (HQ)
100 Carillon Pkwy Ste 100 # 100 (33716-1208)
PHONE......................727 578-8100
Firat Gezen, *CEO*
Dan Chien, *President*
Michael Chin, *Regional Mgr*
Charles Hall, *Exec VP*
Tim McAuliffe, *Vice Pres*
◆ EMP: 100 EST: 1948
SALES (corp-wide): 38.4B **Publicly Held**
SIC: 3728 3812 Military aircraft equipment & armament; search & navigation equipment
PA: General Dynamics Corporation
11011 Sunset Hills Rd
Reston VA 20190
703 876-3000

(G-15059)
GENERAL DYNMICS ORD TCTCAL SYS
3340 Scherer Dr N Ste E (33716-1013)
PHONE......................727 578-8243
Firat Gezen, *Principal*
Timothy Bagniefski, *Principal*
Karyn Bruneau, *Principal*

Caroline Keller, *Principal*
Mark Peterson, *Principal*
EMP: 7 EST: 1996
SALES (est): 460.2K **Privately Held**
WEB: www.gd-ots.com
SIC: 3728 Aircraft parts & equipment

(G-15060)
GENERAL DYNMICS ORD TCTCAL SYS (HQ)
100 Carillon Pkwy (33716-1207)
PHONE......................727 578-8100
Michael S Wilson, *President*
Michael Morris, *Maint Spvr*
Tony Bonahoom, *Opers Staff*
Chris Feather, *Opers Staff*
Chris Jackson, *Mfg Staff*
◆ EMP: 230 EST: 1996
SQ FT: 150,000
SALES (est): 525.2MM
SALES (corp-wide): 38.4B **Publicly Held**
WEB: www.gd-ots.com
SIC: 3483 3482 2892 3489 Ammunition, except for small arms; small arms ammunition; explosives; ordnance & accessories
PA: General Dynamics Corporation
11011 Sunset Hills Rd
Reston VA 20190
703 876-3000

(G-15061)
GIEBNER ENTERPRISES INC
Also Called: Com-Ten Industries
4760 Brittany Dr S Apt 20 (33715-1673)
PHONE......................727 520-1200
Betty Giebner, *President*
Tom Giebner, *Treasurer*
▲ EMP: 15 EST: 1960
SQ FT: 12,000
SALES (est): 498.9K **Privately Held**
WEB: www.com-ten.com
SIC: 3829 Physical property testing equipment

(G-15062)
GLOBAL PRINTING SOLUTIONS INC
2569 25th Ave N (33713-3918)
PHONE......................727 458-3483
EMP: 6 EST: 2018
SALES (est): 389.5K **Privately Held**
WEB: www.seegps.com
SIC: 2752 Commercial printing, offset

(G-15063)
GO 2 PRINT NOW INC
Also Called: G2pn.com
2390 26th Ave N (33713-4040)
P.O. Box 8429, Seminole (33775-8429)
PHONE......................800 500-4276
Kymberly Wostbrock, *President*
Chris Dunn, *Production*
Sandy Zink, *Personnel*
EMP: 25 EST: 2000
SALES (est): 5.2MM **Privately Held**
WEB: www.g2pn.com
SIC: 2759 Commercial printing

(G-15064)
GODWIN AND SINGER INC
1415 Burlington Ave N (33705-1579)
PHONE......................727 896-8631
Steven Trimm, *President*
Linda Trimm, *Vice Pres*
Linda Trimms, *Vice Pres*
EMP: 9 EST: 1945
SQ FT: 3,570
SALES (est): 931.3K **Privately Held**
WEB: www.godwinsinger.com
SIC: 3599 7538 Machine shop, jobbing & repair; engine repair, except diesel: automotive

(G-15065)
GOLDBERG SYSTEMS LLC
575 24th Ave Se (33705-3309)
PHONE......................843 513-5277
Stefan Goldberg,
EMP: 7 EST: 2014
SALES (est): 1.9MM
SALES (corp-wide): 761.2K **Privately Held**
WEB: www.goldberg-systems.com
SIC: 3566 Speed changers, drives & gears

PA: Goldberg Systems Gmbh
Landsberger Str. 155
Munchen BY
895 795-9651

(G-15066)
GREAT AMERCN NATURAL PDTS INC
Also Called: Bulk Food Grocers
4121 16th St N (33703-5607)
PHONE......................727 521-4372
Ron Hamilton, *President*
Karan Martinotti, *Controller*
EMP: 19 EST: 1970
SQ FT: 2,640
SALES (est): 3.7MM **Privately Held**
WEB: www.greatamerican.biz
SIC: 2833 5499 Vitamins, natural or synthetic: bulk, uncompounded; health & dietetic food stores

(G-15067)
GREENCORE LLC
970 Tyrone Blvd N (33710-6333)
PHONE......................727 251-9837
Arnie Cummings, *Vice Pres*
Holle R Chiappo, *Mng Member*
EMP: 5 EST: 2008
SQ FT: 1,000
SALES (est): 510.4K **Privately Held**
WEB: www.greencore.com
SIC: 2891 Cement, except linoleum & tile

(G-15068)
GULFCOAST SAILING INC
1354 20th St N (33713-5743)
PHONE......................727 823-1968
Tom M Barry, *President*
EMP: 7 EST: 1998
SALES (est): 656K **Privately Held**
SIC: 2394 Sails: made from purchased materials

(G-15069)
GULL TOOL & MACHINE INC
3033 47th Ave N Frnt (33714-3191)
PHONE......................727 527-0808
John J Gill, *President*
EMP: 5 EST: 1973
SQ FT: 3,500
SALES (est): 390.3K **Privately Held**
SIC: 3599 3519 Machine shop, jobbing & repair; marine engines

(G-15070)
GUNNS WELDING & FABRICATING
4729 96th St N (33708-3738)
PHONE......................727 393-5238
Joanne Gunn, *President*
Robert Gunn Jr, *Vice Pres*
Judy Larson, *Treasurer*
EMP: 5 EST: 1988
SQ FT: 5,000
SALES (est): 562.5K **Privately Held**
SIC: 3599 7692 1799 3441 Custom machinery; machine shop, jobbing & repair; welding repair; welding on site; fabricated structural metal; tube fabricating (contract bending & shaping)

(G-15071)
H & T GLOBAL CIRCUIT FCTRY LLC
Also Called: H&T Global Circuits
2510 Terminal Dr S (33712-1669)
P.O. Box 17744, Clearwater (33762-0744)
PHONE......................727 327-6236
Dan Schutte, *Business Mgr*
Tom Miller, *Plant Mgr*
William Rice, *Warehouse Mgr*
Steven Garcia, *Opers Staff*
Tamara Jordan, *Purchasing*
◆ EMP: 70 EST: 2001
SQ FT: 35,000
SALES (est): 15.2MM **Privately Held**
WEB: www.htglobalcircuits.com
SIC: 3672 Printed circuit boards

(G-15072)
HALKEY-ROBERTS CORPORATION (HQ)
2700 Halkey Roberts Pl N (33716-4103)
PHONE......................727 471-4200
David Battat, *President*

Alan King, *Vice Pres*
Lewis P Lecceardone, *Vice Pres*
John H Lucius, *Vice Pres*
Karen Prescott, *Purch Mgr*
▲ EMP: 200 EST: 1945
SQ FT: 142,000
SALES (est): 116.7MM
SALES (corp-wide): 165MM **Publicly Held**
WEB: www.halkeyroberts.com
SIC: 3842 Surgical appliances & supplies
PA: Atrion Corporation
1 Allentown Pkwy
Allen TX 75002
972 390-9800

(G-15073)
HEALTH AND BEAUTY MFG LLC ✪
7205 30th Ave N (33710-2915)
PHONE......................727 565-0797
Adam Oliver, *Mng Member*
EMP: 5 EST: 2022
SALES (est): 357.2K **Privately Held**
SIC: 2844 Face creams or lotions

(G-15074)
HERITAGE MANUFACTURING SVCS
4365 22nd St N (33714-4144)
PHONE......................727 906-5599
Jason Bedell, *Principal*
EMP: 7 EST: 2011
SALES (est): 118.6K **Privately Held**
SIC: 3443 Metal parts

(G-15075)
HIGHROLLA EMPIRE LLC ✪
7901 4th St N Ste 300 (33702-4399)
PHONE......................954 743-5324
Andre Clarke,
EMP: 14 EST: 2022
SALES (est): 575.3K **Privately Held**
SIC: 2782 Record albums

(G-15076)
HINE AUTOMATION LLC
12495 34th St N Ste B (33716-1833)
PHONE......................813 749-7519
Karl Pearson, *Opers Staff*
Anthony Williams, *Purch Mgr*
Becky Burner, *Buyer*
John Boozer, *Engineer*
Brendon Cordon, *Engineer*
EMP: 7 EST: 2009
SALES (est): 2.4MM **Privately Held**
WEB: www.hineautomation.com
SIC: 3674 Wafers (semiconductor devices)

(G-15077)
HOME ELMENTS ST PETERSBURG INC
790 Cordova Blvd Ne (33704-3040)
PHONE......................727 510-5700
Reed Sherri, *Principal*
EMP: 7 EST: 2014
SALES (est): 223.4K **Privately Held**
SIC: 2819 Industrial inorganic chemicals

(G-15078)
HOT TUB PARTS LLC
6190 45th St N Ste A (33714-1011)
PHONE......................727 573-9611
Brian K Wiley,
▼ EMP: 6 EST: 2008
SALES (est): 632.5K **Privately Held**
WEB: www.hottubparts.com
SIC: 3088 Hot tubs, plastic or fiberglass

(G-15079)
HYDRON TECHNOLOGIES INC
9843 18th St N Ste 150 (33716-4208)
PHONE......................727 342-5050
Helen Canetano, *CEO*
Richard Banakus, *Ch of Bd*
▲ EMP: 9 EST: 1948
SQ FT: 7,000
SALES (est): 323.1K **Privately Held**
SIC: 2844 Toilet preparations

(G-15080)
I3 MICROSYSTEMS INC
9900 16th St N (33716-4230)
PHONE......................727 235-6532
James Matthews, *President*

Michelle Eldred, *Vice Pres*
EMP: 42 **EST:** 2013
SALES (est): 10MM
SALES (corp-wide): 120.8MM **Privately Held**
WEB: www.i3electronics.com
SIC: 3672 Printed circuit boards
PA: I3 Electronics, Inc.
100 Eldredge St
Binghamton NY 13901
607 238-7077

(G-15081)
ICARE INDUSTRIES INC (PA)
4399 35th St N Ste 100 (33714-3700)
PHONE....................727 512-3000
James S Payne, *President*
Scott S Payne, *Vice Pres*
Robert Stevens, *Vice Pres*
Cy Stankiewicz, *CFO*
Greg Gehrig, *Financial Exec*
EMP: 150 **EST:** 1968
SQ FT: 72,000
SALES (est): 60.9MM **Privately Held**
WEB: www.icare.com
SIC: 3851 5995 Ophthalmic goods; contact lenses, prescription

(G-15082)
IDEAL PUBLISHING CO INC
Also Called: Lightening Print
3063 Lown St N (33713-2930)
PHONE....................727 321-0785
John Kavanagh, *President*
EMP: 7 **EST:** 1971
SQ FT: 6,750
SALES (est): 375.6K **Privately Held**
WEB: www.lightningprint.net
SIC: 2752 Commercial printing, offset

(G-15083)
IMAGE EXPERTS INC
4556 36th Ave N (33713-1154)
PHONE....................727 488-7556
James E Warren Jr, *President*
Jason Devins, *CFO*
EMP: 7 **EST:** 2005
SALES (est): 163.6K **Privately Held**
WEB: www.imageexperts.com
SIC: 2711 Commercial printing & newspaper publishing combined

(G-15084)
INFRASTRUCTURE REPAIR SYSTEMS
3113 Lown St N (33713-2932)
PHONE....................727 327-4216
William Higman, *Principal*
Rosetta Higman, *Principal*
John Scoville, *Manager*
EMP: 5 **EST:** 1997
SQ FT: 3,000
SALES (est): 348.9K **Privately Held**
WEB: www.irsi.net
SIC: 3259 Liner brick or plates for sewer/tank lining, vitrified clay

(G-15085)
INNOVATIVE BASE TECH LLC
Also Called: Ultra Base Systems
5030 Seminole Blvd (33708-3300)
PHONE....................727 391-9009
Cassandra Felt, *Controller*
David R Barlow, *Mng Member*
EMP: 7 **EST:** 2008
SQ FT: 1,500
SALES (est): 1MM **Privately Held**
WEB: www.ultrabasesystems.com
SIC: 3089 Flat panels, plastic

(G-15086)
INTELLITECH INC
11801 28th St N Ste 5 (33716-1813)
PHONE....................727 914-7000
Barbara H Biller, *President*
Andy Biller, *Vice Pres*
EMP: 24 **EST:** 1995
SQ FT: 12,000
SALES (est): 4.1MM **Privately Held**
WEB: www.intellitech-inc.com
SIC: 3565 Packaging machinery

(G-15087)
J & D OLDJA LLC
4424 34th St N (33714-3712)
PHONE....................727 526-3240

Tonia Warner, *Office Mgr*
John D Oldja, *Mng Member*
EMP: 10 **EST:** 2010
SALES (est): 831.6K **Privately Held**
SIC: 2434 Wood kitchen cabinets

(G-15088)
J & J MARINE SERVICE INC
Also Called: Quickload Custom Built Trlrs
2922 46th Ave N (33714-3814)
PHONE....................813 741-2190
John D Nowling, *President*
EMP: 6 **EST:** 1981
SALES (est): 602.6K **Privately Held**
SIC: 3799 7539 Boat trailers; trailer repair

(G-15089)
JABIL ADVNCED MECH SLTIONS INC
10560 Dr M Lth Kng Jr St Martin (33716)
PHONE....................727 577-9749
Timothy L Main, *CEO*
Emanuele Cavallaro, *Senior VP*
EMP: 34 **EST:** 2010
SALES (est): 3.8MM
SALES (corp-wide): 29.2B **Publicly Held**
SIC: 3672 Printed circuit boards
PA: Jabil Inc.
10800 Roosevelt Blvd N
Saint Petersburg FL 33716
727 577-9749

(G-15090)
JABIL CIRCUIT
9700 18th St N (33716-4201)
PHONE....................727 577-9749
EMP: 5
SALES (est): 672.1K **Privately Held**
SIC: 3672 Printed Circuit Boards

(G-15091)
JABIL CIRCUIT LLC (HQ)
10560 Dr Mlk Jr St N (33716)
PHONE....................727 577-9749
Mark T Mondello, *CEO*
Tim L Main, *Ch of Bd*
William E Peters, *President*
Amy Crawford, *Partner*
Forbes I Alexander, *Principal*
▲ **EMP:** 4 **EST:** 2002
SALES (est): 526.4MM
SALES (corp-wide): 29.2B **Publicly Held**
SIC: 3672 Circuit boards, television & radio printed
PA: Jabil Inc.
10800 Roosevelt Blvd N
Saint Petersburg FL 33716
727 577-9749

(G-15092)
JABIL CIRCUIT LLC
3201 34th St S (33711-3828)
PHONE....................727 577-9749
Daniel Woerner, *Project Mgr*
Samantha McIntyre, *Buyer*
Lewis Carpenter, *Engineer*
Mauricio Zaragoza, *Engineer*
Sheri King, *HR Admin*
EMP: 64
SALES (corp-wide): 29.2B **Publicly Held**
SIC: 3672 Printed circuit boards
HQ: Jabil Circuit, Llc
10560 Dr Mlk Jr St N
Saint Petersburg FL 33716
727 577-9749

(G-15093)
JABIL DEF & AROSPC SVCS LLC (HQ)
10500 Dr Mrtn Lther King (33716-3718)
PHONE....................727 577-9749
Mark T Mondello, *CEO*
William D Muir J, *COO*
William Muir, *COO*
Joseph A McGee, *Exec VP*
Sergio A Cadavid, *Senior VP*
EMP: 47 **EST:** 2004
SALES (est): 50.9MM
SALES (corp-wide): 29.2B **Publicly Held**
SIC: 3672 Printed circuit boards
PA: Jabil Inc.
10800 Roosevelt Blvd N
Saint Petersburg FL 33716
727 577-9749

(G-15094)
JABIL DEF & AROSPC SVCS LLC (HQ)
10560 Dr Mlk Jr St N (33716)
PHONE....................727 577-9749
EMP: 18
SALES (est): 14.9MM
SALES (corp-wide): 22.1B **Publicly Held**
SIC: 3672 Mfg Printed Circuit Boards
PA: Jabil Inc.
10560 Dr Martin Luther
Saint Petersburg FL 33716
727 577-9749

(G-15095)
JABIL INC (PA)
10800 Roosevelt Blvd N (33716-2307)
PHONE....................727 577-9749
Steven D Borges, *CEO*
Kenneth S Wilson, *CEO*
Mark T Mondello, *Ch of Bd*
Thomas A Sansone, *Vice Ch Bd*
Robert L Katz, *Exec VP*
EMP: 1344 **EST:** 1966
SALES (est): 29.2B **Publicly Held**
WEB: www.jabil.com
SIC: 3672 Printed circuit boards

(G-15096)
JABIL INC
10500 Dr Mlk Jr St N Dock (33716)
PHONE....................727 577-9749
EMP: 41
SALES (corp-wide): 27.2B **Publicly Held**
SIC: 3672 Printed Circuit Boards
PA: Jabil Inc.
10560 Dr Mrtn Lther King
Saint Petersburg FL 33716
727 577-9749

(G-15097)
JABIL INC
Also Called: Jabil Luxembourg Manufacturing
1300 Dr Marti Luthe King (33705-1002)
PHONE....................727 803-3110
Courtney Ryan, *Exec VP*
Manny Vazquez, *Engineer*
Marty Rodriguez, *Project Engr*
Ron Anderson, *Human Resources*
Sarah Crudo, *Manager*
EMP: 200
SALES (corp-wide): 29.2B **Publicly Held**
WEB: www.jabil.com
SIC: 3672 Printed circuit boards
PA: Jabil Inc.
10800 Roosevelt Blvd N
Saint Petersburg FL 33716
727 577-9749

(G-15098)
JABIL INC
10500 Dr Mrtn Lther King (33716-3718)
PHONE....................727 577-9749
Thomas Toner, *Counsel*
Chinseng Chuah, *Project Mgr*
Howard Yang, *Project Mgr*
Mike Torregrossa, *Opers Mgr*
Mauricio Mena, *Mfg Mgr*
EMP: 75
SALES (corp-wide): 29.2B **Publicly Held**
WEB: www.jabil.com
SIC: 3672 Printed circuit boards
PA: Jabil Inc.
10800 Roosevelt Blvd N
Saint Petersburg FL 33716
727 577-9749

(G-15099)
JACKIE Z STYLE CO ST PETE LLC
Also Called: Jackiezstyleco
113 2nd Ave N (33701-3315)
PHONE....................727 258-4849
Jackie Zumba, *Owner*
EMP: 9 **EST:** 2012
SALES (est): 544.3K **Privately Held**
WEB: www.jackiezstyle.com
SIC: 2326 5621 Men's & boys' work clothing; women's clothing stores

(G-15100)
JANE AND GEORGE INDUSTRIES
4197 49th Ave S (33711-4619)
PHONE....................727 698-4903

Nathan E Dameron, *Principal*
EMP: 9 **EST:** 2016
SALES (est): 120.1K **Privately Held**
SIC: 3999 Manufacturing industries

(G-15101)
JMI-DNIELS PHARMACEUTICALS INC
2517 25th Ave N (33713-3918)
PHONE....................727 323-5151
Brian A Markison, *President*
Joseph Squicciarino, *CFO*
Joe Bayman, *Manager*
James W Elrod, *Admin Sec*
EMP: 242 **EST:** 2010
SALES (est): 3.2MM
SALES (corp-wide): 81.2B **Publicly Held**
SIC: 2834 Pharmaceutical preparations
HQ: King Pharmaceuticals Llc
501 5th St
Bristol TN 37620

(G-15102)
JOANNE JAMES RUSSELL
2166 Blossom Way S (33712-6016)
PHONE....................805 467-3331
Joanne Russell, *Principal*
EMP: 8 **EST:** 2004
SALES (est): 224.3K **Privately Held**
SIC: 2084 Wines

(G-15103)
KEG CONNECT LLC
100 2nd Ave S Ste 701 (33701-4360)
PHONE....................727 821-8752
J Thomas I Williams II, *Principal*
EMP: 5 **EST:** 2014
SALES (est): 349.6K **Privately Held**
WEB: www.elease.com
SIC: 2082 Malt beverages

(G-15104)
KING PHARMACEUTICALS LLC
2540 26th Ave N (33713-3929)
PHONE....................423 989-8000
Elaine Strauss, *Vice Pres*
Mike Lambert, *Mfg Staff*
Trent Barnard, *Sales Staff*
Sarah Belcher, *Sales Staff*
Michael Homer, *Sales Staff*
EMP: 60
SALES (corp-wide): 81.2B **Publicly Held**
SIC: 2834 Pharmaceutical preparations
HQ: King Pharmaceuticals Llc
501 5th St
Bristol TN 37620

(G-15105)
KOZUBA & SONS DISTILLERY INC
1960 5th Ave S (33712-1324)
PHONE....................813 857-8197
Zbigniew Kozuba, *President*
▲ **EMP:** 6 **EST:** 2015
SALES (est): 1.1MM **Privately Held**
WEB: www.kozubadistillery.com
SIC: 2085 Distilled & blended liquors

(G-15106)
KRAFT HEINZ FOODS COMPANY
3901 52nd Ave N (33714-2336)
PHONE....................727 459-4527
Christopher Heinz, *Branch Mgr*
EMP: 7
SALES (corp-wide): 26B **Publicly Held**
WEB: www.kraftheinzcompany.com
SIC: 2033 Canned fruits & specialties
HQ: Kraft Heinz Foods Company
1 Ppg Pl Ste 3400
Pittsburgh PA 15222
412 456-5700

(G-15107)
L3 AVIATION PRODUCTS INC
Also Called: L3 Technologies
490 1st Ave S Ste 600 (33701-4287)
PHONE....................941 371-0811
Frank Doran, *President*
Bruce Coffee, *Branch Mgr*
Michelle Crawford, *Software Engr*
Christian Cunningham, *Commercial*
EMP: 140
SALES (corp-wide): 17.8B **Publicly Held**
WEB: avionics.cas.l3harris.com
SIC: 3769 Guided missile & space vehicle parts & aux eqpt, rsch & dev

▲ = Import ▼=Export
◆ =Import/Export

HQ: L3 Aviation Products, Inc.
5353 52nd St Se
Grand Rapids MI 49512
616 949-6600

(G-15108)
L3 TECHNOLOGIES INC
490 1st Ave S (33701-4204)
PHONE....................941 371-0811
Jennifer Ford, *Manager*
EMP: 11
SALES (corp-wide): 17.8B **Publicly Held**
WEB: www.l3harris.com
SIC: 3812 Search & navigation equipment
HQ: L3 Technologies, Inc.
600 3rd Ave Fl 34
New York NY 10016
321 727-9100

(G-15109)
LEGACY VULCAN LLC
1020 31st St S (33712-1925)
PHONE....................727 321-4667
Paul Beavin, *Branch Mgr*
EMP: 8 **Publicly Held**
SIC: 3273 Ready-mixed concrete
HQ: Legacy Vulcan, Llc
1200 Urban Center Dr
Vestavia AL 35242
205 298-3000

(G-15110)
LEISURE ACTIVITIES USA LLC
2399 26th Ave N (33713-4039)
PHONE....................727 417-7128
Yi Cao, *President*
EMP: 7 EST: 2017
SALES (est): 356.5K **Privately Held**
WEB: www.leisureactivitiesusa.com
SIC: 3944 Games, toys & children's vehicles

(G-15111)
LENSTEC INC (PA)
1765 Commerce Ave N (33716-4207)
PHONE....................727 571-2272
John Clough, *President*
Margaret N Clough, *Vice Pres*
Bill Hanley, *Vice Pres*
Rick Harrison, *QC Mgr*
Briankirk Graham, *Engineer*
EMP: 19 EST: 1993
SQ FT: 23,000
SALES (est): 5.4MM **Privately Held**
WEB: www.lenstec.com
SIC: 3827 Optical instruments & apparatus

(G-15112)
LILLIAN BAY MEDICAL INC
260 1st Ave S Ste 200 (33701-4364)
PHONE....................941 815-7373
Brad M Beatty, *President*
EMP: 12 EST: 2020
SALES (est): 553.1K **Privately Held**
WEB: www.lillianbaymedical.com
SIC: 2836 Biological products, except diagnostic

(G-15113)
LPI INC
6101 45th St N (33714-1038)
PHONE....................702 403-8555
David Bonior, *Principal*
Frey Louis Jr, *Principal*
EMP: 11 EST: 2018
SALES (est): 214.7K **Privately Held**
WEB: www.lpiinc.com
SIC: 3088 Plastics plumbing fixtures

(G-15114)
LUCKE GROUP INC
Also Called: Fastsigns
408 33rd Ave N Ste A (33704-1384)
PHONE....................727 525-4949
Gary Lucke, *President*
EMP: 6 EST: 1997
SQ FT: 4,600
SALES (est): 727.4K **Privately Held**
WEB: www.fastsigns.com
SIC: 3993 Signs & advertising specialties

(G-15115)
LUMASTREAM INC (PA)
2201 1st Ave S (33712-1219)
PHONE....................727 827-2805
Eric Higgs, *Ch of Bd*

George Gordon, *President*
Rob Kapusta, *Chairman*
Chris Booth, *Vice Pres*
Mike Gaydos, *Vice Pres*
▲ EMP: 20 EST: 2009
SALES (est): 4.5MM **Privately Held**
WEB: www.lumastream.com
SIC: 3646 Commercial indusl & institutional electric lighting fixtures

(G-15116)
M VICTORIA ENTERPRISES INC
Also Called: 4th St Print Shack
9109 4th St N (33702-3129)
PHONE....................727 576-8090
Michelle L Grant, *President*
EMP: 10 EST: 2008
SALES (est): 254.6K **Privately Held**
SIC: 2752 Commercial printing, offset

(G-15117)
MARCO POLO PUBLICATIONS INC
360 Central Ave Ste 1260 (33701-3865)
PHONE....................866 610-9441
James Plouf, *President*
David Plouf, *Vice Pres*
Wendy Lahr-Bees, *Marketing Staff*
EMP: 6 EST: 1996
SALES (est): 801.2K **Privately Held**
WEB: www.marcopolopublications.com
SIC: 2759 Publication printing

(G-15118)
MARINE ELECTRONICS ENGINE
4801 96th St N (33708-3740)
PHONE....................727 459-5593
EMP: 8 EST: 2010
SALES (est): 108.8K **Privately Held**
SIC: 3519 Marine engines

(G-15119)
MARINE INDUSTRIAL PAINT CO INC
4590 60th Ave N (33714-1035)
PHONE....................727 527-3382
Gregory T Deininger, *President*
Patricia Deininger, *Corp Secy*
Jerome Deininger, *Vice Pres*
Steven Deininger, *Vice Pres*
Carson Deininger, *Technical Staff*
EMP: 16 EST: 1962
SQ FT: 10,000
SALES (est): 2.6MM **Privately Held**
WEB: www.tuf-top.com
SIC: 2851 Paints & paint additives

(G-15120)
MARINETEK NORTH AMERICA INC
111 2nd Ave Ne Ste 360 (33701-3580)
PHONE....................727 498-8741
Richard Murray, *President*
Harri Weckstrom, *Vice Pres*
Henri Markus, *CFO*
Jukka Saarikko, *CFO*
Deborah Brook, *Treasurer*
◆ EMP: 12 EST: 2012
SALES (est): 8.5MM **Privately Held**
WEB: www.marinetek.net
SIC: 3448 Prefabricated metal buildings
PA: Marinetek Group Oy
Mittalinja 2
Vantaa 01260

(G-15121)
MARK WALTERS LLC
1126 15th Ave N (33704-4120)
PHONE....................727 742-3091
Mark J Walters, *Principal*
EMP: 7 EST: 2007
SALES (est): 122.1K **Privately Held**
WEB: www.waltersco.com
SIC: 2741 Miscellaneous publishing

(G-15122)
MAXI-BLAST OF FLORIDA INC
Also Called: Econo-Blast
11000 Gandy Blvd N (33702-1423)
P.O. Box 13027 (33733-3027)
PHONE....................727 572-0909
Robert A Donaldson, *President*
Dale Fisher, *Vice Pres*
EMP: 8 EST: 1980
SQ FT: 10,000

SALES (est): 1.3MM **Privately Held**
SIC: 3291 3089 Abrasive products; plastic processing

(G-15123)
MB WELDING INC
7360 46th Ave N (33709-2504)
PHONE....................727 548-0923
Michele L Barga, *Principal*
EMP: 12 EST: 2010
SALES (est): 399.9K **Privately Held**
SIC: 7692 Welding repair

(G-15124)
MC GRAPHICS LLC
1527 102nd Ave N (33716-5049)
PHONE....................727 579-1527
Michael Graff, *CEO*
EMP: 1 EST: 1989
SQ FT: 87,500
SALES (est): 3.6MM
SALES (corp-wide): 121.9MM **Privately Held**
SIC: 2752 Commercial printing, offset
PA: Sandy Alexander, Inc.
200 Entin Rd
Clifton NJ 07014
973 470-8100

(G-15125)
MCKENNY PRINTING ENTP INC
Also Called: Speedpro Imaging St Petersburg
2748 25th St N (33713-3942)
PHONE....................727 420-4944
Michael McKenny, *CEO*
Jenny Prado, *Accounting Mgr*
EMP: 5 EST: 2015
SALES (est): 871.3K **Privately Held**
SIC: 3993 5999 7336 3577 Signs & advertising specialties; displays & cutouts, window & lobby; banners, flags, decals & posters; graphic arts & related design; graphic displays, except graphic terminals

(G-15126)
MILLIMETER WAVE PRODUCTS INC
Also Called: Center Technologies
2007 Gandy Blvd N # 1310 (33702-2169)
PHONE....................727 563-0034
Mark Smith, *President*
Ariana Nimani, *Engineer*
Lokesh Saggam, *Project Engr*
▲ EMP: 25 EST: 1996
SQ FT: 8,000
SALES (est): 3.2MM **Privately Held**
WEB: www.miwv.com
SIC: 3663 Microwave communication equipment; space satellite communications equipment; satellites, communications

(G-15127)
MILLS & MURPHY SFTWR SYSTEMS
618 94th Ave N (33702-2408)
P.O. Box 56689 (33732-6689)
PHONE....................727 577-1236
F Edward Murphy, *President*
Scott J Mills, *Vice Pres*
EMP: 19 EST: 1991
SQ FT: 5,500
SALES (est): 566.7K **Privately Held**
WEB: www.millsmur.com
SIC: 7372 Prepackaged software

(G-15128)
MODERN TCHNCAL MOLDING DEV LLC
Also Called: MTM&d
2600 72nd St N (33710-2929)
PHONE....................727 343-2942
Dave S Massie, *President*
John Basley, *General Mgr*
Dave Gunthrop, *QC Mgr*
EMP: 17 EST: 2008
SQ FT: 22,000
SALES (est): 2.7MM **Privately Held**
WEB: www.mtmd.com
SIC: 3089 Injection molding of plastics; injection molded finished plastic products

(G-15129)
MOLLYS SUDS LLC
7490 30th Ave N A (33710-2304)
PHONE....................678 361-5456
Monica M Leonard, *President*
Rick Leonard, *Vice Pres*
Lisa Kimball, *Marketing Staff*
EMP: 6 EST: 2011
SALES (est): 904.8K **Privately Held**
WEB: www.mollyssuds.com
SIC: 2841 2842 Soap & other detergents; laundry cleaning preparations

(G-15130)
MOMMY & ME MOLDS LLC
1359 Monterey Blvd Ne (33704-2354)
PHONE....................727 460-0335
Sally Dumas, *Mng Member*
EMP: 7 EST: 2008
SALES (est): 177.9K **Privately Held**
SIC: 3544 Industrial molds

(G-15131)
MOTHER KOMBUCHA LLC
Also Called: Agua Bucha
4360 28th St N (33714-3924)
PHONE....................727 767-0408
Vic Donati, *Partner*
Josh Rumschlag, *Partner*
Elizabeth Vanneste, *Partner*
Stephanie Davenport, *Sales Mgr*
Carly Craven, *Sales Staff*
EMP: 10 EST: 2014
SQ FT: 13,000
SALES (est): 1.6MM **Privately Held**
WEB: www.motherkombucha.com
SIC: 2099 Tea blending

(G-15132)
MOTOR MAGNETICS INC
2801 72nd St N (33710-2903)
PHONE....................727 873-3180
Nancy Preis, *President*
Edward Schiff, *Vice Pres*
Victor Marino, *Purchasing*
Richard Horbal MD, *Treasurer*
Denise Layman, *Manager*
▲ EMP: 24 EST: 1974
SQ FT: 10,000
SALES (est): 5.3MM **Privately Held**
WEB: www.motormagnetics.com
SIC: 3621 Motors, electric

(G-15133)
MTS MEDICATION TECH INC (HQ)
2003 Gandy Blvd N Ste 800 (33702-2167)
PHONE....................727 576-6311
Todd E Siegel, *CEO*
William G Shields, *President*
Matthew C Hicks, *Corp Secy*
Michael D Stevenson, *COO*
Robert A Martin, *Vice Pres*
▲ EMP: 230 EST: 1986
SQ FT: 132,500
SALES (est): 49.2MM **Publicly Held**
WEB: www.mts-mt.com
SIC: 3565 3089 Packaging machinery; blister or bubble formed packaging, plastic

(G-15134)
MTS PACKAGING SYSTEMS INC (PA)
2003 Gandy Blvd N Ste 800 (33702-2167)
PHONE....................727 576-6311
Todd E Siegel, *President*
Selm Robin E, *Principal*
Michael Stevenson, *COO*
Michael P Conroy, *CFO*
Stephanie Mueller, *Human Res Dir*
▼ EMP: 125 EST: 1992
SALES (est): 11MM **Privately Held**
SIC: 3089 Blister or bubble formed packaging, plastic

(G-15135)
MULTI-PANELS CORPORATION
360 Central Ave Ste 800 (33701-3984)
PHONE....................800 723-8620
Sten Sorensen, *CEO*
▼ EMP: 6 EST: 2016
SALES (est): 500K **Privately Held**
WEB: www.multi-panels.com
SIC: 3089 Corrugated panels, plastic

(G-15136)
NASCO AEROSPACE AND ELEC LLC
3232 44th Ave N (33714-3810)
PHONE...................................727 344-7554
Woody Hewett, *QC Mgr*
Vanessa Porter, *Accounts Exec*
Danny Casanova, *Sales Staff*
Jami Davis, *Sales Staff*
Tracey Geyer, *Sales Staff*
EMP: 13
SALES (corp-wide): 23.8MM **Privately Held**
WEB: www.nascosales.com
SIC: 3452 3674 3728 3676 Bolts, nuts, rivets & washers; semiconductors & related devices; aircraft parts & equipment; electronic resistors
PA: Nasco Aerospace And Electronics Llc
3232 44th Ave N
Saint Petersburg FL 33714
727 344-7554

(G-15137)
NDH MEDICAL INC
11001 Roosevelt Blvd N # 150
(33716-2348)
PHONE...................................727 570-2293
Geary A Havran, *President*
EMP: 5 EST: 1986
SQ FT: 6,000
SALES (est): 1.1MM **Privately Held**
WEB: www.ndhmedical.com
SIC: 3841 Surgical instruments & apparatus

(G-15138)
NEW DAWN COFFEE COMPANY INC
2336 5th Ave S (33712-1631)
PHONE...................................727 321-5155
Terese Delangis, *President*
EMP: 6 EST: 1985
SQ FT: 14,000
SALES (est): 464K **Privately Held**
WEB: www.newdawncoffee.com
SIC: 2095 2099 Coffee roasting (except by wholesale grocers); tea blending

(G-15139)
NI-CHRO PLATING CORP
Also Called: M and P Plating
700 37th St S (33711-2119)
PHONE...................................727 327-5118
Peter Valantiejus, *President*
John Kutch, *Vice Pres*
EMP: 5 EST: 1972
SQ FT: 3,000
SALES (est): 660.2K **Privately Held**
SIC: 3471 Chromium plating of metals or formed products; plating of metals or formed products

(G-15140)
NORTHEAST WATER RECLAMATION
Also Called: Northast Wtr Rclmtion Fclities
1160 62nd Ave Ne (33702-7626)
PHONE...................................727 893-7779
Steve Leavitt, *Director*
EMP: 7 EST: 1918
SALES (est): 89.8K **Privately Held**
SIC: 2899 Water treating compounds

(G-15141)
NUTRACEUTICALS FACTORY LLC ◆
11860 31st Ct N (33716-1805)
PHONE...................................727 692-7294
Patricia Ripetta, *Mng Member*
Hugo Juarez Weigandt, *Mng Member*
EMP: 8 EST: 2021
SALES (est): 715K **Privately Held**
WEB: www.nutraceuticalsfactory.com
SIC: 2023 Dietary supplements, dairy & non-dairy based

(G-15142)
NYPRO HEALTHCARE LLC
10560 Dr Martin Luther (33716-3718)
PHONE...................................727 577-9749
EMP: 20 EST: 2019
SALES: 3.8MM
SALES (corp-wide): 29.2B **Publicly Held**
SIC: 3672 Printed circuit boards

PA: Jabil Inc.
10800 Roosevelt Blvd N
Saint Petersburg FL 33716
727 577-9749

(G-15143)
NYPRO INC
10560 Dr Mlj Jr St N Martin (33716)
PHONE...................................727 577-9749
Alejandro Sanchez, *Mfg Mgr*
Hector Rodriguez, *Production*
Alejandro Avila, *Engineer*
Bruce Bedard, *Engineer*
Colm Browne, *Engineer*
EMP: 13
SALES (corp-wide): 29.2B **Publicly Held**
WEB: www.nypromold.com
SIC: 3089 3559 7389 8711 Injection molding of plastics; robots, molding & forming plastics; design, commercial & industrial; engineering services
HQ: Nypro Inc.
101 Union St
Clinton MA 01510
978 365-8100

(G-15144)
OAKHURST MARKETING INC
Also Called: Oakhurst Signs
2400 31st St S (33712-3350)
PHONE...................................727 532-8255
Josh Buttitta, *President*
Adam Prescott, *Business Mgr*
Joe Centrone, *COO*
Nicholas Reaume, *Vice Pres*
Liana Rollins, *Project Mgr*
EMP: 7 EST: 2005
SALES (est): 1.3MM **Privately Held**
WEB: www.oakhurstsigns.com
SIC: 3993 7336 1799 Signs, not made in custom sign painting shops; commercial art & graphic design; sign installation & maintenance

(G-15145)
OERLIKON USA INC
10050 16th St N (33716-4219)
PHONE...................................727 577-4999
EMP: 19 EST: 1975
SALES (est): 586.3K **Privately Held**
WEB: www.oerlikonoc.com
SIC: 3674 Semiconductors & related devices

(G-15146)
OLDJA ENTERPRISES INC
4424 34th St N (33714-3712)
PHONE...................................727 526-3240
EMP: 7 EST: 2019
SALES (est): 445.5K **Privately Held**
WEB: www.oldjaenterprises.com
SIC: 2434 Wood kitchen cabinets

(G-15147)
OMALLEY MANUFACTURING INC
Also Called: O'Malley Valve Co.
4228 8th Ave S (33711-2029)
P.O. Box 12766 (33733-2766)
PHONE...................................727 327-6817
Richard Wheeler, *President*
EMP: 8 EST: 1910
SQ FT: 8,000
SALES (est): 943K **Privately Held**
WEB: www.omalley.com
SIC: 3451 3432 Screw machine products; faucets & spigots, metal & plastic

(G-15148)
PAINASSIST INC
6199 54th St S (33715-2408)
PHONE...................................248 875-4222
Pramod Kerkar, *Principal*
EMP: 8 EST: 2012
SALES (est): 623.3K **Privately Held**
WEB: www.epainassist.com
SIC: 7372 Application computer software

(G-15149)
PEPSI ST PETE
Also Called: Pepsico
4451 34th St N (33714-3711)
PHONE...................................727 527-8113
EMP: 17 EST: 2016

SALES (est): 6MM **Privately Held**
WEB: www.pepsico.com
SIC: 2086 Carbonated soft drinks, bottled & canned

(G-15150)
PINELLAS PROVISION CORPORATION
Also Called: Centerpoint Meats and Prov
201 16th St S (33705-1635)
PHONE...................................727 822-2701
Todd J Reese, *President*
Daniel P Reese, *Vice Pres*
Randy Cohen, *Manager*
EMP: 23 EST: 1972
SQ FT: 15,000
SALES (est): 14MM **Privately Held**
SIC: 2013 5147 Sausages & other prepared meats; meats, fresh

(G-15151)
PJ DESIGNS INC (PA)
Also Called: Peggy Jennings Design
1515 Park St N (33710-4345)
PHONE...................................727 525-0599
Herb Kosterlitz, *CEO*
James Jennings, *President*
Peggy Jennings, *President*
EMP: 30 EST: 1980
SALES (est): 4.2MM **Privately Held**
SIC: 2335 2331 2339 2341 Dresses, paper: cut & sewn; blouses, women's & juniors': made from purchased material; slacks: women's, misses' & juniors'; nightgowns & negligees: women's & children's; robes & dressing gowns

(G-15152)
PLASMA-THERM INC
1150 16th St N (33705-1149)
PHONE...................................856 753-8111
Ronald Deferrari, *President*
David Hawkins, *Technical Staff*
Jason Dearth, *Analyst*
EMP: 29 EST: 1991
SALES (est): 494.7K **Privately Held**
WEB: www.plasmatherm.com
SIC: 3674 Semiconductors & related devices
PA: Plasma-Therm, Llc
10050 16th St N
Saint Petersburg FL 33716

(G-15153)
PLASMA-THERM LLC (PA)
10050 16th St N (33716-4219)
PHONE...................................727 577-4999
Abdul Lateef, *CEO*
Abdul C Latee, *CEO*
Edward Ostan, *President*
James Pollock, *COO*
Jim Garstka, *Vice Pres*
▲ EMP: 138 EST: 2008
SQ FT: 60,639
SALES (est): 55.3MM **Privately Held**
WEB: www.plasmatherm.com
SIC: 3674 Semiconductors & related devices

(G-15154)
POND INDUSTRIES INC
1942 Iowa Ave Ne (33703-3426)
PHONE...................................727 526-5483
Susan D Poniatowski, *Principal*
EMP: 7 EST: 2010
SALES (est): 232.4K **Privately Held**
SIC: 3999 Manufacturing industries

(G-15155)
POPSTOPS MARKETING INC
111 2nd Ave Ne Ste 1201 (33701-3443)
PHONE...................................800 209-4571
J Scott Fenimore, *President*
EMP: 8 EST: 2017
SQ FT: 3,000
SALES (est): 867.6K **Privately Held**
SIC: 3559 Frame straighteners, automobile (garage equipment)

(G-15156)
POWER PRINTING OF FLORIDA
4001 35th St N (33714-3734)
EMP: 6 EST: 1992
SALES (est): 344.6K **Privately Held**
SIC: 2732 Book Printing

(G-15157)
POWER PRINTING OF FLORIDA
Also Called: Sir Speedy
956 1st Ave N (33705-1502)
PHONE...................................727 823-1162
Jerry Powers, *President*
Zachary Miller, *Graphic Designe*
EMP: 12 EST: 1987
SQ FT: 5,300
SALES (est): 2.5MM **Privately Held**
WEB: www.sirspeedystpete.com
SIC: 2752 Commercial printing, lithographic

(G-15158)
POWERCHORD INC (PA)
360 Central Ave Fl 5 (33701-3832)
PHONE...................................727 823-1530
William Volmuth, *CEO*
Patrick J Schunk, *President*
Kirstyn Cline, *Partner*
Garbis Bedoian, *General Mgr*
Courtney Smith, *Vice Pres*
EMP: 41 EST: 1999
SALES (est): 11.6MM **Privately Held**
WEB: www.powerchord.com
SIC: 7372 Business oriented computer software

(G-15159)
PRECISION CERAMICS USA INC
9843 18th St N Ste 120 (33716-4208)
PHONE...................................727 388-5060
Steve Swallow, *President*
David Ostrow, *Vice Pres*
Kizzan Amer, *VP Bus Dvlpt*
Sally Dumas, *Administration*
EMP: 12 EST: 2009
SALES (est): 4.8MM
SALES (corp-wide): 931.6K **Privately Held**
WEB: www.precision-ceramics.com
SIC: 3253 Wall tile, ceramic
HQ: Mcgeoch Technology Limited
86 Lower Tower Street
Birmingham W MIDLANDS B19 3

(G-15160)
PRECISION METAL PARTS INC
4725 28th St N (33714-3115)
PHONE...................................727 526-9165
John P Garrity, *President*
Cheryl Gallagher, *Marketing Staff*
Dan Murphy, *Technical Staff*
EMP: 18 EST: 1947
SQ FT: 16,000
SALES (est): 1.2MM **Privately Held**
WEB: www.precisionperformanceinc.com
SIC: 3451 3541 Screw machine products; machine tools, metal cutting type

(G-15161)
PRINTING FOR A CAUSE LLC
360 Central Ave Ste 800 (33701-3984)
PHONE...................................786 496-0637
EMP: 25
SQ FT: 1,200
SALES: 5.1MM **Privately Held**
SIC: 2752 2741 2731 Internet Publishing And Broadcasting Lithographic Commercial Printing Books-Publishing/Printing

(G-15162)
PRIVATE LABEL SKIN NA LLC
Also Called: World Product Solutions
2260 118th Ave N (33716-1929)
PHONE...................................877 516-2200
Brian Crowdis, *General Mgr*
Cole Wooten, *Business Mgr*
Vahid Kasliwala, *COO*
Theresa Gay, *Project Mgr*
Fahreta Arnautovic, *Production*
EMP: 165 EST: 2012
SALES (est): 22.5MM **Privately Held**
SIC: 2844 7336 Toilet preparations; package design

(G-15163)
PROFILE RACING INC
Also Called: Profile Tool & Gear
4803 95th St N (33708-3725)
PHONE...................................727 392-8307
James Alley, *President*
Nancy Alley, *Vice Pres*
▲ EMP: 36 EST: 1968
SQ FT: 18,000

SALES (est): 6.6MM **Privately Held**
WEB: www.profileracing.com
SIC: 3714 3751 3462 Gears, motor vehicle; bicycles & related parts; iron & steel
forgings

(G-15164)
**PROGRESS FUELS
CORPORATION (DH)**
1 Progress Plz Fl 11 (33701-4322)
PHONE..................................727 824-6600
Fax: 727 824-6605
▲ EMP: 70 EST: 1976
SQ FT: 24,500
SALES (est): 654.5MM
SALES (corp-wide): 23.5B **Publicly Held**
SIC: 1221 Bituminous Coal/Lignite Surface
Mining
HQ: Progress Energy, Inc.
410 S Wilmington St
Raleigh NC 27601
704 382-3853

(G-15165)
PROSUN INTERNATIONAL LLC
2442 23rd St N (33713-4018)
PHONE..................................727 825-0400
Tom Henkemans, *President*
Jennifer Henkemans, *COO*
Mireille Doffegnies, *Vice Pres*
Akshay Kharwadkar, *Engineer*
Kaitlyn Grady, *Sales Staff*
◆ EMP: 49 EST: 2002
SQ FT: 75,000
SALES (est): 8.6MM **Privately Held**
WEB: www.prosun.com
SIC: 3648 Sun tanning equipment, incl.
tanning beds

(G-15166)
PROTECT ALL COATING INC
2458 36th Ave N (33713-1823)
PHONE..................................727 278-7454
Clifton Davis, *CEO*
Jennifer Davis, *Vice Pres*
EMP: 6 EST: 2004
SALES (est): 499.1K **Privately Held**
SIC: 3479 Metal coating & allied service

(G-15167)
**QUALITY INDUSTRIAL CHEM
INC**
Also Called: St Pete Auto Aids
3161 118th Ave N (33716-1865)
PHONE..................................727 573-5760
Russell C Profitt, *President*
EMP: 10 EST: 1974
SQ FT: 8,000
SALES (est): 728.1K **Privately Held**
SIC: 2842 5087 2891 Cleaning or polish-
ing preparations; service establishment
equipment; carwash equipment & sup-
plies; adhesives & sealants

(G-15168)
QUANTUM SPATIAL INC (HQ)
Also Called: Nv5geospatial
10033 Dr Mrtn Lther King (33716-3830)
PHONE..................................920 457-3631
Peter Lamontagne, *President*
Adam Meyer, *Accounts Mgr*
Leeann Deslauriers MBA, *Marketing Staff*
Alexa Ramirez, *Manager*
Edelina Naydenova, *Technical Staff*
EMP: 100 EST: 1969
SQ FT: 15,000
SALES (est): 54MM
SALES (corp-wide): 706.7MM **Publicly
Held**
WEB: www.datem.com
SIC: 2741 8713 Maps: publishing & print-
ing; surveying services
PA: Nv5 Global, Inc.
200 S Park Rd Ste 350
Hollywood FL 33021
954 495-2112

(G-15169)
RAYTHEON COMPANY
7401 22nd Ave N Bldg D (33710-3804)
PHONE..................................310 647-9438
Thomas Kennedy, *CEO*
Joe Tuckness, *Engineer*
Jan Yang, *Engineer*
W Greg Henson, *Branch Mgr*
W Henson, *Branch Mgr*

EMP: 28
SALES (corp-wide): 64.3B **Publicly Held**
WEB: www.rtx.com
SIC: 3812 Radar systems & equipment;
sonar systems & equipment
HQ: Raytheon Company
870 Winter St
Waltham MA 02451
781 522-3000

(G-15170)
REAL KETONES LLC ✪
111 2nd Ave Ne Ste 1401 (33701-3480)
PHONE..................................801 244-8610
Paul Peach, *Vice Pres*
Gary Millet, *Mng Member*
EMP: 10 EST: 2021
SALES (est): 2.1MM
SALES (corp-wide): 20MM **Privately
Held**
WEB: www.realketones.com
SIC: 2833 5499 Inorganic medicinal
chemicals: bulk, uncompounded; dietetic
foods
PA: Axcess Global , Llc
2157 S Lincoln St
Salt Lake City UT 84106
801 244-8610

(G-15171)
**RESTORATIVE CARE AMERICA
INC (PA)**
Also Called: Rcai
12221 33rd St N (33716-1841)
PHONE..................................727 573-1595
C E Hess, *President*
Joe Wheeler, *Marketing Staff*
Nigel Horsley, *Commissioner*
EMP: 91 EST: 1975
SQ FT: 35,000
SALES (est): 14MM **Privately Held**
WEB: www.rcai.com
SIC: 3842 Braces, orthopedic; orthopedic
appliances

(G-15172)
**REV-TECH MFG SOLUTIONS
LLC**
9900 18th St N Ste 105 (33716-4224)
PHONE..................................727 577-4999
Hector Pujols, *Principal*
EMP: 20 EST: 2011
SALES (est): 1.1MM **Privately Held**
WEB: www.revtechms.com
SIC: 3999 3441 Beekeepers' supplies;
fabricated structural metal

(G-15173)
REVTECH
10050 16th St N (33716-4219)
PHONE..................................727 369-1750
Louis Gomez, *Manager*
EMP: 11 EST: 2017
SALES (est): 563.7K **Privately Held**
WEB: www.revtechms.com
SIC: 3599 Machine shop, jobbing & repair

(G-15174)
RHYTHM HEALTHCARE LLC
3300 Tyrone Blvd N (33710-2340)
PHONE..................................877 843-6464
Douglas Francis, *CEO*
EMP: 16 EST: 2020
SALES (est): 3.5MM **Privately Held**
WEB: www.rhythmhc.com
SIC: 3841 Surgical & medical instruments

(G-15175)
**SAINT PETERSBURG CABINETS
INC**
2547 24th Ave N (33713-4320)
PHONE..................................727 327-4800
Zoran Milic, *President*
Dobrinka Milic, *Treasurer*
EMP: 5 EST: 1978
SQ FT: 4,000
SALES (est): 469.2K **Privately Held**
WEB: www.thestpetersburgcabinetco.com
SIC: 2514 2511 Kitchen cabinets: metal;
bed frames, except water bed frames:
wood

(G-15176)
SANDY-ALEXANDER INC
Also Called: Modern Graphic Arts
1527 102nd Ave N (33716-5049)
PHONE..................................727 579-1527
Steve Sargent, *President*
Eric Reinitz, *General Mgr*
Paul Vogelsang, *General Mgr*
Larry Westlake, *Exec VP*
Peter Stillo, *Vice Pres*
EMP: 100
SALES (corp-wide): 121.9MM **Privately
Held**
WEB: www.sandyinc.com
SIC: 2752 Commercial printing, litho-
graphic
PA: Sandy Alexander, Inc.
200 Entin Rd
Clifton NJ 07014
973 470-8100

(G-15177)
SCI UNDERCAR INC (PA)
2447 5th Ave S (33712-1632)
PHONE..................................727 327-2278
Scott McKalvey, *President*
▲ EMP: 10 EST: 1990
SQ FT: 9,000
SALES (est): 1.8MM **Privately Held**
SIC: 3714 Motor vehicle brake systems &
parts

(G-15178)
SCRIBE MANUFACTURING INC
3001 Tech Dr N (33716-1001)
PHONE..................................727 536-7895
EMP: 131
SALES (corp-wide): 17MM **Privately
Held**
SIC: 3951 Pens & mechanical pencils
PA: Scribe Manufacturing, Inc.
14421 Myerlake Cir
Clearwater FL 33760
727 524-7482

(G-15179)
**SEATING INSTALLATION GROUP
LLC**
Also Called: Sig
12100 31st Ct N (33716-1827)
PHONE..................................727 289-7652
Leah O'Dor,
Eugene O'Dor,
EMP: 13 EST: 2013
SQ FT: 1,500
SALES (est): 1.7MM **Privately Held**
WEB: www.si-gp.com
SIC: 2531 Stadium seating

(G-15180)
SENSIDYNE LP
1000 112th Cir N Ste 100 (33716-2358)
PHONE..................................727 530-3602
Howard Mills, *Partner*
Wes Davis, *Partner*
Glenn Warr, *Partner*
Dave McGill, *Regional Mgr*
Elaine Huber, *Production*
◆ EMP: 95 EST: 1983
SQ FT: 40,000
SALES (est): 25.7MM
SALES (corp-wide): 264.8MM **Privately
Held**
WEB: www.sensidyne.com
SIC: 3823 5084 Industrial instrmnts
msrmnt display/control process variable;
industrial machinery & equipment
HQ: Schauenburg Management, Inc.
1000 112th Cir N Ste 100
Saint Petersburg FL 33716

(G-15181)
SENSOR SYSTEMS LLC
2800 Anvil St N (33710-2943)
PHONE..................................727 347-2181
Charles Nunziata, *Vice Pres*
Ned Schiff, *Vice Pres*
Abel Elmazouri, *Chief Engr*
Jerry Mirsky, *Chief Engr*
Ryan Peterson, *Engineer*
▼ EMP: 120 EST: 1998
SALES (est): 23.1MM **Privately Held**
WEB: www.sensorsllc.com
SIC: 3829 Measuring & controlling devices

(G-15182)
SERVICE BINDERY ENTPS INC
Also Called: Service Bindery of Pinellas
3228 Morris St N (33713-2734)
PHONE..................................727 823-9866
Richard L Love, *President*
EMP: 11 EST: 1985
SQ FT: 7,200
SALES (est): 573.1K **Privately Held**
WEB: www.servicebindery.com
SIC: 2789 2675 Binding only: books, pam-
phlets, magazines, etc.; die-cut paper &
board

(G-15183)
SHUKLA MEDICAL INC
8300 Sheen Dr (33709-2222)
PHONE..................................732 474-1769
Rahul Shukla, *President*
Adam Gosikwolfe, *Engineer*
Jamie Gilroy, *Natl Sales Mgr*
Siddharth Desai, *Planning*
EMP: 24 EST: 1999
SALES (est): 6.8MM
SALES (corp-wide): 30.3MM **Privately
Held**
WEB: www.shuklamedical.com
SIC: 3842 Surgical appliances & supplies
PA: S.S. White Technologies Inc.
8300 Sheen Dr
Saint Petersburg FL 33709
727 626-2800

(G-15184)
SIMPLY RELIABLE INC
10460 Roosevelt Blvd N (33716-3821)
PHONE..................................800 209-9332
John Coffin, *President*
Chris Jaffe, *Vice Pres*
Jonathan Knapp, *CTO*
EMP: 5 EST: 2012
SALES (est): 614.1K **Privately Held**
WEB: www.simplyreliable.com
SIC: 7372 Business oriented computer
software

(G-15185)
SINGLETARY SYSTEMS INC
5264 62nd Ave S (33715-2403)
P.O. Box 111, Millbury MA (01527-0111)
PHONE..................................508 865-4445
Douglas Backman, *President*
▲ EMP: 36 EST: 1946
SALES (est): 6.6MM **Privately Held**
WEB: www.ivstands.com
SIC: 3842 Surgical appliances & supplies

(G-15186)
SKIN COMBAT LLC
5200 Seminole Blvd (33708-3356)
PHONE..................................727 517-3376
James F Armstrong Sr, *Principal*
EMP: 7 EST: 2010
SALES (est): 112.5K **Privately Held**
SIC: 2844 Toilet preparations

(G-15187)
SLIPAWAY CERAMICS INC
236 87th Ave Ne (33702-3804)
PHONE..................................727 577-1936
Linda Wibberg, *Vice Pres*
EMP: 7 EST: 2013
SALES (est): 124.3K **Privately Held**
WEB: www.slipawayceramics.com
SIC: 3269 Pottery products

(G-15188)
SNUG HARBOR DINGHIES INC
Also Called: Biking Boat Works Company,
The
10121 Snug Harbor Rd Ne (33702-1917)
PHONE..................................727 578-0618
Gerald Dalrymple, *President*
Kara Kessler, *Vice Pres*
Eric Rikansrud, *Vice Pres*
EMP: 10 EST: 1986
SQ FT: 10,932
SALES (est): 156.2K **Privately Held**
SIC: 3732 Boat building & repairing

(G-15189)
SOLSEEN LLC
Also Called: Big T Printing
2801 16th St N (33704-2516)
PHONE..................................727 322-3131
Todd Moore, *Principal*

David Sistrunk, *Production*
Matthew Parke, *Sales Staff*
EMP: 7 **EST:** 2012
SQ FT: 4,500
SALES (est): 915.6K **Privately Held**
WEB: www.bigtprinting.com
SIC: 2759 Screen printing

(G-15190)
SOUTHEASTERN MARINE POWER LLC
7398 46th Ave N (33709-2504)
PHONE....................727 545-2700
Cameron Gilly, *General Mgr*
Joanne Johannesson, *Treasurer*
Dan Johannesson,
Eric K Nelson,
▼ **EMP:** 19 **EST:** 1984
SALES (est): 2.2MM **Privately Held**
WEB: www.semarinepower.com
SIC: 3625 5551 Marine & navy auxiliary controls; boat dealers; outboard motors

(G-15191)
SOUTHERN INTEREST CO INC
Also Called: Doyle Ploch Sailmakers
2233 3rd Ave S (33712-1217)
PHONE....................727 471-2040
EMP: 18
SQ FT: 5,000
SALES (est): 1.4MM **Privately Held**
SIC: 2394 Mfg Canvas/Related Products

(G-15192)
SOUTHERN STRL STL FLA INC
1000 31st St S (33712-1925)
PHONE....................727 327-7123
Timothy A Richman, *President*
Brian McGovern, *Vice Pres*
Matthew P Richman, *Vice Pres*
Ken Techton, *Plant Mgr*
Cindy Hughlett, *Project Mgr*
EMP: 15 **EST:** 2015
SALES (est): 2.7MM **Privately Held**
WEB: www.southernstpete.com
SIC: 3441 Fabricated structural metal

(G-15193)
SOUTHERN SUPPLY AND MFG CO
Also Called: Gold Seal Cutlery
1501 22nd St N (33713-5615)
P.O. Box 10066 (33733-0066)
PHONE....................727 323-7099
Ralph O'Brien Jr, *President*
Candace Burner, *Corp Secy*
▲ **EMP:** 25 **EST:** 1927
SQ FT: 10,000
SALES (est): 2.1MM **Privately Held**
WEB: www.goldseal.com
SIC: 3421 Shears, hand; scissors, hand

(G-15194)
SPACE MACHINE & ENGRG CORP
2327 16th Ave N (33713-5625)
PHONE....................727 323-2221
Allen Loyd, *President*
Ted Marston, *Vice Pres*
Gary Lamachia, *Opers Mgr*
Joe Holub, *QC Mgr*
Barrett Mattingly, *QC Mgr*
▲ **EMP:** 46 **EST:** 1962
SQ FT: 12,000
SALES (est): 9.9MM **Privately Held**
WEB: www.space-machine.com
SIC: 3761 Guided missiles & space vehicles

(G-15195)
SPEEDPRO IMAGING ST PETERSBURG
5111 Queen Palm Ter Ne (33703-6306)
PHONE....................727 266-0956
Vernard McKenny, *President*
EMP: 5 **EST:** 2016
SALES (est): 322.3K **Privately Held**
WEB: www.speedpro.com
SIC: 3993 7389 3577 7336 Signs & advertising specialties; displays & cutouts, window & lobby; advertising, promotional & trade show services; graphic displays, except graphic terminals; graphic arts & related design; banners, flags, decals & posters

(G-15196)
SS WHITE TECHNOLOGIES INC (PA)
8300 Sheen Dr (33709-2222)
PHONE....................727 626-2800
Rahul B Shukla, *President*
Steve Grimes, *Managing Dir*
Bernard Marx, *Vice Pres*
Thomas Sarnoski, *Vice Pres*
Cecilia CHI, *Human Res Mgr*
▲ **EMP:** 170 **EST:** 1844
SQ FT: 90,000
SALES (est): 30.3MM **Privately Held**
WEB: www.sswhite.net
SIC: 3568 Shafts, flexible

(G-15197)
ST PETERSBURG DIST CO LLC
Also Called: Brookhaven Beverage Company
800 31st St S (33712-1923)
PHONE....................727 581-1544
Eugene Davis, *Production*
Samuel Hopkins, *Controller*
Clara Robbins, *Manager*
Dominic C Iafrate,
Dominic Iafrate,
EMP: 13 **EST:** 2013
SALES (est): 4.9MM **Privately Held**
WEB: www.stpetersburgdistillery.com
SIC: 2085 Distilled & blended liquors

(G-15198)
STABIL CONCRETE PRODUCTS LLC
4451 8th Ave S (33711-1903)
PHONE....................727 321-6000
Ruth Hardy, *Vice Pres*
Jeff Nolan, *Vice Pres*
Brett Flint, *Plant Mgr*
Tyler Thomas, *Project Mgr*
Diane Sanguedolce, *Opers Staff*
EMP: 56 **EST:** 2006
SALES (est): 9.2MM **Privately Held**
WEB: www.stabilconcrete.com
SIC: 3272 Concrete products

(G-15199)
STALLION KING LLC
7901 4th St N Ste 4691 (33702-4305)
PHONE....................321 503-7368
Kyrie Danger, *President*
EMP: 8 **EST:** 2018
SALES (est): 426.9K **Privately Held**
SIC: 7372 Educational computer software

(G-15200)
STEMLER CORPORATION
Also Called: Viking Cases
1873 64th Ave N (33702-7130)
PHONE....................727 577-1216
Arthur Stemler, *CEO*
Bruce Stemler, *President*
Shirley Stemler, *Admin Sec*
Carol K Strickland, *Asst Sec*
EMP: 30 **EST:** 1975
SQ FT: 12,000
SALES (est): 609K **Privately Held**
WEB: www.thestemlercorporation.com
SIC: 2449 3161 3412 Shipping cases & drums, wood: wirebound & plywood; cases, carrying; metal barrels, drums & pails

(G-15201)
SUNCOAST RESEARCH LABS INC
2901 Anvil St N (33710-2911)
P.O. Box 47254 (33743-7254)
PHONE....................727 344-7627
Robert Beaman, *President*
Bob Beaman, *Vice Pres*
Kyle Beaman, *Vice Pres*
Cherie Beaman, *Treasurer*
EMP: 10 **EST:** 1983
SQ FT: 16,000
SALES (est): 2.2MM **Privately Held**
SIC: 2842 Specialty cleaning preparations

(G-15202)
SUNCOAST TRENDS INC
2860 21st Ave N (33713-4204)
PHONE....................727 321-4948
Rosanna Carl, *President*
Todd Carl, *Vice Pres*
EMP: 6 **EST:** 1975

SQ FT: 6,600
SALES (est): 747.7K **Privately Held**
SIC: 2331 2393 2329 2339 Blouses, women's & juniors': made from purchased material; shirts, women's & juniors': made from purchased materials; bags & containers, except sleeping bags: textile; men's & boys' sportswear & athletic clothing; sportswear, women's; girls' & children's outerwear

(G-15203)
SUPERMEDIA LLC
Also Called: Verizon
10200 Mrtn Lther King St (33716-3717)
P.O. Box 42025 (33742-4025)
PHONE....................727 576-1300
Laura Strickland, *Branch Mgr*
EMP: 75
SQ FT: 101,472
SALES (corp-wide): 1.4B **Publicly Held**
SIC: 2741 7313 Telephone & other directory publishing; radio, television, publisher representatives
HQ: Supermedia Llc
2200 W Airfield Dr
Dfw Airport TX 75261
972 453-7000

(G-15204)
SUPERMEDIA LLC
9620 Exec Ctr Dr N Ste 10 (33702-2429)
PHONE....................972 453-7000
Tommy Lanford, *Manager*
EMP: 16
SALES (corp-wide): 1.4B **Publicly Held**
SIC: 2741 Directories, telephone: publishing only, not printed on site
HQ: Supermedia Llc
2200 W Airfield Dr
Dfw Airport TX 75261
972 453-7000

(G-15205)
SURFACE ENGRG & ALLOY CO INC (PA)
Also Called: Extreme Coatings
2895 46th Ave N (33714-3811)
PHONE....................727 528-3734
Curtis K Kadau, *President*
Michelle Heusinger, *General Mgr*
Craig Travers, *Prdtn Mgr*
Kim Perez, *Sales Staff*
Travis White, *Manager*
◆ **EMP:** 72 **EST:** 1996
SQ FT: 16,000
SALES (est): 24.6MM **Privately Held**
WEB: www.surfaceengineering.com
SIC: 3699 Welding machines & equipment, ultrasonic

(G-15206)
SYLIOS CORP (PA)
735 Arlington Ave N # 308 (33701-3606)
P.O. Box 521 (33731-0521)
PHONE....................727 821-6200
Anderson Wayne, *President*
EMP: 10 **EST:** 2014
SALES (est): 2.5MM **Privately Held**
WEB: www.sylios.com
SIC: 1382 Oil & gas exploration services

(G-15207)
TAKEN FOR GRANITE
4481 Pompano Dr Se (33705-4354)
PHONE....................727 235-1559
Davy Williams, *President*
EMP: 5 **EST:** 2003
SALES (est): 307.7K **Privately Held**
SIC: 3281 Granite, cut & shaped

(G-15208)
TAMPA BAY COATINGS INC
3228 Morris St N (33713-2734)
PHONE....................727 823-9866
Richard Love, *President*
EMP: 11 **EST:** 2005
SALES (est): 152.7K **Privately Held**
SIC: 2672 Coated & laminated paper

(G-15209)
TAMPA BAY SPORTS ENTRMT LLC (PA)
490 1st Ave S (33701-4204)
PHONE....................727 893-8111
Jeff Vinik, *Chairman*

Kerry O'Reilly, *Mktg Dir*
Anne Putnam, *Marketing Staff*
Jean Mitotes, *Advt Staff*
Jessica Petroski, *Advt Staff*
EMP: 93 **EST:** 2010
SALES (est): 134.8MM **Privately Held**
WEB: www.tampabay.com
SIC: 2711 Newspapers, publishing & printing

(G-15210)
TAYLOR MEDIA LLC
Also Called: Penny Hoarder, The
490 1st Ave S Ste 800 (33701-4287)
PHONE....................727 317-5800
Kyle Taylor, *CEO*
Molly Moorhead, *Editor*
Loren Colson, *Controller*
Curt Dailey, *Advt Staff*
Darrell Davis, *Manager*
EMP: 121 **EST:** 2012
SQ FT: 23,000
SALES (est): 14.9MM
SALES (corp-wide): 177.9K **Privately Held**
WEB: www.thepennyhoarder.com
SIC: 2741 Miscellaneous publishing
HQ: Link Clear Technologies Llc
5202 W Dglas Corrigan Way
Salt Lake City UT 84116
801 424-0018

(G-15211)
TECHNO-SOLIS INC
Also Called: Techno Solis USA
301 20th St S (33712-1315)
PHONE....................727 823-6766
Sebastian Bourgeois, *President*
Sebastien Bourgeois, *Engineer*
Eddy Sanchez, *Engineer*
Stephen Messerschmidt, *Sales Staff*
Steve Messerschmidt, *Sales Staff*
EMP: 10 **EST:** 1976
SQ FT: 11,821
SALES (est): 2.6MM **Privately Held**
WEB: www.techno-solisusa.com
SIC: 3613 Panel & distribution boards & other related apparatus

(G-15212)
TIMES HOLDING CO (DH)
Also Called: Tampa Bay Times Storefront
490 1st Ave S (33701-4223)
P.O. Box 1121 (33731-1121)
PHONE....................727 893-8111
Andrew Barnes, *Ch of Bd*
Amanda Dearmon, *Editor*
R Micheal Carroll, *Treasurer*
Jessica Sharp, *Sales Staff*
Lindsey McCormick, *Sales Staff*
EMP: 61 **EST:** 1959
SALES (est): 36.7MM
SALES (corp-wide): 14.9MM **Privately Held**
WEB: www.poynter.org
SIC: 2721 2711 Magazines: publishing & printing; newspapers, publishing & printing
HQ: Times Publishing Company
490 1st Ave S
Saint Petersburg FL 33701
727 893-8111

(G-15213)
TIMES MEDIA SERVICES INC
490 1st Ave S (33701-4223)
PHONE....................727 893-8111
Paul C Tash, *President*
EMP: 37 **EST:** 2017
SALES (est): 1MM
SALES (corp-wide): 14.9MM **Privately Held**
WEB: www.seniorlivingonline.com
SIC: 2711 Newspapers, publishing & printing
HQ: Times Publishing Company
490 1st Ave S
Saint Petersburg FL 33701
727 893-8111

(G-15214)
TIMES PUBLISHING COMPANY (HQ)
490 1st Ave S (33701-4223)
P.O. Box 1121 (33731-1121)
PHONE....................727 893-8111

Paul Tash, *Ch of Bd*
Corty Andrew P, *Vice Pres*
Jana Jones, *CFO*
Robert Ahlgren, *VP Human Res*
Mariel Westervelt, *Software Dev*
◆ **EMP:** 700 **EST:** 1884
SQ FT: 224,000
SALES (est): 52.9MM
SALES (corp-wide): 14.9MM **Privately Held**
WEB: www.tampabay.com
SIC: 2711 2721 Commercial printing & newspaper publishing combined; magazines: publishing & printing
PA: The Poynter Institute For Media Studies Inc
801 3rd St S
Saint Petersburg FL 33701
727 821-9494

(G-15215)
TRAILBLAZERAI INC
10460 Rsvelt Blvd N 298 (33716-3821)
PHONE..............................727 859-2732
Gregory Perry, *CEO*
EMP: 5 **EST:** 2018
SALES (est): 500K **Privately Held**
SIC: 3761 Guided missiles & space vehicles, research & development

(G-15216)
TREND MAGAZINES INC (DH)
Also Called: Florida Trend Magazine
490 1st Ave S Ste 800 (33701-4287)
P.O. Box 611 (33731-0611)
PHONE..............................727 821-5800
Andrew Corty, *President*
Mark Howard, *Principal*
Kristie Stotts, *Business Mgr*
Lynda Keever, *Vice Pres*
Jill South, *Prdtn Mgr*
EMP: 30 **EST:** 1958
SQ FT: 8,000
SALES (est): 10.1MM
SALES (corp-wide): 14.9MM **Privately Held**
WEB: www.floridatrend.com
SIC: 2721 Magazines: publishing only, not printed on site
HQ: Times Publishing Company
490 1st Ave S
Saint Petersburg FL 33701
727 893-8111

(G-15217)
TRI-TECH OF FLORIDA INC
5151 Park St N (33709-1094)
P.O. Box 12729 (33733-2729)
PHONE..............................727 544-8836
Glenn Maller, *President*
Thomas Logan, *Vice Pres*
EMP: 16 **EST:** 1962
SQ FT: 16,000
SALES (est): 1.1MM **Privately Held**
SIC: 3444 3728 Sheet metalwork; aircraft parts & equipment

(G-15218)
TUF TOP COATINGS
4590 60th Ave N (33714-1035)
PHONE..............................727 527-3382
EMP: 12
SQ FT: 10,000
SALES (est): 967.6K **Privately Held**
SIC: 2851 Mfg Paints/Allied Products

(G-15219)
UNIVERSAL LABELING SYSTEMS INC (PA)
3501 8th Ave S (33711-2201)
PHONE..............................727 327-2123
Douglas Hall, *President*
Jane Marie Hall, *Vice Pres*
Frank Jones, *Prdtn Mgr*
Jay Lossa, *Design Engr*
Eileen Gamble, *CFO*
EMP: 46 **EST:** 1968
SQ FT: 35,000
SALES (est): 10.3MM **Privately Held**
WEB: www.universal1.com
SIC: 3565 Labeling machines, industrial

(G-15220)
UNIVERSAL NETWORKING SVCS CO
200 2nd Ave S Ste 432 (33701-4313)
PHONE..............................281 825-9790
Andrea Berg, *CEO*
Waite Ave, *Vice Pres*
EMP: 5 **EST:** 2013
SALES (est): 314.2K **Privately Held**
SIC: 3629 Electronic generation equipment

(G-15221)
UNIVERSAL STNCLING MKG SYSTEMS
205 15th Ave S (33701-5607)
P.O. Box 871 (33731-0871)
PHONE..............................727 894-3027
Donald C Wright Jr, *President*
Karen Surdyk, *Vice Pres*
Stephen M Surdyk, *Vice Pres*
David Daily, *IT Specialist*
EMP: 26 **EST:** 1904
SQ FT: 10,500
SALES (est): 3MM **Privately Held**
WEB: www.marking-systems.com
SIC: 3953 3555 Stencil machines (marking devices); printing trades machinery

(G-15222)
US NATURAL GAS CORP
735 Arlington Ave N # 308 (33701-3606)
PHONE..............................727 482-1505
Wayne Anderson, *Ch of Bd*
Jim Anderson, *Vice Pres*
Chuck Kretchman, *CFO*
EMP: 6 **EST:** 2008
SALES (est): 622.3K **Privately Held**
SIC: 1381 1311 Drilling oil & gas wells; crude petroleum & natural gas

(G-15223)
VANGUARD SYSTEMS CORP
10460 Roosevelt Blvd N (33716-3821)
PHONE..............................727 528-0121
EMP: 6 **EST:** 2012
SALES (est): 352.7K **Privately Held**
WEB: www.vanguardsystemscorp.com
SIC: 3089 Injection molding of plastics

(G-15224)
VERIDIEN CORPORATION (PA)
1100 4th St N Ste 202 (33701-1790)
PHONE..............................727 576-1600
Russell D Van Zandt, *Ch of Bd*
Rene A Gareau, *Vice Ch Bd*
Sheldon C Fenton, *President*
Albina Otte, *Director*
EMP: 10 **EST:** 1991
SQ FT: 6,000
SALES (est): 1.4MM **Privately Held**
WEB: www.veridien.com
SIC: 2842 Sanitation preparations, disinfectants & deodorants

(G-15225)
VETTE BRAKES & PRODUCTS INC
7490 30th Ave N (33710-2304)
P.O. Box 47861 (33743-7861)
PHONE..............................727 345-5292
Angelo Gonzalez, *President*
Josephine Gonzalez, *Vice Pres*
Alan Gonzalez, *Director*
Gary Gonzalez, *Director*
EMP: 23 **EST:** 1977
SQ FT: 22,000
SALES (est): 1MM **Privately Held**
WEB: vette-brakes-and-products.tumblr.com
SIC: 3714 3493 Motor vehicle brake systems & parts; steel springs, except wire

(G-15226)
VICTORS TRIM MOLDING CROWN BAS
6142 38th Ave N (33710-1722)
PHONE..............................727 403-6057
Victor Menendez, *President*
EMP: 7 **EST:** 2006
SALES (est): 85.2K **Privately Held**
SIC: 3089 Injection molding of plastics

(G-15227)
VICTUS CAPITAL ENTERPRISES INC (PA)
1780 102nd Ave N Ste 500 (33716-3603)
PHONE..............................727 442-6677
Al Zwan, *President*
Millie Calderon, *Controller*
Ken Stamey, *Accountant*
Thomas Newhart, *VP Sales*
EMP: 17 **EST:** 1990
SALES (est): 3.4MM **Privately Held**
SIC: 3661 3825 Fiber optics communications equipment; digital test equipment, electronic & electrical circuits

(G-15228)
VIVA 5 LLC (DH)
Also Called: Growve
239 2nd Ave S Ste 200 (33701-4333)
PHONE..............................561 239-2239
Brian Baer, *President*
Vic Peroni, *COO*
Mark Jaggi, *CFO*
EMP: 20 **EST:** 2006
SALES (est): 22.3MM
SALES (corp-wide): 62.9MM **Privately Held**
WEB: www.viva5corp.com
SIC: 2833 Vitamins, natural or synthetic: bulk, uncompounded

(G-15229)
WEEKLY CHALLENGER NEWSPAPER
2500 Dr Mrtn Lther King J (33705-3554)
P.O. Box 35130 (33705-0503)
PHONE..............................727 896-2922
Ethel Johnson, *Owner*
Lyn Johnson, *Publisher*
EMP: 11 **EST:** 1967
SQ FT: 500
SALES (est): 492.5K **Privately Held**
WEB: www.theweeklychallenger.com
SIC: 2711 Newspapers, publishing & printing

(G-15230)
WEST COAST SHUTTERS SUNBURST
128 19th St S Ste B (33712-1307)
PHONE..............................727 894-0044
Joseph Fecera, *President*
Lisa Fecera, *Vice Pres*
EMP: 13 **EST:** 1990
SQ FT: 9,000
SALES (est): 2MM **Privately Held**
WEB: www.westcoastshutters.com
SIC: 3442 5023 5211 Shutters, door or window: metal; window covering parts & accessories; door & window products

(G-15231)
WEST PHRM SVCS FLA INC
5111 Park St N (33709-1009)
PHONE..............................727 546-2402
Don Morel, *CEO*
Fredrick S McCleery, *President*
Michael A Anderson, *Vice Pres*
Fred McCleery, *Vice Pres*
Gabor Wendler, *Purch Dir*
◆ **EMP:** 351 **EST:** 1993
SQ FT: 44,500
SALES (est): 80.2MM
SALES (corp-wide): 2.8B **Publicly Held**
WEB: www.westpharma.com
SIC: 2834 Pharmaceutical preparations
PA: West Pharmaceutical Services, Inc.
530 Herman O West Dr
Exton PA 19341
610 594-2900

(G-15232)
WHITEHOUSE CUSTOM SCRN PR
7183 30th Ave N (33710-2913)
PHONE..............................727 321-7398
Phyllis Race, *Sales Staff*
EMP: 6 **EST:** 2020
SALES (est): 517.7K **Privately Held**
SIC: 2759 Screen printing

(G-15233)
WILLIAM LEUPOLD SR
Also Called: Architectural and Woodworking
3291 40th Ave N (33714-4512)
PHONE..............................727 527-7400
William Leupold, *Principal*
Blanca Bonilla, *Manager*
EMP: 9 **EST:** 2001
SALES (est): 358.6K **Privately Held**
SIC: 2431 Millwork

(G-15234)
WILLIAMS JEWELRY AND MFG CO
3152 Morris St N (33713-2937)
P.O. Box 136178, Clermont (34713-6178)
PHONE..............................727 823-7676
Denise W Ferreira, *President*
EMP: 8 **EST:** 1883
SALES (est): 684.4K **Privately Held**
WEB: www.wjewelry.com
SIC: 3911 3999 2448 Medals, precious or semiprecious metal; pins (jewelry), precious metal; plaques, picture, laminated; cargo containers, wood

(G-15235)
WILLY WALT INC
2390 26th Ave N (33713-4040)
PHONE..............................727 209-2872
Mark Ingles, *Owner*
EMP: 7 **EST:** 2008
SALES (est): 131.9K **Privately Held**
WEB: www.willywalt.com
SIC: 2752 Commercial printing, offset

(G-15236)
WOOD ONE LLC
2416 52nd Ave N (33714-2604)
PHONE..............................727 639-5620
Patrick C Smith, *Principal*
EMP: 7 **EST:** 2015
SALES (est): 412.6K **Privately Held**
WEB: www.woodone.us
SIC: 2431 Millwork

(G-15237)
WOOVFU INC ✪
7901 4th St N Ste 300 (33702-4399)
PHONE..............................719 301-1661
Bill Havre, *CEO*
EMP: 13 **EST:** 2021
SALES (est): 583.4K **Privately Held**
SIC: 2273 Door mats: paper, grass, reed, coir, sisal, jute, rags, etc.

(G-15238)
WORKING COW HOMEMADE INC
4711 34th St N Unit F (33714-3060)
PHONE..............................727 572-7251
Timothy Pappas, *President*
Sonia Pappas, *Vice Pres*
▼ **EMP:** 15 **EST:** 1991
SQ FT: 4,400
SALES (est): 1.4MM **Privately Held**
WEB: www.workingcow.com
SIC: 2024 Ice cream & frozen desserts

(G-15239)
WPS SKINCARE LLC
Also Called: World Product Solution
2260 118th Ave N (33716-1929)
PHONE..............................877 516-2200
EMP: 95 **EST:** 2019
SALES (est): 5.8MM **Privately Held**
SIC: 2844 Toilet preparations

(G-15240)
YOGURTOLOGY
3043 4th St N (33704-2104)
PHONE..............................727 895-1393
EMP: 8 **EST:** 2011
SALES (est): 140.3K **Privately Held**
SIC: 2024 Ice cream, bulk

(G-15241)
YOURMEMBERSHIPCOM INC (PA)
9620 Exec Ctr Dr N Ste 20 (33702-2429)
PHONE..............................727 827-0046
Sharon Love, *President*
Oscar Cunanan, *Partner*
Brenda Brieserhands, *General Mgr*
Tamer Ali, *Vice Pres*

Patrice Cunningham, *Vice Pres*
EMP: 24 **EST:** 2012
SALES (est): 13MM **Privately Held**
WEB: www.yourmembership.com
SIC: 7372 Application computer software; operating systems computer software

(G-15242)
YSI INC (DH)
Also Called: Integrated Systems & Services
9843 18th St N Ste 1200 (33716-4208)
PHONE.............:.............727 565-2201
Rick Omlor, *President*
Shawn Sneddon, *Engineer*
Leon Erdman, *CFO*
Thomas Goucher, *Technical Staff*
Susan Miller, *Admin Sec*
EMP: 12 **EST:** 1988
SQ FT: 20,250
SALES (est): 5.1MM **Publicly Held**
WEB: www.ysi.com
SIC: 3826 Analytical instruments
HQ: Ysi Incorporated
　　　1700 Brannum Ln 1725
　　　Yellow Springs OH 45387
　　　937 767-7241

(G-15243)
YUNG PAYPER CHASERS ENTRMT LLC
695 Central Ave (33701-3669)
PHONE...................................727 239-2880
Lorenzo Arscott,
EMP: 10 **EST:** 2020
SALES (est): 261K **Privately Held**
SIC: 2741 Music book & sheet music publishing

(G-15244)
ZD REALTY LLC
2135 13th Ave N (33713-4001)
PHONE...................................866 672-1212
Dan Camm, *Regl Sales Mgr*
Carine Genicot, *Sales Staff*
James P Markus, *Mng Member*
▲ **EMP:** 17 **EST:** 2007
SALES (est): 3.9MM **Privately Held**
SIC: 3861 Cameras & related equipment

(G-15245)
ZULKIFAL KIANI LLC
7901 4th St N (33702-4305)
PHONE...................................765 291-4529
Zulkifal Kiani,
EMP: 15
SALES (est): 518K **Privately Held**
SIC: 3911 Jewelry apparel

San Antonio
Pasco County

(G-15246)
C & M MILLWORK INC
30450 Commerce Dr (33576-8002)
PHONE...................................352 588-5050
George Curry, *Vice Pres*
Allen Curry, *Office Mgr*
EMP: 12 **EST:** 1980
SQ FT: 20,000
SALES (est): 844K **Privately Held**
WEB: www.cmmillwork.com
SIC: 2431 Millwork

(G-15247)
FROG PUBLICATIONS INC
11820 Uradco Pl Ste 105 (33576-7140)
PHONE...................................352 588-2082
Mary Jo Hand, *President*
Dennis Hand, *Vice Pres*
▲ **EMP:** 8 **EST:** 1975
SQ FT: 1,000
SALES (est): 1MM **Privately Held**
WEB: www.frog.com
SIC: 2741 Miscellaneous publishing

(G-15248)
HARRISON METALS INC
11640 Corporate Lake Blvd (33576-8084)
PHONE...................................352 588-2436
John W Harris III, *President*
Bill H Harris, *Manager*
Jan Harris, *Manager*
EMP: 8 **EST:** 2006

SALES (est): 1.7MM **Privately Held**
WEB: www.harrisonmetals.com
SIC: 3441 Fabricated structural metal

(G-15249)
METALFAB INC (PA)
28212 Rice Rd (33576-7855)
P.O. Box 1184 (33576-1184)
PHONE...................................352 588-9901
Walter M Ruda, *President*
Carol Knapp, *Office Mgr*
EMP: 9 **EST:** 1997
SALES (est): 1.4MM **Privately Held**
WEB: www.metalfab-inc.com
SIC: 3444 Sheet metalwork

(G-15250)
PATRIOT FOUNDATION SYSTEMS LLC
30427 Commerce Dr (33576-8003)
PHONE...................................352 668-4842
Warren Neumann, *CEO*
Jason Neumann, *President*
Ed Latour, *Vice Pres*
Jennifer Odom, *CFO*
▲ **EMP:** 5 **EST:** 2011
SQ FT: 12,000
SALES (est): 800K **Privately Held**
WEB: www.patriotfoundations.com
SIC: 3531 Construction machinery attachments

(G-15251)
PYROTECNICO OF FLORIDA LLC
30435 Commerce Dr Ste 102
(33576-8031)
P.O. Box 1030 (33576-1030)
PHONE...................................352 588-5086
Douglas Aller, *Principal*
Paul Gaffney, *Facilities Mgr*
Pat White, *Facilities Mgr*
Miranda Ithaca, *Production*
Coltt Nelson, *Manager*
▲ **EMP:** 10 **EST:** 2001
SALES (est): 209.3K **Privately Held**
SIC: 2899 Chemical preparations

(G-15252)
S & R FASTENER CO INC
Also Called: International Epoxies Sealers
30241 Commerce Dr (33576-8056)
P.O. Box 185 (33576-0185)
PHONE...................................352 588-0768
Peter Albert, *Sales Staff*
Alan Wolf, *Sales Staff*
Rick Rogers, *Manager*
EMP: 18
SQ FT: 20,800
SALES (corp-wide): 10.7MM **Privately Held**
WEB: www.srfast.com
SIC: 2891 Epoxy adhesives
PA: S & R Fastener Co., Inc.
　　　30241 Commerce Dr
　　　San Antonio FL 33576
　　　352 588-0768

Sanderson
Baker County

(G-15253)
GRIFFIS TIMBER INC
11625 Willie Griffis Rd (32087-2289)
P.O. Box 8 (32087-0008)
PHONE...................................904 275-2372
Penny G Croft, *President*
EMP: 9 **EST:** 1975
SQ FT: 2,400
SALES (est): 237.5K **Privately Held**
SIC: 2411 Timber, cut at logging camp

(G-15254)
INSTEEL WIRE PRODUCTS COMPANY
Also Called: Wiremil Division
1 Wiremill Rd (32087)
PHONE...................................904 275-2100
Joice Davis, *Branch Mgr*
EMP: 58

SALES (corp-wide): 590.6MM **Publicly Held**
WEB: www.insteel.com
SIC: 3272 3496 Concrete products; miscellaneous fabricated wire products
HQ: Insteel Wire Products Company
　　　1373 Boggs Dr
　　　Mount Airy NC 27030
　　　336 719-9000

(G-15255)
SANDERSON PIPE CORPORATION (PA)
1 Enterprise Blvd (32087-9501)
P.O. Box 700 (32087-0700)
PHONE...................................904 275-3289
Barry Ian King, *President*
Frank Traina, *Exec VP*
Bob Eberle, *Vice Pres*
Bob Jones, *Purch Mgr*
Alex McDaniel, *IT/INT Sup*
▼ **EMP:** 49 **EST:** 1996
SALES (est): 26.3MM **Privately Held**
WEB: www.sandersonpipe.com
SIC: 3084 Plastics pipe

Sanford
Seminole County

(G-15256)
A COMPLETE SIGN SERVICE INC
2530 S Snford Ave Ste 106 (32773)
PHONE...................................407 328-7714
John Redding, *Principal*
EMP: 6 **EST:** 2006
SALES (est): 434.9K **Privately Held**
SIC: 3993 Signs & advertising specialties

(G-15257)
A W R CABINETS INC
4155 Saint Johns Pkwy # 1800
(32771-6398)
PHONE...................................407 323-1415
Stephen Elliot, *President*
EMP: 10 **EST:** 2000
SQ FT: 3,000
SALES (est): 500K **Privately Held**
WEB: www.awrcabinets.com
SIC: 2434 7319 Wood kitchen cabinets; display advertising service

(G-15258)
ACME CAP & CLOTHING INC
Also Called: Acme Cap & Branding
221 Bellagio Cir (32771-5001)
PHONE...................................407 321-5100
Felix G Quintana, *President*
Kara Hamby, *Principal*
Bill Miller, *Principal*
Kara Leggett, *Asst Mgr*
EMP: 6 **EST:** 2003
SALES (est): 570K **Privately Held**
WEB: www.acmecap.com
SIC: 2395 Embroidery products, except schiffli machine

(G-15259)
AEROTEC ALUMINIUM INC
1696 N Beardall Ave (32771-9684)
PHONE...................................407 324-5400
Kimberly Mooers, *President*
EMP: 7 **EST:** 2010
SALES (est): 633.4K **Privately Held**
WEB: www.aerotechaluminum.com
SIC: 3446 Architectural metalwork

(G-15260)
AGRIUM ADVANCED TECH US INC
2451 Old Lake Mary Rd (32771-4103)
PHONE...................................407 302-2024
EMP: 10
SALES (corp-wide): 16B **Privately Held**
SIC: 2873 Mfg Nitrogenous Fertilizers
HQ: Agrium Advanced Technologies (U.S.) Inc.
　　　2915 Rocky Mountain Ave # 400
　　　Loveland CO 80538
　　　970 292-9000

(G-15261)
ALPHA TECHNOLOGY USA CORP
Also Called: Futurecow
5401 Penn Ave (32773)
PHONE...................................407 571-2060
Kevin Dole, *President*
Kevin Cole, *Principal*
Karl Ruf, *Facilities Mgr*
Vincent Cloyd, *Engineer*
Darrin Fatter, *Regl Sales Mgr*
▲ **EMP:** 15 **EST:** 2008
SALES (est): 4.1MM **Privately Held**
SIC: 3523 Farm machinery & equipment

(G-15262)
ALT THUYAN
Also Called: H M D
2025 Wp Ball Blvd (32771-7211)
PHONE...................................407 302-3655
Thuyan Alt, *President*
Justin Alt, *Vice Pres*
EMP: 8 **EST:** 2005
SALES (est): 358.9K **Privately Held**
SIC: 2844 Manicure preparations

(G-15263)
AMERICAN BRONZE FOUNDRY INC (PA)
Also Called: Decorators Resource Centl Fla
1650 E Lake Mary Blvd (32773-7130)
PHONE...................................407 328-8090
Charles L Wambold, *President*
Renee Wambold, *Principal*
◆ **EMP:** 18 **EST:** 1991
SQ FT: 22,000
SALES (est): 2.4MM **Privately Held**
WEB: www.americanbronze.com
SIC: 3366 Bronze foundry

(G-15264)
AMERICAN TECHNOLOGY PDTS INC
211 Northstar Ct (32771-6674)
PHONE...................................407 960-1722
Sajjad Jaffer, *President*
EMP: 15 **EST:** 2012
SALES (est): 1.9MM **Privately Held**
WEB: www.serverdiskdrives.com
SIC: 3674 Semiconductors & related devices

(G-15265)
AMICK CSTM WOODCRAFT & DESIGN
1450 Kastner Pl Ste 112 (32771-8005)
PHONE...................................407 324-8525
Scott L Amick, *President*
EMP: 8 **EST:** 1990
SALES (est): 758K **Privately Held**
WEB: amick-custom-woodcraft-design-in-sanford-fl.cityfos.com
SIC: 2499 2541 2517 2434 Decorative wood & woodwork; wood partitions & fixtures; wood television & radio cabinets; wood kitchen cabinets; cabinet & finish carpentry

(G-15266)
ARGONIDE CORPORATION
291 Power Ct (32771-9406)
PHONE...................................407 322-2500
Frederick Tepper, *CEO*
Luisa Bacca, *Business Mgr*
Yuly Prada, *Research*
Stuart Frank, *Marketing Mgr*
Debra Hull, *Marketing Staff*
▲ **EMP:** 10 **EST:** 1994
SQ FT: 15,000
SALES (est): 1.5MM **Privately Held**
WEB: www.argonide.com
SIC: 3499 Fire- or burglary-resistive products

(G-15267)
ASTRUMSAT COMMUNICATIONS LLC
1919 W 1st St (32771-1648)
PHONE...................................954 368-9980
David Horacek, *President*
Michele Loguidice, *Director*
EMP: 5 **EST:** 2010
SALES (est): 2.4MM **Privately Held**
SIC: 3663 Satellites, communications

▲ = Import ▼=Export
◆ =Import/Export

(G-15268)
ATLAS SOUTHEAST PAPERS INC
3401 Saint Johns Pkwy (32771-6363)
PHONE....................................407 330-9118
Peter Leibman, *President*
Patrick Fodale, *CFO*
Robert Pistilli, *Treasurer*
Anne Higgins, *Manager*
◆ **EMP:** 90 **EST:** 2014
SALES (est): 21.2MM
SALES (corp-wide): 2.8B **Privately Held**
WEB: www.atlaspapermills.com
SIC: 2621 Tissue paper
HQ: Resolute Fp Florida Inc.
3301 Nw 107th St
Miami FL 33167
800 562-2860

(G-15269)
AUTOMATIC COAX AND CABLE INC
4060 Saint Johns Pkwy (32771-6374)
PHONE....................................407 322-7622
Glenda D Martinet, *President*
Glenn Harbor, *General Mgr*
Henry Porrata, *QC Mgr*
Kim Casper, *Engineer*
Cliff Cochran, *Executive*
EMP: 45 **EST:** 1998
SQ FT: 8,000
SALES (est): 7.3MM **Privately Held**
WEB: www.autocoax.com
SIC: 3679 Harness assemblies for electronic use: wire or cable

(G-15270)
BADGER WOODWORKS LLC
3800 Entp Way Ste 1160 (32771)
PHONE....................................386 860-9600
Damon Kruid, *Mng Member*
EMP: 15 **EST:** 2020
SALES (est): 980.9K **Privately Held**
WEB: www.badgerww.com
SIC: 2431 Millwork

(G-15271)
BATTER TO PLATTER LLC
Also Called: Jar Joy
2660 Jewett Ln (32771-1678)
PHONE....................................203 309-7632
Sarah Whalley,
James Finck,
Alan Hunte,
Shaun Hunte,
Kathryn Whalley,
EMP: 14 **EST:** 2018
SALES (est): 1.2MM **Privately Held**
SIC: 2051 Cakes, pies & pastries

(G-15272)
BENADA EXTRUSIONS LLC ✪
2540 Jewett Ln (32771-1687)
PHONE....................................407 323-3300
Mark McDonel, *President*
Natalia Alfonzo, *Accountant*
EMP: 13 **EST:** 2022
SALES (est): 355K **Privately Held**
SIC: 3354 Aluminum extruded products

(G-15273)
BIZCARD XPRESS SANFORD LLC
1744 Rinehart Rd (32771-6590)
PHONE....................................407 688-8902
Fortunato Morello Jr,
EMP: 6 **EST:** 2010
SALES (est): 429.8K **Privately Held**
SIC: 2752 Commercial printing, offset

(G-15274)
BOMBARDIER TRNSP HLDNGS USA IN
801 Sunrail Dr (32771-0001)
PHONE....................................407 450-4855
Gregg Nissly, *Manager*
Caren Steller, *Manager*
EMP: 26 **Privately Held**
SIC: 3721 Aircraft
HQ: Bombardier Transportation (Holdings) Usa Inc.
1501 Lebanon Church Rd
Pittsburgh PA 15236
412 655-5700

(G-15275)
BOSS LASER LLC
608 Trestle Pt (32771-8200)
PHONE....................................407 878-0880
Todd Rice, *President*
Daniel L Fox II, *Co-Owner*
Oliver M Pinnock, *Vice Pres*
Brittany Raspo, *Purchasing*
Ashley Cirrincione, *Sales Staff*
▲ **EMP:** 52 **EST:** 2012
SALES (est): 10.6MM **Privately Held**
WEB: www.bosslaser.com
SIC: 3699 Laser systems & equipment; laser welding, drilling & cutting equipment

(G-15276)
CALIGIURI CORPORATION
Also Called: Empress Sissi
518 Central Park Dr (32771-6672)
P.O. Box 471485, Lake Monroe (32747-1485)
PHONE....................................407 324-4441
Miguel Caligiuri, *President*
Karina Caligiuri, *Vice Pres*
EMP: 35 **EST:** 1990
SQ FT: 15,000
SALES (est): 2.9MM **Privately Held**
WEB: www.empresssissi.com
SIC: 2053 Frozen bakery products, except bread

(G-15277)
CAPSMITH INC (PA)
2240 Old Lake Mary Rd (32771-4178)
PHONE....................................407 328-7660
Daniel C Smith, *President*
Danny Smith, *General Mgr*
Marsha Smith, *Treasurer*
Tom Spence, *Comptroller*
Adam Allen, *Sales Mgr*
◆ **EMP:** 23 **EST:** 1985
SQ FT: 12,000
SALES (est): 4.4MM **Privately Held**
WEB: www.capsmith.com
SIC: 2261 2395 2759 Screen printing of cotton broadwoven fabrics; embroidery & art needlework; screen printing

(G-15278)
CEMEX MATERIALS LLC
2210 W 25th St (32771-4137)
PHONE....................................407 322-8862
Bill Sloniger, *Plant Mgr*
Greg Vanlanot, *Plant Mgr*
Ed Hollback, *Terminal Mgr*
Bryan Meskill, *Branch Mgr*
EMP: 40
SQ FT: 1,778 **Privately Held**
SIC: 3273 3271 Ready-mixed concrete; concrete block & brick
HQ: Cemex Materials Llc
1720 Centrepark Dr E # 100
West Palm Beach FL 33401
561 833-5555

(G-15279)
CENTRAL FLORIDA PUBLISHING INC (PA)
700 W Fulton St (32771-1102)
P.O. Box 1057 (32772-1057)
PHONE....................................407 323-5204
Patrick A Tubbs, *CEO*
Robert Mason, *President*
Lawrence Blunk, *COO*
Tom Thomas, *CFO*
EMP: 18 **EST:** 1996
SQ FT: 21,000
SALES (est): 3.3MM **Privately Held**
WEB: www.centralfloridapublishing.com
SIC: 2791 2711 2741 2721 Typesetting; newspapers, publishing & printing; miscellaneous publishing; periodicals

(G-15280)
CENTRO DE DIAGNOSTICO
Also Called: Centro Ddgnstico Y Tratamiento
253 Bellagio Cir (32771-5001)
PHONE....................................407 865-7020
Robert B Haghgou, *Principal*
Nathan Cook, *Vice Pres*
Lisa Ferguson, *Vice Pres*
Lisa Wilk, *Vice Pres*
Hushang S Haghgou, *Director*
EMP: 5 **EST:** 1997
SQ FT: 7,000

SALES (est): 598.8K **Privately Held**
SIC: 2834 Pharmaceutical preparations

(G-15281)
CENTRYS LLC
750 Monroe Rd (32771-8877)
PHONE....................................407 476-4786
EMP: 30
SALES: 5MM **Privately Held**
SIC: 3699 Mfg Electrical Equipment/Supplies

(G-15282)
CHIANTIS
685 Towne Center Blvd (32771-7494)
PHONE....................................407 484-6510
Nick Majaika, *Manager*
EMP: 7 **EST:** 2012
SALES (est): 168K **Privately Held**
WEB: www.chiantispizza.com
SIC: 2033 Pizza sauce: packaged in cans, jars, etc.

(G-15283)
CHOCOLATE COMPASS LLC
5899 Pearl Estates Ln (32771-8520)
PHONE....................................407 600-0145
Harry Jenkins, *Owner*
EMP: 6 **EST:** 2016
SALES (est): 471K **Privately Held**
WEB: www.chocolatecompass.com
SIC: 2026 Milk, chocolate

(G-15284)
CIRCUITRONICS LLC
223 Hickman Dr Ste 101 (32771-8212)
PHONE....................................407 322-8300
Bipin Patel, *President*
EMP: 15 **EST:** 1995
SQ FT: 15,000
SALES (est): 2.9MM **Privately Held**
WEB: www.circuitronics.org
SIC: 3672 8711 Printed circuit boards; engineering services

(G-15285)
CLOUDKISS BEVERAGES INC
3031 S Mellonville Ave (32773-8744)
PHONE....................................407 324-8500
Thomas Barfell, *CEO*
Thomas Kirkeminde, *President*
Don Knudsen, *CFO*
Miller Cooper, *Admin Sec*
EMP: 38 **EST:** 1991
SQ FT: 81,000
SALES (est): 3.4MM **Privately Held**
SIC: 2086 Soft drinks: packaged in cans, bottles, etc.; carbonated beverages, non-alcoholic: bottled & canned

(G-15286)
COBHAM SATCOM
1538 Tropic Park Dr (32773-6323)
PHONE....................................407 650-9054
Brian Anderson, *Sales Mgr*
Scott Lewis, *Supervisor*
George Tong, *Director*
EMP: 20 **EST:** 2013
SALES (est): 9.7MM
SALES (corp-wide): 2.6MM **Privately Held**
SIC: 3812 Search & navigation equipment
HQ: Cobham Limited
Tringham House
Bournemouth
120 288-2020

(G-15287)
COMMERCIAL WOOD DESIGNS INC
257 Power Ct (32771-9406)
PHONE....................................407 302-9063
Jairo Fernandez, *President*
Tanya Fernandez, *Vice Pres*
Chris Lipscomb, *Opers Dir*
EMP: 19 **EST:** 2004
SQ FT: 9,000
SALES (est): 2.9MM **Privately Held**
WEB: www.commercialwooddesigns.com
SIC: 2491 Millwork, treated wood

(G-15288)
COMPAK COMPANIES LLC
Also Called: Celebration Cup
751 Cornwall Rd (32773-5856)
PHONE....................................321 249-9590

Robert L Johnson, *President*
Carl Buford, *Vice Pres*
Buford Carl, *Vice Pres*
Joeann McClandon, *Mng Member*
Nellie Nazario, *Executive Asst*
▲ **EMP:** 16 **EST:** 2003
SQ FT: 47,000
SALES (est): 5.1MM **Privately Held**
WEB: www.celebrationcup.com
SIC: 3089 Cups, plastic, except foam

(G-15289)
COMPASS PUBLISHING LLC
671 Progress Way (32771-6989)
P.O. Box 952674, Lake Mary (32795-2674)
PHONE....................................407 328-0970
Andrea Tolbert,
Andy Tolbert,
EMP: 5 **EST:** 2004
SALES (est): 416.2K **Privately Held**
SIC: 2741 Miscellaneous publishing

(G-15290)
COMPRO SOLUTION
1670 Tropic Park Dr (32773-6335)
PHONE....................................407 733-4130
Mehboob N Ali, *President*
Arifa Suleman, *Sales Mgr*
Parpia Arifa, *Sales Staff*
EMP: 5 **EST:** 2004
SALES (est): 413.5K **Privately Held**
WEB: www.comprosolution.com
SIC: 3577 Computer peripheral equipment

(G-15291)
CONSOLIDATED LABEL CO
2001 E Lake Mary Blvd (32773-7140)
PHONE....................................407 339-2626
Joel R Carmany, *President*
Blake Garrett, *President*
Janaye Melsha, *President*
Greg Solodko, *COO*
Annette Carmany, *Vice Pres*
▼ **EMP:** 200 **EST:** 1980
SQ FT: 80,000
SALES (est): 41.2MM **Privately Held**
WEB: www.consolidatedlabel.com
SIC: 2752 2679 Commercial printing, offset; labels, paper: made from purchased material

(G-15292)
CONTROLOGIX LLC
Also Called: Clx Engineering
361 S White Cedar Rd (32771-6650)
PHONE....................................407 878-2774
Kevin Wilcox, *President*
Mike Sigler, *Vice Pres*
Stephanie Brown, *Project Mgr*
Cory Charles, *Engineer*
Terry Gallagher, *Marketing Staff*
EMP: 52 **EST:** 1998
SQ FT: 10,000
SALES (est): 10MM **Privately Held**
WEB: www.clxengineering.com
SIC: 3823 Computer interface equipment for industrial process control

(G-15293)
COOPER-STANDARD AUTOMOTIVE INC
3551 W 1st St (32771-8852)
PHONE....................................321 233-5563
Josue Ramos, *Manager*
EMP: 25
SALES (corp-wide): 2.3B **Publicly Held**
WEB: www.cooperstandard.com
SIC: 3714 Motor vehicle parts & accessories
HQ: Cooper-Standard Automotive Inc.
40300 Traditions Dr
Northville MI 48168
248 596-5900

(G-15294)
COOPER-STANDARD AUTOMOTIVE INC
501 Cornwall Rd Ste 2773 (32773-5879)
PHONE....................................407 330-3323
Gerald Dunkleman, *Plant Mgr*
EMP: 75
SALES (corp-wide): 2.3B **Publicly Held**
WEB: www.cooperstandard.com
SIC: 3465 Body parts, automobile: stamped metal

HQ: Cooper-Standard Automotive Inc.
40300 Traditions Dr
Northville MI 48168
248 596-5900

(G-15295)
COVERALL ALUMINUM INC
1980 Dolgner Pl Ste 1068 (32771-9231)
PHONE..............................321 377-7874
Peter Wojtas, *President*
EMP: 10 **EST:** 1999
SALES (est): 929.5K **Privately Held**
SIC: 3479 Aluminum coating of metal products

(G-15296)
CRANKSHAFT REBUILDERS INC
1200 Albright Rd (32771-1670)
PHONE..............................407 323-4870
Dan Hunt, *President*
Larry J Eriksson, *Principal*
EMP: 56 **EST:** 1963
SQ FT: 56,000
SALES (est): 5.1MM **Privately Held**
WEB: www.crankshaftrebuilders.com
SIC: 3599 3714 Crankshafts & camshafts, machining; motor vehicle parts & accessories

(G-15297)
CRITICAL DISPOSABLES INC
700 Martin L King Jr Blvd (32771-9531)
PHONE..............................407 330-1154
Autry O V Debusk, *President*
◆ **EMP:** 20 **EST:** 1981
SQ FT: 20,000
SALES (est): 2.4MM
SALES (corp-wide): 3.6MM **Privately Held**
SIC: 3841 3845 Surgical & medical instruments; electromedical equipment
PA: De Royal
200 Debusk Ln
Powell TN 37849
865 938-7828

(G-15298)
CRYSTAL PHOTONICS INC (PA)
5525 Benchmark Ln (32773-8115)
PHONE..............................407 328-9111
Bruce Chai, *President*
Yiting Fei, *Research*
Caroline C Chai, *Treasurer*
Shen Jen, *Technology*
▲ **EMP:** 30 **EST:** 1995
SQ FT: 76,000
SALES (est): 7.5MM **Privately Held**
WEB: www.jccsoc.com
SIC: 3823 Industrial instrmnts msrmnt display/control process variable

(G-15299)
DANIELS WHL SIGN & PLAS INC
5224 W State Road 46 (32771-9230)
PHONE..............................386 736-4918
Daniel Singer,
EMP: 9 **EST:** 2006
SALES (est): 250.9K **Privately Held**
WEB: www.wholesalesignsuperstore.com
SIC: 3993 Signs & advertising specialties

(G-15300)
DAVID RUSSELL ANODIZING
2501 Mccracken Rd (32771-1602)
PHONE..............................407 302-4041
David Russell, *Owner*
▼ **EMP:** 9 **EST:** 1998
SQ FT: 21,000
SALES (est): 892.7K **Privately Held**
WEB: www.davidrussellanodizing.com
SIC: 3471 Anodizing (plating) of metals or formed products

(G-15301)
DECIMAL LLC
121 Central Park Pl (32771-6633)
PHONE..............................407 330-3300
Richard Sweat, *President*
Gus Rathgeber, *COO*
Mary Snyder, *Project Mgr*
Eliezer Torres, *Project Mgr*
Justin Moon, *Prdtn Mgr*
EMP: 50 **EST:** 1986
SQ FT: 36,000

SALES (est): 11.6MM **Privately Held**
WEB: www.dotdecimal.com
SIC: 3842 5047 Personal safety equipment; hospital equipment & furniture

(G-15302)
DEEP OCEAN WOODWORKS INC
Also Called: Wood Arts of India
6289 Bordeaux Cir (32771-6489)
PHONE..............................407 687-2773
Milan Desai, *Principal*
EMP: 7 **EST:** 2017
SALES (est): 105.2K **Privately Held**
SIC: 2431 Millwork

(G-15303)
DEL AIR ELECTRIC CO
201 Tech Dr (32771-6627)
PHONE..............................407 531-1173
EMP: 7 **EST:** 2015
SALES (est): 205K **Privately Held**
WEB: www.delair.com
SIC: 3699 1731 Electrical equipment & supplies; electrical work

(G-15304)
DESIGN CUSTOM MILLWORK INC
130 Tech Dr (32771-6662)
P.O. Box 150419, Altamonte Springs (32715-0419)
PHONE..............................407 878-1267
James Blackburn, *President*
Fred Gemeinhardt, *Vice Pres*
EMP: 25 **EST:** 1999
SQ FT: 8,000
SALES (est): 4MM **Privately Held**
WEB: www.designcustommillworkinc.com
SIC: 2431 Millwork

(G-15305)
DIGIPORTAL SOFTWARE INC
5224 W State Road 46 (32771-9230)
PHONE..............................407 333-2488
EMP: 7 **EST:** 2001
SALES (est): 1MM **Privately Held**
WEB: www.digiportal.com
SIC: 7372 Business oriented computer software

(G-15306)
DISRUPTOR MANUFACTURING
311 Specialty Pt (32771-6624)
PHONE..............................407 900-2868
Alfred Lockyer, *Owner*
David Owen, *Managing Dir*
EMP: 8 **EST:** 2018
SALES (est): 1.1MM **Privately Held**
SIC: 3999 Manufacturing industries

(G-15307)
DNT SOFTWARE CORP
1710 Beacon Dr (32771-9723)
PHONE..............................407 323-0987
Deering N Treppard, *President*
EMP: 5 **EST:** 2000
SALES (est): 356.3K **Privately Held**
SIC: 7372 Prepackaged software

(G-15308)
EARNEST PRODUCTS INC
Also Called: Earnest Metal Fabrication
2000 E Lake Mary Blvd (32773-7133)
PHONE..............................407 831-1588
Bryan H Earnest, *President*
Ken Fadden, *QC Mgr*
Ilias Lamrani, *Engineer*
Mark Greenlaw, *CFO*
Ron Compton, *Human Resources*
EMP: 98 **EST:** 1992
SQ FT: 60,000
SALES (est): 29.7MM **Privately Held**
WEB: www.earnestproducts.com
SIC: 3444 Sheet metalwork

(G-15309)
EAST 46TH AUTO SALES INC
Also Called: East 46th Trailor Sales
3710 E State Road 46 (32771-9159)
PHONE..............................407 322-3100
Charles Brannon, *President*
Patricia Brannon, *Admin Sec*
EMP: 10 **EST:** 1984
SQ FT: 7,800

SALES (est): 1MM **Privately Held**
WEB: www.east46trailers.com
SIC: 3799 5511 3792 Horse trailers, except fifth-wheel type; trucks, tractors & trailers: new & used; travel trailers & campers

(G-15310)
ELECTRONIC COMPONENTS FAS INC
1305 Hstric Gldsboro Blvd (32771-2759)
PHONE..............................407 328-8111
Oscar Redden, *Principal*
Jackie Quinn, *Principal*
Roslyn Redden, *Principal*
Terrell Redden, *Principal*
EMP: 5 **EST:** 2019
SALES (est): 303.4K **Privately Held**
SIC: 3728 Aircraft parts & equipment

(G-15311)
ELECTROTEK INC
201 Steeplechase Cir (32771-9511)
PHONE..............................321 231-6846
Tammy Michelle O Connell, *Principal*
EMP: 6 **EST:** 2012
SALES (est): 513.5K **Privately Held**
WEB: www.sierraelectrotek.com
SIC: 3672 Printed circuit boards

(G-15312)
ELLIS & ASSOCIATES OF SANFORD
Also Called: Computer Center of Sanford
915 W 1st St Ste B (32771-1125)
P.O. Box 2746 (32772-2746)
PHONE..............................407 322-1128
EMP: 5
SQ FT: 1,500
SALES (est): 611.3K **Privately Held**
SIC: 7372 Prepackaged Software Services

(G-15313)
EVERGREEN SWEETENERS INC
2200 Country Club Rd (32771-4053)
PHONE..............................407 323-4250
Tom Girdner, *Vice Pres*
Craig Green, *Vice Pres*
Michele Jones, *Office Mgr*
Tom Robinson, *Branch Mgr*
Neil Toppin, *Supervisor*
EMP: 13
SALES (corp-wide): 10.3MM **Privately Held**
WEB: www.esweeteners.com
SIC: 2099 Sugar
PA: Evergreen Sweeteners, Inc.
1936 Hollywood Blvd # 20
Hollywood FL 33020
954 381-7776

(G-15314)
EXCALIBUR COACH SVC & SLS LLC
1830 Bobby Lee Pt (32771-8075)
PHONE..............................407 302-9139
Doug Stolfo, *Officer*
EMP: 6 **EST:** 2006
SALES (est): 964.7K **Privately Held**
WEB: www.excaliburservice.com
SIC: 3792 Trailer coaches, automobile

(G-15315)
FATHERS TABLE LLC (PA)
Also Called: Father's Table, The
2100 Country Club Rd (32771-4051)
P.O. Box 1509 (32772-1509)
PHONE..............................407 324-1200
Cheryl Lawton, *Vice Pres*
Michael Bishop, *Opers Mgr*
David Nelson, *Prdtn Mgr*
Alexis Dorman, *Production*
Daizy Torres, *Production*
EMP: 250 **EST:** 1999
SALES (est): 114.6MM **Privately Held**
WEB: www.thefatherstable.com
SIC: 2099 Food preparations

(G-15316)
FEA INC
Also Called: Freedom Enterprise & Associate
5333 Pen Ave (32773-9468)
PHONE..............................407 330-3535
Ann E King, *President*
Howard King, *General Mgr*

EMP: 12 **EST:** 2001
SQ FT: 5,000
SALES (est): 2.2MM **Privately Held**
WEB: www.feawaterjet.com
SIC: 3711 Military motor vehicle assembly

(G-15317)
FLORIDA CONTAINER SERVICES
3795 S Sanford Ave (32773-6001)
PHONE..............................407 302-2197
Kurt Till, *Manager*
EMP: 10 **EST:** 2008
SALES (est): 778.3K **Privately Held**
WEB: www.floridashippingcontainers.com
SIC: 3272 Garbage boxes, concrete

(G-15318)
FLORIDA CRAFT DISTRIBUTORS LLC
2650 Jewett Ln (32771-1678)
PHONE..............................813 528-7902
Judith A Forsley, *Mng Member*
EMP: 14 **EST:** 2014
SALES (est): 630.2K **Privately Held**
WEB: www.floridacraftdistributors.com
SIC: 2082 Beer (alcoholic beverage)

(G-15319)
FLORIDA EXTRUDERS INTL INC
2540 Jewett Ln (32771-1687)
P.O. Box 14213, Fort Lauderdale (33302-4213)
PHONE..............................407 323-3300
Joel G Lehman, *President*
Joel Lehman, *President*
Luis Giammattei, *Design Engr*
◆ **EMP:** 65 **EST:** 1989
SQ FT: 400,000
SALES (est): 5.3MM **Privately Held**
WEB: www.floridaextruders.com
SIC: 3354 Aluminum extruded products

(G-15320)
FREEPORT FOUNTAINS LLC
1510 Kastner Pl Ste 3 (32771-9308)
PHONE..............................407 330-1150
Joel Wolcott, *Principal*
Kim Vollet, *Business Mgr*
Joel M Wolcott, *Chief Engr*
Robert Vasquez, *Design Engr*
Diane Vollet, *Sales Staff*
EMP: 20 **EST:** 1981
SALES (est): 3.7MM **Privately Held**
WEB: www.freeportfountains.com
SIC: 3272 Fountains, concrete

(G-15321)
FUELS UNLIMITED INC
509 S French Ave (32771-1875)
P.O. Box 259 (32772-0259)
PHONE..............................407 302-3193
Karen Violet, *Principal*
EMP: 7 **EST:** 2006
SALES (est): 199.8K **Privately Held**
SIC: 1382 Oil & gas exploration services

(G-15322)
FURNITURE DESIGN OF CENTL FLA
Also Called: Furniture Design Gallery
219 Hickman Dr (32771-8201)
PHONE..............................407 330-4430
Ebrahim Hamzeloui, *President*
Mohammad Hamzeloui, *Vice Pres*
EMP: 13 **EST:** 1985
SQ FT: 15,500
SALES (est): 842.7K **Privately Held**
WEB: www.furnituredesigngallery.com
SIC: 2511 2521 Wood household furniture; cabinets, office: wood

(G-15323)
G & R MACHINE INC
701 Cornwall Rd Ste A (32773-7334)
PHONE..............................407 324-1600
Matthew Silvey, *Principal*
EMP: 5 **EST:** 1999
SALES (est): 407.7K **Privately Held**
SIC: 3542 Forging machinery & hammers

▲ = Import ▼ =Export
◆ =Import/Export

(G-15324)
GATOR DOCK & MARINE LLC
Also Called: CMI International
2880 S Mellonville Ave (32773-9686)
PHONE....................407 323-0190
Marlene Fowler, *Office Mgr*
John E Irvine, *Mng Member*
Michael S Crane,
Jon W Fleischman,
Randolph Fortener,
▼ EMP: 16 EST: 1987
SALES (est): 5.2MM
SALES (corp-wide): 91.9MM **Privately
Held**
WEB: www.gatordock.com
SIC: 3999 1629 Dock equipment & sup-
plies, industrial; dock construction
HQ: Cmi Limited Co.
605 Molly Ln Ste 150
Woodstock GA 30189

(G-15325)
GENEVA FOODS LLC (PA)
2664 Jewett Ln (32771-1678)
P.O. Box 720691, Atlanta GA (30358-2691)
PHONE....................407 302-4751
Tom Bandemer, *Mng Member*
Peter A Corteville,
▲ EMP: 14 EST: 1983
SQ FT: 12,000
SALES (est): 2MM **Privately Held**
SIC: 2099 Food preparations

(G-15326)
**GLEMAN SONS CSTM
WOODWORKS LLC**
110 Tech Dr (32771-6625)
PHONE....................407 314-9638
Adrian Gleman, *Manager*
EMP: 10 EST: 2017
SALES (est): 707.4K **Privately Held**
WEB: www.glemanandsons.com
SIC: 2431 Millwork

(G-15327)
GREEN CREATIVE LLC
519 Codisco Way (32771-6618)
PHONE....................866 774-5433
Michael P Santoni, *Treasurer*
Cole Zucker, *Mng Member*
Guillaume Vidal,
Neil Yeargin,
▲ EMP: 50 EST: 2011
SALES (est): 10.9MM
SALES (corp-wide): 1.2B **Privately Held**
WEB: www.greencreative.com
SIC: 3646 Commercial indusl & institu-
tional electric lighting fixtures
PA: Harbour Group Ltd.
7733 Forsyth Blvd Fl 23
Saint Louis MO 63105
314 727-5550

(G-15328)
GREYFIELD HOLDINGS INC (PA)
900 Central Park Dr (32771-6634)
PHONE....................407 830-8861
Bradley Osleger, *President*
Keith Treadwell, *General Mgr*
Kenneth Osleger, *Principal*
Ben Scott, *Opers Staff*
Louis Gonzalez, *Production*
▲ EMP: 17 EST: 1991
SQ FT: 11,000
SALES (est): 6MM **Privately Held**
SIC: 3993 Electric signs

(G-15329)
H & M PRINTING INC
Also Called: Magnolia Press
104 Loren Ct (32771-6321)
PHONE....................407 831-8030
Mary Hargon, *President*
Michael Patrick Hargon, *Vice Pres*
Michael Daven Port, *Vice Pres*
Debby Knorowski, *Sales Staff*
EMP: 17 EST: 1973
SQ FT: 8,000
SALES (est): 2.2MM **Privately Held**
SIC: 2796 2752 2789 Platemaking serv-
ices; commercial printing, offset; book-
binding & related work

(G-15330)
**HEAVY HWY INFRASTRUCTURE
LLC**
2210 W 25th St (32771-4137)
P.O. Box 2161 (32772-2161)
PHONE....................407 323-8853
Leo L Borde, *General Mgr*
Jennifer Flores, *Mng Member*
John Piecguch,
EMP: 75 EST: 2014
SQ FT: 1,000
SALES (est): 12.8MM **Privately Held**
WEB: www.floridahii.com
SIC: 3272 Floor slabs & tiles, precast con-
crete

(G-15331)
HERNON MANUFACTURING INC
121 Tech Dr (32771-6663)
PHONE....................407 322-4000
Harry Arnon, *President*
Gustavo De, *General Mgr*
Karen Arnon, *Exec VP*
Gary Butler, *Plant Mgr*
Roberto Flores, *Plant Mgr*
▲ EMP: 71 EST: 1978
SQ FT: 30,000
SALES (est): 14.4MM **Privately Held**
WEB: www.hernon.com
SIC: 3089 2891 Tissue dispensers, plas-
tic; epoxy adhesives

(G-15332)
HILL DERMACEUTICALS INC
2650 S Mellonville Ave (32773-9311)
PHONE....................407 323-1887
Jerry S Roth, *President*
Sharon Dudash, *General Mgr*
Jerry Roth, *General Mgr*
Susan G Roth, *Corp Secy*
Jeff Tabatabai, *Opers Staff*
EMP: 35 EST: 1979
SQ FT: 27,000
SALES (est): 8.3MM **Privately Held**
WEB: www.hillderm.com
SIC: 2834 Pharmaceutical preparations

(G-15333)
HILL LABS INC
2650 S Mellonville Ave (32773-9311)
PHONE....................407 323-1887
Jerry Roth, *President*
EMP: 35 EST: 1989
SALES (est): 4.4MM **Privately Held**
SIC: 2834 Pharmaceutical preparations

(G-15334)
**ICORP-IFOAM SPECIALTY
PRODUCTS**
250 Power Ct (32771-9404)
P.O. Box 470036, Lake Monroe (32747-
0036)
PHONE....................407 328-8500
Phillip Landers, *President*
Chet Vansyckel, *Opers Staff*
EMP: 6 EST: 1991
SQ FT: 6,800
SALES (est): 1MM **Privately Held**
WEB: www.sniffnstop.com
SIC: 3086 Plastics foam products

(G-15335)
**INDOOR TRAMPOLINE ARENA
INC**
Also Called: Reboundersz Purchasing Dev
605 Hickman Cir (32771-6904)
P.O. Box 952949, Lake Mary (32795-2949)
PHONE....................321 222-1300
Marcus E Gurley, *CEO*
Melvin Horn, *COO*
Kiki Rosas, *Director*
EMP: 13 EST: 2010
SQ FT: 11,000
SALES (est): 918.4K **Privately Held**
WEB: www.rebounderzfranchise.com
SIC: 3949 Trampolines & equipment

(G-15336)
INDUSTRIAL SCAN INC
223 Hickman Dr Ste 109 (32771-8212)
PHONE....................407 322-3664
Ishwar Singh, *President*
Vicki Hart, *Manager*
EMP: 17 EST: 1991
SQ FT: 15,000

SALES (est): 2.3MM **Privately Held**
WEB: www.industrialscan.com
SIC: 3577 8711 Optical scanning devices;
designing: ship, boat, machine & product

(G-15337)
INITIAL MARINE CORPORATION
650 Hickman Cir (32771-6929)
PHONE....................407 321-1340
Steven Stepp, *President*
▼ EMP: 24
SALES (est): 604.5K **Privately Held**
SIC: 3732 Motorboats, inboard or out-
board: building & repairing

(G-15338)
INNOVATIVE SIGNS INC
957 Penfield Cv (32773-8165)
P.O. Box 951851, Lake Mary (32795-1851)
PHONE....................407 830-5155
Bart Baker, *President*
Bart H Baker, *President*
Jeffrey Gardner, *Manager*
Lisa Garvin, *CIO*
Wendy J Baker, *Admin Sec*
EMP: 5 EST: 1984
SALES (est): 503.7K **Privately Held**
WEB: www.innovativesigns.com
SIC: 3993 Signs, not made in custom sign
painting shops

(G-15339)
**INTEGRTED DSIGN DEV CNTL
FLA I**
410 W 4th St (32771-1840)
PHONE....................407 268-4300
Tiffany Kath, *President*
Russel Kath, *Vice Pres*
Russell Kath, *Manager*
EMP: 6 EST: 2005
SQ FT: 8,000
SALES (est): 504.6K **Privately Held**
WEB: www.iddfl.com
SIC: 3599 3489 3451 7389 Machine
shop, jobbing & repair; ordnance & acces-
sories; screw machine products; design,
commercial & industrial

(G-15340)
**INVACARE FLORIDA
CORPORATION**
2101 E Lake Mary Blvd (32773-7141)
PHONE....................407 321-5630
A Malachi Mixon III, *CEO*
Gerald B Blouch, *President*
Jerome E Fox, *Vice Pres*
Anthony C Laplaca, *Admin Sec*
Fernando Baerga, *Administration*
◆ EMP: 300 EST: 1996
SALES (est): 78.9MM
SALES (corp-wide): 872.4MM **Publicly
Held**
SIC: 3842 Surgical appliances & supplies
PA: Invacare Corporation
1 Invacare Way
Elyria OH 44035
440 329-6000

(G-15341)
J & J INTERNATIONAL CORP
Also Called: Action Label
240 Power Ct Ste 132 (32771-9400)
PHONE....................407 349-7114
Jim Schenk, *President*
EMP: 26 EST: 1997
SQ FT: 5,000
SALES (est): 4.6MM **Privately Held**
WEB: www.actionlabel.com
SIC: 2671 2752 Packaging paper & plas-
tics film, coated & laminated; commercial
printing, lithographic

(G-15342)
**JAMAR CNSTR FABRICATION
INC**
119 Commerce Way (32771-3085)
PHONE....................321 400-0333
Mark Pick, *Principal*
EMP: 9 EST: 2017
SALES (est): 217.3K **Privately Held**
WEB: www.jamarfab.com
SIC: 3441 Fabricated structural metal

(G-15343)
JAMCO INDUSTRIAL INC
3800 Entp Way Ste 1110 (32771)
PHONE....................866 848-5400
Abbas Jamal, *President*
Tim Jamal, *Vice Pres*
Imtiaz Jamal, *Director*
EMP: 11 EST: 2012
SALES (est): 991.2K **Privately Held**
WEB: www.jamco1.com
SIC: 3537 Forklift trucks

(G-15344)
JAMES G DOWLING
1375 Palm Way (32773-6807)
PHONE....................407 509-9484
James G Dowling, *Owner*
EMP: 7 EST: 2003
SALES (est): 265.6K **Privately Held**
SIC: 1442 Construction sand & gravel

(G-15345)
JONES COMMUNICATIONS INC
312 W 1st St Ste 503 (32771-1206)
PHONE....................407 448-6615
Jim Jones, *President*
Bill Davis, *Vice Pres*
EMP: 7 EST: 2009
SALES (est): 530.8K **Privately Held**
SIC: 3531 Construction machinery

(G-15346)
JRS LIMB TREE & FARM LLC
297 Grant Line Rd (32771-9091)
PHONE....................407 383-4843
Gerald F Williams Jr, *Manager*
EMP: 7 EST: 2016
SALES (est): 217.8K **Privately Held**
SIC: 3842 Limbs, artificial

(G-15347)
JRT MANUFACTURING LLC
421 Cornwall Rd (32773-5871)
PHONE....................321 363-4133
Charles Chuck Johnson, *Purch Mgr*
David Thomson,
Maria Thomson,
EMP: 10 EST: 2013
SQ FT: 25,000
SALES (est): 1.9MM **Privately Held**
WEB: www.jrtmanufacturingllc.com
SIC: 3672 Printed circuit boards

(G-15348)
KEMCO INDUSTRIES LLC
70 Keyes Ave (32773-6074)
PHONE....................407 322-1230
Ty S Kracht, *CEO*
Ty Kracht, *General Mgr*
Tye Kraft, *General Mgr*
Ted Swartzlander, *COO*
Bynne Harris, *Project Mgr*
▼ EMP: 80 EST: 1988
SQ FT: 55,000
SALES (est): 17.4MM **Privately Held**
WEB: www.kemco.com
SIC: 3441 3625 3613 3444 Fabricated
structural metal; relays & industrial con-
trols; switchgear & switchboard appara-
tus; sheet metalwork; engraving service

(G-15349)
KENNY SKYLIGHTS LLC
5294 Tower Way (32773-8201)
PHONE....................407 330-5150
Lee Walls,
EMP: 8 EST: 2005
SALES (est): 405.3K **Privately Held**
SIC: 3211 Skylight glass

(G-15350)
KID-U-NOT INC
1201 Central Park Dr (32771-6638)
PHONE....................407 324-2112
Linda T Rubel, *President*
Trish Edwards, *Sales Staff*
◆ EMP: 50 EST: 1989
SQ FT: 40,000
SALES (est): 6.8MM **Privately Held**
WEB: www.wekidunot.com
SIC: 2396 Screen printing on fabric articles

(G-15351)
LEGACY VULCAN LLC
4150 Maverick Ct (32771-6902)
PHONE....................407 321-5323

Lawrence McIntyre, *Manager*
EMP: 7 **Publicly Held**
SIC: 3273 Ready-mixed concrete
HQ: Legacy Vulcan, Llc
1200 Urban Center Dr
Vestavia AL 35242
205 298-3000

(G-15352)
LOGGERHEAD DISTILLERY LLC
124 W 2nd St (32771-1212)
PHONE..................................321 800-8566
Colby Theisen, *Mng Member*
EMP: 8 **EST:** 2018
SALES (est): 262.6K **Privately Held**
WEB: www.loggerheaddistillery.com
SIC: 2085 Distilled & blended liquors

(G-15353)
MARKET READY
1721 Missouri Ave (32771-9722)
PHONE..................................407 324-4273
Daniel Liebelt, *Principal*
EMP: 7 **EST:** 2010
SALES (est): 244.7K **Privately Held**
SIC: 3273 Ready-mixed concrete

(G-15354)
MATHEWS ASSOCIATES INC
Also Called: Battery Assemblers
220 Power Ct (32771-9530)
PHONE..................................407 323-3390
Daniel Perreault, *CEO*
Philip Perreault, *President*
Judy J Perreault, *Treasurer*
▲ **EMP:** 160 **EST:** 1980
SQ FT: 20,000
SALES (est): 24.5MM **Privately Held**
WEB: www.maifl.com
SIC: 3691 3629 3812 3672 Batteries, rechargeable; electronic generation equipment; search & navigation equipment; printed circuit boards

(G-15355)
MBF INDUSTRIES INC
210 Tech Dr (32771-6662)
PHONE..................................407 323-9414
John W Baker III, *President*
Jim Long, *General Mgr*
Nilsson Natasha, *Managing Dir*
Tom Vanderluitgaren, *Vice Pres*
Dean Feller, *Production*
EMP: 35 **EST:** 1992
SQ FT: 32,000
SALES (est): 7.7MM **Privately Held**
WEB: www.mbfindustries.com
SIC: 3799 Trailers & trailer equipment

(G-15356)
MCCARTHY FABRICATION LLC
201 N Maple Ave Ste 2 (32771-1106)
P.O. Box 1543 (32772-1543)
PHONE..................................407 943-4909
Eli Ramirez, *Project Mgr*
Charles C McCarthy, *Mng Member*
Elliott Ramirez, *Manager*
EMP: 17 **EST:** 2018
SALES (est): 1.9MM **Privately Held**
WEB: www.mccarthyfabricationllc.com
SIC: 3441 Fabricated structural metal

(G-15357)
MCES LLC
2499 Old Lake Mary Rd # 102 (32771-4192)
PHONE..................................321 363-4977
Carlos Gonzalez, *Mng Member*
Shug Brandell, *Director*
EMP: 8 **EST:** 2010
SALES (est): 894.4K **Privately Held**
WEB: www.mymces.com
SIC: 3571 7699 3577 Electronic computers; agricultural equipment repair services; decoders, computer peripheral equipment

(G-15358)
METAL WORKS BY GAL
5650 S Sanford Ave (32773-9431)
PHONE..................................407 486-7198
Gal Schwartz, *Principal*
EMP: 9 **EST:** 2010
SALES (est): 333.3K **Privately Held**
SIC: 3444 Sheet metalwork

(G-15359)
MOBILE SPECIALTIES INC
Also Called: Mobile Walkways
1683 N Beardall Ave # 117 (32771-9616)
P.O. Box 622363, Oviedo (32762-2363)
PHONE..................................407 878-5469
Dennis Towell, *CEO*
▼ **EMP:** 8 **EST:** 2007
SQ FT: 11,000
SALES (est): 932.3K **Privately Held**
WEB: www.industrialcrewquarters.com
SIC: 3534 Walkways, moving

(G-15360)
MOBILITE CORPORATION
2101 E Lake Mary Blvd (32773-6099)
PHONE..................................407 321-5630
Gerald B Blouch, *President*
EMP: 28 **EST:** 1979
SQ FT: 113,000
SALES (est): 1.5MM
SALES (corp-wide): 872.4MM **Publicly Held**
SIC: 2514 3841 Beds, including folding & cabinet, household: metal; inhalation therapy equipment
PA: Invacare Corporation
1 Invacare Way
Elyria OH 44035
440 329-6000

(G-15361)
MOTHER EARTH STONE LLC
4035 Maronda Way (32771-6503)
P.O. Box 470996, Lake Monroe (32747-0996)
PHONE..................................407 878-2854
Clint Coleman, *Mng Member*
EMP: 12 **EST:** 2010
SALES (est): 1MM **Privately Held**
WEB: mother-earth-stone-llc.business.site
SIC: 3281 3272 1771 Cut stone & stone products; concrete products, precast; concrete work

(G-15362)
NATIVE VANILLA LLC
1255 W Airport Blvd (32773-4996)
PHONE..................................407 724-1995
Daniel Edmiston, *Principal*
EMP: 10 **EST:** 2018
SALES (est): 1MM **Privately Held**
WEB: www.nativevanilla.com
SIC: 2099 Food preparations

(G-15363)
NULINE SENSORS LLC
210 Specialty Pt (32771-6641)
PHONE..................................407 473-0765
Jim Monsor, *CEO*
Eve Gould, *Senior Buyer*
George Cadena, *Engineer*
Audrey Mohlenhoff, *Electrical Engi*
William McEllen, *Agent*
EMP: 8 **EST:** 2013
SQ FT: 15,450
SALES (est): 1MM **Privately Held**
WEB: www.nulinesensors.com
SIC: 3841 5047 3845 Diagnostic apparatus, medical; patient monitoring equipment; diagnostic equipment, medical; arc lamp units, electrotherapeutic (except IR & UV)

(G-15364)
OMEGA MEDICAL IMAGING LLC
3400 Saint Johns Pkwy # 1020 (32771-6769)
PHONE..................................407 323-9400
Brian Fleming, *CEO*
Robert McNeill, *Mfg Staff*
Brandon Diviaio, *Engineer*
Joshua Sterling, *Software Engr*
Linda Robb, *Admin Asst*
EMP: 24 **EST:** 1990
SQ FT: 17,000
SALES (est): 5.7MM **Privately Held**
WEB: www.omegamedicalimaging.com
SIC: 3844 5047 X-ray apparatus & tubes; hospital equipment & furniture

(G-15365)
ONE RESONANCE SENSORS LLC
101 Gordon St (32771-6323)
PHONE..................................407 637-0771

Pablo Prado, *CEO*
Gregory Holifield,
Will McEllen,
EMP: 10 **EST:** 2011
SALES (est): 838.7K **Privately Held**
WEB: www.industrialnmr.com
SIC: 3674 Semiconductors & related devices

(G-15366)
ONLINE LABELS LLC (PA)
2001 E Lake Mary Blvd (32773-7140)
PHONE..................................407 936-3900
David Carmany, *President*
Matt Hamilton, *General Mgr*
Joseph Lyday, *Plant Supt*
Davis Amber, *Engineer*
Matthew Stoltz, *Accountant*
▼ **EMP:** 48 **EST:** 1999
SALES (est): 23.3MM **Privately Held**
WEB: www.onlinelabels.com
SIC: 2672 5999 Adhesive papers, labels or tapes: from purchased material; packaging materials: boxes, padding, etc.

(G-15367)
ONSIGHT INDUSTRIES LLC
Also Called: Commercial Signage
900 Central Park Dr (32771-6634)
PHONE..................................407 830-8861
Brad Osleger,
EMP: 100 **EST:** 2017
SALES (est): 11.8MM **Privately Held**
WEB: www.onsightindustries.com
SIC: 3993 Signs & advertising specialties

(G-15368)
OWENS DISTRIBUTORS INC
2850 W Airport Blvd (32771-1610)
P.O. Box 1358 (32772-1358)
PHONE..................................407 302-8602
Peter Owens, *President*
Susan M Owens, *Vice Pres*
Susan Owens, *Vice Pres*
Greg Duncan, *Warehouse Mgr*
Milton Kingsley, *Warehouse Mgr*
EMP: 20 **EST:** 1994
SQ FT: 20,000
SALES (est): 4.2MM **Privately Held**
WEB: www.owensdistributors.com
SIC: 2841 Detergents, synthetic organic or inorganic alkaline; dishwashing compounds

(G-15369)
PARAGON PRODUCTS INC
Also Called: Creative Printing & Publishing
2300 Old Lake Mary Rd (32771-4189)
PHONE..................................407 302-9147
Richard Roy, *President*
Barbara Dizon, *Marketing Staff*
EMP: 20 **EST:** 1971
SQ FT: 5,500
SALES (est): 3.3MM **Privately Held**
WEB: www.cpponline.com
SIC: 2752 Commercial printing, offset

(G-15370)
PAULS TWING DSPTCH CNTL FLA I
1919 W 1st St (32771-1648)
PHONE..................................407 323-4446
Paul A Lanza, *President*
EMP: 16 **EST:** 2003
SALES (est): 446K **Privately Held**
SIC: 3799 Towing bars & systems

(G-15371)
PHOENIX DEWATERING INC
1980 Cameron Ave (32771-9674)
P.O. Box 952742, Lake Mary (32795-2742)
PHONE..................................407 330-7015
Terry Miles, *President*
James Miles, *Corp Secy*
EMP: 16 **EST:** 1994
SALES (est): 2.3MM **Privately Held**
SIC: 3561 3533 Pumps & pumping equipment; water well drilling equipment

(G-15372)
POWELL WOODWORKING LLC
5150 Sage Cedar Pl (32771-9339)
PHONE..................................407 883-9181
Marc R Powell, *Manager*
EMP: 12 **EST:** 2017

SALES (est): 955.1K **Privately Held**
WEB: www.powellwoodworking.net
SIC: 2431 Millwork

(G-15373)
PRE-CAST SPECIALTIES INC
Also Called: Pcsi
3850 E Lake Mary Blvd (32773-6609)
PHONE..................................954 781-4040
Fred A Cianelli, *President*
Gene Leach, *COO*
John Meyer, *Project Mgr*
Alfred A Cianelli Jr, *Treasurer*
Alfred Cianelli, *Treasurer*
◆ **EMP:** 200 **EST:** 1971
SQ FT: 14,949
SALES (est): 21.8MM **Privately Held**
WEB: www.precastspecialties.com
SIC: 3272 Concrete products, precast

(G-15374)
PRE-CAST SPECIALTIES LLC (PA)
Also Called: Precast Specialties
3850 E Lake Mary Blvd (32773-6609)
PHONE..................................954 781-4040
Margie Metzgar, *Purch Mgr*
Dean Jenness Locke, *Mng Member*
EMP: 5 **EST:** 2015
SALES (est): 10.4MM **Privately Held**
WEB: www.precastspecialties.com
SIC: 3272 Concrete products, precast

(G-15375)
PRECISION QULTY MACHINING INC
710 Golden Spike Ln (32771-8213)
PHONE..................................407 831-7240
Bob Ryan, *President*
Patrick Quinn, *Vice Pres*
EMP: 7 **EST:** 2002
SALES (est): 670.6K **Privately Held**
SIC: 3599 Custom machinery

(G-15376)
PREMIERE MANUFACTURING CO LLC ✪
1480 Mrtin Lther King Jr (32771-9570)
PHONE..................................407 747-3955
Justin G Gaudi, *Mng Member*
EMP: 9 **EST:** 2021
SALES (est): 546K **Privately Held**
SIC: 3484 Machine guns or machine gun parts, 30 mm. & below

(G-15377)
PRESCIENT LOGISTICS LLC
Also Called: Repscrubs
576 Monroe Rd Ste 1304 (32771-8819)
PHONE..................................407 547-2680
Bryan Zediker, *Vice Pres*
Jennifer Feuer, *Human Res Mgr*
Mark Madsen, *Regl Sales Mgr*
Andrew Derksen, *Sales Staff*
Carlie Sutherland, *Marketing Staff*
EMP: 10 **EST:** 2013
SQ FT: 6,500
SALES (est): 500K **Privately Held**
WEB: www.repscrubs.com
SIC: 2389 Hospital gowns

(G-15378)
PRINTER PIX
353 Gordon St (32771-6325)
PHONE..................................863 273-3447
Roshanali Daya, *Principal*
EMP: 8 **EST:** 2011
SALES (est): 93.5K **Privately Held**
SIC: 2752 Commercial printing, offset

(G-15379)
QUANTUMFLY ENTERPRISES INC
Also Called: Manufacturing
2664 Jewett Ln (32771-1678)
PHONE..................................407 807-7050
David Carrier, *CEO*
David P Carrier, *President*
Edwards Linda, *General Mgr*
Roseann Di, *Regional Mgr*
Edward Ross, *Vice Pres*
EMP: 31 **EST:** 2007
SQ FT: 10,000

▲ = Import ▼ =Export
◆ =Import/Export

SALES (est): 5.4MM **Privately Held**
WEB: www.quantumflo.com
SIC: 3561 Industrial pumps & parts

(G-15380)
RAINBOW POOL SUPPLY INC
2920 W Airport Blvd (32771-4818)
PHONE..................................407 324-9616
Jean Riese, *Principal*
EMP: 10 EST: 2008
SALES (est): 244.1K **Privately Held**
SIC: 3089 Plastic processing

(G-15381)
RILEY & COMPANY INC (PA)
5491 Benchmark Ln (32773-6433)
PHONE..................................407 265-9963
Larry Riley, *President*
Audrey Bowman, *General Mgr*
Gerson Velez, *Vice Pres*
Keith Hawkins, *Project Mgr*
Maria Torres, *Manager*
EMP: 12 EST: 2000
SQ FT: 10,000
SALES (est): 2.8MM **Privately Held**
WEB: www.rileyandco.com
SIC: 3999 Atomizers, toiletry

(G-15382)
ROWE MANUFACTURING LLC
722 Golden Spike Ln (32771-8213)
PHONE..................................407 324-5757
Gerald L Rowe Jr,
Donna Rowe,
EMP: 13 EST: 2002
SQ FT: 4,150
SALES (est): 2MM **Privately Held**
WEB: www.rowemfgllc.com
SIC: 3599 Machine shop, jobbing & repair

(G-15383)
RUGBY ROAD CORP
Also Called: Newer Spreader
3941 Saint Johns Pkwy (32771-6373)
PHONE..................................407 328-5474
Rick Gaughan, *President*
Bonita S Gaughan, *Principal*
EMP: 6 EST: 2005
SQ FT: 5,000
SALES (est): 756.6K **Privately Held**
SIC: 3523 Spreaders, fertilizer

(G-15384)
RUSSELL BROS ALUM ANDZING CTIN
Also Called: Russell Bros Alum Anodizing
1001 Cornwall Rd (32773-5873)
PHONE..................................407 323-5619
Charles Russell, *President*
EMP: 12 EST: 1980
SQ FT: 5,000
SALES (est): 137.9K **Privately Held**
WEB: www.davidrussellanodizing.com
SIC: 3471 Anodizing (plating) of metals or formed products

(G-15385)
SEMINOLE COUNTY PUBLIC SCHOOLS
1722 W Airport Blvd (32771-4000)
PHONE..................................407 320-0393
Joel Renda, *Manager*
Kris Sefried, *Teacher*
EMP: 32
SALES (corp-wide): 718.7MM **Privately Held**
WEB: www.scps.us
SIC: 2732 Book printing
HQ: Seminole County Public Schools
400 E Lake Mary Blvd
Sanford FL 32773
407 320-0000

(G-15386)
SIMPLY GROUP II LLC
Also Called: Simplynas
4366 Ronald Reagan Blvd (32773-6315)
PHONE..................................407 960-4690
Fatema Mawji, *CEO*
Tony Salazar,
EMP: 6 EST: 2010
SALES (est): 1.9MM **Privately Held**
WEB: www.simplynas.com
SIC: 3572 Computer storage devices

(G-15387)
SNK AMERICA INC
Also Called: Somec
3551 W State Road 46 (32771-8852)
PHONE..................................407 831-7766
Kevin Lousch, *Officer*
EMP: 10 EST: 2013
SALES (est): 1MM **Privately Held**
WEB: www.someccontainers.com
SIC: 3541 Machine tools, metal cutting type

(G-15388)
SOFIE CO
136 Commerce Way (32771-3091)
PHONE..................................407 321-9076
Timothy Stone, *President*
Chris Williams, *General Mgr*
Kirk McCall, *Manager*
Todd Bejian,
EMP: 28
SQ FT: 8,050 **Privately Held**
WEB: www.sofie.com
SIC: 2834 Pharmaceutical preparations
HQ: Sofie Co.
21000 Atl Blvd Ste 730
Dulles VA 20166

(G-15389)
SOUTHERN MFG & FABRICATION LLC
2000 E Lake Mary Blvd (32773-7133)
PHONE..................................407 894-8851
Bryan H Earnest, *Principal*
David Ayers, *Natl Sales Mgr*
Jennie Niven, *Sales Staff*
Deron McFarland, *Manager*
Jeremy Huffman, *Director*
EMP: 12 EST: 2011
SALES (est): 2MM **Privately Held**
WEB: www.southernmfg.com
SIC: 3443 Tanks, standard or custom fabricated: metal plate

(G-15390)
ST JOHNS OPTICAL SYSTEMS LLC
101 Gordon St (32771-6323)
PHONE..................................407 280-3787
Gregory Holifield,
Ronald Driggers,
EMP: 5 EST: 2013
SALES (est): 328.6K **Privately Held**
WEB: www.stjohnsopticalsystems.com
SIC: 3826 Laser scientific & engineering instruments

(G-15391)
STEEL PLUS SERVICE CENTER INC
2525 Magnolia Ave (32773-5135)
PHONE..................................407 328-7169
Frank Brooklyn, *President*
EMP: 6 EST: 1992
SQ FT: 2,400
SALES (est): 527.6K **Privately Held**
SIC: 7692 7539 Welding repair; trailer repair

(G-15392)
SUNSTATE AWNG GRPHIC DSIGN INC
50 Keyes Ave (32773-6074)
PHONE..................................407 260-6118
Mark A Nelen, *Ch of Bd*
Alan M Hanley, *President*
EMP: 26 EST: 1989
SQ FT: 8,000
SALES (est): 4.7MM **Privately Held**
WEB: www.sunstateawning.com
SIC: 2394 Awnings, fabric: made from purchased materials

(G-15393)
SUPERCHIPS INC
1790 E Airport Blvd (32773-6805)
PHONE..................................407 585-7000
Ron Turcotte, *President*
Craig Ancel, *Engineer*
Chris Rookey, *Engineer*
Guadalupe Soto, *CFO*
Karen Server, *Admin Sec*
EMP: 36 EST: 1992
SQ FT: 25,000

SALES (est): 1.9MM **Privately Held**
WEB: www.superchips.com
SIC: 3571 Electronic computers

(G-15394)
T J SALES ASSOCIATES INC
4355 Saint Johns Pkwy (32771-6381)
PHONE..................................407 328-0777
Randy Lusigman, *Manager*
EMP: 8
SALES (corp-wide): 2.7MM **Privately Held**
SIC: 3699 Laser systems & equipment
PA: T J Sales Associates Inc
3155 State Route 10 # 204
Denville NJ 07834
407 328-0777

(G-15395)
TEAM SOLUTIONS DENTAL LLC
2675 S Design Ct (32773-8120)
PHONE..................................407 542-1552
Jamie McNeely, *Facilities Mgr*
Daniel Lengert, *Engineer*
Julie Magnus, *Cust Mgr*
Matt Doolittle, *Marketing Staff*
Craig Moore, *Director*
EMP: 80 EST: 2013
SALES (est): 5.4MM **Privately Held**
WEB: www.tsdlab.com
SIC: 3999 Manufacturing industries

(G-15396)
TESSERACT SENSORS LLC
101 Gordon St (32771-6323)
PHONE..................................407 385-2498
Monica Nguyen, *Electrical Engi*
Gil C Barrett Jr,
EMP: 11 EST: 2010
SALES (est): 919.7K **Privately Held**
SIC: 3674 Radiation sensors

(G-15397)
TNR TECHNICAL INC (PA)
301 Central Park Dr (32771-6692)
PHONE..................................407 321-3011
Wayne Thaw, *CEO*
Mitchell Thaw, *President*
Anne Provost, *CFO*
Daniel Rivera, *Sales Staff*
◆ EMP: 13 EST: 1979
SQ FT: 8,000
SALES (est): 4.5MM **Privately Held**
WEB: www.tnrtechnical.com
SIC: 3691 3692 Storage batteries; dry cell batteries, single or multiple cell

(G-15398)
TORO COMPANY
3000 S Mellonville Ave # 422 (32773-9351)
PHONE..................................407 321-2901
Steve Perkins, *Branch Mgr*
EMP: 16
SALES (corp-wide): 3.9B **Publicly Held**
WEB: www.thetorocompany.com
SIC: 3523 3524 Fertilizing, spraying, dusting & irrigation machinery; lawn & garden equipment
PA: The Toro Company
8111 Lyndale Ave S
Bloomington MN 55420
952 888-8801

(G-15399)
TORTILLERIA LAMEXICANA 7 INC
2715 S Orlando Dr (32773-5311)
PHONE..................................407 324-3100
Meguel Hornho, *President*
EMP: 10 EST: 2005
SALES (est): 558.3K **Privately Held**
SIC: 2099 Tortillas, fresh or refrigerated

(G-15400)
TOS MANUFACTURING INC
Also Called: Deskrafters
4280 Saint Johns Pkwy (32771-6378)
PHONE..................................407 330-3880
Roger Morin, *President*
EMP: 11 EST: 1992
SQ FT: 10,000
SALES (est): 136.8K **Privately Held**
SIC: 2521 Wood office furniture

(G-15401)
U C CABINET INC
222 Hickman Dr (32771-6917)
PHONE..................................407 322-0968
Joseph Scheuering, *President*
James C Scheuering, *Vice Pres*
Jeffrey T Scheuering, *Vice Pres*
John R Scheuering, *Vice Pres*
Joseph R Scheuering Jr, *Vice Pres*
EMP: 6 EST: 1981
SQ FT: 1,500
SALES (est): 463.6K **Privately Held**
SIC: 2434 Wood kitchen cabinets

(G-15402)
VENTURE CIRCLE ENTERPRISES LLC
140 Maritime Dr (32771-6320)
P.O. Box 6068, Winter Park (32793-6068)
PHONE..................................407 678-7489
Tina Coalburn, *Purchasing*
Ivor Singer, *Mng Member*
Ivor A Singer Jr,
▲ EMP: 12 EST: 1987
SALES (est): 2MM **Privately Held**
WEB: www.creativeimagesvce.com
SIC: 3429 5023 Builders' hardware; home furnishings

(G-15403)
VENTURE CIRCLE INTL LLC
140 Maritime Dr (32771-6320)
PHONE..................................407 677-6004
Marc N Lieberman,
Sheldon Rosenberg,
EMP: 15 EST: 2017
SALES (est): 1.3MM **Privately Held**
WEB: www.venturecirclellc.com
SIC: 3231 Framed mirrors

(G-15404)
VERTICAL AVIATION TECH INC
1609 Hangar Rd Bldg 332 (32773-6826)
PHONE..................................407 322-9488
Brad Clark, *President*
Bethany Wallace, *Assistant*
▼ EMP: 12 EST: 1988
SQ FT: 12,000
SALES (est): 1.9MM **Privately Held**
WEB: www.vertical-aviation.com
SIC: 3721 4581 Helicopters; aircraft servicing & repairing

(G-15405)
VIZCOM ENTERPRISES LLC
1265 Upsala Rd Ste 1133 (32771-5700)
PHONE..................................407 324-8338
Eliud Vizcarrondo, *Principal*
EMP: 7 EST: 2014
SALES (est): 258.8K **Privately Held**
SIC: 3993 Signs & advertising specialties

(G-15406)
WATERFALL INDUSTRIES INC
Also Called: Benchmark of Florida
915 Cornwall Rd (32773-7312)
PHONE..................................407 330-2003
Anthony Di Ottavio, *President*
Glen R Moller, *Vice Pres*
Anthony Lupo, *CIO*
◆ EMP: 12 EST: 1991
SQ FT: 72,000
SALES (est): 2.4MM **Privately Held**
WEB: www.discoveryworldfurniture.com
SIC: 2511 5021 1542 1541 Wood household furniture; waterbeds; beds & bedding; household furniture; nonresidential construction; industrial buildings & warehouses

(G-15407)
WATTS TECHNOLOGIES LLC
Also Called: Queteq
2647 N Design Ct (32773-8119)
PHONE..................................407 512-5750
John Watts, *Mng Member*
EMP: 10 EST: 2019
SALES (est): 1.3MM **Privately Held**
WEB: www.watts.com
SIC: 3629 Electronic generation equipment

(G-15408)
WAYNE METAL PRODUCTS INC
5461 Benchmark Ln (32773-6433)
PHONE..................................407 321-7168

Wayne J Holmes, *President*
Glen R Holmes, *Vice Pres*
EMP: 5 **EST:** 1955
SQ FT: 5,000
SALES (est): 375.9K **Privately Held**
WEB: www.waynemetalproductsinc.com
SIC: 3843 3841 Sterilizers, dental; surgical & medical instruments

(G-15409)
WE RE ORGANIZED
1441 Kastner Pl Unit 111 (32771-8514)
PHONE..................................407 323-5133
Rick Goolsby, *Owner*
Dwaine Massey, *Owner*
EMP: 6 **EST:** 2006
SALES (est): 494.6K **Privately Held**
SIC: 2434 Wood kitchen cabinets

(G-15410)
WEST END
202 Sanford Ave (32771-1342)
PHONE..................................407 322-7475
John Lejarzar, *Principal*
EMP: 20 **EST:** 2007
SALES (est): 3.1MM **Privately Held**
WEB: www.drinkatwestend.com
SIC: 2599 Bar, restaurant & cafeteria furniture

(G-15411)
XYLEM WATER SOLUTIONS USA INC
455 Harvest Time Dr (32771-9572)
PHONE..................................407 880-2900
Tommy Ortiz, *Sales Staff*
Jane Dobson, *Branch Mgr*
EMP: 76 **Publicly Held**
WEB: www.xylem.com
SIC: 3561 Pumps & pumping equipment
HQ: Xylem Water Solutions U.S.A., Inc.
   4828 Prkwy Plz Blvd 200
   Charlotte NC 28217

(G-15412)
YESCO SIGN AND LIGHTING
1940 Dolgner Pl (32771-9225)
PHONE..................................407 321-3577
James Abbott, *Manager*
EMP: 9 **EST:** 2015
SALES (est): 205.4K **Privately Held**
WEB: www.yesco.com
SIC: 3993 Signs & advertising specialties

Sanibel
Lee County

(G-15413)
CAPTIVA CURRENT INC
Also Called: Santa Bell Capitav Group
2340 Periwinkle Way (33957-3221)
P.O. Box 809 (33957-0809)
PHONE..................................239 574-1110
Valerie Harring, *Editor*
EMP: 12 **EST:** 1973
SALES (est): 260.3K **Privately Held**
WEB: www.captivacurrent.com
SIC: 2711 Newspapers: publishing only, not printed on site

(G-15414)
CT HYDRAULICS INC
Also Called: Cooper
1845 Ardsley Way (33957-4110)
PHONE..................................724 342-3089
Kyle Klaric, *Managing Dir*
▲ **EMP:** 11 **EST:** 2008
SALES (est): 967K **Privately Held**
WEB: www.cthydraulic.com
SIC: 3429 Manufactured hardware (general)

(G-15415)
IBTM ENGINEERING INC
1291 Par View Dr (33957-6401)
P.O. Box 1679, Telluride CO (81435-1679)
PHONE..................................239 246-1876
Edward Merralls, *President*
EMP: 6 **EST:** 2003
SALES (est): 365K **Privately Held**
SIC: 3694 Engine electrical equipment

(G-15416)
LORKEN PUBLICATIONS INC (PA)
Also Called: Island Sun Newspaper
1640 Periwinkle Way Ste 2 (33957-4401)
PHONE..................................239 395-1213
Lorin Arundel, *Principal*
EMP: 5 **EST:** 1993
SQ FT: 1,200
SALES (est): 905.2K **Privately Held**
SIC: 2711 Newspapers: publishing only, not printed on site

(G-15417)
S 3 MARKETING GROUP LLC
1663 Bunting Ln (33957-4214)
PHONE..................................317 491-3398
Steve Cunningham, *Mng Member*
EMP: 45 **EST:** 2002
SALES (est): 2.7MM **Privately Held**
SIC: 2396 Apparel & other linings, except millinery

(G-15418)
SANTIVA CHRONICLE LLC
1420 Albatross Rd (33957-3604)
PHONE..................................239 472-0559
David Staver, *Principal*
EMP: 7 **EST:** 2013
SALES (est): 222.2K **Privately Held**
WEB: www.santivachronicle.com
SIC: 2711 Newspapers, publishing & printing

(G-15419)
TOTI MEDIA INC
2422 Palm Ridge Rd # 103 (33957-3202)
P.O. Box 1227 (33957-1227)
PHONE..................................239 472-0205
Daniela Jaeger, *President*
Gysbertus H Tober, *President*
Roeland Pells, *Corp Secy*
Daniella Jaeger, *Vice Pres*
Brian Stromlund, *Vice Pres*
▼ **EMP:** 5 **EST:** 1996
SQ FT: 983
SALES (est): 1.4MM **Privately Held**
WEB: www.totimedia.com
SIC: 2721 Magazines: publishing only, not printed on site
PA: Sidney Nominees Limited
   In Care Of: Bienheim Trust (Bvi) Limited
   Road Town

Santa Rosa Beach
Walton County

(G-15420)
A WSCO
1411 Driftwood Point Rd (32459-8035)
PHONE..................................937 263-1053
Janine Knapp, *Vice Pres*
Michael E Knapp, *Admin Sec*
EMP: 8 **EST:** 2014
SALES (est): 439.2K **Privately Held**
WEB: www.awsco.com
SIC: 2431 Millwork

(G-15421)
AMERICAN WOODWORK SPECIALTY CO
Also Called: A W S C O
1411 Driftwood Point Rd (32459-8035)
PHONE..................................937 263-1053
Michael E Knapp, *President*
Janine A Knapp, *Treasurer*
EMP: 15 **EST:** 1951
SALES (est): 978.4K **Privately Held**
SIC: 2431 3442 3231 Window frames, wood; metal doors, sash & trim; products of purchased glass

(G-15422)
CAPSTORM LLC
3906 Us Highway 98 W # 1159 (32459-4026)
PHONE..................................314 403-2143
Gregory Smith, *Vice Pres*
Rebecca Gray, *VP Bus Dvlpt*
Mary Smith, *Mng Member*
Mary D Smith, *Mng Member*
Gregory B Smith,

EMP: 6 **EST:** 2015
SALES (est): 1MM **Privately Held**
WEB: www.capstorm.com
SIC: 7372 Business oriented computer software

(G-15423)
COASTAL CRANE AND RIGGING INC
54 Pisces Dr (32459-5400)
PHONE..................................850 460-1766
EMP: 9 **EST:** 2016
SALES (est): 319.8K **Privately Held**
WEB: www.coastalcranerigging.com
SIC: 3531 3536 5082 5084 Cranes; cranes, industrial plant; cranes, construction; cranes, industrial

(G-15424)
EMERALD COAST CABINETS INC
Also Called: Canac Kitchens Northwest Fla
5597 Us Highway 98 W # 101 (32459-3282)
PHONE..................................850 267-2290
Nick Zargari, *President*
EMP: 11 **EST:** 1991
SQ FT: 1,700
SALES (est): 309.5K **Privately Held**
WEB:
www.emeraldcoastcabinetdesigns.com
SIC: 2434 Wood kitchen cabinets

(G-15425)
EMERALD COAST MEDIA & MKTG
Also Called: Walton Son Newspapers
790 N County Highway 393 (32459-7018)
P.O. Box 2363 (32459-2363)
PHONE..................................850 267-4555
Fax: 850 267-0929
EMP: 23 **EST:** 1996
SALES (est): 1.3MM
SALES (corp-wide): 2.3B **Privately Held**
SIC: 2711 Newspapers-Publishing/Printing
HQ: Freedom Communications, Inc.
   625 N Grand Ave
   Santa Ana CA 92701
   714 796-7000

(G-15426)
GRMS SERVICING LLC
249 Mack Bayou Loop Ste 30 (32459)
P.O. Box 2548 (32459-2548)
PHONE..................................850 278-1000
Reynolds Henderson, *Manager*
EMP: 5 **EST:** 2010
SALES (est): 351.3K **Privately Held**
SIC: 1389 Roustabout service

(G-15427)
HEY MAMA WINES INC
332 Calle Escada (32459-3698)
PHONE..................................479 530-3057
Lauren Wilkins, *Principal*
Larisa Courtien, *Director*
EMP: 9 **EST:** 2019
SALES (est): 586.7K **Privately Held**
WEB: www.heymamawines.com
SIC: 2084 Wines

(G-15428)
LS INDUSTRIES LLC
31 White Heron Dr (32459-8525)
PHONE..................................850 278-6215
Lincoln Shaw, *Principal*
EMP: 9 **EST:** 2010
SALES (est): 63.4K **Privately Held**
WEB: www.lsindustries.com
SIC: 3999 Manufacturing industries

(G-15429)
NORTH FLORIDA BRICK PAVERS LLC
664 E Shipwreck Rd (32459-8003)
PHONE..................................850 255-0336
Roderick J Booker, *Principal*
EMP: 7 **EST:** 2008
SALES (est): 443K **Privately Held**
SIC: 3531 Pavers

(G-15430)
PHOENIX CATASTROPHE SVCS LLC
5417 E County Highway 30a (32459-6561)
PHONE..................................918 321-2100
Mike Rice, *Mng Member*
Jeff Bleything,
Tim Bleything,
Shane Pratt,
EMP: 19 **EST:** 2018
SALES (est): 37.9MM **Privately Held**
SIC: 3589 Water treatment equipment, industrial

(G-15431)
QTRONICS INC
279 Santa Rosa St (32459-3803)
PHONE..................................850 267-0102
Mike Griffin, *President*
EMP: 5 **EST:** 1992
SALES (est): 381.1K **Privately Held**
WEB: www.gricor.com
SIC: 3571 Personal computers (microcomputers)

(G-15432)
SOUTH WALTON PHARMACY LLC
2050 W County Highway 30a # 106 (32459-0187)
PHONE..................................850 622-3313
George Thomas Flowers, *President*
EMP: 7 **EST:** 2017
SALES (est): 470.6K **Privately Held**
WEB: www.visitsouthwalton.com
SIC: 2833 Medicinal chemicals

(G-15433)
SRB SERVICING LLC
249 Mack Bayou Loop # 302 (32459-7197)
P.O. Box 1350 (32459-1350)
PHONE..................................850 278-1000
Jackie Mauro, *Principal*
Scott Covell, *Nurse*
EMP: 5 **EST:** 2008
SALES (est): 804.4K **Privately Held**
WEB: www.srbservicing.com
SIC: 1389 Roustabout service

(G-15434)
WAY BRIGHT SIGN SYSTEMS
93 Dune Lakes Cir E305 (32459-8393)
P.O. Box 293, Watertown TN (37184-0293)
PHONE..................................615 480-4602
Chris Henderson, *President*
EMP: 8 **EST:** 2014
SALES (est): 78K **Privately Held**
SIC: 3993 Signs & advertising specialties

Sarasota
Manatee County

(G-15435)
A BETTER CHOICE MARINE LLC
8050 N Tamiami Trl (34243-2057)
PHONE..................................941 264-5019
Russell G Douglas, *Manager*
EMP: 7 **EST:** 2019
SALES (est): 385.3K **Privately Held**
WEB: www.betterchoicemarine.com
SIC: 3731 Shipbuilding & repairing

(G-15436)
ABC HAMMERS
7216 21st St E (34243-3903)
PHONE..................................708 343-9900
EMP: 6 **EST:** 2019
SALES (est): 394.7K **Privately Held**
WEB: www.abchammers.com
SIC: 3423 Hand & edge tools

(G-15437)
ACH SOLUTION USA INC
1165 Commerce Blvd N (34243-5056)
PHONE..................................941 355-9488
Steven Broadbent, *General Mgr*
EMP: 7 **EST:** 2018
SALES (est): 332.4K **Privately Held**
WEB: www.ach-solution.at
SIC: 3714 Motor vehicle parts & accessories

(G-15438)
ADVANCED HOUSEHOLD MGT INC
Also Called: Olewo USA
6408 Parkland Dr Ste 103 (34243-5410)
P.O. Box 110298, Lakewood Rch (34211-0004)
PHONE................................941 322-9638
INA Schielke, *Director*
John Schielke, *Director*
EMP: 8 **EST:** 2014
SALES (est): 276.7K **Privately Held**
SIC: 2048 5999 Feed supplements; pet food

(G-15439)
ALFA LAVAL INC
2359 Trailmate Dr (34243-4041)
PHONE................................941 727-1900
Arthur McCutthan, *Branch Mgr*
John Hall, *Manager*
EMP: 17 **Privately Held**
WEB: www.alfalaval.com
SIC: 3491 3433 Industrial valves; heating equipment, except electric
HQ: Alfa Laval Inc.
    5400 Intl Trade Dr
    Richmond VA 23231
    866 253-2528

(G-15440)
ALNITAK CORPORATION
6791 Whitfield Indus Ave (34243-5415)
PHONE................................941 727-1122
Andrew Sewell, *President*
Anthony Dertouzos, *Vice Pres*
Mark Marshik, *Manager*
EMP: 10 **EST:** 1992
SQ FT: 8,150
SALES (est): 1.2MM **Privately Held**
WEB: www.alnitak.com
SIC: 3599 Machine shop, jobbing & repair

(G-15441)
ARCHER PHARMACEUTICALS INC
2040 Whitfield Ave (34243-3956)
PHONE................................941 752-2949
Michael Mullan, *President*
Nicole Russ, *General Mgr*
Fiona Crawford, *Vice Pres*
Parka Dodd, *CFO*
Peter N Townshend, *Admin Sec*
EMP: 10 **EST:** 2008
SALES (est): 1.2MM **Privately Held**
WEB: www.archerpharmaceuticals.com
SIC: 2834 Pharmaceutical preparations

(G-15442)
ARMORIT PRECISION LLC
2280 Trailmate Dr Ste 103 (34243-4078)
PHONE................................941 751-1292
Floyd Asbury,
EMP: 10 **EST:** 2007
SQ FT: 12,000
SALES (est): 497.4K **Privately Held**
WEB: www.armorit.com
SIC: 3545 Precision tools, machinists'

(G-15443)
ARMORIT PRECISON
6423 Parkland Dr (34243-4035)
PHONE................................941 751-6635
Floyd Asbury, *Sales Executive*
EMP: 7 **EST:** 2018
SALES (est): 98.1K **Privately Held**
WEB: www.armorit.com
SIC: 3599 Machine shop, jobbing & repair

(G-15444)
ATHCO INC (PA)
1009 Tallevast Rd (34243-3259)
PHONE................................941 351-1600
Stuart Goldman, *CEO*
David Berger, *Ch of Bd*
Jerry Beckerman, *President*
◆ **EMP:** 25 **EST:** 1990
SQ FT: 39,000
SALES (est): 5.8MM **Privately Held**
SIC: 2339 2329 2369 Athletic clothing: women's, misses' & juniors'; men's & boys' sportswear & athletic clothing; girls' & children's outerwear

(G-15445)
BENZ RESEARCH AND DEV LLC
6447 Parkland Dr (34243-4035)
P.O. Box 1839 (34230-1839)
PHONE................................941 758-8256
Steve Grant, *Engineer*
Neal Mangin, *Engineer*
Rekash Vasant, *Engineer*
Lorrie Pomroy, *Office Mgr*
Patrick H Benz,
EMP: 36 **EST:** 1980
SQ FT: 35,000
SALES (est): 8.4MM **Privately Held**
WEB: www.benzrd.com
SIC: 3827 Lenses, optical: all types except ophthalmic

(G-15446)
BERRY GLOBAL INC
7350 26th Ct E (34243-3947)
PHONE................................941 355-7166
Carrie Branham, *Human Res Mgr*
John Rogers, *Branch Mgr*
John Medcalf, *Maintence Staff*
EMP: 79 **Publicly Held**
WEB: www.berryglobal.com
SIC: 3089 3081 Bottle caps, molded plastic; unsupported plastics film & sheet
HQ: Berry Global, Inc.
    101 Oakley St
    Evansville IN 47710

(G-15447)
BEST BRAND BOTTLERS INC
6620 19th St E Unit 109 (34243-4056)
PHONE................................941 755-1941
Ken A Lewis, *Principal*
EMP: 11 **EST:** 2011
SALES (est): 612.5K **Privately Held**
WEB: www.bestbrandbottlers.com
SIC: 2099 Food preparations

(G-15448)
BHD PRECISION PRODUCTS INC
2120 Whitfield Park Loop (34243-4013)
PHONE................................941 753-0003
Howard A Hughes, *Principal*
EMP: 7 **EST:** 2018
SALES (est): 399.2K **Privately Held**
SIC: 3499 Fabricated metal products

(G-15449)
BIOLIFE LLC
8163 25th Ct E (34243-2800)
PHONE................................941 360-1300
Gloria Dipuma, *Vice Pres*
Kelly Keene, *Vice Pres*
Claudia Masselink, *Vice Pres*
Kurt Vadelund, *Vice Pres*
Ken Wiglund, *Facilities Mgr*
EMP: 39 **EST:** 1998
SQ FT: 20,000
SALES (est): 12.2MM **Privately Held**
WEB: www.biolife.com
SIC: 2834 Powders, pharmaceutical

(G-15450)
CAPACITY INC
Also Called: Go Puck
2240 72nd Ave E (34243-3985)
P.O. Box 1766, Tallevast (34270-1766)
PHONE................................855 440-7825
Samuel Fuller, *Principal*
EMP: 18 **EST:** 2012
SALES (est): 2.6MM **Privately Held**
SIC: 3621 1731 Storage battery chargers, motor & engine generator type; electrical work

(G-15451)
CAPSTONE CG LLC
6348 17th Street Cir E (34243-5426)
PHONE................................941 371-3321
Robert Lodge, *President*
Wilbur Hopper, *Principal*
Shane Rogers, *Principal*
EMP: 13 **EST:** 2016
SALES (est): 957.7K **Privately Held**
SIC: 3449 Fabricated bar joists & concrete reinforcing bars; bars, concrete reinforcing: fabricated steel; curtain wall, metal

(G-15452)
CC SPORTSWEAR INC
Also Called: Windy City Apparel
2331 Whtfield Indus Way Un (34243)
PHONE................................941 351-4205
Thomas Carollo, *CEO*
Stacey Carollo, *President*
EMP: 7 **EST:** 2014
SALES (est): 660.8K **Privately Held**
WEB: www.windycityapparel.org
SIC: 2759 2395 Screen printing; embroidery & art needlework

(G-15453)
CE HOOTON SALES LLC
1901 Whitfield Park Loop (34243-4150)
P.O. Box 110346, Lakewood Rch (34211-0005)
PHONE................................305 255-9722
Gray Mullins, *Chief Engr*
Linda J Long,
A G Mullins,
Bert Mullins,
Nancy Mullins,
EMP: 10 **EST:** 1963
SALES (est): 730.3K **Privately Held**
WEB: www.cehootonsales.com
SIC: 3589 Water treatment equipment, industrial

(G-15454)
CHISM MANUFACTURING SVCS LLC
Also Called: CMS
6416 Parkland Dr (34243-4038)
PHONE................................941 896-9671
David Chism, *Mng Member*
EMP: 10 **EST:** 2012
SQ FT: 12,000
SALES (est): 1.5MM **Privately Held**
SIC: 3621 3441 Exciter assemblies (motor or generator parts); tower sections, radio & television transmission

(G-15455)
CHRIS CRAFT CORPORATION
Also Called: Chris-Craft
8161 15th St E (34243-2709)
PHONE................................941 351-4900
Stephen F Heese, *President*
Steve Callahan, *Vice Pres*
Jeff Ellis, *Vice Pres*
Gavan Hunt, *Vice Pres*
Geoffrey Wedlock, *Facilities Mgr*
◆ **EMP:** 250 **EST:** 2001
SQ FT: 128,800
SALES (est): 33.2MM
SALES (corp-wide): 3.6B **Publicly Held**
WEB: www.chriscraft.com
SIC: 3732 Boats, fiberglass: building & repairing
PA: Winnebago Industries, Inc.
    13200 Pioneer Trl Ste 150
    Eden Prairie MN 55347
    952 829-8600

(G-15456)
COAST CONTROLS INC
7500 Commerce Ct (34243-3217)
PHONE................................941 355-7555
Kyle Koontz, *President*
Thomas Marks, *President*
Alicia Snow, *Admin Asst*
EMP: 18 **EST:** 1992
SQ FT: 11,000
SALES (est): 3MM **Privately Held**
WEB: www.coastcontrols.com
SIC: 3823 3625 Industrial instrmnts msrmnt display/control process variable; relays & industrial controls

(G-15457)
COATING APPLICATION TECH INC
1851 67th Ave E (34243-4149)
PHONE................................781 850-5080
Joseph W Selbeck, *Principal*
EMP: 10 **EST:** 2016
SALES (est): 961.3K **Privately Held**
WEB: www.coatingapplication.com
SIC: 2851 Paints & allied products

(G-15458)
CONTAINER HANDLING SOLUTIONS
1349 W University Pkwy (34243-2704)
PHONE................................941 359-2095
Michael Burkart, *President*
EMP: 8 **EST:** 1997
SALES (est): 1MM **Privately Held**
SIC: 3535 Conveyors & conveying equipment

(G-15459)
CONTEMPORARY CABINETS GULF CST
2245 Whitfield Indus Way (34243-4065)
PHONE................................941 758-3060
Brian Wade, *President*
EMP: 7 **EST:** 2007
SALES (est): 795.9K **Privately Held**
SIC: 2434 Wood kitchen cabinets

(G-15460)
CONVEYOR CONCEPTS CORPORATION
2323 Whitfield Park Ave (34243-4032)
PHONE................................941 751-1200
Bernard J Moltchan, *President*
Raymond Moltchan, *Vice Pres*
EMP: 7 **EST:** 2002
SQ FT: 13,000
SALES (est): 864.5K **Privately Held**
WEB: www.conveyorconceptsinc.com
SIC: 3535 Conveyors & conveying equipment

(G-15461)
COOPER NOTIFICATION INC
7246 16th St E Unit 105 (34243-6817)
PHONE................................941 487-2300
Kenneth V Camarco, *President*
Randal S Heara, *President*
James T Burrell, *Vice Pres*
David Lorey, *Vice Pres*
Tyler W Johnson, *Treasurer*
▲ **EMP:** 68 **EST:** 1993
SQ FT: 5,000
SALES (est): 6.4MM **Privately Held**
SIC: 3663 Radio broadcasting & communications equipment
HQ: Cooper Industries Unlimited Company
    41a Drury Street
    Dublin D02 C

(G-15462)
COPALO INC
Also Called: Y F Yachts
6510 19th St E (34243-4187)
PHONE................................941 753-7828
Wylie Nagler, *President*
▼ **EMP:** 105 **EST:** 1992
SQ FT: 70,000
SALES (est): 25.9MM
SALES (corp-wide): 40MM **Privately Held**
WEB: www.yellowfin.com
SIC: 3732 Boats, fiberglass: building & repairing; yachts, building & repairing
PA: Warbird Marine Holdings, Llc
    4700 Nw 132nd St
    Opa Locka FL 33054
    844 341-2504

(G-15463)
COVOCUP LLC
6621 19th St E (34243-4181)
PHONE................................855 204-5106
John Walters, *COO*
EMP: 6 **EST:** 2011
SALES (est): 354.7K **Privately Held**
WEB: www.covodrinkware.com
SIC: 3089 Injection molding of plastics; tumblers, plastic

(G-15464)
CRUISE CAR INC
1227 Hardin Ave (34243-5024)
PHONE................................941 929-1630
Adam Sulimirski, *President*
Greg Hyde, *COO*
Nathan Kalin, *Exec VP*
Tom McCoy, *Sales Staff*
Susan Lebourgeois, *Office Mgr*
◆ **EMP:** 12 **EST:** 2004
SQ FT: 8,816

SALES (est): 2.5MM **Privately Held**
WEB: www.cruisecarinc.com
SIC: 3799 Cars, off-highway: electric

(G-15465)
CUTTING EDGE MOLDINGS LLC
Also Called: Cutting Edge Archtctral Mldngs
7116 24th Ct E (34243-3993)
PHONE.................................734 649-1500
Melvyn Keshishian, *Mng Member*
Sandra Brennan, *Officer*
EMP: 9 EST: 2010
SALES (est): 916.2K **Privately Held**
WEB: www.cuttingedgemoldings.com
SIC: 3299 Moldings, architectural: plaster
of paris

(G-15466)
D & B MACHINE INC
1855 61st St (34243-2232)
PHONE.................................941 355-8002
David L Frostad, *CEO*
Rick Siferd, *Purch Mgr*
Betty D Chromy-Frostad, *CFO*
EMP: 45 EST: 1991
SQ FT: 14,800
SALES (est): 7.1MM **Privately Held**
WEB: www.dandbmachine.com
SIC: 3599 Machine shop, jobbing & repair

(G-15467)
DANKER LABORATORIES INC
Also Called: Danker Labs
1144 Tallevast Rd Ste 106 (34243-6213)
PHONE.................................941 758-7711
Jeri Struve, *President*
Connie Rodewald, *Treasurer*
Gwen Norris, *Mktg Dir*
EMP: 19 EST: 1958
SQ FT: 5,200
SALES (est): 1.8MM **Privately Held**
SIC: 3851 5048 Contact lenses; contact
lenses

(G-15468)
DENTSPLY SIRONA INC
7290 26th Ct E (34243-3963)
PHONE.................................262 752-4040
Chad Hartness, *Sales Staff*
Nicole Patten, *Sales Staff*
Dan Riegelman, *Branch Mgr*
Jeffrey Ramirez, *Manager*
Kevin Barney, *Supervisor*
EMP: 31
SALES (corp-wide): 4.2B **Publicly Held**
WEB: www.sirona.es
SIC: 3843 Dental equipment & supplies
PA: Dentsply Sirona Inc.
13320 Balntyn Corp Pl
Charlotte NC 28277
844 848-0137

(G-15469)
DENTSPLY SIRONA INC
Also Called: Dentsply Raintree Glenroe
7290 26th Ct E (34243-3963)
PHONE.................................941 527-4450
Patrick Francis, *District Mgr*
Rony Mayer, *Business Mgr*
Matthew Minnick, *Production*
Johana Villegas, *Production*
Serina Damesworth, *Engineer*
EMP: 72
SALES (corp-wide): 4.2B **Publicly Held**
WEB: www.sirona.es
SIC: 3843 Dental equipment & supplies
PA: Dentsply Sirona Inc.
13320 Balntyn Corp Pl
Charlotte NC 28277
844 848-0137

(G-15470)
DISCOUNT AWNINGS INC
6620 19th St E Unit 111 (34243-4056)
PHONE.................................941 753-5700
Steven Judd, *President*
Kimberley Judd, *Vice Pres*
EMP: 7 EST: 1988
SQ FT: 2,750
SALES (est): 631.3K **Privately Held**
WEB: www.discountawningsinc.com
SIC: 2394 Awnings, fabric: made from pur-
chased materials

(G-15471)
DOWE GALLAGHER
AEROSPACE
7425 16th St E (34243-6807)
PHONE.................................941 256-2179
EMP: 7 EST: 2017
SALES (est): 109.6K **Privately Held**
SIC: 3721 Aircraft

(G-15472)
DUKANE SEACOM INC
7135 16th St E Ste 101 (34243-6818)
PHONE.................................941 739-3200
Anish Patel, *President*
EMP: 208 EST: 2009
SQ FT: 4,500
SALES (est): 13.7MM **Publicly Held**
WEB: www.dukaneseacom.com
SIC: 3728 3519 Aircraft power transmis-
sion equipment; controls, remote, for
boats
HQ: Heico Electronic Technologies Corp.
3000 Taft St
Hollywood FL 33021
954 987-6101

(G-15473)
DULOND TOOL & ENGINEERING
INC
2306 Whitfield Park Loop (34243-4045)
P.O. Box 308, Tallevast (34270-0308)
PHONE.................................941 758-4489
Jeffrey Benson, *President*
Gregory J Brunette, *Vice Pres*
EMP: 13 EST: 1975
SQ FT: 12,500
SALES (est): 3.2MM **Privately Held**
WEB: www.dulond-tool-engineering-inc.sbcon-
tract.com
SIC: 3599 Machine shop, jobbing & repair

(G-15474)
ENCORE INC
6487 Parkland Dr Ste 111 (34243-4001)
PHONE.................................941 359-3599
Margaret Bennett, *President*
▲ EMP: 16 EST: 1987
SQ FT: 5,000
SALES (est): 2.6MM **Privately Held**
WEB: www.revivepremium.com
SIC: 3842 Surgical appliances & supplies

(G-15475)
EPOXY EXPERTS LLC
819 Lillian Ln (34243-1003)
PHONE.................................941 565-3785
Stephanie Sullivan, *President*
Shawn Sullivan, *Vice Pres*
Walter Sanders, *CFO*
EMP: 7 EST: 2016
SALES (est): 78K **Privately Held**
SIC: 2851 Paints & allied products

(G-15476)
FAMILY OF SMITH INC (PA)
Also Called: Coast Laser Center
5899 Whitfield Ave # 104 (34243-6152)
PHONE.................................941 726-0873
Stephen J Smith, *President*
EMP: 5 EST: 2006
SALES (est): 669.8K **Privately Held**
SIC: 3841 Surgical lasers

(G-15477)
FLORIDA SNCAST
HELICOPTERS LLC
Also Called: Rotor Works
8191 N Tamiami Trl # 104 (34243-2052)
PHONE.................................941 355-1525
William Cooper, *Owner*
Brian Cooper,
Robin Cooper,
Sarah Cooper,
EMP: 10 EST: 2003
SALES (est): 1MM **Privately Held**
WEB: www.floridasuncoasthelicopters.com
SIC: 3721 5088 4522 7363 Helicopters;
helicopter parts; flying charter service;
pilot service, aviation

(G-15478)
FLOWERS BKG CO
BRADENTON LLC (HQ)
Also Called: Flowers Bakery
6490 Parkland Dr (34243-4036)
P.O. Box 20539, Bradenton (34204-0539)
PHONE.................................941 758-5656
Marta J Turner, *Exec VP*
Bill Steeves, *Controller*
Ken Warber, *Sales Dir*
Todd Thompson, *Sales Staff*
Michael Lord, *Mng Member*
EMP: 207 EST: 1984
SQ FT: 40,000
SALES (est): 37.6MM
SALES (corp-wide): 4.3B **Publicly Held**
WEB: www.flobradconf.com
SIC: 2051 Bread, all types (white, wheat,
rye, etc): fresh or frozen; rolls, bread type:
fresh or frozen
PA: Flowers Foods, Inc.
1919 Flowers Cir
Thomasville GA 31757
229 226-9110

(G-15479)
G G SCHMITT & SONS INC
7230 15th St E (34243-3276)
PHONE.................................717 394-3701
Ronald Schmitt, *President*
Jim Haynes, *Division Mgr*
Gervase A Schmitt, *Vice Pres*
Steve Schmitt, *Vice Pres*
Brian Barr, *Plant Mgr*
▲ EMP: 135 EST: 1951
SALES (est): 22.4MM
SALES (corp-wide): 4B **Publicly Held**
WEB: www.ggschmitt.com
SIC: 3429 3743 Marine hardware; railroad
equipment
PA: Patrick Industries, Inc.
107 W Franklin St
Elkhart IN 46516
574 294-7511

(G-15480)
GANNET TECHNOLOGIES LLC
7135 16th St E Ste 115 (34243-6818)
PHONE.................................941 870-3444
Richard Greenwell, *Administration*
EMP: 10 EST: 2017
SALES (est): 628.8K **Privately Held**
WEB: www.gannettechnologies.com
SIC: 3812 Search & navigation equipment

(G-15481)
GATOR STAMPINGS INTL INC
6610 33rd St E (34243-4123)
PHONE.................................941 753-9598
Paul Cronen, *President*
Christie Borda Lescano, *Corp Secy*
John Cronen, *Vice Pres*
Elizabeth Martin, *Purch Mgr*
Maria Carlos, *Purch Agent*
EMP: 80 EST: 1987
SQ FT: 57,000
SALES (est): 22.7MM **Privately Held**
WEB: www.gatorstamping.com
SIC: 3469 Stamping metal for the trade

(G-15482)
GENERAL PNEUMATICS
INFLATION
2236 72nd Ave E (34243-3985)
PHONE.................................941 216-3500
Timothy Longano, *General Mgr*
Tim Longino, *General Mgr*
Steven Fournier, *Mng Member*
EMP: 5 EST: 2015
SALES (est): 379.2K **Privately Held**
WEB: www.gpinflation.com
SIC: 3324 Aerospace investment castings,
ferrous

(G-15483)
GLENROE TECHNOLOGIES INC
7290 26th Ct E (34243-3963)
PHONE.................................941 554-5262
Charles Robbins, *Manager*
EMP: 13 EST: 2016
SALES (est): 374.9K **Privately Held**
SIC: 3843 Dental equipment & supplies

(G-15484)
GLOBAL ORDNANCE LLC (PA)
2150 Whitfield Ave (34243-3925)
PHONE.................................941 549-8388
Marc Morales, *CEO*
Carrie Morales, *President*
Lee Jackson, *Vice Pres*
Kelly Hartman, *Senior Engr*
Patrick Martin, *Controller*
EMP: 26 EST: 2013
SQ FT: 45,000
SALES (est): 173.3MM **Privately Held**
WEB: www.global-ordnance.com
SIC: 3482 3483 3484 3489 Small arms
ammunition; ammunition, except for small
arms; small arms; ordnance & acces-
sories; brokers' services

(G-15485)
GOBCZYNSKIS PRINTERY INC
Also Called: Printery, The
6452 Parkland Dr (34243-4036)
P.O. Box 110403, Lakewood Rch (34211-
0006)
PHONE.................................941 758-5734
Gene Gobczynski, *President*
Janet Gobczynski, *Corp Secy*
EMP: 8 EST: 1986
SQ FT: 5,612
SALES (est): 665.1K **Privately Held**
WEB: www.thesarasotaprintery.com
SIC: 2752 Commercial printing, offset

(G-15486)
GOGPS USA INC
7152 15th St E (34243-3203)
PHONE.................................941 751-2363
Simon Williams, *President*
EMP: 14 EST: 2012
SALES (est): 6.7MM
SALES (corp-wide): 487K **Privately Held**
WEB: www.gogps.com
SIC: 3663 Radio & TV communications
equipment
PA: Go Gps
1100 South Service Rd Suite 422
Stoney Creek ON L8E 0
866 964-6477

(G-15487)
GREG VALLEY
Also Called: Superior Shutters
2010 Whitfield Park Loop (34243-4006)
P.O. Box 110703, Lakewood Rch (34211-
0009)
PHONE.................................941 739-6628
Greg Valley, *Owner*
EMP: 10 EST: 1996
SQ FT: 8,000
SALES (est): 500K **Privately Held**
SIC: 2431 5023 5211 Window shutters,
wood; window furnishings; screens, door
& window

(G-15488)
GT MACHINING
1400 Commerce Blvd Ste G (34243-5071)
PHONE.................................941 809-5735
Bob Peterka, *Principal*
EMP: 9 EST: 2007
SALES (est): 348.7K **Privately Held**
WEB: www.kenklakdo.com
SIC: 3599 Machine shop, jobbing & repair

(G-15489)
HELI AVIATION FLORIDA LLC
8191 N Tmami Trail Hngar Hangar (34243)
PHONE.................................941 355-1525
Niclas Herle, *Mng Member*
EMP: 6 EST: 2012
SQ FT: 10,000
SALES (est): 493.2K **Privately Held**
WEB: www.heliaf.com
SIC: 3721 7363 4512 0783 Helicopters;
pilot service, aviation; helicopter carrier,
scheduled; tree trimming services for pub-
lic utility lines; flying charter service

(G-15490)
HELIOS TECHNOLOGIES INC
1155 Commerce Blvd N (34243-5056)
PHONE.................................941 351-6648
Sarah Kelp, *Research*
Aneel Craciun, *Manager*
Gene McIntyre, *Manager*
Mike Gaidosh, *Maintence Staff*

▲ = Import ▼=Export
◆ =Import/Export

EMP: 24
SALES (corp-wide): 869.1MM **Publicly Held**
WEB: www.heliostechnologies.com
SIC: 3492 Fluid power valves & hose fittings
PA: Helios Technologies, Inc.
7456 16th St E
Sarasota FL 34243
941 362-1200

(G-15491)
HELIOS TECHNOLOGIES INC (PA)
7456 16th St E (34243-6800)
PHONE...............................941 362-1200
Tricia Fulton, *President*
EMP: 166 EST: 1970
SALES: 869.1MM **Publicly Held**
WEB: www.heliostechnologies.com
SIC: 3492 Control valves, fluid power: hydraulic & pneumatic

(G-15492)
HELIOS TECHNOLOGIES INC
701 Tallevast Rd (34243-3212)
PHONE...............................941 328-1769
Allen Carlson, *President*
EMP: 107
SQ FT: 58,351
SALES (corp-wide): 869.1MM **Publicly Held**
WEB: www.heliostechnologies.com
SIC: 3492 Control valves, fluid power: hydraulic & pneumatic
PA: Helios Technologies, Inc.
7456 16th St E
Sarasota FL 34243
941 362-1200

(G-15493)
HELIOS TECHNOLOGIES INC
1500 W University Pkwy (34243-2217)
PHONE...............................941 362-1200
Clyde G Nixon, *President*
Sarah Kelp, *Research*
Stuart Boyd, *Engineer*
Katherine Duffy, *Engineer*
Marcus Spanolios, *Engineer*
EMP: 17
SALES (corp-wide): 869.1MM **Publicly Held**
WEB: www.heliostechnologies.com
SIC: 3492 3494 Fluid power valves & hose fittings; valves & pipe fittings
PA: Helios Technologies, Inc.
7456 16th St E
Sarasota FL 34243
941 362-1200

(G-15494)
HONEYCOMB COMPANY AMERICA INC
1950 Limbus Ave (34243-3900)
PHONE...............................941 756-8781
Steven J Walker, *President*
Dan G Judge III, *COO*
Terry Sowers, *Facilities Mgr*
Steve Cowart, *Opers Spvr*
Patrick Byers, *Production*
EMP: 112 EST: 1955
SQ FT: 185,000
SALES (est): 22.5MM
SALES (corp-wide): 59MM **Privately Held**
WEB: www.hcoainc.com
SIC: 3728 Panel assembly (hydromatic propeller test stands), aircraft; aircraft body assemblies & parts
HQ: Overall-Honeycomb, Llc
1950 Limbus Ave
Sarasota FL 34243
941 756-8781

(G-15495)
HOVEROUND CORPORATION (PA)
2151 Whitfield Indus Way (34243-4047)
PHONE...............................941 739-6200
Thomas E Kruse, *President*
Scott Davidson, *Editor*
Joyce Boyle, *COO*
Tony N Digiovanni, *Vice Pres*
Jeff Moone, *Vice Pres*
▲ EMP: 303 EST: 1992
SQ FT: 47,000

SALES (est): 99.2MM **Privately Held**
WEB: www.hoveround.com
SIC: 3842 Wheelchairs

(G-15496)
HYDROGEL VISION CORPORATION
Also Called: Extreme H2o
7575 Commerce Ct (34243-3218)
PHONE...............................941 739-1382
Mikael Totterman, *CEO*
Hue Tang, *Production*
Tung Nguyen, *Research*
Jason Leitzman, *Manager*
▲ EMP: 71 EST: 2002
SALES (est): 9.9MM
SALES (corp-wide): 13.8MM **Privately Held**
SIC: 3841 Surgical & medical instruments
PA: Clerio Vision, Inc.
1892 Winton Rd S Ste 140b
Rochester NY 14618
617 216-7881

(G-15497)
ICON WELDING & FABRICATION LLC
8145 27th St E (34243-2874)
PHONE...............................941 822-8822
Michael J Norrito, *President*
EMP: 26 EST: 2013
SALES (est): 3.7MM **Privately Held**
WEB: www.iconmetalcreations.com
SIC: 2431 3446 Staircases, stairs & railings; architectural metalwork

(G-15498)
IDENTITY HOLDING COMPANY LLC
7525 Pennsylvania Ave # 101 (34243-5065)
PHONE...............................941 355-5171
EMP: 56 **Privately Held**
WEB: www.identitygroup.com
SIC: 3953 Marking devices
PA: Identity Holding Company, Llc
1480 Gould Dr
Cookeville TN 38506

(G-15499)
INDUSTRY STANDARD TECHNOLOGY
Also Called: I S T
1868 University Pkwy (34243-2225)
PHONE...............................941 355-2100
Frank Stafford, *President*
EMP: 9 EST: 1984
SQ FT: 5,000
SALES (est): 731.3K **Privately Held**
WEB: www.industrystandardtech.com
SIC: 3629 3571 7629 Electronic generation equipment; personal computers (microcomputers); electronic equipment repair

(G-15500)
INNOVATION MARINE CORPORATION
8011 15th St E (34243-2713)
PHONE...............................941 355-7852
Richard Lamore, *President*
Dennis Mathe, *Vice Pres*
Scott Yow, *Purch Dir*
Derik Bell, *Engineer*
Harry Bell, *Engineer*
◆ EMP: 20 EST: 1983
SQ FT: 28,000
SALES (est): 3MM **Privately Held**
WEB: www.innovation-marine.com
SIC: 3561 3519 Pumps & pumping equipment; internal combustion engines

(G-15501)
INNOVATIVE POWER SOLUTIONS LLC
Also Called: Ips
2250 Whitfield Ave (34243-3926)
PHONE...............................732 544-1075
Gene Terry, *Vice Pres*
Eli Liebermann,
Johnathan Cseh, *Administration*
Santiago Lagunas,
Bill Schatzow,
▲ EMP: 35 EST: 1999

SALES (est): 4.4MM **Privately Held**
WEB: www.ips-llc.com
SIC: 3621 Motors & generators

(G-15502)
INSULATOR SEAL INCORPORATED (HQ)
6460 Parkland Dr (34243-4036)
PHONE...............................941 751-2880
Joe Brownell, *CEO*
Michael A Del Castello, *President*
Mark Russo, *Production*
Jeff Warren, *Manager*
EMP: 40 EST: 1988
SQ FT: 25,000
SALES: 22.2MM
SALES (corp-wide): 104.1MM **Privately Held**
WEB: www.mdcprecision.com
SIC: 3264 3644 Insulators, electrical: porcelain; insulators & insulation materials, electrical
PA: Mdc Precision, Llc
30962 Santana St
Hayward CA 94544
510 265-3500

(G-15503)
J&J SHEET MTAL FABERCATION LLC
728 Winter Garden Dr (34243-1021)
PHONE...............................941 752-0569
Joshua M Cripe, *Principal*
EMP: 7 EST: 2016
SALES (est): 487.2K **Privately Held**
SIC: 3499 Fabricated metal products

(G-15504)
JUST STEEL INC
3100 Whitfield Ave Ste B (34243-3380)
PHONE...............................941 755-7811
Francisco Orduno, *President*
EMP: 10 EST: 1993
SQ FT: 2,500
SALES (est): 1.6MM **Privately Held**
WEB: www.juststeel.net
SIC: 3441 3312 7692 Fabricated structural metal; fence posts, iron & steel; welding repair

(G-15505)
K H S INC
5501 N Washington Blvd (34243-2249)
PHONE...............................941 359-4000
Jeff Piekarski, *Maintenance Dir*
Bonita Cihasky, *Engineer*
Ian Lytwyn, *Engineer*
Oliver Watmough, *Engineer*
Claudio Desouza, *Sales Staff*
▲ EMP: 51 EST: 1996
SALES (est): 43.5MM
SALES (corp-wide): 11B **Privately Held**
SIC: 3565 Packaging machinery
HQ: Khs Gmbh
Juchostr. 20
Dortmund NW 44143
231 569-0

(G-15506)
K PRO SUPPLY CO INC
2135 Whitfield Park Ave (34243-4086)
PHONE...............................941 758-1226
Chris Kerrigan, *President*
Joyce Kerrigan, *Admin Sec*
EMP: 5 EST: 1986
SQ FT: 14,250
SALES (est): 455.8K **Privately Held**
WEB: www.kpropaintballnetting.com
SIC: 2221 Polyethylene broadwoven fabrics

(G-15507)
KEY PACKAGING COMPANY INC
7350 15th St E (34243-3274)
PHONE...............................941 355-2728
E L Smith, *President*
Steve Akel, *Project Mgr*
Joel Thornton, *QC Dir*
Erick Ames, *Engineer*
David Lizotte, *Engineer*
▲ EMP: 50 EST: 1958
SQ FT: 42,000

SALES (est): 10.6MM **Privately Held**
WEB: www.keypackaging.com
SIC: 3086 Cups & plates, foamed plastic; packaging & shipping materials, foamed plastic

(G-15508)
KLUGMAN ENTERPRISES LLC
7410 Linden Ln (34243-5129)
PHONE...............................352 318-9623
Max Klugman, *Owner*
Dhalma I Klugman, *Mng Member*
EMP: 5 EST: 2005
SALES (est): 394.6K **Privately Held**
WEB: klugmanenterpr1.godaddysites.com
SIC: 2599 Carts, restaurant equipment

(G-15509)
LARRICK GROUP INC
1845 57th St (34243-2228)
P.O. Box 758, Oneco (34264-0758)
PHONE...............................941 351-2700
Lauren Danielson, *President*
Vince Scuilla, *COO*
Jonny Johnson, *Production*
Mike Burdick, *Sales Staff*
Tim Cahoon, *Manager*
EMP: 20 EST: 1990
SQ FT: 14,000
SALES (est): 7.3MM **Privately Held**
SIC: 2836 8731 Culture media; commercial physical research

(G-15510)
LASER LENS TEK INC
Also Called: American Photonics
6621 19th St E (34243-4181)
PHONE...............................941 752-5811
Barry Tyler, *President*
William Landers, *Finance Mgr*
Janice Pulomena, *Accounting Mgr*
Lou D 'alessandro, *Sales Staff*
▲ EMP: 12 EST: 2001
SQ FT: 18,000
SALES (est): 2.3MM **Privately Held**
WEB: american-photonics.myshopify.com
SIC: 3827 Optical instruments & lenses

(G-15511)
LATITUDE 235 COFFEE AND TEA (PA)
7245 21st St E (34243-3998)
PHONE...............................941 556-2600
Dimitry Erez, *President*
Holly Erez, *Vice Pres*
Gene Erez, *Director*
◆ EMP: 8 EST: 2003
SALES (est): 1.6MM **Privately Held**
WEB: www.latitudecoffee.com
SIC: 2095 5149 Coffee roasting (except by wholesale grocers); coffee & tea

(G-15512)
LUMISHORE USA LLC
7137 24th Ct E (34243-3992)
PHONE...............................941 405-3302
Eifrion Evans, *CEO*
Chris Myers, *Natl Sales Mgr*
Corinne Fresko, *Marketing Staff*
Gareth Evans, *CTO*
EMP: 11 EST: 2015
SALES (est): 882.7K **Privately Held**
WEB: www.lumishore.com
SIC: 3647 Boat & ship lighting fixtures

(G-15513)
MANATEE TOOL INC
1400 Commerce Blvd Ste Cd (34243-5069)
PHONE...............................941 355-9252
EMP: 5
SALES (est): 376.8K **Privately Held**
SIC: 3599 Machine Shop & Assembly Svcs

(G-15514)
MATRIX24 LABORATORIES LLC
Also Called: Eversafe
1453 Tallevast Rd (34243-5036)
P.O. Box 3954 (34230-3954)
PHONE...............................941 879-3048
Blethen Craig, *Vice Pres*
Greg Blethes,
▼ EMP: 10 EST: 2011
SQ FT: 2,500
SALES (est): 300K **Privately Held**
SIC: 2879 Insecticides & pesticides

(G-15515)
MAXEFF INDUSTRIES INC
1251 Commerce Blvd S (34243-5018)
PHONE..941 893-5804
Gerald Goche, *Principal*
▲ EMP: 7 EST: 2013
SALES (est): 243.8K **Privately Held**
WEB: www.adventechinc.com
SIC: 3999 Manufacturing industries

(G-15516)
MEDONE SURGICAL INC
670 Tallevast Rd (34243-3254)
PHONE..941 359-3129
Bruce A Beckstein, *President*
Lisa S Beckstein, *Vice Pres*
Julie Ovens, *Vice Pres*
Steve Whitt, *Prdtn Mgr*
Len Kendrigan, *Sales Staff*
▲ EMP: 12 EST: 1999
SQ FT: 2,000
SALES (est): 2.4MM **Privately Held**
WEB: www.medone.com
SIC: 3841 5047 Surgical & medical instruments; medical equipment & supplies

(G-15517)
MIO PUBLICATION INC
Also Called: Keels & Wheels
1864 University Pkwy (34243-2225)
P.O. Box 567, Tallevast (34270-0567)
PHONE..941 351-2411
James Dygert, *President*
Judith Dygert, *Treasurer*
EMP: 8 EST: 1978
SQ FT: 16,760
SALES (est): 229.7K **Privately Held**
WEB: www.keelsandwheelsmagazine.com
SIC: 2721 Magazines: publishing only, not printed on site

(G-15518)
MOBILEBITS HOLDINGS CORP (PA)
5901 N Honore Ave Ste 120 (34243-2632)
PHONE..941 225-6115
Kent Kirschner, *CEO*
Cristina M Iturrino, *Counsel*
James Burk, *CFO*
EMP: 5 EST: 2009
SALES (est): 612.1K **Publicly Held**
SIC: 7372 Prepackaged software

(G-15519)
MOISTTECH CORP
6408 Parkland Dr Ste 104 (34243-5410)
PHONE..941 351-7870
John Fordham, *President*
Harold Ribot, *Sales Staff*
Michelle Caulkins, *Marketing Staff*
EMP: 10 EST: 2013
SALES (est): 2.4MM **Privately Held**
WEB: www.moisttech.com
SIC: 3822 Temperature controls, automatic

(G-15520)
MULTI-FLEX LLC
8046 36th Street Cir E (34243-6308)
PHONE..941 360-6500
Peter Rosenquist, *President*
EMP: 7 EST: 1991
SALES (est): 2.3MM
SALES (corp-wide): 11.3B **Publicly Held**
SIC: 3535 Conveyors & conveying equipment
HQ: Se Holdings Llc
1046 W London Park Dr
Forest VA 24551

(G-15521)
MUSTANG VACUUM SYSTEMS INC
7135 16th St E Ste 115 (34243-6818)
PHONE..941 377-1440
Dean Ganzhorn, *CEO*
Richard Greenwell, *President*
Robert Choquette, *Vice Pres*
Brent McGary, *Purchasing*
Ceasar Andolphi, *Engineer*
EMP: 45 EST: 2005
SQ FT: 50,000
SALES (est): 9.7MM **Privately Held**
WEB: www.mustangvac.com
SIC: 3569 Industrial shock absorbers

(G-15522)
N A COMANDULLI LLC
6935 15th St E Units105 (34243-7200)
PHONE..941 870-2878
Ivano Tirapelle, *Mng Member*
▲ EMP: 5 EST: 2013
SALES (est): 1MM
SALES (corp-wide): 23.1MM **Privately Held**
WEB: www.comandulli-na.com
SIC: 2842 Polishing preparations & related products
PA: Comandulli Costruzioni Meccaniche Srl
Via Medaglie D'argento 20
Castelleone CR 26012
037 435-7211

(G-15523)
NADCO TAPES & LABELS INC
2240 72nd Ter E (34243-3997)
PHONE..941 751-6693
Rena J Doniger, *President*
Neil Doniger, *Vice Pres*
EMP: 35 EST: 2004
SALES (est): 6.3MM **Privately Held**
WEB: www.nadco-inc.com
SIC: 2241 2679 Fabric tapes; tags & labels, paper

(G-15524)
NATIONWIDE PRTCTIVE CTING MFRS
7106 24th Ct E (34243-3993)
PHONE..941 753-7500
Dorothy E Ungarelli, *President*
Robert Gocinski, *Vice Pres*
Jarred Dluginski, *Sales Associate*
Steve Ellis, *Technology*
▼ EMP: 28 EST: 1964
SQ FT: 15,000
SALES (est): 6.8MM **Privately Held**
WEB: www.nationwidecoatings.com
SIC: 2851 Paints & allied products

(G-15525)
NATURAL IMMUNOGENICS CORP (PA)
7504 Pennsylvania Ave (34243-5047)
PHONE..888 328-8840
Benjamin Quinto, *Co-President*
Theodore Quinto, *Co-President*
Carol Cotton Riggins, *Controller*
John Brinkman, *Manager*
Martin Coglianese, *Manager*
EMP: 65 EST: 1998
SQ FT: 7,000
SALES (est): 17.3MM **Privately Held**
WEB: www.naturalimmunogenics.com
SIC: 2834 2833 5499 Pharmaceutical preparations; medicinals & botanicals; health foods

(G-15526)
NEW BREED CLOTHING LLC
1120 Magellan Dr (34243-4423)
PHONE..941 773-7406
Nicholas Johnson,
EMP: 9 EST: 2006
SQ FT: 1,100
SALES (est): 390K **Privately Held**
SIC: 2211 Apparel & outerwear fabrics, cotton

(G-15527)
NORMANDIN LLC
2206 72nd Dr E (34243-3988)
PHONE..941 739-8046
Ronnie Cho, *Sales Mgr*
Mark Matter, *Sales Staff*
Scott Normandin, *Manager*
George Tavares, *Manager*
David Normandin,
EMP: 10 EST: 2002
SALES (est): 1.4MM **Privately Held**
SIC: 3444 Sheet metalwork

(G-15528)
ONE BIOTECHNOLOGY COMPANY
1833 57th St Ste A (34243-2228)
P.O. Box 758, Oneco (34264-0758)
PHONE..941 355-8451
Vince Scuilla, *President*
EMP: 12 EST: 1995
SQ FT: 13,000
SALES (est): 357.4K **Privately Held**
WEB: www.bioonesolutions.com
SIC: 2836 Culture media

(G-15529)
OVERALL-HONEYCOMB LLC (HQ)
1950 Limbus Ave (34243-3900)
P.O. Box 2375 (34230-2375)
PHONE..941 756-8781
EMP: 10 EST: 2013
SALES (est): 22.5MM
SALES (corp-wide): 59MM **Privately Held**
WEB: www.hcoainc.com
SIC: 3724 Aircraft engines & engine parts
PA: Overall, Llc
29 Commonwealth Ave # 401
Boston MA 02116
857 263-7961

(G-15530)
PALLET RECALL INC
6755 33rd St E (34243-4129)
PHONE..941 727-1944
Timothy Bragg, *President*
EMP: 7 EST: 1994
SALES (est): 582.1K **Privately Held**
SIC: 2448 Pallets, wood

(G-15531)
PARCUS MEDICAL LLC
6423 Parkland Dr (34243-4035)
PHONE..941 755-7965
Nickolas Henning, *Opers Staff*
David Davis, *Mfg Staff*
Christian Koehler, *Production*
Kevin Burch, *Engineer*
Jeff Hummel, *Accounting Mgr*
EMP: 18 EST: 2007
SALES (est): 8.1MM **Publicly Held**
SIC: 3841 Surgical & medical instruments
PA: Anika Therapeutics, Inc.
32 Wiggins Ave
Bedford MA 01730

(G-15532)
PASSION LABELS & PACKAGING
1223 Tallevast Rd (34243-3271)
PHONE..941 312-5003
Shane Barrett, *Principal*
EMP: 21 EST: 2011
SQ FT: 5,250
SALES (est): 2.6MM **Privately Held**
WEB: www.passionlabels.com
SIC: 2679 5131 2759 Tags & labels, paper; labels, paper: made from purchased material; labels; flexographic printing

(G-15533)
PATRICK INDUSTRIES INC
Also Called: Design Cncepts/Marine Concepts
6805 15th St E (34243-3210)
PHONE..941 556-6311
Robert Long, *Branch Mgr*
EMP: 208
SALES (corp-wide): 4B **Publicly Held**
WEB: www.dcmc-us.com
SIC: 3429 Marine hardware
PA: Patrick Industries, Inc.
107 W Franklin St
Elkhart IN 46516
574 294-7511

(G-15534)
PATRICK INDUSTRIES INC
Also Called: Marine Concepts
6805 15th St E (34243-3210)
PHONE..941 556-6311
EMP: 20
SALES (est): 7.4MM **Privately Held**
SIC: 3732 8711 Boatbuilding/Repairing Engineering Services

(G-15535)
PEEK TRAFFIC CORPORATION
6408 Parkland Dr Ste 102 (34243-5410)
PHONE..941 366-8770
Alejandro Brunell, *CEO*
Rolando Garcia, *COO*
Alejandro Fuentes, *Vice Pres*
Angel Gonzalez, *Prdtn Mgr*
Meliza Garcia, *Purch Mgr*
◆ EMP: 130 EST: 2003
SALES (est): 24.5MM
SALES (corp-wide): 48.9MM **Privately Held**
WEB: www.peektraffic.com
SIC: 3669 Transportation signaling devices
PA: Signal Group, Inc.
5825 N Sam Houston Pkwy W # 220
Houston TX 77086
281 453-0200

(G-15536)
PESTWEST USA LLC
7135 16th St E Ste 124 (34243-6818)
P.O. Box 2234 (34230-2234)
PHONE..941 358-1983
◆ EMP: 9
SQ FT: 5,000
SALES (est): 3.6MM **Privately Held**
SIC: 3699 Mfg Electrical Equipment/Supplies

(G-15537)
PLANT PARTNERS INC
6691 33rd St E Ste B3 (34243-4604)
PHONE..941 752-1039
George Aiello, *Owner*
EMP: 14
SALES (corp-wide): 7.7MM **Privately Held**
WEB: www.tropex.com
SIC: 3579 Mailing, letter handling & addressing machines
PA: Plant Partners, Inc.
3220 Whitfield Ave
Sarasota FL 34243
941 753-5066

(G-15538)
PLATINUM LTG PRODUCTIONS LLC
8051 N Tamiami Trl D10 (34243-2032)
PHONE..941 320-1906
Angela Congdon, *Principal*
EMP: 8 EST: 2016
SALES (est): 2.2MM **Privately Held**
WEB: www.platinumlightingproductions.com
SIC: 3648 Stage lighting equipment

(G-15539)
PREMIER PRFMCE INTERIORS INC
Also Called: Ppi
6304 17th Street Cir E (34243-5424)
PHONE..941 752-6271
Lee Wingard, *President*
Jim Cowan, *Vice Pres*
Jerry Crabtree, *Engineer*
▲ EMP: 30 EST: 2000
SALES (est): 4.4MM **Privately Held**
WEB: www.ppi-fl.com
SIC: 3732 Boat building & repairing

(G-15540)
QUALITY CONTRACT MFG SVCS LLC
Also Called: Qcms
1905 72nd Dr E (34243-8901)
PHONE..941 355-7787
Kevin Beachler,
EMP: 10 EST: 2007
SQ FT: 6,000
SALES (est): 1.1MM **Privately Held**
WEB: www.qcmsfl.com
SIC: 3572 Computer tape drives & components

(G-15541)
RADIANT POWER CORP (DH)
7135 16th St E Ste 101 (34243-6818)
PHONE..941 739-3200
Anish Patel, *President*
Chuck Schofield, *Vice Pres*
Melissa Little, *Buyer*
Carlos L Macau, *Treasurer*
Elizabeth R Letendre, *Asst Sec*
EMP: 57 EST: 1999
SQ FT: 10,000
SALES (est): 38.7MM **Publicly Held**
WEB: www.rpcaero.com
SIC: 3812 5088 3728 3647 Search & navigation equipment; transportation equipment & supplies; aircraft parts & equipment; aircraft lighting fixtures

HQ: Heico Electronic Technologies Corp.
3000 Taft St
Hollywood FL 33021
954 987-6101

(G-15542)
RADIANT POWER IDC LLC
7135 16th St E Ste 101 (34243-6818)
PHONE.....................................760 945-0230
William J Lang, *President*
Matthew K Thomas, *CFO*
John Moyer, *Marketing Staff*
EMP: 50 EST: 1976
SQ FT: 30,000
SALES (est): 27.3MM **Publicly Held**
SIC: 3812 Aircraft control systems, electronic
HQ: Radiant Power Corp.
7135 16th St E Ste 101
Sarasota FL 34243
941 739-3200

(G-15543)
RADIANT-SEACOM REPAIRS CORP
7135 16th St E Ste 101 (34243-6818)
PHONE.....................................941 739-3200
Anish Patel, *President*
EMP: 10 EST: 2017
SALES (est): 3.1MM **Publicly Held**
WEB: www.rpcaero.com
SIC: 3724 Aircraft engines & engine parts
PA: Heico Corporation
3000 Taft St
Hollywood FL 33021

(G-15544)
RAPID COMPOSITES LLC
2216 72nd Dr E (34243-3937)
PHONE.....................................941 322-6647
Alan Taylor, *Mng Member*
EMP: 6 EST: 2012
SQ FT: 5,000
SALES (est): 1.2MM **Privately Held**
WEB: www.rapidcomposites.com
SIC: 2655 3624 7373 8711 Cans, composite: foil-fiber & other; from purchased fiber; fibers, carbon & graphite; systems engineering, computer related; mechanical engineering; electrical or electronic engineering;
PA: Taylor & Lego Holdings, Llc
34655 State Road 70 E
Myakka City FL 34251
941 322-6647

(G-15545)
ROAD SIGNS INC
2017 Whitfield Park Dr (34243-4094)
P.O. Box 2973 (34230-2973)
PHONE.....................................941 321-0695
Keith Bernard, *President*
Carol Bergere, *Principal*
Holly Bergere, *Manager*
EMP: 5 EST: 2005
SALES (est): 498.8K **Privately Held**
WEB: www.nowthatsawrap.com
SIC: 3993 Electric signs

(G-15546)
ROBSON CORPORATION
2231 Whitfield Park Loop (34243-4043)
PHONE.....................................941 753-6935
Gary F Dinsdale, *President*
Mallory J Dinsdale, *Vice Pres*
Craig Abbott, *Sr Project Mgr*
◆ EMP: 50 EST: 1985
SQ FT: 45,000
SALES (est): 6.9MM **Privately Held**
WEB: www.robsonchurchsigns.com
SIC: 3993 Neon signs

(G-15547)
ROCK BOTTOM BOTTLES LLC
1447 Tallevast Rd (34243-5035)
PHONE.....................................901 237-9929
Dustine Keith, *Managing Prtnr*
James Cirillo, *Mng Member*
Michael J Boling Jr,
▲ EMP: 6 EST: 2014
SQ FT: 5,000
SALES (est): 766.1K **Privately Held**
WEB: www.rockbottombottles.com
SIC: 3221 3085 Glass containers; plastics bottles

(G-15548)
SAFRAN POWER UK LTD
Also Called: Labinal Power Systems
2250 Whitfield Ave (34243-3926)
PHONE.....................................941 739-7207
Jorge Ortega, *Exec VP*
EMP: 5 EST: 2013
SQ FT: 2,100
SALES (est): 1.3MM **Privately Held**
WEB: www.labinal-power.com
SIC: 3728 Aircraft parts & equipment

(G-15549)
SAFRAN POWER USA LLC
2250 Whitfield Ave (34243-3926)
PHONE.....................................941 758-7726
David Vollrath, *General Mgr*
Nicolette Midzio, *Buyer*
Jose Calderon, *QC Mgr*
Casey Hodge, *Manager*
EMP: 140
SALES (corp-wide): 650.7MM **Privately Held**
WEB: www.labinal-power.com
SIC: 3728 4581 Aircraft parts & equipment; aircraft maintenance & repair services
HQ: Safran Power Usa, Llc
8380 Darrow Rd
Twinsburg OH 44087
330 487-2000

(G-15550)
SANIT TECHNOLOGIES LLC
Also Called: Durisan
7810 25th Ct E Unit 106 (34243-2841)
PHONE.....................................941 351-9114
Arthur Wein, *Principal*
Andrew Cervasio, *Mng Member*
Troy Daland,
EMP: 32 EST: 2014
SQ FT: 33,259
SALES (est): 80K **Privately Held**
WEB: www.sanittechnologies.com
SIC: 2841 Soap & other detergents; detergents, synthetic organic or inorganic alkaline

(G-15551)
SARASOTA HERALD-TRIBUNE
1800 University Pkwy (34243-2298)
PHONE.....................................941 358-4000
Jim Spear, *Manager*
EMP: 121
SALES (corp-wide): 278.4MM **Privately Held**
WEB: www.heraldtribune.com
SIC: 2711 Newspapers, publishing & printing
HQ: Sarasota Herald-Tribune
801 S Tamiami Trl
Sarasota FL 34236
941 953-7755

(G-15552)
SARASOTA PRECISION ENGRG INC (PA)
2305 72nd Ave E (34243-3952)
PHONE.....................................941 727-3444
Doug Mansfield, *President*
Mike Ontiveros, *Vice Pres*
Pat Clevenger, *Project Mgr*
Nikki Mansfield, *Office Mgr*
▲ EMP: 18 EST: 2003
SQ FT: 20,000
SALES (est): 4.6MM **Privately Held**
WEB: www.spe-inc.com
SIC: 3312 Tool & die steel & alloys

(G-15553)
SCOTT SIGN SYSTEMS INC (HQ)
7525 Pennsylvania Ave C (34243-5065)
P.O. Box 1047, Tallevast (34270-1047)
PHONE.....................................941 355-5171
Brad Wolf, *CEO*
Kathy Hannon, *President*
Brian Mogensen, *CFO*
Stewart Abbott, *Treasurer*
Paul Maggio, *Director*
◆ EMP: 24 EST: 1957
SQ FT: 102,000

(G-15554)
SIEMENS INDUSTRY INC
2650 Tallevast Rd (34243-3912)
PHONE.....................................941 355-2971
Gary Snyder, *Engineer*
A Wayne Coody, *Finance Other*
Al Brown, *Accounts Mgr*
Robert D Tatum, *Systems Staff*
EMP: 71
SALES (corp-wide): 73B **Privately Held**
WEB: www.siemens.com
SIC: 2899 Water treating compounds
HQ: Siemens Industry, Inc.
1000 Deerfield Pkwy
Buffalo Grove IL 60089
847 215-1000

(G-15555)
SIF TECHNOLOGY COMPANY LLC
7245 16th St E Unit 101 (34243-6813)
PHONE.....................................941 225-8363
Mel Cobbin, *Manager*
Bobb Mabbot, *CTO*
Gina Mascio,
EMP: 8 EST: 2010
SALES (est): 463.4K **Privately Held**
SIC: 3571 Computers, digital, analog or hybrid

(G-15556)
SILVER BAY LLC
Also Called: Quasar Light Therapy
1431 Tallevast Rd (34243-5035)
PHONE.....................................941 306-5812
Peter Nesbitt,
EMP: 10 EST: 2008
SALES (est): 887.2K **Privately Held**
SIC: 3845 Laser systems & equipment, medical

(G-15557)
SIMPLIMATIC AUTOMATION
7245 16th St E Unit 114 (34243-6813)
PHONE.....................................941 360-6500
EMP: 8 EST: 2011
SALES (est): 104K **Privately Held**
WEB: www.simplimatic.com
SIC: 3365 Machinery castings, aluminum

(G-15558)
SRQ SIGN PARTNERS LLC
1621 W University Pkwy (34243-2732)
PHONE.....................................941 357-0319
EMP: 7 EST: 2018
SALES (est): 237.8K **Privately Held**
WEB:
www.wholesalechannellettersigns.com
SIC: 3993 Signs & advertising specialties

(G-15559)
STABIL CONCRETE PAVERS LLC
7080 28th Street Ct E (34243-3300)
PHONE.....................................941 739-7823
▲ EMP: 21
SALES (est): 5MM **Privately Held**
SIC: 3531 Mfg Construction Machinery

(G-15560)
STIEBEL ELTRON INC
2060 Whitfield Park Ave (34243-4072)
PHONE.....................................800 826-5537
EMP: 14 **Privately Held**
WEB: www.stiebel-eltron-usa.com
SIC: 3639 Hot water heaters, household
PA: Stiebel Eltron, Inc.
17 West St
West Hatfield MA 01088

(G-15561)
SUN COAST INDUSTRIES LLC
7350 26th Ct E (34243-3947)
PHONE.....................................941 355-7166
Richard Hofmann, *President*

SALES (est): 5.2MM
SALES (corp-wide): 271.1MM **Privately Held**
SIC: 3089 3086 Injection molding of plastics; plastics foam products
PA: Identity Group Holdings Corp.
1480 Gould Dr
Cookeville TN 38506
931 432-4000

Kathy Kruse, *President*
EMP: 60 EST: 1979
SQ FT: 146,000
SALES (est): 5.5MM **Publicly Held**
WEB: www.mysuncoast.com
SIC: 3089 Caps, plastic
HQ: Berry Global, Inc.
101 Oakley St
Evansville IN 47710

(G-15562)
SUN GRAPHIC TECHNOLOGIES INC
Also Called: Sun Screenprinting Lindycal
2310 Whitfield Park Ave (34243-4084)
P.O. Box 807 (34230-0807)
PHONE.....................................941 753-7541
William F Blechta, *President*
Bill Blechta, *Principal*
George E Blechta, *Corp Secy*
Rob Harris, *COO*
Robert Harris, *COO*
EMP: 23 EST: 1978
SQ FT: 16,000
SALES (est): 3.1MM **Privately Held**
WEB: www.sungraphictechnologies.com
SIC: 2759 3993 3953 2752 Screen printing; signs & advertising specialties; marking devices; commercial printing, lithographic

(G-15563)
SUN HYDRAULICS CORPORATION
803 Tallevast Rd (34243-3257)
PHONE.....................................941 362-1300
Stephanie Bivins, *President*
Tim Spears, *Branch Mgr*
EMP: 31
SALES (corp-wide): 869.1MM **Publicly Held**
WEB: www.heliostechnologies.com
SIC: 3492 Fluid power valves & hose fittings
PA: Helios Technologies, Inc.
7456 16th St E
Sarasota FL 34243
941 362-1200

(G-15564)
SUNSHINE TOOL LLC
7245 16th St E Unit 114 (34243-6813)
PHONE.....................................941 351-6330
Steven Reese, *Sales Staff*
John Barrett, *Mng Member*
Bonnie Perkins, *Executive Asst*
EMP: 5 EST: 2007
SALES (est): 1MM **Privately Held**
WEB: www.sunshinemachining.com
SIC: 3559 3535 3599 Robots, molding & forming plastics; robotic conveyors; machine & other job shop work; machine shop, jobbing & repair

(G-15565)
SUPERIOR ELECTRONICS
7519 Pennsylvania Ave # 102 (34243-5015)
PHONE.....................................941 355-9500
Ben Price, *Owner*
EMP: 5 EST: 2006
SALES (est): 385.2K **Privately Held**
SIC: 3679 5065 Harness assemblies for electronic use: wire or cable; electronic parts & equipment

(G-15566)
TALON MARINE
1968 Whitfield Park Ave (34243-4048)
PHONE.....................................941 753-7400
Gary Armington, *Managing Prtnr*
William S Armington, *Partner*
Robert Wilkens, *General Mgr*
EMP: 6 EST: 1978
SQ FT: 18,000
SALES (est): 415.1K **Privately Held**
SIC: 3732 Boats, fiberglass: building & repairing

(G-15567)
TEAKDECKING SYSTEMS INC
7061 15th St E (34243-3243)
PHONE.....................................941 756-0600
Michael G Havey, *Ch of Bd*
Richard Strauss, *President*
Christopher Stokes, *Vice Pres*

David Jackson, *Project Mgr*
Rick Strauss, *Mfg Staff*
EMP: 72 **EST:** 2007
SALES (est): 14.9MM **Privately Held**
WEB: www.teakdecking.com
SIC: 2499 Applicators, wood

(G-15568)
TINTOMETER INC (HQ)
Also Called: Orbeco-Hellige
6456 Parkland Dr (34243-4036)
PHONE............................941 756-6410
Bradley K Martell, *President*
Matthew Meyers, *Materials Mgr*
Cindy Workman, *Warehouse Mgr*
Joan Lambert, *Accountant*
Kyle Follansbee, *Marketing Staff*
▲ **EMP:** 10 **EST:** 1985
SQ FT: 20,000
SALES (est): 4.5MM
SALES (corp-wide): 32MM **Privately Held**
WEB: www.lovibond.com
SIC: 3821 Laboratory apparatus, except heating & measuring
PA: Tintometer Gesellschaft Mit Beschrank-
ter Haftung
Schleefstr. 8-12
Dortmund NW 44287
231 945-100 ..

(G-15569)
TITAN OIL TOOLS LLC
8466 Lockwood Ridge Rd (34243-2951)
PHONE............................941 356-3010
Roy Pandeo, *Manager*
EMP: 8 **EST:** 2013
SALES (est): 1MM **Privately Held**
WEB: www.titanoiltools.com
SIC: 1389 Oil field services

(G-15570)
TORQUE TECHNOLOGIES PRODUCTS
Also Called: Goizper USA
1623 W University Pkwy (34243-2732)
PHONE............................630 462-1188
Bradley H Binks, *President*
Maynard N Wood, *Treasurer*
Jonhnny Jander, *Manager*
Patrick Montgomery, *Manager*
Harry L Binks, *Director*
▲ **EMP:** 5 **EST:** 2005
SALES (est): 1MM **Privately Held**
WEB: www.goizperusa.com
SIC: 3568 Power transmission equipment

(G-15571)
TRIDENT BUILDING SYSTEMS INC
2812 Tallevast Rd (34243-3914)
PHONE............................941 755-7073
Carl Petrat, *President*
Debbie Mavis, *General Mgr*
Cindy L Petrat-Hayden, *Corp Secy*
Willard G Petrat, *Vice Pres*
Heather Kortzendorf, *Project Mgr*
EMP: 170 **EST:** 1986
SQ FT: 52,000
SALES (est): 25.3MM **Privately Held**
WEB: www.tridentbuildingsystems.com
SIC: 3448 Prefabricated metal buildings

(G-15572)
TRINITY GRAPHIC USA INC
885 Tallevast Rd Ste D (34243-3323)
PHONE............................941 355-2636
Robert J Smithson, *CEO*
William Ceperich, *CEO*
Gregory Barba, *President*
Mark Barnard, *Vice Pres*
Simon Smithson, *Vice Pres*
EMP: 18 **EST:** 1987
SQ FT: 6,750
SALES (est): 4.8MM **Privately Held**
WEB: www.trinitygraphic.com
SIC: 3555 2796 Printing plates; platemak-
ing services

(G-15573)
TROJAN FLA POWDR COATING INC
1300 Hardin Ave (34243-5067)
PHONE............................941 351-0500
EMP: 22 **EST:** 2011

SALES (est): 1.1MM **Privately Held**
WEB: www.trojanpowder.com
SIC: 3479 Coating of metals & formed products

(G-15574)
TSM CHAMP LLC
2359 Trailmate Dr (34243-4041)
PHONE............................615 806-7900
Joseph Apuzzo,
EMP: 55 **EST:** 2016
SALES (est): 17.3MM
SALES (corp-wide): 53.1MM **Privately Held**
SIC: 3491 3585 Industrial valves; refriger-
ation & heating equipment
PA: Thermal Solutions Manufacturing, Inc.
25 Century Blvd Ste 210
Nashville TN 37214
800 359-9186

(G-15575)
UFLEX USA INC
6442 Parkland Dr (34243-4038)
PHONE............................941 351-2628
Anna G Gai, *President*
Steven Wasserman, *Sales Staff*
◆ **EMP:** 22 **EST:** 1999
SQ FT: 40,000
SALES (est): 5.5MM **Privately Held**
WEB: www.uflexusa.com
SIC: 3531 5091 Marine related equipment;
boat accessories & parts

(G-15576)
UK SAILMAKERS INC (PA)
Also Called: Uk Sailmakers Sarasota
324 Bernard Ave (34243-1904)
PHONE............................941 365-7245
Greg Knighton, *President*
Alan Capellin, *Principal*
Gregg Knighton, *Principal*
Bob Revou, *Principal*
Travis Odenbach, *Sales Staff*
EMP: 7 **EST:** 2005
SALES (est): 626.5K **Privately Held**
WEB: www.uksailmakers.com
SIC: 3732 Sailboats, building & repairing

(G-15577)
VALINTECH
2260 Whitfield Park Ave (34243-4079)
PHONE............................941 366-8885
Tom Valinth, *Principal*
EMP: 7 **EST:** 2011
SALES (est): 125.5K **Privately Held**
WEB: www.valintech.com
SIC: 3089 Injection molding of plastics

(G-15578)
VOLCANO INDUSTRIES INC
1125 Commerce Blvd N (34243-5056)
PHONE............................770 300-0041
Thomas C Hanson, *Principal*
EMP: 10 **EST:** 2017
SALES (est): 440.2K **Privately Held**
SIC: 3999 Manufacturing industries

(G-15579)
WESCO PARTNERS INC
1125 Commerce Blvd N (34243-5056)
PHONE............................941 484-8224
David O'Halloran, *President*
EMP: 44 **EST:** 1984
SALES (est): 4.4MM **Privately Held**
WEB: wescofountains.blogspot.com
SIC: 3272 3499 3446 Concrete products;
fountains (except drinking); metal; archi-
tectural metalwork
PA: Manufacturing Futures, Inc.
40 Haskell Dr
Cleveland OH 44108
216 903-7993

(G-15580)
WEST COAST SIGNS
2310 Whitfield Indus Way (34243-4062)
PHONE............................941 755-5686
Robin Morrow, *President*
Linda Dunning, *Office Admin*
EMP: 21 **EST:** 1996
SQ FT: 25,000
SALES (est): 992.2K **Privately Held**
SIC: 3993 Electric signs

Sarasota
Sarasota County

(G-15581)
A ALBRTINI CSTM WIN TREATMENTS
Also Called: A Albrtini Cstm Wndows Trtmnts
4023 Sawyer Rd Ofc (34233-1209)
PHONE............................941 925-2556
Ronald Albertini, *President*
EMP: 7 **EST:** 1985
SQ FT: 2,000
SALES (est): 674.4K **Privately Held**
SIC: 2591 Drapery hardware & blinds & shades

(G-15582)
A CAPPELA PUBLISHING INC (PA)
Also Called: Advocate House
913 Tennessee Ln (34234-5712)
P.O. Box 3691 (34230-3691)
PHONE............................941 351-2050
Patrika Vaughn, *President*
EMP: 5 **EST:** 1996
SQ FT: 2,500
SALES (est): 500K **Privately Held**
WEB: www.acappela.com
SIC: 2741 Miscellaneous publishing

(G-15583)
A2Z UNIFORMS INC
999 Cattlemen Rd Unit G (34232-2849)
PHONE............................941 254-3194
Jarek Zaremba, *President*
EMP: 6 **EST:** 1999
SQ FT: 2,400
SALES (est): 811.7K **Privately Held**
WEB: www.a2zuniforms.com
SIC: 2395 5699 Embroidery & art needle-
work; emblems, embroidered; uniforms &
work clothing

(G-15584)
AAP INDUSTRIAL INC
Also Called: Aap Pump and Motor Works
1634 Barber Rd (34240-9393)
PHONE............................941 377-4373
Todd Carter, *Vice Pres*
EMP: 20 **EST:** 2013
SQ FT: 9,000
SALES (est): 2.5MM **Privately Held**
WEB: www.aappumpandmotor.com
SIC: 7694 7699 Electric motor repair;
compressor repair

(G-15585)
ACADEMIC PUBLICATION SVCS INC
3131 Clark Rd Ste 102 (34231-7320)
PHONE............................941 925-4474
John Wolf, *President*
Rhoda Wolf, *CFO*
EMP: 7 **EST:** 1997
SALES (est): 93.5K **Privately Held**
SIC: 2759 2741 Publication printing; mis-
cellaneous publishing

(G-15586)
ACTIVE SOLE
4070 Sawyer Ct (34233-1215)
P.O. Box 1517, Ponte Vedra Beach
(32004-1517)
PHONE............................941 923-4840
Robert Schafer, *Principal*
EMP: 7 **EST:** 2014
SALES (est): 123.6K **Privately Held**
SIC: 2759 Screen printing

(G-15587)
ADHESIVE TECHNOLOGIES FLA LLC
411 Pheasant Way (34236-1915)
PHONE............................941 228-0295
Lawrence Oconnor, *Principal*
EMP: 7 **EST:** 2014
SALES (est): 125.9K **Privately Held**
SIC: 2891 Adhesives

(G-15588)
ADVANCED VACUUM SYSTEMS LLC
2025d Porter Lake Dr (34240-8834)
PHONE............................941 378-4565
Craig Lubkey, *President*
EMP: 8 **EST:** 2005
SALES (est): 347.2K **Privately Held**
WEB: www.avsvacuumsystems.com
SIC: 3999 Chairs, hydraulic, barber &
beauty shop

(G-15589)
AKUWA SOLUTIONS GROUP INC (PA)
6431 Porter Rd Ste 1 (34240)
PHONE............................941 343-9947
Terry Nelson, *CEO*
Karin Nelson, *Vice Pres*
EMP: 10 **EST:** 2000
SQ FT: 2,000
SALES (est): 2MM **Privately Held**
WEB: www.akuwa.com
SIC: 3825 3674 3679 7373 Network ana-
lyzers; integrated circuits, semiconductor
networks, etc.; pulse forming networks;
local area network (LAN) systems integra-
tor

(G-15590)
ALADDIN EQUIPMENT COMPANY
900 Sarasota Center Blvd (34240-8847)
PHONE............................941 371-3732
Lindy L Smith, *Ch of Bd*
Jack McKissock, *President*
Gordon SEC, *Exec VP*
John Miller, *Vice Pres*
Dave Poali, *Purch Mgr*
◆ **EMP:** 55 **EST:** 1950
SQ FT: 108,000
SALES (est): 7.9MM **Privately Held**
WEB: www.aladdin1950.com
SIC: 3589 Swimming pool filter & water
conditioning systems

(G-15591)
ALBRECHT CONSULTING INC
1350 Global Ct (34240-7856)
PHONE............................941 377-7755
Jeff Albrecht, *President*
EMP: 17 **EST:** 1994
SALES (est): 2.7MM **Privately Held**
WEB: www.albrechtcabinets.com
SIC: 2434 Wood kitchen cabinets

(G-15592)
ALL GRANITE & MARBLE CORP
1909 N Washington Blvd (34234-7528)
PHONE............................508 248-9393
Altamiro Abranches, *President*
Ricardo Neves, *Admin Sec*
▲ **EMP:** 6 **EST:** 2004
SALES (est): 628.4K **Privately Held**
WEB:
www.allgraniteandmarblesarasota.com
SIC: 3281 1741 Granite, cut & shaped;
marble, building: cut & shaped; masonry
& other stonework

(G-15593)
ALPHA KITCHEN DESIGN LLC
4141 S Tamiami Trl Ste 9 (34231-3680)
PHONE............................941 351-1659
EMP: 5 **EST:** 2018
SALES (est): 374.3K **Privately Held**
WEB: www.alphakitchendesign.com
SIC: 2434 Wood kitchen cabinets

(G-15594)
ALVIS INDUSTRIES INC
3300 Linden Dr (34232-4938)
PHONE............................941 377-7800
Troy D Alvis, *Principal*
EMP: 8 **EST:** 2004
SALES (est): 374.3K **Privately Held**
WEB: www.alvisindustriesinc.com
SIC: 3999 Manufacturing industries

(G-15595)
ANDROS BOATWORKS INC
202 Industrial Blvd (34234)
PHONE............................941 351-9702
Andrew D Eggebrecht, *President*
Danny Eggebrecht, *Vice Pres*

Donald Eggebrecht, *Vice Pres*
EMP: 10 **EST:** 2005
SQ FT: 22,000
SALES (est): 482.6K **Privately Held**
WEB: www.androsboats.com
SIC: 3732 Motorboats, inboard or outboard: building & repairing

(G-15596)
APOLLO SUNGUARD SYSTEMS INC
4487 Ashton Rd (34233-2284)
PHONE.................................941 925-3000
Kevin Connelly, *President*
Ernesto De Oliveira, *COO*
Danielle Cibello, *Vice Pres*
Valentina D Puscuta, *Controller*
Valentina Puscuta, *Controller*
▲ **EMP:** 15 **EST:** 2001
SQ FT: 10,000
SALES (est): 4MM **Privately Held**
WEB: www.apollosunguard.com
SIC: 2394 3714 5063 Canopies, fabric: made from purchased materials; motor vehicle electrical equipment; electrical apparatus & equipment

(G-15597)
AQUA WHOLESALE INC
1155 Cattlemen Rd Ste B (34232-2836)
PHONE.................................941 341-0847
Larry Eaton, *President*
Sandra K Eaton, *Vice Pres*
John Wilyat, *Purch Mgr*
Sandy Eaton, *Office Mgr*
Susan Harris, *Office Mgr*
▼ **EMP:** 6 **EST:** 2001
SQ FT: 7,500
SALES (est): 891.5K **Privately Held**
WEB: www.aqua-wholesale.com
SIC: 3589 Water treatment equipment, industrial

(G-15598)
AQUARIUS SILK SCREEN INC
5931 Palmer Blvd (34232-2841)
PHONE.................................941 377-3059
Ronald A Ernst, *President*
EMP: 6 **EST:** 1980
SQ FT: 5,400
SALES (est): 593.7K **Privately Held**
SIC: 2261 Screen printing of cotton broadwoven fabrics

(G-15599)
ARCHITCTURAL MBL IMPORTERS INC
2560 12th St (34237-2943)
PHONE.................................941 365-3552
James Newby, *President*
▲ **EMP:** 20 **EST:** 1981
SALES (est): 1.9MM **Privately Held**
WEB: www.architecturalmarbleofflorida.com
SIC: 3281 1743 5032 Household articles, except furniture: cut stone; marble installation, interior; marble building stone

(G-15600)
ARGOS USA LLC
6000 Deacon Pl (34238-2719)
PHONE.................................866 322-4547
EMP: 7 **EST:** 2018
SALES (est): 103.1K **Privately Held**
WEB: www.argos-us.com
SIC: 3273 Ready-mixed concrete

(G-15601)
ASHTON MANUFACTURING LLC
Also Called: Suntech Doors
1633 Northgate Blvd (34234-2117)
PHONE.................................941 351-5529
Joe Zuza, *Prdtn Mgr*
Chris Nelson, *Opers Staff*
Carol Garrison, *Sales Staff*
Terry Ashton,
EMP: 10 **EST:** 2006
SQ FT: 9,300
SALES (est): 1MM **Privately Held**
SIC: 3442 Screen & storm doors & windows

(G-15602)
ASO CORPORATION (HQ)
300 Sarasota Center Blvd (34240-9381)
PHONE.................................941 378-6600

Yasuhiro Kuki, *President*
Wes Kolodziejczyk, *President*
Shawn O 'brien, *General Mgr*
Erin Jones, *Business Mgr*
Robert Bond, *Vice Pres*
EMP: 30 **EST:** 1986
SALES (est): 46.8MM **Privately Held**
WEB: www.asocorp.com
SIC: 3842 Surgical appliances & supplies

(G-15603)
ASPHERICON INC
2601 Cattlemen Rd Ste 301 (34232-6231)
PHONE.................................941 564-0890
Steffen Schneider, *President*
Sabrina Matthias, *President*
Alexander Wolf Zschaebitz, *Principal*
EMP: 14 **EST:** 2013
SALES (est): 2.5MM
SALES (corp-wide): 18.8MM **Privately Held**
WEB: www.aspherricon.com
SIC: 3827 Optical instruments & lenses
PA: Aspherricon Gmbh
Stockholmer Str. 9
Jena TH 07747
364 131-0050

(G-15604)
ATLANTIC CONCRETE PRODUCTS INC
Also Called: Atlantic Steel Fabricators
1701 Myrtle St (34234-4817)
PHONE.................................941 355-2988
Dan Dallas, *Manager*
EMP: 62
SALES (corp-wide): 28MM **Privately Held**
WEB: www.atlanticconcrete.com
SIC: 3272 Concrete products, precast
PA: Atlantic Concrete Products, Inc.
8900 Old Route 13
Bristol PA 19007
215 945-5600

(G-15605)
ATLANTIC TNG LLC
1701 Myrtle St (34234-4817)
P.O. Box 729 (34230-0729)
PHONE.................................941 355-2988
Kristen Dodd, *Production*
Joe Abraham, *Engineer*
Megan Ditcher, *Mng Member*
EMP: 25 **EST:** 2010
SQ FT: 6,000
SALES (est): 5.9MM **Privately Held**
WEB: www.atlantictng.com
SIC: 3272 Concrete products, precast

(G-15606)
AUTISAN INTERNATIONAL INC
612 Lotus Ln (34242-1210)
PHONE.................................941 349-7029
J J Jackson, *President*
EMP: 5 **EST:** 1996
SQ FT: 4,250
SALES (est): 339.1K **Privately Held**
SIC: 2821 Plastics materials & resins

(G-15607)
AUTOMATED VACUUM SYSTEMS INC
2228b Industrial Blvd (34234-3120)
PHONE.................................941 378-4565
Craig Lubkey, *President*
▲ **EMP:** 9 **EST:** 1997
SQ FT: 12,000
SALES (est): 655K **Privately Held**
WEB: www.avsvacuumsystems.com
SIC: 3559 Optical lens machinery

(G-15608)
BALPACK INCORPORATED
5438 Ashton Ct (34233-3403)
PHONE.................................941 371-7323
Pavel Balcar, *President*
Roman Balcar, *Vice Pres*
Eva Balcar, *Admin Sec*
▲ **EMP:** 8 **EST:** 2002
SQ FT: 1,711
SALES (est): 1.8MM **Privately Held**
WEB: www.balpackinc.com
SIC: 3565 Packaging machinery

(G-15609)
BARI ASSOCIATES INC
1805 Apex Rd (34240-2304)
PHONE.................................941 342-9385
Wolfe Taninbaum, *President*
Sylvia Taninbaum, *Vice Pres*
EMP: 13 **EST:** 1965
SQ FT: 4,000
SALES (est): 297.1K **Privately Held**
SIC: 3931 Reeds for musical instruments

(G-15610)
BASECRETE TECHNOLOGIES LLC
8255 Consumer Ct (34240-7862)
PHONE.................................941 312-5142
Kenneth L Pearce, *Sales Staff*
Vito Mariano, *Mng Member*
Kenneth Pearce,
EMP: 18 **EST:** 2015
SALES (est): 2.7MM **Privately Held**
WEB: www.basecreteusa.com
SIC: 3241 Cement, hydraulic

(G-15611)
BELVOIR PUBLICATIONS INC
Also Called: Belvoir Media Group
7820 Holiday Dr (34231-5316)
PHONE.................................941 929-1720
EMP: 74
SALES (corp-wide): 49.9MM **Privately Held**
WEB: www.belvoir.com
SIC: 2731 Book publishing
PA: Belvoir Publications, Inc.
800 Connecticut Ave 4w02
Norwalk CT 06854
203 857-3100

(G-15612)
BLUM & COMPANY INC
5531 Cannes Cir Apt 503 (34231-4082)
PHONE.................................941 922-3239
Carolyn Blum, *Principal*
EMP: 7 **EST:** 2010
SALES (est): 69.2K **Privately Held**
WEB: www.blum.com
SIC: 3577 Computer peripheral equipment

(G-15613)
BLUTEC GLASS FABRICATION LLC
5342 Clark Rd Unit 125 (34233-3227)
PHONE.................................941 232-1600
Robert J Guzzo,
James Guzzo,
EMP: 8 **EST:** 2016
SALES (est): 427.1K **Privately Held**
WEB: www.blutecglass.com
SIC: 2295 5231 Varnished glass & coated fiberglass fabrics; glass

(G-15614)
BOWMAN ANALYTICS INC
5824 Bee Ridge Rd (34233-5065)
PHONE.................................847 781-3523
EMP: 7 **EST:** 2019
SALES (est): 1.1MM **Privately Held**
SIC: 3826 Analytical instruments

(G-15615)
BRESEE WOODWORK INC
Also Called: Elite Woodwork
1795 Desoto Rd (34234-3066)
PHONE.................................941 355-2591
Marc Bresee, *President*
Debbie Bresee, *Treasurer*
EMP: 12 **EST:** 1997
SALES (est): 2.7MM **Privately Held**
WEB: www.elitewood.net
SIC: 2434 1751 Wood kitchen cabinets; carpentry work

(G-15616)
BRETON USA CUSTOMERS SVC CORP
1753 Northgate Blvd (34234-2138)
PHONE.................................941 360-2700
Dario Toncelli, *President*
Kimberly Balychev, *General Mgr*
Magdalena Picardi, *General Mgr*
Gianrico Filippetto, *Vice Pres*
Lorenzo Del Mutolo, *Treasurer*
▲ **EMP:** 15 **EST:** 2004

SALES (est): 3MM **Privately Held**
SIC: 3441 3281 Fabricated structural metal; dimension stone for buildings

(G-15617)
BRONZART FOUNDRY INC
5415 Ashton Ct Unit H (34233-3454)
PHONE.................................941 922-9106
Richard A Frignoca, *President*
Tamzen M Frignoca, *Corp Secy*
▼ **EMP:** 10 **EST:** 1979
SQ FT: 3,500
SALES (est): 1MM **Privately Held**
WEB: www.bronzartfoundry.com
SIC: 3366 Castings (except die): bronze

(G-15618)
BUFFALO WHEELCHAIR INC
4130 S Tamiami Trl (34231-3608)
PHONE.................................941 921-6331
James C Travis, *President*
EMP: 7 **EST:** 2018
SALES (est): 118.9K **Privately Held**
WEB: www.buffalowheelchair.com
SIC: 3842 Wheelchairs

(G-15619)
BUILDERS DOOR AND SUPPLY INC
2022 12th St (34237-2702)
PHONE.................................941 955-2311
David A Johnson, *President*
Coleen Johnson, *Vice Pres*
EMP: 15 **EST:** 1991
SALES (est): 1MM **Privately Held**
WEB: www.buildersdoorandsupply.com
SIC: 2431 5031 3442 Doors, wood; millwork; metal doors, sash & trim

(G-15620)
BULLETIN NET INC
6000 S Tamiami Trl (34231-3950)
PHONE.................................941 468-2569
Bruce Herbert, *President*
EMP: 11 **EST:** 1995
SALES (est): 250.9K **Privately Held**
SIC: 2711 Newspapers, publishing & printing

(G-15621)
BUSHWACKER SPIRITS LLC
3135 Southgate Cir (34239-5515)
PHONE.................................941 200-0818
Carter Echols,
EMP: 10 **EST:** 2020
SALES (est): 1.9MM **Privately Held**
WEB: www.bushwackerspirits.com
SIC: 2085 Distilled & blended liquors

(G-15622)
BYERLY CUSTOM DESIGN INC
743 Gantt Ave (34232-6703)
PHONE.................................941 371-7498
Carl Byerly, *President*
Christopher Byerly, *Vice Pres*
Pam Byerly, *Admin Sec*
EMP: 5 **EST:** 1984
SQ FT: 5,000
SALES (est): 763.7K **Privately Held**
SIC: 2434 Wood kitchen cabinets

(G-15623)
CABINETS BY WFC INC
6092 Clark Center Ave (34238-2716)
PHONE.................................941 355-2703
David L Koffman, *President*
Jeffrey Bloch, *Vice Pres*
Christopher Dowling, *Vice Pres*
Jeffrey P Koffman, *Vice Pres*
Michael R O'Connor, *Vice Pres*
EMP: 10 **EST:** 2017
SALES (est): 232.1K **Privately Held**
SIC: 2434 Wood kitchen cabinets

(G-15624)
CABINETS EXTRAORDINAIRE INC (PA)
7350 S Tamiami Trl (34231-7004)
P.O. Box 21297 (34276-4297)
PHONE.................................941 961-8453
EMP: 7 **EST:** 2018
SALES (est): 226.3K **Privately Held**
WEB: www.cabinetsextra.com
SIC: 2434 Wood kitchen cabinets

(G-15625)
CAE HEALTHCARE INC (DH)
6300 Edgelake Dr (34240-8817)
PHONE.................................941 377-5562
Marc Parent, *CEO*
Michael Bernstein, *President*
Jay Anton, *Vice Pres*
Ray Shuford, *Vice Pres*
Thomas E Whytas, *CFO*
EMP: 27 **EST:** 1994
SQ FT: 76,000
SALES (est): 55.4MM
SALES (corp-wide): 2.6B **Privately Held**
WEB: www.caehealthcare.com
SIC: 3841 Surgical instruments & apparatus
HQ: Cae Healthcare Canada Inc.
8585 Ch De La Cote-De-Liesse
Saint-Laurent QC H4T 1
514 341-6780

(G-15626)
CAE HEALTHCARE USA INC
6300 Edgelake Dr (34240-8817)
PHONE.................................941 377-5562
Marc Parent, *President*
Guillaume Herve, *Vice Pres*
▲ **EMP:** 48 **EST:** 2010
SALES (est): 6.1MM
SALES (corp-wide): 2.6B **Privately Held**
WEB: www.caehealthcare.com
SIC: 3699 Flight simulators (training aids), electronic
PA: Cae Inc
8585 Ch De La Cote-De-Liesse
Saint-Laurent QC H4T 1
514 341-6780

(G-15627)
CAMPHOR TECHNOLOGIES INC
1584 Independence Blvd (34234-2101)
PHONE.................................941 360-0025
Michael Anthony Creaturo, *President*
Steve Reynolds, *Branch Mgr*
▲ **EMP:** 16 **EST:** 1999
SQ FT: 17,000
SALES (est): 2.5MM **Privately Held**
WEB: www.camphortech.com
SIC: 2834 5122 Pharmaceutical preparations; pharmaceuticals

(G-15628)
CAMPUS PUBLICATIONS INC
2975 Bee Ridge Rd Ste D (34239-7100)
PHONE.................................941 780-1326
Carol Moore, *President*
EMP: 8 **EST:** 1999
SQ FT: 800
SALES (est): 685.9K **Privately Held**
WEB: www.campuspublicationsinc.com
SIC: 2741 Miscellaneous publishing

(G-15629)
CANVAS WEST INC
1470 12th St (34236-3313)
PHONE.................................941 355-0780
Michael W Town, *President*
Micheal Town, *Owner*
EMP: 6 **EST:** 1990
SQ FT: 1,500
SALES (est): 493.5K **Privately Held**
SIC: 2394 5999 Canvas & related products; canvas products

(G-15630)
CEMEX CNSTR MTLS FLA LLC
Also Called: Sarasota Cattlemen Rm
622 Cattlemen Rd (34232-6317)
PHONE.................................800 992-3639
Richard A Buckelew, *Branch Mgr*
EMP: 14 **Privately Held**
SIC: 3272 Concrete products, precast
HQ: Cemex Construction Materials Florida, Llc
1501 Belvedere Rd
West Palm Beach FL 33406

(G-15631)
CHELTEC INC
2215 Industrial Blvd (34234-3119)
PHONE.................................941 355-1045
Denise Delancy, *President*
Tom O'Neill, *Vice Pres*
EMP: 7 **EST:** 1996
SQ FT: 9,600

SALES (est): 1.2MM **Privately Held**
WEB: www.cheltec.com
SIC: 2819 Chemicals, high purity: refined from technical grade

(G-15632)
CHOICE TOOL & MOLD LLC
901 Sarasota Center Blvd (34240-7816)
PHONE.................................941 371-6767
James C Westman,
EMP: 19 **EST:** 1996
SALES (est): 2.7MM **Privately Held**
SIC: 3089 Injection molding of plastics
PA: Octex Holdings, Llc
901 Sarasota Center Blvd
Sarasota FL 34240

(G-15633)
CJB INDUSTRIES INC
23 N Blvd Of Presidents (34236-1304)
PHONE.................................941 552-8397
Shaun Douglas, *Principal*
EMP: 10 **EST:** 2012
SALES (est): 287.4K **Privately Held**
WEB: www.cjbindustries.com
SIC: 2899 Chemical preparations

(G-15634)
CLOUD INDUSTRIES
8275 Shadow Pine Way (34238-5619)
PHONE.................................816 213-2730
Paul Shoemaker, *Principal*
EMP: 9 **EST:** 2017
SALES (est): 882.3K **Privately Held**
WEB: www.cloudindustries.com
SIC: 3999 Manufacturing industries

(G-15635)
COASTAL PRINTING INC SARASOTA
4391 Independence Ct (34234-2155)
PHONE.................................941 351-1515
Alan Guttridge, *CEO*
Alan R Guttridge Jr, *President*
Terry Rayner, *COO*
Janet T Guttridge, *Vice Pres*
Andrew Keighley, *Vice Pres*
EMP: 49 **EST:** 1979
SALES (est): 6.2MM **Privately Held**
WEB: www.coastalprint.com
SIC: 2752 2796 2791 Lithographing on metal; platemaking services; typesetting

(G-15636)
COCA-COLA BEVERAGES FLA LLC
2150 47th St (34234-3111)
PHONE.................................941 953-3151
Nathan Gadow, *Manager*
EMP: 9
SALES (corp-wide): 366.5MM **Privately Held**
WEB: www.cocacolaflorida.com
SIC: 2086 5149 Bottled & canned soft drinks; soft drinks
PA: Coca-Cola Beverages Florida, Llc
10117 Princess Palm Ave
Tampa FL 33610
800 438-2653

(G-15637)
COMDIAL REAL ESTATE CO INC
106 Cattlemen Rd (34232-6307)
PHONE.................................941 564-9208
EMP: 3 **EST:** 2006
SALES (est): 3.2MM
SALES (corp-wide): 40MM **Privately Held**
SIC: 3661 Telephones & telephone apparatus
PA: Vertical Communications, Inc.
1000 Holcomb Woods Pkwy # 415
Roswell GA 30076
877 837-8422

(G-15638)
COMMERCIAL INSULATING GLASS CO (PA)
Also Called: C I G
6200 Porter Rd (34240-9696)
PHONE.................................941 378-9100
Jeffery A Winsler, *President*
Rafael Molina, *Plant Mgr*
Frankie Sheppard, *Plant Mgr*
Rebecca Alder, *Buyer*

Mike Estes, *Natl Sales Mgr*
▲ **EMP:** 41 **EST:** 1990
SALES (est): 11.1MM **Privately Held**
WEB: www.cigglass.com
SIC: 3211 3231 Insulating glass, sealed units; products of purchased glass

(G-15639)
COMMERCIAL RFRG DOOR CO INC
Also Called: Styleline Doors
6200 Porter Rd (34240-9696)
PHONE.................................941 371-8110
Jeffrey Winsler, *President*
Rob Winsler, *Vice Pres*
Linda Gabriel, *Controller*
Richard Underwood, *Sales Mgr*
Brian Gill, *Maintence Staff*
EMP: 8 **EST:** 1975
SQ FT: 68,759
SALES (est): 3.9MM **Privately Held**
WEB: www.stylelinedoors.com
SIC: 3442 3231 Metal doors; products of purchased glass

(G-15640)
CONEXUS TECHNOLOGIES INC
1145 Horizon View Dr (34242-3848)
PHONE.................................513 779-5448
▲ **EMP:** 15
SQ FT: 1,200
SALES (est): 3MM **Privately Held**
SIC: 2298 Mfg Cordage/Twine

(G-15641)
CONNECTPRESS LTD
2015 S Tuttle Ave Ste A (34239-4150)
P.O. Box 1418 (34230-1418)
PHONE.................................505 629-0695
Daniel Raker, *President*
EMP: 7 **EST:** 2016
SALES (est): 205.1K **Privately Held**
WEB: www.connectpress.com
SIC: 2741 Miscellaneous publishing

(G-15642)
COOK SPRING CO
233 Sarasota Center Blvd (34240-9380)
PHONE.................................941 377-5766
Randall A Cook, *President*
◆ **EMP:** 75 **EST:** 1954
SQ FT: 90,000
SALES (est): 9.5MM **Privately Held**
WEB: www.cookspring.com
SIC: 3495 Wire springs

(G-15643)
COURTNEY ALLEN ENTERPRISES LLC
1236 16th St (34236-2516)
PHONE.................................571 314-4290
Courtney Allen,
EMP: 10
SALES (est): 413.1K **Privately Held**
SIC: 3537 7389 Trucks: freight, baggage, etc.: industrial, except mining;

(G-15644)
CREATIVE TECH SARASOTA INC
5959 Palmer Blvd (34232-2841)
PHONE.................................941 371-2743
Thomas W Turner, *President*
Michael A Turner, *Corp Secy*
Kenneth Turner, *Vice Pres*
EMP: 13 **EST:** 1969
SQ FT: 12,500
SALES (est): 979.7K **Privately Held**
WEB: www.creative-technology.com
SIC: 2731 2732 Books: publishing & printing; book printing

(G-15645)
CROP LLC
2320 Gulf Gate Dr (34231-5608)
PHONE.................................941 923-8640
Karen L Odierna, *Principal*
EMP: 16 **EST:** 2014
SALES (est): 3.5MM **Privately Held**
WEB: www.cropjuice.com
SIC: 2037 Frozen fruits & vegetables

(G-15646)
CSO SYSTEMS INC
4139 N Washington Blvd (34234-4840)
PHONE.................................941 355-5653

Larry Cavalluzi, *President*
Alina Duncan, *Bookkeeper*
EMP: 16 **EST:** 2000
SQ FT: 100,000
SALES (est): 1.2MM **Privately Held**
SIC: 3993 Signs & advertising specialties

(G-15647)
CUSTOM CABINETS INC
7350 Deer Crossing Ct (34240-7411)
PHONE.................................941 366-0428
Cloyd E Ridenour, *President*
Josh Ridenour, *Vice Pres*
Kathryn Ridenour, *Admin Sec*
EMP: 10 **EST:** 1972
SALES (est): 757.8K **Privately Held**
SIC: 2434 2511 5712 2541 Wood kitchen cabinets; wood household furniture; furniture stores; wood partitions & fixtures

(G-15648)
CUSTOM CLORS POWDERCOATING INC
1930 21st St (34234-7517)
PHONE.................................941 953-7997
Lynn J King, *President*
Tom Parise, *Vice Pres*
EMP: 5 **EST:** 1992
SQ FT: 5,000
SALES (est): 719.6K **Privately Held**
WEB: www.customcolorspowdercoating.com
SIC: 3479 Coating of metals & formed products

(G-15649)
D & R PRINTING LLC
6569 Tarawa Dr (34241-5645)
PHONE.................................941 378-3311
Lori Benvenuto,
EMP: 7 **EST:** 2013
SALES (est): 186.5K **Privately Held**
SIC: 2752 Commercial printing, offset

(G-15650)
DART CONTAINER CORP FLORIDA
Logistical Management
1952 Field Rd Ste B3 (34231-2315)
PHONE.................................941 358-1202
William R Dart, *President*
Kirk Harnish, *Plant Mgr*
Ted Esteves, *Manager*
Marc Mardini, *Manager*
Andrea Correa, *Assistant*
EMP: 23
SALES (corp-wide): 56.1MM **Privately Held**
WEB: www.dartcontainer.com
SIC: 3086 Plastics foam products
PA: Dart Container Corporation Of Florida
500 Hogsback Rd
Mason MI 48854
800 248-5960

(G-15651)
DAYTON INDUSTRIAL CORPORATION
2237 Industrial Blvd (34234-3119)
PHONE.................................941 351-4454
Fax: 941 351-6081
EMP: 5
SQ FT: 2,500
SALES (est): 450K **Privately Held**
SIC: 3663 5065 Mfg Radio Receivers

(G-15652)
DCWFAB LLC
3374 Howell Pl (34232-2317)
PHONE.................................941 320-6095
Daniel Chilton, *Owner*
EMP: 7 **EST:** 2015
SALES (est): 1.2MM **Privately Held**
WEB: www.dcwfab.com
SIC: 7692 Welding repair

(G-15653)
DDI SYSTEM LLC (PA)
1900 Main St (34236-5991)
PHONE.................................203 364-1200
Adam Waller, *CEO*
Michael Van Pelt, *Vice Pres*
Alaina Shneiderovsky, *Project Mgr*
Eric Shoykhetbrod, *Project Mgr*
Alex Esposito, *Business Anlyst*

EMP: 45 EST: 1996
SQ FT: 4,000
SALES (est): 14.2MM Privately Held
WEB: www.ddisystem.com
SIC: 7372 Prepackaged software

(G-15654)
DEFENDER SCREENS INTL LLC
Also Called: Progressive Screens
7839 Fruitville Rd (34240-9280)
PHONE.................................866 802-0400
Arthur James, President
EMP: 50 EST: 2014
SQ FT: 10,000
SALES (est): 7.7MM Privately Held
WEB: www.progressivescreens.com
SIC: 3442 Screen & storm doors & windows

(G-15655)
DELACOM DETECTION SYSTEMS LLC
7463 Roxye Ln (34240-7815)
P.O. Box 50005 (34232-0300)
PHONE.................................941 544-6636
Dennis Akers, CEO
EMP: 8 EST: 2008
SALES (est): 627.4K Privately Held
SIC: 1389 Detection & analysis service, gas

(G-15656)
DESCO
1832 Bayonne St (34231-7702)
PHONE.................................941 284-1160
Donald E Smith, Principal
EMP: 8 EST: 2010
SALES (est): 162.4K Privately Held
SIC: 3999 Manufacturing industries

(G-15657)
DESCO MANUFACTURING INC
4561 Samuel St (34233-3482)
P.O. Box 21448 (34276-4448)
PHONE.................................941 925-7029
Scott McCloud, President
Ruth Sistrunk, Sales Executive
EMP: 12 EST: 1988
SQ FT: 23,000
SALES (est): 1.2MM Privately Held
WEB: www.descospray.com
SIC: 3563 Spraying & dusting equipment

(G-15658)
DESIGN WORKS BY TECH PDTS INC (DH)
Also Called: N A Whittenburg
4500 Carmichael Ave (34234-2133)
PHONE.................................941 355-2703
Burton I Koffman, Ch of Bd
Charles M Custin, President
Milton Koffman, Vice Pres
Richard E Koffman, Vice Pres
David Melin, Vice Pres
◆ EMP: 20 EST: 1952
SQ FT: 75,000
SALES (est): 28.7MM
SALES (corp-wide): 88.7MM Privately Held
WEB: www.floridadesignworks.com
SIC: 3086 5074 5032 5087 Plastics foam products; plumbing fittings & supplies; tile, clay or other ceramic, excluding refractory; upholsterers' equipment & supplies; pillows, bed: made from purchased materials; windows
HQ: Great American Industries Inc
300 Plaza Dr
Vestal NY 13850
607 729-9331

(G-15659)
DOLPHIN PADDLESPORTS INC
6018 S Tamiami Trl (34231-3950)
PHONE.................................941 924-2785
Mark Goodwin, Principal
EMP: 10 EST: 1989
SALES (est): 611K Privately Held
WEB: www.floridakayak.com
SIC: 2499 Oars & paddles, wood

(G-15660)
DONGILI INVESTMENT GROUP INC
Also Called: Label Tape Systems
5563 Marquesas Cir (34233-3332)
P.O. Box 49407 (34230-6407)
PHONE.................................941 927-3003
Paul Santostasi, President
Rosemarie Santostasi, Vice Pres
Gina Synder, Vice Pres
Lisa Castorina, Admin Sec
EMP: 10 EST: 1986
SQ FT: 3,300
SALES (est): 1.3MM Privately Held
WEB: www.labelandtapesystems.com
SIC: 2754 2759 Labels: gravure printing; labels & seals: printing

(G-15661)
DOUGLAS A FISHER INC
Also Called: Ullman Sails Florida
957 N Lime Ave (34237-3510)
PHONE.................................941 951-0189
Douglas A Fisher, President
EMP: 5 EST: 1986
SQ FT: 6,000
SALES (est): 505.3K Privately Held
SIC: 2394 Sails: made from purchased materials

(G-15662)
DRUM CIRCLE DISTILLING LLC
2212 Industrial Blvd (34234-3120)
PHONE.................................941 358-1900
Troy Roberts, Principal
Nanci Roberts, Senior Mgr
▲ EMP: 10 EST: 2009
SALES (est): 477.3K Privately Held
WEB: www.siestakeyrum.com
SIC: 2085 Distillers' dried grains & solubles & alcohol

(G-15663)
DWA INC (PA)
Also Called: Country Store Interiors
5401 Palmer Blvd (34232-2731)
PHONE.................................941 444-1134
Donald W Atha, President
Bonnie Atha, Corp Secy
EMP: 14 EST: 1966
SQ FT: 4,000
SALES (est): 1.8MM Privately Held
WEB: www.countrystoreinteriors.com
SIC: 2591 2211 5714 2392 Venetian blinds; draperies & drapery fabrics, cotton; draperies; household furnishings; curtains & draperies

(G-15664)
EMC TEST DESIGN LLC
5390 Anthony Ln (34233-2447)
P.O. Box 600532, Newton MA (02460-0005)
PHONE.................................508 292-1833
Roman Litovsky,
EMP: 8 EST: 1992
SALES (est): 213.6K Privately Held
WEB: www.emctd.com
SIC: 3825 Test equipment for electronic & electric measurement

(G-15665)
ENGLISH IRONWORKS INC
1960 21st St (34234-7517)
PHONE.................................941 364-9120
Frank Southern, Owner
Penelope Southern, Co-Owner
EMP: 5 EST: 1993
SQ FT: 4,500
SALES (est): 545.9K Privately Held
WEB: www.englishironworks.com
SIC: 3446 Architectural metalwork

(G-15666)
EPIC EXTRUSION INC
8141 Blaikie Ct Ste 3 (34240-8328)
PHONE.................................941 378-0835
Charles F Gasek, President
Pauline Gasek, Vice Pres
EMP: 8 EST: 1982
SQ FT: 3,000
SALES (est): 591.6K Privately Held
SIC: 3089 Injection molding of plastics

(G-15667)
ESTETIKA SKIN & LASER SPE
1463 Tangier Way (34239-5832)
PHONE.................................262 646-9222
Karl Lickteig, Principal
Jessica Schiller, Nurse
EMP: 7 EST: 2007
SALES (est): 134.4K Privately Held
WEB: www.estetikaskin.com
SIC: 3845 Laser systems & equipment, medical

(G-15668)
EVIES GOLF CENTER
4735 Bee Ridge Rd (34233-1415)
PHONE.................................941 377-2399
Michael Evanoff, Owner
EMP: 8 EST: 1999
SQ FT: 3,000
SALES (est): 700.7K Privately Held
WEB: www.eviesgolf.com
SIC: 3949 Driving ranges, golf, electronic

(G-15669)
FAES SRT INC
7619 Trillium Blvd (34241-5207)
PHONE.................................941 960-6742
EMP: 9 EST: 2017
SALES (est): 245.8K Privately Held
SIC: 3714 Motor vehicle parts & accessories

(G-15670)
FALFAS CABINET & STONE LLC
1705 Cattlemen Rd (34232-6261)
PHONE.................................941 960-2065
Jeff Falfas, Principal
EMP: 13 EST: 2015
SALES (est): 934K Privately Held
WEB: www.falfascabinetsandstone.com
SIC: 2434 Wood kitchen cabinets

(G-15671)
FAN AMERICA INC
2235 6th St (34237-2801)
PHONE.................................941 955-9788
Rainer Blomster, President
▲ EMP: 5 EST: 1989
SQ FT: 10,000
SALES (est): 769.4K Privately Held
WEB: www.fanam.com
SIC: 3564 3634 Blowing fans: industrial or commercial; fans, exhaust & ventilating, electric: household

(G-15672)
FANAM INC
2043 Global Ct (34240-7843)
PHONE.................................941 955-9788
Daniel Selberg, President
Rainer Blomster, President
▲ EMP: 6 EST: 2003
SALES (est): 587.2K Privately Held
WEB: www.fanam.com
SIC: 3564 Blowers & fans

(G-15673)
FINECRAFT CUSTOM CABINETRY
6209 Clarity Ct (34240-9620)
PHONE.................................941 378-1901
Paul Martinelli, President
EMP: 5 EST: 1991
SQ FT: 5,000
SALES (est): 462K Privately Held
WEB: www.finecraftcabinetry.com
SIC: 2434 Wood kitchen cabinets

(G-15674)
FIRE FLY FUELS INC
1550 Global Ct (34240-7860)
PHONE.................................941 404-6820
George P Tyson, President
Tammy Fultz, General Mgr
EMP: 7 EST: 2011
SALES (est): 1.2MM Privately Held
WEB: www.fireflyfuel.com
SIC: 2869 Fuels

(G-15675)
FIRST EDITION DESIGN INC
Also Called: First Edition Design Pubg
5202 Old Ashwood Dr (34233-3483)
PHONE.................................941 921-2607
Deborah Gordon, Principal

Cory Levine, Manager
EMP: 8 EST: 2010
SALES (est): 273.8K Privately Held
WEB:
www.firsteditiondesignpublishing.com
SIC: 2731 7336 Book publishing; commercial art & graphic design

(G-15676)
FLORIDA FAMILY MAGAZINE INC
Also Called: Family Magazines
4851 Hoyer Dr (34241-9222)
PHONE.................................941 922-5437
Mary E Winkle, President
Mary Winkle, President
Beth Winkle, Publisher
Paul Winkle, Vice Pres
EMP: 8 EST: 1996
SALES (est): 692.3K Privately Held
SIC: 2721 Magazines: publishing only, not printed on site

(G-15677)
FLORIDA HERITAGE WDWKG LLC
2237 Industrial Blvd (34234-3119)
PHONE.................................941 705-9980
Brandon Semrinec, Principal
EMP: 5 EST: 2016
SALES (est): 430.8K Privately Held
WEB: www.fhwoodworking.com
SIC: 2431 Millwork

(G-15678)
FLORIDA HOMES MAGAZINE
1900 Main St Ste 312 (34236-5927)
PHONE.................................941 227-7331
Julie R Gibson, President
EMP: 6 EST: 2013
SALES (est): 345.4K Privately Held
WEB: www.floridahomesmag.com
SIC: 2721 Magazines: publishing only, not printed on site

(G-15679)
FLORIDA HOMES MAGAZINE LLC
Also Called: Florida Homes & Lifestyle
2345 Bee Ridge Rd Ste 3 (34239-6249)
PHONE.................................941 549-5960
Jules Gibson, Principal
EMP: 5 EST: 2008
SQ FT: 1,250
SALES (est): 388K Privately Held
SIC: 2711 Commercial printing & newspaper publishing combined

(G-15680)
FLORIDA KNIFE CO
1735 Apex Rd (34240-9386)
PHONE.................................941 371-2104
Thomas P Johanning, President
EMP: 18 EST: 1978
SQ FT: 26,000
SALES (est): 2.8MM Privately Held
WEB: www.florida-knife.com
SIC: 3545 3541 3423 Machine knives, metalworking; machine tools, metal cutting type; hand & edge tools

(G-15681)
FLORIDA TAPE & LABELS INC
5717b Lawton Dr (34233-2492)
PHONE.................................941 921-5788
Peter Hosmer, President
Vicki Hosmer, Corp Secy
EMP: 10 EST: 1968
SQ FT: 7,500
SALES (est): 845.4K Privately Held
SIC: 3069 2759 2752 2672 Tape, pressure sensitive: rubber; labels & seals: printing; commercial printing, lithographic; coated & laminated paper; automotive & apparel trimmings

(G-15682)
FOOTE WOODWORKING INC
8347 Midnight Pass Rd (34242-2703)
PHONE.................................941 923-6553
Steven W Foote, Director
EMP: 10 EST: 2001
SALES (est): 158.7K Privately Held
WEB: www.footewoodworking.com
SIC: 2431 Millwork

(G-15683)
FRZ MARINE
3152 Lena Ln (34240-9767)
PHONE..................................941 322-2631
Frederick Hutchinson, *Principal*
EMP: 7 **EST:** 2005
SALES (est): 188.3K **Privately Held**
SIC: 3531 Marine related equipment

(G-15684)
**FUENTES CUSTOM
WOODWORK LLC**
1490 Blvd Of The Arts (34236-2905)
PHONE..................................941 232-0635
Omar Rodriguez, *Manager*
EMP: 7 **EST:** 2015
SALES (est): 629.4K **Privately Held**
WEB: www.fuentescustomwoodwork.com
SIC: 2431 Millwork

(G-15685)
FUJI INTERNATIONAL LLC
6259 Sturbridge Ct (34238-3700)
PHONE..................................941 961-5472
Kenneth W Wade, *Mng Member*
EMP: 17 **EST:** 2006
SALES (est): 477.1K **Privately Held**
SIC: 3542 Machine tools, metal forming
type
PA: Fuji Machine Works Co., Ltd.
1-14-32, Mitejima, Nishiyodogawa-Ku
Osaka OSK 555-0

(G-15686)
FULL CUT TABS LLC
2153 10th St (34237-3430)
PHONE..................................941 316-1510
EMP: 15 **EST:** 2015
SALES (est): 1MM **Privately Held**
WEB: www.fullcuttabs.com
SIC: 2671 Packaging paper & plastics film,
coated & laminated

(G-15687)
G K WOODWORKS
5365 Matthew Ct (34231-6356)
PHONE..................................941 232-3910
George Karabatsos, *Owner*
EMP: 6 **EST:** 2001
SALES (est): 459.2K **Privately Held**
SIC: 2434 Wood kitchen cabinets

(G-15688)
G PHILLIPS AND SONS LLC
8987 Wildlife Loop (34238-4001)
PHONE..................................248 705-5873
Richard Harding,
Michael Harding,
EMP: 10 **EST:** 2011
SALES (est): 10MM **Privately Held**
WEB: www.gpsagrecycle.com
SIC: 2821 Plastics materials & resins

(G-15689)
GAS LIGHT SERVICES INC
4545 Mariotti Ct Unit L (34233-3433)
PHONE..................................941 232-8668
Allen K Albritton, *Principal*
EMP: 8 **EST:** 2008
SALES (est): 149.2K **Privately Held**
SIC: 3648 Gas lighting fixtures

(G-15690)
**GENERAL MACHINE COMPANY
INC**
5207 Malaga Ave (34235-3422)
PHONE..................................941 756-2815
Richard Wilson, *President*
Betty E Wilson, *Corp Secy*
EMP: 6 **EST:** 1981
SQ FT: 4,200
SALES (est): 429.4K **Privately Held**
SIC: 3599 Machine shop, jobbing & repair

(G-15691)
GENIE CAP INC
Also Called: Nwi
4410 Independence Ct (34234-4727)
PHONE..................................941 355-5730
Neide S Santos, *CEO*
EMP: 14 **EST:** 2012
SALES (est): 329.1K **Privately Held**
WEB: www.guardgenie.com
SIC: 3221 Bottles for packing, bottling &
canning: glass

(G-15692)
GETFPV LLC
1060 Goodrich Ave (34236-4305)
PHONE..................................941 444-0021
Tim Nilson, *President*
Andy Graber, *Vice Pres*
Adam Burzynski, *Controller*
Sean Pontzer, *Sales Staff*
EMP: 22 **EST:** 2017
SALES (est): 3.2MM
SALES (corp-wide): 8.4MM **Privately
Held**
WEB: www.getfpv.com
SIC: 3944 Games, toys & children's vehi-
cles
PA: Lumenier Holdco Llc
1060 Goodrich Ave
Sarasota FL 34236
941 444-0021

(G-15693)
GLOBAL SEVEN INC
1936 Grove St (34239-4510)
PHONE..................................973 664-1900
Jonathan Dean, *Principal*
EMP: 7 **EST:** 2018
SALES (est): 176.9K **Privately Held**
SIC: 2899 Chemical preparations

(G-15694)
**GOLF AGRONOMICS SAND &
HLG INC**
2165 17th St (34234-7653)
PHONE..................................800 626-1359
Richard G Colyer, *President*
Dale L Mitchell, *Vice Pres*
EMP: 7 **EST:** 2000
SALES (est): 1.2MM **Privately Held**
SIC: 3523 Soil preparation machinery, ex-
cept turf & grounds

(G-15695)
**GULF COAST BUSINESS
REVIEW**
650 Central Ave Ste 5 (34236-4090)
PHONE..................................941 906-9386
David Beliles, *Chairman*
EMP: 8 **EST:** 1996
SALES (est): 112.9K **Privately Held**
SIC: 2711 Newspapers, publishing & print-
ing

(G-15696)
**GULF COAST SIGNS SARASOTA
INC**
1713 Northgate Blvd (34234-2195)
PHONE..................................941 355-8841
Hidayet L Kutat, *CEO*
Melissa Gross, *Opers Staff*
Bill Eberhart, *Accounts Mgr*
Kathi Johnson, *Supervisor*
Kathi Johnson-Arco, *Admin Asst*
EMP: 30 **EST:** 1975
SQ FT: 15,000
SALES (est): 7MM **Privately Held**
WEB: www.gulfcoastsigns.com
SIC: 3993 Electric signs; displays &
cutouts, window & lobby; letters for signs,
metal; name plates: except engraved,
etched, etc.: metal

(G-15697)
H V PAYNE MFG LLC
164 Cowpen Ln (34240-9704)
PHONE..................................941 773-1112
EMP: 7 **EST:** 2017
SALES (est): 641.5K **Privately Held**
SIC: 3999 Manufacturing industries

(G-15698)
HALIFAX MEDIA GROUP LLC
Also Called: Sarasota Herald Tribune
1777 Main St Ste 200 (34236-5836)
PHONE..................................941 361-4800
Patrick Dorsey, *Publisher*
EMP: 41
SALES (corp-wide): 3.2B **Publicly Held**
WEB: www.gannett.com
SIC: 2711 Newspapers, publishing & print-
ing
HQ: Halifax Media Group, Llc
2339 Beville Rd
Daytona Beach FL 32119
386 265-6700

(G-15699)
HARBOR HOMES
2624 Marlette St (34231-2945)
PHONE..................................941 320-2670
J Brian Bardwick, *Principal*
EMP: 7 **EST:** 2006
SALES (est): 193.7K **Privately Held**
SIC: 2451 Mobile homes, personal or pri-
vate use

(G-15700)
HENSOLDT AVIONICS USA LLC
2480 Fruitville Rd Ste 6 (34237-6204)
PHONE..................................941 306-1328
Joseph Scott, *CEO*
Wesley Osborn, *Engineer*
Herbert Lustig, *Manager*
Triston Hernandez, *Software Engr*
Megan Rich, *Software Dev*
EMP: 7 **EST:** 2008
SQ FT: 4,500
SALES (est): 1MM **Privately Held**
WEB: avionics.hensoldt.net
SIC: 3812 3728 7371 5065 Search &
navigation equipment; aircraft parts &
equipment; computer software develop-
ment & applications; electronic parts &
equipment

(G-15701)
HILTON INTERNATIONAL INDS
6055 Porter Way (34232-6222)
PHONE..................................941 371-2600
Antony Quinn, *President*
Russ Coyle, *Manager*
▲ **EMP:** 22 **EST:** 1958
SQ FT: 11,700
SALES (est): 778.7K **Privately Held**
WEB: www.hiltonind.com
SIC: 3559 3549 Electronic component
making machinery; metalworking machin-
ery

(G-15702)
HOWMEDICA OSTEONICS CORP
Also Called: Striker Orthopedic
8235 Blaikie Ct (34240-8323)
PHONE..................................941 378-4600
Michael Orr, *Sales Associate*
Gianni Dattolico, *Associate*
EMP: 9
SALES (corp-wide): 17.1B **Publicly Held**
SIC: 3842 Surgical appliances & supplies
HQ: Howmedica Osteonics Corp.
325 Corporate Dr
Mahwah NJ 07430
201 831-5000

(G-15703)
I B FURNITURE INC
1236 Porter Rd Unit 4 (34240-9619)
PHONE..................................941 371-5764
Brian Himes, *President*
EMP: 5 **EST:** 1992
SQ FT: 2,500
SALES (est): 414.9K **Privately Held**
WEB: www.corradoknives.com
SIC: 2511 Wood household furniture

(G-15704)
IJKB LLC
502 N Spoonbill Dr (34236-1818)
PHONE..................................941 953-9046
Kenneth B Mooney, *Manager*
EMP: 7 **EST:** 2015
SALES (est): 244K **Privately Held**
SIC: 2211 Gauze

(G-15705)
INFORMA USA INC
101 Paramount Dr Ste 100 (34232-6044)
PHONE..................................561 361-6017
Peter Rigby, *Ch of Bd*
Kenneth B Bohlin, *President*
Christophe Luino, *Managing Dir*
Shabnam Rawal, *Managing Dir*
Patricia Giardina, *Principal*
▲ **EMP:** 825 **EST:** 1987
SQ FT: 32,000
SALES (est): 155.6MM
SALES (corp-wide): 2.4B **Privately Held**
WEB: www.informa.com
SIC: 2731 8742 Pamphlets: publishing
only, not printed on site; business plan-
ning & organizing services

HQ: Informa Group Limited
5 Howick Place
London SW1P

(G-15706)
INTERNATIONAL COMPOSITE
1468 Northgate Blvd (34234-4746)
PHONE..................................206 349-7468
EMP: 5 **EST:** 2016
SALES (est): 454.9K **Privately Held**
WEB: www.ficicomposites.com
SIC: 2821 Plastics materials & resins

(G-15707)
**INTERTAPE POLYMER CORP
(DH)**
Also Called: I P G
100 Paramount Dr Ste 300 (34232-6051)
PHONE..................................888 898-7834
Gregory Yull, *President*
Michael Ladukeqssp, *Business Mgr*
Kris Norberg, *Business Mgr*
Randi Booth, *Senior VP*
Randi Botth, *Senior VP*
▲ **EMP:** 200 **EST:** 1987
SQ FT: 184,000
SALES (est): 509.6MM
SALES (corp-wide): 232MM **Privately
Held**
WEB: www.itape.com
SIC: 2672 Tape, pressure sensitive: made
from purchased materials
HQ: Ipg (Us) Inc.
100 Paramount Dr Ste 300
Sarasota FL 34232
941 727-5788

(G-15708)
IPG (US) HOLDINGS INC (HQ)
Also Called: Intertape Polymer Group
100 Paramount Dr Ste 300 (34232-6051)
PHONE..................................941 727-5788
James Pantelidis, *Ch of Bd*
Jim Bob Carpenter, *President*
Burgess Hildreth, *President*
Gregary Yull, *President*
Randi Booth, *Vice Pres*
◆ **EMP:** 75 **EST:** 1997
SQ FT: 20,000
SALES (est): 571.4MM
SALES (corp-wide): 232MM **Privately
Held**
SIC: 2672 3953 Tape, pressure sensitive:
made from purchased materials; stencils,
painting & marking
PA: Intertape Polymer Group Inc
9999 Boul Cavendish Bureau 200
Saint-Laurent QC H4M 2
514 731-7591

(G-15709)
IPG (US) INC (DH)
100 Paramount Dr Ste 300 (34232-6051)
PHONE..................................941 727-5788
Gregory Yull, *President*
Mary B Thompson, *Vice Pres*
Jeffrey Crystal, *CFO*
Amy Walton, *Human Resources*
EMP: 1 **EST:** 1997
SALES (est): 546.4MM
SALES (corp-wide): 232MM **Privately
Held**
WEB: www.itape.com
SIC: 2672 3953 Tape, pressure sensitive:
made from purchased materials; stencils,
painting & marking
HQ: Ipg (Us) Holdings Inc.
100 Paramount Dr Ste 300
Sarasota FL 34232
941 727-5788

(G-15710)
ITALIAN IDEA SRQ LLC
136 S Pineapple Ave (34236-5727)
PHONE..................................941 330-0525
Christian Delunas, *Mng Member*
EMP: 7 **EST:** 2018
SALES (est): 278.1K **Privately Held**
SIC: 3171 Women's handbags & purses

(G-15711)
J & N STONE INC
6111 Clark Center Ave (34238-2722)
PHONE..................................941 924-6200
EMP: 34

▲ = Import ▼=Export
◆ =Import/Export

SALES (corp-wide): 7.8MM **Privately Held**
SIC: 3272 Mfg Concrete Products
PA: J & N Stone, Inc.
135 Bargain Barn Rd
Davenport FL 33837
863 422-7369

(G-15712)
JAMESTOWN KITCHENS INC
4050 N Washington Blvd (34234-4837)
PHONE..............................941 359-1166
James Gerard, *President*
Brian Higgins, *General Mgr*
EMP: 4 EST: 2009
SQ FT: 3,000
SALES (est): 3MM **Privately Held**
WEB:
www.jamestownkitchenssarasota.com
SIC: 2434 Wood kitchen cabinets

(G-15713)
JDR AND ASSOCIATES INC
5379 Ocean Blvd (34242-3327)
PHONE..............................941 926-1800
Gordon D Hester, *Principal*
EMP: 7 EST: 2017
SALES (est): 156.4K **Privately Held**
SIC: 3089 Injection molding of plastics

(G-15714)
JJ SCREENPRINT LLC
1850 Porter Lake Dr Ste 1 (34240-7802)
PHONE..............................941 587-1801
Jacob E Jock, *Manager*
EMP: 6 EST: 2015
SALES (est): 302.8K **Privately Held**
WEB: www.theorythreads.com
SIC: 2752 Commercial printing, lithographic

(G-15715)
JTE INC
Also Called: Signs By Tomorrow
3959 Sawyer Rd (34233-1218)
PHONE..............................941 925-2605
Tim Eastwood, *President*
Janet Eastwood, *Vice Pres*
EMP: 5 EST: 1991
SALES (est): 432.2K **Privately Held**
SIC: 3993 Signs & advertising specialties

(G-15716)
K & A AUDIO INC
4604 Ashton Rd (34233-3488)
P.O. Box 668, Osprey (34229-0668)
PHONE..............................941 925-7648
Kim Martinelli, *President*
Anthony Milat, *Vice Pres*
EMP: 11 EST: 1995
SALES (est): 899.5K **Privately Held**
WEB: www.kaaudio.com
SIC: 3651 Household audio & video equipment

(G-15717)
KANALFLAKT INC (PA)
1712 Northgate Blvd (34234-2116)
PHONE..............................941 359-3267
Oliver Green, *President*
▲ EMP: 11 EST: 1981
SQ FT: 20,000
SALES (est): 10.7MM **Privately Held**
SIC: 3564 5084 Blowing fans: industrial or commercial; fans, industrial

(G-15718)
KANE-MILLER CORP (PA)
1515 Ringling Blvd # 840 (34236-6781)
PHONE..............................941 346-2003
Stanley B Kane, *CEO*
Harold Oelbaum, *President*
Robert Wininger, *CFO*
Kira Lynn, *Executive*
EMP: 5 EST: 1920
SALES (est): 38.6MM **Privately Held**
WEB: www.kanemillercorp.com
SIC: 2077 Tallow rendering, inedible

(G-15719)
KM PRESS DENTAL CERAMICS LLC
8900 Blind Pass Rd A306 (34242-2905)
PHONE..............................828 299-8500
Kurt D Meinch, *Principal*
EMP: 8 EST: 2015

SALES (est): 114.3K **Privately Held**
SIC: 2741 Miscellaneous publishing

(G-15720)
KOALA TEE INC (USA)
2160 17th St (34234-7654)
PHONE..............................941 954-7700
Jess Manley, *President*
Carmen Manley, *General Mgr*
Barry D Fox, *Vice Pres*
Bert Davis, *Production*
Sheri Hirschberg, *Accounts Mgr*
EMP: 27 EST: 1976
SQ FT: 11,000
SALES (est): 3.1MM **Privately Held**
WEB: www.koalatee.com
SIC: 2759 7336 7389 5199 Screen printing; silk screen design; embroidering of advertising on shirts, etc.; advertising specialties

(G-15721)
KSR PUBLISHING INC
2477 Stickney Point Rd 315b (34231-4022)
PHONE..............................941 388-7050
Kristine S Russell, *President*
Kara Nadeau, *Editor*
Jim Russell, *Sales Mgr*
EMP: 14 EST: 2003
SALES (est): 790.4K **Privately Held**
WEB: www.hpnonline.com
SIC: 2741 Miscellaneous publishing

(G-15722)
LA PERLELLE LLC
17 Fillmore Dr (34236-1425)
PHONE..............................941 388-2458
EMP: 7 EST: 2008
SALES (est): 150K **Privately Held**
WEB: starmandscircle.wordpress.com
SIC: 3423 Jewelers' hand tools

(G-15723)
LEATHER CRAFTSMEN INC (PA)
700 Cocoanut Ave Unit 208 (34236-4997)
PHONE..............................631 752-9000
Howard Schneider, *President*
Joseph Fiore, *Vice Pres*
Dan Hammel, *Sales Staff*
Robert Schneider, *Admin Sec*
Albert Collado, *Technician*
EMP: 70 EST: 1943
SALES (est): 6.9MM **Privately Held**
WEB: www.leathercraftsmen.com
SIC: 2782 Albums

(G-15724)
LEDA PRINTING INC
Also Called: Sir Speedy
3939 S Tamiami Trl (34231-3605)
PHONE..............................941 922-1563
Eileen C Rosenzweig, *President*
Jackie Sanderson, *Vice Pres*
Michael Sanderson, *Admin Sec*
EMP: 25 EST: 1979
SQ FT: 7,500
SALES (est): 4.3MM **Privately Held**
WEB: www.sirspeedy.com
SIC: 2752 2791 2789 2759 Commercial printing, lithographic; typesetting; bookbinding & related work; commercial printing

(G-15725)
LEVELBLOX INC (PA)
6371 Bus Blvd Ste 200 (34240)
PHONE..............................941 907-8822
Gary Macleod, *CEO*
EMP: 1 EST: 2003
SALES (est): 3.9MM **Publicly Held**
WEB: www.levelblox.com
SIC: 7372 Prepackaged software

(G-15726)
LOCATION 3 HOLDINGS LLC
Also Called: Cabinets Extraordinaire
5686 Fruitville Rd (34232-6407)
PHONE..............................941 342-3443
Tracy Cotterill, *Vice Pres*
Dawn Hlasnick, *Human Resources*
Jason L Cotterill, *Mng Member*
Joseph Menna, *Sr Project Mgr*
Dianna Graham, *Manager*
EMP: 12 EST: 2013
SQ FT: 2,300

SALES (est): 15.3MM **Privately Held**
WEB: www.cabinetsextra.com
SIC: 2499 5211 5722 Kitchen, bathroom & household ware: wood; bathroom fixtures, equipment & supplies; kitchens, complete (sinks, cabinets, etc.)
PA: Location 3 Pty Ltd
Shop 3 221 Brisbane Road
Biggera Waters QLD 4216

(G-15727)
LOTUS STRESS RELIEF LLC
2965 Bee Ridge Rd (34239-7194)
PHONE..............................941 706-2778
Marcia W Schulte, *Principal*
Marcia Schulte, *Marketing Staff*
Marciaw Schulte, *Marketing Staff*
EMP: 10 EST: 2008
SALES (est): 3.1MM **Privately Held**
WEB: www.lotusstressrelief.com
SIC: 2833 Medicinals & botanicals

(G-15728)
LUMENIER HOLDCO LLC (PA)
1060 Goodrich Ave (34236-4305)
PHONE..............................941 444-0021
Tim Nilson, *President*
Andy Graber, *Vice Pres*
EMP: 1 EST: 2017
SALES (est): 8.4MM **Privately Held**
WEB: www.getfpv.com
SIC: 3944 3721 Games, toys & children's vehicles; motorized aircraft

(G-15729)
LUMENIER LLC
1060 Goodrich Ave (34236-4305)
PHONE..............................941 444-0021
Tim Nilson, *President*
Andy Graber, *Vice Pres*
EMP: 14 EST: 2017
SALES (est): 4MM
SALES (corp-wide): 8.4MM **Privately Held**
WEB: www.lumenier.com
SIC: 3721 Motorized aircraft
PA: Lumenier Holdco Llc
1060 Goodrich Ave
Sarasota FL 34236
941 444-0021

(G-15730)
LUXE PRINTS LLC
329 Central Ave (34236-4915)
PHONE..............................941 484-4500
EMP: 7 EST: 2020
SALES (est): 527.7K **Privately Held**
WEB: www.artisticphotocanvas.com
SIC: 2752 Commercial printing, lithographic

(G-15731)
M3 BIOPHARMA INC
5437 Manchini St (34238-2153)
PHONE..............................858 603-8296
Matthew Pino, *Administration*
EMP: 7 EST: 2015
SALES (est): 159K **Privately Held**
SIC: 2834 Pharmaceutical preparations

(G-15732)
MAD AT SAD LLC
Also Called: Kombucha 221b.c.
4050 Middle Ave (34234-2111)
PHONE..............................941 203-8854
Jen Seidel, *Sales Staff*
Eric Lundquist, *Mng Member*
Anthony Rechul, *Director*
EMP: 14 EST: 2013
SALES (est): 2.2MM **Privately Held**
WEB: www.kombucha221bc.com
SIC: 2099 Tea blending

(G-15733)
MAGNOLIA CUSTOM CABINETRY LLC
1830 S Osprey Ave Ste 107 (34239-3615)
PHONE..............................941 906-8744
Ryan Abel, *Principal*
EMP: 10 EST: 2015
SALES (est): 369.8K **Privately Held**
WEB: www.magnoliasrq.com
SIC: 2434 Wood kitchen cabinets

(G-15734)
MAINSTREAM FIBER NETWORKS
5124 Redbriar Ct (34238-4322)
PHONE..............................941 807-6100
J Terry Drury, *CEO*
EMP: 6 EST: 2005
SALES (est): 602.9K **Privately Held**
WEB: www.msfiber.net
SIC: 2655 Fiber cans, drums & similar products

(G-15735)
MAKI PRINTING LLC
1173 Palmer Wood Ct (34236-2635)
PHONE..............................941 809-7574
EMP: 16
SALES (corp-wide): 232.2K **Privately Held**
SIC: 2752 Commercial printing, lithographic
PA: Maki Printing, Llc
4130 Boca Pointe Dr
Sarasota FL 34238
941 925-4802

(G-15736)
MAKI PRINTING LLC (PA)
Also Called: Benchmark Blueprinting
4130 Boca Pointe Dr (34238-5572)
PHONE..............................941 925-4802
Raymond Hautamaki, *Principal*
EMP: 8 EST: 2018
SALES (est): 232.2K **Privately Held**
SIC: 2752 Commercial printing, lithographic

(G-15737)
MANASOTA OPTICS INC
Also Called: Moi
1743 Northgate Blvd (34234-2138)
PHONE..............................941 359-1748
Jonah Lowery, *President*
David A Lowery, *Admin Sec*
EMP: 9 EST: 1994
SQ FT: 5,000
SALES (est): 1.3MM **Privately Held**
WEB: www.manasotaoptics.com
SIC: 3827 Optical instruments & apparatus; mirrors, optical

(G-15738)
MANASOTA PALLETS INC
7952 Fruitville Rd (34240-8829)
PHONE..............................941 360-0562
Bryan Sehkay, *Owner*
EMP: 13 EST: 2001
SALES (est): 476.3K **Privately Held**
SIC: 2448 Pallets, wood

(G-15739)
MANTIS SECURITY CORPORATION
1990 Main St Ste 770 (34236-8000)
PHONE..............................571 418-3665
Jeff Afflerbach, *CEO*
Jon Benedict, *Vice Pres*
EMP: 28 EST: 2015
SALES (est): 6.3MM **Privately Held**
WEB: www.mantissecurity.com
SIC: 7372 8748 7373 Application computer software; systems engineering consultant, ex. computer or professional; computer integrated systems design

(G-15740)
MARBELITE INTERNATIONAL CORP
1500 Global Ct (34240-7860)
PHONE..............................941 378-0860
Sam Contrasto, *President*
Marsha Contrasto, *Corp Secy*
▼ EMP: 7 EST: 1992
SQ FT: 16,000
SALES (est): 1.5MM **Privately Held**
WEB: www.marbelite.com
SIC: 2952 5072 Coating compounds, tar; hand tools

(G-15741)
MARCHANT MACHINE CORPORATION
Also Called: Manufcturers Metal Forming Mch
8713 Amaretto Ave (34238-4501)
P.O. Box 138, Beltsville MD (20704-0138)
PHONE.................................301 937-4481
Daryl C Marchant, *President*
Don A Marchant, *Treasurer*
Lois Marchant, *Admin Sec*
EMP: 7 **EST:** 1953
SALES (est): 545.4K **Privately Held**
WEB: www.marchantmachine.com
SIC: 3549 Metalworking machinery

(G-15742)
MDC ENGINEERING INC (PA)
Also Called: Packaging Machines
1701 Desoto Rd (34234-3066)
PHONE.................................941 358-0610
Michelle Bergeron, *President*
Jon Ford, *CFO*
Jim Lyons, *Sales Staff*
▲ **EMP:** 8 **EST:** 2002
SQ FT: 15,000
SALES (est): 3.2MM **Privately Held**
WEB: www.rndautomation.com
SIC: 3565 Vacuum packaging machinery

(G-15743)
MERCANTILE TWO
28 S Blvd Of Presidents (34236-1424)
PHONE.................................941 388-0059
Lauren Pritchard, *Director*
EMP: 8 **EST:** 2016
SALES (est): 226.9K **Privately Held**
SIC: 2721 Magazines: publishing only, not printed on site

(G-15744)
METAL CREATIONS SARASOTA LLC
1985 Cattlemen Rd Unit F (34232-6258)
PHONE.................................941 922-7096
Ramiro Corona,
EMP: 11 **EST:** 2014
SALES (est): 1.1MM **Privately Held**
WEB: www.metalcreationsofsarasota.com
SIC: 3499 3446 1799 7389 Fire- or burglary-resistive products; architectural metalwork; ornamental metal work; design services; sheet metalwork

(G-15745)
MICTRON INC
8130 Fruitville Rd (34240-5204)
PHONE.................................941 371-6564
Myron Weinstein, *President*
Ron Smith, *Corp Secy*
Rolf Kopp, *Vice Pres*
EMP: 23 **EST:** 1962
SQ FT: 20,140
SALES (est): 4.2MM **Privately Held**
WEB: www.mictron.net
SIC: 3599 Machine shop, jobbing & repair

(G-15746)
MIDNITE SON II OF SARASOTA
Also Called: John Measel Cabinets
1257 Porter Rd (34240-9627)
PHONE.................................941 377-6029
John Measel, *President*
EMP: 9 **EST:** 1983
SQ FT: 6,000
SALES (est): 728.4K **Privately Held**
SIC: 2434 Wood kitchen cabinets

(G-15747)
MILES PARTNERSHIP II LLC (PA)
Also Called: See Magazines
6751 Prof Pkwy W Ste 200 (34240)
PHONE.................................941 342-2300
Roger W Miles, *CEO*
David Burgess, *President*
Lauren Bourgoing, *Vice Pres*
Nate Huff, *Vice Pres*
Ryan Thompson, *Vice Pres*
▲ **EMP:** 120 **EST:** 1954
SQ FT: 15,364
SALES (est): 24.7MM **Privately Held**
WEB: www.milespartnership.com
SIC: 2721 Magazines: publishing only, not printed on site; statistical reports (periodicals): publishing only

(G-15748)
MILLER BROTHERS CONTRACTORS
Also Called: Septic Tank Drain Fld/Nsite Sw
990 Cattlemen Rd (34232-2810)
PHONE.................................941 371-4162
Albert E Miller Jr, *President*
Roger Miller, *Principal*
EMP: 10 **EST:** 1968
SQ FT: 1,500
SALES (est): 2.1MM **Privately Held**
WEB: s399930105.initial-website.com
SIC: 3272 Septic tanks, concrete; septic tank cleaning service; septic system construction

(G-15749)
MKM SARASOTA LLC
2363 Industrial Blvd (34234-3121)
PHONE.................................941 358-0383
Raymond Gibson, *President*
Mark Nightingale, *Director*
Marty Myers, *Executive*
EMP: 30 **EST:** 2015
SQ FT: 18,000
SALES (est): 3MM **Privately Held**
WEB: www.mkmsarasotallc.com
SIC: 3451 3599 Screw machine products; machine shop, jobbing & repair

(G-15750)
MODERN SETTINGS LLC
6331 Porter Rd Unit 8 (34240-9701)
PHONE.................................800 645-5585
Harry Bender, *Mng Member*
Charles Binder,
EMP: 7 **EST:** 1951
SQ FT: 22,000
SALES (est): 500.2K **Privately Held**
WEB: www.modernsettings.com
SIC: 3915 Jewelers' findings & materials

(G-15751)
MORNING STAR OF SARASOTA INC
Also Called: Graber Cabinets
1985 Cattlemen Rd Unit A (34232-6258)
PHONE.................................941 371-0392
Todd Schleicher, *President*
Patricia Schleicher, *Corp Secy*
EMP: 9 **EST:** 1969
SQ FT: 7,000
SALES (est): 738.8K **Privately Held**
WEB: www.grabercabinets.com
SIC: 2522 2519 2541 2434 Office chairs, benches & stools, except wood; lawn & garden furniture, except wood & metal; wood partitions & fixtures; wood kitchen cabinets

(G-15752)
MR ALEX PAVERS CORP
4010 Deberry Dr (34233-1229)
PHONE.................................941 726-7273
Alessanco Silva, *Principal*
EMP: 7 **EST:** 2010
SALES (est): 87.1K **Privately Held**
SIC: 3531 Pavers

(G-15753)
MR BONES STUMP GRINDING
5590 Swift Rd (34231-6210)
P.O. Box 19115 (34276-2115)
PHONE.................................941 927-0790
Troy Zengel, *Principal*
EMP: 10 **EST:** 2001
SALES (est): 655.3K **Privately Held**
SIC: 3599 Grinding castings for the trade

(G-15754)
MUMFORD MICRO MCH WORKS LLC
1882 Porter Lake Dr # 103 (34240-7808)
PHONE.................................814 720-7291
Jeremy Mumford, *General Mgr*
EMP: 8 **EST:** 2017
SALES (est): 448.4K **Privately Held**
WEB: www.precisionmicromachine.com
SIC: 3999 Manufacturing industries

(G-15755)
MURSE PROPERTIES LLC
6650 S Tammy Amy Trl (34231)
PHONE.................................941 966-3380
John Murse, *President*

Lucy Murse, *Vice Pres*
EMP: 8 **EST:** 1987
SQ FT: 20,214
SALES (est): 137.6K **Privately Held**
SIC: 2273 5713 Carpets & rugs; rugs

(G-15756)
NATURAL STONE SLTONS FNEST SRS (PA)
2303 17th St (34234-1902)
PHONE.................................941 954-1100
Doris Fox, *Mng Member*
EMP: 21 **EST:** 2010
SALES (est): 3.4MM **Privately Held**
WEB: www.sarasotanss.com
SIC: 3281 1799 Granite, cut & shaped; counter top installation

(G-15757)
NATURES BIOSCIENCE LLC
5020 Clark Rd (34233-3231)
PHONE.................................800 570-7450
EMP: 5 **EST:** 2017
SALES (est): 570.6K **Privately Held**
WEB: www.naturesbioscience.com
SIC: 2834 Pharmaceutical preparations

(G-15758)
NATURES OWN PEST CONTROL INC
1899 Porter Lake Dr # 103 (34240-7897)
PHONE.................................941 378-3334
Mark Studtmann, *President*
Travis Wellbrock, *Vice Pres*
Ida D'Eptorre, *Manager*
EMP: 6 **EST:** 1984
SALES (est): 434.1K **Privately Held**
SIC: 2879 7342 Insecticides & pesticides; pest control services

(G-15759)
NC IV INC
Also Called: NC II
10687 Fruitville Rd (34240-9290)
PHONE.................................941 378-9133
Robert Price, *President*
Mary Price, *Vice Pres*
Michael Hancock, *Accounts Mgr*
◆ **EMP:** 10 **EST:** 1992
SALES (est): 2.3MM **Privately Held**
SIC: 3663 Cable television equipment

(G-15760)
NEAT PRINT INC
Also Called: Divine Coffee Roasters
2147 Porter Lake Dr Ste G (34240-8854)
PHONE.................................941 545-1517
Raca Dejan, *Principal*
EMP: 9 **EST:** 2011
SALES (est): 930.7K **Privately Held**
WEB: www.neatprint.com
SIC: 2752 Commercial printing, lithographic

(G-15761)
NEVER WRONG TOYS & GAMES LLC
2201 Cantu Ct Ste 100 (34232-6254)
PHONE.................................941 371-0909
Eva Wong, *Mng Member*
EMP: 7 **EST:** 2020
SALES (est): 486.5K **Privately Held**
WEB: www.neverwrongtoys.com
SIC: 3944 Games, toys & children's vehicles

(G-15762)
NKEM INC
Also Called: Cymed
1451 Sarasota Center Blvd (34240-7803)
PHONE.................................800 582-0707
Walter Leise, *President*
EMP: 10 **EST:** 2009
SQ FT: 10,640
SALES (est): 363.5K **Privately Held**
SIC: 3841 Surgical & medical instruments

(G-15763)
NUMERATOR TECHNOLOGIES INC
862 Freeling Dr (34242-1025)
P.O. Box 868 (34230-0868)
PHONE.................................941 807-5333
James Turner, *President*
▼ **EMP:** 5 **EST:** 2008

SALES (est): 486K **Privately Held**
WEB: www.numeratortech.com
SIC: 2879 Agricultural chemicals

(G-15764)
NUTRITIOUS YOU LLC
6583 Midnight Pass Rd (34242-2506)
PHONE.................................941 203-5203
Marina Sommers, *Principal*
EMP: 5 **EST:** 2012
SQ FT: 700
SALES (est): 448.9K **Privately Held**
WEB: www.nutritiousyou.com
SIC: 2099 Food preparations

(G-15765)
OBSERVER GROUP INC
Also Called: Longboat Observer
1970 Main St Fl 3 (34236-5923)
P.O. Box 3169 (34230-3169)
PHONE.................................941 383-5509
Matthew G Walsh, *President*
David Beliles, *Chairman*
EMP: 17 **EST:** 1978
SALES (est): 2.3MM **Privately Held**
WEB: www.yourobserver.com
SIC: 2711 Newspapers, publishing & printing

(G-15766)
OBSERVER MEDIA GROUP INC (PA)
Also Called: Observer Group
1970 Main St Fl 3 (34236-5923)
P.O. Box 3169 (34230-3169)
PHONE.................................941 366-3468
Emily Walsh, *President*
Matthew Walsh, *Principal*
Richeal Bair, *Marketing Staff*
Emma Burke, *Advt Staff*
Jennifer Kane, *Advt Staff*
EMP: 40 **EST:** 2004
SALES (est): 13.2MM **Privately Held**
WEB: www.yourobserver.com
SIC: 2711 Commercial printing & newspaper publishing combined; newspapers, publishing & printing

(G-15767)
OBSERVER MEDIA GROUP INC
Also Called: Pelican Press
5011 Ocean Blvd Ste 206 (34242-2638)
PHONE.................................941 349-4949
Dave Honan, *Branch Mgr*
EMP: 40
SALES (corp-wide): 13.2MM **Privately Held**
WEB: www.yourobserver.com
SIC: 2741 2711 Shopping news: publishing & printing; newspapers: publishing only, not printed on site
PA: Observer Media Group, Inc.
1970 Main St Fl 3
Sarasota FL 34236
941 366-3468

(G-15768)
OCTEX HOLDINGS LLC (PA)
901 Sarasota Center Blvd (34240-7816)
PHONE.................................941 371-6767
James C Westman, *CEO*
James Westman, *CEO*
John Hoskins, *President*
Jonathan D Goetze, *Partner*
Josh Palmer, *Vice Pres*
EMP: 46 **EST:** 2009
SQ FT: 60,000
SALES (est): 17.5MM **Privately Held**
WEB: www.octexgroup.com
SIC: 3089 Injection molding of plastics

(G-15769)
OLLO USA LLC
1223 S Tamiami Trl (34239-2208)
PHONE.................................941 366-0600
Edward H Sarbey, *CEO*
John A McCann, *COO*
◆ **EMP:** 8 **EST:** 2011
SQ FT: 12,500
SALES (est): 172.1K **Privately Held**
WEB: www.ollousa.com
SIC: 2789 7389 Display mounting; design services

▲ = Import ▼=Export
◆ =Import/Export

(G-15770)
OMNISYS LLC
Also Called: Voicetech
551 N Cattlemen Rd (34232-6448)
PHONE......................800 325-2017
Robert Buitron, *Software Engr*
Duane Smith, *Director*
Eric Gelsi, *Technician*
EMP: 27 **Privately Held**
WEB: www.omnisys.com
SIC: 3661 Electronic secretary
PA: Omnisys, Llc
15950 Dallas Pkwy Ste 350
Dallas TX 75248

(G-15771)
ORCA COMPOSITES LLC
1468 Northgate Blvd (34234-4746)
PHONE......................206 349-5300
Scott Macindoe, *Principal*
EMP: 21 **EST:** 2016
SALES (est): 3.1MM **Privately Held**
WEB: www.orcacomposites.com
SIC: 2821 Plastics materials & resins

(G-15772)
PACER ELECTRONICS FLORIDA INC (PA)
1555 Apex Rd (34240-9390)
PHONE......................941 378-5774
Joseph Swiatkowski, *CEO*
John M Swiatkowski, *President*
Mary Swiatkowski, *Corp Secy*
Daniel Garcia,
▼ **EMP:** 22 **EST:** 1984
SQ FT: 45,000
SALES (est): 8.6MM **Privately Held**
WEB: www.pacergroup.net
SIC: 3679 5063 Harness assemblies for electronic use: wire or cable; wiring devices

(G-15773)
PALLET DUDE LLC
7952 Fruitville Rd (34240-8829)
PHONE......................941 720-1667
Brian Sehlke, *Manager*
EMP: 10 **EST:** 2016
SALES (est): 990.7K **Privately Held**
SIC: 2448 Pallets, wood

(G-15774)
PAT CLARK CUSTOM WOODWORKING L
5180 Island Date St (34232-5655)
PHONE......................941 376-1387
Patrick L Clark, *Principal*
EMP: 7 **EST:** 2003
SALES (est): 240K **Privately Held**
SIC: 2431 Millwork

(G-15775)
PATRICE INC
1747 Independence Blvd E7 (34234-2146)
P.O. Box 291848, Kerrville TX (78029-1848)
PHONE......................941 359-2577
Patrice Viles, *President*
EMP: 10 **EST:** 1988
SALES (est): 1.1MM **Privately Held**
WEB: secureserver.patricejewelry.com
SIC: 3961 5944 Costume jewelry; jewelry stores

(G-15776)
PATTYS ON MAIN LLC
1400 Main St (34236-5701)
PHONE......................941 650-9080
Rafael Perez, *Principal*
EMP: 8 **EST:** 2011
SALES (est): 269.9K **Privately Held**
WEB: www.pattysonmain.com
SIC: 3421 Table & food cutlery, including butchers'

(G-15777)
PAVERS BY LEANDRO PERALTA CORP
2142 Dodge Ave (34234-8736)
PHONE......................941 323-7338
Leandro E Mojena Peralta, *Principal*
EMP: 8 **EST:** 2013
SALES (est): 237.5K **Privately Held**
SIC: 2951 Asphalt paving mixtures & blocks

(G-15778)
PEARTREE CABINETS & DESIGN LLC
1635 12th St (34236-2605)
PHONE......................941 377-7655
Robert Poirier, *Principal*
EMP: 8 **EST:** 2015
SALES (est): 390.6K **Privately Held**
WEB: www.peartreecabinetsanddesign.com
SIC: 2434 Wood kitchen cabinets

(G-15779)
PEPPER TREE
715 N Wa Blvd Ste B (34236-4256)
PHONE......................941 922-2662
Julie A Howell, *Principal*
EMP: 8 **EST:** 2005
SALES (est): 329.8K **Privately Held**
SIC: 7372 Publishers' computer software

(G-15780)
PEPPERTREE PRESS LLC
6341 Yellow Wood Pl (34241-8319)
PHONE......................941 922-2662
EMP: 8 **EST:** 2006
SALES (est): 80.5K **Privately Held**
WEB: www.peppertreepublishing.com
SIC: 2741 Miscellaneous publishing

(G-15781)
PEPSI-COLA BOTTLING CO TAMPA
7881 Fruitville Rd (34240-9280)
PHONE......................941 378-1058
Michael Lee, *Vice Pres*
Carlos Lozano, *Plant Mgr*
Ahmed Saber, *Plant Mgr*
Carlos Rivera, *Opers Staff*
James Fenton, *Engineer*
EMP: 302
SALES (corp-wide): 70.3B **Publicly Held**
WEB: www.pepsico.com
SIC: 2086 Carbonated soft drinks, bottled & canned
HQ: Pepsi-Cola Bottling Company Of Tampa
11315 N 30th St
Tampa FL 33612
813 971-2550

(G-15782)
PETERSON MANUFACTURING LLC
155 Cattlemen Rd (34232-6397)
PHONE......................941 371-4989
Robert Longo, *Mng Member*
EMP: 20 **EST:** 2019
SALES (est): 1.3MM **Privately Held**
WEB: www.petersonmfg.com
SIC: 3469 3498 Stamping metal for the trade; fabricated pipe & fittings

(G-15783)
PLEASURE INTERIORS LLC
2207 Industrial Blvd (34234-3119)
PHONE......................941 756-9969
EMP: 25
SALES (est): 2.5MM **Privately Held**
SIC: 2431 2499 3553 Mfg Millwork Mfg Wood Products Mfg Woodworking Machinery

(G-15784)
POLY COATINGS OF SOUTH INC
5944 Sandphil Rd (34232-6326)
PHONE......................941 371-8555
Bernard Zapatha, *President*
Elaine Zapatha, *Admin Sec*
EMP: 10 **EST:** 1980
SQ FT: 9,000
SALES (est): 985.9K **Privately Held**
WEB: www.polycoatings.com
SIC: 3471 2851 3399 Finishing, metals or formed products; paints & allied products; laminating steel

(G-15785)
PRECISION GATE & SECURITY INC (PA)
2341 Porter Lake Dr # 205 (34240-7899)
PHONE......................813 404-6278
Christopher A Sparks, *President*
Caitlyn E Sparks, *Vice Pres*
EMP: 9 **EST:** 2018
SALES (est): 2MM **Privately Held**
WEB: www.precisiongate-securityinc.com
SIC: 3446 Gates, ornamental metal

(G-15786)
PRESTIGE GLASS ART LLC
8005 Megan Hammock Way (34240-8244)
PHONE......................941 921-6758
Carol Scherer, *Principal*
▲ **EMP:** 7 **EST:** 2005
SALES (est): 229.1K **Privately Held**
WEB: www.prestigeglassart.com
SIC: 3231 Art glass: made from purchased glass

(G-15787)
PRIME PAVERS INC
7235 Mauna Loa Blvd (34241-5975)
PHONE......................941 320-7878
Mauricio Delima, *Branch Mgr*
EMP: 24 **Privately Held**
WEB: www.primepavers.net
SIC: 2951 Asphalt paving mixtures & blocks
PA: Prime Pavers Inc
1851 57th St
Sarasota FL 34243

(G-15788)
PROFILE PACKAGING INC
Also Called: Paksource Global
1712 Northgate Blvd (34234-2116)
PHONE......................941 359-6678
R Charles Murray, *CEO*
Stuart C Murray, *President*
Tom Richard, *Plant Mgr*
Jon Kramer, *Project Mgr*
Pat Desjardin, *QC Dir*
◆ **EMP:** 40 **EST:** 1996
SQ FT: 48,000
SALES (est): 16.1MM
SALES (corp-wide): 23.7MM **Privately Held**
SIC: 3565 5084 Bag opening, filling & closing machines; packaging machinery & equipment
PA: Pouch Pac Innovations, L.L.C.
1712 Northgate Blvd
Sarasota FL 34234
941 359-6678

(G-15789)
PROTEK ELECTRONICS INC
1781 Independence Blvd (34234-2106)
PHONE......................941 351-4399
Douglas Santoro, *CEO*
Mike Messer, *Production*
Todd Barham, *Marketing Staff*
EMP: 46 **EST:** 1987
SQ FT: 15,000
SALES (est): 5.4MM
SALES (corp-wide): 9.6MM **Privately Held**
SIC: 3679 3672 Electronic circuits; printed circuit boards
PA: Ibis L.L.C.
20416 Harper Ave
Harper Woods MI 48225
313 642-1740

(G-15790)
PROTOTYPE PLASTICS LLC
1523 Edgar Pl (34240-9054)
PHONE......................941 371-3380
EMP: 7 **EST:** 2015
SALES (est): 116K **Privately Held**
SIC: 3089 Plastic containers, except foam

(G-15791)
QUALITY DRIVEN
4023 Sawyer Rd Unit 216 (34233-1276)
PHONE......................941 923-3322
Jeremy A Howe, *Owner*
EMP: 6 **EST:** 2013
SALES (est): 331.6K **Privately Held**
WEB: www.qualitydrivensrq.com
SIC: 7694 Motor repair services

(G-15792)
QUALITY POWDER COATING INC
2025 Porter Lake Dr F (34240-8834)
PHONE......................941 378-0051
Steve Schwart, *Principal*
Troy Newport, *Natl Sales Mgr*
EMP: 17 **EST:** 1998

SALES (est): 814.6K **Privately Held**
SIC: 3471 Finishing, metals or formed products

(G-15793)
RB KANALFLAKT INC
1712 Northgate Blvd (34234-2116)
PHONE......................941 359-3267
Ola Wettergren, *President*
Rainer Blomster, *Principal*
Gerald Engstrom, *Principal*
▲ **EMP:** 39 **EST:** 1981
SALES (est): 1.3MM
SALES (corp-wide): 10.7MM **Privately Held**
SIC: 3564 Blowers & fans
PA: Kanalflakt, Inc
1712 Northgate Blvd
Sarasota FL 34234
941 359-3267

(G-15794)
RECYCLED VINYL
848 Myrtle St (34234-5233)
PHONE......................727 434-1857
Kim Bass, *Principal*
EMP: 7 **EST:** 2010
SALES (est): 89K **Privately Held**
SIC: 3081 7389 Vinyl film & sheet;

(G-15795)
REGIONAL CNSTR RESOURCES INC
66 N Washington Dr (34236-1416)
P.O. Box 1233, Montgomery TX (77356-1233)
PHONE......................713 789-5131
EMP: 20
SQ FT: 4,500
SALES (est): 2.6MM **Privately Held**
SIC: 3446 Mfg Architectural Metalwork

(G-15796)
RFG PETRO SYSTEMS LLC (PA)
32 S Osprey Ave Ste 1 (34236-5843)
PHONE......................941 487-7524
EMP: 7 **EST:** 2012
SALES (est): 2.3MM **Privately Held**
WEB: www.rfgpetrosystems.com
SIC: 3533 Bits, oil & gas field tools: rock

(G-15797)
ROBERTSON TRANSFORMER CO
Also Called: Robertson Worldwide
4152 Independence Ct C2 (34234-2147)
PHONE......................917 603-8530
William Bryant, *CEO*
Dale Marcus, *CFO*
Augusta Nanney, *Controller*
▲ **EMP:** 5 **EST:** 1979
SALES (est): 2.1MM
SALES (corp-wide): 6MM **Privately Held**
SIC: 3612 3621 5063 3641 Fluorescent lighting transformers; motors & generators; electrical apparatus & equipment; ultraviolet lamps
PA: North Point Investments, Inc.
70 W Madison St Ste 3500
Chicago IL 60602
312 977-4386

(G-15798)
ROLITE CO
7841 Birdie Bend Way (34241-2702)
PHONE......................920 251-1006
Elizabeth Heidenberger, *General Mgr*
EMP: 7 **EST:** 2018
SALES (est): 321.2K **Privately Held**
WEB: www.rolitecompany.com
SIC: 2842 Specialty cleaning, polishes & sanitation goods

(G-15799)
ROOF-A-CIDE WEST LLC
1640 Field Rd (34231-2306)
PHONE......................877 258-8998
Irene M Graziosi, *Principal*
EMP: 7 **EST:** 2011
SALES (est): 96.8K **Privately Held**
WEB: www.roof-a-cide-west.com
SIC: 3199 Leather goods

(G-15800)
ROPER INDUSTRIAL PDTS INV CO
6901 Prof Pkwy E Ste 200 (34240)
PHONE................................941 556-2601
Thomas R McNeill Esq, *Principal*
EMP: 17 **EST:** 2014
SALES (est): 2.2MM
SALES (corp-wide): 5.5B **Publicly Held**
SIC: 3823 Industrial instrmnts msrmnt display/control process variable
PA: Roper Technologies, Inc.
　6901 Prof Pkwy E Ste 200
　Sarasota FL 34240
　941 556-2601

(G-15801)
ROPER TECHNOLOGIES INC (PA)
6901 Prof Pkwy E Ste 200 (34240)
PHONE................................941 556-2601
L Neil Hunn, *President*
John K Stipancich, *Exec VP*
Gary Kallman, *Senior VP*
Jason Conley, *Vice Pres*
Wendy Haney, *Vice Pres*
EMP: 21 **EST:** 1981
SQ FT: 29,000
SALES (est): 5.5B **Publicly Held**
WEB: www.ropertech.com
SIC: 3563 3491 3826 3829 Air & gas compressors; valves, automatic control; process control regulator valves; solenoid valves; petroleum product analyzing apparatus; vibration meters, analyzers & calibrators; temperature instruments: industrial process type; computer software systems analysis & design, custom; computer software development

(G-15802)
ROYAL TEES INC
5556 Palmer Blvd (34232-2734)
PHONE................................941 366-0056
Mario Comparetto Jr, *President*
Steven King, *Prdtn Mgr*
Ann Marie Barrena, *Systems Mgr*
EMP: 10 **EST:** 1980
SQ FT: 4,550
SALES (est): 631.2K **Privately Held**
WEB: www.royal-tees.com
SIC: 2261 7389 2396 Screen printing of cotton broadwoven fabrics; textile & apparel services; automotive & apparel trimmings

(G-15803)
RP INTERNATIONAL LLC (PA)
Also Called: Royce
3400 S Tamiami Trl # 300 (34239-6023)
PHONE................................941 894-1228
Harry Anand, *President*
Kevin Palmer, *Vice Pres*
Albert Royce III, *Treasurer*
Mert Nurhan, *Manager*
Roberta Body, *Admin Sec*
▲ **EMP:** 7 **EST:** 2009
SQ FT: 100,000
SALES (est): 4.5MM **Privately Held**
SIC: 2869 Industrial organic chemicals

(G-15804)
S AND S MORRIS LLC
Also Called: Finest Global Products. Com
1630 Assisi Dr (34231-1765)
PHONE................................404 431-7803
Steve Morris, *Principal*
Sarah Hazel, *Vice Pres*
EMP: 10 **EST:** 2016
SQ FT: 3,500
SALES (est): 1.3MM **Privately Held**
SIC: 3599 Flexible metal hose, tubing & bellows

(G-15805)
SAB FUELS INC
2616 Stickney Point Rd (34231-6020)
PHONE................................786 213-3399
Sabbuba Hasan, *Principal*
EMP: 9 **EST:** 2014
SALES (est): 583.5K **Privately Held**
SIC: 2869 Fuels

(G-15806)
SALCO INDUSTRIES INC
263 Field End St (34240-9703)
PHONE................................941 377-7717
Salvatore Caputo, *President*
Theodora Caputo, *Vice Pres*
EMP: 12 **EST:** 1971
SQ FT: 6,000
SALES (est): 1.1MM **Privately Held**
WEB: www.salco.com
SIC: 3699 5065 3825 Security control equipment & systems; security control equipment & systems; instruments to measure electricity

(G-15807)
SANBUR INC
Also Called: Signs In One Day
4118 Bee Ridge Rd (34233-2553)
PHONE................................941 371-7446
Ken Frank, *President*
Niolet Travis, *Electrical Engi*
EMP: 13 **EST:** 1991
SALES (est): 1.6MM **Privately Held**
WEB: www.sarasotasign.com
SIC: 3993 7629 Signs, not made in custom sign painting shops; electrical equipment repair services

(G-15808)
SARAH LOUISE INC
8263 Blaikie Ct (34240-8323)
PHONE................................941 377-9656
Leonard Given, *President*
Jan Gallock, *Exec VP*
Paul Gallock, *Senior VP*
Diane Given, *Vice Pres*
▲ **EMP:** 10 **EST:** 1986
SALES (est): 959.8K **Privately Held**
WEB: www.sarah-louise.com
SIC: 2369 5137 5136 Girls' & children's outerwear; women's & children's clothing; men's & boys' clothing

(G-15809)
SARASOTA ARCHTCTURAL WDWKG LLC
6110 Clark Center Ave (34238-2743)
PHONE................................941 684-1614
Richard A Perrone, *Principal*
EMP: 8 **EST:** 2016
SALES (est): 475.2K **Privately Held**
WEB: www.saww.us
SIC: 2431 Millwork

(G-15810)
SARASOTA BYFRONT PLG ORGNZTION
655 N Tamiami Trl (34236-4045)
PHONE................................941 203-5316
EMP: 7 **EST:** 2017
SALES (est): 114.9K **Privately Held**
WEB: www.thebaysarasota.org
SIC: 2741

(G-15811)
SARASOTA CABINETRY INC
3080 N Washington Blvd # 25 (34234-6245)
PHONE................................941 351-5588
Don Miller, *President*
Gary Miller, *Vice Pres*
EMP: 12 **EST:** 1986
SQ FT: 15,000
SALES (est): 501.4K **Privately Held**
WEB: www.sarasotacabinetryinc.com
SIC: 2434 Wood kitchen cabinets

(G-15812)
SARASOTA COTTAGES LLC
1628 7th St (34236-4121)
P.O. Box 3004 (34230-3004)
PHONE................................941 724-2245
Andrea Seager, *Manager*
EMP: 7 **EST:** 2018
SALES (est): 353.3K **Privately Held**
SIC: 2721 Magazines: publishing only, not printed on site

(G-15813)
SARASOTA HERALD-TRIBUNE (HQ)
801 S Tamiami Trl (34236-7824)
P.O. Box 1719 (34230-1719)
PHONE................................941 953-7755

James Weeks, *President*
Steve Ainsley, *President*
Micheal E Ryan, *Vice Pres*
David Gorham, *Treasurer*
Margaret Garner, *Consultant*
EMP: 300 **EST:** 1925
SQ FT: 20,000
SALES (est): 89.6MM
SALES (corp-wide): 278.4MM **Privately Held**
WEB: www.heraldtribune.com
SIC: 2711 Newspapers, publishing & printing
PA: Halifax Media Holdings, Llc
　901 6th St
　Daytona Beach FL 32117
　386 681-2404

(G-15814)
SARASOTA HERALD-TRIBUNE
1777 Main St Ste 400 (34236-5868)
PHONE................................941 953-7755
Alan Monroe, *Director*
Roxanna Shepherd, *Executive*
EMP: 30
SALES (corp-wide): 278.4MM **Privately Held**
WEB: www.heraldtribune.com
SIC: 2711 7313 7319 Newspapers, publishing & printing; newspaper advertising representative; display advertising service
HQ: Sarasota Herald-Tribune
　801 S Tamiami Trl
　Sarasota FL 34236
　941 953-7755

(G-15815)
SARASOTA SHOWER DOOR COMPANY
Also Called: Quality Enclosures
2025e Porter Lake Dr (34240-8834)
PHONE................................941 378-0051
Manny Schwart, *President*
Paulo Reis, *COO*
Steve Schwart, *Vice Pres*
Derek Couch, *Plant Mgr*
Mike Davis, *Opers Mgr*
◆ **EMP:** 8 **EST:** 1991
SQ FT: 6,000
SALES (est): 1.8MM **Privately Held**
WEB: www.showerdoorsofsarasota.com
SIC: 3231 Doors, glass: made from purchased glass

(G-15816)
SARASOTA SIGNS AND VISUALS
Also Called: Fastsigns
4070 N Washington Blvd (34234-4837)
PHONE................................941 355-5746
Peter Tunberg, *Owner*
Kristen Cruz, *Corp Comm Staff*
EMP: 6 **EST:** 2006
SALES (est): 889.8K **Privately Held**
WEB: www.fastsigns.com
SIC: 3993 5999 7319 Signs & advertising specialties; banners, flags, decals & posters; display advertising service

(G-15817)
SARASOTA-MANATEE ORIGINALS INC
1215 S Tamiami Trl (34239-2208)
PHONE................................941 365-2800
Michael Klauber, *President*
Sarah Firstenberger, *Exec Dir*
EMP: 7 **EST:** 2011
SALES (est): 461.1K **Privately Held**
WEB: www.eatlikealocal.com
SIC: 3421 Table & food cutlery, including butchers'

(G-15818)
SARASOTAS FINEST MBL GRAN INC
550 Mango Ave (34237-6130)
PHONE................................941 365-9697
EMP: 7
SALES (est): 40K **Privately Held**
SIC: 2493 3281 Mfg Reconstituted Wood Products Mfg Cut Stone/Products

(G-15819)
SAVORY STREET
411 N Orange Ave (34236-5003)
PHONE................................941 312-4027
EMP: 8 **EST:** 2010
SALES (est): 575.1K **Privately Held**
SIC: 2051 Mfg Bread/Related Products

(G-15820)
SCIENCE DAILY LLC
4034 Roberts Point Rd (34242-1162)
PHONE................................239 596-2624
Daniel Hogan, *Principal*
EMP: 7 **EST:** 2012
SALES (est): 148.6K **Privately Held**
SIC: 2711 Newspapers, publishing & printing

(G-15821)
SCULLY INDUSTRIES
314 Island Cir (34242-1938)
PHONE................................941 349-5561
Neil Scully, *Principal*
EMP: 7 **EST:** 2008
SALES (est): 140.8K **Privately Held**
WEB: www.scully.com
SIC: 3999 Manufacturing industries

(G-15822)
SEAPRESS INC
Also Called: Mercury Printing
4281 Clark Rd (34233-2405)
PHONE................................941 366-8494
Harry R Pore, *President*
Susan Pore, *Admin Sec*
EMP: 7 **EST:** 1973
SALES (est): 894.2K **Privately Held**
WEB: www.sarasotaprinter.com
SIC: 2752 Commercial printing, offset

(G-15823)
SELECT MACHINERY INC
4590 Ashton Rd (34233-3487)
PHONE................................941 960-1970
Henry P Koelmel, *Director*
EMP: 8 **EST:** 2015
SALES (est): 124.2K **Privately Held**
SIC: 3599 Industrial machinery

(G-15824)
SENTRY PROTECTION TECHNOLOGY
6202 Clarity Ct (34240-9601)
PHONE................................941 306-4949
Arthur James, *President*
EMP: 8 **EST:** 2010
SALES (est): 94.8K **Privately Held**
SIC: 3442 Metal doors, sash & trim

(G-15825)
SERBIN PRINTING INC
1500 N Washington Blvd (34236-2723)
PHONE................................941 366-0755
Mark J Serbin, *President*
Robin Clark, *Vice Pres*
Jim Keen, *Vice Pres*
EMP: 35 **EST:** 1971
SQ FT: 26,500
SALES (est): 5.1MM **Privately Held**
WEB: www.serbinprinting.com
SIC: 2752 Commercial printing, offset

(G-15826)
SIGNARAMA-SARASOTA
4435 S Tamiami Trl (34231-3428)
PHONE................................941 554-8798
Kathy Elliott, *Principal*
EMP: 7 **EST:** 2011
SALES (est): 192.1K **Privately Held**
SIC: 3993 Signs & advertising specialties

(G-15827)
SIGNS PLUS NEW IDS-NEW TECH IN
4242 Mcintosh Ln (34232-5027)
PHONE................................941 378-4262
Robert W Klinger, *President*
Robert H Klinger, *President*
Sally Klinger, *Treasurer*
Bob Blanken, *Manager*
Colin Lane, *Manager*
EMP: 15 **EST:** 1988
SQ FT: 4,000

SALES (est): 3.1MM **Privately Held**
WEB: www.signsplussigns.com
SIC: 3993 Signs & advertising specialties

(G-15828)
SILVER STAR ON LIME LLC
2739 Aspinwall St (34237-5208)
PHONE............................941 312-4566
Victoria J Krone, *Owner*
EMP: 9 **EST:** 2011
SALES (est): 308.5K **Privately Held**
SIC: 3274 Lime

(G-15829)
SIMPLEX MANUFACTURING INC
Also Called: Simplex Tool and Mold
6300 Tower Ln Unit 4 (34240-7837)
PHONE............................941 378-8700
Runar Sigurdsson, *President*
Steve Fennema, *Vice Pres*
Timothy T Gauthier, *Vice Pres*
EMP: 20 **EST:** 1997
SQ FT: 6,700
SALES (est): 1.1MM **Privately Held**
SIC: 3599 3544 Machine shop, jobbing &
repair; special dies, tools, jigs & fixtures

(G-15830)
SLEEPMED INCORPORATED
5432 Bee Ridge Rd Ste 170 (34233-1515)
PHONE............................941 361-3035
EMP: 37
SALES (corp-wide): 7.7MM **Privately
Held**
WEB: www.sleepmedinc.com
SIC: 3841 Surgical & medical instruments
HQ: Sleepmed Incorporated
3330 Cumberland Blvd Se # 800
Atlanta GA 30339

(G-15831)
SMART MATERIAL CORP (PA)
2170 Main St Ste 302 (34237-6040)
P.O. Box 1115, Osprey (34229-1115)
PHONE............................941 870-3337
Thomas Daue, *President*
Madeleine Daue, *Sales Staff*
EMP: 8 **EST:** 2000
SQ FT: 800
SALES (est): 2MM **Privately Held**
WEB: www.smart-material.com
SIC: 3264 3728 3829 Magnets, perma-
nent: ceramic or ferrite; refueling equip-
ment for use in flight, airplane; measuring
& controlling devices

(G-15832)
SPOTLIGHT GRAPHICS INC
6054 Clark Center Ave (34238-2716)
PHONE............................941 929-1500
John H Souza, *President*
Ron Morris, *Electrical Engi*
Arlene Morris, *Treasurer*
Renee Phinney, *Accounts Exec*
Charles Zweil, *Sales Staff*
EMP: 32 **EST:** 1987
SQ FT: 16,000
SALES (est): 7.8MM **Privately Held**
WEB: www.spotlightgraphics.com
SIC: 2752 Commercial printing, offset

(G-15833)
SRQ FABRICATIONS INC
6707 Avenue C (34231-8822)
PHONE............................941 780-5496
EMP: 7 **EST:** 2019
SALES (est): 226.4K **Privately Held**
WEB: www.srqfabrications.com
SIC: 3499 Fabricated metal products

(G-15834)
SRQ STORM PROTECTION LLC
1899 Porter Lake Dr # 105 (34240-7897)
PHONE............................941 341-0334
Jon Reymond, *Mng Member*
EMP: 7 **EST:** 2017
SALES (est): 524.6K **Privately Held**
WEB: www.srqstormprotection.com
SIC: 2431 Blinds (shutters), wood

(G-15835)
SSVM PARTNERS INC
Also Called: Sterling Manufacturing
8293 Consumer Ct (34240-7862)
PHONE............................239 825-6282
Tom Shapiro, *President*

Rhonda Robinson, *Engineer*
Michael Vansyckle, *Engineer*
Steve Shapiro, *Treasurer*
EMP: 75 **EST:** 1990
SQ FT: 25,000
SALES (est): 25.8MM
SALES (corp-wide): 592.8MM **Privately
Held**
SIC: 2541 Counter & sink tops
HQ: Interior Logic Group, Inc.
18565 Jamboree Rd Ste 125
Irvine CA 92612
800 959-8333

(G-15836)
ST ACQUISITIONS LLC
Also Called: Sure Torque
1701 Desoto Rd (34234-3066)
PHONE............................941 753-1095
Francis Caudron, *Purchasing*
Frank Lopez, *Plant Engr*
Bob Burke, *Manager*
Michelle Bergeron,
Robert Szalay, *Master*
EMP: 8 **EST:** 1991
SQ FT: 1,000
SALES (est): 1MM
SALES (corp-wide): 3.2MM **Privately
Held**
WEB: www.mesalabs.com
SIC: 3829 Physical property testing equip-
ment
PA: M.D.C. Engineering, Inc.
1701 Desoto Rd
Sarasota FL 34234
941 358-0610

(G-15837)
STARK ENTERPRISES INC
1964 Barber Rd (34240-9394)
PHONE............................941 341-0319
Rachel Stark Cappelli, *CEO*
EMP: 5 **EST:** 2005
SALES (est): 516.2K **Privately Held**
WEB: www.starkpremium.com
SIC: 3171 Handbags, women's

(G-15838)
STEEL PRODUCTS INC
1821 Myrtle St (34234-4820)
PHONE............................941 351-8128
Tom Losee, *President*
Karen Losee, *Vice Pres*
EMP: 8 **EST:** 1967
SQ FT: 9,000
SALES (est): 841.1K **Privately Held**
WEB: www.steelproductsinc.com
SIC: 7692 3441 Welding repair; fabricated
structural metal

(G-15839)
**STONE TREND INTERNATIONAL
INC**
6244 Clark Center Ave # 3 (34238-1722)
P.O. Box 3018 (34230-3018)
PHONE............................941 927-9113
Jaren Levitt, *President*
Julio Gonzales, *Exec VP*
Sue Kim, *Exec VP*
Theresa Levitt, *Exec VP*
Anthony Ritchie, *Vice Pres*
▲ **EMP:** 25 **EST:** 1995
SQ FT: 10,000
SALES (est): 3.7MM **Privately Held**
SIC: 3281 5032 1411 Cut stone & stone
products; marble building stone; dimen-
sion stone

(G-15840)
STREETWISE MAPS INC (DH)
4376 Independence Ct A (34234-4711)
P.O. Box 10612, Prescott AZ (86304-0612)
PHONE............................941 358-1956
Michael Brown, *President*
EMP: 9 **EST:** 1983
SALES (est): 883.5K
SALES (corp-wide): 1B **Privately Held**
WEB: www.streetwisemaps.com
SIC: 2741 Maps: publishing only, not
printed on site
HQ: Michelin North America, Inc.
1 Parkway S
Greenville SC 29615
864 458-5000

(G-15841)
STUDIO 21 LIGHTING INC
Also Called: Madison Avenue Furniture
1507 Mango Ave (34237-2822)
PHONE............................941 355-2677
Simon T Levell, *President*
◆ **EMP:** 25 **EST:** 1991
SALES (est): 4.4MM **Privately Held**
SIC: 3645 Floor lamps

(G-15842)
**STUDIO LUXE CSTM
CABINETRY LLC**
2035 Constitution Blvd (34231-4108)
PHONE............................941 371-4010
David E Wentzel, *Mng Member*
EMP: 9 **EST:** 2016
SALES (est): 548.6K **Privately Held**
WEB: www.studioluxedesigns.com
SIC: 2434 2514 Wood kitchen cabinets;
kitchen cabinets: metal

(G-15843)
SUNCOAST SIGN SHOP INC
8466 Cookwood Rdg (34231)
PHONE............................941 448-5835
Brian R Gregg, *President*
Gregory R Hornagold, *Corp Secy*
EMP: 8 **EST:** 2008
SALES (est): 180.9K **Privately Held**
WEB:
www.wholesalechannellettersigns.com
SIC: 3993 Signs & advertising specialties

(G-15844)
SUNNIBUNNI
1916 Bay Rd (34239-6903)
PHONE............................941 554-8744
Alexandra Van Wie, *President*
EMP: 8 **EST:** 2017
SALES (est): 487.7K **Privately Held**
WEB: www.sunnibunni.com
SIC: 2024 Ice cream & frozen desserts

(G-15845)
**SUNSET CADILLAC OF
SARASOTA**
2200 Bee Ridge Rd (34239-6201)
PHONE............................941 922-1571
Steve Montanaro, *General Mgr*
Jim Carson, *Director*
Joe Walters, *Director*
Chloe Alvarez, *Administration*
Greg Doan, *Technician*
EMP: 11 **EST:** 2019
SALES (est): 1MM **Privately Held**
WEB: www.sunsetcadillacsarasota.com
SIC: 3089 Automotive parts, plastic

(G-15846)
**SUNSET METAL FABRICATION
INC**
1211 Porter Rd Unit 7 (34240-9621)
PHONE............................386 215-4520
Steve Larimer, *Principal*
EMP: 7 **EST:** 2016
SALES (est): 279.1K **Privately Held**
SIC: 3499 Fabricated metal products

(G-15847)
SWOOGO LLC (PA)
4646 Ashton Rd (34233-3408)
PHONE............................212 655-9810
Leonora Valvo, *President*
Tim Cummins,
Neil Keefe,
EMP: 5 **EST:** 2015
SALES (est): 549.9K **Privately Held**
WEB: www.swoogo.events
SIC: 7372 7389 Business oriented com-
puter software;

(G-15848)
T V HI LITES PENNY SAVER INC
Also Called: Pet Pages
6950 Webber Rd (34240-8665)
P.O. Box 22083 (34276-5083)
PHONE............................941 378-5353
David Deacy, *President*
EMP: 10 **EST:** 1995
SQ FT: 2,000
SALES (est): 156.3K **Privately Held**
WEB: www.petpages.com
SIC: 2721 Magazines: publishing & printing

(G-15849)
TARGET GRAPHICS INC
2053 13th St (34237-2705)
PHONE............................941 365-8809
John P Masio, *President*
EMP: 16 **EST:** 1988
SQ FT: 8,800
SALES (est): 3.2MM **Privately Held**
WEB: www.targetgraphics.net
SIC: 2752 2759 Commercial printing, off-
set; laser printing

(G-15850)
TATTOO FACTORY INC (PA)
Also Called: Tattoo Promotion Factory
2828 Proctor Rd Ste 2 (34231-6423)
PHONE............................941 923-4110
Stephen Bloom, *President*
EMP: 21 **EST:** 1995
SQ FT: 15,000
SALES (est): 1.7MM **Privately Held**
WEB: www.tattoopromotionfactory.com
SIC: 2759 3993 Promotional printing;
signs & advertising specialties

(G-15851)
**TAYLOR & FRANCIS GROUP
LLC**
Accounts Payable Division
1990 Main St Ste 750 (34236-8000)
PHONE............................800 516-0186
Maya Davis, *Marketing Staff*
Myles Stavis, *Marketing Staff*
EMP: 58
SALES (corp-wide): 2.4B **Privately Held**
WEB: www.taylorandfrancis.com
SIC: 2741 Miscellaneous publishing
HQ: Taylor & Francis Group, Llc
6000 Broken Sound Pkwy Nw # 300
Boca Raton FL 33487
561 994-0555

(G-15852)
TAYLOR ELECTRONICS INC
7061b S Tamiami Trl (34231-5559)
P.O. Box 20669 (34276-3669)
PHONE............................941 925-3605
Wilbur Taylor, *President*
Russell M Bailey Jr, *Vice Pres*
Cheryl Taylor, *Treasurer*
Buzz Taylor, *Manager*
Patricia A Bailey, *Admin Sec*
EMP: 10 **EST:** 1936
SALES (est): 1MM **Privately Held**
WEB: www.taylorphaseguard.com
SIC: 3625 Motor controls & accessories

(G-15853)
TAYLOR MADE PLASTICS INC
1561 Global Ct Ste A (34240-7827)
PHONE............................941 926-0200
Kevin Larkin, *President*
Luke Larkin, *Vice Pres*
Joe Barnett, *Admin Sec*
EMP: 8 **EST:** 1995
SQ FT: 8,500
SALES (est): 1.1MM **Privately Held**
SIC: 3084 Plastics pipe

(G-15854)
TIEMPO LLC
1250 S Tamiami Trl (34239-2221)
PHONE............................941 780-9900
Viktor Kolar, *Principal*
EMP: 7 **EST:** 2012
SALES (est): 133.6K **Privately Held**
SIC: 2024 Ice cream & frozen desserts

(G-15855)
**TORRINGTON BRUSH WORKS
INC (PA)**
4377 Independence Ct (34234-4722)
PHONE............................941 355-1499
Michael Grimaldi, *President*
Sidney W Fitzgerald, *President*
John Fitzgerald, *Vice Pres*
Robert Petrovits, *Admin Sec*
◆ **EMP:** 17 **EST:** 1907
SQ FT: 12,500
SALES (est): 3.1MM **Privately Held**
WEB: www.torringtonbrushes.com
SIC: 3991 5085 5719 Brooms & brushes;
paint brushes; brushes, except paint &
varnish; brushes, household or industrial;
brushes, industrial; brushes

(G-15856)
TORTILLERIA DONA CHELA
1155 N Washington Blvd (34236-3407)
PHONE................................941 953-4045
EMP: 6
SALES (est): 436.5K Privately Held
SIC: 2099 Mfg Food Preparations

(G-15857)
TRAFALGER COMMUNICATIONS INC
Also Called: Srq Media Group
331 S Pineapple Ave (34236-7019)
PHONE................................941 365-7702
Lisl Liang, President
Brittany Mattie, Editor
Ashley Grant, Senior VP
Wes Roberts, Vice Pres
Philip Lederer, Senior Editor
EMP: 25 EST: 1997
SQ FT: 6,000
SALES (est): 5MM Privately Held
WEB: www.srqmagazine.com
SIC: 2721 Magazines: publishing only, not printed on site

(G-15858)
TREASURE COVE II INC
8927 S Tamiami Trl (34238-3145)
PHONE................................941 966-2004
Dan Hering, Vice Pres
EMP: 13 EST: 1956
SQ FT: 2,400
SALES (est): 1.1MM Privately Held
WEB: www.treasurecove2.com
SIC: 3299 5947 Non-metallic mineral statuary & other decorative products; gift shop

(G-15859)
ULTRAFAST SYSTEMS LLC
8330 Consumer Ct (34240-7868)
PHONE................................941 360-2161
Alex Gusev, Principal
EMP: 10 EST: 2006
SALES (est): 1.8MM Privately Held
WEB: www.ultrafast.systems
SIC: 3826 Analytical instruments

(G-15860)
UNIQUE TECHNOLOGY INC
1523 Edgar Pl (34240-9054)
PHONE................................941 358-5410
Arthur James, President
Nancy James, Principal
◆ EMP: 23 EST: 1981
SQ FT: 8,000
SALES (est): 3.2MM Privately Held
WEB: www.utindustries.com
SIC: 3442 Metal doors

(G-15861)
UNIQUE TECHNOLOGY INDS LLC
1523 Edgar Pl (34240-9054)
PHONE................................941 358-5410
Michael Tildale,
EMP: 12 EST: 2012
SQ FT: 35,000
SALES (est): 2MM Privately Held
WEB: www.utindustries.com
SIC: 2431 Door screens, wood frame

(G-15862)
UNIROYAL ENGINEERED PDTS LLC (HQ)
1800 2nd St Ste 970 (34236-5992)
PHONE................................941 906-8580
Howard R Curd, CEO
Howard F Curd, President
George L Sanchez, Exec VP
Dave Urbin, Vice Pres
William Cutler, Plant Supt
▲ EMP: 15 EST: 2003
SQ FT: 230,000
SALES (est): 61.7MM
SALES (corp-wide): 71.7MM Publicly Held
WEB: www.naugahyde.com
SIC: 2824 2295 Vinyl fibers; textured yarns, non-cellulosic; leather, artificial or imitation

PA: Uniroyal Global Engineered Products, Inc.
1800 2nd St Ste 970
Sarasota FL 34236
941 906-8580

(G-15863)
UNIROYAL GLOBL ENGNRED PDTS IN (PA)
1800 2nd St Ste 970 (34236-5992)
PHONE................................941 906-8580
Howard R Curd, Ch of Bd
Edmund C King, Ch of Bd
Brent Blanke, Prdtn Mgr
Stephanie Beske, Purch Mgr
Karl Kroening, Engineer
EMP: 12 EST: 1992
SQ FT: 9,010
SALES: 71.7MM Publicly Held
WEB: www.uniroyalglobal.com
SIC: 2824 2396 Vinyl fibers; automotive trimmings, fabric

(G-15864)
UNITED STATES AWNING COMPANY
Also Called: U S Awning
1935 18th St (34234-7508)
PHONE................................941 955-7010
Raymond Hautamaki, President
Ann Hautamaki, Corp Secy
Mark Schamp, Vice Pres
Mark Schwalm, Executive
EMP: 26 EST: 1965
SQ FT: 6,000
SALES (est): 4.3MM Privately Held
WEB: www.unitedstatesawning.com
SIC: 2394 3444 Awnings, fabric: made from purchased materials; awnings, sheet metal

(G-15865)
US PET IMAGING LLC (PA)
Also Called: Imaging For Life
3830 Bee Ridge Rd Ste 100 (34233-1105)
P.O. Box 25487 (34277-2487)
PHONE................................941 921-0383
Neil Bedi,
Inita Bedi,
EMP: 7 EST: 2002
SALES (est): 1.1MM Privately Held
WEB: www.imagingforlife.net
SIC: 2835 In vitro & in vivo diagnostic substances

(G-15866)
VENICE HERALD TRIBUNE
1777 Main St (34236-5845)
PHONE................................941 486-3000
Scott Graves, Principal
EMP: 7 EST: 1927
SALES (est): 101.5K Privately Held
WEB: www.heraldtribune.com
SIC: 2711 Newspapers, publishing & printing

(G-15867)
VILLAR STONE & PAVER WORKS LLC
1140 Seaside Dr (34242-2567)
PHONE................................860 209-2907
Joseph Villar, Principal
EMP: 6 EST: 2007
SALES (est): 488.3K Privately Held
SIC: 3531 Pavers

(G-15868)
VISTA SYSTEM LLC
1800 N East Ave Ste 102 (34234-7600)
PHONE................................941 365-4646
Sam Schneider, General Mgr
Pnina Kedar, Business Mgr
Terry Greer, Marketing Staff
Barak Silber, Manager
Erez Halivni,
◆ EMP: 30 EST: 2000
SQ FT: 11,000
SALES (est): 5.4MM Privately Held
WEB: www.vistasystem.com
SIC: 3993 Signs & advertising specialties

(G-15869)
VOYOMOTIVE LLC
1058 N Tamiami Trl # 108 (34236-2416)
PHONE................................888 321-4633

Peter Yorke, CEO
Harald Ekman, CFO
Adam Sloan, Director
EMP: 12 EST: 2011
SALES (est): 1.1MM Privately Held
WEB: www.voyomotive.com
SIC: 3714 5045 Motor vehicle parts & accessories; computer software

(G-15870)
WEIBEL EQUIPMENT INC
7801 Mainsail Ln (34240-2320)
PHONE................................571 278-1989
Peder Pedersen, President
Peter Muller, Vice Pres
EMP: 5 EST: 1996
SALES (est): 474.6K Privately Held
WEB: www.weibelradars.com
SIC: 3812 Navigational systems & instruments

(G-15871)
WES HOLDINGS CORP
Also Called: De Loach Industries
818 Cattlemen Rd (34232-2811)
PHONE................................941 371-4995
Anthony De Loach, President
Mark Gorrell, Vice Pres
EMP: 15 EST: 1959
SQ FT: 8,000
SALES (est): 2.4MM
SALES (corp-wide): 10.2MM Privately Held
SIC: 3564 3823 Air purification equipment; water quality monitoring & control systems
PA: Water Equipment Services, Inc.
6389 Tower Ln
Sarasota FL 34240
941 371-7617

(G-15872)
WES INDUSTRIES INC (PA)
6389 Tower Ln (34240-8810)
PHONE................................941 371-7617
Anthony Deloach, President
Travis Deloach, Vice Pres
Travis De Loach, Project Engr
EMP: 19 EST: 2013
SALES (est): 3.2MM Privately Held
WEB: www.wesindustries.com
SIC: 3443 1711 Water tanks, metal plate; solar energy contractor

(G-15873)
WF FUEL
300 N Washington Blvd (34236-4236)
PHONE................................941 706-4953
Konstantin Razionov, Manager
EMP: 7 EST: 2013
SALES (est): 247.8K Privately Held
SIC: 2869 Fuels

(G-15874)
WHOLE TOMATO SOFTWARE INC
1990 Main St Ste 750 (34236-8000)
PHONE................................408 323-1590
EMP: 5 EST: 2019
SALES (est): 373.4K Privately Held
WEB: www.wholetomato.com
SIC: 7372 Prepackaged software

(G-15875)
WILLIAM B RUDOW INC
1122 Goodrich Ave (34236-2617)
P.O. Box 2300 (34230-2300)
PHONE................................941 957-4200
David Wertheimer, President
Steven Wertheimer, Vice Pres
▼ EMP: 8 EST: 1946
SQ FT: 5,000
SALES (est): 836.9K Privately Held
WEB: www.suckers.com
SIC: 3089 3555 Injection molded finished plastic products; printing trade parts & attachments

(G-15876)
WINDOW CRAFTSMEN INC
6031 Clark Center Ave (34238-2718)
PHONE................................941 922-1844
Robert Detweiler, President
Steve Gerety, Director
EMP: 20 EST: 1965
SQ FT: 18,000

SALES (est): 2.4MM Privately Held
WEB: www.windowcraftsmen.com
SIC: 3442 3444 3429 Screen & storm doors & windows; sheet metalwork; manufactured hardware (general)

(G-15877)
WINSULATOR CORPORATION
3350 S Osprey Ave (34239-5900)
PHONE................................941 365-7901
Edward Vervane, CEO
EMP: 5 EST: 2005
SALES (est): 327.6K Privately Held
WEB: www.winsulator.com
SIC: 2431 Windows & window parts & trim, wood; windows, storm: wood or metal

(G-15878)
WIRED RITE SYSTEMS INC
1748 Independence Blvd C5 (34234-2150)
PHONE................................707 838-1122
Mark Owades, President
Monika Tomorowicz, General Mgr
Roger Abby, Engineer
▲ EMP: 15 EST: 1990
SQ FT: 10,000
SALES (est): 2.1MM Privately Held
WEB: www.wiredrite.com
SIC: 3612 Control transformers

(G-15879)
WORLD PRECISION INSTRS LLC (PA)
175 Sarasota Center Blvd (34240-8750)
PHONE................................941 371-1003
Karol Macdonald, Vice Pres
Cheryl Halter, CFO
EMP: 31 EST: 2016
SALES (est): 5.1MM Privately Held
WEB: www.wpiinc.com
SIC: 3826 3829 Analytical instruments; measuring & controlling devices

(G-15880)
XE GLOBAL POLSG SYSTEMS LLC
5651 Creekwood Cir (34233-1532)
PHONE................................941 685-9788
Jeffery T Rouwhorst, Manager
EMP: 7 EST: 2011
SALES (est): 155.4K Privately Held
WEB: xeglobalpolishingsystemsllc.yola-site.com
SIC: 3471 Polishing, metals or formed products

(G-15881)
ZIPTEK LLC
1250 S Tamiami Trl # 303 (34239-2221)
PHONE................................941 953-5509
William Bennett, CEO
Ramses Galaz, Info Tech Dir
Leif Olsen, Director
EMP: 12 EST: 2012
SALES (est): 967.3K Privately Held
WEB: www.ziptekglobal.com
SIC: 3841 Surgical & medical instruments

(G-15882)
ZOO HOLDINGS LLC
Also Called: Sign Zoo
4139 N Wa Blvd (34234-4840)
PHONE................................941 355-5653
Jen Aaron, Prdtn Mgr
Melissa Pickelsimer, Accounts Mgr
Jaclyn Rebel, Mktg Dir
Larry Cavalluzzi,
James Marmol, Graphic Designe
EMP: 5 EST: 2004
SALES (est): 1MM Privately Held
WEB: www.signzoo.com
SIC: 3993 Signs & advertising specialties

Satellite Beach
Brevard County

(G-15883)
ARCTIC RAYS LLC
600 Jackson Ct (32937-3933)
PHONE................................321 223-5780
Dirk Fieberg, Mng Member
EMP: 7 EST: 2015

▲ = Import ▼=Export
◆ =Import/Export

SALES (est): 307.2K **Privately Held**
WEB: www.arcticrays.com
SIC: **3429** 3625 3571 Marine hardware; marine & navy auxiliary controls; electronic computers

(G-15884)
CIRCLE REDMONT INC
407 Saint Georges Ct (32937-3839)
PHONE..........................321 259-7374
Frederick J Sandor, *President*
Virginia Hughes, *Vice Pres*
▲ EMP: 16 EST: 1966
SALES (est): 5MM **Privately Held**
WEB: www.glassflooring.com
SIC: **3444** 3231 Skylights, sheet metal; furniture tops, glass: cut, beveled or polished

(G-15885)
J I S ASSOCIATES
445 Cardinal Dr (32937-3707)
PHONE..........................321 777-6829
Vickie Dupont, *Engineer*
EMP: 7 EST: 1988
SALES (est): 90K **Privately Held**
SIC: **3661** Telephone & telegraph apparatus

Sebastian
Brevard County

(G-15886)
AMERICAN SIGN LETTERS
8140 Evernia St Unit 1 (32976-2584)
PHONE..........................772 643-4012
EMP: 8 EST: 2018
SALES (est): 501.2K **Privately Held**
WEB: www.americansignletters.com
SIC: **3993** Signs & advertising specialties

(G-15887)
JODE CORPORATION
9565 Riverview Dr (32976-3142)
PHONE..........................321 684-1769
Debra L Marshall, *President*
EMP: 6 EST: 2002
SALES (est): 434.8K **Privately Held**
SIC: **2211** Apparel & outerwear fabrics, cotton

Sebastian
Indian River County

(G-15888)
BRUNO DANGER CUSTOM CABINETS
761 S Easy St (32958-5022)
PHONE..........................754 366-1302
Bruno P Danger, *Principal*
EMP: 7 EST: 2016
SALES (est): 220.6K **Privately Held**
SIC: **2434** Wood kitchen cabinets

(G-15889)
CASTLE SOFTWARE INC
626 Layport Dr (32958-4412)
PHONE..........................800 345-7606
Steve Hersh, *Vice Pres*
EMP: 5 EST: 2001
SALES (est): 402.3K **Privately Held**
WEB: www.castlelearning.com
SIC: **7372** 8748 Prepackaged software; business consulting

(G-15890)
DOUBLE HEADER FISH CHARTER
706 S Easy St (32958-5023)
PHONE..........................772 388-5741
John M Conlon, *Principal*
EMP: 9 EST: 2010
SALES (est): 175.9K **Privately Held**
SIC: **3542** Headers

(G-15891)
EXPERT PROMOTIONS LLC
Also Called: American Sign
434 Georgia Blvd (32958-4528)
PHONE..........................772 643-4012
Benjamin Furino, *President*

EMP: 17 EST: 2017
SALES (est): 1.2MM **Privately Held**
WEB: www.expertpromotionsllc.com
SIC: **3993** Neon signs

(G-15892)
FORD WIRE AND CABLE CORP
7756 130th St (32958-3613)
PHONE..........................772 388-3660
William S Ford, *CEO*
Laurie Ford Russelburg, *President*
Charlotte Ford, *Corp Secy*
Dale Ford, *Vice Pres*
Steven Ford, *VP Mktg*
▲ EMP: 28 EST: 1986
SQ FT: 40,000
SALES (est): 1.6MM **Privately Held**
SIC: **3357** Building wire & cable, nonferrous

(G-15893)
GATE CFV SOLUTIONS INC
Also Called: Global Agriculture Tech Engrg
100 Sebastian Indus Pl (32958-4627)
PHONE..........................772 388-3387
John R Newton, *CEO*
Gillian N Callaghan, *President*
Gillian Callaghan, *General Mgr*
Peter Brooke, *Research*
Michael Newton, *Director*
EMP: 7 EST: 1998
SQ FT: 7,000
SALES (est): 956.7K **Privately Held**
WEB: www.gatecfv.com
SIC: **3491** 3494 3585 Water works valves; valves & pipe fittings; soda fountain & beverage dispensing equipment & parts

(G-15894)
GRAPH-PLEX CORP
5240 95th St (32958-6372)
PHONE..........................772 766-3866
Denise Rita Webster, *Principal*
EMP: 7 EST: 2018
SALES (est): 244.8K **Privately Held**
WEB: www.graphplex.com
SIC: **3993** Signs & advertising specialties

(G-15895)
IONEMOTO INC
Also Called: Tightails
300 Industrial Cir (32958-3685)
PHONE..........................617 784-1401
Frederic P Baly, *Principal*
EMP: 8 EST: 2017
SALES (est): 1.1MM **Privately Held**
WEB: www.ionemoto.com
SIC: **3714** Motor vehicle parts & accessories

(G-15896)
KATHERINE SCURES
373 Sebastian Blvd (32958-4550)
PHONE..........................772 589-7409
Katherine Scures, *Principal*
EMP: 7 EST: 2011
SALES (est): 148.2K **Privately Held**
WEB: www.gutierrezdentistry.com
SIC: **3843** Enamels, dentists'

(G-15897)
KNIGHT BACON ASSOCIATES
9577 Gator Dr Unit 1 (32958-8562)
PHONE..........................772 388-5115
Jonathan Bacon, *Principal*
Jonathan K Bacon, *Principal*
EMP: 5 EST: 2010
SALES (est): 488.4K **Privately Held**
SIC: **3577** Printers & plotters

(G-15898)
LOPRESTI SPEED MERCHANTS INC
Also Called: Lopresti Aviation
210 Airport Dr E (32958-3957)
PHONE..........................772 562-4757
Tyler Wheeler, *CEO*
Curt Lopresti, *President*
David Lopresti, *Vice Pres*
Alec Surprenant, *Engineer*
▼ EMP: 24 EST: 1991
SQ FT: 19,000
SALES (est): 3.3MM **Privately Held**
WEB: www.flywat.com
SIC: **3728** Aircraft parts & equipment

(G-15899)
MACHO PRODUCTS INC
10045 102nd Ter (32958-7831)
PHONE..........................800 327-6812
Amir K Shadab, *CEO*
Clive R Parker, *CFO*
Ashley Brown, *Marketing Staff*
◆ EMP: 50 EST: 1980
SQ FT: 75,000
SALES (est): 11.9MM **Privately Held**
WEB: www.macho.com
SIC: **3949** Protective sporting equipment

(G-15900)
MC MILLER CO INC
11640 Us Highway 1 (32958-8426)
PHONE..........................772 794-9448
Melvin C Miller II, *Ch of Bd*
Joseph Mekus, *President*
Albert J Hilberts, *Vice Pres*
Kathy Allen, *Sales Staff*
Jessica Carbajal, *Sales Staff*
EMP: 30 EST: 1945
SQ FT: 15,000
SALES (est): 7.1MM **Privately Held**
WEB: www.mcmiller.com
SIC: **3825** 3829 Instruments to measure electricity; measuring & controlling devices

(G-15901)
MDI PRODUCTS LLC
10055 102nd Ter (32958-7831)
PHONE..........................772 228-7371
Clive Parker,
Nancy Grossbart,
Amir Shadab,
▲ EMP: 19 EST: 2000
SALES (est): 801.1K **Privately Held**
WEB: www.mdiproducts.com
SIC: **3089** Injection molding of plastics

(G-15902)
MECHANICAL DESIGN CORP
100 Industrial Park Blvd (32958-5764)
PHONE..........................772 388-8782
Rick Pino, *President*
EMP: 5 EST: 2001
SQ FT: 23,632
SALES (est): 1.2MM **Privately Held**
WEB: www.mechanicaldesigncorp.net
SIC: **1389** Pipe testing, oil field service

(G-15903)
PROFOLD INC
10300 99th Way (32958-7827)
P.O. Box 780929 (32978-0929)
PHONE..........................772 589-0063
Leo A Haydt III, *President*
John Pinchin, *Principal*
Richard A Edmisten, *Director*
John R Pinchin, *Director*
EMP: 28 EST: 1982
SQ FT: 45,000
SALES (est): 1.9MM **Privately Held**
WEB: www.profold.com
SIC: **3554** Folding machines, paper

(G-15904)
SHARK SKINZ
Also Called: Schark Skinz
300 Industrial Park Blvd # 5 (32958-5772)
P.O. Box 22, Grant (32949-0022)
PHONE..........................772 388-9621
David Lee, *Owner*
▲ EMP: 9 EST: 1992
SQ FT: 5,000
SALES (est): 607.1K **Privately Held**
WEB: www.ionemoto.com
SIC: **3714** 3728 5085 5088 Motor vehicle parts & accessories; aircraft body assemblies & parts; bearings; aircraft & parts; motorcycle parts & accessories; aircraft instruments, equipment or parts

(G-15905)
TOTAL PRINT INC
1132 Us Highway 1 (32958-4147)
PHONE..........................772 589-9658
Jeffrey E Fabick, *President*
EMP: 5 EST: 1988
SQ FT: 1,400
SALES (est): 511.4K **Privately Held**
SIC: **2752** Commercial printing, offset; business form & card printing, lithographic

(G-15906)
TRITON SUBMARINES LLC
10055 102nd Ter (32958-7831)
PHONE..........................772 770-1995
Patrick Lahey, *President*
Sue Engen, *Managing Prtnr*
L Bruce Jones, *Partner*
Troy Engen, *General Mgr*
Borja Hidalgo, *Prdtn Mgr*
◆ EMP: 25 EST: 1999
SQ FT: 20,000
SALES (est): 4.6MM **Privately Held**
WEB: www.tritonsubs.com
SIC: **3731** Submarines, building & repairing

(G-15907)
US GENERATOR INC
725 Commerce Center Dr J (32958-3135)
PHONE..........................772 778-0131
William N Broocke, *President*
EMP: 8 EST: 2005
SALES (est): 919.6K **Privately Held**
WEB: www.usgenerator.org
SIC: **3621** 5063 5064 Motors & generators; electrical apparatus & equipment; electrical appliances, major

(G-15908)
VELOCITY INC
200 Airport Dr W (32958-3918)
PHONE..........................772 589-1860
Duane Swing, *CEO*
B Scott Swing, *President*
Chris Parr, *Director*
▲ EMP: 23 EST: 1986
SQ FT: 15,000
SALES (est): 5.3MM **Privately Held**
WEB: www.velocityaircraft.com
SIC: **3721** Airplanes, fixed or rotary wing

(G-15909)
VELOCITY AIRCRAFT INC
200 Airport Dr W (32958-3918)
PHONE..........................772 589-1860
Charles Xia, *Principal*
EMP: 8 EST: 2017
SALES (est): 639.3K **Privately Held**
WEB: www.velocityaircraft.com
SIC: **3728** Aircraft parts & equipment

(G-15910)
VIPER DRONES INC
214 Briarcliff Cir (32958-8693)
PHONE..........................321 427-5837
Leon Shivamber, *Principal*
Leslie Jones, *Principal*
Loretta McKeefery, *Principal*
Tom McKeefery, *Principal*
EMP: 12 EST: 2020
SALES (est): 800.6K **Privately Held**
WEB: www.viper-drones.com
SIC: **3728** Aircraft parts & equipment

(G-15911)
VIPER DRONES LLC
Also Called: My Drone Services
214 Briarcliff Cir (32958-8693)
PHONE..........................205 677-3700
Leon Shivamber, *Principal*
Brad Nichols, *CTO*
EMP: 6 EST: 2016
SALES (est): 439.9K **Privately Held**
WEB: www.viper-drones.com
SIC: **3721** Aircraft

(G-15912)
WHELEN AEROSPACE TECH LLC
210 Airport Dr E (32958-3957)
PHONE..........................800 859-4757
Neil D 'souza, *Engineer*
Michael Lorello, *Engineer*
David Lopresti, *Sales Staff*
Jayde Machado, *Sales Staff*
Bree Wheeler, *Marketing Mgr*
EMP: 11 EST: 2018
SALES (est): 2.4MM **Privately Held**
WEB: www.flywat.com
SIC: **3728** Aircraft parts & equipment

Sebring
Highlands County

(G-15913)
ALPHA GENERAL SERVICES INC
1578 Alpha Rd E (33870-4598)
P.O. Box 3331 (33871-3331)
PHONE..........................863 382-1544
Richard Lapudula, *President*
Paul Suppa, *Vice Pres*
Priscilla Jones, *Office Mgr*
▼ EMP: 20 EST: 1978
SQ FT: 45,000
SALES (est): 3.9MM **Privately Held**
WEB: www.alphageneral.com
SIC: 3089 4952 Septic tanks, plastic; sewerage systems

(G-15914)
AMERIKAN LLC
2006 Fortune Blvd (33870-5502)
PHONE..........................863 314-9417
Chris Koscho, *President*
Gregg Branning, *Vice Pres*
John C Orr, *Vice Pres*
Salvatore Incanno, *Treasurer*
EMP: 24 EST: 2004
SALES (est): 2.8MM **Privately Held**
SIC: 3089 Plastic containers, except foam

(G-15915)
BAPTIST MID-MISSIONS INC
Also Called: Editorial Bautista Independent
3417 Kenilworth Blvd (33870-4469)
PHONE..........................863 382-6350
Darrel Jingst, *Prdtn Mgr*
Tim Fry, *Manager*
Bruce Burkholder, *Director*
Joy Anglea, *Director*
Steve Brennecke, *Administration*
EMP: 10
SQ FT: 3,500
SALES (corp-wide): 16.2MM **Privately Held**
WEB: www.bmm.org
SIC: 2759 Publication printing
PA: Baptist Mid-Missions, Inc.
7749 Webster Rd
Cleveland OH 44130
440 826-3930

(G-15916)
CREATIVE SVCS CENTL FLA INC
Also Called: Creative Printing
2023 Us Highway 27 N (33870-1860)
PHONE..........................863 385-8383
Stephen Kirouac, *President*
Michael Kirouac, *Vice Pres*
Pam Kirouac, *Vice Pres*
EMP: 5 EST: 1985
SALES (est): 487.4K **Privately Held**
SIC: 2752 Commercial printing, offset

(G-15917)
D & N CABINETRY INC
2920 Kenilworth Blvd (33870-4307)
PHONE..........................863 471-1500
Nicholas Hucke, *President*
Tim Pennell, *Engineer*
EMP: 11 EST: 1986
SQ FT: 2,960
SALES (est): 1.7MM **Privately Held**
WEB: www.dncabinetry.com
SIC: 2434 Wood kitchen cabinets

(G-15918)
DARREN THOMAS GLASS CO INC
251 Commercial Ct (33876-6524)
P.O. Box 7822 (33872-0114)
PHONE..........................863 655-9500
Darren Thomas, *President*
Mary Thomas, *Admin Sec*
EMP: 5 EST: 2007
SALES (est): 570K **Privately Held**
WEB: www.neverfogrvwindow.com
SIC: 3231 7536 Products of purchased glass; automotive glass replacement shops

(G-15919)
E-STONE USA CORP
8041 Haywood Taylor Blvd (33870-7505)
PHONE..........................863 655-1273
Andrea Di Giuseppe, *CEO*
Livio Magni, *COO*
◆ EMP: 70 EST: 2014
SALES (est): 11.8MM **Privately Held**
SIC: 3272 5031 Tile, precast terrazzo or concrete; building materials, interior
PA: Trend Group Spa
Piazzale Torquato Fraccon 8
Vicenza VI 36100

(G-15920)
E-STONE USA CORPORATION
472 Webster Turn Dr (33870-7507)
PHONE..........................954 266-6793
EMP: 140
SALES (corp-wide): 46.8MM **Privately Held**
WEB: www.trend-group.com
SIC: 3272 Floor slabs & tiles, precast concrete
HQ: E-Stone Usa Corporation
1565 Nw 36th St
Miami FL 33142

(G-15921)
EVERGLADES FOODS INC
6120 State Road 66 (33875-5942)
PHONE..........................863 655-2214
G Seth Howard, *President*
Mark Gose, *Vice Pres*
Chris Sebring, *Vice Pres*
EMP: 6 EST: 1976
SQ FT: 6,000
SALES (est): 780.5K **Privately Held**
WEB: www.evergladesseasoning.com
SIC: 2099 5141 5499 Seasonings: dry mixes; food brokers; spices & herbs

(G-15922)
EXCALIBUR AIRCRAFT
6439 Tractor Rd (33876-5741)
PHONE..........................863 385-9486
Ray Bratton, *Owner*
EMP: 6 EST: 1997
SALES (est): 938.8K **Privately Held**
WEB: www.excaliburaircraft.com
SIC: 3721 Aircraft

(G-15923)
FNG EXPRESS INC
4343 Schumacher Rd (33872)
PHONE..........................863 471-9669
Dave Francis, *Principal*
EMP: 9 EST: 2005
SALES (est): 280.3K **Privately Held**
SIC: 2741 Miscellaneous publishing

(G-15924)
GATOR SHACK
4651 Us Highway 98 (33876-9561)
PHONE..........................863 381-2222
Steve C Stokes, *President*
EMP: 10 EST: 2012
SALES (est): 344.5K **Privately Held**
WEB: www.gatorshack1.com
SIC: 3421 Table & food cutlery, including butchers'

(G-15925)
GB CABINETS INCORPORATED
3907 Palazzo St (33872-2260)
PHONE..........................863 446-0676
Gary R Barnes, *Owner*
EMP: 7 EST: 2011
SALES (est): 148.4K **Privately Held**
SIC: 2434 Wood kitchen cabinets

(G-15926)
HIGHLAND CABINET INC
Also Called: Highland Cabinet Shop
739 Glenwood Ave (33870-3040)
PHONE..........................863 385-4396
Tom Braswell, *President*
Larry Mercure, *Mfg Staff*
EMP: 5 EST: 1978
SALES (est): 481.3K **Privately Held**
WEB: www.highlandscabinet.com
SIC: 2434 Wood kitchen cabinets

(G-15927)
HUCKE MANUFACTURING INC
Also Called: Advanced Door Concepts
222 Commercial Pl (33876-6526)
PHONE..........................863 655-3667
Margaret Hucke, *President*
Nicholas Hucke, *Vice Pres*
EMP: 6 EST: 2014
SQ FT: 7,500
SALES (est): 628.2K **Privately Held**
WEB: www.advdoor.com
SIC: 2541 Cabinets, lockers & shelving

(G-15928)
KEAVYS CORNER LLC
12413 Us Highway 98 (33876-9489)
PHONE..........................863 658-0235
Stephen Pardee, *CEO*
EMP: 7 EST: 2010
SALES (est): 551.5K **Privately Held**
WEB: www.kvlab.com
SIC: 3821 Laboratory equipment: fume hoods, distillation racks, etc.

(G-15929)
LESCO INC
Also Called: Lesco Service Center
425 Haywood Taylor Blvd (33870-7535)
PHONE..........................863 655-2424
Hal Berry, *Dir Ops-Prd-Mfg*
EMP: 23
SALES (corp-wide): 44B **Publicly Held**
SIC: 2875 Fertilizers, mixing only
HQ: Lesco, Inc.
1385 E 36th St
Cleveland OH 44114
216 706-9250

(G-15930)
LIGHT-TECH INC
8880 W Josephine Rd (33875-7213)
PHONE..........................863 385-6000
Lance A Giller, *President*
Sharon A Giller, *Corp Secy*
Roger Giller, *Vice Pres*
EMP: 7 EST: 1949
SALES (est): 600.1K **Privately Held**
WEB: www.light-tech.com
SIC: 3827 Optical instruments & apparatus

(G-15931)
LOCKWOOD AIRCRAFT CORPORATION
1 Lockwood Ln (33870-7500)
PHONE..........................863 655-4242
EMP: 12 EST: 2006
SALES (est): 317.3K **Privately Held**
SIC: 3728 Aircraft parts & equipment

(G-15932)
MACHINE TECHNOLOGY INC
108 Investment Ct (33876-6617)
PHONE..........................863 298-8001
Chris Nelson, *President*
EMP: 5 EST: 2017
SALES (est): 320.7K **Privately Held**
WEB: www.machine-technology.com
SIC: 3599 Machine shop, jobbing & repair

(G-15933)
ON SITE AG SERVICES
359 S Commerce Ave (33870-3607)
PHONE..........................863 382-7502
Curtis Donovan, *President*
EMP: 10 EST: 2017
SALES (est): 707.2K **Privately Held**
SIC: 3523 Combines (harvester-threshers)

(G-15934)
PARK PLACE MANUFACTURING INC
454 Park St (33870-3225)
PHONE..........................863 382-0126
Ken Wacaster, *President*
EMP: 10 EST: 1997
SALES (est): 466.4K **Privately Held**
WEB: www.parkplacetruss.com
SIC: 3448 2439 Trusses & framing: prefabricated metal; structural wood members

(G-15935)
PARK PLACE TRUSS INC
500 Park St (33870-3227)
PHONE..........................863 382-0126
Keith Wacaster, *President*
EMP: 17 EST: 2003
SALES (est): 1.2MM **Privately Held**
WEB: www.parkplacetruss.com
SIC: 2439 Trusses, wooden roof

(G-15936)
PARK PLACE TRUSS & DESIGN INC ✪
206 W Center Ave (33870-3106)
PHONE..........................863 382-0126
Keith Wacaster, *CEO*
EMP: 28 EST: 2021
SALES (est): 2.6MM **Privately Held**
WEB: www.parkplacetruss.com
SIC: 2439 Trusses, wooden roof

(G-15937)
SCOSTA CORP (PA)
3670 Commerce Center Dr (33870-5538)
PHONE..........................863 385-8242
Scott Stanley II, *President*
Joe Falis, *General Mgr*
Kenny Pagano, *Engineer*
Madeline F Stanley, *Treasurer*
Tanya Davis, *Sales Staff*
EMP: 43 EST: 1979
SALES (est): 10MM **Privately Held**
WEB: www.scostacorp.com
SIC: 2439 Trusses, wooden roof

(G-15938)
SCOSTA CORP
3705 Commerce Center Dr (33870)
PHONE..........................863 385-8242
Scott Stanley, *President*
EMP: 17
SALES (corp-wide): 10MM **Privately Held**
WEB: www.scostacorp.com
SIC: 3448 2439 Trusses & framing: prefabricated metal; structural wood members
PA: Scosta Corp.
3670 Commerce Center Dr
Sebring FL 33870
863 385-8242

(G-15939)
SEA HAWK INDUSTRIES INC
Also Called: Sea Hawk Boats
523 Pear St (33870-3058)
PHONE..........................863 385-1995
Ginger Wyatt, *President*
Mike Wyatt, *Vice Pres*
▼ EMP: 9 EST: 1998
SQ FT: 3,000
SALES (est): 778.6K **Privately Held**
WEB: www.seahawkboats.com
SIC: 3732 Boat building & repairing

(G-15940)
SEBRING CUSTOM TANNING INC
429 Webster Turn Dr (33870-7543)
PHONE..........................863 655-1600
David Travers, *President*
EMP: 7 EST: 1986
SQ FT: 180,000
SALES (est): 972.2K **Privately Held**
WEB: www.sebringcustomtanning.com
SIC: 3111 Tanneries, leather

(G-15941)
SEBRING SEPTIC TANK PRECAST CO
Also Called: Sebring's Precast Products
8037 Associate Blvd (33876-6616)
PHONE..........................863 655-2030
Warren Copeland, *President*
Warren D Copeland, *President*
Sandra B Copeland, *Corp Secy*
EMP: 26 EST: 1978
SQ FT: 5,400
SALES (est): 4.7MM **Privately Held**
WEB: www.sebringprecast.com
SIC: 3272 3523 Septic tanks, concrete; farm machinery & equipment

(G-15942)
SPANCRETE OF FLORIDA LLC
400 Deer Trl E (33876-6500)
PHONE..........................863 655-1515
Toll Free:..........................888 -
Mike Whalen, *President*

EMP: 30 EST: 1999
SALES (est): 3.7MM Privately Held
SIC: 3272 Concrete products, precast

(G-15943)
SPANCRETE SOUTHEAST INC
400 Deer Trl E (33876-6500)
P.O. Box 828, Waukesha WI (53187-0828)
PHONE...................................863 655-1515
John R Nagy, President
Todd Backus, Vice Pres
EMP: 1 EST: 2007
SALES (est): 6.2MM
SALES (corp-wide): 50.9MM Privately
Held
SIC: 3272 Concrete products, precast
PA: The Spancrete Group Inc
N16w23415 Stone Ridge Dr
Waukesha WI 53188
414 290-9000

(G-15944)
STRATONET INC (PA)
935 Mall Ring Rd (33870-8515)
PHONE...................................863 382-8503
Delton E Delaney, President
Arthur Wolfe, Corp Secy
EMP: 9 EST: 1992
SQ FT: 2,000
SALES (est): 1.5MM Privately Held
WEB: www.stratonet.net
SIC: 7372 Prepackaged software

(G-15945)
SUPERSWEET FROG LLC
2932 Us Highway 27 N (33870-1627)
PHONE...................................863 386-4917
Judith Bryan, Principal
EMP: 8 EST: 2014
SALES (est): 365.5K Privately Held
SIC: 2024 Yogurt desserts, frozen

(G-15946)
TECNAM US INC
29536 Flying Fortress Ln (33870-7514)
PHONE...................................863 655-2400
Paolo Pascale, CEO
Giovanni Pascale, Managing Dir
Biagio Silvestro, Prdtn Dir
Fabio Russo, Research
▲ EMP: 9 EST: 2014
SALES (est): 1.6MM Privately Held
SIC: 3721 Aircraft

(G-15947)
THE HC COMPANIES INC
Also Called: Amerikan
2006 Fortune Blvd (33870-5502)
PHONE...................................863 314-9417
EMP: 98
SALES (corp-wide): 447.3MM Privately
Held
WEB: www.hc-companies.com
SIC: 2821 Plastics materials & resins
HQ: The Hc Companies Inc
2450 Edison Blvd Ste 3
Twinsburg OH 44087
440 632-3333

(G-15948)
TRADEWINDS POWER CORP
Also Called: John Deere Authorized Dealer
2717 Alt Us Hwy 27 S (33870-4970)
PHONE...................................863 382-2166
Thomas J Tracey, President
Jorge Rodriguez, Engineer
Caitlin Chason, Sales Staff
Spencer Dickerson, Sales Staff
Michael Waldron, Sales Associate
EMP: 10 Privately Held
WEB: www.deere.com
SIC: 3694 3561 5082 Engine electrical
equipment; pumps & pumping equipment;
construction & mining machinery
HQ: Tradewinds Power Corp.
5820 Nw 84th Ave
Doral FL 33166

(G-15949)
TURF CARE SUPPLY LLC
422 Webster Turn Dr (33870-7507)
PHONE...................................863 655-0700
EMP: 68 Privately Held
WEB: www.turfcaresupply.com
SIC: 2873 Nitrogenous fertilizers

HQ: Turf Care Supply, Llc
50 Pearl Rd Ste 200
Brunswick OH 44212

(G-15950)
WINNTEL USA
Also Called: Winner Group
4014 Vilabella Dr (33872-1554)
PHONE...................................863 451-1789
Ejaj Chowdhury, Owner
EMP: 10 EST: 2010
SALES (est): 91.6K Privately Held
SIC: 2329 Men's & boys' clothing

(G-15951)
YARBROUGH TIRE SVC INC
1532 Sebring Pkwy (33870-5100)
PHONE...................................863 385-1574
Danny Yarbrough, Manager
EMP: 8 EST: 2018
SALES (est): 473.9K Privately Held
SIC: 3714 Motor vehicle parts & accessories

Seffner
Hillsborough County

(G-15952)
BAEZ ENTERPRISES CORP
6315 Morning Star Dr (33584-2901)
PHONE...................................813 317-7277
Frank Felix Baez, President
Erbis Baez, Treasurer
EMP: 11 EST: 2004
SALES (est): 1MM Privately Held
SIC: 3585 Air conditioning equipment,
complete

(G-15953)
CAPTAIN CABINETS LLC
6705 Pemberton View Dr (33584-2423)
PHONE...................................813 685-7179
Leo Hans, Principal
EMP: 7 EST: 2017
SALES (est): 109.3K Privately Held
WEB: www.captcabinets.com
SIC: 2434 Wood kitchen cabinets

(G-15954)
CAST-CRETE USA LLC
6324 County Road 579 (33584-3006)
P.O. Box 24567, Tampa (33623-4567)
PHONE...................................813 621-4641
James Connelly, CEO
Craig Parrino, President
Daniel Cheney, CFO
Sal Deriggi, Natl Sales Mgr
Anthony Livelsberger, Sales Staff
▼ EMP: 99 EST: 1997
SALES (est): 21.2MM Privately Held
WEB: www.castcrete.com
SIC: 3272 5211 Lintels, concrete; lumber
& other building materials

(G-15955)
DE VINCO COMPANY
435 Canning Plant Rd (33584-4645)
P.O. Box 155, Palmetto (34220-0155)
PHONE...................................941 722-1100
Devin Greenlaw, President
Jonathan C Greenlaw, Vice Pres
EMP: 7 EST: 2017
SQ FT: 120,000
SALES (est): 518.3K Privately Held
WEB: www.bulkcookingwines.com
SIC: 2084 Wines

(G-15956)
DEVISE SOLUTIONS LLC
1217 Oakhill St (33584-4909)
PHONE...................................813 760-6393
Mario J Arcicovich, Principal
EMP: 7 EST: 2013
SALES (est): 75K Privately Held
WEB: www.devisesolutions.net
SIC: 3599 Machine shop, jobbing & repair

(G-15957)
EVO MOTORS LLC
11809 E Us Highway 92 (33584-3413)
PHONE...................................813 621-7799
Mike Atir, Manager
EMP: 9 EST: 2012

SALES (est): 2.2MM Privately Held
WEB: www.evomotorsusa.com
SIC: 3594 5521 5511 Motors, pneumatic;
used car dealers; new & used car dealers

(G-15958)
FLORIDA ENGINEERED
CONSTRU (PA)
Also Called: Cast Crete Tampa
6324 County Road 579 (33584-3006)
PHONE...................................813 621-4641
Shea Hughes, CEO
Ralph W Hughes, Ch of Bd
William J Kardash, President
John Stanton, President
Carolyn Potter, Human Resources
◆ EMP: 225 EST: 1955
SQ FT: 10,000
SALES (est): 28.5MM Privately Held
WEB: www.castcrete.com
SIC: 3272 5031 2439 Concrete products,
precast; concrete stuctural support &
building material; building materials, exterior; trusses, wooden roof

(G-15959)
GABLE ENTERPRISES
1008 Lenna Ave (33584-5136)
PHONE...................................727 455-5576
Michael Gable, Owner
EMP: 10 EST: 1982
SALES (est): 432.9K Privately Held
WEB: www.gableenterprises.com
SIC: 3732 3731 Boat building & repairing;
shipbuilding & repairing

(G-15960)
GARDNERS SCREEN
ENCLOSURES
1113 Lake Shore Ranch Dr (33584-5564)
PHONE...................................813 843-8527
Timothy Gardner, Principal
EMP: 12 EST: 2005
SALES (est): 305.8K Privately Held
SIC: 3448 Screen enclosures

(G-15961)
GPM FAB & SUPPLY LLC
1504 Lenna Ave (33584-5122)
P.O. Box 1303 (33583-1303)
PHONE...................................813 689-7107
Henry Lloyd, Mng Member
Lindy Lloyd
EMP: 5 EST: 1989
SQ FT: 8,000
SALES (est): 896.8K Privately Held
WEB: www.gpmfab.com
SIC: 3317 3498 Steel pipe & tubes; fabricated pipe & fittings

(G-15962)
GUNTER SEPTIC TANK MFG
1434 E Dr Mrtn Lther King (33584-4841)
PHONE...................................813 654-1214
Danny Gunter, Owner
Aubery Coleman, Manager
EMP: 5 EST: 1987
SALES (est): 500K Privately Held
WEB: www.gunterseptictanks.com
SIC: 3272 5039 Septic tanks, concrete;
septic tanks

(G-15963)
OLD OAK TRUSS COMPANY
1460 State Rd 574 (33584)
PHONE...................................813 689-6597
David Ledbetter, President
EMP: 8 EST: 1993
SALES (est): 957.8K Privately Held
WEB: oldoaktrusscompany.business.site
SIC: 2439 Trusses, wooden roof

(G-15964)
PIPES R US
12002 E Dr M Lthr Kng Jr Martin Luther
(33584)
PHONE...................................813 661-4420
Hithem Abdelkhader, Owner
EMP: 8 EST: 2008
SALES (est): 256.1K Privately Held
SIC: 3069 Rubber smoking accessories

(G-15965)
TAYLOR COMMUNICATIONS INC
12003 Embarcadero Dr (33584-3455)
PHONE...................................813 689-5099
EMP: 13
SALES (corp-wide): 3.7B Privately Held
WEB: www.taylor.com
SIC: 2761 Manifold business forms
HQ: Taylor Communications, Inc.
1725 Roe Crest Dr
North Mankato MN 56003
866 541-0937

(G-15966)
TSN MANUFACTURING INC
807 Hickory Fork Dr (33584-4755)
PHONE...................................727 709-9802
Tim Ngo, Principal
EMP: 8 EST: 2011
SALES (est): 206.5K Privately Held
WEB: www.tsnmanufacturing.com
SIC: 3999 Manufacturing industries

Seminole
Pinellas County

(G-15967)
ADVA-LITE INC
8285 Bryan Dairy Rd (33777-1350)
PHONE...................................727 369-5319
William A Dolan II, President
Don Pollo, CFO
▲ EMP: 108 EST: 1963
SQ FT: 80,000
SALES (est): 1.1MM
SALES (corp-wide): 23MM Privately
Held
SIC: 3648 3692 2396 Flashlights; primary
batteries, dry & wet; automotive & apparel
trimmings
PA: Camsing Global, Llc
8285 Bryan Dairy Rd
Seminole FL 33777
727 369-5319

(G-15968)
ALLEN SHUFFLEBOARD LLC
6595 Seminole Blvd (33772-6314)
PHONE...................................727 399-8877
Jim Allen, President
Sam Allen, Principal
◆ EMP: 7 EST: 1948
SQ FT: 8,200
SALES (est): 736.6K Privately Held
WEB: www.allenshuffleboard.com
SIC: 3949 7011 2842 Shuffleboards &
shuffleboard equipment; hotels & motels;
specialty cleaning, polishes & sanitation
goods

(G-15969)
ANDERSON PRINTING
SERVICES INC
Also Called: Sir Speedy
7245 Bryan Dairy Rd (33777-1540)
PHONE...................................727 545-9000
Jeffrey Anderson, President
Matt Anderson, Vice Pres
EMP: 22 EST: 1973
SQ FT: 5,300
SALES (est): 2.9MM Privately Held
WEB: www.sirspeedy.com
SIC: 2752 Commercial printing, lithographic

(G-15970)
BAMCO INC
13799 Park Blvd Ste 274 (33776-3402)
PHONE...................................303 886-5992
Mark Ballenger, President
EMP: 8 EST: 2018
SALES (est): 112.6K Privately Held
WEB: www.gobamco.com
SIC: 3444 Sheet metalwork

(G-15971)
BEACH BEACON
9911 Seminole Blvd (33772-2536)
PHONE...................................727 397-5563
Gerard Boutin, Principal
EMP: 14 EST: 2001

SALES (est): 1.1MM **Privately Held**
WEB: www.tbnweekly.com
SIC: 2711 Newspapers, publishing & printing

(G-15972)
COMCEPT SOLUTIONS LLC
13799 Park Blvd Ste 307 (33776-3402)
PHONE..............................727 535-1900
Glenn D Atwell,
Joe D Mattos,
EMP: 20 **EST:** 1993
SALES (est): 5.6MM **Privately Held**
WEB: www.comcept.net
SIC: 3575 7311 7372 Computer terminals, monitors & components; advertising agencies; prepackaged software

(G-15973)
CUSTOM CABINETS
11060 70th Ave (33772-6308)
PHONE..............................727 392-1676
James Warren, *President*
Sandra Davis, *Office Mgr*
EMP: 5 **EST:** 2015
SALES (est): 600K **Privately Held**
WEB: www.advancedcustomcabinets.net
SIC: 2434 Wood kitchen cabinets

(G-15974)
DIGNITAS SOFTWARE DEVELOPMENT
6677 Augusta Blvd (33777-4523)
PHONE..............................727 392-2004
George A Tripp Jr, *Manager*
EMP: 7 **EST:** 2006
SALES (est): 78.4K **Privately Held**
WEB: www.dignitastechnologies.com
SIC: 7372 Prepackaged software

(G-15975)
ELECTRODES INC
10350 62nd Ter (33772-6937)
PHONE..............................727 698-7498
Brian Abbott, *Principal*
EMP: 9 **EST:** 2011
SALES (est): 113.3K **Privately Held**
WEB: www.electrodesinc.com
SIC: 3599 Machine shop, jobbing & repair

(G-15976)
HALMA HOLDINGS INC
8060 Bryan Dairy Rd Ste A (33777-1441)
PHONE..............................973 832-2658
Arnold Moshier, *Officer*
EMP: 38
SALES (corp-wide): 2B **Privately Held**
SIC: 3841 Surgical & medical instruments
HQ: Halma Holdings Inc.
535 Sprngfeld Ave Ste 110
Summit NJ 07901
513 772-5501

(G-15977)
HARLAN J NEWMAN
Also Called: Black Mountain
10490 75th St Ste A (33777-1413)
PHONE..............................727 216-6419
Melissa Newman, *President*
Harlan Newman, *Owner*
▲ **EMP:** 6 **EST:** 1995
SQ FT: 10,000
SALES (est): 613.7K **Privately Held**
WEB: www.blackmountainapparel.com
SIC: 2311 5963 Men's & boys' suits & coats; clothing sales, house-to-house

(G-15978)
INTERNTONAL LINEAR MATRIX CORP
10831 Canal St (33777-1636)
PHONE..............................727 549-1808
Jennifer Foster, *General Mgr*
Jennifer Griffin, *Vice Pres*
EMP: 10 **EST:** 2007
SALES (est): 1MM **Privately Held**
WEB: www.ilmusa.com
SIC: 3699 Linear accelerators

(G-15979)
LIGHTNING PHASE II INC
10700 76th Ct (33777-1440)
PHONE..............................727 539-1800
Andrew Cecere, *Ch of Bd*
Jeff C Sproat, *Vice Pres*

Claire Knafla, *Opers Mgr*
Jon Benjamin, *Engineer*
Matt McNulty, *VP Finance*
EMP: 1 **EST:** 1985
SQ FT: 25,000
SALES (est): 6.5MM
SALES (corp-wide): 23.7B **Publicly Held**
SIC: 7372 7373 7378 Application computer software; computer integrated systems design; computer maintenance & repair
HQ: Elavon, Inc.
2 Concourse Pkwy Ste 800
Atlanta GA 30328

(G-15980)
LONDOS FINE CABINETRY LLC
6901 Bryan Dairy Rd # 130 (33777-1600)
PHONE..............................727 544-2929
Jerimiah Londos, *Mng Member*
Christoffer Londos,
EMP: 6 **EST:** 2012
SQ FT: 5,000
SALES (est): 479.1K **Privately Held**
WEB: www.londosfinecabinetry.com
SIC: 2434 Wood kitchen cabinets

(G-15981)
LORENTE INTERNATIONAL LLC
Also Called: World Class Awards
6950 Bryan Dairy Rd Ste A (33777-1606)
PHONE..............................877 281-6469
Susan Daproza, *Vice Pres*
Cindy Roberson, *Sales Staff*
Kevin Caffey, *Office Mgr*
Alfredo Lorente,
Angela Lorente,
◆ **EMP:** 35 **EST:** 1982
SALES (est): 3.4MM **Privately Held**
WEB: www.lorente.us
SIC: 3993 2396 Advertising novelties; automotive & apparel trimmings

(G-15982)
METAL FRONTS INC
10930 75th St (33777-1432)
PHONE..............................727 547-6700
George Misenhelder, *CEO*
Steven Elsenheimer, *Opers Staff*
EMP: 5 **EST:** 1995
SALES (est): 868.7K **Privately Held**
WEB: www.metalfronts.com
SIC: 3442 Store fronts, prefabricated, metal

(G-15983)
MILES OF SMILES RIDES INC
Also Called: Air-Flo/Erwood Heating and A/C
10530 72nd St Ste 705 (33777-1522)
PHONE..............................727 528-1227
Stuart J Long, *President*
EMP: 10 **EST:** 2007
SALES (est): 1MM **Privately Held**
SIC: 3585 1711 Heating & air conditioning combination units; heating & air conditioning contractors

(G-15984)
MODULAR MOLDING INTL INC
Also Called: M & M Industries
10521 75th St Ste B (33777-1434)
P.O. Box 10412, Largo (33773-0412)
PHONE..............................727 541-1333
Frank Meola, *President*
Mary Ann Meola, *CFO*
EMP: 31 **EST:** 1991
SQ FT: 17,000
SALES (est): 4.7MM **Privately Held**
WEB: www.mm-international.com
SIC: 3089 Injection molding of plastics

(G-15985)
PHOENIX TRANSMISSION PARTS INC (PA)
Also Called: Phoenix Trans Parts
7000 Bryan Dairy Rd A4 (33777-1611)
PHONE..............................727 541-0269
Andrew Smith, *President*
Tony Leverso, *Sales Staff*
EMP: 9 **EST:** 2004
SALES (est): 1.4MM **Privately Held**
WEB: www.phxtransmissionparts.com
SIC: 3714 7537 Motor vehicle parts & accessories; automotive transmission repair shops

(G-15986)
PRECISION RESISTOR CO INC
9442 Laura Anne Dr (33776-1600)
PHONE..............................727 541-5771
Fred A Dusenberry Jr, *President*
Chris Kistler, *General Mgr*
Robert L Wright, *Corp Secy*
EMP: 21 **EST:** 1932
SALES (est): 2.4MM **Privately Held**
WEB: www.precisionresistor.com
SIC: 3676 Electronic resistors

(G-15987)
PREFERRED CUSTOM PRINTING LLC
Also Called: Coconut Tree Btq & Gallery
7000 Bryan Dairy Rd B2 (33777-1612)
PHONE..............................727 443-1900
David L Braun,
Kim Braun,
EMP: 10 **EST:** 2007
SALES (est): 621.7K **Privately Held**
WEB: www.pcpprinting.com
SIC: 2741 2396 Art copy: publishing & printing; fabric printing & stamping

(G-15988)
SSH HOLDING INC
10055 Seminole Blvd (33772-2539)
PHONE..............................678 942-1800
Kirby Sims, *CEO*
Fred Hill III, *COO*
Connie Copelan, *Vice Pres*
Randy Figur, *Vice Pres*
Bruce Kirschner, *Vice Pres*
◆ **EMP:** 73 **EST:** 1993
SALES (est): 12MM
SALES (corp-wide): 536.9MM **Publicly Held**
WEB: www.hpi.net
SIC: 2395 Emblems, embroidered
PA: Superior Group Of Companies, Inc.
10055 Seminole Blvd
Seminole FL 33772
727 397-9611

(G-15989)
STARLITE INC
10861 91st Ter (33772-3045)
P.O. Box 20004, Saint Petersburg (33742-0004)
PHONE..............................727 392-2929
George Darwin, *President*
Tony Darwin, *President*
Barbara Fluharty, *Vice Pres*
Barbara Jowers, *Vice Pres*
George Scheffler Sr, *Vice Pres*
EMP: 14 **EST:** 1983
SALES (est): 2.2MM **Privately Held**
WEB: www.starlite-inc.com
SIC: 2731 Books: publishing & printing; books: publishing only

(G-15990)
STONECRFTERS ARCHTCTRAL PRCAST (PA)
10820 75th St Ste A (33777-1424)
PHONE..............................727 544-1210
Bill Morris, *Partner*
Dennis Nelucci, *Principal*
EMP: 10 **EST:** 1998
SALES (est): 3.2MM **Privately Held**
WEB: www.stonecraftersfl.com
SIC: 3272 3281 Siding, precast stone; cut stone & stone products

(G-15991)
SUPERIOR GROUP COMPANIES INC (PA)
10055 Seminole Blvd (33772-2539)
P.O. Box 4002 (33775-4002)
PHONE..............................727 397-9611
Michael Benstock, *CEO*
Sidney Kirschner, *Ch of Bd*
Andrew D Demott Jr, *COO*
Mor Shvarzman, *Counsel*
Jordan M Alpert, *Senior VP*
◆ **EMP:** 150 **EST:** 1920
SQ FT: 60,000
SALES (est): 536.9MM **Publicly Held**
WEB: www.superiorgroupofcompanies.com
SIC: 2389 3999 7389 Uniforms & vestments; identification badges & insignia; telemarketing services

(G-15992)
SUPERIOR GROUP COMPANIES INC
Universal Cotton Division
10055 Seminole Blvd (33772-2539)
P.O. Box 4002 (33775-4002)
PHONE..............................727 397-9611
Lorraine Becker, *Principal*
Dick Snyder, *Principal*
Michael Benstock, *Branch Mgr*
EMP: 7
SALES (corp-wide): 536.9MM **Publicly Held**
WEB: www.superiorgroupofcompanies.com
SIC: 2211 Laundry nets
PA: Superior Group Of Companies, Inc.
10055 Seminole Blvd
Seminole FL 33772
727 397-9611

(G-15993)
SUPERIOR SURGICAL MFG CO
10055 Seminole Blvd (33772-2539)
P.O. Box 4002 (33775-4002)
PHONE..............................800 727-8643
Michael Benstock, *Principal*
EMP: 11 **EST:** 2007
SALES (est): 259.7K **Privately Held**
SIC: 3842 Surgical appliances & supplies

(G-15994)
TACO METALS LLC
Also Called: Taco Marine
6950 Bryan Dairy Rd Ste A (33777-1606)
PHONE..............................727 224-4282
Charles Upmeyer, *Warehouse Mgr*
Cliston Warren, *Branch Mgr*
EMP: 10
SALES (corp-wide): 4B **Publicly Held**
WEB: www.tacometals.com
SIC: 3089 Plastic boats & other marine equipment
HQ: Taco Metals, Llc
3020 N Commerce Pkwy
Miramar FL 33025
305 652-8566

(G-15995)
TAMPA BAY NEWSPAPERS INC
9911 Seminole Blvd (33772-2536)
PHONE..............................727 397-5563
Dan Autry, *Principal*
EMP: 57 **EST:** 1997
SALES (est): 5MM
SALES (corp-wide): 14.9MM **Privately Held**
WEB: www.tbnweekly.com
SIC: 2711 Newspapers, publishing & printing
HQ: Times Publishing Company
490 1st Ave S
Saint Petersburg FL 33701
727 893-8111

(G-15996)
UNIMED SURGICAL PRODUCTS INC
10401 Belcher Rd S (33777-1415)
PHONE..............................727 546-1900
EMP: 34
SQ FT: 18,000
SALES (est): 4.9MM **Privately Held**
SIC: 3841 Mfg Surgical/Medical Instruments

(G-15997)
VMS USA INC
8060 Cypress Garden Ct (33777-3001)
P.O. Box 7134 (33775-7134)
PHONE..............................727 434-1577
Hans Konle, *President*
Konle Hans, *Principal*
EMP: 10 **EST:** 2012
SQ FT: 7,000
SALES (est): 2.5MM **Privately Held**
WEB: www.vms-usa-inc.com
SIC: 3565 Packaging machinery

(G-15998)
WIDE OPEN ARMORY LLC
8200 113th St Ste 104 (33772-4111)
PHONE..............................727 202-5980
Brian Thomas,
EMP: 5 **EST:** 2012

▲ = Import ▼=Export
◆ =Import/Export

(G-16005)
DURAPOLY INDUSTRIES INC
191 N Highway 314a (34488-5138)
PHONE.................................352 622-3455
Calvin Francis, *President*
Gary F Francis, *Vice Pres*
EMP: 9 **EST:** 1997
SQ FT: 6,000
SALES (est): 988.8K **Privately Held**
WEB: www.durapolyboats.com
SIC: 3443 Water tanks, metal plate

(G-16006)
GEORGIA-PACIFIC LLC
5240 Ne 64th Ave (34488-1340)
PHONE.................................404 652-4000
Fred Jackson, *Manager*
EMP: 50 **Privately Held**
SIC: 2439 Mfg Structural Wood Members

(G-16007)
PETE PETERSON SIGNS INC
11094 Ne Highway 314 (34488-2236)
PHONE.................................352 625-2307
Peter Peterson, *CEO*
Mary Peterson, *Corp Secy*
EMP: 5 **EST:** 1951
SQ FT: 2,275
SALES (est): 480K **Privately Held**
WEB: www.petepetersonsigns.com
SIC: 3993 Electric signs

(G-16008)
STANDARD SAND & SILICA COMPANY
15450 Ne 14th Street Rd (34488-4520)
PHONE.................................352 625-2385
John Smith, *Opers-Prdtn-Mfg*
Charles Wren, *Sales Staff*
EMP: 8
SQ FT: 1,344
SALES (corp-wide): 69.8MM **Privately Held**
WEB: www.standardsand.com
SIC: 1481 Mine & quarry services, non-metallic minerals
PA: Standard Sand & Silica Company
   1850 Us Highway 17 92 N
   Davenport FL 33837
   863 422-7100

Sopchoppy
Wakulla County

(G-16009)
OCOOW LLC
2340 Sopchoppy Hwy (32358-1431)
P.O. Box 554 (32358-0554)
PHONE.................................805 266-7616
Tracie Tinghitella, *Principal*
EMP: 9 **EST:** 2015
SALES (est): 480.3K **Privately Held**
SIC: 2891 Adhesives & sealants

Sorrento
Lake County

(G-16010)
J & S CYPRESS INC
28625 Cypress Mill Rd (32776-9553)
P.O. Box 322 (32776-0322)
PHONE.................................352 383-3864
Ethel Chavis, *President*
EMP: 10 **EST:** 1973
SQ FT: 900
SALES (est): 1MM **Privately Held**
WEB: www.cypressthings.com
SIC: 2421 2511 2434 Sawmills & planing mills, general; wood household furniture; wood kitchen cabinets

(G-16011)
MEACHEM STEEL INC
25546 High Hampton Cir (32776-7739)
PHONE.................................352 735-7333
Lori Dewitt, *CEO*
Carrlynn Dewitt, *Vice Pres*
EMP: 7 **EST:** 1996
SQ FT: 12,000
SALES (est): 660.1K **Privately Held**
SIC: 3441 Fabricated structural metal

SALES (est): 426.5K **Privately Held**
WEB: www.wideopenarmory.com
SIC: 3484 3482 Small arms; small arms ammunition

(G-15999)
XPONDR CORPORATION
10751 75th St (33777-1423)
P.O. Box 3430, Pinellas Park (33780-3430)
PHONE.................................727 541-4149
Lincoln Charlot, *President*
Michael Bryan, *Vice Pres*
◆ **EMP:** 22 **EST:** 1994
SQ FT: 11,000
SALES (est): 2.9MM **Privately Held**
WEB: www.xpondr.com
SIC: 3699 Security control equipment & systems

(G-16000)
ZHONE TECHNOLOGIES INC
7340 Bryan Dairy Rd # 150 (33777-1551)
PHONE.................................510 777-7151
EMP: 11 **EST:** 2016
SALES (est): 3.1MM **Privately Held**
SIC: 3661 Fiber optics communications equipment

Shalimar
Okaloosa County

(G-16001)
EMERALD SAILS
100 Old Ferry Rd (32579-1215)
P.O. Box 800 (32579-0800)
PHONE.................................850 240-4777
Brian Harrison, *Principal*
▲ **EMP:** 9 **EST:** 2010
SALES (est): 129.5K **Privately Held**
WEB: www.canvasrepairsshalimarfl.com
SIC: 3444 Awnings & canopies

(G-16002)
SHALIMAR RACEWAY DBA GULFCOAST
1183 N Eglin Pkwy (32579-1252)
PHONE.................................850 651-7848
EMP: 7 **EST:** 2010
SALES (est): 252.8K **Privately Held**
WEB: www.shalimarflorida.org
SIC: 3644 Raceways

(G-16003)
SIERRA NEVADA CORPORATION
1150 N Eglin Pkwy (32579-1227)
PHONE.................................850 659-3600
Fatih Ozmen, *CEO*
Philip Barcelon, *Software Engr*
Barry Collier, *Technician*
Chase Creamer, *Technician*
EMP: 19
SALES (corp-wide): 2.3B **Privately Held**
WEB: www.sncorp.com
SIC: 3812 3663 3699 Search & navigation equipment; radio & TV communications equipment; countermeasure simulators, electric
PA: Sierra Nevada Corporation
   444 Salomon Cir
   Sparks NV 89434
   775 331-0222

Silver Springs
Marion County

(G-16004)
A-1 CITY WIDE SEWER SVC INC
Also Called: Brown's Septics
6342 E Highway 326 (34488-1151)
P.O. Box 1057 (34489-1057)
PHONE.................................352 236-4456
Raymond W Brown, *President*
Barbara M Brown, *Treasurer*
EMP: 16 **EST:** 1975
SALES (est): 938.2K **Privately Held**
SIC: 3272 Concrete products, precast; septic tanks, concrete

(G-16012)
PRECISION METAL SERVICES INC
33243 Equestrian Trl (32776-9193)
PHONE.................................407 843-3682
Jack Brush, *President*
Heather Brush, *Corp Secy*
EMP: 10 **EST:** 1965
SALES (est): 819.2K **Privately Held**
WEB: www.precisionmetalservices.com
SIC: 3444 3479 Sheet metal specialties, not stamped; painting of metal products

(G-16013)
R F LABORATORIES INC
31355 Bear Pond Dr # 46 (32776-9012)
PHONE.................................920 564-2700
David J Zima, *President*
EMP: 10 **EST:** 1994
SQ FT: 2,000
SALES (est): 180.6K **Privately Held**
WEB: www.rflab.com
SIC: 3663 Pagers (one-way)

(G-16014)
RADIO OEM INC
31355 State Road 46 (32776)
PHONE.................................920 564-6622
David Zima, *CEO*
Tina Zima, *CFO*
EMP: 8 **EST:** 2004
SALES (est): 170K **Privately Held**
SIC: 3651 Electronic kits for home assembly: radio, TV, phonograph

South Bay
Palm Beach County

(G-16015)
FLORIDA CRYSTALS CORPORATION
Also Called: Florida Crystals Food
8501 S Us Hwy 27 Ave (33493-2302)
P.O. Box 9 (33493-0009)
PHONE.................................561 992-5635
Joseph Sommers, *Engineer*
Ricardo Hernandez, *Controller*
Kevin Dick, *Branch Mgr*
Matthew Gilbert, *Manager*
Marcos Zepeda, *Software Dev*
EMP: 369
SALES (corp-wide): 2.1B **Privately Held**
WEB: www.floridacrystals.com
SIC: 2061 2062 Raw cane sugar; cane sugar refining
HQ: Florida Crystals Corporation
   1 N Clematis St Ste 200
   West Palm Beach FL 33401
   561 655-6303

(G-16016)
OKEELANTA CORPORATION
Also Called: Okeelanta Sugar
6 Mile S Of S Bay Hwy 27 (33493)
P.O. Box 86 (33493-8600)
PHONE.................................561 996-9072
Jose Gonzalez, *General Mgr*
Ricardo Lima, *Manager*
EMP: 200
SALES (corp-wide): 2.1B **Privately Held**
WEB: www.floridacrystals.com
SIC: 2061 Raw cane sugar
HQ: Okeelanta Corporation
   1 N Clematis St Ste 200
   West Palm Beach FL 33401
   561 366-5100

(G-16017)
SANCHEZ BROTHERS CORP
Also Called: Sb Pallets
6500 Us Highway 27 S (33493-2203)
P.O. Box 39 (33493-0039)
PHONE.................................561 992-0062
Jorge Sanchez, *President*
▲ **EMP:** 15 **EST:** 1993
SQ FT: 250,000
SALES (est): 2.4MM **Privately Held**
WEB: www.sbpallets.com
SIC: 2448 Pallets, wood

South Daytona
Volusia County

(G-16018)
BELSNICKEL ENTERPRISES INC
901 Valencia Rd (32119-2548)
PHONE.................................386 256-5367
Sally Moyer, *President*
◆ **EMP:** 10 **EST:** 1994
SALES (est): 900K **Privately Held**
WEB: www.thebellpeople.com
SIC: 3931 Bells (musical instruments)

(G-16019)
CENTRAL SIGNS VOLUSIA CNTY INC
497 Buchanan Way (32119-2955)
PHONE.................................386 341-4842
Paul J Payne, *President*
EMP: 9 **EST:** 1964
SALES (est): 134.6K **Privately Held**
SIC: 3993 Signs & advertising specialties

(G-16020)
COUCHMAN PRINTING COMPANY
Also Called: Printing.com
1634 S Ridgewood Ave (32119-8409)
PHONE.................................386 756-3052
Terry Davis, *Owner*
EMP: 7 **EST:** 1947
SQ FT: 3,075
SALES (est): 663K **Privately Held**
WEB: www.printing.com
SIC: 2759 2752 Commercial printing; commercial printing, lithographic

(G-16021)
FLORIDA PLNTN SHUTTERS LLC
Also Called: US Blinds
1725 S Nova Rd Ste A1 (32119-1739)
PHONE.................................386 788-7766
Tom Russel, *President*
EMP: 7 **EST:** 1998
SALES (est): 504.7K **Privately Held**
WEB: www.floridaplantationshutters.com
SIC: 2591 Window blinds

(G-16022)
HOT OFF PRESS
952 Big Tree Rd (32119-2518)
PHONE.................................386 238-8700
Harry Campbell, *Principal*
EMP: 7 **EST:** 2007
SALES (est): 140K **Privately Held**
SIC: 2741 Miscellaneous publishing

(G-16023)
MARIS WORDEN AEROSPACE INC
2001 S Ridgewood Ave (32119-2288)
PHONE.................................514 895-8075
Julia A Maris, *Principal*
EMP: 8 **EST:** 2010
SALES (est): 116.4K **Privately Held**
SIC: 3721 Aircraft

(G-16024)
MERLE HARRIS ENTERPRISES INC
Also Called: Publishers of Seniors Today
724 Big Tree Rd (32119-2754)
PHONE.................................386 677-7060
Merle Harris, *President*
EMP: 5 **EST:** 1976
SQ FT: 1,000
SALES (est): 340K **Privately Held**
WEB: www.seniorstodaynewspaper.com
SIC: 2711 Newspapers, publishing & printing

(G-16025)
ONE HOUR PRINTING
661 Beville Rd Ste 109 (32119-1954)
PHONE.................................386 763-3111
Angela Sabato, *Owner*
EMP: 8 **EST:** 2007
SALES (est): 512.8K **Privately Held**
SIC: 2752 Commercial printing, offset

(G-16026)
PARRILLO INC
Also Called: Permacraft Sign & Trophies Co
1644 S Ridgewood Ave (32119-8410)
PHONE.................................386 767-8011
August Parrillo Sr, *President*
Carmen Parrillo, *Treasurer*
EMP: 6 **EST:** 1972
SQ FT: 10,285
SALES (est): 736.4K **Privately Held**
SIC: 3993 3999 3914 Neon signs;
plaques, picture, laminated; trophies

(G-16027)
RGU COLOR INC
3133 S Ridgewood Ave # 1 (32119-3579)
PHONE.................................386 252-9979
Dennis Fogell, *President*
EMP: 5 **EST:** 2006
SALES (est): 664K **Privately Held**
WEB: www.rgucolor.com
SIC: 2752 Commercial printing, offset

(G-16028)
SIGN-O-SAURUS DAYTONA INC
Also Called: SOS Sign & Lighting Services
2127 S Ridgewood Ave (32119-3015)
PHONE.................................386 322-5222
Angela Kopnicky, *CEO*
Howard G Martin, *President*
EMP: 5 **EST:** 2004
SALES (est): 514.9K **Privately Held**
WEB: www.soscustomsigns.com
SIC: 3993 Signs, not made in custom sign
painting shops

(G-16029)
STANDARD RIVET COMPANY INC
1640 S Segrave St (32119-2122)
PHONE.................................386 872-6477
Stephen Wallace, *President*
Stephen W Wallace, *General Mgr*
Paula Wallace, *Treasurer*
EMP: 10 **EST:** 1888
SQ FT: 34,000
SALES (est): 928.6K **Privately Held**
WEB: www.standardrivet.com
SIC: 3452 3542 Rivets, metal; riveting ma-
chines

(G-16030)
SUPERIOR DASH LLC
1960 S Segrave St (32119-2128)
PHONE.................................386 761-1265
Carl Zimmerman, *President*
EMP: 8 **EST:** 1992
SQ FT: 25,000
SALES (est): 587.4K
SALES (corp-wide): 4.3MM **Privately
Held**
WEB: www.superiordash.com
SIC: 3089 Automotive parts, plastic
PA: Coastal Designs, Inc.
1960 S Segrave St
South Daytona FL 32119
386 761-1265

South Miami
Miami-Dade County

(G-16031)
CAROL CITY OPA LOCKA NEWS
6796 Sw 62nd Ave (33143-3306)
PHONE.................................305 669-7355
Micheal Miller, *CEO*
Albie Barnes, *Accounts Exec*
Bill Kress, *Consultant*
Lori Cohen, *Executive*
EMP: 50 **EST:** 2008
SALES (est): 2.1MM **Privately Held**
SIC: 2711 Newspapers, publishing & print-
ing

(G-16032)
DIVERSITYPRO CORP
6632 Sw 64th Ave (33143-3230)
PHONE.................................305 691-2348
Marc Wolff, *President*
Richard Fernandes, *Treasurer*
Jonathan David, *Admin Sec*
EMP: 55 **EST:** 2000
SQ FT: 70,000

SALES (est): 2.9MM **Privately Held**
SIC: 2676 2673 Sanitary paper products;
bags: plastic, laminated & coated

(G-16033)
EMC SOUTH FLORIDA LLC
Also Called: Forever Yung Altrntive Hlthcar
6075 Sunset Dr Ste 201 (33143-5038)
PHONE.................................786 352-9327
Paul L Guadagno, *President*
EMP: 8 **EST:** 2016
SALES (est): 294.3K **Privately Held**
WEB: www.emcsouthflorida.com
SIC: 3572 Computer storage devices

(G-16034)
GAPV
7800 Sw 57th Ave Ste 219c (33143-5523)
PHONE.................................786 257-1681
Evannan Romero, *Mng Member*
EMP: 7 **EST:** 2015
SALES (est): 158.4K **Privately Held**
SIC: 1389 Oil consultants

(G-16035)
JAM WELDING SERVICE INC
5818 Sw 68th St (33143-3621)
PHONE.................................305 662-3787
Alvaro Espinoza, *President*
Martin Espinosa, *Vice Pres*
Gladys Espinosa, *Admin Sec*
EMP: 11 **EST:** 1992
SQ FT: 2,400
SALES (est): 1MM **Privately Held**
SIC: 7692 Welding repair

(G-16036)
JL WELDING INC
6510 Sw 64th Ct (33143-3204)
PHONE.................................786 442-4319
Joe Lewis Chandler, *President*
Inez Chandler, *Vice Pres*
EMP: 10 **EST:** 1988
SALES (est): 498.2K **Privately Held**
WEB: www.jlweldinginc.net
SIC: 7692 Welding repair

(G-16037)
LENNTECH USA LLC
5975 Sunset Dr Ste 802 (33143-5174)
PHONE.................................877 453-8095
EMP: 11 **EST:** 2019
SALES (est): 2.6MM **Privately Held**
WEB: www.lenntech.com
SIC: 3589 Water treatment equipment, in-
dustrial

(G-16038)
LPS GROUP LLC (PA)
7900 Sw 57th Ave Ph 23 (33143-5546)
PHONE.................................305 668-8780
Frank Landrove, *Vice Pres*
Sidney J Harden Jr, *Vice Pres*
EMP: 5 **EST:** 2000
SALES (est): 1.1MM **Privately Held**
WEB: www.lpsgroup.com
SIC: 7372 Business oriented computer
software

(G-16039)
MILLER PUBLISHING CO INC
Also Called: Home Town News
6796 Sw 62nd Ave (33143-3306)
PHONE.................................305 669-7355
Hope Miller, *President*
Jesus Toledo, *Finance Mgr*
Georgia Tate, *Admin Sec*
EMP: 14 **EST:** 1974
SQ FT: 6,000
SALES (est): 628K **Privately Held**
SIC: 2711 Newspapers, publishing & print-
ing

(G-16040)
MOBILEPOWER LLC
5975 Sunset Dr (33143-5166)
PHONE.................................843 706-6108
Kevin Resnick, *Mng Member*
▲ **EMP:** 9 **EST:** 2010
SQ FT: 1,200
SALES (est): 814.5K **Privately Held**
WEB: www.mobilepower-us.com
SIC: 3714 Motor vehicle parts & acces-
sories

(G-16041)
ORGANABIO LLC
7800 Sw 57th Ave Ste 225 (33143-5523)
PHONE.................................305 676-2586
Justin Irizarry, *CEO*
Priya Baraniak, *Vice Pres*
Laura Malagon, *Vice Pres*
Jordan Greenberg, *Research*
Petra Roulhac, *Manager*
EMP: 15 **EST:** 2018
SALES (est): 2.5MM **Privately Held**
WEB: www.organabio.com
SIC: 2836 Biological products, except diag-
nostic

(G-16042)
PINECREST TRIBUNE
6796 Sw 62nd Ave (33143-3306)
P.O. Box 431970, Miami (33243-1970)
PHONE.................................305 662-2277
Grant Miller, *Partner*
Michael Miller, *Partner*
EMP: 14 **EST:** 2001
SQ FT: 1,447
SALES (est): 533.5K **Privately Held**
SIC: 2711 Newspapers, publishing & print-
ing

(G-16043)
RED KITE GROUP INC
5701 Sunset Dr (33143-5348)
PHONE.................................305 665-7620
Carmen Franchi De Alfaro, *Principal*
EMP: 5 **EST:** 2019
SALES (est): 500.6K **Privately Held**
WEB: www.myredkite.com
SIC: 3944 Kites

(G-16044)
S A GLORIA CORP
6705 S Red Rd Ste 405 (33143-3638)
PHONE.................................305 575-2900
EMP: 222 **Privately Held**
WEB: www.gloria.com.pe
SIC: 2023 Dried & powdered milk & milk
products
HQ: Leche Gloria S.A.
Av. Republica De Panama 2461
Lima LM 13

(G-16045)
SEAL OUTDOORS INC
5900 Sw 56th Ter (33143-2270)
PHONE.................................877 323-7325
Daniela King, *CEO*
Herbert King, *COO*
EMP: 10 **EST:** 2015
SALES (est): 200K **Privately Held**
WEB: www.sealshoecovers.com
SIC: 2385 7389 Waterproof outerwear;
business services

(G-16046)
SOLAR TINT INC
5887 Sw 70th St (33143-3624)
PHONE.................................305 663-4663
Robert Flores, *President*
EMP: 5 **EST:** 1990
SALES (est): 532.8K **Privately Held**
WEB: www.solartintinc.com
SIC: 3479 1799 Painting, coating & hot
dipping; glass tinting, architectural or au-
tomotive

(G-16047)
**SOUTH FLORIDA FINGER
PRINTING**
5900 Sw 73rd St Ste 304 (33143-5162)
PHONE.................................305 661-1636
Marilyn Caplin, *Principal*
EMP: 7 **EST:** 2008
SALES (est): 153.2K **Privately Held**
WEB: www.southfloridafingerprinting.com
SIC: 2759 Commercial printing

(G-16048)
SOUTH FLORIDA INSTITUT
7600 Sw 57th Ave Ste 201 (33143-5408)
PHONE.................................305 668-2853
Rafael Antun MD, *Principal*
EMP: 7 **EST:** 2007
SALES (est): 678K **Privately Held**
WEB: www.lvrsouthflorida.com
SIC: 3826 Laser scientific & engineering
instruments

(G-16049)
**YOUR HOMETOWN NEWSPAPER
INC**
Also Called: Kendall News
6796 Sw 62nd Ave (33143-3306)
P.O. Box 431970, Miami (33243-1970)
PHONE.................................305 669-7355
Michael Miller, *President*
Albie Barnes, *Accounts Exec*
Aaron Guerrero, *Accounts Exec*
EMP: 32 **EST:** 1982
SQ FT: 6,400
SALES (est): 4.5MM **Privately Held**
SIC: 2711 Commercial printing & newspa-
per publishing combined

South Pasadena
Pinellas County

(G-16050)
386 NANOTECH INC
6860 Gulfport Blvd S (33707-2108)
PHONE.................................727 252-9580
Lisa Frick, *President*
Bradley Mescavage, *Vice Pres*
EMP: 12 **EST:** 2007
SALES (est): 994.1K **Privately Held**
WEB: www.386nanotechnology.com
SIC: 2891 Sealants

(G-16051)
**FLORIDA ORANGE GROVES
INC**
Also Called: Florida Orange Groves Winery
1500 Pasadena Ave S (33707-3718)
PHONE.................................727 347-4025
Vincent R Shook, *President*
Lance M Shook, *Exec VP*
Lance Shook, *Exec VP*
Nancy Gorman, *Sales Staff*
Artie Winthrop, *Sales Associate*
EMP: 17 **EST:** 1977
SQ FT: 6,700
SALES (est): 2.4MM **Privately Held**
WEB: www.floridawine.com
SIC: 2084 Wines

Southwest Ranches
Broward County

(G-16052)
AIRIND INCORPORATED
6511 Melaleuca Rd (33330-3830)
PHONE.................................954 252-0900
Robert Charles, *President*
Nancy Charles, *Vice Pres*
EMP: 6 **EST:** 1968
SQ FT: 7,724
SALES (est): 467.9K **Privately Held**
SIC: 3728 Aircraft parts & equipment

(G-16053)
DTF WOODWORKS LLC
5101 Sw 167th Ave (33331-1381)
PHONE.................................954 317-6443
Dale Beswick, *Mng Member*
EMP: 12 **EST:** 1997
SALES (est): 953.8K **Privately Held**
WEB: www.dtfwoodworks.com
SIC: 2431 Doors, wood

(G-16054)
INNEUROCO INC (PA)
19700 Stirling Rd Unit 1 (33332-1345)
PHONE.................................954 742-5988
Marc Litzenberg, *President*
Evan Cohen, *Project Mgr*
Maria Largaespada, *Engineer*
Monique Weller, *Engineer*
Bernardo Navarro, *CFO*
EMP: 20 **EST:** 2014
SALES (est): 5.3MM **Privately Held**
WEB: www.inneuroco.com
SIC: 3841 Catheters

(G-16055)
JBLAZE INC
4910 Sw 172nd Ave (33331-1222)
PHONE.................................954 680-3962
EMP: 5

▲ = Import ▼=Export
◆ =Import/Export

SALES (est): 466.5K **Privately Held**
SIC: 2323 Mfg Men's/Boy's Neckwear

(G-16056)
OSTEEN PLASTIC INC
17539 Sw 59th Ct (33331-2345)
PHONE......................................954 434-4921
Richard Osteen, *President*
EMP: 5 EST: 1971
SALES (est): 419.4K **Privately Held**
SIC: 3544 3523 Special dies, tools, jigs &
fixtures; farm machinery & equipment

(G-16057)
PRO-PUBLISHING INC
18020 Sw 66th St (33331-1860)
PHONE......................................954 888-7726
Aida Corrada-Bertsch, *President*
◆ EMP: 7 EST: 1986
SALES (est): 751.8K **Privately Held**
WEB: www.iconixink.com
SIC: 2731 5961 5192 Books: publishing
only; book club, mail order; books

(G-16058)
SKIN PRO INTERNATIONAL INC
14345 Sunset Ln (33330-3407)
PHONE......................................305 528-9095
Timothy Schmidt, *Principal*
EMP: 7 EST: 2013
SALES (est): 412.8K **Privately Held**
WEB: www.skinpro.com
SIC: 2844 Toilet preparations

Sparr
Marion County

(G-16059)
DMC INDUSTRIES INC
13530 N Jacksonville Rd (32192)
P.O. Box 473 (32192-0473)
PHONE......................................352 620-9322
Dennis M Cauthen, *President*
Diane M Cauthen, *Vice Pres*
EMP: 6 EST: 1993
SALES (est): 947.8K **Privately Held**
WEB: www.dmcindustriesinc.com
SIC: 1389 Construction, repair & disman-
tling services

Spring Hill
Hernando County

(G-16060)
ACCUFORM SIGNS
11119 Holbrook St (34609-3840)
PHONE......................................800 237-1001
Bryan S Glidden, *Principal*
EMP: 10 EST: 2011
SALES (est): 164.7K **Privately Held**
WEB: www.accuform.com
SIC: 3993 Signs & advertising specialties

(G-16061)
AJS ALUMINUM INC
5441 Spring Hill Dr (34606-4563)
PHONE......................................352 688-7631
Andrew Jata, *President*
EMP: 5 EST: 1987
SQ FT: 2,500
SALES (est): 832K **Privately Held**
WEB: www.ajsaluminum.com
SIC: 3334 Primary aluminum

(G-16062)
AMASCOTT LLC
4142 Mariner Blvd (34609-2468)
PHONE......................................352 683-4895
Tetyana Dickson, *Principal*
EMP: 7 EST: 2011
SALES (est): 589.5K **Privately Held**
WEB: www.amascott.com
SIC: 3825 Instruments to measure electric-
ity

(G-16063)
ATLAS INDUSTRIAL SCALES INC
3715 Commercial Way (34606-2303)
PHONE......................................352 610-9989
Douglas Salerno, *Principal*

EMP: 7 EST: 2012
SALES (est): 88.7K **Privately Held**
WEB: www.atlasscales.com
SIC: 3596 Industrial scales

(G-16064)
B & S RIGGING INC
112 Spring Time St (34608-7003)
PHONE......................................727 532-9466
Boguslaw Sokolewicz, *Principal*
EMP: 5 EST: 2009
SALES (est): 349.3K **Privately Held**
WEB: www.bsrigging.com
SIC: 3599 Machine shop, jobbing & repair

(G-16065)
BEAUTIFUL HOMES INC
471 Mariner Blvd (34609-5680)
P.O. Box 11251 (34610-0251)
PHONE......................................800 403-1480
Richard Burkhart, *President*
Mark Lepper, *Corp Secy*
EMP: 5 EST: 2005
SALES (est): 668.2K **Privately Held**
WEB: www.stairpartsusa.com
SIC: 3534 Stair elevators, motor powered

(G-16066)
BUY GOLF GRIPS 4 LESS
11244 Redgate St (34609-3352)
PHONE......................................352 256-7577
Stan Arnold, *Owner*
EMP: 6 EST: 2012
SALES (est): 498.1K **Privately Held**
WEB: www.buygolfgrips4less.com
SIC: 3949 Shafts, golf club

(G-16067)
CAPITAL PUBLISHING INC
7341 Spring Hill Dr (34606-4300)
PHONE......................................813 286-8444
EMP: 7 EST: 1998
SALES (est): 134.1K **Privately Held**
WEB: www.capitalpublishing.com
SIC: 2741 Miscellaneous publishing

(G-16068)
COMMSKI LLC
13342 Whitmarsh St (34609-6163)
PHONE......................................813 501-0111
Mandy Noegel, *Project Mgr*
Karla Lapinski, *Manager*
Nick Berg, *Manager*
EMP: 8 EST: 2012
SALES (est): 1.5MM **Privately Held**
WEB: www.commski.com
SIC: 3357 5063 7373 Fiber optic cable
(insulated); wire & cable; value-added re-
sellers, computer systems

(G-16069)
CUPCAKE HEAVEN
2721 Forest Rd (34606-3377)
PHONE......................................352 610-4433
Denise E Cornelius, *Principal*
EMP: 7 EST: 2009
SALES (est): 243K **Privately Held**
WEB: www.cupcakeheavenspringhill.com
SIC: 2051 Cakes, bakery: except frozen

(G-16070)
D D WELDING
13153 Fish Cove Dr (34609-4254)
PHONE......................................732 998-1100
Dean Dziedzic, *Principal*
EMP: 5 EST: 2016
SALES (est): 46K **Privately Held**
WEB: www.ddwelding.com
SIC: 7692 Welding repair

(G-16071)
FLORIDA STAINLESS STEEL ACC
5601 Cactus Cir (34606-5516)
PHONE......................................727 207-2575
Gary Peterson, *Principal*
EMP: 7 EST: 2010
SALES (est): 96K **Privately Held**
SIC: 3312 Stainless steel

(G-16072)
GRAY INFORMATION SOLUTIONS INC
12812 Coronado Dr (34609-5843)
PHONE......................................352 684-6655

Gary G Gray, *President*
Gary Gray, *President*
Vickie Gray, *Vice Pres*
EMP: 5 EST: 2003
SQ FT: 2,000
SALES (est): 404.6K **Privately Held**
WEB: www.grainformationsolutions.com
SIC: 3825 Network analyzers

(G-16073)
J-KUP CORP
Also Called: Sir Speedy
1260 Lori Dr (34606-4561)
PHONE......................................352 683-5629
Tom Kupcik, *President*
EMP: 12 EST: 2008
SALES (est): 1.3MM **Privately Held**
WEB: www.sirspeedy.com
SIC: 2752 Commercial printing, litho-
graphic

(G-16074)
PHONE WAVE INC
178 Mariner Blvd (34609-5689)
PHONE......................................352 683-8101
Charles Dale Lemons, *COO*
EMP: 11 EST: 2009
SALES (est): 352.4K **Privately Held**
SIC: 3571 Electronic computers

(G-16075)
PROFESSIONAL PAVER RESTORATIONS
3259 Dothan Ave (34609-3123)
PHONE......................................352 797-8411
Eric J Carrasco, *Principal*
EMP: 7 EST: 2010
SALES (est): 162.1K **Privately Held**
SIC: 3531 Pavers

(G-16076)
RAMIREZ CBNETS BLNDS GRAN MR
Also Called: Retail Sales/ Installations
3645 Commercial Way (34606-2318)
PHONE......................................352 606-0049
Edgardo Ramirez, *President*
EMP: 6 EST: 2012
SALES (est): 970.4K **Privately Held**
WEB: springhillcabinets.wix.com
SIC: 1389 1751 2591 2431 Construction,
repair & dismantling services; cabinet &
finish carpentry; cabinet building & instal-
lation; drapery hardware & blinds &
shades; window blinds; blinds (shutters),
wood; kitchen cabinet installation; granite,
cut & shaped

(G-16077)
ROMEO OHANA LLC
Also Called: 808 Island Treats
12501 Drayton Dr (34609-4226)
PHONE......................................808 500-3420
Michael C Romeo, *Mng Member*
EMP: 10 EST: 2018
SALES (est): 814.2K **Privately Held**
SIC: 2024 Ice cream & frozen desserts

(G-16078)
S&H ARCYLIC COATINGS INC
4673 Chamber Ct (34609-1605)
PHONE......................................352 232-1249
Harold G Toms IV, *President*
EMP: 8 EST: 2004
SALES (est): 67.5K **Privately Held**
SIC: 3479 Coating of metals & formed
products

(G-16079)
SIR SPEEDY PRINTING CENTER
1260 Lori Dr (34606-4561)
PHONE......................................352 683-8758
Fax: 352 683-8793
EMP: 12 EST: 2010
SALES (est): 610K **Privately Held**
SIC: 2752 Lithographic Commercial Print-
ing

(G-16080)
SOLLUNAR ENERGY INC
4142 Mariner Blvd Ste 510 (34609-2468)
PHONE......................................352 293-2347
Dale Hobbie, *President*
EMP: 9 EST: 2008
SQ FT: 50,000

SALES (est): 116.9K **Privately Held**
SIC: 3674 Photovoltaic devices, solid state

(G-16081)
SPRING HILL BAKERY LLC
374 Winthrop Dr (34609-2090)
PHONE......................................954 825-3419
Elecia Madaffari, *President*
EMP: 25 EST: 2018
SALES (est): 1MM **Privately Held**
WEB: www.springhillbakery.com
SIC: 2051 Bread, cake & related products

(G-16082)
STALL MASTER COMPANY (PA)
4377 Commercial Way (34606-1963)
PHONE......................................352 279-0089
Michael McHugh, *President*
Lynne McHugh, *Vice Pres*
EMP: 5 EST: 2004
SALES (est): 2.5MM **Privately Held**
WEB: www.stallmaster.com
SIC: 2421 Sawdust, shavings & wood
chips

(G-16083)
TUTELA MONITORING SYSTEMS LLC
485 Mariner Blvd (34609-5680)
PHONE......................................941 462-1067
Steve Peck, *President*
Bruce Anderson, *COO*
EMP: 8 EST: 2005
SALES (est): 2.3MM
SALES (corp-wide): 17.8MM **Privately Held**
WEB: www.tutelamedical.com
SIC: 3823 Industrial instrmnts msrmnt dis-
play/control process variable
PA: Checkit Plc
Broers Building
Cambridge CAMBS CB3 0
180 340-7757

Spring Hill
Pasco County

(G-16084)
DAVID R CASE
18519 Floralton Dr (34610-1307)
PHONE......................................727 808-9330
David Case, *Principal*
EMP: 7 EST: 2011
SALES (est): 112.1K **Privately Held**
SIC: 3523 Farm machinery & equipment

(G-16085)
ISPY EQUITIES LLC
12309 Field Point Way (34603-3366)
PHONE......................................813 731-0676
Lisa Marsala, *Principal*
EMP: 7 EST: 2016
SALES (est): 100.9K **Privately Held**
SIC: 2024 Ice cream & frozen desserts

(G-16086)
LEGGETT & PLATT INCORPORATED
15800 Hudson Ave (34610-7608)
PHONE......................................727 856-3154
EMP: 24
SALES (corp-wide): 4.2B **Publicly Held**
WEB: www.leggett.com
SIC: 2515 Mattresses & bedsprings
PA: Leggett & Platt, Incorporated
1 Leggett Rd
Carthage MO 64836
417 358-8131

(G-16087)
NATURE COAST PRECISION MFG LLC
16706 Wishingwell Ln (34610-4046)
PHONE......................................727 424-3848
Valerie Hager, *Manager*
EMP: 7 EST: 2017
SALES (est): 281.2K **Privately Held**
SIC: 3999 Manufacturing industries

(G-16088)
STRONG TOWER VINEYARD
17810 Forge Dr (34610-3080)
PHONE......................................352 799-7612

Janis McKnight, *Executive Asst*
EMP: 5 **EST:** 2005
SQ FT: 2,648
SALES (est): 334.7K **Privately Held**
WEB: www.strongtowervineyard.com
SIC: 2084 Wines

St Pete Beach
Pinellas County

(G-16089)
ECOTECH WATER LLC
7121 Gulf Blvd (33706-1943)
PHONE..............................877 341-9500
T E Janssen,
EMP: 7 **EST:** 2006
SALES (est): 257.5K **Privately Held**
WEB: www.ecotechwater.com
SIC: 3261 Vitreous plumbing fixtures

(G-16090)
EMERALD TECHNOLOGIES CORP
3807 Belle Vista Dr E (33706-2628)
PHONE..............................773 244-0092
James E Quinn, *Owner*
EMP: 5 **EST:** 1991
SALES (est): 372K **Privately Held**
SIC: 7372 Prepackaged software

(G-16091)
JB THOME & CO INC
1110 Boca Ciega Isle Dr (33706-2544)
PHONE..............................727 642-0588
Heather E Polansky, *Principal*
Heather Thomepolansky, *Vice Pres*
EMP: 7 **EST:** 2018
SALES (est): 273.5K **Privately Held**
WEB: www.bulkspirits.com
SIC: 2085 Distilled & blended liquors

(G-16092)
PUBLIC IMAGE PRINTING INC
5050 Gulf Blvd Ste C (33706-2417)
PHONE..............................727 363-1800
Mark Nathans, *President*
EMP: 8 **EST:** 1987
SALES (est): 500.9K **Privately Held**
WEB: publicimageprinting.4printing.com
SIC: 2752 Commercial printing, offset

(G-16093)
TROPICAL MBC LLC
250 Corey Ave (33706-1857)
PHONE..............................727 498-6511
Reichbach Abraham, *Principal*
EMP: 7 **EST:** 2010
SALES (est): 420.6K **Privately Held**
SIC: 7372 Application computer software

Starke
Bradford County

(G-16094)
10858 OPCO LLC ✪
10858 Se County Road 221 (32091-7853)
PHONE..............................949 697-6737
Sebastian Trujillo,
EMP: 36 **EST:** 2022
SALES (est): 1.4MM **Privately Held**
SIC: 3599 Machine & other job shop work

(G-16095)
ACORE SHELVING & PRODUCTS
1460 Ne State Road 16 (32091-6598)
P.O. Box 67 (32091-0067)
PHONE..............................904 964-4320
Don Thompson Sr, *President*
Hayden Thompson, *Prdtn Mgr*
Joyce C Thompson, *Controller*
EMP: 8 **EST:** 2004
SALES (est): 650K **Privately Held**
WEB: www.acoreshelving.com
SIC: 2541 Cabinets, lockers & shelving

(G-16096)
BRADFORD COUNTY TELEGRAPH INC (PA)
Also Called: Union County Times
135 W Call St (32091-3210)
PHONE..............................904 964-6305

John M Miller, *President*
Anne M Miller, *Vice Pres*
Jewel O'Neal, *Treasurer*
EMP: 12 **EST:** 1877
SQ FT: 4,000
SALES (est): 3.4MM **Privately Held**
WEB: www.bctelegraph.com
SIC: 2711 2752 5943 Newspapers, publishing & printing; commercial printing, offset; office forms & supplies

(G-16097)
CARPORTS ANYWHERE INC
10858 Se County Road 221 (32091-7853)
P.O. Box 776 (32091-0776)
PHONE..............................352 468-1116
Christina Curles, *President*
Sebatian Trujillo, *Manager*
EMP: 14 **EST:** 2015
SALES (est): 3.3MM **Privately Held**
WEB: www.carportsanywhere.com
SIC: 3448 Prefabricated metal buildings

(G-16098)
CHEMOURS COMPANY FC LLC
Florida Plant (32091)
PHONE..............................904 964-1230
David Podmeyer, *Manager*
EMP: 64
SALES (corp-wide): 6.3B **Publicly Held**
WEB: www.chemours.com
SIC: 3532 Mining machinery
HQ: The Chemours Company Fc Llc
　　1007 Market St
　　Wilmington DE 19898
　　302 773-1000

(G-16099)
CHEMOURS COMPANY FC LLC
5222 Treat Rd (32091)
P.O. Box 753 (32091-0753)
PHONE..............................904 964-1200
David J Podmeyer, *Manager*
EMP: 71
SALES (corp-wide): 6.3B **Publicly Held**
WEB: www.chemours.com
SIC: 1446 3295 1041 1031 Industrial sand; minerals, ground or treated; gold ores; lead & zinc ores; copper ores; iron ores
HQ: The Chemours Company Fc Llc
　　1007 Market St
　　Wilmington DE 19898
　　302 773-1000

(G-16100)
DARLING INGREDIENTS INC
Also Called: Hampton Hexane Transfer Stn
11313 Se 52nd Ave (32091-6801)
PHONE..............................904 964-8083
Brad Huffman, *Branch Mgr*
EMP: 7
SALES (corp-wide): 4.7B **Publicly Held**
WEB: www.darlingii.com
SIC: 2077 Animal & marine fats & oils
PA: Darling Ingredients Inc.
　　5601 N Macarthur Blvd
　　Irving TX 75038
　　972 717-0300

(G-16101)
DIVISION 5 FLORIDA INC
Also Called: Division 5 Steel
417 E Weldon St (32091-2365)
P.O. Box 6058 (32091-6058)
PHONE..............................904 964-4513
Kenneth Frisbee, *President*
Mark A Spaur, *Vice Pres*
Justin Pace, *Project Mgr*
Charline Shaw, *Manager*
EMP: 20 **EST:** 1986
SQ FT: 9,000
SALES (est): 5.5MM **Privately Held**
WEB: www.division5steel.com
SIC: 3441 1542 Building components, structural steel; design & erection, combined: non-residential

(G-16102)
GRIFFIN INDUSTRIES LLC
Bakery Feeds
11313 Se 52nd Ave (32091-6801)
PHONE..............................904 964-8083
Pete Weider, *Branch Mgr*
EMP: 59

SALES (corp-wide): 4.7B **Publicly Held**
SIC: 2077 2048 Grease rendering, inedible; tallow rendering, inedible; prepared feeds
HQ: Griffin Industries Llc
　　4221 Alexandria Pike
　　Cold Spring KY 41076
　　859 781-2010

(G-16103)
JONES FIELD SERVICES PAMELA
9904 Nw County Road 229 (32091-5093)
PHONE..............................904 368-9777
Pamela L Thompson, *Principal*
EMP: 5 **EST:** 2014
SALES (est): 303.6K **Privately Held**
SIC: 1311 Crude petroleum & natural gas

(G-16104)
PRESTIGE ALUMINUM RAILING INC
4778 Se 142nd Way (32091-6878)
P.O. Box 366 (32091-0366)
PHONE..............................904 966-2163
James Frisbee, *President*
Mike Cribby, *Vice Pres*
Terry Sorensen, *Vice Pres*
Steve White, *Shareholder*
EMP: 9 **EST:** 1997
SALES (est): 875.9K **Privately Held**
SIC: 3355 Aluminum rail & structural shapes

(G-16105)
STARKE WASTE WTR TRTMNT PLANT
602 Edwards Rd (32091-3802)
PHONE..............................904 964-7999
Fred Magyari, *Principal*
Ricky Thompson, *Director*
EMP: 5 **EST:** 2002
SALES (est): 344.2K **Privately Held**
SIC: 3589 Water treatment equipment, industrial

Steinhatchee
Taylor County

(G-16106)
OUTDOOR PRODUCTS LLC
125 Sw 284th Ave (32359-3107)
PHONE..............................352 473-0886
Jennifer Poppell, *Principal*
EMP: 7 **EST:** 2015
SALES (est): 183.3K **Privately Held**
WEB: www.outdoorproducts.com
SIC: 2329 5699 2339 Men's & boys' sportswear & athletic clothing; customized clothing & apparel; athletic clothing: women's, misses' & juniors'

Stuart
Martin County

(G-16107)
2951 SE DOMINICA HOLDING LLC ✪
Also Called: Ocean Breeze
2979 Se Monroe St (34997-5950)
P.O. Box 279, Palm City (34991-0279)
PHONE..............................772 220-0038
Jose Guch, *Principal*
Jennifer Heinemann, *Vice Pres*
Thomas Rubio, *Mng Member*
Susana Begin,
◆ **EMP:** 15 **EST:** 2021
SQ FT: 14,000
SALES (est): 3.7MM **Privately Held**
WEB: www.oceanbreezeac.com
SIC: 3585 Refrigeration & heating equipment

(G-16108)
A-1 CLEANING CONCEPTS INC
173 Se Norfolk Blvd (34997-5572)
PHONE..............................772 288-7214
Galan Joynes, *CEO*
Heather Joynes, *Manager*
EMP: 5 **EST:** 2002

SALES (est): 450K **Privately Held**
WEB: www.pressurecleaningfl.com
SIC: 3589 High pressure cleaning equipment

(G-16109)
AAA MONTEREY DISCOUNT VACUUM
514 Se Monterey Rd (34994-4408)
PHONE..............................772 288-5233
Cliff Peranio, *President*
Leo Peranio, *President*
EMP: 5 **EST:** 1987
SALES (est): 393.6K **Privately Held**
WEB: www.montereyvacuum.net
SIC: 3635 7629 7623 Household vacuum cleaners; vacuum cleaner repair; refrigeration service & repair

(G-16110)
ACRYFIN COATINGS LLC
901 Nw New Providence Rd (34994-8918)
PHONE..............................772 631-3899
John D Kicklighter, *Manager*
EMP: 8 **EST:** 2016
SALES (est): 737.6K **Privately Held**
WEB: www.acryfin.com
SIC: 2952 Asphalt felts & coatings

(G-16111)
ADVANCED CELL ENGINEERING INC ✪
819 Sw Federal Hwy # 205 (34994-2952)
PHONE..............................772 382-9191
John Kaufman, *President*
Karim Zaghib, *Vice Pres*
EMP: 15 **EST:** 2021
SALES (est): 1MM **Privately Held**
WEB: www.advancedcellengineering.com
SIC: 3691 Storage batteries; batteries, rechargeable

(G-16112)
ADVANCED HURRICANE PROTECTION
4517 Se Commerce Ave (34997-8860)
PHONE..............................772 220-1200
John Zervopoulos, *President*
EMP: 5 **EST:** 1996
SALES (est): 468.3K **Privately Held**
WEB: www.advancedhurricane.net
SIC: 3442 Shutters, door or window: metal

(G-16113)
ADVANTAGE SOFTWARE INC
925 Se Central Pkwy (34994-3904)
PHONE..............................772 288-3266
Greg Seely, *President*
Portia Seely, *Corp Secy*
David Jordan, *VP Opers*
Jonathan Taylor, *Software Engr*
Nicole Bracy, *IT/INT Sup*
EMP: 37 **EST:** 1987
SQ FT: 5,000
SALES (est): 6.4MM **Privately Held**
WEB: www.eclipsecat.com
SIC: 7372 Business oriented computer software

(G-16114)
AMERICAN ENRGY INNOVATIONS LLC
6800 Sw Jack James Dr (34997-6200)
PHONE..............................772 221-9100
Philip Catsman, *Mng Member*
Dominick Lacombe,
EMP: 10 **EST:** 2011
SQ FT: 40,000
SALES (est): 920K **Privately Held**
WEB: www.williscustomyachts.com
SIC: 3728 Aircraft body & wing assemblies & parts

(G-16115)
AMPERSAND GRAPHICS INC
553 Se Monterey Rd (34994-4407)
PHONE..............................772 283-1359
Dennis Clark, *President*
Elaine Clark, *Vice Pres*
Jeremy Savard, *Art Dir*
◆ **EMP:** 19 **EST:** 1977
SQ FT: 6,000

▲ = Import ▼ =Export
◆ =Import/Export

SALES (est): 1.8MM **Privately Held**
WEB: www.ampersand-graphics.com
SIC: **2759** 5199 2396 Screen printing; advertising specialties; automotive & apparel trimmings

(G-16116)
AMPERSAND SHIRT SHACK
553 Se Monterey Rd (34994-4407)
PHONE...................................772 600-8743
Brad Love, *CEO*
Victoria Love, *President*
Jeremy Savard, *Art Dir*
▼ EMP: 10 EST: 2011
SALES (est): 869.8K **Privately Held**
WEB: www.ampersand-graphics.com
SIC: **2759** Screen printing

(G-16117)
ARCHITECTURAL SIGNCRAFTERS
3195 Se Gran Park Way (34997-6701)
PHONE...................................772 600-5032
EMP: 5
SALES (est): 480K **Privately Held**
SIC: **3993** Mfg Signs/Advertising Specialties

(G-16118)
ARTHUR COX
Also Called: A & J Boatworks
4800 Se Anchor Ave (34997-1904)
PHONE...................................772 286-5339
Arthur Cox, *Owner*
EMP: 6 EST: 2003
SALES (est): 345.7K **Privately Held**
SIC: **3732** Boat building & repairing

(G-16119)
BAUSCH AMERICAN TOWERS LLC
6800 Sw Jack James Dr # 3 (34997-6200)
PHONE...................................772 283-2771
C Timothy Bausch,
▲ EMP: 16 EST: 1977
SQ FT: 10,000
SALES (est): 1.2MM **Privately Held**
WEB: www.bauschtowers.com
SIC: **3441** 3732 3446 Fabricated structural metal for ships; boat building & repairing; architectural metalwork; sheet metalwork

(G-16120)
BAUSCH ENTERPRISES INC
3171 Se Waaler St (34997-5923)
P.O. Box 326, Port Salerno (34992-0326)
PHONE...................................772 220-6652
Dana Bausch, *President*
EMP: 10 EST: 1996
SQ FT: 7,000
SALES (est): 1.4MM **Privately Held**
WEB: www.bauschenterprises.com
SIC: **3444** 3732 Sheet metalwork; boat building & repairing

(G-16121)
BE MERRY
320 Se Denver Ave (34994-2138)
PHONE...................................772 324-8289
Anne Falco, *Principal*
EMP: 8 EST: 2012
SALES (est): 452.3K **Privately Held**
SIC: **3421** Table & food cutlery, including butchers'

(G-16122)
BEACHCOMBER FIBRGLS TECH INC
3355 Se Lionel Ter (34997-8870)
PHONE...................................772 283-0200
Michael Cohen, *President*
▼ EMP: 5 EST: 1978
SQ FT: 4,000
SALES (est): 688.8K **Privately Held**
WEB: www.beachfiber.com
SIC: **3089** 5551 3429 Molding primary plastic; marine supplies & equipment; manufactured hardware (general)

(G-16123)
BLAIR PROPELLER MA
3009 Se Monroe St (34997-5981)
PHONE...................................772 283-1453
Todd Blair, *Owner*

EMP: 5 EST: 2018
SALES (est): 1MM **Privately Held**
WEB: www.blairpropeller.com
SIC: **3366** Propellers

(G-16124)
BONADEO BOAT WORKS LLC
4431 Se Commerce Ave (34997-5742)
P.O. Box 328 (34995-0328)
PHONE...................................772 341-9820
Larry Bonadeo,
Tony Bonadeo,
Denise Sovel-Bonadeo,
▼ EMP: 8 EST: 2004
SQ FT: 600
SALES (est): 679.7K **Privately Held**
WEB: www.bonadeoboatworks.com
SIC: **3732** Boat building & repairing

(G-16125)
C & C DIVERSIFIED SERVICES LLC
7954 Sw Jack James Dr (34997-7241)
P.O. Box 517, Indiantown (34956-0517)
PHONE...................................772 597-1022
Brian Critoph, *Manager*
Daniel Cox,
EMP: 9 EST: 2005
SALES (est): 2.2MM **Privately Held**
WEB: www.ccdiversifiedgas.com
SIC: **1311** Crude petroleum & natural gas production

(G-16126)
CEDRUS INC
Also Called: American Stairs
9011 Sw Old Kansas Ave (34997-7218)
PHONE...................................772 286-2082
Mahmoud Mikati, *Ch of Bd*
Jamil Mikati, *President*
Jihad Mikati, *Vice Pres*
Rhonda Roarke, *Admin Sec*
EMP: 20 EST: 1984
SALES (est): 5.2MM **Privately Held**
WEB: www.americanstairparts.com
SIC: **2431** 3446 3442 Staircases & stairs, wood; doors, wood; stairs, staircases, stair treads: prefabricated metal; molding, trim & stripping

(G-16127)
CEMEX MATERIALS LLC
1232 Se Dixie Cutoff Rd (34994-3436)
PHONE...................................772 287-0502
Lester Fultz, *Branch Mgr*
EMP: 137
SQ FT: 2,947 **Privately Held**
SIC: **3273** 5032 5211 Ready-mixed concrete; concrete mixtures; concrete & cinder block
HQ: Cemex Materials Llc
1720 Centrepark Dr E # 100
West Palm Beach FL 33401
561 833-5555

(G-16128)
CFM&D LLC
2550 Se Willoughby Blvd (34994-4701)
PHONE...................................772 220-8938
James E Allen, *Principal*
EMP: 6 EST: 2012
SALES (est): 678.1K **Privately Held**
SIC: **2099** Food preparations

(G-16129)
CHITTUM YACHTS LLC
4953 Se Pine Knoll Way (34997-6995)
PHONE...................................386 589-7224
Hal Chittum, *Manager*
EMP: 21
SALES (corp-wide): 2.6MM **Privately Held**
SIC: **3732** Boat building & repairing
PA: Chittum Yachts, Llc
4577 Sw Cargo Way
Palm City FL 34990
386 589-7224

(G-16130)
CHLORINATORS INC
1044 Se Dixie Cutoff Rd (34994-3436)
P.O. Box 1518 (34995-1518)
PHONE...................................772 288-4854
Diane Haskett, *Ch of Bd*
Michael Chapdelaine, *Regl Sales Mgr*
Charles Rickie, *Sales Staff*

Jill Majka, *Marketing Mgr*
EMP: 36 EST: 1975
SQ FT: 10,600
SALES (est): 7.3MM **Privately Held**
WEB: www.regalchlorinators.com
SIC: **3589** Water treatment equipment, industrial

(G-16131)
CONEHEADS FROZEN CUSTARDS
43 Sw Flagler Ave (34994-2140)
PHONE...................................772 600-7730
Timothy F Stoklosa, *Mng Member*
EMP: 8 EST: 2010
SALES (est): 117.4K **Privately Held**
SIC: **2024** Ice cream, bulk

(G-16132)
CONNECTYX TECHNOLOGIES CORP
850 Nw Federal Hwy # 411 (34994-1019)
P.O. Box 2478, Palm City (34991-2478)
PHONE...................................772 221-8240
Ronn Schuman, *President*
EMP: 8 EST: 2003
SQ FT: 3,000
SALES (est): 1MM
SALES (corp-wide): 1.8MM **Privately Held**
WEB: www.tap4emergency.info
SIC: **7372** Business oriented computer software
PA: Curative Biotechnology, Inc.
850 Nw Federal Hwy
Stuart FL 34994
772 221-8240

(G-16133)
CONSOLIDATED CORDAGE CORP
7849 Sw Ellipse Way (34997-7247)
PHONE...................................561 347-7247
Cathleen Materka, *President*
▲ EMP: 10 EST: 1993
SALES (est): 1.7MM **Privately Held**
WEB: www.consolidatedcordage.com
SIC: **2298** Ropes & fiber cables

(G-16134)
CROWDER CUSTOM RODS INC
Also Called: Crowder Rods
3040 Se Dominica Ter (34997-5716)
P.O. Box 276, Jensen Beach (34958-0276)
PHONE...................................772 220-8108
Robert Crowder, *President*
Matt Potsko, *Vice Pres*
EMP: 9 EST: 1998
SQ FT: 2,500
SALES (est): 678.7K **Privately Held**
WEB: www.crowderrods.com
SIC: **3949** 5941 Fishing equipment; sporting goods & bicycle shops

(G-16135)
CRUNCHI LLC
7671 Sw Ellipse Way (34997-7251)
PHONE...................................772 600-8082
Dante A Weston, *Mng Member*
EMP: 8 EST: 2019
SALES (est): 491.1K **Privately Held**
WEB: www.crunchi.com
SIC: **2844** Toilet preparations

(G-16136)
DAILY RACING ENTERPRISES INC
10922 Sw Hawkview Cir (34997-2710)
PHONE...................................772 287-9106
Duff D Daily, *President*
EMP: 7 EST: 2001
SALES (est): 157.4K **Privately Held**
SIC: **2711** Newspapers, publishing & printing

(G-16137)
DELAWARE CHASSIS WORKS
3513 Se Gran Park Way (34997-8808)
PHONE...................................302 378-3013
Joe Timney, *Owner*
Tonya Turk, *Vice Pres*
EMP: 7 EST: 1979

SALES (est): 494.8K **Privately Held**
WEB: www.delawarechassisworks.com
SIC: **3711** Automobile assembly, including specialty automobiles

(G-16138)
DESIGNER SVCS OF TRSURE CAST I
4515 Se Commerce Ave (34997-8860)
PHONE...................................772 286-0855
Michael Schmidt, *President*
EMP: 5 EST: 1969
SALES (est): 535.6K **Privately Held**
WEB: www.designerservices.com
SIC: **3999** Models, general, except toy

(G-16139)
DOYLE SAILMAKERS INC
900 Se Ocean Blvd (34994-2471)
PHONE...................................772 219-4024
Scott Loomis, *Manager*
EMP: 18
SALES (corp-wide): 6.3MM **Privately Held**
WEB: www.doylesails.com
SIC: **2394** Sails: made from purchased materials
PA: Doyle Sailmakers, Inc.
96 Swampscott Rd Ste 8
Salem MA 01970
978 740-5950

(G-16140)
DRONES SHOP LLC
4406 Se Graham Dr (34997-1544)
PHONE...................................772 224-8118
Matthew Tatem, *Principal*
Sharon Serle, *Vice Pres*
EMP: 7 EST: 2015
SALES (est): 475.1K **Privately Held**
WEB: www.tatemweb.com
SIC: **3728** Target drones

(G-16141)
DYNAMIC PRECISION GROUP INC (PA)
3651 Se Commerce Ave (34997-4967)
PHONE...................................772 287-7770
Greg Bennett, *President*
Jason Mitchell, *Mfg Mgr*
EMP: 45 EST: 2011
SALES (est): 402.2MM **Privately Held**
WEB: www.paradigmprecision.com
SIC: **3724** 3444 Engine mount parts, aircraft; sheet metalwork

(G-16142)
E M P INC
Also Called: Stuart Propeller & Marine
4340 Se Commerce Ave (34997-5726)
PHONE...................................772 286-7343
Edward A Morgan III, *President*
◆ EMP: 7 EST: 1983
SQ FT: 12,750
SALES (est): 843K **Privately Held**
WEB: www.stuartpropeller.net
SIC: **3599** 5088 7692 Propellers, ship & boat: machined; marine propulsion machinery & equipment; welding repair

(G-16143)
ECOSPHERE TECHNOLOGIES INC (PA)
3491 Se Gran Park Way (34997-8804)
PHONE...................................772 287-4846
Dennis McGuire, *Ch of Bd*
Michael Donn Sr, *COO*
Jacqueline McGuire, *Senior VP*
Jamar Blackmon, *Opers Mgr*
David Brooks, *CFO*
EMP: 17 EST: 1998
SQ FT: 14,700
SALES (est): 4.9MM **Publicly Held**
WEB: www.ecospheretech.com
SIC: **3589** Water treatment equipment, industrial

(G-16144)
ENERGYBIONICS LLC
519 Sw Glen Crest Way (34997-7253)
PHONE...................................561 229-4985
Sean Ebersold, *CEO*
EMP: 7 EST: 2012
SALES (est): 779.3K **Privately Held**
SIC: **3571** Minicomputers

(G-16145)
ESPACE INC
135 S River Rd (34996-6311)
PHONE..................................802 735-7546
Greg Wyler, *CEO*
EMP: 35
SALES (est): 1.4MM **Privately Held**
SIC: 3663 7389 Satellites, communications;

(G-16146)
EUROPEAN CUSTOM CASEWORK INC
3063 Se Gran Park Way (34997-6716)
PHONE..................................401 356-0400
Michael Prudhomme, *President*
Yvette Gladu, *Treasurer*
EMP: 5 **EST:** 1987
SALES (est): 484.1K **Privately Held**
WEB: www.europeancustomcasework.com
SIC: 2434 Wood kitchen cabinets

(G-16147)
EVAN LLOYD DESIGNS
3576 Se Dixie Hwy (34997-5245)
P.O. Box 369, Sweet Home OR (97386-0369)
PHONE..................................772 286-7723
EMP: 8
SALES (est): 640K **Privately Held**
SIC: 3911 Mfg Precious Metal Jewelry

(G-16148)
FLAGSHIP MARINE INC
3211 Se Gran Park Way (34997-6702)
PHONE..................................772 781-4242
Thomas C Martland, *President*
▼ **EMP:** 7 **EST:** 1989
SALES (est): 1MM **Privately Held**
WEB: www.flagshipmarine.com
SIC: 3585 3531 3663 Air conditioning equipment, complete; marine related equipment; television closed circuit equipment

(G-16149)
FRESHCO LTD
Also Called: Indian River Select
7929 Sw Jack James Dr (34997-7243)
PHONE..................................772 287-2111
Clifford F Burg, *Partner*
James Burg, *Partner*
Sharon Burg, *Partner*
Wendy Grieve, *Partner*
J Patrick Schirard, *Partner*
EMP: 40 **EST:** 1995
SQ FT: 33,000
SALES (est): 7MM **Privately Held**
WEB: www.freshcopackaging.com
SIC: 2033 Fruits & fruit products in cans, jars, etc.

(G-16150)
G & K ALUMINUM INC
3110 Se Slater St (34997-5703)
PHONE..................................772 283-1297
Gene Rastrelli, *President*
John Rastrelli, *Vice Pres*
▼ **EMP:** 10 **EST:** 1978
SQ FT: 10,000
SALES (est): 879K **Privately Held**
WEB: www.gkaluminum.com
SIC: 3365 3949 3444 Aluminum foundries; sporting & athletic goods; sheet metalwork

(G-16151)
GAME FISHERMAN INC
1384 Nw Coconut Point Ln (34994-9484)
PHONE..................................772 220-4850
Michael T Matlack, *President*
Jeanne Matlack, *Admin Sec*
▲ **EMP:** 10 **EST:** 1984
SALES (est): 1MM **Privately Held**
WEB: www.gamefisherman.com
SIC: 3732 8748 Fishing boats: lobster, crab, oyster, etc.: small; business consulting

(G-16152)
GARLINGTON LANDEWEER MAR INC
3370 Se Slater St (34997-5705)
PHONE..................................772 283-7124
Peter Landeweer, *President*

Evert Landeweer, *Vice Pres*
Mary Jordon, *Sales Dir*
Robb Maas, *Asst Sec*
EMP: 22 **EST:** 1984
SQ FT: 19,000
SALES (est): 10MM **Privately Held**
WEB: www.garlingtonyachts.com
SIC: 3732 Yachts, building & repairing

(G-16153)
GATOR WELDING INC
4597 Se Marie Way (34997-8250)
PHONE..................................561 746-0049
Kenneth Nogal, *President*
Carey Nogal, *Vice Pres*
Alayne Nogal, *Treasurer*
EMP: 11 **EST:** 1967
SALES (est): 873.4K **Privately Held**
WEB: www.gatorwelding.com
SIC: 7692 Welding repair

(G-16154)
GB AIRLINK INC
Also Called: Savi Air
2524 Se Wtham Feld Dr Uni (34996)
PHONE..................................561 593-7284
Michael Donoghue, *CEO*
Gabe Houston, *COO*
EMP: 8 **EST:** 1996
SALES (est): 717.6K **Privately Held**
WEB: www.flysavi.com
SIC: 3721 Aircraft

(G-16155)
GOULD SIGNS INC
3035 Se Waaler St (34997-5948)
P.O. Box 1090, Port Salerno (34992-1090)
PHONE..................................772 221-1218
Donald E Gould, *President*
Joseph Gould, *Vice Pres*
EMP: 9 **EST:** 1982
SQ FT: 6,500
SALES (est): 660K **Privately Held**
SIC: 3993 1799 Electric signs; sign installation & maintenance

(G-16156)
GRAPHIC DESIGNS INTL INC
3161 Se Slater St (34997-5756)
P.O. Box 2431 (34995-2431)
PHONE..................................772 287-0000
Alison Gallagher, *President*
Margaret Holt, *Corp Secy*
Kevin Gallagher, *Vice Pres*
EMP: 14 **EST:** 1994
SQ FT: 3,600
SALES (est): 937.7K **Privately Held**
WEB:
www.graphicdesignsinternational.com
SIC: 3993 Signs & advertising specialties

(G-16157)
GRINDHARD COATINGS INC
7850 Sw Ellipse Way (34997-7246)
PHONE..................................772 221-9986
Austin Weiss, *Principal*
EMP: 9 **EST:** 2017
SALES (est): 135.2K **Privately Held**
SIC: 3479 Metal coating & allied service

(G-16158)
GULFSTREAM ALUM & SHUTTER CORP
1673 Se Pomeroy St (34997-3901)
PHONE..................................772 287-6476
John L O'Brien, *President*
Barbara O'Brien, *Corp Secy*
▼ **EMP:** 21 **EST:** 1979
SQ FT: 20,000
SALES (est): 4.7MM **Privately Held**
WEB: www.gulfshutters.com
SIC: 3442 3448 1751 Louvers, shutters, jalousies & similar items; prefabricated metal buildings; carports: prefabricated metal; screen enclosures; window & door installation & erection

(G-16159)
GULFSTREAM LAND COMPANY LLC
Also Called: Riverwatch Marina & Boatyard
200 Sw Monterey Rd (34994-4612)
PHONE..................................772 286-3456
Erik Bishop, *General Mgr*
Marion Walker, *Office Mgr*
William E Biggs, *Mng Member*

Brett Cherry, *Director*
Arthur E Biggs,
EMP: 17 **EST:** 2001
SALES (est): 675.5K **Privately Held**
SIC: 3731 4493 Shipbuilding & repairing; marinas; boat yards, storage & incidental repair

(G-16160)
GYRO-GALE INC
2981 Se Dominica Ter # 4 (34997-5753)
P.O. Box 2650 (34995-2650)
PHONE..................................772 283-1711
Maged Metwally, *President*
Nagwa Metwally, *Corp Secy*
Asmaa Metwally, *Opers Mgr*
Zeyad Metwally, *VP Engrg*
▼ **EMP:** 6 **EST:** 1976
SQ FT: 3,000
SALES (est): 834.3K **Privately Held**
WEB: www.gyrogalestabilizers.com
SIC: 3499 3537 Stabilizing bars (cargo), metal; cradles, boat

(G-16161)
H2OCEAN LLC (PA)
7938 Sw Jack James Dr (34997-7241)
PHONE..................................866 420-2326
Geri A Kolos, *CFO*
Brandon Ron, *Sales Staff*
Ocean Aid, *Marketing Staff*
Edward Kolos,
◆ **EMP:** 15 **EST:** 2001
SQ FT: 30,000
SALES (est): 10.2MM **Privately Held**
WEB: www.h2ocean.com
SIC: 2844 Mouthwashes

(G-16162)
HANGAR DOOR SPCLSTS DESIGN INC
7876 Sw Jack James Dr (34997-7233)
PHONE..................................772 266-9070
Heather Singleton, *Principal*
EMP: 10
SALES (est): 375.5K **Privately Held**
SIC: 3442 Hangar doors, metal

(G-16163)
HURRICANE MARINE MFG INC
3301 Se Slater St (34997-5706)
PHONE..................................772 260-3950
EMP: 13 **EST:** 2018
SALES (est): 1.4MM **Privately Held**
WEB: www.hurricaneboatlifts.com
SIC: 3999 Manufacturing industries

(G-16164)
I P TEAM INC
701 Nw Federal Hwy # 301 (34994-1061)
PHONE..................................772 398-4664
Randall L Sparks, *CEO*
Jeffrey John, *Vice Pres*
Brigett Matthews, *Prdtn Mgr*
Sparks Andy, *Human Res Mgr*
Michelle Pedro, *Marketing Staff*
EMP: 26 **EST:** 2009
SALES (est): 3.4MM **Privately Held**
WEB: www.teamip.com
SIC: 2759 Screen printing

(G-16165)
IMPERIAL PHOTOENGRAVING
11013 Sw Redwing Dr (34997-2719)
PHONE..................................772 924-1731
Jim D Rueth, *Principal*
EMP: 8 **EST:** 2010
SALES (est): 426.1K **Privately Held**
SIC: 3423 Engravers' tools, hand

(G-16166)
INFRARED ASSOCIATES INC
2851 Se Monroe St (34997-5913)
PHONE..................................772 223-6670
Frederick W Rothe, *President*
Irwin Kudman, *General Mgr*
Danielle Macnamara, *Technical Staff*
EMP: 12 **EST:** 1997
SQ FT: 5,200
SALES (est): 2.1MM **Privately Held**
WEB: www.irassociates.com
SIC: 3823 Infrared instruments, industrial process type

(G-16167)
INTERNATIONAL PRTG AD SPC INC
Also Called: Team Ip
701 Nw Federal Hwy # 301 (34994-1005)
P.O. Box 7609, Port Saint Lucie (34985-7609)
PHONE..................................772 398-4664
Randall L Sparks, *President*
Blaine Isbell, *Vice Pres*
Jill Harrison, *Director*
▲ **EMP:** 40 **EST:** 1992
SALES (est): 5.2MM **Privately Held**
SIC: 2759 Screen printing

(G-16168)
ISOBEV INC (HQ)
1327 Se Dixie Hwy (34994-3438)
PHONE..................................561 701-5385
Marcos Agramont, *President*
EMP: 7 **EST:** 2017
SALES (est): 2.7MM
SALES (corp-wide): 19.1MM **Privately Held**
SIC: 2086 Water, pasteurized: packaged in cans, bottles, etc.
PA: Isodiol International Inc
200 Granville St Suite 2710
Vancouver BC V6C 1
604 409-4409

(G-16169)
JETSTREAM FABRICATION LLC
1880 Se Federal Hwy (34994-3914)
PHONE..................................772 287-3338
Karl Lust, *Manager*
EMP: 5 **EST:** 2008
SALES (est): 342.8K **Privately Held**
SIC: 3499 Fabricated metal products

(G-16170)
JGLC ENTERPRISES LLC
Also Called: Sheet Metal Unlimited
3920 Se Commerce Ave (34997-4958)
PHONE..................................772 223-7393
Lynette Crocker, *Mng Member*
Jose Guth, *Mng Member*
EMP: 24 **EST:** 2006
SALES (est): 3MM **Privately Held**
WEB: www.thehog.com
SIC: 3441 Fabricated structural metal

(G-16171)
JIM SMITH BOATS INC
4396 Se Commerce Ave (34997-5723)
PHONE..................................772 286-9049
John A Vance, *President*
B R Boniface, *Vice Pres*
EMP: 11 **EST:** 1980
SQ FT: 10,000
SALES (est): 1.1MM **Privately Held**
WEB: www.jimsmithboats.com
SIC: 3732 Boat building & repairing

(G-16172)
JOHNSON CONTROLS INC
3101 Se Carnivale Ct (34994-5500)
PHONE..................................772 283-1633
EMP: 16 **Privately Held**
WEB: www.johnsoncontrols.com
SIC: 2531 Seats, automobile
HQ: Johnson Controls, Inc.
5757 N Green Bay Ave
Glendale WI 53209
414 524-1200

(G-16173)
K BAUSCH MFG CORP
2813 Se Monroe St (34997-5904)
PHONE..................................772 485-2426
EMP: 6 **EST:** 2019
SALES (est): 392.1K **Privately Held**
SIC: 3999 Manufacturing industries

(G-16174)
KINANE CORP
Also Called: Minuteman Press
310 Se Denver Ave (34994-2138)
PHONE..................................772 288-6580
Timothy Kinane, *President*
Erica Kinanekelley, *Vice Pres*
EMP: 13 **EST:** 1987
SQ FT: 4,500

SALES (est): 1.5MM **Privately Held**
WEB: www.kinaneprinting.com
SIC: 2752 Commercial printing, offset

(G-16175)
KNIGHT WELDING SUPPLY LLC
3131 Se Waaler St (34997-5923)
PHONE....................................561 889-5342
EMP: 6 EST: 2019
SALES (est): 580.5K **Privately Held**
WEB: www.knightweldingsupply.com
SIC: 7692 Welding repair

(G-16176)
L & H BOATS INC
3350 Se Slater St (34997-5705)
PHONE....................................772 288-2291
Glenn Muller, *President*
Eric Meyer, *President*
John Meyer, *Vice Pres*
Linda Straub, *Treasurer*
Ella Smith, *Admin Sec*
EMP: 7 EST: 1992
SALES (est): 775.3K **Privately Held**
WEB: www.lhboats.com
SIC: 3732 Fishing boats: lobster, crab, oyster, etc.: small

(G-16177)
LARSEN
3 Melody Ln (34996-6708)
PHONE....................................305 989-4043
Louis Larsen, *Principal*
EMP: 8 EST: 2017
SALES (est): 259.3K **Privately Held**
SIC: 3732 Boat building & repairing

(G-16178)
LATA LLC
2447 Se Dixie Hwy (34996-4013)
PHONE....................................772 324-8170
Ramsey B Small, *Principal*
EMP: 8 EST: 2010
SALES (est): 145.8K **Privately Held**
SIC: 3356 Nonferrous rolling & drawing

(G-16179)
LENCO MARINE SOLUTIONS LLC
4700 Se Municipal Ct (34997-8871)
PHONE....................................772 288-2662
Sam Mullinax, *CEO*
Richard Devito, *President*
Todd Smith, *Vice Pres*
Brian Henneman, *Project Mgr*
Kevin Kortum, *Foreman/Supr*
▲ EMP: 33 EST: 1998
SQ FT: 22,000
SALES (est): 14.4MM
SALES (corp-wide): 5.8B **Publicly Held**
WEB: www.lencomarine.com
SIC: 3429 Marine hardware
HQ: Advanced Systems Group Americas Llc
N85w12545 Westbrook Xing
Menomonee Falls WI 53051
262 293-0600

(G-16180)
MACK SALES INC
3129 Se Dominica Ter (34997-5754)
PHONE....................................772 283-2306
Travis Blain, *President*
Collin Mac, *CFO*
Jenny Wagner, *Office Mgr*
▼ EMP: 9 EST: 1988
SALES (est): 1MM **Privately Held**
WEB: www.macksails.com
SIC: 3732 Boat building & repairing

(G-16181)
MAILBOX PUBLISHING INC
Also Called: Ocean Media
2081 Se Ocean Blvd Fl 4 (34996-3350)
PHONE....................................772 334-2121
Glen Fetzner, *CEO*
EMP: 19 EST: 1997
SALES (est): 2.1MM **Privately Held**
SIC: 2721 Magazines: publishing only, not printed on site

(G-16182)
MARINE CUSTOMS UNLIMITED
3355 Se Dixie Hwy (34994-5240)
PHONE....................................772 223-8005
Brian Odonnell, *Owner*

EMP: 10 EST: 2020
SALES (est): 291K **Privately Held**
WEB: www.marinecustoms.com
SIC: 2394 Canvas boat seats

(G-16183)
MARINE DIGITAL INTEGRATORS LLC
7667 Sw Ellipse Way (34997-7251)
PHONE....................................772 210-2403
Yvan Cote, *President*
EMP: 20 EST: 2014
SALES (est): 3.9MM
SALES (corp-wide): 1.8B **Privately Held**
SIC: 3699 Electrical equipment & supplies
HQ: Sierra International Llc
1 Sierra Pl
Litchfield IL 62056
217 324-9400

(G-16184)
MEMON INDUSTRIES LLC
3386 Se Cassell Ln (34997-2513)
PHONE....................................772 204-3131
David A Memon, *Manager*
EMP: 7 EST: 2011
SALES (est): 239.4K **Privately Held**
SIC: 3999 Manufacturing industries

(G-16185)
MINDER RESEARCH INC
3000 Se Waaler St (34997-5937)
P.O. Box 47 (34995-0047)
PHONE....................................772 463-6522
Debbie Druiem, *President*
Janice Melendez, *Controller*
Jennifer Zwicky, *Manager*
▲ EMP: 10 EST: 2013
SALES (est): 1.2MM **Privately Held**
WEB: www.minderresearch.com
SIC: 3714 Motor vehicle parts & accessories

(G-16186)
MR GUTTER CUTTER INC
3102 Se Dixie Hwy (34997-5044)
PHONE....................................772 286-7780
Craig Rice, *President*
EMP: 16 EST: 1985
SQ FT: 5,600
SALES (est): 758.9K **Privately Held**
SIC: 3444 Gutters, sheet metal

(G-16187)
MULTI-COLOR PRINTING INC
1249 Se Dixie Cutoff Rd (34994-3490)
PHONE....................................772 287-1676
Stephen Schmoyer, *President*
EMP: 8 EST: 1968
SALES (est): 712.2K **Privately Held**
WEB: www.gomulticolor.com
SIC: 2752 2791 2789 Commercial printing, offset; typesetting; bookbinding & related work

(G-16188)
MUSCLE LLC ✪
15 Sw Osceola St (34994-2117)
PHONE....................................772 678-6176
Grace Gillespie, *CEO*
EMP: 7 EST: 2022
SALES (est): 266.9K **Privately Held**
SIC: 3556 Distillery machinery

(G-16189)
NEW ENGLAND GRANITE & MARBLE
890 Sw Enterprise Way (34997-7210)
PHONE....................................772 283-8667
Carlos R Salvatierra, *President*
Dayana De Almeida, *Sales Staff*
Francisco Coelho Jr, *Admin Sec*
▲ EMP: 10 EST: 2009
SALES (est): 1.7MM **Privately Held**
WEB: www.newenglandgranite.net
SIC: 3281 1743 Curbing, granite or stone; marble installation, interior

(G-16190)
NITRO LEISURE PRODUCTS INC
Also Called: Nitro Gulf
4490 Se Cheri Ct (34997-5709)
PHONE....................................414 272-5084
J Hanover, *Manager*
EMP: 30

SALES (corp-wide): 68MM **Privately Held**
WEB: www.nitrogolf.com
SIC: 3949 Balls: baseball, football, basketball, etc.
HQ: Nitro Leisure Products Inc
1943 Se Airport Rd
Stuart FL

(G-16191)
OMEGA POWER SYSTEMS INC
4443 Se Commerce Ave (34997-5742)
P.O. Box 406, Port Salerno (34992-0406)
PHONE....................................772 219-0045
Frank Dlouhy, *President*
Michelle Mathis, *Admin Sec*
EMP: 5 EST: 1994
SALES (est): 799.6K **Privately Held**
WEB: www.omegaps.com
SIC: 3643 3825 Lightning protection equipment; electrical energy measuring equipment

(G-16192)
OMT INC
Also Called: Stylecraft Fine Cabinetry
648 Se Monterey Rd (34994-4410)
PHONE....................................772 287-3762
John Waugh, *President*
Cathie Armstrong-Moore, *Vice Pres*
EMP: 8 EST: 1973
SALES (est): 471.3K **Privately Held**
WEB: www.stylecraftfinecabinetry.com
SIC: 2434 Wood kitchen cabinets

(G-16193)
ORGANIC CANE COMPANY INC
923 Se Lincoln Ave (34994-3810)
PHONE....................................561 385-4081
Daniel Consonni, *President*
EMP: 6 EST: 2018
SALES (est): 305.8K **Privately Held**
SIC: 2061 Raw cane sugar

(G-16194)
PACE MACHINE & TOOL INC
7986 Sw Jack James Dr (34997-7241)
PHONE....................................561 747-5444
Monica Dirr, *President*
Ken Desch, *Principal*
Richard Dirr Jr, *Vice Pres*
Mark Van Sleete, *Buyer*
Peter Muller, *Executive*
EMP: 17 EST: 1978
SQ FT: 5,000
SALES (est): 3.5MM **Privately Held**
WEB: www.pacemachine.com
SIC: 3544 Special dies & tools

(G-16195)
PALMER MANUFACTURING CO LLC
3651 Se Commerce Ave (34997-4967)
PHONE....................................772 287-7770
EMP: 11
SALES (corp-wide): 402.2MM **Privately Held**
SIC: 3724 Aircraft engines & engine parts
HQ: Palmer Manufacturing Co., Llc.
243 Medford St
Malden MA 02148
781 321-0480

(G-16196)
PERFORMANCE TECHNOLOGY 2000
1501 Se Decker Ave # 129 (34994-3989)
PHONE....................................772 463-1056
Arthur Scornavacca, *Principal*
EMP: 9 EST: 2004
SALES (est): 898.8K **Privately Held**
SIC: 3825 Internal combustion engine analyzers, to test electronics

(G-16197)
PLATING TECHNOLOGIES INC
2971 Se Dominica Ter # 12 (34997-5713)
PHONE....................................772 220-4201
Lois R Hartzog, *President*
Dee Hartzog, *Vice Pres*
EMP: 8 EST: 1991
SQ FT: 6,000
SALES (est): 749.5K **Privately Held**
SIC: 2819 Industrial inorganic chemicals

(G-16198)
POCKETEC INC
50 Ne Dixie Hwy Ste E7 (34994-1874)
PHONE....................................772 692-8020
Kenneth Featherstone, *Principal*
▲ EMP: 6 EST: 2006
SALES (est): 407.6K **Privately Held**
WEB: www.ladyclassic.com
SIC: 3949 Sporting & athletic goods

(G-16199)
PORT ST LUCIE NEWS
Also Called: Stuart News
1939 Se Federal Hwy (34994-3915)
PHONE....................................772 287-1550
Barrett Sanders, *Editor*
Candace Anderson, *Vice Pres*
David Giles, *Vice Pres*
Cathy Heppler, *Vice Pres*
Carolyn Micheli, *Vice Pres*
EMP: 20 EST: 2010
SALES (est): 940.1K **Privately Held**
SIC: 2711 Newspapers, publishing & printing

(G-16200)
POWER SPORTS TREASURE COAST
Also Called: Treasure Coast Seadoo Yamaha
2212 Se Indian St (34997-4923)
PHONE....................................772 463-6428
Brandon Radcliff, *Owner*
EMP: 7 EST: 2004
SALES (est): 382.5K **Privately Held**
SIC: 3799 All terrain vehicles (ATV)

(G-16201)
PRODUCT DEV EXPERTS INC
2440 Se Federal Hwy # 101 (34994-4531)
PHONE....................................714 366-9000
Anthony Dichiara, *President*
EMP: 11 EST: 2018
SALES (est): 857K **Privately Held**
WEB: www.product-development-experts.com
SIC: 3999 Manufacturing industries

(G-16202)
QUICK PROTECTIVE SYSTEMS INC
421 Sw California Ave # 101 (34994-2905)
P.O. Box 1559 (34995-1559)
PHONE....................................772 220-3315
EMP: 5 EST: 2001
SQ FT: 3,000
SALES: 3MM **Privately Held**
SIC: 3842 Mfg Surgical Appliances/Supplies

(G-16203)
R J MARINE GROUP INC
619 Nw Baker Rd (34994-1032)
PHONE....................................772 232-6590
Cheryl L Bragg, *President*
EMP: 5 EST: 2010
SALES (est): 446.8K **Privately Held**
WEB: www.boemarine.com
SIC: 3429 Marine hardware

(G-16204)
RADIOTRONICS INC
Also Called: Acek9.com
1315 Sw Commerce Way (34997-7231)
PHONE....................................772 600-7574
John J Johnston, *President*
John Johnston, *President*
▲ EMP: 10 EST: 1973
SQ FT: 3,000
SALES (est): 1.1MM **Privately Held**
WEB: www.acek9.com
SIC: 3663 Radio & TV communications equipment

(G-16205)
RAPID INDUSTRIES INC
3100 Se Waaler St (34997-5924)
PHONE....................................772 287-0651
Donald E Rice, *Principal*
Frank Caprio, *Maintence Staff*
EMP: 13 EST: 2013
SALES (est): 401.6K **Privately Held**
WEB: www.rapidindustries.com
SIC: 3999 Manufacturing industries

(G-16206)
RDC MANUFACTURING INC
3353 Se Gran Park Way (34997-8837)
PHONE...................................772 286-6921
Renee D Ciferri, *Principal*
EMP: 7 EST: 2009
SALES (est): 95.4K Privately Held
SIC: 3999 Manufacturing industries

(G-16207)
**REDSLED DBA BULLDOG
EQUIPMENT**
2691 Sw Windship Way (34997-9126)
PHONE...................................954 448-5221
Jason Simione, *President*
Dana Heinsen, *Vice Pres*
EMP: 10 EST: 2001
SQ FT: 8,000
SALES (est): 1.4MM Privately Held
WEB: www.bulldogequipment.us
SIC: 2824 Nylon fibers

(G-16208)
**ROBERT MCKEE ENTERPRISES
INC**
7744 Sw Jack James Dr (34997-7249)
PHONE...................................772 291-2159
Robert McKee, *President*
EMP: 8 EST: 2016
SALES (est): 642.9K Privately Held
WEB: www.mckees37.com
SIC: 2842 Waxes for wood, leather & other
materials

(G-16209)
RONALD M HART INC
Also Called: Earthtnes In Hrmony With Nture
43 Sw Osceola St (34994-2117)
PHONE...................................772 600-8497
Ron M Hart, *President*
EMP: 5 EST: 2003
SALES (est): 652.9K Privately Held
WEB: www.terrafermata.com
SIC: 3269 5261 0781 Art & ornamental
ware, pottery; nurseries; landscape plan-
ning services

(G-16210)
RUPP MARINE INC
4761 Se Anchor Ave (34997-1902)
P.O. Box F, Port Salerno (34992-0167)
PHONE...................................772 286-5300
Herbert E Rupp II, *Ch of Bd*
Ron Karpanty, *Vice Pres*
Scott A Rupp, *Vice Pres*
Scott Rupp, *Vice Pres*
▼ EMP: 13 EST: 1977
SQ FT: 7,600
SALES (est): 2.4MM Privately Held
WEB: www.ruppmarine.com
SIC: 3429 3732 Marine hardware; boat
building & repairing

(G-16211)
RWLA ENTERPRISES LLC
2810 Se Dune Dr Apt 1104 (34996-1931)
PHONE...................................772 334-1248
EMP: 15 EST: 2007
SALES (est): 1.4MM Privately Held
SIC: 2721 Magazine

(G-16212)
SEAROBOTICS CORPORATION
7765 Sw Ellipse Way (34997-7245)
P.O. Box 30909, West Palm Beach (33420-
0909)
PHONE...................................772 742-3700
Donald T Darling, *CEO*
Roger Horn, *Project Mgr*
Lou Dennis, *Engineer*
Geoff Douglass, *Engineer*
Janet Horn, *Planning*
EMP: 22 EST: 1999
SQ FT: 12,000
SALES (est): 4.9MM Privately Held
WEB: www.searobotics.com
SIC: 3812 Search & navigation equipment

(G-16213)
**SEATORQUE CONTROL
SYSTEMS LLC**
2779 Se Monroe St (34997-5958)
PHONE...................................772 220-3020
Peter Stolper, *Mng Member*
James Burke, *Manager*

▲ EMP: 19 EST: 2005
SALES (est): 5.8MM Privately Held
WEB: www.seatorque.com
SIC: 3625 Marine & navy auxiliary controls

(G-16214)
**SEMICONDUCTOR
TECHNOLOGY INC**
3131 Se Jay St (34997-5964)
P.O. Box 474 (34995-0474)
PHONE...................................772 341-0800
EMP: 7 EST: 2019
SALES (est): 389.8K Privately Held
SIC: 3674 Semiconductors & related de-
vices

(G-16215)
SESOLINC GRP INC (PA)
50 Se Ocean Blvd Ste 202 (34994-2222)
PHONE...................................772 287-9090
Harry Ford III, *President*
Courtney Farrell, *General Mgr*
Matthew Bush, *Counsel*
Kaycee Harris, *Sales Mgr*
Michael Joiner, *Director*
▲ EMP: 8 EST: 1993
SQ FT: 1,300
SALES (est): 9MM Privately Held
WEB: www.sesolinc.com
SIC: 3448 2819 Prefabricated metal com-
ponents; industrial inorganic chemicals

(G-16216)
SHEARWATER MARINE FL INC
4519 Se Commerce Ave (34997-8860)
PHONE...................................772 781-5553
James Dragseth, *President*
EMP: 26 EST: 2020
SALES (est): 2.3MM Privately Held
WEB: www.shearwaterfl.com
SIC: 3732 3714 3731 Boat building & re-
pairing; motor vehicle parts & acces-
sories; shipbuilding & repairing

(G-16217)
SHEET METAL UNLIMITED
3920 Se Commerce Ave (34997-4958)
PHONE...................................772 872-7440
EMP: 11 EST: 2018
SALES (est): 1.3MM Privately Held
SIC: 3444 Sheet metalwork

(G-16218)
SHOCKSOCKS LLC
2979 Se Gran Park Way (34997-6715)
PHONE...................................352 258-0496
Ricardo A Romagosa, *Principal*
EMP: 10 EST: 2016
SALES (est): 257K Privately Held
WEB: www.shocksocks.com
SIC: 2759 Screen printing

(G-16219)
SIGNS OF TIME INC
1700 Sw Belgrave Ter (34997-7044)
P.O. Box 1786 (34995-1786)
PHONE...................................772 240-9590
Stephen Fenton, *President*
EMP: 8 EST: 2010
SALES (est): 172.9K Privately Held
SIC: 3993 Signs & advertising specialties

(G-16220)
SIKORSKY AIRCRAFT CORP
2324 Se Liberator Ln (34996-4037)
PHONE...................................772 210-0849
EMP: 7 EST: 2018
SALES (est): 179.2K Privately Held
SIC: 3812 Search & navigation equipment

(G-16221)
SIN PIN INC
600 Nw Dixie Hwy (34994-1118)
PHONE...................................877 805-5665
Majd Ibrahim, *Principal*
EMP: 9 EST: 2011
SALES (est): 125.2K Privately Held
WEB: www.sinpin.com
SIC: 3452 Pins

(G-16222)
**SMITHS INTERCONNECT
GROUP LTD**
8851 Sw Old Kansas Ave (34997-7204)
PHONE...................................805 370-5580

EMP: 7
SALES (corp-wide): 4.1B Privately Held
SIC: 3679 Mfg Electronic Components
HQ: Smiths Interconnect Group Limited
130 Centennial Park
Borehamwood HERTS WD6 3
208 450-8033

(G-16223)
**SMITHS INTRCNNECT
AMERICAS INC**
8851 Sw Old Kansas Ave (34997-7204)
PHONE...................................772 286-9300
Rob Torsiello, *Vice Pres*
Joe Hite, *Safety Mgr*
Tim Meehan, *Director*
Anthea Collier, *Officer*
EMP: 308
SALES (corp-wide): 3.3B Privately Held
WEB: www.smithsinterconnect.com
SIC: 3679 Microwave components; attenu-
ators
HQ: Smiths Interconnect Americas, Inc.
5101 Richland Ave
Kansas City KS 66106
913 342-5544

(G-16224)
**SOLAR ELECTRIC POWER
COMPANY**
Also Called: Sepco
1521 Se Palm Ct (34994-4914)
PHONE...................................772 220-6615
Steven R Robbins, *President*
Steven Burns, *Vice Pres*
Susan Robbins, *Vice Pres*
Matt Cirrito, *Sales Staff*
Shawn Tefft, *Sales Staff*
◆ EMP: 14 EST: 1994
SQ FT: 10,000
SALES (est): 3.4MM Privately Held
WEB: www.sepco-solarlighting.com
SIC: 3674 5063 Photovoltaic devices,
solid state; lighting fixtures, commercial &
industrial

(G-16225)
**SOUTH BCH ORTHTICS
PRSTHTICS I**
7305 Sw Gaines Ave (34997-7332)
PHONE...................................352 512-0262
Mark Selleck, *CEO*
Allen Warman, *Consultant*
EMP: 10 EST: 2013
SALES (est): 348.8K Privately Held
WEB: www.southbeachop.com
SIC: 3842 Orthopedic appliances

(G-16226)
SP SIGN LLC
Also Called: Sign-A-Rama
2201 Se Indian St Unit E4 (34997-4984)
PHONE...................................772 562-0955
Kim Williamson, *Mng Member*
EMP: 10 EST: 2015
SALES (est): 385.8K Privately Held
WEB: www.signarama.com
SIC: 3993 Signs & advertising specialties

(G-16227)
STRATOS AIRPARTS CORP
7897 Sw Jack James Dr (34997-7200)
PHONE...................................772 266-9157
Benjamin Smiley, *President*
EMP: 10 EST: 2018
SALES (est): 700.3K Privately Held
SIC: 3728 Aircraft body & wing assemblies
& parts

(G-16228)
STUART BOATWORKS INC
3515 Se Lionel Ter (34997-8800)
PHONE...................................772 600-7121
Jeffrey E Futch, *President*
Terri L Futch, *Vice Pres*
Hannah Maxwell, *Manager*
EMP: 10 EST: 2008
SALES (est): 1.1MM Privately Held
WEB: www.stuartboatworks.com
SIC: 3732 7389 Boat building & repairing;

(G-16229)
STUART NEWS (DH)
1939 Se Federal Hwy (34994-3915)
P.O. Box 9009 (34995-9009)
PHONE...................................772 287-1550
Bob Brunjes, *President*
EMP: 225 EST: 1976
SALES (est): 47.2MM
SALES (corp-wide): 3.2B Publicly Held
WEB: www.cityofstuart.us
SIC: 2711 Newspapers, publishing & print-
ing
HQ: Journal Media Group, Inc.
333 W State St
Milwaukee WI 53203
414 224-2000

(G-16230)
STUART NEWS
Also Called: Jupiter Courier
1939 Se Federal Hwy (34994-3915)
PHONE...................................772 287-1550
John Maletzke, *Branch Mgr*
EMP: 115
SALES (corp-wide): 3.2B Publicly Held
WEB: www.cityofstuart.us
SIC: 2711 Newspapers, publishing & print-
ing
HQ: The Stuart News
1939 Se Federal Hwy
Stuart FL 34994
772 287-1550

(G-16231)
STUART PRO GREEN
3121 Se Slater St (34997-5751)
PHONE...................................772 286-0510
EMP: 5 EST: 2012
SALES (est): 379.6K Privately Held
WEB: www.progreen.biz
SIC: 3728 Dusting & spraying equipment,
aircraft

(G-16232)
**STUART STAIR & FURNITURE
MFG**
3220 Se Dominica Ter (34997-5758)
PHONE...................................772 287-4097
Carl Stewart, *President*
Elsie Stewart, *Treasurer*
EMP: 8 EST: 1987
SQ FT: 5,500
SALES (est): 971.2K Privately Held
WEB: www.americanstairparts.com
SIC: 2426 2431 Furniture stock & parts,
hardwood; staircases, stairs & railings

(G-16233)
STUART WEB INC
5675 Se Grouper Ave (34997-3103)
PHONE...................................772 287-8022
Thomas Hawken, *President*
Diane K Hawken, *Corp Secy*
Kevin Hawken, *Vice Pres*
◆ EMP: 45 EST: 1981
SQ FT: 14,999
SALES (est): 8.6MM Privately Held
WEB: www.stuartweb.com
SIC: 2752 Commercial printing, offset

(G-16234)
STUART YACHT BUILDERS
450 Sw Salerno Rd (34997-6250)
PHONE...................................561 747-1947
Greg N Burdick, *President*
Nancy G Burdick, *Corp Secy*
Douglas T Newbigin, *Vice Pres*
EMP: 11 EST: 1982
SQ FT: 10,000
SALES (est): 1.4MM Privately Held
SIC: 3732 5091 3949 3441 Yachts, build-
ing & repairing; sporting & recreation
goods; sporting & athletic goods; fabri-
cated structural metal
HQ: Stuart Yacht Corporation
602 Sw Anchorage Way
Stuart FL 34994
772 286-9800

(G-16235)
SUPERIOR KITCHENS INC (PA)
2680 Se Federal Hwy (34994-4535)
PHONE...................................772 286-6801
Marcel Rappold, *President*
Jerry Erbe, *Sales Staff*
Barbara Johnston, *Admin Sec*

EMP: 14 **EST:** 1955
SQ FT: 24,000
SALES (est): 2.8MM **Privately Held**
WEB: www.superiorkitchensinc.com
SIC: 2434 Wood kitchen cabinets

(G-16236)
TALARIA COMPANY LLC
4550 Se Boatyard Ave (34997-1921)
PHONE...................................772 403-5387
Darryl Schmiermund, *Manager*
EMP: 90
SALES (corp-wide): 110.7MM **Privately
Held**
WEB: www.hinckleyyachts.com
SIC: 3732 Boat building & repairing
PA: The Talaria Company Llc
1 Little Harbor Lndg
Portsmouth RI 02871
401 683-7100

(G-16237)
TEAM IP SPORTS LLC
850 Nw Federal Hwy 229 (34994-1019)
PHONE...................................772 398-4664
Randall L Sparks,
Andrew J Sparks,
Bradall E Sparks,
Mary Lou Sparks,
EMP: 14 **EST:** 2004
SALES (est): 1MM **Privately Held**
WEB: www.teamip.com
SIC: 2211 Print cloths, cotton

(G-16238)
TNT TRANSFER INC
7833 Sw Ellipse Way (34997-7247)
PHONE...................................561 594-0123
Gregory N Newton, *President*
George O Macdonald, *Vice Pres*
EMP: 6 **EST:** 2008
SALES (est): 959.4K **Privately Held**
SIC: 3564 Ventilating fans: industrial or
commercial

(G-16239)
**TORTILLERIA GALLO DE ORO
LLC**
3511 Se Dixie Hwy (34997-5244)
PHONE...................................561 818-7829
Manuel E Perez, *Branch Mgr*
EMP: 13
SALES (corp-wide): 359K **Privately Held**
SIC: 2099 Tortillas, fresh or refrigerated
PA: Tortilleria Gallo De Oro Llc
2100 Longwood Rd
West Palm Beach FL

(G-16240)
TREASURE COAST CANVAS
6538 Se Federal Hwy (34997-8315)
PHONE...................................772 210-2588
Cullen Lowery, *Administration*
EMP: 7 **EST:** 2014
SALES (est): 275.8K **Privately Held**
WEB: www.candccanvas.com
SIC: 2394 Awnings, fabric: made from pur-
chased materials

(G-16241)
**TREASURE COAST MACHINES
INC**
3081 Se Slater St (34997-5702)
PHONE...................................772 283-2024
Fax: 772 283-1624
EMP: 18
SALES: 1.5MM **Privately Held**
SIC: 3599 3724 Mfg Industrial Machinery
Mfg Aircraft Engines/Parts

(G-16242)
TRIUMPH GROUP INC
Also Called: Triumph Arstrctres - Vght Coml
1845 Se Airport Rd (34996-4012)
PHONE...................................772 220-5000
Curtis Hoffman, *General Mgr*
Greg Rust, *Vice Chairman*
Jolis Rodriguez, *COO*
Kevin Carney, *Opers Mgr*
Mike Monroy, *Facilities Mgr*
EMP: 400 **Publicly Held**
WEB: www.qarbonaerospace.com
SIC: 3728 Aircraft parts & equipment
PA: Triumph Group, Inc.
899 Cassatt Rd Ste 210
Berwyn PA 19312

(G-16243)
**TURBOCOMBUSTOR
TECHNOLOGY INC (HQ)**
Also Called: Paradigm Precision
3651 Se Commerce Ave (34997-4981)
PHONE...................................772 287-7770
Greg Bennett, *President*
Matthew Pemrick, *General Mgr*
Chaitra Nailadi, *Vice Pres*
John Furnare, *Opers Staff*
Joshua Thayer, *QC Mgr*
▲ **EMP:** 350 **EST:** 1972
SQ FT: 120,000
SALES (est): 101.7MM
SALES (corp-wide): 402.2MM **Privately
Held**
WEB: www.palmermfgco.com
SIC: 3724 3728 3444 Engine mount
parts, aircraft; aircraft parts & equipment;
sheet metalwork
PA: Dynamic Precision Group, Inc.
3651 Se Commerce Ave
Stuart FL 34997
772 287-7770

(G-16244)
UNISOURCE STONE INC
2575 Se Federal Hwy # 101 (34994-4918)
PHONE...................................561 493-0660
Russ Carbone, *President*
Elizabeth Hamill, *Treasurer*
▲ **EMP:** 8 **EST:** 1998
SQ FT: 7,500
SALES (est): 422.3K **Privately Held**
WEB: www.unisourcestone.com
SIC: 3281 Marble, building: cut & shaped

(G-16245)
US PAVERSCAPE INC
1735 Se Federal Hwy (34994-3952)
PHONE...................................772 223-7287
Ray Paulding, *CEO*
◆ **EMP:** 80 **EST:** 2000
SQ FT: 5,832
SALES (est): 13.5MM **Privately Held**
WEB: www.uspaverscape.com
SIC: 3272 Concrete products

(G-16246)
**VIATEK CONSUMER PDTS
GROUP INC (PA)**
Also Called: Viatek Products
2081 Se Ocean Blvd Ste 3a (34996-3326)
PHONE...................................423 402-9010
Lou Lentine, *President*
Zorilee Gascot, *COO*
Angelo Ramsbott, *Vice Pres*
Ryan Wright, *Opers Mgr*
Scott J Sloat, *CFO*
▲ **EMP:** 30 **EST:** 2004
SALES (est): 9.9MM **Privately Held**
WEB: www.viatekproducts.com
SIC: 3634 5013 Electric housewares &
fans; motor vehicle supplies & new parts

(G-16247)
VIESEL FUEL LLC
1000 Se Monterey Cmns # 206
(34996-3342)
PHONE...................................772 781-4300
Michelle Nyberg, *Vice Pres*
Stuart M Lamb, *Mng Member*
Stuart Lamb, *Mng Member*
◆ **EMP:** 30 **EST:** 2009
SALES (est): 4.9MM **Privately Held**
WEB: www.mahoneyes.com
SIC: 2869 Fuels

(G-16248)
**WATERBLASTING
TECHNOLOGIES INC (PA)**
Also Called: Hog Technologies
3920 Se Commerce Ave (34997-4958)
PHONE...................................772 223-7393
James P Crocker, *President*
Michael Nardone, *COO*
Mike Nardone, *COO*
Adam Baldwin, *Vice Pres*
Dave Friday, *Vice Pres*
◆ **EMP:** 71 **EST:** 2005
SALES (est): 32.3MM **Privately Held**
WEB: www.waterblastingtechnologies.com
SIC: 3531 Construction machinery

(G-16249)
**WHITE ALUMINUM
FABRICATION INC**
3195 Se Lionel Ter (34997-8816)
PHONE...................................772 219-3245
Ronald E White, *President*
Victoria White, *Vice Pres*
◆ **EMP:** 50 **EST:** 2000
SQ FT: 15,000
SALES (est): 9.3MM **Privately Held**
WEB: www.whitealuminum.net
SIC: 3355 Aluminum rail & structural
shapes

(G-16250)
**WHITICAR BOAT WORKS INC
(PA)**
3636 Se Old St Lucie Blvd (34996-5155)
P.O. Box 1109 (34995-1109)
PHONE...................................772 287-2883
Jim Dragseth, *President*
John Whiticar, *Treasurer*
Tom Berryhill, *Manager*
Brian Magnant, *Manager*
Calvin Powell, *Supervisor*
EMP: 39 **EST:** 1947
SQ FT: 24,000
SALES (est): 5MM **Privately Held**
WEB: www.whiticar.com
SIC: 3732 5551 Motorized boat, building &
repairing; marine supplies

(G-16251)
**WILLIS CUSTOM YACHTS
LLC ✪**
6800 Sw Jack James Dr # 1 (34997-6200)
PHONE...................................772 221-9100
Doug West, *President*
Mark Willis,
Ron Kirschner,
EMP: 130 **EST:** 2021
SALES (est): 10.3MM **Privately Held**
SIC: 3732 Yachts, building & repairing

(G-16252)
WILLIS MARINE INC
4361 Se Commerce Ave (34997-5728)
PHONE...................................772 283-7189
Mark Willis, *President*
EMP: 5 **EST:** 1990
SQ FT: 5,000
SALES (est): 835.4K **Privately Held**
WEB: www.willismarineinc.com
SIC: 3732 Boat building & repairing

(G-16253)
**WMR CYCLE PERFORMANCE
INC**
Also Called: Cyclelogic Products
7749 Sw Ellipse Way (34997-7245)
PHONE...................................772 426-3000
David Kimmey, *President*
EMP: 5 **EST:** 1998
SQ FT: 2,500
SALES (est): 660K **Privately Held**
SIC: 3751 Motorcycles & related parts; mo-
torcycle accessories

(G-16254)
WWW TCPALM COMPANY
1939 S Federal Hwy (34994)
PHONE...................................772 287-1550
Jeff Haight, *Manager*
Thomas Webber Jr, *Director*
Eric Gates, *Director*
Paulette Hayes, *Technician*
Brian Martin, *Technician*
EMP: 22 **EST:** 2001
SALES (est): 769.1K **Privately Held**
WEB: www.tcpalm.com
SIC: 2711 Newspapers

Summerfield
Marion County

(G-16255)
**A & J COMMERCIAL SEATING
INC**
10485 Se 158th Pl (34491-7648)
PHONE...................................352 288-2022
John Plourde, *President*
Norma Plourde, *Corp Secy*

Tammy Benoit, *Vice Pres*
EMP: 9 **EST:** 1963
SQ FT: 13,000
SALES (est): 470.7K **Privately Held**
WEB: www.ajseating.com
SIC: 2599 2531 Restaurant furniture,
wood or metal; public building & related
furniture

(G-16256)
**ADVANCED WLDG FBRCTION
DSIGN L**
13540 Se 31st Ave (34491-2102)
PHONE...................................352 237-9800
Aaron O'Brien,
Heather O'Brien,
Reynold D Wolter,
Warnieta L Wolter,
EMP: 7 **EST:** 2011
SALES (est): 762.5K **Privately Held**
SIC: 7692 Welding repair

(G-16257)
BEA SUE VINEYARDS INC
Also Called: Dragon Flower Winery
11025 Se Highway 42 (34491-6627)
PHONE...................................352 446-5204
Shannon M Peacock, *President*
EMP: 8 **EST:** 2014
SALES (est): 246.6K **Privately Held**
SIC: 2084 Wines

(G-16258)
CREATIVE CURBING
15340 Se 73rd Ave (34491-4223)
P.O. Box 1259 (34492-1259)
PHONE...................................352 347-3329
Kevin Reedy, *Principal*
EMP: 10 **EST:** 2001
SALES (est): 493.9K **Privately Held**
WEB: www.creativecurbing.net
SIC: 3281 Curbing, paving & walkway
stone

(G-16259)
SOUTH MARION MEATS
13770 S Highway 475 (34491-2020)
PHONE...................................352 245-2096
EMP: 6
SALES (est): 350K **Privately Held**
SIC: 2011 5421 2013 Meat Packing Plant
Ret Meat/Fish Mfg Prepared Meats

(G-16260)
STEPHEN SHIVES
Also Called: S & S Enterprises
14628 Se 95th Ct (34491-3611)
PHONE...................................352 454-6522
Stephen Shives, *Owner*
EMP: 5 **EST:** 2014
SALES (est): 322.6K **Privately Held**
WEB: www.runawaycampers.com
SIC: 3792 Travel trailers & campers

Summerland Key
Monroe County

(G-16261)
**CERTIFIED MOLD TREATMENT
LLC**
17277 Allamanda Dr (33042-3709)
P.O. Box 420311 (33042-0311)
PHONE...................................305 879-1839
Gary V Marsden, *Principal*
EMP: 9 **EST:** 2008
SALES (est): 351.2K **Privately Held**
WEB: www.certifiedmoldtreatment.com
SIC: 3544 Industrial molds

Sumterville
Sumter County

(G-16262)
**ARCOSA TRFFIC LTG
STRCTRES LLC**
1749 Cr 525e (33585-5346)
PHONE...................................352 748-4258
EMP: 50
SALES (corp-wide): 2B **Publicly Held**
WEB: www.arcosatrafficstructures.com
SIC: 3441 Fabricated structural metal

HQ: Arcosa Traffic And Lighting Structures,
Llc
500 N Akard St
Dallas TX 75201
972 942-6500

(G-16263)
FLORIDA DESIGNER CABINETS
INC
1034 S Us 301 (33585-5132)
P.O. Box 98 (33585-0098)
PHONE....................................352 793-8555
Barry Mann, *President*
Barbara Mann, *Corp Secy*
▼ EMP: 12 EST: 1990
SQ FT: 7,000
SALES (est): 1.2MM **Privately Held**
WEB: www.fladc.com
SIC: 2599 2541 2517 2434 Cabinets,
factory; wood partitions & fixtures; wood
television & radio cabinets; wood kitchen
cabinets

(G-16264)
SUWANNEE AMERICAN CEM CO
LLC (HQ)
Also Called: Ash Grove
4750 E C 470 (33585-5342)
P.O. Box 445 (33585-0445)
PHONE....................................352 569-5393
Cary O Cohrs, *President*
Dana B Moran, *Vice Pres*
Billy Edmonds, *Prdtn Mgr*
Darryl Needels, *Purchasing*
Ginger Fredricksen, *Credit Mgr*
EMP: 50 EST: 2006
SALES (est): 56.1MM
SALES (corp-wide): 30.9B **Privately Held**
WEB: www.sacement.com
SIC: 3272 Concrete products
PA: Crh Public Limited Company
Stonemason S Way
Rathfarnham D16 K
140 410-00

Sun City Center
Hillsborough County

(G-16265)
ELITE CAST STONE INC
3805 Gaviota Dr (33573-6707)
PHONE....................................305 904-3032
Hesley Sampaio, *Principal*
EMP: 7 EST: 2015
SALES (est): 235.6K **Privately Held**
SIC: 3272 Concrete products

(G-16266)
PSS COMMUNICATIONS INC
Also Called: Data Line
309 Bryce Ct (33573-6260)
PHONE....................................408 496-3330
Paul R Fales, *CEO*
Marlene C Fales, *President*
Marlene Fales, *CFO*
EMP: 13 EST: 2004
SALES (est): 2.4MM **Privately Held**
SIC: 3661 Telephones & telephone appara-
tus

(G-16267)
SOUTH BAY HOSPITAL
4016 Sun City Center Blvd (33573-5298)
PHONE....................................813 634-3301
Sheldon Barr, *CEO*
Jennifer Wells China, *Chairman*
Cheryl Quimby, *Opers Staff*
Angie Searls, *QA Dir*
Warren Pate, *CFO*
EMP: 392 EST: 1992
SALES (est): 26.5MM **Privately Held**
WEB: www.hcafloridahealthcare.com
SIC: 3821 Chemical laboratory apparatus

Sunny Isles Beach
Miami-Dade County

(G-16268)
ALPHA ADVANTAGE AMERICA
LLC
323 Sunny Isles Blvd Fl 7 (33160-4232)
PHONE....................................305 671-3990
Rios Jose, *CEO*
Jorge Rios, *COO*
Cassandra Freer, *Vice Pres*
Agueda Rios, *CFO*
EMP: 9 EST: 2010
SALES (est): 336.3K **Privately Held**
SIC: 3317 Steel pipe & tubes

(G-16269)
COLA GROUP RIVERSIDE LLC
16047 Collins Ave # 2103 (33160-5557)
PHONE....................................305 940-0277
Louis Cola, *Principal*
EMP: 7 EST: 2011
SALES (est): 129.3K **Privately Held**
SIC: 2086 Soft drinks: packaged in cans,
bottles, etc.

(G-16270)
ECOMBUSTIBLE PRODUCTS
LLC
16690 Collins Ave # 1102 (33160-5687)
PHONE....................................786 565-8610
Jorge D Arevalo, *Mng Member*
Volha Bahdanava, *Mng Member*
EMP: 10 EST: 2013
SALES (est): 716.9K **Privately Held**
WEB: www.ecombustible.com
SIC: 3823 Combustion control instruments

(G-16271)
ECOMKBIZ LLC
16850 Collins Ave Ste 112 (33160-4291)
PHONE....................................786 477-1865
Jeronimo Pineda, *President*
EMP: 10 EST: 2020
SALES (est): 300K **Privately Held**
SIC: 2844 Toilet preparations

(G-16272)
ELIBRO CORPORATION
16699 Collins Ave # 1002 (33160-5408)
PHONE....................................305 466-0155
Eduardo Varela-Cid, *CEO*
Felipe Varela Lucas, *President*
Marlen Lucas, *Administration*
EMP: 18 EST: 2002
SALES (est): 1.6MM **Privately Held**
WEB: www.e-libro.us
SIC: 2731 Book publishing

(G-16273)
ESTRADAS FIBERGLASS MFG
CORP
16900 N Bay Rd Apt 803 (33160-4266)
PHONE....................................954 924-8778
EMP: 6
SQ FT: 2,500
SALES: 675K **Privately Held**
SIC: 3089 Mfg Plastic Products

(G-16274)
ETRONICS4U INC
16850 Collins Ave 112-166 (33160-4238)
PHONE....................................786 303-8429
Eitan Sasson, *Branch Mgr*
EMP: 19
SALES (corp-wide): 229.1K **Privately**
Held
SIC: 3944 Electronic games & toys
PA: Etronics4u, Inc.
21325 Ne 19th Ct
Miami FL 33179
786 546-4501

(G-16275)
GENUINE AD INC
17600 N Bay Rd Apt 406 (33160-2832)
PHONE....................................786 399-6484
Pablo Brochado, *Principal*
EMP: 9 EST: 2008
SALES (est): 285.5K **Privately Held**
SIC: 2759 Commercial printing

(G-16276)
GESCO ICE CREAM VENDING
CORP (PA)
17555 Collins Ave # 2903 (33160-2882)
PHONE....................................718 782-3232
Jeffrey Gesser, *President*
EMP: 10 EST: 1977
SQ FT: 2,000
SALES (est): 1.1MM **Privately Held**
SIC: 2656 Ice cream containers: made
from purchased material

(G-16277)
INOX LLC
Also Called: American Pipes and Tubes Co
19201 Collins Ave Ste 131 (33160-2202)
PHONE....................................305 409-2764
Maksim Tabunou, *CEO*
Siarhei Karankevich,
Victor Savtthouk,
EMP: 5 EST: 2010
SQ FT: 250
SALES (est): 375.9K **Privately Held**
WEB: www.inoxllc.com
SIC: 2421 Furniture dimension stock, soft-
wood

(G-16278)
KAFE PA NOU LLC
17100 N Bay Rd Apt 1514 (33160-3458)
PHONE....................................305 953-3344
Jean Rene Faustin, *Mng Member*
Philippe Andre Jean-Sebastien,
Satya Fabien Dodard,
▲ EMP: 5 EST: 2013
SQ FT: 300
SALES (est): 323K **Privately Held**
SIC: 2095 Roasted coffee

(G-16279)
LAMM INDUSTRIES INC
330 188th St (33160-2411)
PHONE....................................718 368-0181
Vladimir Lamm, *President*
EMP: 6 EST: 1995
SALES (est): 465.2K **Privately Held**
WEB: www.lammindustries.com
SIC: 3651 5731 Audio electronic systems;
radio, television & electronic stores

(G-16280)
NANOTECH ENERGY INC (PA)
323 Sunny Isles Blvd 7thf (33160-4232)
PHONE....................................800 995-5491
Jack Kavanaugh, *CEO*
Edie Gray, *Manager*
Haosen Wang, *Manager*
Maher Kady, *CTO*
Scott Jacobson, *Director*
EMP: 28 EST: 2014
SALES (est): 3MM **Privately Held**
WEB: www.nanotechenergy.com
SIC: 3691 Storage batteries

(G-16281)
REMCODA LLC
18201 Collins Ave # 4501 (33160-5150)
PHONE....................................908 239-4137
EMP: 159
SALES (corp-wide): 7.5MM **Privately**
Held
WEB: www.remcoda.com
SIC: 2992 Oils & greases, blending & com-
pounding
PA: Remcoda, Llc
230 W 39th St Fl 10
New York NY 10018
212 354-1330

(G-16282)
SKAMPAS PERFORMANCE
GROUP
19201 Collins Ave Cu-137 (33160-2202)
PHONE....................................305 974-0047
Morris Laloshi, *Owner*
EMP: 7 EST: 2014
SALES (est): 247.7K **Privately Held**
SIC: 2841 Soap & other detergents

(G-16283)
TERFA LITTER USA INC
17720 N Bay Rd Apt 5a (33160-2806)
PHONE....................................416 358-4495
Jukka Karjalainen, *Principal*
Andrei Sobolevsky, *Vice Pres*

EMP: 10 EST: 2016
SALES (est): 342.2K **Privately Held**
SIC: 3295 8742 7389 Cat box litter; sales
(including sales management) consultant;

(G-16284)
TRANS-RESOURCES LLC
17780 Collins Ave (33160-2827)
PHONE....................................305 933-8301
Rick Chitwood, *Vice Pres*
Oren Shmueli, *Controller*
Mark Hirsh, *Executive*
EMP: 736 EST: 1985
SQ FT: 3,000
SALES (est): 48MM **Privately Held**
WEB: www.valueyourpension.com
SIC: 2873 2819 2879 Nitrogen solutions
(fertilizer); industrial inorganic chemicals;
potasssium nitrate & sulfate; fungicides,
herbicides

Sunrise
Broward County

(G-16285)
AEROSPACE ROTABLES INC
5151 Nw 109th Ave (33351-8003)
PHONE....................................954 452-0056
Marco Villavicencio, *President*
Edmundo Aguilar, *Pastor*
Marlene Villavicencio, *Vice Pres*
Hai Nguyen, *Project Mgr*
Maribel Castro, *Purchasing*
▲ EMP: 14 EST: 1998
SQ FT: 8,000
SALES (est): 2.6MM **Privately Held**
WEB: www.aerospacerotables.com
SIC: 3728 Aircraft body assemblies & parts

(G-16286)
AIM SHUTTERS
5054 N Hiatus Rd (33351-8017)
PHONE....................................954 861-6666
Hector Budejen, *Principal*
EMP: 8 EST: 2010
SALES (est): 113.4K **Privately Held**
SIC: 3442 Metal doors, sash & trim

(G-16287)
AIRSTOX INC
13680 Nw 5th St Ste 140 (33325-6234)
P.O. Box 267520, Fort Lauderdale (33326-
7520)
PHONE....................................954 618-6573
Jeffrey G Thomas, *President*
EMP: 7 EST: 2006
SALES (est): 524.9K **Privately Held**
SIC: 3724 Aircraft engines & engine parts

(G-16288)
ALBER CORP
Also Called: Vertiv
7775 W Oakland Park Blvd (33351-6703)
PHONE....................................954 377-7101
Derek Alber, *President*
S Hassell, *President*
Jeffrey T Blind, *Corp Secy*
Alina Crombie, *Sales Staff*
EMP: 100 EST: 1992
SQ FT: 35,000
SALES (est): 18.6MM
SALES (corp-wide): 5B **Publicly Held**
WEB: www.vertiv.com
SIC: 3825 Battery testers, electrical; elec-
trical energy measuring equipment
HQ: Vertiv Corporation
1050 Dearborn Dr
Columbus OH 43085
614 888-0246

(G-16289)
ALIGN OPTICS INC
4700 N Hiatus Rd Ste 144a (33351-7904)
PHONE....................................954 748-1715
Derek Verma, *President*
▲ EMP: 5 EST: 1997
SQ FT: 2,200
SALES (est): 501.7K **Privately Held**
WEB: www.alignoptics.com
SIC: 3827 Optical instruments & lenses

(G-16290)
ALLERGAN SALES LLC
13800 Nw 2nd St Ste 190 (33325-6243)
PHONE......................787 406-1203
Luis Marrero, *Principal*
Talley Wright, *Business Mgr*
Lori Franke, *Director*
Christina Vituli, *Director*
EMP: 13 **EST:** 2019
SALES (est): 6.7MM **Privately Held**
WEB: www.abbvie.com
SIC: 2834 Pharmaceutical preparations

(G-16291)
ALTUM AEROSPACE
13680 Nw 5th St Ste 140 (33325-6234)
PHONE......................954 618-6573
EMP: 15 **EST:** 2011
SALES (est): 3.2MM **Privately Held**
SIC: 3721 3429 Mfg Aircraft Mfg Hardware

(G-16292)
AMERICAN BIDET COMPANY
10821 Nw 50th St (33351-8091)
P.O. Box 266333, Fort Lauderdale (33326-6333)
PHONE......................954 981-1111
Arnold Cohen, *President*
EMP: 12 **EST:** 1963
SQ FT: 20,000
SALES (est): 973K **Privately Held**
SIC: 3261 Bidets, vitreous china

(G-16293)
ANDRX CORPORATION
13900 Nw 2nd St Ste 100 (33325-6215)
PHONE......................954 585-1770
David Fernandez, *Manager*
EMP: 105 **Privately Held**
WEB: www.andrx.com
SIC: 2834 Pharmaceutical preparations
HQ: Andrx Corporation
     4955 Orange Dr
     Davie FL 33314

(G-16294)
BACKBONE INTERCONNECT LLC
10501 Nw 50th St 104-3 (33351-8012)
PHONE......................954 800-4749
EMP: 23
SQ FT: 2,000
SALES (est): 1MM **Privately Held**
SIC: 3678 3612 3644 3679 Mfg Elec Connectors Mfg Transformers Mfg Nonconductv Wire Dvc Mfg Elec Components

(G-16295)
BENCHMARK CONNECTOR CORP
4501 Nw 103rd Ave (33351-7936)
PHONE......................954 746-9929
David Brand, *President*
Vincent Zarella, *Vice Pres*
Bob Larocca, *Accounts Exec*
Alex Zarrella, *Accounts Exec*
Jose Merced, *Manager*
▲ **EMP:** 41 **EST:** 1997
SQ FT: 16,500
SALES (est): 19MM **Privately Held**
WEB: www.benchmarkconnector.com
SIC: 3678 Electronic connectors

(G-16296)
BJ BURNS INCORPORATED
Also Called: Outlook International Electric
1411 Sawgrs Corp Pkwy (33323-2888)
PHONE......................305 572-9500
Antonio Hyppolite, *President*
Hodari Burns, *Vice Pres*
Frank Telfort, *Vice Pres*
Frantz Telfort, *Vice Pres*
EMP: 25 **EST:** 2000
SALES (est): 1.7MM **Privately Held**
SIC: 3699 1731 5063 Electrical equipment & supplies; general electrical contractor; boxes & fittings, electrical

(G-16297)
BKBL HOLDINGS LTD
Also Called: Quest Drape
5031 N Hiatus Rd (33351-8018)
PHONE......................954 920-6772
Alex Soto, *General Mgr*
EMP: 8

SALES (corp-wide): 19.8MM **Privately Held**
SIC: 2391 Curtains & draperies
PA: Bkbl Holdings, Ltd.
     2591 Dallas Pkwy Ste 201
     Frisco TX 75034
     214 436-4161

(G-16298)
BLIND DEPOT
10794 Nw 53rd St (33351-8031)
PHONE......................954 588-4580
EMP: 7 **EST:** 2020
SALES (est): 145.6K **Privately Held**
WEB: www.blindedpot.com
SIC: 2591 Window blinds

(G-16299)
BLUE LIGHT USA CORP
4625 Nw 103rd Ave (33351-7914)
PHONE......................954 766-4308
F F Chade Yammine, *Principal*
Fabiana Yammine, *Vice Pres*
EMP: 7 **EST:** 2016
SALES (est): 532.7K **Privately Held**
SIC: 2211 5651 Jean fabrics; denims; jeans stores
PA: Y.D. Confeccoes Ltda
     Av. Queiroz Filho 1.560
     Sao Paulo SP 05319

(G-16300)
BOLTON MEDICAL INC
Also Called: Terumo Aortic
799 International Pkwy (33325-6220)
PHONE......................954 838-9699
Oscar Rostigliosi, *CEO*
Allan Buti, *Vice Pres*
Roger Malubay, *Vice Pres*
Jeffrey Mifek, *Vice Pres*
Mark Miles, *Vice Pres*
EMP: 390 **EST:** 1993
SQ FT: 24,000
SALES (est): 79.2MM **Privately Held**
WEB: www.terumoaortic.com
SIC: 3841 Surgical & medical instruments
PA: Terumo Corporation
     2-44-1, Hatagaya
     Shibuya-Ku TKY 151-0

(G-16301)
BUNDY SIGNS LLC
4556 N Hiatus Rd (33351-7987)
PHONE......................954 296-0784
EMP: 7 **EST:** 2018
SALES (est): 606.2K **Privately Held**
WEB: www.bundysigns.com
SIC: 3993 Signs & advertising specialties

(G-16302)
CALIBER SALES ENGINEERING INC (PA)
5373 N Hiatus Rd (33351-8718)
PHONE......................954 430-6234
Sharon Erickson, *President*
David R Mazoff, *President*
Ira Lashinsky, *General Mgr*
Ignacio Sierra, *Purchasing*
Vivian M Alvarez, *Treasurer*
◆ **EMP:** 22 **EST:** 1987
SALES (est): 13.5MM **Privately Held**
WEB: www.calibersales.com
SIC: 3691 Storage batteries

(G-16303)
CAPACITOR AND COMPONENTS LLC
11841 Nw 38th Pl (33323-2691)
PHONE......................954 798-8943
Robert Jasiewicz, *Mng Member*
EMP: 26 **EST:** 2003
SQ FT: 144
SALES (est): 4.3MM
SALES (corp-wide): 93.8B **Publicly Held**
WEB: www.capacitorsupplier.com
SIC: 3679 Electronic circuits
PA: Bank Of America Corporation
     100 N Tryon St Ste 220
     Charlotte NC 28202
     704 386-5681

(G-16304)
CHAMPION NUTRITION INC
Also Called: Champion Performance Products
1301 Sawgrs Corp Pkwy (33323-2813)
PHONE......................954 233-3300
Jose Minski, *CEO*
Reshma Patel, *Vice Pres*
▼ **EMP:** 1 **EST:** 2008
SALES (est): 6.5MM
SALES (corp-wide): 7.1B **Publicly Held**
WEB: www.champion-nutrition.com
SIC: 2099 Food preparations
HQ: Nature's Products, Inc.
     1221 Broadway
     Oakland CA 94612
     954 233-3300

(G-16305)
COASTAL AIRCRAFT PARTS LLC
2999 Nw 115th Ter (33323-1607)
PHONE......................954 980-6929
Arthur Downey, *Principal*
EMP: 6 **EST:** 2006
SALES (est): 313.9K **Privately Held**
WEB: www.coastalaircraftparts.com
SIC: 3999 Airplane models, except toy

(G-16306)
COMPONEXX CORP
789 Shotgun Rd (33326-1940)
P.O. Box 268293, Fort Lauderdale (33326-8293)
PHONE......................954 236-6569
Edwin Diaz, *President*
Max Diaz, *Vice Pres*
Maria Sanchez,
▲ **EMP:** 9 **EST:** 2005
SQ FT: 5,200
SALES (est): 1.3MM **Privately Held**
WEB: www.componexx.com
SIC: 3663 Cable television equipment

(G-16307)
COMPUTATIONAL SYSTEMS INC
Also Called: Emerson Latin America
1300 Concord Ter Ste 400 (33323-2899)
PHONE......................954 846-5030
Dario Kanevsky, *Vice Pres*
Scott Lewis, *Opers Mgr*
Orlando Adriana, *Finance*
Rebecca Earhart, *Sr Project Mgr*
Joe Viers, *Supervisor*
EMP: 149
SALES (corp-wide): 18.2B **Publicly Held**
SIC: 3823 Industrial instrmnts msrmnt display/control process variable
HQ: Computational Systems, Incorporated
     8000 West Florissant Ave
     Saint Louis MO 63136
     314 553-2000

(G-16308)
COUNTWISE LLC (PA)
1149 Sawgrs Corp Pkwy (33323-2847)
PHONE......................954 846-7011
Jacques Stephane, *Sales Executive*
Philip Tomlin, *Sales Executive*
Rik Hideg, *Manager*
Natachia Louis, *Manager*
Joseph Taylor, *Manager*
EMP: 19 **EST:** 2003
SALES (est): 3MM **Privately Held**
WEB: www.countwise.com
SIC: 3824 Tally counters

(G-16309)
CRYSTAL COMMUNICATIONS INC
5600 Nw 102nd Ave Ste M (33351-8709)
PHONE......................954 474-3072
Adam Jacobs, *President*
Michael Vidal, *Vice Pres*
Kim Lee, *Office Mgr*
▲ **EMP:** 8 **EST:** 1998
SALES (est): 1.9MM **Privately Held**
WEB: www.crystalcommunications.net
SIC: 3663 Satellites, communications; television closed circuit equipment

(G-16310)
CRYSTAL POOL SERVICE INC
10718 Nw 53rd St (33351-8025)
PHONE......................954 444-8282

Jeffrey Kohler, *President*
EMP: 9 **EST:** 1989
SALES (est): 948.4K **Privately Held**
WEB: www.crystalpoolsvc.com
SIC: 3589 5091 Commercial cooking & foodwarming equipment; watersports equipment & supplies

(G-16311)
CSI HOME DECOR INC
5365 N Hiatus Rd (33351-8718)
PHONE......................754 301-2147
Paul Dunkley, *Principal*
EMP: 7 **EST:** 2016
SALES (est): 125K **Privately Held**
WEB: www.csihomedecor.com
SIC: 2434 Wood kitchen cabinets

(G-16312)
CUSTOM MOSAICS INC
11110 W Oakland Park Blvd (33351-6808)
PHONE......................954 610-9436
Joe Stephens, *President*
▲ **EMP:** 8 **EST:** 1998
SQ FT: 2,500
SALES (est): 741.6K **Privately Held**
WEB: www.custommosaicsinc.com
SIC: 3253 Mosaic tile, glazed & unglazed: ceramic

(G-16313)
DIGITAL ANTENNA INC
5325 Nw 108th Ave (33351-8755)
PHONE......................954 747-7022
Anthony D Gallagher, *President*
Joanne Gallagher, *Vice Pres*
Joanne Johnson, *Vice Pres*
Brian Fluharty, *Materials Mgr*
John Jones, *VP Engrg*
▲ **EMP:** 12 **EST:** 1993
SQ FT: 22,000
SALES (est): 1.7MM **Privately Held**
WEB: www.digitalantenna.com
SIC: 3679 1629 Antennas, receiving; marine construction

(G-16314)
DP EMB & SCREEN PRINTS INC
3485 N Hiatus Rd (33351-7501)
PHONE......................954 245-5902
Carmen Rivera, *Principal*
EMP: 11 **EST:** 2012
SALES (est): 280.7K **Privately Held**
SIC: 2395 Embroidery & art needlework

(G-16315)
EGM MANUFACTURING CORP
10301 Nw 50th St Ste 102 (33351-8009)
PHONE......................954 440-0445
J Antonio Morales Salinas, *CEO*
Jose Antonio Morales Salinas, *CEO*
Jose Morales, *Mfg Staff*
Rosalia Morales, *Manager*
Rosalia Salinas, *Director*
▲ **EMP:** 18 **EST:** 2013
SALES (est): 461.6K **Privately Held**
WEB: www.egm-mfg.com
SIC: 3999 Barber & beauty shop equipment

(G-16316)
ENTIRE SELECT INC
Also Called: Mon Reve
10857 Nw 50th St (33351-8091)
PHONE......................954 674-2368
Benjamin Perelmuter, *President*
Jun Sheng, *Vice Pres*
EMP: 3 **EST:** 2012
SALES (est): 3.5MM **Privately Held**
SIC: 2331 2321 Women's & misses' blouses & shirts; men's & boys' furnishings

(G-16317)
EQUS LOGISTICS LLC
Also Called: Altum Aerospace
13680 Nw 5th St Ste 140 (33325-6234)
P.O. Box 267520, Fort Lauderdale (33326-7520)
PHONE......................954 618-6573
Viviana Varela, *General Mgr*
Mayra Tapias, *Purchasing*
Camilo Saltos, *Research*
Eda Clevenger, *Sales Staff*
Alejandro Valencia, *Mng Member*
EMP: 10 **EST:** 2009

SQ FT: 1,600
SALES (est): 2MM **Privately Held**
SIC: 3728 Aircraft parts & equipment

(G-16318)
EZVERIFY & VALIDATE LLC
1401 Nw 136th Ave Ste 400 (33323-2861)
PHONE.................................855 398-3981
Tim Ford, *Vice Pres*
EMP: 9 EST: 2016
SALES (est): 260.6K **Privately Held**
SIC: 7372 Prepackaged software

(G-16319)
FOREST RESEARCH INSTITUTE INC
13800 Nw 2nd St Ste 190 (33325-6243)
PHONE.................................954 622-5600
Marco Taglietti MD, *President*
EMP: 22 EST: 2008
SALES (est): 2MM **Privately Held**
SIC: 2834 Pharmaceutical preparations
HQ: Allergan Sales, Llc
2525 Dupont Dr
Irvine CA 92612

(G-16320)
GAYNOR GROUP INC
Also Called: Gem Industries
5030 N Hiatus Rd (33351-8017)
P.O. Box 450061, Fort Lauderdale (33345-0061)
PHONE.................................954 749-1228
Steve Gaynor, *President*
◆ EMP: 6 EST: 1954
SQ FT: 4,100
SALES (est): 829.3K **Privately Held**
SIC: 3541 2999 Buffing & polishing machines; waxes, petroleum: not produced in petroleum refineries

(G-16321)
GLOW BENCH SYSTEMS INTL (PA)
1580 Sawgrs Corp Pkwy # 13 (33323-2859)
PHONE.................................954 315-4615
Danny W Beauchamp, *President*
Rein Luning, *Treasurer*
Elba Hinckley, *Admin Sec*
EMP: 5 EST: 2002
SALES (est): 412.3K **Privately Held**
SIC: 3993 7389 Signs & advertising specialties; advertising, promotional & trade show services

(G-16322)
GRAVITY INK & STITCH INC
2910 Nw 130th Ave Apt 112 (33323-3057)
PHONE.................................954 558-0119
Jayne Schiffres,
EMP: 7 EST: 2016
SALES (est): 66.6K **Privately Held**
WEB: www.gravityinkandstitch.com
SIC: 2395 Embroidery & art needlework

(G-16323)
INTER GARD R&D LLC
15491 Sw 12th St (33326-1991)
PHONE.................................954 476-5574
Alberto Alarcon, *Principal*
EMP: 15 EST: 2008
SALES (est): 1.2MM **Privately Held**
SIC: 3429 Manufactured hardware (general)

(G-16324)
INTERNTNAL NTRCTCALS GROUP INC
Also Called: Ing Phrmctcal Pdts Prvate Lbel
771 Shotgun Rd (33326-1940)
PHONE.................................786 518-2903
Douglas Guardo, *President*
Mario A Villalobos, *Director*
▲ EMP: 8 EST: 2009
SALES (est): 1.3MM **Privately Held**
WEB: www.ingpharmaceutical.net
SIC: 2834 Vitamin preparations

(G-16325)
ITALIAN HAIR EXTENSION INC
Also Called: Blue Butterfly Hair Extensions
10770 Nw 53rd St (33351-8031)
PHONE.................................954 839-5366
Raphael I Arvili, *President*

EMP: 9 EST: 2009
SALES (est): 39.6K **Privately Held**
WEB: www.bbhairextensions.com
SIC: 3999 Hair & hair-based products

(G-16326)
J & J INC
Also Called: Eagle Painting
10062 Nw 50th St (33351-8019)
PHONE.................................954 746-7300
John Field, *President*
Janet Field, *Vice Pres*
▲ EMP: 6 EST: 1992
SQ FT: 1,400
SALES (est): 737.9K **Privately Held**
SIC: 2851 Paints & allied products

(G-16327)
J AND A MAINTENANCE
6220 Nw 15th St (33313-4625)
PHONE.................................754 234-0708
Jean Augustin, *Owner*
EMP: 8 EST: 2003
SALES (est): 164.1K **Privately Held**
WEB: www.res-tek.com
SIC: 3679 Electronic components

(G-16328)
JAMALI INDUSTRIES LLC
1455 Nw 126th Ln (33323-5105)
PHONE.................................954 908-5075
Arash Jamali, *Principal*
EMP: 7 EST: 2016
SALES (est): 358.9K **Privately Held**
SIC: 3999 Manufacturing industries

(G-16329)
JAZWARES LLC (DH)
1067 Shotgun Rd (33326-1906)
PHONE.................................954 845-0800
Judd Zebersky, *CEO*
Laura Zebersky, *President*
Matthew Siesel, *CFO*
▲ EMP: 100 EST: 1997
SQ FT: 4,700
SALES (est): 97.9MM
SALES (corp-wide): 12B **Publicly Held**
WEB: www.jazwares.com
SIC: 3944 5092 Games, toys & children's vehicles; toys & games
HQ: Alleghany Capital Corporation
1411 Broadway Fl 34
New York NY 10018
212 752-1356

(G-16330)
JEM ART INC
Also Called: Stratton Home Decor
801 Shotgun Rd (33326-1946)
PHONE.................................954 966-7078
Evan Merkur, *President*
Sophia Sunjara, *Senior VP*
Juliana Serrano, *Vice Pres*
Michael Siegel, *Vice Pres*
Gabriela Parsons, *Project Mgr*
◆ EMP: 29 EST: 1984
SQ FT: 30,000
SALES (est): 5.2MM **Privately Held**
WEB: www.strattonhomedecor.com
SIC: 2499 Picture frame molding, finished

(G-16331)
JLD MANUFACTURING CORP
Also Called: Jewelry Tray Factory, The
4747 N Nob Hill Rd Ste 8 (33351-4742)
PHONE.................................877 358-5462
Diana Burgos, *President*
EMP: 7 EST: 2010
SALES (est): 1.3MM **Privately Held**
SIC: 3911 Jewelry, precious metal

(G-16332)
JMS DESIGNS OF FLORIDA INC
4550 N Hiatus Rd (33351-7944)
PHONE.................................954 572-6100
Bruce Sharkey, *President*
EMP: 7 EST: 1993
SALES (est): 899.3K **Privately Held**
WEB: www.jmsdesigns.com
SIC: 2759 Commercial printing

(G-16333)
KIKISTEESCOM LLC
Also Called: Clothing
5600 Nw 102nd Ave (33351-8709)
P.O. Box 266376, Fort Lauderdale (33326-6376)
PHONE.................................888 620-4110
Enrique Sznapstajler, *Exec Dir*
EMP: 29 EST: 2018
SALES (est): 1.5MM **Privately Held**
WEB: www.kikistees.com
SIC: 2759 5611 7389 2211 Screen printing; clothing, sportswear, men's & boys'; embroidering of advertising on shirts, etc.; apparel & outerwear fabrics, cotton; T-shirts, custom printed; shorts (outerwear): men's, youths' & boys'

(G-16334)
KLOTH INC
Also Called: Planet
10111 Nw 46th St (33351-7934)
PHONE.................................954 578-5687
Lauren Grossman, *President*
▲ EMP: 7 EST: 2002
SALES (est): 1.1MM **Privately Held**
SIC: 3144 Women's footwear, except athletic

(G-16335)
L A RUST INC
10231 Nw 53rd St (33351-8062)
PHONE.................................954 749-5009
Juan O'Campo, *President*
Loriene O'Campo, *Treasurer*
EMP: 10 EST: 1986
SQ FT: 1,400
SALES (est): 1.1MM **Privately Held**
WEB: www.larust.com
SIC: 3479 Coating, rust preventive

(G-16336)
LEGGETT & PLATT INCORPORATED
Also Called: Gribetz International
13800 Nw 4th St (33325-6207)
PHONE.................................954 846-0300
Steve Bertucci, *Controller*
Teresa Krajick, *Marketing Staff*
Ted Fisk, *Manager*
EMP: 57
SALES (corp-wide): 4.2B **Publicly Held**
WEB: www.leggett.com
SIC: 2515 Mattresses & bedsprings
PA: Leggett & Platt, Incorporated
1 Leggett Rd
Carthage MO 64836
417 358-8131

(G-16337)
LIGHTN UP INC
10401 Nw 53rd St (33351-8014)
PHONE.................................954 797-7778
Stuart Yadgaroff, *President*
Melody Berger, *Office Mgr*
EMP: 10 EST: 1992
SQ FT: 28,000
SALES (est): 11.5MM **Privately Held**
WEB: www.lightnupfl.com
SIC: 3646 Commercial indusl & institutional electric lighting fixtures

(G-16338)
LUI TECHNICAL SERVICES INC
11821 Nw 34th Pl (33323-1233)
PHONE.................................954 803-7610
Luis H Ruiz, *President*
EMP: 6 EST: 2006
SALES (est): 590.7K **Privately Held**
WEB: www.amawebs.com
SIC: 3699 Electrical equipment & supplies

(G-16339)
LUXURY WORLD LLC
4667 Nw 103rd Ave (33351-7916)
PHONE.................................954 746-8776
Isaac Cohen,
Gina Cohen,
EMP: 12 EST: 2009
SALES (est): 310.5K **Privately Held**
SIC: 2844 Toilet preparations

(G-16340)
MDR LLC
14101 Nw 4th St (33325-6209)
PHONE.................................954 845-9500
Denise Elliott, *Marketing Staff*
James B Riley, *Mng Member*
Lily Wang, *Manager*
Cheri Wilson, *Manager*
Carlo Abel, *Producer*
◆ EMP: 150 EST: 1984
SQ FT: 50,000
SALES (est): 15.3MM **Privately Held**
WEB: www.mdr.com
SIC: 2834 Vitamin preparations

(G-16341)
MODERNO PORCELAIN WORKS LLC
13807 Nw 4th St (33325-6214)
PHONE.................................954 607-3535
Douglas Dillard,
EMP: 10
SALES (corp-wide): 24.4MM **Privately Held**
WEB: www.modernoworks.com
SIC: 3281 Cut stone & stone products
HQ: Moderno Porcelain Works, Llc
2506 W Main St
Houston TX 77098
713 360-6837

(G-16342)
MODPROS ELEVATOR INC
10750 Nw 53rd St (33351-8031)
PHONE.................................786 863-0092
EMP: 10 EST: 2019
SALES (est): 712.9K **Privately Held**
SIC: 3534 Elevators & moving stairways

(G-16343)
MONTRES CORUM USA LLC
14050 Nw 14th St Ste 110 (33323-2851)
PHONE.................................954 279-1220
Severin Wunderman,
EMP: 23 EST: 1999
SALES (est): 2.8MM **Privately Held**
SIC: 3873 Watches, clocks, watchcases & parts
HQ: Montres Corum Sarl
Rue Du Petit-Chateau 1
La Chaux-De-Fonds NE 2300
329 670-670

(G-16344)
MOTOR CITY CLASSICS INC
12717 W Sunrise Blvd (33323-0902)
PHONE.................................954 473-2201
Maurice Oujevolk, *President*
Gladys Oujevolk, *Vice Pres*
▲ EMP: 5 EST: 1998
SALES (est): 919.9K **Privately Held**
WEB: www.motorcityclassicsinc.com
SIC: 3364 Nonferrous die-castings except aluminum

(G-16345)
NANO DIMENSION USA INC
Also Called: Nano Dimension 3d
13798 Nw 4th St Ste 315 (33325-6227)
P.O. Box 1227, Santa Clara CA (95052-1227)
PHONE.................................650 209-2866
Simon Fried, *President*
Ziki Peled, *COO*
Jaim Nulman, *Exec VP*
Tal Fridkin, *Marketing Mgr*
EMP: 26 EST: 2017
SALES (est): 10.6MM **Privately Held**
WEB: www.nano-di.com
SIC: 3672 Printed circuit boards
PA: Nano Dimension Ltd
2 Ilan Ramon
Ness Ziona 74036

(G-16346)
NEOPOD SYSTEMS LLC (PA)
Also Called: Juan Bermudez
1329 Shotgun Rd (33326-1935)
PHONE.................................954 603-3100
Daniel Rourke, *Vice Pres*
Ivan Ogburn, *Project Mgr*
Michael Miller, *Opers Staff*
Juan Bermudez,
Charles Ermer,
▼ EMP: 10 EST: 2009

▲ = Import ▼=Export
◆ =Import/Export

SALES (est): 5.1MM **Privately Held**
WEB: www.neopodsystems.com
SIC: 2452 3448 Prefabricated wood buildings; prefabricated metal buildings

(G-16347)
NIPPON MACIWUMEI CO
Also Called: McW Parts
4500 N Hiatus Rd Ste 214 (33351-7984)
PHONE.............................954 533-7747
Camila G Orsi, *President*
EMP: 16 EST: 2019
SALES (est): 1.3MM **Privately Held**
SIC: 3531 Construction machinery

(G-16348)
OCEAN PHARMACEUTICALS INC
5373 N Hiatus Rd (33351-8718)
PHONE.............................954 473-4717
Jeffrey Friedman, *CEO*
Jasara Mohammed, *Director*
EMP: 10 EST: 2010
SALES (est): 673.8K **Privately Held**
SIC: 2834 Pharmaceutical preparations

(G-16349)
OUR CITY MEDIA OF FLORIDA LLC
400 Swgrss Corp Pkwy 200c (33325-6249)
PHONE.............................954 306-1007
Sven Budzisch, *President*
Terrance Jaillet, *Principal*
Gabriela Moscoso, *Office Mgr*
Beverly Perkins, *Manager*
Adrienne Collins, *Executive*
EMP: 10 EST: 2008
SALES (est): 1MM **Privately Held**
WEB: www.ourcitymedia.com
SIC: 2721 Magazines: publishing & printing

(G-16350)
PAAL TECHNOLOGIES HOLDINGS INC ✪
5387 N Nob Hill Rd (33351-4761)
PHONE.............................954 368-5000
Estro M Vitantonio, *President*
EMP: 10 EST: 2021
SALES (est): 2.5MM
SALES (corp-wide): 332.8MM **Privately Held**
SIC: 3677 Electronic coils, transformers & other inductors
PA: Micross Inc.
1810 S Orange Blossom Trl
Apopka FL 32703
407 298-7100

(G-16351)
PERALTA GROUP INC
Also Called: Waterheaterdepot.com
4566 N Hiatus Rd (33351-7987)
PHONE.............................954 502-8100
Victor Peralta, *President*
EMP: 6 EST: 2000
SALES (est): 609.5K **Privately Held**
WEB: www.peraltagroup.com
SIC: 3639 5731 Hot water heaters, household; radio, television & electronic stores

(G-16352)
PIXELS ON TARGET LLC
14050 Nw 14th Ste 170 (33323-2865)
PHONE.............................305 614-0890
Jagrut Patel, *CEO*
Sumeet Suri, *President*
Robert Kendi, *Research*
Brett Boatman, *Engineer*
EMP: 40 EST: 2019
SALES (est): 6MM **Privately Held**
WEB: www.pixelsontarget.com
SIC: 3812 Search & navigation equipment

(G-16353)
PPI INTERNATIONAL CORP
1649 Nw 136th Ave (33323-2802)
PHONE.............................954 838-1008
Caroline J Pandorf, *President*
Warren Pandorf, *CFO*
EMP: 77 EST: 1993
SQ FT: 15,000
SALES (est): 1.3MM **Privately Held**
SIC: 3842 Bulletproof vests

(G-16354)
PREFERRED PCKS PBLICATIONS INC
1335 Shotgun Rd (33326-1935)
P.O. Box 267700, Fort Lauderdale (33326-7700)
PHONE.............................954 377-8000
Lawrence Moorman, *President*
Colleen Moorman, *Treasurer*
Marc Moorman, *Admin Sec*
EMP: 13 EST: 2004
SALES (est): 257.6K **Privately Held**
WEB: www.playbook.com
SIC: 2741 Miscellaneous publishing

(G-16355)
PRIME MERIDIAN TRADING CORP
4624 N Hiatus Rd (33351-7909)
P.O. Box 450358, Fort Lauderdale (33345-0358)
PHONE.............................954 727-2152
Luz A Arbelaez, *President*
Patrick Williams, *Vice Pres*
◆ EMP: 9 EST: 1998
SQ FT: 2,000
SALES (est): 1.6MM **Privately Held**
WEB: www.primemeridian.net
SIC: 3669 5065 3661 Emergency alarms; telephone & telegraphic equipment; telephone equipment; fiber optics communications equipment

(G-16356)
PRINTING AND LABELS INC
5405 Nw 102nd Ave Ste 218 (33351-8743)
PHONE.............................954 578-4411
Kake Andris, *President*
EMP: 9 EST: 2011
SALES (est): 83.9K **Privately Held**
WEB: www.printingandlabels.com
SIC: 2752 Commercial printing, lithographic

(G-16357)
PRINTRUST INC
Also Called: Minuteman Press
10112 W Oakland Park Blvd (33351-6963)
PHONE.............................954 572-0790
Felix Abraham, *President*
EMP: 10 EST: 2015
SALES (est): 252.3K **Privately Held**
WEB: www.minuteman.com
SIC: 2752 Commercial printing, lithographic

(G-16358)
PROWIN INDUSTRIES INC
6120 Nw 11th St (33313-6116)
PHONE.............................954 584-5686
Sandra Rowland, *President*
EMP: 7 EST: 2004
SALES (est): 104.4K **Privately Held**
SIC: 3999 Manufacturing industries

(G-16359)
PULLING INC
12797 Nw 13th St (33323-3135)
PHONE.............................305 224-2469
Julio E Ibanez, *Principal*
EMP: 7 EST: 2010
SALES (est): 87.4K **Privately Held**
SIC: 1389 Construction, repair & dismantling services

(G-16360)
PURPLEFLY PRESS LLC
2301 Nw 93rd Ln (33322-3261)
PHONE.............................954 682-2726
Yanette Mantro, *Branch Mgr*
EMP: 7
SALES (corp-wide): 59.2K **Privately Held**
SIC: 2741 Miscellaneous publishing
PA: Purplefly Press Llc
3225 N Hiatus Rd # 45015
Fort Lauderdale FL

(G-16361)
RAINBOW LGHT NTRTNAL SYSTEMS I (DH)
1301 Sawgrs Corp Pkwy (33323-2813)
PHONE.............................954 233-3300
Jose Minski, *CEO*
Linda Kahler, *President*
Sharon Minski, *Vice Pres*

John Licari, *Manager*
EMP: 5 EST: 1981
SALES (est): 13.5MM
SALES (corp-wide): 7.1B **Publicly Held**
SIC: 2833 2834 5961 Vitamins, natural or synthetic: bulk, uncompounded; pharmaceutical preparations; catalog & mail-order houses
HQ: Nature's Products, Inc.
1221 Broadway
Oakland CA 94612
954 233-3300

(G-16362)
RDE CONNECTORS & CABLES INC
5277 Nw 108th Ave (33351-8070)
PHONE.............................954 746-6400
Reinhard Derksen, *President*
Angelika Derksen, *Vice Pres*
EMP: 10 EST: 1992
SQ FT: 3,000
SALES (est): 2.8MM
SALES (corp-wide): 2.7B **Privately Held**
WEB: www.rde-usa.com
SIC: 3678 Electronic connectors
PA: Phoenix Contact Gmbh & Co. Kg
Flachsmarktstr. 8
Blomberg NW 32825
523 530-0

(G-16363)
RESTORATION GAMES LLC
12717 W Sunrise Blvd (33323-0902)
PHONE.............................954 937-1970
Justin Jacobson,
EMP: 7 EST: 2016
SALES (est): 3MM **Privately Held**
WEB: www.restorationgames.com
SIC: 7372 Prepackaged software

(G-16364)
RITCO FOODS LLC
1671 Nw 144th Ter Ste 107 (33323-2879)
PHONE.............................954 727-3554
Julio C Perez Fuentes, *Mng Member*
Maria A Blanco Perez,
EMP: 6 EST: 2007
SALES (est): 444.8K **Privately Held**
WEB: www.ritcofoods.com
SIC: 2034 5148 5499 Dried & dehydrated fruits; fresh fruits & vegetables; beverage stores

(G-16365)
ROTBURG INSTRUMENTS AMER INC
1560 Sawgrass Corporate (33323-2858)
PHONE.............................954 331-8046
Genaro Cardenas, *President*
EMP: 11 EST: 1998
SALES (est): 237.5K **Privately Held**
WEB: www.rotburg.com
SIC: 3841 Surgical instruments & apparatus

(G-16366)
SKY MEDICAL INC
5229 Nw 108th Ave (33351-8044)
PHONE.............................954 747-3188
Todd Tyrrell, *President*
Tony Tyrrell, *Vice Pres*
Matt Jansen, *Prdtn Mgr*
Christopher Appet, *Sales Staff*
Chris Appet, *Mktg Dir*
EMP: 17 EST: 1996
SQ FT: 8,000
SALES (est): 3.4MM **Privately Held**
WEB: www.skymedicalinc.com
SIC: 3841 3842 Surgical & medical instruments; surgical appliances & supplies

(G-16367)
SLASHER PRINTING CENTER INC
Also Called: Slasher Printing Services
6701 Nw 22nd St (33313-3953)
PHONE.............................305 835-7366
Ainswith Smith, *President*
Bill Ragsdale, *Executive*
EMP: 6 EST: 1976
SALES (est): 524.9K **Privately Held**
SIC: 2759 Commercial printing

(G-16368)
SMOOTHIES RECHARGE
2101 N University Dr (33322-3935)
PHONE.............................954 999-0332
EMP: 7 EST: 2014
SALES (est): 450.2K **Privately Held**
WEB: www.rechargesmoothies.com
SIC: 2037 Frozen fruits & vegetables

(G-16369)
SMURFIT KAPPA PACKAGING LLC (DH)
Also Called: Smurfit Kappa The America's
1301 Intl Pkwy Ste 550 (33323)
PHONE.............................954 838-9738
Sergio Martinez, *Plant Mgr*
Jennie Kaarle, *Project Mgr*
Peter Salazar, *Opers Staff*
Maria Cabre, *Purch Mgr*
Latisha Boles, *Purch Agent*
◆ EMP: 13 EST: 1989
SQ FT: 6,174
SALES (est): 41.3MM **Privately Held**
WEB: www.smurfitkappa.com
SIC: 2653 Boxes, corrugated: made from purchased materials

(G-16370)
SPEC-TEC MANUFACTURING INC
10794 Nw 53rd St (33351-8031)
PHONE.............................954 749-4204
Scott Barrett, *President*
Tracy Barrett, *Corp Secy*
EMP: 5 EST: 1996
SQ FT: 3,000
SALES (est): 744.1K **Privately Held**
SIC: 3669 Emergency alarms

(G-16371)
SRT WIRELESS LLC
1613 Nw 136th Ave Bldg C (33323-2896)
PHONE.............................954 797-7850
Atholl Paton, *QC Mgr*
Nick Glantzis, *Chief Engr*
Jorge Rodriguez, *Engineer*
Ariel Heyliger, *Human Res Mgr*
John Russell, *Chief Mktg Ofcr*
EMP: 5 EST: 2011
SALES (est): 3MM **Privately Held**
WEB: www.srtwireless.net
SIC: 3663 Satellites, communications

(G-16372)
SSE PUBLICATIONS LLC
1 Panther Pkwy (33323-5315)
PHONE.............................954 835-7616
Carol Duncanson, *Principal*
EMP: 10 EST: 2008
SALES (est): 379.5K **Privately Held**
SIC: 2741 Miscellaneous publishing

(G-16373)
STRATA ANALYTICS HOLDG US LLC
1560 Sawgrs Corp Pkwy (33323-2858)
PHONE.............................954 349-4630
Julio Ardiles, *CEO*
Martin Ozores,
Martin Roos, *Advisor*
EMP: 59 EST: 2015
SALES (est): 1.4MM **Privately Held**
WEB: www.strataanalytics.us
SIC: 7372 Business oriented computer software

(G-16374)
STUSH AP USA/STUSH STYLE LLC
2500 N University Dr (33322-3003)
PHONE.............................404 940-3445
Janette Derby-Green, *CEO*
Janette Derby, *Mng Member*
EMP: 11 EST: 2012
SQ FT: 1,500
SALES (est): 920.3K **Privately Held**
SIC: 3144 2331 2335 5136 Women's footwear, except athletic; blouses, women's & juniors': made from purchased material; women's, juniors' & misses' dresses; men's & boys' clothing; women's & children's dresses, suits, skirts & blouses; men's & boys' trousers & slacks

(G-16375)
SUMIFLEX LLC
773 Shotgun Rd (33326-1940)
PHONE..................................954 578-6998
Javier Galarraga, *Mng Member*
EMP: 5 EST: 2012
SALES (est): 716.5K **Privately Held**
WEB: www.sumiflex.com
SIC: 3089 Billfold inserts, plastic

(G-16376)
SUNCOAST COATINGS
Also Called: Benjamin Moore Authorized Ret
10101 Nw 46th St (33351-7934)
PHONE..................................954 306-2149
John Gonzalez, *Principal*
EMP: 8 EST: 2016
SALES (est): 69.4K **Privately Held**
WEB: www.benjaminmoore.com
SIC: 2851 5231 Paints & allied products;
   paint, glass & wallpaper

(G-16377)
SURVIVAL PRODUCTS INC
1655 Nw 136th Ave M (33323-2802)
PHONE..................................954 966-7329
German Alvarez, *CEO*
Peter Loeb, *President*
Donna Rogers, *Vice Pres*
◆ EMP: 9 EST: 1970
SALES (est): 25MM **Privately Held**
WEB: www.avi-aviation.com
SIC: 3728 7929 8711 Aircraft parts &
   equipment; actors; consulting engineer

(G-16378)
SYI INC
Also Called: Secretbandz
10152 Nw 50th St (33351-8026)
PHONE..................................954 323-2483
Shuaib A Khan, *Treasurer*
EMP: 7 EST: 2015
SALES (est): 177.6K **Privately Held**
WEB: www.secretbandz.com
SIC: 2869 2821 Silicones; silicone resins

(G-16379)
TASTYZ LLC
1120 Sunset Strip (33313-6108)
PHONE..................................772 480-5741
Shanoor Commissariat, *Mng Member*
EMP: 9
SALES (est): 633.9K **Privately Held**
SIC: 2099 Food preparations

(G-16380)
TAYLOR COMMUNICATIONS INC
1551 Sawgrs Corp Pkwy 1 (33323-2828)
PHONE..................................954 632-6501
Thomas Dougherty, *General Mgr*
EMP: 13
SALES (corp-wide): 3.7B **Privately Held**
WEB: www.taylor.com
SIC: 2761 Manifold business forms
HQ: Taylor Communications, Inc.
   1725 Roe Crest Dr
   North Mankato MN 56003
   866 541-0937

(G-16381)
TEVA PHARMACEUTICALS
13900 Nw 2nd St (33325-6215)
PHONE..................................954 382-7729
Francisco Garces, *Mfg Staff*
Jennifer Wilson, *VP Bus Dvlpt*
David Monroy, *Finance*
William Roddy, *Security Mgr*
Bernice Mejias, *Manager*
EMP: 11 EST: 2019
SALES (est): 8.9MM **Privately Held**
WEB: www.tevapharm.com
SIC: 2834 Pharmaceutical preparations

(G-16382)
THOR GUARD INC (PA)
Also Called: Thor Guard Weather
1193 Sawgrs Corp Pkwy (33323-2847)
P.O. Box 451987, Fort Lauderdale (33345-1987)
PHONE..................................954 835-0900
Peter L Townsend Sr, *CEO*
Robert Dugan, *President*
EMP: 16 EST: 1988
SQ FT: 8,300
SALES (est): 2.2MM **Privately Held**
WEB: www.thorguard.com
SIC: 3643 Lightning protection equipment

(G-16383)
TONBO IMAGING INC
1351 Sawgrs Corp Pkwy # 104
(33323-2831)
PHONE..................................814 441-0475
Jagret Patel, *CEO*
Sudeep George, *Vice Pres*
Cecilia D'Souza, *CFO*
Ankit Kumar, *CTO*
EMP: 8 EST: 2012
SALES (est): 474K **Privately Held**
WEB: www.tonboimaging.com
SIC: 3826 Magnetic resonance imaging
   apparatus

(G-16384)
TOUCH DYNAMIC INC
5525 N Nob Hill Rd (33351-4708)
PHONE..................................888 508-6824
Craig Paritz, *Principal*
EMP: 13
SALES (corp-wide): 23.1MM **Privately
Held**
WEB: www.touchdynamic.com
SIC: 3575 Computer terminals, monitors &
   components
PA: Touch Dynamic Inc.
   121 Corporate Blvd
   South Plainfield NJ 07080
   732 382-5701

(G-16385)
TSD GROUP CORP
306 International Pkwy B (33325-6273)
PHONE..................................954 940-2111
Maria M Paredes, *President*
Danna Olivo, *Director*
EMP: 13 EST: 2012
SQ FT: 3,000
SALES (est): 971.5K **Privately Held**
SIC: 2911 Aromatic chemical products

(G-16386)
ULTIMATE MACHINING CORPORATION
4741 Nw 103rd Ave (33351-7922)
PHONE..................................954 749-9810
Tommy Foresman Sr, *President*
EMP: 6 EST: 2003
SALES (est): 320K **Privately Held**
SIC: 3599 Machine shop, jobbing & repair

(G-16387)
US PACK GROUP LLC
5011 N Hiatus Rd (33351-8018)
PHONE..................................954 556-1840
Aldo Tavano, *Opers Mgr*
Marco Flores, *Mng Member*
Aarron Hirshbein, *Mng Member*
Cesar Flores, *Director*
Salvador Alcalde, *Shareholder*
EMP: 8 EST: 2010
SQ FT: 15,000
SALES (est): 2MM **Privately Held**
WEB: www.uspackgroup.com
SIC: 3085 Plastics bottles

(G-16388)
VEROCH LLC
10573 Nw 53rd St (33351-8030)
PHONE..................................954 990-7544
Edel Pontes, *Mng Member*
▲ EMP: 7 EST: 2012
SALES (est): 695K **Privately Held**
WEB: www.veroch.com
SIC: 3829 Testing equipment: abrasion,
   shearing strength, etc.

(G-16389)
VERTIV CORPORATION
7775 W Oakland Park Blvd (33351)
PHONE..................................954 377-7101
EMP: 100
SALES (corp-wide): 5B **Publicly Held**
WEB: www.vertiv.com
SIC: 3825 Electrical energy measuring
   equipment
HQ: Vertiv Corporation
   1050 Dearborn Dr
   Columbus OH 43085
   614 888-0246

(G-16390)
VOLAERO UAV DRNES HLDINGS CORP
Also Called: Volaero Drones
5375 N Hiatus Rd (33351-8718)
PHONE..................................954 261-3105
Charles Zwebner, *President*
Kevin Sanders, *Development*
David Abad, *Sales Staff*
Jeff Fidelin, *Senior Mgr*
EMP: 10 EST: 2016
SQ FT: 2,000
SALES (est): 2.3MM **Privately Held**
WEB: www.volaerodrones.com
SIC: 3721 Motorized aircraft

(G-16391)
VPR BRANDS LP (PA)
1141 Sawgrs Corp Pkwy (33323-2847)
PHONE..................................954 715-7001
Kevin Frija, *Ch of Bd*
Soleil C LLC, *General Ptnr*
Daniel Hoff, *COO*
EMP: 6 EST: 2009
SALES (est): 6.2MM **Privately Held**
WEB: www.vprbrands.com
SIC: 2111 Cigarettes

(G-16392)
WIALAN TECHNOLOGIES LLC (PA)
10271 Nw 46th St (33351-7963)
PHONE..................................954 749-3481
Eduardo Garcia, *CEO*
Victor M Tapia, *President*
Reggie Bergeron, *COO*
James Andrew Connolly III, *Admin Sec*
Timothy Peabody,
EMP: 8 EST: 2011
SALES (est): 602.4K **Publicly Held**
WEB: www.wialan.com
SIC: 3663 4813 5045 Airborne radio com-
   munications equipment; ; computer soft-
   ware

(G-16393)
WORLD ELECTRONICS INC
10794 Nw 53rd St (33351-8031)
PHONE..................................954 318-1044
Scott Barrett, *President*
Beate Barrett, *President*
Edward Seltzer, *Principal*
Roy Schwarts, *CFO*
EMP: 9 EST: 1979
SALES (est): 798.3K **Privately Held**
SIC: 3699 Security control equipment &
   systems

(G-16394)
YSL GRAPHICS LLC
4642 N Hiatus Rd (33351-7977)
PHONE..................................954 916-7255
Jose Y Ramirez,
Maria Cortes,
John Lara,
Stephanie Ramirez,
EMP: 8 EST: 2011
SALES (est): 417.9K **Privately Held**
WEB: www.yslsigns.com
SIC: 3993 Signs & advertising specialties

Surfside
Miami-Dade County

(G-16395)
DAIRY FAIRY LLC
9457 Harding Ave (33154-2803)
PHONE..................................305 865-1506
Jessica L Weiss Levison, *Administration*
EMP: 9 EST: 2012
SALES (est): 287.1K **Privately Held**
SIC: 2026 Yogurt

(G-16396)
JIVA CUBES INC
9264 Dickens Ave (33154-3032)
PHONE..................................305 788-1200
Allen Gomberg, *Manager*
EMP: 10 EST: 2013
SALES (est): 552K **Privately Held**
SIC: 3589 Coffee brewing equipment

(G-16397)
NUCOR LLC
8835 Harding Ave (33154-3418)
PHONE..................................786 290-9328
Javier Nunez, *Manager*
EMP: 7 EST: 2015
SALES (est): 173.8K **Privately Held**
WEB: www.nucor.com
SIC: 3312 Blast furnaces & steel mills

(G-16398)
PEEKABOO ORGANICS LLC
8918 Abbott Ave (33154-3431)
PHONE..................................305 527-7162
Jessica Levison, *CEO*
EMP: 1 EST: 2019
SALES (est): 3MM **Privately Held**
WEB: www.eatpeekaboo.com
SIC: 2024 Ice cream & ice milk

(G-16399)
SK WORLDWIDE LLC (PA)
9553 Harding Ave Ste 310 (33154-2510)
PHONE..................................786 360-4842
Jacky Koenig, *President*
Eddy E Silvera, *Principal*
EMP: 5 EST: 2011
SALES (est): 426.8K **Privately Held**
SIC: 3661 Telephones & telephone appara-
   tus

(G-16400)
SKATEBOARD SUPERCROSS LLC
725 92nd St (33154-3019)
PHONE..................................786 529-8187
Jonathan Strauss, *Principal*
EMP: 10 EST: 2014
SALES (est): 944.4K **Privately Held**
WEB: www.skateboardsupercross.com
SIC: 3949 Skateboards

Sweetwater
Miami-Dade County

(G-16401)
DIGIPRINT & DESIGN CORP
1460 Nw 107th Ave Ste R (33172-2734)
P.O. Box 228824, Miami (33222-8824)
PHONE..................................786 464-1770
Guillermo Torres, *Director*
EMP: 7 EST: 2005
SALES (est): 145.8K **Privately Held**
SIC: 3993 Signs & advertising specialties

(G-16402)
FASTKIT CORP
11250 Nw 25th St Ste 100 (33172-1820)
PHONE..................................754 227-8234
Jose Fernandez Jr, *Principal*
EMP: 5 EST: 1986
SALES (est): 326K **Privately Held**
WEB: www.fastkit.com
SIC: 2782 Blankbooks & looseleaf binders

(G-16403)
GLOBALTEK OFFICE SUPPLY INC
Also Called: Globaltek Art & Design
11200 Nw 25th St Ste 123 (33172-1807)
PHONE..................................305 477-2988
Jose Pelucarte, *President*
Oscar Ascanio, *CFO*
Monica Franco, *Controller*
◆ EMP: 9 EST: 2002
SALES (est): 1.7MM **Privately Held**
WEB: www.globaltek.com
SIC: 3861 Toners, prepared photographic
   (not made in chemical plants)

Tallahassee
Leon County

(G-16404)
A J TROPHIES & AWARDS INC (PA)
Also Called: Awards 4u
1387 E Lafayette St (32301-4724)
PHONE..................................850 878-7187
Samuel G Varn, *President*

Nancy C Varn, *Corp Secy*
Richard Baas, *Warehouse Mgr*
Nancy Varn, *CFO*
Cassidy Parsons, *Sales Mgr*
▲ **EMP:** 21 **EST:** 1987
SQ FT: 12,000
SALES (est): 4.1MM **Privately Held**
WEB: www.awards4u.com
SIC: 3914 3993 Trophies; signs & advertising specialties

(G-16405)
ACME BRICK COMPANY
660 Capital Cir Ne (32301-3514)
PHONE.................................850 531-0725
Buster Warmack, *Branch Mgr*
EMP: 10
SALES (corp-wide): 354.6B **Publicly Held**
WEB: www.brick.com
SIC: 3251 Brick & structural clay tile
HQ: Acme Brick Company
3024 Acme Brick Plz
Fort Worth TX 76109

(G-16406)
ADERANT NORTH AMERICA INC
1760 Summit Lake Dr 105 (32317-7942)
PHONE.................................850 224-2200
Jeffrey Desimone, *Database Admin*
Joshua Baker, *Technical Staff*
EMP: 18
SALES (corp-wide): 5.5B **Publicly Held**
WEB: www.aderant.com
SIC: 7372 Prepackaged software
HQ: Aderant North America, Inc.
500 Northridge Rd Ste 800
Atlanta GA 30350
404 720-3600

(G-16407)
AGP HOLDING CORP (PA)
2935 Kerry Forest Pkwy (32309-6825)
P.O. Box 12728 (32317-2728)
PHONE.................................850 668-0006
Herman R Arnold, *CEO*
Kenneth Ellis, *President*
James E Chalmers, *Vice Pres*
Robert W Espy, *Vice Pres*
Deborah K Ellis, *CFO*
EMP: 5 **EST:** 1989
SQ FT: 2,000
SALES (est): 12.7MM **Privately Held**
WEB: www.suncoastbedding.com
SIC: 2499 Beekeeping supplies, wood

(G-16408)
AGRI-PRODUCTS INC (HQ)
3015 N Shnnon Lkes Dr Ste (32309)
P.O. Box 12728 (32317-2728)
PHONE.................................850 668-0006
Arnold Herman R III, *CEO*
James E Chalmers, *President*
H Ross Arnold III, *Corp Secy*
Robert W Espy, *Vice Pres*
Deborah K Ellis, *CFO*
◆ **EMP:** 5 **EST:** 1988
SQ FT: 2,000
SALES (est): 11.2MM **Privately Held**
SIC: 2499 Beekeeping supplies, wood

(G-16409)
ALI KAMAKHI
Also Called: Jareed Online Publishing LLC
5663 Tecumseh Dr (32312-4848)
PHONE.................................850 405-8591
Ali Kamakhi, *Owner*
EMP: 14 **EST:** 2020
SALES (est): 100K **Privately Held**
SIC: 2711 Newspapers: publishing only, not printed on site

(G-16410)
ALL-PRO EQUIPMENT & RENTAL INC
2800 Mahan Dr (32308-5410)
P.O. Box 38355 (32315-8355)
PHONE.................................850 656-0208
Robin Barber, *President*
EMP: 10 **EST:** 2004
SALES (est): 2.3MM **Privately Held**
WEB: www.tallahasseeallpro.com
SIC: 3524 Lawn & garden tractors & equipment

(G-16411)
ANTHONY WRIGHT WELDING
311 Ross Rd (32305-7484)
PHONE.................................850 544-1831
Anthony Wright, *Principal*
EMP: 6 **EST:** 2008
SALES (est): 434.9K **Privately Held**
WEB: www.awrightweldingllc.com
SIC: 7692 Welding repair

(G-16412)
APEXEON BIOMEDICAL LLC
3075 Hawks Landing Dr (32309-7224)
PHONE.................................850 878-2150
Thompson Donald, *Principal*
EMP: 6 **EST:** 2016
SALES (est): 365.5K **Privately Held**
SIC: 2836 Biological products, except diagnostic

(G-16413)
ARCPOINT OF TALLAHASSEE INC (PA)
3520 N Monroe St (32303-2745)
PHONE.................................850 201-2500
Carrie Norris, *Principal*
EMP: 6 **EST:** 2010
SALES (est): 624.9K **Privately Held**
SIC: 2899

(G-16414)
ARGOS USA LLC
1005 Kissimmee St (32310-5324)
PHONE.................................850 576-4141
EMP: 8 **EST:** 2014
SALES (est): 177.8K **Privately Held**
WEB: www.argos-us.com
SIC: 3273 Ready-mixed concrete

(G-16415)
ASYSCO INC
1424 Piedmont Dr E # 100 (32308-7956)
PHONE.................................850 383-2522
Gwendolyn Pettit, *Technical Staff*
EMP: 12 **EST:** 2017
SALES (est): 601.7K **Privately Held**
SIC: 7372 Prepackaged software

(G-16416)
BACKWOODS CROSSING LLC
6725 Mahan Dr (32308-1413)
PHONE.................................850 765-3753
Jesse Rice, *Principal*
EMP: 10 **EST:** 2016
SALES (est): 477.7K **Privately Held**
WEB: www.backwoodscrossing.com
SIC: 2499 Wood products

(G-16417)
BAVA INC
Also Called: Commercial Printing
1403 Maclay Commerce Dr (32312-3963)
PHONE.................................850 893-4799
Keith R Balon, *President*
Ken Van Gordon, *Vice Pres*
EMP: 10 **EST:** 1974
SQ FT: 4,000
SALES (est): 707.8K **Privately Held**
WEB: www.cpctallahassee.com
SIC: 2752 2791 2789 Commercial printing, offset; typesetting; bookbinding & related work

(G-16418)
BE THE SOLUTION INC
1400 Village Square Blvd (32312-1250)
PHONE.................................850 545-2043
Geraldine Phipps, *Principal*
EMP: 5 **EST:** 2009
SALES (est): 370.3K **Privately Held**
WEB: www.bethesolution.us
SIC: 3999 Pet supplies

(G-16419)
BUCKS CORPORATION INC
Also Called: Fastsigns
1920 N Monroe St (32303-4726)
PHONE.................................850 894-2400
John M Buck, *President*
Marilyn M Buck, *Vice Pres*
Thanh Tran, *Sales Staff*
EMP: 10 **EST:** 2000
SQ FT: 1,700

SALES (est): 1.9MM **Privately Held**
WEB: www.fastsigns.com
SIC: 3993 Signs & advertising specialties

(G-16420)
CAPITAL TECHNOLOGY SOLUTIONS
3920 Monterey Pines Trl (32309-6337)
PHONE.................................850 562-3321
Christopher A Lewis, *Principal*
EMP: 8 **EST:** 2002
SALES (est): 179.8K **Privately Held**
WEB: www.technology.jmco.com
SIC: 3652 Pre-recorded records & tapes

(G-16421)
CEMEX CEMENT INC
3440 Weems Rd (32317-7506)
P.O. Box 14596 (32317-4596)
PHONE.................................850 942-4582
Tim Shenuski, *Branch Mgr*
EMP: 103 **Privately Held**
WEB: www.cemexusa.com
SIC: 3271 3273 Blocks, concrete: acoustical; ready-mixed concrete
HQ: Cemex Cement, Inc.
10100 Katy Fwy Ste 300
Houston TX 77043
713 650-6200

(G-16422)
CFS INC
2151 Delta Blvd Ste 101 (32303-4243)
PHONE.................................850 386-2902
Mike Conlan, *CEO*
Marsha Conlan, *President*
William Rodas, *Accounts Mgr*
Michael Dwinell, *Manager*
Jonathan Foskey, *Info Tech Dir*
▼ **EMP:** 10 **EST:** 2000
SQ FT: 4,738
SALES (est): 1.3MM **Privately Held**
WEB: www.cfssolutions.com
SIC: 7372 Business oriented computer software

(G-16423)
CHIEF CABINETS LLC
4329 W Pensacola St Ste 3 (32304-3722)
PHONE.................................850 545-5055
EMP: 7 **EST:** 2016
SALES (est): 252.7K **Privately Held**
WEB: www.chiefcabinets.com
SIC: 2434 Wood kitchen cabinets

(G-16424)
CLEAR VIEW COATINGS LLC
4514 Deslin Ct (32305-6400)
PHONE.................................850 210-0155
Claudine Vieux, *Principal*
EMP: 12 **EST:** 2013
SALES (est): 619.1K **Privately Held**
WEB: www.clearviewcoating.com
SIC: 3479 1721 Etching & engraving; residential painting; exterior residential painting contractor; commercial painting; exterior commercial painting contractor

(G-16425)
CLOTHESLINE INC
1369 E Lafayette St Ste A (32301-4781)
PHONE.................................850 877-9171
David Lachter, *President*
Debra Lachter, *Vice Pres*
Dana Lachter, *Treasurer*
Dana Lachterrivera, *Manager*
Dawn Lachter, *Admin Sec*
EMP: 27 **EST:** 1981
SQ FT: 9,000
SALES (est): 4.8MM **Privately Held**
WEB: www.clothesline.net
SIC: 2396 5651 2395 Screen printing on fabric articles; family clothing stores; emblems, embroidered

(G-16426)
COCA-COLA BOTTLING CO UNTD INC
2050 Maryland Cir (32303-3197)
PHONE.................................850 575-6122
Deank Hank, *Branch Mgr*
EMP: 148
SQ FT: 47,250
SALES (corp-wide): 2B **Privately Held**
WEB: www.coca-cola.com
SIC: 2086 Bottled & canned soft drinks

PA: Coca-Cola Bottling Company United, Inc.
4600 E Lake Blvd
Birmingham AL 35217
205 841-2653

(G-16427)
CONSOLIDATED METAL PRODUCTS
3416 Garber Dr (32303-1114)
PHONE.................................850 576-2167
William C Gadd, *President*
Amy Roberts, *Administration*
EMP: 8 **EST:** 1985
SQ FT: 15,000
SALES (est): 995.7K **Privately Held**
WEB: www.cmpbuildingproducts.com
SIC: 3444 5031 5039 Canopies; sheet metal; lumber, plywood & millwork; building materials, exterior; prefabricated structures

(G-16428)
COPY WELL INC
Also Called: Express Printing
927 N Monroe St (32303-6142)
P.O. Box 16063 (32317-6063)
PHONE.................................850 222-9777
Taroon Shah, *CEO*
Sameera Shah, *Vice Pres*
Salil T Shah, *Admin Sec*
EMP: 6 **EST:** 1986
SQ FT: 4,500
SALES (est): 931K **Privately Held**
SIC: 2752 Commercial printing, offset

(G-16429)
COR INTERNATIONAL (NOT INC)
3204 Hastie Rd (32305-6764)
PHONE.................................850 766-2866
Orazo Whited, *Branch Mgr*
EMP: 7
SALES (corp-wide): 202.4K **Privately Held**
SIC: 2834 Pharmaceutical preparations
PA: Cor International, Inc (Not Inc)
444 Appleyard Dr
Tallahassee FL 32304

(G-16430)
DANFOSS LLC
Also Called: Danfoss Turbocor Compressors
1769 E Paul Dirac Dr (32310-3707)
PHONE.................................850 504-4800
Alex Bruns, *Engineer*
Zhekang Du, *Engineer*
Larry Jogerst, *Engineer*
Bret Olson, *Engineer*
Kurt Funke, *Corp Comm Staff*
EMP: 145 **Privately Held**
WEB: www.danfoss.com
SIC: 3563 3585 Air & gas compressors; refrigeration & heating equipment
HQ: Danfoss, Llc
11655 Crossroads Cir
Baltimore MD 21220
410 931-8250

(G-16431)
DEBRUYNE ENTERPRISE INC
Also Called: Wood Dimensions
5186 Woodlane Cir (32303-6812)
PHONE.................................850 562-0491
Thomas Debruyne, *President*
Mike Brown, *Principal*
EMP: 10 **EST:** 1978
SQ FT: 8,000
SALES (est): 1.4MM **Privately Held**
SIC: 2434 Wood kitchen cabinets

(G-16432)
DREAMSPINNER PRESS LLC
10800 Kilcrease Way (32305-1824)
PHONE.................................800 970-3759
Holly Gerrell, *CEO*
Jocelin Potash, *Editor*
April Arrington, *CFO*
Poppy Dennison, *Marketing Staff*
Katie Obbink, *Librarian*
EMP: 12 **EST:** 2007
SALES (est): 1.8MM **Privately Held**
WEB: www.dreamspinnerpress.com
SIC: 2741 Miscellaneous publishing

(G-16433)
DURRA QUICK PRINT INC
1334 N Monroe St (32303-5527)
PHONE...................................850 681-2900
Sarah F Allen, *President*
EMP: 5 EST: 1983
SQ FT: 3,000
SALES (est): 439.5K **Privately Held**
WEB: www.durraprint.com
SIC: 2752 2759 Commercial printing, off-set; commercial printing

(G-16434)
DURRA-PRINT INC
3044 W Tharpe St (32303-1186)
PHONE...................................850 222-4768
Tim Durrance, *President*
EMP: 23 EST: 1972
SQ FT: 14,000
SALES (est): 1.9MM **Privately Held**
WEB: www.durraprint.com
SIC: 2752 2796 2791 2789 Commercial printing, offset; platemaking services; typesetting; bookbinding & related work; commercial printing

(G-16435)
DVH MACLEOD CORP
Also Called: Sir Speedy
1100 N Monroe St Ste A (32303-6172)
PHONE...................................850 224-6760
David Macleod, *President*
Valerie Macleod, *Corp Secy*
Bernie Jimenez, *Manager*
EMP: 11 EST: 1974
SQ FT: 3,000
SALES (est): 511.5K **Privately Held**
WEB: www.sirspeedy.com
SIC: 2752 2791 Commercial printing, litho-graphic; typesetting

(G-16436)
EMINENT TECHNOLOGY INC
225 E Palmer Ave (32301-5533)
PHONE...................................850 575-5655
Bruce Thigpen, *President*
Will L Stewart, *Vice Pres*
Rob Stewart, *Manager*
EMP: 5 EST: 1982
SQ FT: 9,000
SALES (est): 1.1MM **Privately Held**
WEB: www.eminent-tech.com
SIC: 3651 Loudspeakers, electrodynamic or magnetic; phonograph turntables

(G-16437)
EVERYDAY FEMINISM LLC
75 N Woodward Ave (32313-7500)
PHONE...................................202 643-1001
Jamie Utt, *Credit Staff*
Sandra Kim, *Mng Member*
Derek Ellerman, *Mng Member*
EMP: 6 EST: 2012
SALES (est): 521.7K **Privately Held**
WEB: www.everydayfeminism.com
SIC: 2741 7389 Miscellaneous publishing;

(G-16438)
F S VIEW FLA FLAMBEAU NEWSPPR
277 N Magnolia Dr (32301-2664)
P.O. Box 20208 (32316-0208)
PHONE...................................850 561-6653
Robert Parker, *President*
EMP: 45 EST: 1992
SQ FT: 1,400
SALES (est): 1.1MM **Privately Held**
SIC: 2711 Newspapers, publishing & print-ing

(G-16439)
FIRST COMMUNICATIONS INC
2910 Krry Frest Pkwy Ste (32309)
PHONE...................................850 668-7990
Charles C Livingston Jr, *President*
Michelle Sweeney, *Corp Secy*
Betty Boyett, *Shareholder*
Jeffrey C Livingston, *Shareholder*
EMP: 59 EST: 1993
SALES (est): 3.7MM **Privately Held**
SIC: 3669 3663 4812 Visual communica-tion systems; radio broadcasting & com-munications equipment; receivers, radio communications; radio telephone commu-nication

(G-16440)
FLORIDA BID REPORTING SERVICE
313 Williams St Ste 11 (32303-6231)
P.O. Box 37189 (32315-7189)
PHONE...................................850 539-7522
Wayland D Burgess Jr, *President*
Kila Powell, *Director*
EMP: 10 EST: 1987
SQ FT: 800
SALES (est): 873.1K **Privately Held**
WEB: www.floridabid.com
SIC: 2721 Magazines: publishing only, not printed on site

(G-16441)
FLORIDA PRINT FINISHERS INC
Also Called: Florida Tees
1621 Capital Cir Ne Ste F (32308-5501)
PHONE...................................850 877-8503
James A Walker, *President*
James Walker Jr, *Vice Pres*
EMP: 5 EST: 1967
SALES (est): 349.3K **Privately Held**
SIC: 2789 2675 Trade binding services; die-cut paper & board

(G-16442)
FLOWERS BKG CO THOMASVILLE LLC
3385 S Monroe St (32301-6979)
PHONE...................................229 226-5331
Chris Mulford, *Manager*
EMP: 14
SALES (corp-wide): 4.3B **Publicly Held**
WEB: www.ilovegoats.com
SIC: 2051 Bread, all types (white, wheat, rye, etc): fresh or frozen
HQ: Flowers Baking Co. Of Tyler, Llc
300 S Madison St
Thomasville GA 31792
229 226-5331

(G-16443)
FULL PRESS APPAREL INC
3445 Garber Dr (32303-1115)
PHONE...................................850 222-1003
Daniel Shrine, *President*
Danny Shrine, *President*
Kelley Brewer, *Mktg Coord*
Sonia Jones, *Manager*
Kathy Norman, *Manager*
EMP: 12 EST: 1997
SQ FT: 8,500
SALES (est): 1.5MM **Privately Held**
WEB: www.fullpressapparel.com
SIC: 2759 2396 2395 Screen printing; au-tomotive & apparel trimmings; pleating & stitching

(G-16444)
GANDY PRINTERS INC
1800 S Monroe St (32301-5528)
PHONE...................................850 222-5847
Bernard L Gandy III, *President*
Bernie Gandy, *General Mgr*
EMP: 17 EST: 1970
SQ FT: 10,000
SALES (est): 2.2MM **Privately Held**
WEB: www.gandyprinters.com
SIC: 2752 2789 2759 Commercial print-ing, offset; bookbinding & related work; commercial printing

(G-16445)
GARVIN MANAGEMENT COMPANY INC (PA)
Also Called: Insty-Prints
4042 Sawgrass Cir (32309-2890)
PHONE...................................850 893-4719
William Garvin Sr, *President*
EMP: 5 EST: 1979
SQ FT: 2,600
SALES (est): 569.6K **Privately Held**
WEB: www.instyprints.com
SIC: 2752 7334 Commercial printing, off-set; photocopying & duplicating services

(G-16446)
GENERAL CAPACITOR LLC
132-1 Hamilton Park Dr (32304)
PHONE...................................510 371-2700
Linda Zhong, *CEO*
Hao Chen, *Mng Member*
Jianping Zheng,

▲ EMP: 7 EST: 2011
SALES (est): 182.9K **Privately Held**
SIC: 3629 3675 Capacitors & condensers; electronic capacitors

(G-16447)
GENERAL DYNMICS LAND SYSTEMS I
2930 Commonwealth Blvd (32303-3155)
PHONE...................................850 574-4700
Wynn Koehler, *General Mgr*
Steve Rolph, *General Mgr*
Edward Harris, *Chief*
Dana Pastor, *Regional Mgr*
Michael Bolon, *Vice Pres*
EMP: 354
SALES (corp-wide): 38.4B **Publicly Held**
WEB: www.gdls.com
SIC: 3812 Radio magnetic instrumentation
HQ: General Dynamics Land Systems Inc.
38500 Mound Rd
Sterling Heights MI 48310
586 825-4000

(G-16448)
GEORGESOFT INC
207 W Park Ave Ste B (32301-7715)
PHONE...................................850 329-5517
Kostiantyn Romanchenko, *President*
EMP: 7 EST: 2015
SALES (est): 420.6K **Privately Held**
SIC: 7372 Application computer software

(G-16449)
GET HAMS INC
3396 Lakeshore Dr (32312-1305)
PHONE...................................850 386-7123
Leonard M Taylor, *President*
EMP: 9 EST: 2002
SALES (est): 533.8K **Privately Held**
SIC: 2013 Prepared pork products from purchased pork

(G-16450)
GRAPHIC PRESS CORPORATION
5123a Woodlane Cir Ste A (32303-6862)
PHONE...................................850 562-2262
Dawn Azar Madsen, *President*
Norm Madse, *Vice Pres*
Eric Madsen, *Marketing Mgr*
EMP: 5 EST: 1992
SQ FT: 7,500
SALES (est): 687.1K **Privately Held**
WEB: www.gp-print.com
SIC: 2752 Commercial printing, offset

(G-16451)
GT TECHNOLOGIES INC
2919 Commonwealth Blvd (32303-3156)
PHONE...................................850 575-8181
Ron Krause, *Plant Mgr*
Steve Denolf, *Mfg Staff*
Harold Brown, *QC Mgr*
Daniel Bibish, *Engineer*
David Gosbee, *Engineer*
EMP: 200 **Privately Held**
WEB: www.gttechnologies.com
SIC: 3714 Motor vehicle engines & parts
HQ: Gt Technologies, Inc.
5859 E Executive Dr
Westland MI 48185
734 467-8371

(G-16452)
GT TECHNOLOGIES I INC
2919 Commonwealth Blvd (32303-3156)
PHONE...................................850 575-8181
William E Redmond Jr, *CEO*
Mark Mueller, *General Mgr*
Robert Novo, *Vice Pres*
Douglas J Grierson, *CFO*
Mike Spadarotto, *CFO*
▲ EMP: 203 EST: 2006
SALES (est): 57.4MM
SALES (corp-wide): 1B **Privately Held**
WEB: www.gttechnologies.com
SIC: 3714 Motor vehicle engines & parts
HQ: Gentek, Inc.
90 E Halsey Rd Ste 301
Parsippany NJ 07054
973 515-0900

(G-16453)
GTO ACCESS SYSTEMS LLC
3121 Hartsfield Rd (32303-3149)
PHONE...................................850 575-0176
Shaun Burke, *President*
Joseph A Kelley, *President*
Douglas Waldal, *President*
Steve Ciquero, *Sales Mgr*
Bruce Buehler, *Sales Staff*
◆ EMP: 90 EST: 1987
SQ FT: 75,000
SALES (est): 25.8MM
SALES (corp-wide): 677.2MM **Privately Held**
SIC: 3699 Security devices
HQ: Nice North America Llc
5919 Sea Otter Pl
Carlsbad CA 92010
760 438-7000

(G-16454)
GULF ATLANTIC CULVERT COMPANY
5344 Gateway Dr (32303-6842)
P.O. Box 4002 (32315-4002)
PHONE...................................850 562-2384
Francis Wallace, *President*
James W McCook III, *Corp Secy*
W Howell Jarrard, *Vice Pres*
EMP: 16 EST: 1984
SQ FT: 1,800
SALES (est): 1.2MM **Privately Held**
WEB: www.gaculvert.com
SIC: 3444 3498 3312 Pipe, sheet metal; fabricated pipe & fittings; blast furnaces & steel mills

(G-16455)
GUN VAULT
3305 Capital Cir Ne # 103 (32308-1589)
PHONE...................................850 391-7651
EMP: 5
SALES (est): 400K **Privately Held**
SIC: 3272 Mfg Concrete Products

(G-16456)
H B SHERMAN TRAPS INC
3731 Peddie Dr (32303-1103)
P.O. Box 20267 (32316-0267)
PHONE...................................850 575-8727
Gerald E Phillips, *President*
Rebecca Anne Colon, *Vice Pres*
Rebecca Sciabica, *IT Executive*
Sandra Screws, *Admin Sec*
EMP: 9 EST: 1961
SQ FT: 5,000
SALES (est): 1.1MM **Privately Held**
WEB: www.shermantraps.com
SIC: 3429 Animal traps, iron or steel

(G-16457)
HANGER PRSTHETCS & ORTHO INC
Also Called: Hanger Clinic
2717 Mahan Dr Ste 2 (32308-5499)
PHONE...................................850 216-2392
Sam Liang, *President*
Eric Rancharran, *Manager*
EMP: 8
SALES (corp-wide): 1.1B **Publicly Held**
SIC: 3842 Limbs, artificial; braces, ortho-pedic
HQ: Hanger Prosthetics & Orthotics, Inc.
10910 Domain Dr Ste 300
Austin TX 78758
512 777-3800

(G-16458)
HARBOR ENTPS LTD LBLTY CO
2417 Fleischmann Rd Ste 4 (32308-4505)
PHONE...................................229 403-0756
Todd Vanderbeek, *CFO*
Jackson Rackley, *Branch Mgr*
EMP: 10
SALES (corp-wide): 7.9MM **Privately Held**
WEB: www.harborfedcon.com
SIC: 3312 Structural shapes & pilings, steel
PA: Harbor Fed Con Llc
125 N Broad St Ste 404
Thomasville GA 31792
229 226-0911

(G-16459)
HARVEST PRINT & BUS SVCS INC ✪
1613 Capital Cir Ne (32308-5501)
PHONE..................850 681-2488
Anisur M Rahman, *President*
EMP: 10 EST: 2021
SALES (est): 750.5K Privately Held
WEB: www.harvest-press.com
SIC: 2752 Commercial printing, offset

(G-16460)
HARVEST PRINT MKTG SLTIONS LLC
Also Called: Harvest Printing
1613 Capital Cir Ne (32308-5501)
PHONE..................850 681-2488
Tim Kleman,
Christy Kleman,
EMP: 7 EST: 2017
SALES (est): 1.3MM Privately Held
WEB: www.harvest-press.com
SIC: 2752 Commercial printing, offset

(G-16461)
HARVEST PRTG & COPY CTR INC
1613 Capital Cir Ne (32308-5501)
PHONE..................850 681-2488
Miguel Jimenez, *President*
Theresa Jimenez, *Treasurer*
Ken Bowden, *Technology*
Don Drewek, *Graphic Designe*
EMP: 17 EST: 1985
SQ FT: 9,000
SALES (est): 2.3MM Privately Held
WEB: www.harvest-press.com
SIC: 2752 Commercial printing, offset

(G-16462)
HOMES MEDIA SOLUTIONS LLC (DH)
Also Called: Agent Advantage
325 John Knox Rd Bldg 200 (32303-4114)
PHONE..................850 350-7800
Cindy Elliott, *Agent*
Nicole Eichenberger, *Supervisor*
Manthan Barot, *Software Dev*
Bill Tulko, *Analyst*
EMP: 10 EST: 2015
SALES (est): 12.2MM Privately Held
WEB: www.agentadvantage.com
SIC: 2721 Magazines: publishing only, not printed on site

(G-16463)
JOHN HURST OUTDOOR SVCS LLC
3694 Corinth Dr (32308-4035)
PHONE..................850 556-7459
Johnny H Hurst Jr, *President*
EMP: 5 EST: 2007
SALES (est): 415.7K Privately Held
WEB: www.johnhurstlawncaretallahassee.com
SIC: 2499 Fencing, docks & other outdoor wood structural products

(G-16464)
JUDICIAL & ADM RES ASSOC
Also Called: Florida Law Weekly
1327 N Adams St (32303-5522)
P.O. Box 4284 (32315-4284)
PHONE..................850 222-3171
Neil Young, *President*
Sharon Young, *Vice Pres*
Ernest Page,
Michelle Perruzzi, *Assistant*
Season Stark, *Assistant*
EMP: 15 EST: 1975
SQ FT: 5,000
SALES (est): 1.3MM Privately Held
WEB: www.floridalawweekly.com
SIC: 2721 Magazines: publishing only, not printed on site

(G-16465)
K C W ELECTRIC COMPANY INC
4765 Shelfer Rd (32305-7411)
PHONE..................850 878-2051
Robert E Scribner, *President*
Donald T Scribner, *Vice Pres*
EMP: 5 EST: 1946
SQ FT: 9,000
SALES (est): 462.3K Privately Held
WEB: www.kcwwaterwell.com
SIC: 7694 7699 5531 7549 Electric motor repair; rewinding stators; pumps & pumping equipment repair; automobile air conditioning equipment, sale, installation; automotive maintenance services

(G-16466)
KAMELEON PRESS INC
1925 Benjamin Chaires Rd (32317-7476)
PHONE..................850 566-2522
Kelly K Rysavy, *President*
EMP: 8 EST: 2001
SALES (est): 113K Privately Held
WEB: www.kameleonpress.com
SIC: 2741 Miscellaneous publishing

(G-16467)
KENNY-TS INC
1471 Capital Cir Nw # 10 (32303-1311)
P.O. Box 962 (32302-0962)
PHONE..................850 575-6644
Kenneth Thompson, *President*
Anthony Donaldson, *Corp Secy*
Robert W Thompson, *Shareholder*
EMP: 13 EST: 1998
SQ FT: 2,000
SALES (est): 1MM Privately Held
WEB: www.kennytees.com
SIC: 2759 Screen printing

(G-16468)
LAWRENCE COMMERCIAL SYSTEMS
451 Geddie Rd (32304-8690)
PHONE..................850 574-8723
Richard Lawrence, *Owner*
EMP: 8 EST: 1977
SALES (est): 1.1MM Privately Held
SIC: 3463 Aluminum forgings

(G-16469)
LEON SCREENING & REPAIR INC
1223 Airport Dr (32304-4704)
PHONE..................850 575-2840
Thomas Herring, *President*
Judy Miester, *Admin Sec*
EMP: 15 EST: 1976
SQ FT: 9,000
SALES (est): 1.7MM Privately Held
WEB: www.leonscreening.com
SIC: 3442 5211 Screens, window, metal; windows, storm: wood or metal

(G-16470)
LESLIE INDUSTRIES INC
2454 Centerville Rd (32308-4418)
P.O. Box 13405 (32317-3405)
PHONE..................850 422-0099
Harold C Leslie, *President*
David McGeachy, *Prdtn Mgr*
Sue Morgan, *Accounts Mgr*
EMP: 10 EST: 1981
SQ FT: 3,000
SALES (est): 322.8K Privately Held
WEB: www.leslieindustries.com
SIC: 3448 Buildings, portable: prefabricated metal

(G-16471)
LITHO HAUS PRINTERS INC (PA)
Also Called: Lithohaus Printers
2843 Industrial Plaza Dr A1 (32301-3507)
PHONE..................850 671-6600
Dianne Nagle, *President*
Bill Pickron, *Vice Pres*
Ritchie Pickron, *Manager*
EMP: 9 EST: 1983
SQ FT: 9,500
SALES (est): 2.2MM Privately Held
WEB: www.lithohaus.com
SIC: 2752 Commercial printing, offset

(G-16472)
LOBBY DOCS LLC
3472 Weems Rd (32317-7513)
PHONE..................850 294-0013
James Parsons, *Ch of Bd*
EMP: 7 EST: 2014
SALES (est): 259.3K Privately Held
SIC: 7372 Business oriented computer software

(G-16473)
MAG-TAGS INC
Also Called: Signprinters
4446 Sierra Ct (32309-2293)
PHONE..................850 294-1809
Carolyn Pippenger, *President*
Alan Pippenger, *Admin Sec*
EMP: 6 EST: 1982
SQ FT: 6,000
SALES (est): 390.2K Privately Held
SIC: 3993 Signs, not made in custom sign painting shops

(G-16474)
MAN-TRANS LLC
4920 Woodlane Cir (32303-6810)
PHONE..................850 222-6993
Darryl Moore, *Mng Member*
◆ EMP: 19 EST: 1997
SQ FT: 33,000
SALES (est): 2.4MM Privately Held
WEB: www.manualtransmission.net
SIC: 3568 5063 5085 3714 Power transmission equipment; transformers & transmission equipment; power transmission equipment & apparatus; motor vehicle parts & accessories

(G-16475)
MARLIN COATINGS LLC
3666 Peddie Dr (32303-1126)
PHONE..................850 224-1370
Kyle Rockwell, *Principal*
EMP: 14 EST: 2006
SALES (est): 492.4K Privately Held
SIC: 3479 Metal coating & allied service

(G-16476)
MARQUIS SOFTWARE DEV INC
1625 Summit Lake Dr # 105 (32317-7940)
PHONE..................850 877-8864
Edward Fishback, *President*
Larry Powell, *COO*
Glenn Fishback, *Vice Pres*
Olu Fayemi, *Project Mgr*
Stephen Payne, *Research*
EMP: 100 EST: 1999
SALES (est): 11.8MM Privately Held
WEB: www.marquisware.com
SIC: 7372 Prepackaged software

(G-16477)
MATHERSON ORGANICS LLC
1400 Vlg Sq Blvd 3-85899 (32312-1250)
PHONE..................647 801-6977
William McMacken, *Mng Member*
Michael C Chan,
EMP: 4 EST: 2016
SALES (est): 3MM
SALES (corp-wide): 5.6MM Privately Held
SIC: 2844 Cosmetic preparations
PA: Gloss Ventures Holdings Inc.
1801 Century Park E # 2400
Los Angeles CA 90067
323 542-9699

(G-16478)
MEDAFFINITY CORPORATION
2350 Phillips Rd Apt 1110 (32308-5346)
PHONE..................850 254-9690
Dustin A Holt, *Principal*
Neil Skene, *Vice Chairman*
EMP: 8 EST: 2010
SALES (est): 253.8K Privately Held
WEB: www.medaffinity.com
SIC: 7372 Prepackaged software

(G-16479)
METAL FABRICATION AND
3600 Weems Rd Ste D (32317-7500)
PHONE..................850 205-2300
Chad Anderson, *General Mgr*
Matthew Turner, *Vice Pres*
Stephanie P Turner, *Mng Member*
Len Turner,
Matt Turner,
EMP: 9 EST: 2005
SALES (est): 956.4K Privately Held
WEB: www.metalfabtallahassee.com
SIC: 7692 Welding repair

(G-16480)
MII OIL HOLDING INC
1201 Hays St (32301-2699)
PHONE..................321 200-0039
Armando Mormina, *CEO*
EMP: 242 EST: 2011
SALES (est): 1.2B Privately Held
WEB: www.mii-holding.org
SIC: 1389 Oil field services

(G-16481)
MODERN DIGITAL IMAGING INC
Also Called: Printing.
519 N Monroe St (32301-1259)
PHONE..................850 222-7514
Denise S Perrin, *President*
Tom Perrin, *Owner*
Thomas B Perrin, *Vice Pres*
EMP: 10 EST: 2003
SQ FT: 4,700
SALES (est): 978.3K Privately Held
WEB: www.gomdi.net
SIC: 2752 Commercial printing, offset

(G-16482)
MUNICIPAL CODE CORPORATION (HQ)
1700 Capital Cir Sw (32310-9250)
P.O. Box 2235 (32316-2235)
PHONE..................850 576-3171
George R Langford, *Ch of Bd*
A Lawton Langford, *President*
Ramona Connors, *Editor*
Lauren Coulter, *Editor*
Erin Edwards, *Editor*
EMP: 17 EST: 1951
SQ FT: 40,000
SALES (est): 28.2MM Privately Held
WEB: www.municode.com
SIC: 2741 2721 2731 Directories: publishing & printing; periodicals; book publishing

(G-16483)
NOPETRO LLC
1152 Capital Cir Nw (32304-9234)
PHONE..................305 441-9059
Jonathan Locke, *President*
Jorge Herrera, *Mng Member*
Jose David Santizo, *Manager*
John Del Rossi, *Director*
EMP: 8 EST: 2008
SALES (est): 2.3MM Privately Held
SIC: 1321 Natural gas liquids

(G-16484)
NORTHLAND MANUFACTURING INC
3485 S Monroe St (32301-7200)
P.O. Box 6247 (32314-6247)
PHONE..................850 878-5149
Anita Sandel, *President*
Paul Birdwell, *Vice Pres*
EMP: 6 EST: 1974
SQ FT: 9,000
SALES (est): 719.3K Privately Held
WEB: www.northlandmanufacturing.com
SIC: 2842 Industrial plant disinfectants or deodorants

(G-16485)
OIL FOR AMER EXPLORATION LLC
2903 Royal Isle Dr (32312-4257)
PHONE..................701 690-2407
EMP: 5 EST: 2018
SALES (est): 544.9K Privately Held
SIC: 1382 Oil & gas exploration services

(G-16486)
OOMPHA INC
Also Called: Karmanos Printing & Graphics
1754 Thomasville Rd (32303-5708)
PHONE..................850 222-7210
Beverley Karmanos, *President*
George Karmanos, *Vice Pres*
Amanda Armanos, *Admin Sec*
EMP: 5 EST: 1984
SQ FT: 4,800
SALES (est): 506.7K Privately Held
WEB: www.karmanosprinting.com
SIC: 2752 2791 2789 Commercial printing, offset; typesetting; bookbinding & related work

(G-16487)
PILKINGTON NORTH AMERICA INC
Also Called: Own's Libby Ford
3646 Hartsfield Rd # 110 (32303-1177)
PHONE................................800 759-0940
John Carter, *Manager*
EMP: 7 Privately Held
WEB: www.pilkington.com
SIC: 3211 Flat glass
HQ: Pilkington North America, Inc.
　811 Madison Ave Fl 3
　Toledo OH 43604
　419 247-3731

(G-16488)
PIXE INTERNATIONAL CORP
2306 Domingo Dr (32304-1311)
P.O. Box 2744 (32316-2744)
PHONE................................850 574-6469
J William Nelson, *President*
Becky Selden Hoffman, *Treasurer*
EMP: 8 EST: 1977
SQ FT: 600
SALES (est): 667.6K Privately Held
WEB: www.pixeintl.com
SIC: 3829 5084 Measuring & controlling devices; industrial machinery & equipment

(G-16489)
PREMIER SERVICES OF FL INC
2305 Garland Ct 1 (32303-8341)
PHONE................................678 815-6078
Ladonna Jackson, *Principal*
EMP: 9 EST: 2015
SALES (est): 868.9K Privately Held
SIC: 3714 Motor vehicle engines & parts

(G-16490)
PRINTWORKS
4753 Blountstown Hwy (32304-2773)
PHONE................................850 681-6909
Michael Bartoszewicz, *Principal*
EMP: 6 EST: 2009
SALES (est): 334.2K Privately Held
WEB: www.printworks.info
SIC: 2752 Commercial printing, offset

(G-16491)
PROTEK CUSTOM COATINGS LLC
1320 Gateshead Cir (32317-9548)
PHONE................................850 656-7923
Lynn L Penny, *Principal*
EMP: 7 EST: 2007
SALES (est): 347.3K Privately Held
SIC: 3479 Metal coating & allied service

(G-16492)
RAPID RATER COMPANY
Also Called: Rapid Press, Inc
3626 Cagney Dr (32309-3341)
P.O. Box 13055 (32317-3055)
PHONE................................850 893-7346
Lourdes Madsen, *President*
Natalie Castillo, *Vice Pres*
Henry Madsen, *Vice Pres*
Alan Madsen, *Manager*
EMP: 24 EST: 1959
SQ FT: 10,000
SALES (est): 2.2MM Privately Held
WEB: www.rapidpress.com
SIC: 2741 2752 2759 2789 Technical manuals: publishing & printing; technical papers: publishing & printing; commercial printing, offset; announcements: engraved; envelopes: printing; invitations: printing; stationery: printing; magazines, binding; pamphlets, binding; trade binding services

(G-16493)
REFRESHMENT SERVICES INC
Also Called: Pepsico
3919 W Pensacola St (32304-2837)
PHONE................................850 574-0281
Scott Cason, *General Mgr*
Jason Murphy, *General Mgr*
Al Hudgins, *Branch Mgr*
EMP: 70
SQ FT: 36,021
SALES (corp-wide): 46.9MM Privately Held
WEB: www.refreshmentservicespepsi.com
SIC: 2086 4226 Soft drinks: packaged in cans, bottles, etc.; special warehousing & storage
PA: Refreshment Services, Inc.
　1121 Locust St
　Quincy IL 62301
　217 223-8600

(G-16494)
RIPPEE CONSTRUCTION INC
2107 Delta Way (32303-4224)
PHONE................................850 668-6805
Carol Rippee, *President*
Ellie Bertram, *Manager*
EMP: 6 EST: 1995
SALES (est): 1.7MM Privately Held
WEB: www.rippeeconstruction.com
SIC: 1389 Construction, repair & dismantling services; haulage, oil field

(G-16495)
ROSE PRINTING CO INC
2504 Harriman Cir (32308-0920)
PHONE................................850 339-8093
Charles Rosenberg, *President*
EMP: 11 EST: 2020
SALES (est): 399.6K Privately Held
SIC: 2752 Commercial printing, offset

(G-16496)
ROUND TABLE TOOLS INC
Also Called: King Arthur's Tools
3645 Hartsfield Rd (32303-1142)
PHONE................................850 877-7650
Arthur Aveling, *President*
Pamela Aveling, *Exec VP*
Celeste Tucker, *Administration*
▲ **EMP: 7 EST: 1987**
SQ FT: 7,500
SALES (est): 1MM Privately Held
SIC: 3423 3425 5072 2499 Edge tools for woodworking: augers, bits, gimlets, etc.; saw blades for hand or power saws; hardware; decorative wood & woodwork

(G-16497)
ROWLAND PUBLISHING INC
Also Called: Tallahassee Magazine
1932 Miccosukee Rd (32308-5328)
P.O. Box 1837 (32302-1837)
PHONE................................850 878-0554
Brian Rowland, *President*
McKenzie Burleigh, *Vice Pres*
Daniel Vitter, *Prdtn Mgr*
Mackenzie Ligas, *Sales Staff*
Javis Ogden, *Marketing Mgr*
EMP: 25 EST: 1990
SQ FT: 1,500
SALES (est): 3.8MM Privately Held
WEB: www.rowlandpublishing.com
SIC: 2721 7313 Magazines: publishing only, not printed on site; trade journals: publishing only, not printed on site; magazine advertising representative

(G-16498)
RUVOS LLC (PA)
2252 Klarn Ctr Blvd (32309-3577)
PHONE................................850 254-7270
Andrew Taylor, *COO*
Manuel Ravelo, *Project Mgr*
Carolina Alarcon, *Engineer*
Alex Bello, *Engineer*
Tom Fletcher, *Engineer*
EMP: 8 EST: 2004
SQ FT: 6,600
SALES (est): 2.8MM Privately Held
WEB: www.ruvos.com
SIC: 7372 Business oriented computer software

(G-16499)
SIGNS NOW (PA)
1551 Capital Cir Se Ste 6 (32301-5141)
PHONE................................850 383-6500
Wesley Morgan, *President*
EMP: 5 EST: 1990
SALES (est): 799.3K Privately Held
WEB: www.signsnow.com
SIC: 3993 Signs & advertising specialties

(G-16500)
SKAGFIELD CORPORATION (PA)
Also Called: Skandia Window Fashions
270 Crossway Rd (32305-3460)
P.O. Box 6566 (32314-6566)
PHONE................................850 878-1144
Hilmar O Skagfield, *President*
Larry Sack, *Vice Pres*
Daniel Sullivan, *Vice Pres*
Sarah Sharp-Gilbert, *Plant Mgr*
Sondra Pence, *Production*
▲ **EMP: 86 EST: 1966**
SQ FT: 85,000
SALES (est): 21MM Privately Held
WEB: www.skandiawf.com
SIC: 2591 Window blinds; window shades

(G-16501)
SOUTHEAST REVIEW INC
405 Williams Building (32306-1000)
PHONE................................850 644-4230
Jesse Goolsby, *Manager*
Erin Hoover, *Director*
EMP: 7 EST: 1979
SALES (est): 88.8K Privately Held
WEB: www.southeastreview.org
SIC: 2721 Periodicals

(G-16502)
SPA CONCEPTS INC
Also Called: Sanitation Products of America
3191 W Tharpe St (32303-1133)
PHONE................................850 575-0921
Ajay Chadha, *Principal*
Carl Owenby, *Teacher*
EMP: 16 EST: 2005
SALES (est): 2.1MM Privately Held
WEB:
www.sanitationproductsofamerica.com
SIC: 2842 Specialty cleaning preparations

(G-16503)
SPIRIT SALES CORPORATION
2818 Industrial Plaza Dr D (32301-3557)
PHONE................................850 878-0366
EMP: 6
SQ FT: 750
SALES (est): 325K Privately Held
SIC: 2329 5699 5136 Mfg Men's/Boy's Clothing Ret Misc Apparel/Accessories Whol Men's/Boy's Clothing

(G-16504)
SPRAY BOX LLC
768 Lupine Ln (32308-6256)
PHONE................................850 567-2724
Justin J Wheeless, *Principal*
EMP: 8 EST: 2012
SALES (est): 90.7K Privately Held
WEB: www.thespraybox.com
SIC: 3523 Sprayers & spraying machines, agricultural

(G-16505)
STATE OF FLORIDA
250 Marriott Dr (32301-2983)
PHONE................................850 488-1234
Charlene Feiga, *District Mgr*
Michael Papagikos, *COO*
Sonja Guthrie, *Project Mgr*
Kara Godwin, *Purchasing*
Vilma Rueda, *Research*
EMP: 18 EST: 2019
SALES (est): 9MM Privately Held
WEB: www.flalottery.com
SIC: 3999 Manufacturing industries

(G-16506)
SUBMERSIBLE SYSTEMS LLC
3425 Bannerman Rd 105-4 (32312-7062)
PHONE................................714 842-6566
EMP: 5 EST: 2019
SALES (est): 467.8K Privately Held
WEB: www.submersiblesystems.com
SIC: 3069 Fabricated rubber products

(G-16507)
SYN-TECH SYSTEMS INC (PA)
Also Called: SYNTECH
100 Four Points Way (32305-7091)
P.O. Box 5258 (32314-5258)
PHONE................................850 878-2558
Douglas R Dunlap, *President*
Gene Meadows, *Business Mgr*
Tim Bryant, *Project Mgr*
Heath Spires, *Project Mgr*
Tiffany Simmons, *Opers Staff*
EMP: 180 EST: 1987
SQ FT: 52,000
SALES (est): 31.8MM Privately Held
WEB: www.myfuelmaster.com
SIC: 3571 3569 Electronic computers; liquid automation machinery & equipment

(G-16508)
SYNDICATED PROGRAMMING INC
Also Called: Capital Outlook Newspaper
1363 Mahan Dr (32308-5107)
PHONE................................850 877-0105
Roosevelt Wilson, *President*
EMP: 7 EST: 1987
SALES (est): 587.5K Privately Held
WEB: www.capitaloutlook.com
SIC: 2711 Newspapers, publishing & printing

(G-16509)
SYNERGY BIOLOGICS LLC
2849 Pablo Ave (32308-4288)
PHONE................................850 656-4277
David Hill, *Principal*
EMP: 6 EST: 2015
SALES (est): 450.3K Privately Held
WEB: www.synergybiologics.net
SIC: 2836 Biological products, except diagnostic

(G-16510)
TALLAHASSEE DEMOCRAT
277 N Magnolia Dr (32301-2664)
P.O. Box 990 (32302-0990)
PHONE................................850 599-2100
John Miller, *Founder*
William Griffin, *Production*
Blas Gomez, *Engineer*
Bill Brystiles, *Sales Staff*
Melissa Laird, *Marketing Staff*
EMP: 20 EST: 2018
SALES (est): 1.4MM Privately Held
WEB: www.tallahassee.com
SIC: 2711 Newspapers, publishing & printing

(G-16511)
TALLAHASSEE WELDING & MCH SP
Also Called: Tallahassee Powder Coating
1220 Lake Bradford Rd (32304-4733)
P.O. Box 2472 (32316-2472)
PHONE................................850 576-9596
George A Small, *President*
Allison Small, *Principal*
Kenneth G Small, *Vice Pres*
EMP: 23 EST: 1942
SQ FT: 10,000
SALES (est): 3.5MM Privately Held
WEB: www.tallahasseewelding.com
SIC: 3599 7692 Machine shop, jobbing & repair; welding repair

(G-16512)
TARGET PRINT & MAIL
2843 Industrial Plaza Dr A1 (32301-3537)
PHONE................................850 671-6600
Courtney Carter, *Graphic Designe*
EMP: 10 EST: 2019
SALES (est): 3.1MM Privately Held
WEB: www.targetprintmail.com
SIC: 2752 Commercial printing, offset

(G-16513)
TERMINAL SERVICE COMPANY
2778 W Tharpe St (32303-8614)
P.O. Box 1200 (32302-1200)
PHONE................................850 739-5702
Thomas Panebianco, *President*
Bob Landrum, *Corp Secy*
Donnie Alford, *Vice Pres*
Joe Audie, *Vice Pres*
Donald Gainey, *Purch Agent*
EMP: 167 EST: 1953
SQ FT: 30,000
SALES (est): 2.1MM
SALES (corp-wide): 263.4MM Privately Held
WEB: www.mckenzietanklines.com
SIC: 3713 7539 3715 Tank truck bodies; trailer repair; truck trailers

▲ = Import ▼ =Export
◆ =Import/Export

HQ: Mckenzie Property Management, Inc.
1966 Commonwealth Ln
Tallahassee FL 32303
850 576-1221

(G-16514)
TRAK ENGINEERING INCORPORATED
2901 Crescent Dr (32301-3535)
PHONE..............................850 878-4585
John R Blyth, *President*
Rob Weaver, *Business Mgr*
Katherine M Blyth, *Vice Pres*
James Marlow, *Vice Pres*
Bolong Lui, *Engineer*
EMP: 36 **EST:** 1981
SQ FT: 9,000
SALES (est): 2.7MM **Privately Held**
WEB: www.trakeng.com
SIC: 3824 Fluid meters & counting devices

(G-16515)
TRANE US INC
104-1 Hamilton Park Dr (32304)
PHONE..............................850 574-1726
Tom Watley, *Service Mgr*
Len Martin, *Manager*
EMP: 13 **Privately Held**
WEB: www.trane.com
SIC: 3585 Refrigeration & heating equipment
HQ: Trane U.S. Inc.
800 Beaty St Ste E
Davidson NC 28036
704 655-4000

(G-16516)
TRI COUNTY METALS
3708 Nw Passage (32303-7803)
PHONE..............................850 574-4001
EMP: 7
SALES (corp-wide): 5.6MM **Privately Held**
WEB: www.tricountymetals.com
SIC: 3444 Sheet metalwork
PA: Tri County Metals
301 Se 16th St
Trenton FL 32693
352 463-8400

(G-16517)
TRI-STATE DEMOLITION LLC
5272 Crawfordville Rd (32305-8914)
P.O. Box 5581 (32314-5581)
PHONE..............................850 597-8722
Ryan M Carroll,
Roy L Avery III,
EMP: 8 **EST:** 2019
SALES (est): 595.3K **Privately Held**
WEB: www.tristatedemo.com
SIC: 1081 Metal mining exploration & development services

(G-16518)
TYSON PETROLEUM CONTRS LLC
5311 Tallapoosa Rd (32303-7924)
P.O. Box 180730 (32318-0007)
PHONE..............................850 727-0082
Shannon Tyson, *Manager*
Hunter Tyson,
Marcus Tyson,
EMP: 10 **EST:** 2020
SALES (est): 1MM **Privately Held**
WEB: www.tysonpetroleumcontr.com
SIC: 1389 7389 Construction, repair & dismantling services;

(G-16519)
ULTRA-MAX LLC
3115 Gallimore Dr (32305-6715)
P.O. Box 521 (32302-0521)
PHONE..............................850 728-8442
Ernest Jones,
EMP: 13 **EST:** 2019
SALES (est): 535.6K **Privately Held**
SIC: 2099 Food preparations

(G-16520)
VELOCITY MACHINE WORKS LLC
364 Marpan Ln (32305-0904)
PHONE..............................850 727-5066
Hillar Kalda, *Partner*
Jacob Money, *Info Tech Mgr*

EMP: 10 **EST:** 2013
SALES (est): 834.8K **Privately Held**
WEB: www.velocitymachineworks.com
SIC: 3599 Machine shop, jobbing & repair

(G-16521)
VY SPINE LLC ✪
2236 Capital Cir Ne # 103 (32308-8305)
PHONE..............................866 489-7746
Jordan Hendrickson,
EMP: 9 **EST:** 2021
SALES (est): 353.6K **Privately Held**
WEB: www.vyspine.com
SIC: 3842 Surgical appliances & supplies

(G-16522)
WILLIAMS ORTHTC-PROSTHETIC INC
2360 Centerville Rd (32308-4318)
P.O. Box 15035 (32317-5035)
PHONE..............................850 385-6655
Richard C Williams Jr, *President*
Cathy Williams, *Vice Pres*
Nathan Phillips, *Engineer*
EMP: 9 **EST:** 1952
SQ FT: 3,200
SALES (est): 1.4MM **Privately Held**
WEB: www.williamsoandp.com
SIC: 3842 Orthopedic appliances; limbs, artificial

Tamarac
Broward County

(G-16523)
ALEGRO INDUSTRIES INC
7880 N University Dr # 200 (33321-2124)
PHONE..............................702 943-0978
Mario Gaete, *President*
EMP: 57 **EST:** 2010
SQ FT: 5,000
SALES (est): 6.3MM **Privately Held**
SIC: 3672 Printed circuit boards

(G-16524)
AMERICAN METAL FABRICATION LLC
5476 Nw 59th Pl (33319-2432)
PHONE..............................954 736-9819
Cassandra J Lyle, *Manager*
EMP: 8 **EST:** 2016
SALES (est): 65.7K **Privately Held**
SIC: 3499 Fabricated metal products

(G-16525)
AMERICAN MOLD DETECTIVES INC
8201 Nw 100th Ter (33321-1240)
PHONE..............................954 729-0640
Brian R Andy, *Principal*
EMP: 8 **EST:** 2010
SALES (est): 129.8K **Privately Held**
SIC: 3544 Industrial molds

(G-16526)
AUTHORITY SOFTWARE LLC
7154 N University Dr # 211 (33321-2916)
PHONE..............................877 603-9653
Louis A Mandic, *Mng Member*
Natalie Perez-Mandic, *Mng Member*
Michael Yuen, *Director*
EMP: 6 **EST:** 2006
SALES (est): 579.2K **Privately Held**
WEB: www.authoritysoftware.com
SIC: 7372 Prepackaged software

(G-16527)
AZCUE PUMPS USA INC
10308 W Mcnab Rd (33321-1813)
PHONE..............................954 597-7602
Themis Giachos Sr, *President*
Ana Maria Giachos, *Vice Pres*
Lynn Teti, *Sales Staff*
◆ **EMP:** 5 **EST:** 1997
SALES (est): 501K **Privately Held**
WEB: www.azcuepumps.com
SIC: 3561 Industrial pumps & parts

(G-16528)
D & G CUSTOM CABINETRY INC
5712 Coco Palm Dr (33319-6115)
PHONE..............................954 561-8822
▲ **EMP:** 15

SALES (est): 2.1MM **Privately Held**
SIC: 2434 Mfg Wood Kitchen Cabinets

(G-16529)
DESH-VIDESH MEDIA GROUP INC
10088 W Mcnab Rd (33321-1895)
PHONE..............................954 784-8100
Aruna R Shah, *President*
Sheetal Shah, *Vice Pres*
Raj Shah, *Manager*
Rajni Shah, *Admin Sec*
EMP: 14 **EST:** 1993
SALES (est): 3MM **Privately Held**
WEB: www.deshvidesh.com
SIC: 2721 Magazines: publishing only, not printed on site

(G-16530)
ELECTRICAL CONTROLS INC
Also Called: E C I
9510 Bradshaw Ln (33321-6357)
PHONE..............................954 801-6846
Gregory Anderson, *President*
Elaine Anderson, *Corp Secy*
EMP: 10 **EST:** 1973
SQ FT: 15,000
SALES (est): 467.8K **Privately Held**
SIC: 3613 3625 1731 Panelboards & distribution boards, electric; relays & industrial controls; electronic controls installation

(G-16531)
FLORIDA A&G CO INC
Also Called: Arch Mirror North
10200 Nw 67th St (33321-6404)
P.O. Box 25127, Fort Lauderdale (33320-5127)
PHONE..............................800 432-8132
Leon Silverstein, *President*
Robert Silverstein, *Director*
◆ **EMP:** 1570 **EST:** 1989
SQ FT: 135,000
SALES (est): 61.6MM **Privately Held**
SIC: 3442 5039 Metal doors; glass construction materials

(G-16532)
GRAPHIC AND PRINTING SVCS CORP
Also Called: Image Impressions
5035 Nw 37th Ave (33309-3301)
PHONE..............................954 486-8868
Ray Cheng, *President*
Julianne Cheng, *Director*
▲ **EMP:** 7 **EST:** 1995
SALES (est): 826.9K **Privately Held**
SIC: 2752 2759 Commercial printing, offset; commercial printing

(G-16533)
IQ FORMULATIONS LLC
Also Called: Metabolic Nutrition
10151 Nw 67th St (33321-6400)
PHONE..............................954 533-9256
Jay Cohen, *Mng Member*
▲ **EMP:** 51 **EST:** 2010
SALES (est): 16MM **Privately Held**
WEB: www.iqformulations.com
SIC: 2023 7372 Dietary supplements, dairy & non-dairy based; application computer software

(G-16534)
JCS LIMITED CORPORATION
7611 Nw 70th Ave (33321-5224)
PHONE..............................954 822-2887
Jose E Morales, *President*
EMP: 7 **EST:** 2015
SALES (est): 356.5K **Privately Held**
SIC: 2434 1799 Wood kitchen cabinets; kitchen & bathroom remodeling

(G-16535)
LIGHTFIRE HOLDINGS LLC
Also Called: Kanger Wholesale USA
10601 State St Ste 5 (33321-6420)
PHONE..............................866 375-0541
Muru Kannayan, *CEO*
Jokeswari Kandasamy, *Manager*
EMP: 8 **EST:** 2016
SALES (est): 339.1K **Privately Held**
WEB: www.kangerwholesaleusa.com
SIC: 3634 3911 Cigarette lighters, electric; cigar & cigarette accessories

(G-16536)
METAL BUILDING KINGS
8050 N University Dr (33321-2115)
PHONE..............................412 522-4797
Aaron Troy, *President*
EMP: 9 **EST:** 2016
SQ FT: 1,500
SALES (est): 575.1K **Privately Held**
WEB: www.metalgaragekits.com
SIC: 3448 Prefabricated metal buildings

(G-16537)
MULTIPLE TECH INDUSTRIES INC
7809 W Commercial Blvd (33351-4382)
PHONE..............................561 795-0759
Juan I Alvarado, *Director*
EMP: 7 **EST:** 2001
SALES (est): 124.5K **Privately Held**
SIC: 3999 Manufacturing industries

(G-16538)
NEW VISION PHARMACEUTICALS LLC
10200 Nw 67th St (33321-6404)
PHONE..............................954 721-5000
Alan Petro, *CEO*
Carla Goffstein, *CFO*
EMP: 113 **EST:** 2020
SQ FT: 165,000
SALES (est): 13.4MM **Privately Held**
WEB: www.newvisionpharmaceuticals.com
SIC: 2834 5122 Pharmaceutical preparations; drugs, proprietaries & sundries

(G-16539)
PARASOL FILMS INC
9503 Nw 73rd St (33321-3024)
PHONE..............................954 478-8661
Erik Baquero, *Director*
EMP: 8 **EST:** 2001
SALES (est): 237.5K **Privately Held**
SIC: 2851 Paints & allied products

(G-16540)
RICHLINE GROUP INC
Also Called: Aurafin-Oroamerica
6701 Nob Hill Rd (33321-6402)
PHONE..............................954 718-3200
Michael Milgrom, *President*
Moss Makhoulian, *Vice Pres*
Beppe Monte, *Vice Pres*
Bruce Sasson, *Vice Pres*
Liz Truman, *Vice Pres*
EMP: 300
SALES (corp-wide): 354.6B **Publicly Held**
WEB: www.richlinegroup.com
SIC: 3911 Necklaces, precious metal
HQ: Richline Group, Inc.
1385 Broadway Fl 14
New York NY 10018

(G-16541)
RONAELE MUSTANG INC
5965 Manchester Way (33321-4192)
PHONE..............................954 319-7433
Edward R Monfort, *President*
Suzane Monfort, *Principal*
EMP: 8 **EST:** 2005
SALES (est): 112.9K **Privately Held**
SIC: 3824 Gas meters, domestic & large capacity: industrial

(G-16542)
SHILOH IMPORT/EXPORT LLC
7049 Woodmont Way (33321-2655)
PHONE..............................404 514-4109
Conrad Rowe, *CEO*
EMP: 6 **EST:** 2014
SALES (est): 337.6K **Privately Held**
SIC: 2099 Chili pepper or powder

(G-16543)
SOUTH FLORIDA PARENTING
6501 Nob Hill Rd (33321-6422)
PHONE..............................954 747-3050
Justo Rey, *President*
EMP: 83 **EST:** 1990
SALES (est): 1.1MM **Privately Held**
WEB: www.sun-sentinel.com
SIC: 2721 Magazines: publishing only, not printed on site

HQ: Sun-Sentinel Company, Llc
500 E Broward Blvd # 800
Fort Lauderdale FL 33394
954 356-4000

(G-16544)
WINSTON & SONS INC
9735 Nw 76th St (33321-1954)
PHONE...............................954 562-1984
Frank Winston Jr, *President*
Donna Johnson, *Vice Pres*
Richard Winston, *Treasurer*
Anna Winston, *Admin Sec*
EMP: 10 **EST:** 1974
SQ FT: 15,000
SALES (est): 379.4K **Privately Held**
SIC: 2511 2522 Wood household furniture;
office furniture, except wood

Tampa
Hillsborough County

(G-16545)
1506 N FLORIDA LLC
1505 N Florida Ave (33602-2613)
P.O. Box 800 (33601-0800)
PHONE...............................813 229-0900
Michael Kass, *Manager*
EMP: 6 **EST:** 2010
SALES (est): 363.6K **Privately Held**
WEB: www.garagistemeadery.com
SIC: 2084 Wines

(G-16546)
3B GLOBAL LLC (PA)
Also Called: Oral Stericlean
1202 Race Track Rd (33626)
PHONE...............................813 350-7872
Teresa Birney,
▲ **EMP:** 5 **EST:** 2011
SALES (est): 2.4MM **Privately Held**
WEB: www.go3bglobal.com
SIC: 3843 Sterilizers, dental

(G-16547)
**A JS PRO PERCUSSION
CENTER**
4340 W Hillsborough Ave # 208
(33614-5560)
PHONE...............................813 361-4939
Aj Altieri, *President*
Grace Altieri, *Treasurer*
EMP: 8 **EST:** 1999
SQ FT: 8,000
SALES (est): 463.9K **Privately Held**
WEB: www.propercussion.com
SIC: 3931 Drums, parts & accessories
(musical instruments)

(G-16548)
A&J MANUFACTURING INC
Also Called: Chargriller
5001 W Cypress St (33607-3803)
PHONE...............................912 638-4724
John Simms II, *President*
▲ **EMP:** 45 **EST:** 2007
SALES (est): 4MM **Privately Held**
SIC: 3631 Barbecues, grills & braziers
(outdoor cooking)

(G-16549)
AA CASEY COMPANY
5124 N Nebraska Ave (33603-2364)
PHONE...............................813 234-8831
John A Casey, *President*
Deeann Curci, *Corp Secy*
Richard Casey, *Vice Pres*
Rick Salm, *Buyer*
Manuel Whitworth, *Sales Staff*
EMP: 15 **EST:** 1987
SALES (est): 3.5MM **Privately Held**
WEB: www.aacasey.com
SIC: 3531 Construction machinery

(G-16550)
**AAA-AFFORDABLE PALLETS &
REELS**
2811 N 76th St (33619-2523)
PHONE...............................813 740-8009
EMP: 8
SALES (est): 490K **Privately Held**
SIC: 2448 Mfg Wood Pallets/Skids

(G-16551)
AARONS PALLETS
5006 S 50th St (33619-9515)
PHONE...............................813 627-3225
Aaron Gavrian, *Principal*
EMP: 8 **EST:** 2012
SALES (est): 294.8K **Privately Held**
WEB: www.aaronspallets.com
SIC: 2448 Pallets, wood

(G-16552)
ABAWI FIT LLC
1327 E 7th Ave Ste 204 (33605-3607)
PHONE...............................813 215-1833
Wade Abawi, *CEO*
Jonathan Nimphie, *COO*
EMP: 8 **EST:** 2018
SALES (est): 100K **Privately Held**
SIC: 7372 Application computer software

(G-16553)
ABBEY ROGERS
10150 Highland Manor Dr (33610-9713)
PHONE...............................813 645-1400
William B Simons IV, *President*
John Felter, *Engineer*
Will Thurman, *Teacher*
EMP: 5 **EST:** 2009
SALES (est): 377.5K **Privately Held**
WEB: www.abbeyrogers.com
SIC: 3491 Process control regulator valves

(G-16554)
ABCO INDUSTRIES LLC
5604 W Linebaugh Ave (33624-5071)
PHONE...............................813 605-5900
Adilen Lio,
EMP: 6 **EST:** 2015
SALES (est): 458K **Privately Held**
SIC: 2393 3172 Duffle bags, canvas:
made from purchased materials; personal
leather goods

(G-16555)
ACACIA INC
904 N Rome Ave (33606-1040)
P.O. Box 4527 (33677-4527)
PHONE...............................813 253-2789
Mike Griggs, *President*
◆ **EMP:** 10 **EST:** 1997
SALES (est): 736.2K **Privately Held**
WEB: www.acacia-inc.com
SIC: 3089 Plastics products

(G-16556)
**ACCENTIA
BIOPHARMACEUTICALS (PA)**
324 S Hyde Park Ave # 350 (33606-4127)
PHONE...............................813 864-2554
Francis E O Donnell Jr, *Ch of Bd*
Samuel S Duffey, *President*
Douglas W Calder, *Vice Pres*
Garrison J Hasara, *CFO*
Carlos F Santos PHD, *Officer*
EMP: 15 **EST:** 2002
SQ FT: 7,400
SALES (est): 8.5MM **Privately Held**
WEB: www.accentia.net
SIC: 2834 Pharmaceutical preparations

(G-16557)
**ACCURATE WLDG
FABRICATION LLC**
11029 Clay Pit Rd (33610-9741)
PHONE...............................727 483-3125
Gordon Smith,
EMP: 5 **EST:** 2017
SALES (est): 357.5K **Privately Held**
SIC: 7692 Welding repair

(G-16558)
**ADM II EXHIBITS & DISPLAYS
INC**
5690 W Crenshaw St (33634-3013)
PHONE...............................813 887-1960
Susan Tanonico, *President*
Shannon Bennett, *VP Sls/Mktg*
Tony Ricci, *Marketing Staff*
James Bardin, *Software Engr*
Kat Bedell, *Executive*
EMP: 15 **EST:** 1987
SQ FT: 3,000
SALES (est): 2.3MM **Privately Held**
WEB: www.admtwo.com
SIC: 3993 Signs & advertising specialties

(G-16559)
ADSEVERO LLC
8875 Hdden Rver Pkwy Ste (33637)
PHONE...............................813 508-0616
Oscar Flores, *CEO*
Alain Collins, *Vice Pres*
EMP: 5 **EST:** 2009
SALES (est): 561.4K **Privately Held**
WEB: www.adsevero.com
SIC: 3571 Electronic computers

(G-16560)
**ADVANCED PROSTHETICS
AMER INC**
Also Called: Advanced In Home Prosthetics
15043 Bruce B Downs Blvd (33647-1388)
PHONE...............................813 631-9400
Brandon Courtade, *Branch Mgr*
EMP: 18
SALES (corp-wide): 1.1B **Publicly Held**
SIC: 3842 Surgical appliances & supplies
HQ: Advanced Prosthetics Of America, Inc.
601 Mount Homer Rd
Eustis FL 32726
352 383-0396

(G-16561)
**ADVANCED TECH & TSTG LABS
INC**
17952 Cachet Isle Dr (33647-2702)
PHONE...............................352 871-3802
Lovely Goswami, *President*
Dilip Goswami, *Director*
EMP: 6 **EST:** 1994
SQ FT: 2,000
SALES (est): 1.2MM **Privately Held**
WEB: www.molekule.com
SIC: 3564 Air purification equipment; fil-
ters, air: furnaces, air conditioning equip-
ment, etc.

(G-16562)
AERO SIMULATION INC
8720 E Sligh Ave (33610-9206)
PHONE...............................813 628-4447
Michael Conti, *CEO*
Daniel Deschnow, *Vice Pres*
Kevin Cahill, *Opers Staff*
Luke Archer, *Engineer*
Mike Conti, *Engineer*
EMP: 125 **EST:** 1983
SALES (est): 42.3MM **Privately Held**
WEB: www.aerosimulation.com
SIC: 3699 Flight simulators (training aids),
electronic

(G-16563)
**AFFINITY CHEMICAL
WOODBINE LLC**
4532 W Swann Ave (33609-3722)
PHONE...............................973 873-4070
Tom Drelles, *Plant Supt*
Matthew Reichl, *Analyst*
EMP: 9 **EST:** 2011
SALES (est): 1.7MM **Privately Held**
WEB: www.affinitychemical.com
SIC: 2819 Industrial inorganic chemicals

(G-16564)
**AFLG INVSTMNTS-INDUSTRIALS
LLC (PA)**
701 Suth Hward Ave 106 (33606)
PHONE...............................813 443-8203
Freddy Russian, *Principal*
Anthony Russian, *Assistant VP*
Doug Joseph,
◆ **EMP:** 4 **EST:** 2016
SALES (est): 6MM **Privately Held**
WEB: www.aflgholdings.com
SIC: 3542 3569 Mechanical (pneumatic or
hydraulic) metal forming machines; liquid
automation machinery & equipment

(G-16565)
AGGRESSIVE BOX INC
5444 Pioneer Park Blvd A (33634-4309)
PHONE...............................813 901-9600
Keith Oller, *President*
Aleshia Oller, *Vice Pres*
Bryan Alfonso, *Sales Staff*
Lisa Oller, *Manager*
EMP: 12 **EST:** 1995
SQ FT: 4,000

SALES (est): 3.4MM **Privately Held**
WEB: www.aggressivebox.com
SIC: 2653 Boxes, corrugated: made from
purchased materials

(G-16566)
AGILE RISK MANAGEMENT LLC
Also Called: F-Response
3333 W Kennedy Blvd # 201 (33609-2959)
PHONE...............................800 317-5497
Matthew M Shannon, *Principal*
Matthew J Decker,
Sean Lynch, *Analyst*
EMP: 5 **EST:** 2003
SQ FT: 1,300
SALES (est): 3.1MM **Privately Held**
WEB: www.f-response.com
SIC: 7372 Business oriented computer
software

(G-16567)
AIRITE AIR CONDITIONING INC
Also Called: Honeywell Authorized Dealer
5321 W Crenshaw St (33634-2406)
PHONE...............................813 886-0235
Bruce M Silverman, *President*
Victoria Silverman, *President*
Beth Moberly, *General Mgr*
Michael Venoy, *Exec VP*
Jeff Steiner, *Vice Pres*
EMP: 45 **EST:** 1970
SQ FT: 24,000
SALES (est): 6.9MM **Privately Held**
WEB: www.airiteair.com
SIC: 3444 1711 Sheet metalwork; warm
air heating & air conditioning contractor

(G-16568)
**AJENAT PHARMACEUTICALS
LLC ✪**
203 N Marion St (33602-4914)
PHONE...............................727 471-0850
Jugal Taneja, *Mng Member*
EMP: 200 **EST:** 2022
SALES (est): 15.8MM **Privately Held**
SIC: 2834 Druggists' preparations (phar-
maceuticals)

(G-16569)
AL-FA CABINETS INC
4803 N Grady Ave (33614-6301)
PHONE...............................813 876-4205
Hector Gonzalez Jr, *President*
Caridad Gonzalez, *Treasurer*
Hector Gonzales Sr, *Sales Staff*
EMP: 11 **EST:** 1973
SQ FT: 20,000
SALES (est): 309.3K **Privately Held**
WEB: www.alfacabinets.com
SIC: 2434 2431 Wood kitchen cabinets;
millwork

(G-16570)
ALDALI INC
4821 N Hale Ave (33614-6517)
PHONE...............................877 384-9494
Melissa Morgado, *President*
Melissa Astorquiza, *Exec Dir*
◆ **EMP:** 10 **EST:** 2009
SQ FT: 2,500
SALES (est): 925.6K **Privately Held**
SIC: 2833 Drugs & herbs: grading, grinding
& milling

(G-16571)
ALERE INC
1120 E Kennedy Blvd (33602-3580)
PHONE...............................813 898-5709
Lauri Benson, *Branch Mgr*
EMP: 9
SALES (corp-wide): 43B **Publicly Held**
WEB: www.globalpointofcare.abbott
SIC: 2835 In vitro & in vivo diagnostic sub-
stances
HQ: Alere Inc.
51 Sawyer Rd Ste 200
Waltham MA 02453
781 647-3900

(G-16572)
**ALL COAST MANUFACTURING
INC**
2433 S 86th St Ste F (33619-4909)
PHONE...............................813 626-2264
Jeff George, *President*
Roy George, *Vice Pres*

EMP: 6 **EST:** 1993
SALES (est): 821.3K **Privately Held**
SIC: 3334 Primary aluminum

(G-16573)
ALL NATURALS DIRECT
12191 W Linebaugh Ave (33626-1732)
PHONE.................................813 792-3777
Melony D Rivera, *Owner*
EMP: 9 **EST:** 2013
SALES (est): 339.3K **Privately Held**
SIC: 2032 5963 5149 Ethnic foods:
canned, jarred, etc.; Mexican foods: pack-
aged in cans, jars, etc.; food services, di-
rect sales; specialty food items

(G-16574)
ALLEGRA MARKETING
2705 N Falkenburg Rd (33619-0920)
PHONE.................................813 664-1129
Sam Mancie, *Owner*
Matt Shelley, *Accounts Mgr*
EMP: 8 **EST:** 2017
SALES (est): 590.3K **Privately Held**
WEB: www.allegramarketingprint.com
SIC: 2752 Commercial printing, offset

(G-16575)
**ALLIED FOAM FABRICATORS
LLC (PA)**
216 Kelsey Ln (33619-4300)
PHONE.................................813 626-0090
Alan Rash, *Mng Member*
EMP: 22 **EST:** 2020
SALES (est): 11.6MM **Privately Held**
WEB: www.alliedfoamfab.com
SIC: 3086 Packaging & shipping materials,
foamed plastic

(G-16576)
**ALLIED MANUFACTURING INC
(PA)**
Also Called: Dalpro Commercial Rfrgn
203 Kelsey Ln Ste G (33619-4334)
PHONE.................................813 502-0300
Jeffrey Montelione, *CEO*
Lili Montelione, *COO*
EMP: 5 **EST:** 2016
SALES (est): 1MM **Privately Held**
WEB: www.valprorefrigeration.com
SIC: 3585 Refrigeration & heating equip-
ment

(G-16577)
ALLIED TUBE & CONDUIT
5128 W Hanna Ave (33634-8020)
PHONE.................................813 623-2681
EMP: 7 **EST:** 2016
SALES (est): 151.9K **Privately Held**
WEB: www.alliedeg.us
SIC: 3317 Steel pipe & tubes

(G-16578)
**ALLSTATE LGHTNING
PRTCTION LLC**
7201 Sheldon Rd (33615-2328)
PHONE.................................813 240-2736
Jill Epperson, *Managing Prtnr*
EMP: 6 **EST:** 2014
SALES (est): 473.5K **Privately Held**
WEB: www.allstatelp.com
SIC: 3643 Lightning protection equipment

(G-16579)
ALPHAGRAPHICS US658
105 N Falkenburg Rd Ste D (33619-0902)
PHONE.................................813 689-7788
Art Coley, *President*
EMP: 9 **EST:** 2012
SALES (est): 231.9K **Privately Held**
WEB: www.alphagraphics.com
SIC: 2752 Commercial printing, litho-
graphic

(G-16580)
ALTEC INC
Also Called: Altec Service Center
1041 S 86th St (33619-4916)
PHONE.................................813 372-0058
EMP: 41
SALES (corp-wide): 1.2B **Privately Held**
WEB: www.altec.com
SIC: 3531 Derricks, except oil & gas field

PA: Altec, Inc.
210 Inverness Center Dr
Birmingham AL 35242
205 991-7733

(G-16581)
ALTERED MEDIA INC
100 S Ashley Dr Ste 600 (33602-5300)
PHONE.................................813 397-3892
Rashad Freeman, *CEO*
EMP: 10 **EST:** 2019
SALES (est): 592.7K **Privately Held**
SIC: 2741

(G-16582)
ALTIUM PACKAGING LLC
4961 Distribution Dr (33605-5925)
PHONE.................................813 248-4300
Tony Kalodimos, *Manager*
Jose Hernandez, *Maintence Staff*
EMP: 67
SQ FT: 22,500
SALES (corp-wide): 14.6B **Publicly Held**
WEB: www.altiumpkg.com
SIC: 3089 3085 Plastic containers, except
foam; plastics bottles
HQ: Altium Packaging Llc
2500 Windy Ridge Pkwy Se # 1400
Atlanta GA 30339
678 742-4600

(G-16583)
ALTO RECYCLING LLC
5701 W Linebaugh Ave (33624-5074)
PHONE.................................813 962-0140
Stewart Smith, *President*
EMP: 9 **EST:** 2004
SALES (est): 2MM **Privately Held**
WEB: www.altorecycling.net
SIC: 3559 Recycling machinery

(G-16584)
AMALIE OIL COMPANY (PA)
1601 Mcclosky Blvd (33605-6710)
PHONE.................................813 248-1988
Harry J Barket, *Ch of Bd*
John Osadnick, *Regional Mgr*
Richard Barkett, *COO*
Manny Bonet, *Exec VP*
Anthony Barkett, *Vice Pres*
◆ **EMP:** 103 **EST:** 1957
SQ FT: 135,000
SALES (est): 110.4MM **Privately Held**
WEB: www.amalie.com
SIC: 2992 3085 Lubricating oils; plastics
bottles

(G-16585)
AMC PHARMA USA LLC
201 E Kennedy Blvd (33602-5181)
PHONE.................................813 508-0160
Brett Scott,
EMP: 8
SALES (est): 317.1K **Privately Held**
SIC: 2023 Dietary supplements, dairy &
non-dairy based

(G-16586)
**AMERI PRODU PRODU COMPA
OF PIN**
12157 W Linebaugh Ave # 335
(33626-1732)
PHONE.................................813 925-0144
Joseph Muraco, *President*
Kevin Mullen, *Vice Pres*
EMP: 5 **EST:** 1995
SALES (est): 1.1MM **Privately Held**
WEB: www.americanproducts.com
SIC: 3443 Metal parts

(G-16587)
**AMERICAN BOTTLING
COMPANY**
Also Called: Seven-Up Snapple Southeast
5266 Eagle Trail Dr (33634-1295)
PHONE.................................813 806-2931
John Perry, *Manager*
EMP: 109
SQ FT: 53,997 **Publicly Held**
WEB: www.keurigdrpepper.com
SIC: 2086 Soft drinks: packaged in cans,
bottles, etc.
HQ: The American Bottling Company
6425 Hall Of Fame Ln
Frisco TX 75034

(G-16588)
**AMERICAN CITY BUS
JOURNALS INC**
Also Called: Tampa Bay Business Journal
4890 W Kennedy Blvd # 85 (33609-1851)
P.O. Box 24185 (33623-4185)
PHONE.................................813 873-8225
EMP: 9
SALES (corp-wide): 5B **Privately Held**
SIC: 2711 Newspapers-Publishing/Printing
HQ: American City Business Journals, Inc.
120 W Morehead St Ste 400
Charlotte NC 28202
704 973-1000

(G-16589)
**AMERICAN LOUVERED
PRODUCTS CO**
4910 W Knollwood St (33634-8073)
PHONE.................................813 884-1441
John Saunders, *President*
▲ **EMP:** 18 **EST:** 1959
SALES (est): 1.2MM **Privately Held**
SIC: 2431 Door shutters, wood; doors,
wood

(G-16590)
AMERICAN PRODUCTS INC
Also Called: API
13909 Lynmar Blvd (33626-3124)
PHONE.................................813 925-0144
Joseph Muraco, *President*
Kerri Beals, *General Mgr*
Kerri Muraco, *General Mgr*
Kevin Mullan, *Vice Pres*
Christopher Revoldt, *Prdtn Dir*
EMP: 5 **EST:** 2010
SALES (est): 5.2MM **Privately Held**
WEB: www.americanproducts.com
SIC: 3443 3354 3089 Metal parts; alu-
minum extruded products; extruded fin-
ished plastic products

(G-16591)
**AMERICAN SURGICAL MASK
LLC**
Also Called: American Surgical Mask Co
5508 N 50th St Ste 1000 (33610-4804)
PHONE.................................813 606-4510
Matthew Brandman, *CEO*
Eileen Legler, *Marketing Staff*
Kahora Watanabe,
Charles Young Jr,
EMP: 20 **EST:** 2020
SALES (est): 1.1MM **Privately Held**
SIC: 3841 Surgical instruments & appara-
tus

(G-16592)
AMERICAN VINYL COMPANY
6715 N 53rd St (33610-1905)
PHONE.................................813 663-0157
Eric J Wiborg II, *President*
EMP: 18
SALES (corp-wide): 9.6MM **Privately
Held**
WEB: www.avcplastics.com
SIC: 3312 Pipes & tubes
PA: American Vinyl Company
600 W 83rd St
Hialeah FL 33014
305 687-1863

(G-16593)
**AMORIM CORK COMPOSITES
INC**
6708 Harney Rd (33610-9250)
PHONE.................................800 558-3206
EMP: 35 **Privately Held**
WEB: www.amorimcorkcomposites.com
SIC: 2499 Cork & cork products
HQ: Amorim Cork Composites, Inc.
26112 110th St
Trevor WI 53179
262 862-2311

(G-16594)
**AMPHENOL CUSTOM CABLE
INC (HQ)**
Also Called: Custom Cable Industries
3221 Cherry Palm Dr (33619-8334)
PHONE.................................813 623-2232
Stewart Saad, *President*
Joe Macon, *General Mgr*

Tommy Creacy, *Superintendent*
Jaile Lima, *Vice Pres*
Steve Vickers, *Vice Pres*
EMP: 140 **EST:** 1999
SQ FT: 10,000
SALES (est): 71.9MM
SALES (corp-wide): 10.8B **Publicly Held**
WEB: www.customcable.com
SIC: 3827 3357 Optical instruments &
lenses; fiber optic cable (insulated)
PA: Amphenol Corporation
358 Hall Ave
Wallingford CT 06492
203 265-8900

(G-16595)
AMROB INC
Also Called: Atlantic Printing Ink Company
4719 N Thatcher Ave (33614-6935)
PHONE.................................813 238-6041
Robert C Pettit, *President*
Patrick Laden, *Vice Pres*
Patty Bortstrom, *Manager*
EMP: 6 **EST:** 1985
SQ FT: 10,000
SALES (est): 532.8K **Privately Held**
SIC: 2893 Printing ink

(G-16596)
**ANCHOR GLASS CONTAINER
CORP (PA)**
3001 N Rocky Point Dr E # 300
(33607-5875)
PHONE.................................813 884-0000
Nipesh Shah, *President*
Robert Dugger, *President*
Jason Achterberg, *General Mgr*
William Harper, *General Mgr*
Jason Stephens, *Business Mgr*
◆ **EMP:** 110 **EST:** 1997
SALES (est): 581.3MM **Privately Held**
WEB: www.anchorglass.com
SIC: 3221 Glass containers

(G-16597)
**ANCHOR MACHINE &
FABRICATING**
3905 E 7th Ave (33605-4555)
PHONE.................................813 247-3099
Jerome Majetich, *President*
Cheryl Majetich, *Vice Pres*
EMP: 12 **EST:** 1979
SQ FT: 10,000
SALES (est): 1MM **Privately Held**
WEB: www.anchormachineshop.com
SIC: 3599 3535 Machine shop, jobbing &
repair; conveyors & conveying equipment

(G-16598)
**ANDREWS SALES AGENCY
MANUFACTU**
3104 W San Rafael St (33629-5906)
PHONE.................................813 254-4959
Betty Andrews, *Principal*
EMP: 7 **EST:** 2004
SALES (est): 84.2K **Privately Held**
SIC: 2679 Converted paper products

(G-16599)
AOCLSC INC (HQ)
Also Called: Aocusa
1601 Mcclosky Blvd (33605-6731)
PHONE.................................813 248-1988
Harry Barkett, *President*
Ken Barkett, *CFO*
EMP: 75 **EST:** 2019
SALES (est): 44.2MM
SALES (corp-wide): 110.4MM **Privately
Held**
SIC: 2911 Greases, lubricating
PA: Amalie Oil Company
1601 Mcclosky Blvd
Tampa FL 33605
813 248-1988

(G-16600)
**APOLLO RETAIL SPECIALISTS
LLC (DH)**
4450 E Adamo Dr Ste 501 (33605-5941)
PHONE.................................813 712-2525
Mike Sunderland, *CEO*
Mike Torres, *General Mgr*
Debbie Sutton, *Regional Mgr*
Dustin Hall, *District Mgr*
Alison Schaefer, *District Mgr*

EMP: 55 EST: 2005
SALES (est): 55.4MM
SALES (corp-wide): 255.7MM **Privately Held**
WEB: www.apolloretail.com
SIC: **3432** 7389 2531 7349 Plumbing fixture fittings & trim; bicycle assembly service; assembly hall furniture; building maintenance services

(G-16601)
APPLIED TECHNOLOGIES GROUP INC
Also Called: Automated Integration
333 N Falkenburg Rd B227 (33619-7893)
P.O. Box 777, Brandon (33509-0777)
PHONE..................................813 413-7025
Steve Van Kley, *President*
Steve Kley, *Principal*
EMP: 7 EST: 2013
SQ FT: 5,000
SALES (est): 1.5MM **Privately Held**
WEB: www.uatgroup.com
SIC: **3823** 7373 8742 Industrial instrmnts msrmnt display/control process variable; computer integrated systems design; management consulting services

(G-16602)
AQUATECH MANUFACTURING LLC
7455 E Adamo Dr (33619-3433)
PHONE..................................813 664-0300
Reg Macquarrie, *Mng Member*
Joe Finella,
▲ EMP: 10 EST: 2011
SALES (est): 1.8MM **Privately Held**
SIC: **3589** Water treatment equipment, industrial

(G-16603)
ARGOS CEMENT LLC
2001 Maritime Blvd (33605-6760)
PHONE..................................813 247-4831
◆ EMP: 17 EST: 2014
SALES (est): 2.7MM **Privately Held**
SIC: **3241** Cement, hydraulic

(G-16604)
ARGOS USA LLC
5609 N 50th St (33610-4805)
PHONE..................................813 962-3213
EMP: 32 **Privately Held**
WEB: www.argos-us.com
SIC: **3273** Ready-mixed concrete
HQ: Argos Usa Llc
3015 Windward Plz Ste 300
Alpharetta GA 30005
678 368-4300

(G-16605)
ARIZONA BEVERAGE COMPANY LLC
1909 N Us Highway 301 # 130 (33619-2676)
PHONE..................................516 812-0303
Steve Sullivan, *Sales Dir*
Thomas Deluca, *Manager*
▼ EMP: 10
SALES (corp-wide): 284.6MM **Privately Held**
SIC: **2086** Iced tea & fruit drinks, bottled & canned
HQ: Arizona Beverage Company Llc
60 Crossways Park Dr W # 400
Woodbury NY 11797
516 812-0300

(G-16606)
ARM ALMNUM RLING MNFCTURES LLC
2433 S 86th St Ste F (33619-4909)
PHONE..................................813 626-2264
Jeff George, *Principal*
EMP: 9 EST: 2016
SALES (est): 250.4K **Privately Held**
SIC: **3999** Manufacturing industries

(G-16607)
ARMA HOLDINGS INC
3030 N Rocky Point Dr W # 800 (33607-5859)
PHONE..................................813 402-0667
Todd Schweitzer, *CEO*
Brian Overstreet, *COO*

Charles Broms, *Vice Pres*
Rick Gillies, *CTO*
James Fugit, *Director*
EMP: 12 EST: 2013
SALES (est): 291.1K **Privately Held**
SIC: **3728** 7376 3484 3483 Aircraft parts & equipment; computer facilities management; small arms; ammunition, except for small arms; computer integrated systems design

(G-16608)
ARMOR OIL PRODUCTS LLC
Also Called: Engine Armour Products
1601 Mcclosky Blvd (33605-6731)
PHONE..................................813 248-1988
David A Barkett,
▲ EMP: 6 EST: 2001
SALES (est): 827.2K **Privately Held**
WEB: www.enginearmour.com
SIC: **2992** 5172 Lubricating oils & greases; petroleum products

(G-16609)
ARROW SHEET METAL WORKS INC
2710 N 36th St (33605-3194)
PHONE..................................813 247-2179
Kathy Philippus, *President*
Robert L Philippus, *Vice Pres*
EMP: 27 EST: 1950
SQ FT: 15,000
SALES (est): 4.9MM **Privately Held**
WEB: www.arrowsheetmetal.com
SIC: **3444** Sheet metal specialties, not stamped

(G-16610)
ARXADA LLC
4910 Savarese Cir (33634-2403)
PHONE..................................813 286-0404
Saida Ibrani, *Research*
Theresa Palmer, *Contract Mgr*
Joshua Uyaan, *Manager*
Daniel Kleeman, *Senior Mgr*
Yamir Lopez, *Director*
EMP: 25
SALES (corp-wide): 2.6MM **Privately Held**
WEB: www.lonza.com
SIC: **2834** Pharmaceutical preparations
HQ: Arxada, Llc
412 Mount Kemble Ave # 20
Morristown NJ 07960
201 316-9200

(G-16611)
ASAP MAGAZINE & NEWSPAPER
106 W Haya St (33603-2033)
P.O. Box 7635 (33673-7635)
PHONE..................................813 238-0184
Leo Hooper, *Owner*
EMP: 8 EST: 1996
SALES (est): 392.3K **Privately Held**
SIC: **2711** Newspapers

(G-16612)
ASHBERRY ACQUISITION COMPANY (PA)
Also Called: Ashberry Water Conditioning
5409 S West Shore Blvd (33611-5655)
PHONE..................................813 248-0055
James T McMurray, *President*
William Welch, *Vice Pres*
Sable Lauderdale, *Assistant*
Michelle Johnson, *Clerk*
EMP: 10 EST: 1947
SQ FT: 3,600
SALES (est): 4.1MM **Privately Held**
WEB: www.ashberrywater.com
SIC: **3589** 7359 5999 Water filters & softeners, household type; equipment rental & leasing; water purification equipment

(G-16613)
ASSOCIATED MATERIALS LLC
933 Chad Ln (33619-4331)
PHONE..................................813 621-7058
EMP: 7
SALES (corp-wide): 1.1B **Privately Held**
WEB: www.associatedmaterials.com
SIC: **3089** Plastic containers, except foam

PA: Associated Materials, Llc
3773 State Rd
Cuyahoga Falls OH 44223
330 929-1811

(G-16614)
ATALY INC
Also Called: Ataly Graphics
5828 Johns Rd (33634-4420)
PHONE..................................813 880-9142
Alan Jones, *President*
Wade Carlson, *QC Mgr*
Suzanne Hillabrandt, *Sales Staff*
Nick Jones, *Sales Staff*
Christine H Jones, *Director*
EMP: 40 EST: 1979
SQ FT: 12,000
SALES (est): 5MM **Privately Held**
WEB: www.ataly.com
SIC: **2396** 3993 Screen printing on fabric articles; advertising novelties

(G-16615)
ATITLAN ENTERPRISES LLC
Also Called: Hathaspace
16116 Lake Magdalene Blvd (33613-1249)
PHONE..................................813 362-1909
Marcus Lara, *Mng Member*
Dean Chandra, *Mng Member*
EMP: 8 EST: 2017
SALES (est): 829.7K **Privately Held**
SIC: **3564** Air purification equipment

(G-16616)
ATKORE PLASTIC PIPE CORP
Also Called: Heritage Plastics
5128 W Hanna Ave (33634-8020)
PHONE..................................813 884-2525
RAD Bush, *Production*
Tyler Morrison, *Plant Engr*
Lorene Risen, *Manager*
Steve Ferreri, *Supervisor*
Shannon Johnson, *Maintence Staff*
EMP: 15 **Publicly Held**
WEB: www.heritageplastics.com
SIC: **3084** Plastics pipe
HQ: Atkore Plastic Pipe Corporation
1202 N Bowie Dr
Weatherford TX 76086
817 594-8791

(G-16617)
ATLAS COPCO COMPRESSORS LLC
1100 N 50th St Ste 4e (33619-3248)
PHONE..................................813 247-7231
EMP: 7
SALES (corp-wide): 12.1B **Privately Held**
WEB: www.atlascopco.us
SIC: **3563** Air & gas compressors
HQ: Atlas Copco Compressors Llc
300 Technology Center Way # 550
Rock Hill SC 29730
866 472-1015

(G-16618)
AVATAR PACKAGING INC
5110 W Idlewild Ave (33634-8024)
PHONE..................................813 888-9141
Vance D Fairbanks Jr, *CEO*
Denise M Fairbanks, *President*
Robert J Upcavage, *Vice Pres*
Cody Fairbanks, *Sales Associate*
Cynthia Fairbanks, *Admin Sec*
EMP: 30 EST: 1991
SQ FT: 24,700
SALES (est): 3.6MM **Privately Held**
WEB: www.avatarpackaging.com
SIC: **2653** 5113 Boxes, corrugated: made from purchased materials; corrugated & solid fiber boxes

(G-16619)
AVI-SPL HOLDINGS INC (PA)
6301 Benjamin Rd Ste 101 (33634-5115)
PHONE..................................866 708-5034
John Zettel, *CEO*
Phil Marlowe, *Managing Dir*
Mike Peterson, *Regional Mgr*
Steve Benjamin, *Exec VP*
Dianna Wallace, *Vice Pres*
▼ EMP: 2000 EST: 2008

SALES (est): 1B **Privately Held**
WEB: www.avispl.com
SIC: **3669** 3861 3663 3651 Intercommunication systems, electric; photographic equipment & supplies; radio & TV communications equipment; household audio & video equipment; voice, data & video wiring contractor; electrical appliances, television & radio

(G-16620)
AVI-SPL LLC (DH)
6301 Benjamin Rd Ste 101 (33634-5115)
PHONE..................................813 884-7168
John Zettel, *CEO*
Tim Riek, *President*
Bob Brown, *Business Mgr*
Chris Spence, *Business Mgr*
Steve Benjamin, *Exec VP*
▼ EMP: 258 EST: 1980
SQ FT: 38,000
SALES (est): 509.3MM **Privately Held**
WEB: www.avispl.com
SIC: **3669** 5064 3861 3663 Intercommunication systems, electric; electrical appliances, television & radio; photographic equipment & supplies; radio & TV communications equipment; household audio & video equipment; projection apparatus, motion picture & slide

(G-16621)
AWNINGS BY COVERSOL
5211 W Hillsborough Ave (33634-5308)
PHONE..................................813 251-4774
EMP: 21
SQ FT: 30,000
SALES: 2MM
SALES (corp-wide): 2.3MM **Privately Held**
SIC: **2394** Mfg Canvas/Related Products
PA: Lad Diversified Holdings Llc
15619 Premiere Dr Ste 201
Tampa FL

(G-16622)
AXIOM DIAGNOSTICS INC
4309 W Tyson Ave (33611-3435)
P.O. Box 13275 (33681-3275)
PHONE..................................813 902-9888
Jesse M Carter, *President*
EMP: 6 EST: 1999
SALES (est): 698.7K **Privately Held**
WEB: www.axiomdiagnostics.com
SIC: **3821** Clinical laboratory instruments, except medical & dental

(G-16623)
AXON CIRCUIT INC (PA)
424 S Ware Blvd Ste A (33619-4402)
PHONE..................................407 265-7980
Chandra Patel, *President*
Amrish G Patel, *Vice Pres*
Jayan Sanghani, *Vice Pres*
Suresh Patel, *Treasurer*
Ronnie Shankle, *Sales Mgr*
▲ EMP: 45 EST: 1990
SQ FT: 25,000
SALES (est): 6.2MM **Privately Held**
WEB: www.axoncircuit.com
SIC: **3672** Printed circuit boards

(G-16624)
AZZ POWDER COATING - TAMPA LLC (HQ)
4901 Distribution Dr (33605-5925)
PHONE..................................813 390-2802
David L Bridgforth, *CEO*
EMP: 6 EST: 2011
SALES (est): 1.6MM
SALES (corp-wide): 902.6MM **Publicly Held**
SIC: **3479** 3399 Coating of metals & formed products; powder, metal
PA: Azz Inc.
3100 W 7th St Ste 500
Fort Worth TX 76107
817 810-0095

(G-16625)
B2B SIGN RESOURCE
13359 W Hillsborough Ave # 104 (33635-9543)
PHONE..................................813 855-7446
Dori Hazama, *COO*
EMP: 7 EST: 2018

SALES (est): 750.6K **Privately Held**
WEB: www.b2bsr.com
SIC: 3993 Signs & advertising specialties

(G-16626)
BADER PROSTHETICS & ORTHOTICS
Also Called: Kinetic Research
5513 W Sligh Ave (33634-4431)
PHONE......................................813 962-6100
Wade Bader, *President*
Reid Bader, *Vice Pres*
Valarie Brien, *Vice Pres*
EMP: 15 EST: 1992
SQ FT: 3,000
SALES (est): 1.2MM **Privately Held**
WEB: www.kineticresearch.com
SIC: 3842 Prosthetic appliances

(G-16627)
BALL METAL BEVERAGE CONT CORP
Ball Metal Beverage Cont Div
4700 Whiteway Dr (33617-3424)
PHONE......................................813 980-6073
Drew May, *Superintendent*
Rachel Ford, *Production*
Jesse Bealor, *Purchasing*
Jason Ketchel, *Engrg Mgr*
John Balkcom, *Engineer*
EMP: 253
SALES (corp-wide): 13.8B **Publicly Held**
SIC: 3411 Metal cans
HQ: Ball Metal Beverage Container Corp.
9300 W 108th Cir
Westminster CO 80021

(G-16628)
BARE ARII LLC ✪
10610 N 30th St Apt 13g (33612-6341)
PHONE......................................352 701-6625
Arianna Wade, *Mng Member*
EMP: 7 EST: 2021
SALES (est): 300.6K **Privately Held**
SIC: 3999 Eyelashes, artificial

(G-16629)
BAUSCH & LOMB INCORPORATED
8500 Hidden River Pkwy (33637-1014)
PHONE......................................813 975-7700
Isis Caballer, *Mfg Staff*
Juan Lopez, *Mfg Staff*
Peter Pich, *Production*
Iavor Mihalkov, *Research*
Andrew Sullivan, *Research*
EMP: 201
SALES (corp-wide): 8.6B **Privately Held**
WEB: www.bausch.com
SIC: 3851 Ophthalmic goods
HQ: Bausch & Lomb Incorporated
400 Somerset Corp Blvd
Bridgewater NJ 08807
585 338-6000

(G-16630)
BAY AREA GRAPHICS
4040 E Adamo Dr (33605-5904)
PHONE......................................813 247-2400
Wayne Ricketts, *Partner*
Nanci Ricketts, *Partner*
Jeff Soto, *VP Opers*
EMP: 6 EST: 1985
SQ FT: 5,000
SALES (est): 440.1K **Privately Held**
WEB: www.bayareagraphics.com
SIC: 2752 Commercial printing, offset

(G-16631)
BAY HARBOR SHEET METAL INC
7909 Professional Pl (33637-6747)
P.O. Box 216, Mango (33550-0216)
PHONE......................................813 740-8662
Darrel Peterson, *President*
EMP: 10 EST: 2002
SALES (est): 1.6MM **Privately Held**
WEB: www.bayharborservices.com
SIC: 3444 Sheet metalwork

(G-16632)
BAY NETWORKS INC
6601 Memorial Hwy 200 (33615-4501)
PHONE......................................813 249-8103
EMP: 12 EST: 2008

SQ FT: 5,000
SALES (est): 1.3MM **Privately Held**
SIC: 2211 Cotton Broadwoven Fabric Mill

(G-16633)
BAYTRONICS MANUFACTURING INC
620 E Twiggs St Ste 110 (33602-3938)
PHONE......................................813 434-0401
Timothy Johnson, *President*
EMP: 12 EST: 2011
SALES (est): 291.7K **Privately Held**
SIC: 3559 3825 3674 Semiconductor manufacturing machinery; internal combustion engine analyzers, to test electronics; semiconductors & related devices

(G-16634)
BBJ ENVIRONMENTAL LLC
Also Called: B B J Environmental Solutions
9416 E Broadway Ave (33619-7723)
P.O. Box 110301, Stamford CT (06911-0301)
PHONE......................................813 622-8550
Robert Baker, *CEO*
EMP: 7 EST: 2009
SALES (est): 449.3K **Privately Held**
WEB: www.bbjenviro.com
SIC: 2899 Chemical preparations

(G-16635)
BEACH PRODUCTS INC
Also Called: Beach Pharmaceuticals
3010 W De Leon St Ste 100 (33609-4008)
P.O. Box 13447 (33681-3447)
PHONE......................................813 839-6565
Richard S Jenkins, *President*
Carole C Jenkins, *Treasurer*
Kelly Harrison, *Senior Mgr*
EMP: 7 EST: 1958
SQ FT: 10,000
SALES (est): 1.9MM **Privately Held**
WEB: www.beachlabs.com
SIC: 2834 Pharmaceutical preparations

(G-16636)
BEAUTIFUL CABINETS CORP
1903 W Skagway Ave (33604-1035)
PHONE......................................813 486-9034
Claudia Ardon, *President*
EMP: 7 EST: 2008
SALES (est): 87.6K **Privately Held**
SIC: 2434 Wood kitchen cabinets

(G-16637)
BELLINI SYSTEMS INC
4925 Indpdnc Pkwy Ste 400 (33634-7551)
PHONE......................................813 264-9252
Lauren Bellini, *Admin Sec*
EMP: 8 EST: 2001
SALES (est): 239.6K **Privately Held**
SIC: 7372 Prepackaged software

(G-16638)
BERTRAM YACHTS LLC (DH)
5250 W Tyson Ave (33611-3224)
PHONE......................................813 527-9899
Peter C Truslow,
EMP: 7 EST: 2015
SALES (est): 29MM
SALES (corp-wide): 4.2B **Privately Held**
SIC: 3732 Boat building & repairing
HQ: Baglietto Spa
Viale San Bartolomeo 414
La Spezia SP 19126
018 759-831

(G-16639)
BEVEL EXPRESS & TOPS LAC
6026 Benjamin Rd (33634-5104)
PHONE......................................813 887-3174
Yamileth Sanchez, *Principal*
EMP: 9 EST: 2006
SALES (est): 585.7K **Privately Held**
WEB: www.bevelexpress.com
SIC: 2741 Miscellaneous publishing

(G-16640)
BEVEL TOP SHOP EXPRESS LLC
Also Called: Bevel Express
6022 Benjamin Rd (33634-5104)
PHONE......................................813 299-1250
Neil W Smith Jr,
EMP: 8 EST: 2019

SALES (est): 640.1K **Privately Held**
WEB: www.bevelexpress.com
SIC: 2541 Table or counter tops, plastic laminated

(G-16641)
BEVERAGE BLOCKS INC
218 E Bearss Ave Ste 332 (33613-1625)
PHONE......................................813 309-8711
Michael Patierno, *Chairman*
EMP: 12 EST: 2017
SALES (est): 612.4K **Privately Held**
SIC: 2086 2657 Water, pasteurized: packaged in cans, bottles, etc.; food containers, folding: made from purchased material

(G-16642)
BIG BIZ DIRECT
13922 Monroes Business Pa (33635-6370)
PHONE......................................813 978-0584
EMP: 7 EST: 2010
SALES (est): 286.1K **Privately Held**
WEB: www.mrrc.com
SIC: 2752 Commercial printing, lithographic

(G-16643)
BIG KITCHEN
3719 Corporex Park Dr # 50 (33619-1163)
PHONE......................................813 254-6112
EMP: 10 EST: 2011
SALES (est): 65.1K **Privately Held**
WEB: www.bigkitchen.com
SIC: 2499 Woodenware, kitchen & household

(G-16644)
BIOMEDTECH LABORATORIES INC (PA)
3802 Spectrum Blvd # 154 (33612-9212)
PHONE......................................813 558-2000
Joachim Sasse, *President*
Jutta Sasse, *Vice Pres*
▲ EMP: 6 EST: 1998
SQ FT: 3,500
SALES (est): 1.4MM **Privately Held**
WEB: www.biomedtech.com
SIC: 3471 Electroplating & plating

(G-16645)
BISK EDUCATION INC (PA)
Also Called: Bisk Publishing Company
9417 Princess Palm Ave # 400 (33619-8348)
P.O. Box 31028 (33631-3028)
PHONE......................................813 621-6200
Michael Bisk, *CEO*
David Blinn, *Partner*
Denisse Viale, *Partner*
Clynton Hunt, *Managing Dir*
Nathan M Bisk, *Chairman*
EMP: 227 EST: 1971
SQ FT: 70,000
SALES (est): 124MM **Privately Held**
WEB: www.bisk.com
SIC: 2731 Book publishing

(G-16646)
BLACKLIDGE EMULSIONS INC
2701 E 2nd Ave (33605-5502)
PHONE......................................813 247-5699
Ronald Blacklidge, *Owner*
EMP: 17
SQ FT: 1,712 **Privately Held**
WEB: www.blacklidge.com
SIC: 2951 Road materials, bituminous (not from refineries)
PA: Blacklidge Emulsions, Inc.
12251 Bernard Pkwy # 200
Gulfport MS 39503

(G-16647)
BLASTERS READY JET INC
7815 Professional Pl (33637-6745)
PHONE......................................813 985-4500
Scott F Boos, *President*
Natalie B Elliott, *Vice Pres*
Kris Boos, *Controller*
Frederick Boos, *Admin Sec*
▲ EMP: 21 EST: 2006
SALES (est): 3.3MM **Privately Held**
WEB: www.blasters.net
SIC: 3531 Construction machinery

(G-16648)
BLINGKA INC
3911 Americana Dr (33634-7405)
PHONE......................................800 485-6793
Chandler Rapson, *Chairman*
EMP: 8 EST: 2019
SALES (est): 2.3MM **Privately Held**
SIC: 3944 Video game machines, except coin-operated

(G-16649)
BMC SOFTWARE INC
401 E Jackson St Ste 3300 (33602-5228)
PHONE......................................813 227-4500
Andrew Corbin, *President*
Chris Criollo, *Sales Staff*
Jimmy Hillman, *Sales Staff*
Jason Poole, *Sales Staff*
Sean Coakley, *Manager*
EMP: 10
SALES (corp-wide): 1.5B **Privately Held**
WEB: www.bmc.com
SIC: 7372 Prepackaged software
PA: Bmc Software, Inc.
2103 Citywest Blvd
Houston TX 77042
713 918-8800

(G-16650)
BMP USA INC
8105 Anderson Rd (33634-2319)
P.O. Box 15762 (33684-5762)
PHONE......................................813 443-0757
Xianbin Meng, *President*
Linna Shi, *Vice Pres*
Angela Zhang, *IT/INT Sup*
EMP: 59 EST: 2013
SALES (est): 6.9MM **Privately Held**
WEB: www.bmp-usa.com
SIC: 3585 Refrigeration & heating equipment

(G-16651)
BMS INTERNATIONAL INC
Also Called: Bob's Machine Shop
8802 E Broadway Ave (33619-7702)
PHONE......................................813 247-7040
Greg Pelini, *President*
▲ EMP: 29 EST: 1981
SALES (est): 4.1MM **Privately Held**
WEB: www.bobsmachine.com
SIC: 3429 3732 3537 Manufactured hardware (general); boat building & repairing; industrial trucks & tractors

(G-16652)
BOBS BARRICADES INC
5018 24th Ave S (33619-5340)
PHONE......................................813 886-0518
Terry Chapman, *Manager*
EMP: 28
SALES (corp-wide): 37.2MM **Privately Held**
WEB: www.bobsbarricades.com
SIC: 3499 7353 3291 Barricades, metal; heavy construction equipment rental; abrasive products
PA: Bob's Barricades, Inc.
921 Shotgun Rd
Sunrise FL 33326
954 423-2627

(G-16653)
BOLIVIAN PAVERS LLC
4801 E Hillsborough Ave (33610-4720)
PHONE......................................813 952-0608
Machuca Valdivia, *Principal*
EMP: 8 EST: 2013
SALES (est): 216.3K **Privately Held**
SIC: 2951 Asphalt paving mixtures & blocks

(G-16654)
BOND MEDICAL GROUP INC
3837 Northdale Blvd # 36 (33624-1841)
PHONE......................................813 264-5951
Travis Bond, *President*
Lisa Bond, *Exec VP*
EMP: 19 EST: 2001
SQ FT: 3,000
SALES (est): 1.2MM **Privately Held**
WEB: www.bondmedical.com
SIC: 7372 Prepackaged software

(G-16655)
BOND-PRO INC
1501 E 2nd Ave (33605-5005)
PHONE....................................888 789-4985
Joesph Williams, *Principal*
Frederick Duguay, *Principal*
Roger Hurwitz, *Principal*
Jacques Levy, *Chief*
Jeffrey York, *Exec VP*
EMP: 114 **EST:** 2011
SALES (est): 20MM **Privately Held**
WEB: www.bond-pro.com
SIC: 7372 Application computer software

(G-16656)
BOND-PRO LLC
1501 E 2nd Ave (33605-5005)
PHONE....................................813 413-7576
Larry Maniscalco, *Senior Mgr*
Jesus Benedetti, *Software Dev*
Shreyansh Shah, *Software Dev*
Laura Carrizales, *Sr Consultant*
EMP: 15 **EST:** 2019
SALES (est): 552.6K **Privately Held**
WEB: www.bond-pro.com
SIC: 7372 Application computer software

(G-16657)
BONSAL AMERICAN INC
Also Called: W R Bonsal Plant 44
5455 N 59th St (33610-2011)
PHONE....................................813 621-2427
William A Ashton, *Branch Mgr*
EMP: 7
SQ FT: 20,000
SALES (corp-wide): 30.9B **Privately Held**
SIC: 3272 3241 2899 Dry mixture concrete; cement, hydraulic; chemical preparations
HQ: Bonsal American, Inc.
625 Griffith Rd Ste 100
Charlotte NC 28217
704 525-1621

(G-16658)
BORNT ENTERPRISES INC
Also Called: Superior Design Products
9824 Currie Davis Dr (33619-2651)
PHONE....................................813 623-1492
David Bornt, *President*
Bonnie Bornt, *Vice Pres*
Steve Sdp, *Manager*
Sher Staton, *Manager*
EMP: 35 **EST:** 1980
SQ FT: 15,600
SALES (est): 3.5MM **Privately Held**
WEB: www.superiordesignproducts.com
SIC: 2591 1799 5023 Blinds vertical; window shades; window treatment installation; vertical blinds; window shades

(G-16659)
BRACE INTEGRATED SERVICES INC
8205 E Adamo Dr (33619-3537)
PHONE....................................813 248-6248
Hans Peter Hansen, *Branch Mgr*
EMP: 35
SALES (corp-wide): 2.1B **Privately Held**
WEB: www.brace.com
SIC: 1389 Construction, repair & dismantling services
HQ: Brace Integrated Services, Inc.
2112 S Custer Ave
Wichita KS 67213
316 832-0292

(G-16660)
BRANDON LOCK & SAFE INC
4630 Eagle Falls Pl (33619-9613)
PHONE....................................813 655-4200
Vickie Musall, *President*
Kyle Keffer, *General Mgr*
Larry Musall, *Corp Secy*
Garrett Norris, *Project Mgr*
EMP: 6 **EST:** 1997
SALES (est): 742.8K **Privately Held**
WEB: www.brandonlock.com
SIC: 3429 3499 Locks or lock sets; safes & vaults, metal

(G-16661)
BREEZEMAKER FAN COMPANY INC
1608 N 24th St (33605-5452)
PHONE....................................813 248-5552
Ron Myers, *President*
EMP: 34 **EST:** 1938
SQ FT: 20,000
SALES (est): 1.1MM **Privately Held**
WEB: www.breezemaker-fan.com
SIC: 3564 5084 Blowers & fans; industrial machinery & equipment

(G-16662)
BRISTOL-MYERS SQUIBB COMPANY
4931 George Rd (33634-6201)
PHONE....................................813 881-7000
Chris McDermott, *Opers Staff*
Jelana Bryan, *Accountant*
Tammy Duffey, *Branch Mgr*
Donell Carey, *Manager*
Stacey Martin, *Manager*
EMP: 7
SALES (corp-wide): 46.3B **Publicly Held**
WEB: www.bms.com
SIC: 2834 Pharmaceutical preparations
PA: Bristol-Myers Squibb Company
430 E 29th St Fl 14
New York NY 10016
212 546-4000

(G-16663)
BUILT LLC
602 N Newport Ave (33606-1328)
PHONE....................................813 512-6250
Andrew Watson, *Mng Member*
EMP: 7 **EST:** 2013
SALES (est): 1.2MM **Privately Held**
WEB: www.builtthings.com
SIC: 2514 Household furniture: upholstered on metal frames

(G-16664)
BUSCAR INC
3403 W Morrison Ave (33629-5233)
PHONE....................................813 877-7272
Michael Bustillo, *President*
EMP: 7 **EST:** 2015
SALES (est): 143.3K **Privately Held**
SIC: 3571 7378 Electronic computers; computer maintenance & repair

(G-16665)
BUSINESS JRNL PUBLICATIONS INC (DH)
4350 W Cypress St Ste 800 (33607-4180)
PHONE....................................813 342-2472
Arthur Porter, *Principal*
EMP: 38 **EST:** 1984
SQ FT: 70,000
SALES (est): 127.8MM
SALES (corp-wide): 2.8B **Privately Held**
SIC: 2711 Newspapers: publishing only, not printed on site
HQ: American City Business Journals, Inc.
120 W Morehead St Ste 400
Charlotte NC 28202
704 973-1000

(G-16666)
BYTIO INC ✪
2202 N West Shore Blvd # 2 (33607-5747)
PHONE....................................445 888-9999
Zhuo Yu, *President*
EMP: 100 **EST:** 2022
SALES (est): 3.8MM **Privately Held**
SIC: 3571 Electronic computers

(G-16667)
C & S GRAPHICS INC
Also Called: C & S GRAPHICS, INC. DBA ELECTRIC SIGN COMPANY
1335 W North B St (33606-1615)
PHONE....................................813 251-4411
Edward Croney III, *President*
Betsy Croney, *Office Mgr*
EMP: 5 **EST:** 1987
SQ FT: 10,000
SALES (est): 490.7K **Privately Held**
WEB: www.candsgraphics.com
SIC: 3993 Signs, not made in custom sign painting shops

(G-16668)
C&C BRICK PAVERS INC
8513 N Otis Ave (33604-1249)
PHONE....................................813 716-8291
Natali Cruz, *Principal*
EMP: 8 **EST:** 2010
SALES (est): 602.9K **Privately Held**
WEB: www.ccbrickpavers.com
SIC: 3531 Pavers

(G-16669)
CABINETS MOREUNLIMITED INC
11802 Spanish Lake Dr (33635-6311)
PHONE....................................813 789-4203
Thomas V Magers, *Principal*
EMP: 7 **EST:** 2011
SALES (est): 180.1K **Privately Held**
WEB: www.cabinetsandmoreunlimited.com
SIC: 2434 Wood kitchen cabinets

(G-16670)
CABINETS PLUS OF AMERICA INC
3853 S Lake Dr Unit 164 (33614-2080)
PHONE....................................813 408-0433
John Crescente P, *Principal*
EMP: 7 **EST:** 2018
SALES (est): 204.2K **Privately Held**
WEB: www.cabinetsplusofamerica.com
SIC: 2434 Wood kitchen cabinets

(G-16671)
CADDIE COMPANY INC
Also Called: First Look Display Group
4104 Causeway Vista Dr (33615-5416)
PHONE....................................267 332-0976
John Disantis, *President*
▲ **EMP:** 18 **EST:** 1998
SALES (est): 2MM **Privately Held**
SIC: 2542 Office & store showcases & display fixtures

(G-16672)
CAE USA INC (DH)
Also Called: Cae USA Products
4908 Tampa West Blvd (33634-2411)
P.O. Box 15000 (33684-5000)
PHONE....................................813 885-7481
Dan Gelston, *President*
Stawski Carrie, *Business Mgr*
Pascal Grenier, *Vice Pres*
Dan Sharkey, *Vice Pres*
Davin Brannon, *Project Mgr*
◆ **EMP:** 600 **EST:** 1939
SQ FT: 210,000
SALES (est): 923.9MM
SALES (corp-wide): 2.6B **Privately Held**
WEB: www.cae.com
SIC: 3699 7373 8299 8249 Electronic training devices; flight simulators (training aids), electronic; computer integrated systems design; flying instruction; aviation school; engineering services
HQ: Cae(Us) Inc.
1011 Ct Rd Ste 322
Wilmington DE 19805
813 885-7481

(G-16673)
CALMAC CORPORATION
Also Called: Fastsigns
1801 E Fowler Ave (33612-5556)
PHONE....................................813 493-8700
EMP: 14
SALES (corp-wide): 1.4MM **Privately Held**
SIC: 3993 Signsadv Specs
PA: Calmac Corporation
1506 W Kennedy Blvd Ste A
Tampa FL 33606
813 654-7476

(G-16674)
CAMELOT CABINETS INC
6903 Conaty Dr (33634-4417)
PHONE....................................813 876-9150
John Williams, *President*
EMP: 18 **EST:** 1972
SQ FT: 4,000
SALES (est): 997.8K **Privately Held**
WEB: www.tampabaycabinetry.com
SIC: 2434 Wood kitchen cabinets

(G-16675)
CANARCHY CRAFT
Also Called: Cigar City Brewing
3924 W Spruce St (33607-2441)
PHONE....................................813 348-6363
Neil Callaghan, *General Mgr*
Nick Farhood, *Sales Staff*
Eric Loy, *Manager*
Larry Schriver, *Manager*
Jeromy Dana, *Supervisor*
EMP: 177
SALES (corp-wide): 5.5B **Publicly Held**
WEB: www.oskarblues.com
SIC: 2082 5084 Beer (alcoholic beverage); brewery products manufacturing machinery, commercial
HQ: Canarchy Craft Brewery Collective Llc
1800 Pike Rd Unit B
Longmont CO 80501
303 776-1914

(G-16676)
CAPRI KITCHENS INC
9507 E Us Highway 92 (33610-5990)
PHONE....................................813 623-1424
Billy Isom, *President*
Wanda Switzer, *Vice Pres*
EMP: 10 **EST:** 1970
SQ FT: 1,000
SALES (est): 721.9K **Privately Held**
SIC: 2434 Wood kitchen cabinets

(G-16677)
CAPTIVE-AIRE SYSTEMS INC
4519 George Rd Ste 150 (33634-7354)
PHONE....................................813 448-7884
Alex Gicale, *Branch Mgr*
Woody Brink, *Technical Staff*
EMP: 11
SALES (corp-wide): 503.9MM **Privately Held**
WEB: www.captiveaire.com
SIC: 3444 Sheet metalwork
PA: Captive-Aire Systems, Inc.
4641 Paragon Park Rd # 104
Raleigh NC 27616
919 882-2410

(G-16678)
CARD QUEST INC
7902 W Waters Ave Ste C (33615-1816)
P.O. Box 1915, Elfers (34680-1915)
PHONE....................................813 288-0004
Shannon L Schofield, *President*
Jeffery L Capshaw, *Vice Pres*
▼ **EMP:** 5 **EST:** 2003
SQ FT: 2,000
SALES (est): 3.2MM **Privately Held**
WEB: www.cardquest.com
SIC: 3089 Identification cards, plastic

(G-16679)
CARDINAL HEALTH 414 LLC
3016 Usf Hawthorn Dr (33612)
PHONE....................................813 972-1351
Adam Folesner, *Branch Mgr*
EMP: 7
SALES (corp-wide): 181.3B **Publicly Held**
SIC: 2835 2834 Radioactive diagnostic substances; pharmaceutical preparations
HQ: Cardinal Health 414, Llc
7000 Cardinal Pl
Dublin OH 43017
614 757-5000

(G-16680)
CARE-METIX PRODUCTS INC
121 Kelsey Ln Ste F (33619-4348)
PHONE....................................813 628-8801
Steve Gibbons, *President*
EMP: 15 **EST:** 1998
SALES (est): 2.3MM **Privately Held**
WEB: www.caremetix.com
SIC: 2841 Soap & other detergents

(G-16681)
CARGILL INCORPORATED
2120 Maritime Blvd (33605-6753)
PHONE....................................813 241-4847
Louis Ricard, *Branch Mgr*
EMP: 15
SALES (corp-wide): 42.9B **Privately Held**
WEB: www.cargill.com
SIC: 2048 2899 Prepared feeds; chemical preparations

PA: Cargill, Incorporated
15407 Mcginty Rd W
Wayzata MN 55391
952 742-7575

(G-16682)
CARROLLWOOD CREAMERY
13168 N Dale Mabry Hwy (33618-2406)
PHONE..................................813 926-2023
Jason A Ricci, *Principal*
EMP: 7 EST: 2012
SALES (est): 113.8K **Privately Held**
WEB: www.carrollwoodvillage.com
SIC: 2021 Creamery butter

(G-16683)
CARVALHO NATURALS LLC
5806 Cay Cove Ct (33615-4269)
PHONE..................................813 833-8229
Kathalin Carvalho, *Principal*
EMP: 7 EST: 2017
SALES (est): 220.2K **Privately Held**
WEB: www.carvalhonaturals.com
SIC: 2099 Food preparations

(G-16684)
CASALE DESIGN SOURCE INC
4002 W State St Ste 100 (33609-1223)
PHONE..................................813 873-3653
Denise Casale, *President*
Diane Leone, *Manager*
EMP: 6 EST: 2012
SALES (est): 413.6K **Privately Held**
WEB: www.casaledesignsource.com
SIC: 3253 Ceramic wall & floor tile

(G-16685)
CASINO BAKERY INC
2726 N 36th St (33605-3126)
P.O. Box 5828 (33675-5828)
PHONE..................................813 242-0311
Louis Sanchez Jr, *President*
EMP: 10 EST: 1946
SQ FT: 2,700
SALES (est): 836K **Privately Held**
SIC: 2051 Bread, all types (white, wheat,
rye, etc): fresh or frozen

(G-16686)
CASTOR INC
1701 W Green St (33607-4316)
PHONE..................................813 254-1171
Brian Scott Castor, *President*
Stephen K Castor, *Vice Pres*
Carolyn Newby, *Treasurer*
Alex Castor, *Manager*
▼ EMP: 8 EST: 1977
SQ FT: 7,000
SALES (est): 1.1MM **Privately Held**
WEB: www.castorcabinets.com
SIC: 2434 5712 Wood kitchen cabinets;
cabinet work, custom

(G-16687)
CATALINA FINER FOOD CORP
4709 N Lauber Way (33614-7735)
P.O. Box 15815 (33684-5815)
PHONE..................................813 872-6359
Alejandro Cepero, *President*
Francisco Cepero, *Treasurer*
Justo Luis Cepero, *Admin Sec*
▲ EMP: 47 EST: 1973
SQ FT: 20,000
SALES (est): 9.8MM **Privately Held**
WEB: www.catalinafoods.com
SIC: 2032 2099 2035 Tamales: packaged
in cans, jars, etc.; food preparations; pick-
les, sauces & salad dressings

(G-16688)
CATALINA FINER MEAT CORP
Also Called: Catalina Finer Foods
4710 W Cayuga St (33614-6949)
P.O. Box 15815 (33684-5815)
PHONE..................................813 876-3910
Alejandro Cepero, *President*
Marta Cepero, *Vice Pres*
Justo Luis Cepero, *Treasurer*
Francisco Cepero, *Admin Sec*
EMP: 21 EST: 1982
SQ FT: 7,000
SALES (est): 1.1MM **Privately Held**
SIC: 2013 5147 Sausages & other pre-
pared meats; meats & meat products

(G-16689)
CEDRICK MCDONALD
Also Called: Exotics By Cedrick
4205 N Florida Ave (33603-3870)
PHONE..................................813 279-1442
Cedrick McDonald, *Owner*
EMP: 7 EST: 2016
SALES (est): 65.1K **Privately Held**
WEB: www.exoticsbycedrick.com
SIC: 3144 Dress shoes, women's

(G-16690)
CELIOS CORPORATION
1228 E 7th Ave Ste 313 (33605-3505)
PHONE..................................833 235-4671
Neil Campbell, *CEO*
EMP: 9 EST: 2017
SALES (est): 259.3K **Privately Held**
WEB: www.celios.com
SIC: 3999 Manufacturing industries

(G-16691)
CEMEX INC
5503 E Diana St (33610-1903)
PHONE..................................813 663-9712
Gilberto Perez, *President*
Jesus Benavides, *Treasurer*
Joel Hray, *Accounts Mgr*
Ramiro Morales, *Admin Sec*
EMP: 23 EST: 1991
SALES (est): 5.6MM **Privately Held**
WEB: www.cemexusa.com
SIC: 3273 Ready-mixed concrete

(G-16692)
CEMEX CNSTR MTLS FLA LLC
Also Called: Gypsum Supply - Tampa
9609 Palm River Rd (33619-4433)
PHONE..................................813 621-5575
EMP: 14 **Privately Held**
SIC: 3273 Mfg Ready-Mixed Concrete
HQ: Cemex Construction Materials Florida,
Llc
1501 Belvedere Rd
West Palm Beach FL 33406

(G-16693)
CEMEX MATERIALS LLC
6302 N 56th St (33610-4021)
PHONE..................................813 620-3760
Angie Hinkle, *Manager*
EMP: 69 **Privately Held**
SIC: 3273 Ready-mixed concrete
HQ: Cemex Materials Llc
1720 Centrepark Dr E # 100
West Palm Beach FL 33401
561 833-5555

(G-16694)
CENTREX POWDERCOATING INC
4901 Distribution Dr (33605-5925)
PHONE..................................813 390-2802
Michael K Trout, *President*
EMP: 9 EST: 2003
SALES (est): 791.8K **Privately Held**
SIC: 3479 Coating of metals & formed
products

(G-16695)
CENTURION ARMORING INTL INC
3911 W Eden Roc Cir (33634-7419)
PHONE..................................813 426-3385
Maroun Azzi, *President*
Lena Jammal, *Vice Pres*
▼ EMP: 8 EST: 2010
SALES (est): 177.6K **Privately Held**
WEB: www.centurion-armoring.com
SIC: 3549 Assembly machines, including
robotic

(G-16696)
CENTURION HOLDINGS I LLC
Also Called: Centurion Technologies
324 N Dale Mabry Hwy (33609-1269)
P.O. Box 528, Arnold MO (63010-0528)
PHONE..................................636 349-5425
EMP: 20
SQ FT: 8,000
SALES (est): 2.8MM **Privately Held**
SIC: 3577 Mfg Computer Peripheral Equip-
ment

(G-16697)
CERBERUS CRAFT DISTILLERY LLC
6608 Anderson Rd (33634-4402)
PHONE..................................813 789-1556
Matthew Allen, *Manager*
EMP: 7 EST: 2016
SALES (est): 476.5K **Privately Held**
SIC: 2082 Malt beverages

(G-16698)
CERTANTEED GYPS CILING MFG INC (HQ)
4300 W Cypress St Ste 500 (33607-4157)
PHONE..................................813 286-3900
▼ EMP: 29
SALES (corp-wide): 332.4MM **Privately Held**
SIC: 3275 Mfg Gypsum Products

(G-16699)
CHAD
817 S Macdill Ave (33609-4615)
PHONE..................................727 433-0404
Stephen Myers, *Vice Pres*
Wasson Epps, *Manager*
Daniel Padley, *Manager*
Nathaniel Epps, *Admin Sec*
EMP: 7 EST: 2016
SALES (est): 203.7K **Privately Held**
SIC: 3761 Guided missiles & space vehi-
cles

(G-16700)
CHANNEL INVESTMENTS LLC
Also Called: Tria Beauty
4221 W Boy Scout Blvd # 300
(33607-5765)
PHONE..................................727 599-1360
Sandip Patel,
EMP: 7 EST: 2017
SALES (est): 697K **Privately Held**
SIC: 3845 Laser systems & equipment,
medical

(G-16701)
CHARGEX LLC
4020 W Kennedy Blvd # 10 (33609-2761)
PHONE..................................855 242-7439
Chase Hebeler, *Mng Member*
EMP: 6 EST: 2020
SALES (est): 1.2MM **Privately Held**
WEB: www.lithiumion-batteries.com
SIC: 3691 Storage batteries

(G-16702)
CHOLADOS Y MAS
6729 N Armenia Ave (33604-5715)
PHONE..................................813 935-9262
Maria Shirley Cintron, *Principal*
EMP: 8 EST: 2010
SALES (est): 127.8K **Privately Held**
SIC: 2024 Ice cream, bulk

(G-16703)
CIGAR CITY BREWPUB LLC (PA)
3924 W Spruce St (33607-2441)
PHONE..................................813 348-6363
Michael Haas, *General Mgr*
Justin Clark, *COO*
Madison Roane, *Prdtn Mgr*
Al Alvarez, *CFO*
Joe Burns, *Natl Sales Mgr*
▲ EMP: 6 EST: 2007
SALES (est): 4.3MM **Privately Held**
WEB: www.cigarcitybrewing.com
SIC: 2082 5084 Beer (alcoholic bever-
age); brewery products manufacturing
machinery, commercial

(G-16704)
CIGAR CITY PRINTING
14143 Fennsbury Dr (33624-6941)
PHONE..................................813 843-2751
Elbert Cordero, *Principal*
EMP: 7 EST: 2017
SALES (est): 69.6K **Privately Held**
WEB: www.cigarcitybrewing.com
SIC: 2752 Commercial printing, litho-
graphic

(G-16705)
CIGAR CITY SMOKED SALSA LLC
5106 N 30th St (33610-5102)
PHONE..................................813 421-3340
Roy Kane, *Mng Member*
EMP: 5 EST: 2018
SQ FT: 2,000
SALES (est): 372.9K **Privately Held**
WEB: www.cigarcitysmokedsalsa.com
SIC: 2035 Pickles, sauces & salad dress-
ings

(G-16706)
CINTAS CORPORATION
3601 W Swann Ave Ste 107 (33609-4517)
PHONE..................................813 874-1401
Kenneth Bahng, *Manager*
EMP: 10
SALES (corp-wide): 7.8B **Publicly Held**
WEB: www.cintas.com
SIC: 2326 Work uniforms
PA: Cintas Corporation
6800 Cintas Blvd
Cincinnati OH 45262
513 459-1200

(G-16707)
CIRKUL INC
9210 E Columbus Dr # 110 (33619-2381)
PHONE..................................941 518-8596
Stephen Cucci, *Manager*
EMP: 100
SALES (corp-wide): 106.8MM **Privately Held**
WEB: www.drinkcirkul.com
SIC: 3085 5149 Plastics bottles; groceries
& related products
PA: Cirkul, Inc.
4914 Joanne Kearney Blvd
Tampa FL 33619
941 724-4382

(G-16708)
CIRKUL INC
4545 Madison Indus Ln (33619-9608)
PHONE..................................513 889-6708
Adam Black, *Manager*
EMP: 150
SALES (corp-wide): 106.8MM **Privately Held**
WEB: www.drinkcirkul.com
SIC: 3085 5149 Plastics bottles; groceries
& related products
PA: Cirkul, Inc.
4914 Joanne Kearney Blvd
Tampa FL 33619
941 724-4382

(G-16709)
CKC INDUSTRIES INC (PA)
4908 Savarese Cir (33634-2403)
P.O. Box 151012 (33684-1012)
PHONE..................................813 888-9468
Charles K Cheng, *President*
Anna Cheng, *Admin Sec*
▲ EMP: 9 EST: 1983
SQ FT: 15,000
SALES (est): 985.2K **Privately Held**
WEB: www.ckcindustries.com
SIC: 3829 3672 Temperature sensors, ex-
cept industrial process & aircraft; printed
circuit boards

(G-16710)
CLADDING SYSTEMS INC
3218 E 4th Ave (33605-5716)
PHONE..................................813 250-0786
Elizabeth Lisa Alexander, *President*
Elizabeth G Alexander, *President*
Bill Alexander, *Vice Pres*
William M Alexander, *Vice Pres*
Lee Reese, *Mktg Dir*
◆ EMP: 21 EST: 2000
SQ FT: 1,300
SALES (est): 5MM **Privately Held**
WEB: www.cladsys.com
SIC: 3444 Sheet metalwork

(G-16711)
CLARE INSTRUMENTS (US) INC
Also Called: Seaward Group USA
6304 Benjamin Rd Ste 506 (33634-5128)
PHONE..................................813 886-2775
Rod Taylor, *President*
Frank Belluccia, *General Mgr*

Mark Barron, *Business Mgr*
EMP: 5 **EST:** 2001
SQ FT: 1,500
SALES (est): 2.3MM
SALES (corp-wide): 127.4MM **Privately Held**
WEB: www.seaward-groupusa.com
SIC: 3699 Electrical equipment & supplies
HQ: Seaward Electronic Limited
　　18 Bracken Hill
　　Peterlee CO DURHAM SR8 2
　　191 586-3511

(G-16712)
CLARK CRAIG ENTERPRISES (PA)
Also Called: Fastsigns
3901 W Kennedy Blvd (33609-2721)
PHONE......................813 287-0110
Clark Craig, *President*
Adam Le Blanc, *Sales Staff*
EMP: 7 **EST:** 1996
SQ FT: 3,600
SALES (est): 4.6MM **Privately Held**
SIC: 3993 Signs & advertising specialties

(G-16713)
CLASSIC AUTO A MNFACTORING INC
4901 W Rio Vista Ave A (33634-5356)
PHONE......................813 251-2356
Alfonso L Sedita, *President*
▲ **EMP:** 16 **EST:** 1982
SALES (est): 357.6K **Privately Held**
WEB: www.classicautoair.com
SIC: 3585 Air conditioning, motor vehicle

(G-16714)
CLEANPAK PRODUCTS LLC
Also Called: Clean Pack Products
221 Hobbs St Ste 108 (33619-8068)
PHONE......................813 740-8611
George Brydon, *Human Resources*
John Bartolotti, *Sales Associate*
◆ **EMP:** 5 **EST:** 2006
SQ FT: 10,000
SALES (est): 1MM **Privately Held**
WEB: www.cleanpakproducts.com
SIC: 2899 Chemical preparations

(G-16715)
CLIFTON STUDIO INC
4710 Eisenhower Blvd D (33634-6335)
P.O. Box 273848 (33688-3848)
PHONE......................813 240-0286
Gilbert Bailie, *President*
EMP: 7 **EST:** 1974
SALES (est): 109.6K **Privately Held**
SIC: 3999 Plaques, picture, laminated

(G-16716)
COASTAL WIPERS INC (PA)
Also Called: Landis Service Company
5705 E Hanna Ave (33610-4036)
PHONE......................813 628-4464
Gary H Smiles, *President*
Michelle Smiles, *Vice Pres*
Dennis Bahro, *Manager*
◆ **EMP:** 38 **EST:** 1982
SQ FT: 17,000
SALES (est): 8.6MM **Privately Held**
WEB: www.coastalwipers.com
SIC: 2392 Polishing cloths, plain

(G-16717)
COCA-COLA BEVERAGES FLA LLC
4409 Madison Indus Ln (33619-9610)
PHONE......................813 612-6631
Jim Boyce, *Plant Mgr*
Doug Driscoll, *Branch Mgr*
EMP: 13
SQ FT: 59,200
SALES (corp-wide): 366.5MM **Privately Held**
WEB: www.cocacolaflorida.com
SIC: 2086 5149 Bottled & canned soft drinks; soft drinks
PA: Coca-Cola Beverages Florida, Llc
　　10117 Princess Palm Ave
　　Tampa FL 33610
　　800 438-2653

(G-16718)
COCA-COLA BEVERAGES FLA LLC
9102 Sabal Indus Blvd (33619-8303)
PHONE......................813 623-5411
Ward Sean, *Area Mgr*
Randy Arty, *Branch Mgr*
Jeffrey Cormier, *Supervisor*
Ryan Carter, *CIO*
EMP: 230
SALES (corp-wide): 366.5MM **Privately Held**
WEB: www.cocacolaflorida.com
SIC: 2086 Bottled & canned soft drinks
PA: Coca-Cola Beverages Florida, Llc
　　10117 Princess Palm Ave
　　Tampa FL 33610
　　800 438-2653

(G-16719)
COCA-COLA BEVERAGES FLA LLC (PA)
10117 Princess Palm Ave (33610-8302)
PHONE......................800 438-2653
Troy Taylor, *CEO*
Thomas N Benford, *President*
Jack Palmorn, *General Mgr*
Bernie Roy, *General Mgr*
Laura Detter, *Editor*
EMP: 158 **EST:** 2015
SALES (est): 366.5MM **Privately Held**
WEB: www.cocacolaflorida.com
SIC: 2086 Bottled & canned soft drinks

(G-16720)
COLOR CONCEPTS PRTG DESIGN CO
2602 Tampa East Blvd (33619-3038)
PHONE......................813 623-2921
Robin D Wahler, *President*
Dave Collyer, *Vice Pres*
Donald Barnes, *Shareholder*
Gasper Ciaccio, *Shareholder*
EMP: 15 **EST:** 1986
SQ FT: 15,500
SALES (est): 1.7MM **Privately Held**
WEB: www.colorconcepts.com
SIC: 2752 2791 2789 Commercial printing, offset; typesetting; bookbinding & related work

(G-16721)
COMERINT INC
5125 W Rio Vista Ave (33634-5342)
PHONE......................813 443-2466
Jorge E Ramirez, *President*
EMP: 7 **EST:** 2013
SALES (est): 171.1K **Privately Held**
WEB: www.comerint-inc.com
SIC: 3263 Cookware, fine earthenware

(G-16722)
COMPETITOR GROUP INC
3407 W Dr MI King Jr 10 (33607)
PHONE......................858 450-6510
Justin Sands, *Executive Asst*
EMP: 11 **EST:** 2018
SALES (est): 1.3MM **Privately Held**
SIC: 2741 Miscellaneous publishing

(G-16723)
CONCEPT DESIGN AND PRINTING
7402 N 56th St Ste 810 (33617-7731)
PHONE......................813 516-9798
Syed Haider, *Owner*
EMP: 7 **EST:** 2014
SALES (est): 328.1K **Privately Held**
WEB: www.conceptdp.com
SIC: 2759 Commercial printing

(G-16724)
CONSOLDTED RSURCE RECOVERY INC
1502 N 50th St (33619-3220)
PHONE......................813 262-8404
Deborah Brindley, *Controller*
Cindy Cummings, *Manager*
Toni Lubbers, *Director*
EMP: 27 **Privately Held**
WEB: www.veransa.com
SIC: 2875 1629 Compost; land clearing contractor

PA: Consolidated Resource Recovery, Inc.
　　3025 Whitfield Ave
　　Sarasota FL 34243

(G-16725)
CONTROL SOLUTIONS INC
1406 N 16th St (33605-5126)
PHONE......................813 247-2136
Michael E Vandergriff, *President*
Diana L Vandergriff, *Vice Pres*
EMP: 10 **EST:** 2007
SQ FT: 6,500
SALES (est): 1.4MM **Privately Held**
WEB: www.controlsolutionsinc.com
SIC: 3612 3613 3823 Transformers, except electric; switchgear & switchboard apparatus; industrial instrmnts msrmnt display/control process variable

(G-16726)
CONVICTED PRINTING LLC
4719 N Thatcher Ave (33614-6935)
PHONE......................813 431-6286
EMP: 5 **EST:** 2020
SALES (est): 418.8K **Privately Held**
WEB: www.convictedprinting.com
SIC: 2752 Commercial printing, lithographic

(G-16727)
COOL COMPONENTS INC
904 E Chelsea St (33603-4137)
PHONE......................813 322-3814
David T Lee, *President*
▲ **EMP:** 8 **EST:** 2004
SALES (est): 1MM **Privately Held**
WEB: www.coolcomponents.com
SIC: 3564 Blowers & fans

(G-16728)
CORESENTIAL ENERGY & LIGHTING
1201 N 50th St (33619-3206)
PHONE......................919 602-0849
Robin Conway, *President*
Joe Tumlin, *President*
Jamey Yore, *President*
Barry Enegess, *Vice Chairman*
Jeff Conway, *Vice Pres*
EMP: 40 **EST:** 2011
SALES (est): 3MM **Privately Held**
WEB: www.coresential.com
SIC: 3646 Commercial indusl & institutional electric lighting fixtures

(G-16729)
CORESLAB STRUCTURES TAMPA INC
6301 N 56th St (33610-4020)
PHONE......................602 237-3875
Luigi Franciosa, *President*
Frank Franciosa, *Principal*
Michael Quinlan, *Principal*
Sidney Spiegel, *Principal*
Dominic Franciosa, *Vice Pres*
EMP: 160 **EST:** 1993
SQ FT: 5,000
SALES (est): 46MM
SALES (corp-wide): 27.3MM **Privately Held**
WEB: www.coreslab.com
SIC: 3272 Concrete products, precast
HQ: Coreslab Holdings U S Inc
　　332 Jones Rd Suite 1
　　Stoney Creek ON
　　905 643-0220

(G-16730)
CORIN USA LIMITED INC (DH)
12750 Citrus Park Ln # 120 (33625-3784)
PHONE......................813 977-4469
Stefano Alfonsi, *CEO*
Vaughan Bonny, *Managing Dir*
Russ Mabley, *COO*
Craig Hutchison, *Vice Pres*
Chuck Jaggers, *Vice Pres*
▲ **EMP:** 12 **EST:** 1992
SQ FT: 9,911
SALES (est): 6.8MM
SALES (corp-wide): 2.6MM **Privately Held**
WEB: www.coringroup.com
SIC: 3841 Surgical & medical instruments

HQ: Corin Limited
　　Unit 1-4
　　Cirencester GLOS GL7 1
　　128 565-9866

(G-16731)
CORONA BRUSHES INC
5065 Savarese Cir (33634-2490)
PHONE......................813 885-2525
Gregory Waksman, *President*
Benjamin Waksman, *Vice Pres*
Albert Waksman, *Treasurer*
Neil Trenk, *Sales Mgr*
Joyce McCarthy, *Executive*
◆ **EMP:** 60 **EST:** 1961
SQ FT: 65,000
SALES (est): 9.3MM **Privately Held**
WEB: www.coronabrushes.com
SIC: 3991 Paint brushes; paint rollers

(G-16732)
CORRUGATED INDUSTRIES FLA INC
Also Called: Custom Metal Building Products
1920 N Us Highway 301 (33619-2640)
PHONE......................813 623-6606
Gene Le Bouef Sr, *President*
Gene Lebouef, *President*
▼ **EMP:** 16 **EST:** 1999
SQ FT: 16,000
SALES (est): 8.4MM **Privately Held**
WEB: www.metalroofandwalls.com
SIC: 3444 Sheet metalwork

(G-16733)
COSTA BROOM WORKS INC
3606 E 4th Ave (33605-5835)
P.O. Box 5091 (33675-5091)
PHONE......................813 248-3397
Frank J Costa, *President*
Connie Costa, *Corp Secy*
Mary Costa, *Vice Pres*
◆ **EMP:** 15 **EST:** 1929
SQ FT: 26,000
SALES (est): 840.1K **Privately Held**
SIC: 3991 2392 Brooms; mops, floor & dust

(G-16734)
COVERALL INTERIORS
5102 W Linebaugh Ave (33624-5032)
PHONE......................813 961-8261
Dave Friedel, *Manager*
EMP: 8 **EST:** 2017
SALES (est): 140.4K **Privately Held**
SIC: 2591 Drapery hardware & blinds & shades

(G-16735)
CP ROYALTIES LLC
301 W Platt St (33606-2292)
PHONE......................888 694-9265
Douglas Anacreonte, *Principal*
EMP: 5 **EST:** 2011
SALES (est): 312.9K **Privately Held**
WEB: www.cproyalties.com
SIC: 1382 Oil & gas exploration services

(G-16736)
CRAWFORD MANUFACTURING COMPANY
Also Called: Miller Leasing
8875 Hdden Rver Pkwy Ste (33637)
PHONE......................513 548-6890
Dan J Miller, *President*
Mary Miller, *Admin Sec*
EMP: 18 **EST:** 1959
SQ FT: 2,500
SALES (est): 2.5MM **Privately Held**
WEB: www.crawfordmfg.com
SIC: 3495 Wire springs

(G-16737)
CREATE AND COMPANY INC
Also Called: Createco
1023 E Columbus Dr (33605-3332)
PHONE......................813 393-8778
Kristina M York, *President*
Angela T Davis, *Vice Pres*
David A Valladarez, *Vice Pres*
Shannon Murray, *Director*
EMP: 10 **EST:** 2015
SALES (est): 2.3MM **Privately Held**
WEB: www.createandcompany.com
SIC: 3694 Generators, automotive & aircraft

▲ = Import ▼ =Export
◆ =Import/Export

(G-16738)
CREATIVE BUILDER SERVICES INC
Also Called: Creative Mailbox Designs
6422 Harney Rd Ste F (33610-9162)
PHONE....................813 818-7100
Scott M Tappan, *President*
Melissa Aldawqi, *Business Mgr*
Ronald Ternet, *Prdtn Mgr*
Nicole Arquiett, *Accountant*
EMP: 35 EST: 2016
SALES (est): 3.8MM **Privately Held**
WEB: www.creativemailboxdesigns.com
SIC: 2542 Mail racks & lock boxes, postal service: except wood

(G-16739)
CREATIVE LOAFING INC (HQ)
Also Called: Weekly Planet
1911 N 13th St Ste W200 (33605-3652)
PHONE....................813 739-4800
Marty Petty, *CEO*
Colin Wolf, *Editor*
Scott Harrell, *Chief*
Tammy Bailey, *CFO*
Anthony Carbone, *Executive*
EMP: 50 EST: 1988
SQ FT: 8,000
SALES (est): 27.9MM **Privately Held**
WEB: www.cltampa.com
SIC: 2711 Newspapers: publishing only, not printed on site

(G-16740)
CREATIVE SIGN DESIGNS LLC (PA)
Also Called: Creative Mailbox Sign Designs
12801 Commodity Pl (33626-3104)
PHONE....................800 804-4809
Jamie Harden, *President*
Kelly Crandall, *Co-Owner*
Sam Feldstein, *COO*
Melanie Harden, *Exec VP*
Bryan Vaughn, *Vice Pres*
▲ EMP: 65 EST: 1986
SQ FT: 44,000
SALES (est): 17.7MM **Privately Held**
WEB: www.creativesigndesigns.com
SIC: 3993 Signs & advertising specialties

(G-16741)
CROWE MANUFACTURING
5203 S Lois Ave (33611-3446)
PHONE....................813 334-1921
EMP: 7 EST: 2018
SALES (est): 49.1K **Privately Held**
SIC: 3999 Manufacturing industries

(G-16742)
CROWELL MARINE INC
Also Called: Crowell Companies
7305 N Florida Ave (33604-4837)
PHONE....................813 236-3625
Terri Crowell, *President*
Robert Crowell, *Director*
EMP: 7 EST: 2008
SALES (est): 571.8K **Privately Held**
SIC: 2499 Floating docks, wood

(G-16743)
CROWN EQUIPMENT CORPORATION
Also Called: Crown Lift Trucks
4683 Oak Fair Blvd (33610-7410)
PHONE....................813 628-5500
Randy Bratten, *Sales Staff*
Steve Scholz, *Manager*
Mark Weimer, *Technician*
EMP: 61
SALES (corp-wide): 5.2B **Privately Held**
WEB: www.crown.com
SIC: 3537 Lift trucks, industrial: fork, platform, straddle, etc.
PA: Crown Equipment Corporation
44 S Washington St
New Bremen OH 45869
419 629-2311

(G-16744)
CSBA DIGITAL PRINTING
3601 Bay Heights Way (33611-1548)
PHONE....................813 482-1608
Ricardo Ruiz, *Principal*
EMP: 8 EST: 2013

SALES (est): 137.8K **Privately Held**
WEB: www.csbaonline.org
SIC: 2752 Commercial printing, offset

(G-16745)
CSC TEXTRON
2450 N West Shore Blvd (33607-5741)
PHONE....................813 554-9723
EMP: 6 EST: 2016
SALES (est): 318.9K **Privately Held**
SIC: 3721 Aircraft

(G-16746)
CT NATURAL
2908 W Arch St (33607-5202)
PHONE....................813 996-6443
Florence McCue-Morris, *Principal*
EMP: 7 EST: 2012
SALES (est): 252.9K **Privately Held**
WEB: www.ctnatural.com
SIC: 3599 Boiler tube cleaners

(G-16747)
CUMMINS-WAGNER-FLORIDA LLC (HQ)
9834 Currie Davis Dr (33619-2651)
PHONE....................813 630-2220
Paul Bement, *Engineer*
Daniel Orr, *Sales Staff*
Douglas Ardinger, *Mng Member*
EMP: 11 EST: 2010
SALES (est): 13.3MM
SALES (corp-wide): 78.6MM **Privately Held**
WEB: www.cummins-wagner.com
SIC: 3556 3519 Dehydrating equipment, food processing; internal combustion engines
PA: Cummins-Wagner Company, Inc.
10901 Pump House Rd
Annapolis Junction MD 20701
800 966-1277

(G-16748)
CURRY CABINETRY INC
4831 E Broadway Ave (33605-4703)
PHONE....................813 321-3650
Ann Curry, *President*
Bryan Curry, *Vice Pres*
Matt Alexander, *Opers Staff*
EMP: 22 EST: 2008
SQ FT: 8,000
SALES (est): 3.2MM **Privately Held**
WEB: www.currycabinetry.com
SIC: 2434 Wood kitchen cabinets

(G-16749)
CUSHION SOLUTIONS INCORPORATED
802 N Rome Ave (33606-1038)
PHONE....................813 253-2131
Denis Flagler, *President*
▲ EMP: 6 EST: 2005
SQ FT: 1,000
SALES (est): 628.9K **Privately Held**
WEB: www.cushionsolutions.net
SIC: 2392 Cushions & pillows

(G-16750)
CUSTOM CABINETS BY JENSEN LLC
1704 W Fig St (33606-1626)
PHONE....................813 250-0286
Glenn Jensen, *Manager*
EMP: 8 EST: 2015
SALES (est): 276K **Privately Held**
SIC: 2434 Wood kitchen cabinets

(G-16751)
CUSTOM CRAFT LAMINATES INC
4705 N Manhattan Ave (33614-6921)
PHONE....................813 877-7100
James E Blanton, *President*
Sally J Blanton, *Corp Secy*
EMP: 21 EST: 1968
SQ FT: 20,000
SALES (est): 1.4MM **Privately Held**
WEB: www.mycabinetcompany.com
SIC: 2434 2521 Wood kitchen cabinets; wood office furniture

(G-16752)
CUSTOM DOOR DIRECT LLC
1100 N 50th St Bldg 2 (33619-3233)
PHONE....................813 248-5757
EMP: 10 EST: 2011
SALES (est): 780K **Privately Held**
SIC: 2431 Mfg Millwork

(G-16753)
CUSTOM KLOSETS & CABINETS INC
6403 N 50th St (33610-4004)
PHONE....................813 246-4806
Robin Knapp, *President*
Bradford C Frank, *Principal*
Tom Petrou, *Vice Pres*
Mike Reidy, *Sales Staff*
EMP: 23 EST: 2002
SQ FT: 12,000
SALES (est): 4.7MM **Privately Held**
WEB: www.customclosetsandcabinets.com
SIC: 2434 Vanities, bathroom: wood

(G-16754)
CUSTOM MARBLE WORKS INC
1905 N 43rd St (33605-4644)
PHONE....................813 620-0475
Rick Fincher, *President*
Coy E Fincher, *Corp Secy*
◆ EMP: 43 EST: 1985
SQ FT: 5,000
SALES (est): 2.4MM **Privately Held**
SIC: 3281 3429 3261 2541 Marble, building: cut & shaped; granite, cut & shaped; manufactured hardware (general); vitreous plumbing fixtures; wood partitions & fixtures; dimension stone

(G-16755)
CUSTOM PLASTIC FABRICATORS
6201 Johns Rd Ste 8 (33634-4434)
PHONE....................813 884-5200
Joseph Gregory Bersano, *Owner*
EMP: 8 EST: 2008
SALES (est): 271.7K **Privately Held**
WEB: www.customplasticfab.com
SIC: 3089 Molding primary plastic; netting, plastic; panels, building: plastic; organizers for closets, drawers, etc.: plastic

(G-16756)
CUSTOM QUALITY MFG INC
Also Called: C Q M
5015 Tampa West Blvd (33634-2414)
PHONE....................813 290-0805
Leon Montanbault, *President*
Dolores Alonso, *Corp Secy*
Michelle Mason, *CFO*
Michele Mason, *Finance*
Al Alvarez, *Sales Engr*
▲ EMP: 21 EST: 1996
SQ FT: 10,500
SALES (est): 5MM **Privately Held**
WEB: www.cqm-inc.com
SIC: 3714 Motor vehicle parts & accessories

(G-16757)
CYPRESS FOLDING CARTONS INC
6025 Jet Port Indus Blvd (33634-5161)
PHONE....................813 884-5418
Jon Hartzler, *President*
Lisa Hartzler, *Corp Secy*
Austin Hartzler, *Vice Pres*
EMP: 35 EST: 1981
SQ FT: 19,000
SALES (est): 4.9MM **Privately Held**
WEB: www.cypressfoldingcartons.com
SIC: 2653 2657 Boxes, corrugated: made from purchased materials; folding paperboard boxes

(G-16758)
D G YUENGLING AND SON INC
11111 N 30th St (33612-6439)
PHONE....................813 972-8500
Richard L Yuengling Jr, *President*
Andy Pickerell, *Plant Mgr*
Larry Trakes, *Sales Staff*
Donald Cook, *Manager*
Pete Moquin, *Manager*
EMP: 95

SALES (corp-wide): 53.7MM **Privately Held**
WEB: www.yuengling.com
SIC: 2082 5182 5181 Beer (alcoholic beverage); ale (alcoholic beverage); porter (alcoholic beverage); wine & distilled beverages; beer & ale
PA: D. G. Yuengling And Son, Incorporated
5th & Mahantongo Sts
Pottsville PA 17901
570 628-4890

(G-16759)
DAIRY-MIX INC
Gulf Coast Plastics
9314 Princess Palm Ave (33619-1364)
PHONE....................813 621-8098
Thomas Coryn, *Manager*
EMP: 18
SALES (corp-wide): 27.4MM **Privately Held**
WEB: www.dairymix.com
SIC: 2673 5113 3081 2671 Plastic bags: made from purchased materials; bags, paper & disposable plastic; unsupported plastics film & sheet; packaging paper & plastics film, coated & laminated
PA: Dairy-Mix, Inc.
3020 46th Ave N
Saint Petersburg FL 33714
813 621-8098

(G-16760)
DALANE MACHINING INC
13530 Wright Cir (33626-3028)
PHONE....................813 854-5905
Dale Baird, *President*
Sisk Steve, *General Mgr*
Kyle Tirrell, *Research*
EMP: 26 EST: 1992
SQ FT: 8,500
SALES (est): 3.1MM **Privately Held**
WEB: www.dalanemachining.com
SIC: 3599 Machine shop, jobbing & repair

(G-16761)
DALE MABRY HEATING & METAL CO
4313 W South Ave (33614-6465)
PHONE....................813 877-1574
Fred Besch III, *President*
Becky Cacciatore, *Corp Secy*
Fred Besch Sr, *Vice Pres*
EMP: 6 EST: 1947
SQ FT: 2,200
SALES (est): 798.6K **Privately Held**
WEB: www.dalemabrymetal.com
SIC: 2434 Wood kitchen cabinets

(G-16762)
DARLING INGREDIENTS INC
1001 Orient Rd (33619-3321)
PHONE....................863 425-0065
Don Manning, *Manager*
EMP: 14
SQ FT: 4,152
SALES (corp-wide): 4.7B **Publicly Held**
WEB: www.darlingii.com
SIC: 2077 Animal & marine fats & oils
PA: Darling Ingredients Inc.
5601 N Macarthur Blvd
Irving TX 75038
972 717-0300

(G-16763)
DATA COOLING TECH CANADA LLC
Thermotech Enterprises
5110 W Clifton St (33634-8012)
P.O. Box 15698 (33684-5698)
PHONE....................813 865-4701
Jeff McKee, *General Mgr*
Krister Eriksson, *Branch Mgr*
Christopher Kinney, *Technician*
EMP: 25
SALES (corp-wide): 4.7MM **Privately Held**
WEB: www.thermotech-usa.com
SIC: 3585 Heating & air conditioning combination units
PA: Data Cooling Technologies Canada Llc
3092 Euclid Heights Blvd
Cleveland Heights OH 44118
330 954-3800

(G-16764)
DAVID JACOBS PUBG GROUP LLC
14497 N D Mabry Hwy 135 (33618)
PHONE.............................813 321-4119
Bob Ford, *Vice Pres*
Jacob T Wattam, *Manager*
EMP: 11 EST: 2012
SALES (est): 1.5MM **Privately Held**
WEB: www.davidjacobspg.com
SIC: 2741 Miscellaneous publishing

(G-16765)
DAVIS FRANKLIN PRINTING CO
520 N Willow Ave (33606-1348)
P.O. Box 22362 (33622-2362)
PHONE.............................813 259-2500
Mace Davis, *Owner*
EMP: 7 EST: 1908
SALES (est): 538.2K **Privately Held**
SIC: 2759 Commercial printing

(G-16766)
DAY SHOPPING LLC
10738 Pleasant Knoll Dr (33647-3667)
PHONE.............................321 616-4504
Tiantian Pang,
EMP: 10
SALES (est): 283.4K **Privately Held**
SIC: 2095 7389 Coffee roasting (except by wholesale grocers);

(G-16767)
DAYSTAR INTERNATIONAL INC
917 Terra Mar Dr (33613-2003)
PHONE.............................813 281-0200
Glen Freeman, *President*
Charlotte Murray, *Corp Secy*
Tim Backus, *Vice Pres*
EMP: 7 EST: 1994
SALES (est): 296.1K **Privately Held**
SIC: 2434 1751 2541 Wood kitchen cabinets; finish & trim carpentry; wood partitions & fixtures

(G-16768)
DCG ENTERPRISES LLC
Also Called: Quality Beverage Services
2702 N 35th St (33605-3122)
P.O. Box 15472 (33684-5472)
PHONE.............................813 931-4303
Paul Vadnais,
EMP: 5 EST: 1994
SALES (est): 749.3K **Privately Held**
SIC: 3585 Soda fountain & beverage dispensing equipment & parts

(G-16769)
DDP HOLDINGS LLC (HQ)
4450 E Adamo Dr Ste 501 (33605-5941)
PHONE.............................813 712-2515
Mike Sunderland, *CEO*
Lauren Bishop, *Vice Pres*
EMP: 74 EST: 1992
SQ FT: 5,000
SALES (est): 184.3MM
SALES (corp-wide): 255.7MM **Privately Held**
SIC: 3432 6512 Plumbing fixture fittings & trim; property operation, retail establishment
PA: Palm Beach Capital Fund I, L.P.
　　525 S Flagler Dr Ste 208
　　West Palm Beach FL 33401
　　561 659-9022

(G-16770)
DECOWALL
6001 Johns Rd Ste 342 (33634-4459)
P.O. Box 8281 (33674-8281)
PHONE.............................813 886-5226
Phillip Breakey, *Owner*
EMP: 6 EST: 1979
SQ FT: 1,500
SALES (est): 489.9K **Privately Held**
WEB: www.decowalltampa.com
SIC: 2431 5046 Millwork; commercial equipment

(G-16771)
DESIGN LITHO INC
5205 N Florida Ave (33603-2139)
PHONE.............................813 238-7494
Reg Ide, *President*
EMP: 6 EST: 1979
SQ FT: 6,000
SALES (est): 428.4K **Privately Held**
WEB: www.designlitho.com
SIC: 2752 Commercial printing, offset

(G-16772)
DESTINY & LIGHT INC
Also Called: Salon By Destiny & Light, The
5911 Sheldon Rd (33615-3109)
PHONE.............................813 476-8386
Priscilla M Cruz-Charite, *Vice Pres*
Brown Charite Charite, *Sales Staff*
EMP: 12 EST: 2011
SALES (est): 468.1K **Privately Held**
WEB: www.destinyandlight.com
SIC: 3999 Hair, dressing of, for the trade

(G-16773)
DEVON-AIRE INC
8505 Sunstate St (33634-1311)
P.O. Box 25112 (33622-5112)
PHONE.............................813 884-9544
Harris Giannella, *President*
Darin Dealvarez, *President*
Andres Lendoiro, *Vice Pres*
Robert Della Penna, *Vice Pres*
◆ EMP: 18 EST: 1976
SQ FT: 20,000
SALES (est): 1.6MM **Privately Held**
WEB: www.devonaire.com
SIC: 2329 2339 3144 Riding clothes:, men's, youths' & boys'; riding habits: women's, misses' & juniors'; boots, canvas or leather: women's

(G-16774)
DFA DAIRY BRANDS FLUID LLC
4219 E 19th Ave (33605-3241)
PHONE.............................813 621-7805
George Abel, *Branch Mgr*
EMP: 30
SALES (corp-wide): 19.3B **Privately Held**
SIC: 2026 Fluid milk
HQ: Dfa Dairy Brands Fluid, Llc
　　1405 N 98th St
　　Kansas City KS 66111
　　816 801-6455

(G-16775)
DIANE DAL LAGO LIMITED COMPANY
5915 Memorial Hwy Ste 115 (33615-5008)
PHONE.............................813 374-2473
EMP: 12
SALES (est): 1.2MM **Privately Held**
SIC: 2339 Mfg Women's Sportswear

(G-16776)
DIETZGEN CORPORATION (PA)
121 Kelsey Ln Ste G (33619-4348)
PHONE.............................813 286-4767
Darren Letang, *President*
Darren A Letang, *President*
Bill Eagle, *Plant Mgr*
Joel Jefferson, *Site Mgr*
Mandi Nickerson, *Production*
▼ EMP: 45 EST: 2009
SALES (est): 42.4MM **Privately Held**
WEB: staging.dietzgen.com
SIC: 2679 Paper products, converted

(G-16777)
DIMENSION PHOTO ENGRV CO INC
1507 W Cass St (33606-1207)
PHONE.............................813 251-0244
Douglas Drenberg, *President*
Donald W Drenberg, *Chairman*
Debra Gilmore, *Corp Secy*
Donna Gardner, *Vice Pres*
Jim McMahan, *Sales Staff*
EMP: 20 EST: 1963
SQ FT: 10,000
SALES (est): 3.9MM **Privately Held**
WEB: www.4dimension.com
SIC: 2752 Commercial printing, offset

(G-16778)
DIMENSNAL IMPRSSION HLDNGS INC
Also Called: Dimension Printing
1507 W Cass St (33606-1207)
PHONE.............................813 251-0244
EMP: 10 EST: 2020

SALES (est): 754K **Privately Held**
WEB: www.4dimension.com
SIC: 2752 Commercial printing, offset

(G-16779)
DISBROW CORPORATION (PA)
Also Called: Ad-Co Printing
8412 Sabal Indus Blvd (33619-1327)
PHONE.............................813 621-9444
John Disbrow, *President*
Angela Disbrow, *Admin Sec*
▲ EMP: 7 EST: 1996
SQ FT: 30,000
SALES (est): 3.6MM **Privately Held**
WEB: www.printfast.com
SIC: 2752 Commercial printing, lithographic

(G-16780)
DIVERSFIED LIFTING SYSTEMS INC
6905 Parke East Blvd (33610-9163)
PHONE.............................813 248-2299
Billy Crowe, *President*
David Banks, *Research*
◆ EMP: 22 EST: 1988
SALES (est): 3.5MM **Privately Held**
WEB: www.diversifiedlifting.com
SIC: 3537 3536 Platforms, stands, tables, pallets & similar equipment; hoists, cranes & monorails

(G-16781)
DKA DISTRIBUTING LLC
5010 Tampa West Blvd (33634-2412)
PHONE.............................800 275-4342
Jim Tackenberg,
EMP: 9 EST: 2002
SALES (est): 152K **Privately Held**
WEB: www.dkadistributing.com
SIC: 3639 Major kitchen appliances, except refrigerators & stoves

(G-16782)
DLA DOCUMENT SERVICES
2617 Florida Keys Ave # 25 (33621-5402)
PHONE.............................813 828-4646
William Barrett, *Manager*
EMP: 10 **Publicly Held**
WEB: documentservices.dla.mil
SIC: 2752 9711 Commercial printing, lithographic; national security
HQ: Dla Document Services
　　5450 Carlisle Pike Bldg 9
　　Mechanicsburg PA 17050
　　717 605-2362

(G-16783)
DOCH LLC ✪
14630 Grenadine Dr Apt 7 (33613-2911)
PHONE.............................571 491-7578
Suryanarayana Burri,
EMP: 9 EST: 2021
SALES (est): 350.7K **Privately Held**
SIC: 3491 Valves, automatic control

(G-16784)
DOE & INGALLS FLORIDA OPER LLC
9940 Currie Davis Dr # 13 (33619-2669)
PHONE.............................813 347-4741
Spencer Todd, *President*
EMP: 5 EST: 2005
SQ FT: 10,000
SALES (est): 2.9MM
SALES (corp-wide): 39.2B **Publicly Held**
SIC: 3826 Analytical instruments
HQ: Doe & Ingalls Management, Llc
　　4813 Emperor Blvd Ste 300
　　Durham NC 27703

(G-16785)
DPI INFORMATION INC
8402 Laurel Fair Cir # 209 (33610-7328)
PHONE.............................813 258-8004
Anthony Aguilar, *Principal*
Chris Sharp, *Sales Staff*
EMP: 18 EST: 2008
SALES (est): 1.3MM **Privately Held**
WEB: www.dpiserve.com
SIC: 7372 Operating systems computer software

(G-16786)
DREXEL METALS INC
8641 Elm Fair Blvd (33610-7363)
PHONE.............................727 572-7900
Bryan Partyka, *Branch Mgr*
EMP: 22
SALES (corp-wide): 4.8B **Publicly Held**
WEB: www.drexmet.com
SIC: 2952 5033 Roofing materials; roofing & siding materials
HQ: Drexel Metals, Inc.
　　1234 Gardiner Ln
　　Louisville KY 40213
　　888 321-9630

(G-16787)
DTSYSTEMS INC
4834 W Gandy Blvd (33611-3003)
P.O. Box 46907 (33646-0108)
PHONE.............................813 994-0030
Frank Nicotera, *CEO*
EMP: 5 EST: 2000
SQ FT: 1,200
SALES (est): 878K **Privately Held**
WEB: www.keepontracking.com
SIC: 3577 Optical scanning devices

(G-16788)
DURAMASTER CYLINDERS
5688 W Crenshaw St (33634-3044)
PHONE.............................813 882-0040
Joseph H Greene, *President*
EMP: 9 EST: 1989
SALES (est): 973.3K **Privately Held**
WEB: www.greencocylinders.com
SIC: 3593 5084 3443 Fluid power cylinders, hydraulic or pneumatic; industrial machinery & equipment; fabricated plate work (boiler shop)

(G-16789)
DWM-2021 INC
Also Called: Aafw-Kimco
7810 Professional Pl (33637-6744)
PHONE.............................813 443-0791
John P Mistal, *President*
Kenneth Drummond, *Vice Pres*
Bobby White, *CFO*
EMP: 10 EST: 2008
SQ FT: 12,000
SALES (est): 1.8MM **Privately Held**
WEB: www.americanarchitecturalfoam.com
SIC: 3086 Plastics foam products

(G-16790)
DYNOTEC PLASTIC INC
2211 N 38th St Ste A (33605-4550)
PHONE.............................813 248-5335
Antionio Dodaro, *President*
▼ EMP: 7 EST: 1993
SALES (est): 601.5K **Privately Held**
SIC: 3089 Injection molding of plastics

(G-16791)
E2 WALLS INC
5692 W Crenshaw St (33634-3013)
P.O. Box 270909 (33688-0909)
PHONE.............................813 374-2010
Kenneth P Devars, *President*
Colin C Bowles-Jenner, *Vice Pres*
Donald R Cox, *Vice Pres*
John T Coyle Jr, *Vice Pres*
Kerry P Devars, *Vice Pres*
EMP: 20 EST: 2008
SQ FT: 12,000
SALES (est): 4.2MM **Privately Held**
WEB: www.e2walls.com
SIC: 3275 Gypsum products

(G-16792)
EAG-LED LLC (PA)
Also Called: Eagled Global Lights
12918 Commodity Pl (33626-3119)
PHONE.............................813 463-2420
Jason Pawelsky, *Sales Staff*
Roger Sicotte, *Sales Staff*
Steven Taylor, *Sales Staff*
John Armiger, *Sales Executive*
Andrew Avram, *Sales Executive*
EMP: 44 EST: 2001
SALES (est): 10.9MM **Privately Held**
WEB: www.eag-led.com
SIC: 3648 3641 Floodlights; street lighting fixtures; electric lamps & parts for specialized applications

(G-16793)
EAST BAY MANUFACTURERS INC
100 S Ashley Dr Ste 600 (33602-5300)
P.O. Box 436, Bristol RI (02809-0436)
PHONE...................813 524-9344
Lou Victorino, *President*
Randy Medina, *General Mgr*
Louis Victorino, *General Mgr*
Michael Vitorino, *Production*
▲ EMP: 14 EST: 1994
SQ FT: 10,000
SALES (est): 2.8MM **Privately Held**
WEB: www.eastbaymfg.com
SIC: 3599 Machine shop, jobbing & repair

(G-16794)
EASTMAN KODAK COMPANY
5364 Ehrlich Rd (33624-6979)
PHONE...................813 908-7910
EMP: 72
SALES (corp-wide): 4.1B **Publicly Held**
SIC: 3861 Nonclassified Establishmentmfg
Photo Equip/Supplies & Computer Pe-
ripheral Equipment
PA: Eastman Kodak Company
343 State St
Rochester NY 14650
585 724-4000

(G-16795)
EATON CORPORATION
Also Called: Cutler Hammer
1511 N West Shore Blvd # 1111
(33607-4523)
PHONE...................813 281-8069
EMP: 8 **Privately Held**
SIC: 3634 3699 5063 Mfg Electric House-
wares/Fans Mfg Electrical
Equipment/Supplies Whol Electrical
Equipment
HQ: Eaton Corporation
1000 Eaton Blvd
Cleveland OH 44122
216 523-5000

(G-16796)
EATON LAW
14812 N Florida Ave (33613-1844)
PHONE...................813 264-4800
EMP: 5 EST: 2019
SALES (est): 399.8K **Privately Held**
WEB: www.eaton-law.com
SIC: 3625 Motor controls & accessories

(G-16797)
ED VANCE PRINTING COMPANY INC
Also Called: Dealer Printing Service
6107 Memorial Hwy Ste E7 (33615-4576)
PHONE...................813 882-8888
Edgar V York, *President*
Edward V York, *President*
Jill S York, *Admin Sec*
EMP: 11 EST: 1985
SQ FT: 3,300
SALES (est): 412.2K **Privately Held**
SIC: 2752 2791 2789 Commercial print-
ing, offset; typesetting; bookbinding & re-
lated work

(G-16798)
EDISON CHOUEST OFFSHORE
1130 Mcclosky Blvd (33605-6722)
PHONE...................813 241-2165
EMP: 9 EST: 2019
SALES (est): 303.2K **Privately Held**
WEB: www.chouest.com
SIC: 3731 Shipbuilding & repairing

(G-16799)
ELECTRCAL SYSTEMS CMMNICATIONS
Also Called: Bay Armature and Supply
1601 N 43rd St (33605-5937)
PHONE...................813 248-4275
Donald Kenney, *President*
EMP: 7 EST: 1970
SQ FT: 25,000
SALES (est): 210.1K **Privately Held**
WEB: www.bayarmature.com
SIC: 7694 5063 5999 Electric motor re-
pair; motors, electric; motors, electric

(G-16800)
ELECTUS GLOBAL EDUCATN CO INC
2601 E 7th Ave (33605-4103)
PHONE...................813 885-4122
Osceola H Delgado, *Administration*
EMP: 8 EST: 2015
SALES (est): 193.9K **Privately Held**
WEB: www.lifehubjobs.com
SIC: 7372 Prepackaged software

(G-16801)
ELEMENT SOLUTIONS LLC
Also Called: 24-7 Complete Restoration
13014 N Dale Mbry Hwy (33618-2808)
PHONE...................352 279-3310
Philip Metzler, *Manager*
EMP: 5 EST: 2016
SALES (est): 423.9K **Privately Held**
WEB: www.elementsolutionsac.com
SIC: 2819 Elements

(G-16802)
ELEMENTS RESTORATION LLC
401 N Ashley Dr (33602-4301)
P.O. Box 10516 (33679-0516)
PHONE...................813 330-2035
John R Mauk, *Manager*
Vanessa Willett, *Director*
EMP: 15 EST: 2013
SALES (est): 9.5MM **Privately Held**
WEB: www.erelements.com
SIC: 1389 1522 1542 1799 Construction,
repair & dismantling services; residential
construction; nonresidential construction;
post-disaster renovations

(G-16803)
ELIRPA CORPORATION
17932 Cachet Isle Dr (33647-2702)
PHONE...................813 986-8790
Joseph V Aprile, *Principal*
EMP: 9 EST: 2008
SALES (est): 147.9K **Privately Held**
WEB: www.elirpa.com
SIC: 3273 Ready-mixed concrete

(G-16804)
ELITE WHEEL DISTRIBUTORS INC (PA)
Also Called: Amani
3901 Riga Blvd (33619-1345)
PHONE...................813 673-8393
Hamed Milani, *President*
Kamran Milani, *Vice Pres*
Karla Dominguez, *Bookkeeper*
BJ Moss, *Manager*
◆ EMP: 7 EST: 2008
SALES (est): 7MM **Privately Held**
WEB: www.elitewheelwarehouse.com
SIC: 3312 3011 Wheels; tire & inner tube
materials & related products

(G-16805)
ELOGIC LEARNING LLC
14934 N Florida Ave (33613-1632)
PHONE...................813 901-8600
Mark Anderson, *CEO*
Bill Crandall, *Accounts Exec*
Katie Leahy, *Marketing Staff*
EMP: 35 EST: 2001
SALES (est): 9.2MM
SALES (corp-wide): 30MM **Privately Held**
WEB: www.absorblms.com
SIC: 7372 Educational computer software
PA: Absorb Software Inc
685 Centre St S Suite 2500
Calgary AB T2G 1
403 717-1971

(G-16806)
EMBROIDMECOM INC
Also Called: Fully Promoted
3909 W Kennedy Blvd (33609-2721)
PHONE...................813 878-2400
Ray Titus, *CEO*
EMP: 37 **Privately Held**
WEB: www.fullypromoted.com
SIC: 2395 Embroidery & art needlework;
embroidery products, except schiffli ma-
chine

HQ: Embroidme.Com Inc.
2121 Vista Pkwy
West Palm Beach FL 33411
561 640-7367

(G-16807)
EMC ROOFING LLC
6405 Nikki Ln (33625-1641)
PHONE...................786 597-6604
Ever M Cantillano, *Mng Member*
EMP: 11 EST: 2019
SALES (est): 3.3MM **Privately Held**
SIC: 3572 Computer storage devices

(G-16808)
EMI INDUSTRIES LLC (PA)
Also Called: Edwards Manufacturing
1316 Tech Blvd (33619-7865)
PHONE...................813 626-3166
Mirko Matic, *General Mgr*
Chad Witt, *General Mgr*
Dave Mueller, *COO*
Gerry McDonald, *Exec VP*
Richard Forget, *Project Mgr*
◆ EMP: 130 EST: 1978
SQ FT: 10,000
SALES (est): 53.3MM **Privately Held**
WEB: www.emiindustries.com
SIC: 2541 Wood partitions & fixtures; dis-
play fixtures, wood; store fixtures, wood

(G-16809)
EMK BRICK PAVERS LLC
6505 Secrest Ct (33625-4938)
PHONE...................813 500-9663
EMP: 5 EST: 2018
SALES (est): 312.2K **Privately Held**
WEB: www.emkbrickpavers.com
SIC: 3531 Pavers

(G-16810)
EMPIRE SCIENTIFIC
Also Called: Empire Central
4504 E Hillsborough Ave (33610-5249)
PHONE...................630 510-8636
Jeff English, *Owner*
Bob Slipko, *Purch Mgr*
Robert Slipko, *Manager*
▲ EMP: 5 EST: 2001
SALES (est): 358.4K **Privately Held**
SIC: 3692 Primary batteries, dry & wet

(G-16811)
EMPYRE MUSIC PUBLISHING LLC
1101 N Himes Ave Ste B (33607-5020)
PHONE...................813 873-7700
Darren Howard, *Manager*
EMP: 8 EST: 2011
SALES (est): 102.5K **Privately Held**
SIC: 2741 Miscellaneous publishing

(G-16812)
ENCORE BRANDZ COMPANY
8815 N 15th St (33604-1913)
PHONE...................813 282-7073
Richard Moore, *President*
EMP: 8 EST: 2015
SALES (est): 274.7K **Privately Held**
SIC: 2361 Dresses: girls', children's & in-
fants'

(G-16813)
ENGINE LAB OF TAMPA INC
201 S 78th St (33619-4225)
PHONE...................813 630-2422
Susan Deegan, *President*
David Deegan, *Vice Pres*
EMP: 9 EST: 1994
SQ FT: 15,600
SALES (est): 457.2K **Privately Held**
WEB: www.enginelaboftampa.com
SIC: 3519 7538 Gas engine rebuilding;
engine rebuilding: automotive

(G-16814)
ENGINEERED AIR SYSTEMS INC
Also Called: E A S I
6605 Walton Way (33610-5516)
PHONE...................813 881-9555
Victor Stimans, *Business Mgr*
Bruce Loubet, *Vice Pres*
Bruce Loubet Jr, *Vice Pres*
EMP: 12 EST: 1987

SALES (est): 2.4MM **Privately Held**
WEB: www.engineeredair.com
SIC: 3585 5065 5039 Refrigeration &
heating equipment; telegraph equipment;
air ducts, sheet metal; architectural metalwork

(G-16815)
ENTERRA INC
2801 W Busch Blvd (33618-4500)
PHONE...................813 514-0531
Jeremy Groves, *Principal*
Alexander Tamplon, *CTO*
Roman Dudarev, *Software Dev*
EMP: 11 EST: 2008
SALES (est): 593.8K **Privately Held**
WEB: www.enterra-inc.com
SIC: 2741 Guides: publishing & printing

(G-16816)
ENVIRO FOCUS TECHNOLOGY
6505 Jewel Ave (33619-2903)
PHONE...................813 744-5000
Larry Eagan, *Principal*
▲ EMP: 7 EST: 2011
SALES (est): 280K **Privately Held**
SIC: 3341 Secondary nonferrous metals

(G-16817)
ENVIRO GOLD REF SYSTEMS LLC
Also Called: Egrs
1430 Hobbs St (33619-0928)
PHONE...................813 390-7043
David Caldwell, *Mng Member*
Dylan Caldwel,
EMP: 5 EST: 2019
SALES (est): 389.1K **Privately Held**
WEB: www.egrs24k.com
SIC: 3339 Precious metals

(G-16818)
ENVIROFOCUS TECHNOLOGIES LLC
1901 N 66th St (33619-2901)
PHONE...................813 620-3260
Mark Kutoff, *Mng Member*
Maier Kutoff,
Kevin Murphy,
▲ EMP: 70 EST: 2006
SALES (est): 16.1MM
SALES (corp-wide): 121.8MM **Privately Held**
SIC: 3339 Lead & zinc
PA: Gopher Resource, Llc
2900 Lone Oak Pkwy Ste 14
Eagan MN 55121
651 454-3310

(G-16819)
EPC INC
3629 Queen Palm Dr (33619-1309)
PHONE...................636 443-1999
Tom Ash, *General Mgr*
Michael Thompson, *General Mgr*
Michael McKelvey, *Director*
Parriss Shanno, *Executive*
EMP: 14 EST: 2015
SALES (est): 1.2MM **Privately Held**
WEB: www.epchc.org
SIC: 3571 Electronic computers

(G-16820)
EPPERSON & COMPANY
5202 Shadowlawn Ave (33610-5310)
PHONE...................813 626-6125
James M Abbitt Jr, *President*
Rob Harris, *Vice Pres*
Jeffrey F Rowe, *Vice Pres*
Terry Montefusco, *Controller*
Claudia Huff, *Sales Staff*
▼ EMP: 53 EST: 1956
SQ FT: 25,000
SALES (est): 11.3MM **Privately Held**
WEB: www.metroplaces.com
SIC: 3535 Conveyors & conveying equip-
ment

(G-16821)
ERWIN INC
201 N Franklin St # 2200 (33602-5182)
PHONE...................813 933-3323
James R Hale, *President*
Marjorie Martinez, *Vice Pres*
Harpreet Bains, *Engineer*
Catherine Mystrioti, *Engineer*

Frank Panzarino, *Engineer*
EMP: 15 **EST:** 2016
SALES (est): 1.7MM **Privately Held**
WEB: www.erwin.com
SIC: 7372 Prepackaged software

(G-16822)
**EVOQUA WATER
TECHNOLOGIES LLC**
4711 Oak Fair Blvd (33610-7386)
PHONE.............................813 620-0900
Carol Jones, *Engineer*
Kimberly Callahan, *Sales Staff*
Dave Braykovith, *Manager*
Jason Bleess, *Technician*
EMP: 17
SALES (corp-wide): 1.4B **Publicly Held**
WEB: www.evoqua.com
SIC: 3589 Water treatment equipment, industrial
HQ: Evoqua Water Technologies Llc
210 6th Ave Ste 3300
Pittsburgh PA 15222
724 772-0044

(G-16823)
**EXACTUS PHARMACY
SOLUTIONS INC**
8715 Henderson Rd (33634-1143)
P.O. Box 31422 (33631-3422)
PHONE.............................888 314-3874
Dave Gallitano, *CEO*
Thomas L Tran, *Director*
EMP: 299 **EST:** 2007
SALES (est): 27MM **Publicly Held**
SIC: 2834 Druggists' preparations (pharmaceuticals)
HQ: Wellcare Health Plans, Inc.
8735 Henderson Rd
Tampa FL 33634
813 290-6200

(G-16824)
EXPRESS PRESS INC
107 N Jefferson St (33602-5001)
PHONE.............................813 884-3310
Greg Winchell, *President*
Steve Backhaus, *Vice Pres*
Kevin Hardsock, *Vice Pres*
Thomas Harrison, *Vice Pres*
Laura Regan, *Executive*
EMP: 16 **EST:** 1980
SALES (est): 2.4MM **Privately Held**
WEB: www.eptampa.com
SIC: 2752 Commercial printing, offset

(G-16825)
FABA CABINETS & SUCH LLC
7029 W Hillsborough Ave (33634-4947)
PHONE.............................813 871-1529
Maribel Martinez, *Principal*
EMP: 7 **EST:** 2015
SALES (est): 338.3K **Privately Held**
SIC: 2434 Wood kitchen cabinets

(G-16826)
**FABRICATED PRODUCTS
TAMPA INC**
1100 S 56th St (33619-3763)
PHONE.............................813 247-4001
Michael H Hunt, *President*
M Lynn Hunt, *Corp Secy*
Steven Hunt, *Vice Pres*
EMP: 40 **EST:** 1974
SALES (est): 7.3MM **Privately Held**
WEB: www.fabricatedprod.com
SIC: 3441 Building components, structural steel

(G-16827)
FAOURS MIRROR CORP
Also Called: Faour Glass Technologies
5119 W Knox St Ste A (33634-8093)
PHONE.............................813 884-3297
John Faour, *President*
Paul Suda, *Superintendent*
Aquilla Clark, *Purch Mgr*
Rene Valdes, *Engineer*
Aquilla Clarkmcclarty, *Bookkeeper*
◆ **EMP:** 25 **EST:** 1975
SQ FT: 10,000
SALES (est): 5.5MM **Privately Held**
SIC: 3211 5039 5231 Flat glass; glass construction materials; glass

(G-16828)
FARADAY INC
802 E Whiting St (33602-4136)
PHONE.............................813 536-6104
Clyde Snodgrass, *CEO*
EMP: 10 **EST:** 2014
SQ FT: 1,200
SALES (est): 705.5K **Privately Held**
WEB: www.faradayinc.com
SIC: 2084 Wines

(G-16829)
FAST SIGNS
Also Called: Fastsigns
14618 N Dale Mabry Hwy (33618-2024)
PHONE.............................813 999-4981
Stacey Alexander, *CEO*
EMP: 10 **EST:** 2015
SALES (est): 1MM **Privately Held**
WEB: www.fastsigns.com
SIC: 3993 Signs & advertising specialties

(G-16830)
FEATHERLITE EXHIBITS
1715 E Sewaha St (33612-8677)
PHONE.............................800 229-5533
Mark Lee, *Principal*
EMP: 8 **EST:** 2016
SALES (est): 99.4K **Privately Held**
WEB: www.featherlite.com
SIC: 2541 Wood partitions & fixtures

(G-16831)
FENWALL LLC (PA)
12850 Commodity Pl (33626-3101)
PHONE.............................813 343-5979
Joseph Muraco, *Mng Member*
EMP: 7 **EST:** 2014
SALES (est): 3MM **Privately Held**
WEB: www.fenwalls.com
SIC: 3449 Curtain walls for buildings, steel

(G-16832)
FILTERS PLUS INC
6708 Benjamin Rd Ste 200 (33634-4406)
PHONE.............................813 232-2000
Tom Waites, *President*
Andrew Waites, *Sales Mgr*
Jerry Kautz, *Sales Staff*
Steven P Myers, *Director*
Gary Bergeron, *Technician*
EMP: 5 **EST:** 2004
SALES (est): 1.1MM **Privately Held**
WEB: www.filtersplus.com
SIC: 3564 Filters, air: furnaces, air conditioning equipment, etc.

(G-16833)
**FIRST GRADE FOOD
CORPORATION**
Also Called: Lucky Fortune Cookie
5134 W Hanna Ave (33634-8020)
PHONE.............................813 886-6118
Jimmy Luong, *President*
Tim Luong, *Vice Pres*
◆ **EMP:** 30 **EST:** 1986
SQ FT: 11,000
SALES (est): 2.5MM **Privately Held**
SIC: 2052 2098 Cookies; macaroni & spaghetti

(G-16834)
FIX N FLY DRONES LLC
2105 N Jamaica St (33607-3128)
PHONE.............................321 474-2291
Timothy R Hileman, *Principal*
EMP: 5 **EST:** 2016
SALES (est): 498.5K **Privately Held**
WEB: www.fixnflydrones.com
SIC: 3721 Motorized aircraft

(G-16835)
FLAYCO PRODUCTS INC
4821 N Hale Ave (33614-6517)
P.O. Box 15967 (33684-5967)
PHONE.............................813 879-1356
Jorge Astorquiza, *President*
Teresa Astorquiza, *Corp Secy*
◆ **EMP:** 32 **EST:** 1975
SQ FT: 10,000

SALES (est): 1.5MM **Privately Held**
WEB: www.flayco.com
SIC: 2087 2099 2033 2034 Extracts, flavoring; food colorings; seasonings & spices; barbecue sauce: packaged in cans, jars, etc.; dried & dehydrated soup mixes; pickles, sauces & salad dressings; dry, condensed, evaporated dairy products

(G-16836)
FLEETMATICS
4211 W Boy Scout Blvd # 4 (33607-5724)
PHONE.............................727 483-9016
EMP: 9 **EST:** 2017
SALES (est): 258.1K **Privately Held**
WEB: www.verizonconnect.com
SIC: 7372 Prepackaged software

(G-16837)
FLINT LLC
1212 Maydell Dr (33619-4547)
PHONE.............................813 622-8899
Eric Chang,
EMP: 5 **EST:** 2006
SALES (est): 522.2K **Privately Held**
WEB: www.flintllc.com
SIC: 3679 Electronic circuits

(G-16838)
FLOORS INC
6205 Johns Rd Ste 1 (33634-4492)
P.O. Box 15573 (33684-5573)
PHONE.............................813 879-5720
Michael B Crowley, *President*
Karen Crowley, *Corp Secy*
EMP: 30 **EST:** 1960
SQ FT: 12,000
SALES (est): 3MM **Privately Held**
WEB: www.floorsinc.org
SIC: 2273 1771 Floor coverings, textile fiber; flooring contractor

(G-16839)
**FLORIDA BLOCK & READY MIX
LLC**
5208 36th Ave S (33619-6801)
PHONE.............................813 623-3700
Hprb Romancky, *Branch Mgr*
EMP: 74
SQ FT: 30,504 **Privately Held**
SIC: 3273 Ready-mixed concrete
PA: Florida Block & Ready Mix Llc
12795 49th St N
Clearwater FL 33762

(G-16840)
FLORIDA BOAT LIFT
4821 N Manhattan Ave (33614-6413)
PHONE.............................813 873-1614
Tom Kraemer, *Owner*
EMP: 7 **EST:** 2013
SALES (est): 885.1K **Privately Held**
WEB: www.floridaboatlifts.com
SIC: 3536 Boat lifts

(G-16841)
FLORIDA DACCO/DETROIT INC
3611 W Chestnut St (33607-2556)
PHONE.............................813 879-4131
Rick Wicky, *Manager*
▲ **EMP:** 23 **EST:** 2000
SALES (est): 1.1MM **Privately Held**
SIC: 3714 5013 Motor vehicle parts & accessories; motor vehicle supplies & new parts

(G-16842)
FLORIDA DISTILLERY LLC
Also Called: Florida Cane Distillery, The
501 S Falkenburg Rd C5 (33619-8034)
PHONE.............................813 347-6565
Lee P Nelson,
Patrick O'Brien,
▼ **EMP:** 9 **EST:** 2012
SQ FT: 2,200
SALES (est): 615.1K **Privately Held**
WEB: www.floridacane.com
SIC: 2085 Vodka (alcoholic beverage)

(G-16843)
FLORIDA FISHING PRODUCTS
205 W Ohio Ave (33603-5619)
PHONE.............................239 938-4612
William Nelson, *Principal*
EMP: 7 **EST:** 2017

SALES (est): 226.5K **Privately Held**
WEB: www.floridafishingproducts.com
SIC: 3949 Sporting & athletic goods

(G-16844)
FLORIDA GLASS OF TAMPA BAY
13929 Lynmar Blvd (33626-3124)
PHONE.............................813 925-1330
Joe Muraco, *Principal*
Mary Shields, *CFO*
Marilyn Baker, *Accountant*
▲ **EMP:** 41 **EST:** 1993
SALES (est): 4.4MM **Privately Held**
SIC: 3231 1542 3441 Doors, glass: made from purchased glass; store front construction; fabricated structural metal

(G-16845)
**FLORIDA INDUS SOLUTIONS
LLC**
13773 N Nebraska Ave (33613-3320)
PHONE.............................833 746-7347
Rick Sasser,
Julie Sasser,
EMP: 10 **EST:** 2017
SALES (est): 519.2K **Privately Held**
WEB: www.floridaindustrialsolutions.com
SIC: 3452 Bolts, nuts, rivets & washers

(G-16846)
FLORIDA INK MFG CO INC
Also Called: F I M C O
1715 Temple St (33619-3161)
PHONE.............................813 247-2911
George B Nessmith, *President*
Tiny J Nessmith, *Corp Secy*
John S Nessmith, *Vice Pres*
Scott L Nessmith, *VP Mfg*
EMP: 8 **EST:** 1983
SQ FT: 16,000
SALES (est): 1.1MM **Privately Held**
WEB: www.flaink.com
SIC: 2893 Printing ink

(G-16847)
**FLORIDA LEVEL & TRANSIT CO
INC**
Also Called: Flt Geosystems
5468 56th Cmmrce Pk Blvd (33610-6857)
PHONE.............................813 623-3307
Paul Browning, *Manager*
EMP: 7
SALES (corp-wide): 8.7MM **Privately
Held**
WEB: secure.fltgeosystems.com
SIC: 3829 Measuring & controlling devices
PA: Florida Level & Transit Co., Inc.
809 Progresso Dr
Fort Lauderdale FL 33304
954 763-5300

(G-16848)
FLORIDA MADE DOOR CO (PA)
Also Called: West Bay Door
1 N Dale Mabry Hwy # 950 (33609-2764)
P.O. Box 128, Astatula (34705-0128)
PHONE.............................352 742-1000
Frank L Eger Jr, *President*
Joseph P Eger, *Vice Pres*
Bob Brown, *Controller*
◆ **EMP:** 140 **EST:** 1954
SQ FT: 130,000
SALES (est): 11.4MM **Privately Held**
WEB: www.floridamadedoor.com
SIC: 2431 Doors, wood

(G-16849)
**FLORIDA MARINE JOINER SVC
INC**
4917 Hartford St (33619-6715)
P.O. Box 89729 (33689-0412)
PHONE.............................813 514-1125
William Doyle, *President*
Marsha Doyle,
▲ **EMP:** 15 **EST:** 2012
SALES (est): 1.9MM **Privately Held**
WEB: www.fmjsi.com
SIC: 2431 1751 7699 1742 Millwork; carpentry work; cabinet & finish carpentry; finish & trim carpentry; boat repair; acoustical & insulation work

(G-16850)
FLORIDA MARINE PRODUCTS INC
2001 E 5th Ave (33605-5221)
PHONE.............................813 248-2283
Randolph Urban Pattillo, *President*
Randolph A Pattillo, *Corp Secy*
EMP: 10 EST: 1986
SQ FT: 13,000
SALES (est): 2.3MM **Privately Held**
WEB: www.fmpusa.com
SIC: 3592 Valves

(G-16851)
FLORIDA PLAYGROUND & STEEL CO
4701 S 50th St (33619-9510)
PHONE.............................813 247-2812
Rick Barrs, *President*
▼ EMP: 6 EST: 1942
SQ FT: 8,000
SALES (est): 486.1K **Privately Held**
WEB: www.fla-playground.com
SIC: 3949 Playground equipment

(G-16852)
FLORIDA PRE-FAB INC
2907 Sagasta St (33619-6000)
PHONE.............................813 247-3934
George Levy, *President*
Alexander Levy, *VP Finance*
Alejandro Pose, *CIO*
▼ EMP: 19 EST: 1972
SQ FT: 95,000
SALES (est): 2.3MM **Privately Held**
WEB: www.floridaprefab.com
SIC: 3448 Buildings, portable: prefabricated metal

(G-16853)
FLORIDA PRECISION MCH MET WORK
5904 Lynn Rd (33624-4800)
PHONE.............................813 486-5050
Guillermo Valdes, *Principal*
EMP: 9 EST: 2008
SALES (est): 111.7K **Privately Held**
SIC: 3599 Machine shop, jobbing & repair

(G-16854)
FLORIDA ROCK INDUSTRIES
5920 W Linebaugh Ave (33624-5096)
PHONE.............................305 592-4100
Donald M James, *Branch Mgr*
EMP: 8 **Publicly Held**
WEB: www.flarock.com
SIC: 3999 Barber & beauty shop equipment
HQ: Florida Rock Industries
4707 Gordon St
Jacksonville FL 32216
904 355-1781

(G-16855)
FLORIDA SENTINEL PUBLISHING CO
Also Called: Florida Sentinel Bulletin
2207 E 21st Ave (33605-2043)
P.O. Box 3363 (33601-3363)
PHONE.............................813 248-1921
Blythe Andrews III, *President*
EMP: 27 EST: 1945
SQ FT: 4,900
SALES (est): 4.3MM **Privately Held**
WEB: www.flsentinel.com
SIC: 2711 2752 Newspapers: publishing only, not printed on site; commercial printing, lithographic

(G-16856)
FMC/RHYNO LLC
Also Called: Rhyno Glass
5115 W Knox St (33634-8029)
PHONE.............................813 838-2264
Wyatt Castellvi, *Mng Member*
EMP: 38 EST: 2018
SALES (est): 4.8MM **Privately Held**
SIC: 3211 Flat glass

(G-16857)
FOAM MOLDING LLC
3211 W Beach St (33607-2168)
PHONE.............................813 434-7044
Alexis Hernandez, *Principal*
EMP: 8 EST: 2015

SALES (est): 338.9K **Privately Held**
SIC: 3089 Molding primary plastic

(G-16858)
FOLDERS TABS ET CETERA
4906 Savarese Cir (33634-2403)
PHONE.............................813 884-3651
Joe Torrence, *President*
Debbie Torrence, *Vice Pres*
EMP: 14 EST: 1989
SQ FT: 14,000
SALES (est): 816.9K **Privately Held**
WEB: www.ftec.ws
SIC: 2893 2675 2672 Letterpress or offset ink; die-cut paper & board; coated & laminated paper

(G-16859)
FPC PRINTING INC
201 Kelsey Ln (33619-4310)
PHONE.............................813 626-9430
James L Kendall, *President*
Donice Payne, *President*
A J M Mandt, *Director*
EMP: 116 EST: 1988
SQ FT: 70,000
SALES (est): 7.3MM
SALES (corp-wide): 194.6MM **Publicly Held**
SIC: 2741 Shopping news: publishing & printing
PA: Harte Hanks, Inc.
2 Executive Dr Ste 103
Chelmsford MA 01824
512 434-1100

(G-16860)
FREE PRESS PUBLISHING COMPANY
1010 W Cass St (33606-1307)
PHONE.............................813 254-5888
John N Harrison III, *Ch of Bd*
John Harrison IV, *President*
Joann Klay, *Vice Pres*
EMP: 31 EST: 1911
SQ FT: 17,000
SALES (est): 2.6MM **Privately Held**
WEB: www.einpresswire.com
SIC: 2752 2711 Commercial printing, offset; color lithography; newspapers, publishing & printing

(G-16861)
FRESCO FOODS INC (PA)
Also Called: Eat Fresco
9410 E Broadway Ave (33619-7723)
PHONE.............................813 551-2100
Rob Povolny, *President*
Robert Polvony, *President*
EMP: 22 EST: 2014
SALES (est): 12.7MM **Privately Held**
WEB: www.eatfrescofoods.com
SIC: 2099 Ready-to-eat meals, salads & sandwiches

(G-16862)
FRESH BRANDZ LLC
6201 Johns Rd Ste 11 (33634-4434)
PHONE.............................813 880-7110
Robert Johnson, *CEO*
EMP: 9 EST: 2018
SQ FT: 8,000
SALES (est): 1.7MM **Privately Held**
SIC: 2844 5122 Toilet preparations; toiletries

(G-16863)
FUEL SOLUTIONS LLC
14213 Banbury Way (33624-2620)
PHONE.............................813 969-2506
Bernard Arenas,
Kevin B Banish,
EMP: 8 EST: 2008
SALES (est): 803.2K **Privately Held**
SIC: 2869 Fuels

(G-16864)
FUSE BUILDS LLC
4480 Eagle Falls Pl (33619-9620)
PHONE.............................617 602-4001
EMP: 40
SALES (corp-wide): 60.9MM **Privately Held**
WEB: www.fusebuilds.com
SIC: 1389 Construction, repair & dismantling services

PA: Fuse Builds Llc
65 Allerton St
Roxbury MA 02119
617 602-4001

(G-16865)
FUTURE PLUS OF FLORIDA
Also Called: Batteries Plus
138 S Dale Mabry Hwy (33609-2837)
PHONE.............................612 240-7275
Daniel R Snyder, *Principal*
EMP: 13 EST: 2012
SALES (est): 2.7MM **Privately Held**
SIC: 3692 5531 Primary batteries, dry & wet; batteries, automotive & truck

(G-16866)
FUZION DIGITAL SIGNS
4409 N Clark Ave (33614-7017)
PHONE.............................844 529-0505
EMP: 7 EST: 2015
SALES (est): 309.6K **Privately Held**
SIC: 3999 Manufacturing industries

(G-16867)
FW SHORING COMPANY
Also Called: Professional Shoring & Supply
7532 Malta Ln (33637-6725)
PHONE.............................813 248-2495
Kevin Chandler, *Branch Mgr*
EMP: 7
SALES (corp-wide): 9.9MM **Privately Held**
WEB: www.efficiencyproduction.com
SIC: 3531 Construction machinery
PA: Fw Shoring Company
685 Hull Rd
Mason MI 48854
517 676-8800

(G-16868)
GALLOP GROUP INC
2402 S Ardson Pl (33629-7308)
PHONE.............................813 251-6242
Nancy M Peterson, *Principal*
EMP: 9 EST: 2010
SALES (est): 127.7K **Privately Held**
WEB: www.jamesmanninglaw.com
SIC: 3241 Cement, hydraulic

(G-16869)
GARDNER ASPHALT CORPORATION (DH)
4161 E 7th Ave (33605-4601)
P.O. Box 5449 (33675-5449)
PHONE.............................813 248-2101
Raymond T Hyer, *CEO*
Fernando Navarro, *General Mgr*
Amir Khan, *Vice Pres*
Gustavo Velez, *Plant Mgr*
Jennifer Martinez, *Traffic Mgr*
◆ EMP: 64 EST: 1945
SQ FT: 40,000
SALES (est): 216.7MM
SALES (corp-wide): 913.2MM **Privately Held**
WEB: www.gardner-gibson.com
SIC: 2951 Asphalt paving mixtures & blocks
HQ: Gardner-Gibson, Incorporated
4161 E 7th Ave
Tampa FL 33605
813 248-2101

(G-16870)
GARDNER ASPHALT CORPORATION
Also Called: Gardber-Gibson
4001 E 7th Ave (33605-4506)
PHONE.............................813 248-2101
Mike Hyer, *Sales Staff*
Mike Sullivan, *Sales Staff*
Menlo Scquera, *Manager*
Neil Loftie, *Info Tech Dir*
EMP: 161
SALES (corp-wide): 913.2MM **Privately Held**
WEB: www.gardner-gibson.com
SIC: 3531 Roofing equipment
HQ: Gardner Asphalt Corporation
4161 E 7th Ave
Tampa FL 33605
813 248-2101

(G-16871)
GARDNER-GIBSON MFG INC (DH)
4161 E 7th Ave (33605-4601)
P.O. Box 5449 (33675-5449)
PHONE.............................813 248-2101
Raymond T Hyer Jr, *President*
Rafael Perez, *Plant Mgr*
Imalka Arachchilage, *Research*
Sean W Poole, *Treasurer*
Darminda Ranatunga, *Controller*
◆ EMP: 25 EST: 2000
SALES (est): 114.3MM
SALES (corp-wide): 913.2MM **Privately Held**
WEB: www.gardner-gibson.com
SIC: 2951 2891 2952 Asphalt paving mixtures & blocks; adhesives & sealants; roof cement: asphalt, fibrous or plastic
HQ: Gardner-Gibson, Incorporated
4161 E 7th Ave
Tampa FL 33605
813 248-2101

(G-16872)
GEM ASSET ACQUISITION LLC
Also Called: Gemseal Pavements Pdts - Tampa
5050 Denver St (33619-6812)
PHONE.............................813 630-1695
EMP: 28
SALES (corp-wide): 19.3MM **Privately Held**
SIC: 2951 Asphalt paving mixtures & blocks
PA: Gem Asset Acquisition Llc
1855 Lindbergh St Ste 500
Charlotte NC 28208
704 225-3321

(G-16873)
GEMSEAL PAVEMENT PRODUCTS
5050 Denver St (33619-6812)
PHONE.............................305 328-9159
Carolyn Bradeen, *Office Mgr*
Chris Mariani, *CIO*
EMP: 8 EST: 2017
SALES (est): 957K **Privately Held**
WEB: www.gemsealproducts.com
SIC: 2951 Asphalt paving mixtures & blocks

(G-16874)
GENERAL SAW COMPANY
2902 E Sligh Ave (33610-1412)
PHONE.............................813 231-3167
Timothy Murphy, *President*
EMP: 15 EST: 1990
SQ FT: 14,000
SALES (est): 2.2MM **Privately Held**
WEB: www.gensaw.com
SIC: 3441 Fabricated structural metal

(G-16875)
GENESIS SYSTEMS LLC
3108 N Boundary Blvd # 9 (33621-5050)
PHONE.............................417 499-3301
David J Stuckenberg, *CEO*
Shannon Stuckenberg, *CEO*
Jashal Patel, *Engineer*
Ethan Plumer, *Engineer*
EMP: 9 EST: 2008
SALES (est): 2.1MM **Privately Held**
WEB: www.genesissystems.global
SIC: 3589 Water treatment equipment, industrial

(G-16876)
GERDAU AMERISTEEL CORP (HQ)
4221 W Boy Scout Blvd # 600 (33607-5760)
P.O. Box 31328 (33631-3328)
PHONE.............................813 286-8383
Mario Longhi, *President*
Guilherme C Gerdau Johannpeter, *President*
Rick Szink, *General Mgr*
Tony Klippel, *Superintendent*
Dean Wner, *Superintendent*
◆ EMP: 560 EST: 1956
SALES (est): 1.4B **Privately Held**
SIC: 3312 Blast furnaces & steel mills

(G-16877)
GERDAU AMERISTEEL US INC (DH)
Also Called: Gerdau Long Steel North Amer
4221 W Boy Scout Blvd # 600
(33607-5760)
P.O. Box 31328 (33631-3328)
PHONE................................813 286-8383
Peter J Campo, *CEO*
Guilherme G Johannpeter, *President*
Andre Johannpeter, *Principal*
Franz Olbrich, *Principal*
Darlene Quintilliani, *Principal*
◆ EMP: 300 EST: 1956
SQ FT: 68,310
SALES (est): 1.5B Privately Held
WEB: www.gerdau.com.br
SIC: 3312 3449 3315 Hot-rolled iron &
　steel products; bars, concrete reinforcing:
　fabricated steel; spikes, steel: wire or cut
HQ: Gerdau Usa Inc.
　4221 W Boy Scout Blvd
　Tampa FL 33607
　813 286-8383

(G-16878)
GERDAU USA INC (DH)
Also Called: Gerdau Long Steel America
4221 W Boy Scout Blvd (33607-5743)
PHONE................................813 286-8383
Guilherme Johannpeter, *President*
Peter J Campo, *Vice Pres*
Carl W Czarnik, *Vice Pres*
Rodrigo Ferreira De Souza, *Vice Pres*
Steven Wilkinson, *Maint Spvr*
◆ EMP: 350 EST: 2000
SQ FT: 35,000
SALES (est): 1.5B Privately Held
WEB: www.gerdau.com.br
SIC: 3449 3315 3312 Bars, concrete rein-
　forcing: fabricated steel; spikes, steel:
　wire or cut; welded steel wire fabric; nails,
　steel: wire or cut; hot-rolled iron & steel
　products
HQ: Gerdau Ameristeel Corporation
　1 Gerdau Crt
　Whitby ON L1N 5
　905 668-8811

(G-16879)
GHX INDUSTRIAL LLC
Also Called: Amazon Hose & Rubber
1103 N 50th St (33619-3211)
PHONE................................813 223-7554
Rich Potero, *Principal*
Jim Donlan, *Principal*
George Malgoza, *Principal*
EMP: 8 EST: 2007
SALES (est): 77.4K Privately Held
WEB: www.ghxinc.com
SIC: 3052 Rubber & plastics hose & belt-
　ings

(G-16880)
GLIDER PRINTING LLC
13377 W Hillsborough Ave Uni
(33635-9717)
PHONE................................813 601-8907
Mark Hammonds, *Principal*
EMP: 7 EST: 2016
SALES (est): 323.6K Privately Held
SIC: 2752 Commercial printing, offset

(G-16881)
GLOBAL COMPOSITE USA INC ✪
6608 S West Shore Blvd (33616-1458)
PHONE................................813 898-7987
Matt Major, *President*
EMP: 50 EST: 2021
SALES (est): 1MM Privately Held
SIC: 3999 Manufacturing industries

(G-16882)
GLOBAL FRICTION PRODUCTS INC
2003 S 50th St (33619-5225)
PHONE................................813 241-2700
Billy Peek, *President*
Stacy Peek, *Vice Pres*
EMP: 10 EST: 1996
SQ FT: 2,000
SALES (est): 1.8MM Privately Held
WEB: www.globalfrictionproducts.com
SIC: 3469 Metal stampings

(G-16883)
GLOBAL MEDIA PRESS CORP
6723 N Armenia Ave (33604-5715)
P.O. Box 15657 (33684-5657)
PHONE................................813 857-5898
Mario F Vallejo, *President*
EMP: 7 EST: 2011
SALES (est): 86.7K Privately Held
SIC: 2741 Miscellaneous publishing

(G-16884)
GLOBAL PRODUCTS GROUP LLC (PA)
13760 Reptron Blvd (33626-3040)
PHONE................................866 320-4367
Gene Weitz, *Mng Member*
EMP: 7 EST: 2018
SALES (est): 145.4K Privately Held
WEB: www.globalproductgroup.com
SIC: 3999

(G-16885)
GLOBAL SEASHELL INDUSTRIES LLC
4930 Distribution Dr (33605-5926)
P.O. Box 129, Los Fresnos TX (78566-
0129)
PHONE................................813 677-6674
Elizabeth Harris, *Manager*
◆ EMP: 8 EST: 2010
SALES (est): 814K Privately Held
WEB: www.globalseashell.com
SIC: 3999 Manufacturing industries

(G-16886)
GOLD COAST PRINTING INC
401 E Jackson St Ste 2340 (33602-5226)
PHONE................................813 853-2219
Steven Bicking, *President*
EMP: 7 EST: 2016
SQ FT: 4,000
SALES (est): 142.5K Privately Held
SIC: 2752 Commercial printing, litho-
　graphic

(G-16887)
GOTOBILLING LLC
Also Called: Omnifund
218 E Bearss Ave Ste 368 (33613-1625)
PHONE................................800 305-1534
Steve Roderick, *CEO*
Kayla Diuguid, *Mktg Coord*
Natalie Fairman, *Manager*
Tom Cooper, *Administration*
Scott Miller, *Loan*
EMP: 13 EST: 2007
SALES (est): 1.1MM
SALES (corp-wide): 8.3MM Privately
Held
WEB: www.fortispay.com
SIC: 7372 Business oriented computer
　software
PA: Fortis Payment Systems, Llc
　43155 Main St Ste 2310c
　Novi MI 48375
　248 348-5502

(G-16888)
GRABBER CONSTRUCTION PDTS INC
5835 Barry Rd Ste 107 (33634-3020)
PHONE................................813 249-2281
Jim Briggers, *Manager*
EMP: 7
SALES (corp-wide): 1B Privately Held
WEB: www.grabberpro.com
SIC: 3452 5032 5085 Screws, metal; dry-
　wall materials; fasteners, industrial: nuts,
　bolts, screws, etc.
HQ: Grabber Construction Products, Inc.
　5255 W 11000 N Ste 100
　Highland UT 84003
　801 492-3880

(G-16889)
GRANITE SERVICES INTL INC
Also Called: Pen Power
201 N Franklin St # 1000 (33602-5182)
PHONE................................813 242-7400
Randy Willis, *President*
Mort Smith, *Vice Pres*
Morgan Williams, *CFO*
Mica Segui, *VP Human Res*
EMP: 11 EST: 2002

SALES (est): 9.5MM
SALES (corp-wide): 74.2B Publicly Held
SIC: 3519 7363 8711 Gasoline engines;
　help supply services; engineering serv-
　ices
HQ: Fieldcore Service Solutions Interna-
　tional Llc
　201 N Franklin St # 1000
　Tampa FL 33602
　813 242-7400

(G-16890)
GRANITE WORLD INC
7024 Benjamin Rd (33634-3034)
PHONE................................813 243-6556
Rudolfo Vidal, *President*
Julie Vidal, *Vice Pres*
EMP: 29 EST: 2000
SQ FT: 10,000
SALES (est): 2.7MM Privately Held
WEB: www.graniteworldinc.com
SIC: 3281 1423 Cut stone & stone prod-
　ucts; crushed & broken granite

(G-16891)
GRASS PRO SHOPS INC
303 S Falkenburg Rd (33619-8027)
PHONE................................813 381-3890
Raymond Ham, *President*
James Dombrosky, *Manager*
EMP: 14 EST: 2009
SALES (est): 2.8MM Privately Held
WEB: www.grassproshops.com
SIC: 3537 Industrial trucks & tractors

(G-16892)
GREENCO MANUFACTURING CORP
Also Called: Duramaster
5688 W Crenshaw St Frnt (33634-3043)
PHONE................................813 882-4400
Joseph T Green, *President*
Jaime Howe, *Controller*
EMP: 19 EST: 1970
SQ FT: 20,000
SALES (est): 3MM Privately Held
WEB: www.greencocylinders.com
SIC: 3593 3443 Fluid power cylinders, hy-
　draulic or pneumatic; fabricated plate
　work (boiler shop)

(G-16893)
GRIFFIN INDUSTRIES LLC
1001 Orient Rd (33619-3321)
PHONE................................813 626-1135
Jerome Levy, *General Mgr*
Tom Molini, *General Mgr*
Tim Garris, *Vice Pres*
Mitch Coleman, *Plant Supt*
Dexter Horton, *Plant Mgr*
EMP: 84
SQ FT: 33,078
SALES (corp-wide): 4.7B Publicly Held
SIC: 2077 5199 Tallow rendering, inedible;
　oils, animal or vegetable
HQ: Griffin Industries Llc
　4221 Alexandria Pike
　Cold Spring KY 41076
　859 781-2010

(G-16894)
GRIZZLY PRODUCTS CORP
4406 W Virginia Ave (33614-7742)
P.O. Box 422 (33601-0422)
PHONE................................813 545-3828
Russell P Mathews, *President*
EMP: 10 EST: 2012
SALES (est): 1.4MM Privately Held
WEB: www.grizzlytargets.com
SIC: 3441 Fabricated structural metal

(G-16895)
GROUP TWS LLC
20415 Walnut Grove Ln (33647-3352)
PHONE................................337 499-2928
EMP: 10 EST: 2020
SALES (est): 530.7K Privately Held
SIC: 3851 Protective eyeware

(G-16896)
GULF COAST PAINT & SUPPLIES
Also Called: Abe Paints
1910 N Us Highway 301 (33619-2640)
PHONE................................813 932-3093
EMP: 11 EST: 2018

SALES (est): 1.2MM Privately Held
WEB: www.gulfcoastpaint.com
SIC: 2851 Paints & allied products

(G-16897)
GULF COAST REBAR INC
1301 E 4th Ave (33605-5013)
P.O. Box 75588 (33675-0588)
PHONE................................813 247-1200
Chad E Jones, *President*
EMP: 50
SALES (corp-wide): 9.2MM Privately
Held
WEB: www.gulfcoastrebar.com
SIC: 3449 1541 Bars, concrete reinforc-
　ing: fabricated steel; steel building con-
　struction
PA: Gulf Coast Rebar, Inc.
　4560 Shiloh Mill Blvd
　Jacksonville FL 32246
　904 982-0521

(G-16898)
GULF MARINE REPAIR CORPORATION (PA)
Also Called: G M R
1800 Grant St (33605-6042)
PHONE................................813 247-3153
Aaron Hendry, *President*
Eric F Smith, *Vice Pres*
Claude R Watts, *Vice Pres*
Jim Blackstone, *Facilities Mgr*
Alex Santiago, *Foreman/Supr*
▲ EMP: 184 EST: 1988
SQ FT: 12,500
SALES (est): 27.2MM Privately Held
WEB: www.gulfmarinerepair.com
SIC: 3731 Shipbuilding & repairing

(G-16899)
GULFPORT INDUSTRIES INC
6308 Benjamin Rd Ste 714 (33634-5174)
PHONE................................813 885-1000
Bob Nedic, *Manager*
EMP: 14 EST: 2007
SALES (est): 492.6K Privately Held
WEB: www.gulfport-corp.com
SIC: 2431 3442 5031 Doors, wood; metal
　doors; doors & windows

(G-16900)
GULFSTREAM UNSNKABLE BOATS LLC
Also Called: Gulfstream Yachts
5251 W Tyson Ave (33611-3223)
PHONE................................813 820-6100
Perry Kyra, *Business Mgr*
Molly Edwards, *Purch Mgr*
Huntington James, *Mng Member*
EMP: 12 EST: 2008
SALES (est): 1.5MM Privately Held
SIC: 3732 Boat building & repairing

(G-16901)
GUNN PRTG & LITHOGRAPHY INC
4415 W Dr Martin L King Martin Luther
(33614)
PHONE................................813 870-6010
Clark Gunn, *CEO*
Pat Gunn, *President*
Edna Gunn, *Corp Secy*
EMP: 15 EST: 1985
SQ FT: 10,000
SALES (est): 2.1MM Privately Held
WEB: www.gunnprinting.com
SIC: 2752 Commercial printing, offset

(G-16902)
HALLMARK EMBLEMS INC
2401 N Tampa St (33602-2136)
P.O. Box 172838 (33672-0838)
PHONE................................813 223-5427
Thomas C Burgeson, *President*
Karen Burgeson, *Vice Pres*
Scott Delarco, *Vice Pres*
Ehsan Siddiqui, *Plant Mgr*
▲ EMP: 68 EST: 1981
SQ FT: 44,000
SALES (est): 8.2MM Privately Held
WEB: www.hallmarkemblems.com
SIC: 2399 Aprons, breast (harness)

▲ = Import ▼=Export
◆ =Import/Export

(G-16903)
HAMAN INDUSTRIES INC
Also Called: Tampa Pallet Co
2402 S 54th St (33619-5364)
P.O. Box 310386 (33680-0386)
PHONE...............................813 626-5700
Frederic E Haman, *President*
Carol Haman, *Vice Pres*
EMP: 12 EST: 1954
SQ FT: 6,200
SALES (est): 2.3MM Privately Held
WEB: www.tampapallet.com
SIC: 2441 2448 Nailed wood boxes &
shook; pallets, wood

(G-16904)
HANES-HARRIS DESIGN CONS
Also Called: Sign Art Group, The
6106 N Nebraska Ave Ste A (33604-6877)
PHONE...............................813 237-0202
EMP: 5
SALES (est): 558.6K Privately Held
SIC: 3993 Mfg Signs

(G-16905)
HARCROS CHEMICALS INC
5132 Trenton St (33619-6834)
PHONE...............................813 247-4531
Skye Athey, *Purchasing*
Tom Hillyer, *Branch Mgr*
Gary Dunmeyer, *Manager*
Sue Ernest, *Manager*
Vinay Nair, *Manager*
EMP: 29
SALES (corp-wide): 498.1MM Privately
Held
WEB: www.harcros.com
SIC: 2869 2819 Industrial organic chemi-
cals; industrial inorganic chemicals
PA: Harcros Chemicals Inc.
5200 Speaker Rd
Kansas City KS 66106
913 321-3131

(G-16906)
HARPER LIMBACH LLC
9051 Fla Min Blvd Ste 103 (33634)
PHONE...............................813 207-0057
Robert Wilder, *Safety Dir*
Luis Aguiar, *Opers Mgr*
Rindi Beachel, *Accountant*
Mike McCann, *Branch Mgr*
Robert Leduc, *Manager*
EMP: 13
SALES (corp-wide): 490.3MM Publicly
Held
WEB: www.harperbuildingsystems.com
SIC: 3495 Mechanical springs, precision
HQ: Harper Limbach Llc
5102 W Laurel St Ste 800
Tampa FL 33607
407 321-8100

(G-16907)
HARSCO CORPORATION
Also Called: Reed Minerals Division
5950 Old 41a Hwy (33619-8758)
P.O. Box 2308, Gibsonton (33534-2308)
PHONE...............................717 506-2071
Doug Norris, *Manager*
EMP: 10
SALES (corp-wide): 1.8B Publicly Held
WEB: www.harsco.com
SIC: 3295 3291 2952 Slag, crushed or
ground; abrasive products; asphalt felts &
coatings
PA: Harsco Corporation
350 Poplar Church Rd
Camp Hill PA 17011
717 763-7064

(G-16908)
HATCH TRANSFORMERS INC
Also Called: HATCH LIGHTING
7821 Woodland Center Blvd (33614-2410)
PHONE...............................813 288-8006
Michael Hatch, *CEO*
Dan Garcia, *Exec VP*
Byron Martin, *Warehouse Mgr*
Debbie Kugler, *Purch Agent*
Soufiane Daoudiya, *Electrical Engi*
▲ EMP: 22 EST: 1980
SQ FT: 10,000

SALES (est): 5.4MM Privately Held
WEB: www.hatchlighting.com
SIC: 3612 Lighting transformers, fluores-
cent; lighting transformers, street & airport

(G-16909)
HAWKS NUTS INC
Also Called: Hawks Orgnal Jmbo Bled
Peanuts
4713 N Hale Ave (33614-6515)
PHONE...............................813 872-0900
Mildred M Hawks, *President*
Paul Hawks, *Vice Pres*
EMP: 11 EST: 1995
SQ FT: 50,000
SALES (est): 1.8MM Privately Held
WEB: www.hawksboiledpeanuts.com
SIC: 2076 Peanut oil, cake or meal

(G-16910)
**HAWVER ALUMINUM FOUNDRY
INC**
9526 N Trask St (33624-5137)
P.O. Box 270481 (33688-0481)
PHONE...............................813 961-1497
James A Hawver, *President*
Judith Hawver, *Vice Pres*
EMP: 9 EST: 1969
SQ FT: 8,000
SALES (est): 965.9K Privately Held
WEB: www.hawvercastings.com
SIC: 3366 Copper foundries

(G-16911)
HEAT-PIPE TECHNOLOGY INC
6904 Parke East Blvd (33610-4115)
PHONE...............................813 470-4250
Tom Manenti, *CEO*
Eugene M Toombs, *President*
Gene Toombs IV, *President*
Mazan Awad, *Vice Pres*
Bonnie Daniels, *Vice Pres*
◆ EMP: 30 EST: 1983
SALES (est): 10.9MM
SALES (corp-wide): 354.6B Publicly
Held
WEB: www.heatpipe.com
SIC: 3585 Air conditioning condensers &
condensing units; dehumidifiers electric,
except portable
HQ: Marmon Holdings, Inc.
181 W Madison St Ste 3900
Chicago IL 60602
312 372-9500

(G-16912)
HENDRY CORPORATION
1800 Grant St (33605-6042)
PHONE...............................813 241-9206
Aaron Hendry, *President*
Hal Hendry, *General Mgr*
Dennis E Manelli, *Vice Pres*
Dale West, *CFO*
EMP: 64 EST: 1926
SQ FT: 3,000
SALES (est): 9.4MM Privately Held
WEB: www.hendrymarineindustries.com
SIC: 3731 1629 Shipbuilding & repairing;
marine construction

(G-16913)
**HENDRY MARINE INDUSTRIES
INC**
1800 Grant St (33605-6042)
PHONE...............................813 241-9206
Richard McCreary, *President*
Aaron W Hendry, *Principal*
Eric F Smith, *COO*
Stephanie Koch, *Human Res Dir*
Angela Baylis, *Manager*
EMP: 23 EST: 2011
SALES (est): 1.1MM Privately Held
WEB: www.hendrymarineindustries.com
SIC: 3731 Shipbuilding & repairing

(G-16914)
**HENDRY SHIPYARD JOINT
VENTR 1**
1800 Grant St (33605-6042)
PHONE...............................813 241-9206
Aaron Hendry, *Manager*
EMP: 15 EST: 2012
SALES (est): 470.9K Privately Held
WEB: www.hendrymarineindustries.com
SIC: 3731 Barges, building & repairing

(G-16915)
HERITAGE MEDCALL LLC
202 E Virginia Ave (33603-4821)
PHONE...............................813 221-1000
Donald R Musselman, *CEO*
Justin Franke, *President*
EMP: 13 EST: 2012
SQ FT: 2,500
SALES (est): 2.4MM Privately Held
WEB: www.heritagemedcall.com
SIC: 3669 Emergency alarms

(G-16916)
HIGHLANDS ETHANOL LLC
Also Called: Vercipia Biofuels
2202 N West Shore Blvd (33607-5747)
PHONE...............................813 421-1090
John Doyle, *Vice Pres*
EMP: 6 EST: 2010
SALES (est): 2.3MM
SALES (corp-wide): 157.7B Privately
Held
WEB: www.vercipia.com
SIC: 2869 Ethyl alcohol, ethanol
PA: Bp P.L.C.
1 St. James's Square
London SW1Y
207 496-4000

(G-16917)
**HILL DONNELLY CORPORATION
(PA)**
Also Called: Onesource Information Services
10126 Windhorst Rd (33619-7826)
PHONE...............................800 525-1242
Lee H Hill III, *President*
EMP: 25 EST: 1917
SQ FT: 10,000
SALES (est): 3.9MM Privately Held
SIC: 2741 7331 3572 Telephone & other
directory publishing; direct mail advertis-
ing services; computer storage devices

(G-16918)
HIPPO TAMPA LLC
605 Bosphorous Ave (33606-3915)
PHONE...............................813 391-9152
Gerald Fraser, *Owner*
EMP: 8 EST: 2007
SALES (est): 137.9K Privately Held
SIC: 3089 Garbage containers, plastic

(G-16919)
HOB CORPORATION
Also Called: Palladium Graphics
5604 E 122nd Ave (33617)
PHONE...............................813 988-2272
Jack T O'Brien, *President*
Keith O'Brien, *Vice Pres*
Mary E O'Brien, *Admin Sec*
EMP: 6 EST: 1985
SQ FT: 5,000
SALES (est): 356.1K Privately Held
WEB: www.palladiumgraphics.com
SIC: 2396 3993 2752 2395 Screen print-
ing on fabric articles; signs & advertising
specialties; commercial printing, litho-
graphic; pleating & stitching

(G-16920)
HOME PRIDE CABINETS INC
8503 Sunstate St (33634-1311)
PHONE...............................813 887-3782
Bernie Gaydos, *President*
EMP: 19 EST: 1990
SALES (est): 3.8MM Privately Held
WEB: www.homepridecabinets.com
SIC: 2517 2541 2521 2434 Wood televi-
sion & radio cabinets; wood partitions &
fixtures; wood office furniture; wood
kitchen cabinets

(G-16921)
HONEST HANDS LLC
13907 Carrollwood Vlg Run (33618-2746)
PHONE...............................413 262-3892
Deivis Rodriguez, *Principal*
EMP: 5 EST: 2019
SALES (est): 450.5K Privately Held
WEB: www.honesthandsflorida.com
SIC: 3732 Boat building & repairing

(G-16922)
HORNBLASTERS INC
Also Called: Mini Truckin
6511 N 54th St (33610-1907)
PHONE...............................813 783-8058
Mathew L Heller, *President*
Manny Rizzo, *Sls & Mktg Exec*
EMP: 20 EST: 2002
SALES (est): 3.6MM Privately Held
WEB: www.hornblasters.com
SIC: 3714 5013 5015 5531 Horns, motor
vehicle; springs, shock absorbers &
struts; automotive accessories, used; au-
tomotive accessories

(G-16923)
**HOWARD IMPRINTING MACHINE
CO**
5013 Tampa West Blvd (33634-2414)
P.O. Box 15027 (33684-5027)
PHONE...............................813 884-2398
James Wrobbel, *President*
Bill Wrobbel, *Vice Pres*
Ray J Wrobbel, *Vice Pres*
▲ EMP: 8 EST: 1931
SQ FT: 10,000
SALES (est): 928.3K Privately Held
WEB: www.howardimprinting.com
SIC: 3555 5084 Printing trades machinery;
printing trades machinery, equipment &
supplies

(G-16924)
HOWMEDICA OSTEONICS CORP
Also Called: Stryker Orthopaedics
8731 Florida Mining Blvd (33634-1259)
PHONE...............................813 886-3450
Tommy Edwards, *President*
Kevin Dufford, *Sales Staff*
EMP: 9
SALES (corp-wide): 17.1B Publicly Held
SIC: 3842 Surgical appliances & supplies
HQ: Howmedica Osteonics Corp.
325 Corporate Dr
Mahwah NJ 07430
201 831-5000

(G-16925)
HR EASE INC
2002 N Lois Ave Ste 220 (33607-2395)
PHONE...............................813 414-0040
Susanne Kinsella Gill, *CEO*
Hank Gill, *Principal*
John Tedesco, *Business Mgr*
EMP: 8 EST: 2000
SQ FT: 800
SALES (est): 730K Privately Held
WEB: www.hrease.com
SIC: 7372 Business oriented computer
software

(G-16926)
HTS CONTROLS INC
4918 W Grace St (33607-3806)
P.O. Box 24169 (33623-4169)
PHONE...............................813 287-5512
EMP: 10
SALES (est): 1.2MM
SALES (corp-wide): 34.1MM Privately
Held
SIC: 3625 3621 Mfg Relays/Industrial
Controls Mfg Motors/Generators
PA: Carter & Verplanck, Inc.
4910 W Cypress St
Tampa FL 33607
813 287-0709

(G-16927)
HUSSMANN CORPORATION
Automaten Systems Division
9216 Palm River Rd # 201 (33619-4479)
PHONE...............................813 623-1199
Jason Rose, *Foreman/Supr*
Jim Jacobs, *Branch Mgr*
EMP: 48 Privately Held
WEB: www.hussmann.com
SIC: 3565 Packaging machinery
HQ: Hussmann Corporation
12999 St Charles Rock Rd
Bridgeton MO 63044
314 291-2000

(G-16928)
ICECOLD2 LLC
Also Called: Icecool World
10004 N Dale Mabry Hwy (33618-4494)
PHONE................................855 326-2665
Bhavash Patel, *Mng Member*
Sarah Kimber, *Executive Asst*
EMP: 7 EST: 2014
SALES (est): 231K Privately Held
WEB: www.ecocoolworld.com
SIC: 3585 Air conditioning condensers &
condensing units

(G-16929)
ICI CUSTOM PARTS INC
13911 Bittersweet Way (33625-6426)
PHONE................................813 888-7979
Russell O McKee Sr, *President*
Tammy Lyman, *Corp Secy*
Joanne McKee, *Senior VP*
Balinda K Cardinale, *Treasurer*
Michael L Vaughn, *Admin Sec*
EMP: 16 EST: 2001
SALES (est): 1.5MM Privately Held
WEB: www.icicustomparts.com
SIC: 3589 3625 Dishwashing machines,
commercial; control equipment, electric

(G-16930)
ICON AIRCRAFT INC
825 Severn Ave (33606-4015)
PHONE................................813 387-6603
Warren Curry, *Branch Mgr*
EMP: 16 Privately Held
WEB: www.iconaircraft.com
SIC: 3728 Aircraft parts & equipment
PA: Icon Aircraft, Inc.
2141 Icon Way
Vacaville CA 95688

(G-16931)
IFCO SYSTEMS US LLC (PA)
3030 N Rocky Point Dr W # 300
(33607-5903)
PHONE................................813 463-4103
Candice Herndon, *President*
Russ Bunker, *General Mgr*
Wade Caplinger, *General Mgr*
Tony Flores, *General Mgr*
Brady Grant, *General Mgr*
▼ EMP: 20 EST: 1994
SQ FT: 5,000
SALES (est): 102.7MM Privately Held
WEB: www.ifco.com
SIC: 3081 Packing materials, plastic sheet

(G-16932)
IMAGE DEPOT
Also Called: D & J Logos
2017 E Fowler Ave (33612-5503)
PHONE................................813 685-7116
John Kamenar, *President*
EMP: 9 EST: 1992
SALES (est): 1MM Privately Held
WEB: www.idxbrands.com
SIC: 2759 5099 2395 Advertising
literature: printing; souvenirs; automotive
& apparel trimmings; pleating & stitching

(G-16933)
IMAGE ONE CORPORATION
6202 Benjamin Rd Ste 103 (33634-5184)
PHONE................................813 888-8288
Michael Lutz, *General Mgr*
Kathy Gomez, *Engineer*
Leigh A Corley, *Controller*
Ada Martinez, *HR Admin*
James Alvarez, *Manager*
EMP: 67 EST: 1998
SQ FT: 13,000
SALES (est): 9.4MM Privately Held
WEB: www.image-1.com
SIC: 7372 7374 Prepackaged software;
data processing & preparation

(G-16934)
**IMPACT SAFE GLASS
CORPORATION**
2705 N 35th St (33605-3121)
PHONE................................813 247-5528
Carrie Condon, *President*
EMP: 9 EST: 1999
SALES (est): 228.9K Privately Held
WEB: www.impactsafeglass.com
SIC: 3211 Insulating glass, sealed units

(G-16935)
IN THE NEWS INC
3706 N Ridge Ave (33603-4527)
P.O. Box 30176 (33630-3176)
PHONE................................813 882-8886
Barry J Murante, *President*
Heather Duncan, *General Mgr*
June Lacava, *General Mgr*
Tammy Sand, *General Mgr*
Brett Edwards, *Area Mgr*
EMP: 90 EST: 1987
SALES (est): 10MM Privately Held
WEB: www.inthenewsonline.com
SIC: 3999 5999 2399 Plaques, picture,
laminated; trophies & plaques; banners,
made from fabric

(G-16936)
IN TOUCH ELECTRONICS LLC
13944 Lynmar Blvd Bldg 2 (33626-3123)
PHONE................................813 818-9990
Progeny International,
EMP: 6 EST: 2011
SALES (est): 487.7K Privately Held
WEB: www.intouchdisplays.com
SIC: 3577 Graphic displays, except
graphic terminals

(G-16937)
**INDEPENDENT RESOURCES
INC (PA)**
5010 N Nebraska Ave (33603-2339)
P.O. Box 23489 (33623-3489)
PHONE................................813 237-0945
David J Curbelo, *President*
Daniel R Curbelo Sr, *Chairman*
Jeremy K Starling, *Vice Pres*
Debbie Curbelo, *CFO*
Deborah D Curbelo, *CFO*
EMP: 23 EST: 1977
SQ FT: 6,125
SALES (est): 3.4MM Privately Held
SIC: 2752 5943 5199 2761 Commercial
printing, offset; office forms & supplies;
advertising specialties; manifold business
forms

(G-16938)
INDICALI INC
15310 Amberly Dr Ste 250 (33647-1642)
PHONE................................831 905-4780
Nitin Patel MD, *CEO*
EMP: 5 EST: 1996
SQ FT: 300
SALES (est): 655.7K Privately Held
SIC: 2834 Vitamin, nutrient & hematinic
preparations for human use

(G-16939)
**INDUSTRIAL & MARINE MAINT
INC**
5511 24th Ave S (33619-5372)
P.O. Box 2781, Brandon (33509-2781)
PHONE................................813 622-8338
Larry Chatham, *President*
Chad Duncan, *Vice Pres*
EMP: 9 EST: 1985
SQ FT: 5,000
SALES (est): 895.4K Privately Held
SIC: 7692 3599 Welding repair; machine
shop, jobbing & repair

(G-16940)
**INDUSTRIAL COATING
SOLUTIONS**
7307 Yardley Way (33647-1216)
P.O. Box 48703 (33646-0123)
PHONE................................813 333-8988
George B Bashline Jr, *Principal*
EMP: 8 EST: 2010
SALES (est): 239.6K Privately Held
WEB: www.industrialpaintingsolutions.com
SIC: 3479 Metal coating & allied service

(G-16941)
**INDUSTRIAL GLVANIZERS AMER
INC**
Also Called: Industrial Galvanizers Tampa
9520 E Broadway Ave (33619-7721)
PHONE................................813 621-8990
Mark Mellon, *Branch Mgr*
EMP: 43 Privately Held
WEB: www.valmontcoatings.com
SIC: 3479 Galvanizing of iron, steel or end-
formed products

HQ: Industrial Galvanizers America, Inc.
3535 Halifax Rd Ste A
Petersburg VA 23805

(G-16942)
**INDUSTRIAL PROJECTS
SERVICES**
4102 W Linebaugh Ave # 103
(33624-5296)
P.O. Box 274231 (33688-4231)
PHONE................................813 265-2957
John D Miller, *President*
Louis Galazzo, *Partner*
Blake Miller, *Principal*
EMP: 7 EST: 1993
SQ FT: 8,000
SALES (est): 945.9K Privately Held
WEB: www.industrialprojectsreport.com
SIC: 2721 Trade journals: publishing only,
not printed on site

(G-16943)
INFOR PUBLIC SECTOR INC
Also Called: Fka Enroute Emergency Sys-
tems
3501 E Frontage Rd # 350 (33607-1704)
PHONE................................813 207-6911
Molly Crews, *Vice Pres*
Margaret Moran, *Vice Pres*
Laura Wedin, *Marketing Staff*
Maricel Itchon, *Sr Software Eng*
EMP: 34
SALES (corp-wide): 36.9B Privately Held
SIC: 7372 Prepackaged software
HQ: Infor Public Sector, Inc.
11092 Sun Center Dr
Rancho Cordova CA 95670
916 921-0883

(G-16944)
**INNOVATIVE SOFTWARE TECH
INC**
2802 N Howard Ave (33607-2623)
PHONE................................813 920-9435
William White, *President*
Paul Mazzapica, *Exec VP*
EMP: 18 EST: 2012
SALES (est): 790.1K Privately Held
WEB: www.inivcompanies.com
SIC: 7372 Application computer software

(G-16945)
INNOVATIVE SPINE CARE INC
8333 Gunn Hwy (33626-1608)
PHONE................................813 920-3022
Stephen Watson, *Principal*
EMP: 8 EST: 2012
SALES (est): 639.7K Privately Held
WEB: www.gotspinepain.com
SIC: 3842 Prosthetic appliances

(G-16946)
**INTEGRATED CABLE
SOLUTIONS**
5905 Johns Rd Ste 101 (33634-4513)
PHONE................................813 769-5740
Karen Saoirse, *Mng Member*
Paul Bergfield, *Manager*
Paul Berkfield,
Robert Dill,
EMP: 30 EST: 2003
SQ FT: 8,500
SALES (est): 5.1MM Privately Held
WEB: www.icscable.com
SIC: 3357 Nonferrous wiredrawing & insu-
lating

(G-16947)
**INTEGRITY PRSTHETICS
ORTHOTICS**
12206 Bruce B Downs Blvd (33612-9224)
PHONE................................813 416-5905
Clarence E Crowe, *Principal*
EMP: 7 EST: 2012
SALES (est): 149.4K Privately Held
WEB: www.integritypando.com
SIC: 3842 Orthopedic appliances

(G-16948)
**INTERBAY AIR COMPRESSORS
INC**
Also Called: Honda Generators of Tampa
5110 S West Shore Blvd (33611-5650)
P.O. Box 13442 (33681-3442)
PHONE................................813 831-8213

Manuel Guzman, *President*
▼ EMP: 7 EST: 1982
SQ FT: 6,000
SALES (est): 1.7MM Privately Held
WEB: www.hondageneratorsoftampa.pow-
erdealer.honda.com
SIC: 3563 Air & gas compressors including
vacuum pumps

(G-16949)
**INTERNATIONAL PAPER
COMPANY**
6706 N 53rd St (33610-1906)
P.O. Box 16909 (33687-6909)
PHONE................................813 621-0584
Randy Lawson, *Maintence Staff*
EMP: 58
SALES (corp-wide): 19.3B Publicly Held
WEB: www.internationalpaper.com
SIC: 2653 Boxes, corrugated: made from
purchased materials
PA: International Paper Company
6400 Poplar Ave
Memphis TN 38197
901 419-7000

(G-16950)
**INTERNATIONAL SHIP REPAIR &
MA**
1601 Sahlman Dr (33605-6077)
PHONE................................813 247-1118
Paul Duffy, *President*
George H Lorton, *Principal*
Kateri Rosar, *Accountant*
EMP: 11
SALES (corp-wide): 21.8MM Privately
Held
WEB: www.internationalship.com
SIC: 3731 Shipbuilding & repairing
PA: International Ship Repair & Marine
Services, Inc.
1616 Penny St
Tampa FL 33605
813 247-1118

(G-16951)
INTERTAPE POLYMER CORP
Intertape Polymer Group
9940 Currie Davis Dr (33619-2669)
PHONE................................813 621-8410
Mike McQuire, *Manager*
Sean Struble, *Manager*
EMP: 64
SALES (corp-wide): 232MM Privately
Held
WEB: www.itape.com
SIC: 2672 Tape, pressure sensitive: made
from purchased materials
HQ: Intertape Polymer Corp.
100 Paramount Dr Ste 300
Sarasota FL 34232
888 898-7834

(G-16952)
INTREPID MACHINE INC
12020 Race Track Rd (33626-3109)
PHONE................................813 854-3825
Clinton Ken, *Principal*
EMP: 7 EST: 2016
SALES (est): 145.8K Privately Held
WEB: www.intrepidmachine.com
SIC: 3599 Machine shop, jobbing & repair

(G-16953)
IPVISION SOFTWARE LLC
5905 Johns Rd (33634-4521)
PHONE................................813 728-3175
Mark Felberg, *Mng Member*
EMP: 10 EST: 2006
SALES (est): 649.7K Privately Held
WEB: www.ipvisionsoftware.com
SIC: 7372 Prepackaged software

(G-16954)
ISLAND DESIGNS OUTLET INC
Also Called: Idex International
14501 Mccormick Dr (33626-3023)
PHONE................................813 855-0020
Robert Emerson, *President*
David Heggland, *Director*
▼ EMP: 35 EST: 1989
SQ FT: 11,613

GEOGRAPHIC (vertical tab)

SALES (est): 5MM Privately Held
WEB: www.idexint.net
SIC: 2395 2396 Embroidery products, except schiffli machine; automotive & apparel trimmings

(G-16955)
ISOPRENOIDS LLC
3802 Spectrum Blvd # 153 (33612-9222)
PHONE...................................(813) 785-6446
Ronald Kennedy Keller, *Branch Mgr*
EMP: 28
SALES (corp-wide): 687.9K Privately Held
WEB: www.isoprenoids.com
SIC: 2899 Chemical preparations
PA: Isoprenoids, Llc
  7245 River Forest Ln
  Temple Terrace FL 33617
  813 785-6446

(G-16956)
ITALIAN CAST STONES INC
5418 W Ingraham St (33616-1916)
PHONE...................................(813) 902-8900
Rosy Conto, *President*
Donte Conto, *Vice Pres*
Conto Kevin, *Engineer*
Dante Conto, *Manager*
EMP: 23 EST: 2000
SALES (est): 2.1MM Privately Held
WEB: www.italiancaststone.com
SIC: 3281 3086 Household articles, except furniture; cut stone; plastics foam products

(G-16957)
ITG CIGARS INC
Havatampa Div
3901 Roga Blvd (33619)
PHONE...................................(813) 623-2262
Rory May, *Controller*
Duane Greer, *Branch Mgr*
EMP: 55 Privately Held
WEB: www.altadisusa.com
SIC: 2121 Cigars
HQ: Itg Cigars Inc.
  5900 N Andrews Ave Ste 11
  Fort Lauderdale FL 33309
  954 772-9000

(G-16958)
J C NEWMAN CIGAR CO (PA)
2701 N 16th St (33605-2616)
P.O. Box 2030 (33601-2030)
PHONE...................................(813) 248-2124
Stanford J Newman, *Ch of Bd*
Eric M Newman, *President*
Heather Hill, *COO*
Robert C Newman, *Exec VP*
Rich Dolak, *Vice Pres*
◆ EMP: 100 EST: 1895
SQ FT: 100,000
SALES (est): 34.1MM Privately Held
WEB: www.jcnewman.com
SIC: 2121 5194 Cigars; cigars

(G-16959)
J K & M INK CORPORATION
Also Called: JK&m Ink
4714 N Thatcher Ave (33614-6936)
PHONE...................................(813) 875-3106
Martin J Lenhart, *President*
Mary Lenhart, *Treasurer*
EMP: 6 EST: 1995
SQ FT: 5,700
SALES (est): 827.5K Privately Held
SIC: 2752 Commercial printing, offset

(G-16960)
J W L TRADING COMPANY INC
Also Called: Ameriseam
13801 W Hillsborough Ave (33635-9677)
PHONE...................................(813) 854-1128
James W Larsen, *President*
EMP: 7 EST: 1996
SQ FT: 2,500
SALES (est): 349K Privately Held
WEB: www.ameriseam.com
SIC: 2394 Convertible tops, canvas or boat: from purchased materials

(G-16961)
JADE TACTICAL DISASTER RELIEF
Also Called: Security Hmntrian Rlief Envmtl
3816 W Sligh Ave (33614-3961)
PHONE...................................850 270-4077
Steven Rahl, *President*
Yaritza Rahl, *Vice Pres*
EMP: 138 EST: 2017
SALES (est): 7.7MM Privately Held
SIC: 3812 3721 3711 7381 Search & navigation equipment; aircraft; motor vehicles & car bodies; detective & armored car services; security systems services; charitable organization

(G-16962)
JAK CORPORATE HOLDINGS INC
Also Called: Diji Integrated Press
4920 W Cypress St Ste 100 (33607-3837)
P.O. Box 262573 (33685-2573)
PHONE...................................(813) 289-1660
Kathleen Muraski, *President*
Jeff Murawski, *Vice Pres*
EMP: 10 EST: 1985
SQ FT: 4,000
SALES (est): 926K Privately Held
WEB: www.dijipress.com
SIC: 2752 Commercial printing, offset

(G-16963)
JAMISON INDUSTRIES INC
Also Called: Jamison Paints
7710 N Ola Ave (33604-4067)
PHONE...................................(813) 886-4888
Jamison Derek, *President*
Derek Jamison, *Principal*
EMP: 10 EST: 2013
SALES (est): 550.3K Privately Held
WEB: www.jamisonind.com
SIC: 3599 Machine shop, jobbing & repair

(G-16964)
JAY STRONG LIGHTING INC
2007 W Dekle Ave (33606-3213)
PHONE...................................(813) 253-0490
Jay Strong, *Principal*
EMP: 7 EST: 2010
SALES (est): 136.8K Privately Held
SIC: 3648 Lighting equipment

(G-16965)
JFR HAZARDOUS SERVICES INC
Also Called: Priority Abatement Remediation
16609 Villalenda De Avila (33613-5200)
PHONE...................................716 313-2844
Rani Jones, *President*
EMP: 5 EST: 2018
SALES (est): 306.7K Privately Held
SIC: 1389 Construction, repair & dismantling services

(G-16966)
JKS INDUSTRIES INC (PA)
4644 W Gandy Blvd (33611-3300)
PHONE...................................727 573-1305
Ken Shin, *President*
Kenny Shin, *General Mgr*
Jennifer Shin, *Vice Pres*
EMP: 10 EST: 1992
SQ FT: 12,500
SALES (est): 8.1MM Privately Held
WEB: www.jksindustries.net
SIC: 3499 8742 Strapping, metal; management consulting services

(G-16967)
JLB ENTERPRISES TAMPA INC
Also Called: Tampa Pool Company
4508 Grainary Ave (33624-2127)
PHONE...................................(813) 545-3830
EMP: 7 EST: 2018
SALES (est): 366.7K Privately Held
SIC: 3732 Boat building & repairing

(G-16968)
JOHNSON & JACKSON GL PDTS INC
Also Called: Glass Pros of Tampa
4912 N Manhattan Ave (33614-6420)
PHONE...................................(813) 630-9774
Eric D Johnson, *President*
Eric Johnson, *President*

EMP: 12 EST: 2001
SQ FT: 5,200
SALES (est): 2.2MM Privately Held
SIC: 3449 3442 Curtain wall, metal; curtain walls for buildings, steel; metal doors, sash & trim

(G-16969)
JOHNSON & JOHNSON
Also Called: Johnson & Johnson Global Svcs
8800 Grand Oak Cir # 500 (33637-2006)
PHONE...................................(813) 972-0204
Cory Nedd, *Credit Staff*
Marshella Pounds, *Human Resources*
Anderson Santo, *Branch Mgr*
Jennifer Goetz, *Manager*
Jessica Kuschmeider, *Manager*
EMP: 9
SALES (corp-wide): 93.7B Publicly Held
WEB: www.jnj.com
SIC: 3842 Surgical appliances & supplies
PA: Johnson & Johnson
  1 Johnson And Johnson Plz
  New Brunswick NJ 08933
  732 524-0400

(G-16970)
JOHNSON CONTROLS INC
3802 Sugar Palm Dr Fro (33619-1312)
PHONE...................................(813) 623-1188
Mike Collins, *Principal*
Tim Wilson, *Associate Dir*
Heather Astarita, *Officer*
EMP: 86 Privately Held
WEB: www.johnsoncontrols.com
SIC: 2531 Seats, automobile
HQ: Johnson Controls, Inc.
  5757 N Green Bay Ave
  Glendale WI 53209
  414 524-1200

(G-16971)
JORDAN FLORIDA GROUP
3102 W Harbor View Ave (33611-1919)
PHONE...................................(813) 219-0100
Ivan Jordan, *Owner*
EMP: 10 EST: 2006
SALES (est): 99.7K Privately Held
WEB: jordan-florida-group.ueniweb.com
SIC: 1389 Construction, repair & dismantling services

(G-16972)
JRF TECHNOLOGY LLC
9830 Currie Davis Dr (33619-2651)
PHONE...................................(813) 443-5273
James Rossman, *President*
Richard C Fielder, *Managing Dir*
EMP: 11 EST: 2007
SALES (est): 3.6MM Privately Held
WEB: www.jrftechnology.com
SIC: 2821 Plastics materials & resins

(G-16973)
JUST FOR NETS
4817 N Lois Ave Ste 104 (33614-6570)
P.O. Box 15695 (33684-5695)
PHONE...................................(813) 871-1133
San F Lee, *President*
▼ EMP: 7 EST: 1982
SALES (est): 416.4K Privately Held
WEB: www.justfornets.com
SIC: 3949 Sporting & athletic goods

(G-16974)
KABINETS BY KINSEY INC
3815 N Florida Ave (33603-4909)
PHONE...................................(813) 222-0460
Charles Kinsey, *President*
EMP: 30 EST: 1984
SALES (est): 2.7MM Privately Held
WEB: www.kabinetsbykinsey.com
SIC: 2521 Wood office filing cabinets & bookcases

(G-16975)
KALTEC ELECTRONICS INC
Also Called: Digital Watchdog
5436 W Crenshaw St (33634-3009)
PHONE...................................(813) 888-9555
Jay Kelly, *Engineer*
Louis Riccomini, *Sales Staff*
Karen Horvath, *Branch Mgr*
Chris Plunkett, *CIO*
Patrick Kelly, *Director*
EMP: 14

SALES (corp-wide): 52MM Privately Held
WEB: www.digital-watchdog.com
SIC: 3669 Visual communication systems
PA: Kaltec Electronics, Inc.
  16220 Bloomfield Ave
  Cerritos CA 90703
  813 888-9555

(G-16976)
KAMAJ BUSINESS GROUP INC
601 N Ashley Dr Ste 1 (33602-4334)
PHONE...................................(813) 863-9967
Julius Brown, *CEO*
EMP: 10 EST: 2017
SALES (est): 995.7K Privately Held
SIC: 2329 2339 Athletic (warmup, sweat & jogging) suits: men's & boys'; men's & boys' athletic uniforms; women's & misses' athletic clothing & sportswear

(G-16977)
KAWASUMI LABORATORIES AMER INC
10002 Princess Palm Ave # 324 (33619-1395)
P.O. Box 24355 (33623-4355)
PHONE...................................(813) 630-5554
T Ishikawa, *Principal*
Y Umeki, *Principal*
Tracie Lowe, *Treasurer*
Charles Dolan, *Sales Staff*
Sira Korman, *Sales Staff*
▲ EMP: 17 EST: 1991
SALES (est): 3.3MM Privately Held
WEB: www.kawasumiamerica.com
SIC: 3841 Surgical & medical instruments
HQ: Sb-Kawasumi Laboratories, Inc.
  3-25-4, Tonomachi, Kawasaki-Ku
  Kawasaki KNG 210-0

(G-16978)
KCS PROFESSIONAL COATINGS INC
2603 E Lake Ave (33610-7750)
PHONE...................................(813) 850-6386
Kristin L Crump, *Principal*
EMP: 7 EST: 2012
SALES (est): 92K Privately Held
SIC: 3479 Metal coating & allied service

(G-16979)
KEENE METAL FABRICATORS INC
5912 E Broadway Ave (33619-2816)
PHONE...................................(813) 621-2455
Fred Keene Sr, *Ch of Bd*
Fred P Keene Jr, *President*
Gary Keene, *Corp Secy*
William Keene, *Vice Pres*
EMP: 29 EST: 1948
SQ FT: 6,500
SALES (est): 4.2MM Privately Held
SIC: 3441 3444 Fabricated structural metal; sheet metalwork

(G-16980)
KENFAR CORPORATION
5926 Jet Port Industrial (33634-5158)
PHONE...................................(813) 443-5222
Licio Zanzi, *CEO*
EMP: 5 EST: 1997
SALES (est): 359K Privately Held
SIC: 3556 Ice cream manufacturing machinery

(G-16981)
KEYSTONE COLOR WORKS INC
2411 S Hesperides St (33629-5540)
PHONE...................................(813) 250-1313
Baxter Smith, *President*
Susan Smith, *Principal*
Constance Spencer, *Principal*
EMP: 6 EST: 1919
SQ FT: 20,000
SALES (est): 728.4K Privately Held
SIC: 2865 2816 Color pigments, organic; inorganic pigments

(G-16982)
KEYSTONE RV COMPANY
1201 Old Hopewell Rd # 9 (33619-2608)
PHONE...................................(813) 228-0625
Deth Watson, *Manager*
EMP: 269

SALES (corp-wide): 16.3B **Publicly Held**
WEB: www.keystonerv.com
SIC: **3999** Barber & beauty shop equipment
HQ: Keystone Rv Company
　2642 Hackberry Dr
　Goshen IN 46526

(G-16983)
KEYSTONE STEEL PRODUCTS CO
3101 E 2nd Ave (33605-5705)
P.O. Box 76133 (33675-1133)
PHONE...........................813 248-9828
Michael S Barowski, *President*
▲ EMP: 6 EST: 1968
SQ FT: 15,000
SALES (est): 946.3K **Privately Held**
SIC: **3315** Steel wire & related products

(G-16984)
KEYTROLLER LLC
3907 W Martin Luther King (33614)
PHONE...........................813 877-4500
Ned Mavrommatis, *CFO*
Mike Wilson, *Regl Sales Mgr*
Summers Skip, *Marketing Staff*
Chris Wolfe, *Mng Member*
EMP: 15 EST: 2017
SQ FT: 1,300
SALES (est): 7MM
SALES (corp-wide): 126.2MM **Publicly Held**
WEB: www.powerfleet.com
SIC: **3629 3596 3663 3674** Electronic generation equipment; weighing machines & apparatus; television closed circuit equipment; light emitting diodes; burglar alarm apparatus, electric; industrial machinery & equipment
HQ: I.D. Systems, Inc.
　123 Tice Blvd Ste 101
　Woodcliff Lake NJ 07677

(G-16985)
KEYTROLLER LLC
3907 W Dr Mart Luth Kng B Martin Luther King (33614)
PHONE...........................813 877-4500
▲ EMP: 9
SQ FT: 1,300
SALES (est): 1.6MM **Privately Held**
SIC: **3629** Mfg Electrical Industrial Apparatus

(G-16986)
KIMBALL ELECTRONICS GROUP LLC
13750 Reptron Blvd (33626-3040)
PHONE...........................813 854-2000
Mahmod Zand, *Opers Mgr*
Tim Morris, *Safety Mgr*
Stacy Conard, *Purch Mgr*
Christy Colopy, *Engineer*
Brian Crawford, *Engineer*
EMP: 52
SALES (corp-wide): 1.3B **Publicly Held**
WEB: www.kimballelectronics.com
SIC: **3672** Printed circuit boards
HQ: Kimball Electronics Group, Llc
　1205 Kimball Blvd
　Jasper IN 47546

(G-16987)
KIMBALL ELECTRONICS TAMPA INC
13750 Reptron Blvd (33626-3040)
PHONE...........................813 814-5229
Mahmod Zand, *Opers Mgr*
Andre Alvarado, *Engineer*
Toby Ice, *Engineer*
Tim Morris, *Manager*
EMP: 450
SALES (corp-wide): 1.3B **Publicly Held**
WEB: www.kimballelectronics.com
SIC: **3679 3672** Electronic circuits; printed circuit boards
HQ: Kimball Electronics Tampa Inc
　1205 Kimball Blvd
　Jasper IN 47546
　812 634-4000

(G-16988)
KINETIC RESEARCH INC
5513 W Sligh Ave (33634-4431)
PHONE...........................813 962-6300
Wade Bader, *President*
Reid Bader, *General Mgr*
EMP: 15 EST: 2001
SALES (est): 965.6K **Privately Held**
WEB: www.kineticresearch.com
SIC: **3842** Prosthetic appliances

(G-16989)
KISS POLYMERS LLC
12515 Sugar Pine Way (33624-5712)
P.O. Box 274087 (33688-4087)
PHONE...........................813 962-2703
Cynthia Renee Kent, *Principal*
Jarrod R Kent, *Principal*
Keith Kent, *Principal*
EMP: 10 EST: 2005
SALES (est): 762.1K **Privately Held**
WEB: www.kisspolymers.com
SIC: **2851 3721** Shellac (protective coating); research & development on aircraft by the manufacturer

(G-16990)
KITCHEN AND BATH UNIVERSE INC
Also Called: Cabinet and Stone
6606 N 56th St (33610-1918)
PHONE...........................813 887-5658
Rong Sheng You, *President*
Qing Chan, *Vice Pres*
Kam Ting Wong, *Admin Sec*
◆ EMP: 11 EST: 2010
SQ FT: 3,500
SALES (est): 1.5MM **Privately Held**
WEB: www.cabinetnstoneintl.com
SIC: **2434** Wood kitchen cabinets

(G-16991)
KOHO SOFTWARE INC
Also Called: Quest Desk Solutions
6030 Printery St Unit 103 (33616-1414)
PHONE...........................813 390-1309
William Doucette, *President*
Marc Doucette, *Sales Staff*
Rohany Karya, *Consultant*
EMP: 6 EST: 2014
SALES (est): 538.2K **Privately Held**
WEB: www.kohoconsulting.com
SIC: **7372** Prepackaged software

(G-16992)
KRONOS INCORPORATED
5405 Cypress Center Dr # 300 (33609-1068)
PHONE...........................813 207-1987
Miao Qing, *General Mgr*
Charles Dewitt, *Managing Dir*
Nicole Bello, *Vice Pres*
Claire Richardson, *Vice Pres*
Katelynn Healy, *Project Mgr*
EMP: 8
SALES (corp-wide): 1.1B **Privately Held**
WEB: www.ukg.com
SIC: **7372** Business oriented computer software
HQ: Kronos Incorporated
　900 Chelmsford St
　Lowell MA 01851
　978 250-9800

(G-16993)
KUSSER GRANITEWORKS USA INC
Also Called: Kusser Fountainworks
3109 E 4th Ave (33605-5713)
PHONE...........................813 248-3428
Josef Kusser, *President*
Judy Castle, *Exec VP*
Alan Castle, *Vice Pres*
Adrian Donnelly, *Project Mgr*
Chris George, *Sales Staff*
◆ EMP: 9 EST: 1962
SQ FT: 10,100
SALES (est): 2.9MM **Privately Held**
WEB: www.kusserusa.com
SIC: **3281** Granite, cut & shaped

(G-16994)
L C ACME BARRICADES
2611 S 82nd St (33619-5705)
PHONE...........................813 623-2263

Christian Cunning, *Principal*
Russell Abell, *Regional Mgr*
Thomas Brady, *Regional Mgr*
Michael Moore, *Vice Pres*
Russell Gellhause, *Opers Staff*
EMP: 9 **Privately Held**
WEB: www.acmebarricades.com
SIC: **3499** Barricades, metal
PA: Acme Barricades, L.C.
　9800 Normandy Blvd
　Jacksonville FL 32221

(G-16995)
L3HARRIS TECHNOLOGIES INC
5690 W Cypress St Ste B (33607-1724)
PHONE...........................260 451-6814
EMP: 195
SALES (corp-wide): 11.3B **Publicly Held**
SIC: **3823 3812** Engineering Services
PA: L3harris Technologies, Inc.
　1025 W Nasa Blvd
　Melbourne FL 32919
　321 727-9100

(G-16996)
LA GACETA PUBLISHING INC
Also Called: La Gaceta Tri-Lingual Weekly
3210 E 7th Ave (33605-4302)
PHONE...........................813 248-3921
Roland Manteiga, *President*
Angela Manteiga, *Corp Secy*
EMP: 12 EST: 1922
SQ FT: 20,000
SALES (est): 1.3MM **Privately Held**
WEB: www.lagacetanewspaper.com
SIC: **2711** Newspapers: publishing only, not printed on site

(G-16997)
LABLOGIC SYSTEMS INC
1911 N Us Highway 301 # 140 (33619-2642)
PHONE...........................813 626-6848
Richard Brown, *President*
John Rogus, *Regional Mgr*
Victor Tchiprout, *Exec VP*
Sean Rossiter, *Engineer*
Woodcock Robert, *Human Res Mgr*
EMP: 12 EST: 1990
SQ FT: 5,000
SALES (est): 2MM **Privately Held**
WEB: www.lablogic.com
SIC: **3826** Analytical instruments

(G-16998)
LAKESHORE CUSTOM WOOD PDTS INC
5210 Shadowlawn Ave (33610-5310)
PHONE...........................813 623-2790
Kenneth Sparks, *President*
Chad Oleson, *Vice Pres*
Erika Oleson, *Admin Sec*
EMP: 9 EST: 1980
SQ FT: 4,500
SALES (est): 988.5K **Privately Held**
SIC: **2434** Wood kitchen cabinets

(G-16999)
LANFRANCHI NORTH AMERICA INC
8401 Benjamin Rd Ste A (33634-1203)
PHONE...........................813 901-5333
Davide Danna, *President*
Mario Lanfranchi, *Chairman*
Gisele D Rios, *Manager*
Salvatore Staino, *Manager*
▲ EMP: 15 EST: 2002
SQ FT: 2,800
SALES (est): 3.1MM
SALES (corp-wide): 11.8MM **Privately Held**
SIC: **3565** Packaging machinery
PA: Lanfranchi Srl
　Via Scodoncello 41
　Collecchio PR 43044
　052 154-1011

(G-17000)
LATTERI & SONS INC
Also Called: Latteri & Sons Vault and Monu
305 N Glen Ave (33609-1416)
PHONE...........................813 876-1800
Evelia Latteri, *President*
Anthony Latteri Jr, *Vice Pres*
EMP: 5 EST: 1936
SQ FT: 2,784

SALES (est): 370K **Privately Held**
SIC: **3272 5999** Burial vaults, concrete or precast terrazzo; monuments, finished to custom order

(G-17001)
LAYCOCK SYSTEMS INC
1601 N 43rd St (33605-5937)
PHONE...........................813 248-3555
Charles Snead, *Owner*
▲ EMP: 10 EST: 1982
SQ FT: 23,000
SALES (est): 976.6K **Privately Held**
WEB: www.laycocksystems.com
SIC: **3546** Power-driven handtools

(G-17002)
LEADER TECH INC
Also Called: Heico Company
12420 Race Track Rd (33626-3117)
PHONE...........................813 855-6921
Tracy Kuhns, *President*
Rhonda Dietrich, *Buyer*
Natalia Acostandei, *Engineer*
Josh Chastain, *Engineer*
Scott Lewis, *Engineer*
EMP: 100 EST: 1984
SQ FT: 42,500
SALES (est): 26.4MM **Publicly Held**
WEB: www.leadertechinc.com
SIC: **3469** Metal stampings
HQ: Heico Electronic Technologies Corp.
　3000 Taft St
　Hollywood FL 33021
　954 987-6101

(G-17003)
LEATHER OR NOT
17231 Dona Michelle Dr (33647-3239)
PHONE...........................813 972-9667
Joseph Rehak, *Principal*
EMP: 7 EST: 2001
SALES (est): 129K **Privately Held**
SIC: **3199 2821** Leather goods; vinyl resins

(G-17004)
LEE FISHER INTERNATIONAL INC
Also Called: Just For Nets
3922 W Osborne Ave (33614-6551)
P.O. Box 15695 (33684-5695)
PHONE...........................813 875-6296
San Fu Lee, *President*
Sophia Luo, *Purchasing*
Hsueh Hsiang Lee, *Treasurer*
Raymond Grau, *Sales Staff*
◆ EMP: 25 EST: 1982
SQ FT: 20,000
SALES (est): 5.1MM **Privately Held**
WEB: www.leefisherintl.com
SIC: **2298 2399** Fishing lines, nets, seines: made in cordage or twine mills; fishing nets

(G-17005)
LEGACY COMPONENTS LLC
4613 N Clark Ave (33614-7038)
PHONE...........................813 964-6805
John Donovan, *Accounts Exec*
Steve Stuart, *Sales Staff*
Kenneth Alvarez, *Mng Member*
Brien Berisford, *Manager*
Jason Grajales, *Manager*
EMP: 11 EST: 2011
SALES (est): 5.2MM **Privately Held**
WEB: www.legacycomponents.com
SIC: **3674** Semiconductors & related devices

(G-17006)
LEHIGH CEMENT COMPANY LLC
3920 Pendola Point Rd (33619-9500)
PHONE...........................813 248-4000
Ed Bringman, *Branch Mgr*
EMP: 8
SALES (corp-wide): 21.1B **Privately Held**
WEB: www.lehighwhitecement.com
SIC: **3273** Ready-mixed concrete
HQ: Lehigh Cement Company Llc
　300 E John Carpenter Fwy
　Irving TX 75062
　877 534-4442

(G-17007)
LEHIGH WHITE CEMENT CO LLC
3920 Pendola Point Rd (33619-9500)
PHONE..........................561 812-7441
Gerrhard Milla, *Branch Mgr*
EMP: 140
SALES (corp-wide): 1.8B **Privately Held**
WEB: www.lehighwhitecement.com
SIC: 2891 Adhesives & sealants
HQ: Lehigh White Cement Company, Llc
1601 Forum Pl Ste 1110
West Palm Beach FL 33401
561 812-7439

(G-17008)
LEVENHUK INC (PA)
6021 Catlin Dr (33647-2603)
PHONE..........................800 342-1706
Serge Ulyanenkov, *President*
▲ EMP: 6 EST: 2013
SALES (est): 675.7K **Privately Held**
WEB: www.levenhuk.com
SIC: 3827 Optical instruments & lenses

(G-17009)
LIFE PROTEOMICS INC
8875 Hidden River Pkwy (33637-1035)
PHONE..........................813 864-7646
Robert Brabenec, *President*
EMP: 10 EST: 2008
SALES (est): 725.3K **Privately Held**
SIC: 3829 8731 Measuring & controlling
devices; medical research, commercial

(G-17010)
**LIFEGARD PRFCATION
SYSTEMS LLC**
7028 W Waters Ave Ste 228 (33634-2292)
PHONE..........................813 875-7777
Kenneth E Conley, *Mng Member*
Mancely Conley, *Mng Member*
EMP: 5 EST: 1988
SQ FT: 2,500
SALES (est): 688.7K **Privately Held**
WEB: stores.lifeguardsystems.com
SIC: 3589 Water purification equipment,
household type

(G-17011)
LINDE INC
Also Called: Praxair
6915 E Adamo Dr (33619-3421)
PHONE..........................813 626-3636
Ronnie Creasy, *Branch Mgr*
EMP: 14 **Privately Held**
WEB: www.lindeus.com
SIC: 2813 Industrial gases
HQ: Linde Inc.
10 Riverview Dr
Danbury CT 06810
203 837-2000

(G-17012)
LINPHARMA INC
601 S Fremont Ave (33606-2401)
PHONE..........................888 989-3237
Mario Hofer, *Principal*
EMP: 9 EST: 2013
SALES (est): 1.2MM **Privately Held**
WEB: www.petadolex.com
SIC: 2834 Pharmaceutical preparations

(G-17013)
LIONS INTL MGT GROUP INC
8875 Hidden River Pkwy # 304
(33637-1035)
PHONE..........................813 367-2517
Johnny Adkins, *CEO*
Brittney Nemeth, *Opers Staff*
EMP: 10 EST: 2015
SALES (est): 503K **Privately Held**
SIC: 3088 0781 3711 7342 Plastics
plumbing fixtures; landscape architects;
motor vehicles & car bodies; rest room
cleaning service; protective devices, se-
curity

(G-17014)
LIQUIDCAPSULE MFG LLC
9216 Palm River Rd # 203 (33619-4479)
PHONE..........................813 431-0532
Frederick H Miller,
EMP: 10 EST: 2006

SALES (est): 1.2MM **Privately Held**
WEB: www.liquidcapsule.com
SIC: 2834 Pills, pharmaceutical

(G-17015)
LITHIUM BATTERY CO INTL
4912 W Knox St Ste 100 (33634-8006)
PHONE..........................813 504-0074
Ronald Staron, *General Mgr*
Nathan Staron,
EMP: 10 EST: 2012
SALES (est): 1.6MM **Privately Held**
WEB: www.lithiumbatterycompany.com
SIC: 3625 3629 3621 3691 Truck con-
trols, industrial battery; battery chargers,
rectifying or nonrotating; generators for
storage battery chargers; storage batter-
ies

(G-17016)
LIVELY COMPANY LLC ✪
501 E Jackson St Ste 301 (33602-4929)
PHONE..........................617 737-1199
Damon Brown, *Mng Member*
EMP: 10 EST: 2021
SALES (est): 413.1K **Privately Held**
SIC: 2844 Toothpastes or powders, denti-
frices

(G-17017)
LIVING FUEL INC
1409 W Swann Ave (33606-2532)
P.O. Box 1038 (33601-1038)
PHONE..........................813 254-0777
Kc Craichy, *Principal*
Mark McGee, *Comms Dir*
James Casale, *Director*
Brian Suarez, *Director*
EMP: 9 EST: 2012
SALES (est): 4.8MM **Privately Held**
WEB: www.livingfuel.com
SIC: 2869 Fuels

(G-17018)
LJK & TS PARTNERS INC
Also Called: Bay City X-Press Signs & Prtg
7031 Benjamin Rd Ste E (33634-3015)
PHONE..........................941 661-5675
Libor J Kuzel, *Vice Pres*
EMP: 8 EST: 2017
SALES (est): 260.9K **Privately Held**
SIC: 2752 Commercial printing, litho-
graphic

(G-17019)
LLC BEST BLOCK
5609 N 50th St (33610-4805)
PHONE..........................239 789-3531
EMP: 38
SALES (corp-wide): 2.2MM **Privately
Held**
SIC: 3251 Paving brick, clay
PA: Llc Best Block
2858 Sidney Ave
Orlando FL 32810
239 789-3531

(G-17020)
**LOADMASTER ALUM BOAT
TRLRS INC**
10105 Cedar Run (33619-8003)
PHONE..........................813 689-3096
Pamela L Paulsen, *President*
EMP: 30 EST: 1994
SQ FT: 24,000
SALES (est): 3.5MM **Privately Held**
WEB: www.loadmastertrailer.com
SIC: 3715 5599 Trailer bodies; utility trail-
ers

(G-17021)
LOGAN LABORATORIES LLC
2333 W Hillsborough Ave (33603-1032)
PHONE..........................813 316-4824
Michael Doyle, *CEO*
William Milo, *Vice Pres*
EMP: 5 EST: 2011
SALES (est): 622.3K
SALES (corp-wide): 2.3B **Publicly Held**
WEB: www.surgerypartners.com
SIC: 3821 8071 Clinical laboratory instru-
ments, except medical & dental; medical
laboratories

HQ: Surgery Partners, Inc.
310 Sven Sprng Way Ste 50
Brentwood TN 37027
615 234-5900

(G-17022)
LONZA
5709 Johns Rd Ste 1209 (33634-4315)
PHONE..........................727 608-6802
Barbara Klein, *Manager*
EMP: 14 EST: 2017
SALES (est): 3.5MM **Privately Held**
WEB: www.capsugel.com
SIC: 2834 Pharmaceutical preparations

(G-17023)
LUBOV MANUFACTURING INC
Also Called: Belcher Gear Manufacturing
4747 N West Shore Blvd (33614-6957)
PHONE..........................813 873-2640
Michael Lubov, *President*
EMP: 5 EST: 1990
SALES (est): 466.4K **Privately Held**
SIC: 3566 3462 Gears, power transmis-
sion, except automotive; iron & steel forg-
ings

(G-17024)
LUIS MARTINEZ CIGAR CO
2701 N 16th St (33605-2616)
P.O. Box 76061 (33675-1061)
PHONE..........................800 822-4427
Eric Newman, *President*
Scott Lewis, *Vice Pres*
EMP: 8 EST: 1985
SQ FT: 100,000
SALES (est): 1.5MM
SALES (corp-wide): 34.1MM **Privately
Held**
WEB: www.lmcigars.com
SIC: 2121 Cigars
PA: J. C. Newman Cigar Co.
2701 N 16th St
Tampa FL 33605
813 248-2124

(G-17025)
LUTHER INDUSTRIES LLC
3101 River Grove Dr (33610-1135)
PHONE..........................813 833-5652
Paul Kelly, *General Mgr*
EMP: 10 EST: 2018
SALES (est): 507.8K **Privately Held**
WEB: www.luther-industries.com
SIC: 3999 Manufacturing industries

(G-17026)
LV THOMPSON INC
Also Called: Tamco
5015 E Hillsborough Ave (33610-4814)
PHONE..........................813 248-3456
Leslie V Thompson, *President*
▲ EMP: 125 EST: 1979
SQ FT: 31,000
SALES (est): 25.6MM **Privately Held**
WEB: www.tamcometalroof.com
SIC: 3444 5051 5032 Metal roofing & roof
drainage equipment; metals service cen-
ters & offices; aggregate

(G-17027)
LX HAUSYS AMERICA INC
1820 Massaro Blvd Ste 300 (33619-3014)
PHONE..........................813 249-7658
EMP: 59 **Privately Held**
SIC: 2541 Counter & sink tops
HQ: Lx Hausys America, Inc.
900 Cir 75 Pkwy Se # 1500
Atlanta GA 30339
678 486-8210

(G-17028)
LYNDAN INC
5402 E Hanna Ave (33610-4033)
PHONE..........................813 977-6683
Dana L Guy, *President*
Lynda Carlton, *Corp Secy*
Phyllis M Thornberg, *Director*
EMP: 27 EST: 1981
SQ FT: 20,000
SALES (est): 3.7MM **Privately Held**
WEB: www.lyndan.com
SIC: 2541 2434 2431 Cabinets, except
refrigerated: show, display, etc.: wood;
wood kitchen cabinets; millwork

(G-17029)
**M & N CAPITAL ENTERPRISES
LLC**
Also Called: Tent Renters Supply
5160 W Clifton St (33634-8012)
PHONE..........................800 865-5064
Matthew Perra, *President*
EMP: 23 EST: 2016
SALES (est): 2.6MM **Privately Held**
WEB: www.tentsupply.com
SIC: 2394 Tents: made from purchased
materials

(G-17030)
MAD INC
Also Called: Gutcher's Quickprint
4030 Henderson Blvd (33629-4940)
PHONE..........................813 251-9334
David Gutcher, *President*
Mark Gutcher, *Treasurer*
EMP: 5 EST: 1976
SALES (est): 750K **Privately Held**
WEB: store.gotospark.com
SIC: 2752 Commercial printing, offset

(G-17031)
**MAGELLAN
PHARMACEUTICALS INC**
1202 Tech Blvd Ste 106 (33619-7863)
PHONE..........................813 623-6800
John Cronan, *President*
EMP: 5 EST: 2013
SALES (est): 603.9K **Privately Held**
SIC: 2834 Pharmaceutical preparations

(G-17032)
MAGNUM AUDIO GROUP INC
4504 W Spruce St Apt 112 (33607-5790)
PHONE..........................813 870-2857
Randi Crooks, *President*
Randy Crooks, *President*
David Biggers, *Vice Pres*
Robert Floyd, *Vice Pres*
EMP: 9 EST: 2000
SALES (est): 697.6K **Privately Held**
WEB: www.magnumaudiogroup.com
SIC: 3651 Audio electronic systems

(G-17033)
MAJOR PARTITIONS LTD CORP
405 S Dale Mabry Hwy # 260
(33609-2820)
PHONE..........................813 286-8634
EMP: 30
SQ FT: 300
SALES (est): 2.9MM **Privately Held**
SIC: 2541 Mfg Wood Partitions/Fixtures

(G-17034)
**MANAGEMENT HLTH
SOLUTIONS INC**
Also Called: Syft
5701 E Hillsborough Ave (33610-5423)
P.O. Box 320548, Fairfield CT (06825-
0548)
PHONE..........................888 647-4621
Todd J Plesko, *CEO*
Kevin Kiley, *COO*
Chris Doran, *Senior VP*
Miriam Achour, *Vice Pres*
Rebecca Addison, *Vice Pres*
EMP: 400 EST: 1999
SQ FT: 1,200
SALES (est): 51.1MM
SALES (corp-wide): 107.8MM **Privately
Held**
WEB: www.syftco.com
SIC: 7372 8742 Business oriented com-
puter software; materials mgmt. (purchas-
ing, handling, inventory) consultant
PA: Global Healthcare Exchange, Llc
1315 W Century Dr Ste 100
Louisville CO 80027
720 887-7000

(G-17035)
MANCI GRAPHICS CORP
Also Called: Allegra Print & Imaging Center
2705 N Falkenburg Rd (33619-0920)
PHONE..........................813 664-1129
Linda Manci, *President*
Sam Manci, *Vice Pres*
EMP: 8 EST: 1996
SQ FT: 3,000

SALES (est): 1.4MM **Privately Held**
WEB: www.allegramarketingprint.com
SIC: 2752 Commercial printing, offset

(G-17036)
MANNA PRO PRODUCTS LLC
Also Called: Manna Pro Farm Supply
7000 E Adamo Dr Ste A (33619-3412)
PHONE....................................813 620-9007
Robert Gill Jr, *Vice Pres*
Derrick Hanby, *Branch Mgr*
EMP: 24
SQ FT: 38,164
SALES (corp-wide): 145.5MM **Privately Held**
WEB: www.companapetbrands.com
SIC: 2048 Livestock feeds
PA: Manna Pro Products, Llc
707 Spirit 40 Park Dr # 150
Chesterfield MO 63005
636 681-1700

(G-17037)
MANTUA MANUFACTURING CO
8108 Krauss Blvd B (33619-3009)
PHONE....................................813 621-3714
Jeff Wick, *Vice Pres*
Michael Bosler, *Manager*
EMP: 9
SQ FT: 38,720
SALES (corp-wide): 77.9MM **Privately Held**
WEB: www.bedframes.com
SIC: 2514 3446 2511 3443 Frames for box springs or bedsprings: metal; architectural metalwork; wood household furniture; fabricated plate work (boiler shop)
PA: Mantua Manufacturing Co.
31050 Diamond Pkwy
Solon OH 44139
800 333-8333

(G-17038)
MARCELA CREATIONS INC
1802 W Kennedy Blvd (33606-1645)
PHONE....................................813 253-0556
Dora Boggio, *President*
Raul Boggio MD, *Vice Pres*
Richard Barnes, *CIO*
EMP: 7 EST: 1987
SQ FT: 3,000
SALES (est): 993.4K **Privately Held**
WEB: www.marcelagifts.com
SIC: 3999 Novelties, bric-a-brac & hobby kits

(G-17039)
MARITIME SEC STRTEGIES FLA LLC
5251 W Tyson Ave (33611-3223)
PHONE....................................912 704-0300
John K Ross,
EMP: 5 EST: 2007
SALES (est): 360.6K **Privately Held**
SIC: 3731 Shipbuilding & repairing

(G-17040)
MARK MASTER INC
11111 N 46th St (33617-2009)
PHONE....................................813 988-6000
Kevin A Govin, *CEO*
R Mark Govin, *President*
Luis A Romero, *COO*
Luis Romero, *COO*
Charles Schroeder, *Vice Pres*
▲ EMP: 85 EST: 1933
SQ FT: 40,000
SALES (est): 9.5MM **Privately Held**
WEB: www.markmasterinc.com
SIC: 3953 5943 Marking devices; stationery stores

(G-17041)
MARLON INC
Also Called: Pvc Spiral Supply
8513 Sunstate St (33634-1322)
PHONE....................................813 901-8488
Jack Jackson, *General Mgr*
Larry Jackson, *Manager*
Jerry Roberts, *Manager*
EMP: 10
SALES (corp-wide): 7MM **Privately Held**
WEB: www.pvcspiralsupply.com
SIC: 3089 Plastic processing

PA: Marlon, Inc.
123 E 45th St
Boise ID 83714
208 377-9301

(G-17042)
MARLYN STEEL DECKS INC
6808 Harney Rd (33610-9699)
PHONE....................................813 621-1375
Richard R James, *President*
Jeannie James, *COO*
Chris R James, *Vice Pres*
Jeannie S James, *Vice Pres*
▼ EMP: 10 EST: 1994
SQ FT: 5,000
SALES (est): 2.5MM **Privately Held**
WEB: www.marlynsteel.com
SIC: 3444 Sheet metalwork

(G-17043)
MARLYN STEEL PRODUCTS INC
6808 Harney Rd (33610-9699)
PHONE....................................813 621-1375
Richard R James, *President*
Evelyn K James, *Vice Pres*
Jeannie S James, *Vice Pres*
R Chris James, *Vice Pres*
EMP: 31 EST: 1960
SQ FT: 62,800
SALES (est): 4.9MM **Privately Held**
WEB: www.marlynsteel.com
SIC: 3441 3444 1752 Fabricated structural metal; sheet metalwork; floor laying & floor work

(G-17044)
MARTIN LITHOGRAPH INC
Also Called: Mli Intgrted Graphic Solutions
505 N Rome Ave (33606-1250)
P.O. Box 4240 (33677-4240)
PHONE....................................813 254-1553
Martin Saavedra Jr, *President*
Jennifer Saavedra, *Corp Secy*
Janice Saavedra, *Vice Pres*
EMP: 43 EST: 1970
SQ FT: 27,500
SALES (est): 5MM **Privately Held**
WEB: www.martinlitho.com
SIC: 2752 Commercial printing, offset

(G-17045)
MARTIN SPROCKET & GEAR INC
3201 Queen Palm Dr (33619-1331)
PHONE....................................813 623-1705
Craig Sparks, *Manager*
Roberta Joseph, *Manager*
EMP: 33
SALES (corp-wide): 292.4MM **Privately Held**
WEB: www.martinsprocket.com
SIC: 3566 3568 Gears, power transmission, except automotive; power transmission equipment
PA: Martin Sprocket & Gear, Inc.
3100 Sprocket Dr
Arlington TX 76015
817 258-3000

(G-17046)
MASONITE CORPORATION (HQ)
Also Called: Birchwood Best
1242 E 5th Ave (33605-4904)
PHONE....................................813 877-2726
Howard C Heckes, *President*
Mike Hildebrandt, *General Mgr*
Alex Legall, *Senior VP*
Robert E Lewis, *Senior VP*
Daniel J Shirk, *Senior VP*
▲ EMP: 100 EST: 1925
SALES (est): 1.5B
SALES (corp-wide): 2.6B **Publicly Held**
WEB: www.masonite.com
SIC: 2431 3469 Doors, wood; doors & door parts & trim, wood; stamping metal for the trade
PA: Masonite International Corporation
1242 E 5th Ave
Tampa FL 33605
813 877-2726

(G-17047)
MASONITE CORPORATION
Also Called: Birchwood Best
1205 E 5th Ave (33606-4903)
PHONE....................................715 354-3441

EMP: 99
SALES (corp-wide): 2.6B **Publicly Held**
WEB: www.thebirchwood.com
SIC: 2431 Doors, wood; doors & door parts & trim, wood
HQ: Masonite Corporation
1242 E 5th Ave
Tampa FL 33605
813 877-2726

(G-17048)
MASONITE HOLDINGS INC
201 N Franklin St Ste 300 (33602-5105)
PHONE....................................813 877-2726
Fred Lynch, *President*
Sharon McRae, *Project Mgr*
Mark Albrighton, *Director*
◆ EMP: 11 EST: 1991
SQ FT: 4,000
SALES (est): 5MM
SALES (corp-wide): 2.6B **Publicly Held**
WEB: www.masonite.com
SIC: 2431 3442 Doors, wood; metal doors
PA: Masonite International Corporation
1242 E 5th Ave
Tampa FL 33605
813 877-2726

(G-17049)
MASONITE INTERNATIONAL CORP
5502 Pioneer Park Blvd (33634-4455)
PHONE....................................813 889-3861
Mitch Elkis, *General Mgr*
Matthew Clark, *Vice Pres*
Harold Thomas, *Plant Supt*
Rick McCoy, *Manager*
Kelly Hughes, *Manager*
EMP: 28
SALES (corp-wide): 2.6B **Publicly Held**
WEB: www.masonite.com
SIC: 2431 3442 Doors, wood; window & door frames
PA: Masonite International Corporation
1242 E 5th Ave
Tampa FL 33605
813 877-2726

(G-17050)
MASONITE INTERNATIONAL CORP (PA)
1242 E 5th Ave (33605-4904)
PHONE....................................813 877-2726
Robert J Byrne, *Ch of Bd*
Howard C Heckes, *President*
Christopher O Ball, *President*
Robin Hagen, *President*
Lamont Hayes, *President*
◆ EMP: 100 EST: 1925
SQ FT: 88,000
SALES: 2.6B **Publicly Held**
WEB: www.masonite.com
SIC: 2431 3442 Doors, wood; metal doors

(G-17051)
MASONITE INTERNATIONAL CORP
1242 E 5th Ave (33605-4904)
PHONE....................................813 877-2726
Jim Scali, *Branch Mgr*
Melissa Curtiss, *Manager*
Ian Petty, *Software Dev*
EMP: 50
SALES (corp-wide): 2.6B **Publicly Held**
WEB: www.masonite.com
SIC: 2431 Doors, wood
PA: Masonite International Corporation
1242 E 5th Ave
Tampa FL 33605
813 877-2726

(G-17052)
MASONITE US CORPORATION
Also Called: Masonite International
1242 E 5th Ave (33605-4904)
PHONE....................................813 877-2726
Ken Sreeman, *President*
Steve Swartzmiller, *Senior VP*
Jim Kingry, *Vice Pres*
David Perkins, *Vice Pres*
Kurt Lillie, *Opers Staff*
EMP: 65 EST: 2004
SALES (est): 8.9MM **Privately Held**
WEB: www.masonite.com
SIC: 2431 Doors, wood

(G-17053)
MASSACHUSETTS BAY CLAM CO INC
13605 W Hillsborough Ave (33635-9653)
P.O. Box 208, Oldsmar (34677-0208)
PHONE....................................813 855-4599
Fax: 813 855-3944
EMP: 10
SQ FT: 6,000
SALES (est): 980K **Privately Held**
SIC: 2092 2022 Mfg Fresh/Frozen Packaged Fish Mfg Cheese

(G-17054)
MASSEYS METALS
2251 Massaro Blvd (33619-3021)
P.O. Box 89297 (33689-0404)
PHONE....................................813 626-8275
James R Massey, *President*
Juanita Massey, *Corp Secy*
Alan Massey, *Vice Pres*
Cris Massey, *Vice Pres*
EMP: 42 EST: 1971
SQ FT: 25,600
SALES (est): 4.9MM **Privately Held**
WEB: www.masseymetalscompany.com
SIC: 3444 Sheet metal specialties, not stamped

(G-17055)
MATCHWARE INC (PA)
511 W Bay St Ste 460 (33606-2770)
PHONE....................................800 880-2810
Ulrik Merrild, *President*
Brandon Conrad, *General Mgr*
Christina Daniels, *COO*
Nick Aliantro, *Accountant*
Brady Friedman, *Sales Staff*
◆ EMP: 5 EST: 2001
SALES (est): 1.1MM **Privately Held**
WEB: www.matchware.com
SIC: 7372 Prepackaged software

(G-17056)
MATERIAL CONVEYING MAINT INC (PA)
4901 30th Ave S (33619-6061)
PHONE....................................813 740-1111
Nelson G Castellano, *President*
Venera Campanelli, *Exec Dir*
EMP: 7 EST: 2014
SALES (est): 2.4MM **Privately Held**
WEB: www.gomcmi.com
SIC: 3535 Conveyors & conveying equipment

(G-17057)
MAY & WELL INC
8907 Regents Park Dr # 390 (33647-3401)
PHONE....................................813 333-5806
Zhiqing Han, *Principal*
EMP: 9 EST: 2010
SALES (est): 135.4K **Privately Held**
SIC: 2655 Fiber shipping & mailing containers

(G-17058)
MAYWORTH SHOWCASE WORKS INC
12711 N Armenia Ave (33612-3901)
PHONE....................................813 251-1558
John W Mayworth Jr, *President*
Don Scranton, *Vice Pres*
EMP: 6 EST: 1920
SALES (est): 474.8K **Privately Held**
SIC: 2431 2541 Millwork; wood partitions & fixtures

(G-17059)
MC CONNIE ENTERPRISES INC
Also Called: Mc Connie Fence
4707 30th Ave S (33619-6033)
PHONE....................................813 247-3827
Andreas Mc Connie, *President*
Helga E Mc Connie, *Corp Secy*
Paul Hughes, *Commercial*
EMP: 5 EST: 1973
SQ FT: 3,700
SALES (est): 941.5K **Privately Held**
WEB: www.mcconniefence.com
SIC: 2499 2298 Fencing, wood; fishing lines, nets, seines: made in cordage or twine mills

(G-17060)
MCMULLEN ROAD LLC
12941 Memorial Hwy (33635-9529)
P.O. Box 1916, Oldsmar (34677-6916)
PHONE....................................813 854-3100
Jamie Burge, *CFO*
Michael Williams,
Benjamin Williams,
EMP: 25 **EST:** 2010
SQ FT: 80,000
SALES (est): 7.6MM
SALES (corp-wide): 31.1MM **Privately Held**
WEB: www.millwork360.net
SIC: 2431 Millwork
PA: The Marwin Company Inc
        107 Mcqueen St
        West Columbia SC 29172
        803 776-2396

(G-17061)
MDCO INC
Also Called: Electronic Manufacturing Co
13440 Wright Cir (33626-3026)
PHONE....................................813 855-4068
Norman Blais, *President*
EMP: 11 **EST:** 1980
SQ FT: 10,000
SALES (est): 1.4MM **Privately Held**
SIC: 3679 Electronic circuits

(G-17062)
MEC CRYO LLC ✪
4430 E Adamo Dr Ste 305 (33605-5933)
PHONE....................................813 644-3764
Patrick Donovan, *Mng Member*
Benjamin Lacrosse,
EMP: 30 **EST:** 2021
SALES (est): 2.4MM **Privately Held**
SIC: 3559 Cryogenic machinery, industrial

(G-17063)
MEMPHIS METAL MANUFACTURING CO
10811 Barbados Isle Dr (33647-2792)
P.O. Box 11271, Memphis TN (38111-0271)
PHONE....................................901 276-6363
William B Mason III, *President*
Jake Taylor, *Manager*
EMP: 10 **EST:** 1945
SALES (est): 686K **Privately Held**
WEB: www.memphis-metal.com
SIC: 3444 Sheet metalwork

(G-17064)
MERCHANTS METALS INC
Meadow Burke Products
2835 Overpass Rd Ste 100 (33619-1323)
PHONE....................................813 333-5515
Jose Martinez, *General Mgr*
Dave Kelly, *Vice Pres*
David Lampi, *Vice Pres*
Garrett Kendle, *Opers Mgr*
David Underwood, *Opers Mgr*
EMP: 100
SQ FT: 67,684
SALES (corp-wide): 1B **Privately Held**
WEB: www.merchantsmetals.com
SIC: 3315 Wire & fabricated wire products
HQ: Merchants Metals Llc
        3 Ravinia Dr Ste 1750
        Atlanta GA 30346
        770 741-0300

(G-17065)
MERCHANTS METALS LLC
4921 Joanne Kearney Blvd (33619-8603)
PHONE....................................813 980-0938
Billy Howell, *Manager*
EMP: 10
SALES (corp-wide): 1B **Privately Held**
WEB: www.merchantsmetals.com
SIC: 3496 Fencing, made from purchased wire
HQ: Merchants Metals Llc
        3 Ravinia Dr Ste 1750
        Atlanta GA 30346
        770 741-0300

(G-17066)
MERIT FASTENER CORPORATION
5416 56th Cmmerce Pk Blvd (33610-6857)
PHONE....................................813 626-3748
Linda Anderson, *Vice Pres*

Bob Groom, *Opers Mgr*
Nicole Hess, *Purchasing*
Donna Young, *Technical Staff*
EMP: 8
SALES (corp-wide): 5.6MM **Privately Held**
WEB: www.meritfasteners.com
SIC: 3599 3491 Machine & other job shop work; industrial valves
PA: Merit Fastener Corporation
        2510 N Ronald Reagan Blvd
        Longwood FL 32750
        407 331-4815

(G-17067)
METAL PROCESSORS INC
200 S Falkenburg Rd (33619-8041)
P.O. Box 3087, Brandon (33509-3087)
PHONE....................................813 654-0050
Lance C Cowieson, *President*
Leslie A Godwin, *Corp Secy*
Bill Winnette, *Purchasing*
EMP: 40 **EST:** 1982
SQ FT: 93,000
SALES (est): 5.1MM **Privately Held**
WEB: www.metalprocessors.com
SIC: 3312 Blast furnaces & steel mills

(G-17068)
METALCRAFT SERVICES TAMPA INC
10706 N 46th St (33617-3480)
PHONE....................................813 558-8700
Gene E Pleus, *President*
Gene Pleus, *President*
Scott Yeo, *General Mgr*
Shane Pratt, *QC Mgr*
Dan Huff, *Manager*
EMP: 15 **EST:** 1987
SQ FT: 4,000
SALES (est): 3MM **Privately Held**
WEB: www.metalcraftservices.com
SIC: 3441 Fabricated structural metal

(G-17069)
METPAR CORP
Also Called: Comres Industries
7211 Anderson Rd (33634-3001)
PHONE....................................813 249-0391
EMP: 17
SALES (corp-wide): 24.8MM **Privately Held**
WEB: www.metpar.com
SIC: 3446 Partitions & supports/studs, including accoustical systems
PA: Metpar Corp.
        95 State St
        Westbury NY 11590
        516 333-2600

(G-17070)
METRO LIFE MEDIA INC
Also Called: Orlando Metro Magazine
3404 S Omar Ave (33629-8214)
PHONE....................................813 745-3658
Stephen P Parag II, *President*
Ronda M Parag, *Manager*
EMP: 8 **EST:** 2005
SALES (est): 810.3K **Privately Held**
WEB: www.tampabaywed.com
SIC: 2721 Magazines: publishing & printing

(G-17071)
MICROSOFT CORPORATION
5426 Bay Center Dr # 700 (33609-3477)
PHONE....................................813 281-3900
Dan Anderson, *Partner*
Jason Mills, *Partner*
Jasone Cerasia, *General Mgr*
Eric Crawford, *Vice Pres*
Douglas Harman, *Project Mgr*
EMP: 12
SALES (corp-wide): 198.2B **Publicly Held**
WEB: www.microsoft.com
SIC: 7372 Application computer software
PA: Microsoft Corporation
        1 Microsoft Way
        Redmond WA 98052
        425 882-8080

(G-17072)
MILBANK MANUFACTURING CO
3214 Queen Palm Dr (33619-1304)
PHONE....................................813 623-2681
EMP: 9 **EST:** 2017

SALES (est): 140.8K **Privately Held**
WEB: www.milbankworks.com
SIC: 3999 Manufacturing industries

(G-17073)
MINCO LLC
2931 W Wallcraft Ave (33611-1650)
PHONE....................................813 340-7769
Michael Plucinski, *Principal*
Lisa Garcia, *Manager*
EMP: 8 **EST:** 2012
SALES (est): 148.9K **Privately Held**
WEB: www.mincoinc.com
SIC: 3599 Machine shop, jobbing & repair

(G-17074)
MINK MILLI LLC
610 E Zack St Ste 110-407 (33602-3972)
PHONE....................................813 606-0416
Dominique Harrell, *Mng Member*
EMP: 12
SALES (est): 604.3K **Privately Held**
SIC: 2339 7389 Women's & misses' accessories;

(G-17075)
MINUTEMAN INDUSTRIES INC
Also Called: Minuteman Systems & Alarms
1407 E 5th Ave (33605-5021)
P.O. Box 3474, Apollo Beach (33572-1004)
PHONE....................................813 248-1776
Terry Grewer, *President*
EMP: 5 **EST:** 1975
SQ FT: 3,600
SALES (est): 719.7K **Privately Held**
WEB: www.minutemanst.com
SIC: 3669 5065 Burglar alarm apparatus, electric; electronic parts & equipment

(G-17076)
MINUTEMAN PRESS
5519 Hanley Rd (33634-4900)
PHONE....................................813 884-2476
Manny Fernandez, *Principal*
EMP: 15 **EST:** 1992
SALES (est): 678.2K **Privately Held**
WEB: www.minutemanpress.com
SIC: 2752 Commercial printing, lithographic

(G-17077)
MITEK INC
1801a Massaro Blvd (33619-3013)
PHONE....................................813 675-1224
Jose Ibarra, *Plant Mgr*
Lydia Moring, *Human Resources*
Peter Garcia, *Manager*
Pedro Calzada, *Manager*
Anthony Sierra, *Manager*
EMP: 78
SALES (corp-wide): 354.6B **Publicly Held**
WEB: www.mii.com
SIC: 3443 3429 3542 Truss plates, metal; manufactured hardware (general); machine tools, metal forming type
HQ: Mitek Inc.
        16023 Swingley Ridge Rd
        Chesterfield MO 63017

(G-17078)
MITEK USA INC
1801a Massaro Blvd (33619-3013)
PHONE....................................813 906-3122
EMP: 8 **EST:** 2017
SALES (est): 136K **Privately Held**
WEB: www.mitek-us.com
SIC: 3443 Truss plates, metal

(G-17079)
MMO INDUSTRIES INC
4710 Eisenhower Blvd A1 (33634-6335)
PHONE....................................727 452-8665
Kenley Matheny, *Principal*
EMP: 9 **EST:** 2016
SALES (est): 207.8K **Privately Held**
SIC: 3999 Manufacturing industries

(G-17080)
MOBILE MEALS
8909 Magnolia Chase Cir (33647-2220)
PHONE....................................813 907-6325
Elizabeth Mekdeci, *Executive*
EMP: 8 **EST:** 2009

SALES (est): 169K **Privately Held**
WEB: www.mobilemeals.com
SIC: 2099 Food preparations

(G-17081)
MOLDING DEPOT INC
3707 W Carmen St (33609-1303)
P.O. Box 10067 (33679-0067)
PHONE....................................813 348-4837
John L Rosende, *President*
Chris Rosende, *Vice Pres*
EMP: 36 **EST:** 2000
SALES (est): 1.8MM **Privately Held**
WEB: www.mouldingdepot.com
SIC: 3089 Molding primary plastic

(G-17082)
MOLEKULE INC
3802 Spectrum Blvd # 143 (33612-9212)
PHONE....................................352 871-3803
Lovely Goswami, *President*
Phil Myers, *Engineer*
EMP: 140
SALES (corp-wide): 2.9MM **Privately Held**
WEB: www.molekule.com
SIC: 3822 3829 Air flow controllers, air conditioning & refrigeration; measuring & controlling devices
PA: Molekule, Inc.
        1301 Folsom St
        San Francisco CA 94103
        352 871-3803

(G-17083)
MOMENRY INC
100 S Ashley Dr Ste 600 (33602-5300)
PHONE....................................318 668-0888
EMP: 11
SALES (est): 239.1K **Privately Held**
SIC: 7372 Prepackaged Software Services

(G-17084)
MONSTERTECH CORPORATION ✪
Also Called: Monster Tech USA
4498 Eagle Falls Pl (33619-9620)
PHONE....................................813 898-0405
Oliver Rasche, *President*
EMP: 49 **EST:** 2021
SALES (est): 2.3MM **Privately Held**
SIC: 3291 3334 Abrasive metal & steel products; primary aluminum

(G-17085)
MOROCCAN KHLII INC
808 N Macdill Ave (33609-1532)
PHONE....................................813 699-0096
Hicham H Tadlaoui, *CEO*
EMP: 7 **EST:** 2011
SALES (est): 108.9K **Privately Held**
WEB: www.moroccanjerky.com
SIC: 2013 Beef, dried: from purchased meat; snack sticks, including jerky: from purchased meat

(G-17086)
MOSAIC COMPANY (PA)
101 E Kennedy Blvd # 2500 (33602-3650)
PHONE....................................800 918-8270
Gregory L Ebel, *Ch of Bd*
James C O'Rourke, *President*
Bruce M Bodine Jr, *Senior VP*
Mark J Isaacson, *Senior VP*
Christopher A Lewis, *Senior VP*
◆ **EMP:** 260 **EST:** 2004
SALES (est): 12.3B **Publicly Held**
WEB: www.mosaicco.com
SIC: 2874 2819 Phosphatic fertilizers; phosphates; muriate of potash, not from mines

(G-17087)
MOSAIC GLOBAL SALES LLC (DH)
Also Called: Mosaic Company, The
101 E Kennedy Blvd # 250 (33602-5179)
PHONE....................................763 577-2700
Joc Orourke, *President*
Matthew Berg, *Superintendent*
Don Jernstrom, *Business Mgr*
Jon Faletto, *Counsel*
Bruce Bodine, *Senior VP*
EMP: 47 **EST:** 2014
SALES (est): 46.6MM **Publicly Held**
SIC: 2874 Phosphatic fertilizers

HQ: Mosaic Crop Nutrition, Llc
3033 Campus Dr
Minneapolis MN 55441
763 577-2700

(G-17088)
MP TENNIS INC (PA)
14843 N Dale Mabry Hwy (33618-2027)
PHONE....................813 961-8844
Mike Pratt, *President*
Amy Bovard, *Vice Pres*
EMP: 5 **EST:** 1998
SALES (est): 897K **Privately Held**
WEB: www.mptennis-sports.com
SIC: 3949 Tennis equipment & supplies

(G-17089)
MXN INC
Also Called: Sir Speedy
10120 Woodberry Rd (33619-8006)
PHONE....................813 654-3173
James Mixon, *President*
EMP: 5 **EST:** 1992
SQ FT: 1,500
SALES (est): 423.3K **Privately Held**
WEB: www.sirspeedy.com
SIC: 2752 Commercial printing, litho-
graphic

(G-17090)
MY CLONE SOLUTION
4532 W Kennedy Blvd 183 (33609-2042)
PHONE....................813 442-9925
Brook Borup, *Principal*
Brandy Chanthapho, *Mktg Coord*
Sarah Farnan, *Manager*
EMP: 10 **EST:** 2014
SALES (est): 749.8K **Privately Held**
WEB: www.myclonesolution.com
SIC: 7372 Prepackaged software

(G-17091)
MY REVIEWERS LLC
Also Called: Myreviewers
3802 Spectrum Blvd 8 (33612-9212)
PHONE....................813 404-9734
Joseph Moxley, *Mng Member*
EMP: 5 **EST:** 2013
SALES (est): 369K **Privately Held**
SIC: 7372 Educational computer software

(G-17092)
MYAREA NETWORK INC
500 E Kennedy Blvd # 101 (33602-4934)
PHONE....................800 830-7994
Scott Conlon, *CEO*
Gregory C Cummins Jr, *President*
Gregory Cummins, *Vice Pres*
Amanda RE, *Vice Pres*
David J Annis, *Treasurer*
EMP: 15 **EST:** 2015
SALES (est): 1.8MM **Privately Held**
WEB: www.myareanetwork.com
SIC: 2741 8742 ; marketing consulting
services

(G-17093)
MYERS PRINTING INC
5601 N Florida Ave (33604-6911)
PHONE....................813 237-0288
Phillip Myers, *President*
EMP: 5 **EST:** 1985
SALES (est): 486.3K **Privately Held**
SIC: 2752 Commercial printing, offset

(G-17094)
MYMD PHARMACEUTICALS FLA INC
900 W Platt St Ste 200 (33606-2173)
PHONE....................813 864-2566
Chris Chapman M D, *President*
Josh Silverman, *Chairman*
Paul Rivard, *Vice Pres*
Sonny Jones, *VP Opers*
Adam Kaplin MD PH D, *Officer*
EMP: 12 **EST:** 2016
SALES (est): 2MM **Privately Held**
WEB: www.mymd.com
SIC: 2834 Pharmaceutical preparations

(G-17095)
N-EAR PRO INC
Also Called: N Ear Pro
4821 N Grady Ave (33614-6513)
PHONE....................877 290-4599
EMP: 40

SQ FT: 2,000
SALES (est): 1.2MM **Privately Held**
SIC: 3842 Mfg Surgical Appliances/Sup-
plies

(G-17096)
N3XT L3VEL 2 POINT 0 LLC ✪
1248 E Hillsborough Ave (33604-7201)
PHONE....................863 777-3778
Julius Jones, *Mng Member*
Davon Jackson Jr, *Mng Member*
John Rowland Jr, *Mng Member*
EMP: 11 **EST:** 2021
SALES (est): 717.9K **Privately Held**
SIC: 2211 Lawns, cotton

(G-17097)
N3XT UP EXOTIC LLC ✪
1248 E Hillsborough Ave (33604-7201)
PHONE....................863 777-3778
Stanley Dillard,
EMP: 7 **EST:** 2021
SALES (est): 269K **Privately Held**
SIC: 3199 Dog furnishings: collars,
leashes, muzzles, etc.: leather

(G-17098)
NATIONAL CARWASH SOLUTIONS INC
5624 56th Cmmerce Pk Blvd (33610-6836)
PHONE....................813 973-3507
Tracy Beer, *Manager*
EMP: 35
SALES (corp-wide): 209.4MM **Privately Held**
WEB: www.ryko.com
SIC: 3589 Car washing machinery
PA: National Carwash Solutions, Inc.
1500 Se 37th St
Grimes IA 50111
800 284-7956

(G-17099)
NATIONAL CUSTOM INSIGNIA INC
8875 Hdden Rver Pkwy Ste (33637)
P.O. Box 1190, Oldsmar (34677-1190)
PHONE....................813 313-2561
William Witrak, *President*
Bill Michaels, *Vice Pres*
EMP: 10 **EST:** 1996
SALES (est): 516.6K **Privately Held**
WEB: www.lapelpins.com
SIC: 3915 Jewelers' materials & lapidary
work

(G-17100)
NATIONAL CYLINDER HEAD EXCHANG
4408 N Thatcher Ave (33614-7631)
PHONE....................813 870-6340
Charles Lantry, *President*
EMP: 7 **EST:** 1983
SQ FT: 2,500
SALES (est): 600K **Privately Held**
SIC: 3593 3599 Fluid power cylinders, hy-
draulic or pneumatic; machine shop, job-
bing & repair

(G-17101)
NATIONAL DIESEL ENGINE INC
253 S 78th St (33619-4225)
PHONE....................810 516-6855
Steve Spencer, *President*
EMP: 10 **EST:** 2010
SALES (est): 537.9K **Privately Held**
WEB: www.nationaldieselengineinc.com
SIC: 3519 Diesel engine rebuilding

(G-17102)
NATIONAL HEALTH ALLIANCE LLC
500 N West Shore Blvd # 640
(33609-1910)
PHONE....................727 504-3915
Manindra K Garg,
EMP: 7 **EST:** 2013
SALES (est): 474K **Privately Held**
SIC: 2833 Vitamins, natural or synthetic:
bulk, uncompounded

(G-17103)
NATIONWIDE INDUSTRIES INC (PA)
Also Called: Nwi Enterprises
3505 Cragmont Dr (33619-8340)
PHONE....................813 988-2628
Christopher Kliefoth, *President*
David Lord, *Engineer*
Erik Timothy, *Engineer*
Marc Poirier, *CFO*
Rachel Tiller, *Controller*
◆ **EMP:** 17 **EST:** 1990
SALES (est): 13.8MM **Privately Held**
WEB: www.nationwideindustries.com
SIC: 3442 1799 3315 Metal doors, sash &
trim; fence construction; fence gates
posts & fittings: steel

(G-17104)
NAVIERA COFFEE MILLS INC
Also Called: El Molino Coffee
2012 E 7th Ave (33605-3902)
P.O. Box 5036 (33675-5036)
PHONE....................813 248-2521
Danilo V Fernandez, *President*
Carmelina Fernandez, *Vice Pres*
Marge Raymond, *Comptroller*
EMP: 20 **EST:** 1921
SQ FT: 10,000
SALES (est): 1.9MM **Privately Held**
WEB: www.elmolinocoffee.com
SIC: 2095 Coffee roasting (except by
wholesale grocers)

(G-17105)
NCI
11327 Countryway Blvd (33626-2610)
PHONE....................813 749-1799
EMP: 7 **EST:** 2018
SALES (est): 204.6K **Privately Held**
SIC: 3825 Instruments to measure electric-
ity

(G-17106)
NEBRASKA PRINTING INC
3849 W Azeele St (33609-3921)
PHONE....................813 870-6871
Charles Cuervo Jr, *CEO*
Greg Nelson, *Principal*
Mark Mercer, *CFO*
Ralph Chille, *Director*
EMP: 21 **EST:** 1932
SALES (est): 1MM **Privately Held**
WEB: www.nebcofl.com
SIC: 2752 Commercial printing, offset

(G-17107)
NEURO20 TECHNOLOGIES CORP ✪
3802 Spectrum Blvd # 111 (33612-9212)
PHONE....................813 990-7138
Dennis Schmitt, *CEO*
EMP: 8 **EST:** 2021
SALES (est): 528.3K **Privately Held**
WEB: www.neuro20.com
SIC: 3812 5047 5091 Defense systems &
equipment; medical & hospital equipment;
fitness equipment & supplies

(G-17108)
NEWSPAPER PRINTING COMPANY
5210 S Lois Ave (33611-3445)
PHONE....................813 839-0035
John L Tevlin, *President*
Herb Facas, *President*
Bryan Waterhouse, *President*
Janice Brooks, *Controller*
Kimberly Araca, *Human Res Mgr*
▼ **EMP:** 200 **EST:** 1984
SQ FT: 12,000
SALES (est): 31.5MM **Privately Held**
WEB: www.npcprinting.com
SIC: 2752 Commercial printing, offset

(G-17109)
NEXT GENERATION HOME PDTS INC
Also Called: Nextgen
701 S Howard Ave (33606-2473)
PHONE....................727 834-9400
Bob Dolatowski, *President*
David M Schifino, *Admin Sec*
▲ **EMP:** 6 **EST:** 2001
SQ FT: 6,000

SALES (est): 578.4K **Privately Held**
SIC: 3825 5065 Frequency meters: electrical, mechanical & electronic; electronic
parts

(G-17110)
NIC4 INC
111 Kelsey Ln Ste D (33619-4357)
PHONE....................877 455-2131
Chad Gatlin, *CEO*
Bill Harrington, *Engineer*
Darren Gibbons, *Director*
EMP: 19 **EST:** 2011
SALES (est): 7.5MM
SALES (corp-wide): 7.3MM **Privately
Held**
WEB: www.networkinv.com
SIC: 3663 4899 Space satellite communi-
cations equipment; satellite earth stations
PA: Network Innovations Inc
4424 Manilla Rd Se
Calgary AB T2G 4
403 287-5000

(G-17111)
NIGHTSCENES INC
Also Called: Qssi
12802 Commodity Pl (33626-3101)
P.O. Box 1169, Oldsmar (34677-1169)
PHONE....................813 855-9416
Johnie R Edens, *President*
Rick Edens, *President*
Mary D Edens, *Vice Pres*
◆ **EMP:** 10 **EST:** 1992
SALES (est): 1.6MM **Privately Held**
SIC: 3648 Outdoor lighting equipment

(G-17112)
NPC OF TAMPA INC
5210 S Lois Ave (33611-3445)
PHONE....................813 839-0035
John L Tevlin Jr, *President*
Jennifer L Dal Sasso, *Treasurer*
Cheryl L Tevlin, *Admin Sec*
EMP: 12 **EST:** 1992
SQ FT: 66,984
SALES (est): 150.8K **Privately Held**
WEB: www.npcprinting.com
SIC: 2721 2789 2711 Magazines: publish-
ing & printing; bookbinding & related
work; magazines, binding; commercial
printing & newspaper publishing com-
bined

(G-17113)
NUTRACEUTICAL CORPORATION
Also Called: Aubrey Organics
5046 W Linebaugh Ave (33624-5030)
PHONE....................813 877-4186
Curt Valva, *President*
John Dalessandro, *Chief Mktg Ofcr*
Jimmy Hubbard, *Manager*
EMP: 28
SALES (corp-wide): 319.3MM **Privately
Held**
WEB: www.nutraceutical.com
SIC: 2844 Cosmetic preparations
HQ: Nutraceutical Corporation
222 S Main St Fl 16
Salt Lake City UT 84101

(G-17114)
OCEANA SOFTWARE LLC
5202 Quarrystone Ln (33624-2506)
PHONE....................813 335-6966
Jeffrey L Odell, *Principal*
EMP: 7 **EST:** 2002
SALES (est): 416.2K **Privately Held**
SIC: 7372 Prepackaged software

(G-17115)
ODYSSEY MANUFACTURING CO (PA)
1484 Massaro Blvd (33619-3006)
PHONE....................813 635-0339
Marvin T Rakes, *President*
Stephen W Sidelko, *Vice Pres*
Randy Hancock, *Plant Supt*
Butch Dempsey, *Plant Mgr*
Michael Azzarella, *Project Mgr*
EMP: 45 **EST:** 1998
SQ FT: 17,722

SALES (est): 15MM **Privately Held**
WEB: www.odysseymanufacturing.com
SIC: 2842 Bleaches, household: dry or liq-
uid

(G-17116)
ODYSSEY MANUFACTURING CO
5361 Hartford St (33619-6819)
PHONE................................813 635-0339
Pat Allmand, *General Mgr*
EMP: 10
SALES (corp-wide): 15MM **Privately
Held**
WEB: www.odysseymanufacturing.com
SIC: 2812 Chlorine, compressed or lique-
fied
PA: Odyssey Manufacturing Co.
1484 Massaro Blvd
Tampa FL 33619
813 635-0339

(G-17117)
OLD 97 COMPANY (HQ)
4829 E 7th Ave (33605-4703)
PHONE................................813 246-4180
Frank Ferola, *President*
EMP: 11 EST: 1955
SALES (est): 13.9MM
SALES (corp-wide): 33.3MM **Privately
Held**
SIC: 2844 Toilet preparations
PA: The Stephan Co
2211 Reach Rd Ste B4
Williamsport PA 17701
800 634-1996

(G-17118)
OLD HERITAGE MEDCALL INC
202 E Virginia Ave (33603-4821)
PHONE................................813 221-1000
Donald R Musselman, *President*
Jerry Patterson, *Vice Pres*
EMP: 13 EST: 1987
SQ FT: 2,500
SALES (est): 1.5MM **Privately Held**
WEB: www.heritagemedcall.com
SIC: 3669 Emergency alarms

(G-17119)
**OLD MEETING HOUSE HOME
MADE IC**
901 S Howard Ave (33606-2418)
PHONE................................813 254-0977
Mathew Hoffman,
EMP: 10 EST: 2003
SALES (est): 720.7K **Privately Held**
SIC: 2024 Ice cream & frozen desserts

(G-17120)
**OLDCASTLE ARCHITECTURAL
INC**
5603 Anderson Rd (33614-5313)
PHONE................................813 886-7761
James R Bird, *President*
Rose Huges, *Admin Sec*
EMP: 36 EST: 1966
SQ FT: 2,600
SALES (est): 2.1MM **Privately Held**
WEB: www.oldcastlecoastal.com
SIC: 3272 Concrete products; dry mixture
concrete

(G-17121)
**OLDCASTLE
BUILDINGENVELOPE INC**
Also Called: HGP Industries
5115 Hartford St (33603-6815)
PHONE................................813 247-3184
Scott Reynolds, *Manager*
EMP: 100
SQ FT: 68,195
SALES (corp-wide): 1.5B **Privately Held**
WEB: www.obe.com
SIC: 3231 5231 Tempered glass: made
from purchased glass; insulating glass:
made from purchased glass; glass
PA: Oldcastle Buildingenvelope, Inc.
5005 Lyndon B Johnson Fwy
Dallas TX 75244
214 273-3400

(G-17122)
**OLDCASTLE
BUILDINGENVELOPE INC**
8655 Elm Fair Blvd (33610-7363)
PHONE................................813 663-0949
John Weber, *Principal*
Robert Holzworth, *Human Res Mgr*
EMP: 34
SALES (corp-wide): 1.5B **Privately Held**
WEB: www.obe.com
SIC: 3231 5231 Tempered glass: made
from purchased glass; insulating glass:
made from purchased glass; glass
PA: Oldcastle Buildingenvelope, Inc.
5005 Lyndon B Johnson Fwy
Dallas TX 75244
214 273-3400

(G-17123)
OLDCASTLE COASTAL
5455 N 59th St (33610-2011)
PHONE................................813 621-2427
Frank Ketchum, *Owner*
Jason Barr, *Vice Pres*
Chris Forbes, *Plant Mgr*
Spencer Korb, *Plant Mgr*
Curtis Gorham, *Site Mgr*
EMP: 12 EST: 2018
SALES (est): 2.3MM **Privately Held**
SIC: 3272 Concrete products

(G-17124)
OLDCASTLE COASTAL INC
Coloroc Materials
5603 Anderson Rd (33614-5313)
PHONE................................813 886-7761
Craig Akers, *Sales Staff*
Doug McCall, *Manager*
EMP: 8
SALES (corp-wide): 30.9B **Privately Held**
WEB: www.oldcastlecoastal.com
SIC: 3272 Concrete products
HQ: Oldcastle Coastal, Inc.
4630 WoodInd Corp Blvd
Tampa FL 33614

(G-17125)
OLDCASTLE COASTAL INC
8910 N 12th St (33604-1811)
PHONE................................813 932-1007
Kevin Cintle, *Manager*
EMP: 7
SALES (corp-wide): 30.9B **Privately Held**
WEB: www.oldcastlecoastal.com
SIC: 3272 Covers, catch basin: concrete
HQ: Oldcastle Coastal, Inc.
4630 WoodInd Corp Blvd
Tampa FL 33614

(G-17126)
OLDCASTLE COASTAL INC (DH)
4630 WoodInd Corp Blvd (33614-2415)
PHONE................................813 367-9780
Tim Ortman, *President*
Jason Barr, *Vice Pres*
Bill Braswell, *Vice Pres*
Judy Paredes, *Human Res Dir*
EMP: 219 EST: 2003
SQ FT: 45,000
SALES (est): 102.8MM
SALES (corp-wide): 30.9B **Privately Held**
WEB: www.oldcastlecoastal.com
SIC: 3272 Covers, catch basin: concrete
HQ: Crh Americas, Inc.
900 Ashwood Pkwy Ste 600
Atlanta GA 30338
770 804-3363

(G-17127)
OPEN PALM PRESS INC
3839 W Kennedy Blvd (33609-2719)
PHONE................................813 870-3839
EMP: 7 EST: 2019
SALES (est): 134.6K **Privately Held**
WEB: www.openpalmlaw.com
SIC: 2741 Miscellaneous publishing

(G-17128)
**ORNAMNTAL DESIGN
IRONWORKS INC**
4706 N Falkenburg Rd (33610-5918)
PHONE................................813 626-8449
Michael Ward, *President*
Darlene Yerby, *Admin Sec*
EMP: 20 EST: 1950

SQ FT: 5,000
SALES (est): 2.4MM **Privately Held**
WEB: www.odi-tampa.com
SIC: 3446 3444 Architectural metalwork;
sheet metalwork

(G-17129)
**ORTEGA CUSTOM CABINETS
INC**
7006 Hazelhurst Ct (33615-2945)
PHONE................................813 403-7101
Uziel Ortega Martinez, *President*
EMP: 5 EST: 2010
SALES (est): 326.7K **Privately Held**
WEB: www.ortegacustomcabinets.com
SIC: 2434 Wood kitchen cabinets

(G-17130)
**ORTHOPEDIC DESIGNS N AMER
INC**
5912 Breckenridge Pkwy F (33610-4200)
PHONE................................813 443-4905
Chuck Masek, *President*
Nathan Masek, *Manager*
Brad Bender, *Director*
Steven Lozier, *Representative*
EMP: 5 EST: 2009
SALES (est): 810.7K **Privately Held**
WEB: www.odi-na.com
SIC: 3841 Bone plates & screws; bone
rongeurs; bone drills

(G-17131)
OSG AMERICA LLC
302 Knights Run Ave # 1200 (33602-5962)
PHONE................................813 209-0600
Myles R Itkin, *President*
Henry P Flinter, *CFO*
EMP: 173 EST: 2007
SALES (est): 2MM
SALES (corp-wide): 359MM **Publicly
Held**
WEB: www.osg.com
SIC: 3731 Shipbuilding & repairing
HQ: Osg America L.P.
302 Knights Run Ave # 12
Tampa FL 33602

(G-17132)
OTOC LLC
4035 Priory Cir (33618-2711)
PHONE................................813 265-8352
F Coto, *Principal*
EMP: 8 EST: 2007
SALES (est): 105.6K **Privately Held**
SIC: 3061 Mechanical rubber goods

(G-17133)
**OUTDOOR AMERICA IMAGES
INC (PA)**
Also Called: Oai
4545 W Hillsborough Ave (33614-5441)
PHONE................................813 888-8796
Michael A Garcia, *President*
Michael Garcia, *Principal*
Austin Marks, *Project Mgr*
Shawn Scalise, *Prdtn Mgr*
Nora Zoto, *Buyer*
▲ EMP: 21 EST: 1989
SQ FT: 35,000
SALES (est): 8MM **Privately Held**
SIC: 2399 7336 Banners, made from fab-
ric; graphic arts & related design

(G-17134)
OUTPUT PRINTING CORP
Also Called: Allegra Print Imging Dwntwn Tm
107 N Jefferson St (33602-5001)
PHONE................................813 228-8800
Joel Routman, *President*
Jeff Routman, *Opers Staff*
Nancy Routman, *Treasurer*
Jason Routman, *Marketing Staff*
EMP: 10 EST: 1989
SQ FT: 4,000
SALES (est): 1.9MM **Privately Held**
WEB: www.allegramarketingprint.com
SIC: 2752 2791 2789 Commercial print-
ing, offset; typesetting; bookbinding & re-
lated work

(G-17135)
OUTREACH CORPORATION
Also Called: Sales
1208 E Kennedy Blvd (33602-3504)
PHONE................................888 938-7356
EMP: 244
SALES (corp-wide): 61.5MM **Privately
Held**
WEB: www.outreach.io
SIC: 7372 Business oriented computer
software
PA: Outreach Corporation
333 Elliott Ave W Ste 500
Seattle WA 98119
206 235-3672

(G-17136)
PACA FOODS LLC
5212 Cone Rd (33610-5302)
PHONE................................813 628-8228
Michael Shepardson, *CEO*
Steve De Luca, *Controller*
EMP: 30 EST: 1991
SQ FT: 50,000
SALES (est): 4.8MM **Privately Held**
WEB: www.pacafoods.com
SIC: 2099 Food preparations

(G-17137)
PACIFIC DIE CAST INC (PA)
Also Called: Duraguard Products
12802 Commodity Pl (33626-3101)
P.O. Box 369, Oldsmar (34677-0369)
PHONE................................813 316-2221
Johnie R Edens, *President*
Shannon Edens, *Vice Pres*
Paul Markee, *Sales Staff*
Mary D Edens, *Admin Sec*
▲ EMP: 10 EST: 2000
SQ FT: 97,000
SALES (est): 12.7MM **Privately Held**
SIC: 3544 Special dies & tools

(G-17138)
PACIRA BIOSCIENCES INC (PA)
5401 W Knnedy Blvd Lncoln (33609)
PHONE................................813 553-6680
David Stack, *Ch of Bd*
Vincent Yu, *President*
Scott Braunstein, *Vice Pres*
Ron Ellis, *Vice Pres*
Vladimir Kharitonov, *Vice Pres*
EMP: 129 EST: 2007
SQ FT: 53,000
SALES (est): 541.5MM **Publicly Held**
WEB: www.pacira.com
SIC: 2834 Pharmaceutical preparations

(G-17139)
**PACIRA PHARMACEUTICALS
INC ✪**
5401 W Knnedy Blvd Lncoln Lincoln
(33609)
PHONE................................813 553-6680
David Stack, *CEO*
EMP: 624 EST: 2022
SALES (est): 92.9MM **Publicly Held**
SIC: 2834 Pharmaceutical preparations
PA: Pacira Biosciences, Inc.
5401 W Knnedy Blvd Lncoln
Tampa FL 33609

(G-17140)
**PACKAGING CORPORATION
AMERICA**
Also Called: PCA
1450 Massaro Blvd (33619-3006)
PHONE................................813 626-7006
Joseph Reese, *Sales Staff*
Joe Andrews, *Branch Mgr*
EMP: 65
SALES (corp-wide): 7.7B **Publicly Held**
WEB: www.packagingcorp.com
SIC: 2631 2653 Container board; con-
tainer, packaging & boxboard; corrugated
& solid fiber boxes
PA: Packaging Corporation Of America
1 N Field Ct
Lake Forest IL 60045
847 482-3000

(G-17141)
PADGETT COMMUNICATIONS INC
5005 W Laurel St Ste 103 (33607-3896)
PHONE.................................727 323-5800
Todd Padgett, *President*
Rebecca Brice, *Project Mgr*
Trina Landers, *Project Mgr*
Jessica Sullens, *Office Mgr*
Robyn McCoy, *Director*
EMP: 27 EST: 1994
SALES (est): 4.1MM **Privately Held**
WEB: www.pcipro.com
SIC: 3669 5045 3651 Intercommunication systems, electric; computers, peripherals & software; household audio & video equipment

(G-17142)
PANE RUSTICA BAKERY & CAFE
3225 S Macdill Ave (33629-8171)
PHONE.................................813 902-8828
Karen Kruszewski, *Owner*
EMP: 10 EST: 1999
SALES (est): 1.2MM **Privately Held**
WEB: www.panerusticabakery.com
SIC: 2051 5461 Bakery: wholesale or wholesale/retail combined; bakeries

(G-17143)
PANGENEX CORPORATION (PA)
9950 Princess Palm Ave (33619-8302)
PHONE.................................352 346-4045
Jeffrey M Roman, *President*
EMP: 5 EST: 2008
SALES (est): 833.1K **Privately Held**
SIC: 2023 Dietary supplements, dairy & non-dairy based

(G-17144)
PANTOGRAMS INC
4537 S Dale Mabry Hwy (33611-1425)
PHONE.................................813 839-5697
Scott Colman, *President*
Jen Lasky, *Manager*
◆ EMP: 9 EST: 2015
SQ FT: 13,000
SALES (est): 319.6K **Privately Held**
WEB: www.pantograms.com
SIC: 3552 Embroidery machines

(G-17145)
PANTOGRAMS MFG CO INC
Also Called: EMB Supplies
4537 S Dale Mabry Hwy (33611-1425)
PHONE.................................813 839-5697
John Colman, *CEO*
Larry Sheppard, *Principal*
Linda Colman, *Corp Secy*
Aaron McMahon, *Warehouse Mgr*
Brandon Epperson, *Manager*
▲ EMP: 38 EST: 1979
SQ FT: 12,000
SALES (est): 2.3MM **Privately Held**
WEB: www.pantograms.com
SIC: 3552 2397 7371 Embroidery machines; schiffli machine embroideries; computer software development

(G-17146)
PARADISE INC (PA)
5110 W Poe Ave (33629-7527)
PHONE.................................813 752-1155
Melvin S Gordon, *Ch of Bd*
Randy S Gordon, *President*
Mark H Gordon, *Exec VP*
Tracy W Schulis, *Senior VP*
Paul M Long, *Vice Pres*
▲ EMP: 66 EST: 1961
SQ FT: 350,000
SALES (est): 20.1MM **Privately Held**
WEB: www.paradisefruitco.com
SIC: 2064 3089 Fruits: candied, crystallized, or glazed; molding primary plastic

(G-17147)
PARADISE OAKS WOODWORKING INC
218 E Bearss Ave Ste 378 (33613-1625)
PHONE.................................863 206-0858
Yvonne Mixon, *Principal*
EMP: 7 EST: 2018
SALES (est): 112.1K **Privately Held**
WEB: www.paradiseoaksrv.com
SIC: 2431 Millwork

(G-17148)
PARAGON GLOBL SUP SLUTIONS LLC
301 W Platt St Ste 98 (33606-2292)
PHONE.................................813 745-9902
Charles Fletcher, *President*
EMP: 13 EST: 2012
SQ FT: 200
SALES (est): 1MM **Privately Held**
WEB: www.paragonglobalsupply.com
SIC: 3069 3089 Rubber automotive products; injection molding of plastics

(G-17149)
PARAGON WATER SYSTEMS INC
13805 Monroe Park (33635-6369)
PHONE.................................727 538-4704
George Lutich, *President*
John H Douglas, *President*
Peter Cicchetto, *COO*
Syed Shah, *Vice Pres*
Dorine Delaval, *Engineer*
▲ EMP: 39 EST: 1988
SQ FT: 20,000
SALES (est): 25.9MM
SALES (corp-wide): 652.7MM **Privately Held**
WEB: www.paragonwater.com
SIC: 3589 Water filters & softeners, household type
PA: Culligan International Company
9399 W Higgins Rd # 1100
Rosemont IL 60018
847 430-2800

(G-17150)
PARALLEL FLORIDA LLC
2203 N Lois Ave Ste M275 (33607-2698)
PHONE.................................404 920-4890
William Wrigley, *CEO*
James Whitcomb, *CFO*
Adrian Odougherty, *Admin Sec*
EMP: 1000 EST: 2015
SALES (est): 168.8MM **Privately Held**
SIC: 2834 Vitamin, nutrient & hematinic preparations for human use
HQ: Surterra Holdings Inc.
116 E 4th St
Ocilla GA 31774
229 457-9498

(G-17151)
PATIO PRODUCTS MFG LLC
9706 E Us Highway 92 (33610-5930)
PHONE.................................813 664-0158
Larry Stephens, *President*
EMP: 17 EST: 2010
SQ FT: 17,500
SALES (est): 1.9MM **Privately Held**
WEB: www.patioproductsmfg.com
SIC: 3442 Metal doors

(G-17152)
PDMA CORPORATION
5909 Hampton Oaks Pkwy C (33610-9581)
PHONE.................................813 621-6463
Timothy R Owen, *President*
Fred Baker, *Vice Pres*
Todd Gunderson, *Vice Pres*
Pak Wong, *Vice Pres*
David McKinnon, *Project Mgr*
EMP: 45 EST: 1983
SQ FT: 13,000
SALES (est): 13.7MM **Privately Held**
WEB: www.pdma.com
SIC: 3825 7389 Test equipment for electronic & electric measurement; industrial & commercial equipment inspection service

(G-17153)
PEAK NUTRITIONAL PRODUCTS LLC
5525 Johns Rd Ste 905 (33634-4514)
PHONE.................................813 884-4989
Rob Trautschold, *Purchasing*
Mike Connors, *Sales Staff*
Robert J Lebeau, *Mng Member*
Vesselina Iltcheva, *Manager*
Ted Jackson, *Director*
▲ EMP: 40 EST: 2011

SALES (est): 8.3MM **Privately Held**
WEB: www.peaknutritionalproducts.com
SIC: 2023 2834 Dietary supplements, dairy & non-dairy based; proprietary drug products

(G-17154)
PEARCEY ENTERPRISE
7806 N 52nd St (33617-8108)
PHONE.................................904 235-3096
Randall Pearcey, *Principal*
Michael Chapman, *Project Leader*
EMP: 7 EST: 2010
SALES (est): 128K **Privately Held**
WEB: www.pearceyreport.com
SIC: 2711 Newspapers, publishing & printing

(G-17155)
PEPSI-COLA BOTTLING CO TAMPA (DH)
11315 N 30th St (33612-6495)
PHONE.................................813 971-2550
Brenda C Barnes, *President*
Gerrett Hall, *Warehouse Mgr*
Jackie Chapman, *Maint Spvr*
Tony Allen, *Opers Staff*
Rachel Root, *Mfg Staff*
◆ EMP: 200 EST: 1936
SALES (est): 265.2MM
SALES (corp-wide): 70.3B **Publicly Held**
WEB: www.pepsico.com
SIC: 2086 Carbonated soft drinks, bottled & canned
HQ: Pepsi-Cola Metropolitan Bottling Company, Inc.
700 Anderson Hill Rd
Purchase NY 10577
914 767-6000

(G-17156)
PERCH SECURITY INC
4110 George Rd Ste 200 (33634-7411)
PHONE.................................844 500-1810
Aharon Chenin, *CEO*
Natalie Suarez, *Partner*
David Powell, *Vice Pres*
Gary Dobkin, *Opers Staff*
Mark Shamshoian, *Controller*
EMP: 50 EST: 2017
SALES (est): 10.3MM
SALES (corp-wide): 105.8MM **Privately Held**
WEB: www.perchsecurity.com
SIC: 7372 Application computer software
PA: Connectwise, Llc
400 N Tampa St Ste 130
Tampa FL 33602
813 463-4700

(G-17157)
PETNET SOLUTIONS INC
9204 Florida Palm Dr (33619-4352)
PHONE.................................813 627-0022
Chris Connely, *Branch Mgr*
EMP: 7
SALES (corp-wide): 73B **Privately Held**
WEB: www.siemens.com
SIC: 2835 Radioactive diagnostic substances
HQ: Petnet Solutions, Inc.
810 Innovation Dr
Knoxville TN 37932
865 218-2000

(G-17158)
PETROTECH SERVICES INC
1807 E 2nd Ave (33605-5201)
PHONE.................................813 248-0743
EMP: 88 **Privately Held**
SIC: 3498 Fabricated pipe & fittings
PA: Petrotech Services Inc
4041 Maritime Blvd
Tampa FL 33605

(G-17159)
PETROTECH SERVICES INC (PA)
4041 Maritime Blvd (33605-6849)
P.O. Box 76235 (33675-1235)
PHONE.................................813 248-0743
Gloria Kane, *President*
Lawrence Kane, *Treasurer*
EMP: 6 EST: 1991
SQ FT: 2,000

SALES (est): 3.3MM **Privately Held**
SIC: 3498 3441 Fabricated pipe & fittings; fabricated structural metal

(G-17160)
PGT AMERICAN INC (PA)
5330 Ehrlich Rd Ste 102 (33624-6977)
PHONE.................................813 962-4400
Gary E Lestrange, *President*
EMP: 6 EST: 2002
SALES (est): 1.3MM **Privately Held**
WEB: www.pgtcabinets.com
SIC: 2434 Wood kitchen cabinets

(G-17161)
PHIL & BRENDA JOHNSON INC
Also Called: Sir Speedy
5609 E Hillsborough Ave (33610-5414)
PHONE.................................813 623-5478
Phil Johnson, *President*
Brenda Johnson, *Vice Pres*
EMP: 13 EST: 1983
SQ FT: 4,000
SALES (est): 1.8MM **Privately Held**
WEB: tampafl390.sirspeedy.com
SIC: 2752 Commercial printing, lithographic

(G-17162)
PHIL LAU
Also Called: International Specialist
16309 Millan De Avila (33613-1090)
P.O. Box 271430 (33688-1430)
PHONE.................................813 631-8643
Phil Lau, *Owner*
Christopher Lau, *Vice Pres*
Kayla Lau, *CFO*
▲ EMP: 10 EST: 1971
SALES (est): 699.9K **Privately Held**
SIC: 3679 Electronic components

(G-17163)
PHILLYS FAMOUS WATER ICE INC
Also Called: Philly Swirl
1102 N 28th St (33605-6246)
PHONE.................................813 248-8644
Craig Millican, *General Mgr*
James Askin, *Transportation*
Pete Caspari, *Chief Engr*
Kathy Knox, *CFO*
Rick Marquez, *Controller*
EMP: 110 EST: 2006
SALES (est): 23MM
SALES (corp-wide): 1.1B **Publicly Held**
SIC: 2024 Ices, flavored (frozen dessert)
PA: J & J Snack Foods Corp.
6000 Central Hwy
Pennsauken NJ 08109
856 665-9533

(G-17164)
PHILS CAKE BOX BAKERIES INC
Also Called: Alessi Bakery
4705 W Cayuga St (33614-6948)
PHONE.................................813 348-0128
Gary Horstmann, *COO*
Tarek Ibrahim, *COO*
Jacquie Pissanos, *Vice Pres*
Jenny Hafner, *Opers Staff*
Curtis Hall, *Purchasing*
EMP: 94
SALES (corp-wide): 34.4MM **Privately Held**
WEB: www.alessibakery.com
SIC: 2051 Bakery: wholesale or wholesale/retail combined
PA: Phil's Cake Box Bakeries, Inc.
5202 Eagle Trail Dr
Tampa FL 33634
813 348-0128

(G-17165)
PHOTOENGRAVING INC (PA)
Also Called: Truplate
502 N Willow Ave (33606-1338)
PHONE.................................813 253-3427
Edward L Dalton Jr, *President*
Joe Velazquez, *Vice Pres*
Rachel Dalton, *Treasurer*
▲ EMP: 30 EST: 1953
SQ FT: 20,000

SALES (est): 2.9MM **Privately Held**
WEB: www.photoengravinginc.com
SIC: **3861** 2752 2796 Plates, photographic (sensitized); commercial printing, lithographic; platemaking services

(G-17166)
PIP PRINTING 622 INC
10428 N Florida Ave (33612-6709)
PHONE.............................813 935-8113
John J Driscoll, *Director*
EMP: 5 EST: 2001
SALES (est): 514.8K **Privately Held**
WEB: www.pip.com
SIC: **2752** Commercial printing, offset

(G-17167)
PITNEY BOWES INC
600 N West Shore Blvd # 810
(33609-1041)
P.O. Box 867, Hartford CT (06143-0867)
PHONE.............................813 639-1110
Joyce Taylor, *Manager*
Mark Margait, *Technician*
EMP: 100
SALES (corp-wide): 3.6B **Publicly Held**
WEB: www.pitneybowes.com
PA: Pitney Bowes Inc.
3001 Summer St
Stamford CT 06905
203 356-5000

(G-17168)
PLASTICS AMERICA INC
8501 E Adamo Dr (33619-3510)
PHONE.............................813 620-3711
Bob Belzer, *President*
Dave Modisette, *Vice Pres*
Chris Wiggins, *Treasurer*
EMP: 6 EST: 1991
SQ FT: 5,000
SALES (est): 588.5K **Privately Held**
WEB: www.plasticsamerica.com
SIC: **2821** 5162 5085 Plastics materials & resins; plastics sheets & rods; industrial supplies

(G-17169)
POMPANETTE LLC
Pompanette Gray
7712 Cheri Ct (33634-2419)
PHONE.............................813 885-2182
Richard Truell, *President*
Mark Carpenter, *General Mgr*
Craig Erb, *Materials Mgr*
Paul Adams, *Purch Agent*
Michael Haber, *Branch Mgr*
EMP: 34
SQ FT: 132,230
SALES (corp-wide): 34.2MM **Privately Held**
WEB: www.pompanette.com
SIC: **3732** 3089 3949 3429 Boats, rigid: plastics; boats, nonrigid: plastic; sporting & athletic goods; manufactured hardware (general); products of purchased glass
PA: Pompanette, Llc
73 Southwest St
Charlestown NH 03603
717 569-2300

(G-17170)
POWERSPORTS 911 INC
5911 Benjamin Center Dr (33634-5239)
PHONE.............................813 769-2468
Ryan Heath, *President*
EMP: 7 EST: 2016
SALES (est): 1.6MM
SALES (corp-wide): 5.3MM **Privately Held**
SIC: **3751** Motorcycles & related parts
PA: Web River Group, Inc.
5911 Benjamin Center Dr
Tampa FL 33634
813 769-2451

(G-17171)
PPG ARCHITECTURAL FINISHES INC
Also Called: Glidden Professional Paint Ctr
3102 W Kennedy Blvd (33609-3005)
PHONE.............................813 877-5841
EMP: 7
SALES (corp-wide): 15.3B **Publicly Held**
SIC: **2891** Mfg Adhesives/Sealants

HQ: Ppg Architectural Finishes, Inc.
1 Ppg Pl
Pittsburgh PA 15272
412 434-3131

(G-17172)
PPG INC
Also Called: Promo Printing Group
5133 W Cypress St (33607-1701)
PHONE.............................813 831-9902
William Gillespie, *President*
Steven W Richter, *Vice Pres*
◆ EMP: 10 EST: 1998
SQ FT: 2,000
SALES (est): 1.9MM **Privately Held**
WEB: www.promoprintinggroup.com
SIC: **2752** Commercial printing, offset

(G-17173)
PRECIOUS METALS BUYERS LLC (PA)
6201 Johns Rd Ste 5 (33634-4434)
PHONE.............................813 880-9544
Jorge Rodriguez, *Principal*
EMP: 5 EST: 2010
SALES (est): 324.2K **Privately Held**
SIC: **3339** Precious metals

(G-17174)
PRECIOUS METALS BUYERS LLC
7028 W Waters Ave (33634-2292)
PHONE.............................813 417-7857
Jorge Rodriguez, *Branch Mgr*
EMP: 17
SALES (corp-wide): 324.2K **Privately Held**
SIC: **3339** Precious metals
PA: Precious Metals Buyers, Llc
6201 Johns Rd Ste 5
Tampa FL 33634
813 880-9544

(G-17175)
PRECISION AMMUNITION LLC
5402 E Diana St (33610-1926)
PHONE.............................813 626-0077
Daniel L Powers Jr, *Mng Member*
▲ EMP: 8 EST: 2000
SQ FT: 16,000
SALES (est): 851.6K **Privately Held**
SIC: **3482** Small arms ammunition

(G-17176)
PRECISION ERS
7710 N 30th St (33610-1118)
PHONE.............................813 257-0900
Wayne Chafin, *Buyer*
Susan Garcia, *Sales Staff*
Chase Morrison, *Technician*
Timothy Watson, *Technician*
EMP: 17 EST: 2017
SALES (est): 1.1MM **Privately Held**
SIC: **3599** Machine shop, jobbing & repair

(G-17177)
PREMDOR FINANCE LLC
1 N Dale Mabry Hwy # 950 (33609-2764)
PHONE.............................813 877-2726
EMP: 8 EST: 2009
SALES (est): 104.1K **Privately Held**
SIC: **2431** Doors, wood

(G-17178)
PREMIER PALLETS INC
5805 Breckenridge Pkwy A (33610-4250)
PHONE.............................813 986-4889
Scott Shaw, *President*
Michele Shaw, *Vice Pres*
Timothy Arnold, *Sales Staff*
EMP: 5 EST: 1993
SALES (est): 1.1MM **Privately Held**
WEB: www.premier-pallets.com
SIC: **2448** Pallets, wood

(G-17179)
PRIDE FLORIDA
1913 N Us Highway 301 # 100
(33619-2644)
PHONE.............................813 621-9262
Doug Rickel, *Exec Dir*
EMP: 10 EST: 2007
SALES (est): 266.1K **Privately Held**
SIC: **3842** 5047 Wheelchairs; medical & hospital equipment

(G-17180)
PRIMAL INNOVATION TECH LLC
10150 Highland Manor Dr # 200
(33610-9712)
PHONE.............................407 558-9366
Gregory Holifield,
Gregory Holifield,
EMP: 10 EST: 2012
SALES (est): 710.8K **Privately Held**
WEB: www.primalinnotech.com
SIC: **3661** 8748 7372 Telephone & telegraph apparatus; communications consulting; prepackaged software

(G-17181)
PRIMO WATER CORPORATION
4221 W Boy Scout Blvd (33607-5743)
PHONE.............................844 237-7466
Thomas Harrington, *CEO*
Jerry Fowden, *Ch of Bd*
Jon Kathol, *Vice Pres*
Brian Soltis, *Vice Pres*
Allison Cerqueda, *Accountant*
EMP: 8880 EST: 1955
SALES (est): 2.3B **Privately Held**
WEB: www.primowater.com
SIC: **2086** Bottled & canned soft drinks

(G-17182)
PRINCETON TOOL SOUTH LLC
9009 King Palm Dr (33619-8364)
PHONE.............................813 600-8143
Pamela K Bevington, *Principal*
EMP: 17 EST: 2018
SALES (est): 1MM **Privately Held**
WEB: www.princetontool.com
SIC: **3599** Machine shop, jobbing & repair

(G-17183)
PRINT ETC INC
13121 Canopy Creek Dr (33625-5902)
PHONE.............................813 972-2800
Dennis Kinard, *Owner*
EMP: 8 EST: 2006
SALES (est): 733.8K **Privately Held**
WEB: lutz-fl.minutemanpress.com
SIC: **2752** Commercial printing, offset

(G-17184)
PRINTERS PRIDE INC
Also Called: Bob S Busy Bee Printing
7211 N Dale Mabry Hwy (33614-2669)
PHONE.............................813 932-8683
Beth Seiler Waxler, *President*
Liz Chevalier, *Manager*
EMP: 8 EST: 1976
SALES (est): 838.7K **Privately Held**
SIC: **2752** Commercial printing, offset

(G-17185)
PRINTING SERVICES PLUS LLC
Also Called: Tampa Printing Solutions
100 S Ashley Dr (33602-5304)
P.O. Box 21722 (33622-1722)
PHONE.............................813 279-1903
Jason Scott, *Mng Member*
EMP: 19 EST: 2020
SALES (est): 1.1MM **Privately Held**
WEB: www.printingservicesplus.com
SIC: **2752** 2759 3999 2711 Commercial printing, lithographic; commercial printing, offset; commercial printing; newspapers: printing; manufacturing industries; commercial printing & newspaper publishing combined

(G-17186)
PRO-TECH COATINGS INC
3201 E 3rd Ave (33605-5711)
PHONE.............................813 248-1477
Arthur Quade, *Ch of Bd*
Dale Quade, *President*
John Jones, *Office Mgr*
EMP: 8 EST: 1980
SQ FT: 7,500
SALES (est): 1.1MM **Privately Held**
SIC: **2851** 2992 Epoxy coatings; lubricating oils & greases

(G-17187)
PROBIORA HEALTH LLC
6302 Benjamin Rd Ste 409 (33634-5116)
PHONE.............................214 850-2519
Peter Maroon, *Sales Dir*
Tanya McKinley, *Senior Mgr*
Christine Koski,

Belinda O'Halloran,
EMP: 12 EST: 2016
SALES (est): 1MM **Privately Held**
WEB: www.probiorahealth.com
SIC: **2844** Oral preparations

(G-17188)
PRODUCT DEV PARTNERS LLC
Also Called: Pd Partners
6291 W Linebaugh Ave (33625-5639)
P.O. Box 13449 (33681-3449)
PHONE.............................813 908-6775
Gregory Moore, *Manager*
Steve Jenkins,
EMP: 12 EST: 2000
SALES (est): 3.5MM **Privately Held**
SIC: **2834** Pharmaceutical preparations

(G-17189)
PROFESSIONAL PRODUCTS
4949 Marbrisa Dr Apt 102 (33624-6300)
PHONE.............................323 754-1287
Brian Wald, *Principal*
Michelle Wyman, *Manager*
EMP: 9 EST: 2005
SALES (est): 505.6K **Privately Held**
WEB: www.professional-products.com
SIC: **3714** Manifolds, motor vehicle

(G-17190)
PROMO PRINTING GROUP INC
3210 S Dale Mabry Hwy (33629-7816)
PHONE.............................813 541-3509
Rob Barcus, *VP Opers*
Bill Gillespie, *Representative*
EMP: 8 EST: 2017
SALES (est): 158.5K **Privately Held**
WEB: www.promoprintinggroup.com
SIC: **2752** Commercial printing, offset

(G-17191)
PROXIMITY MILLS LLC
Also Called: Top 10 Floors
4020 W Kennedy Blvd # 10 (33609-2761)
PHONE.............................813 251-3060
Zach Kennedy, *Managing Prtnr*
Charlie Kennedy, *Mng Member*
John V Weller,
▲ EMP: 17 EST: 2008
SALES (est): 638.9K **Privately Held**
SIC: **2273** Carpets & rugs

(G-17192)
PURAGLOBE FLORIDA LLC
4420 Pendola Point Rd (33619-9689)
PHONE.............................813 247-1754
Matt Bulley,
EMP: 61
SALES (corp-wide): 5.6MM **Privately Held**
WEB: www.puraglobe.com
SIC: **1389** Servicing oil & gas wells
PA: Puraglobe Florida, Llc
435 Devon Park Dr
Wayne PA 19087
813 247-1754

(G-17193)
PURE SOLUTIONS INC
14100 Mccormick Dr (33626-3018)
PHONE.............................813 925-1098
James Powers, *CEO*
Jennifer Cook, *COO*
Charles Powers, *COO*
▲ EMP: 20 EST: 2001
SQ FT: 15,500
SALES (est): 4.1MM **Privately Held**
WEB: www.purefactorsusa.com
SIC: **2869** 5499 Perfumes, flavorings & food additives; health & dietetic food stores

(G-17194)
PURE-CHLOR SYSTEMS FLORIDA INC
Also Called: Alfaparf Milano
8200 Nw 33rd St Ste 109 (33614)
PHONE.............................305 437-9937
Davide Cortinovis, *CEO*
Jaskulski Mark, *President*
Barry Billingsley, *Business Mgr*
Mark Jaskulski, *COO*
Roberto Franchina, *Vice Pres*
▼ EMP: 15 EST: 1998

SALES (est): 7.6MM
SALES (corp-wide): 306.4MM **Privately Held**
SIC: **2844** Hair coloring preparations
HQ: Alfa Parf Group Spa
Via Ciserano Snc
Osio Sotto BG 24046

(G-17195)
PUT YOUR NAME ON IT LLC
Also Called: Minisportsballs.com
16057 Tampa Palms Blvd W # 4
(33647-2001)
PHONE....................813 972-1460
Mike Howard, *Controller*
Nancy Kahn,
EMP: 5 EST: 2001
SALES (est): 714.6K **Privately Held**
WEB: www.minisportsballs.com
SIC: **2759** 3069 3993 7389 Imprinting;
balloons; advertising & toy: rubber; adver-
tising novelties; advertising, promotional
& trade show services; advertising spe-
cialties

(G-17196)
PYRAMID IMAGING INC
945 E 11th Ave (33605-3531)
PHONE....................813 984-0125
Rex Lee, *President*
Christine Lee, *COO*
Chris Lee, *Opers Mgr*
Heather Conyers, *Manager*
EMP: 9 EST: 2001
SQ FT: 1,800
SALES (est): 1.4MM **Privately Held**
WEB: www.pyramidimaging.com
SIC: **3827** 8711 3823 Optical instruments
& lenses; engineering services; industrial
instrmnts msrmnt display/control process
variable

(G-17197)
QPS COMPANIES INC (PA)
Also Called: Olympic Case Co
9110 King Palm Dr Ste 101 (33619-8312)
PHONE....................813 246-5525
John S Jackoboice II, *CEO*
John Jackoboice II, *President*
Will Staver, *Purchasing*
Michelle Karakash, *Treasurer*
Otis Jackoboice, *VP Sales*
EMP: 40 EST: 1996
SQ FT: 18,000
SALES (est): 9.2MM **Privately Held**
SIC: **2449** 3161 Shipping cases & drums,
wood: wirebound & plywood; luggage

(G-17198)
QUAD/GRAPHICS INC
Tampa Division
4646 S Grady Ave (33611-2219)
PHONE....................813 837-3436
Nate Lewis, *Area Mgr*
Ron Garrison, *Branch Mgr*
Ben Ronny, *Med Doctor*
John Turner, *Supervisor*
EMP: 62
SALES (corp-wide): 2.9B **Publicly Held**
WEB: www.quad.com
SIC: **2752** 2789 2759 Commercial print-
ing, offset; bookbinding & related work;
commercial printing
PA: Quad/Graphics Inc.
N61w23044 Harrys Way
Sussex WI 53089
414 566-6000

(G-17199)
QUALITY BUILDING CONTROLS INC
Also Called: Albireo Energy
10011 Williams Rd (33624-5047)
PHONE....................813 885-5005
Jerry Dohse, *President*
Dan Whittemore, *Project Mgr*
Brian Helmbold, *Supervisor*
Lorenis Rios, *Admin Asst*
Bryan Smith, *Technician*
EMP: 20 EST: 1997
SQ FT: 3,000
SALES (est): 3MM **Privately Held**
WEB: www.qualitybuildingcontrols.com
SIC: **3613** Control panels, electric

(G-17200)
QUALITY ENGINEERED PRODUCTS CO
4506 Quality Ln (33634-6324)
P.O. Box 22213 (33622-2213)
PHONE....................813 885-1693
Burton Bernstein, *President*
Andrew Bernstein, *Vice Pres*
Nina Bernstein, *Treasurer*
▼ EMP: 23 EST: 1961
SQ FT: 18,000
SALES (est): 4.4MM **Privately Held**
WEB: www.qepco.biz
SIC: **2431** 3442 5031 Doors, wood; win-
dow & door frames; doors & windows

(G-17201)
QUALITY METAL FABRICATORS INC
2610 E 5th Ave (33605-5504)
PHONE....................813 831-7320
Earl Roberts, *President*
Jason Burgess, *Vice Pres*
Earl Roberts III, *Vice Pres*
Steven Roberts, *Vice Pres*
Brian Fields, *Manager*
EMP: 38 EST: 1983
SQ FT: 7,500
SALES (est): 5.8MM **Privately Held**
WEB: www.qmfgroup.com
SIC: **3441** Fabricated structural metal

(G-17202)
QUALITY STEEL FABRICATORS INC
4544 Hartford St (33619-6708)
PHONE....................813 247-7110
Dale Auten, *President*
John Auten, *Vice Pres*
Shane Culberson, *Prdtn Mgr*
EMP: 10 EST: 1986
SQ FT: 15,000
SALES (est): 1.7MM **Privately Held**
WEB: www.qualitysteelfab.com
SIC: **3441** Fabricated structural metal

(G-17203)
QUARTZO LLC
5115 Shadowlawn Ave (33610-5399)
PHONE....................888 813-3442
Ernesto Sanchez,
EMP: 12 EST: 2018
SALES (est): 1.1MM **Privately Held**
WEB: www.quartzousa.com
SIC: **3281** Building stone products

(G-17204)
QUICKSILVER PRTG & COPYING INC
3816a W Sligh Ave (33614-3961)
PHONE....................813 888-6811
Andy Wardrop, *President*
Victoria Wardrop, *Vice Pres*
EMP: 6 EST: 1978
SALES (est): 710.5K **Privately Held**
SIC: **2752** Commercial printing, offset

(G-17205)
R & J CUSTOM CABINETS INC
3907 W Cayuga St (33614-7048)
PHONE....................813 871-5779
Richard Smith, *President*
Jeff Gamble, *Treasurer*
Brian Robertson, *Admin Sec*
EMP: 7 EST: 2002
SQ FT: 5,000
SALES (est): 708.9K **Privately Held**
WEB: www.rjcustomcabinets.com
SIC: **2434** Wood kitchen cabinets

(G-17206)
RACE PERFORMANCE MACHINE SHOP
4707 N Lois Ave (33614-7046)
PHONE....................813 443-8225
Reinaldo Suarez, *Owner*
EMP: 7 EST: 2010
SALES (est): 554.3K **Privately Held**
WEB: raysperformance.business.site
SIC: **3599** Machine shop, jobbing & repair

(G-17207)
RAVEN FOREST OPERATING LLC
13014 N Dale Mbry Hwy # 736
(33618-2808)
PHONE....................727 497-2727
Tony Ferguson,
EMP: 10 EST: 2020
SALES (est): 504.2K **Privately Held**
SIC: **1381** Drilling oil & gas wells

(G-17208)
RB CUSTOM WELDING LLC
5210 E 10th Ave (33619-2710)
PHONE....................813 280-9860
EMP: 8
SALES (est): 40.4K **Privately Held**
SIC: **7692** 1799 Welding Repair Trade
Contractor

(G-17209)
RCR COFFEE COMPANY INC (PA)
402 N 22nd St (33605-6086)
PHONE....................813 248-6264
Richard Perez, *CEO*
Denise Reddick, *President*
Mary Jean Perez, *Vice Pres*
Lucas Reddick, *Warehouse Mgr*
Ron Perez, *Treasurer*
EMP: 30 EST: 1966
SQ FT: 60,000
SALES (est): 3.9MM **Privately Held**
SIC: **2095** 5149 Coffee roasting (except by
wholesale grocers); groceries & related
products; tea; coffee, green or roasted;
cocoa

(G-17210)
REAH GROUP LLC
2721 W Gray St (33609-1732)
PHONE....................727 423-0668
Annemarie Hare, *Principal*
Robert Emmerson, *Mng Member*
EMP: 5 EST: 2016
SALES (est): 600K **Privately Held**
SIC: **2591** Drapery hardware & blinds &
shades

(G-17211)
REFRESCO BEVERAGES US INC
4506 Acline Dr E (33605-5909)
PHONE....................813 241-0147
Martin Cooke, *President*
Darin Clark, *Plant Mgr*
Tamika Hare, *Project Mgr*
Michael Gasper, *Project Engr*
Tham Le, *Finance Mgr*
EMP: 120 **Privately Held**
WEB: www.primowatercorp.com
SIC: **2086** 5149 Carbonated beverages,
nonalcoholic: bottled & canned; groceries
& related products
PA: Refresco Beverages Us Inc.
8118 Woodland Center Blvd
Tampa FL 33614

(G-17212)
REFRESCO BEVERAGES US INC (PA)
8118 Woodland Center Blvd (33614-2403)
P.O. Box 201810, San Antonio TX (78220-
8810)
PHONE....................813 313-1800
Brad Goist, *CEO*
Stephen Corby, *Managing Dir*
Monica Consonery, *Exec VP*
Shayron Barnes-Selby, *Vice Pres*
Ridha Boussetta, *Vice Pres*
◆ EMP: 140 EST: 1991
SQ FT: 10,600
SALES (est): 1B **Privately Held**
WEB: www.refresco-na.com
SIC: **2086** Soft drinks: packaged in cans,
bottles, etc.

(G-17213)
REFRESCO US HOLDING INC (DH)
8118 Woodland Center Blvd (33614-2403)
PHONE....................813 313-1863
Brad Goist, *President*
Barbara Vance, *Production*
Jean Glover, *Human Resources*
Jennifer Lester, *Human Resources*

EMP: 12 EST: 2016
SQ FT: 5,000
SALES (est): 1.3B **Privately Held**
SIC: **2086** Carbonated beverages, nonal-
coholic: bottled & canned

(G-17214)
REIMINK PRINTING INC
Also Called: AlphaGraphics
4209 W Kennedy Blvd (33609-2230)
PHONE....................813 289-4663
Marsha Reimink, *President*
EMP: 6 EST: 1984
SQ FT: 3,000
SALES (est): 871.4K **Privately Held**
WEB: www.alphagraphics.com
SIC: **2752** 7334 7331 2791 Commercial
printing, lithographic; photocopying & du-
plicating services; mailing service; type-
setting; bookbinding & related work;
posters; publishing & printing

(G-17215)
RELIATEX INC
6004 Bonacker Dr (33610-4879)
PHONE....................813 621-6021
Judy Lister, *Sales Staff*
Cuquy Fairbanks, *Marketing Staff*
Donald J Miller, *Systems Mgr*
EMP: 29
SALES (corp-wide): 27.1MM **Privately
Held**
WEB: www.reliatex.com
SIC: **3069** 2221 Foam rubber; broadwo-
ven fabric mills, manmade
PA: Reliatex, Inc.
2201 Nw 72nd Ave
Miami FL 33122
305 592-3220

(G-17216)
RESIDENTIAL ACOUSTICS LLC
Also Called: Commercial Acoustics
6122 Benjamin Rd (33634-5106)
PHONE....................813 922-2390
Walker Peek, *CEO*
Nick Cupp, *Accounts Mgr*
Dylan C McCandless,
EMP: 15 EST: 2013
SALES (est): 1.3MM **Privately Held**
WEB: www.residential-acoustics.com
SIC: **2391** Curtains & draperies

(G-17217)
RESTORATIVE PRODUCTS INC
13560 Wright Cir (33626-3028)
PHONE....................813 342-4432
Craig Turtzo, *President*
EMP: 7 EST: 1992
SQ FT: 6,000
SALES (est): 387.4K **Privately Held**
SIC: **3842** Braces, orthopedic; splints,
pneumatic & wood

(G-17218)
RETREAT
123 S Hyde Park Ave (33606-1929)
P.O. Box 13109 (33681-3109)
PHONE....................813 254-2014
Richard Calderoni, *Principal*
EMP: 7 EST: 2007
SALES (est): 647.5K **Privately Held**
WEB: www.retreattampa.com
SIC: **2064** Candy bars, including chocolate
covered bars

(G-17219)
RICHLAND TOWERS INC
400 N Ashley Dr Ste 2500 (33602-4348)
PHONE....................813 286-4140
Neil S Atkinson, *President*
Jack H Bray, *Chairman*
Anthony Flores, *Vice Pres*
Dale A West, *Vice Pres*
EMP: 34 EST: 1996
SQ FT: 10,000
SALES (est): 2.3MM **Privately Held**
SIC: **3441** 6552 Tower sections, radio &
television transmission; subdividers & de-
velopers

(G-17220)
RIDAN INDUSTRIES LLC
301 W Platt St Ste 339 (33606-2292)
PHONE....................813 258-8334
J Kevin Barile,

Diane Fenimore,
EMP: 8 **EST:** 2004
SALES (est): 500.4K **Privately Held**
SIC: 3441 Tower sections, radio & television transmission

(G-17221)
RINALDI PRINTING COMPANY
Also Called: Rinaldi Printing & Packaging
4514 E Adamo Dr (33605-5967)
PHONE.................................813 569-0033
William S Rinaldi Sr, *Ch of Bd*
William S Rinaldi Jr, *President*
Steve Rinaldi Sr, *Chairman*
Steve Kimbler, *Vice Pres*
Greg Bennett, *Production*
EMP: 46 **EST:** 1905
SQ FT: 36,000
SALES (est): 7.6MM **Privately Held**
WEB: www.rinaldiprinting.com
SIC: 2752 2759 Commercial printing, offset; letterpress printing

(G-17222)
RIPA & ASSOCIATES INC
1409 Tech Blvd Ste 1 (33619-7830)
PHONE.................................813 623-6777
Frank P Ripa, *CEO*
Chris Laface, *President*
Adam Hopkins, *Superintendent*
Robert Houston, *Superintendent*
Kevin Smith, *Superintendent*
EMP: 139 **EST:** 1998
SALES (est): 25.6MM **Privately Held**
WEB: www.ripaconstruction.com
SIC: 2261 Roller printing of cotton broadwoven fabrics

(G-17223)
RIVERHAWK FAST SEA FRAMES LLC
5251 W Tyson Ave (33611-3223)
PHONE.................................912 484-3112
Mark Hornsby, *CEO*
EMP: 6 **EST:** 2008
SALES (est): 515.8K **Privately Held**
WEB: rhfsf.urnge.net
SIC: 3731 Shipbuilding & repairing

(G-17224)
RLS (USA) INC
7802 Woodland Center Blvd (33614-2409)
PHONE.................................561 596-0556
Gruner Werner, *CEO*
Mark Elliott, *Principal*
Gerhardus Van Niererk, *Director*
John Chapman, *Admin Sec*
EMP: 503 **EST:** 2019
SALES (est): 50.5MM **Privately Held**
SIC: 2834 Pharmaceutical preparations

(G-17225)
RMR DISTRIBUTORS INC
9610 Norwood Dr (33624-5115)
PHONE.................................813 908-1141
Robert M Russo, *President*
Tim Parham, *Administration*
EMP: 25 **EST:** 1993
SQ FT: 10,000
SALES (est): 2.8MM **Privately Held**
WEB: www.designsbyrmr.com
SIC: 2759 Screen printing

(G-17226)
ROBBINS MANUFACTURING COMPANY (PA)
Also Called: Robbins Lumber
1003 E 131st Ave (33612-4436)
P.O. Box 17939 (33682-7939)
PHONE.................................813 971-3030
Dionel E Cotanda, *President*
Laurence W Hall Jr, *Chairman*
Peter Shuman, *Exec VP*
William E Brown, *Vice Pres*
Jerome Robbins II, *Vice Pres*
◆ **EMP:** 120 **EST:** 1938
SQ FT: 6,000
SALES (est): 77MM **Privately Held**
WEB: www.robbinslumber.com
SIC: 2491 5031 Wood preserving; lumber, plywood & millwork

(G-17227)
ROBBINS MANUFACTURING COMPANY
1003 E 131st Ave (33612-4436)
PHONE.................................888 558-8199
Bruce Lee, *Branch Mgr*
EMP: 260
SALES (corp-wide): 77MM **Privately Held**
WEB: www.robbinslumber.com
SIC: 2491 Poles, posts & pilings: treated wood
PA: Robbins Manufacturing Company Inc
1003 E 131st Ave
Tampa FL 33612
813 971-3030

(G-17228)
ROBERTSON BILLIARD SUPS INC
Also Called: Billiards & Barstools
1721 N Franklin St (33602-2623)
PHONE.................................813 229-2778
Tom Rodgers, *President*
Debra Robertson Rodgers, *Corp Secy*
Stephen Rodgers, *Manager*
Charles Robertson Sr, *Shareholder*
◆ **EMP:** 7 **EST:** 1930
SQ FT: 15,000
SALES (est): 837.9K **Privately Held**
WEB: www.robertsonbilliards.com
SIC: 3949 5091 5941 Billiard & pool equipment & supplies, general; billiard equipment & supplies; pool & billiard tables

(G-17229)
ROCK BROTHERS BREWING LLC
1901 N 15th St (33605-3659)
PHONE.................................917 324-8175
Kevin Lilly, *Branch Mgr*
EMP: 24
SALES (corp-wide): 247.9K **Privately Held**
WEB: www.rockbrothersbrewing.com
SIC: 2082 Malt beverages
PA: Rock Brothers Brewing, Llc
410 S Cedar Ave
Tampa FL

(G-17230)
ROCKWELL AUTOMATION INC
5820 W Cypress St Ste E (33607-1785)
P.O. Box 999, Lithia (33547-0999)
PHONE.................................813 466-6400
Lee Swank, *Technical Staff*
EMP: 12 **Publicly Held**
WEB: www.rockwellautomation.com
SIC: 3625 Relays & industrial controls
PA: Rockwell Automation, Inc.
1201 S 2nd St
Milwaukee WI 53204

(G-17231)
ROLLERCOAT INDUSTRIES INC
Also Called: Roller Coat Industries
10135 E Us Highway 92 (33610-5965)
PHONE.................................813 621-4668
Joseph L Lancaster, *CEO*
Robert S Lancaster, *Corp Secy*
Mike Lancaster, *Director*
▼ **EMP:** 30 **EST:** 1979
SQ FT: 16,000
SALES (est): 4.9MM **Privately Held**
WEB: www.rollercoat.com
SIC: 3991 Paint rollers

(G-17232)
ROMARK LABORATORIES LC
542 Severn Ave (33606-4046)
PHONE.................................813 282-8544
Jean Francois Rossignol, *Ch of Bd*
Marc S Ayers, *President*
Marc D Lebovitz, *Principal*
Celine Rossignol, *COO*
Matthew Bardin, *Vice Pres*
▲ **EMP:** 45 **EST:** 1993
SALES (est): 21.3MM **Privately Held**
WEB: www.romark.com
SIC: 2834 Pharmaceutical preparations

(G-17233)
ROSS SLADE INC
5024 W Nassau St (33607-3815)
PHONE.................................813 250-0488
William M Slade, *President*
Frederick A Burris, *Principal*
Providence Slade, *Principal*
Jeff D Ross, *Vice Pres*
Justin Bartlett, *Sales Engr*
EMP: 5 **EST:** 2002
SQ FT: 1,100
SALES (est): 2.5MM **Privately Held**
WEB: www.sladerossinc.com
SIC: 3585 Heating & air conditioning combination units

(G-17234)
ROUTE4ME INC
1010 N Florida Ave (33602-3895)
P.O. Box 3014, Fort Lee NJ (07024-9014)
PHONE.................................888 552-9045
Dan Khasis, *CEO*
George Shchegolev, *COO*
Edward Canale, *Sales Staff*
Sean Stenson, *Director*
Robert Tillman, *Bd of Directors*
EMP: 20 **EST:** 2010
SALES (est): 2MM **Privately Held**
WEB: www.route4me.com
SIC: 7372 7389 Business oriented computer software;

(G-17235)
ROYAL CUP INC
3502 Queen Palm Dr Ste A (33619-1391)
PHONE.................................813 664-8902
Scott Scotty, *Vice Pres*
Bill Hann, *Manager*
EMP: 7
SALES (corp-wide): 243.1MM **Privately Held**
WEB: www.royalcupcoffee.com
SIC: 2095 5149 2099 2087 Roasted coffee; coffee & tea; food preparations; flavoring extracts & syrups
PA: Royal Cup Inc.
160 Cleage Dr
Birmingham AL 35217
205 849-5836

(G-17236)
RSC INDUSTRIES INC
Also Called: Robert's Saw Company
5451 W Waters Ave (33634-1214)
PHONE.................................813 886-4711
Robert L Scamardo, *President*
▲ **EMP:** 21 **EST:** 1970
SQ FT: 8,000
SALES (est): 724.2K **Privately Held**
WEB: www.rscsharpening.com
SIC: 3425 7699 Saw blades & handsaws; knife, saw & tool sharpening & repair

(G-17237)
RUBENS CUSTOM CABINETS INC
1310 W Termino St (33612-7760)
PHONE.................................813 510-8397
Betsy A Urrea, *President*
EMP: 7 **EST:** 2017
SALES (est): 246.9K **Privately Held**
SIC: 2434 Wood kitchen cabinets

(G-17238)
RUSTIC STEEL CREATIONS INC
3919 N Highland Ave (33603-4723)
PHONE.................................813 222-0016
Dominique C Martinez, *President*
Dominique Martinez, *President*
EMP: 8 **EST:** 2004
SQ FT: 4,450
SALES (est): 961.6K **Privately Held**
WEB: www.rusticsteel.com
SIC: 3446 Stairs, staircases, stair treads: prefabricated metal

(G-17239)
S I P CORPORATION
Also Called: Universal Gear
7210 Anderson Rd Ste A (33634-3010)
PHONE.................................813 884-8300
Mark Pilger, *President*
Michele Pilger, *CFO*
EMP: 10 **EST:** 1902
SQ FT: 8,000

SALES (est): 1.2MM **Privately Held**
WEB: www.sipgrinder.com
SIC: 3546 3566 Grinders, portable: electric or pneumatic; gears, power transmission, except automotive

(G-17240)
S&J 34102 INC
Also Called: Ark Natural Product For Pets
609 E Jackson St Ste 100 (33602-4933)
PHONE.................................239 592-9388
Susan D Weiss, *President*
Joni Bott, *Vice Pres*
Lera Koch, *Marketing Staff*
Ark Naturals, *Marketing Staff*
Cheryl Kuzman, *Office Mgr*
▲ **EMP:** 8 **EST:** 1996
SALES (est): 1.5MM **Privately Held**
SIC: 2834 Vitamin, nutrient & hematinic preparations for human use

(G-17241)
S&S CRAFTSMEN INC
Also Called: Ssi Wood Products
6404 E Columbus Dr (33619-1659)
P.O. Box 76123 (33675-1123)
PHONE.................................813 247-4429
Thomas M Stenglein, *President*
Leonard J Rosende Jr, *Vice Pres*
Billy Jarboe II, *Sales Staff*
◆ **EMP:** 15 **EST:** 1979
SQ FT: 40,000
SALES (est): 3.3MM **Privately Held**
WEB: www.ssiwoodproducts.com
SIC: 2431 Moldings, wood: unfinished & prefinished

(G-17242)
SACHI TECH INC
Also Called: Pikmykid, Kidio
5005 W Laurel St Ste 204 (33607-3836)
PHONE.................................813 649-8028
Saravana Bhava, *CEO*
Pat Bhava, *General Mgr*
Dionne Bohne, *Vice Pres*
Rey Bermudez, *Engineer*
Dee Bohne, *VP Sales*
EMP: 12 **EST:** 2014
SALES (est): 1.6MM **Privately Held**
WEB: www.pikmykid.com
SIC: 7372 7371 Prepackaged software; software programming applications

(G-17243)
SAF AEROSPACE LLC
8006 N Highland Ave (33604-4006)
PHONE.................................813 376-0883
Patrick Marsh,
EMP: 6 **EST:** 2013
SALES (est): 309.3K **Privately Held**
SIC: 3724 3728 7389 Aircraft engines & engine parts; aircraft parts & equipment;

(G-17244)
SAHLMAN HOLDING COMPANY INC (PA)
1601 Sahlman Dr (33605-6077)
P.O. Box 5009 (33675-5009)
PHONE.................................813 248-5726
Charles W Sahlman, *President*
Herbert J Wiesen, *Corp Secy*
Marchant A Williams, *Vice Pres*
EMP: 5 **EST:** 1987
SQ FT: 10,100
SALES (est): 2.5MM **Privately Held**
WEB: www.ceosahlmanseafood.com
SIC: 2092 0913 Seafoods, fresh: prepared; shrimp, catching of

(G-17245)
SAND DOLLAR PRINTING INC
Also Called: LDI Printing and Signs
3910 N Us Highway 301 # 250
(33619-1283)
PHONE.................................813 740-1953
Jason Lamoore, *President*
EMP: 5 **EST:** 1999
SALES (est): 539.8K **Privately Held**
SIC: 2752 Commercial printing, lithographic

(G-17246)
SANTANAS PWRSPRTS SMALL ENG RP
7941 N Armenia Ave (33604-3830)
PHONE.................................813 658-3530

Eusebio Santana, *President*
EMP: 5 EST: 2011
SALES (est): 491.1K **Privately Held**
WEB: www.santanaspowersports.com
SIC: 3524 7699 5261 7629 Lawnmowers, residential: hand or power; professional instrument repair services; lawn mower repair shop; lawn & garden equipment; lawn & garden supplies; generator repair

(G-17247)
SANTOS FROZEN FOODS INC
2746 W Main St (33607-3317)
P.O. Box 4431 (33677-4431)
PHONE.................................813 875-4901
Geraldine Rosner, *President*
Kenneth Rosner, *Vice Pres*
Delores Zambito, *Treasurer*
EMP: 10 EST: 1962
SQ FT: 3,000
SALES (est): 798.2K **Privately Held**
SIC: 2092 2099 Crabcakes, frozen; crabmeat, frozen; potatoes, peeled for the trade

(G-17248)
SCR PRECISION TUBE BENDING INC
5407 24th Ave S (33619-5370)
PHONE.................................813 622-7091
Patricia M Shafer, *President*
▲ **EMP:** 12 EST: 1986
SQ FT: 10,000
SALES (est): 2.2MM **Privately Held**
WEB: www.scrprecision.com
SIC: 3498 Tube fabricating (contract bending & shaping)

(G-17249)
SECURE BIOMETRIC CORPORATION
Also Called: Global Biometric
2909 W Bay Court Ave (33611-1601)
P.O. Box 10188 (33679-0188)
PHONE.................................813 832-1164
Michael Shapiro, *CEO*
EMP: 8 EST: 2002
SALES (est): 505K **Privately Held**
SIC: 3699 Security devices

(G-17250)
SENIOR VOICE AMERICA INC
3820 Northdale Blvd 205a (33624-1855)
PHONE.................................813 444-1011
Timm Harmon, *Principal*
Lourdes Saenz, *Creative Dir*
EMP: 9 EST: 2012
SALES (est): 292K **Privately Held**
WEB: www.seniorvoiceamerica.com
SIC: 2711 Newspapers, publishing & printing

(G-17251)
SERIGRAPHIC ARTS INC
6806 Parke East Blvd (33610-4144)
PHONE.................................813 626-1070
David W Johnson, *President*
David D Bennett, *Vice Pres*
EMP: 16 EST: 1971
SQ FT: 20,000
SALES (est): 2.3MM **Privately Held**
WEB: www.serigraphicarts.com
SIC: 2759 7389 5199 Screen printing; laminating service; advertising specialties

(G-17252)
SERVICE D N D DUMPSTER
7909 Professional Pl (33637-6747)
PHONE.................................813 989-3867
Darrel Peterson, *President*
EMP: 7 EST: 2016
SALES (est): 155.9K **Privately Held**
SIC: 3443 Dumpsters, garbage

(G-17253)
SEXTANT MARKETING LLC
1860 N Avnida Rpblica De (33605)
PHONE.................................800 691-9980
Jessica Banich MBA, *Vice Pres*
Trudi Kessler, *Assoc VP*
Regan Blessinger, *Marketing Mgr*
Kristin Boulette, *Marketing Mgr*
Jose Clark-Hilery, *Director*
EMP: 14 EST: 2015

SALES (est): 5MM **Privately Held**
WEB: www.sextantmktg.com
SIC: 3812 Sextants

(G-17254)
SGS DESIGNS INC
1515 W Cypress St (33606-1013)
PHONE.................................813 258-2691
James Avery, *President*
Ryan Avery, *Vice Pres*
EMP: 7 EST: 1996
SQ FT: 4,000
SALES (est): 752.5K **Privately Held**
WEB: www.sgsdesignsinc.com
SIC: 2759 Screen printing

(G-17255)
SHAFERS CLSSIC RPRDUCTIONS INC
Also Called: SCR
5407 24th Ave S (33619-5370)
PHONE.................................813 622-7091
Warren Shafer, *President*
Patricia Shafer, *Vice Pres*
Keri Siderio, *Marketing Mgr*
Shane Majetich, *Manager*
Juan Concepcion, *Info Tech Dir*
▲ **EMP:** 9 EST: 1984
SQ FT: 3,000
SALES (est): 1.1MM **Privately Held**
WEB: www.shafersclassic.com
SIC: 3714 5531 3498 Motor vehicle parts & accessories; automotive & home supply stores; fabricated pipe & fittings

(G-17256)
SHEAFFER BOATS INC
3916 W South Ave (33614-6552)
PHONE.................................813 872-7644
Ben Sheaffer, *President*
EMP: 5 EST: 2000
SALES (est): 345.7K **Privately Held**
SIC: 3732 Boat building & repairing

(G-17257)
SHEAFFER MARINE INC
Also Called: Boat Doctor, The
3916 W South Ave (33614-6552)
PHONE.................................813 872-7311
Benjamin R Sheaffer, *President*
Sheri Ellis, *CFO*
EMP: 10 EST: 1967
SQ FT: 3,000
SALES (est): 1.1MM **Privately Held**
WEB: www.sheaffermarine.com
SIC: 3732 Yachts, building & repairing

(G-17258)
SHEFFIELD STEEL CORPORATION
Also Called: Gerdau Ameristeel
4221 W Boy Scout Blvd # 600 (33607-5760)
PHONE.................................918 245-1335
Mario Longhi, *CEO*
Philip Casey, *Ch of Bd*
Neil McCullouhs, *Vice Pres*
▲ **EMP:** 156 EST: 1929
SQ FT: 616,548
SALES (est): 26.4MM **Privately Held**
SIC: 3312 Bars & bar shapes, steel, cold-finished: own hot-rolled
HQ: Gerdau Ameristeel Us Inc.
　4221 W Boy Scout Blvd # 600
　Tampa FL 33607
　813 286-8383

(G-17259)
SHELL PRODUCERS CORP
1200 Sertoma Dr (33605-6050)
PHONE.................................813 247-3153
Aaron Hendry, *President*
EMP: 16 EST: 1997
SALES (est): 1.6MM
SALES (corp-wide): 27.2MM **Privately Held**
SIC: 3731 Shipbuilding & repairing
PA: Gulf Marine Repair Corporation
　1800 Grant St
　Tampa FL 33605
　813 247-3153

(G-17260)
SHIPPING DEPOT INC
4835 W Cypress St (33607-4716)
PHONE.................................813 347-2494

Cecilia M Reid, *Principal*
EMP: 20 EST: 2005
SALES (est): 1.3MM **Privately Held**
WEB: www.ashippingdepot.com
SIC: 3714 PVC valves

(G-17261)
SHIRLEY SIMON & ASSOCIATES LLC
Also Called: TNT
4951b E Adamo Dr Ste 216 (33605-5913)
PHONE.................................813 247-2100
Matthew Simon, *Mng Member*
EMP: 5 EST: 2011
SQ FT: 1,500
SALES (est): 500K **Privately Held**
SIC: 3711 Truck tractors for highway use, assembly of

(G-17262)
SHIRTS & CAPS INC
Also Called: Classb.com
9437 Corporate Lake Dr (33634-2359)
PHONE.................................813 788-7026
Eric H Hilferding, *President*
Eric Hilferding, *President*
Terry Hilferding, *Prdtn Mgr*
Robert H Hilferding, *Treasurer*
Robert Hilferding, *Treasurer*
▲ **EMP:** 14 EST: 1982
SQ FT: 2,400
SALES (est): 1.3MM **Privately Held**
WEB: www.classb.com
SIC: 2396 5651 7389 3993 Screen printing on fabric articles; unisex clothing stores; engraving service; signs & advertising specialties; pleating & stitching

(G-17263)
SIGN A RAMA
Also Called: Sign-A-Rama
3118 Belmore Rd (33618-3629)
PHONE.................................813 264-0022
Michael Pearson, *Principal*
▼ **EMP:** 9 EST: 2008
SALES (est): 116.7K **Privately Held**
SIC: 3993 Signs & advertising specialties

(G-17264)
SIGN SOLUTIONS OF TAMPA BAY
3921 W Dr M Lthr Kng Jr Martin Luther (33614)
PHONE.................................813 269-5990
Ron Neave, *President*
EMP: 5 EST: 2001
SALES (est): 483.8K **Privately Held**
WEB: www.signsolutionstb.com
SIC: 3993 Signs, not made in custom sign painting shops

(G-17265)
SIGN SYSTEMS GRPHIC DSIGNS INC
5031 W Grace St (33607-3807)
PHONE.................................813 281-2400
Thomas F Weber, *President*
Karen Kunkle, *Vice Pres*
Kelly Kline, *Manager*
EMP: 7 EST: 1987
SQ FT: 6,901
SALES (est): 927.1K **Privately Held**
WEB: www.signsystemstampa.com
SIC: 3993 Signs, not made in custom sign painting shops; electric signs

(G-17266)
SIGNATURE GRANITE INC
3904 S 51st St (33619-6802)
PHONE.................................813 443-5597
Eddie Beltran, *President*
EMP: 10 EST: 2011
SALES (est): 588.4K **Privately Held**
SIC: 3281 Granite, cut & shaped

(G-17267)
SIGNODE INDUSTRIAL GROUP LLC
14025 Riveredge Dr (33637-2089)
PHONE.................................866 347-1820
EMP: 16
SALES (est): 541K **Privately Held**
SIC: 2671 Resinous impregnated paper for packaging

(G-17268)
SIGNS OF AMERICA TAMPA CORP
4025 W Waters Ave (33614-1976)
PHONE.................................813 243-9243
EMP: 6 EST: 2019
SALES (est): 348.9K **Privately Held**
WEB: signs-of-america-tampa-corp.business.site
SIC: 3993 Signs & advertising specialties

(G-17269)
SIGNS USA INC
4123 W Hillsborough Ave (33614-5609)
PHONE.................................813 901-9333
Thomas R Miano, *President*
Janet Miano, *Vice Pres*
Angela Swartz, *Executive*
EMP: 10 EST: 1994
SQ FT: 3,700
SALES (est): 1.5MM **Privately Held**
WEB: www.signsusainc.com
SIC: 3993 Signs & advertising specialties

(G-17270)
SITECRAFTERS OF FLORIDA INC
3242 Henderson Blvd # 200 (33609-3094)
PHONE.................................813 258-4696
Jeffrey Hardeman, *President*
Wayne Futch, *Principal*
Steve Howell, *Manager*
EMP: 35 EST: 2003
SALES (est): 5.1MM **Privately Held**
WEB: www.sitecraftersfl.com
SIC: 3993 Signs & advertising specialties

(G-17271)
SKINUTRA INC
5136 W Clifton St (33634-8012)
PHONE.................................813 992-1742
John S Patneaude, *Principal*
EMP: 9 EST: 2014
SALES (est): 206.7K **Privately Held**
WEB: www.skinutra.com
SIC: 2834 Vitamin, nutrient & hematinic preparations for human use

(G-17272)
SLEEP INTERNATIONAL LLC (PA)
5223 16th Ave S (33619-5386)
PHONE.................................813 247-5337
Adam Weinman, *President*
Patrick Murphy, *CFO*
◆ **EMP:** 49 EST: 2011
SALES (est): 10.6MM **Privately Held**
SIC: 2515 Mattresses & bedsprings

(G-17273)
SLOAN HEALTH PRODUCTS LLC (PA)
500 N West Shore Blvd # 640 (33609-1910)
PHONE.................................727 504-3915
Manindra Garg, *Mng Member*
EMP: 6 EST: 2008
SALES (est): 1.1MM **Privately Held**
WEB: www.sloanhealthproducts.com
SIC: 2844 Cosmetic preparations

(G-17274)
SMART GUIDES
20013 Outpost Point Dr (33647-3560)
PHONE.................................813 534-0940
Frank Curtin, *Principal*
EMP: 7 EST: 2007
SALES (est): 145.8K **Privately Held**
SIC: 7372 8742 Business oriented computer software; management consulting services

(G-17275)
SMARTSCIENCE LABORATORIES INC
13760 Reptron Blvd (33626-3040)
PHONE.................................813 925-8454
Gene C Weitz, *President*
Dave Johnson, *Vice Pres*
▲ **EMP:** 15 EST: 1998
SQ FT: 30,000

SALES (est): 9.9MM **Privately Held**
WEB: www.smartsciencelabs.com
SIC: 2834 8742 Pharmaceutical preparations; manufacturing management consultant

(G-17276)
SMITHS INTERCONNECT INC (HQ)
4726 Eisenhower Blvd (33634-6309)
PHONE.................................813 901-7200
Richard Pea, *President*
Vince Novo, *Prdtn Mgr*
Jose Gil, *Mfg Staff*
Eric Behm, *Production*
Rolando Penabrade, *Engineer*
▼ **EMP:** 176 **EST:** 1960
SQ FT: 120,000
SALES (est): 35.8MM
SALES (corp-wide): 3.3B **Privately Held**
WEB: www.smithsinterconnect.com
SIC: 3812 3661 3663 3669 Search & navigation equipment; telephone station equipment & parts, wire; airborne radio communications equipment; intercommunication systems, electric; printed circuit boards; modules, solid state
PA: Smiths Group Plc
4th Floor
London SW1Y
207 004-1600

(G-17277)
SMITHS INTERCONNECT INC
Also Called: Channel Microwave
4726 Eisenhower Blvd (33634-6309)
PHONE.................................813 901-7200
Mike Kujawa, *General Mgr*
EMP: 229
SALES (corp-wide): 3.3B **Privately Held**
WEB: www.smithsinterconnect.com
SIC: 3679 Microwave components
HQ: Smiths Interconnect, Inc.
4726 Eisenhower Blvd
Tampa FL 33634
813 901-7200

(G-17278)
SOE SOFTWARE CORPORATION
Also Called: Scytl
1111 N West Shore Blvd # 300
(33607-4703)
PHONE.................................813 490-7150
Marc Fartello, *CEO*
Branden Elwell, *General Mgr*
Daniel Navas, *Vice Pres*
Richard Catahan, *Project Mgr*
Jack Farmer, *Warehouse Mgr*
EMP: 26 **EST:** 2002
SALES (est): 9MM **Privately Held**
WEB: www.scytl.us
SIC: 7372 Business oriented computer software

(G-17279)
SOL DAVIS PRINTING INC
5205 N Lois Ave (33614-6550)
PHONE.................................813 353-3609
Sol Davis, *President*
David Most, *Prdtn Mgr*
EMP: 15 **EST:** 1999
SQ FT: 8,500
SALES (est): 1.8MM **Privately Held**
WEB: www.soldavisprinting.com
SIC: 2752 Commercial printing, offset

(G-17280)
SOLSTICE SLEEP PRODUCTS INC
500 S Falkenburg Rd (33619-8043)
PHONE.................................813 438-8830
Jim McGrath, *Controller*
Adrian Jones, *Sales Staff*
Kim George, *Marketing Staff*
Manuel Gonzalez, *Manager*
Eb Walthall, *Manager*
EMP: 21
SALES (corp-wide): 23.9MM **Privately Held**
WEB: www.jamisonbedding.com
SIC: 2221 Bedding, manmade or silk fabric
PA: Solstice Sleep Products, Inc.
3720 W Broad St
Columbus OH 43228
614 279-8850

(G-17281)
SOLUTION PUBLISHING LLC
2701 N Rocky Point Dr # 180
(33607-5917)
PHONE.................................813 291-0840
EMP: 12 **EST:** 2001
SALES (est): 73.1K **Privately Held**
WEB: www.solpub.com
SIC: 2721 Periodicals

(G-17282)
SOPHIX SOLUTIONS INC
1228 E 7th Ave Ste 225 (33605-3505)
PHONE.................................813 837-9555
Mark Eckerty,
Robert S Fleming Jr,
Gregory T Moore,
EMP: 6 **EST:** 2004
SALES (est): 722.8K **Privately Held**
WEB: www.sophix.net
SIC: 7372 Business oriented computer software

(G-17283)
SOUTHEAST COMPOUNDING PHRM LLC
3906 Cragmont Dr (33619-8305)
PHONE.................................813 644-7700
Jeff Steele,
Geoff Becker,
Warren Cal Gray Jr,
Milton Larrea,
Frank Ruddy,
EMP: 8 **EST:** 2012
SALES (est): 1MM **Privately Held**
WEB: www.southeastcompounding.com
SIC: 2834 Pharmaceutical preparations

(G-17284)
SOUTHEAST DAIRY PROCESSORS INC
Also Called: Flavor Right Foods SE
3811 E Columbus Dr (33605-3220)
P.O. Box 5088 (33675-5088)
PHONE.................................813 620-1516
William B Tiller, *President*
Donald Tiller Jr, *Vice Pres*
Vickie Osborne, *Treasurer*
EMP: 29 **EST:** 1988
SQ FT: 25,000
SALES (est): 19.4MM
SALES (corp-wide): 29.7MM **Privately Held**
SIC: 2026 Milk processing (pasteurizing, homogenizing, bottling); half & half
PA: Flavor Right Foods Group, Inc.
2517 E Chambers St
Phoenix AZ 85040
602 232-2570

(G-17285)
SOUTHEAST MANUFACTURING INC
4921 E 7th Ave (33605-4705)
PHONE.................................866 550-2511
Karen Ruel, *Principal*
EMP: 7 **EST:** 2010
SALES (est): 72.4K **Privately Held**
SIC: 3999 Manufacturing industries

(G-17286)
SOUTHEAST PRINT PROGRAMS INC
5023 W Rio Vista Ave (33634-5316)
PHONE.................................813 885-3203
EMP: 46
SQ FT: 5,000
SALES (est): 2.2MM **Privately Held**
SIC: 2752 7331 Commercial Printing, Lithographic

(G-17287)
SOUTHEASTERN SEATING INC
903 E 17th Ave (33605-2532)
PHONE.................................813 273-9858
Eugene J Freeman, *President*
Jerry Freidman, *President*
Nick Freeman, *Sales Staff*
Richard Barnes, *CIO*
Jerry Angel, *Technician*
EMP: 15 **EST:** 1999
SQ FT: 15,000

SALES (est): 4.2MM **Privately Held**
WEB: www.seseating.com
SIC: 2531 2452 7359 Stadium furniture; prefabricated wood buildings; equipment rental & leasing

(G-17288)
SOUTHERN MFG TECH INC
5910 Johns Rd (33634-4422)
PHONE.................................813 888-8151
Roy Sweatman, *CEO*
Joe Paciella, *Mfg Spvr*
Gordon Dunn, *Engineer*
Sithea Ean, *Plant Engr*
Shannon Sweatman, *Human Res Dir*
EMP: 100 **EST:** 1983
SQ FT: 20,000
SALES (est): 20.7MM **Privately Held**
WEB: www.smt-tampa.com
SIC: 3599 Machine shop, jobbing & repair

(G-17289)
SOUTHERN STATES MOTIVE PWR INC
6601 E Adamo Dr (33619-3415)
PHONE.................................813 621-3338
J Jeffrey Fischer, *Manager*
EMP: 10 **EST:** 2012
SALES (est): 604.6K **Privately Held**
SIC: 3691 Storage batteries

(G-17290)
SOUTHERN STATES TOYOTA LIFT (PA)
Also Called: Florida Lift Systems
115 S 78th St (33619-4220)
PHONE.................................904 764-7662
Jeffrey Fischer, *President*
Halsey Keats, *Vice Pres*
Kirk Alderman, *Safety Dir*
Darrell Donart, *Parts Mgr*
Guy Heyl, *CFO*
◆ **EMP:** 98 **EST:** 1954
SQ FT: 37,000
SALES (est): 87.9MM **Privately Held**
WEB: www.sstlift.com
SIC: 3537 5511 7359 Forklift trucks; automobiles, new & used; industrial truck rental

(G-17291)
SOUTHERN WINDING SERVICE INC
5302 Saint Paul St (33619-6100)
PHONE.................................813 621-6555
Francis O Jobe, *Ch of Bd*
Leo M Letourneau, *President*
Leo Letourneau, *General Mgr*
Laura Chirichigno, *CFO*
▲ **EMP:** 26 **EST:** 1948
SQ FT: 15,000
SALES (est): 1.9MM **Privately Held**
WEB: www.southernwinding.com
SIC: 7694 Electric motor repair

(G-17292)
SOUTHPRINT CORP
6816 N River Blvd (33604-5444)
PHONE.................................813 237-8000
Jack Barnes, *CEO*
Patricia Brannon, *President*
Shirley Worsham, *Vice Pres*
EMP: 8 **EST:** 1968
SQ FT: 20,000
SALES (est): 358.2K **Privately Held**
WEB: www.southprintcorp.com
SIC: 2752 Commercial printing, offset

(G-17293)
SPEEDLINE ATHLETIC WEAR INC
1804 N Habana Ave (33607-3345)
P.O. Box 4150 (33677-4150)
PHONE.................................813 876-1375
Steven Malzone, *President*
Denis Malzone, *Vice Pres*
Buddy Carter, *Sales Executive*
▲ **EMP:** 39 **EST:** 1936
SQ FT: 60,000
SALES (est): 6.6MM **Privately Held**
WEB: www.speedlineathletic.com
SIC: 2329 2339 Men's & boys' athletic uniforms; uniforms, athletic: women's, misses' & juniors'

(G-17294)
SPEEDLINE TEAM SPORTS INC
1804 N Habana Ave (33607-3345)
PHONE.................................813 876-1375
Steven Malzone, *President*
Steve Malzone, *Principal*
Shane Davis, *Manager*
John Oliva, *Director*
EMP: 11 **EST:** 2013
SALES (est): 2MM **Privately Held**
WEB: www.speedlineathletic.com
SIC: 2329 2339 Men's & boys' sportswear & athletic clothing; men's & boys' athletic uniforms; women's & misses' outerwear; women's & misses' athletic clothing & sportswear; uniforms, athletic: women's, misses' & juniors'

(G-17295)
SPHERE ACCESS INC (PA)
400 N Ashley Dr Ste 1775 (33602-4338)
PHONE.................................336 501-6159
Osama Sabbah, *CEO*
Kathryn Freeman, *Vice Pres*
EMP: 15 **EST:** 2018
SALES (est): 2.6MM **Privately Held**
WEB: www.sphereaccess.com
SIC: 7372 6799 Business oriented computer software; venture capital companies

(G-17296)
SPORT PRODUCTS OF TAMPA INC
8721 Ashworth Dr (33647-2269)
PHONE.................................813 630-5552
Willis J Collier, *President*
EMP: 8 **EST:** 1986
SALES (est): 248.7K **Privately Held**
WEB: www.sportproductsoftampainc.com
SIC: 2221 3069 3949 2339 Nylon broadwoven fabrics; wet suits, rubber; sporting & athletic goods; women's & misses' outerwear

(G-17297)
SRS SOFTWARE LLC
Also Called: SRS Health Software
4221 W Boy Scout Blvd # 200
(33607-5745)
PHONE.................................201 802-1300
Khal Rai, *President*
Robert Harmonay, *COO*
Daniel McGraw, *Senior VP*
Keegan Dowling, *Vice Pres*
Lester Parada, *Vice Pres*
EMP: 8 **EST:** 2013
SALES (est): 2.3MM **Privately Held**
WEB: www.srs-health.com
SIC: 7372 Prepackaged software
PA: Nextech Systems, Llc
4221 W Boy Scout Blvd # 350
Tampa FL 33607

(G-17298)
STANDARD INDUSTRIES INC
Also Called: GAF Materials
5138 Madison Ave (33619-9641)
PHONE.................................813 248-7000
Stewart McCallum, *Finance Other*
Charles AMS, *Regl Sales Mgr*
Darrell S Norrington, *Branch Mgr*
Mike Finster, *Manager*
EMP: 95
SALES (corp-wide): 5.8B **Privately Held**
WEB: www.gaf.com
SIC: 2493 2952 2951 Insulation & roofing material, reconstituted wood; asphalt felts & coatings; asphalt paving mixtures & blocks
HQ: Standard Industries Inc.
1 Campus Dr
Parsippany NJ 07054

(G-17299)
STANLEY CHAIR COMPANY INC
5110 W Hanna Ave (33634-8088)
PHONE.................................813 884-1436
Burton Osiason, *President*
Carol A Osiason, *Vice Pres*
Neal Osiason, *Vice Pres*
Randy Osiason, *Vice Pres*
◆ **EMP:** 33 **EST:** 1946
SQ FT: 45,000
SALES (est): 2.5MM **Privately Held**
WEB: www.stanleychair.com
SIC: 2512 Upholstered household furniture

(G-17300)
STAR QUALITY INC
4006 W Crest Ave (33614-6540)
PHONE..............................813 875-9955
Maximo Sanchez, *President*
Denise Sanchez, *Treasurer*
EMP: 16 EST: 1984
SQ FT: 31,000
SALES (est): 1.9MM **Privately Held**
WEB: www.registrar-transfers.com
SIC: 2521 2434 Cabinets, office: wood;
bookcases, office: wood; vanities, bath-
room: wood

(G-17301)
STELLARNET INC
14390 Carlson Cir (33626-3003)
PHONE..............................813 855-8687
Will Pierce, *President*
Katy Wisner, *Office Mgr*
EMP: 10 EST: 1991
SALES (est): 2.3MM **Privately Held**
WEB: www.shopstellarnet.com
SIC: 3826 3829 Spectrometers; measur-
ing & controlling devices

(G-17302)
STEPHEN GOULD CORPORATION
5132 Tampa West Blvd A (33634-2420)
PHONE..............................813 886-8460
Lane Miller, *Principal*
Hillary Fish, *Accounts Exec*
EMP: 16
SALES (corp-wide): 951.9MM **Privately Held**
WEB: www.stephengould.com
SIC: 2621 3086 2671 Wrapping & pack-
aging papers; plastics foam products;
packaging paper & plastics film, coated &
laminated
PA: Stephen Gould Corporation
35 S Jefferson Rd
Whippany NJ 07981
973 428-1500

(G-17303)
STERIS CORPORATION
3903 Northdale Blvd 120e (33624-1885)
PHONE..............................813 852-8002
Brian Bennetti, *District Mgr*
Barrett Vaughn, *Prdtn Mgr*
Nick Caley, *Opers Staff*
James Niemeyer, *Engineer*
Marc Garofani, *Asst Controller*
EMP: 123 **Privately Held**
WEB: www.steris.com
SIC: 3842 Surgical appliances & supplies
HQ: Steris Corporation
5960 Heisley Rd
Mentor OH 44060
440 354-2600

(G-17304)
STM INDUSTRIES LLC
9524 N Trask St (33624-5137)
PHONE..............................813 854-3544
Leland Holland, *Mng Member*
Katharine Holland,
EMP: 17 EST: 2017
SALES (est): 1.2MM **Privately Held**
WEB: www.stmindustries.com
SIC: 2821 5999 Plastics materials &
resins; fiberglass materials, except insula-
tion

(G-17305)
STREET ELEMENTS MAGAZINE INC
3902 E Powhatan Ave (33610-3753)
PHONE..............................813 935-5894
Kevin Campbell, *Principal*
EMP: 11 EST: 2007
SALES (est): 255.1K **Privately Held**
WEB: www.streetelementsmagazine.com
SIC: 2721 Magazines: publishing only, not
printed on site

(G-17306)
SULLENBERGER INC
Also Called: Shellie Desk
8949 Maislin Dr (33637-6708)
PHONE..............................813 988-4525
Robert Sullenberger, *President*
Donna R Sullenberger, *Treasurer*

Brett Sullenberger, *Director*
Carla Casey, *Admin Sec*
EMP: 14 EST: 1985
SQ FT: 24,000
SALES (est): 1.5MM **Privately Held**
SIC: 2522 2521 Office furniture, except
wood; wood office furniture

(G-17307)
SUN COAST SURGICAL & MED SUP
2711 N 58th St (33619-1628)
PHONE..............................813 881-0065
Ron E Dial, *Owner*
Steve Dial, *Co-Owner*
EMP: 5 EST: 2007
SALES (est): 496.4K **Privately Held**
WEB: www.suncoastsurgical.com
SIC: 3841 Surgical & medical instruments

(G-17308)
SUN COATINGS LLC
Also Called: Sun Coatings, Inc.
4701 E 7th Ave (33605-4701)
PHONE..............................727 531-4100
Michael Hyer, *President*
Eric Sifferlen, *Vice Pres*
John Stitzel, *Vice Pres*
Ken Lewis, *Plant Mgr*
Sven Doerge, *Treasurer*
▲ EMP: 30 EST: 1971
SALES (est): 12.9MM
SALES (corp-wide): 913.2MM **Privately Held**
WEB: www.suncoatings.com
SIC: 2851 Paints & paint additives
PA: Innovative Chemical Products Group,
Llc
150 Dascomb Rd
Andover MA 01810
978 623-9980

(G-17309)
SUN METALS SYSTEMS INC
5008 Tampa West Blvd (33634-2412)
PHONE..............................813 889-0718
James G Hatton, *CEO*
Shalle Van Horn, *President*
James G Hatton III, *Vice Pres*
Jim Woolsey, *QC Mgr*
◆ EMP: 20 EST: 1999
SQ FT: 75,000
SALES (est): 4.1MM **Privately Held**
WEB: www.sunmetalssystems.com
SIC: 3442 Metal doors, sash & trim

(G-17310)
SUN-PAC MANUFACTURING INC
14201 Mccormick Dr (33626-3063)
PHONE..............................813 925-8787
Gary Henderson, *CEO*
Theresa Henderson, *Managing Dir*
Mike Heintz, *Manager*
Riggs Heather, *Admin Asst*
EMP: 40 EST: 2000
SALES (est): 6MM **Privately Held**
WEB: www.sunpacmanufacturing.com
SIC: 2023 Dietary supplements, dairy &
non-dairy based

(G-17311)
SUNCOAST CARTONS & CRATING LLC
5601 Airport Blvd (33634-5305)
P.O. Box 56017, Saint Petersburg (33732-
6017)
PHONE..............................813 242-8477
Maria Brooks, *President*
William Brooks, *Vice Pres*
EMP: 8 EST: 2001
SQ FT: 7,500
SALES (est): 800K **Privately Held**
SIC: 2653 Boxes, corrugated: made from
purchased materials

(G-17312)
SUNCOAST ELECTRIC MTR SVC INC
2502 E 5th Ave (33605-5518)
PHONE..............................813 247-4104
William P Bannar, *President*
Caryl Giordano, *Admin Sec*
▼ EMP: 12 EST: 1990
SQ FT: 5,000

SALES (est): 2.2MM **Privately Held**
WEB: www.suncoastelectricmotor.com
SIC: 7694 5999 Electric motor repair; mo-
tors, electric

(G-17313)
SUNCOAST REBUILD CENTER INC
2717 N 58th St (33619-1628)
PHONE..............................813 238-3433
Glenn McCabe, *President*
Peter McCabe, *Vice Pres*
Ricky Mullins, *Sales Staff*
EMP: 10 EST: 1988
SALES (est): 999.9K **Privately Held**
WEB: www.suncoastrebuilding.com
SIC: 3568 3714 Power transmission
equipment; transmissions, motor vehicle

(G-17314)
SUNCOAST SIGNS INC
9601 E Us Highway 92 (33610-5927)
PHONE..............................813 664-0699
Scott Robinson, *President*
Karen Robinson, *Admin Sec*
EMP: 8 EST: 1985
SALES (est): 987.5K **Privately Held**
WEB: www.suncoastsigns.com
SIC: 3993 7532 5099 Signs, not made in
custom sign painting shops; truck painting
& lettering; signs, except electric

(G-17315)
SUNCOAST SPECIALTY PRTG INC
Also Called: Printing.com
6401 N River Blvd (33604-6021)
PHONE..............................813 951-0899
Brice A Wolford, *Principal*
EMP: 7 EST: 2010
SALES (est): 134.3K **Privately Held**
WEB: www.suncoastspecialtyprinting.com
SIC: 2759 Commercial printing

(G-17316)
SUPERMEDIA LLC
5102 W Laurel St (33607-3854)
PHONE..............................813 402-3753
Joann Leanza, *Branch Mgr*
EMP: 13
SALES (corp-wide): 1.4B **Publicly Held**
SIC: 2741 Telephone & other directory
publishing
HQ: Supermedia Llc
2200 W Airfield Dr
Dfw Airport TX 75261
972 453-7000

(G-17317)
SURF OUTFITTER
1413 S Howard Ave Ste 104 (33606-3176)
PHONE..............................813 489-4587
Daniel Hater, *Administration*
EMP: 7 EST: 2013
SALES (est): 118.4K **Privately Held**
WEB: www.surfoutfitter.com
SIC: 2369 2329 Bathing suits &
swimwear: girls', children's & infants';
men's & boys' sportswear & athletic cloth-
ing

(G-17318)
SYNDAVER LABS INC (PA)
8506 Benjamin Rd Ste C (33634-1242)
PHONE..............................813 600-5530
Christopher Sakezles, *President*
James Sicardi, *Buyer*
Terence Terenzi, *CFO*
Malia Correa, *Sales Staff*
Moira Gustin, *Sales Staff*
EMP: 35 EST: 2009
SALES (est): 10MM **Privately Held**
WEB: www.syndaver.com
SIC: 3842 Surgical appliances & supplies

(G-17319)
SYPRIS ELECTRONICS LLC (HQ)
10421 University Ctr Dr (33612-6422)
PHONE..............................813 972-6000
Timothy Harris, *District Mgr*
Aaron McCarthy, *COO*
Lawrence Bernicky, *Vice Pres*
Lance Martinez, *Opers Mgr*
David Bailey, *Buyer*
▲ EMP: 107 EST: 1965
SQ FT: 50,000

SALES (est): 62.3MM
SALES (corp-wide): 97.4MM **Publicly Held**
WEB: www.sypriselectronics.com
SIC: 3672 3679 Printed circuit boards;
electronic circuits
PA: Sypris Solutions, Inc.
101 Bullitt Ln Ste 450
Louisville KY 40222
502 329-2000

(G-17320)
T C DELIVERIES
7002 Parke East Blvd (33610-4132)
PHONE..............................813 881-1830
Stan Pascarelli, *Opers Staff*
Kevin McMahon, *Manager*
EMP: 8 EST: 2016
SALES (est): 253.2K **Privately Held**
SIC: 2893 Printing ink

(G-17321)
T DISNEY TRUCKING & GRADING
9250 Bay Plaza Blvd # 311 (33619-4465)
PHONE..............................813 443-6258
EMP: 27
SQ FT: 1,500
SALES: 15MM **Privately Held**
SIC: 3713 Mfg Truck/Bus Bodies

(G-17322)
TAE TRANS ATLANTIC ELEC INC (PA)
Also Called: Empire Scientific
4504 E Hillsborough Ave (33610-5249)
P.O. Box 817, Deer Park NY (11729-0981)
PHONE..............................631 595-9206
Janet English, *President*
Jeffrey English, *Vice Pres*
Spencer Slipko, *Vice Pres*
▲ EMP: 23 EST: 1965
SQ FT: 1,500
SALES (est): 3.4MM **Privately Held**
SIC: 3692 5063 Primary batteries, dry &
wet; batteries

(G-17323)
TAIKA LOGISTICS LLC
401 E Jackson St (33602-5233)
PHONE..............................813 945-2911
EMP: 7
SALES (est): 302.2K **Privately Held**
SIC: 3537 Truck trailers, used in plants,
docks, terminals, etc.

(G-17324)
TAMPA AMALGAMATED STEEL CORP
5215 Saint Paul St (33619-6117)
P.O. Box 2031 (33601-2031)
PHONE..............................813 621-0550
Tommy E Craddock, *President*
John E Craddock, *Corp Secy*
Robert E Craddock, *Vice Pres*
Robert Craddock, *Vice Pres*
Dale Damgaard, *Engineer*
EMP: 18 EST: 1964
SQ FT: 40,000
SALES (est): 5.4MM **Privately Held**
SIC: 3441 7692 Building components,
structural steel; welding repair

(G-17325)
TAMPA ARMATURE WORKS INC
Also Called: Taw Tampa Service Center
440 S 78th St (33619-4223)
P.O. Box 3381 (33601-3381)
PHONE..............................813 612-2600
John Sushko, *Production*
Mike Wherley, *Controller*
Jim Peplow, *Finance*
Al Jackson, *Accounts Mgr*
Robin Morton, *Office Mgr*
EMP: 104
SALES (corp-wide): 169.6MM **Privately Held**
WEB: www.tawinc.com
SIC: 7694 3621 5063 Electric motor re-
pair; motors & generators; motors, elec-
tric; generators; electrical supplies
PA: Tampa Armature Works, Inc.
6312 S 78th St
Riverview FL 33578
813 621-5661

▲ = Import ▼=Export
◆ =Import/Export

(G-17326)
TAMPA BAY MACHINING INC
13601 Mccormick Dr (33626-3049)
PHONE..................................813 855-8456
Jeff Kefauver, *President*
Mike Christy, *Vice Pres*
Tammy Coe, *Vice Pres*
EMP: 49 **EST:** 1981
SQ FT: 25,000
SALES (est): 4.5MM **Privately Held**
WEB: www.tampabaymachining.com
SIC: 3599 Machine shop, jobbing & repair

(G-17327)
TAMPA BAY POWDER COATING INC
9601 Norwood Dr Ste B (33624-5300)
PHONE..................................813 964-5667
David Nelson, *Principal*
EMP: 8 **EST:** 2018
SALES (est): 454.4K **Privately Held**
WEB:
www.buffaloavenuepowdercoating.com
SIC: 3479 Coating of metals & formed products

(G-17328)
TAMPA BAY POWERSPORTS LLC
13521 N Florida Ave (33613-3214)
PHONE..................................813 968-7888
Drew Hall, *Parts Mgr*
Mansor Thomas, *Sales Mgr*
John Scott, *Sales Staff*
Laurie Stanford, *Office Mgr*
Rodin Younessi,
EMP: 35 **EST:** 2005
SALES (est): 2.5MM **Privately Held**
SIC: 3751 5571 Motorcycles, bicycles & parts; motorcycle dealers

(G-17329)
TAMPA BAY PRESS INC
4710 Eisenhower Blvd B12 (33634-6308)
PHONE..................................813 886-1415
John Hedler, *President*
EMP: 20 **EST:** 1987
SQ FT: 18,000
SALES (est): 1.3MM **Privately Held**
WEB: www.tampabay.org
SIC: 2752 Commercial printing, offset

(G-17330)
TAMPA BRASS AND ALUMINUM CORP
Also Called: T B A
8511 Florida Mining Blvd (33634-1200)
PHONE..................................813 885-6064
Sam Leto Jr, *Ch of Bd*
Christopher S Leto, *President*
Jason Leto, *COO*
Tim Hemphill, *Plant Mgr*
Ken Sowers, *Project Mgr*
▲ **EMP:** 105 **EST:** 1957
SQ FT: 64,500
SALES (est): 39.2MM **Privately Held**
WEB: www.tampabrass.com
SIC: 3369 3599 Nonferrous foundries; machine shop, jobbing & repair

(G-17331)
TAMPA CONTRACTORS SUPPLY INC
Also Called: Alliance Contractors Supply
5017 N Coolidge Ave (33614-6421)
PHONE..................................813 418-7284
Jerry Monts De Oca, *President*
EMP: 21 **EST:** 2011
SQ FT: 26,000
SALES (est): 2.3MM **Privately Held**
SIC: 2431 Millwork

(G-17332)
TAMPA FIBERGLASS INC
4209 Raleigh St (33619-6059)
PHONE..................................813 248-6828
Stephen Cook, *President*
Brian Cook, *Vice Pres*
Patricia Cook, *Vice Pres*
Edie Restall, *Office Mgr*
Colton McCleave, *Maintence Staff*
EMP: 19 **EST:** 1972
SQ FT: 1,000
SALES (est): 651.7K **Privately Held**
WEB: www.tampafiberglass.com
SIC: 3589 1799 Water treatment equipment, industrial; fiberglass work

(G-17333)
TAMPA MEDIA GROUP INC
Also Called: Tampa Tribune Company, The
202 S Parker St (33606-2379)
P.O. Box 31101, Saint Petersburg (33731-1107)
PHONE..................................813 259-7711
EMP: 200
SALES (corp-wide): 83.3MM **Privately Held**
SIC: 2711 Newspapers-Publishing/Printing
PA: Tampa Media Group, Inc.
202 S Parker St
Tampa FL 33606
813 259-7711

(G-17334)
TAMPA MEDIA GROUP INC (PA)
Also Called: Tampa Tribune, The
202 S Parker St (33606-2379)
PHONE..................................813 259-7711
Robert Loring, *Principal*
Gary Alcock, *Principal*
EMP: 400 **EST:** 2012
SALES (est): 88.4MM **Privately Held**
WEB: www.tampabay.com
SIC: 2711 Newspapers, publishing & printing

(G-17335)
TAMPA MEDIA GROUP LLC
Also Called: Tbo
202 S Parker St (33606-2379)
PHONE..................................813 259-7100
Cyrus Nikou,
Robert Loring,
EMP: 7 **EST:** 2013
SALES (est): 208.8K **Privately Held**
WEB: www.tampabay.com
SIC: 2711 2721 Newspapers, publishing & printing; commercial printing & newspaper publishing combined; periodicals

(G-17336)
TAMPA METAL WORKS INC
6601 N 50th St (33610-1843)
PHONE..................................813 628-9223
Charles S Allen, *President*
Tim Jenkins, *Vice Pres*
EMP: 11 **EST:** 1987
SALES (est): 1.5MM **Privately Held**
WEB: www.tampametalworksinc.com
SIC: 3444 Sheet metalwork

(G-17337)
TAMPA PRINTING COMPANY
4907 N Florida Ave (33603-2119)
PHONE..................................813 612-7746
F Michael Bittman, *President*
Barbara Tomlinson, *Admin Sec*
EMP: 27 **EST:** 1911
SALES (est): 1.9MM **Privately Held**
WEB: www.813tampaprinting.com
SIC: 2752 2791 2759 Commercial printing, offset; typesetting; commercial printing

(G-17338)
TAMPA SHEET METAL COMPANY
1402 W Kennedy Blvd (33606-1847)
PHONE..................................813 251-1845
John L Jiretz, *President*
Carolyn Murphy, *Mktg Dir*
EMP: 31 **EST:** 1920
SQ FT: 24,000
SALES (est): 3.4MM **Privately Held**
WEB: tampasheetmeta.wpengine.com
SIC: 3444 Sheet metalwork

(G-17339)
TAMPA SHIP LLC
1130 Mcclosky Blvd (33605-6722)
P.O. Box 310, Galliano LA (70354-0310)
PHONE..................................813 248-9310
Brian Leblanc, *Production*
Patrick O'Donnell, *Purch Mgr*
Costel Anton, *Purchasing*
Mark Layman, *Purchasing*
Gary J Chouest, *Mng Member*
▲ **EMP:** 327 **EST:** 2008
SQ FT: 15,000
SALES (est): 49.1MM **Privately Held**
WEB: www.tampabayship.com
SIC: 3731 Shipbuilding & repairing

(G-17340)
TAMPA STEEL ERECTING COMPANY
5127 Bloomingdale Ave (33619-9662)
PHONE..................................813 677-7184
Robert J Clark Jr, *President*
Donna Carter, *Corp Secy*
John M Clark, *Vice Pres*
Ronald Teope, *Controller*
EMP: 74 **EST:** 1945
SQ FT: 180,000
SALES (est): 12.9MM **Privately Held**
WEB: www.tampasteelerecting.com
SIC: 3441 Fabricated structural metal

(G-17341)
TARIN SERVICES LLC
5404 24th Ave S (33619-5369)
PHONE..................................803 526-9643
Armando Tarin, *Principal*
EMP: 6 **EST:** 2010
SALES (est): 488.1K **Privately Held**
SIC: 7692 Automotive welding

(G-17342)
TAW PAYROLL INC
440 S 78th St (33619-4223)
PHONE..................................813 621-5661
J A Turner Sr, *Principal*
EMP: 20 **EST:** 2010
SALES (est): 624.9K **Privately Held**
SIC: 7694 Electric motor repair

(G-17343)
TAYLOR COMMUNICATIONS INC
5131 Tampa West Blvd (33634-2408)
PHONE..................................813 886-5511
Brian Freund, *Production*
Gary Reeves, *Manager*
Brenda Lynch, *Manager*
Sara Mason, *Manager*
Traci Jurek, *Admin Sec*
EMP: 46
SALES (corp-wide): 3.7B **Privately Held**
WEB: www.taylor.com
SIC: 2761 2672 Manifold business forms; coated & laminated paper
HQ: Taylor Communications, Inc.
1725 Roe Crest Dr
North Mankato MN 56003
866 541-0937

(G-17344)
TECHNOLGY TRAINING ASSOCIATES
Also Called: Club Information Systems
1412 Tech Blvd (33619-7865)
PHONE..................................813 249-0303
Mike Higgins, *President*
Thomas Howard, *Exec VP*
Janet Taylor, *Technology*
Jodda Perry, *IT/INT Sup*
Jan Taylor, *Training Dir*
EMP: 24 **EST:** 1997
SALES (est): 2.8MM **Privately Held**
WEB: www.tta.club
SIC: 7372 Business oriented computer software

(G-17345)
TECO DIVERSIFIED INC (DH)
702 N Franklin St (33602-4429)
P.O. Box 111 (33601-0111)
PHONE..................................813 228-4111
Steve Winistorfer, *President*
Gordan L Gillette, *CFO*
Isabel Mato, *Finance*
Melody Goedert, *Human Res Mgr*
Victoria Bernal, *Manager*
▼ **EMP:** 4 **EST:** 1981
SALES (est): 344.3MM
SALES (corp-wide): 4.5B **Privately Held**
SIC: 1221 Bituminous coal & lignite-surface mining
HQ: Teco Energy, Inc.
702 N Franklin St
Tampa FL 33602
813 228-1111

(G-17346)
TELEPHONY PARTNERS LLC
Also Called: Acuity Technologies
5215 W Laurel St Ste 210 (33607-1728)
PHONE..................................813 769-4690
Josh Anderson, *CEO*
Ronna Terzado, *Partner*
Kris Mathey, *Vice Pres*
Kristopher Mathey, *Vice Pres*
Jack Plating, *Vice Pres*
EMP: 31 **EST:** 2002
SALES (est): 3.5MM **Privately Held**
WEB: www.acuitytech.com
SIC: 7372 7389 Business oriented computer software; telephone services

(G-17347)
TELEXPRESS LA MUSICA INC
6310 N Armenia Ave Ste A (33604-5777)
PHONE..................................813 879-1914
Lillian Hernandez, *Principal*
EMP: 9 **EST:** 2007
SALES (est): 510.9K **Privately Held**
SIC: 2741 Miscellaneous publishing

(G-17348)
TEN STAR SUPPLY CO INC
Also Called: Ten Star Promotions
7902 Hopi Pl (33634-2418)
PHONE..................................813 254-6921
Donna Killoren, *CEO*
Jack Killoren, *President*
EMP: 8 **EST:** 1956
SQ FT: 3,500
SALES (est): 970.2K **Privately Held**
WEB: www.tenstarsupply.com
SIC: 2759 Screen printing

(G-17349)
TETRA PROCESS TECHNOLOGY
5415 W Sligh Ave Ste 102 (33634-4488)
PHONE..................................813 886-9331
▼ **EMP:** 8
SALES (est): 523.7K **Privately Held**
SIC: 3589 Mfg Service Industry Machinery

(G-17350)
TEXTRON AVIATION INC
Also Called: Hawker Beechcraft Services
2450 N West Shore Blvd # 2 (33607-5741)
PHONE..................................813 878-4500
Joe Defrancisdis, *Manager*
Sebastian Cerrada, *Technician*
Ramsis Nixon, *Technician*
EMP: 30
SALES (corp-wide): 12.3MM **Publicly Held**
WEB: www.txtav.com
SIC: 3721 Aircraft; non-motorized & lighter-than-air aircraft
HQ: Textron Aviation Inc.
1 Cessna Blvd
Wichita KS 67215
316 517-6000

(G-17351)
THERMAL MATRIX INTL LLC
101 E Kennedy Blvd # 322 (33602-5179)
PHONE..................................813 222-3274
Richard Salem, *CEO*
Robert McDaniel, *General Mgr*
Chris Jadick, *Vice Pres*
EMP: 12 **EST:** 2008
SALES (est): 412.7K **Privately Held**
WEB: www.thermalmatrix.com
SIC: 3827 Optical instruments & lenses

(G-17352)
TIGER CUSTOM CABINETS INC
6032 Crestridge Rd (33634-4922)
PHONE..................................813 748-7286
Jose Diaz-Rodriguez, *Principal*
EMP: 7 **EST:** 2011
SALES (est): 127.5K **Privately Held**
SIC: 2434 Wood kitchen cabinets

(G-17353)
TIMELESS TREASURES DOLL CLUB
12020 Steppingstone Blvd (33635-6252)
PHONE..................................813 854-6208
Judy Smith, *President*
Kathleen Short, *Treasurer*
EMP: 30 **EST:** 2014

SALES (est): 835.6K **Privately Held**
SIC: 3942 Miniature dolls, collectors'

(G-17354)
TIMES HOLDING CO
1000 N Ashley Dr Ste 700 (33602-3700)
PHONE.................................813 226-3300
EMP: 283
SALES (corp-wide): 14.9MM **Privately Held**
WEB: www.poynter.org
SIC: 2711 Newspapers, publishing & printing
HQ: Times Holding Co.
　　490 1st Ave S
　　Saint Petersburg FL 33701
　　727 893-8111

(G-17355)
TITAN DEALER SERVICES LLC
2911 W Bay Court Ave (33611-1601)
PHONE.................................813 839-7406
Michael Martin, *Principal*
EMP: 7 EST: 2016
SALES (est): 87.1K **Privately Held**
SIC: 3441 Fabricated structural metal

(G-17356)
TL FAHRINGER CO INC
Also Called: T L Fahringer
10103 Cedar Run (33619-8003)
P.O. Box 1412, Brandon (33509-1412)
PHONE.................................813 681-2373
Elizabeth Fahringer, *CEO*
Jennifer Fahringer, *Vice Pres*
John Zaso, *Opers Mgr*
EMP: 8 EST: 1977
SQ FT: 8,400
SALES (est): 1.2MM **Privately Held**
WEB: www.fahringer.com
SIC: 3728 3549 3548 3496 Aircraft parts
　& equipment; metalworking machinery;
　welding apparatus; miscellaneous fabricated wire products

(G-17357)
TL SHEET METAL INC
4203 N Lauber Way Ste 8 (33614)
P.O. Box 8838 (33674-8838)
PHONE.................................813 871-3780
Tom Williams, *President*
Mary Williams, *Vice Pres*
EMP: 6 EST: 1988
SQ FT: 6,500
SALES (est): 871.3K **Privately Held**
SIC: 3441 Fabricated structural metal

(G-17358)
TLD LLC
14512 N Nebraska Ave (33613-1429)
PHONE.................................813 927-7554
Terri M Casteel, *Principal*
EMP: 6 EST: 2015
SALES (est): 328.4K **Privately Held**
SIC: 3321 Gray iron castings

(G-17359)
TMG MANUFACTURING CORP
5517 W Sligh Ave Ste 100 (33634-4507)
PHONE.................................813 464-2299
Joseph Bloomfield, *President*
Patricia Mansour, *CFO*
EMP: 14 EST: 2003
SALES (est): 3.3MM **Privately Held**
WEB: www.tmgmfg.com
SIC: 3532 Concentration machinery (metallurgical or mining)

(G-17360)
TONERTYPE INC
5100 W Cypress St (33607-1702)
PHONE.................................813 915-1300
David T Shaver, *President*
Clyde C Shaver, *Vice Pres*
Jim Manwell, *Manager*
Carolyn Shaver, *Manager*
Paul Tiller, *Technician*
▼ EMP: 28 EST: 1995
SQ FT: 11,500
SALES (est): 3.4MM **Privately Held**
WEB: www.tonertypeprint.com
SIC: 3861 2759 Printing equipment, photographic; commercial printing

(G-17361)
TOPGOLF INTERNATIONAL INC
10690 Palm River Rd (33619-4571)
PHONE.................................813 298-1811
Mj Owen, *Opers Staff*
Juliana St Thomas, *Opers Staff*
Sergio Tibavisky, *Opers Staff*
Celina Romera, *Marketing Staff*
David Shrimpton, *Office Mgr*
EMP: 7
SALES (corp-wide): 3.1B **Publicly Held**
WEB: www.topgolf.com
SIC: 3949 Driving ranges, golf, electronic
HQ: Topgolf International, Inc.
　　8750 N Cntl Expy Ste 1200
　　Dallas TX 75231
　　214 377-0663

(G-17362)
TOTAL SPCALTY PUBLICATIONS LLC (PA)
Also Called: Corporate Sports & Entrmt
1715 N West Shore Blvd # 266
(33607-3931)
PHONE.................................813 405-2610
Shawn Ferris, *Sales Staff*
Derrick Phillips, *Sales Staff*
Rick Castillo, *Advt Staff*
Eric Kenny, *Advt Staff*
Isabella Rodriguez, *Advt Staff*
EMP: 6 EST: 2009
SALES (est): 528.1K **Privately Held**
WEB: www.tspnational.com
SIC: 2741 Miscellaneous publishing

(G-17363)
TOTALPRINT USA
5100 W Cypress St (33607-1702)
PHONE.................................855 915-1300
EMP: 7 EST: 2017
SALES (est): 364K **Privately Held**
WEB: www.totalprintusa.com
SIC: 2752 5044 5112 3577 Commercial
　printing, lithographic; office equipment;
　laserjet supplies; printers, computer

(G-17364)
TRANE US INC
902 N Himes Ave (33609-1330)
P.O. Box 18547 (33679-8547)
PHONE.................................813 877-8251
Don Smeller, *Project Mgr*
Seve Hewitt, *Sales Staff*
Douglas Cone, *Branch Mgr*
Tim Barnes, *Manager*
Jim Shaw, *Manager*
EMP: 91 **Privately Held**
WEB: www.trane.com
SIC: 3585 Refrigeration & heating equipment
HQ: Trane U.S. Inc.
　　800 Beaty St Ste E
　　Davidson NC 28036
　　704 655-4000

(G-17365)
TRANE US INC
4720 E Adamo Dr (33605-5916)
P.O. Box 18547 (33679-8547)
PHONE.................................813 877-8253
Patrick Lavoy, *Branch Mgr*
EMP: 15 **Privately Held**
WEB: www.trane.com
SIC: 3585 Refrigeration & heating equipment
HQ: Trane U.S. Inc.
　　800 Beaty St Ste E
　　Davidson NC 28036
　　704 655-4000

(G-17366)
TRANSPRTATION CTRL SYSTEMS INC
1030 S 86th St (33619-4946)
PHONE.................................813 630-2800
Steve Gillis, *President*
John T Gillis, *President*
Scott Gillis, *Vice Pres*
Steven Gillis, *Vice Pres*
Ulysses Belmont, *VP Opers*
▼ EMP: 32 EST: 1976
SALES (est): 13.1MM **Privately Held**
WEB: www.tcstraffic.com
SIC: 3669 Traffic signals, electric

(G-17367)
TREPKO INC
4893 W Waters Ave Ste C-F (33634-1314)
PHONE.................................813 443-0794
Jesper Hanson, *President*
Jesus Perez, *Sales Staff*
EMP: 15 EST: 2014
SALES (est): 2.3MM
SALES (corp-wide): 47.2MM **Privately Held**
WEB: www.trepko.com
SIC: 3565 Packaging machinery
HQ: Trepko A/S
　　Energivej 30
　　Ballerup 2750
　　439 922-44

(G-17368)
TRI INC
107 S Willow Ave (33606-1945)
PHONE.................................813 267-1201
Brian Marshall, *President*
EMP: 10 EST: 2007
SALES (est): 630.4K **Privately Held**
SIC: 3299 Moldings, architectural: plaster of paris

(G-17369)
TRIAL EXHIBITS INC (PA)
1177 W Cass St (33606-1308)
PHONE.................................813 258-6153
Jack Stein, *President*
Benjamin B Broome, *Regional Mgr*
Benjamin Broome, *Regional Mgr*
Kathleen Stein, *Vice Pres*
Jeremiah Hodges, *CFO*
EMP: 8 EST: 1989
SALES (est): 2.7MM **Privately Held**
WEB: www.trialexhibitsinc.com
SIC: 3999 7336 Preparation of slides &
　exhibits; commercial art & graphic design

(G-17370)
TRIPLE J MARKETING LLC
301 W Platt St (33606-2292)
PHONE.................................813 247-6999
EMP: 21
SQ FT: 10,000
SALES (est): 1.2MM **Privately Held**
SIC: 3695 Mfg Magnetic/Optical Recording Media

(G-17371)
TROPICAL ENTERPRISES INTL INC (PA)
Also Called: Tmarketing Products
8625 Florida Mining Blvd (33634-1261)
PHONE.................................813 837-9800
Kimberly Canavian, *President*
Sarah Cross, *Principal*
Melissa Dweyer, *Principal*
Maycee Mullarkey, *Principal*
Mark Oki, *Principal*
EMP: 21 EST: 2000
SALES (est): 4.6MM **Privately Held**
WEB: www.tropicallabs.com
SIC: 2844 Face creams or lotions

(G-17372)
TRUE GRIT ABRASIVES INC
7015 E 14th Ave (33619-2921)
PHONE.................................813 247-5219
Arthur Thorn, *President*
Richard Toe, *President*
Geraldine Mann, *Vice Pres*
Omid Zee, *Executive*
▼ EMP: 17 EST: 1979
SQ FT: 10,000
SALES (est): 1.5MM **Privately Held**
WEB: www.truegritabrasives.com
SIC: 3291 5085 Abrasive products; abrasives

(G-17373)
TRUECARE24 INC
8270 Woodland Center Blvd (33614-2401)
PHONE.................................240 434-0963
Bimohit Bawa, *CEO*
Leonid Popov, *President*
Kevin Fitzgerald, *Opers Mgr*
Philip Trageser, *Accounts Mgr*
Ivan Barkar, *Manager*
EMP: 33 EST: 2015

SALES (est): 2.9MM **Privately Held**
WEB: www.truecare24.com
SIC: 7372 7371 Application computer software; custom computer programming services

(G-17374)
TRUESOUTH MARINE CORP
4810 Culbreath Isles Rd (33629-4827)
PHONE.................................813 286-0716
William McCoy, *President*
EMP: 5 EST: 2014
SALES (est): 305.6K **Privately Held**
SIC: 3732 Yachts, building & repairing

(G-17375)
TRUVOICE TELECOM INC
3102 Cherry Palm Dr # 145 (33619-8316)
PHONE.................................888 448-5556
Stephen Jones, *CEO*
Alan Hickey, *Director*
EMP: 5 EST: 2016
SALES (est): 2.2MM **Privately Held**
WEB: www.truvoicetelecom.com
SIC: 3661 Headsets, telephone

(G-17376)
TRYANA LLC
Also Called: Metals Supermarket
4901 W Rio Vista Ave A (33634-5356)
PHONE.................................813 467-9916
Brian Thompson, *Mng Member*
EMP: 5 EST: 2014
SALES (est): 612K **Privately Held**
WEB: www.metalsupermarkets.com
SIC: 3441 Fabricated structural metal

(G-17377)
TSN MANUFACTURING
4011 E 21st Ave (33605-2307)
PHONE.................................813 740-1876
Tim Ngo, *President*
EMP: 8 EST: 2010
SALES (est): 171.4K **Privately Held**
WEB: www.tsnmanufacturing.com
SIC: 3999 Manufacturing industries

(G-17378)
TTI HOLDINGS INC (PA)
2710 E 5th Ave (33605-5522)
PHONE.................................813 623-2675
David D Hale, *CEO*
Brian S Albert, *CEO*
Calvin H Reed, *President*
Dale Ison, *COO*
Jason Bahamonde, *Vice Pres*
◆ EMP: 2 EST: 1994
SQ FT: 100,000
SALES (est): 56.1MM **Privately Held**
SIC: 3443 3446 3441 Tanks, standard or
　custom fabricated: metal plate; stairs,
　staircases, stair treads: prefabricated
　metal; fabricated structural metal

(G-17379)
TWO PAPER CHASERS LLC
3214 W San Miguel St (33629-5949)
PHONE.................................813 251-5090
Paul A Carlisle, *Principal*
EMP: 9 EST: 2007
SALES (est): 125.4K **Privately Held**
SIC: 2653 Corrugated & solid fiber boxes

(G-17380)
TYS VARIETY CO
8330 N Florida Ave (33604-3006)
P.O. Box 3717, Brandon (33509-3717)
PHONE.................................813 643-1515
Anthony McMurray, *Owner*
EMP: 5 EST: 2011
SALES (est): 331.5K **Privately Held**
WEB: www.tysvariety.com
SIC: 2395 Embroidery & art needlework

(G-17381)
U B CORP
9829 Wilsky Blvd (33615-1399)
PHONE.................................813 884-1463
Cynthia Fairbanks, *President*
Robert J Upcavage, *President*
Lawrence J Bauer Jr, *CFO*
David Gluck, *Treasurer*
Cynthia M Fairbanks, *Sales Executive*
EMP: 9 EST: 1968
SQ FT: 20,000

SALES (est): 2MM **Privately Held**
WEB: www.ubcorp.com
SIC: 3663 Microwave communication
equipment

(G-17382)
UDC USA INC (PA)
Also Called: Ultra Defense
100 S Ashley Dr Ste 1620 (33602-5392)
PHONE...................................813 281-0200
Matthew Herring, *CEO*
Brian Roush, *Opers Staff*
Paul Sealy, *Production*
Heather Chase, *Office Mgr*
Meghan Fonte, *Program Mgr*
◆ EMP: 23 EST: 2008
SALES (est): 4.6MM **Privately Held**
WEB: www.udcusa.com
SIC: 3728 8711 7373 Aircraft parts &
equipment; aircraft assemblies, sub-
assemblies & parts; engineering services;
systems integration services

(G-17383)
UFP TAMPA LLC
Also Called: Universal Forest Products
1003 E 131st Ave (33612-4436)
PHONE...................................813 971-3030
Justin Elwell, *Vice Pres*
EMP: 36 EST: 2017
SALES (est): 9.1MM
SALES (corp-wide): 8.6B **Publicly Held**
SIC: 2491 Millwork, treated wood
PA: Ufp Industries, Inc.
2801 E Beltline Ave Ne
Grand Rapids MI 49525
616 364-6161

(G-17384)
**ULTRA-PURE BOTTLED WATER
INC**
5202 S Lois Ave (33611-3431)
PHONE...................................813 835-7873
Lawrence Cacciatore, *President*
Rita Chapman, *Prdtn Mgr*
Larry Cacciatore, *CFO*
Brandy Wilson, *Office Mgr*
Domenick V Traina, *Admin Sec*
◆ EMP: 15 EST: 1998
SQ FT: 18,500
SALES (est): 4.5MM **Privately Held**
WEB: www.nameyourbottle.com
SIC: 2086 5149 5499 5963 Water, pas-
teurized: packaged in cans, bottles, etc.;
water, distilled; water: distilled mineral or
spring; bottled water delivery

(G-17385)
ULTRASONICS AND MAGNETICS
Also Called: Q Sea
5275 Causeway Blvd Ste 2 (33619-6134)
PHONE...................................813 740-1800
Frank Aguilar, *Manager*
EMP: 21 **Privately Held**
SIC: 1389 Testing, measuring, surveying &
analysis services
PA: Ultrasonics And Magnetics Corp
405 Lake Village Blvd
Slidell LA 70461

(G-17386)
ULTROID TECHNOLOGIES INC
3140 W Kennedy Blvd (33609-3075)
PHONE...................................877 858-0555
Michael Knox, *CEO*
Wycliffe McIntosh, *CEO*
EMP: 7 EST: 2005
SALES (est): 824.2K **Privately Held**
SIC: 3841 Surgical & medical instruments

(G-17387)
UNCLE JOHNS PRIDE LLC
Also Called: Crofton & Sons
10250 Woodberry Rd (33619-8008)
PHONE...................................813 685-7745
Denny Simmers, *CFO*
Ben Newlon, *Controller*
Deborah Gonzalez, *Human Res Mgr*
Angela Lewis, *Manager*
Mark Beswick,
EMP: 72 EST: 2015
SQ FT: 45,000
SALES (est): 14.4MM **Privately Held**
WEB: www.unclejohnspride.com
SIC: 2013 Smoked meats from purchased
meat

PA: Blue Planet Holdings Llc
1738 Clarendon Pl
Lakeland FL 33803
863 559-1236

(G-17388)
**UNIFORM NAMETAPE COMPANY
INC**
5701 S Dale Mabry Hwy (33611-4229)
PHONE...................................813 839-6737
John P Colman, *President*
Travis Bell, *General Mgr*
Linda L Colman, *Corp Secy*
EMP: 9 EST: 1973
SQ FT: 3,000
SALES (est): 923.4K **Privately Held**
WEB: www.uniformnametape.com
SIC: 2395 Embroidery products, except
schiffli machine

(G-17389)
UNIPRESS CORPORATION
3501 Queen Palm Dr (33619-1392)
PHONE...................................813 623-3731
Peter Hamlin, *President*
Ronnie Lechowicz, *Production*
Gary C Johnson, *Treasurer*
Jim Groshans, *Regl Sales Mgr*
Robb Johnson, *Manager*
▼ EMP: 80 EST: 1982
SQ FT: 75,000
SALES (est): 26.4MM **Privately Held**
WEB: www.unipresscorp.com
SIC: 3582 Pressing machines, commercial
laundry & drycleaning; drycleaning equip-
ment & machinery, commercial

(G-17390)
**UNITED ARMOUR PRODUCTS
LLC**
1601 N 39th St (33605-5852)
PHONE...................................813 767-9624
David Barkett, *Mng Member*
George Chaconas,
EMP: 7 EST: 2012
SQ FT: 50,000
SALES (est): 550K **Privately Held**
WEB: www.unitedarmour.com
SIC: 2992 Lubricating oils; brake fluid (hy-
draulic): made from purchased materials

(G-17391)
UNITED ELECTRIC MOTOR INC
Also Called: ARC United Electric Motor
905 E Ida St (33603-4317)
P.O. Box 669, Seffner (33583-0669)
PHONE...................................813 238-7872
Robert Burk, *CEO*
EMP: 8 EST: 1974
SQ FT: 3,000
SALES (est): 837.5K **Privately Held**
WEB: www.unitedelectricmotortampafl.com
SIC: 7694 5063 5999 Electric motor re-
pair; motors, electric; motors, electric

(G-17392)
UNITED GRANITE INC
3906 S 51st St (33619-6802)
PHONE...................................813 391-4323
Johana Perez Marquez, *President*
Jesus Perez Marquez, *Vice Pres*
EMP: 16 EST: 2013
SALES (est): 2.4MM **Privately Held**
WEB: www.unitedgraniteus.com
SIC: 3441 Fabricated structural metal

(G-17393)
**UNIVERSAL HM HLTH INDUS
SUPS I**
7320 E Fletcher Ave (33637-0916)
P.O. Box 290314 (33687-0314)
PHONE...................................813 493-7904
Anthony R Smith, *President*
EMP: 5 EST: 1988
SQ FT: 30,000
SALES (est): 1.3MM **Privately Held**
WEB: www.universalhomehealth.com
SIC: 3842 2389 3841 5047 Personal
safety equipment; hospital gowns; surgi-
cal & medical instruments; medical equip-
ment & supplies

(G-17394)
**UNIVERSAL SCREEN GRAPHICS
INC**
4897 W Waters Ave Ste H (33634-1318)
PHONE...................................813 623-5335
Tim Packrall, *President*
Kim Johnson, *Vice Pres*
Dianne Packrall, *Office Mgr*
EMP: 23 EST: 1991
SQ FT: 8,500
SALES (est): 5.3MM **Privately Held**
WEB: www.usgfla.com
SIC: 2759 2791 2396 Screen printing;
typesetting; automotive & apparel trim-
mings

(G-17395)
UR CABINETS
4042 W Kennedy Blvd (33609-2750)
PHONE...................................813 434-6454
EMP: 7 EST: 2018
SALES (est): 236.2K **Privately Held**
WEB: www.urcabinets.com
SIC: 2434 Wood kitchen cabinets

(G-17396)
URBAN METALS LLC
Also Called: TAMPA STEEL & SUPPLY
1301 N 26th St (33605-5534)
PHONE...................................813 241-2801
Troy A Underwood,
EMP: 19 EST: 2018
SALES (est): 2.4MM **Privately Held**
WEB: www.tampasteel.com
SIC: 3312 5051 Bars & bar shapes, steel,
hot-rolled; metals service centers & of-
fices

(G-17397)
US CHINA MINING GROUP INC
15310 Amberly Dr Ste 250 (33647-1642)
PHONE...................................813 514-2873
Guoqing Yue, *Ch of Bd*
Hongwen LI, *President*
Xinyu Peng, *CFO*
EMP: 92 EST: 2004
SALES (est): 3.5MM **Privately Held**
WEB: www.uschinamining.com
SIC: 1241 Coal mining exploration & test
boring

(G-17398)
US ORTHOTICS INC
8605 Palm River Rd (33619-4317)
PHONE...................................813 621-7797
Anthony E Velazquez, *President*
EMP: 15 EST: 1979
SQ FT: 10,000
SALES (est): 2MM **Privately Held**
WEB: www.usorthotics.com
SIC: 3842 Orthopedic appliances

(G-17399)
USA RARE EARTH LLC (PA)
1001 Water St Ste 600 (33602-5464)
PHONE...................................813 867-6155
Thayer Smith, *Mng Member*
Mordechai Gutnick,
Douglas Newby,
EMP: 14 EST: 2019
SALES (est): 4.3MM **Privately Held**
WEB: www.usare.com
SIC: 1479 1099 3499 1081 Lithium min-
eral mining; rare-earth ores mining; mag-
nets, permanent: metallic; metal mining
services

(G-17400)
UTOPIC SOFTWARE LLC (PA)
1213 E 6th Ave (33605-4905)
P.O. Box 55612, Saint Petersburg (33732-
5612)
PHONE...................................813 444-2231
Scott Davis, *Vice Pres*
Adrienne Deveaux, *Manager*
Robert Whirley,
EMP: 25 EST: 2010
SALES (est): 3.1MM **Privately Held**
WEB: www.utopicsoftware.com
SIC: 7372 Prepackaged software

(G-17401)
UVISORS
4919 W Bartlett Dr (33603-1606)
PHONE...................................813 716-1113

Todd Jackson, *Principal*
EMP: 8 EST: 2012
SALES (est): 112.3K **Privately Held**
SIC: 2657 Paperboard backs for blister or
skin packages

(G-17402)
VALCO GROUP INC
Also Called: Roll A Way
2203 N Lois Ave Ste 937 (33607-2318)
PHONE...................................813 870-0482
John Coffill, *President*
John Coffioll, *Chairman*
Lynn Conlen, *Admin Sec*
EMP: 150 EST: 1997
SQ FT: 68,000
SALES (est): 13.8MM **Privately Held**
SIC: 3442 Shutters, door or window: metal;
sash, door or window: metal

(G-17403)
VAN GOGH SIGNS & DISPLAYS
5020 N Florida Ave (33603-2122)
PHONE...................................813 849-7446
John Miller, *Owner*
EMP: 7 EST: 2005
SALES (est): 91.3K **Privately Held**
SIC: 3993 Signs & advertising specialties

(G-17404)
VECOM USA LLC
4803 George Rd Ste 300 (33634-6234)
PHONE...................................813 901-5300
J Vanstarrenburg,
Robert H Baaij,
Stephen Eifert,
EMP: 6 EST: 2004
SQ FT: 2,250
SALES (est): 973.9K **Privately Held**
WEB: www.irwincar.com
SIC: 3669 Intercommunication systems,
electric

(G-17405)
**VECTOR ENGINEERING & MFG
CORP**
16320 Burniston Dr (33647-2763)
PHONE...................................708 474-3900
Daryl P Sullivan, *President*
▲ EMP: 18 EST: 1964
SALES (est): 427K **Privately Held**
WEB: www.vectorenger.com
SIC: 3599 3536 Machine shop, jobbing &
repair; hoists, cranes & monorails

(G-17406)
**VECTOR-SOLUTIONSCOM INC
(PA)**
Also Called: Vector Solutions
4890 W Kennedy Blvd # 30 (33609-1851)
PHONE...................................813 207-0012
Marc Scheipe, *CEO*
Denise Segalla, *CEO*
Kelly Cook, *Partner*
Kris Russell, *Editor*
John-Michael Larry, *Regional Mgr*
EMP: 38 EST: 2016
SALES (est): 86.7MM **Privately Held**
WEB: www.vectorsolutions.com
SIC: 7372 Educational computer software

(G-17407)
VERIFIED LABEL & PRINT INC
7905 Hopi Pl (33634-2418)
PHONE...................................813 290-7721
Raymond Sikorski, *President*
Raymond H Sikorski, *President*
Pamela Haley, *Project Mgr*
EMP: 18 EST: 1995
SQ FT: 4,500
SALES (est): 3.9MM **Privately Held**
WEB: www.verifiedlabel.com
SIC: 2752 5199 Commercial printing, off-
set; advertising specialties

(G-17408)
VERSATILE PACKAGERS LLC
933 Chad Ln Ste C (33619-4331)
PHONE...................................813 664-1171
Larry Gordon, *Opers Staff*
Scott Krajcir, *QC Mgr*
Debbie Wood, *Manager*
Misty Wood, *Manager*
Julian Bossong,
EMP: 14 EST: 2009

SALES (est): 5.7MM **Privately Held**
WEB: www.versatilepackagers.com
SIC: **2679** Wrappers, paper (unprinted): made from purchased material

(G-17409)
VERSEA DIAGNOSTICS LLC ✪
1000 N Florida Ave (33602-3808)
PHONE................................800 397-0670
Steve Porada,
EMP: 28 EST: 2022
SALES (est): 1.6MM **Privately Held**
SIC: **3821** Clinical laboratory instruments, except medical & dental

(G-17410)
VERSEA HOLDINGS INC
1000 N Florida Ave (33602-3808)
PHONE................................800 397-0670
Sean Fetcho, *CEO*
Stephen Porada, *COO*
Colby Fox, *Exec VP*
Joe Magnemi, *CFO*
Chris Duncan, *Ch Credit Ofcr*
EMP: 22 EST: 2019
SALES (est): 2.5MM **Privately Held**
WEB: www.versea.com
SIC: **2834** Pharmaceutical preparations

(G-17411)
VERTIMAX LLC
8108 Benjamin Rd Ste 201 (33634-2302)
PHONE................................800 699-5867
Al Marez, *COO*
Michael Wehrell, *Mng Member*
Jason Hyber, *Manager*
Maureen O'Rourke,
◆ EMP: 9 EST: 1988
SQ FT: 2,500
SALES (est): 5.3MM **Privately Held**
WEB: www.vertimax.com
SIC: **3949** 8331 Exercise equipment; skill training center

(G-17412)
VGCM LLC
Also Called: Tampa Yard
3510 Pendola Point Rd (33619-9525)
PHONE................................813 247-7625
Myron Cantin, *Branch Mgr*
Burton Hershel, *Manager*
EMP: 10 **Publicly Held**
SIC: **1411** Dimension stone
HQ: Vgcm, Llc
　　1200 Urban Center Dr
　　Vestavia AL 35242

(G-17413)
VGCM LLC
Also Called: Port Canaveral Yard
2001 Maritime Blvd (33605-6760)
PHONE................................813 620-4889
Janette Hintze, *Vice Pres*
James Pease, *Manager*
EMP: 50 **Publicly Held**
SIC: **1411** Dimension stone
HQ: Vgcm, Llc
　　1200 Urban Center Dr
　　Vestavia AL 35242

(G-17414)
VIASAT INC
Also Called: Field Office
4211 W Boy Scout Blvd # 550 (33607-5928)
PHONE................................813 880-5000
Fred Rhyne, *Principal*
Joel Babbitt, *Vice Pres*
John Ross, *Engineer*
Thomas Garner, *Software Engr*
Courtney Tilque, *Administration*
EMP: 21
SALES (corp-wide): 2.7B **Publicly Held**
WEB: www.viasat.com
SIC: **3663** Radio & TV communications equipment
PA: Viasat, Inc.
　　6155 El Camino Real
　　Carlsbad CA 92009
　　844 702-3199

(G-17415)
VICKERY AND COMPANY
7911 Professional Pl (33637-6747)
P.O. Box 48229 (33646-0119)
PHONE................................813 987-2100

Dennis W Barber, *President*
Lindsay Barber, *Vice Pres*
Holly Barber, *Sales Staff*
EMP: 10 EST: 1944
SQ FT: 3,000
SALES (est): 1.6MM **Privately Held**
WEB: www.vickerycompany.com
SIC: **3561** 5074 Pumps, domestic: water or sump; heating equipment (hydronic)

(G-17416)
VIDEO DISPLAY CORPORATION
13948 Lynmar Blvd (33626-3123)
PHONE................................813 854-2259
Ronald D Ordway, *Branch Mgr*
EMP: 21
SALES (corp-wide): 7MM **Publicly Held**
WEB: www.videodisplay.com
SIC: **3679** Liquid crystal displays (LCD)
PA: Video Display Corporation
　　5155 King St
　　Tucker GA 32926
　　800 241-5005

(G-17417)
VIGO IMPORTING COMPANY
Also Called: Can-America
4701 Tony Alessi Sr Ave (33614-5499)
P.O. Box 15584 (33684-5584)
PHONE................................813 884-3491
Anthony Alessi Jr, *President*
Alfred Alessi, *Vice Pres*
Fred Alessi, *Vice Pres*
Emilio Settecasi, *Prdtn Dir*
Dave Regalado, *Plant Mgr*
◆ EMP: 187 EST: 1947
SQ FT: 165,000
SALES (est): 43.1MM **Privately Held**
WEB: www.vigo-alessi.com
SIC: **2099** 2079 5149 5141 Rice, uncooked: packaged with other ingredients; bread crumbs, not made in bakeries; olive oil; specialty food items; groceries, general line

(G-17418)
VULCAN MACHINE INC
Also Called: Vulcan Machine -2020
4201 Byshore Blvd Unit 18 (33611)
PHONE................................813 664-0032
James W Williams, *President*
EMP: 34 EST: 2020
SALES (est): 1.8MM **Privately Held**
SIC: **3599** Machine shop, jobbing & repair

(G-17419)
VULCAN MATERIALS COMPANY
2001 Maritime Blvd (33605-6760)
PHONE................................205 298-3000
Phil Dieulio, *Branch Mgr*
EMP: 17 **Publicly Held**
WEB: www.vulcanmaterials.com
SIC: **3273** Ready-mixed concrete
PA: Vulcan Materials Company
　　1200 Urban Center Dr
　　Vestavia AL 35242

(G-17420)
W & W MANUFACTURING CO
4504 E Hillsborough Ave (33610-5249)
PHONE................................516 942-0011
Jeffrey Weitzman, *President*
Saundrice Lucas, *Administration*
▲ EMP: 16 EST: 1975
SALES (est): 1.9MM **Privately Held**
WEB: www.ww-manufacturing.com
SIC: **3691** 3825 3663 Storage batteries; instruments to measure electricity; radio & TV communications equipment

(G-17421)
W D WILSON INC (PA)
Also Called: Wilson Mscllneous Fabrications
3005 S 54th St (33619-6105)
PHONE................................813 626-6989
William D Wilson, *President*
Jackie Wilson, *Treasurer*
EMP: 5 EST: 1985
SQ FT: 4,800
SALES (est): 1.8MM **Privately Held**
SIC: **3429** 3441 3446 3444 Marine hardware; fabricated structural metal; architectural metalwork; sheet metalwork; fabricated plate work (boiler shop)

(G-17422)
WASHINGTON CL INC
Also Called: Washington Free Weekly
810 N Howard Ave (33606-1027)
PHONE................................813 739-4800
Richard Gilbert, *CEO*
▲ EMP: 32 EST: 2007
SALES (est): 1.4MM **Privately Held**
SIC: **2711** Newspapers: publishing only, not printed on site
HQ: Creative Loafing, Inc.
　　1911 N 13th St Ste W200
　　Tampa FL 33605

(G-17423)
WAVE TECH PLUS CORP
11940 Race Track Rd (33626-3107)
PHONE................................813 855-7007
Dale Barclift, *Branch Mgr*
EMP: 12
SALES (corp-wide): 2.8MM **Privately Held**
WEB: www.datatelsupply.com
SIC: **3661** Telephone & telegraph apparatus
PA: Wave Tech Plus Corp
　　700 Stevens Ave Ste C
　　Oldsmar FL 34677
　　813 854-2134

(G-17424)
WEEKLY PLANET OF SARASOTA INC
Also Called: Creative Loafing Sarasota
810 N Howard Ave (33606-1027)
PHONE................................813 739-4800
Angela Lafon, *Principal*
EMP: 26 EST: 2008
SALES (est): 1MM **Privately Held**
SIC: **2711** Newspapers, publishing & printing
HQ: Creative Loafing, Inc.
　　1911 N 13th St Ste W200
　　Tampa FL 33605

(G-17425)
WEEKLY SCHULTE VALDES
1635 N Tampa St Ste 100 (33602-2629)
PHONE................................813 221-1154
Christopher Schulte, *Principal*
Chris Schulte, *Mng Member*
Lauren Agnone, *Admin Asst*
Nellie Pawlowski, *Legal Staff*
Karla Vaughn, *Legal Staff*
EMP: 19 EST: 2009
SALES (est): 5.2MM **Privately Held**
WEB: www.wsvlegal.com
SIC: **2711** Newspapers

(G-17426)
WERE IN STITCHES
14807 N Florida Ave (33613-1825)
P.O. Box 2137, Lutz (33548-2137)
PHONE................................813 264-4804
Molly Berberich, *President*
Peter Berberich, *Vice Pres*
▼ EMP: 6 EST: 1993
SQ FT: 1,500
SALES (est): 423.1K **Privately Held**
WEB: www.wereinstitches.com
SIC: **2395** Embroidery products, except schiffli machine

(G-17427)
WEST CENTRAL SIGNS INC
Also Called: Sign Star
3502 Queen Palm Dr Ste C (33619-1391)
PHONE................................813 980-6763
Daniel V Powell, *President*
Theresa Powell, *Corp Secy*
Andrew Powell, *Vice Pres*
Robert D Powell, *Vice Pres*
Terri Mitchell, *Manager*
▼ EMP: 45 EST: 1983
SALES (est): 5.9MM **Privately Held**
WEB: www.signstar.net
SIC: **3993** Neon signs

(G-17428)
WESTERN INTL GAS CYLINDERS INC
1502 Orient Rd (33619-3332)
P.O. Box 151006 (33684-1006)
PHONE................................813 635-9321
Brian Griffin, *Principal*

Jerald Vann, *Plant Mgr*
EMP: 7 **Privately Held**
WEB: www.work4western.com
SIC: **1382** Oil & gas exploration services
HQ: Western International Gas & Cylinders, Inc.
　　7173 Highway 159 E
　　Bellville TX 77418
　　979 413-2100

(G-17429)
WF BRICK PAVERS INC
12704 Tar Flower Dr (33626-2340)
PHONE................................813 506-1941
Wender R Fonseca, *President*
EMP: 7 EST: 2012
SALES (est): 470.9K **Privately Held**
WEB: www.wfbrickpavers.com
SIC: **3531** Pavers

(G-17430)
WHITE MOP WRINGER COMPANY
10702 N 46th St (33617-3480)
PHONE................................813 971-2223
Jeff Baker, *VP Mfg*
Thomas R Halluska, *CFO*
R Halluska, *CFO*
Bob Eukovich, *VP Sales*
Bob Schneider, *VP Sales*
EMP: 248 EST: 1986
SQ FT: 130,000
SALES (est): 10.2MM **Privately Held**
SIC: **3589** Commercial cleaning equipment; vacuum cleaners & sweepers, electric: industrial; floor washing & polishing machines, commercial; mop wringers

(G-17431)
WHITECAP PROMOTIONS LLC
2523 Cozumel Dr (33618-1901)
PHONE................................813 960-4918
Brandon Jones,
Jim Denison,
EMP: 6 EST: 2010
SALES (est): 394.2K **Privately Held**
SIC: **2759** Promotional printing

(G-17432)
WILLSONET INC
Also Called: Cyber Security Solutions
2502 N Rocky Point Dr # 820 (33607-1421)
PHONE................................813 336-8175
Horacio Maysonet, *CEO*
Thomas Williams, *CTO*
EMP: 30 EST: 2015
SALES (est): 2.4MM **Privately Held**
SIC: **7372** 7373 7371 7379 Prepackaged software; computer integrated systems design; custom computer programming services; computer related consulting services

(G-17433)
WOOD PRODUCT SERVICES INC
2417 N 70th St (33619-2931)
P.O. Box 18063 (33679-8063)
PHONE................................813 248-2221
Pedro Jimenez, *President*
Maria Jeminz, *Vice Pres*
EMP: 32 EST: 1998
SQ FT: 10,675
SALES (est): 3.2MM **Privately Held**
SIC: **2439** Trusses, wooden roof

(G-17434)
WOODWORKS OF TAMPA BAY LLC
333 N Falkenburg Rd B209 (33619-7892)
PHONE................................813 330-5836
Karen Hall,
EMP: 7 EST: 2016
SALES (est): 81.3K **Privately Held**
WEB: www.woodworksoftampa.com
SIC: **2431** Millwork

(G-17435)
WORKFORCE AUDIO INC
4821 N Grady Ave (33614-6513)
PHONE................................866 360-6416
Mark Engel, *CEO*
EMP: 20 EST: 2018
SQ FT: 4,500

SALES (est): 1.2MM **Privately Held**
SIC: 3679 Electronic components

(G-17436)
WORKWEAR OUTFITTERS LLC
Vf
4408 W Linebaugh Ave (33624-5245)
P.O. Box 22041 (33622-2041)
PHONE......................336 424-6000
Ed Doran, *President*
Guillaume Eprinchard, *Partner*
Irene Kim, *Partner*
George N Derhofer, *Principal*
David Wagner, *Exec VP*
EMP: 187
SALES (corp-wide): 2B **Privately Held**
WEB: www.redkap.com
SIC: 2329 2339 Athletic (warmup, sweat &
jogging) suits: men's & boys'; women's &
misses' athletic clothing & sportswear
HQ: Workwear Outfitters, Llc
545 Marriott Dr Ste 200
Nashville TN 37214
615 565-5000

(G-17437)
WORKWEAR OUTFITTERS LLC
Also Called: Vf
6422 Harney Rd Ste F (33610-9162)
PHONE......................813 969-6481
EMP: 13
SALES (corp-wide): 2B **Privately Held**
WEB: www.redkap.com
SIC: 2326 Work apparel, except uniforms
HQ: Workwear Outfitters, Llc
545 Marriott Dr Ste 200
Nashville TN 37214
615 565-5000

(G-17438)
WORLD POLITICS REVIEW LLC
825 S Orleans Ave (33606-2938)
P.O. Box 10398 (33679-0398)
PHONE......................202 903-8398
Hampton Stephens, *Principal*
Judah Grunstein, *Manager*
EMP: 10 EST: 2016
SALES (est): 345.2K **Privately Held**
WEB: www.worldpoliticsreview.com
SIC: 2721 Periodicals

(G-17439)
WORLDGLASS CORPORATION
5600 Airport Blvd Ste C (33634-5315)
PHONE......................813 609-2453
Dan Daniels, *President*
David Daniels, *Opers Staff*
EMP: 8 EST: 2007
SALES (est): 1.6MM **Privately Held**
SIC: 3231 3751 Products of purchased
glass; bicycles & related parts

(G-17440)
**WORLDWIDE DOOR
COMPONENTS INC (PA)**
Also Called: World Wide Hardware
5017 N Coolidge Ave (33614-6421)
P.O. Box 262049 (33685-2049)
PHONE......................813 870-0003
Jerry Monts De Oca, *President*
Mark Wheeler, *Sales Staff*
◆ EMP: 45 EST: 1985
SQ FT: 26,000
SALES (est): 9.5MM **Privately Held**
WEB: www.4everframe.com
SIC: 3442 Metal doors, sash & trim

(G-17441)
**WORTHINGTON INDUSTRIES
LLC**
17501 Preserve Walk Ln (33647-3465)
PHONE......................813 979-1000
Deborah H Need, *Principal*
EMP: 8 EST: 2015
SALES (est): 149.7K **Privately Held**
WEB: www.worthingtonindustries.com
SIC: 3999 Manufacturing industries

(G-17442)
WOW BUSINESS
400 N Tampa St Ste 1000 (33602-4714)
PHONE......................813 301-2620
EMP: 10 EST: 2017
SALES (est): 982.2K **Privately Held**
WEB: www.wowforbusiness.com
SIC: 2431 Doors, wood

(G-17443)
WURTH WOOD GROUP INC
5102 W Hanna Ave (33634-8020)
PHONE......................800 432-1149
EMP: 10 EST: 2018
SALES (est): 632K **Privately Held**
WEB: www.wurthwoodgroup.com
SIC: 2499 Extension planks, wood

(G-17444)
WWS CONTRACTING LLC ✪
142 W Platt St (33606-2315)
PHONE......................813 868-3100
Tim Miller,
EMP: 30 EST: 2021
SALES (est): 1.1MM **Privately Held**
SIC: 3589 Car washing machinery

(G-17445)
XCELIENCE LLC
5415 W Laurel St (33607-1729)
PHONE......................813 286-0404
Derek G Hennecke, *President*
Sharon L Burgess, *Senior VP*
Theodore S Koontz, *Vice Pres*
Douglas J O'Dowd, *CFO*
EMP: 50
SALES (corp-wide): 346.8MM **Privately
Held**
WEB: www.lonza.com
SIC: 2834 Powders, pharmaceutical; solu-
tions, pharmaceutical
HQ: Xcelience, Llc
4910 Savarese Cir
Tampa FL 33634

(G-17446)
XCELIENCE LLC (HQ)
4910 Savarese Cir (33634-2403)
PHONE......................813 286-0404
Derek G Hennecke, *CEO*
Lindon Fellows, *COO*
Sharon L Burgess, *Senior VP*
Joseph Iacobucci, *Vice Pres*
Paul F Skultety-Phd, *Vice Pres*
EMP: 12 EST: 2006
SQ FT: 50,000
SALES (est): 24.7MM
SALES (corp-wide): 346.8MM **Privately
Held**
WEB: www.lonza.com
SIC: 2834 Chlorination tablets & kits (water
purification)
PA: Lonza Usa Inc.
412 Mount Kemble Ave 200s
Morristown NJ 07960
201 316-9200

(G-17447)
XCELIENCE HOLDINGS LLC
4910 Savarese Cir (33634-2403)
PHONE......................813 286-0404
Derek G Hennecke, *President*
Lindon Fellows, *COO*
Douglas J O'Dowd, *CFO*
Douglas O 'dowd, *CFO*
▲ EMP: 446
SALES (est): 6.3MM
SALES (corp-wide): 346.8MM **Privately
Held**
SIC: 2834 Chlorination tablets & kits (water
purification)
HQ: Capsugel Holdings Us, Inc.
412 Mount Kemble Ave 200s
Morristown NJ 07960

(G-17448)
YOGURTOLOGY
3017 W Gandy Blvd (33611-2825)
PHONE......................813 839-4200
Nikki Manecke, *General Mgr*
EMP: 8 EST: 2013
SALES (est): 243K **Privately Held**
SIC: 2026 Yogurt

(G-17449)
YOGURTOLOGY
12400 N Dale Mabry Hwy B (33618-3493)
PHONE......................813 969-2500
EMP: 7 EST: 2012
SALES (est): 254.1K **Privately Held**
SIC: 2026 Yogurt

(G-17450)
YOGURTOLOGY
7889 Gunn Hwy (33626-1611)
PHONE......................813 926-9090
Dianne Heady, *Branch Mgr*
EMP: 8 EST: 2011
SALES (est): 226.6K **Privately Held**
SIC: 2026 Yogurt

(G-17451)
**YORK INTERNATIONAL
CORPORATION**
8633 Elm Fair Blvd (33610-7363)
PHONE......................813 663-9332
Dennis Murphy, *Manager*
EMP: 12 **Privately Held**
WEB: www.shumakerwilliams.com
SIC: 3585 Refrigeration & heating equip-
ment
HQ: York International Corporation
631 S Richland Ave
York PA 17403
800 481-9738

(G-17452)
YOUR NAME PRINTING
6502 N 54th St (33610-1908)
PHONE......................813 621-2400
Christine M Fitzgibbon, *Owner*
Scott E Poindexter, *Owner*
EMP: 6 EST: 2018
SALES (est): 377.4K **Privately Held**
WEB: www.yournameprinting.com
SIC: 2752 Commercial printing, offset

(G-17453)
**YOUR NAME PRTG ENVLOPE
MFG INC**
6502 N 54th St (33610-1908)
PHONE......................813 621-2408
Christine Fitzgibbon, *President*
Scott Poindexter, *Vice Pres*
EMP: 7 EST: 1997
SQ FT: 8,200
SALES (est): 1.6MM **Privately Held**
WEB: www.yournameprinting.com
SIC: 2621 Stationery, envelope & tablet pa-
pers

(G-17454)
Z & L PARTNERS INC
Also Called: Image360 South Tampa
4920 W Cypress St Ste 100 (33607-3837)
PHONE......................813 639-0066
Zachary R Davis, *President*
Leslie M Davis, *Vice Pres*
Zach Davis, *Info Tech Mgr*
EMP: 5 EST: 2002
SQ FT: 2,000
SALES (est): 497.4K **Privately Held**
SIC: 3993 Signs & advertising specialties

(G-17455)
ZENNERGY LLC
3918 N Highland Ave (33603-4724)
PHONE......................813 382-3460
John Venzon, *CEO*
Stephen Tarte, *Chairman*
Jeff Tarte, *Exec VP*
Jorge Santos, *Opers Staff*
Sheila Tarte, *CFO*
EMP: 8 EST: 2015
SALES (est): 611.5K **Privately Held**
WEB: www.zennergyllc.com
SIC: 3492 3531 Control valves, fluid
power: hydraulic & pneumatic; backhoe
mounted, hydraulically powered attach-
ments

Tarpon Springs
Pinellas County

(G-17456)
**A & B OF TARPON
CORPORATION**
40200 Us Highway 19 N (34689-4836)
PHONE......................727 940-5333
Ibrahim Abde, *Principal*
Don Neher, *COO*
EMP: 8 EST: 2012
SALES (est): 126.9K **Privately Held**
SIC: 3565 Packaging machinery

(G-17457)
ALTA PHARMA LLC
1245 N Florida Ave (34689-2003)
PHONE......................727 942-7645
George Bobotas, *Manager*
EMP: 8 EST: 2010
SALES (est): 232K **Privately Held**
SIC: 2834 Pharmaceutical preparations

(G-17458)
**B&B CUSTOM SHEET METAL
INC**
770 N Grosse Ave Ste B (34689-4001)
PHONE......................727 938-8083
James A Housh, *President*
Matthew B Housh, *Vice Pres*
Rebecca M Housh, *CFO*
EMP: 6 EST: 2004
SALES (est): 524.6K **Privately Held**
WEB: www.bbcustomsheetmetal.com
SIC: 3444 Sheet metalwork

(G-17459)
**BOB LAFERRIERE AIRCRAFT
INC**
2769 Saint Andrews Blvd (34688-6312)
PHONE......................727 709-2704
Robert J Laferriere, *Principal*
EMP: 7 EST: 2010
SALES (est): 70.2K **Privately Held**
SIC: 3721 Aircraft

(G-17460)
**C DYER DEVELOPMENT GROUP
LLC**
1125 Lake St (34689-5512)
PHONE......................727 423-6169
Chasen Dyer, *Principal*
EMP: 9 EST: 2015
SALES (est): 230.9K **Privately Held**
WEB: www.cdyerdevelopmentgroup.com
SIC: 3842 Traction apparatus

(G-17461)
CASCO SERVICES INC
Also Called: Architectural Metal Works
153 E Oakwood St (34689-3645)
PHONE......................727 942-1888
Conrad Shrader, *President*
Heather Seiter, *Admin Sec*
EMP: 15 EST: 1988
SQ FT: 9,000
SALES (est): 834.4K **Privately Held**
SIC: 3446 Architectural metalwork

(G-17462)
**CREATIVE WDWKG CONCEPTS
INC**
905 Rivo Pl (34689-4141)
PHONE......................727 937-4165
William M Shadrick, *President*
Daniel Beltram, *Corp Secy*
Harry Roenick, *Vice Pres*
Mark Pikulski, *Opers Staff*
EMP: 25 EST: 1984
SQ FT: 20,000
SALES (est): 4.1MM **Privately Held**
WEB: www.cwcwood.com
SIC: 2431 2521 Millwork; cabinets, office:
wood

(G-17463)
CRUSTYS BREAD BAKERY
438 Athens St (34689-3161)
PHONE......................727 937-9041
Monica L Canales, *Principal*
EMP: 8 EST: 2002
SQ FT: 3,550
SALES (est): 167.6K **Privately Held**
WEB: crustybreadbakery.myfreesites.net
SIC: 2051 Bread, cake & related products

(G-17464)
DECON USA
15 Central Ct (34689-3209)
PHONE......................440 610-5009
EMP: 7 EST: 2014
SALES (est): 159.8K **Privately Held**
WEB: www.jordahlusa.com
SIC: 3444 Sheet metalwork

(G-17465)
DELICAE GOURMET LLC
1310 E Lake Dr (34688-8110)
PHONE.................................727 942-2502
Barbara Macaluso, *Owner*
Meg Scott, *Sales Staff*
EMP: 7 **EST:** 1997
SQ FT: 4,000
SALES (est): 943.3K **Privately Held**
WEB: www.delicaegourmet.com
SIC: 2099 Food preparations

(G-17466)
DEMELLE BIOPHARMA LLC
1245 N Florida Ave (34689-2003)
PHONE.................................908 240-8939
George Bobotas,
Maria Bobotas,
Demetra Dukas,
Abdel A Fawzy,
Eleni Lelekis,
EMP: 5 **EST:** 2008
SALES (est): 335K **Privately Held**
WEB: www.demellebiopharma.com
SIC: 2834 7389 Pharmaceutical preparations;

(G-17467)
DORADO CUSTOM BOATS LLC
1400 L And R Indus Blvd (34689-6807)
PHONE.................................727 786-3800
Andrea Garcia, *Controller*
EMP: 8 **EST:** 2011
SALES (est): 499.6K **Privately Held**
WEB: www.doradocustomboats.com
SIC: 3732 Boat building & repairing

(G-17468)
DUCKWORTH STEEL BOATS INC
1051 Island Ave (34689-6917)
PHONE.................................727 934-2550
Ernest Duckworth, *President*
Paul J Raymond, *Admin Sec*
EMP: 5 **EST:** 1979
SQ FT: 10,000
SALES (est): 651K **Privately Held**
WEB: duckboats.tripod.com
SIC: 3732 Boat building & repairing

(G-17469)
EAGLE ATHLETIC WEAR INC (PA)
Also Called: Graphics Screen Printing & EMB
720 E Tarpon Ave (34689-4250)
PHONE.................................727 937-6147
Imar Tzekas, *Ch of Bd*
Jim Ismaili, *President*
John Ismaili, *Vice Pres*
EMP: 10 **EST:** 1982
SQ FT: 13,000
SALES (est): 803.3K **Privately Held**
SIC: 2396 2395 5199 Screen printing on fabric articles; embroidery products, except schiffli machine; advertising specialties

(G-17470)
ENG MANUFACTURING INC
773 Wesley Ave (34689-6711)
PHONE.................................727 942-3868
Emanuel Ginnis, *President*
Jeannette Ginnis, *CFO*
Janelle McCarthy, *Natl Sales Mgr*
EMP: 6 **EST:** 2002
SALES (est): 687.8K **Privately Held**
WEB: www.engwelding.com
SIC: 7692 1622 Welding repair; bridge, tunnel & elevated highway

(G-17471)
F O F PLASTICS INC
1614 Tallahassee Dr (34689-2242)
PHONE.................................727 937-2144
EMP: 6
SALES (est): 480K **Privately Held**
SIC: 2821 Mfg Plastic Products

(G-17472)
FLORIDA DREDGE AND DOCK LLC
1040 Island Ave (34689-6916)
PHONE.................................727 942-7888
Chet Fletcher, *Senior VP*
Messinger Bruce, *Vice Pres*
Travis Fletcher, *Manager*
Don Fletcher, *Executive*
William D Fletcher,
EMP: 28 **EST:** 2006
SQ FT: 2,000
SALES (est): 2.6MM **Privately Held**
WEB: www.floridadredge.com
SIC: 3731 Dredges, building & repairing

(G-17473)
GAUSE BUILT MARINE INC
728 Wesley Ave Ste 10 (34689-6749)
PHONE.................................727 937-9113
David Gause, *Principal*
EMP: 13 **EST:** 2002
SALES (est): 907.3K **Privately Held**
WEB: www.gausebuiltboats.com
SIC: 3732 Sailboats, building & repairing

(G-17474)
HENDERSON PRESTRESS CON INC
822 Anclote Rd (34689-6699)
PHONE.................................727 938-2828
Dirk V Henderson, *President*
EMP: 10 **EST:** 1987
SQ FT: 2,000
SALES (est): 1.5MM **Privately Held**
WEB: www.hendersonprestressedconcrete.com
SIC: 3272 Piling, prefabricated concrete

(G-17475)
HOPKINS MANUFACTURING CO
855 Pine St (34689-5902)
PHONE.................................620 591-8229
EMP: 7 **EST:** 2018
SALES (est): 94.6K **Privately Held**
WEB: www.hopkinsmfg.com
SIC: 3999 Manufacturing industries

(G-17476)
HTH ENGINEERING INC
Also Called: Start Stop.com
825 Cypress Trail Dr (34688-9044)
P.O. Box 855, Elfers (34680-0855)
PHONE.................................727 939-8853
Joe Winner, *President*
EMP: 20 **EST:** 1987
SALES (est): 1.8MM **Privately Held**
WEB: www.startstop.com
SIC: 3579 5044 Dictating machines; dictating machines

(G-17477)
HYDROGEN INNOVATIONS CO
39650 Us Highway 19 N (34689-7902)
PHONE.................................727 386-8805
Antonios Valamontes, *Ch of Bd*
EMP: 5
SALES (est): 383.6K **Privately Held**
SIC: 2813 7389 Hydrogen;

(G-17478)
IMAGINE THAT INC
Also Called: Architectural Metal Works
155 E Oakwood St (34689-3645)
PHONE.................................813 728-8324
Kristy Seiter, *President*
EMP: 11 **EST:** 2015
SALES (est): 943.1K **Privately Held**
WEB: www.imaginethatinmetal.com
SIC: 3441 Fabricated structural metal

(G-17479)
JABM ADVISORS INC
2839 Grey Oaks Blvd (34688-8159)
PHONE.................................727 458-3755
Kevin Jajuga, *Principal*
EMP: 7 **EST:** 2019
SALES (est): 247.5K **Privately Held**
SIC: 3732 Boat building & repairing

(G-17480)
LIQUID ED INC
740 Wesley Ave (34689-6710)
PHONE.................................727 943-8616
Russell G Armitage, *President*
Russell G Armitade, *President*
EMP: 5 **EST:** 1984
SQ FT: 8,000
SALES (est): 553.5K **Privately Held**
SIC: 3949 5091 Golf equipment; golf equipment

(G-17481)
M & C ASSEMBLIES INC
904 Live Oak St (34689-4140)
P.O. Box 1738, Oldsmar (34677-1738)
PHONE.................................800 462-7779
Dixie Eklund, *CEO*
A Clifton Cannon Jr, *President*
Daniel Whittle, *Vice Pres*
Brynr Garnett, *Sales Mgr*
EMP: 600 **EST:** 1991
SQ FT: 11,000
SALES (est): 26.6MM **Privately Held**
WEB: www.mcassemblies.com
SIC: 3432 Plastic plumbing fixture fittings, assembly

(G-17482)
MARRAKECH INC
Also Called: Express
720 Wesley Ave Ste 11 (34689-6746)
PHONE.................................727 942-2218
Shirley Cooperman, *President*
Steen Sigmund, *Vice Pres*
◆ **EMP:** 8 **EST:** 1979
SALES (est): 971.7K **Privately Held**
WEB: www.marrak.com
SIC: 2752 Commercial printing, offset

(G-17483)
NEIGHBORHOOD NEWS & LIFESTYLES
220 S Safford Ave (34689-3648)
PHONE.................................727 943-0551
Tim Selby, *President*
EMP: 11 **EST:** 2006
SALES (est): 310.6K **Privately Held**
WEB: www.tbnewsandlifestyles.com
SIC: 2711 Newspapers, publishing & printing

(G-17484)
OXZGEN INC
40180 Us Highway 19 N (34689-8334)
PHONE.................................844 569-9436
EMP: 10 **EST:** 2002
SALES (est): 145K **Privately Held**
WEB: www.oxzgen.com
SIC: 3999

(G-17485)
PAPOUS CRAFT DISTILLERY LLC
Also Called: Tarpon Springs Distillery
605 N Pinellas Ave (34689-3343)
PHONE.................................813 766-9539
Barry Butler, *President*
EMP: 7 **EST:** 2018
SALES (est): 439.6K **Privately Held**
WEB: www.tarponspringsdistillery.net
SIC: 2085 Distilled & blended liquors

(G-17486)
PDM LLC
147 Athenian Way (34689-6209)
PHONE.................................317 605-6656
Joseph Miller, *Branch Mgr*
EMP: 39 **Privately Held**
WEB: www.pdmcpas.com
SIC: 2951 Asphalt paving mixtures & blocks
PA: Pdm Llc
　61 Coral Dr
　Key Largo FL 33037

(G-17487)
PLASTIC CONCEPTS LTD INC
1456 L And R Indus Blvd (34689-6808)
P.O. Box 400 (34688-0400)
PHONE.................................727 942-6684
Peter Karantonis, *President*
EMP: 14 **EST:** 1990
SQ FT: 18,000
SALES (est): 497K **Privately Held**
SIC: 3089 Injection molding of plastics

(G-17488)
PRECISION AUTO TINT DSIGN CORP
Also Called: Precision Window Films
746 Haven Pl (34689-4809)
PHONE.................................727 385-8788
Christopher Paine, *President*
EMP: 5 **EST:** 2008

SALES (est): 600K **Privately Held**
SIC: 3993 1799 3211 Signs & advertising specialties; fiberglass work; flat glass

(G-17489)
READING TRUCK BODY LLC
1476 L And R Indus Blvd (34689-6809)
PHONE.................................727 943-8911
Alan Farash, *President*
Stephanie Lane, *Human Resources*
EMP: 20
SALES (corp-wide): 1.4B **Privately Held**
WEB: www.readingtruck.com
SIC: 3713 7532 5531 Truck bodies (motor vehicles); body shop, trucks; automotive accessories; automotive parts
HQ: Reading Truck Body, Llc
　201 Hancock Blvd
　Reading PA 19611
　610 775-3301

(G-17490)
READING TRUCK BODY LLC
1476 L&R Industrial Blvd (34689)
PHONE.................................727 943-8911
Alan Farash, *President*
EMP: 25
SALES (corp-wide): 1.4B **Privately Held**
WEB: www.readingtruck.com
SIC: 3713 3444 Truck beds; truck bodies (motor vehicles); sheet metalwork
HQ: Reading Truck Body, Llc
　201 Hancock Blvd
　Reading PA 19611
　610 775-3301

(G-17491)
SEITER ENTERPRISES INC
155 E Oakwood St (34689-3645)
P.O. Box 3116, Holiday (34692-0116)
PHONE.................................813 728-8324
Kristy Seiter, *President*
EMP: 10 **EST:** 2009
SALES (est): 291.8K **Privately Held**
SIC: 3441 Fabricated structural metal

(G-17492)
SOUTHERN COATINGS OF TS LLC
1109 Sunset Dr (34689-2288)
PHONE.................................727 858-6586
Nomiki Kambourakis, *Principal*
EMP: 7 **EST:** 2018
SALES (est): 360.3K **Privately Held**
SIC: 3479 Metal coating & allied service

(G-17493)
SPONGE MERCHANT INTERNATIONAL
1028 Peninsula Ave (34689-2126)
PHONE.................................727 919-3523
George Billiris, *Principal*
EMP: 8 **EST:** 2001
SALES (est): 94.1K **Privately Held**
SIC: 3842 Sponges, surgical

(G-17494)
STAMAS YACHT INC
300 Pampas Ave (34689-3299)
PHONE.................................727 937-4118
John P Stamas, *President*
George P Stamas, *Treasurer*
Pete Stamas, *Med Doctor*
EMP: 70 **EST:** 1952
SQ FT: 100,000
SALES (est): 8.9MM **Privately Held**
WEB: www.stamas.com
SIC: 3732 Boats, fiberglass: building & repairing

(G-17495)
SUN-ROCK INC
904 Anclote Rd (34689-6627)
PHONE.................................727 938-0013
Edmund Windstrup, *President*
Dan Windstrup, *Vice Pres*
Barbara Windstrup, *Treasurer*
EMP: 13 **EST:** 1969
SQ FT: 6,400
SALES (est): 1MM **Privately Held**
WEB: www.sun-rock.com
SIC: 3299 Moldings, architectural: plaster of paris

(G-17496)
TARPON STNLESS FABRICATORS INC
Also Called: T S F
911 Rivo Pl Ste B (34689-4141)
PHONE.....................727 942-1821
Daniel Beltram, *President*
EMP: 36 **EST:** 1987
SQ FT: 17,000
SALES (est): 3.7MM **Privately Held**
SIC: 3444 Restaurant sheet metalwork

(G-17497)
TROPIC SIGNS INC
Also Called: Tropic Shirts
716 Wesley Ave Ste 5 (34689-6724)
P.O. Box 2027 (34688-2027)
PHONE.....................727 942-4129
Gaver M Powers, *CEO*
Kathy Powers, *Vice Pres*
▼ **EMP:** 7 **EST:** 2003
SQ FT: 5,000
SALES (est): 231K **Privately Held**
SIC: 3993 Neon signs

(G-17498)
VAC CUBES INC
536 E Tarpon Ave Ste 5 (34689-4344)
PHONE.....................727 944-3337
Susan Kroupa, *President*
Larry Kroupa, *Treasurer*
Nicholas Kroupa, *Treasurer*
EMP: 6 **EST:** 1985
SALES (est): 472.8K **Privately Held**
WEB: www.vac-cube.com
SIC: 3563 Air & gas compressors including vacuum pumps

(G-17499)
WEEHOO INC
803 Whitcomb Blvd (34689-2649)
PHONE.....................720 477-3700
Stephen M Rodgers, *Principal*
▲ **EMP:** 5 **EST:** 2008
SALES (est): 891.3K **Privately Held**
WEB: www.rideweehoo.com
SIC: 3429 Bicycle racks, automotive

(G-17500)
WEST FLORIDA PRECISION MCH LLC
728 Anclote Rd (34689-6703)
PHONE.....................727 939-0030
Chip Mortensen, *President*
Charles E Mortensen Jr, *President*
Dan Mortensen, *Enigneer*
Carlton R Swick, *Mng Member*
Dan Mortesen, *Manager*
EMP: 11 **EST:** 2009
SQ FT: 11,000
SALES (est): 2.5MM **Privately Held**
WEB: www.wfpmachine.com
SIC: 3599 Machine shop, jobbing & repair

Tavares
Lake County

(G-17501)
1ST VERTICAL BLIND COMPANY
Also Called: 1st Vertical Blind Factory
207 E Burleigh Blvd (32778-2403)
PHONE.....................352 343-3363
Joseph Pesce, *President*
William Larry Edwards, *Vice Pres*
Gwen Pesce, *Treasurer*
EMP: 6 **EST:** 1983
SALES (est): 423.1K **Privately Held**
SIC: 2591 Blinds vertical

(G-17502)
ACROTURN INDUSTRIES USA LLC
4640 Lake Industrial Blvd (32778-9510)
PHONE.....................754 205-7178
Slavko Grguric, *CEO*
EMP: 10 **EST:** 2014
SALES (est): 274.3K **Privately Held**
WEB: www.acroturn.com
SIC: 3999 Manufacturing industries

(G-17503)
ANGLE TRUSS CO INC
29652 State Road 19 (32778-4248)
P.O. Box 1091 (32778-1091)
PHONE.....................352 343-7477
Mario Caropreso, *President*
Paul Caropreso, *Treasurer*
EMP: 11 **EST:** 1975
SQ FT: 1,100
SALES (est): 2.3MM **Privately Held**
SIC: 2439 Trusses, wooden roof

(G-17504)
EAGLE QUALITY COMPONENTS LLC
280 Hummer Way (32778-9761)
P.O. Box 1618 (32778-1618)
PHONE.....................352 516-4838
Anthony Soos, *Mng Member*
EMP: 13 **EST:** 2011
SQ FT: 7,000
SALES (est): 1.3MM **Privately Held**
WEB: www.eaglequality.net
SIC: 3599 Machine shop, jobbing & repair

(G-17505)
ELITE FIRE PROTECTION INC
4145 County Road 561 (32778-9371)
PHONE.....................352 639-4119
Christopher James Whigham, *CEO*
EMP: 17 **EST:** 2015
SALES (est): 1.2MM **Privately Held**
WEB: www.elitefirefl.com
SIC: 3569 Firefighting apparatus & related equipment; sprinkler systems, fire: automatic

(G-17506)
EXPERT MOLD REMOVAL INC
14929 Lenze Dr (32778-9786)
PHONE.....................407 925-6443
Roger Lewis, *Principal*
EMP: 9 **EST:** 2010
SALES (est): 143K **Privately Held**
WEB: www.expertmoldtestingfl.com
SIC: 3544 Industrial molds

(G-17507)
FLORIDA TRIDENT TRADING LLC
Also Called: Florida Trading Company
3801 State Road 19 (32778-4234)
PHONE.....................352 253-1400
Fax: 352 253-1402
EMP: 14
SQ FT: 14,000
SALES (est): 2.1MM **Privately Held**
SIC: 3732 Boatbuilding/Repairing

(G-17508)
GELANDER INDUSTRIES INC
611 Southridge Indl Dr (32778)
PHONE.....................352 343-3100
Kim Sechler, *President*
Robert J Sechler, *Vice Pres*
▼ **EMP:** 16 **EST:** 1986
SQ FT: 3,200
SALES (est): 4.1MM **Privately Held**
WEB: www.gelanderindustries.com
SIC: 3446 Railings, prefabricated metal

(G-17509)
GREASE TEC HOLDING LLC
28615 Lake Indus Blvd (32778-9741)
PHONE.....................352 742-2440
Hank Fisher, *President*
EMP: 6 **EST:** 1994
SQ FT: 1,500
SALES (est): 473.5K **Privately Held**
SIC: 2079 Cooking oils, except corn: vegetable refined

(G-17510)
GWS TOOL LLC (DH)
Also Called: Gw Schultz Tool
595 County Road 448 (32778-6109)
PHONE.....................352 343-8778
Rick McIntyre, *CEO*
Greg Schultz, *President*
Chris Schulte, *General Mgr*
Adam Lafferty, *Exec VP*
Drew Strauchen, *Vice Pres*
▲ **EMP:** 23 **EST:** 1990
SQ FT: 16,000

SALES (est): 21.8MM
SALES (corp-wide): 10.8B **Privately Held**
WEB: www.gwstoolgroup.com
SIC: 3545 3479 Diamond cutting tools for turning, boring, burnishing, etc.; etching & engraving
HQ: Gws Tool Holdings, Llc
595 County Road 448
Tavares FL 32778
352 343-8778

(G-17511)
GWS TOOL HOLDINGS LLC (HQ)
Also Called: Gws Tool Group
595 County Road 448 (32778-6109)
PHONE.....................352 343-8778
Rick McIntyre, *CEO*
David Novak, *Engineer*
Lynne Burnham, *Human Resources*
EMP: 58 **EST:** 2014
SALES (est): 69.3MM
SALES (corp-wide): 10.8B **Privately Held**
WEB: www.gwstoolgroup.com
SIC: 3545 Precision measuring tools
PA: Sandvik Ab
Hogbovagen 45
Sandviken 811 3
262 600-00

(G-17512)
HDH AGRI PRODUCTS LLC
27536 County Road 561 (32778-9460)
PHONE.....................352 343-3484
Helen A Sanders,
Paul R Leonard,
▼ **EMP:** 6 **EST:** 2006
SALES (est): 711.4K **Privately Held**
WEB: www.hdhagriproducts.com
SIC: 3565 Packaging machinery

(G-17513)
J F V DESIGNS INC
Also Called: Veneer Source
220 Southridge Indus Dr (32778-9126)
PHONE.....................321 228-7469
Jeffrey Vaida, *President*
EMP: 10 **EST:** 1992
SQ FT: 6,000
SALES (est): 915.2K **Privately Held**
WEB: www.jfvdesigns.com
SIC: 2521 Wood office furniture

(G-17514)
JWO INDUSTRIES INC
510 E Alfred St Ste A (32778-3308)
PHONE.....................352 551-6943
Jason M West, *President*
EMP: 10 **EST:** 2016
SALES (est): 245.6K **Privately Held**
SIC: 3999 Manufacturing industries

(G-17515)
KIRTECH ENTERPRISES INC
Also Called: Blue Sky Die Company
28210 Lake Indus Blvd (32778-9742)
PHONE.....................352 742-7222
Rudolph Kirst, *President*
Marilyn Kirst, *Corp Secy*
EMP: 12 **EST:** 1984
SQ FT: 12,000
SALES (est): 1.8MM **Privately Held**
WEB: www.blueskydie.com
SIC: 3544 Special dies & tools

(G-17516)
LEGACY VULCAN CORP
Also Called: Vulcan Materials
27222 County Road 561 (32778-9459)
P.O. Box 176, Astatula (34705-0176)
PHONE.....................352 742-2122
EMP: 9
SALES (corp-wide): 2.9B **Publicly Held**
SIC: 1442 Construction Sand/Gravel
HQ: Legacy Vulcan, Llc
1200 Urban Center Dr
Vestavia AL 35242
205 298-3000

(G-17517)
M A K MANUFACTURING INC
13742 County Road 448 (32778-9422)
PHONE.....................352 343-5881
Leonard Barrett, *Owner*
EMP: 7 **EST:** 1995

SALES (est): 232.5K **Privately Held**
WEB: www.makmanufacturing.com
SIC: 3535 Conveyors & conveying equipment

(G-17518)
MILLWORK PLUS INC
262 Hummer Way (32778-9761)
P.O. Box 14 (32778-0014)
PHONE.....................352 343-2121
Roy A Comer Jr, *President*
EMP: 6 **EST:** 2000
SALES (est): 505.7K **Privately Held**
WEB: www.millworkplus.us
SIC: 2431 Millwork

(G-17519)
MITTS AND MERRILL LP
28623 Lake Indus Blvd (32778-9741)
PHONE.....................352 343-7001
Maschinfabrik Fromag, *Partner*
Jim Barrett, *General Mgr*
▲ **EMP:** 7 **EST:** 1992
SQ FT: 10,000
SALES (est): 2.6MM
SALES (corp-wide): 1.8MM **Privately Held**
WEB: www.mitts-merrill.com
SIC: 3541 3545 3544 Machine tools, metal cutting: exotic (explosive, etc.); machine tool accessories; special dies, tools, jigs & fixtures
HQ: Maschinenfabrik Fromag Gmbh & Co. Kg
Am Klingelbach 2
Frondenberg/Ruhr NW 58730
237 375-60

(G-17520)
PALMATE LLC
Also Called: Florida Extracts
200 County Road 448 (32778-6123)
PHONE.....................352 508-7800
Jeff Field, *President*
EMP: 24 **EST:** 2019
SALES (est): 2.5MM **Privately Held**
WEB: www.palmate.com
SIC: 2833 2834 Medicinals & botanicals; extracts of botanicals: powdered, pilular, solid or fluid

(G-17521)
PROGRESSIVE AERODYNE INC
3801 State Road 19 (32778-4234)
PHONE.....................352 253-0108
Kerry Richter, *President*
Paige Lynette, *Vice Pres*
Wayne Richter, *Admin Sec*
Gerald Strauss, *Technician*
EMP: 9 **EST:** 1993
SQ FT: 10,000
SALES (est): 1MM **Privately Held**
WEB: www.searey.com
SIC: 3721 Aircraft

(G-17522)
SENTINEL CMMNCTONS NEWS VNTRES
Also Called: Lake Sentinel
2012 Classique Ln (32778-5787)
PHONE.....................352 742-5900
Denise Lewis, *Manager*
EMP: 9
SALES (corp-wide): 4.6B **Publicly Held**
SIC: 2711 2741 Commercial printing & newspaper publishing combined; miscellaneous publishing
HQ: Sentinel Communications News Ventures Inc.
633 N Orange Ave
Orlando FL 32801
407 420-5000

(G-17523)
SOUTHRIDGE OUTDOOR STORAGE
595 County Road 448 (32778-6109)
PHONE.....................352 516-5598
Lauren Schultz, *Principal*
EMP: 8 **EST:** 2005
SALES (est): 233.2K **Privately Held**
SIC: 3599 Industrial machinery

(G-17524)
SPENCER FABRICATIONS INC
29511 County Road 561 (32778-9492)
PHONE.................................352 343-0014
Greg S Leonard, *President*
Mark E Fogarty, *Principal*
Jay Persaud, *COO*
Kawal G Persaud, *COO*
Paula M Andrews, *Vice Pres*
EMP: 20 **EST:** 1994
SALES (est): 5.1MM **Privately Held**
WEB: www.spenfab.com
SIC: 3443 3444 3441 Fabricated plate work (boiler shop); sheet metalwork; fabricated structural metal

(G-17525)
TRIDENT PONTOONS INC
28240 Lake Indus Blvd (32778-9742)
PHONE.................................352 253-1400
Robert H Cunningham III, *Principal*
EMP: 8 **EST:** 2012
SALES (est): 782.3K **Privately Held**
WEB: www.tridentpontoons.com
SIC: 3731 Ferryboats, building & repairing

(G-17526)
US CONVEYOR SOLUTIONS INC
3714 County Road 561 (32778-9497)
PHONE.................................352 343-0085
Larry Schumacher, *President*
EMP: 15 **EST:** 2001
SQ FT: 7,500
SALES (est): 3.2MM **Privately Held**
WEB: www.us-conveyor.com
SIC: 3535 Conveyors & conveying equipment

(G-17527)
US SECURITY DEFENSE CORP
1181 E Alfred St (32778-3474)
P.O. Box 590122, Orlando (32859-0122)
PHONE.................................407 979-1478
Angel Rodriguez, *CEO*
EMP: 50 **EST:** 2019
SALES (est): 2.5MM **Privately Held**
SIC: 3484 Guns (firearms) or gun parts, 30 mm. & below

(G-17528)
V-BRO PRODUCTS LLC
28114 County Road 561 (32778-9463)
PHONE.................................352 267-6235
Scott Brockie, *Managing Prtnr*
Joshua Stein, *Opers Staff*
Jason Wilson, *Engineer*
David Mills, *Sales Staff*
Cris Dimitriou, *Manager*
▲ **EMP:** 10 **EST:** 2004
SALES (est): 1.7MM **Privately Held**
SIC: 3536 Davits

(G-17529)
VISION CONVEYOR INC
32834 Lakeshore Dr (32778-5036)
PHONE.................................352 343-3300
Audie M Newman, *Vice Pres*
EMP: 11 **EST:** 2015
SALES (est): 787.7K **Privately Held**
WEB: www.visionconveyor.com
SIC: 3441 Fabricated structural metal

(G-17530)
WALKER STAINLESS EQP CO LLC
27620 County Road 561 (32778-9410)
PHONE.................................352 343-2606
Jerry Stokes, *Manager*
EMP: 7
SALES (corp-wide): 1.8B **Publicly Held**
WEB: www.onewabash.com
SIC: 3443 Fabricated plate work (boiler shop)
HQ: Walker Stainless Equipment Company Llc
625 W State St
New Lisbon WI 53950
608 562-7500

Tavernier
Monroe County

(G-17531)
HURRICANE MARINE MFG S INC
88665 Old Hwy (33070-4005)
PHONE.................................305 735-4461
Mike Hajec, *President*
EMP: 8 **EST:** 2017
SALES (est): 289.3K **Privately Held**
SIC: 3999 Manufacturing industries

(G-17532)
THECLIPCOM INC
91766 Overseas Hwy (33070-2642)
PHONE.................................305 599-3871
Beau Bennett, *President*
EMP: 5 **EST:** 1995
SALES (est): 611.4K **Privately Held**
WEB: www.theclip.com
SIC: 3317 Steel pipe & tubes

(G-17533)
WHITE SQUARE CHEMICAL INC
91760 Overseas Hwy (33070-2642)
P.O. Box 1907, Islamorada (33036-1907)
PHONE.................................302 212-4555
Nicholas Hawkins, *Principal*
Adama Blanco, *COO*
Adam Blanco, *Exec Dir*
EMP: 8 **EST:** 2013
SALES (est): 339.2K **Privately Held**
WEB: www.wsqchem.com
SIC: 3843 Dental equipment & supplies

Temple Terrace
Hillsborough County

(G-17534)
360 O AND P INC
5311 E Fletcher Ave (33617-1147)
PHONE.................................813 985-5000
Greg S Bauer, *Principal*
Darin Lewis, *Opers Staff*
EMP: 8 **EST:** 2007
SALES (est): 176.8K **Privately Held**
WEB: www.360oandp.com
SIC: 3842 Surgical appliances & supplies

(G-17535)
BRISTOL-MYERS SQUIBB COMPANY
11854 Skylake Pl (33617-1621)
PHONE.................................212 546-4000
Beatrice Anduze-Faris, *Vice Pres*
Michelle Terrell, *Opers Staff*
David Torres, *Human Resources*
John Barbieri, *Manager*
Hetvi Solanki, *IT/INT Sup*
EMP: 46
SALES (corp-wide): 46.3B **Publicly Held**
WEB: www.bms.com
SIC: 2834 Pharmaceutical preparations
PA: Bristol-Myers Squibb Company
430 E 29th St Fl 14
New York NY 10016
212 546-4000

(G-17536)
CIRCOR INTERNATIONAL INC
Also Called: Cpc-Cryolab
12501 Telecom Dr (33637-0906)
PHONE.................................813 978-1000
Sandy Petersen, *Senior Buyer*
Lynne Price-Regan, *Senior Buyer*
Gus Camacho, *Manager*
Jason Carpenter, *Manager*
Douglas Hunter, *Manager*
EMP: 7
SALES (corp-wide): 758.6MM **Publicly Held**
WEB: www.circor.com
SIC: 3491 Industrial valves
PA: Circor International, Inc.
30 Corporate Dr Ste 200
Burlington MA 01803
781 270-1200

(G-17537)
FLORIDA HEALTH CARE NEWS INC
215 Bullard Pkwy (33617-5511)
PHONE.................................813 989-1330
Barry Levine, *President*
Michelle Brooks, *Creative Dir*
Nerissa Johnson MBA, *Graphic Designe*
EMP: 21 **EST:** 1987
SALES (est): 4.7MM **Privately Held**
WEB: www.ifoundmydoctor.com
SIC: 2711 Newspapers, publishing & printing

(G-17538)
FLORIDA SPRAYERS INC (PA)
8808 Venture Cv Ste 101 (33637-6703)
PHONE.................................813 989-0500
Joseph C Fowler, *President*
Betty A Fowler, *Corp Secy*
EMP: 5 **EST:** 1985
SQ FT: 7,000
SALES (est): 1MM **Privately Held**
WEB: www.floridasprayers.com
SIC: 3523 5083 Sprayers & spraying machines, agricultural; agricultural machinery

(G-17539)
LESLIE CONTROLS INC (HQ)
Also Called: Circor
12501 Telecom Dr (33637-0903)
PHONE.................................813 978-1000
David A Bloss Sr, *President*
Alan R Carlsen, *Vice Pres*
Len Hamel, *Export Mgr*
Jason Carpenter, *Buyer*
Antonio Roberson, *Engineer*
◆ **EMP:** 180 **EST:** 1900
SQ FT: 150,000
SALES (est): 54.7MM
SALES (corp-wide): 758.6MM **Publicly Held**
WEB: www.lesliecontrols.com
SIC: 3491 3433 3822 3593 Automatic regulating & control valves; valves, automatic control; pressure valves & regulators, industrial; solenoid valves; steam heating apparatus; auto controls regulating residntl & coml environmt & applncs; fluid power cylinders & actuators; valves & pipe fittings; fluid power valves & hose fittings
PA: Circor International, Inc.
30 Corporate Dr Ste 200
Burlington MA 01803
781 270-1200

(G-17540)
M & B PRODUCTS INC (PA)
8601 Harney Rd (33637-6605)
PHONE.................................813 988-2211
Dale McClellan, *President*
Mary McClellan, *Corp Secy*
Thomas Hammerschmidt, *Vice Pres*
Howard Hutchinson, *Vice Pres*
Beatrjce Lovelace, *Vice Pres*
◆ **EMP:** 169 **EST:** 1987
SQ FT: 9,600
SALES (est): 54MM **Privately Held**
WEB: www.mbproducts.com
SIC: 2033 Fruit juices: packaged in cans, jars, etc.

(G-17541)
P & J GRAPHICS INC
11407 Cerca Del Rio Pl (33637-2618)
PHONE.................................813 626-3243
Peter K Goltermann, *President*
Jean Ann Goltermann, *Principal*
Fritz Goltermann, *Vice Pres*
EMP: 10 **EST:** 1987
SALES (est): 845.7K **Privately Held**
WEB: www.pandjgraphics.com
SIC: 2752 Commercial printing, offset

(G-17542)
PHOENIX ENTERPRISES FLA LLC
Also Called: Pro-Tools
7616 Industrial Ln (33637-6715)
PHONE.................................813 986-9000
Cynthia Mullen, *President*
EMP: 10 **EST:** 2015
SQ FT: 20,000

SALES (est): 670.6K **Privately Held**
SIC: 3542 Bending machines

(G-17543)
PRO-COPY INC
5219 E Fowler Ave (33617-2190)
P.O. Box 16489, Tampa (33687-6489)
PHONE.................................813 988-5900
Jon E Statham, *President*
Summer Gambrell, *General Mgr*
Summer Shibley, *General Mgr*
Joan Statham, *Treasurer*
EMP: 20 **EST:** 1987
SALES (est): 2.5MM **Privately Held**
WEB: www.pro-copy.com
SIC: 2752 Commercial printing, offset

(G-17544)
RENAISSANCE STEEL LLC
6508 E Fowler Ave (33617-2406)
PHONE.................................941 773-7290
Don Ball,
Bill Bishop,
Don Wallace,
EMP: 20 **EST:** 2004
SQ FT: 65,000
SALES (est): 1.1MM **Privately Held**
SIC: 3312 Plate, steel

(G-17545)
SEMILAB USA LLC (PA)
Also Called: Semilab Sdi
12415 Telecom Dr (33637-0912)
PHONE.................................813 977-2244
Andrew Findley, *CEO*
Marshall Wilson, *Research*
Amy Mueller, *Admin Sec*
EMP: 34 **EST:** 1988
SALES (est): 10.9MM **Privately Held**
WEB: www.semilab.com
SIC: 3699 3825 3674 Electrical equipment & supplies; instruments to measure electricity; semiconductors & related devices

(G-17546)
SUNCOAST PALLETS INC
11506 Cerca Del Rio Pl (33617-2621)
PHONE.................................813 988-1623
EMP: 8
SALES (est): 947.5K **Privately Held**
SIC: 2448 Mfg Wood Pallets/Skids

(G-17547)
SUNSHINE PEANUT COMPANY (PA)
7405 Temple Terrace Hwy A (33637-5786)
P.O. Box 290153, Tampa (33687-0153)
PHONE.................................813 988-6987
Jeff Turbeville, *President*
Jeff J Turbeville, *President*
Allison Turbeville, *Vice Pres*
Ernest S Turbeville Jr, *Vice Pres*
Sonny Turbeville, *CFO*
EMP: 8 **EST:** 2005
SALES (est): 4MM **Privately Held**
WEB: www.sunshinepeanut.com
SIC: 2099 Food preparations

(G-17548)
VURAM INC ◐
12802 Tampa Oaks Blvd # 241 (33637-1915)
PHONE.................................813 421-8000
Akhila Natarajan, *President*
Arjun Devadas, *Technical Staff*
EMP: 16 **EST:** 2021
SALES (est): 2.7MM **Privately Held**
SIC: 7372 Business oriented computer software

(G-17549)
WESTCOAST BRACE & LIMB INC (PA)
Also Called: West Coast Brace & Limb
5311 E Fletcher Ave (33617-1147)
PHONE.................................813 985-5000
Greg S Bauer, *President*
Christopher Pardo, *COO*
Chris Wilson, *Project Mgr*
Manny Baez, *Purch Agent*
Greg Bender, *Mktg Dir*
EMP: 15 **EST:** 1981
SQ FT: 5,000

▲ = Import ▼=Export
◆ =Import/Export

SALES (est): 4.7MM **Privately Held**
WEB: www.wcbl.com
SIC: 3842 Limbs, artificial; braces, ortho-
pedic

Tequesta
Palm Beach County

(G-17550)
GILBANE BOATWORKS LLC
19137 Se Federal Hwy # 1 (33469-1755)
PHONE..................................561 744-2223
John Kennedy, *Manager*
Matthew R Gilbane,
EMP: 6 EST: 2008
SALES (est): 452.1K **Privately Held**
WEB: www.gilbaneboatworks.com
SIC: 3732 Boat building & repairing

(G-17551)
**PALM BEACH SMOOTHIES COM
INC**
150 N Us Highway 1 Ste 5 (33469-2726)
P.O. Box 4313, Jupiter (33469-1020)
PHONE..................................561 379-8647
Brian Van Brock, *Principal*
EMP: 8 EST: 2009
SALES (est): 108.8K **Privately Held**
SIC: 2037 Frozen fruits & vegetables

The Villages
Lake County

(G-17552)
A BAR CODE BUSINESS INC
505 Sunbelt Rd Ste 8 (32159-5607)
PHONE..................................352 750-0077
Steven Belford, *President*
Elizabeth Shaw, *Corp Secy*
Erik Russell, *Info Tech Mgr*
▼ EMP: 6 EST: 1993
SQ FT: 400
SALES (est): 835.2K **Privately Held**
WEB: www.abarcodebusiness.com
SIC: 2759 Labels & seals: printing

The Villages
Sumter County

(G-17553)
C F PRINT LTD INC
3174 Dressendorfer Dr (32163-4215)
PHONE..................................631 567-2110
EMP: 10
SALES (est): 963.8K **Privately Held**
SIC: 2752 Lithographic Commercial Print-
ing

(G-17554)
E I DU PONT DE NEMOURS & CO
Also Called: Dupont
2555 Flintshire Ave (32162-5043)
PHONE..................................352 205-8103
EMP: 7
SALES (corp-wide): 15.6B **Publicly Held**
WEB: www.dupont.com
SIC: 2879 Agricultural chemicals
HQ: E. I. Du Pont De Nemours And Com-
pany
974 Centre Rd Bldg 735
Wilmington DE 19805
302 485-3000

(G-17555)
GOLDYS BOX CO
3267 Trussler Ter (32163-0020)
PHONE..................................954 648-1623
Howard Goldberg, *President*
EMP: 7 EST: 2005
SALES (est): 142.8K **Privately Held**
SIC: 2652 Setup paperboard boxes

(G-17556)
MAJIC STAIRS INC
744 Abaco Path (32163-6001)
PHONE..................................352 255-1390
EMP: 62

SALES (corp-wide): 1MM **Privately Held**
WEB: www.majicstairsinc.com
SIC: 3446 Stairs, staircases, stair treads:
prefabricated metal
PA: Majic Stairs Inc.
120 Cypress Rd
Ocala FL 34472
352 446-6295

(G-17557)
**STREETROD PRODUCTIONS
INC**
Also Called: Streetrod Productions Florida
11962 County Road 101 (32162-9335)
PHONE..................................352 751-3953
Heidi Ressler, *General Mgr*
EMP: 9 **Privately Held**
WEB: www.streetrodgolfcars.com
SIC: 3799 Golf carts, powered
PA: Streetrod Productions, Inc.
809 S Front St
Montezuma IA 50171

(G-17558)
**TWO MERMAIDS VILLAGES LLC
(PA)**
Also Called: Two Mermaids Swim & Resort
Wr
1039 Canal St (32162-1686)
PHONE..................................352 259-4722
David Ring,
Tina Ring,
EMP: 5 EST: 2009
SALES (est): 456.5K **Privately Held**
WEB: www.twomermaidsvillages.com
SIC: 2253 Knit outerwear mills

(G-17559)
WEBELECTRIC PRODUCTS INC
333 Colony Blvd (32162-6084)
PHONE..................................440 389-5647
Lawrence T Mazza, *Principal*
EMP: 8 EST: 2012
SALES (est): 129.4K **Privately Held**
WEB: www.webelectricproducts.com
SIC: 3714 Motor vehicle parts & acces-
sories

Thonotosassa
Hillsborough County

(G-17560)
A1 PALLETS LLC
11802 N Us Highway 301 (33592-2950)
P.O. Box 82864, Tampa (33682-2864)
PHONE..................................813 598-9165
EMP: 7 EST: 2017
SALES (est): 266K **Privately Held**
SIC: 2448 Pallets, wood

(G-17561)
**COMMERCIAL DUCT SYSTEMS
LLC**
9707 Williams Rd (33592-3554)
PHONE..................................877 237-3828
Marcia Thompson, *CFO*
Gary Gibson, *Sales Staff*
Marsha Thompson, *Mng Member*
Daniel Smith, *Manager*
Rodney Parrish, *CIO*
▼ EMP: 100 EST: 2005
SQ FT: 90,000
SALES (est): 10MM **Privately Held**
WEB: www.commercialduct.com
SIC: 3714 Air conditioner parts, motor vehi-
cle

(G-17562)
HITMASTER GRAPHICS LLC
Also Called: Dtg ASAP
12206 Hazen Ave (33592-2704)
PHONE..................................267 269-8220
Lynette McKown, *Vice Pres*
Allen D Cenal,
William Garvin,
Stuart A McKown,
EMP: 15 EST: 2008
SALES (est): 1.8MM **Privately Held**
WEB: www.hitmastergraphics.com
SIC: 2759 2395 Screen printing; embroi-
dery & art needlework

(G-17563)
NESTLE USA INC
Also Called: Nestle Professional
11471 N Us Highway 301 # 10
(33592-3532)
PHONE..................................813 273-5355
Jonathan Jackman, *Branch Mgr*
Rachel Goldberg, *Manager*
EMP: 385
SALES (corp-wide): 92.3B **Privately Held**
WEB: www.nestleusa.com
SIC: 2023 Dry, condensed, evaporated
dairy products
HQ: Nestle Usa, Inc.
1812 N Moore St Ste 118
Arlington VA 22209
703 682-4600

(G-17564)
NESTLE USA INC
Also Called: Nestle Professional Vitality
11441 N Us Highway 301 (33592-3533)
PHONE..................................813 301-4638
EMP: 187
SALES (corp-wide): 92.3B **Privately Held**
WEB: www.nestleusa.com
SIC: 2064 Candy & other confectionery
products
HQ: Nestle Usa, Inc.
1812 N Moore St Ste 118
Arlington VA 22209
703 682-4600

Titusville
Brevard County

(G-17565)
A SIGN
3670 S Hopkins Ave (32780-5707)
PHONE..................................321 264-0077
Mark Frank, *Principal*
EMP: 9 EST: 2007
SALES (est): 471.5K **Privately Held**
WEB: www.asigncompany.com
SIC: 3993 Signs & advertising specialties

(G-17566)
A1A SPORTBIKE LLC
Also Called: Core Moto
1500 Shepard Dr (32780-7953)
PHONE..................................321 806-3995
Luke McCracken,
EMP: 11 EST: 2006
SALES (est): 550.4K **Privately Held**
SIC: 3751 Motorcycle accessories

(G-17567)
ABA-CON INC
11 S Brown Ave (32796-3329)
P.O. Box 308 (32781-0308)
PHONE..................................321 567-4967
Stephen Reaves, *Vice Pres*
Arden Ballard, *Project Mgr*
Mary Ballard, *CFO*
Lo Whitten, *Treasurer*
Ed Fogle, *Sales Staff*
EMP: 10 EST: 2008
SQ FT: 3,500
SALES (est): 1.6MM **Privately Held**
WEB: www.aba-con.com
SIC: 3795 Tanks & tank components

(G-17568)
**ACCURATE POWDER COATING
INC**
1417 Chaffee Dr Ste 10 (32780-7931)
PHONE..................................321 269-6972
Tony Banks, *Owner*
EMP: 7 EST: 2005
SALES (est): 507.6K **Privately Held**
WEB: www.accuratepowdercoating.net
SIC: 3479 Coating of metals & formed
products

(G-17569)
**AERO ELECTRONICS SYSTEMS
INC**
411 S Park Ave (32796-7621)
P.O. Box 547 (32781-0547)
PHONE..................................321 269-0478
Joanne Murell Griffin, *President*
Michael Moody, *Opers Mgr*
Mike Zeiger, *Engineer*

Sheri Wilson, *Controller*
Kristina Farrell, *Manager*
EMP: 7 EST: 2003
SQ FT: 20,000
SALES (est): 4.1MM **Privately Held**
WEB: www.aeroelectronics.net
SIC: 3679 Harness assemblies for elec-
tronic use: wire or cable

(G-17570)
**AERO SEATING TECHNOLOGIES
LLC**
Also Called: Embraer Aero Seating Tech
1600 Armstrong Dr (32780-7964)
PHONE..................................321 264-5600
EMP: 8 EST: 2019
SALES (est): 633.2K **Privately Held**
SIC: 3714 Motor vehicle parts & acces-
sories

(G-17571)
**ANDERSON MFG &
UPHOLSTERY INC**
1427 Chaffee Dr Ste 4 (32780-7951)
PHONE..................................321 267-7028
Tena Anderson, *President*
EMP: 8 EST: 1997
SQ FT: 500
SALES (est): 920.1K **Privately Held**
WEB: www.amfg.us
SIC: 2211 Upholstery fabrics, cotton

(G-17572)
**APPLE RUSH COMPANY INC
(PA)**
1419 Chaffee Dr Ste 4 (32780-7933)
PHONE..................................888 741-3777
David Anthony Torgerud, *CEO*
EMP: 6 EST: 2008
SALES (est): 2.8MM **Privately Held**
SIC: 2033 Fruit juices: packaged in cans,
jars, etc.

(G-17573)
BLUE POINT FABRICATION INC
3340 Lillian Blvd (32780-9636)
PHONE..................................321 269-0073
Thomas G Benyon, *President*
Mark Gabbot, *Vice Pres*
EMP: 14 EST: 1997
SALES (est): 925.3K **Privately Held**
WEB: www.bluepointfabrication.com
SIC: 7692 Welding repair

(G-17574)
BOEING COMPANY
100 Boeing Way (32780-8046)
PHONE..................................312 544-2000
Bruce Melmick, *Vice Pres*
Hal Baker, *Engineer*
Patrick Hon, *Engineer*
Brenda Isaza, *Engineer*
Melanie Weber, *Engineer*
EMP: 17
SQ FT: 85,774
SALES (corp-wide): 62.2B **Publicly Held**
WEB: www.boeing.com
SIC: 3721 Airplanes, fixed or rotary wing
PA: The Boeing Company
929 Long Bridge Dr
Arlington VA 22202
703 414-6338

(G-17575)
**BREVARD ALUMINUM CNSTR
CO**
4655 Calle Corto (32780-6723)
PHONE..................................321 383-9255
Larry Rhoades, *Owner*
EMP: 5 EST: 1986
SQ FT: 800
SALES (est): 632.5K **Privately Held**
WEB: www.brevardaluminuminc.com
SIC: 3442 Screens, window, metal

(G-17576)
BRINSEA PRODUCTS INC
704 N Dixie Ave (32796-2017)
PHONE..................................321 267-7009
Frank Pearce, *President*
Pascale Deffieux-Pearce, *Vice Pres*
Diana Marquis, *Treasurer*
▲ EMP: 5 EST: 1996
SQ FT: 4,883

SALES (est): 668.4K **Privately Held**
WEB: www.brinsea.com
SIC: 3523 5191 Incubators & brooders, farm; farm supplies

(G-17577)
C & R DESIGNS INC
Also Called: Print123.com
1227 Garden St (32796-3310)
PHONE....................321 383-2255
Christine Bean, *Owner*
Ryen Bean, *Co-Owner*
EMP: 5 **EST:** 1989
SQ FT: 10,000
SALES (est): 480.2K **Privately Held**
WEB: www.print123.com
SIC: 2789 7336 3571 2752 Bookbinding & related work; commercial art & graphic design; electronic computers; commercial printing, lithographic; die-cut paper & board

(G-17578)
C & R DESIGNS PRINTING LLC
Also Called: Print123.com
415 Main St (32796-3531)
PHONE....................321 383-2255
Ryen A Bean, *Mng Member*
Christine C Bean, *Owner*
EMP: 6 **EST:** 2012
SALES (est): 377K **Privately Held**
SIC: 2789 7336 3571 Bookbinding & related work; commercial art & graphic design; electronic computers

(G-17579)
C SPEED LLC
6855 Tico Rd Ste 103 (32780-8000)
PHONE....................321 336-7939
EMP: 9
SALES (corp-wide): 4.9MM **Privately Held**
SIC: 3812 Mfg Search/Navigation Equipment
PA: C Speed, Llc
    316 Commerce Blvd
    Liverpool NY 13088
    315 453-1043

(G-17580)
CEMEX MATERIALS LLC
511 Garden St (32796-3404)
PHONE....................321 636-5121
Dwayne Marabolo, *Branch Mgr*
EMP: 27 **Privately Held**
SIC: 3271 Blocks, concrete or cinder: standard
HQ: Cemex Materials Llc
    1720 Centrepark Dr E # 100
    West Palm Beach FL 33401
    561 833-5555

(G-17581)
CENTRAL SAND INC
6855 Tico Rd Unit 8 (32780-8000)
PHONE....................321 632-0308
Dale L Morris, *President*
Lori L Morris, *Corp Secy*
EMP: 8 **EST:** 1982
SALES (est): 1.7MM **Privately Held**
WEB: www.centralsanddredging.com
SIC: 1442 Construction sand mining

(G-17582)
COMPOSITE HOLDINGS INC (PA)
805 Marina Rd (32796-2837)
PHONE....................321 268-9625
Jeffrey W Gray, *CEO*
Harley Mc Donald, *Ch of Bd*
Matt Mc Donald, *President*
Gerard Beutler, *Partner*
Dana Greenwood, *Plant Mgr*
▲ **EMP:** 46 **EST:** 1993
SQ FT: 100,000
SALES (est): 9.4MM **Privately Held**
WEB: www.compositeholdings.openfos.com
SIC: 3732 3711 3089 2823 Boat building & repairing; motor vehicles & car bodies; plastic boats & other marine equipment; cellulosic manmade fibers

(G-17583)
CONTROLS ON DEMAND LLC
3834 S Hopkins Ave (32780-5753)
PHONE....................321 362-5485

Joshua Thomas, *CEO*
EMP: 12 **EST:** 2016
SALES (est): 731.8K **Privately Held**
WEB: www.codelectrical.com
SIC: 3822 Auto controls regulating residntl & coml environmt & applncs

(G-17584)
D & D MANUFACTURING LLC (PA)
2655 Cherrywood Ln (32780-5909)
P.O. Box 560962, Rockledge (32956-0962)
PHONE....................321 652-4509
Dale Polk, *Mng Member*
Debra Akridge,
EMP: 10 **EST:** 2008
SALES (est): 3.4MM **Privately Held**
SIC: 3496 Mats & matting

(G-17585)
FIRST SHOT MOLD AND TOOL
1125 White Dr (32780-9603)
PHONE....................321 269-0031
John Vogt, *Owner*
▲ **EMP:** 5 **EST:** 1994
SQ FT: 6,000
SALES (est): 523.1K **Privately Held**
SIC: 3089 Injection molding of plastics

(G-17586)
GALAXY MEDALS INC
1125 White Dr (32780-9603)
PHONE....................321 269-0840
Phyllis Jankowski, *President*
David Summers, *Vice Pres*
Duane Summers, *Vice Pres*
Denise E Summers, *Admin Sec*
EMP: 7 **EST:** 1970
SQ FT: 22,000
SALES (est): 916.4K **Privately Held**
WEB: www.galaxymedals.com
SIC: 3961 Costume jewelry

(G-17587)
GENH2 INC ☉
1325 White Dr (32780-9605)
PHONE....................321 223-5950
Cody D Bateman, *CEO*
EMP: 7 **EST:** 2021
SALES (est): 233.1K **Privately Held**
WEB: www.discoverhydrogen.com
SIC: 2813 Hydrogen

(G-17588)
GENH2 CORP ☉
1325 White Dr (32780-9605)
PHONE....................530 654-3642
Cody Bateman, *President*
EMP: 23 **EST:** 2021
SALES (est): 2.7MM **Privately Held**
SIC: 2813 Hydrogen

(G-17589)
GRAPHIC REPRODUCTIONS INC
Also Called: Graphic Press
2214 Garden St Ste B (32796-2581)
PHONE....................321 267-1111
Leonard Piotrowski, *President*
EMP: 7 **EST:** 1976
SQ FT: 2,200
SALES (est): 975.7K **Privately Held**
WEB: www.graphicpressfla.com
SIC: 2752 Commercial printing, offset

(G-17590)
HELLS BAY BOATWORKS LLC
1520 Chaffee Dr (32780-7922)
PHONE....................321 383-8223
J Bryan Broderick, *CEO*
Curtis Suggs, *Plant Mgr*
Randy McBride, *Sales Mgr*
Bryan Broderick, *Sales Staff*
Hal Chittum, *Mktg Dir*
◆ **EMP:** 28 **EST:** 2002
SALES (est): 5MM **Privately Held**
WEB: www.hellsbayboatworks.com
SIC: 3732 Boats, fiberglass: building & repairing

(G-17591)
HELLS BAY MARINE INC
Also Called: Hell's Bay Boatworks
1520 Chaffee Dr (32780-7922)
PHONE....................321 383-8223

Chris Peterson, *President*
Al Keller, *Marketing Staff*
▼ **EMP:** 33 **EST:** 2006
SQ FT: 25,000
SALES (est): 6.3MM **Privately Held**
WEB: www.hellsbayboatworks.com
SIC: 3732 Boats, fiberglass: building & repairing

(G-17592)
INTEGRITY BUSINESS SVCS INC (PA)
Also Called: Fine Line Printing & Graphics
3700 S Hopkins Ave Ste E (32780-5786)
PHONE....................321 267-9294
Lee Descalzo, *President*
EMP: 5 **EST:** 1989
SQ FT: 1,400
SALES (est): 908.7K **Privately Held**
SIC: 2752 Commercial printing, offset

(G-17593)
INVENTIS NORTH AMERICA INC
2503 S Wa Ave Ste 586 (32780-5015)
PHONE....................844 683-6847
Massimo Martinelli, *President*
EMP: 5 **EST:** 2018
SALES (est): 431.2K **Privately Held**
SIC: 3845 Audiological equipment, electromedical

(G-17594)
JSSA INC
Also Called: Synergy Metal Finishing
895 Buffalo Rd (32796-2601)
PHONE....................321 383-7798
John K Smith, *President*
Sandra F Smith, *Vice Pres*
Tammy Benson, *Office Mgr*
EMP: 45 **EST:** 2006
SQ FT: 16,000
SALES (est): 5.5MM **Privately Held**
WEB: www.synergymetalfinishing.com
SIC: 3471 Electroplating of metals or formed products

(G-17595)
K J C O INC (PA)
481 Ambleside Dr (32780-2329)
PHONE....................954 401-4299
Ken Jackson, *President*
EMP: 6 **EST:** 1983
SQ FT: 4,000
SALES (est): 815.8K **Privately Held**
SIC: 3599 Machine shop, jobbing & repair

(G-17596)
K-O CONCEPTS INC
1200 White Dr Ste D (32780-9611)
PHONE....................407 296-7788
Mindy L Ritz-Owen, *CEO*
EMP: 7 **EST:** 1995
SQ FT: 9,000
SALES (est): 1MM **Privately Held**
WEB: www.k-oconcepts.com
SIC: 3845 Laser systems & equipment, medical

(G-17597)
KAVI SKIN SOLUTIONS INC
3520 South St (32780-2918)
PHONE....................415 839-5156
Ben Cohn, *Manager*
EMP: 20
SALES (corp-wide): 2.6MM **Privately Held**
WEB: www.kaviskin.com
SIC: 2834 Pharmaceutical preparations
PA: Kavi Skin Solutions, Inc.
    700 Larkspur Landing Cir
    Larkspur CA 94939
    415 839-5156

(G-17598)
KNIGHT VISION LLLP
701 Columbia Blvd (32780-7902)
PHONE....................321 607-9900
C Reed Knight Jr, *General Ptnr*
Michael Adkins, *Info Tech Mgr*
EMP: 10 **EST:** 2007
SALES (est): 444.6K **Privately Held**
SIC: 3827 Gun sights, optical

(G-17599)
KNIGHTS MANUFACTURING COMPANY
701 Columbia Blvd (32780-7902)
PHONE....................321 607-9900
C Reed Knight Jr, *President*
Gary Perry, *COO*
Ken Greenslade, *Vice Pres*
Paul Pikel, *Export Mgr*
Wendy Miller, *Purch Mgr*
EMP: 55 **EST:** 1992
SQ FT: 60,000
SALES (est): 9.5MM **Privately Held**
SIC: 3484 8734 8731 Guns (firearms) or gun parts, 30 mm. & below; testing laboratories; commercial physical research

(G-17600)
MADART
3635 S Ridge Cir (32796-1866)
PHONE....................321 961-9264
Megan Duncanson, *Principal*
EMP: 7 **EST:** 2011
SALES (est): 70.9K **Privately Held**
WEB: www.madartdesigns.com
SIC: 3229 Art, decorative & novelty glassware

(G-17601)
MARBLE DESIGNS OF FL INC
1975 Silver Star Rd (32796-5118)
PHONE....................321 269-6920
Jeff Hackney, *President*
EMP: 6 **EST:** 1984
SQ FT: 10,000
SALES (est): 689.3K **Privately Held**
WEB: www.marbledesignsofflorida.com
SIC: 3281 5211 Marble, building: cut & shaped; masonry materials & supplies

(G-17602)
MARIMBA COCINA MEXICANA II INC
3758 S Washington Ave (32780-5739)
PHONE....................321 268-6960
Ana L Martinez, *Principal*
EMP: 10 **EST:** 2013
SALES (est): 271.3K **Privately Held**
SIC: 3931 Marimbas

(G-17603)
OLYMPIAN LED INC
3620 S Hopkins Ave (32780-5733)
PHONE....................321 747-3220
Braden P O'Keefe, *President*
EMP: 5 **EST:** 2014
SQ FT: 3,620
SALES (est): 602.1K **Privately Held**
WEB: www.olympianled.com
SIC: 3993 Electric signs

(G-17604)
PARAGON PLASTICS INC
1401 Armstrong Dr (32780-7950)
PHONE....................321 631-6212
David Trout, *President*
▼ **EMP:** 23 **EST:** 1995
SQ FT: 25,000
SALES (est): 6.7MM **Privately Held**
WEB: www.paragonplastics.com
SIC: 3089 Plastic hardware & building products; plastic processing

(G-17605)
PC OF TITUSVILLE INC
701 Columbia Blvd (32780-7902)
PHONE....................321 267-1161
Reed Knight, *Director*
EMP: 31 **EST:** 2004
SALES (est): 1.4MM **Privately Held**
SIC: 3471 Plating of metals or formed products

(G-17606)
PCM PRODUCTS INC
1225 White Dr (32780-9630)
PHONE....................321 267-7500
Paul Richards, *President*
Liv E Richards, *Treasurer*
EMP: 24 **EST:** 1977
SQ FT: 20,000
SALES (est): 3.2MM **Privately Held**
WEB: www.pcmproducts.com
SIC: 3479 Etching, photochemical

(G-17607)
PHARMCO LABORATORIES INC
3520 South St (32780-2918)
PHONE....................................321 268-1313
Robert L Cohn, *President*
Ben Cohn, *VP Opers*
▲ EMP: 6 EST: 1979
SQ FT: 22,000
SALES (est): 1.1MM **Privately Held**
WEB: www.pharmcolabs.com
SIC: 2899 2833 Chemical preparations;
medicinals & botanicals

(G-17608)
PIER 220 INC
2 A Max Brewer Mem Pkwy (32796-2884)
P.O. Box 5779 (32783-5779)
PHONE....................................321 264-2011
EMP: 8 EST: 2018
SALES (est): 441.7K **Privately Held**
WEB: www.pier220.com
SIC: 2092 Fresh or frozen packaged fish

(G-17609)
PRECISION SHAPES INC (PA)
8835 Grissom Pkwy (32780-7904)
P.O. Box 5099 (32783-5099)
PHONE....................................321 269-2555
Susan Palma, *President*
Jesse Palma, *Business Mgr*
Cheryl Cleveland, *Vice Pres*
Colleen Watson, *QC Mgr*
Omar Carambot, *Manager*
EMP: 44 EST: 1941
SQ FT: 30,000
SALES (est): 9.1MM **Privately Held**
WEB: www.precisionshapes.net
SIC: 3452 3451 3724 3599 Bolts, nuts,
rivets & washers; screw machine prod-
ucts; aircraft engines & engine parts; ma-
chine shop, jobbing & repair; aircraft
hardware; aircraft body & wing assem-
blies & parts

(G-17610)
RAIDER OUTBOARDS INC
1885 Armstrong Dr (32780-7947)
PHONE....................................321 383-9585
George E Woodruff, *President*
Christopher D Woodruff, *Vice Pres*
Michael Woodruff, *Admin Sec*
EMP: 30 EST: 2002
SQ FT: 5,300
SALES (est): 5.5MM **Privately Held**
SIC: 3519 Marine engines

(G-17611)
RENZETTI INC
8800 Grissom Pkwy (32780-7999)
PHONE....................................321 267-7705
Andrew Renzetti, *President*
Lily Renzetti, *Vice Pres*
▲ EMP: 10 EST: 1974
SQ FT: 16,119
SALES (est): 1.3MM **Privately Held**
WEB: www.renzetti.com
SIC: 3949 3599 Fishing equipment; flies,
fishing: artificial; machine shop, jobbing &
repair

(G-17612)
RESPONSIVE MACHINING INC
1650 Chaffee Dr (32780-7922)
PHONE....................................321 225-4011
Helen McCourt, *President*
Suzanne M Hall, *President*
David K Hall, *Vice Pres*
Tanya Severson, *Controller*
EMP: 10 EST: 1996
SQ FT: 5,600
SALES (est): 976.3K **Privately Held**
WEB: www.responsivemachining.com
SIC: 7692 3444 3599 Welding repair;
sheet metalwork; machine & other job
shop work

(G-17613)
RICHARD C GOOD
Also Called: Specialty Packaging & Display
1125 White Dr (32780-9603)
P.O. Box 234, Sharpes (32959-0234)
PHONE....................................321 639-6383
Richard C Good, *Owner*
EMP: 5 EST: 1985
SALES (est): 414.9K **Privately Held**
SIC: 2657 Folding paperboard boxes

(G-17614)
RICHARD K PRATT LLC
Also Called: Pratt Plastics
1325 White Dr (32780-9605)
PHONE....................................321 482-9494
Danielle D Pratt, *Principal*
Richard Pratt,
EMP: 7 EST: 2015
SALES (est): 512.7K **Privately Held**
SIC: 3999 Manufacturing industries

(G-17615)
ROCK RIDGE MATERIALS INC
Also Called: Statewide Materials
1525 White Dr (32780-9629)
PHONE....................................321 268-8455
Christine Ruth, *Principal*
William Campbell, *Director*
EMP: 16 EST: 2014
SALES (est): 4.6MM **Privately Held**
WEB: www.swmagg.com
SIC: 1422 5211 1423 1429 Crushed &
broken limestone; sand & gravel; crushed
& broken granite; riprap quarrying; dump
truck haulage; stone, crushed or broken

(G-17616)
**SOUTHERN INNOVATIVE
ENERGY INC**
4373 Fletcher Ln Ste 2 (32780-2857)
PHONE....................................321 747-9205
Kim Mercanti, *Senior Partner*
Raymond Giamporcaro, *Admin Sec*
EMP: 9 EST: 2011
SALES (est): 550.4K **Privately Held**
SIC: 3561 3494 3511 Pumps & pumping
equipment; valves & pipe fittings; plumb-
ing & heating valves; steam turbine gen-
erator set units, complete

(G-17617)
SRM BLINDS INC
4303 Kenneth Ct (32780-5976)
PHONE....................................321 269-5332
Steven Michell, *Principal*
EMP: 9 EST: 2007
SALES (est): 171.8K **Privately Held**
SIC: 2591 Window blinds

(G-17618)
STARLINE EDUCATION INC
414 Garden St (32796-2848)
PHONE....................................808 631-1818
Sandra Combs, *Principal*
EMP: 8 EST: 2017
SALES (est): 465.7K **Privately Held**
WEB: www.starlinepress.com
SIC: 2731 Book publishing

(G-17619)
**STINGER FIBERGLASS
DESIGNS INC**
1525 Armstrong Dr (32780-7950)
PHONE....................................321 268-1118
Arthur J Schricker, *President*
EMP: 13 EST: 2001
SALES (est): 985.9K **Privately Held**
WEB: www.americansportscar.com
SIC: 3732 Boats, fiberglass: building & re-
pairing

(G-17620)
STORMQUANT INC
1431 Chaffee Dr Ste 1 (32780-7957)
PHONE....................................408 840-2003
Tripp Purvis, *CEO*
EMP: 10 EST: 2019
SALES (est): 961.7K **Privately Held**
WEB: www.stormquant.com
SIC: 3812 7371 8999 Radar systems &
equipment; software programming appli-
cations; weather forecasting

(G-17621)
**SUN ELECTRONIC SYSTEMS
INC**
1845 Shepard Dr (32780-7920)
PHONE....................................321 383-9400
Gary Clifford, *President*
Veronica Clifford, *Corp Secy*
Maria Fisher, *Purch Mgr*
Deanna Jeffery, *Sales Staff*
EMP: 14 EST: 1980
SQ FT: 13,000

SALES (est): 2.4MM **Privately Held**
WEB: www.sunelectronics.com
SIC: 3625 3826 Electric controls & control
accessories, industrial; environmental
testing equipment

(G-17622)
THUNDERBIRD PRESS INC
205 N Mantor Ave (32796-4606)
PHONE....................................321 269-7616
Shearer Kennedy, *President*
Scott Kennedy, *Vice Pres*
Dave Forrest, *Sales Mgr*
EMP: 10 EST: 1975
SQ FT: 4,280
SALES (est): 959.5K **Privately Held**
WEB: www.thunderbird-press.com
SIC: 2752 Commercial printing, offset

(G-17623)
**TOWNSEND CERAMICS &
GLASS INC**
Also Called: Townsend's
3535 South St (32780-2906)
PHONE....................................321 269-5671
John Townsend, *President*
Ann Townsend, *Corp Secy*
Kelvin Townsend, *Vice Pres*
EMP: 10 EST: 1969
SQ FT: 13,000
SALES (est): 496.1K **Privately Held**
SIC: 3269 5947 Figures: pottery, china,
earthenware & stoneware; gift, novelty &
souvenir shop

(G-17624)
TRUSSWOOD INC
3620 Bobbi Ln (32780-2917)
PHONE....................................321 383-0366
Jean Francois Langelier, *President*
Tracey Zelman, *Sales Staff*
Charles Thibault, *Executive*
Chad Voorhees, *Associate*
EMP: 60 EST: 1999
SQ FT: 6,000
SALES (est): 8.1MM **Privately Held**
WEB: www.trusswood.net
SIC: 2439 Trusses, wooden roof

(G-17625)
US APPLIED PHYS ICS GROUP
1650 Chaffee Dr (32780-7922)
PHONE....................................321 567-7270
EMP: 9 EST: 2017
SALES (est): 1MM **Privately Held**
SIC: 3674 Semiconductors & related de-
vices

(G-17626)
**US APPLIED PHYSICS GROUP
LLC**
7065 Challenger Ave (32780-8201)
PHONE....................................321 607-9023
Richard McCourt, *President*
James Hoffman, *Mng Member*
EMP: 6 EST: 2014
SALES (est): 484.3K **Privately Held**
SIC: 3674 Diodes, solid state (germanium,
silicon, etc.)

(G-17627)
WINDSOR WINDOW COMPANY
Woodgrain Distribution
1450 Shepard Dr (32780-7921)
PHONE....................................321 385-3880
Robert Mickle, *Division Mgr*
Tony Means, *Site Mgr*
Ryan Dame, *Manager*
EMP: 12 **Privately Held**
WEB: www.woodgrain.com
SIC: 2431 3442 Moldings, wood: unfin-
ished & prefinished; moldings & trim, ex-
cept automobile: metal
HQ: Windsor Window Company
300 Nw 16th St
Fruitland ID 83619
800 452-3801

Treasure Island
Pinellas County

(G-17628)
VINE AND GRIND LLC
Also Called: Vine & Grind
111 107th Ave Ste 1 (33706-4722)
PHONE....................................727 420-3122
Jared Leal, *Principal*
EMP: 5 EST: 2016
SALES (est): 370.9K **Privately Held**
WEB: www.vineandgrind.com
SIC: 3599 Grinding castings for the trade

Trenton
Gilchrist County

(G-17629)
AYERS PUBLISHING INC
Also Called: Ayers Office Supply
207 N Main St (32693-3439)
P.O. Box 127 (32693-0127)
PHONE....................................352 463-7135
John M Ayers II, *President*
Carrie A Mizell, *Principal*
EMP: 5 EST: 1934
SALES (est): 486.7K **Privately Held**
WEB: www.gilchristcountyjournal.net
SIC: 2711 5943 Newspapers: publishing
only, not printed on site; commercial print-
ing & newspaper publishing combined; of-
fice forms & supplies

(G-17630)
COMPOSITE-FX SALES LLC
9069 Se County Road 319 (32693-2660)
PHONE....................................352 538-1624
Dwight Junkin, *Principal*
EMP: 9 EST: 2006
SALES (est): 646.2K **Privately Held**
WEB: www.composite-fx.com
SIC: 3728 Aircraft parts & equipment

(G-17631)
XTREME POWDER COATING INC
5679 Sw County Road 341 (32693-6214)
PHONE....................................352 219-3807
Terry Throop, *Principal*
EMP: 7 EST: 2017
SALES (est): 99.8K **Privately Held**
SIC: 3479 Metal coating & allied service

Trinity
Pasco County

(G-17632)
**ADVANCED DAGNSTC
SOLUTIONS INC**
3633 Little Rd Ste 103 (34655-1815)
PHONE....................................352 293-2810
Jim Arnold Jr, *CEO*
Brandon M Womack, *President*
EMP: 12 EST: 2011
SALES (est): 521.6K **Privately Held**
WEB: www.advdiagnostic.com
SIC: 3841 Diagnostic apparatus, medical

(G-17633)
CAPITOL CONVEYORS INC
1429 Warrington Way (34655-7219)
PHONE....................................727 314-7474
Robert Dersham, *CEO*
EMP: 9 EST: 2007
SQ FT: 900
SALES (est): 1.2MM **Privately Held**
WEB: www.capitolconveyorsinc.com
SIC: 3535 Conveyors & conveying equip-
ment

(G-17634)
CLRS SOLUTIONS LLC
1723 Winsloe Dr (34655-4941)
PHONE....................................612 481-9244
Chad D Henning,
EMP: 5 EST: 2017
SALES (est): 900K **Privately Held**
SIC: 1442 Construction sand & gravel

(PA)=Parent Co (HQ)=Headquarters (DH)=Div Headquarters
✿ = New Business established in last 2 years

2022 Harris Florida
Manufacturers Directory

GEOGRAPHIC

(G-17635)
ENODIS HOLDINGS INC (DH)
2227 Welbilt Blvd (34655-5130)
PHONE..............................727 375-7010
David McCulloch, *CEO*
EMP: 50 **EST:** 2009
SALES (est): 32.8MM
SALES (corp-wide): 2.6MM **Privately Held**
SIC: 3589 Commercial cooking & food-warming equipment
HQ: Welbilt, Inc.
2227 Welbilt Blvd
Trinity FL 34655
727 375-7010

(G-17636)
FACTS ENGINEERING LLC
8049 Photonics Dr (34655-5128)
PHONE..............................727 375-8888
Rick Walker, *Vice Pres*
Kyle Culpepper, *Project Mgr*
Kevin Cochran, *Engineer*
Jose Estrada, *Engineer*
Eric Gatch, *Engineer*
▲ **EMP:** 50 **EST:** 1986
SQ FT: 20,000
SALES (est): 9.7MM **Privately Held**
WEB: www.facts-eng.com
SIC: 3823 3625 Industrial process control instruments; relays & industrial controls

(G-17637)
GARRETT TIN & BROTHER INC
2536 Palesta Dr (34655-5156)
PHONE..............................727 236-5434
Garrett S Tin, *Principal*
EMP: 7 **EST:** 2008
SALES (est): 128.6K **Privately Held**
SIC: 3356 Tin

(G-17638)
KYSOR INDUSTRIAL CORPORATION (DH)
Also Called: Kysor Warren
2227 Welbilt Blvd (34655-5130)
PHONE..............................727 376-8600
Richard Osborne, *President*
Kirk Goss, *Vice Pres*
Donald Holmes, *Treasurer*
◆ **EMP:** 12 **EST:** 1925
SQ FT: 8,000
SALES (est): 432.4MM
SALES (corp-wide): 2.6MM **Privately Held**
SIC: 3714 3585 Motor vehicle engines & parts; heaters, motor vehicle; radiators & radiator shells & cores, motor vehicle; air conditioner parts, motor vehicle; refrigeration equipment, complete
HQ: Welbilt, Inc.
2227 Welbilt Blvd
Trinity FL 34655
727 375-7010

(G-17639)
LUTZ FUEL INC
7821 Lachlan Dr (34655-5147)
PHONE..............................727 376-3013
Chris Bruckner, *Principal*
EMP: 8 **EST:** 2012
SALES (est): 212.3K **Privately Held**
SIC: 2869 Fuels

(G-17640)
MEOPTA USA INC
Also Called: Tyrolit Company
7826 Photonics Dr (34655-5127)
PHONE..............................631 436-5900
Gerald J Rausnitz, *President*
David Rausnitz, *COO*
Daniela Trtik, *Vice Pres*
Jim Lane, *Engineer*
Egon Rausnitz, *Treasurer*
▲ **EMP:** 140 **EST:** 1957
SQ FT: 41,500
SALES (est): 27.5MM **Privately Held**
WEB: www.meopta.com
SIC: 3827 Lenses, optical: all types except ophthalmic
PA: Cong Dao Nguyen
U Rezne 374
Zelezna Ruda

(G-17641)
WELBILT INC (DH)
2227 Welbilt Blvd (34655-5130)
PHONE..............................727 375-7010
William C Johnson, *President*
Stan Ioffe, *President*
Nick Patterson, *President*
Graham Sams, *President*
Tom Kurgan, *General Mgr*
EMP: 218 **EST:** 1902
SALES (est): 1.5B
SALES (corp-wide): 2.6MM **Privately Held**
WEB: www.welbilt.com
SIC: 3589 3585 Commercial cooking & foodwarming equipment; food warming equipment, commercial; ice making machinery; cold drink dispensing equipment (not coin-operated)
HQ: Ali Group North America Corporation
101 Corporate Woods Pkwy
Vernon Hills IL 60061
847 215-6565

(G-17642)
WESTRAN CORPORATION
2227 Welbilt Blvd (34655-5130)
PHONE..............................727 375-7010
David Frase, *Principal*
EMP: 23 **EST:** 2010
SALES (est): 7.4MM
SALES (corp-wide): 2.6MM **Privately Held**
SIC: 3585 Refrigeration & heating equipment
HQ: Welbilt, Inc.
2227 Welbilt Blvd
Trinity FL 34655
727 375-7010

Tyndall Afb
Bay County

(G-17643)
AERO TECH SERVICE ASSOC INC
1311 Florida Ave (32403-5207)
PHONE..............................850 286-1378
Mike Garrett, *Manager*
EMP: 17 **Privately Held**
WEB: www.atsainc.com
SIC: 3721 Autogiros
PA: Aero Tech Service Associates, Inc.
909 S Meridian Ave # 200
Oklahoma City OK 73108

Umatilla
Lake County

(G-17644)
CHASE METALS INC
38051 State Road 19 (32784-8357)
PHONE..............................352 669-1254
Brent C Creasman, *President*
Alan D Twibel, *Vice Pres*
Alan Twibel, *Vice Pres*
EMP: 21 **EST:** 2001
SALES (est): 756.6K **Privately Held**
SIC: 3541 Lathes

(G-17645)
COFFIN CABINETRY & TRIM MICHAE
91 S Pine Ave (32784-9096)
PHONE..............................352 217-3729
Michael Coffin, *Principal*
EMP: 7 **EST:** 2011
SALES (est): 252.4K **Privately Held**
SIC: 2434 Wood kitchen cabinets

(G-17646)
DOERFLER MANUFACTURING INC
235 N Central Ave (32784-7565)
PHONE..............................763 772-3728
George A Doerfler, *President*
EMP: 5 **EST:** 2008
SQ FT: 7,000
SALES (est): 758.3K **Privately Held**
WEB: www.doerflermfg.com
SIC: 2844 Face creams or lotions

(G-17647)
MERCER PRODUCTS COMPANY INC
37235 State Road 19 (32784-8070)
PHONE..............................352 357-0057
Gerry Glatz, *Vice Pres*
EMP: 7 **EST:** 1958
SALES (est): 12.8MM
SALES (corp-wide): 686.3MM **Privately Held**
SIC: 3089 Plastic hardware & building products
HQ: Burke Industries (Delaware), Inc.
2250 S 10th St
San Jose CA 95112
408 297-3500

(G-17648)
ORLANDO MTAL BLDG ERECTORS LLC
17540 Se 294th Court Rd (32784-7311)
P.O. Box 2469 (32784-2469)
PHONE..............................407 917-9762
Vance Harris, *President*
EMP: 18 **EST:** 2017
SALES (est): 1.2MM **Privately Held**
WEB: www.orlandometalbuildingerectors.com
SIC: 3448 Prefabricated metal buildings

(G-17649)
OUTPOST NORTH LAKE
131 N Central Ave (32784-7568)
P.O. Box 1099 (32784-1099)
PHONE..............................352 669-2430
Matt Newby, *Owner*
EMP: 5 **EST:** 1979
SQ FT: 2,270
SALES (est): 327K **Privately Held**
WEB: www.thenorthlakeoutpost.com
SIC: 2711 Newspapers, publishing & printing

(G-17650)
PLASTIC COMPOSITES INC ◐
630 Goodbar Ave (32784-7628)
PHONE..............................352 669-5822
John Purland, *Principal*
EMP: 10 **EST:** 2021
SALES (est): 860K **Privately Held**
SIC: 3089 Plastic processing

(G-17651)
SPECIALTY FABRICATION WLDG INC
680 Goodbar Ave (32784-7628)
P.O. Box 981 (32784-0981)
PHONE..............................352 669-9353
Michael Purvis, *President*
Cott Purvis, *Vice Pres*
Karen Purvis, *Admin Sec*
EMP: 15 **EST:** 2004
SALES (est): 1.1MM **Privately Held**
SIC: 7692 Welding repair

(G-17652)
STERLING EQP MFG CENTL FLA INC
803 Line St (32784-8671)
PHONE..............................352 669-3255
Pete Rogers, *President*
Greg Rogers, *Vice Pres*
Wade Rogers, *Vice Pres*
EMP: 5 **EST:** 1976
SQ FT: 10,000
SALES (est): 669.7K **Privately Held**
WEB: www.sterlingequipment.us
SIC: 3465 Moldings or trim, automobile: stamped metal

University Park
Manatee County

(G-17653)
DUMPSTERMAXX
5265 University Pkwy # 101 (34201-3012)
PHONE..............................805 552-6299
Rafael M Calle Jr, *Manager*
EMP: 6 **EST:** 2017
SALES (est): 513.9K **Privately Held**
WEB: www.dumpstermaxx.com
SIC: 3443 Dumpsters, garbage

Valparaiso
Okaloosa County

(G-17654)
AMERICAN ATHLETIC UNIFORMS INC
90 Eastview Ave (32580-1375)
PHONE..............................850 729-1205
Roger Noel, *President*
Geraldine Noel, *Vice Pres*
Gerri Noel, *Manager*
EMP: 10 **EST:** 1987
SQ FT: 4,400
SALES (est): 1MM **Privately Held**
WEB: aau-inc.mybigcommerce.com
SIC: 2329 2339 Athletic (warmup, sweat & jogging) suits: men's & boys'; sportswear, women's

(G-17655)
BAYOU OUTDOOR EQUIPMENT
Also Called: Schwabs Enterprises
489 Valparaiso Pkwy (32580-1274)
PHONE..............................850 729-2711
Jim Allen, *Owner*
EMP: 12 **EST:** 1999
SALES (est): 962.2K **Privately Held**
SIC: 3546 Saws & sawing equipment

(G-17656)
BAYOU PRINTING INC
Also Called: Ccp Bayou Printing
113 S John Sims Pkwy (32580-1211)
PHONE..............................850 678-5444
Philip Pink, *President*
EMP: 10 **EST:** 1982
SQ FT: 2,045
SALES (est): 500K **Privately Held**
SIC: 2752 2741 2791 2789 Commercial printing, offset; newsletter publishing; yearbooks: publishing & printing; typesetting; bookbinding & related work

(G-17657)
BRADLEY INDUS TEXTILES INC
101 S John Sims Pkwy (32580-1211)
P.O. Box 254 (32580-0254)
PHONE..............................850 678-6111
Anthony S Bradley, *President*
EMP: 10 **EST:** 1977
SALES (est): 954.1K **Privately Held**
WEB: www.bradleygeosynthetics.com
SIC: 2999 2221 Coke; broadwoven fabric mills, manmade

(G-17658)
COCA-COLA BOTTLING CO UNTD INC
647 Valparaiso Pkwy (32580-1135)
PHONE..............................850 678-9370
Ed Hall, *Branch Mgr*
EMP: 78
SQ FT: 28,528
SALES (corp-wide): 2B **Privately Held**
WEB: www.coca-cola.com
SIC: 2086 Bottled & canned soft drinks
PA: Coca-Cola Bottling Company United, Inc.
4600 E Lake Blvd
Birmingham AL 35217
205 841-2653

(G-17659)
CUSTOM FBRCATIONS FREEPORT INC
479 Old Florida Sr 10 Rd (32580-1427)
PHONE..............................850 729-0500
William Moulton, *President*
Lenore Moulton, *Corp Secy*
EMP: 10 **EST:** 2000
SQ FT: 3,200
SALES (est): 1.2MM **Privately Held**
WEB: www.water91306.com
SIC: 3355 1799 1791 2431 Aluminum rail & structural shapes; rails, rolled & drawn, aluminum; ornamental metal work; structural steel erection; staircases, stairs & railings

(G-17660)
FULL CIRCLE INTEGRATION LLC
127b N John Sims Pkwy (32580-1005)
PHONE..............................504 615-5501

Paul M Topp, *CEO*
Grant Martin, *COO*
Michael Hayes, *Marketing Staff*
EMP: 11 **EST:** 2009
SQ FT: 3,000
SALES (est): 1.3MM **Privately Held**
WEB: www.innoventormilitary.com
SIC: 3812 8711 3721 Defense systems &
equipment; engineering services; aircraft

(G-17661)
KENS GAS PIPING INC
419 Adams Ave Ste A (32580-1257)
PHONE..................................850 897-4149
Kenneth C Corbitt, *Owner*
EMP: 7 **EST:** 2014
SALES (est): 511.8K **Privately Held**
SIC: 1382 Oil & gas exploration services

Valrico
Hillsborough County

(G-17662)
AXRDHAM CORP
2134 Ridgemore Dr (33594-3200)
PHONE..................................813 653-9588
▲ **EMP:** 6
SQ FT: 2,400
SALES (est): 346.5K **Privately Held**
SIC: 2099 Mfg Food Preparations

(G-17663)
FABRICATED WIRE PRODUCTS INC
401 Lutie Dr (33594-2926)
P.O. Box 671, Dover (33527-0671)
PHONE..................................813 802-8463
Byrd Chad L, *Principal*
EMP: 9 **EST:** 2014
SALES (est): 481.4K **Privately Held**
WEB: www.harborcountrybike.com
SIC: 3496 Miscellaneous fabricated wire
products

(G-17664)
FLORIDA DISTILLERY LLC
1625 Emerald Hill Way (33594-5009)
PHONE..................................813 892-5431
Sarah M Nelson, *Principal*
EMP: 8 **EST:** 2012
SALES (est): 167.4K **Privately Held**
WEB: www.floridacane.com
SIC: 2085 Distilled & blended liquors

(G-17665)
HOLLOW METAL INC
2803 Park Meadow Dr (33594-4654)
PHONE..................................813 246-4112
Norris Gordon, *President*
EMP: 13 **EST:** 1995
SALES (est): 1.2MM **Privately Held**
SIC: 3442 Sash, door or window: metal

(G-17666)
IMD SOFTWARE INC
5203 Sand Trap Pl (33596-8291)
PHONE..................................813 685-2138
Yicheng Huang, *Principal*
EMP: 7 **EST:** 2014
SALES (est): 52.1K **Privately Held**
SIC: 7372 Prepackaged software

(G-17667)
LINCOLN TACTICAL LLC
1319 Brahma Dr (33594-4914)
PHONE..................................813 419-3110
Ryan Thomas,
Tiffany Thomas,
EMP: 10 **EST:** 2011
SALES (est): 224.1K **Privately Held**
WEB: www.lincolntactical.net
SIC: 3465 Body parts, automobile:
stamped metal

(G-17668)
MAJESTIC METALS INC
1807 N Waterman Dr (33594-5434)
PHONE..................................813 380-6885
Jason Martin, *Branch Mgr*
EMP: 10

SALES (corp-wide): 5.3MM **Privately Held**
WEB: www.majesticmetalsinc.com
SIC: 3448 Prefabricated metal buildings
PA: Majestic Metals, Inc.
192 American Way
Madison MS 39110
601 856-3600

(G-17669)
RAE LAUNO CORPORATION
Also Called: Gourmet Cup
2606 Durant Oaks Dr (33596-5932)
PHONE..................................813 242-4281
Benjamin Rayfield, *President*
Eric Rayfield, *Vice Pres*
▲ **EMP:** 9 **EST:** 1997
SALES (est): 490.1K **Privately Held**
SIC: 2095 5149 Roasted coffee; coffee,
green or roasted

(G-17670)
TITAN TRAILERS LLC
2406 E State Road 60 (33595-8001)
PHONE..................................813 298-8597
Noah Winter,
EMP: 7 **EST:** 2018
SALES (est): 137K **Privately Held**
WEB: www.titantrailers.com
SIC: 3999 Manufacturing industries

Venice
Sarasota County

(G-17671)
ABSOLUTE ALUMINUM INC
Also Called: Absolute Aluminum & Cnstr
1220 Ogden Rd (34285-5530)
PHONE..................................941 497-7777
Dale E Desjardins Jr, *President*
Rodger Manuel, *Opers Mgr*
Valerie Cervantes, *Production*
Paul White, *Engineer*
Joe Clarkson, *Sales Staff*
EMP: 78 **EST:** 1988
SQ FT: 29,000
SALES (est): 26.9MM **Privately Held**
WEB: www.absolutealuminum.com
SIC: 3354 Aluminum extruded products

(G-17672)
ABSOLUTE WINDOW AND DOOR INC
177 Center Rd (34285-5572)
PHONE..................................941 485-7774
Shawn Garathy, *President*
EMP: 9 **EST:** 2000
SQ FT: 3,000
SALES (est): 1MM **Privately Held**
WEB: www.absolutewindowanddoor.net
SIC: 2431 1751 5211 Doors, wood; win-
dow & door (prefabricated) installation;
windows, storm: wood or metal

(G-17673)
ACE BOAT LIFTS LLC (PA)
2211 S Tamiami Trl (34293-5016)
PHONE..................................941 493-8100
Kristy Tingle,
EMP: 20 **EST:** 1959
SQ FT: 5,000
SALES (est): 2.5MM **Privately Held**
WEB: www.aceboatlifts.com
SIC: 3536 Boat lifts

(G-17674)
AES SERVICES INC
575 Bluebell Rd (34293-3162)
PHONE..................................941 237-1446
Angelina E Sigmon, *Principal*
EMP: 9 **EST:** 2013
SALES (est): 175K **Privately Held**
WEB: www.aes.com
SIC: 1381 Drilling oil & gas wells

(G-17675)
AMBO FOODS LLC
727 Commerce Dr Unit C (34292-1723)
PHONE..................................941 485-4400
Bo Martinsen, *Mng Member*
Anne M Chalmers,
EMP: 8 **EST:** 2008

SALES (est): 459.4K **Privately Held**
WEB: www.omegacookie.com
SIC: 2052 Cookies

(G-17676)
AMBO HEALTH LLC
Also Called: Omega3 Innovations
727 Commerce Dr (34292-1723)
PHONE..................................866 414-0188
Mayelise Martinsen, *Director*
Anne-Marie Chalmers,
Bo Martinsen,
EMP: 9 **EST:** 2008
SALES (est): 1MM **Privately Held**
WEB: www.omega3innovations.com
SIC: 2834 Druggists' preparations (phar-
maceuticals)

(G-17677)
AMERICAN ARCHTCTURAL MLLWK LLC
248 James St (34285-5529)
PHONE..................................844 307-9571
Maria West,
EMP: 17 **EST:** 2012
SALES (est): 3.7MM **Privately Held**
WEB: www.millworkusa.com
SIC: 2431 Millwork

(G-17678)
BUDDY BRIDGE INC
751 Us Highway 41 Byp S (34285-4311)
PHONE..................................941 586-8281
EMP: 24
SALES (corp-wide): 350.9K **Privately Held**
WEB: www.bridgebuddy.net
SIC: 2759 Playing cards: printing
PA: Buddy Bridge Inc
350 Sorrento Ranches Dr
Nokomis FL 34275
941 488-0799

(G-17679)
CAMCORP INDUSTRIES INC
170 Rich St (34292-3107)
PHONE..................................941 488-5000
David Demarest, *President*
Dorian Demarest, *Vice Pres*
EMP: 6 **EST:** 1986
SQ FT: 5,000
SALES (est): 903.3K **Privately Held**
WEB: www.camcorponline.com
SIC: 3599 3444 Machine shop, jobbing &
repair; sheet metalwork

(G-17680)
CRANE CO
730 Commerce Dr (34292-1726)
PHONE..................................941 480-9101
Donald Borden, *Branch Mgr*
EMP: 15
SQ FT: 39,906
SALES (corp-wide): 3.1B **Privately Held**
WEB: www.craneco.com
SIC: 3589 Water treatment equipment, in-
dustrial; water purification equipment,
household type
HQ: Redco Corporation
100 1st Stamford Pl
Stamford CT 06902
203 363-7300

(G-17681)
CRANE ENVIRONMENTAL INC
Also Called: Crane Environmental Products
730 Commerce Dr (34292-1726)
PHONE..................................941 480-9101
Thomas J Perlitz, *President*
Rita Graham, *Manager*
▼ **EMP:** 150 **EST:** 1991
SALES (est): 10MM
SALES (corp-wide): 3.1B **Privately Held**
SIC: 3589 Water treatment equipment, in-
dustrial; water purification equipment,
household type
HQ: Redco Corporation
100 1st Stamford Pl
Stamford CT 06902
203 363-7300

(G-17682)
D-R MEDIA AND INVESTMENTS LLC
Also Called: Publishing
300 Tamiami Trl S (34285-2422)
PHONE..................................941 207-1602
David Dunn-Rankin, *CEO*
Michael Ruppel, *CFO*
EMP: 70 **EST:** 2018
SALES (est): 5.9MM **Privately Held**
WEB: www.d-rmedia.com
SIC: 2711 7922 Commercial printing &
newspaper publishing combined; enter-
tainment promotion

(G-17683)
DILLS ENTERPRISES LLC
Also Called: UNI Glide Trailer
301 Seaboard Ave (34285-4623)
PHONE..................................941 493-1993
Robert Dills,
EMP: 5 **EST:** 1986
SQ FT: 32,000
SALES (est): 622.3K **Privately Held**
SIC: 3715 3444 2451 Truck trailers; sheet
metalwork; mobile homes

(G-17684)
DRAKON COATINGS INDUSTRIES INC
167 Progress Cir (34285-5537)
PHONE..................................810 875-3874
Doug Behrendt, *President*
Ryan Blomberg, *Treasurer*
EMP: 5 **EST:** 2015
SALES (est): 390.5K **Privately Held**
WEB: www.drakoncoatings.com
SIC: 3399 Powder, metal

(G-17685)
DYNAMIC VISIONS INC
355 Center Ct (34285-5506)
PHONE..................................941 497-1984
William J Gill, *President*
Sara Gill, *Vice Pres*
EMP: 42 **EST:** 1988
SQ FT: 75,000
SALES (est): 2.4MM **Privately Held**
SIC: 3081 3211 Vinyl film & sheet; con-
struction glass

(G-17686)
DYNAMIS EPOXY LLC
415 E Venice Ave (34285-4632)
PHONE..................................941 488-3999
John Caramanian, *President*
EMP: 5 **EST:** 2006
SALES (est): 497.9K **Privately Held**
WEB: www.dcdynamis.com
SIC: 2891 2851 1771 Epoxy adhesives;
marine paints; epoxy coatings; concrete
repair

(G-17687)
DYNAMIS INC
415 E Venice Ave (34285-4632)
PHONE..................................941 488-3999
John Caramanian, *President*
Cheryl Caramanian, *General Mgr*
EMP: 9 **EST:** 1947
SQ FT: 10,000
SALES (est): 1.6MM **Privately Held**
WEB: www.dcdynamis.com
SIC: 2851 Lacquers, varnishes, enamels &
other coatings

(G-17688)
EMCEE ELECTRONICS INC (PA)
520 Cypress Ave (34285-4603)
PHONE..................................941 485-1515
David Corzilius, *President*
Allan Barberio, *General Mgr*
Donna Neu, *Vice Pres*
EMP: 20 **EST:** 1958
SQ FT: 10,000
SALES (est): 4MM **Privately Held**
WEB: www.emcee-electronics.com
SIC: 3823 3829 Industrial instrmnts
msrmnt display/control process variable;
measuring & controlling devices

(G-17689)
EMCEE ELECTRONICS INC
223 Warfield Ave (34285-4640)
PHONE..................................941 485-1515

Steve King, *Branch Mgr*
EMP: 10
SALES (corp-wide): 4MM **Privately Held**
WEB: www.emcee-electronics.com
SIC: 3825 Measuring instruments & meters, electric
PA: Emcee Electronics, Inc.
520 Cypress Ave
Venice FL 34285
941 485-1515

(G-17690)
ENZYMEDICA INC (PA)
771 Commerce Dr Ste 3 (34292-1731)
PHONE..............................941 505-5565
Scott Sensenbrenner, *CEO*
Lou Destefano, *Principal*
Thomas G Bohager, *Chairman*
Paul Davison, *Exec VP*
Gary Trimble, *Exec VP*
EMP: 36 **EST:** 1998
SQ FT: 14,000
SALES (est): 11MM **Privately Held**
WEB: www.enzymedica.com
SIC: 2899 Gelatin capsules

(G-17691)
FLEX INNOVATIONS LLC
313 Seaboard Ave Unit B (34285-4668)
PHONE..............................866 310-3539
Dan B Asher, *Principal*
EMP: 10 **EST:** 2015
SALES (est): 715.6K **Privately Held**
WEB: www.flexinnovations.com
SIC: 3999 Manufacturing industries

(G-17692)
FLORIDA MATTRESS WHOLESALE
527 Us Highway 41 Byp N (34285-6040)
PHONE..............................941 244-2139
Paul Dunford, *President*
EMP: 7 **EST:** 2017
SALES (est): 119.3K **Privately Held**
SIC: 2515 Mattresses & foundations

(G-17693)
GENERAL RUBBER CORPORATION
Also Called: Technical Sales & Engineering
405 Commercial Ct Ste C (34292-1653)
PHONE..............................941 412-0001
EMP: 13 **Publicly Held**
WEB: www.general-rubber.com
SIC: 3069 Mallets, rubber; tubing, rubber; valves, hard rubber
HQ: General Rubber Corporation
2201 E Ganley Rd
Tucson AZ 85706
520 889-2979

(G-17694)
GLASPRO
Also Called: Zap Skim'ers
101 Pond Cypress Rd (34292-1736)
PHONE..............................941 488-4586
Robert H Smetts, *President*
Dave Scott, *Opers Mgr*
Karen Stewart, *Mktg Dir*
◆ **EMP:** 28 **EST:** 1989
SQ FT: 25,000
SALES (est): 5MM **Privately Held**
WEB: www.zapskimboards.com
SIC: 3949 Surfboards

(G-17695)
GULF BREEZE APPAREL LLC
616 Cypress Ave (34285-4605)
PHONE..............................941 488-8337
Chad Jacob, *Manager*
EMP: 7 **EST:** 2009
SALES (est): 631.6K **Privately Held**
WEB: www.gulfbreezeapparel.com
SIC: 2759 Screen printing

(G-17696)
H & H SIGNS INC
426 E Venice Ave (34285-4631)
PHONE..............................941 485-0556
John Hinshaw, *President*
EMP: 5 **EST:** 1996
SQ FT: 2,200
SALES (est): 474.8K **Privately Held**
WEB:
SIC: 3993 Signs, not made in custom sign painting shops

(G-17697)
HARN RO SYSTEMS INC
310 Center Ct (34285-5505)
PHONE..............................941 488-9671
James A Harn, *President*
Joe Chapman, *General Mgr*
Julia E Nemeth-Harn, *Vice Pres*
Jon Harn, *Project Engr*
Andrey Kharitonenko, *Project Engr*
▲ **EMP:** 22 **EST:** 1972
SQ FT: 40,000
SALES (est): 5.7MM **Privately Held**
WEB: www.harnrosystems.com
SIC: 3589 Water treatment equipment, industrial

(G-17698)
HOPE TECHNICAL SALES & SVCS
692 Sawgrass Bridge Rd (34292-4480)
PHONE..............................941 412-1204
Jack Diggs, *Owner*
EMP: 5 **EST:** 1998
SALES (est): 361.1K **Privately Held**
SIC: 3714 Bumpers & bumperettes, motor vehicle

(G-17699)
HUNT VENTURES INC
232 Bahama St (34285-2450)
PHONE..............................941 375-3699
Darin J Hunt, *Principal*
EMP: 10 **EST:** 2005
SALES (est): 2.2MM **Privately Held**
WEB: www.luminarysource.com
SIC: 1382 Oil & gas exploration services

(G-17700)
INLINE FILLING SYSTEMS LLC
216 Seaboard Ave (34285-4618)
PHONE..............................941 486-8800
Samuel Lubus, *President*
Derek Forte, *Sales Mgr*
Scott Anderson, *Sales Staff*
◆ **EMP:** 30 **EST:** 1996
SQ FT: 26,000
SALES (est): 10.2MM
SALES (corp-wide): 3.2B **Publicly Held**
WEB: www.fillers.com
SIC: 3565 Bag opening, filling & closing machines
PA: The Middleby Corporation
1400 Toastmaster Dr
Elgin IL 60120
847 741-3300

(G-17701)
JOHN FRANKLIN MOWERY
100 W Venice Ave Ste E (34285-1928)
P.O. Box 489 (34284-0489)
PHONE..............................202 468-8644
John F Mowery, *Principal*
EMP: 7 **EST:** 2016
SALES (est): 462.1K **Privately Held**
WEB: www.restorepaper.com
SIC: 2621 Book paper

(G-17702)
K V WATER EQUIPMENT & KRANE CO
Also Called: Krane Environmental
730 Commerce Dr (34292-1726)
PHONE..............................941 723-0707
Don Borden, *President*
EMP: 21 **EST:** 1993
SQ FT: 10,000
SALES (est): 439.6K **Privately Held**
SIC: 3589 Water purification equipment, household type

(G-17703)
KENT MFG FLA KEYS INC
248 James St (34285-5529)
PHONE..............................941 488-0355
Ronald K Drobisch, *Principal*
EMP: 9 **EST:** 2016
SALES (est): 119.2K **Privately Held**
SIC: 3999 Manufacturing industries

(G-17704)
LEARNING FOR LIFE PRESS LLC
165 Morning Star Rd (34285-6006)
PHONE..............................352 234-0472
Dale Simpson, *Principal*

EMP: 8 **EST:** 2014
SALES (est): 119.2K **Privately Held**
WEB: www.learningforlife.org
SIC: 2741 Miscellaneous publishing

(G-17705)
LOAD BANKS DIRECT LLC
309 Nassau St N (34285-1420)
P.O. Box 631287, Cincinnati OH (45263-1287)
PHONE..............................859 554-2522
Martin Glover, *President*
EMP: 12 **EST:** 2012
SQ FT: 10,000
SALES (est): 2.1MM **Privately Held**
WEB: www.loadbanksdirect.com
SIC: 3699 Electrical equipment & supplies

(G-17706)
MARITIME CUSTOM DESIGNS INC
170 Rich St (34292-3107)
PHONE..............................941 716-0255
Timothy McChesney, *President*
EMP: 9 **EST:** 2004
SALES (est): 156.9K **Privately Held**
SIC: 3089 Plastic boats & other marine equipment

(G-17707)
NICKOLS CBINETRY WOODWORKS INC
765 U S 41 Byp S Bypass S (34285)
PHONE..............................941 485-7894
Gary Nickols, *President*
EMP: 8 **EST:** 2003
SALES (est): 451.5K **Privately Held**
WEB: www.nickolscabinetry.com
SIC: 2434 Wood kitchen cabinets

(G-17708)
OLIVE FLORIDA OIL COMPANY
307 W Venice Ave Ste A (34285-2005)
PHONE..............................941 483-1865
Arnish Patel, *CEO*
EMP: 8 **EST:** 2009
SALES (est): 233K **Privately Held**
WEB: www.floridaoliveoil.com
SIC: 2079 Olive oil

(G-17709)
ORCHID ENVY
339 W Venice Ave (34285-2004)
PHONE..............................941 485-1122
Natalee McKinney, *Principal*
EMP: 7 **EST:** 2016
SALES (est): 112.2K **Privately Held**
WEB: www.orchidenvy.com
SIC: 2323 Men's & boys' neckwear

(G-17710)
PACKARD & COMPANY INC
787 Commerce Dr (34292-1747)
PHONE..............................941 451-8201
Gary Packard, *Principal*
EMP: 8 **EST:** 2016
SALES (est): 167.2K **Privately Held**
WEB: www.packardandco.com
SIC: 2434 Wood kitchen cabinets

(G-17711)
PARADISE CABLE INDUSTRIES
723 Commerce Dr Unit H (34292-1742)
PHONE..............................941 488-6092
Jon Bossoli, *President*
Tim Alexander, *Vice Pres*
EMP: 13 **EST:** 2011
SALES (est): 1.5MM **Privately Held**
WEB: www.paradisecableind.com
SIC: 3679 Harness assemblies for electronic use: wire or cable

(G-17712)
RAYNETCRM LLC
121 Ginger Rd (34293-1521)
PHONE..............................813 489-9565
Ales Seifert,
Jaroslav Bazala,
Dusan Galik,
Lukas Rajsky,
EMP: 18 **EST:** 2014
SALES (est): 676.5K **Privately Held**
WEB: www.raynetcrm.com
SIC: 7372 Business oriented computer software

(G-17713)
RICHARD MEER INVESTMENTS INC
Also Called: Buddy's Pizza
822 Pinebrook Rd (34285-7103)
PHONE..............................941 484-6551
Ailene Charlton, *President*
Larry Delor, *Vice Pres*
EMP: 9 **EST:** 1981
SALES (est): 311.7K **Privately Held**
SIC: 2032 5812 Italian foods: packaged in cans, jars, etc.; Italian restaurant; pizza restaurants

(G-17714)
SCENTSTIONAL SOAPS CANDLES INC
730 Commerce Dr (34292-1726)
PHONE..............................941 485-1443
Stephen Morrison, *President*
Amy Morrison, *Vice Pres*
Melanie Schuth, *Executive*
▲ **EMP:** 14 **EST:** 1998
SALES (est): 5.8MM **Privately Held**
WEB: www.scentsational-products.com
SIC: 2841 3999 5199 5999 Soap & other detergents; candles; candles; candle shops

(G-17715)
SINOFRESH HEALTHCARE INC (PA)
2357 S Tamiami Trl Unit 3 (34293-5022)
PHONE..............................941 270-2627
Thomas Fitzgerald, *Ch of Bd*
David R Olund, *President*
EMP: 9 **EST:** 1999
SQ FT: 2,500
SALES (est): 1.6MM **Privately Held**
WEB: www.buysinofresh.com
SIC: 2834 Drugs affecting parasitic & infective diseases

(G-17716)
SOMATICS LLC
720 Commerce Dr Unit 101 (34292-1750)
PHONE..............................847 234-6761
Richard Abrams,
EMP: 7 **EST:** 1984
SQ FT: 1,400
SALES (est): 888.5K **Privately Held**
WEB: www.thymatron.com
SIC: 3845 Electromedical equipment

(G-17717)
SOUTHERN SPRING & STAMPING INC (PA)
401 Substation Rd (34285-6077)
PHONE..............................941 488-2276
Linda Deaterly, *CEO*
Jeff Deaterly, *President*
Dee Deaterly, *Principal*
EMP: 50 **EST:** 1957
SQ FT: 40,000
SALES (est): 12MM **Privately Held**
WEB: www.southernspring.com
SIC: 3495 3496 3469 3493 Precision springs; miscellaneous fabricated wire products; metal stampings; steel springs, except wire

(G-17718)
SPERRY MARKETING GROUP INC
Also Called: Sperry Manufacturing
107 Corporation Way (34285-5524)
PHONE..............................941 483-4667
Steve Perry, *President*
▲ **EMP:** 11 **EST:** 1986
SQ FT: 15,000
SALES (est): 1.2MM **Privately Held**
SIC: 2392 Tablecloths: made from purchased materials, pads & padding, table: except asbestos, felt or rattan; chair covers & pads: made from purchased materials

(G-17719)
STEVE PRINTER INC
601 Cypress Ave (34285-4606)
PHONE..............................941 375-8657
Steve Smallwood, *President*
EMP: 8 **EST:** 2009

▲ = Import ▼=Export
◆ =Import/Export

SALES (est): 124.2K **Privately Held**
SIC: 2752 Commercial printing, offset

(G-17720)
SUN COAST MEDIA GROUP INC
Venice Gondolier Sun
200 E Venice Ave Fl 1 (34285-1941)
P.O. Box 2390, Port Charlotte (33949)
PHONE...............................941 207-1000
Bob Vedder, *Principal*
Robin Marotta, *Prdtn Mgr*
Marty Blubaugh, *Production*
Ken Shelby, *Production*
Lennie Kevin, *Sales Staff*
EMP: 60
SALES (corp-wide): 333.5MM **Privately Held**
WEB: www.yoursun.com
SIC: 2711 Newspapers, publishing & printing
HQ: Sun Coast Media Group, Inc.
23170 Harborview Rd
Port Charlotte FL 33980
941 206-1300

(G-17721)
SUNS UP OF SWF LLC
191 Lee Rd (34292-2523)
PHONE...............................301 470-2678
Mark Graham, *Manager*
EMP: 6 **EST:** 2011
SALES (est): 687.3K **Privately Held**
WEB: www.fixmycasablancafan.com
SIC: 3634 Ceiling fans

(G-17722)
TIDEWATER INCENTIVES GROUP LTD
Also Called: Tidewater Promotions
5292 Layton Dr (34293-8821)
PHONE...............................410 734-0691
Caleb Frick, *Principal*
Veronica Fantom, *Sales Staff*
Vicki Frick, *Sales Staff*
Mathilde Frick, *Info Tech Mgr*
EMP: 10 **EST:** 1992
SALES (est): 1.6MM **Privately Held**
WEB: www.markedpromo.com
SIC: 2759 5199 Screen printing; advertising specialties

(G-17723)
TOMATOES & OLIVE OIL LLC
1055 Us Highway 41 Byp S (34285-4343)
PHONE...............................941 822-9709
Morgan Glickman, *Principal*
EMP: 7 **EST:** 2016
SALES (est): 276.7K **Privately Held**
SIC: 2079 Olive oil

(G-17724)
TOP HAT FOOD SERVICES LLC
11799 Granite Woods Loop (34292-4113)
PHONE...............................630 825-2800
Katherine Rini, *Manager*
EMP: 8 **EST:** 2018
SALES (est): 237.5K **Privately Held**
SIC: 2024 5812 Yogurt desserts, frozen; frozen yogurt stand

(G-17725)
TURBINE WELD INDUSTRIES LLC
402 Substation Rd (34285-6076)
PHONE...............................941 485-5113
David Venarge, *Principal*
Michael Halpin, *Principal*
Beth Laurenson, *Principal*
EMP: 40 **EST:** 2019
SALES (est): 2.6MM **Privately Held**
WEB: www.turbineweld.com
SIC: 3724 Aircraft engines & engine parts

(G-17726)
USSI LLC
752 Commerce Dr Ste 15 (34292-1744)
PHONE...............................941 244-2408
EMP: 15
SALES (est): 571.5K **Privately Held**
SIC: 2891 Mfg Adhesives/Sealants

(G-17727)
VAPRZONE LLC
448 Us Highway 41 Byp N (34285-6056)
PHONE...............................941 882-4841

Michael Brown, *Mng Member*
Penelope A Brown,
Joseph Gonzalez,
EMP: 8 **EST:** 2013
SALES (est): 678.1K **Privately Held**
WEB: www.vaprzone.com
SIC: 2899 2111 Oils & essential oils; cigarettes

(G-17728)
VENICE GRANIT & MARBLE INC
159 Progress Cir (34285-5537)
PHONE...............................941 483-4363
Charles Custin, *President*
Jeffrey Koffman, *Vice Pres*
▲ **EMP:** 7 **EST:** 1999
SALES (est): 511.2K **Privately Held**
WEB: www.kitchenbathinternational.com
SIC: 3281 2541 Table tops, marble; counter & sink tops

Venus
Highlands County

(G-17729)
STORAGE AND CANOPY INC
990 Us Highway 27 S (33960-2200)
PHONE...............................863 840-4005
George Munne, *Principal*
EMP: 7 **EST:** 2017
SALES (est): 573.6K **Privately Held**
WEB: www.storageandcanopy.com
SIC: 3448 Carports: prefabricated metal

Vero Beach
Indian River County

(G-17730)
2204 AVENUE X LLC
1275 Us Highway 1 Unit 2 (32960-4706)
PHONE...............................407 619-1410
Robin Filosa, *President*
Alexander Filosa, *Principal*
Mary Ann Filosa, *Vice Pres*
Lisa Filosa, *Treasurer*
EMP: 6 **EST:** 2015
SALES (est): 320K **Privately Held**
SIC: 3679 Electronic components

(G-17731)
AA PERFORMANCE
955 13th Ln (32960-4732)
PHONE...............................772 672-1164
EMP: 7 **EST:** 2013
SALES (est): 169.6K **Privately Held**
SIC: 3714 Motor vehicle parts & accessories

(G-17732)
ACTION PRINTERS INC
2571 Stockbridge Sq Sw (32962-4217)
PHONE...............................772 567-4377
Kim E Barrett, *President*
Sharon K Schroeder, *Vice Pres*
EMP: 8 **EST:** 1961
SQ FT: 5,500
SALES (est): 795.6K **Privately Held**
WEB: www.actionprinters.net
SIC: 2752 Commercial printing, offset

(G-17733)
ALL PHASE WELDING LLC
8356 E 98th Ave (32967-2819)
PHONE...............................772 834-2980
Leslie Fletcher, *Principal*
EMP: 7 **EST:** 2017
SALES (est): 234.6K **Privately Held**
SIC: 7692 Welding repair

(G-17734)
ALUMA TOWER COMPANY INC (HQ)
1639 Old Dixie Hwy (32960-3656)
P.O. Box 2806 (32961-2806)
PHONE...............................772 567-3423
Robert A Main Jr, *President*
Amelia Dickey, *Vice Pres*
John Hall, *Vice Pres*
David Pascale, *Vice Pres*
Sharen Conley, *Opers Staff*
▼ **EMP:** 20 **EST:** 1974

SQ FT: 18,000
SALES (est): 15MM
SALES (corp-wide): 41.2MM **Privately Held**
WEB: www.alumatower.com
SIC: 3441 Tower sections, radio & television transmission
PA: Main, Robert A & Sons Holding Company Inc
20-21 Wagaraw Rd
Fair Lawn NJ 07410
201 447-3700

(G-17735)
ALUMA TOWER COMPANY INC
926 Old Dixie Hwy (32960-4357)
PHONE...............................772 567-3423
John Hall, *Vice Pres*
Joseph Blume, *Sales Engr*
EMP: 15
SALES (corp-wide): 41.2MM **Privately Held**
WEB: www.alumatower.com
SIC: 3441 Tower sections, radio & television transmission
HQ: Aluma Tower Company, Inc.
1639 Old Dixie Hwy
Vero Beach FL 32960
772 567-3423

(G-17736)
APPROVED TURBO COMPONENTS INC
663 2nd Ln (32962-2951)
PHONE...............................559 627-3600
Michael Rogers, *President*
▲ **EMP:** 10 **EST:** 1998
SALES (est): 911K **Privately Held**
WEB: www.approvedturbo.com
SIC: 3724 Turbo-superchargers, aircraft

(G-17737)
ATLAS ORGNICS INDIAN RIVER LLC
925 74th Ave Sw (32968-9755)
PHONE...............................772 563-9336
Joseph McMillin, *Mng Member*
Gary Nihard,
EMP: 10 **EST:** 2019
SALES (est): 711.9K **Privately Held**
SIC: 2875 Compost

(G-17738)
AUTOPAX INC
6602 Liberty Pl (32966-8991)
PHONE...............................772 563-0131
John Inglis, *Owner*
EMP: 7 **EST:** 2008
SALES (est): 94.7K **Privately Held**
SIC: 3086 Packaging & shipping materials, foamed plastic

(G-17739)
B & F WASTE SOLUTIONS LLC
Also Called: Anytime Waste
4901 Bethel Creek Dr F (32963-1276)
P.O. Box 690729 (32969-0729)
PHONE...............................772 336-1113
Beatrice Sartor, *Mng Member*
EMP: 5 **EST:** 2011
SQ FT: 1,200
SALES (est): 500K **Privately Held**
SIC: 3443 Industrial vessels, tanks & containers

(G-17740)
BLACK DIAMOND SYSTEMS CORP (PA)
1305 Cape Pointe Cir (32963-3995)
PHONE...............................917 539-7309
David Brand, *CFO*
EMP: 26 **EST:** 2019
SALES (est): 28MM **Privately Held**
SIC: 3571 Electronic computers

(G-17741)
BLACKHAWK CONSTRUCTION CO INC (PA)
Also Called: Blackhawk Quarry Co of Fla
3060 Airport West Dr (32960-1993)
PHONE...............................321 258-4957
Andrew Machata, *President*
Adele Machata, *Vice Pres*
EMP: 17 **EST:** 1965
SQ FT: 11,000

SALES (est): 2.8MM **Privately Held**
WEB: www.blackhawkconstructionaz.com
SIC: 1499 Shell mining

(G-17742)
BLOCK ENGINEERING INCORPORATED (PA)
308 Lady Palm Ter (32963-4256)
PHONE...............................508 251-3100
Petros Kotidis, *CEO*
George M Baker, *Ch of Bd*
Daniel J Cavicchio Jr, *President*
Bob Schildkraut, *Principal*
Erik Deutsch, *Vice Pres*
EMP: 6 **EST:** 1960
SQ FT: 20,000
SALES (est): 2.3MM **Privately Held**
WEB: www.blockeng.com
SIC: 3826 Analytical instruments

(G-17743)
BREWER INTERNATIONAL INC
605 90th Ave (32968-9751)
P.O. Box 690037 (32969-0037)
PHONE...............................772 562-0555
Jesse Cruz, *President*
Stephen Brewer, *President*
James Brewer, *Vice Pres*
Nancy Healy, *Accountant*
Linda Brewer, *Administration*
EMP: 10 **EST:** 1970
SQ FT: 14,000
SALES (est): 2.5MM **Privately Held**
WEB: www.brewerint.com
SIC: 2879 2842 3999 Agricultural chemicals; specialty cleaning preparations; barber & beauty shop equipment

(G-17744)
BRICK PAVERS BY MENDOZA INC (PA)
1235 S Us Highway 1 (32962-6450)
PHONE...............................772 925-1666
Elias Mendoza-Hernandez, *President*
Pedro Martinez, *Vice Pres*
David Mendoza, *Vice Pres*
EMP: 5 **EST:** 2014
SALES (est): 556.7K **Privately Held**
SIC: 2951 Asphalt paving mixtures & blocks

(G-17745)
BRICK PAVERS BY MENDOZA INC
1986 21st St Sw (32962-7915)
PHONE...............................772 408-2005
J Carmen Mendoza-Hernandez, *Manager*
EMP: 74
SALES (corp-wide): 556.7K **Privately Held**
SIC: 2951 Asphalt paving mixtures & blocks
PA: Brick Pavers By Mendoza Inc
1235 S Us Highway 1
Vero Beach FL 32962
772 925-1666

(G-17746)
BRYANTS PRECISION M F G CORP
Also Called: Bryant Machine Shop
1803 Wilbur Ave (32960-5567)
P.O. Box 2844 (32961-2844)
PHONE...............................772 569-2319
Brenda Bryant, *President*
L Dale Bryant Jr, *General Mgr*
EMP: 28 **EST:** 1984
SQ FT: 8,000
SALES (est): 4.9MM **Privately Held**
WEB: www.bryantprecision.net
SIC: 3599 Machine shop, jobbing & repair

(G-17747)
BUCK PILE INC
2801 Ocean Dr Ste 101 (32963-2016)
PHONE...............................772 492-1056
Christopher Smoot, *President*
Sarah Smoot, *Vice Pres*
Alex Smoot, *Manager*
Elizabeth Foster, *Admin Sec*
EMP: 7 **EST:** 1984
SQ FT: 1,500

SALES (est): 663.5K **Privately Held**
WEB: www.pilebuck.com
SIC: **2711** 2731 Newspapers: publishing only, not printed on site; books: publishing only

(G-17748)
CABINETREE COLLECTION INC
860 35th Ct Sw (32968-5062)
PHONE..................................772 569-4761
Douglas Hampel, *President*
EMP: 10 EST: 1991
SQ FT: 5,000
SALES (est): 989.5K **Privately Held**
WEB: www.cabinetreecollection.com
SIC: **2434** Wood kitchen cabinets

(G-17749)
CONNECT SLUTIONS WORLDWIDE LLC
Also Called: Symbee/Symbee Connect
1602 Indian Bay Dr (32963-2210)
PHONE..................................407 492-9370
Lance Guthrie, *Principal*
Jerry Perkins, *Mng Member*
EMP: 5 EST: 2019
SALES (est): 554.5K **Privately Held**
WEB: www.connectbestsolutionsllc.com
SIC: **7372** 7389 Prepackaged software;

(G-17750)
CONRAD PICKEL STUDIO INC
7777 20th St (32966-1314)
PHONE..................................772 567-1710
R Paul Pickel, *President*
Kristi Pickel, *Corp Secy*
Lisa Pickel, *Vice Pres*
▲ EMP: 9 EST: 1946
SQ FT: 4,000
SALES (est): 1MM **Privately Held**
WEB: www.pickelstudio.com
SIC: **3231** Stained glass: made from purchased glass; mosaics, glass: made from purchased glass

(G-17751)
CONSTRUCTCONNECT INC
2001 9th Ave Ste 204 (32960-6415)
PHONE..................................772 770-6003
Dave Conway, *Branch Mgr*
EMP: 200
SALES (corp-wide): 5.5B **Publicly Held**
WEB: www.isqft.com
SIC: **2721** Magazines: publishing only, not printed on site
HQ: Constructconnect, Inc.
　3825 Edwards Rd Ste 800
　Cincinnati OH 45209
　800 364-2059

(G-17752)
CUSTOM WALL SYSTEMS INC
9495 22nd St (32966-3056)
PHONE..................................772 408-3006
Mark Unterreiner, *Principal*
EMP: 9 EST: 2016
SALES (est): 389.2K **Privately Held**
SIC: **3299** Stucco

(G-17753)
EMERGE INTERACTIVE INC (PA)
5375 Sol Rue Cir (32967-7025)
PHONE..................................772 563-0570
John C Belknap, *Ch of Bd*
David C Warren, *President*
Robert E Drury, *Exec VP*
Mark S Fox, *Exec VP*
Marvin L Slosman, *Exec VP*
EMP: 23 EST: 1994
SQ FT: 10,798
SALES (est): 1.4MM **Privately Held**
SIC: **3556** Food products machinery; meat processing machinery

(G-17754)
FLOAT-ON CORPORATION
1925 98th Ave (32966-3034)
PHONE..................................772 569-4440
L Ralph Poppell, *President*
Timothy R Poppell, *Vice Pres*
▼ EMP: 22 EST: 1967
SQ FT: 30,208
SALES (est): 4.3MM **Privately Held**
WEB: www.floaton.com
SIC: **3799** 3444 Boat trailers; sheet metalwork

(G-17755)
FLORIDA SHUTTERS INC
1055 Commerce Ave (32960-5772)
PHONE..................................772 569-2200
Thomas L Pease, *President*
Dale Brown, *Purchasing*
John Morris, *Sales Staff*
Miles Wright, *Sales Staff*
Jill Pease, *Admin Sec*
▼ EMP: 45 EST: 1979
SQ FT: 18,000
SALES (est): 5.1MM **Privately Held**
WEB: www.floridashuttersinc.com
SIC: **3444** 3442 2394 1799 Awnings, sheet metal; shutters, door or window: metal; awnings, fabric: made from purchased materials; awning installation

(G-17756)
FROSTING
2915 Cardinal Dr (32963-1916)
PHONE..................................772 234-2915
Barbaralee C Monday, *Principal*
EMP: 8 EST: 2009
SALES (est): 505.3K **Privately Held**
WEB: www.frostingverobeach.com
SIC: **2051** Bakery: wholesale or wholesale/retail combined

(G-17757)
G D PALLETS LLC
695 S Us 1 (32962-4508)
PHONE..................................772 713-8251
EMP: 6 EST: 2018
SALES (est): 302K **Privately Held**
SIC: **2448** Pallets, wood

(G-17758)
H317 LOGISTICS LLC
9019 Somerset Bay Ln # 402 (32963-5603)
PHONE..................................404 307-1621
Douglas H Lynn Jr, *Mng Member*
Mark Bragg,
Charles Pethel,
EMP: 6 EST: 2014
SQ FT: 16,000
SALES (est): 561.5K **Privately Held**
SIC: **2512** Upholstered household furniture

(G-17759)
HDL THERAPEUTICS INC
601 21st St Ste 300 (32960-0860)
PHONE..................................772 453-2770
Michael M Matin, *CEO*
Michael Sheridan, *Vice Pres*
EMP: 10 EST: 2016
SALES (est): 1MM **Privately Held**
WEB: www.hdltherapeutics.com
SIC: **3841** Medical instruments & equipment, blood & bone work

(G-17760)
HYBRID SOURCES INC
2950 43rd Ave (32960-1914)
PHONE..................................772 563-9100
Richard A Vogel, *CEO*
Arleen N Vogel, *President*
Patricia Amoroso, *Principal*
Richard Barnes, *Engineer*
Richard Vogel, *Info Tech Mgr*
▼ EMP: 18 EST: 1985
SQ FT: 5,000
SALES (est): 3.4MM **Privately Held**
WEB: www.hybridsources.com
SIC: **3674** Integrated circuits, semiconductor networks, etc.

(G-17761)
I WENTWORTH INC
645 Beachland Blvd (32963-1725)
PHONE..................................561 231-7544
A D Teaze, *Principal*
EMP: 7 EST: 2009
SALES (est): 112.4K **Privately Held**
SIC: **2782** Blankbooks & looseleaf binders

(G-17762)
IMPERIAL IMPRINTING LLC
8815 92nd Ct (32967-3543)
PHONE..................................772 633-8256
Tera Adams, *Principal*
EMP: 6 EST: 2016
SALES (est): 402.7K **Privately Held**
WEB: www.imperialimprinting.com
SIC: **2759** Screen printing

(G-17763)
INDIAN RIVER ALL-FAB INC
1119 18th Pl (32960-3649)
PHONE..................................772 778-0032
John R Cooper, *President*
EMP: 7 EST: 1987
SQ FT: 4,500
SALES (est): 998.5K **Privately Held**
SIC: **3599** Machine shop, jobbing & repair

(G-17764)
INEOS NEW PLANET BIOENERGY LLC
925 74th Ave Sw (32968-9755)
PHONE..................................772 794-7900
Peter Williams, *CEO*
David King, *President*
Mark Niederschulte, *COO*
Martin Olavesen, *CFO*
Annie Collins, *Persnl Dir*
▲ EMP: 24 EST: 2009
SALES (est): 3.4MM
SALES (corp-wide): 782.2K **Privately Held**
SIC: **2821** Plastics materials & resins
HQ: Jupeng Bio Sa
　C/O Fabien Gillioz, Avocat, etude
　Ochsner & Associes
　GenCve GE 1204
　216 241-721

(G-17765)
INQUIRER NEWSPAPERS INC
2046 Treasure Coast Plz (32960-0927)
PHONE..................................772 257-6230
John Patrick, *Director*
EMP: 22 EST: 2011
SALES (est): 511.9K **Privately Held**
SIC: **2711** Newspapers, publishing & printing

(G-17766)
IOMARTCLOUD INC
601 21st St (32960-0801)
PHONE..................................954 880-1680
Angus Macsween, *CEO*
Richard Logan, *CFO*
William Strain, *CTO*
EMP: 7 EST: 2013
SQ FT: 3,000
SALES (est): 1.6MM
SALES (corp-wide): 140.2MM **Privately Held**
SIC: **7372** Business oriented computer software
PA: Iomart Group Plc
　Lister Pavilion
　Glasgow G20 0
　141 931-6400

(G-17767)
IRONSIDE PRESS
1001 20th Pl (32960-5359)
P.O. Box 2196 (32961-2196)
PHONE..................................772 569-8484
Olske Forbes, *Principal*
Laurel Arendell, *Manager*
Melissa Legg, *Executive Asst*
EMP: 5 EST: 1987
SALES (est): 1MM **Privately Held**
WEB: www.ironsidepress.net
SIC: **2752** Commercial printing, offset

(G-17768)
JIM BAIRD CABINETS
1020 11th Pl Ste 1 (32960-2139)
PHONE..................................772 569-0936
Jim Baird, *President*
EMP: 5 EST: 1984
SALES (est): 485.8K **Privately Held**
WEB: www.jimbairdcabinets.com
SIC: **2434** Vanities, bathroom: wood

(G-17769)
JOHANNSEN BOAT WORKS INC
690 4th Pl Ste D (32962-1671)
P.O. Box 2311 (32961-2311)
PHONE..................................772 567-4612
Mark Johannsen, *President*
Suzanne Johannsen, *Vice Pres*
▼ EMP: 5 EST: 1978
SALES (est): 431.6K **Privately Held**
WEB: www.trinka.com
SIC: **3732** Boats, fiberglass: building & repairing

(G-17770)
KAMCO INDUSTRIES LLC
5720 Us Highway 1 (32967-7531)
PHONE..................................772 299-1401
Keith A Moskowitz, *Manager*
EMP: 9 EST: 2016
SALES (est): 130K **Privately Held**
SIC: **3999** Manufacturing industries

(G-17771)
KREATECK INTERNATIONAL CORP
1707 20th St (32960-3567)
PHONE..................................772 925-1216
Rocio Coronado, *President*
Brenda Coronado, *Vice Pres*
Luis Coronado, *Vice Pres*
Sergio Coronado, *Vice Pres*
EMP: 7 EST: 2004
SALES (est): 382.5K **Privately Held**
WEB: www.kreateck.com
SIC: **7372** 7373 8731 Prepackaged software; computer integrated systems design; computer (hardware) development

(G-17772)
LEMNATURE AQUAFARMS USA INC
455 146th Ave (32968-9680)
PHONE..................................772 207-4794
Frank Jimenez, *CEO*
Anne-Marie Parker, *Business Mgr*
Wayde Douglas, *Maint Spvr*
Lucille Forbes, *Purchasing*
Riki Montgomery, *QC Mgr*
EMP: 128 EST: 2013
SALES (est): 3.5MM **Privately Held**
WEB: www.lemnatureusa.com
SIC: **2869** 6794 Industrial organic chemicals; patent buying, licensing, leasing
PA: Parabel Ltd
　Near Royal Orchid Sheikh Zayed Road
　Abu Dhabi

(G-17773)
LINDEN-BEALS CORP
Also Called: ABC Printing Company
1547 20th St (32960-3563)
PHONE..................................772 562-0624
Frederick J Linden, *President*
Chris Beals, *Principal*
Harriet Linden, *Treasurer*
Sally L Beals, *Admin Sec*
EMP: 8 EST: 1975
SQ FT: 2,300
SALES (est): 972.9K **Privately Held**
WEB: www.abcprintingirc.com
SIC: **2752** 7334 2791 2789 Commercial printing, offset; photocopying & duplicating services; typesetting; bookbinding & related work

(G-17774)
LINENMASTER LLC
601 21st St Ste 300 (32960-0860)
PHONE..................................772 212-2710
James Adler,
EMP: 20 EST: 2019
SALES (est): 1.1MM **Privately Held**
WEB: www.linenmaster.com
SIC: **7372** Prepackaged software

(G-17775)
LITTERBIN LLC
669 2nd Ln (32962-2951)
PHONE..................................772 633-7184
Michael W Rogers, *Administration*
EMP: 8 EST: 2016
SALES (est): 313.9K **Privately Held**
WEB: www.litterbin.net
SIC: **2673** Trash bags (plastic film): made from purchased materials

(G-17776)
MAXRODON MARBLE INC
2250 Old Dixie Hwy Se (32962-7407)
P.O. Box 881 (32961-0881)
PHONE..................................772 562-7543
Ralph P Hamilton, *President*
Kathy Hamilton, *Treasurer*
EMP: 6 EST: 1974
SALES (est): 300K **Privately Held**
SIC: **3272** Art marble, concrete; window sills, cast stone

(G-17777)
MELANIE R BUSH PAVERS
8316 106th Ave (32967-3639)
PHONE..............................772 501-7295
Melanie Bush, *Principal*
EMP: 7 **EST:** 2013
SALES (est): 122.3K **Privately Held**
WEB: www.mrbpavers.com
SIC: 2951 Asphalt paving mixtures & blocks

(G-17778)
MORNING STAR PERSONALIZED AP
Also Called: New Wave Designs
621 2nd Ln (32962-2939)
PHONE..............................772 569-8412
Natall Barsalou, *President*
Joseph Brown, *President*
EMP: 8 **EST:** 1983
SQ FT: 6,000
SALES (est): 500K **Privately Held**
WEB: www.morningstarshirts.com
SIC: 2759 Screen printing

(G-17779)
MOULTON PUBLICATIONS INC
Also Called: Vero Beach Magazine
956 20th St Ste 101 (32960-6423)
PHONE..............................772 234-8871
Beth Moulton, *President*
Susan Haller, *Accounts Exec*
Jennifer Croom, *Manager*
Lisa Diggins, *CIO*
Renee Brady, *Art Dir*
EMP: 9 **EST:** 1996
SALES (est): 1.3MM **Privately Held**
SIC: 2721 Magazines: publishing only, not printed on site

(G-17780)
NATIONAL AEROSPACE GROUP INC
928 36th Ct Sw (32968-4963)
P.O. Box 690575 (32969-0575)
PHONE..............................817 226-0315
Sujan Ghimire, *President*
EMP: 9 **EST:** 2017
SALES (est): 533K **Privately Held**
WEB: www.nationalaerogroup.com
SIC: 3728 Aircraft parts & equipment

(G-17781)
NOVURANIA OF AMERICA INC
2105 S Us Highway 1 (32962-7402)
PHONE..............................772 567-9200
Robert Collada, *President*
Carlo Cozzio, *COO*
Flavia Pellegrini, *Exec VP*
Sylvia Collada, *Treasurer*
Barbara Mixson, *Manager*
◆ **EMP:** 73 **EST:** 1990
SALES (est): 13.8MM
SALES (corp-wide): 16.9MM **Privately Held**
WEB: www.novurania.com
SIC: 3732 Boat building & repairing
PA: Novurania Spa
Via Circonvallazione 3
Tione Di Trento TN 38079
046 532-1551

(G-17782)
NURSERYMENS SURE-GRO CORP
4390 Us Highway 1 (32967-1507)
PHONE..............................772 770-0462
Lawrence R Walker, *President*
EMP: 7 **EST:** 1974
SQ FT: 6,000
SALES (est): 908K **Privately Held**
WEB: www.suregro.net
SIC: 2873 2874 Nitrogenous fertilizers; phosphatic fertilizers

(G-17783)
NYLACARB CORP
1725 98th Ave (32966-3032)
PHONE..............................772 569-5999
Scott Cooley, *President*
Daug Cooley, *Vice Pres*
Frank Cooley Jr, *Vice Pres*
EMP: 25 **EST:** 1987
SQ FT: 27,000

SALES (est): 6.6MM **Privately Held**
WEB: www.nylacarb.com
SIC: 3089 Injection molding of plastics

(G-17784)
PAVER TECHNOLOGIES LLC
2110 Captains Walk (32963-2821)
PHONE..............................772 213-8905
Tim Berry, *Principal*
Timothy Berry,
Paulo Alberto,
Rick Berry,
Brian Dahl,
EMP: 7 **EST:** 2016
SALES (est): 369.1K **Privately Held**
WEB: www.pavertech.com
SIC: 2951 5032 Paving blocks; paving mixtures; paving materials; paving mixtures

(G-17785)
PCP TACTICAL LLC
3895 39th Sq (32960-1812)
P.O. Box 643401 (32964-3401)
PHONE..............................772 473-3472
Thomas L Corr, *Manager*
Charles A Padgett,
EMP: 6 **EST:** 2010
SALES (est): 1MM **Privately Held**
SIC: 3482 Small arms ammunition

(G-17786)
PIPER AIRCRAFT INC (PA)
2926 Piper Dr (32960-1964)
PHONE..............................772 567-4361
Simon Caldecott, *CEO*
Timothy Gazzola, *Project Mgr*
Somkit Carter, *Mfg Spvr*
Piper Gilbert, *Production*
Becky Matthews, *Production*
EMP: 824 **EST:** 1937
SQ FT: 1,000,000
SALES (est): 228.8MM **Privately Held**
WEB: www.piper.com
SIC: 3721 3728 Airplanes, fixed or rotary wing; aircraft parts & equipment

(G-17787)
PLANT FOODS INC
5051 41st St (32967-1901)
P.O. Box 1089 (32961-1089)
PHONE..............................772 567-5741
Robert Geary III, *President*
Edward J Geary, *Exec VP*
Mj Connelly, *Treasurer*
David Geary, *Admin Sec*
▼ **EMP:** 28 **EST:** 1985
SQ FT: 7,500
SALES (est): 10.8MM **Privately Held**
WEB: www.plantfoodsinc.com
SIC: 2875 2653 Fertilizers, mixing only; boxes, corrugated: made from purchased materials

(G-17788)
PRECISION CERAMIC & STONE LLC
810 33rd Ct Sw (32968-8807)
P.O. Box 356 (32961-0356)
Grant Cooper, *Principal*
EMP: 8 **EST:** 2013
SALES (est): 280.1K **Privately Held**
SIC: 3269 Mfg Pottery Products

(G-17789)
PUSHER INTAKES INC
9100 16th Pl (32966-7568)
PHONE..............................772 212-9290
Elizabeth Allenbaugh, *Mng Member*
EMP: 14 **EST:** 2008
SALES (est): 1.3MM **Privately Held**
WEB: www.pusherintakes.com
SIC: 3714 Motor vehicle parts & accessories

(G-17790)
QOL MEDICAL LLC (PA)
3405 Ocean Dr (32963-1620)
PHONE..............................772 584-3640
Frederick Cooper, *CEO*
William Dupere, *COO*
Kevin Rooney, *Exec VP*
Jackson Tubbs, *Production*
Alexander Behani, *Engineer*
EMP: 2 **EST:** 2005

SALES (est): 5.3MM **Privately Held**
WEB: www.qolmed.com
SIC: 2834 Pills, pharmaceutical

(G-17791)
QUIK TEK INC
2046 Treasure Coast Plz (32960-0927)
PHONE..............................772 501-3471
Don Biscoe, *Principal*
EMP: 7 **EST:** 2016
SALES (est): 92.3K **Privately Held**
WEB: www.quiktekmachining.com
SIC: 3599 Machine shop, jobbing & repair

(G-17792)
R & L MANUFACTURING INC
5021 41st St Unit 2 (32967-1965)
PHONE..............................772 770-9300
EMP: 10
SQ FT: 8,000
SALES (est): 1.5MM **Privately Held**
SIC: 3565 Mfg Packaging Machinery

(G-17793)
RIGHT TO BEAR ARMS LLC
1225 S Us Highway 1 (32962-6450)
PHONE..............................772 794-1188
Chris Clarke, *Owner*
EMP: 5 **EST:** 2018
SALES (est): 317.1K **Privately Held**
WEB: www.howdydesignco.com
SIC: 3484 Small arms

(G-17794)
ROBOMOW USA INC
9050 16th Pl Ste 1 (32966-7583)
P.O. Box 1329, Roseland (32957-1329)
PHONE..............................844 762-6669
Udi Peless, *CEO*
Karsten Beck, *COO*
EMP: 5 **EST:** 2013
SQ FT: 1,000
SALES (est): 570K **Privately Held**
WEB: www.robomow.com
SIC: 3524 Grass catchers, lawn mower

(G-17795)
ROURKE EDUCATIONAL MEDIA LLC
2145 14th Ave Ste 2 (32960-4409)
P.O. Box 820 (32961-0820)
PHONE..............................772 234-6001
James Colandrea, *President*
Keli Sipperley, *Editor*
Craig Lopetz, *Vice Pres*
Deborah Watson, *Manager*
Rhea Magaro, *Art Dir*
▲ **EMP:** 16 **EST:** 2000
SALES (est): 2.1MM **Privately Held**
WEB: www.rourkeeducationalmedia.com
SIC: 2731 Books: publishing only

(G-17796)
ROURKE RAY PUBLISHING CO INC
Also Called: Rourke Publishing Group
1701 Highway A1a Ste 300 (32963-2263)
PHONE..............................772 234-6001
James Colandrea, *President*
Steve Oehler, *Administration*
EMP: 9 **EST:** 1980
SQ FT: 1,500
SALES (est): 670K **Privately Held**
SIC: 2731 Book clubs: publishing only, not printed on site

(G-17797)
SEBASTIAN SEA PRODUCTS IN
1800 Us Highway 1 (32960-0903)
PHONE..............................772 321-3997
Joseph Fenyak, *Principal*
EMP: 7 **EST:** 2006
SALES (est): 86.1K **Privately Held**
SIC: 3999 Manufacturing industries

(G-17798)
SEE-RAY PLUMBING INC
2020 Old Dixie Hwy Se (32962-7256)
PHONE..............................772 489-2474
Raymond F Causley, *President*
Raymond Causley, *President*
AMI-Jo Causley, *Vice Pres*
EMP: 26 **EST:** 2006

SALES (est): 4.9MM **Privately Held**
WEB: www.seerayplumbing.com
SIC: 3088 2842 Bathroom fixtures, plastic; drain pipe solvents or cleaners

(G-17799)
SHAVER PROPERTIES INC
Also Called: Shaver Millwork
6010 Old Dixie Hwy Ste K (32967-7539)
PHONE..............................772 569-3466
Robert A Shaver, *President*
Jason A Shaver, *Corp Secy*
Mark A Shaver, *Vice Pres*
▼ **EMP:** 30 **EST:** 1980
SQ FT: 26,000
SALES (est): 1.4MM **Privately Held**
WEB: www.shavermillwork.com
SIC: 2431 Doors, wood; blinds (shutters), wood

(G-17800)
SNOWS CUSTOM FURNITURE INC
4009 Us Highway 1 (32960-1552)
PHONE..............................772 794-4430
Steven C Long, *President*
EMP: 6 **EST:** 2005
SALES (est): 594.1K **Privately Held**
WEB: www.snowcabinetry.com
SIC: 2434 Wood kitchen cabinets

(G-17801)
SPEECH BIN
1965 25th Ave (32960-3062)
PHONE..............................772 770-0006
Joseph M Binney, *CEO*
Jan Binney, *President*
EMP: 10 **EST:** 1984
SQ FT: 5,000
SALES (est): 989.8K **Privately Held**
SIC: 2731 Books: publishing & printing

(G-17802)
SPINNAKER VERO INC
Also Called: Minuteman Press
983 12th St Ste A (32960-6726)
PHONE..............................772 567-4645
Steven Brunk, *President*
Carlene M Brunk, *Corp Secy*
Christina Cassell, *Cust Mgr*
Geoff Krysl, *Manager*
EMP: 10 **EST:** 2007
SQ FT: 15,000
SALES (est): 2MM **Privately Held**
WEB: www.minutemanpress.com
SIC: 2752 Commercial printing, lithographic

(G-17803)
STEPHS WOODWORKING LLC
6065 21st St Sw (32968-9427)
PHONE..............................772 571-2661
Elena Bouyssou, *Principal*
EMP: 7 **EST:** 2014
SALES (est): 140.4K **Privately Held**
SIC: 2431 Millwork

(G-17804)
SUPPLY CHAIN TECHNOLOGIES LLC
Also Called: Sct Software
601 21st St Ste 300 (32960-0860)
P.O. Box 644381 (32964-4381)
PHONE..............................732 282-1000
David Henig, *CEO*
Rahul Agarwal, *President*
EMP: 12 **EST:** 2006
SALES (est): 1.2MM **Privately Held**
WEB: www.sctsoftware.com
SIC: 7372 Business oriented computer software

(G-17805)
SWEET CREATIONS BY L S YOUNG
953 Old Dixie Hwy Ste B11 (32960-4373)
PHONE..............................772 584-7206
Lori Young, *Principal*
EMP: 8 **EST:** 2011
SALES (est): 425.7K **Privately Held**
WEB: www.sweetcreationsverobeach.com
SIC: 2051 Bakery: wholesale or wholesale/retail combined

(G-17806)
THEFT PROTECTION COM CORP
Also Called: Compuclamp
656 Broadway St (32960-5116)
PHONE..................................772 231-6677
Lawrence P Westfield, *President*
EMP: 10 EST: 1994
SALES (est): 740.4K Privately Held
SIC: 3699 Security devices

(G-17807)
TIE COLLECTION LLC
8071 Westfield Cir (32966-5146)
PHONE..................................305 323-1420
Dainelys Torres, *Mng Member*
EMP: 7 EST: 2014
SALES (est): 455.2K Privately Held
SIC: 2241 5611 Tie tapes, woven or braided; tie shops

(G-17808)
TONY WILLIAM SITKO
Also Called: Latitude 27 Canvas
2306 7th Ave (32960-5166)
PHONE..................................772 321-6361
Tony W Sitko, *Principal*
EMP: 8 EST: 2007
SALES (est): 129.2K Privately Held
WEB: latitude-27-canvas.business.site
SIC: 2211 Canvas

(G-17809)
TOX MANUFACTURING GROUP LLC
2145 Sanford Ct (32963-2808)
PHONE..................................310 909-4937
EMP: 11 EST: 2014
SALES (est): 600.1K Privately Held
SIC: 2252 Socks

(G-17810)
UNIQUE MARBLE INC
780 8th Ct (32962-1647)
PHONE..................................772 766-4432
Fred Chavis, *President*
Manuel Dimech, *Vice Pres*
EMP: 10 EST: 1981
SQ FT: 13,750
SALES (est): 637.7K Privately Held
WEB: www.bridgesbyclassen.com
SIC: 3281 5211 Cut stone & stone products; bathroom fixtures, equipment & supplies

(G-17811)
UNITED JICE COMPANIES AMER INC
Also Called: Juiceco
505 66th Ave Sw (32968-9371)
PHONE..................................772 562-5442
Steve Bogen, *CEO*
Marc Craen, *COO*
Colton Greg, *Plant Mgr*
Brenda Motley, *Controller*
Jennifer Pappadouplos, *Human Res Mgr*
◆ EMP: 60 EST: 2002
SQ FT: 2,000
SALES (est): 14.9MM Privately Held
WEB: www.perriconefarms.com
SIC: 2033 Fruit juices: packaged in cans, jars, etc.

(G-17812)
UNIVERSAL WOOD DESIGN
1708 Old Dixie Hwy # 102 (32960-0440)
PHONE..................................772 569-5389
Arthur Noriega, *President*
EMP: 10 EST: 1981
SQ FT: 8,000
SALES (est): 651.9K Privately Held
WEB: www.universalwooddesign.com
SIC: 2434 2431 Wood kitchen cabinets; millwork

(G-17813)
US SUBMARINES INC (PA)
9015 17th Pl (32966-6601)
PHONE..................................208 687-9057
L Bruce Jones, *President*
Ellis C Adams, *Vice Pres*
Craig Barnett, *Marketing Staff*
EMP: 15 EST: 1993
SQ FT: 15,000

SALES (est): 1.6MM Privately Held
WEB: www.tritonsubs.com
SIC: 3731 Submarines, building & repairing

(G-17814)
VERO BEACH PRINTING INC
3280 Quay Dock Rd (32967-5955)
P.O. Box 1059 (32961-1059)
PHONE..................................772 562-4267
Alvin Walker, *President*
EMP: 6 EST: 1952
SQ FT: 3,200
SALES (est): 446.3K Privately Held
WEB: www.verobeach.com
SIC: 2752 Commercial printing, offset

(G-17815)
VERO NEWS
1240 Olde Doubloon Dr (32963-2453)
PHONE..................................772 234-5727
Milton Benjamin, *Principal*
EMP: 9 EST: 2001
SALES (est): 93.8K Privately Held
WEB: www.veronews.com
SIC: 2711 Newspapers, publishing & printing

(G-17816)
VUTEC CORPORATION
Also Called: Wiremaid Products Division
4420 Old Dixie Hwy (32967-1372)
PHONE..................................954 545-9000
Howard Sinkoff, *President*
Allan Axman, *Vice Pres*
Kevin R Baisely, *Vice Pres*
Kevin Baisley, *Vice Pres*
Raul Passalacqua, *Vice Pres*
◆ EMP: 125 EST: 1950
SALES (est): 22.1MM Privately Held
WEB: www.vutec.com
SIC: 3861 3496 Screens, projection; miscellaneous fabricated wire products

(G-17817)
WESTROM SOFTWARE
903 7th Ave (32960-5991)
PHONE..................................866 480-1879
Bill Westrom, *CEO*
Richard Moore, *Technical Staff*
EMP: 9 EST: 2011
SALES (est): 306.3K Privately Held
WEB: www.westromsoftware.com
SIC: 7372 Application computer software

(G-17818)
WHIGHAM CITRUS PACKING HOUSE
Also Called: Whigham Citrus Pkg Hse McHy
10525 State Road 60 (32966-3210)
P.O. Box 690185 (32969-0185)
PHONE..................................772 569-7190
Daniel Whigham, *President*
EMP: 5 EST: 1960
SQ FT: 20,000
SALES (est): 415.1K Privately Held
SIC: 3556 Packing house machinery

(G-17819)
WHITE ROSE INSTALLATION
1266 14th Ave Sw (32962-5323)
PHONE..................................772 562-6698
Laurie Rose, *President*
EMP: 10 EST: 2004
SALES (est): 700K Privately Held
SIC: 3444 Sheet metalwork

Virginia Gardens
Miami-Dade County

(G-17820)
CITY PUBLICATIONS SOUTH FL
6501 Nw 36th St Ste 300 (33166-6963)
PHONE..................................305 495-3311
Rob Doughty, *Principal*
EMP: 7 EST: 2016
SALES (est): 141.9K Privately Held
WEB: www.citypubnationwide.com
SIC: 2741 Miscellaneous publishing

(G-17821)
DARMIVEN INC
6355 Nw 36th St Ste 506 (33166-7058)
PHONE..................................305 871-1157
Mariangel Caicoya, *President*
Carlos E Obregon, *President*
Felipe J Gonzalez, *Treasurer*
▼ EMP: 7 EST: 1994
SALES (est): 1.4MM Privately Held
WEB: degouveia-web.sharepoint.com
SIC: 2731 8742 Book publishing; management consulting services
PA: Continental Publishing Company Inc
C/O Arias Fabrega & Fabrega
Panama City

(G-17822)
DISTRIBUIDORA CONTINENTAL SA
Also Called: Overseas Publishing Management
6355 Nw 36th St Ste 506 (33166-7058)
PHONE..................................305 374-4474
EMP: 10 Privately Held
SIC: 2711 2721 Newspapers; magazines: publishing only, not printed on site
PA: Distribuidora Continental S.A.
Final Av. San Martin,
Caracas D.F.

(G-17823)
E T PLASTERING INC
3831 Nw 58th Ct (33166-5728)
PHONE..................................305 874-7082
Emilio Trenzado, *President*
Anna C Trenzado, *Admin Sec*
▼ EMP: 10 EST: 1983
SALES (est): 910.1K Privately Held
SIC: 3541 3299 1742 Lathes; stucco; plastering, drywall & insulation

(G-17824)
ET PUBLISHING INTERNATIONAL (PA)
Also Called: Editorial Televisa Publishing
6355 Nw 36th St (33166-7009)
PHONE..................................305 871-6400
Rodrigo Edwards, *President*
Rodrigo S Sepulveda Edwards Mc, *President*
Marcia Morgado, *Editor*
Jorge Lutteroth Echegoyen Mv, *Vice Pres*
Jose Antonio Garcia Gonzalez M, *Vice Pres*
◆ EMP: 80 EST: 1963
SQ FT: 150,000
SALES (est): 19.7MM Privately Held
WEB: www.televisapublishing.com
SIC: 2721 Magazines: publishing only, not printed on site

Wauchula
Hardee County

(G-17825)
DEBUT DEVELOPMENT LLC
897 S 6th Ave Ste 1 (33873-3309)
PHONE..................................863 448-9081
Kristin Giuliani, *Mng Member*
Vanessa Thomas, *Mng Member*
Kristin A Giuliani,
EMP: 20 EST: 2015
SQ FT: 4,000
SALES (est): 1.6MM Privately Held
WEB: www.debutdevelopmentllc.com
SIC: 3842 3999 Cosmetic restorations; atomizers, toiletry

(G-17826)
EZPRODUCTS INTERNATIONAL INC
612 N Florida Ave (33873-3041)
P.O. Box 1289 (33873-1289)
PHONE..................................863 735-0813
David H Brown, *Principal*
Diane Rue, *Vice Pres*
EMP: 7 EST: 2004
SQ FT: 2,800
SALES (est): 1MM Privately Held
WEB: www.ezpi.us
SIC: 3471 Cleaning, polishing & finishing

(G-17827)
FRANZ A ULLRICH JR
Also Called: Ullrich's
514 N Florida Ave (33873-2110)
PHONE..................................863 773-4653
Franz A Ullrich Jr, *Owner*
EMP: 6 EST: 1938
SALES (est): 319.2K Privately Held
WEB: www.hiflowpumpandmachine.com
SIC: 7692 3523 Welding repair; farm machinery & equipment

(G-17828)
HERALD-ADVOCATE PUBLISHING CO
115 S 7th Ave (33873-2801)
P.O. Box 338 (33873-0338)
PHONE..................................863 773-3255
James R Kelly, *President*
Jean Kelly, *Vice Pres*
Mildred Kelly, *Director*
EMP: 9 EST: 1941
SQ FT: 4,500
SALES (est): 853.5K Privately Held
WEB: www.theheraldadvocate.com
SIC: 2711 2752 2761 2759 Commercial printing & newspaper publishing combined; commercial printing, offset; manifold business forms; commercial printing

(G-17829)
JLT CUSTOM WORKS INC
2239 Greenleaf Rd (33873-8200)
PHONE..................................863 245-3371
Jose Torres, *President*
Darlene Torres, *Admin Sec*
EMP: 40 EST: 2012
SALES (est): 1.5MM Privately Held
WEB: www.jltcustomworks.com
SIC: 1459 0781 Brucite mining; landscape services

(G-17830)
UTILITECH INC
130 W Main St (33873-2820)
P.O. Box 536 (33873-0536)
PHONE..................................863 767-0600
Brent Stephens, *President*
Matthew Thompson, *Vice Pres*
EMP: 11 EST: 2014
SALES (est): 1MM Privately Held
WEB: www.utili-tech.net
SIC: 7372 7371 8243 Application computer software; business oriented computer software; utility computer software; computer software systems analysis & design, custom; software training, computer

Wausau
Washington County

(G-17831)
BERNICE I FINCH
Also Called: B Finch Logging
1867 6th Ave (32463)
P.O. Box 123 (32463-0123)
PHONE..................................850 638-0082
Bernice I Finch, *Owner*
Geraldine Finch, *Co-Owner*
EMP: 6 EST: 1958
SALES (est): 362K Privately Held
SIC: 2411 Logging

Webster
Sumter County

(G-17832)
BOYETT TIMBER INC
45260 Lcchee Clay Sink Rd (33597)
PHONE..................................352 583-2138
Tim Boyett, *President*
EMP: 8 EST: 1990
SQ FT: 600
SALES (est): 1.3MM Privately Held
WEB: www.boyetttimbermulch.com
SIC: 2421 2426 2499 Lumber: rough, sawed or planed; lumber, hardwood dimension; mauls, wood

(G-17833)
ROBBINS MANUFACTUING CO
12904 Sr 471 (33597-5114)
P.O. Box 295 (33597-0295)
PHONE..................352 793-2443
EMP: 70
SALES (est): 437.7K Privately Held
SIC: 2421 Sawmill/Planing Mill

Weeki Wachee
Hernando County

(G-17834)
A 1 FABRICATIONS INC
12440 Charlton Dr (34614-1914)
PHONE..................352 410-0752
Beverly Earle, Principal
EMP: 7 EST: 2011
SALES (est): 87.5K Privately Held
SIC: 3089 Injection molding of plastics

(G-17835)
CARDBOARD ONLY INC
11080 Wdlnd Waters Blvd (34613)
PHONE..................352 345-5060
William P Drinkwater, Principal
EMP: 7 EST: 2008
SALES (est): 69.1K Privately Held
SIC: 2631 Cardboard

(G-17836)
ECLIPSE EHR SOLUTIONS LLC
11242 Commercial Way (34614-3063)
PHONE..................352 488-0081
Michael Norworth, Manager
EMP: 14 EST: 2018
SQ FT: 2,520
SALES (est): 828.7K Privately Held
WEB: www.eclipsepracticemanage-
mentsoftware.com
SIC: 7372 Business oriented computer
software

(G-17837)
FLORIDA NORTH INC
10294 Maybird Ave (34613-3610)
PHONE..................352 606-2408
Sara Nelson, Principal
EMP: 7
SALES (corp-wide): 1.6MM Privately
Held
WEB: www.floridanorth.com
SIC: 3949 Swimming pools, plastic
PA: Florida North, Inc.
134 Vanderwerken Rd
Sloansville NY 12160
518 868-2888

(G-17838)
MICROTEX ELECTRONICS INC
13191 Kingfisher Rd (34614-2106)
P.O. Box 950372, Lake Mary (32795-0372)
PHONE..................386 426-1922
John E Knight, President
John Knight, President
Elaine Knight, Vice Pres
EMP: 5 EST: 1994
SALES (est): 316K Privately Held
WEB: www.microtex.net
SIC: 3545 Micrometers

Weirsdale
Marion County

(G-17839)
FINE WOODWORKS
15145 Se 175th St (32195-3120)
PHONE..................954 448-9206
Robert Ives, Principal
EMP: 7 EST: 2010
SALES (est): 85.3K Privately Held
SIC: 2431 Millwork

Welaka
Putnam County

(G-17840)
LAKEVIEW DIRT CO INC
Also Called: Ldc
105 Beechers Point Dr (32193-3426)
PHONE..................904 824-2586
Greg A Wilson, President
Gary Wilson, Vice Pres
EMP: 20 EST: 1985
SALES (est): 2.3MM Privately Held
WEB: www.lakeviewdirt.com
SIC: 1422 1794 Crushed & broken lime-
stone; excavation & grading, building con-
struction

Wellington
Palm Beach County

(G-17841)
5 STAR BUILDERS INC
Also Called: Five Star Builders W Palm Bch
3180 Frlane Frms Rd Ste 2 (33414)
PHONE..................561 795-1282
Art Beyer, President
James T Williamson, Vice Pres
EMP: 5 EST: 1996
SALES (est): 1MM Privately Held
SIC: 3523 Barn stanchions & standards

(G-17842)
ADVANCED THERMAL TECH INC
(DH)
Also Called: Be Aerospace
1400 Corporate Center Way (33414-2158)
PHONE..................561 791-5000
Amin J Khoury, Ch of Bd
Olivia Bowers, General Mgr
Gerardo Portillo, Project Mgr
Christopher Yarber, Project Mgr
James Merkley, Mfg Mgr
▲ EMP: 29 EST: 1997
SQ FT: 20,000
SALES (est): 19.2MM
SALES (corp-wide): 64.3B Publicly Held
WEB: www.beaerospace.com
SIC: 3728 Aircraft parts & equipment
HQ: B/E Aerospace, Inc.
1400 Corporate Center Way
Wellington FL 33414
410 266-2048

(G-17843)
ARYA GROUP LLC
11858 Forest Hill Blvd (33414-6291)
PHONE..................561 792-9992
EMP: 8 EST: 2017
SALES (est): 890.1K Privately Held
SIC: 3431 Metal sanitary ware

(G-17844)
B/E AEROSPACE INC (DH)
Also Called: Rockwell Collins
1400 Corporate Center Way (33414-2158)
PHONE..................410 266-2048
Stephen Timm, CEO
Edward Gager, President
William Godecker, President
Terry Coutee, Chief
Jon Buff, Business Mgr
▲ EMP: 30 EST: 1987
SQ FT: 31,300
SALES (est): 1.6B
SALES (corp-wide): 64.3B Publicly Held
WEB: www.beaerospace.com
SIC: 2531 3728 3647 Seats, aircraft; air-
craft parts & equipment; aircraft lighting
fixtures

(G-17845)
BLUE HORSESHOE RES GROUP
LLC
9348 Via Elegante (33411-6556)
PHONE..................561 429-2030
Mark Cohen, Principal
EMP: 7 EST: 2014
SALES (est): 253.1K Privately Held
WEB: search.sunbiz.org
SIC: 3462 Horseshoes

(G-17846)
CAPTAIN ZOOM PRODUCTS INC
10653 Stable Ln Apt 204 (33414-4460)
PHONE..................561 989-9119
Robert Stiller, President
Cynthia S Stiller, Admin Sec
EMP: 7 EST: 2004
SALES (est): 405.1K Privately Held
WEB: www.captainzoom.com
SIC: 3652 Compact laser discs, prere-
corded

(G-17847)
CASABLANCA POLO CO
3500 Frlane Frms Rd Ste 5 (33414)
PHONE..................832 668-6804
Stephen L Alexander, President
Alejandro V Temperley, Vice Pres
EMP: 8 EST: 2002
SALES (est): 87.9K Privately Held
WEB: www.casablancapolo.com
SIC: 2353 Helmets, jungle cloth: wool lined

(G-17848)
CHILI PRODUKT KFT
9850 Scribner Ln (33414-6486)
PHONE..................954 655-4111
Zsolt Bucko, CEO
EMP: 40 EST: 2020
SALES (est): 1.2MM Privately Held
WEB: www.spice-paprika.com
SIC: 2099 Spices, including grinding

(G-17849)
CLASSIC INDUSTRIES INC
3111 Fortune Way (33414-8712)
PHONE..................561 855-4609
Jessica Brown, President
EMP: 9 EST: 2015
SALES (est): 301.6K Privately Held
WEB: www.classicindustries.com
SIC: 3999 Manufacturing industries

(G-17850)
EXCES INTERNATIONAL LLC
3460 Frlane Frms Rd Ste 1 (33414)
PHONE..................561 880-8920
EMP: 7 EST: 2019
SALES (est): 653.3K Privately Held
WEB: www.equilineamerica.com
SIC: 2323 Men's & boys' neckwear

(G-17851)
FIRST CLASS LIAISONS LLC
2470 Wellington Green Dr (33414-9321)
PHONE..................954 882-8634
Amieke Reid, CEO
EMP: 7 EST: 2017
SALES (est): 360K Privately Held
SIC: 3441 Railroad car racks, for transport-
ing vehicles: steel

(G-17852)
GONZALEZ AEROSPACE
SERVICES
1035 S State Road 7 # 313 (33414-6134)
PHONE..................561 227-1575
Jose Gonzalez, Principal
EMP: 7 EST: 2016
SALES (est): 110.9K Privately Held
SIC: 3721 Aircraft

(G-17853)
INNOVATE AUDIO VISUAL INC
3460 Frlane Frms Rd Ste 1 (33414)
PHONE..................561 249-1117
Juan Villacirica, President
Amy Fiorillo, CFO
EMP: 7
SALES (est): 566.9K Privately Held
WEB: www.innovate-av.com
SIC: 3861 Photographic equipment & sup-
plies

(G-17854)
LAKE POINT RESTORATION LLC
12012 South Shore Blvd # 10
(33414-6507)
PHONE..................561 924-9100
Bonnie Owen, Controller
Harold D Rusbridge, Mng Member
Danny Pridgen, Administration
Francis J Laird IV,
EMP: 26 EST: 2007

SALES (est): 7.4MM Privately Held
WEB: www.lakepointrestoration.com
SIC: 1422 Crushed & broken limestone

(G-17855)
NEWSPAPER PUBLISHERS INC
Also Called: Town Crier Newspaper
12794 Frest Hl Blvd Ste 3 (33414)
PHONE..................561 793-7606
Phyllis Manning, President
Barry Manning, Publisher
Joshua Manning, Admin Sec
EMP: 20 EST: 1998
SALES (est): 2.2MM Privately Held
WEB: www.gotowncrier.com
SIC: 2711 Newspapers: publishing only,
not printed on site

(G-17856)
NOA INTERNATIONAL INC
Also Called: Rock & Roll
3066 Payson Way (33414-3401)
PHONE..................954 835-5258
Paul J Johansson, President
Paul D Johansson, Vice Pres
EMP: 5 EST: 2010
SALES (est): 341.3K Privately Held
WEB: www.noainternationalinc.com
SIC: 3842 Wheelchairs

(G-17857)
ONTYTE LLC
3460 Fairlane Farms Rd # 15
(33414-8755)
PHONE..................561 880-8920
Paul Yanke,
Ashley Yanke,
▲ EMP: 7 EST: 2009
SALES (est): 250.6K Privately Held
WEB: www.ontyte.com
SIC: 3199 Stirrups, wood or metal

(G-17858)
REAL EXTRACT VENTURES INC
2200 Merriweather Way (33414-6428)
PHONE..................561 371-3532
Sajid Ahmed, President
EMP: 7 EST: 2017
SALES (est): 81.2K Privately Held
SIC: 2836 Extracts

(G-17859)
REKORD SERVICES LLC
11603 Waterbend Ct (33414-8849)
PHONE..................706 401-1791
Rafal Krawczuk, Mng Member
EMP: 18 EST: 2020
SALES (est): 693.3K Privately Held
SIC: 1389 Construction, repair & disman-
tling services

(G-17860)
REV PERSONAL CARE LLC
2905 Payson Way (33414-3409)
PHONE..................832 217-8585
Fabian Maclaren,
David Giuliano,
EMP: 6 EST: 2017
SQ FT: 6,000
SALES (est): 319.6K Privately Held
SIC: 2844 Cosmetic preparations

(G-17861)
SHADE EXPERTS USA LLC
11117 Alameda Bay Ct (33414-8811)
PHONE..................561 422-3200
Jeff Costa, Managing Prtnr
Mariza Costa, Principal
EMP: 7 EST: 2015
SALES (est): 115.6K Privately Held
WEB: www.theshadeexpertsusa.com
SIC: 3999 Manufacturing industries

(G-17862)
SHEAS SALSA LLC
11328 Regatta Ln (33449-7420)
PHONE..................954 371-7781
Shea C Osteen, Manager
EMP: 5 EST: 2017
SALES (est): 378.9K Privately Held
SIC: 2099 Dips, except cheese & sour
cream based

(G-17863)
SHINING TREE INC
2952 Payson Way (33414-3409)
PHONE................................855 688-7987
EMP: 10 EST: 2014
SALES (est): 370K **Privately Held**
SIC: 2041 5149 Flour And Other Grain Mill Products, Nsk

(G-17864)
SIGNCRAFT LLC
3694 Old Lighthouse Cir (33414-8843)
PHONE................................561 543-0034
Linda Prusiecki, *President*
Robin Intoppa, *Vice Pres*
Brian K Waxman,
EMP: 7 EST: 2007
SQ FT: 20,000
SALES (est): 212.1K **Privately Held**
WEB: www.signcraftsm.com
SIC: 3993 Signs & advertising specialties

(G-17865)
SIGNS SUPREME INC
17224 Gulf Pine Cir (33414-6360)
PHONE................................561 795-0111
Valerie Walton, *President*
Douglas Walton, *Vice Pres*
▲ EMP: 7 EST: 1999
SQ FT: 8,000
SALES (est): 176K **Privately Held**
SIC: 3993 Signs & advertising specialties

(G-17866)
SOUTHEAST CARBON WORKS INC
1243 Canyon Way (33414-3143)
PHONE................................561 422-1798
Jorge Ferrin, *Principal*
EMP: 9 EST: 2014
SALES (est): 95.6K **Privately Held**
SIC: 3714 Motor vehicle parts & accessories

(G-17867)
TROIKA GROUP INC
12300 South Shore Blvd # 20 (33414-6509)
PHONE................................561 313-1119
EMP: 5 EST: 2019
SALES (est): 351.9K **Privately Held**
SIC: 3341 Secondary nonferrous metals

(G-17868)
WATTS ONE LLC
13670 Doubletree Trl (33414-4017)
PHONE................................305 606-1816
Jose Blanco, *Manager*
EMP: 12 EST: 2012
SALES (est): 1.1MM **Privately Held**
WEB: www.watts.com
SIC: 3491 Industrial valves

(G-17869)
WHITE HORSE FASHION CUISINE
14440 Pierson Rd (33414-7673)
PHONE................................561 847-4549
EMP: 8 EST: 2014
SALES (est): 114.6K **Privately Held**
WEB: www.olisfashioncuisine.com
SIC: 2299 Textile goods

Wesley Chapel
Pasco County

(G-17870)
BELT MAINTENANCE GROUP INC (PA)
27658 Cashford Cir # 102 (33544-6959)
PHONE................................813 907-9316
Alba Benitez, *President*
Carl Debord, *Vice Pres*
EMP: 6 EST: 2004
SQ FT: 17,000
SALES (est): 2.4MM **Privately Held**
WEB: www.beltmaintenance.com
SIC: 3496 Conveyor belts

(G-17871)
BOOST LAB INC
31050 Chatterly Dr (33543-6811)
PHONE................................813 443-0531
Kirk Riollano, *Principal*
Ryan Hostetler, *Production*
EMP: 10 EST: 2010
SALES (est): 248.2K **Privately Held**
SIC: 3714 Motor vehicle parts & accessories

(G-17872)
COREYCO LLC
6253 Candlewood Dr (33544-5834)
PHONE................................813 469-1203
Tracey Munroe, *Mng Member*
Corey Munroe,
John E Munroe,
EMP: 9 EST: 2008
SALES (est): 1.6MM **Privately Held**
WEB: www.coreyco.net
SIC: 3273 Ready-mixed concrete

(G-17873)
DATAMENTORS LLC (PA)
Also Called: V12 Data
2319 Oak Myrtle Ln # 101 (33544-6329)
PHONE................................813 960-7800
Andrew Frawley, *CEO*
Anders Ekman, *President*
Sasa Zorovic, *COO*
Peg Kuman, *Exec VP*
Michelle Taves, *Exec VP*
EMP: 35 EST: 1999
SQ FT: 5,000
SALES (est): 16MM **Privately Held**
WEB: www.v12data.com
SIC: 7372 Business oriented computer software

(G-17874)
ELEMENTS OF STYLEZ
30040 State Road 54 (33543-4500)
PHONE................................813 575-8416
Daniel Quintana, *Principal*
EMP: 8 EST: 2018
SALES (est): 2.1MM **Privately Held**
WEB: elements-of-stylez-barber-shop.business.site
SIC: 2819 Industrial inorganic chemicals

(G-17875)
FIRST WINDOWS INCORPORATED
27524 Cashford Cir (33544-6947)
PHONE................................813 508-9388
Eric Rodriguez, *Principal*
EMP: 5 EST: 2017
SALES (est): 489.3K **Privately Held**
SIC: 3442 Window & door frames

(G-17876)
FLORIDA STL FRAME TRUSS MFG LL
2312 Cypress Cv Ste 101 (33544-6785)
PHONE................................813 460-0006
Khamir H Patel, *Mng Member*
Hardevbhai D Patel, *Mng Member*
EMP: 9 EST: 2018
SALES (est): 1MM **Privately Held**
WEB: www.fsftm.com
SIC: 3312 Bars & bar shapes, steel, cold-finished: own hot-rolled

(G-17877)
FORCE IMAGING GROUP LLC
Also Called: Thermalroll
1936 Bruce B Downs Blvd (33544-9262)
PHONE................................888 406-2120
Blaise Collura,
EMP: 6 EST: 2012
SALES (est): 739.8K **Privately Held**
WEB: www.forceimaging.com
SIC: 2679 Tags & labels, paper

(G-17878)
GRAPHICS PDTS EXCELLENCE INC
Also Called: Clear Vision Signs and Systems
5335 Emory Dr (33543-4640)
PHONE................................813 884-1578
Joseph Torrence, *Principal*
Deborah Torrence, *CFO*
EMP: 13 EST: 2003

SALES (est): 1MM **Privately Held**
WEB: www.gpxtabs.com
SIC: 3993 Signs & advertising specialties

(G-17879)
ILER GROUP INC
Also Called: Fleetistics
15310 Amberly Dr Ste 250 (33544)
PHONE................................877 467-0326
Eron Iler, *President*
Amy Anderson, *VP Finance*
Amy Anderson Iler, *VP Finance*
Hope Duke, *Bookkeeper*
Brandon Santiago, *Sales Staff*
EMP: 7 EST: 2001
SQ FT: 2,500
SALES (est): 1.6MM **Privately Held**
WEB: www.ilergroup.com
SIC: 3531 5012 Trucks, off-highway; trucks, commercial

(G-17880)
KERICURE INC
Also Called: Tough Seal
26620 Easy St (33544-5711)
PHONE................................855 888-5374
Kerriann Greenhalgh, *CEO*
Kerriann R Greenhalgh, *President*
EMP: 10 EST: 2011
SALES (est): 1MM **Privately Held**
WEB: www.kericure.com
SIC: 3842 Surgical appliances & supplies

(G-17881)
LOCAL BIZ SPOT INC (PA)
Also Called: Bizzspot
26747 Saxony Way (33544-6486)
PHONE................................866 446-1790
Ryan Anderson, *President*
Brad Anderson, *Vice Pres*
EMP: 5 EST: 2008
SALES (est): 407.9K **Privately Held**
WEB: www.bizzspot.com
SIC: 3993 Signs & advertising specialties

(G-17882)
LULULEMON
28211 Paseo Dr Ste 160 (33543-5380)
PHONE................................813 973-3879
EMP: 7 EST: 1998
SALES (est): 42.5K **Privately Held**
SIC: 2389 Apparel & accessories

(G-17883)
NATURES POWER AND ENERGY LLC
30131 Clearview Dr (33545-3010)
PHONE................................813 907-6279
Walter Rooney,
Dave Beruska,
Paul Cooper,
Dorraine Rooney,
EMP: 10 EST: 2012
SALES (est): 523.9K **Privately Held**
WEB: www.naturespowerandenergy.us
SIC: 3699 7389 High-energy particle physics equipment;

(G-17884)
NEBULA LED LIGHTING SYSTEMS OF
28832 Falling Leaves Way (33543-5761)
PHONE................................813 907-0001
Mark J Rosenberg, *Mng Member*
EMP: 5 EST: 2007
SALES (est): 1MM
SALES (corp-wide): 1.1MM **Privately Held**
SIC: 3674 5063 Light emitting diodes; lighting fixtures
PA: M R Enterprises Llc
31314 Heatherstone Dr
Wesley Chapel FL 33543
813 924-0303

(G-17885)
OLIVE TREE II
2653 Bruce B Downs Blvd (33544-9206)
PHONE................................813 991-8781
EMP: 7 EST: 2016
SALES (est): 945.9K **Privately Held**
WEB: www.theolivetreestore.com
SIC: 2079 Olive oil

(G-17886)
PRIMETIME INDUSTRIES LLC
32671 Natural Bridge Rd (33543-7209)
PHONE................................813 781-0196
Joshua Boddiford, *Partner*
EMP: 2 EST: 2018
SALES (est): 3.1MM **Privately Held**
SIC: 3842 5084 Personal safety equipment; safety equipment

(G-17887)
SUN VALLEY TECH SOLUTIONS INC
31437 Heatherstone Dr (33543-6877)
PHONE................................480 463-4101
Joshua Lee, *President*
Jennifer Lee, *CFO*
EMP: 7 EST: 2006
SALES (est): 346.2K **Privately Held**
SIC: 7372 Application computer software

(G-17888)
TRANSPORT PC USA INC
Also Called: Gator Freds
1423 Baythorn Dr (33543-7804)
PHONE................................813 264-1700
Alfredo Medina, *President*
Sandra Perez Medina, *President*
EMP: 8 EST: 2003
SALES (est): 737.7K **Privately Held**
SIC: 3599 Carnival machines & equipment, amusement park

(G-17889)
TROPICAL PAVER SEALING
4834 Windingbrook Trl (33544-7482)
PHONE................................727 786-4011
Amanda Wyandt, *Mng Member*
EMP: 6 EST: 2014
SALES (est): 404.7K **Privately Held**
WEB: www.tropicalpaversealing.com
SIC: 3531 7389 Pavers;

(G-17890)
ULTRASONIC TECHNOLOGIES INC
27247 Breakers Dr (33544-6612)
PHONE................................813 973-1702
Sergei Ostapenko, *CEO*
Charles Causey, *Engineer*
▼ EMP: 8 EST: 1997
SALES (est): 913.2K **Privately Held**
WEB: www.ultrasonictech.com
SIC: 3629 Electronic generation equipment

(G-17891)
WESLEY CHAPEL FUEL INC
27616 Wesley Chapel Blvd (33544-4200)
PHONE................................813 907-9994
Richard Elkhoury, *Principal*
EMP: 12 EST: 2010
SALES (est): 10.5MM **Privately Held**
SIC: 2869 Fuels

West Melbourne
Brevard County

(G-17892)
AMERICAN PRESSURE SYSTEMS INC
7608 Emerald Dr (32904-1166)
PHONE................................321 914-0827
Tad Hoskins, *President*
Ford Hoskins, *Vice Pres*
EMP: 8 EST: 2010
SALES (est): 655.6K **Privately Held**
WEB: www.americanpressuresystems.com
SIC: 3589 High pressure cleaning equipment

(G-17893)
AXIOM MANUFACTURING INC
962 Hailey St (32904-8204)
PHONE................................321 223-3394
Jonah King, *President*
EMP: 7 EST: 2016
SALES (est): 115.3K **Privately Held**
WEB: www.axman.com
SIC: 3999 Manufacturing industries

(G-17894)
BK TECHNOLOGIES INC (HQ)
7100 Technology Dr (32904-1525)
PHONE.....................................321 984-1414
John M Suzuki, *CEO*
E Gray Payne, *Ch of Bd*
Timothy A Vitou, *President*
Henry R Willis, *COO*
Cindy Kippley MBA, *Vice Pres*
▲ EMP: 11 EST: 1947
SQ FT: 54,000
SALES: 49.3MM
SALES (corp-wide): 45.3MM **Publicly Held**
WEB: www.bktechnologies.com
SIC: 3663 Radio broadcasting & communications equipment
PA: Bk Technologies Corporation
7100 Technology Dr
West Melbourne FL 32904
321 984-1414

(G-17895)
BK TECHNOLOGIES CORPORATION (PA)
7100 Technology Dr (32904-1525)
PHONE.....................................321 984-1414
John M Suzuki, *CEO*
D Kyle Cerminara, *Ch of Bd*
Timothy A Vitou, *President*
Henry R Willis, *COO*
Scott Malmanger, *CFO*
EMP: 11 EST: 1947
SQ FT: 54,000
SALES: 45.3MM **Publicly Held**
WEB: www.bktechnologies.com
SIC: 3663 Radio broadcasting & communications equipment

(G-17896)
CEDARS FOOD INC
2110 Dairy Rd Ste 101 (32904-5200)
PHONE.....................................321 724-2624
Eddin Chams, *Principal*
EMP: 11 EST: 2012
SALES (est): 446.2K **Privately Held**
WEB: www.cedarsfoods.com
SIC: 2015 Poultry slaughtering & processing

(G-17897)
COB INDUSTRIES INC
6909 Vickie Cir (32904-2252)
P.O. Box 361175, Melbourne (32936-1175)
PHONE.....................................321 723-3200
Cletus M O'Brien, *President*
Veronica O'Brien, *Vice Pres*
Kurt Brown, *Sales Staff*
▲ EMP: 7 EST: 1965
SQ FT: 11,000
SALES (est): 1.4MM **Privately Held**
WEB: www.cob-industries.com
SIC: 3544 3423 Special dies & tools; mechanics' hand tools

(G-17898)
DOCTOR GRANITE AND CABINETS
3532 Chica Cir (32904-6836)
PHONE.....................................321 368-1779
Ronald J Isaza, *Principal*
EMP: 9 EST: 2015
SALES (est): 378.4K **Privately Held**
SIC: 2434 Wood kitchen cabinets

(G-17899)
ELEMENT MTLS TECH JUPITER LLC
Also Called: Element Melbourne
7780 Technology Dr (32904-1575)
PHONE.....................................321 327-8985
Jo Wetz, *Principal*
Mike Mather, *Principal*
EMP: 12 EST: 2013
SALES (est): 2.4MM
SALES (corp-wide): 782.6MM **Privately Held**
SIC: 2819 Elements
PA: Element Materials Technology Group Limited
3rd Floor
London WC2E
203 540-1820

(G-17900)
GATCHELL VIOLINS COMPANY INC
1377 W New Haven Ave (32904-3901)
PHONE.....................................321 733-1499
Allen Gatchell, *Owner*
▲ EMP: 10 EST: 2003
SALES (est): 986.2K **Privately Held**
WEB: www.gatchellviolins.com
SIC: 3931 Violins & parts; violas & parts

(G-17901)
IMPRESSIVE PAVERS INC
2883 Glasbern Cir (32904-8080)
PHONE.....................................321 508-9991
Kenneth L Goetz Jr, *Principal*
EMP: 8 EST: 2014
SALES (est): 244K **Privately Held**
SIC: 2951 Asphalt paving mixtures & blocks

(G-17902)
UNITED SPACE COAST CABLES INC
7703 Tech Dr Ste 100 (32904)
PHONE.....................................321 952-1040
Bryan Holm, *President*
Denise Shaw, *President*
David Brownell, *Buyer*
Brian Comstock, *Manager*
Andre Bessette, *Director*
EMP: 40 EST: 2011
SALES (est): 6.6MM **Privately Held**
WEB: www.unitedscc.com
SIC: 3699 Electrical equipment & supplies

(G-17903)
ZPACKS CORP
7703 Technology Dr (32904-1573)
PHONE.....................................321 215-5658
Joseph E Valesko, *President*
Will Wood, *Director*
EMP: 16 EST: 2014
SALES (est): 3.2MM **Privately Held**
WEB: www.zpacks.com
SIC: 3172 Personal leather goods

West Miami
Miami-Dade County

(G-17904)
DABY PRODUCTS CARISEN
5757 Sw 8th St (33144-5060)
PHONE.....................................305 559-3018
Daby Sully, *Principal*
EMP: 7 EST: 1997
SALES (est): 125K **Privately Held**
SIC: 2844 Cosmetic preparations

West Palm Beach
Palm Beach County

(G-17905)
5HP INVESTMENTS LLC
Also Called: Minuteman Press
2822 S Dixie Hwy (33405-1543)
PHONE.....................................561 655-5355
Daniel Hernandez,
Raquel Presas,
EMP: 15 EST: 2014
SALES (est): 3.7MM **Privately Held**
WEB: www.minutemanpress.com
SIC: 2752 Commercial printing, lithographic

(G-17906)
5NINE SOFTWARE INC
1555 Palm Bch Lkes Blvd S (33401)
PHONE.....................................561 898-1100
Karen Armor, *CEO*
Morgan Holm, *Vice Pres*
Konstantin Malkov, *CTO*
EMP: 25 EST: 2009
SQ FT: 1,500
SALES (est): 4.9MM
SALES (corp-wide): 196.2MM **Privately Held**
WEB: www.acronis.com
SIC: 7372 Prepackaged software

HQ: Acronis International Gmbh
Eurohaus
Schaffhausen SH
526 302-800

(G-17907)
A GS MICA AND CUSTOM WDWRK LLC
5307 East Ave (33407-2363)
PHONE.....................................561 351-5429
Timothy H Kenney, *Administration*
EMP: 7 EST: 2014
SALES (est): 172.6K **Privately Held**
SIC: 2431 Millwork

(G-17908)
A PALLET CO INC
9750 Galleon Dr (33411-1806)
PHONE.....................................561 798-1564
Rocco Zito, *President*
EMP: 8 EST: 2002
SALES (est): 631.4K **Privately Held**
WEB: www.apallet.net
SIC: 2448 Pallets, wood

(G-17909)
A&M CLEANING SOLUTIONS LLC
4400 N Terrace Dr (33407-3738)
PHONE.....................................786 559-7093
Margo H Mitchell,
EMP: 10 EST: 2020
SALES (est): 438.6K **Privately Held**
SIC: 3589 Commercial cleaning equipment

(G-17910)
A1 BALERS AND COMPATORS LLC
13476 Orange Blvd (33412-2102)
PHONE.....................................561 792-3399
Lizza Serrano, *Mng Member*
EMP: 11 EST: 2006
SALES (est): 1.2MM **Privately Held**
SIC: 3589 Water treatment equipment, industrial

(G-17911)
ACE MARKING DEVICES CORP
Also Called: Ace Rubber Stamp
3308 S Dixie Hwy (33405-1949)
P.O. Box 6425 (33405-6425)
PHONE.....................................561 833-4073
Walter Zajkowski Jr, *President*
Gertrude Zajkowski, *Corp Secy*
David J Zajkowski, *Vice Pres*
EMP: 7 EST: 1940
SQ FT: 1,600
SALES (est): 515.5K **Privately Held**
WEB: www.usacustom.com
SIC: 3953 5943 Embossing seals & hand stamps; office forms & supplies

(G-17912)
ACS OF WEST PALM BEACH INC
1300 N Florida Mango Rd # 14 (33409-5259)
PHONE.....................................561 844-5790
Matthew McClellan, *President*
Sam Cabrera, *General Mgr*
EMP: 8 EST: 2014
SALES (est): 1MM **Privately Held**
SIC: 2674 Vacuum cleaner bags: made from purchased materials

(G-17913)
ACTION MFG & SUP WPB LLC
2711 Vista Pkwy Ste B5 (33411-2732)
PHONE.....................................239 574-3443
Lena Pilgrim, *Vice Pres*
Justin Marshall, *Sales Staff*
EMP: 9 EST: 2013
SALES (est): 598.9K **Privately Held**
WEB: www.actionmfg.com
SIC: 3589 Water treatment equipment, industrial

(G-17914)
ACTION WEEKLY CORP
Also Called: Semenario Accion
3708 Georgia Ave (33405-2125)
PHONE.....................................561 586-8699
Maria Triana, *President*
EMP: 5 EST: 1997

SALES (est): 437.2K **Privately Held**
SIC: 2721 8661 Magazines: publishing only, not printed on site; religious organizations

(G-17915)
ADVATECH CORPORATION
250 S Australian Ave # 1504 (33401-5018)
PHONE.....................................732 803-8000
Gerald F Richman, *President*
Michael Spiegel, *Vice Pres*
Richard Margulies, *CFO*
EMP: 7 EST: 1990
SALES (est): 757.1K **Privately Held**
SIC: 3589 Water treatment equipment, industrial

(G-17916)
AFRIKIN LLC (PA)
2408 Florida St (33406-4407)
PHONE.....................................646 296-3613
Alfonso Brooks, *Mng Member*
EMP: 7 EST: 2017
SALES (est): 1.5MM **Privately Held**
WEB: store.afrikin.org
SIC: 2741 Art copy: publishing & printing

(G-17917)
ALCHIBA INC
505 S Flagler Dr Ste 900 (33401-5948)
PHONE.....................................561 832-9292
James Clark, *Officer*
EMP: 7 EST: 2011
SALES (est): 96.3K **Privately Held**
SIC: 7372 Prepackaged software

(G-17918)
ALERT TOWING INC
Also Called: Alert Manufacturing
8166 140th Ave N (33412-2619)
PHONE.....................................561 586-5504
Paul Lobsinger, *President*
Christina Lane, *Vice Pres*
EMP: 16 EST: 1989
SALES (est): 906.9K **Privately Held**
SIC: 3711 Wreckers (tow truck), assembly of

(G-17919)
ALI TAMPOSI PUBLISHING INC
2106 Chagall Cir (33409-7526)
PHONE.....................................561 306-6597
EMP: 7 EST: 2015
SALES (est): 59K **Privately Held**
WEB: www.alitamposi.com
SIC: 2741 Misc Publishing

(G-17920)
ALTERNATIVE DAILY
400 Clematis St Ste 203 (33401-5322)
PHONE.....................................561 628-4711
Stephen Steranka, *Principal*
David Sigler, *CFO*
Steve Steranka, *Marketing Staff*
EMP: 9 EST: 2017
SALES (est): 362.7K **Privately Held**
WEB: www.thealternativedaily.com
SIC: 2711 Newspapers

(G-17921)
ALTERNATIVE SIGN GROUP INC
8955 120th Ave N (33412-2634)
PHONE.....................................561 722-9272
Joe Adinolfe, *Vice Pres*
David Lanter, *Administration*
EMP: 7 EST: 2014
SALES (est): 495K **Privately Held**
WEB: www.asgsign.com
SIC: 3993 Signs & advertising specialties

(G-17922)
AMERICAN AWNING COMPANY INC
537 Pine Ter (33405-2697)
PHONE.....................................561 832-7123
Dale Di Persico, *President*
Daniel Di Persico, *Vice Pres*
Stephany Di Persico, *Exec Dir*
Dawn Mattei, *Admin Sec*
EMP: 20 EST: 1955
SALES (est): 1.8MM **Privately Held**
WEB: www.americanawning.com
SIC: 2394 Awnings, fabric: made from purchased materials

(G-17923)
AMERICAN CAB CONNECTION LLC
Also Called: St John Designs
16107 74th Ave N (33418-7411)
PHONE.................................561 676-5875
Lawrence A Cathy, *Manager*
EMP: 7 **EST:** 2017
SALES (est): 180.7K **Privately Held**
WEB: www.stjohndesigns.com
SIC: 2434 Wood kitchen cabinets

(G-17924)
APPLIED SOFTWARE INC
737 Sandy Point Ln (33410-3427)
P.O. Box 30698 (33420-0698)
PHONE.................................215 297-9441
Janis Josephson, *President*
Marisa Josephson, *Vice Pres*
EMP: 8 **EST:** 1973
SQ FT: 4,000
SALES (est): 863.6K **Privately Held**
WEB: www.asisoft.com
SIC: 7372 Application computer software

(G-17925)
ARCHITECTURAL DETAIL & WDWKG
2617 Pinewood Ave (33407-5436)
PHONE.................................561 835-4005
Christian Hentschl, *President*
Mathew Mayfield, *Vice Pres*
EMP: 6 **EST:** 1993
SQ FT: 3,000
SALES (est): 994.8K **Privately Held**
WEB: www.adwwinc.com
SIC: 2431 Millwork

(G-17926)
ARCOAT COATINGS CORPORATION
2351 Vista Pkwy Ste 500 (33411-6728)
PHONE.................................561 422-9900
Richard Jaffin, *Branch Mgr*
EMP: 21
SALES (corp-wide): 4.8MM **Privately Held**
WEB: www.arcoat.com
SIC: 3479 Coating of metals & formed products
PA: Arcoat Coatings Corporation
615 Broadway
Hastings On Hudson NY 10706
914 478-9400

(G-17927)
ARMBRUST AVIATION GROUP INC
Also Called: World Jet Fuel Report
8895 N Military Trl # 201 (33410-6220)
PHONE.................................561 355-8488
John H Armbrust, *President*
Pauline H Armbrust, *Vice Pres*
Carol Ward, *Accounting Dir*
Andrea Caballero, *Mktg Coord*
David Broderick, *Exec Dir*
EMP: 20 **EST:** 1986
SQ FT: 3,000
SALES (est): 2.5MM **Privately Held**
WEB: www.armbrustaviation.com
SIC: 2731 8748 2721 Book publishing; business consulting; periodicals

(G-17928)
ART OF PRINTING INC
1500 N Fl Mango Rd Ste 4 (33409-5208)
PHONE.................................561 640-7344
EMP: 6
SALES (est): 719.9K **Privately Held**
SIC: 2759 Commercial Printing

(G-17929)
ARTWORKS INTERNATIONAL
420 6th St (33401-3908)
PHONE.................................561 833-9165
Sioban Torres, *Owner*
▲ **EMP:** 9 **EST:** 2006
SALES (est): 200.8K **Privately Held**
SIC: 2499 5023 Picture frame molding, finished; frames & framing, picture & mirror

(G-17930)
ASSOCIATED INTR DESGR SVC INC
4300 Georgia Ave (33405-2522)
PHONE.................................561 655-4926
Sara Petti, *President*
Richard Petti, *Vice Pres*
Scott McNutt, *Manager*
EMP: 18 **EST:** 1974
SQ FT: 6,500
SALES (est): 2.2MM **Privately Held**
WEB: www.associateddesignerservice.com
SIC: 2211 2512 2392 2391 Draperies & drapery fabrics, cotton; living room furniture: upholstered on wood frames; bedspreads & bed sets: made from purchased materials; curtains & draperies

(G-17931)
AZUL STONE LLC
920 Fern St (33401-5718)
PHONE.................................561 655-9385
Ihab Nasser, *Principal*
Ayman A Nasser, *Mng Member*
EMP: 7 **EST:** 2014
SALES (est): 1.2MM **Privately Held**
WEB: www.azulstone.com
SIC: 1411 5032 Limestone & marble dimension stone; granite dimension stone; marble building stone

(G-17932)
B E PRESSURE SUPPLY INC
Also Called: Be Pressure Supply
5483 Leaper Dr (33407-7000)
PHONE.................................561 688-9246
John Pankow,
Nick Braber,
◆ **EMP:** 10 **EST:** 1992
SALES (est): 1.3MM **Privately Held**
WEB: www.bepowerequipment.com
SIC: 3569 Blast cleaning equipment, dustless

(G-17933)
B G SERVICE COMPANY INC
1400 Alabama Ave Ste 15 (33401-7048)
P.O. Box 2259 (33402-2259)
PHONE.................................561 659-1471
John Frost, *Ch of Bd*
Timothy Frost, *President*
Ashwinee Basani, *QC Mgr*
Tim Frost, *VP Bus Dvlpt*
Mary Frost, *Treasurer*
EMP: 39 **EST:** 1964
SQ FT: 19,000
SALES (est): 7.1MM **Privately Held**
WEB: www.bgservice.com
SIC: 3643 3694 Current-carrying wiring devices; engine electrical equipment; ignition apparatus, internal combustion engines

(G-17934)
B M H CONCRETE INC
6811 Belvedere Rd (33413-1012)
P.O. Box 18453 (33416-8453)
PHONE.................................561 615-0011
Jay Major Callaway Jr, *President*
EMP: 10 **EST:** 1999
SALES (est): 965.2K **Privately Held**
WEB: www.bmhconcrete.com
SIC: 3273 Ready-mixed concrete

(G-17935)
B&K COUNTRY FEEDS LLC
912 Jamaican Dr (33415-3816)
PHONE.................................561 701-1852
Beverly Rys,
EMP: 5 **EST:** 2018
SALES (est): 335.2K **Privately Held**
SIC: 2048 Prepared feeds

(G-17936)
BABCOCK & WILCOX COMPANY
6501 N Jog Rd (33412-2413)
PHONE.................................561 478-3800
Clyde Herrell, *Branch Mgr*
Mike Davis, *Manager*
Joe Mendenhall, *Supervisor*
EMP: 8
SALES (corp-wide): 723.3MM **Publicly Held**
WEB: www.babcock.com
SIC: 3511 Steam turbines

HQ: The Babcock & Wilcox Company
1200 E Market St Ste 650
Akron OH 44305
330 753-4511

(G-17937)
BALTIC MARBLE INC
4180 Brook Cir W (33417-8203)
PHONE.................................561 436-3774
Edvinas Budzinauskas, *President*
EMP: 7 **EST:** 2001
SALES (est): 143.8K **Privately Held**
SIC: 1411 Marble, dimension-quarrying

(G-17938)
BAMA PRINTING LLC
2257 Vista Pkwy Ste 11 (33411-2726)
PHONE.................................561 855-7641
John Vanginhoven, *Mng Member*
Mark Vanginhoven, *Mng Member*
EMP: 30 **EST:** 2012
SALES (est): 1.9MM **Privately Held**
WEB: www.printbama.com
SIC: 2752 Commercial printing, offset

(G-17939)
BDC FLORIDA LLC
Also Called: Native Outfitters
1300 N Florida Mango Rd # 30 (33409-5259)
PHONE.................................561 249-0900
Gene Caiazzo,
EMP: 14 **EST:** 2017
SALES (est): 1.1MM **Privately Held**
WEB: www.nativeoutfitters.com
SIC: 2361 2329 T-shirts & tops: girls', children's & infants'; men's & boys' sportswear & athletic clothing; men's & boys' athletic uniforms; windbreakers: men's, youths' & boys'

(G-17940)
BECARRO INTERNATIONAL CORP (PA)
Also Called: Sondra Roberts
917 S Military Trl Ste C3 (33415-3928)
PHONE.................................561 737-5585
Robert Camche, *President*
Glenn Camche, *Vice Pres*
Robyn Albaum, *Sales Mgr*
◆ **EMP:** 2 **EST:** 2003
SQ FT: 10,000
SALES (est): 3.9MM **Privately Held**
SIC: 3171 Handbags, women's

(G-17941)
BEE WELDING INC
Also Called: Bee Access Products
2145 Indian Rd (33409-3221)
PHONE.................................561 616-9003
John Belmonte, *President*
Brian Andrews, *Vice Pres*
Tom Dejong, *Vice Pres*
Patrick Hickey, *Vice Pres*
Sam Brown, *Warehouse Mgr*
▲ **EMP:** 18 **EST:** 1986
SALES (est): 5.1MM **Privately Held**
WEB: www.beeaccess.com
SIC: 7692 Welding repair

(G-17942)
BEESFREE INC
Also Called: Bees Vita Plus
2101 Vista Pkwy Ste 122 (33411-2706)
PHONE.................................561 939-4860
Andrea Festuccia, *Ch of Bd*
David W Todhunter, *President*
Juan Carlos Trabucco, *Director*
EMP: 5 **EST:** 2011
SALES (est): 711.6K **Privately Held**
WEB: www.beesfree.biz
SIC: 2899 Chemical preparations

(G-17943)
BEST METAL WORK
3301 Elec Way Ste A (33407)
PHONE.................................561 842-1960
Glenn Simmons, *Owner*
EMP: 8 **EST:** 2007
SALES (est): 364.5K **Privately Held**
WEB: www.pbironman.com
SIC: 3599 Machine shop, jobbing & repair

(G-17944)
BIO BUBBLE PETS LLC
1400 Centrepark Blvd # 860 (33401-7421)
PHONE.................................561 998-5350
Steven Berlin, *Vice Pres*
Al Venezia,
▲ **EMP:** 11 **EST:** 2010
SALES (est): 9.7MM
SALES (corp-wide): 291.8MM **Privately Held**
WEB: www.biobubblepets.com
SIC: 3089 Plastic processing
PA: Peerless Clothing Inc
8888 Boul Pie-Ix
Montreal QC H1Z 4
514 593-9300

(G-17945)
BIONITROGEN HOLDINGS CORP (PA)
Also Called: Hidenet Scrities Architectures
1400 Centrepark Blvd # 860 (33401-7402)
PHONE.................................561 600-9550
Graham Copley, *CEO*
Bryan B Kornegay Jr, *President*
Ernesto Ernie Iznaga, *Vice Pres*
EMP: 5 **EST:** 1990
SALES (est): 982.2K **Privately Held**
WEB: www.bionitrogen.com
SIC: 2873 Nitrogenous fertilizers

(G-17946)
BIOSCULPTURE TECHNOLOGY INC (PA)
1701 S Flagler Dr Apt 607 (33401-7341)
PHONE.................................561 651-7816
Robert L Cucin MD, *CEO*
Robert L D, *CEO*
Jack Meskunas, *CFO*
Deborah Salerno, *CFO*
Gayer Cucin, *Treasurer*
EMP: 23 **EST:** 2001
SQ FT: 3,500
SALES (est): 2.5MM **Privately Held**
WEB: www.biosculpturetechnology.com
SIC: 3841 Surgical & medical instruments

(G-17947)
BIRDSALL MARINE DESIGN INC
530 Nottingham Blvd (33405-2635)
PHONE.................................561 832-7879
Robert P Birdsall, *President*
▼ **EMP:** 20 **EST:** 1979
SQ FT: 14,000
SALES (est): 3.9MM **Privately Held**
WEB: www.birdsallmarine.com
SIC: 3429 5961 3732 3444 Marine hardware; mail order house, order taking office only; boat building & repairing; sheet metalwork

(G-17948)
BLAST OFF EQUIPMENT INC
2350 S Military Trl (33415-7544)
PHONE.................................561 964-6199
Vickie Finnegan, *President*
EMP: 10 **EST:** 1984
SQ FT: 5,000
SALES (est): 2MM **Privately Held**
WEB: www.blastoffequipment.com
SIC: 3589 High pressure cleaning equipment

(G-17949)
BLUMER & STANTON ENTPS INC (PA)
5112 Georgia Ave (33405-3192)
PHONE.................................561 585-2525
Roger Stanton, *President*
Marcille S Irwin, *Vice Pres*
Marcille Irwin, *Vice Pres*
William W Stanton, *Vice Pres*
William Stanton, *Vice Pres*
EMP: 12 **EST:** 1995
SQ FT: 30,000
SALES (est): 4.9MM **Privately Held**
WEB: www.blumerandstanton.com
SIC: 2431 Millwork

(G-17950)
BLUMER & STANTON INC
5112 Georgia Ave (33405-3192)
PHONE.................................561 585-2525
Roger Stanton, *President*
Marcille S Irwin, *Vice Pres*

Marcille Irwin, *Vice Pres*
Charles A Stanton, *Vice Pres*
William W Stanton, *Vice Pres*
▼ **EMP:** 18 **EST:** 1946
SQ FT: 30,000
SALES (est): 1.8MM
SALES (corp-wide): 4.9MM **Privately Held**
WEB: www.blumerandstanton.com
SIC: 2431 Millwork
PA: Blumer & Stanton Enterprises, Inc.
5112 Georgia Ave
West Palm Beach FL 33405
561 585-2525

(G-17951)
BOB KLINE QUALITY METAL INC
2511 Division Ave (33407-5345)
PHONE..................561 659-4245
Robert M Kline, *President*
Bobby Kline, *Manager*
EMP: 5 **EST:** 1976
SQ FT: 2,200
SALES (est): 805.5K **Privately Held**
WEB: bob-kline-quality-metal-inc.hub.biz
SIC: 3444 7692 Sheet metal specialties, not stamped; welding repair

(G-17952)
BT GLASS & MIRROR INC
3748 Prospect Ave Ste 4 (33404-3488)
PHONE..................561 841-7676
Scott Taylor, *President*
EMP: 6 **EST:** 1999
SQ FT: 32,000
SALES (est): 671.6K **Privately Held**
SIC: 3231 1793 Mirrored glass; glass & glazing work

(G-17953)
BUDDY PAULS INC
301 Clematis St Ste 300 (33401-4611)
PHONE..................561 578-9813
Bryan Williams, *CEO*
EMP: 5 **EST:** 2008
SALES (est): 300K **Privately Held**
SIC: 2087 Flavoring extracts & syrups

(G-17954)
BUSH BROTHERS PROVISION CO
1931 N Dixie Hwy (33407-6007)
PHONE..................561 832-6666
Harry Bush, *President*
Billy Bush, *Vice Pres*
Doug Bush, *Vice Pres*
John Bush, *Opers Staff*
Dante Vargas, *Research*
▼ **EMP:** 25 **EST:** 1925
SQ FT: 27,000
SALES (est): 5.6MM **Privately Held**
WEB: www.bush-brothers.com
SIC: 2013 5147 Sausages & other prepared meats; meats, fresh

(G-17955)
CADENCE KEEN INNOVATIONS INC
Also Called: Cki Solutions
1655 Palm Bch Lkes Blvd S (33401)
PHONE..................561 249-2219
Sam Montross, *CEO*
Steven Gordon, *President*
Bojana Dorsey, *Business Mgr*
Faye Lizotte, *Sales Staff*
Catalina Lluis, *Admin Asst*
EMP: 6 **EST:** 1996
SQ FT: 2,200
SALES (est): 1MM **Privately Held**
WEB: www.ckisolutions.us
SIC: 2514 Beds, including folding & cabinet, household: metal

(G-17956)
CAROLINA CLUBS INC
11064 68th St N (33412-1831)
PHONE..................561 753-6948
Kevin Lane, *President*
George Lane, *Principal*
Thomas Lane, *Vice Pres*
Karen Lane, *Treasurer*
EMP: 5 **EST:** 1990
SALES (est): 483.3K **Privately Held**
WEB: www.carolinaclubs.com
SIC: 3949 Baseball equipment & supplies, general

(G-17957)
CC CONTROL CORP
5760 Corporate Way (33407-2004)
PHONE..................561 293-3975
Luis L Garcia, *President*
Matthew Skidmore, *Vice Pres*
EMP: 20 **EST:** 1980
SQ FT: 13,200
SALES (est): 10.2MM **Privately Held**
WEB: www.cccontrolcorp.com
SIC: 3625 Electric controls & control accessories, industrial

(G-17958)
CEMEX CNSTR MTLS ATL LLC (DH)
1501 Belvedere Rd (33406-1501)
PHONE..................561 833-5555
Fernando A Gonzalez, *CEO*
Maher Al-Haffar, *Exec VP*
Mauricio Doehner, *Exec VP*
Jaime Elizondo, *Vice Pres*
Joaqun Estrada, *Vice Pres*
▲ **EMP:** 49 **EST:** 1988
SALES (est): 81.1MM **Privately Held**
SIC: 3272 Concrete products
HQ: Cemex, Inc.
10100 Katy Fwy Ste 300
Houston TX 77043
713 650-6200

(G-17959)
CEMEX CNSTR MTLS FLA LLC
Also Called: Mat Div-Palm Beach Maint Shop
1021 N Railroad Ave (33401-3305)
PHONE..................561 832-6646
Chuck Carew, *Branch Mgr*
EMP: 10
SQ FT: 7,896 **Privately Held**
SIC: 3444 5032 3273 5211 Sheet metalwork; concrete mixtures; ready-mixed concrete; concrete & cinder block
HQ: Cemex Construction Materials Florida, Llc
1501 Belvedere Rd
West Palm Beach FL 33406

(G-17960)
CEMEX CNSTR MTLS FLA LLC (DH)
1501 Belvedere Rd (33406-1501)
PHONE..................561 833-5555
Gonzalo Galindo, *President*
Kelly C Anderson, *Vice Pres*
Greg Hazle, *Vice Pres*
Jim Reed, *Human Res Mgr*
Thomas Edgeller,
▼ **EMP:** 16 **EST:** 2008
SALES (est): 525.2MM **Privately Held**
SIC: 3273 Ready-mixed concrete
HQ: Cemex, Inc.
10100 Katy Fwy Ste 300
Houston TX 77043
713 650-6200

(G-17961)
CEMEX CNSTR MTLS PCF LLC (DH)
1501 Belvedere Rd (33406-1501)
PHONE..................561 833-5555
Rob Cutter, *President*
▲ **EMP:** 45 **EST:** 2008
SALES (est): 595.1MM **Privately Held**
SIC: 3272 Concrete products
HQ: Cemex, Inc.
10100 Katy Fwy Ste 300
Houston TX 77043
713 650-6200

(G-17962)
CEMEX MATERIALS LLC (DH)
1720 Centrepark Dr E # 100 (33401-7405)
P.O. Box 24635 (33416-4635)
PHONE..................561 833-5555
Duncan Gage, *President*
Karl Watson, *President*
Lauren Dickinson, *Credit Staff*
Martha Laurent, *Credit Staff*
Francy Pinto, *Credit Staff*
◆ **EMP:** 200 **EST:** 1981
SALES (est): 1.9B **Privately Held**
SIC: 3271 3273 3272 1422 Blocks, concrete or cinder: standard; ready-mixed concrete; pipe, concrete or lined with concrete; crushed & broken limestone

HQ: Cemex, Inc.
10100 Katy Fwy Ste 300
Houston TX 77043
713 650-6200

(G-17963)
CEMEX MATERIALS LLC
9111 Southern Blvd (33411-3626)
PHONE..................561 793-1442
David Clark, *Branch Mgr*
Jeff Porter, *Manager*
EMP: 118 **Privately Held**
SIC: 3271 3273 3272 1422 Blocks, concrete or cinder: standard; ready-mixed concrete; concrete products; crushed & broken limestone
HQ: Cemex Materials Llc
1720 Centrepark Dr E # 100
West Palm Beach FL 33401
561 833-5555

(G-17964)
CENTURION RESIDENTIAL INDS
3819 Heath Cir N (33407-3180)
PHONE..................561 574-1483
Laverne Ferguson, *Director*
EMP: 10 **EST:** 2001
SALES (est): 133.6K **Privately Held**
SIC: 3999 Manufacturing industries

(G-17965)
CHANNEL INDUSTRIES INC
Also Called: Pelican Pumps
511 29th St (33407-5115)
P.O. Box 65, Canal Point (33438-0065)
PHONE..................561 214-0637
James Goldie, *President*
Christine Goldie, *Vice Pres*
Craig White, *Engineer*
EMP: 12 **EST:** 1941
SQ FT: 10,000
SALES (est): 1.5MM **Privately Held**
SIC: 3561 7699 7692 Pumps & pumping equipment; farm machinery repair; welding repair

(G-17966)
CHIKITAS LLC
2269 S Military Trl (33415-7579)
PHONE..................561 401-5033
Rosa H Moody, *Principal*
EMP: 6 **EST:** 2016
SALES (est): 329.2K **Privately Held**
SIC: 2024 Ice cream & frozen desserts

(G-17967)
CLINICAL CHMSTRY SPCLISTS CORP
Also Called: Ir Clinical
6901 Okeechobee Blvd D5-L3 (33411-2511)
PHONE..................919 554-1424
Larry Denney, *CEO*
◆ **EMP:** 10 **EST:** 2012
SQ FT: 3,000
SALES (est): 577.1K **Privately Held**
SIC: 3841 Diagnostic apparatus, medical

(G-17968)
COASTAL MILLWORKS INC
3810 Consumer St Ste 2 (33404-1710)
PHONE..................561 881-7755
John B Maffett, *President*
Mary R Maffett, *Corp Secy*
Carl Tourigny, *Project Mgr*
Tony Perez, *Prdtn Mgr*
Matt Carothers, *Supervisor*
EMP: 40 **EST:** 1990
SQ FT: 26,000
SALES (est): 10.9MM **Privately Held**
WEB: www.coastalmillworks.com
SIC: 2431 Millwork

(G-17969)
COHAGAN ENGINEERING INC
5307 East Ave Ste 6 (33407-2356)
PHONE..................561 842-7779
Brent Cohagan, *President*
Traver Maselli, *Vice Pres*
EMP: 5 **EST:** 2008
SALES (est): 498.7K **Privately Held**
WEB: www.cohaganengineering.com
SIC: 3599 Machine shop, jobbing & repair

(G-17970)
COLLINS AEROSPACE (PA)
777 S Flagler Dr Ste 1800 (33401-6279)
PHONE..................704 423-7000
Stephen Timm, *President*
Caitlin Tulaney, *Partner*
Daniel Scott, *General Mgr*
Sun Lee, *Business Mgr*
Clay Stephens, *Business Mgr*
EMP: 11 **EST:** 2019
SALES (est): 4.8MM **Privately Held**
WEB: www.rockwellcollins.com
SIC: 3728 Aircraft parts & equipment

(G-17971)
COMMUNITY MGT SYSTEMS LLC
701 Nrthpint Pkwy Ste 150 (33407)
PHONE..................561 214-4780
Kirk Kanjian,
EMP: 9 **EST:** 2003
SALES (est): 420.3K **Privately Held**
SIC: 7372 Application computer software

(G-17972)
CONTRACTING CNC MACHINING INC
8360 Currency Dr Ste 7 (33404-1714)
PHONE..................561 494-0703
Michael Vernsey, *President*
EMP: 7 **EST:** 2006
SALES (est): 942.3K **Privately Held**
SIC: 3965 Fasteners, buttons, needles & pins

(G-17973)
CORAL REEF CAST STONE INC
Also Called: Jhr Management
6100 Georgia Ave (33405-3950)
P.O. Box 540549, Greenacres (33454-0549)
PHONE..................561 586-1900
Rhoda Meyers, *President*
▼ **EMP:** 14 **EST:** 1995
SQ FT: 14,447
SALES (est): 759K **Privately Held**
WEB: www.coralreefcaststone.com
SIC: 3272 Stone, cast concrete

(G-17974)
COVERT ARMOR LLC
1101 Clare Ave Ste 2 (33401-6967)
PHONE..................561 459-8077
Cathie Nash, *Finance*
Robert Barnard, *Marketing Staff*
EMP: 9 **EST:** 2018
SALES (est): 471K **Privately Held**
WEB: www.covertarmor.com
SIC: 3949 Sporting & athletic goods

(G-17975)
CROWN SEAMLESS GUTTERS INC
7880 Coconut Blvd (33412-2256)
PHONE..................561 748-9919
Joshua Muller, *President*
Jason Brackett, *General Mgr*
Richard Muller, *Vice Pres*
Sara Muller, *Admin Sec*
EMP: 22 **EST:** 1976
SALES (est): 1.1MM **Privately Held**
WEB: www.crownseamlessgutters.net
SIC: 3444 1711 Gutters, sheet metal; heating & air conditioning contractors

(G-17976)
DB DOORS INC
Also Called: First Impression Doors & More
346 Pike Rd Ste 6 (33411-3819)
PHONE..................561 798-6684
Darren Dobkins, *President*
Greg Dobkins, *Sales Staff*
▼ **EMP:** 11 **EST:** 2003
SALES (est): 2MM **Privately Held**
WEB: www.fidminc.com
SIC: 2431 Millwork

(G-17977)
DELTA MG
4440 S Tiffany Dr Ste 8 (33407)
PHONE..................561 840-0577
Danilo Alcantara, *President*
Eliseo Fancane, *Vice Pres*
EMP: 6 **EST:** 2007

SALES (est): 642.3K **Privately Held**
WEB: www.deltamg.com
SIC: 2499 Tiles, cork

(G-17978)
DIAMOND ADVERTISING &
MKTG
Also Called: South Florida Time
1200 S Flagler Dr Apt 106 (33401-6701)
P.O. Box 222 (33402-0222)
PHONE....................................561 833-5129
Audrey Diamonds, *Owner*
Cy Caine, *Director*
Robin Diamand, *Director*
EMP: 10 EST: 2003
SALES (est): 685.7K **Privately Held**
SIC: 2721 Magazines: publishing & printing

(G-17979)
DIGITAL ASSET MGT GROUP
LLC ✪
1645 Palm Bch Lkes Blvd S (33401)
PHONE....................................877 507-5777
John Marz, *Mng Member*
EMP: 10 EST: 2021
SALES (est): 1.5MM **Privately Held**
SIC: 3571 Electronic computers

(G-17980)
DISCOVERY TANK TESTING INC
1209 Gateway Rd Ste 203 (33403-1929)
P.O. Box 14207, North Palm Beach
(33408-0207)
PHONE....................................561 840-1666
Jerry Pellegrino, *President*
EMP: 5 EST: 1987
SQ FT: 1,800
SALES (est): 625.3K **Privately Held**
WEB: www.discoverytanktesting.com
SIC: 1389 Testing, measuring, surveying &
analysis services

(G-17981)
DOVETAILS A PRECISION
5325 Georgia Ave (33405-3551)
PHONE....................................561 818-6323
Howard Griffith, *President*
EMP: 7 EST: 2004
SALES (est): 122.2K **Privately Held**
SIC: 3423 Carpenters' hand tools, except
saws: levels, chisels, etc.

(G-17982)
DUNCANSON DYNASTY INC
Also Called: Soft Water Techs
801 Northpoint Pkwy # 97 (33407-1812)
PHONE....................................561 288-1349
Roddrick E Duncanson Sr, *President*
EMP: 7 EST: 2017
SALES (est): 182.7K **Privately Held**
SIC: 2899 Water treating compounds

(G-17983)
DURACELL COMPANY
515 N Flagler Dr Ste 1600 (33401-4346)
PHONE....................................561 494-7550
Carolina Martinize, *Branch Mgr*
Zdenka Cumano, *Consultant*
EMP: 30
SALES (corp-wide): 354.6B **Publicly
Held**
WEB: www.duracell.com
SIC: 3691 Storage batteries
HQ: The Duracell Company
135 S Lasalle St Ste 2250
Chicago IL 60603
203 796-4000

(G-17984)
DYNAMIC METALS LLC
340 Pike Rd (33411-3837)
PHONE....................................561 629-7304
Jesus Lara,
EMP: 10 EST: 2015
SALES (est): 498.2K **Privately Held**
SIC: 3444 Roof deck, sheet metal

(G-17985)
EASTERN METAL SUPPLY NC
INC
4268 Westroads Dr (33407-1201)
PHONE....................................800 432-2204
Jill Harvey, *Buyer*
Kevin Parkes, *Controller*
Isabel Linares, *Manager*

EMP: 13 **Privately Held**
WEB: www.easternmetal.com
SIC: 3441 Fabricated structural metal
PA: Eastern Metal Supply Of North Car-
olina, Inc.
2925 Stewart Creek Blvd
Charlotte NC 28216

(G-17986)
ECOSMART SURFACE &
COATING TEC
1313 S Killian Dr (33403-1918)
PHONE....................................402 319-1607
EMP: 8 EST: 2014
SALES (est): 110.3K **Privately Held**
SIC: 3479 Metal coating & allied service

(G-17987)
ENGINEERED EQUIPMENT
CORP
777 S Flagler Dr Ste 800 (33401-6161)
PHONE....................................561 839-4008
Ronald Regan, *Principal*
EMP: 12 EST: 2018
SALES (est): 907K **Privately Held**
WEB: www.engineeredequipmentcorp.com
SIC: 2521 Panel systems & partitions
(free-standing), office: wood

(G-17988)
ETC PALM BEACH LLC
1800 Okeechobee Rd # 100 (33409-5207)
PHONE....................................561 881-8118
Andrea Avila, *Project Mgr*
Pasquale Ramella, *Project Mgr*
Paul Biava, *Mng Member*
Lisa Carta, *Executive*
Peter Sheptak, *Technician*
EMP: 70 EST: 2017
SALES (est): 9MM **Privately Held**
WEB: www.etcsimplify.com
SIC: 3699 Security control equipment &
systems

(G-17989)
EUROPEAN CABINETS &
DESIGN LLC
4050 Westgate Ave (33409-4732)
PHONE....................................561 684-1440
EMP: 5 EST: 2019
SALES (est): 524.5K **Privately Held**
WEB:
www.europeancabinetsanddesign.com
SIC: 2434 Wood kitchen cabinets

(G-17990)
EVOLUTION METALS CORP
Also Called: Metals & Mining
516 S Dixie Hwy (33401-5810)
PHONE....................................561 531-2314
David Wilcox, *CEO*
EMP: 20 EST: 2020
SALES (est): 1.3MM **Privately Held**
WEB: www.evolution-metals.com
SIC: 1081 Metal mining services; metal
mining exploration & development serv-
ices

(G-17991)
EXCEL PALM BEACH LLC
351 N Jog Rd (33413-1712)
PHONE....................................616 864-6650
Sophia M Banks, *Manager*
EMP: 7 EST: 2017
SALES (est): 103.9K **Privately Held**
SIC: 3714 Motor vehicle parts & acces-
sories

(G-17992)
EXCELL CABINET CORP
8233 Gator Ln (33411-3702)
PHONE....................................561 628-9059
Vijai Nancoo, *Principal*
EMP: 7 EST: 2007
SALES (est): 142.8K **Privately Held**
SIC: 2434 Wood kitchen cabinets

(G-17993)
F D SIGNWORKS LLC
Also Called: Identifire Safety
941 S Military Trl F5 (33415-3980)
PHONE....................................561 248-6323
Matthew Hyman, *Principal*
EMP: 9 EST: 2014

SALES (est): 687.6K **Privately Held**
WEB: www.identifiresafety.com
SIC: 3993 Signs & advertising specialties

(G-17994)
FACTORYMART INC
3875 Fiscal Ct Ste 400 (33404-1707)
PHONE....................................561 202-9820
John Didonato, *Principal*
John Kilburg, *Vice Pres*
EMP: 10 EST: 2011
SALES (est): 211.6K **Privately Held**
WEB: www.factorymart.com
SIC: 2752 Commercial printing, offset

(G-17995)
FERRIN SIGNS INC
945 26th St (33407-5314)
PHONE....................................561 802-4242
Ralph Lashells, *President*
Dan May, *Vice Pres*
Danielle Hannon, *Project Mgr*
William Bennett, *Accounts Exec*
Tim Lewzader, *Accounts Exec*
EMP: 22 EST: 1991
SQ FT: 18,000
SALES (est): 3.4MM **Privately Held**
WEB: www.ferrinsigns.com
SIC: 3993 Electric signs

(G-17996)
FINE LINE PAVERS INC
6480 Bischoff Rd (33413)
PHONE....................................561 389-9819
Edgar W Garcia, *Principal*
EMP: 6 EST: 2008
SALES (est): 475.7K **Privately Held**
WEB: www.finelinepaversinc.com
SIC: 3531 Pavers

(G-17997)
FIRST IMPRSSION DOORS
MORE INC
346 Pike Rd Ste 6 (33411-3819)
PHONE....................................561 798-6684
Steven L Gross, *President*
Darren R Dobkins, *Vice Pres*
Susan M Gross, *Admin Sec*
EMP: 5 EST: 2013
SALES (est): 968.8K **Privately Held**
WEB: www.fidminc.com
SIC: 2431 Millwork

(G-17998)
FLAVORWORKS INC
10130 Northlake Blvd (33412-1101)
PHONE....................................561 588-8246
Jonathan Pierce, *President*
▼ EMP: 22 EST: 1998
SQ FT: 15,400
SALES (est): 2.8MM **Privately Held**
WEB: www.flavorworksfoodgroup.com
SIC: 2099 Food preparations

(G-17999)
FLORIDA CRYSTAL REFINERY
INC (DH)
1 N Clematis St Ste 200 (33401-5551)
P.O. Box 1059, Palm Beach (33480-1059)
PHONE....................................561 366-5200
Alfonso Fanjul Jr, *Ch of Bd*
Jose Fanjul, *President*
Donald W Carson, *Vice Pres*
Rick Blomqvist, *Treasurer*
Ricardo Martinez, *Controller*
▼ EMP: 5 EST: 1978
SQ FT: 9,000
SALES (est): 21.4MM
SALES (corp-wide): 2.1B **Privately Held**
WEB: www.floridacrystalscorp.com
SIC: 2062 Cane sugar refining
HQ: Okeelanta Corporation
1 N Clematis St Ste 200
West Palm Beach FL 33401
561 366-5100

(G-18000)
FLORIDA CRYSTALS
CORPORATION (HQ)
1 N Clematis St Ste 200 (33401-5551)
P.O. Box 4671 (33402-4671)
PHONE....................................561 655-6303
Alfonso Fanjul, *Ch of Bd*
Armando A Tabernilla, *Principal*
Jose F Fanjul Jr, *Vice Chairman*

Dolly Davis, *Counsel*
Jose Fanjul, *Vice Pres*
▲ EMP: 100 EST: 1962
SALES (est): 561.8MM
SALES (corp-wide): 2.1B **Privately Held**
WEB: www.floridacrystalscorp.com
SIC: 2061 2062 2044 4911 Raw cane
sugar; cane sugar refining; rice milling;
electric services
PA: Fanjul Corp.
1 N Clematis St Ste 200
West Palm Beach FL 33401
561 655-6303

(G-18001)
FLORIDA CRYSTALS
CORPORATION
626 N Dixie Hwy (33401-3918)
PHONE....................................561 366-5000
Rafael Gregorich, *Superintendent*
Woody O 'neal, *Superintendent*
Steven Pincus, *Counsel*
Benjamin Sadler, *Counsel*
Connie Matthews, *Vice Pres*
EMP: 469
SALES (corp-wide): 2.1B **Privately Held**
WEB: www.floridacrystals.com
SIC: 2061 2062 0133 Raw cane sugar;
cane sugar refining; sugarcane & sugar
beets
HQ: Florida Crystals Corporation
1 N Clematis St Ste 200
West Palm Beach FL 33401
561 655-6303

(G-18002)
FLORIDA CRYSTALS
CORPORATION
Also Called: Purchasing Department
1 N Clematis St Ste 400 (33401-5552)
PHONE....................................561 515-8080
Larry Grayson, *Superintendent*
Jeffrey Lampton, *Regional Mgr*
Jeremy Surpin, *Regional Mgr*
David Tack, *Project Mgr*
Mark Lichtenstein, *Maint Spvr*
EMP: 101
SALES (corp-wide): 2.1B **Privately Held**
WEB: www.floridacrystals.com
SIC: 2061 2062 2044 4911 Raw cane
sugar; cane sugar refining; rice milling;
electric services
HQ: Florida Crystals Corporation
1 N Clematis St Ste 200
West Palm Beach FL 33401
561 655-6303

(G-18003)
FLORIDA CRYSTALS FOOD
CORP
1 N Clematis St Ste 200 (33401-5551)
PHONE....................................561 366-5100
Armando A Tabernilla, *Principal*
Ed Starr, *Regional Mgr*
Stacey Griffith, *Sales Staff*
▲ EMP: 670 EST: 2011
SALES (est): 5.2MM
SALES (corp-wide): 2.1B **Privately Held**
WEB: www.floridacrystalscorp.com
SIC: 2061 Raw cane sugar
HQ: Florida Crystals Corporation
1 N Clematis St Ste 200
West Palm Beach FL 33401
561 655-6303

(G-18004)
FLORIDA DESIGN MFG ASSOC
INC
7430 Pine Tree Ln (33406-6821)
P.O. Box 10505 (33419-0505)
PHONE....................................561 533-0733
John Shanks, *President*
EMP: 10 EST: 1997
SQ FT: 6,000
SALES (est): 951.6K **Privately Held**
SIC: 2542 1799 Counters or counter dis-
play cases: except wood; counter top in-
stallation

(G-18005)
FLORIDA MICROELECTRONICS
LLC
Also Called: F M E
1601 Hill Ave Ste E (33407-2233)
PHONE....................................561 845-8455

Tony Byk, *General Mgr*
Barbara Sanabria, *Buyer*
Amy Ferreira, *CFO*
Brian Shiau, *Mng Member*
Leonard Levie, *Mng Member*
EMP: 35 **EST:** 2005
SQ FT: 45,000
SALES (est): 4MM
SALES (corp-wide): 10.9MM **Privately Held**
WEB: www.fortemicro.com
SIC: 3679 Electronic circuits
PA: Fme Technologies, Llc
  1601 Hill Ave
  West Palm Beach FL 33407
  561 845-8455

(G-18006)
FLORIDA SUGAR DISTRIBUTORS (DH)
1 N Clematis St Ste 310 (33401-5551)
PHONE..................561 655-6303
Alfonso Fanjul, *Ch of Bd*
Rick Blomquist, *Vice Pres*
EMP: 20 **EST:** 1994
SQ FT: 5,200
SALES (est): 26MM
SALES (corp-wide): 2.1B **Privately Held**
SIC: 2062 Cane sugar refining
HQ: Florida Crystals Corporation
  1 N Clematis St Ste 200
  West Palm Beach FL 33401
  561 655-6303

(G-18007)
FORCE ENTERPRISES COATINGS LLC
1130 Quaye Lake Cir # 106 (33411-5089)
PHONE..................561 480-7298
Richard Alloe, *Principal*
EMP: 13 **EST:** 2016
SALES (est): 4MM **Privately Held**
SIC: 3559 Fiber optics strand coating machinery

(G-18008)
FOUR WD CONSULTING & PUBG LLC
2721 Vista Pkwy (33411-6722)
PHONE..................561 969-7412
Thomas Ryan, *Principal*
EMP: 6 **EST:** 2017
SALES (est): 679.5K **Privately Held**
SIC: 2741 Miscellaneous publishing

(G-18009)
FOUR X FOUR ORGANICS
5331 Ruth Dr (33415-1939)
PHONE..................561 687-1514
Janel Horne, *Principal*
EMP: 7 **EST:** 2010
SALES (est): 225K **Privately Held**
SIC: 2844 Toilet preparations

(G-18010)
FOVICO INC
Also Called: Aqua Solutions
15908 77th Trl N (33418-1854)
PHONE..................561 624-5400
Forrest R Vincent, *President*
EMP: 14 **EST:** 2008
SALES (est): 871K **Privately Held**
SIC: 3589 Water treatment equipment, industrial

(G-18011)
FOWLERS SHEET METAL INC
4716 Georgia Ave (33405-2897)
PHONE..................561 659-3309
Brenda Fowler, *President*
Brian Fowler, *Vice Pres*
Daniel Fowler, *Admin Sec*
EMP: 13 **EST:** 1980
SQ FT: 2,500
SALES (est): 2.5MM **Privately Held**
WEB: www.fowlerssheetmetal.com
SIC: 3444 Sheet metalwork

(G-18012)
FRANK THEODORE JOHANSON
Also Called: Florida Generators
1317 S Killian Dr (33403-1918)
PHONE..................800 607-0690
Frank Theodore Johanson, *Owner*
EMP: 10 **EST:** 2011

SALES (est): 615.6K **Privately Held**
SIC: 3825 Integrating electricity meters

(G-18013)
FRITZ COMMERCIAL PRINTING INC
5401 S Dixie Hwy (33405-3232)
PHONE..................561 585-6869
Fritz Jean-Louis, *President*
EMP: 6 **EST:** 2006
SALES (est): 359.2K **Privately Held**
SIC: 2759 Commercial printing

(G-18014)
FULLY PROMOTED
1369 N Military Trl (33409-6016)
PHONE..................561 615-8655
EMP: 7 **EST:** 2018
SALES (est): 345.6K **Privately Held**
WEB: www.fullypromoted.com
SIC: 2395 Embroidery & art needlework

(G-18015)
GEORGE GILLESPIE LLC
15611 78th Dr N (33418-1857)
PHONE..................561 744-6191
George C Gillespie Jr, *President*
EMP: 8 **EST:** 2010
SALES (est): 377.7K **Privately Held**
SIC: 2434 Wood kitchen cabinets

(G-18016)
GEORGIA MKTG & SIGN CO LLC
Also Called: Signarama - Woodstock
2121 Vista Pkwy (33411-2706)
PHONE..................800 286-8671
Steve Dabbs,
EMP: 7 **EST:** 2011
SQ FT: 1,500
SALES (est): 457.5K **Privately Held**
WEB: www.signarama.com
SIC: 3993 Signs & advertising specialties

(G-18017)
GF & ASSOCIATE GROUP LLC
7750 Okeechobee Blvd (33411-2104)
PHONE..................954 593-4788
Tony Chester,
EMP: 8
SALES (est): 687.3K **Privately Held**
SIC: 3537 7389 Trucks: freight, baggage, etc.: industrial, except mining;

(G-18018)
GIZMOS LION SHEET METAL INC
1648 Donna Rd (33409-5202)
PHONE..................561 684-8480
EMP: 13 **EST:** 2019
SALES (est): 772.5K **Privately Held**
SIC: 3444 Sheet metalwork

(G-18019)
GRAPHICS DESIGNER INC
Also Called: Sign-A-Rama
2353 N Military Trl C (33409-2904)
PHONE..................561 687-7993
Lino Defeo, *President*
EMP: 11 **EST:** 1990
SALES (est): 1.5MM **Privately Held**
SIC: 3993 2752 2671 Signs & advertising specialties; commercial printing, lithographic; packaging paper & plastics film, coated & laminated

(G-18020)
GREEN TOUCH INDUSTRIES INC
100 Us Highway 1 (33403-3550)
P.O. Box 30614, Palm Beach Gardens (33420-0614)
PHONE..................561 659-5525
Dan Keegan, *Owner*
▲ **EMP:** 8 **EST:** 2011
SALES (est): 847.9K **Privately Held**
WEB: www.trailerracks.com
SIC: 3999 Manufacturing industries

(G-18021)
GROWHEALTHY HOLDINGS LLC
324 Datura St (33401-5414)
P.O. Box 708, Lake Wales (33859-0708)
PHONE..................863 223-8882
Don Clifford, *CEO*

EMP: 14 **EST:** 2014
SALES (est): 7.8MM
SALES (corp-wide): 86.6MM **Privately Held**
WEB: www.growhealthy.com
SIC: 2834 Pharmaceutical preparations
PA: Ianthus Capital Holdings, Inc
  22 Adelaide St W Suite 2740
  Toronto ON M5H 4
  416 591-1525

(G-18022)
HDD LLC
412 Clematis St (33401-5312)
PHONE..................561 346-9054
Hessan Musallet, *Manager*
EMP: 7 **EST:** 2013
SALES (est): 259.8K **Privately Held**
SIC: 2084 Wines, brandy & brandy spirits

(G-18023)
HERPEL INC (PA)
6400 Georgia Ave (33405-4220)
PHONE..................561 585-5573
Frederick Herpel, *President*
Joan McDonald, *Admin Sec*
▼ **EMP:** 9 **EST:** 1948
SQ FT: 20,000
SALES (est): 2.1MM **Privately Held**
WEB: www.herpelcaststone.com
SIC: 3272 Tile, precast terrazzo or concrete; cast stone, concrete

(G-18024)
HIGHWAY SFETY MTR VHCLES FLA D
Also Called: Motor Services Region 9
470 Columbia Dr Ste E200 (33409-1949)
PHONE..................561 640-6826
Diane Buck, *Administration*
EMP: 11
SALES (corp-wide): 104.1B **Privately Held**
WEB: www.flhsmv.gov
SIC: 3469 9621 Automobile license tags, stamped metal;
HQ: Florida Department Of Highway Safety And Motor Vehicles
  2900 Apalachee Pkwy
  Tallahassee FL 32399

(G-18025)
HOLLAND PUMP COMPANY (PA)
7312 Westport Pl (33413-1661)
PHONE..................561 697-3333
Thomas Vossman, *CEO*
Bill Blodgett, *Chairman*
Eugene Lant, *Vice Pres*
Dennis Olsen, *Opers Mgr*
Keno Cox, *CFO*
◆ **EMP:** 7 **EST:** 1978
SQ FT: 21,000
SALES (est): 20.1MM **Privately Held**
WEB: www.hollandpump.com
SIC: 3561 7359 Pumps & pumping equipment; equipment rental & leasing

(G-18026)
HONEYCOMMCORE LLC (PA)
15771 80th Dr N (33418-1837)
PHONE..................561 747-2678
William M Marvel,
▲ **EMP:** 5 **EST:** 2004
SQ FT: 10,000
SALES (est): 1.3MM **Privately Held**
WEB: www.aluminum-honeycomb.com
SIC: 3999 Honeycomb foundations (beekeepers' supplies)

(G-18027)
HOWIES INSTANT PRINTING INC
1572 Palm Bch Lakes Blvd (33401-2338)
PHONE..................561 686-8699
EMP: 10
SQ FT: 2,500
SALES (est): 1.1MM **Privately Held**
SIC: 2752 2759 Offset Printing & Commercial Printing

(G-18028)
I-POP INC
475 N Cleary Rd Unit 4 (33413-1626)
PHONE..................561 567-9000
Devorah Leo, *CEO*
Steven Leo, *President*
EMP: 32 **EST:** 2013

SALES (est): 850K **Privately Held**
WEB: www.rsc-ny.com
SIC: 2531 Assembly hall furniture

(G-18029)
IACONO IRON LLC
163 N Cleary Rd Ste C5 (33413-1645)
PHONE..................561 640-1696
Guy Iacono,
EMP: 7 **EST:** 2014
SALES (est): 106.5K **Privately Held**
WEB: www.iaconometals.com
SIC: 3446 Ornamental metalwork

(G-18030)
IMAGE INTERNATIONAL INC
8040 Belvedere Rd Ste 1 (33411-3202)
PHONE..................561 793-9560
Janna Levendofsky, *President*
EMP: 7 **EST:** 2002
SALES (est): 507.4K **Privately Held**
SIC: 2844 Cosmetic preparations

(G-18031)
INCITY SECURITY INC
Also Called: Incity Property Management
3560 Inv Ln Ste 102 (33404)
PHONE..................561 306-9228
John Sizer, *President*
EMP: 17 **EST:** 2012
SALES (est): 5MM **Privately Held**
SIC: 3861 2085 5063 1731 Cameras & related equipment; gin (alcoholic beverage); rum (alcoholic beverage); alarm systems; burglar alarm systems; computer installation; computer software; modems, monitors, terminals & disk drives: computers
PA: Intercity Alarms And Security Systems (Pty) Ltd
  4 Sandberg St
  GP 2094

(G-18032)
INDIAN RIVER BIODIESEL LLC
1810 Okeechobee Rd Ste A (33409-5237)
PHONE..................321 586-7670
Christopher C Burdett,
EMP: 7 **EST:** 2016
SALES (est): 143.5K **Privately Held**
WEB: www.indianriverbiodiesel.com
SIC: 2911 Diesel fuels

(G-18033)
INNOVA HOME LLC
6200 S Dixie Hwy (33405-4329)
PHONE..................561 855-2450
Michel McNabb, *Mng Member*
EMP: 11 **EST:** 2015
SALES (est): 932K **Privately Held**
SIC: 2084 Wines, brandy & brandy spirits

(G-18034)
INSANEJOURNALCOM
2372 Pinewood Ln (33415-7330)
PHONE..................561 315-9311
Jason Vervlied, *Owner*
EMP: 7 **EST:** 2011
SALES (est): 87.8K **Privately Held**
WEB: www.insanejournal.com
SIC: 2741 Miscellaneous publishing

(G-18035)
INTEGRA CONNECT LLC (PA)
501 S Flagler Dr Ste 600 (33401-5914)
PHONE..................800 742-3069
Charles Saunders, *CEO*
Emily Phillips, *Partner*
John Connolly, *Senior VP*
Christian Herrick, *Vice Pres*
Lynne Jones, *Vice Pres*
EMP: 12 **EST:** 2013
SQ FT: 1,000
SALES (est): 98MM **Privately Held**
WEB: www.integraconnect.com
SIC: 7372 Business oriented computer software

(G-18036)
ISLA INSTRUMENTS LLC
13884 71st Pl N (33412-2127)
PHONE..................561 603-4685
Bradley Holland,
EMP: 9 **EST:** 2016

SALES (est): 260K **Privately Held**
WEB: www.islainstruments.com
SIC: **3931** Musical instruments

(G-18037)
J & I VENTURES INC
Also Called: Ocean Tech
4390 Westroads Dr Ste 2 (33407-1226)
PHONE.................................561 845-0030
Jack P Bates, *President*
Jesse Underhill, *Production*
▲ EMP: 22 EST: 2004
SALES (est): 1.9MM **Privately Held**
SIC: **3069** Wet suits, rubber

(G-18038)
J A CUSTOM
3042 Ike Rd Ste 17 (33411)
PHONE.................................561 615-4680
Jorge A Angel Jr, *Owner*
EMP: 8 EST: 2010
SALES (est): 77.3K **Privately Held**
SIC: **3441 3446** Fabricated structural
metal; ornamental metalwork

(G-18039)
JDJSIS INC
8645 N Military Trl # 501 (33410-6296)
PHONE.................................561 732-2388
Anthony Accaputo, *Principal*
EMP: 7 EST: 2010
SALES (est): 95.5K **Privately Held**
SIC: **2759** Commercial printing

(G-18040)
JKA PUMP SPECIALISTS
5407 N Haverhill Rd 344-345 (33407-7008)
PHONE.................................561 686-4455
▲ EMP: 8 EST: 2012
SALES (est): 895.4K **Privately Held**
WEB: www.jkapump.com
SIC: **3561** Industrial pumps & parts

(G-18041)
JNG LIGHTING
9905 Baywinds Dr Apt 2302 (33411-6308)
PHONE.................................561 707-2028
Jakub A Gryczan, *Principal*
EMP: 7 EST: 2008
SALES (est): 107.1K **Privately Held**
SIC: **3648** Lighting equipment

(G-18042)
JSR WELLNESS INC
5500 Village Blvd Ste 202 (33407-1961)
PHONE.................................561 748-2477
Jordan Rubin, *CEO*
Rich Petti, *COO*
Jeff Brams, *Vice Pres*
Teresa Miller, *Vice Pres*
Erik Schmitt, *Vice Pres*
▲ EMP: 79 EST: 2000
SQ FT: 20,000
SALES (est): 16.9MM **Privately Held**
SIC: **2834** Vitamin, nutrient & hematinic
preparations for human use

(G-18043)
**JUSTICE GOVERNMENT SUPPLY
INC**
555 Pacific Grove Dr # 2 (33401-8312)
PHONE.................................954 559-3038
Grady Renville, *CEO*
Steven Pietro, *President*
EMP: 5 EST: 2016
SALES (est): 467.6K **Privately Held**
WEB: www.jgsfoods.com
SIC: **2011** Meat packing plants

(G-18044)
K AND G FOOD SERVICES LLC
Also Called: Pbg Golf Restaurant
9500 Sandhill Crane Dr (33412-6301)
PHONE.................................954 857-9283
Gustavo Seminario, *Principal*
Eddie Guillen, *Opers Staff*
Matt Marken, *Corp Comm Staff*
Tim Ford, *Manager*
Yves Rosena, *Manager*
EMP: 7 EST: 2015
SALES (est): 112.4K **Privately Held**
SIC: **2099 5141** Food preparations; food
brokers

(G-18045)
K&T STONEWORKS INC
101 N Benoist Farms Rd (33411-3743)
PHONE.................,.................561 798-8486
Karen Kendall, *President*
◆ EMP: 9 EST: 1997
SALES (est): 1.3MM **Privately Held**
WEB: www.ktstoneworks.com
SIC: **3272** Stone, cast concrete

(G-18046)
K12 PRINT INC
3875 Fiscal Ct Ste 400 (33404-1707)
PHONE.................................800 764-7600
John Didonato, *President*
John Kilburg, *Vice Pres*
EMP: 9 EST: 2017
SALES (est): 1MM **Privately Held**
WEB: www.k12print.com
SIC: **2752** Commercial printing, offset

(G-18047)
**KINGMAN CSTM STAIRS & TRIM
LLC**
436 Lytle St (33405-4622)
PHONE.................................561 547-9888
Frederick D Kingman, *Principal*
EMP: 9 EST: 2006
SALES (est): 395.2K **Privately Held**
WEB: www.kingmanstairsandfloors.com
SIC: **3272** Floor slabs & tiles, precast con-
crete

(G-18048)
**L & L ORNA ALUM IRONWORKS
INC**
5601 Georgia Ave (33405-3709)
PHONE.................................561 547-5605
Gina Perez, *President*
Leo Perez, *Owner*
▼ EMP: 12 EST: 1992
SALES (est): 1.8MM **Privately Held**
WEB: www.lironworks.com
SIC: **3446** Architectural metalwork

(G-18049)
**LA PERRADA DEL GORDO
BOCA LLC**
2650 S Military Trl (33415-7514)
PHONE.................................561 968-6978
Miguel A Martinez, *Mng Member*
Elizabeth Novoa, *Mng Member*
Nelson G Villalba, *Mng Member*
EMP: 9 EST: 2007
SALES (est): 2.1MM **Privately Held**
WEB: www.laperradadelgordo.com
SIC: **3411** Food & beverage containers

(G-18050)
LAKE PARK AUTO MACHINE INC
404 Foresta Ter (33415-2614)
PHONE.................................561 848-6197
Fax: 561 848-9514
EMP: 6
SQ FT: 1,800
SALES (est): 709K **Privately Held**
SIC: **3599** Machine Shop Jobbing And Re-
pair

(G-18051)
**LAKEWOOD MANUFACTURING
CO INC ✪**
Also Called: Lakewood Manufacutring
10696 Grande Blvd (33412-1309)
P.O. Box 2185, Westminster MD (21158-
7185)
PHONE.................................443 398-5015
Doug Widlake, *President*
▲ EMP: 150 EST: 2021
SALES (est): 9.9MM **Privately Held**
WEB: www.lakewood-manufacturing.com
SIC: **2511 5712** Wood household furniture;
furniture stores; unfinished furniture

(G-18052)
LAND MARINE SERVICE INC
2590 W Edgewater Dr (33410-2436)
PHONE.................................561 626-2947
Jim Jesteadt, *Owner*
EMP: 6 EST: 1996
SALES (est): 441.1K **Privately Held**
SIC: **3732** Boats, fiberglass: building & re-
pairing

(G-18053)
LARRYS RIGS
2460 Sunset Dr (33415-7428)
PHONE.................................561 967-7791
EMP: 7
SALES (est): 130K **Privately Held**
SIC: **3949** Manufactures Fishing Rigs

(G-18054)
LAVISH ICE CREAM LLC ✪
500 S Australian Ave # 60 (33401-6223)
PHONE.................................561 408-1616
Bianca N McDaniel, *President*
EMP: 15 EST: 2021
SALES (est): 1MM **Privately Held**
SIC: **2024** Ice cream & frozen desserts

(G-18055)
**LEHIGH WHITE CEMENT CO LLC
(DH)**
1601 Forum Pl Ste 1110 (33401-8104)
PHONE.................................561 812-7439
Daniel Harrington, *CEO*
Kirk Nielsen, *VP Sls/Mktg*
EMP: 9 EST: 1897
SALES (est): 50.6MM
SALES (corp-wide): 1.8B **Privately Held**
WEB: www.lehighwhitecement.com
SIC: **2891** Cement, except linoleum & tile
HQ: Cementir Holding N.V.
Corso Di Francia 200
Roma RM 00191
063 249-3305

(G-18056)
LEVATAS
1250 Elizabeth Ave Ste 3 (33401-6929)
PHONE.................................561 622-4511
Chris Neilsen, *Owner*
Orlando Allgeier, *QC Mgr*
Rick Blalock, *Engineer*
David Newmon, *Engineer*
Santiago Valdarrama, *Engineer*
EMP: 63 EST: 2013
SALES (est): 5MM **Privately Held**
WEB: www.levatas.com
SIC: **2741**

(G-18057)
LEVINSON BUILT LLC
1638 Donna Rd (33409-5202)
PHONE.................................561 712-9882
Matthew Levinson, *Branch Mgr*
EMP: 7
SALES (corp-wide): 1.4MM **Privately
Held**
WEB: www.levinsonbuilt.com
SIC: **3442** Screen & storm doors & win-
dows
PA: Levinson Built, Llc
1638 Donna Rd
West Palm Beach FL 33409
561 712-9882

(G-18058)
LION INK PRINT INC
8091 N Military Trl Ste 7 (33410-6351)
Rural Route 404 Winter (33410)
PHONE.................................561 358-8925
Edward Maldonado, *CEO*
Amalfia C Maldonado, *Principal*
EMP: 8 EST: 2010
SALES (est): 243.6K **Privately Held**
WEB: www.lioninkprint.com
SIC: **2752** Commercial printing, litho-
graphic

(G-18059)
LION SHEET METAL INC
1648 Donna Rd (33409-5202)
PHONE.................................561 840-0540
Paul Ditocco, *Owner*
▼ EMP: 13 EST: 2007
SALES (est): 1.4MM **Privately Held**
WEB: www.lionsm.com
SIC: **3444** Sheet metalwork

(G-18060)
LOGUS MANUFACTURING CORP
Also Called: Logus Microwave
1711 Longwood Rd Ste A (33409-6491)
PHONE.................................561 842-3550
Tom Hack, *President*
Nancy Yerkes, *General Mgr*
Barry O 'connell, *Engineer*
Barry Oconnell, *Engineer*
Don Tarca, *Engineer*
EMP: 46 EST: 1961
SQ FT: 34,000
SALES (est): 11.5MM **Privately Held**
WEB: www.logus.com
SIC: **3679 5065 3825 3678** Microwave
components; electronic parts & equip-
ment; instruments to measure electricity;
electronic connectors; current-carrying
wiring devices; nonferrous wiredrawing &
insulating

(G-18061)
M&D SIGNS
2898 Forest Hill Blvd (33406-5959)
PHONE.................................561 296-3636
Mike Gonzalez, *Manager*
EMP: 7 EST: 2006
SALES (est): 135.7K **Privately Held**
SIC: **3993** Signs & advertising specialties

(G-18062)
MAIN TAPE CO INC
521 27th St (33407-5458)
PHONE.................................561 248-8867
Alan Faille, *Principal*
Bethann Belardo, *Accountant*
Troy Marshall, *Sales Mgr*
EMP: 8 EST: 2012
SALES (est): 214K **Privately Held**
WEB: www.maintape.com
SIC: **3842** Surgical appliances & supplies

(G-18063)
MAKO HOSE & RUBBER CO
8331 Mc Allister Way 100a (33411-3713)
PHONE.................................561 795-6200
John Cobb, *President*
Kim Cobb, *Corp Secy*
Manuel R Perez, *Vice Pres*
▼ EMP: 5 EST: 1990
SQ FT: 5,500
SALES (est): 1MM **Privately Held**
WEB: www.makohose.com
SIC: **3069 3492** Sheeting, rubber or rub-
berized fabric; hose & tube fittings & as-
semblies, hydraulic/pneumatic

(G-18064)
MARBON INC
10723 Ibis Reserve Cir (33412-1341)
PHONE.................................561 822-9999
Edward Bonieski, *President*
Paul Vassalotti, *Vice Pres*
Vera Bonieski, *Treasurer*
EMP: 14 EST: 1994
SQ FT: 37,000
SALES (est): 559.3K **Privately Held**
WEB: www.marbon.com
SIC: **3272** Cast stone, concrete

(G-18065)
**MARINE HDWR SPECIALISTS
INC**
3570 Consumer St Ste 1 (33404-1740)
PHONE.................................561 766-1987
Bernard G Sykes, *Principal*
EMP: 7 EST: 2016
SALES (est): 74.5K **Privately Held**
SIC: **3429** Marine hardware

(G-18066)
MARK PLATING CO
441 25th St (33407-5407)
PHONE.................................561 655-4370
Kevin Hendrickson, *President*
Kristi Hendrickson, *Partner*
Shirley Hendrickson, *Partner*
EMP: 6 EST: 1977
SQ FT: 1,800
SALES (est): 695.8K **Privately Held**
WEB: www.markplating.com
SIC: **3471** Plating of metals or formed
products

(G-18067)
MARKET INK USA INC
1000 S Military Trl Ste D (33415-4774)
PHONE.................................561 502-3438
Jonatan Guzman, *President*
Jose Dominguez, *Vice Pres*
EMP: 7 EST: 2011
SALES (est): 175.7K **Privately Held**
WEB: www.marketink.net
SIC: **2752** Commercial printing, offset

▲ = Import ▼=Export
◆ =Import/Export

(G-18068)
MASON WAYS INDSTRCTBLE PLAS LL
580 Village Blvd Ste 330 (33409-1953)
PHONE..............................561 478-8838
Debbie Shrake, *Vice Pres*
Judd Ettinger,
Shelly Ettinger,
Anna Swartz,
EMP: 20 EST: 1978
SQ FT: 2,000
SALES (est): 4.6MM **Privately Held**
WEB: www.masonways.com
SIC: 3089 Pallets, plastic

(G-18069)
MATRIX COATINGS CORP
3575 Investment Ln (33404-1728)
PHONE..............................561 848-1288
Larry Sloan, *President*
Dave Barbato, *Principal*
Terry Sloan, *Principal*
EMP: 12 EST: 2019
SALES (est): 1MM **Privately Held**
WEB: www.matrixcoat.com
SIC: 3479 Coating of metals & formed products

(G-18070)
MATRIX COATINGS INC
3575 Investment Ln (33404-1728)
PHONE..............................561 848-1288
Jack Thygesen, *President*
EMP: 9 EST: 2002
SQ FT: 20,000
SALES (est): 1.4MM **Privately Held**
WEB: www.musselbuster.com
SIC: 3479 Coating of metals & formed products

(G-18071)
MDH GRAPHIC SERVICES INC
5001 Georgia Ave (33405-3101)
PHONE..............................561 533-9000
George W Davison, *President*
EMP: 10 EST: 1978
SQ FT: 3,800
SALES (est): 822.1K **Privately Held**
WEB: www.mdhprinting.com
SIC: 2752 Commercial printing, offset

(G-18072)
MEGAMAXMONEY LLC
931 Village Blvd (33409-1803)
PHONE..............................561 523-4458
Matthew Okosodo, *Branch Mgr*
EMP: 12 **Privately Held**
SIC: 2844 Perfumes & colognes; shampoos, rinses, conditioners: hair; face creams or lotions; lipsticks
PA: Megamaxmoney, Llc
4843 Palmbrooke Cir
West Palm Beach FL 33417

(G-18073)
MEGAMAXMONEY LLC (PA)
4843 Palmbrooke Cir (33417-7540)
PHONE..............................561 523-4458
Matthew Okosodo,
EMP: 7 EST: 2018
SALES (est): 129.4K **Privately Held**
SIC: 2844 5122 Perfumes & colognes; shampoos, rinses, conditioners: hair; face creams or lotions; lipsticks; cosmetics, perfumes & hair products

(G-18074)
MEMO LABS INC
8390 Currency Dr Ste 4 (33404-1745)
PHONE..............................561 842-0586
Barbara Daniels, *Ch of Bd*
Jack Daniels, *President*
Bob Carter, *Vice Pres*
Bernice Czapkewicz, *Admin Sec*
▲ EMP: 10 EST: 1981
SQ FT: 4,000
SALES (est): 754K **Privately Held**
SIC: 3672 Printed circuit boards

(G-18075)
MERCHANTS METALS LLC
1601 Hill Ave Ste B (33407-2233)
PHONE..............................561 478-0059
David Hickaersos, *Manager*
EMP: 8

SALES (corp-wide): 1B **Privately Held**
WEB: www.merchantsmetals.com
SIC: 3496 Fencing, made from purchased wire; mesh, made from purchased wire; concrete reinforcing mesh & wire
HQ: Merchants Metals Llc
3 Ravinia Dr Ste 1750
Atlanta GA 30346
770 741-0300

(G-18076)
MESTIZO PERUVIAN CUISINE LLC
511 Northwood Rd (33407-5817)
PHONE..............................561 469-1164
Bruce Parrish, *Administration*
EMP: 8 EST: 2019
SALES (est): 453.2K **Privately Held**
WEB: www.mestizoperuvian.com
SIC: 2092 Fresh or frozen packaged fish

(G-18077)
MICA CRAFT & DESIGN INC
3905 Investment Ln Ste 15 (33404-1700)
PHONE..............................561 863-5354
Paul Sharone, *President*
Diane Sharone, *Corp Secy*
EMP: 15 EST: 1984
SQ FT: 7,000
SALES (est): 1MM **Privately Held**
WEB: www.micacraftanddesign.com
SIC: 3429 2434 Furniture builders' & other household hardware; wood kitchen cabinets

(G-18078)
MICROGERM DEFENSE LLC
2257 Vista Pk Way Ste 22 (33411)
PHONE..............................561 309-0842
Amin Rahi, *Branch Mgr*
EMP: 20
SALES (corp-wide): 119.9K **Privately Held**
WEB: www.microgermdefense.com
SIC: 3812 Defense systems & equipment
PA: Microgerm Defense, Llc
8577 Estate Dr
West Palm Beach FL

(G-18079)
MICROSALT INC
515 N Flagler Dr Ste P300 (33401-4326)
PHONE..............................877 825-0655
Victor Hugo Manzanilla, *CEO*
EMP: 12 EST: 2020
SALES (est): 1.5MM **Privately Held**
SIC: 2899 Salt

(G-18080)
MOBILE AUTO SOLUTIONS LLC ✪
1578 Quail Dr Apt 10 (33409-4757)
PHONE..............................561 903-5328
Marquisha Wright,
EMP: 8 EST: 2021
SALES (est): 120K **Privately Held**
WEB: www.autosolutionfl.com
SIC: 2273 7389 Automobile floor coverings, except rubber or plastic;

(G-18081)
MR GRAPHIC PRTG & SIGNS LLC
2300 Palm Bch Lkes Blvd S (33409)
PHONE..............................561 424-1724
Nabil A Gabriel, *Manager*
EMP: 7 EST: 2018
SALES (est): 467.8K **Privately Held**
WEB: www.mrgraphic.org
SIC: 3993 Signs & advertising specialties

(G-18082)
MUELLER INDUSTRIES INC
525 Okeechobee Blvd # 860 (33401-6331)
PHONE..............................901 753-3200
Mark Manni, *Manager*
EMP: 8 **Publicly Held**
WEB: www.muellerindustries.com
SIC: 3351 Copper & copper alloy pipe & tube
PA: Mueller Industries, Inc.
150 Schilling Blvd # 100
Collierville TN 38017

(G-18083)
N2W SOFTWARE INC
500 S Australian Ave # 910 (33401-6220)
PHONE..............................561 225-2483
Jason Judge, *CEO*
Ohad Kritz, *COO*
Andrew Langsam, *COO*
Elizabeth Lewis, *Engineer*
Elliott Bell, *Accounts Mgr*
EMP: 14 EST: 2012
SQ FT: 3,000
SALES (est): 5.2MM
SALES (corp-wide): 62.3MM **Privately Held**
WEB: www.n2ws.com
SIC: 7372 Utility computer software
HQ: Veeam Software Group Gmbh
Lindenstrasse 16
Baar ZG 6340
417 667-131

(G-18084)
NATIONAL DIRECT SIGNS LLC
777 S Flagler Dr (33401-6161)
PHONE..............................561 320-2102
Daniela Skeen, *Mng Member*
EMP: 50 EST: 2017
SALES (est): 2.3MM **Privately Held**
WEB: www.nationaldirectsigns.com
SIC: 3993 Signs & advertising specialties

(G-18085)
NATIONAL MOLD TESTING
1057 Siena Oaks Cir E (33410-5133)
PHONE..............................561 626-7418
Allan Tann, *Principal*
EMP: 7 EST: 2004
SALES (est): 111.2K **Privately Held**
WEB: www.nationalmoldtesting.com
SIC: 3544 Industrial molds

(G-18086)
NATURES EARTH PRODUCTS INC
2200 N Fl Mango Rd # 403 (33409-6468)
PHONE..............................561 688-8101
Kenyon Allen Simard, *CEO*
Fred Burckbuchler, *Vice Pres*
Jana Simardparker, *Mng Member*
▼ EMP: 20 EST: 1993
SQ FT: 6,000
SALES (est): 3.6MM **Privately Held**
WEB: www.naturesearth.com
SIC: 3297 Cement refractories, nonclay

(G-18087)
NAZTEC INTERNATIONAL GROUP LLC
263 N Jog Rd (33413-1712)
PHONE..............................561 802-4110
Pazhoor Mohamed, *Branch Mgr*
EMP: 13
SALES (corp-wide): 3MM **Privately Held**
WEB: www.naztecgroup.com
SIC: 3579 Voting machines
PA: Naztec International Group, Llc
8983 Okeechobee Blvd # 202
West Palm Beach FL 33411
561 802-4110

(G-18088)
NAZTEC INTERNATIONAL GROUP LLC (PA)
Also Called: Smartpoll Election Solutions
8983 Okeechobee Blvd # 202 (33411-5115)
PHONE..............................561 802-4110
Sadiq Shariff, *COO*
Saeeda Mohamed, *Vice Pres*
Sal Pazhoor, *Mng Member*
▲ EMP: 10 EST: 2003
SQ FT: 3,500
SALES (est): 3MM **Privately Held**
WEB: www.naztecgroup.com
SIC: 3579 7379 5049 5013 Voting machines; computer related consulting services; engineers' equipment & supplies; automotive supplies & parts

(G-18089)
NEPTUNE PETROLEUM LLC
3974 Okeechobee Blvd # 2 (33409-4043)
PHONE..............................561 684-2844
EMP: 8 EST: 2007

SALES (est): 740K **Privately Held**
SIC: 1311 Crude Petroleum/Natural Gas Production

(G-18090)
NEW HOPE SUGAR COMPANY
1 N Clematis St (33401-5550)
PHONE..............................561 366-5120
Oscar R Hernandez, *Principal*
EMP: 10 EST: 2007
SALES (est): 224.5K **Privately Held**
SIC: 2099 Food preparations

(G-18091)
NEWSMAX MEDIA INC
1501 Nrthpint Pkwy Ste 10 (33407)
PHONE..............................561 686-1165
Solange Reyner, *Editor*
Andy Brown, *Senior VP*
Elliot Jacobson, *Senior Mgr*
EMP: 10
SALES (corp-wide): 127.9MM **Privately Held**
SIC: 2721 2741 Periodicals; miscellaneous publishing
PA: Newsmax Media, Inc.
750 Park Of Commerce Dr # 100
Boca Raton FL 33487
561 686-1165

(G-18092)
NIKIANI INC
Also Called: Buggy Guard
717 Maritime Way (33410-3425)
PHONE..............................305 606-1104
Annette M Atteridge, *President*
Christopher B Atteridge, *Vice Pres*
▲ EMP: 5 EST: 2005
SQ FT: 1,000
SALES (est): 484.4K **Privately Held**
WEB: www.nikiani.com
SIC: 3944 Strollers, baby (vehicle)

(G-18093)
NITV FEDERAL SERVICES LLC
11400 Fortune Cir (33414-8741)
PHONE..............................561 798-6280
Jim Kane, *Marketing Staff*
David Hughes, *Exec Dir*
EMP: 6 EST: 2003
SALES (est): 792.7K **Privately Held**
WEB: www.cvsa1.com
SIC: 3669 Communications equipment

(G-18094)
NOVO AERO SERVICES LLC
6965 Vista Pkwy N Ste 16 (33411-6757)
PHONE..............................786 319-8637
Petr Kraus, *General Mgr*
Leonardo Novo, *Principal*
Kimberly Novo, *Vice Pres*
EMP: 9 EST: 2014
SALES (est): 1.1MM **Privately Held**
WEB: www.novoaeroservices.com
SIC: 3728 Aircraft parts & equipment

(G-18095)
OIL WATER SEPARATOR TECH LLC
7020 Georgia Ave Ste A (33405-4568)
PHONE..............................561 693-3250
Thomas D Bieneman, *Mng Member*
EMP: 5 EST: 2013
SALES (est): 300.9K **Privately Held**
WEB: www.owstech.com
SIC: 3822 Hydronic controls

(G-18096)
OKEECHOBEE PETROLEUM LLC
6970 Okeechobee Blvd (33411-2508)
PHONE..............................561 478-1083
Paula Lean, *Principal*
EMP: 10 EST: 2008
SALES (est): 536.5K **Privately Held**
SIC: 2911 Petroleum refining

(G-18097)
OKEELANTA CORPORATION (HQ)
Also Called: Florida Crystals
1 N Clematis St Ste 200 (33401-5551)
P.O. Box 1059, Palm Beach (33480-1059)
PHONE..............................561 366-5100
Alfonso Fanjul Jr, *Ch of Bd*

Jose Fanjul, *President*
Evelyn Hopkins, *Counsel*
Nicole Rocco, *Counsel*
Donald W Carson, *Exec VP*
◆ **EMP:** 35 **EST:** 1984
SQ FT: 9,000
SALES (est): 131.2MM
SALES (corp-wide): 2.1B **Privately Held**
WEB: www.bellegladechamber.com
SIC: 2061 2062 Raw cane sugar; cane
sugar refining
PA: Fanjul Corp.
　1 N Clematis St Ste 200
　West Palm Beach FL 33401
　561 655-6303

(G-18098)
OLIVERI WOODWORKING INC
3001 Tuxedo Ave (33405-1031)
PHONE..................561 478-7233
Vincent Oliveri, *President*
EMP: 24 **EST:** 1988
SALES (est): 1.5MM **Privately Held**
WEB: www.oliverimillworks.com
SIC: 2431 5211 3442 Woodwork, interior
& ornamental; cabinets, kitchen; moldings
& trim, except automobile: metal

(G-18099)
ONE STOP GENERATOR SHOP INC
3600 Inv Ln Ste 104 (33404)
PHONE..................561 840-0009
Jon Andio, *President*
EMP: 8 **EST:** 2007
SALES (est): 1.7MM **Privately Held**
WEB: www.1stopgeneratorshop.com
SIC: 3621 Motors & generators

(G-18100)
OTIS ELEVATOR COMPANY
5500 Village Blvd (33407-1961)
PHONE..................561 618-4831
Jorge Castillo, *Counsel*
EMP: 500
SALES (corp-wide): 14.3B **Publicly Held**
WEB: www.otis.com
SIC: 3534 1796 7699 Elevators & equipment; escalators, passenger & freight;
walkways, moving; installing building
equipment; elevator installation & conversion; miscellaneous building item repair
services; elevators: inspection, service &
repair
HQ: Otis Elevator Company
　1 Carrier Pl
　Farmington CT 06032
　860 676-6000

(G-18101)
OXBOW CALCING LLC
1601 Forum Pl Ph 2 (33401-8104)
PHONE..................580 874-2201
Jonathan Bartley, *Project Engr*
Rick Thurlow, *Regl Sales Mgr*
Paul Koenig, *Manager*
EMP: 59 **EST:** 2015
SALES (est): 10.2MM **Privately Held**
WEB: www.oxbow.com
SIC: 2911 Petroleum refining

(G-18102)
OXBOW CALCING USA INC (DH)
1601 Forum Pl Ste 1400 (33401-8104)
PHONE..................580 874-2201
Steve Fried, *Exec VP*
Zachary Shipley, *CFO*
EMP: 107 **EST:** 1998
SALES (est): 41.5MM
SALES (corp-wide): 859.6MM **Privately Held**
WEB: www.oxbow.com
SIC: 2999 Coke (not from refineries), pe-
troleum

(G-18103)
OXBOW CARBON LLC (DH)
1601 Forum Pl Ste 1400 (33401-8104)
PHONE..................561 907-5400
William I Koch, *CEO*
Gord McIntosh, *Exec VP*
Roy J Schorsch, *Exec VP*
William D Parmelee, *CFO*
Sharon Anderson, *Accounting Mgr*
EMP: 800 **EST:** 2006

SALES (est): 741MM
SALES (corp-wide): 859.6MM **Privately Held**
WEB: www.oxbow.com
SIC: 1241 2062 5052 Coal mining serv-
ices; coke, calcined petroleum: made
from purchased materials; coal
HQ: Oxbow Corporation
　1601 Forum Pl Ste 1400
　West Palm Beach FL 33401
　561 907-5400

(G-18104)
OXBOW ENTERPRISES INTL LLC
1601 Forum Pl Ste 1400 (33401-8104)
PHONE..................561 907-5400
EMP: 5
SALES (est): 499.1K **Privately Held**
SIC: 1241 2999 5052 Coal mining serv-
ices; coke, calcined petroleum: made
from purchased materials; coal

(G-18105)
OZ NATURALS LLC
319 Clematis St Ste 700 (33401-4622)
PHONE..................561 602-2932
Mike Small, *CFO*
Samer Marwani, *Sales Staff*
Richard C Romero,
▲ **EMP:** 5 **EST:** 2015
SALES (est): 754.7K **Privately Held**
WEB: www.oznaturals.com
SIC: 2844 Toilet preparations

(G-18106)
P B C CULTURAL COUNSEL
1555 Palm Bch Lakes Blvd (33401-2323)
PHONE..................561 471-2903
Rena Blades, *CEO*
Rina Blades, *President*
Sonya Davis, *Vice Pres*
EMP: 10 **EST:** 2005
SALES (est): 909.7K **Privately Held**
SIC: 2836 Culture media

(G-18107)
PALM BEACH CAST STONE INC
Also Called: Palm Beach Limestone
809 N Railroad Ave (33401-3301)
PHONE..................561 835-4085
Steve Ford, *President*
Jeannie Foss, *Regional Mgr*
▼ **EMP:** 45 **EST:** 1984
SALES (est): 5.1MM **Privately Held**
WEB: www.pbcaststone.com
SIC: 3272 Cast stone, concrete

(G-18108)
PALM BEACH EMBROIDERY USA INC
8645 N Military Trl (33410-6294)
PHONE..................561 506-6307
Robert L Marzullo, *Principal*
EMP: 5 **EST:** 2014
SALES (est): 495.9K **Privately Held**
WEB: www.palmbeachembroidery.com
SIC: 2395 Embroidery products, except
schiffli machine

(G-18109)
PALM BEACH IRON WORKS INC
7768 Belvedere Rd (33411-3896)
PHONE..................561 683-1816
Jim Roy Higgins Jr, *President*
Elsie S Higgins, *Corp Secy*
Jim Roy Higgins Sr, *Vice Pres*
Swallows Tim, *Sales Staff*
▼ **EMP:** 22 **EST:** 1973
SQ FT: 25,000
SALES (est): 3.7MM **Privately Held**
WEB: www.pbiron.com
SIC: 3441 Fabricated structural metal

(G-18110)
PALM BEACH LIQUIDATION COMPANY (PA)
Also Called: Naples Illustrated
1000 N Dixie Hwy Ste C (33401-3349)
P.O. Box 3344, Palm Beach (33480-1544)
PHONE..................561 659-0210
Michele Hurtado, *Editor*
Ronald Woods, *Chairman*
Karen Powell, *COO*
Kassandre Kallen, *Production*

Dina Turner, *Sls & Mktg Exec*
EMP: 26 **EST:** 1952
SQ FT: 4,500
SALES (est): 5MM **Privately Held**
WEB: www.palmbeachmedia.com
SIC: 2721 Magazines: publishing only, not
printed on site

(G-18111)
PALM BEACH NEWSPAPERS INC
Also Called: Palm Beach Daily News
2751 S Dixie Hwy (33405-1298)
P.O. Box 1151, Palm Beach (33480-1151)
PHONE..................561 820-3800
Michael Brockman, *Partner*
V B Breckenridge, *Treasurer*
Joyce Harr, *Branch Mgr*
EMP: 158
SALES (corp-wide): 1.6MM **Privately Held**
SIC: 2721 2711 2741 Magazines: publish-
ing & printing; newspapers, publishing &
printing; miscellaneous publishing
HQ: Palm Beach Newspapers, Inc.
　6205-A Pchtree Dnwody Rd
　Atlanta GA 30328
　678 645-0000

(G-18112)
PALM PRINT INC
Also Called: Sir Speedy
919 N Dixie Hwy (33401-3329)
PHONE..................561 833-9661
Yuda Raz, *President*
Shauna Makrealeas, *General Mgr*
EMP: 12 **EST:** 1981
SQ FT: 3,600
SALES (est): 1.9MM **Privately Held**
WEB: www.thepalmbeachprinter.com
SIC: 2752 Commercial printing, litho-
graphic

(G-18113)
PASSPORT PBLCATIONS MEDIA CORP
Also Called: Palm Bch Pssport Pblctons Mdia
1555 Palm Beach Lakes Blv (33401-2335)
PHONE..................561 615-3900
Robert Kirschner, *President*
Peter Greenberg, *Publisher*
Patrick Gamble, *Editor*
John Thomason, *Editor*
Angelo Lopresti, *COO*
EMP: 20 **EST:** 1989
SQ FT: 4,000
SALES (est): 5.6MM **Privately Held**
WEB: www.passportpublications.com
SIC: 2721 7311 Magazines: publishing
only, not printed on site; advertising agen-
cies

(G-18114)
PATHFNDERS PALM BCH-MRTIN CNTY
Also Called: Palm Beach Post
2751 S Dixie Hwy (33405-1233)
PHONE..................561 820-4262
Janie Fogt, *President*
Tom Elia, *Editor*
Jim Hayward, *Editor*
Dominic Pugliese, *Editor*
Carol Rose, *Editor*
EMP: 41 **EST:** 2010
SALES (est): 111.4K **Privately Held**
WEB: www.palmbeachpost.com
SIC: 2711 Newspapers, publishing & print-
ing

(G-18115)
PAUL HIMBER INC
5324 Georgia Ave (33405-3520)
P.O. Box 6007 (33405-6007)
PHONE..................561 586-3741
Paul Himber, *President*
Elizabeth A Himber, *Vice Pres*
EMP: 10 **EST:** 1979
SQ FT: 5,000
SALES (est): 682K **Privately Held**
WEB: www.paulhimberinc.com
SIC: 2391 5023 Draperies, plastic & tex-
tile: from purchased materials; draperies

(G-18116)
PAW PRINT CO
1593 Trotter Ct (33414-1063)
PHONE..................561 753-5588
Peter Wiesner, *Vice Pres*
EMP: 6 **EST:** 2006
SALES (est): 446.3K **Privately Held**
WEB: www.pawprintsco.com
SIC: 2752 Commercial printing, offset

(G-18117)
PEAKTOP TECHNOLOGIES INC
1727 Okeechobee Rd (33409-5225)
PHONE..................561 598-6005
Jeff Robins, *President*
Greg Shutte, *Vice Pres*
Mark Wilson, *Vice Pres*
▲ **EMP:** 12 **EST:** 2003
SQ FT: 1,000
SALES (est): 122.8K **Privately Held**
SIC: 3089 Watering pots, plastic

(G-18118)
PETER T AMANN
Also Called: Poly Systems Co
8111 Garden Rd Ste G (33404-1751)
PHONE..................561 848-2770
Peter T Amann, *Owner*
EMP: 6 **EST:** 1972
SQ FT: 6,600
SALES (est): 486.6K **Privately Held**
SIC: 2732 5162 2678 5199 Pamphlets:
printing only, not published on site; plas-
tics materials & basic shapes; tablets &
pads, book & writing: from purchased ma-
terials; packaging materials

(G-18119)
PETROLEUM MARINE LLC
15985 Meadow Wood Dr (33414-9027)
PHONE..................561 422-9018
Karen A Doyle,
EMP: 6 **EST:** 2003
SALES (est): 621.8K **Privately Held**
WEB:
www.petroleummarineconstruction.com
SIC: 2911 Petroleum refining

(G-18120)
PHIL ROWE SIGNS INC
805 N Dixie Hwy (33401-3327)
PHONE..................561 832-8688
Stephen Rowe, *President*
Allayne Rowe, *Admin Sec*
EMP: 5 **EST:** 1949
SQ FT: 3,500
SALES (est): 378.5K **Privately Held**
SIC: 3993 Signs & advertising specialties

(G-18121)
PINEAPPLE GROVE WOODWORKS INC
3740 Prospect Ave (33404-3445)
PHONE..................561 676-1287
EMP: 9 **EST:** 2017
SALES (est): 440.2K **Privately Held**
SIC: 2431 Millwork

(G-18122)
PLASMA CREATIONS LLC
6014 14th Pl S (33415-4500)
PHONE..................561 324-8214
James Faucett, *Principal*
EMP: 5 **EST:** 2015
SALES (est): 772.9K **Privately Held**
WEB: www.plasmacreationsllc.com
SIC: 2836 Plasmas

(G-18123)
POMA CORPORATION
9040 Belvedere Rd (33411-3636)
PHONE..................561 790-5799
Patrick Whelan, *Ch of Bd*
David Zajac, *President*
Roger Seitz, *Purch Dir*
EMP: 52 **EST:** 1983
SQ FT: 52,000
SALES (est): 836.5K **Privately Held**
WEB: www.pomametals.com
SIC: 3355 3442 Rails, rolled & drawn, alu-
minum; storm doors or windows, metal

▲ = Import ▼=Export
◆ =Import/Export

GEOGRAPHIC

(G-18124)
PORATH FINE CABINETRY INC
3101 Tuxedo Ave (33405-1033)
PHONE.............................561 616-9400
Shaul Porath, *President*
EMP: 15 EST: 1991
SQ FT: 78,000
SALES (est): 1.6MM **Privately Held**
WEB: www.porathcabinets.com
SIC: 2434 Wood kitchen cabinets

(G-18125)
PRECISION EQUIPMENT CO INC
197 65th Ter N (33413-1715)
PHONE.............................561 689-4400
Henry J Goyette, *President*
Annette Goyette, *Vice Pres*
EMP: 9 EST: 1996
SQ FT: 7,000
SALES (est): 758.1K **Privately Held**
SIC: 3799 Trailers & trailer equipment

(G-18126)
PRECISION TURBINES INC (PA)
11250 Aviation Blvd Ste 4 (33412-0007)
PHONE.............................561 447-0032
Robert L Spahr, *President*
Susannah Forbes, *Human Resources*
Paul Capes, *Program Mgr*
EMP: 9 EST: 2007
SQ FT: 300
SALES (est): 2.2MM **Privately Held**
WEB: www.precisionturbines.aero
SIC: 3724 Aircraft engines & engine parts

(G-18127)
PREMIER PALLET RECYCLER LLC
1230 Gateway Rd Ste 1 (33403-1956)
PHONE.............................561 722-0457
James A Wilson, *Principal*
EMP: 7 EST: 2016
SALES (est): 87.5K **Privately Held**
WEB: www.premier-pallets.com
SIC: 2448 Pallets, wood

(G-18128)
PRESSURE SYSTEMS INNVTIONS LLC
3750 Investment Ln Ste 4 (33404-1765)
PHONE.............................561 249-2708
John Pankow, *Mng Member*
EMP: 11 EST: 2012
SALES (est): 1.5MM **Privately Held**
WEB:
www.pressuresystemsinnovations.com
SIC: 3699 5063 Cleaning equipment, ultrasonic, except medical & dental; electrical supplies

(G-18129)
PRESTIGE/AB READY MIX LLC (PA)
7228 Westport Pl Ste C (33413-1683)
PHONE.............................561 478-9980
Brian Mahoney,
Patti-Lee D'Ausilio, *Admin Sec*
Beat Kahail,
EMP: 20 EST: 2002
SALES (est): 11.2MM **Privately Held**
SIC: 3273 Ready-mixed concrete

(G-18130)
PROTO PLUS INC
350 Tall Pines Rd Ste B (33413-1700)
PHONE.............................561 471-5325
Steve L Price, *President*
Zozislaw Kozirl, *Vice Pres*
EMP: 5 EST: 2003
SALES (est): 430.9K **Privately Held**
WEB: www.protoplusinc.com
SIC: 3599 Machine shop, jobbing & repair

(G-18131)
PURAGEN LLC (DH)
Also Called: Oxbow Activated Carbon LLC
1601 Forum Pl Ste 1400 (33401-8104)
P.O. Box 4444, Oceanside CA (92052-4444)
PHONE.............................561 907-5400
Kenneth Schaeffer, *President*
Kimberly Walsh, *Vice Pres*
◆ EMP: 25 EST: 1998
SQ FT: 10,000

SALES (est): 24.7MM
SALES (corp-wide): 859.6MM **Privately Held**
WEB: www.puragen.com
SIC: 2819 5052 Charcoal (carbon), activated; coal

(G-18132)
PURE LABS LLC
240 10th St 1 (33401-3502)
PHONE.............................561 659-2229
Robin Case, *Principal*
EMP: 8 EST: 2008
SALES (est): 526.1K **Privately Held**
WEB: www.gopurebeauty.com
SIC: 2844 Toilet preparations

(G-18133)
PURECOAT INTERNATIONAL LLC (PA)
3301 Elec Way Ste B (33407)
P.O. Box 4406 (33402-4406)
PHONE.............................561 844-0100
George Bognar, *President*
Ron Keohan, *Prdtn Mgr*
Rob Sagehorn, *Purchasing*
Anjela Throckmorton, *QC Mgr*
Brenda Gleason, *Manager*
EMP: 24 EST: 1987
SQ FT: 39,500
SALES (est): 6.3MM **Privately Held**
WEB: www.purecoat.com
SIC: 3471 Electroplating of metals or formed products

(G-18134)
QHSLAB INC
901 Nrthpint Pkwy Ste 302 (33407)
PHONE.............................929 379-6503
Troy Grogan, *Ch of Bd*
EMP: 5 EST: 1983
SALES (est): 1.4MM **Privately Held**
WEB: www.usaqcorp.com
SIC: 3841 7372 Surgical & medical instruments; prepackaged software

(G-18135)
QUALITY READY MIX INC (PA)
1720 Centrepark Dr E # 100 (33401-7405)
PHONE.............................561 833-5555
Cemex Constmaterialssouth, *Principal*
EMP: 7 EST: 2012
SALES (est): 22.5MM **Privately Held**
WEB: www.qualityreadymix.org
SIC: 3273 Ready-mixed concrete

(G-18136)
R & R DOOR AND TRIM INC
8111 Garden Rd Ste J (33404-1751)
P.O. Box 9491 (33419-9491)
PHONE.............................561 844-5496
Robert M Danculovich, *President*
EMP: 5 EST: 1988
SQ FT: 5,000
SALES (est): 453.3K **Privately Held**
WEB: www.rrdoorandtrim.com
SIC: 2431 5031 Doors, wood; doors & windows; millwork

(G-18137)
R DORIAN MILLWORKS LLC
2361 Vista Pkwy Ste 7 (33411-2780)
PHONE.............................561 863-9125
Paul Reilly, *Manager*
EMP: 10 EST: 2015
SALES (est): 937.1K **Privately Held**
SIC: 2431 Millwork

(G-18138)
REDDY ICE CORPORATION
7719 Garden Rd (33404-3415)
PHONE.............................561 881-9501
Wayne Macmullen, *General Mgr*
EMP: 13
SQ FT: 21,200 **Privately Held**
WEB: www.reddyice.com
SIC: 2097 Manufactured ice
HQ: Reddy Ice Llc
5710 Lbj Fwy Ste 300
Dallas TX 75240
214 526-6740

(G-18139)
REICH METAL FABRICATORS INC
5405 Webster Ave (33405-3203)
P.O. Box 6036 (33405-6036)
PHONE.............................561 585-3173
James Bailey, *President*
John Childs, *Vice Pres*
Marion Bailey, *Admin Sec*
▼ EMP: 30 EST: 1918
SQ FT: 12,000
SALES (est): 1.9MM **Privately Held**
SIC: 3442 3446 Metal doors, sash & trim; architectural metalwork

(G-18140)
REWARD LIGHTING NET LLC
6000 Georgia Ave Ste 10 (33405-3946)
PHONE.............................561 832-1819
John J J Shea, *Principal*
EMP: 5 EST: 2015
SALES (est): 346K **Privately Held**
WEB: www.rewardlight.com
SIC: 3648 Lighting equipment

(G-18141)
RICH ICE CREAM CO
2915 S Dixie Hwy (33405-1585)
PHONE.............................561 833-7585
Randall Rich, *President*
John P Rich, *Chairman*
Renee Farias, *Business Mgr*
Martha R Rich, *Corp Secy*
Donald A Rich, *Vice Pres*
▼ EMP: 134 EST: 1946
SQ FT: 10,000
SALES (est): 25.3MM **Privately Held**
WEB: www.richicecream.com
SIC: 2024 Ice cream, bulk

(G-18142)
RIZO INDUSTRIES INC
310 Hemlock Rd (33409-6214)
PHONE.............................561 420-2548
A Alejandro Rizo Trian, *Principal*
EMP: 12 EST: 2019
SALES (est): 530.7K **Privately Held**
WEB: www.rizoindustries.com
SIC: 3999 Manufacturing industries

(G-18143)
ROBERT ST CROIX SCULPTURE STU
1400 Alabama Ave Ste 6 (33401-7048)
PHONE.............................561 835-1753
Robert St Croix, *Owner*
EMP: 6 EST: 1996
SALES (est): 734K **Privately Held**
WEB: www.robertstcroix.com
SIC: 3366 Copper foundries

(G-18144)
ROCKET TOWNE INC
412 Tall Pines Rd (33413-1717)
PHONE.............................561 478-1274
Jack Lucas, *President*
EMP: 9 EST: 2001
SALES (est): 624.9K **Privately Held**
SIC: 2899 Pyrotechnic ammunition: flares, signals, rockets, etc.

(G-18145)
RONMAR INDUSTRIES INC
8990 Lakes Blvd (33412-1550)
PHONE.............................561 630-8035
Marvin Starger, *President*
Ronny Starger, *Vice Pres*
EMP: 9 EST: 1965
SQ FT: 7,000
SALES (est): 412.6K **Privately Held**
WEB: www.ronmarequine.com
SIC: 2399 2353 3143 3144 Horse & pet accessories, textile; saddle cloth; hats & caps; boots, dress or casual: men's; boots, canvas or leather: women's; men's & boys' furnishings

(G-18146)
RORO INC
300 S Australian Ave # 16 (33401-5083)
PHONE.............................561 909-6220
EMP: 28 EST: 2003
SALES (est): 3.7MM **Privately Held**
SIC: 3496 Conveyor belts

(G-18147)
RSC MOLDING INC
475 N Cleary Rd Unit 4 (33413-1626)
PHONE.............................516 351-9871
Deborah Leo, *President*
Stephen Leo, *Vice Pres*
Tony Chan, *Engineer*
Bob Vanhorn, *VP Business*
Kelley White, *Clerk*
EMP: 14 EST: 2006
SALES (est): 726.8K
SALES (corp-wide): 4.2MM **Privately Held**
SIC: 3089 Injection molding of plastics
PA: Retail Solution Center, Inc.
475 N Cleary Rd Unit 4
West Palm Beach FL 33413
516 771-7000

(G-18148)
SB SIGNS INC
Also Called: Signs By Tomorrow
1300 N Florida Mango Rd # 20 (33409-5259)
PHONE.............................561 688-9100
Scott Bedford, *President*
Dave Tripp, *Sales Staff*
Mary Lou Bedford, *Admin Sec*
EMP: 5 EST: 1997
SQ FT: 2,300
SALES (est): 451K **Privately Held**
WEB: www.sbsigns.net
SIC: 3993 Signs & advertising specialties

(G-18149)
SETTY ENTERPRISES INC
Also Called: B T I
4128 Westroads Dr # 225 (33407-1253)
PHONE.............................561 844-3711
Swamy N Setty, *President*
Kiran Setty, *Vice Pres*
Shashi Setty, *Vice Pres*
EMP: 17 EST: 1994
SQ FT: 12,000
SALES (est): 2.5MM **Privately Held**
SIC: 3728 3599 Aircraft body assemblies & parts; machine shop, jobbing & repair

(G-18150)
SHANKER INDUSTRIES REALTY INC (PA)
3900 Fiscal Ct Ste 100 (33404-1726)
PHONE.............................631 940-9889
John Shanker, *President*
Francine Shanker, *Exec VP*
Frances Shanker, *Vice Pres*
▲ EMP: 5 EST: 1896
SALES (est): 1MM **Privately Held**
SIC: 3446 Ornamental metalwork

(G-18151)
SHOPWORKS LLC
1101 N Olive Ave (33401-3513)
PHONE.............................561 491-6000
Denise Brooks, *Marketing Staff*
Greg Stevens, *Manager*
Jay Malanga, *CTO*
Omar Castillo, *Technical Staff*
EMP: 9 EST: 1996
SALES (est): 1.1MM **Privately Held**
WEB: www.shopworx.com
SIC: 7372 Prepackaged software

(G-18152)
SIGN A RAMA INC (HQ)
Also Called: Sign-A-Rama
2121 Vista Pkwy (33411-2706)
PHONE.............................561 640-5570
Ray Titus, *CEO*
Brian Kinney, *President*
Matt Vaughn, *Managing Prtnr*
Phil Loftis, *General Mgr*
Gary Lengel, *Exec VP*
▼ EMP: 45 EST: 1986
SQ FT: 20,500
SALES (est): 53.4MM **Privately Held**
WEB: www.signaramaworthington.com
SIC: 3993 Signs & advertising specialties

(G-18153)
SILENT STANDBY POWER SUP LLC
3866 Prospect Ave Ste 5 (33404-3343)
PHONE.............................954 253-9557
Frank Freedman, *Mng Member*

EMP: 8 EST: 2009
SALES (est): 880.4K **Privately Held**
WEB: www.indoorgenerator.com
SIC: 3621 Power generators

(G-18154)

SILK SAFARI INC
613 Madeline Dr (33413-3421)
PHONE..........................561 689-3882
Jodie Quackenbush, *Treasurer*
EMP: 7 EST: 2016
SALES (est): 96.8K **Privately Held**
SIC: 3272 Concrete products

(G-18155)

SIMPLIFIED FABRICATORS INC
9040 Belvedere Rd (33411-3636)
PHONE..........................561 335-3488
Jean Chardon, *President*
EMP: 35 EST: 2017
SALES (est): 4.2MM **Privately Held**
SIC: 3713 Truck bodies & parts

(G-18156)

SOCKETS & SPECIALS INC
Also Called: Fastener Specialties Mfg Co
7110 Georgia Ave (33405-4556)
PHONE..........................561 582-7022
Richard Perkaus Jr, *President*
Donna Perkaus, *Vice Pres*
EMP: 15 EST: 1975
SQ FT: 4,500
SALES (est): 1MM **Privately Held**
WEB: www.fastenerspecialties.com
SIC: 3452 Screws, metal

(G-18157)

SOFTWARE PRODUCT SOLUTIONS LLC
12713 Westport Cir (33414-5537)
PHONE..........................561 798-6727
Joseph Carrigan, *Principal*
EMP: 5 EST: 2007
SALES (est): 322.7K **Privately Held**
SIC: 7372 Prepackaged software

(G-18158)

SOLITRON DEVICES INC
3301 Electronics Way C (33407-4697)
PHONE..........................561 848-4311
Tim Eriksen, *CEO*
David W Pointer, *Ch of Bd*
Mark W Matson, *President*
Joanne Crumbley, *General Mgr*
John Hunt, *Finance*
EMP: 74 EST: 1959
SQ FT: 47,000
SALES: 12.2MM **Privately Held**
WEB: www.solitrondevices.com
SIC: 3674 3676 Integrated circuits, semiconductor networks, etc.; electronic resistors

(G-18159)

SOUTH ESTRN PRSTRESSED CON INC
860 N Benoist Farms Rd (33411-3749)
P.O. Box 3768 (33402-3768)
PHONE..........................561 793-1177
Martin E Murphy Sr, *President*
EMP: 12 EST: 1966
SQ FT: 1,000
SALES (est): 139.4K
SALES (corp-wide): 1.1MM **Privately Held**
WEB: www.seprestressed.com
SIC: 3272 Prestressed concrete products
PA: Jamco, Inc.
1615 Clare Ave
West Palm Beach FL 33401
561 655-3634

(G-18160)

SOUTH FLORIDA FIELD TECHS INC
1598 Newhaven Point Ln (33411-6624)
PHONE..........................954 325-6548
John Randolph, *Director*
EMP: 8 EST: 2010
SALES (est): 417.4K **Privately Held**
SIC: 3732 Boat building & repairing

(G-18161)

STATE LIGHTING CO INC
405 4th Way (33407-6670)
PHONE..........................561 371-9529
Perry S Weisberg, *President*
EMP: 5 EST: 2009
SALES (est): 482.8K **Privately Held**
SIC: 3648 Lighting equipment

(G-18162)

STATEMENTS 2000 LLC
1374 N Killian Dr Ste A (33403-1901)
PHONE..........................561 249-1587
Jon Cohen, *Principal*
EMP: 7 EST: 2010
SALES (est): 962.9K **Privately Held**
WEB: www.statements2000.com
SIC: 3446 Architectural metalwork

(G-18163)

STELLAR SIGNS GRAP
5401 N Haverhill Rd (33407-7005)
PHONE..........................561 721-6060
EMP: 5 EST: 2019
SALES (est): 515.6K **Privately Held**
WEB: www.stellar-signs.com
SIC: 3993 Signs & advertising specialties

(G-18164)

STEVEN K BAKUM INC
Also Called: Sir Speedy
4634 S Dixie Hwy (33405-2932)
PHONE..........................561 804-9110
Steven K Bakum, *President*
Theresa Bakum, *Vice Pres*
EMP: 6 EST: 1982
SQ FT: 3,000
SALES (est): 889.1K **Privately Held**
WEB: www.sirspeedy.com
SIC: 2752 2791 2789 Commercial printing, lithographic; typesetting; bookbinding & related work

(G-18165)

STICK WITH US DELIVERY SVC LLC ✪
1481 7th St (33401-3042)
PHONE..........................561 425-4910
Tony Frith, *Principal*
EMP: 8 EST: 2021
SALES (est): 344.4K **Privately Held**
SIC: 3441 7389 Railroad car racks, for transporting vehicles: steel;

(G-18166)

STILL WATER INDUSTRIES INC
8400 Garden Rd Ste A (33404-1773)
PHONE..........................561 845-6033
John S Rey, *President*
Jeff Rey, *Vice Pres*
EMP: 7 EST: 1995
SQ FT: 12,800
SALES (est): 689.8K **Privately Held**
SIC: 2541 2517 Cabinets, except refrigerated: show, display, etc.: wood; home entertainment unit cabinets, wood

(G-18167)

STORM DEPOT PALM BEACH LLC
1202 S Congress Ave Ste A (33406-5402)
PHONE..........................561 721-9800
Frank Roca, *Partner*
EMP: 10 EST: 2005
SALES (est): 646.8K **Privately Held**
WEB: www.hurricaneshutterswestpalmbeach.com
SIC: 2431 Awnings, blinds & shutters, wood

(G-18168)

STRAIGHT LINE MLLWK & SUP INC
1315 N Jog Rd Ste 101 (33413-1022)
PHONE..........................561 422-0444
Neil Haset, *President*
▼ EMP: 11 EST: 2012
SALES (est): 2MM **Privately Held**
WEB: www.slcmi.com
SIC: 2431 Millwork

(G-18169)

SUNSHINE LTD TAPE & LABEL SPC
Also Called: Sunshine Tape & Label
516 24th St (33407-5404)
PHONE..........................561 832-9656
Larry Susauter, *President*
Joe Lindall, *Vice Pres*
Joseph Shalle, *Vice Pres*
EMP: 19 EST: 1985
SQ FT: 7,000
SALES (est): 1MM **Privately Held**
SIC: 2672 Tape, pressure sensitive: made from purchased materials

(G-18170)

SUNSHINE PRINTING INC (PA)
Also Called: Preferred Printing & Graphics
2605 Old Okeechobee Rd (33409-4146)
PHONE..........................561 478-2602
Dennis Watrous, *President*
Tim Gonyer, *Vice Pres*
Kevin Watrous, *Vice Pres*
▲ EMP: 16 EST: 1983
SQ FT: 7,500
SALES (est): 2MM **Privately Held**
WEB: www.preferredprinting.net
SIC: 2752 2791 2789 Commercial printing, offset; typesetting; bookbinding & related work

(G-18171)

SUPERIOR LEAF INC
Also Called: Superleaf
523 Ogston St Ste A (33405-2610)
P.O. Box 540403, Greenacres (33454-0403)
PHONE..........................561 480-2464
EMP: 7 EST: 2014
SQ FT: 3,500
SALES (est): 75K **Privately Held**
WEB: www.superiorleaf.com
SIC: 2621 Specialty papers

(G-18172)

SV MICROWAVE INC
2400 Cntre Pk W Dr Ste 10 (33409)
PHONE..........................561 840-1800
Subi Katragadda, *CEO*
Andrew Dinsdale, *Business Mgr*
Heri Aponte, *Vice Pres*
Laura Lopez, *Vice Pres*
Jeannette Roldan, *Vice Pres*
EMP: 150 EST: 1992
SQ FT: 20,000
SALES (est): 55.2MM
SALES (corp-wide): 10.8B **Publicly Held**
SIC: 3679 5065 3678 Microwave components; electronic parts & equipment; electronic connectors
PA: Amphenol Corporation
358 Hall Ave
Wallingford CT 06492
203 265-8900

(G-18173)

SWEET MIX LLC
2644 Starwood Cir (33406-5196)
PHONE..........................561 227-8332
Fabian Maly, *Principal*
EMP: 5 EST: 2019
SALES (est): 334.6K **Privately Held**
SIC: 3273 Ready-mixed concrete

(G-18174)

SYSTEM 48 PLUS INC
3866 Prospect Ave Ste 1 (33404-3343)
PHONE..........................561 844-5305
Max Houss, *Director*
EMP: 8 EST: 1998
SALES (est): 240.9K **Privately Held**
WEB: www.ladybirdworldcom.wordpress.com
SIC: 3599 Industrial machinery

(G-18175)

T M TOOLING INC
7341 Westport Pl Ste B (33413-1604)
PHONE..........................561 712-0903
Lindi Meier, *President*
Terry Meier, *Vice Pres*
EMP: 21 EST: 1985
SQ FT: 9,500
SALES (est): 1.3MM **Privately Held**
WEB: www.tmtooling.com
SIC: 3599 Machine shop, jobbing & repair

(G-18176)

TEE LINE CORP
11883 62nd Ln N (33412-2052)
PHONE..........................786 350-9526
Upton Coke, *Principal*
EMP: 19 EST: 2012
SALES (est): 1.2MM **Privately Held**
SIC: 2759 Screen printing

(G-18177)

THERMO ARL US INC (PA)
Also Called: Baird
1400 Northpoint Pkwy # 50 (33407-1976)
PHONE..........................800 532-4752
Marc Casper, *CEO*
Robert Boyd,
Dan Shine,
EMP: 30 EST: 2001
SALES (est): 7.2MM **Privately Held**
SIC: 3826 3829 3827 Spectrometers; measuring & controlling devices; optical instruments & lenses

(G-18178)

THERMO ELECTRON NORTH AMER LLC (DH)
1400 Nrthpint Pkwy Ste 10 (33407)
PHONE..........................561 688-8700
Seth H Hoogasian, *Senior VP*
Kenneth J Apicerno, *Vice Pres*
Christie Baldizar, *Engineer*
Christy Green, *Sales Staff*
Frank Trensch, *Director*
EMP: 46 EST: 2002
SQ FT: 22,750
SALES (est): 127MM
SALES (corp-wide): 39.2B **Publicly Held**
SIC: 3826 Analytical instruments
HQ: Thermo Fisher Scientific West Palm Holdings Llc
168 3rd Ave
Waltham MA 02451
781 622-1000

(G-18179)

THERMO FISHER SCIENTIFIC INC
1400 Nrthpint Pkwy Ste 10 (33407)
P.O. Box 11448 (33419-1448)
PHONE..........................561 688-8700
Kenneth Gray, *Vice Pres*
Bob Brister, *Sales Staff*
Karl Kastner, *Sales Staff*
Ronald George, *Business Anlyst*
Timothy Fahrenholz, *Technical Staff*
EMP: 307
SALES (corp-wide): 39.2B **Publicly Held**
WEB: www.thermofisher.com
SIC: 3826 5049 Analytical instruments; scientific instruments
PA: Thermo Fisher Scientific Inc.
168 3rd Ave
Waltham MA 02451
781 622-1000

(G-18180)

TIMES MICROWAVE SYSTEMS INC
2400 Cntre Pk W Dr Ste 10 (33409)
PHONE..........................203 949-8400
Marc Degan, *Opers Mgr*
EMP: 10
SALES (corp-wide): 10.8B **Publicly Held**
WEB: www.timesmicrowave.com
SIC: 3357 Nonferrous wiredrawing & insulating
HQ: Times Microwave Systems, Inc.
358 Hall Ave
Wallingford CT 06492
203 949-8400

(G-18181)

TITAN AMERICA LLC
9151 Weisman Way (33411-3603)
PHONE..........................800 396-3434
EMP: 11
SALES (corp-wide): 177.9K **Privately Held**
WEB: www.titanamerica.com
SIC: 3241 Cement, hydraulic
HQ: Titan America Llc
5700 Lake Wright Dr # 300
Norfolk VA 23502
757 858-6500

2022 Harris Florida
Manufacturers Directory

▲ = Import ▼=Export
◆ =Import/Export

(G-18182)
TITAN NATURAL FOCUS CORP
2701 Vista Pkwy (33411-5614)
PHONE...................................305 778-7005
Marcel Brunner, *CEO*
Golnesa Brunner, *Marketing Staff*
EMP: 9 **EST:** 2015
SALES (est): 117.7K **Privately Held**
WEB: www.titannaturalfocus.com
SIC: 2086 Bottled & canned soft drinks

(G-18183)
TNT CUSTOM CABINETRY INC
11093 49th St N (33411-8014)
PHONE...................................561 662-0964
Thomas Harper Brannigan, *Principal*
EMP: 8 **EST:** 2004
SALES (est): 506.6K **Privately Held**
WEB: www.tntcustombuilders.com
SIC: 2434 Wood kitchen cabinets

(G-18184)
TOLLIVER ALUMINUM SERVICE INC
Also Called: Tolliver Powder Coating
6810 Georgia Ave (33405-4520)
PHONE...................................561 582-8939
Brandon Greer, *President*
Eric Lebano, *General Mgr*
Wayne Frinkle, *Personnel*
▼ **EMP:** 18 **EST:** 1999
SQ FT: 15,000
SALES (est): 2.7MM **Privately Held**
WEB: www.tolliverpc.com
SIC: 3479 Coating of metals & formed products

(G-18185)
TOTALLY GLASS & BLINDS LLC
1027 Egremont Dr (33406-5032)
PHONE...................................561 929-6125
Marcel Llerena Alvarez, *Manager*
EMP: 8 **EST:** 2010
SALES (est): 222.5K **Privately Held**
SIC: 2591 Window blinds

(G-18186)
TRANE US INC
6965 Vista Pkwy N Ste 11 (33411-6757)
PHONE...................................561 683-1521
Lou Zaccone, *Branch Mgr*
EMP: 38 **Privately Held**
WEB: www.trane.com
SIC: 3585 Refrigeration & heating equipment
HQ: Trane U.S. Inc.
800 Beaty St Ste E
Davidson NC 28036
704 655-4000

(G-18187)
TRU CANE SUGAR CORP
1 N Clematis St Ste 200 (33401-5551)
PHONE...................................561 833-1731
EMP: 7 **EST:** 2019
SALES (est): 739K **Privately Held**
SIC: 2061 Raw cane sugar

(G-18188)
TULIPAN BAKERY INC (PA)
740 Belvedere Rd (33405-1108)
PHONE...................................561 832-6107
Jose Allione, *President*
Stella Allione, *Vice Pres*
EMP: 8 **EST:** 1971
SQ FT: 2,400
SALES (est): 843.1K **Privately Held**
WEB: www.tulipanbakery.com
SIC: 2051 5812 Bakery: wholesale or wholesale/retail combined; cafeteria

(G-18189)
U S COMPOSITES INC
5101 Georgia Ave (33405-3103)
PHONE...................................561 588-1001
Mark Ananos, *President*
▼ **EMP:** 5 **EST:** 2000
SALES (est): 999.1K **Privately Held**
WEB: www.uscomposites.com
SIC: 2821 Plastics materials & resins

(G-18190)
UFG GROUP INC (PA)
Also Called: United Franchise Group
2121 Vista Pkwy (33411-2706)
PHONE...................................561 425-6829
Raymond Titus, *President*
James Prendamano, *General Mgr*
Kyle Bostwick, *Regional Mgr*
Michael Glick, *Regional Mgr*
Charles Kowanetz, *Regional Mgr*
EMP: 8 **EST:** 2005
SALES (est): 92.8MM **Privately Held**
WEB: www.unitedfranchisegroup.com
SIC: 3993 Signs & advertising specialties

(G-18191)
ULTRA AIRCONDITIONING INC
801 Nrthpint Pkwy Ste 106 (33411-)
P.O. Box 1343, Boynton Beach (33425-1343)
PHONE...................................877 333-0189
Dalisa Schoburgh, *CEO*
EMP: 10 **EST:** 2015
SALES (est): 653.1K **Privately Held**
SIC: 1389 Construction, repair & dismantling services

(G-18192)
UNITED STRINGS INTL LLC
352 Tall Pines Rd Ste G (33413-1737)
PHONE...................................561 790-4191
Jorge F Monteiro, *Principal*
▲ **EMP:** 6 **EST:** 2012
SALES (est): 372K **Privately Held**
WEB: www.larchetbrasil.com
SIC: 3949 Arrows, archery

(G-18193)
US TRUSS INC
3400 45th St (33407-1844)
PHONE...................................561 686-4000
Erol Tuzcu, *President*
Kemal Aldemir, *Engineer*
EMP: 41 **EST:** 1990
SQ FT: 35,000
SALES (est): 5.4MM **Privately Held**
WEB: www.ustruss.com
SIC: 2439 Trusses, wooden roof

(G-18194)
VAPORBRANDS INTERNATIONAL INC
40 Easthampton B (33417-1907)
PHONE...................................352 573-6130
James Hodge, *Branch Mgr*
EMP: 19
SALES (corp-wide): 99.6K **Privately Held**
WEB: www.ecitemotors.com
SIC: 2111 Cigarettes
PA: Vaporbrands International, Inc.
8002 Mohawk Trl
Spring Hill FL
352 777-5284

(G-18195)
VERTARIB INC (PA)
Also Called: Thermacon
9005 Southern Blvd (33411-3625)
PHONE...................................877 815-8610
Alan Dinow, *CEO*
▼ **EMP:** 25 **EST:** 2009
SQ FT: 10,000
SALES (est): 3.8MM **Privately Held**
WEB: www.vertarib.com
SIC: 3443 Tank towers, metal plate

(G-18196)
VESTA T HETHERINGTON
Also Called: Vesta's
5411 S Olive Ave (33405-3344)
PHONE...................................561 588-9933
Vesta T Hetherington, *Owner*
EMP: 7 **EST:** 2014
SALES (est): 156.7K **Privately Held**
SIC: 3511 Turbines & turbine generator sets

(G-18197)
VIRAG DISTRIBUTION LLC
Also Called: Virag Biosciences
700 S Rosemary Ave # 204 (33401-6313)
PHONE...................................844 448-4724
Koutsogiannis Vas, *Mng Member*
EMP: 7 **EST:** 2019

SALES (est): 712.7K **Privately Held**
WEB: www.virag.bio
SIC: 3999

(G-18198)
VITAL SOLUTIONS LLC
3755 Fiscal Ct Ste 2 (33404-1704)
PHONE...................................561 848-1717
Ali Burnett, *Accounts Mgr*
Michelle Haas,
EMP: 5 **EST:** 2011
SQ FT: 6,000
SALES (est): 466.1K **Privately Held**
WEB: www.vitaloxide.com
SIC: 2836 Antitoxins

(G-18199)
VITAL USA INC
525 S Flagler Dr Ste 301 (33401-5932)
PHONE...................................561 282-6074
Irwin Gross, *CEO*
Robert Faber, *CFO*
Mark Haig Khachaturi, *CTO*
EMP: 12 **EST:** 2017
SQ FT: 3,100
SALES (est): 1.6MM **Privately Held**
WEB: www.wellvii.com
SIC: 3841 Surgical & medical instruments
PA: Arc Devices Limited
C/O Ion Equity Limited 15 Pembroke Street Lower
Dublin

(G-18200)
VR PRESERVE DEVELOPMENT LLC
1804 N Dixie Hwy Ste A (33407-6570)
PHONE...................................561 370-3617
Joseph Visconti, *President*
EMP: 30 **EST:** 2010
SALES (est): 495.2K **Publicly Held**
SIC: 2731 Book publishing
PA: Twin Vee Powercats, Inc.
3101 S Us Highway 1
Fort Pierce FL 34982

(G-18201)
WAFER WORLD INC
1100 Tech Pl Ste 104 (33407)
PHONE...................................561 842-4441
Sean Quinn, *President*
◆ **EMP:** 14 **EST:** 1985
SQ FT: 2,800
SALES (est): 2.2MM **Privately Held**
WEB: www.waferworld.com
SIC: 3674 Integrated circuits, semiconductor networks, etc.

(G-18202)
WALLACE INDUSTRIES INC
316 Valencia Rd (33401-7932)
PHONE...................................561 833-8554
Paul R Kludt, *President*
EMP: 8 **EST:** 2011
SALES (est): 233K **Privately Held**
SIC: 3999 Manufacturing industries

(G-18203)
WE MIX YOU MATCH INC
6524 Patricia Dr (33413-3402)
PHONE...................................561 615-0253
Dr Connie L Ingram, *President*
EMP: 9 **EST:** 2005
SALES (est): 108.7K **Privately Held**
SIC: 3273 Ready-mixed concrete

(G-18204)
WHITE COUNTY STONE LLC
135 Churchill Rd (33405-4143)
PHONE...................................415 516-0849
Peter Lombardi, *Mng Member*
EMP: 31 **EST:** 2017
SALES (est): 900K **Privately Held**
SIC: 1429 Boulder, crushed & broken-quarrying

(G-18205)
WICKED POLISHING INC
11254 67th Pl N (33412-1807)
PHONE...................................561 255-7554
Joshua W Camp, *Principal*
EMP: 7 **EST:** 2014
SALES (est): 120.3K **Privately Held**
WEB: wickedpolishing.webs.com
SIC: 3471 Polishing, metals or formed products

(G-18206)
WILD PRINTS LLC
12415 76th Rd N (33412-2277)
PHONE...................................561 800-6536
Michelle Brennan, *Mng Member*
EMP: 7 **EST:** 2013
SALES (est): 742.3K **Privately Held**
WEB: www.wildprints561.com
SIC: 2752 Commercial printing, lithographic

(G-18207)
WINDSOR & YORK INC
7233 Southern Blvd (33413-1648)
P.O. Box 2617, Palm Beach (33480-2617)
PHONE...................................561 687-8424
Peter B Newton, *President*
Linda Flower, *President*
EMP: 5 **EST:** 1996
SALES (est): 312.4K **Privately Held**
SIC: 2295 Leather, artificial or imitation

(G-18208)
WOOD U ENVISION
4252 Westroads Dr (33407-1219)
PHONE...................................561 601-1973
Thomas Fasig, *Owner*
EMP: 6 **EST:** 2017
SALES (est): 308.9K **Privately Held**
SIC: 2434 Wood kitchen cabinets

(G-18209)
YONDER WOODWORKS INC
4901 Georgia Ave (33405-3113)
PHONE...................................561 547-5777
Prior Powers, *President*
Judy Powers, *Owner*
EMP: 5 **EST:** 1985
SQ FT: 8,000
SALES (est): 558.9K **Privately Held**
WEB: www.yonderwoodworks.net
SIC: 2511 Wood household furniture

West Park
Broward County

(G-18210)
AK INDUSTRIES LLC
3530 Sw 47th Ave (33023-5553)
PHONE...................................954 662-7038
Donald Sarmento, *Principal*
EMP: 8 **EST:** 2012
SALES (est): 146.3K **Privately Held**
WEB: www.akindustries.com
SIC: 3999 Manufacturing industries

(G-18211)
EBCO ENVMTL BINS & CNTRS INC
2101 Sw 56th Ter (33023-3011)
PHONE...................................954 967-9999
Eduardo Brandao, *President*
Sonia Toro, *Admin Sec*
▼ **EMP:** 17 **EST:** 1994
SALES (est): 593K **Privately Held**
SIC: 3589 Garbage disposers & compactors, commercial

(G-18212)
GNJ MANUFACTURING INC
5811 Hallandale Bch Blvd (33023-5243)
PHONE...................................305 651-8644
Eric Gavara, *President*
▲ **EMP:** 35 **EST:** 1998
SQ FT: 30,000
SALES (est): 4MM **Privately Held**
WEB: www.gnjmanufacturing.com
SIC: 3911 5999 Jewelry apparel; mobile telephones & equipment

(G-18213)
HOLLYWOOD IRON WORKS INC
2313 Sw 57th Ter (33023-4026)
PHONE...................................954 962-0556
Joseph Caparelli, *President*
Ernest Caparelli, *President*
Irma Caparelli, *Director*
▼ **EMP:** 10 **EST:** 1970
SQ FT: 12,000
SALES (est): 3.2MM **Privately Held**
WEB: www.hollywoodiron.com
SIC: 3312 3441 Structural shapes & pilings, steel; fabricated structural metal

(G-18214)
IT PACS PRO SOFTWARE INC
5612 Pembroke Rd Ste A (33023-2304)
PHONE..................................954 678-1270
Robert Daniel, *Principal*
EMP: 6 EST: 2015
SALES (est): 338.6K **Privately Held**
WEB: www.itpacspro.com
SIC: 7372 Educational computer software

(G-18215)
MIAMI TRUCOLOR OFFSET SVC CO
2211 Sw 57th Ter (33023-3024)
PHONE..................................954 962-5230
Donald Melton, *President*
EMP: 9 EST: 1962
SQ FT: 20,000
SALES (est): 890.8K **Privately Held**
SIC: 2752 2796 Commercial printing, off-set; color separations for printing

(G-18216)
SHORELINE FOUNDATION INC
Also Called: Sfi
2781 Sw 56th Ave (33023-4166)
PHONE..................................954 985-0981
James A Royo, *President*
Fred Maxwell, *General Mgr*
Barry Reed, *Corp Secy*
John McGee, *Vice Pres*
Efrain D 'aleccio, *Safety Dir*
◆ EMP: 110 EST: 1986
SQ FT: 3,960
SALES (est): 23.3MM **Privately Held**
WEB: www.shorelinefoundation.com
SIC: 3448 1629 Prefabricated metal build-ings; pile driving contractor

Weston
Broward County

(G-18217)
911 EQUIPMENT INC (PA)
2645 Executive Park Dr (33331-3624)
PHONE..................................954 217-1745
Franco L Tortolani, *President*
Francisco Ramos, *Vice Pres*
▼ EMP: 8 EST: 2003
SALES (est): 2.5MM **Privately Held**
WEB: www.equipment911.com
SIC: 3569 Firefighting apparatus & related equipment

(G-18218)
954 SAVINGS MAGAZINE
405 Sailboat Cir (33326-1505)
PHONE..................................954 900-4649
EMP: 5
SALES (est): 334.3K **Privately Held**
SIC: 2721 Periodicals-Publishing/Printing

(G-18219)
ABC INTERCARGO LLC
2700 Glades Cir Ste 124 (33327-9100)
PHONE..................................954 908-5200
Leyde Janeth Pardo, *Exec Dir*
Freddy Godoy Leon, *Director*
Maria I Gonzalez,
EMP: 8 EST: 2011
SALES (est): 1.2MM **Privately Held**
WEB: www.abcintercargo.com
SIC: 3728 Aircraft parts & equipment

(G-18220)
ACTAVIS LABORATORIES FL INC
2945 W Corp Lks Blvd (33331-3626)
PHONE..................................954 358-6100
Laura Jolley, *Human Resources*
Janet Vaughn, *Branch Mgr*
EMP: 10 **Privately Held**
WEB: www.actavis.com
SIC: 2834 Pharmaceutical preparations
HQ: Actavis Laboratories Fl, Inc.
　　5 Giralda Farms
　　Madison NJ 07940
　　862 261-7000

(G-18221)
AFFINEON LIGHTING
16709 Amber Lk (33331-3165)
PHONE..................................407 448-3434

Teddy Van Bemmel, *Partner*
EMP: 7 EST: 2008
SALES (est): 236K **Privately Held**
SIC: 3646 Commercial indusl & institu-tional electric lighting fixtures

(G-18222)
AMINSA CORP
612 Bald Cypress Rd (33327-2456)
PHONE..................................954 865-1289
EMP: 6 EST: 2018
SALES (est): 414.4K **Privately Held**
WEB: www.aminsausa.com
SIC: 3441 Fabricated structural metal

(G-18223)
ANDRX CORPORATION
2915 Weston Rd (33331-3654)
PHONE..................................954 217-4500
Danys Martinez, *Production*
Debi Abelow, *Technology*
Donna Thompson, *Representative*
EMP: 231 **Privately Held**
WEB: www.andrx.com
SIC: 2834 Pharmaceutical preparations
HQ: Andrx Corporation
　　4955 Orange Dr
　　Davie FL 33314

(G-18224)
APACHE SHEET METAL
631 Stanton Ln (33326-4501)
PHONE..................................954 214-4468
Thomas Corette, *Owner*
EMP: 8 EST: 1984
SALES (est): 350K **Privately Held**
SIC: 3444 Sheet metalwork

(G-18225)
APOTEX CORP (DH)
2400 N Commerce Pkwy # 400
(33326-3253)
PHONE..................................954 384-8007
Jeff Watson, *President*
Bernard C Sherman, *Chairman*
Jim Young, *Exec VP*
Jack Kay, *Vice Pres*
Paul Martin, *Project Mgr*
▲ EMP: 50 EST: 1992
SALES (est): 81.1MM
SALES (corp-wide): 1.1B **Privately Held**
WEB: www.apotex.com
SIC: 2834 Pharmaceutical preparations
HQ: Apotex Holdings Inc.
　　150 Signet Dr
　　North York ON M9L 1
　　416 749-9300

(G-18226)
ARGUS INTERNATIONAL INC
318 Indian Trce (33326-2996)
PHONE..................................305 888-4881
Alfonso Hernandez, *President*
Roberto B Bequillard, *President*
Frederick Bustamante, *Admin Sec*
◆ EMP: 50 EST: 1989
SALES (est): 1.1MM **Privately Held**
SIC: 2331 Blouses, women's & juniors': made from purchased material
PA: Central American Cutting Center S.A. De C.V.
　　Zona Franca Miramar
　　Comalapa

(G-18227)
BANG ENERGY LLC
1600 N Park Dr (33326-3278)
PHONE..................................954 641-0570
John H Owoc, *Mng Member*
EMP: 18 EST: 2016
SALES (est): 1.7MM **Privately Held**
SIC: 2086 5651 Bottled & canned soft drinks; unisex clothing stores

(G-18228)
BEANO PUBLISHING LLC
1575 N Park Dr Ste 100 (33326-3230)
PHONE..................................954 689-8339
Rafael Wynn, *CFO*
Bryan Taylor,
Dina Taylor,
EMP: 10 EST: 2000
SALES (est): 1.1MM **Privately Held**
WEB: www.beanopublishing.com
SIC: 2741 Miscellaneous publishing

(G-18229)
BIGG D ENTERTAINMENT LLC
904 Stillwater Ct (33327-2130)
PHONE..................................917 204-0292
Derrick Baker,
EMP: 5 EST: 2005
SALES (est): 500K **Privately Held**
SIC: 2741 Music book & sheet music pub-lishing

(G-18230)
BIORESOURCE TECHNOLOGY LLC
1800 N Commerce Pkwy # 1 (33326-3221)
PHONE..................................954 792-5222
David Reichenbach, *President*
Ron Dilling, *COO*
Michael Leblanc, *Manager*
Thomas Hunter, *Director*
EMP: 20 EST: 2003
SQ FT: 23,000
SALES (est): 5.4MM
SALES (corp-wide): 58.8MM **Privately Held**
WEB: www.brt-us.com
SIC: 2836 Biological products, except diag-nostic
HQ: Oy Medix Biochemica Ab
　　Klovinpellontie 3
　　Espoo 02180
　　954 768-0

(G-18231)
CACAO FRUIT COMPANY
1500 Weston Rd Ste 200 (33326-3264)
PHONE..................................954 449-8704
Joseph W Montgomery III, *President*
EMP: 6 EST: 2017
SALES (est): 309.8K **Privately Held**
WEB: www.cacaofruitco.com
SIC: 2099 Food preparations

(G-18232)
CANVAS FOODS CORP
19266 Seneca Ave (33332-2437)
PHONE..................................786 529-8041
Ignacio Aguerrevere, *Principal*
EMP: 7 EST: 2016
SALES (est): 246.1K **Privately Held**
SIC: 2211 Canvas

(G-18233)
CNH INDUSTRIAL AMERICA LLC
3265 Meridian Pkwy # 124 (33331-3523)
PHONE..................................954 389-9779
EMP: 15
SALES (corp-wide): 28B **Privately Held**
SIC: 3523 Mfg Farm Equipments
HQ: Cnh Industrial America Llc
　　700 State St
　　Racine WI 60527
　　262 636-6011

(G-18234)
CONTRACT MFG SOLUTIONS INC
Also Called: Cmsi
1880 N Commerce Pkwy # 1 (33326-3223)
PHONE..................................954 424-9813
Edwin Aguilera, *President*
Don Lisiewski, *Principal*
Zana Maldonado, *Principal*
Kristin Aguilera, *Corp Secy*
EMP: 16 EST: 2001
SALES (est): 653.5K **Privately Held**
WEB: www.nikaousa.com
SIC: 3841 Surgical & medical instruments

(G-18235)
CROSS ATLANTIC COMMODITIES INC (PA)
Also Called: Cxac
4581 Weston Rd Ste 273 (33331-3141)
PHONE..................................954 678-0698
Jorge Bravo, *President*
EMP: 5 EST: 1998
SALES (est): 957.3K **Publicly Held**
WEB: www.crossac.com
SIC: 2024 5143 Ice cream & frozen desserts; ice cream & ices

(G-18236)
D V M PHARMACEUTICALS INC
3040 Universal Blvd (33331-3573)
PHONE..................................305 575-6950

Jane H Hsiao, *CEO*
EMP: 75 EST: 1975
SALES (est): 12.3MM **Privately Held**
SIC: 2834 Veterinary pharmaceutical preparations
HQ: Ivax Corporation
　　4400 Biscayne Blvd
　　Miami FL 33137
　　305 329-3795

(G-18237)
DIAMOND MOBA AMERICAS INC
2731 Executive Park Dr # 4 (33331-3619)
PHONE..................................954 384-5828
Dennis Glanert, *Production*
Troy Sigriest, *CFO*
Jose Gorosabel, *Manager*
▼ EMP: 100 EST: 2010
SQ FT: 1,500
SALES (est): 40MM **Privately Held**
WEB: www.moba.net
SIC: 3565 Packaging machinery
HQ: Moba Group B.V.
　　Stationsweg 117
　　Barneveld 3771
　　342 455-655

(G-18238)
DOUBLE J OF BROWARD INC (PA)
Also Called: Ritchie Swimwear
1800 N Commerce Pkwy # 2 (33326-3221)
PHONE..................................954 659-8880
Richard Berger, *CEO*
Michael Berger, *President*
Nina Berger, *Corp Secy*
◆ EMP: 23 EST: 1979
SQ FT: 13,000
SALES (est): 6MM **Privately Held**
SIC: 2339 5699 Bathing suits: women's, misses' & juniors'; athletic clothing: women's, misses' & juniors'; bathing suits; sports apparel

(G-18239)
ECLIPSE DEVELOPMENT LLC
Also Called: Eclipse Products
170 Lakeview Dr Apt 204 (33326-2541)
PHONE..................................520 370-7358
Daniel J Bailey, *Mng Member*
EMP: 16 EST: 2018
SALES (est): 1.1MM **Privately Held**
SIC: 2541 5112 5943 Store & office dis-play cases & fixtures; stationery & office supplies; office forms & supplies

(G-18240)
FASSI EQUIPMENT INC
Also Called: Fassiequipment.com
2800 Glades Cir Ste 127 (33327-2278)
PHONE..................................954 385-6555
Ricardo Fassi, *President*
◆ EMP: 6 EST: 2000
SQ FT: 2,000
SALES (est): 902.4K **Privately Held**
WEB: www.fassidigital.com
SIC: 2759 Screen printing

(G-18241)
FASSIDIGITALCOM INC
2800 Gldes Crcles Ste 127 (33327)
PHONE..................................954 385-6555
Riccardo Fassi, *President*
Maria Eugenia Fassi, *Vice Pres*
EMP: 9 EST: 2015
SALES (est): 179.8K **Privately Held**
WEB: www.fassidigital.com
SIC: 2759 7336 Screen printing; commer-cial art & graphic design

(G-18242)
FLORIDA FRESHNER CORP
1138 Sunflower Cir (33327-2105)
PHONE..................................954 349-0348
Jack Benmaor, *Principal*
EMP: 7 EST: 2010
SALES (est): 136.6K **Privately Held**
WEB: www.floridafreshner.com
SIC: 3999 Manufacturing industries

▲ = Import ▼=Export
◆ =Import/Export

(G-18243)
FOREST RESEARCH INSTITUTE INC
2915 Weston Rd (33331-3627)
PHONE.................................631 436-4600
William J Candee, *Ch of Bd*
Marco Taglietti, *Vice Pres*
EMP: 18 EST: 2008
SALES (est): 802.1K Privately Held
SIC: 2834 Pharmaceutical preparations

(G-18244)
FRANJA CORP
1515 Veracruz Ln (33327-1735)
PHONE.................................954 659-1950
Javier Oviedo, *President*
Diana Rueas, *Principal*
Diana Rojas, *Marketing Staff*
EMP: 5 EST: 2001
SALES (est): 347.3K Privately Held
WEB: www.tusanteojos.com
SIC: 2721 Magazines: publishing & printing

(G-18245)
G & G LATIN BUSINESS INC
16668 Saddle Club Rd (33326-1816)
PHONE.................................954 385-8085
Glenys Garcia, *President*
EMP: 7 EST: 2008
SALES (est): 501K Privately Held
SIC: 2099 Food preparations

(G-18246)
GASEOUS FUEL SYSTEMS CORP
Also Called: GFS
3360 Entp Ave Ste 180 (33331)
PHONE.................................954 693-9475
Kenneth Green, *CEO*
Jason Green, *President*
George Aguilera, *Vice Pres*
Warren J Roy, *CFO*
Arpesh Mehta, *Director*
EMP: 6 EST: 1998
SALES (est): 1MM Privately Held
SIC: 2869 Fuels

(G-18247)
GFS CORP
3360 Entp Ave Ste 180 (33331)
PHONE.................................954 693-9657
Kerry Hackney, *Vice Pres*
Scott A Greenwald, *Mng Member*
Jen Hupf, *Manager*
EMP: 33 EST: 1992
SALES (est): 3.2MM Privately Held
WEB: www.gfs-corp.com
SIC: 3519 Diesel engine rebuilding; governors, pump, for diesel engines

(G-18248)
GOLD-REP CORPORATION
Also Called: Sigillu
750 Heritage Dr (33326-4539)
PHONE.................................954 892-5868
Felipe Yungman, *CEO*
Douglas Haskins, *Manager*
EMP: 5 EST: 2010
SALES (est): 401.5K Privately Held
SIC: 7372 Prepackaged software

(G-18249)
GRAMPUS ENTERPRISES INC
Also Called: Grampus Tech
2800 Glades Cir Ste 109 (33327-2270)
PHONE.................................305 491-9827
Jim Fang, *President*
Jack Cai, *Exec Dir*
MEI Fang, *Director*
▲ **EMP: 5 EST: 1999**
SALES (est): 429.5K Privately Held
SIC: 3827 Optical instruments & lenses

(G-18250)
GWMF HOLDINGS LLC
16791 Royal Poinciana Dr (33326-1542)
PHONE.................................305 788-1473
Aryel Rivero,
Vanessa Clavijo,
EMP: 14 EST: 2014
SALES (est): 1.8MM Privately Held
SIC: 2679 Gift wrap & novelties, paper

(G-18251)
GYROSOLAR CORP
2655 Edgewater Dr (33332-3400)
PHONE.................................954 554-9990
Eukeni Urrechaga, *President*
EMP: 9 EST: 2015
SALES (est): 545.1K Privately Held
SIC: 3334 Aluminum ingots & slabs

(G-18252)
HAAS LASER TECHNOLOGIES INC
1612 Eastlake Way (33326-2734)
PHONE.................................954 529-7273
Gilbert Haas, *President*
Michelle Gelenites, *Admin Asst*
EMP: 7 Privately Held
WEB: www.haaslti.com
SIC: 3826 Laser scientific & engineering instruments
PA: Haas Laser Technologies Inc.
     37 Ironia Rd Ste 1
     Flanders NJ 07836

(G-18253)
IANOROD JB LLC
Also Called: Juiceblendz
4579 Weston Rd (33331-3141)
PHONE.................................954 217-3014
Iliana Ianotto, *Mng Member*
Michael Lawand, *Director*
EMP: 16 EST: 2011
SALES (est): 859K Privately Held
SIC: 2023 Dietary supplements, dairy & non-dairy based
PA: Grafiplast Ca
     Av Principal Con Calle E
     Charallave

(G-18254)
ILIAD BIOTECHNOLOGIES LLC
4581 Weston Rd Ste 260 (33331-3141)
PHONE.................................954 336-0777
Keith Rubin MD, *CEO*
Ken Solovay, *COO*
EMP: 9 EST: 2012
SALES (est): 487.5K Privately Held
WEB: www.iliadbio.com
SIC: 2836 Vaccines

(G-18255)
INCEPTRA LLC (PA)
1900 N Commerce Pkwy (33326-3236)
PHONE.................................954 442-5400
Timothy Peterson, *CEO*
Daniel J Smith, *President*
Manish Barlingay, *Engineer*
Peter Duckworth, *Engineer*
Aamer Khan, *Engineer*
EMP: 21 EST: 2004
SALES (est): 13.8MM Privately Held
WEB: www.inceptra.com
SIC: 7372 7373 8243 Prepackaged software; computer integrated systems design; operator training, computer

(G-18256)
INSIGHT SOFTWARE LLC (HQ)
Also Called: My Vision Express
3265 Meridian Pkwy # 112 (33331-3505)
PHONE.................................305 495-0022
Chris Cummings, *COO*
Luis Necuze, *Manager*
Gloria Marquez, *Technical Staff*
Yadian Ojito, *Sr Software Eng*
Jennifer Childress, *Director*
EMP: 100 EST: 2004
SQ FT: 1,500
SALES (est): 26.9MM
SALES (corp-wide): 394.4MM Privately Held
WEB: www.eyecareleaders.com
SIC: 7372 Prepackaged software
PA: Eli Global, Llc
     2222 Sedwick Rd
     Durham NC 27713
     972 448-9084

(G-18257)
ITELECOM USA INC
Also Called: Go Lighting Service
1422 Canary Island Dr (33327-2348)
PHONE.................................305 557-4660
Marcelo Lefort, *President*
Juan Bauza, *Business Mgr*
Christopher Zanyk, *Vice Pres*

Leonardo Bustos, *Treasurer*
Jesse Revilla, *Manager*
EMP: 7 EST: 2010
SALES (est): 709.3K Privately Held
WEB: www.itelecomusa.com
SIC: 3663 3674 7349 8748 Satellites, communications; light emitting diodes; lighting maintenance service; telecommunications consultant; systems software development services

(G-18258)
IVAX TEVA
2945 W Corp Lks Blvd A (33331-3626)
PHONE.................................954 384-5316
Zulma Morris, *Vice Pres*
EMP: 7 EST: 2008
SALES (est): 228.8K Privately Held
SIC: 2834 Pharmaceutical preparations

(G-18259)
JOHNSON CONTROLS INC
3300 Corporate Ave (33331-3504)
PHONE.................................954 233-3000
Mark Faucher, *Manager*
EMP: 10 Privately Held
WEB: www.johnsoncontrols.com
SIC: 3822 Building services monitoring controls, automatic
HQ: Johnson Controls, Inc.
     5757 N Green Bay Ave
     Glendale WI 53209
     414 524-1200

(G-18260)
JURITIS USA LLC
2500 Weston Rd Ste 105 (33331-3616)
PHONE.................................954 529-2168
Marcelo De Azeredo Souccar,
EMP: 9 EST: 2017
SALES (est): 461.4K Privately Held
WEB: www.juritis.com
SIC: 7372 Business oriented computer software

(G-18261)
JV&H CORPORATION
2200 N Commerce Pkwy # 20 (33326-3258)
PHONE.................................954 305-9043
Aldo J Barona Herrera, *President*
Rosa V Aguinaga Villacreses, *Vice Pres*
Paola A Barona, *Treasurer*
EMP: 7 EST: 2015
SALES (est): 1.7MM Privately Held
WEB: www.jv-h.com
SIC: 3565 5199 Packaging machinery; packaging materials

(G-18262)
KOOKIE KLLECTION KOSMETICS LLC
Also Called: Cosmetics
2645 Executive Park Dr (33331-3624)
PHONE.................................888 811-1657
Franshetta Sisney, *Mng Member*
EMP: 10 EST: 2019
SALES (est): 377.1K Privately Held
SIC: 2844 3999 Cosmetic preparations; face creams or lotions; candles

(G-18263)
LIFESTYLE PUBLICATIONS LLC
1675 Market St Ste 203 (33326-3681)
PHONE.................................954 217-1165
Gary Israel, *Publisher*
David Sherman, *Principal*
Jill Horowitz, *Vice Pres*
Sally Nicholas, *Associate*
EMP: 8 EST: 2017
SALES (est): 247.9K Privately Held
WEB: www.lifestylepubs.com
SIC: 2741 Miscellaneous publishing

(G-18264)
LOLLIPOPS AND GUMDROPS INC
2459 Greenbrier Ct (33327-1440)
PHONE.................................954 389-7032
Pam Van Dam, *Principal*
EMP: 7 EST: 2010
SALES (est): 78.7K Privately Held
SIC: 2064 Lollipops & other hard candy

(G-18265)
LOUIS POULSEN USA INC
Also Called: Poulsen Lighting
3260 Meridian Pkwy (33331-3502)
PHONE.................................954 349-2525
Kent S Pedersen, *President*
Claus Brix, *Vice Pres*
Liane Barr, *Regl Sales Mgr*
Tom Wong, *Regl Sales Mgr*
◆ **EMP: 60 EST: 1985**
SQ FT: 14,400
SALES (est): 24.9MM
SALES (corp-wide): 60K Privately Held
WEB: www.louispoulsen.com
SIC: 3645 3646 5063 Residential lighting fixtures; commercial indusl & institutional electric lighting fixtures; lighting fixtures
HQ: Louis Poulsen A/S
     Kuglegardsvej 19
     Kobenhavn K 1434
     703 314-14

(G-18266)
MAKO SURGICAL CORP (HQ)
Also Called: Stryker Mako
3365 Enterprise Ave (33331-3524)
PHONE.................................866 647-6256
Kevin A Lobo, *Ch of Bd*
Menashe R Frank, *Senior VP*
Duncan Moffat, *Vice Pres*
Sean Farrell, *Engineer*
Alan Fitzpatrick, *Engineer*
▲ **EMP: 315 EST: 2004**
SQ FT: 68,000
SALES (est): 137MM
SALES (corp-wide): 17.1B Publicly Held
SIC: 3842 Orthopedic appliances; trusses, orthopedic & surgical
PA: Stryker Corporation
     2825 Airview Blvd
     Portage MI 49002
     269 385-2600

(G-18267)
MEDSTONE PHARMA LLC
3300 Corp Ave Ste 114 (33331)
PHONE.................................305 777-7872
Rudolph Lavecchia, *President*
Patrice Michel, *Vice Pres*
EMP: 5 EST: 2016
SQ FT: 800
SALES (est): 557.8K Privately Held
WEB: www.medstonepharma.com
SIC: 2834 Pharmaceutical preparations
PA: Paragon Enterprises, Inc.
     3300 Corp Ave Ste 114
     Weston FL 33331

(G-18268)
MONTEBANA FUELS LLC
1565 Sandpiper Cir (33327-1664)
PHONE.................................954 385-5374
Jesus Flores, *Principal*
EMP: 7 EST: 2011
SALES (est): 146.8K Privately Held
SIC: 2869 Fuels

(G-18269)
MUNDI INTL TRADING CORP
1971 Landing Way (33326-2381)
PHONE.................................305 205-0062
Ivan Moran, *President*
Tracie Moran, *Vice Pres*
EMP: 5 EST: 2003
SALES (est): 436.7K Privately Held
SIC: 2295 Coated fabrics, not rubberized

(G-18270)
MVS INTERNATIONAL INC
702 Willow Bend Rd (33327-1826)
PHONE.................................954 727-3383
Maricel De Michele, *President*
Juan Iliopulos, *Vice Pres*
EMP: 6 EST: 2006
SQ FT: 2,000
SALES (est): 417.2K Privately Held
WEB: www.mvsinternational.net
SIC: 2086 5963 2066 Water, pasteurized: packaged in cans, bottles, etc.; fruit drinks (less than 100% juice): packaged in cans, etc.; snacks, direct sales; chocolate & cocoa products

(G-18271)
NATIONAL STONEWORKS LLC
Also Called: US Granite and Quartz
3360 Entp Ave Ste 100 (33331)
PHONE................................954 349-1609
Everett Parris, *Controller*
Mitchel Hires, *Mng Member*
Fred Hires,
▲ EMP: 50 EST: 2009
SALES (est): 25MM Privately Held
WEB: www.constructionresourceusa.com
SIC: 3281 2434 Table tops, marble; wood
kitchen cabinets
PA: Cr Home, Llc
196 Rio Cir
Decatur GA 30030

(G-18272)
NETWORKS ASSETS LLC
Also Called: Starbridge Networks
3265 Meridian Pkwy # 134 (33331-3523)
PHONE................................954 334-1390
Enrique Diaz, *Mng Member*
Cristina Kellert,
▲ EMP: 16 EST: 2003
SQ FT: 5,000
SALES (est): 825.5K Privately Held
WEB: www.networksassets.com
SIC: 3661 Telephones & telephone appara-
tus

(G-18273)
NKC ELECTRONICS INC
2875 Kinsington Cir (33332-1865)
PHONE................................954 471-8368
Tony Kim, *President*
▲ EMP: 9 EST: 2007
SALES (est): 109.1K Privately Held
WEB: www.nkcelectronics.com
SIC: 3699 Electronic training devices

(G-18274)
NORTHRICH FLORIDA LLC
Also Called: Nationwide Coils & Coatings
2111 N Commerce Pkwy (33326-3238)
PHONE................................954 678-6602
Robert Evans,
Walter Dickinson,
EMP: 11 EST: 2017
SALES (est): 1.5MM Privately Held
WEB: www.northrich.com
SIC: 3585 Air conditioning equipment,
complete

(G-18275)
ORACLE ESSENCE INC
1341 St Tropez Cir (33326-3015)
P.O. Box 267910 (33326-7910)
PHONE................................786 258-8153
Greg Toth, *Branch Mgr*
EMP: 9
SALES (corp-wide): 117.7K Privately
Held
WEB: www.oracleessence.com
SIC: 7372 Prepackaged software
PA: Oracle Essence, Inc.
4700 N Hiatus Rd
Sunrise FL

(G-18276)
ORIGINAL IMPRESSIONS LLC
Also Called: Oi Distribution
2965 W Corp Lks Blvd (33331-3626)
PHONE................................305 233-1322
Ismael Diaz, *President*
Ivan Alvarez, *Prdtn Mgr*
Jose Santos, *Purch Agent*
Ivan Melcon, *Human Res Dir*
Mayda Guerra, *Human Res Mgr*
▼ EMP: 190 EST: 1982
SALES (est): 35.6MM
SALES (corp-wide): 54.2MM Privately
Held
SIC: 2752 7331 7371 8732 Commercial
printing, offset; direct mail advertising
services; computer software development
& applications; market analysis or re-
search
PA: Postal Center International, Inc.
2965 W Corp Lks Blvd
Weston FL 33331
954 321-5644

(G-18277)
OXIGENO NITROGENO INC
Also Called: Tex Medical
16200 Golf Club Rd (33326-1696)
PHONE................................954 659-3881
Rosa A Sanchez, *President*
Estebaldo J Martinez, *Vice Pres*
EMP: 9 EST: 2013
SALES (est): 233.5K Privately Held
SIC: 3443 Industrial vessels, tanks & con-
tainers

(G-18278)
PACKAGING & RESOURCES INC
19245 S Gardenia Ave (33332-4401)
P.O. Box 266271, Fort Lauderdale (33326-
6271)
PHONE................................954 288-9678
Juan Arenas, *President*
◆ EMP: 5 EST: 1999
SALES (est): 659.2K Privately Held
WEB: www.packres.com
SIC: 3221 Bottles for packing, bottling &
canning: glass

(G-18279)
POWER GRID PROS INC
618 Heritage Dr (33326-4538)
PHONE................................716 378-1419
Jonathan Woodworth, *President*
Jean Paul Combeau, *Vice Pres*
Guy Combeau, *Treasurer*
Deborah Limburg, *Admin Sec*
EMP: 5 EST: 2018
SALES (est): 750K Privately Held
SIC: 3613 Fuses, electric

(G-18280)
PROFESSIONAL LABORATORIES INC
Also Called: Pro-Lab
1675 N Commerce Pkwy (33326-3205)
P.O. Box 267730, Fort Lauderdale (33326-
7730)
PHONE................................954 384-4446
James McDonnell, *CEO*
Bob Irvine, *Vice Pres*
Todd Marine, *Vice Pres*
Ron Romero, *Project Mgr*
Matt Adams, *CFO*
EMP: 42 EST: 1998
SQ FT: 30,000
SALES (est): 7.9MM Privately Held
WEB: www.prolabinc.com
SIC: 3826 Environmental testing equip-
ment

(G-18281)
R-DA TRADING LLC
2893 Executive Park Dr (33331-3664)
PHONE................................954 278-6983
Carlos A Gutierrez, *Mng Member*
Josue D Rivas, *Mng Member*
EMP: 9 EST: 2012
SALES (est): 870.4K Privately Held
SIC: 2834 2869 Pharmaceutical prepara-
tions; perfumes, flavorings & food addi-
tives

(G-18282)
REDUCTION INTERNATIONAL LLC
2700 Glades Cir Ste 134 (33327-2210)
PHONE................................954 905-5999
Carlos Garcia, *Mng Member*
EMP: 7 EST: 2007
SALES (est): 466.8K Privately Held
WEB: www.reductioninternational.com
SIC: 3559 Plastics working machinery

(G-18283)
ROCKWELL AUTOMATION INC
2200 N Commerce Pkwy # 107
(33326-3258)
PHONE................................954 306-7900
Luis Gamboa, *Marketing Staff*
Willy Moeller, *Manager*
EMP: 7 Publicly Held
WEB: www.rockwellautomation.com
SIC: 3625 Relays & industrial controls
PA: Rockwell Automation, Inc.
1201 S 2nd St
Milwaukee WI 53204

(G-18284)
ROYAL INDUSTRIES INC
16621 Royal Poinciana Ct (33326-1717)
PHONE................................954 871-6807
Jaime Rosado, *Principal*
EMP: 9 EST: 2018
SALES (est): 118.3K Privately Held
WEB: www.royalindustries.com
SIC: 3999 Manufacturing industries

(G-18285)
S V BAGS AMERICA INC
1563 Sandpiper Cir (33327-1646)
PHONE................................954 577-9091
Claude Levy, *President*
Elliot Levy, *Vice Pres*
▼ EMP: 5 EST: 2000
SALES (est): 421.6K Privately Held
WEB: www.grupoelliot.com
SIC: 2674 5162 Paper bags: made from
purchased materials; plastics materials

(G-18286)
SCUTTI AMERICA INC
2700 Glades Cir Ste 160 (33327-2296)
PHONE................................954 384-2377
Heriberto Sprecace, *President*
Alejandro Carrizales, *Vice Pres*
Rosa A Barquero, *Treasurer*
Maria Isabel Carrizales, *Admin Sec*
EMP: 9 EST: 2000
SALES (est): 755K Privately Held
WEB: www.scuttiamerica.com
SIC: 3531 Cement silos (batch plant)

(G-18287)
SUPERSONIC IMAGINE INC
2625 Weston Rd (33331-3614)
PHONE................................954 660-3528
Bernard Dorenboos, *President*
Elisabeth Winter, *Treasurer*
Claire Phalippou, *Controller*
EMP: 8 EST: 2007
SQ FT: 300
SALES (est): 8.4MM
SALES (corp-wide): 22MM Privately
Held
WEB: www.supersonicimagine.com
SIC: 3845 Ultrasonic scanning devices,
medical
PA: Supersonic Imagine
Zac De L Enfant
Aix En Provence 13290
960 418-623

(G-18288)
THALO ASSIST LLC
2893 Executive Park Dr # 203
(33331-3664)
PHONE................................786 340-6892
Henry Cristo, *Mng Member*
EMP: 7 EST: 2018
SALES (est): 250K Privately Held
WEB: www.thaloassist.com
SIC: 7372 4724 Application computer soft-
ware; travel agencies

(G-18289)
THERETBICOM INC
725 Tanglewood Cir (33327-1839)
PHONE................................917 796-1443
Maurice White, *Principal*
EMP: 7 EST: 2016
SALES (est): 91.5K Privately Held
SIC: 2834 Pharmaceutical preparations

(G-18290)
THERMABAND INC
2502 Eagle Watch Ln (33327-1402)
PHONE................................248 497-1665
Debbie Dickinson, *CEO*
Markea Dickinson, *COO*
EMP: 8 EST: 2019
SALES (est): 746K Privately Held
WEB: www.thermaband.com
SIC: 7372 Application computer software

(G-18291)
THETRADEBAYCOM LLC
451 Conservation Dr (33327-2474)
PHONE................................954 607-2405
Alfredo E Valenzuela,
Gabriela G Ugarte,
EMP: 9 EST: 2015
SALES (est): 555K Privately Held
SIC: 2092 Shrimp, frozen: prepared

(G-18292)
TIGO INC
Also Called: Expose Yourself USA
16522 Ruby Lk (33331-3176)
PHONE................................954 935-5990
Cheryl Tiapago, *President*
Brooke Bradshaw, *General Mgr*
Marco Tiapago, *Vice Pres*
▼ EMP: 34 EST: 2006
SALES (est): 3.7MM Privately Held
WEB: www.exposeyourselfusa.com
SIC: 3993 Signs & advertising specialties

(G-18293)
UKG INC
1485 N Park Dr (33326-3215)
PHONE................................954 331-7000
Aron AIN, *CEO*
Cezar Camara, *Engineer*
Adriana Quintero, *Accounting Mgr*
Janice Gessa, *Accountant*
Thomas Lohmeyer, *Accountant*
EMP: 80
SALES (corp-wide): 1.1B Privately Held
WEB: www.ukg.com
SIC: 7372 Business oriented computer
software
HQ: Ukg Inc.
900 Chelmsford St Ste 212
Lowell MA 01851

(G-18294)
UKG INC
Also Called: Ultimate Kronos Group
2000 Ultimate Way (33326-3643)
PHONE................................954 331-7000
EMP: 121
SALES (corp-wide): 1.1B Privately Held
WEB: www.ukg.com
SIC: 7372 Business oriented computer
software
HQ: Ukg Inc.
900 Chelmsford St Ste 212
Lowell MA 01851

(G-18295)
UNITE PARENT CORP (PA)
2000 Ultimate Way (33326-3643)
PHONE................................800 432-1729
Scott Scherr, *Ch of Bd*
Ryan Chai, *Counsel*
Bethanie Haynes, *Counsel*
Robert Kennedy, *Vice Pres*
John Machado, *Vice Pres*
EMP: 11 EST: 2019
SALES (est): 1.1B Privately Held
SIC: 7372 Business oriented computer
software

(G-18296)
URBAPRINT LLC
649 Conservation Dr (33327-2468)
PHONE................................786 502-3223
Adriana Perrotta, *President*
Samantha Alvarez, *Manager*
EMP: 7 EST: 2016
SALES (est): 173.1K Privately Held
WEB: www.urbaprint.com
SIC: 2752 Commercial printing, litho-
graphic

(G-18297)
VLEX 1450 LLC
1199 Hidden Valley Way (33327-1819)
PHONE................................954 218-5443
Andreina Manzo, *Principal*
EMP: 6 EST: 2014
SALES (est): 356K Privately Held
SIC: 2741 Miscellaneous publishing

(G-18298)
WISE GAS FUEL CARD LLC
1058 Bluewood Ter (33327-2056)
PHONE................................954 636-4291
Christine A Slager, *Principal*
EMP: 7 EST: 2010
SALES (est): 176.5K Privately Held
SIC: 2869 Fuels

(G-18299)
XIKAR INC
3350 Entp Ave Ste 120 (33331)
PHONE................................816 474-7555
Michael J Giordano, *CEO*
Michael Cellucci, *President*
Anthony D'Eri, *Business Mgr*

Deanna Scott, *Business Mgr*
Tim Webster, *COO*
◆ **EMP:** 30 **EST:** 1996
SALES (est): 50MM
SALES (corp-wide): 50.7MM **Privately Held**
WEB: www.xikar.com
SIC: 3999 Cigarette & cigar products & accessories
PA: Quality Importers Trading Company, Llc
3350 Entp Ave Ste 120
Weston FL 33331
888 795-4839

(G-18300)
ZEROLL CO (HQ)
3355 Entp Ave Ste 160 (33331)
P.O. Box 999, Fort Pierce (34954-0999)
PHONE..................................772 461-3811
O Neal Asbury, *CEO*
▲ **EMP:** 24 **EST:** 1935
SQ FT: 25,000
SALES (est): 1MM
SALES (corp-wide): 208MM **Privately Held**
WEB: www.zeroll.com
SIC: 3469 Utensils, household: metal, except cast
PA: Greenfield World Trade, Inc.
3355 Entp Ave Ste 160
Fort Lauderdale FL 33331
954 202-7419

Westville
Holmes County

(G-18301)
L AND D LOGGING
701 Sandspur Rd (32464-2632)
PHONE..................................850 859-1013
Woodie L Dupree Jr, *Principal*
EMP: 6 **EST:** 2008
SALES (est): 427.3K **Privately Held**
SIC: 2411 Logging camps & contractors

Wewahitchka
Gulf County

(G-18302)
TUCKER TRCKG LOG JHNNY E TCKER
2371 County Road 381 (32465-5502)
PHONE..................................850 258-1982
Eddie Belle White, *Principal*
EMP: 6 **EST:** 2009
SALES (est): 485.9K **Privately Held**
SIC: 2411 Logging

(G-18303)
WHITFIELD TIMBER COMPANY INC (PA)
101 N Highway 71 (32465-9507)
P.O. Box 674 (32465-0674)
PHONE..................................850 639-5556
Theodore L Whitfield, *President*
Doris Kay Whitfield, *Treasurer*
EMP: 30 **EST:** 1975
SQ FT: 4,000
SALES (est): 4.5MM **Privately Held**
SIC: 2411 2421 Pulpwood contractors engaged in cutting; sawmills & planing mills, general

White Springs
Hamilton County

(G-18304)
B&M LOGGING INC
10616 Se County Road 135 (32096-1604)
PHONE..................................386 397-1145
Tammy Ogburn, *President*
EMP: 8 **EST:** 1993
SALES (est): 815.5K **Privately Held**
SIC: 2411 Logging camps & contractors

(G-18305)
BTR LOGGING INC
10249 Se 161st Ave (32096-2210)
P.O. Box 180 (32096-0180)
PHONE..................................386 397-0730
Byron Ogburn, *President*
EMP: 8 **EST:** 2016
SALES (est): 256K **Privately Held**
SIC: 2411 Logging camps & contractors

(G-18306)
HIZER MACHINE MFG INC
12137 Se Us Highway 41 (32096-2501)
P.O. Box E (32096-0279)
PHONE..................................386 755-3155
James Hizer, *President*
Katheryn Hizer, *Treasurer*
EMP: 6 **EST:** 1998
SQ FT: 1,600
SALES (est): 671.8K **Privately Held**
SIC: 3561 Pumps & pumping equipment

(G-18307)
WHITE SPRINGS AG CHEM INC
Also Called: Pcs Phosphate/White Springs
15843 Se 78th St (32096-2703)
P.O. Box 300 (32096-0300)
PHONE..................................386 397-8101
William J Doyle, *CEO*
Prentiss Adams, *Manager*
Al Murphy, *Officer*
◆ **EMP:** 900 **EST:** 1994
SQ FT: 1,200
SALES (est): 320.7MM
SALES (corp-wide): 27.7B **Privately Held**
SIC: 1475 2874 Phosphate rock; phosphates
HQ: Potash Corporation Of Saskatchewan Inc.
122 1st Ave S Suite 500
Saskatoon SK S7K 7
306 933-8500

Wildwood
Sumter County

(G-18308)
ALUMNE MANUFACTURING INC
801 Industrial Dr (34785-4710)
PHONE..................................352 748-3229
Lester D Yancey, *President*
Anita Yancey, *Vice Pres*
Barbara Rusin, *Bookkeeper*
EMP: 6 **EST:** 1989
SQ FT: 30,000
SALES (est): 680.8K **Privately Held**
WEB: www.alumne.com
SIC: 3715 Truck trailers

(G-18309)
BOB & LEES CABINETS
4386 Warm Springs Ave (34785-8058)
PHONE..................................352 748-3553
John S Smith, *Partner*
Robert L Wagner, *Partner*
EMP: 15 **EST:** 1971
SALES (est): 1.7MM **Privately Held**
SIC: 2542 2434 Cabinets: show, display or storage: except wood; wood kitchen cabinets

(G-18310)
CEMEX CNSTR MTLS FLA LLC
Also Called: Gypsum Supply - Wildwood
4270 County Road 124a (34785-7617)
PHONE..................................352 330-1115
Jennifer Lee, *Branch Mgr*
EMP: 10 **Privately Held**
SIC: 3273 Ready-mixed concrete
HQ: Cemex Construction Materials Florida, Llc
1501 Belvedere Rd
West Palm Beach FL 33406

(G-18311)
GLOBAL TIRE RCYCL OF SMTER CNT
1201 Industrial Dr (34785-5202)
PHONE..................................352 330-2213
Robert Bjork, *Vice Pres*
EMP: 30 **EST:** 1996
SQ FT: 48,000

SALES (est): 1.8MM **Privately Held**
WEB: www.gtrcrumbrubber.com
SIC: 3069 Reclaimed rubber & specialty rubber compounds
PA: Global Tire Recycling Inc
1201 Industrial Dr
Wildwood FL 34785

(G-18312)
GLOBAL TIRE RECYCLING INC (PA)
1201 Industrial Dr (34785-5202)
PHONE..................................352 330-2213
Mark Bailey, *President*
Samuels Richards, *Sr Consultant*
D Watson, *Sr Consultant*
▼ **EMP:** 15 **EST:** 1996
SQ FT: 38,520
SALES (est): 5.1MM **Privately Held**
SIC: 3069 Reclaimed rubber & specialty rubber compounds

(G-18313)
INSPIRED CLOSETS CENTRAL FL
3107 E State Road 44 (34785-7401)
PHONE..................................352 748-0770
EMP: 5 **EST:** 2020
SALES (est): 391K **Privately Held**
SIC: 2541 Wood partitions & fixtures

(G-18314)
JENNIFER YODER SUNG
Also Called: T & D Screen Enclosures
9235 County Road 128d (34785-9177)
PHONE..................................352 748-6655
Lorraine Ferri, *Principal*
EMP: 7 **EST:** 2010
SALES (est): 344.8K **Privately Held**
SIC: 3448 Screen enclosures

(G-18315)
LITTORAL MARINE LLC
Also Called: Crevalle Boats
1520 Industrial Dr (34785-9418)
PHONE..................................352 400-4222
Roger B Taylor Jr, *COO*
Mike Hankins, *Vice Pres*
Engels Nick, *Vice Pres*
Hugh Dailey, *CFO*
Nick Engels, *Executive*
EMP: 35 **EST:** 2013
SQ FT: 40,000
SALES (est): 9MM **Privately Held**
WEB: www.crevalleboats.com
SIC: 3732 Boat building & repairing

(G-18316)
OLDCASTLE INFRASTRUCTURE INC
Also Called: Utility Vault
1410 Industrial Dr (34785-5204)
P.O. Box 238 (34785-0238)
PHONE..................................800 642-1540
James Wimington, *General Mgr*
EMP: 10
SALES (corp-wide): 30.9B **Privately Held**
WEB: www.oldcastleinfrastructure.com
SIC: 3272 Concrete products
HQ: Oldcastle Infrastructure, Inc.
7000 Central Pkwy Ste 800
Atlanta GA 30328
770 270-5000

(G-18317)
PRINT ALL PROMOTIONS LLC
18202 Sandalwood Dr 18 (34785-9706)
PHONE..................................800 971-3209
Sheryl Ryan, *Principal*
EMP: 6 **EST:** 2008
SALES (est): 303.4K **Privately Held**
WEB: www.printallpromotions.com
SIC: 2752 Commercial printing, lithographic

(G-18318)
PROGRESS RAIL SERVICES CORP
4198 E County Road 462 (34785-8760)
PHONE..................................352 748-8008
Steve Hunt, *Manager*
EMP: 12

SALES (corp-wide): 50.9B **Publicly Held**
WEB: www.progressrail.com
SIC: 3559 Recycling machinery; cryogenic machinery, industrial
HQ: Progress Rail Services Corporation
1600 Progress Dr
Albertville AL 35950
256 505-6421

(G-18319)
RINKER MATERIALS
4270 County Road 124a (34785-7617)
PHONE..................................352 330-1115
Kurt Milliman, *Principal*
EMP: 7 **EST:** 2008
SALES (est): 99.1K **Privately Held**
SIC: 3273 Ready-mixed concrete

(G-18320)
SALTY BOATS RJL INC
900 Industrial Dr (34785-4711)
PHONE..................................863 802-0543
Donald J Lacharite, *Principal*
EMP: 9 **EST:** 2014
SALES (est): 485.6K **Privately Held**
WEB: www.stumpnockerboats.com
SIC: 3732 Boat building & repairing

(G-18321)
STONE CENTRAL OF CENTRAL FLA
3200 Ne 37th Pl (34785-7832)
PHONE..................................352 689-0075
Philip Shibler, *President*
Jennifer G Shibler, *Vice Pres*
EMP: 11 **EST:** 2005
SQ FT: 7,000
SALES (est): 1MM **Privately Held**
WEB: www.stonecentralinc.com
SIC: 3272 Cast stone, concrete

(G-18322)
SYMRNA READY MIX
8302 Ne 44th Dr (34785-9183)
PHONE..................................352 330-1001
EMP: 7 **EST:** 2017
SALES (est): 154.2K **Privately Held**
WEB: www.smyrnareadymix.com
SIC: 3273 Ready-mixed concrete

(G-18323)
T AND M WOODWORKING INC
3321 Ne 37th Pl (34785-7851)
PHONE..................................352 748-6655
Nathan Yoder, *President*
EMP: 7 **EST:** 2016
SALES (est): 235.4K **Privately Held**
SIC: 2431 Millwork

(G-18324)
TDSE INC
3151 Ne 37th Pl (34785-7800)
PHONE..................................352 399-6413
Matthew L Yoder, *President*
EMP: 50 **EST:** 2018
SALES (est): 4.5MM **Privately Held**
SIC: 3448 Screen enclosures

(G-18325)
TEREX CORPORATION
Also Called: Telelect East
3400 Ne 37th Pl (34785-7848)
PHONE..................................352 330-4044
EMP: 8
SALES (corp-wide): 7B **Publicly Held**
SIC: 3537 Mfg Industrial Trucks/Tractors
PA: Terex Corporation
200 Nyala Farms Rd Ste 2
Westport CT 06850
203 222-7170

(G-18326)
XPRESS MATERIALS LLC
8302 Ne 44th Dr (34785-9183)
PHONE..................................352 748-2200
Claude Graham,
Dan Graham,
Jeff Graham,
Jim Graham,
EMP: 19 **EST:** 2003
SALES (est): 1.3MM **Privately Held**
SIC: 3273 Ready-mixed concrete

Williston
Levy County

(G-18327)
A & N CORPORATION
Also Called: Ancorp
707 Sw 19th Ave (32696-2427)
PHONE................352 528-4100
Daniel N Vaudreuil, *President*
Glenn W Vaudreuil, *Vice Pres*
Jon Rohrer, *Project Mgr*
Rick Shroyer, *QC Mgr*
Kim Folken, *Engineer*
◆ EMP: 90 EST: 1965
SQ FT: 42,000
SALES (est): 29.5MM **Privately Held**
WEB: www.ancorp.com
SIC: 3494 Valves & pipe fittings

(G-18328)
A AND H LOGGING INC
333 Se 4th Ave (32696-2647)
P.O. Box 986 (32696-0986)
PHONE................352 528-3868
Art Nussel, *President*
EMP: 5 EST: 1988
SALES (est): 430.4K **Privately Held**
SIC: 2411 0811 Logging camps & contractors; timber tracts

(G-18329)
AMERICAN COMPOSITES ENGRG
20751 Ne Highway 27 (32696-3109)
PHONE................352 528-5007
Ronny Walker, *Principal*
EMP: 29
SALES (corp-wide): 4.3MM **Privately Held**
WEB: www.nacomposites.com
SIC: 3089 Plastic containers, except foam
HQ: American Composites Engineering Inc
1090 W Saint James St
Tarboro NC 27886

(G-18330)
B4 ENTERPRISES INC
241 S Main St (32696-2657)
P.O. Box 848 (32696-0848)
PHONE................352 529-1114
Matthew Brooks, *Principal*
EMP: 6 EST: 2019
SALES (est): 428.1K **Privately Held**
SIC: 3993 Signs & advertising specialties

(G-18331)
BREEDEN PULPWOOD INC
Off Hwy 41 (32696)
P.O. Box 421 (32696-0421)
PHONE................352 528-5243
James E Breeden, *President*
Lisa Breeden, *Treasurer*
EMP: 12 EST: 1969
SALES (est): 769.2K **Privately Held**
SIC: 2411 Pulpwood contractors engaged in cutting

(G-18332)
HARRISON LOGGING
17701 Nw 133rd Court Rd (32696-4417)
PHONE................352 591-2779
William C Harrison Jr, *President*
EMP: 22 EST: 1971
SALES (est): 1.1MM **Privately Held**
WEB: www.harrisonloggingco.com
SIC: 2411 Logging camps & contractors

(G-18333)
HOWELL LOGGING & LAND CLEARING
20253 Ne 20th St (32696-7333)
PHONE................352 528-2698
Tarrel Howell, *Owner*
▼ EMP: 6 EST: 2002
SQ FT: 2,301
SALES (est): 510K **Privately Held**
WEB: www.alpinecarpetcleaning.us
SIC: 2411 Logging camps & contractors

(G-18334)
RJ STAAB STONE CO
824 N Main St (32696-1706)
PHONE................352 377-3313
Ronald J Staab, *Vice Pres*
EMP: 9 EST: 2012
SALES (est): 560.7K **Privately Held**
WEB: www.rjstaabstonecompany.com
SIC: 3272 Concrete products, precast

(G-18335)
SHADOW TRAILERS INC
951 Sw 21st Pl (32696-2453)
PHONE................352 529-2190
Larry R Pruitt, *CEO*
Chris Roe, *Engineer*
Janet Williams, *Manager*
EMP: 45 EST: 2003
SALES (est): 9.7MM **Privately Held**
WEB: www.shadowtrailer.com
SIC: 3715 Trailers or vans for transporting horses

(G-18336)
WILLISTON TIMBER CO INC
4351 Ne 176th Ave (32696-4807)
PHONE................352 528-2699
Eddie Hodge, *President*
John Hodge, *Vice Pres*
Julie Hodge, *Treasurer*
Christine Hodge, *Admin Sec*
EMP: 50 EST: 1977
SQ FT: 6,000
SALES (est): 7.5MM **Privately Held**
SIC: 2421 Sawmills & planing mills, general

Wilton Manors
Broward County

(G-18337)
CUSTOM DOORS & SPECIALTIES INC
2637 N Andrews Ave (33311-2509)
PHONE................954 763-4214
John Ouelette, *Director*
EMP: 9 EST: 2001
SALES (est): 106.6K **Privately Held**
SIC: 2431 Doors & door parts & trim, wood

(G-18338)
DM OIL CORP
1450 Ne 26th St (33305-1322)
PHONE................954 835-5468
Brune A Diaz Mercado, *Principal*
EMP: 7 EST: 2012
SALES (est): 125.1K **Privately Held**
SIC: 1382 Oil & gas exploration services

(G-18339)
FLOOR AND BATH SOLUTIONS
2718 N Dixie Hwy (33334-3727)
PHONE................954 368-6698
EMP: 7 EST: 2015
SALES (est): 140K **Privately Held**
WEB: www.floorandbathsolution.com
SIC: 3469 Tile, floor or wall: stamped metal

(G-18340)
GENESIS HEALTH INSTITUTE INC
1001 Ne 26th St (33305-1243)
PHONE................954 561-3175
Ferdinand Cabrera, *President*
Dimitri Bakoulis, *COO*
EMP: 9 EST: 2007
SALES (est): 1.3MM **Privately Held**
WEB: www.ghinstitute.com
SIC: 2834 Dermatologicals

(G-18341)
GNEKOW FAMILY WINERY LLC
132 Ne 21st Ct (33305-1010)
PHONE................209 463-0697
Sean Gnekow,
Rudy Gnekow,
EMP: 17 EST: 1996
SALES (est): 1.4MM **Privately Held**
WEB: www.campusoakswines.com
SIC: 2084 Wines

(G-18342)
SOUTHFLORIDAGAYNEWSCOM
2520 N Dixie Hwy (33305-1247)
PHONE................954 530-4970
Jason Parsley, *Chief*
Norm Kent, *Manager*
EMP: 20 EST: 2013
SALES (est): 1.3MM **Privately Held**
WEB: www.southfloridagaynews.com
SIC: 2711 Newspapers, publishing & printing

(G-18343)
TEE-HEE CORP
Also Called: Menchies Frz Ygurt Five Points
2607 N Dixie Hwy (33334-3724)
PHONE................754 200-4962
Melissa Kushner, *Principal*
EMP: 7 EST: 2010
SALES (est): 151.1K **Privately Held**
SIC: 2759 Screen printing

(G-18344)
VENICE QUARTERS INC
Also Called: Hotspot Magazine of Florida
2435 N Dixie Hwy (33305-2239)
PHONE................954 318-3483
Cleto J Beuren, *President*
Brian Burda, *Business Mgr*
Peter J Clark, *Vice Pres*
EMP: 23 EST: 1998
SALES (est): 4MM **Privately Held**
SIC: 2721 8742 Magazines: publishing only, not printed on site; marketing consulting services

Wimauma
Hillsborough County

(G-18345)
SEA FORCE IX INC
1403 Pinetree Cir (33598-7612)
PHONE................941 721-9009
Ronald Rookstool, *Owner*
Chris Mackenzie, *Purch Mgr*
Gail Rookstool, *Office Mgr*
Sydney Kline, *Consultant*
Ronald R Rookstool, *CIO*
EMP: 28 EST: 2004
SALES (est): 2.6MM **Privately Held**
WEB: www.seaforceboats.com
SIC: 3732 Yachts, building & repairing

(G-18346)
SOUTH BAY HOME SERVICES LLC
4832 Sandy Glen Way (33598-2502)
PHONE................813 260-4708
EMP: 7 EST: 2018
SALES (est): 248K **Privately Held**
WEB: www.handymansuncitycenter.com
SIC: 3732 Boat building & repairing

Windermere
Orange County

(G-18347)
ALPHA OMEGA COMMERCIAL LIMITED (PA)
5820 Nature View Dr (34786-5130)
PHONE................407 925-7913
Sandro Motta, *President*
Sonia Motta, *Vice Pres*
◆ EMP: 1 EST: 2018
SQ FT: 750
SALES (est): 8MM **Privately Held**
WEB: www.omegaalpha.us
SIC: 2032 Ethnic foods: canned, jarred, etc.

(G-18348)
BLACK DAMND DRILL GRINDERS INC
8776 Danforth Dr (34786-9425)
PHONE................978 465-3799
Ha Phung, *President*
Frank Kiritsy, *Vice Pres*
▲ EMP: 10 EST: 1930
SALES (est): 982K **Privately Held**
WEB: www.blackdiamondgrinder.com
SIC: 3599 5084 Machine shop, jobbing & repair; industrial machinery & equipment

(G-18349)
DELUXE GEMS LLC
13506 Summerport Vlg Pkwy (34786-7366)
PHONE................407 513-2004
Rajees S Khan, *Manager*
EMP: 7 EST: 2007
SALES (est): 380.8K **Privately Held**
WEB: www.deluxegems.com
SIC: 3911 Jewelry, precious metal

(G-18350)
ELEMENT STUDIOS
3328 Wax Berry Ct (34786-7842)
PHONE................407 968-2192
James Wasson, *Principal*
EMP: 7 EST: 2010
SALES (est): 118.1K **Privately Held**
SIC: 2819 Industrial inorganic chemicals

(G-18351)
FUELMYSCHOOL
4344 Indian Deer Rd (34786-3181)
PHONE................407 952-1030
Krista Monteleone, *Principal*
EMP: 9 EST: 2011
SALES (est): 238.7K **Privately Held**
WEB: www.fuelmyschool.com
SIC: 2869 Fuels

(G-18352)
GOENGINEER INC
9100 Wndermere Rd Ste 208 (34786)
PHONE................800 688-3234
EMP: 8
SALES (corp-wide): 81.4MM **Privately Held**
WEB: www.goengineer.com
SIC: 7372 Prepackaged software
PA: Goengineer, Inc.
739 E Fort Union Blvd
Midvale UT 84047
801 359-6100

(G-18353)
ICON EMBROIDERY INC
2833 Butler Bay Dr N (34786-6113)
PHONE................407 858-0886
Charles Wilson, *President*
EMP: 5 EST: 1991
SQ FT: 20,000
SALES (est): 520.9K **Privately Held**
WEB: www.iecshirt.com
SIC: 2339 2329 2396 2395 Sportswear, women's; men's & boys' sportswear & athletic clothing; automotive & apparel trimmings; pleating & stitching

(G-18354)
IPRO FORCE LLC
6929 Corley Ave (34786-9483)
PHONE................603 766-8716
Molly Schwartz, *Owner*
EMP: 7 EST: 2015
SALES (est): 97.9K **Privately Held**
WEB: www.neomarkets.com
SIC: 2911 Petroleum refining

(G-18355)
JAMUNA1 LLC
4654 River Gem Ave (34786-3180)
PHONE................407 313-5927
Manish Parikh, *President*
Amish Parikh, *Manager*
EMP: 7 EST: 2014
SALES (est): 286.9K **Privately Held**
SIC: 3589 Service industry machinery

(G-18356)
JETSPARES INTERNATIONAL INC
10650 Chase Rd Bldg 5 (34786-8972)
PHONE................407 876-3978
Toby Silverton, *President*
Jonathan Jomes, *President*
▲ EMP: 8 EST: 1985
SQ FT: 6,000
SALES (est): 699.9K **Privately Held**
SIC: 3728 Aircraft parts & equipment

(G-18357)
KABRIT REPAIR SERVICES LLC ✪
9118 Panzani Pl (34786-8136)
PHONE................407 714-1470

GEOGRAPHIC

Tralonnie Tisdale,
EMP: 15 **EST:** 2021
SALES (est): 266.3K **Privately Held**
SIC: 1389 Construction, repair & dismantling services

(G-18358)
LA GENOMICS LLC
5939 Blakeford Dr (34786-5601)
PHONE.................................407 909-1120
Jose Clavier, *Principal*
EMP: 8 **EST:** 2016
SALES (est): 92.9K **Privately Held**
SIC: 2835 Microbiology & virology diagnostic products

(G-18359)
LOGSDON AND ASSOCIATES INC
13049 Lake Roper Ct (34786-5822)
PHONE.................................407 292-0084
Curtis A Logsdon, *President*
Cynthia M Logsdon, *Vice Pres*
Ryan Logsdon, *Opers Staff*
EMP: 5 **EST:** 1990
SALES (est): 464.3K **Privately Held**
WEB: www.logsdonandassociates.com
SIC: 2394 5031 Canopies, fabric: made from purchased materials; skylights, all materials

(G-18360)
MATRIX MARKETING SOLUTIONS INC
13629 Lake Cawood Dr (34786-7002)
PHONE.................................407 654-5736
Sean Irvine, *Principal*
EMP: 11 **EST:** 2002
SALES (est): 231K **Privately Held**
WEB: www.matrixmarketinggroup.com
SIC: 2752 Commercial printing, lithographic

(G-18361)
MCCOLL DISPLAY SOLUTIONS
8416 Iron Mountain Trl (34786-9478)
PHONE.................................813 333-6613
Kimberly Bellis, *Principal*
EMP: 8 **EST:** 2014
SALES (est): 433.1K **Privately Held**
WEB: www.mccolldisplay.com
SIC: 3993 Signs & advertising specialties

(G-18362)
MILLENIA FROYO LLC
9066 Harbor Isle Dr (34786-8350)
PHONE.................................407 694-9938
Ariff Khimani, *Principal*
EMP: 9 **EST:** 2010
SALES (est): 232.1K **Privately Held**
SIC: 2024 Yogurt desserts, frozen

(G-18363)
PURE WATER CHANGES INC
7775 Maslin St (34786-6346)
PHONE.................................407 699-2837
Bobby G Pinson Jr, *President*
EMP: 10 **EST:** 2017
SALES (est): 1MM **Privately Held**
WEB: www.purewaterchanges.com
SIC: 3589 Water treatment equipment, industrial

(G-18364)
QUICKWOOD LLC
13506 Summerport Vlg Pkwy
(34786-7366)
PHONE.................................866 888-5858
EMP: 5 **EST:** 2019
SALES (est): 472.5K **Privately Held**
WEB: www.quickwood.com
SIC: 3553 Woodworking machinery

(G-18365)
RUKE INC
1226 Main St (34786-8702)
PHONE.................................239 292-2553
Victoria Ruke, *Principal*
EMP: 9 **EST:** 2017
SALES (est): 115K **Privately Held**
SIC: 3714 Motor vehicle parts & accessories

(G-18366)
SKYLINK TECHNOLOGY INC
1707 Whitney Isles Dr (34786-6068)
P.O. Box 1542 (34786-1542)
PHONE.................................609 689-9200
Alan Meeh, *Principal*
Robert Newmark, *Principal*
Thomas Young Jr, *Principal*
Cyrus Chiu, *Engineer*
Michael Fang, *Sr Software Eng*
EMP: 9 **EST:** 1996
SQ FT: 6,000
SALES (est): 1.3MM **Privately Held**
WEB: www.skylinktechnology.com
SIC: 3559 Electronic component making machinery

(G-18367)
TIMBERWOLF ORGANICS LTD LBLTY
13506 Summerport Vlg Pkwy
(34786-7366)
PHONE.................................407 877-8779
Mark Heyward, *CEO*
Heather Winkler, *Administration*
EMP: 11 **EST:** 2007
SALES (est): 1.3MM **Privately Held**
SIC: 3999 Pet supplies

(G-18368)
US THRILLRIDES LLC
11536 Lake Butler Blvd (34786-7815)
PHONE.................................407 909-8898
EMP: 9 **EST:** 2003
SALES (est): 941.4K **Privately Held**
WEB: www.usthrillrides.com
SIC: 3599 7996 Mfg Industrial Machinery Amusement Park

(G-18369)
VIPER 4X4
11924 Perspective Dr (34786-6511)
PHONE.................................305 468-9818
Nelson Suarez, *Principal*
Trautman Fred, *Director*
▼ **EMP:** 11 **EST:** 2010
SALES (est): 1.1MM **Privately Held**
WEB: www.vpr4x4.com
SIC: 3799 All terrain vehicles (ATV)

(G-18370)
WATERBRICK INTERNATIONAL INC
13506 Smmrport Vlg Pkwy S (34786-7366)
P.O. Box 770969, Winter Garden (34777-0969)
PHONE.................................877 420-9283
Kevin Adams, *President*
▼ **EMP:** 5 **EST:** 2008
SALES (est): 510.6K **Privately Held**
WEB: www.waterbrick.org
SIC: 3089 5091 8322 5085 Plastic & fiberglass tanks; boats, canoes, watercrafts & equipment; temporary relief service; packing, industrial

(G-18371)
WINDERMERE NANNIES LLC
6526 Old Brick Rd Ste 120 (34786-5839)
PHONE.................................407 782-2057
Katelyn Arias,
EMP: 12 **EST:** 2020
SALES (est): 120K **Privately Held**
WEB: www.windermerenannies.com
SIC: 7372 7361 Application computer software; employment agencies

Winter Garden
Orange County

(G-18372)
ADVANCED DRAINAGE SYSTEMS INC
115 N West Crown Point Rd (34787-2948)
PHONE.................................407 654-3989
Ken Smith, *Manager*
John Trivento, *Manager*
Lynn Hawk, *Executive Asst*
Joseph Hurt, *Products*
EMP: 126
SQ FT: 55,528

SALES (corp-wide): 2.7B **Publicly Held**
WEB: www.adspipe.com
SIC: 3084 5051 Plastics pipe; pipe & tubing, steel
PA: Advanced Drainage Systems, Inc.
4640 Trueman Blvd
Hilliard OH 43026
614 658-0050

(G-18373)
ANUVIA PLANT NUTRIENTS CORP
113 S Boyd St (34787-3501)
PHONE.................................689 407-3430
Amy Yoder, *CEO*
Chris Larson, *Senior VP*
Brett Bell, *Vice Pres*
Dan Froehlich, *Vice Pres*
Michael Hoger, *Vice Pres*
EMP: 5 **EST:** 2008
SALES (est): 1MM **Privately Held**
WEB: www.anuviaplantnutrients.com
SIC: 2873 Nitrogenous fertilizers

(G-18374)
ARCANA TILEWORKS
1226 Wntr Gdn Vnlnd Rd # 100
(34787-4451)
PHONE.................................407 492-0668
Nancy T Krug, *Owner*
EMP: 5 **EST:** 2006
SALES (est): 419.3K **Privately Held**
WEB: www.arcanatileworks.com
SIC: 3253 Floor tile, ceramic

(G-18375)
BALSYS TECHNOLOGY GROUP INC
930 Carter Rd Ste 228 (34787-4105)
PHONE.................................407 656-3719
Larry Lamoray, *President*
EMP: 5 **EST:** 2000
SQ FT: 6,000
SALES (est): 647.8K **Privately Held**
SIC: 3663 Television broadcasting & communications equipment

(G-18376)
BARRIER-1 INC
640 Garden Commerce Pkwy
(34787-5708)
PHONE.................................877 224-5850
Richard Koon, *President*
John R Van Horn, *Corp Secy*
EMP: 17 **EST:** 2003
SALES (est): 1.9MM **Privately Held**
WEB: www.barrier1.com
SIC: 3272 Concrete products, precast

(G-18377)
CANDELA CONTROLS INC
751 Business Park Blvd # 101
(34787-5704)
PHONE.................................407 654-2420
Bill Ellis, *President*
Dale Ward, *General Mgr*
Carol Cimino, *Project Mgr*
Mark Colvin, *Project Mgr*
Kacey Conn, *Project Mgr*
EMP: 38 **EST:** 1999
SQ FT: 10,000
SALES (est): 7.3MM **Privately Held**
WEB: www.candelacontrols.com
SIC: 3646 3648 Commercial indusl & institutional electric lighting fixtures; lighting equipment

(G-18378)
CEMEX CEMENT INC
201 Hennis Rd (34787-2410)
PHONE.................................407 877-9623
Frank Craddock, *Vice Pres*
EMP: 103 **Privately Held**
WEB: www.cemexusa.com
SIC: 3273 Ready-mixed concrete
HQ: Cemex Cement, Inc.
10100 Katy Fwy Ste 300
Houston TX 77043
713 650-6200

(G-18379)
CERTIFIED WHL EXTERIOR PDTS
902 Carter Rd Ste 300 (34787-4144)
PHONE.................................407 654-7170

Karen E Smith, *President*
Michael P Smith, *Vice Pres*
EMP: 5 **EST:** 2001
SQ FT: 4,400
SALES (est): 488.1K **Privately Held**
WEB: www.cwproductsinc.com
SIC: 2821 5072 Vinyl resins; builders' hardware

(G-18380)
CHOCTAW TRADING CO INC
Also Called: Choctaw Willy
99 W Plant St (34787-3139)
PHONE.................................407 905-9917
Ken Kelly, *President*
Wayne Bird, *President*
EMP: 10 **EST:** 1989
SALES (est): 283.8K **Privately Held**
SIC: 2033 5812 Barbecue sauce: packaged in cans, jars, etc.; eating places

(G-18381)
CONCEPT SOFTWARE INC
Also Called: Softwarekey.com
1319 Green Frest Ct Ste 4 (34787)
P.O. Box 770459 (34777-0459)
PHONE.................................321 250-6670
Michael Wozniak, *President*
Regina Nax, *Opers Staff*
EMP: 6 **EST:** 1991
SALES (est): 1MM **Privately Held**
WEB: www.softwarekey.com
SIC: 7372 8748 Prepackaged software; systems analysis & engineering consulting services

(G-18382)
DACKOR INC
Also Called: Dackor 3d Laminates
310 E Crown Point Rd (34787-2998)
PHONE.................................407 654-5013
Mark V Viers, *President*
Yumi Viers, *Treasurer*
Jennifer Atkins, *Manager*
Scott Edwards, *Representative*
▲ **EMP:** 12 **EST:** 2003
SALES (est): 2.3MM **Privately Held**
WEB: www.dackor.com
SIC: 2435 Hardwood veneer & plywood

(G-18383)
EASY PAVERS CORP
334 Windford Ct (34786-6061)
PHONE.................................407 967-0511
Aldemir Arpini, *Principal*
EMP: 7 **EST:** 2013
SALES (est): 119.4K **Privately Held**
SIC: 2951 Asphalt paving mixtures & blocks

(G-18384)
EDASHOP INC
Also Called: Anacom Electronica
15388 Arcadia Bluff Loop (34786-8158)
PHONE.................................786 565-9197
Carlos Eugenio Lion, *President*
Gus Salinas, *General Mgr*
EMP: 10 **EST:** 1995
SALES (est): 1.1MM **Privately Held**
WEB: www.edashop.com
SIC: 7372 5063 Prepackaged software; electrical apparatus & equipment

(G-18385)
EXPRESS SIGNS & GRAPHICS INC
547 Garden Heights Dr (34787-2218)
PHONE.................................407 889-4433
Phillip Zabukovec, *President*
David Zabukovec, *Treasurer*
Tabitha Zabukovec, *Admin Sec*
EMP: 16 **EST:** 1993
SQ FT: 4,500
SALES (est): 1.1MM **Privately Held**
SIC: 3993 5199 2752 Electric signs; advertising specialties; commercial printing, lithographic

(G-18386)
FLORIDA METAL-CRAFT INC
47 S Dillard St (34787-3116)
P.O. Box 771179 (34777-1179)
PHONE.................................407 656-1100
Thomas Burnett, *President*
Robert Burnett, *Vice Pres*
EMP: 13 **EST:** 1931

SQ FT: 10,000
SALES (est): 1.7MM **Privately Held**
WEB: www.floridametalcraft.com
SIC: 3444 3599 Sheet metalwork; machine shop, jobbing & repair

(G-18387)
GALLANT INC
1267 Wntr Gdn Vnlnd Rd # 230
(34787-6701)
PHONE.................................800 330-1343
▲ EMP: 8
SQ FT: 1,800
SALES (est): 1.4MM **Privately Held**
SIC: 3069 7389 8742 5094 Mfg Fabrcatd Rubber Prdt Business Services Mgmt Consulting Svcs Whol Jewelry/Precs Stone Mfg Men/Boy Work Clothng

(G-18388)
HANCOR INC
115 N West Crown Point Rd (34787-2948)
PHONE.................................863 655-5499
Ron Buckley, *Principal*
EMP: 38
SALES (corp-wide): 2.7B **Publicly Held**
SIC: 2821 3084 Polyurethane resins; plastics pipe
HQ: Hancor, Inc.
4640 Trueman Blvd
Hilliard OH 43026
614 658-0050

(G-18389)
HEALTHLINE MEDICAL PDTS INC
1065 E Story Rd (34787-3732)
PHONE.................................407 656-0704
Jim Magnuson, *President*
▲ EMP: 17 EST: 1994
SQ FT: 100,000
SALES (est): 1.3MM **Privately Held**
SIC: 3842 5047 Surgical appliances & supplies; medical equipment & supplies

(G-18390)
HILL PRINTING INC
1220 Wntr Gdn Vnlnd Rd # 104
(34787-6373)
PHONE.................................407 654-4282
Kenneth L Hill, *President*
EMP: 9 EST: 1996
SQ FT: 2,000
SALES (est): 999.3K **Privately Held**
WEB: www.hillprinting.com
SIC: 2752 Post cards, picture: lithographed; commercial printing, offset

(G-18391)
HOLLYWOOD HOUNDZ LLC
4101 Briar Gate Ln (34787-5521)
PHONE.................................407 614-2108
Alexandre Lima, *Principal*
EMP: 8 EST: 2016
SALES (est): 365.5K **Privately Held**
SIC: 2499 Wood products

(G-18392)
INGELUB CORP
12935 W Colonial Dr (34787-4101)
PHONE.................................407 656-8800
Helmer Alarcon, *Principal*
EMP: 8
SALES (corp-wide): 736.7K **Privately Held**
SIC: 3569 Filters
PA: Ingelub Corp
7519 Tattant Blvd
Windermere FL

(G-18393)
KOMATSU MINING CORP
3253 Hidden Lake Dr (34787-5427)
PHONE.................................407 491-0758
Rhonda Straub, *Manager*
EMP: 21 **Privately Held**
WEB: www.mining.komatsu
SIC: 3532 Mining machinery
HQ: Komatsu Mining Corp.
311 E Greenfield Ave
Milwaukee WI 53204
414 670-8454

(G-18394)
KONADOCKS LLC
230 Deer Island Rd (34787-9457)
P.O. Box 784267 (34778-4267)
PHONE.................................407 909-0606
Jose Martin, *Finance Mgr*
Brian Hall,
EMP: 6 EST: 2017
SALES (est): 496.8K **Privately Held**
SIC: 2499 Applicators, wood

(G-18395)
LEK TECHNOLOGY CONSULTANTS INC
12788 Gillard Rd (34787-5224)
P.O. Box 783635 (34778-3635)
PHONE.................................407 877-6505
Wade Lowe, *President*
Firpo Guerrero, *Engineer*
Ricardo Nahmens, *Sales Mgr*
David Schmuki, *Technician*
EMP: 5 EST: 2002
SALES (est): 1MM **Privately Held**
WEB: www.lekcomp.com
SIC: 3571 Computers, digital, analog or hybrid

(G-18396)
LIFECO FOODS NORTH AMERICA
855 E Plant St Ste 1700 (34787-3167)
PHONE.................................321 348-5896
Nabil Belizario, *CEO*
EMP: 8 EST: 2018
SALES (est): 159K **Privately Held**
SIC: 2099 Food preparations
PA: Life Company Industria Alimenticia Eireli
Av. Sao Francisco De Assis 1490
Hortolandia SP 13183

(G-18397)
LOTTS CONCRETE PRODUCTS INC
510 E Bay St (34787-3115)
P.O. Box 771255 (34777-1255)
PHONE.................................407 656-2112
Johnnie P Lott Jr, *President*
Willer D Lott, *Corp Secy*
Belinda Fleming, *Vice Pres*
Chelsea Sengel, *Bookkeeper*
April Dunigan, *Human Resources*
▼ EMP: 50 EST: 1963
SALES (est): 14.9MM **Privately Held**
WEB: www.lottsconcrete.com
SIC: 3272 Concrete products

(G-18398)
MOTOR COACH INDS INTL INC
1155 Elboc Way (34787-4487)
PHONE.................................407 246-1414
EMP: 19
SALES (corp-wide): 2.3B **Privately Held**
SIC: 3714 Mfg Motor Vehicle Parts & Accessories
HQ: Motor Coach Industries International, Inc.
200 E Oakton St
Des Plaines IL 60018
847 285-2000

(G-18399)
OBSERVER GROUP
446 N Dillard St (34787-2861)
PHONE.................................407 654-5500
EMP: 8 EST: 2013
SALES (est): 251.8K **Privately Held**
WEB: www.orangeobserver.com
SIC: 2711 Newspapers, publishing & printing

(G-18400)
PRINT ADMINISTRATE
1273 Winter Gdn (34787-6702)
PHONE.................................407 877-5923
Buddy Carpenito, *Partner*
EMP: 8 EST: 2017
SALES (est): 70.5K **Privately Held**
WEB: www.printadministrate.com
SIC: 2752 Commercial printing, lithographic

(G-18401)
PRODALIM USA INC (HQ)
355 9th St (34787-3651)
PHONE.................................407 656-1000
Tsahi I Berezovsky, *President*
Ran Harpaz, *Counsel*
Eusebio Navarro, *Prdtn Mgr*
Makwan Ahmad, *Production*
Heraldo Haynes, *Production*
EMP: 1 EST: 2017
SALES (est): 6.7MM
SALES (corp-wide): 63.6MM **Privately Held**
WEB: www.prodalim.com
SIC: 2086 Carbonated beverages, nonalcoholic: bottled & canned

(G-18402)
QUALITY PRECAST & COMPANY
Also Called: R and R Rebar
416 E Bay St (34787-3112)
P.O. Box 625, Fruitland Park (34731-0625)
PHONE.................................407 877-1000
Mike Phelps, *President*
John Waldron, *Sales Staff*
EMP: 15 EST: 1969
SALES (est): 315.8K **Privately Held**
WEB: www.qualityprecast.com
SIC: 3272 Concrete products, precast

(G-18403)
RIEGL USA INC
14707 W Colonial Dr (34787-4220)
PHONE.................................407 248-9927
James Van Rens, *President*
Mylinh Truong, *Opers Staff*
Vladimir Kadatskiy, *Engineer*
Tan Nguyen, *Engineer*
Kelly Martin, *Finance*
EMP: 21 EST: 1993
SQ FT: 8,000
SALES (est): 7.9MM **Privately Held**
WEB: www.rieglusa.com
SIC: 3812 3823 3599 3829 Search & navigation equipment; controllers for process variables, all types; custom machinery; measuring & controlling devices

(G-18404)
SLR RIFLEWORKS LLC
1232 Wntr Gdn Vnlnd Rd (34787-4453)
PHONE.................................855 757-7435
EMP: 7 EST: 2018
SALES (est): 771.1K **Privately Held**
WEB: www.slrrifleworks.com
SIC: 3489 Ordnance & accessories

(G-18405)
SUNCITI INDUSTRIES INC
3402 Rex Dr (34787-9799)
PHONE.................................407 877-8081
Philip Bruno, *Director*
EMP: 9 EST: 2001
SALES (est): 220.7K **Privately Held**
WEB: www.fathervapor.com
SIC: 3999 Manufacturing industries

(G-18406)
VENOM ALLSTARS LLC
1205 Crown Park Cir (34787-2417)
PHONE.................................407 575-3484
Nguyen Khang, *Principal*
EMP: 7 EST: 2015
SALES (est): 81.8K **Privately Held**
WEB: www.venomallstars.com
SIC: 2836 Venoms

(G-18407)
VICX LLC
Also Called: Majic Nails
1273 Wntr Gdn Vnlnd Rd (34787-6702)
PHONE.................................407 674-2073
Rodrigo Cabral, *Principal*
EMP: 16 EST: 2010
SALES (est): 1MM **Privately Held**
SIC: 3999 Fingernails, artificial
PA: Magic Nails Comercio De Cosmeticos Importacao E Exportacao Ltda
Av. Salvador Allende 6700
Rio De Janeiro RJ 22790

(G-18408)
WASTE MANAGEMENT INC FLORIDA
5400 Rex Dr (34787-9164)
PHONE.................................954 984-2000
David Myhan, *President*
EMP: 25
SALES (corp-wide): 17.9B **Publicly Held**
SIC: 1499 1422 4953 Gemstone & industrial diamond mining; crushed & broken limestone; sanitary landfill operation
PA: Waste Management, Inc.
800 Capitol St Ste 3000
Houston TX 77002
713 512-6200

(G-18409)
WINTER GARDEN TIMES INC
Also Called: West Orange Times
661 Garden Commerce Pkwy
(34787-5714)
P.O. Box 770309 (34777-0309)
PHONE.................................407 656-2121
Dawn Willis, *President*
Troy Herring, *Editor*
Hannah Swayze, *Editor*
Allison Brunelle, *Opers Staff*
Ann Carpenter, *Executive*
EMP: 23 EST: 1913
SALES (est): 1MM **Privately Held**
WEB: www.orangeobserver.com
SIC: 2711 Newspapers, publishing & printing

Winter Haven
Polk County

(G-18410)
90-MINUTE BOOKS LLC
302 Martinique Dr (33884-1707)
PHONE.................................863 318-0464
Stuart Bell,
EMP: 6 EST: 2015
SALES (est): 300K **Privately Held**
WEB: www.90minutebooks.com
SIC: 2731 Books: publishing only

(G-18411)
ACME DYNAMICS INC (PA)
545 Avenue K Se (33880-4215)
PHONE.................................813 752-3137
Joseph A Murphy, *President*
Christopher Irwin, *Exec VP*
◆ EMP: 10 EST: 1957
SQ FT: 19,197
SALES (est): 1.7MM **Privately Held**
WEB: www.acmedynamics.com
SIC: 3561 Pumps, oil well & field

(G-18412)
AJC TILING SOLUTIONS LLC
607 Evergreen Pl Sw (33880-2006)
PHONE.................................863 274-1962
Adrian Clay, *Manager*
EMP: 9
SALES (est): 495.1K **Privately Held**
SIC: 3069 7389 Flooring, rubber: tile or sheet;

(G-18413)
AJS FABRICATION LLC
5754 State Road 542 W # 2 (33880-5151)
PHONE.................................863 514-9630
Anthony Jay Detrick, *Owner*
EMP: 7 EST: 2017
SALES (est): 299.2K **Privately Held**
WEB: www.ajsfabrication.com
SIC: 7692 Welding repair

(G-18414)
ALFREDO WELDING SERVICE LLC
5599 Commercial Blvd (33880-1009)
PHONE.................................954 770-8744
EMP: 6 EST: 2019
SALES (est): 503.9K **Privately Held**
SIC: 7692 Welding repair

(G-18415)
ALUMINUM TANK INDUSTRIES INC
36 Spirit Lake Rd (33880-1245)
PHONE...............................863 401-9474
Daniel Lamonica, *President*
EMP: 7 EST: 2004
SALES (est): 1MM Privately Held
WEB: www.atitank.com
SIC: 3443 Fabricated plate work (boiler shop)

(G-18416)
AMERICAN VULKAN CORPORATION (DH)
Also Called: Shrieve Chemical Co Chemi
2525 Dundee Rd (33884-1169)
P.O. Box 673 (33882-0673)
PHONE...............................863 324-2424
Thomas Falz, *President*
Wayne Dowers, *Vice Pres*
Thomas Lehner, *Vice Pres*
Eric Mower, *Vice Pres*
Michael McClure, *Production*
◆ EMP: 37 EST: 1971
SQ FT: 40,000
SALES (est): 24.6MM
SALES (corp-wide): 1.9MM Privately
Held
WEB: vulkancom.b-cdn.net
SIC: 3568 Shafts; flexible; couplings, shaft: rigid, flexible, universal joint, etc.
HQ: Vulkan Kupplungs- Und Getriebebau
Bernhard Hackforth Gmbh & Co. Kg
Heerstr. 66
Herne NW 44653
232 592-20

(G-18417)
ANTWON PUBLISHING COMPANY INC
806 Ware Ave Ne (33881-1767)
PHONE...............................863 508-0825
Macy Butler, *Principal*
EMP: 7 EST: 2009
SALES (est): 4.9K Privately Held
SIC: 2741 Miscellaneous publishing

(G-18418)
ARDS AWNING & UPHOLSTERY INC
503 5th St Sw (33880-3306)
PHONE...............................863 293-2442
David Ard, *President*
Randall Ard, *Vice Pres*
EMP: 17 EST: 1961
SQ FT: 49,000
SALES (est): 1.3MM Privately Held
WEB: www.ardsawnings.com
SIC: 2394 7641 2211 Awnings, fabric: made from purchased materials; canvas covers & drop cloths; furniture upholstery repair; draperies & drapery fabrics, cotton

(G-18419)
B&M RC RACING
4336 Shadow Wood Way (33880-1531)
PHONE...............................313 518-3999
Michael L King, *Owner*
EMP: 8 EST: 2019
SALES (est): 225K Privately Held
SIC: 3542 Gear rolling machines

(G-18420)
BAXTER CUSTOM FABRICATION INC
133 Browning Cir (33884-2334)
PHONE...............................863 289-9819
Kevin Baxter, *Principal*
EMP: 7 EST: 2014
SALES (est): 226.1K Privately Held
SIC: 3499 Novelties & giftware, including trophies

(G-18421)
BLACK OAK INDUSTRIES INC
9518 Waterford Oaks Blvd (33884-3297)
PHONE...............................863 307-1566
Lisa A Bates, *Principal*
Emily Dale, *Manager*
EMP: 9 EST: 2017
SALES (est): 628K Privately Held
SIC: 3999 Manufacturing industries

(G-18422)
BOLAND PRODUCTION SUPPLY INC
507 Burns Ln (33884-1148)
PHONE...............................863 324-7784
John M Boland, *President*
David Hay, *General Mgr*
David S Hays, *General Mgr*
John S Boland, *Vice Pres*
Ardis L Boland, *Admin Sec*
EMP: 7 EST: 1993
SQ FT: 3,000
SALES (est): 809K Privately Held
WEB: bolandfx-com.3dcartstores.com
SIC: 2892 2899 7819 5099 Secondary high explosives; flares, fireworks & similar preparations; equipment & prop rental, motion picture production; firearms & ammunition, except sporting; paper shells: empty, blank or loaded: 30 mm. & below

(G-18423)
BORDEN DAIRY COMPANY FLA LLC
1000 6th St Sw (33880-3334)
PHONE...............................863 298-9742
Jeff Monroe, *Division Mgr*
Mike Slaughter, *Finance*
EMP: 39
SALES (corp-wide): 766.1MM Privately Held
SIC: 2026 5143 5142 2037 Fermented & cultured milk products; dairy products, except dried or canned; packaged frozen goods; frozen fruits & vegetables
HQ: Borden Dairy Company Of Florida, Llc
308 Avenue G Sw
Winter Haven FL 33880

(G-18424)
BROWN INTERNATIONAL CORP LLC
333 Avenue M Nw (33881-2405)
P.O. Box 713 (33882-0713)
PHONE...............................863 299-2111
Victor Onchi, *Senior VP*
J P Devito, *Vice Pres*
Clarissa Albarran, *Engineer*
Richard Lucas, *Engineer*
Elizabeth Webb, *Engineer*
◆ EMP: 5 EST: 2005
SALES (est): 5.9MM
SALES (corp-wide): 82.6MM Privately Held
WEB: www.brown-intl.com
SIC: 2033 Fruit juices: fresh; vegetable juices: fresh
HQ: Atlas Pacific Engineering Company
1 Atlas Ave
Pueblo CO 81001
719 948-3040

(G-18425)
BRUNS MFG HOMES
10 Spirit Lake Rd (33880-1245)
PHONE...............................863 294-4949
Jim Burn, *Owner*
EMP: 7 EST: 2006
SALES (est): 118.4K Privately Held
SIC: 3999 Manufacturing industries

(G-18426)
BURR PRINTING CO INC
Also Called: Larry Burr Printing Co
4212 Hammond Dr (33881-9701)
P.O. Box 980 (33882-0980)
PHONE...............................863 294-3166
George Burr IV, *President*
EMP: 5 EST: 1930
SQ FT: 2,600
SALES (est): 719.3K Privately Held
SIC: 2752 3953 2791 Lithographing on metal; commercial printing, offset; marking devices; typesetting

(G-18427)
C & S PLASTICS
1550 5th St Sw (33880-3729)
PHONE...............................863 294-5628
Chris Cooper, *President*
Jeremy Ledford, *Prdtn Mgr*
EMP: 28 EST: 1987
SQ FT: 5,600

SALES (est): 5MM Privately Held
WEB: www.candsplastics.com
SIC: 3084 3429 3089 Plastics pipe; furniture hardware; extruded finished plastic products

(G-18428)
C C CALHOUN INC
3750 W Lake Hamilton Dr (33881-9261)
P.O. Box 1877, Dundee (33838-1877)
PHONE...............................863 292-9511
Charles M Carnes, *President*
Lawrence Cahoon, *Corp Secy*
Gary Carnes, *Vice Pres*
EMP: 17 EST: 1996
SALES (est): 8MM Privately Held
WEB: www.cccalhoun.com
SIC: 1442 1459 Sand mining; clays, except kaolin & ball

(G-18429)
CARIBBEAN DISTILLERS LLC
2200 3rd St Nw (33881-1402)
P.O. Box 1447, Lake Alfred (33850-1447)
PHONE...............................863 508-1175
Alberto Rivera, *Senior VP*
◆ EMP: 22 EST: 2011
SALES (est): 2.5MM Privately Held
SIC: 2085 Distilled & blended liquors

(G-18430)
CENTRAL FLA BUS SOLUTIONS INC
Also Called: Propak Software
150 3rd St Sw (33880-2979)
P.O. Box 1056 (33882-1056)
PHONE...............................863 297-9293
John R Sauer, *President*
Chengyu Chang, *Vice Pres*
Richard H Montney Jr, *Vice Pres*
EMP: 25 EST: 1992
SQ FT: 4,000
SALES (est): 2.4MM Privately Held
SIC: 7372 Business oriented computer software

(G-18431)
CERTAINTEED CORPORATION (DH)
Also Called: Certainteed Machine Works
101 Hatfield Rd (33880-1325)
PHONE...............................863 294-3206
Blair Gaida, *President*
Richard Anderson, *Manager*
Ron Hutson, *Maintence Staff*
EMP: 14 EST: 1936
SQ FT: 60,000
SALES (est): 6MM
SALES (corp-wide): 340.6MM Privately Held
WEB: www.certainteed.com
SIC: 3564 Blowing fans: industrial or commercial
HQ: Certainteed Llc
20 Moores Rd
Malvern PA 19355
610 893-5000

(G-18432)
CHILTON SIGNS & DESIGNS LLC
549 Pope Ave Nw (33881-4678)
PHONE...............................863 438-0880
Christopher Chilton, *Administration*
EMP: 6 EST: 2019
SALES (est): 742.7K Privately Held
WEB: www.chiltonsigns.com
SIC: 3993 Signs & advertising specialties

(G-18433)
CUSTOM FLANGE PIPE LLC
3700 W Lake Hamilton Dr (33881-9261)
PHONE...............................863 353-6602
Tom Klingensmith,
EMP: 10 EST: 2017
SALES (est): 1.3MM Privately Held
SIC: 3321 Cast iron pipe & fittings

(G-18434)
DC APPAREL INC
3260 Dundee Rd (33884-1102)
PHONE...............................863 325-9273
Francis D McCrystal, *President*
Chris Broyles, *Vice Pres*
EMP: 5 EST: 2007

SALES (est): 659.8K Privately Held
WEB: www.dcapparelinc.com
SIC: 2759 Screen printing

(G-18435)
EXPRESS PRTG WINTER HAVEN INC
757 Cypress Gardens Blvd (33880-4712)
PHONE...............................863 294-3286
Mark Alford, *Principal*
EMP: 8 EST: 2006
SALES (est): 83.9K Privately Held
SIC: 2752 Commercial printing, lithographic

(G-18436)
FLORIDA AIRBOAT PROPELLER
602 Burns Ln (33884-1149)
PHONE...............................863 324-1653
Tim Wagman, *President*
Billy Wagman, *Vice Pres*
Roberta Wagman, *Treasurer*
Louise Wagman, *Admin Sec*
EMP: 7 EST: 1994
SALES (est): 858.2K Privately Held
WEB: www.floridaairboatpropellers.com
SIC: 3366 Copper foundries

(G-18437)
FLORIDA CAN MANUFACTURING LLC
100 Florida Can Way (33880)
PHONE...............................863 356-5260
Carlos M De La Cruz Sr,
Julio S Bravo,
Alberto De La Cruz,
Jose Rivera,
EMP: 5 EST: 2019
SALES (est): 1.5MM Privately Held
WEB: www.floridacan.com
SIC: 3411 Can lids & ends, metal

(G-18438)
FLORIDA CENTRAL EXTRUSION INC
3700 Dundee Rd Unit 9 (33884-1190)
P.O. Box 1852, Dundee (33838-1852)
PHONE...............................863 324-2541
Pat Sabin, *Owner*
John P Sabin, *Owner*
EMP: 6 EST: 1985
SQ FT: 6,800
SALES (est): 564.1K Privately Held
SIC: 3089 Injection molding of plastics

(G-18439)
FOOD PARTNERS INC
340 W Central Ave Ste 200 (33880-2967)
P.O. Box 1478 (33882-1478)
PHONE...............................863 298-8771
Webb Tanner, *President*
Syed Bukhari, *Opers Staff*
Shelly Prickett, *Finance*
Angie Peebles, *Sales Mgr*
Rhonda Freeman, *Accounts Mgr*
◆ EMP: 10 EST: 1999
SQ FT: 2,000
SALES (est): 50MM Privately Held
WEB: www.foodpartners.com
SIC: 2037 Fruit juices, frozen

(G-18440)
FORTERRA PIPE & PRECAST LLC
1285 Lucerne Loop Rd Ne (33881-9607)
PHONE...............................863 401-6800
Antonio Kalinish, *Branch Mgr*
EMP: 59 Privately Held
WEB: www.forterrabp.com
SIC: 3272 Concrete products, precast
HQ: Forterra Pipe & Precast, Llc
511 E John Carpenter Fwy
Irving TX 75062
469 458-7973

(G-18441)
FOUR PURLS
1226 7th St Nw (33881-2303)
PHONE...............................863 293-6261
Laura Lee Dobratz, *Principal*
EMP: 5 EST: 2010
SALES (est): 406.9K Privately Held
WEB: www.fourpurls.com
SIC: 2281 Crochet yarn, spun

(G-18442)
GATEHOUSE MEDIA LLC
Also Called: News Chief
455 6th St Nw (33881-4061)
P.O. Box 1440 (33882-1440)
PHONE..........................863 401-6900
Robin Quillon, *Principal*
Sam Caruso, *Manager*
Jennifer Eichorn, *Manager*
EMP: 94
SQ FT: 24,000
SALES (corp-wide): 3.2B **Publicly Held**
WEB: www.gannett.com
SIC: 2721 2741 2711 Periodicals; miscellaneous publishing; newspapers
HQ: Gatehouse Media, Llc
175 Sullys Trl Ste 203
Pittsford NY 14534
585 598-0030

(G-18443)
GLOBAL GL LC
Also Called: Greased Lightning
343 Hamilton Shores Dr Ne (33881-5711)
PHONE..........................863 551-1079
EMP: 5
SQ FT: 6,000
SALES (est): 907.5K **Privately Held**
SIC: 2911 2843 Petroleum Refiner Mfg Surface Active Agents

(G-18444)
HARRINGTON CORPORATION
1101 Snively Ave (33880)
PHONE..........................863 326-6130
Mike Harrington, *Branch Mgr*
Eddie Johnson, *Manager*
EMP: 17
SALES (corp-wide): 33.6MM **Privately Held**
WEB: www.harcofittings.com
SIC: 3491 Water works valves
PA: The Harrington Corporation
3721 Cohen Pl
Lynchburg VA 24501
434 845-7094

(G-18445)
HI TECH CONSTRUCTION SVC INC
5540 Commercial Blvd (33880-1008)
P.O. Box 878 (33882-0878)
PHONE..........................863 968-0731
Carl Allen Bryan, *President*
Sara Bryan, *Vice Pres*
EMP: 23 EST: 1996
SQ FT: 6,000
SALES (est): 2.4MM **Privately Held**
SIC: 2452 Modular homes, prefabricated, wood

(G-18446)
HIGH PERFORMANCE SYSTEMS INC
1201 Amercn Superior Blvd (33880-5553)
PHONE..........................863 294-5566
Richard Muto, *President*
Tony Piedra, *Vice Pres*
John Taylor, *Vice Pres*
Jackie Trautwein, *Purchasing*
◆ EMP: 21 EST: 1991
SQ FT: 120,000
SALES (est): 937.5K **Privately Held**
WEB: www.hpscoatings.com
SIC: 3479 Coating of metals & formed products

(G-18447)
KOMMERCIAL REFRIGERATION INC
810 Hillside Ct N (33881-9773)
PHONE..........................863 299-3000
John Waldman, *President*
Cheryl Waldman, *Admin Sec*
EMP: 5 EST: 1987
SQ FT: 400
SALES (est): 660K **Privately Held**
WEB: www.kommercialrefrigeration.com
SIC: 3585 1711 Air conditioning equipment, complete; refrigeration contractor

(G-18448)
KR WARD INC
Also Called: A Ward Design
1000 Hoover Rd (33884-2801)
PHONE..........................863 325-9070
Kevin R Ward, *President*
EMP: 7 EST: 2003
SQ FT: 1,000
SALES (est): 959.5K **Privately Held**
SIC: 2434 Wood kitchen cabinets

(G-18449)
LAPORTE INV HOLDINGS INC
Also Called: Sign Effex
512 6th St Nw (33881-4009)
PHONE..........................863 294-4498
Wayne M Laporte, *President*
Kimberly K Laporte, *Vice Pres*
EMP: 9 EST: 2013
SQ FT: 1,000
SALES (est): 827.3K **Privately Held**
SIC: 3993 6719 Signs & advertising specialties; investment holding companies, except banks

(G-18450)
MABEL LAKE LOOP LLC
2503 Partridge Dr (33884-3033)
PHONE..........................863 326-7144
Richard A Chilton, *Manager*
EMP: 7 EST: 2010
SALES (est): 83.8K **Privately Held**
SIC: 3489 Ordnance & accessories

(G-18451)
MECHANICAL DYNAMICS INC
1116 5th St Sw (33880-3725)
PHONE..........................863 292-0709
Jeff Hughes, *President*
Lee Pointer, *Project Mgr*
EMP: 19 EST: 1995
SQ FT: 5,000
SALES (est): 4.5MM **Privately Held**
WEB: www.mechanicaldynamics.com
SIC: 3441 Fabricated structural metal

(G-18452)
MESSNER PUBLICATIONS INC
Also Called: Messner Printing
3250 Dundee Rd (33884-1113)
PHONE..........................863 318-1595
Jeff Messner, *President*
Jerry Messner Jr, *VP Opers*
Ann Messner, *Production*
Scott Messner, *VP Sales*
Chuck Aiken, *Sales Mgr*
EMP: 18 EST: 2001
SALES (est): 2.3MM **Privately Held**
WEB: www.4lpi.com
SIC: 2741 Miscellaneous publishing

(G-18453)
OWENS CORNING SALES LLC
3327 Queens Cove Loop (33880-5012)
PHONE..........................863 291-3046
Kelly Beerman, *Chairman*
EMP: 40 **Publicly Held**
WEB: www.owenscorning.com
SIC: 3296 3229 Fiberglass insulation; insulation: rock wool, slag & silica minerals; acoustical board & tile, mineral wool; roofing mats, mineral wool; glass fibers, textile; yarn, fiberglass
HQ: Owens Corning Sales, Llc
1 Owens Corning Pkwy
Toledo OH 43659
419 248-8000

(G-18454)
PACKAGING CORPORATION AMERICA
Also Called: PCA/Winter Haven 394
2155 42nd St Nw (33881-1947)
PHONE..........................863 967-0641
Matthew Pyles, *Superintendent*
Kenneth Lynn, *Production*
Gordon Hare, *Cust Mgr*
Larry Fairchild, *Branch Mgr*
EMP: 212
SALES (corp-wide): 7.7B **Publicly Held**
WEB: www.packagingcorp.com
SIC: 2653 Boxes, corrugated: made from purchased materials

PA: Packaging Corporation Of America
1 N Field Ct
Lake Forest IL 60045
847 482-3000

(G-18455)
PEAVY ENTERPRISES INC
Also Called: Speciality Wood Sales
4204 Recker Hwy (33880-1235)
P.O. Box 1736, Auburndale (33823-1736)
PHONE..........................863 297-6513
EMP: 8 EST: 1999
SALES (est): 243.4K **Privately Held**
SIC: 2452 Prefabricated wood buildings

(G-18456)
PEPSI-COLA METRO BTLG CO INC
5023 Recker Hwy (33880-1234)
PHONE..........................863 551-4500
Michael Sales, *Manager*
EMP: 15
SALES (corp-wide): 70.3B **Publicly Held**
WEB: www.pepsico.com
SIC: 2086 Soft drinks: packaged in cans, bottles, etc.
HQ: Pepsi-Cola Metropolitan Bottling Company, Inc.
700 Anderson Hill Rd
Purchase NY 10577
914 767-6000

(G-18457)
PETERS STRUCTURAL PRODUCTS
1320 Hidden Creek Ct (33880-5029)
PHONE..........................863 229-5275
Robert Peters, *Principal*
EMP: 7 EST: 2016
SALES (est): 77.8K **Privately Held**
WEB: www.petersstructuralproducts.com
SIC: 3441 Fabricated structural metal

(G-18458)
POLK COUNTY DEMOCRAT (PA)
99 3rd St Nw (33881-4609)
PHONE..........................863 533-4183
Loyal Frisbie, *President*
S L Frisbie IV, *Vice Pres*
Alan Walrond, *CFO*
Mary G Frisbie, *Treasurer*
Gary Peach, *Accounts Exec*
EMP: 17 EST: 1946
SQ FT: 12,600
SALES (est): 2.2MM **Privately Held**
SIC: 2711 Commercial printing & newspaper publishing combined

(G-18459)
PRECISION PLASTICS GROUP INC
Also Called: C & S Plastics
1635 7th St Sw (33880-3818)
PHONE..........................863 299-6639
Christopher Cooper, *CEO*
Don Millman, *Vice Pres*
Eric Yarbrough, *Maintence Staff*
EMP: 30 EST: 2017
SALES (est): 2.9MM **Privately Held**
WEB: www.candsplastics.com
SIC: 3089 Injection molding of plastics

(G-18460)
PREFERRED PALLETS LLC
4353 Fussell Ln (33880-4848)
PHONE..........................863 401-9517
EMP: 8
SALES (est): 732.5K **Privately Held**
SIC: 2448 Mfg Wood Pallets/Skids

(G-18461)
PRO TRIM OF CENTRAL FLORIDA
2456 Hartridge Point Dr W (33881-1288)
PHONE..........................863 294-4646
Tommy Matthews, *Owner*
EMP: 5 EST: 2004
SALES (est): 432.6K **Privately Held**
SIC: 3465 Body parts, automobile: stamped metal

(G-18462)
PRODUCTION SYSTEM ENGINEERING
3204 E Lake Hamilton Dr (33881)
PHONE..........................863 299-7330
Gary Niemann, *President*
Randy Grulke, *General Mgr*
Meredith Niemann, *Vice Pres*
Meridth Niemann, *Shareholder*
EMP: 10 EST: 1978
SQ FT: 12,000
SALES (est): 802.2K **Privately Held**
SIC: 3565 Packaging machinery

(G-18463)
PROGRAPHIX INC
2614 Avenue G Nw (33880-2139)
PHONE..........................863 298-8081
Deanna Morris, *President*
EMP: 5 EST: 2001
SQ FT: 5,000
SALES (est): 450K **Privately Held**
WEB: www.pgaustin.com
SIC: 2759 Screen printing

(G-18464)
RAY GRAPHICS INC
Also Called: Raygraphics
1895 Executive Rd (33884-1123)
PHONE..........................863 325-0911
Carol Morrow, *President*
EMP: 7 EST: 1988
SQ FT: 2,500
SALES (est): 443.6K **Privately Held**
WEB: www.raygraphicsapparel.com
SIC: 2759 2396 2395 Screen printing; automotive & apparel trimmings; embroidery products, except schiffli machine

(G-18465)
S S DESIGNS INC
5558 Commercial Blvd (33880-1008)
P.O. Box 834 (33882-0834)
PHONE..........................863 965-2576
Bob Carter, *President*
Benjamin Carter, *Vice Pres*
Kevin Ray, *Vice Pres*
Cynthia Zimmerman, *Vice Pres*
Doug Heminger, *Adv Mgr*
EMP: 85 EST: 1976
SQ FT: 100,000
SALES (est): 12MM **Privately Held**
WEB: www.ssdesigns.net
SIC: 2396 2395 Screen printing on fabric articles; embroidery products, except schiffli machine

(G-18466)
SABCON UNDERGROUND LLC
1730 Dundee Rd (33884-1018)
PHONE..........................863 268-8225
Kellie Burns, *Mng Member*
EMP: 23 EST: 2016
SALES (est): 2.8MM **Privately Held**
SIC: 1381 Directional drilling oil & gas wells

(G-18467)
SALVA ENTERPRISES INC
Also Called: Advantage Plastics
654 Post Ave Sw (33880-4353)
P.O. Box 2590 (33883-2590)
PHONE..........................863 291-4407
John Salva, *President*
EMP: 13 EST: 1995
SQ FT: 5,000
SALES (est): 3.9MM **Privately Held**
WEB: www.advplasticsny.com
SIC: 3089 Injection molding of plastics; plastic processing
PA: Orchard Creek Capital, Llc
133 W Main St Ste 290
Northville MI 48167
248 308-3671

(G-18468)
SOLAR ENERGY SPECIALIST CORP
1130 1st St S (33880-3903)
PHONE..........................863 514-9532
Tanesha L Bouthner, *President*
EMP: 9 EST: 2016
SALES (est): 514.2K **Privately Held**
WEB: www.solarandenergyspecialists.com
SIC: 3433 Solar heaters & collectors

▲ = Import ▼=Export
◆ =Import/Export

(G-18469)
SOUTHAST PROTEIN PURVEYORS LLC
604 Lake Elizabeth Dr (33884-1434)
P.O. Box 1024, Auburndale (33823-1024)
PHONE...................................912 354-2770
Jay Javetz, *Mng Member*
Stephen Saterbo,
EMP: 4 **EST:** 2005
SQ FT: 2,000
SALES (est): 15MM **Privately Held**
SIC: 2013 Frozen meats from purchased meat

(G-18470)
STACY LEE MONTGOMERY
Also Called: Stacy's Printing
6320 Cypress Gardens Blvd (33884-3176)
PHONE...................................863 662-3163
Stacy Lee Montgomery, *Owner*
EMP: 7 **EST:** 2016
SALES (est): 277.8K **Privately Held**
SIC: 2752 Commercial printing, offset

(G-18471)
SUPERIOR PALLETS LLC
4353 Fussell Ln (33880-4848)
PHONE...................................863 875-4041
EMP: 7
SALES (est): 418.7K **Privately Held**
SIC: 2448 Mfg Wood Pallets/Skids

(G-18472)
SUPERIOR UNLIMITED ENTPS INC
Also Called: Cypress Signs
160 Spirit Lake Rd (33880-1242)
PHONE...................................863 294-1683
Donie Bowman, *President*
Bruce Mc Whirter, *Plant Mgr*
Mark Bowman, *Treasurer*
EMP: 9 **EST:** 1977
SQ FT: 4,000
SALES (est): 980.6K **Privately Held**
WEB: www.cypresssigns.com
SIC: 3993 7699 Signs, not made in custom sign painting shops; professional instrument repair services

(G-18473)
TARGET MARINE INC
Also Called: Target Marine Manufacturers
125 Bomber Rd (33880-5666)
PHONE...................................863 293-3592
Charles Monts De Oca, *President*
EMP: 11 **EST:** 1980
SALES (est): 67.1K **Privately Held**
SIC: 3732 Boats, fiberglass: building & repairing

(G-18474)
TENSIK INC
3955 W Lake Hamilton Dr (33881-9272)
PHONE...................................954 937-9505
Eduardo Fuenmayor, *CEO*
EMP: 5 **EST:** 2019
SALES (est): 410.5K **Privately Held**
WEB: www.tensikusa.com
SIC: 3531 Concrete plants

(G-18475)
TRAVIS LH LLC
Also Called: Lh Travis
1800 42nd St Nw (33881-1948)
PHONE...................................863 967-0628
Erica Hamilton,
EMP: 10 **EST:** 2020
SALES (est): 1MM **Privately Held**
WEB: www.lhtravis.com
SIC: 3569 Lubrication equipment, industrial

(G-18476)
UNITED ADHESIVE PRODUCTS INC
4202 Hammond Dr (33881-9701)
PHONE...................................863 698-9484
Jennifer Schaal, *Principal*
EMP: 8 **EST:** 2016
SALES (est): 275.8K **Privately Held**
SIC: 2891 Adhesives

(G-18477)
VASS HOLDINGS INC (PA)
146 Avenue B Nw (33881-4506)
P.O. Box 1707 (33882-1707)
PHONE...................................863 295-5664
Howard Levasseur Jr, *President*
Billy Graham, *Warehouse Mgr*
Marylin Riggs, *CFO*
EMP: 4 **EST:** 1993
SQ FT: 1,800
SALES (est): 27.8MM **Privately Held**
SIC: 2899 Chemical preparations

(G-18478)
WM G ROE & SONS INC
Also Called: Noble Worldwide Fla Citrus Sls
500 Avenue R Sw (33880-3871)
P.O. Box 900 (33882-0900)
PHONE...................................863 294-3577
Quentin J Roe, *President*
Allison Lee, *Principal*
William G Roe II, *Vice Pres*
April Porter, *CFO*
Dan Arnold, *Sales Staff*
▼ **EMP:** 500 **EST:** 1927
SQ FT: 40,000
SALES (est): 53.7MM **Privately Held**
WEB: www.noblecitrus.com
SIC: 2033 Fruit juices: fresh

(G-18479)
YAUCHLER PROPERTIES LLC
119 Avenue D Se (33880-3525)
PHONE...................................863 662-5570
Eugene P Yauchler, *Principal*
EMP: 15 **EST:** 2008
SALES (est): 1MM **Privately Held**
SIC: 3589 Swimming pool filter & water conditioning systems

Winter Park
Orange County

(G-18480)
ACCORD INDUSTRIES LLC (HQ)
Also Called: Concrete Products-Division
4001 Forsyth Rd (32792-6833)
P.O. Box 35430, Charlotte NC (28235-5430)
PHONE...................................407 671-6989
Mr Michael Kline, *Vice Pres*
Debbie Deford, *CFO*
Diane Wiggins,
◆ **EMP:** 95 **EST:** 1990
SQ FT: 2,500
SALES (est): 16.5MM
SALES (corp-wide): 66.4MM **Privately Held**
WEB: www.universal100.com
SIC: 3084 3444 3317 3272 Plastics pipe; sheet metalwork; steel pipe & tubes; prestressed concrete products
PA: Alliance Holdings, Inc.
100 Witmer Rd Ste 170
Horsham PA 19044
215 706-0873

(G-18481)
ACE CUSTOM SIGNS OF WINTER PK
922 Orange Ave (32789-4707)
PHONE...................................407 257-6475
EMP: 9 **EST:** 2019
SALES (est): 497.6K **Privately Held**
WEB:
www.acecustomsignsofwinterpark.com
SIC: 3993 Signs & advertising specialties

(G-18482)
AI2 INC
1400 Bonnie Burn Cir (32789-5703)
PHONE...................................407 645-3234
Roger D Ray, *Director*
Jennifer R Clark, *Admin Sec*
EMP: 8 **EST:** 2001
SALES (est): 112.9K **Privately Held**
SIC: 7372 Educational computer software

(G-18483)
ALPHA CARD COMPACT MEDIA LLC
941 W Morse Blvd Ste 100 (32789-3781)
PHONE...................................407 698-3592
Ian Whitfield,
EMP: 7 **EST:** 2018
SALES (est): 641.5K **Privately Held**
WEB: www.alpha-cards.com
SIC: 2759 Card printing & engraving, except greeting

(G-18484)
AM2F ENERGY INC
501 N Orlando Ave 313-256 (32789-7313)
PHONE...................................407 505-1127
Juyoung Kim, *President*
Yoonjung Kim, *Vice Pres*
EMP: 8 **EST:** 2011
SALES (est): 170.9K **Privately Held**
WEB: www.am2fenergy.com
SIC: 2992 Lubricating oils & greases

(G-18485)
API TECH NORTH AMERICA INC
941 W Morse Blvd Ste 100 (32789-3781)
PHONE...................................929 255-1231
EMP: 14 **EST:** 2019
SALES (est): 673.9K **Privately Held**
SIC: 3674 Semiconductors & related devices

(G-18486)
AQUA ENGINEERING & EQP INC
7206 Aloma Ave (32792-7102)
PHONE...................................407 599-2123
Marianne Brizio, *President*
▲ **EMP:** 11 **EST:** 2000
SQ FT: 1,800
SALES (est): 1.4MM **Privately Held**
WEB: www.aquariumwaterfilters.com
SIC: 3589 5074 Water treatment equipment, industrial; water purification equipment

(G-18487)
ARCHITCTRAL SHTMTL FBRCTORS IN
Also Called: Asmf
2720 Forsyth Rd Ste 200 (32792-8212)
PHONE...................................407 672-9086
Jeremiah Dice, *President*
Matthew David Dice, *Manager*
EMP: 5 **EST:** 2005
SQ FT: 5,000
SALES (est): 374.6K **Privately Held**
SIC: 3444 Sheet metalwork

(G-18488)
ARSENAL INDUSTRIES LLC
750 S Orlando Ave Ste 200 (32789-4872)
PHONE...................................407 506-2698
Jennifer Dunham, *Principal*
Jason Rottenberg, *General Ptnr*
EMP: 11 **EST:** 2017
SALES (est): 783.2K **Privately Held**
WEB: www.arsenalgrowth.com
SIC: 3999 Manufacturing industries

(G-18489)
ARSENAL VENTURE PARTNERS FLA
750 S Orlando Ave Ste 200 (32789-4872)
PHONE...................................407 838-1400
Jason Rottenberg, *General Ptnr*
Amy Brooks, *Finance Dir*
Christopher Fountas, *Director*
John Nolan, *Advisor*
EMP: 10 **EST:** 2012
SALES (est): 354.7K **Privately Held**
SIC: 3999 Manufacturing industries

(G-18490)
BINDERY LLC
611 N Wymore Rd Ste 100 (32789-2848)
PHONE...................................407 647-7777
Larry J Herring, *Principal*
EMP: 7 **EST:** 2001
SALES (est): 156.3K **Privately Held**
SIC: 2789 Bookbinding & related work

(G-18491)
BONNIER CORPORATION (DH)
480 N Orlando Ave Ste 236 (32789-2918)
PHONE...................................407 628-4802
David Ritchie, *CEO*
David Benz, *Publisher*
Andrew Leisner, *Publisher*
David Morel, *Publisher*
Parker Stair, *Publisher*
EMP: 200 **EST:** 2007
SALES (est): 616.8MM **Privately Held**
WEB: www.bonniercorp.com
SIC: 2721 Magazines: publishing only, not printed on site

(G-18492)
BOONE BAIT CO INC
1501 Minnesota Ave (32789-4622)
P.O. Box 2966 (32790-2966)
PHONE...................................407 975-8775
Peter F Foley, *President*
▲ **EMP:** 15 **EST:** 1953
SQ FT: 14,000
SALES (est): 671.9K **Privately Held**
WEB: www.boonebait.com
SIC: 3949 5941 Lures, fishing: artificial; sporting goods & bicycle shops

(G-18493)
C & M MANUFACTURING LLC
4212 Metric Dr (32792-6819)
PHONE...................................407 673-9601
Chad J Berecz, *Manager*
EMP: 7 **EST:** 2017
SALES (est): 230K **Privately Held**
WEB: www.cm-manufacturing.com
SIC: 3999 Barber & beauty shop equipment

(G-18494)
C E S WIRELESS TECH CORP
931 S Semoran Blvd # 200 (32792-5396)
PHONE...................................407 681-0869
Pat Lohan, *President*
William Mercurio, *Chairman*
Ada Gaston, *Corp Secy*
EMP: 27 **EST:** 1974
SQ FT: 15,000
SALES (est): 1MM **Privately Held**
WEB: www.gpswirelesstechnologies.com
SIC: 3663 Mobile communication equipment

(G-18495)
C&A LOZARO INC
3000 N Goldenrod Rd (32792-8708)
PHONE...................................407 671-8809
Diego Lozano, *President*
EMP: 8 **EST:** 2005
SALES (est): 110.9K **Privately Held**
SIC: 2024 Ice cream & frozen desserts

(G-18496)
CABINET SYSTEMS CENTL FLA INC
2716 Forsyth Rd Ste 114 (32792-8204)
PHONE...................................407 678-0994
Jeff Hebert, *President*
Dennis Jones, *Vice Pres*
EMP: 6 **EST:** 1983
SQ FT: 5,200
SALES (est): 484.1K **Privately Held**
SIC: 2434 Wood kitchen cabinets

(G-18497)
CATO STEEL CO
3928 Forsyth Rd (32792-6813)
PHONE...................................407 671-3333
Allen McCormick, *President*
Mike McCormick, *Office Mgr*
Tracy Gironda, *Admin Asst*
EMP: 17 **EST:** 1963
SQ FT: 2,500
SALES (est): 2MM **Privately Held**
WEB: www.catosteel.com
SIC: 3444 3441 Sheet metalwork; fabricated structural metal

(G-18498)
CHAMPION SHTMTL FABRICATION
6450 University Blvd B2 (32792-7434)
PHONE...................................407 509-7439
Patrick Madden, *President*
▲ **EMP:** 7 **EST:** 2011
SALES (est): 606.3K **Privately Held**
SIC: 3499 Fire- or burglary-resistive products

(G-18499)
CHIN & CHIN ENTERPRISES INC
3580 Aloma Ave Ste 5 (32792-4011)
PHONE...................................407 478-8726
Luong Moc Tran, *President*

James Chin, *Vice Pres*
Thomas Chin, *Vice Pres*
David Hansen, *Vice Pres*
EMP: 15 EST: 2003
SQ FT: 750
SALES (est): 305K **Privately Held**
SIC: 2599 Food wagons, restaurant

(G-18500)
CONTROL MICRO SYSTEMS INC
4420 Metric Dr Ste A (32792-6961)
PHONE.................................407 679-9716
Timothy Miller, *President*
Victor Rivera, *Buyer*
Jason Dembkoski, *Engineer*
Ryan Karnemaat, *Engineer*
Mark Machovec, *Engineer*
▲ **EMP: 49 EST:** 1983
SQ FT: 25,000
SALES (est): 15MM **Privately Held**
WEB: www.cmslaser.com
SIC: 3699 Laser systems & equipment

(G-18501)
CUP PLUS USA
4440 Metric Dr (32792-6933)
PHONE.................................321 972-1968
Lawrence Griller, *Principal*
▲ **EMP: 8 EST:** 2010
SALES (est): 109.8K **Privately Held**
SIC: 2821 Plastics materials & resins

(G-18502)
CUSTOM COMFORT MEDTEK LLC
3939 Forsyth Rd Ste A (32792-6835)
P.O. Box 4779 (32793-4779)
PHONE.................................407 332-0062
Doug D Patton, *Vice Pres*
Cindy Aymat, *Sales Staff*
Peter Gaughn, *Mng Member*
◆ **EMP: 20 EST:** 1987
SQ FT: 50,000
SALES (est): 3.3MM **Privately Held**
WEB: www.customcomfort.com
SIC: 2599 Hospital furniture, except beds; hospital beds

(G-18503)
DAILY BUZZ
3260 University Blvd (32792-7431)
PHONE.................................407 673-5400
Steve Bailey, *Principal*
EMP: 7 EST: 2007
SALES (est): 109.1K **Privately Held**
WEB: www.dailybuzznow.com
SIC: 2711 Newspapers, publishing & printing

(G-18504)
DAIN M BAYER
2333 Chantilly Ave (32789-1341)
PHONE.................................407 647-0679
Timothy Bayer, *Principal*
EMP: 8 EST: 2001
SALES (est): 253.1K **Privately Held**
SIC: 2834 Pharmaceutical preparations

(G-18505)
DARK LAKE SOFTWARE INC
Also Called: Dark Lake Systems
1229 Wading Waters Cir (32792-3162)
PHONE.................................407 602-8046
Bradley Foley, *Principal*
Madison Fang, *Software Dev*
EMP: 15 EST: 2010
SALES (est): 1.6MM **Privately Held**
WEB: www.darklakesoftware.com
SIC: 7372 Application computer software

(G-18506)
DIGITAL PRINTING SOLUTIONS INC
6438 University Blvd # 12 (32792-7417)
PHONE.................................407 671-8715
Kevin Johnson, *President*
Terry Sutton, *Vice Pres*
Randy Dexter, *Technician*
EMP: 47 EST: 2001
SQ FT: 23,000
SALES (est): 5MM **Privately Held**
WEB: www.dpscan.com
SIC: 2752 Commercial printing, offset

(G-18507)
DIVERSIFIED MINING INC
2178 Crandon Ave (32789-3382)
PHONE.................................407 923-3194
Jefferson A Bootes, *President*
EMP: 7 EST: 2011
SALES (est): 155.6K **Privately Held**
SIC: 1241 Coal mining services

(G-18508)
DMC COMPONENTS INTL LLC
Also Called: Data Image
4202 Metric Dr (32792-6819)
PHONE.................................407 478-4064
Michael P Dathe, *CEO*
Bill Reichert, *Sales Executive*
▲ **EMP: 7 EST:** 1999
SALES (est): 1.2MM **Privately Held**
WEB: www.dataimagelcd.com
SIC: 3679 3699 Liquid crystal displays (LCD); electrical equipment & supplies

(G-18509)
DREWLU ENTERPRISES INC
Also Called: Printing USA
3500 Aloma Ave Ste D9 (32792-4005)
PHONE.................................407 478-7872
Jean Horning, *President*
Dean A Horning, *Vice Pres*
EMP: 7 EST: 1986
SALES (est): 1.1MM **Privately Held**
WEB: www.onesourceonestop.com
SIC: 2752 Commercial printing, offset

(G-18510)
EVERYTHING COMMUNICATES INC
Also Called: Sign-A-Rama
1740 State Road 436 # 104 (32792-1932)
P.O. Box 1077, Flagler Beach (32136-1077)
PHONE.................................407 578-6616
Amy S Marvin, *President*
Ross M Marvin, *Vice Pres*
EMP: 8 EST: 2004
SALES (est): 731.8K **Privately Held**
WEB: www.signarama.com
SIC: 3993 Signs & advertising specialties

(G-18511)
F C MACHINE CORPORATION
4212 Metric Dr (32792-6819)
PHONE.................................407 673-9601
Frank Cordi, *President*
Michele Cordi, *Admin Sec*
EMP: 8 EST: 1990
SQ FT: 3,000
SALES (est): 736.2K **Privately Held**
WEB: www.fcmachineshop.com
SIC: 3599 Machine shop, jobbing & repair

(G-18512)
FAITHFUL HEART FROYO LLC
2405 Whitehall Cir (32792-4752)
PHONE.................................407 325-3052
Laura S Williams, *Principal*
EMP: 7 EST: 2014
SALES (est): 225.5K **Privately Held**
SIC: 2024 Yogurt desserts, frozen

(G-18513)
HERFF JONES INC
Also Called: Herff Jones
112 N Wymore Rd (32789-3453)
PHONE.................................407 647-4373
Joe K Slaughter, *President*
Matthew R Barth, *Vice Pres*
Mark D Dillman, *Vice Pres*
Larry T Hill, *Vice Pres*
Kenneth G Langlois, *Vice Pres*
EMP: 6 EST: 1994
SQ FT: 2,299
SALES (est): 769.9K **Privately Held**
WEB: www.herfforlando.com
SIC: 2752 Commercial printing, lithographic

(G-18514)
HORIZON DUPLICATION INC
Also Called: Horizon Media Express
841 Nicolet Ave Ste 5 (32789-4618)
PHONE.................................407 767-5000
Peter Schimpf, *President*
Ann Stuart, *CFO*
Anita Castado, *Marketing Staff*

EMP: 7 EST: 1991
SQ FT: 10,000
SALES (est): 774.6K **Privately Held**
WEB: www.horizonmediaexpress.com
SIC: 3695 5735 Computer software tape & disks: blank, rigid & floppy; compact discs

(G-18515)
INFRARED SYSTEMS DEV CORP
7319 Sandscove Ct Ste 4 (32792-6979)
PHONE.................................407 679-5101
Andrew Duran, *President*
Jeffrey Bueltmann, *Vice Pres*
Carlene Duran, *Vice Pres*
EMP: 14 EST: 1997
SQ FT: 6,500
SALES (est): 2MM **Privately Held**
WEB: www.infraredsystems.com
SIC: 3826 Laser scientific & engineering instruments

(G-18516)
J BRISTOL LLC
2715 Norris Ave (32789-6667)
PHONE.................................407 488-6744
Jason P Bristol, *Manager*
EMP: 7 EST: 2016
SALES (est): 190.9K **Privately Held**
SIC: 2621 Paper mills

(G-18517)
JUICE CULTURE LLC
805 S Orlando Ave Ste H (32789-4869)
PHONE.................................407 312-8079
Raquel Hair, *Principal*
EMP: 7 EST: 2015
SALES (est): 185.6K **Privately Held**
SIC: 3585 Soda fountain & beverage dispensing equipment & parts

(G-18518)
LAC INC
3580 Aloma Ave Ste 1 (32792-4011)
PHONE.................................407 671-6610
Lacey Sharp, *Principal*
EMP: 10 EST: 2005
SALES (est): 255.8K **Privately Held**
SIC: 3552 Embroidery machines

(G-18519)
LEGACY PUBLISHING SERVICES
1883 Lee Rd (32789-2102)
PHONE.................................407 647-3787
▲ **EMP: 8**
SALES: 350K **Privately Held**
SIC: 2731 Books-Publishing/Printing

(G-18520)
LUCKY DOG SCREEN PRINTING MG
2716 Forsyth Rd Ste 105 (32792-8204)
PHONE.................................407 629-8838
Susan Marcus, *President*
EMP: 7 EST: 1995
SALES (est): 183.3K **Privately Held**
WEB: www.luckydogfl.com
SIC: 2759 7389 Screen printing; embroidering of advertising on shirts, etc.

(G-18521)
LUONG MOC III INC
3580 Aloma Ave Ste 5 (32792-4011)
PHONE.................................407 478-8726
Luong Moc Tran, *President*
EMP: 50
SALES (est): 3.6MM **Privately Held**
SIC: 2599 Food wagons, restaurant

(G-18522)
METRO DEFENSE SERVICES INC
3001 Aloma Ave 227 (32792-3752)
PHONE.................................407 285-2304
Bruce Chatterton, *President*
EMP: 7 EST: 2007
SALES (est): 80.3K **Privately Held**
SIC: 3812 Defense systems & equipment

(G-18523)
METROPOLIS GRAPHICS INC
805 S Orlando Ave Ste D (32789-4869)
PHONE.................................407 740-5455
Darrell Robinson, *President*
EMP: 8 EST: 1989

SQ FT: 1,000
SALES (est): 1.2MM **Privately Held**
WEB: www.metropolisgraphics.com
SIC: 2759 5199 Screen printing; advertising specialties

(G-18524)
MICROJIG INC
7212 Sandscove Ct (32792-6908)
PHONE.................................855 747-7233
Henry Wang, *President*
Steve Thomas, *Finance*
Bruce Wang, *Director*
EMP: 7 EST: 2001
SALES (est): 1.1MM **Privately Held**
WEB: www.microjig.com
SIC: 3423 Hand & edge tools

(G-18525)
MIKES PRINT SHOP INC
2118 Poinciana Rd (32792-1827)
PHONE.................................407 718-4964
Michael P Schuermann, *President*
EMP: 9 EST: 1970
SALES (est): 502.4K **Privately Held**
WEB: www.flprinting.net
SIC: 2752 2791 2789 2672 Commercial printing, offset; typesetting; bookbinding & related work; coated & laminated paper

(G-18526)
NIVCOE INTERNATIONAL DEV
2020 W Fairbanks Ave # 102 (32789-4522)
PHONE.................................321 282-3666
Reginal Ovince, *President*
EMP: 15 EST: 2007
SALES (est): 3MM **Privately Held**
SIC: 1389 Construction, repair & dismantling services

(G-18527)
ONEZENO LLC
3300 University Blvd # 218 (32792-7435)
PHONE.................................407 539-1665
Jason S Rimes, *Principal*
EMP: 5 EST: 2018
SALES (est): 307.9K **Privately Held**
SIC: 7372 Prepackaged software

(G-18528)
PLAYOFF TECHNOLOGIES LLC
Also Called: Sponsor Locker
1430 Elizabeth Dr (32789-2733)
PHONE.................................407 497-2202
Charles E Harris, *CEO*
EMP: 7 EST: 2013
SALES (est): 408.7K **Privately Held**
WEB: www.playofftech.com
SIC: 7372 Prepackaged software

(G-18529)
QUICK CANS INC
7034 Arbor Ct (32792-7529)
PHONE.................................407 415-1361
James M Urichko, *Principal*
EMP: 7 EST: 2010
SALES (est): 93.5K **Privately Held**
SIC: 3089 Garbage containers, plastic

(G-18530)
REDBERD PRINTING
803 S Orlando Ave (32789-4868)
PHONE.................................407 622-2292
Peter R Cleeveley, *Principal*
EMP: 9 EST: 2009
SALES (est): 75.1K **Privately Held**
WEB: www.redbirdprinting.com
SIC: 2752 Commercial printing, offset

(G-18531)
REDBIRD PRINTING
803 S Orlando Ave Ste J (32789-4868)
PHONE.................................904 654-8371
Cleeveley R John, *CFO*
EMP: 7 EST: 2017
SALES (est): 247.1K **Privately Held**
WEB: www.redbirdprinting.com
SIC: 2752 Commercial printing, offset

(G-18532)
REGAL CABINETS INC
3903 Forsyth Rd (32792-6834)
PHONE.................................407 678-1003
Faramarz Sadri, *President*
EMP: 10 EST: 1995
SQ FT: 10,519

SALES (est): 955.4K **Privately Held**
WEB: www.regalcabinetsfl.com
SIC: 2434 Wood kitchen cabinets

(G-18533)
REV AMBLANCE GROUP ORLANDO INC (DH)
Also Called: Wheeled Coach Industries
2737 Forsyth Rd (32789-6673)
P.O. Box 677339, Orlando (32867-7339)
PHONE....................407 677-7777
Robert L Collins, *President*
Joe Leggett, *President*
Donald Lynn Collins, *Corp Secy*
Grisell Carballido, *Vice Pres*
Dino Cusamano, *Vice Pres*
◆ EMP: 360 EST: 1975
SQ FT: 200,000
SALES (est): 95.8MM **Publicly Held**
WEB: www.wheeledcoach.com
SIC: 3711 Ambulances (motor vehicles), assembly of
HQ: Collins Industries, Inc.
15 Compound Dr
Hutchinson KS 67502
620 663-5551

(G-18534)
SIGHTHOUND INC
520 N Orlando Ave Apt 1 (32789-7317)
PHONE....................407 974-5694
Rj Burnham, *CEO*
Stephen Neish, *President*
Linda Mattedi, *Human Res Mgr*
Scott Swazey, *CTO*
Brent Richardson, *Software Dev*
EMP: 49 EST: 2012
SQ FT: 900
SALES (est): 4.5MM **Privately Held**
WEB: www.sighthound.com
SIC: 7372 Application computer software

(G-18535)
SIGNS NOW INC
1003 S Orlando Ave (32789-4850)
PHONE....................407 628-2410
Michelle Gonzalez, *President*
Juan Gonzalez, *Vice Pres*
EMP: 5 EST: 1990
SALES (est): 388.3K **Privately Held**
WEB: www.signsnow.com
SIC: 3993 Signs & advertising specialties

(G-18536)
SIGNWAY INC
2964 Forsyth Rd (32792-6690)
P.O. Box 195486, Winter Springs (32719-5486)
PHONE....................407 696-7446
Steve Bryan, *President*
Jeff Bryan, *Vice Pres*
EMP: 5 EST: 2001
SALES (est): 528.3K **Privately Held**
WEB: www.signwayinc.com
SIC: 3993 Signs, not made in custom sign painting shops

(G-18537)
SIMETRI INC
Also Called: Trauma Tattoos
937 S Semoran Blvd # 100 (32792-5316)
PHONE....................321 972-9980
Angela Alban Naranjo, *President*
EMP: 20 EST: 2011
SQ FT: 5,500
SALES (est): 3.5MM **Privately Held**
WEB: www.simetri.us
SIC: 3999 Mannequins

(G-18538)
SONNYS STRINGS INC
311 E Morse Blvd Apt 1-3 (32789-3833)
PHONE....................407 862-4905
Sonia Glatting, *President*
▲ EMP: 8 EST: 1972
SQ FT: 600
SALES (est): 224.8K **Privately Held**
SIC: 3961 Costume jewelry, ex. precious metal & semiprecious stones

(G-18539)
SPINENET LLC
1300 Minnesota Ave # 200 (32789-4800)
PHONE....................321 439-1806
King Floyd, *President*
EMP: 7 EST: 2006

SALES (est): 409.8K **Privately Held**
WEB: www.spinenetllc.com
SIC: 3842 Implants, surgical

(G-18540)
STAY SMART CARE LLC
941 W Morse Blvd (32789-3734)
PHONE....................321 682-7113
Alan Young, *Officer*
Mark Feinberg,
EMP: 5 EST: 2018
SALES (est): 480.6K **Privately Held**
WEB: www.staysmartcare.com
SIC: 7372 Application computer software
PA: Feinberg Health Partners, Llc
941 W Morse Blvd
Winter Park FL 32789
321 682-7113

(G-18541)
SUPERIOR PRINTERS INC
Also Called: Superior Quick Print
1884 W Fairbanks Ave (32789-4502)
P.O. Box 2238 (32790-2238)
PHONE....................407 644-3344
C Edward Sengel, *President*
Teresa Sengel, *Vice Pres*
EMP: 53 EST: 1975
SQ FT: 10,000
SALES (est): 5.1MM **Privately Held**
WEB: www.superiorprinters.net
SIC: 2752 Commercial printing, offset

(G-18542)
T BEATTIE ENTERPRISES
Also Called: American Heritage Press
7208 Aloma Ave Ste 300 (32792-7134)
PHONE....................407 679-2000
Richard Beattie, *President*
EMP: 19 EST: 1969
SQ FT: 3,600
SALES (est): 616.3K **Privately Held**
SIC: 2752 Commercial printing, offset

(G-18543)
TAPINFLUENCE INC
480 N Orlando Ave Ste 200 (32789-2918)
PHONE....................720 726-4071
Promise Phelon, *CEO*
Brian Brady, *Director*
EMP: 21 EST: 2009
SALES (est): 3MM **Publicly Held**
WEB: www.tapinfluence.com
SIC: 7372 Business oriented computer software
PA: Izea Worldwide, Inc.
1317 Edgewater Dr 1880
Orlando FL 32804

(G-18544)
TENNESSEE TOOL AND FIXTURE LLC
1750 Barcelona Way (32789-5672)
PHONE....................931 954-5316
Scott Neidig, *Business Mgr*
Rob Brooks, *Mng Member*
EMP: 11 EST: 2017
SALES (est): 727.2K **Privately Held**
WEB: www.tntool.com
SIC: 3544 Special dies & tools

(G-18545)
TIGART WELDING LLC
1468 Auburn Green Loop (32792-6182)
PHONE....................407 371-1820
Michael Vig, *Principal*
EMP: 7 EST: 2019
SALES (est): 450.2K **Privately Held**
SIC: 7692 Welding repair

(G-18546)
TITANIUM PERFORMANCE LLC
1233 Valley Creek Run (32792-8156)
PHONE....................407 712-5770
Ty Sochacki, *Principal*
EMP: 6 EST: 2015
SALES (est): 329.2K **Privately Held**
SIC: 3356 Titanium

(G-18547)
U S HARDWARE SUPPLY INC
4675 Metric Dr (32792-6980)
PHONE....................407 657-1551
Nissim Astrouck, *President*
EMP: 22 EST: 1981
SQ FT: 30,000

SALES (est): 4.8MM **Privately Held**
WEB: www.ushardwaresupply.com
SIC: 3714 3429 3469 3542 Motor vehicle parts & accessories; clamps, couplings, nozzles & other metal hose fittings; metal stampings; machine tools, metal forming type; bolts, nuts, rivets & washers

(G-18548)
URECON SYSTEMS INC
4046 N Goldenrod Rd 162 (32792-8911)
PHONE....................321 638-2364
EMP: 150
SALES (est): 1.3MM **Privately Held**
SIC: 2295 Mfg Coated Fabrics

(G-18549)
URECON SYSTEMS INC
7136 Smallow Run (32792)
PHONE....................904 695-3332
Gregg Gaylard, *President*
Maurice Tousignant, *President*
Christian Phenix, *Vice Pres*
Nicole Stojc, *Controller*
EMP: 46 EST: 1994
SALES (est): 508.7K
SALES (corp-wide): 4B **Privately Held**
WEB: www.urecon.com
SIC: 3321 Cast iron pipe & fittings
HQ: Gf Piping Systems Canada Ltd
75 Boul Dupont
Coteau-Du-Lac QC J0P 1
450 455-0961

(G-18550)
WILSONS MACHINE PRODUCTS INC
1844 Kentucky Ave (32789-4529)
PHONE....................407 644-2020
Douglas T Stevenson, *President*
Douglas Stevenson, *Mfg Staff*
Sherry Gaidry, *CFO*
EMP: 38 EST: 1947
SQ FT: 10,400
SALES (est): 5MM **Privately Held**
WEB: www.wilsons-machine.com
SIC: 3599 Machine shop, jobbing & repair

(G-18551)
WINTER PARK DISTILLING CO LLC
1288 Orange Ave (32789-4940)
P.O. Box 2878 (32790-2878)
PHONE....................407 801-2714
EMP: 12 EST: 2017
SALES (est): 358.5K **Privately Held**
WEB: www.wpdistilling.com
SIC: 2085 Distilled & blended liquors

(G-18552)
WINTER PARK PUBLISHING CO LLC
201 W Canton Ave Ste 125b (32789-3172)
PHONE....................941 320-6627
EMP: 8 EST: 2018
SALES (est): 724.3K **Privately Held**
WEB: www.winterparkmag.com
SIC: 2741 Miscellaneous publishing

(G-18553)
WORKING MOTHER MEDIA INC
Also Called: Diversity Best Practices
480 N Orlando Ave Ste 236 (32789-2918)
PHONE....................212 351-6400
Carol Evans, *President*
Joan Labarge, *Publisher*
Michele Siegel, *Research*
Michele Zito, *Research*
Nancy Colter, *CFO*
EMP: 51 EST: 2001
SALES (est): 11.9MM **Privately Held**
SIC: 2721 4813 Magazines: publishing only, not printed on site;
HQ: Bonnier Corporation
480 N Orlando Ave Ste 236
Winter Park FL 32789

(G-18554)
WORLD PUBLICATIONS INC
460 N Orlando Ave Ste 200 (32789-2920)
PHONE....................407 628-4802
Terry L Snow, *Principal*
EMP: 5 EST: 2011

SALES (est): 554.3K **Privately Held**
SIC: 2721 Magazines: publishing only, not printed on site

(G-18555)
YEAGER MANUFACTURING TECH LLC
7005 Stapoint Ct (32792-6696)
PHONE....................407 573-7033
Zachary Yeager, *President*
EMP: 12 EST: 2018
SALES (est): 1.1MM **Privately Held**
WEB: www.yeagermanufacturing.com
SIC: 3999 3499 Manufacturing industries; fabricated metal products

(G-18556)
ZEL TECH TRINING SOLUTIONS LLC
7123 University Blvd (32792-6722)
PHONE....................757 722-5565
Jack L Ezzell II, *CEO*
Jim Grant, *President*
William Barfield, *General Mgr*
Lynn Taylor, *CFO*
Mike Chesser, *Analyst*
EMP: 34 EST: 2012
SALES (est): 5.8MM **Privately Held**
WEB: www.zeltech.com
SIC: 3541 Machine tools, metal cutting type

Winter Springs
Seminole County

(G-18557)
ACCESS-ABLE TECHNOLOGIES INC
360 Old Sanford Oviedo Rd (32708-2664)
PHONE....................407 834-2999
Kenneth B Mc Garvey, *President*
Christie Mc Garvey, *Vice Pres*
Carolyn Mc Garvey, *Treasurer*
Ken McGarvey, *Human Res Mgr*
EMP: 5 EST: 1993
SQ FT: 3,600
SALES (est): 732K **Privately Held**
WEB: www.accessabletech.com
SIC: 2295 Sealing or insulating tape for pipe: coated fiberglass

(G-18558)
ADAPTIVE INSIGHTS INC
1401 Town Plaza Ct (32708-6222)
PHONE....................800 303-6346
Ivan Marchenko, *Engineer*
Shirvan Basdeo, *Sr Consultant*
EMP: 46 **Publicly Held**
SIC: 7372 Business oriented computer software
HQ: Adaptive Insights Llc
2300 Geng Rd Ste 100
Palo Alto CA 94303
650 528-7500

(G-18559)
AIREHEALTH INC (PA)
1511 E State Road 434 # 2 (32708-5644)
PHONE....................407 280-4107
Stacie Ruth, *CEO*
Frank O 'neill, *Engineer*
Matt Weed, *Development*
Kayla Mangan, *Finance*
Kirstie Hines, *Marketing Staff*
EMP: 7 EST: 2018
SALES (est): 1.3MM **Privately Held**
WEB: www.aire.health
SIC: 3845 Respiratory analysis equipment, electromedical

(G-18560)
BARCODE AUTOMATION INC
207 N Moss Rd Ste 105 (32708-2591)
PHONE....................407 327-2177
Doug Jarrett, *President*
Elizabeth Seibert, *Vice Pres*
Elizabeth B Seibert, *Opers Mgr*
Jim Pope, *Opers Staff*
Ryan Waxberg, *Marketing Staff*
EMP: 10 EST: 1996
SALES (est): 1.2MM **Privately Held**
WEB: www.barcode-automation.com
SIC: 3625 Control equipment, electric

(G-18561)
BOB VIOLETT MODELS INC
Also Called: B V M
3481 State Road 419 (32708-2667)
PHONE....................................407 327-6333
Robert Violet, *President*
▲ EMP: 20 EST: 1982
SQ FT: 8,500
SALES (est): 2.3MM **Privately Held**
WEB: www.bvmjets.com
SIC: 3944 Craft & hobby kits & sets

(G-18562)
CLASSIC SCREEN
1021 Chesterfield Cir (32708-4711)
PHONE....................................407 699-2473
Mike McIntyre, *Principal*
EMP: 7 EST: 2015
SALES (est): 92.3K **Privately Held**
SIC: 2752 Commercial printing, lithographic

(G-18563)
CUSTOM CFT WINDOWS &
DOORS INC
1436 Northern Way (32708-3848)
PHONE....................................407 834-5400
George Lawlor, *President*
EMP: 12 EST: 1984
SQ FT: 20,640
SALES (est): 436.1K **Privately Held**
SIC: 3442 3444 3231 2431 Window &
door frames; sheet metalwork; products
of purchased glass; millwork; door & window products; doors & windows

(G-18564)
DANIEL LAMPERT
COMMUNICATIONS
Also Called: Dlc
101 Brookshire Ct (32708-6303)
P.O. Box 151719, Altamonte Springs
(32715-1719)
PHONE....................................407 327-7000
Daniel Lampert, *President*
EMP: 10 EST: 1998
SALES (est): 531.6K **Privately Held**
SIC: 7372 Prepackaged software

(G-18565)
EQUITY GROUP USA INC
1129 Citrus Oaks Run (32708-4800)
PHONE....................................407 421-6464
Carlos Lafont, *President*
EMP: 5 EST: 2006
SALES (est): 733.9K **Privately Held**
WEB: www.egroupu.com
SIC: 3357 2411 3496 Nonferrous wiredrawing & insulating; rails, fence: round or
split; mesh, made from purchased wire

(G-18566)
GREYFIELD HOLDINGS INC
711 Ironwood Ct (32708-5900)
PHONE....................................407 927-4476
Kenneth W Osleger, *Branch Mgr*
EMP: 14
SALES (corp-wide): 6MM **Privately Held**
SIC: 3993 Signs & advertising specialties
PA: Greyfield Holdings Inc.
900 Central Park Dr
Sanford FL 32771
407 830-8861

(G-18567)
HBYS ENTERPRISES LLC
Also Called: Pin Creator, The
1170 Tree Swallow Dr # 347 (32708-2826)
PHONE....................................855 290-9900
Jeff Steiner,
EMP: 10 EST: 2009
SALES (est): 544.9K **Privately Held**
SIC: 3999 Identification badges & insignia

(G-18568)
IPAC INC
Also Called: Interntnal Pckg Athntic Cisine
1270 Belle Ave Unit 115 (32708-1905)
PHONE....................................407 699-7507
Steve Adamission, *President*
Paul Adamission, *Vice Pres*
Seth Van Der Stelt, *Manager*
EMP: 5 EST: 1995
SQ FT: 3,000

SALES (est): 1.2MM **Privately Held**
WEB: www.copack.com
SIC: 2099 Tortillas, fresh or refrigerated

(G-18569)
IRADIMED CORPORATION
1025 Willa Springs Dr (32708-5235)
PHONE....................................407 677-8022
Roger Susi, *Ch of Bd*
Lynn Neuhardt, *Vice Pres*
Marybeth Smith, *Vice Pres*
Raymond Ascue, *Mfg Mgr*
Mikel Solis, *Opers Spvr*
▲ EMP: 110 EST: 1992
SQ FT: 23,100
SALES (est): 41.8MM **Privately Held**
WEB: www.iradimed.com
SIC: 3841 Diagnostic apparatus, medical

(G-18570)
ITI ENGINEERING LLC
1081 Willa Springs Dr (32708-5235)
PHONE....................................866 245-9356
Kevin Speed, *President*
Kevin Lebeau, *Vice Pres*
Caity Ayers, *Project Mgr*
Corey Barnes, *Engineer*
Jerry Bracken, *Engineer*
EMP: 40 EST: 2003
SQ FT: 24,000
SALES (est): 10.2MM **Privately Held**
WEB: www.itiengineering.com
SIC: 3728 5045 7371 7373 Aircraft parts
& equipment; computers, peripherals &
software; custom computer programming
services; computer integrated systems
design; data processing & preparation;
engineering services
PA: Sv-Aero Holdings, Llc
1775 W Hibiscus Blvd # 20
Melbourne FL 32901
321 984-1671

(G-18571)
LATIN GODDESS PRESS INC
872 Leopard Trl (32708-4147)
PHONE....................................917 703-1356
Bermudez Anibal, *Principal*
EMP: 8 EST: 2015
SALES (est): 244.4K **Privately Held**
SIC: 2741 Miscellaneous publishing

(G-18572)
LINQS INC
1511 E State Road 434 # 2 (32708-5644)
PHONE....................................321 244-2626
Ozkan Erdem, *President*
Ozkan M Erdem, *President*
Ken Arkin, *Business Mgr*
EMP: 10 EST: 2010
SALES (est): 667.5K **Privately Held**
WEB: www.linqsdata.com
SIC: 7372 Business oriented computer
software

(G-18573)
MICROSIMULATORS INC
1612 White Dove Dr (32708-3864)
PHONE....................................407 696-8722
David J Smith Sr, *CEO*
R Spencer Hughes, *Vice Pres*
EMP: 9 EST: 1999
SALES (est): 769.6K **Privately Held**
SIC: 3699 Flight simulators (training aids),
electronic

(G-18574)
PREMIX-MARBLETITE MFG CO
325 Old Sanford Oviedo Rd (32708-2627)
PHONE....................................407 327-0830
Henry Dye, *Manager*
EMP: 13
SQ FT: 1,905
SALES (corp-wide): 387.6MM **Privately Held**
WEB: www.pmmproducts.com
SIC: 3299 3275 Stucco; gypsum products
HQ: Premix-Marbletite Manufacturing Co
Inc
1259 Nw 21st St
Pompano Beach FL 33069
954 970-6540

(G-18575)
PRO CO INC
910 Belle Ave Ste 1000 (32708-2968)
PHONE....................................321 422-0900
Brian Mullins, *President*
William Grabe, *Vice Pres*
Cheryl Helmly, *Sales Staff*
EMP: 5 EST: 1989
SQ FT: 2,000
SALES (est): 1.1MM **Privately Held**
WEB: www.pro-co.com
SIC: 3625 Control equipment, electric

(G-18576)
PROGRAM WORKS INC
1511 E State Road 434 # 2001
(32708-5646)
P.O. Box 4225, Sanford (32772-4225)
PHONE....................................407 489-4140
Carol Beyner, *Principal*
EMP: 11 EST: 2011
SALES (est): 602.5K **Privately Held**
WEB: www.workschedule.net
SIC: 7372 Prepackaged software

(G-18577)
QUANTUM CARE R&D LLC
1339 Palo Alto Ct (32708-4839)
PHONE....................................407 365-1179
Gary Kersey, *Principal*
EMP: 7 EST: 2013
SALES (est): 310.6K **Privately Held**
SIC: 3572 Computer storage devices

(G-18578)
STREAMLINE TECHNOLOGIES
INC
1900 Town Plaza Ct (32708-6208)
PHONE....................................407 679-1696
Gregory Sauter, *President*
EMP: 6 EST: 1984
SALES (est): 1.1MM **Privately Held**
WEB: www.streamnologies.com
SIC: 7372 7371 Application computer software; computer software development &
applications

(G-18579)
T T PUBLICATIONS INC
Also Called: Tow Times
203 W State Road 434 A (32708-2598)
P.O. Box 522020, Longwood (32752-2020)
PHONE....................................407 327-4817
Dave Jones, *President*
Tim Jackson, *Editor*
Peter Aspesi, *Treasurer*
Dennis Brewer, *Treasurer*
Sissy Figliolia, *Advt Staff*
EMP: 25 EST: 1983
SQ FT: 3,000
SALES (est): 3.1MM **Privately Held**
WEB: www.towtimes.com
SIC: 2721 Magazines: publishing only, not
printed on site

(G-18580)
UNLIMITED WELDING INC
235 Old Sanford Oviedo Rd (32708-2651)
PHONE....................................407 327-3333
Bonnie Smith, *President*
Brian Smith, *Vice Pres*
Nicky Marjama, *Credit Mgr*
Luis Matos, *Manager*
EMP: 30 EST: 1988
SQ FT: 22,000
SALES (est): 9MM **Privately Held**
WEB: www.unlimitedwelding.com
SIC: 3441 7692 Fabricated structural
metal; welding repair

(G-18581)
WALT DITTMER AND SONS INC
Also Called: Dittmer Architectural Aluminum
1006 Shepard Rd (32708-2018)
PHONE....................................407 699-1755
Dana S Callan, *President*
Walter J Dittmer, *Vice Pres*
Dennis Laskowski, *Safety Mgr*
Rick Carroll, *Technology*
Shelli Smith, *Director*
EMP: 36 EST: 1962
SQ FT: 26,000

SALES (est): 12.2MM **Privately Held**
WEB: www.dittdeck.com
SIC: 3354 3089 Shapes, extruded aluminum; plastic hardware & building products

(G-18582)
WILLIAMS MINERALS CO INC
168 Seville Chase Dr (32708-3920)
PHONE....................................304 897-6003
Brenda J Williams, *President*
Keith A Williams, *Vice Pres*
EMP: 6 EST: 1975
SALES (est): 377.1K **Privately Held**
SIC: 2517 5099 Wood television & radio
cabinets; novelties, durable

Yalaha
Lake County

(G-18583)
HOLLYWOOD DESIGN &
CONCEPTS
26534 Bloomfield Ave (34797-3426)
PHONE....................................954 458-4634
David L Wade, *President*
Julie Elsbury, *Vice Pres*
EMP: 12 EST: 1994
SQ FT: 8,000
SALES (est): 491.6K **Privately Held**
SIC: 3446 3444 Stairs, staircases, stair
treads: prefabricated metal; railings, bannisters, guards, etc.: made from metal
pipe; sheet metalwork

Yulee
Nassau County

(G-18584)
50 HWY 17 S INC
850822 Us Highway 17 (32097-6826)
P.O. Box 1033 (32041-1033)
PHONE....................................904 225-1077
Matt Clarkston, *President*
EMP: 8 EST: 2005
SALES (est): 295.3K **Privately Held**
SIC: 3949 Bowling alleys & accessories

(G-18585)
A M RAYONIER PRODUCTS INC
1 Rayonier Way (32097-0002)
PHONE....................................904 261-3611
CA McDonald, *Manager*
EMP: 300
SALES (corp-wide): 1.4B **Publicly Held**
WEB: www.ryamglobal.com
SIC: 2679 Pressed fiber products from
wood pulp: from purchased goods
HQ: Rayonier A.M. Products Inc.
1301 Riverplace Blvd
Jacksonville FL 32207
904 357-9100

(G-18586)
AB AMPERE INDUSTRIAL
PANELS
96266 Dowling Dr (32097-6319)
PHONE....................................904 379-4168
Sharon M Caserta, *Principal*
EMP: 7 EST: 2012
SALES (est): 227.8K **Privately Held**
SIC: 3825 Electrical power measuring
equipment

(G-18587)
ALM TECHNOLOGIES INC
Also Called: Definitive Design
850816 Us Highway 17 (32097-6826)
P.O. Box 707 (32041-0707)
PHONE....................................904 849-7212
Michael J Piscatella, *President*
Steve Crow, *Vice Pres*
Jake Costello, *Engineer*
Robin Mosley, *Administration*
EMP: 25 EST: 2011
SQ FT: 14,000
SALES (est): 4.6MM **Privately Held**
WEB: www.almtechnologiesinc.com
SIC: 3324 3728 Aerospace investment
castings, ferrous; aircraft parts & equipment

▲ = Import ▼=Export
◆ =Import/Export

(G-18588)
FIRST COAST FABRICATION INC
96144 Nassau Pl (32097-8626)
P.O. Box 1800 (32041-1800)
PHONE....................904 849-7426
Christopher D Wolfe, *President*
Christopher Wolfe, *President*
Douglas H Wolfe, *President*
K Patsy Wolfe, *Treasurer*
EMP: 8 **EST:** 1979
SQ FT: 9,000
SALES (est): 1.6MM **Privately Held**
WEB:
www.carolinafosterkidsfoundation.org
SIC: 7692 3599 Welding repair; machine shop, jobbing & repair

(G-18589)
FLORIDA MCH WORKS LTD PARTNR
86412 Gene Lassere Blvd (32097-3379)
P.O. Box 2710 (32041-2710)
PHONE....................904 225-2090
Rebecca Armstrong, *Managing Prtnr*
Mike Gall, *Engineer*
Bill Skipper, *Sales Staff*
Frank Showers, *Manager*
Roy Kunkle, *Prgrmr*
EMP: 10 **EST:** 2002
SQ FT: 38,000
SALES (est): 2.2MM **Privately Held**
WEB: www.floridamachineworks.com
SIC: 3599 Machine shop, jobbing & repair

(G-18590)
GILMAN BUILDING PRODUCTS LLC
581705 White Oak Rd (32097-2169)
PHONE....................904 548-1000
EMP: 10 **EST:** 2019
SALES (est): 777.8K **Privately Held**
SIC: 2421 Sawmills & planing mills, general

(G-18591)
MASONITE INTERNATIONAL CORP
86554 Gene Lassere Blvd (32097-3382)
PHONE....................904 225-3889
Dan Cook, *Principal*
Derek Steele, *QC Mgr*
Renee Peters, *Human Resources*
Fred Hiller, *Sales Staff*
Tim Botelho, *Software Dev*
EMP: 67
SALES (corp-wide): 2.6B **Publicly Held**
WEB: www.masonite.com
SIC: 2431 3469 Doors, wood; stamping metal for the trade
PA: Masonite International Corporation
1242 E 5th Ave
Tampa FL 33605
813 877-2726

(G-18592)
RAYONIER INC
Fernandina Mill Division
1 Rayonier Way (32097-0002)
PHONE....................904 277-1343
Steve Olsen, *Manager*
Seth Walker, *Manager*
EMP: 41
SALES (corp-wide): 1.1B **Publicly Held**
WEB: www.rayonier.com
SIC: 2611 2823 Pulp mills; cellulosic man-made fibers
PA: Rayonier Inc.
1 Rayonier Way
Yulee FL 32097
904 357-9100

(G-18593)
SCIENCE FIRST LLC
86475 Gene Lassere Blvd (32097-3378)
PHONE....................904 225-5558
Aaron Bell, *President*
Mark Eidemueller, *Vice Pres*
Robert Exon, *Foreman/Supr*
Lori Chorbak, *Purch Mgr*
Derick Douglas, *Engineer*
◆ **EMP:** 35 **EST:** 2016

SALES (est): 5.2MM **Privately Held**
WEB: www.sciencefirst.com
SIC: 3999 Education aids, devices & supplies

(G-18594)
SOYTHANE TECHNOLOGIES INC
Also Called: Expandothane
850709 Us Highway 17 (32097-3984)
P.O. Box 879 (32041-0879)
PHONE....................904 225-1047
Fred A Akel, *President*
▲ **EMP:** 11 **EST:** 2009
SALES (est): 331.1K **Privately Held**
WEB: www.soythane.com
SIC: 2851 Polyurethane coatings

Zellwood
Orange County

(G-18595)
ANUVIA PLANT NTRNTS HLDNGS LLC
6751 W Jones Ave (32798)
P.O. Box 220 (32798-0220)
PHONE....................352 720-7070
EMP: 6
SALES (est): 567K **Privately Held**
SIC: 2873 Nitrogenous Fertilizers, Nsk

(G-18596)
CC WELDING & CONSTRUCTION LLC
Also Called: C&C Company
5960 W Jone Ave (32798)
PHONE....................407 884-7474
Carol Adkins, *Mng Member*
EMP: 5 **EST:** 2011
SALES (est): 414.3K **Privately Held**
WEB: www.cwpartners.com
SIC: 3441 Fabricated structural metal

(G-18597)
CHEMICAL SYSTEMS ORLANDO INC
Also Called: Chemical Systems of Florida
6429 W Jones Ave (32798)
P.O. Box 810 (32798-0810)
PHONE....................407 886-2329
George A Thein, *President*
Gary Loughmiller, *General Mgr*
Kathy Marschner, *Controller*
Ethan Long, *Accounts Mgr*
Jeffrey Long, *Director*
EMP: 1 **EST:** 1979
SALES (est): 3.5MM **Privately Held**
WEB: www.chemicalsystems.com
SIC: 2899 2842 Chemical preparations; specialty cleaning, polishes & sanitation goods

(G-18598)
GOHO ENTERPRISES INC
Also Called: Auto Kare
3351 Laughlan Rd (32798)
P.O. Box 610 (32798-0610)
PHONE....................407 884-0770
Douglas Gondera, *President*
Timothy Hoatson, *Treasurer*
EMP: 10 **EST:** 1979
SALES (est): 699.6K **Privately Held**
SIC: 2842 5169 Specialty cleaning, polishes & sanitation goods; chemicals & allied products

(G-18599)
K & M TRUSS INC
2844 N Ornge Blssom Trl (32798)
P.O. Box 1138 (32798-1138)
PHONE....................407 880-4551
Micheal Farvis, *President*
EMP: 8 **EST:** 2006
SQ FT: 900
SALES (est): 837.1K **Privately Held**
WEB: www.kmtruss.com
SIC: 2439 Trusses, wooden roof

(G-18600)
ZELLWIN FARMS COMPANY (PA)
6052 Jones Ave (32798)
P.O. Box 188 (32798-0188)
PHONE....................407 886-9241

Glen Rogers, *President*
Suzanne P Roberts, *Corp Secy*
M C Jorgenson, *Vice Pres*
Kennedy Charles W, *Vice Pres*
Thomas L Youngs, *Vice Pres*
▲ **EMP:** 50 **EST:** 1947
SALES (est): 23MM **Privately Held**
WEB: www.zellwin.com
SIC: 2671 Packaging paper & plastics film, coated & laminated

Zephyrhills
Pasco County

(G-18601)
ALL CRAFT MARINE LLC
Also Called: Century Boats
40047 County Road 54 (33540-7951)
P.O. Box 2859 (33539-2859)
PHONE....................813 236-8879
Bryan Lucius, *Senior VP*
Thomas A Alsup, *Vice Pres*
Frederick H Brown Jr, *CFO*
Skip Sorenson, *Mng Member*
EMP: 44 **EST:** 2004
SALES (est): 9.9MM **Privately Held**
WEB: www.centuryboats.com
SIC: 3732 Motorized boat, building & repairing

(G-18602)
ALTIUM PACKAGING LLC
4330 20th St (33542-6703)
PHONE....................813 782-2695
Dan Sarris, *Plant Mgr*
EMP: 45
SALES (corp-wide): 14.6B **Publicly Held**
WEB: www.altiumpkg.com
SIC: 3089 Plastic containers, except foam
HQ: Altium Packaging Llc
2500 Windy Ridge Pkwy Se # 1400
Atlanta GA 30339
678 742-4600

(G-18603)
AQUA FLOAT CO
37100 Geiger Rd (33542-1863)
PHONE....................320 524-2782
Robert Claggett, *Owner*
EMP: 6 **EST:** 2014
SALES (est): 402K **Privately Held**
WEB: www.aquafloat.com
SIC: 3728 Aircraft parts & equipment

(G-18604)
AVIATION INSTRUMENT TECH INC (PA)
39520 Aviation Ave (33542-5293)
PHONE....................813 783-3361
Dave Teichman, *President*
Ken Gulla, *VP Bus Dvlpt*
Jeffrey Rosenberg, *CFO*
▲ **EMP:** 9 **EST:** 1997
SALES (est): 2.5MM **Privately Held**
WEB: www.aircraftinstruments.com
SIC: 3699 3812 4581 Flight simulators (training aids), electronic; aircraft control instruments; aircraft maintenance & repair services

(G-18605)
BET-ER-MIXING
38508 A Ave (33542-6014)
P.O. Box 5577, Hudson (34674-5577)
PHONE....................813 779-2774
Terry White, *Principal*
EMP: 12 **EST:** 2003
SQ FT: 784
SALES (est): 749.2K **Privately Held**
WEB: www.betermix.com
SIC: 3273 Ready-mixed concrete

(G-18606)
BIG DOGS MOBILE POLISHING LLC
37310 Stanford Ave (33541-3641)
PHONE....................813 312-6892
David C Foor, *Manager*
EMP: 8 **EST:** 2016
SALES (est): 317.2K **Privately Held**
SIC: 3471 Polishing, metals or formed products

(G-18607)
CALIBER COATING INC
39615 Dawson Chase Dr (33540-7342)
PHONE....................813 928-1461
Christopher Stubbs, *Principal*
EMP: 7 **EST:** 2018
SALES (est): 129.9K **Privately Held**
SIC: 3479 Metal coating & allied service

(G-18608)
CENTRAL STATE AGGREGATES LLC
41150 Yonkers Blvd (33541)
P.O. Box 100, Crystal Springs (33524-0100)
PHONE....................813 788-0454
Dan Coy, *Sales Staff*
Brandell Kemble, *Manager*
EMP: 14 **EST:** 2007
SALES (est): 5.5MM **Privately Held**
WEB: www.csagg.com
SIC: 1411 Dimension stone

(G-18609)
CISAM LLC
32789 Eiland Blvd (33545-5268)
PHONE....................813 404-4180
EMP: 7 **EST:** 2018
SALES (est): 207.7K **Privately Held**
WEB: www.cisamservice.com
SIC: 3559 Special industry machinery

(G-18610)
CRAZY 4 SIGNS LLC
4819 Allen Rd (33541-3553)
PHONE....................813 239-3085
Deborah Patel, *Principal*
EMP: 6 **EST:** 2015
SALES (est): 337K **Privately Held**
WEB: www.crazy4signs.com
SIC: 3993 Signs & advertising specialties

(G-18611)
DADS POWDER COATING
40420 Free Fall Ave (33542-5801)
PHONE....................813 715-6561
Cameron Shaun Evans, *Principal*
EMP: 7 **EST:** 2014
SALES (est): 911K **Privately Held**
SIC: 3479 Coating of metals & formed products

(G-18612)
DIXIE RESTORATIONS LLC
2212 Hilda Ann Rd (33540-7206)
PHONE....................813 785-2159
EMP: 6 **EST:** 2018
SALES (est): 471.5K **Privately Held**
SIC: 3089 Automotive parts, plastic

(G-18613)
ELEVATED DUMPSTERS LLC
37550 Phelps Rd (33541-7434)
PHONE....................813 732-6338
Frank J Brassart, *President*
EMP: 7 **EST:** 2017
SALES (est): 245.4K **Privately Held**
SIC: 3443 Dumpsters, garbage

(G-18614)
FIREDRAKE INC
39309 Air Park Rd (33542-5240)
PHONE....................813 713-8902
John Cooley, *President*
EMP: 9 **EST:** 1985
SQ FT: 3,500
SALES (est): 500K **Privately Held**
WEB: www.firedrakeinc.com
SIC: 3082 7389 3993 3544 Unsupported plastics profile shapes; lettering service; signs & advertising specialties; special dies, tools, jigs & fixtures

(G-18615)
FLUSHING AMUSEMENT INC
40423 Air Time Ave (33542-5837)
PHONE....................813 780-7900
Lenin Budloo, *President*
Annette Budloo, *Treasurer*
EMP: 5 **EST:** 1987
SQ FT: 7,500
SALES (est): 367K **Privately Held**
WEB: www.flushingmfg.com
SIC: 3999 Coin-operated amusement machines

(G-18616)
GILLETTE SIGN & LIGHTING INC
1609 Warbler St (33540-3383)
P.O. Box 924, Dade City (33526-0924)
PHONE..........................352 256-2225
Wyatt Gillette, *Principal*
EMP: 8 **EST:** 2015
SALES (est): 247.8K **Privately Held**
SIC: 3993 Signs & advertising specialties

(G-18617)
INSTACRETE MOBILE CONCRETE
6253 Candlewood Dr (33544-5834)
PHONE..........................813 956-3741
John E Munroe, *President*
EMP: 11 **EST:** 2004
SALES (est): 272.9K **Privately Held**
SIC: 3273 Ready-mixed concrete

(G-18618)
JOYCE TELECTRONICS CORP
40421 Chancey Rd Ste 101 (33542-1507)
PHONE..........................727 461-3525
Peter Joyce, *President*
Christopher Joyce, *Vice Pres*
Michael J Joyce, *Vice Pres*
Penny Joyce, *Treasurer*
EMP: 15 **EST:** 1950
SALES (est): 2.2MM **Privately Held**
WEB: www.orbitalcorp.net
SIC: 3679 Headphones, radio

(G-18619)
LATHAM PLASTICS INC
40119 County Road 54 (33540-7953)
PHONE..........................813 783-7212
EMP: 7 **EST:** 2017
SALES (est): 128.6K **Privately Held**
SIC: 3089 Plastics products

(G-18620)
LINVILLE ENTERPRISES LLC
38333 5th Ave (33542-4978)
PHONE..........................813 782-1558
Jane Linville, *Principal*
Danny Linville,
EMP: 5 **EST:** 2010
SALES (est): 310.4K **Privately Held**
SIC: 2711 Newspapers, publishing & printing

(G-18621)
MAGUIRES WELDING SERVICES INC
38736 Pretty Pond Rd (33540-1423)
P.O. Box 651 (33539-0651)
PHONE..........................813 382-3558
Daniel Neal, *Principal*
EMP: 6 **EST:** 2008
SALES (est): 423.4K **Privately Held**
WEB: www.htwc.biz
SIC: 7692 Welding repair

(G-18622)
ORBITAL CORPORATION OF TAMPA
40421 Chancey Rd Ste 101 (33542-1507)
PHONE..........................813 782-7300
Josh Thakrar, *President*
EMP: 5 **EST:** 1994
SQ FT: 4,000
SALES (est): 3MM **Privately Held**
WEB: www.orbitalcorp.net
SIC: 3315 Cable, steel: insulated or armored

(G-18623)
PASCO VISION CENTER
Also Called: Pusateri, Thomas J MD
38038 North Ave (33542-7468)
PHONE..........................813 788-7656
Stephanie Papello, *Principal*
EMP: 9 **EST:** 1999
SALES (est): 590K **Privately Held**
SIC: 3851 Eyeglasses, lenses & frames

(G-18624)
PERFECT REFLECTIONS INC
7708 Avocet Dr (33544-2638)
PHONE..........................813 991-4361
Greg Saunders, *Principal*
EMP: 8 **EST:** 2005
SALES (est): 151.6K **Privately Held**
SIC: 3229 Pressed & blown glass

(G-18625)
PICKET FENCE CHILDRENS
4931 Allen Rd (33541-3527)
PHONE..........................813 713-8589
Robin Beldin, *Principal*
EMP: 7 **EST:** 2016
SALES (est): 86.9K **Privately Held**
SIC: 2273 Carpets & rugs

(G-18626)
PIERGATE LLC
35377 Condominium Blvd (33541-7337)
PHONE..........................813 938-9170
Sameh A Hassan, *Principal*
EMP: 9 **EST:** 2016
SALES (est): 921.2K **Privately Held**
WEB: www.piergate.com
SIC: 3652 Pre-recorded records & tapes

(G-18627)
PLAZA MATERIALS CORP
41150 Yonkers Blvd (33541)
P.O. Box 100, Crystal Springs (33524-0100)
PHONE..........................813 788-0454
Marcus Jobes, *President*
EMP: 66 **EST:** 1990
SQ FT: 7,000
SALES (est): 3.8MM
SALES (corp-wide): 545.9MM **Privately Held**
SIC: 1411 Dimension stone
PA: Yonkers Contracting Co Inc
　　969 Midland Ave
　　Yonkers NY 10704
　　914 965-1500

(G-18628)
REPUBLIC NEWSPAPERS INC
Zephyrhills News
38333 5th Ave (33542-4978)
P.O. Box 638 (33539-0638)
PHONE..........................813 782-1558
Linda Wood, *Controller*
Janet Gillis, *Loan Officer*
David Walters, *Advt Staff*
EMP: 8
SQ FT: 3,451 **Privately Held**
WEB: www.republicnewspapers.com
SIC: 2711 Newspapers, publishing & printing
PA: Republic Newspapers, Inc.
　　11863 Kingston Pike
　　Knoxville TN 37934

(G-18629)
RESORT WINDOW TREATMENTS INC
5157 Gall Blvd (33542-4964)
PHONE..........................813 355-4877
Nancy Bradford, *President*
Steve Bradford, *Vice Pres*
EMP: 5 **EST:** 1998
SQ FT: 10,000
SALES (est): 377.5K **Privately Held**
SIC: 2591 Drapery hardware & blinds & shades

(G-18630)
SPECIALTY POWDER COATING LLC
7640 Chenkin Rd (33540-1937)
PHONE..........................813 782-2720
Bonnie L Brock, *President*
Bonnie Brock, *Principal*
EMP: 5 **EST:** 2014
SALES (est): 591.3K **Privately Held**
WEB: www.specialtypowdercoating.com
SIC: 3479 Coating of metals & formed products

(G-18631)
STATEWIDE CSTM CBINETS FLA INC
38535 Palm Grove Dr (33542-7360)
PHONE..........................813 788-3856
Jerry H Moates III, *President*
Rhonda Moates, *Corp Secy*
EMP: 8 **EST:** 1969
SQ FT: 1,000
SALES (est): 1.5MM **Privately Held**
WEB: www.statewidecabinets.com
SIC: 2434 Wood kitchen cabinets

(G-18632)
SUNRISE MANUFACTURING INTL INC
4035 Correia Dr (33542-7116)
PHONE..........................813 780-7369
Henri Pohjolainen, *President*
EMP: 11 **EST:** 2004
SALES (est): 2.8MM **Privately Held**
WEB: www.skydivewings.com
SIC: 3542 Metal container making machines: cans, etc.

(G-18633)
SWANS FEED MILL
8916 Fort King Rd (33541-7421)
PHONE..........................813 782-6969
James Swan, *Partner*
Steven E Swan, *Partner*
Wolfred Swan, *Partner*
EMP: 5 **EST:** 1972
SQ FT: 3,600
SALES (est): 413.9K **Privately Held**
SIC: 2048 Prepared feeds

(G-18634)
TACTICAL PRCHUTE DLVRY SYSTEMS
4035 Correia Dr (33542-7116)
PHONE..........................813 782-7482
Henri Pohjolainen, *President*
Nina Luoto, *General Mgr*
EMP: 10 **EST:** 2007
SALES (est): 527.6K **Privately Held**
WEB: www.tpdsairborne.com
SIC: 3999 2399 Barber & beauty shop equipment; parachutes

(G-18635)
TEKNA MANUFACTURING LLC
39248 South Ave (33542-5254)
P.O. Box 3263 (33539-3263)
PHONE..........................813 782-6700
Phillip P Janca, *President*
Janet Lessnau, *Managing Dir*
Carol R Janca, *Vice Pres*
◆ **EMP:** 8 **EST:** 2012
SALES (est): 6MM **Privately Held**
WEB: www.hyperbaric-chamber.com
SIC: 3999 Atomizers, toiletry

(G-18636)
WHEELBLAST INC
3951 Copeland Dr (33542-8403)
PHONE..........................813 715-7117
Micheal B Lynch, *President*
Tami Carbone, *Prdtn Mgr*
▲ **EMP:** 25 **EST:** 1973
SQ FT: 20,000
SALES (est): 4.7MM **Privately Held**
WEB: www.wheelblastinc.com
SIC: 3479 Coating of metals & formed products

(G-18637)
ZEPHYR FEED COMPANY INC
40140 Lynbrook Dr (33540-7902)
P.O. Box 2679 (33539-2679)
PHONE..........................813 782-1578
Lois Linville, *President*
Danny Linville, *President*
Terry Linville, *Corp Secy*
EMP: 7 **EST:** 1968
SQ FT: 12,000
SALES (est): 748.1K **Privately Held**
SIC: 2048 Chicken feeds, prepared

(G-18638)
ZEPHYRHILLS CORP
Also Called: Zephyrhills Water
4330 20th St (33542-6703)
PHONE..........................813 778-0595
Charlie Crouso, *Principal*
▼ **EMP:** 56 **EST:** 2010
SALES (est): 33.1MM
SALES (corp-wide): 1.3B **Privately Held**
WEB: www.zephyrhillswater.com
SIC: 2086 Bottled & canned soft drinks
HQ: Bluetriton Brands, Inc.
　　900 Long Ridge Rd Bldg 2
　　Stamford CT 06902

Zolfo Springs
Hardee County

(G-18639)
CIRCLE C TIMBER INC
2086 Fish Branch Rd (33890-2701)
PHONE..........................863 735-0383
Garit W Cooper, *President*
Krystle A Cooper, *Corp Secy*
EMP: 6 **EST:** 2006
SALES (est): 559.6K **Privately Held**
SIC: 2411 Logging camps & contractors

(G-18640)
MANCINI PACKING COMPANY
Also Called: Manicini Foods
3500 Mancini Pl (33890-4710)
P.O. Box 157 (33890-0157)
PHONE..........................863 735-2000
Maria Prieto, *Production*
J D Mancini MD, *Director*
Margaret Mancini, *Director*
Mary Mancini, *Director*
Anthony Mancini MD, *Shareholder*
▲ **EMP:** 100 **EST:** 1922
SQ FT: 64,000
SALES (est): 13.4MM **Privately Held**
WEB: www.mancinifoods.com
SIC: 2033 Canned fruits & specialties

(G-18641)
NEWVIDA PRODUCTS LLC
4757 Sweetwater Rd (33890-2736)
PHONE..........................863 781-9232
Marlon Pendergrass, *Principal*
EMP: 8 **EST:** 2014
SALES (est): 335.9K **Privately Held**
SIC: 3999 Manufacturing industries

SIC INDEX

SIC NO	PRODUCT

A

3291 Abrasive Prdts
2891 Adhesives & Sealants
3563 Air & Gas Compressors
3585 Air Conditioning & Heating Eqpt
3721 Aircraft
3724 Aircraft Engines & Engine Parts
3728 Aircraft Parts & Eqpt, NEC
2812 Alkalies & Chlorine
3363 Aluminum Die Castings
3354 Aluminum Extruded Prdts
3365 Aluminum Foundries
3355 Aluminum Rolling & Drawing, NEC
3353 Aluminum Sheet, Plate & Foil
3483 Ammunition, Large
3826 Analytical Instruments
2077 Animal, Marine Fats & Oils
2389 Apparel & Accessories, NEC
2387 Apparel Belts
3446 Architectural & Ornamental Metal Work
7694 Armature Rewinding Shops
3292 Asbestos products
2952 Asphalt Felts & Coatings
3822 Automatic Temperature Controls
3581 Automatic Vending Machines
3465 Automotive Stampings
2396 Automotive Trimmings, Apparel Findings, Related Prdts

B

2673 Bags: Plastics, Laminated & Coated
2674 Bags: Uncoated Paper & Multiwall
3562 Ball & Roller Bearings
2836 Biological Prdts, Exc Diagnostic Substances
1221 Bituminous Coal & Lignite: Surface Mining
2782 Blankbooks & Looseleaf Binders
3312 Blast Furnaces, Coke Ovens, Steel & Rolling Mills
3564 Blowers & Fans
3732 Boat Building & Repairing
3452 Bolts, Nuts, Screws, Rivets & Washers
2732 Book Printing, Not Publishing
2789 Bookbinding
2731 Books: Publishing & Printing
3131 Boot & Shoe Cut Stock & Findings
2342 Brassieres, Girdles & Garments
2051 Bread, Bakery Prdts Exc Cookies & Crackers
3251 Brick & Structural Clay Tile
3991 Brooms & Brushes
3995 Burial Caskets
2022 Butter

C

3578 Calculating & Accounting Eqpt
2064 Candy & Confectionery Prdts
2033 Canned Fruits, Vegetables & Preserves
2032 Canned Specialties
2394 Canvas Prdts
3624 Carbon & Graphite Prdts
3955 Carbon Paper & Inked Ribbons
3592 Carburetors, Pistons, Rings & Valves
2273 Carpets & Rugs
2823 Cellulosic Man-Made Fibers
3241 Cement, Hydraulic
3253 Ceramic Tile
2043 Cereal Breakfast Foods
2022 Cheese
1479 Chemical & Fertilizer Mining
2899 Chemical Preparations, NEC
2361 Children's & Infants' Dresses & Blouses
3261 China Plumbing Fixtures & Fittings
2066 Chocolate & Cocoa Prdts
2111 Cigarettes
2121 Cigars
3255 Clay Refractories
1459 Clay, Ceramic & Refractory Minerals, NEC
1241 Coal Mining Svcs
3479 Coating & Engraving, NEC
2095 Coffee
3316 Cold Rolled Steel Sheet, Strip & Bars
3582 Commercial Laundry, Dry Clean & Pressing Mchs
2759 Commercial Printing
2754 Commercial Printing: Gravure
2752 Commercial Printing: Lithographic
3646 Commercial, Indl & Institutional Lighting Fixtures
3669 Communications Eqpt, NEC
3577 Computer Peripheral Eqpt, NEC
3572 Computer Storage Devices

3575 Computer Terminals
3271 Concrete Block & Brick
3272 Concrete Prdts
3531 Construction Machinery & Eqpt
1442 Construction Sand & Gravel
2679 Converted Paper Prdts, NEC
3535 Conveyors & Eqpt
2052 Cookies & Crackers
3366 Copper Foundries
1021 Copper Ores
2298 Cordage & Twine
2653 Corrugated & Solid Fiber Boxes
3961 Costume Jewelry & Novelties
2261 Cotton Fabric Finishers
2211 Cotton, Woven Fabric
1311 Crude Petroleum & Natural Gas
1423 Crushed & Broken Granite
1422 Crushed & Broken Limestone
1429 Crushed & Broken Stone, NEC
3643 Current-Carrying Wiring Devices
2391 Curtains & Draperies
3087 Custom Compounding Of Purchased Plastic Resins
3281 Cut Stone Prdts
3421 Cutlery
2865 Cyclic-Crudes, Intermediates, Dyes & Org Pigments

D

3843 Dental Eqpt & Splys
2835 Diagnostic Substances
2675 Die-Cut Paper & Board
3544 Dies, Tools, Jigs, Fixtures & Indl Molds
1411 Dimension Stone
2047 Dog & Cat Food
3942 Dolls & Stuffed Toys
2591 Drapery Hardware, Window Blinds & Shades
2381 Dress & Work Gloves
2034 Dried Fruits, Vegetables & Soup
1381 Drilling Oil & Gas Wells

E

3263 Earthenware, Whiteware, Table & Kitchen Articles
3634 Electric Household Appliances
3641 Electric Lamps
3694 Electrical Eqpt For Internal Combustion Engines
3629 Electrical Indl Apparatus, NEC
3699 Electrical Machinery, Eqpt & Splys, NEC
3845 Electromedical & Electrotherapeutic Apparatus
3313 Electrometallurgical Prdts
3675 Electronic Capacitors
3677 Electronic Coils & Transformers
3679 Electronic Components, NEC
3571 Electronic Computers
3678 Electronic Connectors
3676 Electronic Resistors
3471 Electroplating, Plating, Polishing, Anodizing & Coloring
3534 Elevators & Moving Stairways
3431 Enameled Iron & Metal Sanitary Ware
2677 Envelopes
2892 Explosives

F

2241 Fabric Mills, Cotton, Wool, Silk & Man-Made
3499 Fabricated Metal Prdts, NEC
3498 Fabricated Pipe & Pipe Fittings
3443 Fabricated Plate Work
3069 Fabricated Rubber Prdts, NEC
3441 Fabricated Structural Steel
3399 Fabricated Textile Prdts, NEC
2295 Fabrics Coated Not Rubberized
2297 Fabrics, Nonwoven
3523 Farm Machinery & Eqpt
3965 Fasteners, Buttons, Needles & Pins
1061 Ferroalloy Ores, Except Vanadium
2875 Fertilizers, Mixing Only
2655 Fiber Cans, Tubes & Drums
2091 Fish & Seafoods, Canned & Cured
2092 Fish & Seafoods, Fresh & Frozen
3211 Flat Glass
2087 Flavoring Extracts & Syrups
2045 Flour, Blended & Prepared
2041 Flour, Grain Milling
3824 Fluid Meters & Counters
3593 Fluid Power Cylinders & Actuators
3594 Fluid Power Pumps & Motors
3492 Fluid Power Valves & Hose Fittings
2657 Folding Paperboard Boxes

3556 Food Prdts Machinery
2099 Food Preparations, NEC
2053 Frozen Bakery Prdts
2037 Frozen Fruits, Juices & Vegetables
2038 Frozen Specialties
2371 Fur Goods
2599 Furniture & Fixtures, NEC

G

3944 Games, Toys & Children's Vehicles
3524 Garden, Lawn Tractors & Eqpt
3053 Gaskets, Packing & Sealing Devices
2369 Girls' & Infants' Outerwear, NEC
3221 Glass Containers
3231 Glass Prdts Made Of Purchased Glass
1041 Gold Ores
3321 Gray Iron Foundries
2771 Greeting Card Publishing
3769 Guided Missile/Space Vehicle Parts & Eqpt, NEC
3764 Guided Missile/Space Vehicle Propulsion Units & parts
3761 Guided Missiles & Space Vehicles
2861 Gum & Wood Chemicals
3275 Gypsum Prdts

H

3423 Hand & Edge Tools
3425 Hand Saws & Saw Blades
3171 Handbags & Purses
3429 Hardware, NEC
2426 Hardwood Dimension & Flooring Mills
2435 Hardwood Veneer & Plywood
2353 Hats, Caps & Millinery
3433 Heating Eqpt
3536 Hoists, Cranes & Monorails
2252 Hosiery, Except Women's
2251 Hosiery, Women's Full & Knee Length
2392 House furnishings: Textile
3142 House Slippers
3639 Household Appliances, NEC
3651 Household Audio & Video Eqpt
3631 Household Cooking Eqpt
2519 Household Furniture, NEC
3633 Household Laundry Eqpt
3632 Household Refrigerators & Freezers
3635 Household Vacuum Cleaners

I

2097 Ice
2024 Ice Cream
2819 Indl Inorganic Chemicals, NEC
3823 Indl Instruments For Meas, Display & Control
3569 Indl Machinery & Eqpt, NEC
3567 Indl Process Furnaces & Ovens
3537 Indl Trucks, Tractors, Trailers & Stackers
2813 Industrial Gases
2869 Industrial Organic Chemicals, NEC
3543 Industrial Patterns
1446 Industrial Sand
3491 Industrial Valves
2816 Inorganic Pigments
3825 Instrs For Measuring & Testing Electricity
3519 Internal Combustion Engines, NEC
3462 Iron & Steel Forgings
1011 Iron Ores

J

3915 Jewelers Findings & Lapidary Work
3911 Jewelry: Precious Metal

K

2253 Knit Outerwear Mills
2254 Knit Underwear Mills
2259 Knitting Mills, NEC

L

3821 Laboratory Apparatus & Furniture
2258 Lace & Warp Knit Fabric Mills
1031 Lead & Zinc Ores
3952 Lead Pencils, Crayons & Artist's Mtrls
2386 Leather & Sheep Lined Clothing
3151 Leather Gloves & Mittens
3199 Leather Goods, NEC
3111 Leather Tanning & Finishing
3648 Lighting Eqpt, NEC
3274 Lime
3996 Linoleum & Hard Surface Floor Coverings, NEC
2085 Liquors, Distilled, Rectified & Blended

S I C

SIC NO	PRODUCT
2411	Logging
2992	Lubricating Oils & Greases
3161	Luggage

M

SIC NO	PRODUCT
2098	Macaroni, Spaghetti & Noodles
3545	Machine Tool Access
3541	Machine Tools: Cutting
3542	Machine Tools: Forming
3599	Machinery & Eqpt, Indl & Commercial, NEC
3322	Malleable Iron Foundries
2083	Malt
2082	Malt Beverages
2761	Manifold Business Forms
3999	Manufacturing Industries, NEC
3953	Marking Devices
2515	Mattresses & Bedsprings
3829	Measuring & Controlling Devices, NEC
3586	Measuring & Dispensing Pumps
2011	Meat Packing Plants
3568	Mechanical Power Transmission Eqpt, NEC
2833	Medicinal Chemicals & Botanical Prdts
2329	Men's & Boys' Clothing, NEC
2323	Men's & Boys' Neckwear
2325	Men's & Boys' Separate Trousers & Casual Slacks
2321	Men's & Boys' Shirts
2311	Men's & Boys' Suits, Coats & Overcoats
2322	Men's & Boys' Underwear & Nightwear
2326	Men's & Boys' Work Clothing
3143	Men's Footwear, Exc Athletic
3412	Metal Barrels, Drums, Kegs & Pails
3411	Metal Cans
3442	Metal Doors, Sash, Frames, Molding & Trim
3497	Metal Foil & Leaf
3398	Metal Heat Treating
2514	Metal Household Furniture
1081	Metal Mining Svcs
3469	Metal Stampings, NEC
3549	Metalworking Machinery, NEC
2026	Milk
2023	Milk, Condensed & Evaporated
2431	Millwork
3296	Mineral Wool
3295	Minerals & Earths: Ground Or Treated
3532	Mining Machinery & Eqpt
3496	Misc Fabricated Wire Prdts
2741	Misc Publishing
3449	Misc Structural Metal Work
1499	Miscellaneous Nonmetallic Mining
2451	Mobile Homes
3061	Molded, Extruded & Lathe-Cut Rubber Mechanical Goods
3716	Motor Homes
3714	Motor Vehicle Parts & Access
3711	Motor Vehicles & Car Bodies
3751	Motorcycles, Bicycles & Parts
3621	Motors & Generators
3931	Musical Instruments

N

SIC NO	PRODUCT
1321	Natural Gas Liquids
2711	Newspapers: Publishing & Printing
2873	Nitrogenous Fertilizers
3297	Nonclay Refractories
3644	Noncurrent-Carrying Wiring Devices
3364	Nonferrous Die Castings, Exc Aluminum
3463	Nonferrous Forgings
3369	Nonferrous Foundries: Castings, NEC
3357	Nonferrous Wire Drawing
3299	Nonmetallic Mineral Prdts, NEC
1481	Nonmetallic Minerals Svcs, Except Fuels

O

SIC NO	PRODUCT
2522	Office Furniture, Except Wood
3579	Office Machines, NEC
1382	Oil & Gas Field Exploration Svcs
1389	Oil & Gas Field Svcs, NEC
3533	Oil Field Machinery & Eqpt
3851	Ophthalmic Goods
3827	Optical Instruments
3489	Ordnance & Access, NEC
3842	Orthopedic, Prosthetic & Surgical Appliances/Splys

P

SIC NO	PRODUCT
3565	Packaging Machinery
2851	Paints, Varnishes, Lacquers, Enamels
2671	Paper Coating & Laminating for Packaging
2672	Paper Coating & Laminating, Exc for Packaging
3554	Paper Inds Machinery

SIC NO	PRODUCT
2621	Paper Mills
2631	Paperboard Mills
2542	Partitions & Fixtures, Except Wood
2951	Paving Mixtures & Blocks
3951	Pens & Mechanical Pencils
2844	Perfumes, Cosmetics & Toilet Preparations
2721	Periodicals: Publishing & Printing
3172	Personal Leather Goods
2879	Pesticides & Agricultural Chemicals, NEC
2911	Petroleum Refining
2834	Pharmaceuticals
3652	Phonograph Records & Magnetic Tape
1475	Phosphate Rock
2874	Phosphatic Fertilizers
3861	Photographic Eqpt & Splys
2035	Pickled Fruits, Vegetables, Sauces & Dressings
3085	Plastic Bottles
3086	Plastic Foam Prdts
3083	Plastic Laminated Plate & Sheet
3084	Plastic Pipe
3088	Plastic Plumbing Fixtures
3089	Plastic Prdts
3082	Plastic Unsupported Profile Shapes
3081	Plastic Unsupported Sheet & Film
2821	Plastics, Mtrls & Nonvulcanizable Elastomers
2796	Platemaking & Related Svcs
2395	Pleating & Stitching For The Trade
3432	Plumbing Fixture Fittings & Trim, Brass
3264	Porcelain Electrical Splys
2096	Potato Chips & Similar Prdts
3269	Pottery Prdts, NEC
2015	Poultry Slaughtering, Dressing & Processing
3546	Power Hand Tools
3612	Power, Distribution & Specialty Transformers
3448	Prefabricated Metal Buildings & Cmpnts
2452	Prefabricated Wood Buildings & Cmpnts
7372	Prepackaged Software
2048	Prepared Feeds For Animals & Fowls
3229	Pressed & Blown Glassware, NEC
3692	Primary Batteries: Dry & Wet
3399	Primary Metal Prdts, NEC
3339	Primary Nonferrous Metals, NEC
3334	Primary Production Of Aluminum
3331	Primary Smelting & Refining Of Copper
3672	Printed Circuit Boards
2893	Printing Ink
3555	Printing Trades Machinery & Eqpt
2999	Products Of Petroleum & Coal, NEC
2531	Public Building & Related Furniture
2611	Pulp Mills
3561	Pumps & Pumping Eqpt

R

SIC NO	PRODUCT
3663	Radio & T V Communications, Systs & Eqpt, Broadcast/Studio
3671	Radio & T V Receiving Electron Tubes
3743	Railroad Eqpt
3273	Ready-Mixed Concrete
2493	Reconstituted Wood Prdts
3695	Recording Media
3625	Relays & Indl Controls
3645	Residential Lighting Fixtures
2044	Rice Milling
2384	Robes & Dressing Gowns
3547	Rolling Mill Machinery & Eqpt
3351	Rolling, Drawing & Extruding Of Copper
3356	Rolling, Drawing-Extruding Of Nonferrous Metals
3021	Rubber & Plastic Footwear
3052	Rubber & Plastic Hose & Belting

S

SIC NO	PRODUCT
2068	Salted & Roasted Nuts & Seeds
2656	Sanitary Food Containers
2676	Sanitary Paper Prdts
2013	Sausages & Meat Prdts
2421	Saw & Planing Mills
3596	Scales & Balances, Exc Laboratory
2397	Schiffli Machine Embroideries
3451	Screw Machine Prdts
3812	Search, Detection, Navigation & Guidance Systs & Instrs
3341	Secondary Smelting & Refining Of Nonferrous Metals
3674	Semiconductors
3589	Service Ind Machines, NEC
2652	Set-Up Paperboard Boxes
3444	Sheet Metal Work
3731	Shipbuilding & Repairing
2079	Shortening, Oils & Margarine
3993	Signs & Advertising Displays

SIC NO	PRODUCT
2262	Silk & Man-Made Fabric Finishers
2221	Silk & Man-Made Fiber
1044	Silver Ores
3914	Silverware, Plated & Stainless Steel Ware
3484	Small Arms
3482	Small Arms Ammunition
2841	Soap & Detergents
2086	Soft Drinks
2436	Softwood Veneer & Plywood
2075	Soybean Oil Mills
2842	Spec Cleaning, Polishing & Sanitation Preparations
3559	Special Ind Machinery, NEC
2429	Special Prdt Sawmills, NEC
3566	Speed Changers, Drives & Gears
3949	Sporting & Athletic Goods, NEC
2678	Stationery Prdts
3511	Steam, Gas & Hydraulic Turbines & Engines
3325	Steel Foundries, NEC
3324	Steel Investment Foundries
3317	Steel Pipe & Tubes
3493	Steel Springs, Except Wire
3315	Steel Wire Drawing & Nails & Spikes
3691	Storage Batteries
3259	Structural Clay Prdts, NEC
2439	Structural Wood Members, NEC
2061	Sugar, Cane
2062	Sugar, Cane Refining
2843	Surface Active & Finishing Agents, Sulfonated Oils
3841	Surgical & Medical Instrs & Apparatus
3613	Switchgear & Switchboard Apparatus
2824	Synthetic Organic Fibers, Exc Cellulosic
2822	Synthetic Rubber (Vulcanizable Elastomers)

T

SIC NO	PRODUCT
3795	Tanks & Tank Components
3661	Telephone & Telegraph Apparatus
2393	Textile Bags
2269	Textile Finishers, NEC
2299	Textile Goods, NEC
3552	Textile Machinery
2284	Thread Mills
3011	Tires & Inner Tubes
2131	Tobacco, Chewing & Snuff
3799	Transportation Eqpt, NEC
3792	Travel Trailers & Campers
3713	Truck & Bus Bodies
3715	Truck Trailers
2791	Typesetting

V

SIC NO	PRODUCT
3494	Valves & Pipe Fittings, NEC
2076	Vegetable Oil Mills
3647	Vehicular Lighting Eqpt

W

SIC NO	PRODUCT
3873	Watch & Clock Devices & Parts
2385	Waterproof Outerwear
3548	Welding Apparatus
7692	Welding Repair
2046	Wet Corn Milling
2084	Wine & Brandy
3495	Wire Springs
2331	Women's & Misses' Blouses
2335	Women's & Misses' Dresses
2339	Women's & Misses' Outerwear, NEC
2337	Women's & Misses' Suits, Coats & Skirts
3144	Women's Footwear, Exc Athletic
2341	Women's, Misses' & Children's Underwear & Nightwear
2441	Wood Boxes
2449	Wood Containers, NEC
2511	Wood Household Furniture
2512	Wood Household Furniture, Upholstered
2434	Wood Kitchen Cabinets
2521	Wood Office Furniture
2448	Wood Pallets & Skids
2499	Wood Prdts, NEC
2491	Wood Preserving
2517	Wood T V, Radio, Phono & Sewing Cabinets
2541	Wood, Office & Store Fixtures
3553	Woodworking Machinery
2231	Wool, Woven Fabric

X

SIC NO	PRODUCT
3844	X-ray Apparatus & Tubes

Y

SIC NO	PRODUCT
2281	Yarn Spinning Mills
2282	Yarn Texturizing, Throwing, Twisting & Winding Mills

SIC INDEX

SIC NO	PRODUCT

10 metal mining

1011 Iron Ores
1021 Copper Ores
1031 Lead & Zinc Ores
1041 Gold Ores
1044 Silver Ores
1061 Ferroalloy Ores, Except Vanadium
1081 Metal Mining Svcs

12 coal mining

1221 Bituminous Coal & Lignite: Surface Mining
1241 Coal Mining Svcs

13 oil and gas extraction

1311 Crude Petroleum & Natural Gas
1321 Natural Gas Liquids
1381 Drilling Oil & Gas Wells
1382 Oil & Gas Field Exploration Svcs
1389 Oil & Gas Field Svcs, NEC

14 mining and quarrying of nonmetallic minerals, except fuels

1411 Dimension Stone
1422 Crushed & Broken Limestone
1423 Crushed & Broken Granite
1429 Crushed & Broken Stone, NEC
1442 Construction Sand & Gravel
1446 Industrial Sand
1459 Clay, Ceramic & Refractory Minerals, NEC
1475 Phosphate Rock
1479 Chemical & Fertilizer Mining
1481 Nonmetallic Minerals Svcs, Except Fuels
1499 Miscellaneous Nonmetallic Mining

20 food and kindred products

2011 Meat Packing Plants
2013 Sausages & Meat Prdts
2015 Poultry Slaughtering, Dressing & Processing
2022 Butter
2022 Cheese
2023 Milk, Condensed & Evaporated
2024 Ice Cream
2026 Milk
2032 Canned Specialties
2033 Canned Fruits, Vegetables & Preserves
2034 Dried Fruits, Vegetables & Soup
2035 Pickled Fruits, Vegetables, Sauces & Dressings
2037 Frozen Fruits, Juices & Vegetables
2038 Frozen Specialties
2041 Flour, Grain Milling
2043 Cereal Breakfast Foods
2044 Rice Milling
2045 Flour, Blended & Prepared
2046 Wet Corn Milling
2047 Dog & Cat Food
2048 Prepared Feeds For Animals & Fowls
2051 Bread, Bakery Prdts Exc Cookies & Crackers
2052 Cookies & Crackers
2053 Frozen Bakery Prdts
2061 Sugar, Cane
2062 Sugar, Cane Refining
2064 Candy & Confectionery Prdts
2066 Chocolate & Cocoa Prdts
2068 Salted & Roasted Nuts & Seeds
2075 Soybean Oil Mills
2076 Vegetable Oil Mills
2077 Animal, Marine Fats & Oils
2079 Shortening, Oils & Margarine
2082 Malt Beverages
2083 Malt
2084 Wine & Brandy
2085 Liquors, Distilled, Rectified & Blended
2086 Soft Drinks
2087 Flavoring Extracts & Syrups
2091 Fish & Seafoods, Canned & Cured
2092 Fish & Seafoods, Fresh & Frozen
2095 Coffee
2096 Potato Chips & Similar Prdts
2097 Ice
2098 Macaroni, Spaghetti & Noodles
2099 Food Preparations, NEC

21 tobacco products

2111 Cigarettes
2121 Cigars
2131 Tobacco, Chewing & Snuff

22 textile mill products

2211 Cotton, Woven Fabric
2221 Silk & Man-Made Fiber
2231 Wool, Woven Fabric
2241 Fabric Mills, Cotton, Wool, Silk & Man-Made
2251 Hosiery, Women's Full & Knee Length
2252 Hosiery, Except Women's
2253 Knit Outerwear Mills
2254 Knit Underwear Mills
2258 Lace & Warp Knit Fabric Mills
2259 Knitting Mills, NEC
2261 Cotton Fabric Finishers
2262 Silk & Man-Made Fabric Finishers
2269 Textile Finishers, NEC
2273 Carpets & Rugs
2281 Yarn Spinning Mills
2282 Yarn Texturizing, Throwing, Twisting & Winding Mills
2284 Thread Mills
2295 Fabrics Coated Not Rubberized
2297 Fabrics, Nonwoven
2298 Cordage & Twine
2299 Textile Goods, NEC

23 apparel and other finished products made from fabrics and similar material

2311 Men's & Boys' Suits, Coats & Overcoats
2321 Men's & Boys' Shirts
2322 Men's & Boys' Underwear & Nightwear
2323 Men's & Boys' Neckwear
2325 Men's & Boys' Separate Trousers & Casual Slacks
2326 Men's & Boys' Work Clothing
2329 Men's & Boys' Clothing, NEC
2331 Women's & Misses' Blouses
2335 Women's & Misses' Dresses
2337 Women's & Misses' Suits, Coats & Skirts
2339 Women's & Misses' Outerwear, NEC
2341 Women's, Misses' & Children's Underwear & Nightwear
2342 Brassieres, Girdles & Garments
2353 Hats, Caps & Millinery
2361 Children's & Infants' Dresses & Blouses
2369 Girls' & Infants' Outerwear, NEC
2371 Fur Goods
2381 Dress & Work Gloves
2384 Robes & Dressing Gowns
2385 Waterproof Outerwear
2386 Leather & Sheep Lined Clothing
2387 Apparel Belts
2389 Apparel & Accessories, NEC
2391 Curtains & Draperies
2392 House furnishings: Textile
2393 Textile Bags
2394 Canvas Prdts
2395 Pleating & Stitching For The Trade
2396 Automotive Trimmings, Apparel Findings, Related Prdts
2397 Schiffli Machine Embroideries
2399 Fabricated Textile Prdts, NEC

24 lumber and wood products, except furniture

2411 Logging
2421 Saw & Planing Mills
2426 Hardwood Dimension & Flooring Mills
2429 Special Prdt Sawmills, NEC
2431 Millwork
2434 Wood Kitchen Cabinets
2435 Hardwood Veneer & Plywood
2436 Softwood Veneer & Plywood
2439 Structural Wood Members, NEC
2441 Wood Boxes
2448 Wood Pallets & Skids
2449 Wood Containers, NEC
2451 Mobile Homes
2452 Prefabricated Wood Buildings & Cmpnts
2491 Wood Preserving
2493 Reconstituted Wood Prdts
2499 Wood Prdts, NEC

25 furniture and fixtures

2511 Wood Household Furniture
2512 Wood Household Furniture, Upholstered
2514 Metal Household Furniture
2515 Mattresses & Bedsprings
2517 Wood T V, Radio, Phono & Sewing Cabinets
2519 Household Furniture, NEC
2521 Wood Office Furniture
2522 Office Furniture, Except Wood
2531 Public Building & Related Furniture
2541 Wood, Office & Store Fixtures
2542 Partitions & Fixtures, Except Wood
2591 Drapery Hardware, Window Blinds & Shades
2599 Furniture & Fixtures, NEC

26 paper and allied products

2611 Pulp Mills
2621 Paper Mills
2631 Paperboard Mills
2652 Set-Up Paperboard Boxes
2653 Corrugated & Solid Fiber Boxes
2655 Fiber Cans, Tubes & Drums
2656 Sanitary Food Containers
2657 Folding Paperboard Boxes
2671 Paper Coating & Laminating for Packaging
2672 Paper Coating & Laminating, Exc for Packaging
2673 Bags: Plastics, Laminated & Coated
2674 Bags: Uncoated Paper & Multiwall
2675 Die-Cut Paper & Board
2676 Sanitary Paper Prdts
2677 Envelopes
2678 Stationery Prdts
2679 Converted Paper Prdts, NEC

27 printing, publishing, and allied industries

2711 Newspapers: Publishing & Printing
2721 Periodicals: Publishing & Printing
2731 Books: Publishing & Printing
2732 Book Printing, Not Publishing
2741 Misc Publishing
2752 Commercial Printing: Lithographic
2754 Commercial Printing: Gravure
2759 Commercial Printing
2761 Manifold Business Forms
2771 Greeting Card Publishing
2782 Blankbooks & Looseleaf Binders
2789 Bookbinding
2791 Typesetting
2796 Platemaking & Related Svcs

28 chemicals and allied products

2812 Alkalies & Chlorine
2813 Industrial Gases
2816 Inorganic Pigments
2819 Indl Inorganic Chemicals, NEC
2821 Plastics, Mtrls & Nonvulcanizable Elastomers
2822 Synthetic Rubber (Vulcanizable Elastomers)
2823 Cellulosic Man-Made Fibers
2824 Synthetic Organic Fibers, Exc Cellulosic
2833 Medicinal Chemicals & Botanical Prdts
2834 Pharmaceuticals
2835 Diagnostic Substances
2836 Biological Prdts, Exc Diagnostic Substances
2841 Soap & Detergents
2842 Spec Cleaning, Polishing & Sanitation Preparations
2843 Surface Active & Finishing Agents, Sulfonated Oils
2844 Perfumes, Cosmetics & Toilet Preparations
2851 Paints, Varnishes, Lacquers, Enamels
2861 Gum & Wood Chemicals
2865 Cyclic-Crudes, Intermediates, Dyes & Org Pigments
2869 Industrial Organic Chemicals, NEC
2873 Nitrogenous Fertilizers
2874 Phosphatic Fertilizers
2875 Fertilizers, Mixing Only
2879 Pesticides & Agricultural Chemicals, NEC
2891 Adhesives & Sealants
2892 Explosives
2893 Printing Ink
2899 Chemical Preparations, NEC

29 petroleum refining and related industries

2911 Petroleum Refining
2951 Paving Mixtures & Blocks
2952 Asphalt Felts & Coatings
2992 Lubricating Oils & Greases
2999 Products Of Petroleum & Coal, NEC

S I C

SIC NO	PRODUCT

30 rubber and miscellaneous plastics products

3011 Tires & Inner Tubes
3021 Rubber & Plastic Footwear
3052 Rubber & Plastic Hose & Belting
3053 Gaskets, Packing & Sealing Devices
3061 Molded, Extruded & Lathe-Cut Rubber Mechanical Goods
3069 Fabricated Rubber Prdts, NEC
3081 Plastic Unsupported Sheet & Film
3082 Plastic Unsupported Profile Shapes
3083 Plastic Laminated Plate & Sheet
3084 Plastic Pipe
3085 Plastic Bottles
3086 Plastic Foam Prdts
3087 Custom Compounding Of Purchased Plastic Resins
3088 Plastic Plumbing Fixtures
3089 Plastic Prdts

31 leather and leather products

3111 Leather Tanning & Finishing
3131 Boot & Shoe Cut Stock & Findings
3142 House Slippers
3143 Men's Footwear, Exc Athletic
3144 Women's Footwear, Exc Athletic
3151 Leather Gloves & Mittens
3161 Luggage
3171 Handbags & Purses
3172 Personal Leather Goods
3199 Leather Goods, NEC

32 stone, clay, glass, and concrete products

3211 Flat Glass
3221 Glass Containers
3229 Pressed & Blown Glassware, NEC
3231 Glass Prdts Made Of Purchased Glass
3241 Cement, Hydraulic
3251 Brick & Structural Clay Tile
3253 Ceramic Tile
3255 Clay Refractories
3259 Structural Clay Prdts, NEC
3261 China Plumbing Fixtures & Fittings
3263 Earthenware, Whiteware, Table & Kitchen Articles
3264 Porcelain Electrical Splys
3269 Pottery Prdts, NEC
3271 Concrete Block & Brick
3272 Concrete Prdts
3273 Ready-Mixed Concrete
3274 Lime
3275 Gypsum Prdts
3281 Cut Stone Prdts
3291 Abrasive Prdts
3292 Asbestos products
3295 Minerals & Earths: Ground Or Treated
3296 Mineral Wool
3297 Nonclay Refractories
3299 Nonmetallic Mineral Prdts, NEC

33 primary metal industries

3312 Blast Furnaces, Coke Ovens, Steel & Rolling Mills
3313 Electrometalurgical Prdts
3315 Steel Wire Drawing & Nails & Spikes
3316 Cold Rolled Steel Sheet, Strip & Bars
3317 Steel Pipe & Tubes
3321 Gray Iron Foundries
3322 Malleable Iron Foundries
3324 Steel Investment Foundries
3325 Steel Foundries, NEC
3331 Primary Smelting & Refining Of Copper
3334 Primary Production Of Aluminum
3339 Primary Nonferrous Metals, NEC
3341 Secondary Smelting & Refining Of Nonferrous Metals
3351 Rolling, Drawing & Extruding Of Copper
3353 Aluminum Sheet, Plate & Foil
3354 Aluminum Extruded Prdts
3355 Aluminum Rolling & Drawing, NEC
3356 Rolling, Drawing-Extruding Of Nonferrous Metals
3357 Nonferrous Wire Drawing
3363 Aluminum Die Castings
3364 Nonferrous Die Castings, Exc Aluminum
3365 Aluminum Foundries
3366 Copper Foundries
3369 Nonferrous Foundries: Castings, NEC
3398 Metal Heat Treating
3399 Primary Metal Prdts, NEC

34 fabricated metal products, except machinery and transportation equipment

3411 Metal Cans
3412 Metal Barrels, Drums, Kegs & Pails
3421 Cutlery
3423 Hand & Edge Tools
3425 Hand Saws & Saw Blades
3429 Hardware, NEC
3431 Enameled Iron & Metal Sanitary Ware
3432 Plumbing Fixture Fittings & Trim, Brass
3433 Heating Eqpt
3441 Fabricated Structural Steel
3442 Metal Doors, Sash, Frames, Molding & Trim
3443 Fabricated Plate Work
3444 Sheet Metal Work
3446 Architectural & Ornamental Metal Work
3448 Prefabricated Metal Buildings & Cmpnts
3449 Misc Structural Metal Work
3451 Screw Machine Prdts
3452 Bolts, Nuts, Screws, Rivets & Washers
3462 Iron & Steel Forgings
3463 Nonferrous Forgings
3465 Automotive Stampings
3469 Metal Stampings, NEC
3471 Electroplating, Plating, Polishing, Anodizing & Coloring
3479 Coating & Engraving, NEC
3482 Small Arms Ammunition
3483 Ammunition, Large
3484 Small Arms
3489 Ordnance & Access, NEC
3491 Industrial Valves
3492 Fluid Power Valves & Hose Fittings
3493 Steel Springs, Except Wire
3494 Valves & Pipe Fittings, NEC
3495 Wire Springs
3496 Misc Fabricated Wire Prdts
3497 Metal Foil & Leaf
3498 Fabricated Pipe & Pipe Fittings
3499 Fabricated Metal Prdts, NEC

35 industrial and commercial machinery and computer equipment

3511 Steam, Gas & Hydraulic Turbines & Engines
3519 Internal Combustion Engines, NEC
3523 Farm Machinery & Eqpt
3524 Garden, Lawn Tractors & Eqpt
3531 Construction Machinery & Eqpt
3532 Mining Machinery & Eqpt
3533 Oil Field Machinery & Eqpt
3534 Elevators & Moving Stairways
3535 Conveyors & Eqpt
3536 Hoists, Cranes & Monorails
3537 Indl Trucks, Tractors, Trailers & Stackers
3541 Machine Tools: Cutting
3542 Machine Tools: Forming
3543 Industrial Patterns
3544 Dies, Tools, Jigs, Fixtures & Indl Molds
3545 Machine Tool Access
3546 Power Hand Tools
3547 Rolling Mill Machinery & Eqpt
3548 Welding Apparatus
3549 Metalworking Machinery, NEC
3552 Textile Machinery
3553 Woodworking Machinery
3554 Paper Inds Machinery
3555 Printing Trades Machinery & Eqpt
3556 Food Prdts Machinery
3559 Special Ind Machinery, NEC
3561 Pumps & Pumping Eqpt
3562 Ball & Roller Bearings
3563 Air & Gas Compressors
3564 Blowers & Fans
3565 Packaging Machinery
3566 Speed Changers, Drives & Gears
3567 Indl Process Furnaces & Ovens
3568 Mechanical Power Transmission Eqpt, NEC
3569 Indl Machinery & Eqpt, NEC
3571 Electronic Computers
3572 Computer Storage Devices
3575 Computer Terminals
3577 Computer Peripheral Eqpt, NEC
3578 Calculating & Accounting Eqpt
3579 Office Machines, NEC
3581 Automatic Vending Machines
3582 Commercial Laundry, Dry Clean & Pressing Mchs
3585 Air Conditioning & Heating Eqpt
3586 Measuring & Dispensing Pumps
3589 Service Ind Machines, NEC
3592 Carburetors, Pistons, Rings & Valves
3593 Fluid Power Cylinders & Actuators
3594 Fluid Power Pumps & Motors
3596 Scales & Balances, Exc Laboratory
3599 Machinery & Eqpt, Indl & Commercial, NEC

36 electronic and other electrical equipment and components, except computer

3612 Power, Distribution & Specialty Transformers
3613 Switchgear & Switchboard Apparatus
3621 Motors & Generators
3624 Carbon & Graphite Prdts
3625 Relays & Indl Controls
3629 Electrical Indl Apparatus, NEC
3631 Household Cooking Eqpt
3632 Household Refrigerators & Freezers
3633 Household Laundry Eqpt
3634 Electric Household Appliances
3635 Household Vacuum Cleaners
3639 Household Appliances, NEC
3641 Electric Lamps
3643 Current-Carrying Wiring Devices
3644 Noncurrent-Carrying Wiring Devices
3645 Residential Lighting Fixtures
3646 Commercial, Indl & Institutional Lighting Fixtures
3647 Vehicular Lighting Eqpt
3648 Lighting Eqpt, NEC
3651 Household Audio & Video Eqpt
3652 Phonograph Records & Magnetic Tape
3661 Telephone & Telegraph Apparatus
3663 Radio & T V Communications, Systs & Eqpt, Broadcast/Studio
3669 Communications Eqpt, NEC
3671 Radio & T V Receiving Electron Tubes
3672 Printed Circuit Boards
3674 Semiconductors
3675 Electronic Capacitors
3676 Electronic Resistors
3677 Electronic Coils & Transformers
3678 Electronic Connectors
3679 Electronic Components, NEC
3691 Storage Batteries
3692 Primary Batteries: Dry & Wet
3694 Electrical Eqpt For Internal Combustion Engines
3695 Recording Media
3699 Electrical Machinery, Eqpt & Splys, NEC

37 transportation equipment

3711 Motor Vehicles & Car Bodies
3713 Truck & Bus Bodies
3714 Motor Vehicle Parts & Access
3715 Truck Trailers
3716 Motor Homes
3721 Aircraft
3724 Aircraft Engines & Engine Parts
3728 Aircraft Parts & Eqpt, NEC
3731 Shipbuilding & Repairing
3732 Boat Building & Repairing
3743 Railroad Eqpt
3751 Motorcycles, Bicycles & Parts
3761 Guided Missiles & Space Vehicles
3764 Guided Missile/Space Vehicle Propulsion Units & parts
3769 Guided Missile/Space Vehicle Parts & Eqpt, NEC
3792 Travel Trailers & Campers
3795 Tanks & Tank Components
3799 Transportation Eqpt, NEC

38 measuring, analyzing and controlling instruments; photographic, medical an

3812 Search, Detection, Navigation & Guidance Systs & Instrs
3821 Laboratory Apparatus & Furniture
3822 Automatic Temperature Controls
3823 Indl Instruments For Meas, Display & Control
3824 Fluid Meters & Counters
3825 Instrs For Measuring & Testing Electricity
3826 Analytical Instruments
3827 Optical Instruments
3829 Measuring & Controlling Devices, NEC
3841 Surgical & Medical Instrs & Apparatus
3842 Orthopedic, Prosthetic & Surgical Appliances/Splys
3843 Dental Eqpt & Splys
3844 X-ray Apparatus & Tubes
3845 Electromedical & Electrotherapeutic Apparatus
3851 Ophthalmic Goods
3861 Photographic Eqpt & Splys
3873 Watch & Clock Devices & Parts

39 miscellaneous manufacturing industries

3911 Jewelry: Precious Metal
3914 Silverware, Plated & Stainless Steel Ware
3915 Jewelers Findings & Lapidary Work
3931 Musical Instruments
3942 Dolls & Stuffed Toys
3944 Games, Toys & Children's Vehicles
3949 Sporting & Athletic Goods, NEC
3951 Pens & Mechanical Pencils

SIC NO	PRODUCT
3952	Lead Pencils, Crayons & Artist's Mtrls
3953	Marking Devices
3955	Carbon Paper & Inked Ribbons
3961	Costume Jewelry & Novelties
3965	Fasteners, Buttons, Needles & Pins
3991	Brooms & Brushes

SIC NO	PRODUCT
3993	Signs & Advertising Displays
3995	Burial Caskets
3996	Linoleum & Hard Surface Floor Coverings, NEC
3999	Manufacturing Industries, NEC

SIC NO	PRODUCT
73 business services	
7372	Prepackaged Software
76 miscellaneous repair services	
7692	Welding Repair
7694	Armature Rewinding Shops

S I C

SIC SECTION

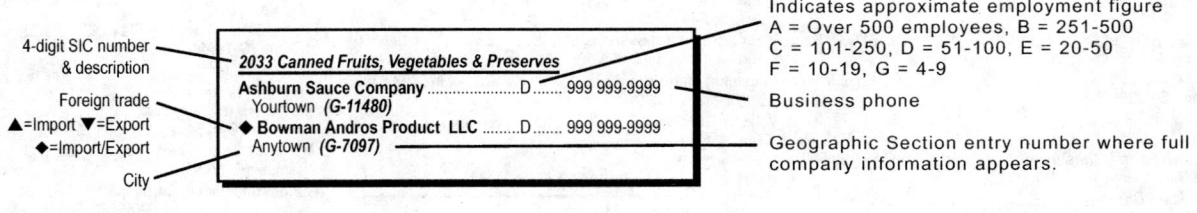

01 AGRICULTURAL PRODUCTION-CROPS

0132 Tobacco

◆ Colonial Wholesale Distrg Inc ....D...... 813 621-8880
Tampa (G-17496)

0133 Sugarcane & Sugar Beets

◆ A Duda & Sons Inc ....D 407 365-2111
Oviedo (G-13536)
◆ Flo Sun Land Corporation ....D...... 561 655-6303
Palm Beach (G-13655)
Florida Crystals Corporation ....B... 561 366-5000
West Palm Beach (G-19145)
Hilliard Brothers Florida Ltd ....E... 863 983-5111
Clewiston (G-1904)
Hundley Farms Inc ....D... 561 996-6855
Belle Glade (G-359)
King Ranch Inc ....C... 561 996-7257
South Bay (G-16481)
▲ Palm Beach Aggregates LLC ....E... 561 795-6550
Loxahatchee (G-8424)
▲ United States Sugar Corp ....A... 863 983-8121
Clewiston (G-1912)

0134 Irish Potatoes

◆ 4 Star Tomato Inc ....E... 941 722-0596
Bradenton (G-1048)
▲ Alger Farms Inc ....D... 305 247-4334
Homestead (G-5553)
Black Gold Farms ....B...... 386 776-1472
Live Oak (G-8308)

0139 Field Crops, Except Cash Grains, NEC

Anutra Super Grain LLC ....D...... 321 221-0233
Lakeland (G-7800)
▼ Bills Nursery Inc ....E...... 305 246-3878
Homestead (G-5557)
C & B Farms Inc ....D...... 863 983-8269
Clewiston (G-1897)
Trulieve Inc ....C...... 844 878-5438
Tallahassee (G-17159)

0161 Vegetables & Melons

◆ 4 Star Tomato Inc ....E....... 941 722-0596
Bradenton (G-1048)
◆ A Duda & Sons Inc ....D... 407 365-2111
Oviedo (G-13536)
▲ Alger Farms Inc ....D...... 305 247-4334
Homestead (G-5553)
▲ Alpine Fresh LLC ....D...... 305 594-9117
Doral (G-3114)
Astin Ranch Inc ....E... 813 650-8448
Riverview (G-15244)
◆ Ayco Farms Inc ....E... 954 788-6800
Pompano Beach (G-14746)
▲ B & W Quality Growers LLC ....C....... 772 571-0514
Fellsmere (G-3506)
Berry Red Farms LLC ....D... 813 716-3949
Plant City (G-14546)
C & B Farms Inc ....D... 863 983-8269
Clewiston (G-1897)
◆ Chiquita Brands Intl Inc ....A... 954 924-5700
Dania (G-2405)
▼ Custom-Pak Inc ....D... 239 657-4421
Immokalee (G-5654)

◆ Duda Farm Fresh Foods Inc ....B... 407 365-2111
Oviedo (G-13546)
Farm-Op Inc ....E... 239 657-4421
Estero (G-3456)
Farm-Op Inc ....E... 239 657-4421
Immokalee (G-5656)
Farm-Op Inc ....D... 239 774-6936
Naples (G-11108)
▲ Four Star Tomato Inc ....E... 941 747-8780
Bradenton (G-1105)
Generation Fresh LLC ....D... 912 537-3575
Delray Beach (G-2953)
▼ Heller Bros Packing Corp ....D... 407 656-2124
Winter Garden (G-19570)
Hundley Farms Inc ....D... 561 996-6855
Belle Glade (G-359)
▼ Hunsader Farms Inc ....D... 941 322-1195
Bradenton (G-1123)
Hyatt Farms LLC ....D... 863 393-9699
Lake Wales (G-7686)
J & J AG Products Inc ....D... 863 983-2900
Clewiston (G-1905)
◆ M & M Farm Incorporated ....E... 305 233-8224
Miami (G-9887)
▲ Mack Farms Inc ....D... 863 692-1200
Lake Wales (G-7692)
▼ Pacific Tomato Growers Ltd ....B... 941 729-8410
Palmetto (G-13925)
Sam S Accursio Sons Farms Inc ....D... 305 246-3455
Homestead (G-5603)
Schroeder Manatee Inc ....D... 941 755-1637
Lakewood Ranch (G-8030)
Scotlynn USA Division Inc ....C... 239 210-3000
Fort Myers (G-4585)
Statewide Harvesting & Hlg LLC ....E... 863 439-4225
Dundee (G-3373)
The Smith Group LLC ....D... 904 692-3307
Hastings (G-5190)
Villages Grown LLC ....D... 352 775-7333
The Villages (G-18667)

0171 Berry Crops

Astin Farms Inc ....E... 813 650-8448
Plant City (G-14544)
Astin Ranch Inc ....E... 813 650-8448
Riverview (G-15244)
Berry Red Farms LLC ....D... 813 716-3949
Plant City (G-14546)

0172 Grapes

▲ Seavin Inc ....E... 352 394-8627
Clermont (G-1886)

0174 Citrus Fruits

◆ A Duda & Sons Inc ....D ... 407 365-2111
Oviedo (G-13536)
▲ Ben Hill Griffin Inc ....D... 863 635-2281
Frostproof (G-4818)
◆ Bernard Egan & Company ....D... 772 465-7555
Fort Pierce (G-4682)
C Elton Crews Incorporated ....E... 863 453-3040
Avon Park (G-289)
◆ Cherrylake Inc ....B... 352 429-2171
Groveland (G-5088)
◆ Chiquita Brands Intl Inc ....A... 954 924-5700
Dania (G-2405)
◆ Duda Farm Fresh Foods Inc ....B... 407 365-2111
Oviedo (G-13546)

Edsall Groves Inc ....D... 772 562-3724
Vero Beach (G-18853)
Evans Properties Inc ....E... 863 763-4869
Vero Beach (G-18857)
◆ Haines Cy Citrus Growers Assn ....D... 863 422-4924
Haines City (G-5149)
Happiness Farms Inc ....D... 863 465-0044
Lake Placid (G-7666)
▼ Heller Bros Packing Corp ....D... 407 656-2124
Winter Garden (G-19570)
Hilliard Brothers Florida Ltd ....E... 863 983-5111
Clewiston (G-1904)
▲ Holly Hill Fruit Pdts Co Inc ....D... 863 422-1131
Davenport (G-2444)
IMG Enterprises Inc ....D... 352 429-2171
Groveland (G-5093)
Jack M Berry Inc ....C... 863 675-2769
Alva (G-121)
Lykes Bros Inc ....D... 863 465-4127
Lake Placid (G-7668)
Lykes Bros Inc ....E... 863 763-3041
Okeechobee (G-11873)
McArthur Farms Inc ....C... 863 763-4673
Okeechobee (G-11874)
Mountain Lake Corporation ....D... 863 676-3494
Lake Wales (G-7694)
Oakley Groves Inc ....D... 863 638-1435
Lake Wales (G-7696)
▼ Pacific Tomato Growers Ltd ....B... 941 729-8410
Palmetto (G-13925)
◆ Peace River Citrus Pdts Inc ....D... 772 492-4050
Vero Beach (G-18905)
Rolling Meadow Ranch Inc ....E... 863 696-2409
Lake Wales (G-7699)
Sanchez Citrus Inc ....E... 863 533-4395
Bartow (G-336)
Southern Grdn Citrus Nurs LLC ....B... 352 472-9185
Trenton (G-18720)
Woolfolk Myers Grove Cretaking ....E... 863 676-0521
Lake Wales (G-7705)

0175 Deciduous Tree Fruits

◆ Chiquita Brands Intl Inc ....A... 954 924-5700
Dania (G-2405)

0179 Fruits & Tree Nuts, NEC

◆ Chiquita Brands Intl Inc ....A... 954 924-5700
Dania (G-2405)

0181 Ornamental Floriculture & Nursery Prdts

A-1 Florida Sod Inc ....E... 863 424-6222
Davenport (G-2434)
◆ Acosta Farms Inc ....D... 305 253-2649
Miami (G-9074)
Agri-Starts Inc ....D... 407 889-8055
Apopka (G-151)
▼ Albin Hagstrom & Son Inc ....C... 386 749-2521
Pierson (G-14495)
Alpha Foliage Inc ....E... 305 245-2220
Homestead (G-5554)
Ameri-Companies Management Inc ...D... 707 422-5100
West Palm Beach (G-19030)
Aris Horticulture Inc ....D... 239 728-2535
Alva (G-120)
Boran Ranch & Sod Farm Inc ....E... 863 993-2455
Arcadia (G-224)
◆ Cherrylake Inc ....B... 352 429-2171
Groveland (G-5088)

S I C

▲ Clinton Nurseries Florida Inc ....B 850 539-5022
Havana (G-5191)
Continental Farms LLC ....D 305 591-8886
Doral (G-3162)
◆ Costa Farms LLC ....A 305 247-3248
Miami (G-9422)
Costa Farms LLC ....C 800 327-7074
Miami (G-9423)
Costa Farms LLC ....A 305 971-7750
Miami (G-9424)
D & D Tree Farm & Nursery Inc ....D 407 827-0944
Lake Buena Vista (G-7458)
◆ Driftwood Gardens Inc ....D 407 889-5166
Apopka (G-174)
◆ Engelmann Holding Company ....C 407 886-3434
Miami (G-9522)
Floral Acres LLC ....E 561 499-2655
Boynton Beach (G-990)
▲ Florida Aquatic Nurseries Inc ....E 954 472-5120
Davie (G-2482)
▼ Frank Underhill ....D 386 749-2211
Barberville (G-306)
Green Point Research LLC ....E 954 500-4367
Fort Lauderdale (G-3836)
Hanley Landscape Services Inc ....E 561 793-9269
Loxahatchee (G-8422)
Happiness Farms Inc ....D 863 465-0044
Lake Placid (G-7666)
IMG Enterprises Inc ....D 352 429-2171
Groveland (G-5093)
▲ Kerrys Nursery Inc ....D 305 247-7096
Homestead (G-5586)
Kerrys Nursery Inc ....E 305 247-7096
Apopka (G-194)
Kerrys Nursery Inc ....D 407 886-6122
Apopka (G-195)
King Ranch Inc ....C 561 996-7257
South Bay (G-16481)
Knox Nursery Inc ....E 407 654-1972
Winter Garden (G-19576)
M & P Concrete Products Inc ....D 561 498-4125
Delray Beach (G-2987)
▲ Manatee Fruit Company ....B 941 722-3279
Palmetto (G-13922)
Marian Farms Inc ....C 352 429-4151
Groveland (G-5098)
Mazzoni Farms Inc ....C 561 638-0681
Boynton Beach (G-1012)
▲ Oglesby Plants Intl Inc ....C 850 762-3229
Altha (G-116)
Paff Landscape Inc ....E 352 796-1876
Brooksville (G-1304)
▲ Palm Beach Aggregates LLC ....E 561 795-6550
Loxahatchee (G-8424)
Pursley Inc ....C 800 683-7584
Bradenton (G-1167)
R Plants Inc ....C 305 257-9883
Homestead (G-5598)
Railroad Nursery Inc ....D 305 245-4595
Homestead (G-5599)
Rock City Nursery & Ldscpg ....E 772 589-5835
Wabasso (G-18955)
▲ Rockledge Gardens Inc ....E 321 636-7662
Rockledge (G-15363)
S and K Sod Company Inc ....E 407 892-3400
Saint Cloud (G-15532)
Simpson Nurseries LAA ....D 850 997-5054
Monticello (G-10937)
Southern Grdn Citrus Nurs LLC ....B 352 472-9185
Trenton (G-18720)
▲ Sutton Ferneries Incorporated ....D 305 477-4776
Doral (G-3328)
Travis Resmondo Sod Inc ....C 863 676-6109
Dundee (G-3374)
Verzaal Family Partnership ....E 561 498-3930
Delray Beach (G-3031)

0182 Food Crops Grown Under Cover

Astin Farms Inc ....E 813 650-8448
Plant City (G-14544)
▲ B & W Quality Growers LLC ....C 772 571-0514
Fellsmere (G-3506)
Farm-Op Inc ....E 239 657-4421
Estero (G-3456)
Gargiulo Inc ....C 239 597-3131
Immokalee (G-5657)
◆ J & C Enterprises Inc ....E 305 255-5100
Doral (G-3246)
Kalera Inc ....B 407 574-8204
Orlando (G-12719)

Leasa Industries Co Inc ....D 305 696-0651
Miami (G-9854)
Monterey Mushrooms LLC ....B 407 886-0449
Zellwood (G-19824)
Plant Agricultural Systems LLC ....E 954 618-8350
Fort Lauderdale (G-4052)
Speedling Incorporated ....E 352 793-6700
Bushnell (G-1328)
Villages Grown LLC ....E 352 775-7333
The Villages (G-18667)

0191 Crop Farming, Misc

Agoro Carbon Alliance Us Inc ....D 813 816-6387
Tampa (G-17251)
Black Gold Farms ....B 386 776-1472
Live Oak (G-8308)
Costa Farms LLC ....C 407 880-6412
Apopka (G-169)
Costa Farms LLC ....C 863 735-0139
Wauchula (G-18958)
Curaleaf Florida LLC ....E 305 247-3248
Cutler Bay (G-2363)
▲ Estrada & Sons Inc ....D 863 735-0124
Ona (G-11937)
▼ Excel Farms Inc ....C 305 246-0030
Homestead (G-5571)
Garcia Family Farm LLC ....E 863 983-0050
Clewiston (G-1902)
H & A Farms LLC ....D 321 239-3137
Mount Dora (G-10952)
L&M Farms North Florida LLC ....D 919 981-8086
East Palatka (G-3400)
Lykes Bros Inc ....E 863 763-3041
Okeechobee (G-11873)
◆ Manuel Diaz Farms Inc ....D 305 258-8440
Homestead (G-5591)
Margiric Farm LLC ....C 772 409-1166
Fort Pierce (G-4719)
Optimum Icd Holdings LLC ....D 912 526-3575
Delray Beach (G-3001)
◆ Pavilo Cnf LLC ....D 305 247-3248
Miami (G-10104)
Pebbledale Farms Inc ....E 863 445-1053
Ona (G-11938)
◆ Pero Family Farms LLC ....D 561 498-4533
Delray Beach (G-3003)
▲ Roseville Farms LLC ....E 407 884-4559
Apopka (G-207)
Rouge River Farms Inc ....C 863 983-2691
Clewiston (G-1908)
Sunny Sweet Farms Inc ....B 863 773-6322
Bowling Green (G-955)
Taeyang Farms Inc ....E 201 562-4846
Hastings (G-5189)
▲ Tkm Farms Inc ....E 561 996-1980
Belle Glade (G-364)
Tkm-Bengard Farms LLC ....A 561 996-1980
Belle Glade (G-365)
▲ Wish Farms Inc ....D 813 752-5111
Plant City (G-14593)
Wish Farms Inc ....C 813 752-5111
Plant City (G-14594)

02 AGRICULTURAL PRODUCTION-LIVESTOCK AND ANIMAL SPECIALTIES

0212 Beef Cattle, Except Feedlots

Boran Ranch & Sod Farm Inc ....E 863 993-2455
Arcadia (G-224)
Chapman Fruit Co Inc ....E 863 773-3161
Wauchula (G-18957)
Clark Family Farm LLC ....E 386 462-1188
Alachua (G-5)
Coldwell Bnkers Wlter Wllams R ....E 904 268-3000
Jacksonville (G-5976)
General Citrus Systems ....D 863 299-2111
Winter Haven (G-19630)
Hilliard Brothers Florida Ltd ....D 863 983-5111
Clewiston (G-1904)
Live Oak ....E 352 854-2691
Ocala (G-11714)
Lykes Bros Inc ....E 863 763-3041
Okeechobee (G-11873)
Schroeder Manatee Inc ....D 941 755-1637
Lakewood Ranch (G-8030)

0241 Dairy Farms

▲ Alliance Dries A Fla Gen Prtnr ...C 352 463-6613
Trenton (G-18715)
Borden Dairy Company Fla LLC ....D 352 622-1539
Ocala (G-11644)
Danone Us Inc ....B 321 439-5327
Orlando (G-12400)
Florida Sunny Dairy Inc ....D 305 885-5745
Hialeah (G-5264)
▲ Florida Sunny Dairy Inc ....D 813 471-0236
Tampa (G-17698)
Gustafsons Family Entps Inc ....B 904 284-3750
Green Cove Springs (G-5056)
JM Larson Inc ....D 863 763-7330
Okeechobee (G-11870)
McArthur Farms Inc ....C 863 763-4673
Okeechobee (G-11874)
New Dairy Opco LLC ....E 850 784-9006
Panama City (G-14048)
North Florida Holsteins LC ....E 352 463-7174
Bell (G-353)
White Construction Company Inc ...D 352 493-1444
Chiefland (G-1487)

0252 Chicken Egg Farms

Cal-Maine Foods Inc ....E 352 458-9000
Dade City (G-2381)
Cal-Maine Foods Inc ....E 407 892-9849
Kenansville (G-7153)
Hillandale LLC ....C 352 429-3631
Groveland (G-5092)

0272 Horse & Other Equine Production

Live Oak ....E 352 854-2691
Ocala (G-11714)
Salamander Farms LLC ....A 561 753-8110
West Palm Beach (G-19351)

0273 Animal Aquaculture Farms

American Mariculture Inc ....D 239 260-4720
Saint James City (G-15541)

0279 Animal Specialties, NEC

Godwins Gatorland Inc ....D 407 855-5496
Orlando (G-12577)

0291 Animal Production, NEC

Big Dog Ranch Rescue Inc ....C 561 719-1754
Palm Beach Gardens (G-13693)
Bonnie Blue Ranch LLC ....D 813 391-6037
Brandon (G-1217)
Russakis Investments LLC ....D 772 465-5355
Fort Pierce (G-4737)
Schroeder-Manatee Ranch Inc ....E 941 755-1637
Lakewood Ranch (G-8031)

07 AGRICULTURAL SERVICES

0711 Soil Preparation Svcs

Masci Corporation ....D 386 322-4111
Port Orange (G-15081)
Masci General Contractor Inc ....D 386 322-4500
Port Orange (G-15082)
Southeast Spreading Co LLC ....B 239 332-2595
Naples (G-11300)
Triest AG Group Inc ....E 941 722-5587
Palmetto (G-13935)

0721 Soil Preparation, Planting & Cultivating Svc

Aquatic Vegetation Control Inc ....E 561 845-5525
Riviera Beach (G-15278)
Blue Goose Growers LLC ....D 772 461-3020
Fort Pierce (G-4685)
Cooperative Producers Inc ....D 239 369-2169
Felda (G-3505)
Dobsons Woods and Water Inc ....E 407 841-0030
Ocoee (G-11811)
▲ Earthbalance Corporation ....D 941 426-7878
North Port (G-11568)
Echo Inc ....D 239 543-3246
North Fort Myers (G-11472)
Kahn Grove Service Co ....E 863 385-6136
Sebring (G-16404)
Paff Landscape Inc ....E 352 796-1876
Brooksville (G-1304)

Proscape Inc ....C 407 438-7442
Orlando **(G-13070)**

Sanchez Citrus Inc ....E 863 533-4395
Bartow **(G-336)**

Statewide Harvesting & Hlg LLC ....E 863 439-4225
Dundee **(G-3373)**

0722 Crop Harvesting By Machine

4 J Harvesting Inc ....E 239 728-3419
Alva **(G-119)**

Everglades AG Svcs Inc ....D 863 675-8500
Labelle **(G-7425)**

Peace River Packing Company ....E 863 285-7164
Fort Meade **(G-4241)**

▲ Sugarland Harvesting Co ....E 863 673-2055
Moore Haven **(G-10942)**

Texas Aquatic Harvesting Inc ....E 863 696-7200
Lake Wales **(G-7702)**

0723 Crop Preparation, Except Cotton Ginning

◆ 4 Star Tomato Inc ....E 941 722-0596
Bradenton **(G-1048)**

◆ Bernard Egan & Company ....D 772 465-7555
Fort Pierce **(G-4682)**

◆ Brooks Tropicals Holding Inc ....C 305 247-3544
Homestead **(G-5562)**

Chapman Fruit Co Inc ....E 863 773-3161
Wauchula **(G-18957)**

Dlf Packing LLC ....D 772 257-8003
Fort Pierce **(G-4695)**

◆ Dundee Citrus Growers Assn ....C 863 439-1574
Dundee **(G-3372)**

Eco Produce Inc ....E 754 366-0878
Plantation **(G-14635)**

Edsall Groves Inc ....D 772 562-3724
Vero Beach **(G-18853)**

Egan Fruit Packing LLC ....D 772 571-0700
Fellsmere **(G-3507)**

Finfrock Enterprises Inc ....E 407 293-4000
Apopka **(G-181)**

▼ Florida Classic Growers Inc ....D 863 439-1600
Lake Hamilton **(G-7554)**

Florida Orngic Aquaculture LLC ....E 772 783-5103
Fellsmere **(G-3508)**

▲ Fresh Express Incorporated ....E 407 612-5000
Windermere **(G-19542)**

Fresko Foods LLC ....E 305 696-6401
Miami **(G-9611)**

◆ Garland LLC ....E 305 636-1607
Miami **(G-9619)**

Goodson Farms Inc ....E 813 634-5060
Balm **(G-305)**

◆ Haines Cy Citrus Growers Assn ....D 863 422-4924
Haines City **(G-5149)**

Hunt Bros Cooperative ....E 863 676-9471
Lake Wales **(G-7684)**

▼ Oslo Citrus Growers Assn ....E 772 562-2301
Vero Beach **(G-18902)**

▼ Packers of Indian River Ltd ....C 772 464-6575
Vero Beach **(G-18903)**

Peace River Packing Company ....E 863 285-7164
Fort Meade **(G-4241)**

Sanchez Citrus Inc ....E 863 533-4395
Bartow **(G-336)**

◆ Southern Grdns Ctrus Proc Corp .....D 863 983-3030
Clewiston **(G-1911)**

Utopia Packing LLC ....E 941 322-2483
Myakka City **(G-10987)**

Woolfolk Myers Grove Cretaking ....E 863 676-0521
Lake Wales **(G-7705)**

0741 Veterinary Livestock Svcs

Humane Society of Broward Cnty ....D 954 989-3977
Fort Lauderdale **(G-3882)**

Julington Creek Anmal Hosp Inc ....E 904 268-6731
Jacksonville **(G-6393)**

0742 Veterinary Animal Specialties

Affilted Vterinary Specialists ....D 321 207-9134
Maitland **(G-8498)**

Animal Hospital of Pensacola ....E 850 202-2020
Pensacola **(G-14217)**

Arbor Pet Hospital LLC ....E 954 565-1896
Wilton Manors **(G-19520)**

Baycare Health System Inc ....D 727 395-2600
Largo **(G-8080)**

Bluepearl Florida LLC ....B 813 936-8809
Tampa **(G-17370)**

Bluepearl Florida LLC ....B 813 571-3303
Brandon **(G-1216)**

Bluepearl Management LLC ....A 813 936-8809
Tampa **(G-17371)**

Bluepearl Operations LLC ....B 813 549-7688
Sarasota **(G-16106)**

Bluepearl Operations LLC ....B 352 672-6718
Gainesville **(G-4844)**

Bluepearl Operations LLC ....D 813 933-8944
Tampa **(G-17372)**

Bluepearl Vet LLC ....B 813 936-8809
Tampa **(G-17373)**

Board of Governors State Unive ....B 352 392-2235
Gainesville **(G-4845)**

Board of Governors State Unive ....D 352 512-0886
Ocala **(G-11642)**

Calusa Veterinary Center ....E 561 999-3000
Boca Raton **(G-491)**

Cleveland Heights Animal Hosp ....E 863 646-2995
Lakeland **(G-7837)**

Custom Veterinary Services LLC ....E 305 255-1910
Miami **(G-9447)**

Dr Robert C Buzzetti Dvm ....E 561 638-8282
Oakland Park **(G-11594)**

Ellie Vet LLC ....E 239 945-2800
Cape Coral **(G-1389)**

Equine Medical Center Ocala Pl ....E 352 873-7830
Ocala **(G-11678)**

Gainesville Animal Hosp Inc ....E 352 332-5366
Gainesville **(G-4899)**

Goldendoodles of Miami Corp ....E 305 927-4551
Miami **(G-9646)**

Gomara Animal Clinic Inc ....D 305 857-0096
Miami **(G-9649)**

Humane Society of Broward Cnty ....D 954 989-3977
Fort Lauderdale **(G-3882)**

Julington Creek Anmal Hosp Inc ....E 904 268-6731
Jacksonville **(G-6393)**

Lloyd S Meisels P A ....C 954 753-1800
Coral Springs **(G-2268)**

Miami Vterinary Specialists PA ....E 305 665-2820
Miami **(G-9984)**

Milton J McKelvie Dvm PA ....D 239 574-2868
Cape Coral **(G-1414)**

Newberry Anmal Hosp 39th Ave I ....E 352 372-5391
Gainesville **(G-4956)**

Ovh Operating LLC ....D 727 391-9784
Seminole **(G-16457)**

Palm Beach Equine Clinic LLC ....D 561 793-1599
Wellington **(G-18986)**

Peterson Smith Equine Hosp LLC ....D 352 237-6151
Ocala **(G-11760)**

Pets Choice Inc ....E 239 936-0177
Fort Myers **(G-4541)**

Simmons & Fullerton Dvm PA ....E 850 385-5141
Tallahassee **(G-17100)**

South Florida Ent Assoc PA ....E 305 599-1101
Doral **(G-3318)**

South Florida Wildlife Center ....E 954 524-4302
Fort Lauderdale **(G-4140)**

Southast Vtrinary Referral Ctr ....D 305 666-4142
South Miami **(G-16518)**

Southeast Veterinary Svc Inc ....D 904 823-1270
Jacksonville **(G-6752)**

Teigland Frnklin Brkken Dvms I ....E 954 680-5886
Cooper City **(G-2015)**

Veternary Healthcare Assoc Inc ....E 863 324-3340
Winter Haven **(G-19670)**

Vtrinary Southern Partners LLC ....A 941 366-1222
Parrish **(G-14118)**

0751 Livestock Svcs, Except Veterinary

Goldendoodles of Miami Corp ....E 305 927-4551
Miami **(G-9646)**

0752 Animal Specialty Svcs, Exc Veterinary

County of Brevard ....D 321 253-6608
Melbourne **(G-8854)**

Gainesville Animal Hosp Inc ....E 352 332-5366
Gainesville **(G-4899)**

Goldendoodles of Miami Corp ....E 305 927-4551
Miami **(G-9646)**

Guardian Angels Med Svc Dogs I ....B 352 425-1981
Williston **(G-19512)**

Payson Pk Thrghbred Trning Ctr ....E 772 597-3555
Indiantown **(G-5681)**

Primate Products LLC ....D 239 867-2020
Miami **(G-10142)**

Simmons & Fullerton Dvm PA ....E 850 385-5141
Tallahassee **(G-17100)**

Southeastern Guide Dogs Inc ....D 941 729-5665
Palmetto **(G-13928)**

Sunset Services Inc ....E 352 241-6329
Clermont **(G-1893)**

Windy City Paws LLC ....E 773 791-5021
Key West **(G-7257)**

0761 Farm Labor Contractors & Crew Leaders

Harvestco LLC ....E 863 659-1188
Lake Placid **(G-7667)**

Sebring Citrus Inc ....C 863 840-5741
Avon Park **(G-297)**

Statewide Harvesting & Hlg LLC ....E 863 439-4225
Dundee **(G-3373)**

0762 Farm Management Svcs

Blue Goose Growers LLC ....D 772 461-3020
Fort Pierce **(G-4685)**

◆ Brooks Tropicals Holding Inc ....C 305 247-3544
Homestead **(G-5562)**

Estes Citrus Inc ....E 772 569-5022
Vero Beach **(G-18856)**

Greenes Citrus Management Inc ....E 772 778-4220
Vero Beach **(G-18862)**

Grove Services Inc of Miami ....D 305 248-1924
Homestead **(G-5577)**

◆ Haines Cy Citrus Growers Assn ....D 863 422-4924
Haines City **(G-5149)**

Hunt Bros Service Inc ....E 863 676-9471
Lake Wales **(G-7685)**

Jack M Berry Inc ....C 863 675-2769
Alva **(G-121)**

Nelson & Company Inc ....E 407 365-6631
Oviedo **(G-13562)**

Peace River Packing Company ....E 863 285-7164
Fort Meade **(G-4241)**

▲ Phillip Rucks Citrus Nurs Inc ....D 863 635-1948
Frostproof **(G-4822)**

Schirard Citrus Inc ....D 772 466-0112
Fort Pierce **(G-4738)**

▲ Sun AG LLC ....D 772 571-1147
Fellsmere **(G-3509)**

United States Sugar Corp ....A 863 902-2501
Clewiston **(G-1914)**

0781 Landscape Counseling & Planning

ABM Onsite Services - West Inc ....C 813 886-0001
Tampa **(G-17225)**

Agriscape Inc ....D 239 948-3300
Bonita Springs **(G-893)**

Alexanders Property Maint Inc ....D 727 535-7314
Largo **(G-8073)**

All American Facility Maint ....D 954 322-9909
Sunrise **(G-16734)**

Amera-Tech Inc ....E 239 561-9184
Naples **(G-11007)**

Ameriscape Usa Inc ....D 813 948-3938
Thonotosassa **(G-18669)**

Annco Maintenance Inc ....D 561 881-8038
Riviera Beach **(G-15277)**

Arazoza Brothers Corporation ....E 305 246-3223
Miami **(G-9165)**

Batallan Enterprises Inc ....D 561 805-8687
West Palm Beach **(G-19048)**

Big Tree Inc ....E 239 694-9700
Fort Myers **(G-4292)**

Big Yellow Enterprises Inc ....E 813 920-4881
Odessa **(G-11834)**

Blue Landscape Contg Group LLC ....C 239 566-2583
Naples **(G-11034)**

Boynton Landscape Company Inc ....D 561 655-5900
West Palm Beach **(G-19056)**

Brickman Group Ltd LLC ....A 954 434-1957
Fort Lauderdale **(G-3649)**

Brightview Companies LLC ....C 813 994-2309
Lutz **(G-8432)**

Brightview Companies LLC ....C 813 243-5399
Tampa **(G-17387)**

Brightview Companies LLC ....C 305 863-0025
Medley **(G-8708)**

Brightview Golf Maint Inc ....E 561 716-8304
West Palm Beach **(G-19063)**

Brightview Landscape Dev Inc ....C 813 628-8116
Seffner **(G-16423)**

Brightview Landscape Dev Inc ....C 305 258-8011
Homestead **(G-5561)**

Brightview Landscape Dev Inc ....D 941 794-0476
Bradenton **(G-1068)**

S
I
C

Brightview Landscape Svcs Inc C 904 725-2552
Jacksonville *(G-5878)*
Brightview Landscape Svcs Inc C 813 641-3672
Ruskin *(G-15396)*
Brightview Landscape Svcs Inc D 352 401-9145
Fruitland Park *(G-4823)*
Brightview Landscape Svcs Inc D 772 220-3676
Stuart *(G-16596)*
Brightview Landscape Svcs Inc C 407 292-9600
Orlando *(G-12205)*
Brightview Landscape Svcs Inc D 407 292-9600
Kissimmee *(G-7272)*
Brightview Landscape Svcs Inc C 941 249-9831
Port Charlotte *(G-15024)*
Brightview Landscape Svcs Inc C 904 292-0716
Jacksonville *(G-5879)*
Brightview Landscape Svcs Inc C 561 495-6330
Delray Beach *(G-2921)*
Brightview Landscape Svcs Inc D 850 622-6280
Destin *(G-3084)*
Brightview Landscape Svcs Inc B 813 621-6619
Tampa *(G-17388)*
Brightview Landscape Svcs Inc B 407 292-9600
Orlando *(G-12206)*
Brightview Landscape Svcs Inc C 941 756-2939
Sarasota *(G-16024)*
Brightview Landscapes LLC E 561 626-1240
West Palm Beach *(G-19064)*
Brightview Landscapes LLC D 239 947-0122
Fort Myers *(G-4296)*
Buccaneer Landscape MGT Corp D 727 209-0383
Pinellas Park *(G-14509)*
Carroll Bradford Incorporated E 407 647-9420
Orlando *(G-12246)*
Cfl Landscapes LLC D 321 352-7228
Apopka *(G-165)*
Chen Moore and Associates Inc D 954 730-0707
Fort Lauderdale *(G-3686)*
Cloverleaf Landscape Assoc Inc E 239 454-3577
Fort Myers *(G-4316)*
Cnc Management Group Inc E 305 250-4907
Miami *(G-9383)*
Commercial Companies Inc D 407 938-9600
Eustis *(G-3492)*
Commercial Industrial Corp E 352 840-0161
Ocala *(G-11665)*
Corradino Group Inc D 800 887-5551
Doral *(G-3166)*
Crawford Landscaping Group LLC D 888 581-5151
Naples *(G-11081)*
Crosspoint Ldscp & Design Inc E 813 765-1325
Tampa *(G-17553)*
CSS Landscaping Inc E 904 262-5389
Jacksonville *(G-6028)*
Cutting Edge Industries Inc E 561 218-4981
Pompano Beach *(G-14791)*
Delray Garden Center Inc E 561 243-6869
Delray Beach *(G-2944)*
Dixie Landscape LLC D 305 884-5700
Medley *(G-8721)*
Duval Landscape Maint LLC C 904 233-3388
Jacksonville *(G-6094)*
Dynaserv Florida LLC E 954 476-7888
Davie *(G-2477)*
Earthscpes Complete Ldscpg Inc E 813 982-1399
Thonotosassa *(G-18672)*
Edgewood Landscape & Nurs Inc D 863 453-7300
Avon Park *(G-290)*
▼ **Edsa Inc** D 954 524-3330
Fort Lauderdale *(G-3768)*
Edsa Inc E 407 425-3330
Orlando *(G-12455)*
Esposito Nursery Inc C 850 386-2114
Tallahassee *(G-16942)*
Executive Landscaping Inc E 850 478-2312
Pensacola *(G-14301)*
Facility Resources Inc E 352 347-5898
Summerfield *(G-16686)*
Five Star Ldscpg Irrgation Inc E 352 748-8000
The Villages *(G-18657)*
Florida Commercial Care Inc D 813 972-4962
Kissimmee *(G-7309)*
Florida Exotic A Ldscp Co Inc E 772 286-2924
Palm City *(G-13789)*
Florida Landscape Cons Inc D 813 886-7755
Tampa *(G-17689)*
Fran-Car Corporation E 561 741-9777
Jupiter *(G-7074)*
Girard Environmental Svcs Inc E 954 640-5478
Fort Lauderdale *(G-3819)*
Girard Environmental Svcs Inc E 407 708-5856
Sanford *(G-15946)*
Green Acres Lawn Yard Mint Inc E 239 348-2261
Naples *(G-11142)*
Green Effex LLC E 239 774-5263
Naples *(G-11143)*
Greenpoint Inc E 904 429-9781
Saint Augustine *(G-15447)*
Greenspire & Associates Inc E 239 598-2391
Naples *(G-11146)*
Griffin Ken Landscaping Contrs E 850 932-9304
Gulf Breeze *(G-5116)*
Hazeltine Nurseries Inc C 941 485-1272
Venice *(G-18784)*
Jerry Davis Ldscpg Sls & Svc E 407 855-1922
Orlando *(G-12703)*
Jlt Custom Works Inc E 863 245-3371
Wauchula *(G-18962)*
Johnson Engineering Inc D 239 334-0046
Fort Myers *(G-4454)*
Juniper Landscaping Inc A 239 561-5980
Fort Myers *(G-4455)*
Juniper Landscaping Fla LLC A 239 561-5980
Fort Myers *(G-4456)*
Kam Services Inc E 352 429-0049
Groveland *(G-5095)*
Keith and Associates Inc D 954 788-3400
Pompano Beach *(G-14837)*
Keyestone Intrlcking Pav Cntr E 239 793-4422
Naples *(G-11190)*
Landcare Group Inc D 386 586-3321
Bunnell *(G-1322)*
Landcare Landscaping Inc E 813 676-6000
Tampa *(G-17932)*
Lawn Mdic Ldscpg Irrgation LLC E 813 759-9263
Plant City *(G-14568)*
Lawnscapes Bay County Inc E 850 763-2975
Panama City *(G-14034)*
Livetrends Design Group LLC D 407 814-4907
Apopka *(G-198)*
Magnolia Group Ldscp Dev LLC E 813 642-7722
Tampa *(G-17975)*
Mainscape Inc C 239 348-8810
Naples *(G-11202)*
Marc Plant Outlet Store Inc E 305 294-9526
Key West *(G-7227)*
Matthews Design Group LLC E 904 826-1334
Saint Augustine *(G-15466)*
Millennium Lawn & Ldscp Inc D 813 920-8041
Odessa *(G-11850)*
Miller Legg & Associates Inc D 954 436-7000
Fort Lauderdale *(G-3973)*
Natures Care Orlando LLC D 407 362-1649
Longwood *(G-8386)*
Nottely Management Inc E 941 379-0272
Sarasota *(G-16246)*
ODonnell Landscapes Inc C 239 992-8842
Estero *(G-3471)*
Orchidman Ldscp Artisans Corp E 786 271-0332
Miami *(G-10078)*
Paff Landscape Inc E 352 796-1876
Brooksville *(G-1304)*
Paradise Lawns and Ldscpg Inc D 321 543-8111
Cocoa *(G-1945)*
Pda Landscaping Services Inc E 786 908-7159
Hialeah *(G-5309)*
Pink and Green LLC E 954 552-9725
Southwest Ranches *(G-16530)*
Prestige Property Maintenance E 954 584-3465
Davie *(G-2507)*
Prince Land Services Inc E 863 422-5207
Haines City *(G-5153)*
Pro Lawn Care Plus Inc E 561 820-2443
West Palm Beach *(G-19333)*
Progreen Services LLC D 888 377-4144
Greenacres *(G-5078)*
Prosser Inc D 904 739-3655
Jacksonville *(G-6619)*
Renfroe & Jackson Inc D 239 455-5020
Naples *(G-11281)*
Rock City Nursery & Ldscpg E 772 589-5835
Wabasso *(G-18955)*
Russell Landscape Group Inc C 850 622-1381
Santa Rosa Beach *(G-16013)*
SFM Landscape Services LLC C 305 818-2424
Hialeah Gardens *(G-5350)*
Southern Blossoms Inc E 305 234-3356
Miami *(G-10307)*
Sunny Grove Ldscpg & Nurs Inc C 239 992-1818
Fort Myers *(G-4613)*
Sunshine Land Design Inc C 772 283-2648
Stuart *(G-16673)*
Superior Ldscpg & Lawn Svc Inc D 305 634-0717
Miami *(G-10351)*
Total Prprty Mint Ldscpg II LL E 407 342-2366
Sanford *(G-15989)*
Tree Amigos Outdoor Svcs Inc D 904 778-1030
Orange Park *(G-12022)*
Tremron LLC D 863 603-0995
Lakeland *(G-7989)*
Tremron LLC D 407 834-0997
Altamonte Springs *(G-108)*
Tremron LLC D 954 418-0000
Pompano Beach *(G-14928)*
Tri County Ldscp Contrs Inc E 352 399-2647
Summerfield *(G-16691)*
Urban Resource/Group Inc D 772 778-3300
Vero Beach *(G-18930)*
Vazquez Citrus & Hauling Inc C 863 465-5003
Lake Placid *(G-7670)*
Visualscape Inc D 305 362-2404
Hialeah *(G-5335)*
W L Jenkins Company D 904 261-5364
Fernandina Beach *(G-3544)*
West Bay Landscape Inc D 941 753-8225
Bradenton *(G-1202)*
Xtreme Green Landscaping Inc E 386 283-0005
Palm Coast *(G-13848)*
Yellowstone Landscape Inc D 386 437-6211
Bunnell *(G-1326)*
Yellowstone Landscape Inc D 407 872-1266
Winter Park *(G-19794)*
Yellowstone Lndscp-Stheast LLC D 904 268-2626
Jacksonville *(G-6951)*
Yellowstone Lndscp-Stheast LLC D 941 251-8080
Bradenton *(G-1209)*
Yellowstone Lndscp-Stheast LLC D 407 396-0529
Davenport *(G-2451)*
Yellowstone Lndscp-Stheast LLC D 386 248-3298
Daytona Beach *(G-2692)*

0782 Lawn & Garden Svcs

A Cut Above Ldscp & Maint Inc E 561 795-1995
Loxahatchee *(G-8417)*
A2b Lawn & Maintenance Service E 407 703-2929
Apopka *(G-145)*
Agro-Iron Inc E 813 645-6911
Ruskin *(G-15393)*
Al Hoffers Pest Protection E 954 753-1222
Coral Springs *(G-2222)*
Amera-Tech Inc E 239 561-9184
Naples *(G-11007)*
Ameri - Pride Inc D 727 447-2186
Clearwater *(G-1517)*
◆ **Amerigrow Rcyclng-Dlray Ltd PR** D 561 499-8148
Delray Beach *(G-2905)*
Aquatic Vegetation Control Inc E 561 845-5525
Riviera Beach *(G-15278)*
Arrow Exterminators Inc E 239 596-6545
Naples *(G-11015)*
Arrow Exterminators Inc D 352 373-3642
Gainesville *(G-4840)*
Azalea Oaks Inc E 352 753-2388
Leesburg *(G-8232)*
Bay Landscape & Palm Svc LLC E 850 233-0809
Panama City Beach *(G-14089)*
▼ **Bermuda Landscape & Design Inc** D 561 762-8817
West Palm Beach *(G-19052)*
Big Yellow Enterprises Inc E 813 920-4881
Odessa *(G-11834)*
Bill Hatfield Enterprises Inc E 407 736-8727
Orlando *(G-12187)*
Bloomings Ldscp & Lawn Maint D 941 927-9765
Sarasota *(G-16105)*
Blue Landscape Contg Group LLC C 239 566-2583
Naples *(G-11034)*
Boynton Landscape Company Inc E 561 655-5900
West Palm Beach *(G-19057)*
Bradford Landscaping D 727 546-4149
Kenneth City *(G-7161)*
Brightview Landscape Svcs Inc C 904 725-2552
Jacksonville *(G-5878)*
Brightview Landscape Svcs Inc C 813 641-3672
Ruskin *(G-15396)*
Brightview Landscape Svcs Inc C 904 292-0716
Jacksonville *(G-5879)*
Brightview Landscape Svcs Inc B 813 621-6619
Tampa *(G-17388)*
Brightview Landscape Svcs Inc B 407 292-9600
Orlando *(G-12206)*

Brightview Landscape Svcs Inc ....C 941 756-2939
Sarasota (G-16024)

Carc-Dvcate For Ctzens With Ds ....C 386 752-1880
Lake City (G-7517)

Central Florida Ldscpg Inc.................D 813 623-1771
Tampa (G-17447)

Challenge Entps N Fla Inc ....B 904 284-9859
Green Cove Springs (G-5048)

◆ Cherrylake Inc..................................B 352 429-2171
Groveland (G-5088)

Coastal Landscape & Maint Inc ....D 561 640-5930
West Palm Beach (G-19096)

Complete Property Maint Inc ....E 561 744-3333
Jupiter (G-7060)

Complete Property Maint Inc ....E 561 744-3333
Coconut Creek (G-1983)

Coral Reef Tropical Pools Inc ....D 305 367-2005
Key Largo (G-7174)

Cornerstone Tree Farm Inc ....E 813 440-2741
Dade City (G-2383)

County of Brevard.............................E 321 952-4529
Melbourne (G-8860)

Creative North Inc............................D 754 204-7039
Weston (G-19454)

D & S Pallets Inc.............................D 727 540-0061
Clearwater (G-1600)

Deangelo Brothers LLC ....D 904 262-2001
Jacksonville (G-6052)

Delray Garden Center Inc ....E 561 243-6869
Delray Beach (G-2944)

Dixie Landscape LLC ....D 305 884-5700
Medley (G-8721)

Dixie Landscape Co Inc ....C 561 964-1356
Lake Worth (G-7722)

Dora Landscaping Company ....D 407 886-3103
Apopka (G-173)

Environmental SEC Okaloosa ....E 850 474-4000
Cantonment (G-1338)

Evans Holdings LLC ....E 239 643-6124
Naples (G-11106)

Everglades Envmtl Care Inc ....D 305 828-8282
Miami (G-9534)

Floralawn Inc.................................E 863 668-0494
Lakeland (G-7867)

Forest Country Club Inc ....E 239 482-6818
Fort Myers (G-4397)

Fresh Cut Lawn Service Inc ....E 407 298-0911
Orlando (G-12547)

Garden Couture Inc ....E 561 469-8261
West Palm Beach (G-19158)

Global Greenz LLC.............................E 321 725-8013
Malabar (G-8605)

▲ Grasshoppers Ldscp & Design ....D 561 638-2356
Delray Beach (G-2957)

Greenpoint Inc.................................E 904 429-9781
Saint Augustine (G-15447)

Greenscapes Southwest Fla LLC ....C 239 643-4471
Naples (G-11145)

Greenturf Services Inc.......................E 813 933-2647
Tampa (G-17755)

Griffin Ken Landscaping Contrs...........E 850 932-9304
Gulf Breeze (G-5116)

Ground Level Inc..............................C 863 581-5122
Bowling Green (G-952)

Groundtek Central Florida LLC ....E 407 877-7473
Ocoee (G-11815)

Halls Higher Quality LLC.....................E 352 396-4940
Clermont (G-1873)

Harrison Home Services In ....E 786 553-6421
Boca Raton (G-619)

Images of Green Inc...........................E 772 781-1406
Stuart (G-16631)

ISS C & S Building Maint Corp ....D 352 372-8753
Gainesville (G-4924)

▼ Jcl Maintenance Services Inc ....E 954 985-5783
West Park (G-19432)

Jsm Services Inc...............................D 813 917-6319
Bartow (G-323)

Juniper Landscaping Fla LLC...............C 407 275-6200
Orlando (G-12716)

Juniper Landscaping Fla LLC...............A 239 561-5980
Fort Myers (G-4456)

Keller Outdoor Inc.............................C 407 330-2750
Sanford (G-15957)

Kyle Enterprises Inc ....D 352 394-3213
Clermont (G-1878)

Landcare Landscaping Inc..................E 813 676-6000
Tampa (G-17932)

Landcare USA LLC ....D 561 734-3404
Boynton Beach (G-1006)

Landform Central Florida Inc...............E 407 298-3036
Orlando (G-12751)

Landscape Mint Prfssionals Inc ....D 813 757-6500
Dover (G-3369)

Landscape Svc Prfessionals Inc ....D 954 721-6920
Coral Springs (G-2265)

Lawn Care Company LLC ....D 407 697-7757
Kissimmee (G-7345)

Len-Tran Inc....................................E 941 745-2101
Bradenton (G-1128)

Leo Jr Lawn Irrgation Svcs Inc.............D 239 348-8090
Naples (G-11196)

Lopefra Corp....................................D 305 266-3896
Doral (G-3263)

LSP Nursery Inc...............................E 321 724-6176
Palm Bay (G-13628)

Luke Brothers Inc.............................E 727 937-6448
Fort Lauderdale (G-3949)

M & P Concrete Products Inc...............D 561 498-4125
Delray Beach (G-2987)

◆ Manuel Diaz Farms Inc....................D 305 258-8440
Homestead (G-5591)

Masse & Associates Inc ....E 561 495-7784
Delray Beach (G-2990)

Massey Services..............................E 941 629-6669
Port Charlotte (G-15047)

Massey Services Inc..........................D 813 246-5001
Tampa (G-17998)

Massey Services Inc..........................E 407 846-6620
Kissimmee (G-7354)

Massey Services Inc..........................E 386 756-6696
South Daytona (G-16490)

Massey Services Inc..........................D 850 222-2508
Tallahassee (G-17035)

Massey Services Inc..........................E 352 357-7415
Eustis (G-3497)

McCall Service Nw LLC ....E 904 389-5561
Jacksonville (G-6476)

MDI Property Maintenance Inc.............D 954 720-3336
Boynton Beach (G-1013)

Millennium Lawn & Ldscp Inc...............D 813 920-8041
Odessa (G-11850)

▼ Naders Pest Raiders Inc ....E 904 285-0091
Ponte Vedra Beach (G-14994)

Natures Care Orlando LLC ....D 407 362-1649
Longwood (G-8386)

Natures Keeper Inc...........................E 772 467-1230
Fort Pierce (G-4724)

Oasis Landscape Services Inc ....E 352 373-9530
Gainesville (G-4970)

OHara Landscape & Maint Inc ....D 561 655-9011
West Palm Beach (G-19291)

P & L Lawn Maintenance Inc................D 407 273-9123
Orlando (G-13000)

Paff Landscape Inc...........................E 352 796-1876
Brooksville (G-1304)

Pickhardt Sarasota Inc ....D 941 803-4021
Sarasota (G-16265)

Pink and Green LLC...........................E 954 552-9725
Southwest Ranches (G-16530)

Precision Turf Inc.............................E 904 262-6089
Jacksonville (G-6613)

Prestige Property Maintenance ....E 954 584-3465
Davie (G-2507)

Prince Land Services Inc ....E 863 422-5207
Haines City (G-5153)

Pro Lawn Care Plus Inc ....E 561 820-2443
West Palm Beach (G-19333)

Professional Turf Managers ....E 352 753-3498
Lady Lake (G-7439)

Progreen Services LLC ....D 888 377-4144
Greenacres (G-5078)

Proscape Inc....................................C 407 438-7442
Orlando (G-13070)

Quality By Design Inc.........................E 352 483-2299
Leesburg (G-8268)

R & R Maintenance Inc.......................E 904 292-9100
Jacksonville (G-6629)

Raulerson & Son Inc..........................E 813 985-6886
Tampa (G-18202)

Rew Landscape Corp.........................E 407 328-9425
Debary (G-2705)

▲ Rockledge Gardens Inc ....E 321 636-7662
Rockledge (G-15363)

Save-On Entps Sarasota Co Inc ....C 941 488-8897
Venice (G-18803)

Schroeder Manatee Inc ....E 941 746-8873
Bradenton (G-1176)

Seacrest Services Inc........................C 561 697-4990
West Palm Beach (G-19354)

Senlex Environmental LLC ....E 800 284-0394
Miami (G-10259)

Siljan Corp......................................E 561 499-8148
Delray Beach (G-3016)

Southeast Spreading Co LLC ....B 239 332-2595
Naples (G-11300)

Southern Grdn Citrus Nurs LLC...........B 352 472-9185
Trenton (G-18720)

Squires Enterprises Inc......................D 305 255-7000
Miami (G-10320)

Sr Landscaping LLC...........................C 813 985-9381
Tampa (G-18323)

Stahlmn-England Irrigation Inc.............D 239 514-1200
Naples (G-11306)

Sterling Silver Scape Sod Inc...............D 407 846-3225
Kissimmee (G-7390)

Sun State Nursery & Ldscpg Inc ....D 904 260-0822
Jacksonville (G-6806)

Sunflower Ldscpg & Maint Inc...............C 561 498-1611
Delray Beach (G-3021)

Sunshine Land Design Inc ....C 772 283-2648
Stuart (G-16673)

Superior Ldscpg & Lawn Svc Inc ....D 305 634-0717
Miami (G-10351)

T J Turf Farm Inc..............................E 239 352-5988
Naples (G-11316)

T J Turf Farm Inc..............................D 561 496-4200
Delray Beach (G-3022)

Tallahassee Nurseries Inc ....E 850 385-2162
Tallahassee (G-17142)

Texas Aquatic Harvesting Inc ....E 863 696-7200
Lake Wales (G-7702)

Three Seasons Lawn & Landscape ......E 727 847-1553
New Port Richey (G-11406)

Tip-Top Enterprises Inc ....D 305 255-8198
Miami (G-10392)

Top Cut Lawn Services Inc ....D 561 649-1335
Lake Worth (G-7755)

Total Lawn Care ....D 904 771-8889
Green Cove Springs (G-5065)

Tranquil Water Scapes ....D 561 582-4667
Palm Beach Gardens (G-13777)

Tree Amigos Outdoor Svcs Inc ....D 904 778-1030
Orange Park (G-12022)

Tropical Touch Gardens Ctr Inc ....E 954 252-9884
Fort Lauderdale (G-4190)

Trugreen Chemlawn............................D 239 694-1311
Fort Myers (G-4632)

Truly Nolen of America Inc..................E 407 425-2222
Orlando (G-13316)

Turf Sales of Florida LLC ....E 561 996-6716
South Bay (G-16482)

United States Service Inds Fla..............D 352 561-4551
Lady Lake (G-7442)

US Lawns Inc....................................D 407 246-1630
Orlando (G-13360)

US Lawns of SE Orlando ....E 407 453-0437
Kissimmee (G-7404)

Victoria Grdns Hmwnrs Assoc In ....D 386 785-2700
Deland (G-2887)

Weber Environmental Svcs Inc ....C 863 551-1820
Winter Haven (G-19672)

Westcoast Ldscp & Lawns LLC.............E 727 544-6300
Pinellas Park (G-14538)

Wolfer Landscape Services Inc ....E 954 581-3555
Davie (G-2537)

Yellowstone Landscape Inc ....E 386 437-6211
Bunnell (G-1326)

Yellowstone Landscape Inc ....D 407 872-1266
Winter Park (G-19794)

Yellowstone Ldscp - Sthast LLC............C 772 200-4571
Port Saint Lucie (G-15177)

0783 Ornamental Shrub & Tree Svc

A+ Envrnmental Restoration LLC ....E 863 494-7585
Arcadia (G-222)

A-1 Florida Sod Inc...........................E 863 424-6222
Davenport (G-2434)

Arbor Pros Expert Tree Co LLC............E 850 445-6505
Tallahassee (G-16881)

B&J Services of Sebring LLC ....E 863 414-2063
Valrico (G-18748)

Davey Tree Expert Company ....D 407 644-4695
Winter Park (G-19711)

Davey Tree Expert Company ....D 904 768-8733
Jacksonville (G-6047)

EDJ Service LLC...............................E 954 791-4167
Davie (G-2478)

Enviro Tree Service LLC......................D 407 641-6154
Apopka (G-179)

Green Effex LLC ....E 239 774-5263
Naples (G-11143)

Juniper Landscaping Fla LLC ....A 239 561-5980
Fort Myers (G-4456)

Lewis Tree Service Inc ....C 305 508-2437
Miami (G-9866)

◆ Manuel Diaz Farms Inc ....D 305 258-8440
Homestead (G-5591)

National Storm Recovery Inc ....C 407 886-8733
Astatula (G-237)

Prestige Property Maintenance ....E 954 584-3465
Davie (G-2507)

Sr Landscaping LLC ....C 813 985-9381
Tampa (G-18323)

Trugreen Chemlawn ....D 239 694-1311
Fort Myers (G-4632)

Weber Environmental Svcs Inc ....C 863 551-1820
Winter Haven (G-19672)

Wood Resource Recovery LLC ....E 352 671-7845
Ocala (G-11798)

08 FORESTRY

0811 Timber Tracts

Clari Tree Farm Inc ....E 305 345-2707
Homestead (G-5563)

◆ Coastal Forest Resources Co ....B 850 539-6432
Havana (G-5192)

D & D Tree Farm & Nursery Inc ....D 407 827-0944
Lake Buena Vista (G-7458)

LD Plante Inc ....E 407 831-0777
Altamonte Springs (G-69)

Loeks Peace Plenty Palms E LLC .....E 239 283-1329
Bokeelia (G-885)

M A Rigoni Inc ....E 850 584-7030
Perry (G-14491)

◆ Manuel Diaz Farms Inc ....D 305 258-8440
Homestead (G-5591)

Marshall Tree Farm Inc ....D 352 528-3880
Morriston (G-10943)

Schroeder Manatee Inc ....D 941 755-1637
Lakewood Ranch (G-8030)

0831 Forest Prdts

48forty Solutions LLC ....C 321 319-8541
Orlando (G-12030)

Fraser West Inc ....C 904 290-6460
Lake Butler (G-7503)

0851 Forestry Svcs

Agriclture Cnsmr Svcs Fla Dept ....D 850 638-6250
Chipley (G-1488)

◆ Coastal Forest Resources Co ....B 850 539-6432
Havana (G-5192)

Prestige Property Maintenance ....E 954 584-3465
Davie (G-2507)

Southern Pine Insptn Bur Inc ....E 850 434-2611
Pensacola (G-14445)

09 FISHING, HUNTING, AND TRAPPING

0919 Marine Fishing, Misc

◆ Veethree Electronics & Mar LLC .....D 941 538-7775
Bradenton (G-1199)

0921 Finfish Farming & Fish Hatcheries

▲ 5-D Tropical Inc ....D 813 986-4560
Plant City (G-14542)

Columbia Properties Stuart LLC ....D 772 225-3700
Stuart (G-16608)

Ekk-Will Tropical Fish Frm Inc ....D 813 677-5475
Ruskin (G-15400)

Research Aquaculture Inc ....E 561 344-2717
Boca Raton (G-771)

0971 Hunting & Trapping

Stillwater Preserve Dev LLC ....C 813 500-6854
Lithia (G-8306)

10 METAL MINING

1011 Iron Ores

Chemours Company Fc LLC ....D 904 964-1200
Starke (G-16575)

1021 Copper Ores

Chemours Company Fc LLC ....D 904 964-1200
Starke (G-16575)

Goldfield Cnsld Mines Co ....D 321 724-1700
Melbourne (G-8893)

1031 Lead & Zinc Ores

Chemours Company Fc LLC ....D 904 964-1200
Starke (G-16575)

1041 Gold Ores

Chemours Company Fc LLC ....D 904 964-1200
Starke (G-16575)

Goldfield Cnsld Mines Co ....D 321 724-1700
Melbourne (G-8893)

1044 Silver Ores

Goldfield Cnsld Mines Co ....D 321 724-1700
Melbourne (G-8893)

1061 Ferroalloy Ores, Except Vanadium

▲ Georgian American Alloys Inc ....E 305 375-7560
Miami (G-9627)

1081 Metal Mining Svcs

Emr Inc ....E 850 897-0210
Niceville (G-11446)

Nyrstar Us Inc ....D 954 400-6464
Fort Lauderdale (G-4022)

12 COAL MINING

1221 Bituminous Coal & Lignite: Surface Mining

▲ Progress Fuels Corporation ....D 727 824-6600
Saint Petersburg (G-15811)

◆ Teco Energy Inc ....E 813 228-1111
Tampa (G-18412)

1222 Bituminous Coal: Underground Mining

◆ Oxbow Carbn Mnrl Holdings Inc ....E 561 907-5400
West Palm Beach (G-19298)

◆ Teco Energy Inc ....E 813 228-1111
Tampa (G-18412)

1241 Coal Mining Svcs

Mosaic ....D 863 860-1328
Lakeland (G-7928)

Oxbow Carbon LLC ....A 561 907-5400
West Palm Beach (G-19299)

US China Mining Group Inc ....D 813 514-2873
Tampa (G-18483)

13 OIL AND GAS EXTRACTION

1311 Crude Petroleum & Natural Gas

Breitburn Operating LP ....C 850 675-1704
Jay (G-7010)

Carpenter Co ....D 863 687-9494
Lakeland (G-7826)

1381 Drilling Oil & Gas Wells

Boeing Distribution Svcs Inc ....C 305 925-2600
Hialeah (G-5224)

Centerline Drctnal Drlg Svc In ....C 863 674-0913
Labelle (G-7424)

Precision Directional Drlg LLC ....E 941 320-8308
Bradenton (G-1164)

1382 Oil & Gas Field Exploration Svcs

Seacor Marine LLC ....D 954 523-2200
Fort Lauderdale (G-4111)

1389 Oil & Gas Field Svcs, NEC

Avco Materials and Svcs Inc ....E 727 233-2043
Hudson (G-5627)

Brace Integrated Services Inc ....E 813 248-6248
Tampa (G-17383)

Buena Vista Construction Co ....E 407 828-2104
Lake Buena Vista (G-7455)

D & S Pallets Inc ....D 727 540-0061
Clearwater (G-1600)

Envirowaste Services Group Inc ....D 305 637-9665
Palmetto Bay (G-13940)

Fuse Builds LLC ....E 617 602-4001
Tampa (G-17720)

Genos Construction Inc ....D 234 303-3427
Dade City (G-2389)

Hoerbiger America Holding Inc ....B 954 422-9850
Deerfield Beach (G-2751)

Hoerbiger America Holding Inc ....A 954 422-9850
Deerfield Beach (G-2752)

Legacy Cnstr Rmdlg Clg Svcs LL ....E 800 638-9646
Hallandale Beach (G-5176)

Mll Oil Holding Inc ....C 321 200-0039
Tallahassee (G-17047)

Muelby Construction Services ....E 561 376-7614
North Palm Beach (G-11554)

▲ Offshore Inland Mar Olfld Svcs ....C 251 443-5550
Pensacola (G-14392)

Puraglobe Florida LLC ....D 813 247-1754
Tampa (G-18183)

Weldcorp Industries ....E 561 339-7713
Jupiter (G-7151)

Williams Industrial Svcs LLC ....C 904 696-9994
Jacksonville (G-6935)

14 MINING AND QUARRYING OF NONMETALLIC MINERALS, EXCEPT FUELS

1411 Dimension Stone

◆ Custom Marble Works Inc ....E 813 620-0475
Tampa (G-17560)

LW Rozzo Inc ....E 954 435-8501
Pembroke Pines (G-14167)

Plaza Materials Corp ....D 813 788-0454
Zephyrhills (G-19847)

Vgcm LLC ....E 813 620-4889
Tampa (G-18506)

Youngquist Brothers Rock Inc ....D 239 267-6000
Fort Myers (G-4665)

1422 Crushed & Broken Limestone

◆ Cemex Materials LLC ....C 561 833-5555
West Palm Beach (G-19078)

Cemex Materials LLC ....C 352 435-0783
Okahumpka (G-11860)

Cemex Materials LLC ....C 305 558-0315
Miami (G-9343)

Cemex Materials LLC ....C 561 793-1442
West Palm Beach (G-19079)

Cemex Materials LLC ....C 561 743-4039
Jupiter (G-7056)

◆ Florida Rock Industries ....C 904 355-1781
Jacksonville (G-6201)

Harlis R Ellington Cnstr Inc ....E 386 496-2134
Lake Butler (G-7504)

Vecellio & Grogan Inc ....D 305 822-5322
Hialeah (G-5334)

1442 Construction Sand & Gravel

Campbell Sand & Gravel Co ....D 850 256-4112
Century (G-1474)

Charlotte County Min & Mtl Inc ....E 239 567-1800
Punta Gorda (G-15197)

Titan America LLC ....D 954 523-9790
Fort Lauderdale (G-4177)

Vecellio & Grogan Inc ....D 305 822-5322
Hialeah (G-5334)

1446 Industrial Sand

Chemours Company Fc LLC ....D 904 964-1200
Starke (G-16575)

1459 Clay, Ceramic & Refractory Minerals, NEC

◆ Entec Polymers LLC ....D 407 875-9595
Orlando (G-12469)

Jlt Custom Works Inc ....E 863 245-3371
Wauchula (G-18962)

1475 Phosphate Rock

◆ White Springs AG Chem Inc ....A 386 397-8101
White Springs (G-19489)

1481 Nonmetallic Minerals Svcs, Except Fuels

Fcs Holdings Inc ....E 352 793-5151
Center Hill (G-1473)

Schroeder Manatee Inc ....D 941 755-1637
Lakewood Ranch *(G-8030)*

1499 Miscellaneous Nonmetallic Mining

Charlotte County Min & Mtl Inc ....E 239 567-1800
Punta Gorda *(G-15197)*

Marion Rock Inc ....E 352 687-2023
Ocala *(G-11725)*

15 BUILDING CONSTRUCTION-GENERAL CONTRACTORS AND OPERATIVE BUILDERS

1521 General Contractors, Single Family Houses

911 Restoration Inc ....E 954 747-7000
Sunrise *(G-16729)*

A - Plus Homes Inc ....D 352 624-0120
Ocala *(G-11622)*

ACR Family Construction Inc ....E 352 429-0304
Groveland *(G-5083)*

Adams Homes Northwest Fla Inc ....D 850 934-0470
Pensacola *(G-14211)*

All Southwest Construction LLC ....E 239 410-8184
Fort Myers *(G-4264)*

◆ Allied Home Improvement Inc ....E 305 949-7444
Wilton Manors *(G-19519)*

American Classic Homes LLC ....D 904 351-0308
Jacksonville *(G-5778)*

Amicon Dg Inc ....D 305 573-8030
Miami *(G-9149)*

Anglers Club Inc ....E 305 367-2382
Key Largo *(G-7171)*

Armex Construction Inc ....E 239 645-1517
Cape Coral *(G-1376)*

Arthur Rutenberg Homes Inc ....D 727 536-5900
Clearwater *(G-1526)*

Ashton Orlando Residential LLC ....E 407 647-3700
Lake Mary *(G-7569)*

Austen Builders Inc ....E 305 805-8166
Hialeah *(G-5221)*

Balfour Beatty Cnstr LLC ....D 214 451-1000
Orlando *(G-12174)*

Bcbe Construction LLC ....E 239 643-3343
Naples *(G-11026)*

Berman Construction LLC ....D 407 522-7140
Orlando *(G-12184)*

Birken Construction Inc ....E 904 518-6154
Jacksonville *(G-5862)*

Bluewater Builders Inc ....D 954 753-7233
Coral Springs *(G-2233)*

Braswell Eg Construction Inc ....E 305 296-0305
Key West *(G-7195)*

Bruce Williams Homes Inc ....E 941 748-8834
Bradenton *(G-1069)*

Buccaneer Motel Corporation ....D 239 261-1148
Naples *(G-11042)*

Burgoon Berger Construction ....E 321 723-0388
Palm Bay *(G-13610)*

▲ Burkhardt Construction Inc ....E 561 659-1400
West Palm Beach *(G-19068)*

C Pearson Builders LLC ....E 813 525-9095
Tallahassee *(G-16898)*

Capling Leveling Inc ....D 863 612-1000
Labelle *(G-7423)*

Catalfumo Cnstr & Dev Inc ....D 954 421-4200
Deerfield Beach *(G-2720)*

CB Structures Inc ....E 954 977-4211
Pompano Beach *(G-14768)*

Cdc Builders Inc ....E 305 261-4100
Miami *(G-9340)*

Cemex Construction Mtls Inc ....C 813 409-6280
Tampa *(G-17440)*

Centex Homes Inc ....D 941 343-4545
Estero *(G-3447)*

Centex Real Estate Corporation ....D 813 886-4700
Tampa *(G-17444)*

Century Homebuilders LLC ....E 305 883-8117
Doral *(G-3149)*

Certified Foundations Inc ....E 863 859-3889
Lakeland *(G-7829)*

Certified Restoration Dryclean ....C 904 814-7428
Jacksonville *(G-5930)*

Chris Barbara Development Co ....E 561 312-2717
Palm Beach Gardens *(G-13705)*

Chris-Tel Co Southwest Fla Inc ....E 239 226-0500
Fort Myers *(G-4310)*

Clark & Logan Inc ....E 727 446-2184
Clearwater *(G-1571)*

Coastal Reconstruction Group ....E 877 708-5501
Longwood *(G-8351)*

Codina Partners LLC ....C 305 529-1300
Coral Gables *(G-2074)*

◆ Companies of R & S Inc ....E 305 256-6666
Miami *(G-9396)*

Complete Alum Gen Contrs Inc ....D 941 379-9886
Sarasota *(G-16128)*

Connery Corporation ....E 772 231-1224
Vero Beach *(G-18849)*

Continental Home Health Care ....D 954 309-8567
Coconut Creek *(G-1984)*

Continental Properties Inc ....E 561 689-4766
West Palm Beach *(G-19107)*

Contrcting Spcalists Inc - S E ....D 954 786-3223
Pompano Beach *(G-14782)*

▲ Cornerstone Group Inc ....C 305 443-8288
Hollywood *(G-5418)*

County of Pinellas ....D 727 582-3100
Clearwater *(G-1589)*

Craft Construction Company LLC ....E 954 532-3078
Pompano Beach *(G-14788)*

Crisafulli Builders Inc ....E 321 507-4893
Merritt Island *(G-9025)*

Croom Construction Company ....D 772 562-7474
Vero Beach *(G-18850)*

Curington Contracting LLC ....E 352 732-7839
Ocala *(G-11671)*

D Garrett Construction Inc ....E 239 643-2900
Naples *(G-11087)*

D N Construction Company Inc ....D 305 888-3119
Hialeah *(G-5250)*

Dales Decking Inc ....E 561 747-4679
Jupiter *(G-7062)*

Damex Corporation ....E 941 624-3100
Port Charlotte *(G-15028)*

▼ Danielle Fence Mfg Co Inc ....D 863 425-3182
Mulberry *(G-10975)*

Danis Builders LLC ....C 904 221-1081
Jacksonville *(G-6044)*

Db Civil Construction LLC ....E 386 256-7460
Ormond Beach *(G-13484)*

Dbk Inc ....D 386 860-2050
Debary *(G-2701)*

Debartolo Cnstr Svcs LLC ....E 813 676-7677
Tampa *(G-17580)*

Deeb Construction & Dev Co ....D 727 376-6831
New Port Richey *(G-11371)*

Divco Construction Corp ....E 239 592-7222
Naples *(G-11095)*

Edgewater Cnstr Group Inc ....E 305 463-7700
Miami *(G-9505)*

Elias Bros Group Pntg Cntg Inc ....D 239 643-1624
Naples *(G-11101)*

Emerald Coast Constructors Inc ....E 850 780-6113
Pensacola *(G-14287)*

Equix Energy Services LLC ....C 850 878-1212
Midway *(G-10800)*

Erosion Control Specialist ....E 850 481-8370
Lynn Haven *(G-8468)*

Fireservice Inc ....D 239 936-1033
Fort Myers *(G-4372)*

First Home Builders Fla LLC ....C 239 458-8000
Cape Coral *(G-1392)*

Flores-Hager and Assoc Inc ....D 386 676-9999
Daytona Beach *(G-2589)*

Florida Catastrophe Co LLC ....D 407 295-5440
Orlando *(G-12521)*

Fluharty-Monroe Cnstr Inc ....E 239 240-7455
Fort Myers *(G-4392)*

▲ Focus Construction LLC ....D 954 384-9330
Fort Lauderdale *(G-3800)*

Forrest Inc ....D 904 794-2547
Saint Augustine *(G-15444)*

Foshee Construction Co Inc ....E 352 394-7211
Minneola *(G-10831)*

Framecor LLC ....E 727 259-7691
Saint Petersburg *(G-15680)*

Franz Inc ....E 954 428-8181
Deerfield Beach *(G-2742)*

G L Homes Florida Corp ....C 954 753-1730
Sunrise *(G-16772)*

Garmon Construction Corp ....E 305 260-2112
Miami *(G-9620)*

Gates Butz Instnl Cnstr LLC ....E 239 593-3777
Bonita Springs *(G-915)*

Gates Group LLC ....D 239 593-3777
Bonita Springs *(G-916)*

Go-Tilt Construction LLC ....E 561 391-2450
Deerfield Beach *(G-2745)*

Group 5 Construction Inc ....E 954 859-9477
Margate *(G-8651)*

Gryphon Construction LLC ....C 954 626-0451
Fort Lauderdale *(G-3842)*

Hd Roofing and Cnstr LLC ....E 407 401-5173
Longwood *(G-8364)*

Highwoods Contracting Corp ....E 813 477-7786
Land O Lakes *(G-8050)*

Hill Group Inc ....E 772 567-9154
Vero Beach *(G-18871)*

Holiday Builders Inc ....E 321 610-5156
Melbourne *(G-8907)*

Home Builders Institute ....D 863 452-3883
Avon Park *(G-293)*

Home Improvement Services ....E 352 728-8818
Leesburg *(G-8247)*

Hughes Construction Inds Inc ....E 561 320-6332
Boca Raton *(G-636)*

Icon Building Inc ....E 239 643-3689
Naples *(G-11172)*

Indian River Colony Club Inc ....C 321 255-6000
Melbourne *(G-8911)*

Integrated Construction LLC ....D 904 356-6715
Jacksonville *(G-6324)*

Intervest Cnstr Orlando Inc ....C 386 788-0820
Daytona Beach *(G-2619)*

Intervest Construction Jax Inc ....E 386 788-0820
Daytona Beach *(G-2620)*

Issa Homes Inc ....E 407 566-4772
Kissimmee *(G-7329)*

J & D Mechanical LLC ....D 239 288-5834
Fort Myers *(G-4453)*

J & K Underground Cnstr LLC ....E 904 738-9889
Jacksonville *(G-6969)*

J Malever Construction Co ....E 352 429-9507
Groveland *(G-5094)*

JAM Shell Builders Inc ....E 954 893-5900
Oakland Park *(G-11601)*

Jarod Construction Svcs Inc ....E 305 343-1164
Miami *(G-9784)*

Jaxi Builders Inc ....D 305 599-0700
Doral *(G-3251)*

JO Delotto & Sons Inc ....D 813 935-2191
Tampa *(G-17897)*

John Cannon Homes Inc ....D 941 924-5935
Sarasota *(G-16205)*

Jr Davis Construction Co Inc ....A 407 870-0066
Kissimmee *(G-7334)*

▲ Jsw of Palm Beach Inc ....D 561 588-4460
Lake Worth Beach *(G-7771)*

K Hovnnian Windward Homes LLC ....D 813 885-7744
Tampa *(G-17906)*

Kbf Renovations Inc ....E 813 269-7257
New Port Richey *(G-11391)*

Kenyon Company LLC ....D 904 777-0833
Jacksonville *(G-6403)*

Kohly Construction Inc ....C 305 255-2624
Miami *(G-9834)*

Krystal Companies LLC ....E 904 838-8003
Jacksonville *(G-6409)*

L7 Construction Inc ....E 321 972-9325
Longwood *(G-8376)*

Lamb Construction Group Inc ....D 954 687-0301
Bonita Springs *(G-927)*

Landstar Development Corp ....E 305 461-2440
Plantation *(G-14664)*

Lane Construction Corporation ....D 407 331-3100
Maitland *(G-8552)*

Lee Wetherington Homes Inc ....E 941 922-3480
Sarasota *(G-16218)*

◆ Lennar Homes Inc ....C 305 559-4000
Miami *(G-9859)*

Lennar Homes Inc ....C 813 388-6877
Tampa *(G-17941)*

Leola Construction Inc ....C 813 397-6100
Gibsonton *(G-5036)*

▼ Levis Inc ....E 305 854-1919
Miami *(G-9865)*

Lifetime Enclosures Inc ....E 904 647-4580
Jacksonville *(G-6437)*

London Bay Construction Inc ....D 239 592-1400
Naples *(G-11199)*

Lott Energy LLC ....E 407 656-2335
Orlando *(G-12781)*

Lowes Home Centers LLC ....E 352 330-3458
Wildwood *(G-19503)*

M Pete McNabb Inc ....D 941 907-6771
Lakewood Ranch *(G-8026)*

M/I Homes of Orlando LLC	D	407 531-5100
Lake Mary (G-7608)		
Manhattan Construction Fla Inc	C	813 675-1960
Tampa (G-17983)		
Manhattan Construction Fla Inc	E	239 643-6000
Naples (G-11203)		
Marand Builders Inc	D	904 247-3211
Jacksonville Beach (G-6994)		
Marino Construction Group Inc	E	305 359-5269
Key West (G-7228)		
Marlin Construction Group LLC	E	239 331-5252
Fort Myers (G-4502)		
Maronda Systems Inc Florida	B	407 321-0064
Sanford (G-15963)		
Masterpiece Homes & Prpts Inc	D	407 833-0150
Lake Mary (G-7609)		
Mattamy Homes Corporation	C	407 215-6293
Maitland (G-8556)		
Meritage Homes Florida Inc	A	561 847-7514
West Palm Beach (G-19262)		
Miranda Contracting LLC	E	904 388-1121
Jacksonville (G-6506)		
Mirasol Realty Sales Office	E	561 622-1730
Maitland (G-8559)		
Mocca Construction LLC	D	305 441-2348
Miami (G-10009)		
Naples Executive Builders Inc	E	239 403-1714
Naples (G-11229)		
Nassau Pools Construction Inc	E	239 643-0990
Naples (G-11243)		
Net Construction Inc	C	305 888-3177
Medley (G-8761)		
Nexxus Solutions Group LLC	D	407 378-3631
Orlando (G-12914)		
Nova Ht Renovation & Cnstr LLC	E	727 481-2079
Treasure Island (G-18712)		
Oak Construction Co Inc	E	954 583-9625
Fort Lauderdale (G-4023)		
Odc Construction LLC	E	813 374-2288
Tampa (G-18094)		
▲ Odc Construction LLC	D	407 447-5999
Orlando (G-12926)		
Omni Construction LLC	D	239 260-7584
Naples (G-11252)		
On-Site Cnstr Solutions Corp	E	305 297-3517
Miami (G-10071)		
OR dicky Smith & Co Inc	D	904 220-7600
Jacksonville (G-6566)		
Orlando Trim Carpenters Inc	C	407 564-3700
Orlando (G-12987)		
Park & Eleazer Cnstr LLC	E	727 216-6591
Clearwater (G-1753)		
PCL Construction Services Inc	D	407 466-6292
Miami (G-10105)		
▲ Pegasus Builders Inc	E	561 790-3116
Wellington (G-18987)		
Perrone Construction Inc	E	941 924-6900
Sarasota (G-16263)		
Phoenix Homes Inc	E	239 732-1844
Naples (G-11262)		
Ponderosa Builders Inc	E	850 243-7696
Fort Walton Beach (G-4799)		
Powertown Line Cnstr LLC	C	813 374-9298
Seffner (G-16432)		
Premier Construction & Dev Inc	E	850 514-1000
Tallahassee (G-17073)		
Prime Investors Developers LLC	E	954 392-8788
Hollywood (G-5496)		
Prince Land Services Inc	E	863 422-5207
Haines City (G-5153)		
Principles Construction Inc	E	754 800-7110
Pompano Beach (G-14881)		
Providence Homes Inc	E	904 262-9898
Jacksonville (G-6620)		
Pulte Homes Corporation	E	904 288-8166
Jacksonville (G-6623)		
Pulte Homes of Texas Lp	E	813 653-2092
Lithia (G-8303)		
R C C Associates Inc	D	954 429-3700
Deerfield Beach (G-2787)		
Randall Cnstr Holdings Inc	C	407 464-7776
Apopka (G-205)		
Ranger Construction Inds Inc	D	561 793-9400
Winter Garden (G-19592)		
▼ Redland Company Inc	D	305 247-3226
Homestead (G-5601)		
Reece Builders and Alum Co Inc	E	727 522-3035
Saint Petersburg (G-15826)		
Regency Cnstr Palm Bch Cnty Co	D	586 741-8000
West Palm Beach (G-19341)		

Reliable Homes Inc	E	941 766-8028
Punta Gorda (G-15218)		
Richardson Enterprises	E	850 678-2584
Valparaiso (G-18747)		
▼ Richmond American Homes Fla LP	C	904 541-2300
Orange Park (G-12014)		
Ridge Energy Savers Inc	E	863 676-2665
Lake Wales (G-7698)		
Rigoberto Sanchez Jr Inc	E	407 837-0427
Haines City (G-5155)		
Roadway Construction LLC	E	786 842-3952
Miami (G-10217)		
Rockwell Building Systems LLC	E	813 425-2734
Riverview (G-15269)		
Rose Fence Company	E	407 382-5000
Orlando (G-13127)		
Royal Plus Inc	E	407 790-4883
Winter Springs (G-19810)		
S&R Louisiana LLC	E	850 332-5316
Pensacola (G-14424)		
Saj Construction Services LLC	E	305 828-8111
Hialeah (G-5319)		
▲ Sands Construction Co Inc	E	772 546-2111
Hobe Sound (G-5369)		
Scenario Cockram USA Inc	C	407 613-2949
Orlando (G-13169)		
▼ Sears Home Imprv Pdts Inc	B	407 767-0990
Longwood (G-8400)		
Seda Construction Company	D	904 724-7800
Jacksonville (G-6707)		
Sema Construction Inc	E	407 563-7900
Orlando (G-13185)		
Seretta Construction Inc	E	407 290-9440
Apopka (G-209)		
Shellco Construction Corp	C	561 684-5755
West Palm Beach (G-19360)		
Sierra Paul J Construction Inc	E	813 228-6661
Tampa (G-18284)		
Site and Utility LLC	E	850 439-5734
Pensacola (G-14437)		
Solarhomepros Inc	C	973 524-8404
Orlando (G-13213)		
Southeast Charters Cnstr Inc	E	954 979-9078
Fort Lauderdale (G-4142)		
Sovereign Construction Svcs	E	754 220-6982
Pompano Beach (G-14908)		
Sovran Building Systems Inc	E	850 297-1990
Tallahassee (G-17109)		
Squipeek Inc	E	321 507-8139
Bartow (G-339)		
Star Construction LLC	E	815 703-1874
Estero (G-3479)		
Starlink Cnstr Utilities LLC	E	813 926-8846
Tampa (G-18332)		
▼ Storm Smart Bldg Systems LLC	D	239 938-1000
Fort Myers (G-4608)		
Storm Team Construction Inc	E	614 367-6930
Jupiter (G-7140)		
Superior Cnstr Southeast LLC	C	904 292-4240
Jacksonville (G-6817)		
Swell Construction Co	C	407 971-0434
Oviedo (G-13573)		
Synergy Contracting Group Inc	E	727 287-6320
Clearwater (G-1812)		
Tan Land Development Inc	E	941 359-9000
Sarasota (G-16063)		
Taylor Morrison Home Corp	D	239 947-2173
Estero (G-3481)		
Taylor Morrison Inc	E	941 371-3008
Sarasota (G-16346)		
Thomas May Construction Co	E	904 272-4808
Orange Park (G-12021)		
Tiki Huts Inc	D	305 259-9232
Miami (G-10390)		
Timo Brothers Inc	E	239 949-0405
Bonita Springs (G-946)		
Titus Construction Group Inc	E	407 362-5940
Orlando (G-13294)		
Toll Brothers Inc	E	904 217-0739
Saint Johns (G-15550)		
Toll Brothers Inc	E	386 246-3808
Edgewater (G-3415)		
Tomp Construction Inc	C	321 424-6051
North Miami Beach (G-11535)		
Trax Company	E	757 741-2630
Orlando (G-13306)		
Traylor Industrial LLC	C	941 621-8027
Punta Gorda (G-15223)		
Triton Construction Group LLC	E	813 781-1969
Tampa (G-18448)		

True Builders Inc	E	863 647-1800
Plant City (G-14589)		
Tumbleson White Cnstr Inc	E	352 373-8883
Gainesville (G-5017)		
United Coachworks Inc	D	407 328-0190
Sanford (G-15991)		
United Roofg & Cnstr Svcs Inc	C	727 900-2617
Saint Petersburg (G-15881)		
US Aluminum Services Corp	E	407 237-3128
Orlando (G-13359)		
US Brick & Block Systems Inc	D	954 792-1312
Dania (G-2421)		
◆ Villages of Lake-Sumter Inc	A	352 753-2270
Lady Lake (G-7447)		
Wall Systems Inc Southwest Fla	E	239 643-1921
Naples (G-11340)		
Watson Civil Construction Inc	E	904 297-1800
Saint Augustine (G-15512)		
Weekley Homes LLC	D	850 236-3468
Panama City (G-14086)		
Weekley Homes LLC	E	850 708-1778
Panama City (G-14087)		
Weekley Homes LLC	B	407 865-9992
Altamonte Springs (G-113)		
Westfall Construction Inc	D	813 264-5690
Tampa (G-18544)		
Willis A Smith Cnstr Inc	E	941 366-3116
Lakewood Ranch (G-8042)		
Woolems Inc	D	561 835-0401
West Palm Beach (G-19427)		
Worthington Communities Inc	E	239 561-4666
Fort Myers (G-4658)		
Wpc III Inc	D	407 644-8923
Sanford (G-15996)		
Wright Construction Group Inc	E	239 481-5000
Fort Myers (G-4661)		
Zom Inc	D	407 644-6300
Orlando (G-13472)		

1522 General Contractors, Residential Other Than Single Family

Aacg Inc	E	352 467-7000
Dade City (G-2380)		
▼ All Weather Contractors Inc	D	904 781-7060
Jacksonville (G-5767)		
▲ Allen Concrete & Masonry Inc	C	239 566-1661
Naples (G-11006)		
American Land Lease Inc	E	352 795-7603
Homosassa (G-5616)		
Anglers Club Inc	E	305 367-2382
Key Largo (G-7171)		
Aquarius Building Inc	C	305 824-1324
Miami Lakes (G-10705)		
Armex Construction Inc	E	239 645-1517
Cape Coral (G-1376)		
Ashton Orlando Residential LLC	E	407 647-3700
Lake Mary (G-7569)		
Atlantic PCF Communities LLC	C	305 357-4700
Miami (G-9187)		
Axios Construction Svcs LLC	E	321 352-6829
Fern Park (G-3510)		
▲ Bcc Construction Inc	D	407 865-5771
Mount Dora (G-10946)		
Beach House Development Partnr	E	727 803-9400
Saint Petersburg (G-15596)		
Beattie Development Corp	E	239 257-3295
Cape Coral (G-1378)		
Benderson Properties Inc	D	941 359-8303
University Park (G-18737)		
Bestmarck Capital MGT LLC	E	305 741-3298
Miami (G-9250)		
Britton-Harr Contracting LLC	E	727 432-0637
Tampa (G-17390)		
Buccaneer Motel Corporation	D	239 261-1148
Naples (G-11042)		
C E D Construction Partners	D	407 741-8500
Maitland (G-8510)		
C&N Foundation Tech LLC	C	352 588-0910
San Antonio (G-15908)		
Camden Development Inc	C	407 650-2093
Orlando (G-12229)		
Capmen Construction Co Inc	E	954 427-1490
Coconut Creek (G-1982)		
Carlisle Development Group LLC	D	305 476-8118
Miami (G-9324)		
Cgc Inc	E	904 783-4119
Jacksonville (G-5932)		
Chris Barbara Development Co	E	561 312-2717
Palm Beach Gardens (G-13705)		

Cks Masonry & Concrete Inc ....E 407 366-6229
 Oviedo (G-13544)

CMR Construction & Roofing LLC .....D 855 905-1827
 Lantana (G-8060)

Concrete Lumber Enterprises ....D 305 226-5525
 Miami (G-9403)

▲ Cornerstone Group Inc ....C 305 443-8288
 Hollywood (G-5418)

Craft Creation Inc ....E 954 927-3353
 Hollywood (G-5424)

Crescent Heights Inc ....D 305 374-5700
 Miami (G-9439)

Csci LLC ....D 561 330-7155
 Boynton Beach (G-979)

Current Builders Inc ....C 954 977-4211
 Pompano Beach (G-14790)

▲ Cvc Hospitality Inc ....E ... /.. 407 299-7619
 Winter Garden (G-19564)

Dbk Inc ....D 386 860-2050
 Debary (G-2701)

DEANGELIS DIAMOND CONSTRUCTION C
 239 594-1994
 Naples (G-11092)

Deeb Construction & Dev Co ....D 727 376-6831
 New Port Richey (G-11371)

Delant Construction Co ....D 305 591-8394
 Miami (G-9467)

Diamond Resorts Intl Inc ....A 407 226-1000
 Orlando (G-12422)

DMS Contractors LLC ....D 305 627-3276
 Fort Lauderdale (G-3761)

Dream Finders Homes LLC ....D 904 644-7670
 Jacksonville (G-6084)

Dykstra Construction LLC ....E 813 707-0082
 Lakeland (G-7853)

Elias Brothers Gen Contr Inc ....C 239 293-2442
 Naples (G-11102)

Emerald Coast Constructors Inc ....E 850 780-6113
 Pensacola (G-14287)

Emr Inc ....E 850 897-0210
 Niceville (G-11446)

Facility and Construction Mgt ....D 754 321-0764
 Fort Lauderdale (G-3781)

Fallsafe Solutions LLC ....E 239 260-4120
 Fort Myers (G-4367)

Favergray Company ....E 904 208-2023
 Jacksonville Beach (G-6985)

Ffd Development Company LLC ....E 407 903-7970
 Orlando (G-12507)

First Florida Constructors LLC ....D 305 665-1146
 Miami (G-9559)

G & E Florida Contractors Inc ....C 954 961-0078
 Fort Lauderdale (G-3812)

G C Contractor Services LLC ....E 386 257-6199
 Daytona Beach (G-2599)

Gables Construction Inc ....C 561 997-9700
 Boca Raton (G-594)

Greystar Management Svcs LP ....C 813 887-4200
 Tampa (G-17758)

Hartzell Pntg & Waterproofing ....E 954 957-9761
 Pompano Beach (G-14820)

Haskell Company Inc ....B 904 791-4500
 Jacksonville (G-6262)

Home2 Suites By Hilton Naples ....E 239 598-2222
 Naples (G-11167)

Horizon Bay Management LLC ....D 813 287-3900
 Tampa (G-17841)

Intervest Cnstr Orlando Inc ....C 386 788-0820
 Daytona Beach (G-2619)

Island One Inc ....C 407 859-8900
 Orlando (G-12690)

J Kokolakis Contracting Inc ....E 631 589-4983
 Tarpon Springs (G-18587)

J Kokolakis Contracting Inc ....D 727 942-2211
 Tarpon Springs (G-18588)

Jaxi Builders Inc ....D 305 599-0700
 Doral (G-3251)

▲ JCQ Services Inc ....E 407 889-4944
 Orlando (G-12702)

Jomar Development & Cnstr Inc ....E 727 584-6405
 Clearwater (G-1687)

▲ Jsw of Palm Beach Inc ....D 561 588-4460
 Lake Worth Beach (G-7771)

K D Construction Florida LLC ....C 954 344-4515
 Pompano Beach (G-14836)

Kalos Services Inc ....E 352 243-7088
 Clermont (G-1877)

KB Home Orlando LLC ....E 407 587-3400
 Orlando (G-12723)

Kbf Renovations Inc ....E 813 269-7257
 New Port Richey (G-11391)

▲ Kimmins Corp ....E 813 248-3878
 Tampa (G-17924)

Km Development Corp ....D 941 907-9799
 Sarasota (G-16212)

Lacerte Builders Inc ....E 954 784-8804
 Pompano Beach (G-14840)

Led Enterprise Inc ....E 407 674-8259
 Orlando (G-12759)

Live Oak Contracting LLC ....E 904 497-1500
 Jacksonville (G-6441)

Malak LLC ....E 407 601-7675
 Orlando (G-12805)

Marino Construction Group Inc ....E 305 359-5269
 Key West (G-7228)

MBC Capital Investment Corp ....D 813 477-2725
 Lithia (G-8302)

Net Construction Inc ....C 305 888-3177
 Medley (G-8761)

Ocean Properties Ltd ....C 603 559-2100
 Delray Beach (G-2999)

Odebrecht of America Inc ....D 305 704-5800
 Miami (G-10062)

▼ Oec Usa Inc ....E 305 341-8800
 Miami (G-10063)

Olen Residential Realty Corp ....D 561 732-0633
 Boynton Beach (G-1022)

Orange & Blue Construction Inc ....E 561 994-7266
 Boca Raton (G-731)

Park & Eleazer Cnstr LLC ....E 727 216-6591
 Clearwater (G-1753)

Picerne Construction Corp ....E 407 772-0200
 Altamonte Springs (G-91)

Picerne Development Corp Fla ....D 407 772-0200
 Altamonte Springs (G-92)

Pioneer Screen LLC ....E 772 283-9197
 Stuart (G-16657)

Ponderosa Builders Inc ....E 850 243-7696
 Fort Walton Beach (G-4799)

Pro Construction llc ....D 850 225-5354
 Pensacola (G-14414)

R T Moore Co Inc ....C 239 479-7873
 Fort Myers (G-4560)

Rapid Home Solutions Inc ....E 407 334-4752
 Cape Coral (G-1422)

Reboliz Construction Inc ....D 305 226-5525
 Miami (G-10186)

Recromax LLC ....E 407 842-1430
 Lake Mary (G-7632)

Reliance Construction Co LLC ....E 561 613-5423
 Delray Beach (G-3012)

Restorations Unlimited LLC ....D 954 418-3000
 Hollywood (G-5507)

Rlh Construction LLC ....E 407 384-1908
 Oviedo (G-13568)

Ryka LLC ....E 407 709-4539
 Celebration (G-1470)

Sealand Contractors Corp ....E 561 997-6715
 Boca Raton (G-789)

Senoma Inc ....E 954 979-6364
 Deerfield Beach (G-2795)

Southeast Charters Cnstr Inc ....E 954 979-9078
 Fort Lauderdale (G-4142)

Stellar Contracting Inc ....B 904 260-2900
 Jacksonville (G-6789)

Summit Contractors Inc ....E 904 292-3300
 Jacksonville (G-6804)

Terremark Construction Svcs ....E 786 333-4151
 Miami (G-10379)

Thomas Riley Artisans Guild Inc ....E 239 591-3203
 Naples (G-11323)

▲ United Subcontractors Inc ....E 651 225-6300
 Daytona Beach (G-2684)

Universal Roofing Group Inc ....D 407 295-7403
 Jacksonville (G-6891)

Universal Roofing Group Inc ....D 407 901-4444
 Orlando (G-13350)

Viking Cnstr Corp SW Fla ....E 239 574-3000
 Cape Coral (G-1432)

Vintage Estate Homes LLC ....D 321 610-3924
 Melbourne (G-9003)

▼ Walker & Company Inc ....E 407 645-0500
 Winter Park (G-19785)

Zilber Ltd ....E 941 907-9799
 Sarasota (G-16371)

1531 Operative Builders

3201 Hotel LLC ....E 305 535-3009
 Miami Beach (G-10536)

A G Spanos Construction Inc ....E 904 714-9101
 Jacksonville (G-5719)

ACC All Contractors Inc ....E 305 842-6338
 Doral (G-3100)

▼ Aqua Sun Investments Inc ....E 386 677-0573
 Ormond Beach (G-13477)

Calatlantic Group Inc ....D 407 645-6500
 Winter Park (G-19692)

▲ Cnl Apf Partners LP ....C 407 650-1000
 Orlando (G-12327)

Divco Construction Corp ....E 239 592-7222
 Naples (G-11095)

DR Horton Inc ....E 904 268-2845
 Saint Johns (G-15545)

DR Horton Inc ....D 239 225-2600
 Fort Myers (G-4348)

DR Horton Inc ....E 813 740-9720
 Tampa (G-17602)

DR Horton Inc ....D 407 850-5200
 Orlando (G-12438)

DR Horton Inc ....D 954 949-3000
 Coconut Creek (G-1986)

Dream Finders Holdings LLC ....B 904 644-7670
 Jacksonville (G-6082)

Dream Finders Homes Inc ....E 904 644-7670
 Jacksonville (G-6083)

Edgewater Beach Resort LLC ....B 850 235-4044
 Panama City (G-13995)

Icon Building Inc ....E 239 643-3689
 Naples (G-11172)

Kast Construction Company LLC ....C 561 689-2910
 West Palm Beach (G-19225)

KB Home Orlando LLC ....D 407 587-3800
 Orlando (G-12722)

KB Home Orlando LLC ....E 407 587-3400
 Orlando (G-12723)

Lennar Corporation ....A 305 559-4000
 Miami (G-9858)

Lennar Homes Inc ....C 813 388-6877
 Tampa (G-17941)

Manhattan Construction Fla Inc ....E 239 643-6000
 Naples (G-11203)

Nvr Inc ....E 407 276-5169
 Windermere (G-19547)

Schroeder Manatee Inc ....E 941 755-1637
 Lakewood Ranch (G-8030)

Scottsdale Co ....E 239 261-6100
 Naples (G-11295)

Seda Construction Company ....D 904 724-7800
 Jacksonville (G-6707)

Sonesta Intl Hotels Corp ....E 305 529-2828
 Miami (G-10294)

Tbhc Inc ....C 888 422-9445
 Orlando (G-13271)

Transatlantic Asset Wealth LLC ....E 850 960-5061
 Gulf Breeze (G-5137)

Verbena LLC ....E 305 854-7100
 Miami (G-10464)

▲ WCI Communities Inc ....E 239 947-2600
 Fort Myers (G-4650)

Weekley Homes LLC ....D 904 547-2982
 Saint Johns (G-15551)

Weekley Homes LLC ....E 850 236-3468
 Panama City (G-14086)

Weekley Homes LLC ....D 850 708-1778
 Panama City (G-14087)

Weekley Homes LLC ....B 407 865-9992
 Altamonte Springs (G-113)

Williams Scotsman Inc ....C 561 922-0501
 West Palm Beach (G-19426)

1541 General Contractors, Indl Bldgs & Warehouses

A E New Jr Inc ....D 850 472-1001
 Pensacola (G-14207)

A&A Skyline Construction LLC ....E 813 894-2200
 Temple Terrace (G-18626)

Albertelli Construction Inc ....E 904 493-3028
 Jacksonville (G-5763)

All Steel Consultants Inc ....E 941 727-1444
 Palmetto (G-13902)

▲ Allen Concrete & Masonry Inc ....C 239 566-1661
 Naples (G-11006)

Auld & White Constructors LLC ....C 904 296-2555
 Jacksonville (G-5823)

Barr & Barr Inc ....E 813 591-4545
 Tampa (G-17339)

Bengoa Construction Inc ....E 954 589-0541
 Hollywood (G-5403)

Blue Cord Design and Cnstr LLC ....E 407 425-1390
 Orlando (G-12191)

Bollenback Builders Inc ....E 813 855-2656
Oldsmar *(G-11895)*

Bowman Steel LLC ....C 239 303-9739
Sebring *(G-16390)*

Brasfield & Gorrie LLC ....E 407 562-4500
Winter Park *(G-19688)*

Buccaneer Motel Corporation.............D 239 261-1148
Naples *(G-11042)*

Burke Construction Group Inc ....E 305 468-6604
Doral *(G-3142)*

Caladesi Construction Co ....E 727 585-9945
Largo *(G-8084)*

Catalfumo Cnstr & Dev Inc ....D 954 421-4200
Deerfield Beach *(G-2720)*

CCC Group Inc ....C 863 533-1494
Mulberry *(G-10972)*

Cck Construction Services Inc ....D 407 472-9700
Winter Garden *(G-19561)*

Certified Indus Mint Wldg Fbrc ....E 863 425-1000
Plant City *(G-14549)*

Chris Barbara Development Co ....E 561 312-2717
Palm Beach Gardens *(G-13705)*

Cloud 9 Services Inc ....E 407 481-2750
Orlando *(G-12324)*

Creighton Cnstr & MGT LLC ....D 239 210-0455
Fort Myers *(G-4331)*

Dixie Southern Industrial Inc ....D 863 984-1900
Polk City *(G-14726)*

Duvekot Corporation ....E 305 716-9775
Fort Lauderdale *(G-3766)*

Ed Taylor Construction Inc ....C 813 623-3724
Tampa *(G-17615)*

Emerald Coast Constructors Inc ....E 850 780-6113
Pensacola *(G-14287)*

Eveland Brothers Inc ....E 727 573-1107
Clearwater *(G-1628)*

Grace & Naeem Uddin Inc ....E 954 693-0620
Sunrise *(G-16776)*

Gulf Coast Indus Maint LLC ....D 863 354-9195
Mulberry *(G-10980)*

Gulf Coast Rebar Inc ....E 813 247-1200
Tampa *(G-17771)*

Haskell Company Inc ....B 904 791-4500
Jacksonville *(G-6262)*

HJ High Construction Company.............E 407 422-8171
Orlando *(G-12652)*

Iap World Services Inc ....E 321 784-7100
Cape Canaveral *(G-1367)*

Integrated Apartment Svcs Inc ....E 904 551-4992
Jacksonville *(G-6323)*

Iveys Construction Inc ....C 321 453-3812
Merritt Island *(G-9035)*

James A Cummings Inc ....D 954 484-1532
Fort Lauderdale *(G-3903)*

▲ Jsw of Palm Beach Inc ....D 561 588-4460
Lake Worth Beach *(G-7771)*

Kennedy Construction Svcs Inc ....E 407 658-6310
Orlando *(G-12724)*

Kenyon & Partners Inc ....E 813 241-6568
Tampa *(G-17915)*

Legacy Foods LLC ....E 386 672-5659
Ormond Beach *(G-13507)*

Lemartec Group LLC ....D 305 273-8676
Miami *(G-9857)*

Martin County School District ....E 772 219-1255
Stuart *(G-16639)*

McCree Inc ....E 407 898-4821
Orlando *(G-12840)*

▼ Met-Con Inc ....D 321 632-4880
Cocoa *(G-1944)*

Metro Property Services Inc ....E 904 399-1020
Jacksonville *(G-6501)*

Milton J Wood Company ....C 863 648-0775
Lakeland *(G-7925)*

Milton J Wood Company ....E 941 746-3031
Bradenton *(G-1147)*

Mitchell G Hancock Inc.............E 863 467-8468
Okeechobee *(G-11875)*

P J Callaghan Company Inc ....E 727 573-2505
Saint Petersburg *(G-15784)*

Paul Davis National LLC ....E 888 222-4122
Jacksonville *(G-6589)*

Perry Charles Partners Inc.............D 352 333-9292
Gainesville *(G-4977)*

Platinum Strl Restoration Inc.............E 305 908-8764
Hollywood *(G-5494)*

Probitas Technology Inc ....D 813 200-5625
South Pasadena *(G-16523)*

R C Stevens Construction Co.............E 407 299-3800
Winter Garden *(G-19591)*

Reintjes Services Inc ....D 863 595-0961
Winter Haven *(G-19654)*

Richard K Davis Construction ....E 772 461-8335
Fort Pierce *(G-4734)*

Rlh Construction LLC ....E 407 384-1908
Oviedo *(G-13568)*

Rodda Construction Inc ....D 863 669-0990
Lakeland *(G-7956)*

SE Cline Construction Inc ....D 386 446-6426
Palm Coast *(G-13839)*

Semco Construction Inc ....D 863 533-7193
Bartow *(G-337)*

Sharpe Inc ....E 850 433-2179
Pensacola *(G-14434)*

Sierra Paul J Construction Inc.............E 813 228-6661
Tampa *(G-18284)*

Skanska USA Cvil Southeast Inc.............D 757 420-4140
Maitland *(G-8577)*

Sperry & Associates Inc ....E 850 562-1101
Tallahassee *(G-17111)*

Stearns Cnrad Schmidt Cnslting.............D 813 621-0080
Tampa *(G-18334)*

Stellar Companies Inc ....C 904 899-9393
Jacksonville *(G-6788)*

◆ Stellar Group Incorporated ....C 904 260-2900
Jacksonville *(G-6791)*

Stiles Corporation ....C 954 627-9150
Fort Lauderdale *(G-4156)*

Symx Infrastructure LLC ....C 305 442-8577
Coral Gables *(G-2192)*

Taylor Industrial Cnstr Inc ....E 386 792-3060
Live Oak *(G-8320)*

Terhaar Cronley Gen Contrs Inc ....E 850 433-7007
Pensacola *(G-14458)*

Topbuild Home Services Inc ....C 386 304-2200
Daytona Beach *(G-2677)*

Tutor Perini Building Corp ....E 954 733-4211
Fort Lauderdale *(G-4192)*

Vanson Enterprises Inc ....E 407 647-2334
Winter Park *(G-19783)*

Viking Pure Solutions LLC ....E 386 428-9800
Port Orange *(G-15094)*

Walbridge Aldinger LLC ....C 813 622-8900
Tampa *(G-18518)*

Weitz Company LLC ....D 561 686-5511
West Palm Beach *(G-19416)*

▼ West Construction Inc ....E 561 588-2027
Lantana *(G-8072)*

Whiting-Turner Contracting Co ....E 702 491-9463
Orlando *(G-13431)*

Willis A Smith Cnstr Inc.............E 941 366-3116
Lakewood Ranch *(G-8042)*

Worthmann LLC ....D 386 454-5591
High Springs *(G-5356)*

1542 General Contractors, Nonresidential & Non-indl Bldgs

1st Chice Facilities Svcs Corp ....D 941 758-1915
Sarasota *(G-16016)*

A E New Jr Inc ....D 850 472-1001
Pensacola *(G-14207)*

Aacg Inc ....E 352 467-7000
Dade City *(G-2380)*

ABI Companies Inc ....D 813 289-8808
Tampa *(G-17223)*

ACC All Contractors Inc ....E 305 842-6338
Doral *(G-3100)*

▼ Adler Phillips Cnstr Inc ....E 305 392-4000
Sweetwater *(G-16856)*

Aerial Companies Inc ....C 239 643-7625
Naples *(G-11002)*

AG Contractors Fl LLC ....D 305 503-9869
Miami *(G-9101)*

All Steel Consultants Inc ....E 941 727-1444
Palmetto *(G-13902)*

Ally Building Solutions LLC ....D 904 647-7604
Orlando *(G-12099)*

American Cnstr & Engrg Co ....E 305 604-8998
Pinecrest *(G-14497)*

Ames 1 LLC ....E 907 344-0067
Edgewater *(G-3408)*

Anderson-Moore Cnstr Corp ....D 561 753-7400
West Palm Beach *(G-19036)*

Anf Group Inc ....E 954 693-9900
Davie *(G-2457)*

Aquarius Building Inc ....C 305 824-1324
Miami Lakes *(G-10705)*

◆ Astaldi Construction Corp ....C 954 423-8766
Davie *(G-2459)*

Atlantic Cast Rest Mech Svcs L ....E 305 633-4327
Miami *(G-9185)*

Auld & White Constructors LLC ....C 904 296-2555
Jacksonville *(G-5823)*

▲ Autobilders Gen Contg Svcs Inc ....D 561 622-3515
West Palm Beach *(G-19044)*

Axios Construction Svcs LLC ....E 321 352-6829
Fern Park *(G-3510)*

B&M West Cnstr Co Texas Ltd ....E 863 519-4441
Bartow *(G-310)*

Balfour Beatty Cnstr LLC ....B 954 585-4000
Plantation *(G-14606)*

Barr & Barr Inc ....E 813 591-4545
Tampa *(G-17339)*

Batson-Cook Company ....D 904 268-0094
Jacksonville *(G-5843)*

Batson-Cook Company ....E 813 221-7575
Tampa *(G-17343)*

Bbmk Contracting LLC ....E 954 928-3870
Boca Raton *(G-444)*

Bcl Civil Contractors Inc ....E 850 871-1516
Panama City *(G-13968)*

Beauchamp Construction Co Inc ....E 305 445-0819
Coral Gables *(G-2049)*

Bella Construction Key W Inc ....E 305 292-9888
Key West *(G-7193)*

Benderson Properties Inc ....D 941 359-8303
University Park *(G-18737)*

Biltmore Construction Co Inc ....D 727 585-2084
Clearwater *(G-1548)*

Bollenback Builders Inc ....E 813 855-2656
Oldsmar *(G-11895)*

Brasfield & Gorrie LLC ....E 904 256-6826
Jacksonville *(G-5877)*

Brasfield & Gorrie LLC ....E 407 562-4500
Winter Park *(G-19688)*

Braswell Eg Construction Inc ....E 305 296-0305
Key West *(G-7195)*

Brillant Crtive Fbrication LLC ....D 239 774-3333
Orlando *(G-12207)*

Britton-Harr Contracting LLC ....E 727 432-0637
Tampa *(G-17390)*

Building Restoration Tech Inc ....E 209 273-1209
Deerfield Beach *(G-2717)*

Burke Construction Group Inc ....E 305 468-6604
Doral *(G-3142)*

C & R General Contactors Inc.............E 904 596-3255
Jacksonville *(G-5888)*

Caladesi Construction Co ....E 727 585-9945
Largo *(G-8084)*

Camcon Group LLC ....E 786 801-1503
Miami *(G-9306)*

Capmen Construction Co Inc ....E 954 427-1490
Coconut Creek *(G-1982)*

Carousel Dev & Restoration Inc ....D 561 272-3700
Delray Beach *(G-2926)*

Carr and Collier Inc ....D 352 314-3625
Leesburg *(G-8235)*

Castle Constructors Company ....D 407 888-1195
Lake Mary *(G-7574)*

Catalfumo Cnstr & Dev Inc ....C 561 694-3000
Palm Beach Gardens *(G-13699)*

Catalfumo Cnstr & Dev Inc ....D 954 421-4200
Deerfield Beach *(G-2720)*

Catalfumo Construction Inc.............D 561 627-2875
Palm Beach Gardens *(G-13700)*

CB Constructors Inc ....D 954 977-4211
Pompano Beach *(G-14767)*

CB Structures Inc ....E 954 977-4211
Pompano Beach *(G-14768)*

CCC Group Inc ....C 863 533-1494
Mulberry *(G-10972)*

Cck Construction Services Inc ....D 407 472-9700
Winter Garden *(G-19561)*

Cdc Builders Inc ....E 305 261-4100
Miami *(G-9340)*

Central Florida Store Svcs Inc ....E 407 288-3526
Sanford *(G-15933)*

Cesar Glass and Cnstr Inc ....D 919 796-3341
Valrico *(G-18751)*

Cgc Inc ....E 904 783-4119
Jacksonville *(G-5932)*

Childers Construction Company.............E 850 222-2281
Tallahassee *(G-16911)*

Chris-Tel Co Southwest Fla Inc ....E 239 226-0500
Fort Myers *(G-4310)*

Clancy & Theys Construction Co ....D 407 578-1449
Winter Garden *(G-19562)*

Clark & Logan Inc ....E 727 446-2184
Clearwater *(G-1571)*

Clark McCrthy Hlthcare Prtners	D	813 636-4422	Tampa (G-17486)
Cleveland Construction Inc	C	239 643-8000	Naples (G-11057)
Commercial Metal Building Svcs	E	954 492-0661	Oakland Park (G-11590)
Commons Medical Dev Inc	E	407 425-8454	Orlando (G-12349)
◆ Companies of R & S Inc	E	305 256-6666	Miami (G-9396)
Compass Construction Inc	E	239 542-7118	Cape Coral (G-1385)
Complete Property Services Inc	E	727 793-9777	Tampa (G-17507)
Concrete Lumber Enterprises	D	305 226-5525	Miami (G-9403)
▲ Condotte America Inc	C	305 670-7585	Medley (G-8716)
Conlan Company	B	904 309-8000	Jacksonville (G-5997)
Constructions & Svc Solutions	E	716 852-1219	Orange Park (G-11984)
Core Construction Svcs Fla LLC	E	504 731-3143	University Park (G-18740)
Correctional Properties LLC	D	561 893-0101	Boca Raton (G-531)
Craft Construction Company LLC	D	954 532-3078	Pompano Beach (G-14788)
Craft Creation Inc	E	954 927-3353	Hollywood (G-5424)
Creighton Cnstr & MGT LLC	D	239 210-0455	Fort Myers (G-4331)
Crescent Heights Inc	D	305 374-5700	Miami (G-9439)
Croom Construction Company	D	772 562-7474	Vero Beach (G-18850)
Culpepper Construction Co Inc	C	850 224-3146	Tallahassee (G-16926)
Curington Contracting LLC	E	352 732-7839	Ocala (G-11671)
Curran Young Construction LLC	E	239 829-8378	Bonita Springs (G-908)
D & A Construction Group Inc	E	407 960-4032	Altamonte Springs (G-43)
D Garrett Construction Inc	E	239 643-2900	Naples (G-11087)
D Stephenson Construction Inc	E	954 315-7020	Fort Lauderdale (G-3747)
Danis Construction LLC	E	904 724-6045	Jacksonville (G-6045)
David Nelson Construction Co	C	727 784-7624	Palm Harbor (G-13859)
Dbk Inc	D	386 860-2050	Debary (G-2701)
DE Murphy Constructors Inc	D	941 955-5990	Sarasota (G-16137)
◆ Dean Steel Buildings Inc	D	239 334-1051	Fort Myers (G-4342)
DEANGELIS DIAMOND CONSTRUCTION	C	239 594-1994	Naples (G-11092)
Delant Construction Co	D	305 591-8394	Miami (G-9467)
Diaz/Fritz Group Inc	E	813 254-0072	Temple Terrace (G-18632)
Don Facciobene Inc	D	321 727-7100	Palm Bay (G-13617)
Dykstra Construction LLC	E	813 707-0082	Lakeland (G-7853)
Ed Taylor Construction Inc	C	813 623-3724	Tampa (G-17615)
Ehc Inc	E	239 254-6050	Fort Myers (G-4355)
Emerald Coast Constructors Inc	E	850 780-6113	Pensacola (G-14287)
Emerald Construction Corp	E	954 241-2583	Dania (G-2412)
Encon Inc	D	813 354-0446	Tampa (G-17631)
Ervin Bishop Construction Inc	E	813 996-6560	Land O Lakes (G-8046)
ESA South Inc	E	850 937-8505	Cantonment (G-1339)
Esa-Morette Jv LLC	E	850 937-8520	Cantonment (G-1340)
Eveland Brothers Inc	E	727 573-1107	Clearwater (G-1628)
Evergreen Construction MGT	D	352 227-1460	Mount Dora (G-10949)
Facchina Construction Fla LLC	C	305 341-4900	Medley (G-8731)

Facility and Construction Mgt	D	754 321-0764	Fort Lauderdale (G-3781)
Favergray Company	E	904 208-2023	Jacksonville Beach (G-6985)
First Florida Constructors LLC	D	305 665-1146	Miami (G-9559)
Flagler Real Estate Dev Corp	C	305 520-2300	Coral Gables (G-2108)
Flores-Hager and Assoc Inc	D	386 676-9999	Daytona Beach (G-2589)
Florida Catastrophe Co LLC	D	407 295-5440	Orlando (G-12521)
▲ Florida Glass of Tampa Bay	E	813 925-1330	Tampa (G-17681)
Florida Lemark Corporation	E	305 593-1442	Doral (G-3201)
Florida Masonry Cnstr Co	E	813 626-4518	Tampa (G-17690)
Florida Structural Group Inc	E	239 437-6007	Fort Myers (G-4390)
Ford Construction Company	E	904 992-9133	Jacksonville Beach (G-6987)
Formcrete LLC	C	305 248-5885	Florida City (G-3561)
Forrest Inc	D	904 794-2547	Saint Augustine (G-15444)
Fort Partners LLC	E	305 571-8228	Fort Lauderdale (G-3805)
Gates Butz Instnl Cnstr LLC	E	239 593-3777	Bonita Springs (G-915)
Geo Design Services Inc	D	561 893-0101	Boca Raton (G-600)
Golden Sands Gen Contrs Inc	E	305 633-3336	Lakeland (G-7875)
Golden Sands Gen Contrs Inc	E	305 633-3336	Coral Gables (G-2114)
Grace & Naeem Uddin Inc	E	954 693-0620	Sunrise (G-16776)
Great Dane Petro Contrs Inc	E	954 792-1334	Fort Lauderdale (G-3833)
Greg Construction Co	E	352 503-2092	Homosassa (G-5617)
Gryphon Construction LLC	C	954 626-0451	Fort Lauderdale (G-3842)
Gulf Bay Hotel Inc	E	239 732-9300	Naples (G-11148)
Gulf Building LLC	C	954 492-9191	Fort Lauderdale (G-3845)
H A Contracting Corp	E	305 591-9212	Doral (G-3219)
▲ Haley Construction Inc	D	386 944-0470	Ormond Beach (G-13498)
Haskell Company Inc	B	904 791-4500	Jacksonville (G-6262)
Hawkins Construction Inc	D	727 937-2690	Tarpon Springs (G-18585)
Hedrick Brothers Cnstr Co Inc	C	561 689-8880	West Palm Beach (G-19176)
Hennessy Cnstr Svcs Corp	E	727 821-3223	Saint Petersburg (G-15706)
Hensel Phelps Construction Co	E	850 306-2285	Crestview (G-2324)
HG Cnstr Dev & Inv Inc	D	786 845-8999	Miami (G-9699)
HJ High Construction Company	E	407 422-8171	Orlando (G-12652)
Hoar Construction LLC	E	407 650-8100	Orlando (G-12653)
I Wpc Inc	C	407 644-8923	Sanford (G-15951)
I9tecc LLC	D	305 916-9090	Homestead (G-5584)
Iconstructors LLC	D	813 287-9000	Tampa (G-17851)
Intertech Cnstr Corp Amer Inc	E	954 893-1900	Coral Springs (G-2261)
Ironrock Commercial Cnstr LLC	E	407 915-6676	Sanford (G-15953)
Ironwood Construction Co Inc	D	850 539-8888	Havana (G-5195)
Iveys Construction Inc	C	321 453-3812	Merritt Island (G-9035)
J & D Mechanical LLC	D	239 288-5834	Fort Myers (G-4453)
J Kokolakis Contracting Inc	E	631 589-4983	Tarpon Springs (G-18587)
J Kokolakis Contracting Inc	D	727 942-2211	Tarpon Springs (G-18588)
▼ J McGarvey Cnstr Co Inc	D	239 992-8940	Bonita Springs (G-924)

J R S Construction Inc	E	407 862-6966	Longwood (G-8371)
J Raymond & Associates Inc	D	407 339-2988	Longwood (G-8372)
J Raymond Construction Corp	E	407 862-6966	Longwood (G-8373)
J2 Solutions Inc	E	941 492-3266	Venice (G-18787)
JAM Shell Builders Inc	E	954 893-5900	Oakland Park (G-11601)
James A Cummings Inc	D	954 484-1532	Fort Lauderdale (G-3903)
Jasper Steward LLC	E	754 600-9127	Pembroke Pines (G-14157)
Jaxi Builders Inc	D	305 599-0700	Doral (G-3251)
▼ Jjw Construction Inc	C	954 970-0211	Fort Lauderdale (G-3908)
JO Delotto & Sons Inc	D	813 935-2191	Tampa (G-17897)
Johnson-Laux Construction LLC	D	407 770-2180	Winter Garden (G-19575)
JP Donovan Construction Inc	D	321 383-1171	Rockledge (G-15353)
▲ Jsw of Palm Beach Inc	D	561 588-4460	Lake Worth Beach (G-7771)
Keller Mechanical & Engrg Inc	E	863 686-0947	Lakeland (G-7894)
Kellogg & Kimsey Inc	E	941 927-7700	Sarasota (G-16209)
Kendale Design/Build LLC	D	904 384-8611	Jacksonville (G-6401)
Kenyon & Partners Inc	E	813 241-6568	Tampa (G-17915)
Km Development Corp	D	941 907-9799	Sarasota (G-16212)
Kohly Construction Inc	D	305 255-2624	Miami (G-9834)
Krane Development Inc	D	813 875-4600	Tampa (G-17931)
Krystal Companies LLC	E	904 838-8003	Jacksonville (G-6409)
L & R Structural Corp Inc	D	305 220-8200	Miami (G-9838)
◆ Land-Ron Inc	E	407 816-7035	Orlando (G-12750)
Landstar Development Corp	E	305 461-2440	Plantation (G-14664)
Lema Construction Inc	E	727 563-0298	Saint Petersburg (G-15746)
▼ Levis Inc	E	305 854-1919	Miami (G-9865)
▲ Link Construction Group Inc	D	305 665-9826	Doral (G-3260)
Live Oak Contracting LLC	E	904 497-1500	Jacksonville (G-6441)
Lord & Son Construction Inc	E	850 863-5158	Fort Walton Beach (G-4787)
▲ Lotspeich Company Inc	D	305 624-7777	Hialeah (G-5292)
Lotspeich Company Inc	D	786 298-0899	Pembroke Pines (G-14164)
Lott Energy LLC	E	407 656-2335	Orlando (G-12781)
Lynn Kaufman Construction Inc	D	561 361-6700	Delray Beach (G-2985)
M E Construction Inc	D	321 723-5661	Orlando (G-12798)
M E Construction Inc	D	321 723-5661	Melbourne (G-8925)
▼ M M Parrish Construction Co	D	352 378-1571	Gainesville (G-4938)
Macdade Construction Inc	E	407 964-1099	Sanford (G-15962)
Malak LLC	E	407 601-7675	Orlando (G-12805)
Mallen Construction Inc	E	904 880-5580	Jacksonville (G-6464)
Manhattan Construction Company	D	813 675-1960	Tampa (G-17982)
Manhattan Construction Fla Inc	E	239 643-6000	Naples (G-11203)
Marcobay Construction Inc	D	863 680-2293	Lakeland (G-7912)
Matcon Construction Svcs Inc	D	813 600-5555	Tampa (G-18001)
Mattair Construction Co Inc	E	850 433-7538	Pensacola (G-14355)
MBC Capital Investment Corp	D	813 477-2725	Lithia (G-8302)

MBR Construction Inc ....E 954 771-2130
Fort Lauderdale (G-3962)

McCree Inc ....C 407 898-4821
Orlando (G-12840)

▼ McGarvey Construction Co Inc ....D 239 738-7800
Fort Myers (G-4505)

McIntyre Elwell Strmmer Gen CN ....D 941 377-6800
Sarasota (G-16227)

Mead Construction Inc ....E 321 255-3920
Melbourne (G-8928)

Mena Cosmetics Inc ....C 786 822-5922
Miami (G-9934)

▼ Merkury Corporation ....E 305 758-9888
Miami (G-9936)

Metro Property Services Inc ....E 904 399-1020
Jacksonville (G-6501)

Metro Service Group Inc ....D 504 520-8331
Pensacola (G-14364)

Mills Corporation ....D 954 846-2300
Sunrise (G-16799)

▼ Milton J Wood Company ....D 904 353-5527
Jacksonville (G-6505)

Miranda Contracting LLC ....E 904 388-1121
Jacksonville (G-6506)

Moss & Associates LLC ....C 864 254-9450
Orlando (G-12881)

Moss & Associates LLC ....C 727 410-3229
Tampa (G-18055)

Moss & Associates LLC ....C 407 730-5550
Orlando (G-12882)

◆ Moss & Associates LLC ....D 954 524-5678
Wilton Manors (G-19531)

▼ Mrg Glazing Contractors Inc ....C 305 470-8284
Medley (G-8760)

N W F Contractors Inc ....E 850 862-5376
Fort Walton Beach (G-4793)

Naples Executive Builders Inc ....E 239 403-1714
Naples (G-11229)

◆ Nassal Company ....D 407 648-0400
Orlando (G-12894)

NDC Construction Company ....E 941 747-1062
Bradenton (G-1150)

Net Construction Inc ....C 305 888-3177
Medley (G-8761)

Nexxus Solutions Group LLC ....D 407 378-3631
Orlando (G-12914)

Nhcs LLC ....E 407 574-2164
Groveland (G-5100)

Nni Construction Co ....E 954 870-7792
Fort Lauderdale (G-4000)

Ohl - Arellano Construction Co ....D 305 994-9901
Medley (G-8764)

OR dicky Smith & Co Inc ....D 904 220-7600
Jacksonville (G-6566)

P J Callaghan Company Inc ....E 727 573-2505
Saint Petersburg (G-15784)

Papico Construction Inc ....E 772 288-1826
Palm City (G-13795)

Park & Eleazer Cnstr LLC ....E 727 216-6591
Clearwater (G-1753)

Parkinson-Beauchamp JV ....D 305 445-0819
Coral Gables (G-2165)

Parrish McCall Constructors ....D 352 378-1571
Gainesville (G-4974)

Pat Cook Construction Inc ....E 941 749-1959
Bradenton (G-1159)

Pate Construction Company Inc ....D 772 288-1600
Stuart (G-16656)

PCL Civil Constructors Inc ....E 813 264-9500
Tampa (G-18126)

PCL Construction Inc ....E 813 264-9500
Tampa (G-18127)

PCL Construction Services Inc ....D 407 363-0059
Orlando (G-13016)

▲ Pegasus Builders Inc ....E 561 790-3116
Wellington (G-18987)

Pemberton Building Inc ....E 561 842-5137
Lake Park (G-7661)

Perry Charles Partners Inc ....D 352 333-9292
Gainesville (G-4977)

Pinkerton & Laws Florida Inc ....E 321 400-6161
Orlando (G-13031)

Pinkerton Laws Cnstr Orlndo In ....D 321 400-6161
Orlando (G-13032)

▲ Plaza Cnstr Group Fla LLC ....D 786 693-8700
Miami (G-10128)

Prbc Inc ....D 813 282-7275
Tampa (G-18160)

Prbc Inc ....E 850 668-6710
Tallahassee (G-17071)

Prime Investors Developers LLC ....E 954 392-8788
Hollywood (G-5496)

Pro Construction llc ....D 850 225-5354
Pensacola (G-14414)

Questar Construction Inc ....E 941 376-3310
Sarasota (G-16278)

R C C Associates Inc ....E 954 429-3700
Deerfield Beach (G-2787)

R C Stevens Construction Co ....E 407 299-3800
Winter Garden (G-19591)

Regency Cnstr Palm Bch Cnty Co ....D 586 741-8000
West Palm Beach (G-19341)

Register Roofing & Sheet Metal ....D 904 215-8533
Jacksonville (G-6650)

Restorations Unlimited LLC ....D 954 418-3000
Hollywood (G-5507)

Rlh Construction LLC ....E 407 384-1908
Oviedo (G-13568)

RMC Property Group LLC ....E 800 728-5379
Tampa (G-18228)

Rodda Construction Inc ....D 863 669-0990
Lakeland (G-7956)

Rooney Holdings Inc ....D 239 403-0375
Naples (G-11288)

Ruby Builders Inc ....E 407 293-8217
Orlando (G-13147)

Rycon Construction Inc ....E 954 851-9494
Sunrise (G-16819)

Ryka LLC ....E 407 709-4539
Celebration (G-1470)

SA Casey Construction Inc ....E 407 240-6775
Orlando (G-13157)

Scherer Construction Svcs LLC ....D 407 894-7661
Ocoee (G-11822)

Schmid Construction Inc ....D 352 243-3720
Clermont (G-1885)

School Dst of Osceola Cnty FL ....C 407 518-2964
Kissimmee (G-7380)

Scottsdale Co ....E 239 261-6100
Naples (G-11295)

SE Cline Construction Inc ....D 386 446-6426
Palm Coast (G-13839)

Sembler Company ....D 727 384-6000
Saint Petersburg (G-15841)

Sembler Family Partnr 41 Ltd ....D 727 384-6000
Saint Petersburg (G-15842)

Semco Construction Inc ....D 863 533-7193
Bartow (G-337)

Sharpe Inc ....E 850 433-2179
Pensacola (G-14434)

Sierra Paul J Construction Inc ....E 813 228-6661
Tampa (G-18284)

Skanska USA Building Inc ....D 813 294-4174
Tampa (G-18291)

Skanska USA Building Inc ....E 407 541-4700
Orlando (G-13204)

Skanska USA Building Inc ....D 954 920-5167
Fort Lauderdale (G-4131)

Soares Da Costa Contractor LLC ....B 407 502-5535
Orlando (G-13209)

Southeast Charters Cnstr Inc ....E 954 979-9078
Fort Lauderdale (G-4142)

Southland Construction Inc ....C 407 889-9844
Apopka (G-212)

Sovereign Construction Svcs ....E 754 220-6982
Pompano Beach (G-14908)

Spectrum Contracting Inc ....D 239 643-2772
Naples (G-11302)

Sperry & Associates Inc ....E 850 562-1101
Tallahassee (G-17111)

Spruce Creek Gols LLC ....D 352 347-3700
Summerfield (G-16690)

Stellar Companies Inc ....C 904 899-9393
Jacksonville (G-6788)

Stellar Contracting Inc ....B 904 260-2900
Jacksonville (G-6789)

◆ Stellar Group Incorporated ....C 904 260-2900
Jacksonville (G-6791)

Stiles Corporation ....C 954 627-9150
Fort Lauderdale (G-4156)

Stobs Bros Construction Co ....E 305 751-1692
Miami Shores (G-10776)

Strongcore Group LLC ....D 305 539-0680
South Miami (G-16519)

Suffolk Construction Co Inc ....D 305 374-1107
Miami (G-10337)

Suffolk Construction Co Inc ....C 561 282-3000
West Palm Beach (G-19376)

▼ Summit Construction Inc ....E 850 660-1019
Santa Rosa Beach (G-16015)

Summit Contracting Group Inc ....C 904 268-5515
Jacksonville (G-6803)

Summit Contractors Inc ....E 904 292-3300
Jacksonville (G-6804)

Symx Infrastructure LLC ....C 305 442-8577
Coral Gables (G-2192)

T & G Corporation ....D 305 592-0552
Orlando (G-13263)

TDS Construction Inc ....D 941 795-6100
Bradenton (G-1190)

Tecta America South Fla Inc ....D 954 419-9339
Deerfield Beach (G-2803)

Tenex Enterprises Inc ....E 954 788-8100
Pompano Beach (G-14919)

Terhaar Cronley Gen Contrs Inc ....E 850 433-7007
Pensacola (G-14458)

Terremark Construction Svcs ....E 786 333-4151
Miami (G-10379)

▲ Thornton Construction Co Inc ....D 305 649-1995
Opa Locka (G-11956)

Total Concrete Repairs Inc ....E 904 768-2700
Jacksonville (G-6861)

Triangle Associates Inc ....E 305 817-8443
Davie (G-2531)

Tru - Proof Inc ....E 305 270-6111
Miami (G-10412)

True Builders Inc ....E 863 647-1800
Plant City (G-14589)

Tumbleson White Cnstr Inc ....E 352 373-8883
Gainesville (G-5017)

Turner Construction Company ....E 786 621-9000
Miami (G-10421)

Turner Construction Company ....E 407 210-2500
Orlando (G-13319)

Turner Construction Company ....D 407 210-2500
Orlando (G-13320)

▲ United Subcontractors Inc ....E 651 225-6300
Daytona Beach (G-2684)

Valiant Power South LLC ....D 561 578-4682
Hobe Sound (G-5371)

▼ Veitia Padron Inc ....E 305 669-8575
Miami (G-10462)

Viking Cnstr Corp SW Fla ....E 239 574-3000
Cape Coral (G-1432)

Vmg Construction Inc ....D 407 347-9536
Winter Garden (G-19599)

Vogel Bros Building Co ....E 608 241-5454
Lakeland (G-7994)

Vulcan Group LLC ....D 305 967-6344
Miami (G-10486)

Walbridge Aldinger LLC ....C 813 622-8900
Tampa (G-18518)

▼ Walker & Company Inc ....E 407 645-0500
Winter Park (G-19785)

Wall Systems Inc Southwest Fla ....E 239 643-1921
Naples (G-11340)

Weitz Company LLC ....D 561 686-5511
West Palm Beach (G-19416)

▼ West Construction Inc ....E 561 588-2027
Lantana (G-8072)

◆ Wharton-Smith Inc ....C 407 321-8410
Sanford (G-15993)

Wharton-Smith Inc ....C 813 288-0068
Tampa (G-18550)

Whites Site Development Inc ....D 407 302-1549
Sanford (G-15994)

Whitesell-Green Inc ....E 850 434-5311
Pensacola (G-14473)

Whiting-Turner Contracting Co ....D 407 601-3004
Orlando (G-13430)

Whiting-Turner Contracting Co ....B 813 287-9700
Tampa (G-18553)

Whiting-Turner Contracting Co ....E 702 491-9463
Orlando (G-13431)

Williams & Rowe Company Inc ....E 904 387-2333
Jacksonville (G-6934)

Williams Company - Southeast ....D 407 295-2530
Maitland (G-8600)

Willis A Smith Cnstr Inc ....E 941 366-3116
Lakewood Ranch (G-8042)

Worthmann LLC ....D 386 454-5591
High Springs (G-5356)

Wpc III Inc ....D 407 644-8923
Sanford (G-15996)

Wright Construction Corp ....D 239 481-5000
Fort Myers (G-4660)

Wright Construction Group Inc ....E 239 481-5000
Fort Myers (G-4661)

Zarco Construction LLC ....E 305 970-9520
Coral Gables (G-2214)

16 HEAVY CONSTRUCTION OTHER THAN BUILDING CONSTRUCTION-CONTRACTORS

1611 Highway & Street Construction

AAA Top Quality Asphalt LLC ....E 863 226-0404
Mulberry *(G-10967)*

Acosta Tractors Inc ....E 305 556-0473
Hialeah *(G-5212)*

Acplm Inc ....E 813 633-0548
Tampa *(G-17230)*

Ajax Paving Industries Fla LLC ....B 239 936-9444
Fort Myers *(G-4256)*

Ajax Paving Industries Fla LLC ....B 941 729-5114
Odessa *(G-11831)*

All American Driveway Inc ....E 305 420-5458
Doral *(G-3109)*

Allstate Paving Inc ....D 407 277-5247
Orlando *(G-12098)*

American Sand & Xcavation Inc ....E 850 763-4300
Lynn Haven *(G-8467)*

Anderson Columbia Co Inc ....D 850 526-4440
Marianna *(G-8670)*

Anderson Columbia Co Inc ....B 386 752-7585
Lake City *(G-7511)*

Anderson Columbia Co Inc ....E 352 542-7942
Old Town *(G-11886)*

Andrews Paving Inc ....E 386 462-1115
Gainesville *(G-4836)*

Archer Western Contractors LLC ....D 813 849-7500
Tampa *(G-17301)*

Asphalt Paving Systems Inc ....E 321 632-6552
Rockledge *(G-15333)*

Associated Cnstr Pdts Inc ....D 813 973-4425
Lutz *(G-8430)*

Atlantic Civil Constrs Corp ....E 407 277-8410
Orlando *(G-12148)*

Atlantic Sthern Pav Slcting LL ....E 954 581-5805
Plantation *(G-14604)*

Bella Construction Key W Inc ....E 305 292-9888
Key West *(G-7193)*

Bergeron Land Development Inc ....D 954 680-6100
Fort Lauderdale *(G-3638)*

Better Roads Inc ....E 239 597-2181
Bonita Springs *(G-898)*

Blackrock Milling LLC ....E 813 251-6455
Tampa *(G-17365)*

Blue Ox Enterprises LLC ....D 407 339-4800
Sanford *(G-15921)*

Boykin Construction Inc ....E 352 394-5993
Minneola *(G-10830)*

Brevard Concrete Paving Inc ....E 321 543-0607
Cape Canaveral *(G-1352)*

Brewer Paving & Dev Inc ....D 321 636-4645
Cocoa *(G-1921)*

C & M Road Builders Inc ....C 941 758-1933
Sarasota *(G-16025)*

C W Roberts Contracting Inc ....C 850 785-4675
Panama City *(G-13974)*

Capps Land MGT & Mtl LLC ....E 904 693-8644
Jacksonville *(G-5900)*

Carlo John Inc ....D 239 481-1643
Fort Myers *(G-4301)*

Cemex Materials LLC ....C 407 293-5126
Apopka *(G-162)*

▲ Central Fla Eqp Rentals Inc ....C 305 883-7518
Medley *(G-8713)*

Central Southern Cnstr Corp ....E 904 503-2353
Jacksonville *(G-5925)*

Cheyenne Associates Inc ....E 352 279-2488
Brooksville *(G-1280)*

Chris-Tel Co Southwest Fla Inc ....E 239 226-0500
Fort Myers *(G-4310)*

Ciraco Underground Inc ....D 352 347-2035
Belleview *(G-373)*

City of Riviera Beach ....E 561 845-4076
Riviera Beach *(G-15289)*

▼ Clark Hunt Construction Inc ....E 727 441-1559
Clearwater *(G-1572)*

Cobra Construction Inc ....D 800 697-1724
Boynton Beach *(G-977)*

Community Asphalt Corp ....B 305 829-0700
Hialeah *(G-5245)*

▲ Condotte America Inc ....C 305 670-7585
Medley *(G-8716)*

Cone & Graham Inc ....D 813 623-2856
Tampa *(G-17512)*

Construct Group Corp ....D 305 824-8845
Miami Lakes *(G-10718)*

Construction Svc Co Fla Inc ....E 850 897-8030
Niceville *(G-11443)*

Couch Brick Pavers Inc ....D 727 645-6909
Lutz *(G-8436)*

Cougar Cutting Inc ....D 239 275-9334
Fort Myers *(G-4328)*

Counts Construction Co Inc ....D 352 629-3506
Ocala *(G-11669)*

County of Pinellas ....D 727 464-8900
Clearwater *(G-1591)*

Craggs Construction Co ....D 352 622-7175
Ocala *(G-11670)*

Cronin Construction Corp ....E 407 339-5120
Altamonte Springs *(G-42)*

D&C Parking Lot Maint Inc ....E 407 986-5585
Orlando *(G-12395)*

DAB Constructors Inc ....C 352 447-5488
Inglis *(G-5683)*

Dana Site Dev & Pav Inc ....E 941 722-4913
Palmetto *(G-13910)*

Deeb Construction & Dev Co ....D 727 376-6831
New Port Richey *(G-11371)*

DMS Contractors LLC ....D 305 627-3276
Fort Lauderdale *(G-3761)*

Doug Connor Inc ....D 321 259-8349
Melbourne *(G-8873)*

Downrite Engineering Corp ....B 305 232-2340
Miami *(G-9487)*

Dragados Usa Inc ....D 954 668-2015
Fort Lauderdale *(G-3764)*

Dragados Usa Inc ....D 305 423-7600
Coral Gables *(G-2095)*

Felix Associates Florida Inc ....D 772 220-2722
Stuart *(G-16622)*

Florida Blacktop Inc ....E 954 979-5757
Pompano Beach *(G-14807)*

Florida Dickerson Inc ....C 772 429-4444
Fort Pierce *(G-4701)*

Florida North Construction Inc ....D 850 674-5730
Clarksville *(G-1503)*

Florida Roads Contracting Inc ....C 904 714-0041
Jacksonville *(G-6200)*

Florida Safety Contractors Inc ....E 813 982-9172
Thonotosassa *(G-18673)*

Forrest Excavating Inc ....E 813 336-4999
Odessa *(G-11841)*

Forsberg Construction Inc ....D 941 637-8500
Punta Gorda *(G-15204)*

Frederick Derr and Company Inc ....D 941 355-8575
Sarasota *(G-16171)*

Gac Contractors Inc ....D 850 772-1370
Panama City *(G-14014)*

Gac Contractors Inc ....C 850 785-4675
Panama City *(G-14015)*

Gator Grading & Paving LLC ....E 941 751-3900
Palmetto *(G-13913)*

Genesis Con Structures LLC ....E 904 406-8443
Green Cove Springs *(G-5053)*

Global Contracting Group LLC ....D 352 748-3324
Wildwood *(G-14997)*

◆ Gonzalez & Sons Equipment Inc ......C 305 822-5455
Hialeah *(G-5267)*

Goodson Paving Inc ....E 321 631-5523
Cocoa *(G-1939)*

Goss Foundations Inc ....E 407 831-1690
Altamonte Springs *(G-54)*

Guettler Brothers Cnstr LLC ....E 772 461-8345
Fort Pierce *(G-4708)*

Gulf-Atlantic Constructors Inc ....E 850 477-0588
Pensacola *(G-14320)*

Gum Creek Farms Inc ....E 850 892-0291
Defuniak Springs *(G-2833)*

▼ H & R Paving Inc ....D 305 261-3005
Miami *(G-9673)*

Hale Contracting Inc ....E 850 575-2506
Midway *(G-10802)*

Halifax Paving Inc ....C 386 676-0200
Ormond Beach *(G-13501)*

Hardrives of Delray Inc ....C 561 278-0456
Delray Beach *(G-2963)*

Heaton Brothers Cnstr Co Inc ....E 850 453-1253
Pensacola *(G-14322)*

Heritage Utilities LLC ....D 239 348-2636
Naples *(G-11162)*

Hewitt Contracting Company Inc ....D 352 787-5651
Okahumpka *(G-11861)*

HG Cnstr Dev & Inv Inc ....D 786 845-8999
Miami *(G-9699)*

Highway Safety Devices Inc ....D 813 759-1559
Tampa *(G-17822)*

Hlp Hot-In-Place Paving LLC ....E 727 327-4900
Gulfport *(G-5141)*

Holley Paving LLC ....E 813 968-4200
Tampa *(G-17833)*

Homestead Con & Draing Inc ....E 305 248-9649
Homestead *(G-5580)*

Horizon Contractors Inc ....E 305 828-2050
Hialeah *(G-5275)*

▼ Hubbard Construction Company ......C 407 645-5500
Winter Park *(G-19734)*

Hubbard Construction Company ....C 407 855-3535
Orlando *(G-12668)*

Hubbard Construction Company ....C 904 786-1020
Jacksonville *(G-6303)*

Hubbard Construction Company ....E 813 689-7983
Tampa *(G-17844)*

Hubbard Group Inc ....D 407 645-5500
Winter Park *(G-19735)*

James C Hall Company Inc ....E 407 327-4930
Winter Springs *(G-19806)*

James Construction Group LLC ....C 863 428-2313
Bartow *(G-322)*

Jimmie Crwder Excvtg Land Clri ....C 850 576-7176
Tallahassee *(G-17010)*

Jmhc Inc ....C 407 865-7600
Orlando *(G-12708)*

John C Hipp Cnstr Eqp Co ....E 386 462-2047
Alachua *(G-9)*

Jorgensen Contract Svcs LLC ....B 904 268-0410
Jacksonville *(G-6390)*

Jvd Construction Inc ....E 407 767-8853
Casselberry *(G-1450)*

JW Cheatham LLC ....D 561 471-4100
West Palm Beach *(G-19224)*

Kamminga & Roodvoets Inc ....E 813 623-3031
Tampa *(G-17908)*

Keystone Intrlcking Pav Cntr ....E 239 793-4422
Naples *(G-11190)*

Kodiak Contracting & Dev LLC ....E 407 788-9720
Longwood *(G-8375)*

Landmark Paving LLC ....E 407 359-1172
Oviedo *(G-13555)*

Lead Engineering Contrs LLC ....D 305 615-3272
Miami *(G-9853)*

Leos Concrete Specialties ....D 321 951-7638
Palm Bay *(G-13626)*

Leware Construction Co Fla Inc ....C 352 787-1616
Leesburg *(G-8258)*

M & M Asphalt Maintenance Inc ....D 561 588-0949
Delray Beach *(G-2986)*

M of Tallahassee Inc ....D 850 528-2038
Tallahassee *(G-17028)*

Marks Brothers Inc ....D 305 805-6900
Palmetto Bay *(G-13946)*

Marshall Bros Cnstr Engrg Inc ....E 850 596-4526
Panama City *(G-14041)*

Martin Construction Inc ....C 863 439-4655
Lake Hamilton *(G-7555)*

Masci Corporation ....D 386 322-4111
Port Orange *(G-15081)*

Masci General Contractor Inc ....D 386 322-4500
Port Orange *(G-15082)*

McLeod Land & Equipment Inc ....C 941 355-0784
Sarasota *(G-16041)*

Mercon Construction Company ....E 407 260-6710
Winter Springs *(G-19808)*

Metric Civil Constructors LLC ....E 904 329-3506
Jacksonville *(G-6500)*

Mid State Paving Co Inc ....E 863 965-2861
Auburndale *(G-257)*

Middlesex Asphalt LLC ....C 407 206-0078
Orlando *(G-12866)*

Midsouth Paving Inc ....D 850 433-3001
Pensacola *(G-14365)*

Mill-It Corporation ....E 407 661-1181
Altamonte Springs *(G-78)*

Mora Engineering Contrs Inc ....D 954 752-8065
Casselberry *(G-1452)*

Msb Services LLC ....E 941 747-7100
Bradenton *(G-1149)*

MTM Contractors Inc ....D 727 528-0178
Pinellas Park *(G-14529)*

N W F Contractors Inc ....E 850 862-5376
Fort Walton Beach *(G-4793)*

Nash Plumbing and Mech LLC ....C 352 748-1454
Wildwood *(G-19504)*

Odebrecht Construction Inc ....C 305 341-8800
Coral Gables *(G-2160)*

Orlando Line Striping Sltons LL ....E 407 990-1178
Orlando *(G-12973)*

P & S Paving Inc ....C 386 258-7911
Daytona Beach *(G-2647)*

Panhandle Grading & Paving Inc ....D 850 478-5250
Pensacola *(G-14399)*

Pave-Rite Inc ....E 352 621-1600
Lecanto *(G-8224)*

Pavex Corporation ....E 954 428-8712
Miami *(G-10103)*

PCL ....C 813 264-9500
Tampa *(G-18125)*

PCL Civil Constructors Inc ....E 813 264-9500
Tampa *(G-18126)*

Pcs Civil Inc ....C 813 868-7719
Tampa *(G-18128)*

Peavy & Son Cnstr Co Inc ....D 850 539-5019
Havana *(G-5198)*

Persant Construction Co Inc ....D 305 234-0627
Miami *(G-10112)*

Pfi-Con LLC ....E 813 880-9100
Tampa *(G-18141)*

Phillips & Jordan Inc ....A 813 783-1132
San Antonio *(G-15909)*

Phoenix Construction Svcs Inc ....C 850 265-4210
Lynn Haven *(G-8470)*

Pontchartrain Partners LLC ....D 504 872-3199
Cocoa *(G-1948)*

Poole & Kent Company Florida ....D 305 325-1930
Miami *(G-10134)*

Powers Development Group Inc ....D 904 619-9355
Macclenny *(G-8478)*

Prime Construction Group Inc ....D 407 856-8180
Orlando *(G-13057)*

Properties Elgant Dstnction LL ....D 561 364-9675
Boynton Beach *(G-1029)*

R Cobb Construction Co Inc ....E 727 781-8617
Palm Harbor *(G-13878)*

◆ Ranger Construction Inds Inc ....B 561 793-9400
West Palm Beach *(G-19336)*

Ranger Construction Inds Inc ....D 772 464-6460
Fort Pierce *(G-4732)*

Ranger Construction Inds Inc ....E 321 725-2700
Malabar *(G-8606)*

Ranger Construction Inds Inc ....E 386 761-8383
Daytona Beach *(G-2657)*

Rcs Construction Centl Fla Inc ....E 321 239-4350
Clermont *(G-1884)*

▼ Redland Company Inc ....D 305 247-3226
Homestead *(G-5601)*

RL James Inc General Contr ....D 941 758-8557
Bradenton *(G-1172)*

Roads Inc of Nwf ....C 850 968-0991
Cantonment *(G-1341)*

Roberts and Roberts Inc ....E 850 210-0350
Tallahassee *(G-17088)*

Robinson Industries Inc ....C 305 573-8334
North Miami *(G-11509)*

S Applebaum & Associates Inc ....D 305 836-8678
Miami *(G-10229)*

Safety Contractors Inc ....E 904 355-6331
Jacksonville *(G-6687)*

Salser Construction LLC ....D 352 861-4563
Ocala *(G-11773)*

Sauer Construction LLC ....D 904 262-6444
Jacksonville *(G-6692)*

▲ Signal Group Inc ....E 561 744-3206
Coral Springs *(G-2285)*

Sikes Concrete Inc ....E 850 265-4564
Panama City *(G-14070)*

Smith & Company Inc ....C 772 777-2662
Port Saint Lucie *(G-15166)*

Southeastern Engrg Contrs Inc ....D 305 557-4226
Hialeah *(G-5323)*

Southern Road & Bridge LLC ....C 727 940-5395
Tarpon Springs *(G-18592)*

Southland Construction Inc ....D 407 889-9844
Apopka *(G-212)*

Stage Door II Inc ....E 407 294-8878
Apopka *(G-215)*

Stone Age Pavers Inc ....D 954 380-2392
Pompano Beach *(G-14911)*

Strongcore Group LLC ....D 305 539-0680
South Miami *(G-16519)*

Structral Prsrvtion Systems LL ....D 941 758-9090
Saint Petersburg *(G-15861)*

Suncoast Paving Inc ....E 727 938-2411
Tarpon Springs *(G-18594)*

Superior Cnstr Southeast LLC ....C 904 292-4240
Jacksonville *(G-6818)*

Superior Interlocking Pav Inc ....E 239 593-5077
Naples *(G-11313)*

Surface Management Corporation ....E 904 751-1587
Jacksonville *(G-6819)*

Surfside Pavers Inc ....E 772 770-3890
Vero Beach *(G-18924)*

Tenex Enterprises Inc ....E 954 788-8100
Pompano Beach *(G-14919)*

Terra Excavating Inc ....C 727 497-8106
Saint Petersburg *(G-15874)*

Thad Construction Co Inc ....E 386 253-3963
Daytona Beach *(G-2675)*

The De Moya Group Inc ....D 305 828-9661
Hialeah *(G-5333)*

Total Concrete Repairs Inc ....E 904 768-2700
Jacksonville *(G-6861)*

Traffic Control Devices Inc ....E 407 869-5300
Altamonte Springs *(G-107)*

Transportation Structures Inc ....E 813 899-4411
Tampa *(G-18437)*

▲ Tucker Paving Inc ....E 863 299-2262
Winter Haven *(G-19668)*

Turtle Infrstrcture Prtners LL ....D 727 518-0962
Largo *(G-8157)*

Turtle Southeast LLC ....D 727 518-0962
Largo *(G-8158)*

US Brick & Block Systems Inc ....E 954 792-1312
Dania *(G-2421)*

V A Paving Inc ....E 321 636-2896
Cocoa *(G-1959)*

V E Whitehurst & Sons Inc ....E 352 528-6052
Williston *(G-19515)*

Vallencourt Cnstr Co Inc ....C 904 291-9330
Green Cove Springs *(G-5066)*

Vecellio Group Inc ....D 561 793-2102
Palm Beach *(G-13675)*

VJ Usina Contracting Inc ....D 904 829-6727
Saint Augustine *(G-15511)*

Vos Utility LLC ....E 305 522-5137
Miami *(G-10484)*

Vulcan Group LLC ....D 305 967-6344
Miami *(G-10486)*

W Jackson & Sons Cnstr Co ....C 954 973-3060
Pompano Beach *(G-14940)*

Waterfront Services Inc ....D 561 721-2902
West Palm Beach *(G-19413)*

Watson Construction Co LLC ....E 352 472-9157
Newberry *(G-11434)*

Wdg Construction Inc ....B 317 536-6500
Saint Petersburg *(G-15892)*

Weekley Asphalt Paving Inc ....C 954 680-8005
Southwest Ranches *(G-16531)*

Weitz Company LLC ....A 561 686-5511
West Palm Beach *(G-19415)*

White Construction Company Inc ....D 352 493-1444
Chiefland *(G-1487)*

Williams Paving Co Inc ....D 305 882-1950
Fort Lauderdale *(G-4225)*

Woodruff & Sons Inc ....D 941 756-1871
Bradenton *(G-1207)*

Wpc Management Partners LLC ....C 407 644-8923
Maitland *(G-8602)*

Zahlene Enterprises Inc ....D 305 805-6858
Medley *(G-8801)*

1622 Bridge, Tunnel & Elevated Hwy Construction

Archer Western Contractors LLC ....D 813 849-7500
Tampa *(G-17301)*

◆ Astaldi Construction Corp ....C 954 423-8766
Davie *(G-2459)*

Charley Toppino & Sons Inc ....D 305 296-5606
Key West *(G-7199)*

Charlotte County Seawalls Inc ....E 941 629-4900
Port Charlotte *(G-15026)*

▲ Condotte America Inc ....C 305 670-7585
Medley *(G-8716)*

Cone & Graham Inc ....D 813 623-2856
Tampa *(G-17512)*

Continental Heavy Civil Corp ....C 786 250-5851
Miami *(G-9407)*

Dalco Inc ....D 561 686-3948
West Palm Beach *(G-19116)*

Emr Inc ....E 850 897-0210
Niceville *(G-11446)*

Gosalia Concrete Constrs Inc ....D 813 443-0984
Brandon *(G-1234)*

◆ Hjc Jax Inc ....D 904 355-5885
Jacksonville *(G-6282)*

Johnson Bros Corp A Southland ....A 407 248-9208
Orlando *(G-12710)*

M&J Cnstrction Pnllas Cnty Inc ....E 727 938-6478
Tarpon Springs *(G-18589)*

Misener Marine Inc ....C 813 839-8441
Tampa *(G-18042)*

Mitchell & Stark Cnstr Co Inc ....C 239 597-2165
Naples *(G-11216)*

Odebrecht of America Inc ....D 305 704-5800
Miami *(G-10062)*

▼ Oec Usa Inc ....E 305 341-8800
Miami *(G-10063)*

PCL Civil Constructors Inc ....E 813 264-9500
Tampa *(G-18126)*

Pontchartrain Partners LLC ....D 504 872-3199
Cocoa *(G-1948)*

R B M Contracting Services LLC ....E 850 622-1434
Freeport *(G-4816)*

Ranger Construction Inds Inc ....E 386 761-8383
Daytona Beach *(G-2657)*

Ric-Man Construction Fla Inc ....D 954 426-1221
Deerfield Beach *(G-2788)*

◆ Rizzani De Eccher (usa) Inc ....C 305 866-9917
Bay Harbor Islands *(G-348)*

Sema Construction Inc ....C 407 563-7900
Orlando *(G-13185)*

Skanska USA Cvil Southeast Inc ....C 757 420-4140
Maitland *(G-8577)*

The Murphy Construction Co ....D 561 655-3634
West Palm Beach *(G-19385)*

Zep Construction Inc ....D 239 267-8778
Fort Myers *(G-4666)*

1623 Water, Sewer & Utility Line Construction

Accelrted Cmmnctions Cnstr LLC ....D 850 733-9000
Gulf Breeze *(G-5104)*

Acosta Tractors Inc ....E 305 556-0473
Hialeah *(G-5212)*

ADS Drying Systems LLC ....D 888 898-0699
Tampa *(G-17238)*

Advanced Communications Tech ....E 561 771-6677
Jupiter *(G-7045)*

Advanced Pace Technologies LLC ....E 352 593-5140
Clermont *(G-1856)*

AJ Johns Inc ....D 904 641-2055
Jacksonville *(G-5759)*

Allstate Paving Inc ....D 407 277-5247
Orlando *(G-12098)*

American Civil Construction ....E 386 847-3079
Bunnell *(G-1321)*

American Metering Services Inc ....E 941 358-1253
Sarasota *(G-16021)*

American Prsian Engners Cnstrs ....E 407 522-0530
Orlando *(G-12115)*

American Sand & Xcavation Inc ....E 850 763-4300
Lynn Haven *(G-8467)*

Andrew Site Work LLC ....E 239 226-1606
Fort Myers *(G-4276)*

Andrews Paving Inc ....E 386 462-1115
Gainesville *(G-4836)*

Atlantic Development Cocoa Inc ....E 321 639-8788
Cocoa *(G-1915)*

Atlantic Tower Services Inc ....D 407 423-9071
Orlando *(G-12150)*

Atlas Solutions Inc ....D 941 812-1764
Bradenton *(G-1054)*

Bcl Civil Contractors Inc ....E 850 871-1516
Panama City *(G-13968)*

▲ Belvedere Contracting Inc ....E 561 747-6637
Jupiter *(G-7050)*

Blue Ox Land Services Inc ....C 407 339-4800
Sanford *(G-15922)*

Blue Streak LLC ....D 786 615-3693
Miami *(G-9261)*

Bore Tech Utilities & Maint ....D 305 297-8162
Miami *(G-9269)*

Boykin Construction Inc ....E 352 394-5993
Minneola *(G-10830)*

Cabana Construction Co Inc ....E 239 332-1665
Fort Myers *(G-4298)*

Capps Land MGT & Mtl LLC ....E 904 693-8644
Jacksonville *(G-5900)*

Centerline Utilities Inc ....C 561 689-3917
Palm City *(G-13785)*

Central Fla Excvtg & Fill Dirt ....D 813 757-6783
Saint Petersburg *(G-15619)*

Central Florida Undgrd Inc ....D 407 260-9000
Altamonte Springs *(G-34)*

Central Southern Cnstr Corp ....E 904 503-2353
Jacksonville *(G-5925)*

Company	Code	Phone
Certified Envmtl Svcs Inc Jacksonville (G-5929)	D	904 695-1911
Chaz Equipment Company Inc Wellington (G-18976)	E	561 333-2109
City of Boca Raton Boca Raton (G-511)	D	561 338-7309
City of Deerfield Beach Deerfield Beach (G-2724)	C	954 480-4270
City of Miami Beach Miami Beach (G-10572)	C	305 673-7080
City of North Port North Port (G-11567)	D	941 426-9500
City of Palm Bay Palm Bay (G-13615)	D	321 952-3400
▼ Clark Hunt Construction Inc Clearwater (G-1572)	E	727 441-1559
Construction Svc Co Fla Inc Niceville (G-11443)	E	850 897-8030
Core & Main Inc Lakeland (G-7845)	B	863 868-8279
County of Martin Stuart (G-16612)	D	772 221-1442
Coventina - Pttg Jv LLC Riverview (G-15253)	C	813 509-0669
Cronin Construction Corp Altamonte Springs (G-42)	E	407 339-5120
D & L Telecommunications LLC Pompano Beach (G-14792)	E	954 941-7288
Dalco Inc West Palm Beach (G-19116)	D	561 686-3948
Dallas 1 Corporation Thonotosassa (G-18671)	C	813 986-1922
Danella Cnstr Corp FL Inc Melbourne (G-8864)	D	321 253-6136
Danella Utility Cnstr Inc West Palm Beach (G-19117)	D	561 327-5320
David Mancini & Sons Inc Pompano Beach (G-14793)	D	954 977-3556
David Nelson Construction Co Palm Harbor (G-13859)	C	727 784-7624
DBE Management Inc Loxahatchee (G-8421)	C	561 508-3708
Deeb Construction & Dev Co New Port Richey (G-11371)	D	727 376-6831
Dejonge Excavating Contrs Inc Venice (G-18777)	E	941 485-7799
Deme Construction LLC Sarasota (G-16030)	E	941 755-5900
Dewitt Excavation LLC Winter Garden (G-19565)	C	407 656-1799
Dns Contracting LLC Jacksonville (G-6075)	D	904 724-6430
Don Luchetti Construction Inc Melbourne (G-8872)	E	321 779-8681
Downrite Engineering Corp Miami (G-9487)	B	305 232-2340
Dp Development LLC Palm Springs (G-13891)	E	561 650-1333
Draftpros LLC Miami Lakes (G-10723)	C	786 641-5131
Ds Boring LLC Odessa (G-11838)	E	813 920-8610
Dycom Industries Inc Palm Beach Gardens (G-13722)	E	561 627-7171
EM Entps Gen Contrs Inc Tampa (G-17626)	E	813 241-9000
Emr Inc Niceville (G-11446)	E	850 897-0210
Equix Energy Services LLC Midway (G-10800)	C	850 878-1212
Fairwind Inc Orlando (G-12487)	D	281 812-4150
Felix Associates Florida Inc Stuart (G-16622)	D	772 220-2722
Fh Construction Marion LLC Ocala (G-11680)	D	352 236-3355
Fishel Company Plant City (G-14556)	D	813 764-0256
Florida All Site & Utilities Jacksonville (G-6187)	D	904 268-1811
Florida Gas & Electric Corp Dade City (G-2385)	D	813 996-0019
◆ Florida Keys Elc Coop Assn Inc Tavernier (G-18624)	D	305 852-2431
Florida North Construction Inc Clarksville (G-1503)	E	850 674-5730
Forsberg Construction Inc Punta Gorda (G-15204)	D	941 637-8500
General Contracting Svcs Inc Port Charlotte (G-15037)	E	941 697-2047
▼ Genesis Water Technologies Inc Maitland (G-8535)	D	321 280-2742
▲ Globetec Construction LLC Pompano Beach (G-14816)	C	305 599-1800
Goff Communications Inc Sarasota (G-16035)	E	941 955-7106
◆ Gonzalez & Sons Equipment Inc Hialeah (G-5267)	C	305 822-5455
Goodson Paving Inc Cocoa (G-1939)	E	321 631-5523
Gossamer Crossing Inc Vero Beach (G-18859)		916 335-8018
Guettler Brothers Cnstr LLC Fort Pierce (G-4708)	E	772 461-8345
Gulf Coast Underground Inc Fort Myers (G-4429)	E	239 274-9504
Gulf Coast Utility Contrs LLC Panama City (G-14023)	D	850 265-9166
Gulfcoast Boring Pipeline Inc Lakeland (G-7880)	E	863 686-2263
Gulfcoast Utility Constrs Inc Saint Petersburg (G-15701)	E	727 328-7882
Haleakala Construction Inc Naples (G-11152)	D	239 598-1968
Harty Tractor Services Inc Orange City (G-11966)	E	386 775-1005
Haskell Company Inc Jacksonville (G-6262)	B	904 791-4500
Haskins Inc Bonita Springs (G-919)	E	239 947-1846
Hawkins Tommy Sons Pav Contrs Fort Pierce (G-4710)	E	772 464-7587
Hazen Construction LLC New Smyrna Beach (G-11417)	D	386 322-8700
Heart Utlties Jacksonville Inc Jacksonville (G-6272)	E	904 695-3383
Heliservice LLC Apopka (G-187)	E	407 964-1070
HG Cnstr Dev & Inv Inc Miami (G-9699)	D	786 845-8999
Horizon Contractors Inc Hialeah (G-5275)	E	305 828-2050
Hubbard Construction Company Orlando (G-12668)	C	407 855-3535
▼ Hubbard Construction Company Winter Park (G-19734)	C	407 645-5500
Hubbard Group Inc Winter Park (G-19735)	D	407 645-5500
▼ International Underground Corp Jacksonville (G-6329)	E	904 353-0050
Irby Construction Company Longwood (G-8370)	D	407 696-4999
Ivy H Smith Company LLC Orlando (G-12692)	D	407 855-1801
J B Coxwell Contracting Inc Jacksonville (G-6336)	C	904 786-1120
Jackson Land Development LLC Pompano Beach (G-14830)	E	954 973-3060
▲ Jacksonville Electric Auth Jacksonville (G-6353)	A	904 665-6000
Jade Communications Inc Boca Raton (G-647)	E	561 997-8552
▼ Jeffry Knight Inc Clearwater (G-1683)	E	727 524-6235
Jensen Undgrd Utilities Inc Naples (G-11182)	C	239 597-0060
Jmhc Inc Orlando (G-12708)	C	407 865-7600
Johnson - Davis Incorporated Lantana (G-8065)	C	561 588-1170
Johnson Bros Corp A Southland Lake Worth (G-7738)	A	813 643-3459
Johnson Bros Corp A Southland Orlando (G-12710)	A	407 248-9208
Jvs Contracting Inc Tampa (G-17904)	C	813 514-8229
Jwj Inc Ocala (G-11703)	E	352 732-0550
KDI Underground and Dev Inc Sebring (G-16405)	D	863 385-8834
Kearney Construction Co LLC Riverview (G-15259)	B	813 621-0855
Killebrew Inc Lakeland (G-7897)	E	863 701-0273
Kimmins Contracting Corp Tampa (G-17923)	B	813 248-3878
Kline Construction Co Inc Saint Augustine (G-15460)	E	609 652-0929
L & R Contracting Inc Panama City (G-14033)	E	850 784-9979
Landmasters Development Inc Melbourne (G-8920)	E	321 724-1697
M of Tallahassee Inc Tallahassee (G-17028)	D	850 528-2038
Maj Contracting Inc Fort Myers (G-4500)	E	239 332-7989
Makotek Inc Longwood (G-8378)	D	407 521-0402
Marshall Bros Cnstr Engrg Inc Panama City (G-14041)	E	850 596-4526
Masci Corporation Port Orange (G-15081)	D	386 322-4111
Masci General Contractor Inc Port Orange (G-15082)	D	386 322-4500
▲ Mastec Inc Coral Gables (G-2138)	C	305 599-1800
Mastec International Holding Coral Gables (G-2139)		305 599-1800
Mastec North America Inc Tampa (G-17999)	E	813 621-0881
Mastec North America Inc Coral Gables (G-2142)	C	305 599-1800
Mastec North America Inc Pensacola (G-14353)	D	850 478-6227
Mastec North America Inc Tallahassee (G-17036)	B	850 562-2135
Mercon Construction Company Winter Springs (G-19808)	E	407 260-6710
Metric Civil Constructors LLC Jacksonville (G-6500)	E	904 329-3506
Metro Equipment Service Inc Miami (G-9945)	E	305 740-3303
Mid State Paving Co Inc Auburndale (G-257)	C	863 965-2861
Miller Pipeline LLC Ocala (G-11734)	D	352 236-3355
Mitchell & Stark Cnstr Co Inc Naples (G-11216)	C	239 597-2165
Mora Engineering Contrs Inc Casselberry (G-1452)	D	954 752-8065
Multiband Engrg Wrless Ssthat Sarasota (G-16241)	B	941 378-0080
Noble Resources Corporation Clearwater (G-1739)	E	813 241-6968
Partridge Well Drilling Co Inc Jacksonville (G-6581)	D	904 355-3323
Pepper Contracting Svcs Inc Clearwater (G-1756)	C	813 868-7719
Persant Construction Co Inc Miami (G-10112)	D	305 234-0627
Petroleum and Cnstr Svcs Inc Pompano Beach (G-14876)	E	954 942-1117
▼ Phoenix Products Inc Jacksonville (G-6599)	D	904 354-1858
Pipeline Contractors Inc Starke (G-16580)	E	904 964-2019
Pipeline Distribution Inc Plantation (G-14694)	E	954 816-3164
Pipeline Utilities Inc West Palm Beach (G-19326)	C	561 842-8833
Pontchartrain Partners LLC Cocoa (G-1948)	E	504 872-3199
Powers Development Group Inc Macclenny (G-8478)	D	904 619-9355
Prime Construction Group Inc Orlando (G-13057)	D	407 856-8180
Prince Land Inc Jupiter (G-7126)	D	561 320-9969
Quality Cable Contractors Inc Orlando (G-13077)	E	407 246-0606
Rainey Construction Company Wildwood (G-19508)	B	352 748-0955
Ram-Tech Construction Inc Homestead (G-5600)	E	305 259-7853
Rcs Construction Centl Fla Inc Clermont (G-1884)	E	321 239-4350
Ric-Man Construction Fla Inc Deerfield Beach (G-2788)	D	954 426-1221
Ric-Man International Inc Pompano Beach (G-14884)	E	954 426-1042
Rio-Bak Corporation Wellington (G-18988)	D	561 791-9721
Ripa & Associates LLC Tampa (G-18226)	D	813 623-6777
Rohl Networks LP Jupiter (G-7136)	E	561 316-2290
Rowland Inc Pinellas Park (G-14534)	D	727 545-3815
Ryan Incorporated Southern Deerfield Beach (G-2791)	D	954 427-5599

Sandco Inc ....C...... 850 402-1111 Tallahassee *(G-17092)*	▲ American Engineering Pdts Corp ......D...... 305 825-9800 Hialeah *(G-5216)*	◆ Hi-Tide Sales Inc ....E...... 772 461-4660 Fort Pierce *(G-4711)*
Service Electric Company ....D...... 352 431-3648 Leesburg *(G-8273)*	American Sand & Xcavation Inc ....E...... 850 763-4300 Lynn Haven *(G-8467)*	◆ Hjc Jax Inc ....D...... 904 355-5885 Jacksonville *(G-6282)*
Shenandoah General Cnstr LLC ....E...... 954 975-0098 Pompano Beach *(G-14897)*	American Track Generations LLC ....D...... 863 425-4561 Mulberry *(G-10968)*	Hydro Rock Company Inc ....E...... 239 267-5300 Fort Myers *(G-4446)*
Smart Comm Systems LLC ....B...... 813 325-3267 Apollo Beach *(G-140)*	Armond Cassil RR Cnstr Inc ....E...... 586 754-4200 Jacksonville *(G-5807)*	Interrail Signal Incorporated ....D...... 904 268-6411 Jacksonville *(G-6330)*
Sol Florida Systems Inc ....E...... 305 262-8404 Doral *(G-3315)*	Bellingham Marine Inds Inc ....E...... 904 358-3362 Jacksonville *(G-5855)*	▲ Jackson-Cook Lc ....E...... 850 576-4187 Tallahassee *(G-17009)*
Solomon Construction Co Quincy ....E...... 561 349-5715 Delray Beach *(G-3018)*	Bergeron Land Development Inc ....D...... 954 680-6100 Fort Lauderdale *(G-3638)*	Jasper Steward LLC ....E...... 754 600-9127 Pembroke Pines *(G-14157)*
Spectrum Underground Inc ....E...... 941 342-6708 Sarasota *(G-16328)*	Blue Goose Construction LLC ....D...... 772 461-3020 Fort Pierce *(G-4684)*	Jcal Holdings LLC ....E...... 561 687-5005 Lake Worth Beach *(G-7770)*
Spivey Utility Construction Co ....D...... 813 926-8846 Odessa *(G-11856)*	Blue Goose Growers LLC ....D...... 772 461-3020 Fort Pierce *(G-4685)*	JEI Site Development Inc ....E...... 407 673-0011 Winter Park *(G-19741)*
Stage Door II Inc ....E...... 407 294-8878 Apopka *(G-215)*	Brasfield & Gorrie LLC ....E...... 407 562-4500 Winter Park *(G-19688)*	Jimmie Crwder Excvtg Land Clri ....C...... 850 576-7176 Tallahassee *(G-17010)*
Stevens & Layton Inc ....D...... 239 693-1400 Fort Myers *(G-4607)*	Bul-Hed Corporation ....E...... 863 804-0044 Bartow *(G-313)*	Jims Log & Land Clearing Inc ....D...... 407 349-0206 Geneva *(G-5035)*
Sullivan Bros Inc ....D...... 561 848-5536 Riviera Beach *(G-15321)*	Caladesi Construction Co ....E...... 727 585-9945 Largo *(G-8084)*	Johnson Bros Corp A Southland ....A...... 407 248-9208 Orlando *(G-12710)*
Sunshine Land Design Inc ....C...... 772 283-2648 Stuart *(G-16673)*	Cardinal Contractors Inc ....E...... 941 377-8555 Bradenton *(G-1071)*	Jon M Hall Company LLC ....D...... 407 215-0410 Sanford *(G-15955)*
Symx Infrastructure LLC ....C...... 305 442-8577 Coral Gables *(G-2192)*	Certified Constrs Svcs Inc ....B...... 850 682-8953 Crestview *(G-2313)*	Jr Davis Construction Co Inc ....A...... 407 870-0066 Kissimmee *(G-7334)*
T & T Pipeline Co Inc ....E...... 407 290-5509 Orlando *(G-13264)*	Charlotte County Seawalls Inc ....E...... 941 629-4900 Port Charlotte *(G-15026)*	KDI Underground and Dev Inc ....D...... 863 385-8834 Sebring *(G-16405)*
T B Landmark Construction Inc ....D...... 904 751-1016 Jacksonville *(G-6826)*	City of Hollywood ....E...... 954 921-3288 Hollywood *(G-5414)*	Keller North America Inc ....D...... 727 572-7740 Clearwater *(G-1693)*
Taylor Industrial Cnstr Inc ....E...... 386 792-3060 Live Oak *(G-8320)*	City of Tampa ....E...... 813 259-1693 Tampa *(G-17480)*	Kelly Brothers Inc ....E...... 239 482-7300 Fort Myers *(G-4458)*
Terra Excavating Inc ....C...... 727 497-8106 Saint Petersburg *(G-15874)*	Conch Republic Marine LLC ....D...... 305 439-0202 Key Largo *(G-7173)*	Landform Central Florida Inc ....E...... 407 298-3036 Orlando *(G-12751)*
Thad Construction Co Inc ....D...... 386 253-3963 Daytona Beach *(G-2675)*	Construction Svc Co Fla Inc ....E...... 850 897-8030 Niceville *(G-11443)*	Landirr Incorporated ....D...... 407 330-2892 Sanford *(G-15960)*
Tim-Prep Inc ....E...... 904 289-7000 Jacksonville *(G-6854)*	Continental Heavy Civil Corp ....C...... 786 250-5851 Miami *(G-9407)*	Lee Mar Building & Cnstr Corp ....E...... 239 481-2613 Fort Myers *(G-4478)*
Total Concrete Repairs Inc ....E...... 904 768-2700 Jacksonville *(G-6861)*	County of Brevard ....D...... 321 255-4400 Melbourne *(G-8856)*	Lopefra Corp ....D...... 305 266-3896 Doral *(G-3263)*
Trawick Construction Co LLC ....C...... 850 638-0429 Chipley *(G-1494)*	Cronin Construction Corp ....E...... 407 339-5120 Altamonte Springs *(G-42)*	Lowell Dunn Company ....E...... 305 821-8300 Hialeah Gardens *(G-5345)*
Underground Utilities Group ....E...... 239 334-4427 Fort Myers *(G-4634)*	David Barron Land Dev Inc ....C...... 239 425-0260 Fort Myers *(G-4340)*	▼ Ls Energia Inc ....E...... 954 281-7022 Plantation *(G-14668)*
United Brothers Dev Corp ....D...... 904 262-3227 Jacksonville *(G-6884)*	DB Construction Services Inc ....D...... 813 248-6358 Tampa *(G-17576)*	M of Tallahassee Inc ....E...... 850 528-2038 Tallahassee *(G-17028)*
US Water Services Corp ....D...... 727 848-8292 New Port Richey *(G-11408)*	Deme Construction LLC ....E...... 941 755-5900 Sarasota *(G-16030)*	Maccurrach Golf Cnstr Inc ....C...... 904 646-1581 Jacksonville *(G-6458)*
USA Strctral Stl Fndations Inc ....E...... 941 747-7038 Sarasota *(G-16068)*	Dixie Industrial LLC ....D...... 904 781-9500 Jacksonville *(G-6073)*	Manson Construction Co ....D...... 206 762-0850 Jacksonville *(G-6465)*
▲ Utility Board of The Cy Key W ....D...... 305 295-1000 Key West *(G-7255)*	Dobsons Woods and Water Inc ....E...... 407 841-0030 Ocoee *(G-11811)*	Marine Contracting Group Inc ....E...... 941 505-0221 Punta Gorda *(G-15213)*
Utility Service Co Inc ....E...... 850 932-5342 Gulf Breeze *(G-5138)*	Don Luchetti Construction Inc ....E...... 321 779-8681 Melbourne *(G-8872)*	Marks Brothers Inc ....D...... 305 805-6900 Palmetto Bay *(G-13946)*
Vallencourt Cnstr Co Inc ....C...... 904 291-9330 Green Cove Springs *(G-5066)*	Doug Connor Inc ....E...... 321 259-8349 Melbourne *(G-8873)*	Martin Construction Inc ....E...... 863 439-4655 Lake Hamilton *(G-7555)*
VJ Usina Contracting Inc ....D...... 904 829-6727 Saint Augustine *(G-15511)*	Duncan Swall Dock Boat Lift LL ....D...... 941 954-1555 Sarasota *(G-16143)*	Meadors Construction Co Inc ....D...... 904 695-9290 Jacksonville *(G-6487)*
Vos Utility LLC ....E...... 305 522-5137 Miami *(G-10484)*	Earthworks Northeast Fla Inc ....E...... 904 653-2800 Macclenny *(G-8476)*	Mercon Construction Company ....E...... 407 260-6710 Winter Springs *(G-19808)*
W C Roese Contracting Inc ....D...... 813 628-4395 Tampa *(G-18516)*	▼ Ebsary Foundation Co ....D...... 305 325-0530 Miami *(G-9499)*	▼ Messier Land Developing Inc ....E...... 561 616-9819 West Palm Beach *(G-19265)*
W Jackson & Sons Cnstr Co ....C...... 954 973-3060 Pompano Beach *(G-14940)*	Ecosystem Technologies Inc ....D...... 239 337-5310 Fort Myers *(G-4351)*	Metric Civil Constructors LLC ....E...... 904 329-3506 Jacksonville *(G-6500)*
Watson Construction Co LLC ....E...... 352 472-9157 Newberry *(G-11434)*	Ehc Inc ....E...... 239 254-6050 Fort Myers *(G-4355)*	Metro Service Group Inc ....D...... 504 520-8331 Pensacola *(G-14364)*
Wdg Construction Inc ....B...... 317 536-6500 Saint Petersburg *(G-15892)*	Florida Floats Inc ....C...... 904 358-3362 Jacksonville *(G-6192)*	Midcoast Cnstr Entps LLC ....E...... 813 855-7900 Tarpon Springs *(G-18590)*
Westra Construction Corp ....C...... 941 721-0862 Palmetto *(G-13937)*	Gac Contractors Inc ....D...... 850 772-1370 Panama City *(G-14014)*	Misener Marine Inc ....C...... 813 839-8441 Tampa *(G-18042)*
Woodruff & Sons Inc ....C...... 941 756-1871 Bradenton *(G-1207)*	Glenn T Warren & Company Inc ....E...... 850 674-8159 Blountstown *(G-385)*	Mora Engineering Contrs Inc ....D...... 954 752-8065 Casselberry *(G-1452)*
Wpc Industrial Contractors LLC ....E...... 904 268-0099 Jacksonville *(G-6945)*	▲ Globaltech Inc ....E...... 561 997-6433 Boca Raton *(G-609)*	Orion Marine Construction Inc ....D...... 813 839-8441 Tampa *(G-18106)*
▼ Young & Son Inc ....D...... 850 729-1321 Niceville *(G-11460)*	Grade Services Incorporated ....D...... 941 729-2292 Palmetto *(G-13915)*	◆ Orion Marine Construction Inc ....E...... 813 839-8441 Tampa *(G-18107)*
Youngs Communications Co Inc ....D...... 321 723-6025 Melbourne *(G-9011)*	Greenpoint Inc ....E...... 904 429-9781 Saint Augustine *(G-15447)*	Overland Contracting Inc ....B...... 919 329-8449 Sebastian *(G-16374)*
Zahlene Enterprises Inc ....E...... 305 805-6858 Medley *(G-8801)*	Grundy Marine Construction Co ....E...... 904 738-8717 Ponte Vedra Beach *(G-14984)*	Persant Construction Co Inc ....D...... 305 234-0627 Miami *(G-10112)*
Zorrn Company Inc ....E...... 352 236-4550 Ocala *(G-11800)*	Harrack Trckg Land Claring Inc ....E...... 321 638-4636 Cocoa *(G-1940)*	Pga Tour National Headquarters ....D...... 904 285-3700 Ponte Vedra Beach *(G-15000)*
1629 Heavy Construction, NEC	Harty Tractor Services Inc ....E...... 386 775-1005 Orange City *(G-11966)*	Powers Development Group Inc ....D...... 904 619-9355 Macclenny *(G-8478)*
Acosta Tractors Inc ....E...... 305 556-0473 Hialeah *(G-5212)*	Hendry Corporation ....D...... 813 241-9206 Tampa *(G-17815)*	Q & Q Inc ....E...... 863 665-6197 Lakeland *(G-7947)*
AJ Johns Inc ....D...... 904 641-2055 Jacksonville *(G-5759)*	Herzog Contracting Corp ....C...... 816 233-9001 Melbourne *(G-8904)*	R B M Contracting Services LLC ....E...... 850 622-1434 Freeport *(G-4816)*
▲ Allen Concrete & Masonry Inc ....C...... 239 566-1661 Naples *(G-11006)*	Hewitt Contracting Company Inc ....D...... 352 787-5651 Okahumpka *(G-11861)*	Ranger Construction Inds Inc ....C...... 386 761-8383 Daytona Beach *(G-2657)*

Ridgdill & Son Inc ... E ... 863 983-3136
Clewiston *(G-1907)*
Rio-Bak Corporation ... D ... 561 791-9721
Wellington *(G-18988)*
RTD Construction Inc ... D ... 813 783-9119
Zephyrhills *(G-19848)*
RW Summers RR Contr Inc ... D ... 863 533-8107
Bartow *(G-334)*
▲ Ryan Incorporated Mining ... D ... 954 427-5599
Deerfield Beach *(G-2790)*
Ryangolf Corporation ... E ... 954 571-2088
Deerfield Beach *(G-2792)*
Sandco Inc ... C ... 850 402-1111
Tallahassee *(G-17092)*
Sarasota Land Services Inc ... E ... 941 744-0211
Bradenton *(G-1175)*
Sawcross Inc ... E ... 904 751-7500
Jacksonville *(G-6695)*
◆ Scanship Americas Inc ... E ... 954 651-6205
Davie *(G-2513)*
Scottsdale Co ... E ... 239 261-6100
Naples *(G-11295)*
SE Cline Construction Inc ... D ... 386 446-6426
Palm Coast *(G-13839)*
Sean M Gerrits Inc ... E ... 352 795-7170
Crystal River *(G-2352)*
◆ Shoreline Foundation Inc ... C ... 954 985-0981
West Park *(G-19434)*
Siemens Energy Inc ... E ... 941 807-2847
Lakewood Ranch *(G-8032)*
◆ Siemens Generation Services Co ... C ... 407 736-2000
Orlando *(G-13196)*
Skanska USA Cvil Southeast Inc ... D ... 757 420-4140
Maitland *(G-8577)*
Smith & Company Inc ... C ... 772 777-2662
Port Saint Lucie *(G-15166)*
South East Indus Sls & Svc Inc ... D ... 813 247-2780
Apollo Beach *(G-141)*
▲ Southeastern Cnstr & Maint Inc ... C ... 863 428-1511
Mulberry *(G-10982)*
Standard Concrete Products Inc ... C ... 813 831-9520
Tampa *(G-18328)*
Superior Golf Concepts Inc ... E ... 561 744-6536
Jupiter *(G-7142)*
Superior Ldscpg & Lawn Svc Inc ... D ... 305 634-0717
Miami *(G-10351)*
Thad Construction Co Inc ... E ... 386 253-3963
Daytona Beach *(G-2675)*
The Murphy Construction Co ... D ... 561 655-3634
West Palm Beach *(G-19385)*
TLC Diversified Inc ... E ... 941 722-0621
Palmetto *(G-13934)*
◆ Total Golf Construction Inc ... E ... 772 562-1177
Vero Beach *(G-18927)*
Underwater Mechanix Svcs LLC ... D ... 913 909-8874
Jacksonville *(G-6882)*
Vallencourt Cnstr Co Inc ... C ... 904 291-9330
Green Cove Springs *(G-5066)*
VJ Usina Contracting Inc ... D ... 904 829-6727
Saint Augustine *(G-15511)*
Walbridge Aldinger LLC ... C ... 813 622-8900
Tampa *(G-18518)*
▼ Waterfront Property Svcs LLC ... D ... 727 527-1300
Clearwater *(G-1836)*
Watson Construction Co LLC ... E ... 352 472-9157
Newberry *(G-11434)*
Wdg Construction Inc ... B ... 317 536-6500
Saint Petersburg *(G-15892)*
Whites Site Development Inc ... D ... 407 302-1549
Sanford *(G-15994)*
Williamson Sons Mar Cnstr Inc ... E ... 239 283-0341
Cape Coral *(G-1435)*
▼ Wog Technologies Inc ... D ... 561 429-6889
Greenacres *(G-5082)*
WPC Industrial Contractors ... E ... 904 268-0099
Jacksonville *(G-6944)*
Xgd Systems LLC ... D ... 772 286-3419
Stuart *(G-16681)*
Xorail Inc ... C ... 904 443-0083
Jacksonville *(G-6949)*
Zahlene Enterprises Inc ... E ... 305 805-6858
Medley *(G-8801)*

17 CONSTRUCTION-SPECIAL TRADE CONTRACTORS

1711 Plumbing, Heating & Air Conditioning Contractors

15 Lightyears Inc ... E ... 855 438-1515
Longwood *(G-8333)*
1st Fire & Security ... E ... 772 794-2220
Vero Beach *(G-18826)*
5 Star Refrigeration & AC Inc ... C ... 352 345-4813
Brooksville *(G-1262)*
A & P Air Conditioning Corp ... D ... 305 556-7849
Hialeah *(G-5211)*
A/C Warehouse Inc ... D ... 941 753-1651
Bradenton *(G-1049)*
AA Advance Air Inc ... C ... 954 742-3553
Pompano Beach *(G-14730)*
Able Air Inc ... D ... 321 242-7400
Melbourne *(G-8804)*
ACR Sales and Service Inc ... E ... 407 299-9190
Apopka *(G-146)*
▲ Acres & Son Plumbing Inc ... E ... 239 597-5031
Naples *(G-10998)*
Acres & Son Plumbing Inc ... D ... 239 598-0800
Naples *(G-10999)*
Action Cooling & Heating Inc ... E ... 239 768-7005
Fort Myers *(G-4249)*
Advanced Air and Rfrgn Inc ... E ... 239 768-5558
Fort Myers *(G-4251)*
Advanced Mechanical Services ... E ... 407 291-3199
Orlando *(G-12057)*
Advanced Refrigeration & A Inc ... C ... 407 679-0644
Orlando *(G-12058)*
Advanced Refrigeration & A Inc ... E ... 407 679-0644
Oldsmar *(G-11890)*
Advanced Roofing Inc ... D ... 813 885-5811
Tampa *(G-17241)*
Advanced Systems Inc ... E ... 954 921-2224
Hollywood *(G-5387)*
Advantage Plumbing Inc ... E ... 407 323-7515
Longwood *(G-8336)*
Air Cndtioning By Wiegold Sons ... D ... 239 597-8774
Naples *(G-11004)*
Air Design Systems Inc ... D ... 850 434-5592
Pensacola *(G-14213)*
Air Flow Designs Inc ... D ... 904 276-4060
Jacksonville *(G-5756)*
Air Flow Designs Inc ... D ... 813 962-2797
Tampa *(G-17252)*
Air Flow Designs Inc ... E ... 407 831-3600
Casselberry *(G-1440)*
Air Masters Tampa Bay Inc ... D ... 813 234-2419
Tampa *(G-17254)*
Air Mechanical & Service Corp ... C ... 813 875-0782
Tampa *(G-17255)*
Airite Air Conditioning Inc ... E ... 813 886-0235
Tampa *(G-17257)*
Airstron Inc ... E ... 813 309-2514
Tampa *(G-17258)*
Airstron Inc ... D ... 954 923-1654
Fort Lauderdale *(G-3585)*
Aknew2 Inc ... D ... 813 623-5818
Tampa *(G-17261)*
All American Facility Maint ... D ... 954 322-9909
Sunrise *(G-16734)*
All Fire Services Inc ... D ... 954 367-3607
Hollywood *(G-5390)*
▼ All Weather Contractors Inc ... D ... 904 781-7060
Jacksonville *(G-5767)*
▼ All Year Cooling and Htg Inc ... D ... 888 829-6391
Coral Springs *(G-2224)*
Alta Refrigeration Inc ... D ... 863 619-7101
Lakeland *(G-7794)*
◆ Alternate Energy Tech LLC ... E ... 904 297-9369
Green Cove Springs *(G-5046)*
American Air & Heat Inc ... E ... 407 359-9501
Oviedo *(G-13540)*
American Fire Sprnklr Svcs LLC ... E ... 305 628-0100
Miami Gardens *(G-10678)*
American Plumbing Sarasota Inc ... D ... 941 377-4010
Sarasota *(G-16086)*
American Rsdntial Svcs Ind Inc ... B ... 305 235-7223
Cutler Bay *(G-2358)*
◆ Anchor Tampa Inc ... D ... 813 879-8685
Tampa *(G-17286)*
Anthony Torri Plumbing Inc ... D ... 352 330-5900
Wildwood *(G-19490)*
Aqua Services Inc ... D ... 941 366-7676
Sarasota *(G-16092)*

Arnett Heating & AC Inc ... E ... 904 829-3071
Saint Augustine *(G-15425)*
Arrow Plumbing Corporation ... E ... 941 365-0778
Sarasota *(G-16093)*
Arrow Plumbing Services LLC ... E ... 941 365-0778
Sarasota *(G-16094)*
ARS ... D ... 813 623-2665
Tampa *(G-17308)*
ARS of Florida Inc ... E ... 561 744-8458
Lake Worth Beach *(G-7764)*
Arthur A Schleman Plbg Co Inc ... E ... 813 971-7619
Tampa *(G-17309)*
Aspen Air Conditioning Inc ... D ... 561 395-1500
Boca Raton *(G-428)*
Atlantic Key Energy LLC ... C ... 407 988-0273
Orlando *(G-12149)*
Averett Septic Tank Co Inc ... E ... 863 665-1748
Lakeland *(G-7806)*
Avis Plumbing and AC Inc ... E ... 239 542-4421
Cape Coral *(G-1377)*
Aztil Inc ... D ... 561 433-2197
West Palm Beach *(G-19046)*
B & C Fire Safety Inc ... E ... 850 862-7812
Fort Walton Beach *(G-4753)*
B & I Contractors Inc ... C ... 239 332-4646
Fort Myers *(G-4286)*
Babes Plumbing ... E ... 941 488-2402
Nokomis *(G-11461)*
Balanced Mechanical Svcs LLC ... E ... 352 351-5560
Ocala *(G-11636)*
Barker Electric AC & Htg Inc ... D ... 772 562-2103
Vero Beach *(G-18839)*
Bay Climate Ctrl & Rfrgn LLC ... E ... 850 797-5918
Niceville *(G-11440)*
Bayonet Plbg Htg Ar-Cndtning L ... D ... 727 868-4636
Hudson *(G-5629)*
Bayou Mechanical Inc ... C ... 850 682-2784
Crestview *(G-2311)*
Bch Mechanical LLC ... C ... 727 546-3561
Largo *(G-8083)*
BCI Mechanical Inc ... D ... 321 726-8000
Melbourne *(G-8825)*
Bcl Civil Contractors Inc ... E ... 850 871-1516
Panama City *(G-13968)*
Bears Plumbing South Fla Inc ... E ... 239 597-2951
Naples *(G-11028)*
Bensons Heating and AC Inc ... D ... 850 562-3132
Tallahassee *(G-16889)*
Big Yellow Enterprises Inc ... E ... 813 920-4881
Odessa *(G-11834)*
Bill Wllams Ar-Cndtning Htg In ... E ... 904 387-0491
Jacksonville *(G-5859)*
Bingham On-Site Sewers Inc ... D ... 813 659-0003
Dover *(G-3366)*
Blueline Mechanical LLC ... E ... 727 540-0255
Clearwater *(G-1549)*
Blume Mechanical LLC ... E ... 727 544-5993
Clearwater *(G-1550)*
Bonnell Inc ... D ... 727 573-4650
Clearwater *(G-1551)*
Bordeau Plumbing Inc ... E ... 407 410-0160
Tavares *(G-18600)*
Boreal LLC ... B ... 786 621-8250
Doral *(G-3139)*
Boyd Brothers Service Inc ... D ... 941 627-8881
Punta Gorda *(G-15192)*
Boyd Plumbing Company Inc ... E ... 850 968-0711
Cantonment *(G-1334)*
Brighton Air Conditioning Inc ... E ... 954 977-5095
Pompano Beach *(G-14755)*
Brightview Landscape Dev Inc ... D ... 941 794-0476
Bradenton *(G-1068)*
Broward Water Consultants Inc ... E ... 954 941-9153
Pompano Beach *(G-14760)*
Brownies Septic and Plbg LLC ... E ... 407 841-4321
Orlando *(G-12211)*
Buckeye Plumbing Inc ... C ... 561 793-3169
Royal Palm Beach *(G-15381)*
Cailis Mechanical Corp ... E ... 954 252-0263
Davie *(G-2467)*
Caloosa Cooling Lee County LLC ... E ... 239 226-0202
Fort Myers *(G-4299)*
Campbell Plbg Cntrs Sthast Inc ... C ... 904 387-9996
Jacksonville *(G-5894)*
Captive-Aire Systems Inc ... C ... 407 682-0317
Groveland *(G-5085)*
Casey Hyman Plumbing Inc ... E ... 850 477-0388
Pensacola *(G-14250)*
Central Air Conditioning Inc ... E ... 954 428-0033
Deerfield Beach *(G-2723)*

Central Air Control Inc ....E 305 822-1551	Dixie Plumbing Inc ....E 561 746-4504	Gulfcoast Air Systems Inc ....E 813 689-2082
Hialeah (G-5231)	Jupiter (G-7063)	Tampa (G-17775)
Central Florida Ldscpg Inc ....D 813 623-1771	Don Harris Plumbing Co Inc ....E 904 772-0900	Hcmsmm Millian Corporation ....D 727 862-2100
Tampa (G-17447)	Jacksonville (G-6078)	Hudson (G-5641)
Certified Air Contractors Inc ....E 904 389-7950	Doug Hambels Plumbing Inc ....E 321 242-9562	Heichel Plumbing Inc ....D 407 656-7073
Jacksonville (G-5928)	Melbourne (G-8874)	Winter Garden (G-19569)
Certified Envmtl Svcs Inc ....D 904 695-1911	Douglas Orr Plumbing Inc ....C 305 887-1687	Hill York Service Company LLC ....D 561 689-7355
Jacksonville (G-5929)	Miami Springs (G-10780)	West Palm Beach (G-19177)
Certified Mechanical Co Inc ....E 407 294-1564	Drain Mechanics LLC ....E 321 351-2033	Hill York Service Company LLC ....E 954 525-4200
Apopka (G-164)	Palm Bay (G-13618)	Fort Lauderdale (G-3860)
Champ Plumbing Corp ....E 305 638-7777	DT Burns Enterprises Inc ....E 941 744-5552	Hilliard AC & Htg ....E 352 622-9390
Miami (G-9355)	Bradenton (G-1089)	Ocala (G-11699)
Climate Control Mech Svcs Inc ....E 352 291-0185	Duck Duck Rooter LLC ....E 954 608-7783	Hobbs Plumbing Inc ....E 850 235-8859
Ocala (G-11663)	Jacksonville (G-6086)	Lynn Haven (G-8469)
Climate Design AC Inc ....E 727 572-9100	Dynafire LLC ....D 407 740-0232	▼ Hughes Supply Inc ....D 239 334-2205
Clearwater (G-1580)	Casselberry (G-1447)	Fort Myers (G-4445)
Climate Pros LLC ....D 954 540-9344	E C Stokes Mech Contr Inc ....E 561 737-1310	Hunter Colg Htg Inc Wther Engr ......E 321 727-2542
Tamarac (G-17184)	Lake Worth Beach (G-7766)	Melbourne (G-8910)
Climate Pros LLC ....E 904 362-0377	Eagerton Plumbing Company Inc .....E 904 388-0761	Hys Holding Corp ....D 866 525-4200
Daytona Beach (G-2560)	Jacksonville (G-6097)	Fort Lauderdale (G-3885)
CM Hvac Holdings LLC ....D 813 247-2665	East Coast Mechanical Inc ....C 561 585-9850	◆ Hyvac Inc ....E 954 427-3811
Tampa (G-17490)	Boynton Beach (G-985)	Deerfield Beach (G-2756)
Cnc Management Group Inc ....E 305 250-4907	Ehota Inc ....D 954 902-4299	I V&S Incorporated ....C 888 528-3688
Miami (G-9383)	Fort Lauderdale (G-3769)	Pinellas Park (G-14525)
Coastal Cooling Inc ....E 239 432-9833	Emr Inc ....E 850 897-0210	Industrial Fire & Safety Inc ....E 727 573-1556
Fort Myers (G-4317)	Niceville (G-11446)	Saint Petersburg (G-15718)
Coastal Mechanical Svcs LLC ....C 813 764-8105	Encon Inc ....D 813 354-0446	Integrated Apartment Svcs Inc ....E 904 551-4992
Riverview (G-15250)	Tampa (G-17631)	Jacksonville (G-6323)
Coastal Mechanical Svcs LLC ....C 407 284-1550	Energy Air Inc ....C 813 750-1283	J & D Heating and AC Inc ....D 239 985-7299
Orlando (G-12334)	Plant City (G-14552)	Fort Myers (G-4452)
Coastal Mechanical Svcs LLC ....C 321 725-3061	▼ Energy Air Inc ....C 407 886-3729	J & K Mechanical LLC ....D 305 278-7171
Melbourne (G-8847)	Orlando (G-12467)	Miami (G-9778)
Coastal Plumbing & Mech Corp ....D 239 643-0025	Engineered Air LLC ....E 954 599-5800	J R Long Inc ....E 813 988-4810
Naples (G-11062)	Pompano Beach (G-14800)	Tampa (G-17881)
Comfort Control Services Inc ....E 772 785-9010	Engineered Cooling Svcs LLC ....D 850 432-7656	▲ JA Croson LLC ....E 352 729-7100
Port Saint Lucie (G-15130)	Pensacola (G-14291)	Sorrento (G-16475)
Comfort Systems USA Sthast Inc .....D 850 484-4999	Envirnmntal Dsign Systems Cntl ......E 813 269-0832	JA Green Plumbing & Mech Inc ....D 813 251-3233
Pensacola (G-14263)	Tampa (G-17636)	Tampa (G-17883)
▲ Comprehensive Energy Svcs Inc ...D 407 682-1313	Evans Holdings LLC ....E 239 643-6124	Jack Joyner Enterprises Inc ....D 727 447-6100
Longwood (G-8353)	Naples (G-11106)	Clearwater (G-1680)
Conditioned Air Co Naples LLC ....B 239 643-2445	F R T Inc ....E 352 728-6053	Jackson Total Service Inc ....E 239 643-0923
Naples (G-11075)	Leesburg (G-8243)	Naples (G-11181)
Conserv Building Services LLC ....D 727 541-5503	▲ Farmer & Irwin Corp ....C 561 842-5316	James Marlin Inc ....E 813 689-0817
Largo (G-8087)	Riviera Beach (G-15294)	Valrico (G-18754)
Consolidated Water Group LLC ....E 352 291-5900	Fcs Inc ....E 727 576-1111	Jax Refrigeration Inc ....D 904 249-1400
Ocala (G-11668)	Clearwater (G-1634)	Jacksonville Beach (G-6991)
Constructive Resource Inc ....E 954 488-3868	Ferran Services & Contg Inc ....C 407 422-3551	JB Electric and Solar LLC ....E 321 305-6068
Altamonte Springs (G-39)	Orlando (G-12506)	Cocoa (G-1941)
Cool Bear Services LLC ....D 561 572-3636	Ferran Services & Contg Inc ....C 407 422-3551	Jennings Company Inc ....E 334 289-4517
Delray Beach (G-2934)	Port Orange (G-15075)	Pensacola (G-14333)
▲ Cool-Breeze AC Corp ....D 305 226-2665	Fire & Life Safety America Inc ....D 804 222-1381	John C Cassidy AC Inc ....D 561 863-6750
Miami (G-9412)	Sanford (G-15939)	Riviera Beach (G-15302)
Coolair Conditioning Inc ....E 239 275-7077	First Qlty Plbg Irrigation Inc ....E 386 775-0909	Johnson Cntrls Fire Prtction L ....A 561 988-7200
Fort Myers (G-4325)	Orange City (G-11962)	Boca Raton (G-653)
Cortez Heating and AC Inc ....E 941 755-5211	Florida Delta Mechanical Inc ....E 727 545-7957	Johnson Controls Inc ....E 561 881-7200
Palmetto (G-13909)	Tampa (G-17677)	West Palm Beach (G-19217)
Cox Fire Protection Inc ....D 813 247-4777	Foodservice Refrigeration Inc ....D 954 917-9765	Jorda Enterprises Inc ....D 305 597-7080
Tampa (G-17545)	Pompano Beach (G-14812)	Doral (G-3253)
Cox Heating & AC Inc ....E 727 442-6158	Forrest Inc ....D 904 794-2547	Juniper Landscaping Fla LLC ....C 407 275-6200
Clearwater (G-1595)	Saint Augustine (G-15444)	Orlando (G-12716)
Crd Electrical Service LLC ....D 407 944-0191	Franz Inc ....E 954 428-8181	Kalos Services Inc ....E 352 243-7088
Kissimmee (G-7291)	Deerfield Beach (G-2742)	Clermont (G-1877)
CSC ....E 813 289-9309	Franzese Plumbing Inc ....D 239 574-4121	Keith Lawson Company Inc ....D 850 562-7711
Thonotosassa (G-18670)	Cape Coral (G-1395)	Tallahassee (G-17014)
Csn Power and MGT Firm LLC ....D 813 252-5515	Freedom Fire Protection of Cen ....E 407 328-1663	Keith Mc Neill Plumbing Contr ....E 850 562-5504
Wesley Chapel (G-18995)	Sanford (G-15942)	Tallahassee (G-17015)
Cunningham Oil Company Inc ....E 386 253-7621	Frenchs Air Conditioning Inc ....D 813 626-4630	Keller Mechanical & Engrg Inc ....E 863 686-0947
Daytona Beach (G-2571)	Tampa (G-17713)	Lakeland (G-7894)
Custom Air Inc ....D 941 371-0833	▲ Gay Frank Services Inc ....D 407 293-2642	Kelly Brothers Sheet Metal Inc ....E 850 878-1148
Sarasota (G-16135)	Orlando (G-12563)	Tallahassee (G-17017)
Custom Drilling Services Inc ....E 863 425-9600	Gold Coast Usa Inc ....C 321 405-2870	Kenyon & Partners Inc ....E 813 241-6568
Mulberry (G-10974)	Palm Bay (G-13621)	Tampa (G-17915)
Custom Mechanical Inc ....D 561 844-1004	Good 3nergy LLC ....A 866 990-9052	Keystone Mechanical Inc ....E 407 298-0970
Lake Park (G-7658)	Orlando (G-12582)	Longwood (G-8374)
Cyvsa International Inc ....E 954 674-3444	Good Air Inc ....E 954 964-6355	L Pugh & Associates Inc ....E 850 478-2777
Miramar (G-10850)	West Park (G-19431)	Pensacola (G-14339)
D G Meyer Inc ....D 386 253-7774	Greens Energy Services Inc ....E 407 282-5000	Lakeside Heating Coolg & Plbg ....D 813 444-9474
Daytona Beach (G-2572)	Orlando (G-12600)	Land O Lakes (G-8051)
Darleys Plumbing Inc ....D 904 727-1484	Ground Services Intl Inc ....A 813 884-4915	Larrabee Air Conditioning Inc ....E 305 887-1573
Jacksonville (G-6046)	Tampa (G-17762)	Medley (G-8752)
David Gray Plumbing Inc ....D 904 724-7211	Grunau Company Inc ....D 407 857-1800	Larry Batchelor Mechanical LLC ......D 850 862-4796
Jacksonville (G-6048)	Orlando (G-12609)	Fort Walton Beach (G-4786)
Debonair Mechanical Inc ....D 305 826-2240	Gulf Coast Plbg of Centl Fla ....D 813 246-5341	Lilley Air Conditioning Inc ....E 863 644-0496
Miami Lakes (G-10719)	Tampa (G-17770)	Lakeland (G-7908)
Del-Air Heating AC & Rfrgn Inc ....B 866 796-4874	Gulf Mechanical Contrs LLC ....E 352 460-4176	Limbach Company LP ....C 714 653-7000
Sanford (G-15935)	Leesburg (G-8246)	Tampa (G-17955)
Del-Air Heating AC & Rfrgn Inc ....E 352 394-1220	Gulf Plumbing Inc ....D 305 662-6844	Lindstrom Air Conditioning Inc ....C 954 420-5300
Clermont (G-1864)	Miami (G-9671)	Pompano Beach (G-14843)
Dhr McHncal Srvces-Orlando Inc ......E 727 868-9800	Gulf Shore Cooling Inc ....D 239 939-1137	Lindstrom Brothers AC Inc ....E 954 420-5300
Hudson (G-5636)	Fort Myers (G-4431)	Pompano Beach (G-14844)

Lipten Company LLC	E	800 860-0790	
Groveland (G-5097)			
Longs Air Conditioning Inc	E	863 465-7771	
Avon Park (G-294)			
▼ Ls Energia Inc	E	954 281-7022	
Plantation (G-14668)			
Lsci Inc	E	727 571-4141	
Seminole (G-16455)			
Lt Plumbing LLC	E	941 729-1111	
Palmetto (G-13920)			
Lunex Power Inc	D	813 540-8807	
Tampa (G-17966)			
M & P Concrete Products Inc	D	561 498-4125	
Delray Beach (G-2987)			
Mabry Brothers Inc	C	239 482-1122	
Fort Myers (G-4499)			
Madd Services Inc	E	561 494-5062	
Wellington (G-18984)			
Maintenx Intl Svc MGT Group In	B	813 254-1656	
Tampa (G-17979)			
Manny & Lou Plbg Contrs Inc	D	305 666-7511	
Miami (G-9896)			
Marios Air Conditioning & Htg	D	727 843-9598	
Brooksville (G-1299)			
Massive Air Inc	D	954 900-5936	
Lauderdale Lakes (G-8178)			
Master Craft Plbg Contrs Inc	D	386 252-7047	
Daytona Beach (G-2632)			
Mc Mechanical AC Svcs Inc	E	727 540-0400	
Clearwater (G-1709)			
Mc Natt Plumbing Inc	D	813 971-6100	
Tampa (G-18007)			
McDonald Air & Sheet Metal Inc	D	407 295-0220	
Orlando (G-12841)			
McDusky Inc	D	239 437-7040	
Fort Myers (G-4504)			
McMullen AC Rfrgn Inc	E	727 527-0000	
Saint Petersburg (G-15757)			
McNatt Plumbing Company Inc	E	813 971-6100	
Tampa (G-18011)			
Mechanical AC Corp	E	561 848-6227	
West Palm Beach (G-19259)			
Mechanical Svcs Centl Fla Inc	C	407 857-3510	
Orlando (G-12850)			
Meeks Plumbing Inc	E	772 569-2285	
Vero Beach (G-18894)			
Meraki Solar LLC	D	850 378-1257	
Pensacola (G-14361)			
Merritt Island Air & Heat Inc	D	321 452-5665	
Merritt Island (G-9039)			
Miami Air Mechanical Inc	D	305 592-5780	
Doral (G-3273)			
Miami-Dade Cnty Pub Schols-158	C	305 235-2329	
Miami (G-9994)			
◆ Mid-State SMS LLC	B	727 573-7828	
Lakeland (G-7923)			
▲ Midway Services Inc	C	727 573-9500	
Clearwater (G-1721)			
Mike Scott Plumbing Inc	E	866 314-4443	
Hernando (G-5208)			
Millers Plumbing and Mech Inc	E	850 386-4622	
Tallahassee (G-17048)			
Mills Air Inc	D	407 292-4357	
Orlando (G-12872)			
▼ Milton J Wood Company	D	904 353-5527	
Jacksonville (G-6505)			
Mirasol Fafco Solar Inc	E	941 484-0130	
Sarasota (G-16234)			
MMS Mechanical Services Inc	E	352 376-5221	
Gainesville (G-4950)			
Modern Mechanical Services LLC	E	800 572-0852	
Fort Myers (G-4517)			
Modern Plumbing Industries Inc	D	407 327-6000	
Winter Springs (G-19809)			
Mor Ppm Inc	B	386 325-4666	
Palatka (G-13595)			
Morgan Air Conditioning LLC	E	813 500-7765	
Lutz (G-8450)			
Munns Sales & Service Inc	D	352 241-2039	
Fruitland Park (G-4824)			
N&M Cooling and Heating Inc	C	941 921-5581	
Sarasota (G-16243)			
Nagelbush Mechanical Inc	C	954 736-3000	
Fort Lauderdale (G-3988)			
Nash Plumbing and Mech LLC	C	352 748-1454	
Wildwood (G-19504)			
Newberg Irrigation Inc	D	727 521-6620	
Saint Petersburg (G-15776)			
Newberrys Refrigeration Inc	E	863 688-8871	
Lakeland (G-7931)			

◆ Norca AC & Rfrgn Corp	D	305 558-1422	
Miami Lakes (G-10749)			
Nuccio Heating & AC Inc	E	813 961-7895	
Tampa (G-18091)			
OHara Landscape & Maint Inc	D	561 655-9011	
West Palm Beach (G-19291)			
Olympia Plumbing Corp	D	305 821-8111	
Miami (G-10068)			
One Energy Service LLC	D	404 681-7717	
Winter Park (G-19756)			
One Stop Cooling & Heating LLC	B	407 629-6920	
Winter Park (G-19757)			
Palm Beach Pluming Inc	E	561 478-0303	
Lake Worth (G-7744)			
Pampering Plumber Inc	D	727 232-8400	
Odessa (G-11852)			
Partridge Well Drilling Co Inc	E	904 355-3323	
Jacksonville (G-6581)			
Peaden LLC	C	850 872-1004	
Panama City (G-14054)			
Pinellas Plumbing Inc	D	727 768-0100	
Clearwater (G-1758)			
Pipeline Mechanical Inc	E	352 385-0195	
Mount Dora (G-10959)			
Piper Fire Protection Inc	E	813 221-5101	
Tampa (G-18155)			
Piper Fire Protection Inc	E	941 377-2100	
Sarasota (G-16268)			
Piper Fire Protection Inc	D	727 581-9339	
Clearwater (G-1759)			
Plumbing Experts Inc	E	561 368-5111	
Delray Beach (G-3007)			
Plumbing Mart Florida Inc	D	561 392-2410	
Deerfield Beach (G-2784)			
Poole & Kent Company Florida	C	239 325-9985	
Naples (G-11265)			
Precision Air Systems Inc	E	561 791-3980	
West Palm Beach (G-19330)			
Precision Plumbing Services	D	239 481-2300	
Fort Myers (G-4548)			
Precisionair	E	352 624-4000	
Ocala (G-11762)			
Pride AC & Appl Inc	E	954 977-7433	
Pompano Beach (G-14880)			
Pro-Air Mechanical Inc	E	407 339-4333	
Longwood (G-8393)			
Pro-Tech AC & Plbg Svc Inc	E	407 291-1644	
Orlando (G-13062)			
Professional Plumbing Corp	C	305 822-8282	
Hialeah (G-5312)			
Progressive Plumbing Inc	C	352 394-7171	
Clermont (G-1883)			
Pure Air Control Services Inc	E	727 572-4550	
Clearwater (G-1767)			
Q & Q Inc	E	863 665-6197	
Lakeland (G-7947)			
Quality AC Co Inc	D	954 984-4329	
Fort Lauderdale (G-4071)			
Quality Plbg Gainesville Inc	D	352 377-1009	
Gainesville (G-4983)			
R & R Maintenance Inc	D	904 292-9100	
Jacksonville (G-6629)			
R T Moore Co Inc	C	317 291-1052	
Sarasota (G-16279)			
Rapid Global Technologies Inc	E	407 739-1157	
Orlando (G-13081)			
Reliant Roofing LLC	D	904 657-0880	
Jacksonville (G-6653)			
▼ Research Irrigation Inc	E	305 825-3341	
Medley (G-8774)			
Reyes Fc Services Corp	E	305 600-9484	
Hialeah (G-5316)			
Rf Group LLC	D	904 278-0339	
Jacksonville (G-6660)			
Ridge Energy Savers Inc	E	863 676-2665	
Lake Wales (G-7698)			
RJ Kielty Plbg Htg Coolg Inc	D	727 863-5486	
New Port Richey (G-11403)			
Robinhood Solar LLC	E	610 509-3209	
Haines City (G-5156)			
Rodan Fire Sprinklers Inc	D	813 621-1357	
Lithia (G-8304)			
S & S Air Conditioning Inc	E	954 321-6186	
Fort Lauderdale (G-4097)			
▲ Sansone LLC	D	954 428-8919	
Haverhill (G-5200)			
Sasso Air Conditioning Inc	E	561 249-4636	
Lake Worth Beach (G-7773)			
Sauer Construction LLC	D	904 262-6444	
Jacksonville (G-6693)			

Sauer Construction LLC	D	904 262-6444	
Jacksonville (G-6692)			
Sauer Incorporated	C	904 262-6444	
Jacksonville (G-6694)			
Sawyer Air Conditioning Inc	D	904 781-4440	
Jacksonville (G-6696)			
Schmitt Inc	E	727 868-9531	
Hudson (G-5648)			
Schmitt Inc	E	352 683-7606	
Spring Hill (G-16546)			
Schwenn Services & Contg LLC	E	407 895-7550	
Winter Garden (G-19593)			
Scotto Plumbing Service Inc	D	727 581-5828	
Clearwater (G-1784)			
Sean McCutcheons AC & Htg Inc	E	941 921-7208	
Sarasota (G-16313)			
Senica Air Conditioning Inc	E	727 856-0058	
Spring Hill (G-16557)			
Service Experts LLC	D	561 655-7700	
West Palm Beach (G-19358)			
Service Experts LLC	D	239 768-2665	
Fort Myers (G-4589)			
Service Experts LLC	E	305 264-2020	
Doral (G-3308)			
Service Experts LLC	E	386 734-0515	
Deland (G-2880)			
Service Experts LLC	E	352 732-7320	
Ocala (G-11778)			
Service Experts LLC	D	321 635-9946	
Cocoa (G-1952)			
Service First LLC	D	850 863-1982	
Fort Walton Beach (G-4804)			
Shaw Mechanical Services LLC	E	407 835-7880	
Longwood (G-8405)			
Shelleys Septic Tank Inc	D	407 889-8042	
Zellwood (G-19826)			
Shine and Company Inc	E	386 454-2034	
High Springs (G-5355)			
SI Goldman Company Inc	C	407 830-5000	
Longwood (G-8406)			
▲ Simpson Mechanical Inc	E	813 558-0858	
Tampa (G-18285)			
Smith Services Inc	E	866 592-8268	
Vero Beach (G-18920)			
Smyth Air Conditioning Inc	E	561 533-6066	
Lake Worth Beach (G-7774)			
▲ Snyder Co	D	904 641-0600	
Jacksonville (G-6736)			
Soltys Plumbing LLC	E	561 243-2218	
Boca Raton (G-810)			
South Seminole Sheet Metal Inc	C	407 464-7776	
Apopka (G-211)			
Southeast Mech Contrs LLC	C	954 981-3600	
West Park (G-19435)			
Southeast Mech Systems Inc	E	904 262-1066	
Jacksonville (G-6751)			
Southern Comfort Htg Coolg Inc	D	941 358-1539	
South Daytona (G-16495)			
▼ Southern Equipment Corporation	D	813 251-1839	
Tampa (G-18309)			
Southern Erectors Inc	E	850 944-0013	
Pensacola (G-14444)			
Southern Fire Control Inc	E	954 858-1600	
Fort Lauderdale (G-4147)			
Southern Fire Prtction Orlndo	D	407 320-1990	
Sanford (G-15982)			
Southwest Plumbing Service	E	305 232-6203	
Miami (G-10311)			
Spegal Plumbing LLC	C	321 256-1234	
Apopka (G-213)			
Sprinklrmtic Fire Prtction Sys	E	954 327-3686	
Davie (G-2520)			
Stahlmn-England Irrigation Inc	D	239 514-1200	
Naples (G-11306)			
Striper Home Services LLC	E	772 359-3115	
Doral (G-3322)			
Summers Fire Sprinklers Inc	D	561 393-6718	
Boca Raton (G-826)			
Summers Fire Sprinklers Inc	E	786 313-0522	
Hialeah (G-5326)			
▼ Summit Construction Inc	E	850 660-1019	
Santa Rosa Beach (G-16015)			
Sunshine Land Design Inc	C	772 283-2648	
Stuart (G-16673)			
▲ Suntech Plumbing Corp	D	305 328-3898	
Doral (G-3324)			
Suntuity Solar Ltd Lblty Co	D	863 417-8600	
Lakeland (G-7984)			
Suntuity Solar Ltd Lblty Co	D	855 786-8848	
Orlando (G-13251)			

S I C

Suojanen Plumbers Inc .... E 813 926-0707
Odessa *(G-11857)*
Superior Heating-Cooling Corp .... E 941 488-5359
Venice *(G-18809)*
Superior Htg & Coolg MGT Inc .... E 813 854-3449
Oldsmar *(G-11927)*
Superior Mech Systems Inc .... E 727 548-1711
Pinellas Park *(G-14536)*
Svcs In Advanced Fire Prtction .... E 850 244-2026
Fort Walton Beach *(G-4806)*
▼ Sybac Solar LLC .... D 863 229-1081
Orlando *(G-13257)*
System Service & Engrg Inc .... E 850 441-3458
Lynn Haven *(G-8472)*
Tasco Plumbing Corp .... C 305 455-1377
Hialeah *(G-5328)*
The Boyd Plbg Residential LLC .... E 850 471-9650
Cantonment *(G-1343)*
Thermal Concepts Inc .... B 305 940-0381
Davie *(G-2528)*
▲ Thermal Dynamics Intl Inc .... D 239 415-3601
Fort Myers *(G-4625)*
Thermo Cool Cooling & Htg LLC .... D 352 326-5530
Fruitland Park *(G-4825)*
Thigpen Heating & Cooling Inc .... D 904 353-5726
Jacksonville *(G-6848)*
Three GS Inc .... E 772 778-2818
Fort Pierce *(G-4744)*
Titan Fire Systems LLC .... E 321 453-2212
Cocoa *(G-1958)*
TI Services Inc .... E 813 641-2730
Ruskin *(G-15404)*
Total Air Care Inc .... D 904 282-5050
Madison *(G-8491)*
Total Appliance & AC RPS Inc .... C 954 900-6868
Hallandale Beach *(G-5186)*
Total Comfort Heat and AC Inc .... D 386 672-8494
Ormond Beach *(G-13528)*
Total Comfort Heat and AC Inc .... D 386 672-8894
Ormond Beach *(G-13529)*
Total Comfort Heat and AC Inc .... D 386 672-8494
New Smyrna Beach *(G-11427)*
Touchton Plumbing Contrs Inc .... E 904 389-9299
Jacksonville *(G-6870)*
Trane US Inc .... E 407 660-1111
Maitland *(G-8590)*
Tri Cnty Air Cndtnng-Hting Inc .... D 941 625-1638
North Venice *(G-11578)*
Tropical Plumbing & Septic .... E 407 568-0111
Orlando *(G-13313)*
True Builders Inc .... E 863 647-1800
Plant City *(G-14589)*
Tudi Mechanical Systems Inc .... E 813 635-0100
Tampa *(G-18452)*
TWC Services Inc .... D 407 695-6700
Sanford *(G-15990)*
Ufp Operating Inc .... E 407 504-0922
Orlando *(G-13329)*
United AC & Htg Co .... D 727 531-0496
Largo *(G-8159)*
United Mechanical LLC .... D 239 939-4502
Fort Myers *(G-4637)*
Universal Fabricators LLC .... E 850 968-5252
Cantonment *(G-1344)*
Universal Fire Systems Inc .... E 813 662-9200
Tampa *(G-18466)*
Unlimited Solar Technology .... E 954 982-4761
Hollywood *(G-5546)*
Vause Mechanical Contg Inc .... E 850 575-4563
Tallahassee *(G-17169)*
VSC Fire & Security Inc .... D 727 456-5200
Seminole *(G-16464)*
Water Works Plumbing Corp .... E 239 574-2326
Cape Coral *(G-1434)*
Watson Construction Group .... E 904 737-6337
Jacksonville *(G-6920)*
Wayne Atmtc Fire Sprnklers Inc .... D 239 433-3030
Fort Myers *(G-4647)*
Wayne Atmtc Fire Sprnklers Inc .... C 407 656-3030
Ocoee *(G-11828)*
Wayne Atmtc Fire Sprnklers Inc .... D 813 630-0303
Tampa *(G-18527)*
Wayne Atmtc Fire Sprnklers Inc .... D 904 268-3030
Jacksonville *(G-6923)*
Wayne Atmtc Fire Sprnklers Inc .... D 954 917-3030
Deerfield Beach *(G-2814)*
Wdr Mechanical Contractors Inc .... D 850 432-0160
Pensacola *(G-14468)*
Weather Control AC Inc .... E 239 936-0333
Fort Myers *(G-4651)*
Weather Engineers Inc .... D 904 356-3963
Jacksonville *(G-6924)*
Wentco Inc .... D 239 694-2700
Fort Myers *(G-4653)*
Wentzels Heating & AC Inc .... E 941 924-8120
Sarasota *(G-16363)*
Westbrook Management Corp .... D 407 841-3310
Orlando *(G-13420)*
Westbrook Service Corporation .... C 407 841-3310
Orlando *(G-13421)*
▼ Wiginton Corporation .... D 407 585-3200
Sanford *(G-15995)*
Wiginton Corporation .... E 813 514-4487
Tampa *(G-18555)*
Wiginton Corporation .... E 904 262-6107
Jacksonville *(G-6933)*
William R Nash Inc .... E 305 885-8155
Miramar *(G-10916)*
William R Nash Inc .... D 561 394-5614
Boca Raton *(G-876)*
◆ William R Nash LLC .... C 864 208-1810
Tamarac *(G-17208)*
▼ Windmill Sprinkler Company Inc .... E 954 763-3411
Fort Lauderdale *(G-4226)*
Wm F McDonough Plumbing Inc .... E 941 753-6436
Sarasota *(G-16074)*
Wright Company .... D 850 434-6728
Pensacola *(G-14478)*
WW Gay Fire Protection Inc .... C 904 387-7973
Jacksonville *(G-6946)*
WW Gay Mechanical Contr Inc .... A 904 388-2696
Jacksonville *(G-6947)*
WW Gay Mechanical Contr Inc .... D 407 841-4670
Orlando *(G-13452)*
WW Gay Mechanical Contr Inc .... C 352 372-3963
Gainesville *(G-5034)*
Wyatt-Fitzgibbons Shtmtl Inc .... E 863 683-7759
Lakeland *(G-8012)*
Ximeno Plumbing Inc .... D 305 829-4050
Medley *(G-8800)*
Y and T Management Inc .... E 305 255-8919
Miami *(G-10523)*
▲ Youngquist Brothers LLC .... B 239 489-4444
Fort Myers *(G-4664)*
Zicaro Services Inc .... E 561 265-1132
Boynton Beach *(G-1046)*

1721 Painting & Paper Hanging Contractors

Aerial Companies Inc .... C 239 643-7625
Naples *(G-11002)*
Akca LLC .... D 813 752-4471
Plant City *(G-14543)*
Anthony Michaels Painting .... E 407 331-9000
Longwood *(G-8341)*
Artistry Painting Company Inc .... E 941 484-3805
Venice *(G-18765)*
B & G Painting Inc .... D 813 882-6000
Tampa *(G-17331)*
Champion Pntg Spclty Svcs Corp .... E 954 462-9079
Fort Lauderdale *(G-3683)*
Coast To Coast Gen Contrs Inc .... D 954 920-3900
Hollywood *(G-5416)*
Corrosion Ctrl Specialists Inc .... E 813 677-2899
Tampa *(G-17525)*
Elias Bros Group Pntg Cntg Inc .... D 239 643-1624
Naples *(G-11101)*
Elias Brothers Gen Contr Inc .... C 239 293-2442
Naples *(G-11102)*
Fausnight Stripe and Line Inc .... E 407 261-5446
Longwood *(G-8359)*
Five Arrows Inc .... E 407 872-7555
Orlando *(G-12515)*
▲ Five Arrows Inc .... D 813 972-4945
Tampa *(G-17668)*
Flores-Hager and Assoc Inc .... D 386 676-9999
Daytona Beach *(G-2589)*
▼ Gemstone LLC .... E 305 294-3233
Key West *(G-7208)*
Gustafson Industries Inc .... E 561 732-0656
Boynton Beach *(G-993)*
Harpy Corporation .... D 954 771-1594
Fort Lauderdale *(G-3848)*
Hartzell Construction Inc .... E 954 957-9762
Pompano Beach *(G-14819)*
Hartzell Pntg & Waterproofing .... E 954 957-9761
Pompano Beach *(G-14820)*
Interior Txtres of Palm Bches .... D 561 768-9512
Jupiter *(G-7089)*
JB Pntg & Waterproofing Inc .... D 954 574-0000
Deerfield Beach *(G-2759)*
Joshua W Kennedy Entps LLC .... E 904 383-7721
Jacksonville *(G-6391)*
Krystal Companies LLC .... E 904 838-8003
Jacksonville *(G-6409)*
L & T Brothers Inc .... E 727 742-1492
Largo *(G-8125)*
▼ M & R & Sons Inc .... E 561 391-7507
Boca Raton *(G-681)*
Merit Professional Coatings .... E 813 979-6146
Tampa *(G-18027)*
Metro Property Services Inc .... E 904 399-1020
Jacksonville *(G-6501)*
Mousseri Painting Inc .... E 561 793-5701
Wellington *(G-18985)*
Murphy Painters Inc .... E 954 626-0540
Fort Lauderdale *(G-3982)*
Noel Painting of Usa LLC .... C 239 466-7343
Fort Myers *(G-4524)*
Paintmaster Inc .... E 941 953-2500
Clearwater *(G-1752)*
Paramount Painting & Svcs Inc .... E 813 715-9699
Tampa *(G-18121)*
Pass Painting Co Inc .... E 305 751-7855
Miami Gardens *(G-10696)*
Plummer Pntg Waterproofing Inc .... D 407 585-0210
Winter Park *(G-19762)*
Pod LLC .... E 855 707-2468
Tampa *(G-18158)*
Principles Construction Inc .... E 754 800-7110
Pompano Beach *(G-14881)*
Pristine Painting of Tampa Bay .... E 813 701-4671
Tampa *(G-18173)*
Pritts Inc .... D 954 733-7663
Fort Lauderdale *(G-4062)*
Pro-Max Restoration & Pnt Corp .... E 305 253-7900
Miami *(G-10146)*
Proietto Painting Inc .... D 954 772-3898
Oakland Park *(G-11610)*
Rainbow Colors Inc .... E 561 737-3566
Boynton Beach *(G-1033)*
Restore Construction Group Inc .... D 954 985-5353
West Park *(G-19433)*
RL James Inc General Contr .... E 239 936-6002
Fort Myers *(G-4574)*
▲ S & S Pntg & Waterproofing LLC .... E 954 917-5554
Pompano Beach *(G-14887)*
S David & Co LLC .... D 904 636-7788
Jacksonville *(G-6683)*
Seminole Equipment Inc .... E 727 944-4481
Tarpon Springs *(G-18591)*
Southern Road & Bridge LLC .... C 727 940-5395
Tarpon Springs *(G-18592)*
Specialized Property Svcs Inc .... D 813 246-4274
Tampa *(G-18318)*
Spectrum Contracting Inc .... D 239 643-2772
Naples *(G-11302)*
Spraggins Contract Interiors .... E 407 295-4150
Orlando *(G-13226)*
▲ Surface Technologies Corp .... D 904 241-1501
Jacksonville *(G-6820)*
Tom White Inc .... D 727 578-5819
Saint Petersburg *(G-15876)*
Tru Colors Contracting Inc .... E 954 973-5600
Pompano Beach *(G-14930)*
Trutwin Industries Inc .... D 239 489-4223
Fort Myers *(G-4633)*
Wilson Kehoe & Miller Corp .... E 727 584-7742
Largo *(G-8164)*

1731 Electrical Work

1st Fire & Security .... E 772 794-2220
Vero Beach *(G-18826)*
21st Century Elec Contrs Inc .... D 954 974-5412
Pompano Beach *(G-14728)*
A & B Electric Company Inc .... D 407 293-5984
Apopka *(G-144)*
A & G Electrical Tech Inc .... E 352 588-0400
San Antonio *(G-15907)*
A & W Electric Hollywood Inc .... D 954 527-5599
Fort Lauderdale *(G-3571)*
A Randys Electric Inc .... E 727 573-1400
Clearwater *(G-1508)*
A/C Electric Svc of SW FL .... E 239 597-2634
Naples *(G-10994)*
AAA Electrical Contractors Inc .... E 727 847-2357
Port Richey *(G-15096)*
ABC Communications Corporation .... E 954 321-9000
Plantation *(G-14597)*
ABC Electric Service Inc .... E 239 936-3355
Fort Myers *(G-4246)*

Access Control Tech Inc ....E 407 422-8850
Orlando *(G-12045)*

Acra Electric Inc ....E 239 542-1624
Cape Coral *(G-1372)*

Adkins Electric Inc............................D 904 765-1622
Jacksonville *(G-5738)*

ADT Holdings Inc ....,A 888 298-9274
Boca Raton *(G-402)*

Advanced Cable Connection Inc ....D 813 978-0101
Tampa *(G-17240)*

Advanced Communications Tech ....E 561 771-6677
Jupiter *(G-7045)*

Advanced Control Corp Inc ....D 954 491-6660
Fort Lauderdale *(G-3579)*

Advanced Lighting Inc ....E 407 508-1774
Davenport *(G-2435)*

Advanced Power Tech Group LLC........C 888 964-4487
Pompano Beach *(G-14734)*

Aei Electrical Cnstr Inc ....E 863 619-6909
Lakeland *(G-7786)*

Afc Electric Inc ....E 239 992-5757
Bonita Springs *(G-892)*

Aggressive Electric Inc ....E 904 781-8905
Jacksonville *(G-5752)*

Airo Cable Construction Inc ....E 904 399-2260
Jacksonville *(G-5758)*

All American Facility Maint ....D 954 322-9909
Sunrise *(G-16734)*

All Phase Electric & Maint Inc.............C 813 876-7074
Tampa *(G-17263)*

All United Contracting Inc ....E 904 728-4429
Jacksonville *(G-5766)*

Allbrite Electrical Contrs ....D 954 583-6788
Coral Springs *(G-2225)*

Alliance Power Solutions Inc...............E 813 470-7200
Tampa *(G-17265)*

Allstate Electrical Contrs Inc ....C 904 296-2700
Jacksonville *(G-5769)*

American Electrical Contg Inc ....D 904 737-9046
Jacksonville *(G-5781)*

American Ltg Signalization Inc.............C 813 719-2211
Dover *(G-3365)*

◆ Anchor Tampa Inc ....D 813 879-8685
Tampa *(G-17286)*

▼ AP Sound LLC ....D 850 432-5780
Pensacola *(G-14219)*

Apg Electric Inc ....C 863 688-0600
Lakeland *(G-7801)*

▼ Apg Electric Inc ....C 727 530-0077
Clearwater *(G-1523)*

Apg Electric Inc ....C 772 567-5778
Vero Beach *(G-18832)*

Arlington Electric Inc........................E 772 287-1353
Stuart *(G-16589)*

Armstrong Electric Company ....D 850 432-2371
Pensacola *(G-14220)*

Associated Companies Inc ....C 863 294-9292
Winter Haven *(G-19606)*

Atci Communications Inc ....E 305 620-0062
Miami *(G-9183)*

Atlas Wireless & Telecom Inc ....E 703 608-1315
Temple Terrace *(G-18629)*

▼ Audio Advisors Inc ....D 561 478-3100
West Palm Beach *(G-19043)*

▲ Automation Logistics Corp ....D 813 855-8600
Oldsmar *(G-11893)*

Automted Bldg Ctrl Systems Inc ....E 813 879-8222
Tampa *(G-17322)*

Av-Worx LLC ....D 844 428-9679
West Palm Beach *(G-19045)*

Avatel Technologies Inc.....................E 813 314-2111
Brandon *(G-1213)*

Aveco Electrical Inc ....E 863 225-5912
Lakeland *(G-7805)*

▼ AVI-Spl Holdings Inc ....A 866 708-5034
Tampa *(G-17325)*

B & I Contractors Inc ....C 239 332-4646
Fort Myers *(G-4286)*

Baroco Electric Cnstr Co ....D 850 465-2008
Pensacola *(G-14229)*

Bass-Nted Fire SEC Systems Inc ....C 954 785-7800
Pompano Beach *(G-14750)*

Bates Electric Inc ....D 813 888-7050
Tampa *(G-17342)*

Bayou Mechanical Inc ....C 850 682-2784
Crestview *(G-2311)*

Bayshore Electric Inc ....E 386 252-2287
Daytona Beach *(G-2550)*

Beachem Brothers Electric Inc.............D 941 365-1919
Port Charlotte *(G-15023)*

▲ Beaumont Electric Co Inc ....C 239 643-4515
Naples *(G-11031)*

BL Smith Electric Inc........................D 863 439-7401
Dundee *(G-3371)*

Bore Tech Utilities & Maint ....D 305 297-8162
Miami *(G-9269)*

Borrell Electric Co Inc ....C 813 223-2727
Tampa *(G-17381)*

▼ Boys Electrical Contrs LLC ....C 321 727-3887
Melbourne *(G-8830)*

Bradford Electric Inc.........................D 561 747-0656
Jupiter *(G-7051)*

Bright Future Electric LLC ....E 941 752-0939
Sarasota *(G-16023)*

Bright Future Electric LLC ....E 407 654-0155
Ocoee *(G-11807)*

Bright Future Electric LLC ....E 850 622-3005
Santa Rosa Beach *(G-16006)*

Bryant Electric ....D 305 599-2700
Doral *(G-3140)*

C & F Elc Fort Lauderdale Inc ....E 954 791-1114
Plantation *(G-14610)*

C and C Power Line Inc ....C 904 751-6020
Jacksonville *(G-5889)*

▼ C Davis Electric Co Inc ....C 954 432-4334
Miramar *(G-10843)*

Cable Electrical Services Inc ....E 407 880-9400
Apopka *(G-160)*

Cable Wiring Specialist Inc ....D 954 893-0918
Hollywood *(G-5412)*

Calkins Electric Cnstr Co ....E 386 734-6751
Deland *(G-2845)*

Capri Industries Inc ....D 904 810-0899
Palm Coast *(G-13814)*

Carl Hankins Inc..............................E 813 977-7270
Tampa *(G-17421)*

Carpenter Electric Inc ....D 561 640-0400
Mangonia Park *(G-8607)*

Carter Electric Inc ....D 407 814-2677
Apopka *(G-161)*

Carter Electrical MGT Co Inc ....E 386 255-1418
Daytona Beach *(G-2557)*

Central Cntrs Hghlnds Cnty Inc............D 863 465-3587
Lake Placid *(G-7665)*

Central Florida Elc Ocala Inc ....E 352 622-8850
Ocala *(G-11656)*

Century Fire Prtction - Advnce ....D 954 970-3746
Pompano Beach *(G-14770)*

Certified Air Contractors Inc ....E 904 389-7950
Jacksonville *(G-5928)*

Certified Thrmgraphic Svcs Inc............D 321 953-2900
Palm Bay *(G-13612)*

Champion Electrical Contg LLC ....D 561 296-4144
Jupiter *(G-7057)*

Chrome Electric LLC ....D 321 267-0990
Titusville *(G-18683)*

Ciraco Electric LLC..........................D 352 629-5976
Ocala *(G-11661)*

CMI Services LLC ....E 850 638-0406
Chipley *(G-1490)*

Coastal Electric Company Fla ....D 904 645-0026
Jacksonville *(G-5971)*

Coltin Electric Inc............................D 850 904-6052
Destin *(G-3053)*

Comdesign Infrstrcture Sltons ....D 727 578-6700
Saint Petersburg *(G-15632)*

Command Ctrl Cmmnctons Engrg L.....D 813 620-0051
Tampa *(G-17502)*

Commercial Elec Contg Inc ....E 727 328-1700
Saint Petersburg *(G-15634)*

Commercial Fire Cmmnctons Inc...........D 727 530-4521
Clearwater *(G-1582)*

Community Electric Collier Inc.............E 239 262-3438
Naples *(G-11072)*

Comnet Communications LLC ....E 904 464-0114
Jacksonville *(G-5992)*

Complete Electric Inc ....D 772 388-0533
Sebastian *(G-16377)*

▲ Comprehensive Energy Svcs Inc .....D 407 682-1313
Longwood *(G-8353)*

Compulink Cble Assmblies Fla I ....E 727 579-1500
Saint Petersburg *(G-15640)*

Compulink Installation Svcs S..............D 954 938-9977
Fort Lauderdale *(G-3711)*

Controls Systems Contg Inc................E 786 472-3499
Doral *(G-3164)*

County Electric Inc ....E 954 565-2400
Oakland Park *(G-11592)*

County of Manatee ....D 941 747-3011
Bradenton *(G-1086)*

Crd Electrical Service LLC ....D 407 944-0191
Kissimmee *(G-7291)*

Curry Controls Company ....D 863 646-5781
Lakeland *(G-7847)*

Cv Technology Inc ....E 561 694-9588
Jupiter *(G-7061)*

Cypress Communications Inc ....E 561 640-9224
West Palm Beach *(G-19115)*

D L Williams Electric Co Inc................E 904 262-8005
Jacksonville *(G-6039)*

D&S Electrical Tech LLC ....D 813 254-5160
Tampa *(G-17566)*

Dale R Yox Inc ....E 352 794-7368
Crystal River *(G-2345)*

DAndrea Enterprises ....E 727 536-3535
Largo *(G-8094)*

Dato Electric Inc ....D 305 883-7319
Fort Lauderdale *(G-3753)*

Deberry Electric Co Inc ....E 904 757-8424
Jacksonville *(G-6053)*

Delgado Electric Inc..........................E 813 876-4782
Tampa *(G-17585)*

Doyle Electric Services Inc ....D 813 630-4600
Tampa *(G-17601)*

Dycom Industries Inc.........................D 561 627-7171
Palm Beach Gardens *(G-13722)*

E Harold Wilson Inc ....E 863 682-0158
Lakeland *(G-7854)*

East Coast Mechanical Inc ....E 561 585-9850
Boynton Beach *(G-985)*

Edlen Elec Exhbtion Svcs Inc O ....E 407 854-9991
Orlando *(G-12454)*

Edmonson Electric Inc ....C 813 910-3403
Land O Lakes *(G-8045)*

Edwards Electric Corp........................E 561 683-7066
West Palm Beach *(G-19129)*

▲ EF Lea Electrical Contr Inc ....E 904 355-7885
Jacksonville *(G-6105)*

Ehota Inc ....D 954 902-4299
Fort Lauderdale *(G-3769)*

Elcon Electric Incorporated ....E 800 446-8915
Deerfield Beach *(G-2739)*

Electrcal Cnstr Cmmnctions Inc............E 727 545-8468
Largo *(G-8098)*

Electric Maint & Cnstr Inc ....D 813 886-3733
Tampa *(G-17619)*

Electric Services Inc ....C 352 787-1322
Leesburg *(G-8242)*

Electric Solutions Un Ltd LLC ....E 321 281-8075
Orlando *(G-12457)*

Electrical Consulting Svcs Inc..............D 954 994-8468
West Palm Beach *(G-19130)*

Electrical Energy Systems Inc..............D 954 994-9442
Tamarac *(G-17188)*

Electrical Engrg Entps Inc ....E 813 740-9601
Tampa *(G-17621)*

Electrical Inv Group LLC ....E 941 756-5465
Bradenton *(G-1091)*

Electro Design Engineering Inc............C 813 621-0121
Riverview *(G-15256)*

Elite Electrical Contrs Inc..................D 239 561-1314
Fort Myers *(G-4356)*

Emergency Systems Inc ....E 904 388-3975
Jacksonville *(G-6112)*

Empire Elc Maint & Svc Inc ....D 305 264-9982
Miami *(G-9520)*

Empire Electrical Contrs LLC ....E 407 930-3736
Orlando *(G-12463)*

Empire Erectors & Elec Co Inc ....E 772 234-5288
Vero Beach *(G-18855)*

Encompass Elec Tech N Fla ....C 904 281-0600
Jacksonville *(G-6116)*

Encon Inc.......................................D 813 354-0446
Tampa *(G-17631)*

Energy Electric Inc ....E 813 932-7146
Tampa *(G-17633)*

Energycare LLC ....C 888 870-1933
Largo *(G-8099)*

Engineered Environments Inc ....E 561 282-4111
Riviera Beach *(G-15292)*

Engineered Services Inc ....E 772 223-2320
Stuart *(G-16619)*

Enterprise Elec Contg Inc ....C 305 884-6540
Miami *(G-9524)*

Erickson Electrical Contrs Inc..............E 904 641-9090
Jacksonville *(G-6129)*

Erwin Electric Inc ....D 813 701-2300
Tampa *(G-17639)*

Esi Maintenance Inc..........................E 561 262-4207
Crystal River *(G-2346)*

S
I
C

▼ Etc-Maronet Inc	D	561 881-8118
North Palm Beach (G-11545)		
Feldman Brothers Elec Sup Co	E	954 345-6884
Coral Springs (G-2251)		
Ferran Services & Contg Inc	C	407 422-3551
Orlando (G-12506)		
Fine Line Construction & Elc	D	954 786-8006
Pompano Beach (G-14803)		
Fire & Life Safety America Inc	D	804 222-1381
Sanford (G-15939)		
▼ Fire Alarm Systems & SEC Inc	E	954 327-8670
Davie (G-2480)		
Firetronics Inc	D	407 774-6900
Altamonte Springs (G-46)		
Fishel Company	D	352 429-4007
Groveland (G-5091)		
Florida Fire and Sound Inc	E	407 298-8812
Longwood (G-8360)		
◆ Florida Keys Elc Coop Assn Inc	D	305 852-2431
Tavernier (G-18624)		
Florida Keys Electric Inc	D	305 296-4028
Key West (G-7205)		
Florida LLC Integrated Systems	E	813 925-1007
Oldsmar (G-11903)		
Forrest Inc	D	904 794-2547
Saint Augustine (G-15444)		
Fortune Electrical Cnstr LLC	E	239 674-3171
Fort Myers (G-4402)		
FOS Fiber Optics Inc	D	727 572-1310
Odessa (G-11842)		
Franz Inc	E	954 428-8181
Deerfield Beach (G-2742)		
Fred Newton Electric Company	E	407 277-1719
Orlando (G-12544)		
Frontier Florida LLC	B	941 953-4760
Sarasota (G-16172)		
Fuellgraf Electric Co Tenn Inc	E	724 282-4800
Fort Myers (G-4405)		
Fusion Electric & Engrg LLC	E	239 494-4881
Bonita Springs (G-914)		
Galaxy Home Solutions Inc	C	352 748-4868
Wildwood (G-19496)		
Gerelco Electrical Contrs Inc	C	772 340-5998
Port Saint Lucie (G-15138)		
Globe Electrical Contrs Inc	E	904 810-0900
Saint Augustine (G-15446)		
Gmaa Inc	A	407 788-3717
Altamonte Springs (G-53)		
Goodson Electric Inc	E	941 722-1255
Palmetto (G-13914)		
Grassland Enterprises Inc	E	407 298-2494
Orlando (G-12595)		
Greenway Electrical Svcs LLC	E	407 532-2778
Apopka (G-186)		
Guardian Alarm Florida LLC	E	561 547-4550
Lantana (G-8064)		
Gulf Atlantic Elec Constrs Inc	E	850 622-2225
Santa Rosa Beach (G-16009)		
Gulf Electric Company	E	813 626-6280
Thonotosassa (G-18674)		
Hamker Enterprises Corporation	E	305 247-8281
Homestead (G-5578)		
Hank Lowry Electric Inc	E	407 855-0035
Orlando (G-12616)		
Harris-Mcburney Company	C	813 626-7171
Tampa (G-17794)		
Hawkins Service Company	E	813 871-6610
Riverview (G-15257)		
Henderson Electric Inc	E	850 243-2223
Fort Walton Beach (G-4779)		
Hicks Electric Inc	E	407 831-4881
Altamonte Springs (G-59)		
Highway Safety Devices Inc	C	239 489-4114
Fort Myers (G-4438)		
Himes Electric Company Inc	D	813 909-1927
Lutz (G-8443)		
Honshy Electric Co Inc	C	305 264-5500
Miami (G-9718)		
Horsepower Electric Inc	D	305 819-4060
Hialeah (G-5276)		
Horton/Jones Elec Contrs Inc	E	954 564-4220
Wilton Manors (G-19525)		
Hypower LLC	C	888 978-9300
Fort Lauderdale (G-3884)		
Hypower Inc	E	954 574-9392
Deerfield Beach (G-2755)		
Hypower Inc	E	954 972-6367
Pompano Beach (G-14825)		
Industrial Energy Services Inc	C	850 941-7621
Pensacola (G-14327)		
Industrial Fire & Safety Inc	E	727 573-1556
Saint Petersburg (G-15718)		
Infinite Communications Inc	D	336 516-0536
Saint Johns (G-15546)		
Irby Construction Company	D	407 696-4999
Longwood (G-8370)		
J & K Electric Inc	D	727 323-2288
Saint Petersburg (G-15730)		
J Crompton Electric Inc	E	561 588-6559
West Palm Beach (G-19211)		
J H Ham Engineering Inc	E	863 646-1448
Lakeland (G-7890)		
Jackson Total Service Inc	E	239 643-0923
Naples (G-11181)		
Jade Communications Inc	E	561 997-8552
Boca Raton (G-647)		
Jajo Inc	C	316 267-6700
Doral (G-3249)		
James W Knight Electric Inc	E	813 248-3877
Tampa (G-17890)		
▼ JC&a Electrical Contrs Inc	D	305 594-2775
Miami (G-9786)		
Jeff & Jerrys Electric Inc	C	407 933-7771
Kissimmee (G-7331)		
▼ Jeffry Knight Inc	E	727 524-6235
Clearwater (G-1683)		
Jerry Pybus Electric Inc	D	850 784-2766
Panama City (G-14032)		
Jn Electric Tampa Bay Inc	D	813 948-1608
Tampa (G-17896)		
John J Rack Inc	E	561 391-3550
Boca Raton (G-652)		
◆ Johnson Cntrls SEC Sltions LLC	B	561 264-2071
Boca Raton (G-654)		
Johnson Controls Inc	E	407 291-1971
Orlando (G-12711)		
Jsc Systems Inc	E	850 656-1705
Tallahassee (G-17012)		
Jsc Systems Inc	E	352 378-9777
Jacksonville (G-6392)		
Jsc Systems Inc	E	904 737-3511
Gainesville (G-4930)		
K&K Electric Inc	D	407 323-6300
Sanford (G-15956)		
Keller Mechanical & Engrg Inc	E	863 686-0947
Lakeland (G-7894)		
Keylite Power and Ltg Corp	E	305 232-9910
Miami (G-9826)		
Kinbro Inc	E	407 698-6950
Wauchula (G-18963)		
Kirkwood Electric Inc	E	239 574-3449
Cape Coral (G-1404)		
▲ Knight Electric Company Inc	E	561 689-3500
Riviera Beach (G-15305)		
Konnect Communications Inc	D	954 842-4532
Hollywood (G-5465)		
Kreg Electric Incorporated	E	954 786-1642
Pompano Beach (G-14839)		
Latour Enterprizes Inc	E	386 252-0573
Daytona Beach (G-2625)		
Lenhart Electric Company	E	352 748-5818
Wildwood (G-19502)		
Lighting Resources Usa Inc	E	386 738-7228
Deland (G-2867)		
▲ Lightning Electric Inc	E	561 965-2323
West Palm Beach (G-19239)		
Longs Air Conditioning Inc	E	863 465-7771
Avon Park (G-294)		
Loveland Electric Inc	E	561 882-0401
West Palm Beach (G-19242)		
▼ Ls Energia Inc	E	954 281-7022
Plantation (G-14668)		
Lsci Inc	E	727 571-4141
Seminole (G-16455)		
Mabry Brothers Inc	E	239 482-1122
Fort Myers (G-4499)		
Maddox Electric Company Inc	C	407 934-8084
Winter Garden (G-19580)		
Malone Elec Solutions LLC	D	561 242-0680
West Palm Beach (G-19248)		
Mardant Elec Cnstr Co Inc	E	904 363-0200
Jacksonville (G-6466)		
Mastec North America Inc	B	850 562-2135
Tallahassee (G-17036)		
McDonald Electric Service Inc	E	904 356-9473
Jacksonville (G-6481)		
Meisner Electric Inc	C	561 243-2020
Boca Raton (G-688)		
Merit Electric Company Inc	D	727 536-5945
Largo (G-8135)		
Metro Electrical Services Inc	E	850 222-2804
Tallahassee (G-17045)		
Miami-Dade Cnty Pub Schols-158	C	305 235-2329
Miami (G-9994)		
Michael J Looney Inc	D	941 474-3104
Englewood (G-3438)		
Mid-State Inc	E	352 376-0793
Gainesville (G-4946)		
Midstate Electric Ocala LLC	D	352 622-3208
Ocala (G-11733)		
▲ Midway Services Inc	C	727 573-9500
Clearwater (G-1721)		
Millennium Entps Unlimited Inc	E	407 420-2001
Orlando (G-12869)		
Millennium Tech Group Inc	E	407 996-2399
Orlando (G-12870)		
Miller Electric Company	D	904 388-8000
Jacksonville (G-6504)		
Miller Electric Company	E	954 761-2110
Fort Lauderdale (G-3972)		
Miller Electric Company	E	407 328-5220
Altamonte Springs (G-79)		
Miller Electrical Service Inc	C	407 648-8540
Orlando (G-12871)		
Mills Electric Service Inc	E	954 640-5262
Fort Lauderdale (G-3974)		
Milwaukee Electric Tool Corp	E	305 592-0860
Doral (G-3276)		
MJM Electric Inc	D	813 248-1711
Tampa (G-18045)		
Mm Electric Cfl Inc	E	321 228-2832
Orlando (G-12874)		
Morton Electric Inc	B	407 830-1000
Sanford (G-15966)		
Mr Electric & Associates Inc	E	954 792-6710
Plantation (G-14679)		
N&M Cooling and Heating Inc	C	941 921-5581
Sarasota (G-16243)		
NCN Electric Inc	E	941 488-0005
Venice (G-18794)		
New Energy Service Inc	C	321 269-1124
Titusville (G-18697)		
North Ridge Electric Inc	E	954 782-3663
Pompano Beach (G-14870)		
On-Line Electric	D	813 662-0362
Brandon (G-1246)		
Owen Electric Company Inc	C	904 824-9954
Saint Augustine (G-15476)		
Palmer Electric Company	B	407 646-8700
Winter Park (G-19759)		
Pcg Securities LLC	E	978 902-0352
Wesley Chapel (G-19005)		
Phones 4 Less LLC	E	786 496-0618
Weston (G-19475)		
Pike Electric LLC	C	239 561-2201
Fort Myers (G-4542)		
Pikes Electric Inc	E	352 748-6251
Wildwood (G-19506)		
Plumbing Experts Inc	E	561 368-5111
Delray Beach (G-3007)		
Pmh Group Inc	E	863 299-3695
Bartow (G-330)		
Pomeroy Electric Incorporated	C	954 427-0705
Deerfield Beach (G-2785)		
Power Design Inc	B	727 210-0492
Saint Petersburg (G-15804)		
Powerserve Technologies Inc	D	561 840-1441
Jupiter (G-7125)		
Preston-Link Electric Inc	D	352 373-3516
Gainesville (G-4981)		
Primary Electrical Contrs Inc	E	954 434-2646
Fort Pierce (G-4730)		
Proton Electric Service LLC	E	561 547-0027
Riviera Beach (G-15314)		
Quality Cable Contractors Inc	E	407 246-0606
Orlando (G-13077)		
Quinco Electrical Inc	C	407 478-6005
Winter Park (G-19766)		
Quinco Services Inc	E	407 857-6133
Winter Park (G-19767)		
R & R Electric North Fla Inc	E	904 764-5555
Jacksonville (G-6628)		
R&C It Hdwr & Sftwr Dist Corp	E	954 368-3793
Fort Lauderdale (G-4077)		
Randall Electrical Contrs Inc	E	321 269-1124
Titusville (G-18701)		
Rauland-Borg Corp Florida	E	407 830-6175
Altamonte Springs (G-96)		
Rayco Electric Inc	D	941 747-1968
Bradenton (G-1168)		

Regency Electric Company Inc ....C 904 281-0600
Jacksonville *(G-6647)*
Richard L Oreair & Company ....D 904 764-2524
Jacksonville *(G-6662)*
Rising Force Security LLC ....D 407 205-6633
Melbourne *(G-8971)*
Riskwatch International LLC ....D 941 500-4525
Sarasota *(G-16284)*
Roadrunner Electric Inc ....E 305 267-1013
Miami *(G-10216)*
◆ Robert Forbis Inc ....D 239 598-2000
Naples *(G-11285)*
S & S Electric Co Inc ....D 727 489-3000
Oldsmar *(G-11925)*
Sanders Brothers Electric Inc ....D 850 857-0701
Pensacola *(G-14428)*
Schmitt Inc ....E 352 683-7606
Spring Hill *(G-16546)*
Schmitt Inc ....E 727 868-9531
Hudson *(G-5648)*
Seabreeze Electric Inc ....D 941 255-5968
Port Charlotte *(G-15059)*
Service Complete Electric Inc ....D 407 679-3500
Oviedo *(G-13569)*
Service Electric Company ....D 352 431-3648
Leesburg *(G-8273)*
Service Electric Usa LLC ....D 850 602-4226
Pensacola *(G-14433)*
Service Minds LLC ....E 941 960-7878
Sarasota *(G-16055)*
Shine and Company Inc ....E 386 454-2034
High Springs *(G-5355)*
▲ Siemens Energy Inc ....C 407 736-5988
Casselberry *(G-1457)*
◆ Siemens Generation Services Co ....C 407 736-2000
Orlando *(G-13196)*
▲ Signal Group Inc ....E 561 744-3206
Coral Springs *(G-2285)*
▼ Signal Tech Installation Corp ....D 954 327-2434
Pompano Beach *(G-14898)*
Sinns & Thomas Elec Contrs Inc ....D 407 696-6042
Winter Springs *(G-19811)*
Sir Electric Inc ....C 561 738-9000
Boynton Beach *(G-1037)*
Smartwatch SEC & Sound LLC ....E 352 383-2479
Orlando *(G-13208)*
Soc LLC ....E 321 501-2809
Melbourne *(G-8974)*
Soma Global Inc ....E 855 750-7662
Tampa *(G-18304)*
Sonitrol of Tallahassee Inc ....E 850 222-3676
Tallahassee *(G-17103)*
South Lake Electric & Cnstr Co ....E 352 429-2624
Groveland *(G-5101)*
Southast Undgrd Utilities Corp ....E 954 583-8745
Sunrise *(G-16829)*
Statewide Elec Contrs Inc ....E 305 971-8864
Miami *(G-10328)*
◆ Stellar Energy Americas Inc ....E 904 260-2044
Jacksonville *(G-6790)*
Strada Services Inc ....C 321 421-7783
Melbourne *(G-8985)*
Structred Cbling Solutions Inc ....E 305 628-9445
Miramar *(G-10903)*
Structured Media Group Inc ....E 407 323-8607
Sanford *(G-15983)*
Stryker Electrical Contg Inc ....D 772 219-3389
Palm City *(G-13804)*
Summit Electrical Contrs Inc ....E 904 741-4898
Jacksonville *(G-6805)*
▼ Sun Electric Works Inc ....E 561 757-4403
Deerfield Beach *(G-2802)*
Superior Electrical Contrs Inc ....D 305 477-6328
Doral *(G-3326)*
T & M Electric Clay County Inc ....D 904 272-0272
Orange Park *(G-12020)*
Talon Security Inc ....E 850 728-1535
Midway *(G-10808)*
TCS Group Inc ....E 954 846-8787
Coral Springs *(G-2290)*
Tecc Inc ....E 407 330-2900
Osteen *(G-13535)*
Technical Management Assoc Inc ....D 724 282-4800
Fort Myers *(G-4623)*
Tektron Electrical Systems ....E 561 615-3111
West Palm Beach *(G-19380)*
Telecom Engineering Cons ....D 305 592-4328
Doral *(G-3331)*
Telecore Inc ....B 954 492-9277
Fort Lauderdale *(G-4172)*

Terrys Electric Inc ....C 407 572-2100
Kissimmee *(G-7397)*
Terrys Electric Inc ....D 407 572-2100
West Palm Beach *(G-19384)*
Thomas Services Inc ....D 630 519-3265
West Palm Beach *(G-19387)*
Thunder Electrical Contrs Inc ....D 305 669-1776
Miami *(G-10389)*
Tirone Electric Inc ....D 954 989-7162
Hollywood *(G-5537)*
Titan Elec Svcs Sthwest Fla LL ....E 239 800-3233
North Fort Myers *(G-11477)*
Titan Electric Southeast LLC ....E 407 677-4080
Orlando *(G-13293)*
Topaz Lighting Company LLC ....D 904 924-8850
Jacksonville *(G-6860)*
Total Comfort Heat and AC Inc ....D 386 672-8494
Ormond Beach *(G-13528)*
Total Electric Contracting LLC ....D 239 278-0002
Fort Myers *(G-4628)*
Total Electric Svc Tampa Inc ....E 813 899-4948
Tampa *(G-18426)*
Traffic Control Devices Inc ....E 407 869-5300
Altamonte Springs *(G-107)*
Transtec Systems Inc ....E 718 679-0484
Miramar *(G-10905)*
Traylor Electric Company Inc ....E 954 421-3300
Coconut Creek *(G-2007)*
Tri-City Electrical Contrs Inc ....C 954 586-4393
Pompano Beach *(G-14929)*
Tri-City Electrical Contrs Inc ....C 813 622-7180
Tampa *(G-18443)*
Tri-City Electrical Contrs Inc ....B 407 788-3500
Altamonte Springs *(G-109)*
Tri-City Electrical Contrs Inc ....C 239 768-5566
Fort Myers *(G-4630)*
Tri-County Electric Inc ....E 727 723-3400
Dunedin *(G-3392)*
Triage Partners LLC ....D 813 801-9869
Tampa *(G-18445)*
Try-Cor Electric Inc ....D 407 839-4699
Orlando *(G-13317)*
Under Power Corp ....E 305 468-9900
Miami *(G-10432)*
United Signs & Signals Inc ....D 352 742-1904
Tavares *(G-18620)*
◆ Unlimited Elec Contrs Corp ....C 954 481-8250
Fort Lauderdale *(G-4201)*
Vans Electric Lake Worth Inc ....E 561 588-3854
West Palm Beach *(G-19406)*
Vengroff Williams & Assoc Inc ....C 941 363-5200
Sarasota *(G-16358)*
Victoria Electric Inc ....E 786 547-4909
Miami *(G-10471)*
▼ Wards Marine Electric Inc ....E 954 523-2815
Fort Lauderdale *(G-4219)*
Water Equipment Services Inc ....D 941 371-7617
Sarasota *(G-16361)*
Wayne Atmtc Fire Sprnklers Inc ....E 954 917-3030
Deerfield Beach *(G-2814)*
Wentco Inc ....D 239 694-2700
Fort Myers *(G-4653)*
West Florida Elc Coop Assn Inc ....E 850 263-3231
Graceville *(G-5043)*
Weston Trawick Inc ....E 850 514-0003
Tallahassee *(G-17173)*
◆ Westside Electric Incorporated ....E 904 741-8001
Jacksonville *(G-6931)*
▼ Wilco Electrical LLC ....E 305 248-9911
Miami *(G-10504)*
Windemuller Technical Svcs Inc ....E 941 355-8822
Sarasota *(G-16366)*
Wiring Technologies Inc ....D 407 862-6290
Altamonte Springs *(G-115)*
Youngs Communications Co Inc ....D 321 723-6025
Melbourne *(G-9011)*
Youngs Electrical Contg Inc ....E 239 574-1288
Cape Coral *(G-1436)*
Zio Group LLC ....E 407 622-2262
Winter Park *(G-19795)*

1741 Masonry & Other Stonework

▲ 3 C Construction Corp ....D 305 638-5511
Miami *(G-9056)*
Advanced Masonry Assoc LLC ....C 941 926-3155
Sarasota *(G-16077)*
AF Masonry Inc ....E 813 967-6039
Dover *(G-3364)*
All American Driveway Inc ....E 305 420-5458
Doral *(G-3109)*

◆ Allan Spear Construction LLC ....D 352 337-0773
Gainesville *(G-4833)*
Apex Pavers Inc ....E 772 419-5151
Stuart *(G-16588)*
Argos USA LLC ....E 941 351-9611
Sarasota *(G-16022)*
Associated Cnstr Pdts Inc ....D 813 973-4425
Lutz *(G-8430)*
Bob Miller Masonry Inc ....D 941 377-5376
Sarasota *(G-16108)*
Bradley Masonry Inc ....E 850 432-3958
Pensacola *(G-14239)*
Carroll Bradford Incorporated ....E 407 647-9420
Orlando *(G-12246)*
Central Broward Cnstr Inc ....E 954 491-2772
Fort Lauderdale *(G-3677)*
Certified Foundations Inc ....E 863 859-3889
Lakeland *(G-7829)*
Coast To Coast Gen Contrs Inc ....D 954 920-3900
Hollywood *(G-5416)*
Cocoa Inc ....E 407 425-9095
Orlando *(G-12338)*
Commercial Con Systems LLC ....D 239 592-1101
Naples *(G-11071)*
D Lenn Masonry Contrs Inc ....E 850 433-7396
Pensacola *(G-14281)*
▼ Doyle Masonry Inc ....E 772 464-2378
Fort Pierce *(G-4696)*
Dz Block Inc ....E 352 399-2746
The Villages *(G-18656)*
EL Shearer Con Masonary Inc ....E 727 548-7959
Pinellas Park *(G-14515)*
Ervin Bishop Construction Inc ....E 813 996-6560
Land O Lakes *(G-8046)*
Florida Masonry Cnstr Co ....E 813 626-4518
Tampa *(G-17690)*
General Masonry NW Florida Inc ....E 850 244-2901
Fort Walton Beach *(G-4773)*
Gilbert Byrd Masnry Contrs Inc ....E 727 541-2662
Largo *(G-8112)*
Hommes Masonry Inc ....E 407 654-2648
Winter Garden *(G-19571)*
Industrial Concrete LLC ....E 407 654-6100
Clermont *(G-1875)*
Jackson Stoneworks LLC ....E 352 372-6600
Gainesville *(G-4925)*
Kd Construction Consulting Inc ....E 305 661-2505
Miami *(G-9814)*
Keller North America Inc ....C 813 884-3441
Tampa *(G-17912)*
Keller North America Inc ....C 305 592-8181
Miami *(G-9815)*
Keller North America Inc ....C 813 884-3441
Tampa *(G-17913)*
◆ LHP Group Inc ....E 305 759-4141
Miami *(G-9867)*
Masonry Builders Inc ....E 813 287-1731
Tampa *(G-17997)*
Masonry Incorporated ....D 850 893-9873
Tallahassee *(G-17034)*
NCM Collier County Inc ....C 239 566-1601
Naples *(G-11248)*
Ogden Brothers Cnstr Inc ....E 239 592-9960
Naples *(G-11251)*
Pardue Masonry of Central Fla ....D 813 948-3205
Tampa *(G-18122)*
Pepper Contracting Svcs Inc ....C 813 868-7719
Clearwater *(G-1756)*
Pompano Masonry Corporation ....D 407 428-1182
Orlando *(G-13042)*
Pompano Masonry Corporation ....C 954 946-3033
Pompano Beach *(G-14878)*
Premier Restoration Cnstr Inc ....E 352 385-9106
Mount Dora *(G-10960)*
◆ Premier Stoneworks LLC ....E 561 330-3737
Delray Beach *(G-3010)*
R D Masonry Inc ....D 904 992-6468
Jacksonville *(G-6630)*
▲ Ramos Marble and Granite Inc ....E 813 253-2620
Tampa *(G-18200)*
◆ Real Stone & Granite Corp ....E 772 489-9964
Fort Pierce *(G-4733)*
Reintjes Services Inc ....E 863 595-0961
Winter Haven *(G-19653)*
Reintjes Services Inc ....E 386 752-9506
Lake City *(G-7542)*
Reintjes Services Inc ....E 863 595-0961
Winter Haven *(G-19654)*
▼ Ron Kendall Masonry Inc ....D 561 793-5924
West Palm Beach *(G-19345)*

Ron Kendall Masonry Inc ....D...... 904 272-4436
Orange Park *(G-12015)*

Seminole Masonry LLC ....E...... 407 971-2464
Sanford *(G-15979)*

Stevens Masonry LLC ....E...... 904 823-1115
Saint Augustine *(G-15504)*

Sunshine Structures Inc ....D...... 239 303-1001
Lehigh Acres *(G-8293)*

T & T Cnstr Centl Fla Inc ....B...... 407 831-5506
Casselberry *(G-1461)*

▲ Titan Stone LLC ....D...... 954 977-1001
Pompano Beach *(G-14921)*

Tom Brunton Masonry Inc ....E...... 941 408-1821
Venice *(G-18812)*

Tom White Inc ....D...... 727 578-5819
Saint Petersburg *(G-15876)*

US Brick & Block Systems Inc ....D...... 954 792-1312
Dania *(G-2421)*

Wavecrest Masonry Inc ....C...... 352 860-0560
Inverness *(G-5701)*

Westcoast Strl Con Masnry Inc ....D...... 239 590-6408
Fort Myers *(G-4655)*

1742 Plastering, Drywall, Acoustical & Insulation Work

AA Stucco & Drywall Inc ....B...... 239 598-1100
Naples *(G-10995)*

Acousti Engineering Co Fla ....E...... 386 462-9900
Alachua *(G-1)*

Acousti Engineering Co Fla ....E...... 850 434-0264
Pensacola *(G-14210)*

Acousti Engineering Co Fla ....D...... 904 781-9355
Jacksonville *(G-5732)*

Acousti Engineering Co Fla ....D...... 813 620-0718
Tampa *(G-17229)*

Acousti Engineering Co Fla ....D...... 239 332-1610
Fort Myers *(G-4248)*

Acousti Engineering Co Fla ....D...... 305 887-0740
Medley *(G-8701)*

Acousti Engineering Co Fla ....E...... 321 636-4042
Rockledge *(G-15331)*

Acousti Engineering Co Fla ....E...... 850 576-0102
Tallahassee *(G-16868)*

Aerial Companies Inc ....C...... 239 643-7625
Naples *(G-11002)*

Alpha Insul & Waterproofing ....E...... 407 379-9300
Longwood *(G-8339)*

American Commercial Insul LLC ....D...... 386 304-2222
Daytona Beach *(G-2541)*

American Insulators LLC ....E...... 904 268-4588
Jacksonville *(G-5786)*

American National Insul Inc ....A...... 386 304-2200
Daytona Beach *(G-2543)*

Andersen Interior Contg Inc ....C...... 941 845-3200
Palmetto *(G-13903)*

ASAP Shell Contracting Inc ....D...... 727 289-7721
Tampa *(G-17310)*

Atlantis Drywall & Framing LLC ....D...... 407 834-6767
Longwood *(G-8343)*

B & H Interiors Inc ....E...... 904 725-4142
Jacksonville *(G-5830)*

Baylor Construction Inc ....E...... 386 253-8976
Holly Hill *(G-5379)*

Bergolla Inc ....E...... 305 887-3088
Hialeah *(G-5223)*

Brant & Son Inc ....D...... 407 658-1925
Orlando *(G-12199)*

Builder Services Group Inc ....E...... 407 295-5316
Orlando *(G-12218)*

▼ Builder Services Group Inc ....D...... 386 304-2222
Daytona Beach *(G-2556)*

Builder Services Group Inc ....E...... 772 589-1514
Fort Pierce *(G-4688)*

Builder Services Group Inc ....E...... 941 485-5471
Venice *(G-18768)*

Builder Services Group Inc ....E...... 352 799-0051
Brooksville *(G-1276)*

Builder Services Group Inc ....E...... 407 678-9451
Winter Park *(G-19690)*

C2 Construction Services Inc ....D...... 571 379-5684
Edgewater *(G-3409)*

Carlisos Construction Inc ....D...... 813 447-6046
Tampa *(G-17422)*

Central Florida Drywall & Plst ....D...... 352 376-6606
Gainesville *(G-4853)*

Commercial Contg Systems Inc ....E...... 941 351-4633
Sarasota *(G-16125)*

Daniel Insulation LLC ....E...... 727 572-8990
Clearwater *(G-1601)*

DMS Contractors LLC ....D...... 305 627-3276
Fort Lauderdale *(G-3761)*

Fallsafe Solutions LLC ....C...... 239 260-4120
Fort Myers *(G-4367)*

Fickling Brothers Inc ....D...... 904 359-0314
Jacksonville *(G-6154)*

Ford Drywall & Stucco Inc ....E...... 239 649-6962
Naples *(G-11122)*

Garrard Carpentry Inc ....D...... 863 967-3992
Winter Haven *(G-19629)*

Hanlon Acoustical Ceilings LLC ....E...... 813 930-0023
Tampa *(G-17787)*

Herndon Construction Service ....D...... 813 854-3117
Oldsmar *(G-11906)*

Ingram Enterprises Inc ....D...... 850 576-6448
Tallahassee *(G-17003)*

Interior Txtres of Palm Bches ....D...... 561 768-9512
Jupiter *(G-7089)*

J S Plastering Inc ....D...... 321 725-7751
Melbourne *(G-8913)*

Jack Vgel Smulated Brick Stone ....E...... 561 659-3400
West Palm Beach *(G-19212)*

JE Abercrombie Inc ....D...... 904 724-4411
Jacksonville *(G-6382)*

Jims Drywall Inc ....D...... 904 824-0836
Saint Augustine *(G-15458)*

▼ Keenan Hpkins Schmidt Stwell C ......D...... 813 628-9330
Tampa *(G-17910)*

Kenpat (central Florida) LLC ....D...... 407 464-7070
Apopka *(G-192)*

Kenpat Usa LLC ....D...... 407 464-7070
Apopka *(G-193)*

Lee Drywall Inc ....D...... 239 939-9779
Fort Myers *(G-4477)*

Lotspeich Co Florida Inc ....E...... 954 978-2388
Fort Lauderdale *(G-3946)*

Low Country Insulation Inc ....E...... 561 394-9155
Boca Raton *(G-676)*

M & R Drywall Inc ....E...... 954 788-8966
Pompano Beach *(G-14846)*

Marvin Hauesler Interiors Inc ....E...... 727 573-5408
Clearwater *(G-1708)*

Master Plaster Inc ....E...... 954 922-9396
Hollywood *(G-5473)*

Miller Insul & Acoustics Inc ....E...... 941 751-4991
Palmetto *(G-13923)*

▲ Msei Inc ....B...... 813 628-5566
Orlando *(G-12886)*

Paramount Drywall Inc ....D...... 305 403-4818
Miami *(G-10094)*

Paul Johnson Drywall Inc ....E...... 407 365-3303
Oviedo *(G-13564)*

▲ Pedersen Lathing & Plastering ....E...... 772 879-3911
Palm City *(G-13796)*

Performance Contracting Inc ....E...... 863 644-4738
Lakeland *(G-7940)*

Pro-Crete Systems Inc ....E...... 727 527-2424
Largo *(G-8143)*

Protective Barriers LLC ....E...... 239 693-5937
Fort Myers *(G-4556)*

Raynor Company Group ....E...... 727 581-4558
Oldsmar *(G-11922)*

Ridge Energy Savers Inc ....E...... 863 676-2665
Lake Wales *(G-7698)*

Rue Quality Systems Inc ....E...... 407 330-6109
Sanford *(G-15976)*

▲ Service Partners LLC ....E...... 804 515-7400
Daytona Beach *(G-2661)*

Southern Acoustics Inc ....E...... 407 696-4448
Casselberry *(G-1458)*

Southern Quality Plst Inc ....D...... 727 399-0028
Largo *(G-8152)*

Southwest Cnstr Svcs Inc ....C...... 239 491-2567
Lehigh Acres *(G-8290)*

SPI LLC ....E...... 813 621-5371
Tampa *(G-18321)*

Starcevich Systems Inc ....D...... 407 855-0022
Orlando *(G-13235)*

Tailored Foam of Florida LLC ....E...... 407 332-0333
Sanford *(G-15984)*

Technology Contractors Inc ....E...... 305 971-1163
Miami *(G-10369)*

Terracon Group Inc ....D...... 305 635-4698
Coral Gables *(G-2196)*

Topbuild Corp ....C...... 386 304-2200
Daytona Beach *(G-2676)*

Truteam of California Inc ....E...... 386 304-2200
Daytona Beach *(G-2680)*

▲ United Subcontractors Inc ....E...... 651 225-6300
Daytona Beach *(G-2684)*

United Subcontractors Inc ....D...... 863 655-2261
Fort Myers *(G-4640)*

United Subcontractors Inc ....D...... 561 276-0177
West Palm Beach *(G-19399)*

United Subcontractors Inc ....D...... 239 334-8002
Fort Myers *(G-4641)*

US Greenfiber LLC ....E...... 813 627-0331
Tampa *(G-18486)*

US Walls & Ceilings Inc ....D...... 407 445-8861
Orlando *(G-13362)*

Wal-Mark Contracting Group LLC ....E...... 941 342-6900
Sarasota *(G-16360)*

Wal-Mark Contracting Group LLC ....D...... 813 348-4711
Tampa *(G-18517)*

Wall Systems Inc ....E...... 813 254-4356
Tampa *(G-18519)*

Wall Systems Inc Southwest Fla ....E...... 239 643-1921
Naples *(G-11340)*

Wb Interiors LLC ....E...... 239 244-9492
Fort Myers *(G-4649)*

Wilco Enterprises Inc ....E...... 352 629-8157
Ocala *(G-11797)*

Williams Consolidated I Ltd ....C...... 386 304-2200
Daytona Beach *(G-2690)*

1743 Terrazzo, Tile, Marble & Mosaic Work

▼ Amazon USA Enterprise Corp ....E...... 561 278-5552
Delray Beach *(G-2903)*

At Your Service Clg Group Inc ....E...... 941 360-6796
Sarasota *(G-16096)*

Bella Tile & Marble Corp ....E...... 239 643-3624
Naples *(G-11032)*

◆ Century Tile and Marble Inc ....E...... 954 973-1020
Fort Lauderdale *(G-3679)*

Creative Terrazzo Systems Inc ....C...... 954 767-6372
Southwest Ranches *(G-16528)*

Creative Tile Concepts Inc ....D...... 239 513-0200
Naples *(G-11082)*

◆ D&B Tile and Related Entps Inc ....E...... 954 845-1110
Sunrise *(G-16761)*

▲ European Marble Co ....D...... 941 955-9536
Sarasota *(G-16153)*

Fred Nickel Tile Inc ....E...... 352 347-9988
Ocala *(G-11694)*

▲ Greer Tile Company ....D...... 407 296-4600
Orlando *(G-12602)*

Horizon Tile & Crpt Southeast ....E...... 561 744-1018
Jupiter *(G-7088)*

◆ Mosaics of America Inc ....D...... 772 468-8453
Fort Pierce *(G-4722)*

Namm Group Inc ....E...... 954 968-1700
Pompano Beach *(G-14864)*

Paragon Industries Inc ....E...... 954 917-8002
Deerfield Beach *(G-2782)*

▲ Ramos Marble and Granite Inc ....E...... 813 253-2620
Tampa *(G-18200)*

◆ Real Stone & Granite Corp ....E...... 772 489-9964
Fort Pierce *(G-4733)*

Steward-Mellon Company LLC ....E...... 813 621-3577
Tampa *(G-18338)*

◆ Stone-Mart MBL Trvrtine Group ....D...... 813 885-6900
Tampa *(G-18339)*

▲ United Stone Installation Inc ....E...... 239 597-7773
Naples *(G-11333)*

1751 Carpentry Work

Acousti Engineering Co Fla ....D...... 904 781-9355
Jacksonville *(G-5732)*

Advanced Woodworking Inds LLC ....E...... 954 634-3100
Oakland Park *(G-11583)*

American Builders Supply Inc ....D...... 863 294-0611
Winter Haven *(G-19604)*

American Builders Supply Inc ....D...... 321 674-9207
Melbourne *(G-8814)*

American Woodmark Corporation ....B...... 407 857-9081
Orlando *(G-12117)*

◆ Arso Enterprises Inc ....E...... 305 681-2020
Opa Locka *(G-11940)*

Aws Carpenter Contractors Inc ....E...... 813 855-1006
Oldsmar *(G-11894)*

Baylor Construction Inc ....E...... 386 253-8976
Holly Hill *(G-5379)*

▼ Broten Garage Door Sales LLC ....D...... 954 946-5555
Pompano Beach *(G-14756)*

Capital City Lumber Co Inc ....E...... 850 385-0315
Tallahassee *(G-16902)*

Carpenter Contractors Amer Inc ....A...... 863 294-6449
Winter Haven *(G-19613)*

Central Florida Drywall & Plst ....D...... 352 376-6606
Gainesville *(G-4853)*

D & M Trim Inc ....E 904 284-3753
Green Cove Springs *(G-5050)*
▼ Dab Door Company Inc ....E 305 556-6624
Hialeah *(G-5251)*
◆ Door Systems South Florida Inc ....E 561 479-2039
Pompano Beach *(G-14797)*
Dorr Houzzer USA LLC ....E 561 444-9496
Pompano Beach *(G-14798)*
Fallsafe Solutions LLC ....C 239 260-4120
Fort Myers *(G-4367)*
Flores-Hager and Assoc Inc ....D 386 676-9999
Daytona Beach *(G-2589)*
Florida Crpnters Rgnal Cncil T ....D 954 739-9200
Fort Lauderdale *(G-3795)*
Florida West Cabinets Inc ....E 850 474-3986
Pensacola *(G-14312)*
Garrard Carpentry Inc ....D 863 967-3992
Winter Haven *(G-19629)*
Glenco Industries I LLC ....E 407 888-0651
Orlando *(G-12574)*
GM&p Consulting Glazing Contrs ....E 305 638-5151
Miami *(G-9643)*
H B S Inc ....E 772 567-7461
Vero Beach *(G-18863)*
Hughes Trim LLC ....D 863 206-6048
Orlando *(G-12669)*
Isec Incorporated ....D 813 422-5100
Tampa *(G-17876)*
Jims Drywall Inc ....E 904 824-0836
Saint Augustine *(G-15458)*
▲ Jsw of Palm Beach Inc ....D 561 588-4460
Lake Worth Beach *(G-7771)*
Ka Operations LLC ....D 954 753-3501
Coral Springs *(G-2264)*
Keane Architectural Wdwrk Inc ....E 954 574-9915
Coconut Creek *(G-1994)*
Omega Garage Doors Inc ....E 941 627-0150
Venice *(G-18795)*
Overhead Door Co Orlando Inc ....E 407 830-5600
Longwood *(G-8390)*
Performance Door and Hdwr Inc ....E 407 932-2115
Kissimmee *(G-7374)*
Precision Holdings Brevard Inc ....A 321 225-3500
Titusville *(G-18699)*
Properties Elgant Dstnction LL ....D 561 364-9675
Boynton Beach *(G-1029)*
R B M Contracting Services LLC ....E 850 622-1434
Freeport *(G-4816)*
RG Framing Inc ....E 386 281-3053
Ormond Beach *(G-13518)*
Robert Chalk Framing Inc ....E 904 692-1374
Elkton *(G-3426)*
S M I Cabinetry Inc ....E 407 841-0292
Orlando *(G-13155)*
▼ Structural Roof Systems Inc ....E 954 484-9663
Fort Lauderdale *(G-4157)*
Sunbelt Home Solutions Inc ....E 941 259-3827
Sarasota *(G-16337)*
Topbuild Corp ....C 386 304-2200
Daytona Beach *(G-2676)*
Universal Window Solutions LLC ....E 941 752-7473
Sarasota *(G-16066)*
Viking Cnstr Corp SW Fla ....E 239 574-3000
Cape Coral *(G-1432)*
Wall Systems Inc Southwest Fla ....E 239 643-1921
Naples *(G-11340)*
Windowwall LLC ....E 813 649-8959
Tampa *(G-18562)*

1752 Floor Laying & Other Floor Work, NEC

A B Property Services Inc ....D 786 320-5305
Miami *(G-9060)*
◆ A B Property Services Inc ....D 800 432-2115
Miami *(G-9061)*
◆ Absolute Hardwood Flooring Inc ....D 561 833-5720
West Palm Beach *(G-19019)*
Acousti Engineering Co Fla ....E 850 576-0102
Tallahassee *(G-16868)*
Acousti Engineering Co Fla ....E 386 462-9900
Alachua *(G-1)*
Acousti Engineering Co Fla ....D 904 781-9355
Jacksonville *(G-5732)*
Acousti Engineering Co Fla ....D 813 620-0718
Tampa *(G-17229)*
Bella Tile & Marble Corp ....E 239 643-3624
Naples *(G-11032)*
◆ Chadwell Supply Inc ....D 888 341-2423
Tampa *(G-17453)*
Cianos Tile & Marble Inc ....E 239 267-8453
Fort Myers *(G-4312)*
Floor Technologies Inc ....E 305 818-9530
Hialeah *(G-5262)*
Lotspeich Co Florida Inc ....C 954 978-2388
Fort Lauderdale *(G-3946)*
Shaw Contract Flrg Svcs Inc ....D 813 254-7278
Tampa *(G-18274)*
Shaw Contract Flrg Svcs Inc ....D 813 833-9134
Tampa *(G-18275)*
Shaw Contract Flrg Svcs Inc ....E 800 845-0649
Jacksonville *(G-6719)*
Spraggins Inc ....C 407 295-4150
Orlando *(G-13225)*
Steam-S-Way Inc ....E 561 966-0765
Riviera Beach *(G-15319)*
Steward-Mellon Company LLC ....E 813 621-3577
Tampa *(G-18338)*
▲ Wayne Wiles Floorcoverings Inc ....E 239 267-7600
Fort Myers *(G-4648)*

1761 Roofing, Siding & Sheet Metal Work

A-1 Duran Roofing Inc ....D 305 470-9570
Miami *(G-9063)*
A-1 Property Svcs Group Inc ....E 786 419-5041
Miami *(G-9064)*
Ad-Ler Roofing Inc ....E 239 936-8226
Fort Myers *(G-4250)*
Aderhold Roofing Corporation ....E 813 856-1797
Tampa *(G-17235)*
Advanced Roofg Sheetmetal LLC ....D 239 939-4412
Fort Myers *(G-4252)*
Advanced Roofing Inc ....D 561 743-6952
Jupiter *(G-7046)*
Advanced Roofing Inc ....D 813 885-5811
Tampa *(G-17241)*
◆ Advanced Roofing Inc ....C 954 522-6868
Fort Lauderdale *(G-3580)*
Advanced Roofing Inc ....D 904 826-3860
Saint Augustine *(G-15420)*
Agantic Group LLC ....D 904 329-7004
Jacksonville *(G-5751)*
Alans Roofing Inc ....E 352 754-8880
Brooksville *(G-1266)*
All American Roofing Inc ....E 954 772-7663
Fort Lauderdale *(G-3591)*
Allied Roofing Inc ....E 813 875-2727
Tampa *(G-17268)*
American Rofg Jacksonville LLC ....E 904 385-4375
Jacksonville *(G-5791)*
AMS Inc ....E 561 848-2277
Pompano Beach *(G-14740)*
Architectural Sheet Metal Inc ....D 407 855-7183
Orlando *(G-12130)*
Arcon Industries Inc ....E 954 979-9400
Pompano Beach *(G-14741)*
Arnett Heating & AC Inc ....E 904 829-3071
Saint Augustine *(G-15425)*
Arrys Roofing Service Inc ....E 727 938-9565
Tarpon Springs *(G-18579)*
Atlantic Roofg II Vero Bch Inc ....E 772 492-8493
Vero Beach *(G-18837)*
Barber & Associates Inc ....D 904 744-4067
Jacksonville *(G-5840)*
Barker Electric AC & Htg Inc ....D 772 562-2103
Vero Beach *(G-18839)*
Bbg Contracting Group Inc ....D 904 766-5800
Jacksonville *(G-5846)*
Bbmk Contracting LLC ....E 954 928-3870
Boca Raton *(G-444)*
Bel-Mac Roofing Inc ....E 850 267-0900
Santa Rosa Beach *(G-16005)*
Best Chice Roofg Centl Fla LLC ....E 407 350-4380
Kissimmee *(G-7271)*
Best Roofing Services LLC ....C 954 941-9111
Fort Lauderdale *(G-3641)*
Biscayne Construction Co Inc ....E 305 688-7663
Davie *(G-2461)*
Bob Hilson & Company Inc ....C 305 248-2227
Homestead *(G-5560)*
Bonner Roofing & Shtmtl Co ....E 407 321-9333
Sanford *(G-15924)*
C & S Roofing Co ....D 352 489-4274
Dunnellon *(G-3395)*
Campany Roof Maintenance LLC ....D 561 881-3560
West Palm Beach *(G-19072)*
Cardinal Roofg & Siding of Fla ....E 772 335-9550
Port Saint Lucie *(G-15125)*
Carroll Bradford Incorporated ....E 407 647-9420
Orlando *(G-12246)*
Central Air Control Inc ....E 305 822-1551
Hialeah *(G-5231)*
Certified Contg Group Inc ....E 954 781-7663
Pompano Beach *(G-14771)*
CFS Roofing Services LLC ....C 239 561-2600
Fort Myers *(G-4307)*
Chappelle Roofing LLC ....D 941 567-6039
Saint Petersburg *(G-15622)*
Charles A Roy Roofing Inc ....E 941 746-0008
Palmetto *(G-13906)*
Childers Rofg Shtmtl A Tcta AM ....D 904 696-8550
Jacksonville *(G-5943)*
CMR Construction & Roofing LLC ....D 855 905-1827
Lantana *(G-8060)*
Code Red Roofers Inc ....E 561 622-6343
Stuart *(G-16607)*
Collis Roofing Inc ....A 321 441-2300
Longwood *(G-8352)*
Colonial Roofing Inc ....D 239 458-1000
Lehigh Acres *(G-8278)*
Constructomax Corporation ....E 813 520-8957
Tampa *(G-17517)*
Core Roofing Systems Inc ....E 407 434-7170
Orlando *(G-12368)*
Crown Roofing LLC ....D 941 312-2592
Sarasota *(G-16134)*
Crowther Roofg Shtmtl Fla Inc ....C 239 337-1300
Fort Myers *(G-4334)*
David Farsaci Inc ....E 239 261-1363
Naples *(G-11088)*
▼ Daybreak Inc ....D 386 487-1040
Lake City *(G-7524)*
Decktight Roofing Services Inc ....C 954 970-8565
Fort Lauderdale *(G-3757)*
Denard Moore Cnstr Co Inc Fla ....E 863 425-4947
Mulberry *(G-10977)*
◆ Design Containers Inc ....E 904 764-6541
Jacksonville *(G-6064)*
Dynasty Building Solutions LLC ....E 813 321-3269
Tampa *(G-17607)*
Eco-Logical Roofing LLC ....E 407 821-5311
Orlando *(G-12450)*
Edwards Roofing Company Inc ....E 850 478-0230
Pensacola *(G-14286)*
Elias Brothers Gen Contr Inc ....C 239 293-2442
Naples *(G-11102)*
Elite Roofg & Restoration LLC ....E 239 900-9714
Bonita Springs *(G-910)*
Elo Restoration ....E 407 605-6060
Orlando *(G-12458)*
Elo Restoration Inc ....D 904 528-0188
Jacksonville *(G-6109)*
Evergreen Building and Cnstr ....E 888 393-0547
Ponte Vedra *(G-14963)*
Ferber Sheet Metal Works Inc ....C 904 356-3042
Jacksonville *(G-6152)*
Fiddlers Roofing Inc ....E 407 366-2300
Orlando *(G-12508)*
Florida Sthern Rofg Shtmtl Inc ....E 941 782-0409
Sarasota *(G-16034)*
Forrest Inc ....D 904 794-2547
Saint Augustine *(G-15444)*
G & W Roofing and Sheet Metal ....E 386 427-2798
Edgewater *(G-3411)*
G and G Roofing Cnstr Inc ....E 321 301-4470
Rockledge *(G-15345)*
Garabar Inc ....E 561 215-6620
Lake Worth Beach *(G-7768)*
▲ Gary W Curry Inc ....E 941 921-9111
Sarasota *(G-16173)*
Grace Roofg & Shtmtl Entp LLC ....E 954 733-7332
Coral Springs *(G-2256)*
Gulf Wstn Roofg & Shtmtl Inc ....C 239 949-9200
Bonita Springs *(G-918)*
▼ Gulfstream Roofing Inc ....E 561 276-9531
Delray Beach *(G-2960)*
Gustafson Industries Inc ....E 561 732-0656
Boynton Beach *(G-993)*
Guy Brothers Roofing & Siding ....E 850 434-1785
Pensacola *(G-14321)*
Hartford South LLC ....C 407 857-9392
Orlando *(G-12621)*
Hi-Tech Roofg & Sheetmetal Inc ....E 561 586-3110
Lake Worth Beach *(G-7769)*
Icon Building Inc ....E 239 643-3689
Naples *(G-11172)*
Infinity Roofing & Shtmtl Inc ....E 954 917-7107
Fort Lauderdale *(G-3891)*
Iroofing LLC ....C 754 244-4121
Hallandale *(G-5162)*
Island Roofing LLC ....D 239 778-4050
Naples *(G-11180)*

SIC

JA Taylor Roofing Inc ....E 772 466-4040
Fort Pierce (G-4714)

Johnson Rofg Cnstrctn/R L Cmpb .....E 904 224-1996
Jacksonville (G-6388)

Jpj Companies LLC ....D 561 747-1990
West Palm Beach (G-19222)

Kaiser Siding & Roofing LLC ....E 239 351-2576
Naples (G-11186)

Kelly Roofing LLC ....D 239 435-0014
Naples (G-11188)

Kelly Sheet Metal Inc ....E 850 878-1101
Tallahassee (G-17018)

Lamb Construction Group Inc ....D 954 687-0301
Bonita Springs (G-927)

Lewis Walker Roofing Inc ....E 866 959-7663
Lake City (G-7535)

Lido Holdings Inc ....D 561 863-6550
West Palm Beach (G-19235)

Lsci Inc ....E 727 571-4141
Seminole (G-16455)

Manson Roofing Inc ....E 941 748-5403
Bradenton (G-1143)

McCurdy - Walden Inc ....D 904 783-9000
Jacksonville (G-6480)

McDonald Air & Sheet Metal Inc .....D 407 295-0220
Orlando (G-12841)

McEnany Contracting Inc ....C 863 588-4130
Lake Alfred (G-7451)

McEnany Roofing Inc ....D 813 988-1669
Temple Terrace (G-18641)

Mechanical Svcs Centl Fla Inc ....C 407 857-3510
Orlando (G-12850)

Metro Property Services Inc ....E 904 399-1020
Jacksonville (G-6501)

Mullets Aluminum Products Inc ....D 941 371-3502
Sarasota (G-16240)

Murton Roofing Corp ....D 305 592-5385
Deerfield Beach (G-2774)

Nations Roof of Florida LLC ....A 407 649-1333
Winter Garden (G-19582)

Nationwide Gen Cntg Nthrn VA L .....E 407 717-9055
Orlando (G-12900)

Neth & Son Inc ....E 407 855-9096
Orlando (G-12908)

Nolands Roofing Inc ....C 352 242-4322
Clermont (G-1880)

◆ Norca AC & Rfrgn Corp ....D 305 558-1422
Miami Lakes (G-10749)

▼ North American Roofg Svcs LLC ....A 800 551-5602
Tampa (G-18087)

North American Roofing Co Inc ....E 317 875-5434
Tampa (G-18088)

P & A Roofing and Shtmtl Inc ....E 407 650-9541
Orlando (G-12999)

Patnode Roofing Inc ....E 239 693-9091
Fort Myers (G-4535)

Perfection Archtctrl Sys LLC ....E 407 671-6225
Orlando (G-13022)

Perry Roofing Inc ....D 800 487-6637
Gainesville (G-4978)

Petersen-Dean Inc ....D 407 857-1757
Orlando (G-13025)

Pinnacle Roofing Contrs Inc ....D 904 880-6005
Jacksonville (G-6603)

Pioneer Roofing Company Inc ....D 954 920-7688
Hollywood (G-5492)

Pritts Inc ....D 954 733-7663
Fort Lauderdale (G-4062)

Professional Roofg NW Fla Inc ....D 850 478-7887
Pensacola (G-14415)

Protex Roofing LLC ....D 813 654-7663
Tampa (G-18179)

Quality Roofing Inc ....C 813 620-4797
Tampa (G-18188)

R/J Group Inc ....E 386 760-0764
Port Orange (G-15085)

Ramcon LLC ....D 813 663-9667
Tampa (G-18199)

Reliant Roofing LLC ....E 904 657-0880
Jacksonville (G-6653)

Resilient Roofing Inc ....E 407 682-5066
Longwood (G-8395)

RF Lusa & Sons Shtmtl Inc ....D 863 682-0798
Lakeland (G-7953)

Robert Binns Roofing Inc ....E 863 967-1382
Winter Haven (G-19657)

Roof Concepts Inc ....E 772 344-3717
Port Saint Lucie (G-15161)

Roof Master of Central Florida ....E 407 872-3200
Orlando (G-13125)

Roof System Services Inc ....D 954 522-6868
Fort Lauderdale (G-4094)

Roofco LLC ....E 407 516-0653
Orlando (G-13126)

RSI of Florida LLC ....D 954 960-0224
Pompano Beach (G-14886)

Rss Roofing Svcs Solutions LLC ......E 407 426-0400
Orlando (G-13146)

Sack Roofing Inc ....C 352 430-2773
Lady Lake (G-7441)

Scott Smith Roofing Inc ....E 352 867-0044
Ocala (G-11776)

South Seminole Sheet Metal Inc ......C 407 464-7776
Apopka (G-211)

▲ Southern Coast Enterprises Inc ......E 954 426-3312
Deerfield Beach (G-2800)

Southern Roofing Company Inc ......D 813 251-5252
Tampa (G-18310)

Springr-Ptrson Rofg Shtmtl Inc ....D 800 244-1163
Eaton Park (G-3405)

Star Pntg & Waterproofing Inc ....E 305 770-0143
West Park (G-19436)

Storm Team Construction Inc ....E 614 367-6930
Jupiter (G-7140)

Stratus Cnstr & Roofg LLC ....E 407 625-5866
Maitland (G-8581)

▼ Structural Waterproofing Inc ....D 407 645-2021
Maitland (G-8582)

Sutter Roofing Company Florida ......C 941 377-1000
Sarasota (G-16341)

Target Roofing and Shtmtl Inc ....E 239 332-5707
Fort Myers (G-4622)

Tarheel Roofing ....D 727 823-3455
Saint Petersburg (G-15872)

Taylor Contracting & Roofg Inc ....E 954 989-8338
Fort Lauderdale (G-4167)

Taylor Made Roofing ....D 904 849-7758
Yulee (G-19822)

Tecta America South Fla Inc ....D 954 419-9339
Deerfield Beach (G-2803)

Tecta America Southeast LLC ....D 407 330-9303
Sanford (G-15986)

Therma Seal Roof Systems LLC ......E 561 223-2096
Fort Lauderdale (G-4175)

▼ Thermoset Roofing Corp ....C 954 984-9099
Pompano Beach (G-14920)

Thl Enterprises Inc ....D 813 236-7500
Tampa (G-18419)

▲ Tim Graboski Roofing Inc ....C 561 276-8252
Deerfield Beach (G-2805)

Tip Top Roofing Company Inc ....E 407 660-2212
Orlando (G-13292)

▲ Titan Specialty Cnstr Inc ....D 850 916-7660
Milton (G-10827)

Topbuild Corp ....D 386 304-2200
Daytona Beach (G-2676)

Total Home Properties Inc ....E 321 452-9223
Rockledge (G-15375)

Trans Coastalconstruction Co ....E 561 835-9522
West Palm Beach (G-19391)

Triple M Roofing Corp ....E 954 524-7000
Fort Lauderdale (G-4185)

Ucms LLC ....C 239 321-5886
Lehigh Acres (G-8294)

Universal Roofing Group Inc ....D 407 295-7403
Jacksonville (G-6891)

Universal Roofing Group Inc ....D 407 901-4444
Orlando (G-13350)

Voss Incorporated ....E 904 396-1546
Jacksonville (G-6912)

Wallin Roofing Co Inc ....E 305 421-2072
Deerfield Beach (G-2813)

Weiss & Woolrich Contg Co ....D 954 419-9339
Deerfield Beach (G-2815)

West Coast Florida Entps Inc ....C 239 433-9777
Fort Myers (G-4654)

Wolverine Roofing LLC ....E 561 660-5844
Lake Park (G-7662)

1771 Concrete Work

▲ 3 C Construction Corp ....D 305 638-5511
Miami (G-9056)

ABC Concrete Cutting Inc ....E 954 523-4848
Pompano Beach (G-14732)

▼ Adonel Con Pmpg Fnshg S Fla In ...D 305 392-5416
Miami (G-9078)

Aerial Companies Inc ....C 239 643-7625
Naples (G-11002)

Agantic Group LLC ....D 904 329-7004
Jacksonville (G-5751)

Ajax Paving Industries Fla LLC ....B 941 729-5114
Odessa (G-11831)

All American Driveway Inc ....E 305 420-5458
Doral (G-3109)

All Terrain Tractor Svc Inc ....D 386 218-6969
Sanford (G-15915)

◆ Allan Spear Construction LLC ......D 352 337-0773
Gainesville (G-4833)

Alto Construction Co Inc ....D 813 241-2586
Tampa (G-17275)

Amaralto Concrete Pump Inc ....D 305 553-0200
Miami (G-9132)

American Cnstr & Engrg Co ....E 305 604-8998
Pinecrest (G-14497)

Anderson Columbia Co Inc ....E 352 542-7942
Old Town (G-11886)

B E T Er Mix Holding Inc ....D 727 862-2239
Hudson (G-5628)

Baker Concrete Cnstr Inc ....A 305 884-7793
Fort Lauderdale (G-3626)

Baker Concrete Cnstr Inc ....E 407 736-9900
Orlando (G-12170)

Barreiro Concrete Corporation ....D 305 258-7004
Princeton (G-15185)

◆ Bauer Foundation Corp ....C 727 536-4748
Odessa (G-11833)

Berkel & Company Contrs Inc ....D 352 365-4308
Okahumpka (G-11859)

Bng Construction Inc ....D 407 688-1747
Sanford (G-15923)

Bonness Inc ....D 239 597-6221
Naples (G-11038)

Burkett Stucco Inc ....E 813 972-1000
Lutz (G-8433)

▲ C & C Concrete Pumping Inc ......E 305 885-1522
Medley (G-8709)

C & C Pumping Services Inc ....D 352 429-7867
Groveland (G-5084)

C & H Concrete Cnstr Inc ....D 941 255-0975
Arcadia (G-225)

Case Atlantic Co ....E 727 572-7740
Clearwater (G-1560)

Cck Construction Services Inc ....D 407 472-9700
Winter Garden (G-19561)

Ceco Concrete Construction LLC ....D 813 622-8080
Boca Raton (G-502)

Ceco Concrete Construction LLC ....C 813 622-8080
Tampa (G-17435)

▲ Cellucrete Corp ....E 305 826-2960
Hialeah (G-5230)

Certified Foundations Inc ....E 863 859-3889
Lakeland (G-7829)

Coast To Coast Gen Contrs Inc ....D 954 920-3900
Hollywood (G-5416)

Cobra Construction Inc ....D 800 697-1724
Boynton Beach (G-977)

Cocoa Inc ....D 407 425-9095
Orlando (G-12338)

Commercial Con Systems LLC ......D 239 592-1101
Naples (G-11071)

Commercial Concrete Contrs ....D 813 920-7231
Odessa (G-11837)

Commercial Forming Corp South .....C 954 970-7671
Pompano Beach (G-14779)

Concrete Lumber Enterprises ....D 305 226-5525
Miami (G-9403)

Concrete Profiles Inc ....D 904 642-0055
Jacksonville (G-5996)

Concrete Prtction Rstrtion LLC ....C 954 505-3977
Oakland Park (G-11591)

Concrete Pumping Eqp Co Inc ....E 407 843-0247
Orlando (G-12359)

Concrete Services LLC ....D 561 742-3049
Boynton Beach (G-978)

Connery Corporation ....E 772 231-1224
Vero Beach (G-18849)

Conshor Inc ....D 239 992-3720
Fort Myers (G-4323)

Contech Construction LLC ....E 407 905-4662
Orlando (G-12362)

Cornerstone Cnstr Svcs Inc ....E 407 299-3299
Orlando (G-12369)

Cougar Cutting Inc ....D 239 275-9334
Fort Myers (G-4328)

Cpr Contracting LLC ....E 904 723-3500
Jacksonville (G-6009)

Cross Entps Centl Fla Inc ....E 407 843-0247
Orlando (G-12386)

Custom Concrete of Tampa Bay ....E 813 672-8868
Riverview (G-15254)

D and D Cnstr & Remodel LLC ....E 561 330-8100
Boynton Beach *(G-981)*

Dana Site Dev & Pav Inc ....E 941 722-4913
Palmetto *(G-13910)*

Daniello & Associates Inc ....E 561 835-4788
West Palm Beach *(G-19118)*

◆ Diversfied Cnstr Rstration Inc ....E 305 246-4306
Miami *(G-9481)*

Don Kings Concrete Inc ....E 407 977-9001
Winter Springs *(G-19803)*

EL Shearer Con Masonary Inc ....E 727 548-7959
Pinellas Park *(G-14515)*

▲ Expo Marble & Granite Inc ....E 954 943-9006
Pompano Beach *(G-14802)*

Finfrock Dsgn-Mnfctr-Cnstruct ....D 407 293-4000
Apopka *(G-180)*

▲ Five Star Ceramics Group Inc ....E 305 820-1414
Miami *(G-9564)*

Flores-Hager and Assoc Inc ....D 386 676-9999
Daytona Beach *(G-2589)*

Florida Blacktop Inc ....E 954 979-5757
Pompano Beach *(G-14807)*

▼ Florida Concrete Unlimited Inc ....C 305 232-3296
Miami *(G-9571)*

Florida Lemark Corporation ....D 305 593-1442
Doral *(G-3202)*

Foam By Design Inc ....E 727 561-7479
Clearwater *(G-1644)*

Forrest Inc ....D 904 794-2547
Saint Augustine *(G-15444)*

Full-Tilt Contracting LLC ....C 407 910-1400
Sanford *(G-15943)*

Gator Concrete and Masonry Inc ....D 813 714-8141
Dade City *(G-2387)*

Genesis Con Structures LLC ....E 904 406-8443
Green Cove Springs *(G-5053)*

Genesis Concrete LLC ....E 904 422-2824
Green Cove Springs *(G-5054)*

Guettler Brothers Cnstr LLC ....E 772 461-8345
Fort Pierce *(G-4708)*

Hawkins Tommy Sons Pav Contrs ....E 772 464-7587
Fort Pierce *(G-4710)*

Helicon Fndtion Repr Systems I ....D 813 567-1065
Tampa *(G-17814)*

HG Cnstr Dev & Inv Inc ....D 786 845-8999
Miami *(G-9699)*

Homestead Paving Co ....D 305 258-1972
Homestead *(G-5582)*

Hoopers Concrete & Cnstr LLC ....E 352 777-4986
Tarpon Springs *(G-18586)*

Jaxi Builders Inc ....D 305 599-0700
Doral *(G-3251)*

Jett Concrete Inc ....D 904 276-3488
Orange Park *(G-11998)*

Jimmie Crwder Excvtg Land Clri ....C 850 576-7176
Tallahassee *(G-17010)*

Jims Concrete Brevard Inc ....C 904 886-4743
Jacksonville *(G-6387)*

Jvd Construction Inc ....E 407 767-8853
Casselberry *(G-1450)*

Krj Holdings Inc ....E 407 290-9440
Apopka *(G-196)*

Landmark Services S W Fla Inc ....D 941 358-8393
Bradenton *(G-1127)*

Lenard Powell Inc ....E 352 748-4259
Wildwood *(G-19501)*

M & M Asphalt Maintenance Inc ....D 561 588-0949
Delray Beach *(G-2986)*

Masci Corporation ....D 386 322-4111
Port Orange *(G-15081)*

Masci General Contractor Inc ....D 386 322-4500
Port Orange *(G-15082)*

McLeod Land & Equipment Inc ....C 941 355-0784
Sarasota *(G-16041)*

Miguel Lopez Jr Inc ....E 305 884-0767
Miami *(G-10003)*

MJS Concrete Inc ....E 407 349-5972
Oviedo *(G-13561)*

Mora Engineering Contrs Inc ....D 954 752-8065
Casselberry *(G-1452)*

Mosley & Son Construction ....E 772 287-6962
Stuart *(G-16646)*

Mullins Concrete Pumping Inc ....E 727 544-1308
Clearwater *(G-1731)*

Mvp Construction Services Inc ....E 954 956-8001
Margate *(G-8659)*

Namm Group Inc ....E 954 968-1700
Pompano Beach *(G-14864)*

Nichols Concrete Equipment Co ....D 850 267-2463
Santa Rosa Beach *(G-16011)*

Ogden Brothers Cnstr Inc ....D 239 592-9960
Naples *(G-11251)*

Pardue Masonry of Central Fla ....D 813 948-3205
Tampa *(G-18122)*

Pate Construction Company Inc ....D 772 288-1600
Stuart *(G-16656)*

Phoenix Coatings Inc ....D 850 857-4740
Pensacola *(G-14413)*

Pioneer Sales & Service Inc ....E 813 985-5100
Temple Terrace *(G-18645)*

Pioneer Screen LLC 772 283-9197
Stuart *(G-16657)*

Precision Concrete Cutting ....E 954 484-1110
Lauderdale Lakes *(G-8182)*

Pro-Max Restoration & Pnt Corp ....E 305 253-7900
Miami *(G-10146)*

Properties Elgant Dstnction LL ....D 561 364-9675
Boynton Beach *(G-1029)*

R F Concrete Construction Inc ....E 772 567-3356
Vero Beach *(G-18910)*

▼ R W Harris Inc ....E 727 572-9200
Clearwater *(G-1771)*

Ranger Construction Inds Inc ....C 386 761-8383
Daytona Beach *(G-2657)*

Regency Cnstr Palm Bch Cnty Co ....D 586 741-8000
West Palm Beach *(G-19341)*

Restocon Corporation ....E 813 643-2202
Tampa *(G-18221)*

Restore Construction Group Inc ....D 954 985-5353
West Park *(G-19433)*

Rio-Bak Corporation ....D 561 791-9721
Wellington *(G-18988)*

RL James Inc General Contr ....E 239 936-6002
Fort Myers *(G-4574)*

Rti Restoration Technology Inc ....D 954 583-6048
Davie *(G-2512)*

Rubaroc Usa Inc ....E 214 295-7366
Sanford *(G-15975)*

S Applebaum & Associates Inc ....D 305 836-8678
Miami *(G-10229)*

Snapp Industries Inc ....E 305 635-0687
Miami *(G-10288)*

Southwest Cnstr Svcs Inc ....C 239 491-2567
Lehigh Acres *(G-8290)*

Speedy Con Cutng Centl Fla Inc ....E 888 345-7155
Fort Lauderdale *(G-4148)*

Speedy Concrete Cutting Inc ....D 813 246-4455
San Antonio *(G-15910)*

Stancel Concrete Incorporated ....D 239 437-7051
Fort Myers *(G-4604)*

Star Pntg & Waterproofing Inc ....E 305 770-0143
West Park *(G-19436)*

Steelmaster Industries Inc ....E 386 345-0391
Oak Hill *(G-11580)*

Structral Prsrvtion Systems LL ....E 954 975-0344
Pompano Beach *(G-14912)*

Sunshine Structures Inc ....D 239 303-1001
Lehigh Acres *(G-8293)*

▲ Superior Asphalt Inc ....D 941 755-2850
Bradenton *(G-1187)*

T & D Concrete Inc ....B 352 748-2111
Wildwood *(G-19509)*

T & T Cnstr Centl Fla Inc ....B 407 831-5506
Casselberry *(G-1461)*

Tincher Concrete Construction ....D 239 267-7766
Fort Myers *(G-4626)*

Trident Surfacing Inc ....E 305 620-4220
Miami Lakes *(G-10769)*

USA Services of Florida Inc ....E 407 339-1800
Longwood *(G-8413)*

Victory Concrete Contrs Inc ....D 561 227-9577
Lake Worth Beach *(G-7776)*

Vmg Construction Inc ....D 407 347-9536
Winter Garden *(G-19599)*

Walker Contracting Group Inc ....D 239 229-3774
Naples *(G-11339)*

Waterfront Services Inc ....E 561 721-2902
West Palm Beach *(G-19413)*

Wavecrest Masonry Inc ....C 352 860-0560
Inverness *(G-5701)*

Westcoast Strl Con Masnry Inc ....D 239 590-6408
Fort Myers *(G-4655)*

Wilson Kehoe & Miller Corp ....E 727 584-7742
Largo *(G-8164)*

Woodland Construction Co Inc ....C 561 743-0490
Jupiter *(G-7152)*

1781 Water Well Drilling

Custom Drilling Services Inc ....E 863 425-9600
Mulberry *(G-10974)*

Drillpro LLC ....E 407 426-7885
Orlando *(G-12441)*

Kustom US Inc ....E 904 268-4555
Jacksonville *(G-6411)*

Malcolm Drilling Company Inc ....D 305 374-8618
Pompano Beach *(G-14848)*

Partridge Well Drilling Co Inc ....E 904 355-3323
Jacksonville *(G-6581)*

▲ Youngquist Brothers LLC ....B 239 489-4444
Fort Myers *(G-4664)*

1791 Structural Steel Erection

▲ Ambor Structures Inc ....C 651 528-8774
North Port *(G-11563)*

American Bridge Company ....D 813 254-4127
Tampa *(G-17276)*

Bowman Steel LLC ....E 239 303-9739
Sebring *(G-16390)*

Central Maintenance & Wldg Inc ....C 813 229-0012
Lithia *(G-8298)*

Coastal Steel Inc ....D 321 632-8228
Cocoa *(G-1925)*

Curry Steel Inc ....E 863 984-1900
Polk City *(G-14725)*

Dixie Southern Industrial Inc ....D 863 984-1900
Polk City *(G-14726)*

East Coast Met Structures Corp ....E 561 766-2579
Lantana *(G-8062)*

▼ Fence Masters Inc ....E 305 635-7777
Miami *(G-9551)*

Fitzlord Inc ....D 904 731-2041
Jacksonville *(G-6181)*

Florida Atlantic Contrs Inc ....E 352 669-9750
Umatilla *(G-18734)*

◆ Florida Wldg Fbrctors Erectors ....D 954 971-4800
Parkland *(G-14107)*

Full-Tilt Contracting LLC ....C 407 910-1400
Sanford *(G-15943)*

Hodges Erectors Inc ....E 305 234-3467
Medley *(G-8742)*

Hodges Erectors Inc ....E 305 234-3467
Palmetto Bay *(G-13944)*

Industrial Steel LLC ....E 321 267-2341
Titusville *(G-18689)*

Iveys Construction Inc ....C 321 453-3812
Merritt Island *(G-9035)*

▲ Jackson-Cook Lc ....E 850 576-4187
Tallahassee *(G-17009)*

John Bowman Inc ....C 239 303-9739
Sebring *(G-16403)*

▼ Met-Con Inc ....D 321 632-4880
Cocoa *(G-1944)*

Morrow Steel Erectors Inc ....D 813 715-0404
Zephyrhills *(G-19843)*

Morrow Steel Fabricators Inc ....D 813 715-0404
Zephyrhills *(G-19844)*

NCM Collier County Inc ....C 239 566-1601
Naples *(G-11248)*

Ogden Brothers Cnstr Inc ....D 239 592-9960
Naples *(G-11251)*

Oracle Elevator Holdco Inc ....E 800 526-6115
Tampa *(G-18105)*

R&D Steel Erectors LLC ....E 904 529-9474
Fleming Island *(G-3556)*

Seminole Machine & Welding Inc ....D 727 586-0599
Largo *(G-8150)*

Shelby Erectors Inc ....D 954 275-3123
Tampa *(G-18276)*

Southern Erectors Inc ....D 850 944-0013
Pensacola *(G-14444)*

Steel Worx Solutions LLC ....E 407 580-8585
Groveland *(G-5102)*

Steelmaster Industries Inc ....E 386 345-0391
Oak Hill *(G-11580)*

▼ Sunshine Crane Rental Corp ....E 407 880-2222
Apopka *(G-216)*

Titan Florida LLC ....D 954 481-2800
Deerfield Beach *(G-2806)*

▲ V & M Erectors Inc ....D 954 443-1220
Pembroke Pines *(G-14197)*

Vasco Builders Inc ....E 813 968-2120
Lutz *(G-8464)*

1793 Glass & Glazing Work

▼ A Christian Glass & Mirror Co ....E 561 278-3385
Delray Beach *(G-2897)*

▼ Ad Investment Group LLC ....C 954 784-6900
Miramar *(G-10834)*

◆ Arso Enterprises Inc ....E 305 681-2020
Opa Locka *(G-11940)*

Asd Specialties Inc ....E 305 685-0611
Miami Lakes (G-10707)

◆ Cgi Windows and Doors Inc ....C 305 592-1965
Hialeah (G-5234)

◆ Continental Glass Systems LLC .....D 305 231-1101
Hialeah (G-5247)

Countryside Glass & Mirror Inc .....D 727 738-6000
Saint Petersburg (G-15646)

▼ Crawford-Tracey Corp ....D 954 698-6888
Deerfield Beach (G-2730)

▼ Dash-Door & Closer Service Inc ...E 305 477-1164
Doral (G-3171)

▲ Gamma Usa Inc ....E 305 633-2403
Doral (G-3207)

▼ Glass Systems Inc ....E 407 841-7330
Orlando (G-12573)

H B S Inc ....E 772 567-7461
Vero Beach (G-18863)

Harmon Inc ....E 813 635-0649
Orlando (G-12619)

Lake Glass & Mirror Inc ....E 352 787-4700
Leesburg (G-8250)

Miller Glass & Glazing Inc ....E 954 784-6601
Pompano Beach (G-14858)

▼ Mrg Glazing Contractors Inc ......C 305 470-8284
Medley (G-8760)

RL James Inc General Contr ....E 239 936-6002
Fort Myers (G-4574)

▼ Tropical Glass & Cnstr Co ....E 305 757-0651
Miami (G-10410)

◆ West Tampa Glass Company ....D 813 247-5528
Tampa (G-18543)

1794 Excavating & Grading Work

814 Sand Inc ....D 850 814-7263
Panama City (G-13953)

All Terrain Tractor Svc Inc ....D 386 218-6969
Sanford (G-15915)

Allens Excavation Inc ....E 850 421-6872
Tallahassee (G-16874)

Allstate Paving Inc ....D 407 277-5247
Orlando (G-12098)

American Civil Construction ....E 386 847-3079
Bunnell (G-1321)

American Sand & Xcavation Inc ......E 850 763-4300
Lynn Haven (G-8467)

Andrews Paving Inc ....E 386 462-1115
Gainesville (G-4836)

BJ Excavating Entps Inc ....E 239 643-3478
Naples (G-11033)

Blue Ox Land Services Inc ....C 407 339-4800
Sanford (G-15922)

Bradanna Inc ....E 239 417-2300
Naples (G-11040)

C & C Loader Service Inc ....E 561 790-3308
Loxahatchee (G-8419)

▲ Central Fla Eqp Rentals Inc ......C 305 883-7518
Medley (G-8713)

Central Fla Excvtg & Fill Dirt ......D 813 757-6783
Saint Petersburg (G-15619)

Cliffs Trucking Inc ....E 561 793-0322
West Palm Beach (G-19095)

Continental Heavy Civil Corp ....C 786 250-5851
Miami (G-9407)

Counts Construction Co Inc ....D 352 629-3506
Ocala (G-11669)

Dana Site Dev & Pav Inc ....E 941 722-4913
Palmetto (G-13910)

David Nelson Construction Co ....C 727 784-7624
Palm Harbor (G-13859)

Dejonge Excavating Contrs Inc ......E 941 485-7799
Venice (G-18777)

Deme Construction LLC ....E 941 755-5900
Sarasota (G-16030)

Dns Contracting LLC ....D 904 724-6430
Jacksonville (G-6075)

Downrite Engineering Corp ....B 305 232-2340
Miami (G-9487)

E T Mackenzie of Florida Inc ....D 941 756-6760
Bradenton (G-1090)

Earthworks of Florida LLC ....D 904 653-2800
Macclenny (G-8477)

Eden Site Development Inc ....E 407 265-1113
Longwood (G-8358)

Forrest Excavating Inc ....E 813 336-4999
Odessa (G-11841)

Garys Grading Inc ....D 407 892-3690
Saint Cloud (G-15522)

Glenn T Warren & Company Inc .....E 850 674-8159
Blountstown (G-385)

Groundtek Central Florida LLC ......E 407 877-7473
Ocoee (G-11815)

Guettler Brothers Cnstr LLC ....E 772 461-8345
Fort Pierce (G-4708)

Gulf-Atlantic Constructors Inc ......E 850 477-0588
Pensacola (G-14320)

Harlis R Ellington Cnstr Inc ....E 386 496-2134
Lake Butler (G-7504)

Harty Tractor Services Inc ....E 386 775-1005
Orange City (G-11966)

J B Coxwell Contracting Inc ....C 904 786-1120
Jacksonville (G-6336)

Jax Dirtworks Inc ....E 904 683-3124
Atlantic Beach (G-242)

Jimmie Crwder Excvtg Land Clri .....C 850 576-7176
Tallahassee (G-17010)

Kamminga & Roodvoets Inc ....E 813 623-3031
Tampa (G-17908)

Lundquist Excavating Inc ....D 407 847-3716
Kissimmee (G-7351)

Martin Construction Inc ....E 863 439-4655
Lake Hamilton (G-7555)

Masci Corporation ....D 386 322-4111
Port Orange (G-15081)

Masci General Contractor Inc ....D 386 322-4500
Port Orange (G-15082)

Master Excavators Inc ....C 305 238-0119
Miami (G-9908)

McLeod Land & Equipment Inc ......C 941 355-0784
Sarasota (G-16041)

Mid State Paving Co Inc ....E 863 965-2861
Auburndale (G-257)

Middlesex Asphalt LLC ....C 407 206-0078
Orlando (G-12866)

Palm Beach Grading Inc ....C 772 678-4029
Stuart (G-16655)

R & S Excavation Inc ....E 850 379-8449
Hosford (G-5621)

Ram-Tech Construction Inc ....E 305 259-7853
Homestead (G-5600)

Ridgdill & Son Inc ....E 863 983-3136
Clewiston (G-1907)

Ronco Consulting Corporation ....A 571 551-2934
Jupiter (G-7137)

Ryan Incorporated Southern ....D 954 427-5599
Deerfield Beach (G-2791)

Sandco Inc ....C 850 402-1111
Tallahassee (G-17092)

Sarasota Land Services Inc ....E 941 744-0211
Bradenton (G-1175)

Sayar Enterprises Inc ....E 904 727-7483
Jacksonville (G-6697)

Seminole Excavation & Sup Inc ......E 407 834-8091
Longwood (G-8402)

Site and Utility LLC ....E 850 439-5734
Pensacola (G-14436)

South Florida Excavation Inc ....D 239 596-8111
Naples (G-11299)

Southern Waste Systems LLC ....C 561 582-6688
Davie (G-2518)

Terra Excavating Inc ....C 727 497-8106
Saint Petersburg (G-15874)

USA Grading Inc ....E 941 505-9837
Marco Island (G-8639)

W C Roese Contracting Inc ....D 813 628-4395
Tampa (G-18516)

Wetherington Tractor Svc Inc ....D 813 752-4510
Plant City (G-14592)

Wrights Excavating Inc ....E 407 892-1070
Saint Cloud (G-15540)

▼ Young & Son Inc ....E 850 729-1321
Niceville (G-11460)

1795 Wrecking & Demolition Work

Allens Excavation Inc ....E 850 421-6872
Tallahassee (G-16874)

Allied Demolition Inc ....E 954 868-9990
Miami (G-9124)

American Sand & Xcavation Inc ......E 850 763-4300
Lynn Haven (G-8467)

Best-TEC Asb Abatement Inc ....E 904 695-9900
Boynton Beach (G-964)

Bg Group LLC ....D 561 998-7997
Lake Worth (G-7715)

Bg Group LLC ....E 561 998-7997
Delray Beach (G-2914)

Central Environmental Svcs Inc ......E 407 295-7005
Orlando (G-12261)

Cougar Cutting Inc ....D 239 275-9334
Fort Myers (G-4328)

Cross Environmental Svcs Inc ....E 813 783-1688
Zephyrhills (G-19827)

▼ D P C General Contractors Inc .....E 305 325-0447
Miami (G-9448)

Honc Destruction Inc ....E 239 772-2378
Fort Myers (G-4442)

Jimmie Crwder Excvtg Land Clri .....C 850 576-7176
Tallahassee (G-17010)

JP Services Sarasota LLC ....E 941 587-4362
Sarasota (G-16039)

▲ Kimmins Corp ....E 813 248-3878
Tampa (G-17924)

Metro Service Group Inc ....E 504 520-8331
Pensacola (G-14364)

Northstar Contg Group Inc ....C 813 684-4400
Riverview (G-15262)

Northstar Dem & Remediation LP .....D 407 855-2365
Orlando (G-12917)

Northstar Dem & Remediation LP .....D 850 474-4077
Pensacola (G-14389)

Pece Mind Environmental Inc ....D 407 568-3456
Orlando (G-13017)

Ross & Logan Industries Inc ....D 904 378-9700
Jacksonville (G-6676)

▼ Sonny Glasbrenner Inc ....E 727 573-1110
Saint Petersburg (G-15849)

Southern Waste Systems LLC ....C 561 582-6688
Davie (G-2518)

Terra Excavating Inc ....C 727 497-8106
Saint Petersburg (G-15874)

Woodruff & Sons Inc ....C 941 756-1871
Bradenton (G-1207)

1796 Installation Or Erection Of Bldg Eqpt & Machinery, NEC

Assurance Power Systems LLC ......E 561 886-0470
Delray Beach (G-2912)

▲ Automation Logistics Corp ....D 813 855-8600
Oldsmar (G-11893)

▲ Central Moving & Storage Inc ......E 407 219-9779
Orlando (G-12284)

Diverse Co ....E 863 425-4251
Mulberry (G-10978)

Fieldcore Service Inc ....C 813 242-7400
Tampa (G-17657)

Lipten Company LLC ....E 800 860-0790
Groveland (G-5097)

▼ Ls Energia Inc ....E 954 281-7022
Plantation (G-14668)

Oracle Elevator Holdco Inc ....E 800 526-6115
Tampa (G-18105)

Otis Elevator Company ....B 561 618-4831
West Palm Beach (G-19296)

Otis Elevator Company ....C 305 816-5740
Fort Lauderdale (G-4036)

Page Mechanical Group LLC ....C 239 275-4406
Fort Myers (G-4532)

Pro Serv Industrial Contrs LLC ......E 407 324-5666
Sanford (G-15974)

Schindler Elevator Corporation ......E 904 880-4922
Jacksonville (G-6698)

T Mowery Enterprises Inc ....E 850 526-4111
Marianna (G-8686)

Taylor Industrial Cnstr Inc ....E 386 792-3060
Live Oak (G-8320)

The Siebold Company Inc ....D 954 340-3005
Coral Springs (G-2292)

Thomas Services Inc ....D 630 519-3265
West Palm Beach (G-19387)

Tk Elevator Corporation ....D 813 287-1744
Tampa (G-18422)

Tk Elevator Corporation ....D 850 477-0015
Pensacola (G-14460)

▲ United Subcontractors Inc ....E 651 225-6300
Daytona Beach (G-2684)

Water Equipment Services Inc ....D 941 371-7617
Sarasota (G-16361)

1799 Special Trade Contractors, NEC

1-800-Boardup Inc ....E 904 758-8000
Jacksonville Beach (G-6972)

A & G Concrete Pools Inc ....E 772 467-6626
Port Saint Lucie (G-15120)

Aacg Inc ....E 352 467-7000
Dade City (G-2380)

ABG Caulking Contractors Inc ....D 407 846-6868
Kissimmee (G-7261)

Academy Home Kitchen & Bath ......E 239 410-7080
North Fort Myers (G-11471)

Company	Code	Phone
Aerial Companies Inc	C	239 643-7625
Naples (G-11002)		
◆ Aerial Rigging Inc	C	863 607-9100
Lakeland (G-7787)		
AG Contractors Fl LLC	D	305 503-9869
Miami (G-9101)		
Air Flow Designs Inc	E	407 831-3600
Casselberry (G-1440)		
Air Qlity Innvtive Sltions LLC	E	407 574-5268
Orlando (G-12086)		
AK Glazing Contractors Inc	E	954 673-6532
Davie (G-2454)		
◆ Allied Home Improvement Inc	E	305 949-7444
Wilton Manors (G-19519)		
American Eagle Scaffolding Inc	E	561 826-8458
Boca Raton (G-414)		
▼ American Envmtl Cont Corp	D	863 666-3020
Lakeland (G-7798)		
American Pools & Spas Inc	E	407 847-9322
Orlando (G-12114)		
American Rofg Jacksonville LLC	E	904 385-4375
Jacksonville (G-5791)		
American Sand & Xcavation Inc	E	850 763-4300
Lynn Haven (G-8467)		
Anchor Sndblst & Coatings LLC	D	813 247-4140
Tampa (G-17285)		
Apex Pavers Inc	E	772 419-5151
Stuart (G-16588)		
Aqua Blue Pools Centl Fla Inc	D	321 777-2812
Melbourne (G-8817)		
Aquarius Building Inc	C	305 824-1324
Miami Lakes (G-10705)		
Armex Construction Inc	E	239 645-1517
Cape Coral (G-1376)		
Artistry Painting Company Inc	E	941 484-3805
Venice (G-18765)		
▲ Ashbritt Inc	E	954 725-6992
Deerfield Beach (G-2712)		
Atlas Signs Holdings Inc	D	561 863-6659
Riviera Beach (G-15281)		
Bergeron Emergency Svcs Inc	E	954 680-6100
Fort Lauderdale (G-3637)		
Best-TEC Asb Abatement Inc	E	904 695-9900
Boynton Beach (G-964)		
▼ Blasters Inc	E	813 985-4500
Tampa (G-17366)		
Blue Ribbon Cleaning Co Inc	E	352 624-3444
Ocala (G-11641)		
Blue Team Restoration LLC	C	561 246-4016
Boca Raton (G-452)		
▲ Bobs Pool Service Inc	E	407 834-7100
Casselberry (G-1444)		
Bornt Enterprises Inc	E	813 623-1492
Tampa (G-17380)		
▲ C T Windows LLC	E	407 857-9237
Orlando (G-12223)		
C W Roberts Contracting Inc	C	850 785-4675
Panama City (G-13974)		
C-Squared Certif Gen Contr Inc	D	941 345-3093
Sarasota (G-16026)		
Caribbean Pool Service & Repr	D	561 842-7482
Riviera Beach (G-15287)		
Carter Fence Company Inc	D	239 353-4102
Naples (G-11047)		
Ceco Concrete Construction LLC	C	813 622-8080
Tampa (G-17435)		
Certified Contg Group Inc	E	954 781-7663
Pompano Beach (G-14771)		
Certified Pool Mechanics Inc	E	239 992-9096
Fort Myers (G-4306)		
Ces Synergies Inc	C	813 783-1688
Crystal Springs (G-2356)		
▼ Classic Marcite Inc	E	407 521-6260
Orlando (G-12313)		
Coast To Coast Gen Contrs Inc	D	954 920-3900
Hollywood (G-5416)		
◆ Comanco Environmental Corp	E	813 988-8829
Plant City (G-14550)		
Commercial Contg Systems Inc	E	941 351-4633
Sarasota (G-16125)		
Commercial Maint Systems Inc	E	813 805-0512
Clearwater (G-1583)		
Connery Corporation	E	772 231-1224
Vero Beach (G-18849)		
Coral Reef Tropical Pools Inc	D	305 367-2005
Key Largo (G-7174)		
Corrosion Ctrl Specialists Inc	E	813 677-2899
Tampa (G-17525)		
Cosugas LLC	E	954 916-7500
Sunrise (G-16759)		

Company	Code	Phone
Cox Building Corporation	D	850 234-7800
Panama City (G-13990)		
Cross Construction Company Inc	E	813 909-7061
Lutz (G-8437)		
Cross Construction Company Inc	C	813 907-1013
Lutz (G-8438)		
Cross Environmental Svcs Inc	E	954 583-9528
Davie (G-2473)		
Cross Environmental Svcs Inc	E	813 783-1688
Zephyrhills (G-19827)		
Cross Environmental Svcs Inc	D	813 782-3512
Zephyrhills (G-19828)		
Custom Wldg & Fabrication Inc	D	863 967-1000
Auburndale (G-253)		
D & A Construction Group Inc	E	407 960-4032
Altamonte Springs (G-43)		
▼ D P C General Contractors Inc	E	305 325-0447
Miami (G-9448)		
▼ Danielle Fence Mfg Co Inc	D	863 425-3182
Mulberry (G-10975)		
▼ Davis Fence Company Inc	E	305 593-8590
Miami (G-9461)		
Delta Petroleum and Indus Inc	D	561 840-1446
West Palm Beach (G-19120)		
▲ Dillon Pools Inc	E	954 668-2000
Miramar (G-10853)		
◆ Diversfied Cnstr Rstration Inc	E	305 246-4306
Miami (G-9481)		
DMS Contractors LLC	D	305 627-3276
Fort Lauderdale (G-3761)		
Drawdy Brothers Cnstr II Inc	B	407 679-6382
Orlando (G-12439)		
Dykstra Construction LLC	E	813 707-0082
Lakeland (G-7853)		
Elias Bros Group Pntg Cntg Inc	D	239 643-1624
Naples (G-11101)		
▼ Entera Inc	E	850 763-7982
Panama City (G-14001)		
▼ Entera LLC	E	850 763-1184
Panama City (G-14002)		
ESA South Inc	E	850 937-8505
Cantonment (G-1339)		
Essig Pools Inc	E	305 949-0000
Miramar (G-10857)		
▲ Expo Marble & Granite Inc	E	954 943-9006
Pompano Beach (G-14802)		
F & H Contractors Inc	E	352 795-0525
Haines City (G-5147)		
Federal Rent-A-Fence Inc	E	386 775-8444
Orange City (G-11961)		
▼ Fence Masters Inc	E	305 635-7777
Miami (G-9551)		
Fickling Brothers Inc	D	904 359-0314
Jacksonville (G-6154)		
◆ Fire Stop Systems Inc	C	239 774-3343
Naples (G-11111)		
Fire Stop Systems LLC	E	239 774-3343
Naples (G-11112)		
▲ Five Arrows Inc	D	813 972-4945
Tampa (G-17668)		
Flood Zone Restoration LLC	E	844 863-3279
Port Charlotte (G-15035)		
Florida Commercial Care Inc	D	813 972-4962
Kissimmee (G-7309)		
▼ Florida Shutters Inc	E	772 569-2200
Vero Beach (G-18858)		
Fresh Cut Lawn Service Inc	E	407 298-0911
Orlando (G-12547)		
Frs Envrnmntal Remediation Inc	E	813 623-1557
Tampa (G-17719)		
Gac Contractors Inc	C	850 227-9826
Port Saint Joe (G-15116)		
General Caulking Coatings Inc	D	305 652-1020
Miami (G-9624)		
Geopolymer Solutions LLC	D	954 234-8881
Delray Beach (G-2954)		
Glenco Industries I LLC	E	407 888-0651
Orlando (G-12574)		
Global Maritek Systems Inc	D	904 827-8466
Saint Augustine (G-15445)		
Granite Wave Inc	E	786 718-8935
Hialeah (G-5268)		
H and J Contracting Inc	D	561 791-1953
Wellington (G-18982)		
Hardwick Fence LLC	E	904 599-8644
Saint Augustine (G-15449)		
Hartshorn Custom Contg Inc	E	813 620-0931
Temple Terrace (G-18635)		
Heritage Insur Holdings Inc	D	407 282-4421
Orlando (G-12635)		

Company	Code	Phone
HG Cnstr Dev & Inv Inc	D	786 845-8999
Miami (G-9699)		
Highway Safety Devices Inc	D	813 759-1559
Tampa (G-17822)		
Hubbard Construction Company	C	407 855-3535
Orlando (G-12668)		
Hydrotech Pools Inc	E	239 595-7808
Naples (G-11171)		
Icon Building Inc	E	239 643-3689
Naples (G-11172)		
Illinois Avenue Partners LLC	E	727 532-8255
Saint Petersburg (G-15716)		
Image Janitorial Services Inc	C	561 627-8748
West Palm Beach (G-19196)		
Infinite Pool Finishes LLC	E	239 466-7665
Fort Myers (G-4449)		
Insul-Coat Inc	E	407 647-3541
Winter Park (G-19737)		
▲ International Gran & Stone LLC	E	813 920-6500
Odessa (G-11845)		
▼ Interstate Signcrafters LLC	D	561 547-3760
Boynton Beach (G-1002)		
Jackson Stoneworks LLC	E	352 372-6600
Gainesville (G-4925)		
Jaret Construction LLC	E	407 810-3313
Saint Cloud (G-15527)		
Jcal Holdings LLC	E	561 687-5005
Lake Worth Beach (G-7770)		
K T Carter Contracting Inc	E	904 354-9999
Jacksonville (G-6394)		
Kbf Renovations Inc	E	813 269-7257
New Port Richey (G-11391)		
▲ Kimmins Corp	E	813 248-3878
Tampa (G-17924)		
Konopka Services Inc	E	561 793-6404
West Palm Beach (G-19228)		
Landmark Pools Inc	E	813 792-1331
Odessa (G-11848)		
Lang Environmental Inc	E	813 622-8311
Tampa (G-17934)		
Led Enterprise Inc	E	407 674-8259
Orlando (G-12759)		
▲ Liberty Aluminum Co	E	239 369-3000
Lehigh Acres (G-8288)		
Lotspeich Co Florida Inc	C	954 978-2388
Fort Lauderdale (G-3946)		
Louden Bonded Pools Inc	E	772 465-2700
Fort Pierce (G-4718)		
LRE Ground Services Inc	C	352 796-0229
Brooksville (G-1298)		
Malak LLC	E	407 601-7675
Orlando (G-12805)		
Marquis Kitchens & Baths Inc	C	850 267-2290
Santa Rosa Beach (G-16010)		
Master Line Kitchen LLC	E	305 256-5955
Palmetto Bay (G-13947)		
McEnany Roofing Inc	D	813 988-1669
Temple Terrace (G-18641)		
McW Acquisition LLC	E	954 974-0770
Pompano Beach (G-14852)		
Metro Property Services Inc	E	904 399-1020
Jacksonville (G-6501)		
◆ Miami Beach Awning Co	E	305 576-2029
Miami (G-9955)		
Micon Scaffolding LLC	E	305 456-1220
Opa Locka (G-11951)		
Moorecars LLC	E	678 472-9114
Boynton Beach (G-1018)		
Nassau Pools Construction Inc	E	239 643-0990
Naples (G-11243)		
National Service Source Inc	C	321 328-1032
Melbourne (G-8947)		
▲ Natural Stone Concepts LLC	E	239 263-1930
Naples (G-11246)		
Nettie Bayou Industries Inc	E	941 625-5056
Port Charlotte (G-15051)		
Norris & Samon Pump Service	E	727 323-4422
Saint Petersburg (G-15779)		
Northstar Contg Group Inc	C	813 684-4400
Riverview (G-15262)		
Northstar Dem & Remediation LP	D	407 855-2365
Orlando (G-12917)		
Northstar Dem & Remediation LP	D	850 474-4077
Pensacola (G-14389)		
One Stop Pool Pros Inc	D	800 880-6919
Hallandale Beach (G-5178)		
Org By Design Inc	E	352 748-0770
Wildwood (G-19505)		
Outsource Option LLC	E	407 493-7928
Orlando (G-12994)		

S
I
C

Paramount Painting & Svcs Inc	E	813 715-9699
Tampa *(G-18121)*		
Phoenix Coatings Inc	D	850 857-4740
Pensacola *(G-14413)*		
Pinnacle Pool Construction	E	239 596-1600
Naples *(G-11264)*		
◆ Play/Space Services Inc	E	888 653-7529
Melbourne *(G-8959)*		
Plummer Pntg Waterproofing Inc	D	407 585-0210
Winter Park *(G-19762)*		
Poma Metals Corp	E	772 283-0099
Palm City *(G-13798)*		
▲ Premier Bathrooms Usa Inc	D	386 761-1830
South Daytona *(G-16493)*		
Proietto Painting Inc	D	954 772-3898
Oakland Park *(G-11610)*		
Project Combo Inc	E	708 465-0028
Naples *(G-11274)*		
Properties Elgant Dstnction LL	D	561 364-9675
Boynton Beach *(G-1029)*		
Protective Barriers LLC	E	239 693-5937
Fort Myers *(G-4556)*		
Pyro Solutions Inc	D	813 986-7680
Plant City *(G-14576)*		
Quality Cable Contractors Inc	E	407 246-0606
Orlando *(G-13077)*		
Quality Roofing Inc	C	813 620-4797
Tampa *(G-18188)*		
R & B Metalworks	E	941 723-1975
Palmetto *(G-13926)*		
R & S Assembly Inc	D	561 793-6029
West Palm Beach *(G-19334)*		
R B M Contracting Services LLC	E	850 622-1434
Freeport *(G-4816)*		
Rainey Construction Company	B	352 748-0955
Wildwood *(G-19508)*		
◆ Real Stone & Granite Corp	E	772 489-9964
Fort Pierce *(G-4733)*		
Regency Cnstr Palm Bch Cnty Co	B	586 741-8000
West Palm Beach *(G-19341)*		
Reintjes Services Inc	D	386 752-9506
Lake City *(G-7542)*		
Remove It Pros Inc	E	239 333-7678
Bonita Springs *(G-937)*		
Restocon Corporation	E	813 643-2202
Tampa *(G-18221)*		
Restore Construction Group Inc	D	954 985-5353
West Park *(G-19433)*		
RL James Inc General Contr	E	239 936-6002
Fort Myers *(G-4574)*		
◆ Rolladen Inc	E	954 454-4114
Hallandale Beach *(G-5181)*		
Rose Fence Company	E	407 382-5000
Orlando *(G-13127)*		
Ross & Logan Industries Inc	D	904 378-9700
Jacksonville *(G-6676)*		
◆ Rountree Trnspt & Rigging Inc	E	904 781-1033
Jacksonville *(G-6677)*		
RSI of Florida LLC	D	954 960-0224
Pompano Beach *(G-14886)*		
Scotfam Inc	E	904 246-2666
Jacksonville Beach *(G-7001)*		
Sears Roebuck and Co	C	305 594-2400
Doral *(G-3307)*		
Sears Roebuck and Co	C	561 731-3635
Boynton Beach *(G-1034)*		
Sears Roebuck and Co	C	954 370-2800
Plantation *(G-14704)*		
Security MGT Partners Inc	E	863 425-5626
Mulberry *(G-10981)*		
SI Goldman Company Inc	C	407 830-5000
Longwood *(G-8406)*		
Sign Acquisition LLC	D	631 273-4800
Boynton Beach *(G-1036)*		
Simpson Environmental Svcs LLC	D	352 583-2509
Dade City *(G-2396)*		
Southern Road & Bridge LLC	C	727 940-5395
Tarpon Springs *(G-18592)*		
Southern Staircase Inc	D	239 949-7040
Bonita Springs *(G-943)*		
Southern Waste Systems LLC	C	561 582-6688
Davie *(G-2518)*		
Star Pntg & Waterproofing Inc	E	305 770-0143
West Park *(G-19436)*		
▲ Stone Spirit Inc	E	407 770-0077
Orlando *(G-13240)*		
Strauss Investments Inc	E	850 575-7981
Tallahassee *(G-17116)*		
Strongcore Group LLC	D	305 539-0680
South Miami *(G-16519)*		

▼ Structural Waterproofing Inc	D	407 645-2021
Maitland *(G-8582)*		
▼ Sun Fiberglass Products Inc	E	352 540-9420
Brooksville *(G-1313)*		
Sundance Archtectural Pdts LLC	E	407 297-1337
Orlando *(G-13249)*		
Sunrise Systems Brevard Inc	E	321 636-1618
Cocoa *(G-1957)*		
▼ Sunshine Crane Rental Corp	E	407 880-2222
Apopka *(G-216)*		
Sunshine Kitchens LLC	D	954 591-2030
Miami *(G-10348)*		
Super Restoration Svc Co LLC	E	305 233-0500
Doral *(G-3325)*		
Superior Rigging and Erct Co	C	407 858-2925
Orlando *(G-13252)*		
Superior Structures Inc	D	813 884-2636
Tampa *(G-18348)*		
▲ Surface Technologies Corp	D	904 241-1501
Jacksonville *(G-6820)*		
Suwannee Ir Works & Fence Inc	D	386 935-3466
O Brien *(G-11579)*		
Sweetwater Restoration Inc	E	904 880-1919
Saint Johns *(G-15549)*		
Synergy Contracting Group Inc	E	727 287-6320
Clearwater *(G-1812)*		
Therma Seal Roof Systems LLC	E	561 223-2096
Fort Lauderdale *(G-4175)*		
Triton Global Petroleum Ltd	E	954 639-0005
Fort Lauderdale *(G-4186)*		
US Federal Contr Registration	E	727 576-6358
Clearwater *(G-1828)*		
USA Fence Company	E	941 753-5585
Bradenton *(G-1197)*		
Velocity Restorations LLC	E	850 434-6769
Cantonment *(G-1345)*		
Wegman Associates Inc	D	407 850-9191
Orlando *(G-13414)*		
Wellington Royal Kit & Gran	E	561 798-2212
West Palm Beach *(G-19418)*		
West Coast Florida Entps Inc	D	239 433-9777
Fort Myers *(G-4654)*		
▼ West Construction Inc	E	561 588-2027
Lantana *(G-8072)*		
Western Waterproofing Co Amer	E	407 647-4175
Winter Park *(G-19786)*		
Whitesell-Green Inc	E	850 434-5311
Pensacola *(G-14473)*		
Wilco Enterprises Inc	E	352 629-8157
Ocala *(G-11797)*		
Wilson Kehoe & Miller Corp	E	727 584-7742
Largo *(G-8164)*		
Windward Island Cnstr Pool Spa	E	239 219-6462
Fort Myers *(G-4656)*		
Wrk Lab Inc	E	305 400-8101
Doral *(G-3362)*		
Wsh - Florida LLC	E	717 268-4776
Saint Petersburg *(G-15901)*		
Zicaro Services Inc	E	561 265-1132
Boynton Beach *(G-1046)*		
Zpacez LLC	D	413 272-8720
North Miami *(G-11514)*		

40 RAILROAD TRANSPORTATION

4011 Railroads, Line-Hauling Operations

Atlas Railroad Construction Co	C	412 677-2020
Jacksonville *(G-5819)*		
Bay Line Railroad LLC	D	850 747-4034
Panama City *(G-13966)*		
Bayline Railroad LLC	D	850 785-5141
Panama City *(G-13967)*		
Brightline Holdings LLC	B	305 521-4800
Miami *(G-9284)*		
CSX Corporation	D	904 279-6744
Jacksonville *(G-6029)*		
CSX Corporation	D	904 359-3200
Jacksonville *(G-6030)*		
▲ CSX Transportation Inc	E	904 359-3100
Jacksonville *(G-6033)*		
CSX Transportation Inc	E	863 967-3533
Auburndale *(G-252)*		
CSX Transportation Inc	D	904 381-4030
Jacksonville *(G-6034)*		
Florida East Coast Railway LLC	D	904 538-6100
Jacksonville *(G-6190)*		
Florida East Coast Railway LLC	D	305 889-1958
Miami *(G-9573)*		
Florida East Coast Railway LLC	D	305 889-5654
Miami *(G-9574)*		

Florida East Coast Railway LLC	D	904 538-6100
Fort Lauderdale *(G-3796)*		
Florida East Coast Railway LLC	E	904 279-3129
Jacksonville *(G-6191)*		
Florida Gulf & Atlantic RR LLC	D	850 207-5305
Tallahassee *(G-16970)*		
Fruit Growers Express Co Inc	D	904 356-2791
Jacksonville *(G-6210)*		
Genesee & Wyoming Inc	D	904 596-1045
Jacksonville *(G-6225)*		
Norfolk Southern Railway Co	C	904 366-1401
Jacksonville *(G-6546)*		
Patriot Rail Company LLC	D	904 423-2540
Jacksonville *(G-6584)*		
Railamerica Trnsp Corp	C	904 538-6100
Jacksonville *(G-6633)*		
Railusa LLC	D	561 617-8052
Boca Raton *(G-764)*		
South Carolina Central RR Co	E	203 202-8904
Jacksonville *(G-6746)*		
Talleyrand Terminal RR Co	E	904 634-1884
Jacksonville *(G-6830)*		

41 LOCAL AND SUBURBAN TRANSIT AND INTERURBAN HIGHWAY PASSENGER TRANSPORTATION

4111 Local & Suburban Transit

ABC Taxi	E	813 872-8294
Tampa *(G-17222)*		
All Points Services Inc	E	305 253-9076
Miami *(G-9119)*		
Aventura Limosne Trnsp Svc Inc	E	305 651-3337
Miami *(G-9194)*		
Cargo Services Inc	E	305 870-9666
Miami *(G-9318)*		
Central Fla Rgional Trnsp Auth	A	407 841-2279
Orlando *(G-12272)*		
City of Tallahassee	C	850 891-5044
Tallahassee *(G-16918)*		
Coach Crafters Inc	E	352 742-8111
Tavares *(G-18602)*		
Community Cnnctons Trnsprttons	E	407 579-4302
Orlando *(G-12350)*		
County of Brevard	D	321 635-7815
Cocoa *(G-1934)*		
County of Miami-Dade	D	786 469-5675
Miami *(G-9430)*		
Deugro (usa) Inc	E	814 520-8152
Doral *(G-3177)*		
First Transit Inc	D	850 215-1854
Panama City *(G-14007)*		
First Transit Inc	E	850 595-0501
Pensacola *(G-14305)*		
First Transit Inc	E	305 681-5757
Hialeah *(G-5260)*		
First Transit Inc	C	305 876-7123
Miami *(G-9561)*		
First Transit Inc	E	305 673-7688
Miami Beach *(G-10593)*		
Geo Transport Inc	D	561 893-0101
Boca Raton *(G-604)*		
Hillsborough Transit Authority	B	813 623-5835
Tampa *(G-17828)*		
Hillsbrugh Area Rgnal Trnst Au	B	813 623-5835
Tampa *(G-17829)*		
Jacksonville Trnsp Auth	B	904 630-3181
Jacksonville *(G-6368)*		
Jacksonville Trnsp Auth	D	904 630-3137
Jacksonville *(G-6369)*		
Jetstream Ground Services Inc	D	561 746-3282
Jupiter *(G-7090)*		
Lakeland Area Mass Transit Dst	C	863 688-7433
Lakeland *(G-7899)*		
Maruti Transit Group LLC	E	407 412-5613
Orlando *(G-12825)*		
Mears Destination Services Inc	A	407 422-4561
Orlando *(G-12849)*		
Miami-Dade Cnty Pub Schols-158	E	305 234-3365
Miami *(G-9992)*		
Mv Transportation Inc	B	407 858-5615
Orlando *(G-12890)*		
Pinellas Sncast Trnst Auth Inc	A	727 540-1800
Saint Petersburg *(G-15801)*		
Prestige Trnsp Svc LLC	E	305 387-4777
Miami *(G-10140)*		

Silver Airways LLC	C	954 985-1500	
Hollywood *(G-5520)*			
South Fla Regional Trnsp Auth	C	954 942-7245	
Pompano Beach *(G-14902)*			
Super Shuttle	C	727 572-1111	
Clearwater *(G-1807)*			
Supershuttle International Inc	D	727 799-2222	
Clearwater *(G-1808)*			
Transdev On Demand Inc	A	407 888-9220	
Orlando *(G-13302)*			

4119 Local Passenger Transportation: NEC

A1a Airport & Limosne Svc Inc	D	561 622-2222	
Boca Raton *(G-391)*			
All County Ambulance Inc	D	772 465-1111	
Fort Pierce *(G-4678)*			
Ambitrans Medical Trnspt Inc	C	941 743-3665	
Port Charlotte *(G-15020)*			
American Med	E	305 296-2401	
Tavernier *(G-18622)*			
Americare Ambulance Svc Inc	D	813 930-0911	
Seffner *(G-16421)*			
Aqua Utilities Florida Inc	E	352 245-9293	
Ocala *(G-11632)*			
Aventura Limosne Trnsp Svc Inc	E	305 651-3337	
Miami *(G-9194)*			
B & L Service Inc	C	954 565-8900	
Fort Lauderdale *(G-3623)*			
Boyce Trans Inc	D	561 391-4762	
Boca Raton *(G-478)*			
Campanile Motor Services Inc	D	305 893-9850	
Miami *(G-9308)*			
Carey Chffeur Svcs Jcksonville	D	904 246-3741	
Jacksonville *(G-5905)*			
Central Florida Ambulance Inc	E	407 292-8777	
Orlando *(G-12281)*			
City Cab Company of Orlando	C	407 422-4561	
Orlando *(G-12304)*			
Cnc Management Group Inc	E	305 250-4907	
Miami *(G-9383)*			
Coastal Hlth Systems Brvard In	D	321 631-1448	
Rockledge *(G-15339)*			
Community Cnnctons Trnsprttons	E	407 579-4302	
Deltona *(G-3038)*			
Crisis Center of Tampa Bay Inc	C	813 964-1964	
Tampa *(G-17551)*			
Destination MCO Inc	D	407 422-2522	
Orlando *(G-12414)*			
Dolphin Trnsp Specialists Inc	D	239 530-0100	
Naples *(G-11096)*			
Dynamic Tours and Trnsp Inc	C	407 351-7777	
Orlando *(G-12446)*			
East Coast Trnsp Co N Fla LLC	E	904 525-8600	
Jacksonville *(G-6101)*			
First 2 Aid Ems Inc	D	407 777-4322	
Kissimmee *(G-7307)*			
First Class Limousine Svcs Inc	D	352 259-9398	
Lady Lake *(G-7431)*			
Fort Lauderdale Trnsp Inc	E	954 462-7287	
Fort Lauderdale *(G-3804)*			
Good Wheels Inc	D	239 768-2900	
Fort Lauderdale *(G-3825)*			
Harbor Cy Vlntr Amblance Squad	C	321 723-8480	
Melbourne *(G-8898)*			
Innovtive Trnspt Lgstics Sltion	D	850 291-0215	
Pensacola *(G-14329)*			
Jax Patient Care Inc	E	904 309-9902	
Jacksonville *(G-6378)*			
Key Lrgo Vlntr Ambulance Corps	E	305 451-2766	
Key Largo *(G-7184)*			
Lake Emergency Med Svcs Inc	E	352 383-4554	
Tavares *(G-18613)*			
Leopard Transport Inc	E	352 812-1670	
Ocala *(G-11709)*			
Liberty Ambulance Service Inc	D	904 721-0008	
Jacksonville *(G-6432)*			
Life Alert Emrgncy Rsponse Inc	D	954 491-8511	
Fort Lauderdale *(G-3940)*			
Lifefleet Southeast Inc	D	813 885-3955	
Tampa *(G-17948)*			
Limousines South Florida Inc	D	954 463-0845	
Fort Lauderdale *(G-3944)*			
Limousines South Florida Inc	C	305 633-0891	
Miami *(G-9872)*			
Loyal Rideshare Corporation	D	289 407-9421	
New Smyrna *(G-11413)*			
M C T Express Inc	E	305 779-0505	
Miami *(G-9888)*			
Marion Senior Services Inc	D	352 620-3501	
Ocala *(G-11726)*			

Mears Destination Services Inc	A	407 422-4561	
Orlando *(G-12849)*			
Medfleet Inc	D	727 849-6849	
Clearwater *(G-1710)*			
Medfleet LLC	C	727 849-6849	
Hudson *(G-5645)*			
Medical Air Services Assn Inc	E	954 334-8263	
Plantation *(G-14672)*			
Medics Ambulance Service Inc	E	954 763-1776	
Pompano Beach *(G-14854)*			
Minority Mobile System Inc	E	305 669-4550	
Miami *(G-10006)*			
Modivcare Solutions LLC	B	904 737-8022	
Jacksonville *(G-6513)*			
Mt Medical Florida Inc	D	843 284-6331	
Jacksonville *(G-6521)*			
Naples Trnsp & Tours LLC	D	239 262-7300	
Naples *(G-11241)*			
National Health Transport Inc	C	305 636-5555	
Miami *(G-10029)*			
Nature Cast Emrgncy Med Fndtio	C	352 249-4700	
Lecanto *(G-8223)*			
Owl Inc	C	904 679-4555	
Jacksonville *(G-6572)*			
Positive Mobility Inc	E	863 655-0030	
Sebring *(G-16411)*			
Rainbow Limousine Inc	B	407 688-2229	
Deltona *(G-3043)*			
Rural/Metro Corp Florida	E	352 569-1012	
Orlando *(G-13149)*			
S&S Exotics LLC	D	929 230-4963	
Coral Springs *(G-2282)*			
Seven-One-Seven Prkg Svcs Inc	A	813 228-7722	
Tampa *(G-18273)*			
Super Shuttle	C	727 572-1111	
Clearwater *(G-1807)*			
West Coast Southern Med Svcs	E	941 748-7162	
Bradenton *(G-1203)*			
Wheelchair Transport Svc Inc	D	727 586-2811	
Clearwater *(G-1839)*			

4121 Taxi Cabs

ABC Taxi	E	813 872-8294	
Tampa *(G-17222)*			
B & L Service Inc	E	661 589-9080	
Wilton Manors *(G-19521)*			
B & L Service Inc	C	954 565-8900	
Fort Lauderdale *(G-3623)*			
Bay Area Metro LLC	E	727 507-2667	
Clearwater *(G-1533)*			
City Cab Company of Orlando	C	407 422-4561	
Orlando *(G-12304)*			
Gulf Coast Transportation	E	813 251-3107	
Tampa *(G-17772)*			
Yellow Cab Central Florida Inc	E	352 241-2000	
Lady Lake *(G-7444)*			
Yellow Cab Company of Orlando	D	407 422-4561	
Orlando *(G-13468)*			

4131 Intercity & Rural Bus Transportation

City of Tallahassee	C	850 891-5044	
Tallahassee *(G-16918)*			
Greyhound Lines Inc	E	305 358-0692	
Miami *(G-9665)*			
Hillsborough Transit Authority	B	813 623-5835	
Tampa *(G-17828)*			
TWC Services Inc	E	954 489-0104	
Pompano Beach *(G-14932)*			

4141 Local Bus Charter Svc

A&S Transportation Inc	C	239 434-0777	
Naples *(G-10993)*			
Carnival Corporation	A	305 599-2600	
Doral *(G-3145)*			
Dynamic Tours and Trnsp Inc	C	407 351-7777	
Orlando *(G-12446)*			
First Class Coach Company Inc	D	727 526-9086	
Saint Petersburg *(G-15669)*			
Mears Destination Services Inc	A	407 422-4561	
Orlando *(G-12849)*			
Quality Transport Services Inc	D	954 791-2505	
Fort Lauderdale *(G-4073)*			

4142 Bus Charter Service, Except Local

Astro Travel & Tours Inc	E	850 514-1793	
Tallahassee *(G-16885)*			
Carnival Corporation	A	305 599-2600	
Doral *(G-3145)*			

Connexxions Bus Inc	E	917 940-1334	
Orlando *(G-12360)*			
Escot Bus Lines LLC	C	727 545-2088	
Largo *(G-8101)*			
First Class Coach Company Inc	D	727 526-9086	
Saint Petersburg *(G-15669)*			
Quality Transport Services Inc	D	954 791-2505	
Fort Lauderdale *(G-4073)*			

4151 School Buses

A&S Transportation Inc	C	239 434-0777	
Naples *(G-10993)*			
Atlantic School Bus Corp	B	904 598-2880	
Jacksonville *(G-5817)*			
Broward County Public Schools	E	754 321-4460	
Oakland Park *(G-11586)*			
First Student Inc	C	904 751-9828	
Jacksonville *(G-6176)*			
Marion County Public Schools	C	352 671-7000	
Ocala *(G-11720)*			
School Bd of Okeechobee Cnty	B	863 462-5146	
Avon Park *(G-296)*			
School Board Orange County Fla	A	407 521-2344	
Orlando *(G-13170)*			
School Dst Putnam Cnty Fla	E	386 329-0553	
Palatka *(G-13600)*			
St Johns County School Dst	C	904 547-7810	
Saint Augustine *(G-15501)*			
Volusia County School District	D	386 822-6743	
Deland *(G-2890)*			

4173 Bus Terminal & Svc Facilities

City of Miami Beach	D	305 673-7616	
Miami Beach *(G-10573)*			
Dade County Expressway Auth	E	305 637-3277	
Miami *(G-9450)*			
Menzies Aviation (texas) Inc	C	407 851-5636	
Orlando *(G-12856)*			

42 MOTOR FREIGHT TRANSPORTATION AND WAREHOUSING

4212 Local Trucking Without Storage

1-800-Pack-rat LLC	D	800 722-5728	
West Palm Beach *(G-19015)*			
3 ES Corp	E	352 216-6644	
Ocala *(G-11621)*			
AAA Cooper Transportation	D	904 355-4722	
Jacksonville *(G-5721)*			
AAA Cooper Transportation	D	305 887-8811	
Medley *(G-8699)*			
AAA Cooper Transportation	D	954 978-0455	
Pompano Beach *(G-14731)*			
Aadvantage Relocation Inc	D	850 478-0082	
Pensacola *(G-14209)*			
Advan Disp Serv Soli Wast of P	E	407 464-2264	
Apopka *(G-147)*			
All My Sons Mvg Stor Ft Myers	E	239 334-0700	
Fort Myers *(G-4262)*			
American Loading Services	E	239 471-8293	
Cape Coral *(G-1374)*			
◆ **American Van Lines Inc**	E	954 630-0316	
Pompano Beach *(G-14739)*			
Anthym Logistics LLC	E	954 366-1204	
Tampa *(G-17290)*			
▲ **Armstrong Relocation Fla LLC**	E	954 956-0059	
Pompano Beach *(G-14743)*			
Averitt Express Inc	D	904 387-1423	
Jacksonville *(G-5828)*			
Baggage Airline Guest Svcs Inc	A	407 447-5547	
Orlando *(G-12166)*			
Burnsed Trucking Inc	D	772 467-2620	
Fort Pierce *(G-4689)*			
Bynum Transport Inc	C	863 967-3244	
Auburndale *(G-250)*			
C & W Global Inc	C	407 877-2600	
Winter Garden *(G-19559)*			
C & W Trucking Inc	C	407 877-2600	
Winter Garden *(G-19560)*			
C Diamond Transport Inc	E	352 728-5361	
Leesburg *(G-8234)*			
Capps Land MGT & Mtl LLC	E	904 693-8644	
Jacksonville *(G-5900)*			
Charles Silliman Trucking	D	813 247-4131	
Tampa *(G-17461)*			
Choice Environmental Svcs Inc	E	954 797-7974	
Fort Lauderdale *(G-3691)*			

CLC Hauling Inc ....E 727 848-7723
Hudson (G-5633)
◆ Cliff Berry Inc ....E 954 763-3390
Fort Lauderdale (G-3701)
Coastal Courier Inc ....E 407 679-6640
Winter Park (G-19706)
Coastal Waste & Recycl Fla Inc ......C 954 947-4000
Pompano Beach (G-14776)
Conser Mvg Stor Jcksnville LLC ......E 904 786-0242
Jacksonville (G-5998)
County of Brevard ....D 321 633-2042
Melbourne (G-8857)
Cross Street Service Inc ....E 904 781-2299
Jacksonville (G-6013)
Cypress Truck Lines Inc ....B 813 837-9998
Tampa (G-17564)
▲ Davidson Forwarding Company .....D 904 390-7100
Jacksonville (G-6049)
Davis Express Inc ....D 800 874-4270
Starke (G-16576)
Dhl Network Operations USA Inc .....E 954 888-7000
Plantation (G-14630)
Edward Zengel & Son Ex Inc ....D 239 768-0044
Fort Myers (G-4354)
Exclusive Enterprises Inc ....E 850 878-5548
Midway (G-10801)
Fedex Freight Inc ....E 561 684-7629
West Palm Beach (G-19137)
Fedex Ground Package Sys Inc ....C 305 887-7151
Medley (G-8732)
First Cast Dlvry Svc Prtners L ....D 904 657-3297
Jacksonville (G-6968)
Fleetgistics Holdings LLC ....D 407 843-6505
Orlando (G-12516)
Florida Beauty Flora Inc ....D 305 487-7777
Miami (G-9568)
◆ Florida Beauty Flora Inc ....C 305 503-1200
Miami (G-9569)
Florida Fertilizer Company Inc ....E 863 773-4159
Wauchula (G-18960)
Florida Food Tankers Inc ....D 863 676-2588
Lake Wales (G-7682)
Florida Topmoving Apollo Beach .....E 813 365-7438
Apollo Beach (G-137)
Freehold Cartage Inc ....D 863 533-4599
Bartow (G-318)
FSR Trucking Inc ....C 561 624-1931
West Palm Beach (G-19156)
Gator Freightways Inc ....C 863 984-4811
Lakeland (G-7873)
Glb Trucking LLC ....E 305 974-6239
Miami Gardens (G-10684)
Harlis R Ellington Cnstr Inc ....E 386 496-2134
Lake Butler (G-7504)
Harris Sanitation Inc ....C 321 409-6600
Melbourne (G-8899)
Harrison Trucking LLC ....D 256 734-1598
Panama City (G-14026)
Harte-Hanks Logistics LLC ....C 954 429-3771
Deerfield Beach (G-2747)
Homedeliverylink Inc ....D 813 620-3400
Brandon (G-1238)
IBC Messenger Inc ....D 305 591-8900
Doral (G-3233)
In Touch Logistics LLC ....E 305 398-4930
Miami Gardens (G-10689)
Integrity Ex Logistics LLC ....C 888 374-5138
Tampa (G-17870)
J W Watson Trucking Inc ....E 813 626-4553
Tampa (G-17882)
Jasons Hauling Inc ....D 813 872-8440
Tampa (G-17891)
Jlb Logistics Inc ....E 800 875-2463
Riverview (G-15258)
Jones Transportation LLC ....E 786 281-3402
Miami (G-9801)
Jsm Airport Services LLC ....C 352 383-2600
Tavares (G-18612)
L T L Express Inc ....E 305 882-0966
Miami (G-9840)
▲ Laney & Duke Terminal Whse Inc ....E 904 798-3500
Jacksonville (G-6420)
Larry Young Enterprises Inc ....E 941 637-3723
Punta Gorda (G-15211)
Lazaro Delivery Corporation ....E 305 629-8948
Miami (G-9851)
Mansari LLC ....D 813 391-6628
Tampa (G-17985)
May Trucking Company ....C 850 478-5550
Pensacola (G-14357)

Merica Delivery Services LLC ....E 239 849-1117
Sun City Center (G-16704)
Metropolitan Delivery Corp ....D 305 385-5551
Miami (G-9946)
Mjd Trucking Inc ....D 954 761-9871
Fort Lauderdale (G-3975)
Move Pro ....A 225 283-5048
Port Orange (G-15084)
Mr Subs of Melbourne - LLC ....E 321 473-8477
Melbourne (G-8943)
National Freight Inc ....E 407 826-3524
Orlando (G-12899)
North Florida Hauling LLC ....E 866 751-2371
Medley (G-8762)
Patco Transport Inc ....E 352 330-0708
Coleman (G-2012)
Patriot Trnsp Holdg Inc ....E 904 858-9100
Jacksonville (G-6586)
Paw Trucking Inc ....E 727 862-5956
Port Richey (G-15108)
Pece of Mind Environmental ....D 407 568-3456
Orlando (G-13018)
Peluso Movers Inc ....E 239 643-3303
Naples (G-11259)
Petro Tech Hauling Inc ....D 815 468-8280
Cocoa (G-1947)
Phb Inc ....C 904 570-9948
East Palatka (G-3401)
Pritchett Trucking Inc ....B 386 496-2630
Lake Butler (G-7509)
Quick Delivery Inc ....E 954 771-7292
Oakland Park (G-11611)
Red Arrow Express Inc ....E 313 454-7491
Largo (G-8144)
Republic Svcs Fla Ltd Partnr ....D 954 583-1830
Lauderhill (G-8206)
◆ Rountree Trnspt & Rigging Inc ....E 904 781-1033
Jacksonville (G-6677)
Rowland Transportation Inc ....C 352 567-2002
Dade City (G-2394)
Rsb Enterprises Inc ....E 866 616-7540
Jacksonville (G-6680)
Ryder System Inc ....A 305 500-3726
Medley (G-8776)
Sabal Transport Inc ....C 863 533-0871
Bartow (G-335)
Saia Motor Freight Line LLC ....D 561 845-6447
West Palm Beach (G-19350)
Schwend Inc ....E 352 588-2220
Dade City (G-2395)
SE Independent Dlvry Svcs Inc ....C 877 686-3737
Lakeland (G-7963)
Shelton Trucking Service Inc ....D 850 762-3201
Altha (G-117)
Silver Star Express Inc ....C 954 447-5000
Miramar (G-10895)
Smarter Moving Solutions LLC ....E 352 448-9095
Tampa (G-18296)
Smith Trucking Company Inc ....D 904 940-1226
Saint Augustine (G-15494)
Southeastern Freight Lines Inc ....C 813 986-2900
Thonotosassa (G-18676)
Southeastern Freight Lines Inc ....C 904 798-7000
Jacksonville (G-6753)
Southeastern Freight Lines Inc ....D 305 889-0501
Miami (G-10306)
Southeastern Freight Lines Inc ....E 407 855-1540
Orlando (G-13220)
Southland Waste Systems of Ga ......C 904 731-1732
Jacksonville (G-6766)
Star Distribution Systems Inc ....D 813 659-1002
Lakeland (G-7978)
Statewide Harvesting & Hlg LLC ....E 863 439-4225
Dundee (G-3373)
▲ Suddath Rlction Systems of Orl ......C 407 843-6683
Orlando (G-13243)
Suddath Rlction Systems of Pal ....D 904 390-7100
Jacksonville (G-6800)
Suddath Rlction Systems of Pal ....E 407 843-6683
Orlando (G-13244)
Suddath Van Lines Inc ....E 904 256-5540
Jacksonville (G-6802)
◆ Technlgy Cnsrvation Group Inc ....D 352 527-2534
Lecanto (G-8226)
Tempest Transportation Inc ....E 305 503-1200
Miami (G-10376)
Tisma Trucking Company LLC ....E 561 543-3661
West Palm Beach (G-19388)
Titan America LLC ....D 407 656-3313
Clermont (G-1895)

Trans-Phos Inc ....C 863 534-1575
Mulberry (G-10983)
Transplastics Inc ....D 813 630-5826
Tampa (G-18436)
Transportation America Inc ....D 305 308-8110
Miami (G-10403)
Trash Butler LLC ....D 813 500-7291
Tampa (G-18439)
Treasure Coast Refuse ....E 772 562-6620
Palm Bay (G-13642)
◆ U & ME Transfer Inc ....E 561 832-6156
West Palm Beach (G-19394)
United FL Transport Corp ....D 386 872-3142
Daytona Beach (G-2683)
US Van Lines Incorporated ....E 904 278-0708
Jacksonville (G-6899)
Usher Land & Timber Inc ....E 352 493-4221
Chiefland (G-1486)
Valiant Delivery Service LLC ....E 407 697-1814
Orlando (G-13366)
Van Nobel Lines Inc ....D 305 620-2002
Miami (G-10458)
Waste Pro Usa Inc ....D 850 365-1900
Milton (G-10829)
Watson Delivery Service LLC ....E 407 620-8269
Maitland (G-8599)
Withers/ Sddath Rlction System ....D 954 920-5445
Miami (G-10510)
▼ Young & Son Inc ....D 850 729-1321
Niceville (G-11460)
Zariz Transport Inc ....C 561 418-7200
Boca Raton (G-883)

4213 Trucking, Except Local

A & A Transfer & Storage Inc ....D 850 244-7661
Fort Walton Beach (G-4750)
A & A Transfer & Storage Inc ....E 904 786-0242
Jacksonville (G-5717)
AAA Cooper Transportation ....D 813 899-1306
Temple Terrace (G-18627)
AAA Cooper Transportation ....E 407 851-7900
Orlando (G-12038)
AAA Cooper Transportation ....D 904 355-4722
Jacksonville (G-5721)
AAA Cooper Transportation ....D 305 887-8811
Medley (G-8699)
AAA Cooper Transportation ....E 239 332-5581
Fort Myers (G-4245)
AAA Cooper Transportation ....E 850 576-1146
Tallahassee (G-16867)
AAA Cooper Transportation ....E 352 873-0137
Ocala (G-11624)
AAA Cooper Transportation ....E 850 479-2556
Pensacola (G-14208)
AAA Cooper Transportation ....D 954 978-0455
Pompano Beach (G-14731)
AAA Cooper Transportation ....E 772 429-2797
Fort Pierce (G-4675)
Abco Transportation Inc ....E 352 583-2777
Ocala (G-11625)
American Heritage Relocation ....E 904 390-7100
Jacksonville (G-5784)
Amerijet Holdings Inc ....D 800 927-6059
Miami Springs (G-10777)
Arlington Salvage & Wrecker Co ....E 904 744-4933
Jacksonville (G-5806)
Armellini Industries Inc ....B 772 287-0575
Palm City (G-13784)
Armellini Pierson Terminal Inc ....E 386 749-2044
Pierson (G-14496)
Armellini Pierson Terminal Inc ....E 305 592-5933
Miami (G-9171)
Arnold Transportation Svcs Inc ....E 904 262-4285
Jacksonville (G-5808)
ATF Services Lc ....D 305 885-6464
Hialeah Gardens (G-5340)
Atlantic Logistics LLC ....E 904 886-1110
Jacksonville (G-5816)
Averitt Express Inc ....D 561 842-9771
Riviera Beach (G-15282)
Averitt Express Inc ....D 239 332-4259
Fort Myers (G-4284)
Averitt Express Inc ....D 904 387-1423
Jacksonville (G-5828)
B E C Trucking Corp ....D 786 293-1158
Miami (G-9199)
Benton Express Inc ....D 813 621-5541
Tampa (G-17360)
Bestway Refrigerated Svc Inc ....E 407 889-3862
Apopka (G-158)

Beyel Bros Crane Rigging S Fla ....E 561 798-5776
  Riviera Beach *(G-15283)*
Boasso America Corporation ....E 904 475-0336
  Jacksonville *(G-5873)*
▲ Boasso Global Inc............C 813 797-3271
  Tampa *(G-17376)*
Bonded Transportation Inc ....D 850 438-4694
  Pensacola *(G-14238)*
◆ Brandon Transfer & Storage Co ....E 561 683-5000
  West Palm Beach *(G-19060)*
Brown Integrated Logistics Inc ....E 904 783-8323
  Jacksonville *(G-5885)*
Buchanan Hauling & Rigging Inc ....B 407 859-5171
  Orlando *(G-12213)*
▼ Bulk Express Transport Inc ....D 305 637-5567
  Miami *(G-9293)*
Bynum Transport Inc ....C 863 967-3244
  Auburndale *(G-250)*
C & W Global Inc ....C 407 877-2600
  Winter Garden *(G-19559)*
C & W Trucking Inc ....C 407 877-2600
  Winter Garden *(G-19560)*
C Diamond Transport Inc ....E 352 728-5361
  Leesburg *(G-8234)*
C Hayne Herndon & Co Inc ....E 863 422-3115
  Davenport *(G-2436)*
▲ Central Moving & Storage Inc ....E 407 219-9779
  Orlando *(G-12284)*
Centurion Auto Logistics Inc ....E 904 798-6740
  Jacksonville *(G-5926)*
▲ Centurion Auto Logistics Inc ....D 904 766-8500
  Jacksonville *(G-5927)*
Charles Silliman Trucking ....D 813 247-4131
  Tampa *(G-17461)*
Commercial Relocation Group ....E 954 532-5330
  Deerfield Beach *(G-2726)*
Consulttive Sls Prfssonals LLC ....E 954 510-4541
  Coral Springs *(G-2239)*
Cowan Systems Inc ....B 904 695-1234
  Jacksonville *(G-6006)*
◆ Crowley Logistics Inc ....C 904 727-2200
  Jacksonville *(G-6018)*
CSX Intermodal Terminals Inc ....C 904 359-3100
  Jacksonville *(G-6031)*
Cypress Truck Lines Inc ....B 813 837-9998
  Tampa *(G-17564)*
Cypress Truck Lines Inc ....E 904 353-8641
  Jacksonville *(G-6038)*
Davis Express Inc ....D 800 874-4270
  Starke *(G-16576)*
Diel-Jerue Inc ....E 352 732-9221
  Ocala *(G-11674)*
Estes Express Lines ....D 561 863-3535
  Riviera Beach *(G-15293)*
Estes Express Lines ....E 352 567-4111
  Wesley Chapel *(G-18997)*
Estes Express Lines ....E 407 293-2881
  Groveland *(G-5090)*
Estes Express Lines ....D 305 882-8847
  Miami *(G-9533)*
Estes Express Lines ....C 904 384-2277
  Jacksonville *(G-6134)*
Estes Express Lines Inc ....D 941 322-1054
  Fort Myers *(G-4361)*
Exxact Express Incorporated ....E 863 682-4101
  Lakeland *(G-7858)*
Exxact Transport Inc ....D 863 682-1799
  Lakeland *(G-7859)*
Fedex Freight Inc ....E 561 684-7629
  West Palm Beach *(G-19137)*
Fedex Freight Corporation ....A 863 687-4545
  Lakeland *(G-7864)*
Fedex Ground Package Sys Inc ....E 800 463-3339
  Orlando *(G-12501)*
Fedex Ground Package Sys Inc ....C 850 797-1492
  Niceville *(G-11447)*
First Coast Logistics Svcs Inc ....B 904 757-6008
  Jacksonville *(G-6169)*
Firstfleet Inc ....C 813 740-9564
  Tampa *(G-17664)*
Fort Myers Trucking Inc ....D 239 458-7424
  Fort Myers *(G-4401)*
Freehold Cartage Inc ....D 863 533-4599
  Bartow *(G-318)*
Freshpoint North Florida Inc ....C 904 764-7681
  Orlando *(G-12549)*
Fsr Logistics Corp ....D 561 624-1931
  West Palm Beach *(G-19155)*
Gac Transco Inc ....E 813 248-2101
  Tampa *(G-17724)*

Gator Freightways Inc ....D 407 578-8553
  Orlando *(G-12562)*
Gator Freightways Inc ....D 904 783-9470
  Jacksonville *(G-6222)*
Gator Freightways Inc ....C 863 984-4811
  Lakeland *(G-7873)*
Gator Freightways Inc ....C 954 432-2600
  Pembroke Pines *(G-14152)*
Gator Freightways Inc ....D 772 468-0027
  Fort Pierce *(G-4706)*
Gator Freightways Inc ....D 850 576-0138
  Tallahassee *(G-16986)*
Gator Freightways Inc ....D 850 983-0063
  Milton *(G-10816)*
General Transystems Inc ....D 352 521-3033
  Dade City *(G-2388)*
Glt Transportation Group LLC ....B 305 726-0275
  Miami Springs *(G-10783)*
Gold Coast Freightways Inc ....D 305 687-3560
  Fort Lauderdale *(G-3823)*
◆ Gonzalez & Sons Equipment Inc ....C 305 822-5455
  Hialeah *(G-5267)*
Gruden Acquisition Inc ....A 813 569-7131
  Tampa *(G-17765)*
Harte-Hanks Logistics LLC ....C 954 429-3771
  Deerfield Beach *(G-2747)*
Hellmann Wrldwide Lgistics Inc ....E 305 629-2703
  Doral *(G-3227)*
Hirschbach Motor Lines Inc ....B 813 659-0206
  Dover *(G-3367)*
Holman Dist Ctr Ore Inc ....D 904 696-1369
  Jacksonville *(G-6284)*
Honey Transport Inc ....D 407 889-9726
  Apopka *(G-190)*
Hopper Dispatch Inc ....E 386 487-6000
  Lake City *(G-7532)*
Indian River Transport Co ....C 863 324-2430
  Winter Haven *(G-19634)*
J B Hunt Transport Inc ....E 407 926-2228
  Orlando *(G-12694)*
John L Shadd Trucking Inc ....D 386 496-2631
  Lake Butler *(G-7505)*
Joule Yacht Transport Inc ....D 727 573-2627
  Clearwater *(G-1689)*
Justin Davis Enterprises Inc ....D 850 929-4584
  Tampa *(G-17903)*
L&S Logistic Services Inc ....C 407 582-0900
  Orlando *(G-12745)*
Landstar Global Logistics Inc ....E 786 475-7575
  Doral *(G-3257)*
Landstar Global Logistics Inc ....E 813 417-6487
  Orlando *(G-12753)*
▲ Landstar Ligon Inc ....C 904 398-9400
  Jacksonville *(G-6416)*
Landstar Ranger Inc ....C 800 872-9400
  Jacksonville *(G-6417)*
◆ Landstar System Holdings Inc ....A 904 398-9400
  Jacksonville *(G-6418)*
▲ Laney & Duke Terminal Whse Inc ....E 904 798-3500
  Jacksonville *(G-6420)*
Larry Young Enterprises Inc ....E 941 637-3723
  Punta Gorda *(G-15211)*
Maccabees Trucking Inc ....B 786 859-7872
  Orlando *(G-12801)*
Marathon Xpress Inc ....D 305 381-5155
  Miami *(G-9897)*
Marten Transport Ltd ....C 813 620-4603
  Tampa *(G-17995)*
Matheson Trucking Inc ....E 407 251-9695
  Orlando *(G-12832)*
Mc Tyre Trucking Company Inc ....C 407 859-5171
  Orlando *(G-12836)*
McCartney Enterprises LLC ....E 786 725-8660
  Jacksonville *(G-6477)*
McKenzie Property MGT Inc ....D 850 576-1221
  Tallahassee *(G-17039)*
Mid State Moving & Storage Co ....D 727 535-1423
  Clearwater *(G-1719)*
Midwest Transport Inc ....D 813 241-6841
  Tampa *(G-18038)*
Moore Freight Lines Inc ....E 352 567-3502
  Dade City *(G-2392)*
National Freight Inc ....E 407 826-3524
  Orlando *(G-12899)*
Old Ls Inc ....D 863 686-6872
  Lakeland *(G-7933)*
PAT Auto Transport Inc ....D 850 474-8850
  Pensacola *(G-14401)*
Patriot Transportation Inc Fla ....C 877 704-1776
  Jacksonville *(G-6585)*

Pece of Mind Environmental ....D 407 568-3456
  Orlando *(G-13018)*
Peninsula Trucking Inc ....C 352 735-3553
  Sorrento *(G-16476)*
Phoenix Trnsp & Logistics Inc ....D 407 459-4912
  Orlando *(G-13027)*
PM Transport of Florida Inc ....E 305 247-3248
  Goulds *(G-5042)*
Pritchett Trucking Inc ....B 386 496-2630
  Lake Butler *(G-7509)*
Proficient Auto Transport Inc ....D 904 772-1175
  Jacksonville *(G-6618)*
PS Logistics LLC ....D 904 782-3535
  Lawtey *(G-8210)*
Purdy Brothers Trucking LLC ....E 321 396-3000
  Zellwood *(G-19825)*
▲ Quality Carriers Inc ....D 800 282-2031
  Tampa *(G-18186)*
R & E Carriers Inc ....C 888 769-4779
  Miami *(G-10178)*
Raven Transport Company Inc ....C 904 880-1515
  Jacksonville *(G-6635)*
Reads Moving Systems Fla Inc ....D 904 733-2626
  Jacksonville *(G-6641)*
Rinaudo Enterprises Inc ....D 904 783-0000
  Jacksonville *(G-6664)*
Rons Transport LLC ....D 954 300-2435
  Plantation *(G-14702)*
◆ Rountree Trnspt & Rigging Inc ....E 904 781-1033
  Jacksonville *(G-6677)*
Rowland Transportation Inc ....C 352 567-2002
  Dade City *(G-2394)*
Sabal Transport Inc ....E 863 533-0871
  Bartow *(G-335)*
Saia Motor Freight Line LLC ....D 850 576-1102
  Tallahassee *(G-17091)*
Saia Motor Freight Line LLC ....D 239 334-3454
  Fort Myers *(G-4578)*
Saia Motor Freight Line LLC ....E 850 432-4528
  Pensacola *(G-14426)*
Saia Motor Freight Line LLC ....D 352 854-8240
  Ocala *(G-11772)*
Saia Motor Freight Line LLC ....D 561 845-6447
  West Palm Beach *(G-19350)*
Schwend Inc ....E 352 588-2220
  Dade City *(G-2395)*
Service Trucking Inc ....C 352 357-1300
  Eustis *(G-3500)*
Shelton Trucking Service Inc ....D 850 762-3201
  Altha *(G-117)*
Smith Transportation Svcs LLC ....E 954 718-5555
  Tampa *(G-18299)*
Sorensen Moving & Stor Co Inc ....D 407 447-2773
  Orlando *(G-13215)*
Southeastern Freight Lines Inc ....C 813 986-2900
  Thonotosassa *(G-18676)*
Southeastern Freight Lines Inc ....C 904 798-7000
  Jacksonville *(G-6753)*
Southeastern Freight Lines Inc ....D 407 855-1540
  Orlando *(G-13220)*
Southeastern Freight Lines Inc ....D 954 783-6140
  Pompano Beach *(G-14905)*
Southeastern Freight Lines Inc ....D 305 889-0501
  Miami *(G-10306)*
Southeastern Freight Lines Inc ....E 352 351-2313
  Ocala *(G-11780)*
Southeastern Freight Lines Inc ....D 239 332-8686
  Punta Gorda *(G-15220)*
Southeastern Freight Lines Inc ....E 850 484-8889
  Pensacola *(G-14442)*
Star Enterprise Transport LLC ....D 305 720-9942
  Jacksonville *(G-6785)*
Suddath Rlction Systems of Jck ....D 904 256-5540
  Jacksonville *(G-6799)*
▲ Suddath Rlction Systems of Orl ....C 407 843-6683
  Orlando *(G-13243)*
Suddath Rlction Systems of Pal ....D 407 843-6683
  Orlando *(G-13244)*
Suddath Rlction Systems of St ....C 727 573-0000
  Clearwater *(G-1800)*
▲ Suddath Van Lines Inc ....B 904 390-7100
  Jacksonville *(G-6801)*
Suddath Van Lines Inc ....E 904 256-5540
  Jacksonville *(G-6802)*
Sunbelt Transport LLC ....E 800 311-1022
  Jacksonville *(G-6807)*
Sunstate Carriers Inc ....C 352 343-6711
  Tavares *(G-18619)*
Super Transport Inc ....D 561 241-0100
  Boca Raton *(G-832)*

S I C

T L A Inc E 727 572-8841
Clearwater *(G-1815)*

Tankstar Usa Inc E 904 714-0850
Jacksonville *(G-6834)*

Tforce Freight Inc E 407 877-8444
Ocoee *(G-11826)*

Tforce Freight Inc D 305 883-3389
Miami *(G-10382)*

▲ **Time Definite Services Inc** D 800 466-8040
Sumterville *(G-16698)*

Titan America LLC D 407 656-3313
Clermont *(G-1895)*

Titan America LLC C 305 364-2200
Medley *(G-8789)*

Total Logistics Online LLC D 904 417-0950
Elkton *(G-3427)*

Trailer Bridge Inc D 904 751-7100
Jacksonville *(G-6872)*

Transplastics Inc D 813 630-5826
Tampa *(G-18436)*

Transpremier LLC D 407 905-4433
Orlando *(G-13304)*

Transprttion Svcs Unlmited Inc D 305 888-2623
Doral *(G-3337)*

Transsystems Inc D 863 421-7879
Haines City *(G-5159)*

U S Xpress Inc A 423 510-3000
Jacksonville *(G-6880)*

United Parcel Service Inc E 904 730-0398
Jacksonville *(G-6886)*

Valrico Ventures Inc E 888 305-1750
Seffner *(G-16435)*

Walpole Inc D 813 623-1702
Tampa *(G-18520)*

▲ **Walpole Inc** C 863 763-5593
Okeechobee *(G-11884)*

Walpole Leasing Corporation E 813 623-1702
Tampa *(G-18521)*

Watson Construction Co LLC E 352 472-9157
Newberry *(G-11434)*

▲ **Wes-Flo Co Inc** E 813 626-2171
Tampa *(G-18542)*

Windy Hill Foliage Inc E 352 589-0225
Eustis *(G-3504)*

Xpo Logistics Freight Inc E 850 997-4217
Monticello *(G-10938)*

Xpo Logistics Freight Inc D 904 783-6307
Jacksonville *(G-6950)*

Xpo Logistics Freight Inc D 813 653-3116
Tampa *(G-18572)*

Xpo Logistics Freight Inc D 561 842-1971
Riviera Beach *(G-15330)*

Yarnall Warehouse & Transf Inc D 941 365-3060
Sarasota *(G-16368)*

4214 Local Trucking With Storage

A & A Transfer & Storage Inc D 850 244-7661
Fort Walton Beach *(G-4750)*

A Alpha Transportation Inc D 410 488-9200
Jacksonville *(G-5718)*

A-Turner Moving & Storage Inc E 352 372-0406
Gainesville *(G-4828)*

Aadvantage Relocation Inc D 850 478-0082
Pensacola *(G-14209)*

Air Land Forwarders Inc E 904 390-7100
Jacksonville *(G-5757)*

Alltrust Moving & Storage Inc E 888 879-9997
Miami *(G-9127)*

Arlington Salvage & Wrecker Co E 904 744-4933
Jacksonville *(G-5806)*

Beltmann Group Incorporated E 407 295-0636
Orlando *(G-12180)*

Bonded Transportation Inc D 850 438-4694
Pensacola *(G-14238)*

◆ **Brandon Transfer & Storage Co** E 561 683-5000
West Palm Beach *(G-19060)*

▲ **Central Moving & Storage Inc** E 407 219-9779
Orlando *(G-12284)*

Covan World-Wide Moving Inc D 850 262-1552
Pensacola *(G-14272)*

Covan World-Wide Moving Inc D 850 785-0501
Panama City *(G-13987)*

CSI Enterprises Inc C 239 947-5169
Bonita Springs *(G-907)*

Cypress Truck Lines Inc B 813 837-9998
Tampa *(G-17564)*

Eagle Moving Systems Inc D 904 278-0708
Jacksonville *(G-6099)*

East Cast Trdg Import Export L E 561 308-0766
Lake Worth *(G-7724)*

Empire Office Inc D 813 543-5050
Tampa *(G-17630)*

Glb Trucking LLC E 305 974-6239
Miami Gardens *(G-10684)*

Green Energy Contracting LLC D 850 537-4043
Holt *(G-5551)*

Grimes Logistics Services Inc E 904 786-5711
Jacksonville *(G-6242)*

Mid State Moving & Storage Co D 727 535-1423
Clearwater *(G-1719)*

Ofab Inc D 352 629-0040
Ocala *(G-11757)*

Postal Fleet Services Inc A 904 824-2007
Saint Augustine *(G-15483)*

SE Independent Dlvry Svcs Inc D 813 623-5400
Seffner *(G-16433)*

◆ **Sentry Household Shipping Inc** E 904 858-1200
Jacksonville *(G-6710)*

Sorensen Moving & Stor Co Inc D 407 447-2773
Orlando *(G-13215)*

◆ **Star Distribution Systems Inc** C 813 659-1002
Plant City *(G-14584)*

Suddath Global Logistics LLC D 904 858-1234
Jacksonville *(G-6798)*

Suddath Rlction Systems of Boc C 954 596-4000
Deerfield Beach *(G-2801)*

Suddath Rlction Systems of Jck D 904 256-5540
Jacksonville *(G-6799)*

Suddath Rlction Systems of St C 727 573-0000
Clearwater *(G-1800)*

▲ **Suddath Van Lines Inc** B 904 390-7100
Jacksonville *(G-6801)*

Sunset Moving & Storage Inc D 772 233-4460
Palm City *(G-13806)*

Sutters Transport LLC E 941 371-2596
Sarasota *(G-16342)*

Wegman Associates Inc C 954 438-9980
Medley *(G-8797)*

▲ **Wes-Flo Co Inc** E 813 626-2171
Tampa *(G-18542)*

Yarnall Warehouse & Transf Inc D 941 365-3060
Sarasota *(G-16368)*

4215 Courier Svcs, Except Air

24 Seven Enterprises Inc C 315 399-9728
Bradenton *(G-1047)*

ARC Couriers LLC C 678 773-2192
Fort Myers *(G-4278)*

▲ **ATI Systems International Inc** D 561 939-7000
Boca Raton *(G-433)*

Aura Logistics LLC C 813 652-2903
Deerfield Beach *(G-2714)*

Boyett Enterprises LLC C 904 448-8000
Jacksonville *(G-5876)*

Cag Logistics MGT Svcs LLC B 813 860-4558
Tampa *(G-17410)*

Chapters Health System Inc D 813 664-0684
Tampa *(G-17460)*

Coastal Courier Inc E 407 679-6640
Winter Park *(G-19706)*

Crews and Co Logistics LLC D 404 337-9663
Windermere *(G-19538)*

Expert Messenger Inc D 727 343-8863
Pinellas Park *(G-14517)*

Export Freight & Brokers Inc E 305 592-7343
Doral *(G-3197)*

Federal Express Corporation C 954 497-2700
Fort Lauderdale *(G-3784)*

Federal Express Corporation D 954 316-7651
Fort Lauderdale *(G-3783)*

Fedex Smartpost Inc D 407 859-8747
Orlando *(G-12502)*

Garda CL Southwest Inc C 213 383-3611
Boca Raton *(G-595)*

Garryowen Dsp LLC D 321 356-0329
Windermere *(G-19543)*

Integrated Dlvry Solutions Inc E 941 725-1468
Lakewood Ranch *(G-8018)*

◆ **Interntnal Bonded Couriers Inc** D 305 591-8080
Doral *(G-3245)*

M & D Belanger Inc E 727 430-6191
Clearwater *(G-1703)*

My Parcel Pro LLP D 561 729-3081
West Palm Beach *(G-19275)*

Palm Beach Logistics LLC D 813 629-1974
West Palm Beach *(G-19314)*

Pso Inc E 305 470-9977
Miami *(G-10156)*

Quality Express Delivery Inc E 904 783-3335
Jacksonville *(G-6625)*

Silver Star Express Inc C 954 447-5000
Miramar *(G-10895)*

United Parcel Service Inc A 800 742-5877
Orlando *(G-13334)*

United Parcel Service Inc E 800 742-5877
Chipley *(G-1495)*

United Parcel Service Inc D 813 881-8950
Tampa *(G-18461)*

United Parcel Service Inc E 352 799-7550
Brooksville *(G-1318)*

United Parcel Service Inc D 800 742-5877
Tallahassee *(G-17163)*

United Parcel Service Inc D 727 571-8045
Clearwater *(G-1827)*

United Parcel Service Inc C 352 371-7162
Gainesville *(G-5018)*

United Parcel Service Inc E 321 725-8036
Melbourne *(G-8998)*

United Parcel Service Inc C 305 238-0134
Miami *(G-10438)*

United Parcel Service Inc A 904 693-0020
Jacksonville *(G-6885)*

United Parcel Service Inc E 561 640-3417
West Palm Beach *(G-19398)*

United Parcel Service Inc E 800 742-5877
Rockledge *(G-15377)*

United Parcel Service Inc E 954 525-2761
Lauderhill *(G-8208)*

United Parcel Service Inc E 954 489-1675
Oakland Park *(G-11618)*

United Parcel Service Inc C 813 241-1033
Tampa *(G-18463)*

United Parcel Service Inc E 772 778-6505
Vero Beach *(G-18929)*

United Parcel Service Inc E 904 825-1944
Saint Augustine *(G-15508)*

United Parcel Service Inc E 800 742-5877
Fort Walton Beach *(G-4807)*

United Parcel Service Inc E 850 747-8483
Panama City *(G-14082)*

United Parcel Service Inc E 407 826-0175
Orlando *(G-13339)*

Venecia Logistica LLC D 813 405-7288
Tampa *(G-18500)*

Watermark Dlvry Solutions LLC D 732 995-3882
Sarasota *(G-16072)*

Williams United Logistics LLC D 315 664-8620
Lawtey *(G-8211)*

4221 Farm Product Warehousing & Storage

◆ **Econocaribe Inc** C 305 693-5133
Miami *(G-9500)*

Econoline Storage Corp E 305 693-5133
Miami *(G-9502)*

4222 Refrigerated Warehousing & Storage

Burris Logistics D 904 265-5990
Jacksonville *(G-5887)*

Burris Logistics C 863 682-1442
Lakeland *(G-7821)*

Central Fla Frzr & Whses LLC E 352 031-6629
Leesburg *(G-8236)*

Citrosuco North America Inc C 863 696-7400
Lake Wales *(G-7679)*

Floral Logistics Miami Inc D 305 487-7777
Miami *(G-9566)*

◆ **Freedom Fresh LLC** C 305 715-5700
Medley *(G-8734)*

Grimes Logistics Services Inc E 904 786-5711
Jacksonville *(G-6242)*

▲ **Imeson Distribution Center Inc** E 904 751-5500
Jacksonville *(G-6312)*

Industrial Fuels LLC E 904 786-8038
Jacksonville *(G-6317)*

Mid Florida Freezer Warehouses E 407 886-7730
Apopka *(G-202)*

Publix Super Markets Inc A 904 781-8600
Jacksonville *(G-6622)*

◆ **Southeast Frozen Foods Co LP** E 954 882-1044
Miramar *(G-10899)*

Total Logistics Online LLC D 904 417-0950
Elkton *(G-3427)*

4225 General Warehousing & Storage

A & A Transfer & Storage Inc E 904 786-0242
Jacksonville *(G-5717)*

Aldi Inc C 561 640-8000
Royal Palm Beach *(G-15380)*

Amazoncom Inc D 813 645-7980
Ruskin *(G-15394)*

Amazoncom Inc	E	803 529-9581
Lakeland (G-7795)		
Ambassador Services Inc	C	321 783-9623
Port Canaveral (G-15013)		
◆ American Cnsldtion Lgstics Inc	D	305 769-2112
Miami (G-9137)		
Amerisourcebergen Corporation	D	407 259-5568
Orlando (G-12119)		
Amerisourcebergen Drug Corp	E	407 454-6600
Orlando (G-12120)		
Attorneys Title Fund Svcs LLC	E	407 240-4440
Orlando (G-12152)		
Bedabox LLC	D	855 222-4601
Fort Lauderdale (G-3634)		
BJs Wholesale Club Inc	D	904 378-4300
Jacksonville (G-5863)		
Blaine Larsen Farms Inc	D	352 732-4445
Ocala (G-11640)		
Boeing Company	B	321 853-6647
Cape Canaveral (G-1351)		
Brown Integrated Logistics Inc	E	904 783-8323
Jacksonville (G-5885)		
Bruce Bachman Enterprises	E	863 293-1151
Eloise (G-3429)		
▲ Central Moving & Storage Inc	E	407 219-9779
Orlando (G-12284)		
Commercial Warehousing Inc	E	863 967-1940
Winter Haven (G-19618)		
Costco Wholesale Corporation	E	561 273-2520
West Palm Beach (G-19109)		
Cousin Corporation of America	E	727 536-3568
Largo (G-8091)		
▲ Cubesmart LP	B	610 535-5700
Boynton Beach (G-980)		
Dhl Network Operations USA Inc	E	954 888-7000
Plantation (G-14630)		
Eclipse Advantage LLC	D	321 250-6380
Melbourne (G-8877)		
Escambia County School Dst	D	850 469-5435
Pensacola (G-14296)		
Extra Space Storage LLC	E	772 465-9460
Fort Pierce (G-4698)		
Freshone Foods LLC	E	817 881-2479
Tampa (G-17714)		
Great Space Self Storage Bonit	E	239 992-8987
Bonita Springs (G-917)		
Grimes Logistics Services Inc	E	904 786-5711
Jacksonville (G-6242)		
▲ H & M Warehousing Jacksonville	B	904 768-3403
Jacksonville (G-6252)		
Holman Dist Ctr Ore Inc	D	904 696-1369
Jacksonville (G-6284)		
Home Depot USA Inc	C	770 433-8211
Jacksonville (G-6288)		
Honc Industries Inc	E	239 283-5454
Saint James City (G-15542)		
▲ Imeson Distribution Center Inc	E	904 751-5500
Jacksonville (G-6312)		
◆ International Whse Svcs Inc	E	954 763-7551
Fort Lauderdale (G-3899)		
Kroger Co	C	859 630-6559
Groveland (G-5096)		
Landstar System Inc	C	904 398-9400
Jacksonville (G-6419)		
▲ Laney & Duke Terminal Whse Inc	E	904 798-3500
Jacksonville (G-6420)		
Las Vegas Self Storage	C	904 992-9000
Jacksonville (G-6423)		
Life Storage LP	C	727 446-1888
Clearwater (G-1697)		
Lowes Home Centers LLC	C	863 635-8300
Frostproof (G-4821)		
Lutfi Investment Co Inc	D	407 506-1200
Orlando (G-12792)		
Manatee County Port Authority	D	941 722-6621
Palmetto (G-13921)		
Martin-Brower Company LLC	D	407 583-0693
Orlando (G-12821)		
Mid Florida Freezer Warehouses	E	407 886-7730
Apopka (G-202)		
Neiman Marcus Group LLC	D	954 447-1600
Miramar (G-10881)		
Nordstrom Inc	E	352 384-2111
Gainesville (G-4958)		
Orlando Health Inc	E	407 841-5252
Orlando (G-12963)		
Pods LLC	B	727 538-6300
Clearwater (G-1760)		
Pods Enterprises LLC	C	727 538-6300
Clearwater (G-1761)		

Pods of Seattle LLC	B	727 538-6300
Clearwater (G-1762)		
Portus Services LLC	C	904 751-8801
Jacksonville (G-6608)		
Publix Super Markets Inc	A	904 781-8600
Jacksonville (G-6622)		
Publix Super Markets Inc	A	863 680-5229
Lakeland (G-7946)		
Publix Super Markets Inc	A	941 923-4929
Sarasota (G-16276)		
Publix Super Markets Inc	A	954 429-0122
Deerfield Beach (G-2786)		
Publix Super Markets Inc	A	561 369-7900
Boynton Beach (G-1030)		
◆ Quantum Storage Systems	D	305 687-0405
North Miami Beach (G-11531)		
Reads Moving Systems Fla Inc	D	904 733-2626
Jacksonville (G-6641)		
◆ Saddle Creek Corporation	B	863 665-0966
Lakeland (G-7958)		
Sams West Inc	E	863 667-1136
Lakeland (G-7961)		
▲ Seaboard Tampa Terminals Inc	E	813 628-4003
Tampa (G-18258)		
▲ Seaboard Whse Terminals Ltd	E	305 633-8587
Miami (G-10251)		
South Florida Materials Corp	E	561 793-2102
West Palm Beach (G-19372)		
◆ Star Distribution Systems Inc	C	813 659-1002
Plant City (G-14584)		
Storage Rentals of America	D	941 877-6603
Lehigh Acres (G-8291)		
Sunset Moving & Storage Inc	D	772 233-4460
Palm City (G-13806)		
Supply Chain Shipping LLC	E	786 347-3484
Doral (G-3327)		
▲ Team Dgd Inc	E	888 219-4544
Miami (G-10365)		
▲ Tech Packaging of Tampa Inc	E	813 664-1171
Tampa (G-18409)		
The H T Hackney Co	E	305 685-6232
Miami (G-10384)		
The H T Hackney Co	E	813 621-0100
Tampa (G-18418)		
Total Logistics Online LLC	D	904 417-0950
Elkton (G-3427)		
True Grade LLC	D	305 800-8783
Miami (G-10414)		
U-Stor Management Corporation	D	904 276-4553
Orange Park (G-12023)		
Ultimate Storage Inc	E	386 274-2378
Daytona Beach (G-2682)		
Value Storage Ltd	C	941 358-7715
Sarasota (G-16069)		
Walgreen Co	C	407 856-8633
Orlando (G-13391)		
Walgreen Co	E	407 240-1143
Orlando (G-13392)		
Walmart Inc	B	321 504-0120
Cocoa (G-1961)		
Walmart Inc	B	863 298-1000
Winter Haven (G-19671)		
Walmart Inc	B	863 491-6502
Arcadia (G-235)		
Wegman Associates Inc	D	407 850-9191
Orlando (G-13414)		
Winn-Dixie Stores Inc	B	954 783-2700
Coconut Creek (G-2008)		
Yarnall Warehouse & Transf Inc	D	941 365-3060
Sarasota (G-16368)		

4226 Special Warehousing & Storage, NEC

Ample Storage	D	321 725-3141
Melbourne (G-8815)		
Archive America Limited	D	305 633-8587
Miami (G-9166)		
▲ Boasso Global Inc	C	813 797-3271
Tampa (G-17376)		
Doculex Inc	E	863 297-3691
Winter Haven (G-19622)		
Glb Trucking LLC	E	305 974-6239
Miami Gardens (G-10684)		
H Lee Mfft Cncr Ctr & RES	C	813 745-4644
Tampa (G-17783)		
Interntnal Data Depository Inc	E	305 477-7388
Miami (G-9773)		
Lawson Industries Inc	E	561 735-0608
Boynton Beach (G-1007)		
Martin Operating Partnr LP	E	813 247-5063
Tampa (G-17996)		

Mid-Flrida Lbr Acqisitions Inc	E	863 533-0155
Bartow (G-328)		
Publix Super Markets Inc	A	904 781-8600
Jacksonville (G-6622)		
Publix Super Markets Inc	A	941 923-4929
Sarasota (G-16276)		
Publix Super Markets Inc	A	561 369-7900
Boynton Beach (G-1030)		
Refreshment Services Inc	D	850 574-0281
Tallahassee (G-17084)		
Scientific Record MGT Inc	E	954 966-2345
Sunrise (G-16823)		
Target Corporation	C	407 366-5907
Oviedo (G-13574)		
Value Store It Management Inc	E	305 819-8850
Fort Lauderdale (G-4208)		
Walgreen Co	C	407 856-8633
Orlando (G-13391)		
Westrec Marina Management Inc	D	954 926-0300
Dania (G-2422)		

4231 Terminal & Joint Terminal Maint Facilities

AAA Cooper Transportation	D	813 899-1306
Temple Terrace (G-18627)		
Benton Express Inc	D	813 621-5541
Tampa (G-17360)		
Estes Express Lines	D	305 882-8847
Miami (G-9533)		
Estes Express Lines	C	904 384-2277
Jacksonville (G-6134)		
GA Fd Svcs Pinellas Cnty LLC	D	386 274-5600
Daytona Beach (G-2600)		
Marley International LLC	D	386 246-7640
Gibsonton (G-5037)		
Southeastern Freight Lines Inc	D	407 855-1540
Orlando (G-13220)		

44 WATER TRANSPORTATION

4412 Deep Sea Foreign Transportation Of Freight

Amerijet International Inc	E	954 320-5300
Miami Springs (G-10778)		
◆ Antillean Marine Shipping Corp	E	305 633-6361
Miami (G-9155)		
Balearia Caribbean Ltd Corp	D	305 331-8302
Fort Lauderdale (G-3627)		
Birdsall Inc	E	561 881-3900
Riviera Beach (G-15284)		
Crowley Holdings Inc	D	904 727-2200
Jacksonville (G-6016)		
▲ Crowley Marine Services Inc	A	904 717-2200
Jacksonville (G-6020)		
◆ Crowley Maritime Corporation	D	904 727-2200
Jacksonville (G-6021)		
Crowley Petroleum Services Inc	D	904 727-2200
Jacksonville (G-6022)		
Crowley Technical Services LLC	B	904 727-2200
Jacksonville (G-6025)		
Lykes Bros Steamship Co Inc	A	813 276-4600
Tampa (G-17969)		
◆ Marine Transport MGT Inc	D	904 727-2200
Jacksonville (G-6467)		
▼ North ATL Intl Ocean Crier Inc	E	786 233-9586
Pompano Beach (G-14867)		
Overseas Shipholding Group Inc	D	813 209-0600
Tampa (G-18115)		
Red Oak Logistics Inc	E	904 693-0606
Jacksonville (G-6642)		
◆ Resolve Marine Group Inc	D	954 764-8700
Fort Lauderdale (G-4087)		
Seaboard Marine Ltd Inc	C	305 863-4444
Miami (G-10250)		
Seaboard Solutions Inc	D	305 863-4591
Medley (G-8779)		
Seabulk Overseas Transport Inc	D	954 523-2200
Fort Lauderdale (G-4107)		
◆ Seacor Holdings Inc	E	954 523-2200
Fort Lauderdale (G-4109)		
Seacor Island Lines LLC	C	954 920-9292
Fort Lauderdale (G-4110)		
Trailer Bridge Inc	D	904 751-7100
Jacksonville (G-6872)		
Tropical Shipg Cnstr Ltd LLC	E	305 805-7400
Medley (G-8793)		
Tropical Shipping Usa LLC	A	561 863-5737
Riviera Beach (G-15327)		

Vessel Management Service Inc..........D....... 904 727-2200
Jacksonville (G-6906)

4424 Deep Sea Domestic Transportation Of Freight

Crowley Holdings Inc ....D....... 904 727-2200
Jacksonville (G-6016)
◆ Crowley Maritime Corporation ....D....... 904 727-2200
Jacksonville (G-6021)
Crowley Petroleum Services Inc ....D....... 904 727-2200
Jacksonville (G-6022)
Crowley Technical Services LLC ....B....... 904 727-2200
Jacksonville (G-6025)
Global Marine Travel LLC ....E....... 954 761-9595
Fort Lauderdale (G-3821)
◆ Marine Transport MGT Inc ....D....... 904 727-2200
Jacksonville (G-6467)
Marine Transportation Svcs Inc..........D....... 850 769-1459
Panama City (G-14040)
▲ Maritrans Operating Company LP..D....... 813 209-0600
Tampa (G-17991)
McAllister Towing Florida Inc ....D....... 904 751-6228
Jacksonville (G-6475)
▼ North ATL Intl Ocean Crier Inc ....E....... 786 233-9586
Pompano Beach (G-14867)
OSG America Operating Co LLC ....E....... 813 209-0600
Tampa (G-18111)
Overseas Shipholding Group Inc ....D....... 813 209-0600
Tampa (G-18115)
Seabulk International Inc ....D....... 954 828-1701
Fort Lauderdale (G-4106)
◆ Seacor Holdings Inc..........................E....... 954 523-2200
Fort Lauderdale (G-4109)
◆ Teco Energy Inc ....E....... 813 228-1111
Tampa (G-18412)

4432 Freight Transportation On The Great Lakes

▼ North ATL Intl Ocean Crier Inc ....E....... 786 233-9586
Pompano Beach (G-14867)

4449 Water Transportation Of Freight, NEC

Kirby Inland Marine LP ....D....... 305 579-5013
Miami (G-9830)
◆ Mobro Marine Inc..............................D....... 866 313-9670
Green Cove Springs (G-5059)
▼ North ATL Intl Ocean Crier Inc ....E....... 786 233-9586
Pompano Beach (G-14867)
◆ Park Street Imports LLC ....C....... 305 967-7440
Miami (G-10097)
◆ Seacor Holdings Inc..........................E....... 954 523-2200
Fort Lauderdale (G-4109)
▲ USS Vessel Management LLC ....E....... 732 635-2705
Fort Lauderdale (G-4207)

4481 Deep Sea Transportation Of Passengers

Carnival Corporation ....A....... 305 599-2600
Doral (G-3145)
Carnival Corporation ....A....... 305 599-2600
Doral (G-3146)
◆ Carnival Corporation ....E....... 305 406-7255
Hialeah (G-5229)
Carnival Corporation ....D....... 305 913-4802
Miami (G-9327)
Carnival Corporation ....D....... 305 913-4802
Miami (G-9328)
◆ Crystal Cruises LLC..........................C....... 786 971-1000
Fort Lauderdale (G-3744)
Magical Cruise Company Limited ....B....... 407 566-3500
Kissimmee (G-7352)
◆ MSC Cruises (usa) Inc ....D....... 954 772-6262
Fort Lauderdale (G-3978)
Ncl (bahamas Ltd A Bermuda Co ....A....... 305 436-4000
Miami (G-10034)
Ncl Corporation Ltd ....A....... 305 436-4000
Miami (G-10035)
Norwegian Crise Line Hldngs Lt..........A....... 305 436-4000
Miami (G-10054)
Paradise Cruise Line Operator ....D....... 954 414-1320
Deerfield Beach (G-2781)
Prestige Cruises Intl Inc ....C....... 305 514-2300
Miami (G-10139)
Royal Caribbean Cruises Ltd................A....... 305 539-6000
Miramar (G-10892)
Star Clippers Ltd Corp.........................D....... 305 553-9405
Miami (G-10327)

Valerie Wilson Travel Inc ....E....... 904 285-2222
Ponte Vedra Beach (G-15011)

4489 Water Transport Of Passengers, NEC

Carnival PLC.......................................B....... 305 599-2600
Doral (G-3147)
Magical Cruise Company Limited ....B....... 407 566-3500
Kissimmee (G-7352)
National State Pk Cncssons Inc ....D....... 772 595-6429
Fort Pierce (G-4723)
Nautical Ventures Group Inc................D....... 954 926-5250
Fort Lauderdale (G-3995)
Poseidon Ferry LLC.............................E....... 833 443-3779
Miami (G-10135)
Sarabay Marine Inc ....D....... 941 794-1235
Cortez (G-2299)
Seadream Yacht Club Limited ....C....... 305 631-6100
Miami (G-10252)
SMS Intrntnal Shore Oprtons US...........C....... 305 290-3000
Miami (G-10286)

4491 Marine Cargo Handling

▲ Amports Inc ....B....... 904 652-2962
Jacksonville (G-5795)
Canaveral Port Authority......................C....... 321 783-7831
Cape Canaveral (G-1356)
◆ Cliff Berry Inc....................................E....... 954 763-3390
Fort Lauderdale (G-3701)
◆ Crowley Liner Services Inc ....A....... 904 727-2200
Jacksonville (G-6017)
◆ Crowley Logistics Inc ....C....... 904 727-2200
Jacksonville (G-6018)
Eller-Ito Stevedoring Co LLC ....A....... 305 379-3700
Miami (G-9516)
Florida Trnsp Svcs Inc.........................D....... 954 462-9159
Fort Lauderdale (G-3798)
Hirsch Stevedoring LLC ....D....... 954 952-5991
Fort Lauderdale (G-3864)
Offshore Marine Towing Inc ....E....... 954 783-7821
Pompano Beach (G-14872)
Port of Palm Beach District...................E....... 561 842-4201
Riviera Beach (G-15313)
Ports America Florida Inc ....D....... 813 242-1900
Tampa (G-18159)
◆ Resolve Marine Group Inc ....D....... 954 764-8700
Fort Lauderdale (G-4087)
South Florida Cont Trml LLC ....C....... 305 347-3800
Miami (G-10301)
Southeast Unloading LLC ....D....... 904 491-6800
Fernandina Beach (G-3542)
Tampa Port Authority ....D....... 813 905-7678
Tampa (G-18401)
Worldwide Trmnals Frnndina LLC..........D....... 904 261-0753
Fernandina Beach (G-3545)

4492 Towing & Tugboat Svcs

Beyel Bros Crane Rigging S Fla ....E....... 561 798-5776
Riviera Beach (G-15283)
Crowley Holdings Inc ....D....... 904 727-2200
Jacksonville (G-6016)
◆ Crowley Liner Services Inc ....A....... 904 727-2200
Jacksonville (G-6017)
◆ Crowley Maritime Corporation ....D....... 904 727-2200
Jacksonville (G-6021)
Crowley Technical Services LLC ....B....... 904 727-2200
Jacksonville (G-6025)
Crows Nest Rest & Tav Inc...................D....... 941 484-7661
Venice (G-18775)
Dann Ocean Towing Inc ....D....... 813 251-5100
Tampa (G-17571)
Hvide Marine Services Inc....................B....... 954 523-2200
Fort Lauderdale (G-3883)
Lightship Tankers IV LLC ....E....... 954 523-2200
Fort Lauderdale (G-3942)
Lightship Tankers V LLC ....C....... 954 523-2200
Fort Lauderdale (G-3943)
McAllister Towing Florida Inc ....D....... 904 751-6228
Jacksonville (G-6475)
◆ Mobro Marine Inc.............................D....... 866 313-9670
Green Cove Springs (G-5059)
Offshore Marine Towing Inc ....E....... 954 783-7821
Pompano Beach (G-14872)
◆ Resolve Marine Group Inc ....D....... 954 764-8700
Fort Lauderdale (G-4087)
Seabulk International Inc ....D....... 954 828-1701
Fort Lauderdale (G-4106)
Seabulk Towing Inc ....A....... 813 248-1123
Tampa (G-18259)
Wireless Maritime Services LLC............D....... 954 883-2400
Miramar (G-10917)

4493 Marinas

▲ Bayshore Restaurant Management..D....... 305 854-7997
Miami (G-9230)
BCM-CHI Eden Rock Tenants LP...........B....... 305 531-0000
Miami (G-9232)
Bluepoints Intl Fisheries ....D....... 321 799-2860
Cape Canaveral (G-1350)
Brandy Marinas Inc ....D....... 561 688-9288
West Palm Beach (G-19061)
◆ Broward Yard & Marine LLC..............D....... 954 927-4119
Dania (G-2404)
Cape Marine Services Inc ....E....... 321 783-8410
Cape Canaveral (G-1359)
Clewiston Marina Inc ....E....... 863 983-3151
Clewiston (G-1900)
Crp LMC Rb LLC ....E....... 954 713-0341
Fort Lauderdale (G-3742)
Earthmark Companies LLC ....C....... 813 645-3291
Ruskin (G-15399)
Evergldes Hsptlity Resorts LLC ....C....... 239 695-4224
Fort Myers (G-4362)
Flyhopco LLC ....E....... 954 791-3800
Fort Lauderdale (G-3799)
▲ Galati Yacht Sales LLC ....D....... 941 778-0755
Anna Maria (G-125)
Gilberts Boat Storage Inc.....................D....... 305 451-1133
Key Largo (G-7177)
Harborwalk Marina Services ....B....... 850 650-2400
Destin (G-3061)
Hickory Pass Marina LLC ....D....... 786 796-1257
North Miami (G-11495)
Hilton Ft Lauderdale Marina.................C....... 305 463-4000
Fort Lauderdale (G-3861)
Holiday Isle Resort & Marina ....D....... 305 664-2321
Islamorada (G-5704)
Jones Boat Yard Inc ....D....... 305 635-0891
Miami (G-9800)
Marco River Marina Inc........................E....... 239 394-2502
Marco Island (G-8634)
▼ Marina Lauderdale Inc ....D....... 954 523-8507
Fort Lauderdale (G-3957)
Marinemax of Sarasota LLC ....E....... 941 388-4411
Sarasota (G-16226)
◆ Moorings Club Inc.............................D....... 772 231-1004
Vero Beach (G-18896)
Msb of Destin Inc ....E....... 850 837-0404
Destin (G-3069)
Nautical Ventures Group Inc.................D....... 954 926-5250
Fort Lauderdale (G-3995)
Old Port Cove Holdings Inc ....D....... 561 844-2504
Riviera Beach (G-15310)
▼ Palm Beach Yacht Club Assoc ....E....... 561 655-1944
West Palm Beach (G-19318)
Pirates Cove Resort and Marina ....D....... 772 223-5048
Stuart (G-16658)
Plantation Resort Inc............................D....... 352 795-4211
Crystal River (G-2350)
Ponces By Sea Inc ....D....... 904 824-4347
Saint Augustine (G-15482)
Rahn Bahia Mar Mgmt Inc ....E....... 954 764-2233
Fort Lauderdale (G-4080)
Rochester Resorts Inc..........................D....... 239 472-5161
Captiva (G-1439)
▲ Rolly Marine Service Inc....................E....... 954 583-5300
Fort Lauderdale (G-4093)
Rybovich Boat Company LLC ....C....... 561 844-1800
West Palm Beach (G-19349)
Sands Harbor Inc ....D....... 954 942-9100
Pompano Beach (G-14890)
Sarabay Marine Inc ....D....... 941 794-1235
Cortez (G-2299)
Sebastian Inlet Marina Trdg Co ....D....... 772 388-8588
Sebastian (G-16381)
Sh Marinas 6000 LLC ....E....... 305 292-3121
Key West (G-7245)
◆ Spencer Boat Co Inc ....E....... 561 844-1800
West Palm Beach (G-19373)
Suntex Marina Investors LLC ....D....... 561 582-4422
Lantana (G-8070)
Suntex Marina Investors LLC ....D....... 772 257-0315
Vero Beach (G-18923)
Tannex Development Corp....................A....... 305 294-4000
Key West (G-7250)
Twin Harbors Inc ....D....... 305 451-8500
Key Largo (G-7190)
Useppa Inn and Dock Co Ltd ....D....... 239 283-1061
Bokeelia (G-886)
Useppa Island Club Inc ....E....... 239 283-5005
Bokeelia (G-887)

Westrec Marina Management Inc ....D...... 954 926-0300
Dania **(G-2422)**

4499 Water Transportation Svcs, NEC

3d Marine Usa Inc ....D...... 954 885-9850
Hollywood **(G-5384)**

Fcs Inc..........E...... 727 576-1111
Clearwater **(G-1634)**

Offshore Marine Towing Inc ....E...... 954 783-7821
Pompano Beach **(G-14872)**

Psycheceutical Bioscience Inc..........E...... 904 215-7601
Green Cove Springs **(G-5061)**

Resolve Americas Holdings Inc ....E...... 954 764-8700
Fort Lauderdale **(G-4086)**

◆ Resolve Marine Group Inc ....D...... 954 764-8700
Fort Lauderdale **(G-4087)**

Treasure Salvors Inc..........E...... 305 296-6533
Key West **(G-7253)**

45 TRANSPORTATION BY AIR

4512 Air Transportation, Scheduled

Aerolineas Argentinas SA Inc..........D...... 305 254-1038
Miami **(G-9096)**

Airtran Airways Inc ....D...... 407 856-9220
Orlando **(G-12089)**

Airtran Holdings Inc..........D...... 407 318-5600
Orlando **(G-12090)**

◆ America Central Corp..........D...... 305 871-1587
Miami **(G-9134)**

American Airlines Inc ....C...... 305 520-3192
Coral Gables **(G-2031)**

Amerijet Holdings Inc..........D...... 800 927-6059
Miami Springs **(G-10777)**

Capital Cargo Intl Arln Inc..........C...... 407 855-2004
Orlando **(G-12230)**

Cargo Force Inc..........D...... 305 740-3252
Miami **(G-9316)**

Cargo Services Inc..........E...... 305 599-9333
Miami **(G-9320)**

Cargo Transportation Svcs Inc..........E...... 954 718-5555
Sunrise **(G-16755)**

Embraer Aircraft Holding Inc..........C...... 954 359-3700
Fort Lauderdale **(G-3770)**

Federal Express Corporation..........D...... 954 316-7651
Fort Lauderdale **(G-3783)**

Gulf Air Group Inc..........C...... 850 682-8411
Crestview **(G-2322)**

◆ IBC Airways Inc..........E...... 954 848-2300
Fort Lauderdale **(G-3886)**

Interntnal Cnsld Arln Group SA..........E...... 305 267-7747
Miami **(G-9772)**

Jacksonville Aviation Auth..........C...... 904 741-3751
Jacksonville **(G-6351)**

Jetblue Airways Corporation..........C...... 407 541-8958
Orlando **(G-12704)**

Latam Airlines Group SA Inc..........A...... 786 265-6050
Miami **(G-9849)**

National Air Cargo Group Inc..........E...... 407 429-9767
Sanford **(G-15968)**

National Air Cargo Group Inc..........D...... 407 283-6200
Orlando **(G-12896)**

Pan American World Airways..........D...... 786 305-7887
Miami **(G-10089)**

Piedmont Airlines Inc..........C...... 386 253-9976
Daytona Beach **(G-2652)**

Piedmont Airlines Inc..........C...... 352 377-7661
Gainesville **(G-4980)**

Psa Airlines Inc..........D...... 304 224-9335
Pensacola **(G-14416)**

Signature Flight Support LLC..........D...... 407 825-6999
Orlando **(G-13198)**

Silver Airways LLC..........C...... 954 985-1500
Hollywood **(G-5520)**

Sky King Inc..........D...... 310 689-1651
Lakeland **(G-7969)**

Sky Lease I Inc..........B...... 305 871-0130
Miami **(G-10281)**

Skyscanner Inc..........E...... 786 239-4931
Miami **(G-10284)**

South African Airways Soc Ltd..........D...... 800 722-9675
Plantation **(G-14711)**

Southern Airways Corporation..........A...... 901 672-7820
Palm Beach **(G-13671)**

Southern Airways Express LLC..........B...... 954 660-6897
Palm Beach **(G-13672)**

▲ Spirit Airlines Inc..........A...... 954 447-7920
Miramar **(G-10902)**

United Airlines Inc..........E...... 407 825-4498
Orlando **(G-13332)**

United Airlines Inc..........D...... 800 525-0280
Orlando **(G-13331)**

United Parcel Service Inc..........E...... 407 851-6965
Orlando **(G-13336)**

United Parcel Service Inc..........E...... 407 851-7250
Orlando **(G-13337)**

United Parcel Service Inc..........D...... 305 477-4361
Miami **(G-10439)**

United Parcel Service Inc..........D...... 954 316-7867
Fort Lauderdale **(G-4194)**

United Parcel Service Inc..........D...... 407 377-9200
Orlando **(G-13338)**

United Parcel Service Inc..........D...... 800 742-5877
Tampa **(G-18462)**

United Parcel Service Inc..........E...... 561 840-7060
Riviera Beach **(G-15328)**

United Parcel Service Inc..........D...... 954 971-0393
Pompano Beach **(G-14935)**

United Parcel Service Inc..........E...... 352 368-3767
Ocala **(G-11792)**

4513 Air Courier Svcs

Amerijet International Inc..........E...... 954 320-5300
Miami Springs **(G-10778)**

▲ ATI Systems International Inc..........D...... 561 939-7000
Boca Raton **(G-433)**

Cag Logistics MGT Svcs LLC..........B...... 813 860-4558
Tampa **(G-17410)**

▼ Columbia Intl Trnspt Inc..........D...... 786 370-4553
Miami **(G-9391)**

◆ Dpwn Holdings (usa) Inc..........B...... 954 888-7000
Plantation **(G-14634)**

Federal Express Corporation..........C...... 786 388-2791
Miami **(G-9547)**

Federal Express Corporation..........D...... 800 463-3339
Orlando **(G-12500)**

Federal Express Corporation..........C...... 954 497-2700
Fort Lauderdale **(G-3784)**

Federal Express Corporation..........C...... 786 265-6570
Miami **(G-9548)**

Federal Express Corporation..........D...... 954 316-7651
Fort Lauderdale **(G-3783)**

Fedex Corporation..........E...... 954 978-3399
Coconut Creek **(G-1987)**

Fedex Corporation..........E...... 954 978-6888
Margate **(G-8645)**

▲ Global Mail Inc..........C...... 800 805-9306
Weston **(G-19461)**

▲ Laparkan Airways Inc..........D...... 305 836-4393
Miami **(G-9845)**

◆ Skyworld Intl Couriers Inc..........D...... 786 265-4800
Doral **(G-3313)**

United Parcel Service Inc..........D...... 800 742-5877
Port Richey **(G-15114)**

United Parcel Service Inc..........D...... 407 438-9874
Orlando **(G-13335)**

United Parcel Service Inc..........E...... 352 799-7550
Brooksville **(G-1318)**

United Parcel Service Amer Inc..........D...... 888 742-5877
Miami Gardens **(G-10700)**

Zoom International Couriers..........E...... 305 592-3972
Miami **(G-10531)**

4522 Air Transportation, Nonscheduled

Avid Palm Beach LLC..........E...... 561 855-0050
Fort Pierce **(G-4680)**

Banyan Air Services Inc..........C...... 954 491-3170
Fort Lauderdale **(G-3628)**

▼ Bell Textron Miami Inc..........D...... 954 491-5071
Fort Lauderdale **(G-3635)**

Cargo Holdings Intl Inc..........D...... 407 517-0293
Orlando **(G-12239)**

Cargo Services Inc..........E...... 305 599-9333
Miami **(G-9320)**

Centurion Air Cargo Inc..........D...... 305 871-0130
Miami Springs **(G-10779)**

Craft Charter LLC..........D...... 310 848-3636
Opa Locka **(G-11943)**

D3 Air & Space Operations Inc..........D...... 904 217-3887
Saint Augustine **(G-15437)**

▲ Epic Aviation Inc..........D...... 386 957-1458
New Smyrna Beach **(G-11416)**

Exclusive Charter Service Inc..........E...... 516 967-8526
West Palm Beach **(G-19135)**

Executive Air Charter Boca Rat..........E...... 786 409-2546
Opa Locka **(G-11945)**

Global Jet Charters LLC..........E...... 954 771-1795
Fort Lauderdale **(G-3820)**

Hop-A-Jet Worldwide Jet..........D...... 954 771-5779
Fort Lauderdale **(G-3870)**

◆ Jamaica Air Freighters Ltd Co..........E...... 305 470-8989
Doral **(G-3250)**

National Jets Inc..........E...... 954 359-9400
Fort Lauderdale **(G-3990)**

Personal Jet Charter Inc..........E...... 954 776-4515
Fort Lauderdale **(G-4048)**

Rockhill Group Inc..........C...... 850 754-0400
Molino **(G-10929)**

Sunrise Aviation Inc..........E...... 214 906-5635
Ormond Beach **(G-13526)**

Tropic Ocean Airways LLC..........D...... 954 210-5569
Fort Lauderdale **(G-4189)**

Ultra Aviation Services Inc..........C...... 304 876-8901
Miami **(G-10429)**

Windsor Jet Management..........D...... 954 938-9508
Fort Lauderdale **(G-4227)**

Winfair Holdings Delaware..........D...... 954 565-6633
Fort Lauderdale **(G-4228)**

4581 Airports, Flying Fields & Terminal Svcs

AAR Aircraft Services Inc..........E...... 305 871-2104
Miami **(G-9065)**

ABM Aviation Inc..........D...... 678 313-2106
Orlando **(G-12042)**

Ace Aviation Services Corp..........E...... 954 771-5779
Fort Lauderdale **(G-3576)**

Acpjets LLC..........C...... 561 686-5551
Lake Worth **(G-7707)**

◆ Aero Seating Technologies LLC......E...... 626 286-1130
Melbourne **(G-8811)**

Air General Inc..........D...... 407 851-4000
Orlando **(G-12085)**

Air General Inc..........E...... 813 875-9595
Tampa **(G-17253)**

Aircraft Service Intl Inc..........C...... 954 760-1841
Fort Lauderdale **(G-3584)**

Airgroup Dynamics Inc..........E...... 321 235-0859
Orlando **(G-12087)**

Amerijet Holdings Inc..........D...... 800 927-6059
Miami Springs **(G-10777)**

Ametek Hsa Inc..........D...... 305 599-8855
Doral **(G-3121)**

Atlantic AVI Fbo Holdings LLC..........E...... 561 368-1110
Boca Raton **(G-434)**

Atlantic Aviation Corporation..........E...... 407 894-7331
Orlando **(G-12147)**

Atlas Aerospace ACC Inc..........E...... 817 267-1371
Doral **(G-3126)**

Atlas Aerospace ACC LLC..........E...... 305 717-9951
Doral **(G-3127)**

Atlas Aviation Tampa Inc..........E...... 813 251-1752
Tampa **(G-17318)**

Aviation Inflatables Inc..........D...... 954 749-3500
Sunrise **(G-16744)**

Aviation Main Services Inc..........E...... 305 871-4766
Miami **(G-9195)**

Aviation Partners Group Inc..........E...... 941 637-6530
Punta Gorda **(G-15190)**

Avocet Aviation Services Llc..........E...... 407 585-6201
Sanford **(G-15920)**

Banyan Air Services Inc..........C...... 954 491-3170
Fort Lauderdale **(G-3628)**

◆ Barfield Inc..........C...... 305 894-5300
Miami **(G-9222)**

Barfield Inc..........C...... 305 436-5464
Doral **(G-3133)**

▲ Barfield Aero LLC..........D...... 305 436-5464
Doral **(G-3134)**

◆ Blue Aerospace LLC..........D...... 954 718-4404
Tamarac **(G-17181)**

▼ Boeing US Trng Ad Flgt Svcs LL.....B...... 786 265-4741
Virginia Gardens **(G-18953)**

Boeing US Trning Flght Svcs LL..........A...... 786 265-4702
Virginia Gardens **(G-18954)**

Cae Doss Aviation Inc..........D...... 904 778-1611
Jacksonville **(G-5892)**

Capital Cargo Intl Arln Inc..........C...... 407 855-2004
Orlando **(G-12230)**

Cargo Force Inc..........D...... 305 740-3252
Miami **(G-9316)**

Cargo Services Inc..........E...... 305 874-2450
Miami **(G-9319)**

Centurion Air Cargo Inc..........C...... 305 871-0130
Miami Springs **(G-10779)**

Charlotte County Airport Auth..........E...... 941 639-4119
Punta Gorda **(G-15196)**

Chromalloy Component Svcs Inc..........E...... 850 244-7684
Fort Walton Beach **(G-4758)**

▲ Chromalloy Gas Turbine LLC..........A...... 561 935-3571
Palm Beach Gardens **(G-13706)**

City of Fort Lauderdale ....D...... 954 828-4955
   Fort Lauderdale *(G-3696)*

Com-Jet Corp ....E...... 305 592-3283
   Doral *(G-3157)*

Commercial Jet Inc ....C...... 305 341-5150
   Miami *(G-9393)*

County Miami Dade AVI Dept .....A...... 305 869-4244
   Miami *(G-9426)*

County of Broward ....C...... 866 435-9355
   Fort Lauderdale *(G-3720)*

County of Pinellas ....C...... 727 453-7850
   Clearwater *(G-1592)*

Craig Air Center Inc ....E...... 904 641-0300
   Jacksonville *(G-6010)*

Crestview Aerospace LLC ....A...... 850 682-2746
   Crestview *(G-2316)*

D3 Air & Space Operations Inc ...D...... 904 217-3887
   Saint Augustine *(G-15437)*

Dae Aviation Services Inc ....E...... 305 530-3800
   Miami *(G-9452)*

Daytona Beach Intl Arprt ....D...... 386 248-8030
   Daytona Beach *(G-2574)*

Dolphin Aviation Inc ....E...... 941 355-2902
   Sarasota *(G-16031)*

Efco USA Inc ....E...... 305 876-0026
   Doral *(G-3187)*

Elitejetscom LLC ....D...... 239 900-9000
   Naples *(G-11104)*

FIT Aviation LLC ....E...... 321 674-6501
   Melbourne *(G-8887)*

Flightline Group Inc ....E...... 850 574-4444
   Tallahassee *(G-16954)*

Flightstar Aircraft Svcs LLC ....B...... 904 741-0300
   Jacksonville *(G-6185)*

Florida Institute Tech Inc ....A...... 321 674-8000
   Melbourne *(G-8889)*

Fma Hospitality LP I ....D...... 239 210-7200
   Fort Myers *(G-4395)*

◆ GA Telesis LLC ....D...... 954 676-3111
   Fort Lauderdale *(G-3816)*

GA Telesis LLC ....D...... 305 492-0084
   Miami *(G-9615)*

Gama Aviation Engineering Inc ...B...... 954 489-9001
   Fort Lauderdale *(G-3817)*

Gulf Air Group Inc ....C...... 850 682-8411
   Crestview *(G-2322)*

Haeco Airframe Services LLC .....D...... 386 758-3000
   Lake City *(G-7528)*

Haeco Americas LLC ....D...... 386 758-3000
   Lake City *(G-7529)*

▲ High Standard Aviation Inc .....E...... 305 599-8855
   Doral *(G-3229)*

▲ Homyn Enterprises Corp ....D...... 305 870-9720
   Miami *(G-9717)*

Iap World Services Inc ....E...... 321 784-7100
   Cape Canaveral *(G-1367)*

Iap Worldwide Services Inc ....D...... 321 784-7100
   Cape Canaveral *(G-1368)*

Jacksonville Aviation Auth ....C...... 904 741-3751
   Jacksonville *(G-6351)*

Jasper Steward LLC ....E...... 754 600-9127
   Pembroke Pines *(G-14157)*

Jet Aviation Associates Ltd ....E...... 561 233-7200
   West Palm Beach *(G-19213)*

▲ Jet Aviation Specialists LLC ....C...... 305 681-0160
   Miami *(G-9790)*

▲ Jet Repair Center Inc ....E...... 786 281-2119
   Doral *(G-3252)*

Jetstream Ground Services Inc ....D...... 561 746-3282
   Jupiter *(G-7090)*

Journey Aviation LLC ....E...... 561 826-9400
   Boca Raton *(G-655)*

Landmark Aviation Miami LLC .....E...... 305 874-1477
   Orlando *(G-12752)*

Learjet Inc ....E...... 954 622-1200
   Fort Lauderdale *(G-3933)*

Lee County Port Authority ....D...... 239 590-4800
   Fort Myers *(G-4474)*

Marathon Aviation Assoc LLC .....E...... 305 743-1995
   Marathon *(G-8622)*

Maximus Global Services Llc ......D...... 786 953-4294
   Doral *(G-3271)*

Melbourne Airport Shuttle ....E...... 321 724-1600
   Melbourne *(G-8933)*

Menzies Aviation (texas) Inc ......D...... 407 825-1616
   Orlando *(G-12855)*

Menzies Aviation (texas) Inc ......C...... 407 851-5636
   Orlando *(G-12856)*

Miami Air International Inc ....B...... 305 676-3600
   Miami *(G-9950)*

Miami-Dade Aviation Department ....E...... 305 876-7000
   Miami *(G-9987)*

MSI Aviation LLC ....E...... 407 645-2500
   Maitland *(G-8562)*

Naples Airport Authority ....D...... 239 643-0733
   Naples *(G-11223)*

National Air Cargo Group Inc ......E...... 407 283-6211
   Orlando *(G-12895)*

National Jets Inc ....E...... 954 359-9400
   Fort Lauderdale *(G-3990)*

▼ North ATL Intl Ocean Crier Inc ....E...... 786 233-9586
   Pompano Beach *(G-14867)*

Oxford Electronics Inc ....E...... 407 373-6953
   Orlando *(G-12998)*

Pacific Scientific Company ....E...... 305 215-6982
   Medley *(G-8768)*

Panama Cty-Bay Cnty Arprt Indu ....E...... 850 763-6751
   Panama City *(G-14052)*

Pemco World Air Services Inc .....B...... 813 322-9600
   Tampa *(G-18133)*

Personal Jet Charter Inc ....E...... 954 776-4515
   Fort Lauderdale *(G-4048)*

Power Avionics Inc ....E...... 305 599-7745
   Fort Lauderdale *(G-4055)*

▼ Premier Aircraft Sales Inc ....E...... 954 771-0411
   Fort Lauderdale *(G-4057)*

Privatesky Aviation Svcs Inc ....E...... 239 225-6100
   Fort Myers *(G-4553)*

Regions Security Services Inc .....D...... 305 517-1266
   Miami *(G-10196)*

Rockhill Group Inc ....E...... 850 754-0400
   Molino *(G-10929)*

Safe Fuel Systems LLC ....E...... 954 929-7233
   Hialeah *(G-5318)*

Safran Power Usa LLC ....C...... 941 758-7726
   Sarasota *(G-16050)*

Sanford Airport Authority ....D...... 407 585-4000
   Sanford *(G-16052)*

Sarasota Manatee Airport Auth ....C...... 941 359-2770
   Sarasota *(G-16053)*

Senlex Environmental LLC ....E...... 800 284-0394
   Miami *(G-10259)*

Servisair USA & Carribean ....A...... 239 768-6696
   Fort Myers *(G-4590)*

Sheltair of Clearwater Inc ....D...... 954 771-2210
   Oakland Park *(G-11613)*

Sherwood Avionics and ACC Inc ....E...... 305 477-2994
   Opa Locka *(G-11955)*

Signature Flight Support LLC ......D...... 407 825-6999
   Orlando *(G-13198)*

Signature Flight Support LLC ......D...... 407 648-7200
   Orlando *(G-13199)*

Skyborne Airline Academy Inc .....D...... 772 564-7600
   Vero Beach *(G-18919)*

Skybridge Aviation LLC ....E...... 813 579-1221
   Tampa *(G-18292)*

Skywarrior Flight Training LLC .....E...... 850 433-6114
   Pensacola *(G-14438)*

◆ Southeast Aerospace Inc ....C...... 321 255-9877
   Melbourne *(G-8975)*

Southeast Toyota Distrs LLC ....C...... 954 429-2390
   Fort Lauderdale *(G-4145)*

Sunrise Aviation Inc ....E...... 214 906-5635
   Ormond Beach *(G-13526)*

Superior Aircraft Services Inc .....B...... 561 242-4996
   West Palm Beach *(G-19378)*

Support Aviation LLC ....C...... 407 731-4118
   Altamonte Springs *(G-103)*

Swissport Cargo Services LP ......C...... 305 869-9480
   Miami *(G-10355)*

Swissport Usa Inc ....D...... 305 526-6245
   Miami *(G-10356)*

Swissport Usa Inc ....D...... 407 825-2862
   Orlando *(G-13255)*

Swissport Usa Inc ....D...... 407 409-7527
   Orlando *(G-13256)*

Tbi Airport Management Inc ....D...... 407 585-4500
   Sanford *(G-15985)*

Thrust Tech Accessories Inc ....E...... 954 984-0450
   Fort Lauderdale *(G-4176)*

▼ Turbopower LLC ....C...... 305 820-3225
   Opa Locka *(G-11958)*

Ultra Aviation Services Inc ....D...... 305 876-0091
   Miami *(G-10428)*

Vulcan Group LLC ....D...... 305 967-6344
   Miami *(G-10486)*

Wayman Maintenance LLC ....E...... 786 574-5232
   Pembroke Pines *(G-14201)*

Western Global Airlines LLC ....B...... 941 907-6810
   Estero *(G-3488)*

Xojet Aviation LLC ....D...... 866 669-6538
   Fort Lauderdale *(G-4236)*

47 TRANSPORTATION SERVICES

4724 Travel Agencies

45 Buyers Group Inc ....D...... 561 272-9666
   Delray Beach *(G-2896)*

Advantage Travel Lc ....D...... 863 686-1400
   Lakeland *(G-7785)*

Amadeus Globl Oprtons Amrcas I ....D...... 305 499-6000
   Doral *(G-3115)*

American Ex Trvl Rlted Svcs In ....C...... 954 503-3000
   Fort Lauderdale *(G-3601)*

American Ex Trvl Rlted Svcs In ....B...... 239 417-5699
   Naples *(G-11008)*

Assist-Card of Florida Inc ....D...... 786 437-0100
   Miami *(G-9177)*

Auto Club Group ....A...... 813 289-5000
   Tampa *(G-17321)*

Bags ....E...... 404 201-5716
   Orlando *(G-12167)*

Barrington-Hall Corporation ....E...... 954 720-0475
   Fort Lauderdale *(G-3630)*

Bookingcom ....D...... 407 587-3900
   Orlando *(G-12194)*

Bookit Operating LLC ....E...... 850 234-8887
   Panama City Beach *(G-14090)*

Bookohotel US LLC ....D...... 786 581-4146
   Coral Gables *(G-2057)*

Celebrity Cruises Inc ....C...... 888 751-7804
   Miami *(G-9342)*

◆ Club Med Sales Inc ....C...... 305 925-9000
   Miami *(G-9379)*

Corporate Travel Cons II LLC ......D...... 800 842-8763
   Miami Beach *(G-10576)*

CP Franchising LLC ....D...... 954 344-8060
   Coral Springs *(G-2245)*

Cruisecom Inc ....C...... 954 266-6601
   Dania *(G-2408)*

Cruises Inc ....D...... 888 282-1249
   Fort Lauderdale *(G-3743)*

◆ Crystal Cruises LLC ....C...... 786 971-1000
   Fort Lauderdale *(G-3744)*

Cuddlynest LLC ....E...... 321 830-3576
   Orlando *(G-12391)*

Customer Svc Netwrk Group LLC ....D...... 954 839-6052
   Fort Lauderdale *(G-3746)*

Despegarcom Usa Inc ....C...... 877 893-3988
   Miami *(G-9474)*

Disney Cruise Vacations Inc ....B...... 407 566-3687
   Lake Monroe *(G-7656)*

Educational Opportunities Inc ......D...... 863 648-0383
   Mulberry *(G-10979)*

Escalabeds Group LLC ....E...... 305 707-6761
   Miami *(G-9532)*

Fast Lane Travel Inc ....E...... 813 343-3001
   Oldsmar *(G-11902)*

Florida Trism Indust Mktg Corp ....D...... 850 728-5878
   Tallahassee *(G-16982)*

Forest Travel Agency Inc ....E...... 305 932-5560
   Miami *(G-9598)*

Fti North America Inc ....E...... 407 345-5119
   Orlando *(G-12553)*

Global Marine Travel LLC ....E...... 954 761-9595
   Fort Lauderdale *(G-3821)*

Global Travel Intl Inc ....C...... 407 660-7800
   Maitland *(G-8536)*

Global Trvl Intl Worldwide Inc ......E...... 407 660-7800
   Maitland *(G-8537)*

Go Travel Inc ....D...... 407 423-5300
   Orlando *(G-12576)*

Great Bay Corp ....E...... 305 530-9700
   Miami *(G-9661)*

Holbrook Travel Inc ....D...... 352 377-7111
   Gainesville *(G-4917)*

Hurley Travel Experts Inc ....E...... 239 594-7400
   Naples *(G-11169)*

Interval Servicing Intl Co ....E...... 954 485-5400
   Fort Lauderdale *(G-3900)*

Iworld of Travel Ltd ....D...... 212 661-1193
   Fort Lauderdale *(G-3901)*

Jetsmarter Inc ....D...... 888 984-7538
   Fort Lauderdale *(G-3906)*

Lazy Days RV Center Inc ....B...... 813 246-4999
   Seffner *(G-16428)*

Lexyl Travel Technologies LLC .....E...... 800 898-1347
   West Palm Beach *(G-19233)*

Live For A Moment Inc ....D...... 561 331-1611
   Miami Beach *(G-10608)*

Luxe Travel Management Inc ....E 561 395-1414
Boca Raton *(G-678)*

Magical Cruise Company Limited ....E 800 951-3532
Lake Buena Vista *(G-7466)*

Miami Airport LLC ....B 305 265-3835
Miami *(G-9952)*

◆ Oceania Cruises Inc ....D 305 514-2300
Miami *(G-10061)*

◆ On-Board Media Inc ....D 305 673-0400
Doral *(G-3281)*

Online Vacation Center Inc ....E 954 377-6400
Fort Lauderdale *(G-4029)*

Paradise Cruise Line Operator ....D 954 414-1320
Deerfield Beach *(G-2781)*

Pga Tour Experiences ....D 904 940-9570
Ponte Vedra *(G-14968)*

Preferred Travel of Naples ....E 239 261-1177
Naples *(G-11268)*

Princess Cruise Lines Ltd ....A 954 525-8520
Fort Lauderdale *(G-4059)*

Princess Cruise Lines Ltd ....A 954 797-4112
Fort Lauderdale *(G-4060)*

Regent Seven Seas Cruises Inc ....C 844 473-4368
Miami *(G-10193)*

Royal Caribbean Cruises Ltd.............E 305 539-6000
Miami *(G-10220)*

◆ Royal Caribbean Cruises Ltd ....A 305 539-6000
Miami *(G-10221)*

◆ Silversea Cruises Ltd ....C 800 722-9955
Miami *(G-10272)*

Special T Travel Service Inc................E 407 896-8680
Casselberry *(G-1460)*

Springhill Suites Tampa N/Tamp ....E 813 558-0300
Tampa *(G-18322)*

Star Clippers Ltd Corp ....D 305 553-9405
Miami *(G-10327)*

Starship Cruise Lines LLC ....E 813 223-7999
Clearwater *(G-1795)*

Stylus Transportation Corp.................D 321 631-8183
Daytona Beach *(G-2669)*

Stylus Transportation Corp.................E 561 439-2223
Riviera Beach *(G-15320)*

Tampa Bay Cnvntion Vstors Bur ....B 813 223-1111
Tampa *(G-18365)*

Total Travel Enterprises Inc ....E 305 817-9339
Coral Gables *(G-2198)*

Tourico Holidays Inc ....C 407 667-8700
Altamonte Springs *(G-106)*

Travel Planners Intl Inc ....E 407 331-3888
Maitland *(G-8592)*

Travelxchange Inc..............................D 305 890-4428
Miami *(G-10406)*

Unique Travel Palm Beach Inc.............E 561 495-5775
Delray Beach *(G-3026)*

▲ Universal Studios Vacation Co ....A 407 224-7000
Orlando *(G-13351)*

Vacation VIP LLC ....E 321 802-6011
Melbourne Beach *(G-9014)*

Valerie Wilson Travel Inc ....E 904 285-2222
Ponte Vedra Beach *(G-15011)*

Virgin Incoming Service Inc................E 407 856-1177
Orlando *(G-13377)*

Vistana Sgnture Expriences Inc ....E 800 601-8699
Orlando *(G-13384)*

Walmart Inc.......................................B 941 497-2523
Venice *(G-18822)*

Walmart Inc.......................................C 407 397-7000
Kissimmee *(G-7408)*

Walmart Inc.......................................C 321 242-1601
Melbourne *(G-9005)*

Walt Disney Travel Co Inc ....C 407 939-7411
Orlando *(G-13394)*

Wmph Incorporated ....D 561 243-2100
Delray Beach *(G-3035)*

World Travel Partners Orlando ....E 407 839-0027
Orlando *(G-13448)*

4725 Tour Operators

Berkley Group Inc ....D 954 563-2444
Fort Lauderdale *(G-3639)*

Carnival Corporation ....A 305 599-2600
Doral *(G-3145)*

Carnival Corporation ....A 305 599-2600
Doral *(G-3146)*

◆ Carnival Corporation ....E 305 406-7255
Hialeah *(G-5229)*

Clewiston Marina Inc ....E 863 983-3151
Clewiston *(G-1900)*

◆ Club Med Sales Inc.........................C 305 925-9000
Miami *(G-9379)*

Dynamic Tours and Trnsp Inc...............C 407 351-7777
Orlando *(G-12446)*

EDIson&ford Winter Estates ....E 239 334-7419
Fort Myers *(G-4353)*

Fti North America Inc ....C 407 345-5119
Orlando *(G-12553)*

Historic Tours America Inc....................D 305 292-8909
Key West *(G-7211)*

Holbrook Travel Inc.............................D 352 377-7111
Gainesville *(G-4917)*

Hotel Connections Inc ....E 201 830-2800
Miami *(G-9723)*

Lazy Days RV Center Inc......................D 813 246-4999
Seffner *(G-16428)*

Magical Cruise Company Limited ....E 800 951-3532
Lake Buena Vista *(G-7466)*

Maracaibo & Orlando Ex LLC ....C 321 274-6635
Daytona Beach *(G-2630)*

◆ MSC Cruises (usa) Inc ....D 954 772-6262
Fort Lauderdale *(G-3978)*

Old Town Trlley Turs St Agstin ....B 904 826-0380
Saint Augustine *(G-15474)*

Paradise Cruise Line Operator ....D 954 414-1320
Deerfield Beach *(G-2781)*

Saint Agstine Historical Tours ....D 305 292-8900
Key West *(G-7242)*

Stylus Transportation Corp..................E 954 522-1516
Miami *(G-10336)*

Travel Opportunities Inc.......................E 954 563-2444
Fort Lauderdale *(G-4181)*

Travel Planners Intl Inc ....E 407 331-3888
Maitland *(G-8592)*

Virgin Incoming Service Inc..................E 407 856-1177
Orlando *(G-13377)*

Walt Disney Travel Co Inc ....C 407 939-7411
Orlando *(G-13394)*

4729 Passenger Transportation Arrangement, NEC

▲ ME Productions...............................E 954 458-4000
Hallandale *(G-5163)*

Qatar Airways Group ....E 305 876-1775
Miami *(G-10170)*

Shuttleport Trnsp Svcs LLC..................A 954 359-3636
Fort Lauderdale *(G-4125)*

Silver Airways LLC ....C 954 985-1500
Hollywood *(G-5520)*

United Airlines Inc...............................D 800 525-0280
Orlando *(G-13331)*

4731 Freight Forwarding & Arrangement

21 Air LLC ....E 786 233-6758
Doral *(G-3093)*

◆ A Custom Brokerage Inc..................E 305 805-6797
Doral *(G-3097)*

AAA Cooper Transportation ....D 954 978-0455
Pompano Beach *(G-14731)*

Adcom Express Inc.............................D 813 887-3747
Tampa *(G-17234)*

Aeropost Inc......................................A 305 592-5534
Doral *(G-3105)*

Air Express Intl USA Inc ....E 407 851-7520
Orlando *(G-12084)*

Air General Inc ....D 407 851-4000
Orlando *(G-12085)*

Ajc Logistics LLC...............................D 877 331-0794
Jacksonville *(G-5760)*

Alba Wheels Up Intl LLC ....E 305 499-9994
Miami *(G-9112)*

▲ Allyn International Svcs Inc ....D 239 267-4261
Fort Myers *(G-4269)*

▲ Alpha Brokers Corporation ....D 305 594-9290
Miami *(G-9129)*

▲ American Cargo Logistics Inc ....E 904 741-4990
Jacksonville *(G-5777)*

Amerijet International Inc......................E 954 320-5300
Miami Springs *(G-10778)*

Amerijet International Inc......................E 954 320-5300
Miami *(G-9148)*

◆ Aqua Gulf Xpress Inc ....E 954 360-6900
Deerfield Beach *(G-2710)*

Aqua Gulf Xpress Inc..........................E 904 359-0076
Jacksonville *(G-5801)*

Armellini Industries Inc ....B 772 287-0575
Palm City *(G-13784)*

Armellini Pierson Terminal Inc ....E 386 749-2044
Pierson *(G-14496)*

◆ Asecomer International Corp ....E 305 599-2115
Medley *(G-8706)*

Assetco Freight Brokers Inc ....E 888 662-4928
Miami *(G-9175)*

Assetco Global Forwarding Inc ....E 786 449-4020
Miami *(G-9176)*

◆ Atec Systems Ltd ....E 407 740-5565
Altamonte Springs *(G-28)*

AV Logistics LLC................................D 904 269-4700
Fleming Island *(G-3549)*

Bedabox LLC.....................................D 855 222-4601
Fort Lauderdale *(G-3634)*

Bernuth Agencies Inc ....E 305 637-8916
Miami *(G-9246)*

◆ Blue-Grace Logistics LLC ....C 800 697-4477
Riverview *(G-15246)*

Brown Integrated Logistics Inc ....E 904 783-8323
Jacksonville *(G-5885)*

◆ Caribbean Shipping Svcs Inc ....D 904 247-0031
Jacksonville *(G-5906)*

◆ Caribtrans Logistics LLC..................E 305 696-1200
Miami *(G-9322)*

Carroll Fulmer Holding Corp ....E 352 429-5000
Groveland *(G-5086)*

Carroll Fulmer Logistics Corp ....D 352 429-5000
Groveland *(G-5087)*

▲ Central Moving & Storage Inc ....E 407 219-9779
Orlando *(G-12284)*

Centurion Deliveries LLC ....D 786 537-0516
Miami *(G-9348)*

Ceva Logistics LLC.............................B 904 928-1400
Jacksonville *(G-5931)*

Cht Holdings Inc ....D 954 900-3986
Fort Lauderdale *(G-3692)*

◆ Clover Systems LLC ....E 305 592-4300
Doral *(G-3153)*

CMA - Cgm Caribbean Inc ....E 305 477-0216
Miami *(G-9380)*

CMA Cgm (caribbean) LLC ....D 305 398-3600
Miami *(G-9381)*

▼ Coastal Intl Logistics LLC ....E 904 589-3010
Jacksonville *(G-5972)*

▼ Columbia Intl Trnspt Inc ....D 786 370-4553
Miami *(G-9391)*

Concepts In Freight Inc ....E 305 468-3255
Doral *(G-3160)*

Convey Express Inc............................E 561 674-3029
Orlando *(G-12366)*

Corporate Traffic Inc...........................D 904 727-0051
Jacksonville *(G-6002)*

Corporate Transportation Inc ....D 904 224-7287
Jacksonville *(G-6003)*

Crowley American Transport ....D 904 727-2200
Jacksonville *(G-6014)*

Crowley Government Svcs Inc ....D 904 727-2200
Jacksonville *(G-6015)*

◆ Crowley Liner Services Inc...............A 904 727-2200
Jacksonville *(G-6017)*

◆ Crowley Logistics Inc ....C 904 727-2200
Jacksonville *(G-6018)*

Crowley Marine Services Inc ....B 904 727-2475
Jacksonville *(G-6019)*

Crowley Puerto Rico Svcs Inc ....D 904 727-2200
Jacksonville *(G-6023)*

Crowley Solutions Inc ....D 904 727-4176
Jacksonville *(G-6024)*

Crowley Trucking Inc...........................E 904 727-2200
Jacksonville *(G-6026)*

Curv Logistics Group Inc ....E 305 255-4061
Cutler Bay *(G-2364)*

Cw Carriers Usa Inc ....D 813 621-5057
Tampa *(G-17561)*

Data2logistics LLC.............................E 239 936-2800
Fort Myers *(G-4338)*

Data2logistics LLC.............................C 239 936-2800
Fort Myers *(G-4339)*

Dedicated Carriers Inc ....E 813 884-8466
Tampa *(G-17583)*

Dfds International Corporation ....D 305 477-6800
Doral *(G-3178)*

Dhl Aviation Americas Inc ....C 954 626-4272
Plantation *(G-14629)*

◆ Distributors Transport Inc ....E 407 851-1615
Orlando *(G-12430)*

Dm World Transportation LLC...............E 407 738-1655
Longwood *(G-8357)*

◆ Dpwn Holdings (usa) Inc ....B 954 888-7000
Plantation *(G-14634)*

◆ Econocaribe Inc ....C 305 693-5133
Miami *(G-9500)*

◆ Econocaribe Consolidators Inc ....C 305 693-5133
Miami *(G-9501)*

S I C

Elite Team Logistics LLC ....B 727 612-6762
Seminole (G-16446)

Ella Bay Logistics LLC ....E 239 214-7723
Marco Island (G-8628)

◆ Evolution Logistics Corp ....E 305 591-7713
Medley (G-8729)

Expedited World Cargo Inc ....E 305 392-5085
Doral (G-3194)

Expeditors Intl Wash Inc ....D 305 592-9410
Doral (G-3195)

Expeditors Intl Wash Inc ....D 305 599-1973
Doral (G-3196)

Expeditors Intl Wash Inc ....D 407 816-0186
Orlando (G-12481)

Export Freight & Brokers Inc ....E 305 592-7343
Doral (G-3197)

Exxact Express Incorporated ....E 863 682-4101
Lakeland (G-7858)

◆ Faith Freight Forwarding Corp ....E 305 265-5400
Coral Gables (G-2104)

▼ Fast Track Wrldwide Lgstics In ......E 305 728-7801
Doral (G-3199)

Fedex Crossborder LLC ....E 813 839-0561
Saint Petersburg (G-15665)

Fedex Freight Inc ....D 813 621-1071
Tampa (G-17654)

Flower Logistics ....E 305 418-9906
Miami (G-9592)

Forward Air Corporation ....D 863 583-4607
Lakeland (G-7871)

◆ Four Star Cargo Inc ....D 305 717-6200
Miami (G-9604)

Four Towers Logistics Corp ....E 305 513-3324
Miami (G-9605)

Freightcenter Inc ....E 727 450-7800
Palm Harbor (G-13863)

◆ G & G Marine Inc ....D 954 920-9292
Fort Lauderdale (G-3813)

◆ Garces & Garces Crgo Svcs Inc ....E 305 477-4766
Doral (G-3208)

Gemcap Investments LLC ....E 305 551-5626
Miami (G-9623)

Geodis Wilson Usa Inc ....B 305 718-9320
Doral (G-3209)

Glb Trucking LLC ....E 305 974-6239
Miami Gardens (G-10684)

▼ Global Cargo Corporation ....E 305 513-8555
Doral (G-3211)

Global Entps & Logistics Inc ....D 954 302-2296
Miami (G-9634)

Grc Intermediate Holdco LLC ....E 954 969-2336
Margate (G-8650)

Grimes Logistics Services Inc ....E 904 786-5711
Jacksonville (G-6243)

Hamburg Sud North America Inc ....E 954 761-2656
Fort Lauderdale (G-3847)

Hapag-Lloyd (america) LLC ....C 732 562-1800
Tampa (G-17789)

Hellmann Wrldwide Lgistics Inc ....C 305 406-4500
Doral (G-3226)

Hellmann Wrldwide Lgistics Inc ....E 305 629-2703
Doral (G-3227)

Helmsman Freight Solutions LLC ....D 305 421-1800
Coral Gables (G-2122)

Hoegh Autoliners Inc ....E 904 516-4800
Jacksonville (G-6283)

Hts Logistics LLC ....D 877 874-3164
Jacksonville (G-6302)

◆ Hyde Shipping Corporation ....C 305 913-4933
Hialeah (G-5279)

Iap World Services Inc ....E 321 784-7100
Cape Canaveral (G-1367)

Ics Delivery Solutions LLC ....D 704 258-8584
Palmetto (G-13917)

◆ Ils Cargo Corp ....E 305 718-3799
Medley (G-8743)

Inland Transport Inc ....D 407 858-3039
Orlando (G-12681)

Innovel Solutions Inc ....A 954 779-1391
Fort Lauderdale (G-3895)

Integrity Ex Logistics LLC ....C 888 374-5138
Tampa (G-17870)

Interport Logistics Llc ....D 305 477-1910
Miami (G-9776)

Interstate Transport Inc ....D 727 822-9999
Saint Petersburg (G-15724)

Ips Worldwide LLC ....D 386 672-7727
Ormond Beach (G-13505)

▲ Iqor Global Services LLC ....B 727 369-0100
Saint Petersburg (G-15725)

▲ JA Flower Service Inc ....B 305 592-5198
Miami (G-9779)

JD Associates LLC ....E 386 740-0159
Deland (G-2864)

Jit Express Inc ....E 786 221-0200
Miami (G-9794)

Jlb Logistics Inc ....E 800 875-2463
Riverview (G-15258)

◆ John Cassidy International Inc ....E 305 836-6216
Miami (G-9797)

John J Jerue Truck Broker Inc ....E 863 607-5600
Lakeland (G-7892)

Kintetsu World Express USA Inc ....D 813 964-0031
Tampa (G-17927)

Komyo America Co Inc ....E 904 751-0063
Jacksonville (G-6408)

Kuehne & Nagel Inc Frt Fwdng ....E 407 240-7395
Orlando (G-12741)

Kuehne + Nagel Inc ....C 407 240-7395
Orlando (G-12742)

Kw International Inc ....D 310 747-1530
Medley (G-8751)

Lan Cargo SA ....A 786 265-6000
Miami (G-9843)

Landstar Global Logistics Inc ....E 904 390-4751
Jacksonville (G-6415)

Laparkan Airways Inc ....E 305 870-9949
Miami (G-9844)

▲ Laparkan Airways Inc ....E 305 836-4393
Miami (G-9845)

◆ Laparkan Trading Ltd Company ....E 305 836-4393
Miami (G-9846)

Larry Young Enterprises Inc ....E 941 637-3723
Punta Gorda (G-15211)

Logical Brokerage Corp ....D 786 207-2150
Miami Beach (G-10611)

Logistics Frt Solutions Inc ....D 833 744-7537
Doral (G-3261)

Luxor Trnsp & Drv Away LLC ....D 866 315-3029
Orlando (G-12793)

M J M Quality Transportation ....D 407 855-0296
Orlando (G-12799)

Maccabees Trucking Inc ....B 786 859-7872
Orlando (G-12801)

Magellan Trnspt Logistics Inc ....C 904 620-0311
Jacksonville (G-6461)

Magic Transport Inc ....E 305 887-2424
Medley (G-8753)

Mainfreight International Inc ....E 786 336-8199
Miami (G-9894)

◆ Marlins Consolidators Inc ....E 305 592-1669
Miami (G-9903)

Martinez Group Enterprises LLC ....E 321 356-8663
Orlando (G-12822)

Maruti Fleet & Mgmt LLC ....B 407 412-5613
Orlando (G-12823)

Maruti Transit Group LLC ....E 407 412-5613
Orlando (G-12825)

Mc-N-Law Inc ....E 904 765-0437
Jacksonville (G-6474)

McCartney Trucking LLC ....E 786 320-5080
North Miami Beach (G-11530)

Medical Trnspt Solutions Inc ....E 954 888-8682
Pembroke Pines (G-14171)

▲ Mercator Shipping Ltd ....E 305 887-0900
Medley (G-8756)

Miami Intl Frt Solutions LLC ....D 305 685-0035
Miami Lakes (G-10745)

Myrthil Carrier Service LLC ....D 813 481-2192
Miami (G-10023)

National Freight Inc ....E 407 518-9263
Kissimmee (G-7360)

Net Links Enterprises LLC ....E 727 579-0700
Saint Petersburg (G-15774)

Nippon Express USA Inc ....E 305 592-6109
Miami (G-10049)

Nobel Relocation Maryland LLC ....E 305 620-2002
Miami Gardens (G-10694)

Norfolk Southern Corporation ....D 904 366-1496
Jacksonville (G-6545)

▼ North ATL Intl Ocean Crier Inc ....E 786 233-9586
Pompano Beach (G-14867)

Off The Docks LLC ....D 727 239-6299
Clearwater (G-1744)

Optimal US Logistics LLC ....B 727 325-2909
Clearwater (G-1749)

▲ OSG Ship Management Inc ....E 813 209-0600
Tampa (G-18112)

◆ Panalpina Inc ....D 305 894-1300
Miami (G-10090)

Panalpina Inc ....D 305 894-1300
Miami (G-10091)

Panama City Port Authority ....E 850 769-6683
Panama City (G-14050)

◆ Pas Cargo Usa Inc ....D 305 994-7232
Hialeah Gardens (G-5348)

Plains Dedicated LLC ....E 720 259-7140
Champions Gate (G-1477)

Pods of Seattle LLC ....B 727 538-6300
Clearwater (G-1762)

Priano Marchelli Usa LLC ....E 786 452-0633
Doral (G-3295)

Quality Express Delivery Inc ....D 904 783-3335
Jacksonville (G-6625)

R+l Global Inc ....E 239 337-8700
Fort Myers (G-4561)

Reed Transport Services Inc ....E 800 606-4471
Tampa (G-18207)

Rhenus Logistics LLC ....D 786 235-7800
Miami (G-10212)

Royal Bengal Logistics Inc ....E 954 228-7277
Coral Springs (G-2281)

▼ Rudy Export Corp ....E 305 599-0029
Miami (G-10225)

Saddle Creek Trnsp Inc ....C 863 665-0966
Lakeland (G-7959)

Schenker Inc ....D 305 639-5200
Miami (G-10247)

Scott Logistics Corp ....E 904 900-2125
Jacksonville (G-6700)

Scs Logistics LLC ....E 305 592-5333
Doral (G-3305)

◆ Seafreight Agencies Inc ....E 305 592-6060
Doral (G-3306)

▲ Senator Intl Frt Fwdg LLC ....E 305 593-5520
Medley (G-8781)

Shipco Transport Inc ....D 305 591-3900
Medley (G-8782)

Shipmonk Inc ....B 855 222-4601
Fort Lauderdale (G-4123)

Ss Delivery Systems Llc ....E 561 504-3422
Miami (G-10321)

Star Freight LLC ....E 904 781-4788
Jacksonville (G-6786)

Suddath Rlction Systems of Jck ....D 904 256-5540
Jacksonville (G-6799)

▲ Suddath Van Lines Inc ....B 904 390-7100
Jacksonville (G-6801)

Suncoast Air Trnsp Inc ....D 407 876-2739
St Pete Beach (G-16571)

Sunteck Holdings LLC ....D 800 759-7910
Jacksonville (G-6813)

Sunteck Transport Co Llc ....E 561 988-9456
Jacksonville (G-6814)

Sunteck Transport Group LLC ....C 561 988-9456
Jacksonville (G-6815)

Sunteck/Tts Integration II ....E 561 988-9456
Jacksonville (G-6816)

Supply Chain Shipping LLC ....E 786 347-3484
Doral (G-3327)

Swissport Usa Inc ....D 239 822-2751
Fort Myers (G-4618)

Syncreon America Inc ....E 321 443-1175
Orlando (G-13260)

▲ Team Dgd Inc ....E 888 219-4544
Miami (G-10365)

◆ Ten Pubco Inc ....A 239 949-4450
Bonita Springs (G-945)

▲ Time Definite Services Inc ....D 800 466-8040
Sumterville (G-16698)

Tobico Transportation LLP ....D 972 483-2330
Cape Coral (G-1429)

Total Military Management Inc ....C 904 739-9940
Jacksonville (G-6863)

Total Quality Logistics LLC ....C 800 580-3101
Tampa (G-18428)

Total Quality Logistics LLC ....D 513 831-2600
Dania Beach (G-2432)

Total Quality Logistics LLC ....C 513 831-2600
Jacksonville (G-6865)

Total Quality Logistics LLC ....C 513 831-2600
Tampa (G-18429)

Total Quality Logistics LLC ....C 800 580-3101
Orlando (G-13298)

Total Quality Logistics LLC ....D 800 580-3101
Miami (G-10398)

Tote Maritime Puerto Rico LLC ....E 904 855-1260
Jacksonville (G-6866)

◆ Tote Maritime Puerto Rico LLC ....D 904 855-1260
Jacksonville (G-6867)

Tote Maritime Puerto Rico LLC..........E 904 751-2110
Jacksonville (G-6868)
◆ Traffic Tech Intl US LLC ....E 866 642-6832
Medley (G-8792)
Transflo Express LLC ....E 813 386-6000
Tampa (G-18434)
Transprttion MGT Solutions Inc ....E 954 433-8549
Pembroke Pines (G-14196)
Tropical Shipg Cnstr Ltd LLC ....E 305 805-7400
Medley (G-8793)
Veritas Dispatch LLC ....E 305 399-8848
Miami (G-10465)
▼ Veterans Trading Company Inc ....E 352 438-0084
Ocala (G-11794)
Wal-Mart Transportation LLC ....E 863 256-1649
Davenport (G-2450)
◆ Wetherill Associates Inc ....C 800 877-3340
Miramar (G-10915)
◆ Wrt World Enterprises Inc ....E 305 884-3700
Medley (G-8799)
Wwl Vehicle Svcs Americas Inc ....E 904 751-5720
Jacksonville (G-6948)
Xipron Inc ....E 305 330-6250
Miami (G-10520)
Xoom Cargo Inc ....E 305 803-6819
Pembroke Pines (G-14205)
Xpo Global Forwarding Inc ....D 630 795-1300
Miami (G-10521)
Xpo Logistics Freight Inc ....C 407 812-5479
Orlando (G-13466)
Xpo Logistics Freight Inc ....C 305 428-1800
Miami Lakes (G-10772)
Yusen Logistics Americas Inc ....E 904 485-1937
Jacksonville (G-6964)
Zoom International Couriers ....E 305 592-3972
Miami (G-10531)

4783 Packing & Crating Svcs

American Packing & Crating LLC..........C 954 467-8948
Fort Lauderdale (G-3604)
Beaver Street Fisheries Inc ....C 904 354-5661
Jacksonville (G-5850)
▲ Davidson Forwarding Company ....D 904 390-7100
Jacksonville (G-6049)
Goodwill Cntl Southern Ind Inc ....E 850 877-6840
Tallahassee (G-16990)
▲ Homyn Enterprises Corp ....D 305 870-9720
Miami (G-9717)

4785 Fixed Facilities, Inspection, Weighing Svcs Transptn

Central Florida Exwy Auth ....E 407 690-5000
Orlando (G-12283)
Dade County Expressway Auth ....E 305 637-3277
Miami (G-9450)
Envirowaste Services Group Inc ....D 305 637-9665
Palmetto Bay (G-13940)
Florida Turnpike Enterprise ....E 407 532-3999
Ocoee (G-11813)
Maruti Mobility Management Inc ....D 866 678-0222
Orlando (G-12824)
Mortgage Contracting Svcs LLC ....E 813 387-1100
Tampa (G-18053)

4789 Transportation Svcs, NEC

A & P Consulting Transporta ....E 786 332-3681
Medley (G-8698)
All Railroad Services Corp ....C 904 296-3434
Saint Augustine (G-15422)
All Stars Tours and Trnsp LLC ....D 954 226-7828
Fort Lauderdale (G-3594)
Alstom Signaling Operation LLC ....C 321 435-7021
Melbourne (G-8813)
◆ American Rll-On Rll-Off Crier ....E 201 571-0401
Ponte Vedra Beach (G-14972)
APL Logistics Ltd ....E 305 468-3054
Miami (G-9160)
◆ Apollo Export Warehouse Inc..........C 305 592-8790
Miami (G-9161)
◆ Asecomer International Corp ....E 305 599-2115
Medley (G-8706)
Caaj Corporation ....E 407 977-8681
Chuluota (G-1498)
Cassel Logistics LLC......................E 361 946-9474
Palm Coast (G-13815)
Cdc Transport LLC..........................D 305 687-7277
Pembroke Pines (G-14137)
Cleveland Clinic Martin Health ....E 772 287-5200
Stuart (G-16605)

Dhpartners Inc................................C 305 403-3136
Laud By Sea (G-8166)
Drummac Inc..................................C 904 241-4999
Atlantic Beach (G-240)
Dual Logistics Dispatch LLC ....D 800 221-5796
Miami Gardens (G-10681)
Eclipse Advantage LLC ....C 321 250-6380
Melbourne (G-8877)
Evergreen Transportation LLC ....E 407 732-0911
Kissimmee (G-7304)
Evolved Source Solutions Corp ....C 239 288-9470
Lehigh Acres (G-8282)
Farias Transportation Inc ....C 407 955-1101
Orlando (G-12493)
Federal Express Corporation..............D 954 316-7651
Fort Lauderdale (G-3783)
Fort Lauderdale Trnsp Inc ....A 954 237-2961
Fort Lauderdale (G-3802)
Gateway Warehouse Inc....................E 904 751-8880
Jacksonville (G-6221)
Hts Logistics LLC ....D 877 874-3164
Jacksonville (G-6302)
Icare Home LLC ....C 407 221-8571
Oviedo (G-13553)
Intermodal Support Svcs Inc ....D 904 858-1587
Jacksonville (G-6327)
Latitude Lngtude Logistics LLC ....D 904 327-9773
Ormond Beach (G-13506)
Lightning Trnspt Logistics LLC ....D 813 444-5144
Tampa (G-17954)
◆ Linea Peninsular Inc ....E 850 785-0397
Panama City (G-14036)
Lorry Mf Group LLC ....E 727 219-9304
Saint Petersburg (G-15749)
▲ Maritime Container Svcs Inc ....B 305 885-1288
Medley (G-8754)
Maruti Transportation Group ....D 407 412-5613
Orlando (G-12826)
MB Freight Corp ....E 845 430-8090
Seffner (G-16431)
Movingplace LLC ....C 904 849-3882
Lutz (G-8451)
Nba Recovery LLC ....D 863 605-6363
Kissimmee (G-7421)
Propak Logistics Inc........................E 407 730-9228
Orlando (G-13069)
Rcc Auto Transport Ltd ....E 877 873-5512
Miami (G-10184)
Scotlynn USA Division Inc ....C 239 210-3000
Fort Myers (G-4585)
Skyhop Global LLC ....D 518 428-1762
Fort Lauderdale (G-4132)
Stonewall Lgstics Slutions LLC ....E 931 257-8891
Venice (G-18806)
Sunny Tiger Logistics LLC ....C 540 841-3454
Fort Pierce (G-4742)
Sweetwater Transportation LLC ....D 904 874-6512
Jacksonville (G-6821)
▲ Team Dgd Inc..............................E 888 219-4544
Miami (G-10365)
Transportation Cons Amer Inc ....C 954 917-9515
Pompano Beach (G-14926)
Transportation Florida Dept ....D 386 943-5456
Deland (G-2883)
Tropical Shipping Usa LLC ....A 561 863-5737
Riviera Beach (G-15327)
Unity Transport Service LLC ....E 904 472-8756
Jacksonville (G-6890)
VIP Transport LLC..........................E 209 874-6643
Wilton Manors (G-19534)
Watco Companies Inc ....D 904 786-1700
Jacksonville (G-6918)
Zuni Go LLC ....E 305 258-9864
Homestead (G-5614)

48 COMMUNICATIONS

4812 Radiotelephone Communications

All Cellular S FL LLC ....E 954 227-1722
Coral Springs (G-2223)
AT&T Corp ....D 305 255-8451
Palmetto Bay (G-13938)
AT&T Corp ....D 904 282-1508
Middleburg (G-10791)
Big Bang Enterprises Inc ....A 954 800-3892
Coral Springs (G-2231)
Callstar Inc....................................E 727 346-4400
Saint Petersburg (G-15609)
Cane Wireless Inc ....E 954 757-0876
Pompano Beach (G-14764)

◆ Cellantenna Corporation ....E 954 340-7053
Coral Springs (G-2236)
Cellco Partnership ....D 727 784-8090
Palm Harbor (G-13854)
Cellco Partnership ....D 239 774-5540
Naples (G-11049)
Cellco Partnership ....D 904 223-1795
Jacksonville (G-5921)
Cellco Partnership ....D 561 630-0400
Palm Beach Gardens (G-13704)
Cellco Partnership ....D 561 369-8633
Boynton Beach (G-972)
Cellco Partnership ....D 850 916-4900
Gulf Breeze (G-5111)
Cellco Partnership ....D 941 360-1374
Sarasota (G-16027)
Cellco Partnership ....D 239 939-4335
Fort Myers (G-4304)
Cellco Partnership ....D 904 880-8282
Jacksonville (G-5922)
Cellco Partnership ....D 954 704-4700
Pembroke Pines (G-14138)
Cellco Partnership ....D 954 561-5999
Fort Lauderdale (G-3675)
Cellco Partnership ....D 305 251-1174
Cutler Bay (G-2360)
Cellco Partnership ....D 239 573-1934
Cape Coral (G-1382)
Cellco Partnership ....D 813 632-2216
Tampa (G-17438)
Cellco Partnership ....D 407 823-7751
Orlando (G-12251)
Cellco Partnership ....D 850 478-1311
Pensacola (G-14254)
Cellco Partnership ....D 850 969-1248
Pensacola (G-14255)
Cellco Partnership ....D 407 823-7751
Deland (G-2846)
Cellco Partnership ....D 813 938-1112
Ruskin (G-15397)
Cellco Partnership ....D 407 343-0516
Kissimmee (G-7277)
Cellco Partnership ....D 904 276-1620
Orange Park (G-11979)
Cellco Partnership ....D 352 796-9919
Brooksville (G-1279)
Cellco Partnership ....D 850 526-7700
Panama City (G-13978)
Cellco Partnership ....D 941 756-2356
Bradenton (G-1074)
Cooper General Global Svcs Inc ....C 305 418-4440
Doral (G-3165)
Eurostar Intl Corp ....E 305 639-2160
Doral (G-3191)
First Communications Inc ....D 850 668-7990
Tallahassee (G-16952)
Florida Embarq Inc ....E 407 390-8002
Kissimmee (G-7310)
Frontier Florida LLC ....B 863 284-0532
Lakeland (G-7872)
GP Mobile LLC ....C 386 366-8615
South Daytona (G-16488)
GP Mobile LLC ....C 813 670-2100
Zephyrhills (G-19835)
Gtp Infrastructure III LLC ....D 561 886-5854
Boca Raton (G-611)
Hello Mobile Telecom LLC ....E 888 954-9556
Dania (G-2416)
Interop Technologies LLC ....D 239 425-6845
Fort Myers (G-4451)
Island Technology Networks Inc ....D 909 249-1150
Jacksonville (G-6334)
Jjr Media Inc..................................D 954 336-3545
Tallahassee (G-17011)
Jupiter Tequesta Rptr Grp..................D 561 746-7421
Jupiter (G-7108)
Lenhart Electric Company ....E 352 748-5818
Wildwood (G-19502)
Likewize Corp ....C 305 921-1237
Miami (G-9871)
Marconi Wireless Holdings LLC ....D 561 290-5631
West Palm Beach (G-19250)
Mastec Network Solutions LLC ....C 866 545-1782
Coral Gables (G-2140)
Mastec Network Solutions LLC ....E 866 545-1782
Coral Gables (G-2141)
Mobile Store Operators LLC ....D 786 701-8117
Cutler Bay (G-2371)
National Connection Corp..................E 786 970-7325
Miami (G-10027)

New Cingular Wireless Svcs Inc..........D...... 561 775-4341
North Palm Beach *(G-11555)*

New Cingular Wireless Svcs Inc..........C...... 407 496-9287
Orlando *(G-12910)*

New Cingular Wireless Svcs Inc..........E...... 786 268-7400
Pinecrest *(G-14500)*

New Cingular Wireless Svcs Inc..........E...... 954 474-5252
Plantation *(G-14684)*

New Cingular Wireless Svcs Inc..........D...... 305 598-2621
Miami *(G-10040)*

New Cingular Wireless Svcs Inc..........E...... 850 484-3636
Pensacola *(G-14383)*

New Cingular Wireless Svcs Inc..........E...... 954 894-2926
Hollywood *(G-5481)*

New Cingular Wireless Svcs Inc..........E...... 954 730-2305
Fort Lauderdale *(G-3998)*

New Cingular Wireless Svcs Inc..........E...... 561 883-0633
Boca Raton *(G-712)*

Nextraq LLC..........E...... 678 762-6800
Tampa *(G-18082)*

Panhandle Alarm & Tele Co Inc..........E...... 850 478-2108
Pensacola *(G-14398)*

Pcs Mobile Solutions LLC..........D...... 813 321-6555
Oldsmar *(G-11920)*

Q Link Wireless LLC..........B...... 855 754-6543
Dania *(G-2418)*

▲ Quality One Wireless LLC..........C...... 407 857-3737
Orlando *(G-13078)*

Qxc Communications Inc..........E...... 561 708-1500
Boca Raton *(G-762)*

Round Room LLC..........E...... 850 926-8255
Crawfordville *(G-2304)*

Sac Wireless LLC..........C...... 561 337-0101
Pompano Beach *(G-14889)*

Safelink Wireless..........A...... 305 715-6500
Medley *(G-8778)*

Sprint Communications Co LP..........C...... 954 979-4279
Coconut Creek *(G-2006)*

Sprint Communications Co LP..........C...... 407 388-1515
Winter Springs *(G-19812)*

Sprint Communications Co LP..........C...... 352 264-7887
Gainesville *(G-5007)*

Sprint Communications Co LP..........C...... 954 385-3770
Davie *(G-2521)*

T & R Cellular Inc..........E...... 727 515-0388
Clearwater *(G-1814)*

Tcc Cellular Connection..........C...... 941 896-4329
Bradenton *(G-1189)*

◆ Tracfone Wireless Inc..........C...... 305 715-6500
Medley *(G-8791)*

Transfer To Inc..........D...... 305 393-8923
Hollywood *(G-5540)*

Verizon Data Services LLC..........B...... 813 978-4180
Temple Terrace *(G-18648)*

Wireless Lifestyle LLC..........E...... 954 538-0101
Pembroke Pines *(G-14204)*

Wireless Partners LLC..........E...... 614 777-9410
Sarasota *(G-16367)*

Wireless Partners LLC..........E...... 863 644-3388
Mulberry *(G-10984)*

4813 Telephone Communications, Except Radio

230 Third Avenue..........D...... 781 839-2800
Jacksonville *(G-5712)*

4g Antenna Shop Inc..........E...... 850 449-8888
Vero Beach *(G-18827)*

▼ Acceller Inc..........E...... 786 837-6819
Vero Beach *(G-18828)*

▲ Airespring Inc..........D...... 818 786-8990
Clearwater *(G-1516)*

America Online Latin Amer Inc..........E...... 954 689-3000
Fort Lauderdale *(G-3598)*

Amtec LLC..........E...... 561 999-9181
Boca Raton *(G-420)*

Anew Broadband Inc..........E...... 305 392-1649
Coral Gables *(G-2032)*

Arise Virtual Solutions Inc..........A...... 954 392-2600
Miramar *(G-10839)*

Blackstone America Inc..........C...... 305 639-9590
Miami *(G-9260)*

Brck Inc..........D...... 678 557-6266
Orlando *(G-12200)*

BTS Group Inc..........E...... 305 358-5850
Miami *(G-9292)*

Businessmallcom Inc..........E...... 727 409-2302
Clearwater *(G-1554)*

Cable Wrless Cmmunications LLC..........C...... 305 424-9547
Miami *(G-9302)*

Caprock Communications Corp..........E...... 305 627-6001
Miami *(G-9311)*

Cima Telecom Inc..........E...... 305 261-7778
Coral Gables *(G-2068)*

Cogeco US (miami) LLC..........C...... 305 861-8069
North Bay Village *(G-11467)*

Cogent Cmmunications Group Inc..........E...... 202 295-4200
Boca Raton *(G-520)*

Cogent Cmmunications Group Inc..........C...... 786 295-8177
Miami *(G-9385)*

Coleman Technologies Inc..........E...... 407 481-8600
Orlando *(G-12343)*

Columbus Networks Usa Inc..........E...... 786 274-7400
North Miami Beach *(G-11520)*

Comtech Mobile Datacom LLC..........E...... 240 686-3300
Orlando *(G-12356)*

Consult Pr Inc..........E...... 561 444-7265
West Palm Beach *(G-19106)*

Core Hosting Corporation..........E...... 833 224-2673
Tampa *(G-17520)*

Cyxtera Data Centers Inc..........A...... 305 537-9500
Coral Gables *(G-2084)*

Datalot Inc..........E...... 855 328-2568
Delray Beach *(G-2938)*

Despegarcom Usa Inc..........E...... 877 893-3988
Miami *(G-9474)*

Devstreet Inc..........E...... 954 880-8965
Plantation *(G-14628)*

Dsl Internet Corporation..........D...... 305 779-7777
Coral Gables *(G-2096)*

Embarq Mid-Atlantic MGT Svcs..........D...... 407 933-0360
Kissimmee *(G-7299)*

Embarq Mid-Atlantic MGT Svcs..........D...... 239 590-0440
Fort Myers *(G-4357)*

Equinix Inc..........E...... 650 598-6204
Tampa *(G-17637)*

Flexential Corp..........E...... 904 279-1777
Jacksonville *(G-6184)*

Flexential Corp..........E...... 954 736-2700
Fort Lauderdale *(G-3793)*

Florida Advantone Inc..........E...... 954 671-6500
Plantation *(G-14642)*

Florida Embarq Inc..........E...... 239 336-2142
Naples *(G-11117)*

Florida Embarq Inc..........D...... 407 889-6448
Winter Park *(G-19724)*

Florida Embarq Inc..........D...... 239 772-9100
Cape Coral *(G-1394)*

Florida Keys Lobster House..........E...... 305 743-5516
Marathon *(G-8619)*

Fort Pierce Utilities Auth..........C...... 772 466-1600
Fort Pierce *(G-4703)*

Friendfinder Networks Inc..........D...... 408 745-5400
Delray Beach *(G-2951)*

Frontier Florida LLC..........B...... 941 953-4760
Sarasota *(G-16172)*

Frontier Florida LLC..........B...... 727 443-9528
Seminole *(G-16448)*

Frontier Florida LLC..........B...... 863 284-0532
Lakeland *(G-7872)*

Frontier Florida LLC..........A...... 813 626-8545
Tampa *(G-17718)*

Frontier Florida LLC..........B...... 727 443-9237
Clearwater *(G-1650)*

Full Spectrum Telecom Inc..........C...... 727 532-2500
Clearwater *(G-1652)*

Globenet Cbos Sbmrnos Amer Inc..........E...... 561 314-0500
Fort Lauderdale *(G-3822)*

GP Mobile LLC..........C...... 941 254-6400
Bradenton *(G-1114)*

GP Mobile LLC..........C...... 727 350-2200
Saint Petersburg *(G-15692)*

Groupware International Inc..........E...... 407 522-9400
Orlando *(G-12608)*

Grupo Ngn Inc..........C...... 954 800-8586
Coral Springs *(G-2257)*

Hostdimecom Inc..........D...... 407 467-2053
Orlando *(G-12663)*

Hostgatorcom LLC..........C...... 713 574-5287
Jacksonville *(G-6300)*

Hotwire Communications LLC..........D...... 800 355-5668
Orlando *(G-12666)*

Iap World Services Inc..........E...... 321 784-7100
Cape Canaveral *(G-1367)*

Ifx Cmmunications Ventures Inc..........D...... 305 512-1100
Hollywood *(G-5459)*

Incomm Agent Solutions Inc..........C...... 305 381-7729
North Miami Beach *(G-11497)*

Innerhost Inc..........E...... 305 717-6600
Doral *(G-3240)*

Intellicall Operator Svcs Inc..........C...... 904 273-2440
Ponte Vedra Beach *(G-14985)*

Intermedia Communications Inc..........D...... 321 263-0451
Maitland *(G-8544)*

Intermedia Communications Inc..........D...... 954 745-2800
Fort Lauderdale *(G-3897)*

Launch That LLC..........E...... 407 965-5755
Orlando *(G-12754)*

Leadrev Holding LLC..........E...... 866 902-5323
Gulf Breeze *(G-5120)*

Lhs Investments Inc..........E...... 904 448-6901
Jacksonville *(G-6431)*

Mastec North America Inc..........E...... 407 265-2398
Longwood *(G-8380)*

Maxihost LLC..........E...... 712 481-2400
Miami *(G-9910)*

MCI Communications Svcs LLC..........D...... 850 997-0204
Monticello *(G-10934)*

MCI Communications Svcs LLC..........D...... 239 275-6719
Fort Myers *(G-4508)*

Mediacom Southeast LLC..........A...... 850 934-7700
Gulf Breeze *(G-5127)*

Millicom Intl Svcs LLC..........D...... 305 445-4100
Coral Gables *(G-2150)*

Mobile Store Operators LLC..........E...... 954 722-7974
North Lauderdale *(G-11481)*

Neoris Usa Inc..........E...... 305 728-6000
Miami *(G-10038)*

Netdirective Technologies Inc..........D...... 321 757-8909
Melbourne *(G-8948)*

Network Tallahassee Inc..........E...... 850 671-4007
Tallahassee *(G-17053)*

Network Telephone LLC..........B...... 850 432-4855
Pensacola *(G-14382)*

North American Telecom Corp..........D...... 954 449-8000
Fort Lauderdale *(G-4001)*

Now Communications Inc..........C...... 888 612-4226
Orlando *(G-12920)*

Omalas Inc..........E...... 305 248-3777
Homestead *(G-5593)*

Orlando Telephone Company Inc..........E...... 407 996-8900
Orlando *(G-12986)*

Partsbase Inc..........C...... 561 953-0700
Boca Raton *(G-745)*

Pe-Nexus LLC..........B...... 786 837-0866
Miami *(G-10106)*

Pnv Inc..........B...... 954 324-3900
Coral Springs *(G-2278)*

Qwest Corporation..........E...... 813 354-8122
Tampa *(G-18193)*

Qxc Communications Inc..........E...... 561 708-1500
Boca Raton *(G-762)*

Registercom Inc..........C...... 877 454-5213
Jacksonville *(G-6651)*

Retail Ecommerce Ventures LLC..........C...... 650 328-0100
Miami Beach *(G-10647)*

Round Room LLC..........E...... 850 926-8255
Crawfordville *(G-2304)*

Siesta Telecom Inc..........C...... 941 342-1712
Sarasota *(G-16318)*

Southeastern Services Inc..........D...... 904 653-4727
Macclenny *(G-8479)*

Southerntier Telecom Inc..........E...... 330 550-2733
Cape Coral *(G-1425)*

Sprint Communications Co LP..........C...... 954 385-3770
Davie *(G-2521)*

Star2star Holdings LLC..........B...... 941 234-0001
Sarasota *(G-16057)*

Studio98 LLC..........E...... 727 888-1211
Clearwater *(G-1799)*

Supra Telecom & Info Systems..........D...... 786 455-4200
Miramar *(G-10904)*

Targetsolutions Learning LLC..........D...... 972 309-4000
Tampa *(G-18407)*

Telefnica Globl Sltons USA Inc..........B...... 305 925-5300
Miami *(G-10371)*

Telefonica USA..........D...... 305 925-5300
Miami *(G-10373)*

Telxius Cable Usa Inc..........E...... 305 925-5298
Miami *(G-10375)*

▲ Terremark Worldwide Inc..........D...... 305 961-3200
Miami *(G-10380)*

Todo1 Services Inc..........E...... 786 331-0001
Medley *(G-8790)*

Trace Systems Inc..........C...... 727 457-4395
Tampa *(G-18431)*

◆ Tracfone Wireless Inc..........C...... 305 715-6500
Medley *(G-8791)*

Transworld Network LLC..........D...... 813 891-4700
Oldsmar *(G-11931)*

Ultimate Connection The Inc ....D...... 941 206-7800
Port Charlotte *(G-15066)*
United States Agency ....C...... 305 437-7001
Miami *(G-10441)*
Verizon Business Global LLC ....E...... 407 318-7377
Orlando *(G-13372)*
Verizon Business Global LLC ....E...... 904 358-6497
Jacksonville *(G-6905)*
Verizon Business Global LLC ....E...... 305 460-2118
Doral *(G-3353)*
Verizon Business Global LLC ....E...... 407 244-3001
Orlando *(G-13373)*
Verizon New England Inc ....B...... 813 978-7629
Lutz *(G-8465)*
Verizon New York Inc ....C...... 954 917-1109
Pompano Beach *(G-14938)*
Verizon New York Inc ....A...... 813 664-2660
Tampa *(G-18503)*
Verizon Pennsylvania LLC ....B...... 407 926-0065
Orlando *(G-13374)*
Verizon Washington DC Inc ....E...... 786 662-6028
Miami *(G-10466)*
Windstream Communications LLC ....C...... 904 731-3973
Jacksonville *(G-6936)*
Windstream Communications LLC ....C...... 407 581-6359
Maitland *(G-8601)*
Windstream Florida LLC ....D...... 386 364-2400
Live Oak *(G-8321)*
Windstream Nuvox LLC ....E...... 407 472-1700
Orlando *(G-13437)*
Working Mother Media Inc ....D...... 212 351-6400
Winter Park *(G-19793)*
Xacti LLC ....D...... 561 948-6425
Boca Raton *(G-879)*
Xponet Corporation ....E...... 703 629-6599
Orlando *(G-13467)*
Yupi Internet Inc ....C...... 305 604-0366
Miami Beach *(G-10675)*

4822 Telegraph & Other Message Communications

Full Spectrum Telecom Inc ....C...... 727 532-2500
Clearwater *(G-1652)*
◆ **Globe Wireless LLC** ....D...... 321 309-1300
Merritt Island *(G-9029)*
Intermex Wire Transfer LLC ....C...... 305 671-8000
Miami *(G-9762)*
Pnv Inc ....B...... 954 324-3900
Coral Springs *(G-2278)*
Swn Communications Inc ....D...... 866 939-0911
Ormond Beach *(G-13527)*
▲ **Vigo Remittance Corp** ....C...... 954 625-6878
Fort Lauderdale *(G-4213)*

4832 Radio Broadcasting Stations

Abe Entercom Holdings LLC ....B...... 305 521-5100
Miami *(G-9068)*
Beasley Broadcast Group Inc ....E...... 561 392-8164
Boca Raton *(G-446)*
Beasley Broadcast Group Inc ....C...... 239 263-5000
Naples *(G-11029)*
Beasley Broadcasting MGT Corp ....D...... 239 495-2100
Estero *(G-3444)*
▲ **Beasley FM Acquisition Corp** ....E...... 305 654-1770
Miami *(G-9236)*
Beasley Radio Inc ....E...... 239 263-5000
Naples *(G-11030)*
Caracol Broadcasting Inc ....C...... 305 285-1260
Coral Gables *(G-2062)*
Chesapeake-Portsmouth ....E...... 904 470-4615
Jacksonville *(G-5941)*
City of Lakeland ....B...... 863 834-8123
Lakeland *(G-7836)*
Community Broadcasters LLC ....E...... 850 654-1000
Fort Walton Beach *(G-4759)*
Community Communications Inc ....E...... 407 273-2300
Orlando *(G-12351)*
Coral Rdge Mnistries Media Inc ....E...... 954 977-9661
Fort Lauderdale *(G-3717)*
Cox Radio Inc ....E...... 407 295-5858
Orlando *(G-12381)*
Cox Radio Inc ....E...... 727 579-2000
Saint Petersburg *(G-15647)*
Cox Radio Inc ....E...... 904 245-8500
Jacksonville *(G-6007)*
Cox Radio Inc ....E...... 954 584-7117
Hollywood *(G-5423)*
Diocese St Petersburg Inc ....E...... 813 289-8040
Tampa *(G-17592)*

Dominion Video Satellite Inc ....D...... 239 963-3200
Naples *(G-11097)*
Entercom Media Corp ....E...... 561 616-4600
West Palm Beach *(G-19134)*
Fort Myers Broadcasting Co ....C...... 239 334-1131
Fort Myers *(G-4399)*
Infinity Brdcstg Corp of Fla ....E...... 727 579-1925
Saint Petersburg *(G-15720)*
Miami-Dade Cnty Pub Schols-158 ......E...... 305 995-1717
Miami *(G-9993)*
New Life Christian Fellowship ....C...... 904 223-5270
Jacksonville *(G-6539)*
Office of Cuba Broadcasting ....C...... 305 437-7001
Miami *(G-10064)*
Pamal Broadcasting Ltd ....E...... 850 478-6011
Pensacola *(G-14397)*
Renda Broadcasting Corporation ......E...... 904 721-3696
Jacksonville *(G-6656)*
Sirius XM Radio Inc ....C...... 954 571-4300
Deerfield Beach *(G-2798)*
Spanish Broadcasting Sys Inc ....D...... 305 441-6901
Miami *(G-10312)*
St Johns Golf Community ....E...... 904 940-3200
Saint Augustine *(G-15502)*
Universal Media Enterprises ....E...... 561 848-0811
West Palm Beach *(G-19403)*
Univision Radio Florida LLC ....E...... 305 447-1140
Doral *(G-3347)*
Wjct Inc ....D...... 904 353-7770
Jacksonville *(G-6938)*
Wsua Broadcasting Corporation ....D...... 305 285-1260
Miami *(G-10517)*
Wusf Pubhic Broadcasting Admin ....E...... 813 905-6900
Tampa *(G-18569)*

4833 Television Broadcasting Stations

◆ **AMC Networks Latin America LLC** ....E...... 305 445-4350
Coral Gables *(G-2029)*
America-Cv Network LLC ....B...... 305 592-4141
Hialeah Gardens *(G-5338)*
BBC Worldwide Ltd ....D...... 305 461-6999
Coral Gables *(G-2048)*
Blab Network Inc ....E...... 850 432-8982
Pensacola *(G-14237)*
CBS Broadcasting Inc ....D...... 850 474-4011
Pensacola *(G-14251)*
CBS Broadcasting Inc ....D...... 305 591-4444
Miami *(G-9338)*
CBS Operations Inc ....D...... 727 576-4444
Saint Petersburg *(G-15618)*
Community Communications Inc ....E...... 407 273-2300
Orlando *(G-12351)*
Coral Rdge Mnistries Media Inc ....E...... 954 977-9661
Fort Lauderdale *(G-3717)*
Diamond Sports Net Florida LLC ....C...... 954 375-3634
Fort Lauderdale *(G-3760)*
Diversified Communications ....E...... 352 377-2020
Gainesville *(G-4876)*
Dominion Video Satellite Inc ....D...... 239 963-3200
Naples *(G-11097)*
Espn Productions Inc ....B...... 704 973-5067
Saint Petersburg *(G-15663)*
EW Scripps Company ....D...... 239 574-3636
Cape Coral *(G-1390)*
First Coast News ....E...... 904 633-8862
Jacksonville *(G-6170)*
Florida W Cast Pub Brdcstg Inc ....E...... 813 254-9338
Tampa *(G-17700)*
Fort Myers Broadcasting Co ....C...... 239 334-1131
Fort Myers *(G-4399)*
Fox Television Stations LLC ....C...... 407 644-3535
Lake Mary *(G-7594)*
Freedom Broadcasting Fla Inc ....B...... 561 844-1212
West Palm Beach *(G-19154)*
Gol Tv Inc ....D...... 305 861-2501
Miami *(G-9645)*
Golf Channel Inc ....B...... 407 355-4653
Orlando *(G-12580)*
Graham Media Group Florida Inc ....C...... 904 399-4000
Jacksonville *(G-6239)*
Graham Media Group Orlando Inc ....C...... 407 291-6000
Orlando *(G-12586)*
Gray Media Group Inc ....E...... 850 234-7777
Panama City *(G-14019)*
Gray Media Group Inc ....D...... 850 893-6666
Tallahassee *(G-16992)*
HBO Ole Partners ....C...... 954 514-5000
Sunrise *(G-16783)*
Hearst Properties Inc ....D...... 407 645-2222
Winter Park *(G-19730)*

Ion Media Networks Inc ....D...... 561 659-4122
West Palm Beach *(G-19207)*
Miami-Dade Cnty Pub Schls-158 ....E...... 305 995-1717
Miami *(G-9993)*
Mtv Networks Latin America Inc ....C...... 305 534-9936
Miami Beach *(G-10632)*
Nbcuniversal LLC ....E...... 407 350-9622
Orlando *(G-12901)*
Newsmax Broadcasting LLC ....C...... 561 686-1165
Boca Raton *(G-717)*
▲ **Newsmax Media Inc** ....C...... 561 686-1165
Boca Raton *(G-718)*
Sinclair Broadcast Group Inc ....E...... 561 844-1212
Mangonia Park *(G-8611)*
Sinclair Media II Inc ....C...... 850 456-3333
Pensacola *(G-14435)*
South Florida Pbs Inc ....E...... 305 949-8321
Boynton Beach *(G-1038)*
Southern Brdcast Corp Sarasota ....D...... 941 923-6397
Sarasota *(G-16323)*
Spanish Broadcasting Sys Inc ....D...... 305 441-6901
Miami *(G-10312)*
▲ **Sunbeam Television Corporation** ....C...... 305 751-6692
North Bay Village *(G-11470)*
Tegna Inc ....D...... 703 854-6000
Jacksonville *(G-6845)*
Telefutura Corp ....D...... 305 421-1900
Doral *(G-3332)*
Telemndo Cmmncations Group Inc ......E...... 813 319-4949
Tampa *(G-18414)*
Telemndo Cmmncations Group Inc ......D...... 305 882-8200
Hialeah *(G-5329)*
Telemndo Cmmncations Group Inc ......D...... 407 888-2288
Orlando *(G-13279)*
Telemundo Network Group LLC ....D...... 305 882-8709
Hialeah *(G-5330)*
Telemundo Productions Inc ....D...... 305 884-8200
Hialeah *(G-5331)*
Telemundo Studios Miami LLC ....D...... 305 774-0033
Miami *(G-10374)*
United States Agency ....C...... 305 437-7001
Miami *(G-10441)*
Univision ABC News Network LLC ....E...... 305 894-1483
Doral *(G-3342)*
Univision Holdings Inc ....A...... 305 592-8913
Doral *(G-3343)*
Univision Networks Studios Inc ....C...... 305 471-3900
Doral *(G-3344)*
Univision Productions ....A...... 212 455-5200
Doral *(G-3345)*
Univision Radio Inc ....E...... 305 500-9844
Doral *(G-3346)*
Walt Disney Co ....E...... 407 938-1948
Orlando *(G-13393)*
Waterman Broadcasting Corp Fla ....D...... 239 939-2020
Fort Myers *(G-4646)*
Wfts ....C...... 813 354-2800
Tampa *(G-18549)*
Wfts ....D...... 561 655-5455
West Palm Beach *(G-19423)*
Wftv Inc ....C...... 407 841-9000
Orlando *(G-13427)*
Wjct Inc ....D...... 904 353-7770
Jacksonville *(G-6938)*
Wplg Inc ....D...... 954 364-2500
Pembroke Park *(G-14127)*
Wtwc Inc ....D...... 850 893-4140
Tallahassee *(G-17179)*
Wxel Public Broadcasting Corp ....E...... 561 737-8000
Boynton Beach *(G-1044)*
Wzvn TV ABC 7 ....C...... 239 939-2020
Fort Myers *(G-4663)*

4841 Cable & Other Pay TV Svcs

Blue Stream Communications LLC ....C...... 954 752-7244
Coral Springs *(G-2232)*
Bright House Networks LLC ....E...... 352 465-3031
Citrus Springs *(G-1501)*
Broadstar Communications LLC ....D...... 561 472-5022
West Palm Beach *(G-19065)*
Brothers Mdia Group Hldngs LLC ....C...... 904 280-2673
Jacksonville *(G-5884)*
Cable TV Installation Svc Inc ....E...... 813 630-5500
Apollo Beach *(G-132)*
Cogeco US (miami) LLC ....C...... 305 861-8069
North Bay Village *(G-11467)*
Cogeco US Finance LLC ....C...... 305 861-8069
North Bay Village *(G-11468)*
Comcast of Florida ....D...... 844 386-6796
Pompano Beach *(G-14778)*

Cypress Communications Inc ....D 813 221-7500	Sidus Space Inc ....E 321 613-5620	Florida Power & Light Company ....D 305 770-7900
Tampa *(G-17562)*	Merritt Island *(G-9044)*	Miami Lakes *(G-10730)*
Digital Reception Services Inc..........D 813 623-2999	Spectrio LLC ....E 800 584-4653	Florida Power & Light Company ....D 561 479-4553
Tampa *(G-17591)*	Tampa *(G-18319)*	Boca Raton *(G-586)*
Florida LLC Integrated Systems..........E 813 925-1007	Sr Technologies Inc ....C 954 797-7850	Florida Power & Light Company ....D 239 262-1322
Oldsmar *(G-11903)*	Sunrise *(G-16830)*	Naples *(G-11119)*
Futuretv LLC ....D 718 536-9017	Sun-Sentinel Company LLC ....E 305 810-5000	Florida Power & Light Company ....C 954 321-2018
Miami *(G-9613)*	Miami *(G-10340)*	Plantation *(G-14644)*
HBO Latin America Prod Svcs Lc ....E 954 217-5300	Swn Communications Inc ....D 866 939-0911	Florida Power & Light Company ....D 561 575-6314
Sunrise *(G-16782)*	Ormond Beach *(G-13527)*	Jupiter *(G-7072)*
HBO Ole Partners ....D 305 648-8100	Synect LLC ....E 425 497-9688	Florida Power & Light Company ....C 561 301-8698
Coral Gables *(G-2120)*	Orlando *(G-13261)*	West Palm Beach *(G-19149)*
Hemisphere Media Group Inc ....D 305 421-6364	Tower Cloud Inc ....E 727 471-5600	Florida Power & Light Company ....C 772 468-4111
Coral Gables *(G-2123)*	Saint Petersburg *(G-15877)*	Jensen Beach *(G-7015)*
Lamberts Cable Splicing Co LLC ....D 813 659-5270	Truenet Communications Corp ....D 904 777-9052	Florida Power & Light Company ....D 904 824-7665
Plant City *(G-14567)*	Jacksonville *(G-6876)*	Saint Augustine *(G-15442)*
Mediacom LLC ....E 850 203-1703	US Metropolitan Telecom LLC ....D 239 244-0242	Florida Power & Light Company ....D 850 244-4741
Gulf Breeze *(G-5126)*	Bonita Springs *(G-947)*	Fort Walton Beach *(G-4770)*
Mediacom Southeast LLC..........A 850 934-7700	Wfdc Univision Communicat ....E 202 237-2744	Florida Power & Light Company ....E 850 593-6421
Gulf Breeze *(G-5127)*	Doral *(G-3357)*	Sneads *(G-16474)*
Metrocom Cable Inc ....D 954 491-1399	Wind Talker Innovations Inc ....D 253 883-3615	Florida Power & Light Company ....D 954 442-6300
Oakland Park *(G-11604)*	Lakeland *(G-8006)*	Hollywood *(G-5438)*
Mtv Networks Latin America Inc..........C 305 534-9936		Florida Power & Light Company ....D 305 599-4000
Miami Beach *(G-10632)*		Miami *(G-9581)*
▲ Newsmax Media Inc ....C 561 686-1165	**49 ELECTRIC, GAS, AND SANITARY**	Florida Power & Light Company ....D 386 586-6410
Boca Raton *(G-718)*	**SERVICES**	Palm Coast *(G-13823)*
Orlando Telephone Company Inc..........E 407 996-8900		Florida Power & Light Company ....D 561 742-2000
Orlando *(G-12986)*	*4911 Electric Svcs*	Boynton Beach *(G-991)*
Pcg Securities LLC ....E 978 902-0352	A & G Electrical Tech Inc ....E 352 588-0400	Florida Power & Light Company ....E 561 994-8227
Wesley Chapel *(G-19005)*	San Antonio *(G-15907)*	Boca Raton *(G-587)*
Pnv Inc ....B 954 324-3900	Atlantic City Electric Company ....E 863 425-5411	Florida Power & Light Company ....D 561 616-1617
Coral Springs *(G-2278)*	Mulberry *(G-10971)*	West Palm Beach *(G-19150)*
Saveologycom LLC..........D 954 657-9614	C and C Power Line Inc ....C 904 751-6020	Florida Power & Light Company ....D 386 329-5130
Margate *(G-8665)*	Jacksonville *(G-5889)*	Palatka *(G-13587)*
Spectrum MGT Holdg Co LLC ....D 239 424-9438	Choctawhatchee Elc Coop Inc ....C 850 892-2111	Florida Power & Light Company ....C 239 693-4206
Cape Coral *(G-1426)*	Defuniak Springs *(G-2827)*	Fort Myers *(G-4385)*
Time Warner Cable Entps LLC ....E 407 295-9119	City of Gainesville ....C 352 334-2660	Florida Power & Light Company ....E 386 252-1541
Orlando *(G-13288)*	Gainesville *(G-4860)*	Daytona Beach *(G-2597)*
Wideopenwest Networks LLC..........D 727 239-0211	City of Jacksonville ....C 904 665-6000	Florida Power & Light Company ....D 407 694-3143
Pinellas Park *(G-14539)*	Jacksonville *(G-5961)*	Juno Beach *(G-7032)*
	City of Jacksonville Beach ....E 904 247-6281	Florida Power & Light Company ....D 561 904-3627
4899 Communication Svcs, NEC	Jacksonville *(G-5962)*	Jupiter *(G-7073)*
	City of Lakeland ....C 863 834-6600	Florida Power & Light Company ....B 561 691-7171
AMI Paper Inc ....A 561 997-7733	Lakeland *(G-7834)*	Miami *(G-9582)*
Boca Raton *(G-418)*	City of Lakeland ....C 863 834-6300	Florida Power & Light Company ....D 772 337-7081
Assoction Pblc-Sfty-Cmmnctons..........E 386 322-2500	Lakeland *(G-7833)*	Port Saint Lucie *(G-15135)*
Daytona Beach *(G-2547)*	City of Ocala ....D 352 629-2489	Florida Power & Light Company ....D 941 628-3319
Beacon LLC ....D 800 627-1265	Ocala *(G-11662)*	North Port *(G-11570)*
Pompano Beach *(G-14753)*	City of Tallahassee ....D 850 891-5100	Florida Power & Light Company ....B 941 639-1106
Cardworks Servicing LLC ....C 321 275-7900	Tallahassee *(G-16917)*	Punta Gorda *(G-15203)*
Lake Mary *(G-7573)*	City of Tallahassee ....D 850 891-4968	Florida Power & Light Company ....D 850 265-2185
▼ Computer Sciences Raytheon ....A 321 494-5272	Tallahassee *(G-16919)*	Panama City *(G-14011)*
Patrick Afb *(G-14119)*	Clay Electric Cooperative Inc ....C 352 473-8000	Florida Power & Light Company ....C 941 776-5234
Digisat International Inc ....E 321 676-5250	Keystone Heights *(G-7258)*	Parrish *(G-14115)*
Melbourne *(G-8871)*	Clay Electric Cooperative Inc ....D 904 272-2456	Florida Power & Light Company ....D 850 872-3236
E Solutions Corporation ....B 813 301-2600	Orange Park *(G-11981)*	Panama City *(G-14012)*
Tampa *(G-17609)*	Clay Electric Cooperative Inc ....E 386 328-1432	Florida Power & Light Company ....B 561 697-8000
Edd Helms Group Inc ....E 305 653-2520	Palatka *(G-13586)*	West Palm Beach *(G-19151)*
Sunrise *(G-16767)*	Clay Electric Cooperative Inc ....C 352 372-8543	Florida Power & Light Company ....C 386 575-5263
Etags Inc ....D 888 633-5332	Gainesville *(G-4865)*	Debary *(G-2703)*
Fort Lauderdale *(G-3776)*	Clay Electric Cooperative Inc ....E 386 752-7447	Florida Power & Light Company ....E 863 444-8463
Figgers Health ....D 800 223-5435	Lake City *(G-7520)*	Arcadia *(G-230)*
Lauderhill *(G-8196)*	Cogentrix Energy Power MGT LLC ....D 904 751-4000	Florida Power & Light Company ....D 850 429-2600
Fremantlemedia Latin Amer Inc ....D 305 267-0821	Jacksonville *(G-5975)*	Pensacola *(G-14310)*
Miami *(G-9610)*	Consumer Energy Solutions Inc ....D 727 724-5811	Florida Power & Light Company ....D 305 430-1103
Geoeye LLC ....C 813 254-6900	Clearwater *(G-1586)*	Miami Lakes *(G-10731)*
Tampa *(G-17732)*	▲ Covanta Dade Rnwable Enrgy LLC ....C 305 593-7000	Florida Power & Light Company ....D 305 442-8770
Gtp Infrastructure Issuer III..........C 561 886-5854	Doral *(G-3168)*	Miami *(G-9583)*
Boca Raton *(G-612)*	Covanta Energy LLC ....E 727 919-3339	Florida Power & Light Company ....D 850 478-5900
High Wire Networks Inc ....B 407 512-9102	Hernando *(G-5205)*	Pensacola *(G-14311)*
Boca Raton *(G-628)*	Duke Energy Florida LLC ....D 352 748-8740	Florida Power & Light Company ....D 954 797-5000
Impsat Fiber Networks LLC ....E 954 779-7171	Wildwood *(G-19494)*	Lauderhill *(G-8197)*
Wilton Manors *(G-19526)*	E S I Geothermal Inc ....D 561 691-7171	Florida Power & Light Company ....C 305 442-0388
Informa Marine Holdings Inc ....C 800 940-7642	Juno Beach *(G-7029)*	Homestead *(G-5574)*
Fort Lauderdale *(G-3892)*	Electrical Alliance Corp ....E 305 280-9150	Florida Power & Light Company ....D 305 246-1300
▲ Intelsat Corporation ....A 305 445-5536	Miami *(G-9513)*	Homestead *(G-5575)*
Coral Gables *(G-2131)*	Energy Professionals LLC ....D 877 343-9044	Florida Power & Light Company ....C 305 442-8770
Kbr Wyle Services LLC ....D 904 696-5209	Clearwater *(G-1624)*	Miami *(G-9584)*
Jacksonville *(G-6397)*	Entegra Power Group LLC ....E 813 301-4900	Florida Power & Light Company ....D 239 415-1310
Lhs Investments Inc ....E 904 448-6901	Tampa *(G-17634)*	Fort Myers *(G-4386)*
Jacksonville *(G-6431)*	Escambia River Elc Coop Inc ....D 850 675-4521	Florida Power & Light Company ....C 561 881-3412
Nexgen Agency Inc ....D 954 708-2896	Jay *(G-7011)*	Riviera Beach *(G-15295)*
Deerfield Beach *(G-2776)*	▲ Florida Crystals Corporation ....D 561 655-6303	Florida Power & Light Company ....D 772 595-1227
Nextnet Communications LLC..........D 786 544-1100	West Palm Beach *(G-19144)*	Fort Pierce *(G-4702)*
Miami *(G-10046)*	Florida Crystals Corporation ....C 561 515-8080	Florida Power & Light Company ....D 386 239-5924
Richland Twers - Nashville LLC ....E 813 286-4140	West Palm Beach *(G-19146)*	Daytona Beach *(G-2598)*
Tampa *(G-18225)*	◆ Florida Keys Elc Coop Assn Inc ....D 305 852-2431	Florida Power & Light Company ....D 239 332-9137
Satcom Direct Inc ....C 321 777-3000	Tavernier *(G-18624)*	Fort Myers *(G-4387)*
Melbourne *(G-8973)*	Florida Municipal Power Agency ....D 407 355-7767	Florida Power & Light Company ....D 321 690-5221
SBA Communications Corporation ....C 561 995-7670	Orlando *(G-12532)*	Cocoa *(G-1937)*
Boca Raton *(G-781)*		

Florida Power & Light Company ....D...... 772 597-1386
Indiantown *(G-5676)*

Florida Power & Light Company ....C...... 786 229-1216
Miami *(G-9585)*

Florida Power & Light Company ....E...... 386 329-4600
East Palatka *(G-3398)*

Florida Power & Light Company ....D...... 305 229-7857
Miami *(G-9586)*

Florida Power & Light Company ....C...... 772 223-4200
Palm City *(G-13790)*

Florida Power & Light Company ....E...... 772 597-7245
Indiantown *(G-5677)*

Florida Power & Light Company ....D...... 305 377-6135
Miami *(G-9587)*

Florida Power & Light Company ....C...... 386 763-6021
Ormond Beach *(G-13494)*

Florida Power & Light Company ....D...... 772 287-5400
Stuart *(G-16624)*

Florida Public Utilities Co ....E...... 352 447-2790
Fernandina Beach *(G-3527)*

Florida Public Utilities Co ....E...... 352 447-2790
West Palm Beach *(G-19152)*

Florida Public Utilities Co ....E...... 904 261-3663
Fernandina Beach *(G-3528)*

Florida Public Utilities Co ....E...... 850 526-0179
Marianna *(G-8675)*

Gainesville Regional Utilities ....B...... 352 334-3400
Gainesville *(G-4900)*

Glades Electric Coop Inc ....E...... 863 946-0061
Moore Haven *(G-10941)*

Iap World Services Inc ....E...... 321 784-7100
Cape Canaveral *(G-1367)*

Indiantown Cogen Fding Corp ....D...... 772 597-6500
Indiantown *(G-5678)*

Indiantown Cogeneration LP ....E...... 772 597-6500
Indiantown *(G-5679)*

Infinite Energy Holdings Inc ....C...... 352 240-4121
Gainesville *(G-4919)*

Jacksonville Electric Auth ....B...... 904 665-6460
Jacksonville *(G-6352)*

▲ Jacksonville Electric Auth ....A...... 904 665-6000
Jacksonville *(G-6353)*

Jacksonville Electric Auth ....D...... 904 665-6000
Jacksonville *(G-6354)*

Jacksonville Electric Auth ....C...... 904 665-7945
Jacksonville *(G-6355)*

Jacksonville Electric Auth ....E...... 904 665-6000
Jacksonville *(G-6356)*

Jacksonville Electric Auth ....D...... 904 665-8700
Jacksonville *(G-6357)*

Jacksonville Electric Auth ....E...... 904 665-6970
Jacksonville *(G-6358)*

Jacksonville Electric Auth ....D...... 904 696-1503
Jacksonville *(G-6359)*

Kissimmee Utility Authority ....C...... 407 933-7777
Kissimmee *(G-7340)*

Kissimmee Utility Authority ....D...... 407 933-7777
Kissimmee *(G-7341)*

Kissimmee Utility Authority ....D...... 407 933-7777
Intercession City *(G-5685)*

Kissimmee Utility Authority ....D...... 407 933-7777
Kissimmee *(G-7342)*

Lee County Electric Coop Inc ....B...... 800 599-2356
Fort Myers *(G-4472)*

Lee County Electric Coop Inc ....D...... 239 995-2121
Fort Myers *(G-4473)*

Mader Electric Inc ....E...... 941 351-5858
Bradenton *(G-1131)*

▲ Nextera Energy Marketing LLC ....C...... 561 691-7171
Juno Beach *(G-7036)*

▲ Nextera Energy Oper Svcs LLC ....B...... 561 691-7171
Juno Beach *(G-7037)*

◆ Nextera Energy Resources LLC ....D...... 561 691-7171
Juno Beach *(G-7038)*

▲ Nextera Enrgy Duane Arnold LLC .....A...... 561 691-7171
Juno Beach *(G-7039)*

Nextera Enrgy US Prtners Hldng ....D...... 561 691-7171
Juno Beach *(G-7040)*

NRG Florida LP ....D...... 407 891-2186
Saint Cloud *(G-15528)*

▲ Orlando Utilities Commission ....B...... 407 246-2121
Orlando *(G-12988)*

Orlando Utilities Commission ....B...... 407 423-9100
Orlando *(G-12989)*

Orlando Utilities Commission ....D...... 407 423-9100
Orlando *(G-12991)*

Peace River Electric Coop Inc ....D...... 800 282-3824
Wauchula *(G-18964)*

Polk Power Partners LP ....E...... 863 533-9073
Bartow *(G-332)*

Seminole Electric Coop Inc ....B...... 813 963-0994
Palatka *(G-13601)*

▲ Seminole Electric Coop Inc ....C...... 813 963-0994
Tampa *(G-18264)*

Service Electric Usa LLC ....D...... 850 602-4226
Pensacola *(G-14433)*

Sumter Electric Coop Inc ....C...... 352 793-3801
Sumterville *(G-16697)*

Sumter Electric Coop Inc ....E...... 352 602-4617
Eustis *(G-3501)*

Sumter Electric Coop Inc ....E...... 352 357-5600
Eustis *(G-3502)*

Sumter Electric Coop Inc ....D...... 352 793-3801
Ocala *(G-11783)*

Sumter Electric Coop Inc ....D...... 352 429-2195
Groveland *(G-5103)*

Talquin Electric Coop Inc ....E...... 850 627-7651
Quincy *(G-15234)*

Talquin Electric Coop Inc ....E...... 850 562-2115
Tallahassee *(G-17153)*

Tampa Electric Company ....D...... 813 382-3517
Riverview *(G-15273)*

◆ Tampa Electric Company ....B...... 813 228-1111
Tampa *(G-18375)*

Tampa Electric Company ....D...... 386 329-5406
Palatka *(G-13603)*

Tampa Electric Company ....D...... 904 739-1211
Jacksonville *(G-6833)*

Tampa Electric Company ....C...... 813 627-2808
Tampa *(G-18376)*

Tampa Electric Company ....C...... 352 754-1461
Brooksville *(G-1315)*

Tampa Electric Company ....C...... 813 241-9206
Tampa *(G-18377)*

Tampa Electric Company ....C...... 813 223-0800
Tampa *(G-18378)*

Tampa Electric Company ....D...... 305 262-7630
Miami *(G-10363)*

Tampa Electric Company ....C...... 813 630-6518
Tampa *(G-18379)*

Teco Coalbed Methane Fla Inc ....A...... 813 228-4111
Tampa *(G-18411)*

◆ Teco Energy Inc ....E...... 813 228-1111
Tampa *(G-18412)*

Tri-County Electric Coop ....E...... 850 973-2285
Madison *(G-8492)*

West Florida Elc Coop Assn Inc ....E...... 850 263-3231
Graceville *(G-5043)*

Withlacoochee River Elc Coop ....D...... 352 567-5133
Dade City *(G-2399)*

4922 Natural Gas Transmission

Aqua Utilities Florida Inc ....D...... 239 394-3880
Marco Island *(G-8626)*

Florida Public Utilities Co ....E...... 352 447-2790
Fernandina Beach *(G-3527)*

Pivotal Utility Holdings Inc ....C...... 800 993-7546
Doral *(G-3290)*

4923 Natural Gas Transmission & Distribution

Core-Mark Distributors Inc ....C...... 650 589-9445
Tampa *(G-17521)*

▲ Okaloosa Gas District ....C...... 850 729-4700
Valparaiso *(G-18746)*

4924 Natural Gas Distribution

▲ 2g Energy Inc ....E...... 904 579-3217
Saint Augustine *(G-15417)*

Atlantic Energy LLC ....E...... 800 917-9133
Deerfield Beach *(G-2713)*

Centerpint Enrgy Hston Elc LLC ....C...... 321 267-2155
Titusville *(G-18681)*

City of Leesburg ....E...... 352 728-9840
Leesburg *(G-8240)*

Fort Pierce Utilities Auth ....C...... 772 466-1600
Fort Pierce *(G-4703)*

Gainesville Regional Utilities ....B...... 352 334-3400
Gainesville *(G-4900)*

Infinite Energy Holdings Inc ....C...... 352 240-4121
Gainesville *(G-4919)*

Lake Apopka Natural Gas Dst ....E...... 407 656-2734
Winter Garden *(G-19578)*

▲ Okaloosa Gas District ....C...... 850 729-4700
Valparaiso *(G-18746)*

Peoples Gas ....A...... 727 824-0990
Tampa *(G-18137)*

Pivotal Utility Holdings Inc ....D...... 321 638-3426
Rockledge *(G-15360)*

Pivotal Utility Holdings Inc ....C...... 800 993-7546
Doral *(G-3290)*

Radiant Oil Co Inc ....D...... 305 634-2634
Miami *(G-10179)*

St Joe Natural Gas Co Inc ....E...... 850 229-8216
Port Saint Joe *(G-15119)*

Supreme Energy Inc ....D...... 973 678-1800
Sarasota *(G-16340)*

◆ Tampa Electric Company ....B...... 813 228-1111
Tampa *(G-18375)*

◆ Teco Energy Inc ....E...... 813 228-1111
Tampa *(G-18412)*

4925 Gas Production &/Or Distribution

Liberty Power Delaware LLC ....D...... 866 769-3799
Fort Lauderdale *(G-3939)*

4931 Electric & Other Svcs Combined

▲ 2g Energy Inc ....E...... 904 579-3217
Saint Augustine *(G-15417)*

City of Clewiston ....E...... 863 983-1454
Clewiston *(G-1899)*

City of Lakeland ....C...... 863 834-6300
Lakeland *(G-7833)*

▲ Covanta Palm Bch Rsrce Rcvery ....C...... 561 616-6216
West Palm Beach *(G-19111)*

Energy Authority Inc ....D...... 904 356-3900
Jacksonville *(G-6117)*

Fort Pierce Utilities Auth ....C...... 772 466-1600
Fort Pierce *(G-4703)*

Genplant On-Site Energy LLC ....D...... 904 907-7503
Green Cove Springs *(G-5055)*

Mastec North America Inc ....B...... 850 562-2135
Tallahassee *(G-17036)*

Orlando Utilities Commission ....B...... 407 423-9100
Orlando *(G-12989)*

Orlando Utilities Commission ....C...... 407 423-9100
Orlando *(G-12990)*

Orlando Utilities Commission ....D...... 407 423-9100
Orlando *(G-12991)*

▲ Orlando Utilities Commission ....B...... 407 246-2121
Orlando *(G-12988)*

4932 Gas & Other Svcs Combined

Energy Authority Inc ....D...... 904 356-3900
Jacksonville *(G-6117)*

4939 Combination Utilities, NEC

City of Boynton Beach ....D...... 561 742-6400
Boynton Beach *(G-974)*

Gainesville Regional Utilities ....B...... 352 334-3400
Gainesville *(G-4900)*

Gainesvlle Regional Utilities ....C...... 352 334-3400
Gainesville *(G-4905)*

Gainesvlle Regional Utilities ....C...... 352 334-3434
Gainesville *(G-4906)*

Jacksonville Electric Auth ....D...... 904 665-8700
Jacksonville *(G-6357)*

▲ Orlando Utilities Commission ....B...... 407 246-2121
Orlando *(G-12988)*

Reedy Creek Improvement Dst ....D...... 407 824-4913
Lake Buena Vista *(G-7471)*

4941 Water Sply

Aqua Utilities Florida Inc ....C...... 386 740-7174
Apopka *(G-154)*

Aqua Utilities Florida Inc ....D...... 239 394-3880
Marco Island *(G-8626)*

Bonita Springs Utilities Inc ....C...... 239 390-4817
Bonita Springs *(G-900)*

Broward Cnty Wtr Wstwater Svcs ....B...... 954 831-3250
Pompano Beach *(G-14759)*

City of Boca Raton ....D...... 561 338-7309
Boca Raton *(G-511)*

City of Boynton Beach ....D...... 561 742-6400
Boynton Beach *(G-974)*

City of Clearwater ....D...... 727 562-4538
Clearwater *(G-1568)*

City of Jacksonville Beach ....E...... 904 247-6281
Jacksonville *(G-5962)*

City of Palm Bay ....C...... 321 952-3471
Palm Bay *(G-13614)*

City of Plantation ....D...... 954 452-2544
Plantation *(G-14618)*

City of Port St Lucie ....C...... 772 873-6400
Port Saint Lucie *(G-15127)*

City of Tampa ....E...... 813 274-8121
Tampa *(G-17484)*

▲ Clay County Utilities Auth Inc ....C 904 272-5999
  Middleburg **(G-10795)**
County of Brevard ....E 321 633-2014
  Melbourne **(G-8858)**
County of Miami-Dade ....A 305 665-7477
  Miami **(G-9429)**
County of Pinellas ....C 727 582-2300
  Largo **(G-8089)**
Destin Water Users Inc ....D 850 837-6146
  Destin **(G-3059)**
Emerald Coast Utilities Auth ....C 850 458-1658
  Cantonment **(G-1337)**
Emerald Coast Utilities Auth ....B 850 476-5110
  Pensacola **(G-14288)**
Envirnmntal Prtection Fla Dept ....D 352 821-1489
  Umatilla **(G-18733)**
Florida Cmnty Svcs Corp Wlton ....D 850 231-5114
  Santa Rosa Beach **(G-16008)**
Florida Keys Aqueduct Auth ....D 305 296-2454
  Homestead **(G-5572)**
Florida Keys Aqueduct Auth ....D 305 296-2454
  Key West **(G-7203)**
Florida Keys Aqueduct Auth ....D 305 296-2454
  Key West **(G-7204)**
Fort Pierce Utilities Auth ....C 772 466-1600
  Fort Pierce **(G-4703)**
Gainesville Regional Utilities ....B 352 334-3400
  Gainesville **(G-4900)**
Hillsborough County Public Util ....D 813 272-5977
  Tampa **(G-17827)**
Holley-Navarre Water Systems ....D 850 939-2427
  Navarre **(G-11352)**
Jacksonville Electric Auth ....E 904 665-6970
  Jacksonville **(G-6358)**
Mountain Lake Corporation ....D 863 676-3494
  Lake Wales **(G-7694)**
Northwest Florida Wtr Mgt Dst ....D 850 539-5999
  Havana **(G-5197)**
Okeechobee Utility Authority ....E 863 763-9460
  Okeechobee **(G-11877)**
▲ Orlando Utilities Commission ....B 407 246-2121
  Orlando **(G-12988)**
Orlando Utilities Commission ....B 407 423-9100
  Orlando **(G-12989)**
Orlando Utilities Commission ....B 407 423-9100
  Orlando **(G-12991)**
Pace Water System Inc ....E 850 994-5129
  Milton **(G-10820)**
Peace Rver Mnsota Rgnal Wtr Su .....E 863 993-4565
  Arcadia **(G-233)**
Saint Lucie West Services Dst ....E 772 340-0220
  Port Saint Lucie **(G-15164)**
Seacoast Utility Authority ....C 561 627-2900
  Palm Beach Gardens **(G-13772)**
◆ South Fla Wtr MGT Dst Lsg Corp .....B 561 686-8800
  West Palm Beach **(G-19369)**
South Fla Wtr MGT Dst Lsg Corp ....D 863 983-1431
  Clewiston **(G-1910)**
South Fla Wtr MGT Dst Lsg Corp ....C 561 791-4100
  West Palm Beach **(G-19370)**
South Fla Wtr MGT Dst Lsg Corp ....C 561 753-2400
  West Palm Beach **(G-19371)**
South Fla Wtr MGT Dst Lsg Corp ....C 305 513-3420
  Doral **(G-3317)**
South Fla Wtr MGT Dst Lsg Corp ....E 407 858-6100
  Orlando **(G-13216)**
South Fla Wtr MGT Dst Lsg Corp ....D 863 462-5280
  Okeechobee **(G-11879)**
South Fla Wtr MGT Dst Lsg Corp ....E 239 338-2929
  Fort Myers **(G-4597)**
Southwest Florida Wtr Mgt Dst ....B 352 796-7211
  Brooksville **(G-1311)**
Southwest Florida Wtr Mgt Dst ....D 813 985-7481
  Tampa **(G-18312)**
Southwest Florida Wtr MGT Dst ....D 941 377-3722
  Sarasota **(G-16326)**
St Johns River Water MGT Dst ....D 386 329-4500
  Palatka **(G-13602)**
St Johns Water Management Dst ....D 904 730-6270
  Jacksonville **(G-6772)**
Suwannee River Water MGT Dst ....D 386 362-1001
  Live Oak **(G-8319)**
Tampa Bay Wtr A Rgnal Wtr Sup ....E 727 796-2355
  Clearwater **(G-1816)**
Tohopekaliga Water Authority ....C 407 944-5000
  Kissimmee **(G-7399)**

4952 Sewerage Systems

Aqua Utilities Florida Inc ....C 386 740-7174
  Apopka **(G-154)**

Aqua Utilities Florida Inc ....D 239 394-3880
  Marco Island **(G-8626)**
Bonita Springs Utilities Inc ....C 239 390-4817
  Bonita Springs **(G-900)**
City New Port Richey ....E 727 841-4568
  New Port Richey **(G-11370)**
City of Clearwater ....E 727 562-4538
  Clearwater **(G-1570)**
City of Hialeah ....D 305 556-3800
  Hialeah **(G-5241)**
City of Lakeland ....D 863 834-8277
  Lakeland **(G-7835)**
City of Saint Petersburg ....C 813 920-5252
  Odessa **(G-11835)**
City of Saint Petersburg ....D 727 893-7261
  Saint Petersburg **(G-15627)**
Destin Water Users Inc ....D 850 837-6146
  Destin **(G-3059)**
Emerald Coast Utilities Auth ....B 850 476-5110
  Pensacola **(G-14288)**
Florida Cmnty Svcs Corp Wlton ....D 850 231-5114
  Santa Rosa Beach **(G-16008)**
Lake Worth Drainage District ....D 561 737-3835
  Delray Beach **(G-2975)**
Pace Water System Inc ....E 850 994-5129
  Milton **(G-10820)**
Seacoast Utility Authority ....C 561 627-2900
  Palm Beach Gardens **(G-13772)**
▲ Tucker Paving Inc ....E 863 299-2262
  Winter Haven **(G-19668)**

4953 Refuse Systems

27 Recycling LLC ....E 305 637-2750
  Miami **(G-9055)**
▼ A1 Assets Inc ....D 407 339-7030
  Lake Mary **(G-7558)**
Aaction Recycling Corporation ....C 904 356-8869
  Jacksonville **(G-5722)**
Advan Disp Serv Soli Wast of P ....E 407 464-2264
  Apopka **(G-147)**
Advanced Disposal Services ....E 904 737-7900
  Ponte Vedra **(G-14945)**
Advanced Disposal Services Inc ....C 904 737-7900
  Ponte Vedra **(G-14946)**
Advanced Disposal Services Inc ....D 407 358-6481
  Lakeland **(G-7783)**
Advanced Disposal Svcs S LLC ....E 904 737-7900
  Ponte Vedra **(G-14947)**
Advanced Dspsal Svcs Bickfoot ....E 904 737-7900
  Ponte Vedra **(G-14948)**
Advanced Dspsal Svcs Blue Rdge .....E 904 737-7900
  Ponte Vedra **(G-14949)**
Advanced Dspsal Svcs Brmngham .....C 904 737-7900
  Ponte Vedra **(G-14950)**
Advanced Dspsal Svcs Crnbry Cr ....E 904 737-7900
  Ponte Vedra **(G-14951)**
Advanced Dspsal Svcs Cypress A .....E 904 737-7900
  Ponte Vedra **(G-14952)**
Advanced Dspsal Svcs Emrald Pk .....E 904 737-7900
  Ponte Vedra **(G-14953)**
Advanced Dspsal Svcs Evrgrn Ln .....E 904 737-7900
  Ponte Vedra **(G-14954)**
Advanced Dspsal Svcs Hsier Lnd .....E 904 737-7900
  Ponte Vedra **(G-14955)**
Advanced Dspsal Svcs Jcksnvlle ....C 904 783-7000
  Jacksonville **(G-5741)**
Advanced Dspsal Svcs Jcksnvlle ....C 904 695-0500
  Green Cove Springs **(G-5045)**
Advanced Dspsal Svcs Jcksnvlle ....C 904 827-1005
  Saint Augustine **(G-15419)**
Advanced Dspsal Svcs Mple Hl L .....E 904 737-7900
  Ponte Vedra **(G-14956)**
Advanced Dspsal Svcs Oak Rdge .....E 904 737-7900
  Ponte Vedra **(G-14957)**
Advanced Dspsal Svcs Rlling Hl ....E 904 737-7900
  Ponte Vedra **(G-14958)**
Advanced Dspsal Svcs Sttline L ....C 904 879-2301
  Callahan **(G-1329)**
Advanced Dspsal Svcs Wstn PA I .....E 904 737-7900
  Ponte Vedra **(G-14959)**
Alachua County ....D 352 374-5245
  Gainesville **(G-4832)**
◆ Amerigrow Rcyclng-Dlray Ltd PR .....D 561 499-8148
  Delray Beach **(G-2969)**
▲ Angelos Aggregate Mtls Ltd ....E 727 581-1544
  Lutz **(G-8429)**
Arbor Hills Landfill Inc ....E 904 737-7900
  Ponte Vedra **(G-14960)**
Bcr Environmental Corporation ....E 904 819-9170
  Jacksonville **(G-5847)**

Best-TEC Asb Abatement Inc ....E 904 695-9900
  Boynton Beach **(G-964)**
Bullbag Corporation ....E 203 996-7516
  Pompano Beach **(G-14762)**
Ces Synergies Inc ....C 813 783-1688
  Crystal Springs **(G-2356)**
Choice Environmental Svcs Inc ....D 305 653-2684
  Miami **(G-9366)**
Choice Environmental Svcs Inc ....E 954 797-7974
  Fort Lauderdale **(G-3691)**
Choice Environmental Svcs Inc ....E 954 582-9300
  Pompano Beach **(G-14772)**
City of Delray Beach ....E 561 243-7318
  Delray Beach **(G-2928)**
City of Gainesville ....D 352 393-6601
  Gainesville **(G-4862)**
City of Hialeah ....D 305 687-2625
  Hialeah **(G-5240)**
City of Jacksonville ....E 904 384-8028
  Jacksonville **(G-5957)**
City of St Cloud ....D 407 957-7267
  Saint Cloud **(G-15519)**
City of Tampa ....C 813 348-1111
  Tampa **(G-17481)**
◆ Cliff Berry Inc ....E 954 763-3390
  Fort Lauderdale **(G-3701)**
Coastal Waste & Recycl Fla Inc ....C 954 947-4000
  Pompano Beach **(G-14776)**
Coastal Wste Rcycl Bay Cnty In ....E 850 769-4304
  Panama City **(G-13985)**
Coastal Wste Rcycl Brward Cnty ....C 954 947-4000
  Pompano Beach **(G-14777)**
Coastal Wste Rcycl Cntl Fla LL ....D 407 905-9200
  Orlando **(G-12335)**
Commercial Metals Company ....E 407 293-6584
  Apopka **(G-168)**
County of Brevard ....D 321 633-1888
  Cocoa **(G-1932)**
County of Broward ....E 954 765-4202
  Fort Lauderdale **(G-3725)**
County of Walton ....E 850 892-8180
  Defuniak Springs **(G-2829)**
▲ Covanta Dade Rnwable Enrgy LLC ..C 305 593-7000
  Doral **(G-3168)**
Covanta Energy LLC ....E 727 919-3339
  Hernando **(G-5205)**
▲ Covanta Hillsborough Inc ....E 813 684-5688
  Tampa **(G-17542)**
▲ Covanta Palm Bch Rsrce Rcvery .....E 561 616-6216
  West Palm Beach **(G-19111)**
Crush Supply LLC ....E 386 320-0615
  Debary **(G-2700)**
D & S Pallets Inc ....D 727 540-0061
  Clearwater **(G-1600)**
Dade Recycling Center Inc ....E 305 826-0707
  Hialeah **(G-5252)**
East Bay Sanitation Inc ....D 813 265-0292
  Tampa **(G-17610)**
Ecologic Waste Management LLC .....C 561 624-4000
  Palm Beach Gardens **(G-13723)**
◆ Electronic Recycling Ctr Inc ....E 305 482-9100
  Miami **(G-9514)**
Empire Tire of Edgewater LLC ....E 407 250-5875
  Orlando **(G-12464)**
Envirocycle Inc ....D 954 792-8177
  Fort Lauderdale **(G-3774)**
FCR Florida Inc ....E 239 731-3700
  Fort Myers **(G-4369)**
Florida Refuse Services Inc ....E 863 421-9854
  Haines City **(G-5148)**
Garbage Grbbers Vlet Trash Inc ....E 512 815-8497
  Altamonte Springs **(G-52)**
Gel Corporation ....D 386 775-5385
  Orange City **(G-11965)**
◆ Global Investment Recovery Inc ....C 813 549-0864
  Tampa **(G-17737)**
Goodwill Cntl Southern Ind Inc ....E 850 877-6840
  Tallahassee **(G-16990)**
Greentree Landfill LLC ....E 914 421-4900
  Ponte Vedra **(G-14964)**
Hagan Holding Company ....E 727 327-8467
  Saint Petersburg **(G-15702)**
Harris Sanitation Inc ....C 321 409-6600
  Melbourne **(G-8899)**
Jones Road Landfill and Recycl ....E 904 483-2180
  Jacksonville **(G-6389)**
▲ JR Capital Corp ....C 954 543-9800
  Pompano Beach **(G-14835)**
Kbh Recycling LLC ....E 407 870-1688
  Kissimmee **(G-7336)**

▲ Lee Covanta Inc ....E...... 239 337-2200
Fort Myers *(G-4475)*

Lgl Recycling LLC ....E...... 561 582-6688
West Palm Beach *(G-19234)*

Liberty Tire Services LLC.............E...... 772 465-0477
Port Saint Lucie *(G-15145)*

Lighting Resources LLC ....D...... 352 509-3001
Ocala *(G-11712)*

Magnum Environmental Services ....D...... 954 785-2320
Pompano Beach *(G-14847)*

Marathon Garbage Service Inc ....E...... 305 743-5165
Marathon *(G-8623)*

Marpan Recycling LLC ....E...... 850 216-1006
Tallahassee *(G-17032)*

Metro Service Group Inc ....D...... 504 520-8331
Pensacola *(G-14364)*

▲ Miami Waste Paper Co Inc ....E...... 305 325-0860
Miami *(G-9985)*

Nates Sanitation Service Inc..........E...... 850 769-4304
Panama City *(G-14045)*

Omni Waste Osceola County LLC......C...... 407 891-3720
Saint Cloud *(G-15530)*

Orlando Waste Paper Co Inc...........D...... 407 299-1380
Orlando *(G-12992)*

OSteen Brothers Inc ....D...... 352 495-3238
Archer *(G-236)*

Pece of Mind Environmental............D...... 407 568-3456
Orlando *(G-13018)*

Perma-Fix of Florida Inc ....D...... 352 373-6066
Gainesville *(G-4976)*

◆ Recycling Revolution LLC ....E...... 561 488-1305
Boca Raton *(G-766)*

▲ Refuse Services Inc ....C...... 904 260-1592
Jacksonville *(G-6645)*

◆ Royce Corporation ....E...... 305 937-1099
Miami *(G-10224)*

Siljan Corp ....E...... 561 499-8148
Delray Beach *(G-3016)*

Solid Waste Auth Palm Bch Cnty ......E...... 561 697-2700
Delray Beach *(G-3017)*

Solid Waste Auth Palm Bch Cnty ......E...... 561 533-6021
Lantana *(G-8069)*

Solid Waste Auth Palm Bch Cnty ......E...... 561 687-1100
West Palm Beach *(G-19364)*

Solid Waste Auth Palm Bch Cnty ......C...... 561 640-4000
West Palm Beach *(G-19366)*

Solid Waste Auth Palm Bch Cnty ......E...... 561 640-4000
Belle Glade *(G-362)*

Solid Waste Auth Palm Bch Cnty ......E...... 561 625-9108
Jupiter *(G-7138)*

Solomon Construction Co Quincy ......E...... 850 575-1636
Tallahassee *(G-17101)*

Southland Environmental Svcs.........D...... 904 825-0991
Saint Augustine *(G-15495)*

Southland Environmental Svcs.........E...... 863 665-1489
Lakeland *(G-7974)*

Southland Environmental Svcs.........D...... 904 354-8107
Jacksonville *(G-6764)*

Southland Waste Systems Inc ....D...... 904 731-2456
Jacksonville *(G-6765)*

Stream Recycling Solutions LLC ....E...... 813 694-2587
Plant City *(G-14586)*

Sunburst Sanitation Corp ....D...... 561 478-9590
West Palm Beach *(G-19377)*

Synergy Recycl Centl Fla LLC ....E...... 863 419-0556
Winter Haven *(G-19665)*

Synergy Recycling LLC ....D...... 866 492-6789
Miami *(G-10357)*

◆ Technlgy Cnsrvation Group Inc .....D...... 352 527-2534
Lecanto *(G-8226)*

◆ US Ecology Tampa Inc ....E...... 813 623-5302
Tampa *(G-18484)*

USA Services of Florida Inc ....E...... 407 339-1800
Longwood *(G-8413)*

Veolia Envmtl Svcs N Amer Corp ....C...... 352 351-5624
Ocala *(G-11793)*

Wallbusters Recycling Inc ....E...... 772 334-2707
Jensen Beach *(G-7026)*

Waste Away LLC ....E...... 866 999-2929
Tampa *(G-18524)*

Waste Management Inc Florida ....D...... 904 450-5572
Jacksonville *(G-6916)*

Waste Management Inc Florida ....E...... 954 984-2072
Melbourne *(G-9008)*

Waste Pro of Florida Inc ....E...... 407 869-8800
Longwood *(G-8415)*

Waste Pro of Florida Inc ....C...... 386 788-8890
Daytona Beach *(G-2688)*

Waste Pro of Florida Inc ....B...... 954 967-4200
Pembroke Pines *(G-14199)*

Waste Pro of Florida Inc ....D...... 352 624-3100
Ocala *(G-11795)*

Waste Pro of Florida Inc ....C...... 904 731-7288
Jacksonville *(G-6917)*

Waste Pro Usa Inc ....D...... 561 688-8912
West Palm Beach *(G-19412)*

Waste Pro Usa Inc ....D...... 954 967-4200
Pembroke Pines *(G-14200)*

Waste Pro Usa Inc ....D...... 850 365-1900
Milton *(G-10829)*

Waste Pro Usa Inc ....D...... 386 758-7800
Lake City *(G-7552)*

Waste Pro Usa Inc ....D...... 941 355-9600
Sarasota *(G-16071)*

Water Medic Cape Coral Inc...........E...... 239 541-2581
Cape Coral *(G-1433)*

Wca of Florida LLC ....D...... 713 292-2400
Orange City *(G-11972)*

Wca Waste Corporation ....D...... 352 377-0800
Gainesville *(G-5029)*

Wca Waste Corporation ....D...... 386 774-6162
Orange City *(G-11973)*

Wca Waste Corporation ....E...... 407 843-7990
Orlando *(G-13411)*

Wheelabrator McKay Bay Inc ....E...... 800 682-0026
Tampa *(G-18551)*

▲ Wheelabrator South Broward Inc ....D...... 954 321-6343
Davie *(G-2536)*

◆ Wm North Broward Inc ....D...... 954 973-4370
Coconut Creek *(G-2009)*

4959 Sanitary Svcs, NEC

Advanced Disposal Services ....E...... 904 737-7900
Ponte Vedra *(G-14945)*

Bingham On-Site Sewers Inc ....D...... 813 659-0003
Dover *(G-3366)*

Carlson Environmental Cons PC.........D...... 863 634-7185
West Palm Beach *(G-19074)*

City of Boynton Beach ....D...... 561 742-6400
Boynton Beach *(G-974)*

◆ Cliff Berry Inc ....E...... 954 763-3390
Fort Lauderdale *(G-3701)*

County of Putnam ....E...... 386 329-0368
East Palatka *(G-3397)*

Ecosystem Technologies Inc ....E...... 239 337-5310
Fort Myers *(G-4351)*

EE&g Construction & Elec LLC ....E...... 305 374-8300
Miami Lakes *(G-10725)*

Emerald Coast Utilities Auth ....B...... 850 476-5110
Pensacola *(G-14288)*

Florida Keys Mosquito Ctrl Dst ....E...... 305 292-7190
Key West *(G-7206)*

Gem Technology Intl Corp ....C...... 305 447-1344
Miami *(G-9622)*

Hagan Holding Company ....E...... 727 327-8467
Saint Petersburg *(G-15702)*

Lee County Mosquito Ctrl Dst ....D...... 239 694-2174
Lehigh Acres *(G-8285)*

Magnum Environmental Services ....D...... 954 785-2320
Pompano Beach *(G-14847)*

Moretrench Industrial Inc ....C...... 813 831-1871
Riverview *(G-15261)*

Pasco County Mosquito Ctrl Dst ....E...... 727 376-4568
Odessa *(G-11853)*

Perma-Fix of Florida Inc ....D...... 352 373-6066
Gainesville *(G-4976)*

◆ Seacor Holdings Inc ....E...... 954 523-2200
Fort Lauderdale *(G-4109)*

Southern Cat Inc ....D...... 850 215-2280
Panama City *(G-14073)*

Tri-County Sweeping Svcs Inc..........D...... 954 797-0101
Davie *(G-2530)*

True Builders Inc ....E...... 863 647-1800
Plant City *(G-14589)*

USA Services of Florida Inc ....E...... 407 339-1800
Longwood *(G-8413)*

Witt OBriens LLC ....E...... 954 523-2200
Fort Lauderdale *(G-4229)*

4961 Steam & Air Conditioning Sply

◆ Eair LLC ....E...... 305 500-9898
Medley *(G-8724)*

Edd Helms Group Inc ....E...... 305 653-2520
Sunrise *(G-16767)*

4971 Irrigation Systems

Ameri - Pride Inc ....D...... 727 447-2186
Clearwater *(G-1517)*

Arazoza Brothers Corporation ....E...... 305 246-3223
Miami *(G-9165)*

Juniper Landscaping Fla LLC...........A...... 239 561-5980
Fort Myers *(G-4456)*

Oasis Landscape Services Inc ....E...... 352 373-9530
Gainesville *(G-4970)*

Orlando Utilities Commission...........B...... 407 423-9100
Orlando *(G-12989)*

Orlando Utilities Commission...........D...... 407 423-9100
Orlando *(G-12991)*

Prince Land Services Inc ....E...... 863 422-5207
Haines City *(G-5153)*

Senninger Irrigation Inc...............E...... 407 877-5655
Clermont *(G-1887)*

Superior Ldscpg & Lawn Svc Inc.........D...... 305 634-0717
Miami *(G-10351)*

Tohopekaliga Water Authority ....C...... 407 944-5000
Kissimmee *(G-7399)*

Treasure Cast Irrgtion Ldscp L ....D...... 772 546-4535
Hobe Sound *(G-5370)*

50 WHOLESALE TRADE¨DURABLE GOODS

5012 Automobiles & Other Motor Vehicles Wholesale

ABC Bus Inc ....D...... 407 656-7977
Oakland *(G-11581)*

Adesa Inc ....C...... 407 328-7300
Sanford *(G-15913)*

▼ Adesa Florida LLC ....C...... 904 764-1004
Jacksonville *(G-5736)*

Adesa Florida LLC ....C...... 813 620-3600
Tampa *(G-17236)*

Adesa-South Florida LLC ....C...... 352 351-5100
Ocala *(G-11628)*

▼ Americas Auto Actn Pnscola Inc ....D...... 850 944-1945
Pensacola *(G-14215)*

APS East Coast Inc ....E...... 904 751-4391
Jacksonville *(G-5799)*

APS East Coast Inc ....E...... 904 652-2962
Jacksonville *(G-5800)*

◆ Atlantic Ford Truck Sales Inc ....C...... 305 652-2336
Miami *(G-9186)*

Automotive Webmercials LLC ....E...... 561 571-3323
Boca Raton *(G-435)*

◆ Bill Seidle Imports Inc ....C...... 954 463-9533
Doral *(G-3137)*

◆ Boomerang Consulting Group LLC ......D...... 352 368-2451
Ocala *(G-11643)*

Brico LLC ....D...... 561 797-2400
West Palm Beach *(G-19062)*

Carmen Cargo Express Inc ....E...... 407 380-2627
Orlando *(G-12243)*

◆ College Auto Sales Florida LLC ....E...... 305 694-0000
Miami *(G-9387)*

Courtesy Auto Group Inc ....C...... 407 767-1690
Longwood *(G-8354)*

▼ Dick Baird Inc ....D...... 407 831-1318
Longwood *(G-8356)*

East Coast Auto Cons LLC ....C...... 561 533-5331
Boynton Beach *(G-984)*

◆ Em Sil Enterprises Inc ....E...... 954 979-9422
Pompano Beach *(G-14799)*

Flammer Ford Spring Hill Inc..........E...... 352 686-8255
Spring Hill *(G-16535)*

▼ Florida Auction Services Corp........A...... 386 255-2500
Daytona Beach *(G-2590)*

Florida Kenworth LLC ....E...... 863 668-9525
Lakeland *(G-7868)*

General Truck Eqp & Trlr Sls ....E...... 904 389-5541
Jacksonville *(G-6224)*

◆ Globe Trailer Mfg Inc ....D...... 941 753-2199
Bradenton *(G-1112)*

▼ Greenway Ford Inc ....C...... 407 275-3200
Orlando *(G-12601)*

Group 1 Automotive Inc ....C...... 305 952-5900
North Miami *(G-11494)*

Jacksonville Auto Auction Inc ....E...... 904 764-7653
Jacksonville *(G-6350)*

JM Family Enterprises Inc.............B...... 954 429-2418
Deerfield Beach *(G-2762)*

◆ JM Family Enterprises Inc ....A...... 954 429-2000
Deerfield Beach *(G-2761)*

Koons Ford LLC ....C...... 954 443-7000
Pembroke Pines *(G-14159)*

◆ Lambretta South Inc ....E...... 954 785-4820
Deerfield Beach *(G-2765)*

Lazydays Holdings Inc ....D...... 352 330-3800
Wildwood *(G-19499)*

▼ Lehman Hyundai Subaru Inc ....C 305 653-7111
Miami *(G-9855)*

Lipton Nothing But Truck ....D 954 735-4486
Oakland Park *(G-11602)*

Manheim Actons Gvrnment Svcs L ......C 407 438-1000
Orlando *(G-12806)*

Manheim Actons Gvrnment Svcs L ......C 813 247-1666
Tampa *(G-17984)*

▼ Manheims Grter Orlndo Auto Act ....B 407 438-1000
Orlando *(G-12807)*

Matthews Bus Alliance Inc ....D 407 219-3820
Orlando *(G-12833)*

Matthews Buses Florida Inc ....E 407 219-3820
Orlando *(G-12834)*

▼ Mazda of North Miami ....D 305 654-3825
Miami *(G-9912)*

Motor Coach Inds Intl Inc ....D 407 654-6363
Winter Garden *(G-19581)*

Motorsports of Orlando LLC ....D 407 328-1212
Sanford *(G-15967)*

New Auto Toy Store Inc ....D 954 463-1700
Fort Lauderdale *(G-3997)*

▼ Ocean Auto Center Inc ....D 786 464-1100
Doral *(G-3280)*

Performnce Ptrbilt Tllhssee LL ....E 850 574-0732
Midway *(G-10806)*

Prestige Ford Inc ....D 321 248-6235
Mount Dora *(G-10961)*

▼ R D K Truck Sales & Svc Inc ....E 813 241-0711
Tampa *(G-18195)*

Rush Truck Centers Florida Inc ....E 786 433-7600
Miami *(G-10227)*

▼ South Orlando Imports Inc ....E 407 851-8510
Orlando *(G-13217)*

Ten-8 Fire & Safety LLC ....E 877 989-7660
Bradenton *(G-1191)*

Treasure Coast Auto Auction ....E 321 626-0576
Fort Pierce *(G-4745)*

◆ Trucks & Parts of Tampa LLC ....D 813 247-6637
Tampa *(G-18449)*

Uma Holdings Inc ....E 786 587-1349
Hollywood *(G-5545)*

Worldwide Intl Trade LLC ....E 305 414-9774
Hollywood *(G-5549)*

Your Auction Inc ....C 727 572-8800
Saint Petersburg *(G-15905)*

5013 Motor Vehicle Splys & New Parts Wholesale

◆ American Battery Company Inc ....E 954 583-2470
Fort Lauderdale *(G-3600)*

American Racing Supply Inc ....D 407 740-7406
Winter Park *(G-19685)*

▼ Asbury Jax Ford LLC ....C 904 725-3060
Jacksonville *(G-5809)*

Atlantic Dodge Inc ....E 904 797-4383
Saint Augustine *(G-15426)*

◆ Atlantic Ford Truck Sales Inc ....C 305 652-2336
Miami *(G-9186)*

Automotive Parts & Machine ....D 305 254-8356
Miami *(G-9193)*

Autopart International Inc ....E 954 722-0606
Lauderhill *(G-8188)*

▲ Baccus Global LLC ....E 561 361-4900
Boca Raton *(G-440)*

▲ Battery Usa Inc ....E 863 665-6317
Lakeland *(G-7813)*

Central Auto Parts Inc ....E 407 841-7440
Orlando *(G-12259)*

▲ Club Assist US LLC ....B 407 322-7033
Lake Mary *(G-7577)*

▲ Coast To Coast International ....E 813 980-6166
Tampa *(G-17493)*

Dealer General Supply Co LLC ....C 407 374-1615
Lakeland *(G-7850)*

Derive Power LLC ....D 407 774-2447
Sanford *(G-15936)*

▲ Eastern Industries Inc ....D 850 769-1200
Panama City *(G-13993)*

◆ Em Sil Enterprises Inc ....E 954 979-9422
Pompano Beach *(G-14799)*

▼ Esserman Nissan Ltd ....D 305 626-2600
Miami Gardens *(G-10682)*

▼ Fleet Acquisitions LLC ....D 813 621-1734
Tampa *(G-17669)*

◆ Foreign Parts Distributors Inc ....D 305 885-8646
Miami *(G-9594)*

Fort Myers Auto & Indus Sup ....E 239 936-3917
Fort Myers *(G-4398)*

◆ Gar-P Industries Inc ....E 305 888-7252
Medley *(G-8736)*

General Truck Eqp & Trlr Sls ....E 904 389-5541
Jacksonville *(G-6224)*

▲ Gilmore Products Inc ....C 407 425-1236
Orlando *(G-12570)*

Hercules Tire & Rubber Company ......D 305 887-8876
Doral *(G-3228)*

◆ Herko International Inc ....E 305 971-4997
Miami *(G-9697)*

▼ Hollywood Chrysler Plymuth Inc ......D 954 342-5080
Hollywood *(G-5451)*

Horizon Global Americas Inc ....C 904 964-7311
Starke *(G-16577)*

HR Lewis Petroleum Co ....E 904 356-0731
Jacksonville *(G-6301)*

▼ Ideal Automotive & Truck ACC ....E 954 493-9800
Fort Lauderdale *(G-3887)*

Ieh Auto Parts LLC ....E 863 686-4123
Lakeland *(G-7884)*

◆ Integrated Supply Network LLC ....C 800 966-8478
Lakeland *(G-7886)*

Jim Quinlan Chevrolet Co ....D 727 222-0034
Clearwater *(G-1684)*

◆ JM Family Enterprises Inc ....A 954 429-2000
Deerfield Beach *(G-2761)*

◆ Keystone Auto Inds FL Inc ....E 305 885-6500
Medley *(G-8749)*

Lkq Corporation ....E 954 991-4636
Davie *(G-2497)*

Lkq Corporation ....D 352 746-3011
Crystal River *(G-2348)*

Miami Powertrain LLC ....E 305 600-6261
Miami *(G-9980)*

◆ Miami World Parts Inc ....C 305 635-7008
Miami *(G-9986)*

▲ Midas International LLC ....C 561 383-3100
Palm Beach Gardens *(G-13754)*

◆ Mile Marker International Inc ....D 800 886-8647
Pompano Beach *(G-14857)*

Motorsports of Orlando LLC ....D 407 328-1212
Sanford *(G-15967)*

Mulberry Motor Parts Inc ....E 863 676-6057
Lake Wales *(G-7695)*

◆ National Auto Parts Whse LLC ....E 305 953-7270
Miami *(G-10026)*

◆ Nationwide Lift Trucks Inc ....E 954 922-4645
Hollywood *(G-5479)*

◆ Nestor Sales LLC ....C 727 544-6114
Largo *(G-8139)*

Pantropic Power Inc ....E 239 337-4222
Fort Myers *(G-4533)*

Parts House Lllp ....D 904 209-0892
Saint Augustine *(G-15478)*

Parts House Lllp ....D 239 425-0830
Fort Myers *(G-4534)*

◆ Primero Auto Parts Inc ....E 305 696-3333
Miami *(G-10144)*

Quality Trailer Products LP ....E 813 659-2948
Plant City *(G-14577)*

▼ Reed Motors Inc ....C 407 297-7333
Orlando *(G-13091)*

▼ Sen-Dure Products Inc ....D 954 973-1260
Fort Lauderdale *(G-4115)*

▼ Southast Pwr Systems Tampa Inc ......E 813 623-1551
Tampa *(G-18307)*

◆ Southeast Power Group Inc ....D 305 592-9745
Doral *(G-3319)*

▼ Southeast Power Systems Inc ....D 407 293-7971
Orlando *(G-13219)*

▼ St Lucie Battery & Tire Co ....D 772 461-1746
Fort Pierce *(G-4740)*

▼ Steele Truck Center Inc ....D 239 334-7300
Fort Myers *(G-4606)*

Suburban Fla Accessory Ctr LLC ......C 813 574-1070
Tampa *(G-18342)*

◆ Sunbelt Auto Parts Group Inc ....E 305 599-9200
Davie *(G-2524)*

◆ Sunbelt Chemicals Corp ....D 386 446-4595
Palm Coast *(G-13841)*

T R S ....D 407 298-5490
Orlando *(G-13267)*

Tamargo Holdings Corp ....E 786 361-7446
Miami *(G-10362)*

◆ Tbc Corporation ....A 561 383-3100
Palm Beach Gardens *(G-13774)*

▲ Topline Automotive Engrg Inc ....D 352 799-4668
Brooksville *(G-1316)*

Tph Acquisition Lllp ....E 305 625-3332
Opa Locka *(G-11957)*

◆ Tph Acquisition Lllp ....D 904 731-3034
Jacksonville *(G-6871)*

▼ Tradewinds Power Corp ....D 305 592-9745
Doral *(G-3336)*

Universal Parts Warehouse Inc ....E 407 847-2005
Kissimmee *(G-7403)*

◆ Voxx International Corporation ....B 800 645-7750
Orlando *(G-13389)*

Warren Equipment Inc ....E 813 752-5126
Plant City *(G-14591)*

◆ Wetherill Associates Inc ....C 800 877-3340
Miramar *(G-10915)*

Wurth USA Inc ....E 407 856-8386
Orlando *(G-13451)*

Zuma & Sons Distributors Corp ....E 305 887-0089
Medley *(G-8802)*

5014 Tires & Tubes Wholesale

◆ Barrons Wholesale Tire LLC ....D 904 696-1200
Jacksonville *(G-5842)*

◆ Big O Tires LLC ....D 561 383-3000
Palm Beach Gardens *(G-13694)*

Carrolls LLC ....D 800 282-9026
Tampa *(G-17427)*

Carrolls LLC ....E 800 342-2450
Jacksonville *(G-5911)*

Carrolls LLC ....E 800 432-5695
Orlando *(G-12247)*

Conlan Tire Co LLC ....D 863 777-2410
Mulberry *(G-10973)*

Florida Tire Inc ....D 352 536-1177
Clermont *(G-1870)*

Hercules Tire & Rubber Company ......D 305 887-8876
Doral *(G-3228)*

◆ Jca Ventures Inc ....E 305 887-9015
Medley *(G-8748)*

▼ St Lucie Battery & Tire Co ....D 772 461-1746
Fort Pierce *(G-4740)*

◆ Tbc Corporation ....A 561 383-3100
Palm Beach Gardens *(G-13774)*

◆ Tire Group International LLC ....D 305 696-0096
Miami *(G-10393)*

Tire Outlet Direct LLC ....D 904 696-0580
Jacksonville *(G-6856)*

Treadmaxx Tire Distrs Inc ....E 813 247-5855
Tampa *(G-18441)*

Treadmaxx Tire Distrs LLC ....E 904 260-8700
Jacksonville *(G-6875)*

Treadmaxx Tire Distrs LLC ....E 407 841-3325
Orlando *(G-13307)*

5015 Motor Vehicle Parts, Used Wholesale

▲ Battery Usa Inc ....E 863 665-6317
Lakeland *(G-7813)*

Chuck Latham Associates Inc ....B 305 477-1356
Miami *(G-9369)*

Lkq Corporation ....E 352 746-3011
Crystal River *(G-2348)*

Luxury Orlando Imports Inc ....D 888 903-4311
Orlando *(G-12794)*

TT&r Enterprises Inc ....D 904 226-0335
Jacksonville *(G-6878)*

5021 Furniture Wholesale

◆ Berwin Inc ....E 954 499-6677
Miramar *(G-10840)*

Clarklift of Florida LLC ....D 813 874-2008
Orlando *(G-12311)*

Commercial Design Services Inc ....E 813 886-0580
Tampa *(G-17503)*

Educatnal Fnding Resources Inc ....D 954 388-1915
Hollywood *(G-5430)*

Empire Office Inc ....D 813 543-5050
Tampa *(G-17630)*

◆ Florida Seating Inc ....E 727 540-9802
Clearwater *(G-1643)*

Gulf Coast Off Pdts Inc NW Fla ......E 850 434-5588
Pensacola *(G-14318)*

H A Friend & Company Inc ....E 847 746-1248
Boynton Beach *(G-994)*

Hotel Superstore ....C 561 371-2661
Mascotte *(G-8696)*

◆ Leaders Holding Company ....D 727 538-5577
Largo *(G-8128)*

▲ List Industries Inc ....C 954 429-9155
Deerfield Beach *(G-2768)*

List Plymouth LLC ....D 954 429-9155
Deerfield Beach *(G-2769)*

▲ Mac Marketing LLC ....E 386 423-2223
Edgewater *(G-3413)*

◆ **Office Furniture Warehouse Inc** ....E 954 968-4700
Pompano Beach *(G-14871)*

Pltv Alliance LLC ....E 702 290-5552
Boca Raton *(G-752)*

S P Richards Company ....E 305 769-0565
Miami *(G-10230)*

S P Richards Company ....D 813 626-6009
Tampa *(G-18242)*

▲ **Sleep Studio LLC** ....E 212 679-6679
Miami *(G-10285)*

Soflo Mattress Inc ....E 844 654-5935
Tampa *(G-18300)*

▲ **Southern Hsptality Whl Ret Inc** ....E 813 717-7895
Plant City *(G-14583)*

▲ **Sun Wholesale Supply Inc** ....C 727 524-3299
Clearwater *(G-1801)*

▲ **Total Office Solutions Inc** ....D 904 353-4020
Jacksonville *(G-6864)*

▲ **Uniters North America LLC** ....D 877 336-3041
West Palm Beach *(G-19401)*

Workscapes Inc ....E 305 400-8101
Miami *(G-10513)*

Wrk Lab Inc ....E 305 400-8101
Doral *(G-3362)*

5023 Home Furnishings Wholesale

Acousti Engineering Co Fla ....D 813 620-0718
Tampa *(G-17229)*

▲ **All Glass Inc** ....D 407 702-0403
Niceville *(G-11437)*

Archipelago Inc ....C 212 334-9460
North Miami Beach *(G-11516)*

Ascot Enterprises Inc ....D 352 687-2151
Ocala *(G-11635)*

▼ **Blackton Inc** ....D 407 898-2661
Orlando *(G-12189)*

Bornt Enterprises Inc ....E 813 623-1492
Tampa *(G-17380)*

◆ **Cain & Bultman Inc** ....D 904 356-4812
Jacksonville *(G-5893)*

◆ **Carico International Inc** ....C 954 973-3900
Fort Lauderdale *(G-3670)*

Carpet Company III Inc ....E 407 888-8008
Orlando *(G-12244)*

▲ **Cazabak of Miami Inc** ....D 305 817-6600
Plantation *(G-14613)*

CPI Group LLC ....E 813 254-6112
Tampa *(G-17546)*

▲ **CPI Manufacturing Co Inc** ....E 954 961-9100
Fort Lauderdale *(G-3737)*

◆ **Cromer Company** ....E 305 373-5414
Hialeah Gardens *(G-5341)*

▲ **Cvc Hospitality Inc** ....E 407 299-7619
Winter Garden *(G-19564)*

◆ **Delta Picture Frame Co Inc** ....E 305 592-6456
Miami *(G-9471)*

◆ **Epoca International LLC** ....E 561 353-3900
Boca Raton *(G-567)*

Foodware LLC ....D 973 295-3830
Medley *(G-8733)*

Freeman Expositions LLC ....C 214 445-1000
Orlando *(G-12546)*

◆ **Geoglobal Partners LLC** ....D 561 598-6000
Riviera Beach *(G-15296)*

▲ **Gfx Inc** ....E 305 499-9789
Miami *(G-9629)*

Globaltexusa LLC ....E 305 751-2343
Miami *(G-9638)*

◆ **Harbor Linen LLC** ....D 305 805-8085
Medley *(G-8741)*

◆ **Healthtex Distributors Inc** ....D 305 633-7900
Miami *(G-9690)*

Homegoods Inc ....E 305 598-3919
Miami *(G-9715)*

House of Floors Palm Beach Inc ....E 561 571-8000
Boca Raton *(G-635)*

J & R United Industries Inc ....E 305 933-7100
Opa Locka *(G-11947)*

▲ **M & C Enterprises Sebring Inc** ....E 407 293-2969
Orlando *(G-12797)*

◆ **Michael Aram Inc** ....E 201 758-2551
West Palm Beach *(G-19268)*

Old Time Pottery LLC ....E 407 438-5103
Orlando *(G-12927)*

Old Time Pottery LLC ....D 954 486-4883
Tamarac *(G-17201)*

Old Time Pottery LLC ....D 813 627-8448
Tampa *(G-18098)*

Old Time Pottery LLC ....D 850 650-3401
Destin *(G-3070)*

Old Time Pottery LLC ....D 407 644-1460
Casselberry *(G-1453)*

Old Time Pottery LLC ....D 239 278-1141
Fort Myers *(G-4526)*

Old Time Pottery LLC ....D 407 877-0412
Ocoee *(G-11819)*

◆ **Ortega Industries and Mfg** ....D 305 688-0090
Opa Locka *(G-11952)*

Over Top Inc ....E 954 424-0076
Davie *(G-2503)*

Royal Foam US LLC ....E 904 345-5400
Jacksonville *(G-6678)*

▲ **Sobel Westex** ....D 702 735-4973
Miami *(G-13210)*

Sobel Westex ....D 954 942-5777
Pompano Beach *(G-14900)*

◆ **Southland Floors LLC** ....E 954 974-4700
Pompano Beach *(G-14907)*

▲ **Sun Wholesale Supply Inc** ....C 727 524-3299
Clearwater *(G-1801)*

◆ **Suncrest Supply Inc** ....E 561 804-1700
Riviera Beach *(G-15322)*

◆ **Unique Wholesale Distrs LLC** ....D 954 975-0227
Pompano Beach *(G-14934)*

◆ **Vertilux Limited** ....D 305 593-9494
Medley *(G-8795)*

Wildcard Systems Inc ....D 954 851-0700
Sunrise *(G-16848)*

World Image Corp ....E 954 472-9884
Plantation *(G-14722)*

Zulay LLC ....D 727 386-9117
Clearwater *(G-1846)*

5031 Lumber, Plywood & Millwork Wholesale

◆ **A&M Supply Corporation** ....D 727 541-6631
Pinellas Park *(G-14502)*

Acousti Engineering Co Fla ....D 813 620-0718
Tampa *(G-17229)*

◆ **Advantage Trim & Lumber Co Inc** .....E 941 388-9299
Sarasota *(G-16019)*

Affordble Wndows Dors Tmpa Bay .....E 727 437-0017
Clearwater *(G-1515)*

Alco Windows and Doors ....E 888 877-2526
Doral *(G-3108)*

Alside Inc ....E 813 621-7058
Tampa *(G-17273)*

American Builders Supply Inc ....D 239 989-0893
Fort Myers *(G-4272)*

American Builders Supply Inc ....D 321 257-0300
Sanford *(G-15917)*

American Woodmark Corporation ....B 407 857-9081
Orlando *(G-12117)*

◆ **Arso Enterprises Inc** ....E 305 681-2020
Opa Locka *(G-11940)*

Artemis Holdings LLC ....C 904 284-5611
Green Cove Springs *(G-5047)*

Associated Hardwoods LLC ....C 813 984-9111
Tampa *(G-17314)*

Awp Windows and Doors ....C 305 887-2646
Pompano Beach *(G-14745)*

Bluelinx Corporation ....D 813 621-1352
Tampa *(G-17369)*

Bluelinx Corporation ....E 305 769-5875
Miami *(G-9262)*

Bluelinx Corporation ....E 770 953-7000
Lake City *(G-7515)*

Boise Cascade Company ....D 850 626-4042
Milton *(G-10812)*

Brazilian Lumber LLC ....E 877 203-2004
Miami *(G-9276)*

◆ **Brothers Two Wndows Screns Inc** .....E 305 235-8110
Miami *(G-9289)*

Builders Firstsource - Fla LLC ....D 941 575-2250
Punta Gorda *(G-15193)*

Builders Frstsrce - Sthast Gro ....D 561 798-2026
Riviera Beach *(G-15286)*

◆ **Builders Hardware Inc** ....D 800 966-7753
Tampa *(G-17399)*

Busato Millwork Inc ....D 954 691-8991
Deerfield Beach *(G-2718)*

Cape Lumber Company ....D 239 332-1753
Cape Coral *(G-1380)*

Cedar Creek LLC ....E 863 967-1131
Auburndale *(G-251)*

◆ **Century Plumbing Wholesale Inc** .....E 305 261-4731
Miami *(G-9350)*

Cgi Windows & Doors Holdings ....B 305 593-6590
Hialeah *(G-5233)*

◆ **Chadwell Supply Inc** ....D 888 341-2423
Tampa *(G-17453)*

Chadwell Supply Missouri Inc ....C 888 341-2423
Tampa *(G-17454)*

◆ **Companies of R & S Inc** ....E 305 256-6666
Miami *(G-9396)*

Cook & Boardman Group LLC ....C 941 587-6654
Seminole *(G-16444)*

Dirt Cheap Building Sups LLC ....C 850 477-4916
Pensacola *(G-14283)*

Dyke Industries Inc ....E 305 888-7779
Medley *(G-8723)*

◆ **E-Stone USA Corp** ....D 863 655-1273
Sebring *(G-16393)*

▲ **EF San Juan Incorporated** ....E 850 722-4830
Youngstown *(G-19813)*

Fas Windows and Doors LLC ....D 866 737-7173
Tampa *(G-17651)*

Faswd LLC ....E 877 289-0825
Orlando *(G-12496)*

▲ **Florida Building Products LLC** ....E 561 627-2112
Palm Beach Gardens *(G-13730)*

◆ **Florida Engineered Constru** ....C 813 621-4641
Seffner *(G-16425)*

◆ **Florida Lumber Company** ....E 305 635-6412
Miami *(G-9579)*

◆ **FPG Wholesale Inc** ....C 305 266-2296
Miami *(G-9608)*

▼ **G Proulx LLC** ....E 954 327-3465
Fort Lauderdale *(G-3814)*

◆ **Gancedo Lumber Co Inc** ....C 305 836-7030
Miami *(G-9618)*

Georgia-Pacific LLC ....D 386 328-9210
Palatka *(G-13589)*

Gleckler LLC ....E 904 357-5402
Jacksonville *(G-6232)*

Gulfside Supply Inc ....E 941 484-9721
Nokomis *(G-11462)*

◆ **Hartman Windows and Doors LLC** ..D 561 296-9600
Riviera Beach *(G-15298)*

Hd Supply Inc ....E 407 852-3900
Orlando *(G-12625)*

Home Energy Advisors Inc ....D 727 282-4110
Saint Petersburg *(G-15710)*

Imeca East LLC ....D 786 693-6535
Miami Gardens *(G-10688)*

International Beams LLC ....E 941 552-9914
Sarasota *(G-16201)*

Jeld-Wen Inc ....D 407 944-9939
Kissimmee *(G-7332)*

Jeld-Wen Inc ....D 407 343-8596
Kissimmee *(G-7333)*

Joyner Lumber & Supply Co ....E 863 682-8101
Lakeland *(G-7893)*

JW Logistics Corp ....E 863 419-4222
Haines City *(G-5150)*

Labrador & Fundora Corporation ....E 305 888-4151
Hialeah *(G-5288)*

Lawson Industries Inc ....E 813 740-0033
Tampa *(G-17936)*

Lowes Home Centers LLC ....C 352 365-2223
Leesburg *(G-8260)*

Lowes Home Centers LLC ....C 386 418-6060
Alachua *(G-10)*

Lowes Home Centers LLC ....D 561 883-1215
Boca Raton *(G-677)*

Lowes Home Centers LLC ....E 954 680-8667
Southwest Ranches *(G-16529)*

Lowes Home Centers LLC ....D 850 932-0762
Gulf Breeze *(G-5123)*

Lowes Home Centers LLC ....C 863 299-2819
Winter Haven *(G-19644)*

Lowes Home Centers LLC ....C 813 558-6760
Tampa *(G-17961)*

Lowes Home Centers LLC ....C 407 452-1100
Kissimmee *(G-7350)*

Lowes Home Centers LLC ....C 386 719-6622
Lake City *(G-7536)*

Lowes Home Centers LLC ....D 239 596-2570
Naples *(G-11200)*

Lowes Home Centers LLC ....D 386 774-7000
Orange City *(G-11968)*

Lowes Home Centers LLC ....C 407 788-4305
Altamonte Springs *(G-72)*

Lowes Home Centers LLC ....C 850 575-1435
Tallahassee *(G-17026)*

Lowes Home Centers LLC ....D 407 977-9599
Oviedo *(G-13556)*

Lowes Home Centers LLC ....C 727 547-9335
Pinellas Park *(G-14527)*

Lowes Home Centers LLC ....C 941 756-1822
Bradenton *(G-1129)*

Lowes Home Centers LLC ....C....... 561 733-1397
Boynton Beach (G-1008)

Lowes Home Centers LLC ....D....... 321 631-0696
Rockledge (G-15356)

Lowes Home Centers LLC ....C....... 352 592-0176
Spring Hill (G-16541)

Lowes Home Centers LLC ....C....... 772 283-4229
Stuart (G-16637)

Lowes Home Centers LLC ....E....... 954 578-0246
Sunrise (G-16793)

Lowes Home Centers LLC ....C....... 904 277-5000
Fernandina Beach (G-3535)

Lowes Home Centers LLC ....D....... 813 659-4040
Plant City (G-14570)

Lowes Home Centers LLC ....D....... 352 259-6500
Lady Lake (G-7438)

Lowes Home Centers LLC ....C....... 407 430-4060
Sanford (G-15961)

Lowes Home Centers LLC ....C....... 727 724-3557
Clearwater (G-1701)

Lowes Home Centers LLC ....E....... 954 346-3993
Coral Springs (G-2270)

Lowes Home Centers LLC ....C....... 239 433-9255
Fort Myers (G-4497)

Lowes Home Centers LLC ....C....... 863 701-9800
Lakeland (G-7911)

Lowes Home Centers LLC ....C....... 321 953-2880
Melbourne (G-8924)

Lowes Home Centers LLC ....C....... 727 859-9450
New Port Richey (G-11392)

Lowes Home Centers LLC ....D....... 954 630-9550
Wilton Manors (G-19529)

Lowes Home Centers LLC ....C....... 407 532-6884
Orlando (G-12783)

Lowes Home Centers LLC ....C....... 386 671-9112
Ormond Beach (G-13508)

Lowes Home Centers LLC ....D....... 386 788-8566
Port Orange (G-15080)

Lowes Home Centers LLC ....C....... 727 822-8220
Saint Petersburg (G-15751)

Lowes Home Centers LLC ....D....... 772 564-6955
Vero Beach (G-18889)

Lowes Home Centers LLC ....C....... 772 692-7745
Jensen Beach (G-7019)

Lowes Home Centers LLC ....C....... 561 795-3808
Royal Palm Beach (G-15384)

Lowes Home Centers LLC ....D....... 850 913-1600
Panama City (G-14037)

Lowes Home Centers LLC ....C....... 561 207-9037
Lake Park (G-7660)

Lowes Home Centers LLC ....C....... 727 588-1200
Largo (G-8132)

Lowes Home Centers LLC ....C....... 850 423-7400
Crestview (G-2325)

Lowes Home Centers LLC ....D....... 954 624-1900
Pembroke Pines (G-14166)

Lowes Home Centers LLC ....C....... 904 682-7667
Orange Park (G-12002)

Lowes Home Centers LLC ....C....... 954 545-7381
Pompano Beach (G-14845)

Lowes Home Centers LLC ....E....... 352 237-7600
Ocala (G-11715)

Lowes Home Centers LLC ....D....... 386 326-5340
Palatka (G-13593)

Lowes Home Centers LLC ....D....... 352 860-5800
Inverness (G-5696)

Lowes Home Centers LLC ....C....... 813 838-9000
Zephyrhills (G-19841)

Lowes Home Centers LLC ....C....... 850 526-6440
Marianna (G-8681)

Lowes Home Centers LLC ....C....... 941 525-1000
Venice (G-18792)

Lowes Home Centers LLC ....C....... 352 385-3600
Mount Dora (G-10956)

Lowes Home Centers LLC ....D....... 904 696-4063
Jacksonville (G-6447)

Lowes Home Centers LLC ....C....... 386 785-2430
De Land (G-2695)

Lowes Home Centers LLC ....C....... 352 754-6320
Brooksville (G-1297)

Lowes Home Centers LLC ....C....... 863 451-4000
Sebring (G-16406)

Lowes Home Centers LLC ....D....... 863 519-4000
Bartow (G-325)

Lowes Home Centers LLC ....C....... 813 313-1424
Riverview (G-15260)

Lowes Home Centers LLC ....B....... 352 367-8900
Gainesville (G-4937)

Lowes Home Centers LLC ....C....... 321 779-7960
Indian Harbour Beach (G-5671)

Lowes Home Centers LLC ....C....... 941 421-1041
Port Charlotte (G-15045)

Lowes Home Centers LLC ....C....... 386 330-5760
Live Oak (G-8314)

Lowes Home Centers LLC ....D....... 239 458-6440
Cape Coral (G-1410)

Lowes Home Centers LLC ....C....... 813 793-9152
Brandon (G-1243)

Lowes Home Centers LLC ....C....... 305 820-4192
Hialeah (G-5293)

Lowes Home Centers LLC ....D....... 850 636-3920
Panama City (G-14038)

Lowes Home Centers LLC ....E....... 239 494-9000
Estero (G-3469)

Lowes Home Centers LLC ....C....... 321 207-2860
Fern Park (G-3514)

Lowes Home Centers LLC ....D....... 850 316-3359
Pensacola (G-14350)

Lowes Home Centers LLC ....C....... 941 961-6261
Sarasota (G-16223)

Lowes Home Centers LLC ....C....... 863 734-5000
Lake Wales (G-7691)

Lowes Home Centers LLC ....C....... 863 551-3070
Auburndale (G-256)

Lowes Home Centers LLC ....C....... 863 422-9116
Haines City (G-5151)

Lowes Home Centers LLC ....C....... 305 508-3020
Homestead (G-5589)

Lowes Home Centers LLC ....C....... 407 905-3900
Winter Garden (G-19579)

Lowes Home Centers LLC ....C....... 386 585-6000
Palm Coast (G-13833)

Lowes Home Centers LLC ....C....... 321 327-6906
Palm Bay (G-13627)

Lowes Home Centers LLC ....D....... 407 814-2760
Apopka (G-199)

Lowes Home Centers LLC ....C....... 561 471-4828
West Palm Beach (G-19243)

Lowes Home Centers LLC ....D....... 941 257-2200
North Port (G-11573)

Lowes Home Centers LLC ....D....... 386 960-9031
Deltona (G-3042)

Lowes Home Centers LLC ....C....... 904 589-3022
Middleburg (G-10797)

Lowes Home Centers LLC ....D....... 786 319-5126
Miami (G-9882)

▲ M & C Enterprises Sebring Inc ....E....... 407 293-2969
Orlando (G-12797)

Metrie Inc ....E....... 407 826-0335
Orlando (G-12862)

MI Windows and Doors Inc ....E....... 813 855-2690
Oldsmar (G-11912)

▲ Millwork Sales Orlando LLC ....C....... 770 799-0345
Orlando (G-12873)

▼ Millwork Sls Ryal Palm Bch LLC ......E....... 561 472-6497
Royal Palm Beach (G-15386)

▼ Mrg Glazing Contractors Inc ....C....... 305 470-8284
Medley (G-8760)

Nachon Enterprises Inc ....D....... 305 888-5236
Hialeah (G-5303)

Natures Source Products Inc..............E....... 386 628-5064
Lake City (G-7537)

Newsouth Win Sltons Bnita Sprn ....C....... 239 949-4300
Bonita Springs (G-929)

Newsouth Window Solutions LLC........D....... 813 626-6000
Tampa (G-18078)

Newsouth Window Solutions LLC........A....... 941 925-4000
Bradenton (G-1152)

Noroestana De Exprtaciones Cxa ....E....... 305 639-6772
Doral (G-3279)

Novo Distribution LLC ....B....... 863 413-9200
Lakeland (G-7932)

ODonnell Impact Wndows Storm ....E....... 772 408-0200
Stuart (G-16654)

Paradise Exteriors LLC ....D....... 561 732-0300
Boynton Beach (G-1026)

Primesource Building Pdts Inc ....E....... 407 888-3115
Orlando (G-13059)

◆ Quality Plywood Spc Inc..................E....... 727 572-0500
Clearwater (G-1769)

Raymond Building Supply LLC ....C....... 239 348-7272
Naples (G-11278)

Rayonier Inc ....D....... 904 357-9100
Yulee (G-19820)

◆ Rayonier Prfmce Fibers LLC ....E....... 912 427-5000
Jacksonville (G-6636)

Rayonier Trs Holdings Inc..................C....... 904 357-9100
Jacksonville (G-6637)

Ro-Mac Lumber & Supply Inc ....C....... 352 787-4545
Leesburg (G-8270)

◆ Robbins Manufacturing Company ....C....... 813 971-3030
Tampa (G-18231)

◆ Rolladen Inc ....E....... 954 454-4114
Hallandale Beach (G-5181)

Rollsheld Hrricane Shutter Mfr ....E....... 727 451-7655
Clearwater (G-1778)

▲ S&P Architectural Products Inc ....D....... 954 968-3701
Pompano Beach (G-14888)

◆ Sheridan Lumber Inc ....E....... 954 920-8079
Hollywood (G-5519)

▼ Smith & Deshields Inc ....D....... 561 395-0808
Boca Raton (G-809)

Southern Fuelwood Inc ....E....... 352 472-4324
Newberry (G-11432)

Southern Milling & Lumber Inc...........D....... 863 682-1605
Lakeland (G-7973)

▼ Stuart Paint and Supply Inc ....D....... 772 334-2700
Jensen Beach (G-7024)

◆ Sun Power Marine Inc ....E....... 305 594-0797
Miami (G-10339)

Sunmaster of Naples Inc ....E....... 239 261-3581
Naples (G-11310)

▲ Tampa Intl Forest Pdts LLC.............E....... 813 880-7300
Tampa (G-18388)

▼ Tm Windows LLC ....D....... 954 781-4430
Pompano Beach (G-14923)

TP Brands International Inc ....E....... 941 882-3224
Osprey (G-13534)

Tri-Excellence Inc ....E....... 727 539-6455
Largo (G-8156)

Trusses Unlimited Inc ....E....... 904 355-6611
Ponte Vedra Beach (G-15010)

▼ Ufp Auburndale LLC ....E....... 863 965-2566
Auburndale (G-260)

▲ US Block Windows Inc ....E....... 850 473-0555
Pensacola (G-14461)

USG Corporation.............................D....... 305 688-8744
Miami (G-10454)

V Oakvest Inc ....C....... 941 758-2424
Bradenton (G-1198)

▲ Weekes Logan Forest Products ......D....... 813 253-3445
Tampa (G-18529)

◆ Wholesale Building Pdts LLC ....E....... 954 927-1475
Hollywood (G-5548)

Woodsman Kitchens & Floors Inc.......D....... 904 641-8336
Jacksonville (G-6942)

5032 Brick, Stone & Related Construction Mtrls Wholesale

◆ A B Property Services Inc ....D....... 800 432-2115
Miami (G-9061)

A-1 Block Corporation ....E....... 407 422-3768
Orlando (G-12034)

Argos USA LLC ....E....... 941 351-9611
Sarasota (G-16022)

◆ Brastile Inc ....E....... 800 881-1031
Miami (G-9275)

◆ C L Industries Inc ....E....... 800 333-2660
Orlando (G-12222)

Campbell Sand & Gravel Co ....D....... 850 256-4112
Century (G-1474)

◆ Ccp Management Inc ....D....... 904 398-7177
Jacksonville (G-5917)

Cement Industries Inc ....D....... 239 332-1440
Fort Myers (G-4305)

Cemex Corp ....C....... 800 992-3639
Grant (G-5044)

Cemex Materials LLC ....C....... 386 775-0790
Deland (G-2847)

Cemex Materials LLC ....C....... 772 287-0502
Stuart (G-16602)

Cemex Materials LLC ....C....... 941 722-4578
Palmetto (G-13905)

Cemex Materials LLC ....D....... 954 523-9978
Fort Lauderdale (G-3676)

Cemex Materials LLC ....C....... 954 431-7655
Pembroke Pines (G-14139)

Conrad Yelvington Distrs Inc ....E....... 386 257-5504
Daytona Beach (G-2563)

◆ Coverings Etc Inc ....E....... 305 757-6000
Miami (G-9434)

Crh Americas Inc ....C....... 239 334-8022
Fort Myers (G-4332)

Crh Americas Inc ....B....... 941 957-3933
Sarasota (G-16133)

▼ G Proulx LLC ....E....... 954 327-3465
Fort Lauderdale (G-3814)

Gosalia Concrete Constrs Inc ....E....... 813 443-0984
Tampa (G-17744)

Granite Express Inc ....D..... 941 373-1452
Sarasota *(G-16178)*

◆ Iberia Tiles Corporation ....D..... 305 591-3880
Miami *(G-9738)*

◆ International Materials LLC ....D..... 561 705-0350
Delray Beach *(G-2972)*

◆ J & J Imports Fabrication Inc ....D..... 904 826-0602
Ponte Vedra Beach *(G-14986)*

◆ John Abell Corporation................E..... 305 253-4440
Cutler Bay *(G-2369)*

▲ LV Thompson Inc ....C..... 813 248-3456
Tampa *(G-17968)*

Medley Block Industries Corp ....D..... 305 888-8822
Medley *(G-8755)*

◆ Megatrade Corporation ....E..... 305 592-5599
Deerfield Beach *(G-2772)*

Mosaic ....E..... 863 491-1003
Arcadia *(G-231)*

Paramount Global Surfaces Inc..........C..... 310 712-1850
Miami *(G-10095)*

Paver Systems LLC ....E..... 407 859-9117
Orlando *(G-13015)*

Pinnacle Concrete LLC..................D..... 904 273-0882
Jacksonville Beach *(G-7000)*

Ridgdill & Son Inc ....E..... 863 983-3136
Clewiston *(G-1907)*

Stone Crazy Inc ....E..... 407 290-5790
Orlando *(G-13239)*

Suwannee American Cem Co LLC ....D..... 386 935-5000
Branford *(G-1259)*

T M G International LLC ....E..... 863 421-8008
Winter Haven *(G-19666)*

◆ Trinity Tile Group LLC ....E..... 352 369-0444
Ocala *(G-11788)*

◆ Trinity Tile Group Ocala LLC ....E..... 352 482-1600
Ocala *(G-11789)*

◆ Wholesale Building Pdts LLC ....E..... 954 927-1475
Hollywood *(G-5548)*

5033 Roofing, Siding & Insulation Mtrls Wholesale

Biscayne Construction Co Inc...........E..... 305 688-7663
Davie *(G-2461)*

▼ Blackton Inc.........................D..... 407 898-2661
Orlando *(G-12189)*

Carpenter Co ....D..... 863 682-2188
Lakeland *(G-7825)*

Carpenter Co ....D..... 863 687-9494
Lakeland *(G-7826)*

▼ G Proulx LLC ....E..... 954 327-3465
Fort Lauderdale *(G-3814)*

◆ Gulfside Supply Inc ....D..... 813 636-9808
Tampa *(G-17776)*

Hd Supply Inc ....E..... 407 852-3900
Orlando *(G-12625)*

Kingspan Insulation LLC................D..... 305 921-0100
Opa Locka *(G-11949)*

North Amrcn Spray Foam Plymers ......E..... 800 713-1646
Saint Petersburg *(G-15780)*

◆ Sunniland Corporation ....C..... 407 322-2421
Longwood *(G-8407)*

Topbuild Corp ....C..... 386 304-2200
Daytona Beach *(G-2676)*

USG Corporation.......................D..... 305 688-8744
Miami *(G-10454)*

◆ Wholesale Building Pdts LLC ....E..... 954 927-1475
Hollywood *(G-5548)*

5039 Construction Materials, NEC Wholesale

Accu-Span Truss Co ....E..... 407 321-1440
Longwood *(G-8335)*

Acousti Engineering Co Fla.............D..... 239 332-1610
Fort Myers *(G-4248)*

◆ Aldora Aluminum & GL Pdts Inc ......E..... 954 441-5057
Miami *(G-9114)*

American Loading Services.............E..... 239 471-8293
Cape Coral *(G-1374)*

American Structural Corporate ....E..... 305 801-6631
Hialeah *(G-5218)*

Atlantic Steel Inc ....E..... 407 599-3822
Longwood *(G-8342)*

▲ Bedard Holdings LLC ....D..... 904 268-8000
Jacksonville *(G-5851)*

Conspec Materials of Orlando ....E..... 813 885-4324
Tampa *(G-17516)*

▼ Equipco Manufacturing Inc ....E..... 305 513-8540
Miami *(G-9529)*

◆ Florida A&G Co Inc ....A..... 800 432-8132
Tamarac *(G-17190)*

▼ G Proulx LLC ....E..... 954 327-3465
Fort Lauderdale *(G-3814)*

◆ Interglass Corp ....E..... 305 885-4442
Miami *(G-9758)*

Oldcastle Buildingenvelope Inc..........C..... 305 651-6630
Miami *(G-10066)*

Simpson Strong-Tie Company Inc ....E..... 904 693-2762
Jacksonville *(G-6728)*

◆ Suncrest Supply Inc ....E..... 561 804-1700
Riviera Beach *(G-15322)*

▼ US Wholesale Pipe & Tube Inc ....E..... 727 945-9060
Holiday *(G-5377)*

◆ Wholesale Building Pdts LLC ....E..... 954 927-1475
Hollywood *(G-5548)*

Williams Scotsman Inc ....C..... 813 626-2862
Tampa *(G-18556)*

Williams Scotsman Inc ....E..... 954 450-9222
Pembroke Pines *(G-14203)*

5043 Photographic Eqpt & Splys Wholesale

▼ AVI-Spl LLC ....B 813 884-7168
Tampa *(G-17326)*

◆ B & G PTL Enterprises Inc ....E..... 954 977-4060
Pompano Beach *(G-14747)*

◆ Ces Plus Inc ....D..... 305 232-8182
Doral *(G-3151)*

F & E Trading LLC.....................D..... 305 717-0036
Medley *(G-8730)*

◆ Lexjet LLC ....D..... 941 330-1210
Sarasota *(G-16219)*

South Florida Photo Co Inc.............D..... 863 683-7858
Lakeland *(G-7970)*

5044 Office Eqpt Wholesale

Advanced Dcument Solutions Inc........D..... 407 412-6929
Orlando *(G-12054)*

◆ Canon Financial Services Inc..........C..... 561 997-3100
Boca Raton *(G-496)*

Canon Solutions America Inc ....C..... 561 997-3100
Boca Raton *(G-497)*

Copyfax Inc ....E..... 904 296-1600
Jacksonville *(G-6001)*

Delta Business Solutions Inc ....E..... 954 885-0102
Miramar *(G-10852)*

Dex Imaging LLC......................C..... 813 288-8080
Tampa *(G-17590)*

Fba Holding Inc ....E..... 321 733-1020
Melbourne *(G-8884)*

H A Friend & Company Inc ....E..... 847 746-1248
Boynton Beach *(G-994)*

Halsey & Griffith Inc ....E..... 305 623-1921
Miami Gardens *(G-10685)*

Imagine Technology Group Inc ....A 813 960-5508
Tampa *(G-17858)*

◆ Intercom Group Inc ....E..... 954 978-2121
Pompano Beach *(G-14827)*

Konica Minolta Business Soluti ....E..... 813 287-1102
Tampa *(G-17930)*

Mr Copy Service Inc...................D..... 904 448-9447
Fort Myers *(G-4519)*

Odp Corporation ....A 561 438-4800
Boca Raton *(G-726)*

◆ Office Depot LLC ....A 561 438-4800
Boca Raton *(G-727)*

◆ OfficeMax Incorporated ....B 800 463-3768
Boca Raton *(G-728)*

◆ Safemark Systems LP ....E..... 407 299-0044
Orlando *(G-13159)*

Safemark Systems LP ....C..... 407 581-2101
Orlando *(G-13160)*

▼ Saxon Business Systems Inc ....D..... 305 362-0100
Miami Lakes *(G-10759)*

School Board Palm Beach County ....A 561 684-5206
West Palm Beach *(G-19353)*

Tavistock Corporation ....E..... 407 876-8800
Windermere *(G-19549)*

Team Bamf LLC ....C..... 954 917-5510
Fort Lauderdale *(G-4168)*

Toshiba Bus Solutions USA Inc..........C..... 954 428-1300
Deerfield Beach *(G-2807)*

▲ Xerox Business Solutions Inc ....E..... 813 960-5508
Tampa *(G-18571)*

5045 Computers & Peripheral Eqpt & Software Wholesale

360fly Inc ....E..... 954 849-3673
Fort Lauderdale *(G-3568)*

A5 Solutions Group Inc ....D..... 305 927-2988
Weston *(G-19438)*

Aci Worldwide Inc ....B 305 894-2200
Coral Gables *(G-2021)*

Acordis International Corp ....E..... 954 620-0072
Miramar *(G-10833)*

◆ Allplus Computer Systems Corp ......E..... 305 436-3993
Doral *(G-3111)*

Arctos Mission Solutions LLC ....E..... 813 609-5591
Tampa *(G-17303)*

Arma Global Corporation ....D..... 866 554-9333
Tampa *(G-17306)*

◆ Bluestar Latin America Inc ....E..... 954 485-1931
Miramar *(G-10841)*

Canon Financial Services Inc ....C..... 561 997-3100
Boca Raton *(G-495)*

Cash Management Solutions Inc.........E..... 727 524-1103
Clearwater *(G-1561)*

Colorvision International Inc ....B 407 851-0103
Orlando *(G-12346)*

Compro Computer Services Inc ....E..... 321 727-2211
Melbourne *(G-8849)*

Compusa Inc ....E..... 954 428-6928
Deerfield Beach *(G-2727)*

Compusoft ....E..... 305 520-9218
Tallahassee *(G-16921)*

Connectwisecom Inc ....C..... 813 935-7100
Tampa *(G-17515)*

▲ Convergence Technologies Inc ....E..... 630 887-1000
Riviera Beach *(G-15290)*

▲ Dalbani Corporation America ....D..... 305 716-1016
Miami *(G-9455)*

Datex Inc ....E..... 727 571-4159
Clearwater *(G-1603)*

Dbk Concepts Inc......................C..... 305 596-7226
Miami *(G-9463)*

Decurtis LLC ....E..... 407 965-1395
Orlando *(G-12410)*

Dhs Associates Inc ....E..... 904 213-0448
Orange Park *(G-11985)*

Distritech LLC ....E..... 305 517-3730
Miami *(G-9480)*

Enotice Inc ....E..... 405 266-7679
Miami *(G-9523)*

▲ Ferris Marketing Inc ....D..... 239 244-2808
Naples *(G-11109)*

◆ Flytec Computers Inc ....E..... 305 471-5142
Doral *(G-3204)*

▲ General Dynamics Itronix Corp ....B 954 846-3400
Sunrise *(G-16774)*

Genisys Software Inc ....E..... 763 391-6133
Sanford *(G-15944)*

▲ Image Access Inc ....E..... 561 995-8334
Boca Raton *(G-639)*

Ingram Micro Inc ....E..... 305 593-5900
Doral *(G-3236)*

Ingram Micro Mobility ....E..... 305 593-5900
Doral *(G-3237)*

◆ Intcomex Inc ....B 305 477-6230
Medley *(G-8744)*

◆ Intcomex Holdings LLC ....E..... 305 477-6230
Medley *(G-8745)*

Integrated Cmpt Solutions Inc..........D..... 850 205-7501
Tallahassee *(G-17007)*

Intermemory Corp ....E..... 305 597-9710
Miami *(G-9761)*

◆ Intracom USA Inc ....E..... 813 855-0550
Oldsmar *(G-11908)*

Iron Eaglex Inc ....E..... 813 230-1066
Tampa *(G-17874)*

ITI Engineering LLC ....E..... 866 245-9356
Winter Springs *(G-19805)*

Kofax Inc ....B 954 888-7800
Plantation *(G-14662)*

◆ Lexjet LLC ....E..... 941 330-1210
Sarasota *(G-16219)*

Loanlogics Inc ....C..... 215 367-5500
Jacksonville *(G-6443)*

Lucayan Tech Solutions LLC ....E..... 813 252-2219
Tampa *(G-17964)*

◆ Mayortec Corp ....E..... 305 592-0055
Doral *(G-3272)*

▲ Moredirect Inc ....E..... 561 237-3300
Boca Raton *(G-699)*

Muck Rack LLC ....C..... 212 500-1883
Miami Beach *(G-10633)*

Odp Corporation ....A 561 438-4800
Boca Raton *(G-726)*

◆ Office Depot LLC ....A 561 438-4800
Boca Raton *(G-727)*

◆ OfficeMax Incorporated ....B 800 463-3768
Boca Raton *(G-728)*

Pace Systems Group Inc	E	904 564-9690	
Jacksonville Beach (G-6999)			
Pilgrim Quality Solutions	D	813 915-1663	
Tampa (G-18150)			
Posabilities Inc	E	239 337-4767	
Fort Myers (G-4544)			
Redvectorcom LLC	E	866 546-1212	
Tampa (G-18206)			
Ringlogix LLC	E	305 800-8647	
Miami Lakes (G-10757)			
Rosen Hotel Investments Inc	E	407 996-9840	
Orlando (G-13133)			
Saphire Entertainment Group	E	305 771-2326	
Coral Gables (G-2182)			
Six3 Advanced Systems Inc	C	941 907-8803	
Lakewood Ranch (G-8041)			
◆ Software Brokers America Inc	C	305 477-6230	
Medley (G-8784)			
Teamviewer Us Inc	E	800 951-4573	
Clearwater (G-1819)			
Tech Data Corporation	A	727 539-7429	
Clearwater (G-1820)			
Tech Data Corporation	C	727 539-7429	
Miami (G-10366)			
Tech Data Corporation	C	727 539-7429	
Clearwater (G-1821)			
◆ Tech Data Product MGT Inc	B	727 539-7429	
Clearwater (G-1822)			
Tesseract Operating LLC	C	978 250-9800	
Orlando (G-13282)			
▲ Tubelite Fl LLC	E	407 884-0477	
Apopka (G-220)			
Tyler Business Systems Inc	E	727 536-5588	
Clearwater (G-1826)			
Valgenesis Inc	E	510 445-0505	
Tampa (G-18493)			
Xbyte Technologies Inc	E	941 358-9770	
Bradenton (G-1208)			
▲ Xerox Business Solutions Inc	E	813 960-5508	
Tampa (G-18571)			
Xos Technologies Inc	D	407 404-5500	
Maitland (G-8603)			

5046 Commercial Eqpt, NEC Wholesale

▼ Allpoints Warehousing Eqp Co	D	813 246-5800	
Tampa (G-17269)			
◆ Americas Export Corporation	D	561 515-8080	
Miami (G-9147)			
◆ Baring Industries Inc	E	954 327-6700	
Fort Lauderdale (G-3629)			
Beltram Edge Tool Supply Inc	E	813 239-1136	
Tampa (G-17357)			
Beltram South Inc	D	239 334-1101	
Fort Myers (G-4290)			
▼ Beltram South Inc	E	239 334-1101	
Fort Myers (G-4291)			
Blue Ribbon Cleaning Co Inc	E	352 624-3444	
Ocala (G-11641)			
C & D Industrial Maint LLC	E	833 776-5833	
Bradenton (G-1070)			
Compass Group Usa Inc	A	305 624-5100	
Miami (G-9397)			
Complete Prchute Solutions Inc	D	386 736-3862	
Deland (G-2851)			
Cues Inc	C	407 849-0190	
Orlando (G-12392)			
Durante Equipment LLC	E	561 806-3666	
Hollywood (G-5429)			
◆ General Hotel & Rest Sup Corp	D	305 885-8651	
Miami Lakes (G-10733)			
◆ Greenfield World Trade Inc	D	954 202-7419	
Fort Lauderdale (G-3837)			
Hotel Superstore	C	561 371-2661	
Mascotte (G-8696)			
Jetro Holdings LLC	B	904 733-1005	
Jacksonville (G-6384)			
◆ Johnson-Lancaster & Assoc Inc	E	727 796-5622	
Clearwater (G-1686)			
Juldav Distributors Inc	D	813 251-2421	
Tampa (G-17902)			
Knapheide Trck Eqp Southeast	C	407 857-2040	
Orlando (G-12734)			
◆ Louis Wohl & Sons Inc	E	813 985-8870	
Tampa (G-17960)			
▲ Mettler Toledo Florida Inc	E	813 626-8127	
Tampa (G-18032)			
Modular Mailing Systems Inc	E	813 549-5340	
Tampa (G-18049)			
◆ N Land Sea Distributing Inc	D	800 432-7652	
Pompano Beach (G-14863)			

▼ One Fat Frog Incorporated	D	407 480-3409	
Orlando (G-12929)			
Pantropic Power Inc	E	239 337-4222	
Fort Myers (G-4533)			
Restaurant Depot LLC	E	813 247-7900	
Tampa (G-18220)			
Strategic Equipment LLC	D	813 873-2402	
Tampa (G-18341)			
◆ Sun Power Marine Inc	E	305 594-0797	
Miami (G-10339)			
Synergy Rents LLC	C	844 796-3749	
Pompano Beach (G-14915)			
Synergy Rents LLC	E	239 334-4987	
Fort Myers (G-4620)			
Synergy Rents LLC	E	941 780-9444	
Sarasota (G-16062)			
Sysco Guest Supply LLC	D	407 857-9023	
Orlando (G-13262)			
◆ Taylor Ultimate Services LLC	E	954 217-9100	
Weston (G-19481)			
◆ Tube Light Company Inc	E	800 505-4900	
Apopka (G-219)			
Tubelite Holdings LLC	C	800 505-4900	
Apopka (G-221)			

5047 Medical, Dental & Hospital Eqpt & Splys Wholesale

Access Mediquip LLC	C	877 985-4850	
Lake Mary (G-7560)			
◆ Accurate Biomed Services Inc	E	800 376-5660	
Ocala (G-11626)			
◆ Acorn Stairlifts Inc	B	407 650-0216	
Orlando (G-12049)			
Adler Instrument Company	E	770 263-7888	
Brooksville (G-1264)			
Aerocare Holdings LLC	A	407 206-0040	
Orlando (G-12073)			
Agiliti Health Inc	E	407 295-1422	
Orlando (G-12078)			
Allegheny Medical Systems LLC	E	561 998-3474	
Boca Raton (G-411)			
Alphapromed LLC	E	855 444-4073	
Tampa (G-17271)			
Amerisourcebergen Corporation	D	407 259-5568	
Orlando (G-12119)			
Arthrex Inc	C	239 552-5051	
Fort Myers (G-4281)			
▲ Associated Medical Products	D	904 646-0199	
Jacksonville (G-5811)			
▲ Atls Medical Supply Inc	A	772 398-5842	
Port Saint Lucie (G-15122)			
Audina Hearing Instruments Inc	D	407 331-0077	
Longwood (G-8344)			
Benco Dental Supply Co	E	407 263-7125	
Ormond Beach (G-13480)			
Benco Dental Supply Co	D	904 783-4094	
Jacksonville (G-5856)			
Beneficial Marketing Inc	E	954 981-0900	
West Park (G-19429)			
Cardinal Health 200 LLC	E	614 757-5000	
Weston (G-19447)			
Care Plus Oxygen Inc	E	407 206-0040	
Orlando (G-12237)			
Carefree Health Services Inc	E	561 279-1811	
Delray Beach (G-2925)			
Carewell Family Inc	E	305 431-1833	
Coral Gables (G-2063)			
Childrens Home Medical Eqp Inc	B	407 513-3030	
Orlando (G-12298)			
Darby Dental Supply LLC	D	800 448-7323	
Coral Springs (G-2246)			
Decimal LLC	E	407 330-3300	
Sanford (G-15934)			
Direct Shield Medical Supplies	E	800 517-5994	
Pompano Beach (G-14794)			
Dr Turri	D	352 729-3377	
Clermont (G-1867)			
Eastern Medical Eqp Distrs Inc	E	786 332-5111	
Doral (G-3185)			
▲ Electrostim Medical Svcs Inc	B	800 588-8383	
Tampa (G-17622)			
Elite Medical Technologies LLC	E	317 965-7522	
Indian Shores (G-5674)			
◆ EM Adams Inc	D	772 468-6550	
Fort Pierce (G-4697)			
▲ Erchonia Corporation LLC	E	321 473-1251	
Melbourne (G-8883)			
◆ Essential Medical Supply Inc	E	407 770-0710	
Orlando (G-12476)			

First Nation Group LLC	E	850 389-8448	
Niceville (G-11448)			
▲ Flow Metrix Inc	E	954 835-2300	
Weston (G-19460)			
G E Walker Inc	D	813 623-2481	
Tampa (G-17721)			
▲ Genicon LLC	E	407 657-4851	
Orlando (G-12567)			
Geosurgical LLC	E	800 535-6385	
Clearwater (G-1654)			
Grifols Usa LLC	B	305 593-6163	
Doral (G-3218)			
▲ Gulf South Medical Supply Inc	E	904 332-3000	
Jacksonville (G-6249)			
Habana Hospital Pharmacy Inc	E	813 872-7771	
Tampa (G-17784)			
HCA North Fla Sup Chain Svcs	E	904 378-7000	
Jacksonville (G-6264)			
Henry Schein Inc	D	904 380-3230	
Jacksonville (G-6275)			
Hotel Superstore	C	561 371-2661	
Mascotte (G-8696)			
Howmedica Osteonics Corp	E	269 389-8959	
Davie (G-2492)			
▲ Inovo Inc	D	239 491-3516	
Lehigh Acres (G-8284)			
Intermed Group Inc	E	561 586-3667	
Alachua (G-7)			
▲ KLS-Martin LP	E	904 641-7746	
Jacksonville (G-6407)			
Knight Dental Group Inc	B	813 854-3333	
Oldsmar (G-11910)			
Leesar Inc	B	239 939-8800	
Fort Myers (G-4495)			
Lensar LLC	D	888 536-7271	
Orlando (G-12762)			
Liberator Medical Supply Inc	C	772 287-2414	
Stuart (G-16636)			
Liberty Medical LLC	E	772 398-5800	
Fort Lauderdale (G-3937)			
Liberty Medical Supply Inc	E	800 695-2500	
Fort Lauderdale (G-3938)			
Major Medical Supply Inc	E	407 822-4600	
Orlando (G-12804)			
Managed Care North America Inc	D	954 730-7131	
Fort Lauderdale (G-3954)			
◆ McKesson Mdcl-Srgcal Top Hldng	D	904 332-3000	
Jacksonville (G-6486)			
▲ Med-Care Medical Inc	C	954 794-0634	
Deerfield Beach (G-2771)			
Medassist-Op Inc	E	813 342-4432	
Tampa (G-18016)			
Medical Ctr Hm Hlth Care Svcs	A	850 431-6868	
Tallahassee (G-17040)			
▼ Medical Technology Assoc Inc	D	727 548-8600	
Pinellas Park (G-14528)			
◆ Megalabs Usa LLC	E	305 663-2129	
Miami (G-9933)			
◆ Mercedes Medical LLC	C	941 355-3333	
Bradenton (G-1145)			
▲ Mercury Enterprises Inc	D	727 573-0088	
Clearwater (G-1713)			
Mp Totalcare Supply Inc	D	614 855-6300	
Clearwater (G-1729)			
Mrb Acquisition Corp	D	866 387-2668	
Daytona Beach (G-2639)			
MSC Group Inc	D	904 646-0199	
Jacksonville (G-6519)			
Mwi Veterinary Supply Inc	C	407 438-2350	
Orlando (G-12892)			
◆ Nds Surgical Imaging LLC	D	408 776-0085	
Bradenton (G-1151)			
Neumanns Home Medical Eqp Inc	E	407 822-4600	
Orlando (G-12909)			
New World Holdings Inc	E	561 888-4939	
Delray Beach (G-2995)			
Oculus Surgical Inc	E	772 236-2622	
Port St Lucie (G-15180)			
◆ Olympus Latin America Inc	D	305 266-2332	
Miami (G-10069)			
One Home Medical Equipment LLC	C	855 441-6900	
Miramar (G-10884)			
Orchid Medical Inc	D	866 888-6724	
Orlando (G-12938)			
Orion Medical Enterprises Inc	E	305 651-3261	
Miami (G-10080)			
Orthofix Medical Inc	E	352 672-6992	
Gainesville (G-4972)			
Oscor Inc	C	727 937-2511	
Palm Harbor (G-13874)			

Patterson Dental Supply Inc ....D 904 741-4480
Jacksonville (G-6587)

Patterson Dental Supply Inc ....D 904 779-2838
Jacksonville (G-6588)

Perfusioncom Inc ....C 888 499-5672
Fort Myers (G-4540)

Philips Med Systems Clvland In ....E 813 626-8280
Tampa (G-18144)

Philips Med Systems Clvland In ....D 800 722-9377
Gainesville (G-4979)

Pikes Peak Holdings Inc ....E 352 854-8080
Ocala (G-11761)

Priority Healthcare Dist Inc ....C 407 833-7000
Lake Mary (G-7625)

◆ Professional Products Inc ....C 850 892-5731
Defuniak Springs (G-2839)

Prohealth Select Inc ....E 800 488-0279
Jupiter (G-7128)

▲ Q-Med Corporation ....D 954 316-1212
Fort Lauderdale (G-4069)

Quality Assured Services Inc ....C 407 563-2860
Orlando (G-13076)

Respitek Inc ....E 813 626-3333
Tampa (G-18219)

Rgh Enterprises Inc ....E 904 378-8940
Jacksonville (G-6661)

▼ Rotech Healthcare Inc ....C 407 822-4600
Orlando (G-13140)

Rotech Home Medical Care Inc ....D 407 822-4600
Orlando (G-13141)

▲ Soule Co ....D 813 907-6000
Lutz (G-8458)

◆ Steripack (usa) Limited LLC ....E 863 648-2333
Lakeland (G-7979)

◆ Stone Medical Group LLC ....E 561 998-2402
Boca Raton (G-822)

Summit Medical Supplies Inc ....E 386 214-0227
Tallahassee (G-17117)

◆ Sunoptic Technologies LLC ....D 877 677-2832
Jacksonville (G-6809)

▲ Terumo Latin America Corp ....E 305 477-4822
Coral Gables (G-2197)

◆ Trividia Health Inc ....B 954 677-8201
Fort Lauderdale (G-4188)

Ugm Global Inc ....D 772 634-8279
Miami (G-10427)

United Medco Inc ....E 954 947-4300
Coral Springs (G-2295)

United States Phrm Group LLC ....B 954 903-5000
Sunrise (G-16841)

US Med Direct LLC ....B 305 436-6033
Doral (G-3350)

Usine Rotec Inc ....D 407 227-1153
Orlando (G-13364)

▲ Venus Concept USA Inc ....E 888 907-0115
Weston (G-19484)

▲ Veterans Medical Supply Inc ....E 727 517-4428
Saint Petersburg (G-15886)

Vitas Healthcare Corporation ....E 561 496-2378
Delray Beach (G-3032)

▲ Warehouse Goods LLC ....E 877 865-2260
Boca Raton (G-868)

Watermark Medical Inc ....A 561 283-1191
West Palm Beach (G-19414)

West Coast Med Resources LLC ....E 727 392-2800
Clearwater (G-1837)

Zimmer Biomet CMF Thoracic LLC ......C 574 267-6639
Jacksonville (G-6966)

5048 Ophthalmic Goods Wholesale

Abb-Diversified Holding Corp ....E 800 852-8089
Coral Springs (G-2216)

Abb/Con-Cise Optical Group LLC ....B 303 506-1836
Coral Springs (G-2217)

Alvaco Trading Company ....D 800 852-8089
Coral Springs (G-2226)

Bausch & Lomb Incorporated ....C 727 724-6600
Clearwater (G-1532)

▲ Eyekon Medical Inc ....E 727 793-0170
Clearwater (G-1629)

Grandvision USA Ret Holdg Corp ....E 305 794-4780
Miramar (G-10860)

Insight Optical Mfg Co Fla Inc ....E 305 557-9004
Hialeah (G-5281)

▲ Neoptx LLC ....D 954 441-9611
Miramar (G-10882)

5049 Professional Eqpt & Splys, NEC Wholesale

▼ Ace Educational Supplies Inc ....E 954 680-8172
Fort Lauderdale (G-3577)

Advanced Dcument Solutions Inc ....D 407 412-6929
Orlando (G-12054)

▼ Air Science Usa LLC ....E 239 489-3200
Fort Myers (G-4255)

▲ Aspex Eyewear Inc ....D 954 433-7296
Hollywood (G-5393)

▲ Brinkmann Instruments Inc ....D 813 316-4700
Riverview (G-15247)

▼ Compuquip Technologies LLC ....D 786 416-6143
Doral (G-3159)

▼ Lengemann Corporation ....E 352 669-2111
Altoona (G-118)

▲ Pyramid Paper Company ....E 800 792-2644
Tampa (G-18185)

Red Hawk Fire & Security LLC ....E 954 791-1313
Miami (G-10188)

Thermo Fisher Scientific Inc ....B 561 688-8700
West Palm Beach (G-19386)

5051 Metals Service Centers

▲ AA Metals Inc ....E 407 377-0246
Orlando (G-12037)

Advanced Drainage Systems Inc ....C 407 654-3989
Winter Garden (G-19552)

Allied Crawford Lakeland Inc ....E 863 667-4966
Lakeland (G-7793)

Alro Steel Corporation ....E 407 678-2576
Orlando (G-12101)

Alro Steel Corporation ....C 561 997-6766
Boca Raton (G-413)

Bell Steel Company ....D 850 432-1545
Pensacola (G-14233)

▲ Berman Bros Inc ....D 904 353-3694
Jacksonville (G-5857)

▲ Bob Dean Supply Inc ....E 239 332-1131
Fort Myers (G-4293)

Bowman Steel LLC ....C 239 303-9739
Sebring (G-16390)

◆ Certified Slings Inc ....E 407 831-7449
Casselberry (G-1446)

Chaparral Steel Midlothian LP ....A 813 319-4883
Tampa (G-17456)

Chatham Steel Corporation ....E 407 859-0310
Orlando (G-12290)

Coastal Steel Group Inc ....D 407 827-4309
Cocoa (G-1926)

Commercial Metals Company ....B 904 266-4261
Jacksonville (G-5982)

Consolidated Pipe & Sup Co Inc ....C 407 293-2001
Orlando (G-12361)

◆ Corpac Steel Products Corp ....C 305 933-8599
Miami (G-9419)

◆ Diploma Holdings Inc ....C 727 796-1300
Clearwater (G-1607)

◆ Eastern Metal Supply Inc ....C 561 533-6061
Lake Worth Beach (G-7767)

Flag Intrmediate Holdings Corp ....A 954 202-4000
Fort Lauderdale (G-3791)

◆ Future Metals LLC ....D 954 724-1400
Tamarac (G-17191)

Infra-Metals Co ....E 813 626-6005
Tampa (G-17865)

Kloeckner Metals Corporation ....D 954 785-2850
Pompano Beach (G-14838)

Kloeckner Metals Corporation ....D 813 247-4511
Tampa (G-17929)

▼ Lehman Pipe and Plbg Sup Inc ....E 305 576-3054
Miami (G-9856)

Lloyd Industries Inc ....D 904 541-1655
Orange Park (G-12001)

▲ LV Thompson Inc ....C 813 248-3456
Tampa (G-17968)

◆ McNichols Company ....D 877 884-4653
Tampa (G-18012)

McNichols Company ....D 813 243-1800
Tampa (G-18013)

Metals USA Building Pdts LP ....D 352 787-7766
Groveland (G-5099)

▼ Modern Welding Company Fla Inc ...D 407 843-1270
Orlando (G-12875)

ONeal Steel LLC ....E 813 621-2036
Jacksonville (G-6562)

Phoenix Corporation ....E 813 626-8999
Tampa (G-18147)

Plenums Inc ....E 727 521-3567
Pinellas Park (G-14532)

Primus Pipe and Tube Inc ....D 352 748-9276
Wildwood (G-19507)

R&D Steel Erectors LLC ....E 904 529-9474
Fleming Island (G-3556)

▼ Robbins Engineering Inc ....E 813 972-1135
Tampa (G-18230)

Royce Electronic Sales Inc ....E 407 869-4700
Casselberry (G-1455)

Skyline Steel Inc ....E 954 640-9146
Fort Lauderdale (G-4133)

▼ Smith & Deshields Inc ....D 561 395-0808
Boca Raton (G-809)

◆ Southwestern Suppliers Inc ....D 813 626-2193
Tampa (G-18313)

Southwire Company LLC ....C 850 423-4680
Crestview (G-2332)

◆ Steel Resources LLC ....E 305 459-4000
Miami (G-10330)

Stephens Pipe & Steel LLC ....C 321 952-7932
Melbourne (G-8981)

Taco Metals LLC ....E 727 577-3377
Seminole (G-16463)

Taco Metals LLC ....E 407 339-1190
Longwood (G-8409)

◆ Tampa Bay Steel Corporation ....C 813 621-4738
Tampa (G-18369)

▲ Tampa Intl Forest Pdts LLC ....E 813 880-7300
Tampa (G-18388)

Trinity Construction Pdts Inc ....D 407 886-5896
Apopka (G-218)

▼ US Wholesale Pipe & Tube Inc ....E 727 945-9060
Holiday (G-5377)

◆ W & O Supply Inc ....D 904 354-3800
Jacksonville (G-6914)

5052 Coal & Other Minerals & Ores Wholesale

◆ IMI Fuels LLC ....D 561 705-0350
Delray Beach (G-2970)

◆ Oxbow Carbn Mnrl Holdings Inc ......E 561 907-5400
West Palm Beach (G-19298)

Oxbow Carbon LLC ....A 561 907-5400
West Palm Beach (G-19299)

◆ Oxbow Energy Solutions LLC ....C 561 907-4300
West Palm Beach (G-19301)

5063 Electrl Apparatus, Eqpt, Wiring Splys Wholesale

AA Electric SE Inc ....E 863 665-6941
Lakeland (G-7780)

Accurate Power and Tech Inc ....E 352 735-8285
Eustis (G-3490)

American Ltg Signalization Inc ....D 904 886-4300
Jacksonville (G-5787)

◆ American Plumbing Supply Co ....E 305 532-3447
Miami Beach (G-10548)

Anixter Inc ....E 407 240-1888
Orlando (G-12123)

Anixter Power Solutions Inc ....D 813 621-9649
Tampa (G-17288)

Austen Generators Inc ....E 305 805-8166
Hialeah (G-5222)

◆ B & G PTL Enterprises Inc ....E 954 977-4060
Pompano Beach (G-14747)

Bass-Nted Fire SEC Systems Inc ....E 954 785-7800
Pompano Beach (G-14750)

Beck Electric Supply ....B 850 398-8468
Crestview (G-2312)

▲ Boca Flasher Inc ....E 561 989-5338
Deerfield Beach (G-2716)

Bore Tech Utilities & Maint ....D 305 297-8162
Miami (G-9269)

▲ Cableorganizer Acquisition LLC ....E 954 642-7090
Fort Lauderdale (G-3664)

Carrier Fire SEC Americas Corp ....B 828 428-2157
Palm Beach Gardens (G-13697)

▼ Champion Controls Inc ....E 954 318-3090
Fort Lauderdale (G-3682)

Composite Motors Inc ....E 352 799-2599
Brooksville (G-1282)

Crawford Electric Supply Co ....E 407 949-3500
Maitland (G-8521)

Curry Controls Company ....D 863 646-5781
Lakeland (G-7847)

Dale R Yox Inc ....E 352 794-7368
Crystal River (G-2345)

Dbk Concepts Inc ....C 305 596-7226
Miami (G-9463)

S
I
C

Ddci Inc	D	407 814-0225
Orlando *(G-12407)*		
Digisat International Inc	E	321 676-5250
Melbourne *(G-8871)*		
E Harold Wilson Inc	E	863 682-0158
Lakeland *(G-7854)*		
◆ Electric Supply of Tampa LLC	D	813 872-1894
Tampa *(G-17620)*		
◆ Electrical Supplies Inc	D	305 702-6001
Hialeah Gardens *(G-5342)*		
Englander Enterprises Inc	E	727 461-4755
Clearwater *(G-1625)*		
◆ Farreys Wholesale Hdwr Co Inc	D	305 947-5451
North Miami *(G-11489)*		
▲ Faulhaber Micromo LLC	E	727 572-0131
Clearwater *(G-1633)*		
▼ Fire Alarm Systems & SEC Inc	E	954 327-8670
Davie *(G-2480)*		
Frontier Florida LLC	A	813 620-2518
Tampa *(G-17717)*		
▼ Frontier Lighting Inc	E	727 447-7676
Clearwater *(G-1651)*		
◆ Gdi Technology Inc	D	305 969-2047
Miami *(G-9621)*		
▼ Generx Generators LLC	E	813 814-5900
Oldsmar *(G-11904)*		
▲ Gfx Inc	E	305 499-9789
Miami *(G-9629)*		
◆ Global Exports USA Inc	D	305 371-9200
Miami *(G-9635)*		
Glomar Corporation	E	305 624-2044
Miami *(G-9640)*		
Graybar Electric Company Inc	D	407 841-4810
Orlando *(G-12596)*		
Graybar Electric Company Inc	E	904 356-7611
Jacksonville *(G-6240)*		
Graybar Electric Company Inc	E	305 520-4800
Medley *(G-8740)*		
Graybar Electric Company Inc	E	813 259-4123
Tampa *(G-17748)*		
Graybar Electric Company Inc	E	561 841-5055
Riviera Beach *(G-15297)*		
Graybar Electric Company Inc	E	321 768-7661
Melbourne *(G-8895)*		
Green Applications LLC	E	954 900-2290
Fort Lauderdale *(G-3835)*		
Home Depot Inc	C	713 862-5550
Jacksonville *(G-6285)*		
Home Depot USA Inc	B	904 421-1400
Jacksonville *(G-6291)*		
Hughes Supply Inc	A	727 573-7793
Clearwater *(G-1674)*		
▼ Hughes Supply Inc	D	239 334-2205
Fort Myers *(G-4445)*		
▲ Industrial Lighting Pdts LLC	D	407 478-3759
Sanford *(G-15952)*		
Integrated SEC Systems Inc	D	305 324-8800
Miami *(G-9754)*		
◆ International Elec Sls Corp	E	305 591-8390
Miami *(G-9763)*		
◆ Intracom USA Inc	E	813 855-0550
Oldsmar *(G-11908)*		
Jackman Williams LLC	E	407 377-6886
Orlando *(G-12697)*		
Johnson Controls Inc	D	954 538-1601
Miramar *(G-10871)*		
▼ K & M Electric Supply Inc	E	561 842-4911
Riviera Beach *(G-15303)*		
Light Bulb Depot 5 LLC	E	904 727-6787
Jacksonville *(G-6438)*		
◆ Louis Poulsen USA Inc	E	954 349-2525
Weston *(G-19465)*		
Magnaluxus Inc	B	855 624-6258
Old Town *(G-11887)*		
▲ Martin Professional Inc	E	954 858-1800
Weston *(G-19466)*		
Master LLC	D	786 840-0949
Pembroke Pines *(G-14168)*		
Mathes Electric Supply Co Inc	E	850 432-4161
Pensacola *(G-14354)*		
▼ Mercedes Electric Supply Inc	E	305 887-5550
Medley *(G-8757)*		
North Amrcn Sbstation Svcs LLC	D	407 788-3717
Altamonte Springs *(G-83)*		
Osram Sylvania Inc	D	502 315-2545
Palm Beach Gardens *(G-13759)*		
▼ Pacer Marine Inc	E	941 378-5774
Sarasota *(G-16255)*		
Palmer Electric Company	B	407 646-8700
Winter Park *(G-19759)*		

◆ Pantropic Power Inc	D	305 477-3329
Doral *(G-3287)*		
▼ Peninsular Electric Distrs Inc	D	561 832-1626
West Palm Beach *(G-19322)*		
Quality Cable Contractors Inc	E	407 246-0606
Orlando *(G-13077)*		
Rexel Inc	A	229 249-8337
Tallahassee *(G-17087)*		
Rexel Usa Inc	E	813 249-3200
Tampa *(G-18223)*		
Rexel Usa Inc	E	407 849-6532
Orlando *(G-13106)*		
Rexel Usa Inc	E	954 977-2600
Pompano Beach *(G-14883)*		
Rexel Usa Inc	E	305 597-1940
Miami *(G-10210)*		
Safe Touch Inc	C	850 385-9544
Tallahassee *(G-17090)*		
Scis Air Security Corporation	D	786 725-4492
Miami *(G-10249)*		
◆ SEES Incorporated	D	954 971-1115
Pompano Beach *(G-14895)*		
◆ Siemens Energy Inc	A	407 736-2000
Orlando *(G-13195)*		
Solutions Manufacturing LLC	D	321 848-0848
Rockledge *(G-15368)*		
Sonepar Distribution Neng Inc	D	407 949-3500
Maitland *(G-8578)*		
Sonepar USA Holdings Inc	D	407 343-7800
Kissimmee *(G-7387)*		
Sonepar USA Holdings Inc	C	305 949-6336
North Miami Beach *(G-11532)*		
▼ South Dade Electrical Sup Inc	D	305 238-7131
Miami *(G-10297)*		
◆ South Dade Lighting Inc	E	305 233-8020
Miami *(G-10298)*		
Surge Suppression LLC	E	850 654-5559
Brooksville *(G-1314)*		
T R S	D	407 298-5490
Orlando *(G-13267)*		
◆ Tampa Armature Works Inc	A	813 621-5661
Riverview *(G-15272)*		
Tampa Armature Works Inc	D	904 757-7790
Jacksonville *(G-6831)*		
Tampa Armature Works Inc	C	813 612-2600
Tampa *(G-18361)*		
◆ Taw Miami Service Center Inc	E	305 884-1717
Medley *(G-8788)*		
◆ The Swatch Group U S Inc	D	201 271-1400
Miami *(G-10385)*		
Topaz Lighting Company LLC	D	772 778-1197
Vero Beach *(G-18926)*		
Westinghouse Lighting Corp	C	215 671-2000
Jacksonville *(G-6930)*		
World Electric Supply Inc	E	954 979-1960
Pompano Beach *(G-14943)*		
▲ World Electric Supply Inc	E	904 378-4000
Jacksonville *(G-6943)*		
World Electric Supply Inc	E	239 274-8111
Fort Myers *(G-4657)*		

5064 Electrical Appliances, TV & Radios Wholesale

Aamp Holdings Inc	D	727 572-9255
Clearwater *(G-1509)*		
◆ Aamp of Florida Inc	E	727 572-9255
Clearwater *(G-1510)*		
▼ AP Sound LLC	D	850 432-5780
Pensacola *(G-14219)*		
◆ Ard Distributors Inc	E	305 624-0106
Miami *(G-9167)*		
▼ AVI-Spl Holdings Inc	A	866 708-5034
Tampa *(G-17325)*		
▼ AVI-Spl LLC	B	813 884-7168
Tampa *(G-17326)*		
Century/Aaa Ltd	E	305 362-2666
Hialeah *(G-5232)*		
▲ Dalbani Corporation America	D	305 716-1016
Miami *(G-9455)*		
◆ Famous Tate Electric Co	D	813 931-8455
Tampa *(G-17648)*		
Ferguson Enterprises LLC	E	407 856-5161
Orlando *(G-12505)*		
◆ First Coast Supply Inc	D	904 388-1217
Jacksonville *(G-6172)*		
Home-Tech Service Inc	C	941 751-9992
Bradenton *(G-1122)*		
▼ Jair Electronics Corporation	E	305 594-7361
Doral *(G-3248)*		

▼ Johns Appliance City Inc	D	386 760-2776
South Daytona *(G-16489)*		
◆ King of Fans Inc	E	954 484-7500
Fort Lauderdale *(G-3922)*		
Lowes Home Centers LLC	C	352 365-2223
Leesburg *(G-8260)*		
Lowes Home Centers LLC	C	386 418-6060
Alachua *(G-10)*		
Lowes Home Centers LLC	D	561 883-1215
Boca Raton *(G-677)*		
Lowes Home Centers LLC	C	954 680-8667
Southwest Ranches *(G-16529)*		
Lowes Home Centers LLC	C	850 932-0762
Gulf Breeze *(G-5123)*		
Lowes Home Centers LLC	C	863 299-2819
Winter Haven *(G-19644)*		
Lowes Home Centers LLC	C	813 558-6760
Tampa *(G-17961)*		
Lowes Home Centers LLC	C	407 452-1100
Kissimmee *(G-7350)*		
Lowes Home Centers LLC	C	386 719-6622
Lake City *(G-7536)*		
Lowes Home Centers LLC	D	239 596-2570
Naples *(G-11200)*		
Lowes Home Centers LLC	D	386 774-7000
Orange City *(G-11968)*		
Lowes Home Centers LLC	C	407 788-4305
Altamonte Springs *(G-72)*		
Lowes Home Centers LLC	C	850 575-1435
Tallahassee *(G-17026)*		
Lowes Home Centers LLC	D	407 977-9599
Oviedo *(G-13556)*		
Lowes Home Centers LLC	C	727 547-9335
Pinellas Park *(G-14527)*		
Lowes Home Centers LLC	C	941 756-1822
Bradenton *(G-1129)*		
Lowes Home Centers LLC	C	561 733-1397
Boynton Beach *(G-1008)*		
Lowes Home Centers LLC	D	321 631-0696
Rockledge *(G-15356)*		
Lowes Home Centers LLC	C	352 592-0176
Spring Hill *(G-16541)*		
Lowes Home Centers LLC	D	772 283-4229
Stuart *(G-16637)*		
Lowes Home Centers LLC	E	954 578-0246
Sunrise *(G-16793)*		
Lowes Home Centers LLC	C	904 277-5000
Fernandina Beach *(G-3535)*		
Lowes Home Centers LLC	C	813 659-4040
Plant City *(G-14570)*		
Lowes Home Centers LLC	D	352 259-6500
Lady Lake *(G-7438)*		
Lowes Home Centers LLC	C	407 430-4060
Sanford *(G-15961)*		
Lowes Home Centers LLC	C	727 724-3557
Clearwater *(G-1701)*		
Lowes Home Centers LLC	E	954 346-3993
Coral Springs *(G-2270)*		
Lowes Home Centers LLC	C	239 433-9255
Fort Myers *(G-4497)*		
Lowes Home Centers LLC	C	863 701-9800
Lakeland *(G-7911)*		
Lowes Home Centers LLC	C	321 953-2880
Melbourne *(G-8924)*		
Lowes Home Centers LLC	C	727 859-9450
New Port Richey *(G-11392)*		
Lowes Home Centers LLC	E	954 630-9550
Wilton Manors *(G-19529)*		
Lowes Home Centers LLC	C	407 532-6884
Orlando *(G-12783)*		
Lowes Home Centers LLC	C	386 671-9112
Ormond Beach *(G-13508)*		
Lowes Home Centers LLC	D	386 788-8566
Port Orange *(G-15080)*		
Lowes Home Centers LLC	C	727 822-8220
Saint Petersburg *(G-15751)*		
Lowes Home Centers LLC	D	772 564-6955
Vero Beach *(G-18889)*		
Lowes Home Centers LLC	C	772 692-7745
Jensen Beach *(G-7019)*		
Lowes Home Centers LLC	C	561 795-3808
Royal Palm Beach *(G-15384)*		
Lowes Home Centers LLC	D	850 913-1600
Panama City *(G-14037)*		
Lowes Home Centers LLC	C	561 207-9037
Lake Park *(G-7660)*		
Lowes Home Centers LLC	C	727 588-1200
Largo *(G-8132)*		
Lowes Home Centers LLC	C	850 423-7400
Crestview *(G-2325)*		

Lowes Home Centers LLC	D	954 624-1900	
Pembroke Pines (G-14166)			
Lowes Home Centers LLC	C	904 682-7667	
Orange Park (G-12002)			
Lowes Home Centers LLC	C	954 545-7381	
Pompano Beach (G-14845)			
Lowes Home Centers LLC	E	352 237-7600	
Ocala (G-11715)			
Lowes Home Centers LLC	D	386 326-5340	
Palatka (G-13593)			
Lowes Home Centers LLC	D	352 860-5800	
Inverness (G-5696)			
Lowes Home Centers LLC	C	813 838-9000	
Zephyrhills (G-19841)			
Lowes Home Centers LLC	C	850 526-6440	
Marianna (G-8681)			
Lowes Home Centers LLC	C	941 525-1000	
Venice (G-18792)			
Lowes Home Centers LLC	C	352 385-3600	
Mount Dora (G-10956)			
Lowes Home Centers LLC	D	904 696-4063	
Jacksonville (G-6447)			
Lowes Home Centers LLC	C	386 785-2430	
De Land (G-2695)			
Lowes Home Centers LLC	C	352 754-6320	
Brooksville (G-1297)			
Lowes Home Centers LLC	C	863 451-4000	
Sebring (G-16406)			
Lowes Home Centers LLC	C	863 519-4000	
Bartow (G-325)			
Lowes Home Centers LLC	C	813 313-1424	
Riverview (G-15260)			
Lowes Home Centers LLC	B	352 367-8900	
Gainesville (G-4937)			
Lowes Home Centers LLC	C	321 779-7960	
Indian Harbour Beach (G-5671)			
Lowes Home Centers LLC	C	941 421-1041	
Port Charlotte (G-15045)			
Lowes Home Centers LLC	C	386 330-5760	
Live Oak (G-8314)			
Lowes Home Centers LLC	D	239 458-6440	
Cape Coral (G-1410)			
Lowes Home Centers LLC	C	813 793-9152	
Brandon (G-1243)			
Lowes Home Centers LLC	C	305 820-4192	
Hialeah (G-5293)			
Lowes Home Centers LLC	D	850 636-3920	
Panama City (G-14038)			
Lowes Home Centers LLC	E	239 494-9000	
Estero (G-3469)			
Lowes Home Centers LLC	C	321 207-2860	
Fern Park (G-3514)			
Lowes Home Centers LLC	D	850 316-3359	
Pensacola (G-14350)			
Lowes Home Centers LLC	C	941 961-6261	
Sarasota (G-16223)			
Lowes Home Centers LLC	C	863 734-5000	
Lake Wales (G-7691)			
Lowes Home Centers LLC	D	863 551-3070	
Auburndale (G-256)			
Lowes Home Centers LLC	C	863 422-9116	
Haines City (G-5151)			
Lowes Home Centers LLC	C	305 508-3020	
Homestead (G-5589)			
Lowes Home Centers LLC	C	407 905-3900	
Winter Garden (G-19579)			
Lowes Home Centers LLC	C	386 585-6000	
Palm Coast (G-13833)			
Lowes Home Centers LLC	C	321 327-6906	
Palm Bay (G-13627)			
Lowes Home Centers LLC	D	407 814-2760	
Apopka (G-199)			
Lowes Home Centers LLC	D	941 257-2200	
North Port (G-11573)			
Lowes Home Centers LLC	D	386 960-9031	
Deltona (G-3042)			
Lowes Home Centers LLC	C	904 589-3022	
Middleburg (G-10797)			
Lowes Home Centers LLC	E	786 319-5126	
Miami (G-9882)			
Mar-Cone Appliance Parts Co	C	813 247-4410	
Tampa (G-17989)			
Miele Incorporated	E	305 445-1336	
Coral Gables (G-2149)			
Munters Corporation	D	517 676-7070	
Fort Myers (G-4520)			
◆ Newtech Electronics Inds Inc	E	305 628-0900	
Miami (G-10045)			
Panasonic Do Brasil Ltda	E	305 377-9224	
Miami (G-10092)			

Peaden LLC	C	850 872-1004	
Panama City (G-14054)			
◆ Precision Trading Corp	E	305 592-4500	
Medley (G-8771)			
◆ Regal Worldwide Trading LLC	E	305 714-7425	
Medley (G-8773)			
Setzers & Company Inc	E	904 731-4100	
Jacksonville (G-6714)			
Sharp Electronics Corporation	D	305 779-5817	
Miami Lakes (G-10761)			
Skg Marketing LLC	E	786 954-3800	
Doral (G-3311)			
◆ Sony Latin America Inc	D	858 942-2400	
Miami (G-10295)			
Tampa Bay Systems Sales Inc	E	813 877-8253	
Tampa (G-18371)			
Techni-Car Inc	C	800 886-0022	
Oldsmar (G-11930)			

5065 Electronic Parts & Eqpt Wholesale

Abacus Industries Inc	E	800 701-8152	
Naples (G-10996)			
Abstract Electronics Inc	C	727 540-0236	
Clearwater (G-1512)			
Access Control Tech Inc	E	407 422-8850	
Orlando (G-12045)			
Acopian Technical Company	D	321 727-1172	
Melbourne (G-8808)			
Addvantage Triton LLC	E	786 787-7000	
Miami (G-9076)			
Addvantage Triton LLC	E	786 787-7000	
Miami (G-9077)			
◆ Advanced Media Tech Inc	D	954 427-5711	
Deerfield Beach (G-2707)			
All American Semiconductor LLC	E	305 626-4183	
Miami (G-9117)			
◆ Allplus Computer Systems Corp	E	305 436-3993	
Doral (G-3111)			
America II Electronics LLC	C	727 573-0900	
Saint Petersburg (G-15566)			
America II Group LLC	E	800 767-2637	
Saint Petersburg (G-15567)			
American Tchncal Ceramics Corp	D	904 724-2000	
Jacksonville (G-5793)			
Asa-Tron Inc	D	786 744-7011	
Hollywood (G-5392)			
Atci Communications Inc	E	305 620-0062	
Miami (G-9183)			
Atlas Property Management Svcs	D	305 718-4038	
Doral (G-3128)			
Auvidatel Inc	E	863 288-8844	
Winter Haven (G-19607)			
Avnet Inc	E	954 493-8111	
Fort Lauderdale (G-3622)			
◆ Benq Latin America Corp	E	305 421-1200	
Doral (G-3136)			
◆ Blu Products Inc	C	305 715-7171	
Doral (G-3138)			
Brightstar Global Group Inc	A	305 421-6000	
Melbourne (G-8707)			
Call One Inc	D	321 783-2400	
Cape Canaveral (G-1354)			
◆ Camrose Trading Inc	C	305 594-4666	
Miami (G-9309)			
▲ Cellworks International Inc	E	407 951-7251	
Altamonte Springs (G-33)			
Cinch Cnnctivity Solutions Inc	D	321 308-4100	
Melbourne (G-8842)			
Communications Intl Inc	D	772 569-5355	
Vero Beach (G-18847)			
Compulink Corporation	B	727 579-1500	
Saint Petersburg (G-15641)			
Copyfax Inc	E	904 296-1600	
Jacksonville (G-6001)			
▲ CT Group LLC	E	305 715-7171	
Doral (G-3170)			
▼ Dedc Inc	D	813 626-5195	
Tampa (G-17582)			
▲ Digitalpersona Inc	D	561 622-1650	
Palm Beach Gardens (G-13717)			
◆ Diploma Holdings Inc	C	727 796-1300	
Clearwater (G-1607)			
Direct Components Inc	E	813 835-3883	
Tampa (G-17593)			
◆ Domital Corporation	E	305 594-0873	
Fort Lauderdale (G-3762)			
Englander Enterprises Inc	E	727 461-4755	
Clearwater (G-1625)			
◆ Four S Group Inc	E	305 666-7474	
Coral Gables (G-2110)			

G G B Industries Inc	D	239 643-4400	
Naples (G-11127)			
▲ Ghekko Networks Inc	D	800 736-4397	
Saint Petersburg (G-15687)			
Graybar Electric Company Inc	E	904 356-7611	
Jacksonville (G-6240)			
Hammond Electronics Inc	D	407 521-6202	
Orlando (G-12613)			
▲ Hopper Radio of Florida Inc	D	954 659-2028	
Boca Raton (G-633)			
▲ Image Access Inc	E	561 995-8334	
Boca Raton (G-639)			
Integrated SEC Systems Inc	D	305 324-8800	
Miami (G-9754)			
▲ Interconnect Cable Tech Corp	C	352 796-1716	
Brooksville (G-1296)			
◆ International SEC & Trdg Corp	D	305 594-4141	
Doral (G-3243)			
◆ Intradeco Inc	D	305 264-6022	
Medley (G-8747)			
JC Global Inc	D	800 260-8830	
Odessa (G-11846)			
◆ JI Audio Inc	C	954 443-1100	
Miramar (G-10870)			
Jsc Systems Inc	E	850 656-1705	
Tallahassee (G-17012)			
▲ Kai Limited	C	954 957-8586	
Fort Lauderdale (G-3915)			
▲ Kemet Electronics Corporation	D	864 963-6700	
Fort Lauderdale (G-3919)			
Logus Manufacturing Corp	E	561 842-3550	
West Palm Beach (G-19240)			
▲ Metra Electronics Corporation	B	386 257-1186	
Holly Hill (G-5382)			
▲ Micro Ram Electronics Inc	E	813 854-5500	
Oldsmar (G-11913)			
Mitel Technologies Inc	C	954 427-8787	
Boca Raton (G-696)			
◆ Modern Entp Solutions Inc	E	813 673-8886	
Tampa (G-18047)			
◆ Nac Group Inc	B	727 576-0550	
Saint Petersburg (G-15770)			
▲ Nac Semi Inc	D	866 651-2901	
Saint Petersburg (G-15771)			
Net-Tec LLC	C	786 605-0644	
Pembroke Pines (G-14173)			
▲ Nexxtworks Inc	E	727 725-0400	
Tampa (G-18084)			
Orlando Bus Tele Systems Inc	D	407 996-9000	
Orlando (G-12942)			
Pace Micro Tech Support Svcs	D	561 995-2610	
Boca Raton (G-736)			
◆ Pdi Communications Inc	E	561 998-0600	
Boca Raton (G-747)			
▲ Pro Sound Inc	E	305 891-1000	
North Miami (G-11507)			
◆ Protel Inc	D	863 644-5558	
Lakeland (G-7942)			
Radial South LP	B	719 948-1900	
Melbourne (G-8965)			
▲ Senelco Iberia Inc	A	561 912-6000	
Deerfield Beach (G-2794)			
Shadow Technologies Inc	E	321 207-0112	
Longwood (G-8404)			
Sharp Electronics Corporation	D	305 779-5817	
Miami Lakes (G-10761)			
▼ Shields Environmental Inc	E	407 936-0025	
Sanford (G-15980)			
◆ Solution Box LLC	E	305 722-3825	
Miami (G-10292)			
◆ Sony Latin America Inc	D	858 942-2400	
Miami (G-10295)			
Sourceability North Amer LLC	E	786 329-4001	
Doral (G-3316)			
Southeastern Lsg & Eqp Corp	E	904 448-5112	
Jacksonville (G-6755)			
Sr Technologies Inc	C	954 797-7850	
Sunrise (G-16830)			
◆ Strax Holdings Inc	E	305 468-1770	
Doral (G-3321)			
Sv Microwave Inc	C	561 840-1800	
West Palm Beach (G-19379)			
Telxius Cable Usa Inc	E	305 925-5298	
Miami (G-10375)			
▼ Tem Systems Inc	E	954 577-6044	
Sunrise (G-16836)			
▲ Tm Wireless Comm Svcs Inc	D	305 421-9938	
Doral (G-3333)			
Traka Usa LLC	E	407 681-4001	
Orlando (G-13301)			

▼ Veterans Trading Company Inc ......E 352 438-0084
Ocala (G-11794)

Vibe Enterprise Inc ......E 305 723-1640
Doral (G-3354)

▼ Videoscope Inc ......E 305 436-1684
Doral (G-3355)

Voalte Inc ......D 941 312-2830
Sarasota (G-16359)

▼ Vology Inc ......E 813 280-1300
Clearwater (G-1835)

▼ Voxx International Corporation ......B 800 645-7750
Orlando (G-13389)

Ware Group Inc ......E 850 576-5922
Tallahassee (G-17172)

▲ Wes-Garde Components Group Inc .E 863 644-7564
Lakeland (G-8005)

5072 Hardware Wholesale

◆ American Fasteners Corporation ......D 305 885-1717
Miami (G-9139)

◆ Builders Hardware Inc ......E 800 966-7753
Tampa (G-17399)

▼ Central Lock & Hardware Sup Co ...E 305 947-4853
Miami (G-9346)

Colony Hardware Corporation ......D 561 585-2113
Lake Worth (G-7718)

◆ Deco Truss Company Inc ......E 305 257-1910
Homestead (G-5569)

Energy Hardware Holdings LLC ......E 850 266-2323
Pensacola (G-14290)

◆ Farreys Wholesale Hdwr Co Inc ......D 305 947-5451
North Miami (G-11489)

▲ Florida Pneumatic Mfg Corp ......E 561 744-9500
Jupiter (G-7071)

Florida Tool & Fasteners Inc ......C 239 768-2658
Fort Myers (G-4391)

Home Depot Inc ......C 713 862-5550
Jacksonville (G-6285)

Home Depot USA Inc ......B 904 421-1400
Jacksonville (G-6291)

Integrated SEC Systems Inc ......D 305 324-8800
Miami (G-9754)

◆ Integrated Supply Network LLC ......C 800 966-8478
Lakeland (G-7886)

◆ Interstate Screw Corp ......E 305 888-8700
Hialeah (G-5282)

◆ Lars LLC ......D 305 635-3300
Miami (G-9847)

Mid-West Wholesale Hardware Co ...D 407 661-1140
Longwood (G-8383)

Mil-Spec Industries Inc ......E 561 544-4500
Oakland Park (G-11605)

Nachon Enterprises Inc ......D 305 888-5236
Hialeah (G-5303)

Pcg Securities LLC ......E 978 902-0352
Wesley Chapel (G-19005)

▲ Perko Inc ......A 305 621-7525
Miami (G-10111)

◆ QEP Co Inc ......D 561 994-5550
Boca Raton (G-761)

◆ Sewell Hardware Company Inc ......E 561 832-7171
West Palm Beach (G-19359)

◆ Sheridan Lumber Inc ......E 954 920-8079
Hollywood (G-5519)

▼ Smith & Deshields Inc ......D 561 395-0808
Boca Raton (G-809)

▲ Toptech Systems Inc ......C 407 332-1774
Longwood (G-8410)

True Value Company ......C 863 665-1549
Lakeland (G-7991)

Tyson Bolt & Sup Co Tampa Inc ......E 813 248-1111
Tampa (G-18455)

◆ Wurth Action Bolt & Tool Co ......E 800 423-0700
Lake Worth Beach (G-7778)

5074 Plumbing & Heating Splys Wholesale

◆ American Plumbing Supply Co ......E 305 532-3447
Miami Beach (G-10548)

◆ Bond Plumbing Supply Inc ......E 305 634-0656
Miami (G-9268)

◆ Carico International Inc ......E 954 973-3900
Fort Lauderdale (G-3670)

City of Hialeah ......E 305 556-7205
Hialeah (G-5239)

Consolidated Elec Distrs Inc ......D 941 413-0403
Palmetto (G-13908)

Constructive Resource Inc ......E 954 488-3868
Altamonte Springs (G-39)

Discovery Mktg & Distrg Inc ......B 813 664-0009
Tampa (G-17594)

▼ Enviro Water Solutions LLC ......D 877 842-1635
Deland (G-2858)

Ferguson Enterprises LLC ......E 407 856-5161
Orlando (G-12505)

Ferguson Enterprises LLC ......E 904 348-5354
Jacksonville (G-6153)

Ferguson Enterprises LLC ......E 954 726-3951
Tamarac (G-17189)

▼ Florida Industrial Pdts Inc ......E 407 240-0600
Tampa (G-17688)

Home Depot Inc ......C 713 862-5550
Jacksonville (G-6285)

Home Depot USA Inc ......B 904 421-1400
Jacksonville (G-6291)

▼ Hughes Supply Inc ......D 239 334-2205
Fort Myers (G-4445)

Hughes Supply Inc ......A 352 401-3700
Ocala (G-11702)

Hydrologic Distribution Co ......D 727 608-1800
Pinellas Park (G-14524)

◆ Pentair Aqatic Eco-Systems Inc ......D 407 886-7575
Apopka (G-204)

Royalaire Mechanical Svcs Inc ......C 813 749-2370
Oldsmar (G-11924)

Solar Power One LLC ......E 833 765-2778
Miami (G-10291)

◆ Spears Coastline Plastics LLC ......A 888 225-5909
Yulee (G-19821)

◆ Uma Distributors LLC ......E 407 339-8267
Altamonte Springs (G-110)

Village of Wellington ......D 561 790-0794
Wellington (G-18990)

Ware Group Inc ......E 850 576-5922
Tallahassee (G-17172)

Watermill Express LLC ......E 813 988-1111
Tampa (G-18525)

Winsupply Inc ......D 386 255-2200
Crystal River (G-2355)

▼ Wool Wholesale Plumbing Supply ...D 954 763-3632
Fort Lauderdale (G-4231)

5075 Heating & Air Conditioning Eqpt & Splys Wholesale

Air Design Systems Inc ......D 850 434-5592
Pensacola (G-14213)

▼ Baker Distributing Company LLC ....C 904 407-4500
Jacksonville (G-5833)

Carrier Enterprise LLC ......C 407 299-9800
Orlando (G-12245)

◆ Carrier Interamerica Corp ......D 305 805-4500
Miami (G-9329)

Coastline Distribution LLC ......D 813 885-7641
Tampa (G-17494)

Con-Air Industries Inc ......D 407 298-5733
Orlando (G-12357)

Cyvsa International Inc ......D 954 674-3444
Miramar (G-10850)

Daikin Applied Americas Inc ......E 407 816-6350
Orlando (G-12397)

Daikin Applied Americas Inc ......E 813 621-8440
Tampa (G-17568)

Daikin Applied Americas Inc ......E 954 862-8550
Davie (G-2475)

◆ Daikin Applied Latin Amer LLC ......D 305 716-8631
Miami (G-9453)

Dometic Corporation ......C 954 973-2477
Pompano Beach (G-14796)

◆ FHP Manufacturing Company ......B 954 776-5471
Fort Lauderdale (G-3785)

◆ Gemaire Distributors LLC ......D 954 246-2665
Deerfield Beach (G-2744)

▼ Hughes Supply Inc ......D 239 334-2205
Fort Myers (G-4445)

◆ Nortek Globl Hvac Ltin Amer In ......D 305 593-9061
Miramar (G-10883)

Parker Davis Hvac Intl Inc ......E 305 513-4488
Doral (G-3288)

▼ R S K Corporation ......E 800 909-7276
Clearwater (G-1770)

◆ Refricenter of Miami Inc ......D 305 477-8880
Miami (G-10192)

◆ Saeg Engineering Group LLC ......E 305 716-8631
Miami (G-10231)

▼ Tampa Bay Systems Sales Inc ......D 813 877-8251
Tampa (G-18370)

The Ware Group LLC ......E 863 665-4045
Lakeland (G-7988)

The Ware Group LLC ......D 407 849-0573
Orlando (G-13286)

Trane US Inc ......E 407 660-1111
Maitland (G-8590)

◆ Tropic Supply Inc ......D 954 835-6010
Sunrise (G-16840)

Tropic Supply Inc ......E 386 258-8337
Daytona Beach (G-2679)

Ware Group Inc ......E 904 354-0282
Jacksonville (G-6915)

Ware Group Inc ......E 850 576-5922
Tallahassee (G-17172)

Watsco Inc ......C 904 407-4371
Jacksonville (G-6919)

5078 Refrigeration Eqpt & Splys Wholesale

ACR Sales and Service Inc ......E 407 299-9190
Apopka (G-146)

▼ Baker Distributing Company LLC ...C 904 407-4500
Jacksonville (G-5833)

Clarios LLC ......E 904 241-4679
Jacksonville Beach (G-6981)

▲ Gram Equipment of America Inc ......E 813 248-1978
Tampa (G-17746)

◆ Nortek Globl Hvac Ltin Amer In ......D 305 593-9061
Miramar (G-10883)

◆ Refricenter of Miami Inc ......E 305 477-8880
Miami (G-10192)

Ridge Energy Savers Inc ......E 863 676-2665
Lake Wales (G-7698)

◆ Saeg Engineering Group LLC ......E 305 716-8631
Miami (G-10231)

▼ Southern Rfrgn Engineers Inc ......E 305 825-2063
Hialeah (G-5324)

▲ Thermo King of Southeast LLC ......E 407 293-7158
Winter Garden (G-19595)

◆ Tropic Supply Inc ......D 954 835-6010
Sunrise (G-16840)

5082 Construction & Mining Mach & Eqpt Wholesale

Alta Construction Eqp Fla LLC ......C 305 477-2442
Miami (G-9130)

▲ Atlantic Insulation Inc ......D 904 354-2217
Jacksonville (G-5814)

Beard Equipment Company ......E 850 476-0277
Pensacola (G-14230)

◆ Caterpillar Americas Svcs Co ......E 305 476-6800
Miramar (G-10845)

City of Pinellas Park ......E 727 541-0767
Pinellas Park (G-14512)

Cross Match Technologies Inc ......D 561 622-1665
Palm Beach Gardens (G-13713)

◆ Dobbs Equipment LLC ......D 561 848-6618
Riviera Beach (G-15291)

Dobbs Equipment LLC ......D 239 334-3627
Fort Myers (G-4345)

ER Jahna Industries Inc ......E 863 676-9431
Lake Wales (G-7681)

Florida Contractor Rentals Inc ......E 386 274-1002
Daytona Beach (G-2591)

Glacius Holdings Inc ......E 305 900-9891
Miami (G-9631)

▼ Industrial Tractor Company Inc ......D 904 296-5000
Jacksonville (G-6318)

Jama Southeast Region ......D 904 741-1905
Jacksonville (G-6372)

◆ Kelly Tractor Co ......C 305 592-5360
Doral (G-3254)

Kelly Tractor Co ......E 863 983-8177
Clewiston (G-1906)

Kelly Tractor Co ......D 239 693-9233
Fort Myers (G-4460)

King Products and Eqp LLC ......D 786 514-3476
Miami (G-9829)

Liebherr Cranes Inc ......D 305 817-7521
Hialeah (G-5290)

◆ Linder Industrial Machinery Co ......D 813 754-2727
Plant City (G-14569)

Linder Industrial Machinery Co ......E 954 433-2800
Pembroke Pines (G-14162)

Lopefra Corp ......E 305 266-3896
Doral (G-3263)

Magna CM Inc ......E 954 862-3614
Davie (G-2498)

Marathon Electrical Contrs Inc ......D 850 737-2677
Fort Walton Beach (G-4789)

▼ Nationwide Equipment Company ......E 904 924-2500
Jacksonville Beach (G-6996)

Onpower Services LLC ......E 239 288-7965
Fort Myers (G-4528)

Pantropic Power Inc ....D 954 797-7972
Fort Lauderdale (G-4040)
Phillips Manufacturing Co ....D 813 319-0931
Tampa (G-18145)
Prince Contracting LLC ....E 813 699-5900
Tampa (G-18171)
Retail Contractors of PR ....D 352 503-9900
Port Richey (G-15111)
◆ Ring Power Corporation ....B 904 201-7400
Saint Augustine (G-15486)
Ring Power Corporation ....D 941 359-6000
Sarasota (G-16048)
Ring Power Corporation ....D 813 671-3123
Riverview (G-15266)
Ring Power Corporation ....C 813 671-3700
Riverview (G-15267)
Ring Power Corporation ....E 352 797-9500
Brooksville (G-1307)
Ring Power Corporation ....C 407 855-6195
Orlando (G-13110)
Ring Power Corporation ....E 850 562-2121
Midway (G-10807)
▼ Rpc Inc ....B 904 737-7730
Saint Augustine (G-15487)
Sealand Contractors Corp ....E 561 997-6715
Boca Raton (G-789)
◆ Sims Crane & Equipment Co ....C 813 626-8102
Tampa (G-18286)
Sims Crane & Equipment Co ....D 407 851-2930
Orlando (G-13203)
Sims Crane & Equipment Co ....E 800 573-0780
Medley (G-8783)
◆ SMS International Corp ....A 813 754-2727
Plant City (G-14579)
Steven Stratton Stucco ....D 386 325-7155
East Palatka (G-3402)
Synergy Rents LLC ....E 386 274-1002
Daytona Beach (G-2671)
Thompson Tractor Co Inc ....E 850 785-4007
Panama City (G-14079)
Titan America LLC ....D 407 656-3313
Clermont (G-1895)
▼ Trekker Tractor LLC ....D 561 296-9710
Lake Worth (G-7757)

5083 Farm & Garden Mach & Eqpt Wholesale

◆ Alaso USA Corp ....D 863 606-0033
Lakeland (G-7790)
B&W Enterprise LLC ....E 863 617-5889
Lakeland (G-7809)
Beard Equipment Company ....E 850 476-0277
Pensacola (G-14230)
Capling Leveling Inc ....D 863 612-1000
Labelle (G-7423)
Florida Fertilizer Company Inc ....E 863 773-4159
Wauchula (G-18960)
▼ Florida Outdoor Equipment Inc ....E 407 295-5010
Orlando (G-12533)
▼ Glade Grove Sup Inc Blle Glade ....E 561 996-3949
Belle Glade (G-357)
▼ Grant Sprinklers Inc ....C 407 995-9095
Sanford (G-15947)
Griffin Ken Landscaping Contrs ....E 850 932-9304
Gulf Breeze (G-5116)
◆ Hector Turf Inc ....D 954 428-1229
Deerfield Beach (G-2750)
Horizon Distributors Inc ....E 941 371-4221
Sarasota (G-16187)
James Irrigation Inc ....E 813 659-0201
Dover (G-3368)
Jerry Pate Turf Irrigation Inc ....D 850 479-4653
Pensacola (G-14334)
◆ Kelly Tractor Co ....C 305 592-5360
Doral (G-3254)
Kelly Tractor Co ....E 863 983-8177
Clewiston (G-1906)
◆ Kilpatrick Company Inc ....E 561 533-1450
Boynton Beach (G-1004)
◆ Kilpatrick Irrigation Sup Co ....E 561 533-1450
Boynton Beach (G-1005)
Pace Inc ....E 863 686-1606
Lakeland (G-7934)
▲ Roberts Supply Inc ....E 407 657-5555
Winter Park (G-19771)
▼ Tesco South Incorporated ....D 954 429-3200
Deerfield Beach (G-2804)
Trail Saw & Mower Service Inc ....E 407 293-1861
Orlando (G-13300)
Treasure Coast Irrigation and ....D 321 676-3755
Palm Bay (G-13641)

▼ Trekker Tractor LLC ....E 305 821-2273
Davie (G-2529)
Weber Environmental Svcs Inc ....C 863 551-1820
Winter Haven (G-19672)
◆ Wincorp International Inc ....E 305 887-4000
Medley (G-8798)

5084 Industrial Mach & Eqpt Wholesale

▼ Adams Air & Hydraulics Inc ....D 813 626-4128
Tampa (G-17233)
▼ ADM Ventures Inc ....E 813 621-4671
Tampa (G-17237)
▲ Aircel LLC ....E 865 681-7066
Naples (G-11005)
▼ Allpoints Warehousing Eqp Co ....D 813 246-5800
Tampa (G-17269)
American Industrial Plas LLC ....E 386 274-5335
Daytona Beach (G-2542)
◆ Architectural Panel Pdts Inc ....E 561 265-0707
Delray Beach (G-2908)
Argo Turboserve Corporation ....E 954 861-4000
Pompano Beach (G-14742)
Axyz Ohio Valley Region Inc ....D 813 620-3105
Tampa (G-17328)
▼ Barneys Pumps Inc ....D 863 665-8500
Lakeland (G-7812)
Binder Machinery Co Inc ....E 772 546-9777
Hobe Sound (G-5361)
◆ Bmg Conveyor Services Fla Inc ....E 813 247-3620
Tampa (G-17374)
▲ Bob Dean Supply Inc ....E 239 332-1131
Fort Myers (G-4293)
◆ Bolivar Trading Inc ....E 954 442-4545
Miramar (G-10842)
C & D Industrial Maint LLC ....E 833 776-5833
Bradenton (G-1070)
Canarchy Craft ....C 813 348-6363
Tampa (G-17413)
Canariis Corporation ....D 813 621-8643
Riverview (G-15248)
Capital Machine Tech Inc ....E 813 621-9751
Tampa (G-17415)
◆ Caterpillar Americas Svcs Co ....E 305 476-6800
Miramar (G-10845)
◆ Certified Slings Inc ....E 407 831-7449
Casselberry (G-1446)
◆ Chemical Containers Inc ....E 863 638-2117
Lake Wales (G-7678)
Cintas Corporation No 2 ....C 407 423-4222
Orlando (G-12301)
Cintas Corporation No 2 ....D 561 686-1444
West Palm Beach (G-19086)
Clarklift of Florida LLC ....D 407 855-1062
Apopka (G-167)
Clarklift of Florida LLC ....E 813 874-2008
Orlando (G-12311)
◆ Compressed Air Systems Inc ....E 800 626-8177
Tampa (G-17509)
◆ Costex Corporation ....C 305 592-9769
Miami (G-9425)
Crown Equipment Corporation ....D 954 786-8889
Pompano Beach (G-14789)
▲ Crumpton Welding Sup & Eqp Inc ....E 813 248-8150
Tampa (G-17554)
▼ Cspi Inc ....C 813 626-1101
Tampa (G-17555)
Curry Controls Company ....D 863 646-5781
Lakeland (G-7847)
▼ Custom Industrial Products Inc ....E 321 728-3355
Melbourne (G-8861)
▼ Dash-Door & Closer Service Inc ....E 305 477-1164
Doral (G-3171)
Deland Genco Acquisition Inc ....D 386 469-0070
Deland (G-2855)
Don Mays Corp ....E 800 888-4971
Tampa (G-17599)
E & M Equipment Corp ....E 305 824-1700
Hialeah (G-5255)
Ed Colton Sotec LLC ....E 904 246-6202
Atlantic Beach (G-241)
Elliott Company ....E 904 757-7600
Jacksonville (G-6107)
▼ Equipco Manufacturing Inc ....E 305 513-8540
Miami (G-9529)
▲ Faulhaber Micromo LLC ....D 727 572-0131
Clearwater (G-1633)
Florida Handling Systems Inc ....E 863 534-1212
Bartow (G-317)
◆ Four S Group Inc ....E 305 666-7474
Coral Gables (G-2110)

Gas Turbine Efficiency LLC ....E 407 304-5200
Orlando (G-12560)
▼ Got- Rackcom Inc ....E 813 246-5800
Tampa (G-17745)
▼ Grant Sprinklers Inc ....C 407 995-9095
Sanford (G-15947)
Guardian Fueling Technologies ....E 239 210-2053
Fort Myers (G-4426)
▼ Gulf Controls Company Inc ....D 813 884-0471
Tampa (G-17773)
Hlg Capital Partners III LP ....A 305 379-2322
Miami (G-9703)
◆ High Reach Company LLC ....E 321 275-2100
Sanford (G-15950)
Hoist Material Handling Inc ....D 708 552-2736
Fort Myers (G-4439)
◆ Hugo Motor-Services Stamp Inc ....B 954 763-3660
Fort Lauderdale (G-3879)
▼ Industrial Tractor Company Inc ....D 904 296-5000
Jacksonville (G-6318)
International Baler Corp ....E 904 358-3812
Jacksonville (G-6328)
▲ Jamco Inc ....D 407 302-5400
Sanford (G-15954)
◆ Kelly Tractor Co ....C 305 592-5360
Doral (G-3254)
Lipten Company LLC ....E 800 860-0790
Groveland (G-5097)
Lloyd Industries Inc ....D 904 541-1655
Orange Park (G-12001)
Ludeca Inc ....D 305 591-8935
Doral (G-3266)
▲ Marble Today Inc ....E 386 326-6580
Palatka (G-13594)
◆ Marine Exhaust Systems Inc ....E 561 848-1238
Riviera Beach (G-15307)
Mecca Resources Inc ....D 239 591-3777
Naples (G-11206)
Motion Industries Inc ....E 954 845-1040
Sunrise (G-16800)
Mowrey Elevator Co Fla Inc ....D 850 526-4111
Marianna (G-8684)
◆ National Lift Truck Svc Inc ....E 954 462-6500
Pompano Beach (G-14865)
◆ Nationwide Lift Trucks Inc ....E 954 922-4645
Hollywood (G-5479)
Oracle Elevator Company ....E 954 986-0991
Fort Lauderdale (G-4033)
Oracle Elevator Holdco Inc ....D 954 986-0991
Fort Lauderdale (G-4034)
Otis Elevator Company ....E 850 473-1244
Pensacola (G-14396)
Otis Elevator Company ....D 904 296-6847
Jacksonville (G-6570)
Otis Elevator Company ....E 407 438-3633
Orlando (G-12993)
◆ Pantropic Power Inc ....D 305 477-3329
Doral (G-3287)
Pantropic Power Inc ....E 239 337-4222
Fort Myers (G-4533)
Parker-Hannifin Corporation ....D 904 475-3600
Jacksonville (G-6580)
Pete Store LLC ....C 954 584-3200
Davie (G-2504)
▼ Phoenix Products Inc ....D 904 354-1858
Jacksonville (G-6599)
◆ Plasco LLC ....E 305 625-4222
Miami Lakes (G-10754)
◆ Profile Packaging Inc ....E 941 359-6678
Sarasota (G-16274)
Progress Rail Services Corp ....D 239 643-3013
Naples (G-11272)
PSi Waste Equipment Svcs Inc ....E 352 742-4774
Tavares (G-18616)
Pump Tech Equipment Services ....E 954 448-4393
Fort Lauderdale (G-4066)
◆ Raymond Handling Cons Lc ....E 863 577-5438
Lakeland (G-7949)
▲ Residential Elevators Inc ....C 850 926-6022
Crawfordville (G-2303)
Retro Elevator Corporation ....E 727 895-8144
Saint Petersburg (G-15832)
Ring Power Corporation ....C 904 737-7730
Jacksonville (G-6665)
Ring Power Corporation ....E 850 562-2121
Midway (G-10807)
Ring Power Corporation ....E 904 714-2612
Jacksonville (G-6666)
Ring Power Corporation ....D 352 732-2800
Ocala (G-11768)

S
I
C

Ring Power Corporation	C	407 855-6195
Orlando *(G-13110)*		
Ring Power Corporation	D	407 857-1973
Orlando *(G-13111)*		
Ring Power Corporation	D	386 755-3997
Lake City *(G-7544)*		
Ring Power Corporation	D	321 952-3001
Palm Bay *(G-13637)*		
◆ Ring Power Corporation	B	904 201-7400
Saint Augustine *(G-15486)*		
▼ Rios Con Pmpg & Rentl Inc	E	305 888-7909
Medley *(G-8775)*		
▲ Ross Mixing Inc	E	772 337-0900
Port Saint Lucie *(G-15162)*		
▲ Ryan Incorporated Mining	D	954 427-5599
Deerfield Beach *(G-2790)*		
◆ SEES Incorporated	E	954 971-1115
Pompano Beach *(G-14895)*		
◆ Sensidyne LP	D	727 530-3602
Saint Petersburg *(G-15846)*		
◆ Ship Supply of Florida Inc	E	305 681-7447
Miromar Lakes *(G-10928)*		
◆ Southeast Power Group Inc	D	305 592-9745
Doral *(G-3319)*		
Star Transportation Co	D	813 659-1002
Plant City *(G-14585)*		
Sun Hydraulics LLC	D	941 362-1200
Sarasota *(G-16060)*		
▼ Sun Lift Inc	D	954 971-9440
Pompano Beach *(G-14914)*		
T Mowery Enterprises Inc	E	850 526-4111
Marianna *(G-8686)*		
Tencarva Machinery Company LLC	E	863 665-7867
Lakeland *(G-7987)*		
Texas Aquatic Harvesting Inc	E	863 696-7200
Lake Wales *(G-7702)*		
◆ Thompson Pump and Mfg Co Inc	D	386 767-7310
Port Orange *(G-15091)*		
Thompson Tractor Co Inc	E	850 471-6700
Pensacola *(G-14459)*		
Tk Elevator Corporation	C	561 791-4311
Riviera Beach *(G-15325)*		
Tk Elevator Corporation	D	239 334-2511
Fort Myers *(G-4627)*		
Tk Elevator Corporation	D	904 260-4656
Jacksonville *(G-6857)*		
Tk Elevator Corporation	D	954 971-6500
Pompano Beach *(G-14922)*		
Tk Elevator Corporation	D	941 755-5198
Bradenton *(G-1194)*		
Tk Elevator Corporation	D	850 477-0015
Pensacola *(G-14460)*		
Tomahawk Robotics Inc	E	321 888-3490
Melbourne *(G-8995)*		
◆ Tradewinds Power Corp	D	305 592-9745
Doral *(G-3336)*		
◆ Traeger Brothers and Assoc Inc	D	305 371-5551
Miami *(G-10399)*		
◆ Trans-Market Sales & Eqp Inc	D	813 988-6146
Tampa *(G-18432)*		
Wastewater Solutions LLC	E	954 483-9269
Lake Worth *(G-7760)*		
Wilkinson Hi-Rise LLC	C	954 342-4400
Fort Lauderdale *(G-4224)*		
◆ Worldwide Wholesale Forklifts	E	954 768-9875
Fort Lauderdale *(G-4234)*		
▼ Zeppelin Systems Usa Inc	D	813 920-7434
Odessa *(G-11858)*		

5085 Industrial Splys Wholesale

Abb Inc-Coral Springs Relays	B	919 856-2360
Coral Springs *(G-2215)*		
◆ Advantus Corp	C	904 482-0091
Jacksonville *(G-5744)*		
◆ All American Containers Inc	E	305 887-0797
Medley *(G-8703)*		
Alro Steel Corporation	C	561 997-6766
Boca Raton *(G-413)*		
Alternatives For Industry Inc	D	800 789-0200
Sarasota *(G-16020)*		
Argo Turboserve Corporation	E	954 861-4000
Pompano Beach *(G-14742)*		
◆ Assembly Fasteners Inc	E	407 880-4777
Apopka *(G-155)*		
Atlantic Firebrick Sup Co Inc	E	904 355-8333
Jacksonville *(G-5813)*		
▲ Bernd Group Inc	E	727 733-0122
Dunedin *(G-3379)*		
▲ Bob Dean Supply Inc	E	239 332-1131
Fort Myers *(G-4293)*		

◆ Bridgestone Hosepower LLC	D	904 264-1267
Orange Park *(G-11976)*		
Century Fasteners Corp	E	813 886-5770
Tampa *(G-17450)*		
▼ Chemical Containers Inc	E	863 638-2117
Lake Wales *(G-7678)*		
CKS Packaging Inc	C	407 423-0333
Orlando *(G-12308)*		
Clover Imaging Group LLC	A	518 859-4121
Jacksonville *(G-5968)*		
David Farsaci Inc	E	239 261-1363
Naples *(G-11088)*		
◆ Diploma Holdings Inc	C	727 796-1300
Clearwater *(G-1607)*		
▲ Fastening Specialists Inc	E	407 888-9099
Orlando *(G-12495)*		
▼ Fleet Acquisitions LLC	E	813 621-1734
Tampa *(G-17669)*		
Flotech Inc	D	478 956-5551
Jacksonville *(G-6204)*		
◆ HB Sealing Products Inc	C	727 796-1300
Clearwater *(G-1662)*		
▼ Hoerbiger Service Inc	D	281 955-5888
Deerfield Beach *(G-2753)*		
▼ Hofmann & Leavy Inc	D	954 698-0000
Deerfield Beach *(G-2754)*		
▼ Hughes Supply Inc	D	239 334-2205
Fort Myers *(G-4445)*		
Industrial Cont Srvcs-Lkland L	E	863 967-3388
Auburndale *(G-255)*		
▲ Industrial Cont Svcs - FL LLC	D	407 930-4182
Zellwood *(G-19823)*		
Industrial Eqp & Engrg Co In	D	407 886-5533
Apopka *(G-191)*		
▲ International Fasteners Inc	E	813 241-0203
Tampa *(G-17871)*		
ITR America LLC	D	813 559-8650
Tampa *(G-17878)*		
▼ Lehman Pipe and Plbg Sup Inc	E	305 576-3054
Miami *(G-9856)*		
Ludeca Inc	D	305 591-8935
Doral *(G-3266)*		
Matthews International Corp	C	407 886-5533
Apopka *(G-201)*		
Mil-Spec Industries Inc	E	561 544-4500
Oakland Park *(G-11605)*		
▲ Millennium Fasteners Inc	E	813 247-4007
Tampa *(G-18040)*		
Motion Industries Inc	D	954 845-1040
Sunrise *(G-16800)*		
▲ National Std Parts Assoc Inc	D	850 456-5771
Pensacola *(G-14375)*		
▼ Nestor Sales LLC	C	727 544-6114
Largo *(G-8139)*		
Orion Solutions LLC	E	904 394-0934
Jacksonville *(G-6569)*		
▼ Orlando Drum Co	E	407 855-0208
Orlando *(G-12948)*		
◆ Pantropic Power Inc	D	305 477-3329
Doral *(G-3287)*		
◆ QEP Co Inc	D	561 994-5550
Boca Raton *(G-761)*		
Ram Tool & Supply Co Inc	E	813 621-0891
Tampa *(G-18198)*		
◆ Rubber & Accessories Inc	D	863 665-6115
Lakeland *(G-7957)*		
Southeastern Paper Group LLC	C	904 693-7000
Jacksonville *(G-6756)*		
▼ Stihl Southeast Inc	D	407 240-7900
Orlando *(G-13237)*		
▼ Supplyone Tampa Bay Inc	E	727 573-1822
Clearwater *(G-1809)*		
◆ Traeger Brothers and Assoc Inc	D	305 371-5551
Miami *(G-10399)*		
▼ Tube Light Company Inc	E	800 505-4900
Apopka *(G-219)*		
▲ Tubelite Fl LLC	E	407 884-0477
Apopka *(G-220)*		
◆ W & O Supply Inc	D	904 354-3800
Jacksonville *(G-6914)*		
▲ White Aluminum Products LLC	D	352 787-3622
Leesburg *(G-8276)*		
Wise El Santo Company	D	904 693-8781
Jacksonville *(G-6937)*		

5087 Service Establishment Eqpt & Splys Wholesale

◆ All Florida Paper LLC	C	305 835-6060
Medley *(G-8704)*		

Anderson Ventures Inc	D	727 897-9151
Saint Petersburg *(G-15570)*		
◆ Bar Productscom Inc	D	727 584-2093
Largo *(G-8076)*		
◆ Beauty Elements Corp	D	305 430-4400
Miami Lakes *(G-10711)*		
◆ Beyond Serendipity Inc	D	954 572-2500
Sunrise *(G-16746)*		
▼ Blasters Inc	E	813 985-4500
Tampa *(G-17366)*		
Blue Ribbon Cleaning Co Inc	E	352 624-3444
Ocala *(G-11641)*		
◆ Cheney Bros Inc	A	561 845-4700
Riviera Beach *(G-15288)*		
◆ Commercial Laundries Inc	D	305 592-7990
Doral *(G-3158)*		
Csi International Inc	A	305 672-8724
Miami Beach *(G-10580)*		
Dade Paper & Bag Co	C	407 859-1020
Orlando *(G-12396)*		
▼ East Continental Supplies LLC	D	305 887-0158
Hialeah *(G-5256)*		
▼ Elegant Beauty Supplies 15	E	954 921-9129
Hollywood *(G-5431)*		
Elite Beauty International LLC	E	813 884-8900
Tampa *(G-17623)*		
Florida Alarm & SEC Tech LLC	E	321 455-9377
Merritt Island *(G-9028)*		
◆ Goodwill Inds Suthwest Fla Inc	C	239 995-2106
Fort Myers *(G-4421)*		
Hd Supply Facilities Maint Ltd	D	863 682-1073
Lakeland *(G-7882)*		
I AM King of Cuts LLC	D	239 225-5972
Fort Myers *(G-4447)*		
Imperial Bag & Paper Co LLC	D	813 621-3091
Tampa *(G-17862)*		
Industrial Shredders LLC	E	941 755-2621
Sarasota *(G-16037)*		
Jal Chemical Co Inc	E	407 293-3055
Orlando *(G-12699)*		
◆ Jensen Usa Inc	C	850 271-5959
Panama City *(G-14031)*		
Johnson Cntrls Fire Prtction L	A	561 988-7200
Boca Raton *(G-653)*		
Lewis Dk LLC	E	727 580-4981
Saint Petersburg *(G-15747)*		
Margaritaville Enterprises LLC	A	866 215-9015
Orlando *(G-12808)*		
◆ Micro Matic Usa Inc	E	352 544-1081
Brooksville *(G-1301)*		
Moorecars LLC	D	678 472-9114
Boynton Beach *(G-1018)*		
OHanrahan Consultants Inc	E	727 531-3375
Largo *(G-8141)*		
Osceola Supply Inc	E	850 580-9800
Midway *(G-10805)*		
Pyramid II Jantr Sups & Eqp	D	239 939-4496
Fort Myers *(G-4557)*		
Sharon Hinson	E	321 305-5586
Cocoa *(G-1953)*		
St Johns Cnty Bd Commissioners	E	904 209-0400
Saint Augustine *(G-15500)*		
St Moritz Building Svcs Inc	D	904 504-8514
Jacksonville *(G-6774)*		
▼ Supplyone Tampa Bay Inc	E	727 573-1822
Clearwater *(G-1809)*		
Ware Oil & Supply Company Inc	D	850 838-1852
Perry *(G-14494)*		

5088 Transportation Eqpt & Splys, Except Motor Vehicles Wholesale

AAR Corp	D	630 227-2000
Medley *(G-8700)*		
▼ Aba Aviation Resources Inc	D	786 845-9539
Doral *(G-3098)*		
▼ Aero Precision Industries LLC	C	954 953-3854
Miramar *(G-10836)*		
◆ Aeroservicios Usa Inc	D	305 637-3040
Miami *(G-9097)*		
Aerospares 2000 Inc	D	305 440-1007
Doral *(G-3106)*		
▲ Aersale Inc	D	305 764-3200
Coral Gables *(G-2025)*		
▲ Aersale Holdings Inc	D	305 764-3200
Coral Gables *(G-2026)*		
◆ Africair Inc	D	305 255-6973
Miami *(G-9100)*		
◆ Air Cost Control Us LLC	E	954 991-4667
Sunrise *(G-16733)*		

Airborne Maint Engrg Svcs Inc..........C.... 813 322-9617
Tampa *(G-17256)*

Asrc Aerospace Corp..........B.... 321 867-1462
Kennedy Space Center *(G-7154)*

Atlas Aerospace ACC Inc..........E.... 817 267-1371
Doral *(G-3126)*

AVI Trading Llc..........D.... 954 749-3500
Sunrise *(G-16742)*

Banyan Air Services Inc..........C.... 954 491-3170
Fort Lauderdale *(G-3628)*

Barfield Precision Elec LLC..........C.... 305 436-5464
Doral *(G-3135)*

▼ Bell Textron Miami Inc..........D.... 954 491-5071
Fort Lauderdale *(G-3635)*

Boeing Distribution Svcs Inc..........C.... 305 925-2600
Hialeah *(G-5224)*

Boeing Distribution Svcs Inc..........A.... 305 925-2600
Hialeah *(G-5225)*

▼ Boeing Distribution Svcs X Inc..........D.... 305 925-2600
Hialeah *(G-5226)*

Calfland Traders Inc..........D.... 239 598-3130
Naples *(G-11044)*

◆ Dasi LLC..........C.... 305 234-2333
Doral *(G-3172)*

Demax Trading Inc..........E.... 305 491-5598
Bal Harbour *(G-298)*

◆ Diversfied Mar Pdts A Cal Ltd..........E.... 954 581-1188
Pompano Beach *(G-14795)*

◆ Duty Free Air and Ship Sup LLC..........E.... 305 654-9200
Miami *(G-9492)*

Ed Colton Sotec LLC..........E.... 904 246-6202
Atlantic Beach *(G-241)*

Embraer Executive Jet Svcs LLC..........C.... 321 751-5050
Melbourne *(G-8881)*

Future Aviation Inc..........D.... 239 225-0101
Fort Myers *(G-4406)*

◆ General Propeller Company Inc..........E.... 941 748-1527
Bradenton *(G-1109)*

Hamilton Sunstrand AVI Svcs..........D.... 954 433-3588
Miramar *(G-10862)*

Innovative Marine Elec Inc..........E.... 954 467-2695
Fort Lauderdale *(G-3894)*

◆ ITW GSE Inc..........D.... 941 721-1000
Palmetto *(G-13919)*

Jt Power LLC..........E.... 561 272-5402
Boynton Beach *(G-1003)*

◆ Kellstrom Aerospace LLC..........E.... 847 233-5800
Miami Lakes *(G-10738)*

L3harris Technologies Inc..........D.... 321 727-4000
Melbourne *(G-8919)*

◆ Lewis Marine Supply Inc..........D.... 954 523-4371
Fort Lauderdale *(G-3936)*

Lewis Marine Supply Inc..........E.... 727 536-1955
Largo *(G-8129)*

◆ Man Engines & Components Inc..........E.... 954 946-9092
Pompano Beach *(G-14849)*

◆ Marine Exhaust Systems Inc..........D.... 561 848-1238
Riviera Beach *(G-15307)*

▼ Med-Craft Inc..........E.... 305 594-7444
Miami *(G-9927)*

◆ Miami Cordage LLC..........E.... 305 636-3000
Miami *(G-9965)*

◆ N Land Sea Distributing Inc..........D.... 800 432-7652
Pompano Beach *(G-14863)*

N Land Sea Distributing Inc..........E.... 941 764-0214
Lake Suzy *(G-7672)*

◆ National Marine Suppliers Inc..........D.... 954 764-0975
Fort Lauderdale *(G-3991)*

◆ Nivel Parts & Mfg Co LLC..........E.... 904 741-6161
Jacksonville *(G-6544)*

Radiant Power Corp..........D.... 941 739-3200
Sarasota *(G-16047)*

◆ Regional One Inc..........E.... 305 754-4212
Miami *(G-10195)*

◆ Relli Technology Inc..........D.... 561 886-0200
Boca Raton *(G-768)*

▲ Schroth Safety Products LLC..........D.... 954 784-3178
Fort Lauderdale *(G-4101)*

▲ Silver Wings Aerospace Inc..........E.... 305 258-5950
Princeton *(G-15188)*

◆ Southeast Aerospace Inc..........C.... 321 255-9877
Melbourne *(G-8975)*

◆ Southern Cross Aviation LLC..........E.... 954 377-0320
Fort Lauderdale *(G-4146)*

◆ Sun Power Marine Inc..........E.... 305 594-0797
Miami *(G-10339)*

TEAM JAS INC..........E.... 904 292-2328
Jacksonville *(G-6841)*

Triumph Instruments Inc..........E.... 954 772-4559
Fort Lauderdale *(G-4187)*

◆ Trueaero LLC..........D.... 772 925-8026
Sebastian *(G-16384)*

▲ Vas Aero Services LLC..........C.... 561 998-9330
Boca Raton *(G-859)*

◆ Veethree Electronics & Mar LLC..........E.... 941 538-7775
Bradenton *(G-1199)*

▲ Velocity Arspc - Fort Ldrdale..........E.... 954 772-4559
Fort Lauderdale *(G-4210)*

Wartsila Voyage Americas Inc..........E.... 321 426-9715
Melbourne *(G-9006)*

◆ West Marine Inc..........C.... 831 728-2700
Fort Lauderdale *(G-4223)*

X5 Company LLC..........E.... 407 575-1780
Doral *(G-3363)*

◆ ZF Marine Propulsion Systms..........D.... 954 441-4040
Miramar *(G-10919)*

5091 Sporting & Recreational Goods & Splys Wholesale

Ack LLC..........E.... 561 863-5191
West Palm Beach *(G-19020)*

◆ Diversfied Mar Pdts A Cal Ltd..........E.... 954 581-1188
Pompano Beach *(G-14795)*

Florida Solar Distributors Inc..........D.... 407 699-9960
Sanford *(G-15941)*

Folsom Corporation..........D.... 201 529-3550
Odessa *(G-11840)*

▲ Gamo Outdoor Usa Inc..........E.... 479 636-1200
Davie *(G-2483)*

▼ Golf Ventures Inc..........E.... 863 665-5800
Lakeland *(G-7877)*

◆ Hornerxpress Inc..........D.... 954 772-6966
Fort Lauderdale *(G-3872)*

▼ Hydro Spa Parts and ACC Inc..........D.... 727 573-9611
Saint Petersburg *(G-15713)*

Jerrys Enterprises Inc..........D.... 239 472-9300
Sanibel *(G-16001)*

▲ Mp Direct Inc..........D.... 727 572-8443
Clearwater *(G-1728)*

◆ N Land Sea Distributing Inc..........D.... 800 432-7652
Pompano Beach *(G-14863)*

▼ Nautical Acquisitions Corp..........D.... 727 541-6664
Largo *(G-8138)*

Outsource Option LLC..........E.... 407 493-7928
Orlando *(G-12994)*

Paradise Fishing Inc..........D.... 305 395-1416
Key West *(G-7237)*

Porpoise Pool & Patio Inc..........C.... 727 531-8913
Clearwater *(G-1763)*

◆ Seabring Marine Industries Inc..........E.... 352 528-2628
Williston *(G-19514)*

▲ Sun Wholesale Supply Inc..........C.... 727 524-3299
Clearwater *(G-1801)*

◆ Uma Distributors LLC..........E.... 407 339-8267
Altamonte Springs *(G-110)*

5092 Toys & Hobby Goods & Splys Wholesale

Alliance Entertainment LLC..........D.... 954 255-4000
Sunrise *(G-16735)*

Brady Starburst LLC..........D.... 954 874-1100
Davie *(G-2463)*

Game Depot LLC..........C.... 305 230-4766
Doral *(G-3206)*

▲ Jazwares LLC..........D.... 954 845-0800
Sunrise *(G-16790)*

Jazwares Holdco Inc..........C.... 954 845-0800
Sunrise *(G-16791)*

◆ Just Play LLC..........D.... 800 317-3245
Boca Raton *(G-656)*

Larose Industries LLC..........E.... 800 272-9278
Jacksonville *(G-6422)*

◆ Safari Programs Inc..........D.... 305 621-1000
Jacksonville *(G-6685)*

Stylus Worldwide LLC..........E.... 844 878-9587
Boca Raton *(G-825)*

◆ Valsan of Miami Inc..........E.... 305 324-0102
Miami *(G-10457)*

5093 Scrap & Waste Materials Wholesale

▼ Allied Recycling Inc..........E.... 239 332-7766
Fort Myers *(G-4268)*

Commercial Metals Company..........D.... 904 786-2771
Jacksonville *(G-5981)*

Commercial Metals Company..........E.... 407 293-6584
Apopka *(G-168)*

Crown Shredding LLC..........D.... 386 767-1133
South Daytona *(G-16485)*

Emerald Waste Services LLC..........E.... 850 236-1440
Panama City *(G-13999)*

◆ Exotech Inc..........E.... 954 917-1919
Pompano Beach *(G-14801)*

Ferrous Processing and Trdg Co..........E.... 305 638-0040
Miami *(G-9553)*

▼ Florida Express Envmtl LLC..........E.... 352 629-4349
Ocala *(G-11683)*

Icahn Enterprises LP..........E.... 305 422-4100
Sunny Isles Beach *(G-16720)*

Nar Electronics Solutions LLC..........D.... 305 691-5575
Miami *(G-10025)*

Orlando Waste Paper Co Inc..........D.... 407 299-1380
Orlando *(G-12992)*

Price & Pierce Intl Inc..........E.... 212 301-0004
Fort Myers *(G-4552)*

Single Stream Recyclers LLC..........D.... 941 552-6715
Sarasota *(G-16319)*

Skinner Waste Solutions LLC..........E.... 904 239-7222
Jacksonville *(G-6730)*

◆ Technlogy Cnsrvation Group Inc..........D.... 352 527-2534
Lecanto *(G-8226)*

Trademark Metals Recycling LLC..........D.... 239 337-5865
Fort Myers *(G-4629)*

5094 Jewelry, Watches, Precious Stones Wholesale

Bijoux Terner LLC..........C.... 786 477-4308
Miami *(G-9255)*

Blue Nile Inc..........D.... 540 636-7177
Tampa *(G-17367)*

Cartier International Del Corp..........C.... 305 448-4111
Coral Gables *(G-2064)*

◆ Cousin Corporation of America..........C.... 727 536-3568
Largo *(G-8090)*

◆ Dfc Services Corp..........E.... 954 971-9393
Fort Lauderdale *(G-3759)*

▲ Free Enterprise Company Llc..........D.... 407 851-8585
Orlando *(G-12545)*

◆ Invicta Watch Company Amer Inc..........E.... 954 921-2444
Hollywood *(G-5461)*

▲ Mp Direct Inc..........D.... 727 572-8443
Clearwater *(G-1728)*

OCon Enterprise Inc..........D.... 954 920-6700
Hollywood *(G-5487)*

◆ Richemont Ltin Amer Crbbean LL..........E.... 305 448-4111
Coral Gables *(G-2177)*

▲ Roma Industries LLC..........C.... 727 545-9009
Largo *(G-8146)*

SPD Group Inc..........E.... 954 782-5000
Lighthouse Point *(G-8297)*

◆ The Swatch Group U S Inc..........D.... 201 271-1400
Miami *(G-10385)*

◆ Valsan of Miami Inc..........E.... 305 324-0102
Miami *(G-10457)*

5099 Durable Goods: NEC Wholesale

Albert Uster Imports Inc..........D.... 954 923-0858
Hollywood *(G-5388)*

▲ All American Cntrs Tampa LLC..........E.... 813 248-2023
Tampa *(G-17262)*

◆ All American Containers Inc..........C.... 305 887-0797
Medley *(G-8703)*

Alliance Entertainment LLC..........D.... 954 255-4000
Sunrise *(G-16735)*

◆ Allison USA Inc..........E.... 305 856-2888
Miami *(G-9126)*

Am-Med Diabetic Supplies Inc..........E.... 561 900-3548
Delray Beach *(G-2902)*

▼ AVI-Spl Global LLC..........A.... 813 884-7168
Tampa *(G-17324)*

Bee Electronics Inc..........D.... 772 468-7477
Fort Pierce *(G-4681)*

Dgg Tactical Supply Inc..........D.... 904 777-4801
Jacksonville *(G-6065)*

Ed Colton Sotec LLC..........E.... 904 246-6202
Atlantic Beach *(G-241)*

European Center Inc..........E.... 561 747-4539
Jupiter *(G-7066)*

▼ First Coast Supply Inc..........E.... 904 388-1217
Jacksonville *(G-6172)*

▼ Florida Express Envmtl LLC..........E.... 352 629-4349
Ocala *(G-11683)*

▲ Group III International Inc..........D.... 954 984-1607
Pompano Beach *(G-14818)*

◆ Lifesaving Systems Corporation..........E.... 813 645-2748
Apollo Beach *(G-139)*

S I C

◆ Mercury Luggage Mfg Co	D	904 733-9595
Jacksonville (G-6496)		
◆ Music Arts Enterprises Inc Mae	E	954 581-2203
Fort Lauderdale (G-3986)		
Onsite Safety Inc	D	407 671-7363
Oviedo (G-13563)		
Plevo LLC	E	888 577-5386
Miami (G-10129)		
Price & Pierce Intl Inc	E	212 301-0004
Fort Myers (G-4552)		
Rayonier Inc	D	904 357-9100
Yulee (G-19820)		
▼ Redmont Sign LLC	E	941 378-4242
Sarasota (G-16281)		
▲ Safariland LLC	D	904 741-5400
Jacksonville (G-6686)		
Saferite Solutions Inc	E	407 675-5286
Orlando (G-13161)		
Safety Guys LLC	B	954 463-9811
Fort Lauderdale (G-4098)		
▲ Safety Products Inc	E	863 665-8224
Lakeland (G-7960)		
▲ Scooterbug Inc	D	781 933-3120
Orlando (G-13171)		
Scott-Mcrae Auto Group Inc	D	904 388-7006
Jacksonville (G-6702)		
Sherwood Southeast LLC	D	407 816-1978
Orlando (G-13192)		
Summit Safety LLC	E	352 521-7171
Brooksville (G-1312)		
Ten-8 Fire & Safety LLC	E	877 989-7660
Bradenton (G-1191)		
Tractor Supply Company	E	850 682-0945
Crestview (G-2336)		
◆ Travelpro International LLC	D	561 998-2824
Boca Raton (G-845)		
◆ Travelpro Products Inc	D	561 998-2824
Boca Raton (G-846)		
◆ Troy Industries Inc	D	305 324-1742
Doral (G-3339)		
◆ Valsan of Miami Inc	E	305 324-0102
Miami (G-10457)		
Wheels Up Private Jets LLC	D	786 501-1127
Coral Gables (G-2210)		
▲ Y-Not Design & Mfg Inc	D	305 479-2627
Hialeah (G-5337)		

51 WHOLESALE TRADE¨NONDURABLE GOODS

5111 Printing & Writing Paper Wholesale

Florida Trade Graphics Inc	E	954 786-2000
Pompano Beach (G-14811)		
◆ Lexjet LLC	D	941 330-1210
Sarasota (G-16219)		
Mac Papers Inc	D	305 362-9699
Hialeah (G-5294)		
◆ Mac Papers LLC	D	904 348-3300
Jacksonville (G-6457)		
Mac Papers LLC	E	407 370-5595
Orlando (G-12800)		
◆ Perez Trading Company Inc	C	305 769-0761
Miami (G-10109)		

5112 Stationery & Office Splys Wholesale

Advanced Dcument Solutions Inc	D	407 412-6929
Orlando (G-12054)		
◆ Advantus Corp	C	904 482-0091
Jacksonville (G-5744)		
Apex Office Products Inc	E	813 871-2010
Tampa (G-17295)		
▼ Broward Paper and Packg Inc	D	954 776-6272
Oakland Park (G-11587)		
Essendant Co	E	800 342-8073
Jacksonville (G-6132)		
Essendant Co	D	305 863-6300
Medley (G-8726)		
Essendant Inc	D	407 354-1523
Orlando (G-12475)		
Gulf Coast Off Pdts Inc NW Fla	E	850 434-5588
Pensacola (G-14318)		
H A Friend & Company Inc	E	847 746-1248
Boynton Beach (G-994)		
◆ Herko International Inc	E	305 971-4997
Miami (G-9697)		
◆ Levenger Company	D	561 276-2436
Delray Beach (G-2977)		
◆ Lexjet LLC	D	941 330-1210
Sarasota (G-16219)		

◆ Mac Papers LLC	D	904 348-3300
Jacksonville (G-6457)		
Mac Papers LLC	E	407 370-5595
Orlando (G-12800)		
O D International Inc	D	561 438-4480
Delray Beach (G-2997)		
Office Club Inc	A	561 438-4800
Delray Beach (G-3000)		
◆ OfficeMax Incorporated	B	800 463-3768
Boca Raton (G-728)		
◆ Pilot Corporation of America	D	904 565-7600
Jacksonville (G-6602)		
◆ Refurbished Office Furn Inc	E	877 763-4400
Tampa (G-18209)		
S P Richards Company	E	305 769-0565
Miami (G-10230)		
S P Richards Company	D	813 626-6009
Tampa (G-18242)		
Sun Print Management LLC	E	727 945-0255
Holiday (G-5375)		
Universal Designs Inc	E	386 740-4700
Deland (G-2884)		

5113 Indl & Personal Svc Paper Wholesale

◆ All Florida Paper LLC	C	305 835-6060
Medley (G-8704)		
Atlas Paper Mills LLC	C	305 835-8046
Hialeah (G-5220)		
◆ Beyond Serendipity Inc	D	954 572-2500
Sunrise (G-16746)		
▼ Broward Paper and Packg Inc	D	954 776-6272
Oakland Park (G-11587)		
◆ Cheney Bros Inc	A	561 845-4700
Riviera Beach (G-15288)		
▼ Coronet Ppr Pdts Entps Fla LLC	E	305 688-6601
Miami (G-9418)		
◆ Dade Paper & Bag LLC	B	305 805-2600
Medley (G-8719)		
Dade Paper & Bag Co	C	407 859-1020
Orlando (G-12396)		
Hj Express Shippers	E	786 408-5942
Miami (G-9707)		
Imperial Bag & Paper Co LLC	D	813 621-3091
Tampa (G-17862)		
◆ Konie Cups International Inc	E	786 337-7967
Medley (G-8750)		
Mac Papers LLC	D	305 362-9699
Hialeah (G-5295)		
Mac Papers LLC	D	813 247-3461
Tampa (G-17970)		
McLane Foodservice Dist Inc	C	863 687-2189
Lakeland (G-7915)		
▼ Oren International Inc	E	850 433-9080
Pensacola (G-14395)		
◆ Perez Trading Company Inc	C	305 769-0761
Miami (G-10109)		
Price & Pierce Intl Inc	E	212 301-0004
Fort Myers (G-4552)		
Procter & Gamble Distrg LLC	E	904 477-8034
Jacksonville (G-6617)		
Procter & Gamble Distrg LLC	B	407 282-4926
Orlando (G-13064)		
◆ Riverside Paper Co Inc	E	305 722-0110
Miami (G-10215)		
▼ Supplyone Tampa Bay Inc	E	727 573-1822
Clearwater (G-1809)		
Sygma Network Inc	D	407 816-2470
Orlando (G-13258)		
Sysco Guest Supply LLC	E	407 857-9023
Orlando (G-13262)		
◆ Sysco South Florida Inc	A	305 651-5421
Medley (G-8787)		
Veritiv Operating Company	D	770 391-8200
Jacksonville (G-6904)		
▲ Vistapak Industries Inc	E	352 702-3770
Leesburg (G-8275)		
Zuma & Sons Distributors Corp	E	305 887-0089
Medley (G-8802)		

5122 Drugs, Drug Proprietaries & Sundries Wholesale

Airborne Inc	E	800 590-9794
Bonita Springs (G-894)		
◆ Alberto Crtes Csmt Prfumes Inc	E	305 358-0680
Miami (G-9113)		
▼ Alfa Vitamins Laboratories Inc	D	305 597-6410
Miami (G-9116)		
Amatheon Animal Health LLC	E	800 399-8387
Doral (G-3117)		

Amerisourcebergen Corporation	D	407 259-5568
Orlando (G-12119)		
Amerisourcebergen Drug Corp	E	407 454-6600
Orlando (G-12120)		
▲ Anda Inc	B	954 217-4500
Weston (G-19440)		
▲ Andrx Corporation	E	954 585-1400
Davie (G-2456)		
◆ Aso LLC	C	941 379-0300
Sarasota (G-16095)		
◆ B & G PTL Enterprises Inc	E	954 977-4060
Pompano Beach (G-14747)		
Be Powerful LLC	D	954 926-0900
Fort Lauderdale (G-3632)		
Beekman 1802 Inc	E	407 351-5656
Orlando (G-12176)		
Benecard Central Fill FL LLC	C	888 907-0070
Bonita Springs (G-897)		
◆ Bio-Engnred Spplmnts Ntrtn Inc	C	561 994-8335
Boca Raton (G-451)		
◆ Bpi Sports LLC	E	954 926-0900
Fort Lauderdale (G-3647)		
Cardinal Health Inc	E	813 972-1564
Tampa (G-17418)		
Children & Families Fla Dept	C	850 663-7274
Chattahoochee (G-1479)		
▲ Cosmetic Dermatology LLC	E	305 406-0411
Coral Gables (G-2080)		
▼ Creative Beauty Group LLC	E	305 471-0660
Doral (G-3169)		
Curascript Inc	E	888 773-7376
Lake Mary (G-7583)		
Curascript Inc	C	407 852-4903
Orlando (G-12393)		
Designs For Health Inc	E	860 623-6314
Palm Coast (G-13818)		
◆ Duty Free Air and Ship Sup LLC	E	305 654-9200
Miami (G-9492)		
Easyscripts Westchester Llc	E	305 537-3288
Miami (G-9498)		
▼ Elegant Beauty Supplies 15	E	954 921-9129
Hollywood (G-5431)		
Elite Beauty International LLC	E	813 884-8900
Tampa (G-17623)		
Family Medicine & Rehab Inc	D	904 771-1116
Jacksonville (G-6145)		
GE Healthcare Inc	D	414 247-1437
Fort Myers (G-4412)		
Instanatural LLC	E	800 290-6932
Orlando (G-12684)		
▲ Ion Labs Inc	B	727 527-1072
Largo (G-8121)		
Kroger Specialty Pharmacy Inc	D	407 936-2900
Lake Mary (G-7605)		
▲ Krs Global Biotechnology Inc	E	888 502-2050
Boca Raton (G-662)		
Ksf Acquisition Corporation	E	561 231-6548
Palm Beach Gardens (G-13745)		
▲ Labelm Usa Inc	E	305 624-2456
Miami Lakes (G-10739)		
◆ LOreal Trvl Ret Americas Inc	C	305 262-7500
Miami (G-9881)		
Lupin Research Inc	E	800 466-1450
Coral Springs (G-2271)		
▲ Luxury Brand Partners LLC	D	305 600-1305
Miami (G-9886)		
Mason Distributors Inc	E	305 428-6800
Miami Lakes (G-10742)		
◆ McKesson Mdcl-Srgcal Top Hldng	D	904 332-3000
Jacksonville (G-6486)		
▲ Med-Care Medical Inc	C	954 794-0634
Deerfield Beach (G-2771)		
▲ Miracle Line Inc	D	954 583-4732
Plantation (G-14676)		
▲ Monat Global Corp	B	305 392-2999
Doral (G-3277)		
▲ Nailtiques Cosmetic Corp	E	772 643-7040
Sebastian (G-16379)		
Natural Vitality Holdg Co LLC	E	800 446-7462
Sunrise (G-16801)		
New Vision Pharmaceuticals LLC	C	954 721-5000
Tamarac (G-17200)		
Newbeauty Media Group LLC	E	561 961-7600
Boca Raton (G-713)		
◆ Nicolas Vlllba Wholesalers Inc	D	305 638-4450
Miami Gardens (G-10693)		
Nutranext LLC	D	954 233-3300
Sunrise (G-16804)		
Opa Laboratories LLC	E	786 360-2426
Hialeah (G-5304)		

Optum Infusion Svcs 202 Inc ....E 877 342-9352
Jacksonville *(G-6565)*

Paragon Enterprises Inc ....E 954 389-1700
Weston *(G-19473)*

Parlux Holdings Inc ....D 954 442-5453
Miramar *(G-10886)*

Performspecialty LLC ....A 407 335-1458
Orlando *(G-13023)*

Petmed Express Inc ....C 561 526-4444
Delray Beach *(G-3005)*

◆ Pevonia International LLC ....E 386 239-8980
Daytona Beach *(G-2651)*

Pharmalogic Holdings Corp ....E 561 416-0085
Boca Raton *(G-749)*

▲ Pharmerica Long-Term Care LLC ....B 877 874-2768
Tampa *(G-18143)*

Plasma Biolife Services L P ....E 904 248-3972
Jacksonville *(G-6605)*

Priority Healthcare Dist Inc ....C 407 833-7000
Lake Mary *(G-7625)*

Procter & Gamble Distrg LLC ....E 904 477-8034
Jacksonville *(G-6617)*

Procter & Gamble Distrg LLC ....B 407 282-4926
Orlando *(G-13064)*

Propharma Inc ....E 305 594-7645
Miami *(G-10153)*

◆ Purity Wholesale Grocers Inc ....D 561 997-8302
Boca Raton *(G-760)*

Resilience Government Svcs Inc ....D 386 462-9663
Alachua *(G-12)*

Sancilio & Company Inc ....E 561 847-2302
Riviera Beach *(G-15316)*

▲ Sancilio & Company Inc ....D 561 847-2302
Riviera Beach *(G-15317)*

Santo Remedio LLC ....E 404 312-4217
Doral *(G-3303)*

Sincerus Florida LLC ....D 800 604-5032
Pompano Beach *(G-14899)*

◆ Smt Duty Free Inc ....E 305 477-0515
Doral *(G-3314)*

Titleist Technologies LLC ....E 352 324-7024
Howey In The Hills *(G-5626)*

Unifirst-First Aid Corporation ....D 800 634-7680
Fort Myers *(G-4635)*

Unifirst-First Aid Corporation ....D 800 634-7680
Fort Myers *(G-4636)*

▲ Universal Handicraft Inc ....E 305 627-9370
Miami Beach *(G-10670)*

Uspharma Ltd ....D 954 817-4418
Miami Lakes *(G-10770)*

Vitamedmd LLC ....C 800 728-0009
Boca Raton *(G-867)*

◆ Vogue International LLC ....E 727 216-1600
Clearwater *(G-1834)*

Welldynerx LLC ....D 888 479-2000
Lakeland *(G-8004)*

Wellspring Pharmaceutical Corp ....D 941 312-4727
Sarasota *(G-16073)*

5131 Piece Goods, Notions & Dry Goods Wholesale

Ascend Prfmce Mtls Oprtons LLC ....A 850 968-7000
Cantonment *(G-1333)*

◆ Bay Rag Corporation ....E 305 693-6868
Miami *(G-9228)*

Stark Scalamandre Fabric LLC ....D 954 929-4900
Hollywood *(G-5534)*

Three Sheep LLC ....E 616 215-1848
Miami *(G-10388)*

5136 Men's & Boys' Clothing & Furnishings Wholesale

◆ Aetg LLC ....E 305 634-4766
Miami *(G-9098)*

American Eagle Trade Group LLC ....D 305 634-4766
Miami *(G-9138)*

◆ Bay Rag Corporation ....E 305 693-6868
Miami *(G-9228)*

Broder Bros Co ....E 407 859-3661
Orlando *(G-12208)*

Chateau Bodywear USA Inc ....E 514 274-7505
Fort Lauderdale *(G-3684)*

◆ Cromer Company ....E 305 373-5414
Hialeah Gardens *(G-5341)*

◆ Daniel Lord Sportswear Inc ....E 954 318-6000
Sunrise *(G-16762)*

Dgg Tactical Supply Inc ....D 904 777-4801
Jacksonville *(G-6065)*

▲ Entertainment Retail Entps LLC ....E 407 649-6552
Apopka *(G-178)*

◆ ICO Companies Inc ....C 888 380-5646
Miami Gardens *(G-10687)*

◆ Intradeco Inc ....D 305 264-6022
Medley *(G-8747)*

▲ Isaco International Corp ....E 305 594-4455
Bal Harbour *(G-299)*

◆ JI Kaya Inc ....E 305 888-3962
Miami *(G-9795)*

Milway Corporation ....E 305 946-0000
Pompano Beach *(G-14859)*

◆ Mitchell-Proffitt Company ....E 904 783-3177
Jacksonville *(G-6508)*

◆ Sportailor Inc ....D 305 754-3255
Miami *(G-10315)*

◆ Tsf Sportswear LLC ....E 954 691-9050
Pompano Beach *(G-14931)*

5137 Women's, Children's & Infants Clothing Wholesale

American Eagle Trade Group LLC ....D 305 634-4766
Miami *(G-9138)*

◆ Atlantic Hosiery Inc ....E 305 428-1111
Opa Locka *(G-11941)*

◆ Bay Rag Corporation ....E 305 693-6868
Miami *(G-9228)*

▲ Benetton Trading Usa Inc ....E 305 604-9000
Miami Beach *(G-10555)*

Broder Bros Co ....E 407 859-3661
Orlando *(G-12208)*

Chateau Bodywear USA Inc ....E 514 274-7505
Fort Lauderdale *(G-3684)*

◆ Cromer Company ....E 305 373-5414
Hialeah Gardens *(G-5341)*

▲ Entertainment Retail Entps LLC ....E 407 649-6552
Apopka *(G-178)*

◆ Gator of Florida Inc ....C 813 877-8267
Tampa *(G-17726)*

▲ Luemme Inc ....E 800 451-5393
Miami *(G-9885)*

Milway Corporation ....E 954 946-0000
Pompano Beach *(G-14859)*

Procter & Gamble Distrg LLC ....E 904 477-8034
Jacksonville *(G-6617)*

Procter & Gamble Distrg LLC ....B 407 282-4926
Orlando *(G-13064)*

◆ Sportailor Inc ....D 305 754-3255
Miami *(G-10315)*

◆ Tsf Sportswear LLC ....D 954 691-9050
Pompano Beach *(G-14931)*

5139 Footwear Wholesale

◆ Bay Rag Corporation ....E 305 693-6868
Miami *(G-9228)*

Nettleton Shoes Since 1879 Inc ....D 800 925-2238
Juno Beach *(G-7035)*

Shoes For Crews Inc ....E 561 683-5090
Boca Raton *(G-797)*

Shoes For Crews LLC ....D 407 608-7710
Orlando *(G-13193)*

◆ Shoes For Crews LLC ....E 561 683-5090
Boca Raton *(G-798)*

◆ Unisa Diem Inc ....D 305 591-9397
Doral *(G-3340)*

5141 Groceries, General Line Wholesale

Acosta Sales Co Inc ....C 904 363-6812
Jacksonville *(G-5730)*

Acosta Sales Co Inc ....C 813 626-2600
Temple Terrace *(G-18628)*

▼ Acosta Sales Co Inc ....C 904 281-9800
Jacksonville *(G-5731)*

Advantage Lgstics Suthwest Inc ....C 786 440-5336
Miami *(G-9094)*

Advantage Sales & Mktg Inc ....D 904 296-8886
Jacksonville *(G-5743)*

◆ American Foods LLC ....D 727 848-1010
Port Richey *(G-15097)*

◆ Associated Grocers Florida Inc ....B 954 876-3000
Pompano Beach *(G-14744)*

B & B Corporate Holdings Inc ....D 813 621-6411
Tampa *(G-17330)*

◆ Beaver Street Fisheries Inc ....C 904 354-5661
Jacksonville *(G-5849)*

Brothers Trading Co Inc ....D 561 392-8530
Boca Raton *(G-482)*

Btb Food Service Inc ....E 754 701-8154
Margate *(G-8643)*

C&S Wholesale Grocers Inc ....C 904 695-5100
Jacksonville *(G-5890)*

C&S Wholesale Grocers Inc ....B 305 769-6600
Miami *(G-9299)*

C&S Wholesale Grocers Inc ....B 413 247-8247
Plant City *(G-14547)*

◆ Carisam-Samuel Meisel FL Inc ....D 305 591-3993
Doral *(G-3144)*

Cheney Bros Inc ....A 352 291-7800
Ocala *(G-11658)*

◆ Cheney Bros Inc ....A 561 845-4700
Riviera Beach *(G-15288)*

Cheney Bros Inc ....C 941 505-5885
Punta Gorda *(G-15200)*

◆ Colonial Wholesale Distrg Inc ....D 813 621-8880
Tampa *(G-17496)*

Corrections Florida Department ....E 904 368-2500
Raiford *(G-15238)*

David Oppenheimer and Co I LLC ....E 813 264-5669
Tampa *(G-17575)*

Detwilers Farm Market Inc ....D 941 378-2727
Sarasota *(G-16138)*

◆ Dismex Food Inc ....D 305 238-6146
Miami *(G-9479)*

El Mira Sol Inc ....D 813 754-5857
Plant City *(G-14551)*

Florida Food Service Inc ....D 352 372-3514
Gainesville *(G-4891)*

◆ Food Supply Inc ....D 386 763-7500
South Daytona *(G-16487)*

Global Distributors Inc ....E 305 638-8954
Miami *(G-9633)*

Gordon Food Service Inc ....D 813 703-6500
Plant City *(G-14559)*

Gordon Food Service Inc ....C 305 685-5851
Miami *(G-9652)*

Gordon Food Service Inc ....A 305 685-5851
Miami *(G-9653)*

Goya Foods of Florida LLC ....D 305 592-4093
Miami *(G-9655)*

Gracekennedy Foods (usa) LLC ....C 305 884-1100
Medley *(G-8739)*

I Sales Group Inc ....E 305 333-3420
Sunrise *(G-16786)*

Import Mex Distributors Inc ....E 561 881-5581
Riviera Beach *(G-15300)*

Infinity Foods LLC ....E 305 333-4244
Hialeah *(G-5280)*

▼ International Grocers Inc ....D 305 597-1550
Miami *(G-9765)*

Jerrys Famous Deli Inc ....C 305 672-1861
Miami Beach *(G-10605)*

◆ Jetro Cash Carry Entps of Fla ....C 305 326-0409
Miami *(G-9791)*

Kenneth O Lester Company Inc ....C 352 378-8844
Gainesville *(G-4931)*

Maximum Marketing Inc ....E 954 725-3700
Pompano Beach *(G-14850)*

McLane Foodservice Inc ....C 863 256-1700
Haines City *(G-5152)*

McLane Foodservice Dist Inc ....D 407 857-3960
Orlando *(G-12846)*

McLane/Suneast Inc ....A 254 771-7500
Kissimmee *(G-7355)*

◆ Merchants Export LLC ....E 561 863-7171
Riviera Beach *(G-15309)*

◆ Niagara Distributors Inc ....E 954 925-6775
Hollywood *(G-5482)*

North America Duty Free Inc ....D 954 962-3432
Hollywood *(G-5484)*

Oliva International Foods LLC ....C 305 638-5161
Miami *(G-10067)*

Performance Food Group Inc ....E 305 953-4900
Miami *(G-10110)*

Publix Super Markets Inc ....A 904 781-8600
Jacksonville *(G-6622)*

Publix Super Markets Inc ....A 941 923-4929
Sarasota *(G-16276)*

Publix Super Markets Inc ....A 954 429-0122
Deerfield Beach *(G-2786)*

Publix Super Markets Inc ....A 561 369-7900
Boynton Beach *(G-1030)*

◆ Purity Wholesale Grocers Inc ....D 561 997-8302
Boca Raton *(G-760)*

Restaurant Depot LLC ....C 954 577-0470
Davie *(G-2509)*

◆ Roma Food Group Inc ....C 305 888-1355
Miami *(G-10218)*

Sanwa Growers Inc ....D 813 234-8428
Tampa *(G-18249)*

S I C

Sellethics Marketing Group Inc ....C 904 423-2070
Jacksonville *(G-6708)*

◆ Ship Supply of Florida Inc ....E 305 681-7447
Miromar Lakes *(G-10928)*

Sygma Network Inc ....C 407 816-2470
Orlando *(G-13258)*

▲ Sysco Central Florida Inc ....B 407 877-8500
Ocoee *(G-11825)*

◆ Sysco Southeast Florida LLC ....E 561 842-1999
Riviera Beach *(G-15324)*

▲ Sysco West Coast Florida Inc ....A 941 721-1450
Palmetto *(G-13931)*

▲ Tama Corporation ....E 305 592-1717
Doral *(G-3329)*

The H T Hackney Co ....D 850 981-5700
Milton *(G-10826)*

The H T Hackney Co ....D 352 377-3933
Gainesville *(G-5012)*

▲ Transnational Foods Inc ....E 305 365-9652
Miami *(G-10401)*

Transnational Foods LLC ....D 305 365-9652
Miami *(G-10402)*

Tri Venture Marketing LLC ....D 863 648-1881
Lakeland *(G-7990)*

Trujillo & Sons Inc ....D 305 696-8701
Miami *(G-10416)*

◆ Trujillo & Sons Inc ....D 305 696-8701
Miami *(G-10417)*

US Foods Inc ....E 561 998-2221
Boca Raton *(G-854)*

US Foods Inc ....E 561 994-8500
Boca Raton *(G-855)*

US Foods Inc ....D 813 621-6677
Tampa *(G-18485)*

US Foods Inc ....C 863 683-4373
Lakeland *(G-7992)*

US Foods Inc ....C 386 677-2240
Port Orange *(G-15093)*

◆ Vigo Importing Company ....C 813 884-3491
Tampa *(G-18507)*

Vini Plus Inc ....D 305 597-8697
Doral *(G-3356)*

◆ Yu Brothers Inc ....D 305 688-2228
Miami *(G-10527)*

Zuma & Sons Distributors Corp ....E 305 887-0089
Medley *(G-8802)*

5142 Packaged Frozen Foods Wholesale

◆ Allapattah Industries Inc ....E 305 324-5900
Miami *(G-9120)*

▲ Aquanita LLC ....E 305 444-8661
Miami *(G-9162)*

◆ Beaver Street Fisheries Inc ....C 904 354-5661
Jacksonville *(G-5849)*

Beaver Street Fisheries Inc ....C 904 354-5661
Jacksonville *(G-5850)*

Borden Dairy Company Fla LLC ....E 863 298-9742
Winter Haven *(G-19610)*

◆ Colorado Boxed Beef Co ....A 863 967-0636
Lakeland *(G-7842)*

GA Fd Svcs Pinellas Cnty LLC ....D 954 972-8884
Fort Lauderdale *(G-3815)*

Gem Freshco LLC ....D 772 595-0070
Fort Pierce *(G-4707)*

Goya Foods Inc ....D 800 432-4692
Doral *(G-3214)*

Goya Foods Inc ....D 407 816-7776
Doral *(G-3215)*

◆ Jetro Cash Carry Entps of Fla ....C 305 326-0409
Miami *(G-9791)*

◆ L & J General Intl Corp ....E 305 638-5161
Miami *(G-9837)*

Lantmannen Unibake Usa Inc ....C 727 823-1113
Saint Petersburg *(G-15743)*

Martin-Brower Company LLC ....D 407 583-0693
Orlando *(G-12821)*

McLane Foodservice Dist Inc ....C 863 687-2189
Lakeland *(G-7915)*

McLane Foodservice Dist Inc ....C 407 857-3960
Orlando *(G-12846)*

◆ Mercadagro International Corp ....C 786 507-0540
Miami *(G-9935)*

◆ Merchants Export LLC ....E 561 863-7171
Riviera Beach *(G-15309)*

▼ Miami Beef Company Inc ....E 305 621-3252
Miami Lakes *(G-10744)*

◆ Miami Purveyors Inc ....E 305 262-6170
Miami *(G-9981)*

◆ Procurement Systems Inc ....D 954 931-9787
Fort Lauderdale *(G-4063)*

Publix Super Markets Inc ....A 954 429-0122
Deerfield Beach *(G-2786)*

◆ Quirch Foods LLC ....B 305 691-3535
Coral Gables *(G-2173)*

Restaurant Depot LLC ....C 954 577-0470
Davie *(G-2509)*

◆ Southeast Frozen Foods Co LP ....E 954 882-1044
Miramar *(G-10899)*

▲ Southern Belle Frozen Foods ....D 904 768-1591
Jacksonville *(G-6761)*

◆ Sysco South Florida Inc ....A 305 651-5421
Medley *(G-8787)*

US Foods Inc ....C 386 677-2240
Port Orange *(G-15093)*

Weyand Food Distributors Inc ....E 813 236-5923
Tampa *(G-18548)*

5143 Dairy Prdts, Except Dried Or Canned Wholesale

American Foods Intl LLC ....E 877 894-7675
Aventura *(G-264)*

Borden Dairy Company Fla LLC ....D 407 849-6202
Orlando *(G-12195)*

Borden Dairy Company Fla LLC ....E 813 805-0825
Tampa *(G-17379)*

▼ Borden Dairy Company Fla LLC ....D 863 297-7300
Winter Haven *(G-19611)*

Borden Dairy Company Fla LLC ....E 561 845-6492
Riviera Beach *(G-15285)*

Borden Dairy Company Fla LLC ....E 904 786-4464
Jacksonville *(G-5874)*

Borden Dairy Company Fla LLC ....E 863 298-9742
Winter Haven *(G-19610)*

▼ Dakin Dairy Farms Inc ....E 941 322-2802
Myakka City *(G-10985)*

◆ Dean Dairy Holdings LLC ....E 305 795-7700
Miami *(G-9465)*

Dean Dairy Holdings LLC ....D 305 576-2880
Miami *(G-9466)*

Dean Dairy Holdings LLC ....D 239 334-1114
Fort Myers *(G-4341)*

▲ Deconna Ice Cream Company Inc ....E 352 591-1530
Reddick *(G-15239)*

Dfa Dairy Brands Fluid LLC ....C 407 894-4941
Orlando *(G-12418)*

◆ Freshpoint South Florida Inc ....C 954 917-7272
Pompano Beach *(G-14814)*

McArthur Next LLC ....E 609 499-3601
Miami *(G-9916)*

McLane Foodservice Dist Inc ....C 407 857-3960
Orlando *(G-12846)*

◆ Merchants Export LLC ....E 561 863-7171
Riviera Beach *(G-15309)*

▲ Mothers Milk Inc ....E 954 471-4429
Davie *(G-2500)*

New Dairy Opco LLC ....E 850 574-1331
Tallahassee *(G-17055)*

Rubix Foods LLC ....E 904 268-8999
Jacksonville *(G-6681)*

Saputo Inc ....D 813 756-0120
Plant City *(G-14578)*

▲ Schratter Foods Incorporated ....D 305 651-8884
Miami *(G-10248)*

Southeast Milk Inc ....D 352 245-2437
Belleview *(G-375)*

◆ Sunny Morning Foods Inc ....E 954 735-3447
Fort Lauderdale *(G-4162)*

Sunrise Fresh Produce LLC ....D 904 366-1368
Jacksonville *(G-6810)*

◆ Sysco South Florida Inc ....A 305 651-5421
Medley *(G-8787)*

◆ Tropical Foods LLC ....E 305 477-5811
Doral *(G-3338)*

Tzion Group LLC ....E 954 673-0843
Miami *(G-10424)*

5144 Poultry & Poultry Prdts Wholesale

McLane Foodservice Dist Inc ....C 407 857-3960
Orlando *(G-12846)*

◆ Quirch Foods LLC ....B 305 691-3535
Coral Gables *(G-2173)*

Sea Breeze Food Service Inc ....D 904 356-9905
Jacksonville *(G-6703)*

◆ Sunny Morning Foods Inc ....E 954 735-3447
Fort Lauderdale *(G-4162)*

Sysco Intl Fd Group Inc ....E 904 371-5734
Jacksonville *(G-6824)*

◆ Sysco Intl Fd Group Inc ....D 813 707-6161
Plant City *(G-14587)*

▼ Sysco Jacksonville Inc ....B 904 781-5070
Jacksonville *(G-6825)*

◆ Sysco South Florida Inc ....A 305 651-5421
Medley *(G-8787)*

Tzion Group LLC ....E 954 673-0843
Miami *(G-10424)*

◆ Wincorp International Inc ....E 305 887-4000
Medley *(G-8798)*

5145 Confectionery Wholesale

▼ Barnard Nut Company Inc ....D 305 836-9999
Miami *(G-9223)*

◆ Colombina Candy Company Inc ......D 786 265-1920
Miami *(G-9389)*

▼ Convenent Whlslers of Amer Inc ....E 954 351-0080
Fort Lauderdale *(G-3716)*

Frito-Lay North America Inc ....D 727 319-4173
Seminole *(G-16447)*

GF Pretzels LLC ....E 703 362-3188
Stuart *(G-16626)*

Las Olas Confections & Snacks ....C 305 940-4900
Fort Lauderdale *(G-3930)*

▲ Lisy Corp ....D 305 836-6001
Apopka *(G-197)*

▼ Monel Inc ....E 305 635-7331
Miami *(G-10013)*

◆ Rex Discount Inc ....D 305 633-6650
Miami *(G-10209)*

Snackcrate Inc ....C 850 341-9555
Pensacola *(G-14440)*

Snackworks Inc ....D 941 751-3333
Bradenton *(G-1180)*

Summit Naturals Inc ....D 425 280-1696
Orlando *(G-13247)*

Tropical Nut & Fruit Co ....D 407 843-8141
Orlando *(G-13312)*

Yummy Snacks Inc ....D 954 225-2535
Margate *(G-8669)*

Zuma & Sons Distributors Corp ....E 305 887-0089
Medley *(G-8802)*

5146 Fish & Seafood Wholesale

◆ Alfa International Seafood Inc ....E 305 888-6789
Medley *(G-8702)*

◆ Bama Sea Products Inc ....D 727 327-3474
Saint Petersburg *(G-15584)*

◆ Bay-N-Gulf Inc ....D 727 321-0425
Saint Petersburg *(G-15591)*

Captains Fine Foods LLC ....E 727 822-0615
Saint Petersburg *(G-15610)*

◆ Collier County Produce Inc ....D 239 280-3713
Naples *(G-11064)*

Coxs Wholesale Seafood LLC ....C 305 448-4424
Miami Beach *(G-10577)*

Daytona Beach Cold Storage Co ....D 386 763-7500
South Daytona *(G-16486)*

◆ Gamma Seafood Corporation ....E 305 888-6789
Medley *(G-8735)*

Halperns Steak Seafood Co LLC ....B 407 423-8550
Orlando *(G-12612)*

Harbor Docks Inc ....C 850 837-2506
Destin *(G-3060)*

▼ Jowdy Industries Inc ....E 561 586-2212
West Palm Beach *(G-19221)*

Klf Fisheries LLC ....D 305 451-3782
Key Largo *(G-7186)*

Leavins Seafood Inc ....E 850 653-8823
Apalachicola *(G-128)*

Local + Turtle LLC ....E 813 570-8222
Tampa *(G-17959)*

Merrick Seafood Company ....D 239 542-8080
Cape Coral *(G-1412)*

◆ Mowi Usa LLC ....E 305 591-8550
Medley *(G-8759)*

New England Whl Fish Lbster In ....E 772 334-6666
Stuart *(G-16649)*

◆ North Star Seafood LLC ....C 305 696-7183
Medley *(G-8763)*

Olr Investment Corp ....E 407 849-0534
Orlando *(G-12928)*

Patti Joe Seafood Company ....D 850 432-3315
Pensacola *(G-14403)*

Pfg Specialty Inc ....C 407 851-4001
Orlando *(G-13026)*

◆ Quirch Foods LLC ....B 305 691-3535
Coral Gables *(G-2173)*

◆ Raffield Fisheries Inc ....E 850 229-8229
Port Saint Joe *(G-15117)*

◆ Regal Springs Trading Company ......D 954 283-9035
Miramar *(G-10890)*

Samuels Son Safood S Coast LLC ....C...... 407 401-8898
  Orlando *(G-13165)*
Sea Breeze Food Service Inc ....D...... 904 356-9905
  Jacksonville *(G-6703)*
Sg Seafood Holdings Inc ....B...... 954 377-3400
  Fort Lauderdale *(G-4118)*
Stokes Fish Company ....E...... 352 787-4335
  Leesburg *(G-8274)*
◆ Tampa Bay Fisheries Inc ....B...... 813 752-8883
  Dover *(G-3370)*
Tampa Bay Fisheries Inc ....B...... 904 783-8800
  Jacksonville *(G-6832)*
▲ Tampa Maid Foods LLC ....B...... 863 687-4411
  Lakeland *(G-7986)*
▲ True Grade LLC ....E...... 305 800-8783
  Miami *(G-10413)*
◆ True World Foods Miami LLC ....E...... 305 687-4303
  Miami *(G-10415)*
Tzion Group LLC ....E...... 954 673-0843
  Miami *(G-10424)*
◆ Water Street Seafood Inc ....E...... 850 653-8902
  Apalachicola *(G-131)*
Webbs Seafood Inc ....E...... 850 753-3267
  Youngstown *(G-19814)*

5147 Meats & Meat Prdts Wholesale

▲ Berry Veal Corp ....E...... 561 736-1993
  Boynton Beach *(G-963)*
▲ Boars Head Provisions Co Inc ....D...... 941 955-0994
  Sarasota *(G-16107)*
▼ Charlies Pastries Inc ....E...... 954 583-3979
  Lauderhill *(G-8190)*
◆ Colorado Boxed Beef Co ....A...... 863 967-0636
  Lakeland *(G-7842)*
Global Distributors Inc ....E...... 305 638-8954
  Miami *(G-9633)*
Jerrys Famous Deli Inc ....C...... 305 672-1861
  Miami Beach *(G-10605)*
◆ Jetro Cash Carry Entps of Fla ....C...... 305 326-0409
  Miami *(G-9791)*
Local + Turtle LLC ....E...... 813 570-8222
  Tampa *(G-17959)*
◆ Martinez Distributors Corp ....D...... 305 882-8282
  Miami *(G-9907)*
McLane Foodservice Dist Inc ....C...... 863 687-2189
  Lakeland *(G-7915)*
McLane Foodservice Dist Inc ....C...... 407 857-3960
  Orlando *(G-12846)*
▼ Meat Traders Inc ....E...... 813 253-0865
  Tampa *(G-18015)*
◆ Miami Purveyors Inc ....E...... 305 262-6170
  Miami *(G-9981)*
Penn Dutch Food Center II Inc ....B...... 954 974-3900
  Fort Lauderdale *(G-4045)*
◆ Quirch Foods LLC ....B...... 305 691-3535
  Coral Gables *(G-2173)*
Quirch Foods LLC ....C...... 305 691-3535
  Medley *(G-8772)*
Restaurant Depot LLC ....C...... 954 577-0470
  Davie *(G-2509)*
▲ Rey/Chavez Distributor Corp ....D...... 305 696-4677
  Miami *(G-10211)*
Sanwa Fresh Produce Co LLC ....C...... 813 642-5166
  Tampa *(G-18247)*
▲ Sanwa Growers Inc ....D...... 813 642-5159
  Tampa *(G-18248)*
Sanwa Growers Inc ....D...... 813 234-8428
  Tampa *(G-18249)*
Sea Breeze Food Service Inc ....D...... 904 356-9905
  Jacksonville *(G-6703)*
▼ Sysco Jacksonville Inc ....B...... 904 781-5070
  Jacksonville *(G-6825)*
◆ Sysco South Florida Inc ....A...... 305 651-5421
  Medley *(G-8787)*
Tzion Group LLC ....E...... 954 673-0843
  Miami *(G-10424)*

5148 Fresh Fruits & Vegetables Wholesale

◆ A Duda & Sons Inc ....D...... 407 365-2111
  Oviedo *(G-13536)*
◆ Alpine Fresh LLC ....D...... 305 594-9117
  Doral *(G-3114)*
◆ American Fruit & Produce Corp ....D...... 305 681-1880
  Opa Locka *(G-11939)*
Apple Core Inc ....D...... 561 471-0848
  West Palm Beach *(G-19038)*
◆ Ayco Farms Inc ....E...... 954 788-6800
  Pompano Beach *(G-14746)*
Ben Hill Griffin Inc ....D...... 863 635-2251
  Frostproof *(G-4819)*

Brian Pzyckis Frm Fresh Prod L ....D...... 727 823-2916
  Saint Petersburg *(G-15605)*
◆ Brooks Tropicals Holding Inc ....C...... 305 247-3544
  Homestead *(G-5562)*
◆ Caribe Food Corp ....D...... 305 835-7110
  Miami *(G-9321)*
CH Robinson Worldwide Inc ....C...... 561 999-0200
  Sunrise *(G-16756)*
Chapman Fruit Co Inc ....E...... 863 773-3161
  Wauchula *(G-18957)*
◆ Chiquita Brands LLC ....C...... 954 924-5801
  Dania *(G-2406)*
◆ Collier County Produce Inc ....D...... 239 280-3713
  Naples *(G-11064)*
Coosemans Tampa Inc ....C...... 813 238-9500
  Tampa *(G-17519)*
◆ Del Monte Fresh Produce Co ....C...... 305 520-8400
  Coral Gables *(G-2092)*
◆ Del Monte Fresh Produce NA Inc ......C...... 305 520-8400
  Coral Gables *(G-2093)*
◆ Dimare Ruskin Inc ....D...... 813 645-3241
  Apollo Beach *(G-134)*
▲ Dimare Tampa Inc ....D...... 813 671-8200
  Riverview *(G-15255)*
Downtown Discount Produce Inc ....D...... 321 308-0275
  Melbourne *(G-8875)*
◆ Duda Farm Fresh Foods Inc ....B...... 407 365-2111
  Oviedo *(G-13546)*
Estes Citrus Inc ....E...... 772 569-5022
  Vero Beach *(G-18856)*
Falkner Produce Inc ....E...... 941 322-2016
  Myakka City *(G-10986)*
Farm Cut LLC ....C...... 813 754-3321
  Plant City *(G-14555)*
Florida Potato & Onion LLC ....E...... 813 719-2660
  Plant City *(G-14557)*
◆ Freedom Fresh LLC ....C...... 305 715-5700
  Medley *(G-8734)*
Fresh Distribution LLC ....E...... 888 373-7461
  Fort Lauderdale *(G-3806)*
◆ Freshpoint Inc ....E...... 407 858-0046
  Maitland *(G-8534)*
◆ Freshpoint Central Florida Inc ....C...... 407 383-8427
  Orlando *(G-12548)*
Freshpoint North Florida Inc ....C...... 904 764-7681
  Orlando *(G-12549)*
◆ Freshpoint South Florida Inc ....C...... 954 917-7272
  Pompano Beach *(G-14814)*
◆ Gargiulo Inc ....E...... 239 597-3131
  Naples *(G-11128)*
Gargiulo Inc ....C...... 850 875-4020
  Quincy *(G-15230)*
◆ Garland LLC ....C...... 305 636-1607
  Miami *(G-9619)*
Generation Fresh LLC ....D...... 912 537-3575
  Delray Beach *(G-2953)*
◆ Haines Cy Citrus Growers Assn ....D...... 863 422-4924
  Haines City *(G-5149)*
▲ Harvest Sensations LLC ....D...... 305 591-8173
  Doral *(G-3222)*
HD Budd Farms Inc ....E...... 813 752-2434
  Plant City *(G-14562)*
▲ Herbs Unlimited Inc ....D...... 305 477-8833
  Miami *(G-9696)*
◆ Hortifrut Imports Inc ....D...... 239 552-4453
  Estero *(G-3465)*
Indrio Brands LLC ....D...... 772 978-0056
  Vero Beach *(G-18878)*
Indrio Brands LLC ....C...... 772 226-3500
  Vero Beach *(G-18879)*
◆ Jalaram Produce Inc ....D...... 305 245-0083
  Homestead *(G-5585)*
King Fresh Tomatoes Inc ....E...... 863 307-9652
  Bartow *(G-324)*
Leasa Industries Co Inc ....D...... 305 696-0651
  Miami *(G-9854)*
◆ Leroy Smith Inc ....E...... 772 567-3421
  Vero Beach *(G-18887)*
▼ Mac Edwards Produce & Co Inc ....C...... 305 326-7223
  Doral *(G-3268)*
▲ Marjon Specialty Foods Inc ....C...... 813 752-3482
  Plant City *(G-14572)*
McLane Foodservice Dist Inc ....C...... 407 857-3960
  Orlando *(G-12846)*
◆ Merchants Export LLC ....E...... 561 863-7171
  Riviera Beach *(G-15309)*
◆ New Limeco LLC ....C...... 305 258-1611
  Princeton *(G-15187)*
◆ Pero Family Farms Food Co LLC ....D...... 561 498-4533
  Delray Beach *(G-3004)*

Ppinc LLC ....D...... 954 458-1010
  Fort Lauderdale *(G-4056)*
▼ Premier Citrus Packers LLC ....C...... 772 794-0302
  Vero Beach *(G-18906)*
▲ RC Treatt Inc ....D...... 863 668-9500
  Lakeland *(G-7950)*
Sanwa Fresh Produce Co LLC ....C...... 813 642-5166
  Tampa *(G-18247)*
▲ Sanwa Growers Inc ....D...... 813 642-5159
  Tampa *(G-18248)*
◆ Seald Sweet LLC ....E...... 772 569-2244
  Vero Beach *(G-18916)*
◆ Six LS Packing Company Inc ....E...... 239 657-3117
  Immokalee *(G-5662)*
◆ Sun Commodities Inc ....C...... 954 972-8383
  Pompano Beach *(G-14913)*
Sunfresh Produce Inc ....D...... 941 475-7336
  Englewood *(G-3433)*
Sunrise Fresh Produce LLC ....D...... 904 366-1368
  Jacksonville *(G-6810)*
▼ Taylor & Fulton Packing LLC ....C...... 941 729-3883
  Palmetto *(G-13932)*
Todds Quality Tomatoes Inc ....E...... 407 323-1380
  Sanford *(G-15988)*
Tom Lange Company Intl Inc ....C...... 305 901-1223
  Vero Beach *(G-18925)*
▼ Tomato Thyme Corporation ....C...... 813 672-7707
  Wimauma *(G-19535)*
▼ Tomatoes of Ruskin Inc ....C...... 813 645-6431
  Ruskin *(G-15405)*
Tri Venture Marketing LLC ....D...... 863 648-1881
  Lakeland *(G-7990)*
Villages Grown LLC ....C...... 352 775-7333
  The Villages *(G-18667)*
West Coast Tomato LLC ....A...... 941 722-4545
  Palmetto *(G-13936)*
Weyand & Son Inc ....D...... 813 234-2151
  Tampa *(G-18547)*
Weyand Food Distributors Inc ....E...... 813 236-5923
  Tampa *(G-18548)*

5149 Groceries & Related Prdts, NEC Wholesale

▼ Acosta Sales Co Inc ....C...... 904 281-9800
  Jacksonville *(G-5731)*
◆ American Beverage Depot LLC ....E...... 305 882-0199
  Medley *(G-8705)*
◆ AMLL Corporation ....E...... 305 885-9785
  Hialeah Gardens *(G-5339)*
Antonellas Wholesale Inc ....E...... 305 548-5061
  Miami *(G-9156)*
Arizona Beverages USA LLC ....C...... 516 812-0303
  Lakeland *(G-7803)*
◆ Asr Group International Inc ....C...... 914 963-2400
  West Palm Beach *(G-19041)*
Atlantic Bakery Ltd ....E...... 561 276-0013
  Delray Beach *(G-2913)*
◆ Badia Spices Inc ....C...... 305 629-8000
  Doral *(G-3131)*
Bagel King Wholesale Inc ....E...... 407 660-2000
  Orlando *(G-12165)*
Bakemark USA LLC ....E...... 800 282-0565
  Tampa *(G-17332)*
Bakemark USA LLC ....E...... 305 685-0700
  Miami *(G-9200)*
Bakery Express Central Fla Inc ....C...... 407 826-5711
  Orlando *(G-12173)*
Base Culture LLC ....E...... 844 697-2536
  Clearwater *(G-1531)*
◆ Best Value Food Products LLC ....E...... 305 691-0700
  Miami *(G-9249)*
Bittersweet Financial Corp ....C...... 786 605-0350
  Miami *(G-9259)*
▲ Caribbean Supercenter Inc ....E...... 407 523-1308
  Orlando *(G-12240)*
Castellon Coffee LLC ....C...... 786 878-2030
  Miami *(G-9334)*
◆ Cheney Bros Inc ....A...... 561 845-4700
  Riviera Beach *(G-15288)*
Cheney Ofs Inc ....A...... 407 292-3223
  Orlando *(G-12293)*
Cirkul Inc ....D...... 941 724-4382
  Tampa *(G-17474)*
Cirkul Inc ....D...... 941 518-8596
  Tampa *(G-17475)*
Cirkul Inc ....C...... 513 889-6708
  Tampa *(G-17476)*
▲ Coastal Beverage Ltd ....D...... 239 643-4343
  Naples *(G-11061)*

Coca-Cola Beverages Fla LLC ....C 407 295-9290
Orlando *(G-12336)*

Coca-Cola Beverages Fla LLC ....B 904 786-2720
Jacksonville *(G-5974)*

Coca-Cola Bottling Co Untd Inc ....C 850 478-4800
Pensacola *(G-14261)*

◆ Conchita Foods Inc ....D 305 888-9703
Medley *(G-8715)*

Croissants De France Inc ....E 305 294-2624
Key West *(G-7201)*

Deland Bakery Inc ....D 386 734-7553
Deland *(G-2854)*

Dominos Pizza LLC ....E 352 429-5555
Groveland *(G-5089)*

▼ Dp Distribution LLC ....A 305 777-6108
Medley *(G-8722)*

▲ Garden of Life LLC ....C 561 748-2477
West Palm Beach *(G-19159)*

Garrison Natural Spring Water ....E 516 349-8866
Fort Myers *(G-4407)*

Global Widget LLC ....C 800 589-9098
Tampa *(G-17739)*

Golden Seed LLC ....C 786 354-7359
Medley *(G-8738)*

Gordon Food Service Inc ....D 305 507-2950
Miami *(G-9651)*

▲ Herbs Unlimited Inc ....D 305 477-8833
Miami *(G-9696)*

Iberia Foods Corp ....E 305 863-8840
Miami *(G-9737)*

Indrio Brands LLC ....C 772 226-3500
Vero Beach *(G-18879)*

▲ Infinite Herbs LLC ....D 305 599-9255
Doral *(G-3235)*

◆ Interntnal Crise Fd Ht Spplers ....E 305 653-2042
Medley *(G-8746)*

Joffreys Coffee & Tea Co ....D 813 250-0404
Tampa *(G-17898)*

▲ Johnson Brothers Florida Inc ....C 813 832-4477
Tampa *(G-17900)*

▲ K A S Inc ....E 813 628-8182
Tampa *(G-17905)*

Kahwa Management LLC ....D 727 388-1340
Saint Petersburg *(G-15739)*

Kehe Distributors LLC ....C 800 223-2910
Jacksonville *(G-6399)*

▲ Lisy Corp ....D 305 836-6001
Apopka *(G-197)*

Martin-Brower Company LLC ....D 407 583-0693
Orlando *(G-12821)*

McLane Company Inc ....C 407 816-7600
Orlando *(G-12845)*

McLane Foodservice Dist Inc ....C 863 687-2189
Lakeland *(G-7915)*

ME Thompson Inc ....D 863 667-3732
Lakeland *(G-7916)*

▼ Monel Inc ....E 305 635-7331
Miami *(G-10013)*

Nelson Family Farms Inc ....E 772 464-2100
Fort Pierce *(G-4725)*

▲ New Southern Food Distrs Inc ....E 352 620-0205
Ocala *(G-11742)*

◆ Niagara Distributors Inc ....E 954 925-6775
Hollywood *(G-5482)*

North & South Wholesalers LLC ....E 305 638-4550
Miami Gardens *(G-10695)*

P & L Foods Inc ....E 239 369-5200
Lehigh Acres *(G-8289)*

Pepsi-Cola Metro Btlg Co Inc ....C 904 733-1627
Jacksonville *(G-6596)*

Pepsico Inc ....D 305 593-7500
Medley *(G-8770)*

Phillips Feed Service Inc ....E 813 754-2302
Plant City *(G-14574)*

▲ Phils Cake Box Bakeries Inc ....D 813 348-0128
Tampa *(G-18146)*

Pj Food Service Inc ....D 407 851-3595
Orlando *(G-13033)*

◆ Prime Line Distributors Inc ....E 954 925-4500
Fort Lauderdale *(G-4058)*

Procter & Gamble Distrg LLC ....E 904 477-8034
Jacksonville *(G-6617)*

Procter & Gamble Distrg LLC ....B 407 282-4926
Orlando *(G-13064)*

Qzina Specialty Foods Inc ....C 954 590-4000
Hollywood *(G-5500)*

▲ RC Treatt Inc ....D 863 668-9500
Lakeland *(G-7950)*

Refresco Beverages US Inc ....C 813 241-0147
Tampa *(G-18208)*

◆ Rex Discount Inc ....D 305 633-6650
Miami *(G-10209)*

◆ Roma Food Group Inc ....C 305 888-1355
Miami *(G-10218)*

Sarvis Incorporated ....B 407 890-9303
Orlando *(G-13168)*

◆ Scff LLC ....D 305 592-0008
Miami *(G-10246)*

▲ Schratter Foods Incorporated ....D 305 651-8884
Miami *(G-10248)*

Shasta Beverages Intl Inc ....E 954 581-0922
Plantation *(G-14706)*

◆ Ship Supply of Florida Inc ....E 305 681-7447
Miromar Lakes *(G-10928)*

Southern Bakeries Inc ....C 863 682-1155
Lakeland *(G-7971)*

◆ Sunny Morning Foods Inc ....E 954 735-3447
Fort Lauderdale *(G-4162)*

Sysco Intl Fd Group Inc ....C 904 371-5734
Jacksonville *(G-6824)*

▼ Sysco Intl Fd Group Inc ....D 813 707-6161
Plant City *(G-14587)*

▼ Sysco Jacksonville Inc ....B 904 781-5070
Jacksonville *(G-6825)*

▼ Sysco South Florida Inc ....A 305 651-5421
Medley *(G-8787)*

▲ Sysco West Coast Florida Inc ....A 941 721-1450
Palmetto *(G-13931)*

Tierra Nueva Fine Cocoa LLC ....E 786 364-4444
Miami Gardens *(G-10698)*

◆ Tropical Foods LLC ....E 305 477-5811
Doral *(G-3338)*

Tropical Nut & Fruit Co ....D 407 843-8141
Orlando *(G-13312)*

▲ True Grade LLC ....E 305 800-8783
Miami *(G-10413)*

Unfi Distribution Company LLC ....D 952 828-4529
Quincy *(G-15235)*

Unfi Distribution Company LLC ....E 952 828-4529
Quincy *(G-15236)*

US Foods Inc ....E 561 994-8500
Boca Raton *(G-855)*

◆ Vigo Importing Company ....C 813 884-3491
Tampa *(G-18507)*

◆ Vitality Foodservice Inc ....E 813 301-4600
Tampa *(G-18510)*

◆ Walton & Post Inc ....E 305 591-1111
Medley *(G-8796)*

Waste Pro Usa Inc ....D 321 837-0055
Cocoa *(G-1962)*

Watermill Express LLC ....E 813 988-1111
Tampa *(G-18525)*

Zuma & Sons Distributors Corp ....E 305 887-0089
Medley *(G-8802)*

5153 Grain & Field Beans Wholesale

Bakemark USA LLC ....E 305 685-0700
Miami *(G-9200)*

▲ Balos Foods LLC ....E 786 454-2800
Coral Gables *(G-2041)*

Bunge North America Inc ....E 305 648-4300
Miami *(G-9294)*

Central States Enterprises LLC ....E 386 755-7443
Lake City *(G-7519)*

Columbia Grn & Ingredients Inc ....E 386 755-7700
Lake City *(G-7521)*

5159 Farm-Prdt Raw Mtrls, NEC Wholesale

Moss & Associates LLC ....C 305 444-8164
Miami *(G-10018)*

5162 Plastics Materials & Basic Shapes Wholesale

◆ Entec Polymers LLC ....D 407 875-9595
Orlando *(G-12469)*

◆ Farco Plastics Supply Inc ....E 727 572-7722
Clearwater *(G-1632)*

Imperial Bag & Paper Co LLC ....D 813 621-3091
Tampa *(G-17862)*

◆ Muehlstein International Ltd ....D 203 855-6000
Orlando *(G-12889)*

Piedmont Plastics Inc ....E 386 274-4627
Daytona Beach *(G-2653)*

◆ Plasco LLC ....E 305 625-4222
Miami Lakes *(G-10754)*

◆ Rapid Industrial Plas Co Inc ....C 407 875-9595
Orlando *(G-13082)*

◆ Ravago Americas LLC ....A 407 773-7777
Orlando *(G-13083)*

Universal Designs Inc ....E 386 740-4700
Deland *(G-2884)*

5169 Chemicals & Allied Prdts, NEC Wholesale

Advanced Biocide Tech Inc ....E 954 530-1292
Sunrise *(G-16732)*

◆ Allchem Industries Holdg Corp ....D 352 378-9696
Gainesville *(G-4834)*

◆ Allied Universal Corp ....E 305 888-2623
Doral *(G-3110)*

Amz Holding Corp ....C 863 578-1206
Mulberry *(G-10969)*

◆ Arr-Maz Custom Chemicals Inc ....D 863 578-1206
Mulberry *(G-10970)*

Ascend Prfmce Mtls Oprtons LLC ....A 850 968-7000
Cantonment *(G-1333)*

Barentz North America LLC ....E 561 995-0070
Boca Raton *(G-442)*

Brenntag Mid-South Inc ....E 407 851-9003
Orlando *(G-12201)*

Brenntag Mid-South Inc ....E 813 247-7354
Tampa *(G-17386)*

◆ Ccp Management Inc ....D 904 398-7177
Jacksonville *(G-5917)*

◆ Cheney Bros Inc ....A 561 845-4700
Riviera Beach *(G-15288)*

Drew Marine USA Inc ....E 305 770-7120
Miami *(G-9489)*

Duraedge Products Incorporated ....C 866 867-0052
Vero Beach *(G-18851)*

Dyco Paints Inc ....E 727 381-1229
Tampa *(G-17606)*

Ecological Laboratories Inc ....E 239 573-6650
Cape Coral *(G-1388)*

▼ Fleet Acquisitions LLC ....D 813 621-1734
Tampa *(G-17669)*

Florida Hosp Hm Care Svc Ctr ....E 407 691-8202
Orlando *(G-12526)*

Hi-TEC Laboratories Inc ....E 850 835-6822
Freeport *(G-4815)*

Illinois Tool Works Inc ....D 863 665-3338
Lakeland *(G-7885)*

▼ Interstate Chemical Inc ....E 863 607-6700
Lakeland *(G-7887)*

◆ Jci Jones Chemicals Inc ....E 941 330-1537
Sarasota *(G-16203)*

Kimera Labs Inc ....E 305 454-7836
Miramar *(G-10872)*

Lifesafe Services LLC ....E 904 730-4800
Jacksonville *(G-6436)*

◆ Mapei Corporation ....C 954 246-8888
Deerfield Beach *(G-2770)*

Medical Ctr Hm Hlth Care Svcs ....A 850 431-6868
Tallahassee *(G-17040)*

Mosaic ....E 863 491-1003
Arcadia *(G-231)*

◆ Nebula Glass International Inc ....E 954 975-3233
Pompano Beach *(G-14866)*

Nuco2 Inc ....C 772 221-1754
Stuart *(G-16651)*

Nuco2 Supply LLC ....C 772 221-1754
Stuart *(G-16653)*

Procter & Gamble Distrg LLC ....E 904 477-8034
Jacksonville *(G-6617)*

Procter & Gamble Distrg LLC ....B 407 282-4926
Orlando *(G-13064)*

Pyramid II Jantr Sups & Eqp ....E 239 939-4496
Fort Myers *(G-4557)*

Ravago Chemical Dist Inc ....E 508 770-0076
Orlando *(G-13084)*

◆ Rex Discount Inc ....D 305 633-6650
Miami *(G-10209)*

◆ Sewell Hardware Company Inc ....E 561 832-7171
West Palm Beach *(G-19359)*

▲ Sun Wholesale Supply Inc ....C 727 524-3299
Clearwater *(G-1801)*

◆ Sunbelt Chemicals Corp ....D 386 446-4595
Palm Coast *(G-13841)*

▼ Supplyone Tampa Bay Inc ....E 727 573-1822
Clearwater *(G-1809)*

◆ Yara North America Inc ....D 813 222-5700
Tampa *(G-18574)*

5171 Petroleum Bulk Stations & Terminals

Crowley Holdings Inc ....D 904 727-2200
Jacksonville *(G-6016)*

◆ Crowley Maritime Corporation ....D 904 727-2200
Jacksonville *(G-6021)*

Mplx Terminals LLC ....E 813 247-1459
Tampa *(G-18058)*

Ritco Inc ....E 517 439-1920
Ocala *(G-11769)*

5172 Petroleum & Petroleum Prdts Wholesale

Allied AVI Fueling Miami Inc ....E 305 871-7001
Miami *(G-9123)*

Associated Energy Group LLC...........D 305 913-5253
Miami *(G-9178)*

Atlas Aviation Tampa Inc ....E 813 251-1752
Tampa *(G-17318)*

Automated Petroleum & Enrgy Co ....E 813 681-4279
Lake Worth *(G-7713)*

Banyan Air Services Inc ....C 954 491-3170
Fort Lauderdale *(G-3628)*

▼ Blaylock Oil Co ....E 305 247-7249
Homestead *(G-5559)*

BP Products North America Inc...........C 813 248-3191
Tampa *(G-17382)*

Crowley Holdings Inc ....D 904 727-2200
Jacksonville *(G-6016)*

◆ Crowley Maritime Corporation ....D 904 727-2200
Jacksonville *(G-6021)*

CSI Enterprises Inc ....C 239 947-5169
Bonita Springs *(G-907)*

Deull Fuel Co ....E 561 624-0293
Palm Beach Gardens *(G-13716)*

ESP Fueling LLC ....E 305 336-9995
Hialeah *(G-5258)*

First Coast Energy LLP ....D 904 596-3200
Jacksonville *(G-6168)*

Florida Petroleum Corporation ....E 904 237-9739
Jacksonville Beach *(G-6986)*

Guardian Fueling Tech LLC ....D 904 680-0860
Jacksonville *(G-6246)*

Guardian Fueling Tech LLC ....D 954 432-0622
Hialeah *(G-5269)*

Guardian Fueling Tech LLC ....D 407 321-0130
Sanford *(G-15948)*

Guardian Fueling Technologies ....E 850 466-3050
Pensacola *(G-14316)*

Jess Petroleum Inc ....E 954 426-1482
Coconut Creek *(G-1992)*

Land & Sea Petro Holdings Inc............E 954 978-3835
Fort Lauderdale *(G-3928)*

Man Energy Solutions USA Inc ....D 954 960-6700
Fort Lauderdale *(G-3953)*

Mplx Terminals LLC ....D 540 494-4152
Jacksonville *(G-6518)*

National Jets Inc ....E 954 359-9400
Fort Lauderdale *(G-3990)*

Om SAI Petroleum Inc ....E 321 213-3692
Cocoa Beach *(G-1976)*

◆ Port Consolidated Inc ....D 954 522-1182
Fort Lauderdale *(G-4054)*

Reladyne Inc ....E 305 652-2944
Miami *(G-10198)*

Seaboard Distribution Inc ....E 863 815-4424
Lakeland *(G-7965)*

▼ Sentinel Lubricants Inc ....D 305 625-6400
Miami *(G-10260)*

Sun Aviation Inc ....E 772 562-2857
Vero Beach *(G-18921)*

Triton Global Petroleum Ltd ....E 954 639-0005
Fort Lauderdale *(G-4186)*

Tropic Oil Company LLC ....E 863 676-3910
Lake Wales *(G-7703)*

◆ World Fuel Services Inc ....C 305 428-8000
Doral *(G-3359)*

World Fuel Services Corp ....B 305 428-8000
Doral *(G-3360)*

World Fuel Svcs Corp AVI Sppor..........E 305 428-8000
Doral *(G-3361)*

5181 Beer & Ale Wholesale

Bernie Little Distributors Inc..............D 863 665-3615
Eaton Park *(G-3404)*

◆ Brown Distributing Company Inc......C 561 655-3791
West Palm Beach *(G-19067)*

Burkhardt Distributing Co Inc............D 352 377-9092
Saint Augustine *(G-15432)*

Burkhardt Distributing Co Inc............D 904 829-3008
Gainesville *(G-4850)*

▼ Carroll Distributing Company ....C 321 636-2377
Melbourne *(G-8839)*

▲ Champion Brands Inc ....C 904 268-1220
Jacksonville *(G-5935)*

▲ City Beverages LLC ....C 407 851-7100
Orlando *(G-12303)*

▲ Coastal Beverage Ltd ....D 239 643-4343
Naples *(G-11061)*

▲ Cone Distributing Inc..................C 352 732-4111
Ocala *(G-11667)*

Cone Distributing Inc ....D 850 576-4176
Tallahassee *(G-16922)*

D G Yuengling and Son Inc ....D 813 972-8500
Tampa *(G-17565)*

Daytona Beverages LLC...................D 386 274-4005
Daytona Beach *(G-2578)*

▲ Eagle Brands Wedco Ltd Partnr ....C 305 599-2337
Miami *(G-9494)*

▲ Gold Cast Egle Dstrg Ltd Lblty ....C 941 355-7685
Lakewood Ranch *(G-8039)*

Gold Coast Beverage LLC................A 305 591-9800
Doral *(G-3213)*

▲ Grantham Distributing Co Inc..........D 407 299-6446
Orlando *(G-12594)*

▲ Great Bay Distributors Inc ....C 727 584-8626
Saint Petersburg *(G-15693)*

Great Bay Distributors Inc ....C 727 584-8626
Saint Petersburg *(G-15694)*

▲ J J Taylor Distrg Tampa Bay ....C 813 247-4000
Tampa *(G-17880)*

L C Busch-Transou ....D 352 401-0993
Ocala *(G-11706)*

L C Busch-Transou ....C 850 539-2539
Midway *(G-10804)*

▲ Lewis Bear Company Inc ....D 850 434-8612
Pensacola *(G-14346)*

Motorworks Brewing LLC ....E 941 567-6218
Bradenton *(G-1148)*

North Florida Sales Co Inc ....D 904 645-0283
Jacksonville *(G-6549)*

Peace River Distributing Inc ....D 941 637-9799
Punta Gorda *(G-15215)*

▲ Pepin Distributing Company ....D 813 626-6176
Tampa *(G-18139)*

Premier Beverage Company LLC.........C 239 561-0340
Fort Myers *(G-4549)*

▲ Premier Beverage Company LLC ......C 954 436-9200
Miramar *(G-10887)*

Quality Brands Inc ....D 386 738-3808
De Land *(G-2696)*

Restaurant Depot LLC ....C 954 577-0470
Davie *(G-2509)*

Rmet Holdings Inc ....D 305 591-9800
Homestead *(G-5602)*

Rmet Holdings Inc ....D 954 943-3950
Pompano Beach *(G-14885)*

◆ Rmet Holdings Inc ....D 305 567-3582
Coral Gables *(G-2180)*

Rmet Holdings Inc ....D 305 567-3582
Palm Beach *(G-13668)*

Rmet Holdings Inc ....E 772 461-8227
Fort Pierce *(G-4736)*

Rmet Holdings Inc ....D 305 293-3186
Key West *(G-7241)*

Silver Eagle Distributors Ltd ....D 305 230-2337
Homestead *(G-5605)*

Southern Glzers Wine Sprits LL ....B 863 413-8200
Lakeland *(G-7972)*

▲ SR Perrott Inc ....C 386 672-2975
Ormond Beach *(G-13525)*

▲ Stephens Distributing Company ......D 954 989-4350
Fort Lauderdale *(G-4154)*

Suncoast Beverage Sales Lllp............E 239 334-3520
Fort Myers *(G-4612)*

Suncoast Beverage Sales Lllp............D 239 334-3520
Punta Gorda *(G-15222)*

Wayne Densch Inc ....C 407 323-5600
Sanford *(G-15992)*

5182 Wine & Distilled Alcoholic Beverages Wholesale

Aroma Boca Inc...........................D 954 252-2600
Cooper City *(G-2013)*

◆ Bacardi USA Inc ....D 305 573-8600
Coral Gables *(G-2040)*

◆ Caribbean Distillers LLC...............C 863 956-1116
Lake Alfred *(G-7448)*

◆ Carisam-Samuel Meisel FL Inc.........D 305 591-3993
Doral *(G-3144)*

Cavatappi Distribution LLC...............B 305 625-4171
Miami *(G-9336)*

Cone Distributing Inc.....................D 850 576-4176
Tallahassee *(G-16922)*

Country Vintner Inc.......................D 804 752-3670
Boca Raton *(G-535)*

D G Yuengling and Son Inc ....D 813 972-8500
Tampa *(G-17565)*

Diageo North America Inc ....C 305 269-4500
Miami *(G-9475)*

◆ Duty Free Air and Ship Sup LLC ....E 305 654-9200
Miami *(G-9492)*

▲ Grantham Distributing Co Inc..........D 407 299-6446
Orlando *(G-12594)*

◆ International Operations Svcs ....D 305 591-1763
Miami *(G-9768)*

▲ Johnson Brothers Florida Inc..........C 813 832-4477
Tampa *(G-17900)*

Liquor Management LLC ....E 954 358-9463
Fort Lauderdale *(G-3945)*

Mast-Jaegermeister Us Inc ....D 813 994-2114
Wesley Chapel *(G-19002)*

Mexcor Inc ....C 713 979-0066
Medley *(G-8758)*

North America Duty Free Inc ....D 954 962-3432
Hollywood *(G-5484)*

◆ Palm Bay International Inc ....D 561 893-9998
Boca Raton *(G-738)*

◆ Pernod Rcard Amrcas Trvl Ret I.........E 954 940-9000
Fort Lauderdale *(G-4047)*

▲ Premier Beverage Co....................D 813 672-6161
Tampa *(G-18163)*

Premier Beverage Company LLC.........C 407 852-5200
Orlando *(G-13049)*

▲ Premier Beverage Company LLC ......B 954 436-9200
Miramar *(G-10887)*

Republic Nat Distrg Co LLC...............A 904 714-7200
Jacksonville *(G-6658)*

◆ Rmet Holdings Inc......................B 305 567-3582
Coral Gables *(G-2180)*

Shaw-Ross Intl Importers LLC............E 954 430-5020
Miramar *(G-10894)*

◆ Smt Duty Free Inc ....C 305 477-0515
Doral *(G-3314)*

◆ Southern Glzers Wine Sprits LL........A 866 375-9555
Miami *(G-10309)*

Southern Glzers Wine Sprits LL...........C 954 680-4600
Miramar *(G-10900)*

Southern Glzers Wine Sprits LL...........B 863 413-8200
Lakeland *(G-7972)*

▲ Southern Trademark Holdg Inc........D 954 430-5020
Miramar *(G-10901)*

▲ Vicente Gandia Pla ....C 310 699-8559
Miami *(G-10470)*

Vineyard Brands LLC ....E 305 271-8971
Miami *(G-10474)*

Vineyard Wine Company LLC.............D 407 942-0066
Longwood *(G-8414)*

5191 Farm Splys Wholesale

Ausoil International Corp ....D 954 249-8060
Miami *(G-9191)*

Branch Properties Inc.....................D 352 732-4143
Ocala *(G-11646)*

Chemplast International Corp.............B 813 286-8680
Tampa *(G-17464)*

Dolime Minerals Company ....C 863 533-0721
Bartow *(G-316)*

Florida Fertilizer Company Inc ....E 863 773-4159
Wauchula *(G-18960)*

◆ Geoglobal Partners LLC ....D 561 598-6000
Riviera Beach *(G-15296)*

▼ Golf Ventures Inc ....E 863 665-5800
Lakeland *(G-7877)*

◆ Harrells LLC ....E 863 687-2774
Lakeland *(G-7881)*

Harrells Horticultural ....D 800 282-8007
Avon Park *(G-292)*

▲ Hazera Seeds USA Inc ....E 954 834-5192
Deerfield Beach *(G-2748)*

◆ Howard Fert & Chem Co Inc ....D 407 855-1841
Orlando *(G-12667)*

▲ Knox Nursery Inc ....D 407 654-1972
Winter Garden *(G-19577)*

Marian Farms Inc ....C 352 429-4151
Groveland *(G-5098)*

▲ Mayo Fertilizer Incorporated ....E 386 294-2024
Mayo *(G-8697)*

Ocala Breeders Sales Co Inc ....E 352 629-8686
Ocala *(G-11747)*

◆ Pioneer Ag-Chem Inc ....E 772 464-9300
Fort Pierce *(G-4729)*

◆ Southern AG Insecticides Inc............E 941 722-3285
Palmetto *(G-13929)*

◆ Sunniland Corporation ....C 407 322-2421
Longwood (G-8407)

◆ Syfrett Feed Co Inc...............................E 863 763-5586
Okeechobee (G-11880)

Tractor Supply Company ....E 727 372-3450
New Port Richey (G-11407)

Triest AG Group Inc..............................E 941 722-5587
Palmetto (G-13935)

◆ Wincorp International Inc ....E 305 887-4000
Medley (G-8798)

◆ Yara North America Inc ....D 813 222-5700
Tampa (G-18574)

5192 Books, Periodicals & Newspapers Wholesale

Choice Books Northern VA Inc...............D 352 523-2959
Dade City (G-2382)

Florida Schl Bk Depository Inc..............E 904 781-7191
Jacksonville (G-6202)

Globetech Media LLC ....E 954 893-0003
Hollywood (G-5443)

Hudson Group (hg) Retail LLC ....E 954 463-4931
Fort Lauderdale (G-3878)

Jim Pattison Industries Ltd ....E 904 783-2350
Jacksonville (G-6386)

Newsbank Inc ....E 800 762-8182
Naples (G-11249)

▲ Source Interlink Dist LLC ....A 239 949-4450
Bonita Springs (G-942)

◆ Spanish House Inc ....E 305 503-1191
Medley (G-8786)

▼ Spanish Peri & Bk Sls Inc ....D 305 592-3919
Doral (G-3320)

Tng GP ....A 786 501-7207
Doral (G-3334)

5193 Flowers, Nursery Stock & Florists' Splys Wholesale

AG 3 Inc ....D 352 589-8055
Eustis (G-3491)

▼ Albin Hagstrom & Son Inc.................C 386 749-2521
Pierson (G-14495)

◆ Allure Farms Inc ....E 305 883-7781
Doral (G-3112)

Alpha Foliage Inc ....E 305 245-2220
Homestead (G-5554)

▲ American Farms LLC ....C 239 455-0300
Naples (G-11009)

Armellini Industries Inc ....B 772 287-0575
Palm City (G-13784)

Arziki Nursery LLC ....E 954 648-6875
Homestead (G-5555)

Azalea Oaks Inc ....E 352 753-2388
Leesburg (G-8232)

▼ Berkeley Florist Supply Co Inc ....E 305 638-4141
Miami (G-9243)

▲ Bouquet Collection Inc ....D 305 594-4981
Miami (G-9271)

Brantley Lake Plant Corp ....E 407 869-6545
Winter Garden (G-19558)

▲ Colour Republic LLC ....D 305 463-9000
Doral (G-3156)

▼ Connectaflor LLC ....D 305 629-4000
Doral (G-3161)

▼ Continental Flowers Inc ....E 305 594-4214
Doral (G-3163)

◆ Deleons Management Inc ....D 305 238-6028
Goulds (G-5041)

◆ Deroose Plants Inc ....E 407 889-5228
Apopka (G-172)

▲ Earthbalance Corporation ....D 941 426-7878
North Port (G-11568)

▲ Elite Flower Services Inc ....D 305 436-7400
Miami (G-9515)

Emerald Farms Inc ....E 305 463-8381
Miami (G-9518)

Equiflor Corporation ....D 305 594-4445
Doral (G-3189)

▼ Esprit-Miami Inc ....E 305 591-2244
Doral (G-3190)

▼ Everbloom Growers Inc ....D 305 248-1478
Homestead (G-5570)

◆ Falcon Farms Inc ....B 305 477-8088
Miami (G-9542)

▲ Fernlea Nurseries Inc ....D 772 287-1160
Palm City (G-13788)

◆ Foremostco Inc ....E 305 592-8986
Miami (G-9596)

Grays Ornamentals Inc ....D 561 496-6442
Delray Beach (G-2958)

▲ Hammerhead Group LLC ....E 305 436-1415
Doral (G-3221)

Harrells Nursery Inc ....E 813 752-0931
Plant City (G-14560)

Hidden Acres Nursery Inc ....E 863 385-1325
Sebring (G-16399)

Holmberg Farms Inc ....C 813 689-3601
Lithia (G-8299)

Kerrys Nursery Inc ....D 407 886-6122
Apopka (G-195)

▲ Knox Nursery Inc ....D 407 654-1972
Winter Garden (G-19577)

Knox Nursery Inc ....E 407 654-1972
Winter Garden (G-19576)

Liner Source Inc ....E 888 812-3020
Eustis (G-3496)

◆ Loops Nurs & Greenhouses Inc...........D 904 772-0880
Saint Johns (G-15547)

May Nursery Inc ....E 850 539-6495
Havana (G-5196)

Millennium Lawn & Ldscp Inc ....D 813 920-8041
Odessa (G-11850)

◆ Napco Marketing Corp ....D 904 737-8500
Jacksonville (G-6525)

Nordlie - Tampa Bay Inc ....E 813 239-0599
Tampa (G-18086)

◆ Passion Growers LLC ....D 855 967-6737
Miami (G-10099)

Plantas Y Flores Ornamentales ....A 305 810-5959
Miami (G-10126)

◆ Plants In Design Inc ....E 305 232-6567
Miami (G-10127)

Queens Flowers Corp ....D 305 591-2113
Miami (G-10173)

R Plants Inc ....C 305 257-9883
Homestead (G-5598)

▲ Riverdale Farms LLC ....E 305 592-5760
Doral (G-3299)

Royal Flowers Inc ....E 305 477-4483
Doral (G-3303)

Silver Vase Inc ....E 407 814-0339
Apopka (G-210)

◆ Silver Vase Inc ....E 305 248-0821
Homestead (G-5606)

Simpson Nurseries LAA ....E 850 997-5054
Monticello (G-10936)

◆ Southern Hsptality Whl Ret Inc ....E 813 717-7895
Plant City (G-14583)

Starling Nursery Inc ....E 386 804-2842
Seville (G-16466)

◆ Sun Bulb Company Inc ....E 863 494-5896
Arcadia (G-234)

Sun State Nursery & Ldscpg Inc ....D 904 260-0822
Jacksonville (G-6806)

◆ Sunburst Farms Inc ....C 305 594-4300
Miami (G-10341)

◆ Superior Foliage Inc ....E 305 245-0828
Miami (G-10350)

▼ Tiki Exports Inc ....E 386 467-2550
Crescent City (G-2309)

United Nursery LLC ....E 786 243-0905
Homestead (G-5611)

▲ USA Bouquet LLC ....C 786 437-6500
Doral (G-3351)

Verdego LLC ....E 386 437-3122
Saint Augustine (G-15509)

Verzaal Family Partnership ....E 561 498-3930
Delray Beach (G-3031)

▲ Windmill Farms Nurseries Inc ....D 863 735-0904
Zolfo Springs (G-19859)

5194 Tobacco & Tobacco Prdts Wholesale

◆ Carisam-Samuel Meisel FL Inc...........D 305 591-3993
Doral (G-3144)

▼ Convenent Whlslers of Amer Inc ....E 954 351-0080
Fort Lauderdale (G-3716)

Dbpr ....E 305 470-6787
Doral (G-3173)

◆ Inter-Continental Cigar Corp ....E 954 450-1994
Miramar (G-10869)

◆ International Operations Svcs ....D 305 591-1763
Miami (G-9768)

◆ J C Newman Cigar Co ....D 813 248-2124
Tampa (G-17879)

▲ Jetro Cash Carry Entps of Fla ....C 305 326-0409
Miami (G-9791)

Restaurant Depot LLC ....E 954 577-0470
Davie (G-2509)

Seminole Tribe of Florida Inc ....D 954 961-2800
Hollywood (G-5517)

◆ Smt Duty Free Inc ....E 305 477-0515
Doral (G-3314)

Swisher International Inc ....A 904 503-7452
Jacksonville (G-6822)

Zuma & Sons Distributors Corp ....E 305 887-0089
Medley (G-8802)

5198 Paints, Varnishes & Splys Wholesale

Bens Paint Supply LLC ....D 386 252-3817
Daytona Beach (G-2552)

Falls of Neuse Management LLC............A 850 785-3413
Panama City (G-14004)

Sherwin-Williams Company ....E 407 859-4260
Orlando (G-13191)

Sherwin-Williams Company ....E 863 293-6492
Winter Haven (G-19661)

5199 Nondurable Goods, NEC Wholesale

▲ 5-D Tropical Inc ....D 813 986-4560
Plant City (G-14542)

ABB Enterprise Software Inc ....E 407 732-2719
Lake Mary (G-7559)

Advantage Sales & Mktg Inc ....D 904 296-8886
Jacksonville (G-5743)

◆ Al-Dan Trading Inc ....D 305 620-2090
Miami Gardens (G-10677)

◆ Altrua Global Solutions Inc ....D 850 562-4564
Tallahassee (G-16876)

Amera 2009 LLC ....E 407 558-9101
Orlando (G-12105)

American Eagle Trade Group LLC...........D 305 634-4766
Miami (G-9138)

◆ Americas Export Corporation ....D 561 515-8080
Miami (G-9147)

Bay Promo LLC ....E 813 439-9638
Tampa (G-17347)

◆ Beauty Elements Corp ....D 305 430-4400
Miami Gardens (G-10711)

Bellagio Export LLC ....E 786 317-4889
Miami (G-9239)

◆ Bufkor Incorporated ....D 727 572-9991
Safety Harbor (G-15407)

◆ Camrose Trading Inc ....C 305 594-4666
Miami (G-9309)

▲ Camsing Global LLC ....E 727 369-5319
Seminole (G-16440)

Carrilon Miami Beach Hotel ....B 305 514-7000
Miami (G-9330)

Cartier International Del Corp ....C 305 448-4111
Coral Gables (G-2064)

Central Garden & Pet Company ....E 813 889-7161
Tampa (G-17448)

Chewy Inc ....A 786 320-7111
Dania Beach (G-2425)

◆ Commercial Services Intl Inc ....E 954 971-9393
Fort Lauderdale (G-3707)

▼ Convenent Whlslers of Amer Inc ....E 954 351-0080
Fort Lauderdale (G-3716)

◆ Dependable Packg Solutions LLC ....D 305 624-8338
Miami Lakes (G-10720)

Evergreen Packaging LLC ....C 813 752-2150
Plant City (G-14553)

Fanatics Mounted Memories Inc ....E 866 578-9115
Jacksonville (G-6147)

◆ Flexsol Packg Corp Pompano Bch ....B 800 325-7740
Pompano Beach (G-14806)

◆ Florida Malnove Incorporated ....C 904 696-1600
Jacksonville (G-6186)

Florida General Trading Inc ....D 352 631-1193
Ocala (G-11684)

▲ Florida State Distributors ....E 407 841-8344
Orlando (G-12534)

Gomez Packaging Company LLC............E 863 688-1200
Lakeland (G-7878)

▲ Great Innovations LLC ....E 954 747-3300
Miramar (G-10861)

Griffin Industries LLC ....D 813 626-1135
Tampa (G-17760)

Harmon Inc ....E 813 635-0649
Orlando (G-12619)

Hilex Poly Co LLC ....D 904 783-9985
Jacksonville (G-6279)

HRT Supply Inc ....E 786 228-7642
Miami (G-9726)

◆ Intradeco Inc ....D 305 264-6022
Medley (G-8747)

▼ Kaluz LLC ....E 786 991-2260
Miami (G-9810)

L&M Warehouse & Pkg N Fla LLC ......E 904 692-2027
Elkton (G-3424)

◆ Levy Advertising Entps Inc ....E 305 592-5389
Doral (G-3259)

▲ Lisle Liquidation Corporation ....E 630 968-8900
Orlando (G-12772)

◆ London Commercial Dist LLC ....E 305 477-5141
Doral (G-3262)

Mac Papers Inc ....E 305 362-9699
Hialeah (G-5294)

◆ Mo Money Associates LLC ....C 850 432-6301
Pensacola (G-14366)

◆ On-Rite Company Inc ....D 954 677-0404
Fort Lauderdale (G-4027)

Palladio Us LLC ....D 877 336-3040
West Palm Beach (G-19305)

Palm Beach Imports Inc ....D 888 437-5135
West Palm Beach (G-19312)

◆ Paradies Gifts Inc ....C 407 290-5288
Sanford (G-15969)

◆ Perez Trading Company Inc ....D 305 769-0761
Miami (G-10109)

◆ Pet Supermarket Inc ....C 954 351-0834
Sunrise (G-16809)

Phillips Feed Service Inc ....E 813 754-2302
Plant City (G-14574)

Plastipak Packaging Inc ....E 813 759-2503
Plant City (G-14575)

▲ Pouch Pac Innovations LLC ....E 941 359-6678
Sarasota (G-16272)

▲ Premiums Prmotions Imports Inc ....E 888 451-3905
Daytona Beach (G-2654)

Proampac Orlando Inc ....D 407 859-7780
Orlando (G-13063)

◆ Purity Wholesale Grocers Inc ....E 561 997-8302
Boca Raton (G-760)

▲ R J Roberts & Co ....D 800 521-6022
Pompano Beach (G-14882)

Renaissance Trading Inc ....D 561 994-0600
Boca Raton (G-770)

Rialto International Llc ....E 305 639-3401
Miami (G-10214)

◆ Richemont Ltin Amer Crbbean LL ....E 305 448-4111
Coral Gables (G-2177)

▲ Rifle LLC ....E 407 622-7679
Winter Park (G-19770)

Sarvis Incorporated ....B 407 890-9303
Orlando (G-13168)

▲ Soule Co ....D 813 907-6000
Lutz (G-8458)

Spc Export Corp. ....E 786 942-9798
Miami (G-10313)

▲ Stein Mart Buying Corp ....C 904 346-1500
Jacksonville (G-6787)

Sunflora Inc ....E 727 235-0720
Palmetto (G-13930)

Te Distributors Inc ....E 407 745-7533
Orlando (G-13275)

▲ Tjm Promos Inc ....E 352 291-5334
Ocala (G-11787)

◆ Traffic Brick Networks LLC ....E 561 304-9470
Deerfield Beach (G-2808)

US Bus & Trdg Overseas Inc ....D 786 557-4927
Miami (G-10451)

Vitro Molecular Labs LLC ....E 305 267-7979
Miami (G-10482)

◆ Wincorp International Inc ....E 305 887-4000
Medley (G-8798)

▲ Y-Not Design & Mfg Inc ....D 305 479-2627
Hialeah (G-5337)

60 DEPOSITORY INSTITUTIONS

6011 Federal Reserve Banks

Federal Reserve Bank Atlanta ....C 904 632-1000
Jacksonville (G-6151)

Federal Reserve Bank Atlanta ....C 305 591-2065
Doral (G-3200)

6021 National Commercial Banks

▲ Amerant Bank National Assn ....D 305 460-8701
Coral Gables (G-2030)

American Bank Payments LLC ....E 708 382-1913
Fort Lauderdale (G-3599)

American Banking Company ....D 904 288-8933
Jacksonville (G-5775)

Banco Davivienda SA Corp. ....E 305 372-9909
Miami (G-9203)

Bank America National Assn ....E 813 393-4942
Tampa (G-17335)

Bank America National Assn ....E 954 384-6204
Weston (G-19443)

Bankshares Corp Niceville ....E 850 678-3110
Niceville (G-11439)

Bny Mellon National Assn ....C 305 604-6099
Miami Beach (G-10559)

Bny Mellon National Assn ....D 239 919-5500
Naples (G-11035)

Bny Mellon National Assn ....D 954 476-7090
Plantation (G-14609)

Bny Mellon National Assn ....D 813 405-1220
Tampa (G-17375)

Centerstate Bank ....B 863 551-5160
Winter Haven (G-19615)

Citibank FSB ....E 786 235-9248
Key Biscayne (G-7165)

Citigroup Inc. ....C 212 559-1000
Tampa (G-17477)

Citigroup Inc. ....D 904 954-2067
Jacksonville (G-5950)

Citigroup Inc. ....B 904 954-0340
Jacksonville (G-5951)

▲ City National Bank of Florida ....C 305 577-7333
Miami (G-9371)

Comerica Bank and Trust Fsb ....C 561 961-6600
Boca Raton (G-521)

◆ Eastern National Bank ....D 305 995-5800
Miami (G-9497)

First Nat Bnk of Wauchula ....E 863 773-4136
Wauchula (G-18959)

First National Bank of Mt Dora ....E 352 383-2111
Mount Dora (G-10950)

First National Bankers Bank ....E 407 541-1620
Lake Mary (G-7591)

Florida Capital Bank Nat Assn ....C 352 692-5280
Gainesville (G-4885)

Florida Capital Group Inc ....C 904 472-2730
Jacksonville (G-6188)

Fpb Bancorp Inc. ....E 772 398-1388
Port Saint Lucie (G-15136)

Highlands Independent Bank ....E 863 385-8700
Sebring (G-16400)

Home Federal Bank Hollywood ....E 954 458-2626
Hallandale Beach (G-5174)

Mayors Bank Corp ....E 229 683-3411
Fernandina Beach (G-3537)

Merrill Lynch Prce Fnner Smith ....D 305 995-9232
Miami (G-9939)

Merrill Lynch Prce Fnner Smith ....D 305 530-3600
Miami (G-9940)

N A Bankunited ....C 305 231-6400
Miami Lakes (G-10747)

Safra National Bank New York ....D 305 682-3800
Miami (G-10234)

▲ Seacoast Nat Bnk A Nat Bnkg As .....C 772 288-6086
Stuart (G-16668)

Sofidel America Corp ....A 863 547-1100
Haines City (G-5157)

South State Corporation ....E 352 368-6800
Ocala (G-11779)

SunTrust Bank ....E 407 944-4540
Kissimmee (G-7393)

Synchrony Financial ....D 480 707-4747
Altamonte Springs (G-104)

Synchrony Financial ....D 937 534-2000
Altamonte Springs (G-105)

Truist Bank ....E 954 766-2110
Fort Lauderdale (G-4191)

Truist Bank ....D 407 237-4153
Orlando (G-13314)

Truist Bank ....E 407 563-3811
Orlando (G-13315)

United Bancorporation Ala Inc ....E 850 994-2301
Milton (G-10828)

UPS Capital Business Credit ....E 305 577-7540
Miami (G-10449)

USI Insurance Services Nat Inc ....E 813 639-3000
Tampa (G-18491)

USI Insurance Services Nat Inc ....E 954 832-9492
Fort Lauderdale (G-4206)

We Florida Financial ....D 954 522-2705
Pembroke Pines (G-14202)

Wells Fargo Bank National Assn ....D 772 569-5500
Vero Beach (G-18948)

Wells Fargo Bank National Assn ....E 954 784-5700
Pompano Beach (G-14941)

Wells Fargo Capital Fin LLC ....E 239 254-2200
Naples (G-11341)

6022 State Commercial Banks

Ameris Bank ....D 850 926-5211
Crawfordville (G-2300)

Banco Itau International ....E 786 564-2639
Miami (G-9206)

Bank of Tampa ....E 813 998-2600
Tampa (G-17336)

Bank of Tampa ....D 813 998-2660
Brandon (G-1214)

Bankunited Inc. ....C 305 569-2000
Miami Lakes (G-10709)

Bankunited National Assn ....D 305 231-6400
Miami Lakes (G-10710)

Bradesco BAC Florida Bank ....E 305 789-7090
Miami (G-9272)

Bradesco BAC Florida Bank ....E 305 789-7000
Coral Gables (G-2058)

Brannen Bank ....E 352 726-1221
Inverness (G-5688)

Capital City Bank ....D 850 402-7700
Tallahassee (G-16900)

Capital City Bank Group Inc ....C 850 671-0300
Tallahassee (G-16901)

Centennial Bank ....B 954 315-5500
Pompano Beach (G-14769)

Center State Bank ....E 772 299-6857
Vero Beach (G-18843)

Center State Bank ....C 863 676-4328
Lake Wales (G-7676)

Centerstate Bank ....B 863 551-5160
Winter Haven (G-19615)

Central Bank ....E 813 929-4477
Tampa (G-17445)

City National Bank of Florida ....B 305 448-6500
Miami (G-9372)

Community Bank and Trust Fla ....D 352 369-1000
Ocala (G-11666)

Community Bank South Fla Inc ....C 305 245-2211
Homestead (G-5565)

▲ Continental National Bank ....D 305 642-2440
Miami (G-9408)

Drummond Community Bank ....E 352 493-2277
Chiefland (G-1483)

Eagle National Holding Company ....E 305 418-6000
Doral (G-3184)

Fidelity Bank of Florida ....E 321 452-0011
Merritt Island (G-9027)

Fifth Third Bank ....C 941 792-5000
Bradenton (G-1097)

Fifth Third Bank ....C 941 739-1500
Bradenton (G-1098)

First A National Banking Assn ....E 850 997-2591
Monticello (G-10931)

First City Bank of Florida ....D 850 244-5151
Fort Walton Beach (G-4768)

First Federal Bank ....D 386 755-0600
Lake City (G-7525)

First Nat Bnk Polk Cnty Inc ....A 863 956-2500
Lake Alfred (G-7449)

▲ First National Bank NW Fla ....E 850 769-3207
Panama City (G-14005)

First Republic Bank ....C 561 529-8388
Jupiter (G-7069)

First State Bank of Fla Keys ....D 305 296-8535
Key West (G-7202)

First-Citizens Bank & Trust Co ....C 813 228-8300
Tampa (G-17663)

Florida First City Banks Inc ....D 850 244-5151
Fort Walton Beach (G-4769)

Grove Bank & Trust ....D 305 858-6666
Miami (G-9666)

Heritage Southeast Bank ....D 904 474-6153
Jacksonville (G-6276)

Iberiabank Corporation ....D 561 615-1657
Royal Palm Beach (G-15383)

Inter-Mrcan Fdral Sav Ln Assn ....D 786 476-9530
Miami (G-9755)

International Finance Bank ....E 305 648-8800
Miami (G-9764)

N A Terrabank ....E 305 448-4898
Miami (G-10024)

▲ Ocean Bank ....A 305 448-2265
Miami (G-10059)

Peoples Bank ....D 727 786-6677
Saint Petersburg (G-15796)

Plus International Bank ....E 305 358-4690
Miami (G-10130)

Premier Community Bank of Fla ....E 239 415-7566
Fort Myers (G-4550)

S
I
C

Premier Community Bank of Fla .... E 727 549-1202
Clearwater *(G-1764)*

Seacoast Bank Florida Inc .... D 407 321-3233
Lake Mary *(G-7638)*

Seacoast Banking Corp Florida .... A 772 287-4000
Stuart *(G-16667)*

Seacoast Nat Bnk A Nat Bnkg As ....D 561 544-8400
Boca Raton *(G-788)*

Seacoast National Bank .... E 727 800-5134
Saint Petersburg *(G-15840)*

Skylake Bankshares Inc .... D 305 364-4230
Miami Lakes *(G-10762)*

▲ Skylake State Bank .... D 305 364-4264
Miami Lakes *(G-10763)*

South State Bank National Assn .... E 863 291-3900
Winter Haven *(G-19662)*

South State Corporation .... E 941 776-5040
Bradenton *(G-1181)*

South State Corporation .... C 904 348-3100
Jacksonville *(G-6747)*

South State Corporation .... D 904 301-2250
Jacksonville *(G-6748)*

South State Corporation .... E 954 784-7979
Pompano Beach *(G-14903)*

South State Corporation .... E 813 779-7735
Zephyrhills *(G-19850)*

South State Corporation .... E 352 368-6800
Ocala *(G-11779)*

▲ Sun American Bank .... E 305 421-6800
Coral Gables *(G-2191)*

Tallahassee State Bank .... E 850 576-1182
Tallahassee *(G-17144)*

Tampa Bay Banking Company .... D 813 872-1200
Tampa *(G-18364)*

United Bancorporation Ala Inc .... E 850 994-2301
Milton *(G-10828)*

United Southern Bank .... E 352 589-2121
Eustis *(G-3503)*

Warrington Bank .... E 850 455-7351
Pensacola *(G-14467)*

Wauchula State Bank .... D 863 773-4151
Wauchula *(G-18966)*

We Florida Financial .... D 954 522-2705
Pembroke Pines *(G-14202)*

6029 Commercial Banks, NEC

A Bb Power .... D 610 691-7555
Lake Mary *(G-7557)*

American Banking Company .... D 904 288-8933
Jacksonville *(G-5775)*

Banco Itau SA .... C 305 372-1596
Miami *(G-9207)*

Banesco USA .... D 305 347-8300
Miami *(G-9208)*

Centerstate Bank .... B 863 551-5160
Winter Haven *(G-19615)*

City National Bank of Florida .... D 305 274-8382
Miami *(G-9373)*

Commerce Bank Investment Svcs .... E 305 460-8599
Coral Gables *(G-2077)*

Hsbc Finance Corporation .... C 954 785-4900
Pompano Beach *(G-14824)*

▲ Intercredit Bank National Assn .... E 786 369-2577
Coral Gables *(G-2132)*

Old Harbor Bank .... E 727 797-0696
Clearwater *(G-1745)*

South State Corporation .... E 352 368-6800
Ocala *(G-11779)*

United Southern Bank .... E 352 589-2121
Eustis *(G-3503)*

We Florida Financial .... D 954 522-2705
Pembroke Pines *(G-14202)*

6035 Federal Savings Institutions

Bankunited Capital .... C 305 569-2000
Coral Gables *(G-2042)*

Chemical Bank .... E 904 996-3330
Neptune Beach *(G-11355)*

Everbank Funding LLC .... A 904 281-6000
Jacksonville *(G-6136)*

Federal Trust Bank .... D 407 324-1881
Sanford *(G-15938)*

First A National Banking Assn .... E 850 219-7200
Tallahassee *(G-16949)*

First Bank of Puerto Rico .... E 305 577-6000
Miami *(G-9558)*

First Federal Bank .... E 904 398-7859
Jacksonville *(G-6174)*

First International Exch Group .... C 336 733-2000
Fort Lauderdale *(G-3788)*

Premier Community Bank of Fla .... E 727 549-1202
Clearwater *(G-1764)*

Raymond James Bank Nat Assn .... D 727 567-8000
Saint Petersburg *(G-15817)*

Raymond James Fincl Svcs Inc .... D 727 567-1000
Saint Petersburg *(G-15819)*

Southwest Florida Regional .... C 615 344-9551
Largo *(G-8153)*

Tiaa Fsb .... C 904 245-7267
Jacksonville *(G-6850)*

Tiaa Fsb .... E 904 623-8408
Jacksonville *(G-6851)*

Tiaa Fsb Holdings Inc .... B 904 281-6000
Jacksonville *(G-6852)*

6036 Savings Institutions, Except Federal

Banco Popular De Puerto Rico .... E 850 784-3939
Panama City *(G-13958)*

Banco Popular De Puerto Rico .... E 850 769-3939
Panama City *(G-13959)*

6061 Federal Credit Unions

121 Financial Credit Union .... D 800 342-2352
Jacksonville *(G-5711)*

Achieva Credit Union .... E 727 431-7680
Dunedin *(G-3376)*

Addition Financial Credit Un .... E 407 896-9411
Lake Mary *(G-7563)*

Baptist Health South Fla Fcu .... D 305 662-8122
South Miami *(G-16497)*

Brightstar Credit Union .... E 954 486-2728
Sunrise *(G-16751)*

Brightstar Credit Union .... E 954 590-3920
Margate *(G-8642)*

Buckeye Cmnty Federal Cr Un .... E 850 223-7100
Perry *(G-14487)*

Campus USA Credit Union .... D 352 335-9090
Newberry *(G-11430)*

Citizens State Bank .... E 850 584-4411
Perry *(G-14488)*

Community Credit Union Florida .... E 321 637-3184
Rockledge *(G-15341)*

Community First Credit Un Fla .... D 904 354-8537
Jacksonville *(G-5985)*

Community First Credit Un Fla .... C 904 371-7967
Jacksonville *(G-5986)*

Community South Credit Union .... E 850 638-8376
Chipley *(G-1491)*

Connect Credit Union .... E 954 730-2047
Fort Lauderdale *(G-3712)*

▲ Dade County Federal Credit Un .... C 305 471-5080
Sweetwater *(G-16858)*

Educational Federal Credit Un .... E 305 251-7544
Miami *(G-9506)*

Educational Federal Credit Un .... C 305 270-5200
Miami *(G-9507)*

Educational Federal Credit Un .... D 305 379-0621
Miami *(G-9508)*

Educational Federal Credit Un .... E 305 556-4311
Miami Lakes *(G-10724)*

Eglin Federal Credit Union .... D 850 862-0111
Hurlburt Field *(G-5650)*

Eglin Federal Credit Union .... D 850 862-0111
Niceville *(G-11445)*

Eglin Federal Credit Union .... E 850 863-3517
Fort Walton Beach *(G-4763)*

Eglin Federal Credit Union .... E 850 682-6688
Crestview *(G-2320)*

Eglin Federal Credit Union .... D 850 862-0111
Mary Esther *(G-8688)*

Envision Credit Union .... E 850 942-9000
Tallahassee *(G-16941)*

▲ Fairwinds Credit Union .... D 407 277-5045
Orlando *(G-12489)*

Fairwinds Credit Union .... D 407 365-6611
Oviedo *(G-13548)*

Fairwinds Financial Svcs Inc .... D 407 282-6039
Orlando *(G-12490)*

First Choice Credit Union .... E 561 641-0100
West Palm Beach *(G-19142)*

First Florida Credit Union .... E 904 359-6800
Jacksonville *(G-6175)*

Florida Credit Union .... D 352 237-8222
Gainesville *(G-4887)*

Focus Credit Union .... E 850 526-9710
Chattahoochee *(G-1481)*

▲ G T E Federal Credit Union .... C 813 871-2690
Tampa *(G-17722)*

G T E Federal Credit Union .... B 813 871-2690
Tampa *(G-17723)*

Gold Coast Federal Credit Un .... E 561 969-9231
Palm Springs *(G-13893)*

Grow Financial Federal Cr Un .... E 813 969-2655
Tampa *(G-17763)*

Grow Financial Federal Cr Un .... C 813 837-2451
Tampa *(G-17764)*

Grow Financial Federal Cr Un .... E 941 827-4100
Bradenton *(G-1116)*

Grow Financial Federal Cr Un .... D 727 822-5220
Saint Petersburg *(G-15699)*

Grow Financial Federal Cr Un .... E 813 837-2451
Brandon *(G-1235)*

Guardians Credit Union .... D 561 686-4006
West Palm Beach *(G-19168)*

Gulf Winds Credit Union .... E 850 562-6702
Tallahassee *(G-16993)*

Gulf Winds Federal Credit Un .... E 850 479-9601
Pensacola *(G-14319)*

Innovations Federal Credit Un .... E 850 233-4400
Panama City *(G-14030)*

Insight Financial Credit Union .... D 407 426-6000
Orlando *(G-12683)*

Ithink Financial Credit Union .... C 561 982-4700
Delray Beach *(G-2973)*

Jax Federal Credit Union .... E 904 475-8000
Jacksonville *(G-6375)*

Launch Federal Credit Union .... E 321 455-9400
Merritt Island *(G-9037)*

League Sthastern Cr Unions Inc .... D 866 231-0545
Tallahassee *(G-17021)*

McCoy Federal Credit Union .... D 407 855-5452
Orlando *(G-12838)*

Midflorida Federal Credit Un .... D 352 369-1000
Ocala *(G-11732)*

Orlando Credit Union .... D 407 835-3500
Orlando *(G-12946)*

Pen-Air Federal Credit Union .... D 850 505-7811
Pensacola *(G-14405)*

Power Financial Credit Union .... E 954 538-4400
Pembroke Pines *(G-14175)*

Priority One Credit Union Fla .... E 954 335-5100
Sunrise *(G-16812)*

Publix Emplyees Federal Cr Un .... C 863 683-6404
Lakeland *(G-7945)*

Space Coast Credit Union .... C 321 752-2222
Melbourne *(G-8977)*

Suncoast Credit Union .... D 813 621-7511
Lehigh Acres *(G-8292)*

Sunshine State Credit Un Inc .... D 850 219-7825
Tallahassee *(G-17124)*

Sunstate Federal Credit Union .... D 352 381-5200
Gainesville *(G-5009)*

Tampa Bay Federal Credit Union .... D 813 247-4414
Tampa *(G-18367)*

Trax Federal Credit Union .... E 813 800-8729
Tampa *(G-18440)*

Tropical Financial Credit Un .... C 888 261-8328
Miramar *(G-10907)*

Tyndall Federal Credit Union .... D 850 747-4150
Panama City *(G-14080)*

Tyndall Federal Credit Union .... E 850 769-9999
Panama City *(G-14081)*

University Credit Union .... D 786 425-5000
Miami *(G-10443)*

USF Federal Credit Union .... D 813 569-2000
Tampa *(G-18489)*

Vystar Credit Union .... B 904 777-6000
Jacksonville *(G-6913)*

6062 State Credit Unions

Campus USA Credit Union .... D 352 335-9090
Newberry *(G-11430)*

Fairwinds Credit Union .... C 407 857-9237
Orlando *(G-12488)*

First Commerce Credit Union .... E 850 488-0035
Tallahassee *(G-16951)*

Florida Central Credit Union .... E 813 879-3333
Tampa *(G-17673)*

Insight Financial Credit Union .... D 407 426-6000
Orlando *(G-12683)*

6081 Foreign Banks, Branches & Agencies

PA Advisors Ltd .... D 305 530-1031
Miami *(G-10084)*

6082 Foreign Trade & Intl Banks

Banco De Crdito E Invrsones SA .... D 305 347-3330
Miami *(G-9204)*

Banco De Sabadell SA .... D 305 350-1200
Miami Lakes *(G-10708)*

Banco De Sabadell SA.................E...... 305 350-1200
Miami *(G-9205)*

6091 Nondeposit Trust Facilities

Charles Schwab Corporation................D...... 800 435-9050
The Villages *(G-18654)*
Db USA Corporation ....A...... 904 515-8260
Jacksonville *(G-6050)*
Db USA Corporation ....A...... 904 997-9947
Jacksonville *(G-6051)*
Raymond James Fincl Svcs Inc ....D...... 727 567-1000
Saint Petersburg *(G-15819)*

6099 Functions Related To Deposit Banking, NEC

Bny Mellon National Assn.................C...... 305 810-2900
Miami *(G-9265)*
Cashela Inc.................E...... 786 370-6436
Miami *(G-9332)*
Certegy Gaming Services Inc ....C...... 800 363-3321
Saint Petersburg *(G-15620)*
Clearent LLC.................D...... 561 684-5352
West Palm Beach *(G-19093)*
Garda CL Technical Svcs Inc.................D...... 561 939-7000
Boca Raton *(G-596)*
Girosol Corp.................E...... 305 944-1424
North Miami Beach *(G-11524)*
Intermex Wire Transfer LLC ....C...... 305 671-8000
Miami *(G-9762)*
▲ NYCE Corporation ....D...... 201 865-9000
Orlando *(G-12922)*
Paya Eft Inc.................D...... 850 344-4500
Fort Walton Beach *(G-4796)*
Populus Financial Group Inc ....E...... 352 323-0031
Leesburg *(G-8267)*
Star Systems Inc.................B...... 321 263-3000
Maitland *(G-8579)*

61 NONDEPOSITORY CREDIT INSTITUTIONS

6111 Federal Credit Agencies

Educare Financial Inc.................E...... 813 960-7206
Tampa *(G-17616)*
Navient Solutions LLC.................C...... 386 752-0068
Lake City *(G-7538)*
Navient Solutions LLC.................C...... 813 281-3170
Tampa *(G-18069)*
Sherloq Group Inc.................D...... 813 273-7833
Tampa *(G-18277)*

6141 Personal Credit Institutions

Advantage Vehicle Fing LLC.................C...... 877 858-3855
Orlando *(G-12062)*
Asset Acceptance LLC.................C...... 813 569-0400
Riverview *(G-15243)*
Centerone Financial Svcs LLC ....D...... 954 429-2200
Deerfield Beach *(G-2722)*
Cnac.................E...... 904 338-9996
Jacksonville *(G-5969)*
▲ Cnl Financial Group Inc.................D...... 407 650-1000
Orlando *(G-12328)*
Cobon International LLC ....E...... 786 373-3819
Miami *(G-9384)*
Debt Shield Inc.................E...... 888 397-7546
Melbourne *(G-8866)*
Farm Credit Northwest Fla Aca ....E...... 850 526-4910
Marianna *(G-8674)*
Farm Credit of Florida ....C...... 561 965-9001
Royal Palm Beach *(G-15382)*
Farm Credit of Florida Aca.................D...... 386 462-4201
Alachua *(G-6)*
Furtenburg Inc.................C...... 800 934-1950
Boca Raton *(G-593)*
General Electric Company ....B...... 239 275-2700
Fort Myers *(G-4413)*
Grow Financial Federal Cr Un.................D...... 813 837-2451
Brandon *(G-1235)*
Mid-Atlantic Finance Co Inc.................D...... 727 535-1554
Clearwater *(G-1720)*
Nicholas Financial Inc.................D...... 727 726-0763
Clearwater *(G-1738)*
One Park Financial LLC.................E...... 800 617-2020
Miami *(G-10072)*
Premium Assignment Corporation ....D...... 850 893-1191
Tallahassee *(G-17074)*
Sears Roebuck and Co.................C...... 305 594-2400
Doral *(G-3307)*

Sears Roebuck and Co ....C...... 561 731-3635
Boynton Beach *(G-1034)*
Sears Roebuck and Co.................C...... 954 370-2800
Plantation *(G-1034)*
▲ Smart Choice Auto Group Inc.................D...... 321 269-9680
Titusville *(G-18704)*
Southern Auto Finance Company ....D...... 954 497-1000
Pompano Beach *(G-14906)*
SpeeDee Cash Management Co Inc ....D...... 850 682-0475
Crestview *(G-2333)*
Standard Premium Fin MGT Corp ....D...... 305 232-7040
Miami *(G-10326)*
Summit Financial Corp.................D...... 954 961-0749
Fort Lauderdale *(G-4159)*
World Omni Financial Corp.................C...... 954 429-2200
Deerfield Beach *(G-2821)*

6153 Credit Institutions, Short-Term Business

Ally Financial Inc.................D...... 904 370-1800
Jacksonville *(G-5770)*
Altc Funding LLC.................D...... 800 362-8837
Fort Myers *(G-4271)*
Arf Financial LLC.................E...... 954 689-4044
Sunrise *(G-16738)*
Bankers Healthcare Group LLC.................C...... 954 384-9119
Davie *(G-2460)*
Bfs Capital Inc.................E...... 866 905-4334
Coral Springs *(G-2230)*
Capital Funding Tech Inc ....E...... 754 264-4371
Davie *(G-2468)*
Davinci Worldwide Inc.................D...... 866 535-5231
Orlando *(G-12405)*
Eprodigy Financial LLC.................E...... 888 782-2510
Sunny Isles Beach *(G-16718)*
Expocredit LLC.................E...... 305 347-9222
Miami *(G-9539)*
Flexshopper Inc.................D...... 855 353-9289
Boca Raton *(G-576)*
Hamilton Group Funding Inc ....D...... 850 994-5853
Sunrise *(G-16778)*
Hamilton Home Loans Inc.................B...... 954 241-2800
Sunrise *(G-16779)*
Idea 247 Inc.................E...... 855 900-7838
Miami *(G-9742)*
Lsq Funding Group LC.................E...... 407 206-0022
Orlando *(G-12789)*
Lsq Group LLC.................D...... 407 206-0022
Orlando *(G-12790)*
Nicholas Financial Inc.................D...... 727 726-0763
Clearwater *(G-1738)*
Novus Capital Funding LLC.................E...... 888 466-6615
Saint Petersburg *(G-15782)*
Nuvell Financial Services LLC.................B...... 904 886-5223
Jacksonville *(G-6555)*
Premium Assignment Corporation ....D...... 850 893-1191
Tallahassee *(G-17074)*
Raymond Jmes Affrdbl Hsing Inv ....E...... 727 573-3800
Saint Petersburg *(G-15822)*
Sun Capital Inc.................D...... 561 995-9615
Boca Raton *(G-829)*
White Oak Commercial Fin LLC ....E...... 954 660-7599
Boca Raton *(G-872)*
Wofco Funding Corp ....C...... 954 429-2000
Deerfield Beach *(G-2819)*

6159 Credit Institutions, Misc Business

County of Broward.................D...... 954 357-7800
Fort Lauderdale *(G-3723)*
Credito Real USA Finance LLC.................E...... 954 475-5915
Fort Lauderdale *(G-3740)*
Ford Motor Credit Company LLC ....E...... 800 416-9461
Tampa *(G-17705)*
Gaddis Capital Corporation ....B...... 954 565-8900
Wilton Manors *(G-19524)*
Scott-Mcrae Auto Group Inc ....D...... 904 354-4000
Jacksonville *(G-6701)*
South Fla Regional Plg Council ....E...... 954 924-3653
Hollywood *(G-5532)*
Sun Capital Inc.................D...... 561 995-9615
Boca Raton *(G-829)*
VA Leasing Corp ....E...... 305 591-7707
Doral *(G-3352)*
World Omni Financial Corp.................C...... 954 429-2200
Deerfield Beach *(G-2821)*

6162 Mortgage Bankers & Loan Correspondents

A&D Mortgage LLC.................E...... 305 760-7000
Hollywood *(G-5386)*
Agamerica Lending LLC.................E...... 863 607-9500
Lakeland *(G-7788)*
Alkan Mortgage Corporation ....D...... 321 473-6080
Rockledge *(G-15332)*
Amerant Mortgage LLC.................D...... 844 200-8638
Miami *(G-9133)*
American Mortgage Ln Svcs LLC.................D...... 407 331-4700
Orlando *(G-12111)*
Amerinational Cmnty Svcs LLC ....E...... 813 282-4800
Tampa *(G-17280)*
Avatar Communities Inc.................D...... 305 442-7000
Kissimmee *(G-7418)*
Bluegreen Vacations Holdg Corp.................D...... 561 912-8000
Boca Raton *(G-457)*
Builders Choice Mortgage LLC ....E...... 561 395-6900
Boca Raton *(G-487)*
Caliber Home Loans Inc.................D...... 321 609-0789
Orlando *(G-12227)*
Caliber Home Loans Inc.................D...... 850 832-3210
Panama City *(G-13975)*
Caliber Home Loans Inc.................D...... 561 805-8598
West Palm Beach *(G-19070)*
Caliber Home Loans Inc.................D...... 305 789-6630
Miami *(G-9305)*
Capital International Fincl.................E...... 305 442-1256
Coral Gables *(G-2061)*
Capital Markets Coop LLC.................D...... 904 543-0052
Jacksonville *(G-5898)*
Chase Manhattan Mortgage Corp.................D...... 727 372-2162
New Port Richey *(G-11369)*
Chase Manhattan Mortgage Corp.................C...... 904 620-6834
Jacksonville *(G-5939)*
Christensen Financial Inc.................C...... 407 869-0008
Altamonte Springs *(G-36)*
Cimarron Mortgage Company ....E...... 727 373-3033
Clearwater *(G-1566)*
Columbus Capital Lending LLC ....E...... 305 271-8005
Miami *(G-9392)*
Community Loan Servicing LLC ....C...... 305 854-8880
Coral Gables *(G-2079)*
Consumer Real Estate Fin Co.................D...... 440 526-5000
Fort Lauderdale *(G-3715)*
Crosscountry Mortgage LLC ....E...... 239 254-2260
Naples *(G-11083)*
Crosscountry Mortgage LLC ....E...... 561 414-2832
Delray Beach *(G-2935)*
Crosscountry Mortgage LLC ....E...... 561 693-4782
Palm Beach Gardens *(G-13714)*
Crosscountry Mortgage LLC ....E...... 813 431-7843
Tampa *(G-17552)*
Crosscountry Mortgage LLC ....E...... 239 250-9373
Naples *(G-11084)*
Crosscountry Mortgage LLC ....E...... 772 202-5109
Fort Pierce *(G-4692)*
Crosscountry Mortgage LLC ....E...... 407 990-0235
Winter Park *(G-19710)*
Ditech Financial LLC.................B...... 813 249-6988
Tampa *(G-17595)*
Ditech Financial LLC.................B...... 904 363-2444
Jacksonville *(G-6071)*
Embrace Home Loans Inc.................E...... 407 733-6425
Melbourne *(G-8880)*
Equity Loans LLC.................E...... 800 236-9416
Orlando *(G-12474)*
Everhome Mortgage Company ....B...... 904 281-6000
Jacksonville *(G-6137)*
FBC Mortgage LLC.................E...... 866 413-2563
Orlando *(G-12499)*
Florida Housing Finance Corp.................C...... 850 488-4197
Tallahassee *(G-16972)*
▲ Freedom Mortgage Corporation ....E...... 855 690-5900
Boca Raton *(G-591)*
Group One Mortgage Inc.................E...... 561 745-1200
Jupiter *(G-7085)*
Guaranteed Rate Inc.................C...... 813 830-3586
Clearwater *(G-1657)*
Guaranteed Rate Inc.................C...... 954 629-6151
Fort Lauderdale *(G-3844)*
Guaranteed Rate Inc.................C...... 954 727-8200
Plantation *(G-14652)*
Hamilton Home Loans Inc.................D...... 954 241-8313
Sunrise *(G-16780)*
Home Financing Center Rlty Inc.................E...... 305 777-1100
Coral Gables *(G-2127)*
Integrity HM Ln Centl Fla Inc.................D...... 407 688-8268
Lake Mary *(G-7602)*

SIC

Jet Homeloans LLC ....E 904 479-7468
Jacksonville (G-6383)

▲ Kalin Enterprises Inc ....E 941 923-5638
Sarasota (G-16208)

Lender Processing Service ....E 904 854-5462
Jacksonville (G-6427)

Lenderlive Network LLC ....D 303 226-8000
Jacksonville (G-6428)

Lennar Mortgage Llc ....E 727 791-2111
Miami (G-9860)

Loandepot Inc ....B 678 221-2820
Palm Coast (G-13832)

Loandepotcom LLC ....A 904 513-7950
Jacksonville Beach (G-6993)

Mattamy Home Funding LLC ....D 321 214-1043
Maitland (G-8555)

Merrill Lynch Credit Corp ....D 904 218-6000
Jacksonville (G-6497)

Mortgage Information Services ....C 305 817-7700
Miramar (G-10878)

Mortgage300 Corporation ....E 888 826-0944
North Palm Beach (G-11552)

Ocwen Financial Corporation .....B 561 682-8000
West Palm Beach (G-19286)

Ocwen Loan Servicing LLC ....B 561 682-8000
West Palm Beach (G-19287)

Ocwen Loan Servicing LLC ....C 407 737-5000
Orlando (G-12925)

Opteum Financial Services LLC ...C 772 231-1245
Vero Beach (G-18899)

P2p Staffing Corp ....B 407 218-8999
Orlando (G-13003)

Paramunt Rsdntial Mrtg Group I ...E 305 972-2120
Kissimmee (G-7372)

Paramunt Rsdntial Mrtg Group I ...E 239 659-1660
Naples (G-11255)

Principal Residential Mortgage ....B 772 781-2575
Stuart (G-16660)

R P Funding Inc ....C 321 397-4420
Lake Mary (G-7629)

Reverse Mortgage Funding LLC ...C 321 259-7880
Melbourne (G-8970)

Ross Mortgage Corporation ......E 954 598-0958
Davie (G-2511)

Service Finance Company LLC ....D 866 254-0497
Boca Raton (G-795)

Sprout Mortgage LLC ....B 516 393-2650
Port St Lucie (G-15182)

Success Mortgage Partners Inc ...E 954 641-8203
Pembroke Pines (G-14192)

Success Mortgage Partners Inc ...E 352 242-1535
Montverde (G-10940)

Success Mortgage Partners Inc ...E 772 678-7711
Palm City (G-13805)

Van Dyk Mortgage Corporation ...E 727 395-9095
Clearwater (G-1830)

Walker & Dunlop LLC ....E 954 389-7822
Fort Lauderdale (G-4218)

Walter Mortgage Company LLC ...B 813 421-7600
Tampa (G-18522)

Walter Reverse Acquisition LLC ...D 813 421-7600
Tampa (G-18523)

Watson Mortgage Corp ....E 904 645-7111
Jacksonville (G-6921)

6163 Loan Brokers

Attorneys Mortgage Services .....E 321 639-6841
Fort Lauderdale (G-3618)

Bolsanet Inc ....D 305 533-1541
Miami (G-9267)

Chase Manhattan Mortgage Corp ...C 904 620-6834
Jacksonville (G-5939)

City National Bank of Florida .....B 305 448-6500
Miami (G-9372)

▲ Cnl Apf Partners LP ....C 407 650-1000
Orlando (G-12327)

Continental Properties Inc ....E 561 689-4766
West Palm Beach (G-19107)

Homebuyers Financial LLC ....C 954 978-5350
Coconut Creek (G-1990)

I3 Lending Inc ....E 888 975-1374
Longwood (G-8365)

Insight Financial Credit Union ....D 407 426-6000
Orlando (G-12683)

Lending Hand Mortgage Inc ......E 813 908-9281
Tampa (G-17940)

Lennar Corporation ....A 305 559-4000
Miami (G-9858)

Main Street Mrtg Co Ltd Partnr ...E 727 825-3800
Saint Petersburg (G-15753)

Merrill Lynch Credit Corp ....D 904 218-6000
Jacksonville (G-6497)

Mid-Atlantic Finance Co Inc ......D 727 535-1554
Clearwater (G-1720)

Mortgage Works Unlimited Inc ....E 561 841-5955
Palm Beach Gardens (G-13756)

Novus Capital Funding LLC ....E 888 466-6615
Saint Petersburg (G-15782)

Pen-Air Federal Credit Union .....D 850 505-7811
Pensacola (G-14465)

Popular Mortgage Corp ....C 305 470-8585
Doral (G-3292)

Sunbelt Lending Services Inc .....E 727 723-8884
Clearwater (G-1802)

Tallahassee State Bank ....E 850 576-1182
Tallahassee (G-17144)

Tampa Bay Federal Credit Union ...D 813 247-4414
Tampa (G-18367)

Tes Notary LLC ....C 407 627-0469
Miami (G-10381)

Watson Mortgage Corp ....E 904 645-7111
Jacksonville (G-6921)

Wcs Lending LLC ....E 561 241-5200
Hollywood (G-5547)

62 SECURITY AND COMMODITY BROKERS, DEALERS, EXCHANGES, AND SERVICES

6211 Security Brokers & Dealers

Acceptance Capital Mrtg Corp ....E 352 684-8425
Spring Hill (G-16532)

Allen & Company Florida LLC ....E 863 688-9000
Lakeland (G-7791)

American Bancshares Mrtg LLC ...C 305 817-2163
Miami Lakes (G-10702)

Amundi Pioneer Distributor ....E 305 982-1550
Miami (G-9152)

Assuredpartners Inc ....B 407 804-5222
Lake Mary (G-7570)

Avm LP ....D 561 544-4600
Boca Raton (G-438)

Bass Underwriters Inc ....E 954 473-4488
Plantation (G-14607)

Benchmark Intl Sls Spclist LLC ...E 813 898-2350
Tampa (G-17358)

Blg Spain LLC ....C 305 854-8880
Coral Gables (G-2056)

Brickell 21 Capital MGT Inc ......E 786 300-2302
Miami (G-9278)

Cbiz Retirement Consulting Inc ...D 407 475-1765
Maitland (G-8511)

Charles Schwab Corporation .....D 800 435-9050
The Villages (G-18654)

Charles Schwab Corporation .....D 941 833-9236
Venice (G-18772)

Comvest Advisors LLC ....E 561 727-2000
West Palm Beach (G-19102)

Comvest Group Holdings LP ......D 561 727-2000
West Palm Beach (G-19103)

Cortez Connect Inc ....E 941 773-9319
Parrish (G-14113)

Digital Risk Mortgage Svcs LLC ...D 407 215-2900
Maitland (G-8525)

Excelta Corporation ....C 386 986-4399
Palm Coast (G-13821)

Fasha Corporation ....E 505 991-9115
Orlando (G-12494)

Fifth Third Securities Inc ....E 813 251-4283
Tampa (G-17659)

Fmsbonds Inc ....C 561 368-5284
Boca Raton (G-589)

Foundry Commercial LLC ....D 407 540-7700
Orlando (G-12542)

Goldman Sachs & Co LLC ....D 305 755-1000
Miami (G-9648)

HIG Capital Inc ....E 305 379-2322
Miami (G-9700)

▲ HIG Capital LLC ....D 305 379-2322
Miami (G-9701)

▲ Hig Capital Management Inc ....E 305 379-2322
Miami (G-9702)

Hig Capital Partners III LP ....A 305 379-2322
Miami (G-9703)

Ifc Holdings Inc ....E 813 289-0722
Tampa (G-17855)

Institutional Banking Svcs NA .....D 954 889-5827
Boca Raton (G-642)

Merrill Lynch Pierce Fenner ......E 561 514-4800
West Palm Beach (G-19263)

Merrill Lynch Pierce Fenner ......D 904 273-3800
Ponte Vedra Beach (G-14991)

Merrill Lynch Pierce Fenner ......E 352 374-1000
Gainesville (G-4942)

Merrill Lynch Prce Fnner Smith ...C 239 263-1400
Naples (G-11213)

Merrill Lynch Prce Fnner Smith ...E 954 349-7609
Weston (G-19468)

Merrill Lynch Prce Fnner Smith ...C 561 393-4500
Boca Raton (G-689)

Merrill Lynch Prce Fnner Smith ...C 352 374-1000
Gainesville (G-4943)

Merrill Lynch Prce Fnner Smith ...D 407 909-2112
Orlando (G-12859)

Merrill Lynch Prce Fnner Smith ...C 305 347-2600
Miami (G-9937)

Merrill Lynch Prce Fnner Smith ...C 407 645-1212
Winter Park (G-19750)

Merrill Lynch Prce Fnner Smith ...C 850 434-7083
Pensacola (G-14362)

Merrill Lynch Prce Fnner Smith ...E 407 420-2525
Orlando (G-12860)

Merrill Lynch Prce Fnner Smith ...E 407 839-2525
Orlando (G-12861)

Merrill Lynch Prce Fnner Smith ...D 727 462-2321
Clearwater (G-1715)

Merrill Lynch Prce Fnner Smith ...C 305 577-6900
Miami (G-9938)

Merrill Lynch Prce Fnner Smith ...D 305 442-1122
Coral Gables (G-2145)

Merrill Lynch Prce Fnner Smith ...B 904 634-6000
Jacksonville (G-6498)

Merrill Lynch Prce Fnner Smith ...C 954 916-2800
Plantation (G-14673)

Merrill Lynch Prce Fnner Smith ...C 561 655-7720
Palm Beach (G-13664)

Merrill Lynch Prce Fnner Smith ...C 954 537-3800
Fort Lauderdale (G-3968)

Merrill Lynch Prce Fnner Smith ...C 239 481-3330
Fort Myers (G-4511)

Merrill Lynch Prce Fnner Smith ...D 904 273-3812
Ponte Vedra Beach (G-14992)

Merrill Lynch Prce Fnner Smith ...D 941 413-4520
Lakewood Ranch (G-8027)

Merrill Lynch Prce Fnner Smith ...D 727 824-7300
Saint Petersburg (G-15764)

Merrill Lynch Prce Fnner Smith ...D 561 514-4800
West Palm Beach (G-19264)

Merrill Lynch Prce Fnner Smith ...C 305 933-6200
Miami (G-9941)

Merrill Lynch Prce Fnner Smith ...C 772 231-2000
Vero Beach (G-18895)

Merrill Lynch Prce Fnner Smith ...D 407 333-8300
Lake Mary (G-7611)

Merrill Lynch Prce Fnner Smith ...D 561 276-1600
Delray Beach (G-2992)

Merrill Lynch Prce Fnner Smith ...C 772 223-6700
Stuart (G-16642)

Merrill Lynch Prce Fnner Smith ...C 813 273-8500
Tampa (G-18028)

Merrill Lynch Prce Fnner Smith ...C 727 799-5646
Clearwater (G-1716)

Merrill Lynch Prce Fnner Smith ...C 386 274-2739
Daytona Beach (G-2635)

Merrill Lynch Prce Fnner Smith ...B 904 218-9943
Jacksonville (G-6499)

Merrill Lynch Prce Fnner Smith ...C 941 365-1300
Sarasota (G-16229)

Merrill Lynch Prce Fnner Smith ...C 813 273-8639
Lakeland (G-7918)

Merrill Lynch Prce Fnner Smith ...C 850 599-8969
Tallahassee (G-17044)

Merrill Lynch Prce Fnner Smith ...D 888 243-2144
Bonita Springs (G-928)

Merrill Lynch Prce Fnner Smith ...D 352 350-2700
The Villages (G-18661)

Merrill Lynch Prce Fnner Smith ...E 954 357-4500
Fort Lauderdale (G-3969)

Merrill Lynch Prce Fnner Smith ...D 941 746-1123
Bradenton (G-1146)

Merrill Lynch Prce Fnner Smith ...D 850 864-6100
Fort Walton Beach (G-4791)

Merrill Lynch Prce Fnner Smith ...D 941 484-2641
Venice (G-18793)

Merrill Lynch Prce Fnner Smith ...C 941 637-4300
Punta Gorda (G-15214)

Money Concepts Capital Corp ....D 561 472-2000
Palm Beach Gardens (G-13755)

Morgan & Morgan PA......................E...... 352 204-4720
  Gainesville *(G-4951)*
Morgan Stnley Smith Barney LLC........C...... 772 283-7170
  Stuart *(G-16645)*
Morgan Stnley Smith Barney LLC........C...... 561 650-7500
  West Palm Beach *(G-19273)*
Morgan Stnley Smith Barney LLC........D...... 863 382-1818
  Sebring *(G-16409)*
Morgan Stnley Smith Barney LLC........D...... 850 470-8012
  Gulf Breeze *(G-5128)*
Morgan Stnley Smith Barney LLC........C...... 800 490-5412
  Winter Park *(G-19751)*
Morgan Stnley Smith Barney LLC........C...... 305 672-5900
  Miami Beach *(G-10625)*
Morgan Stnley Smith Barney LLC........C...... 305 460-7800
  Coral Gables *(G-2152)*
Morgan Stnley Smith Barney LLC........C...... 561 391-8282
  Boca Raton *(G-700)*
Mutual America Life Insur Co.............E...... 212 224-1600
  Boca Raton *(G-705)*
Newbridge Financial Inc..................D...... 954 334-3450
  Boca Raton *(G-714)*
Newbridge Securities Corp................D...... 877 447-9625
  Boca Raton *(G-715)*
Newport Group Securities Inc............D...... 407 333-2905
  Lake Mary *(G-7615)*
North Florida Financial....................E...... 850 562-9075
  Tallahassee *(G-17058)*
Ocwen Mortgage Servicing Inc..........E...... 561 682-8000
  West Palm Beach *(G-19288)*
Patient Matters LLC.......................C...... 407 872-7969
  Orlando *(G-13013)*
Patriot Underwriting Agency ....B...... 954 727-7004
  Fort Lauderdale *(G-4042)*
Raymond James & Associates Inc......A...... 727 567-1000
  Saint Petersburg *(G-15816)*
Raymond James Financial Inc...........C...... 727 567-1000
  Saint Petersburg *(G-15818)*
Raymond James Fincl Svcs Inc.........D...... 727 567-1000
  Saint Petersburg *(G-15819)*
Raymond James Trust Company ....D...... 727 567-2300
  Saint Petersburg *(G-15821)*
Schlitt Insurance Services Inc...........E...... 772 567-1188
  Vero Beach *(G-18914)*
Smart Financial Operations LLC.........E...... 407 960-4686
  Orlando *(G-13207)*
Summit Fincl Svcs Group Inc............D...... 561 338-2800
  Boca Raton *(G-828)*
Templeton Worldwide Inc.................A...... 954 527-7500
  Fort Lauderdale *(G-4173)*
Templeton/Franklin Inv Svcs ....D...... 954 761-9357
  Fort Lauderdale *(G-4174)*
Tradestation Group Inc....................D...... 954 652-7000
  Plantation *(G-14715)*
Tradestation Securities Inc...............D...... 954 652-7000
  Plantation *(G-14716)*

6221 Commodity Contracts Brokers & Dealers

Barkley Financial Corp.....................E...... 310 207-8000
  Boca Raton *(G-443)*
Fintec Group Inc............................D...... 305 669-4440
  South Miami *(G-16502)*
Merrill Lynch Pierce Fenner ....E...... 352 374-1000
  Gainesville *(G-4942)*
Merrill Lynch Prce Fnner Smith..........C...... 813 273-8639
  Lakeland *(G-7918)*
◆ Park Street Imports LLC................C...... 305 967-7440
  Miami *(G-10097)*

6282 Investment Advice

Affiliated Managers Group Inc............D...... 800 345-1100
  West Palm Beach *(G-19023)*
American Financial Network Inc..........E...... 561 202-8406
  West Palm Beach *(G-19032)*
AON Investments USA Inc................E...... 813 636-3070
  Tampa *(G-17293)*
Arete Advisors LLC ....E...... 646 907-9767
  Boynton Beach *(G-961)*
Assurance Fincl Partners LLC...........C...... 954 874-4600
  Sunrise *(G-16740)*
Bear Atlantic Group LLC ....E...... 305 507-5545
  Miami *(G-9235)*
Capstone Fincl Partners LLC.............D...... 904 394-2610
  Jacksonville *(G-5901)*
Carnes Capital Corporation ....E...... 239 254-2500
  Naples *(G-11046)*
Certified Financial Group Inc.............E...... 407 869-5608
  Altamonte Springs *(G-35)*

Charles Schwab Corporation.............D...... 800 435-9050
  The Villages *(G-18654)*
▲ Community Loan Servicing LLC .....A...... 305 854-8880
  Coral Gables *(G-2078)*
Dfc Global Corp.............................C...... 941 408-7386
  Venice *(G-18778)*
Eagle Boston Inv MGT Inc................D...... 727 573-8768
  Saint Petersburg *(G-15657)*
Fasha Corporation.........................E...... 505 991-9115
  Orlando *(G-12494)*
Florida Penn ....E...... 561 750-1187
  Boca Raton *(G-584)*
Francois Investments Inc..................D...... 305 495-7553
  Miami *(G-9609)*
Gamco Investors Inc......................D...... 561 671-2100
  Palm Beach *(G-13656)*
Global Fncl Private Capitl LLC ....D...... 941 918-0507
  Sarasota *(G-16177)*
Granite Associates LP....................E...... 845 295-2400
  Naples *(G-11141)*
Gruden Acquisition Inc....................A...... 813 569-7131
  Tampa *(G-17765)*
I G H -Gpii Inc..............................C...... 305 379-2322
  Miami *(G-9736)*
Icv Partners LLC...........................C...... 917 282-2533
  Miami *(G-9741)*
Interntnal Assets Advisory LLC ....D...... 407 254-1500
  Orlando *(G-12687)*
Italian Rose Garlic Pdts LLC.............C...... 561 863-5556
  Riviera Beach *(G-15301)*
Jvb Financial Group LLC ....E...... 561 416-5876
  Boca Raton *(G-657)*
Keys To Success Financial LLC.........E...... 754 202-6681
  Pembroke Pines *(G-14158)*
Life of South ....C...... 904 350-9660
  Jacksonville *(G-6434)*
Lighthouse Partners LLC.................D...... 561 741-0820
  Palm Beach Gardens *(G-13748)*
Ljake Financial Group Llc.................E...... 407 698-5253
  Orlando *(G-12774)*
Marina Funding Group Inc................D...... 561 989-5423
  West Palm Beach *(G-19252)*
Merrill Lynch Prce Fnner Smith..........C...... 561 393-4500
  Boca Raton *(G-689)*
Merrill Lynch Prce Fnner Smith..........B...... 904 634-6000
  Jacksonville *(G-6498)*
Mesirow Financial Inc.....................E...... 305 416-3333
  Miami *(G-9943)*
Money Concepts Capital Corp...........D...... 561 472-2000
  Palm Beach Gardens *(G-13755)*
Morgan Stnley Smith Barney LLC........C...... 305 937-7100
  Miami *(G-10015)*
Morgan Stnley Smith Barney LLC........C...... 305 379-1000
  Miami *(G-10016)*
National Financial Svcs LLC..............A...... 239 596-3303
  Naples *(G-11244)*
North Florida Financial....................E...... 850 562-9075
  Tallahassee *(G-17058)*
Ntech Investment MGT LLC..............D...... 561 775-1100
  West Palm Beach *(G-19280)*
Park Hill Group Inc.........................D...... 561 997-1111
  Boca Raton *(G-743)*
Polen Capital Management LLC ....D...... 561 241-2425
  Boca Raton *(G-754)*
Raymond James Fincl Svcs Inc ....D...... 727 567-1000
  Saint Petersburg *(G-15819)*
Second Chance Credit LLC...............E...... 786 502-8844
  Coral Gables *(G-2183)*
▲ Silver Hill Financial LLC................C...... 305 854-8880
  Coral Gables *(G-2187)*
Slavic Investment Corporation ....C...... 561 241-9244
  Boca Raton *(G-807)*
Statetrust Capital LLC ....D...... 833 942-1334
  Boca Raton *(G-819)*
Summit Brokerage Services Inc ....D...... 561 338-2800
  Boca Raton *(G-827)*
Templeton Worldwide Inc ....A...... 954 527-7500
  Fort Lauderdale *(G-4173)*
Templeton/Franklin Inv Svcs ....D...... 954 761-9357
  Fort Lauderdale *(G-4174)*
Weiss Research Inc ....C...... 561 627-3300
  Jupiter *(G-7150)*

6289 Security & Commodity Svcs, NEC

Depository Trust Clearing Corp...........A...... 212 855-1000
  Tampa *(G-17588)*
Financl-Nfrmtn-Tchnologies LLC.........D...... 813 288-1980
  Tampa *(G-17660)*
Hernandez Consulting LLC................E...... 786 348-2061
  Miami *(G-9698)*

Madison Security Group Inc...............B...... 978 459-5911
  West Palm Beach *(G-19245)*

63 INSURANCE CARRIERS

6311 Life Insurance Carriers

Accurate Insur Solutions Inc.............E...... 813 994-4114
  Wesley Chapel *(G-18992)*
American Bankers Lf Asrn Fla............D...... 305 253-2244
  Miami *(G-9135)*
▼ American Bnkrs Insrce Grp Inc ....C...... 305 253-2244
  Miami *(G-9136)*
American Gen Lf Accident Insur ....E...... 850 656-8207
  Tallahassee *(G-16879)*
American Heritage Lf Insur Co ....C...... 904 992-1776
  Jacksonville *(G-5782)*
American Heritage Lf Inv Corp ....B...... 904 992-1776
  Jacksonville *(G-5783)*
American Insurance Agencies Di.........D...... 941 954-5700
  Lakewood Ranch *(G-8035)*
American Pioneer Life Insur Co ....D...... 407 628-1776
  Lake Mary *(G-7566)*
American Security Insurance Co..........E...... 727 556-2900
  Saint Petersburg *(G-15568)*
American Security Insurance Co..........C...... 305 253-2244
  Miami *(G-9142)*
Aplifi Inc.....................................D...... 954 788-0700
  Fort Lauderdale *(G-3612)*
Assurant Inc ....B...... 515 226-2200
  Miami *(G-9180)*
Assurant Inc ....D...... 305 253-2244
  Miami *(G-9181)*
Auto Club Group ....A...... 813 289-5000
  Tampa *(G-17321)*
Baldwin Krystyn Shrman Prtners.........B...... 813 984-3200
  Tampa *(G-17333)*
Bowen McLtte Britt Brevard LLC.........E...... 407 647-1616
  Maitland *(G-8506)*
Citizens Property Insur Corp ....C...... 813 374-4592
  Tampa *(G-17479)*
Citizens Property Insur Corp ....C...... 904 296-6105
  Jacksonville *(G-5953)*
Citizens Property Insur Corp ....B...... 904 296-6105
  Jacksonville *(G-5954)*
Citizens Property Insur Corp ....C...... 904 380-6187
  Jacksonville *(G-5955)*
Citizens Property Insur Corp ....D...... 888 685-1555
  Tallahassee *(G-16915)*
Fortegra Group LLC.......................A...... 866 961-9529
  Jacksonville *(G-6209)*
Great-West Lf Annuity Insur Co..........E...... 863 256-5593
  Davenport *(G-2441)*
Guardian Life Insur Co of Amer...........E...... 904 296-1944
  Jacksonville *(G-6247)*
Guardian Life Insur Co of Amer...........D...... 239 561-2900
  Fort Myers *(G-4427)*
Mutual America Life Insur Co ....E...... 212 224-1600
  Boca Raton *(G-705)*
Nassau Life Insurance Co Kans ....C...... 407 628-1776
  Lake Mary *(G-7614)*
National Insurance Agency Inc...........E...... 305 253-2244
  Miami *(G-10030)*
National Planning Corporation ....E...... 305 371-6333
  Miami *(G-10031)*
New York Life Insurance Co...............C...... 407 999-0291
  Maitland *(G-8565)*
New York Life Insurance Co...............B...... 813 288-5500
  Tampa *(G-18076)*
New York Life Insurance Co...............E...... 954 772-5200
  Sunrise *(G-16803)*
Northwestern Mutual.......................D...... 561 948-6548
  Boca Raton *(G-722)*
Northwestern Mutual ....D...... 772 562-5698
  Vero Beach *(G-18898)*
Onesource Group Inc ....E...... 727 447-6481
  Clearwater *(G-1747)*
Online Insurance Quotes Inc ....E...... 888 438-0588
  Miami *(G-10075)*
Pennsylvania Life Insurance Co..........C...... 800 275-6667
  Lake Mary *(G-7621)*
Saveologycom LLC........................D...... 954 657-9614
  Margate *(G-8665)*
Southern Fidelity Insurance Co...........E...... 850 521-0742
  Tallahassee *(G-17106)*
Standard Insurance Company ....C...... 813 879-2900
  Tampa *(G-18329)*
Ulysses Caremark Holding Corp.........B...... 407 444-4100
  Lake Mary *(G-7650)*
Unitedhealthcare Insurance Co..........A...... 813 818-3310
  Oldsmar *(G-11932)*

Voyager Service Warranties Inc ....C 305 253-2244
Miami (G-10485)

Washington National Insur Co ....B 321 633-9210
Melbourne (G-9007)

Welcome Funds Inc ....E 561 826-1829
Boca Raton (G-870)

6321 Accident & Health Insurance

Ahca ....D 850 414-0355
Tallahassee (G-16872)

▼ American Bnkrs Insrce Grp Inc .....C 305 253-2244
Miami (G-9136)

American Eldercare N Fla LLC ....C 850 462-1380
Tallahassee (G-16878)

American Gen Lf Accident Insur ....E 850 656-8207
Tallahassee (G-16879)

American Heritage Lf Insur Co ....C 904 992-1776
Jacksonville (G-5782)

American Heritage Lf Inv Corp ....B 904 992-1776
Jacksonville (G-5783)

American Insurance Agencies Di ....D 941 954-5700
Lakewood Ranch (G-8035)

American Pioneer Life Insur Co ....D 407 628-1776
Lake Mary (G-7566)

Amerisys Inc ....E 407 949-3100
Oviedo (G-13542)

AON Benfield Inc ....D 305 961-6000
Miami (G-9157)

Chubb US Holdings Inc ....C 305 670-9935
Miami (G-9368)

Enstar (us) Inc ....D 727 217-2900
Saint Petersburg (G-15662)

Evolutons Hlthcare Systems Inc ....D 727 938-2222
New Port Richey (G-11372)

Firefghters Emplyee Bneft Fund ....E 561 969-6663
West Palm Beach (G-19140)

First American Financial ....B 321 525-1571
Melbourne (G-8885)

Florida Health Care Plan Inc ....D 386 445-7073
Palm Coast (G-13822)

Florida Health Solution Corp ....E 305 269-2004
Miami (G-9577)

Franco Signor LLC ....C 888 959-0692
Bradenton (G-1106)

Legacy Healing Ctr Margate LLC ....E 518 209-7229
Fort Lauderdale (G-3934)

Mfb Financial Inc ....D 904 461-1800
Saint Augustine (G-15468)

Mmm of Florida Inc ....D 844 212-9858
Miami (G-10008)

Mutual America Life Insur Co ....E 212 224-1600
Boca Raton (G-705)

Nassau Life Insurance Co Kans ....C 407 628-1776
Lake Mary (G-7614)

Online Insurance Quotes Inc ....E 888 438-0588
Miami (G-10075)

Optimum Healthcare Inc ....B 866 245-5360
Tampa (G-18104)

Palamerican Security Inc ....C 727 550-1085
Saint Petersburg (G-15786)

Pennsylvania Life Insurance Co ....C 800 275-6667
Lake Mary (G-7621)

Physicians United Plan Inc ....E 888 827-5787
Tallahassee (G-17069)

Prudentrx LLC ....D 813 833-9861
Tampa (G-18182)

Simply Healthcare Holdings Inc ....E 877 915-0551
Miami (G-10275)

Tobias & Associates Inc ....D 866 611-0519
Boca Raton (G-841)

Unitedhealthcare Insurance Co ....A 813 818-3310
Oldsmar (G-11932)

Universal Health Care Inc ....D 866 690-4842
Tallahassee (G-17166)

US Health Exchange LLC ....C 786 574-9683
Doral (G-3349)

Wellcare Prescr Insur Inc ....C 813 290-6200
Tampa (G-18541)

Xn Holdings Inc ....E 561 368-2408
Boca Raton (G-880)

6324 Hospital & Medical Svc Plans Carriers

Adva Holdings LLC ....C 941 313-3300
Lakewood Ranch (G-8034)

AFLAC Benefits Solutions Inc ....D 877 864-0625
Tampa (G-17243)

▼ American Bnkrs Insrce Grp Inc .....C 305 253-2244
Miami (G-9136)

Amerigroup Corporation ....C 561 750-8866
Plantation (G-14600)

Avmed Inc ....B 352 372-8400
Gainesville (G-4841)

Avmed Inc ....B 407 539-0007
Orlando (G-12161)

Blue Cross Blue Shield Fla Inc ....D 904 905-0000
Jacksonville (G-5871)

▲ Careplus Health Plans Inc ....D 877 245-7930
Miramar (G-10844)

Centene Corporation ....D 407 351-9625
Orlando (G-12253)

Centurion of Florida LLC ....A 850 692-2314
Tallahassee (G-16910)

Cigna Dental Health Inc ....B 954 514-6600
Plantation (G-14615)

Coastal Ansthesiology Cons LLC ....D 904 819-4478
Saint Augustine (G-15435)

Coastal Community Health Inc ....D 904 376-4050
Jacksonville (G-5970)

Comprehensive Health MGT Inc ....E 813 290-6200
Tampa (G-17508)

▼ Coventry Health Care Fla Inc ....E 954 858-3000
Plantation (G-14626)

Delta Dental of California ....E 904 448-0106
Jacksonville (G-6059)

Delta Dental of California ....D 407 660-9034
Maitland (G-8523)

Dentalplanscom Inc ....D 954 923-1487
Plantation (G-14627)

Dentaquest of Florida Inc ....A 305 443-3111
Doral (G-3176)

Evolutons Hlthcare Systems Inc ....D 727 938-2222
New Port Richey (G-11372)

Florida Amerigroup Inc ....B 813 830-6900
Tampa (G-17670)

Florida Health Care Plan Inc ....B 386 615-4022
Daytona Beach (G-2593)

Florida Health Care Plan Inc ....D 321 567-7500
Titusville (G-18685)

Freedom Health Inc ....D 813 506-6000
Tampa (G-17711)

Health First Health Plans Inc ....C 321 434-5600
Rockledge (G-15348)

Health First Shared Svcs Inc ....A 321 434-4300
Rockledge (G-15350)

Health Network Group LLC ....D 800 200-9416
West Palm Beach (G-19175)

Health Options Inc ....D 904 564-5700
Jacksonville (G-6270)

Healthchoice Inc ....A 407 481-7100
Orlando (G-12630)

Healthspring of Florida Inc ....D 305 229-7461
Doral (G-3225)

Humana Government Business Inc .....A 305 222-2000
Miami (G-9732)

Humana Inc ....C 321 421-1521
Miramar (G-10865)

Humana Inc ....C 386 676-1800
Daytona Beach (G-2614)

Humana Inc ....E 305 512-9381
Hialeah (G-5277)

Humana Inc ....E 941 346-1968
Sarasota (G-16188)

Humana Inc ....C 904 567-6726
Dade City (G-2390)

Humana Inc ....D 954 267-0000
Fort Lauderdale (G-3881)

Humana Inc ....D 561 496-6000
Delray Beach (G-2968)

Humana Inc ....E 305 626-5499
Miramar (G-10866)

Humana Inc ....C 800 526-1489
Miramar (G-10867)

Humana Inc ....D 561 969-1244
Palm Springs (G-13894)

Humana Inc ....D 904 376-1000
Jacksonville (G-6306)

Humana Pharmacy Inc ....A 502 580-3733
Hialeah (G-5278)

Liberty Dental Plan Corp ....D 888 352-7924
Tampa (G-17944)

Managed Care North America Inc ......D 954 730-7131
Fort Lauderdale (G-3954)

One Call Medical Inc ....D 973 257-1000
Jacksonville (G-6560)

Preferred Care Partners Inc ....B 305 670-8440
Miami (G-10136)

Preferred Medical Plan Inc ....D 305 324-5585
Coral Gables (G-2171)

Public Hlth Trust of Mm-Dade C ....B 305 585-1152
Miami (G-10163)

Quality Health Plans NY Inc ....E 813 463-0099
Tampa (G-18187)

▲ Sacred Heart Health System Inc ....A 850 416-1600
Pensacola (G-14425)

Solstice Benefits Inc ....C 954 370-1700
Plantation (G-14710)

South Fla Cmnty Care Ntwrk LLC ......C 954 622-3226
Sunrise (G-16828)

Total Health Choice Inc ....E 305 408-5700
Miami (G-10397)

United Healthcare of Florida ....C 407 659-6900
Maitland (G-8593)

Unitedhealthcare Insurance Co ....A 305 238-9111
Cutler Bay (G-2378)

Unitedhealthcare Insurance Co ....A 813 818-3310
Oldsmar (G-11932)

Well Care Hmo Inc ....C 813 290-6200
Tampa (G-18531)

Wellcare Health Insur NY Inc ....E 800 308-2571
Tampa (G-18532)

Wellcare Health Plans Inc ....B 813 290-6200
Tampa (G-18533)

Wellcare Health Plans Inc ....D 813 206-3405
Tampa (G-18534)

Wellcare Health Plans NJ Inc ....B 813 290-6200
Tampa (G-18535)

Wellcare Hlth Insur Co KY Inc ....C 813 290-6200
Tampa (G-18538)

Wellcare of Kansas Inc ....C 813 290-6200
Tampa (G-18538)

Wellcare of Maine Inc ....E 800 960-2530
Tampa (G-18539)

Zelis Payments Inc ....C 877 828-8770
Saint Petersburg (G-15906)

6331 Fire, Marine & Casualty Insurance

Allied Intl Holdings Inc ....C 727 367-6900
Saint Petersburg (G-15563)

▼ American Bnkrs Insrce Grp Inc .....C 305 253-2244
Miami (G-9136)

American Strategic Insur Corp ....C 727 821-8765
Saint Petersburg (G-15569)

Ameritrust Insurance Corp ....D 941 924-4444
Sarasota (G-16090)

Amtrust North America of Fla ....C 561 962-9300
Boca Raton (G-421)

Asi Assurance Corp ....A 727 821-8765
Saint Petersburg (G-15575)

Asi Preferred Insurance Corp ....A 727 821-8765
Saint Petersburg (G-15576)

Asi Select Auto Insurance Corp ....C 727 821-8765
Saint Petersburg (G-15577)

Asi Services Inc ....A 727 821-8765
Saint Petersburg (G-15579)

Asi Underwriters Corp ....C 727 821-8765
Saint Petersburg (G-15580)

Associated Industries Insur Co ....C 800 866-1234
Boca Raton (G-430)

Assurance Managing Gen Agents ......E 954 761-3470
Fort Lauderdale (G-3614)

Assurant Inc ....,D 305 253-2244
Miami (G-9181)

Auto Club Group ....A 813 289-5000
Tampa (G-17321)

Baldwin Krystyn Shrman Prtners ....B 813 984-3200
Tampa (G-17333)

Bankers Insurance Services Inc ....B 727 823-4000
Saint Petersburg (G-15586)

Bankers Surety Services Inc ....C 727 823-4000
Saint Petersburg (G-15588)

Bridgefield Casualty Insur Co ....E 863 665-6060
Lakeland (G-7818)

Bristol West Holdings Inc ....B 954 316-5200
Davie (G-2464)

Broadspire Services Inc ....A 954 452-4000
Sunrise (G-16752)

Citizens Property Insur Corp ....B 904 296-6105
Jacksonville (G-5954)

Commercial Risk Management Inc ......E 813 289-3900
Tampa (G-17504)

Employers Preferred Insur Co ....C 561 840-7171
North Palm Beach (G-11544)

Fcci Insurance Company ....B 941 907-3224
Sarasota (G-16159)

▲ Fednat Holding Company ....D 800 293-2532
Sunrise (G-16679)

Fidelity National Fincl Inc ....A 904 854-8100
Jacksonville (G-6162)

Frontline Unlmted Insur Mngers ....E 877 744-5224
Lake Mary (G-7596)

Guarantee Insurance Group Inc ....D...... 954 670-2900
Plantation (G-14651)

Hci Group Inc ....C...... 813 849-9500
Tampa (G-17800)

Heritage Insur Holdings Inc ....D...... 727 362-7202
Clearwater (G-1664)

Liberty Mutual Holding Corp ....D...... 561 793-2300
Wellington (G-18983)

Lloyds Asi Inc ....A...... 727 821-8765
Saint Petersburg (G-15748)

Mercury Insurance Company Fla ....B...... 727 561-4000
Clearwater (G-1714)

National Cncil On Cmpnstn Insr ....A...... 561 893-1000
Boca Raton (G-708)

National Flood Services LLC ....A...... 406 756-8656
Coral Springs (G-2273)

Ncci Holdings Inc ....A...... 561 893-1000
Boca Raton (G-710)

Ngm Insurance Company ....C...... 904 380-7282
Jacksonville (G-6543)

Onesource Group Inc ....E...... 727 447-6481
Clearwater (G-1747)

Pmsi LLC ....B...... 813 626-7788
Tampa (G-18156)

Program Underwriters LLC ....E...... 954 796-4800
Plantation (G-14698)

Progressive Bayside Insur Co ....A...... 855 347-3939
Riverview (G-15263)

Progressive Corporation ....D...... 407 765-6275
Tampa (G-18176)

Progressive Southeastern Insur ....A...... 813 487-1000
Riverview (G-15264)

Servicelink Holdings LLC ....A...... 904 854-8100
Jacksonville (G-6713)

Summit Consulting LLC ....B...... 863 665-6060
Lakeland (G-7981)

Summit Holding Southeast Inc ....D...... 863 665-6060
Lakeland (G-7983)

United Automobile Insurance Co ....C...... 305 940-7299
Miami (G-10435)

United Insurance Holdings Corp ....D...... 727 895-7737
Saint Petersburg (G-15879)

United Property Cslty Insur Co............C...... 727 895-7737
Saint Petersburg (G-15880)

Wright National Flood Insur Co ....B...... 800 820-3242
Saint Petersburg (G-15900)

Zenith Insurance Company ....D...... 941 906-5158
Sarasota (G-16370)

6351 Surety Insurance Carriers

▼ American Bnkrs Insrce Grp Inc ....C.... 305 253-2244
Miami (G-9136)

American Heritage Lf Insur Co ....C.... 904 992-1776
Jacksonville (G-5782)

American Heritage Lf Inv Corp ....B.... 904 992-1776
Jacksonville (G-5783)

Bowen McLtte Britt Brevard LLC..........E.... 407 647-1616
Maitland (G-8506)

Cinch Home Services Inc ....B.... 954 835-1900
Boca Raton (G-509)

Cross Country HM Holdings Inc..........E.... 954 835-1900
Boca Raton (G-539)

Home Buyers Warranty Corp VI ....D.... 954 585-6500
Plantation (G-14654)

Rasi Home Insurance Corp ....A.... 866 274-8765
Saint Petersburg (G-15815)

6361 Title Insurance

Atif Inc.....................................C.... 407 240-4440
Orlando (G-12146)

Atif Inc.....................................D.... 904 731-2644
Jacksonville (G-5812)

Atif Inc.....................................C.... 239 278-3434
Fort Myers (G-4283)

Attorneys Title Fund Svcs LLC............E.... 727 736-4884
Palm Harbor (G-13851)

Chicago Title Insurance Co..................C.... 904 854-8100
Jacksonville (G-5942)

Chicago Title Insurance Co..................A.... 772 221-3853
Stuart (G-16603)

Commonwealth Land Title Insur ....E.... 904 928-0014
Jacksonville (G-5984)

Commonwealth Land Title Insur ....D.... 813 254-2101
Tampa (G-17506)

Doma Title Insurance Inc ....C.... 800 374-8475
Miami (G-9485)

Fidelity Nat Title Insur Co ....C.... 888 934-3354
Jacksonville (G-6160)

Fidelity Nat Title Insur Co NY..............A.... 954 236-5563
Plantation (G-14640)

Fidelity National Europe LLC.................D.... 904 854-8100
Jacksonville (G-6161)

Fidelity National Fincl Inc ....A.... 904 854-8100
Jacksonville (G-6162)

First American Title Insur Co ....C.... 727 549-3200
Largo (G-8105)

First American Title Insur Co ....D.... 407 691-5200
Maitland (G-8531)

Miller South Milhausen ....E.... 352 241-9131
Clermont (G-1879)

Old Republic Nat Title Insur ....C.... 813 228-0555
Tampa (G-18097)

Old Republic Nat Title Insur ....D.... 904 354-7112
Jacksonville (G-6558)

Old Republic Nat Title Insur ....E.... 941 365-3122
Sarasota (G-16251)

Old Republic Nat Title Insur ....D.... 954 421-4599
Deerfield Beach (G-2779)

Reltco Inc ....D.... 813 855-0009
Tampa (G-18213)

Resort Title Agency Inc ....E.... 561 912-8070
Boca Raton (G-773)

Servicelink Holdings LLC ....A.... 904 854-8100
Jacksonville (G-6713)

Stillwter Property Cslty Insur ....D.... 866 373-5663
Jacksonville (G-6796)

6371 Pension, Health & Welfare Funds

American Maritime Off Bldg FL ....E.... 954 920-4247
Dania Beach (G-2423)

American Mrtime Offcers Bldg C...........E.... 954 920-4247
Dania (G-2402)

City of Clearwater ....E.... 727 562-4800
Clearwater (G-1569)

City of Plantation ....C.... 954 797-2200
Plantation (G-14616)

Connectyourcare LLC ....C.... 877 292-4040
Saint Petersburg (G-15643)

Florida Retirement Division ....C.... 850 488-5541
Tallahassee (G-16978)

Frankcrum 9 Inc ....D.... 727 799-1229
Clearwater (G-1648)

National Sourcing Inc ....E.... 813 281-0013
Tampa (G-18068)

Nationsbenefits LLC ....B.... 877 439-2665
Plantation (G-14681)

6399 Insurance Carriers, NEC

4warranty Corporation ....D.... 800 867-2216
Jacksonville (G-5715)

Abco Premium Finance Inc...................E.... 305 461-2555
Coral Gables (G-2019)

Advanced Marketing & Proc Inc...........B.... 800 253-2850
Saint Petersburg (G-15559)

Advocate Health LLC........................D.... 800 709-5513
Venice (G-18761)

Asi Select Auto Insurance Corp ....C.... 727 821-8765
Saint Petersburg (G-15577)

Assurant Inc ....D.... 305 253-2244
Miami (G-9181)

Federal Warranty Service Corp ....B.... 813 977-7600
Tampa (G-17653)

Healthplan Holdings Inc ....A.... 813 289-1000
Tampa (G-17808)

Iws Acquisition Corporation ....D.... 561 981-7000
Boca Raton (G-646)

Phoenix Amercn Warranty Co Inc ....D.... 305 266-5665
Miami (G-10117)

PMC Home & Auto Insur Co LLC...........C.... 800 253-2850
Saint Petersburg (G-15803)

Security Frst Insur Hldngs LLC..............D.... 877 333-9992
Ormond Beach (G-13521)

United Service Protection ....C.... 727 556-2900
Saint Petersburg (G-15882)

64 INSURANCE AGENTS, BROKERS, AND SERVICE

6411 Insurance Agents, Brokers & Svc

1st Capital Financial Inc ....E.... 954 623-6164
Margate (G-8640)

Aai Runoff Inc ....E.... 813 933-6691
Tampa (G-17221)

Absolute Best Insurance LLC................E.... 561 420-0280
Greenacres (G-5068)

Acrisure LLC ....D.... 305 670-6111
Miami (G-9075)

Adcahb Life Group Inc ....E.... 954 753-8080
Pompano Beach (G-14733)

Adjusters Best Claims Svcs LLC ....E.... 904 744-5990
Jacksonville (G-5737)

Aequicap Program Administrator ....C.... 954 493-6565
Fort Lauderdale (G-3581)

Agency Marketing Svcs Co Inc..............E.... 727 384-1036
Saint Petersburg (G-15560)

AJK Enterprises Inc ....E.... 813 558-9560
Tampa (G-17259)

All Claims USA Inc ....C.... 561 306-1408
Boca Raton (G-409)

Allied Amercn Adjusting Co LLC ....E.... 800 794-2529
Tampa (G-17267)

Allied World Assurance Inc ....E.... 305 866-7808
Miami (G-9125)

American Gen Lf Accident Insur ....E.... 352 787-2953
Leesburg (G-8228)

American Heritg Licensed Insur ....C.... 904 992-1776
Jacksonville (G-5785)

American Intgrity Insur Group ....C.... 813 880-7000
Tampa (G-17277)

Amerisure Insurance Company ....E.... 813 282-5820
Tampa (G-17281)

Amstar Insurance Company ....D.... 305 264-8582
Miami (G-9151)

Anthem Lakes LLC ....D.... 904 583-5399
Jacksonville (G-5798)

AON Risk Services Inc Florida ....C.... 305 372-9950
Miami (G-9158)

AON Risk Svcs Companies Inc ....E.... 305 372-9950
Miami (G-9159)

ARA Insurance Group Inc ....E.... 305 779-2447
Miami (G-9164)

▲ Arthur J Gallagher & Co Fla ....E.... 305 592-6080
Miami (G-9174)

Arthur J Gllgher Risk MGT Svcs ....E.... 941 757-0020
Lakewood Ranch (G-8014)

Arthur J Gllgher Risk MGT Svcs ....D.... 239 262-7171
Naples (G-11016)

Ascendant Commercial Insur Inc............C.... 305 820-4360
Coral Gables (G-2034)

Ascendant Underwriters LLC ....E.... 305 820-4360
Coral Gables (G-2035)

Asi Select Insurance Corp ....B.... 727 821-8765
Saint Petersburg (G-15578)

Asi Underwriters Texas Inc ....A.... 727 821-8765
Saint Petersburg (G-15581)

Assuredpartners Inc ....E.... 802 448-4600
Sanford (G-15918)

Assuredpartners Inc ....B.... 407 804-5222
Lake Mary (G-7570)

Assuredpartners NI LLC......................E.... 502 894-2100
Lake Mary (G-7571)

Asurion Services LLC........................A.... 850 423-7200
Crestview (G-2310)

Atlas Mortgage & Insurance Co............E.... 941 366-8424
Sarasota (G-16097)

Auditwerx Risk and Adv Svs LLC ....E.... 866 446-4038
Tampa (G-17320)

Auto-Owners Insurance Company ....E.... 772 219-3465
Stuart (G-16591)

B-Engaged Inc ....C.... 727 447-6481
Clearwater (G-1530)

Baldwin Krystyn Shrman Prtners ....D.... 813 707-8652
Lakeland (G-7811)

Baldwin Risk Partners LLC ....A.... 866 279-0698
Tampa (G-17334)

Banack Insurance Agency Inc ....E.... 772 562-3369
Vero Beach (G-18838)

Bankers Financial Corporation...............A.... 727 823-4000
Saint Petersburg (G-15585)

Bankers Intl Fincl Corp.......................D.... 727 823-4000
Saint Petersburg (G-15587)

◆ Bateman Gordon & Sands Inc...........E.... 954 941-0900
Pompano Beach (G-14751)

Bay National Title Company ....D.... 727 449-8733
Clearwater (G-1535)

Beacon Group Inc ....E.... 561 994-9994
Boca Raton (G-445)

Bear Atlantic Group LLC ....E.... 305 507-5545
Miami (G-9235)

Bell LLC ....E.... 813 261-7755
Tampa (G-17356)

Ben Brown Insurance Agency ....E.... 941 366-9373
Sarasota (G-16100)

Benefytt Technologies Inc ....E.... 877 376-5831
Tampa (G-17359)

Bliss and Glennon Inc ....D.... 904 350-9660
Jacksonville (G-5870)

Bluestar Retirement Svcs Inc ....D.... 904 273-5220
Ponte Vedra Beach (G-14977)

Bmi Financial Group Inc	D	305 443-2898	
Miami (G-9264)			
Bowen McLtte Britt Brevard LLC	E	407 647-1616	
Maitland (G-8506)			
Boyd Insur & Investments Svc	D	941 745-8300	
Bradenton (G-1061)			
Bradley Stinson & Associates	E	877 761-2332	
Fort Lauderdale (G-3648)			
Brandon Pest Control Inc	D	863 602-5988	
Lakeland (G-7817)			
Bridgefield Employers Insur Co	C	863 665-6060	
Lakeland (G-7819)			
Bristol West Insurance Svc Inc	D	954 893-8866	
Davie (G-2465)			
Bristol West Insurance Svc Inc	B	954 316-5200	
Davie (G-2466)			
◆ Brown & Brown Inc	B	386 252-9601	
Daytona Beach (G-2555)			
Brown & Brown Inc	E	954 776-2222	
Fort Lauderdale (G-3659)			
Brown & Brown Inc	D	407 660-8282	
Maitland (G-8507)			
Brown & Brown Florida Inc	E	813 226-1300	
Tampa (G-17392)			
Brp Group Inc	D	866 279-0698	
Tampa (G-17393)			
Businessfirst Insurance Co	D	863 665-6060	
Lakeland (G-7822)			
Butler Pappas Weihmuller Katz	C	813 281-1900	
Tampa (G-17404)			
Capitol Preferred Insur Co Inc	E	850 521-0742	
Tallahassee (G-16905)			
Carisk Behavioral Health Inc	D	305 514-5300	
Miami (G-9323)			
Carolina Casualty Insurance Co	C	904 363-0900	
Jacksonville (G-5908)			
Cbg Health LLC	E	251 250-2223	
Cantonment (G-1335)			
Cecil W Powell and Company	D	904 353-3181	
Jacksonville (G-5920)			
Celedinas Agency	E	561 514-5646	
Palm Beach Gardens (G-13703)			
Chase Insurance Agency Inc	E	954 792-4300	
Plantation (G-14614)			
Chubb US Holdings Inc	C	305 670-9935	
Miami (G-9368)			
Cigna Health Corporation	B	904 306-5520	
Jacksonville (G-5948)			
Cigna Healthcare Florida Inc	A	215 761-1000	
Tampa (G-17471)			
Citi Investor Services Inc	D	877 846-1796	
Melbourne (G-8845)			
Citizens Property Insur Corp	C	904 296-6105	
Jacksonville (G-5952)			
Citizens Property Insur Corp	C	904 296-6105	
Jacksonville (G-5953)			
Citizens Property Insur Corp	C	904 380-6187	
Jacksonville (G-5955)			
CL Acquisition Holdings Ltd	E	813 886-6571	
Tampa (G-17485)			
Coastal Hmwners Insur Spclist	C	954 958-1211	
Fort Lauderdale (G-3703)			
Comp Options Insurance Co Inc	E	888 207-4215	
Jacksonville (G-5993)			
Complex Clims MGT Slutions LLC	E	844 672-6070	
Dunedin (G-3382)			
Corbin Executive Group Inc	E	813 963-1669	
Lutz (G-8435)			
Coventbridge (usa) Inc	C	904 641-7300	
Jacksonville (G-6004)			
Cramer Jhnson Wggins Assoc Inc	D	407 849-0044	
Orlando (G-12382)			
Crystal Frank & Co Inc	E	305 421-0900	
Miami (G-9443)			
Cunningham Lindsey US LLC	C	863 401-3380	
Winter Haven (G-19620)			
Cunningham Lindsey US LLC	C	813 830-7100	
Tampa (G-17557)			
Cypress Property Cslty Insur	E	904 992-4492	
Jacksonville (G-6037)			
Dan Bonsanti Inc	E	305 595-8260	
Miami (G-9456)			
David Platt & Associates Inc	D	954 426-6571	
Deerfield Beach (G-2733)			
Demetree Insurance Svcs Inc	C	904 398-5656	
Jacksonville (G-6062)			
Dhl Enterprises Inc	E	850 994-9211	
Milton (G-10814)			
DLS Insurance Group Inc	E	833 357-4671	
Sweetwater (G-16859)			

E-Ins LLC	E	727 578-3663	
Saint Petersburg (G-15656)			
E-Telequote Insurance Inc	D	727 601-4000	
Clearwater (G-1614)			
Eig Two Inc	E	239 649-1444	
Naples (G-11100)			
Elbardi Intl Triangle LLC	E	305 406-1583	
Cutler Bay (G-2366)			
Elite Insurance Partners LLC	E	800 845-2484	
Palm Harbor (G-13861)			
Emmitt Combs and Co Rlty Inc	E	407 614-8336	
Winter Garden (G-19566)			
Ereceivables Inc	E	954 893-1390	
Coral Springs (G-2250)			
Erj Insurance Group Inc	B	305 885-4216	
Miami (G-9530)			
Excelsior Benefits LLC	D	407 629-6664	
Maitland (G-8529)			
Falck Global Assistance LLC	D	855 659-6672	
Lake Mary (G-7589)			
Fcci Agency Inc	C	941 907-3224	
Sarasota (G-16157)			
Fcci Group Inc	B	941 907-3224	
Sarasota (G-16158)			
Fcci Insurance Group Inc	B	941 907-2515	
Sarasota (G-16160)			
Fcci Mutual Insurance Holdg Co	B	941 907-3224	
Sarasota (G-16161)			
Fcci Services Inc	B	941 907-3224	
Sarasota (G-16162)			
▲ Fednat Holding Company	D	800 293-2532	
Sunrise (G-16769)			
Fia Liquidation Company Inc	E	772 283-0003	
Stuart (G-16623)			
Fidelity Nat Indemnity Insur	C	888 333-2120	
Jacksonville (G-6158)			
Financial Reinsurance Inc	E	386 677-4453	
Ormond Beach (G-13491)			
First Call Iq Inc	D	877 405-3763	
Fort Lauderdale (G-3787)			
First General Insurance Co	E	305 817-0303	
Miami Lakes (G-10729)			
Fisher-Brown Incorporated	D	850 432-7474	
Pensacola (G-14306)			
Florida Farm Bur Gen Insur Co	D	352 378-1321	
Gainesville (G-4890)			
Florida Farm Bur Gen Insur Co	A	727 466-6390	
Saint Petersburg (G-15678)			
Florida Insur Guaranty Assn	E	850 386-9200	
Tallahassee (G-16973)			
Florida Peninsula Holdings LLC	D	561 210-0370	
Boca Raton (G-583)			
Florida Prfrred Administrators	C	941 748-8555	
Bradenton (G-1104)			
Florida Specialty Managing	E	941 210-5670	
Longboat Key (G-8324)			
Fortegra Financial Corporation	D	866 961-9529	
Jacksonville (G-6208)			
Fortun Insurance Inc	D	305 445-3535	
Coral Gables (G-2109)			
Frank H Furman Inc	E	954 946-6720	
Pompano Beach (G-14813)			
Frank Winston Crum Insur Co	D	727 799-1150	
Clearwater (G-1646)			
Frontline Insur Managers Inc	E	407 444-5224	
Lake Mary (G-7595)			
Frontline Unlmted Insur Mngers	E	877 744-5224	
Lake Mary (G-7596)			
Granada Insurance Company Inc	E	305 554-0353	
Miami (G-9657)			
Greene-Hazel & Associates Inc	E	904 398-1234	
Jacksonville (G-6241)			
Guarantee Insurance Company	C	954 556-1600	
Fort Lauderdale (G-3843)			
Guarantee Insurance Company	D	321 257-1300	
Lake Mary (G-7597)			
Guarantee Insurance Group Inc	D	954 670-2900	
Plantation (G-14651)			
Gulfshore Insurance Inc	D	239 261-3646	
Naples (G-11151)			
H&A Legacy Inc	A	904 355-1700	
Jacksonville (G-6253)			
H&A Legacy Inc	C	904 548-2333	
Yulee (G-19817)			
Haa Preferred Partners LLC	C	305 260-9987	
Miami (G-9674)			
Hadley & Lyden Inc	E	407 679-8181	
Winter Park (G-19728)			
Hammer Construction Corp	E	786 618-0116	
Miami (G-9678)			

Harbor Group Consulting LLC	D	212 245-0001	
Miami (G-9681)			
Harrington Health Services Inc	A	800 237-7767	
Tampa (G-17793)			
Hci Group Inc	C	813 849-9500	
Tampa (G-17800)			
Health E Systems LLC	B	813 463-1235	
Tampa (G-17802)			
Health First ADM Plans Inc	D	321 434-4300	
Rockledge (G-15347)			
Health Insurance Assoc LLC	B	800 985-9449	
Port Orange (G-15078)			
Health Line One LLC	E	800 606-1671	
Deerfield Beach (G-2749)			
Healthcare Solutions Inc	E	866 810-4332	
Tampa (G-17807)			
Healthplan Svcs Insur Agcy LLC	A	813 289-1000	
Tampa (G-17810)			
Herbie Wiles Insurance Inc	E	904 829-2201	
Saint Augustine (G-15451)			
Holland Financial Inc	E	386 671-1245	
Ormond Beach (G-13504)			
Hub International Limited	D	305 444-2324	
Miami (G-9730)			
Hub International Limited	E	850 386-1111	
Tallahassee (G-16998)			
▼ Hull & Company LLC	E	954 527-4855	
Hollywood (G-5458)			
Humana Health Insur Co Fla Inc	C	502 580-1000	
Miramar (G-10864)			
Ican Benefit Group LLC	D	800 530-4226	
Boca Raton (G-638)			
Ifc Holdings Inc	E	813 289-0722	
Tampa (G-17855)			
Iler Wall and Shonter Insur	D	727 327-7070	
Saint Petersburg (G-15715)			
Ingham & Company	E	305 671-2200	
Miami (G-9748)			
Insurance Care Direct Inc	D	866 792-5976	
Deerfield Beach (G-2757)			
Insurance Center Inc	E	561 433-1492	
West Palm Beach (G-19202)			
Insurance Center Inc	E	904 645-0006	
Jacksonville (G-6322)			
Insurance Office America Inc	C	407 314-6190	
Longwood (G-8367)			
Insurance Risk Services Inc	E	407 302-9004	
Lake Mary (G-7601)			
Ioa Group LLC	E	800 243-6899	
Longwood (G-8368)			
Ira Nuview Inc	D	407 367-3472	
Longwood (G-8369)			
J P Perry Insurance Inc	E	904 268-7310	
Jacksonville (G-6337)			
John Galt Insurance Agcy Corp	E	954 281-7070	
Fort Lauderdale (G-3910)			
Johns Eastern Company Inc	C	941 907-3100	
Lakewood Ranch (G-8019)			
Joseph D Johnson & Company	D	407 843-1120	
Orlando (G-12714)			
Kemper Independence Insur Co	B	904 245-5600	
Jacksonville (G-6400)			
▲ Keyes Coverage LLC	D	954 724-7000	
Fort Lauderdale (G-3920)			
Knox Insurance	C	904 797-2177	
Saint Augustine (G-15461)			
Legacy Insur Assoc Unlmted Inc	E	561 877-1922	
Boca Raton (G-668)			
Lighthouse Management LLC	C	407 982-7646	
Orlando (G-12769)			
Lions Share Holding Inc	E	813 229-8021	
Tampa (G-17958)			
Ljake Financial Group Llc	E	407 698-5253	
Orlando (G-12774)			
Lozano Insurance Adjusters Inc	E	904 493-9220	
Jacksonville (G-6448)			
Lynx Services LLC	B	800 806-2573	
Fort Myers (G-4498)			
Macduff Underwriters Inc	E	386 366-6300	
Daytona Beach (G-2629)			
Macneill Group Inc	C	954 331-4800	
Sunrise (G-16794)			
Main Street America Group Inc	C	877 927-5672	
Jacksonville (G-6462)			
Major American Mktg Intl Co	E	866 729-1274	
Miami (G-9895)			
Marsh & McLennan Agency LLC	B	914 397-1600	
Doral (G-3270)			
McGriff Insurance Services Inc	E	727 327-7070	
Saint Petersburg (G-15755)			

McGriff Insurance Services Inc ....E 850 386-2143
Tallahassee (G-17038)

McGriff Insurance Services Inc ....E 239 433-4535
Fort Myers (G-4507)

McGriff Insurance Services Inc ....E 727 803-8121
Tampa (G-18009)

ME Wilson Company LLC ....E 813 229-8021
Tampa (G-18014)

Medmal Direct Insurance Co..............E 904 482-4068
Jacksonville (G-6491)

Medwatch Inc ....D 407 333-8166
Lake Mary (G-7610)

Merrill Lynch Prce Fnner Smith..........D 352 350-2700
The Villages (G-18661)

MetLife Financial Services ....E 850 478-9841
Pensacola (G-14363)

Mfb Financial Inc............................D 904 461-1800
Saint Augustine (G-15468)

Mfkks LLC......................................C 888 354-5050
Fort Myers (G-4512)

Miami Intl Arprt Crgo Fclties ....E 305 856-3333
Miami (G-9973)

Midamrica ADM Rtrment Sltons L ......D 863 688-4500
Lakeland (G-7924)

Morris & Reynolds Inc ....E 305 238-1000
Miami (G-10017)

Nation Group Inc ....E 352 840-0999
Ocala (G-11741)

National Flood Services LLC ....A 406 756-8656
Coral Springs (G-2273)

Nations Insur Solutions LLC ....E 786 528-8692
Miami (G-10032)

Nationsbenefits LLC........................B 877 439-2665
Plantation (G-14681)

Nationwide Mutual Insurance Co ....D 352 377-8500
Gainesville (G-4954)

Nationwide Mutual Insurance Co ....E 877 669-6877
Clearwater (G-1733)

Nboa Marine Insurance Agency ....E 941 360-6777
Sarasota (G-16244)

Ncci ....E 561 893-1000
Boca Raton (G-709)

Network Insurance ....E 727 726-0726
Clearwater (G-1735)

Newport Retirement Svcs Inc ....C 407 333-2905
Lake Mary (G-7617)

Nexxus Solutions Group LLC ....D 407 378-3631
Orlando (G-12914)

North American Risk Svcs Inc ....C 407 875-1700
Altamonte Springs (G-82)

North Florida Financial ....E 850 562-9075
Tallahassee (G-17058)

Northwestern Mutual ....D 772 562-5698
Vero Beach (G-18898)

Nsure Insurance Services Inc ....E 561 288-9700
Boca Raton (G-724)

Old Dominion Insurance Company ......C 904 642-3000
Jacksonville (G-6557)

Old Republic Nat Title Insur ....D 954 421-4599
Deerfield Beach (G-2779)

Olympus Managed Health Care ....D 305 530-8600
Miami (G-10070)

Onesource Group Inc ....E 727 447-6481
Clearwater (G-1747)

Orchid Insurance ....E 772 299-0046
Vero Beach (G-18900)

Oriental Pension Cons Inc ....B 561 392-5149
Boca Raton (G-733)

Ormond Re Group Inc ....E 386 677-4453
Ormond Beach (G-13514)

Pagidem LLC ....E 888 201-3105
Boca Raton (G-737)

Pboa Inc ....E 941 955-0793
Sarasota (G-16260)

Peoples Trust Insurance Co..............A 561 417-1148
Deerfield Beach (G-2783)

Poe & Brown Inc ....D 407 352-0374
Orlando (G-13040)

Preferred Managing Agency LLC ....D 850 521-0742
Tallahassee (G-17072)

Primepay of Florida Inc ....E 813 890-0415
Tampa (G-18170)

Proassurance Casualty Company........E 813 969-2010
Tampa (G-18174)

Program Management Services ....E 407 331-3838
Lake Mary (G-7626)

Program Underwriters LLC ....E 954 796-4800
Plantation (G-14698)

Progressive Insurance Agcy Inc ....D 239 434-5500
Naples (G-11273)

Progrssive Auto Pro Insur Agcy..........B 813 487-1000
Riverview (G-15265)

Rai Automation Services Inc ....E 850 386-1115
Tallahassee (G-17078)

Raymond James Insur Group Inc........D 727 567-1000
Saint Petersburg (G-15820)

Relation Insur Svcs Fla Inc ....E 772 287-7650
Jacksonville (G-6652)

Relation Insur Svcs Fla Inc ....D 800 431-2221
Stuart (G-16662)

Riemer Insurance Group Inc ....E 954 454-3145
Hallandale Beach (G-5179)

Rivertrust Solutions Inc ....C 423 535-3257
Jacksonville (G-6670)

Rodes Roper & Love Insur Agcy..........A 321 757-6185
Melbourne (G-8972)

Safeway Insurance Company ....E 305 932-7096
Miami (G-10233)

Schlitt Insurance Services Inc ....E 772 567-1188
Vero Beach (G-18914)

Security First Managers LLC ....D 386 523-2302
Ormond Beach (G-13520)

Sedgwick Claims MGT Svcs Inc ....C 407 829-2172
Lake Mary (G-7639)

Seeman Holtz Group Inc ....E 561 241-3121
Boca Raton (G-792)

Seitlin & Company ....D 305 591-0090
Fort Lauderdale (G-4112)

Shapiro Insurance Inc ....E 850 386-6933
Tallahassee (G-17099)

Shelly Middlebrooks Oleary Inc..........E 904 354-7711
Jacksonville (G-6722)

Sihle Insurance Group Inc ....D 407 869-0962
Altamonte Springs (G-98)

Skyway Claims Services LLC ....E 727 895-7737
Saint Petersburg (G-15847)

Slavic Integrated ADM Inc ....E 561 241-9244
Boca Raton (G-806)

Specialty Claim Services LLC ....E 407 937-0481
Winter Park (G-19775)

Squaremouth Inc ....E 727 564-9203
Saint Petersburg (G-15852)

Stahl & Associates Insurance ....E 727 391-9791
Saint Petersburg (G-15859)

Star & Shield Services LLC ....E 866 942-9822
Lake Mary (G-7642)

Star Casualty Insurance Co ....E 305 262-4733
Coral Gables (G-2189)

State Farm General Insur Co ....E 727 821-6607
Saint Petersburg (G-15860)

State Farm Life Insurance Co ....D 321 727-3992
Palm Bay (G-13639)

Stillwater Insurance Svcs Inc ....D 904 997-7408
Jacksonville (G-6795)

Summit Consulting LLC ....B 863 665-6060
Lakeland (G-7981)

Summit Holding Corporation ....B 863 665-6060
Lakeland (G-7982)

Sunshine SEC Insur Agcy Inc ....A 727 821-8765
Saint Petersburg (G-15867)

T Agency ....E 941 474-4511
Englewood (G-3440)

T Dougie Inc ....E 954 735-5555
Pompano Beach (G-14917)

Teachers Insur Annity Assn AME........C 866 842-2442
Jacksonville (G-6840)

Team Focus Insurance Group LLC ......B 954 331-4800
Sunrise (G-16835)

Tech-Cor LLC ....D 954 482-4067
Fort Lauderdale (G-4171)

Thomas Cothron Agency ....E 352 694-9800
Ocala (G-11785)

Thomas Financial Group ....E 813 273-9416
Tampa (G-18420)

Thrifty Insurance Agency Inc ....E 239 301-7000
Estero (G-3484)

Tiaa Fsb ....E 904 623-8214
Jacksonville (G-6849)

Tri-Insurance Underwriters Inc ....E 954 889-3328
Hollywood (G-5542)

▼ United Auto Insur Group Inc ....D 305 940-5022
Miami Gardens (G-10699)

Universal Insur Holdings Inc ....D 954 958-1200
Fort Lauderdale (G-4198)

Universal Insur Managers Inc ....D 941 378-8851
Sarasota (G-16353)

Universal Protection Plans Inc ....E 954 958-1200
Fort Lauderdale (G-4199)

Universal Risk Advisors ....C 954 958-1203
Fort Lauderdale (G-4200)

US Assure Inc ....B 904 398-3907
Jacksonville (G-6897)

USI Insurance Services Nat Inc ....E 305 443-4886
Coral Gables (G-2203)

USI Insurance Services Nat Inc ....E 561 655-5500
West Palm Beach (G-19404)

USI Insurance Services Nat Inc ....E 407 627-0640
Orlando (G-13363)

USI Insurance Services Nat Inc ....E 561 368-2777
Boca Raton (G-858)

Valuteachers Inc ....E 678 683-4032
Ponte Vedra (G-14971)

Vault Insurance ....D 844 368-2858
Saint Petersburg (G-15885)

Vaxcare Corporation ....E 407 480-5970
Orlando (G-13370)

Vengroff Williams & Assoc Inc ....C 941 363-5200
Sarasota (G-16358)

Wallace Welch & Willingham Inc ....D 727 522-7777
Saint Petersburg (G-15891)

Weekes & Callaway Inc ....D 561 278-0448
Delray Beach (G-3034)

Welcome Funds Inc ....E 561 826-1829
Boca Raton (G-870)

West Made Holdings LLC..................E 855 937-9276
Fort Lauderdale (G-4222)

West Point Underwriters LLC ....D 727 507-7565
Pinellas Park (G-14537)

Weston Insurance MGT LLC ....E 888 800-5002
Coral Gables (G-2209)

Williams Stzzone Insur Agcy In ....E 321 868-2000
Melbourne (G-9010)

Willis North America Inc....................E 813 712-7000
Tampa (G-18557)

Willis of Florida Inc ....B 863 293-2787
Winter Haven (G-19673)

Willis of Florida Inc ....B 407 805-3005
Tampa (G-18558)

Willis of Florida Inc ....B 352 378-2511
Gainesville (G-5032)

Willis of Florida Inc ....B 305 854-1330
Miami (G-10507)

Willis RE Inc ....A 305 373-8460
Miami (G-10508)

Windhaven Insurance Company ....E 800 919-9114
Tallahassee (G-17177)

Worldwide Insurance Agency LLC ......E 407 616-7894
Orlando (G-13449)

Wright Nat Flood Insur Svcs LL ....D 727 803-2040
Saint Petersburg (G-15899)

Zenith Insurance Company ....D 941 906-5158
Sarasota (G-16370)

65 REAL ESTATE

6512 Operators Of Nonresidential Bldgs

2125 Bscyne Nvel Coworking LLC ....D 312 283-3683
Miami (G-9053)

3201 Hotel LLC ....E 305 535-3009
Miami Beach (G-10536)

3290 Sunrise Investments Inc............C 954 791-7927
Fort Lauderdale (G-3567)

37 N Ornge Novel Coworking LLC ......D 312 283-3683
Orlando (G-12028)

6/10 Corporation ....E 863 299-1195
Winter Haven (G-19602)

Ameri-Tech Realty Inc ....C 727 726-8000
Clearwater (G-1518)

Asm Global Parent Inc......................D 850 432-0800
Pensacola (G-14221)

Atrium Hotels Inc ....A 321 773-9260
Melbourne (G-8820)

B & B Cash Grocery Stores Inc ....E 813 621-6411
Tampa (G-17329)

B & B Corporate Holdings Inc ....D 813 621-6411
Tampa (G-17330)

▲ Bayshore Restaurant Management ..D 305 854-7997
Miami (G-9230)

Biltmore Hotel Ltd Partnership............B 305 445-1926
Coral Gables (G-2054)

Bmlrw ....D 904 388-2225
Jacksonville (G-5872)

Castle Management Inc ....E 800 337-5850
Plantation (G-14611)

Castle Management Inc ....B 239 498-5455
Estero (G-3446)

Charltte Hbr Event Cnfrnce Ctr............E 941 639-5833
Punta Gorda (G-15199)

City of Fort Lauderdale......................D 954 828-5380
Fort Lauderdale (G-3695)

Coconut Point Town Center LLC.........D...... 239 992-1386	Premiere Prpts of Suthwest Fla.........D...... 239 261-6161	Brookside Properties Inc.........C...... 813 632-0677
Estero (G-3448)	Naples (G-11270)	Tampa (G-17391)
▲ Colonnade Partners Ltd.........E...... 305 441-2600	Premium Outlet Partners LP.........C...... 407 238-7787	Camden Development Inc.........C...... 407 650-2093
Coral Gables (G-2075)	Orlando (G-13051)	Orlando (G-12229)
Compass Research LLC.........E...... 352 261-0901	R I - Fadjem Inc.........D...... 904 268-8080	Canterbury Towers Inc.........D...... 813 837-1083
The Villages (G-18655)	Jacksonville (G-6631)	Tampa (G-17414)
Complete Property Maint Inc.........E...... 954 973-3333	Rauch Waver Norfleet Kurtz Inc.........D...... 954 771-4400	Carlisle At Lantana Ltd Partnr.........C...... 561 533-9440
Lake Worth (G-7720)	Fort Lauderdale (G-4082)	Lantana (G-8059)
Continental Property Svcs Inc.........D...... 866 286-6219	Realty Capital Management Inc.........E...... 407 843-7070	Caroline Square Realty.........D...... 904 743-1277
South Daytona (G-16484)	Maitland (G-8572)	Jacksonville (G-5909)
Cooper Realty Company.........D...... 239 482-2900	RMC Property Group LLC.........E...... 800 728-5379	Carpenters Home Estates Inc.........B...... 863 858-3847
Fort Myers (G-4326)	Tampa (G-18228)	Lakeland (G-7827)
Coral Springs Trade Center Ltd.........C...... 954 753-9500	Sandpiper Resort Prpts Inc.........E...... 305 925-9229	Cathedral Court Inc.........B...... 904 807-1218
Coral Springs (G-2242)	Miami (G-10238)	Jacksonville (G-5913)
Cornfeld Group.........D...... 954 986-1070	Sembler Company.........D...... 727 384-6000	Cathedral Fndtion Jcksnvlle In.........E...... 904 807-1203
Hollywood (G-5419)	Saint Petersburg (G-15841)	Jacksonville (G-5914)
County of Orange.........C...... 407 345-9800	So - Trails LLC.........D...... 386 275-1601	Christian Mssnary Alnce Fndtio.........A...... 239 466-1111
Orlando (G-12378)	Ormond Beach (G-13524)	Fort Myers (G-4311)
Crexent LLC.........E...... 954 862-1440	Southern Restaurant Group Inc.........D...... 850 837-1637	Church St Hsing Partners I LLC.........E...... 407 648-1623
Davie (G-2472)	Destin (G-3090)	Orlando (G-12300)
Dania Entertainment Center LLC.........C...... 954 920-1511	Southern Restaurant Group Inc.........E...... 850 837-2022	City View Apartments Inc.........D...... 305 371-8300
Dania Beach (G-2426)	Destin (G-3078)	Miami (G-9375)
Ddp Holdings LLC.........D...... 813 712-2515	Strata Properties LLC.........E...... 904 677-9505	Clear Harbor Ltd.........A...... 203 869-0900
Tampa (G-17577)	Jacksonville (G-6797)	West Palm Beach (G-19092)
Design Professional LLC.........E...... 954 920-7997	▲ Sunbeam Television Corporation.........C...... 305 751-6692	Collier Companies Inc.........D...... 352 375-2152
Dania (G-2410)	North Bay Village (G-11470)	Gainesville (G-4866)
Draftpros LLC.........E...... 786 641-5131	Sunrise Mills Ltd Partnership.........E...... 954 846-2300	Concord Management Ltd.........C...... 407 741-8600
Miami Lakes (G-10723)	Sunrise (G-16832)	Maitland (G-8519)
Edison Mall Business Trust.........C...... 239 939-1933	Tampa Bay Prfrmg Arts Ctr Inc.........B...... 813 222-1000	Concord Management Ltd.........C...... 407 277-8636
Fort Myers (G-4352)	Tampa (G-18368)	Orlando (G-12358)
Faculty Clinic Inc.........B...... 904 549-3700	Tb Mall At UTC LLC.........E...... 941 552-7000	Concord Management Ltd.........B...... 407 350-5957
Jacksonville (G-6143)	Sarasota (G-16064)	Kissimmee (G-7287)
First Cast Prpts Jcksnvlle Inc.........E...... 904 553-0069	TWC Holding Company.........E...... 813 281-8888	Concord Management Company Inc.........C...... 727 220-2483
Jacksonville (G-6166)	Tampa (G-18454)	Palm Harbor (G-13855)
Florida Care Properties Inc.........E...... 239 652-5604	Whitman Family Properties Lllp.........D...... 305 866-0311	Coral Oaks.........D...... 727 787-3333
North Fort Myers (G-11473)	Bal Harbour (G-304)	Palm Harbor (G-13856)
Florida Data Bank Inc.........E...... 863 273-3263	Wilson Management Company.........D...... 813 281-8888	▲ Cornerstone Group Inc.........C...... 305 443-8288
Winter Haven (G-19628)	Tampa (G-18561)	Hollywood (G-5418)
Florida Income Fund III Ptr.........C...... 239 481-2011	Yanni Ventures Inc.........D...... 904 829-6581	Cornfeld Group.........D...... 954 986-1070
Fort Myers (G-4383)	Saint Augustine (G-15514)	Hollywood (G-5419)
Florida Mall Associates Ltd.........D...... 407 851-6255	Yuengling Center.........D...... 813 974-3111	E R Management Inc.........D...... 407 671-2400
Orlando (G-12530)	Tampa (G-18575)	Winter Park (G-19717)
Forbes/Cohen Properties LLC.........E...... 239 598-1605		East Ridge Retirement Vlg Inc.........C...... 305 238-2623
Naples (G-11121)		Cutler Bay (G-2365)
Forbes/Cohen Properties LLC.........E...... 561 775-7750	## 6513 Operators Of Apartment Buildings	Emeritus Corporation.........D...... 941 756-5571
Palm Beach Gardens (G-13731)		Bradenton (G-1092)
Gallagher Property & Cslty LLC.........E...... 305 663-6270	3201 Hotel LLC.........E...... 305 535-3009	Encore Capital Management LLC.........E...... 561 961-1000
Palmetto Bay (G-13942)	Miami Beach (G-10536)	Boca Raton (G-566)
Gerald D Ross.........D...... 305 621-5801	Acts Rtrmnt-Life Cmmnties Inc.........C...... 561 487-5500	Evanglcal Lthran Good Smrtan S.........D...... 386 253-6791
Miami Gardens (G-10683)	Boca Raton (G-397)	Daytona Beach (G-2586)
Gerald D Ross.........D...... 954 776-4880	Acts Rtrmnt-Life Cmmnties Inc.........C...... 561 362-8377	First Svc Residential Fla Inc.........D...... 305 919-8885
Fort Lauderdale (G-3818)	Boca Raton (G-398)	Sunny Isles Beach (G-16719)
Holiday Isle Resort & Marina.........D...... 305 664-2321	Acts Rtrmnt-Life Cmmnties Inc.........C...... 561 487-1270	Flagler Street Associates.........D...... 305 373-5283
Islamorada (G-5704)	Boca Raton (G-399)	Miami (G-9565)
Hyatt Corporation.........A...... 239 444-1234	Acts Rtrmnt-Life Cmmnties Inc.........B...... 772 562-7400	▼ Florida Cnfrnce Svnth-Day Advn.........D...... 407 644-5000
Bonita Springs (G-923)	Vero Beach (G-18829)	Altamonte Springs (G-49)
Hyatt Corporation.........B...... 305 358-1234	Acts Rtrmnt-Life Cmmnties Inc.........C...... 772 770-1900	Florida Landarama Inc.........E...... 561 968-7368
Miami (G-9735)	Vero Beach (G-18830)	Greenacres (G-5071)
Inclusive Properties LLC.........E...... 202 820-3676	Advent Christian Village Inc.........D...... 386 658-3333	Florida Presbyterian Homes Inc.........B...... 863 688-5521
Fort Lauderdale (G-3890)	Live Oak (G-8307)	Lakeland (G-7869)
Jim Wilson & Associates Inc.........B...... 850 244-2172	Allapttah Trace Apartments Ltd.........A...... 203 869-0900	Fountains At Lee Vista LLC.........A...... 844 591-4235
Mary Esther (G-8689)	West Palm Beach (G-19027)	Orlando (G-12543)
JJ Gumberg Co.........D...... 954 537-2700	Allegro Senior Living LLC.........E...... 561 253-8161	Freedom Village of Sun Cy Ctr.........C...... 813 633-1992
Fort Lauderdale (G-3907)	Jupiter (G-7047)	Sun City Center (G-16703)
Jon M Hall Company LLC.........D...... 407 215-0410	Alliance Residential LLC.........E...... 904 247-0122	Genmar Realty Group Inc.........D...... 305 865-8011
Sanford (G-15955)	Jacksonville Beach (G-6974)	Bay Harbor Islands (G-346)
Key Hospitality & Healthcare.........D...... 305 293-1818	Ambassador Ht Coop Apartments.........D...... 561 582-2511	Goodwill Indstres-Suncoast Inc.........D...... 727 523-1512
Key West (G-7219)	Palm Beach (G-13646)	Tampa (G-17742)
Lutfi Investment Co Inc.........D...... 407 506-1200	American Cmpus Cmmnties Oprtin.........D...... 407 366-7474	Grep Southeast LLC.........D...... 954 332-3600
Orlando (G-12792)	Oviedo (G-13541)	Fort Lauderdale (G-3839)
M&C Hotel Interests Inc.........C...... 904 396-5100	American Cmpus Cmmnties Oprtin.........E...... 407 482-9990	Greystar Management Svcs LP.........C...... 813 887-4200
Jacksonville (G-6456)	Orlando (G-12107)	Tampa (G-17758)
▲ Midas International LLC.........C...... 561 383-3100	American Cmpus Cmmnties Oprtin.........D...... 407 384-7080	Gumenick Properties LLC.........E...... 305 672-2412
Palm Beach Gardens (G-13754)	Orlando (G-12108)	Miami Beach (G-10598)
Millennium Two LLC.........D...... 561 981-8500	American Cmpus Communities Inc.........D...... 850 309-0100	Harbor Retirement Assoc LLC.........D...... 239 566-8077
Boca Raton (G-694)	Tallahassee (G-16877)	Naples (G-11155)
Mj Ocala Hotel Associates.........C...... 352 854-1400	American Landmark LLC.........D...... 561 512-5691	Harbours Edge.........C...... 561 272-7979
Ocala (G-11736)	Lake Park (G-7657)	Delray Beach (G-2962)
Newport Hospitality LLC.........C...... 305 949-1300	American MGT Group N Fla LLC.........E...... 904 378-0144	HI Resorts Inc.........C...... 813 229-6686
Sunny Isles Beach (G-16726)	Jacksonville (G-5788)	Tampa (G-17818)
North Beach Investment Inc.........E...... 904 824-1806	Arbor Place Apartments Ltd.........C...... 727 369-5800	Highlands Viera West II LLC.........C...... 770 437-5226
Saint Augustine (G-15473)	Tampa (G-17300)	Melbourne (G-8906)
Orange Lake Country Club Rlty.........E...... 407 239-0000	Barkley Place Ltd Partnership.........E...... 239 939-3553	Housing Partnership Inc.........D...... 561 841-3500
Kissimmee (G-7363)	Fort Myers (G-4288)	Riviera Beach (G-15299)
Parkway Prprty Investments LLC.........D...... 407 650-0593	Bay Village of Sarasota Inc.........C...... 941 966-5493	Hunters Run Partners Ltd.........E...... 813 269-2900
Orlando (G-13009)	Sarasota (G-16098)	Tampa (G-17847)
Port of Palm Beach District.........E...... 561 842-4201	Bayco Development Company.........C...... 850 526-3191	IMT Capital LLC.........C...... 954 456-8787
Riviera Beach (G-15313)	Marianna (G-8671)	Miramar (G-10868)
Power Studios.........D...... 305 576-1336	Bridge Property Management LLC.........E...... 407 523-4252	International Residential.........D...... 305 866-2122
Miami Beach (G-10640)	Orlando (G-12202)	Miami (G-9769)
	Brisas Del Mar LLC.........D...... 305 377-2020	
	Miami (G-9286)	

Lake Deer Apartments I LLC ....C 863 299-4467
Winter Haven *(G-19640)*
Lake Hse Wst-Flrida Gen Partnr ....E 941 312-5100
Sarasota *(G-16213)*
Landmark APT Tr Holdings LP ....E 813 281-2907
Tampa *(G-17933)*
Liberty Healthcare of Oklahoma............E 239 262-8006
Naples *(G-11197)*
Life Care Centers America Inc ....C 863 318-8646
Winter Haven *(G-19643)*
Lifespace Communities Inc ....B 561 775-3230
Juno Beach *(G-7033)*
Lifespace Communities Inc ....E 561 272-7979
Delray Beach *(G-2982)*
Lifespace Communities Inc ....B 561 454-2000
Delray Beach *(G-2979)*
Lourds-Nreen McKeen Rsdnce For......B 561 655-8544
West Palm Beach *(G-19241)*
Lynd Company ....B 904 720-5266
Jacksonville *(G-6455)*
Macarthur Park Apartments LLC...........D 305 460-9900
Miami *(G-9889)*
Mahaffey & Associates Florida ....D 813 968-6666
Lutz *(G-8446)*
Manatee Cove Apartments LLC ....D 321 728-8488
Melbourne *(G-8927)*
Manor Cre- Lely Plms Nples FL ....B 239 775-7661
Naples *(G-11204)*
Mayflower Retirement Ctr Inc ....C 407 672-1620
Winter Park *(G-19748)*
Merrill Gardens LLC..................................E 407 786-5637
Altamonte Springs *(G-76)*
Merritt Island Rhf Housing ....B 321 452-1233
Merritt Island *(G-9040)*
Methodist Home For Aging Corp...........E 850 215-4663
Panama City *(G-14042)*
Museum Walk Apartments LLC ....D 305 535-8284
Miami Beach *(G-10634)*
North Beach Investment Inc ....E 904 824-1806
Saint Augustine *(G-15473)*
Oakland Management Corp ....D 954 472-6922
Plantation *(G-14685)*
Orlando Lutheran Towers Inc ....C 407 872-7088
Orlando *(G-12975)*
Park of Palms Inc ....D 352 473-6100
Keystone Heights *(G-7259)*
Pelican Sound Apartments Inc ....D 727 579-9232
Saint Petersburg *(G-15795)*
Picerne Management Corporation ....D 407 772-0200
Altamonte Springs *(G-93)*
Pinnacle At Abbey Park Ltd ....D 305 854-7100
Miami *(G-10124)*
Pinnacle Realty Management Co...........E 305 258-4832
Homestead *(G-5594)*
Plymouth Harbor Incorporated ....B 941 365-2600
Sarasota *(G-16270)*
Presbytrian Rtrment Cmmnties I ....D 941 748-4161
Bradenton *(G-1165)*
Presbytrian Rtrment Cmmnties I ....E 904 388-9376
Jacksonville *(G-6615)*
Princeton Groves Village LLC ....E 786 504-2632
Homestead *(G-5595)*
Properties of Hamilton Inc ....D 305 576-6575
Miami *(G-10152)*
Prudent Property Managers Inc.............D 305 673-8425
Miami *(G-10155)*
Ram Partners LLC......................................D 850 913-9666
Panama City *(G-14059)*
Realty Lv Inc..C 727 797-4424
Clearwater *(G-1774)*
Related Companies of Fla Inc ....D 305 460-9900
Miami *(G-10199)*
Related Management Corporation ....D 561 640-5794
West Palm Beach *(G-19343)*
Royal American Management Inc...........E 850 769-8981
Panama City *(G-14067)*
Sandhill Cove Properties Inc ....C 772 678-7875
Palm City *(G-13799)*
Satchmo Properties LLC ....E 305 661-2000
Miami *(G-10242)*
Senior Lifestyle Corporation ....D 305 255-6402
Miami *(G-10258)*
Shell Point Retirement Comm ....E 239 454-2175
Fort Myers *(G-4593)*
Southwest Fla Rtrement Ctr Inc ....C 941 484-9753
Venice *(G-18805)*
Spring Haven Retirement LLC ....C 863 293-0072
Winter Haven *(G-19663)*
St Joseph Garden Courts Inc ....E 407 382-0808
Orlando *(G-13231)*

Stadium Tower LLC ....E 786 517-8800
Miami *(G-10324)*
Stoltz Realty Co..D 561 395-9800
Boca Raton *(G-821)*
Summer Lakes Apartments II Ltd..........A 203 869-0900
Naples *(G-11309)*
Sun City Operations Inc ....E 813 633-3333
Sun City *(G-16699)*
Sunchase American Ltd ....E 850 385-9955
Tallahassee *(G-17118)*
Sunnyside Prpts Sarasota Inc ....C 941 371-2729
Sarasota *(G-16339)*
T & P Enterprises Bay Cnty Inc ....E 850 234-2502
Panama City *(G-14078)*
Tate Development Corp ....E 561 498-3277
Delray Beach *(G-3024)*
Trimark Properties ....E 352 376-6223
Gainesville *(G-5016)*
Vero Retirement Associates LLC ....D 772 299-7900
Vero Beach *(G-18940)*
Vicars Landing ....E 904 273-1734
Ponte Vedra Beach *(G-15012)*
Vida Buena Estate Inc ....E 321 351-3082
Melbourne *(G-8999)*
Watermark Rtrment Cmmnties Inc ....D 727 381-5411
South Pasadena *(G-16525)*
Watermark Rtrment Cmmnties Inc ....D 941 929-2400
Sarasota *(G-16362)*
Wesley Manor Inc ....C 904 287-7300
Jacksonville *(G-6971)*
Westminister Suncoast ....D 727 867-1131
Saint Petersburg *(G-15896)*
Westport Snior Lving Inv Fund...............C 941 798-8200
Bradenton *(G-1206)*
Wilson Co Inc ....B 727 945-0886
Holiday *(G-5378)*
Wilson Management Company ....C 407 737-8383
Orlando *(G-13434)*
Wn Legacy Residential llc........................E 386 631-1234
Lake Worth *(G-7763)*

6514 Operators Of Dwellings, Except Apartments

Booker Creek Apartments Ltd ....A 203 869-0900
West Palm Beach *(G-19055)*
Florida Presbyterian Homes Inc ....C 863 688-5521
Lakeland *(G-7869)*
Island One Resorts Mgt Corp ....D 407 239-8811
Winter Garden *(G-19574)*
Island One Resorts Mgt Corp ....D 407 238-0007
Kissimmee *(G-7327)*
Lutheran Haven Inc..................................C 407 365-5676
Oviedo *(G-13557)*
Pinnacle An American MGT Svcs............C 407 949-0800
Maitland *(G-8567)*
Potential Property Realty LLC ....E 305 260-6300
Weston *(G-19477)*
Spruce Creek Gols LLC.............................D 352 347-3700
Summerfield *(G-16690)*
Strongcore Group LLC..............................D 305 539-0680
South Miami *(G-16519)*

6515 Operators of Residential Mobile Home Sites

American Rsdntial Cmmnties LLC........A 352 331-4400
Gainesville *(G-4835)*
Cypress Lakes Associates Ltd ....E 863 859-1431
Lakeland *(G-7848)*
Genesis Investments Inc ....C 727 372-8808
Odessa *(G-11844)*
Lee Corporation ....E 239 498-2220
Estero *(G-3467)*
Sun Cove of Kissimmee Inc...................D 407 933-5870
Kissimmee *(G-7391)*
Travelers Rest Resort Inc.......................E 352 588-2013
Dade City *(G-2398)*
Venice Isle Home Owners Inc ....D 941 488-9648
Venice *(G-18815)*
Yes Management LLC................................D 904 693-2707
Jacksonville *(G-6953)*

6519 Lessors Of Real Estate, NEC

Buffalo-Marine Associates......................B 941 359-8303
University Park *(G-18739)*
Crexent LLC...E 954 862-1440
Davie *(G-19033)*
Douglas Gardens Holdg Corp Inc ....D 305 751-8626
Miami *(G-9486)*

Eola Capital LLC..E 904 356-1978
Jacksonville *(G-6124)*
First Svc Residential Fla Inc ....D 727 299-9555
Saint Petersburg *(G-15671)*
Florida Fontainebleau Ht LLC.................B 305 538-2000
Miami *(G-9576)*
Globally Connected Agency ....E 786 322-5119
Saint Petersburg *(G-15689)*
Grand Cypress Florida LP ....C 407 239-4700
Orlando *(G-12589)*
Mill Creek Residential Tr LLC ....D 561 998-4451
Boca Raton *(G-693)*
N Atkins Amer Holdings Corp.................B 813 282-7275
Tampa *(G-18064)*
National Realty Brevard Inc ....E 321 259-7624
Melbourne *(G-8946)*
Realty Exchange LLC ....E 386 693-4854
Flagler Beach *(G-3547)*
SBA Das & Small Cells LLC ....E 561 995-7670
Boca Raton *(G-782)*
SBA Leasing Inc..E 561 995-7670
Boca Raton *(G-783)*
SBA Properties LLC..................................D 561 995-7670
Boca Raton *(G-784)*
SBA Senior Finance II LLC ....E 561 995-7670
Boca Raton *(G-785)*
Select Hotels Group LLC..........................C 863 413-1122
Lakeland *(G-7966)*
Seven-One-Seven Prkg Svcs Inc............A 813 228-7722
Tampa *(G-18273)*
Showcase Prpts Investments Inc............D 321 783-5000
Cape Canaveral *(G-1370)*
Spottswood Companies Inc......................C 305 294-6100
Key West *(G-7246)*
Ulliby LLC..E 866 670-9187
Tampa *(G-18456)*
Wellpath Rcovery Solutions LLC ....E 772 597-9375
Indiantown *(G-5682)*

6531 Real Estate Agents & Managers

A & V Reality Trnsp LLC...........................E 305 509-8467
Doral *(G-3096)*
Abbott Realty Services Inc.......................C 850 837-3700
Destin *(G-3046)*
Abbott Realty Services Inc.......................E 850 837-6575
Destin *(G-3048)*
Abbott Realty Services Inc.......................C 850 267-9194
Destin *(G-3083)*
Abbott Realty Services Inc.......................E 850 837-4700
Destin *(G-3047)*
Active Data Technologies Inc ....E 561 988-9669
Boca Raton *(G-395)*
Adlene Ezzekmi PA ....E 786 556-4960
Miami Beach *(G-10542)*
▼ Adler Phillips Cnstr Inc..........................E 305 392-4000
Sweetwater *(G-16856)*
Advantage Realty of Sarasota ....D 941 371-8558
Sarasota *(G-16078)*
Advenir Inc ....E 305 948-3535
Aventura *(G-263)*
Affinity Management Svcs LLC ....E 305 325-4243
Doral *(G-3107)*
Agpm North Carolina LLC.........................E 407 447-1780
Orlando *(G-12080)*
Akam On-Site Inc ....D 561 994-4870
Dania *(G-2400)*
American Heritage Relocation..................E 904 390-7100
Jacksonville *(G-5784)*
▼ American Metro/Study Corp...................E 561 835-9235
West Palm Beach *(G-19033)*
American Realty of NW Fla ....E 850 651-2454
Shalimar *(G-16468)*
American Rlty Invstmnts Ctrus ....E 352 746-3600
Beverly Hills *(G-377)*
Aqua Sun Investments Inc ....E 386 441-1111
Ormond Beach *(G-13478)*
Aqua Sun Investments Inc ....E 386 672-3550
Ormond Beach *(G-13479)*
ARC Resorts LLC..D 321 320-8830
Orlando *(G-12129)*
Armor Realty Tallahassee Inc ....D 850 559-5388
Tallahassee *(G-16882)*
Arnold Colliers Inc ....E 727 442-7184
Clearwater *(G-1525)*
Associates Boca Raton Inc.......................D 561 279-7800
Delray Beach *(G-2911)*
Avesta Homes LLC....................................B 813 444-1600
Tampa *(G-17323)*
Avia Emmet RE Ltd Lblty Co ....E 954 394-8056
Sunrise *(G-16743)*

Baptist Clay Timeshare	E	904 516-1000		
Fleming Island (G-3550)				
Barclay Group Hldings Ltd Lllp	E	727 733-7585		
Tampa (G-17337)				
Bay National Title Company	D	727 449-8733		
Clearwater (G-1535)				
Berkadia Proprietary Holdg LLC	C	407 218-5688		
Orlando (G-12183)				
Berkley Group Inc	D	954 563-2444		
Fort Lauderdale (G-3639)				
Blue Goose Growers LLC	D	772 461-3020		
Fort Pierce (G-4685)				
Blue Moon Estate Sls Palm Bch	D	305 769-8088		
Key Biscayne (G-7164)				
Bluegreen Vacations Corp	A	561 912-8000		
Surfside (G-16852)				
Booker Creek Apartments Ltd	A	203 869-0900		
West Palm Beach (G-19055)				
Booking Ninjas	E	917 600-2345		
Miami Beach (G-10560)				
Branca Realty	E	772 882-9583		
Fort Pierce (G-4687)				
Breakers of Fort Wlton Bch Cnd	E	850 244-9127		
Fort Walton Beach (G-4756)				
Brickell Brokers Corporation	C	305 438-7777		
Miami (G-9279)				
Bridge Real Estate Group LLC	C	561 826-3917		
Saint Petersburg (G-15606)				
Brown Hrris Stevens Avatar LLC	D	305 666-1800		
Miami (G-9290)				
Cagan Management Group Inc	E	407 846-9446		
Kissimmee (G-7273)				
Camelot & Associates Inc	D	321 799-0221		
Cape Canaveral (G-1355)				
Campbell Property MGT & RE Inc	E	954 427-8770		
Deerfield Beach (G-2719)				
Capstone Tropical Holdings Inc	E	727 835-3188		
Port Richey (G-15099)				
Carson & Associates Ltd Inc	E	941 346-7166		
Sarasota (G-16117)				
Castle Management LLC	A	954 792-6000		
Plantation (G-14612)				
Cathedral Fndtion Jcksnvlle In	E	904 807-1203		
Jacksonville (G-5914)				
CB Richard Ellis	E	407 404-5000		
Orlando (G-12249)				
Cbre Inc	E	904 296-3000		
Jacksonville (G-5916)				
Central Fla Investments Inc	E	407 354-3040		
Orlando (G-12265)				
Centric Realty Services LLC	E	407 421-9391		
Orlando (G-12285)				
Century 21 Commander Realty	E	850 769-8326		
Panama City (G-13979)				
Cfh Group LLC	E	305 779-8040		
Miami (G-9352)				
Champagne & Parisi LLC	D	561 235-7800		
Boca Raton (G-505)				
Champagne & Parisi LLC	E	561 998-9015		
Boca Raton (G-506)				
Charles Rutenberg Realty	D	407 622-2122		
Winter Park (G-19704)				
Charles Rutenberg Realty Inc	A	614 352-4612		
Clearwater (G-1565)				
Chris Creegan LLC	D	407 622-1111		
Maitland (G-8514)				
Citrus Hill Investment Prpts	D	352 746-0744		
Hernando (G-5204)				
Classic Rsdence MGT Ltd Partnr	A	954 943-1936		
Pompano Beach (G-14774)				
Club Serendipity LLC	D	561 510-0903		
Deerfield Beach (G-2725)				
▲ Cnl Apf Partners LP	C	407 650-1000		
Orlando (G-12327)				
Codina Klein Realty Inc	D	305 520-2322		
Coral Gables (G-2073)				
Codina Partners LLC	C	305 529-1300		
Coral Gables (G-2074)				
Coldwell Banker Realestate	D	407 696-7279		
Winter Springs (G-19800)				
Coldwell Banker Residential RE	E	863 644-7561		
Lakeland (G-7841)				
Coldwell Banker Schmitt	E	305 743-5181		
Marathon (G-8615)				
Coldwell Bnkers Wlter Wllams R	E	904 268-3000		
Jacksonville (G-5976)				
Coldwell Bnkr Prperty Showcase	C	386 736-2066		
Deland (G-2850)				
Coldwell Bnkr Rsdntial Rfrral	A	727 381-2345		
Saint Petersburg (G-15631)				

Colonial Country Club	E	239 768-7217
Fort Myers (G-4319)		
Colonnade Properties LLC	E	212 632-6915
West Palm Beach (G-19097)		
Commercial Inc	E	407 648-2787
Orlando (G-12348)		
Compass Real Estate LLC	E	727 867-0161
Saint Petersburg (G-15639)		
Consolidated Community MGT Inc	D	954 718-9903
Tamarac (G-17186)		
Continental Properties Inc	E	561 689-4766
West Palm Beach (G-19107)		
Continntal RE Cmpnies Coml Prp	D	305 854-7342
Miami (G-9409)		
Contravest Management Company	D	407 333-0066
Altamonte Springs (G-41)		
Corcoran Group Inc	B	561 472-6400
Palm Beach Gardens (G-13710)		
Corcoran Group Inc	A	561 655-9081
Palm Beach (G-13652)		
Cornfeld Group	D	954 986-1070
Hollywood (G-5419)		
County of Broward	C	954 357-6830
Fort Lauderdale (G-3731)		
Courtelis Company	D	305 261-4330
Miami (G-9431)		
Cresa South Florida LLC	C	954 676-1835
Miami (G-9437)		
Current Capital Management Inc	E	954 966-8181
Hollywood (G-5426)		
Cushman & Wakefield Fla Inc	D	813 223-6300
Tampa (G-17559)		
Cushman & Wakefield Fla Inc	E	305 371-4411
Miami (G-9446)		
Daily Management Inc	B	407 396-9086
Kissimmee (G-7293)		
Daily Management Inc	C	954 385-8599
Weston (G-19455)		
Dale E Peterson Realty Inc	D	850 654-4747
Destin (G-3055)		
Demetree Brothers Inc	D	904 398-7350
Jacksonville (G-6061)		
Dimension One Management Inc	D	904 642-1759
Jacksonville (G-6068)		
Diocese St Augustine Inc	E	904 824-2806
Jacksonville (G-6069)		
Dlc Residential LLC	C	954 455-0336
Aventura (G-267)		
Douglas Elliman Real Estate	E	561 245-2635
Boca Raton (G-556)		
Dresi LLC	E	407 917-0007
Winter Park (G-19716)		
Eagle Harbor At Fleming Island	E	904 269-4000
Orange Park (G-11986)		
East West Partners MGT Co	D	904 291-7200
Orange Park (G-11987)		
Edgewater Beach Resort LLC	C	850 235-4044
Panama City (G-13996)		
El-Ad National Properties LLC	C	954 846-7800
Plantation (G-14637)		
Elite International Realty	E	305 940-6611
Aventura (G-268)		
Energy RE Solutions LLC	D	701 713-6606
Sarasota (G-16151)		
Executive Hotel Management Inc	D	561 733-3731
Ocean Ridge (G-11801)		
Faithful Heritage Holdings Inc	D	352 372-1447
Gainesville (G-4882)		
Fannie Hillman & Assoc Inc	D	407 644-1234
Winter Park (G-19722)		
Feick Corporation	D	305 271-8550
Miami (G-9549)		
Ferdinandsen Enterprises Inc	E	407 770-1748
Kissimmee (G-7306)		
Fidelity Nat Title Insur Co	C	888 934-3354
Jacksonville (G-6160)		
Fidelity National Fincl Inc	A	904 854-8100
Jacksonville (G-6162)		
Fip Realty Services LLC	D	786 419-4539
Miami (G-9556)		
First Home Builders Fla LLC	C	239 458-8000
Cape Coral (G-1392)		
First International Exch Group	C	336 733-2000
Fort Lauderdale (G-3788)		
First Service Realty Inc	C	305 551-1518
Miami (G-9560)		
First Svc Residential Fla Inc	D	727 299-9555
Saint Petersburg (G-15671)		
First Svc Residential Fla Inc	E	407 389-4900
Altamonte Springs (G-48)		

First Svc Residential Fla Inc	C	954 925-8200
Hollywood (G-5436)		
Firstservice Residential Inc	E	954 926-2934
Dania Beach (G-2427)		
FL Sunshine Services Tampa LLC	D	727 838-8000
Port Richey (G-15102)		
Flexxspace Management LLC	E	407 926-8275
Orlando (G-12517)		
Florida Assn of Realtors	E	407 438-1400
Orlando (G-12518)		
Florida Best Realty	D	305 792-0800
Miami (G-9570)		
Florida Landarama Inc	E	561 968-7368
Greenacres (G-5071)		
Florida Penn Capital Corp	E	561 750-1030
Boca Raton (G-585)		
Florida Realty & Co LLC	E	239 500-8000
Naples (G-11120)		
Florida Realty of Miami Corp	E	305 598-5488
Miami (G-9589)		
Forest Oaks Care Center	D	352 683-3323
Spring Hill (G-16537)		
Fortune International Rlty Inc	C	305 856-2600
Miami (G-9600)		
Fortune Intl Equity Corp	D	305 351-1000
Miami (G-9601)		
Foundry Commercial LLC	D	407 540-7700
Orlando (G-12542)		
Fountins Cndominium Operations	E	561 434-2480
Lake Worth (G-7731)		
Foxfire Realty Inc	D	352 732-3344
Ocala (G-11693)		
Funnel Leasing Inc	D	833 971-2734
Odessa (G-11843)		
Get Connexions Inc	E	844 259-8599
Jacksonville (G-6229)		
GII Real Estate Partners Inc	D	407 233-1900
Orlando (G-12575)		
Goldman Properties Wynwood LLC	E	305 531-4411
Miami (G-9647)		
Grand Haven Realty LLC	E	386 447-0800
Palm Coast (G-13825)		
Grand Realty America Corp	A	305 931-7878
Miami (G-9658)		
Greenacre Properties Inc	D	813 600-1100
Tampa (G-17751)		
Greensmart Inc	D	352 214-4646
Gainesville (G-4909)		
Greystar Management Svcs LP	C	407 514-2658
Orlando (G-12604)		
Greystar Management Svcs LP	C	813 887-4200
Tampa (G-17758)		
Greystar Rs Group LLC	A	407 377-0600
Orlando (G-12605)		
Gulf Coast Commercial Corp	D	239 597-8777
Naples (G-11150)		
Harbour Cove Associates LP	D	305 371-5500
Miami (G-9683)		
Highwoods Realty Ltd Partnr	D	919 872-4924
Orlando (G-12641)		
Highwoods Realty Ltd Partnr	D	813 876-7000
Tampa (G-17823)		
Holding Co of Villages Inc	C	352 753-2270
The Villages (G-18659)		
Home Buyers Warranty Corp VI	D	954 585-6500
Plantation (G-14654)		
Home Town Realty Limited Inc	E	407 448-2073
Orlando (G-12662)		
Homeasap LLC	E	904 549-7619
Jacksonville (G-6293)		
Horizon Bay Management LLC	E	813 287-3900
Tampa (G-17841)		
Horizon Realty Management	E	904 641-1232
Jacksonville (G-6298)		
Htg Management LLC	E	305 860-8188
Miami (G-9728)		
Icahn Enterprises LP	E	305 422-4100
Sunny Isles Beach (G-16720)		
Il Marianna LLC Lcg	E	850 477-7044
Pensacola (G-14326)		
Illustrated Properties Inc	D	561 626-7000
Palm Beach Gardens (G-13739)		
In2place Investments Inc	D	813 672-6030
Apollo Beach (G-138)		
Incore Residential LLC	E	239 275-8320
Fort Myers (G-4448)		
Inland Property Management Inc	E	813 621-4359
Tampa (G-17867)		
Inman Group LLC	E	510 658-9252
Tallahassee (G-17004)		

Insignia/Esg Ht Partners Inc ....B 813 221-7474
Tampa *(G-17868)*
Interinvestments Realty Inc ....D 305 220-1101
Miami *(G-9759)*
Interval Holding Company Inc ....A 305 666-1861
South Miami *(G-16504)*
Intracoastal Real Estate Group.......B 954 812-1102
Sunny Isles Beach *(G-16722)*
Investmnt Equity Illus Prprts ....C 561 626-5100
Palm Beach Gardens *(G-13742)*
Island One Resorts Mgt Corp ....D 407 396-1300
Kissimmee *(G-7328)*
Islander Bch CLB Cndo Assn Vls.......E 386 427-7100
New Smyrna Beach *(G-11419)*
J&G Florida Enterprises LC ....D 321 207-0511
Altamonte Springs *(G-66)*
Jcr Management LLC.......E 727 397-0441
N Redngtn Bch *(G-10989)*
Jcr Management LLC.......E 727 397-0441
Indian Shores *(G-5675)*
▲ **Jeremiahs Intl Trdg Co Inc** ....C 727 321-5728
Saint Petersburg *(G-15731)*
Jetty East Condo Assn Inc.......E 850 837-2141
Destin *(G-3065)*
Jim White & Associates Inc ....E 727 367-3795
Treasure Island *(G-18710)*
Jmg Realty Inc.......C 561 451-4949
Coconut Creek *(G-1993)*
John R Wood Inc.......B 239 592-1011
Naples *(G-11184)*
John T Ferreira & Son Inc ....E 904 261-3077
Fernandina Beach *(G-3533)*
Jones Lang Lasalle Inc.......E 407 982-8550
Orlando *(G-12712)*
K & P Clearwater Estate LLC ....C 727 281-9500
Clearwater *(G-1692)*
K M D Executives Inc.......E 727 823-8000
Treasure Island *(G-18711)*
Keyes Company ....E 772 225-2222
Jensen Beach *(G-7018)*
Kroll Realty Co Inc ....E 954 771-7200
Fort Lauderdale *(G-3924)*
Kw Property MGT Consulting LLC ....A 239 495-3428
Bonita Springs *(G-926)*
Kw Property MGT Consulting LLC ....D 305 476-9188
Doral *(G-3256)*
Lake Nona Real Estate Services.......E 407 851-9091
Orlando *(G-12749)*
Landqwest Coml Orlando LLC ....E 239 275-4922
Fort Myers *(G-4469)*
Lang Realty Inc ....E 561 998-0100
Boca Raton *(G-666)*
Leary Management Group.......E 407 597-3100
Kissimmee *(G-7347)*
Leland Management Inc ....D 727 451-7900
Tampa *(G-17938)*
Leland Management Inc ....D 904 223-7224
Jacksonville *(G-6426)*
Lifespace Communities Inc ....C 561 272-7979
Delray Beach *(G-2981)*
Lincoln Harris LLC.......D 850 479-4355
Pensacola *(G-14348)*
Lnr Partners LLC.......E 305 695-5600
Miami Beach *(G-10609)*
Lofty Asset Management Inc ....E 904 730-9300
Jacksonville *(G-6444)*
Louis D Musica Jr ....D 407 298-6410
Orlando *(G-12782)*
Louis Skye Realty Inc.......C 954 529-9203
Coral Springs *(G-2269)*
Luxpro Inc.......E 844 589-7761
Bradenton *(G-1130)*
Macken Realty Inc.......E 305 933-3800
Hollywood *(G-5470)*
Magical Memories MGT Inc.......D 407 390-8200
Kissimmee *(G-7353)*
Makpow Marketing & Investments ....A 407 633-1568
Port Saint Lucie *(G-15147)*
Marcus Mllchap RE Inv Svcs Ind ....C 786 522-7000
Miami *(G-9899)*
Markus & Miller Chap Inc.......D 954 245-3400
Fort Lauderdale *(G-3960)*
Marriott Vctons Worldwide Corp ....C 407 206-6000
Orlando *(G-12820)*
Masterpiece Realty LLC ....E 772 340-2700
Port Saint Lucie *(G-15152)*
Mattamy Homes Corporation.......A 407 599-2228
Maitland *(G-8557)*
May Management Services Inc.......E 904 461-9708
Saint Augustine *(G-15467)*

McKinley Associates Inc.......E 407 291-4499
Orlando *(G-12844)*
McKinley Inc.......A 727 341-0186
Gulfport *(G-5142)*
Mdlv LLC.......E 305 666-0562
Coral Gables *(G-2143)*
Meridian Asset Services LLC.......C 727 914-2317
Saint Petersburg *(G-15762)*
Meridian Management Corp.......E 904 285-3400
Delray Beach *(G-2991)*
Meridian Trust LLC ....E 954 495-4631
Hallandale Beach *(G-5177)*
Miami Condo Solution Group Inc.......E 786 361-7289
Miami *(G-9963)*
Miami Riverfront Partners LLC ....D 781 794-1000
Miami *(G-9982)*
Michael Snders Securities Corp.......E 941 951-6660
Sarasota *(G-16232)*
Mountain Lake Corporation ....D 863 676-3494
Lake Wales *(G-7694)*
MSI Property Management Inc.......E 954 345-4991
Parkland *(G-14110)*
Mv Realty Pbc LLC.......E 561 819-2100
Delray Beach *(G-2994)*
Nafl Investments Ltd.......D 239 262-2600
Naples *(G-11222)*
Naples Realty Services Inc ....C 239 262-4333
Naples *(G-11239)*
National HM MGT Solutions LLC.......D 305 854-1711
Coral Gables *(G-2155)*
National Realty Brevard Inc ....E 321 259-7624
Melbourne *(G-8946)*
Nationwide Apprisal Netwrk LLC ....E 813 749-8841
Oldsmar *(G-11915)*
New ERA Electric Inc.......E 305 909-3126
Miami *(G-10041)*
Newport Property Ventures Ltd ....C 305 446-0010
Miami *(G-10044)*
Northwest Fla Investments Inc ....D 850 748-0065
Navarre *(G-11353)*
Olde Carriage Realty Inc ....E 904 824-3398
Saint Augustine *(G-15475)*
Opendoor Labs Inc ....D 888 352-7075
Orlando *(G-12933)*
Opulence International.......E 305 615-1376
Fort Lauderdale *(G-4030)*
Opulence Intl Rlty LLC ....E 954 308-4300
Fort Lauderdale *(G-4031)*
Orion Administration Inc.......E 305 790-3589
Miami *(G-10079)*
Osmany Mondaca PA ....D 305 396-9003
Miami *(G-10082)*
Owens Renz & Lee Co Inc.......C 407 681-2000
Orlando *(G-12995)*
Owens Realty Network LLC ....B 407 681-2000
Orlando *(G-12996)*
Owners Property MGT Corp Inc ....C 813 287-1091
Plant City *(G-14573)*
Palm Realty of Pasco Inc ....D 727 372-2121
Port Richey *(G-15106)*
Parc Group Inc ....D 904 992-9750
Jacksonville *(G-6577)*
Pepine Realty ....E 352 219-3845
Gainesville *(G-4975)*
Phoenix Organization Inc.......C 561 988-2036
Boca Raton *(G-750)*
Pinnacle 441 LLC ....E 305 854-7100
Miami *(G-10123)*
Pinnacle Realty Management Co.......E 206 215-9700
Patrick Afb *(G-14122)*
Pinnacle Realty Management Co.......D 407 660-1130
Maitland *(G-8568)*
Platinum Coast Mgt & Rlty ....D 321 242-2900
Melbourne *(G-8958)*
Platinum Elite Realty LLC ....E 239 931-9779
Fort Myers *(G-4543)*
Ponte Vedra Club Realty Inc ....D 904 285-4884
Ponte Vedra Beach *(G-15002)*
Potential Property Realty LLC ....E 305 260-6300
Weston *(G-19477)*
Precedent Management LLC.......E 786 452-1807
Doral *(G-3294)*
Premiere Plus Realty Co ....E 239 732-7837
Naples *(G-11269)*
Premiere Plus Realty Co ....E 239 206-2777
Fort Myers *(G-4551)*
Premiere Prpts of Suthwest Fla.......D 239 261-6161
Naples *(G-11270)*
Premiere Sothebys Intl Realty ....A 239 403-2200
Naples *(G-11271)*

Prime Management Group Inc.......C 561 429-8477
West Palm Beach *(G-19332)*
Prime Management Group Inc ....E 561 734-5675
Boca Raton *(G-756)*
Progressive Mgt Amer Inc.......D 850 664-6000
Destin *(G-3071)*
Property Management Resources.......D 561 969-2700
Greenacres *(G-5079)*
Proplogix LLC ....D 941 444-7142
Sarasota *(G-16046)*
Prudential Florida W C I Rlty.......D 239 394-2505
Marco Island *(G-8637)*
Prudential Florida W C I Rlty.......D 561 278-7370
Delray Beach *(G-3011)*
RA Nass Management Company.......C 386 740-7355
Deland *(G-2877)*
Rawlings Realty Inc ....E 239 482-7785
Fort Myers *(G-4565)*
RE Max of Lee County II Inc.......D 239 242-2022
Cape Coral *(G-1423)*
RE Summerville Group LLC.......E 208 370-9177
Miramar Beach *(G-10925)*
Re/Max Marketing Specialists.......D 352 686-0540
Spring Hill *(G-16545)*
Real Equity Partners Inc.......E 407 862-8000
Altamonte Springs *(G-97)*
Realty Exchange LLC ....E 386 693-4854
Flagler Beach *(G-3547)*
Realty Lv Inc.......C 727 797-4424
Clearwater *(G-1774)*
Realvest Equity Partners LLC.......E 407 875-6935
Orlando *(G-13086)*
Related Cervera Realty Inc.......D 561 651-1000
West Palm Beach *(G-19342)*
Related Management Corporation ....D 561 640-5794
West Palm Beach *(G-19343)*
Remax Professionals Inc ....E 352 375-1002
Gainesville *(G-4987)*
Renaissance At Brickell LLC ....E 786 391-3908
Miami *(G-10200)*
Reunion Wyndh Grand Golf & Spa.......E 407 662-1000
Reunion *(G-15242)*
Richman Property Services Inc.......E 727 581-9800
Clearwater *(G-1776)*
Robert Slack LLC ....E 800 210-6610
Ocala *(G-11771)*
Royal American Hospitality Inc ....E 850 230-4618
Panama City Beach *(G-14102)*
Royal American Management Inc.......E 850 769-8981
Panama City *(G-14067)*
Ryan Scott LLC ....D 954 630-3434
Fort Lauderdale *(G-4096)*
San Ann Oil Company ....D 813 286-2323
Tampa *(G-18246)*
Satchmo Properties LLC ....E 305 661-2000
Miami *(G-10242)*
Schmidt RE Fla - Morris LLC ....E 941 255-3497
Port Charlotte *(G-15058)*
Seacrest Services Inc.......C 561 697-4990
West Palm Beach *(G-19354)*
Sentry Management Inc.......E 386 423-7796
New Smyrna Beach *(G-11422)*
Sentry Management Inc.......D 407 788-6700
Longwood *(G-8403)*
Servicelink Holdings LLC.......A 904 854-8100
Jacksonville *(G-6713)*
Shorewalk Vacation Villas LLC.......E 941 794-9800
Bradenton *(G-1179)*
Showcase Prpts Investments Inc.......D 321 783-5000
Cape Canaveral *(G-1370)*
Silver Bch CLB A Fla Ltd Prtnr ....E 386 252-9681
Daytona Beach *(G-2662)*
Sky Resort Management LLC ....C 407 581-2151
Orlando *(G-13205)*
Smith & Associates Realtors ....D 813 839-3800
Tampa *(G-18298)*
Southeast Housing LLC ....D 904 270-8870
Jacksonville *(G-6750)*
Southeast Realty Connection.......E 954 783-1088
Pompano Beach *(G-14904)*
Southwest Property Management.......D 239 261-3440
Naples *(G-11301)*
Specialty MGT Co Centl Fla ....E 407 647-2622
Altamonte Springs *(G-101)*
Star Island Resort & Club.......D 407 997-8000
Kissimmee *(G-7389)*
Stephen D Snow LLC.......D 561 291-1783
Lake Worth *(G-7753)*
Sterling Companies LLC ....E 850 269-8000
Destin *(G-3079)*

Employee Codes: A=Over 500 employees, B=251-500
C=101-250, D=51-100, E=20-50, F=10-19, G=4-9

2022 Harris Florida
Manufacturers Directory

747

Stirling Intl Rlty Inc	E	407 333-1900
Orlando (G-13238)		
Stoltz Realty Co	D	561 395-9800
Boca Raton (G-821)		
Suitor & Associates Inc	E	239 437-0340
Fort Myers (G-4610)		
Sun Publications Florida Inc	D	321 402-0257
Kissimmee (G-7392)		
Sunchase American Ltd	E	850 385-9955
Tallahassee (G-17118)		
Sunstream Inc	E	239 765-9400
Fort Myers Beach (G-4673)		
Sunvest Realty	C	407 847-8200
Kissimmee (G-7394)		
Synergy Properties Inc	C	813 221-3344
Tampa (G-18356)		
Tavistock Corporation	E	407 876-8800
Windermere (G-19549)		
Telemar Inc	C	321 773-2468
Indian Harbour Beach (G-5672)		
Tempus Intl Mktg Entps	D	407 363-1717
Orlando (G-13280)		
Tempus Intl Mktg Entps	B	407 363-1717
Kissimmee (G-7396)		
Testing Matters Inc	E	888 272-1633
Sunrise (G-16838)		
Timbers Resort Management LLC	E	970 510-6796
Winter Park (G-19778)		
Travel + Leisure Co	C	407 626-5200
Orlando (G-13305)		
TWC Holding Company	E	813 281-8888
Tampa (G-18454)		
United RE Infinity LLC	D	239 288-2424
Fort Myers (G-4638)		
United Realty Group Inc	E	954 450-2000
Plantation (G-14718)		
▲ Urban Retail Properties LLC	E	561 394-6433
Boca Raton (G-853)		
Vesta Property Services Inc	A	904 355-1831
Jacksonville (G-6907)		
Vestcor Structures Inc	E	904 260-3030
Jacksonville (G-6908)		
VIP Realty Group Inc	C	239 489-1100
Fort Myers (G-4643)		
Visionary Destin Inc	D	850 650-9998
Destin (G-3081)		
Vistana Management Inc	D	407 239-3100
Orlando (G-13383)		
Voxtur Appraisal Services LLC	E	888 852-5380
Tampa (G-18513)		
Voxtur Appraisal Services LLC	C	800 778-4915
Tampa (G-18514)		
Walgreen Co	E	407 933-8101
Kissimmee (G-7407)		
Watermark Realty Inc	E	954 693-0100
Sunrise (G-16845)		
Watson Realty Corp	E	904 596-5960
Jacksonville (G-6922)		
▲ WCI Communities Inc	D	239 947-2600
Fort Myers (G-4650)		
Weller Workforce LLC	C	727 498-8823
Saint Petersburg (G-15893)		
Williams Island Property Owner	C	305 935-5555
Miami (G-10506)		
Woolbright Development Inc	D	561 989-2240
Boca Raton (G-877)		
Wrh Realty Services Inc	C	727 892-3000
Saint Petersburg (G-15898)		
Wyndham Resort Dev Corp	C	866 495-1924
Orlando (G-13456)		
Wyndham Vacation Ownership Inc	C	407 370-5200
Orlando (G-13457)		
Wyndham Vacation Resorts Inc	C	850 837-8866
Destin (G-3091)		
Wyndham Vacation Resorts Inc	C	407 351-2641
Orlando (G-13459)		
Wyndham Vacation Resorts Inc	C	407 238-3100
Orlando (G-13460)		
Wyndham Vacation Resorts Inc	C	954 233-7500
Pompano Beach (G-14944)		
Yellowfin Realty Group LLC	D	813 229-8862
Riverview (G-15275)		
Zom Development Inc	D	954 779-7950
Fort Lauderdale (G-4240)		
Zom Development Inc	C	305 674-5880
Miami Beach (G-10676)		
Zom Development Inc	E	407 644-6300
Orlando (G-13473)		

6541 Title Abstract Offices

Americas Title Corp	E	813 225-1231
Tampa (G-17279)		
Atif Inc	B	407 240-3863
Fort Myers (G-4282)		
Atif Inc	C	407 240-4440
Orlando (G-12146)		
Attorneys Title Fund Svcs LLC	E	386 788-9869
Port Orange (G-15069)		
Attorneys Title Fund Svcs LLC	E	305 459-2640
Doral (G-3129)		
Attorneys Title Fund Svcs LLC	E	305 459-2640
Doral (G-3130)		
Attorneys Title Fund Svcs LLC	E	813 740-1900
Tampa (G-17319)		
Attorneys Title Fund Svcs LLC	C	407 240-3863
Orlando (G-12151)		
Attorneys Title Fund Svcs LLC	E	954 771-0150
Fort Lauderdale (G-3619)		
Attorneys Title Fund Svcs LLC	E	772 879-1770
Port Saint Lucie (G-15123)		
Attorneys Title Fund Svcs LLC	E	407 240-4440
Orlando (G-12152)		
Buyers Title Inc	D	954 915-8450
Fort Lauderdale (G-3661)		
Chicago Title Insurance Co	A	772 221-3853
Stuart (G-16603)		
Fidelity Nat Title Insur Co	C	888 934-3354
Jacksonville (G-6160)		
First American Title	C	866 808-9092
Clearwater (G-1636)		
First American Title Insur Co	E	850 402-4101
Tallahassee (G-16950)		
First American Title Insur Co	D	407 691-5200
Maitland (G-8531)		
Inspired Title Services LLC	E	407 439-0137
Maitland (G-8542)		
Landcastle Title Group LLC	C	407 961-5560
Altamonte Springs (G-68)		
MLS Title LLC	E	239 768-7050
Fort Myers (G-4516)		
Nationwide Title Clearing LLC	A	727 771-4000
Palm Harbor (G-13871)		
Red Vision Systems Inc	D	352 331-8242
Gainesville (G-4985)		
Select MGT Resources LLC	E	904 538-0694
Jacksonville Beach (G-7002)		
St Joe Title Services LLC	B	727 360-7913
St Pete Beach (G-16570)		
St Joe Title Services LLC	B	407 926-4383
Orlando (G-13230)		
Sunstate Title Agency Inc	E	352 567-1141
Zephyrhills (G-19851)		
Timeshare Closing Services LLC	C	407 370-2373
Orlando (G-13289)		
Universal Land Title LLC	C	561 767-3120
Boynton Beach (G-1041)		
Universal Land Title S Fla Ltd	D	561 689-8200
West Palm Beach (G-19402)		
Vantage Point Title Inc	E	727 483-9112
Clearwater (G-1831)		

6552 Land Subdividers & Developers

◆ A Duda & Sons Inc	D	407 365-2111
Oviedo (G-13536)		
A M J Inc of Gainesville	E	352 371-8100
Gainesville (G-4827)		
▼ Adler Phillips Cnstr Inc	E	305 392-4000
Sweetwater (G-16856)		
Ahs Development Group LLC	C	305 255-5527
Miami (G-9104)		
Ahs Residential LLC	E	305 255-5527
Miami (G-9105)		
Amelia Island Company	A	904 261-6161
Fernandina Beach (G-3521)		
▲ American Engineering Pdts Corp	D	305 825-9800
Hialeah (G-5216)		
Anglers Club Inc	E	305 367-2382
Key Largo (G-7171)		
Avatar Properties Inc	D	407 933-5000
Kissimmee (G-7419)		
Barclay Group Hldings Ltd Lllp	E	727 733-7585
Tampa (G-17337)		
◆ Big O Tires LLC	D	561 383-3000
Palm Beach Gardens (G-13694)		
Bluegreen Vacations Corp	A	561 912-8000
Surfside (G-16852)		
Briar Team LLC	C	407 321-2773
Sanford (G-15927)		

Carlisle Group Inc	D	305 476-8118
Miami (G-9325)		
Catalfumo Cnstr & Dev Inc	C	561 694-3000
Palm Beach Gardens (G-13699)		
Central Fla Investments Inc	E	407 354-3040
Orlando (G-12265)		
Central Site Development LLC	C	813 621-7800
Brandon (G-1221)		
Codina Partners LLC	C	305 529-1300
Coral Gables (G-2074)		
Collier Enterprises	E	239 261-5307
Naples (G-11065)		
Commons Medical Dev Inc	E	407 425-8454
Orlando (G-12349)		
Concord Mlstone Plus Ltd Prtne	E	561 394-9260
Boca Raton (G-524)		
Construction Developers Inc	A	305 936-9802
Miami (G-9405)		
▲ Cornerstone Group Inc	C	305 443-8288
Hollywood (G-5418)		
Courtelis Company	D	305 261-4330
Miami (G-9431)		
Crescent Heights America Inc	D	305 374-5700
Miami (G-9438)		
Cypress Gulf Development Corp	E	813 241-6200
Oldsmar (G-11899)		
Dale E Peterson Realty Inc	D	850 654-4747
Destin (G-3055)		
David Barron Land Dev Inc	C	239 425-0260
Fort Myers (G-4340)		
Deer Creek Inc	E	863 424-2839
Davenport (G-2439)		
Del Webb Corporation	C	239 304-2835
Ave Maria (G-262)		
Del Webb Corporation	E	904 217-0005
Ponte Vedra (G-14962)		
Demetree Brothers Inc	D	904 398-7350
Jacksonville (G-6061)		
Devlin Group Inc	E	904 543-0026
Jacksonville Beach (G-6983)		
Divosta Homes LP	D	561 691-9050
Palm Beach Gardens (G-13719)		
Dolphin Mall Associates LP	E	305 365-7446
Miami (G-9484)		
Dune FL Land I Sub LLC	E	813 288-8078
Tampa (G-17603)		
Eagle Harbor At Fleming Island	E	904 269-4000
Orange Park (G-11986)		
Earthmark Companies LLC	D	239 415-6200
Fort Myers (G-4350)		
East West Partners MGT Co	C	904 291-7200
Orange Park (G-11987)		
◆ Fanjul Corp	D	561 655-6303
West Palm Beach (G-19136)		
◆ Flo Sun Land Corporation	D	561 655-6303
Palm Beach (G-13655)		
Gate Lands Company	B	904 737-7220
Jacksonville (G-6216)		
Glen Lakes Realty LLC	D	352 597-9000
Weeki Wachee (G-18968)		
Goldman Properties Wynwood LLC	E	305 531-4411
Miami (G-9647)		
Gunnstruction Inc	E	321 455-6498
Merritt Island (G-9030)		
Hobe Sound Associates Inc	E	772 546-4600
Hobe Sound (G-5364)		
▲ Holiday Inn Club Vacations Inc	A	407 239-0000
Orlando (G-12656)		
Homeasap LLC	E	904 549-7619
Jacksonville (G-6293)		
Indian River Colony Club Inc	C	321 255-6000
Melbourne (G-8911)		
James C Hall Company Inc	E	407 327-4930
Winter Springs (G-19806)		
Jax Utilities Management Inc	D	904 779-5353
Jacksonville (G-6379)		
Kearney Construction Co LLC	B	813 621-0855
Riverview (G-15259)		
◆ Keystone Holdings Group LLC	A	305 567-1577
Miami (G-9827)		
Lansbrook Group Inc	E	727 784-7675
Palm Harbor (G-13869)		
Len-Angeline LLC	E	813 288-8078
Tampa (G-17939)		
Lennar Corporation	A	305 559-4000
Miami (G-9858)		
Lexington Community Assn Inc	C	239 437-0404
Fort Myers (G-4496)		
Lwr Development LLC	D	941 755-6574
Lakewood Ranch (G-8025)		

M L Partnership.................................C...... 904 285-6514
  Ponte Vedra Beach *(G-14990)*

Newport Partners...............................D...... 407 333-2905
  Lake Mary *(G-7616)*

North Brook Holdings LLC...................E...... 813 288-8078
  Tampa *(G-18089)*

Oak & Stone......................................E...... 813 288-8078
  Tampa *(G-18092)*

Oak Run Associates Ltd.....................C...... 352 414-4309
  Ocala *(G-11744)*

Ocean Properties Ltd.........................C...... 603 559-2100
  Delray Beach *(G-2999)*

Palm Beach Polo Inc..........................D...... 561 798-7000
  West Palm Beach *(G-19316)*

Parc Group Inc...................................D...... 904 992-9750
  Jacksonville *(G-6577)*

Pasteur Med Miami Grdns LLC.............C...... 305 722-8565
  Miami *(G-10100)*

Peter D Cummings & Assoc Inc...........E...... 561 630-6110
  Palm Beach Gardens *(G-13763)*

Powers Development Group Inc...........D...... 904 619-9355
  Macclenny *(G-8478)*

Premiere Prpts of Suthwest Fla...........D...... 239 261-6161
  Naples *(G-11270)*

Pursley Inc..C...... 800 683-7584
  Bradenton *(G-1167)*

Rayonier Inc......................................D...... 904 357-9100
  Yulee *(G-19820)*

Real Sub LLC.....................................A...... 863 688-1188
  Lakeland *(G-7951)*

Realvest Equity Partners LLC.............E...... 407 875-6935
  Orlando *(G-13086)*

Related Companies of Fla Inc..............D...... 305 460-9900
  Miami *(G-10199)*

Ronto Management Group Inc..............D...... 239 649-6310
  Naples *(G-11287)*

Royal American Development...............B...... 305 259-3407
  Miami *(G-10219)*

Schroeder Manatee Inc.......................D...... 941 755-1637
  Lakewood Ranch *(G-8030)*

Scottsdale Co....................................E...... 239 261-6100
  Naples *(G-11295)*

Seminole Tribe of Florida Inc...............A...... 813 627-7625
  Tampa *(G-18265)*

Signet Enterprises LLC.......................D...... 904 350-1314
  Jacksonville *(G-6727)*

Spanish Trace Housing Ltd..................A...... 203 869-0900
  Tampa *(G-18315)*

Sunrise Mills Ltd Partnership..............E...... 954 846-2300
  Sunrise *(G-16832)*

Tampa Innkeepers LLC........................D...... 813 971-8930
  Tampa *(G-18387)*

Tesoro Club LLC.................................E...... 772 345-4010
  Port Saint Lucie *(G-15171)*

◆ Turnberry Associates.......................D...... 305 937-6262
  Miami *(G-10418)*

TWC Holding Company........................E...... 813 281-8888
  Tampa *(G-18454)*

Vector Group Ltd.................................D...... 305 579-8000
  Miami *(G-10461)*

Verbena LLC......................................E...... 305 854-7100
  Miami *(G-10464)*

◆ Villages of Lake-Sumter Inc.............A...... 352 753-2270
  Lady Lake *(G-7447)*

Vineyards Development Corp...............D...... 239 353-1551
  Naples *(G-11337)*

Westfield Development Corp Fla...........D...... 813 282-1616
  Tampa *(G-18545)*

Williams Island Associates..................E...... 305 935-5555
  Aventura *(G-285)*

Windsor...D...... 772 388-8430
  Vero Beach *(G-18949)*

Wynne Building Corporation................C...... 305 235-3175
  Miami *(G-10518)*

Zom Development Inc..........................D...... 954 779-7950
  Fort Lauderdale *(G-4240)*

Zom Development Inc..........................C...... 305 674-5880
  Miami Beach *(G-10676)*

6553 Cemetery Subdividers & Developers

Cemetery Management Inc...................B...... 813 626-3161
  Tampa *(G-17439)*

Codina Management LLC.....................E...... 305 529-1300
  Doral *(G-3155)*

Dignity Memorial................................E...... 407 647-1100
  Winter Park *(G-19713)*

Diocese St Petersburg Inc...................D...... 727 572-4355
  Clearwater *(G-1606)*

Jacksonville Jewish Center..................D...... 904 292-1000
  Jacksonville *(G-6363)*

Pershing Industries Inc.......................D...... 305 821-1421
  Miami Lakes *(G-10753)*

67 HOLDING AND OTHER INVESTMENT OFFICES

6712 Offices Of Bank Holding Co's

FBC Bancorp Inc.................................E...... 407 246-7772
  Orlando *(G-12498)*

Marine Bancorp Florida Inc..................D...... 772 231-6611
  Vero Beach *(G-18891)*

Orion Bancorp Inc...............................D...... 239 434-6974
  Naples *(G-11253)*

Raymond James Fincl Svcs Inc............D...... 727 567-1000
  Saint Petersburg *(G-15819)*

6719 Offices Of Holding Co's, NEC

Aamp Holdings Inc..............................D...... 727 572-9255
  Clearwater *(G-1509)*

Abb-Diversified Holding Corp...............E...... 800 852-8089
  Coral Springs *(G-2216)*

Acquiescent Holdings Inc....................E...... 877 983-2443
  Sarasota *(G-16018)*

Advanced Disposal Svcs S LLC............E...... 904 737-7900
  Ponte Vedra *(G-14947)*

Agro-Iron Inc......................................E...... 863 648-9555
  Lakeland *(G-7789)*

◆ Altadis Holdings USA Inc..................D...... 954 772-9000
  Fort Lauderdale *(G-3597)*

Amports Midco Inc..............................A...... 904 265-6272
  Jacksonville *(G-5796)*

Apak LLC...E...... 727 546-8974
  Clearwater *(G-1522)*

Askari Holding Corp............................D...... 904 780-2021
  Jacksonville *(G-5810)*

Bch-A Orlando Holdings LLC................D...... 407 313-1234
  Orlando *(G-12175)*

Best Doctors Insur Svcs LLC................C...... 305 269-2521
  Miami *(G-9248)*

Buccaneer Holdings LLC.....................A...... 813 637-5000
  Tampa *(G-17395)*

Cenvill Recreation Inc.........................C...... 561 640-7511
  West Palm Beach *(G-19081)*

Cheddars Restaurant Holdg Corp.........E...... 214 596-6700
  Orlando *(G-12292)*

▲ Cnl Financial Group Inc...................D...... 407 650-1000
  Orlando *(G-12328)*

Comvest Group Holdings LP.................D...... 561 727-2000
  West Palm Beach *(G-19103)*

Cross Match Holdings Inc....................D...... 561 622-1650
  Palm Beach Gardens *(G-13712)*

Cv Family Enterprises Inc....................C...... 407 842-7000
  Kissimmee *(G-7292)*

Dar Holdings Inc.................................E...... 305 235-1604
  Miami *(G-9457)*

Diverse Holdings LLC..........................E...... 561 805-1500
  Boca Raton *(G-555)*

Doral Carolina Ale House LLC..............D...... 919 851-0858
  Doral *(G-3179)*

Doublejo Tribe Inc..............................E...... 786 267-8061
  Fort Lauderdale *(G-3763)*

Fh Construction Marion LLC.................D...... 352 236-3355
  Ocala *(G-11680)*

Fish Tale Investments Inc....................D...... 239 949-2583
  Estero *(G-3457)*

Florida Bc Holdings LLC......................C...... 407 273-7383
  Orlando *(G-12519)*

Greylind Corp.....................................E...... 334 389-6955
  Seminole *(G-16449)*

Health Grid Holding Company...............D...... 844 367-4743
  Orlando *(G-12629)*

Health Holdings Company LLC..............C...... 305 913-9444
  Coral Gables *(G-2121)*

Hencorp Becstone LC..........................E...... 305 373-9000
  Miami *(G-9694)*

Herban Holdings Inc............................D...... 305 249-1239
  Miami *(G-9695)*

Icbd Holdings LLC...............................C...... 833 575-2500
  West Palm Beach *(G-19195)*

IEM Holdings Group Inc.......................C...... 904 365-4393
  Jacksonville *(G-6309)*

J&J Produce Holdings Inc....................C...... 561 422-9777
  City of Westlake *(G-1502)*

Jae Miami Dade LLC............................A...... 561 997-6002
  Pompano Beach *(G-14832)*

Las Palmas Inv Tr Holdings LLC...........E...... 305 913-5440
  Miami *(G-9848)*

Lincoln Merger Sub Two LLC................A...... 561 438-4800
  Boca Raton *(G-673)*

Lsq Group LLC...................................D...... 407 206-0022
  Orlando *(G-12790)*

▲ Manitwoc Fdsrvice Cmpanies LLC...D...... 727 375-7010
  Trinity *(G-18727)*

McFarlin Group Inc..............................C...... 407 425-3170
  Orlando *(G-12843)*

Medical Developers LLC.......................E...... 239 461-8589
  Fort Myers *(G-4510)*

Modani Holdings LLC...........................E...... 786 362-5516
  Miami *(G-10010)*

Msk RE Holdings LLC..........................D...... 386 233-9009
  Orange City *(G-11969)*

New World Holdings Inc.......................E...... 561 888-4939
  Delray Beach *(G-2995)*

OBrien Imports Ft Myers Inc.................D...... 239 277-1222
  Fort Myers *(G-4525)*

Optimum Icd Holdings LLC...................D...... 912 526-3575
  Delray Beach *(G-3001)*

Palm Coast Data Holdco Inc.................B...... 386 445-4662
  Bunnell *(G-1324)*

Pb Parent Holdco LP...........................A...... 800 927-8610
  Saint Petersburg *(G-15792)*

Pershard Clipper LLC...........................D...... 317 417-8284
  Greenacres *(G-5077)*

▲ Riverdale Farms LLC........................E...... 305 592-5760
  Doral *(G-3299)*

Rutherford Med Holdings LLC...............D...... 904 636-5600
  Jacksonville *(G-6682)*

Ryan Holdings Inc...............................D...... 321 268-2000
  Titusville *(G-18702)*

Senoma Inc..E...... 954 979-6364
  Deerfield Beach *(G-2795)*

Simply Chosen Wealth MGT...................C...... 786 872-4948
  Miami *(G-10274)*

Simply Healthcare Holdings Inc............E...... 877 915-0551
  Miami *(G-10275)*

Triton Group Holdings LLC...................B...... 561 401-2099
  Jupiter *(G-7147)*

Tropical Shipg Cnstr Hldngs Lt.............A...... 561 881-3900
  Riviera Beach *(G-15326)*

V P Holdings Inc.................................A...... 727 393-1270
  Saint Petersburg *(G-15883)*

Viewpost Holdings LLC........................C...... 407 515-6700
  Orlando *(G-13375)*

Wellspring Usa LLC.............................D...... 407 232-7130
  Orlando *(G-13416)*

You Technology Inc.............................C...... 877 787-1187
  Delray Beach *(G-3036)*

6722 Management Investment Offices

Affiliated Managers Group Inc.............D...... 800 345-1100
  West Palm Beach *(G-19023)*

Alliancebernstein LP...........................C...... 305 358-2253
  Hialeah *(G-5215)*

Alliancebernstein LP...........................B...... 561 820-2100
  West Palm Beach *(G-19028)*

Bainbridge Communities MGT Inc.........E...... 407 349-8864
  Casselberry *(G-1443)*

Bayview Fncl Small Bus Fnding.............B...... 305 854-8880
  Coral Gables *(G-2046)*

Bayview Lnding Group Hldngs LL...........A...... 305 854-8880
  Coral Gables *(G-2047)*

Bear Atlantic Group LLC......................E...... 305 507-5545
  Miami *(G-9235)*

Eagle Small Cap Stock Fund................D...... 800 237-3101
  Saint Petersburg *(G-15658)*

Falcone Group LLC..............................D...... 561 961-1000
  Boca Raton *(G-572)*

Florida Sheriffs Risk MGT Fund............D...... 850 320-6880
  Tallahassee *(G-16980)*

Franklin Tmpleton Inv Svcs LLC............C...... 727 299-8712
  Saint Petersburg *(G-15681)*

Icahn Enterprises LP...........................E...... 305 422-4100
  Sunny Isles Beach *(G-16720)*

Jacksonville Police and........................C...... 904 255-7373
  Jacksonville *(G-6365)*

Merrill Lynch Prce Fnner Smith.............B...... 904 634-6000
  Jacksonville *(G-6498)*

Raymond James & Associates Inc.........A...... 727 567-1000
  Saint Petersburg *(G-15816)*

Signet LLC...C...... 904 350-1314
  Jacksonville *(G-6725)*

6726 Unit Investment Trusts, Face-Amount Certificate Offices

Ae Industrial Partners LP.....................E...... 561 372-7820
  Boca Raton *(G-405)*

Atlantic Land & Imprv Co Inc................D...... 904 359-3100
  Jacksonville *(G-5815)*

Fcp Investors Inc ....D...... 813 222-8000
Tampa (G-17652)
Iap Worldwide Services Inc ....D...... 321 784-7100
Cape Canaveral (G-1368)
Industry Fintech Inc ....D...... 646 854-9996
Miami (G-9747)
Stillwell Holdings LLC ....C...... 646 580-6581
Miami (G-10333)
Transmrica Blckrock Globl Allc .....C...... 888 233-4339
Saint Petersburg (G-15878)

6732 Education, Religious & Charitable Trusts

Adrienne Arsht Center Tr Inc ....E...... 786 468-2223
Miami (G-9089)
Childrens Trust ....D...... 305 571-5700
Miami (G-9365)

6733 Trusts Except Educational, Religious & Charitable

Bankunited Statutory Trust Xi ......A...... 305 569-2000
Coral Gables (G-2043)
Dlc Capital Management LLC ....E...... 516 996-9369
Miami Beach (G-10584)
▲ Fiduciary Trust Intl of S ....C...... 305 372-1260
Coral Gables (G-2106)
Hill Ward Henderson Prof Assn ......C...... 813 221-3900
Tampa (G-17824)
Investors Trust ADM LLC ....D...... 305 603-1400
Miami (G-9777)
Lee Memorial Health System ....C...... 239 418-2000
Fort Myers (G-4487)
Maracaibo & Orlando Ex LLC ....D...... 321 274-6635
Daytona Beach (G-2630)
Mills Mehr & Associates Inc ....D...... 727 669-0140
Clearwater (G-1722)
Osceola Lead Gnrtion Hldngs LL .....E...... 813 703-2406
Tampa (G-18109)
Public Hlth Tr Miami Dade Cnty .....B...... 305 547-2500
Miami (G-10160)
Public Hlth Trust of Mm-Dade C .....B...... 305 251-2500
Palmetto Bay (G-13949)
Public Hlth Trust of Mm-Dade C .....B...... 305 585-1152
Miami (G-10163)
Public Hlth Trust of Mm-Dade C .....A...... 786 466-3000
Miami (G-10166)
Public Hlth Trust of Mm-Dade C .....A...... 305 585-1111
Miami (G-10167)
Public Hlth Trust of Mm-Dade C .....B...... 786 466-8003
Miami (G-10168)
State Board of ADM Fla ....C...... 850 488-4406
Tallahassee (G-17113)
Trust Hills Company Ltd ....D...... 833 464-4557
Boca Raton (G-848)
Trustees Mease Hospital Inc ....C...... 727 725-6226
Safety Harbor (G-15416)
U S Trust Company Fla Sav Bnk .....D...... 561 653-5984
Palm Beach (G-13674)
United Fincl Resources Corp ....E...... 941 214-0454
University Park (G-18743)
University Community Hosp Inc ......D...... 813 971-6000
Tampa (G-18476)
Vanguard Alliance Land Trustee .....E...... 727 819-2773
Tarpon Springs (G-18596)

6794 Patent Owners & Lessors

1-800-Boardup Inc ....E...... 904 758-8000
Jacksonville Beach (G-6972)
Actikare Inc ....E...... 888 451-5273
Tampa (G-17231)
▲ Adecco Usa Inc ....C...... 904 360-2000
Jacksonville (G-5735)
Ahcglobal Inc ....E...... 954 341-5600
Coral Springs (G-2220)
American Recruiters Inc ....E...... 954 493-9200
Coral Springs (G-2227)
Assignment America Llc ....C...... 561 998-2232
Boca Raton (G-429)
Barnies Coffee & Tea Co Inc ....D...... 305 259-0524
Miami (G-9224)
◆ Benihana Inc ....D...... 305 593-0770
Miami (G-9240)
Benihana National Corporation ......C...... 305 593-0770
Miami (G-9241)
Buddys Newco LLC ....D...... 813 623-5461
Orlando (G-12215)
◆ Burger King Corporation ....B...... 305 378-3000
Miami (G-9296)

▲ Burger King Holdings Inc ....D...... 305 378-3000
Miami (G-9297)
Checkers Drive-In Rest Inc ....C...... 813 283-7000
Tampa (G-17462)
Coverall North America Inc ....B...... 561 922-2500
Deerfield Beach (G-2729)
Csi Companies Inc ....D...... 904 338-9515
Jacksonville (G-6027)
◆ Darden Restaurants Inc ....A...... 407 245-4000
Orlando (G-12402)
Dollar Thrifty Auto Group Inc ......A...... 239 301-7000
Estero (G-3452)
Earl of Sandwich (usa) LLC ....E...... 407 903-5500
Orlando (G-12448)
First Watch Restaurants Inc ....D...... 941 907-9800
Bradenton (G-1099)
Front Burner Brands Inc ....D...... 813 881-0055
Tampa (G-17716)
Half-Full Holdings Inc ....E...... 954 801-9597
Hallandale Beach (G-5172)
Happy Tax Franchising LLC ....C...... 844 426-1040
Miami Beach (G-10599)
▲ Hard Rock Cafe Intl USA Inc .....B...... 954 488-7800
Davie (G-2485)
Hc (usa) Inc ....D...... 561 361-7600
Boca Raton (G-622)
▼ Hertz Corporation ....A...... 239 301-7000
Estero (G-3460)
Ideal Image Development Corp .....C...... 813 286-8100
Tampa (G-17854)
Interfoods of America Inc ....A...... 305 670-0746
Miami (G-9757)
Lemnature Aquafarms Usa Inc .....C...... 772 207-4794
Vero Beach (G-18886)
Medical Doctor Associates LLC .....D...... 561 998-2232
Boca Raton (G-686)
▲ Melting Pot Restaurants Inc ......D...... 813 881-0055
Tampa (G-18022)
Merit Professional Coatings ....E...... 813 979-6146
Tampa (G-18027)
▲ Midas Inc ....C...... 561 383-3100
Palm Beach Gardens (G-13753)
▲ Midas International LLC ....C...... 561 383-3100
Palm Beach Gardens (G-13754)
Money Mailer LLC ....C...... 714 889-3800
Cape Coral (G-1416)
Mriglobal ....E...... 321 722-1556
Palm Bay (G-13629)
Our Town Inc ....D...... 800 497-8360
Clearwater (G-1751)
Parabel Inc ....E...... 321 409-7415
Melbourne (G-8956)
Planet Hollywood Intl Inc ....C...... 407 903-5500
Orlando (G-13034)
Pods Enterprises LLC ....C...... 727 538-6300
Clearwater (G-1761)
Pods of Seattle LLC ....B...... 727 538-6300
Clearwater (G-1762)
▲ Pollo Operations Inc ....E...... 305 671-1225
Miami (G-10132)
Porpoise Pool & Patio Inc ....C...... 727 531-8913
Clearwater (G-1763)
Preferred Care At Home ....E...... 561 455-2627
Delray Beach (G-3009)
◆ Ripley Entertainment Inc ....E...... 407 345-8010
Orlando (G-13113)
Ruths Hospitality Group Inc ....C...... 407 333-7440
Winter Park (G-19773)
▲ Sfn Group Inc ....E...... 954 308-7600
Fort Lauderdale (G-4117)
Shulas Steak Houses Lllp ....E...... 954 393-1924
Fort Lauderdale (G-4124)
Thrifty LLC ....D...... 239 301-7000
Estero (G-3482)
◆ Tnb Inc ....E...... 407 444-6322
Sanford (G-15987)
◆ Tracfone Wireless Inc ....C...... 305 715-6500
Medley (G-8791)
Ubreakifix Co ....B...... 877 320-2237
Orlando (G-13322)
US Lawns Inc ....D...... 407 246-1630
Orlando (G-13360)
Valpak Direct Mktg Systems Inc .....A...... 727 399-3175
Saint Petersburg (G-15884)
Wyndham Resort Dev Corp ....C...... 866 495-1924
Orlando (G-13456)

6798 Real Estate Investment Trusts

Adler Group Inc ....D...... 305 392-4000
Sweetwater (G-16855)

C W Investment Group Ltd Inc .....E...... 305 220-6748
Miami (G-9298)
Duke Construction Ltd Partnr ....E...... 407 241-0000
Orlando (G-12445)
Gables Construction Inc ....C...... 561 997-9700
Boca Raton (G-594)
Geo Group Inc ....E...... 561 992-9505
South Bay (G-16480)
Lion Gables Realty Ltd Partnr ......D...... 561 997-9700
Boca Raton (G-674)
Orange Lake Country Club Rlty ......E...... 407 239-0000
Kissimmee (G-7363)
Parkway Inc ....E...... 407 650-0593
Orlando (G-13008)
RAD Diversified Reit Inc ....D...... 949 606-2225
Tampa (G-18196)
Rayonier Inc ....D...... 904 357-9100
Yulee (G-19820)
Regency Centers Corporation ......C...... 904 598-7000
Jacksonville (G-6646)
United Shares Real Estate LLC .....D...... 407 996-1290
Orlando (G-13341)

6799 Investors, NEC

Agmus Ventures Inc ....D...... 407 243-1846
Orlando (G-12079)
Airspan Networks Holdings Inc .....E...... 917 592-7979
Boca Raton (G-406)
Alinian Capital Group LLC ....A...... 954 495-2040
Fort Lauderdale (G-3590)
Alliancebernstein LP ....C...... 813 314-3300
Tampa (G-17266)
Ameriform Acquisition Co LLC .....D...... 248 454-1977
Naples (G-11012)
Amzak Capital Management Llc .....C...... 561 953-4164
Boca Raton (G-422)
Anzu Partners LLC ....E...... 941 773-1615
Tampa (G-17292)
Apollo Funding LLC ....E...... 561 290-4000
Palm Beach Gardens (G-13685)
Assuredpartners Inc ....B...... 407 804-5222
Lake Mary (G-7570)
Aua Prvate Equity Partners LLC .....B...... 212 231-8600
West Palm Beach (G-19042)
Boston Diagnostic Imaging ....C...... 407 656-6040
Ocoee (G-11806)
Capital Confirmation Inc ....C...... 561 404-1015
Delray Beach (G-2924)
Cnl Securities Corp ....D...... 407 399-2310
Orlando (G-12329)
Cnl Strategic Capital LLC ....D...... 407 650-1000
Orlando (G-12330)
Collier Entps Gainesville Inc ....C...... 352 375-2152
Gainesville (G-4867)
Compass Resorts LLC ....E...... 850 269-1005
Destin (G-3054)
Comvest Group Holdings LP ....D...... 561 727-2000
West Palm Beach (G-19103)
Crm Holdings & Investments ....E...... 561 491-9503
Lake Worth (G-7721)
Fcp Investors Inc ....D...... 813 222-8000
Tampa (G-17652)
Gem Capital Multiservice LLC ......E...... 407 686-0281
Saint Cloud (G-15523)
Gqg Partners LLC ....D...... 754 218-5500
Fort Lauderdale (G-3828)
Hammock Bch Acqstion Group LLC ...D...... 866 841-0287
Palm Coast (G-13827)
Inomax LLC ....A...... 561 868-6060
West Palm Beach (G-19201)
Interntional A Trnspt Assn Inc ......C...... 305 264-7772
Miami (G-9771)
Lutfi Investment Co Inc ....D...... 407 506-1200
Orlando (G-12792)
Macquarie Global Svcs USA LLC .....E...... 212 231-1000
Jacksonville (G-6459)
MBC Capital Investment Corp ....D...... 813 477-2725
Lithia (G-8302)
McTempo Investments Inc ....D...... 727 572-9999
Saint Petersburg (G-15758)
My Community Homes LLC ....E...... 305 390-8435
Miami Lakes (G-10746)
New Urban Forestry LLC ....D...... 706 389-0398
Orlando (G-12911)
Palm Beach Capital Fund I LP ....D...... 561 659-9022
West Palm Beach (G-19309)
Ri/Bbnm Acquisition Corp ....D...... 954 769-7000
Fort Lauderdale (G-4091)
Rialto Capital Advisors LLC ....D...... 305 485-2077
Miami (G-10213)

Royal Palm Companies LLC .... E 786 363-9050
Miami *(G-10222)*
RV Investment Group LLC .... E 772 300-1000
Vero Beach *(G-18912)*
Starz Acquisition LLC .... E 239 482-7829
Fort Myers *(G-4605)*
Sun Capital Partners Inc .... D 561 394-0550
Boca Raton *(G-830)*
Sun Land Capital Corporation .... E 954 684-5684
Pembroke Pines *(G-14193)*
Sunbelt Acquisition II Fla LLC .... E 321 631-1003
Rockledge *(G-15373)*
Surgical Capital Solutions .... E 727 784-3500
Clearwater *(G-1810)*
Sy-Klone Holdings Incorporated .... E 904 448-6563
Jacksonville *(G-6823)*
T3 Trading Group LLC .... C 561 961-4455
Boca Raton *(G-834)*
Targhee Energy LLC .... E 720 778-2013
Coral Gables *(G-2194)*
Trivest Fund III LP .... E 305 858-2200
Coral Gables *(G-2199)*

70 HOTELS, ROOMING HOUSES, CAMPS, AND OTHER LODGING PLACES

7011 Hotels, Motels & Tourist Courts

1 Hotel South Beach Inc .... C 305 604-1000
Miami Beach *(G-10533)*
1600 Collins Avenue LLC .... D 305 695-7400
Miami Beach *(G-10534)*
1701 Collins Miami Oper Co LLC .... D 305 674-1701
Miami Beach *(G-10535)*
18001 Holdings LLC .... D 305 692-5600
Sunny Isles Beach *(G-16711)*
211 Tampa Lessee LLC .... E 813 204-3000
Tampa *(G-17210)*
2301 SE 17th St LLC .... B 954 525-6666
Fort Lauderdale *(G-3564)*
315 Flagler Qozb Owner LLC .... E 954 769-9982
Fort Lauderdale *(G-3566)*
3420 Collins Avenue LLC .... D 305 534-8800
Miami Beach *(G-10537)*
3900 NW LLC .... D 305 871-3800
Miami *(G-9057)*
401 North Wabash Ave Hotel Con .... D 305 592-2000
Doral *(G-3094)*
5 Star Hospitality LLC .... E 561 719-4317
North Palm Beach *(G-11540)*
6 Continents Travel Netwrk LLC .... C 888 508-4805
Pembroke Pines *(G-14128)*
6515 Idrive Resort LLC .... B 407 996-0900
Orlando *(G-12031)*
700 Corp .... E 954 563-2451
Fort Lauderdale *(G-3570)*
8040 Palm Pkwy Trs LLC .... E 407 635-8500
Orlando *(G-12032)*
900 North Atlantic Ave LLC .... D 386 947-7300
Daytona Beach *(G-2538)*
905 N Fla Ave Prprty Owner LLC .... E 813 225-1700
Tampa *(G-17215)*
A-R HHC Orlndo Cnvntion Ht LLC .... B 407 313-4300
Orlando *(G-12035)*
A1a Acquisition Group Ltd LLP .... D 321 323-1100
Cape Canaveral *(G-1347)*
A1a Clipper LLC .... B 954 524-5551
Fort Lauderdale *(G-3572)*
A1a Trader LLC .... C 954 467-1111
Fort Lauderdale *(G-3573)*
Aaditya Inc .... D 407 645-5600
Orlando *(G-12039)*
▲ AB Green Raleigh Operator Inc .... D 305 534-6300
Miami Beach *(G-10541)*
Abbott Realty Services Inc .... C 850 837-4700
Destin *(G-3047)*
Abe Group Enterprise Inc .... D 954 767-8700
Fort Lauderdale *(G-3575)*
Accor North America Inc .... C 786 364-6180
Doral *(G-3101)*
Accord Hotels Inc .... E 561 848-1188
Riviera Beach *(G-15276)*
Accorhotels .... E 786 483-2954
Doral *(G-3102)*
Ad1 Global Viera LLC .... E 321 255-0077
Melbourne *(G-8810)*
Ad1 Lbv2 Hotels De LLC .... C 407 239-1115
Orlando *(G-12050)*
Ad1 Pb Airport Hotels LLC .... E 561 659-3880
West Palm Beach *(G-19021)*
Ad1 Urban Sw LLC .... D 407 584-0441
Orlando *(G-12051)*
Admirals Inn Ltd .... D 863 318-1456
Winter Haven *(G-19603)*
Advanced Care Hospitalists Pl .... E 863 816-5884
Lakeland *(G-7782)*
Advantus Leisure Management .... C 727 446-2200
Dunedin *(G-3377)*
Affiliated American Inns IV LP .... D 904 940-9500
Saint Augustine *(G-15421)*
Affiliated American Inns Ltd .... E 904 940-9500
Jacksonville *(G-5749)*
AFP 103 Corp .... D 305 261-3800
Miami *(G-9099)*
Ahi Jacksonville-1 Inv LLC .... E 404 497-4111
Jacksonville *(G-5754)*
Airport Hotel Group Ltd .... E 305 262-5400
Miami *(G-9108)*
Airport Regency Management Inc .... E 305 441-1600
Miami *(G-9109)*
Aku Tiki Ltd .... D 386 252-9631
Daytona Beach *(G-2539)*
Albion Associates .... D 305 913-1000
Miami Beach *(G-10545)*
Alden Enterprises Inc .... E 727 360-7081
St Pete Beach *(G-16558)*
Alena Hospitality Ucf LLC .... E 407 275-9000
Orlando *(G-12091)*
Alexander Condominuim Assn Inc .... C 305 341-6500
Miami Beach *(G-10546)*
Alfieres .... D 954 772-1331
Fort Lauderdale *(G-3589)*
Alfond Inn .... E 407 998-8090
Winter Park *(G-19683)*
Alico Land Development Inc .... D 239 226-2000
Fort Myers *(G-4260)*
Alico Lodging LLC .... D 239 561-1550
Fort Myers *(G-4261)*
All Sunny Hotels .... E 954 358-2300
Fort Lauderdale *(G-3595)*
Almar Hotel Corp .... D 305 261-4230
Doral *(G-3113)*
Altamonte Hotel Associates LLC .... D 407 830-1985
Altamonte Springs *(G-25)*
Amber Group Inc .... C 407 933-0700
Kissimmee *(G-7417)*
Ameeunc Inc .... D 352 795-3111
Crystal River *(G-2339)*
Amelia Ccrc Island LLC .... D 904 277-1088
Fernandina Beach *(G-3519)*
Amelia Island Company .... C 904 261-6161
Fernandina Beach *(G-3521)*
Amelia Omni Island LLC .... B 904 261-6161
Amelia Island *(G-122)*
Amelia Omni Island LLC .... B 904 432-2204
Fernandina Beach *(G-3522)*
American Hospitality Assn .... E 407 862-7111
Altamonte Springs *(G-26)*
American-International Ht Corp .... E 727 391-4000
N Redngtn Bch *(G-10988)*
Amrit & Sons I LLC .... C 850 438-4922
Pensacola *(G-14216)*
Andretti Thrill Park .... E 321 956-6706
Melbourne *(G-8816)*
Anglers Boutique Resort LLC .... E 786 594-5888
Miami Beach *(G-10550)*
Ap/Aim Westshore Suites LLC .... D 813 875-1555
Tampa *(G-17294)*
Apex Hospitality LLP .... E 239 278-3949
Fort Myers *(G-4277)*
Apple Six Hospitality MGT Inc .... D 407 444-1000
Heathrow *(G-5202)*
Apple Ten Florida Services Inc .... E 321 868-1841
Cape Canaveral *(G-1349)*
Apple Ten Svcs Gainesville Inc .... E 804 727-6337
Gainesville *(G-4837)*
Aqua Sun Investments Inc .... E 386 441-1111
Ormond Beach *(G-13478)*
Aqua Sun Investments Inc .... E 386 672-3550
Ormond Beach *(G-13479)*
Arcadia Holding Co Inc .... E 863 494-5900
Arcadia *(G-223)*
Arden Fund II Ict Operator LLC .... D 813 286-4400
Tampa *(G-17304)*
Arep II Gh Holding LLC .... D 352 384-3419
Gainesville *(G-4839)*
Arin Enterprises Llc .... E 863 683-5095
Lakeland *(G-7802)*
Army & Air Force Exchange Svc .... D 850 882-8761
Eglin A F B *(G-3416)*
Ashford Trs Five LLC .... D 305 296-2991
Key West *(G-7191)*
Ashford Trs Lessee II LLC .... D 727 894-5000
Saint Petersburg *(G-15574)*
Ashford Trs Pool C1 LLC .... E 407 465-0075
Orlando *(G-12135)*
Ashford Trs Pool C1 LLC .... D 954 343-2225
Weston *(G-19442)*
Atlantic Beach Country CLB Inc .... D 904 372-2222
Atlantic Beach *(G-239)*
Atlantic Hotel Partners LLC .... C 954 567-8020
Fort Lauderdale *(G-3616)*
Atlantic View Partners Ltd .... E 305 522-3311
Miami *(G-9188)*
Atrium Hotels Inc .... C 904 940-8000
Saint Augustine *(G-15427)*
Atrium Hotels Inc .... A 321 773-9260
Melbourne *(G-8820)*
Atrium Trs I LP .... C 954 753-5598
Coral Springs *(G-2228)*
AV Fairfield Inn Stes .... E 407 351-7000
Orlando *(G-12154)*
Avakar Lkeland Hospitality LLC .... E 863 688-7972
Lakeland *(G-7804)*
Aventura Beach Associates Ltd .... C 305 932-2233
Hallandale Beach *(G-5164)*
Avista Properties Ix Inc .... D 407 465-8150
Orlando *(G-12160)*
B & P Partnership .... E 904 741-4000
Jacksonville *(G-5831)*
B Hotels and Resorts LLC .... C 954 564-1000
Fort Lauderdale *(G-3624)*
B Z K Key West Partners Ltd .... D 305 294-5541
Key West *(G-7192)*
Babaji Shvram USA Holdings Inc .... E 904 737-8000
Jacksonville *(G-5832)*
Bahia Cabana Ltd .... D 954 524-1555
Fort Lauderdale *(G-3625)*
Bahia Sun Associates .... E 813 645-3291
Ruskin *(G-15395)*
Banana Bay Inc .... E 305 743-3648
Marathon *(G-8614)*
Baxters Realty Inc .... E 850 648-5757
Mexico Beach *(G-9052)*
Bay Hotel LLC .... E 813 874-6700
Tampa *(G-17346)*
Bay Inn Incorporated .... D 239 597-8777
Naples *(G-11025)*
Baymeadows Lodging Inc .... D 904 562-4920
Jacksonville *(G-5845)*
BCM-CHI Eden Rock Tenants LP .... B 305 531-0000
Miami *(G-9232)*
Bd-Morr Hotel LLC .... D 305 398-1806
Miami Beach *(G-10553)*
Beach Hotel Associates LLC .... C 305 672-2000
Miami Beach *(G-10554)*
Beach Tennis Resort III Inc .... D 904 471-6606
Saint Augustine *(G-15429)*
Beachcomber Hotel .... C 954 941-7830
Pompano Beach *(G-14752)*
Beaches Hospitality LLC .... D 904 223-0222
Jacksonville *(G-5848)*
Beechwood Lakeland Hotel LLC .... E 863 647-0066
Lakeland *(G-7815)*
Beluga Hospitality LLC .... C 407 996-3400
Orlando *(G-12181)*
Belv Partners LP .... A 407 352-4000
Orlando *(G-12182)*
Benderson Properties Inc .... D 941 359-8303
University Park *(G-18737)*
Bent Creek Golf Vlg Condo Assn .... E 865 436-3947
Winter Garden *(G-19557)*
Bentleys Boutique Hotel .... E 941 966-2121
Osprey *(G-13531)*
Berkley Group Inc .... E 954 563-2444
Fort Lauderdale *(G-3640)*
Best Western Aku Tiki Inn .... D 386 252-9631
Daytona Beach Shores *(G-2693)*
Best Western Ambassador .... E 941 480-9898
Venice *(G-18766)*
Best Western International .... D 407 828-2424
Lake Buena Vista *(G-7454)*
Best Western-Ocala Park Centre .... E 352 237-4848
Ocala *(G-11639)*
Betsy Ross Hotel Corp .... D 844 539-2840
Miami Beach *(G-10556)*
Betsy Ross Owner LLC .... E 305 531-6100
Miami Beach *(G-10557)*

BF Saul Property Company ....D 954 484-2214	C&P Global Enterprise Inc ....E 407 851-1113	Charles Bernard Ltd ....C 305 531-7494
Fort Lauderdale (G-3642)	Orlando (G-12224)	Miami Beach (G-10566)
BF Saul Property Company ....E 561 994-2107	Calflo Inc ....E 352 629-7041	Chartwell Hospitality ....D 850 654-9383
Boca Raton (G-449)	Ocala (G-11648)	Destin (G-3051)
BF Saul Property Company ....D 561 994-7232	Calpac Inc ....E 941 388-2161	Chartwell Hospitality LLC ....B 850 654-8611
Boca Raton (G-450)	Sarasota (G-16114)	Destin (G-3052)
Bgs Group Inc ....D 321 632-4561	Calpac Inc ....C 941 484-8471	Chateaubleau Inn Inc ....E 305 448-2634
Cocoa (G-1917)	Venice (G-18769)	Coral Gables (G-2066)
Biltmore Hotel Ltd Partnership ....B 305 445-1926	Calypso Cay Vacation Villas ....E 407 997-1600	Chatham Lugano LLC ....E 954 564-4400
Coral Gables (G-2054)	Kissimmee (G-7274)	Fort Lauderdale (G-3685)
Birchwood Inn LLC ....E 727 896-1080	Calypso Resort Towers ....E 850 636-5004	Chatham Maitland Hs LLC ....E 407 875-8777
Saint Petersburg (G-15598)	Panama City (G-13976)	Maitland (G-8513)
Birmingham Hospitality Corp ....E 850 934-3609	Cambridge Trs Inc ....E 727 222-7881	Cheeca Holdings LLC ....D 305 664-4651
Gulf Breeze (G-5110)	Fort Lauderdale (G-3666)	Islamorada (G-5703)
Bluegreen Communities Inc ....C 561 912-8000	Canada House Resort Ltd ....E 954 942-8200	Chesapeake Motel and Villas ....E 305 664-4662
Boca Raton (G-453)	Pompano Beach (G-14763)	Vero Beach (G-18844)
Bluegreen Land and Realty Inc ....C 561 912-8000	Candlewood Suites ....D 904 296-1287	▲ Chesterfield Hotel Pb LLC ....D 561 659-5800
Boca Raton (G-454)	Jacksonville (G-5896)	Palm Beach (G-13650)
Bluegreen New Jersey LLC ....C 561 912-8000	Cape Caribe Association Inc ....E 321 328-2550	Chisholm Properties S Bch Inc ....C 305 532-7715
Boca Raton (G-455)	Cape Canaveral (G-1357)	Miami Beach (G-10567)
Bluegreen Vacations Corp ....E 904 940-2000	Capitol City Travel Center Inc ....E 850 997-3538	CIP 2014 Ginesville Tenant LLC ....D 352 375-2400
Saint Augustine (G-15431)	Lloyd (G-8323)	Gainesville (G-4857)
Bluegreen Vacations Corp ....E 407 905-4119	Capt Hirams Resort ....E 772 589-4345	CIP 2014 Tampa Tenant LLC ....D 813 225-1234
Orlando (G-12192)	Sebastian (G-16373)	Tampa (G-17473)
Bluegreen Vacations Corp ....E 561 998-3311	Caravan Hotel Properties LLC ....D 407 581-5041	Cko Mgt LLC ....E 662 781-5100
Boca Raton (G-456)	Orlando (G-12233)	Tallahassee (G-16920)
Bluegreen Vacations Holdg Corp ......D 561 912-8000	◆ Carisam-Samuel Meisel FL Inc .....D 305 591-3993	Cl1 Orlando LLC ....D 407 660-9000
Boca Raton (G-457)	Doral (G-3144)	Maitland (G-8516)
Bluegreen Vctons Unlimited Inc ....D 561 912-8000	Carnival Corporation ....A 305 599-2600	Cl2 Orlando LLC ....B 407 396-7000
Surfside (G-16853)	Doral (G-3146)	Kissimmee (G-7285)
Boca Raton Hotel MGT LLP ....D 561 368-5200	Carrilon Miami Beach Hotel ....B 305 514-7000	Clarion Hotel Universal ....D 407 351-5009
Boca Raton (G-464)	Miami (G-9330)	Orlando (G-12309)
Boca Suites LLC ....E 561 393-5308	Carroll Properties ....D 239 472-4123	Clear Hospitality Group LLC ....E 727 573-3334
Boca Raton (G-471)	Sanibel (G-15999)	Clearwater (G-1573)
Bon Aire Motel Inc ....E 727 360-5596	Cas Holdings LLC ....E 863 299-9251	Clevelander Restaurant Inc ....C 305 531-3485
St Pete Beach (G-16559)	Winter Haven (G-19614)	Miami Beach (G-10574)
Bonaventure Resort & Spa LLC ....B 954 389-3300	Casa Marina Hotel and Rest Inc ....D 904 270-0025	Clewiston Marina Inc ....E 863 983-3151
Weston (G-19444)	Jacksonville Beach (G-6980)	Clewiston (G-1900)
Bonita Springs Hs LLC ....D 239 949-5913	Casa Marina Owner LLC ....D 305 296-3535	Club At Hammock Beach LLC ....B 855 485-1419
Bonita Springs (G-899)	Key West (G-7197)	Palm Coast (G-13816)
Bosta Co Inc ....E 954 454-2220	Casa Tua Partners Ltd ....D 305 604-2024	Club Continental Inc ....D 904 264-6070
Hallandale Beach (G-5167)	Miami Beach (G-10565)	Orange Park (G-11982)
Bostons Inc ....E 561 278-3364	Casablanca Inn Incorporated ....E 904 829-0928	Club Exploria LLC ....D 352 242-1100
Delray Beach (G-2918)	Saint Augustine (G-15433)	Clermont (G-1862)
Boykin Mgt Co Ltd Lblty Co ....D 321 779-1996	Casablanca of Key West Inc ....D 305 296-0815	◆ Club Med A Cayman Islands Corp ...C 305 925-9000
Indialantic (G-5664)	Key West (G-7198)	Coral Gables (G-2071)
Boykin Mgt Co Ltd Lblty Co ....D 321 777-5000	Casino Miami LLC ....E 305 633-6400	Club Med Management Svcs Inc ......D 305 925-9168
Indialantic (G-5665)	Miami (G-9333)	Miami (G-9378)
Brazilian Court Management ....C 561 655-7740	Cbm One Hotels LP ....E 813 229-1100	Club Med Sales Inc ....C 772 398-5003
Palm Beach (G-13649)	Tampa (G-17432)	Port Saint Lucie (G-15129)
Bre Hotels & Resorts LLC ....C 239 472-5111	Ccmh Tampa AP LLC ....D 813 879-5151	◆ Club Med Sales Inc ....C 305 925-9000
Captiva (G-1437)	Tampa (G-17433)	Miami (G-9379)
Bre Imagination Ht Owner LLC ....C 813 879-4800	Celebration Hotel Ltd ....E 407 566-6000	Clubcorp Usa Inc ....D 813 972-1991
Tampa (G-17385)	Kissimmee (G-7276)	Tampa (G-17489)
Bre/Baton Operating Lessee LLC ......E 561 447-3000	Central Fla Investments Inc ....D 407 355-1000	Cmp I Miami Doral Owner LLC ....E 305 477-8118
Boca Raton (G-480)	Ocoee (G-11808)	Doral (G-3154)
Bre/Clearwater Owner LLC ....C 727 461-3222	Central Fla Investments Inc ....C 407 396-8523	Cni Thl Ops LLC ....E 407 856-8896
Clearwater (G-1552)	Kissimmee (G-7278)	Orlando (G-12326)
Bre/Cocoa Beach Owner LLC ....A 321 799-0003	Central Fla Investments Inc ....E 407 851-2278	Coco Key Ht Wtr Rsort - Orlndo ....E 407 351-2626
Cocoa Beach (G-1963)	Orlando (G-12266)	Orlando (G-12337)
Bre/Key Largo Owner LLC ....D 305 852-5553	Central Fla Investments Inc ....B 407 345-0000	Cocoa Beach Motel Inc ....C 321 784-0000
Key Largo (G-7172)	Ocoee (G-11809)	Cape Canaveral (G-1362)
Bre/Sanibel Inn Owner LLC ....E 239 472-3181	Central Fla Investments Inc ....D 407 352-8051	Collegiate Village Inn Inc ....E 407 422-8191
Sanibel (G-15997)	Orlando (G-12267)	Winter Park (G-19707)
Bre/Suth Seas Resort Owner LLC ......D 239 472-5111	Central Fla Investments Inc ....D 407 396-2500	Colonial Galt Ocean Ltd Partnr ....C 954 565-6611
Captiva (G-1438)	Kissimmee (G-7279)	Fort Lauderdale (G-3704)
Brighton Seminole Bingo ....D 863 467-9998	Central Fla Investments Inc ....D 407 345-0000	▲ Colonnade Partners Ltd ....E 305 441-2600
Okeechobee (G-11863)	Orlando (G-12268)	Coral Gables (G-2075)
Brookside Inc ....E 239 774-3200	Central Fla Investments Inc ....E 407 354-3040	Colony Hotel Inc ....C 561 655-5430
Naples (G-11041)	Orlando (G-12265)	Palm Beach (G-13651)
Bsrep III Fort Ldrdale Trs LLC ....C 954 463-4000	Central Fla Investments Inc ....C 863 422-7511	Columbia Properties Stuart LLC ....D 772 225-3700
Fort Lauderdale (G-3660)	Haines City (G-5146)	Stuart (G-16608)
Bsrep III Pbg Resort Trs LLC ....B 561 627-2000	Century National Properties ....C 813 289-1950	Columbia Properties Tampa LLC ....C 813 623-6363
Palm Beach Gardens (G-13696)	Tampa (G-17451)	Tampa (G-17497)
Buccaneer Motel Corporation ....D 239 261-1148	CFI Resorts Management Inc ....A 407 997-6604	▲ Columbia Prpts Orlando LLC ....B 407 856-0100
Naples (G-11042)	Kissimmee (G-7282)	Orlando (G-12347)
Buena Vista Suites ....D 407 239-8588	CFI Resorts Management Inc ....E 407 351-3350	Columbia Prpts Westshore LLC ....C 813 287-2555
Orlando (G-12216)	Orlando (G-12287)	Tampa (G-17498)
Buffalo-Orlando I LLC ....E 407 363-9332	Cgi 1100 Biscayne MGT LLC ....E 786 577-9700	Comfort Inn ....E 904 225-2600
Orlando (G-12217)	Miami (G-9353)	Yulee (G-19815)
Bundschu Investments ....E 239 472-1700	Ch Orlando Hotel Partners LLC ....E 407 581-5600	Comfort Inn & Executive Suites ....E 239 353-9500
Sanibel (G-15998)	Orlando (G-12288)	Naples (G-11070)
Bvp Tenant LLC ....A 407 827-2727	Chaffee Lodging LLC ....C 904 693-4400	Comfort Inn & Suites ....E 954 315-2900
Lake Buena Vista (G-7456)	Jacksonville (G-5933)	Fort Lauderdale (G-3705)
By The Sea Resorts Inc ....C 850 234-6644	Chaffee Pt Hospitalities LLC ....E 904 783-8277	Comfort Inn & Suites ....E 727 323-3100
Panama City Beach (G-14091)	Jacksonville (G-5934)	Saint Petersburg (G-15633)
C & N of Palm Beach Inc ....E 561 582-7878	Chand Enterprises Inc ....E 321 632-5721	Comfort Inn North ....E 727 796-0135
Lantana (G-8058)	Cocoa (G-1923)	Clearwater (G-1581)
C E Brooks Investments Inc ....D 407 659-0030	Charles Bernard Ltd ....D 305 532-3311	Comfort Suites Tamarac ....E 954 343-1322
Maitland (G-8509)	Miami (G-9357)	Tamarac (G-17185)

Comfort Suites-Airport E 904 741-0505 Jacksonville *(G-5978)*
Commonwealth Hotels LLC D 813 875-1555 Tampa *(G-17505)*
Como Traymore LLC E 305 695-3600 Miami *(G-9395)*
Compass Resorts LLC E 850 269-1005 Destin *(G-3054)*
Concord Ppf Spg Ddland Opco LL D 305 668-4490 Miami *(G-9402)*
Concord Sierra Nli WPB Ht LLC D 561 665-4001 West Palm Beach *(G-19104)*
Concord Tampa Westshore LLC E 813 353-0555 Tampa *(G-17510)*
Conrad Miami E 305 503-6500 Miami *(G-9404)*
Cooper Realty Company D 239 482-2900 Fort Myers *(G-4326)*
Coral Bch Hotels & Resorts Inc D 239 449-1800 Naples *(G-11077)*
Coral Park Co E 305 371-4400 Miami *(G-9414)*
Coral Park Co C 305 667-5611 Miami *(G-9415)*
Country Inns Stes By Crlson In E 850 306-2020 Crestview *(G-2314)*
Courtyard By Marriott E 239 275-8600 Fort Myers *(G-4329)*
Courtyard By Marriott E 305 642-8200 Miami *(G-9432)*
Courtyard By Marriott E 813 661-9559 Tampa *(G-17541)*
Courtyard By Mrrott Fort Ldrda E 954 342-8333 Dania *(G-2407)*
Courtyard Management Corp E 407 240-7200 Orlando *(G-12379)*
Courtyard Management Corp E 727 572-8484 Clearwater *(G-1593)*
Courtyard Management Corp LLC E 850 222-8822 Tallahassee *(G-16924)*
Courtyard Miami Coconut Grove D 305 858-2500 Miami *(G-9433)*
Courtyard Orlndo Lk Bena Vsta D 407 938-9001 Orlando *(G-12380)*
CP Jacksonville LLC C 904 296-2222 Jacksonville *(G-6008)*
CP Sanibel LLC B 239 466-4000 Fort Myers *(G-4330)*
Craven Properties Ltd Inc D 904 471-2575 Saint Augustine *(G-15436)*
Crest Hotel & Apartments E 305 531-0321 Miami Beach *(G-10578)*
Crestview Hospitality LLC E 850 682-1481 Crestview *(G-2318)*
Cri Hotel Income Partners LP E 727 573-3334 Clearwater *(G-1596)*
Cri-Leslie LLC D 813 281-8900 Tampa *(G-17549)*
Crossroads Hospitality Co LLC D 407 313-3030 Orlando *(G-12387)*
Cs Hospitality LLC C 954 427-7700 Deerfield Beach *(G-2732)*
CSC Mayfair Land Ltd Partnr E 305 770-6665 Miami *(G-9444)*
Csfb2001-Fl2 Hrp LLC C 407 828-2828 Lake Buena Vista *(G-7457)*
Csps Hotel Inc E 813 933-7275 Tampa *(G-17556)*
CT Hix Orlando LLC E 407 581-7900 Orlando *(G-12389)*
Cuidad De Nstros Angeles I LLC E 954 485-0500 Lauderhill *(G-8193)*
Cypress Hotel Melbourne Ltd D 321 723-5320 Melbourne *(G-8862)*
Cypress Pnte Rsort II Cndo Ass C 407 238-2300 Orlando *(G-12394)*
Cypress Street Hotel LLC C 813 873-8675 Tampa *(G-17563)*
D&R Hospitality Inc D 850 398-8100 Crestview *(G-2319)*
Dad 2605 N Hwy A1a Mlbrne Owne E 321 777-4100 Melbourne *(G-8863)*
Dale Mabry Associates LLC D 813 877-6181 Tampa *(G-17569)*
Dale Mabry Investment Co Inc D 813 877-6721 Tampa *(G-17570)*
Dalmar E 954 945-9500 Fort Lauderdale *(G-3748)*
Dania Entertainment Center LLC C 954 920-1511 Dania Beach *(G-2426)*
Danmar Inc D 561 368-9500 Boca Raton *(G-543)*
Daves New National LLC D 305 423-7201 Miami Beach *(G-10582)*
Days Inn C 954 463-2500 Fort Lauderdale *(G-3754)*
Days Inn D 352 493-9400 Chiefland *(G-1482)*
Days Inn - Cocoa Beach E 321 784-2550 Cocoa Beach *(G-1969)*
Days Inn Gainesville Univ D 352 376-2222 Gainesville *(G-4874)*
Days Inn North Beach E 305 866-1631 Miami *(G-9462)*
Days Inn of Wildwood E 352 874-3807 Wildwood *(G-19493)*
Days Inns Worldwide Inc D 239 348-1700 Naples *(G-11091)*
Days Inns Worldwide Inc C 407 396-1400 Kissimmee *(G-7294)*
Daytona Beach Owner Opco LLC B 386 254-8200 Daytona Beach *(G-2576)*
Daytona Beach Resort LLC C 386 672-3770 Daytona Beach *(G-2577)*
Daytona Hospitality II LLC D 561 334-4274 Daytona Beach *(G-2580)*
Daytona Hotel Corporation E 407 240-5555 Orlando *(G-12406)*
Deauville Hotel Management LLC C 305 865-8511 Miami Beach *(G-10583)*
Decade Glfcast Ht Partners Ltd D 727 281-3100 Clearwater Beach *(G-1847)*
Decade Properties Inc E 727 595-9484 Indian Rocks Beach *(G-5673)*
Deerfield Hotel One LLC E 954 570-8888 Deerfield Beach *(G-2735)*
Destination Daytona LLC D 386 671-7104 Ormond Beach *(G-13485)*
Dev Hospitality Inc E 727 299-9800 Clearwater *(G-1604)*
Dev Krupa Inc E 813 490-9090 Tampa *(G-17589)*
Diamond Rsrts Cntrlzed Svcs US D 407 238-2500 Orlando *(G-12423)*
Diamondhead Island Bch Rsort L D 239 765-7654 Fort Myers Beach *(G-4667)*
Dimension Development Two LLC E 318 352-9519 Destin *(G-3086)*
Diplomat Properties Ltd Partnr A 954 602-6000 Hollywood *(G-5428)*
Diplomate Inc C 407 396-6000 Kissimmee *(G-7295)*
Disney Destinations LLC B 407 824-2222 Orlando *(G-12426)*
Disney Destinations LLC B 407 390-5234 Kissimmee *(G-7296)*
Disney Destinations LLC B 407 934-4000 Lake Buena Vista *(G-7459)*
Disney Vacation Dev Inc B 407 566-3800 Kissimmee *(G-7297)*
Disneyland International C 321 939-7013 Lake Buena Vista *(G-7461)*
Djont/Cmb Orsouth Leasing LLC D 407 352-1400 Orlando *(G-12432)*
Djont/Jpm Hsptlity Lsg Spe LLC E 305 634-5000 Miami *(G-9482)*
Djont/Jpm Orlando Leasing LLC D 407 851-6400 Orlando *(G-12433)*
DK Orlando AC LLC D 407 635-2300 Orlando *(G-12434)*
Dl-Dw Holdings LLC B 813 643-5900 Brandon *(G-1224)*
Dolphin Holdings Limited Inc D 727 363-6482 St Pete Beach *(G-16560)*
Don Ce Sar Resort Hotel Ltd D 727 360-1881 St Pete Beach *(G-16561)*
Doral Golf Resort & Spa E 305 592-2000 Doral *(G-3180)*
Doral Hotel Enterprise LLC E 786 272-7200 Doral *(G-3181)*
Doubletree By Hilton Orlando E E 407 996-0796 Orlando *(G-12437)*
Doubltree By Hlton Ht Tllhssee D 850 224-5000 Tallahassee *(G-16935)*
Downtown Miami Hotel LLC C 305 374-0000 Miami *(G-9488)*
Dp Luxury Ventures LLC D 305 931-7700 Sunny Isles Beach *(G-16716)*
Drap Florida LLC E 904 997-9190 Jacksonville *(G-6081)*
Driftwood Hospitality MGT LLC C 561 207-2700 North Palm Beach *(G-11543)*
Drury Hotels Company LLC E 407 354-3305 Orlando *(G-12443)*
Drury Hotels Company LLC E 573 334-8281 Gainesville *(G-4878)*
Drury Hotels Company LLC E 407 560-6111 Lake Buena Vista *(G-7462)*
Drv Hotel Partners Lllp E 561 622-7799 Palm Beach Gardens *(G-13721)*
DSI Sunrise LLC D 954 335-4533 Fort Lauderdale *(G-3765)*
Durgama Inc E 904 737-1700 Jacksonville *(G-6092)*
Duval Partners LLC D 850 224-6000 Tallahassee *(G-16937)*
Dvi Cardel West Palm Beach Ht D 561 655-0404 West Palm Beach *(G-19125)*
Dylan II Inc D 850 626-9060 Milton *(G-10815)*
Eagle Landings of Jax LLC C 904 741-4404 Jacksonville *(G-6098)*
East India Trading Co E 407 647-1072 Winter Park *(G-19719)*
Economos Properties Inc A 305 538-3373 Miami *(G-9503)*
Economos Properties Inc C 561 361-2504 Boca Raton *(G-564)*
Eden Roc Lllp B 305 674-5558 Miami Beach *(G-10587)*
EDG Hspitality Miami Arprt LLC E 305 636-7000 Miami *(G-9504)*
EDG Hsptlity Orlndo Cnvntion C D 407 351-4091 Orlando *(G-12452)*
Edgewater Beach Resort LLC B 850 235-4044 Panama City *(G-13995)*
Ehp Plantation Ventures LLC D 954 424-3300 Plantation *(G-14636)*
Elmira Miami LLC C 305 534-6300 Miami Beach *(G-10589)*
Embassy Investments IV LLC D 386 255-2577 Ormond Beach *(G-13487)*
Embassy Suites D 831 393-1115 Orlando *(G-12460)*
Embassy Suites Dwntwn Orlando E 407 841-1000 Orlando *(G-12461)*
Embassy Suites Hotel D 813 875-1555 Tampa *(G-17627)*
Embassy Suites Hotel Inc D 561 622-1000 Palm Beach Gardens *(G-13724)*
Embassy Suites Miami Airport E 305 634-5000 Miami *(G-9517)*
Emerald Breze Rsort Group 2 LL D 850 362-1000 Fort Walton Beach *(G-4764)*
Emerald Coast Hospitality Svc D 850 319-7215 Tampa *(G-17628)*
Enchantment LLC E 727 443-7652 Clearwater *(G-1623)*
Enclave At Orlando Condo Assn D 407 351-1155 Orlando *(G-12466)*
Encore Hospitality LLC C 813 287-0778 Tampa *(G-17632)*
Enn Leasing Company Inc D 239 790-3500 Fort Myers *(G-4359)*
Enn Sarasota 3 LLC C 941 358-3385 Sarasota *(G-16152)*
Enterprise Hotels Orlando Inc D 407 996-9999 Orlando *(G-12471)*
Epic Hotel LLC E 305 424-5226 Miami *(G-9527)*
Epoch-Flrida Cpitl Ht Prtners E 407 997-1400 Kissimmee *(G-7300)*
ESA P Prtfolio Oper Lessee LLC D 941 246-0133 Port Charlotte *(G-15032)*
Esha Hospitality Inc E 850 944-8442 Pensacola *(G-14299)*
Excel Hotel Inc D 727 367-1902 St Pete Beach *(G-16562)*
Excelsior Hspitality Entps LLC E 407 985-1988 Orlando *(G-12480)*
Expo Hotel Associates Ltd D 954 778-9977 Aventura *(G-269)*
Express Shop Investments LLC D 407 290-2710 Orlando *(G-12482)*
Extra Holidays E 800 989-1574 Orlando *(G-12483)*
F A C Hotel Ltd Partnership E 239 948-0699 Bonita Springs *(G-912)*
Fairfeld Inn Stes St Agstine I E 904 810-6882 Saint Augustine *(G-15439)*

S I C

Company		Phone	Location (Ref)
Fairfield Inn	E	561 748-5252	Jupiter (G-7068)
Fairfield Inn & Suites	D	352 861-8400	Ocala (G-11679)
Fairfield Inn By Marriott	E	305 643-0055	Miami (G-9540)
Fairfield Inn Suites Crestview	E	850 689-0074	Crestview (G-2321)
Falkenburg Hotel LLC	E	813 497-4590	Tampa (G-17645)
Farna Inc	D	863 858-4481	Lakeland (G-7862)
Faro Blnco Resort Holdings LLC	D	305 743-1234	Marathon (G-8618)
Felcor St Pete Leasing Spe LLC	C	727 824-8072	Saint Petersburg (G-15666)
First Choice Properties Corp	B	904 281-0900	Jacksonville (G-6167)
FL Grande LLC	D	954 463-4000	Fort Lauderdale (G-3790)
Flagler Vlg Hsptlity Group II	E	954 766-8800	Fort Lauderdale (G-3792)
Flamingo Motel	D	850 234-2232	Panama City (G-14008)
Flautt-Cornerstone Bay Pt LLC	C	850 236-6005	Panama City (G-14009)
Flocal Inc	E	386 736-3100	Deland (G-2861)
Florencia Park LLC	D	727 892-9900	Saint Petersburg (G-15673)
Florida Fontainebleau Ht LLC	B	305 538-2000	Miami (G-9576)
Florida Hotels & Rest Inc	D	407 425-4455	Orlando (G-12528)
Florida Motor Lodge Inc	E	561 395-5225	Boca Raton (G-582)
Florida Pritikin Center Inc	D	305 935-7131	Doral (G-3203)
Floridays Orlando Resort Condo	E	407 238-7700	Orlando (G-12536)
FM Hotel Company Ltd	D	239 482-2900	Fort Myers (G-4393)
FM Hotel/Office Venture LP Ltd	E	239 275-6000	Fort Myers (G-4394)
Fma Hospitality LP I	D	239 210-7200	Fort Myers (G-4395)
FMB Associates Ltd Partnership	E	239 463-6000	Fort Myers Beach (G-4668)
Focus Enterprises Inc	E	941 907-9155	Sarasota (G-16169)
Forbes Place Hotel II LLC	E	407 240-1000	Orlando (G-12538)
Fort Lauderdale Hospitality	E	954 587-3105	Fort Lauderdale (G-3801)
Fort Myers Florida Assoc Pl	D	239 690-9537	Fort Myers (G-4400)
Fortune Hotels Inc	D	727 367-6461	St Pete Beach (G-16563)
Fortune Hotels Inc	A	727 363-2235	St Pete Beach (G-16564)
Fountainhead Sebring Inc	E	863 655-7200	Sebring (G-16397)
Four Pnts By Shrton Cral Gbles	E	305 567-0534	Miami (G-9603)
Four Points Hotel Miami Beach	E	305 532-8501	Miami Beach (G-10595)
Freeman Hsslwnder Rsort Prpts	C	239 541-5000	Cape Coral (G-1396)
Fru Management Inc	D	305 532-3311	Miami (G-9612)
Fs Orlando LLC	B	407 313-6868	Golden Oak (G-5039)
Fs Orlando II LLC	B	407 313-7777	Golden Oak (G-5040)
Ft Lauderdale Es Leasing LLC	D	954 527-2700	Fort Lauderdale (G-3808)
Ft Lauderdale Falcon Ht LLC	E	954 772-5400	Fort Lauderdale (G-3809)
Ft Pierce Enterprises Inc	D	772 465-7000	Fort Pierce (G-4705)
Ftrc Hotel Partners L P	C	407 396-2229	Kissimmee (G-7314)
G/B/H Five Star LLC	D	407 597-5500	Orlando (G-12557)
G/B/H Four Star LLC	C	407 597-3722	Orlando (G-12558)
Galleon At Key West Inc	E	305 295-0207	Key West (G-7207)
Gardens Pointe Development LLC	E	561 694-5833	West Palm Beach (G-19160)
Gaylord Plms Rsort Cnvntion CT	B	407 586-0000	Kissimmee (G-7315)
Gdc Orlando Hotel Owner LLC	E	407 380-3500	Orlando (G-12564)
Geeta Hospitality Incorporated	D	937 642-3777	Naples (G-11129)
George Gary & Barbara Brown	B	386 252-6252	Daytona Beach (G-2602)
Georgia Bluegreen Corporation	E	561 912-7810	Boca Raton (G-605)
Gfii Dvi Crdel Flgler Crtyard	D	305 500-9600	Medley (G-8737)
Ghm Lido Hi LLC	E	941 388-5555	Sarasota (G-16175)
Gibson Inn	D	850 653-2191	Apalachicola (G-127)
Gilberts Boat Storage Inc	E	305 451-1133	Key Largo (G-7177)
Giovanni Enterprises Inc	E	386 677-8060	Ormond Beach (G-13496)
Give Kids World Inc	C	407 396-1114	Kissimmee (G-7318)
GNB Properties Inc	D	321 777-3552	Satellite Beach (G-16372)
Golden Gate Inn Cntry CLB Inc	D	239 455-9498	Naples (G-11134)
Golden Gate Inn Cntry CLB Prtn	D	239 643-6655	Naples (G-11135)
Golden Gate Inn Cntry CLB Prtn	D	239 353-9500	Naples (G-11136)
Golden Sands Gen Contrs Inc	E	863 984-7500	Lakeland (G-7876)
Gordon River Hotel Assoc LLC	E	239 649-5800	Fort Myers (G-4422)
Gospel Crusade Inc	E	941 746-2882	Bradenton (G-1113)
Governors Inn Cndo Assction In	E	850 681-6855	Orlando (G-12584)
Grand Bohemian Ltd	D	407 996-9999	Orlando (G-12587)
Grand Bohemian Hotel	D	407 316-0300	Orlando (G-12588)
Grand Cypress Florida LP	D	407 239-4700	Orlando (G-12589)
Grand Cypress Florida LP	D	407 239-4700	Orlando (G-12591)
Grand Plaza Resorts Inc	E	727 367-1902	St Pete Beach (G-16565)
Grand Prix Altamonte LLC	E	407 788-7991	Altamonte Springs (G-55)
Grand Prix Ft Lauderdale LLC	D	954 772-7770	Fort Lauderdale (G-3829)
Grand Prix Naples LLC	E	239 261-8000	Naples (G-11140)
Grande Pelican Beach Inc	E	954 568-9431	Fort Lauderdale (G-3830)
Grandview Ht Ltd Partnr Ohio	C	407 856-0100	Orlando (G-12593)
Grant Alliance LLC	E	727 450-1200	Dunedin (G-3386)
Gray Star Investments Inc	E	352 742-1600	Tavares (G-18607)
Great Vcation Destinations Inc	D	561 912-8000	Orlando (G-12597)
Green Comet LLC	E	305 673-0401	Miami Beach (G-10597)
Greenlinks	E	239 732-5532	Naples (G-11144)
Greyfield Inn Corp Not A Fla	E	904 261-6408	Fernandina Beach (G-3529)
Gringteam Inc	D	321 783-9222	Cocoa Beach (G-1971)
Gringteam Inc	D	954 764-2233	Fort Lauderdale (G-3840)
Gringteam Inc	D	407 934-1000	Lake Buena Vista (G-7463)
Gringteam Inc	D	954 427-7700	Deerfield Beach (G-2746)
Gringteam Inc	D	954 565-3800	Fort Lauderdale (G-3841)
Gringteam Inc	D	813 888-8800	Tampa (G-17761)
Gringteam Inc	D	321 783-9222	Cocoa Beach (G-1972)
Grove Hotel Group Ltd	E	305 448-2800	Miami (G-9667)
Gs Development LLC	D	850 236-8988	Panama City Beach (G-14096)
Gsnp Corporation	D	813 832-4656	Tampa (G-17766)
Gulf Coast Commercial Corp	D	239 280-2777	Naples (G-11149)
Gumenick Properties LLC	E	305 672-2412	Miami Beach (G-10598)
Gvi-Ip Tampa Hotel Tenant LLC	B	813 874-1234	Tampa (G-17777)
H L Murphy Inc	D	305 294-2917	Key West (G-7209)
H O Hospitality LP	E	407 869-9000	Altamonte Springs (G-56)
H&S Development LLC	D	850 932-6800	Pensacola Beach (G-14481)
Haggerty Novi Owner LLC	E	248 349-4000	Coral Gables (G-2117)
Hammock Beach Resort MGT LLC	C	386 246-5500	Palm Coast (G-13828)
Hampton Inn	E	904 363-7150	Jacksonville (G-6255)
Hampton Inn	E	407 888-2995	Orlando (G-12614)
Hampton Inn	D	407 396-8700	Kissimmee (G-7319)
Hampton Inn Orlnd-Suth Unvrsal	D	407 345-1112	Orlando (G-12615)
Hampton Inn Suites Clearwater	E	727 572-7456	Clearwater (G-1660)
Hampton Inn W PLM Bch Cntrl	E	561 472-7333	West Palm Beach (G-19171)
Harbor Mstr Svcs Corp of Lngbo	D	800 858-0836	Longboat Key (G-8326)
Harbor Resort Hotel LLC	E	941 637-6770	Punta Gorda (G-15207)
Harbour Island Owner LLC	E	813 229-5000	Tampa (G-17790)
Hardage Hotels I LLC	D	813 281-5677	Tampa (G-17791)
Harp Hotels Inc	D	863 414-5161	Boca Raton (G-618)
Harris Rosen Enterprises Inc	D	407 351-1600	Orlando (G-12620)
Haten Bisheouly and Mazzawi	D	305 245-1260	Homestead (G-5579)
Hcp Grsvenor Orlando Owner LLC	B	407 828-4444	Lake Buena Vista (G-7464)
Health Dst Ht Partners LLC	D	305 575-5300	Miami (G-9688)
Heartland Hotel Corporation	C	727 540-0050	Saint Petersburg (G-15705)
HEI Hospitality LLC	C	561 392-4600	Boca Raton (G-627)
Helping Hnds Superior Care LLC	E	866 521-7606	New Port Richey (G-11382)
Henderson Beach Resort LLC	C	850 424-4000	Destin (G-3062)
Henderson Beach Resort Ht LLC	B	855 741-2777	Destin (G-3063)
HHC Florida LLC	D	561 266-9910	Delray Beach (G-2965)
HI Development Corp	C	305 885-1941	Miami Springs (G-10784)
HI Development Corp	D	727 577-9200	Clearwater (G-1665)
HI Development Corp	D	352 376-1661	Gainesville (G-4913)
HI Resorts Inc	C	813 229-6686	Tampa (G-17818)
Hialeah Hotel Inc	C	305 823-2000	Hialeah (G-5273)
Hialeah Lcp Operating Group	E	305 825-1000	Hialeah Gardens (G-5343)
Hiex Orlando Conway Ltd	D	407 581-7900	Orlando (G-12639)
Highbeach Inc	E	561 278-6241	Highland Beach (G-5357)
Highpointe Hospitability Inc	D	850 939-9400	Gulf Breeze (G-5118)
Highpointe Hospitability Inc	D	850 432-0202	Pensacola (G-14323)
Highpointe Hospitability Inc	E	850 478-1123	Pensacola (G-14324)
Hilton Ft Lauderdale Marina	C	305 463-4000	Fort Lauderdale (G-3861)
Hilton Garden Inn	C	407 363-9332	Orlando (G-12643)
Hilton Garden Inn	E	772 871-6850	Port Saint Lucie (G-15142)
Hilton Garden Inn Jacksonville	E	904 396-6111	Jacksonville (G-6280)
Hilton Garden Inns MGT LLC	D	407 703-4493	Apopka (G-188)

▲ **Hilton Grand Vacations CLB LLC** D 407 354-1500
Orlando *(G-12644)*

Hilton Grand Vacations Co LLC D 407 465-5000
Orlando *(G-12645)*

Hilton Grand Vacations Co LLC D 407 722-3100
Orlando *(G-12646)*

▲ **Hilton Grand Vacations Co LLC** D 407 722-3100
Orlando *(G-12647)*

Hilton Grand Vacations Inc B 407 613-3100
Orlando *(G-12648)*

Hilton Grdn Inn Key Wst/The Ke E 305 320-0920
Key West *(G-7210)*

Hilton Resorts Corporation D 407 722-3218
Orlando *(G-12649)*

Hilton St Agstine Hstric Byfro D 904 429-0216
Saint Augustine *(G-15452)*

Hilton Univ Fla Cnfrnce Ctr Gn E 352 371-3600
Gainesville *(G-4915)*

Hilton West Palm Beach D 561 231-9600
West Palm Beach *(G-19178)*

Historical Prpts Ltd Lblty Co C 904 824-3383
Saint Augustine *(G-15453)*

Hit Portfolio II Misc Trs LLC D 904 741-6550
Jacksonville *(G-6281)*

Hit Portfolio II Trs LLC D 407 248-2232
Orlando *(G-12650)*

Hit Portfolio II Trs LLC D 407 354-4447
Orlando *(G-12651)*

Holiday Inn D 407 862-4455
Altamonte Springs *(G-60)*

Holiday Inn CLB Vctons Rsrvton E 407 395-6538
Orlando *(G-12655)*

▲ **Holiday Inn Club Vacations Inc** A 407 239-0000
Orlando *(G-12656)*

Holiday Inn Express D 239 542-2121
Cape Coral *(G-1399)*

Holiday Inn Hotel & Suites E 407 581-9001
Orlando *(G-12657)*

Holiday Inn Marathon E 305 289-0222
Marathon *(G-8620)*

Holiday Inn Sunspree Resort D 850 234-1111
Panama City *(G-14029)*

Holiday Isle Resort & Marina D 305 664-2321
Islamorada *(G-5704)*

Holiday Village Sandpiper Inc B 772 398-5100
Miami *(G-9710)*

Hollywood Resorts Company E 954 563-2444
Fort Lauderdale *(G-3867)*

Homewood Stes By Hlton Jcksnvl E 904 396-6888
Jacksonville *(G-6294)*

Homewood Suites Port Richey E 727 819-1000
Port Richey *(G-15105)*

Homosassa Riverside Resort LLC D 352 628-0622
Homosassa *(G-5618)*

Hospitality Partners LLC D 561 640-9000
West Palm Beach *(G-19188)*

◆ **Hospitality Purveyors Inc** E 305 667-9725
Miami *(G-9720)*

Hospitality Receiver LLC E 561 886-1804
Boca Raton *(G-634)*

Host Hotels & Resorts LP E 305 649-5000
Miami *(G-9721)*

Host Hotels & Resorts LP E 813 221-4900
Tampa *(G-17842)*

Host Hotels & Resorts LP E 305 374-3900
Miami *(G-9722)*

Host Hotels & Resorts LP E 954 766-6123
Fort Lauderdale *(G-3874)*

Host Hotels & Resorts LP E 904 277-1100
Fernandina Beach *(G-3531)*

Hostmark Investors Ltd Partnr B 813 879-4800
Tampa *(G-17843)*

Hotel 14501 Hotel Opco LP E 954 874-1250
Miramar *(G-10863)*

Hotel Cardozo Inc D 786 577-7600
Miami Beach *(G-10600)*

Hotel Entps of Port Charlotte E 813 494-9069
Port Charlotte *(G-15042)*

Hotel Genpar Ltd E 305 468-1400
Doral *(G-3232)*

Hotel Mgt of Port Charlotte E 941 627-5600
Punta Gorda *(G-15208)*

Hotel Miami LLC E 305 636-1600
Miami *(G-9724)*

Hotel Resort Company A 561 627-2000
Palm Beach Gardens *(G-13738)*

Hotel Riu Plaza Miami Beach E 305 673-5333
Miami Beach *(G-10601)*

Hotel Shelley LLC E 305 531-3341
Miami Beach *(G-10602)*

Hotel Trail LLC E 216 990-1363
Orlando *(G-12664)*

Hotel West Palm Bch Opco L L C E 561 689-6888
West Palm Beach *(G-19189)*

▲ **Hotelbeds Usa Inc** D 407 926-5344
Orlando *(G-12665)*

Hotelex Airport LLC E 305 779-0900
Miami *(G-9725)*

Hotels of Key Largo Inc E 305 451-2121
Key Largo *(G-7179)*

Howard Johnson C 954 781-2200
Laud By Sea *(G-8167)*

Howard Johnson D 239 936-3229
Fort Myers *(G-4444)*

Hst Downtown Miami LLC D 303 358-4555
Miami *(G-9727)*

Hutchinson Island Corporation D 772 229-1000
Jensen Beach *(G-7017)*

Hyatt Beach House Resort E 305 293-5050
Key West *(G-7213)*

Hyatt Corporation B 305 358-1234
Miami *(G-9735)*

Hyatt Corporation D 305 441-1234
Coral Gables *(G-2128)*

Hyatt Corporation A 239 444-1234
Bonita Springs *(G-923)*

Hyatt Corporation A 407 239-1234
Orlando *(G-12673)*

Hyatt Corporation C 813 874-1234
Tampa *(G-17849)*

Hyatt Corporation B 407 825-1234
Orlando *(G-12674)*

Hyatt Corporation B 904 588-1234
Jacksonville *(G-6307)*

Hyatt Corporation D 954 616-1234
Weston *(G-19462)*

Hyatt Corporation C 727 373-1234
Clearwater *(G-1677)*

Hyatt Corporation E 561 330-3530
Delray Beach *(G-2969)*

Hyatt Equities LLC D 904 588-1234
Jacksonville *(G-6308)*

Hyatt Equities LLC D 407 352-4000
Orlando *(G-12675)*

Hyatt Hotels Management Corp D 941 953-1234
Sarasota *(G-16189)*

Hyatt Vacation Ownership Inc D 800 464-9288
Saint Petersburg *(G-15712)*

I-O-T-L Inc D 863 471-9400
Sebring *(G-16402)*

IA Lodging W Palm Bch Cntrpark E 561 207-1800
West Palm Beach *(G-19192)*

Icon Orlando LLC D 407 601-7907
Orlando *(G-12677)*

IL Lugano LLC E 954 226-5115
Fort Lauderdale *(G-3888)*

Ilg LLC D 305 666-1861
South Miami *(G-16503)*

Impact Properties II LLC E 813 287-0907
Tampa *(G-17860)*

Impact Properties Inc E 813 281-0000
Tampa *(G-17861)*

Indian Creek Hotel Inc E 305 531-2727
Miami *(G-9746)*

Indsar Hospitality LLC E 941 487-3800
Sarasota *(G-16192)*

Inland Amrcn Gnesville Trs LLC D 352 371-3600
Gainesville *(G-4921)*

Inn Hampton & Suites A 904 997-9100
Jacksonville *(G-6321)*

Inn of Lake City Inc C 386 752-3901
Lake City *(G-7533)*

Inn On Bay Inc D 305 865-7100
North Bay Village *(G-11469)*

Inn Suites C 941 474-5544
Englewood *(G-3430)*

Innisfree Hotels Inc B 850 916-2999
Pensacola Beach *(G-14482)*

Innisfree Hotels Inc C 850 934-3609
Gulf Breeze *(G-5119)*

Innkeeper Hospitality Vi Inc D 561 655-9001
Palm Beach *(G-13658)*

Innkeeper Hospitality Vii D 561 655-9001
Palm Beach *(G-13659)*

Innkeepers Hospitality III Inc E 561 655-9001
Palm Beach *(G-13660)*

International Hotel Co LLC E 305 374-4752
Doral *(G-3242)*

International Residential D 305 866-2122
Miami *(G-9769)*

International Sports Club Corp D 954 485-0500
Lauderhill *(G-8201)*

Interstate Hotels & Resorts D 407 828-8888
Lake Buena Vista *(G-7465)*

Interstate Hotels Resorts Inc E 407 239-0444
Orlando *(G-12689)*

Interstate MGT & Inv Corp C 904 321-1111
Fernandina Beach *(G-3532)*

Iq16 Tampa Gateway Blvd LLC D 813 630-4321
Seffner *(G-16427)*

Irnm Hotel Investors LLC D 850 477-0711
Pensacola *(G-14331)*

Island Grand Resort A Tradewi A 727 363-2358
St Pete Beach *(G-16566)*

Island Harbor Beach Club Ltd E 941 697-0566
Placida *(G-14540)*

Island Hospitality MGT LLC C 850 243-8116
Fort Walton Beach *(G-4783)*

Island Hospitality MGT LLC E 407 875-8777
Maitland *(G-8545)*

Island Hospitality MGT LLC D 407 788-7991
Altamonte Springs *(G-65)*

Island Hospitality MGT LLC D 954 922-0011
Hollywood *(G-5462)*

Island Hospitality MGT LLC E 561 471-8700
West Palm Beach *(G-19210)*

Island Hospitality MGT LLC E 239 261-8000
Naples *(G-11179)*

Island House 1989 Inc E 305 294-6284
Key West *(G-7215)*

Island Inn Company D 239 472-1561
Sanibel *(G-16000)*

Island One Resorts Mgt Corp D 407 238-0007
Kissimmee *(G-7327)*

Islander Motel E 305 664-2031
Islamorada *(G-5705)*

J A M M 18 Inc D 305 532-2362
Miami Beach *(G-10604)*

J J C Investments Inc D 407 396-7666
Kissimmee *(G-7330)*

Jabo LLC D 239 463-8607
Fort Myers Beach *(G-4669)*

Jai Sachchidanand Hospitality E 352 375-1550
Gainesville *(G-4927)*

Jairamki LLC E 813 835-6262
Tampa *(G-17889)*

Jalaram Hotels Inc D 904 741-1997
Jacksonville *(G-6371)*

James Hotels LLC D 727 799-1181
Clearwater *(G-1681)*

Jasmine Hospitality Inc D 407 313-3100
Orlando *(G-12701)*

Jax Airport Hotel LLC D 904 741-1997
Jacksonville *(G-6374)*

Jax Lodging Inc D 904 741-4911
Jacksonville *(G-6377)*

Jaya Hotels Inc D 386 365-1988
Live Oak *(G-8313)*

Jefast Pelican Grand I LLC E 954 568-9431
Fort Lauderdale *(G-3904)*

JHM Lake Buena Vista Hotel Ltd C 407 239-1115
Orlando *(G-12706)*

John J Grother E 941 627-8900
Port Charlotte *(G-15043)*

Johnson Resort Properties - FL D 305 296-6595
Key West *(G-7217)*

Jupiter Hotel LLC E 561 575-7201
Jupiter *(G-7096)*

Jupiter Resort LLC C 561 746-2511
Jupiter *(G-7106)*

▲ **JV Associates Inc** B 561 582-2800
Palm Beach *(G-13661)*

JW Marrott Orlndo Bnnet Creek E 407 789-0999
Orlando *(G-12717)*

JW Marrott Orlndo Grande Lakes E 407 206-2300
Orlando *(G-12718)*

K & P Clearwater Estate LLC C 727 281-9500
Clearwater *(G-1692)*

Kaysons Enterprises Inc E 407 855-5360
Orlando *(G-12721)*

Kelco FB Tallahassee LLC E 850 402-9400
Tallahassee *(G-17016)*

Kelco/FB Ocean Point LLC D 786 528-2500
Sunny Isles Beach *(G-16723)*

Kenne Ops LLC D 954 659-2234
Weston *(G-19464)*

▲ **Kessler Enterprise Inc** E 407 996-9999
Orlando *(G-12725)*

Kessler Hotels Ltd E 407 996-9999
Orlando *(G-12726)*

S I C

Key Ambassador Inc Key West *(G-7218)*	E	305 296-3500
Key Clearwater LLC Clearwater Beach *(G-1848)*	E	727 218-1088
Key Clearwater LLC Clearwater Beach *(G-1849)*	E	727 218-1090
Key Club Associates Ltd Partnr Longboat Key *(G-8327)*	D	941 383-0292
Key Hospitality & Healthcare Key West *(G-7219)*	D	305 293-1818
Key Largo Bay Beach LLC Key Largo *(G-7181)*	C	305 451-8500
Key Largo Management Corp Key Largo *(G-7182)*	E	305 451-2121
Key Largo Management Corp Key Largo *(G-7183)*	C	888 731-9056
Key West Beverage Inc Key West *(G-7220)*	E	305 296-2991
Key West Reach Owner LLC Key West *(G-7223)*	D	305 296-5000
Keys Hotel Operator Inc Marathon *(G-8621)*	B	305 743-7000
Khp IV Key Largo Trs LLC Key Largo *(G-7185)*	D	305 852-5553
Kinsman Hotel Associates Inc Ocala *(G-11705)*	D	352 237-8000
Kjl Hotel Realty LLC Fort Myers *(G-4464)*	D	239 997-5511
Kjl Hotel Realty LLC Sanford *(G-15959)*	D	407 320-0845
Kjl Hotel Realty LLC Bradenton *(G-1126)*	D	941 238-0800
Kjl Hotel Realty LLC Madison *(G-8486)*	D	850 973-2020
Kjl Hotel Realty LLC Doral *(G-3255)*	D	305 593-6366
Kjl Hotel Realty LLC Kissimmee *(G-7343)*	D	407 997-3300
Kjl Hotel Realty LLC Orlando *(G-12733)*	D	407 839-1983
Kjl Hotel Realty LLC Midway *(G-10803)*	D	850 514-2222
Kjl Hotel Realty LLC Jacksonville *(G-6406)*	D	904 741-4980
Kjl Hotel Realty LLC Fort Pierce *(G-4715)*	D	772 409-1740
Kjl Hotel Realty LLC Edgewater *(G-3412)*	D	386 427-7101
Kjl Hotel Realty LLC Sebastian *(G-16378)*	D	772 388-9300
Kjl Hotel Realty LLC Bowling Green *(G-953)*	D	863 773-2378
Kornerstone Equities Inc Bonita Springs *(G-925)*	E	239 949-5913
Kpa/GP Ft Walton Beach LLC Fort Walton Beach *(G-4784)*	D	850 243-8116
Kpa/GP Ft Walton Beach LLC Fort Walton Beach *(G-4785)*	D	850 244-9226
Kpc Lakeview Development LLC West Palm Beach *(G-19229)*	D	561 655-1454
Krishna Assoc of Titusville Titusville *(G-18692)*	C	321 269-4480
L Governor Motel Mexico Beach *(G-9051)*	E	850 648-5757
La Hacienda I LP Fort Myers *(G-4466)*	C	239 466-0012
La Playa LLC Naples *(G-11192)*	B	239 597-3123
La Quinta Inn Gainesville *(G-4932)*	E	352 332-6466
La Siesta Resort Inc Islamorada *(G-5706)*	E	305 664-2132
Labree Inc Orlando *(G-12747)*	E	407 239-7100
Ladbroke Hotels USA Corp Miami *(G-9842)*	E	305 218-7217
Lago Mar Properties Inc Fort Lauderdale *(G-3927)*	C	954 523-6511
Lakeshore Hospitality LLC Tallahassee *(G-17020)*	E	850 597-7000
Lakeside Center II Edens LLC Boca Raton *(G-664)*	D	561 482-7070
Lakeside Corp of Mt Dora Inc Mount Dora *(G-10954)*	D	352 383-4101
Lakeside Operating Partnr LP Kissimmee *(G-7344)*	D	407 396-2222
Lakeville Partners LLC Winter Haven *(G-19642)*	D	863 292-2100
Landcom Hospitality MGT Inc Jacksonville *(G-6414)*	E	904 396-7770

Lani Kai Island Resort Fort Myers Beach *(G-4670)*	D	239 463-3111
Las Olas Company Inc Fort Lauderdale *(G-3929)*	D	954 467-0671
Lauderdale Partners LLC Plantation *(G-14665)*	E	954 370-2220
Lax Hotel LLC Orlando *(G-12755)*	C	407 240-1000
Laxmi Augusta Nat Ht II Ltd Orlando *(G-12756)*	E	407 816-5533
Laxmi Austrian Hotel Ltd Orlando *(G-12757)*	E	407 226-0288
Laxmi Realty Inc Dania *(G-2417)*	E	954 921-6500
Lbvks LP Orlando *(G-12758)*	D	407 239-4500
Lcp Hleah Grdns Hspitality LLC Hialeah Gardens *(G-5344)*	E	305 825-1000
Lcp Tampa East Investment LLC Tampa *(G-17937)*	D	813 623-6363
Ledgeburn Enterprises Inc Kissimmee *(G-7348)*	E	407 396-1212
Leesburg Associates LP Leesburg *(G-8253)*	D	352 787-5151
Legacy Vacation Club LLC Orlando *(G-12761)*	C	407 238-1700
Legacy Vacation Club LLC Kissimmee *(G-7349)*	C	407 997-5000
▲ Lehill Partners LLC Naples *(G-11195)*	D	239 597-3232
Leslie A Lurken Jacksonville *(G-6429)*	D	904 741-1997
Lexdevcojax LLC Coral Springs *(G-2266)*	D	954 575-2668
Lh Daytona Operating LLC Daytona Beach *(G-2626)*	D	386 767-7350
Lh Tampa Operating LLC Tampa *(G-17943)*	B	813 286-4400
Liberty Tampa Investments LLC Tampa *(G-17945)*	D	813 280-2000
Lido Beach Resort Inc Sarasota *(G-16220)*	E	941 388-2161
Lighthouse Cove Resort Inc Pompano Beach *(G-14841)*	E	954 941-3410
Little Palm Island Assoc Ltd Summerland Key *(G-16694)*	D	305 872-2524
Little Sabine Inc Gulf Breeze *(G-5121)*	C	850 916-9755
Little Sabine Investment Group Gulf Breeze *(G-5122)*	E	850 934-5400
Little Torch Resort Inc Bokeelia *(G-884)*	E	305 872-2157
Liveco Inc Miami *(G-9877)*	D	305 854-2070
Lmr Inc Miami *(G-9879)*	D	305 531-5771
Lnt Hotel I Ops LLC Orlando *(G-12776)*	D	407 865-9165
Lodge At Ponte Vedra Beach Ltd Ponte Vedra Beach *(G-14988)*	C	904 285-1111
Lodging Resources Inc Fernandina Beach *(G-3534)*	D	800 772-3359
Loews Hotels & Co Orlando *(G-12778)*	E	407 503-7000
Loews Hotels Holding Corp Orlando *(G-12779)*	D	407 503-3000
▲ Loews Miami Bch Ht Oper Co Inc Miami Beach *(G-10610)*	A	305 604-5427
Loews Orlando Ht Partner LLC Orlando *(G-12780)*	B	407 503-9000
Logan Acquisitions Corporation Sarasota *(G-16222)*	D	941 388-2161
Longboat Key Marina Associates Longboat Key *(G-8328)*	E	941 383-0930
Louque Hospitality Corporation Perry *(G-14490)*	E	850 223-3000
Lq Management LLC Hollywood *(G-5468)*	D	954 922-2295
Lq Management LLC Doral *(G-3265)*	D	305 436-0830
Lq Management LLC Ocala *(G-11716)*	E	352 861-1137
Lq Management LLC Tallahassee *(G-17027)*	D	850 385-7172
Lq Management LLC Clearwater *(G-1702)*	E	727 572-7222
Lq Management LLC Orlando *(G-12788)*	D	407 857-9215
Lq Management LLC Fort Lauderdale *(G-3947)*	E	954 485-7900

Lq Management LLC Tampa *(G-17963)*	E	813 684-4007
Lq Management LLC Fort Lauderdale *(G-3948)*	D	954 484-6909
Lq Management LLC Miami *(G-9883)*	E	305 871-1777
Lr Jax LLC Jacksonville *(G-6449)*	E	904 355-6664
Lr Miami Airport Hotel LLC Miami *(G-9884)*	D	401 946-4600
Lutfi Investment Co Inc Orlando *(G-12792)*	D	407 506-1200
Luv-Kush Enterprises Inc Okeechobee *(G-11872)*	E	863 357-7100
Lvp Hmi Ft Lauderdale LLC Hollywood *(G-5469)*	E	954 922-0011
M & D Partnership Clearwater *(G-1704)*	D	727 799-0100
M Resort Hotel LLC Sunny Isles Beach *(G-16724)*	C	305 503-6000
M&C Hotel Interests Inc Jacksonville *(G-6456)*	C	904 396-5100
M&C Hotel Interests Inc Fort Lauderdale *(G-3951)*	C	954 463-2500
M-10505 Doral Hotel Owner LLC Doral *(G-3267)*	E	305 718-4144
Magic City Casino Miami *(G-9891)*	D	305 649-3000
Magna Hospitality Group Lc Plantation *(G-14670)*	C	954 472-5600
Mahudi Investment Corp Orlando *(G-12803)*	E	305 592-2712
Maine Crse Hsptality Group Inc Clearwater Beach *(G-1850)*	D	207 865-6105
Mainsail Central LLC Tampa *(G-17976)*	E	813 243-2600
Mainsail Epicurean Hotel Lllp Tampa *(G-17977)*	E	813 999-8700
Mainsail Lodging & Dev LLC Tampa *(G-17978)*	E	813 243-2609
Majestic Hotel Corp Miami Beach *(G-10612)*	E	305 538-1411
Malkus Inc Deland *(G-2868)*	D	386 736-3440
Marco Beach Hotel Inc Marco Island *(G-8632)*	C	239 394-5000
Marco Beach Ocean Resort Mgt Marco Island *(G-8633)*	C	239 393-1400
Margartvlle Hllywood Bch Rsort Hollywood *(G-5472)*	E	954 874-4444
Marina At Nples Bay Rsort Assn Naples *(G-11205)*	D	239 530-1199
Marina Bay Rsort Cndo Assn Inc Fort Walton Beach *(G-4790)*	D	850 244-5132
Marina Beach Associates Inc Saint Petersburg *(G-15754)*	D	727 867-1151
Marriott Orlando *(G-12812)*	D	407 238-1300
Marriott Orlando *(G-12813)*	A	407 206-2300
Marriott Orlando *(G-12814)*	D	407 238-6200
Marriott Port Saint Lucie *(G-15150)*	E	772 871-2929
Marriott Orlando *(G-12815)*	D	407 238-6800
Marriott Hotel Services Inc Miami Beach *(G-10613)*	E	786 264-4720
Marriott Hotel Services Inc Miami *(G-9905)*	C	305 649-5000
Marriott Hotel Services Inc Tampa *(G-17994)*	B	813 221-4950
Marriott International Inc Miami *(G-9906)*	E	305 374-3900
Marriott International Inc West Palm Beach *(G-19253)*	C	561 803-1915
Marriott International Inc Miami Lakes *(G-10741)*	D	305 556-6665
Marriott International Inc Marco Island *(G-8635)*	C	239 394-2511
Marriott International Inc Lakeland *(G-7913)*	C	863 688-7700
Marriott Intl Hotels Inc Lakeland *(G-7914)*	C	800 906-2871
Marriott Ovrseas Owners Svcs C Orlando *(G-12816)*	E	407 206-6000
◆ Marriott Ownership Resorts Inc Orlando *(G-12817)*	A	863 688-7700
Marriott Resorts Title Company Orlando *(G-12818)*	C	407 206-6000

Company	Code	Phone
Marriott Resorts Travel Co Inc	C	407 206-6000
Orlando (G-12819)		
Marriott Suites Resort	D	727 596-1100
Clearwater (G-1707)		
Marriott Vctons Worldwide Corp	C	407 206-6000
Orlando (G-12820)		
Marriott Villas At Doral		305 629-3400
Doral (G-3269)		
Marriotts Beachplace Towers	E	954 525-4440
Fort Lauderdale (G-3961)		
Marriotts Oceana Palms	E	561 227-3600
Riviera Beach (G-15308)		
▲ Maruti Hotels LLC	E	813 985-8525
Temple Terrace (G-18640)		
Mastercorp Inc	B	877 426-3275
Orlando (G-12830)		
Mayfair House Hotel LLC	C	305 441-0000
Miami (G-9911)		
MB Florida Limited LLC	C	305 538-8666
Miami Beach (G-10614)		
MCM Corp	C	305 531-5831
Miami Beach (G-10615)		
McOwc Marriott Hotels RES	E	407 239-4200
Orlando (G-12847)		
MCR Orlando Tenant LLC	D	407 354-1500
Orlando (G-12848)		
Mdm Brickell Hotel Group Ltd	C	305 329-3500
Miami (G-9924)		
Mdm Hotel Group Ltd	D	305 670-1035
Miami (G-9925)		
Mdm Hotel Group Ltd	D	305 670-1220
Miami (G-9926)		
Melbourne FL 0716 LLC	E	321 345-4186
West Melbourne (G-19013)		
Melbourne Hotel XI Owner LLC	D	321 768-0200
Melbourne (G-8935)		
Melbourne Ocean Club Hotel	C	321 773-9260
Melbourne (G-8937)		
Meldon Enterprises Inc	D	352 629-7300
Ocala (G-11728)		
Melia Orlando Suite Hotel At	E	407 964-7000
Celebration (G-1468)		
Menin Hotels	D	305 704-3615
Miami Beach (G-10617)		
Menna Brothers Number Two Inc	E	727 322-0770
Saint Petersburg (G-15760)		
Meristar Hotels and Resorts	D	407 351-5050
Orlando (G-12858)		
Merritt Hospitality	C	407 830-1985
Altamonte Springs (G-77)		
Mersina LLC	E	800 446-4656
Hollywood (G-5477)		
Mfm Services LLC	E	904 240-1345
Jacksonville (G-6502)		
Mgc Fort Pierce Corporation	E	772 464-5000
Fort Pierce (G-4721)		
MGM Hotels LLC	D	352 629-9500
Ocala (G-11729)		
MGM Resorts LLC	C	321 255-0077
Melbourne (G-8939)		
Mhf Las Olas Operating VI LLC	E	954 524-9595
Fort Lauderdale (G-3970)		
Mhg of Tmpa - Wstshore Fla 3 L	D	813 289-2700
Tampa (G-18034)		
Mhg Tampa Avion Park Hm LP	E	813 282-1950
Tampa (G-18035)		
Mhi Hospitality Trs LLC	D	813 289-1950
Tampa (G-18036)		
Mia Hospitality LLC	E	786 566-9468
Miami (G-9948)		
Mia Lejeune LLC	E	305 667-1003
Miami (G-9949)		
Miami Airport Complex II LLC	E	305 649-5000
Miami (G-9951)		
Miami Airport LLC	B	305 265-3835
Miami (G-9952)		
Miami Airways Motel	E	305 883-4700
Miami Springs (G-10786)		
Miami Beach Resort	C	305 532-3600
Miami Beach (G-10620)		
Miami Convention Hotel Corp	D	305 374-3000
Miami (G-9964)		
Miami Hilton	E	305 265-3832
Miami (G-9971)		
Miami Hotel Enterprise LLC	E	786 272-7250
Doral (G-3274)		
Miami Hotels	D	305 513-0777
Doral (G-3275)		
▼ Miami International Airport Ht	E	305 871-4100
Miami (G-9972)		

Company	Code	Phone
Mic Atlantis LLC	E	954 590-1000
Pompano Beach (G-14856)		
Miccosukee Resort & Gaming	D	877 242-6464
Miami (G-10000)		
Mid-Beach Management Inc	C	305 531-7494
Miami Beach (G-10624)		
Mid-Florida Hotels Inc	D	352 732-3131
Ocala (G-11730)		
Millenium Investment Group LLC	D	305 825-1000
Hialeah Gardens (G-5347)		
Millennium Twr Cndo Ht Assn In	B	305 358-3535
Miami (G-10004)		
Miramar Lodging LLC	D	954 438-7700
Miramar (G-10877)		
Miranjali LLC	E	754 221-0600
Dania Beach (G-2429)		
Misccosukee Tribe of Indians	E	305 228-8380
Miami (G-10007)		
▲ Mission Inn Resorts Inc	C	352 324-3101
Howey In The Hills (G-5623)		
Mj Ocala Hotel Associates	C	352 854-1400
Ocala (G-11736)		
Mj Ocala Hotel Associates	C	352 854-1400
Ocala (G-11736)		
Mlq Sgr Reo LLC	D	904 285-7777
Ponte Vedra Beach (G-14993)		
Mmi Hospitality Group Inc	D	904 741-3500
Jacksonville (G-6509)		
Mmi Hospitality Group Inc	D	352 375-2400
Gainesville (G-4949)		
Mocny Limited Partnership Lllp	E	407 656-5050
New Smyrna Beach (G-11420)		
Mohini Hospitality LLC	D	904 824-6181
Saint Augustine (G-15469)		
Moody Nat Orlando R Mt LLC	E	407 273-2084
Orlando (G-12877)		
Morgans Hotel Group MGT LLC	C	305 514-1500
Miami Beach (G-10626)		
Morgans Hotel Group MGT LLC	D	305 695-3226
Miami Beach (G-10627)		
Morgans Hotel Group MGT LLC	B	305 672-2000
Miami Beach (G-10628)		
Morlin Hospitality Group LLC	E	954 418-4000
Coconut Creek (G-1996)		
Motel 6 Tampa Fairground	E	813 623-5121
Tampa (G-18056)		
Motel 6 West	E	877 770-9801
Pensacola (G-14369)		
Mountain Lake Corporation	D	863 676-3494
Lake Wales (G-7694)		
MPK Investments Inc	E	407 239-9550
Tampa (G-12884)		
Msci 2007-Iq16 Lodging 100 LLC	E	386 254-8200
Daytona Beach (G-2642)		
Msr Hotels & Resorts Inc	D	407 888-9339
Orlando (G-12888)		
Murphco of Florida Inc	E	813 903-6000
Tampa (G-18061)		
Murphco of Florida Inc	D	904 217-5191
Orange Park (G-12005)		
Murphco of Florida Inc	E	863 292-3000
Winter Haven (G-19648)		
Murphco of Florida Inc	E	850 536-2000
Tallahassee (G-17051)		
Murphco of Florida Inc	D	850 562-7200
Tallahassee (G-17052)		
Mvhf LLC	D	678 292-4962
Hollywood (G-5478)		
Mvw Services Corporation	E	407 206-6000
Orlando (G-12891)		
Naples CFC Enterprises Ltd	D	239 643-8002
Naples (G-11224)		
Naples Golf and Beach Club Inc	B	239 261-2222
Naples (G-11230)		
Naples Hilton & Towers	D	239 430-4900
Naples (G-11232)		
Naples Hotel Co	E	239 261-6046
Naples (G-11233)		
Nard Inc	E	813 973-1665
Zephyrhills (G-19846)		
Natha Govan Inc	E	352 373-6500
Gainesville (G-4953)		
National Realty Holdings Inc	D	727 360-1811
St Pete Beach (G-16567)		
Nautilus Inn	E	386 254-8600
Daytona Beach (G-2643)		
Navnish Corporation	D	386 752-7891
Lake City (G-7539)		
Navy Exchange Service Command	E	904 772-6000
Jacksonville (G-6528)		

Company	Code	Phone
NAVY UNITED STATES DEPARTMENT	C	904 542-1295
Jacksonville (G-6531)		
NAVY UNITED STATES DEPARTMENT	D	904 542-2182
Jacksonville (G-6530)		
Neptune Inn Inc	D	239 463-6141
Fort Myers Beach (G-4671)		
Nesc LLC	D	727 442-4772
Clearwater Beach (G-1851)		
New Tampa Hotels LLC	E	813 910-7171
Tampa (G-18075)		
Newport Hospitality LLC	C	305 949-1300
Sunny Isles Beach (G-16726)		
Nf II Miami South Op Co LLC	E	305 265-0144
Miami (G-10048)		
Nf III Ft Lauderdale Op Co LLC	E	954 636-1700
Fort Lauderdale (G-3999)		
Nicklaus Investment Entps	E	727 360-1748
St Pete Beach (G-16568)		
Noble Hse Hotels & Resorts Ltd	A	305 296-7701
Key West (G-7231)		
Noble Hse Hotels & Resorts Ltd	E	561 557-5840
West Palm Beach (G-19277)		
Noble Hse Hotels & Resorts Ltd	C	305 295-7012
Key West (G-7232)		
Noble Investment Group LLC	E	305 269-1922
Miami (G-10050)		
Noble Investment Group LLC	D	813 221-4224
Tampa (G-18085)		
North Redington Bch Assoc Ltd	D	727 391-4000
N Redngtn Bch (G-10990)		
North-South Ltd	E	561 279-9900
Delray Beach (G-2996)		
Norwich Aventura I LLC	D	786 590-5100
Aventura (G-276)		
Npi Gcd West 38 LLC	E	352 378-1100
Gainesville (G-4967)		
Oak Plantation Resort & Suites	E	407 847-8200
Kissimmee (G-7361)		
Oakspring Inc	E	352 629-7021
Ocala (G-11746)		
Ocala Inn Cash Inc	D	352 629-0091
Ocala (G-11753)		
Ocean Drive Clevelander Inc	D	305 531-3485
Miami Beach (G-10636)		
Ocean Equities Ltd	E	954 931-9375
Laud By Sea (G-8168)		
Ocean Partners Associates Lllp	E	321 784-4800
Cocoa Beach (G-1974)		
Ocean Partners Associates Lllp	E	321 799-4099
Cocoa Beach (G-1975)		
Ocean Pointe	D	561 682-0500
Palm Beach Shores (G-13781)		
Ocean Properties	E	305 292-4320
Key West (G-7233)		
Ocean Properties Ltd	D	941 747-3727
Bradenton (G-1155)		
Ocean Properties Ltd	E	561 274-3200
Delray Beach (G-2998)		
Ocean Properties Ltd	E	813 639-9600
Tampa (G-18093)		
Ocean Properties Ltd	C	603 559-2100
Delray Beach (G-2999)		
Ocean Properties Ltd	D	603 559-2100
Treasure Island (G-18713)		
Ocean Properties Ltd	D	941 747-3727
Bradenton (G-1156)		
Ocean Properties Ltd	E	407 239-6900
Orlando (G-12924)		
Ocean Properties Ltd	E	561 737-4600
Boca Raton (G-725)		
Ocean Properties Ltd	D	941 383-2451
Longboat Key (G-8330)		
Ocean Properties Ltd	E	941 747-3727
Bradenton (G-1157)		
Ocean Properties Ltd	D	561 278-6241
Highland Beach (G-5358)		
Ocean Properties Ltd	E	772 337-2200
Port Saint Lucie (G-15154)		
Ocean Properties Ltd	D	941 388-5555
Sarasota (G-16249)		
Oceanfront Lodging II Inc	E	904 435-3535
Jacksonville Beach (G-6997)		
Old Island Hotels Inc	E	305 294-5702
Key West (G-7235)		
Old Key West Resort	E	407 827-1672
Lake Buena Vista (G-7467)		
Omni Hotels Corporation	E	904 261-6161
Amelia Island (G-123)		
Omni Hotels Corporation	C	904 355-6664
Jacksonville (G-6559)		

Omni-Chmpionsgate Resort Ht LP	C	407 390-6664	
Champions Gate *(G-1476)*			
Oprock Boynton Trs LLC	E	561 737-4600	
Boca Raton *(G-730)*			
Oprock Hollywood Trs LLC	C	954 924-2202	
Hollywood *(G-5488)*			
Oprock Key West Trs LLC	E	305 292-9800	
Key West *(G-7236)*			
Oprock Longboat Trs LLC	E	941 383-2451	
Longboat Key *(G-8331)*			
Oprock Port St Lucie Trs LLC	E	772 337-2200	
Port Saint Lucie *(G-15155)*			
Oprock Tampa Trs LLC	E	813 639-9600	
Tampa *(G-18102)*			
Optimal Wllness Physicians Ctr	E	786 279-6295	
Aventura *(G-277)*			
Orange Lake Holdings LLP	C	407 239-0000	
Kissimmee *(G-7364)*			
Orange Park Yacht Club LLC	E	904 854-1500	
Orange Park *(G-12009)*			
Orl Crown Plaza Universal	D	407 355-0550	
Orlando *(G-12939)*			
Orlando Hotel Associates LLC	C	407 351-3333	
Orlando *(G-12970)*			
Orlando Hotel Group LLC	E	407 993-3999	
Winter Garden *(G-19587)*			
Orlando Investment Corporation	C	407 248-2277	
Orlando *(G-12972)*			
Orlando Marriott Downtown	E	407 843-6664	
Aventura *(G-278)*			
Orlando Marriott Lake Mary	C	407 995-1100	
Lake Mary *(G-7618)*			
Orlando Metro Resort LLC	E	407 581-2000	
Orlando *(G-12977)*			
Owner Services	E	407 513-6578	
Orlando *(G-12997)*			
Oyster By/Pinte Condo Assn Inc	E	772 589-6513	
Sebastian *(G-16380)*			
P T T Management Co	E	904 269-8887	
Orange Park *(G-12010)*			
Pacifica Daytona LLC	D	386 252-4120	
Daytona Beach *(G-2648)*			
Packing House By-Products Co	D	352 324-3101	
Howey In The Hills *(G-5624)*			
Palace Resorts LLC	C	305 374-4752	
Doral *(G-3286)*			
Pallas LLC	C	727 572-7800	
Saint Petersburg *(G-15787)*			
Pallas Inc	C	727 572-7800	
Saint Petersburg *(G-15788)*			
Palm Ave Hsptlity Holdings LLC	C	941 316-0808	
Sarasota *(G-16256)*			
Palm Bay Hotel Venture LLC	A	321 725-2952	
Palm Bay *(G-13635)*			
Palm Bch Shres Rsort Vction VI	E	561 863-4000	
Palm Beach Shores *(G-13782)*			
▲ Palm Bch Stging Prod By Brkers	D	561 655-6611	
Palm Beach *(G-13665)*			
Palm Plaza D B S Inc	E	386 767-1711	
Daytona Beach *(G-2649)*			
Palmetto Hsptlity Gnsvlle II L	D	352 264-0000	
Gainesville *(G-4973)*			
Palmlor LLC	D	561 582-2585	
Palm Beach *(G-13666)*			
Palms South Beach Inc	C	305 534-0505	
Miami *(G-10088)*			
Pan American Venture Fund LLC	D	561 827-2048	
Boynton Beach *(G-1025)*			
Pan American Venture Fund LLC	D	800 366-5437	
Kissimmee *(G-7371)*			
Panama City Beach Hotel LLC	E	850 234-5722	
Panama City Beach *(G-14100)*			
▲ Panthers Brhc LLC	D	888 543-1277	
Boca Raton *(G-740)*			
Panthers Brhc LLC	A	561 447-3059	
Boca Raton *(G-741)*			
Panthers Rpn LLC	D	239 403-2000	
Naples *(G-11254)*			
Paradise Hotels Florida LLC	D	941 487-3800	
Sarasota *(G-16257)*			
Paradise Lakes Inc	D	813 949-9327	
Lutz *(G-8454)*			
Paradise of Port Richey Inc	C	727 849-2789	
Port Richey *(G-15107)*			
Parallel Hotels Inc	C	850 877-4437	
Tallahassee *(G-17063)*			
Paramand Investment Group Inc	D	407 323-6500	
Sanford *(G-15970)*			
Paramount Hospitality MGT LLC	C	407 238-7700	
Orlando *(G-13005)*			

Park Hotels & Resorts Inc	D	407 827-4000	
Lake Buena Vista *(G-7468)*			
Park Hotels & Resorts Inc	D	407 834-2400	
Altamonte Springs *(G-87)*			
Park Hotels & Resorts Inc	E	904 731-3555	
Jacksonville *(G-6579)*			
Park Hotels & Resorts Inc	E	561 994-8200	
Boca Raton *(G-744)*			
Park Hotels & Resorts Inc	E	407 313-4300	
Orlando *(G-13006)*			
Park Pl Hospitality Group Inc	C	904 491-4911	
Fernandina Beach *(G-3541)*			
Parliament Partners Inc	D	407 423-7227	
Orlando *(G-13010)*			
Parvati Inc	C	904 264-5107	
Orange Park *(G-12011)*			
Patten Receivables Fin Corp VI	D	561 912-7810	
Boca Raton *(G-746)*			
Pb Surf Ltd	E	850 932-6800	
Gulf Breeze *(G-5132)*			
Pbg Hotel LLC	D	804 777-9000	
Palm Beach Gardens *(G-13762)*			
Peacock Hotel LLC	D	850 319-2359	
Mary Esther *(G-8691)*			
Peacock Hotel LLC	D	850 581-7000	
Mary Esther *(G-8692)*			
Pegasus Hotel Associates LLC	D	813 282-3636	
Tampa *(G-18130)*			
Pegasus Hotel LLC	E	561 242-9066	
Orlando *(G-13020)*			
Pelican Beach Hotel Ltd	D	954 568-9431	
Fort Lauderdale *(G-4043)*			
Pelican Cove Resort Condo Assn	D	305 664-4435	
Islamorada *(G-5708)*			
Pelican Grnd Bch Rsort Cndo As	D	954 556-7575	
Fort Lauderdale *(G-4044)*			
▲ Pelican On Ocean Inc	D	305 532-6410	
Miami Beach *(G-10637)*			
Pensacola Bay Ltd Hward Jhnson	D	850 478-4499	
Pensacola *(G-14406)*			
Perry South Beach Hotel	C	305 604-1000	
Miami Beach *(G-10638)*			
Pestana Miami LLC	D	305 531-5635	
Miami Beach *(G-10639)*			
Peter A Thompson Trustee	D	863 424-1880	
Davenport *(G-2446)*			
Pfeffer & Marin Management	D	305 888-3661	
Miami Springs *(G-10787)*			
Pfl Vii LLC	E	954 772-1331	
Fort Lauderdale *(G-4050)*			
Pga National Resort & Spa	A	561 627-2000	
West Palm Beach *(G-19323)*			
PH Hotel Inc	D	305 372-0313	
Miami *(G-10114)*			
Phg Jacksonville LLC	E	904 741-3500	
Jacksonville *(G-6598)*			
Phillips Palm Beach Inc	D	561 659-3880	
West Palm Beach *(G-19324)*			
PHM Providence LLC	D	561 242-9066	
Royal Palm Beach *(G-15388)*			
Phr Stpfl LLC	D	401 946-4600	
Saint Petersburg *(G-15798)*			
Phr Stpfl Opco Sub LLC	E	401 946-4600	
Saint Petersburg *(G-15799)*			
Phvif II Plantation LLC	E	954 382-4500	
Plantation *(G-14693)*			
Phvif Miami LLC	D	786 439-0866	
Miami *(G-10118)*			
Pier House Joint Venture	D	305 296-4600	
Key West *(G-7238)*			
Pierre Resort LLC	E	407 313-3500	
Orlando *(G-13030)*			
Pinelands - Kendall Hotel LLC	E	786 837-2100	
Miami *(G-10121)*			
Pines Hotel Group Ltd	E	954 441-4242	
Pembroke Pines *(G-14174)*			
Pinnacle Inc	D	407 805-9111	
Lake Mary *(G-7624)*			
Pirates Cove Resort and Marina	D	772 223-5048	
Stuart *(G-16658)*			
Pk Domestic Lessee LLC	E	305 262-1000	
Miami *(G-10125)*			
Plantation Hotel Assoc LLC	D	954 423-4339	
Plantation *(G-14696)*			
Plantation Resort Inc	D	352 795-4211	
Crystal River *(G-2350)*			
Platinum Hospitality Group LLC	D	407 396-7969	
Orlando *(G-13037)*			
Playa Largo Resort & Spa	D	305 853-1001	
Key Largo *(G-7188)*			

Pnk Investments Inc	D	407 363-0332	
Orlando *(G-13039)*			
Point Orlndo Rsort Cndo Assn I	D	407 956-2000	
Orlando *(G-13041)*			
Ponces By Sea Inc	D	904 824-4347	
Saint Augustine *(G-15482)*			
Ponte Vedra Corporation	C	904 285-1111	
Ponte Vedra Beach *(G-15003)*			
Ponte Vedra Lodge Inc	C	904 273-9500	
Ponte Vedra Beach *(G-15004)*			
Poonam Inc	E	407 438-2121	
Orlando *(G-13043)*			
Port Hotel and Marina	E	352 795-3111	
Crystal River *(G-2351)*			
Premier Hospitality Mgt Group	D	863 688-8080	
Lakeland *(G-7941)*			
Premier Hotel Corporation	D	904 928-9116	
Jacksonville *(G-6614)*			
President Hotel	D	305 538-2882	
Miami Beach *(G-10641)*			
Prh 1300 Hotel LLC	E	305 533-1350	
Miami *(G-10141)*			
Prince Bush Hotels Inc	C	305 803-7455	
Hollywood *(G-5497)*			
Prisa Lhc LLC	D	407 828-8888	
Lake Buena Vista *(G-7469)*			
Provident Doral Resorts LLC	E	305 597-8600	
Doral *(G-3297)*			
Pyramid Advisors Ltd Partnr	E	954 424-3300	
Plantation *(G-14699)*			
Q Club Hotel LLC	C	954 414-2222	
Fort Lauderdale *(G-4068)*			
Qbd Properties LLC	E	954 561-7530	
Fort Lauderdale *(G-4070)*			
Quadrum Miami Beach LLC	E	305 503-5700	
Miami Beach *(G-10643)*			
Quality Hotel On Beach	D	727 442-7171	
Clearwater *(G-1768)*			
R I - Fadjem Inc	D	904 268-8080	
Jacksonville *(G-6631)*			
R S & R S Inc	E	904 829-3435	
Elkton *(G-3425)*			
Rabella Hospitality Inc	E	321 821-9009	
Melbourne *(G-8964)*			
Radsk Associates Ltd	C	727 595-1611	
Clearwater Beach *(G-1852)*			
Ragans Motel II Inc	D	850 973-8546	
Madison *(G-8489)*			
Ragans Motel Inc	D	850 973-3330	
Madison *(G-8490)*			
Rahn Bahia Mar LLC	C	954 627-6309	
Fort Lauderdale *(G-4079)*			
Railyard Hotel LLC	D	850 210-0008	
Tallahassee *(G-17079)*			
Rajn Hotels LLC	E	352 867-1347	
New Port Richey *(G-11402)*			
Ramada Inn Hollywood Beach	E	954 921-0990	
Hollywood *(G-5503)*			
Rap Ventures Inc	D	727 393-6700	
Saint Petersburg *(G-15814)*			
Rbhv Jacksonville LLC	D	904 564-4772	
Jacksonville *(G-6638)*			
Rc/Pb LLC	B	561 533-6000	
Lantana *(G-8066)*			
Rd & Rd Corporation	D	305 248-3155	
Florida City *(G-3562)*			
Red Roof Inns Inc	D	352 336-3311	
Gainesville *(G-4984)*			
Red Roof Inns Inc	E	904 296-1006	
Jacksonville *(G-6643)*			
Red Roof Inns Inc	D	850 476-7960	
Pensacola *(G-14419)*			
Red Roof Inns Inc	E	305 871-4221	
Miami *(G-10189)*			
Red Roof Inns Inc	E	239 774-3117	
Naples *(G-11279)*			
Red Roof Inns Inc	E	561 697-7710	
West Palm Beach *(G-19340)*			
Reema Hospitality Inc	D	321 956-6200	
Melbourne *(G-8967)*			
Remington Hotel Corporation	D	407 465-0075	
Orlando *(G-13096)*			
Remington Hotel Corporation	D	904 899-1485	
Jacksonville *(G-6654)*			
Remington Hotel Corporation	C	407 352-1100	
Orlando *(G-13097)*			
Remington Hotel Corporation	D	941 746-1141	
Bradenton *(G-1169)*			
Remington Hotel Corporation	E	727 894-5000	
Saint Petersburg *(G-15828)*			

Remington Hotel Corporation................D....... 305 296-2991
Key West *(G-7239)*
Renaissance Hotel MGT Co LLC...........C....... 727 894-1000
Saint Petersburg *(G-15829)*
Renaissance Hotel Operating Co..........A....... 407 351-5555
Orlando *(G-13098)*
Renaissance Hotel Operating Co..........B....... 305 531-0000
Miami Beach *(G-10644)*
Renassnce Orlndo Hotel-Airport...........E....... 407 240-1000
Orlando *(G-13100)*
Renthotel Florida Inc..............................E....... 407 396-4000
Kissimmee *(G-7377)*
Residence Inn By Marriott LLC.............E....... 305 604-6070
Miami Beach *(G-10646)*
Residence Inn By Marriott LLC.............E....... 407 313-3600
Orlando *(G-13102)*
Residence Inn By Marriott LLC.............E....... 386 252-3949
Daytona Beach *(G-2660)*
Residence Inn By Marriott LLC.............E....... 305 285-9303
Miami *(G-10204)*
Residence Inn By Marriott LLC.............D....... 301 380-3000
Orlando *(G-13103)*
Residence Inn By Marriott LLC.............D....... 321 723-5740
Melbourne *(G-8969)*
Residence Inn Tallahassee.....................D....... 850 329-9080
Tallahassee *(G-17086)*
Resort At Snger Island Prpts I...............B....... 561 340-1700
Riviera Beach *(G-15315)*
Resort Hospitality Entps Ltd..................B....... 850 234-3484
Panama City *(G-14064)*
Resort Hospitality Entps Ltd..................C....... 850 234-3484
Panama City *(G-14065)*
Resort Hospitality Entps Ltd..................C....... 850 234-3484
Panama City *(G-14066)*
Resort Hotels of Key Largo...................D....... 305 451-2121
Key Largo *(G-7189)*
Resort On Cocoa Beach Assn Inc...........D....... 321 783-4000
Cocoa Beach *(G-1977)*
Resortquest International Inc................E....... 850 301-3421
Fort Walton Beach *(G-4800)*
Resortquest RE Fla LLC.........................A....... 850 837-3700
Destin *(G-3074)*
Resorts World Omni LLC........................D....... 305 374-6664
Miami *(G-10206)*
Reunion Club of Orlando LLC.................B....... 407 662-1000
Reunion *(G-15240)*
Reunion West Club LLC.........................E....... 407 308-0519
Reunion *(G-15241)*
Reunion Wyndh Grand Golf & Spa.........E....... 407 662-1000
Reunion *(G-15242)*
Rhp Operations Gp LLC.........................A....... 407 586-6000
Kissimmee *(G-7378)*
Ritz-Carlton..D....... 407 206-2300
Orlando *(G-13116)*
Ritz-Carlton Dev Co Inc..........................C....... 407 206-6000
Orlando *(G-13117)*
Ritz-Carlton Hotel Company LLC...........C....... 239 254-3392
Naples *(G-11282)*
Ritz-Carlton Hotel Company LLC...........E....... 407 393-4900
Orlando *(G-13118)*
Ritz-Carlton Hotel Company LLC...........A....... 407 206-2400
Orlando *(G-13119)*
Ritz-Carlton Hotel Company LLC...........A....... 786 276-4000
Miami Beach *(G-10648)*
Ritz-Carlton Hotel Company LLC...........A....... 305 365-4500
Key Biscayne *(G-7169)*
Ritz-Carlton Hotel Company LLC...........C....... 904 277-1100
Amelia Island *(G-124)*
Ritz-Carlton Hotel Company LLC...........B....... 239 598-3300
Naples *(G-11283)*
Ritz-Carlton Hotel Company LLC...........B....... 561 691-8700
Jupiter *(G-7135)*
Ritz-Carlton Sarasota.............................B....... 941 309-2000
Sarasota *(G-16285)*
▲ **Riutel Beach Inc**.................................C....... 305 534-9330
Miami Beach *(G-10649)*
Riverwalk Hotels LLC.............................D....... 904 396-5100
Jacksonville *(G-6671)*
Rlj Dbt Key West Lessee LLC................D....... 305 293-1818
Key West *(G-7240)*
Rlj II - C Miramar Lessee LLC................E....... 954 450-1801
Miramar *(G-10891)*
Rochester Resorts Inc............................D....... 239 472-5161
Captiva *(G-1439)*
Rockresorts International LLC...............D....... 305 664-4651
Islamorada *(G-5709)*
Roop LLC..D....... 904 772-7771
Jacksonville *(G-6675)*
Rose Management Properties.................D....... 954 456-8333
Hallandale Beach *(G-5182)*
Rosemary Bch Cottage Rentl Co............E....... 850 231-2900
Rosemary Beach *(G-15379)*
Rosen 7600 Inc..C....... 407 996-1600
Orlando *(G-13129)*
Rosen 9000 Inc..B....... 407 996-8585
Orlando *(G-13130)*
Rosen 9939 Inc..A....... 407 996-9939
Orlando *(G-13131)*
Rosen Centre Inc.....................................A....... 407 996-9840
Orlando *(G-13132)*
Rosen Hotels and Resorts Inc...............B....... 407 996-1706
Orlando *(G-13134)*
Rosen International Inc..........................D....... 407 996-4444
Orlando *(G-13135)*
Rosen Plaza Inc.......................................B....... 407 996-9700
Orlando *(G-13137)*
Rosen Shingle Creek Community...........D....... 407 996-9939
Orlando *(G-13138)*
Rosen Vista Inc..C....... 407 996-7300
Orlando *(G-13139)*
Roya International Ht Inv LLC................E....... 850 275-0300
Fort Walton Beach *(G-4801)*
Royal American Hospitality Inc..............E....... 850 230-4618
Panama City Beach *(G-14102)*
Royal Flridian Resort Assn Inc...............D....... 386 672-7550
Ormond Beach *(G-13519)*
Royal Mansion Condo Assn Inc..............E....... 321 784-8484
Cape Canaveral *(G-1369)*
Royal Palms...E....... 407 238-6200
Orlando *(G-13142)*
Royal Place Owner LLC...........................D....... 407 827-2727
Lake Buena Vista *(G-7473)*
Rp Hotel Operating Co Inc......................E....... 786 276-0142
Miami Beach *(G-10651)*
RS Motel Corp...D....... 386 752-9350
Lake City *(G-7546)*
Rsllc-Orlando Downtown Ht LLC.............D....... 407 425-4455
Orlando *(G-13144)*
Rt-Destin Associates LLC........................D....... 850 337-7000
Destin *(G-3087)*
Rushlake Hotels (usa) Inc......................B....... 407 396-4500
Kissimmee *(G-7379)*
▲ **Saddlebrook Resorts Inc**....................A....... 813 973-1111
Wesley Chapel *(G-19006)*
Safety Harbor Resort and Spa................C....... 727 726-1161
Safety Harbor *(G-15411)*
Safety Harbor Spa & Fitnes Ctr..............E....... 727 726-1161
Safety Harbor *(G-15412)*
Sagamore Partners Ltd............................C....... 305 535-8088
Miami Beach *(G-10652)*
SAI Shyam Hotels LLC............................D....... 239 288-1372
North Fort Myers *(G-11476)*
SAI Sumukh LLC.......................................E....... 904 899-9000
Jacksonville *(G-6688)*
Saint Ptrsburg Clrwter Arprt A................D....... 727 577-9100
Clearwater *(G-1780)*
Salamander Farms LLC............................A....... 561 753-8110
West Palm Beach *(G-19351)*
Salamander Innisbrook LLC....................C....... 727 942-2000
Palm Harbor *(G-13879)*
Sand Key Associates Ltd Partnr.............C....... 727 595-1611
Clearwater Beach *(G-1853)*
Sandcastle Hotel Inc.................................B....... 941 388-2181
Sarasota *(G-16292)*
Sandestin Beach Hotel Ltd.......................D....... 850 622-9595
Destin *(G-3088)*
Sandestin Investments LLC......................A....... 850 267-6630
Destin *(G-3089)*
Sandpearl Resort LLC..............................B....... 727 441-2425
Clearwater *(G-1782)*
Sandpiper Gulf Resort Inc........................D....... 239 463-5721
Fort Myers Beach *(G-4672)*
Sands Harbor Inc.......................................D....... 954 942-9100
Pompano Beach *(G-14890)*
Sarasota Motor Inn....................................D....... 941 355-7747
Sarasota *(G-16054)*
Sarona Orlando Lee LLC..........................E....... 407 851-6400
Orlando *(G-13167)*
Sarp Inc..D....... 904 829-5643
Saint Augustine *(G-15490)*
Savoy Hotel Partners LLP.........................D....... 305 532-0200
Miami Beach *(G-10653)*
Sawgrass Hotel Opco LLC........................D....... 954 846-0400
Sunrise *(G-16822)*
SBE Hotel Management LLC....................E....... 305 794-8823
Miami *(G-10243)*
SC Collins LLC...E....... 305 674-5674
Miami Beach *(G-10654)*
SC Hotel Property LLC..............................E....... 786 482-2318
Surfside *(G-16854)*
Sea Club Ocean Resort Ht Inc.................E....... 954 564-3211
Fort Lauderdale *(G-4105)*
Sea Grdens Bch Tnnis Rsort - O.............A....... 954 943-6200
Pompano Beach *(G-14892)*
Sea View Hotel Inc.....................................D....... 305 866-4441
Bal Harbour *(G-300)*
Seaboard Associates Ltd Partnr..............C....... 305 296-7701
Key West *(G-7243)*
Seascape Resorts Inc................................D....... 850 837-9181
Miramar Beach *(G-10926)*
Sebastian Inlet Marina Trdg Co................D....... 772 388-8588
Sebastian *(G-16381)*
Select Hotels Group LLC...........................C....... 813 979-1922
Tampa *(G-18263)*
Select Hotels Group LLC...........................D....... 863 413-1122
Lakeland *(G-7966)*
Select Hotels Group LLC...........................E....... 407 816-7800
Orlando *(G-13182)*
Select Hotels Group LLC...........................D....... 239 495-1395
Estero *(G-3474)*
Select Title..E....... 407 345-1172
Orlando *(G-13184)*
Seminole Hard Rock Ht & Casino.............A....... 954 327-7625
Fort Lauderdale *(G-4113)*
Seminole Tribe Fla Hard Rock..................A....... 954 327-7625
Fort Lauderdale *(G-4114)*
Seminole Tribe of Florida Inc...................C....... 954 378-7840
Coconut Creek *(G-2002)*
Seminole Tribe of Florida Inc...................D....... 954 797-5425
Davie *(G-2515)*
Seminole Tribe of Florida Inc...................B....... 800 218-0007
Immokalee *(G-5660)*
Seminole Tribe of Florida Inc...................A....... 813 627-7625
Tampa *(G-18265)*
Senyar Miami Holding LLC.......................C....... 305 503-4400
Miami *(G-10261)*
Setai South Beach LLC.............................C....... 305 520-6000
Miami Beach *(G-10656)*
Sewaca Inc..C....... 305 294-5511
Key West *(G-7244)*
SF Hotels Inc...C....... 305 260-8951
Miami *(G-10265)*
Shalimar Nights Inc....................................E....... 850 651-9999
Shalimar *(G-16472)*
Shaner Hotel Group Ltd Partnr..................D....... 904 247-6782
Jacksonville *(G-6718)*
Shaner Slect Svcs Htels IV LLC................D....... 904 826-4068
Saint Augustine *(G-15493)*
Shelborne Beach Hotel Inc........................C....... 305 531-1271
Miami Beach *(G-10657)*
Shelborne Beach Resort.............................E....... 305 531-8416
Miami Beach *(G-10658)*
Shelini Hsptlity Ft Ldrdale LL......................E....... 954 767-8700
Fort Lauderdale *(G-4120)*
Shephards Beach Resort Inc......................D....... 727 442-5107
Clearwater *(G-1787)*
Shephards Beach Resort Inc......................E....... 727 441-6875
Clearwater *(G-1788)*
Sheraton Bal Hrbour Bch Resort................B....... 305 390-2629
Bal Harbour *(G-301)*
Sheraton LLC..E....... 954 424-3300
Plantation *(G-14707)*
Sheraton LLC..E....... 407 238-5000
Orlando *(G-13190)*
Shiraz Management LLC.............................C....... 561 684-9400
West Palm Beach *(G-19361)*
Shiv Shakti Investments Inc........................E....... 850 522-5200
Panama City *(G-14069)*
Shivam Neptune LLC....................................E....... 904 249-2777
Neptune Beach *(G-11358)*
Shiwani Investment Corp..............................D....... 904 964-7600
Starke *(G-16582)*
Shorewalk Vacation Villas LLC...................E....... 941 794-9800
Bradenton *(G-1179)*
Shreeji Hotel Group LLC..............................D....... 321 638-0604
Cocoa *(G-1954)*
Shreeji L L C..E....... 386 615-1280
Ormond Beach *(G-13522)*
SHS Resort LLC..B....... 727 726-1161
Safety Harbor *(G-15413)*
Shubh Hotels Boca LLC................................E....... 561 997-9500
Boca Raton *(G-799)*
Sierra Kyngs Heath LLC................................C....... 407 597-4000
Kissimmee *(G-7385)*
Sierra Land Group Inc...................................A....... 407 238-8000
Orlando *(G-13197)*
Signia By Hlton Orlndo Bnnet C....................D....... 407 597-3600
Orlando *(G-13200)*
Silver Lake Resort Ltd...................................D....... 407 397-1300
Kissimmee *(G-7386)*

S
I
C

Simpler Corporation ....E 321 799-3460
Cocoa Beach *(G-1978)*

Sirata Beach Resort LLC ....C 727 363-5100
St Pete Beach *(G-16569)*

Sita Rami & Sons Inc ....D 239 936-1311
Fort Myers *(G-4594)*

Six Continents Hotels Inc ....B 305 577-1000
Miami *(G-10279)*

Sky Resort Management LLC ....C 407 581-2151
Orlando *(G-13205)*

Skyline Hotels LLC ....D 407 658-9008
Orlando *(G-13206)*

Sobeny Partners LLC ....D 615 457-8906
Miami Beach *(G-10660)*

Soho House Beach House LLC ....D 786 507-7900
Miami Beach *(G-10661)*

Sokolov Ltd ....D 305 673-3337
Miami Beach *(G-10662)*

Sol Group Corp ....D 305 350-9828
Miami *(G-10290)*

Solus Quorum Tampa LLC ....C 813 289-8200
Tampa *(G-18303)*

Sonesta Intl Hotels Corp ....E 305 529-2828
Miami *(G-10294)*

▲ South Beach Properties LLP ....E 305 674-8200
Miami Beach *(G-10663)*

South Fla Hsptlity Invstmnts I ....E 954 484-9290
Oakland Park *(G-11614)*

South Pacific Entps Ltd Partnr ....E 561 793-3000
Royal Palm Beach *(G-15390)*

South Park Hospitality LLC ....E 407 226-3999
Orlando *(G-13218)*

Southeast Hospitality Corp ....D 954 525-8115
Fort Lauderdale *(G-4143)*

Southeast Hotels LLC ....E 352 508-5344
Tavares *(G-18618)*

Southeastern Hotel Partnership ....D 850 477-7155
Pensacola *(G-14443)*

Spectrum Hotels Inc ....E 407 226-0900
Orlando *(G-13224)*

Springhill Stes Convention Ctr ....E 407 345-9073
Orlando *(G-13228)*

Springhill Suites ....E 850 932-3678
Pensacola Beach *(G-14483)*

Springhill Suites Tampa N/Tamp ....E 813 558-0300
Tampa *(G-18322)*

Ssp-Pensacola Lodging LLC ....D 850 316-4226
Pensacola *(G-14447)*

St Augustine Resorts Inc ....D 904 471-2555
Saint Augustine *(G-15497)*

St Petersburg Harbour View Ht ....B 727 894-5000
Saint Petersburg *(G-15857)*

St Regis Bal Harbour Hotel ....E 305 993-3300
Bal Harbour *(G-302)*

Stanford Lake Hotel Inc ....D 561 483-3600
Boca Raton *(G-817)*

Star Hospitality MGT Inc ....E 941 347-8918
Punta Gorda *(G-15221)*

Star Island Development Corp ....C 407 997-8000
Kissimmee *(G-7388)*

Star Island Resort & Club ....D 407 997-8000
Kissimmee *(G-7389)*

Star Resorts Inc ....E 954 566-7500
Fort Lauderdale *(G-4150)*

Starwood Hotels & Resorts ....C 770 661-0252
Bal Harbour *(G-303)*

Starwood Latin America Inc ....E 786 999-6300
North Miami Beach *(G-11533)*

Staybrdge Stes Tampa E Brandon ....D 813 227-4000
Tampa *(G-18333)*

Stes Country Inn By Rdsson Inc ....D 850 249-4747
Panama City Beach *(G-14104)*

Stirling Coed Road LLC ....E 954 924-9204
Dania *(G-2419)*

Stirling Hosptality LLC ....E 954 922-0011
Hollywood *(G-5536)*

Stirling Hotel Dania Beach ....D 954 920-9696
Dania *(G-2420)*

Streamline Hotel ....E 386 947-7470
Daytona Beach *(G-2668)*

Streamsong Resort ....D 863 428-1000
Bowling Green *(G-954)*

Studio City Hotel Ventures LLC ....D 407 351-2100
Orlando *(G-13241)*

Sugar Loaf Lodge Tavern Inc ....E 305 745-3211
Summerland Key *(G-16695)*

Summit Hotel Trs 048 LLC ....D 407 370-4720
Orlando *(G-13245)*

Summit Hotel Trs 051 LLC ....E 407 351-0627
Orlando *(G-13246)*

Summit Hotel Trs 088 LLC ....D 239 418-1844
Fort Myers *(G-4611)*

Summit Hotel Trs 101 LLC ....D 813 247-6700
Tampa *(G-18343)*

Summit Hotel Trs 130 LLC ....C 305 269-1922
Miami *(G-10338)*

Summit Hotel Trs 134 LLC ....D 954 524-8733
Fort Lauderdale *(G-4160)*

Sun Cove of Kissimmee Inc ....D 407 933-5870
Kissimmee *(G-7391)*

Sun Ray Village Owners Assn ....D 850 932-4300
Gulf Breeze *(G-5134)*

Sunbelt - Ipf LLC ....D 850 505-7500
Pensacola *(G-14449)*

Sunbelt Hotel Enterprises Inc ....E 850 857-7744
Pensacola *(G-14450)*

Sunbrite Inc ....E 941 746-2505
Bradenton *(G-1183)*

Sunrise Hsptlity Pnscola Bch L ....E 850 932-5331
Gulf Breeze *(G-5135)*

Sunset Key Cottages ....D 305 292-5300
Key West *(G-7248)*

Sunstream Inc ....D 239 649-7333
Naples *(G-11312)*

Sunstream Inc ....C 239 765-1155
Fort Myers Beach *(G-4674)*

Super 8 Motel ....D 239 275-3500
Fort Myers *(G-4615)*

Superior Concierge Service LLC ....E 716 244-0643
Clermont *(G-1894)*

Surf Club of Marco Inc ....E 239 642-5800
Marco Island *(G-8638)*

Surya Inc ....D 850 689-2378
Crestview *(G-2334)*

Suzanne Chalet Properties Inc ....D 863 676-6011
Lake Wales *(G-7701)*

Swh Hotel LLC ....E 850 654-2677
Destin *(G-3080)*

▲ Swire Brickell Key Hotel Ltd ....A 305 913-8288
Miami *(G-10354)*

Swvp Sawgrass Mills LLC ....E 954 851-1020
Sunrise *(G-16833)*

T B H Corporation ....D 850 433-3336
Pensacola *(G-14455)*

T F Properties ....D 321 725-7500
Indialantic *(G-5668)*

T H Orlando Limited ....E 407 859-7700
Orlando *(G-13266)*

Tallahassee Ri LLC ....E 850 329-9080
Tallahassee *(G-17143)*

Tallmar Inc ....E 561 276-7441
Delray Beach *(G-3023)*

Tampa Airport Hotel LLC ....D 813 289-8200
Tampa *(G-18360)*

Tampa Back Bay Real Estate LLC ......E 813 350-4020
Tampa *(G-18362)*

Tampa East Hotel Holdings LLC ....D 813 626-6700
Tampa *(G-18374)*

Tampa Hospitality LLC ....E 813 872-0044
Tampa *(G-18384)*

Tampa Hotel LLC ....D 813 877-6061
Tampa *(G-18385)*

Tampa Ht Prtners Mstr Tnnts LL ....D 813 221-9555
Tampa *(G-18386)*

Tampa Innkeepers LLC ....D 813 971-8930
Tampa *(G-18387)*

Tampa Intl Tenant Corp ....C 813 877-9200
Tampa *(G-18389)*

Tampa Road Ht Holdings I LLC ....D 813 925-8887
Oldsmar *(G-11928)*

Tannex Development Corp ....A 305 294-4000
Key West *(G-7250)*

Tantallon Orlando LLC ....D 407 859-1500
Orlando *(G-13268)*

Tar Brax Corporation ....D 305 296-6595
Key West *(G-7251)*

Tavistock Hotel Collection LLC ....D 407 675-2000
Orlando *(G-13269)*

Tb Isle Resort LP ....D 305 932-6200
Aventura *(G-282)*

Tbhc Inc ....C 888 422-9445
Orlando *(G-13271)*

Td Lake Buena Vista Hotel LLC ....D 407 387-9999
Orlando *(G-13274)*

Telemar Inc ....C 321 773-2468
Indian Harbour Beach *(G-5672)*

Terremark Brickell II Ltd ....B 305 358-3535
Miami *(G-10378)*

Tesoro Club LLC ....E 772 345-4010
Port Saint Lucie *(G-15171)*

Tgc Hospitality LLC ....B 305 821-1130
Miami Lakes *(G-10767)*

Thi IV Miami Lessee LLC ....D 305 871-3800
Miami *(G-10386)*

Thi IV Pbg Lessee LLC ....E 561 622-2260
Palm Beach Gardens *(G-13776)*

Tides Real Estate LLC ....C 305 604-5070
Miami Beach *(G-10667)*

Timbers Resort Management LLC ......E 970 510-6796
Winter Park *(G-19778)*

Tishman Dolphin Ltd Partnr ....B 407 938-3000
Lake Buena Vista *(G-7474)*

Tishman Dolphin Ltd Partnr ....E 407 934-4000
Lake Buena Vista *(G-7475)*

Tishman Dolphin Ltd Partnr ....B 954 602-8500
Hollywood *(G-5538)*

Titusville Lodging Assoc LLP ....E 321 383-0200
Titusville *(G-18705)*

Touchmark Hotel Group LLC ....E 904 696-3333
Jacksonville *(G-6869)*

Tournment Plyers CLB Tampa Bay ....C 813 949-0090
Lutz *(G-8462)*

TownePlace Management LLC ....D 407 507-1300
Winter Garden *(G-19597)*

TownePlace Management LLC ....D 305 512-0946
Doral *(G-3335)*

TownePlace Sites Ft Lauderdale ....E 954 484-2214
Fort Lauderdale *(G-4179)*

Tpg Boca Raton LLC ....C 561 368-5252
Boca Raton *(G-842)*

Tralodge Inc ....D 407 396-4222
Kissimmee *(G-7401)*

Travel + Leisure Co ....C 407 626-5200
Orlando *(G-13305)*

Travel Lodge Kissimmee ....E 407 846-2221
Kissimmee *(G-7402)*

Travel Traders Hotels Inc ....E 786 388-2511
Miami *(G-10405)*

Travelkey LLC ....C 305 292-8539
Key West *(G-7252)*

Travelodge Colonial Gtwy Inn ....D 727 367-2711
St Pete Beach *(G-16572)*

Travelodge Inn and Suites ....E 904 741-4600
Jacksonville *(G-6874)*

Tri-King Inc ....D 727 367-1961
Treasure Island *(G-18714)*

Trianon Hotel Co ....E 239 263-8900
Naples *(G-11329)*

Trident Allied Assoc II LLC ....E 954 334-9233
Fort Lauderdale *(G-4184)*

Tristar Lodging Inc ....E 386 763-4299
Daytona Beach *(G-2678)*

Tropical Breeze Resort of Sies ....E 941 349-1125
Sarasota *(G-16351)*

◆ Turnberry Associates ....D 305 937-6262
Miami *(G-10418)*

Turnberry Ht Group Miami Inc ....D 305 937-0805
Miami *(G-10419)*

TWC Hotel LLC ....E 813 591-6900
Wesley Chapel *(G-19009)*

Twin Harbors Inc ....D 305 451-8500
Key Largo *(G-7190)*

Ucf Associates Ltd Partnership ....C 407 277-7676
Orlando *(G-13323)*

Ucf Hotel Venture ....B 407 503-9000
Orlando *(G-13325)*

Ucf Hotel Venture II ....E 407 503-9000
Orlando *(G-13326)*

Ucf Hotel Venture III ....E 407 503-5000
Orlando *(G-13327)*

Ucf III Associates Ltd Partnr ....E 407 243-6100
Orlando *(G-13328)*

Union Mnagment Tallahassee LLC ....D 850 422-0071
Tallahassee *(G-17161)*

United Hotel Group LLC ....E 321 636-7110
Rockledge *(G-15376)*

United New Albany Corporation ....E 561 776-3923
Juno Beach *(G-7041)*

United States Sugar Corp ....B 863 983-8172
Clewiston *(G-1913)*

University Hospitality II LLC ....E 407 737-7303
Orlando *(G-13356)*

US Army Shds Green Resort Afrc ......B 407 824-3400
Lake Buena Vista *(G-7477)*

Uscr Management LLC ....C 813 971-4710
Boca Raton *(G-857)*

Vacation Capital Group MGT ....E 407 307-2794
Miami *(G-10455)*

Vacation Club Services Inc ....E 407 370-3661
Miami *(G-10456)*

Vacation Vllas At Fntsywrld Tm.............D....... 407 396-1808
Kissimmee (G-7405)
Van Tampa Plaza Hotel Inc.....................D....... 813 289-1950
Tampa (G-18495)
Varad Hospitality LLC.............................D....... 772 287-6900
Stuart (G-16675)
Ved Hotels Inc..E....... 321 269-5510
Titusville (G-18706)
Velogan Inc...E....... 772 231-2300
Vero Beach (G-18931)
Venture Hsptality Partners Ltd ....E....... 850 863-3467
Fort Walton Beach (G-4808)
Vero Hotel LLC ....D....... 772 231-5666
Vero Beach (G-18937)
Vero Mar Development Ltd.....................E....... 772 231-5666
Vero Beach (G-18938)
Viera Hospitality LLC.............................E....... 321 255-6868
Melbourne (G-9001)
Vinay Inc...E....... 727 525-1800
Saint Petersburg (G-15887)
Vinayak Properties LLC.........................E....... 941 355-9000
Sarasota (G-16070)
Virosa Inc..E....... 407 722-8380
Orlando (G-13378)
Visionary Destin Inc................................D....... 850 650-9998
Destin (G-3081)
Visioners Hospitality LLC ....E....... 850 392-1093
Panama City (G-14084)
Vista CP Orlando LP ....E....... 607 760-8855
Orlando (G-13380)
Vista Myrtle Beach Hotel LP ....D....... 607 722-4469
Deerfield Beach (G-2812)
Vistana Development Inc ....B....... 407 239-3000
Orlando (G-13381)
Vistana Hawaii Management Inc............E....... 407 903-4242
Orlando (G-13382)
Vistana Vacation Ownership Inc............C....... 407 239-3100
Orlando (G-13385)
Vl West Building Corp ....D....... 954 739-4000
Fort Lauderdale (G-4215)
Vwi-Tampa East LLC...............................D....... 813 623-6363
Tampa (G-18515)
W A P Inc..E....... 850 234-2142
Panama City (G-14085)
W Fort Lauderdale Hotel ....D....... 954 414-8200
Fort Lauderdale (G-4217)
W2007 Eqi Jcksnvlle Bch Prtnr ....E....... 904 241-2311
Jacksonville Beach (G-7006)
W2007 Eqi Jcksnvlle Bch Prtnr ....E....... 904 241-2311
Jacksonville Beach (G-7007)
Walco Associates Inc ....D....... 305 592-5440
Miami (G-10487)
◆ Wallace Corporation...........................E....... 305 538-2331
Miami (G-10488)
Walt Disney World Co.............................E....... 407 855-8341
Orlando (G-13395)
Walt Disney World Information..............A....... 407 824-4321
Lake Buena Vista (G-7478)
▲ Walt Disney World Resort ....A....... 407 939-6000
Lake Buena Vista (G-7479)
Walt Dsney Prks Resorts US Inc ....A....... 407 824-1378
Lake Buena Vista (G-7480)
Walt Dsney Prks Resorts US Inc ....A....... 407 824-3200
Orlando (G-13398)
Walt Dsney Prks Resorts US Inc ....A....... 407 827-7962
Lake Buena Vista (G-7482)
Walt Dsney Prks Resorts US Inc ....A....... 407 827-3505
Lake Buena Vista (G-7483)
Walt Dsney Prks Resorts US Inc ....C....... 407 934-6000
Lake Buena Vista (G-7484)
Walt Dsney Prks Resorts US Inc ....C....... 407 824-5905
Lake Buena Vista (G-7485)
Walt Dsney Prks Resorts US Inc ....A....... 407 939-1000
Lake Buena Vista (G-7486)
Walt Dsney Prks Resorts US Inc ....A....... 407 939-3463
Lake Buena Vista (G-7489)
Walt Dsney Prks Resorts US Inc ....E....... 407 824-6429
Orlando (G-13402)
Walt Dsney Prks Resorts US Inc ....A....... 407 934-7000
Orlando (G-13404)
Walt Dsney Prks Resorts US Inc ....A....... 407 938-4000
Lake Buena Vista (G-7493)
Walt Dsney Prks Resorts US Inc ....A....... 407 824-3000
Lake Buena Vista (G-7494)
Walt Dsney Prks Resorts US Inc ....D....... 407 934-5000
Orlando (G-13405)
Walt Dsney Prks Resorts US Inc ....B....... 407 824-1253
Orlando (G-13406)
Walt Dsney Prks Resorts US Inc ....A....... 407 824-4321
Orlando (G-13407)
Walt Dsney Prks Resorts US Inc ....A....... 407 397-6000
Lake Buena Vista (G-7495)
Walt Dsney Prks Resorts US Inc ....A....... 407 824-2000
Lake Buena Vista (G-7496)
Walt Dsney Prks Resorts US Inc ....A....... 772 234-2000
Vero Beach (G-18946)
Walt Dsney Prks Resorts US Inc ....A....... 407 824-4026
Lake Buena Vista (G-7497)
Walt Dsney Prks Resorts US Inc ....A....... 321 939-7013
Orlando (G-13408)
Walt Dsney Prks Resorts US Inc ....C....... 407 828-3550
Lake Buena Vista (G-7498)
Walt Dsney Prks Resorts US Inc ....A....... 407 827-1100
Lake Buena Vista (G-7500)
Walt Dsney Prks Resorts US Inc ....A....... 407 824-2900
Lake Buena Vista (G-7501)
▲ Walt Dsney Prks Resorts US Inc ......A....... 407 824-2222
Lake Buena Vista (G-7487)
Walt Dsney Prks Resorts US Inc ....B....... 407 934-3400
Lake Buena Vista (G-7499)
Waramaug Tallahassee LLC...................E....... 850 325-1103
Tallahassee (G-17171)
Washington Aveassociates LLC............E....... 305 725-7486
Miami Beach (G-10673)
Wc Hospitality LLC ....E....... 407 260-8200
Daytona Beach (G-2689)
Welbro Heathrow Ht Assoc LLC............C....... 407 995-1100
Lake Mary (G-7654)
West Gate Company................................E....... 305 532-8831
Miami Beach (G-10674)
West Group Laplaya LLC ....D....... 239 597-3123
Naples (G-11342)
West Key Inn ....E....... 772 388-8588
Sebastian (G-16385)
West Palm Beach Hotel LLC ....D....... 561 689-6888
West Palm Beach (G-19419)
West Wind Assoc Sanibel Ltd................E....... 239 472-1541
Sanibel (G-16003)
Westbay Investment Development........D....... 305 374-5100
Miami (G-10500)
Westgate Planet Hllywd Las Veg...........B....... 407 351-3350
Orlando (G-13422)
Westgate Resorts LLC...........................B....... 407 351-3351
Orlando (G-13423)
▲ Westgate Resorts Ltd ....B....... 407 351-3350
Orlando (G-13424)
Westin Hotels Ltd Partnership...............B....... 305 441-2600
Coral Gables (G-2208)
▼ Westin Shrton Vcation Svcs Inc ....B....... 407 903-4640
Orlando (G-13425)
Westshore Hotel Owner LLC ....D....... 813 875-1555
Tampa (G-18546)
Westview Resorts Corp.... ....D....... 954 389-6750
Hillsboro Beach (G-5360)
White Lodging Services Corp................D....... 305 296-5700
Key West (G-7256)
White Lodging Services Corp................D....... 954 723-0300
Plantation (G-14720)
Whiteco Industries Inc............................C....... 954 472-2252
Plantation (G-14721)
Wifl Associates LLC ....E....... 813 971-7676
Tampa (G-18554)
Wilmarc of Florida Inc ....E....... 321 269-9100
Titusville (G-18708)
Wim Fwb Ri LLC......................................E....... 850 301-1369
Fort Walton Beach (G-4813)
Windsor Hospitality LLC ....E....... 407 313-4100
Orlando (G-13436)
Witham Family Ltd Partnership.............E....... 954 428-0650
Deerfield Beach (G-2818)
Wls Holdings LLC ....E....... 772 344-7814
Port St Lucie (G-15184)
World Center Marriott.............................C....... 407 238-8980
Orlando (G-13447)
Worldgate Resort Kissimmee ....C....... 407 396-1400
Kissimmee (G-7412)
Ww Lbv Inc...E....... 407 396-8806
Kissimmee (G-7413)
Ww Lbv Inc...E....... 407 396-4222
Kissimmee (G-7414)
Wyndham Bonnet Creek Hotel LLC ......B....... 407 390-2300
Orlando (G-13453)
Wyndham International Inc....................B....... 407 355-3609
Orlando (G-13454)
Wyndham Plms Mstr Cmnty Assn I.......E....... 407 390-1991
Kissimmee (G-7415)
Wyndham Resort Dev Corp ....C....... 866 495-1924
Orlando (G-13456)
Wyndham Vacation Resorts Inc ....C....... 850 837-8866
Destin (G-3091)
Wyndham Vacation Resorts Inc ....C....... 407 351-2641
Orlando (G-13459)
Wyndham Vacation Resorts Inc ....C....... 407 238-3100
Orlando (G-13460)
Wyndham Vacation Resorts Inc ....C....... 954 233-7500
Pompano Beach (G-14944)
Wyndham Worldwide Inc ....B....... 407 370-5200
Orlando (G-13461)
Wyndham Wrldwide Oprations Inc........C....... 973 753-6000
Orlando (G-13462)
Wynne Building Corporation ....C....... 305 235-3175
Miami (G-10518)
X Fund Properties LLC ....D....... 407 351-1000
Orlando (G-13463)
Xenia Hotels & Resorts Inc ....E....... 407 246-8100
Orlando (G-13465)
Yanni Ventures Inc..................................D....... 904 829-6581
Saint Augustine (G-15514)
Yes Hotel Services Inc...........................E....... 407 504-4400
Orlando (G-13469)
Yogeshwar Hospitality Inc ....D....... 904 378-1530
Jacksonville (G-6954)
Young MNS Chrstn Assn of Grter..........D....... 727 895-9622
Saint Petersburg (G-15904)
Younglim Inc..E....... 407 438-2121
Orlando (G-13470)
Yrg Hotel Group III LLC ....C....... 407 531-3555
Lake Mary (G-7655)
Zen Hospitality LLC ....E....... 850 472-1400
Pensacola (G-14480)

7021 Rooming & Boarding Houses

Earthmark Companies LLC....................C....... 813 645-3291
Ruskin (G-15399)
NAVY UNITED STATES DEPARTMENT..D....... 904 542-2182
Jacksonville (G-6530)
NAVY UNITED STATES DEPARTMENT..C....... 904 542-1295
Jacksonville (G-6531)

7032 Sporting & Recreational Camps

Board of Trstees of The Fla An..............E....... 352 787-4345
Leesburg (G-8233)
Caliente Resorts LLC.............................D....... 813 996-3700
Land O Lakes (G-8044)
Central Fla Yung MNS Chrstn As...........C....... 407 679-9622
Winter Park (G-19698)
Central Fla Yung MNS Chrstn As...........C....... 321 433-7770
Cocoa (G-1922)
Central Fla Yung MNS Chrstn As...........C....... 407 847-7413
Kissimmee (G-7281)
Central Fla Yung MNS Chrstn As...........C....... 352 343-1144
Tavares (G-18601)
City of Mount Dora..................................E....... 352 735-7183
Mount Dora (G-10948)
Eckerd Youth Alternatives Inc ....D....... 727 461-2990
Clearwater (G-1616)
Eckerd Youth Alternatives Inc ....D....... 727 461-2990
Brooksville (G-1283)
Envirnmntal Prtection Fla Dept ....D....... 863 696-1112
Lake Wales (G-7680)
Greater Daytona Bch Area YMCA..........D....... 386 255-8773
Deland (G-2863)
Greater Dytona Bch Area Yung M..........D....... 386 532-9622
Deltona (G-3039)
Jacksonville Fc Inc..................................E....... 904 223-3606
Jacksonville (G-6360)
Lake Arora Chrstn Assembly Inc...........E....... 863 696-1102
Lake Wales (G-7687)
Pestana Miami LLC.................................E....... 305 531-5635
Miami Beach (G-10639)
Riviera Day Camp Inc ....E....... 305 666-1856
Coral Gables (G-2179)
Saddlebrook Intl Tennis Inc ....D....... 813 973-1111
Zephyrhills (G-19849)
Safe Children Coalition Inc ....B....... 941 955-8194
Sarasota (G-16290)
Sun Cove of Kissimmee Inc...................D....... 407 933-5870
Kissimmee (G-7391)
Tampa Metropolitan Area YMCA............C....... 813 684-1371
Valrico (G-18759)
Tampa Mtro Area Yung MNS Chrst.........C....... 813 866-9622
Tampa (G-18395)
Tampa Mtro Area Yung MNS Chrst.........D....... 813 224-9622
Tampa (G-18396)
Tampa Mtro Area Yung MNS Chrst.........C....... 352 521-0484
Dade City (G-2397)
Tampa Mtro Area Yung MNS Chrst.........E....... 813 222-1334
Tampa (G-18397)
Tampa Mtro Area Yung MNS Chrst.........D....... 813 229-9622
Tampa (G-18399)

Tampa Mtro Area Yung MNS Chrst........D...813 780-9622
  Zephyrhills (G-19852)
Time2shine Academy Inc ....E...202 430-3039
  Saint Augustine (G-15506)
Trinity Bptst Ch of Jcksnvlle........D...352 473-4226
  Melrose (G-9015)
Twister Gymnastics West Boca ......E...561 750-6001
  Boca Raton (G-849)
Volusia Flagler Family ....E...386 736-6000
  Deland (G-2891)
YMCA of Palm Beaches ....D...561 967-3573
  Palm Springs (G-13901)
YMCA of Treasure Coast ....E...772 221-9622
  Stuart (G-16683)
YMCA Southwest Florida Inc ....D...941 475-1234
  Englewood (G-3442)
Young MNS Christn Assn NW Fla......E...850 432-8327
  Pensacola (G-14479)
Young MNS Chrstn Assn of Flrda........C...904 355-1436
  Jacksonville (G-6957)
Young MNS Chrstn Assn of Flrda........C...904 259-0898
  Macclenny (G-8480)
Young MNS Chrstn Assn of Flrda........C...904 471-9622
  Saint Augustine (G-15515)
Young MNS Chrstn Assn of Flrda........C...904 464-3901
  Jacksonville (G-6960)
Young MNS Chrstn Assn of Flrda........C...904 296-3220
  Fernandina Beach (G-3546)
Young MNS Chrstn Assn of Mrtin........C...772 286-4444
  Stuart (G-16684)
Young MNS Chrstn Assn of Sncas........D...312 932-1200
  Clearwater (G-1844)
Young MNS Chrstn Assn of Sncas........C...727 394-9622
  Seminole (G-16465)
Young MNS Chrstn Assn of Sncas........D...727 787-9622
  Palm Harbor (G-13887)
Young MNS Chrstn Assn of Sncas........C...352 688-9622
  Spring Hill (G-16556)
Young MNS Chrstn Assn of Sncas........D...727 461-9622
  Clearwater (G-1845)
Young MNS Chrstn Assn of Sncas........D...727 772-9622
  Palm Harbor (G-13888)
Young MNS Chrstn Assn of Sncas........D...727 844-0332
  New Port Richey (G-11411)
Young MNS Chrstn Assn S Fla In ......E...305 643-2626
  Miami (G-10524)
Young MNS Chrstn Assn S Fla In ......D...305 635-9622
  Miami (G-10525)
Young MNS Chrstn Assn S Fla In ......E...305 248-5189
  Homestead (G-5613)

7033 Trailer Parks & Camp Sites

Century Realty Funds Inc................D...863 424-2839
  Davenport (G-2438)
Clewiston Marina Inc ....E...863 983-3151
  Clewiston (G-1900)
Cornetts Sprit of Suwannee Inc........D...386 364-1683
  Live Oak (G-8309)
Dixie Plaza ....E...863 993-2221
  Arcadia (G-228)
Envirnmntal Prtection Fla Dept ......D...352 466-3397
  Micanopy (G-10790)
Envirnmntal Prtection Fla Dept ......D...386 454-1853
  High Springs (G-5352)
Fla Dpt Envirnmntal Prtection ......D...850 227-1327
  Port Saint Joe (G-15115)
Ginnie Spring Outdoors LLC ......E...386 454-7188
  High Springs (G-5353)
Gospel Crusade Inc ....E...941 746-2882
  Bradenton (G-1113)
Hometown America MGT Corp ......C...352 796-8016
  Brooksville (G-1295)
Kampgrounds of America Inc ......E...239 774-5455
  Naples (G-11187)
Kampgrounds of America Inc ......E...727 392-2233
  Saint Petersburg (G-15740)
Kampgrounds of America Inc ......E...305 745-3549
  Summerland Key (G-16693)
Ldrv Holdings Corp ....D...813 246-4777
  Seffner (G-16430)
N H C F L 8 LP ....D...813 792-7160
  Odessa (G-11851)
North Beach Investment Inc ......E...904 824-1806
  Saint Augustine (G-15473)
Peter A Thompson Trustee ......D...863 424-1880
  Davenport (G-2446)
Royalty Resorts Corporation ......D...941 371-2505
  Sarasota (G-16287)
Sun Communities Inc ....D...941 371-2505
  Sarasota (G-16335)

T & P Enterprises Bay Cnty Inc......E...850 234-2502
  Panama City (G-14078)
Travelers Rest Resort Inc......E...352 588-2013
  Dade City (G-2398)
Twin Harbors Inc ....D...305 451-8500
  Key Largo (G-7190)
Walt Dsney Prks Resorts US Inc......D...863 605-3995
  Orlando (G-13401)
Whiteys Fish Camp Inc................E...904 269-4198
  Orange Park (G-12024)

7041 Membership-Basis Hotels

Club Continental Inc ....D...904 264-6070
  Orange Park (G-11982)
Collegiate Village Inn Inc................D...407 380-6000
  Orlando (G-12344)
Episcpal Cnfrnce Ctr Dcese of ......D...941 776-1018
  Parrish (G-14114)
Flagler System Inc ....C...561 655-6611
  Palm Beach (G-13654)
Florence Villa Cmnty Dev Corp ......E...863 299-3263
  Winter Haven (G-19627)
Lake Arora Chrstn Assembly Inc........C...863 696-1102
  Lake Wales (G-7687)
Life Concepts Inc ....D...813 423-7700
  Tampa (G-17946)
Lodging Resources Inc ....D...800 772-3359
  Fernandina Beach (G-3534)
NAVY UNITED STATES DEPARTMENT..D...904 542-2182
  Jacksonville (G-6530)
NAVY UNITED STATES DEPARTMENT..C...904 542-1295
  Jacksonville (G-6531)
Oceanfront Lodging II Inc ....E...904 435-3535
  Jacksonville Beach (G-6997)
Wyndham Vacation Resorts Inc ....D...407 370-5200
  Orlando (G-13458)

72 PERSONAL SERVICES

7211 Power Laundries, Family & Commercial

Acme Laundry and Cleaners Inc ......E...407 841-2301
  Orlando (G-12048)
Crothall Services Group ....A...407 656-6888
  Clermont (G-1863)
Cys Linen Service Inc................E...305 887-9441
  Hialeah (G-5248)
Deluxe Laundry & Dry Clrs Inc ......E...904 387-0415
  Jacksonville (G-6060)
Florida Avenue Clrs & Ldry Inc........C...813 238-1453
  Tampa (G-17672)
Orlando Cleaners LLC ....D...407 481-2000
  Orlando (G-12943)
Vicks Cleaners Inc ....E...850 432-8351
  Pensacola (G-14463)

7212 Garment Pressing & Cleaners' Agents

595 Repair Shop LLC ....D...954 357-1480
  Davie (G-2452)
Combined Services Inc ....C...305 685-7219
  Miami Lakes (G-10717)
Crown Hlth Care Ldry Svcs LLC......B...844 383-7500
  Pensacola (G-14279)
Deluxe Laundry & Dry Clrs Inc ......E...904 387-0415
  Jacksonville (G-6060)
Imperium Fabricare LLC ....E...239 775-7232
  Naples (G-11174)

7213 Linen Sply

Alsco Inc ....E...941 366-5950
  Sarasota (G-16085)
Alsco Inc ....D...904 354-6675
  Jacksonville (G-5771)
Alsco Inc ....D...407 841-4661
  Orlando (G-12102)
Alsco Inc ....D...954 979-2600
  Pompano Beach (G-14738)
Bay Linen Inc ....C...727 573-7608
  Clearwater (G-1534)
Cintas Corporation No 2................D...561 686-1444
  West Palm Beach (G-19086)
Crown Hlth Care Ldry Svcs LLC..........C...850 433-2600
  Pensacola (G-14278)
Florida Linen Services LLC................D...954 784-8125
  Pompano Beach (G-14810)
Gold Coast Linen Services LLC........E...561 832-3841
  West Palm Beach (G-19166)
Over Top Inc ....E...954 424-0076
  Davie (G-2503)

Rfid Corporation ....E...386 672-3932
  Holly Hill (G-5383)

7215 Coin Operated Laundries & Cleaning

Crown Hlth Care Ldry Svcs LLC........B...863 608-9537
  Lakeland (G-7846)
CSC Serviceworks Inc ....E...954 392-5800
  Miramar (G-10849)
Elite Laundry Services Fla Inc ......C...305 887-6799
  Medley (G-8725)
Five Star Laundry MGT II LLC........E...407 586-2145
  Kissimmee (G-7308)
Mariottis Cleaning Centers ....E...904 829-2414
  Saint Augustine (G-15465)

7216 Dry Cleaning Plants, Except Rug Cleaning

Acme Laundry and Cleaners Inc ......E...407 841-2301
  Orlando (G-12048)
Agemy Family Corporation ....D...813 925-0900
  Tampa (G-17245)
Carden Inc ....E...407 740-8837
  Debary (G-2699)
Cys Linen Service Inc ....E...305 887-9441
  Hialeah (G-5248)
Deluxe Laundry & Dry Clrs Inc ......E...904 387-0415
  Jacksonville (G-6060)
Ehrlich Road Cleaners & Ldry ......D...813 968-4599
  Tampa (G-17617)
Florida Avenue Clrs & Ldry Inc........C...813 238-1453
  Tampa (G-17672)
Glidewell Corporation ....D...321 632-1007
  Cocoa (G-1938)
Mariottis Cleaning Centers ....E...904 829-2414
  Saint Augustine (G-15465)
Orlando Cleaners LLC ....C...407 447-6701
  Winter Garden (G-19584)
Orlando Cleaners LLC ....D...407 481-2000
  Orlando (G-12943)
Scott S Custom Cleaners Inc ......E...727 584-8382
  Belleair Bluffs (G-372)
Sir Galloway Dry Cleaners Inc ......D...305 252-2000
  Miami (G-10277)
Sir Galloway Dry Cleaners Inc ......D...305 665-5050
  South Miami (G-16513)
Sudsies Inc ....E...305 864-3279
  Miami Beach (G-10664)
Vicks Cleaners Inc ....E...850 432-8351
  Pensacola (G-14463)

7217 Carpet & Upholstery Cleaning

CC & Ss Inc ....E...229 228-1512
  Tallahassee (G-16907)
CC & Ss Inc ....E...352 622-5885
  Ocala (G-11653)
Cole Industries Inc ....E...850 433-8100
  Pensacola (G-14262)
Complete Cleaning Serv of Irc........D...772 562-3585
  Vero Beach (G-18848)
Cubix Inc ....E...407 373-7412
  Orlando (G-12390)
Gellner Enterprises Inc ....D...407 291-4717
  Apopka (G-184)
Image Janitorial Services Inc........C...561 627-8748
  West Palm Beach (G-19196)
Joshua W Kennedy Entps LLC ......E...904 383-7721
  Jacksonville (G-6391)
Mega Service Solutions Inc ......D...813 501-5001
  Tampa (G-18021)
Mussallem Oriental Rugs Inc ......E...904 731-4785
  Jacksonville (G-6524)
Progressive Business Inc ....E...954 370-7778
  Davie (G-2508)
Senoma Inc ....E...954 979-6364
  Deerfield Beach (G-2795)
Stanley Stmer Crpt Clg of Clli ......D...239 597-8104
  Naples (G-11307)
Steam-S-Way Inc ....E...561 966-0765
  Riviera Beach (G-15319)
Super Restoration Svc Co LLC........E...305 233-0500
  Doral (G-3325)

7218 Industrial Launderers

Cintas Corporation No 2................E...813 623-3474
  Tampa (G-17472)
Cintas Corporation No 2................E...386 274-2715
  Daytona Beach (G-2559)
Cintas Corporation No 2................C...407 423-4222
  Orlando (G-12301)

Crown Linen LLC	C	305 691-4048
Miami (G-9441)		
Crown Linen LLC	C	305 691-4048
Orlando (G-12388)		
Five Star Laundry MGT II LLC	E	407 586-2145
Kissimmee (G-7308)		
Mbgc LLC	D	305 851-8281
Miami (G-9913)		
Orlando Health Inc	D	407 656-6888
Clermont (G-1881)		
Supreme Linen Services Inc	E	305 822-6667
Hialeah (G-5327)		
Unifirst Corporation	E	813 621-4741
Tampa (G-18459)		
Van Dyne-Crotty Co	E	954 979-2600
Pompano Beach (G-14937)		

7219 Laundry & Garment Svcs, NEC

Ehrlich Road Cleaners & Ldry	D	813 968-4599
Tampa (G-17617)		
Hotelier Consulting Svcs LLC	C	305 823-2139
Miami Lakes (G-10736)		
Orlando Health Inc	D	407 656-6888
Clermont (G-1881)		

7221 Photographic Studios, Portrait

Bryn-Alan Studios Inc	C	813 286-8216
Tampa (G-17394)		
Devore Design LLC	E	407 500-7427
Clermont (G-1865)		
Rekcut Photographic Inc	D	904 829-6541
Saint Augustine (G-15485)		
Smiles Beach Photo LLC	E	850 249-3349
Panama City (G-14071)		
Walmart Inc	C	407 957-4333
Saint Cloud (G-15538)		
Walmart Inc	D	850 526-0064
Marianna (G-8687)		
Walmart Inc	C	386 734-5468
De Land (G-2697)		

7231 Beauty Shops

1st Lady Nails	E	561 471-0551
West Palm Beach (G-19016)		
Aacardi Inc	E	727 343-0074
Saint Petersburg (G-15555)		
◆ Beauty Elements Corp	D	305 430-4400
Miami Lakes (G-10711)		
Belk Inc	C	904 363-1100
Jacksonville (G-5854)		
Benes Intl Schl Buty Inc	E	727 848-8415
New Port Richey (G-11368)		
Bliss Salon In Destin LLC	E	850 424-7884
Destin (G-3050)		
Bosta Co Inc	E	954 454-2220
Hallandale Beach (G-5167)		
Bridgeview Investements LLC	E	727 466-1703
Clearwater (G-1553)		
Cartoon Cuts LP	E	561 383-6500
Wellington (G-18973)		
Central Fla Drmtology Assoc PA	E	407 481-2620
Orlando (G-12264)		
Compass Rose Foundation Inc	E	904 328-5600
Jacksonville (G-5995)		
Creative Hairdressers Inc	A	813 854-5746
Tampa (G-17547)		
Creative Hairdressers Inc	A	386 774-5070
Orange City (G-11960)		
◆ Creative Nail Design Inc	C	760 599-2900
Jacksonville (G-6011)		
Eeg Inc	E	954 742-4111
Lauderhill (G-8195)		
Hc Salon Holdings Inc	D	954 920-8595
Hollywood (G-5446)		
Hc Salon Holdings Inc	D	386 734-9341
De Land (G-2694)		
Hc Salon Holdings Inc	D	904 264-9065
Orange Park (G-11994)		
Hc Salon Holdings Inc	D	772 770-1531
Vero Beach (G-18866)		
Hc Salon Holdings Inc	D	407 788-8119
Altamonte Springs (G-57)		
Hc Salon Holdings Inc	D	407 656-9500
Winter Garden (G-19568)		
Hc Salon Holdings Inc	D	904 223-1455
Jacksonville (G-6263)		
Hc Salon Holdings Inc	D	305 936-8749
Aventura (G-272)		
Hc Salon Holdings Inc	D	863 422-9496
Davenport (G-2443)		

Hc Salon Holdings Inc	D	407 891-9272
Saint Cloud (G-15524)		
Hc Salon Holdings Inc	D	772 770-1048
Vero Beach (G-18867)		
Hc Salon Holdings Inc	D	407 893-8150
Orlando (G-12622)		
Hc Salon Holdings Inc	D	561 798-1226
West Palm Beach (G-19172)		
Hc Salon Holdings Inc	D	561 697-2847
West Palm Beach (G-19173)		
Ideal Image Development Corp	C	813 286-8100
Tampa (G-17854)		
Indian River State College	E	772 419-5695
Stuart (G-16633)		
Jon Ric Intl Salon & Spas	C	386 734-1234
Deland (G-2865)		
Jon Ric Intl Salon & Spas	C	954 345-5222
Coral Springs (G-2262)		
Kavonyas Beauti Brows Entp LLC	D	863 656-3087
Winter Haven (G-19639)		
Lakeland Ob-Gyn PA	E	863 688-1528
Lakeland (G-7902)		
ME Bath Spa Experience LLC	E	954 436-1251
Pembroke Pines (G-14169)		
Natures Elite Inc	E	800 986-6402
Hollywood (G-5480)		
Orlando Oral Facial Surgery PA	E	407 522-0464
Ocoee (G-11821)		
Orlando Oral Facial Surgery PA	E	407 333-3011
Lake Mary (G-7619)		
Penney Opco LLC	E	954 472-2500
Plantation (G-14692)		
Penney Opco LLC	C	863 858-7900
Lakeland (G-7939)		
Penney Opco LLC	D	239 574-9111
Cape Coral (G-1420)		
Penney Opco LLC	C	305 823-9880
Hialeah (G-5310)		
Peter of London	D	305 274-1166
Miami (G-10113)		
◆ Pevonia International LLC	E	386 239-8980
Daytona Beach (G-2651)		
Riverchase Dermatology	E	941 488-7727
Venice (G-18800)		
Springline Corp	E	407 365-9568
Orlando (G-13229)		
Taisa Cotton Services	E	386 218-9030
Deltona (G-3044)		
Tsp Institute Inc	E	904 647-4575
Jacksonville (G-6877)		
Tsp Institute Inc	E	727 460-4883
Winter Park (G-19781)		
Walmart Inc	C	386 734-5468
De Land (G-2697)		
Xander Blue Salon LLC	E	407 628-2583
Deland (G-2895)		

7241 Barber Shops

Hairuwear Inc	D	954 835-2200
Sunrise (G-16777)		
Jon Ric Intl Salon & Spas	C	954 345-5222
Coral Springs (G-2262)		

7251 Shoe Repair & Shoeshine Parlors

Speedy Car Wash Inc	E	850 785-9274
Panama City (G-14075)		

7261 Funeral Svcs & Crematories

Baldwin-Fairchild Fnrl Homes	D	407 656-2233
Winter Garden (G-19556)		
Baldwin-Fairchild Fnrl Homes	D	407 886-1461
Apopka (G-157)		
Caballero Rvero Wdlawn Fnrl Hm	E	305 221-8282
Miami (G-9301)		
Cemetery Management Inc	B	813 626-3161
Tampa (G-17439)		
Curlew Hills Memory Grdns Inc	E	727 789-2000
Palm Harbor (G-13857)		
Faith Chapel Funeral Svcs LLC	E	850 937-8118
Pensacola (G-14303)		
Faithful Heritage Holdings Inc	D	352 372-1447
Gainesville (G-4882)		
Florida Mortuary Services Inc	A	305 325-1171
Miami (G-9580)		
Funeral Services Inc	E	850 425-1340
Tallahassee (G-16985)		
Keystone Group Holdings Inc	C	813 237-2900
Tampa (G-17917)		
Keystone Group Holdings Inc	D	813 225-4650
Orlando (G-12728)		

Miami Memorial LLC	C	305 274-8972
Miami (G-9978)		
Pershing Industries Inc	D	305 821-1421
Miami Lakes (G-10753)		
SCI Funeral Services Fla Inc	E	813 645-3231
Ruskin (G-15403)		

7291 Tax Return Preparation Svcs

Andersen Tax LLC	C	561 805-6550
West Palm Beach (G-19035)		
Bastion Capital Investment	E	305 431-8531
Miami (G-9227)		
Deloitte & Touche LLP	D	561 962-7700
Boca Raton (G-550)		
Grant Thornton LLP	C	954 768-9900
Fort Lauderdale (G-3831)		
Happy Tax Franchising LLC	C	844 426-1040
Miami Beach (G-10599)		
Insurance Center Inc	E	904 645-0006
Jacksonville (G-6322)		
Jackson Hewitt Inc	E	941 378-7163
Sarasota (G-16202)		
Prime Capital Services Inc	D	727 791-0077
Clearwater (G-1765)		
Ratliffs Ex Txes Cnsulting LLC	E	850 591-1682
Tallahassee (G-17081)		
Royalty Tax Services Inc	E	954 228-7467
Winter Park (G-19772)		

7299 Miscellaneous Personal Svcs, NEC

2345 Wilton Drive LLC	E	954 765-6968
Wilton Manors (G-19518)		
250 W State Road 84 LLC	E	954 525-5641
Fort Lauderdale (G-3565)		
Admirals Inn Ltd	D	863 318-1456
Winter Haven (G-19603)		
Alto Usa LLC	E	214 435-8632
Miami (G-9131)		
American Debt Counseling Inc	D	954 227-7221
Sunrise (G-16736)		
Ameripark LLC	B	954 681-4264
Fort Lauderdale (G-3605)		
Associated Cnstr Pdts Inc	D	813 973-4425
Lutz (G-8430)		
Atomic Tattoos - Tampa Bay LLC	D	727 787-4444
Clearwater (G-1527)		
Atrium Trs I LP	C	954 753-5598
Coral Springs (G-2228)		
Auto Titles of America LLC	E	941 739-8841
Bradenton (G-1055)		
Avista Properties Ix Inc	D	407 465-8150
Orlando (G-12160)		
Beachcomber Hotel	C	954 941-7830
Pompano Beach (G-14752)		
Biltmore Hotel Ltd Partnership	B	305 445-1926
Coral Gables (G-2054)		
Buena Vista Suites	D	407 239-8588
Orlando (G-12216)		
Can Do Building Services Inc	E	305 885-1011
Miami (G-9310)		
Caravan Hotel Properties LLC	D	407 581-5041
Orlando (G-12233)		
Caretnders Vsting Svcs Dst 6 L	C	941 360-6974
Bradenton (G-1072)		
Caretnders Vsting Svcs Dst 7 L	A	321 308-0321
Palm Bay (G-13611)		
Cec Entertainment LLC	E	407 382-6528
Orlando (G-12250)		
Ceviche Restaurant Inc	D	321 281-8140
Orlando (G-12286)		
Challenge Entps N Fla Inc	B	904 284-9859
Green Cove Springs (G-5048)		
City Nights Valet Inc	C	407 849-0670
Orlando (G-12305)		
Cko Mgt LLC	E	662 781-5100
Tallahassee (G-16920)		
Club Continental Inc	D	904 264-6070
Orange Park (G-11982)		
Club Med Sales Inc	C	772 398-5003
Port Saint Lucie (G-15129)		
Collegiate Village Inn Inc	E	407 422-8191
Winter Park (G-19707)		
Colorvision International Inc	B	407 851-0103
Orlando (G-12346)		
Columbia Properties Tampa LLC	C	813 623-6363
Tampa (G-17497)		
▲ Columbia Prpts Orlando LLC	B	407 856-0100
Orlando (G-12347)		
Comfort Inn & Suites	E	727 323-3100
Saint Petersburg (G-15633)		

SIC

Concord Management Ltd..........B.....407 350-5957
Kissimmee *(G-7287)*

Consoldted Cr Cnsling Svcs Inc.......D.....954 484-3328
Plantation *(G-14623)*

Consumer Attorney Rec Svcs LLC.......D.....850 549-3335
Pensacola *(G-14267)*

Courtesy Valet Corporation.......D.....844 727-5872
Seminole *(G-16445)*

Creditguard of America Inc.......D.....561 948-7961
Boca Raton *(G-537)*

Crystal Rver Safood Oyster Bar.......E.....904 284-4933
Green Cove Springs *(G-5049)*

D & D Fitness Corporation.......E.....850 942-9712
Tallahassee *(G-16928)*

Days Inn.......D.....352 493-9400
Chiefland *(G-1482)*

Disney Destinations LLC.......B.....407 934-4000
Lake Buena Vista *(G-7459)*

Doubltree By Hlton Ht Tllhssee.......D.....850 224-5000
Tallahassee *(G-16935)*

Emerald Breze Rsort Group 2 LL.......D.....850 362-1000
Fort Walton Beach *(G-4764)*

Fairwinds Credit Union.......C.....407 857-9237
Orlando *(G-12488)*

Florida Entersport Corp.......D.....352 332-2695
Gainesville *(G-4889)*

Florida Hotels & Rest Inc.......D.....407 425-4455
Orlando *(G-12528)*

Fort Lauderdale Trnsp Inc.......A.....954 237-2961
Fort Lauderdale *(G-3802)*

Fort Lauderdale Trnsp Inc.......B.....954 359-0200
Fort Lauderdale *(G-3803)*

Gables Construction Inc.......C.....864 643-5038
Wilton Manors *(G-19523)*

Gainesvlle Hlth Fitnes Ctr Inc.......C.....352 374-4634
Gainesville *(G-4903)*

Golden Egle Golf Cntry CLB Inc.......E.....850 893-7700
Tallahassee *(G-16989)*

Golfvisions Management Inc.......C.....863 676-2422
Lake Wales *(G-7683)*

Goodwin Property Maint LLC.......E.....904 463-6722
Jacksonville *(G-6236)*

Grand Cypress Florida LP.......C.....407 239-4700
Orlando *(G-12589)*

Hair Club For Men LLC.......A.....561 367-7600
Boca Raton *(G-615)*

Hair Club For Men Ltd Inc.......D.....561 361-7600
Boca Raton *(G-616)*

Hc (usa) Inc.......D.....561 361-7600
Boca Raton *(G-622)*

Holiday Inn Hotel & Suites.......E.....407 581-9001
Orlando *(G-12657)*

Home Energy Advisors Inc.......D.....727 282-4110
Saint Petersburg *(G-15710)*

Hyatt Corporation.......A.....407 239-1234
Orlando *(G-12673)*

Image Janitorial Services Inc.......C.....561 627-8748
West Palm Beach *(G-19196)*

Indsar Hospitality LLC.......C.....941 487-3800
Sarasota *(G-16192)*

Interstate Hotels Resorts Inc.......D.....407 351-1000
Orlando *(G-12688)*

Irnm Hotel Investors LLC.......D.....850 477-0711
Pensacola *(G-14331)*

Kaoz Inc.......E.....850 473-0072
Pensacola *(G-14336)*

Kastellum Group LLC.......E.....813 523-2362
Odessa *(G-11847)*

Kent Security Services Inc.......C.....239 430-9315
Naples *(G-11189)*

▲ Kent Security Services Inc.......C.....305 919-9400
North Miami *(G-11501)*

Kent Security Services Inc.......C.....904 371-1906
Jacksonville *(G-6402)*

Kent Security Services Inc.......C.....305 919-9400
Miami *(G-9823)*

Key Parking Services Inc.......B.....305 948-7773
Miami *(G-9825)*

Kinetic Renovations LLC.......E.....937 321-1576
Mary Esther *(G-8690)*

Lakeside Terrace.......C.....561 483-8338
Boca Raton *(G-665)*

Lani Kai Island Resort.......D.....239 463-3111
Fort Myers Beach *(G-4670)*

▲ Lighthouse Cr Foundation Inc.......D.....866 342-0000
Largo *(G-8130)*

Louies Back Yard Inc.......E.....305 294-1061
Key West *(G-7224)*

Lpga Intl Girls Golf CLB.......D.....386 274-5742
Daytona Beach *(G-2628)*

Magna Hospitality Group Lc.......C.....954 472-5600
Plantation *(G-14670)*

Maintenx Intl Svc MGT Group In.......B.....813 254-1656
Tampa *(G-17979)*

Memories Unlimited Inc.......C.....407 872-3838
Orlando *(G-12854)*

Merritt Hospitality.......C.....407 830-1985
Altamonte Springs *(G-77)*

Mol Investments LLC.......E.....305 222-1984
Miami *(G-10012)*

Muvico Theaters Inc.......E.....954 946-8416
Pompano Beach *(G-14862)*

Naples Community Hospital Inc.......B.....239 436-6770
Naples *(G-11226)*

Netlook Inc.......D.....904 642-8757
Jacksonville *(G-6536)*

Park Hotels & Resorts Inc.......D.....407 827-4000
Lake Buena Vista *(G-7468)*

Pink Frog Company Inc.......D.....689 258-6031
Lake Mary *(G-7623)*

Practice Solutions Inc.......E.....865 982-2653
Orlando *(G-13046)*

Pristine & Clean Inc.......E.....407 896-6366
Orlando *(G-13061)*

R & R Smith Enterprises Inc.......E.....813 626-3663
Tampa *(G-18194)*

Red Lobster Hospitality LLC.......D.....407 295-2791
Orlando *(G-13087)*

Regions Security Services Inc.......D.....305 517-1266
Miami *(G-10196)*

Renuity Inc.......A.....855 399-3257
Coral Gables *(G-2174)*

Resort Hospitality Entps Ltd.......C.....850 234-3484
Panama City *(G-14066)*

Rosie OGradys Inc.......C.....850 434-6211
Pensacola *(G-14423)*

Ruths Hospitality Group Inc.......C.....407 226-3900
Orlando *(G-13151)*

Sacino & Sons Inc.......E.....727 328-1555
Saint Petersburg *(G-15835)*

Sanlan Rv & Golf Resort Inc.......C.....863 667-1988
Lakeland *(G-7962)*

Sarasota Restaurant Entps Inc.......C.....941 366-0007
Sarasota *(G-16310)*

Seascape Resorts Inc.......C.....850 837-9181
Miramar Beach *(G-10926)*

Seven-One-Seven Prkg Svcs Inc.......A.....813 228-7722
Tampa *(G-18273)*

Shiraz Management LLC.......C.....561 684-9400
West Palm Beach *(G-19361)*

Shortys Inc.......E.....305 595-1622
Davie *(G-2517)*

Sight & Sound Productions LLC.......E.....904 645-7880
Jacksonville *(G-6724)*

Skybridge Aviation LLC.......E.....813 579-1221
Tampa *(G-18292)*

South Cast Rstoration Pntg LLC.......C.....954 596-1334
Coconut Creek *(G-2005)*

Southern Dunes Golf &.......D.....863 421-4653
Haines City *(G-5158)*

Southern Parking Inc.......B.....954 454-2530
Hallandale Beach *(G-5185)*

Sunrise Hsptlty Pnscola Bch L.......E.....850 932-5331
Gulf Breeze *(G-5135)*

Sunshine Babysitting Inc.......E.....888 609-8979
Maitland *(G-8584)*

Sunshine Valet LLC.......E.....813 609-2808
Tampa *(G-18347)*

Tax Defense Network LLC.......C.....800 691-5390
Jacksonville *(G-6835)*

◆ Traffic Brick Networks LLC.......E.....561 304-9470
Deerfield Beach *(G-2808)*

Transform Sr HM Imprv Pdts LLC.......E.....407 551-5883
Longwood *(G-8412)*

Triple Play Usa LLC.......E.....941 927-6200
Sarasota *(G-16350)*

Two R Productions Inc.......E.....305 220-4366
Miami *(G-10423)*

Ultra Events Mia LLC.......C.....561 631-2971
Wellington *(G-18989)*

Vmm Enterprises Inc.......E.....727 298-0808
Clearwater *(G-1833)*

73 BUSINESS SERVICES

7311 Advertising Agencies

Affiliated Media Group Inc.......E.....904 642-8902
Jacksonville *(G-5750)*

Alma Advertising LLC.......D.....305 529-4300
Miami *(G-9128)*

American Airship Company LLC.......D.....352 353-4824
Williston *(G-19511)*

APT Professional Services LLC.......E.....813 202-8060
Tampa *(G-17297)*

Beber Silverstein Productions.......E.....305 856-9800
Miami *(G-9237)*

Benedict Advg & Mktg Inc.......E.....386 255-1222
Daytona Beach *(G-2551)*

Bfz Holdings Pittsburgh Inc.......E.....305 423-8300
Miami *(G-9252)*

Britepool Inc.......E.....310 699-8346
Winter Park *(G-19689)*

▲ Brown Prker Demarinis Advg Inc.......E.....561 276-7701
Delray Beach *(G-2922)*

Campbell-Ewald Company.......C.....305 200-8700
Coral Gables *(G-2059)*

Cartier International Del Corp.......C.....305 448-4111
Coral Gables *(G-2064)*

Charisma Media.......D.....407 333-0600
Lake Mary *(G-7576)*

Chatter-Buzz Media LLC.......E.....321 236-2899
Orlando *(G-12291)*

Comcast Spotlight LP.......E.....904 733-8489
Jacksonville *(G-5977)*

Comcast Spotlight LP.......E.....561 653-4900
West Palm Beach *(G-19099)*

Consani Development LLC.......D.....850 869-7528
Hialeah *(G-5246)*

Cross Agency.......E.....904 642-8902
Jacksonville *(G-6012)*

D & S Advertising Services.......E.....954 327-9164
Davie *(G-2474)*

Dalton Agency Inc.......E.....904 398-5222
Jacksonville *(G-6041)*

Digitas Inc.......E.....703 226-2832
Miami *(G-9477)*

Dunn & Co Inc.......E.....813 350-7990
Tampa *(G-17604)*

Endeavor Business Media LLC.......E.....941 388-7050
Sarasota *(G-16150)*

Fkq Marketing Inc.......D.....727 539-8800
Clearwater *(G-1637)*

Focus III Inc.......E.....813 908-8600
Tampa *(G-17703)*

Fry/Hammond/Barr Incorporated.......E.....407 849-0100
Orlando *(G-12551)*

Glue Iq LLC.......D.....305 239-9440
Miami *(G-9641)*

Gustazos Orlando LLC.......D.....787 246-3886
Miami *(G-9672)*

Gut Agency LLC.......C.....305 742-4469
Coral Gables *(G-2116)*

Healthcare Inc.......C.....786 252-0129
Miami *(G-9689)*

Hispanic Group Corporation.......E.....305 477-5483
Doral *(G-3231)*

Homes Media Solutions LLC.......C.....877 363-4442
Boca Raton *(G-631)*

Hunter Hmrsmith Assoc Advg Inc.......E.....305 895-8430
North Miami *(G-11496)*

Ignited Services LLC.......C.....618 969-0406
Niceville *(G-11452)*

Igt Services Inc.......E.....305 573-2800
Miami *(G-9743)*

Imperial Distributing Company.......D.....813 630-5888
Tampa *(G-17863)*

Izea Worldwide Inc.......D.....407 674-6911
Orlando *(G-12693)*

Jamdel Inc.......E.....561 314-4810
Boca Raton *(G-648)*

K Pp Inc.......E.....813 496-7000
Tampa *(G-17907)*

Kjh III Inc.......E.....561 620-4774
Boca Raton *(G-661)*

Knight Images Inc.......E.....407 206-1011
Orlando *(G-12736)*

Kobie Marketing Inc.......C.....727 822-5353
Saint Petersburg *(G-15742)*

L M Berry and Company.......E.....352 622-5166
Ocala *(G-11707)*

Lien Solutions LLC.......E.....844 905-4300
Miami *(G-9868)*

Media 8 LLC.......E.....786 623-5500
Miami *(G-9928)*

Mediabrains Inc.......E.....239 594-3200
Naples *(G-11207)*

Mediagistic Inc.......E.....813 477-6462
Tampa *(G-18019)*

Mindshare Usa LLC.......C.....786 264-7687
Miami *(G-10005)*

Money Pages of Florida Inc	E	904 306-0086	
Jacksonville (G-6514)			
Newlink Cmmnications Group LLC	E	305 532-7950	
Miami (G-10043)			
Otent Inc	C	954 862-2400	
Fort Lauderdale (G-4035)			
Our Town Inc	E	800 497-8360	
Clearwater (G-1751)			
Push Incorporated	E	407 841-2299	
Orlando (G-13073)			
Quikfillrx LLC	C	904 265-5476	
Jacksonville (G-6627)			
Rabinovici & Associates Inc	E	305 655-0021	
Hollywood (G-5501)			
Rci Next Generation Inc	E	561 686-6800	
Jupiter (G-7131)			
Red Rocket Studios LLC	E	407 895-9358	
Orlando (G-13088)			
Reed Brennan Media Associates	E	407 894-7300	
Orlando (G-13090)			
Republica LLC	E	305 442-0977	
Miami (G-10202)			
Robin Shepherd Studios Inc	E	904 359-0981	
Jacksonville (G-6673)			
Star Group Communications Inc	D	561 807-8828	
Boca Raton (G-818)			
Starmark Global Inc	E	305 665-5225	
Coral Gables (G-2190)			
Starmark International Inc	E	954 874-9000	
Fort Lauderdale (G-4151)			
Tinsley Advertising & Mktg Inc	D	305 856-6060	
Miami (G-10391)			
US Media Consulting LLC	E	305 722-5500	
North Miami Beach (G-11536)			
Visionamics Inc	E	561 405-6894	
Boca Raton (G-863)			
Voxxi	E	786 507-4717	
Coral Gables (G-2207)			
White Shark Media Inc	D	305 728-4828	
Miami (G-10503)			
Zimmerman Advertising LLC	B	954 644-4000	
Fort Lauderdale (G-4239)			
▼ Zimmerman Agency LLC	D	850 877-8896	
Tallahassee (G-17180)			

7312 Outdoor Advertising Svcs

Bill Salter Advertising Inc	E	850 994-4611	
Milton (G-10811)			
Clear Channel Outdoor LLC	D	305 592-6250	
Doral (G-3152)			
Clear Channel Outdoor LLC	D	407 298-6410	
Orlando (G-12318)			
Cyclehop LLC	E	773 340-4080	
Miami Beach (G-10581)			
Metropolitan Advertising Co	E	813 872-8502	
Tampa (G-18030)			
▲ National Mobile Billboards LLC	E	954 777-9998	
Fort Lauderdale (G-3993)			

7313 Radio, TV & Publishers Adv Reps

Caracol Broadcasting Inc	C	305 285-1260	
Coral Gables (G-2062)			
Comcast Spotlight LP	D	904 733-8489	
Jacksonville (G-5977)			
Diversified Communications	E	352 377-2020	
Gainesville (G-4876)			
Forum Publishing Group Inc	D	239 643-3933	
Naples (G-11125)			
Gatehouse Media LLC	D	386 681-2573	
Daytona Beach (G-2601)			
Gatehouse Media LLC	D	561 820-4663	
West Palm Beach (G-19161)			
Gut Agency LLC	C	305 742-4469	
Coral Gables (G-2116)			
Majority Strategies LLC	E	904 567-2008	
Jacksonville (G-6463)			
Multimedia Platforms Inc	E	954 440-4678	
Fort Lauderdale (G-3980)			
Prism Data LLC	B	727 287-0426	
Clearwater (G-1766)			
Showcase Publications Inc	E	863 687-4377	
Lakeland (G-7968)			
Supermedia LLC	D	727 576-1300	
Saint Petersburg (G-15868)			
USA Distributors Inc	E	305 225-3742	
Miami (G-10453)			

7319 Advertising, NEC

Direct Mail Express Inc	B	386 271-3000	
Daytona Beach (G-2583)			

Distribution Services Inc	A	561 997-7733	
Boca Raton (G-554)			
Grc Intermediate Holdco LLC	E	954 969-2336	
Margate (G-8650)			
Harte-Hnks Drct Mrktng/Fllrto	D	410 636-6660	
Jacksonville (G-6261)			
Mediacom Worldwide LLC	E	786 264-7611	
Miami (G-9929)			
Onmedia Communications Co Inc	D	850 916-6813	
Gulf Breeze (G-5131)			
Rebel Anthemz LLC	E	954 477-6461	
Saint Petersburg (G-15825)			
Sloane Media Inc	E	954 442-8365	
Hollywood (G-5521)			
Transfirst Media Inc	E	407 926-4055	
Orlando (G-13303)			
Travel Guide LLC	D	407 673-3466	
Maitland (G-8591)			

7322 Adjustment & Collection Svcs

Account Receivable MGT Fla Inc	E	877 726-8505	
Jacksonville (G-5726)			
Asset Acceptance LLC	C	813 569-0400	
Riverview (G-15243)			
Associated Cr & Collectn Bur	E	321 636-3880	
Rockledge (G-15334)			
Assurance Fincl Partners LLC	C	954 874-4600	
Sunrise (G-16740)			
Bca Financial Services Inc	C	305 909-2200	
Palmetto Bay (G-13939)			
Bell LLC	E	813 261-7755	
Tampa (G-17356)			
Broward Adjustment Services	E	954 565-6682	
Fort Lauderdale (G-3652)			
Capstone Corporation	E	813 885-7766	
Tampa (G-17416)			
Challenge Health Network Inc	E	954 839-8080	
Fort Lauderdale (G-3681)			
Convergent Resources Inc	D	561 862-1640	
Boca Raton (G-527)			
Debtication Inc Corporate	D	561 353-5680	
Boca Raton (G-549)			
Diversified Consultants Inc	C	904 641-4572	
Jacksonville (G-6072)			
Douglas Knight & Assoc Inc	E	941 744-1042	
Bradenton (G-1088)			
Enhanced Recovery Company LLC	A	904 371-1005	
Jacksonville (G-6120)			
Enhanced Recovery Company LLC	A	904 680-2591	
Orange Park (G-11988)			
Gulf Coast Collection Bur Inc	D	941 927-6999	
Sarasota (G-16180)			
Heldan Jax Inc	D	904 733-3033	
Jacksonville (G-6273)			
Hunter Warfield Inc	C	813 283-4500	
Tampa (G-17846)			
Iqor US Inc	A	646 274-3030	
Saint Petersburg (G-15727)			
Legal Mediation Practice Inc	E	904 388-7929	
Jacksonville (G-6425)			
Managed Care Solutions Inc	C	877 450-0330	
Plantation (G-14671)			
Medical Data Systems Inc	C	863 382-6050	
Sebring (G-16407)			
Mfp Inc	C	727 446-0018	
Sarasota (G-16231)			
Ncb Management Services Inc	D	904 737-2485	
Jacksonville (G-6532)			
One Advantage LLC	E	888 891-1269	
Doral (G-3282)			
Phillips & Cohen Assoc Ltd	D	954 660-8400	
Lauderdale Lakes (G-8181)			
Protocol Recovery Service Inc	D	770 425-8865	
Panama City (G-14058)			
Royal Merc Tr Corp of Amer	E	772 220-1300	
Stuart (G-16663)			
Sherloq Group Inc	D	813 273-7833	
Tampa (G-18277)			
United Collection Bureau Inc	C	954 236-6030	
Davie (G-2532)			
Vengroff Williams Inc	B	941 363-5200	
Sarasota (G-16357)			
Vengroff Williams & Assoc Inc	B	941 363-5200	
Sarasota (G-16358)			

7323 Credit Reporting Svcs

American Credit Auditors LLC	D	904 425-9575	
Jacksonville (G-5780)			
Applicant Insight Inc	C	727 807-2010	
New Port Richey (G-11364)			

Cortera Inc	C	877 569-7376	
Boca Raton (G-533)			
Dun & Bradstreet Inc	D	954 835-0114	
Sunrise (G-16765)			
Dun & Bradstreet Corporation	B	904 648-6350	
Jacksonville (G-6087)			
▲ Dun & Bradstreet Inc	B	904 648-6350	
Jacksonville (G-6088)			
Lumbermens Cr Assn Ocala Inc	D	954 771-2100	
Oakland Park (G-11603)			

7331 Direct Mail Advertising Svcs

230 Third Avenue	D	781 839-2800	
Jacksonville (G-5712)			
Advanced Xrgrphics Imging Syst	E	407 351-0232	
Orlando (G-12061)			
American Mktg Mailing Svcs Inc	D	813 886-5597	
Tampa (G-17278)			
Amsive LLC	C	813 855-4274	
Tampa (G-17282)			
Ccr Holdings Inc	C	305 591-0024	
Miami (G-9339)			
Cox Target Media Inc	A	727 399-3000	
Saint Petersburg (G-15648)			
Direct Impressions Inc	E	239 549-4484	
Cape Coral (G-1387)			
Direct Mail Express Inc	B	386 271-3000	
Daytona Beach (G-2583)			
Direct Mail Systems Inc	D	727 573-1985	
Saint Petersburg (G-15655)			
Dunhill Intl List Co Inc	E	561 998-7800	
Boca Raton (G-559)			
Fulfillment Partners Inc	E	407 660-8606	
Orlando (G-12554)			
Grc Intermediate Holdco LLC	E	954 969-2336	
Margate (G-8650)			
Harte-Hnks Drct Mrktng/Fllrto	D	410 636-6660	
Jacksonville (G-6261)			
Kessler Creative LLC	E	904 346-3898	
Jacksonville (G-6404)			
Lighthouse List Company Inc	E	954 489-3008	
Pompano Beach (G-14842)			
Mail Unlimited Inc	E	407 657-9333	
Winter Park (G-19746)			
Majority Strategies LLC	E	904 567-2008	
Jacksonville (G-6463)			
▲ MBI Direct Mail Inc	D	386 736-9998	
Deland (G-2869)			
Midlantic Mktg Solutions Inc	E	386 274-1227	
Daytona Beach (G-2638)			
Money Mailer LLC	C	714 889-3800	
Cape Coral (G-1416)			
Ncp Solutions LLC	D	205 849-5200	
Jacksonville (G-6533)			
Nordis Inc	D	954 323-5500	
Coral Springs (G-2275)			
▼ Original Impressions LLC	C	305 233-1322	
Weston (G-19472)			
▲ Postal Center Intl Inc	D	954 321-5644	
Weston (G-19476)			
Primenet Drct Mktg Sltons LLC	D	727 447-6245	
Largo (G-8142)			
Pronto Post Inc	D	305 621-7900	
Hialeah (G-5313)			
Rme LLC	C	813 885-8200	
Tampa (G-18229)			
Solvera Inc	E	954 963-2200	
Fort Lauderdale (G-4135)			
Southeast Print Programs Inc	E	813 885-3203	
Tampa (G-18308)			
Southwest Direct Inc	D	239 768-9588	
Fort Myers (G-4599)			
Tc Specialties Co	E	813 881-1830	
Tampa (G-18408)			
Tc Specialties Co	E	407 855-8262	
Orlando (G-13272)			
Tc Specialties Co	E	904 281-2604	
Jacksonville (G-6839)			
Thinkdirect Mktg Group Inc	B	727 914-0300	
Clearwater (G-1823)			
V P Holdings Inc	A	727 393-1270	
Saint Petersburg (G-15883)			
Valassis Direct Mail Inc	C	305 341-9500	
Miami Lakes (G-10771)			
Valpak Direct Mktg Systems Inc	A	727 399-3175	
Saint Petersburg (G-15884)			
Wilen Press Lc	D	954 246-5000	
Deerfield Beach (G-2816)			
Worldata Infocenter Inc	D	561 241-3000	
Boca Raton (G-878)			

S I C

7334 Photocopying & Duplicating Svcs

Advanced Data Solutions Inc ....E....... 813 855-3545
Oldsmar *(G-11889)*

American Blueprinting Sup Inc ....D....... 407 644-5366
Winter Park *(G-19684)*

▼ Ashby & Ashby Inc ....D....... 813 886-0065
Tampa *(G-17312)*

Bay Reprographics Inc ....E....... 813 286-8520
Tampa *(G-17348)*

Exela Enterprise Solutions Inc ....E....... 850 549-3748
Pensacola *(G-14302)*

Exela Enterprise Solutions Inc ....E....... 850 942-1308
Tallahassee *(G-16943)*

OfficeMax North America Inc ....D....... 386 752-7830
Lake City *(G-7541)*

OfficeMax North America Inc ....E....... 941 925-4579
Sarasota *(G-16250)*

Target Copy Gainesville Inc ....D....... 352 372-2233
Gainesville *(G-5011)*

▼ Triangle Reprographics Inc ....D....... 407 843-1492
Orlando *(G-13309)*

7335 Commercial Photography

Devore Design LLC ....E....... 407 500-7427
Clermont *(G-1865)*

Ideal Image Development Inc ....E....... 813 347-9152
Tampa *(G-17853)*

Ideal Image Development Inc ....E....... 813 982-3420
Brandon *(G-1240)*

Image Quest Worldwide Inc ....C....... 702 283-9568
Daytona Beach *(G-2616)*

Pro Image Solutions Inc ....E....... 407 774-4884
Longwood *(G-8392)*

7336 Commercial Art & Graphic Design

A-Plus Prtg & Graphic Ctr Inc ....E....... 954 327-7315
Plantation *(G-14596)*

Adsync Technologies Inc ....D....... 850 497-6969
Pensacola *(G-14212)*

◆ Altrua Global Solutions Inc ....D....... 850 562-4564
Tallahassee *(G-16876)*

Amazing7 Studios ....D....... 800 867-3168
Oldsmar *(G-11891)*

▲ Blue Ocean Press Inc ....E....... 954 973-1819
Fort Lauderdale *(G-3646)*

Bungalow Scenic Studios Inc ....E....... 407 401-9191
Orlando *(G-12220)*

Chatter Buzz Media LLC ....E....... 321 236-2899
Orlando *(G-12291)*

Creative Drive Inc ....B....... 866 924-4410
Hollywood *(G-5425)*

Ferguson and Ferguson ....D....... 407 422-2362
Orlando *(G-12504)*

Fortune Financial Inc ....E....... 305 629-2644
Miami *(G-9599)*

Graphic Masters Inc ....D....... 800 230-3873
Miami *(G-9659)*

▼ Graphics Type Color Entps Inc ....E....... 305 591-7600
Miami *(G-9660)*

Group 4 Design Inc ....E....... 904 353-5900
Jacksonville *(G-6244)*

Jardon & Howard Tech Inc ....D....... 407 381-7797
Orlando *(G-12700)*

Joy Rockwell Enterprises Inc ....C....... 727 442-6440
Clearwater *(G-1690)*

Kent White and Associates Inc ....A....... 727 515-3004
Tampa *(G-17914)*

Kessler Creative LLC ....E....... 904 346-3898
Jacksonville *(G-6404)*

Live Design Inc ....E....... 786 513-9807
Coral Springs *(G-2267)*

Majority Strategies LLC ....E....... 904 567-2008
Jacksonville *(G-6463)*

Media 1 Signs Inc ....E....... 407 331-6161
Longwood *(G-8382)*

Presentation Resource Inc ....E....... 904 398-8179
Jacksonville *(G-6616)*

Private Label Skin Na LLC ....C....... 877 516-2200
Saint Petersburg *(G-15809)*

Prosser Inc ....D....... 904 739-3655
Jacksonville *(G-6619)*

Purple Rock Scissors LLC ....E....... 407 936-1749
Winter Park *(G-19765)*

Shr Communications LLC ....D....... 786 420-7631
Doral *(G-3309)*

Synect LLC ....E....... 425 497-9688
Orlando *(G-13261)*

Timothy R West ....E....... 321 314-2493
Orlando *(G-13291)*

Visually Inc ....D....... 416 838-7047
Boca Raton *(G-864)*

7338 Secretarial & Court Reporting Svcs

All Office Suppt Lee & Collier ....E....... 239 939-2200
Fort Myers *(G-4263)*

County of Broward ....C....... 954 831-7740
Fort Lauderdale *(G-3724)*

Deposition Solutions LLC ....D....... 888 811-3408
West Palm Beach *(G-19121)*

J L G Medical Inc ....B....... 813 286-1977
Oldsmar *(G-11909)*

Litigation Svcs & Tech Fla LLC ....E....... 772 563-0227
Vero Beach *(G-18888)*

Medscribe Info Systems Inc ....E....... 239 430-0068
Naples *(G-11210)*

Polk County Florida ....B....... 863 534-4000
Bartow *(G-331)*

Sclafani Williams ....E....... 407 420-2200
Kissimmee *(G-7381)*

Universal Court Reporting Inc ....E....... 954 712-2600
Fort Lauderdale *(G-4196)*

US Legal Support Inc ....D....... 904 425-1290
Orlando *(G-13361)*

◆ Wincorp International Inc ....E....... 305 887-4000
Medley *(G-8798)*

7342 Disinfecting & Pest Control Svcs

Advanced Biocide Tech Inc ....E....... 954 530-1292
Sunrise *(G-16732)*

Al Hoffers Pest Protection ....E....... 954 753-1222
Coral Springs *(G-2222)*

Al-Flex Exterminators Inc ....E....... 305 552-0141
Miami *(G-9111)*

Alford Wildlife & Pest MGT LLC ....E....... 239 245-7482
Fort Myers *(G-4258)*

Amera-Tech Inc ....E....... 239 561-9184
Naples *(G-11007)*

Anchor Pest Control Inc ....E....... 850 435-7696
Cantonment *(G-1332)*

Arrow Exterminators Inc ....E....... 239 596-6545
Naples *(G-11015)*

Arrow Exterminators Inc ....E....... 352 373-3642
Gainesville *(G-4840)*

Arrow Exterminators Inc ....D....... 772 562-5944
Vero Beach *(G-18834)*

Arrow Exterminators Inc ....D....... 941 629-3033
Port Charlotte *(G-15021)*

Arrow Exterminators Inc ....E....... 561 393-2808
Boca Raton *(G-426)*

Arrow Exterminators Inc ....C....... 561 533-3864
Lake Worth *(G-7710)*

B & B Exterminating Co ....E....... 904 389-3323
Jacksonville *(G-5829)*

Brandon Pest Control Inc ....D....... 863 602-5988
Lakeland *(G-7817)*

Bug Out Service Inc ....E....... 904 743-8272
Jacksonville *(G-5886)*

Bugs Extrmntors Trmt Pest Svcs ....E....... 954 489-8354
Pompano Beach *(G-14761)*

Capelouto Termite & Pest Ctrl ....D....... 850 656-1166
Tallahassee *(G-16899)*

Caughtem Critters ....D....... 954 300-9488
Fort Lauderdale *(G-3674)*

Centex Home Services Co LLC ....C....... 813 890-0444
Tampa *(G-17443)*

Deans Pest Control Inc ....D....... 352 787-5300
Leesburg *(G-8241)*

Ecoshield Pest Ctrl Miami LLC ....E....... 305 330-4755
Deerfield Beach *(G-2738)*

El Toro Exterminator Fla Inc ....E....... 305 594-4767
Sweetwater *(G-16861)*

Environmental SEC Okaloosa ....E....... 850 474-4000
Cantonment *(G-1338)*

Flood Zone Restoration LLC ....E....... 844 863-3279
Port Charlotte *(G-15035)*

Florida Keys Mosquito Ctrl Dst ....D....... 305 453-1290
Key Largo *(G-7176)*

Florida Pest Control & Chem Co ....C....... 352 376-2661
Gainesville *(G-4895)*

Green Effex LLC ....E....... 239 774-5263
Naples *(G-11143)*

Haskell Trmt & Pest Ctrl Inc ....D....... 813 239-1790
Tampa *(G-17795)*

Hulett Environmental Svcs Inc ....D....... 561 686-7171
West Palm Beach *(G-19190)*

Larue Pest Management Inc ....E....... 239 369-6121
Fort Myers *(G-4471)*

Massey Services ....E....... 941 629-6669
Port Charlotte *(G-15047)*

▲ Massey Services Inc ....D....... 407 645-2500
Orlando *(G-12828)*

Massey Services Inc ....E....... 386 756-6696
South Daytona *(G-16490)*

Massey Services Inc ....D....... 850 222-2508
Tallahassee *(G-17035)*

Massey Services Inc ....E....... 407 898-7378
Orlando *(G-12829)*

Massey Services Inc ....E....... 352 357-7415
Eustis *(G-3497)*

Massey Services Inc ....E....... 407 846-6620
Kissimmee *(G-7354)*

McCall Service Nw LLC ....E....... 904 389-5561
Jacksonville *(G-6476)*

Mosquitonix ....D....... 941 360-1630
Sarasota *(G-16042)*

▼ Naders Pest Raiders Inc ....E....... 904 285-0091
Ponte Vedra Beach *(G-14994)*

Nolen Nozzle Inc ....D....... 561 844-3544
West Palm Beach *(G-19278)*

Oasis Landscape Services Inc ....E....... 352 373-9530
Gainesville *(G-4970)*

Pestguard Commercial Svcs Inc ....E....... 941 358-3863
Sarasota *(G-16264)*

Pickhardt Sarasota Inc ....D....... 941 803-4021
Sarasota *(G-16265)*

Quick Fumigation Inc ....D....... 305 266-0559
Miami *(G-10175)*

Rentokil North America Inc ....D....... 813 886-1363
Winter Haven *(G-19655)*

Rentokil North America Inc ....D....... 904 525-8782
Jacksonville *(G-6657)*

Rentokil North America Inc ....C....... 954 961-4700
Fort Lauderdale *(G-4084)*

Rentokil North America Inc ....D....... 813 877-6144
Tampa *(G-18215)*

Rentokil North America Inc ....D....... 239 432-2783
Fort Myers *(G-4567)*

Security Pest Inc ....D....... 904 786-8260
Jacksonville *(G-6705)*

Shield Pest Control Inc ....E....... 305 247-1771
Homestead *(G-5604)*

Springer Pest Solutions ....D....... 515 262-9229
Gulf Breeze *(G-5133)*

Terminix Intl Co Ltd Partnr ....D....... 386 756-0801
Daytona Beach *(G-2673)*

Tri-S Inc ....E....... 813 935-5565
Tampa *(G-18444)*

Trugreen Chemlawn ....D....... 239 694-1311
Fort Myers *(G-4632)*

Truly Nolen of America Inc ....E....... 407 425-2222
Orlando *(G-13316)*

Turner Pest Control LLC ....C....... 352 216-7473
Ocala *(G-11790)*

Turner Pest Control LLC ....C....... 904 355-5300
Jacksonville *(G-6879)*

Weber Environmental Svcs Inc ....C....... 863 551-1820
Winter Haven *(G-19672)*

7349 Building Cleaning & Maintenance Svcs, NEC

24 Hours Inc ....D....... 772 200-0072
Palm City *(G-13783)*

4m Building Solutions Inc ....A....... 904 355-2741
Jacksonville *(G-5714)*

A & K Energy Conservation Inc ....C....... 352 567-1999
Dade City *(G-2379)*

A-Stellar Prprty Mint Ldscpg I ....E....... 813 270-9637
Pinellas Park *(G-14503)*

A1 Orange Cleaning Svc Co Inc ....E....... 407 422-1040
Orlando *(G-12036)*

ABF/CFM Joint Venture ....D....... 800 351-7380
Jacksonville *(G-5723)*

Able Business Services Inc ....D....... 305 636-5099
Miami *(G-9069)*

ABM Janitorial Services Inc ....E....... 352 259-7717
The Villages *(G-18651)*

ABM Janitorial Services Inc ....E....... 813 837-4257
Tampa *(G-17224)*

ABM Janitorial Services Inc ....C....... 407 523-9442
Orlando *(G-12043)*

ABM Janitorial Services Inc ....E....... 904 737-2755
Jacksonville *(G-5724)*

ABM Jnitorial Svcs - Nthrn Cal ....C....... 239 498-1270
Bonita Springs *(G-891)*

ABM Onsite Services - West Inc ....C....... 813 886-0001
Tampa *(G-17225)*

ABM Security Services Inc ....D....... 561 395-5773
Orlando *(G-12044)*

Company	Code	Phone
Aci Facility Maintenance Inc ......E...... 407 999-9797		
Tampa (G-17228)		
Acl Cleaning Systems LLC ......C...... 954 854-0046		
Fort Lauderdale (G-3578)		
Advanced Power Tech Group LLC ......C...... 888 964-4487		
Pompano Beach (G-14734)		
Age Wise Inc ......E...... 386 212-2778		
Orlando (G-12076)		
AK Building Services Inc ......E...... 561 471-8817		
Fort Lauderdale (G-3587)		
AK Building Services Inc ......B...... 561 471-8817		
Fort Lauderdale (G-3588)		
All American Facility Maint ......D...... 954 322-9909		
Sunrise (G-16734)		
All Jani Inc ......E...... 786 344-9118		
Miami (G-9118)		
American Maintenance LLC ......E...... 561 317-3219		
Lake Worth (G-7708)		
▲ American Sls MGT Orgnztion LLC ......A...... 305 269-2700		
Miami (G-9143)		
AMS Trading Inc ......E...... 954 776-2000		
Fort Lauderdale (G-3607)		
Apollo Retail Specialists LLC ......D...... 813 712-2525		
Tampa (G-17296)		
At Your Service Clg Group Inc ......E...... 941 360-6796		
Sarasota (G-16096)		
Batallan Enterprises Inc ......D...... 561 805-8687		
West Palm Beach (G-19048)		
Blue Ribbon Cleaning Co Inc ......E...... 352 624-3444		
Ocala (G-11641)		
Bore Tech Utilities & Maint ......D...... 305 297-8162		
Miami (G-9269)		
Broward County Public Schools ......D...... 754 321-4691		
Oakland Park (G-11585)		
Building Maintenance Svcs Inc ......D...... 407 830-9002		
Winter Park (G-19691)		
Building Tech Engineers Inc ......E...... 407 423-1600		
Orlando (G-12219)		
Ccnl LLC ......E...... 239 936-7700		
Fort Myers (G-4302)		
Central Fla Facilities MGT LLC ......D...... 321 200-2671		
Longwood (G-8350)		
Challenge Entps N Fla Inc ......B...... 904 284-9859		
Green Cove Springs (G-5048)		
City Facilities MGT FL LLC ......B...... 904 655-0484		
Jacksonville (G-5956)		
City of Jacksonville ......E...... 904 630-3525		
Jacksonville (G-5959)		
City of Port Orange ......E...... 386 506-5577		
Port Orange (G-15071)		
Clean America Corp ......E...... 941 722-1078		
Palmetto (G-13907)		
Clean-Mark Group Inc ......C...... 416 364-0677		
Boca Raton (G-518)		
Cleanevent Usa Inc ......C...... 407 856-7676		
Orlando (G-12317)		
Cleaning Systems Inc ......D...... 954 341-0000		
Fort Lauderdale (G-3700)		
Cole Industries Inc ......C...... 850 433-8100		
Pensacola (G-14262)		
Commercial Kit Exhaust Clg Inc ......E...... 904 642-3606		
Jacksonville (G-5980)		
Commercial Services Inc ......E...... 904 642-3606		
Jacksonville (G-5983)		
Complete Cleaning Serv of Irc ......D...... 772 562-3585		
Vero Beach (G-18848)		
Complete Property Maint Inc ......E...... 561 744-3333		
Coconut Creek (G-1983)		
County of Escambia ......E...... 850 595-3190		
Pensacola (G-14271)		
County of Miami-Dade ......D...... 305 510-3596		
Miami (G-9428)		
Coverall North America Inc ......B...... 561 922-2500		
Deerfield Beach (G-2729)		
Creative Management Tech Inc ......B...... 321 799-4022		
Rockledge (G-15343)		
Crestwood Services Inc ......D...... 954 570-1165		
Deerfield Beach (G-2731)		
Crystal Building Services Inc ......E...... 407 862-4093		
Apopka (G-170)		
Crystal Clean S LLC ......E...... 239 936-7700		
Fort Myers (G-4335)		
Csi International Inc ......A...... 954 308-4300		
Fort Lauderdale (G-3745)		
Cyclone National LLC ......E...... 251 219-8889		
Pensacola (G-14280)		
D & A Building Services Inc ......D...... 407 831-5388		
Longwood (G-8355)		
Destin VIP Cleaning LLC ......E...... 850 533-1136		
Destin (G-3058)		

Company	Code	Phone
Diversified Maint Systems LLC ......D...... 800 351-1557		
Tampa (G-17596)		
Diversified MGT Group LLC ......E...... 305 772-3612		
Macclenny (G-8475)		
Drake Auto Rcndtning DBA White ......E...... 321 795-9800		
Winter Park (G-19715)		
Duval County Public Schools ......E...... 904 381-3980		
Jacksonville (G-6093)		
Efco USA Inc ......E...... 305 876-0026		
Doral (G-3187)		
Elite Property Services Inc ......E...... 239 566-9797		
Naples (G-11103)		
Encompass Onsite ......B...... 954 318-2477		
Fort Lauderdale (G-3772)		
Entire Maint Solutions Inc ......E...... 888 516-0003		
Miami (G-9526)		
Ermc II LP ......D...... 863 471-0733		
Sebring (G-16395)		
Esi Maintenance Inc ......E...... 561 262-4207		
Crystal River (G-2346)		
Eulen America Inc ......A...... 954 703-1918		
Fort Lauderdale (G-3777)		
Executive Management Svcs Inc ......B...... 239 437-1110		
Fort Myers (G-4364)		
Executive Management Svcs Inc ......C...... 813 626-8886		
Tampa (G-17641)		
Executive Management Svcs Inc ......E...... 239 437-1111		
Fort Myers (G-4365)		
Fantastic Five Inc ......D...... 727 847-3000		
Port Richey (G-15101)		
Flood Pros of Swfl Corp ......D...... 239 321-5554		
Fort Myers (G-4376)		
Flood Pros of Swfl Corp ......D...... 888 595-1105		
Tallahassee (G-17054)		
Florida Center Bldg Maint LLC ......D...... 407 578-4333		
Orlando (G-12522)		
Florida Cleaning Systems Inc ......B...... 407 268-4035		
Lake Mary (G-7592)		
Florida Commercial Care Inc ......D...... 813 972-4962		
Kissimmee (G-7309)		
Fresh Cut Lawn Service Inc ......E...... 407 298-0911		
Orlando (G-12547)		
Gca Services Group Inc ......C...... 850 640-2572		
Panama City (G-14016)		
Gca Services Group Inc ......A...... 904 630-6660		
Jacksonville (G-6223)		
Goodwin Property Maint LLC ......E...... 904 463-6722		
Jacksonville (G-6236)		
Greene Kleen South Florida Inc ......C...... 305 234-2981		
Doral (G-3217)		
Grosvenor Building Svcs LLC ......B...... 407 292-3383		
Orlando (G-12607)		
Harvard Maintenance Inc ......B...... 954 484-7765		
Fort Lauderdale (G-3849)		
Harvard Maintenance Inc ......B...... 305 351-7300		
Miami (G-9684)		
Harvard Services Group Inc ......B...... 954 484-7765		
Miami (G-9685)		
HCC C LLc ......D...... 321 388-6262		
Orlando (G-12624)		
Heveron Group Inc ......D...... 772 569-0799		
Vero Beach (G-18870)		
High Sources Inc ......C...... 813 585-0313		
Tampa (G-17819)		
Hotel Cleaning Services Inc ......A...... 407 846-4671		
Kissimmee (G-7323)		
Image Janitorial Services Inc ......C...... 561 627-8748		
West Palm Beach (G-19196)		
ISS C & S Building Maint Corp ......D...... 352 372-8753		
Gainesville (G-4924)		
Jaaj Building Maintenance Corp ......E...... 954 479-1407		
Doral (G-3247)		
Jasper Steward LLC ......E...... 754 600-9127		
Pembroke Pines (G-14157)		
Jetstream Ground Services Inc ......D...... 561 746-3282		
Jupiter (G-7090)		
Jimco Maintenance Inc ......D...... 941 485-5985		
Venice (G-18789)		
Jjdac Inc ......E...... 502 419-5231		
Naples (G-11183)		
Joshua W Kennedy Entps LLC ......E...... 904 383-7721		
Jacksonville (G-6391)		
Jupiter Hills Club Inc ......E...... 561 747-2829		
Jupiter (G-7095)		
Kent Holding Group Inc ......E...... 305 919-9400		
North Miami (G-11500)		
Kings Service Solutions LLC ......C...... 407 704-8542		
Orlando (G-12731)		
Klino Enterprises Corp ......D...... 786 308-6353		
Miami (G-9832)		

Company	Code	Phone
Krystal Companies LLC ......E...... 904 838-8003		
Jacksonville (G-6409)		
Led Enterprise Inc ......E...... 407 674-8259		
Orlando (G-12759)		
Lll Services Company ......D...... 904 448-4011		
Jacksonville (G-6442)		
Magic Janitorial Services Inc ......E...... 786 845-9930		
Miami (G-9893)		
Maintenx Intl Svc MGT Group In ......B...... 813 254-1656		
Tampa (G-17979)		
Mega Service Solutions Inc ......D...... 813 501-5001		
Tampa (G-18021)		
Merry Maids Ltd Partnership ......E...... 321 632-5014		
Cocoa (G-1943)		
Mfm Services LLC ......E...... 904 240-1345		
Jacksonville (G-6502)		
Miami-Dade Cnty Pub Schls-158 ......D...... 305 995-4000		
Miami (G-9990)		
Miami-Dade Cnty Pub Schls-158 ......C...... 305 235-2329		
Miami (G-9994)		
Milton J Wood Company ......E...... 941 746-3031		
Bradenton (G-1147)		
MMS Mechanical Services Inc ......E...... 352 376-5221		
Gainesville (G-4950)		
Moorecars LLC ......E...... 678 472-9114		
Boynton Beach (G-1018)		
National Building Maint LLC ......C...... 813 877-7467		
Tampa (G-18066)		
National Doorstep Pickup ......D...... 844 278-8727		
Tampa (G-18067)		
New Century Cleaning Svcs Inc ......E...... 850 894-6226		
Tallahassee (G-17054)		
New Life Facility Services Inc ......D...... 863 686-1300		
Lakeland (G-7930)		
Newventure Jacksonville Inc ......E...... 904 732-7270		
Jacksonville (G-6541)		
Non-Core Bus Solutions LLC ......D...... 919 755-9026		
Clearwater (G-1740)		
Orange Industrial Services LLC ......D...... 863 519-0831		
Bartow (G-329)		
Outsource Option LLC ......E...... 407 493-7928		
Orlando (G-12994)		
Overtime Building Maintenance ......D...... 561 659-9791		
West Palm Beach (G-19297)		
Parkway Maintenance & Mgt Co ......E...... 727 799-3270		
Clearwater (G-1754)		
Parkway Maintenance & Mgt Co ......E...... 352 873-0848		
Ocala (G-11759)		
Pasco County Schools ......E...... 727 774-7900		
New Port Richey (G-11398)		
Personnel Services Inc ......A...... 954 735-5330		
Lauderdale Lakes (G-8180)		
Pro Clean Building Maint Inc ......E...... 407 740-5554		
Maitland (G-8569)		
Radius Gge Inc ......D...... 239 948-9820		
Fort Myers (G-4564)		
Red Coats Inc ......D...... 813 443-5124		
Tampa (G-18205)		
Red Coats Inc ......D...... 301 654-4360		
Sunrise (G-16813)		
Red Coats Inc ......C...... 321 775-1595		
Melbourne (G-8966)		
Red Coats Inc ......E...... 305 716-0920		
Doral (G-3298)		
Rev 1 Power Services Inc ......D...... 813 657-2404		
Brandon (G-1253)		
S&K Building Services LLC ......E...... 239 541-0222		
Fort Myers (G-4576)		
Safeguard Services Inc ......E...... 954 963-4900		
Pembroke Pines (G-14182)		
Seacrest Services Inc ......C...... 561 697-4990		
West Palm Beach (G-19354)		
Seminole Coml Clg Mint Svcs FL ......D...... 480 748-6296		
Hollywood (G-5515)		
Senlex Environmental LLC ......E...... 800 284-0394		
Miami (G-10259)		
Service Keepers Maint Inc ......E...... 305 751-2261		
Miami (G-10263)		
SFM Janitorial Services LLC ......B...... 305 818-2424		
Hialeah Gardens (G-5349)		
SFM Services Inc ......E...... 305 818-2424		
Hialeah Gardens (G-5351)		
Southeast Service Corporation ......B...... 954 561-0401		
Fort Lauderdale (G-4144)		
Southern Cleaning Service Inc ......A...... 904 260-3100		
Jacksonville (G-6762)		
Southern Management Corp ......C...... 850 983-5262		
Milton (G-10825)		
Space Coast Launch Svcs LLC ......C...... 321 853-0312		
Canaveral As (G-1331)		

SIC

St Johns Cnty Bd Commissioners ......E 904 209-0400
  Saint Augustine *(G-15500)*

St Moritz Building Svcs Inc ......D 904 504-8514
  Jacksonville *(G-6774)*

Steward-Mellon Company LLC ......E 813 621-3577
  Tampa *(G-18338)*

Stockton Maintenance Group Inc ......E 561 684-8922
  West Palm Beach *(G-19375)*

Sunflower Ldscpg & Maint Inc ......C 561 498-1611
  Delray Beach *(G-3021)*

Sunshine Window Cleaning Inc ......B 954 772-0884
  Oakland Park *(G-11615)*

Super Restoration Svc Co LLC ......E 305 233-0500
  Doral *(G-3325)*

▼ Swisher Hygiene Inc ......E 203 682-8331
  Fort Lauderdale *(G-4163)*

T N M Services Inc ......E 954 942-8768
  Pompano Beach *(G-14918)*

Tektron Electrical Systems ......E 561 615-3111
  West Palm Beach *(G-19380)*

TMI Company Store Holding LLC ......D 813 871-9700
  Tampa *(G-18424)*

Total Facility Maintenance Inc ......D 904 313-5046
  Jacksonville *(G-6862)*

Total Facility Solutions ......D 305 418-8533
  Miami *(G-10396)*

Transportation Florida Dept ......E 352 848-2600
  Brooksville *(G-1317)*

Triangle Services Inc ......C 954 929-0509
  Fort Lauderdale *(G-4183)*

Turbine Generator Maint Inc ......E 239 573-1233
  Cape Coral *(G-1430)*

United States Service Inds Fla ......D 850 877-4314
  Tallahassee *(G-17165)*

United States Service Inds Inc ......A 239 334-1865
  Fort Myers *(G-4639)*

Vista Building Maint Svcs Inc ......E 305 869-4334
  Miami *(G-10476)*

Vista Building Maint Svcs Inc ......C 305 552-1973
  Miami *(G-10477)*

Watson Construction Group ......E 904 737-6337
  Jacksonville *(G-6920)*

Wilcin Enterprises Inc ......C 239 596-9880
  Naples *(G-11343)*

Ww Entrprses Southwest Fla Inc ......D 239 277-0330
  Fort Myers *(G-4662)*

Xtremely Clean Jantr Svcs LLC ......D 863 660-9199
  Tampa *(G-18573)*

7352 Medical Eqpt Rental & Leasing

American Homepatient Inc ......C 800 284-2006
  Clearwater *(G-1519)*

Analgesic Healthcare Inc ......E 813 915-8367
  Tampa *(G-17283)*

▲ Associated Medical Products ......D 904 646-0199
  Jacksonville *(G-5811)*

Baycare Home Care Inc ......B 727 394-6461
  Largo *(G-8082)*

Bayshore Dura Medical Inc ......E 305 821-1202
  Miami *(G-9229)*

Cambria Medical Supply Inc ......E 407 822-4600
  Orlando *(G-12228)*

Childrens Home Medical Eqp Inc ......B 407 513-3030
  Orlando *(G-12298)*

Community Home Oxygen Inc ......E 407 822-4600
  Orlando *(G-12353)*

Dade Medical Inc ......D 305 485-0804
  Miramar *(G-10851)*

Eastern Medical Eqp Distrs Inc ......E 786 332-5111
  Doral *(G-3185)*

▲ Electrostim Medical Svcs Inc ......B 800 588-8383
  Tampa *(G-17622)*

Fletchers Medical Supplies Inc ......C 904 387-4481
  Jacksonville *(G-6183)*

Hlg Capital Partners III LP ......A 305 379-2322
  Miami *(G-9703)*

Liberator Medical Supply Inc ......C 772 287-2414
  Stuart *(G-16636)*

Lincare Inc ......E 904 288-8188
  Jacksonville *(G-6439)*

MSC Group Inc ......D 904 646-0199
  Jacksonville *(G-6519)*

Neumanns Home Medical Eqp Inc ......E 407 822-4600
  Orlando *(G-12909)*

Orion Medical Enterprises Inc ......E 305 651-3261
  Miami *(G-10080)*

Quality Biomedical Inc ......D 727 547-6000
  Pinellas Park *(G-14533)*

Surf Drugs Inc ......D 305 948-6429
  Pembroke Park *(G-14126)*

Watermark Medical Inc ......A 561 283-1191
  West Palm Beach *(G-19414)*

7353 Heavy Construction Eqpt Rental & Leasing

Allegiance Crane & Eqp LLC ......C 239 288-7939
  Fort Myers *(G-4265)*

Allegiance Crane & Eqp LLC ......D 954 973-3030
  Pompano Beach *(G-14737)*

Beyel Bros Crane Rigging S Fla ......E 561 798-5776
  Riviera Beach *(G-15283)*

◆ Beyel Brothers Inc ......D 321 632-2000
  Cocoa *(G-1916)*

Beyel Brothers Inc ......E 407 438-8600
  Orlando *(G-12185)*

▲ Central Fla Eqp Rentals Inc ......C 305 883-7518
  Medley *(G-8713)*

Charley Toppino & Sons Inc ......D 305 296-5606
  Key West *(G-7199)*

◆ Crane Rental Corporation ......D 407 277-5000
  Orlando *(G-12383)*

Deep South Crane Rentals Inc ......E 850 944-5810
  Pensacola *(G-14282)*

Deme Construction LLC ......E 941 755-5900
  Sarasota *(G-16030)*

Florida Contractor Rentals Inc ......E 386 274-1002
  Daytona Beach *(G-2591)*

Georges Crane Service Inc ......E 305 513-0188
  Miami *(G-9626)*

Gold Coast Crane Service Inc ......E 954 525-4186
  Hollywood *(G-5444)*

▼ Herc Rentals Inc ......C 800 654-6659
  Bonita Springs *(G-920)*

◆ High Reach Company LLC ......E 321 275-2100
  Sanford *(G-15950)*

▲ Jackson-Cook Lc ......E 850 576-4187
  Tallahassee *(G-17009)*

Kelly Tractor Co ......D 239 693-9233
  Fort Myers *(G-4460)*

◆ Kelly Tractor Co ......E 305 592-5360
  Doral *(G-3254)*

◆ Linder Industrial Machinery Co ......D 813 754-2727
  Plant City *(G-14569)*

Linder Industrial Machinery Co ......E 954 433-2800
  Pembroke Pines *(G-14162)*

▼ Nationwide Equipment Company ......E 904 924-2500
  Jacksonville Beach *(G-6996)*

◆ Pantropic Power Inc ......D 305 477-3329
  Doral *(G-3287)*

Pantropic Power Inc ......E 239 337-4222
  Fort Myers *(G-4533)*

Ram-Tech Construction Inc ......E 305 259-7853
  Homestead *(G-5600)*

Ring Power Corporation ......E 352 797-9500
  Brooksville *(G-1307)*

Ring Power Corporation ......C 407 855-6195
  Orlando *(G-13110)*

Ring Power Corporation ......D 386 755-3997
  Lake City *(G-7544)*

Ring Power Corporation ......D 321 952-3001
  Palm Bay *(G-13637)*

◆ Ring Power Corporation ......B 904 201-7400
  Saint Augustine *(G-15486)*

Ring Power Corporation ......E 850 562-2121
  Midway *(G-10807)*

Robins & Morton Group ......E 407 299-1105
  Orlando *(G-13121)*

◆ Sims Crane & Equipment Co ......E 813 626-8102
  Tampa *(G-18286)*

Sims Crane & Equipment Co ......D 407 851-2930
  Orlando *(G-13203)*

Sims Crane & Equipment Co ......E 800 573-0780
  Medley *(G-8783)*

Sims Crane Service LLC ......E 813 575-6400
  Tampa *(G-18287)*

▼ Sunshine Crane Rental Corp ......E 407 880-2222
  Apopka *(G-216)*

Synergy Rents LLC ......E 386 274-1002
  Daytona Beach *(G-2671)*

Thompson Tractor Co Inc ......E 850 471-6700
  Pensacola *(G-14459)*

Trekker Tractor LLC ......E 407 367-2633
  Haines City *(G-5160)*

United Rentals North Amer Inc ......E 904 636-6336
  Jacksonville *(G-6887)*

7359 Equipment Rental & Leasing, NEC

Abbott Realty Services Inc ......C 850 534-0296
  Santa Rosa Beach *(G-16004)*

ABC Party Rentals Inc ......D 305 592-1223
  Doral *(G-3099)*

▼ ADM Ventures Inc ......E 813 621-4671
  Tampa *(G-17237)*

Aercap Inc ......D 954 760-7777
  Fort Lauderdale *(G-3582)*

Aercap Group Services Inc ......C 305 406-3090
  Doral *(G-3104)*

▲ Aersale Holdings Inc ......D 305 764-3200
  Coral Gables *(G-2026)*

Agiliti Inc ......E 952 893-3259
  Orlando *(G-12077)*

Agiliti Inc ......E 904 425-7013
  Jacksonville *(G-5753)*

Agiliti Inc ......E 954 437-2695
  Miramar *(G-10837)*

Alsco Inc ......E 954 979-2600
  Pompano Beach *(G-14738)*

Around Clock A/C Service LLC ......C 954 742-5544
  Sunrise *(G-16739)*

Atlas Party Rental Inc ......E 305 392-0699
  Miami *(G-9190)*

◆ Atlas Party Rental Inc ......E 561 436-9525
  Boynton Beach *(G-962)*

Ayoub and Associates Inc ......E 239 643-1334
  Naples *(G-11023)*

Beard Equipment Company ......E 850 476-0277
  Pensacola *(G-14230)*

Bedabox LLC ......D 855 222-4601
  Fort Lauderdale *(G-3634)*

Beltram Edge Tool Supply Inc ......E 813 239-1136
  Tampa *(G-17357)*

Better Barricades Inc Florida ......E 386 427-4971
  New Smyrna Beach *(G-11414)*

▲ Bobs Barricades Inc ......E 954 423-2627
  Sunrise *(G-16748)*

Brown Integrated Logistics Inc ......E 904 783-8323
  Jacksonville *(G-5885)*

Buddys Newco LLC ......D 813 623-5461
  Orlando *(G-12215)*

Chep Cont Poling Solutions Inc ......C 866 855-2437
  Orlando *(G-12294)*

Choose 2 Rent LLC ......E 800 622-6484
  Miami *(G-9367)*

Cintas Corporation No 2 ......C 407 423-4222
  Orlando *(G-12301)*

Clarklift of Florida LLC ......E 813 874-2008
  Orlando *(G-12311)*

▼ Compressed Air Systems Inc ......C 800 626-8177
  Tampa *(G-17509)*

▼ Compuquip Technologies LLC ......D 786 416-6143
  Doral *(G-3159)*

Consolidated Water Group LLC ......E 352 291-5900
  Ocala *(G-11668)*

County of Broward ......C 954 357-5170
  Pembroke Pines *(G-14144)*

Dave Carter and Associates ......D 352 732-2992
  Ocala *(G-11672)*

Deep South Crane Rentals Inc ......E 850 944-5810
  Pensacola *(G-14282)*

Doodie Calls Inc ......E 813 800-7667
  Osprey *(G-13532)*

Embraer Aircraft Holding Inc ......E 954 359-3700
  Fort Lauderdale *(G-3770)*

Eventmakers International LLC ......E 772 286-1841
  Stuart *(G-16621)*

Eventstar Corp ......E 305 969-0191
  Medley *(G-8727)*

◆ Eventstar Structures Corp ......E 786 367-0028
  Medley *(G-8728)*

Flexshopper Inc ......D 855 353-9289
  Boca Raton *(G-576)*

General Citrus Systems ......D 863 299-2111
  Winter Haven *(G-19630)*

▼ Glade Grove Sup Inc Blle Glade ......D 561 996-3949
  Belle Glade *(G-357)*

▼ Herc Rentals Inc ......C 800 654-6659
  Bonita Springs *(G-920)*

Hertz Corporation ......E 239 552-5800
  Naples *(G-11163)*

▼ Hertz Corporation ......A 239 301-7000
  Estero *(G-3460)*

Home Depot USA Inc ......C 386 760-6498
  Port Orange *(G-15079)*

Home Depot USA Inc ......C 904 824-3657
  Saint Augustine *(G-15454)*

Home Depot USA Inc ......C 305 293-1313
  Key West *(G-7212)*

Home Depot USA Inc ......C 813 933-0302
  Tampa *(G-17836)*

Home Depot USA Inc ....C 561 683-7221
West Palm Beach *(G-19182)*
Home Depot USA Inc ....D 941 358-3360
University Park *(G-18742)*
Home Depot USA Inc ....C 561 478-0783
West Palm Beach *(G-19183)*
Home Depot USA Inc ....C 904 781-6208
Jacksonville *(G-6286)*
Home Depot USA Inc ....C 239 793-2203
Naples *(G-11165)*
Home Depot USA Inc ....D 727 943-5048
Holiday *(G-5373)*
Home Depot USA Inc ....D 954 971-0643
Coconut Creek *(G-1989)*
Home Depot USA Inc ....C 407 977-8566
Oviedo *(G-13550)*
Home Depot USA Inc ....D 941 625-0783
Port Charlotte *(G-15040)*
Home Depot USA Inc ....C 954 922-7886
Hollywood *(G-5454)*
Home Depot USA Inc ....C 904 727-7574
Jacksonville *(G-6287)*
Home Depot USA Inc ....C 954 961-1761
Hollywood *(G-5455)*
Home Depot USA Inc ....D 813 888-7111
Tampa *(G-17837)*
Home Depot USA Inc ....C 813 655-3871
Brandon *(G-1237)*
Home Depot USA Inc ....C 727 541-3606
Pinellas Park *(G-14522)*
Home Depot USA Inc ....C 727 399-9959
Seminole *(G-16450)*
Home Depot USA Inc ....C 407 275-5771
Orlando *(G-12659)*
Home Depot USA Inc ....D 239 947-5868
Bonita Springs *(G-921)*
Home Depot USA Inc ....C 850 350-9001
Tallahassee *(G-16996)*
Home Depot USA Inc ....D 954 252-1048
Davie *(G-2489)*
Home Depot USA Inc ....C 904 766-2818
Jacksonville *(G-6289)*
Home Depot USA Inc ....C 786 388-9108
Miami *(G-9713)*
Home Depot USA Inc ....C 772 878-4206
Port Saint Lucie *(G-15143)*
Home Depot USA Inc ....D 954 971-2743
North Lauderdale *(G-11479)*
Home Depot USA Inc ....D 305 643-3777
Miami *(G-9714)*
Home Depot USA Inc ....D 954 747-8226
Sunrise *(G-16785)*
Home Depot USA Inc ....C 850 650-4175
Destin *(G-3064)*
Home Depot USA Inc ....C 407 865-5410
Altamonte Springs *(G-61)*
Home Depot USA Inc ....C 904 220-0822
Jacksonville *(G-6290)*
Home Depot USA Inc ....D 407 226-1066
Orlando *(G-12660)*
Home Depot USA Inc ....C 352 242-1870
Clermont *(G-1874)*
Home Depot USA Inc ....C 727 347-1833
Saint Petersburg *(G-15708)*
Home Depot USA Inc ....C 954 763-1932
Fort Lauderdale *(G-3869)*
Home Depot USA Inc ....C 386 445-2497
Palm Coast *(G-13831)*
Home Depot USA Inc ....C 863 293-6574
Winter Haven *(G-19633)*
Home Depot USA Inc ....C 813 788-1642
Zephyrhills *(G-19839)*
Home Depot USA Inc ....C 407 880-4778
Apopka *(G-189)*
Home Depot USA Inc ....D 305 883-7748
Hialeah *(G-5274)*
Home Depot USA Inc ....C 407 498-0606
Saint Cloud *(G-15525)*
Home Depot USA Inc ....C 407 859-3500
Orlando *(G-12661)*
Home Depot USA Inc ....E 386 325-5857
Palatka *(G-13591)*
Home Depot USA Inc ....D 727 581-2093
Largo *(G-8116)*
Home Depot USA Inc ....C 941 377-1900
Sarasota *(G-16185)*
Home Depot USA Inc ....C 813 879-1000
Tampa *(G-17838)*
Home Depot USA Inc ....C 305 940-6503
North Miami Beach *(G-11529)*
Home Depot USA Inc ....C 561 364-9600
Boynton Beach *(G-997)*
Home Depot USA Inc ....C 727 669-5993
Clearwater *(G-1667)*
Home Depot USA Inc ....C 561 793-7048
West Palm Beach *(G-19184)*
Home Depot USA Inc ....C 954 978-6100
Pompano Beach *(G-14823)*
Home Depot USA Inc ....C 904 464-0046
Jacksonville *(G-6292)*
Home Depot USA Inc ....D 239 597-1515
Naples *(G-11166)*
Home Depot USA Inc ....C 813 960-0051
Tampa *(G-17839)*
Home Depot USA Inc ....C 863 688-6800
Lakeland *(G-7883)*
Home Depot USA Inc ....C 305 234-2700
Cutler Bay *(G-2368)*
Home Depot USA Inc ....C 954 733-3030
Oakland Park *(G-11600)*
Home Depot USA Inc ....C 813 835-9565
Tampa *(G-17840)*
Home Depot USA Inc ....D 954 385-9418
Davie *(G-2490)*
Home Depot USA Inc ....D 321 453-5855
Merritt Island *(G-9032)*
Home Depot USA Inc ....D 954 437-2902
Pembroke Pines *(G-14154)*
Home Depot USA Inc ....C 239 656-3033
Cape Coral *(G-1400)*
Home Depot USA Inc ....C 407 935-9600
Kissimmee *(G-7322)*
Home Depot USA Inc ....D 727 784-3800
Clearwater *(G-1668)*
Home Depot USA Inc ....C 727 898-1100
Saint Petersburg *(G-15709)*
Home Depot USA Inc ....C 850 422-2777
Tallahassee *(G-16997)*
Home Depot USA Inc ....D 904 269-3117
Orange Park *(G-11995)*
Home Depot USA Inc ....B 352 596-7699
Spring Hill *(G-16540)*
Home Depot USA Inc ....D 561 747-6561
Jupiter *(G-7087)*
▲ International Lease Fin Corp ....E 310 788-1999
Miami *(G-9766)*
◆ Kelly Tractor Co ....C 305 592-5360
Doral *(G-3254)*
▼ Lengemann Corporation ....E 352 669-2111
Altoona *(G-118)*
Lmg Inc ....B 407 850-0505
Orlando *(G-12775)*
Lopefra Corp ....D 305 266-3896
Doral *(G-3263)*
Lynx Fbo Destin LLC ....A 850 424-6890
Destin *(G-3067)*
Modular Mailing Systems Inc ....E 813 549-5340
Tampa *(G-18049)*
◆ Music Arts Enterprises Inc Mae ....E 954 581-2203
Fort Lauderdale *(G-3986)*
◆ Mwi Corporation ....E 954 426-1500
Deerfield Beach *(G-2775)*
National Cnstr Rentals Inc ....E 407 381-2727
Orlando *(G-12897)*
National Equipment Corp ....E 904 466-4321
Jacksonville *(G-6526)*
◆ Nationwide Lift Trucks Inc ....E 954 922-4645
Hollywood *(G-5479)*
Neff Corporation ....D 888 458-2768
Temple Terrace *(G-18643)*
Pot-O-Gold Rentals LLC ....D 850 995-3375
Pace *(G-13581)*
Power Rental Asset Co LLC ....B 860 305-9440
Jacksonville *(G-6610)*
Powers Radiator Inc ....E 239 332-0036
Fort Myers *(G-4545)*
Presentation Resource Inc ....E 904 398-8179
Jacksonville *(G-6616)*
Production Resource Group LLC ....E 407 996-4200
Orlando *(G-13065)*
◆ Regional One Inc ....E 305 754-4212
Miami *(G-10195)*
Rent Lease Group LLC ....E 786 579-0800
Miami Beach *(G-10645)*
Rent My Wedding LLC ....E 800 465-8020
Miami *(G-10201)*
Rent—Cnter Frnchsing Intl Inc ....D 407 847-7368
Kissimmee *(G-7376)*
Ring Power Corporation ....E 352 797-9500
Brooksville *(G-1307)*
Ring Power Corporation ....E 850 562-2121
Midway *(G-10807)*
Rockhill Group Inc ....C 850 754-0400
Molino *(G-10929)*
Safety Systems Barricades ....D 305 591-2687
Miami *(G-10232)*
▲ Scooterbug Inc ....D 781 933-3120
Orlando *(G-13171)*
Sky One Holdings LLC ....E 561 886-5093
Boca Raton *(G-805)*
Somerset Aviation LLC ....D 561 573-5434
Fort Lauderdale *(G-4136)*
Sonco Corporation ....E 813 971-9990
Tampa *(G-18305)*
South East Indus Sls & Svc Inc ....D 813 247-2780
Apollo Beach *(G-141)*
◆ Southern States Toyota Lift ....D 904 764-7662
Tampa *(G-18311)*
▼ Sun Lift Inc ....D 954 971-9440
Pompano Beach *(G-14914)*
Sun Print Management LLC ....E 727 945-0255
Holiday *(G-5375)*
Sunrise Aviation Inc ....E 214 906-5635
Ormond Beach *(G-13526)*
Terminal Investment Corp ....E 904 751-6631
Jacksonville *(G-6846)*
Thompson Tractor Co Inc ....E 850 785-4007
Panama City *(G-14079)*
▼ Trekker Tractor LLC ....D 561 296-9710
Lake Worth *(G-7757)*
Unique & Exquisite Rentals LLC ....D 863 302-1580
Winter Haven *(G-19669)*
United Rentals North Amer Inc ....E 305 888-1919
Miami *(G-10440)*
United Rentals North Amer Inc ....E 904 636-6336
Jacksonville *(G-6887)*
United Site Services Fla LLC ....D 941 741-8194
Jacksonville *(G-6888)*
Vacation Property Group LLC ....E 850 653-6710
Eastpoint *(G-3403)*
▲ Vas Aero Services LLC ....C 561 998-9330
Boca Raton *(G-859)*
Verizon Credit Inc ....E 813 229-6000
Temple Terrace *(G-18647)*
Vulcan Group LLC ....D 305 967-6344
Miami *(G-10486)*
Williams Communications Inc ....E 850 385-1121
Tallahassee *(G-17176)*

7361 Employment Agencies

360 Healthcare Staffing LLC ....B 877 360-7823
Tampa *(G-17211)*
5 Star Globl Rcrtment Prtners ....E 205 410-8933
Tallahassee *(G-16865)*
A & Associates Inc ....E 561 533-5303
West Palm Beach *(G-19018)*
A Quality Staffing LLC ....B 727 314-4811
Seminole *(G-16436)*
AB Closing Corporation ....E 407 243-6006
Orlando *(G-12040)*
Accountable Health Staff Inc ....B 321 441-3362
Melbourne *(G-8806)*
Accountable Healthcare ....D 561 235-7813
Boca Raton *(G-393)*
Accountble Hlthcare Stffing In ....E 561 235-7810
Boca Raton *(G-394)*
Ace Staffing Inc ....D 407 273-7753
Orlando *(G-12046)*
Ad-Vance Recruiting LLC ....D 941 556-0811
Bradenton *(G-1050)*
▲ Adecco Usa Inc ....C 904 360-2000
Jacksonville *(G-5735)*
Alach/Brdford Rgnal Wrkfrce Bd ....E 352 955-2245
Gainesville *(G-4831)*
Alegiant Services LLC ....D 407 389-0036
Oviedo *(G-13539)*
All Surce Recruiting Group Inc ....B 954 752-6025
Tampa *(G-17264)*
Alterntive Hmmking With A Hart ....D 941 488-2248
Venice *(G-18763)*
American Recruiters Inc ....E 954 493-9200
Coral Springs *(G-2227)*
American Traveler Staff Prof L ....A 561 391-1811
Boca Raton *(G-415)*
American Trvler Stffing Prfssn ....D 561 391-1811
Boca Raton *(G-416)*
AMG Healthcare Services Inc ....C 305 255-1400
Doral *(G-3122)*
Anistar Technologies LLC ....A 813 286-9888
Tampa *(G-17287)*

Aquent LLC	D	407 916-9119
Orlando (G-12128)		
AR International Entps Inc	E	786 955-6946
Weston (G-19441)		
Avant Connections LLC	A	954 999-2405
Coral Springs (G-2229)		
Avant Hlthcare Prfssionals LLC	C	407 681-2999
Casselberry (G-1442)		
Aws Inc	D	407 205-0500
Orlando (G-12164)		
Bay View	D	904 829-3475
Saint Augustine (G-15428)		
Baycare Home Care Inc	E	941 727-9880
Bradenton (G-1056)		
Baycare Home Care Inc	E	352 795-4495
Crystal River (G-2341)		
Bayforce Tech Solutions Inc	C	813 386-0663
Tampa (G-17353)		
Be Active Corp	D	347 893-4481
Fort Lauderdale (G-3631)		
Better Healthcare Intl	E	954 473-4082
Sunrise (G-16745)		
Capital Staffing Solutions Inc	E	904 395-8346
Jacksonville (G-5899)		
Carc-Dvcate For Ctzens With Ds	C	386 752-1880
Lake City (G-7517)		
Careers Usa Inc	A	407 875-8000
Winter Park (G-19695)		
Careers Usa Inc	A	407 894-7700
Orlando (G-12238)		
Careers Usa Inc	C	561 995-7000
Boca Raton (G-498)		
Careersource Palm Bch Cnty Inc	D	561 340-1060
West Palm Beach (G-19073)		
Carter Aston Inc	C	904 527-5601
Jacksonville (G-5912)		
Cherokee Nation Businesses	C	813 881-0819
Tampa (G-17465)		
CHG Medical Staffing Inc	D	800 866-0407
Boca Raton (G-508)		
Child & Fmly Support Svcs Inc	D	610 469-2566
Parrish (G-14112)		
City of Gainesville	D	352 334-5077
Gainesville (G-4861)		
Club Staffing Inc	B	800 875-8999
Boca Raton (G-519)		
Cochhbha Enterprises Inc	D	954 572-6802
Sunrise (G-16757)		
Comphealth Associates Inc	E	954 343-5800
Fort Lauderdale (G-3709)		
Constrction Rcrters Amer Stffi	B	954 533-1689
Davie (G-2470)		
Contemprary Nrsing Sltions Inc	B	703 354-5151
Sarasota (G-16131)		
Contract Specialties Group Ltd	D	321 956-8009
Melbourne (G-8852)		
Countrywide Payroll & Hr	E	877 257-6662
Orlando (G-12373)		
Crescent Staffing Inc	E	561 585-1700
North Palm Beach (G-11542)		
Cross Country Healthcare Inc	A	561 998-2232
Boca Raton (G-538)		
Cross Country Staffing Inc	D	561 998-2232
Boca Raton (G-540)		
Csi Companies Inc	D	904 338-9515
Jacksonville (G-6027)		
Cybervision Inc	E	201 585-9809
Sunny Isles Beach (G-16715)		
Dak Resources Inc	D	904 371-1962
Jacksonville (G-6040)		
Dial-A-Nurse Inc	D	239 434-8000
Naples (G-11094)		
Douglas Steven Associates Inc	E	954 385-8595
Sunrise (G-16764)		
Eca Staffing Solutions Inc	D	904 686-1380
Ponte Vedra Beach (G-14981)		
Edge Information MGT Inc	E	321 722-3343
Melbourne (G-8878)		
EE&sg LLC	B	786 646-9288
Miami (G-9509)		
Emphire Staffing Inc	C	305 262-7280
Miami (G-9519)		
Emphire Staffing Inc	E	954 424-3173
Plantation (G-14638)		
Employment Simplified Inc	E	888 246-6066
Palm City (G-13786)		
Executive Ldrship Slutions Inc	E	239 225-0361
Fort Myers (G-4363)		
Executive Prsnnel Slutions LLC	E	954 630-1575
Oakland Park (G-11595)		
Express Emplyment Prfssnals LL	D	904 707-9946
Jacksonville (G-6140)		
Famoso Inc	C	772 335-8280
Port Saint Lucie (G-15134)		
Flexit Inc	E	954 397-9395
Plantation (G-14641)		
Florida Hosp Hm Care Svc Ctr	D	407 691-8202
Orlando (G-12526)		
Florida Paratitioners LLC	C	954 791-6146
Fort Lauderdale (G-3797)		
Florida Peopleready Inc	C	407 944-1440
Kissimmee (G-7312)		
Florida Peopleready Inc	C	727 524-6699
Largo (G-8110)		
Florida Premier Staffing Inc	D	813 830-2079
Tampa (G-17695)		
Fortiline Drivers LLC	C	205 895-8667
Lakeland (G-7870)		
Frankcrum 1 Inc	C	727 799-1229
Clearwater (G-1647)		
Frankcrum 9 Inc	C	727 799-1229
Clearwater (G-1648)		
Frankcrum Corporate Inc	C	727 799-1229
Clearwater (G-1649)		
Gdkn Corporation	B	954 985-6650
Hollywood (G-5441)		
Genesis Medical Staffing Inc	E	402 898-1113
Clearwater (G-1653)		
Genoa Employment Solutions Inc	C	954 604-6056
Sunrise (G-16775)		
GL Staffing Services Inc	E	786 242-5150
Palmetto Bay (G-13943)		
GL Staffing Services Inc	E	786 409-5456
Doral (G-3210)		
GL Staffing Services Inc	E	407 930-7125
Orlando (G-12572)		
GL Staffing Services Inc	E	954 973-8350
Margate (G-8649)		
GL Staffing Services Inc	E	954 893-7717
West Park (G-19430)		
GL Staffing Services Inc	E	772 419-5002
Stuart (G-16627)		
GL Staffing Services Inc	D	305 885-2500
Hialeah (G-5265)		
GL Staffing Services Inc	D	305 885-2500
Hialeah (G-5266)		
Global Staff USA Inc	E	305 978-3098
Miami (G-9637)		
Granite Prof Technical Svcs	A	813 242-2300
Tampa (G-17747)		
Gsh Health Inc	C	863 551-3900
Auburndale (G-254)		
Gulf Coast Workforce Dev Bd	E	850 913-3285
Panama City (G-14024)		
Halifax Home Health	E	386 322-4700
Port Orange (G-15077)		
Harmony Healthcare LLC	A	813 321-6877
Tampa (G-17792)		
Hayes Locums LLC	C	888 837-3172
Fort Lauderdale (G-3850)		
Hays Talent Solutions LLC	C	813 936-7004
Tampa (G-17796)		
Hays US Corporation	E	813 936-7004
Tampa (G-17797)		
Health Advocates Network Inc	D	561 437-4880
Boca Raton (G-623)		
Health Matters Inc	E	352 597-4084
Spring Hill (G-16539)		
Healthcare Scouts Inc	D	800 708-0605
Maitland (G-8540)		
Healthcare Spport Staffing Inc	C	407 478-0332
Maitland (G-8541)		
Healthcare Systems Inc	C	772 770-1100
Vero Beach (G-18868)		
Hire Quest LLC	A	954 491-0919
Fort Lauderdale (G-3863)		
Hq Aero Management (fl) Inc	D	407 977-1570
Oviedo (G-13551)		
Hutco Inc	B	813 221-0123
Tampa (G-17848)		
IM Slzbcher Ctr For Hmless I	E	904 359-0457
Jacksonville (G-6310)		
Imethods LLC	E	888 306-2261
Jacksonville (G-6313)		
Incepture Inc	D	904 905-4407
Jacksonville (G-6314)		
Innovent Global Inc	D	561 444-3152
West Palm Beach (G-19200)		
Innovtive Systems Group Fla In	D	407 481-9580
Orlando (G-12682)		
Intellapro LLC	D	954 589-1234
Saint Petersburg (G-15722)		
Interactive Resources LLC	E	904 821-8960
Jacksonville (G-6325)		
Interim Hlthcare of N Cntl Fla	C	352 326-0400
Leesburg (G-8248)		
Interim Hlthcare of N Cntl Fla	C	352 378-0333
Gainesville (G-4923)		
Inverted Hlthcare Stffing Fla	E	954 281-9475
Pompano Beach (G-14829)		
Iplacement Inc	A	407 373-0878
Winter Park (G-19740)		
J&L Worldwide Solutions LLC	D	407 692-4239
Orlando (G-12695)		
Jackson Therapy Partners LLC	A	877 896-3660
Orlando (G-12698)		
Jaykay Inc	C	800 442-5441
Tavares (G-18609)		
Jobletics Pro Cstl Hospitality	E	305 975-9956
Miami (G-9796)		
K B Staffing LLC	E	863 875-5721
Winter Haven (G-19638)		
Kforce Clinical Research Llc	D	813 552-2927
Tampa (G-17918)		
Kforce Global Solutions Inc	A	813 552-3990
Tampa (G-17919)		
Kforce Inc	A	813 552-5000
Tampa (G-17920)		
Kforce Services Corp	D	813 552-3734
Tampa (G-17921)		
Kforcecom Inc	A	813 552-5000
Tampa (G-17922)		
Landrum Companies Inc	C	850 476-5100
Pensacola (G-14341)		
Landrum Humn Rsrce Cmpnies Inc	E	850 476-5100
Pensacola (G-14342)		
Life Care Home Hlth Svcs Corp	B	561 272-5866
Delray Beach (G-2978)		
Little Hvana Actvties Ntrtn CT	D	305 858-0887
Miami (G-9876)		
Local Staff LLC	C	800 347-2264
Boca Raton (G-675)		
Loyal Source Worldwide Inc	B	407 306-8441
Orlando (G-12786)		
Loyal Srce Government Svcs LLC	A	407 306-8441
Orlando (G-12787)		
Magellan Solutions USA Inc	C	650 897-5147
Melbourne (G-8926)		
Mainline Professional Svcs LLC	C	850 219-5000
Tallahassee (G-17030)		
Management Health Systems LLC	C	954 739-4247
Sunrise (G-16795)		
Mantech Mgh Inc	D	813 552-5000
Tampa (G-17987)		
Marcum Search LLC	D	305 995-9600
Miami (G-9898)		
McVt Inc	E	561 998-2232
Boca Raton (G-684)		
Medical Ctr Hm Hlth Care Svcs	A	850 431-6868
Tallahassee (G-17040)		
Medical Doctor Associates LLC	D	561 998-2232
Boca Raton (G-686)		
Medsource LLC	D	727 469-8940
Safety Harbor (G-15410)		
Mission Critical Group LLC	E	904 422-9731
Jacksonville (G-6507)		
Mission Search Intl Inc	E	800 410-2009
Tampa (G-18044)		
Modis Inc	C	813 379-3718
Tampa (G-18048)		
Msstaff LLC	C	561 322-1300
Boca Raton (G-702)		
Mswstaffing LLC	E	772 519-2066
Fort Lauderdale (G-3979)		
National Computer Services	E	904 321-0050
Fernandina Beach (G-3539)		
National Sourcing Inc	C	813 281-0013
Tampa (G-18068)		
National Staffing Solutions	A	863 299-5015
Winter Haven (G-19649)		
Nightingale Nurses LLC	E	561 314-0140
Boca Raton (G-720)		
North Broward Hospital Dst	C	954 785-2990
Pompano Beach (G-14868)		
Nursecore Management Svcs LLC	B	727 796-2299
Clearwater (G-1741)		
Nursecore Management Svcs LLC	B	941 951-6080
Sarasota (G-16248)		
Oasis Hr Solutions II Inc	D	561 227-6500
West Palm Beach (G-19283)		

Oasis Outsourcing LLC ....C 561 227-6500
West Palm Beach (G-19284)
Oasis Staffing Inc ....D 904 281-0220
Jacksonville (G-6556)
Optimum Healthcare It LLC ....C 904 373-0831
Jacksonville Beach (G-6998)
Osceola Staffing Holdings LLC ....E 813 792-6559
Tampa (G-18110)
P2p Staffing Corp ....A 954 507-4860
Fort Lauderdale (G-4037)
P2p Staffing Corp ....D 954 656-8600
Boca Raton (G-735)
Panhandle Labor Solutions LLC ....D 850 449-7871
Pensacola (G-14400)
Paul Betancur ....D 561 312-6295
Orlando (G-13014)
PC Management Inc ....E 239 335-1320
Bonita Springs (G-930)
Perfusioncom Inc ....C 888 499-5672
Fort Myers (G-4540)
Platinum Hr Management LLC ....D 954 634-4256
Fort Lauderdale (G-4053)
Pontoon Solutions Inc ....D 855 881-1533
Jacksonville (G-6607)
Power Resources Fincl Svcs Inc ....E 954 281-5590
Pembroke Pines (G-14176)
Pro Image Solutions Inc ....E 407 774-4884
Longwood (G-8392)
Pro Med Healthcare Svcs LLC ....C 727 209-0639
Saint Petersburg (G-15810)
Pro Med Healthcare Svcs LLC ....E 863 299-5015
Auburndale (G-259)
Professional Contrs Svcs Inc ....E 305 871-1119
Miami (G-10149)
Professnal Stffing Svcs Group ....E 407 878-3900
Altamonte Springs (G-94)
Progressive Employer Servicesi ....E 941 925-2990
Sarasota (G-16045)
Ramnarain II LLC ....E 407 855-8586
Orlando (G-13080)
Randstad Professionals Us LLC ....D 305 265-5300
Miami (G-10183)
Randstad Professionals Us LLC ....C 904 296-2424
Jacksonville (G-6634)
Reflectxion Resources Inc ....A 407 833-8815
Lake Mary (G-7633)
Resource Emplyment Sltions LLC ....E 866 412-6535
Orlando (G-13104)
Resume Express Inc ....E 561 567-5853
Lantana (G-8068)
Richard P Rita Personnel Syste ....E 863 583-7482
Lakeland (G-7954)
S2 Hr Solutions 1a LLC ....D 727 565-2950
Hollywood (G-5512)
Scribeamerica LLC ....B 954 908-8600
Fort Lauderdale (G-4103)
Senior Home Care Inc ....D 863 682-6182
Lakeland (G-7967)
Sherloq Group Inc ....D 813 273-7833
Tampa (G-18277)
Shiftpixy Inc ....D 888 798-9100
Miami (G-10268)
Shotrock Productions Inc ....D 407 614-6160
Sanford (G-15981)
Skiltrek LLC ....E 866 620-2612
Jacksonville Beach (G-7003)
Skybridge Resources LLC ....D 813 579-1220
Tampa (G-18294)
Skybridge Tactical LLC ....E 813 204-1195
Tampa (G-18295)
South East Personnel Lsg Inc ....C 866 800-0785
Holiday (G-5374)
Southwest Fla Wrkfrce Dev Bd I ....E 239 225-2500
Fort Myers (G-4600)
Southwest Florida ....E 941 235-5900
Port Charlotte (G-15061)
Spec Personnel LLC ....D 813 331-8025
Tampa (G-18316)
Special Counsel Inc ....B 904 737-3436
Jacksonville (G-6770)
Spectra Personnel Services ....B 888 316-1168
Lake Mary (G-7640)
Staff America Inc ....C 352 432-0080
Ocala (G-11782)
Staffing Specifix Inc ....E 305 974-1850
Miami (G-10325)
Strategic Direct Solutions LLC ....E 972 355-7500
Largo (G-8154)
STS Federal LLC ....E 407 965-2596
Oviedo (G-13572)

STS Workforce Solutions Inc ....D 800 800-2400
Jensen Beach (G-7023)
Sunbelt Staffing LLC ....B 813 471-0152
Oldsmar (G-11926)
Sunwest Peo Florida Vi Inc ....D 941 925-2990
Sarasota (G-16061)
Superbeo LLC ....E 614 256-7047
Miami (G-10349)
TBA Management Consulting LLC ....E 786 276-2345
Miami Beach (G-10665)
Tech Usa Inc ....D 407 667-7000
Maitland (G-8586)
Tech Usa Inc ....B 813 287-2679
Tampa (G-18410)
Tech Usa Inc ....C 954 492-2345
Fort Lauderdale (G-4170)
Techtrueup LLC ....D 813 393-9393
Naples (G-11317)
Travel Staff LLC ....D 800 347-2264
Boca Raton (G-844)
Tri-State Employment Svc Inc ....C 754 223-2956
Fort Lauderdale (G-4182)
Trinet Hr I Inc ....A 813 620-3376
Tampa (G-18447)
Triumph Staffing Assoc Inc ....E 305 722-4500
Miami (G-10409)
Triumph Staffing Assoc Inc ....E 954 634-0777
Hollywood (G-5544)
▲ United Nursing Services Inc ....D 561 478-8788
West Palm Beach (G-19397)
United Nursing Services Inc ....C 239 596-6003
Naples (G-11332)
Universal Select Inc ....A 904 786-1166
Jacksonville (G-6892)
Vaco LLC ....C 305 790-4774
Coral Gables (G-2204)
Vaco LLC ....D 561 304-4142
West Palm Beach (G-19405)
Vaco LLC ....C 321 445-2100
Maitland (G-8596)
Vaco LLC ....D 813 749-2050
Tampa (G-18492)
Valintry Services LLC ....D 800 360-1407
Winter Park (G-19782)
Vcarve Inc ....E 850 205-8278
Tallahassee (G-17170)
Velocity Resource Group LLC ....D 630 848-0888
Tampa (G-18498)
Vendorpass Inc ....A 877 699-2297
Jacksonville (G-6903)
Veredus Holdings Inc ....A 813 936-7004
Tampa (G-18501)
Virtual Resource MGT Corp ....C 239 948-1147
Estero (G-3487)
Visiting Nurse Assn Fla Inc ....D 352 592-9800
Weeki Wachee (G-18970)
Weatherby Locums Inc ....D 954 343-3050
Fort Lauderdale (G-4220)
Wilson Human Capital Group ....C 813 600-4303
Tampa (G-18560)
Workers Temporary Staffing Inc ....A 352 742-3357
Tavares (G-18621)
Workfrce Dev Bd of Trsure Cast ....D 866 482-4473
Port Saint Lucie (G-15176)
Worksquare LLC ....E 305 577-4482
Miami (G-10515)
Worldstaff Usa Corp ....E 786 431-1537
Miami (G-10516)

7363 Help Supply Svcs

A & Associates Inc ....E 561 533-5303
West Palm Beach (G-19018)
Adecco Inc ....D 866 528-0707
Jacksonville (G-5733)
▲ Adecco Usa Inc ....C 904 360-2000
Jacksonville (G-5735)
Airplanes Inc ....B 772 232-2305
Jensen Beach (G-7012)
Ajilon LLC ....C 973 331-3890
Jacksonville (G-5761)
Ajilon LLC ....B 206 467-0700
Jacksonville (G-5762)
All Care Consultants Inc ....E 954 748-2800
Fort Lauderdale (G-3592)
Allocation Services Inc ....D 407 389-1303
Longwood (G-8338)
Alternative Resources Corp ....B 813 639-7650
Tampa (G-17274)
Ameri-Force Management Svcs ....B 904 633-9918
Jacksonville (G-5773)

Ameri-Force Professional Svcs ....A 800 522-8998
Jacksonville (G-5774)
▲ American Sls MGT Orgnztion LLC ...A 305 269-2700
Miami (G-9143)
American Traveler Staff Prof L ....A 561 391-1811
Boca Raton (G-415)
American Trvler Stffing Prfssn ....D 561 391-1811
Boca Raton (G-416)
Arcadia Health Services Inc ....E 727 579-9414
Saint Petersburg (G-15572)
Arcadia Health Svcs Mich Inc ....D 727 579-9414
Saint Petersburg (G-15573)
Assignment America Llc ....C 561 998-2232
Boca Raton (G-429)
Associatesmd Medical Group Inc ....D 844 954-3627
Davie (G-2458)
Atlas Aviation Tampa Inc ....E 813 251-1752
Tampa (G-17318)
Big Bang Enterprises Inc ....B 305 539-3810
Coral Gables (G-2052)
CHG Healthcare Services Inc ....A 954 870-5139
Fort Lauderdale (G-3688)
CHS Middle East LLC ....D 321 783-2720
Cape Canaveral (G-1361)
CMI Services LLC ....E 850 638-0406
Chipley (G-1490)
Cochhbha Enterprises Inc ....D 954 572-6802
Sunrise (G-16757)
Comforce Solutions Inc ....A 813 349-1777
Tampa (G-17501)
Comphealth Associates Inc ....E 954 343-5800
Fort Lauderdale (G-3709)
Constrction Rcrters Amer Stffi ....B 954 533-1689
Davie (G-2470)
Consultis Funding Inc ....C 407 805-9040
Lake Mary (G-7580)
Crg Corporation ....D 727 767-9887
Saint Petersburg (G-15651)
Cross Country Healthcare Inc ....A 561 998-2232
Boca Raton (G-538)
Dalpar Corporation ....E 850 362-6426
Fort Walton Beach (G-4761)
Dcr Workforce Inc ....D 561 998-3737
Boca Raton (G-548)
Debbies Staffing Services Inc ....A 813 314-2229
Tampa (G-17581)
Dental Tmprries Unlimited Group ....D 239 417-1739
Naples (G-11093)
Diaz Fontanez & Associates LLC ....E 800 201-0406
Miami (G-9476)
Document Storage Systems Inc ....C 813 985-1900
Tampa (G-17598)
Driver Solutions LLC ....D 813 563-6012
Apollo Beach (G-136)
Emerald Labor Source LLC ....E 772 220-3200
Stuart (G-16616)
Employee Leasing Solutions Inc ....A 407 562-1424
Lake Mary (G-7588)
Employee Leasing Solutions Inc ....D 941 746-6567
Bradenton (G-1094)
Event Services America Inc ....A 954 435-3600
Miramar (G-10858)
Express Care Belleview LLC ....D 352 347-7396
Belleview (G-374)
Famoso Inc ....C 772 335-8280
Port Saint Lucie (G-15134)
Fasthire Staffing Inc ....D 813 692-4733
Temple Terrace (G-18633)
Fasttrack Staffing Inc ....C 352 748-0045
Wildwood (G-19495)
Fieldcore Svc Sltions Intl LLC ....D 813 242-7400
Tampa (G-17658)
First Coast Workforce Dev Inc ....E 904 213-3800
Fleming Island (G-3553)
Florida Peopleready Inc ....C 407 944-1440
Kissimmee (G-7312)
Florida Peopleready Inc ....C 727 524-6699
Largo (G-8110)
Florida Premier Staffing Inc ....D 813 830-2079
Tampa (G-17695)
Genesiscare Usa Inc ....C 239 931-7333
Fort Myers (G-4414)
Gevity Hr LP ....A 941 748-4540
Lakewood Ranch (G-8016)
Gevity Hr Inc ....A 941 741-4300
Lakewood Ranch (G-8017)
GL Staffing Services Inc ....D 954 893-7717
West Park (G-19430)
GL Staffing Services Inc ....D 772 419-5002
Stuart (G-16627)

GL Staffing Services Inc	D	305 885-2500
Hialeah (G-5265)		
GL Staffing Services Inc	D	305 885-2500
Hialeah (G-5266)		
Glotel Inc	E	312 612-7480
Oakland Park (G-11597)		
Granite Prof Technical Svcs	A	813 242-2300
Tampa (G-17747)		
Healthcare Scouts Inc	D	800 708-0605
Maitland (G-8540)		
Hire Velocity LLC	E	813 286-7240
Lutz (G-8444)		
Iap Global Services LLC	D	321 784-7100
Cape Canaveral (G-1366)		
Icbd Holdings LLC	C	833 575-2500
West Palm Beach (G-19195)		
In Touch Logistics LLC	E	305 398-4930
Miami Gardens (G-10689)		
Indelible Solutions LLP	D	850 321-5168
Jacksonville (G-6316)		
Inner-Parish Security Corp	D	985 542-7960
Pensacola (G-14328)		
Innovtive Systems Group Fla In	D	407 481-9580
Orlando (G-12682)		
Inphynet Hospital Services	D	954 475-1300
Tamarac (G-17194)		
Instore Group LLC	C	407 616-4418
Ocoee (G-11817)		
Integrated Retail Services LLC	D	786 360-0015
Coral Gables (G-2130)		
Integrity Rsurces Staffing Inc	D	813 788-4011
Zephyrhills (G-19840)		
Interim Health Care of N Fla	D	850 474-0767
Pensacola (G-14330)		
Interim Healthcare Inc	C	800 338-7786
Sunrise (G-16787)		
Interim Hlthcare of N Cntl Fla	C	352 326-0400
Leesburg (G-8248)		
Interim Hlthcare of N Cntl Fla	D	352 378-0333
Gainesville (G-4923)		
ISS C & S Building Maint Corp	D	352 372-8753
Gainesville (G-4924)		
Jaykay Inc	C	800 442-5441
Tavares (G-18609)		
John Paul USA	D	415 905-6088
Miami (G-9798)		
Kforce Inc	A	813 552-5000
Tampa (G-17920)		
L C Ramnarain	D	407 855-8586
Orlando (G-12744)		
Labor Finders	E	561 627-6507
Palm Beach Gardens (G-13746)		
Labor Finders of Miami Inc	E	954 581-7774
Fort Lauderdale (G-3926)		
Labor Ready Southeast III LP	A	407 648-8868
Orlando (G-12746)		
Labor Ready Southeast III LP	A	772 286-5522
Stuart (G-16634)		
Luke & Associates Inc	B	321 452-4601
Rockledge (G-15357)		
Magellan Solutions USA Inc	C	650 897-5147
Melbourne (G-8926)		
Management Health Systems LLC	C	954 739-4247
Sunrise (G-16795)		
Maxim Healthcare Services Inc	D	352 360-7291
Leesburg (G-8261)		
Maxim Healthcare Services Inc	D	239 931-6777
Fort Myers (G-4503)		
Maxim Healthcare Services Inc	C	813 887-4100
Tampa (G-18003)		
Maxim Healthcare Services Inc	D	850 473-0323
Pensacola (G-14356)		
Maxim Healthcare Services Inc	C	813 877-8711
Tampa (G-18004)		
Maxim Healthcare Services Inc	D	305 556-8901
Miami Lakes (G-10743)		
Maxim Healthcare Services Inc	D	813 877-8711
Tampa (G-18005)		
Maxim Healthcare Services Inc	C	813 289-0760
Tampa (G-18006)		
Medical Ctr Hm Hlth Care Svcs	A	850 431-6868
Tallahassee (G-17040)		
Melbourne Flight Training LLC	E	321 345-3194
Melbourne (G-8934)		
Meridian Healthcare Group Inc	D	850 325-7777
Tallahassee (G-17042)		
Msn Incorporated	D	954 714-6064
Oakland Park (G-11607)		
Msstaff LLC	D	407 825-9009
Belle Isle (G-367)		

Msstaff LLC	C	561 322-1300
Boca Raton (G-702)		
National Computer Services	E	904 321-0050
Fernandina Beach (G-3539)		
National Staffing Solutions	D	888 830-1050
Winter Park (G-19752)		
Nesco Inc	B	813 654-7444
Tampa (G-18070)		
Nn & R Enterprises	E	352 373-3919
Gainesville (G-4957)		
Novel Engineering Inc	E	321 392-0911
Melbourne (G-8951)		
Outsource Inc	E	407 774-1951
Altamonte Springs (G-86)		
Payroll Management Inc	D	850 243-5604
Fort Walton Beach (G-4797)		
Personnel Services Inc	A	954 735-5330
Lauderdale Lakes (G-8180)		
Poch Staffing Inc	B	813 414-0334
Tampa (G-18157)		
Pontoon Solutions Inc	D	855 881-1533
Jacksonville (G-6607)		
Powell Supportive Services Inc	E	813 335-4891
Land O Lakes (G-8053)		
Randstad Professionals Us LLC	C	954 308-7600
Fort Lauderdale (G-4081)		
Rcg Global Services Inc	C	407 999-9594
Orlando (G-13085)		
Resource Acqstion MGT Svcs Inc	D	239 390-9886
Fort Myers (G-4569)		
Resource Acqstion MGT Svcs Inc	D	813 880-7133
Tampa (G-18218)		
Resource Emplyment Sltions LLC	E	866 412-6535
Orlando (G-13104)		
Rockhill Group Inc	D	850 754-0400
Molino (G-10929)		
Select Staffing	D	305 477-6688
Miami (G-10257)		
Sfn Group Inc	A	904 808-1500
Saint Augustine (G-15492)		
Sfn Group Inc	A	305 265-5300
Miami (G-10266)		
▲ Sfn Group Inc	B	954 308-7600
Fort Lauderdale (G-4117)		
Shotrock Productions Inc	D	407 614-6160
Sanford (G-15981)		
Skybridge Aviation LLC	E	813 579-1221
Tampa (G-18292)		
South Louisiana Mar Contg LLC	D	337 316-4601
Panama City (G-14072)		
Special Counsel Inc	E	919 674-2410
Jacksonville (G-6769)		
Spherion Staffing LLC	E	321 255-0222
Melbourne (G-8980)		
Staff America Inc	C	352 432-0080
Ocala (G-11782)		
Staff Builders Hr LLC	C	863 701-8690
Lakeland (G-7977)		
Staffing Sltions Southeast Inc	D	561 994-4600
Boca Raton (G-816)		
STS Aviation Group LLC	D	800 800-2400
Jensen Beach (G-7022)		
Synerfac Inc	D	954 772-3300
Fort Lauderdale (G-4165)		
Techtrueup LLC	D	813 393-9393
Naples (G-11317)		
U C A C Inc	E	561 689-5927
West Palm Beach (G-19395)		
Unifi Aviation LLC	A	813 396-4045
Tampa (G-18457)		
Unifi Aviation LLC	A	904 741-2625
Jacksonville (G-6883)		
Veritashealthcare Inc	C	850 477-2410
Pensacola (G-14462)		
Virtual Resource MGT Corp	C	239 948-1147
Estero (G-3487)		
Visiting Care Florida Inc	C	561 433-8800
Lake Worth (G-7759)		
Workers Temporary Staffing Inc	A	813 882-9819
Tampa (G-18566)		
Workers Temporary Staffing Inc	C	813 637-2220
Tampa (G-18567)		
Workers Temporary Staffing Inc	A	352 742-3357
Tavares (G-18621)		
Workway Inc	E	954 351-3339
Fort Lauderdale (G-4232)		

7371 Custom Computer Programming Svcs

352 Inc	D	352 374-9657
Newberry (G-11428)		

3cinteractive Corp	C	561 443-5505
Boca Raton (G-390)		
404 Fairway Inc	E	561 963-9005
Lake Worth (G-7706)		
5x5 Technologies Inc	E	941 900-4350
Saint Petersburg (G-15554)		
AB Closing Corporation	D	407 243-6006
Orlando (G-12041)		
Abie Inc	E	561 309-1955
Boca Raton (G-392)		
Accenture Federal Services LLC	C	904 899-0290
Jacksonville (G-5725)		
Accrisoft Corporation	E	561 908-6260
Sarasota (G-16076)		
Activengage Inc	C	321 441-7702
Maitland (G-8494)		
Actsoft Inc	D	813 936-2331
Tampa (G-17232)		
Adacel Systems Inc	D	407 581-1560
Orlando (G-12052)		
Adaptive Computing Entps Inc	D	239 330-6083
Naples (G-11000)		
Advanced Answers On Demand Inc	E	954 724-9809
Coral Springs (G-2218)		
Advanced Bus Cmputers Amer Inc	E	904 354-2073
Jacksonville (G-5739)		
Advanced Software Pdts Group	E	239 649-1548
Naples (G-11001)		
Advanced Systems Tech Inc	D	321 235-7500
Orlando (G-12060)		
Afs Technologies Inc	E	602 522-8282
Tampa (G-17244)		
Agilethought LLC	C	877 514-9180
Tampa (G-17250)		
Alegeus Technologies LLC	E	321 251-5333
Maitland (G-8502)		
Allergy Free Labs LLC	E	561 994-3397
Boca Raton (G-412)		
Allvue Systems Holdings Inc	E	305 901-7060
Coral Gables (G-2027)		
Alpha II LLC	C	888 889-6777
Tallahassee (G-16875)		
Alphanet Technologies Inc	E	305 497-5575
Bay Harbor Islands (G-345)		
Amadeus North America Inc	B	305 499-6613
Doral (G-3116)		
Analytics Partners Inc	E	904 322-7736
Tampa (G-17284)		
Apex Covantage LLC	D	703 709-3000
Miami Beach (G-10551)		
Appiskey LLC	D	407 545-4527
Orlando (G-12124)		
AR International Entps Inc	E	786 955-6946
Weston (G-19441)		
Arionkoder Global LLC	E	631 204-6094
Miami (G-9168)		
Arionkoder LLC	D	631 204-6094
Miami (G-9169)		
Asrc Aerospace Corp	B	321 867-1462
Kennedy Space Center (G-7154)		
Assembly Software LLC	D	305 357-6500
Coral Gables (G-2036)		
Auditmacs	D	904 222-8399
Jacksonville (G-5822)		
Auritasllc	E	407 834-8324
Sanford (G-15919)		
Authorify Holdings LLC	C	904 695-9933
Jacksonville (G-5824)		
Avectra Inc	D	703 506-7000
Saint Petersburg (G-15583)		
Axiom Services Inc	E	727 442-7774
Clearwater (G-1529)		
Axpire LLC	D	917 680-7897
Miami (G-9197)		
▼ Aya Associates Inc	D	407 539-1800
Maitland (G-8504)		
Barr Systems Inc	E	352 491-3100
Gainesville (G-4842)		
Bayshore Solutions LLC	E	813 902-0141
Tampa (G-17354)		
Beauteine Limited	D	213 269-5431
North Miami (G-11484)		
BellSouth Entertainment LLC	C	407 425-1267
Orlando (G-12179)		
Bergenske Enterprises Inc	E	866 435-8865
Longwood (G-8346)		
Besweet Creations LLC	E	754 200-4833
Oakland Park (G-11584)		
Bilr LLC	E	212 269-4520
Pinecrest (G-14498)		

Company	Code	Phone
Biomatrix Specialty Phrm LLC ....E .....954 385-7322 Plantation (G-14608)		
Bitdefender Inc ....C .....954 776-6262 Fort Lauderdale (G-3645)		
Bliss Bits Rewards ....D .....407 690-4841 Orlando (G-12190)		
Blue Martini Software Inc ....B .....561 265-2700 Delray Beach (G-2917)		
Bluecloud Services Inc ....B .....813 504-2056 Tampa (G-17368)		
Bluehawk LLC ....D .....561 293-3734 West Palm Beach (G-19054)		
Boom Rewards LLC ....D .....844 278-0072 Weston (G-19445)		
Bridgecr LLC ....E .....561 228-6444 Palm Beach Gardens (G-13695)		
Bst Consultants Inc ....D .....772 341-3834 Jupiter (G-7052)		
Business Info Tech Sltnscom In ......E .....407 363-0024 Orlando (G-12221)		
Bydesign Technologies LLC ....D .....813 253-2235 Tampa (G-17405)		
▲ Cake Corporation ....D .....813 400-2000 Tampa (G-17411)		
Callpass LLC ....E .....877 324-0999 Clearwater (G-1555)		
Cantata Health LLC ....E .....877 532-6347 Jacksonville (G-5897)		
Capital City Services Company ......C .....850 671-0300 Tallahassee (G-16903)		
Caremedic Systems Inc ....D .....952 936-1179 Tampa (G-17420)		
Carley Corporation ....C .....407 894-5575 Orlando (G-12241)		
Carprix LLC ....E .....305 274-2147 Fort Lauderdale (G-3671)		
Cash Management Solutions Inc .....E .....727 524-1103 Clearwater (G-1561)		
CCX Holdings Inc ....E .....941 306-4951 Sarasota (G-16119)		
CD Advantage LLC ....E .....904 722-8200 Jacksonville (G-5918)		
Centralreach LLC ....D .....800 939-5414 Fort Lauderdale (G-3678)		
Checkalt Eras Inc ....C .....305 255-1452 Miami (G-9358)		
City of West Palm Beach ....E .....561 822-1400 West Palm Beach (G-19089)		
Cloud Sherpas LLC ....C .....407 325-3453 Winter Park (G-19705)		
Cole Engineering Services Inc ....C .....407 674-8300 Orlando (G-12342)		
Common Sense Publishing LLC ......C .....561 510-1713 Delray Beach (G-2933)		
Communications Intl Inc ....D .....772 569-5355 Vero Beach (G-18847)		
Computer Associates Intl ....E .....941 552-2700 Sarasota (G-16129)		
Computer Sftwr Sltons Intl LLC .....B .....954 419-1008 Boca Raton (G-523)		
Comsysco Corp ....E .....754 200-5266 Plantation (G-14622)		
Concurrent Real-Time Inc ....D .....954 974-1700 Pompano Beach (G-14781)		
Connectwise LLC ....D .....813 463-4700 Tampa (G-17514)		
Control Data Inc ....D .....317 710-7997 Melbourne (G-8853)		
Cotalker Inc ....E .....954 643-1497 Weston (G-19453)		
Craig Technical Consulting Inc ......E .....321 613-5620 Merritt Island (G-9024)		
Crg Management LLC ....A .....813 517-1653 Tampa (G-17548)		
CSX Technology Inc ....A .....904 633-1000 Jacksonville (G-6032)		
Cybernetics & Systems Inc ....B .....904 359-3100 Jacksonville (G-6036)		
Cybervision Inc ....E .....201 585-9809 Sunny Isles Beach (G-16715)		
D3 Air & Space Operations Inc ......D .....904 217-3887 Saint Augustine (G-15437)		
Darkside Game Studios Inc ....E .....954 341-1112 Fort Lauderdale (G-3749)		
Data Age Business Systems Inc .....E .....727 582-9100 Clearwater (G-1602)		
Data Meaning Services Group ....E .....855 424-3282 Delray Beach (G-2937)		
Data MGT Assoc Brevard Inc ....D .....321 725-8081 Malabar (G-8604)		

Company	Code	Phone
Data Software Services LLC ....B .....877 859-0195 Destin (G-3056)		
Data2intel Corporation ....C .....800 420-1321 Fort Lauderdale (G-3751)		
Datalink LLC ....D .....813 903-1091 Tampa (G-17573)		
Datis Hr Cloud Inc ....D .....813 289-4451 Tampa (G-17574)		
Datson360 LLC ....E .....954 516-8851 Lauderhill (G-8194)		
David Lewis & Associates Inc ....D .....321 872-2016 Melbourne (G-8865)		
Decurtis LLC ....D .....407 965-1395 Orlando (G-12410)		
Dev2017cap LLC ....D .....847 713-0680 Orlando (G-12415)		
Dhs Associates Inc ....D .....904 213-0448 Orange Park (G-11985)		
Diyotta Inc ....E .....704 817-4646 Saint Johns (G-15544)		
Doculex Inc ....E .....863 297-3691 Winter Haven (G-19622)		
Document Storage Systems Inc .....C .....561 284-7173 Juno Beach (G-7028)		
Dogwood MGT Partners LLC ....D .....703 935-2235 Apollo Beach (G-135)		
Donyati LLC ....C .....248 633-4893 Naples (G-11098)		
Drivosity LLC ....E .....407 986-0477 Clermont (G-1868)		
E-Builder Inc ....C .....800 580-9322 Sunrise (G-16766)		
▼ Earthsoft Inc ....D .....850 471-6262 Pensacola (G-14285)		
▲ Easyworkforce Software Inc ......E .....954 383-0887 Miramar (G-10856)		
Ecometry Corporation ....C .....561 265-2700 Delray Beach (G-2948)		
Elitepronet Inc ....E .....561 656-4701 West Palm Beach (G-19131)		
Ellucian Assistance Inc ....D .....407 660-1199 Lake Mary (G-7586)		
Ellucian Inc ....D .....407 660-1199 Lake Mary (G-7587)		
Emason Inc ....D .....727 507-3440 Saint Petersburg (G-15660)		
Emtec Inc ....C .....904 739-7676 Jacksonville (G-6115)		
Energy Toolbase Software Inc ....D .....866 303-7786 Stuart (G-16618)		
Enginring Cmpt Simulations Inc .....D .....407 823-9991 Orlando (G-12468)		
Ensurem II LLC ....D .....727 451-5120 Largo (G-8100)		
Entech Computer Services Inc ....E .....239 573-1000 Fort Myers (G-4360)		
Equisolve Inc ....D .....954 390-6060 Palm City (G-13787)		
Eventtracker Security LLC ....D .....410 953-6776 Fort Lauderdale (G-3779)		
Executive Digital LLC ....D .....305 992-8713 Boca Raton (G-569)		
Experts Inc ....D .....954 493-8040 Fort Lauderdale (G-3780)		
Exscribe Inc ....E .....610 419-2050 Boca Raton (G-570)		
Fischer Intl Identity LLC ....E .....239 643-1500 Naples (G-11113)		
Fischer Intl Systems Corp ....D .....239 643-1500 Naples (G-11114)		
Fiserv Tampa Inc ....E .....813 885-5800 Tampa (G-17666)		
Five Points Tech Group Inc ....E .....941 751-1901 Sarasota (G-16164)		
Flocabulary Inc ....D .....718 852-0105 Dania (G-2414)		
Florida Justice Association ....E .....850 224-9403 Tallahassee (G-16974)		
Force Legion LLC ....E .....305 423-3339 Miami (G-9593)		
Forcura LLC ....D .....800 378-0596 Jacksonville (G-6207)		
Foresight Gps Srl ....E .....305 398-3866 Miami (G-9597)		
Forestech Consulting Inc ....D .....850 385-3667 Tallahassee (G-16983)		
Fortress Information SEC LLC ....C .....407 930-8981 Orlando (G-12700)		
▲ General Dynamics Itronix Corp ...B .....954 846-3400 Sunrise (G-16774)		

Company	Code	Phone
Genisys Software Inc ....E .....763 391-6133 Sanford (G-15944)		
Gladiator Innovations LLC ....E .....773 931-6275 Melbourne (G-8892)		
Global Radar Acquisition LLC ....E .....239 274-0048 Fort Myers (G-4419)		
Globant LLC ....A .....877 215-5230 Miami (G-9639)		
Gold Standard Inc ....D .....813 258-4747 Tampa (G-17740)		
Gotsoccer LLC ....E .....904 571-8058 Jacksonville Beach (G-6988)		
Govworks LLC ....C .....800 963-7000 Miami (G-9654)		
Greenbacks Partnerships LLC ....E .....813 586-0167 Tampa (G-17752)		
Greenway Health ....A .....770 836-3100 Tampa (G-17756)		
Greenway Health ....C .....877 932-6301 Tampa (G-17757)		
Grupo Ngn Inc ....C .....954 800-8586 Coral Springs (G-2257)		
Happy Tax Franchising LLC ....C .....844 426-1040 Miami Beach (G-10599)		
Harris N Computer Corporation ......E .....407 767-0570 Maitland (G-8539)		
Healthaxis LLC ....D .....972 443-5000 Tampa (G-17805)		
HHS Technology Group LLC ....E .....954 400-4180 Fort Lauderdale (G-3858)		
Himagic Limited ....D .....213 631-3453 Doral (G-3230)		
Holovis Inc ....C .....321 204-1850 Orlando (G-12658)		
Honorlock Inc ....E .....844 841-5625 Boca Raton (G-632)		
Horizon Business Services Inc ....D .....239 261-5828 Naples (G-11168)		
Hospice Systems Inc ....E .....727 586-4432 Clearwater (G-1673)		
Housing and Dev Svcs Inc ....D .....954 217-9597 Miami Lakes (G-10737)		
Hte-Ucs Inc ....D .....954 771-8116 Fort Lauderdale (G-3877)		
Huey Magoos Restaurants LLC ......D .....214 293-1564 Hollywood (G-5457)		
Hyland Software Inc ....D .....440 788-5000 Tampa (G-17850)		
Iap Global Services LLC ....D .....321 784-7100 Cape Canaveral (G-1366)		
Iatric Systems Inc ....C .....978 805-4100 Daytona Beach (G-2615)		
Iblesoft Inc ....E .....305 908-7957 Doral (G-3234)		
▼ Idatix Corporation ....E .....727 441-8228 Clearwater (G-1678)		
Idoc Hldngs Inc DBA Chckdup In ....E .....954 439-3700 Plantation (G-14659)		
Immersive Tech Inc ....E .....813 397-1413 Tampa (G-17859)		
Infinity Software Dev Inc ....D .....850 383-1011 Tallahassee (G-17002)		
Info Tech Inc ....C .....352 375-7624 Gainesville (G-4920)		
Information & Cmpt Svcs Inc ....D .....904 399-8500 Jacksonville (G-6319)		
Information & Cmpt Svcs Inc ....D .....904 399-8500 Jacksonville (G-6320)		
Information Svcs Extended Inc ....E .....954 689-6300 Fort Lauderdale (G-3893)		
Infrasafe Holding Inc ....D .....407 859-3350 Orlando (G-12680)		
Innovative Routines Intl Inc ....E .....321 777-8889 Indian Harbour Beach (G-5670)		
Intelli Erp Software Llc ....E .....407 732-7750 Lake Mary (G-7603)		
International Bus Mchs Corp ....A .....239 945-0169 Cape Coral (G-1403)		
Inzoe Limited ....D .....213 269-5420 North Lauderdale (G-11480)		
Ispa Technology LLC ....D .....703 822-4161 Lithia (G-8300)		
It Software Solutions Inc ....E .....954 239-3435 Sunrise (G-16788)		
ITI Engineering LLC ....E .....866 245-9356 Winter Springs (G-19805)		
Jardon & Howard Tech Inc ....D .....407 381-7797 Orlando (G-12700)		
JM Dealer Services Inc ....E .....954 429-2000 Deerfield Beach (G-2760)		

▲ JM Field Marketing Inc Fort Lauderdale **(G-3909)**	E	954 523-1957
Jolt Advantage Group Inc Tampa **(G-17901)**	E	855 238-5658
Jose Sergio De Andrade Galindo Orlando **(G-12713)**	E	800 925-0609
Khameleon Software Llc Temple Terrace **(G-18638)**	D	813 223-4148
Kofax Inc Plantation **(G-14662)**	B	954 888-7800
L C Radise International Riviera Beach **(G-15306)**	E	561 841-0103
Lakeview Center Inc Pensacola **(G-14340)**	C	850 432-1222
Leanswift Solutions Inc Cocoa Beach **(G-1973)**	D	321 474-3760
Lexisnxis Claims Solutions Inc Boca Raton **(G-670)**	A	561 982-5000
Live Design Inc Coral Springs **(G-2267)**	E	786 513-9807
Loanlogics Inc Jacksonville **(G-6443)**	C	215 367-5500
Lockheed Martin Corporation Oldsmar **(G-11911)**	B	813 855-5711
Loyal Rideshare Corporation New Smyrna **(G-11413)**	D	289 407-9421
Lucayan Tech Solutions LLC Tampa **(G-17964)**	E	813 252-2219
Lyndis Group Inc Orlando **(G-12796)**	E	407 273-1001
M2 Systems Corporation Altamonte Springs **(G-73)**	E	407 551-1300
Mad Mobile Inc Tampa **(G-17974)**	D	813 400-2000
Magic Leap Inc Plantation **(G-14669)**	B	954 889-7010
Magicjack Smb Inc West Palm Beach **(G-19247)**	D	800 624-4252
Mainline Info Systems Inc Tallahassee **(G-17029)**	D	850 219-5000
Mangrove Software Inc Tampa **(G-17981)**	D	813 387-3100
Mantech Enterprises Inc Tampa **(G-17986)**	E	813 720-7738
Mass Virtual Inc Orlando **(G-12827)**	D	407 410-9031
Matrixcare Coral Springs **(G-2272)**	D	954 688-5141
Medai Inc Orlando **(G-12851)**	E	321 281-4480
Meditationlive Inc Miami Beach **(G-10616)**	E	415 484-6018
MEI Micro Inc Orlando **(G-12853)**	E	407 514-2619
Mindteck Inc Naples **(G-11215)**	C	239 990-2417
Mindtree Limited Gainesville **(G-4948)**	E	352 433-0760
Mobiletec International Inc Tampa **(G-18046)**	E	813 876-8333
Modis Inc Jacksonville **(G-6511)**	C	800 467-4448
Modis Inc Jacksonville **(G-6512)**	B	904 360-2300
Moovel North America LLC Sarasota **(G-16237)**	D	866 255-0250
Mortgage300 Corporation North Palm Beach **(G-11552)**	E	888 826-0944
Mortgageflex Systems Inc Jacksonville **(G-6516)**	E	904 356-2490
Multisoft Corporation Cape Coral **(G-1417)**	E	239 945-6433
Muscato Corporation Altamonte Springs **(G-80)**	E	407 551-1300
Muscato Group Inc Altamonte Springs **(G-81)**	C	407 551-1300
N-Ix USA Inc Aventura **(G-275)**	A	212 532-8600
N-Space Inc Orlando **(G-12893)**	D	407 352-5333
Nasoft Usa Inc Tampa **(G-18065)**	E	760 410-1210
National Computer Services Fernandina Beach **(G-3539)**	E	904 321-0050
Nci Information Systems Inc Orlando **(G-12902)**	A	407 208-3046
Nearpod Inc Dania Beach **(G-2430)**	D	305 677-5030
Netdirective Technologies Inc Melbourne **(G-8948)**	D	321 757-8909
Neulion College LLC Maitland **(G-8563)**	E	407 936-0800
Nextech Systems LLC Tampa **(G-18080)**	D	813 425-9200
Nextsphere Technologies Inc Tampa **(G-18083)**	C	727 230-9185
Novatus LLC Orlando **(G-12919)**	B	407 745-3070
Novel Engineering Inc Melbourne **(G-8951)**	E	321 392-0911
Now Technologies LLC Fleming Island **(G-3555)**	E	801 362-8437
Nu Info Systems Inc West Palm Beach **(G-19281)**	E	561 693-4500
Nucleus Security Inc Sarasota **(G-16247)**	D	855 235-6139
Okaloosa County Sheriffs Off Shalimar **(G-16470)**	E	850 651-7410
Ole Interactive LLC Coral Gables **(G-2161)**	E	954 702-6325
Omega Whitespace Health LLC Boca Raton **(G-729)**	E	888 794-2266
Omnicomm Systems Inc Fort Lauderdale **(G-4026)**	E	954 473-1254
Opswat Inc Tampa **(G-18103)**	E	415 590-7300
Optimus Bus Transformation LLC Doral **(G-3283)**	E	305 407-2428
▼ Original Impressions LLC Weston **(G-19472)**	C	305 233-1322
Pace Micro Tech Support Svcs Boca Raton **(G-736)**	D	561 995-2610
▲ Pantograms Mfg Co Inc Tampa **(G-18119)**	E	813 839-5697
Parabler Limited West Palm Beach **(G-19319)**	D	213 269-5436
Paradiso Solutions LLC Boca Raton **(G-742)**	D	800 513-5902
Paycargo LLC Coral Gables **(G-2166)**	E	888 250-7778
Payspan Inc Jacksonville **(G-6594)**	D	904 997-6777
Percepta LLC Melbourne **(G-8957)**	C	321 435-1000
Pilgrim Quality Solutions Tampa **(G-18150)**	D	813 915-1663
Pincho Holdings LLC Coral Gables **(G-2168)**	C	206 890-1098
Pinecrest Glades Chrtr Academy Miami **(G-10120)**	D	305 229-6949
Pioneer Technology Group LLC Sanford **(G-15971)**	E	407 321-7434
Pioneer Technology Group LLC Sanford **(G-15972)**	E	407 330-4747
Pixeom Inc Boca Raton **(G-751)**	E	408 844-4044
Pmweb Inc Aventura **(G-279)**	E	617 207-7080
Praxsoft Inc Orlando **(G-13047)**	D	407 903-9396
Prolific Publishing Inc Fort Lauderdale **(G-4065)**	E	310 844-6537
Prolifics Inc Orlando **(G-13068)**	B	212 267-7722
◆ Protel Inc Lakeland **(G-7942)**	D	863 644-5558
Q1 LLC Orlando **(G-13074)**	E	407 857-3737
Qnomy Inc Miami **(G-10171)**	E	212 813-2300
RA It Solutions Inc West Palm Beach **(G-19335)**	D	561 570-4032
Radgov Inc Fort Lauderdale **(G-4078)**	E	954 938-2800
Rainmaker Group Inc Boca Raton **(G-765)**	E	678 578-5700
Red Six Aerospace Inc Orlando **(G-13089)**	E	323 793-8721
Riptide Software Inc Oviedo **(G-13567)**	C	321 296-7724
Rise8 Inc Tampa **(G-18227)**	E	813 575-4080
Riskwatch International LLC Sarasota **(G-16284)**	D	941 500-4525
Rungigs LLC Doral **(G-3301)**	E	877 993-7636
Sal Johnson & Associates Inc Apopka **(G-208)**	E	407 598-1800
Salesmessage Inc Delray Beach **(G-3013)**	E	888 409-2298
Salient Federal-Sgis Inc Orlando **(G-13162)**	E	407 243-9600
Sap International Inc Miami **(G-10241)**	D	305 476-4400
SC Parent Corporation Miami **(G-10244)**	D	703 351-0200
SC Purchaser Corporation Miami **(G-10245)**	D	703 351-0200
Science and MGT Resources Inc Pensacola **(G-14429)**	E	850 473-9010
Scriptlogic Corporation Boca Raton **(G-786)**	D	561 886-2400
Siegent Inc Boca Raton **(G-802)**	E	561 981-9700
Silverlogic LLC Boca Raton **(G-803)**	D	561 569-2366
Skillstorm Commercial Svcs LLC Jacksonville **(G-6729)**	B	904 438-3440
Skinner Waste Solutions LLC Jacksonville **(G-6730)**	D	904 239-7222
Skybridge Aviation LLC Tampa **(G-18292)**	E	813 579-1221
Skylight Inc Sarasota **(G-16320)**	E	919 271-4123
Skyplanner LLC Miami **(G-10283)**	E	305 814-7597
Smartronix LLC Tampa **(G-18297)**	E	813 443-5371
Soft Computer Consultants Inc Clearwater **(G-1790)**	A	727 789-0100
Soft Tech Development Corp Jacksonville **(G-6737)**	E	904 312-9678
Softserve Inc Fort Myers **(G-4596)**	D	239 284-1210
Software Development Inc North Miami **(G-11510)**	D	786 577-3148
Soho Sushi Inc Tampa **(G-18302)**	E	813 873-7646
Solution 6 North America Tallahassee **(G-17102)**	C	850 224-2200
Solutions Company LLC Cocoa Beach **(G-1979)**	D	754 888-5988
Solutions Mbaf LLC Miami **(G-10293)**	D	305 373-0076
Southtech Solutions Inc Sarasota **(G-16325)**	D	941 953-7455
Spirion LLC Saint Petersburg **(G-15851)**	D	646 863-8301
Springbig Inc Boca Raton **(G-813)**	E	561 208-1573
Springshare LLC Miami **(G-10318)**	D	800 451-3160
Sql Sentry LLC Fleming Island **(G-3558)**	E	904 348-0216
SRI Tech Solutions Inc Tampa **(G-18324)**	C	813 423-6501
Star Refining West Palm Beach **(G-19374)**	E	914 764-5180
Star Systems Inc Maitland **(G-8579)**	B	321 263-3000
Starlims Corporation Hollywood **(G-5535)**	D	954 964-8663
Stefanini International Corp Fort Lauderdale **(G-4153)**	D	954 229-9150
Sterling 5 Inc Boca Raton **(G-820)**	E	305 735-3637
Stratis Business Systems Inc Coral Springs **(G-2289)**	D	561 447-7111
Stratus Silver Lining Inc Sarasota **(G-16334)**	D	408 425-0548
▲ Sumtotal Systems LLC Gainesville **(G-5008)**	C	352 264-2800
▲ Sungard Business Systems LLC Jacksonville **(G-6808)**	C	904 399-5888
Sylint Group Inc Sarasota **(G-16343)**	E	941 951-6015
Synergistix Inc Sunrise **(G-16834)**	D	954 707-4200
Synergy Technologies LLC Plantation **(G-14712)**	C	954 775-0064
System Soft Technologies Inc Tampa **(G-18359)**	D	727 723-0801
Tandel Systems Inc Oldsmar **(G-11929)**	E	727 530-1110
Tattoo System Software LLC Jupiter **(G-7143)**	D	863 303-5554
Technologies On Demand Inc Orlando **(G-13277)**	D	321 285-7682
Temenos USA Inc Lake Mary **(G-7646)**	E	407 732-5200

Teracode Inc	D	508 455-5000
Miami *(G-10377)*		
The Gensight Group Inc	D	215 489-9424
Naples *(G-11321)*		
Theoris Orlando	E	321 800-5538
Orlando *(G-13287)*		
Thinkrite Inc	E	954 653-2514
Pembroke Pines *(G-14195)*		
Tiburon Inc	D	858 799-7000
Lake Mary *(G-7647)*		
Tlfo LLC	C	561 988-4200
Boca Raton *(G-839)*		
Toolbox Group LLC	E	407 734-4000
Orlando *(G-13297)*		
▲ Toptech Systems Inc	C	407 332-1774
Longwood *(G-8410)*		
Traka Usa LLC	E	407 681-4001
Orlando *(G-13301)*		
Transnion Risk Altrntive Data	D	561 988-4200
Boca Raton *(G-843)*		
▲ Trivantis Corporation	D	513 929-0188
Deerfield Beach *(G-2809)*		
TRT Interactive USA LLC	E	786 363-0116
Miami *(G-10411)*		
Trustlayer Inc	E	415 358-1199
Brandon *(G-1257)*		
Twixsoft LLC	E	203 273-6988
Miami *(G-10422)*		
Tyler Business Systems Inc	E	727 536-5588
Clearwater *(G-1826)*		
Ultracast LLC	E	786 449-9222
Miami *(G-10430)*		
United States Agency	C	305 437-7001
Miami *(G-10441)*		
United Systems and Sftwr Inc	E	407 875-2120
Lake Mary *(G-7651)*		
V-Count Inc	C	866 549-9360
Miami Beach *(G-10671)*		
Vcarve Inc	E	850 205-8278
Tallahassee *(G-17170)*		
Veriato Inc	D	772 770-5670
West Palm Beach *(G-19408)*		
Vericle Corporation	E	727 266-2235
Clearwater Beach *(G-1855)*		
Veritas Technologies LLC	C	407 357-7199
Lake Mary *(G-7652)*		
Verizon Data Services LLC	A	212 395-1000
Tampa *(G-18502)*		
Victhex Technology Corp	D	651 592-4545
Deerfield Beach *(G-2811)*		
Viewpost North America LLC	C	888 248-9190
Orlando *(G-13376)*		
Vistar Technologies Corp	E	561 792-6644
West Palm Beach *(G-19411)*		
Visualmed Clinical Systems	D	888 567-9447
Boca Raton *(G-865)*		
Visualtouch Pos Solutions LLC	C	855 261-0504
Pompano Beach *(G-14939)*		
Vital Network Services Inc	C	813 818-5100
Clearwater *(G-1832)*		
Voalte Inc	D	941 312-2830
Sarasota *(G-16359)*		
Volunteer CB Blocker LLC	A	727 827-0046
Saint Petersburg *(G-15890)*		
Warkentine Inc	E	405 799-5282
Ocoee *(G-11827)*		
Wbpro LLC	E	407 855-0670
Orlando *(G-13410)*		
Web Benefits Design Corp	D	800 779-8952
Orlando *(G-13412)*		
Web Dev Group Ltd Liability Co	D	866 238-5046
Lakeland *(G-8003)*		
Wellhive Holdings LLC	E	321 339-1946
Melbourne *(G-9009)*		
White Shark Media Inc	D	305 728-4828
Miami *(G-10503)*		
Win Systems Intl Holdings Inc	E	212 206-9325
Miami *(G-10509)*		
Wlt Software Enterprises Inc	E	727 442-9296
Clearwater *(G-1842)*		
Wpi Services LLC	E	877 864-3613
Juno Beach *(G-7042)*		
Xipron Inc	E	305 330-6250
Miami *(G-10520)*		
Yang Enterprises Inc	B	407 365-7374
Oviedo *(G-13578)*		
Yashow Limited	D	213 325-5691
Aventura *(G-286)*		
Yoga Joint Holdings LLC	E	561 543-1174
Sunrise *(G-16850)*		

Zone Health and Fitness Llc	D	352 509-3133
Ocala *(G-11799)*		
Ztscom LLC	E	813 514-4427
Tampa *(G-18577)*		

7372 Prepackaged Software

Aci Worldwide Inc	B	305 894-2200
Coral Gables *(G-2021)*		
Adaptive Insights Inc	E	800 303-6346
Winter Springs *(G-19796)*		
Advantage Software Inc	E	772 288-3266
Stuart *(G-16585)*		
Aeropost Inc	A	305 592-5534
Doral *(G-3105)*		
Apex Covantage LLC	D	703 709-3000
Miami Beach *(G-10551)*		
Aptum Technologies (usa) Inc	D	877 504-0091
Doral *(G-3124)*		
Avt Technology Solutions LLC	C	727 539-7429
Clearwater *(G-1528)*		
Axiom Services Inc	E	727 442-7774
Clearwater *(G-1529)*		
Bio-Tech Medical Software Inc	D	800 797-4711
Fort Lauderdale *(G-3644)*		
Black Knight Inc	B	904 854-5100
Jacksonville *(G-5866)*		
Black Knight Fincl Svcs Inc	C	904 854-5100
Jacksonville *(G-5867)*		
Blue Martini Software Inc	B	561 265-2700
Delray Beach *(G-2917)*		
Bond-Pro Inc	C	888 789-4985
Tampa *(G-17377)*		
Ca Inc	C	305 559-4640
Miami *(G-9300)*		
CB Parent Holdco GP LLC	A	727 827-0046
Saint Petersburg *(G-15617)*		
Citrix Systems Inc	A	954 267-3000
Fort Lauderdale *(G-3693)*		
Computer Associates Intl	E	941 552-2700
Sarasota *(G-16129)*		
Data Access International Inc	D	305 238-0012
Miami *(G-9458)*		
▼ Datacore Software Corporation	E	954 377-6000
Fort Lauderdale *(G-3752)*		
Datamentors LLC	E	813 960-7800
Wesley Chapel *(G-18996)*		
Ddi System LLC	E	203 364-1200
Sarasota *(G-16136)*		
Duos Technologies Group Inc	E	904 652-1601
Jacksonville *(G-6091)*		
Easy Solutions Inc	C	866 524-4782
Doral *(G-3186)*		
Elogic Learning LLC	E	813 901-8600
Tampa *(G-17625)*		
Emason Inc	D	727 507-3440
Saint Petersburg *(G-15660)*		
Emerson Prcess MGT Pwr Wtr Slt	E	941 748-8100
Bradenton *(G-1093)*		
Emphasys Cmpt Solutions Inc	E	305 599-2531
Pembroke Pines *(G-14147)*		
Empower Software Solutions Inc	B	407 233-2000
Orlando *(G-12465)*		
Eventtracker Security LLC	D	410 953-6776
Fort Lauderdale *(G-3779)*		
Fattmerchant Inc	E	855 550-3288
Orlando *(G-12497)*		
Feick Corporation	D	305 271-8550
Miami *(G-9549)*		
Finastra USA Corporation	C	800 989-9009
Lake Mary *(G-7590)*		
Finastra USA Corporation	D	800 394-8778
Orlando *(G-12512)*		
Fis Avantgard LLC	E	484 582-2000
Jacksonville *(G-6177)*		
Fis Capital Markets US LLC	E	877 776-3706
Jacksonville *(G-6178)*		
Fis Financial Systems LLC	B	904 438-6000
Jacksonville *(G-6179)*		
Genisys Software Inc	E	763 391-6133
Sanford *(G-15944)*		
Genius Central Systems Inc	E	800 360-2231
Bradenton *(G-1110)*		
◆ Gleim Publications Inc	D	352 375-0772
Gainesville *(G-4908)*		
Global Recash LLC	D	818 297-4437
Coral Gables *(G-2112)*		
Himgc Limited	D	213 443-8729
Daytona Beach *(G-2612)*		
Image One Corporation	D	813 888-8288
Tampa *(G-17857)*		

Industry Weapon Inc	E	877 344-8450
Oldsmar *(G-11907)*		
Information & Cmpt Svcs Inc	D	904 399-8500
Jacksonville *(G-6319)*		
Inperium Corp	E	305 901-5650
Miami Beach *(G-10603)*		
Insight Software LLC	D	305 495-0022
Weston *(G-19463)*		
Intermedix Corporation	D	954 308-8700
Fort Lauderdale *(G-3898)*		
Intouch Gps LLC	E	877 593-2981
Lakeland *(G-7888)*		
▲ Iq Formulations Llc	E	954 533-9256
Tamarac *(G-17195)*		
Kirchman Corporation	E	877 384-0936
Orlando *(G-12732)*		
Ld Telecommunications Inc	D	954 628-3029
Fort Lauderdale *(G-3932)*		
Link-Systems International Inc	C	813 674-0660
Tampa *(G-17956)*		
Lucayan Tech Solutions LLC	E	813 252-2219
Tampa *(G-17964)*		
Luminar LLC	B	407 900-5259
Orlando *(G-12791)*		
Management Hlth Solutions Inc	B	888 647-4621
Tampa *(G-17980)*		
Marquis Software Dev Inc	D	850 877-8864
Tallahassee *(G-17033)*		
Messangi Corporation	E	305 731-2003
South Miami *(G-16508)*		
Microsoft Corporation	C	425 882-8080
Fort Lauderdale *(G-3971)*		
Modernizing Medicine Inc	C	561 880-2998
Boca Raton *(G-697)*		
Modernzing Mdcine Gstrntrlogy	C	561 880-2998
Boca Raton *(G-698)*		
Multimedia Platforms Inc	E	954 440-4678
Fort Lauderdale *(G-3980)*		
Muscato Corporation	D	407 551-1300
Altamonte Springs *(G-80)*		
N-Ix USA Inc	A	212 532-8600
Aventura *(G-275)*		
Nearpod Inc	D	305 677-5030
Dania Beach *(G-2430)*		
New Generation Computing Inc	D	800 690-0642
Miami Lakes *(G-10748)*		
Nexogy Inc	D	305 358-8952
Coral Gables *(G-2158)*		
Nphase Inc	D	805 750-8580
Atlantic Beach *(G-244)*		
Omnivore Technologies Inc	D	800 293-4058
Clearwater *(G-1746)*		
Oracle Corporation	C	772 337-4141
Port Saint Lucie *(G-15156)*		
Oracle Corporation	B	772 466-0704
Fort Pierce *(G-4728)*		
Oracle Systems Corporation	E	407 458-1200
Orlando *(G-12934)*		
Outreach Corporation	C	888 938-7356
Tampa *(G-18113)*		
Paylocity Holding Corporation	A	407 878-6585
Lake Mary *(G-7620)*		
Perch Security Inc	E	844 500-1810
Tampa *(G-18140)*		
Powerchord Inc	E	727 823-1530
Saint Petersburg *(G-15806)*		
Powerdms Inc	D	407 992-6000
Orlando *(G-13045)*		
Powerline Group Inc	C	631 828-1183
Delray Beach *(G-3008)*		
Profitsword LLC	E	407 909-8822
Orlando *(G-13067)*		
Qgiv Inc	D	888 855-9595
Lakeland *(G-7948)*		
Radixx Solutions Intl Inc	E	407 856-9009
Orlando *(G-13079)*		
Rainmaker Group Inc	D	678 578-5700
Boca Raton *(G-765)*		
Ria Advisory LLC	E	305 496-7405
Coral Gables *(G-2176)*		
Safeboot Corp	D	239 298-7000
Naples *(G-11291)*		
Sarasota County Pub Hosp Dst	A	941 917-9000
Sarasota *(G-16300)*		
Sarasota County Pub Hosp Dst	C	941 917-4041
Sarasota *(G-16302)*		
SC Elearning LLC	D	561 293-2543
Deerfield Beach *(G-2793)*		
SC Parent Corporation	D	703 351-0200
Miami *(G-10244)*		

SC Purchaser Corporation....................D......703 351-0200
  Miami (G-10245)
Sighthound Inc..............................E......407 974-5694
  Winter Park (G-19774)
Signingordercom LLC.........................E......904 300-0104
  Orange Park (G-12018)
Smartcop Inc................................E......850 429-0082
  Pensacola (G-14439)
Smartstart Emplyment Screening.............B......813 377-4343
  Clearwater (G-1789)
Springbig Holdings Inc......................C......800 772-9172
  Boca Raton (G-814)
Strata Analytics Holdg US LLC..............D......954 349-4630
  Sunrise (G-16831)
Superion LLC................................A......407 304-3235
  Lake Mary (G-7643)
System Soft Technologies Inc...............D......727 723-0801
  Tampa (G-18359)
Team Cymru Inc..............................C......847 378-3300
  Lake Mary (G-7645)
Technisys LLC...............................B......305 728-5372
  Miami (G-10368)
Teledyne Flir LLC...........................D......407 816-0091
  Orlando (G-13278)
Thales Esecurity Inc........................C......954 888-6200
  Plantation (G-14714)
Threattrack Security Inc....................C......855 885-5566
  Clearwater (G-1824)
◆ Tom Zosel Associates Inc..................D......847 828-5856
  Naples (G-11325)
Tradestation Technologies Inc..............C......954 652-7000
  Plantation (G-14717)
▲ Trivantis Corporation.....................D......513 929-0188
  Deerfield Beach (G-2809)
Ukg Inc.....................................D......954 331-7000
  Weston (G-19482)
Ukg Inc.....................................D......954 331-7000
  Weston (G-19483)
Ultracast LLC...............................E......786 449-9222
  Miami (G-10430)
Vector-Solutionscom Inc.....................E......813 207-0012
  Tampa (G-18497)
Veeam Software Corporation..................D......614 339-8200
  Davie (G-2535)
◆ Verifone Inc..............................C......800 837-4366
  Coral Springs (G-2296)
▲ Verifone Systems Inc......................C......408 232-7800
  Coral Springs (G-2297)
▲ Webcom Group Inc..........................C......904 680-6600
  Jacksonville (G-6925)

7373 Computer Integrated Systems Design

4th Source LLC..............................B......855 875-4700
  Tampa (G-17212)
AB Closing Corporation......................D......407 243-6006
  Orlando (G-12041)
Accenture Federal Services LLC.............C......904 899-0290
  Jacksonville (G-5725)
Acordis International Corp...................E......954 620-0072
  Miramar (G-10833)
Adsync Technologies Inc.....................D......850 497-6969
  Pensacola (G-14212)
Advanced Systems Tech Inc...................D......407 277-8069
  Orlando (G-12059)
Advent Software Inc.........................E......904 241-2444
  Jacksonville (G-5745)
▼ Allin Interactive Corporation.............E......954 630-1020
  Fort Lauderdale (G-3596)
Amadeus Arprt It Americas Inc..............D......407 370-4664
  Orlando (G-12104)
American Blueprinting Sup Inc..............D......407 644-5366
  Winter Park (G-19684)
Anthology Inc...............................C......561 923-2500
  Boca Raton (G-423)
Asrc Aerospace Corp.........................B......321 867-1462
  Kennedy Space Center (G-7154)
Assured Info Tech Engrg LLC.................D......407 601-7148
  Orlando (G-12143)
Av-Worx LLC.................................D......844 428-9679
  West Palm Beach (G-19045)
▼ Aya Associates Inc........................D......407 539-1800
  Maitland (G-8504)
Beeline Acquisition Corp....................D......904 527-5700
  Jacksonville (G-5852)
Beelinecom Inc..............................C......866 352-5463
  Jacksonville (G-5853)
Beep Inc....................................D......800 640-0316
  Orlando (G-12177)
Black Knight Inc............................B......904 854-5100
  Jacksonville (G-5866)

Caci Inc - Federal..........................E......850 475-9646
  Pensacola (G-14242)
◆ Cae USA Inc...............................A......813 885-7481
  Tampa (G-17408)
Central Dynamics LLC........................C......561 750-3173
  Boca Raton (G-503)
Command Ctrl Cmmnctons Engrg L.............E......813 620-0051
  Tampa (G-17502)
Community Brands Holdco LLC.................D......727 827-0046
  Saint Petersburg (G-15637)
Compro Computer Services Inc...............E......321 727-2211
  Melbourne (G-8849)
Computer Sftwr Sltons Intl LLC.............B......954 419-1008
  Boca Raton (G-523)
▲ Contec Americas Inc.......................D......321 728-0172
  Melbourne (G-8851)
Contender Solutions LLC.....................C......813 279-6280
  Tampa (G-17518)
▲ Convergence Technologies Inc.............D......630 887-1000
  Riviera Beach (G-15290)
Cybear LLC..................................D......561 999-3500
  Boca Raton (G-542)
Cybervision Inc.............................E......201 585-9809
  Sunny Isles Beach (G-16715)
◆ Datamax System Solutions Inc.............E......561 994-1250
  Boca Raton (G-545)
▲ Datamaxx Applied Tech Inc................D......850 558-8000
  Tallahassee (G-16929)
Datamaxx Group Inc..........................D......850 558-8000
  Tallahassee (G-16930)
Datapro Inc.................................D......305 374-0606
  Coral Gables (G-2089)
Dbk Concepts Inc............................C......305 596-7226
  Miami (G-9463)
Dcr System House Inc........................C......561 998-3737
  Boca Raton (G-547)
Dedicated It LLC............................C......561 491-5750
  Lake Park (G-7659)
Dentalrobot Inc.............................D......786 775-1145
  Doral (G-3175)
Disti LLC...................................D......407 206-3390
  Orlando (G-12429)
Dogwood MGT Partners LLC....................D......703 935-2235
  Apollo Beach (G-135)
Dyncorp.....................................E......850 678-7441
  Eglin Afb (G-3418)
Easy Solutions Inc..........................C......866 524-4782
  Doral (G-3186)
Eci Telecom Inc.............................E......954 772-3070
  Fort Lauderdale (G-3767)
Emason Inc..................................D......727 507-3440
  Saint Petersburg (G-15660)
Entech Computer Services Inc...............E......239 573-1000
  Fort Myers (G-4360)
Facility Automtn Solutions Inc.............D......904 446-8100
  Jacksonville (G-6142)
Farfield Systems Inc........................E......410 874-9363
  Sarasota (G-16156)
Fattmerchant Inc............................E......855 550-3288
  Orlando (G-12497)
Fiserv Tampa Inc............................E......813 885-5800
  Tampa (G-17666)
Future Tech Enterprise Inc..................D......631 472-5500
  Fort Lauderdale (G-3811)
General Dynmics Ots Ncvlle Inc.............D......850 897-9700
  Niceville (G-11449)
Greenway Health.............................A......770 836-3100
  Tampa (G-17756)
Greenway Health.............................C......877 932-6301
  Tampa (G-17757)
Iatric Systems Inc..........................C......978 805-4100
  Daytona Beach (G-2615)
Information & Cmpt Svcs Inc.................D......904 399-8500
  Jacksonville (G-6319)
Information & Cmpt Svcs Inc.................C......904 399-8500
  Jacksonville (G-6320)
Innovtive Schdling Hldings Inc.............D......352 334-7283
  Gainesville (G-4922)
Inspired Tech N Fla Inc.....................D......850 402-3700
  Tallahassee (G-17005)
Intellaquest LLC............................D......800 239-7013
  Deerfield Beach (G-2758)
Intelli Erp Software Llc....................E......407 732-7750
  Lake Mary (G-7603)
Interactive Communications Inc.............B......305 807-3500
  Doral (G-3241)
▲ Itec Entertainment LLC...................E......407 226-0200
  Orlando (G-12691)
ITI Engineering LLC.........................E......866 245-9356
  Winter Springs (G-19805)

Keitaro Inc.................................E......813 397-3741
  Tampa (G-17911)
Khameleon Software Llc......................D......813 223-4148
  Temple Terrace (G-18638)
Knight Federal Solutions Inc...............C......407 243-6008
  Orlando (G-12735)
Kofax Inc...................................B......954 888-7800
  Plantation (G-14662)
Lakeview Center Inc.........................D......850 432-1222
  Pensacola (G-14340)
Link2gov Corporation........................D......615 297-2770
  Orlando (G-12770)
LLC Golden Wolf.............................C......240 672-7995
  Lithia (G-8301)
Lmg Inc.....................................B......407 850-0505
  Orlando (G-12775)
Mainline Info Systems Inc...................D......850 219-5000
  Tallahassee (G-17029)
Mastec Network Solutions LLC...............C......866 545-1782
  Coral Gables (G-2140)
Mastec Network Solutions LLC...............E......866 545-1782
  Coral Gables (G-2141)
Merge Healthcare Solutions Inc.............D......386 253-6222
  Daytona Beach (G-2634)
Mindteck Inc................................C......239 990-2417
  Naples (G-11215)
Modcomp Inc.................................D......954 571-4600
  Deerfield Beach (G-2773)
▲ Moredirect Inc............................D......561 237-3300
  Boca Raton (G-699)
Mortgageflex Systems Inc....................D......904 356-2490
  Jacksonville (G-6516)
Muscato Corporation.........................D......407 551-1300
  Altamonte Springs (G-80)
Netsurion LLC...............................E......713 929-0200
  Fort Lauderdale (G-3996)
Netwolves Ecci Corporation..................D......813 579-3200
  Tampa (G-18071)
Network Dynamics Inc........................E......813 818-8597
  Oldsmar (G-11916)
Network Inc.................................D......727 366-6922
  Clearwater (G-1734)
Networks Inc................................E......954 389-3880
  Weston (G-19469)
Newbold Advisors LLC........................E......727 535-2102
  Clearwater (G-1736)
Novopayment Inc.............................E......305 372-8695
  Miami (G-10055)
Onechem Ltd.................................E......305 423-4000
  Miami (G-10074)
Onesourcepcs LLC............................D......888 611-3379
  Pensacola (G-14394)
Ornsoft Corporation.........................D......888 808-9498
  Miami (G-10081)
Pinnacle Software Inc.......................E......954 938-8870
  Fort Lauderdale (G-4051)
Piper Technology LLC........................D......954 989-3778
  Hollywood (G-5493)
Pragma Edge Inc.............................C......224 804-0690
  Jacksonville (G-6611)
Presidio Ntwrked Solutions LLC.............C......407 481-8600
  Orlando (G-13055)
R&C It Hdwr & Sftwr Dist Corp..............E......954 368-3793
  Fort Lauderdale (G-4077)
Radgov Inc..................................E......954 938-2800
  Fort Lauderdale (G-4078)
Revelex Corporation.........................D......561 988-5588
  Boca Raton (G-774)
Serdi-LLC...................................D......240 353-9656
  Saint Cloud (G-15533)
Sharpspring Inc.............................C......888 428-9605
  Gainesville (G-5000)
▼ Shields Environmental Inc................E......407 936-0025
  Sanford (G-15980)
Skillsoft Inc...............................D......603 324-3000
  Boca Raton (G-804)
Soft Computer Consultants Inc..............A......727 789-0100
  Clearwater (G-1790)
Softrim LLC.................................E......239 449-4444
  Estero (G-3477)
Sohard Tech Solutions Inc...................E......321 352-7301
  Orlando (G-13211)
Space Ground System Solutions..............E......321 312-4242
  Melbourne (G-8979)
Studio98 LLC................................E......727 888-1211
  Clearwater (G-1799)
Sykes Enterprises Incorporated.............A......813 274-1000
  Tampa (G-18355)
Synergistix Inc.............................D......954 707-4200
  Sunrise (G-16834)

Synergy Technologies LLC...........C......954 775-0064
  Plantation *(G-14712)*
Systems Intgrtion Mntenace Inc....E......305 624-1113
  Miami *(G-10358)*
T3t Inc...........E......727 577-2200
  Saint Petersburg *(G-15870)*
TCS Group Inc...........E......954 846-8787
  Coral Springs *(G-2290)*
Techtrueup LLC...........C......813 393-9393
  Naples *(G-11317)*
Tecnica Business Systems LLC..........E......305 477-5617
  Doral *(G-3330)*
Tektron Electrical Systems...........E......561 615-3111
  West Palm Beach *(G-19380)*
Telecommunication Systems Inc.....E......321 259-6050
  Melbourne *(G-8993)*
Telecommunication Systems Inc.....E......813 831-6353
  Tampa *(G-18413)*
Thinkrite Inc...........E......954 653-2514
  Pembroke Pines *(G-14195)*
Trax USA Corp...........D......305 662-7400
  Miami *(G-10407)*
Twixsoft LLC...........E......203 273-6988
  Miami *(G-10422)*
Vistana Vacation Ownership Inc..........D......407 447-2701
  Orlando *(G-13386)*
Visual Awareness Technologies..........D......813 207-5055
  Saint Petersburg *(G-15888)*
▲ Vivaticket Inc...........E......407 370-2900
  Orlando *(G-13387)*
Voyce Inc...........C......855 568-6509
  Sunrise *(G-16844)*
Wfp Investments Inc...........E......813 889-8324
  Oldsmar *(G-11935)*
Xponet Corporation...........E......703 629-6599
  Orlando *(G-13467)*
Yang Enterprises Inc...........B......407 365-7374
  Oviedo *(G-13578)*

7374 Data & Computer Processing & Preparation

404 Fairway Inc...........E......561 963-9005
  Lake Worth *(G-7706)*
Accenture LLP...........D......786 425-7000
  Coral Gables *(G-2020)*
Acclaris Inc...........D......813 873-2020
  Tampa *(G-17227)*
ADP Totalsource Co Xxi Inc...........E......800 962-4404
  Miami *(G-9079)*
ADP Totalsource II Inc...........D......305 630-1000
  Miami *(G-9085)*
Advanced Xrgrphics Imging Syst..........E......407 351-0232
  Orlando *(G-12061)*
Alphanet Technologies Inc...........E......305 497-5575
  Bay Harbor Islands *(G-345)*
American Heritage Lf Inv Corp...........B......904 992-1776
  Jacksonville *(G-5783)*
Apptical Corp...........E......800 737-6972
  Boca Raton *(G-424)*
Attainia Inc...........E......866 288-2464
  Jacksonville *(G-5820)*
Automatic Data Processing Inc...........C......305 569-4304
  Coral Gables *(G-2037)*
Avanze Solutions Inc...........A......321 236-9600
  Orlando *(G-12157)*
Bill2pay LLC...........E......904 302-0686
  Jacksonville *(G-5860)*
Black Knight Infoserv LLC...........B......651 234-3500
  Jacksonville *(G-5869)*
Black Knight Infoserv LLC...........E......904 854-5100
  Jacksonville *(G-5868)*
Bradesco BAC Florida Bank...........E......305 789-7000
  Coral Gables *(G-2058)*
Brannen Banks Services Inc...........C......352 726-1221
  Inverness *(G-5689)*
Cag Logistics MGT Svcs LLC...........B......813 860-4558
  Tampa *(G-17410)*
Certegy Transaction Svcs Inc...........D......727 556-9000
  Saint Petersburg *(G-15621)*
Children & Families Fla Dept...........E......850 488-4612
  Tallahassee *(G-16913)*
City of Tampa...........E......813 274-8155
  Tampa *(G-17483)*
Coastal Cloud LLC...........D......800 237-9574
  Palm Coast *(G-13817)*
County of Broward...........C......954 357-8500
  Fort Lauderdale *(G-3733)*
Csg Systems Inc...........C......850 402-6700
  Crawfordville *(G-2301)*

Cyxtera Management Inc...........E......305 537-9500
  Coral Gables *(G-2085)*
Cyxtera Technologies Inc...........D......305 537-9500
  Coral Gables *(G-2086)*
Cyxtera Technologies LLC...........E......305 537-9500
  Coral Gables *(G-2087)*
Data MGT Assoc Brevard Inc...........D......321 725-8081
  Malabar *(G-8604)*
Diagnostic Ctrs Amer - Fla Inc...........D......561 727-2300
  West Palm Beach *(G-19122)*
Digital Reception Services Inc...........E......727 868-3792
  Hudson *(G-5637)*
Digitcom LLC...........D......407 872-9199
  Orlando *(G-12424)*
Electronic Computer Svcs Inc...........D......954 923-4168
  Dania *(G-2411)*
Emason Inc...........D......727 507-3440
  Saint Petersburg *(G-15660)*
Experts Inc...........D......954 493-8040
  Fort Lauderdale *(G-3780)*
Fidelity Information Svcs LLC...........B......877 823-7051
  Saint Petersburg *(G-15668)*
Fidelity Information Svcs LLC...........A......877 776-3706
  Jacksonville *(G-6155)*
Fidelity Information Svcs LLC...........D......407 217-0217
  Orlando *(G-12509)*
Fidelity Intl Resource MGT Inc...........D......904 438-6000
  Jacksonville *(G-6156)*
▼ Fidelity Nat Info Svcs Inc...........A......904 438-6000
  Jacksonville *(G-6159)*
Fis Capital Markets US LLC...........E......877 776-3706
  Jacksonville *(G-6178)*
Fis Financial Systems LLC...........B......904 438-6000
  Jacksonville *(G-6179)*
Fis Payments LLC...........D......813 884-4101
  Tampa *(G-17665)*
Fiserv Tampa Inc...........E......813 885-5800
  Tampa *(G-17666)*
Florida Hospital Ocala Inc...........B......352 351-7200
  Ocala *(G-11690)*
▲ Fsv Payment Systems Inc...........E......904 446-1100
  Jacksonville *(G-6211)*
Fsv Payment Systems Inc...........C......904 446-1100
  Jacksonville *(G-6212)*
Fulfillment Partners Inc...........E......407 660-8606
  Orlando *(G-12554)*
Genisys Software Inc...........E......763 391-6133
  Sanford *(G-15944)*
Harte-Hnks Drect Mrktng/Fllrto..........D......410 636-6660
  Jacksonville *(G-6261)*
Image Api LLC...........C......850 222-1400
  Tallahassee *(G-17000)*
Image API Holdings LLC...........C......850 222-1400
  Tallahassee *(G-17001)*
Image One Corporation...........D......813 888-8288
  Tampa *(G-17857)*
Image Web Design Inc...........E......941 564-9323
  North Port *(G-11571)*
Independent Imaging LLC...........E......561 795-5558
  West Palm Beach *(G-19198)*
Interntional Support Group LLC...........D......954 900-1095
  Pembroke Pines *(G-14155)*
Iqor Holdings Inc...........B......727 369-0100
  Saint Petersburg *(G-15726)*
Iqor US Inc...........A......646 274-3030
  Saint Petersburg *(G-15727)*
Ir4c Inc...........E......863 614-0742
  Lakeland *(G-7889)*
ITI Engineering LLC...........E......866 245-9356
  Winter Springs *(G-19805)*
Izea Worldwide Inc...........D......407 674-6911
  Orlando *(G-12693)*
Link-Systems International Inc...........C......813 674-0660
  Tampa *(G-17956)*
Locus Solutions LLC...........D......561 575-7600
  Palm Beach Gardens *(G-13750)*
Mail Unlimited Inc...........E......407 657-9333
  Winter Park *(G-19746)*
Mediapro Holdings LLC...........E......425 483-4700
  Clearwater *(G-1711)*
Medical Records Corp Maryland...........D......954 687-1163
  Boca Raton *(G-687)*
Metrc LLC...........D......863 583-0228
  Lakeland *(G-7919)*
Mfp Inc...........C......727 446-0018
  Sarasota *(G-16231)*
Mindteck Inc...........C......239 990-2417
  Naples *(G-11215)*
Motionpoint Corporation...........D......954 421-0890
  Coconut Creek *(G-1997)*

MSP Recovery Inc...........D......305 614-2222
  Coral Gables *(G-2154)*
Mvl Group Inc...........A......561 748-0931
  Jupiter *(G-7117)*
NAVY UNITED STATES DEPARTMENT..B......850 452-3501
  Pensacola *(G-14379)*
Naylor LLC...........C......800 369-6220
  Gainesville *(G-4955)*
Neptune Tech Services Inc...........E......904 646-2700
  Jacksonville *(G-6535)*
Nielsen Company (us) LLC...........E......954 753-6043
  Coral Springs *(G-2274)*
Northrop Grumman Systems Corp..........D......850 863-8000
  Fort Walton Beach *(G-4794)*
▲ NYCE Corporation...........D......201 865-9000
  Orlando *(G-12922)*
Outsource America Inc...........C......941 746-4555
  Bradenton *(G-1158)*
Peopleticker LLC...........A......844 887-5501
  Delray Beach *(G-3002)*
Perfectwifi Inc...........E......954 666-0300
  Weston *(G-19474)*
Pharmacy Management Svcs Inc...........A......813 626-7788
  Tampa *(G-18142)*
Pitchpoint Solutions Corp...........E......412 564-0339
  Sarasota *(G-16269)*
Presentation Group Inc...........E......813 228-6400
  Tampa *(G-18165)*
Primenet Drect Mktg Sltons LLC..........D......727 447-6245
  Largo *(G-8142)*
Pronto Post Inc...........D......305 621-7900
  Hialeah *(G-5313)*
Prototype Interactive LLC...........E......305 458-3746
  Miami *(G-10154)*
Rumble Inc...........E......941 210-0196
  Longboat Key *(G-8332)*
Skybooks Inc...........D......904 741-8700
  Jacksonville Beach *(G-7004)*
▲ Sportslinecom...........C......954 351-2120
  Fort Lauderdale *(G-4149)*
Sproutloud Media Networks LLC..........D......877 634-9260
  Davie *(G-2522)*
Surety LLC...........E......239 436-2501
  Naples *(G-11314)*
Tc Specialties Co...........E......904 281-2604
  Jacksonville *(G-6839)*
Telefonica USA...........D......305 925-5300
  Miami *(G-10373)*
The Cherryroad Group Inc...........E......561 226-4466
  Boca Raton *(G-838)*
Tierpont Florida LLC...........C......904 440-7200
  Jacksonville *(G-6853)*
Tirone Electric Inc...........D......954 989-7162
  Hollywood *(G-5537)*
▼ Triangle Reprographics Inc...........D......407 843-1492
  Orlando *(G-13309)*
Umbra Solar Services LLC...........D......954 270-9260
  Coral Springs *(G-2294)*
United Solutions Company...........E......850 942-9186
  Tallahassee *(G-17164)*
US Data Lone Star Inc...........E......651 308-7623
  Miami *(G-10452)*
Valutec Card Solutions Inc...........E......615 550-8209
  Orlando *(G-13367)*
Vastec Inc...........E......813 375-9213
  Tampa *(G-18496)*
Verizon Data Services LLC...........A......212 395-1000
  Tampa *(G-18502)*
▲ Webcom Group Inc...........C......904 680-6600
  Jacksonville *(G-6925)*
Weston Trawick Inc...........E......850 514-0003
  Tallahassee *(G-17173)*
Xtrm Inc...........E......866 367-9289
  Miami *(G-10522)*
Yang Enterprises Inc...........B......407 365-7374
  Oviedo *(G-13578)*

7375 Information Retrieval Svcs

211 Tampa Bay Cares Inc...........E......727 888-5211
  Clearwater *(G-1506)*
Bayshore Solutions LLC...........E......813 902-0141
  Tampa *(G-17354)*
Black Knght Data Analytics LLC..........A......904 854-5100
  Jacksonville *(G-5864)*
Cequint Inc...........E......954 372-9576
  Fort Lauderdale *(G-3680)*
Certegy Transaction Svcs Inc...........D......727 556-9000
  Saint Petersburg *(G-15621)*
Clear Tech Inc...........E......727 347-6770
  Saint Petersburg *(G-15629)*

S
I
C

Cyxtera Data Centers Inc ....A 305 537-9500
  Coral Gables *(G-2084)*

Merge Healthcare Solutions Inc ....C 386 253-6222
  Daytona Beach *(G-2634)*

Mission Critical Group LLC ....E 904 422-9731
  Jacksonville *(G-6507)*

Network Telephone LLC ....B 850 432-4855
  Pensacola *(G-14382)*

Nicole Scheman LLC ....E 813 493-4072
  Saint Petersburg *(G-15777)*

Owl Inc ....C 904 679-4555
  Jacksonville *(G-6572)*

Partsbase Inc ....C 561 953-0700
  Boca Raton *(G-745)*

Peopleticker LLC ....A 844 887-5501
  Delray Beach *(G-3002)*

Perfusioncom Inc ....C 888 499-5672
  Fort Myers *(G-4540)*

Pnv Inc ....B 954 324-3900
  Coral Springs *(G-2278)*

Pro Net Group Inc ....E 407 790-4165
  Maitland *(G-8570)*

Schlesinger Associates NY Inc ....E 407 660-1808
  Maitland *(G-8576)*

Search Engine Partner ....D 561 450-8724
  West Palm Beach *(G-19355)*

◆ Sitel Worldwide Corporation ....C 615 301-7100
  Miami *(G-10278)*

Smartstart Emplyment Screening ......B 813 377-4343
  Clearwater *(G-1789)*

Telefonica USA ....D 305 925-5300
  Miami *(G-10373)*

US Information Search Inc ....A 800 596-4327
  Tampa *(G-18487)*

Veritas Technologies LLC ....C 407 357-7199
  Lake Mary *(G-7652)*

Verizon New England Inc ....B 813 978-7629
  Lutz *(G-8465)*

Yupi Internet Inc ....C 305 604-0366
  Miami Beach *(G-10675)*

7376 Computer Facilities Management Svcs

AB Closing Corporation ....D 407 243-6006
  Orlando *(G-12041)*

Advanced Concepts Entps Inc ....D 850 613-6170
  Shalimar *(G-16467)*

▼ Aya Associates Inc ....D 407 539-1800
  Maitland *(G-8504)*

Cloudhesive LLC ....C 954 613-0520
  Fort Lauderdale *(G-3702)*

County of Volusia ....C 386 736-5922
  Deland *(G-2853)*

Ekkonet Telecom LLC ....E 201 424-2694
  Madeira Beach *(G-8482)*

Ellucian Inc ....D 321 674-8002
  Melbourne *(G-8879)*

Experts Inc ....D 954 493-8040
  Fort Lauderdale *(G-3780)*

Interntional Support Group LLC ......D 954 900-1095
  Pembroke Pines *(G-14155)*

Liberty It Solutions LLC ....B 321 425-4852
  Melbourne *(G-8921)*

Lucayan Tech Solutions LLC ....E 813 252-2219
  Tampa *(G-17964)*

▲ Moredirect Inc ....D 561 237-3300
  Boca Raton *(G-699)*

Muscato Corporation ....D 407 551-1300
  Altamonte Springs *(G-80)*

National Sourcing Inc ....C 813 281-0013
  Tampa *(G-18068)*

Onesourcepcs LLC ....D 888 611-3379
  Pensacola *(G-14394)*

Qualfon Data Svcs Group LLC ....D 877 261-0804
  Casselberry *(G-1454)*

Radgov Inc ....E 954 938-2800
  Fort Lauderdale *(G-4078)*

Synergy Technologies LLC ....C 954 775-0064
  Plantation *(G-14712)*

Yang Enterprises Inc ....B 407 365-7374
  Oviedo *(G-13578)*

7377 Computer Rental & Leasing

Kofax Inc ....B 954 888-7800
  Plantation *(G-14662)*

Kyocera Dcment Sltons Sthast L ......D 407 841-2932
  Orlando *(G-12743)*

Rentex Incorporated ....D 844 675-7689
  Orlando *(G-13101)*

7378 Computer Maintenance & Repair

C & W Enterprises Inc ....E 772 287-5215
  Stuart *(G-16598)*

Compro Computer Services Inc ....E 321 727-2211
  Melbourne *(G-8849)*

Compulink Installation Svcs S ....D 954 938-9977
  Fort Lauderdale *(G-3711)*

▼ Compuquip Technologies LLC ....D 786 416-6143
  Doral *(G-3159)*

Csa Service Solutions LLC ....D 877 487-5360
  Clearwater *(G-1598)*

Dbk Concepts Inc ....C 305 596-7226
  Miami *(G-9463)*

Entech Computer Services Inc ....E 239 573-1000
  Fort Myers *(G-4360)*

Experts Inc ....D 954 493-8040
  Fort Lauderdale *(G-3780)*

Fis Avantgard LLC ....E 484 582-2000
  Jacksonville *(G-6177)*

Ironclad Technology Svcs LLC ....E 813 765-4096
  Tampa *(G-17875)*

Kofax Inc ....B 954 888-7800
  Plantation *(G-14662)*

Kyocera Dcment Sltons Sthast L ......D 407 841-2932
  Orlando *(G-12743)*

Modcomp Inc ....D 954 571-4600
  Deerfield Beach *(G-2773)*

Networks Inc ....E 954 389-3880
  Weston *(G-19469)*

◆ Office Depot LLC ....A 561 438-4800
  Boca Raton *(G-727)*

Piper Technology LLC ....D 954 989-3778
  Hollywood *(G-5493)*

Posabilities Inc ....E 239 337-4767
  Fort Myers *(G-4544)*

◆ Tech-Optics Inc ....E 305 256-3302
  Miami *(G-10367)*

Tektron Electrical Systems ....E 561 615-3111
  West Palm Beach *(G-19380)*

Ubreakifix Co ....B 877 320-2237
  Orlando *(G-13322)*

7379 Computer Related Svcs, NEC

352 Inc ....D 352 374-9657
  Newberry *(G-11428)*

360 Advanced Inc ....E 866 418-1708
  Saint Petersburg *(G-15553)*

A Harold and Associates LLC ....D 904 265-1940
  Jacksonville *(G-5720)*

▼ A1 Assets Inc ....D 407 339-7030
  Lake Mary *(G-7558)*

Aaj Computer Services Inc ....E 954 689-3984
  Fort Lauderdale *(G-3574)*

Ace Digital Marketing Inc ....C 786 358-6347
  Miami *(G-9073)*

Acquiescent Holdings Inc ....E 877 983-2443
  Sarasota *(G-16018)*

Advanced Dcument Solutions Inc ......D 407 412-6929
  Orlando *(G-12054)*

▲ Akimeka LLC ....D 808 442-7100
  Maitland *(G-8500)*

Alison Proquest Inc ....D 772 220-4410
  Stuart *(G-16587)*

▼ Allin Interactive Corporation ....E 954 630-1020
  Fort Lauderdale *(G-3596)*

Amazing7 Studios ....D 800 867-3168
  Oldsmar *(G-11891)*

American Computer Technologies ......D 904 739-7556
  Jacksonville *(G-5779)*

Andromeda Systems Incorporated ......D 904 637-2020
  Jacksonville *(G-5797)*

Andromeda Systems Incorporated ......E 757 340-9070
  Orange Park *(G-11974)*

Appriver LLC ....D 850 932-5338
  Gulf Breeze *(G-5106)*

AR International Entps Inc ....E 786 955-6946
  Weston *(G-19441)*

Arctos Mission Solutions LLC ....E 813 609-5591
  Tampa *(G-17303)*

Arisglobal LLC ....E 609 360-4042
  Coral Gables *(G-2033)*

Arrow Consulting & Design LLC ......D 561 714-7926
  West Palm Beach *(G-19040)*

Atlas International Tech LLC ....B 386 202-4600
  Daytona Beach *(G-2548)*

Avit LLC ....D 888 520-5229
  Tampa *(G-17327)*

Axxiome Americas Inc ....D 212 351-5013
  Miami *(G-9198)*

▼ Aya Associates Inc ....D 407 539-1800
  Maitland *(G-8504)*

Bdo Usa LLP ....C 305 373-5500
  Miami *(G-9233)*

Berean Group International Inc ....E 954 499-6531
  Hollywood *(G-5404)*

Best Worldwide Network ....E 305 891-4700
  North Miami *(G-11485)*

Blm Technologies Florida LLC ....E 800 486-1571
  Pompano Beach *(G-14754)*

Brandt Information Svcs LLC ....E 850 577-4900
  Tallahassee *(G-16895)*

Bridge2 Solutions Inc ....E 386 868-4500
  Daytona Beach *(G-2554)*

Business Info Tech Sltnscom In ......E 407 363-0024
  Orlando *(G-12221)*

C & W Enterprises Inc ....E 772 287-5215
  Stuart *(G-16598)*

Cadence Rx Inc ....E 813 512-7351
  Tampa *(G-17407)*

Castalia Systems LLC ....D 813 748-2283
  Tampa *(G-17429)*

CD Advantage Inc ....E 904 722-8200
  Jacksonville *(G-5918)*

Central Dynamics LLC ....C 561 750-3173
  Boca Raton *(G-503)*

Cgi Federal Inc ....D 904 264-1337
  Orange Park *(G-11980)*

Cgi Technologies Solutions Inc ....E 813 873-8200
  Tampa *(G-17452)*

Champion Solutions Group Inc ....D 800 771-7000
  Boca Raton *(G-507)*

Clearcommerce Corporation ....D 512 832-0132
  Jacksonville *(G-5966)*

Cloudhesive LLC ....C 954 613-0520
  Fort Lauderdale *(G-3702)*

Coastal Cloud LLC ....D 800 237-9574
  Palm Coast *(G-13817)*

Codefirm Solutions LLC ....E 877 756-6985
  Orlando *(G-12339)*

Comcast Enterprise Svcs LLC ....C 800 506-9609
  Tampa *(G-17500)*

Company Combo LLC ....D 866 428-2030
  Orlando *(G-12354)*

Connecton Inc ....D 813 769-1807
  Tampa *(G-17513)*

County of Hillsborough ....E 813 272-4701
  Tampa *(G-17537)*

CPS Graphics Inc ....C 954 975-2220
  Fort Lauderdale *(G-3738)*

Crystal Clear Technologies Inc ....E 727 321-8888
  Saint Petersburg *(G-15652)*

Cybervision Inc ....E 201 585-9809
  Sunny Isles Beach *(G-16715)*

Datacomm Networks Incorporated ......E 800 544-4627
  Tampa *(G-17572)*

Dataprise Inc ....D 786 725-5640
  Miami *(G-9459)*

Dbaccess LLC ....D 312 404-6457
  Hernando *(G-5206)*

Dcr Workforce Inc ....D 561 998-3737
  Boca Raton *(G-548)*

Dedicated It LLC ....D 561 491-5750
  Lake Park *(G-7659)*

Dev2017cap LLC ....D 847 713-0680
  Orlando *(G-12415)*

Digitcom LLC ....D 407 872-9199
  Orlando *(G-12424)*

Disney Worldwide Services Inc ....E 407 934-6375
  Orlando *(G-12428)*

Disney Worldwide Services Inc ....B 321 939-7713
  Kissimmee *(G-7298)*

Dogwood MGT Partners LLC ....D 703 935-2235
  Apollo Beach *(G-135)*

DSM Technology Consultants LLC ......D 863 802-8888
  Lakeland *(G-7852)*

Electronic Computer Svcs Inc ....D 954 923-4168
  Dania *(G-2411)*

Emerging Tech LLC ....E 443 203-8196
  Gainesville *(G-4880)*

Emtec Inc ....C 904 739-7676
  Jacksonville *(G-6115)*

Entech Computer Services Inc ....E 239 573-1000
  Fort Myers *(G-4360)*

Enterprise 24x7 Inc ....D 850 728-3420
  Havana *(G-5193)*

Enterprise Integration Inc ....C 904 733-4916
  Jacksonville *(G-6121)*

Eox Technology Solutions Inc ....E 954 256-0006
  Deerfield Beach *(G-2740)*

Evolution Insight Incorporated	D	321 282-1999
Windermere *(G-19539)*		
Experts Inc	D	954 493-8040
Fort Lauderdale *(G-3780)*		
Extensys Inc	E	813 855-3909
Oldsmar *(G-11901)*		
Fis Avantgard LLC	E	484 582-2000
Jacksonville *(G-6177)*		
Five Points Tech Group Inc	E	941 751-1901
Sarasota *(G-16164)*		
Fnihcs Technology Inc	C	321 621-8854
Boca Raton *(G-590)*		
Forestech Consulting Inc	E	850 385-3667
Tallahassee *(G-16983)*		
Gdkn Corporation	B	954 985-6650
Hollywood *(G-5441)*		
Gem Technology Intl Corp	C	305 447-1344
Miami *(G-9622)*		
General Dynamics Info Tech Inc	D	850 235-2424
Panama City *(G-14017)*		
Geographic Solutions Inc	C	727 786-7955
Palm Harbor *(G-13864)*		
Goldsky Security LLC	E	407 853-8400
Tampa *(G-17741)*		
Guidepoint Security LLC	D	877 889-0132
Saint Petersburg *(G-15700)*		
H2 Performance Consulting Corp	D	850 474-0844
Gulf Breeze *(G-5117)*		
Haku App Corporation	E	305 710-9397
Miami *(G-9676)*		
Hayes E-Gvrnment Resources Inc	D	850 297-0551
Tallahassee *(G-16994)*		
Hte-Ucs Inc	D	954 771-8116
Fort Lauderdale *(G-3877)*		
▲ I-Tech Support Inc	E	407 265-2000
Ocoee *(G-11816)*		
Iatric Systems Inc	C	978 805-4100
Daytona Beach *(G-2615)*		
Icon International Holdings	A	916 339-7985
Aventura *(G-273)*		
Image API Holdings LLC	C	850 222-1400
Tallahassee *(G-17001)*		
Incepture Inc	D	904 905-4407
Jacksonville *(G-6314)*		
Info Tech Inc	C	352 375-7624
Gainesville *(G-4920)*		
Information & Cmpt Svcs Inc	D	904 399-8500
Jacksonville *(G-6319)*		
Information & Cmpt Svcs Inc	E	904 399-8500
Jacksonville *(G-6320)*		
Ingage Networks Inc	E	239 513-0092
Naples *(G-11175)*		
Innovtive Systems Group Fla In	D	407 481-9580
Orlando *(G-12682)*		
Inspired Tech N Fla Inc	D	850 402-3700
Tallahassee *(G-17005)*		
Integrated Solutions MGT Inc	E	813 855-3710
Tampa *(G-17869)*		
Interactive Communications Inc	B	305 807-3500
Doral *(G-3241)*		
Intervisual Technology Inc	E	954 438-1740
Hollywood *(G-5460)*		
Inventory Locator Service LLC	B	305 889-0609
Miami Springs *(G-10785)*		
Isc Inc	E	727 785-0189
Clearwater *(G-1679)*		
It Authorities Inc	E	813 246-5100
Key West *(G-7216)*		
Itelagen Inc	E	877 983-2443
Tampa *(G-17877)*		
Lanlogics LLC	E	561 953-0461
Delray Beach *(G-2976)*		
Lannan Technologies LLC	D	321 271-8273
Saint Augustine *(G-15462)*		
Liberty It Solutions LLC	B	321 425-4852
Melbourne *(G-8921)*		
Lucayan Tech Solutions LLC	E	813 252-2219
Tampa *(G-17964)*		
Mainline Info Systems Inc	D	850 219-5000
Tallahassee *(G-17029)*		
Mantech Mgs Inc	D	813 552-5000
Tampa *(G-17988)*		
Michael Gray & Associates Inc	E	727 791-7890
Clearwater *(G-1717)*		
Millennium Tech Group Inc	E	407 996-2399
Orlando *(G-12870)*		
Nettech Consultants Inc	D	904 992-6970
Jacksonville *(G-6537)*		
Netwolves Network Services LLC	C	813 579-3200
Tampa *(G-18072)*		

Network Dynamics Inc	E	813 818-8597
Oldsmar *(G-11916)*		
Next Level Business Svcs Inc	A	904 267-0528
Seminole *(G-16456)*		
Nextech LLC	E	813 421-2411
Tampa *(G-18079)*		
Nu Info Systems Inc	E	561 693-4500
West Palm Beach *(G-19281)*		
Nwps LLC	D	305 699-5160
Miami *(G-10057)*		
Oao Corporation	A	321 867-2785
Kennedy Space Center *(G-7160)*		
Omega Whitespace Health LLC	E	888 794-2266
Boca Raton *(G-729)*		
Ops Tech Alliance LLC	B	443 223-6115
Clearwater *(G-1748)*		
Orion Solutions LLC	D	904 394-0934
Jacksonville *(G-6569)*		
P3s Corporation	C	210 496-6934
Fort Lauderdale *(G-4038)*		
Payall Payment Systems Inc	B	323 539-3411
Wilton Manors *(G-19533)*		
People Tech & Processes LLC	D	813 498-0486
Tampa *(G-18136)*		
Peopleticker LLC		844 887-5501
Delray Beach *(G-3002)*		
Phacil Inc	B	404 316-0033
Lake Mary *(G-7622)*		
Picsolve Inc	D	407 482-3131
Orlando *(G-13029)*		
Podiatry Network Solutions LLC	D	305 284-7484
Doral *(G-3291)*		
Point of Care Inc	D	305 648-9534
Coral Gables *(G-2169)*		
Polk State Cllege Fndation Inc	C	863 699-2927
Bartow *(G-333)*		
▼ Primestream Corporation	E	305 625-4415
Miami *(G-10145)*		
Prolifics Inc	B	212 267-7722
Orlando *(G-13068)*		
Prov International Inc	D	813 281-2959
Tampa *(G-18180)*		
Providence Tech Solutions LLC	E	904 337-6304
Jacksonville *(G-6621)*		
Qualex Consulting Services Inc	E	305 576-5447
Bay Harbor Islands *(G-347)*		
Radgov Inc	E	954 938-2800
Fort Lauderdale *(G-4078)*		
Raytheon Cyber Solutions Inc	D	321 253-7841
Indialantic *(G-5667)*		
Rcg Global Services Inc	C	407 999-9594
Orlando *(G-13085)*		
RCM Technologies (usa) Inc	B	856 356-4533
Atlantic Beach *(G-245)*		
Reliaquest LLC	E	800 925-2159
Tampa *(G-18212)*		
Ria Advisory LLC	E	305 496-7405
Coral Gables *(G-2176)*		
RMC 2021 LLC	D	850 974-2566
Destin *(G-3075)*		
Rosen Hotel Investments Inc	E	407 996-9840
Orlando *(G-13133)*		
Rosen Mllennium Tech Group Inc	D	407 996-2399
Orlando *(G-13136)*		
Roundtower Technologies LLC	E	561 757-3972
Boca Raton *(G-777)*		
Sanrose Information Svcs Inc	E	850 270-2160
Tallahassee *(G-17093)*		
Save Wire Inc	E	800 277-0088
Naples *(G-11294)*		
Science Applications Intl Corp	E	703 676-4300
Panama City Beach *(G-14103)*		
▲ Signature Consultants LLC	E	954 677-1020
Fort Lauderdale *(G-4129)*		
Six Points LLC	D	321 735-8630
Merritt Island *(G-9045)*		
Skillstorm Commercial Svcs LLC	B	904 438-3440
Jacksonville *(G-6729)*		
Skiltrek LLC	E	866 620-2612
Jacksonville Beach *(G-7003)*		
Snap Technology Corp	E	929 231-9233
Miami *(G-10287)*		
Softrim LLC	E	239 449-4444
Estero *(G-3477)*		
Sogeti USA LLC	D	813 402-7900
Tampa *(G-18301)*		
St Johns Cnty Bd Commissioners	E	904 209-0400
Saint Augustine *(G-15500)*		
Strategic Business Systems Inc	E	727 797-0303
Dunedin *(G-3391)*		

Sykes Acquisition LLC	D	813 274-1000
Tampa *(G-18354)*		
Sykes Enterprises Incorporated	A	813 274-1000
Tampa *(G-18355)*		
Synergy Technologies LLC	C	954 775-0064
Plantation *(G-14712)*		
Synzi LLC	E	888 515-5368
Saint Petersburg *(G-15869)*		
Technical Software Svcs Inc	E	850 469-0086
Pensacola *(G-14457)*		
Telesto Group LLC	E	561 802-7446
West Palm Beach *(G-19381)*		
The Cherryroad Group Inc	C	561 226-4466
Boca Raton *(G-838)*		
Trajectory Inc	E	239 217-6281
Naples *(G-11327)*		
Triage Partners LLC	D	813 801-9869
Tampa *(G-18445)*		
True Group Inc	D	347 675-6994
Tampa *(G-18450)*		
Twixsoft LLC	E	203 273-6988
Miami *(G-10422)*		
▼ United Data Technologies Inc	D	305 882-0435
Miramar *(G-10908)*		
US Utility Suppliers Corp	D	850 290-5456
Pompano Beach *(G-14936)*		
Valintry Services LLC	D	800 360-1407
Winter Park *(G-19782)*		
Venatore LLC	E	813 229-7500
Tampa *(G-18499)*		
Verifract LLC	D	305 908-4479
Miami Beach *(G-10672)*		
Visual Awrness Tchnlgies Cnslt	E	813 207-5055
Tampa *(G-18509)*		
Wca Waste Corporation	E	407 843-7990
Orlando *(G-13411)*		
Weedu Inc	E	954 336-0807
Orlando *(G-13413)*		
Wfp Investments Inc	E	813 889-8324
Oldsmar *(G-11935)*		
Xlm LLC	E	610 937-0088
Saint Johns *(G-15552)*		
Yang Enterprises Inc	B	407 365-7374
Oviedo *(G-13578)*		

7381 Detective & Armored Car Svcs

A & Associates Inc	E	561 533-5303
West Palm Beach *(G-19018)*		
ABM Janitorial Services Inc	E	813 837-4257
Tampa *(G-17224)*		
ABM Security Services Inc	D	561 395-5773
Orlando *(G-12044)*		
ADT Holdings Inc	A	888 298-9274
Boca Raton *(G-402)*		
▲ ADT Security Corporation	B	561 988-3600
Boca Raton *(G-404)*		
Advanced Tactical Security LLC	E	386 304-5106
Edgewater *(G-3407)*		
All Amrcan Invstgators SEC LLC	C	770 500-7476
Lake Mary *(G-7565)*		
All Star Security Services	E	561 306-0991
Boca Raton *(G-410)*		
Allegiance Security Group LLC	C	239 278-0000
Fort Myers *(G-4266)*		
Andy Frain Services Inc	C	407 271-7300
Orlando *(G-12122)*		
Apb Security Services Inc	E	954 420-2250
Deerfield Beach *(G-2709)*		
APS Consultants Inc	E	407 250-5663
Orlando *(G-12127)*		
Arrow Security Corp	E	561 417-0026
Boca Raton *(G-427)*		
▲ ATI Systems International Inc	D	561 939-7000
Boca Raton *(G-433)*		
Barkley Security Agency Inc	E	904 475-1860
Jacksonville *(G-5841)*		
Barkley Security Agency Inc	C	850 627-2151
Quincy *(G-15227)*		
Bryant Security Corporation	C	305 948-0100
North Miami Beach *(G-11518)*		
Budd Group Inc	B	407 658-1187
Orlando *(G-12214)*		
Buena Vsta SEC Prtction Agcy L	C	305 573-6356
Doral *(G-3141)*		
Cambridge Security Svcs Corp	B	239 405-7321
Fort Myers *(G-4300)*		
Cargo Security Company Inc	C	773 457-2720
Miami *(G-9317)*		
Centerra Group LLC	C	941 371-5150
Sarasota *(G-16120)*		

Centerra Group LLC	C	904 398-1640		
Jacksonville (G-5923)				
Centurion Security Group LLC	C	800 800-9151		
Miami (G-9349)				
Children & Families Fla Dept	E	352 330-2177		
Wildwood (G-19491)				
City of Jacksonville	D	904 630-4000		
Jacksonville (G-5958)				
Command Investigations LLC	E	407 468-2394		
Lake Mary (G-7578)				
Contego Investigative Svcs LLC	C	321 249-7600		
Orlando (G-12363)				
Contemporary Services Corp	C	954 435-4544		
Miramar (G-10847)				
Contemporary Services Corp	C	904 630-4012		
Jacksonville (G-6000)				
Contemporary Services Corp	D	407 872-7444		
Orlando (G-12364)				
Contemporary Services Corp	D	850 438-5150		
Pensacola (G-14268)				
Core Security Solutions Inc	E	727 329-0056		
Clearwater (G-1587)				
Coventbridge (usa) Inc	C	904 641-7300		
Jacksonville (G-6005)				
Critical Intervention Svcs Inc	C	727 461-9417		
Clearwater (G-1597)				
Dak Resources Inc	D	904 371-1962		
Jacksonville (G-6040)				
DAK Security Agency Inc	E	305 634-8426		
Miami (G-9454)				
Domestic Protection Svc LLC	E	239 810-5912		
Fort Myers (G-4347)				
Dothan Security Inc	C	813 207-0040		
Tampa (G-17600)				
Dothan Security Inc	C	305 470-0188		
Doral (G-3183)				
Dothan Security Inc	C	904 348-3270		
Jacksonville (G-6079)				
Dunbar Armored Inc	E	239 931-3377		
Fort Myers (G-4349)				
Dunbar Armored Inc	E	727 299-0731		
Clearwater (G-1611)				
Dynamic Security Inc	B	850 471-2667		
Pensacola (G-14284)				
Ebs Security Inc	E	904 354-4242		
Jacksonville (G-6102)				
Elite Guard & Patrol Services	D	305 956-9520		
Sunny Isles Beach (G-16717)				
Ermc II LP	D	863 471-0733		
Sebring (G-16395)				
Event Services America Inc	A	954 435-3600		
Miramar (G-10858)				
Excelsior Defense Inc	D	727 527-9600		
Saint Petersburg (G-15664)				
Excelsior Defense Inc	D	407 277-7732		
Orlando (G-12478)				
Excelsior Defense Inc	D	407 251-3080		
Orlando (G-12479)				
Fam Intrnational Logistics Inc	E	954 252-0166		
Davie (G-2479)				
Feick Security Corporation	E	305 259-3000		
Miami (G-9550)				
Fidelity Security Agency LLC	D	407 542-1529		
Orlando (G-12510)				
Field Force Security Inc	D	305 827-8278		
Miami Lakes (G-10728)				
First Chice RES Invstgtons LLC	E	954 964-1260		
Hollywood (G-5435)				
First Coast Security Svcs Inc	D	904 598-1993		
Jacksonville (G-6171)				
First Coast Security Svcs Inc	E	813 626-6026		
Tampa (G-17662)				
Florida Executive SEC Agcy	C	786 610-0100		
Miami (G-9575)				
Florida Revenue Department	E	305 470-5001		
Hialeah (G-5263)				
Fortitude Security Inc	E	352 577-0929		
Gainesville (G-4898)				
Fox Protective Service Inc	A	813 289-8744		
Tampa (G-17708)				
FPI Security Services Inc	B	305 827-4300		
Pembroke Pines (G-14150)				
Fryar Security Inc	E	407 674-8600		
Orlando (G-12552)				
G4s Holding One Inc	B	561 622-5656		
Jupiter (G-7076)				
G4s Retail Solutions USA Inc	D	561 622-5656		
Jupiter (G-7077)				
G4s Secure Solutions Intl Inc	B	561 622-5656		
Jupiter (G-7078)				
G4s Secure Solutions USA Inc	E	407 207-3221		
Orlando (G-12559)				
G4s Secure Solutions USA Inc	E	904 619-8548		
Jacksonville (G-6214)				
G4s Secure Solutions USA Inc	B	561 622-5656		
Jupiter (G-7079)				
G4s Tchnology Holdings USA Inc	D	561 622-5656		
Jupiter (G-7080)				
G4s Us Inc	D	561 622-5656		
West Palm Beach (G-19157)				
Garda CL Southwest Inc	C	213 383-3611		
Boca Raton (G-595)				
Garda CL Technical Svcs Inc	D	561 939-7000		
Boca Raton (G-596)				
Gardaworld Cash Services	C	561 939-7000		
Boca Raton (G-597)				
Gem Technology Intl Corp	C	305 447-1344		
Miami (G-9622)				
Giddens Security Corp	B	904 384-8071		
Jacksonville (G-6231)				
Gold Finger Entp Intl LLC	C	786 499-3060		
Orlando (G-12578)				
◆ Ibi Intrnational Logistics Inc	E	305 592-0997		
Miami (G-9739)				
◆ Icda Investigations Inc	E	305 635-6200		
Miami (G-9740)				
Inner-Parish Security Corp	E	985 542-7960		
Pensacola (G-14328)				
Interntional SEC MGT Group Inc	C	813 932-7814		
Tampa (G-17872)				
Interntional SEC MGT Group Inc	C	305 443-4311		
Doral (G-3244)				
ISS Action Inc	D	718 978-3000		
Punta Gorda (G-15210)				
Jade Tactical Disaster Relief	C	850 270-4077		
Tampa (G-17887)				
James Alan SEC Invstgtons Agcy	E	954 319-1257		
Celebration (G-1467)				
◆ Johnson Cntrls SEC Sltions LLC	B	561 264-2071		
Boca Raton (G-654)				
Jurney & Associates Inc	C	305 446-3433		
Miami (G-9806)				
Kent Holding Group Inc	E	305 919-9400		
North Miami (G-11500)				
Kent Security Services Inc	C	239 430-9315		
Naples (G-11189)				
▲ Kent Security Services Inc	C	305 919-9400		
North Miami (G-11501)				
Kent Security Services Inc	C	904 371-1906		
Jacksonville (G-6402)				
Kent Security Services Inc	C	305 919-9400		
Miami (G-9823)				
Leon County School Board	C	850 617-5979		
Tallahassee (G-17023)				
Marksman Security Corporation	B	727 536-0088		
Clearwater (G-1706)				
Marksman Security Corporation	B	813 282-4547		
Tampa (G-17992)				
Marksman Security Corporation	C	954 964-6704		
Fort Lauderdale (G-3959)				
Master Security Corp East	C	954 748-2400		
Sunrise (G-16796)				
Maximus Global Services Llc	D	786 953-4294		
Doral (G-3271)				
Mc Roberts Corporation	C	305 373-0605		
Miami (G-9915)				
McCray Global Protection Corp	B	833 832-6647		
Orlando (G-12839)				
McRoberts Protective Agcy Inc	A	305 438-1500		
Miami (G-9923)				
Meridian Invstgative Group Inc	D	800 830-4022		
Saint Petersburg (G-15763)				
Meritus Solutions Group LLC	C	321 603-2133		
Titusville (G-18696)				
Morrison Security Corporation	C	407 855-0056		
Orlando (G-12880)				
National Alliance SEC Agcy Inc	C	727 242-0094		
Clearwater (G-1732)				
National Building Maint LLC	C	813 877-7467		
Tampa (G-18066)				
Navarro Group Ltd Inc	C	754 200-6835		
Plantation (G-14682)				
Nor-Seg Security Services Inc	E	305 650-9666		
Miami (G-10051)				
O S A Global LLC	D	941 896-3148		
Bradenton (G-1153)				
Owl Inc	C	904 679-4555		
Jacksonville (G-6572)				
PG Security Inc	C	954 571-9080		
Boca Raton (G-748)				
PGsecurity Inc	C	305 952-3377		
Miami Gardens (G-10697)				
PGsecurity Inc	C	954 404-9528		
Dania Beach (G-2431)				
Platinum Boss Incorporated	D	818 416-5216		
Saint Petersburg (G-15802)				
Premium Security Services LLC	E	877 437-8495		
Miami (G-10138)				
Pro Guard Security Inc	D	305 247-5085		
Homestead (G-5596)				
Ramco Protective Orlando Inc	C	407 622-7609		
Altamonte Springs (G-95)				
Ramco Protective Orlando Inc	C	904 503-8765		
Saint Augustine (G-15484)				
Ramco Protective Orlando Inc	C	239 237-0048		
Bonita Springs (G-935)				
Rat Pack Wrldwide SEC Cnslt In	E	888 575-7225		
Tampa (G-18201)				
Red Coats Inc	C	321 775-1595		
Melbourne (G-8966)				
Refuge Services Group Inc	D	407 985-1000		
Orlando (G-13093)				
Regions Security Services Inc	C	305 517-1266		
Miami (G-10196)				
Riskwatch International LLC	D	941 500-4525		
Sarasota (G-16284)				
River City Security Svcs Inc	C	904 346-0488		
Jacksonville (G-6667)				
Royal Protection & SEC LLC	E	407 382-0700		
Longwood (G-8397)				
Saeta Guard Services LLC	E	609 705-0213		
Boca Raton (G-780)				
Secure-Pro Security Svcs LLC	D	305 720-9698		
Coral Springs (G-2284)				
Securitas SEC Svcs USA Inc	C	850 244-0014		
Mary Esther (G-8695)				
Securitas SEC Svcs USA Inc	C	239 561-1091		
Fort Myers (G-4588)				
Security Engineers Inc	A	813 870-1241		
Tampa (G-18262)				
Security Indust Spcialists Inc	A	305 219-6350		
Miami Beach (G-10655)				
Security MGT Innovations Inc	C	305 406-2225		
Miami (G-10255)				
Security Oprtons Solutions Inc	E	321 636-8011		
Cocoa (G-1951)				
Security Union Title Insur Co	E	904 854-8997		
Jacksonville (G-6706)				
Security Vault Works Inc	E	954 972-3859		
Pompano Beach (G-14894)				
Securtas Crtcal Infrstrcture S	B	321 984-3636		
Rockledge (G-15367)				
Sentry Event Services Inc	C	813 350-6590		
Tampa (G-18270)				
Seven Hills Security Inc	E	904 215-3144		
Orange Park (G-12017)				
Shergroup Usa LLC	E	407 535-7337		
Celebration (G-1471)				
Sig 9	D	954 774-1117		
Fort Lauderdale (G-4128)				
SOS Security Incorporated	E	904 805-9940		
Jacksonville (G-6745)				
SOS Security LLC	A	561 939-1300		
Fort Lauderdale (G-4137)				
South Florida SEC Group Inc	B	305 432-3501		
Miami (G-10304)				
Spere Inc	E	866 406-2582		
Boynton Beach (G-1039)				
Ssa Security Inc	B	239 437-1632		
Fort Myers (G-4602)				
Ssa Security Inc	A	954 484-0908		
Pompano Beach (G-14909)				
St Moritz Security Svcs Inc	D	863 665-2827		
Lakeland (G-7975)				
Star Guard Security Inc	E	954 734-0876		
Cutler Bay (G-2377)				
Strategic Security Corp	C	646 285-7495		
Sarasota (G-16333)				
Sylint Group Inc	E	941 951-6015		
Sarasota (G-16343)				
Tactical Operations Group LLC	C	561 232-9818		
Boca Raton (G-835)				
Talos Secure Group Inc	E	707 927-5432		
Pensacola (G-14456)				
Tcsc Acquisition LLC	C	305 740-3252		
South Miami (G-16520)				
Titan International SEC Svcs	E	561 296-3893		
West Palm Beach (G-19389)				
Tucker Consulting Corporation	C	904 824-6237		
Saint Augustine (G-15507)				

United Global Security LLC ....D 561 961-9971
Oakland Park (G-11617)
Universal Protection Svc LLC ....C 813 281-0858
Tampa (G-18467)
US Alliance Corp ....D 305 667-8669
Doral (G-3348)
US Alliance Management Inc ....D 407 382-5051
Orlando (G-13358)
US Security Associates Inc ....B 954 351-0190
Fort Lauderdale (G-4204)
US Security Associates Inc ....C 305 592-9747
North Miami (G-11511)
US Security Associates Inc ....B 813 933-4487
Tampa (G-18488)
US Security Associates Inc ....A 407 629-2244
Maitland (G-8595)
US Security Associates Inc ....C 941 351-4007
Sarasota (G-16355)
Veterans SEC Corps Amer Inc ....C 954 731-5161
Fort Lauderdale (G-4212)
Weiser Security Services Inc ....B 504 949-7558
Orlando (G-13415)
Weiser Security Services Inc ....B 239 278-1151
Fort Myers (G-4652)
Weiser Security Services Inc ....C 561 641-4404
Lake Worth (G-7761)
Weiser Security Services Inc ....B 904 786-3955
Jacksonville (G-6926)
Weiser Security Services Inc ....C 727 547-6620
Tampa (G-18530)
Westmoreland Protection Agency ....D 954 318-0532
Sunrise (G-16846)
Xpressguards LLC ....E 561 560-0046
West Park (G-19437)

7382 Security Systems Svcs

ADT Commercial LLC ....D 877 387-0188
Boca Raton (G-401)
ADT Inc ....A 561 988-3600
Boca Raton (G-403)
ADT LLC ....D 772 419-2030
Stuart (G-16584)
ADT LLC ....D 904 701-7148
Saint Augustine (G-15418)
ADT LLC ....A 561 988-3600
Tallahassee (G-16869)
ADT LLC ....D 561 322-4878
Niceville (G-11436)
ADT LLC ....C 863 583-3343
Lakeland (G-7781)
ADT LLC ....C 407 265-1868
Orlando (G-12053)
▲ ADT Security Corporation ....B 561 988-3600
Boca Raton (G-404)
Advantor Systems LLC ....C 407 859-3350
Orlando (G-12063)
Airscan Inc ....C 321 567-9000
Lutz (G-8428)
▲ Alarm Specialist Corporation ....D 800 318-9486
Sarasota (G-16081)
▲ American Sls MGT Orgnztion LLC ...A 305 269-2700
Miami (G-9143)
Americas Security ....E 951 260-7843
Debary (G-2698)
Arqai LLC ....D 239 552-5900
Naples (G-11014)
Atlas Property Management Svcs ....D 305 718-4038
Doral (G-3128)
BA Bull Inc ....D 863 583-3343
Lakeland (G-7810)
Blue Hair Technologies LLC ....D 386 255-1921
Daytona Beach (G-2553)
Bryant Security Corporation ....C 305 948-0100
North Miami Beach (G-11518)
◆ Carrier Fire SEC Americas Corp .....C 561 365-4200
Palm Beach Gardens (G-13698)
Centurion Intl SEC Svcs ....E 305 714-2226
North Miami (G-11486)
Centurion Security Group LLC ....C 800 800-9151
Miami (G-9349)
▲ Comprehensive Energy Svcs Inc ...D 407 682-1313
Longwood (G-8353)
Crime Prvntion SEC Systems LLC ....C 352 376-1499
Gainesville (G-4871)
Cross Match Inc ....E 561 622-1650
Palm Beach Gardens (G-13711)
Dehart Alarm Systems LLC ....E 941 365-1991
Sarasota (G-16029)
Elite Team Logistics LLC ....B 727 612-6762
Seminole (G-16446)

Emergency Systems Inc ....E 904 388-3975
Jacksonville (G-6112)
Eox Technology Solutions Inc ....E 954 256-0006
Deerfield Beach (G-2740)
Fire & Security Holdings LLC ....D 212 915-8888
Boca Raton (G-575)
Focal Point Data Risk LLC ....C 813 402-1208
Tampa (G-17702)
G4s Holding One Inc ....B 561 622-5656
Jupiter (G-7076)
G4s Secure Solutions Intl Inc ....B 561 622-5656
Jupiter (G-7078)
Geo Group Inc ....B 561 893-0101
Boca Raton (G-601)
Goldsky Security LLC ....E 407 853-8400
Tampa (G-17741)
Guardian Alarm Florida LLC ....E 561 547-4550
Lantana (G-8064)
Guardian International Inc ....C 954 926-5200
Hollywood (G-5445)
Guardian Protection Svcs Inc ....D 813 886-3692
Tampa (G-17768)
Hidden Eyes LLC ....E 941 556-0731
Sarasota (G-16184)
Homeland Intelligence Tech ....E 727 776-7424
Largo (G-8117)
▲ Ic Realtime LLC ....E 954 772-5327
Pompano Beach (G-14826)
Infrasafe Holding Inc ....D 407 859-3350
Orlando (G-12680)
Integrated Cyber Solutions LLC ....E 212 634-9534
West Palm Beach (G-19203)
Integrated SEC Systems Inc ....D 305 324-8800
Miami (G-9754)
ISS Action Inc ....D 718 978-3000
Punta Gorda (G-15210)
Jade Tactical Disaster Relief ....C 850 270-4077
Tampa (G-17887)
John F Kennedy Space Center ....A 321 867-3210
Kennedy Space Center (G-7159)
Johnson Cntrls Fire Prtction L ....A 561 988-7200
Boca Raton (G-653)
◆ Johnson Cntrls SEC Sltions LLC .....B 561 264-2071
Boca Raton (G-654)
Jsc Systems Inc ....E 904 737-3511
Gainesville (G-4930)
Kent Holding Group Inc ....C 305 919-9400
North Miami (G-11500)
Knowbe4 Inc ....A 855 566-9234
Clearwater (G-1694)
Legacy Ds Security Services ....E 561 779-5961
West Palm Beach (G-19230)
Life Safety Designs Inc ....E 904 388-1700
Jacksonville (G-6435)
Linx Technologies Global LLC ....E 321 282-8604
Orlando (G-12771)
Lydia Security Monitoring Inc ....E 800 310-1837
Boca Raton (G-679)
Mc2 Inc ....E 407 859-6802
Longwood (G-8381)
Ncipher Security LLC ....D 833 425-1990
Sunrise (G-16802)
▲ Nutech Fire and Security Inc ....D 407 629-7200
Maitland (G-8566)
Panhandle Alarm & Tele Co Inc ....E 850 478-2108
Pensacola (G-14398)
Pcg Securities LLC ....E 978 902-0352
Wesley Chapel (G-19005)
Phillips Fire Sprinklers Inc ....D 954 217-0600
Sunrise (G-16810)
Premier Security Services Inc ....D 727 375-7201
Odessa (G-11854)
Quality Cable Contractors Inc ....E 407 246-0606
Orlando (G-13077)
Quantum Tech Sciences Inc ....A 321 868-0288
Melbourne (G-8963)
Rat Pack Wrldwide SEC Cnslt In ....C 888 575-7225
Tampa (G-18201)
Realtime North America Inc ....D 813 283-0070
Tampa (G-18203)
Red Hawk Fire & Security LLC ....E 954 791-1313
Miami (G-10188)
Redwire LLC ....C 877 371-9473
Tallahassee (G-17083)
Regions Security Services Inc ....D 305 517-1266
Miami (G-10196)
Ronco Consulting Corporation ....A 571 551-2934
Jupiter (G-7137)
Ross Security Systems Inc ....C 813 664-0770
Tampa (G-18237)

Safe Touch Inc ....C 850 385-9544
Tallahassee (G-17090)
Securdyne Systems Intrmdate LL ....A 850 434-2050
Pensacola (G-14431)
Security Monitoring Svcs Inc ....D 407 260-2712
Longwood (G-8401)
▲ Sensormatic Electronics LLC ....B 561 912-6000
Boca Raton (G-794)
Sentry Event Services Inc ....D 727 825-3200
Tampa (G-18271)
Silversphere LLC ....D 386 523-3247
Daytona Beach (G-2663)
◆ Skypatrol LLC ....E 786 331-3300
Doral (G-3312)
Sonitrol of Tallahassee Inc ....E 850 222-3676
Tallahassee (G-17103)
Sonitrol Security Inc ....E 850 222-3676
Tallahassee (G-17104)
Source 1 Solutions Inc ....D 727 538-4114
Clearwater (G-1792)
Strategic Technologies Inc ....D 305 229-6400
Miami (G-10334)
Sunstates Security LLC ....B 561 863-2366
Riviera Beach (G-15323)
Trident Ground Protection LLC ....D 954 306-3956
Oakland Park (G-11616)
Tyco International MGT Co LLC ....D 609 720-4200
Boca Raton (G-850)
◆ Tyco Safety Products Us Inc ....E 561 912-6000
Boca Raton (G-851)
United Security Services ....D 954 596-4411
Deerfield Beach (G-2810)
▲ Vanguard Products Group Inc ....D 813 855-9639
Oldsmar (G-11934)
WW Gay Fire Protection Inc ....C 904 387-7973
Jacksonville (G-6946)

7383 News Syndicates

Tribune Media Services Inc ....D 407 420-6200
Orlando (G-13310)

7384 Photofinishing Labs

Bi-Lo Holdings Foundation Inc ....C 850 939-5627
Navarre (G-11351)
Bi-Lo Holdings Foundation Inc ....C 850 864-3727
Fort Walton Beach (G-4755)
Bi-Lo Holdings Foundation Inc ....B 850 479-9186
Pensacola (G-14234)
Bi-Lo Holdings Foundation Inc ....C 850 626-9800
Milton (G-10810)
Bi-Lo Holdings Foundation Inc ....C 850 994-4240
Pace (G-13580)
Bi-Lo Holdings Foundation Inc ....B 850 473-1012
Pensacola (G-14235)
▼ H & D Graphics Inc ....E 305 594-9906
Hialeah (G-5271)
Procare Pharmacy LLC ....D 407 893-6387
Miami (G-10147)
Rekcut Photographic Inc ....D 904 829-6541
Saint Augustine (G-15485)
South Florida Photo Co Inc ....D 863 683-7858
Lakeland (G-7970)
▲ Timothy J Odonnell Corporation ......E 407 422-0731
Orlando (G-13290)
▼ Triangle Reprographics Inc ....D 407 843-1492
Orlando (G-13309)
Walgreen Co ....E 407 933-8101
Kissimmee (G-7407)
Walgreen Co ....C 407 856-8633
Orlando (G-13391)
Walmart Inc ....C 386 734-5468
De Land (G-2697)
Walmart Inc ....E 386 328-6733
Palatka (G-13606)
Walmart Inc ....C 863 467-7169
Okeechobee (G-11883)
Walmart Inc ....C 352 686-0744
Spring Hill (G-16552)
Walmart Inc ....D 850 526-0064
Marianna (G-8687)
Winn-Dixie Stores Inc ....C 407 380-5445
Orlando (G-13438)
Winn-Dixie Stores Inc ....D 352 528-5302
Williston (G-19517)
Winn-Dixie Stores Inc ....D 863 665-5553
Lakeland (G-8007)
Winn-Dixie Stores Inc ....D 863 644-2214
Lakeland (G-8008)
Winn-Dixie Stores Inc ....D 863 291-3218
Winter Haven (G-19674)

S I C

Winn-Dixie Stores Inc	D	863 859-4611	
Lakeland (G-8009)			
Winn-Dixie Stores Inc	D	863 421-6535	
Haines City (G-5161)			
Winn-Dixie Stores Inc	E	863 683-8352	
Lakeland (G-8010)			
Winn-Dixie Stores Inc	E	386 738-1272	
Deland (G-2892)			
Winn-Dixie Stores Inc	D	850 968-3318	
Cantonment (G-1346)			
Winn-Dixie Stores Inc	D	386 943-6131	
Deland (G-2893)			
Winn-Dixie Stores Inc	D	941 505-9553	
Punta Gorda (G-15225)			
Winn-Dixie Stores Inc	D	850 476-0494	
Pensacola (G-14474)			
Winn-Dixie Stores Inc	E	386 738-5321	
Deland (G-2894)			
Winn-Dixie Stores Inc	D	904 278-2691	
Orange Park (G-12025)			
Winn-Dixie Stores Inc	D	407 282-4527	
Orlando (G-13439)			
Winn-Dixie Stores Inc	E	386 756-4814	
Port Orange (G-15095)			
Winn-Dixie Stores Inc	E	386 574-2698	
Deltona (G-3045)			
Winn-Dixie Stores Inc	D	863 665-4752	
Lakeland (G-8011)			
Winn-Dixie Stores Inc	D	407 339-1593	
Fern Park (G-3517)			
Winn-Dixie Stores Inc	E	352 686-8057	
Spring Hill (G-16553)			
Winn-Dixie Stores Inc	E	863 967-6100	
Auburndale (G-261)			
Winn-Dixie Stores Inc	D	386 439-4301	
Palm Coast (G-13846)			
Winn-Dixie Stores Inc	E	863 439-6047	
Dundee (G-3375)			
Winn-Dixie Stores Inc	D	407 332-8025	
Longwood (G-8416)			
Winn-Dixie Stores Inc	D	407 933-5088	
Kissimmee (G-7411)			
Winn-Dixie Stores Inc	D	850 926-8451	
Crawfordville (G-2307)			
Winn-Dixie Stores Inc	D	407 897-3579	
Orlando (G-13440)			
Winn-Dixie Stores Inc	E	850 627-4686	
Quincy (G-15237)			
Winn-Dixie Stores Inc	D	386 446-4774	
Palm Coast (G-13847)			
Winn-Dixie Stores Inc	D	352 799-2220	
Brooksville (G-1320)			
Winn-Dixie Stores Inc	D	352 666-4600	
Spring Hill (G-16554)			
Winn-Dixie Stores Inc	E	863 676-1223	
Lake Wales (G-7704)			

7389 Business Svcs, NEC

11th Hour Business Centers LLC	E	407 934-4259	
Lake Buena Vista (G-7452)			
24-7 Intouch Guatemala Inc	D	727 259-7676	
Clearwater (G-1507)			
24-7 Intouch Guatemala Inc	D	352 284-2897	
Altamonte Springs (G-15)			
3gimbals LLC	E	703 957-7269	
Miami Beach (G-10538)			
500 Degrees LLC	D	786 615-8265	
Miami (G-9058)			
786 Downtown Inc	D	813 977-6808	
Tampa (G-17214)			
A & Associates Inc	E	561 533-5303	
West Palm Beach (G-19018)			
A&A Skyline Construction LLC	E	813 894-2200	
Temple Terrace (G-18626)			
AAA Communications Inc	E	813 386-3500	
Brandon (G-1211)			
AB Design Group Inc	D	407 774-6078	
Longwood (G-8334)			
ABA Fire Equipment Inc	E	305 573-8273	
Miami (G-9066)			
Abie Inc	D	561 309-1955	
Boca Raton (G-392)			
Ability-Go LLC	C	239 244-8624	
Palm Beach Gardens (G-13677)			
Abts Convention Services Inc	E	305 865-4380	
North Bay Village (G-11466)			
Access Trnspt Svcs Holdg Inc	D	888 748-7575	
Lake Mary (G-7561)			
▲ Acme Barricades LC	E	904 781-1950	
Jacksonville (G-5728)			

Acordis International Corp	E	954 620-0072	
Miramar (G-10833)			
Across Oceans Group Inc	C	561 325-9522	
Palm Beach Gardens (G-13678)			
Ae Opco III LLC	C	727 539-8585	
Clearwater (G-1514)			
Air America AC & Plbg LLC	E	954 973-6599	
Coral Springs (G-2221)			
Al Hoffers Pest Protection	E	954 753-1222	
Coral Springs (G-2222)			
Alignnetworks Inc	E	904 998-0211	
Jacksonville (G-5764)			
All Fire Services Inc	D	954 367-3607	
Hollywood (G-5390)			
All Office Supplt Lee & Collier	E	239 939-2200	
Fort Myers (G-4263)			
All Points Boats Inc	E	954 767-8255	
Fort Lauderdale (G-3593)			
All-American Surveyors Fla Inc	E	904 279-0088	
Jacksonville (G-5768)			
Alorica Customer Care Inc	B	813 663-6000	
Tampa (G-17270)			
Alorica Customer Care Inc	C	941 906-9000	
Sarasota (G-16084)			
Alorica Inc	E	239 344-3846	
Fort Myers (G-4270)			
Alpha Envmtl Mnagementcorp LLC	C	407 542-0300	
Winter Springs (G-19797)			
Als Carrier Express Svcs LLC	D	704 916-9042	
Tampa (G-17272)			
◆ American Beverage Depot LLC	E	305 882-0199	
Medley (G-8705)			
American Maintenance LLC	E	561 317-3219	
Lake Worth (G-7708)			
American Sign Lngage Svcs Corp	C	407 518-7900	
Kissimmee (G-7268)			
American Water Services Inc	E	561 361-4014	
Boca Raton (G-417)			
Americrown Service Corporation	E	386 254-2700	
Daytona Beach (G-2545)			
Anne Rue Interiors Inc	D	407 936-0893	
Lake Mary (G-7567)			
Answer Aide LLC	E	904 719-8500	
Ponte Vedra Beach (G-14973)			
Answerfirst Communications	C	813 882-5307	
Tampa (G-17289)			
Answering Service Care LLC	C	800 430-6511	
Margate (G-8641)			
Antone Hope LLC	E	727 902-1517	
Saint Petersburg (G-15571)			
Anu Industries Inc	E	813 927-7245	
Tampa (G-17291)			
Aplifi Inc	D	954 788-0700	
Fort Lauderdale (G-3612)			
Apollo Retail Specialists LLC	D	813 712-2525	
Tampa (G-17296)			
Applied Research Labs Inc	E	305 624-4800	
Miami Lakes (G-10703)			
Apra Usa Inc	E	786 314-7079	
Doral (G-3123)			
APS of Hollywood LLC	B	954 792-1191	
Plantation (G-14602)			
Aqua Triangle 1 Corporation	E	727 531-0473	
Largo (G-8074)			
Arbitration Forums Inc	C	813 931-4004	
Tampa (G-17299)			
◆ Architectural Panel Pdts Inc	E	561 265-0707	
Delray Beach (G-2908)			
Arep II Gh Holding LLC	D	352 384-3419	
Gainesville (G-4839)			
◆ Armadillo Dist Entps Inc	D	813 600-3920	
Tampa (G-17307)			
Armex Construction Inc	E	239 645-1517	
Cape Coral (G-1376)			
Arquitectonica Intl Corp	D	305 372-1812	
Miami (G-9173)			
Arthur Rutenberg Homes Inc	D	727 536-5900	
Clearwater (G-1526)			
Ascom Nurse Call	D	941 684-5465	
Lakewood Ranch (G-8015)			
Associated Space Design Inc	D	813 223-2293	
Tampa (G-17315)			
◆ Attraction Entrmt Slutions Inc	E	904 260-6689	
Jacksonville (G-5821)			
Auctions By Cellular LLC	E	888 748-2323	
Saint Petersburg (G-15582)			
Avanze Solutions Inc	A	321 236-9600	
Orlando (G-12157)			
Avesi Inc	E	618 795-1619	
Panama City Beach (G-14088)			

Avista Properties Ix Inc	D	407 465-8150	
Orlando (G-12160)			
B & C Fire Safety Inc	E	850 862-7812	
Fort Walton Beach (G-4753)			
B&J Services of Sebring LLC	E	863 414-2063	
Valrico (G-18748)			
Bags	E	404 201-5716	
Orlando (G-12167)			
Balanced Mechanical Svcs LLC	E	352 351-5560	
Ocala (G-11636)			
▲ Bay Area Pools and Spas Inc	D	813 889-9091	
Tampa (G-17345)			
Bca Financial Services Inc	C	305 909-2200	
Palmetto Bay (G-13939)			
Beautiful Naturally Inc	E	800 986-6402	
Hollywood (G-5402)			
Bedabox LLC	E	855 222-4601	
Fort Lauderdale (G-3634)			
Begus Online LLC	D	888 462-6210	
Miami (G-9238)			
Bell and Roper PA	D	407 897-5150	
Orlando (G-12178)			
Bennett Enterprises Inc	D	561 395-1396	
Boca Raton (G-447)			
Bernard LLC	E	855 361-2273	
Holly Hill (G-5380)			
Beyer-Brown & Associates LP	E	407 232-9046	
Orlando (G-12186)			
Bilkey/Llinas Design Assoc Inc	E	561 253-0088	
West Palm Beach (G-19053)			
Black Knght Lnding Sltions Inc	B	904 854-5100	
Jacksonville (G-5865)			
Black Knight Infoserv LLC	E	904 854-5100	
Jacksonville (G-5868)			
▲ Blue Ocean Press Inc	E	954 973-1819	
Fort Lauderdale (G-3646)			
Bmg Money Inc	D	305 851-6134	
Miami (G-9263)			
Braille Works International	E	813 654-4050	
Seffner (G-16422)			
Braxton Jones Inc	E	352 629-1884	
Ocala (G-11647)			
Broward Cnty Cnvention Ctr Inc	E	954 765-5900	
Fort Lauderdale (G-3653)			
BSD Fillmore LLC	D	305 206-2910	
Hollywood (G-5411)			
Bto Commerce Corp	C	689 257-3301	
Orlando (G-12212)			
Buena Vista Suites	E	407 239-8588	
Orlando (G-12216)			
Bureau Veritas Holdings Inc	D	954 236-8100	
Sunrise (G-16753)			
Business Financial Svcs Inc	E	954 757-2525	
Coral Springs (G-2234)			
Byblos Shorecrest	D	786 864-2990	
Miami Beach (G-10564)			
C & D Industrial Maint LLC	E	833 776-5833	
Bradenton (G-1070)			
C A G Inc	E	813 774-4245	
Tampa (G-17406)			
C A S H Incorporated	E	561 994-3334	
Boca Raton (G-489)			
C-Systems & Services Inc	E	954 979-5273	
Coconut Creek (G-1981)			
Calabash Outdoors Inc	E	407 440-2896	
Orlando (G-12226)			
Call 4 Health Inc	E	561 994-3334	
Delray Beach (G-2923)			
Callstar Inc	E	727 346-4400	
Saint Petersburg (G-15609)			
CAM Options Inc	E	407 349-9600	
Longwood (G-8349)			
▲ Cambrdge Intgrted Svcs Group I	E	954 966-4772	
Hollywood (G-5413)			
Captive-Aire Systems Inc	C	407 682-0317	
Groveland (G-5085)			
Car Financial Services Inc	E	407 804-2980	
Lake Mary (G-7572)			
Care Solutions Inc	C	407 249-1002	
Winter Park (G-19694)			
Caretnders Vsting Svcs Gnsvlle	C	352 323-5570	
Clermont (G-1858)			
Carey Group Publishing LLC	D	877 892-2739	
Melbourne Beach (G-9012)			
Caribbean Pool Service & Repr	E	561 842-7482	
Riviera Beach (G-15287)			
Carters Group LLC	C	786 533-2270	
Miami (G-9331)			
Ccmh Tampa AP LLC	D	813 879-5151	
Tampa (G-17433)			

Center For Sales Strategy Inc	E	813 254-2222	Tampa (G-17441)
Centerline Utilities Inc	C	561 689-3917	Palm City (G-13785)
Certegy Payment Solutions LLC	D	800 237-7506	Clearwater (G-1564)
Certified Guaranty Company LLC	E	941 360-3991	Lakewood Ranch (G-8037)
Certified Pool Mechanics Inc	E	239 992-9096	Fort Myers (G-4306)
◆ Challengers Import Export LLC	E	914 338-2924	Orlando (G-12289)
Charles Schwab Corporation	D	800 435-9050	The Villages (G-18654)
◆ Chemco Services Inc	E	850 968-1786	Cantonment (G-1336)
Citicorp Credit Services Inc	A	972 653-4198	Jacksonville (G-5949)
Citigroup Technology Inc	E	866 213-0890	Tampa (G-17478)
City of Fort Lauderdale	D	954 828-5380	Fort Lauderdale (G-3695)
City of Rockledge	E	321 690-3213	Rockledge (G-15338)
City of Tampa	B	813 274-8511	Tampa (G-17482)
Clark Family Farm LLC	E	386 462-1188	Alachua (G-5)
Clearent LLC	D	561 684-5352	West Palm Beach (G-19093)
Clincloud LLC	E	717 357-1569	Orlando (G-12320)
Closetmaid LLC	D	800 874-0008	Ocala (G-11664)
Collins & Dupont Interiors Inc	E	239 948-2400	Bonita Springs (G-903)
Commercial Design Services Inc	E	813 886-0580	Tampa (G-17503)
Commercial Fire LLC	C	904 642-3606	Jacksonville (G-5979)
Commercial Relocation Group	E	954 532-5330	Deerfield Beach (G-2726)
Common Sense Publishing LLC	C	561 510-1713	Delray Beach (G-2933)
Community Brands Holdco LLC	D	727 827-0046	Saint Petersburg (G-15637)
Community Tax LLC	C	800 444-0622	Jacksonville (G-5990)
Complete Bus Sltions Group Inc	E	215 922-2636	Miami (G-9398)
Concept Companies Inc	D	352 333-3233	Gainesville (G-4868)
Connexxions Bus Inc	E	917 940-1334	Orlando (G-12360)
Contact Center Solution LLC	A	786 504-2103	Homestead (G-5567)
▲ Convention Center Net Inc	E	407 685-9000	Orlando (G-12365)
Corporate Amercn Solutions LLC	E	305 434-7227	Miami (G-9420)
Corporate Amercn Solutions LLC	D	305 423-8380	Miami (G-9421)
County of Broward	D	954 831-0892	Pompano Beach (G-14786)
County of Broward	B	954 765-5925	Fort Lauderdale (G-3730)
County of Broward	C	954 786-4201	Pompano Beach (G-14787)
County of Orange	A	407 685-5829	Orlando (G-12376)
County of Orange	C	407 836-5068	Orlando (G-12377)
County of Orange	C	407 345-9800	Orlando (G-12378)
County of Volusia	E	386 239-6427	Daytona Beach (G-2567)
County of Volusia	B	386 254-4500	Daytona Beach (G-2568)
County of Walton	D	850 267-1216	Santa Rosa Beach (G-16007)
Courtyard By Mrrott Fort Ldrda	E	954 342-8333	Dania (G-2407)
Crab Trap	D	850 301-0959	Fort Walton Beach (G-4760)
Creative Kitchen Designs Inc	E	770 355-3380	Milton (G-10813)
Credomatic of Florida Inc	C	305 372-3000	Miami (G-9436)
Cruising Accessories Limited	E	561 318-0000	Boca Raton (G-541)

D & D Tree Farm & Nursery Inc	D	407 827-0944	Lake Buena Vista (G-7458)
Data Search NY Inc	D	239 552-3900	Bonita Springs (G-909)
Daytona Beach Resort LLC	C	386 672-3770	Daytona Beach (G-2577)
Dbaccess LLC	D	312 404-6457	Hernando (G-5206)
Dealers Auction Xchange LLC	E	727 400-3929	Zephyrhills (G-19829)
Deco Productions Inc	E	305 558-0800	Opa Locka (G-11944)
◆ Decorators Unlimited Inc	D	561 625-3000	Palm Beach Gardens (G-13715)
Defense Contract Audit Agency	D	321 752-2400	Melbourne (G-8867)
◆ Denison Yacht Sales Inc	E	954 763-3971	Dania (G-2409)
Denny Ackerman	E	305 232-1717	Miami (G-9472)
Denny Energy LLC	E	407 365-5646	Winter Springs (G-19802)
Dentprosth Digital Inc	E	305 878-9835	Weston (G-19456)
Designshop Services LLC	D	407 251-1800	Orlando (G-12413)
Devore Design LLC	E	407 500-7427	Clermont (G-1865)
Dialamerica Marketing Inc	C	352 854-8860	Ocala (G-11673)
Dialamerica Marketing Inc	B	407 243-9400	Orlando (G-12421)
Digitcom LLC	D	407 872-9199	Orlando (G-12424)
Discovery Mktg & Distrg Inc	D	407 523-0775	Orlando (G-12425)
Diversified Consultants Inc	C	904 641-4572	Jacksonville (G-6072)
Dotcom Marketing Group Inc	D	954 839-8775	Weston (G-19457)
Dowling Graphics Inc	E	727 573-5997	Clearwater (G-1609)
Drb Capital LLC	D	561 995-4200	Boca Raton (G-557)
Dsdr Service Corp	E	954 200-4608	Coral Springs (G-2248)
Dtg2go LLC	D	305 785-4182	Hialeah (G-5253)
Dtg2go LLC	E	727 800-9767	Clearwater (G-1610)
Duchess Designs LLC	D	813 300-0392	Tarpon Springs (G-18582)
Dun & Brdstreet Emrging Bsnsse	C	904 648-6350	Jacksonville (G-6089)
E M I International	B	305 674-7529	Miami Beach (G-10586)
Eagle Product Inspection LLC	D	877 379-1670	Lutz (G-8439)
East Coast Auto Cons LLC	C	561 533-5331	Boynton Beach (G-984)
East Lk Trpon Spcial Fire Ctrl	E	727 784-8668	Palm Harbor (G-13860)
Eat Right Meal Plans LLC	D	813 355-8849	Tampa (G-17611)
Ehota Inc	D	954 902-4299	Fort Lauderdale (G-3769)
El Chilar - Hf LLC	D	407 880-6007	Apopka (G-177)
Elite American Group Inc	E	305 998-8999	Hallandale Beach (G-5168)
Elitepronet Inc	E	561 656-4701	West Palm Beach (G-19131)
Emerging Tech LLC	E	443 203-8196	Gainesville (G-4880)
Encore Funding LLC	E	800 586-7949	West Palm Beach (G-19133)
Endicott Communications Inc	E	305 271-5929	Miami (G-9521)
Endo Group Pllc	E	954 438-4282	Pembroke Pines (G-14148)
Enhanced Recovery Company LLC	A	904 371-1005	Jacksonville (G-6120)
Ephonamationcom Inc	C	714 560-1000	Ocala (G-11677)
Epic Vision LLC	E	404 954-1140	Hastings (G-5188)
Espace Inc	E	802 735-7546	Stuart (G-16620)
Estate Management Services Inc	E	912 261-8882	Jacksonville (G-6133)

Etech Global Services LLC	D	561 627-7988	Palm Beach Gardens (G-13727)
Eventus Marketing LLC	E	305 668-4343	Doral (G-3193)
▲ Everise Inc	D	877 449-6487	Plantation (G-14639)
Evolved Source Solutions Corp	C	239 288-9470	Lehigh Acres (G-8282)
Excellence In Cw Zone A LLC	D	786 271-0641	Miami (G-9536)
▲ Expo Convention Contrs Inc	D	305 751-1234	Miami (G-9538)
Export Freight & Brokers Inc	E	305 592-7343	Doral (G-3197)
EZ Purchase LLC	D	786 501-6313	Aventura (G-270)
Fairweather Group Inc	E	954 481-8787	Deerfield Beach (G-2741)
Family Chrstn Assn of Amer Inc	E	305 573-5527	Opa Locka (G-11946)
Faneuil Inc	B	954 689-6712	Fort Lauderdale (G-3782)
Faneuil Inc	B	813 286-2063	Tampa (G-17649)
Faneuil Inc	A	407 515-4700	Orlando (G-12492)
Faneuil Inc	B	863 646-2231	Lakeland (G-7861)
Farfield Systems Inc	E	410 874-9363	Sarasota (G-16156)
Fasha Corporation	E	505 991-9115	Orlando (G-12494)
Fattmerchant Inc	E	855 550-3288	Orlando (G-12497)
Fba II Inc	E	786 777-1000	Miami (G-9546)
Federal Express Corporation	C	863 646-9127	Lakeland (G-7863)
Fetty Partnership Inc	E	863 510-0141	Lakeland (G-7865)
Fidelity Intl Resource MGT Inc	D	904 438-6000	Jacksonville (G-6156)
Fidelity Nat Card Svcs Inc	D	727 556-9000	Jacksonville (G-6157)
▼ Fidelity Nat Info Svcs Inc	A	904 438-6000	Jacksonville (G-6159)
Finchberry LLC	E	703 663-0237	Gainesville (G-4884)
Firepak Inc	E	305 994-9220	Miami (G-9557)
Fireservice Inc	D	239 936-1033	Fort Myers (G-4372)
First Cast Dlvry Svc Prtners L	D	904 657-3297	Jacksonville (G-6968)
First Contact LLC	D	727 369-0850	Apopka (G-182)
First Contact LLC	D	727 369-0850	Saint Petersburg (G-15670)
First Contact LLC	D	727 369-0850	Altamonte Springs (G-47)
First Family Insurance LLC	D	800 327-0977	Fort Myers (G-4373)
▲ Five Star Ceramics Group Inc	E	305 820-1414	Miami (G-9564)
Five Star Ldscpg Irrgation Inc	E	352 748-8000	The Villages (G-18657)
Florida Business Ctr Acqn Sub	D	954 928-2800	Fort Lauderdale (G-3794)
Florida Business Ctr Acqn Sub	D	561 962-4100	Boca Raton (G-580)
Florida Handling Systems Inc	E	863 534-1212	Bartow (G-317)
Florida Hotels & Rest Inc	D	407 425-4455	Orlando (G-12528)
Florida Plice Bnvlent Assn Inc	D	813 988-0077	Tampa (G-17694)
Florida Power and Design Inc	E	786 393-1857	Miami (G-9588)
Florida West Coast Inc	E	813 759-6060	Plant City (G-14558)
Focus Wealth Strategies LLC	D	813 305-0411	Brandon (G-1232)
Folsom Corporation	D	813 926-3582	Odessa (G-11839)
Fortiline Drivers LLC	D	205 895-8667	Lakeland (G-7870)
▼ Friedmans Premier Systems Inc	D	847 983-6124	Hallandale Beach (G-5170)
Froz-N Inc	E	407 593-8300	Saint Cloud (G-15521)

SIC

Full Sail LLC	E	407 679-0100
Winter Park (G-19725)		
Gables Ah LLC	D	919 851-0858
Miami (G-9617)		
Galati Marine	D	941 778-0755
Bradenton (G-1108)		
Garda CL Southwest Inc	C	213 383-3611
Boca Raton (G-595)		
Geodetic Associates Inc	E	727 345-8903
Saint Petersburg (G-15685)		
Global Axcess Corp	E	904 395-1149
Jacksonville (G-6233)		
◆ Global Exports USA Inc	E	305 371-9200
Miami (G-9635)		
Global Lsure Cpitl Prtners LLC	E	561 228-5381
West Palm Beach (G-19165)		
Go Outdoors Florida LLC	C	888 347-4356
Tallahassee (G-16988)		
God Hands LLC	E	786 587-6563
North Miami (G-11492)		
Gpi Geospatial Inc	E	407 851-7880
Orlando (G-12585)		
Gr Opco LLC	E	786 360-3971
Miami (G-9656)		
Greater Fort Ldrdale Cnvntion	D	954 765-4466
Fort Lauderdale (G-3834)		
Greater Mami Cnvntion Vstors B	D	305 539-3000
Miami (G-9662)		
Greenery Productions Inc	E	407 363-9151
Orlando (G-12599)		
Grohappy LLC	E	863 326-7190
Davenport (G-2442)		
Group 4 Design Inc	E	904 353-5900
Jacksonville (G-6244)		
Grsc Inc	E	772 888-6818
Stuart (G-16628)		
Grupo Corzo Inc	D	305 767-9712
North Miami Beach (G-11525)		
Guardian Angels Med Svc Dogs I	B	352 425-1981
Williston (G-19512)		
Guardian Service Corp	E	866 826-3309
Tampa (G-17769)		
H2a Services & Compliance LLC	D	239 339-3496
Fort Myers (G-4432)		
Hampton West LLC	E	904 517-5939
Jacksonville (G-6256)		
Harrison Home Services In	E	786 553-6421
Boca Raton (G-619)		
Hawkins Roniesha	D	754 246-5432
Coral Springs (G-2260)		
HBO Latin Amer Techequip LLC	C	954 217-5351
Sunrise (G-16781)		
Hello Fla Destination MGT Inc	E	407 425-5300
Orlando (G-12634)		
Hertz Funding Corp	E	239 301-7000
Estero (G-3461)		
Highland Packg Solutions LLC	C	863 425-5757
Plant City (G-14564)		
Highpointe Hospitability Inc	D	850 939-9400
Gulf Breeze (G-5118)		
Hjw Designs Inc	E	321 473-6890
Ponte Vedra (G-14965)		
HMS Global Maritime Inc	D	954 769-9260
Fort Lauderdale (G-3865)		
Holiday Inn Hotel & Suites	E	407 581-9001
Orlando (G-12657)		
▼ Home Entrmt Design S Inc	E	954 923-2335
Hollywood (G-5456)		
Host Hotels & Resorts LP	E	305 374-3900
Miami (G-9722)		
Htg Paradise LLC	E	305 860-8188
Miami (G-9729)		
Hybrid Payments Inc	E	877 755-4829
Naples (G-11170)		
I Sales Group Inc	E	305 333-3420
Sunrise (G-16786)		
Idea Aviation Corporation	E	888 596-9551
Saint Petersburg (G-15714)		
Ifp Securities LLC	B	813 341-0960
Tampa (G-17856)		
Igt Services Inc	E	305 573-2800
Miami (G-9743)		
Incharge Debt Solutions	D	407 291-7770
Orlando (G-12678)		
Independent Purch Coop Inc	D	305 670-0041
Miami (G-9745)		
Industrial Energy Services Inc	C	850 941-7621
Pensacola (G-14327)		
Inkabap Group II LLC	E	407 733-5860
Palm Beach Gardens (G-13741)		

Inktel Cntact Ctr Slutions LLC	C	305 523-1145
Doral (G-3238)		
◆ Inktel Holdings Corp	B	305 523-1100
Doral (G-3239)		
Instiglio Inc	D	562 645-3339
Miami (G-9750)		
▲ Interiors By Steven G Inc	D	954 735-8223
Pompano Beach (G-14828)		
Interius Inc	E	305 935-9526
Miami (G-9760)		
Intermodal Support Svcs Inc	D	904 858-1587
Jacksonville (G-6327)		
Internal Revenue Service	E	727 449-0732
Belleair Bluffs (G-371)		
▲ International Laboratories LLC	C	727 322-7160
Seminole (G-16451)		
International Money Ex Inc	C	305 671-8000
Miami (G-9767)		
Interntnal M2o Fire Prtction S	C	561 506-6277
Lake Worth (G-7735)		
Interntonal Money Ex Sub 2 LLC	D	305 671-8000
Miami (G-9774)		
Interntonal Register Shipg LLC	E	305 323-0274
Miami (G-9775)		
Ipacesetters LLC	C	267 530-6275
Naples (G-11178)		
Ips Worldwide LLC	D	386 672-7727
Ormond Beach (G-13505)		
Irnm Hotel Investors LLC	D	850 477-0711
Pensacola (G-14331)		
Islander Bch CLB Cndo Assn Vls	E	386 427-7100
New Smyrna Beach (G-11419)		
Itc Translations USA Inc	D	561 746-6242
Palm Beach Gardens (G-13744)		
Ivox Solutions LLC	B	772 301-1718
Port Saint Lucie (G-15144)		
Jacksnvlle The Bches Cnvntion	E	904 798-9111
Jacksonville (G-6349)		
Jhs Capital Advisors Inc	E	813 202-7960
Tampa (G-17895)		
▲ JM Field Marketing Inc	E	954 523-1957
Fort Lauderdale (G-3909)		
▲ Jorge M Prez Art Mseum Mm-Dade	D	305 375-3000
Miami (G-9803)		
Judicary Crts of The State Fla	E	850 488-0637
Tallahassee (G-17013)		
K9s For Warriors Inc	D	904 686-1956
Ponte Vedra (G-14966)		
Kam Services Inc	E	352 429-0049
Groveland (G-5095)		
Kelly Roofing LLC	D	239 435-0014
Naples (G-11188)		
▼ Kemco Industries LLC	D	407 322-1230
Sanford (G-15958)		
Keystone Group Holdings Inc	D	813 225-4650
Orlando (G-12728)		
King Fresh Tomatoes Inc	E	863 307-9652
Bartow (G-324)		
▲ Klocke of America Inc	D	239 561-5800
Fort Myers (G-4465)		
L & K Group LLC	E	954 907-5120
Hollywood (G-5466)		
L & T Brothers Inc	E	727 742-1492
Largo (G-8125)		
L Fagan Enterprises Inc	E	321 720-4529
Melbourne (G-8917)		
L&S Diversified LLC	E	407 681-3836
Casselberry (G-1451)		
Lake Wales Care Center Inc	E	863 676-6678
Lake Wales (G-7688)		
Lakeview Center Inc	C	850 432-1222
Pensacola (G-14340)		
LAMA Miami 305 Chapter	D	305 699-4255
Tamarac (G-17197)		
Landrum Prof Emplyer Svcs Inc	D	850 476-5100
Pensacola (G-14343)		
LAS International Corp	E	786 517-5700
Doral (G-3258)		
Lasconi Translation LLC	E	954 226-2779
Margate (G-8655)		
Lee Mmrial Hlth Sys Foundation	B	239 343-6950
Fort Myers (G-4494)		
Leslies Holdings Inc	D	850 494-9233
Pensacola (G-14344)		
Life Care Associates Inc	D	561 743-5966
Jupiter (G-7110)		
Lighthouse Associates Inc	D	561 588-1200
West Palm Beach (G-19238)		
Live Design Inc	E	786 513-9807
Coral Springs (G-2267)		

Livetrends Design Group LLC	D	407 814-4907
Apopka (G-198)		
LLC Golden Wolf	C	240 672-7995
Lithia (G-8301)		
Mad Room LLC	D	305 525-7662
Coral Gables (G-2136)		
Mag Ventures LLC	E	904 207-6094
Jacksonville (G-6460)		
Magellan Solutions USA Inc	C	650 897-5147
Melbourne (G-8926)		
Magna Hospitality Group Lc	C	954 472-5600
Plantation (G-14670)		
Manes Realty Group LLC	D	407 788-6474
Altamonte Springs (G-74)		
Marc-Michaels Intr Design Inc	E	407 629-0441
Winter Park (G-19747)		
Marine Systems Corporation	D	850 249-7774
Panama City Beach (G-14098)		
Marriott International Inc	C	239 394-2511
Marco Island (G-8635)		
Mastercard International Inc	D	914 249-2000
Miami (G-9909)		
Matteico Inc	D	305 822-0244
Hialeah Gardens (G-5346)		
Mbgc LLC	D	305 851-8281
Miami (G-9913)		
Medical Data Systems Inc	C	772 770-2255
Vero Beach (G-18893)		
Memories Unlimited Inc	C	407 872-3838
Orlando (G-12854)		
Merchant One Inc	E	305 538-5240
Miami Beach (G-10618)		
▲ Merrill-Stevens Dry Dock Co	D	305 640-5676
Miami (G-9942)		
Merritt Hospitality	C	407 830-1985
Altamonte Springs (G-77)		
Meteor Education LLC	C	800 699-7516
Gainesville (G-4944)		
Metro Connections Inc	C	407 414-2603
Celebration (G-1469)		
Mfkks LLC	C	888 354-5050
Fort Myers (G-4512)		
Mia Hospitality LLC	D	786 566-9468
Miami (G-9948)		
Miami Chld Hosp Foundation Inc	C	305 666-2889
Miami (G-9962)		
Mica Plus & Sons Inc	D	727 314-9835
Boca Raton (G-692)		
Miccoskee Tribe of Indians Fla	B	305 222-4600
Miami (G-9997)		
Miccosukee Corporation	C	305 223-8380
Miami (G-9998)		
Mid-Florida Medical Svcs Inc	D	863 292-4077
Winter Haven (G-19645)		
Mid-State Rodbusters Inc	D	352 789-6933
Ocala (G-11731)		
Midds Inc	E	561 586-6220
Lake Worth Beach (G-7772)		
◆ Mitsubishi Power Americas Inc	D	407 688-6100
Lake Mary (G-7612)		
Mme Florida LLC	C	904 853-1330
Jacksonville Beach (G-6995)		
Mobile Management Inc	E	352 233-2700
Ocala (G-11738)		
Modivcare Solutions LLC	E	305 471-0441
Miami (G-10011)		
Mothertongue Inc	D	561 354-5530
Miami (G-10019)		
Motionpoint Corporation	D	954 421-0890
Coconut Creek (G-1997)		
Myrthil Carrier Service LLC	D	813 481-2192
Miami (G-10023)		
National Building Insptn Svcs	E	772 287-0444
Stuart (G-16648)		
National Check Trust Inc	C	954 431-5256
Miramar (G-10880)		
National Fire Protection LLC	E	954 739-8107
Fort Lauderdale (G-3989)		
Nationwide Move Management LLC	B	954 580-8200
Margate (G-8660)		
Naval AVI Mseum Foundation Inc	D	850 453-2389
Pensacola (G-14376)		
Ncb Management Services Inc	D	904 737-2485
Jacksonville (G-6532)		
Nemesis - Green Urban Bstro LL	D	786 837-0854
Miami (G-10037)		
Netlook Inc	D	904 642-8757
Jacksonville (G-6536)		
New World Venture NW Florida	D	850 434-7736
Pensacola (G-14386)		

Company	Code	Phone
Next Step Network LLC Boca Raton (G-719)	C	516 780-5534
◆ Niagara Distributors Inc Hollywood (G-5482)	E	954 925-6775
Nopetro LLC Saint Augustine (G-15472)	D	904 460-2897
Norris Ryback Group LLC Lutz (G-8452)	E	813 924-5407
▼ Ntr Holdco LLC Fort Lauderdale (G-4021)	E	954 522-2323
Nv5 Global Inc Hollywood (G-5486)	C	954 495-2112
Ocala Breeders Sales Co Inc Ocala (G-11748)	E	352 237-4667
Ocasa Inc Miami (G-10058)	D	305 591-0634
Ocean Reef Community Assn Key Largo (G-7187)	E	305 367-3067
Office Sense LLC Miami (G-10065)	E	786 220-7170
Okee-B Inc Belle Glade (G-361)	D	561 996-3040
▼ One Call Medical Inc Jacksonville (G-6561)	B	904 646-0199
One Touch Direct LLC Tampa (G-18100)	B	813 549-7500
Ops Tech Alliance LLC Clearwater (G-1748)	B	443 223-6115
Optimal Translation & Trnsp Jacksonville (G-6564)	D	904 646-0199
Optucorp Usa LLC Miami (G-10077)	C	305 964-7262
Orange County Convention Ctr Orlando (G-12936)	E	407 685-9800
▲ Orland/Rnge Cnty Cnvntion Vsto Orlando (G-12940)	C	407 363-5800
Orlando Hotel Group LLC Winter Garden (G-19588)	E	407 993-3011
Orlando Rentco LLC Orlando (G-12980)	E	646 706-1001
Otak Group Inc Yulee (G-19818)	E	904 225-2588
Our Town Inc Clearwater (G-1751)	E	800 497-8360
Outsource Option LLC Orlando (G-12994)	E	407 493-7928
P S C U Service Centers Inc Saint Petersburg (G-15785)	B	727 572-8822
Pallas LLC Saint Petersburg (G-15787)	C	727 572-7800
Palm Beach Cnty Convention Ctr West Palm Beach (G-19310)	D	561 366-3000
▲ Palm Coast Data LLC Bunnell (G-1325)	A	386 445-4662
Palmer Prprty Preservation LLC Fort Lauderdale (G-4039)	E	954 932-3209
Paragon Systems Inc Tampa (G-18120)	A	813 242-4300
Partsfleet Inc Orlando (G-13011)	E	407 843-6505
Patlive Inc Tallahassee (G-17064)	B	800 775-7790
Patlive Inc Tallahassee (G-17065)	D	844 287-3782
Patrick B Appleby Winter Park (G-19760)	D	407 970-8480
Pavetech Inc Miami (G-10102)	E	305 546-3473
Paycargo LLC Coral Gables (G-2166)	E	888 250-7778
Payments Business Corp Plantation (G-14690)	E	954 510-3750
Pdma Corporation Tampa (G-18129)	E	813 621-6463
Peninsula Lifestyle Capital Naples (G-11260)	D	239 494-8633
Percepta LLC Melbourne (G-8957)	C	321 435-1000
Pershard Clipper LLC Greenacres (G-5077)	D	317 417-8284
Pf Collier LLC Naples (G-11261)	E	239 277-1102
▼ Phoenix Products Inc Jacksonville (G-6599)	D	904 354-1858
Pink Frog Company Inc Lake Mary (G-7623)	D	689 258-6031
Pinmar Usa Inc Riviera Beach (G-15312)	E	954 923-8887
Plansource Financial Svcs Inc Orlando (G-13036)	A	877 549-8549
Platinum Strl Restoration Inc Hollywood (G-5494)	E	305 908-8764
Pmweb Inc Aventura (G-279)	E	617 207-7080
Port Chrltte Fclty Oprtons LLC Port Charlotte (G-15055)	D	941 743-4700
Poulos & Bennett LLC Orlando (G-13044)	D	407 487-2594
Power Design Resources LLC Saint Petersburg (G-15805)	E	727 210-0492
Power Resources Fincl Svcs Inc Pembroke Pines (G-14176)	E	954 281-5590
Prc LLC Tampa (G-18161)	A	813 952-1010
Prc LLC Longwood (G-8391)	E	407 682-1556
Precision Rockledge (G-15361)	E	518 892-0640
Precision Fire Systems Inc Sanford (G-15973)	D	407 402-2195
Premc III Inc Orlando (G-13048)	E	407 851-0261
Presentation Resource Inc Jacksonville (G-6616)	E	904 398-8179
Primesouth LLC Windermere (G-19548)	D	803 753-5199
▼ Primestream Corporation Miami (G-10145)	E	305 625-4415
Professnal Trnslating Svcs LLC Coral Gables (G-2172)	C	305 371-7887
Pscu Incorporated Saint Petersburg (G-15812)	A	727 572-8822
Pure Leverage Intl Inc Orange Park (G-12013)	E	904 701-8699
Quality Companies Inc Tallahassee (G-17076)	D	850 576-4880
Quantum Servicing Corproation Tampa (G-18189)	D	813 472-6500
Quest Workspaces Miami (G-10174)	E	305 200-0218
R and M Same Here Inc Fort Lauderdale (G-4075)	E	954 776-1432
R Smith International LLC Boca Raton (G-763)	B	561 245-4350
Radial South LP Melbourne (G-8965)	B	719 948-1900
Rcb Fund Services LLC Lantana (G-8067)	E	203 618-0065
Reads Moving Systems Inc Jacksonville (G-6640)	E	386 255-7400
Recourse Communications Inc West Palm Beach (G-19339)	E	561 686-6800
Red Rhino of Fl Inc Palm Beach Gardens (G-13768)	C	800 737-3418
Reed Healthcare Services Corp Jacksonville (G-6644)	D	904 329-4975
Relogistics Services LLC Alachua (G-11)	E	386 418-0245
Renthotel Florida Inc Kissimmee (G-7377)	E	407 396-4000
▲ Renz Nichols Family Ltd Partnr Saint Petersburg (G-15830)	A	727 573-7848
◆ Resolve Marine Group Inc Fort Lauderdale (G-4087)	E	954 764-8700
Resort Hospitality Entps Ltd Panama City (G-14066)	C	850 234-3484
Results Companies LLC Fort Lauderdale (G-4090)	E	954 921-2400
Revinu Inc Winter Haven (G-19656)	E	863 205-3208
Rgis LLC Pensacola (G-14421)	D	850 476-5051
Rgn-Palm Beach Gardens I LLC Palm Beach Gardens (G-13769)	D	561 337-5200
Rifle Inc Maitland (G-8574)	D	407 622-7679
▲ Rifle LLC Winter Park (G-19770)	E	407 622-7679
Rio Citrus Inc Fort Pierce (G-4735)	E	772 460-1429
Rje Telecom LLC Fort Myers (G-4573)	E	239 936-2904
◆ Robb & Stucky Intl Inc Fort Myers (G-4575)	E	239 415-2800
Rogers Lovelock & Fritz Inc Orlando (G-13123)	D	407 730-8600
Ronco Consulting Corporation Jupiter (G-7137)	A	571 551-2934
Rone Engineering Hialeah (G-5317)	C	214 630-9745
Rosen 9939 Inc Orlando (G-13131)	A	407 996-9939
Rosen Centre Inc Orlando (G-13132)	A	407 996-9840
Rosen Plaza Inc Orlando (G-13137)	B	407 996-9700
Ross Technology Services LLC Palmetto (G-13927)	A	941 479-2162
Royal Foam US LLC Jacksonville (G-6678)	E	904 345-5400
Ryan Hughes Design Inc Tampa (G-18241)	E	727 940-2653
Salsas of Jacksonville Corp Palm Coast (G-13838)	E	386 445-3096
San Crlos Pk Fire Prtction RSC Fort Myers (G-4583)	D	239 489-3114
Sansone Group/Ddr LLC Miami (G-10240)	C	305 416-8194
Seacoast Brokers LLC Palm Beach Gardens (G-13771)	E	561 776-1166
Seamar Divers Inc Medley (G-8780)	D	305 805-6896
Sebring Citrus Inc Avon Park (G-297)	C	863 840-5741
Securdyne Systems Intrmdate LL Pompano Beach (G-14893)	A	754 220-6148
Seminole Cnty Prprty Apprisers Sanford (G-15978)	E	407 665-7560
Seminole Financial Svcs LLC Clearwater (G-1785)	E	727 298-8930
Septic Maxx Delray Beach (G-3015)	E	561 455-2717
SGS North America Inc Miami (G-10267)	E	201 508-3000
SH Pasco Incorporated Odessa (G-11855)	D	727 409-0319
Shepard Exposition Svcs Inc Orlando (G-13189)	C	407 888-9669
Shin Group Inc Sunny Isles Beach (G-16727)	D	954 530-7356
Shinelogics LLC Lutz (G-8457)	E	813 470-0480
Shotrock Productions Inc Sanford (G-15981)	D	407 614-6160
Shuel Enterprises Inc Sarasota (G-16317)	E	941 923-7401
Si America LLC Boca Raton (G-800)	D	561 990-1953
Silverminds LLC Doral (G-3310)	E	904 342-6591
Simply Chosen Inc Miami (G-10273)	C	786 872-4948
Simply Chosen Wealth MGT Miami (G-10274)	C	786 872-4948
Sitel Corporation Tampa (G-18290)	D	402 963-6810
◆ Sitel Worldwide Corporation Miami (G-10278)	C	615 301-7100
Smg Holdings LLC Miami Beach (G-10659)	D	305 674-9809
SMS Intrntnal Shore Oprtons US Miami (G-10286)	C	305 290-3000
South Seaside Enterprises LLC Fort Lauderdale (G-4141)	D	954 656-2153
Southern Mntee Fire Rescue Dst Sarasota (G-16056)	D	941 751-7675
Southstern Archlogical RES Inc Orlando (G-13221)	C	407 236-7711
Spegal Plumbing LLC Apopka (G-213)	C	321 256-1234
▲ Spencer Boat Co Inc West Palm Beach (G-19373)	E	561 844-1800
Sprig Llc Miami (G-10317)	D	305 502-9900
Springleaf Fincl Holdings LLC Apopka (G-214)	B	407 682-2079
Springleaf Fincl Holdings LLC Lake Wales (G-7700)	B	863 293-5615
Sraddha Software Solutions Davie (G-2523)	E	669 301-8146
St Joseph Garden Courts Inc Orlando (G-13231)	E	407 382-0808
Stantec Architecture Inc Orlando (G-13233)	C	301 220-1861
Starcourse International Ltd Sarasota (G-16331)	E	352 702-5447
Steadfast Dlvry Solutions LLC Apollo Beach (G-142)	D	813 422-2824
Stearns Wver Mller Wssler Alhd Miami (G-10329)	C	305 789-3200

S I C

◆ Stellar Energy Americas Inc ....E...... 904 260-2044
   Jacksonville *(G-6790)*

◆ Stellar Group Incorporated ....C...... 904 260-2900
   Jacksonville *(G-6791)*

Sterling Payment Tech LLC ....C...... 813 637-9696
   Tampa *(G-18336)*

Stone Concepts Miami Inc ....D...... 786 309-0660
   Miami Springs *(G-10788)*

Strategic Security Corp ....C...... 646 285-7495
   Sarasota *(G-16333)*

Stratus Audio Inc ....E...... 877 746-4674
   Winter Park *(G-19776)*

Stratus Indemand Inc ....C...... 206 347-8467
   Clearwater *(G-1796)*

Stratus Indemand Inc ....C...... 509 888-3824
   Clearwater *(G-1797)*

Stratus Video LLC ....D...... 727 451-9766
   Clearwater *(G-1798)*

Structured Asset Funding LLC ....D...... 954 445-6060
   Lauderhill *(G-8207)*

Stryker Sstnblity Slutions Inc ....C...... 863 683-8680
   Lakeland *(G-7980)*

Stuart Weitzman Ret Stores LLC ....C...... 212 582-9500
   Fort Lauderdale *(G-4158)*

Studio98 LLC ....E...... 727 888-1211
   Clearwater *(G-1799)*

Studioplus LLC ....E...... 239 476-8888
   Fort Myers *(G-4609)*

Sunrise Wings LLC ....D...... 352 242-0567
   Clermont *(G-1892)*

Superbeo LLC ....E...... 614 256-7047
   Miami *(G-10349)*

◆ Superior Group Companies Inc ....C...... 727 397-9611
   Seminole *(G-16462)*

Surgical Capital Solutions ....E...... 727 784-3500
   Clearwater *(G-1810)*

Susan Gordon ....E...... 800 458-2549
   Miami *(G-10352)*

Sykes Acquisition LLC ....D...... 863 802-3000
   Lakeland *(G-7985)*

Sykes Enterprises Incorporated ....A...... 813 274-1000
   Tampa *(G-18355)*

Synchrony Bank ....A...... 866 419-4096
   Longwood *(G-8408)*

Synchrony Financial ....D...... 480 707-4747
   Altamonte Springs *(G-104)*

T-Concepts Solutions Inc ....E...... 786 301-8090
   Miami *(G-10360)*

Tampa Bay Cnvntion Vstors Bur ....E...... 813 223-1111
   Tampa *(G-18365)*

Tc Specialties Co ....E...... 407 855-8262
   Orlando *(G-13272)*

Tc Specialties Co ....E...... 904 281-2604
   Jacksonville *(G-6839)*

Tcom Nicaragua Virtual Agents ....E...... 951 764-7667
   Orlando *(G-13273)*

Team National Inc ....E...... 954 584-2151
   Davie *(G-2527)*

▼ Tech Packaging Inc ....E...... 904 288-6403
   Jacksonville *(G-6843)*

Techtrueup LLC ....C...... 813 393-9393
   Naples *(G-11317)*

Ted and Stans LLC ....E...... 305 213-2966
   Miami *(G-10370)*

Teleperformance Group Inc ....C...... 786 437-3294
   Miami Beach *(G-10666)*

Testing Matters Inc ....E...... 888 272-1633
   Jupiter *(G-7145)*

Thinkdirect Mktg Group Inc ....B...... 727 914-0300
   Clearwater *(G-1823)*

Tiaa Fsb Holdings Inc ....B...... 904 281-6000
   Jacksonville *(G-6852)*

Time Customer Service Inc ....C...... 352 620-8100
   Ocala *(G-11786)*

Time2shine Academy Inc ....E...... 202 430-3039
   Saint Augustine *(G-15506)*

▲ Tjm Promos Inc ....E...... 352 291-5334
   Ocala *(G-11787)*

Tms Health LLC ....B...... 561 226-5000
   Boca Raton *(G-840)*

Tomaida Inc ....E...... 201 686-2662
   Kissimmee *(G-7400)*

Touch Points Solutions LLC ....D...... 800 722-8783
   Tampa *(G-18430)*

Tpusa Inc ....E...... 954 720-4000
   North Lauderdale *(G-11483)*

Tpusa - Fhcs Inc ....C...... 772 398-2000
   Port Saint Lucie *(G-15173)*

◆ Traffic Brick Networks LLC ....E...... 561 304-9470
   Deerfield Beach *(G-2808)*

Traffic Safety Consultants Inc ....C...... 407 629-9551
   Longwood *(G-8411)*

Trajectory Inc ....E...... 239 217-6281
   Naples *(G-11327)*

Travel + Leisure Co ....C...... 407 626-5200
   Orlando *(G-13305)*

Trendmax LLC ....E...... 856 278-1003
   Sunrise *(G-16839)*

Triloma Seniors Housing LLC ....E...... 888 773-3526
   Winter Park *(G-19779)*

Trinity Council No 4839 ....C...... 561 742-4652
   Boynton Beach *(G-1040)*

▲ Tropicana Products Sales Inc ....D...... 941 747-4461
   Bradenton *(G-1196)*

Tru - Proof Inc ....E...... 305 270-6111
   Miami *(G-10412)*

U S Transnet Corporation ....D...... 386 274-2120
   Daytona Beach *(G-2681)*

Udeliver LLC ....E...... 813 703-0029
   Seffner *(G-16434)*

Ulliby LLC ....E...... 866 670-9187
   Tampa *(G-18456)*

Unifi Management LLC ....D...... 813 514-2797
   Tampa *(G-18458)*

◆ Unique Vacations Inc ....E...... 305 284-1300
   Miami *(G-10433)*

Unirush LLC ....E...... 727 828-3333
   Tampa *(G-18460)*

United States Agency ....C...... 305 437-7001
   Miami *(G-10441)*

United Tranzactions LLC ....C...... 954 431-5256
   Miramar *(G-10909)*

▲ United Trophy Manufacturing ....E...... 407 841-2525
   Orlando *(G-13342)*

Universal Designs Inc ....E...... 386 740-4700
   Deland *(G-2884)*

Universal Inspection Corp ....E...... 954 958-1200
   Fort Lauderdale *(G-4197)*

University of Miami ....D...... 305 284-4877
   Coral Gables *(G-2202)*

US Communications Industries ....E...... 772 468-7477
   Fort Pierce *(G-4747)*

US Remodelers Inc ....C...... 561 994-6081
   Boca Raton *(G-856)*

Usine Rotec Inc ....D...... 407 227-1153
   Orlando *(G-13364)*

Utility Meter Services Inc ....B...... 407 831-6669
   Casselberry *(G-1463)*

Vacation Capital Group MGT ....E...... 407 307-2794
   Miami *(G-10455)*

Valley Tank Testing LLC ....E...... 813 671-9065
   Apollo Beach *(G-143)*

Vertek LLC ....E...... 608 495-1109
   Boca Raton *(G-860)*

Vici Marketing LLC ....E...... 727 451-4964
   Largo *(G-8161)*

▲ Vigo Remittance Corp ....C...... 954 625-6878
   Fort Lauderdale *(G-4213)*

Village Doctors PA ....E...... 386 496-1236
   Lake Butler *(G-7510)*

◆ Villages of Lake-Sumter Inc ....A...... 352 753-2270
   Lady Lake *(G-7447)*

Virtual Dining Concepts LLC ....E...... 407 903-5500
   Orlando *(G-13379)*

Vsp Labs Inc ....C...... 954 975-8600
   Fort Lauderdale *(G-4216)*

Watermark Dlvry Solutions LLC ....D...... 732 995-3882
   Sarasota *(G-16072)*

Wb Interiors LLC ....E...... 239 244-9492
   Fort Myers *(G-4649)*

Wegman Associates Inc ....D...... 407 850-9191
   Orlando *(G-13414)*

West Flagler Associates Ltd ....C...... 305 649-3000
   Miami *(G-10496)*

West Mill Inc ....E...... 941 807-4428
   Bradenton *(G-1205)*

Western Repacking Lllp ....E...... 916 688-8443
   Immokalee *(G-5663)*

Weston Ale House LLC ....D...... 919 851-0858
   Weston *(G-19485)*

Whetstone Holdings LLC ....C...... 305 600-0114
   Doral *(G-3358)*

▼ Wiginton Corporation ....D...... 407 585-3200
   Sanford *(G-15995)*

▼ Wilderness Graphics Inc ....E...... 850 224-6414
   Tallahassee *(G-17175)*

Williams United Logistics LLC ....E...... 315 664-8620
   Lawtey *(G-8211)*

Worklife Financial Inc ....D...... 248 269-0060
   Sarasota *(G-16075)*

World of Conferencing Inc ....E...... 754 206-9966
   Fort Lauderdale *(G-4233)*

World Travel Partners Orlando ....E...... 407 839-0027
   Orlando *(G-13448)*

Ww Zephyrhills LLC ....D...... 813 780-8064
   Zephyrhills *(G-19857)*

Xact Acquisition LLC ....C...... 877 922-8877
   Orlando *(G-13464)*

Xcira LLC ....E...... 813 621-7881
   Tampa *(G-18570)*

▲ Yachting Promotions Inc ....D...... 954 764-7642
   Fort Lauderdale *(G-4237)*

Your Auction Inc ....E...... 727 572-8800
   Saint Petersburg *(G-15905)*

Zenith American Solutions Inc ....C...... 813 666-6900
   Tampa *(G-18576)*

Zeuz LLC ....D...... 305 944-3189
   North Miami Beach *(G-11539)*

Zigong Lntern Group Wrldwide L ....C...... 800 946-5213
   Kissimmee *(G-7416)*

Zulay LLC ....E...... 727 386-9117
   Clearwater *(G-1846)*

Zyscovich Inc ....D...... 305 372-5222
   Miami *(G-10532)*

75 AUTOMOTIVE REPAIR, SERVICES, AND PARKING

7513 Truck Rental & Leasing, Without Drivers

◆ Atlantic Ford Truck Sales Inc ....C...... 305 652-2336
   Miami *(G-9186)*

B & D Transportation Services ....D...... 239 768-1500
   Fort Myers *(G-4285)*

Budget Truck Rental LLC ....B...... 239 732-0439
   Naples *(G-11043)*

Budget Truck Rental LLC ....B...... 321 784-0634
   Cape Canaveral *(G-1353)*

Cross Street Service Inc ....E...... 904 781-2299
   Jacksonville *(G-6013)*

▲ Ferman Chevrolet Tarpon Sprng ....D...... 727 942-4800
   Tarpon Springs *(G-18584)*

General Truck Eqp & Trlr Sls ....E...... 904 389-5541
   Jacksonville *(G-6224)*

▼ Hertz Corporation ....A...... 239 301-7000
   Estero *(G-3460)*

▼ Matthews-Currie Ford Co ....D...... 941 488-6787
   Nokomis *(G-11463)*

Mike Erdman Toyota ....D...... 321 453-1313
   Merritt Island *(G-9041)*

Penske Corporation ....C...... 305 463-6006
   Medley *(G-8769)*

Penske Corporation ....C...... 863 216-5007
   Winter Haven *(G-19650)*

Pritchett Trucking Inc ....B...... 386 496-2630
   Lake Butler *(G-7509)*

◆ Rechtien Intl Trcks Inc ....C...... 305 888-0111
   Miami *(G-10187)*

Rollins Leasing LLC ....C...... 850 434-6663
   Pensacola *(G-14422)*

Rollins Leasing LLC ....D...... 813 623-3751
   Tampa *(G-18235)*

Rountree-Moore Motors LLC ....D...... 386 755-0630
   Lake City *(G-7545)*

Ryder Integrated Logistics Inc ....D...... 305 436-1578
   Miami *(G-10228)*

◆ Ryder Services Corporation ....C...... 305 500-3007
   Doral *(G-3302)*

Ryder System Inc ....A...... 305 500-3726
   Medley *(G-8776)*

◆ Ryder Truck Rental Inc ....A...... 305 500-3726
   Medley *(G-8777)*

Sutherlin Inc ....E...... 321 453-2050
   Merritt Island *(G-9050)*

Terminal Investment Corp ....E...... 904 751-6631
   Jacksonville *(G-6846)*

Thrifty LLC ....D...... 239 301-7000
   Estero *(G-3482)*

Thrifty Rent-A-Car System Inc ....B...... 239 301-7000
   Estero *(G-3485)*

U-Haul Co of Wyoming Inc ....E...... 954 946-4532
   Pompano Beach *(G-14933)*

7514 Passenger Car Rental

212 LLC ....E...... 954 946-2500
   Fort Lauderdale *(G-3563)*

Advantage Opco LLC ....D...... 239 768-7092
   Fort Myers *(G-4253)*

▼ Air and Sea Rent-A-Car Inc ....E...... 954 764-1008
   Jacksonville *(G-5755)*

Alamo Rental (us) Inc ....E 561 951-3706
West Palm Beach (G-19025)

Alamo Rental (us) Inc ....E 239 768-2424
Fort Myers (G-4257)

Avis Rent A Car System Inc ....E 954 431-4217
Fort Lauderdale (G-3621)

Avis Rental Car Systems ....B 407 660-1950
Maitland (G-8503)

Avis Rental Car Systems ....C 863 687-8446
Lakeland (G-7807)

B & D Transportation Services ....D 239 768-1500
Fort Myers (G-4285)

Budget Truck Rental LLC ....B 239 732-0439
Naples (G-11043)

Budget Truck Rental LLC ....B 321 784-0634
Cape Canaveral (G-1353)

Dollar Rent A Car Inc ....E 904 741-4444
Jacksonville (G-6077)

▼ Dollar Rent A Car Inc ....C 239 301-7000
Estero (G-3451)

Dollar Thrifty Auto Group Inc ....A 239 301-7000
Estero (G-3452)

▼ Dtg Operations Inc ....D 239 301-7000
Estero (G-3453)

Enterprise Leasing Co Fla LLC..........E 904 798-0035
Jacksonville (G-6122)

Enterprise Leasing Co Fla LLC..........E 954 564-0824
Fort Lauderdale (G-3773)

◆ Enterprise Leasing Co Fla LLC ......E 813 887-4299
Tampa (G-17635)

Enterprise Lsg Co Orlando LLC.........D 407 447-7999
Orlando (G-12472)

Enterprise Rnt—car Boston LLC.........E 386 437-0350
Palm Coast (G-13820)

Fox Rent A Car Inc ....D 813 337-0950
Tampa (G-17709)

Fox Rent A Car Inc ....D 310 342-5155
Fort Myers (G-4403)

Fox Rent A Car Inc ....D 310 342-5155
Dania (G-2415)

Golds Angel Group Inc ....C 786 350-3804
North Miami (G-11493)

▼ Hertz Corporation ....A 239 301-7000
Estero (G-3460)

Hertz Corporation ....E 239 552-5800
Naples (G-11163)

Hertz Global Holdings Inc ....A 239 301-7000
Estero (G-3462)

Hertz Puerto Rico Holdings Inc ....C 239 301-7000
Estero (G-3463)

▲ Hertz Technologies Inc ....A 239 301-7000
Estero (G-3464)

Marita Car Rental Inc ....D 716 632-4662
Odessa (G-11849)

Mike Erdman Toyota ....D 321 453-1313
Merritt Island (G-9041)

Royal Rent A Car Systems Fla ....E 305 871-3000
Miami (G-10223)

Supa Rentals LLC ....D 954 375-1477
Margate (G-8666)

Thrifty LLC ....D 239 301-7000
Estero (G-3482)

Thrifty Car Sales Inc ....D 239 301-7000
Estero (G-3483)

Thrifty Rent-A-Car System Inc...........B 239 301-7000
Estero (G-3485)

Trac Asia Pacific Inc ....D 239 301-7000
Estero (G-3486)

Van Rental Services LLC ....E 813 282-8619
Tampa (G-18494)

7515 Passenger Car Leasing

Advantage Opco LLC ....D 239 768-7092
Fort Myers (G-4253)

Braman Motor Cars..........................D 561 966-5000
Greenacres (G-5070)

▼ Courtesy Chrysler Jeep ....E 813 620-4300
Tampa (G-17540)

▼ Dadeland Dodge Inc ....D 305 278-9994
Miami (G-9451)

▼ Ed Howard Lincoln Mercury ....E 941 921-4402
Sarasota (G-16144)

◆ Enterprise Leasing Co Fla LLC ......E 813 887-4299
Tampa (G-17635)

▲ Ferman Chevrolet Tarpon Sprng ......D 727 942-4800
Tarpon Springs (G-18584)

Ferman Chevrolet Tarpon Sprng ....D 727 847-5555
New Port Richey (G-11374)

▼ Gordon Stewart Chevrolet Inc ....D 813 969-2600
Tampa (G-17743)

▼ Gulf Management Inc ....C 813 888-8221
Tampa (G-17774)

▼ Hertz Corporation ....A 239 301-7000
Estero (G-3460)

▼ JM Auto Inc ....B 954 972-2200
Margate (G-8654)

Kelley Automotive Inc ....E 954 455-8855
Fort Lauderdale (G-3918)

Lloyd Buick Cadillac ....D 386 252-3755
Daytona Beach (G-2627)

▼ Matthews-Currie Ford Co ....D 941 488-6787
Nokomis (G-11463)

▼ Mazda of North Miami ....D 305 654-3825
Miami (G-9912)

Mike Erdman Toyota ....D 321 453-1313
Merritt Island (G-9041)

▼ Mutz Motors Ltd Partnership ....C 863 682-1100
Lakeland (G-7929)

▼ Rick Case Hyundai Inc ....D 954 581-5885
Plantation (G-14701)

▼ Roger Dean Enterprises Inc ....C 561 683-8100
West Palm Beach (G-19344)

Scott-Mcrae Auto Group Inc ....D 904 354-4000
Jacksonville (G-6701)

Stuart Jeep Inc ....E 772 220-3600
Stuart (G-16672)

Thrifty LLC ....D 239 301-7000
Estero (G-3482)

Thrifty Rent-A-Car System Inc..........D 239 301-7000
Estero (G-3485)

7519 Utility Trailers & Recreational Vehicle Rental

Budget Truck Rental LLC ....B 239 732-0439
Naples (G-11043)

Budget Truck Rental LLC ....B 321 784-0634
Cape Canaveral (G-1353)

◆ Rechtien Intl Trcks Inc ....C 305 888-0111
Miami (G-10187)

Rollins Leasing LLC ....C 850 434-6663
Pensacola (G-14422)

7521 Automobile Parking Lots & Garages

Airport Parking LLC........................E 407 855-5899
Orlando (G-12088)

Ameripark LLC ....B 954 681-4264
Fort Lauderdale (G-3605)

Central Parking System of Conn ....C 305 373-4703
Miami (G-9347)

Central Parking System of Conn ....E 904 356-9841
Jacksonville (G-5924)

City Miami Off St Prkg Auth ....D 305 648-1465
Miami (G-9370)

Courtesy Valet Corporation ....D 844 727-5872
Seminole (G-16445)

First Class Prkg Systems LLC ....C 305 531-4466
North Miami (G-11490)

Fort Lauderdale Trnsp Inc ....B 954 359-0200
Fort Lauderdale (G-3803)

▲ Metromont Corp ....A 863 440-5400
Bartow (G-327)

Miami Parking Authority ....C 305 579-8102
Miami (G-9979)

Moorecars LLC ....E 678 472-9114
Boynton Beach (G-1018)

One Parking Inc ....E 561 833-7222
West Palm Beach (G-19294)

One Parking 700 Inc ....D 561 833-7222
West Palm Beach (G-19295)

Parking Company America Inc ....E 407 251-7555
Orlando (G-13007)

Reef Global Inc ....D 888 695-7275
Miami (G-10191)

Seven-One-Seven Prkg Svcs Inc ....A 813 228-7722
Tampa (G-18273)

Universal Cy Dev Partners Ltd ....D 407 363-8000
Orlando (G-13346)

7532 Top, Body & Upholstery Repair & Paint Shops

◆ Bill Seidle Imports Inc ....C 954 463-9533
Doral (G-3137)

Boyd Group (us) Inc ....D 850 422-3699
Tallahassee (G-16894)

Boyd Group (us) Inc ....E 321 639-3230
Cocoa (G-1919)

Boyd Group (us) Inc ....E 321 804-8354
Longwood (G-8347)

Braman Motor Cars..........................D 561 966-5000
Greenacres (G-5070)

City Collision Gainesville Inc ....E 352 338-3544
Gainesville (G-4858)

Classic Collision LLC ....E 772 879-4447
Port Saint Lucie (G-15128)

Classic Collision LLC ....D 321 768-2605
Palm Bay (G-13616)

Classic Collision LLC ....E 954 837-8333
Pompano Beach (G-14773)

Classic Collision LLC ....D 561 265-2333
Delray Beach (G-2931)

Classic Collision LLC ....D 954 947-5701
Fort Lauderdale (G-3697)

Classic Collision LLC ....D 305 513-4833
Sweetwater (G-16857)

Classic Collision LLC ....E 772 778-0443
Vero Beach (G-18846)

Classic Collision LLC ....E 772 286-2800
Stuart (G-16604)

Classic Collision LLC ....E 954 906-4000
Boca Raton (G-517)

Classic Collision LLC ....D 305 255-2427
Miami (G-9377)

Classic Collision LLC ....E 954 772-0313
Fort Lauderdale (G-3698)

Classic Collision LLC ....E 954 772-0313
Fort Lauderdale (G-3699)

Classic Soft Trim Inc ....E 813 626-7113
Tampa (G-17487)

Countyline Auto Center Inc ....E 954 443-2020
Pembroke Pines (G-14145)

▼ Dadeland Dodge Inc ....D 305 278-9994
Miami (G-9451)

Daytona Bch Lncoln Mercury Inc ....D 386 258-5216
Daytona Beach (G-2573)

▼ Daytona Br-Gd Inc ....C 888 244-7475
Daytona Beach (G-2579)

Don Mealey Chevrolet Inc ....D 352 394-6176
Clermont (G-1866)

Donald Moss Corp ....E 561 996-4203
South Bay (G-16477)

◆ Em Sil Enterprises Inc ....E 954 979-9422
Pompano Beach (G-14799)

▼ Esserman Nissan Ltd ....D 305 626-2600
Miami Gardens (G-10682)

Expressway Motorcars Inc ....C 305 455-1580
Doral (G-3198)

Florida Service Painting Inc ....C 305 364-5092
Miami Lakes (G-10732)

◆ Gar-P Industries Inc ....E 305 888-7252
Medley (G-8736)

▼ Gordon Stewart Chevrolet Inc ....D 813 969-2600
Tampa (G-17743)

H Greg Collision and Service ....D 305 677-0900
Doral (G-3220)

Kelley Automotive Inc ....E 954 455-8855
Fort Lauderdale (G-3918)

Lloyd Buick Cadillac ....D 386 252-3755
Daytona Beach (G-2627)

Master Collision Repair Inc ....E 321 725-7450
West Melbourne (G-19012)

Master Collision Repair Inc ....E 813 933-7641
Tampa (G-18000)

Master Collision Repair Inc ....E 813 907-9481
Lutz (G-8447)

▼ Matthews-Currie Ford Co ....D 941 488-6787
Nokomis (G-11463)

Mazda Motor of America Inc ....C 954 797-1600
Davie (G-2499)

▼ Midway Mall Ford Inc ....C 305 266-3000
Miami (G-10002)

Mullinax Ford South Inc ....E 954 972-7200
Margate (G-8658)

▼ Mutz Motors Ltd Partnership ....C 863 682-1100
Lakeland (G-7929)

Parks Automotive Group Inc ....E 386 734-2184
Deland (G-2876)

Plaza-Lincoln Mercury Inc ....C 352 787-1255
Leesburg (G-8266)

Prestige Ford Inc ....D 321 248-6235
Mount Dora (G-10961)

▼ Reed Motors Inc ....C 407 297-7333
Orlando (G-13091)

Ri/Bb Acquisition Corp ....D 407 277-6639
Orlando (G-13108)

▼ Roger Dean Enterprises Inc ....C 561 683-8100
West Palm Beach (G-19344)

Rountree-Moore Motors LLC ....D 386 755-0630
Lake City (G-7545)

Sonic Automotive - Bondesen ....C 386 734-2661
Deland (G-2881)
South Motor Company Dade Cnty ....C 305 232-0790
Miami (G-10305)
Sun State Ford Inc ....E 407 297-8144
Orlando (G-13248)
▼ Sun State Intl Trcks LLC ....D 813 621-1331
Tampa (G-18344)
Suncoast Motorsports Group Inc ....D 941 366-7800
Sarasota (G-16338)
▼ Terry Taylor Ford Company ....C 386 274-6700
Daytona Beach (G-2674)
▼ Triangle Auto Center Inc ....C 954 966-2160
Hollywood (G-5543)
Tropical Cadillac Oldsmobile ....E 941 755-8922
Bradenton (G-1195)
Venice Nissan Dodge ....E 941 485-1531
Venice (G-18816)
Wade Rulerson Pontiac GMC Trck ....D 352 372-2583
Gainesville (G-5027)
◆ Wayne Ford Akers Inc ....C 561 540-9601
Lake Worth Beach (G-7777)
Weston Auto Inc ....D 954 385-8696
Sunrise (G-16847)
▼ Yardley Car Company ....D 954 327-4000
Plantation (G-14723)

7533 Automotive Exhaust System Repair Shops

▲ Midas Inc ....C 561 383-3100
Palm Beach Gardens (G-13753)
▲ Midas International LLC ....C 561 383-3100
Palm Beach Gardens (G-13754)

7534 Tire Retreading & Repair Shops

Day & Night Tire LLC ....E 863 648-2336
Lakeland (G-7849)
▼ Earl W Colvard Inc ....D 386 734-6447
Deland (G-2857)
▼ Tbc Retail Group Inc ....D 561 383-3000
Palm Beach Gardens (G-13775)

7536 Automotive Glass Replacement Shops

Boyd Group (us) Inc ....E 321 639-3230
Cocoa (G-1919)
Safelite Glass Corp ....D 407 563-4220
Orlando (G-13158)

7537 Automotive Transmission Repair Shops

▼ American Transm Auto Exch ....D 904 396-3766
Jacksonville (G-5794)
Factory Transmissions Inc ....D 407 420-5800
Orlando (G-12486)
◆ Seal Aftermarket Products LLC ......E 954 364-2400
Pembroke Park (G-14125)

7538 General Automotive Repair Shop

595 Repair Shop LLC ....D 954 357-1480
Davie (G-2452)
AAA of Caribbean Inc ....E 813 289-5000
Tampa (G-17219)
▼ Abraham Chevrolet-Tampa Inc ......C 813 238-1610
Tampa (G-17226)
▼ Advantage Stuart Ford Inc ....D 772 287-0955
Stuart (G-16586)
Alan Jay Ford Lincoln Mercury ....E 863 314-5361
Sebring (G-16388)
▼ American Transm Auto Exch ....D 904 396-3766
Jacksonville (G-5794)
An Motors On Federal Hwy LLC ....D 954 390-6400
Fort Lauderdale (G-3609)
▼ Arlington Motor Company Inc ....C 904 721-3000
Jacksonville (G-5805)
◆ Atlantic Ford Truck Sales Inc ....C 305 652-2336
Miami (G-9186)
◆ B O O Inc ....D 954 985-2424
Pembroke Pines (G-14133)
Bartow Ford Co ....C 863 533-0425
Bartow (G-311)
▼ Bgp Auto LLC ....D 386 447-3380
Palm Coast (G-13812)
▼ Bill Currie Ford Inc ....B 813 872-5555
Tampa (G-17364)
Bill Jarrett Ford Inc ....D 863 453-0280
Avon Park (G-288)
◆ Bill Seidle Imports Inc ....C 954 463-9533
Doral (G-3137)
◆ Bill Ussery Motors Body Sp Inc ....C 305 445-8593
Coral Gables (G-2053)

▼ Boast Motors Inc ....D 941 755-8585
Bradenton (G-1060)
Bob Lees Inc ....E 727 822-3981
Saint Petersburg (G-15599)
▼ Bob Steele Chevrolet Inc ....D 321 632-6700
Cocoa (G-1918)
▼ Bob Taylor Chevrolet Inc ....D 239 591-0991
Naples (G-11036)
▼ Boniface and Company Inc ....E 855 821-6650
Melbourne (G-8827)
Boomerang Consulting Group LLC ....D 352 368-2451
Ocala (G-11643)
Braman Motor Cars ....D 561 966-5000
Greenacres (G-5070)
Carmax Inc ....B 407 240-1700
Orlando (G-12242)
Carpenters Campers Inc ....E 850 477-6666
Pensacola (G-14249)
Central Fla Lincoln Mercury ....D 407 841-4550
Orlando (G-12270)
▼ Century Buick Inc ....D 813 872-7746
Tampa (G-17449)
Classic Car Co Inc ....D 407 291-6090
Orlando (G-12312)
▲ Copans Motors Inc ....C 954 946-4020
Pompano Beach (G-14783)
County of Broward ....C 954 357-5471
Fort Lauderdale (G-3727)
County of Orange ....D 407 836-8238
Orlando (G-12374)
County of Volusia ....C 386 254-1595
Daytona Beach (G-2566)
▼ Courtesy Chrysler Jeep ....E 813 620-4300
Tampa (G-17540)
▼ Cox Chevrolet Incorporated ....D 888 350-4514
Bradenton (G-1087)
Cross Street Service Inc ....E 904 781-2299
Jacksonville (G-6013)
▼ Cspi Inc ....C 813 626-1101
Tampa (G-17555)
▼ Dadeland Dodge Inc ....D 305 278-9994
Miami (G-9451)
▼ Desoto Automotive Entps Inc ....D 863 494-4848
Arcadia (G-227)
Dodge Chrysler Jeep Wnter Hven ....D 888 612-3182
Winter Haven (G-19623)
Don Gasgarth Ford Inc ....E 941 625-6141
Port Charlotte (G-15029)
Donald Moss Corp ....E 561 996-4203
South Bay (G-16477)
▼ Duval Motor Company Inc ....C 904 387-6541
Jacksonville (G-6095)
▼ Elder Ford of Tampa LLC ....D 888 218-6746
Tampa (G-17618)
▼ Esserman Nissan Ltd ....D 305 626-2600
Miami Gardens (G-10682)
▼ Family Ford Inc ....C 813 246-3673
Tampa (G-17647)
▲ Ferman Chevrolet Tarpon Sprng ....D 727 942-4800
Tarpon Springs (G-18584)
▼ Ferman Chevrolet Tarpon Sprng ....D 727 847-5555
New Port Richey (G-11374)
Ferman Motor Car Company Inc ......B 813 623-2411
Tampa (G-17655)
Ferman Motor Car Company Inc ......B 813 933-6641
Lutz (G-8441)
Fidelity Manufacturing LLC ....E 352 414-4700
Ocala (G-11681)
Firstgroup America Inc ....B 727 847-8169
New Port Richey (G-11375)
Florida Lincoln North Company ....D 904 642-4100
Jacksonville (G-6193)
Florida Tire Inc ....D 352 536-1177
Clermont (G-1870)
Ford of Ocala Inc ....C 352 732-4800
Ocala (G-11692)
Gator Chrysler Plymouth Inc ....D 321 727-7711
Melbourne (G-8890)
General Truck Eqp & Trlr Sls ....E 904 389-5541
Jacksonville (G-6224)
▼ Gettel Automotive Inc ....C 941 225-7567
Bradenton (G-1111)
▼ Gordon Stewart Chevrolet Inc ....D 813 969-2600
Tampa (G-17743)
Group 1 Automotive Inc ....D 305 952-5900
North Miami (G-11494)
Gt Daytona LLC ....D 386 258-3311
Daytona Beach (G-2604)
▼ Gulf Management Inc ....C 813 888-8221
Tampa (G-17774)

◆ Gus Machado Ford Inc ....C 305 796-7833
Hialeah (G-5270)
Hall-Mark Fire Apparatus Inc ....E 352 629-6305
Ocala (G-11696)
Hanania Automotive Corp ....D 904 777-5600
Jacksonville (G-6257)
▼ Hollywood Chrysler Plymuth Inc ....E 954 342-5080
Hollywood (G-5451)
▼ Hooley Family Management Inc ......E 954 584-2400
Plantation (G-14657)
Interlake Gulf Corp ....E 239 262-0405
Naples (G-11177)
Island Lincoln-Mercury Inc ....D 321 452-9220
Merritt Island (G-9034)
▼ Jarrett-Gordon Ford Inc ....D 863 422-1167
Davenport (G-2445)
Jarrett-Grdon Lincoln Ford Inc ....E 863 294-3571
Winter Haven (G-19637)
Jarrett-Scott Ford Inc ....D 863 686-2318
Plant City (G-14565)
▼ Jon Hall Chevrolet Inc ....C 386 255-4444
Daytona Beach (G-2622)
Justins Diesel & Auto Repr LLC ......D 850 682-6067
Holt (G-5552)
Kelley Automotive Inc ....E 954 455-8855
Fort Lauderdale (G-3918)
Kelly Ford Inc ....D 888 902-6849
Melbourne (G-8915)
King Motor Center Et AI ....E 407 240-3800
Orlando (G-12730)
King Motor Company South Fla ....E 954 421-3330
Deerfield Beach (G-2763)
Knowles On Site Repair Inc ....E 850 994-4211
Pensacola (G-14338)
Kovac Automotive Davie Inc ....E 954 792-7357
Davie (G-2496)
Lane Pontiac-Buick-Gmc Inc ....E 321 724-5263
Indialantic (G-5666)
Larry Dimmitt Cadillac Inc ....C 727 797-7070
Clearwater (G-1695)
▼ Lincoln Pines Ford ....E 954 443-7000
Pembroke Pines (G-14161)
Lloyd Buick Cadillac ....D 386 252-3755
Daytona Beach (G-2627)
Love Automotive Inc ....D 352 341-0018
Inverness (G-5695)
Lucas Investments Inc ....D 904 737-0804
Jacksonville (G-6451)
Lynch Automotive Group Inc ....D 904 642-6060
Jacksonville (G-6454)
▼ Matthews-Currie Ford Co ....D 941 488-6787
Nokomis (G-11463)
▼ Mazda of North Miami ....D 305 654-3825
Miami (G-9912)
Mercedes Benz of Naples ....D 239 643-5007
Naples (G-11212)
Miami Automobile Center Corp ....E 580 226-2628
Miami (G-9953)
▼ Midway Mall Ford Inc ....C 305 266-3000
Miami (G-10002)
Monro Inc ....D 239 643-4415
Naples (G-11217)
▼ Mullinax Ford Central Fla Inc ....D 407 889-7600
Apopka (G-203)
▼ Mullinax Ford-Mercury Inc ....E 888 261-1363
New Smyrna Beach (G-11421)
Murray Ford-Mercury Inc ....D 904 964-7200
Starke (G-16579)
▼ Mutz Motors Ltd Partnership ....C 863 682-1100
Lakeland (G-7929)
◆ Nationwide Lift Trucks Inc ....E 954 922-4645
Hollywood (G-5479)
Nextran Corporation ....D 904 354-3721
Miami (G-10047)
Nextran Corporation ....D 407 240-0452
Orlando (G-12913)
◆ Nextran Corporation ....D 904 354-3721
Jacksonville (G-6542)
Nick Nicholas Ford Inc ....D 352 489-0661
Inverness (G-5697)
◆ Ocean Cadillac Inc ....D 305 864-2271
Miami (G-10060)
Orion Solutions LLC ....E 904 394-0934
Jacksonville (G-6569)
▼ Orlando Automotive LLC ....B 407 240-3800
Orlando (G-12941)
▲ Osman Automotive Company Inc ....D 321 725-1100
Melbourne (G-8954)
Packer Family Ltd Partnr II ....D 561 790-1100
Royal Palm Beach (G-15387)

◆ Packer Family Ltd Partnr II ....C 561 689-6550
West Palm Beach **(G-19303)**

Palm Bay Ford Inc...............................D 321 722-9000
Palm Bay **(G-13633)**

Palm Chevrolet Inc..............................C 352 629-8011
Ocala **(G-11758)**

Paul Clark Ford-Mercury Inc ....E 904 225-3673
Yulee **(G-19819)**

◆ Pblm Inc ....D 561 683-8500
West Palm Beach **(G-19321)**

Pep Boys - Mnny Moe Jack Del L ....E 305 252-7311
Cutler Bay **(G-2374)**

Pep Boys - Mnny Moe Jack Del L ....E 305 557-4498
Hialeah **(G-5311)**

Pep Boys - Mnny Moe Jack Del L ....D 407 339-3385
Altamonte Springs **(G-90)**

Pep Boys - Mnny Moe Jack Del L ....D 407 851-2626
Orlando **(G-13021)**

Pep Boys - Mnny Moe Jack Del L ....E 954 784-7676
Pompano Beach **(G-14875)**

Pep Boys - Mnny Moe Jack Del L ....D 239 939-5447
Fort Myers **(G-4539)**

Pep Boys - Mnny Moe Jack Del L ....E 954 985-9440
Hollywood **(G-5491)**

Plaza-Lincoln Mercury Inc...............C 352 787-1255
Leesburg **(G-8266)**

Potamkin Automotive Group Inc ....B 305 470-8000
Doral **(G-3293)**

Powers Radiator Inc ....E 239 332-0036
Fort Myers **(G-4545)**

Prestige Ford Inc...............................D 321 248-6235
Mount Dora **(G-10961)**

◆ R P M Diesel Engine Co ....D 800 660-6304
Fort Lauderdale **(G-4076)**

▼ R V World Inc of Nokomis ....D 941 966-4800
Nokomis **(G-11465)**

◆ Raneys Truck Parts Inc ....D 352 789-6701
Ocala **(G-11764)**

◆ Rechtien Intl Trcks Inc ....C 305 888-0111
Miami **(G-10187)**

Regency Motor Company Inc ....D 904 725-8000
Jacksonville **(G-6648)**

▼ Rick Case Hyundai Inc ....E 954 581-5885
Plantation **(G-14701)**

Rick Case Sunrise LLC......................E 954 377-7413
Sunrise **(G-16817)**

▼ Roger Dean Enterprises Inc ....C 561 683-8100
West Palm Beach **(G-19344)**

Rountree-Moore Motors LLC...............D 386 755-0630
Lake City **(G-7545)**

Rush Truck Centers Florida Inc............E 786 433-7600
Miami **(G-10227)**

◆ Ryder Services Corporation ....C 305 500-3007
Doral **(G-3302)**

◆ Sam Galloway Ford Inc ....B 888 699-0916
Fort Myers **(G-4582)**

▲ Sarasota 500 LLC...........................D 941 296-6870
Sarasota **(G-16293)**

Saunders Engine and Eqp Co Inc ....D 850 763-7656
Panama City **(G-14068)**

▼ Sawgrass Ford Inc ....C 954 851-9100
Sunrise **(G-16821)**

Scott-Mcrae Auto Group Inc ....D 813 935-8585
Tampa **(G-18252)**

Smith Chevy Oldsmbile Cadillac ....E 479 646-7301
Cocoa **(G-1955)**

▼ Sonic Atomotive-Clearwater Inc ....C 727 799-1234
Clearwater **(G-1791)**

▼ South Orlando Imports Inc ....E 407 851-8510
Orlando **(G-13217)**

▼ Southast Pwr Systems Tampa Inc...E 813 623-1551
Tampa **(G-18307)**

Southast Pwr Systems Tampa Inc........D 239 694-4197
Fort Myers **(G-4598)**

▼ Southeast Power Systems Inc ....E 407 293-7971
Orlando **(G-13219)**

▼ Steele Truck Center Inc ....D 239 334-7300
Fort Myers **(G-4606)**

Steve Moore Chevrolet LLC................C 561 433-5757
Greenacres **(G-5081)**

Stuart Jeep Inc ....E 772 220-3600
Stuart **(G-16672)**

▼ Sun Imports Inc ....D 941 923-3413
Sarasota **(G-16336)**

Suncoast Motorsports Group Inc ....D 941 366-7800
Sarasota **(G-16338)**

▼ Sunrise Ford Company ....D 772 461-6000
Fort Pierce **(G-4743)**

Sutherlin Inc ....E 321 453-2050
Merritt Island **(G-9050)**

Tallahssee Auto Invstors I LLC...........D 850 877-1171
Tallahassee **(G-17145)**

◆ Tbc Retail Group Inc ....D 561 383-3000
Palm Beach Gardens **(G-13775)**

Tc Motorcycles LLC...........................E 904 771-8244
Jacksonville **(G-6838)**

▼ Terry Taylor Ford Company ....C 386 274-6700
Daytona Beach **(G-2674)**

Tom Nehl Truck Company....................E 386 755-9527
Lake City **(G-7549)**

▼ Tom Nehl Truck Company ....C 904 389-3653
Jacksonville **(G-6859)**

▲ Topline Automotive Engrg Inc ....D 352 799-4668
Brooksville **(G-1316)**

University Sales and Service ....D 850 878-3171
Tallahassee **(G-17167)**

Wade Rulerson Pontiac GMC Trck ....D 352 372-2583
Gainesville **(G-5027)**

Wallace International Trucks ....E 239 334-1000
Fort Myers **(G-4645)**

Walmart Inc.......................................C 352 596-0797
Brooksville **(G-1319)**

Walmart Inc.......................................C 863 467-7169
Okeechobee **(G-11883)**

▼ Warren Henry Automobiles Inc.........C 305 690-6010
Miami **(G-10490)**

◆ Wayne Ford Akers Inc ....D 561 540-9601
Lake Worth Beach **(G-7777)**

Webb Automotive Group Inc................E 954 769-7000
Fort Lauderdale **(G-4221)**

Weston Auto Inc.................................D 954 385-8696
Sunrise **(G-16847)**

Wlofm Corp..E 386 362-1112
Live Oak **(G-8322)**

▼ Yardley Car Company ....D 954 327-4000
Plantation **(G-14723)**

▼ Zabatt Engine Services Inc ....D 904 384-4505
Jacksonville **(G-6965)**

7539 Automotive Repair Shops, NEC

All American Air and Elc Inc ....D 352 629-1211
Ocala **(G-11629)**

▼ Amera Trail Inc ....E 407 892-1100
Saint Cloud **(G-15517)**

Atlantic Tower Services Inc ....D 407 423-9071
Orlando **(G-12150)**

Automotive Parts & Machine ....D 305 254-8356
Miami **(G-9193)**

▼ Avalanche Corporation ....D 800 708-0087
Brooksville **(G-1270)**

Boniface-Hiers Motors LLC.................D 321 723-3611
Melbourne **(G-8828)**

Capitol City Travel Center Inc ....D 850 997-3538
Lloyd **(G-8323)**

Carlisle Motors LLC...........................D 727 231-1323
Saint Petersburg **(G-15612)**

Classic Car Co Inc ....D 407 291-6090
Orlando **(G-12312)**

Coachcrafters Inc..............................E 352 742-8111
Tavares **(G-18603)**

Cortez Heating and AC Inc ....D 941 755-5211
Palmetto **(G-13909)**

County of Pinellas..............................D 727 582-2150
Largo **(G-8088)**

Dealer Profit Systems Inc ....C 813 935-1500
Tampa **(G-17579)**

◆ Delray Motors Inc ....C 561 454-1800
Delray Beach **(G-2945)**

Dkw Industries Inc ....E 954 714-8199
Oakland Park **(G-11593)**

Eci Communications Inc ....D 561 416-5880
Boca Raton **(G-563)**

Edd Helms Group Inc ....E 305 653-2520
Sunrise **(G-16767)**

Emerald Coast Rv Center LLC.............D 850 939-1064
Gulf Breeze **(G-5112)**

Ernie Palmer Inc................................D 904 389-4561
Jacksonville **(G-6130)**

Fine Line Construction & Elc...............D 954 786-8006
Pompano Beach **(G-14803)**

Firstgroup America Inc.......................A 954 497-3665
Fort Lauderdale **(G-3789)**

▼ Lehman Hyundai Subaru Inc ....C 305 653-7111
Miami **(G-9855)**

McGee Tire Stores Inc ....D 813 968-2657
Tampa **(G-18008)**

Murphy Cadillac Inc ....E 321 727-2830
Melbourne **(G-8945)**

▼ Ocean Auto Center Inc ....D 786 464-1100
Doral **(G-3280)**

Orange Buick - GMC Truck ....D 407 295-8100
Orlando **(G-12935)**

▼ Orlando Dodge Inc ....D 407 299-1120
Orlando **(G-12947)**

Pep Boys - Mnny Moe Jack Del L ....D 850 457-1907
Pensacola **(G-14412)**

Pep Boys - Mnny Moe Jack Del L ....D 215 430-9000
Tampa **(G-18138)**

▼ Sheehan Pontiac G M A C Inc ....D 954 943-2200
Pompano Beach **(G-14896)**

▼ Southeast Power Systems Inc ....E 407 293-7971
Orlando **(G-13219)**

Suncoast Motorsports Group Inc..........D 941 366-7800
Sarasota **(G-16338)**

Tallahassee Hyundai LLC....................C 850 575-1000
Tallahassee **(G-17127)**

Techni-Car Inc ....C 800 886-0022
Oldsmar **(G-11930)**

Terminal Service Company ....C 850 739-5702
Tallahassee **(G-17155)**

▼ Tom Endicott Buick Inc ....E 954 781-7700
Pompano Beach **(G-14924)**

▼ Tropical Ford Inc ....D 407 851-3800
Orlando **(G-13311)**

Try-Cor Electric Inc ....D 407 839-4699
Orlando **(G-13317)**

Weston Auto Inc.................................D 954 385-8696
Sunrise **(G-16847)**

▼ William Lehman and Assoc Inc .....E 305 652-5252
Miami **(G-10505)**

WW Gay Fire Protection Inc................C 904 387-7973
Jacksonville **(G-6946)**

7542 Car Washes

Anderson Ventures Inc........................D 727 897-9151
Saint Petersburg **(G-15570)**

Blue Beacon USA LP II........................D 772 429-1459
Fort Pierce **(G-4683)**

Car Spa Inc ....C 904 723-5626
Jacksonville **(G-5902)**

Car Wash Partners Inc........................B 407 203-0993
Orlando **(G-12231)**

Car Wash Partners Inc........................C 813 933-6661
Tampa **(G-17417)**

Car Wash Partners Inc........................C 407 207-1294
Orlando **(G-12232)**

Car Wash Partners Inc........................C 407 260-0335
Fern Park **(G-3511)**

Car Wash Partners Inc........................C 407 324-0443
Sanford **(G-15929)**

Car Wash Partners Inc........................E 813 754-0777
Plant City **(G-14548)**

Decker Car Wash Inc ....D 954 396-1317
Fort Lauderdale **(G-3756)**

Golden Gate of Orlando LLC ....D 407 351-1370
Orlando **(G-12579)**

Grand Prix Ltd ....E 727 446-9274
Clearwater **(G-1655)**

Jal Chemical Co Inc ....E 407 293-3055
Orlando **(G-12699)**

Muse Lucky ....E 863 494-0202
Arcadia **(G-232)**

Pelican Car Wash Inc.........................E 727 787-9274
Palm Harbor **(G-13876)**

Pristine & Clean Inc ....E 407 896-6366
Orlando **(G-13061)**

Speedy Car Wash Inc ....E 850 785-9274
Panama City **(G-14075)**

Weston Auto Inc.................................D 954 385-8696
Sunrise **(G-16847)**

7549 Automotive Svcs, Except Repair & Car Washes

A Superior Towing Company ....B 800 793-0841
Davie **(G-2453)**

An Dealership Holding Corp ....D 954 769-7000
Fort Lauderdale **(G-3608)**

Anderson Ventures Inc........................D 727 897-9151
Saint Petersburg **(G-15570)**

Arlington Salvage & Wrecker Co...........D 904 744-4933
Jacksonville **(G-5806)**

Boyd Group (us) Inc ....D 850 422-3699
Tallahassee **(G-16894)**

Broward County Public Schools ....E 754 321-4460
Oakland Park **(G-11586)**

Cae Doss Aviation Inc ....D 904 778-1611
Jacksonville **(G-5892)**

Car Wash Partners Inc........................E 813 754-0777
Plant City **(G-14548)**

City of Saint Petersburg ....D...... 727 893-7286
Saint Petersburg *(G-15628)*

Cjd Northpark LLC ....D...... 407 878-7710
Orlando *(G-12307)*

Donald Moss Corp ....E...... 561 996-4203
South Bay *(G-16477)*

Ed Morse Lakeland LLC ....A...... 863 274-7240
Tampa *(G-17614)*

Humble Imports Inc ....E...... 407 483-4825
Kissimmee *(G-7324)*

Hyundai New Port Richey LLC ....E...... 727 569-0999
New Port Richey *(G-11388)*

Jal Chemical Co Inc ....E...... 407 293-3055
Orlando *(G-12699)*

Jim Jenkins ....E...... 863 688-3244
Lakeland *(G-7891)*

Kauffs of Miami Inc ....D...... 305 685-7593
Opa Locka *(G-11948)*

Off Lease Only Inc ....C...... 561 812-7157
West Palm Beach *(G-19289)*

Overspray Rmval Spcialsts Inc ....E...... 800 835-5858
Sarasota *(G-16253)*

Pep Boys - Mnny Moe Jack Del L ....E...... 954 985-9440
Hollywood *(G-5491)*

Pep Boys - Mnny Moe Jack Del L ....D...... 813 689-0700
Brandon *(G-1249)*

Pep Boys - Mnny Moe Jack Del L ....D...... 407 339-3385
Altamonte Springs *(G-90)*

Pep Boys - Mnny Moe Jack Del L ....E...... 407 851-2626
Orlando *(G-13021)*

Pep Boys - Mnny Moe Jack Del L ....E...... 954 784-7676
Pompano Beach *(G-14875)*

Pep Boys - Mnny Moe Jack Del L ....E...... 305 252-7311
Cutler Bay *(G-2374)*

Pep Boys - Mnny Moe Jack Del L ....E...... 305 557-4498
Hialeah *(G-5311)*

Public Safety Supply LLC ....E...... 888 895-8745
Hialeah *(G-5314)*

Rick Case Enterprises Inc ....A...... 954 622-1706
Sunrise *(G-16816)*

Seabulk Towing Inc ....C...... 954 523-2200
Fort Lauderdale *(G-4108)*

Sears Roebuck and Co ....D...... 305 378-5195
Miami *(G-10253)*

Sears Roebuck and Co ....D...... 850 474-5428
Mary Esther *(G-8694)*

Sunshine Lube ....D...... 239 949-6031
Estero *(G-3480)*

76 MISCELLANEOUS REPAIR SERVICES

7622 Radio & TV Repair Shops

▲ Ghekko Networks Inc ....D...... 800 736-4397
Saint Petersburg *(G-15687)*

Kosse Partners I LLC ....D...... 352 314-0144
Leesburg *(G-8249)*

▼ Lengemann Corporation ....E...... 352 669-2111
Altoona *(G-118)*

National Service Source Inc ....C...... 321 328-1032
Melbourne *(G-8947)*

▲ Pro Sound Inc ....E...... 305 891-1000
North Miami *(G-11507)*

◆ Sound Advice Inc ....C...... 954 922-4434
Fort Lauderdale *(G-4138)*

Techni-Car Inc ....E...... 800 886-0022
Oldsmar *(G-11930)*

Williams Communications Inc ....E...... 850 385-1121
Tallahassee *(G-17176)*

7623 Refrigeration & Air Conditioning Svc & Repair Shop

ACR Sales and Service Inc ....E...... 407 299-9190
Apopka *(G-146)*

Advanced Refrigeration & A Inc ....C...... 407 679-0644
Orlando *(G-12058)*

Advanced Refrigeration & A Inc ....E...... 407 679-0644
Oldsmar *(G-11890)*

Air Advisors Inc ....E...... 561 383-5600
Loxahatchee *(G-8418)*

Air Flow Designs Inc ....D...... 407 831-3600
Saint Cloud *(G-15516)*

Air Masters Tampa Bay Inc ....D...... 813 234-2419
Tampa *(G-17254)*

All American Air and Elc Inc ....D...... 352 629-1211
Ocala *(G-11629)*

◆ Anchor Tampa Inc ....D...... 813 879-8685
Tampa *(G-17286)*

Around Clock A/C Service LLC ....C...... 954 742-5544
Sunrise *(G-16739)*

Aspen Air Conditioning Inc ....D...... 561 395-1500
Boca Raton *(G-428)*

Building Air Services Hvac LLC ....C...... 888 528-3688
Pinellas Park *(G-14510)*

Central Air Conditioning Inc ....E...... 954 428-0033
Deerfield Beach *(G-2723)*

Central Florida Store Svcs Inc ....E...... 407 288-3526
Sanford *(G-15933)*

Century Service Systems Inc ....C...... 954 421-3344
Doral *(G-3150)*

Climate Control Services Inc ....E...... 561 738-9100
Boynton Beach *(G-976)*

CMS Mechanical Services LLC ....E...... 321 727-2865
Melbourne *(G-8846)*

Coastal Mechanical Svcs LLC ....E...... 321 725-3061
Melbourne *(G-8847)*

Con-Air Industries Inc ....D...... 407 298-5733
Orlando *(G-12357)*

Cox Heating & AC Inc ....E...... 727 442-6158
Clearwater *(G-1595)*

Daikin Applied Americas Inc ....E...... 954 862-8550
Davie *(G-2475)*

Del-Air Heating AC & Rfrgn Inc ....E...... 352 394-1220
Clermont *(G-1864)*

Edd Helms Group Inc ....E...... 305 653-2520
Sunrise *(G-16767)*

Envirnmntal Dsign Systems Cntl ....E...... 813 269-0832
Tampa *(G-17636)*

Hill York Service Company LLC ....E...... 954 525-4200
Fort Lauderdale *(G-3860)*

Jadeco Inc ....E...... 813 627-0243
Tampa *(G-17888)*

Kalos Services Inc ....E...... 352 243-7088
Clermont *(G-1877)*

McMullen AC Rfrgn Inc ....E...... 727 527-0000
Saint Petersburg *(G-15557)*

Mechanical Svcs Centl Fla Inc ....C...... 407 857-3510
Orlando *(G-12850)*

▲ Midway Services Inc ....C...... 727 573-9500
Clearwater *(G-1721)*

MMS Mechanical Services Inc ....E...... 352 376-5221
Gainesville *(G-4950)*

Newberrys Refrigeration Inc ....E...... 863 688-8871
Lakeland *(G-7931)*

Nextech Central LLC ....C...... 940 891-3200
Melbourne *(G-8949)*

Pride AC & Appl Inc ....E...... 954 977-7433
Pompano Beach *(G-14880)*

Pro-Air Mechanical Inc ....E...... 407 339-4333
Longwood *(G-8393)*

Quamec Corp ....E...... 305 783-2877
Hialeah *(G-5315)*

Ridge Energy Savers Inc ....E...... 863 676-2665
Lake Wales *(G-7698)*

Royalaire Mechanical Svcs Inc ....C...... 813 749-2370
Oldsmar *(G-11924)*

▼ Southern Rfrgn Engineers Inc ....E...... 305 825-2063
Hialeah *(G-5324)*

Stellar Indus Solutions Inc ....B...... 904 260-2900
Jacksonville *(G-6792)*

Stellar Interactive Solutions ....B...... 904 260-2900
Jacksonville *(G-6793)*

Stellar Rfrgn Contg Inc ....E...... 904 260-2900
Jacksonville *(G-6794)*

▼ Tampa Bay Systems Sales Inc ......D...... 813 877-8251
Tampa *(G-18370)*

Total Appliance & AC RPS Inc ....C...... 954 900-6868
Hallandale Beach *(G-5186)*

Trane US Inc ....E...... 407 660-1111
Maitland *(G-8590)*

Tropic Supply Inc ....E...... 386 258-8337
Daytona Beach *(G-2679)*

United AC & Htg Co ....D...... 727 531-0496
Largo *(G-8159)*

Westbrook Service Corporation ....C...... 407 841-3310
Orlando *(G-13421)*

Whaley Foodservice LLC ....E...... 407 757-0851
Orlando *(G-13428)*

7629 Electrical & Elex Repair Shop, NEC

Abacus Business Solutions Inc ....E...... 727 524-0177
Clearwater *(G-1511)*

Anderson Columbia Co Inc ....E...... 352 542-7942
Old Town *(G-11886)*

Bass-Nted Fire SEC Systems Inc ....E...... 954 785-7800
Pompano Beach *(G-14750)*

Boring Business Systems Inc ....D...... 863 686-3167
Lakeland *(G-7816)*

Central Fla Spech Hring Ctr In ....E...... 863 686-3189
Lakeland *(G-7828)*

Century Service Systems Inc ....C...... 954 421-3344
Doral *(G-3150)*

Dbk Concepts Inc ....C...... 305 596-7226
Miami *(G-9463)*

Disney Worldwide Services Inc ....E...... 407 934-6375
Orlando *(G-12428)*

Electronic Controls Inc ....E...... 321 783-5858
Cape Canaveral *(G-1365)*

Florida Transformer Inc ....C...... 850 892-2711
Defuniak Springs *(G-2830)*

Galaxy Home Solutions Inc ....C...... 352 748-4868
Wildwood *(G-19496)*

GE Medcal Systems Info Tech In ....D...... 561 575-5000
Jupiter *(G-7082)*

Hytec Dealer Services Inc ....C...... 407 297-1001
Orlando *(G-12676)*

IMS / American LLC ....E...... 772 219-4460
Stuart *(G-16632)*

Intermed Nuc Med Inc ....E...... 386 462-5220
Alachua *(G-8)*

◆ ITW GSE Inc ....D...... 941 721-1000
Palmetto *(G-13919)*

▼ Johns Appliance City Inc ....D...... 386 760-2776
South Daytona *(G-16489)*

Kosse Partners I LLC ....D...... 352 314-0144
Leesburg *(G-8249)*

▼ Lengemann Corporation ....E...... 352 669-2111
Altoona *(G-118)*

Lhs Investments Inc ....E...... 904 448-6901
Jacksonville *(G-6431)*

Maddox Electric Company Inc ....C...... 407 934-8084
Winter Garden *(G-19580)*

Mader Electric Inc ....E...... 941 351-5858
Bradenton *(G-1131)*

Maintenx Intl Svc MGT Group In ....B...... 813 254-1656
Tampa *(G-17979)*

Nemesio Office Eqp Distrs ....E...... 305 477-8822
Doral *(G-3278)*

Precision Elctrnic Repr Svcs I ....E...... 813 523-3324
Tampa *(G-18162)*

Professional Aircraft ACC Inc ....C...... 321 267-1040
Titusville *(G-18700)*

Prolec-GE Waukesha Inc ....E...... 407 838-0877
Maitland *(G-8571)*

◆ Pulau Corporation ....C...... 407 380-9191
Orlando *(G-13072)*

Repair Technologies Inc ....E...... 352 596-9121
Weeki Wachee *(G-18969)*

Solutions Manufacturing LLC ....D...... 321 848-0848
Rockledge *(G-15368)*

STS Repair & Modification LLC ....C...... 321 405-3700
Melbourne *(G-8986)*

Telefonica USA ....E...... 786 845-9600
Sweetwater *(G-16862)*

Tempus Enterprise Inc ....E...... 941 316-8800
Sarasota *(G-16065)*

Tri-Tech Electronics Inc ....D...... 407 277-2131
Orlando *(G-13308)*

Ubreakifix Co ....B...... 877 320-2237
Orlando *(G-13322)*

Wood Business Solutions Inc ....D...... 954 493-7422
Sunrise *(G-16849)*

▲ Xerox Business Solutions Inc ....E...... 813 960-5508
Tampa *(G-18571)*

Xtra Aerospace LLC ....D...... 954 318-5073
Miramar *(G-10918)*

▼ Zabatt Engine Services Inc ....D...... 904 384-4505
Jacksonville *(G-6965)*

7631 Watch, Clock & Jewelry Repair

Breitling USA Inc ....E...... 754 218-8880
Sunrise *(G-16750)*

Maurices Jewelers Inc ....E...... 305 253-5740
Pinecrest *(G-14499)*

7641 Reupholstery & Furniture Repair

American Maintenance LLC ....E...... 561 317-3219
Lake Worth *(G-7708)*

Carc-Dvcate For Ctzens With Ds ....C...... 386 752-1880
Lake City *(G-7517)*

◆ Jose Leal Enterprises Inc ....D...... 305 887-9611
Hialeah *(G-5284)*

Joshua W Kennedy Entps LLC ....E...... 904 383-7721
Jacksonville *(G-6391)*

▼ Le Jeune Upholstery Inc ....E...... 305 261-4009
Miami *(G-9852)*

Refurbishing Works LLC ....E...... 407 281-1135
Orlando *(G-13094)*

Wegman Associates Inc..................D....... 407 850-9191
Orlando (G-13414)

7692 Welding Repair

◆ Advanced Machine and Tool Inc.......D....... 772 465-6546
Fort Pierce (G-4677)
▲ Bob Dean Supply Inc......................E....... 239 332-1131
Fort Myers (G-4293)
Central Maintenance & Wldg Inc..........D....... 352 795-2817
Crystal River (G-2342)
Central Maintenance & Wldg Inc..........C....... 813 229-0012
Lithia (G-8298)
Emf Inc..C....... 321 453-3670
Merritt Island (G-9026)
Exact Inc..C....... 904 783-6640
Jacksonville (G-6138)
◆ Florida Wldg Fbrctors Erectors.......D....... 954 971-4800
Parkland (G-14107)
Griffiths Corporation......................D....... 407 851-8342
Orlando (G-12606)
◆ JC Industrial Mfg Corp.................E....... 305 634-5280
Miami (G-9785)
Mid-State Machine & Fabg Corp..........C....... 863 665-6233
Lakeland (G-7922)
◆ Serf Inc......................................E....... 850 476-8203
Cantonment (G-1342)
Taylor Industrial Cnstr Inc..............E....... 386 792-3060
Live Oak (G-8320)

7694 Armature Rewinding Shops

Aircraft Electric Motors Inc...............D....... 305 885-9476
Miami Lakes (G-10701)
Tampa Armature Works Inc.................D....... 904 757-7790
Jacksonville (G-6831)
Tampa Armature Works Inc.................C....... 813 612-2600
Tampa (G-18361)
◆ Taw Miami Service Center Inc..........E....... 305 884-1717
Medley (G-8788)

7699 Repair Shop & Related Svcs, NEC

2401 Ne 2nd St Operations LLC..........D....... 954 943-5100
Pompano Beach (G-14729)
630 Aerospace Inc..........................E....... 754 208-3737
Hialeah (G-5210)
ACR Sales and Service Inc................E....... 407 299-9190
Apopka (G-146)
Adsync Technologies Inc..................D....... 850 497-6969
Pensacola (G-14212)
Advanced Cmpsite Strctres Fla..........E....... 407 585-6111
Sanford (G-15914)
Advanced Disposal Services..............E....... 904 737-7900
Ponte Vedra (G-14945)
◆ Africair Inc.................................D....... 305 255-6973
Miami (G-9100)
Airborne Maint Engrg Svcs Inc..........C....... 813 322-9617
Tampa (G-17256)
▲ Aire-Tech Aviation Repairs Inc........E....... 305 691-6833
Miami (G-9107)
All Points Boats Inc........................D....... 954 767-8255
Fort Lauderdale (G-3593)
Aqua Triangle 1 Corporation..............E....... 727 531-0473
Largo (G-8074)
Aquarius Building Inc......................C....... 305 824-1324
Miami Lakes (G-10705)
▲ Art Headquarters LLC...................B....... 727 573-1417
Largo (G-8075)
Atlantic Firebrick Sup Co Inc............E....... 904 355-8333
Jacksonville (G-5813)
▼ Atlantic Marine Inc.......................E....... 305 826-2202
Hialeah (G-5219)
Averett Septic Tank Co Inc...............E....... 863 665-1748
Lakeland (G-7806)
AVI Trading Llc..............................D....... 954 749-3500
Sunrise (G-16742)
◆ Avp Valve Inc...............................E....... 863 709-0455
Lakeland (G-7808)
Barfield Precision Elec LLC...............C....... 305 436-5464
Doral (G-3135)
▼ Barneys Pumps Inc.......................D....... 863 665-8500
Lakeland (G-7812)
▲ Battery Usa Inc............................E....... 863 665-6317
Lakeland (G-7813)
Beltram Edge Tool Supply Inc............E....... 813 239-1136
Tampa (G-17357)
Bingham On-Site Sewers Inc.............D....... 813 659-0003
Dover (G-3366)
◆ Bmg Conveyor Services Fla Inc.......E....... 813 247-3620
Tampa (G-17374)
▼ Bms Partners LLC.........................E....... 954 436-9905
Hollywood (G-5408)

Boomerang Consulting Group LLC.....D....... 352 368-2451
Ocala (G-11643)
Cable Marine Inc............................E....... 954 462-2822
Fort Lauderdale (G-3662)
Cable Marine Inc............................E....... 954 587-4000
Fort Lauderdale (G-3663)
Cambata Aviation Inc......................E....... 407 585-3413
Sanford (G-15928)
Cei Holding Company......................E....... 215 734-1400
Dunedin (G-3381)
Certified Envmtl Svcs Inc..................D....... 904 695-1911
Jacksonville (G-5929)
Chromalloy Component Svcs Inc........E....... 850 244-7684
Fort Walton Beach (G-4758)
▲ Chromalloy Gas Turbine LLC...........A....... 561 935-3571
Palm Beach Gardens (G-13706)
Clarklift of Florida LLC....................E....... 813 874-2008
Orlando (G-12311)
Clean N Dry Inc..............................E....... 407 216-8000
Orlando (G-12314)
Clean Up Group Inc........................E....... 239 455-2225
Naples (G-11056)
Clean World Global LLC...................E....... 407 574-8353
Orlando (G-12316)
Clean-Mark Group Inc.....................C....... 416 364-0677
Boca Raton (G-518)
Climate Control Services Inc.............E....... 561 738-9100
Boynton Beach (G-976)
CMC Products and Services LLC........E....... 407 574-5830
Orlando (G-12325)
▼ Compressed Air Systems Inc..........E....... 800 626-8177
Tampa (G-17509)
Consensys Imaging Service Inc..........D....... 847 462-2030
Deerfield Beach (G-2728)
Construction Svc Co Fla Inc...............D....... 850 897-8030
Niceville (G-11443)
Copyfax Inc...................................E....... 904 296-1600
Jacksonville (G-6001)
Countryside Property Maint LLC........C....... 352 897-4803
Coral Gables (G-2082)
Crestwood Services Inc...................E....... 954 570-1165
Fort Lauderdale (G-3741)
CRS Facility Services LLC.................C....... 786 425-2888
Miami (G-9442)
Crystal FL Clean LLC.......................D....... 239 936-7700
Fort Myers (G-4336)
Daisy Fresh Commercial Clg Inc........E....... 407 880-0599
Apopka (G-171)
Dallas Airmotive Inc........................C....... 407 206-5247
Orlando (G-12398)
Dallas Airmotive Inc........................D....... 561 568-4462
Boynton Beach (G-982)
Daves Detailing Inc.........................D....... 317 439-5000
Orlando (G-12403)
Daves Detailing Inc.........................E....... 866 535-6500
Orlando (G-12404)
◆ Deangelo Marine Exhaust Inc..........E....... 954 763-3005
Fort Lauderdale (G-3755)
Dejonge Excavating Contrs Inc..........D....... 941 485-7799
Venice (G-18777)
Diverse Co.....................................E....... 863 425-4251
Mulberry (G-10978)
Domsky Enterprises Inc...................E....... 772 220-2288
Stuart (G-16614)
Don Mays Corp...............................E....... 800 888-4971
Tampa (G-17599)
◆ Eastern Aero Marine Inc.................C....... 305 871-4050
Miami (G-9496)
Elliott Company.............................E....... 904 757-7600
Jacksonville (G-6107)
Embraer Training Services LLC..........D....... 954 359-3700
Fort Lauderdale (G-3771)
Envirowaste Services Group Inc........D....... 305 637-9665
Palmetto Bay (G-13940)
Esposito Nursery Inc.......................C....... 850 386-2114
Tallahassee (G-16942)
F & E Aviation Holdings Inc...............C....... 305 871-3758
Miami Springs (G-10781)
Fcs Inc...E....... 727 576-1111
Clearwater (G-1634)
▲ Five Arrows Inc............................D....... 813 972-4945
Tampa (G-17668)
Florida Js Motorsports LLC...............D....... 954 414-4135
Sunrise (G-16771)
▲ Florida North Shipyards Inc............C....... 904 354-3278
Jacksonville (G-6196)
◆ Flotech LLC.................................D....... 904 358-1849
Jacksonville (G-6205)
Flyhopco LLC.................................D....... 954 791-3800
Fort Lauderdale (G-3799)

Future Aviation Inc.........................D....... 239 225-0101
Fort Myers (G-4406)
G E Walker Inc...............................D....... 813 623-2481
Tampa (G-17721)
GA Telesis LLC..............................D....... 305 492-0084
Miami (G-9615)
Gator North Inc..............................E....... 352 787-8050
Leesburg (G-8244)
◆ General Propeller Company Inc........E....... 941 748-1527
Bradenton (G-1109)
Generations At HM Holdings LLC........D....... 727 940-3414
Saint Petersburg (G-15684)
▲ Global Engine Maintenance LLC......D....... 305 717-0951
Doral (G-3212)
◆ Golten Service Company Inc............E....... 305 576-4410
Miramar (G-10859)
◆ Gray Taxidermy Inc.......................D....... 954 785-6456
Pompano Beach (G-14817)
▼ Gulf Controls Company Inc.............D....... 813 884-0471
Tampa (G-17773)
Hamilton Sunstrand AVI Svcs............D....... 954 433-3588
Miramar (G-10862)
Harrison Home Services In................E....... 786 553-6421
Boca Raton (G-619)
Hd American Road LLC....................D....... 407 944-3700
Kissimmee (G-7320)
▲ Heico Corporation........................C....... 954 987-4000
Hollywood (G-5447)
Hlg Capital Partners III LP................A....... 305 379-2322
Miami (G-9703)
▲ Hoerbger Cmprssion Tech Amer H..B....... 954 974-5700
Pompano Beach (G-14822)
▼ Hoerbiger Service Inc....................D....... 281 955-5888
Deerfield Beach (G-2753)
◆ Hugo Motor-Services Stamp Inc.......B....... 954 763-3660
Fort Lauderdale (G-3879)
Independence Rv Sales & Svc............D....... 407 877-7878
Winter Garden (G-19573)
Industrial Eqp & Engrg Co In............D....... 407 886-5533
Apopka (G-191)
Innovative Marine Elec Inc...............E....... 954 467-2695
Fort Lauderdale (G-3894)
International Airmotive Holdg............A....... 561 734-0121
Boynton Beach (G-1001)
◆ ITW GSE Inc.................................D....... 941 721-1000
Palmetto (G-13919)
Jimco Maintenance Inc....................D....... 941 485-5985
Venice (G-18789)
Johnson Controls Inc......................E....... 407 291-1971
Orlando (G-12711)
Jsm & Associates LLC.....................C....... 352 383-2600
Tavares (G-18611)
Keen On Klean...............................E....... 904 748-9060
Jacksonville (G-6398)
◆ Kelly Tractor Co............................C....... 305 592-5360
Doral (G-3254)
▼ Keltner/Rush Ventures Inc..............E....... 239 334-3424
Fort Myers (G-4461)
◆ Kilpatrick Company Inc..................E....... 561 533-1450
Boynton Beach (G-1004)
Kone Inc.......................................D....... 407 492-6649
Orlando (G-12737)
Kone Inc.......................................D....... 954 437-4300
Miramar (G-10873)
Lazydays Holdings Inc.....................D....... 813 246-4999
Seffner (G-16429)
Lewis Dk LLC.................................E....... 727 580-4981
Saint Petersburg (G-15747)
Lipa Management Consulting Inc........E....... 561 379-3601
Palm Beach Gardens (G-13749)
LRE Ground Services Inc..................C....... 352 796-0229
Brooksville (G-1298)
Magnum Environmental Services........D....... 954 785-2320
Pompano Beach (G-14847)
◆ Marine Exhaust Systems Inc............E....... 561 848-1238
Riviera Beach (G-15307)
Matthews International Corp..............C....... 407 886-5533
Apopka (G-201)
McClain International Inc..................D....... 770 964-3361
Hollywood (G-5474)
McJ Professional Clg Svcs Corp..........E....... 954 418-6248
Pompano Beach (G-14851)
▼ Med-Craft Inc..............................E....... 305 594-7444
Miami (G-9927)
◆ Medical Optics LLC.......................D....... 954 838-8600
Tamarac (G-17199)
▲ Mercury Enterprises Inc.................D....... 727 573-0088
Clearwater (G-1713)
▲ Mettler Toledo Florida Inc..............E....... 813 626-8127
Tampa (G-18032)

Mettler-Toledo Hi-Speed Inc..............D..... 800 836-0836
  Lutz (G-8449)
Miami Intl APT Car Fac..............D..... 305 826-1903
  Hialeah (G-5298)
◆ Mid-State SMS LLC..............B..... 727 573-7828
  Lakeland (G-7923)
Millennium Coml Clg Svcs Inc..............E..... 813 925-3565
  Tampa (G-18039)
▼ Millers Boating Center Inc..............E..... 352 620-2435
  Ocala (G-11735)
◆ Mobro Marine Inc..............D..... 866 313-9670
  Green Cove Springs (G-5059)
Mold Zero LLC..............E..... 727 592-8878
  Largo (G-8136)
Mr Copy Service Inc..............E..... 904 448-9447
  Fort Myers (G-4519)
◆ Music Arts Enterprises Inc Mae..............E..... 954 581-2203
  Fort Lauderdale (G-3986)
New Century Cleaning Svcs Inc..............E..... 850 894-6226
  Tallahassee (G-17054)
Oracle Elevator Holdco Inc..............E..... 800 526-6115
  Tampa (G-18105)
Orange Cycle Works Inc..............E..... 407 422-5552
  Orlando (G-12937)
▼ Orlando Drum Co..............E..... 407 855-0208
  Orlando (G-12948)
Otis Elevator Company..............D..... 904 296-6847
  Jacksonville (G-6570)
Otis Elevator Company..............B..... 561 618-4831
  West Palm Beach (G-19296)
Otis Elevator Company..............C..... 305 816-5740
  Fort Lauderdale (G-4036)
▲ Overhaul Accessory Inc..............E..... 305 887-1507
  Medley (G-8765)
Page Mechanical Group LLC..............C..... 239 275-4406
  Fort Myers (G-4532)
Performance Door and Hdwr Inc..............E..... 407 932-2115
  Kissimmee (G-7374)
Phase II Copiers Inc..............E..... 386 676-2098
  Ormond Beach (G-13516)
◆ Plasco LLC..............E..... 305 625-4222
  Miami Lakes (G-10754)
Pro Clean Building Maint Inc..............E..... 407 740-5554
  Maitland (G-8569)
▲ Process Systems Components Inc..E..... 813 888-6300
  Tampa (G-18175)
Professional Aircraft ACC Inc..............E..... 321 267-1040
  Titusville (G-18700)
Purosystems LLC..............E..... 800 775-7876
  Tamarac (G-17203)
◆ Q4 Services Inc..............D..... 407 382-4000
  Orlando (G-13075)
Quality Biomedical Inc..............D..... 727 547-6000
  Pinellas Park (G-14533)
Rick Case Cars Inc..............C..... 954 364-3000
  Davie (G-2510)
▲ Rolly Marine Service Inc..............E..... 954 583-5300
  Fort Lauderdale (G-4093)
Rossiters Harley-Davidson Inc..............E..... 941 342-0040
  Sarasota (G-16286)
RW Raddatz Inc..............E..... 954 480-9327
  Deerfield Beach (G-2789)
Safran Oil Systems LLC..............D..... 239 204-3129
  Fort Myers (G-4577)
Schindler Elevator Corporation..............E..... 904 880-4922
  Jacksonville (G-6698)
Seascape Resorts Inc..............D..... 850 837-9181
  Miramar Beach (G-10926)
Seminole Coml Clg Mint Svcs FL..............D..... 480 748-6296
  Hollywood (G-5515)
▲ Silver Wings Aerospace Inc..............E..... 305 258-5950
  Princeton (G-15188)
Sonofinis Inc..............D..... 407 892-5577
  Saint Cloud (G-15536)
Spectrum Systems Inc..............E..... 850 944-3392
  Pensacola (G-14446)
▲ Spencer Boat Co Inc..............E..... 561 844-1800
  West Palm Beach (G-19373)
Sun Aviation Inc..............E..... 772 562-2857
  Vero Beach (G-18921)
▼ Sun Lift Inc..............D..... 954 971-9440
  Pompano Beach (G-14914)
Sun Nuclear Corp..............C..... 321 259-6862
  Melbourne (G-8987)
Sun Print Management LLC..............E..... 727 945-0255
  Holiday (G-5375)
Supreme Energy Inc..............D..... 973 678-1800
  Sarasota (G-16340)
T & M Cleaning Services LLC..............E..... 954 942-0388
  Pompano Beach (G-14916)

T Mowery Enterprises Inc..............E..... 850 526-4111
  Marianna (G-8686)
Tc Motorcycles LLC..............E..... 904 771-8244
  Jacksonville (G-6838)
TEAM JAS INC..............E..... 904 292-2328
  Jacksonville (G-6841)
▲ Thales Avionics Inc..............D..... 407 812-2600
  Orlando (G-13284)
Tk Elevator Corporation..............D..... 239 334-2511
  Fort Myers (G-4627)
Tk Elevator Corporation..............D..... 813 287-1744
  Tampa (G-18422)
Total Appliance & AC RPS Inc..............C..... 954 900-6868
  Hallandale Beach (G-5186)
Touch Cleaning & Gen Svcs LLC..............E..... 561 929-4388
  Pompano Beach (G-14925)
Treasure Coast Harley-Davidson..............E..... 772 287-3871
  Stuart (G-16674)
▼ Trekker Tractor LLC..............D..... 561 296-9710
  Lake Worth (G-7757)
▲ Velocity Arspc - Fort Ldrdale..............E..... 954 772-4559
  Fort Lauderdale (G-4210)
▼ Vera-Wliiamson Investments Inc..............E..... 954 362-9458
  Pembroke Pines (G-14198)
VHL Aircraft Inc..............E..... 305 592-4178
  Miami (G-10469)
West Marine Products Inc..............C..... 772 828-4170
  Fort Pierce (G-4749)
Whaley Foodservice LLC..............E..... 904 725-7800
  Jacksonville (G-6932)
White River Marine Group LLC..............D..... 407 248-8115
  Orlando (G-13429)
▼ Wiginton Corporation..............D..... 407 585-3200
  Sanford (G-15995)
Xtra Aerospace LLC..............D..... 954 318-5073
  Miramar (G-10918)
▼ Zabatt Engine Services Inc..............D..... 904 384-4505
  Jacksonville (G-6965)
◆ ZF Marine Propulsion Systms..............E..... 954 441-4040
  Miramar (G-10919)

78 MOTION PICTURES

7812 Motion Picture & Video Tape Production

Alliance Entertainment LLC..............D..... 954 255-4000
  Sunrise (G-16735)
and More Entertainment Corp..............E..... 305 773-5563
  Miami (G-9153)
Arrow Sky Media LLC..............E..... 407 720-8019
  Orlando (G-12134)
Bollywood Hollywood Prod Inc..............E..... 732 317-3583
  Miami (G-9266)
CD Advantage Inc..............E..... 904 722-8200
  Jacksonville (G-5918)
Christian Vision Usa Inc..............E..... 305 231-7704
  Miami Lakes (G-10715)
▲ Disney Worldwide Services Inc..............E..... 407 397-3748
  Lake Buena Vista (G-7460)
Hubbard Sight & Sound Av Inc..............E..... 904 645-7880
  Jacksonville (G-6305)
◆ Multi Image Group Inc..............C..... 561 994-3515
  Boca Raton (G-703)
News Group Inc..............E..... 561 870-5259
  Boca Raton (G-716)
Pga Tour Inc..............E..... 904 285-3700
  Saint Augustine (G-15480)
Platinum Television Group Inc..............E..... 954 755-5514
  Coral Springs (G-2277)
Pulse Evolution Corporation..............E..... 772 345-4100
  Jupiter (G-2255)
Red Rocket Studios LLC..............E..... 407 895-9358
  Orlando (G-13088)
◆ Remedy TV + Branded Inc..............E..... 813 229-3600
  Tampa (G-18214)
Set Distribution LLC..............E..... 305 400-3000
  Miami (G-10264)
Simply Chosen Inc..............C..... 786 872-4948
  Miami (G-10273)
Simply Chosen Wealth MGT..............C..... 786 872-4948
  Miami (G-10274)
Sony Pictures TV Advg Sls Co..............E..... 305 358-0711
  Miami (G-10296)
South Florida Pbs Inc..............E..... 305 949-8321
  Boynton Beach (G-1038)
◆ Spanish House Inc..............E..... 305 503-1191
  Medley (G-8786)
US Imagina LLC..............C..... 305 357-6000
  Medley (G-8794)
Walt Dsney Prks Resorts US Inc..............A..... 407 560-5974
  Lake Buena Vista (G-7490)

7819 Services Allied To Motion Picture Prdtn

Imax Corporation..............D..... 813 262-8455
  Saint Petersburg (G-15717)
◆ On-Board Media Inc..............D..... 305 673-0400
  Doral (G-3281)
▲ Pro Sound Inc..............E..... 305 891-1000
  North Miami (G-11507)
▲ Universal City Fla Partners..............D..... 407 363-8000
  Orlando (G-13343)

7822 Motion Picture & Video Tape Distribution

and More Entertainment Corp..............E..... 305 773-5563
  Miami (G-9153)
Fishbowl Productions Inc..............D..... 786 723-6260
  Miami (G-9562)
New Wisdom Agency Prod Corp..............E..... 754 802-9450
  North Miami (G-11505)
Pioneer Production Svcs LLC..............D..... 561 869-3969
  Delray Beach (G-3006)
Tellus Products LLC..............D..... 561 996-5556
  Belle Glade (G-363)

7829 Services Allied To Motion Picture Distribution

Jbtp LLC..............D..... 718 286-7900
  Dania Beach (G-2428)

7832 Motion Picture Theaters, Except Drive-In

Ashbrie Cinema Inc..............E..... 850 393-5258
  Gulf Breeze (G-5107)
Carmike Cinemas LLC..............D..... 863 471-1179
  Sebring (G-16391)
Carmike Cinemas LLC..............D..... 954 946-8416
  Pompano Beach (G-14766)
Carmike Cinemas LLC..............D..... 850 475-2240
  Pensacola (G-14247)
Carmike Cinemas LLC..............E..... 727 942-8476
  Palm Harbor (G-13853)
Carmike Cinemas LLC..............D..... 772 344-3580
  Port St Lucie (G-15178)
Carmike Cinemas LLC..............D..... 561 833-2310
  West Palm Beach (G-19075)
Carmike Cinemas LLC..............E..... 321 369-7884
  West Melbourne (G-19010)
Carmike Cinemas LLC..............E..... 727 502-9573
  Saint Petersburg (G-15614)
Carmike Cinemas LLC..............D..... 813 558-9745
  Tampa (G-17426)
Carmike Cinemas LLC..............D..... 321 775-1210
  Melbourne (G-8837)
Carmike Cinemas LLC..............E..... 305 826-7242
  Hialeah (G-5228)
Carmike Mtion Pctres Pnscola L..............C..... 850 471-1933
  Pensacola (G-14248)
Cinema Holdings LLC..............D..... 239 592-0300
  Naples (G-11053)
Cinema World Inc..............D..... 321 723-5211
  Melbourne (G-8843)
City of Fort Lauderdale..............D..... 954 828-5380
  Fort Lauderdale (G-3695)
Enzian Theater Inc..............D..... 407 629-1088
  Maitland (G-8528)
Hippodrome State Theatre Inc..............E..... 352 373-5968
  Gainesville (G-4916)
Ipic Theaters LLC..............D..... 561 299-3000
  Boca Raton (G-645)
John Gore Theatrical Group Inc..............C..... 954 764-0700
  Fort Lauderdale (G-3911)
L & D Enterprises Orlando Inc..............D..... 407 678-8214
  Winter Park (G-19743)
Marquee Cinemas Inc..............C..... 239 410-5469
  Cape Coral (G-1411)
Mercato Cinema LLC..............D..... 239 592-0300
  Naples (G-11211)
Muvico Theaters Inc..............E..... 954 564-6550
  Fort Lauderdale (G-3987)
Muvico Theaters Inc..............B..... 305 826-7245
  Hialeah (G-5301)
Muvico Theaters Inc..............B..... 954 946-8416
  Pompano Beach (G-14862)
Muvico Theaters Inc..............B..... 727 942-8476
  Palm Harbor (G-13870)
Panhandle Movie Company LLC..............E..... 850 393-5258
  Milton (G-10821)
Regal Cinemas Inc..............D..... 386 673-7828
  Ormond Beach (G-13517)

Regal Cinemas Inc................................E....... 352 336-0414
Gainesville *(G-4986)*
Regal Cinemas Inc................................E....... 239 498-8109
Estero *(G-3473)*
Regal Cinemas Inc................................D....... 813 920-9471
Tampa *(G-18210)*
Regal Cinemas Inc................................E....... 863 676-8894
Lake Wales *(G-7697)*
Regal Cinemas Inc................................E....... 407 977-7206
Oviedo *(G-13566)*
Regal Cinemas Inc................................E....... 239 597-4252
Naples *(G-11280)*
Regal Cinemas Inc................................D....... 407 628-0163
Winter Park *(G-19768)*
Regal Cinemas Inc................................D....... 954 345-4113
Coral Springs *(G-2280)*
Regal Cinemas Inc................................D....... 407 207-4603
Orlando *(G-13095)*
Regal Cinemas Inc................................E....... 352 637-3388
Inverness *(G-5699)*
Regal Cinemas Inc................................E....... 727 862-9567
Port Richey *(G-15110)*
Regal Cinemas Inc................................E....... 407 884-8080
Apopka *(G-206)*
Regal Cinemas Inc................................E....... 850 243-1457
Mary Esther *(G-8693)*
Regal Cinemas Inc................................E....... 954 923-4321
Hollywood *(G-5505)*
Regal Cinemas Inc................................E....... 727 581-7389
Largo *(G-8145)*
Regal Cinemas Inc................................E....... 239 437-2020
Fort Myers *(G-4566)*
Riverview Ops LLC................................D....... 812 945-4006
Riverview *(G-15268)*
Swap Shop Management LLC................E....... 561 965-4518
Palm Springs *(G-13899)*
Theatres Cobb III LLC............................C....... 813 948-5444
Wesley Chapel *(G-19008)*
Theatres Cobb III LLC............................C....... 305 558-3810
Miami Lakes *(G-10768)*
Twin Creeks Cinema LLC........................E....... 850 306-2500
Crestview *(G-2337)*

7833 Drive-In Motion Picture Theaters

3290 Sunrise Investments Inc................C....... 954 791-7927
Fort Lauderdale *(G-3567)*

7841 Video Tape Rental

Adcomm Inc..A....... 850 936-5501
Navarre *(G-11350)*

79 AMUSEMENT AND RECREATION SERVICES

7911 Dance Studios, Schools & Halls

Armour Dance Theatre Inc.....................E....... 305 667-5543
South Miami *(G-16496)*
▲ **Columbia Prpts Orlando LLC**...............B....... 407 856-0100
Orlando *(G-12347)*
Conchita Espinosa Academy Inc...........C....... 305 227-1149
Miami *(G-9401)*
Harid Conservatory Music Inc...............D....... 561 995-0151
Boca Raton *(G-617)*
Miami City Ballet Inc.............................C....... 305 929-7000
Miami Beach *(G-10622)*
▲ **Sarasota Ballet Florida Inc**.................D....... 941 359-0099
Sarasota *(G-16052)*

7922 Theatrical Producers & Misc Theatrical Svcs

Accesso LLC..D....... 407 333-7311
Lake Mary *(G-7562)*
Act IV Ocala Civic Theater.....................D....... 352 732-5920
Ocala *(G-11627)*
Actors Plyhuse Productions Inc............C....... 305 444-9293
Coral Gables *(G-2024)*
Adrienne Arsht Ctr Fndtion Inc.............C....... 305 949-6722
Miami *(G-9090)*
Asm Global Parent Inc...........................D....... 850 432-0800
Pensacola *(G-14221)*
Attorneys Title Fund Svcs LLC..............E....... 727 736-4884
Palm Harbor *(G-13851)*
Avmedia Inc...C....... 407 545-7499
Orlando *(G-12162)*
BBC Worldwide Ltd................................D....... 305 461-6999
Coral Gables *(G-2048)*
◆ **Bgw Design Limited Inc**......................E....... 305 757-7577
Hollywood *(G-5405)*
Caracol Broadcasting Inc......................C....... 305 285-1260
Coral Gables *(G-2062)*
Christian Vision Usa Inc.......................E....... 305 231-7704
Miami Lakes *(G-10715)*
City of Miami Beach................................E....... 305 673-7730
Miami Beach *(G-10570)*
College Core Entrtainments LLC...........E....... 844 256-7991
Riverview *(G-15251)*
Contemporary Services Corp................C....... 954 435-4544
Miramar *(G-10847)*
Cornetts Sprit of Suwannee Inc.............D....... 386 364-1683
Live Oak *(G-8309)*
D-R Media and Investments LLC...........D....... 941 207-1602
Venice *(G-18776)*
Davis-Wick Talent MGT LLC..................E....... 407 369-1614
Margate *(G-8644)*
Disney Destinations LLC.......................B....... 407 824-5252
Orlando *(G-12427)*
Estefan Enterprises Inc.........................E....... 305 695-7037
Miami Beach *(G-10592)*
Eventus Marketing LLC..........................E....... 305 668-4343
Doral *(G-3193)*
▲ **F/X Design Group LLC**.......................E....... 407 877-9600
Ocoee *(G-11812)*
Fantasma Productions Inc......................E....... 561 832-6397
Palm Beach *(G-13653)*
Florida Repertory Theatre Inc...............D....... 239 332-4488
Fort Myers *(G-4389)*
Florida Studio Theatre Inc.....................E....... 941 366-9017
Sarasota *(G-16168)*
Force Legion LLC...................................E....... 305 423-3339
Miami *(G-9593)*
Gold Finger Entp Intl LLC......................C....... 786 499-3060
Orlando *(G-12578)*
Hippodrome State Theatre Inc..............E....... 352 373-5968
Gainesville *(G-4916)*
John Gore Theatrical Group Inc............C....... 954 764-0700
Fort Lauderdale *(G-3911)*
Maltz Jpter Thtre Endwment Inc............E....... 561 743-2666
Jupiter *(G-7112)*
Mutli-Media Production USA..................E....... 561 988-0609
Boca Raton *(G-704)*
Naval AVI Mseum Foundation Inc..........D....... 850 453-2389
Pensacola *(G-14376)*
Next Door Entertainment Inc.................E....... 850 727-4555
Tallahassee *(G-17056)*
North Brward Hosp Dst Chrtble............D....... 954 355-5856
Fort Lauderdale *(G-4009)*
Opryland Productions Inc......................A....... 407 586-0000
Kissimmee *(G-7362)*
Performing Arts Center Auth.................C....... 954 522-5334
Fort Lauderdale *(G-4046)*
Planet Hollywood Orlando Inc...............C....... 407 903-5500
Orlando *(G-13035)*
Prather & Co Inc....................................D....... 239 278-4422
Fort Myers *(G-4546)*
Presentation Resource Inc....................E....... 904 398-8179
Jacksonville *(G-6616)*
▲ **Raymond F Krvis Ctr For The PR**.......C....... 561 832-7469
West Palm Beach *(G-19337)*
Rebekahs Drams Entrmt Prod Svc........B....... 561 840-4071
West Palm Beach *(G-19338)*
Rent My Wedding LLC............................E....... 800 465-8020
Miami *(G-10201)*
Royal Chessmen Inc..............................E....... 954 940-1051
Hollywood *(G-5510)*
Ruth Eckerd Hall Inc..............................E....... 727 791-7060
Clearwater *(G-1779)*
▲ **Sarasota Ballet Florida Inc**.................D....... 941 359-0099
Sarasota *(G-16052)*
Shotrock Productions Inc......................D....... 407 614-6160
Sanford *(G-15981)*
Tampa Bay Prfrmg Arts Ctr Inc.............B....... 813 222-1000
Tampa *(G-18368)*
Tampa Sportservice Inc.........................D....... 813 301-6906
Tampa *(G-18404)*
Tod Booth Production Inc......................D....... 904 641-1212
Jacksonville *(G-6858)*
Venice Theatre.......................................D....... 941 488-1115
Venice *(G-18820)*
▲ **World Triathlon Corporation**...............C....... 813 868-5940
Tampa *(G-18568)*
Xposure Inc..E....... 863 605-2167
Winter Haven *(G-19679)*

7929 Bands, Orchestras, Actors & Entertainers

▲ **Artis-Naples Inc**..................................B....... 239 597-1111
Naples *(G-11017)*
College Core Entrtainments LLC...........E....... 844 256-7991
Riverview *(G-15251)*
Cox Radio Inc...E....... 727 579-2000
Saint Petersburg *(G-15647)*
Davis-Wick Talent MGT LLC..................E....... 407 369-1614
Margate *(G-8644)*
Denivel LLC..E....... 727 375-0236
Trinity *(G-18723)*
Disney Destinations LLC.......................B....... 407 824-5252
Orlando *(G-12427)*
Entertnment Benefits Group LLC..........B....... 702 617-5500
Orlando *(G-12473)*
Entertnment Benefits Group LLC..........E....... 305 907-5020
Miami *(G-9525)*
◆ **Feld Entertainment Inc**.......................C....... 941 721-1200
Palmetto *(G-13912)*
Galaxy Entertainment............................E....... 954 851-9599
Sunrise *(G-16773)*
Gold Finger Entp Intl LLC......................C....... 786 499-3060
Orlando *(G-12578)*
Harvard Scientific Corp.........................C....... 954 630-9724
Oakland Park *(G-11599)*
HBO Digital Latin America LLC.............B....... 786 501-8372
Coral Gables *(G-2119)*
Hob Entertainment LLC.........................B....... 407 934-2583
Orlando *(G-12654)*
Jacksonville Symphony Assn Inc..........D....... 904 354-5657
Jacksonville *(G-6366)*
Joseph Bauer..D....... 941 371-8776
Sarasota *(G-16207)*
Latitude 360 Inc.....................................C....... 904 730-0011
Jacksonville *(G-6424)*
▲ **ME Productions**...................................E....... 954 458-4000
Hallandale *(G-5163)*
Michael Randolph LLC...........................D....... 772 626-7581
Plantation *(G-14675)*
New World Symphony Inc......................E....... 305 673-3330
Miami Beach *(G-10635)*
Next Door Entertainment Inc.................E....... 850 727-4555
Tallahassee *(G-17056)*
Parvarti Corporation..............................E....... 904 570-0798
Jacksonville *(G-6582)*
Productons Entrmt Networks Inc..........D....... 866 661-5588
Miami *(G-10148)*
Pure Play Family Entps Inc....................E....... 727 560-1972
New Port Richey *(G-11400)*
R I - Fadjem Inc.....................................D....... 904 268-8080
Jacksonville *(G-6631)*
Rebekahs Drams Entrmt Prod Svc........B....... 561 840-4071
West Palm Beach *(G-19338)*
Reel Ting Inc..E....... 561 215-7596
Jupiter *(G-7132)*
Rosie OGradys Inc.................................C....... 850 434-6211
Pensacola *(G-14423)*
Seminole Entertainment Inc..................E....... 407 767-2977
Casselberry *(G-1456)*
Song 222 Inc...D....... 954 481-8338
Deerfield Beach *(G-2799)*
Swarm Inc...E....... 305 461-2700
Miami *(G-10353)*
Tampa Bay Prfrmg Arts Ctr Inc.............B....... 813 222-1000
Tampa *(G-18368)*
West Florida Coast Symphony..............D....... 941 953-4252
Sarasota *(G-16364)*

7933 Bowling Centers

Aloma Bowling Center East Inc.............D....... 407 384-0003
Orlando *(G-12100)*
AMF Bowling Centers Inc......................E....... 407 846-8844
Kissimmee *(G-7269)*
AMF Bowling Centers Inc......................E....... 954 432-5500
Pembroke Pines *(G-14130)*
AMF Bowling Centers Inc......................E....... 407 862-2500
Altamonte Springs *(G-27)*
AMF Bowling Centers Inc......................E....... 863 646-5791
Lakeland *(G-7799)*
AMF Bowling Centers Inc......................D....... 386 775-8738
Orange City *(G-11959)*
AMF Bowling Centers Inc......................E....... 941 484-0666
Venice *(G-18764)*
AMF Bowling Centers Inc......................E....... 352 787-3335
Leesburg *(G-8229)*
AMF Bowling Centers Inc......................E....... 941 758-8838
Bradenton *(G-1052)*
AMF Bowling Centers Inc......................E....... 941 921-4447
Sarasota *(G-16091)*
Bird Bowl Partnership...........................E....... 305 221-1221
Miami *(G-9258)*
Bowlero Corp..E....... 407 880-9090
Apopka *(G-159)*

SIC

Coral Lanes Inc ....E 239 772-7244
Cape Coral (G-1386)

Hz Partners Ltd Partnership ....E 561 968-0100
Greenacres (G-5074)

Jax Lanes Inc ....E 904 641-3133
Jacksonville (G-6376)

▲ Martins Capital Inc ....E 352 683-7272
Spring Hill (G-16542)

Pin Chasers Inc ....E 813 877-7418
Tampa (G-18151)

Pin Chasers Inc ....E 813 879-1339
Tampa (G-18152)

Pin Chasers Inc ....D 813 884-1475
Tampa (G-18153)

Schumacker Recreation Co LLC ....D 954 434-9663
Davie (G-2514)

Seminole Lanes Inc ....E 727 392-2271
Largo (G-8149)

7941 Professional Sports Clubs & Promoters

Aragon Group Inc ....D 954 920-1511
Dania Beach (G-2424)

Arena Horse Shows Ocala LLC ....D 239 275-2314
Ocala (G-11633)

Atlanta Nat Leag Bsbal CLB LLC ....D 941 413-5000
North Port (G-11565)

Atp Tour Charities Inc ....E 904 285-8000
Ponte Vedra Beach (G-14975)

Basketball Properties Ltd ....D 786 777-1000
Miami (G-9226)

Boston Red Sox Bsbal CLB Ltd P ....B 239 334-4700
Fort Myers (G-4294)

▲ Buccaneers Team LLC ....C 813 870-2700
Tampa (G-17396)

Epic Productions LLC ....C 954 270-8335
Pembroke Pines (G-14149)

Florida Sports Foundation Inc ....E 850 488-8347
Tallahassee (G-16981)

Football Equities Inc ....E 407 648-4444
Ocoee (G-11814)

Hw Spring Training Complex LLC ....E 844 676-2017
West Palm Beach (G-19191)

International Mtr Spt Assn LLC ....C 386 310-5000
Daytona Beach (G-2617)

Jacksonville Fc Inc ....E 904 223-3606
Jacksonville (G-6360)

Jacksonville Jaguars LLC ....C 904 633-6000
Jacksonville (G-6362)

Jacksonville Sports Group ....D 904 621-0700
Middleburg (G-10796)

Jupiter Stadium Ltd ....C 561 775-1818
Jupiter (G-7107)

Ktb Florida Sports Arena LLC ....C 239 948-7825
Estero (G-3466)

Lightning Hockey LP ....D 813 301-6500
Tampa (G-17953)

Marlins Teamco LLC ....E 305 480-1300
Miami (G-9904)

▲ Miami Dolphins Ltd ....C 954 452-7000
Miami Gardens (G-10691)

Miami Dolphins Ltd ....E 954 452-7000
Miami Gardens (G-10692)

▼ Miami Heat Limited Partnership ....E 786 777-4328
Miami (G-9970)

▼ Miami Marlins LP ....B 305 480-1300
Miami (G-9977)

Minnesota Twins LLC ....C 239 561-1117
Fort Myers (G-4515)

Naimoli Baseball Enterprises ....D 727 825-3137
Saint Petersburg (G-15772)

Northwest Prof Basbal LLC ....E 850 934-8444
Pensacola (G-14390)

Orlando Magic Ltd ....C 407 440-7000
Orlando (G-12976)

Orlando Sports Holdings LLC ....D 855 675-2489
Orlando (G-12984)

Pittsburgh Associates ....E 941 747-3031
Bradenton (G-1161)

Pittsburgh Associates LP ....D 412 321-2827
Bradenton (G-1162)

Polo CLB of Boca Rton Prprty O ....B 561 995-1200
Boca Raton (G-755)

Professnal Glfers Assn of Amer ....C 561 624-8400
Palm Beach Gardens (G-13766)

Tampa Bay Arena LLC ....B 813 301-6500
Tampa (G-18363)

Tampa Bay Rays Baseball Ltd ....C 727 825-3137
Saint Petersburg (G-15871)

▲ Tampa Sports Authority ....E 813 350-6500
Tampa (G-18402)

Walt Dsney Prks Resorts US Inc ....A 407 824-2222
Lake Buena Vista (G-7492)

7948 Racing & Track Operations

Associated Outdoor Club Inc ....D 901 486-9654
Boca Raton (G-431)

Automobile Racing CLB Amer LLC ....E 734 847-6726
Daytona Beach (G-2549)

Bestbet- Jacksonville ....D 904 646-0001
Orange Park (G-11975)

Calder Race Course Inc ....B 305 625-1311
Miami Gardens (G-10679)

Daytona Beach Kennel Club Inc ....C 386 252-6484
Daytona Beach (G-2575)

◆ Daytona Intl Speedway LLC ....E 386 226-2000
Daytona Beach (G-2581)

Gulfstream Park Racg Assn Inc ....D 954 454-7000
Hallandale Beach (G-5171)

Homestead-Miami Speedway LLC ....C 305 230-5000
Homestead (G-5583)

▲ International Speedway Corp ....E 386 254-2700
Daytona Beach (G-2618)

Investment Corp Palm Beach ....A 561 683-2222
West Palm Beach (G-19206)

▲ Investment Corp South Florida ....D 954 454-0605
Hallandale Beach (G-5175)

Jacksonville Kennel Club Inc ....E 904 646-0001
Jacksonville (G-6364)

Jefferson Cnty Kennel CLB Inc ....D 850 997-1000
Monticello (G-10933)

Orange Park Kennel Club Inc ....D 904 646-0001
Orange Park (G-12008)

Ppi Inc ....A 954 972-2000
Pompano Beach (G-14879)

Sanford Orlando Kennel Club ....D 407 830-8752
Longwood (G-8399)

Sarasota Kennel Club Inc ....D 941 355-7515
Sarasota (G-16305)

▲ Sebring Intl Raceway Inc ....E 800 626-7223
Sebring (G-16417)

Southwest Florida Entps Inc ....E 239 992-2411
Miami (G-10310)

Southwest Florida Entps Inc ....B 239 992-2411
Bonita Springs (G-944)

St Petersburg Kennel Club Inc ....C 727 812-3339
Saint Petersburg (G-15858)

▲ Tampa Bay Downs Inc ....A 813 855-4401
Tampa (G-18366)

Washington Cnty Kennel CLB Inc ....D 850 535-4048
Ebro (G-3406)

West Flagler Associates Ltd ....C 305 649-3000
Miami (G-10496)

7991 Physical Fitness Facilities

18001 Holdings LLC ....D 305 692-5600
Sunny Isles Beach (G-16711)

Adventist Hlth Systm/Snbelt In ....D 407 303-4400
Kissimmee (G-7263)

Amelia Island Company ....C 904 261-6161
Fernandina Beach (G-3521)

Bardmoor/Bayou Club Ltd ....D 727 392-1234
Largo (G-8078)

Bath and Tennis Club Inc ....C 561 833-8050
Palm Beach (G-13647)

BCM-CHI Eden Rock Tenants LP ....B 305 531-0000
Miami (G-9232)

Beach Club Inc ....D 561 842-4874
Palm Beach (G-13648)

Central Fla Yung MNS Chrstn As ....D 407 679-9622
Winter Park (G-19698)

Central Fla Yung MNS Chrstn As ....C 321 433-7770
Cocoa (G-1922)

Central Fla Yung MNS Chrstn As ....C 407 847-7413
Kissimmee (G-7281)

Central Fla Yung MNS Chrstn As ....C 352 343-1144
Tavares (G-18601)

Central Fla Yung MNS Chrstn As ....C 407 644-3606
Winter Park (G-19699)

City of Cape Coral ....E 239 574-0557
Cape Coral (G-1384)

Club At Admirals Cove Inc ....C 561 745-5920
Jupiter (G-7059)

Club At Eaglebrooke ....D 863 701-0101
Lakeland (G-7838)

Club of Treasure Island ....E 727 367-4511
Treasure Island (G-18709)

Clubcorp Usa Inc ....D 813 972-1991
Tampa (G-17489)

▲ Colonnade Partners Ltd ....E 305 441-2600
Coral Gables (G-2075)

Contour Nils Hair By Fnit Pnfs ....C 954 472-7733
Plantation (G-14624)

Corporate Fitness Works Inc ....D 727 522-2900
Saint Petersburg (G-15644)

CP Sanibel LLC ....B 239 466-4000
Fort Myers (G-4330)

Crunch LLC ....D 239 208-4253
Estero (G-3450)

Crunch LLC ....D 305 674-8222
Miami Beach (G-10579)

D & D Fitness Corporation ....E 850 385-9712
Tallahassee (G-16927)

D & D Fitness Corporation ....E 850 942-9712
Tallahassee (G-16928)

Delray Club Inc ....D 561 819-6930
Delray Beach (G-2942)

Dkp Enterprises Inc ....D 727 541-7296
Pinellas Park (G-14514)

E3 Fitness Inc ....E 561 750-7945
Boca Raton (G-561)

Elase Medical Spas ....D 407 897-2211
Orlando (G-12456)

Equinox-76th Street Inc ....D 786 497-8200
Coral Gables (G-2102)

Equinox-76th Street Inc ....D 305 273-1988
Miami (G-9528)

Equinox-76th Street Inc ....C 305 673-1172
Miami Beach (G-10591)

Fiddlers Creek Insur Agcy Inc ....E 239 732-3030
Naples (G-11110)

Florida Fontainebleau Ht LLC ....B 305 538-2000
Miami (G-9576)

Florida Hospital Ocala Inc ....C 352 368-7099
Ocala (G-11691)

Forest Oaks Country Club Inc ....D 336 674-2241
Orlando (G-12540)

Gainesvlle Hlth Fitnes Ctr Inc ....C 352 692-2180
Newberry (G-11431)

Gainesvlle Hlth Fitnes Ctr Inc ....C 352 374-4634
Gainesville (G-4903)

Geeta Hospitality Incorporated ....D 937 642-3777
Naples (G-11129)

Golden Gate Inn Cntry CLB Prtn ....D 239 353-9500
Naples (G-11136)

Golds Gym Franchising LLC ....A 727 822-9394
Saint Petersburg (G-15690)

Golf Breeze Aerobics & Fitnes ....E 850 934-0335
Gulf Breeze (G-5115)

Gratiae Soap and Spa Co Inc ....E 239 325-8263
Fort Myers (G-4424)

Greater Daytona Bch Area YMCA ....D 386 255-8773
Deland (G-2863)

Greater Dytona Bch Area Yung M ....D 386 532-9622
Deltona (G-3039)

Health First Shared Svcs Inc ....A 321 434-4300
Rockledge (G-15350)

Health Management Assoc Inc ....D 813 783-1237
Zephyrhills (G-19836)

HI Development Corp ....B 352 376-1661
Gainesville (G-4913)

▲ Hippocrates Health Inst Inc ....E 561 471-8876
West Palm Beach (G-19179)

Hyatt Corporation ....C 813 874-1234
Tampa (G-17849)

Ideal Image Development Inc ....E 813 286-8100
Tampa (G-17852)

IM A Body Exercise Studio ....D 561 626-7711
Palm Beach Gardens (G-13740)

Jewish Cmnty Ctr Grter Orlndo ....D 407 645-5933
Maitland (G-8546)

▲ Johns Island Club Inc ....C 772 231-1700
Vero Beach (G-18882)

Jupiter Resort LLC ....C 561 746-2511
Jupiter (G-7106)

Key Hospitality & Healthcare ....D 305 293-1818
Key West (G-7219)

Lake Region Yacht & Cntry CLB ....E 863 324-4579
Winter Haven (G-19641)

Laurel Oak Country Club Inc ....D 941 378-3608
Sarasota (G-16217)

Life Time Inc ....D 561 208-5900
Boca Raton (G-671)

Life Time Inc ....D 561 208-5924
Boca Raton (G-672)

Lodge At Ponte Vedra Beach Ltd ....C 904 285-1111
Ponte Vedra Beach (G-14988)

M&C Hotel Interests Inc ....C 904 396-5100
Jacksonville (G-6456)

Martin Downs Country Club Inc ....C 772 286-6818
Palm City (G-13792)

Meadows Country Club Inc	C	941 371-6000	Sarasota (G-16228)

Meadows Country Club Inc..........C......941 371-6000
Sarasota (G-16228)
Met LLC..........E......941 388-3991
Sarasota (G-16230)
Mj Ocala Hotel Associates..........C......352 854-1400
Ocala (G-11736)
▲ Moorings Club Inc..........D......772 231-1004
Vero Beach (G-18896)
My Pure Life LLC..........E......561 617-5993
Boca Raton (G-706)
Naples Community Hospital Inc..........B......239 436-6770
Naples (G-11226)
Ocean Properties Ltd..........D......941 747-3727
Bradenton (G-1156)
One Spa World LLC..........E......305 358-9002
Coral Gables (G-2162)
Orangetheory Fitness West Boca..........D......561 488-1955
Boca Raton (G-732)
Palm Beach Polo Inc..........D......561 798-7000
West Palm Beach (G-19316)
Pensacola Country Club Assn..........E......850 455-7364
Pensacola (G-14408)
PH Hotel Inc..........D......305 372-0313
Miami (G-10114)
Porto Vita Villa Grande Club..........E......305 931-7442
Aventura (G-280)
Quail West Foundation Inc..........C......239 593-4100
Naples (G-11276)
Rdc Golf of Florida I Inc..........C......407 333-1450
Lake Mary (G-7631)
Royal Poinciana Golf Club Inc..........C......239 261-3968
Naples (G-11290)
Safe Children Coalition Inc..........B......941 955-8194
Sarasota (G-16290)
Safe Children Coalition Inc..........E......941 371-4799
Sarasota (G-16288)
Seascape Resorts Inc..........D......850 837-9181
Miramar Beach (G-10926)
Sportsplex Inc..........D......904 247-5552
Neptune Beach (G-11359)
Swh Hotel LLC..........E......850 654-2677
Destin (G-3080)
Tampa Metropolitan Area YMCA..........C......813 684-1371
Valrico (G-18759)
Tampa Mtro Area Yung MNS Chrst..........C......813 866-9622
Tampa (G-18395)
Tampa Mtro Area Yung MNS Chrst..........D......813 224-9622
Tampa (G-18396)
Tampa Mtro Area Yung MNS Chrst..........D......352 521-0484
Dade City (G-2397)
Tampa Mtro Area Yung MNS Chrst..........D......813 222-1334
Tampa (G-18397)
Tampa Mtro Area Yung MNS Chrst..........D......813 229-9622
Tampa (G-18399)
Tampa Mtro Area Yung MNS Chrst..........D......813 780-9622
Zephyrhills (G-19852)
The Club..........E......850 696-9556
Gulf Breeze (G-5136)
Town Sports Intl Holdings Inc..........C......212 246-6700
Jupiter (G-7146)
Trustees Mease Hospital Inc..........C......727 772-2222
Palm Harbor (G-13885)
Twin Harbors Inc..........D......305 451-8500
Key Largo (G-7190)
Vero Beach Sports Complex Inc..........E......772 261-3123
Vero Beach (G-18936)
Visionary Destin Inc..........D......850 650-9998
Destin (G-3081)
What Inc..........E......850 224-7625
Tallahassee (G-17174)
Williams Island A Private Club..........D......305 937-7860
Aventura (G-284)
Wycliffe Golf & Cntry CLB Inc..........C......561 964-9200
Wellington (G-18991)
Yf Fc Operations LLC..........C......954 642-5200
Deerfield Beach (G-2822)
YMCA of Palm Beachs..........D......561 967-3573
Palm Springs (G-13901)
YMCA of Treasure Coast..........E......772 221-9622
Stuart (G-16683)
YMCA Southwest Florida Inc..........C......941 492-9622
Venice (G-18823)
YMCA Southwest Florida Inc..........D......941 475-1234
Englewood (G-3442)
Youfit Health Clubs LLC..........C......954 642-5200
Deerfield Beach (G-2823)
Young MNS Christn Assn NW Fla..........E......850 432-8327
Pensacola (G-14479)
Young MNS Chrstn Assn of Flrda..........C......904 355-1436
Jacksonville (G-6957)

Young MNS Chrstn Assn of Flrda..........C......904 259-0898
Macclenny (G-8480)
Young MNS Chrstn Assn of Flrda..........C......904 471-9622
Saint Augustine (G-15515)
Young MNS Chrstn Assn of Flrda..........C......904 464-3901
Jacksonville (G-6960)
Young MNS Chrstn Assn of Flrda..........C......904 296-3220
Fernandina Beach (G-3546)
Young MNS Chrstn Assn of Flrda..........C......904 272-4304
Orange Park (G-12026)
Young MNS Chrstn Assn of Grter..........D......727 895-9622
Saint Petersburg (G-15904)
Young MNS Chrstn Assn of Mrtin..........C......772 286-4444
Stuart (G-16684)
Young MNS Chrstn Assn of Sncas..........D......312 932-1200
Clearwater (G-1844)
Young MNS Chrstn Assn of Sncas..........C......727 394-9622
Seminole (G-16465)
Young MNS Chrstn Assn of Sncas..........D......727 787-9622
Palm Harbor (G-13887)
Young MNS Chrstn Assn of Sncas..........C......352 688-9622
Spring Hill (G-16556)
Young MNS Chrstn Assn of Sncas..........C......727 461-9622
Clearwater (G-1845)
Young MNS Chrstn Assn of Sncas..........D......727 772-9622
Palm Harbor (G-13888)
Young MNS Chrstn Assn of Sncas..........D......727 844-0332
New Port Richey (G-11411)
Young MNS Chrstn Assn S Fla In..........E......305 643-2626
Miami (G-10524)
Young MNS Chrstn Assn S Fla In..........E......305 635-9622
Miami (G-10525)
Young MNS Chrstn Assn S Fla In..........E......305 248-5189
Homestead (G-5613)
Young MNS Chrstn Assn S Fla In..........E......305 248-5189
Homestead (G-5612)
Zone Health and Fitness Llc..........D......352 509-3133
Ocala (G-11799)
▲ Zumba Fitness LLC..........D......954 526-7979
Hallandale Beach (G-5187)

7992 Public Golf Courses

Addison Reserve Cntry CLB Inc..........C......561 637-4004
Delray Beach (G-2898)
Amelia Island Company..........C......904 261-6161
Fernandina Beach (G-3521)
Banyan Golf CLB of Palm Bch In..........E......561 793-2800
West Palm Beach (G-19047)
Bardmoor/Bayou Club Ltd..........D......727 392-1234
Largo (G-8078)
Bloomingdale Golf LLC..........E......813 685-4105
Valrico (G-18749)
Bradenton Country Club Inc..........C......941 792-1600
Bradenton (G-1065)
Brightview Golf Maint Inc..........D......239 275-9815
Fort Myers (G-4295)
Capri Isles Golf Inc..........D......941 488-4099
Venice (G-18771)
▼ Capri Isles Golf Inc..........D......941 484-6621
Venice (G-18770)
Central Fla Investments Inc..........C......863 422-7511
Haines City (G-5146)
City of Boca Raton..........E......561 367-7000
Boca Raton (G-510)
City of Bradenton..........E......941 708-6331
Bradenton (G-1080)
City of Cape Coral..........E......239 573-3100
Cape Coral (G-1383)
City of Delray Beach..........E......561 243-7380
Delray Beach (G-2929)
City of Fort Pierce..........D......772 461-9620
Fort Pierce (G-4690)
City of Largo..........D......727 518-3024
Largo (G-8086)
City of Miami Beach..........D......305 532-3350
Miami (G-9374)
City of Palm Beach Gardens..........D......561 775-2556
West Palm Beach (G-19087)
City of Port Orange..........E......386 756-5449
Port Orange (G-15072)
City of Saint Petersburg..........D......727 551-3333
Saint Petersburg (G-15626)
City of Sarasota..........E......941 955-8097
Sarasota (G-16123)
City of Tallahassee..........D......850 891-3935
Tallahassee (G-16916)
Club At Admirals Cove Inc..........C......561 745-5920
Jupiter (G-7059)
Club At Eaglebrooke..........D......863 701-0101
Lakeland (G-7838)

Countryside Country Club Inc..........D......727 796-2153
Clearwater (G-1588)
Cypress Golf Management LLC..........E......855 557-7500
Apollo Beach (G-133)
Dazi LLC..........D......772 692-3322
Jensen Beach (G-7014)
Dixie Plaza..........E......863 993-2221
Arcadia (G-228)
Dubsdread Golf Course..........D......407 246-2551
Orlando (G-12444)
Dunedin Country Club Inc..........E......727 733-7836
Dunedin (G-3384)
Edward Rack Corporation..........D......954 726-8430
Tamarac (G-17187)
Emerald Golf Inc..........E......954 961-4000
Hollywood (G-5432)
Fairways Golf Corporation..........C......407 589-7200
Lakeland (G-7860)
Falcons Fire Golf Club Inc..........E......407 397-2777
Kissimmee (G-7305)
Forest Glen Golf Cntry CLB MST..........D......239 348-1332
Naples (G-11123)
Forest Oaks Country Club Inc..........D......336 674-2241
Orlando (G-12540)
▲ Gateway Golf & Country CLB Inc..........D......239 561-1036
Fort Myers (G-4410)
Gateway Golf Management Corp..........E......239 561-1200
Fort Myers (G-4411)
Golden Gate Inn Cntry CLB Inc..........D......239 455-9498
Naples (G-11134)
Golf Club of The Everglades..........E......239 643-4241
Naples (G-11137)
Golf Courses..........D......321 255-4606
Melbourne (G-8894)
Golf First LLC..........E......561 622-0036
Jupiter (G-7084)
Golfnow LLC..........D......800 767-3574
Orlando (G-12581)
Golfvisions Management Inc..........C......863 676-2422
Lake Wales (G-7683)
Grand Cypress Florida LP..........C......407 239-4700
Orlando (G-12589)
Green Golf Partners LLC..........E......239 283-5522
Cape Coral (G-1397)
Heritage Plms Golf Cntry CLB I..........D......239 278-9090
Fort Myers (G-4437)
HHCC Inc..........E......352 753-8700
Lady Lake (G-7435)
Hunters Run Prprty Owners Assn..........C......561 735-4002
Boynton Beach (G-999)
Ibis West Palm Partners LP..........C......561 624-8944
West Palm Beach (G-19194)
Igc-Metrowest Golf Club LLC..........D......407 299-8800
Winter Garden (G-19572)
Indian River County..........D......772 770-5000
Vero Beach (G-18876)
Inverrary Golf Club LLC..........C......954 733-7550
Lauderhill (G-8202)
Isleworth Country Club Inc..........B......407 999-2000
Windermere (G-19544)
J & D Properties LLC..........E......954 752-5305
Margate (G-8653)
▲ Johns Island Club Inc..........C......772 231-1700
Vero Beach (G-18882)
▲ Jupiter Golf Club LLC..........D......561 691-8700
Jupiter (G-7093)
Kelly Plantation Golf Club Ltd..........E......850 650-7600
Destin (G-3066)
Key West Golf Club..........E......305 292-1480
Key West (G-7221)
La Playa Golf Club LLC..........D......239 597-2991
Naples (G-11193)
Laurel Oak Country Club Inc..........D......941 378-3608
Sarasota (G-16217)
Loxahatchee Club Inc..........D......561 744-6168
Jupiter (G-7111)
Lpga Intl Girls Golf CLB..........D......386 274-5742
Daytona Beach (G-2628)
Lucas Fairways LLC..........D......904 285-5552
Ponte Vedra Beach (G-14989)
Martin Downs Country Club Inc..........C......772 286-6818
Palm City (G-13792)
Meadowbrook Ekana LLC..........C......407 366-1211
Oviedo (G-13560)
Meadowbrook Golf Group Inc..........D......850 939-4604
Gulf Breeze (G-5124)
Meadowbrook Golf Group Inc..........E......850 476-0611
Pensacola (G-14359)
Meadowbrook Golf Group Inc..........D......850 932-1333
Gulf Breeze (G-5125)

▲ Meadowbrook Golf Group Inc..........D...... 407 589-7200
  Lakeland (G-7917)
Meadowbrook Kissimmee Bay LLC ......C...... 407 348-4653
  Kissimmee (G-7356)
Meadows Country Club Inc ....C...... 941 371-6000
  Sarasota (G-16228)
Miccosukee Golf and Cntry CLB ....E...... 305 382-3930
  Miami (G-9999)
Mlq Sgr Reo LLC ....D...... 904 285-7777
  Ponte Vedra Beach (G-14993)
▲ Moorings Club Inc...........................D...... 772 231-1004
  Vero Beach (G-18896)
Myakka Pnes Golf CLB Englwood ....E...... 941 474-1753
  Englewood (G-3439)
Naples Golf and Beach Club Inc ....B...... 239 261-2222
  Naples (G-11230)
Naples National Golf Club Inc...........D...... 239 775-8743
  Naples (G-11237)
Nittany Trails LLC ....D...... 813 920-6681
  Dunedin (G-3389)
North Shore Golf Club LLC ....E...... 407 277-9277
  Orlando (G-12916)
Oceanside Golf & Cntry CLB Inc ....D...... 386 677-7200
  Ormond Beach (G-13512)
Old Marsh Golf Club Inc ....E...... 561 626-7400
  West Palm Beach (G-19292)
Orange County Nat Golf CLB LLC ....E...... 407 656-2626
  Winter Garden (G-19583)
Orchid Island Golf Bch CLB Inc ....D...... 772 388-2350
  Vero Beach (G-18901)
Packing House By-Products Co ....D...... 352 324-3101
  Howey In The Hills (G-5624)
Palm Bch Nat Golf Cntry CLB In ....E...... 561 965-0044
  Lake Worth (G-7743)
Palm Beach Golf Center Inc ....E...... 561 842-7100
  West Palm Beach (G-19311)
Palm Beach Polo Inc ....D...... 561 798-7000
  West Palm Beach (G-19316)
Pensacola Country Club Assn ....E...... 850 455-7364
  Pensacola (G-14408)
Pga Golf Enterprises Inc ....C...... 561 624-8400
  Palm Beach Gardens (G-13764)
Pga Reserve Inc ....C...... 561 624-8400
  Palm Beach Gardens (G-13765)
Pga Tour Golf Course Prpts ....E...... 904 535-3689
  Ponte Vedra (G-14969)
Pga Tour Holdings Inc ....A...... 904 285-3700
  Ponte Vedra Beach (G-14999)
Pga Tour National Headquarters ....D...... 904 285-3700
  Ponte Vedra Beach (G-15000)
Pga Tour Pub Golf Jacksonville ....D...... 904 779-2100
  Jacksonville (G-6597)
Pine Tree Golf Club Inc......................B...... 561 732-6404
  Boynton Beach (G-1028)
Plantation Golf Cntry CLB Inc ....D...... 941 497-1494
  Venice (G-18797)
Pope Golf LLC ....E...... 941 444-6600
  Sarasota (G-16271)
Professional Course MGT II Ltd ....D...... 305 532-3350
  Miami Beach (G-10642)
Professional Course MGT II Ltd ....E...... 305 868-6502
  Miami (G-10150)
Professional Course Mgt II Ltd ....E...... 305 795-2360
  Pembroke Pines (G-14177)
Quail West Foundation Inc..................C...... 239 593-4100
  Naples (G-11276)
Rdc Golf of Florida I Inc ....C...... 407 333-1450
  Lake Mary (G-7631)
Regatta Bay Investors Ltd ....E...... 850 337-8070
  Destin (G-3073)
Rida Development Corp ....D...... 407 397-2500
  Champions Gate (G-1478)
Rida Development Corp ....D...... 407 787-4653
  Orlando (G-13109)
Ritz-Carlton Hotel Company LLC ....B...... 561 691-8700
  Jupiter (G-7135)
Rodriguez Chi Chi Yuth Fndtion ....E...... 727 723-0516
  Clearwater (G-1777)
Rosen 9939 Inc ....A...... 407 996-9939
  Orlando (G-13131)
Royal Poinciana Golf Club Inc ....C...... 239 261-3968
  Naples (G-11290)
S & S Golf Management Inc ....C...... 407 384-6888
  Orlando (G-13153)
Saint Andrews S Golf CLB Inc ....E...... 941 639-8353
  Punta Gorda (G-15219)
Sandestin Beach Hotel Ltd ....D...... 850 622-9595
  Destin (G-3088)
Sanlan Rv & Golf Resort Inc ....D...... 863 667-1988
  Lakeland (G-7962)

Schroeder Manatee Inc ....E...... 941 907-4700
  Lakewood Ranch (G-8029)
Scratch Golf Company ....D...... 407 321-0010
  Lake Mary (G-7637)
Southern Dunes Golf & ....D...... 863 421-4653
  Haines City (G-5158)
Southern Golf Appraisals Inc ....D...... 954 927-1751
  Hollywood (G-5533)
Southern Sandbaggers LLC ....E...... 850 942-4653
  Tallahassee (G-17107)
Spring Run Golf CLB Cmnty Assn ....D...... 239 949-0707
  Estero (G-3478)
Spruce Creek Country Club Inc ....D...... 386 756-6116
  Port Orange (G-15088)
Sugar Mill Country Club Inc................D...... 386 426-5200
  New Smyrna Beach (G-11426)
Tampa Sports Authority ....D...... 813 673-4317
  Tampa (G-18403)
▲ Tampa Sports Authority ....E...... 813 350-6500
  Tampa (G-18402)
Tournment Plyers CLB At Cheval ....D...... 813 949-0090
  Lutz (G-8461)
Tournment Plyers CLB At Swgras ....C...... 904 273-3230
  Ponte Vedra Beach (G-15009)
Tournment Plyers CLB Tampa Bay ....D...... 813 949-0090
  Lutz (G-8462)
Trump Intl Golf CLB Lc ....C...... 561 682-0700
  Palm Beach (G-13673)
University Athletic Assn Inc ....D...... 352 375-4866
  Gainesville (G-5019)
Venice Golf Association Inc ....E...... 941 488-3948
  Venice (G-18814)
Walt Dsney Prks Resorts US Inc ....A...... 407 939-4653
  Lake Buena Vista (G-7481)
Walt Dsney Prks Resorts US Inc ....B...... 407 934-3400
  Lake Buena Vista (G-7499)
Winston Trails Golf Club Ltd.................E...... 561 439-3700
  Lake Worth (G-7762)

7993 Coin-Operated Amusement Devices & Arcades

Apex Parks Group LLC........................B...... 850 837-8319
  Destin (G-3049)
Cocoa Beach Pier ....D...... 321 783-4050
  Cocoa Beach (G-1966)
Recreation Investments of Fla.............D...... 850 654-4668
  Destin (G-3072)
Rwb Financial LLC.............................D...... 407 363-5919
  Orlando (G-13152)

7996 Amusement Parks

Andretti Thrill Park............................E...... 321 956-6706
  Melbourne (G-8816)
Apex Parks Group LLC........................B...... 850 837-8319
  Destin (G-3049)
City of Deland ....E...... 386 740-6832
  Deland (G-2849)
County of Broward.............................C...... 954 357-5170
  Pembroke Pines (G-14144)
Envirnmntal Prtection Fla Dept ....D...... 954 924-3859
  Dania (G-2413)
Envirnmntal Prtection Fla Dept ....D...... 386 497-1148
  Fort White (G-4814)
Festival Fun Parks LLC ....D...... 305 361-5705
  Miami (G-9554)
Fun Spot of Florida Inc.......................E...... 407 363-3867
  Orlando (G-12555)
Godwins Gatorland Inc ....D...... 407 855-5496
  Orlando (G-12577)
▲ Orlampa Inc ....D...... 863 984-3500
  Polk City (G-14727)
Parc Management LLC ....D...... 904 732-7272
  Jacksonville (G-6578)
Recreation Investments of Fla.............D...... 850 654-4668
  Destin (G-3072)
▲ Sea World LLC ....E...... 407 226-5011
  Orlando (G-13174)
Sea World of Florida LLC.....................A...... 877 434-7268
  Orlando (G-13175)
Sea World of Florida LLC.....................A...... 407 825-2631
  Orlando (G-13176)
Sea World of Florida LLC.....................C...... 407 226-5121
  Orlando (G-13177)
Seaworld Entertainment Inc ....C...... 407 226-5011
  Orlando (G-13178)
Seaworld Parks & Entrmt Inc ....C...... 407 226-5011
  Orlando (G-13179)
Seaworld Parks & Entrmt LLC ....A...... 813 987-5250
  Tampa (G-18260)

Seaworld Parks & Entrmt LLC ....A...... 813 987-5600
  Tampa (G-18261)
Seaworld Parks Entrmt Intl Inc ....C...... 407 226-5011
  Orlando (G-13180)
State of Florida ....C...... 850 922-6007
  Tallahassee (G-17114)
T Old Town LLC ....C...... 407 396-4888
  Kissimmee (G-7395)
Twdc Enterprises 18 Corp ....B...... 407 824-7839
  Orlando (G-13321)
▲ United Trophy Manufacturing ....E...... 407 841-2525
  Orlando (G-13342)
▲ Universal City Fla Partners ....D...... 407 363-8000
  Orlando (G-13343)
Universal City Travel Partners ....A...... 407 363-8000
  Orlando (G-13344)
▲ Universal Cy Dev Partners Ltd ....B...... 407 363-8000
  Orlando (G-13347)
Universal Orlando Online ....D...... 407 363-8000
  Orlando (G-13349)
▲ Universal Studios Vacation Co ....A...... 407 224-7000
  Orlando (G-13351)
Walt Dsney Prks Resorts US Inc ....A...... 321 939-7013
  Orlando (G-13397)
Walt Dsney Prks Resorts US Inc ....C...... 407 824-2330
  Orlando (G-13399)
▲ Walt Dsney Prks Resorts US Inc ....A...... 407 824-2222
  Lake Buena Vista (G-7487)
Walt Dsney Prks Resorts US Inc ....C...... 407 939-5277
  Lake Buena Vista (G-7488)
Walt Dsney Prks Resorts US Inc ....B...... 716 541-7657
  Orlando (G-13400)
Walt Dsney Prks Resorts US Inc ....A...... 407 541-5600
  Kissimmee (G-7409)
Walt Dsney Prks Resorts US Inc ....C...... 708 670-6204
  Lake Buena Vista (G-7491)
Walt Dsney Prks Resorts US Inc ....B...... 407 566-1900
  Celebration (G-1472)
Whiteco Industries Inc.......................C...... 727 791-1799
  Clearwater (G-1840)

7997 Membership Sports & Recreation Clubs

809 Surf Club LLC.............................D...... 305 695-1965
  Miami Beach (G-10539)
Aberdeen Golf & Cntry CLB Inc............E...... 561 738-5976
  Boynton Beach (G-956)
Addison Reserve Cntry CLB Inc............C...... 561 637-4004
  Delray Beach (G-2898)
Adios Golf Club Inc............................E...... 954 574-1456
  Coconut Creek (G-1980)
Aikg LLC ....E...... 770 992-5688
  Orlando (G-12083)
Aqua Utilities Florida Inc ....D...... 850 837-9216
  Miramar Beach (G-10921)
Arnold Plmers Bay HI CLB Lodge ....C...... 407 876-2429
  Orlando (G-12133)
Atlantic Beach Country CLB Inc............D...... 904 372-2222
  Atlantic Beach (G-239)
Atlantis Golf Club Inc ....D...... 561 966-7600
  Lake Worth (G-7712)
Audubon Country Club Assn Inc...........D...... 239 566-2677
  Naples (G-11018)
Ballenisles Country Club Inc ....C...... 561 775-4778
  Palm Beach Gardens (G-13689)
Ballenisles Country Club Inc ....C...... 561 622-0220
  Palm Beach Gardens (G-13690)
Bardmoor/Bayou Club Ltd ....D...... 727 545-3683
  Largo (G-8077)
Bardmoor/Bayou Club Ltd ....D...... 727 392-1234
  Largo (G-8078)
▲ Basketball Properties Inc ....C...... 786 777-1000
  Miami (G-9225)
Bath and Tennis Club Inc ....C...... 561 833-8050
  Palm Beach (G-13647)
Bcc LLC ....D...... 352 796-8236
  Brooksville (G-1274)
Beach Club Inc ....D...... 561 842-4874
  Palm Beach (G-13648)
Bear Lakes Country Club Inc ....D...... 561 478-0001
  West Palm Beach (G-19050)
Bears CLB Fnding Partners LLC ....D...... 561 626-2327
  Jupiter (G-7049)
Bears Paw Country Club Inc ....D...... 239 262-1836
  Naples (G-11027)
Belleview Bltmore Cntry CLB Co ....C...... 727 461-7171
  Belleair (G-368)
Bent Creek Golf Vlg Condo Assn ....E...... 865 436-3947
  Winter Garden (G-19557)
Bent Pine Golf Club Inc ....E...... 772 567-6838
  Vero Beach (G-18841)

Big Five Club Inc	D	305 223-2818	
Miami *(G-9254)*			
Bird Key Yacht Club Inc	E	941 953-4455	
Sarasota *(G-16104)*			
Bluewater Bay Tennis Center Lc	C	850 897-8010	
Niceville *(G-11441)*			
Boca Dunes Country Club Inc	E	561 451-1600	
Boca Raton *(G-460)*			
Boca Grove Golf Tennis CLB Inc	D	561 487-5300	
Boca Raton *(G-461)*			
Boca Lago Country Club Inc	D	561 482-5000	
Boca Raton *(G-462)*			
Boca Pnte Frmer Eqity Mmbers I	B	561 864-8500	
Boca Raton *(G-463)*			
Boca Rio Golf Club Inc	E	561 482-3300	
Boca Raton *(G-470)*			
▲ Boca West Country Club Inc	B	561 488-6990	
Boca Raton *(G-472)*			
Boca Woods Cntry CLB Assn Inc	C	561 487-2800	
Boca Raton *(G-474)*			
Bocaire Country Club Inc	D	561 998-1602	
Boca Raton *(G-476)*			
Boys Girls Clubs Centl Fla Inc	D	407 298-0680	
Orlando *(G-12197)*			
Bradenton Country Club Inc	C	941 792-1600	
Bradenton *(G-1065)*			
Bradenton Yacht Club Inc	E	941 722-5936	
Palmetto *(G-13904)*			
Bre/Baton Operating Lessee LLC	E	561 447-3000	
Boca Raton *(G-480)*			
Broken Sound Club Inc	D	561 241-6800	
Boca Raton *(G-481)*			
Brown Golf Leasing LLC	D	352 372-1458	
Gainesville *(G-4849)*			
Buckhorn Sprng Golf Cntry CLB	D	813 689-7766	
Valrico *(G-18750)*			
Burnt Store Golf & Actvty	E	941 637-1577	
Punta Gorda *(G-15194)*			
Caddie Master Enterprises Inc	D	904 694-0100	
Jacksonville Beach *(G-6979)*			
Calusa Pines Golf Club LLC	D	239 348-2220	
Naples *(G-11045)*			
▼ Capri Isles Golf Inc	D	941 484-6621	
Venice *(G-18770)*			
Carlouel Yacht Club Inc	E	727 446-9162	
Clearwater *(G-1558)*			
Carrollwood Country Club	D	813 961-1381	
Tampa *(G-17428)*			
◆ Cat Cay Yacht Club Inc	E	954 359-9575	
Fort Lauderdale *(G-3672)*			
Cedar Hmmock Golf Cntry CLB In	E	239 793-1134	
Naples *(G-11048)*			
Central Fla Yung MNS Chrstn As	C	407 644-3606	
Winter Park *(G-19699)*			
Central Fla Yung MNS Chrstn As	B	407 644-1509	
Winter Park *(G-19700)*			
Citrus Club Inc	E	407 843-1080	
Orlando *(G-12302)*			
Citrus Hill Golf & Country CLB	D	352 746-6855	
Hernando *(G-5203)*			
City of Cocoa Beach	E	321 868-3351	
Cocoa Beach *(G-1965)*			
City of Delray Beach	E	561 243-7380	
Delray Beach *(G-2929)*			
City of Delray Beach	D	561 243-7360	
Delray Beach *(G-2930)*			
City of Fort Pierce	D	772 461-9620	
Fort Pierce *(G-4690)*			
City of West Palm Beach	E	561 582-2019	
West Palm Beach *(G-19090)*			
Clearwater Country Club Inc	E	727 446-2240	
Clearwater *(G-1575)*			
Clearwater Yacht Club Inc	E	727 447-6000	
Clearwater *(G-1577)*			
Club At Eaglebrooke	D	863 701-0101	
Lakeland *(G-7838)*			
Club At Strand	C	239 592-7710	
Naples *(G-11058)*			
Club Continental Inc	D	904 264-6070	
Orange Park *(G-11982)*			
Club of Treasure Island	E	727 367-4511	
Treasure Island *(G-18709)*			
Club Pelican Bay Inc	D	239 597-2244	
Naples *(G-11059)*			
Club Pelican Bay Inc	D	239 597-1183	
Naples *(G-11060)*			
Clubcorp Golf Florida LLC	D	727 784-8576	
Oldsmar *(G-11897)*			
Clubcorp Usa Inc	D	813 972-1991	
Tampa *(G-17489)*			

Colliers Reserve Cntry CLB Inc	D	239 597-7029	
Naples *(G-11069)*			
Colonial Country Club	E	239 768-2825	
Fort Myers *(G-4318)*			
Colony At Plcan Lnding Fndtion	E	239 992-2100	
Bonita Springs *(G-904)*			
Copperleaf Golf CLB Cmnty Assn	E	239 390-2027	
Estero *(G-3449)*			
▲ Coral Reef Yacht Club	E	305 858-1733	
Miami *(G-9416)*			
Coral Ridge Golf Course Inc	D	954 449-4400	
Fort Lauderdale *(G-3718)*			
Coral Ridge Yacht Club Inc	E	954 566-7886	
Fort Lauderdale *(G-3719)*			
Country CLB At Jacaranda W Inc	D	941 493-2664	
Venice *(G-18774)*			
Country CLB of Coral Sprng Inc	C	954 752-4500	
Pompano Beach *(G-14784)*			
Country CLB of Wnter Haven LLC	E	863 324-6666	
Winter Haven *(G-19619)*			
▲ Country Club At Woodfield Inc	B	561 241-9060	
Boca Raton *(G-534)*			
Country Club of Coral Gables	D	305 448-7464	
Coral Gables *(G-2081)*			
Country Club of Naples Inc	D	239 261-1267	
Naples *(G-11078)*			
Country Club of Orlando Inc	C	407 849-0990	
Orlando *(G-12372)*			
Countryside Country Club Inc	D	727 796-2153	
Clearwater *(G-1588)*			
Countryside Master Assn Inc	D	239 353-1780	
Naples *(G-11079)*			
County of Brevard	C	321 255-4400	
Melbourne *(G-8859)*			
Cove Cay Country Club Inc	D	727 535-1406	
Clearwater *(G-1594)*			
Cresthill Inc	D	407 352-0330	
Orlando *(G-12384)*			
Crown Golf Properties LP	E	727 399-1000	
Largo *(G-8092)*			
Cypress Run Golf Club Inc	E	727 937-3191	
Tarpon Springs *(G-18581)*			
Cypress Wods Golf Cntry CLB Ms	D	239 593-5311	
Naples *(G-11086)*			
Debary Management Corp	D	386 668-1705	
Debary *(G-2702)*			
Deering Bay Ycht Cntry CLB Inc	E	305 256-2500	
Coral Gables *(G-2091)*			
Deerwood Country Club Inc	D	904 641-6100	
Jacksonville *(G-6055)*			
Delaire Country Club Inc	D	561 499-9090	
Delray Beach *(G-2939)*			
Delray Club Inc	D	561 819-6930	
Delray Beach *(G-2942)*			
Delray Dunes Golf & Cntry CLB	D	561 732-1600	
Boynton Beach *(G-983)*			
Destination Residences LLC	C	386 445-0852	
Palm Coast *(G-13819)*			
Doral Park Cntry CLB Assn Inc	D	305 591-8800	
Doral *(G-3182)*			
Dunedin Country Club Inc	E	727 733-7836	
Dunedin *(G-3384)*			
Eagle Creek Golf Cntry CLB Inc	C	239 793-2702	
Naples *(G-11099)*			
Eastpointe Country Club Inc	C	561 626-9651	
West Palm Beach *(G-19127)*			
Epping Forest Yacht Club Inc	D	904 739-7200	
Jacksonville *(G-6127)*			
Esplanade Golf Cntry CLB At Lk	E	941 306-3500	
Bradenton *(G-1094)*			
Esplanade Golf Cntry CLB Nples	E	239 494-8020	
Naples *(G-11105)*			
Estero Country Club Inc	D	239 267-7000	
Estero *(G-3454)*			
Evert Tennis Academy LLC	D	561 488-2001	
Boca Raton *(G-568)*			
Falls Country Club Inc	E	561 964-5700	
Lake Worth *(G-7726)*			
Feather Sound Country Club Inc	D	727 573-5666	
Clearwater *(G-1635)*			
Felcor St Pete Leasing Spe LLC	C	727 824-8072	
Saint Petersburg *(G-15666)*			
Fiddlers Creek Insur Agcy Inc	E	239 732-3030	
Naples *(G-11110)*			
Fiddlesticks Country Club Inc	D	239 768-1024	
Fort Myers *(G-4370)*			
Fiddlesticks Security Inc	C	239 768-1111	
Fort Myers *(G-4371)*			
Field Club Inc	D	941 924-1201	
Sarasota *(G-16163)*			

Flagler System Inc	C	561 655-6611	
Palm Beach *(G-13654)*			
Florida Golf Shop Inc	E	954 972-8140	
Margate *(G-8646)*			
Florida Lemkco Inc	D	352 688-8888	
Miami *(G-9578)*			
Florida Olde Golf Club Inc	E	239 353-4441	
Naples *(G-11118)*			
Florida Windermere Inc	D	407 876-4410	
Windermere *(G-19541)*			
Florida Yacht Club Inc	D	904 387-1653	
Jacksonville *(G-6203)*			
Forest Country Club Inc	D	239 482-8378	
Fort Myers *(G-4396)*			
Forest Country Club Inc	E	239 482-6818	
Fort Myers *(G-4397)*			
Forest Glen Golf Cntry CLB MST	D	239 348-1332	
Naples *(G-11123)*			
Forest Oaks Country Club Inc	D	336 674-2241	
Orlando *(G-12540)*			
▲ Fort Lauderdale Cntry CLB Inc	C	954 587-4700	
Plantation *(G-14645)*			
◆ Fountains Country Club Inc	C	561 642-2700	
Lake Worth *(G-7730)*			
Foxfire Cmnty Assn Cllier Cnty	D	239 643-3139	
Naples *(G-11126)*			
Frenchmans Creek Inc	C	561 622-8300	
Palm Beach Gardens *(G-13732)*			
Frenchmans Rsrve Cntry CLB Inc	D	561 630-0333	
Palm Beach Gardens *(G-13733)*			
Gate Petroleum Company	C	904 737-7220	
Jacksonville *(G-6217)*			
Glades Golf and Cntry CLB Inc	E	239 774-6899	
Naples *(G-11132)*			
Glen Eagle Golf Cntry CLB Inc	D	239 304-1428	
Naples *(G-11133)*			
Glen Herons Recreation Dst	D	239 567-0600	
Fort Myers *(G-4418)*			
Glen Lakes Realty LLC	D	352 597-9000	
Weeki Wachee *(G-18968)*			
Gleneagles Country Club Inc	B	561 495-6336	
Delray Beach *(G-2956)*			
Golden Egle Golf Cntry CLB Inc	E	850 893-7700	
Tallahassee *(G-16989)*			
Golden Gate Inn Cntry CLB Inc	D	239 455-9498	
Naples *(G-11134)*			
Golf Club of Quincy The Inc	D	850 627-8386	
Quincy *(G-15231)*			
Golf Club of The Everglades	E	239 643-4241	
Naples *(G-11137)*			
Golfnow LLC	D	800 767-3574	
Orlando *(G-12581)*			
Golfvisions Management Inc	C	863 676-2422	
Lake Wales *(G-7683)*			
Grand Hbr Golf & Bch CLB Inc	D	772 794-9508	
Vero Beach *(G-18861)*			
Grand Palms Golf and Cntry CLB	E	954 431-8800	
Pembroke Pines *(G-14153)*			
Grasslands Golf and Cntry CLB	D	863 680-1600	
Lakeland *(G-7879)*			
▲ Grey Oaks Country Club Inc	C	239 262-5550	
Naples *(G-11147)*			
Gulf Hrbour Golf Cntry CLB Inc	D	239 433-5111	
Fort Myers *(G-4430)*			
Gulf Stream Golf Club Inc	D	561 276-4421	
Delray Beach *(G-2959)*			
Haile Plantation Cmnty CLB Inc	D	352 335-0055	
Gainesville *(G-4911)*			
Hamilton Harbor Marina Inc	E	239 775-0506	
Naples *(G-11154)*			
Hammock Dunes Club Inc	D	386 445-0747	
Palm Coast *(G-13829)*			
Harbour Rdge Ycht Cntry CLB In	C	772 336-3000	
Palm City *(G-13791)*			
Heritage Golf Group LLC	D	941 922-2800	
Sarasota *(G-16182)*			
Heritage Plms Golf Cntry CLB I	D	239 278-9090	
Fort Myers *(G-4437)*			
Heritage Rdge Golf CLB Hobe Su	E	772 546-2800	
Hobe Sound *(G-5363)*			
Heritage Sprng Cmnty Assn Inc	D	727 372-4866	
Trinity *(G-18726)*			
Hfm Inc	D	772 464-2054	
Port Saint Lucie *(G-15141)*			
HHC Seagate Hamlet LLC	C	561 498-7600	
Delray Beach *(G-2966)*			
HHCC Inc	E	352 753-8700	
Lady Lake *(G-7435)*			
Hideaway Beach Association Inc	E	239 394-5555	
Marco Island *(G-8629)*			

SIC

High Ridge Country Club Inc	E	561 586-3333	
Lake Worth (G-7733)			
Hobe Sound Associates Inc	E	772 546-4600	
Hobe Sound (G-5364)			
Hobe Sound Co Inc	D	772 546-2617	
Hobe Sound (G-5366)			
▲ Holiday Inn Club Vacations Inc	A	407 239-0000	
Orlando (G-12656)			
Hunters Run Prprty Owners Assn	C	561 735-4002	
Boynton Beach (G-999)			
Ibis West Palm Partners LP	E	561 625-8500	
West Palm Beach (G-19193)			
Ieh Gh Management LLC	C	772 794-4380	
Vero Beach (G-18873)			
Imperial Golf Club Inc	D	239 597-8165	
Naples (G-11173)			
Indian Creek Country Club	E	305 866-5751	
Indian Creek Village (G-5669)			
Indian River Colony Club Inc	C	321 255-6000	
Melbourne (G-8911)			
Indian Spring Country Club Inc	E	561 737-5544	
Boynton Beach (G-1000)			
Interlachen Country Club Inc	C	407 657-0850	
Winter Park (G-19739)			
Inverrary Golf Club LLC	C	954 733-7550	
Lauderhill (G-8202)			
Ironhorse Lakes LLC	E	561 624-5550	
West Palm Beach (G-19208)			
Isla Del Sol Ycht Cntry CLB In	D	727 906-4752	
Saint Petersburg (G-15729)			
Island Country Club Inc	D	239 394-3151	
Marco Island (G-8631)			
Isles Yacht Club Inc	D	941 639-7551	
Punta Gorda (G-15209)			
Jacksnville Golf Cntry CLB Inc	D	904 223-5555	
Jacksonville (G-6340)			
▲ Johns Island Club Inc	C	772 231-1700	
Vero Beach (G-18882)			
Jonathans Landing Golf CLB In	C	561 747-7600	
Jupiter (G-7091)			
Jonathans Landing Golf CLB In	D	561 747-5503	
Jupiter (G-7092)			
Jupiter Hills Club Inc	D	561 746-5228	
Jupiter (G-7094)			
Jupiter Island Holdings Inc	B	772 402-4208	
Hobe Sound (G-5367)			
Kasmark Inc	E	352 489-0239	
Dunnellon (G-3396)			
Kelly Greens Master Assn Inc	D	239 466-9570	
Fort Myers (G-4459)			
Key Biscayne Yacht Club Inc	E	305 361-9171	
Miami (G-9824)			
Key Largo Anglers Club Inc	D	305 367-2258	
Key Largo (G-7180)			
Kingsway Country Club Inc	D	941 625-1985	
Lake Suzy (G-7671)			
La Cita Golf and Country Club	D	321 383-5301	
Titusville (G-18693)			
La Cita Management Corp Inc	E	321 383-2582	
Titusville (G-18694)			
La Gorce Country Club Inc	C	305 866-4421	
Miami Beach (G-10606)			
La Playa Golf Club LLC	D	239 597-2991	
Naples (G-11193)			
Lago Mar Membership Assn	D	954 472-7044	
Plantation (G-14663)			
Lake City Country Club LLC	E	386 752-0721	
Lake City (G-7534)			
Lake Jovita Golf Cntry CLB Inc	D	352 588-9200	
Dade City (G-2391)			
Lake Region Yacht & Cntry CLB	E	863 324-4579	
Winter Haven (G-19641)			
Lakeland Yacht & Country Club	D	863 680-2582	
Lakeland (G-7906)			
Lakewood Ranch Golf Co LLC	C	941 755-6574	
Lakewood Ranch (G-8021)			
Lakewood Rnch Golf & Cntry CLB	E	941 907-4700	
Lakewood Rnch (G-8023)			
Lakewood Rnch Golf & Cntry CLB	C	941 907-0194	
Lakewood Ranch (G-8024)			
Landings Ycht Golf Tnnis CLB I	D	239 482-3211	
Fort Myers (G-4468)			
Lansbrook Group Inc	E	727 784-7675	
Palm Harbor (G-13869)			
Lauderdale Yacht Club Inc	D	954 524-5500	
Fort Lauderdale (G-3931)			
Laurel Oak Country Club Inc	D	941 378-3608	
Sarasota (G-16217)			
Little Club Inc	D	561 278-1010	
Delray Beach (G-2984)			

Lone Palm Golf Club LLC	D	863 499-5480	
Lakeland (G-7910)			
Lost Tree Club Inc	D	561 626-1501	
North Palm Beach (G-11550)			
Loxahatchee Club Inc	D	561 744-6168	
Jupiter (G-7111)			
Lpga Intl Girls Golf CLB	D	386 274-5742	
Daytona Beach (G-2628)			
M L Partnership	D	904 285-6514	
Ponte Vedra Beach (G-14990)			
Magnolia Golf Management	E	904 269-9276	
Green Cove Springs (G-5058)			
Manatee Cnty Fmly Yung MNS CHR	B	941 792-7484	
Bradenton (G-1133)			
Mariner Sands Country Club Inc	C	772 283-0202	
Stuart (G-16638)			
Martin Downs Country Club Inc	C	772 286-6818	
Palm City (G-13792)			
Mayacoo Lakes Country Club	E	561 793-1703	
West Palm Beach (G-19255)			
McArthur Golf LLC	D	772 545-3838	
Hobe Sound (G-5368)			
Meadowbrook Ekana LLC	C	407 366-1211	
Oviedo (G-13560)			
Meadowbrook Kissimmee Bay LLC	C	407 348-4653	
Kissimmee (G-7356)			
Meadowood Golf Tennis CLB Inc	D	772 464-4466	
Fort Pierce (G-4720)			
Meadows Country Club Inc	C	941 371-6000	
Sarasota (G-16228)			
Miccosukee Golf and Cntry CLB	E	305 382-3930	
Miami (G-9999)			
Miles Grant Country Club Inc	E	772 286-2220	
Stuart (G-16644)			
Mirasol Club Inc	B	561 775-7800	
West Palm Beach (G-19270)			
Misty Creek Country Club Inc	E	941 921-5258	
Sarasota (G-16235)			
▲ Mizner Country Club Inc	C	561 638-5600	
Delray Beach (G-2993)			
Monarch Country Club Mgt	E	772 286-8447	
Palm City (G-13794)			
▲ Moorings Club Inc	D	772 231-1004	
Vero Beach (G-18896)			
Moorings Cntry CLB of Nples In	D	239 261-1033	
Naples (G-11219)			
Mountain Lake Corporation	D	863 676-3494	
Lake Wales (G-7694)			
Naples Golf and Beach Club Inc	B	239 261-2222	
Naples (G-11230)			
Naples Hritg Golf Cntry CLB In	D	239 417-2555	
Naples (G-11234)			
Naples Lakes Country Club	D	239 919-1150	
Naples (G-11235)			
Naples National Golf Club Inc	D	239 775-8743	
Naples (G-11237)			
Naples Yacht Club Inc	D	239 262-6648	
Naples (G-11242)			
North Central Florida YMCA Inc	D	352 374-9622	
Gainesville (G-4960)			
Oaks Club Corporation	E	941 966-9764	
Osprey (G-13533)			
Ocean Club Community Assn Inc	E	305 361-2876	
Key Biscayne (G-7168)			
Ocean Club of Florida Inc	D	561 734-2440	
Ocean Ridge (G-11802)			
Oceanside Golf & Cntry CLB Inc	D	386 677-7200	
Ormond Beach (G-13512)			
Old Corkscrew Golf CLB MGT LLC	E	239 949-4700	
Estero (G-3472)			
Old Memorial Club Inc	D	813 926-8888	
Tampa (G-18096)			
Old Palm Golf Club Inc	E	866 499-6742	
Palm Beach Gardens (G-13758)			
Old Palm Golf Club Inc	D	561 472-5101	
West Palm Beach (G-19293)			
Olde Hckry Golf Cntry CLB Mstr	D	239 768-2400	
Fort Myers (G-4527)			
Opus Enterprises Ltd	E	954 626-0412	
Fort Lauderdale (G-4032)			
Orchid Island Golf Bch CLB Inc	D	772 388-2350	
Vero Beach (G-18901)			
Pablo Creek Club Inc	E	904 992-2090	
Jacksonville (G-6575)			
Palencia Club	D	904 599-9040	
Saint Augustine (G-15477)			
Palm Aire Resorts Management	D	954 978-3538	
Pompano Beach (G-14874)			
Palm Beach Polo Inc	D	561 798-7000	
West Palm Beach (G-19316)			

▼ Palm Beach Yacht Club Assoc	E	561 655-1944	
West Palm Beach (G-19318)			
Palm-Aire Country Club At Sara	C	941 351-4117	
Sarasota (G-16043)			
Palma Ceia Golf Cntry CLB Inc	C	813 253-3101	
Tampa (G-18118)			
Palmetto-Pine Country Club Inc	E	239 574-4711	
Cape Coral (G-1419)			
▲ Panthers Brhc LLC	C	888 543-1277	
Boca Raton (G-740)			
Pasadena Country Club Dev LLC	D	727 381-7922	
Gulfport (G-5143)			
Pelican Marsh Golf Club Inc	C	239 947-2600	
Naples (G-11258)			
Pelican Pointe Golf Cntry CLB	E	941 492-9776	
Venice (G-18796)			
Pelicans Nest Golf Club Inc	C	239 947-4600	
Bonita Springs (G-932)			
Pensacola Country Club Assn	E	850 455-7364	
Pensacola (G-14408)			
Peridia Prprty Owners Assn Inc	E	941 758-2582	
Bradenton (G-1160)			
Pga Tour Inc	C	904 285-3700	
Saint Augustine (G-15480)			
▲ Pga Tour Inc	A	904 285-3700	
Ponte Vedra Beach (G-14995)			
Pga Tour Inc	A	904 273-7643	
Ponte Vedra Beach (G-14996)			
Pga Tour Inc	D	904 280-2451	
Ponte Vedra Beach (G-14997)			
Pga Tour Inc	C	904 285-3700	
Ponte Vedra Beach (G-14998)			
Pga Tour Holdings Inc	A	904 285-3700	
Ponte Vedra Beach (G-14999)			
Pga Tour National Headquarters	D	904 285-3700	
Ponte Vedra Beach (G-15000)			
Pheasant Run Inc	D	239 992-5100	
Bonita Springs (G-933)			
Pine Island Rdge Cntry CLB Inc	D	954 472-7600	
Davie (G-2505)			
Pine Tree Golf Club Inc	B	561 732-6404	
Boynton Beach (G-1028)			
Plantation At Ponte Vedra Inc	D	904 543-2999	
Ponte Vedra Beach (G-15001)			
Plantation Golf Cntry CLB Inc	D	941 497-1494	
Venice (G-18797)			
Plantation Resort Inc	D	352 795-4211	
Crystal River (G-2350)			
Polo CLB of Boca Rton Prprty O	B	561 995-1200	
Boca Raton (G-755)			
Ponte Vedra Corporation	C	904 285-1111	
Ponte Vedra Beach (G-15003)			
Port Royal Club Inc	C	239 261-7615	
Naples (G-11266)			
Premier Corp Prof Svcs LLC	C	352 324-2001	
Howey In The Hills (G-5625)			
Professional Course MGT II Ltd	D	305 795-2360	
Miami Shores (G-10775)			
Professional Course MGT Inc	E	305 795-2360	
Pembroke Pines (G-14178)			
Professional Turf Maintenance	C	561 744-7849	
Jupiter (G-7127)			
Quail Creek Country Club Inc	C	239 597-2831	
Naples (G-11275)			
Quail Rdge Prprty Owners Assn	E	561 737-5100	
Boynton Beach (G-1031)			
Quail Ridge Country Club Inc	C	561 737-5100	
Boynton Beach (G-1032)			
Quail Valley Golf Club	E	772 299-0093	
Vero Beach (G-18908)			
Quail Valley Golf Club	D	772 492-2020	
Vero Beach (G-18909)			
Quail West Foundation Inc	C	239 593-4100	
Naples (G-11276)			
Rdc Golf Group Inc	E	407 333-1450	
Lake Mary (G-7630)			
Rdc Golf of Florida I Inc	E	407 333-1450	
Lake Mary (G-7631)			
Regatta Bay Investors Ltd	E	850 337-8070	
Destin (G-3073)			
River Strand Golf Cntry CLB In	D	941 708-3837	
Bradenton (G-1171)			
River Wilderness Golf Inc	D	941 776-2691	
Parrish (G-14116)			
Riviera Cntry CLB Cral Gbles F	C	305 661-5331	
Coral Gables (G-2178)			
Rockledge Country Club LLC	E	321 636-6022	
Rockledge (G-15362)			
Rocky Bayou Country Club Inc	E	850 678-3270	
Niceville (G-11457)			

Rotonda West Golf Partners D 941 697-2414
Placida *(G-14541)*
Royal Palm Cntry CLB Nples Inc D 239 793-1167
Naples *(G-11289)*
Royal Palm Yacht Cntry CLB Inc D 561 395-2100
Boca Raton *(G-778)*
Royal Poinciana Golf Club Inc C 239 261-3968
Naples *(G-11290)*
S & S Golf Management Inc C 407 384-6888
Orlando *(G-13153)*
Safe Children Coalition Inc E 941 371-4799
Sarasota *(G-16288)*
Sailfish Club of Florida Inc D 561 844-0206
Palm Beach *(G-13669)*
Sailfish Point Golf Club Inc D 772 225-1500
Stuart *(G-16665)*
Salamander Farms LLC A 561 753-8110
West Palm Beach *(G-19351)*
Salamander Innisbrook LLC C 727 942-2000
Palm Harbor *(G-13879)*
San Jose Country Club C 904 733-1511
Jacksonville *(G-6691)*
Sanctuary Golf Club Inc E 239 472-6223
Sanibel *(G-16002)*
Sanibel Hrbour Ycht CLB Cndo A E 239 333-4200
Fort Myers *(G-4584)*
Santa Rosa Golf & Bch CLB Inc E 850 267-1240
Santa Rosa Beach *(G-16014)*
Sara Bay Country Club Inc D 941 355-7658
Sarasota *(G-16051)*
Sarasota Nat Mstr Assn Inc E 941 496-8676
Venice *(G-18802)*
Sarasota Yacht Club Inc D 941 365-4191
Sarasota *(G-16311)*
Sawgrass Country Club Inc C 904 273-3700
Ponte Vedra Beach *(G-15005)*
Scratch Golf Company D 407 321-0010
Lake Mary *(G-7637)*
Seadream Yacht Club Limited C 305 631-6100
Miami *(G-10252)*
Seagate Beach Club Inc E 561 330-3775
Delray Beach *(G-3014)*
Seminole Lake Golf Course Inc E 727 391-6255
Seminole *(G-16459)*
Serenata Beach Club LLC D 904 823-3368
Ponte Vedra Beach *(G-15006)*
Seven Sprng Golf Cntry CLB Inc D 727 376-0039
New Port Richey *(G-11405)*
Shadow Wood Country Club Inc D 239 992-6000
Estero *(G-3475)*
Shadow Wood Country Club Inc C 239 949-1200
Estero *(G-3476)*
Silver Seas Hotel Inc D 954 942-7244
Lighthouse Point *(G-8296)*
Silverthorn Associates LLC D 352 799-4653
Brooksville *(G-1310)*
Six Lakes Country Club Inc E 239 995-0595
Fort Myers *(G-4595)*
Spring Lake Club Inc D 863 655-0900
Sebring *(G-16419)*
▲ St Andrews Country Club Inc B 561 487-1110
Boca Raton *(G-815)*
St Johns Golf Community E 904 940-3200
Saint Augustine *(G-15502)*
St Petersburg Country CLB Inc D 727 867-2111
Saint Petersburg *(G-15856)*
Stonebrdge Golf Cntry CLB Boca C 561 488-0800
Boca Raton *(G-823)*
Stonebridge Club C 561 488-0800
Boca Raton *(G-824)*
Stonebridge Count Club Commu A D 239 594-5200
Naples *(G-11308)*
Stoneybrook Golf Cntry CLB SRS E 941 966-2711
Sarasota *(G-16332)*
STS Aviation Group LLC D 800 800-2400
Jensen Beach *(G-7022)*
Sugar Mill Country Club Inc D 386 426-5200
New Smyrna Beach *(G-11426)*
Summer Bch Amenities Ventr LLP D 904 277-8015
Fernandina Beach *(G-3543)*
Sun Cove of Kissimmee Inc D 407 933-5870
Kissimmee *(G-7391)*
Suntacc and Company Inc C 352 382-3838
Homosassa *(G-5620)*
Suntree Country Club Inc C 321 242-6230
Melbourne *(G-8988)*
Sweetwater Golf & Country Club D 407 889-4743
Apopka *(G-217)*
Tampa Bay Golf & Cntry CLB LLC D 352 588-5454
San Antonio *(G-15911)*

Tampa Club E 813 229-6028
Tampa *(G-18372)*
Tampa Mtro Area Yung MNS Chrst B 813 962-3220
Tampa *(G-18393)*
Tampa Mtro Area Yung MNS Chrst C 813 839-0210
Tampa *(G-18398)*
Tampa Warriors Hockey Program C 845 637-7421
Parrish *(G-14117)*
Tampa Yacht and Country Club C 813 831-1611
Tampa *(G-18406)*
Tara Golf and Country Club Inc D 941 756-7775
Bradenton *(G-1188)*
Tb Isle Resort LP A 305 933-6512
Sunny Isles Beach *(G-16728)*
Tb Isle Resort LP D 305 932-6200
Aventura *(G-282)*
Tbhc Inc C 888 422-9445
Orlando *(G-13271)*
Temple Ter Golf Cntry CLB Inc D 813 988-1771
Temple Terrace *(G-18646)*
Tequesta Country Club Inc D 561 746-4620
Jupiter *(G-7144)*
The Club At Mediterra Inc D 239 254-3000
Naples *(G-11320)*
▲ The River Club Inc E 941 751-4211
Bradenton *(G-1192)*
Tiburon Golf CLB At RTZ-Crlton E 239 593-2200
Naples *(G-11324)*
Timuquana Country Club C 904 388-2664
Jacksonville *(G-6855)*
Tournment Plyers CLB At Egle T D 954 753-7222
Coral Springs *(G-2293)*
Tournment Plyers CLB At Swgras C 904 273-3230
Ponte Vedra Beach *(G-15009)*
Tournment Plyers CLB Tampa Bay C 813 949-0090
Lutz *(G-8462)*
Tower Club D 954 764-8550
Fort Lauderdale *(G-4178)*
Town Sports Intl Holdings Inc C 212 246-6700
Jupiter *(G-7146)*
Trump Intl Golf CLB Inc D 561 682-0700
West Palm Beach *(G-19392)*
Turtle Creek Club Inc D 561 746-8884
Jupiter *(G-7148)*
Tuscawilla Investors Inc D 321 277-1452
Winter Garden *(G-19598)*
Twin Isles Country Club Inc D 941 637-1232
Punta Gorda *(G-15224)*
Twineagles Club Inc C 239 354-1700
Naples *(G-11331)*
University Park Country C D 941 355-3888
University Park *(G-18744)*
University Pk Cntry CLB Assoc E 941 328-1038
University Park *(G-18745)*
Useppa Inn and Dock Co Ltd D 239 283-1061
Bokeelia *(G-886)*
Vanderbilt Community Assn Inc E 239 348-2662
Naples *(G-11335)*
Vasari Cntry CLB Mstr Assn Inc E 239 596-0645
Bonita Springs *(G-948)*
Venice Golf & Cntry CLB 1 Inc D 941 492-9600
Venice *(G-18813)*
Venice Yacht Club Inc D 941 488-7708
Venice *(G-18821)*
Ventura Cntry CLB Cmnty Hmwner D 407 275-7002
Orlando *(G-13371)*
Vero Beach Country Club Inc D 772 567-3320
Vero Beach *(G-18933)*
Villages Health E 352 674-8905
The Villages *(G-18668)*
◆ Villages of Lake-Sumter Inc A 352 753-2270
Lady Lake *(G-7447)*
Vineyards Country Club Inc D 239 353-1500
Naples *(G-11336)*
Vineyards Golf & Country Club E 239 353-1500
Naples *(G-11338)*
Walt Dsney Prks Resorts US Inc C 407 934-8410
Orlando *(G-13396)*
Wellington Soccer Club Inc E 561 985-8739
Royal Palm Beach *(G-15391)*
Westchester Golf & Country CLB D 561 369-1000
Boynton Beach *(G-1043)*
Weston Hills Country Club C 954 384-4600
Weston *(G-19486)*
Wildcat Run Golf & Country CLB E 239 947-6066
Estero *(G-3489)*
Wilderness Country Club Inc D 239 261-1140
Naples *(G-11344)*
Willoughby Golf Club Inc C 772 220-6000
Stuart *(G-16680)*

Windermere Country Club E 407 876-1112
Orlando *(G-13435)*
Windstar Club Incorporated E 239 775-5233
Naples *(G-11346)*
Winter Park Racquet Club Inc D 407 644-2226
Winter Park *(G-19790)*
Woodmont Country Club Inc D 954 597-9674
Tamarac *(G-17209)*
Worthington Master Assn Inc D 239 495-1750
Bonita Springs *(G-950)*
Worthington Renaissance LLC D 239 561-4170
Fort Myers *(G-4659)*
Wta Tour Inc D 727 895-5000
Saint Petersburg *(G-15902)*
Wycliffe Golf & Cntry CLB Inc C 561 964-9200
Wellington *(G-18991)*
Wyndemere Country Club Inc D 239 263-1700
Naples *(G-11348)*
Yacht & Country Club Inc D 772 287-3736
Stuart *(G-16682)*
YMCA Southwest Florida Inc C 941 492-9622
Venice *(G-18823)*
Young MNS Chrstn Assn of Flrda C 904 731-2006
Jacksonville *(G-6959)*
Young MNS Chrstn Assn of Flrda C 904 272-4304
Orange Park *(G-12026)*
Young MNS Chrstn Assn S Palm B C 561 738-9622
Boynton Beach *(G-1045)*
YWCA South Florida Inc D 305 377-9922
Miami *(G-10528)*

7999 Amusement & Recreation Svcs, NEC

Accesso LLC D 407 333-7311
Lake Mary *(G-7562)*
Aloma Bowling Center East Inc D 407 384-0003
Orlando *(G-12100)*
Amelia Island Cnvntion Vstors E 904 483-0214
Fernandina Beach *(G-3520)*
AMF Bowling Centers Inc E 407 846-8844
Kissimmee *(G-7269)*
AMF Bowling Centers Inc E 954 432-5500
Pembroke Pines *(G-14130)*
Apex Parks Group LLC B 850 837-8319
Destin *(G-3049)*
Aquila Ftns Cnsltng Systms Ltd D 305 400-8444
Miami *(G-9163)*
Aragon Group Inc D 954 920-1511
Dania Beach *(G-2424)*
Attraction Concepts Ltd C 407 351-8800
Orlando *(G-12153)*
Big Kahuna Luau Inc E 305 927-9969
Hollywood *(G-5406)*
Boucher Brothers Miami Bch LLC D 305 674-6878
Miami Beach *(G-10563)*
BSB Mentor LLC E 305 506-0800
Miami *(G-9291)*
Buggy Bus Inc E 305 296-6688
Key West *(G-7196)*
C M C Realty Inc D 727 938-5778
Tarpon Springs *(G-18580)*
Calfland Traders Inc D 239 598-3130
Naples *(G-11044)*
Central Fla Investments Inc C 863 422-7511
Haines City *(G-5146)*
Central Fla Yung MNS Chrstn As C 407 855-2430
Orlando *(G-12277)*
Central Fla Yung MNS Chrstn As C 352 867-1441
Ocala *(G-11655)*
City of Apopka D 407 703-1741
Apopka *(G-166)*
City of Cape Coral E 239 574-0557
Cape Coral *(G-1384)*
City of Clearwater D 727 562-4538
Clearwater *(G-1567)*
City of Clewiston E 863 983-7656
Clewiston *(G-1898)*
City of Delray Beach D 561 243-7360
Delray Beach *(G-2930)*
City of Lakeland B 863 834-8123
Lakeland *(G-7836)*
City of Largo E 727 587-6723
Largo *(G-8085)*
City of Palm Beach Gardens E 561 630-1100
Palm Beach Gardens *(G-13707)*
City of Palm Beach Gardens D 561 775-2556
West Palm Beach *(G-19087)*
City of Saint Petersburg D 727 893-7441
Saint Petersburg *(G-15624)*
▲ Cocoa Beach Surf Company E 321 784-2318
Cocoa Beach *(G-1967)*

Cocoa Beach Surf Company	C	321 799-9930	
Cocoa Beach (G-1968)			
County of Brevard	D	321 633-1874	
Cocoa (G-1931)			
County of Broward	C	954 357-5150	
Hollywood (G-5422)			
County of Miami-Dade	E	305 258-1945	
Homestead (G-5568)			
County of Osceola	E	321 697-3333	
Kissimmee (G-7290)			
Cyclehop LLC	E	773 340-4080	
Miami Beach (G-10581)			
Dazi LLC	D	772 692-3322	
Jensen Beach (G-7014)			
East Cast Zlogical Soc Fla Inc	C	321 254-9453	
Melbourne (G-8876)			
Eller-Ito Stevedoring Co LLC	A	305 379-3700	
Miami (G-9516)			
Envirnmntal Prtection Fla Dept	C	321 984-4852	
Melbourne Beach (G-9013)			
Everblades Food Services LLC	D	239 948-7825	
Estero (G-3455)			
Festival Fun Parks LLC	D	305 361-5705	
Miami (G-9554)			
Fla Dpt Envirnmntal Prtection	C	407 553-4374	
Apopka (G-183)			
Florida Entersport Corp	D	352 332-2695	
Gainesville (G-4889)			
Florida Js Motorsports LLC	D	954 414-4135	
Sunrise (G-16771)			
Florida Olde Golf Club Inc	E	239 353-4441	
Naples (G-11118)			
Florida Panthers Ice Den LLC	D	954 341-9956	
Coral Springs (G-2253)			
Florida State Fair Authority	D	813 740-3500	
Tampa (G-17697)			
Godwins Gatorland Inc	D	407 855-5496	
Orlando (G-12577)			
Golf Management Solutions LLC	D	352 753-3396	
The Villages (G-18658)			
Golf Schools Inc	D	813 634-3331	
Ruskin (G-15402)			
Golfnow LLC	D	800 767-3574	
Orlando (G-12581)			
Grand Cypress Florida LP	D	407 239-1938	
Orlando (G-12590)			
Grand Cypress Florida LP	C	407 239-4700	
Orlando (G-12589)			
Grand Incentives Inc	D	941 552-5070	
Sarasota (G-16036)			
Greater Dytona Bch Area Yung M	D	386 673-9622	
Ormond Beach (G-13497)			
Grove Xxiii Golf Club Inc	D	772 631-2445	
Hobe Sound (G-5362)			
Gulf Exhibition Corp	E	850 243-9046	
Fort Walton Beach (G-4777)			
Gulf World Marine Park	E	850 234-5271	
Panama City (G-14025)			
Hibbett Sports Inc	D	352 372-2484	
Gainesville (G-4914)			
Icahn Enterprises LP	E	305 422-4100	
Sunny Isles Beach (G-16720)			
Ijump LLC	D	954 973-3031	
Coconut Creek (G-1991)			
◆ IMG Academy LLC	C	941 755-1000	
Bradenton (G-1124)			
Investment Corp Palm Beach	A	561 683-2222	
West Palm Beach (G-19206)			
Jacksonville Jewish Center	D	904 292-1000	
Jacksonville (G-6363)			
Jonathans Landing Golf CLB Inc	D	561 747-7600	
Jupiter (G-7091)			
Jungle Queens Inc	D	954 462-5596	
Fort Lauderdale (G-3913)			
Krav Maga of Ft Lauderdal	D	954 567-5686	
Fort Lauderdale (G-3923)			
Leslies Holdings Inc	D	850 494-9233	
Pensacola (G-14344)			
Level Up Sports Facility Inc	D	786 232-0811	
Cutler Bay (G-2370)			
Lion Cntry Safari Inc-Florida	C	561 793-1084	
Loxahatchee (G-8423)			
Lowry Pk Zlgical Soc Tampa Inc	B	813 935-8552	
Tampa (G-17962)			
Lpga Intl Girls Golf CLB	D	386 274-5742	
Daytona Beach (G-2628)			
Magic Ice Usa Inc	C	305 255-4144	
Miami (G-9892)			
◆ Mariner International Trvl Inc	D	888 952-8420	
Clearwater (G-1705)			

Maritime Prof Trning Msters Mt	D	954 525-1014	
Fort Lauderdale (G-3958)			
Meditationlive Inc	E	415 484-6018	
Miami Beach (G-10616)			
Miami Boat Experts Inc	E	305 507-1315	
Miami Beach (G-10621)			
▲ Miami-Dade Cnty Fair Expo Inc	E	305 223-3247	
Miami (G-9989)			
Msb of Destin Inc	E	850 837-0404	
Destin (G-3069)			
National Park Service	D	850 934-2602	
Gulf Breeze (G-5130)			
National State Pk Cncssons Inc	D	772 595-6429	
Fort Pierce (G-4723)			
▲ Nexus Shooting LLC	E	954 587-8005	
Davie (G-2501)			
Ocala Breeders Sales Co Inc	D	352 237-4667	
Ocala (G-11748)			
Ocean Drive Clevelander Inc	D	305 531-3485	
Miami Beach (G-10636)			
Orange Brook Country Club Rest	E	954 967-4653	
Hollywood (G-5489)			
▲ Orlampa Inc	D	863 984-3500	
Polk City (G-14727)			
Orlando Sportsplex Ltd	B	407 916-2550	
Orlando (G-12985)			
Palm Beach Golf Center Inc	E	561 842-7100	
West Palm Beach (G-19311)			
Palm Beach Skate Zone 2012 LLC	E	561 963-5900	
Lake Worth (G-7745)			
Palm Beach Skating Rinks Inc	E	561 434-1222	
Lake Worth (G-7746)			
Pga Tour Pub Golf Jacksonville	D	904 779-2100	
Jacksonville (G-6597)			
Recreation Investments of Fla	D	850 654-4668	
Destin (G-3072)			
Reithoffer Shows Inc	D	813 422-0074	
Gibsonton (G-5038)			
Rineberg Tennis Inc	E	561 395-8604	
Boca Raton (G-775)			
▲ Rodmar Grocers Inc	D	954 929-0131	
Hollywood (G-5508)			
Safety Harbor Spa & Fitnes Ctr	E	727 726-1161	
Safety Harbor (G-15412)			
▲ Sally Industries Inc	E	904 355-7100	
Jacksonville (G-6689)			
Sanlan Rv & Golf Resort Inc	E	863 667-1988	
Lakeland (G-7962)			
Sarasota Jungle Gardens Inc	D	941 355-5305	
Sarasota (G-16304)			
Sarvis Incorporated	B	407 890-9303	
Orlando (G-13168)			
Scratch Golf Company	D	407 321-0010	
Lake Mary (G-7637)			
Seascape Resorts Inc	D	850 837-9181	
Miramar Beach (G-10926)			
Seaworld Parks & Entrmt LLC	A	813 987-5250	
Tampa (G-18260)			
Seaworld Parks & Entrmt LLC	A	813 987-5600	
Tampa (G-18261)			
Seminole Classic Casino	B	954 834-0669	
Coconut Creek (G-2001)			
Seminole Classic Casino	E	954 961-3220	
Hollywood (G-5514)			
Seminole Tribe of Florida Inc	C	954 961-3220	
Hollywood (G-5516)			
Seminole Tribe of Florida Inc	A	813 627-7625	
Tampa (G-18265)			
Seniorbridge Family Companies	C	954 423-2217	
Plantation (G-14705)			
South Fla Fair Palm Bch Cnty E	D	561 793-0333	
West Palm Beach (G-19368)			
Southern Dunes Golf &	D	863 421-4653	
Haines City (G-5158)			
St Larent At Waterpark Pl Corp	E	239 261-3440	
Naples (G-11305)			
Sun Dream Yacht Charters Inc	D	954 765-1460	
Fort Lauderdale (G-4161)			
Surebet Casinos Inc	D	850 438-9647	
Pensacola (G-14453)			
▲ Tampa Bay Downs Inc	A	813 855-4401	
Tampa (G-18366)			
Team Z Entertainment LLC	D	904 300-0070	
Jacksonville (G-6842)			
Theatre of The Sea Inc	E	305 664-2431	
Islamorada (G-5710)			
Time2shine Academy Inc	E	202 430-3039	
Saint Augustine (G-15506)			
Tynda Holdings LLC	B	321 799-0021	
Cape Canaveral (G-1371)			

Volume Services Inc	B	352 378-0120	
Gainesville (G-5026)			
Walt Dsney Prks Resorts US Inc	C	407 560-4870	
Orlando (G-13403)			
Yoga Joint Holdings LLC	E	561 543-1174	
Sunrise (G-16850)			
Young MNS Chrstn Assn S Fla In	E	305 248-5189	
Homestead (G-5612)			
Zigong Lntern Group Wrldwide L	C	800 946-5213	
Kissimmee (G-7416)			
Zoo Miami Foundation Inc	D	305 255-5551	
Miami (G-10530)			
Zoologcal Soc of The Palm Bche	D	561 547-9453	
West Palm Beach (G-19428)			

80 HEALTH SERVICES

8011 Offices & Clinics Of Doctors Of Medicine

21st Century Oncology LLC	D	561 793-6500	
Wellington (G-18971)			
21st Century Oncology LLC	D	863 382-8811	
Port Charlotte (G-15014)			
21st Century Oncology Holdings	E	239 931-7254	
Fort Myers (G-4242)			
24/7 Pediatric Care Ctrs Inc	D	904 249-3373	
Jacksonville Beach (G-6973)			
26health Inc	E	321 800-2874	
Orlando (G-12027)			
A Adlt & Pedtrc Allrgy	E	239 262-0505	
Naples (G-10992)			
A Caring Touch Nursing Svc	D	352 628-0911	
Homosassa (G-5615)			
A Center For Dermatology PA	D	954 977-0270	
Maitland (G-8493)			
Access 2 Hlth Care Physcans LL	D	352 793-1140	
Beverly Hills (G-376)			
Adams David C MD Facms	E	850 654-3376	
Miramar Beach (G-10920)			
Adcs Clinics LLC	C	407 875-2080	
Maitland (G-8495)			
Advanced Ctr For Surgery LLC	C	772 257-3600	
Vero Beach (G-18831)			
Advanced Dermatology MGT Inc	E	954 349-3376	
Weston (G-19439)			
Advanced Dermatology MGT Inc	E	386 322-8310	
Port Orange (G-15068)			
Advanced Dermatology MGT Inc	E	727 344-6851	
Saint Petersburg (G-15558)			
Advanced Dermatology MGT Inc	E	904 503-6999	
Jacksonville (G-5740)			
Advanced Dermatology MGT Inc	E	321 594-5555	
Maitland (G-8496)			
Advanced Imging Port Chrltte L	E	941 235-4646	
Port Charlotte (G-15015)			
Advanced Orthopedic Center	E	941 629-6262	
Port Charlotte (G-15016)			
Advanced Orthpd Spt Medicine	E	352 683-0416	
Spring Hill (G-16533)			
Advanced Urology Assoc Fla Pl	D	772 388-0239	
Sebastian (G-16375)			
Advanced Urology Specialists	C	352 430-0705	
Oxford (G-13579)			
Adventist Health System/Sunbel	D	407 303-2200	
Altamonte Springs (G-17)			
Adventist Hlth Systm/Snbelt In	C	407 898-2343	
Orlando (G-12069)			
Adventist Hlth Systm/Snbelt In	E	407 200-2300	
Oviedo (G-13537)			
Adventist Hlth Systm/Snbelt In	E	407 678-5554	
Winter Park (G-19682)			
Adventist Hlth Systm/Snbelt In	D	407 357-1000	
Orlando (G-12070)			
Adventist Hlth Systm/Snbelt In	C	407 390-1888	
Kissimmee (G-7266)			
Aesculapian Management Co LLC	D	941 955-1108	
Sarasota (G-16079)			
Aesculapian Surgery Center LLC	D	941 379-5884	
Sarasota (G-16080)			
Ahs/Central Texas Inc	A	407 303-6830	
Orlando (G-12082)			
Airsculpt Technologies Inc	C	786 709-9690	
Miami Beach (G-10543)			
Aker Kasten Eye Center Inc	E	561 338-7722	
Boca Raton (G-407)			
Akumin Corp		954 475-2368	
Plantation (G-14598)			
Akumin Holdings Corp	E	954 577-6000	
Plantation (G-14599)			

All Pediatric Care PA ....E 352 688-0100
Spring Hill (G-16534)
Allergy Asthma Care............D....... 904 298-1800
Fleming Island (G-3548)
Allergy Free Labs LLC............E 561 994-3397
Boca Raton (G-412)
Allergy Partners Pllc............D 850 863-1189
Fort Walton Beach (G-4751)
Alliance Medical Assoc Inc............E 352 622-7268
Ocala (G-11630)
Alliance Medical Group Inc............D....... 407 461-7588
Altamonte Springs (G-24)
Am-Med Diabetic Supplies Inc............E 561 900-3548
Delray Beach (G-2902)
Ambrose G Updegraff MD PA ....E 727 551-2020
Saint Petersburg (G-15565)
Ambultory Srgcal Fclty S Fla L............D....... 954 430-1700
Pembroke Pines (G-14129)
American Health Choice Inc ....E 305 860-2333
Doral (G-3118)
American Maintenance LLC............E 561 317-3219
Lake Worth (G-7708)
American Oncology Network LLC........E 866 266-0555
Fort Myers (G-4274)
American Oncology Network LLC........D....... 239 318-6284
Fort Myers (G-4275)
American Radiology Services ....E 239 261-9729
Naples (G-11010)
American Sleep Medicine LLC............E 904 517-5500
Jacksonville (G-5792)
Amicus Medical Group Inc............D....... 954 436-0555
Pembroke Pines (G-14131)
Andrews Institute Asc LLC ....D....... 850 916-8500
Gulf Breeze (G-5105)
Anesco North Broward LLC............D....... 954 485-5666
Fort Lauderdale (G-3610)
Anesthesia Associates Mdpa ....E 630 248-9689
Delray Beach (G-2906)
Anesthesiologists Assoc PA............E 727 845-1736
New Port Richey (G-11363)
Anesthsia Assoc Pnllas Cnty PA............D....... 727 441-1524
Clearwater (G-1521)
Ansthesiology Halifax Assoc PA............B 386 255-1266
Daytona Beach (G-2546)
Ansthsology Panhandle Assoc PA............E 850 477-7042
Pensacola (G-14218)
APC Pediatrics............E 941 209-7680
Bradenton (G-1053)
Arthritis Associates South Fla............E 561 495-0600
Delray Beach (G-2910)
Ascent Medical Group LLC............D....... 954 426-1169
Deerfield Beach (G-2711)
Assoctes In Intrnal Mdicine PA............E 386 445-4700
Palm Coast (G-13810)
Atlantic Urological Assoc PA............D....... 386 445-8530
Palm Coast (G-13811)
Augusta Physicians Group LLC............E 770 874-5400
Pensacola (G-14223)
Aurora Michigan LLC............D....... 561 626-5512
Palm Beach Gardens (G-13687)
Aventura Orthopedic Care Ctr............E 954 455-5655
Hallandale Beach (G-5165)
Aventus Health LLC............D....... 407 547-3546
Orlando (G-12159)
Badolato Fmly Hlth At Sntree L............E 321 242-7425
Melbourne (G-8823)
Baker Hard Osteen Dvnport MD P............E 407 843-9083
Orlando (G-12172)
Ballas Otptient Surgery Ctr LP ....C....... 561 391-7642
Boca Raton (G-441)
▲ Baptist Health South Fla Inc ....C....... 305 596-1960
South Miami (G-16500)
Baptist Health System Inc............B 904 202-2000
Jacksonville (G-5836)
Baptist Health System Inc............C....... 904 376-3707
Jacksonville (G-5837)
Baptist Hospital Miami Inc ....C....... 305 596-6566
Miami (G-9221)
Baptist Hospital Miami Inc ....B 305 598-5990
Miami (G-9219)
Baptist Medical Ctr ....D....... 904 627-2900
Jacksonville Beach (G-6977)
Baptist Pediatrics Inc ....D....... 904 280-1225
Ponte Vedra Beach (G-14976)
Barranco Clinic Inc............D....... 863 299-1251
Winter Haven (G-19608)
Barron Barron & Steiner MD PA ....E 954 989-4700
Hollywood (G-5401)
Barry J Kaplan MD PA............E 352 622-3360
Ocala (G-11637)

Bay Area Heart Center Inc............E 727 526-6624
Saint Petersburg (G-15590)
Bay County Health System LLC ....A 850 769-1511
Panama City (G-13961)
Bay Hospital Inc............C....... 850 747-7100
Panama City (G-13965)
Baycare Health System Inc............C....... 813 870-4064
Tampa (G-17350)
Baycare Health System Inc............A 727 462-7000
Clearwater (G-1538)
Baycare Health System Inc............A 727 820-8200
Clearwater (G-1539)
Bayshore Medical Center............E 941 755-9550
Bradenton (G-1057)
Beneva Family Practice............E 941 365-7390
Sarasota (G-16101)
Beraja Medical Institute............D....... 305 357-1706
Coral Gables (G-2050)
Best Doctors Insur Svcs LLC ....C....... 305 269-2521
Miami (G-9248)
Bio-Mdcal Applications Fla Inc............D....... 352 335-1751
Gainesville (G-4843)
Bloomingdale Medical Assoc PA............E 813 654-1775
Riverview (G-15245)
Board of Gvrnors State Univ Sy ....A 352 265-9928
Gainesville (G-4846)
Boca Raton Orthopedic............E 561 391-5515
Boca Raton (G-465)
Boca Raton Orthpd Group Inc............E 561 391-5515
Boca Raton (G-467)
Bocacare Inc............A 561 483-0072
Boca Raton (G-475)
Bond & Steele Clinic PA............B 863 293-1191
Winter Haven (G-19609)
Borinquen Health Care Ctr Inc............D....... 305 576-6611
Miami (G-9270)
Bosshardt & Marzek Plastic............E 714 865-3262
Sunrise (G-16749)
Boston Diagnostic Imaging ....C....... 407 330-7333
Sanford (G-15925)
Bradenton Cardiology Center............E 941 742-6384
Bradenton (G-1063)
Bradenton Walk-In Med Ctr Inc............C....... 941 753-7843
Bradenton (G-1067)
Brandon Jones Sandall Zeide Kn............D....... 561 967-6500
Palm Springs (G-13889)
Brevard Cardiology Physcn PA ....E 321 449-4175
Merritt Island (G-9018)
Brevard Hmtlogy Onclogy Cons - ....E 321 268-4200
Titusville (G-18679)
Brevard Orthpdic Spine Pain CL ....D....... 321 723-7716
Melbourne (G-8833)
Brevard Physician Assoc Pllc ....C....... 321 837-3820
Melbourne (G-8834)
Bridgeway Center Inc ....D....... 850 833-3975
Fort Walton Beach (G-4757)
Brilliance Living LLC ....E 386 423-0505
New Smyrna Beach (G-11415)
Broward Guardian LLC............C....... 954 276-1512
Hollywood (G-5409)
Broward Surgical Associates ....E 954 491-0900
Fort Lauderdale (G-3658)
Brown Fertility LLC............D....... 407 244-5515
Orlando (G-12210)
Brrh Corporation............E 561 955-4708
Boca Raton (G-483)
Cac-Florida Medical Ctrs LLC............E 305 222-2000
Miami (G-9303)
Cac-Florida Medical Ctrs LLC............E 407 522-2082
Orlando (G-12225)
Can Community Health Inc ....C....... 941 366-0461
Sarasota (G-16115)
▲ Cancer Specialists LLC ....B 904 516-3737
Jacksonville (G-5895)
Cancer Treatment Ctrs Amer Glo ....E 561 923-3151
Boca Raton (G-492)
Cano Health Inc............E 855 226-6633
Medley (G-8710)
Cano Health LLC ....E 855 226-6633
Medley (G-8711)
Cape Coral Eye Center PA ....E 239 542-2020
Cape Coral (G-1379)
Cardiac and Vascular Insitute............D....... 352 375-1212
Gainesville (G-4851)
Cardilogy Assoc Chrltte Cnty P............E 941 206-0228
Punta Gorda (G-15195)
Cardinal Health 200 LLC............E 614 757-5000
Weston (G-19447)
▲ Cardiology Assoc Orlando PA............D....... 321 841-6444
Orlando (G-12234)

Cardiology Associates Stuart............E 772 781-0222
Stuart (G-16600)
Cardiology Partners PL............D....... 561 793-6100
Wellington (G-18972)
Cardiovascular Associates Inc............E 407 846-0626
Kissimmee (G-7275)
Cardiovascular Institute of............E 352 622-4251
Ocala (G-11650)
Cardiovascular Res Ctr S Fla............D....... 305 275-8200
Miami (G-9312)
Cardiovascular Surgeons PA............E 407 425-1566
Orlando (G-12235)
Care One of Florida LLC............E 352 556-5216
Brooksville (G-1277)
Carenow Urgent Care - Wnter Sp ....C....... 321 765-6152
Winter Springs (G-19799)
Carespot of Austin LLC............C....... 954 378-0333
Pembroke Pines (G-14136)
Carespot of Austin LLC............C....... 954 210-5185
Sunrise (G-16754)
Carespot of Austin LLC............C....... 561 740-2273
Boynton Beach (G-970)
Carespot of Austin LLC............C....... 954 379-8342
Coral Springs (G-2235)
Carespot of Austin LLC............C....... 904 406-8240
Middleburg (G-10793)
Carespot of Austin LLC............C....... 954 580-4001
Pompano Beach (G-14765)
Carespot of Austin LLC............C....... 904 757-2008
Jacksonville (G-5903)
Caridad Center Inc............D....... 561 853-1624
Boynton Beach (G-971)
Carillon Surgery Center LLC............B 727 573-5626
Saint Petersburg (G-15611)
Carithers Thrlkel Bakr Cheek C ....E 904 387-6200
Jacksonville (G-5907)
Carlos J Rozas MD PA............E 813 875-9362
Tampa (G-17423)
Catholic Health Services Inc............D....... 954 484-1515
Lauderdale Lakes (G-8169)
Cecil C Aird MD ....E 813 978-9494
Tampa (G-17434)
Celebrtion Orthpdic Spt Mdcine ....D....... 321 939-0222
Celebration (G-1465)
Center For Advanced Eye Care ....E 772 299-1404
Vero Beach (G-18842)
Center For Clon Rectal Surgery ....E 407 303-6626
Orlando (G-12255)
Center For Excellence Eye Care............E 305 595-2141
Miami (G-9344)
Center For Orthopedic Sur............E 954 765-6247
Oakland Park (G-11589)
Center For Sight............E 850 476-9236
Pensacola (G-14256)
Center For Surgery & Digestiv............D....... 305 854-3636
Miami (G-9345)
Centerstone of Florida Inc ....C....... 941 782-4860
Bradenton (G-1077)
Centerwell Snior Prmry Care FL............D....... 866 405-2821
Orlando (G-12258)
Central Fla Crdiolgy Group PA ....D....... 407 841-7151
Orlando (G-12263)
Central Fla Drmtology Assoc PA............E 407 481-2620
Orlando (G-12264)
Central Fla Fmly Hlth Ctr Inc............C....... 407 322-8645
Sanford (G-15930)
Central Fla Inptent Mdcine LLC............C....... 407 647-2346
Lake Mary (G-7575)
Central Florida Cancer Inst............D....... 863 679-2960
Lake Wales (G-7677)
Central Florida Heart Ctr PA ....D....... 352 873-0707
Ocala (G-11657)
Central Florida Hlth Care Inc ....D....... 863 291-5110
Winter Haven (G-19617)
Central Florida Hlth Care Inc ....E 863 635-4891
Frostproof (G-4820)
Centurion Quintana Assoc MD PA ....E 305 759-1300
Miami Shores (G-10773)
Chad Shaykher MD PA ....D....... 305 754-4848
Miami Shores (G-10774)
Charles E Griff Md PA............D....... 561 357-5636
West Palm Beach (G-19082)
Charles J Montgomery MD PA............E 239 261-8383
Naples (G-11050)
Charles R Hollen MD PA............D....... 941 379-5121
Sarasota (G-16121)
Charles S Theofilos MD PA............D....... 772 807-5566
Port Saint Lucie (G-15126)
Chen Medical Aventura Inc ....C....... 305 621-0023
Miami (G-9359)

SIC

Chen Medical Hialeah Inc.....................E.....305 653-1770	Conviva Care Solutions LLC...............C.....561 487-8865	Elevate Psychiatry LLC........................E.....305 908-1115
Miami (G-9360)	Boca Raton (G-528)	Doral (G-3188)
Chen Medical Miami Lakes Inc.........E.....305 556-7500	Coral Springs Ambulatory..................E.....954 227-7760	Emerald Cast Obgyn of Pnhdl LL.....E.....850 769-0338
Hialeah (G-5235)	Coral Springs (G-2240)	Panama City (G-13997)
Children..D.....561 795-3333	Coral Springs Surgical Center..........E.....954 227-7760	Emerald Coast Surgery Ctr LP..........E.....850 863-7887
Loxahatchee (G-8420)	Coral Springs (G-2241)	Fort Walton Beach (G-4766)
Childrens Medical Center PA..............E.....954 378-1500	Core Oncology.....................................D.....805 692-2673	Empath Community Health LLC........C.....727 586-4432
Pembroke Pines (G-14140)	Miami (G-9417)	Clearwater (G-1617)
Childrens Medical Center PA..............E.....954 435-7000	County of Palm Beach........................D.....561 656-6200	Empath Elder Care LLC......................D.....727 586-4432
Pembroke Pines (G-14141)	West Palm Beach (G-19110)	Clearwater (G-1618)
Christian Gonzalez MD LLC...............D.....305 974-5533	Critical Care Newborn Svcs PA.........D.....305 662-8668	Empath Hlth Phrmaceuticals LLC.....C.....727 586-4432
Sunny Isles Beach (G-16714)	Coral Gables (G-2083)	Clearwater (G-1621)
Circles of Care Inc.............................C.....321 722-5200	Daniel G Maico....................................D.....352 331-8902	Empath Medical Services LLC...........E.....727 586-4432
Melbourne (G-8844)	Gainesville (G-4873)	Clearwater (G-1622)
Citrus Health Network Inc.................D.....305 572-7140	Davita Medical Florida Inc................E.....727 824-0780	Encompass Health Corporation.........E.....850 863-7887
Hialeah (G-5238)	Saint Petersburg (G-15653)	Fort Walton Beach (G-4767)
Citrus Regional Surgery Ctr LP.........E.....352 249-0873	Deerfield Bch Otptent Srgcal CT.......E.....954 418-7222	Encompass Health Corporation.........D.....561 367-6090
Lecanto (G-8216)	Deerfield Beach (G-2734)	Boca Raton (G-565)
Citrus Urology Center Inc.................E.....352 527-0102	Defense Health Agency.......................D.....305 437-1148	Endoscopy Center of Ocala Inc.........D.....352 261-0499
Lecanto (G-8217)	Doral (G-3174)	Ocala (G-11676)
City of Plantation.................................D.....954 452-2510	Delray Ambltory Srgcal Lser CT.......D.....561 495-9111	Englewood Community Hosp Inc.........B.....941 475-6571
Plantation (G-14617)	Delray Beach (G-2940)	Englewood (G-3436)
Clearly Derm LLC................................E.....561 739-9595	Delray Center For Recovery Inc.........D.....561 266-8866	Er Svcs Leeland Partnership.............E.....239 369-2101
Boynton Beach (G-975)	Delray Beach (G-2941)	Lehigh Acres (G-8281)
Clearwter Crdvsclar Intrvntnal.........E.....727 445-1992	Delray Eye Associates PA..................D.....561 498-8100	Excel Medical Electronics LLC...........E.....866 573-8807
Clearwater (G-1578)	Delray Beach (G-2943)	Jupiter (G-7067)
Clermont Medical Center PA..............E.....352 394-3195	Denny Ragsdale Md Inc.....................D.....321 432-9564	Eye Associates of Boca Raton............D.....561 391-8300
Clermont (G-1860)	Melbourne (G-8868)	Boca Raton (G-571)
Clermont Radiology LLC......................E.....352 241-6100	Dermatology Center.............................D.....352 637-1310	Eye Associates Tallahassee PA.........D.....850 878-6161
Clermont (G-1861)	Inverness (G-5690)	Tallahassee (G-16944)
Cleveland Clinic Foundation...............E.....561 904-7200	Dermatology Partners of Saint.........D.....727 821-3600	Eye Center North Florida PA.............D.....850 784-3937
Palm Beach Gardens (G-13708)	Saint Petersburg (G-15654)	Panama City (G-14003)
Clinic Building Inc...............................E.....850 785-8557	Destin Surgery Center Ltd.................D.....850 654-5222	Eye Centers of Florida PA.................C.....239 790-2444
Panama City (G-13982)	Destin (G-3057)	Fort Myers (G-4366)
▼ Clinic For Kidney Diseases PA.......E.....904 387-9919	▼ Diabetes Endcrine Ctr Orlndo P.......D.....407 894-3241	Eye Consultant The PA........................E.....941 748-1818
Jacksonville (G-5967)	Orlando (G-12419)	Bradenton (G-1096)
Clinica Las Mercedes Inc...................D.....305 456-7621	Diagnostic Ctrs Amer - Fla Inc.........D.....561 496-6935	Eye Health of Fort Myers Inc.............A.....239 594-7636
Hialeah (G-5243)	Delray Beach (G-2946)	Naples (G-11107)
Clinical Care Associates Inc.............D.....305 649-6077	Diagnostic Ctrs Amer - Fla Inc.........D.....561 727-2300	Eye Health of Fort Myers Inc.............A.....239 458-5800
Coral Gables (G-2070)	West Palm Beach (G-19122)	Cape Coral (G-1391)
Coast Drmtlogy Skin Cncer Ctr.........D.....941 493-7400	Diagnostic Professionals Inc...........C.....954 449-7023	Eye Health of Fort Myers Inc.............A.....941 639-2020
Venice (G-18773)	Plantation (G-14631)	Punta Gorda (G-15201)
Coast Ortho & Sport Medic of S.........D.....941 792-2251	Diagnstic Clinic Med Group Inc.........D.....727 726-8871	Eye Institute of West Florida.............E.....727 584-5748
Bradenton (G-1083)	Clearwater (G-1605)	Largo (G-8103)
Coastal Ansthesiology Cons LLC.......D.....904 819-4478	Diagnstic Clinic Med Group Inc.........B.....727 584-7706	Eye Physicians of Pinellas PA.........E.....727 581-8706
Saint Augustine (G-15435)	Largo (G-8096)	Largo (G-8104)
Coastal Detox Inc.................................D.....888 481-1993	Diagnstic Imaging Holdings Inc.........C.....407 253-7190	Eye Specialist Mid Florida PA...........D.....863 294-3504
Stuart (G-16606)	Orlando (G-12420)	Winter Haven (G-19626)
Coastal Urgent Care LLC....................E.....850 769-6612	Digestive Disease Cons PA................E.....407 830-8661	Eye Surgeons & Consultants PA.......E.....954 894-1500
Panama City (G-13984)	Altamonte Springs (G-44)	Hollywood (G-5433)
Coastal Vsclar Intrvntnal Pllc.........E.....850 479-1805	Digestive Dseases Ctr Fla Pllc.........E.....850 763-5409	▲ FA Hauber MD PA..............................E.....727 847-4448
Pensacola (G-14260)	Panama City (G-13991)	New Port Richey (G-11373)
Cohen Madosky Pinon & Santa.........D.....305 245-1002	Dinesh Khanna MD..............................D.....352 259-2159	Faben Obgyn Inc..................................E.....904 346-0050
Homestead (G-5564)	Lady Lake (G-7430)	Jacksonville (G-6141)
Collier Health Services Inc...............C.....239 658-3000	▼ Diseases Infectious Assoc PA.......E.....941 366-9060	Faith Telehealth Care LLC..................D.....305 928-9727
Immokalee (G-5653)	Sarasota (G-16140)	Aventura (G-271)
Collier Health Services Inc...............E.....239 775-3052	Dmh Real Estate Holdings Inc.........B.....863 494-8401	Family Medicine & Rehab Inc.............D.....904 771-1116
Naples (G-11066)	Arcadia (G-229)	Jacksonville (G-6145)
Collier Nrlogic Specialists Pl...........D.....239 262-1721	Docto Outpa Surge Cente of Jup.......E.....561 799-3388	Family Physicians Group Inc.............D.....407 253-3535
Naples (G-11067)	Palm Beach Gardens (G-13720)	Orlando (G-12491)
Collier Regional Medical Ctr.............E.....239 354-6000	Doctors Imaging Group LLC..............D.....352 331-9729	Family Physicians Winter Pk PA.......D.....407 539-0079
Naples (G-11068)	Gainesville (G-4877)	Winter Park (G-19721)
Community Health Centers Inc.........E.....407 905-8827	Doctors Inlet Ped Primary Care.........E.....904 519-0008	Family Practice At Clayton Crt...........E.....239 275-4799
Winter Garden (G-19563)	Jacksonville (G-6076)	Fort Myers (G-4368)
Community Health South Fla Inc.........E.....305 246-4607	Doctors Same Day Srgery Ctr Lt.........D.....941 342-1303	Family Practice Ctr Plant Cy.............E.....813 754-3504
Florida City (G-3559)	Sarasota (G-16141)	Plant City (G-14554)
Community Health South Fla Inc.........E.....305 743-4000	Donald A Barnhorst Jr........................D.....904 249-3937	Family Practice West Volusia.............D.....386 734-6265
Marathon (G-8616)	Jacksonville Beach (G-6984)	Deland (G-2860)
Community Health South Fla Inc.........B.....305 246-1666	Dpi of Fort Lauderdale........................D.....954 570-5560	Femwell Group Health Inc..................B.....305 854-2899
Homestead (G-5566)	Coconut Creek (G-1985)	Coral Gables (G-2105)
Community Hlth Ctrs Pnllas Inc.........E.....727 824-8100	Dr Rishi Kakar MD..............................D.....888 852-6672	First Cast Hart Vscular Ctr PA...........E.....904 423-0010
Clearwater (G-1584)	Miami Lakes (G-10722)	Jacksonville (G-6164)
Community Hlth Wllness Ctr Mam.......E.....305 541-5245	Drs Arala Lser Cataract Inst PA.........E.....305 558-7895	First Cast Infctous Dsase Cons.........E.....904 264-7132
Miami (G-9394)	Miami (G-9490)	Orange Park (G-11989)
Compass Health Systems PA.............E.....305 891-0050	▲ Drs Mori Bean & Brooks PA.........E.....904 399-5550	First Choice Medical Group LLC.........E.....321 725-2225
North Miami (G-11487)	Jacksonville (G-6085)	Melbourne (G-8886)
Comprehensive Health Svcs LLC.......A.....321 868-8500	Dwic of Tampa Bay Inc......................D.....727 799-2727	First Class Obgyn PA..........................D.....954 507-4494
Cape Canaveral (G-1363)	Clearwater (G-1612)	Weston (G-19459)
Comprehensive Pain Medicine PA.......E.....850 969-9804	Dwic of Tampa Bay Inc......................D.....813 264-1885	Fleming Island Surgery Ctr LLC.........D.....904 644-0700
Plantation (G-14621)	Tampa (G-17605)	Orange Park (G-11990)
Comprhensive Hlth Holdings Inc.........A.....321 783-2720	Ear Nose Throat Srgcal Assoc.........D.....407 644-4883	Florida Cancer Specialists Pl.............D.....407 426-8484
Cape Canaveral (G-1364)	Winter Park (G-19718)	Orlando (G-12520)
Comprhnsive Hmtlogy Onclogy LL.......E.....727 344-6569	Eastern Regional Med Ctr LLC.........B.....215 537-7400	Florida Cancer Specialists Pl.............D.....386 673-2442
Trinity (G-18722)	Boca Raton (G-562)	Ormond Beach (G-13492)
Consulate Management Co LLC.........C.....863 859-1446	Econfina Cardiology Group PA.........D.....850 769-0329	Florida Cancer Specialists Pl.............D.....727 784-6779
Lakeland (G-7844)	Panama City (G-13994)	Clearwater (G-1638)
Consult A Doctor Inc...........................D.....888 688-3628	Edelstein Slinero Llanso MD PA.......E.....305 444-6592	Florida Cancer Specialists Pl.............D.....561 366-4100
Miami Beach (G-10575)	Coral Gables (G-2099)	Wellington (G-18978)
Consulting Cardiologists PC.............E.....860 855-7060	Eiber Radiology Inc...........................D.....305 557-0330	Florida Cardiology PA........................E.....407 645-1847
Fort Pierce (G-4691)	Miami Beach (G-10588)	Winter Park (G-19723)

Florida Cmnty Hlth Ctrs Inc ....E.... 863 763-1951
Okeechobee *(G-11867)*
Florida Cmnty Hlth Ctrs Inc ....E.... 561 844-9443
West Palm Beach *(G-19143)*
Florida Cmnty Hlth Ctrs Inc ....D.... 863 763-7481
Okeechobee *(G-11868)*
Florida Cmnty Hlth Ctrs Inc ....D.... 863 983-7813
Clewiston *(G-1901)*
Florida Cncer Spclsts RES Inst ....D.... 941 766-7222
Port Charlotte *(G-15036)*
Florida Cncer Spclsts RES Inst ....D.... 813 876-0035
Tampa *(G-17674)*
Florida Cncer Spclsts RES Inst ....D.... 727 341-1316
South Pasadena *(G-16522)*
Florida Cncer Spclsts RES Inst ....E.... 941 257-2280
North Port *(G-11569)*
Florida Cncer Spclsts RES Inst ....D.... 352 860-7400
Inverness *(G-5691)*
Florida Cncer Spclsts RES Inst ....D.... 813 982-3460
Brandon *(G-1230)*
Florida Cncer Spclsts RES Inst ....D.... 813 633-3955
Sun City Center *(G-16701)*
Florida Cncer Spclsts RES Inst ....D.... 352 753-9777
Lady Lake *(G-7432)*
Florida Cncer Spclsts RES Inst ....D.... 239 274-2119
Fort Myers *(G-4377)*
Florida Cncer Spclsts RES Inst ....C.... 850 877-8166
Tallahassee *(G-16963)*
Florida Cncer Spclsts RES Inst ....C.... 239 274-8200
Fort Myers *(G-4378)*
Florida Cncer Spclsts RES Inst ....C.... 239 434-2622
Naples *(G-11116)*
Florida Cncer Spclsts RES Inst ....C.... 239 947-3092
Bonita Springs *(G-913)*
Florida Cncer Spclsts RES Inst ....D.... 386 774-7411
Orange City *(G-11963)*
Florida Cncer Spclsts RES Inst ....E.... 727 683-2900
Largo *(G-8106)*
Florida Cncer Spclsts RES Inst ....C.... 239 274-9930
Fort Myers *(G-4379)*
Florida Cncer Spclsts RES Inst ....D.... 352 343-1117
Tavares *(G-18605)*
Florida Cncer Spclsts RES Inst ....E.... 352 394-1150
Clermont *(G-1869)*
Florida Cncer Spclsts RES Inst ....E.... 407 330-1788
Lake Mary *(G-7593)*
Florida Cncer Spclsts RES Inst ....E.... 727 397-9641
Largo *(G-8107)*
Florida Cncer Spclsts RES Inst ....E.... 727 447-8100
Clearwater *(G-1639)*
Florida Cncer Spclsts RES Inst ....D.... 727 842-8411
New Port Richey *(G-11376)*
Florida Cncer Spclsts RES Inst ....E.... 813 253-3879
Tampa *(G-17675)*
Florida Cncer Spclsts RES Inst ....D.... 813 632-6220
Tampa *(G-17676)*
Florida Cncer Spclsts RES Inst ....D.... 813 783-1676
Zephyrhills *(G-19832)*
Florida Cncer Spclsts RES Inst ....D.... 727 868-9208
Hudson *(G-5639)*
Florida Cncer Spclsts RES Inst ....E.... 863 385-1244
Sebring *(G-16396)*
Florida Cncer Spclsts RES Inst ....E.... 941 748-2217
Bradenton *(G-1101)*
Florida Cncer Spclsts RES Inst ....D.... 941 792-1881
Bradenton *(G-1102)*
Florida Cncer Spclsts RES Inst ....D.... 727 842-2795
New Port Richey *(G-11377)*
Florida Cncer Spclsts RES Inst ....C.... 941 362-3460
Sarasota *(G-16165)*
Florida Cncer Spclsts RES Inst ....D.... 239 541-4633
Cape Coral *(G-1393)*
Florida Cncer Spclsts RES Inst ....E.... 727 462-7514
Clearwater *(G-1640)*
Florida Cncer Spclsts RES Inst ....C.... 352 332-3900
Gainesville *(G-4886)*
Florida Cncer Spclsts RES Inst ....D.... 941 377-9993
Sarasota *(G-16166)*
Florida Cncer Spclsts RES Inst ....D.... 239 275-5357
Fort Myers *(G-4381)*
Florida Cncer Spclsts RES Inst ....D.... 941 460-1300
Englewood *(G-3437)*
Florida Cncer Spclsts RES Inst ....D.... 727 216-1143
Saint Petersburg *(G-15675)*
▲ **Florida Cncer Spclsts RES Inst** ....D.... 239 274-8200
Fort Myers *(G-4380)*
Florida Cncer Spclsts RES Inst ....D.... 352 596-1926
Spring Hill *(G-16536)*
Florida Ctr For Gstrenterology ....E.... 727 544-1600
Largo *(G-8108)*
Florida Department Corrections ....B.... 386 496-6000
Lake Butler *(G-7502)*
Florida Dgstive Hlth Spclist L ....D.... 941 757-4810
Bradenton *(G-1103)*
Florida Drmtlogy Skin Cncer Sp ....D.... 813 877-4811
Saint Petersburg *(G-15676)*
Florida Ear & Sinus Center PA ....E.... 941 366-9222
Sarasota *(G-16167)*
Florida Emrgncy Physcans Kang ....A.... 407 875-0555
Maitland *(G-8532)*
Florida Endocrinology & Diabet ....E.... 727 515-2032
Safety Harbor *(G-15408)*
Florida Eye Associates Inc ....E.... 321 727-2020
Melbourne *(G-8888)*
Florida Eye Center ....E.... 813 972-4444
Tampa *(G-17680)*
Florida Eye Clinic Ambulatory ....C.... 407 834-7776
Altamonte Springs *(G-50)*
Florida Gulf CST Ear Nse & Thr ....D.... 239 498-2528
Estero *(G-3458)*
Florida Gulf-To-Bay Anesthsiol ....A.... 813 253-2532
Tampa *(G-17682)*
Florida Health Care Plan Inc ....D.... 386 671-4337
Ormond Beach *(G-13493)*
Florida Health Care Plan Inc ....C.... 386 774-2550
Orange City *(G-11964)*
Florida Health Care Plan Inc ....D.... 386 445-7073
Palm Coast *(G-13822)*
Florida Health Sciences Center ....A.... 813 844-4200
Tampa *(G-17683)*
Florida Heart Associates Pll ....D.... 239 938-2000
Fort Myers *(G-4382)*
Florida Heart Group PA ....C.... 407 894-4474
Orlando *(G-12524)*
Florida Hlth Prfssons Assn Inc ....E.... 352 273-6214
Gainesville *(G-4893)*
Florida Hlth Sciences Ctr Inc ....A.... 813 844-4500
Tampa *(G-17686)*
Florida Hlth Sciences Ctr Inc ....A.... 813 254-0344
Tampa *(G-17685)*
Florida Hlth Sciences Ctr Inc ....A.... 813 236-5100
Tampa *(G-17687)*
Florida Hosp Zephyrhills Inc ....D.... 813 991-5900
Wesley Chapel *(G-18998)*
Florida Hospital Assn Inc ....E.... 407 933-6618
Kissimmee *(G-7311)*
Florida Hospital Assn Inc ....D.... 407 303-1169
Orlando *(G-12527)*
Florida Hospital Med Group Inc ....C.... 407 200-2700
Maitland *(G-8533)*
Florida Hospital Ocala Inc ....C.... 352 351-7200
Ocala *(G-11686)*
Florida Hospital Ocala Inc ....C.... 352 237-9298
Ocala *(G-11687)*
Florida Inst For Crdvsclar Car ....E.... 954 967-6550
Hollywood *(G-5437)*
Florida Ivf Reproductive Assoc ....E.... 954 247-6200
Margate *(G-8647)*
Florida Medical Clinic PA ....B.... 813 780-8440
Zephyrhills *(G-19834)*
Florida Neurology Group LP ....E.... 239 936-3554
Fort Myers *(G-4384)*
Florida Oncology Associates ....E.... 904 388-2619
Jacksonville *(G-6197)*
Florida Oncology Associates Pl ....E.... 904 363-2113
Jacksonville *(G-6198)*
Florida Orthopaedic Institute ....D.... 813 972-8772
Tampa *(G-17691)*
Florida Orthpdic Inst Srgery C ....D.... 727 499-9448
Palm Harbor *(G-13862)*
Florida Orthpdic Inst Srgery C ....D.... 813 558-6850
Valrico *(G-18752)*
Florida Orthpdic Inst Srgery C ....D.... 813 910-3668
Wesley Chapel *(G-18999)*
Florida Orthpdic Inst Srgery C ....D.... 813 910-3669
Brooksville *(G-1287)*
Florida Orthpdic Inst Srgery C ....D.... 813 287-9370
Tampa *(G-17692)*
Florida Orthpdic Inst Srgery C ....D.... 813 657-8448
Brandon *(G-1231)*
Florida Orthpdic Inst Srgery C ....D.... 813 633-5232
Sun City Center *(G-16702)*
Florida Orthpdic Inst Srgery C ....D.... 813 387-9890
Tampa *(G-17693)*
Florida Premier Cardiology ....E.... 561 496-7900
Delray Beach *(G-2949)*
Florida Presbyterian Homes Inc ....C.... 863 688-5521
Lakeland *(G-7869)*
Florida Spine & Joint Inst LLC ....E.... 888 655-7473
Boca Raton *(G-588)*
Florida Spine Specialists LLC ....E.... 954 801-1646
Hollywood *(G-5439)*
Florida Surgery Center ....D.... 407 830-0573
Altamonte Springs *(G-51)*
Florida Urogynecology & Recons ....E.... 888 783-0888
Palm Coast *(G-13824)*
Florida Urology Center PA ....E.... 386 673-5100
Ormond Beach *(G-13495)*
Florida Venice Dermatology ....E.... 941 486-1404
Venice *(G-18781)*
Florida Wellcare Alliance ....E.... 352 746-5111
Hernando *(G-5207)*
Fort Lauderdale Eye Institute ....E.... 954 453-5349
Plantation *(G-14646)*
Fox Medical Center ....D.... 305 595-1300
Miami *(G-9607)*
Frantz Eye Care ....D.... 239 418-0999
Fort Myers *(G-4404)*
Fresenius Vascular Care Inc ....E.... 850 466-3843
Pensacola *(G-14314)*
Gainesvlle Drmtlogy Skin Srger ....D.... 352 332-4442
Gainesville *(G-4902)*
Gainesvlle Intrnal Mdcine Phys ....B.... 352 333-5242
Gainesville *(G-4904)*
Garcia and Assoc Obgyn LLC ....E.... 904 398-7654
Jacksonville *(G-6215)*
Gardens Plastic Surgery ....E.... 561 472-2190
Palm Beach Gardens *(G-13734)*
Gastrntrlogy Assoc Cntl Fla PA ....E.... 407 895-8532
Orlando *(G-12561)*
Gastrntrlogy Assoc Pnscola Inc ....D.... 850 477-8109
Pensacola *(G-14315)*
Gastrntrlogy Assoc Sthwest Fla ....D.... 239 275-8882
Fort Myers *(G-4409)*
Gastro Interology Associates ....E.... 352 563-2450
Crystal River *(G-2347)*
Gastrocare LLP ....E.... 954 344-2522
Coral Springs *(G-2255)*
Gastrocare LLP ....C.... 561 499-8227
Delray Beach *(G-2952)*
Gateway Medical Group LLC ....D.... 863 467-7084
Okeechobee *(G-11869)*
Gateway Radiology Cons PA ....E.... 727 525-2121
Saint Petersburg *(G-15683)*
Genesis Health Inc ....B.... 904 858-7600
Jacksonville *(G-6226)*
Genesiscare Usa Inc ....C.... 239 931-7333
Fort Myers *(G-4414)*
Genesiscare USA Florida LLC ....D.... 239 275-0728
Lehigh Acres *(G-8283)*
Genesiscare USA Florida LLC ....C.... 800 437-1619
Fort Myers *(G-4415)*
Genesiscare USA Florida LLC ....E.... 239 333-0995
Fort Myers *(G-4416)*
Genesiscare USA Florida LLC ....E.... 239 333-0995
Naples *(G-11131)*
Genesiscare USA Florida LLC ....E.... 561 748-2488
Jupiter *(G-7083)*
Genesiscare USA Florida LLC ....D.... 239 939-2616
Fort Myers *(G-4417)*
Gessler Clinic Prof Assn ....C.... 863 294-0670
Winter Haven *(G-19631)*
Gessler Clinic Prof Assn ....D.... 863 382-1000
Winter Haven *(G-19632)*
Glades Medical Group Inc ....E.... 561 394-3088
Boca Raton *(G-608)*
Goldman Vein Institute ....E.... 561 790-4550
Wellington *(G-18981)*
Goodman Crdplmnary Assoc MD PA ....E.... 954 581-6041
Plantation *(G-14649)*
Gorovoy MD Eye Specialist ....E.... 239 939-1444
Fort Myers *(G-4423)*
Greystone Healthcare MGT Corp ....C.... 727 544-1444
Kenneth City *(G-7163)*
Gulf Cast Physcn Prtners PA PC ....E.... 850 476-9000
Pensacola *(G-14317)*
Gulf Coast Dermatology ....D.... 850 215-4170
Panama City *(G-14020)*
Gulf Coast Medical Center PA ....E.... 727 868-2151
Port Richey *(G-15103)*
Gulf Pointe Surgery Center ....D.... 941 235-5800
Port Charlotte *(G-15039)*
H Lee Mffitt Cncer Ctr RES In ....D.... 813 745-7046
Tampa *(G-17778)*
H Lee Mffitt Cncer Ctr RES In ....E.... 813 745-4673
Tampa *(G-17779)*
H Lee Mffitt Cncer Ctr RES In ....D.... 813 745-7852
Tampa *(G-17780)*
H Lee Mffitt Cncer Ctr RES In ....A.... 813 745-4673
Tampa *(G-17781)*

SIC

H Lee Mfft Cncr Ctr & RES	A	813 745-4673	
Tampa (G-17782)			
Halifax Emergency Physicians	E	386 254-2285	
Daytona Beach (G-2606)			
Halifax Health Services LLC	D	386 254-4211	
Daytona Beach (G-2607)			
Halifax Health Services LLC	E	386 523-1212	
Ormond Beach (G-13499)			
Halifax Hlth Care Systems Inc	B	386 425-6000	
Deltona (G-3040)			
Halifax Hlth Care Systems Inc	B	386 254-4107	
Daytona Beach (G-2610)			
Halifax Hlth Care Systems Inc	B	386 425-4400	
Ormond Beach (G-13500)			
Halifax Radiation Oncology	E	386 254-4210	
Daytona Beach (G-2611)			
Harm Reduction Center LLC	E	561 602-5224	
Boynton Beach (G-995)			
Harris Wilcox and Donovan PA	E	904 272-2020	
Orange Park (G-11993)			
Health Care Ctr For Hmless Inc	E	407 428-5751	
Orlando (G-12626)			
Health Diagnostics LLC	C	407 965-1112	
Orlando (G-12628)			
Health First Medical Group LLC	C	321 729-6166	
Melbourne (G-8901)			
Health First Medical Group LLC	B	321 434-4300	
Rockledge (G-15349)			
Health First Medical Group LLC	C	321 725-4500	
Melbourne (G-8902)			
Health First Medical Group LLC	C	321 724-0015	
Palm Bay (G-13623)			
Health First Shared Svcs Inc	A	321 434-4300	
Rockledge (G-15350)			
Health Integrated Inc	C	877 267-7577	
Tampa (G-17803)			
Health Management Assoc Inc	D	239 354-4301	
Naples (G-11158)			
Health Management Assoc Inc	B	239 348-4400	
Naples (G-11159)			
Healthcare Amer Med Group Inc	E	941 752-2700	
Bradenton (G-1118)			
Healthcare Cardon Network LLC	C	904 527-3235	
Jacksonville (G-6271)			
Healthpoint MGT Svcs Inc	E	813 870-3720	
Tampa (G-17811)			
Healthpoint MGT Svcs Inc	E	813 870-4824	
Tampa (G-17812)			
Healthpoint MGT Svcs Inc	E	813 254-7079	
Tampa (G-17813)			
Heart Care Associates	E	561 392-2021	
Boca Raton (G-625)			
Heart Care Cfl PA	E	321 636-6914	
Titusville (G-18686)			
Heart Fmily Hlth Inst of Port	D	772 335-9600	
Port Saint Lucie (G-15140)			
Heart Group P L	E	239 433-8888	
Fort Myers (G-4435)			
Heart Specialists of Sarasota	E	941 917-4250	
Sarasota (G-16181)			
Heart Vsclar Ctr Brdenton Pllc	E	941 761-4448	
Bradenton (G-1119)			
Heart Vscular Ctr of Venice PA	E	941 497-5511	
Venice (G-18785)			
Heidi M McNaney MD PA	E	772 288-2992	
Port St Lucie (G-15179)			
Helen B Bntley Fmly Hlth Ctr I	E	305 447-4950	
Miami (G-9693)			
Henderson Behavioral Hlth Inc	D	954 677-3113	
Fort Lauderdale (G-3857)			
Hepatlogy Onclogy Spclsts Tmpa	E	813 875-3950	
Tampa (G-17816)			
Hernando Endscopy Srgery Ctr I	E	352 596-4999	
Brooksville (G-1289)			
Hess Spinal & Medical Ctrs Inc	E	727 784-5200	
Palm Harbor (G-13866)			
Hess Spinal & Medical Ctrs Inc	E	727 848-9144	
New Port Richey (G-11385)			
HMA Santa Rosa Medical Ctr LLC	D	850 626-7762	
Milton (G-10817)			
Hollywood Diagnostics Ctr Inc	E	954 966-3600	
Hollywood (G-5452)			
Hollywood Drmtlogy Csmtc Srger	E	954 961-1200	
Hollywood (G-5453)			
Hospice Fndtion of The Fla SNC	B	727 586-4432	
Clearwater (G-1671)			
Howard Susan W Faafp MD	E	386 254-4001	
Daytona Beach (G-2613)			
Hutton Medical Services LLC	E	727 441-4777	
Clearwater (G-1676)			

Hyperbaric & Woundcare Inc	D	813 932-1510	
Temple Terrace (G-18636)			
IM Slzbcher Ctr For Hmless I	D	904 359-0457	
Jacksonville (G-6310)			
Ima Evaluations Inc	D	904 731-0085	
Jacksonville (G-6311)			
Impower Inc	C	407 215-0095	
Longwood (G-8366)			
Independent Imaging LLC	E	561 795-5558	
West Palm Beach (G-19198)			
Independent Imaging LLC	E	561 795-5558	
Lake Worth (G-7734)			
Indian River Memorial Hosp Inc	A	772 567-4311	
Vero Beach (G-18877)			
Infants and Children PA	E	561 451-5767	
Boca Raton (G-640)			
Infectious Disease Cons MD PA	D	407 647-3960	
Altamonte Springs (G-63)			
Inpatient Consultants Fla Inc	C	941 486-6927	
Venice (G-18786)			
Inspire Oncology LLC	E	239 429-0400	
Naples (G-11176)			
Institute Crdvsclar Excllnce P	E	352 854-0681	
Williston (G-19513)			
Intensive Care Consortium Inc	E	561 997-0821	
Boca Raton (G-644)			
Intercoastal Medical Group Inc	D	941 342-8892	
Sarasota (G-16196)			
Intercoastal Medical Group Inc	D	941 739-3040	
Bradenton (G-1125)			
Intercoastal Medical Group Inc	D	941 341-0042	
Sarasota (G-16197)			
Intercoastal Medical Group Inc	D	941 379-5884	
Sarasota (G-16198)			
Intercoastal Medical Group Inc	D	941 366-3062	
Sarasota (G-16199)			
Intercoastal Medical Group Inc	E	941 955-1108	
Sarasota (G-16200)			
Interlachen Pediatrics Inc	D	407 767-2477	
Maitland (G-8543)			
Internal Mdcine Assoc Lee Cnty	D	239 936-1343	
Fort Myers (G-4450)			
Internal Mdcine Group Wnter Hv	D	863 294-4404	
Winter Haven (G-19635)			
Internal Mdcine Pdtrics Assoc	E	850 656-2006	
Tallahassee (G-17008)			
Internal Medicine Specialst ME	D	863 294-1999	
Winter Haven (G-19636)			
Irmc Physician Network Urology	E	772 794-9771	
Vero Beach (G-18880)			
Irving Radiology Inc	D	646 725-2800	
Saint Petersburg (G-15728)			
Island Doctors	D	904 388-2820	
Jacksonville (G-6333)			
Island Doctors	E	386 312-0250	
East Palatka (G-3399)			
Jack R Groover MD PA	E	904 398-7205	
Jacksonville (G-6338)			
Jacksonville Bch Surgery Ctr LP	D	904 247-8181	
Jacksonville Beach (G-6989)			
Jacksnvlle Orthpaedic Inst Inc	D	904 733-9948	
Jacksonville (G-6344)			
Jacksnvlle Orthpaedic Inst Inc	D	904 346-3465	
Jacksonville (G-6345)			
Jacksnvlle Orthpaedic Inst Inc	D	904 564-9594	
Jacksonville (G-6346)			
Jacksnvlle Orthpaedic Inst Inc	E	904 388-1400	
Jacksonville (G-6347)			
Jackson County Hospital Dst	B	850 526-2200	
Marianna (G-8680)			
Jacksonville Heart Center PA	D	904 241-7147	
Jacksonville Beach (G-6990)			
Jaffer Medical Group	D	954 433-7344	
Pembroke Pines (G-14156)			
James G Houle MD PA	E	561 750-2100	
Boca Raton (G-649)			
Jeffery A Hunt Do PA	E	813 282-0223	
Tampa (G-17893)			
Jessie Trice Cmnty Hlth Sys In	E	305 693-1213	
Miami (G-9789)			
Jessie Trice Cmnty Hlth Sys In	E	305 887-0004	
Hialeah (G-5283)			
Jewett Orthopaedic Clinic LLC	D	407 647-2287	
Winter Park (G-19742)			
JFK Internal Medicine	E	561 548-1450	
Lake Worth (G-7737)			
John A Ortolani MD PA	E	386 274-2000	
Daytona Beach (G-2621)			
John G Finn MD Facc	E	727 544-1441	
Pinellas Park (G-14526)			

Johns Hpkins All Chld Hosp Inc	E	727 834-5411	
New Port Richey (G-11390)			
Jon R Thogmartin MD PA	E	727 582-6800	
Largo (G-8122)			
Jorge Agoilar Mdpa	D	904 241-8300	
Jacksonville Beach (G-6992)			
Jose L Gallastegui MD	D	727 445-1911	
Clearwater (G-1688)			
Joseph I Fernandez MD PA	E	305 275-5677	
Miami (G-9805)			
Joseph L Riley Anesthesia Asso	E	407 667-0444	
Maitland (G-8548)			
Joseph Onorato MD PC	E	239 500-7546	
Naples (G-11185)			
Juan J Perez MD	E	321 269-5101	
Rockledge (G-15354)			
Jupiter Medical Center Inc	E	561 744-4411	
Jupiter (G-7104)			
Jupiter Otptent Srgery Ctr LLC	D	561 741-1705	
Jupiter (G-7105)			
Kagan Jugan & Associates PA	E	239 936-6778	
Fort Myers (G-4457)			
Karr Krnberg Orthpdic Assoc MD	D	407 846-6004	
Kissimmee (G-7335)			
Kasraeian Urology Pllc	E	904 727-7955	
Jacksonville (G-6396)			
Kendall Regional Med Ctr Inc	A	305 223-3000	
Miami (G-9819)			
Kendall West Surgical Center	E	305 279-0098	
Miami (G-9821)			
Kennedy-White Orthpdic Prtners	E	941 365-0655	
Sarasota (G-16210)			
Kenneth A Berdick MD PA	E	239 334-4157	
Fort Myers (G-4462)			
Kessler Rehabilitation of Fla	E	863 688-6931	
Lakeland (G-7896)			
Kidz Medical Services Inc	D	954 609-0753	
Boca Raton (G-659)			
Kidz Medical Services Inc	D	239 213-0690	
Naples (G-11191)			
Kzmss Again Lllp	D	352 391-5875	
Lady Lake (G-7436)			
Lake Med Imging Brast Ctr At V	C	352 365-2583	
Leesburg (G-8251)			
Lakeland Eye Clinic PA	E	863 688-5604	
Lakeland (G-7900)			
Lakeland FL Endoscopy Asc LLC	E	863 226-0855	
Lakeland (G-7901)			
Lakeland Ob-Gyn PA	E	863 688-1528	
Lakeland (G-7902)			
Lakeland Regional Health	D	863 284-5000	
Lakeland (G-7903)			
Lakeland Srgcal Dgnstc Ctr LLP	D	863 683-2428	
Lakeland (G-7905)			
Lakeside Pediatrics PA	D	863 619-8441	
Lakeland (G-7907)			
Laser LLC	C	941 330-2020	
Sarasota (G-16216)			
Lee Memorial Health System	E	239 939-7375	
Fort Myers (G-4486)			
Legacy Behavioral Hlth Ctr Inc	E	772 257-5264	
Vero Beach (G-18885)			
Leon Flagler Holdings LLC	A	305 631-3900	
Miami (G-9862)			
Leon Medical Centers Inc	D	305 559-2881	
Miami (G-9864)			
Liberty Health Science 360	E	352 485-1153	
Gainesville (G-4934)			
Life & Wellness Med Ctr Corp	D	786 542-5706	
Miami (G-9870)			
Lifestream Behavioral Ctr Inc	D	352 360-6575	
Leesburg (G-8259)			
Lower Keys Medical Ctr Aux Inc	B	305 294-5531	
Key West (G-7226)			
Lyerly Neurosurgery	D	904 388-6518	
Jacksonville (G-6453)			
Madison Cnty Hosp Hlth Systems	C	850 973-2271	
Madison (G-8488)			
Magic Medspa Corp	E	954 332-6243	
Fort Lauderdale (G-3952)			
Magnolia Medical Clinic PA	D	850 243-7681	
Fort Walton Beach (G-4788)			
Manatee Diagnostic Center Ltd	D	941 748-8077	
Bradenton (G-1134)			
Manatee Surgical Center Inc	D	941 745-2727	
Bradenton (G-1141)			
Manatee Surgicare Ltd	E	941 746-1121	
Bradenton (G-1142)			
Marc J Hirsh MD PA	E	561 819-3100	
Delray Beach (G-2989)			

Margarita R Cancio MD PA.....E.....813 251-8444
Tampa ***(G-17990)***

Mariner Health Care Inc.....E.....407 541-2600
Orlando ***(G-12810)***

Marion Community Hospital Inc.....C.....352 401-1000
Ocala ***(G-11719)***

Marion Medical Associates PA.....E.....352 732-3005
Ocala ***(G-11724)***

Mark & Kambour MD PA.....C.....305 669-3471
Miami ***(G-9901)***

Mark J Powers MD P A.....D.....772 335-4770
Port Saint Lucie ***(G-15149)***

Mark Steven Nestor MD PHD PA.....D.....305 933-6716
Miami ***(G-9902)***

Maxim Healthcare Services Inc.....D.....352 360-7291
Leesburg ***(G-8261)***

Mayo Clnic Jcksnvlle A Nnprfit.....D.....904 953-2000
Jacksonville ***(G-6473)***

McCi Holdings LLC.....C.....305 554-7200
Miami ***(G-9917)***

McCi Holdings LLC.....C.....561 966-1000
West Palm Beach ***(G-19257)***

McCi Holdings LLC.....C.....561 744-0287
Jupiter ***(G-7113)***

McCi Holdings LLC.....C.....305 828-5000
Hialeah ***(G-5296)***

McCi Holdings LLC.....C.....561 487-8865
Boca Raton ***(G-683)***

McCi Holdings LLC.....C.....561 626-7604
Palm Beach Gardens ***(G-13752)***

McCi Holdings LLC.....C.....954 597-0135
Tamarac ***(G-17198)***

McCi Holdings LLC.....C.....561 683-4008
West Palm Beach ***(G-19258)***

McCi Holdings LLC.....C.....305 644-4200
Miami ***(G-9918)***

McCi Holdings LLC.....C.....954 971-2266
Coconut Creek ***(G-1995)***

McCi Holdings LLC.....C.....904 282-8000
Middleburg ***(G-10798)***

McCi Holdings LLC.....C.....954 491-1686
Fort Lauderdale ***(G-3963)***

McCi Holdings LLC.....C.....305 662-5200
Miami ***(G-9919)***

McCi Holdings LLC.....C.....561 744-2232
Jupiter ***(G-7114)***

McCi Holdings LLC.....C.....305 635-0335
Miami ***(G-9920)***

McCi Holdings LLC.....C.....904 378-8520
Jacksonville ***(G-6479)***

McCi Holdings LLC.....D.....305 662-5200
Miami ***(G-9921)***

McCi Holdings LLC.....C.....904 265-2050
Jacksonville ***(G-6478)***

McIver Neurologic Clinic.....E.....904 355-6583
Jacksonville ***(G-6484)***

McRoberts & Steiner Chartered.....E.....561 799-5253
Palm City ***(G-13793)***

Mease Cntryside Ambltory Care.....C.....727 725-6111
Safety Harbor ***(G-15409)***

Med Express Urgent Care LLC.....E.....561 333-9331
Royal Palm Beach ***(G-15385)***

Medexpress Urgent Care Bynton.....E.....561 572-3200
Boynton Beach ***(G-1014)***

Medical Ansthsia Pain MGT Cons.....E.....239 332-5344
Fort Myers ***(G-4509)***

Medical Associates Brevard PA.....E.....321 255-1500
Melbourne ***(G-8929)***

Medical Center of Trinity.....E.....727 834-4000
Largo ***(G-8133)***

Medical Center Palm Beach Inc.....D.....561 969-7900
West Palm Beach ***(G-19260)***

Medical Center Palm Beach Inc.....D.....954 974-3111
Fort Lauderdale ***(G-3967)***

Medical Consultants Florida.....D.....305 948-9595
Miami ***(G-9931)***

Medical Ctr Rdlgy Group Drs Cr.....D.....407 423-2581
Orlando ***(G-12852)***

Medical Ctr Srgery Assoc Ltd P.....E.....352 596-2905
Brooksville ***(G-1300)***

Medical Documentatn Syst of AM.....A.....239 592-5660
Naples ***(G-11208)***

Medical Express Corp.....E.....904 281-9723
Jacksonville ***(G-6489)***

Medical Group of South Fla Inc.....E.....561 622-6111
Jupiter ***(G-7115)***

Medical Life Inc.....E.....904 806-3955
Jacksonville ***(G-6490)***

Medical Marijuana Treatment CL.....E.....850 906-5000
Tallahassee ***(G-17041)***

Medical Park Diagnostic Center.....D.....305 279-7275
Miami ***(G-9932)***

Medical Spclsts of Palm Bches.....E.....561 965-8222
West Palm Beach ***(G-19261)***

Medical Spclsts of Palm Bches.....E.....561 737-9227
Boynton Beach ***(G-1015)***

Medical Spclsts of PLM Beachs.....E.....561 434-3900
Lake Worth ***(G-7740)***

Medical Surgical Specialist.....D.....239 354-4301
Naples ***(G-11209)***

Medical Technology Transf Corp.....E.....321 726-3800
Melbourne ***(G-8930)***

Medical Ventures America Pllc.....E.....352 385-4404
Mount Dora ***(G-10957)***

Medical Ventures America Pllc.....E.....352 633-7518
The Villages ***(G-18660)***

Mediquick Urgent Care.....E.....386 597-2829
Palm Coast ***(G-13835)***

Meditationlive Inc.....E.....415 484-6018
Miami Beach ***(G-10616)***

Mednax Inc.....B.....954 384-0175
Sunrise ***(G-16797)***

Melborne Intrnal Mdcine Assoc.....C.....321 725-4500
Melbourne ***(G-8931)***

Memorial Hosp - W Volusia Inc.....D.....863 382-2049
Sebring ***(G-16408)***

Metcare of Florida Inc.....E.....561 805-8500
West Palm Beach ***(G-19266)***

Metcare of Florida Inc.....B.....386 257-1626
Daytona Beach ***(G-2636)***

Metropolitan Hlth Networks Inc.....D.....772 236-2440
Port Saint Lucie ***(G-15153)***

Metropolitan Hlth Networks Inc.....D.....386 676-9690
Daytona Beach ***(G-2637)***

Metropolitan Hlth Networks Inc.....D.....954 581-1900
Plantation ***(G-14674)***

Metropolitan Hlth Networks Inc.....D.....561 842-7293
West Palm Beach ***(G-19267)***

Metropolitan Hlth Networks Inc.....E.....561 238-0928
Jupiter ***(G-7116)***

Metropolitan Hlth Networks Inc.....E.....386 675-4411
Port Orange ***(G-15083)***

Metropolitan Hlth Networks Inc.....D.....954 970-2600
Pompano Beach ***(G-14855)***

▲ **Metropolitan Hlth Networks Inc**.....C.....561 805-8500
Boca Raton ***(G-691)***

Mia Aesthetics Clinic LLC.....E.....305 330-4959
Miami ***(G-9947)***

Miami Beach Cmnty Hlth Ctr Inc.....C.....305 538-8835
North Miami ***(G-11503)***

▲ **Miami Hand Center**.....E.....305 642-4263
Coconut Grove ***(G-2011)***

Miami Intl Cardiology Cons.....E.....305 233-9770
Pembroke Pines ***(G-14172)***

Miami Intl Med Ctr LLC.....E.....786 431-5084
Miami ***(G-9974)***

Miami-Dade Cnty Pub Schols-158.....E.....305 995-1537
Miami ***(G-9995)***

Miami-Hialeah Med Group Inc.....E.....305 696-0842
Hialeah ***(G-5299)***

Miccoskee Tribe of Indians Fla.....B.....305 894-2387
Miami ***(G-9996)***

Michas Vlntn GL Psyc ASC PA.....E.....850 862-3141
Fort Walton Beach ***(G-4792)***

Michele P Winesett.....D.....727 822-4300
Saint Petersburg ***(G-15767)***

Mid-Florida Eye Center PA.....E.....352 735-4214
Mount Dora ***(G-10958)***

Mid-Florida Eye Center PA.....E.....352 787-5900
Leesburg ***(G-8263)***

Mid-Florida Hematolog.....C.....386 734-1013
Deland ***(G-2872)***

Mid-Florida Medical Svcs Inc.....C.....863 965-9327
Auburndale ***(G-258)***

Mid-Flrida Anesthesia Assoc Inc.....C.....772 223-2115
Stuart ***(G-16643)***

Mid-Flrida Crdlgy Spcalists PA.....D.....754 223-3162
Sunrise ***(G-16798)***

Millennium Physician Group LLC.....E.....941 883-8383
Port Charlotte ***(G-15048)***

Millennium Physician Group LLC.....C.....941 883-8383
Port Charlotte ***(G-15049)***

Millennium Physician Group LLC.....E.....239 540-1495
Cape Coral ***(G-1413)***

Millennium Physician Group LLC.....D.....239 561-8033
Fort Myers ***(G-4514)***

Millennium Physician Group LLC.....C.....239 261-5511
Naples ***(G-11214)***

Millennium Physician Group LLC.....E.....941 474-3359
Englewood ***(G-3431)***

Millennium Physician Group LLC.....C.....239 217-4636
North Fort Myers ***(G-11475)***

Millennium Physician Group LLC.....D.....877 856-3774
Fort Myers ***(G-4513)***

Mittleman Eye Center.....E.....561 775-3303
Juno Beach ***(G-7034)***

MK Acharya MD PA.....E.....727 863-5418
Hudson ***(G-5646)***

Morning Light Beauty LLC.....E.....386 405-5054
Lake Mary ***(G-7613)***

Mount Sinai Med Ctr Fla Inc.....D.....305 558-8700
Hialeah ***(G-5300)***

Mount Sinai Med Ctr Fla Inc.....D.....305 441-0910
Coral Gables ***(G-2153)***

Mri Associates of Tampa Inc.....E.....813 886-9999
Tampa ***(G-18059)***

Mri Radiology Network PA.....C.....561 362-9191
Boca Raton ***(G-701)***

Murdock Family Medicine PA.....D.....941 255-3535
Port Charlotte ***(G-15050)***

Musculoskeletal Inst Chartered.....E.....813 633-5232
Sun City Center ***(G-16705)***

Musculoskeletal Inst Chartered.....D.....813 287-9370
Tampa ***(G-18062)***

Musculoskeletal Inst Chartered.....C.....813 978-9700
Temple Terrace ***(G-18642)***

Naples Community Hospital Inc.....B.....239 455-6300
Naples ***(G-11228)***

Naples Ctr For Drmtlogy Csmtc.....D.....239 596-9075
Fort Myers ***(G-4521)***

Naples Hart Rhythm Spclists PA.....E.....239 263-0849
Naples ***(G-11231)***

Naples Medical Center PA.....C.....239 261-5511
Naples ***(G-11236)***

Naples Pathology Associates PA.....D.....239 263-1777
Naples ***(G-11238)***

Nautilus Health Care Group.....A.....765 456-5433
Jacksonville ***(G-6527)***

Navarre Urgent Care LLC.....D.....850 398-8668
Crestview ***(G-2327)***

NAVY UNITED STATES DEPARTMENT.....E.....904 542-7912
Jacksonville ***(G-6529)***

NAVY UNITED STATES DEPARTMENT.....A.....904 542-7300
Orange Park ***(G-12006)***

Nemours Fundation Pension Plan.....C.....352 708-4828
Orlando ***(G-12906)***

Nemours Fundation Pension Plan.....C.....407 380-9115
Orlando ***(G-12907)***

Nemours Fundation Pension Plan.....C.....321 802-6590
Palm Bay ***(G-13630)***

Nemours Fundation Pension Plan.....C.....407 830-5437
Longwood ***(G-8387)***

Nephrology Assoc Centl Fla PA.....C.....407 894-4693
Winter Park ***(G-19753)***

Neurology Assoc Ormond Bch PA.....E.....386 673-2500
Ormond Beach ***(G-13510)***

Neurology Associates PA.....D.....407 647-5996
Maitland ***(G-8564)***

Neuroscience Consultants LLC.....D.....305 595-4041
Miami ***(G-10039)***

Neuroscience Consultants LLC.....C.....786 219-3145
Coral Gables ***(G-2156)***

Nevada Rdtion Thrapy MGT Svcs.....B.....239 931-7275
Fort Myers ***(G-4523)***

New Age Dermatology Inc.....E.....561 721-9510
Jupiter ***(G-7122)***

New Vision Eye Center LLC.....E.....772 257-8700
Vero Beach ***(G-18897)***

Newsom Eye & Laser Center Inc.....E.....813 908-2020
Tampa ***(G-18077)***

Newsom Eye & Laser Center Inc.....D.....863 385-1544
Sebring ***(G-16410)***

Norman H Anderson MD PA.....E.....352 861-0440
Ocala ***(G-11743)***

North Brward Hosp Dst Chrtble.....D.....954 217-5000
Weston ***(G-19470)***

North Brward Hosp Dst Chrtble.....A.....954 344-3000
Coral Springs ***(G-2276)***

North Fla Obstet Gynclgic Ctr.....E.....904 541-3055
Orange Park ***(G-12007)***

North Fla Regional Med Ctr Inc.....D.....352 372-2321
Gainesville ***(G-4962)***

North Fla Regional Med Ctr Inc.....D.....352 375-1999
Gainesville ***(G-4961)***

North Fla Regional Med Ctr Inc.....A.....352 333-4100
Gainesville ***(G-4963)***

North Fla Surgical Pavilion.....E.....352 333-4555
Gainesville ***(G-4965)***

North Fla Wns Physicians PA.....E.....352 332-7222
Gainesville ***(G-4966)***

S I C

North Florida Obgyn & Assoc	E	904 384-3699	Jacksonville (G-6548)
North Florida Surgery Ctr Inc	E	850 494-0048	Pensacola (G-14388)
North Florida Womens Care PA	E	850 877-7241	Tallahassee (G-17059)
North Manatee Health Svc Ctr	D	941 721-2020	Palmetto (G-13924)
North Miami Beach Surgical Ctr	E	305 952-2000	Miami (G-10053)
Northport Emergency Assoc PA	E	941 917-8507	Sarasota (G-16245)
Northshore Medical Center	E	561 988-4611	Boca Raton (G-721)
Northwest Fla Healthcare Inc	B	850 638-3400	Chipley (G-1492)
Notami Hospitals Florida Inc	B	386 719-9000	Lake City (G-7540)
O Roberto Garcia MD PA	D	813 948-0081	Lutz (G-8453)
Oakridge Outpatient Center Inc	E	954 958-0606	Fort Lauderdale (G-4024)
Ob & Gyn Specialists PA	E	407 644-5371	Winter Park (G-19755)
Ob/Gyn Specialist of The Palm	D	561 802-5352	West Palm Beach (G-19285)
Obgyn Associates Inc	E	727 461-2757	Clearwater (G-1743)
Ocala Eye PA	D	352 622-5183	Ocala (G-11749)
Ocala Eye Surgery Center Inc	D	352 873-9311	Ocala (G-11750)
Ocala Family Medical Ctr Inc	D	352 237-4133	Ocala (G-11751)
Ocala Heart Clinic II LLC	D	352 873-0707	Ocala (G-11752)
Ocala Kidney Group Inc	E	352 622-4231	Ocala (G-11754)
Ocala Oncology Center PA	D	352 732-4032	Ocala (G-11755)
Ocalasurg Inc	E	352 237-5906	Ocala (G-11756)
Odylab Inc	D	315 922-1154	Brandon (G-1245)
Omni Healthcare Inc	C	321 724-1171	Palm Bay (G-13631)
Oncology Hematology Associates	E	954 726-0035	Tamarac (G-17202)
One Call Medical Inc	D	973 257-1000	Jacksonville (G-6560)
Orange Park Pediatric Assoc PA	D	904 520-6620	Jacksonville (G-6567)
Orange Park Surgery Center	E	904 272-2550	Jacksonville (G-6568)
Orion Medical Management Inc	D	813 903-9238	Tampa (G-18108)
Orlando Clinic	E	407 843-1180	Orlando (G-12944)
Orlando Health Inc	A	407 649-9111	Orlando (G-12962)
Orlando Health Inc	E	352 726-5830	Inverness (G-5698)
Orlando Health Inc	A	407 351-8500	Orlando (G-12960)
Orlando Health Inc	A	407 767-1200	Longwood (G-8389)
Orlando Heart Specialist PA	E	407 865-5791	Altamonte Springs (G-85)
Orlando Heart Vascular Ctr LLC	D	407 930-8005	Orlando (G-12968)
Orlando Immunology Center PA	E	407 647-3960	Orlando (G-12971)
▲ Orlando Orthopaedic Ctr MD PA	E	407 254-2500	Orlando (G-12978)
Orlando Orthpdic Otptent Srger	D	407 254-2549	Orlando (G-12979)
Ormond Medical Arts	E	386 677-0453	Ormond Beach (G-13513)
Ortho Florida LLC	E	561 939-0800	Boca Raton (G-734)
Orthopaedic Specialists	E	727 942-0552	Palm Harbor (G-13872)
Orthopaedic Surgery Assoc Inc	E	561 395-5733	Boynton Beach (G-1023)
Orthopaedic Surgery Assoc Inc	E	561 395-2117	Boynton Beach (G-1024)
Orthopedic Assoc Cape Coral	E	239 772-4484	Cape Coral (G-1418)
Orthopedic Associates Broward	D	954 476-8800	Plantation (G-14686)

Orthopedic Center Florida Inc	C	386 270-0137	Daytona Beach (G-2645)
Orthopedic Center South Fla PA	D	954 473-6344	Plantation (G-14687)
Orthopedic Clinic Daytona Bch	D	386 252-5534	Daytona Beach (G-2646)
Orthopedic Specialist S Fla	E	305 822-0401	Hialeah (G-5305)
Orthopedic Specialists SW Fla	D	239 334-7000	Fort Myers (G-4529)
Orthopedic Specialties	E	727 938-1935	Palm Harbor (G-13873)
Outpatient Center At Plntn	D	239 343-0776	Fort Myers (G-4531)
Outpatient Surgical Svcs Ltd	C	954 693-8600	Plantation (G-14688)
P A Advantage Dermatology	E	904 717-1001	Jacksonville (G-6573)
Palm Bch Spine Dgnstc Inst Inc	E	561 649-8770	West Palm Beach (G-19307)
Palm Beach Cancer Institute	E	561 366-4100	West Palm Beach (G-19308)
Palm Beach Neurology	E	561 845-0500	West Palm Beach (G-19315)
Palm Beach Orthopaedic Inst PA	E	561 694-7776	Palm Beach Gardens (G-13761)
Palm Harbor Medical Center	E	727 786-1673	Palm Harbor (G-13875)
Palms Medical Group	D	352 463-2374	Trenton (G-18719)
Palms West Hospital Ltd Partnr	D	561 795-5130	Loxahatchee (G-8425)
Pan AM Diagnostic Services	E	407 857-1700	Orlando (G-13004)
Panama City Surgery Center LLC	D	850 769-3191	Panama City (G-14051)
Panhandle Anesthesiologists	D	850 872-0303	Panama City (G-14053)
Park Place Therapeutic Center	E	954 475-4500	Plantation (G-14689)
Parkcreek Surgery Center Lllp	D	954 312-3500	Coconut Creek (G-1999)
Partners Imging Ctr Srsota LLC	E	941 342-0505	Sarasota (G-16258)
Passport Health Inc	E	904 824-0577	Jacksonville (G-6583)
Passport Health LLC	E	941 362-0304	Sarasota (G-16259)
Pasteur Medical Center LLC	E	305 512-0075	Miami (G-10101)
Pasteur Medical Holdings LLC	C	786 422-6821	Miami Lakes (G-10751)
Pathology Group of NW Fla Pllc	E	850 438-1154	Pensacola (G-14402)
Pathology Specialists PA	E	407 422-1377	Orlando (G-13012)
PCA Medical Group Inc	E	877 285-8617	Tampa (G-18124)
Peace River Center For Per Dev	E	863 413-2708	Lakeland (G-7937)
Pediatric Associates of Ne FL	E	954 382-6045	Plantation (G-14691)
Pediatric Center	E	561 777-8419	Boynton Beach (G-1027)
Pediatric Physician Svcs Inc	D	727 767-4313	Saint Petersburg (G-15793)
Pediatric Professional Assoc	D	305 271-1087	Miami (G-10108)
Pediatrics of Brevard PA	E	321 724-5437	Rockledge (G-15359)
Pediatrix Management Svcs Inc	E	954 384-0175	Sunrise (G-16805)
Pediatrix Med Group Fla Inc	E	727 322-4830	Saint Petersburg (G-15794)
Pediatrix Medical Group Ark PA	D	800 243-3839	Sunrise (G-16806)
Pediatrix Medical Group Inc	D	407 841-5218	Orlando (G-13019)
Pediatrix Medical Group Ind PC	E	954 851-1940	Sunrise (G-16807)
Pediatrix Medical Group of Tex	D	954 851-1940	Sunrise (G-16808)
▲ Pensacola Lung Group	D	850 477-9253	Pensacola (G-14411)
Phuphanich Surasak MD	C	813 974-2918	Tampa (G-18148)
Physcians Millennium Group ADM	E	239 573-1606	Cape Coral (G-1421)
Physcians Millennium Group ADM	E	941 743-2277	Port Charlotte (G-15053)

Physician Associates LLC	E	407 381-7387	Oviedo (G-13565)
Physician Associates LLC	E	407 381-7367	Orlando (G-13028)
Physicians Group Services PA	E	904 264-7517	Orange Park (G-12012)
Physicians Group Services PA	E	904 268-2227	Jacksonville (G-6601)
Physicians Winter Haven LLC	E	863 293-8471	Winter Haven (G-19651)
Pinellas Medical Associates PA	E	727 528-6100	Saint Petersburg (G-15800)
Pinnacle Fertility Inc	E	727 638-1296	Tampa (G-18154)
Pioneer Medical Group Pl	C	813 779-6303	Temple Terrace (G-18644)
Planned Parenthood Ne FL Inc	E	904 249-2378	Jacksonville (G-6604)
Plastic Surgery Palm Beach PA	E	561 968-7111	Palm Springs (G-13896)
PMG Cardiology	D	407 647-4890	Sunrise (G-16811)
Poinciana Medical Center Inc	C	407 530-2000	Kissimmee (G-7422)
Pompano Beach Cmnty Med Ctr	E	954 781-2139	Pompano Beach (G-14877)
Portable Medical Diagnostics	E	561 964-3311	West Palm Beach (G-19329)
Premier Cmnty Hlthcare Group I	E	352 518-2000	Dade City (G-2393)
Premier Dermatology LLC	D	941 312-5027	Sarasota (G-16273)
Premiere Medical Clinic	E	850 584-3278	Perry (G-14492)
Presgar Medical Imaging Inc	D	813 977-8756	Lutz (G-8455)
Price Hoffman Stone & Assoc PC	E	727 827-5423	Saint Petersburg (G-15807)
Primary Care of Treasure Coast	E	772 567-6340	Vero Beach (G-18907)
Primary Care Specialists LLC	C	407 275-9014	Orlando (G-13056)
Primary Healthcare Associates	E	407 483-8848	Kissimmee (G-7375)
Princeton Prof Svcs Inc	E	305 258-5670	Orlando (G-13060)
Pro Med Healthcare Svcs LLC	C	727 209-0639	Saint Petersburg (G-15810)
Professional Imaging Cons Inc	D	407 657-7979	Orlando (G-13066)
Professnal Med Admnstrtors Inc	D	561 893-8800	Boca Raton (G-758)
Psych/Care Inc	D	305 630-1400	Miami (G-10157)
Psychological Associates PA	E	850 432-1480	Pensacola (G-14417)
Psychtric Hsptals Hrnndo Cnty	E	352 596-4306	Brooksville (G-1305)
Pulmonary Assn Brandon PA	D	813 681-4413	Brandon (G-1252)
Pulmonary Group South Fla PA	E	305 661-9404	South Miami (G-16512)
Pulmonary Physicians S Fla LLC	E	305 275-4755	Miami (G-10169)
Pulmonary Practice Associates	E	407 321-8230	Orange City (G-11970)
Putnam Cmnty Med Ctr N Fla LLC	E	386 328-5711	Palatka (G-13598)
Qualcare Medical Group Inc	E	954 929-6078	Pembroke Pines (G-14179)
Qualified Emergency Group PA	E	904 854-7911	Jacksonville (G-6624)
Quest Health Solutions LLC	E	877 888-7050	Coral Springs (G-2279)
Quincy Medical Group	E	850 875-3600	Quincy (G-15233)
Radiation Thrapy Svcs Intl Inc	D	239 931-7275	Fort Myers (G-4562)
Radiology Assoc Centl Fla Pl	D	352 365-0777	Leesburg (G-8269)
Radiology Assoc Centl Fla Pl	E	352 787-5858	Lady Lake (G-7440)
Radiology Assoc Clearwater PA	D	727 446-5681	Clearwater (G-1772)
Radiology Assoc Pensacola PA	E	850 438-6784	Pensacola (G-14418)
Radiology Assoc Tallahassee PA	C	850 878-4127	Tallahassee (G-17077)
Radiology Assoc Vnice Englwod	D	941 488-7781	Venice (G-18799)

Radiology Associates	D	727 847-5122	
New Port Richey *(G-11401)*			
Radiology Associates Ocala PA	E	352 671-4300	
Ocala *(G-11763)*			
Radiology Associates of Tampa	E	813 251-5822	
Tampa *(G-18197)*			
Radiology Associates S Fla Inc	D	786 596-5990	
Miami *(G-10180)*			
Radiology Cons Hollywood Inc	D	954 927-1776	
Hollywood *(G-5502)*			
Radiology Group of Baptst Hosp	E	305 596-6595	
Miami *(G-10181)*			
Radiology Imaging Assoc PA	E	386 274-7118	
Daytona Beach *(G-2656)*			
Radiology Partners Inc	A	904 348-3804	
Jacksonville *(G-6632)*			
Radiology Regional Center PA	D	239 936-2316	
Fort Myers *(G-4563)*			
Rai Care Centers Sarasota LLC	D	941 917-6444	
Sarasota *(G-16280)*			
Red Hill Surgery Center LLC	E	850 702-5020	
Tallahassee *(G-17082)*			
Redwood Radiology LLC	B	800 243-3839	
Sunrise *(G-16814)*			
Regional Consultants In Hem	E	904 493-5100	
Jacksonville *(G-6649)*			
Reina Pitisci & Assoc P A	E	813 870-3720	
Tampa *(G-18211)*			
Research To Practice	E	305 377-2828	
Miami *(G-10203)*			
Resolute Anesthesia	E	772 223-2115	
Plantation *(G-14700)*			
Resolute Ansthsia Pain Sltons	E	561 939-5500	
Boca Raton *(G-772)*			
Retina Cons of Southwest Fla	D	239 939-4323	
Fort Myers *(G-4570)*			
Retina Cons of Southwest Fla	E	239 939-4323	
Fort Myers *(G-4571)*			
Retina Cons Southwest Fla	E	239 939-4323	
Fort Myers *(G-4572)*			
Rheumtology Assoc Centl Fla PA	E	407 859-4540	
Orlando *(G-13107)*			
▼ Richard F Lockey MD	E	813 971-9743	
Tampa *(G-18224)*			
Ris Imaging Centers Inc	D	863 688-2334	
Lakeland *(G-7955)*			
Riverchase Dermatology	E	941 488-7727	
Venice *(G-18800)*			
RMA Medical Centers Fla LLC	D	954 918-0369	
Orlando *(G-13120)*			
Robert O Pohl MD PA	E	904 739-0037	
Jacksonville *(G-6672)*			
Ronald F Demeo	E	305 448-6166	
Miami Beach *(G-10650)*			
Rosemont Family Medical Ctr PA	D	407 292-0292	
Orlando *(G-13128)*			
Ruffolo Hooper & Assoc MD PA	D	813 490-7206	
Tampa *(G-18239)*			
Rural Health Care Incorporated	E	386 328-0108	
Palatka *(G-13599)*			
Sacred Heart Health Service	E	850 897-8081	
Crestview *(G-2330)*			
Saint Lucie Surgery Center	E	772 337-3178	
Port Saint Lucie *(G-15163)*			
Saltzman Tnis Pttell Lvin Jcbs	D	954 486-8020	
Lauderdale Lakes *(G-8184)*			
Same Day Surgi Ctr of Orlando	D	407 423-0573	
Orlando *(G-13164)*			
Sarasota Anesthesiologists PA	E	941 366-2360	
Sarasota *(G-16294)*			
Sarasota County Pub Hosp Dst	C	941 917-4500	
Lakewood Ranch *(G-8028)*			
Sarasota County Pub Hosp Dst	C	941 917-1383	
Sarasota *(G-16301)*			
Sarasota Orthopedic Assoc LLC	D	941 951-2663	
Sarasota *(G-16307)*			
Sarasota Physcans Srgcal Ctr L	E	941 556-3515	
Sarasota *(G-16308)*			
Sarasota Plastic Surgery Inc	E	941 366-8897	
Sarasota *(G-16309)*			
▼ Scott D Warren MD PA	E	904 296-1313	
Jacksonville *(G-6699)*			
Sdi Diagnostic Imaging LLC	E	813 348-6900	
Tampa *(G-18253)*			
Sdi Teleradiology Inc	D	813 348-6950	
Tampa *(G-18254)*			
Sebring Health Services LLC	D	863 386-4302	
Sebring *(G-16412)*			
Sebring Health Services LLC	D	863 471-0165	
Sebring *(G-16413)*			

Sebring Health Services LLC	D	863 471-3500	
Sebring *(G-16414)*			
Sebring Health Services LLC	D	863 382-2576	
Sebring *(G-16415)*			
Senior Medical Associates	E	954 870-5671	
Sunrise *(G-16824)*			
Senior Medical Associates Llc	A	954 368-3048	
Oakland Park *(G-11612)*			
SF Gastro Inc	E	561 434-0060	
Lake Worth *(G-7750)*			
Sg Gastro Inc	E	561 738-5772	
Boynton Beach *(G-1035)*			
Shands Jacksonville Medical	E	904 244-4332	
Jacksonville *(G-6715)*			
▲ Shands Tching Hosp Clinics Inc	C	352 265-0111	
Gainesville *(G-4997)*			
Shands Tching Hosp Clinics Inc	D	352 565-3536	
Gainesville *(G-4998)*			
Sheridan Childrens Hosp Svcs	B	954 838-2371	
Sunrise *(G-16825)*			
Sheridan Healthcare Inc	E	720 462-5373	
Fort Lauderdale *(G-4121)*			
Sheridan Healthcare Inc	A	615 665-1283	
Sunrise *(G-16827)*			
Sheridan Healthcare Inc	E	954 389-2700	
Pembroke Pines *(G-14183)*			
Sheridan Healthcorp Inc	A	954 963-6363	
Hollywood *(G-5518)*			
Signet Dgnstics Imging Svcs Gr	E	954 492-8151	
Fort Lauderdale *(G-4130)*			
Signet Dgnstics Imging Svcs Gr	E	904 745-5900	
Jacksonville *(G-6726)*			
Simedhealth LLC	D	352 224-2201	
Gainesville *(G-5001)*			
Simonmed Imaging Florida LLC	E	407 513-9528	
Orlando *(G-13201)*			
Simonmed Imaging Florida LLC	E	407 581-1099	
Orlando *(G-13202)*			
Simonmed Imaging Florida LLC	E	407 206-7372	
Altamonte Springs *(G-99)*			
Sleepmed Incorporated	E	561 283-1191	
Boca Raton *(G-808)*			
Solantic Corporation	E	904 223-2330	
Jacksonville *(G-6741)*			
Solantic Corporation	E	407 581-9672	
Orlando *(G-13212)*			
Solantic Corporation	E	904 854-1700	
Jacksonville *(G-6742)*			
Solantic Corporation	E	786 563-0280	
Hialeah *(G-5321)*			
Solantic Corporation	E	352 888-4449	
Gainesville *(G-5003)*			
Solantic Corporation	E	904 213-0600	
Orange Park *(G-12019)*			
Solantic Corporation	E	407 890-1890	
Oviedo *(G-13570)*			
Soma Medical Center PA	E	561 275-1155	
Lake Worth *(G-7751)*			
Soma Medical Center PA	E	561 360-2034	
Palm Springs *(G-13898)*			
Soma Medical Center PA	E	561 425-5075	
Palm Springs *(G-13897)*			
South Broward Hospital Dst	D	954 457-0500	
Hallandale Beach *(G-5184)*			
South Broward Hospital Dst	C	954 985-1551	
Hollywood *(G-5528)*			
South Broward Hospital Dst	D	954 265-3449	
Hollywood *(G-5529)*			
South Fla Intl Orthopaedics	E	305 247-1701	
Homestead *(G-5607)*			
South Fla Nephrology Group PA	E	954 345-4333	
Coral Springs *(G-2287)*			
South Fla Orthpdics Spt Mdcine	E	772 288-2400	
Stuart *(G-16670)*			
South Fla Pdatric Homecare Inc	C	305 249-5218	
Miami Lakes *(G-10765)*			
South Florida Ent Assoc Inc	D	305 595-6200	
Miami *(G-10302)*			
South Florida Ent Assoc Inc	D	305 667-4515	
South Miami *(G-16514)*			
South Florida Ent Assoc PA	E	954 731-9188	
Lauderdale Lakes *(G-8185)*			
South Florida Ent Assoc PA	E	954 389-1414	
Weston *(G-19479)*			
South Florida Ent Assoc PA	E	305 255-5995	
Palmetto Bay *(G-13951)*			
South Florida Spine Clinic Inc	D	954 567-1332	
Fort Lauderdale *(G-4139)*			
South Lake Anesthesia Svcs PA	C	352 243-9114	
Clermont *(G-1888)*			

Southast Orthpd Spcialists Inc	D	904 634-0640	
Fleming Island *(G-3557)*			
Southast Orthpd Spcialists Inc	C	904 686-1805	
Ponte Vedra Beach *(G-15007)*			
Southast Orthpd Spcialists LLC	D	904 634-0640	
Jacksonville *(G-6749)*			
Southast Vlsia Healthcare Corp	E	386 424-9421	
Edgewater *(G-3414)*			
Southeastern Integrated Med Pl	C	352 376-2608	
Gainesville *(G-5004)*			
Southeastern Integrated Med Pl	E	352 224-2200	
Gainesville *(G-5005)*			
Southeastern Urological Ctr PA	D	850 309-0400	
Tallahassee *(G-17105)*			
Southern Baptist Hosp Fla Inc	B	904 249-0335	
Jacksonville *(G-6758)*			
Southern Baptist Hosp Fla Inc	B	904 241-2990	
Jacksonville Beach *(G-7005)*			
Southern Baptist Hosp Fla Inc	C	904 202-3270	
Jacksonville *(G-6760)*			
Southern Orthpd Specialists PA	D	850 785-4344	
Panama City *(G-14074)*			
Southwestern Regional Med Ctr	B	918 286-5000	
Boca Raton *(G-812)*			
Sovereign Healthcare LLC	D	772 288-0060	
Palm City *(G-13801)*			
Space Cast Hlth Foundation Inc	B	321 452-5340	
Merritt Island *(G-9048)*			
Space Coast Orthopedic Ctr Pl	E	321 459-1446	
Merritt Island *(G-9049)*			
Spinecare Associates LLC	D	727 797-7463	
Clearwater *(G-1793)*			
St Anthonys Primary Care LLC	D	727 561-2450	
Clearwater *(G-1794)*			
St Anthonys Primary Care LLC	C	727 895-5210	
Saint Petersburg *(G-15855)*			
St Lucys Outpatient	E	941 625-1325	
Port Charlotte *(G-15062)*			
St Lukes Surgical Center Inc	B	727 938-2020	
Tarpon Springs *(G-18593)*			
St Marks Surgical Center LLC	E	239 210-0301	
Fort Myers *(G-4603)*			
St Petersburg Pediatric	E	727 392-8033	
Seminole *(G-16461)*			
St Vincents Health System Inc	B	904 262-7211	
Jacksonville *(G-6775)*			
St Vincents Medical Center	A	904 783-2405	
Jacksonville *(G-6780)*			
Stern Drake Isbell & Assoc PA	D	813 348-6900	
Tampa *(G-18337)*			
Stockwell Rsman Pulk Taylor PA	D	850 877-2105	
Tallahassee *(G-17115)*			
STS Federal LLC	C	407 965-2596	
Oviedo *(G-13572)*			
Stuart Cardiology Group PA	D	772 286-9400	
Stuart *(G-16671)*			
▲ Suncoast Cmnty Hlth Ctrs Inc	D	813 349-7567	
Riverview *(G-15270)*			
Suncoast Intrnal Mdcine Cons P	E	727 595-2519	
Largo *(G-8155)*			
Suncoast Orthpd Srgery Spt Mdc	E	941 485-1505	
Venice *(G-18807)*			
Sunil Gupta MD LLC	E	850 476-6759	
Pensacola *(G-14451)*			
Sunil Gupta MD LLC	E	850 476-6759	
Pensacola *(G-14452)*			
Sunrise Detoxification Ctr LLC	E	561 533-0074	
Lake Worth Beach *(G-7775)*			
Sunrise Detoxification Ctr LLC	D	561 318-4401	
Lake Worth *(G-7754)*			
Suntree Internal Medicine	E	321 259-9500	
Melbourne *(G-8989)*			
Surgery Center Key West LLC	E	305 293-1801	
Key West *(G-7249)*			
Surgery Center Mount Dora LLC	E	352 383-1268	
Mount Dora *(G-10963)*			
Surgery Center Naples LLC	E	239 234-2620	
Naples *(G-11315)*			
Surgery Center of Volusia LLC	D	386 760-2888	
Port Orange *(G-15090)*			
Surgery Partners Lake Mary LLC	E	813 569-6500	
Tampa *(G-18349)*			
Surgery Partners Millenia LLC	E	407 529-9139	
Orlando *(G-13253)*			
Surgery Partners Millenia LLC	E	813 569-6500	
Tampa *(G-18350)*			
Surgical Assoc Palm Bch Cnty	E	561 395-2626	
Boca Raton *(G-833)*			
Surgical Care Affiliates LLC	B	321 729-9493	
Melbourne *(G-8991)*			

Surgical Ctr For Exclnce Lllp	E	850 522-1930	
Panama City (G-14077)			
Surgical Spclsts Sthwest Fla P	E	239 936-8555	
Fort Myers (G-4616)			
Symbion Inc	D	941 932-4042	
Sarasota (G-16344)			
Symbion Inc	E	407 302-4770	
Lake Mary (G-7644)			
Symbion Inc	C	239 939-7375	
Fort Myers (G-4619)			
Symbion Inc	E	407 650-0051	
Orlando (G-13259)			
Symbion Inc	D	352 331-1590	
Gainesville (G-5010)			
Symmetry Management Corp	D	954 730-0993	
Fort Lauderdale (G-4164)			
Sypert Institute PA	E	239 432-0774	
Fort Myers (G-4621)			
Tallahssee Dgnstc Imging Ctr A	E	850 656-2261	
Tallahassee (G-17146)			
Tallahssee Orthpd Clinc Fndtio	E	850 878-4250	
Tallahassee (G-17148)			
Tallahssee Orthpd Clnic III Pl	C	850 877-8174	
Tallahassee (G-17149)			
Tallahssee Prmry Care Assoc PA	D	850 297-0114	
Tallahassee (G-17151)			
Tallahssee Prmry Care Assoc PA	C	850 878-6134	
Tallahassee (G-17152)			
Tampa Eye Clinic and Assoc PA	E	813 877-2020	
Tampa (G-18380)			
Tampa Family Health Ctrs Inc	E	813 866-0930	
Tampa (G-18381)			
Tampa Medical Group PA	E	813 879-5485	
Tampa (G-18392)			
Tampa Womens Healthcare PA	D	813 872-8551	
Tampa (G-18405)			
Tenet Healthsystem Medical Inc	D	813 780-8085	
Zephyrhills (G-19853)			
Tenet Healthsystem Medical Inc	C	561 883-7044	
Boca Raton (G-837)			
Tenet Healthsystem Medical Inc	D	561 495-0400	
Delray Beach (G-3025)			
Tenet Healthsystem Medical Inc	E	850 656-4800	
Tallahassee (G-17154)			
Theodore Crowell MD	E	239 566-7676	
Naples (G-11322)			
Tomoka Eye Associates	E	386 672-4244	
Port Orange (G-15092)			
Tomoka Surgery Center LLC	D	386 586-3711	
Palm Coast (G-13844)			
Total Insurance Brokers LLC	E	877 771-6866	
Tampa (G-18427)			
Treasure Coast Cmnty Hlth Inc	D	772 257-8224	
Vero Beach (G-18928)			
Treasure Coast Ob Gyn Inc	D	772 219-1080	
Jensen Beach (G-7025)			
Trinity Surgery Center LLC	D	727 372-4055	
Trinity (G-18730)			
U Empower Incorporated	D	786 318-2337	
Miami (G-10425)			
U S A Medical Services Corp	D	305 275-1500	
Miami (G-10426)			
Umtb Biomedical Inc	E	770 575-5221	
Miami (G-10431)			
Unconditional Love Inc	E	321 259-8928	
Melbourne (G-8997)			
Univeristy of South Florida	D	813 974-4296	
Tampa (G-18465)			
University Fla Fmly Physicians	E	352 265-0111	
Gainesville (G-5021)			
University Med Svc Assn Inc	B	813 974-2201	
Tampa (G-18477)			
University of Fla Jcksnvlle PH	B	904 244-9500	
Jacksonville (G-6893)			
University of Florida Jacksonv	A	904 244-7874	
Jacksonville (G-6894)			
University of Florida Jacksonv	C	904 244-9500	
Jacksonville (G-6895)			
University of Miami	E	305 243-6946	
Miami (G-10444)			
University of Miami	E	305 270-3400	
Miami (G-10448)			
University of Miami Miller	E	239 659-3937	
Naples (G-11334)			
University of South Flori	E	813 974-2201	
Tampa (G-18478)			
University S Fla Med Svcs Sppo	A	813 974-3374	
Tampa (G-18480)			
Urgent Care Ctrs Brvard Cnty L	D	407 200-2273	
Maitland (G-8594)			

Urgentmed Inc	E	954 423-9234	
Davie (G-2534)			
Urology Health Center PC	E	727 842-9561	
Trinity (G-18731)			
Urology Trtmnt Ctr SW Fla PA	E	941 917-8488	
Sarasota (G-16354)			
US Anesthesia Partners Inc	A	321 422-7423	
Fort Myers (G-4642)			
US Anesthesia Partners Inc	B	713 458-4123	
Fort Lauderdale (G-4203)			
Van Houten & Zann Md PA Inc	D	561 734-5080	
Boynton Beach (G-1042)			
Van Nrtwck Brown Htchnson Stk	D	904 355-6583	
Jacksonville (G-6902)			
Vascular Center Orlando PA	E	407 244-8559	
Orlando (G-13369)			
Venice Regional Hospital	E	941 473-5100	
Englewood (G-3441)			
Ventre Medical Associates	E	954 561-6222	
Oakland Park (G-11619)			
Venture Ambltory Srgery Ctr LL	D	305 652-2999	
North Miami Beach (G-11537)			
Vero Radiology Associates Inc	E	772 562-0163	
Vero Beach (G-18939)			
Veterans Health Administration	E	352 674-5000	
The Villages (G-18662)			
Veterans Health Administration	A	386 755-3016	
Lake City (G-7551)			
Veterans Health Administration	A	305 575-7000	
Miami (G-10467)			
Veterans Health Administration	E	239 939-3939	
Cape Coral (G-1431)			
Veterans Health Administration	E	727 398-6661	
Bay Pines (G-351)			
Veterans Health Administration	E	727 869-4100	
New Port Richey (G-11410)			
Veterans Health Administration	E	727 398-9387	
Bay Pines (G-352)			
Veterans Health Administration	A	561 422-7430	
Riviera Beach (G-15329)			
Veterans Health Administration	A	352 271-5000	
Gainesville (G-5024)			
Viera Diagnostic Center	E	321 254-7880	
Melbourne (G-9000)			
Village Pdtrics St Agstine LLC	E	904 217-8461	
Saint Augustine (G-15510)			
Virtual Imaging Services Inc	E	305 596-9992	
Miami (G-10475)			
Vision Care Holdings LLC	E	561 965-9110	
West Palm Beach (G-19409)			
Visual Hlth & Surgical Ctr Inc	E	561 964-0707	
Palm Springs (G-13900)			
Vohra Health Services PA	D	305 614-3348	
Miramar (G-10912)			
Vohra Wund Physicians Mgnt LLC	D	305 614-3348	
Miramar (G-10914)			
Waterford Lakes Wns Hlth Ctr	E	407 207-6768	
Orlando (G-13409)			
Waters Edge Dermatology LLC	D	561 463-5676	
Palm Beach Gardens (G-13780)			
Watson Clinic LLP	B	863 603-4717	
Lakeland (G-7995)			
Watson Clinic LLP	B	813 633-6121	
Ruskin (G-15406)			
Watson Clinic LLP	B	813 788-7867	
Zephyrhills (G-19856)			
Watson Clinic Foundation Inc	B	863 904-6250	
Lakeland (G-7996)			
Watson Clinic Foundation Inc	A	863 680-7000	
Lakeland (G-7997)			
Watson Clinic Foundation Inc	B	863 680-7700	
Lakeland (G-7998)			
Watson Clinic Foundation Inc	B	863 393-9472	
Lakeland (G-7999)			
Watson Clinic Foundation Inc	B	863 647-8011	
Lakeland (G-8000)			
Watson Clinic LLP	B	863 680-7000	
Lakeland (G-8002)			
Watson Clinic LLP	B	863 680-7560	
Lakeland (G-8001)			
Wazni Pllc	E	813 961-1331	
Tampa (G-18528)			
Weitz Ritter & Desolo MD PA	E	305 661-2299	
Miami (G-10493)			
Wellcare of Connecticut Inc	B	813 206-6352	
Tampa (G-18537)			
Wellmax Health Med Ctrs LLC	B	786 552-7800	
Miami (G-10494)			
Wellmed Medical Management Inc	E	772 344-7228	
Port Saint Lucie (G-15174)			

Wellmex Medical Center	E	305 631-8080	
Miami (G-10495)			
West Bay Surgery Center	E	727 585-9500	
Largo (G-8162)			
West Brward Rhmtlogy Assoc Inc	D	954 724-5560	
Tamarac (G-17207)			
West Coast Neonatology Inc	B	727 767-4313	
Saint Petersburg (G-15894)			
West Fla Med Ctr Clnic Ambltor	C	850 969-2121	
Pensacola (G-14469)			
West Florida Med Ctr Clinic PA	B	850 474-8000	
Pensacola (G-14472)			
Weston Otptent Srgical Ctr Ltd	D	954 703-3000	
Weston (G-19487)			
Westside Samaritans Clinic Inc	D	352 872-5171	
Gainesville (G-5030)			
White & Russell PA	E	561 684-6600	
North Palm Beach (G-11560)			
▲ White Wilson Medical Center PA	B	850 863-8100	
Fort Walton Beach (G-4811)			
White Wilson Medical Center PA	D	850 269-6400	
Destin (G-3082)			
White Wilson Medical Center PA	E	850 863-8222	
Fort Walton Beach (G-4812)			
William A Newsom	E	352 377-7733	
Gainesville (G-5031)			
William J Rand MD PA	C	954 545-1217	
Deerfield Beach (G-2817)			
William M Demarchi MD Pa	C	954 840-1666	
Coral Springs (G-2298)			
William P Mack	E	813 681-1122	
Brandon (G-1258)			
Willimson Frrara Gllgher Djsus	E	407 422-3790	
Orlando (G-13433)			
Winnie Plmer Hosp For Wmen Bbi	A	321 843-1110	
Orlando (G-13441)			
Winter Haven Hospital Inc	C	863 292-4060	
Winter Haven (G-19676)			
Winter Haven Hospital Inc	B	863 294-7010	
Winter Haven (G-19678)			
Winter Park Internal Medicine	E	407 645-2334	
Winter Park (G-19789)			
Winter Park Surgery Center LP	E	407 647-5100	
Winter Park (G-19791)			
Winter Pk Healthcare Group Ltd	A	407 646-7000	
Winter Park (G-19792)			
Winter Pk Urlogy Assoc Prof As	E	407 897-3499	
Orlando (G-13442)			
Witus Nsnson Mdrsky Urlogy Ass	D	305 270-6000	
Miami (G-10511)			
Wolverine Anesthesia Cons Inc	E	407 872-2244	
Orlando (G-13444)			
Womans Group	E	813 769-2778	
Tampa (G-18564)			
Womens Care Florida LLC	D	813 286-0033	
Tampa (G-18565)			
Womens Center For Radiology PA	E	407 841-0822	
Orlando (G-13445)			
Womens Health PA	E	850 476-3696	
Pensacola (G-14475)			
Woodlands Med Specialists PA	E	850 444-4707	
Pensacola (G-14476)			
Woodlands Med Specialists PA	D	850 696-4000	
Gulf Breeze (G-5139)			
Yergin Pulmonary Clinic PA	E	904 396-0300	
Jacksonville (G-6952)			

8021 Offices & Clinics Of Dentists

Advanced Dental Group	E	561 689-0872	
West Palm Beach (G-19022)			
Affordable Dentistry Corp	D	239 231-4089	
Naples (G-11003)			
Alan D Shpak DMD Orthdntic Gro	E	772 388-5666	
Saint Petersburg (G-15561)			
Alexander A Gaukhman DMD PA	E	941 234-4455	
Venice (G-18762)			
Barkley Circle Dental Ctr PA	E	239 939-0423	
Fort Myers (G-4287)			
Bells Dental Center Florida PA	E	727 546-4558	
Pinellas Park (G-14506)			
Central Fla Oral Mxllfcial Srg	E	407 843-2261	
Orlando (G-12271)			
Chace & Horvat PA Drs	E	407 644-4404	
Winter Park (G-19703)			
CM Dental Group Inc	E	305 558-9222	
Hialeah (G-5244)			
Coast Dental Services LLC	E	863 937-0190	
Lakeland (G-7839)			
Coast Dental Services LLC	D	813 288-1999	
Tampa (G-17492)			

Community Health Centers Inc............E 407 905-8827
Winter Garden *(G-19563)*

Dab Dental Pllc...........................D 786 252-5995
Tampa *(G-17567)*

Dahya Dentistry LLC....................D 772 461-4330
Fort Pierce *(G-4694)*

Dental Care Alliance LLC...............A 888 876-4531
Lakewood Ranch *(G-8038)*

Dental Professionals III PC.............D 904 448-6122
Jacksonville *(G-6063)*

Dental Team of West Palm Beach ....C 561 488-1688
Boca Raton *(G-552)*

Dentaland PA............................E 305 935-1400
Miami *(G-9473)*

Dentalplanscom Inc....................D 954 923-1487
Plantation *(G-14627)*

Divergent Dental MGT LLC.............E 813 300-6547
Englewood *(G-3434)*

Endodontic Associates ....D 727 372-8814
Trinity *(G-18724)*

Florida Dental Centers PA.............E 727 461-9149
Clearwater *(G-1642)*

Gateway Dental Inc.....................E 954 541-9796
Pembroke Pines *(G-14151)*

Gornstein Enterprises LLC.............C 561 734-2001
Boynton Beach *(G-992)*

Hart Dental Pllc.........................E 954 376-3676
Oakland Park *(G-11598)*

Henry Schein Fincl Svcs LLC...........E 800 262-4119
Naples *(G-11161)*

Interdent Service Corporation ....C 407 566-2222
Kissimmee *(G-7326)*

Interntnal Ctr For Cmplete Dnt ....E 727 822-8701
Saint Petersburg *(G-15723)*

Island Dental Associates PA...........E 305 294-6696
Key West *(G-7214)*

Jenee P Ware Dmd LLC.................E 772 521-7275
Vero Beach *(G-18881)*

Joseph C Mantione DMD PA.............D 727 393-7771
Saint Petersburg *(G-15738)*

Joseph Whitesides DDS.................E 941 564-6127
North Port *(G-11572)*

Lee Dental Care ....E 239 936-3436
Fort Myers *(G-4476)*

Martin Orthodontics PA.................D 352 490-0900
Chiefland *(G-1485)*

Monarch Dental Corp....................E 941 365-9110
Sarasota *(G-16236)*

Monarch Dental Corp....................E 321 253-0606
Melbourne *(G-8941)*

Nacht & Trupkin DDS PA...............E 954 797-4171
Plantation *(G-14680)*

Neal A Stubbs DDS PA.................D 813 685-3511
Brandon *(G-1244)*

North River Dental P A..................E 941 722-0502
Ellenton *(G-3428)*

Ocala Dental Sleep Center LLC.........D 941 809-7475
Port Charlotte *(G-15052)*

Orlando Oral Facial Surgery PA.........E 407 333-3011
Lake Mary *(G-7619)*

Orlando Oral Facial Surgery PA.........E 407 522-0464
Ocoee *(G-11821)*

Orthosynetics Inc........................E 305 278-9914
Cutler Bay *(G-2373)*

▼ Phanord & Associates PA............E 305 685-7863
Miami *(G-10115)*

Pross & Kanter DMD PA................E 813 961-1727
Tampa *(G-18178)*

R Dustin Dxon DMD Hldngs Pllc ....E 941 888-0573
North Port *(G-11577)*

Rural Health Care Incorporated ....E 386 328-0108
Palatka *(G-13599)*

Seda Dental of Jupiter PA..............D 305 643-3040
Miami *(G-10256)*

Seminole Dental Centers................E 407 856-2555
Orlando *(G-13186)*

South Fla Dntstry For Chldren..........D 954 752-7651
Coral Springs *(G-2286)*

South Fla Dntstry For Chldren..........E 561 391-6660
Boca Raton *(G-811)*

STS Federal LLC........................C 407 965-2596
Oviedo *(G-13572)*

SW Florida Oral Surgery ....E 239 936-8151
Fort Myers *(G-4617)*

Tomoka Periodontics and Implan........D 386 446-8444
Palm Coast *(G-13843)*

Tower Dental Inc ....D 239 566-9700
Naples *(G-11326)*

United Dental Group.....................E 321 729-6060
Palm Bay *(G-13643)*

University Dental Group.................E 407 679-5151
Orlando *(G-13355)*

Wayne J Dollard DDS Pllc ....D 561 706-2191
Stuart *(G-16679)*

8031 Offices & Clinics Of Doctors Of Osteopathy

Advanced Dermatology MGT Inc.......E 386 322-8310
Port Orange *(G-15068)*

Carespot of Austin LLC.................C 904 757-2008
Jacksonville *(G-5903)*

Florida Cancer Specialists Pl..........D 727 784-6779
Clearwater *(G-1638)*

Ocala Family Medical Ctr Inc ....D 352 237-4133
Ocala *(G-11751)*

Soma Medical Center PA...............E 561 425-5075
Palm Springs *(G-13897)*

St Vincents Medical Center.............A 904 783-2405
Jacksonville *(G-6780)*

University Community Hosp Inc.........D 813 702-4944
Zephyrhills *(G-19855)*

▲ Upledger Institute Inc ....E 561 622-4334
Palm Beach Gardens *(G-13779)*

8041 Offices & Clinics Of Chiropractors

All Broward Chirprctc & Pain...........E 954 443-2420
Hollywood *(G-5389)*

Complete Care Centers LLC ....E 407 977-3434
Oviedo *(G-13545)*

Dynamic Medical Services Inc.........D 305 226-1721
Hialeah *(G-5254)*

Hess Spinal & Medical Ctrs Inc ....E 813 265-4377
Tampa *(G-17817)*

Hess Spinal & Medical Ctrs Inc ....E 727 784-5200
Palm Harbor *(G-13866)*

Hess Spinal & Medical Ctrs Inc ....E 727 848-9144
New Port Richey *(G-11385)*

John L Keelan DC ....E 321 314-2394
Orlando *(G-12709)*

Medical Center Palm Beach Inc.........D 954 974-3111
Fort Lauderdale *(G-3967)*

Suncoast Total Healthcare LLC.........C 727 848-3377
Port Richey *(G-15112)*

8042 Offices & Clinics Of Optometrists

Center For Sight.........................E 850 476-9236
Pensacola *(G-14256)*

Daniel M Durante Od PA................E 772 692-3232
Jensen Beach *(G-7013)*

Erickson Cstllo Btlr Optmtrist ....E 561 582-3383
Lantana *(G-8063)*

Eye Health of Fort Myers Inc...........A 941 639-2020
Punta Gorda *(G-15201)*

Eye Health of Fort Myers Inc...........A 239 458-5800
Cape Coral *(G-1391)*

Mid-Florida Eye Center PA.............E 352 735-4214
Mount Dora *(G-10958)*

Mid-Florida Eye Center PA.............E 352 787-5900
Leesburg *(G-8263)*

Ocala Eye Surgery Center Inc..........D 352 873-9311
Ocala *(G-11750)*

Practice Innovision Group PA..........D 727 772-1000
Palm Harbor *(G-13877)*

Robert A Davis OD PA..................E 954 432-7711
Pembroke Pines *(G-14181)*

Samuel J Teske Od PA.................E 813 632-2020
Tampa *(G-18245)*

True Eye Experts LLC...................E 239 310-6155
North Fort Myers *(G-11478)*

Vision Care Institute LLC ....A 904 443-1086
Jacksonville *(G-6910)*

Walmart Inc..............................B 772 778-6677
Vero Beach *(G-18945)*

8043 Offices & Clinics Of Podiatrists

Pascarella Hoover Finkelstien ....E 407 339-7759
Altamonte Springs *(G-88)*

8049 Offices & Clinics Of Health Practitioners, NEC

Access Trnspt Svcs Holdg Inc.........D 888 748-7575
Lake Mary *(G-7561)*

Adventist Hlth Systm/Snbelt In.........E 407 303-7600
Orlando *(G-12072)*

Adventist Hlth Systm/Snbelt In.........C 386 671-2138
Ormond Beach *(G-13474)*

All Broward Chirprctc & Pain...........E 954 443-2420
Hollywood *(G-5389)*

All Coast Therapy Services.............D 352 791-1095
Lady Lake *(G-7427)*

American Health Care Inc ....D 352 544-5015
Brooksville *(G-1267)*

American Health Care Inc ....D 352 796-6701
Brooksville *(G-1268)*

Atlas Pyscal Thrapy Spt Mdcine ....E 904 292-0195
Jacksonville *(G-5818)*

Audiology Distribution LLC..............C 561 478-8770
Palm Beach Gardens *(G-13686)*

Beckman & Associates ....D 407 647-4740
Maitland *(G-8505)*

Bio-Mdcal Applications Fla Inc ....D 305 246-5043
Homestead *(G-5558)*

Bioplus Spcialty Phrm Svcs Inc ....E 407 830-8820
Altamonte Springs *(G-30)*

Camen Behavioral Serivces LLC........E 321 972-4039
Casselberry *(G-1445)*

Caretnders Vsting Svcs Ocala L.........B 352 694-8100
Ocala *(G-11651)*

Caretnders Vsting Svcs St Agst.........D 386 615-2053
Ormond Beach *(G-13481)*

Choice Mtters HM Halthcare Inc.........E 904 680-1256
Jacksonville *(G-5946)*

County of Brevard.......................D 321 633-1981
Rockledge *(G-15342)*

County of Hillsborough..................D 813 272-6900
Tampa *(G-17535)*

Emerald Okes Hlth Care Assoc L.......C 941 366-0336
Sarasota *(G-16145)*

Florida Eye Center......................E 813 972-4444
Tampa *(G-17680)*

Florida Hosp Zephyrhills Inc............D 813 991-5900
Wesley Chapel *(G-18998)*

Florida Hospital Ocala Inc..............B 352 368-2238
Ocala *(G-11685)*

Florida Hospital Ocala Inc..............C 352 732-4900
Ocala *(G-11689)*

Florida Kids Therapy Assoc LLC........D 786 732-0384
Cutler Bay *(G-2367)*

Gentiva Health Services Inc............C 407 324-8200
Sanford *(G-15945)*

Gulf Coast Treatment Ctr Inc ....D 850 520-4642
Defuniak Springs *(G-2832)*

Hearinglife Usa Inc.....................D 850 252-4765
Panama City *(G-14027)*

Hearinglife Usa Inc.....................D 352 877-3699
Ocala *(G-11698)*

Hearx West LLC.........................A 561 478-8770
Palm Beach Gardens *(G-13737)*

Hess Spinal & Medical Ctrs Inc ....E 727 848-9144
New Port Richey *(G-11385)*

Integrcare Rhbltation Agcy Inc ....E 954 531-1472
Delray Beach *(G-2971)*

Kessler Rehabilitation of Fla............E 863 688-6931
Lakeland *(G-7896)*

Lake Worth Enterprise LLC.............E 561 586-7404
Lake Worth *(G-7739)*

Lee Dental Care ....E 239 936-3436
Fort Myers *(G-4476)*

Lifespace Communities Inc ....B 561 272-9600
Delray Beach *(G-2980)*

McCi Holdings LLC......................C 904 265-2050
Jacksonville *(G-6478)*

McCi Holdings LLC......................D 954 762-6440
Weston *(G-19467)*

Mederi Crtnders Vs Broward LLC ....C 954 484-4837
Fort Lauderdale *(G-3966)*

Medical Center Palm Beach Inc.........D 954 974-3111
Fort Lauderdale *(G-3967)*

Memorial Hospital Tampa LP ....C 813 873-2673
Tampa *(G-18023)*

Miami-Dade Cnty Pub Schols-158.......E 305 836-0012
Miami *(G-9991)*

Millennium Physician Group LLC........D 877 856-3774
Fort Myers *(G-4513)*

Multilingual Psychotherapy Ctr ....E 561 712-8821
West Palm Beach *(G-19274)*

My Pure Life LLC........................E 561 617-5993
Boca Raton *(G-706)*

New Heights Northeast Fla Inc ....D 904 396-1462
Jacksonville *(G-6538)*

North Brward Hosp Dst Chrtble.........A 954 344-3000
Coral Springs *(G-2276)*

Nutritious Lifestyles LLC ....E 407 894-1444
Orlando *(G-12921)*

Nutropia Inc.............................C 866 877-5433
West Palm Beach *(G-19282)*

Onesourcepcs LLC......................D 888 611-3379
Pensacola *(G-14394)*

S I C

Orlando Health Inc ....C 321 841-3820
Orlando (G-12955)
Orlando Health Inc ....A 407 767-1200
Longwood (G-8389)
Orlando Health Inc ....A 407 649-9111
Orlando (G-12962)
Pinellas Medical Associates PA ......E 727 528-6100
Saint Petersburg (G-15800)
Premier Rehab Management LLC ....D 850 622-0838
Santa Rosa Beach (G-16012)
Pro Med Healthcare Svcs LLC ....C 813 654-3604
Brandon (G-1251)
Pro Med Healthcare Svcs LLC ....C 727 209-0639
Saint Petersburg (G-15810)
Psychological Affiliates Inc ....E 407 740-6838
Winter Park (G-19764)
Psychological Associates PA ....E 850 432-1480
Pensacola (G-14417)
Rehablttion Ctr For Chldren Ad ....D 561 655-7266
Palm Beach (G-13667)
Santiago Inc ....C 954 731-0070
Fort Lauderdale (G-4100)
Sea Crest Health Care MGT LLC ......E 407 658-2046
Orlando (G-13173)
Sea Crest Health Care MGT LLC ......C 352 240-6402
Gainesville (G-4994)
Sea Crest Health Care MGT LLC ......C 850 654-4588
Destin (G-3077)
Seniorbridge Family ....D 305 529-0224
Coral Gables (G-2184)
▲ Sinai Plz Nursing & Rehab Ctr ......C 305 899-4700
Miami (G-10276)
Sleepmed Incorporated ....E 850 314-6574
Fort Walton Beach (G-4805)
Smith Mental Health Assoc LLC ......D 954 321-2296
Plantation (G-14709)
Solex LLC ....E 239 300-4779
Naples (G-11298)
Space Cast Massage Therapy Inc ....E 321 729-9000
West Melbourne (G-19014)
Special Communications LLC ....E 352 371-3680
Gainesville (G-5006)
St Anthnys Physcans Srgery Ctr ......D 727 825-1771
Saint Petersburg (G-15853)
STS Federal LLC ....C 407 965-2596
Oviedo (G-13572)
Sunrise Childrens Services Inc ....E 305 273-3013
Miami (G-10343)
Tenet Healthsystem Medical Inc ......D 954 730-2789
Lauderdale Lakes (G-8187)
Transitions Rehabilitation LLC ....D 813 341-2726
Tampa (G-18435)
United Nursing Services Inc ....C 239 596-6003
Naples (G-11332)
Viva 5 Corporation ....E 801 404-1658
Saint Petersburg (G-15889)
Watson Clinic Foundation Inc ....D 863 680-7700
Lakeland (G-7998)
Wellington Retreat Inc ....D 561 296-5288
Lantana (G-8071)
West Gbles Rhbltation Hosp LLC .....D 305 262-6800
Miami (G-10498)

8051 Skilled Nursing Facilities

1026 Albee Frm Rd Oprtions LLC .....D 941 484-0425
Venice (G-18760)
1120 W Dngan Ave Oprations LLC ....D 407 847-2854
Kissimmee (G-7260)
125 Alma Blvd Operations LLC ....D 321 453-0202
Merritt Island (G-9016)
1445 Howell Ave Operations LLC ......C 352 799-1451
Brooksville (G-1261)
15204 W Clnl Drv Oprations LLC .....D 407 877-2394
Winter Garden (G-19551)
1820 Shore Drv Operations LLC ....E 727 384-9300
South Pasadena (G-16521)
1851 Elkcam Blvd Oprations LLC .....D 386 789-3769
Deltona (G-3037)
1980 Sunset Point Road LLC ....A 727 443-1588
Clearwater (G-1504)
207 Mrshall Drv Operations LLC ......E 850 584-6334
Perry (G-14485)
2600 Highlands Boulevard N LLC .....A 727 781-7123
Palm Harbor (G-13849)
3101 Ginger Drv Operations LLC ......D 850 877-2177
Tallahassee (G-16864)
3735 Evans Ave Operations LLC ....C 239 277-3977
Fort Myers (G-4244)
3865 Tampa Road LLC ....C 813 855-4661
Oldsmar (G-11888)

3920 Rswood Way Operations LLC ....D 407 298-9335
Orlando (G-12029)
4200 Wash St Operations LLC ....D 954 981-6300
Hollywood (G-5385)
4927 Voorhees Road LLC ....A 727 848-3578
New Port Richey (G-11360)
5065 Wallis Rd Operations LLC ....D 561 689-1799
West Palm Beach (G-19017)
518 West Fletcher Avenue ....D 813 265-1600
Tampa (G-17213)
5405 Babcock St Operations LLC .....D 321 722-0660
Palm Bay (G-13607)
6414 13th Rd S Operations LLC ....D 561 478-9900
Greenacres (G-5067)
650 Reed Cnal Rd Oprations LLC .....D 386 767-4831
South Daytona (G-16483)
710 Nrth Sun Drv Oprations LLC ......D 407 805-3131
Lake Mary (G-7556)
777 Ninth St N Operations LLC ....D 239 261-8126
Naples (G-10991)
9311 South Orange Blos Trl Ope ......D 407 858-0455
Orlando (G-12033)
9355 San Jose Blvd Oprtons LLC .....E 904 739-0877
Jacksonville (G-5716)
Abbiejean Russell Care Ctr LLC ....E 772 465-7560
Fort Pierce (G-4676)
Accounting Plus Solutions ....D 321 723-1235
Melbourne (G-8807)
Acts Rtrmnt-Life Cmmnties Inc ....C 561 391-6305
Boca Raton (G-400)
Acts Rtrmnt-Life Cmmnties Inc ....C 561 362-8377
Boca Raton (G-398)
Advanced Hlth & Rehabilitation ....D 727 797-6313
Clearwater (G-1513)
Advent Christian Village Inc ....D 386 658-3333
Live Oak (G-8307)
Adventist Health System/Sunbel ....C 407 303-4000
Winter Garden (G-19553)
Adventist Hlth Systm/Snbelt In ....D 407 200-2511
Altamonte Springs (G-21)
Adventist Hlth Systm/Snbelt In ....C 407 357-1000
Altamonte Springs (G-19)
AG Holdings Inc ....E 386 677-7955
Ormond Beach (G-13475)
AG Holdings Inc ....E 954 987-7180
Orlando (G-12075)
AG Holdings Inc ....E 954 741-6700
Miami (G-9102)
AG Holdings Inc ....C 321 723-3215
Melbourne (G-8812)
Aicc Inc ....C 904 261-5518
Fernandina Beach (G-3518)
Alhambra Nh LLC ....D 727 345-9307
Saint Petersburg (G-15562)
All Snts Cthlic Nrsing HM Rhbl ....D 904 772-1220
Jacksonville (G-5765)
Alliance Cmnty For Rtrment LVI ....D 386 734-0254
Deland (G-2843)
Alliance Foundation Fla Inc ....C 386 257-4400
Daytona Beach (G-2540)
American Health Care Inc ....D 352 796-6701
Brooksville (G-1268)
American Health Care Inc ....D 727 849-6939
New Port Richey (G-11361)
American Nursing Care Inc ....D 863 421-5500
Haines City (G-5144)
American Retirement Corp ....D 727 398-0166
Seminole (G-16438)
American Retirement Corp ....D 863 318-8416
Winter Haven (G-19605)
American Retirement Corp ....D 561 498-0134
Delray Beach (G-2904)
American Retirement Corp ....C 727 934-1000
Tarpon Springs (G-18578)
American Retirement Corp ....D 941 798-8200
Bradenton (G-1051)
American Retirement Corp ....C 941 952-0446
Sarasota (G-16087)
American Retirement Corp ....C 941 366-7667
Sarasota (G-16088)
American Retirement Corp ....E 239 430-3535
Naples (G-11011)
American Retirement Corp ....C 352 750-2817
Lady Lake (G-7428)
American Retirement Corp ....C 727 398-0379
Seminole (G-16439)
American Retirement Corp ....D 727 726-5090
Clearwater (G-1520)
American Retirement Corp ....C 561 733-8444
Boynton Beach (G-960)

American Retirement Corp ....D 386 677-0782
Ormond Beach (G-13476)
American Retirement Corp ....C 904 641-7501
Jacksonville (G-5790)
American Retirement Corp ....C 813 633-1992
Sun City Center (G-16700)
Arbor Company ....D 904 701-7227
Jacksonville (G-5802)
Arbor Trail Rhab Sklled Nrsing ....E 352 637-1130
Inverness (G-5686)
Arcadia Healthcare LLC ....C 863 676-1512
Lake Wales (G-7674)
Ard En Courts ....D 407 696-8400
Winter Springs (G-19798)
Arden Courts Delray Bch FL LLC ......A 561 638-7880
Delray Beach (G-2909)
Arden Crts-Lely Plms Nples FL ....A 239 417-8511
Naples (G-11013)
Atlantic Care Acquisition LLC ....E 772 567-2552
Vero Beach (G-18835)
Auburndale Oaks Care Acqstion ....E 863 967-4125
Auburndale (G-248)
Avante At Charlotte Inc ....C 954 987-7180
Hollywood (G-5394)
Avante At Harrisonburg Inc ....B 540 433-2791
Hollywood (G-5395)
Avante At Inverness Inc ....C 352 726-3141
Inverness (G-5687)
Avante At Lake Worth Inc ....C 561 202-2582
Lake Worth (G-7714)
Avante At Leesburg Inc ....C 352 787-3545
Leesburg (G-8231)
Avante At Lynchburg Inc ....B 434 846-8437
Hollywood (G-5396)
Avante At Melbourne Inc ....C 321 723-3215
Melbourne (G-8821)
Avante At Mt Dora Inc ....D 352 383-4161
Mount Dora (G-10945)
Avante At Orlando Inc ....D 407 671-5400
Orlando (G-12155)
Avante At Roanoke Inc ....C 540 345-8139
Hollywood (G-5397)
Avante At St Cloud Inc ....E 407 892-5121
Saint Cloud (G-15518)
Avante At Waynesboro Inc ....C 540 949-7191
Hollywood (G-5398)
Avante At Wilkesboro Inc ....B 336 667-2365
Hollywood (G-5399)
Avante At Wilson Inc ....B 252 237-8161
Hollywood (G-5400)
Avante Group Inc ....D 954 987-7180
Orlando (G-12156)
Avante Vlla At Jcksnvlle Bch I ....C 904 241-0211
Jacksonville Beach (G-6976)
Ayers Hlth Rhbltation Ctr LLC ....C 352 463-7101
Trenton (G-18716)
Baker County Medical Svcs Inc ....C 904 259-7815
Macclenny (G-8474)
Bay View ....D 904 829-3475
Saint Augustine (G-15428)
Bay Village of Sarasota Inc ....C 941 966-5493
Sarasota (G-16098)
Baya Nrsing Rehabilitation LLC ....D 386 752-7800
Lake City (G-7512)
Baycare Home Care Inc ....D 727 535-8362
Largo (G-8081)
Bayonet Pt Fclty Oprations LLC ....D 727 863-3100
Hudson (G-5630)
Bayside Care ....C 727 209-3600
Saint Petersburg (G-15595)
Bear Creek Nursing Center LLC ....D 727 863-5488
Hudson (G-5631)
Beaver Dam Health Care Center ....E 850 434-2355
Pensacola (G-14231)
Beaver Dam Health Care Center ....E 850 871-6363
Panama City (G-13969)
Belleair East Health Care Ctr ....D 727 585-5491
Clearwater (G-1545)
Blue Ridge Healthcare LLC ....B 786 358-5200
Sunrise (G-16747)
Boca Ciega Center ....D 727 344-4608
Gulfport (G-5140)
Bon Scrs-St Jseph Nrsing Care ....D 941 624-5966
Punta Gorda (G-15191)
Bon Secours-Maria Manor Nurs ....B 727 576-1025
Saint Petersburg (G-15603)
Braden Rver Rhbltation Ctr LLC ....D 941 747-3706
Bradenton (G-1062)
Bradenton Council On Aging LLC ......D 352 376-8821
Bradenton (G-1064)

Brandon Fcilty Operations LLC ....D 813 681-4220
Brandon (G-1218)
Brook Summer Health Care ....D 904 768-1506
Jacksonville (G-5880)
Brookdale Sarasota Midtown ....E 941 954-1911
Sarasota (G-16111)
Brookdale Senior Living Inc ....E 941 955-4646
Sarasota (G-16112)
Brookdale Senior Living Inc ....C 561 282-6014
Lake Worth Beach (G-7765)
Brookins Elderserve Inc ....E 850 309-1982
Tallahassee (G-16896)
Brooks Skilled Nursing Inc ....D 904 345-8100
Jacksonville (G-5881)
Brooks Skilled Nursing Inc ....D 904 296-5645
Jacksonville (G-5882)
Broward Nrsing Rhblttion Ctr L ....C 954 524-5587
Fort Lauderdale (G-3656)
Cana Corporation ....E 727 391-9611
Seminole (G-16441)
Care One of Florida LLC ....E 352 556-5216
Brooksville (G-1277)
Caregivers of Pensacola Inc ....D 850 437-3131
Pensacola (G-14246)
Carpenters Home Estates Inc ....B 863 858-3847
Lakeland (G-7827)
Carrington Place St Pete LLC ....D 727 577-3800
Saint Petersburg (G-15615)
Casa Mora Rehabilitation and E ....C 941 761-1000
Bradenton (G-1073)
Cathedral Gerontology Ctr Inc ....C 904 798-5300
Jacksonville (G-5915)
Catholic Hospice Inc ....C 954 676-5465
Fort Lauderdale (G-3673)
Catholic Hospice Inc ....C 786 260-6462
Miami (G-9335)
Catholic Hospice Inc ....D 305 822-2380
Miami Lakes (G-10714)
Centennial Healthcare Corp ....C 407 872-9393
Orlando (G-12254)
Centennial Healthcare Corp ....C 850 653-8853
Apalachicola (G-126)
Centennial Healthcare Corp ....C 850 674-4311
Blountstown (G-382)
Centennial Healthcare Corp ....C 386 752-7900
Lake City (G-7518)
Centre Pnte Hlth Rhblttion Ctr ....D 850 386-4054
Tallahassee (G-16909)
Century Care Center Inc ....E 850 256-1540
Century (G-1475)
Christian Mssnary Alnce Fndtio ....A 239 466-1111
Fort Myers (G-4311)
City of Marianna ....D 850 482-6865
Marianna (G-8672)
Clear Wtr Care Acquisition LLC ....C 727 461-6613
Clearwater (G-1574)
Clearwter Rhbilitation Ctr LLC ....D 727 443-7639
Clearwater (G-1579)
Community Hspice Nrthast Fla I ....C 904 268-5200
Jacksonville (G-5988)
Concordia of Florida Inc ....B 813 977-4950
Tampa (G-17511)
Consolidated Group Madison Inc ......C 850 973-4880
Madison (G-8485)
Consulate Health Care LLC ....A 407 892-7344
Saint Cloud (G-15520)
Consulate Management Co LLC ....C 941 378-8000
Sarasota (G-16130)
Consulate Management Co LLC ....C 407 527-1550
Tallahassee (G-16923)
Consulate Management Co LLC ....C 727 863-3100
Hudson (G-5635)
Consulate Management Co LLC ....C 407 571-1550
Maitland (G-8520)
Consulate Management Co LLC ....B 850 857-5200
Pensacola (G-14266)
Consulate Management Co LLC ....C 813 681-4220
Brandon (G-1222)
Consulate Management Co LLC ....B 407 931-3336
Kissimmee (G-7288)
Consulate Management Co LLC ....C 239 995-8809
Fort Myers (G-4324)
Consulate Management Co LLC ....C 941 743-4700
Port Charlotte (G-15027)
Consulate Management Co LLC ....C 321 255-9200
Melbourne (G-8850)
Consulate Management Co LLC ....B 904 296-6800
Jacksonville (G-5999)
Conway Lakes Nursing Center ....D 407 384-8838
Orlando (G-12367)

Coral Gables Management Co Inc ......E 305 261-1363
Miami (G-9413)
Countryside Lakes Inc ....D 386 756-3480
Port Orange (G-15073)
Covenant Hospice Inc ....E 850 484-3529
Pensacola (G-14275)
Covenant Living Florida Inc ....C 954 472-2860
Plantation (G-14625)
Cplace of St Pete LLC ....D 727 577-3800
Saint Petersburg (G-15649)
Cross Creek Center LLC ....C 850 474-0570
Pensacola (G-14277)
Cross Key Manor LLC ....E 239 369-2194
Lehigh Acres (G-8279)
Cross Ter Rehabilitation Ctr ....E 727 736-1421
Dunedin (G-3383)
Cypress Cove Care Center LLC ....C 352 795-8832
Crystal River (G-2344)
Cypress Cove Retirement Cmnty ....D 239 415-5100
Fort Myers (G-4337)
Dbi Health Inc ....D 352 430-0017
Lady Lake (G-7429)
Dos Health Management Inc ....C 305 891-1710
North Miami (G-11488)
Dos of Eden Springs LLC ....C 850 926-7181
Crawfordville (G-2302)
Dunns Creek Ltd ....D 904 757-0600
Jacksonville (G-6090)
East Bay Nc LLC ....E 727 530-7100
Clearwater (G-1615)
East Orlndo Hlth Rehab Ctr Inc ....E 407 380-3466
Orlando (G-12449)
East Orlndo Hlth Rehab Ctr Inc ....B 407 880-2266
Apopka (G-175)
East Orlndo Hlth Rehab Ctr Inc ....B 407 862-6263
Apopka (G-176)
East Orlndo Hlth Rehab Ctr Inc ....C 407 975-3000
Zephyrhills (G-19831)
East Orlndo Hlth Rehab Ctr Inc ....B 813 788-4300
Zephyrhills (G-19830)
Eden Park Management Inc ....B 772 223-8777
Stuart (G-16615)
Eden Park Management Inc ....D 772 283-5887
Port Saint Lucie (G-15133)
ELM Realty Inc ....E 561 433-0387
West Palm Beach (G-19132)
Emerald Coast Center ....E 850 243-6134
Fort Walton Beach (G-4765)
Emerald Health Care Inc ....E 904 786-7331
Jacksonville (G-6110)
Emerald Okes Hlth Care Assoc L ....C 941 366-0336
Sarasota (G-6145)
Emerald Shres Hlth Care Assoc ....C 850 871-6363
Panama City (G-13998)
Emeritus Corporation ....C 813 961-1044
Tampa (G-17629)
Emeritus Corporation ....C 941 474-8600
Englewood (G-3435)
Emeritus Corporation ....C 561 736-2424
Boynton Beach (G-986)
Emeritus Corporation ....C 407 977-5250
Oviedo (G-13547)
Emeritus Corporation ....C 813 662-0255
Brandon (G-1226)
Emeritus Corporation ....C 727 576-1234
Pinellas Park (G-14516)
Emeritus Corporation ....C 386 761-1055
Port Orange (G-15074)
Emeritus Corporation ....C 904 296-2384
Jacksonville (G-6113)
Emeritus Corporation ....C 321 733-7111
Melbourne (G-8882)
Emeritus Corporation ....D 727 734-4696
Dunedin (G-3385)
Emeritus Corporation ....C 561 742-0189
Boynton Beach (G-987)
Emeritus Corporation ....C 407 277-7225
Orlando (G-12462)
Emeritus Corporation ....C 904 260-0800
Jacksonville (G-6114)
Emeritus Corporation ....C 239 454-4100
Fort Myers (G-4358)
Emeritus Corporation ....C 352 547-1292
Lecanto (G-8218)
Emeritus Corporation ....C 904 460-9100
Saint Augustine (G-15438)
Emeritus Corporation ....B 407 699-7999
Winter Springs (G-19804)
Emeritus Corporation ....C 954 572-4261
Sunrise (G-16768)

Emeritus Corporation ....C 941 316-0151
Sarasota (G-16147)
Esc-New Port Richey LLC ....A 863 647-1199
Lakeland (G-7856)
Evanglcal Lthran Good Smrtan S ......D 386 253-6791
Daytona Beach (G-2587)
Evanglcal Lthran Good Smrtan S ......D 407 870-1783
Kissimmee (G-7303)
F L C Beneva Nursing Pavillion ....E 941 957-0310
Sarasota (G-16154)
Fair Havens Center LLC ....B 305 887-1565
Miami Springs (G-10782)
Fairway Oaks Center LLC ....D 813 558-6600
Tampa (G-17644)
Fairway Pk Rtrment Fcilty Corp ....E 786 286-4484
Palmetto Bay (G-13941)
Faith Telehealth Care LLC ....D 305 928-9727
Aventura (G-271)
Family Extnded Care Pnta Grda ....E 941 627-5388
Port Charlotte (G-15033)
Fi-Carrollwood Care LLC ....E 813 960-1969
Tampa (G-17656)
Fi-Windsor Woods LLC ....D 727 862-6795
Hudson (G-5638)
Fifth Fla Living Options LLC ....E 850 521-1000
Brandon (G-1228)
Finnish American Rest Home Inc ....D 561 588-4333
Lake Worth (G-7728)
First Cast Hlth Rhblttion Ctr ....E 904 725-8044
Jacksonville (G-6165)
Five Points Health Care Ltd ....D 904 358-6711
Jacksonville (G-6182)
Five Star Quality Care-Fl LLC ....E 239 275-7800
Fort Myers (G-4374)
Five Star Senior Living Inc ....D 239 417-9459
Naples (G-11115)
Five Star Senior Living Inc ....C 954 975-8900
Pompano Beach (G-14805)
Five Star Senior Living Inc ....D 239 278-0078
Fort Myers (G-4375)
Five Star Senior Living Inc ....D 561 369-7919
Boynton Beach (G-989)
Five Star Senior Living Inc ....C 954 752-9500
Coral Springs (G-2252)
Florida Dept Veterans Affairs ....C 386 274-3460
Daytona Beach (G-2592)
Florida Hlth Fclties Corp of P ....A 561 439-8897
West Palm Beach (G-19148)
Florida Presbyterian Homes Inc ....C 863 688-5521
Lakeland (G-7869)
Floridian Fcilty Operations LLC ....D 305 649-2911
Miami (G-9591)
Fountains Senior Prpts of Fla ....B 941 923-5694
Sarasota (G-16170)
Fpc Acquisition Inc ....C 727 669-1616
Clearwater (G-1645)
Fs Tenant Pool I Trust ....E 954 752-9500
Coral Springs (G-2254)
Ft Ladrdale Hlth Rhblation Ctr ....D 954 771-2300
Fort Lauderdale (G-3807)
Gainesvlle Cuncil On Aging Inc ....D 352 376-8821
Gainesville (G-4901)
Gainesvlle Rhblttion Nrsing CT ....E 352 376-2461
Gainesville (G-4907)
Genesis Eldercare Nat Ctrs Inc ....C 813 977-4214
Tampa (G-17728)
Genesis Eldercare Nat Ctrs LLC ....B 352 357-1990
Eustis (G-3493)
Genesis Eldercare Nat Ctrs LLC ....A 407 830-7744
Longwood (G-8361)
Genesis Healthcare LLC ....C 239 261-2554
Naples (G-11130)
Genesis Healthcare LLC ....B 813 855-4661
Oldsmar (G-11905)
Gentiva Health Services Inc ....C 407 324-8200
Sanford (G-15945)
Gold Coast Home Hlth Svcs Inc ....A 954 785-2990
Fort Lauderdale (G-3824)
Grand Palms Alf Operator LLC ....E 941 952-9411
Orlando (G-12592)
Greenbriar Nh LLC ....D 941 747-3786
Bradenton (G-1115)
Greenbrook Nh LLC ....D 727 323-4711
Saint Petersburg (G-15696)
Greystone Healthcare MGT Corp ....B 727 898-5119
Saint Petersburg (G-15697)
Greystone Healthcare MGT Corp ....B 727 323-4711
Saint Petersburg (G-15698)
Greystone Healthcare MGT Corp ....A 941 492-5313
Venice (G-18783)

Gsh Health Inc	C	863 551-3900	**Kendall Health Care Property**	D	305 270-7000	**Lifespace Communities Inc**	B	561 272-9600

Gsh Health Inc............C.....863 551-3900
  Auburndale *(G-254)*

Guardian Care Inc............C.....407 295-5371
  Orlando *(G-12610)*

Gulf Care Inc............B.....239 772-1333
  Cape Coral *(G-1398)*

Gulf Coast Health Care LLC............D.....850 997-1800
  Monticello *(G-10932)*

Gulf Coast Hlth Care Assoc LLC............D.....850 769-7686
  Panama City *(G-14021)*

Halthcare N Solaris Naples LLC............D.....239 919-1142
  Naples *(G-11153)*

Hamilton Health Entps Inc............D.....386 792-1868
  Jasper *(G-7008)*

Hampton Court Nursing Ctr LLC............E.....305 947-3755
  Miami *(G-9679)*

Harbor Retirement Assoc LLC............D.....954 255-5557
  Coral Springs *(G-2259)*

Harbor Retirement Assoc LLC............D.....850 531-0404
  Havana *(G-5194)*

Harbor Retirement Assoc LLC............D.....352 332-4505
  Gainesville *(G-4912)*

Harbor Retirement Assoc LLC............D.....239 566-8077
  Naples *(G-11155)*

Harbor Retirement Assoc LLC............D.....772 778-7727
  Vero Beach *(G-18864)*

HBA Corporation............D.....954 714-2244
  Fort Lauderdale *(G-3851)*

HBA Corporation............C.....386 428-6424
  New Smyrna Beach *(G-11418)*

▲ HBA Corporation............C.....954 731-3350
  Fort Lauderdale *(G-3852)*

HBA Corporation............C.....954 597-3311
  Tamarac *(G-17192)*

HBA Corporation............C.....954 587-3296
  Plantation *(G-14653)*

Hba Management Inc............D.....954 731-3350
  Fort Lauderdale *(G-3853)*

Hcsg Crestwood Crest40............D.....386 328-1472
  Palatka *(G-13590)*

Health Center of Hudson Inc............D.....727 863-1521
  Port Richey *(G-15104)*

Health Center of Imperial Inc............D.....239 591-4800
  Naples *(G-11156)*

Health Center of Naples Inc............D.....239 592-5501
  Naples *(G-11157)*

Health Center-Windermere............E.....407 420-2090
  Orlando *(G-12627)*

Health Facilities Inc............D.....352 463-1222
  Trenton *(G-18718)*

Health Quest Mgt Corp VII............B.....407 679-1515
  Winter Park *(G-19729)*

Health Svcs Bluewater Bay LLC............C.....850 897-5592
  Niceville *(G-11451)*

Healthcare Prpts St Agstine In............C.....904 824-3311
  Saint Augustine *(G-15450)*

Healthpark Care Center............B.....239 343-7300
  Fort Myers *(G-4434)*

Heather Hill Nursing Ctr LLC............D.....727 849-6939
  New Port Richey *(G-11381)*

Hebrew Homes Miami Beach Inc............C.....305 917-1802
  North Miami Beach *(G-11527)*

Heritage Nh LLC............C.....305 945-1404
  North Miami Beach *(G-11528)*

Hernando-Pasco Hospice Inc............D.....813 780-6797
  Zephyrhills *(G-19838)*

Highland Pnes Rhblttion Nrsing............B.....727 446-0581
  Clearwater *(G-1666)*

Hollywood Hlls Rhblttion Ctr L............E.....954 981-5511
  Lighthouse Point *(G-8295)*

Hospice By Sea Inc............A.....561 395-5031
  West Palm Beach *(G-19185)*

Huntington Place LP............B.....321 632-7341
  Rockledge *(G-15352)*

Innovtive Med MGT Slutions LLC............E.....813 635-9500
  Clermont *(G-1876)*

Isle Health NH LLC............D.....904 541-3500
  Orange Park *(G-11997)*

Jackson Heights Nh LLC............D.....305 325-1050
  Miami *(G-9781)*

Jackson Plaza Nursing Home............E.....305 347-3380
  Miami *(G-9783)*

▲ John Knox Village Florida Inc............B.....954 783-4000
  Pompano Beach *(G-14834)*

Joseph Lmorse Health Ctr Inc............A.....561 471-5111
  West Palm Beach *(G-19220)*

Jupiter Medical Center Inc............A.....561 747-2234
  Jupiter *(G-7099)*

Kabirhu Associates LLC............C.....305 653-8427
  Miami *(G-9809)*

Kendall Health Care Property............D.....305 270-7000
  Miami *(G-9816)*

Kendall Hlth Care Property III............D.....305 270-7000
  Miami *(G-9818)*

Kindred Healthcare LLC............D.....561 495-3188
  Delray Beach *(G-2974)*

Kindred Hospitals East LLC............A.....727 894-8719
  Saint Petersburg *(G-15741)*

Kindred Hospitals East LLC............A.....813 839-6341
  Tampa *(G-17926)*

Kissimmee Fclty Operations LLC............D.....407 931-3336
  Kissimmee *(G-7338)*

Lady Lake Nh LLC............D.....352 259-0129
  Lady Lake *(G-7437)*

Lake Park of Madison............E.....850 973-8277
  Madison *(G-8487)*

Lake Region Homes Inc............E.....352 315-7500
  Leesburg *(G-8252)*

Lake Seminole Square Inc............B.....727 391-0500
  Seminole *(G-16452)*

Lake Wales Healthcare LLC............D.....863 676-1512
  Lake Wales *(G-7689)*

Lakeside Nrsing Rehabilitation............C.....904 714-3793
  Jacksonville *(G-6413)*

Landmark Healthcare Inc............D.....850 674-5464
  Blountstown *(G-386)*

Largo Investments & Assoc LLC............C.....727 219-9025
  Largo *(G-8126)*

Lee Memorial Health System............A.....239 343-2000
  Fort Myers *(G-4480)*

▲ Leesburg Health & Rehab LLC............D.....352 728-3020
  Leesburg *(G-8254)*

Leesburg Regional Med Ctr Inc............C.....352 323-5610
  Leesburg *(G-8257)*

Legend Senior Living LLC............D.....941 408-2600
  Venice *(G-18790)*

Legend Senior Living LLC............D.....239 772-2107
  Cape Coral *(G-1408)*

Lehigh Acres NH LLC............D.....239 369-2194
  Lehigh Acres *(G-8286)*

Lexington Mnor At Port Chrltte............D.....941 766-7991
  Port Charlotte *(G-15044)*

Liberty Healthcare of Oklahoma............E.....239 262-8006
  Naples *(G-11197)*

Life Care Centers America Inc............C.....941 360-6411
  Sarasota *(G-16040)*

Life Care Centers America Inc............D.....772 337-4330
  Port Saint Lucie *(G-15146)*

Life Care Centers America Inc............B.....904 264-1950
  Orange Park *(G-11999)*

Life Care Centers America Inc............B.....407 831-3446
  Altamonte Springs *(G-71)*

Life Care Centers America Inc............C.....352 291-4600
  Ocala *(G-11710)*

Life Care Centers America Inc............C.....561 683-3333
  West Palm Beach *(G-19236)*

Life Care Centers America Inc............C.....954 485-6144
  Lauderhill *(G-8205)*

Life Care Centers America Inc............E.....561 626-1125
  Palm Beach Gardens *(G-13747)*

Life Care Centers America Inc............C.....863 318-8646
  Winter Haven *(G-19643)*

Life Care Centers America Inc............C.....239 495-4000
  Estero *(G-3468)*

Life Care Centers America Inc............C.....321 727-0984
  Melbourne *(G-8922)*

Life Care Centers America Inc............C.....904 845-7128
  Hilliard *(G-5359)*

Life Care Centers America Inc............B.....904 332-4546
  Jacksonville *(G-6433)*

Life Care Centers America Inc............B.....407 281-1070
  Orlando *(G-12764)*

Life Care Centers America Inc............C.....561 655-7780
  West Palm Beach *(G-19237)*

Life Care Centers America Inc............C.....850 471-5400
  Pensacola *(G-14347)*

Life Care Centers America Inc............D.....941 639-8771
  Punta Gorda *(G-15212)*

Life Care Centers America Inc............E.....321 952-1818
  Melbourne *(G-8923)*

Life Care Centers America Inc............C.....352 527-1686
  Lecanto *(G-8221)*

Life Care Centers America Inc............C.....904 272-2424
  Orange Park *(G-12000)*

Life Care Ponte Vedra Inc............C.....904 273-1700
  Ponte Vedra Beach *(G-14987)*

Lifespace Communities Inc............C.....561 272-7979
  Delray Beach *(G-2981)*

Lifespace Communities Inc............B.....561 454-2000
  Delray Beach *(G-2979)*

Lifespace Communities Inc............B.....561 272-9600
  Delray Beach *(G-2980)*

Lifestyles 1 Healthcare LLC............D.....727 391-9986
  Seminole *(G-16454)*

Lifestyles and Healthcare Ltd............C.....863 357-2442
  Okeechobee *(G-11871)*

LP Defuniak Springs LLC............D.....850 892-2176
  Defuniak Springs *(G-2836)*

LP Live Oak LLC............D.....386 364-5961
  Live Oak *(G-8315)*

LP Marianna LLC............D.....850 526-2000
  Marianna *(G-8682)*

LP Orange Park LLC............E.....904 272-6194
  Orange Park *(G-12003)*

LP Orlando LLC............D.....407 565-5990
  Apopka *(G-200)*

LP St Petersburg LLC............E.....727 323-3611
  Saint Petersburg *(G-15752)*

Lutheran Haven Inc............D.....407 365-3456
  Oviedo *(G-13558)*

Lutheran Haven Inc............D.....407 365-5676
  Oviedo *(G-13559)*

Lutheran Haven Inc............C.....407 365-5676
  Oviedo *(G-13557)*

M-K of Fernandina Beach LLC............E.....904 261-0771
  Fernandina Beach *(G-3536)*

Manatee Springs Nursing Center............D.....941 753-8941
  Bradenton *(G-1140)*

Manor Oaks Inc............D.....954 771-8400
  Fort Lauderdale *(G-3955)*

Mariner Health Care Inc............E.....407 699-5506
  Winter Springs *(G-19807)*

Mariner Health Care Inc............E.....407 541-2600
  Orlando *(G-12810)*

Mariner Health Care Inc............D.....386 274-4172
  Daytona Beach *(G-2631)*

Mariner Health Care Inc............D.....850 386-4054
  Tallahassee *(G-17031)*

Mariner Health Care Inc............E.....772 337-3565
  Port Saint Lucie *(G-15148)*

Mariner Health Care Inc............E.....321 267-0060
  Titusville *(G-18695)*

Mayflower Retirement Ctr Inc............C.....407 672-1620
  Winter Park *(G-19748)*

Melborne Ter Rstrtive Care Ctr............D.....321 725-6131
  Melbourne *(G-8932)*

Melbourne Terrace Rcc LLC............C.....321 725-3990
  Melbourne *(G-8938)*

Menorah Manor Inc............C.....727 345-2775
  Saint Petersburg *(G-15761)*

▲ Miami Jewish Hlth Systems Inc............A.....305 751-8626
  Miami *(G-9975)*

Mid-South Nursing Homes Inc............C.....407 975-3000
  Maitland *(G-8558)*

Miracle Hl Nrsing Rhblttion CT............C.....850 224-8486
  Tallahassee *(G-17049)*

Monticello Hlth Mgmt LLC............D.....850 997-2313
  Monticello *(G-10935)*

Morton Plant Hospital Assn Inc............E.....727 724-6800
  Clearwater *(G-1725)*

Morton Plant Hospital Assn Inc............A.....727 462-7000
  Clearwater *(G-1724)*

Ms HUD Dixie LLC............C.....850 479-4000
  Pensacola *(G-14371)*

Ms HUD Dixie LLC............D.....321 723-1321
  Melbourne *(G-8944)*

Ms HUD Dixie LLC............C.....386 734-8614
  Deland *(G-2874)*

Ms HUD Dixie LLC............C.....850 267-2887
  Miramar Beach *(G-10924)*

Ms HUD Dixie LLC............C.....850 682-1903
  Crestview *(G-2326)*

Ms HUD Dixie LLC............C.....863 675-1440
  Labelle *(G-7426)*

Ms HUD Dixie LLC............C.....850 430-3400
  Pensacola *(G-14372)*

Ms HUD Dixie LLC............C.....850 932-9257
  Gulf Breeze *(G-5129)*

Ms HUD Dixie LLC............C.....850 430-3300
  Pensacola *(G-14373)*

Ms HUD Dixie LLC............C.....352 357-3565
  Eustis *(G-3499)*

Ms HUD Dixie LLC............C.....305 891-6850
  North Miami *(G-11504)*

Ms HUD Dixie LLC............C.....813 971-2383
  Tampa *(G-18060)*

Ms HUD Dixie LLC............C.....904 964-3383
  Starke *(G-16578)*

Ms HUD Dixie LLC............C.....850 875-3711
  Quincy *(G-15232)*

Ms HUD Dixie LLC.................D...... 386 668-4426
Debary (G-2704)

Ms HUD Dixie LLC.................C...... 561 736-6000
Boynton Beach (G-1019)

Ms HUD Dixie LLC.................C...... 386 362-7860
Live Oak (G-8316)

Ms HUD Dixie LLC.................C...... 407 339-9200
Longwood (G-8384)

Ms HUD Dixie LLC.................C...... 863 465-7200
Lake Placid (G-7669)

Ms HUD Dixie LLC.................C...... 954 979-6401
Margate (G-8657)

Ms HUD Dixie LLC.................C...... 386 252-2600
Daytona Beach (G-2640)

Ms HUD Dixie LLC.................C...... 386 274-4575
Daytona Beach (G-2641)

Ms HUD Dixie LLC.................C...... 772 286-9440
Stuart (G-16647)

Ms HUD Dixie LLC.................C...... 407 847-7200
Kissimmee (G-7359)

Ms HUD Dixie LLC.................C...... 386 437-4168
Bunnell (G-1323)

Ms HUD Dixie LLC.................C...... 407 647-2092
Maitland (G-8561)

Ms HUD Dixie LLC.................C...... 727 442-7106
Clearwater (G-1730)

Ms HUD Dixie LLC.................C...... 800 881-9907
Pensacola (G-14374)

New Port Rchey Fclty Oprtons L........D...... 727 376-1585
New Port Richey (G-11395)

New Port Richey FL Opco LLC........D...... 201 928-7814
New Port Richey (G-11396)

New Rvera Nrsing Rhbltton Ctr........D...... 786 517-6999
Coral Gables (G-2157)

Nhc Healthcare/Pensacola Inc........C...... 850 474-1252
Pensacola (G-14387)

Nhc Hlthcare/Coconut Creek LLC........D...... 954 968-8333
Coconut Creek (G-1998)

Nhs Management LLC........C...... 386 252-3686
Daytona Beach (G-2644)

North Rehab Nh LLC........E...... 727 898-5119
Saint Petersburg (G-15781)

Northport Health Svcs Fla LLC........E...... 321 725-7360
Melbourne (G-8950)

Oak Hmmock At The Univ Fla Inc........C...... 352 548-1000
Gainesville (G-4968)

Oak Tree Health Care........E...... 386 767-4831
South Daytona (G-16491)

Oaks At Avon........B...... 863 453-5200
Avon Park (G-295)

Oaks Nh LLC........C...... 352 378-1558
Gainesville (G-4969)

Ocoee Health Care........C...... 407 877-2272
Ocoee (G-11818)

Okeechbee Council On Aging Inc........C...... 561 924-5561
Pahokee (G-13582)

Oldsmar FL Opco LLC........D...... 813 855-4661
Oldsmar (G-11918)

Orlando Lutheran Towers Inc........C...... 407 515-3801
Orlando (G-12974)

Orlando Lutheran Towers Inc........C...... 407 872-7088
Orlando (G-12975)

Orlando Rhbilitation Group Inc........D...... 407 841-4371
Orlando (G-12981)

Orlando Rhbilitation Group Inc........B...... 407 843-3230
Orlando (G-12982)

Orlando Rhbilitation Group Inc........C...... 352 394-2188
Clermont (G-1882)

Osceola Mental Health Inc........E...... 407 239-0229
Kissimmee (G-7368)

Palace Group........D...... 305 275-2533
Miami (G-10086)

Palm Court Nh LLC........D...... 954 567-0620
Wilton Manors (G-19532)

Palm Garden of Tampa LLC........E...... 813 972-8775
Tampa (G-18117)

Palmetto Sub Acute Care Ctr In........D...... 305 261-1806
Miami (G-10087)

Pavilion At Cres Lk For Nrsing........D...... 386 698-2222
Crescent City (G-2308)

Pavilion At Jcksnvlle For Nrsi........D...... 904 766-7436
Jacksonville (G-6590)

Pelican Bay Coop Hsing Corp........B...... 239 591-0011
Naples (G-11256)

Pembroke Park Healthcare Inc........E...... 954 893-7755
Hollywood (G-5490)

Pensacola Care Incorporated........C...... 850 575-0619
Tallahassee (G-17067)

Pensacola Fclty Operations LLC........E...... 850 857-5200
Pensacola (G-14409)

PHC - Crestview Inc........D...... 850 682-5322
Crestview (G-2329)

Pinecrest Convalescent Ctr LLC........D...... 305 893-1170
North Miami (G-11506)

Pines Nursing Home 2015 LLC........D...... 305 893-5000
Miami (G-10122)

Pines of Sarasota Inc........B...... 941 365-0250
Sarasota (G-16266)

Plymouth Harbor Incorporated........B...... 941 365-2600
Sarasota (G-16270)

Ponce NH LLC........D...... 904 824-3311
Saint Augustine (G-15481)

Ponce Plz Nrsing Rhbltton Ctr........C...... 305 545-6695
Miami (G-10133)

Port Chrltte Fclty Oprtons LLC........D...... 941 743-4700
Port Charlotte (G-15055)

Port Chrltte Rhabilitation Ctr........D...... 941 629-7466
Port Charlotte (G-15056)

Port Saint Lucie MGT LLC........C...... 772 337-1333
Port Saint Lucie (G-15159)

Presbyterian Retirement........B...... 850 878-1136
Tallahassee (G-17075)

Presbytrian Rtrment Cmmnties I........D...... 877 452-2588
Orlando (G-13054)

Presbytrian Rtrment Cmmnties I........C...... 407 841-1310
Orlando (G-13052)

Presbytrian Rtrment Cmmnties I........D...... 407 839-5050
Orlando (G-13053)

Presbytrian Rtrment Cmmnties I........C...... 941 747-1881
Bradenton (G-1166)

Promedica Health System Inc........A...... 941 921-7462
Sarasota (G-16275)

Promedica Health System Inc........A...... 239 561-7700
Fort Myers (G-4555)

Public Hlth Trust of Mm-Dade C........A...... 786 466-3000
Miami (G-10166)

Punta Gorda Associates........D...... 941 639-8771
Punta Gorda (G-15216)

Quality Health Care Center........E...... 941 426-8411
North Port (G-11575)

Quality Health Care Center........D...... 407 877-6636
Winter Garden (G-19590)

Quality Health Facilities Inc........D...... 863 422-8656
Haines City (G-5154)

Regents Park Inc........C...... 561 483-9282
Boca Raton (G-767)

Regents Park At Aventura Inc........C...... 305 932-6360
Miami (G-10194)

Rehabltton Ctr At Jpter Grdns........D...... 561 746-2998
Jupiter (G-7133)

Reliant Health Care Services........D...... 352 860-0200
Inverness (G-5700)

Richmond Health Care Inc........B...... 954 577-3600
Sunrise (G-16815)

River Grdn Hbrew HM For The AG........B...... 904 260-1818
Jacksonville (G-6668)

Riverview Alf Operator LLC........E...... 321 312-4555
Palm Bay (G-13638)

Rockledge Nh LLC........D...... 321 632-0190
Rockledge (G-15365)

RSC Oakmonte Cordova LLC........D...... 407 444-0122
Lake Mary (G-7635)

Sabal Palms Health Care Center........D...... 727 586-4211
Largo (G-8147)

Saint Annes Nrsing Ctr Rsdence........C...... 305 252-0776
Miami (G-10235)

Saint Jhns Rhbltion Hosp Nrsin........D...... 954 486-9676
Lauderdale Lakes (G-8183)

Salem Nursing and Rehab Center........E...... 305 248-1103
Leesburg (G-8271)

Sandra Williams........E...... 850 314-6813
Fort Walton Beach (G-4802)

Santa Rosa Health & Rehab Ctr........D...... 850 623-4661
Milton (G-10823)

Schwartzberg Associates LLC........D...... 352 854-6262
Ocala (G-11775)

Schwartzberg Associates LLC........D...... 772 567-2443
Vero Beach (G-18915)

Schwartzberg Associates LLC........D...... 727 786-6697
Clearwater (G-1783)

Sea Crest Health Care MGT LLC........D...... 850 584-6334
Perry (G-14493)

Sea Crest Health Care MGT LLC........D...... 904 284-5606
Green Cove Springs (G-5063)

Sea Crest Health Care MGT LLC........D...... 239 277-3977
Fort Myers (G-4587)

Sea Crest Health Care MGT LLC........D...... 386 446-6060
Palm Coast (G-13840)

Sea Crest Health Care MGT LLC........D...... 407 877-2394
Winter Garden (G-19594)

Sea Crest Health Care MGT LLC........D...... 850 689-3146
Crestview (G-2331)

Sea Crest Health Care MGT LLC........D...... 239 334-1091
Fort Myers (G-4586)

Sea Crest Health Care MGT LLC........D...... 727 393-8279
Largo (G-8148)

Sea Crest Health Care MGT LLC........C...... 941 474-9371
Englewood (G-3432)

Sea Crest Health Care MGT LLC........C...... 941 484-0425
Venice (G-18804)

Sea Crest Health Care MGT LLC........C...... 813 876-5141
Tampa (G-18257)

Sea Crest Health Care MGT LLC........D...... 352 383-4161
Mount Dora (G-10962)

Sea Crest Health Care MGT LLC........D...... 386 362-7860
Live Oak (G-8317)

Sea Crest Health Care MGT LLC........D...... 850 474-0570
Pensacola (G-14430)

Sea Crest Health Care MGT LLC........C...... 407 298-9335
Orlando (G-13172)

Sea Crest Health Care MGT LLC........C...... 850 877-2177
Tallahassee (G-17095)

Sea Crest Health Care MGT LLC........D...... 321 269-2200
Titusville (G-18703)

Sea Crest Health Care MGT LLC........C...... 352 746-6611
Lecanto (G-8225)

Sea Crest Health Care MGT LLC........C...... 904 739-0877
Jacksonville (G-6704)

Sea Crest Health Care MGT LLC........D...... 239 772-4600
Cape Coral (G-1424)

Sea Crest Health Care MGT LLC........C...... 727 784-2848
Palm Harbor (G-13880)

Sea Crest Health Care MGT LLC........C...... 850 877-4115
Tallahassee (G-17096)

Sea Crest Health Care MGT LLC........D...... 407 658-2046
Orlando (G-13173)

Sea Crest Health Care MGT LLC........D...... 386 767-4831
South Daytona (G-16494)

Sea Crest Health Care MGT LLC........D...... 772 464-5262
Fort Pierce (G-4739)

Sea Crest Health Care MGT LLC........C...... 941 761-3499
Bradenton (G-1177)

Sea Crest Health Care MGT LLC........D...... 863 815-0488
Lakeland (G-7964)

Sea Crest Health Care MGT LLC........C...... 813 265-1600
Tampa (G-18256)

Sea Crest Health Care MGT LLC........D...... 863 983-5123
Clewiston (G-1909)

Sea Crest Health Care MGT LLC........C...... 352 240-6402
Gainesville (G-4994)

Sea Crest Health Care MGT LLC........D...... 407 846-3568
Kissimmee (G-7383)

Sea Crest Health Care MGT LLC........C...... 850 654-4588
Destin (G-3077)

Sea Crest Health Care MGT LLC........C...... 954 981-6300
Hollywood (G-5513)

Sebring Senior Living Inc........C...... 863 385-0161
Sebring (G-16418)

Seminole Properties........D...... 727 398-0166
Seminole (G-16460)

Senior Care Group Inc........D...... 813 968-5093
Tampa (G-18266)

Senior Health-Tnf LLC........D...... 813 238-6406
Tampa (G-18268)

Senior Hlth - Winter Haven LLC........E...... 863 293-3103
Winter Haven (G-19659)

Senior Lifestyle Corporation........E...... 727 781-8686
Palm Harbor (G-13881)

Senior Living I LLC........E...... 727 490-3233
Saint Petersburg (G-15845)

Seniors Management Inc........D...... 352 236-2626
Ocala (G-11777)

Shady Rest Care Pavilion Inc........C...... 239 931-8405
Fort Myers (G-4592)

Signature Healthcare LLC........E...... 386 673-0450
Ormond Beach (G-13523)

▲ Sinai Plz Nursing & Rehab Ctr........C...... 305 899-4700
Miami (G-10276)

Skyler Mississippi Inc........C...... 850 526-3191
Marianna (G-8685)

Skyler Mississippi Inc........C...... 772 286-9440
Stuart (G-16669)

Solaris Halthcare Plant Cy LLC........D...... 239 919-1142
Plant City (G-14580)

Solaris Healthcare Daytona LLC........D...... 239 919-1142
Daytona Beach (G-2666)

Solaris Healthcare Imperl LLC........D...... 239 919-1142
Naples (G-11297)

Solaris Healthcare Osceola LLC........C...... 407 957-3341
Saint Cloud (G-15535)

SIC

Solaris Healthcare Palatka LLC ....C 386 325-0173
Bonita Springs *(G-941)*

Solaris Hlthcare Byonet Pt LLC ....D 239 919-1142
Hudson *(G-5649)*

Solaris Hlthcare Chrltte Hbr L ....D 239 919-1142
Port Charlotte *(G-15060)*

Solaris Hlthcare Lk Bennet LLC ....C 239 919-1142
Ocoee *(G-11823)*

Solaris Hlthcare Mrritt Island ....D 321 454-4035
Merritt Island *(G-9046)*

Solaris Hlthcare Pensacola LLC ....D 239 919-1142
Pensacola *(G-14441)*

Solaris Hlthcare Wndermere LLC ....D 239 919-1142
Orlando *(G-13214)*

South Broward Hospital Dst ....D 954 987-2000
Hollywood *(G-5524)*

South Broward Hospital Dst ....C 954 276-6200
Pembroke Pines *(G-14188)*

South Tmpa Hlth Rhbltation Ctr ....C 813 839-5311
Tampa *(G-18306)*

Southlake Nrsing Rhbltion Ctr ....E 904 268-4953
Jacksonville *(G-6763)*

Sovereign Healthcare LLC ....D 904 797-7583
Saint Augustine *(G-15496)*

Sovereign Healthcare LLC ....D 772 398-2522
Port Saint Lucie *(G-15167)*

Sovereign Healthcare LLC ....D 772 288-0060
Palm City *(G-13801)*

Sovereign Healthcare Tampa LLC ....E 813 261-5500
Tampa *(G-18314)*

Soverign Halthcare Metro W LLC ....D 407 296-8164
Orlando *(G-13223)*

Soverign Halthcare Palm Cy LLC ....D 772 288-0060
Palm City *(G-13802)*

Soverign Hlthcare Jcksnvlle LL ....E 904 766-2297
Jacksonville *(G-6768)*

Soverign Hlthcare Medicana LLC ....A 561 582-5331
Lake Worth *(G-7752)*

Spring Hills Health Care LLC ....D 407 688-1660
Lake Mary *(G-7641)*

Spring Hills Health Care LLC ....D 407 251-8088
Orlando *(G-13227)*

Spring Lake NC LLC ....D 863 294-3055
Winter Haven *(G-19664)*

Springs At Lake Pointe Woods ....D 941 929-2700
Sarasota *(G-16329)*

St Andrews Hlth Rhbltation Ctr ....E 850 763-0446
Panama City *(G-14076)*

St Barnabas Incorporated ....C 724 443-0700
Naples *(G-11304)*

St Ctherine Laboure Manor Inc ....C 904 308-4700
Jacksonville *(G-6771)*

St Mark Village Inc ....B 727 785-2576
Palm Harbor *(G-13882)*

Stacey Health Care Centers Inc ....C 305 548-4020
Miami *(G-10323)*

Stanford Centre ....D 407 260-2433
Altamonte Springs *(G-102)*

Steward Rockledge Hospital Inc ....C 321 752-1000
Melbourne *(G-8984)*

Summerfeld Rtrment Rsdence Ltd ....E 941 751-7200
Bradenton *(G-1182)*

Summerville Senior Living Inc ....E 904 794-9988
Saint Augustine *(G-15505)*

Summerville Senior Living Inc ....E 407 299-2710
Ocoee *(G-11824)*

Summerville Senior Living Inc ....E 386 761-1055
Port Orange *(G-15089)*

Sun Healthcare Group Inc ....C 321 632-7341
Rockledge *(G-15372)*

Sunland-Vero Beach LLC ....E 772 567-5166
Vero Beach *(G-18922)*

Sunnyside Properties ....E 941 371-2729
Venice *(G-18808)*

Sunnyside Prpts Sarasota Inc ....C 941 371-2729
Sarasota *(G-16339)*

Sunrise Connecticut Ave Assn ....A 727 863-5808
Port Richey *(G-15113)*

Sunrise Senior Living LLC ....E 561 392-5940
Boca Raton *(G-831)*

Sunrise Senior Living LLC ....D 239 332-3333
Fort Myers *(G-4614)*

Sunrise Senior Living LLC ....D 727 787-1500
Palm Harbor *(G-13883)*

Sunrise Senior Living LLC ....D 239 593-1923
Naples *(G-11311)*

Sunrise Senior Living LLC ....E 800 646-1409
Parkland *(G-14111)*

Sunrise Senior Living LLC ....D 727 381-5411
South Pasadena *(G-16524)*

Sunrise Senior Living LLC ....D 904 332-0774
Jacksonville *(G-6811)*

Sunrise Senior Living LLC ....E 772 335-9990
Port Saint Lucie *(G-15169)*

Sv/Holly Point Properties Inc ....E 813 839-5311
Tampa *(G-18352)*

Tandem Health Care Miami Inc ....A 305 836-1550
Miami *(G-10364)*

Tender Care Medical Svcs Inc ....E 352 683-6831
Spring Hill *(G-16550)*

Tidewell Hospice Inc ....D 941 441-2000
Venice *(G-18811)*

Towers HM Care Rehabilitation ....D 407 425-2707
Orlando *(G-13299)*

United Living LLC ....A 305 716-0710
Miami *(G-10437)*

V I P Care Pavilion Ltd ....E 954 971-2286
Margate *(G-8668)*

Valencia Hlls Hlth Rhblitation ....E 863 858-4402
Lakeland *(G-7993)*

Venice Regional Hospital ....E 941 492-5313
Venice *(G-18818)*

Vero Bch Fcilty Operations LLC ....D 772 569-5107
Vero Beach *(G-18932)*

Victoria Nrsing Rhbltton Ctr ....C 786 517-6999
Coral Gables *(G-2206)*

Victoria Nrsing Rhbltton Ctr ....C 305 324-8090
Miami *(G-10472)*

Viera NH LLC ....D 321 752-1000
Melbourne *(G-9002)*

Villa Health NH LLC ....D 386 738-3433
Deland *(G-2888)*

Villa Healthcare MGT Inc ....D 847 440-2660
Hobe Sound *(G-5372)*

Village Place NH LLC ....E 941 624-5966
Port Charlotte *(G-15067)*

▲ Vitas Healthcare Corporation ....B 305 374-4143
Miami *(G-10480)*

Waverley Group Inc ....C 352 732-2449
Ocala *(G-11796)*

Waverley Group Inc ....C 904 824-4479
Saint Augustine *(G-15513)*

Waverley Group Inc ....C 352 795-5044
Crystal River *(G-2354)*

Wesley Manor Inc ....C 904 287-7300
Jacksonville *(G-6971)*

Wesley Susanna Health Center ....D 305 556-5654
Hialeah *(G-5336)*

West Altmnte Fclty Oprtons LLC ....D 407 865-8000
Altamonte Springs *(G-114)*

West Broward Acquisition I LLC ....C 954 473-8040
Plantation *(G-14719)*

West Fla Regional Med Ctr Inc ....A 850 494-4000
Pensacola *(G-14470)*

West Gables Health Care Center ....D 305 265-9391
Miami *(G-10497)*

West PLM Bch Fclty Oprns LLC ....D 561 439-8897
West Palm Beach *(G-19422)*

Westcare Gulfcoast - Fla Inc ....D 727 490-6767
Saint Petersburg *(G-15895)*

Westchster Grdns Rhbltton Car ....B 727 785-8335
Clearwater *(G-1838)*

Westminister Suncoast ....D 727 867-1131
Saint Petersburg *(G-15896)*

Westport Snior Lving Inv Fund ....C 941 798-8200
Bradenton *(G-1206)*

Whitehall Boca III Ltd Partnr ....D 561 392-3000
Boca Raton *(G-873)*

Whitehall Opco LLC ....D 561 392-3000
Boca Raton *(G-874)*

Wildwood Snf LLC ....D 352 748-3322
Wildwood *(G-19510)*

Williston Rhbltttion Nrsing Ctr ....E 352 528-3561
Williston *(G-19516)*

Winter Garden Rehab LLC ....C 407 877-6636
Winter Garden *(G-19601)*

Woodland Grove NH LLC ....E 904 245-7620
Jacksonville *(G-6941)*

Woodland Terrace Citrus County ....B 352 249-3100
Hernando *(G-5209)*

WoodInds Care Ctr Alchua Cnty ....E 352 333-0558
Gainesville *(G-5033)*

Zephyr Hven Hlth Rehab Ctr Inc ....D 407 975-3000
Zephyrhills *(G-19858)*

8052 Intermediate Care Facilities

207 Mrshall Drv Operations LLC ....C 850 584-6334
Perry *(G-14484)*

Allegiance Senior Care LLC ....E 407 699-5002
Casselberry *(G-1441)*

American Retirement Corp ....C 727 398-0379
Seminole *(G-16439)*

Andies Inc ....E 954 920-1988
Dania *(G-2403)*

Angelus Inc ....D 727 856-1775
Port Richey *(G-15098)*

Assisted Living Inc ....D 813 350-9040
Tampa *(G-17313)*

Avante At Boca Raton Inc ....B 561 394-6282
Boca Raton *(G-436)*

Avante At Lynchburg Inc ....B 434 846-8437
Hollywood *(G-5396)*

Avante At Roanoke Inc ....C 540 345-8139
Hollywood *(G-5397)*

Avante At Wilson Inc ....B 252 237-8161
Hollywood *(G-5400)*

Avow Hospice Inc ....D 239 280-2272
Naples *(G-11021)*

Avow Hospice Inc ....D 239 261-4404
Immokalee *(G-5651)*

Avow Hospice Inc ....C 239 261-4404
Naples *(G-11022)*

Avow Hospice Inc ....D 239 389-1089
Marco Island *(G-8627)*

Bay Village of Sarasota Inc ....C 941 966-5493
Sarasota *(G-16098)*

Broward Childrens Center Inc ....D 954 943-7336
Pompano Beach *(G-14757)*

Centennial Healthcare Corp ....C 386 752-7900
Lake City *(G-7518)*

Central Florida Communities ....D 321 268-2252
Titusville *(G-18682)*

Central Florida Communities ....D 407 660-8600
Orlando *(G-12282)*

Central Florida Communities ....D 404 233-6500
Winter Park *(G-19702)*

Chapters Health System Inc ....D 813 984-2200
Tampa *(G-17458)*

Chapters Health System Inc ....D 863 687-2103
Lakeland *(G-7830)*

Chapters Health System Inc ....C 813 871-8111
Temple Terrace *(G-18631)*

Chapters Health System Inc ....D 863 533-0203
Bartow *(G-314)*

Chapters Health System Inc ....D 813 634-7621
Ruskin *(G-15398)*

Community Hospice of ....B 904 407-5300
Jacksonville *(G-5987)*

Community Supports Inc ....E 407 645-3211
Winter Park *(G-19708)*

Consulate Management Co LLC ....C 321 255-9200
Melbourne *(G-8850)*

Coral Oaks ....D 727 787-3333
Palm Harbor *(G-13856)*

Council On Aging Vlsia Cnty In ....E 386 253-4700
Daytona Beach *(G-2565)*

Cove At Marsh Landing ....D 904 285-8827
Jacksonville Beach *(G-6982)*

Covenant Hospice Inc ....D 850 575-4998
Tallahassee *(G-16925)*

Cypress Cove Retirement Cmnty ....D 239 415-5100
Fort Myers *(G-4337)*

East Orlndo Hlth Rehab Ctr Inc ....B 813 788-4300
Zephyrhills *(G-19830)*

Emeritus Corporation ....C 941 922-8778
Sarasota *(G-16146)*

Emily Company I I L L C ....E 904 277-8222
Fernandina Beach *(G-3526)*

Encore Senior Living III LLC ....D 561 733-3200
Boynton Beach *(G-988)*

Finnish American Rest Home Inc ....D 561 588-4333
Lake Worth *(G-7728)*

Florida Prfrred Care Dvlpmntal ....D 239 995-5833
Fort Myers *(G-4388)*

Genesis Eldercare Nat Ctrs LLC ....B 352 357-1990
Eustis *(G-3493)*

Group Walter LLC Kbs ....D 904 797-5027
Saint Augustine *(G-15448)*

Gsh Health Inc ....E 863 402-1066
Sebring *(G-16398)*

Guardian Care Inc ....C 407 295-5371
Orlando *(G-12610)*

Gulfside Hospice Inc ....C 727 845-5707
New Port Richey *(G-11380)*

Halifax Health Services LLC ....D 386 597-6306
Palm Coast *(G-13826)*

Harbor Retirement Assoc LLC ....D 904 821-8030
Jacksonville *(G-6259)*

Hcr Manor Care Svcs Fla LLC ....D 419 252-5743
Jacksonville *(G-6265)*

Health Plltive Svcs of Trsure............C......772 403-4500
Stuart *(G-16630)*

Health Quest Mgt Corp VII...............B......407 679-1515
Winter Park *(G-19729)*

Hernando-Pasco Hospice Inc ....D......352 596-8888
Brooksville *(G-1292)*

Hernando-Pasco Hospice Inc ....D......813 355-4830
Zephyrhills *(G-19837)*

Hernando-Pasco Hospice Inc ....D......352 746-5700
Lecanto *(G-8220)*

Hernando-Pasco Hospice Inc ....D......352 518-1400
Wesley Chapel *(G-19000)*

Hernando-Pasco Hospice Inc ....E......727 863-7971
Hudson *(G-5643)*

Hernando-Pasco Hospice Inc ....D......727 817-1804
New Port Richey *(G-11384)*

Horizons Okaloosa County Inc...........E......850 863-8578
Fort Walton Beach *(G-4780)*

Horizons Okaloosa County Inc...........D......850 863-1644
Fort Walton Beach *(G-4781)*

Hospice of St Francis Inc ....E......321 269-4240
Titusville *(G-18687)*

Hospice Palm Beach County Inc.........B......561 364-2463
Boynton Beach *(G-998)*

Hospice Palm Beach County Inc.........C......561 848-5200
West Palm Beach *(G-19187)*

Independent Living Systems LLC.........C......305 262-1292
Miami *(G-9744)*

Lake Hse Wst-Flrida Gen Partnr.........E......941 312-5100
Sarasota *(G-16213)*

Liberty Healthcare of Oklahoma.........E......239 262-8006
Naples *(G-11197)*

Life Care Centers America Inc...........C......863 318-8646
Winter Haven *(G-19643)*

Life Care Centers America Inc...........B......407 281-1070
Orlando *(G-12764)*

Life Care Ponte Vedra Inc ....C......904 273-1700
Ponte Vedra Beach *(G-14987)*

Life Concepts Inc ....D......407 298-8121
Orlando *(G-12766)*

Life Path Hospice ....E......813 984-2200
Temple Terrace *(G-18639)*

Lifespace Communities Inc ....A......407 788-2300
Longwood *(G-8377)*

Lifespace Communities Inc ....B......561 454-2000
Delray Beach *(G-2979)*

Lifespace Communities Inc ....B......561 272-9600
Delray Beach *(G-2980)*

Lifespace Communities Inc ....C......561 272-7979
Delray Beach *(G-2981)*

Lourds-Nreen McKeen Rsdnce For......B......561 655-8544
West Palm Beach *(G-19241)*

Loveland Center Inc ....E......941 493-0016
Venice *(G-18791)*

M-K of Fernandina Beach LLC...........E......904 261-0771
Fernandina Beach *(G-3536)*

Mariner Health Care Inc ....D......386 274-4172
Daytona Beach *(G-2631)*

Marion Hospice County Inc...............D......352 291-5100
Ocala *(G-11722)*

Marion Hospice County Inc...............D......352 307-7550
Summerfield *(G-16687)*

Marion Hospice County Inc...............D......352 873-7400
Ocala *(G-11723)*

Marion Hospice County Inc...............D......352 307-0222
Summerfield *(G-16688)*

Mederi Inc ....D......407 931-0487
Kissimmee *(G-7357)*

Merritt Island Rhf Housing ....B......321 452-1233
Merritt Island *(G-9040)*

Miami Crbral Plsy Rsdntial Svc ....E......305 325-1080
Hialeah *(G-5297)*

Naval Cntning Care Rtrment Fnd ....B......904 246-9900
Atlantic Beach *(G-243)*

New Horizons Northwest Fla Inc.........D......850 474-0667
Pensacola *(G-14384)*

North Central Fla Hospice Inc............D......352 378-2121
Gainesville *(G-4959)*

North Fla Retirement Vlg Inc.............C......352 373-4032
Gainesville *(G-4964)*

Osprey Vlg At Amlia Island Ltd..........C......904 277-3337
Fernandina Beach *(G-3540)*

Palmetto Sub Acute Care Ctr In.........D......305 261-1806
Miami *(G-10087)*

Pensacola Care Incorporated ....C......850 769-7636
Panama City *(G-14055)*

Pensacola Care Incorporated ....C......850 575-0619
Tallahassee *(G-17067)*

Pensacola Care Incorporated ....C......850 862-0108
Fort Walton Beach *(G-4798)*

Pensacola Care Incorporated ....C......813 971-3490
Tampa *(G-18134)*

Pensacola Care Incorporated ....C......850 453-2323
Pensacola *(G-14407)*

Pines of Sarasota Inc ....B......941 365-0250
Sarasota *(G-16266)*

Pines Sarasota Healthcare LLC.........E......941 365-0250
Sarasota *(G-16267)*

Presbytrian Rtrment Cmmnties I.........C......407 841-1310
Orlando *(G-13052)*

Presbytrian Rtrment Cmmnties I.........D......407 839-5050
Orlando *(G-13053)*

Presbytrian Rtrment Cmmnties I.........D......407 647-4083
Winter Park *(G-19763)*

Presbytrian Rtrment Cmmnties I.........C......941 747-1881
Bradenton *(G-1166)*

Princpal Snior Lving Group LLC ....C......321 415-0400
Chuluota *(G-1500)*

Quality Health Facilities Inc ....D......863 422-8656
Haines City *(G-5154)*

RES-Care Inc ....D......239 495-5546
Bonita Springs *(G-938)*

RES-Care Inc ....D......727 793-0500
Clearwater *(G-1775)*

RES-Care Inc ....D......727 551-2900
Saint Petersburg *(G-15831)*

RES-Care Inc ....C......386 755-6104
Lake City *(G-7543)*

Richmond Health Care Inc ....B......954 577-3600
Sunrise *(G-16815)*

River Grdn Hbrew HM For The AG ....D......904 260-1818
Jacksonville *(G-6668)*

Sea Crest Health Care MGT LLC ....D......954 943-5100
Pompano Beach *(G-14891)*

Sea Crest Health Care MGT LLC ....D......863 983-5123
Clewiston *(G-1909)*

Sea Crest Health Care MGT LLC ....D......407 846-3568
Kissimmee *(G-7383)*

Senior Health - Alpine LLC...............C......727 327-1988
Saint Petersburg *(G-15843)*

Senior Hlth - Winter Haven LLC..........E......863 293-3103
Winter Haven *(G-19659)*

Senior Lifestyle Corporation.............E......813 251-6333
Tampa *(G-18269)*

Solantic Corporation ....D......352 240-8000
Gainesville *(G-5002)*

South Tmpa Hlth Rhbltation Ctr ....C......813 839-5311
Tampa *(G-18306)*

Sunbridge Healthcare LLC...............C......727 726-4888
Clearwater *(G-1803)*

Sunnyside Prpts Sarasota Inc ....C......941 371-2729
Sarasota *(G-16339)*

Sunrise Community Inc ....B......305 275-3365
Miami *(G-10345)*

Sunrise Community Inc ....C......813 671-2271
Riverview *(G-15271)*

Sunrise Community Inc ....C......305 341-8400
Miami *(G-10346)*

Sunrise Community Inc ....C......727 896-7117
Tampa *(G-18346)*

Sunrise Community Inc ....C......850 514-8020
Tallahassee *(G-17119)*

Sunrise Community Inc ....C......850 878-3313
Tallahassee *(G-17120)*

Sunrise Community Inc ....C......850 878-3313
Tallahassee *(G-17121)*

Sunrise Community Inc ....C......305 436-0145
Doral *(G-3323)*

Sunrise Community Inc ....C......863 533-0837
Bartow *(G-340)*

Sunrise Community Inc ....C......305 246-0425
Homestead *(G-5609)*

Sunrise Community Inc ....C......727 576-0492
Saint Petersburg *(G-15866)*

Sunrise Community Inc ....C......239 283-3666
Cape Coral *(G-1427)*

Sunrise Community Inc ....C......850 878-0808
Tallahassee *(G-17122)*

Sunrise Community Inc ....C......239 574-0039
Cape Coral *(G-1428)*

Sunrise Community Inc ....C......954 981-6167
Davie *(G-2525)*

Sunrise Community Inc ....C......954 434-8167
Tallahassee *(G-17123)*

Sunrise Community Inc ....C......954 434-8167
Cooper City *(G-2014)*

Tidewell Hospice Inc.....................D......941 487-3100
Sarasota *(G-16347)*

Tidewell Hospice Inc.....................E......941 552-7500
Sarasota *(G-16348)*

Tidewell Hospice Inc.....................D......941 782-4900
Bradenton *(G-1193)*

Tidewell Hospice Inc.....................D......941 845-3000
Palmetto *(G-13933)*

Tidewell Hospice Inc.....................D......941 552-5900
Lakewood Ranch *(G-8033)*

Trustbridge Inc ....D......561 848-5200
West Palm Beach *(G-19393)*

University Behavioral LLC ....B......407 281-7000
Orlando *(G-13353)*

Vitas Healthcare Corp Florida...........B......305 374-4143
Miami *(G-10478)*

Vitas Healthcare Corp Midwest ....B......407 875-0028
Maitland *(G-8597)*

Vitas Healthcare Corporation ....E......863 767-0941
Wauchula *(G-18965)*

Vitas Healthcare Corporation ....B......305 374-4143
Miami *(G-10479)*

Vitas Healthcare Corporation ....D......850 477-5586
Pensacola *(G-14464)*

Vitas Healthcare Corporation ....D......386 248-4000
Daytona Beach *(G-2686)*

Vitas Healthcare Corporation ....E......386 320-5792
Palatka *(G-13605)*

Vitas Healthcare Corporation ....D......863 279-4147
Davenport *(G-2449)*

Vitas Healthcare Corporation ....D......386 225-2000
Palm Coast *(G-13845)*

Vitas Healthcare Corporation ....D......352 589-0927
Mount Dora *(G-10964)*

Vitas Healthcare Corporation ....D......954 704-2700
Miramar *(G-10910)*

Vitas Healthcare Corporation ....D......321 751-6671
Titusville *(G-18707)*

Vitas Healthcare Corporation ....D......305 350-5965
Miramar *(G-10911)*

Vitas Healthcare Corporation ....D......772 301-6475
Stuart *(G-16678)*

Vitas Healthcare Corporation ....C......561 364-1479
Palm Beach *(G-13676)*

Vitas Healthcare Corporation ....C......305 654-3718
North Miami Beach *(G-11538)*

Vitas Healthcare Corporation ....C......321 751-6671
Melbourne *(G-9004)*

Vitas Healthcare Corporation ....D......954 343-9499
Fort Lauderdale *(G-4214)*

Vitas Hospice Services LLC..............A......800 938-4827
Miami *(G-10481)*

Westminster Shores Inc ....C......727 867-2131
Saint Petersburg *(G-15897)*

Westport Snior Lving Inv Fund...........C......941 798-8200
Bradenton *(G-1206)*

Woodhouse Inc ....E......954 786-0344
Pompano Beach *(G-14942)*

8059 Nursing & Personal Care Facilities, NEC

1010 Crpnters Way Oprtions LLC........E......863 815-0488
Lakeland *(G-7779)*

Ace Homecare ....E......863 385-7058
Avon Park *(G-287)*

Advent Christian Village Inc ....D......386 658-3333
Live Oak *(G-8307)*

Adventist Health System/Sunbel.........B......407 975-3800
Orlando *(G-12065)*

Aicc Inc ....C......904 261-5518
Fernandina Beach *(G-3518)*

Avante At Boca Raton Inc ....B......561 394-6282
Boca Raton *(G-436)*

Avante At Charlotte Inc ....B......954 987-7180
Hollywood *(G-5394)*

Avante At Melbourne Inc ....C......321 723-3215
Melbourne *(G-8821)*

Avante At Wilkesboro Inc ....B......336 667-2365
Hollywood *(G-5399)*

Bethamy Living Ctr Ltd Partnr...........C......727 461-6613
Clearwater *(G-1547)*

Bradenton Hlth Care Assoc LLC ....E......941 761-3499
Bradenton *(G-1066)*

Brandywine Cnvalescent Ctr Inc........C......863 293-1989
Winter Haven *(G-19612)*

Bridgeway Center Inc ....B......850 833-3975
Fort Walton Beach *(G-4757)*

Brookwood-Extd Care/Hialeah Gr.......E......305 556-9900
Hialeah *(G-5227)*

Carc-Dvcate For Ctzens With Ds........C......386 752-1880
Lake City *(G-7517)*

Caregiver Services Inc ....D......877 227-3448
Medley *(G-8712)*

Century Care Center Inc..................E......850 256-1540
Century *(G-1475)*

Christian Mssnary Alnce Fndtio	A	239 466-1111	
Fort Myers *(G-4311)*			
Clearwater Snf LLC	E	727 210-2600	
Clearwater *(G-1576)*			
Clearwter Rhbilitation Ctr LLC	D	727 443-7639	
Clearwater *(G-1579)*			
Colonial Care Nh LLC	D	727 544-1444	
Kenneth City *(G-7162)*			
Colonial Inn LLC	E	561 499-2300	
Delray Beach *(G-2932)*			
Community Affrdbl Spprted Lvin	D	941 365-8645	
Sarasota *(G-16126)*			
Concordia of Florida Inc	B	813 977-4950	
Tampa *(G-17511)*			
Consulate Management Co LLC	B	904 296-6800	
Jacksonville *(G-5999)*			
Coral Gables Management Co Inc	E	305 261-1363	
Miami *(G-9413)*			
Cornerstone Hspice Plltive Car	C	352 343-1341	
Tavares *(G-18604)*			
Deerwood Place Assisted Living	B	904 646-4699	
Jacksonville *(G-6056)*			
East Orlndo Hlth Rehab Ctr Inc	B	813 788-4300	
Zephyrhills *(G-19830)*			
Eden Park Management Inc	C	772 283-5887	
Port Saint Lucie *(G-15133)*			
Emeritus Corporation	C	941 922-8778	
Sarasota *(G-16146)*			
Encore Senior Living III LLC	D	561 733-3200	
Boynton Beach *(G-988)*			
Evanglcal Lthran Good Smrtan S	D	407 933-1999	
Kissimmee *(G-7301)*			
Evanglcal Lthran Good Smrtan S	C	407 933-3213	
Kissimmee *(G-7302)*			
Evanglcal Lthran Good Smrtan S	C	386 736-5800	
Deland *(G-2859)*			
Family Extnded Care of Wnter H	E	305 728-1536	
Hialeah *(G-5259)*			
Fi-Bay Pointe LLC	C	727 867-1104	
Saint Petersburg *(G-15667)*			
Finnish American Rest Home Inc	E	561 588-4333	
Lake Worth *(G-7727)*			
Finnish American Rest Home Inc	D	561 588-4333	
Lake Worth *(G-7728)*			
Five Star Senior Living Inc	C	954 975-8900	
Pompano Beach *(G-14805)*			
Florida Dept Veterans Affairs	C	386 755-3016	
Lake City *(G-7526)*			
Florida Hlth Fclties Corp of P	A	561 439-8897	
West Palm Beach *(G-19148)*			
Florida Mentor	E	904 223-4173	
Jacksonville *(G-6194)*			
Florida Presbyterian Homes Inc	C	863 688-5521	
Lakeland *(G-7869)*			
Four Murphys Personal Care LLC	D	727 845-5819	
New Port Richey *(G-11379)*			
Freedom Village Bradenton LLC	A	941 210-6153	
Bradenton *(G-1107)*			
▲ Friends of Ctrus Nture Cast In	C	352 527-2020	
Beverly Hills *(G-378)*			
Gardens At Depugh	E	407 644-6634	
Winter Park *(G-19726)*			
Genesis Eldercare Nat Ctrs Inc	C	813 977-4214	
Tampa *(G-17728)*			
Good Samaritan Medical Ctr Inc	D	469 803-3827	
West Palm Beach *(G-19167)*			
Gulf Care Inc	B	239 772-1333	
Cape Coral *(G-1398)*			
Harbor Retirement Assoc LLC	D	772 778-7727	
Vero Beach *(G-18864)*			
Health Center of Plant Cy Inc	D	813 752-3611	
Plant City *(G-14563)*			
Health First Inc	B	321 434-4335	
Rockledge *(G-15346)*			
Health Quest Mgt Corp VII	B	407 679-1515	
Winter Park *(G-19729)*			
Hebrew Home Sinai Inc	E	305 899-4700	
Miami *(G-9692)*			
Helping Hnds Superior Care LLC	E	866 521-7606	
New Port Richey *(G-11382)*			
Hernando-Pasco Hospice Inc	D	727 841-7356	
New Port Richey *(G-11383)*			
Highlands Lake Center LLC	C	813 518-6600	
Tampa *(G-17820)*			
Holiday Al Systems Sub LLC	D	503 370-7070	
Winter Park *(G-19732)*			
Hope 4 Life	E	813 438-5122	
Brandon *(G-1239)*			
Hospice Palm Beach County Inc	B	561 265-6000	
Delray Beach *(G-2967)*			

Icare Home LLC	C	407 221-8571	
Oviedo *(G-13553)*			
Independent Living Systems LLC	C	305 262-1292	
Miami *(G-9744)*			
Jeft Operating Inc	D	352 343-4464	
Tavares *(G-18610)*			
Lake Park of Madison	E	850 973-8277	
Madison *(G-8487)*			
Lake Wales Medical Centers Inc	A	863 676-1433	
Lake Wales *(G-7690)*			
Laurderhill Manor	E	954 484-1960	
Lauderhill *(G-8204)*			
Lifespace Communities Inc	A	407 788-2300	
Longwood *(G-8377)*			
Lifespace Communities Inc	C	561 272-7979	
Delray Beach *(G-2981)*			
Lourds-Nreen McKeen Rsdnce For	B	561 655-8544	
West Palm Beach *(G-19241)*			
Manor Oaks Inc	D	954 771-8400	
Fort Lauderdale *(G-3955)*			
Mederi Inc	D	407 931-0487	
Kissimmee *(G-7357)*			
Merritt Island Rhf Housing	B	321 452-1233	
Merritt Island *(G-9040)*			
Micor Enterprises Inc	C	727 449-0366	
Clearwater *(G-1718)*			
Naval Cntning Care Rtrment Fnd	B	904 246-9900	
Atlantic Beach *(G-243)*			
P H C Blountstown Inc	D	850 674-5464	
Blountstown *(G-387)*			
Pelican Bay Coop Hsing Corp	B	239 591-0011	
Naples *(G-11256)*			
Ponce Plz Nrsing Rhblttion Ctr	C	305 545-6695	
Miami *(G-10133)*			
Presbytrian Rtrment Cmmnties I	C	941 747-1881	
Bradenton *(G-1166)*			
Prime Care Nurses Inc	C	754 222-9999	
Margate *(G-8663)*			
Ridgecrest Nh LLC	C	386 469-1235	
Deland *(G-2878)*			
Saint Annes Nrsing Ctr Rsdence	C	305 252-0776	
Miami *(G-10235)*			
Salem Nursing and Rehab Center	E	305 248-1103	
Leesburg *(G-8271)*			
Sandhill Cove Properties Inc	C	772 283-7775	
Palm City *(G-13800)*			
Sea Crest Health Care MGT LLC	D	386 446-6060	
Palm Coast *(G-13840)*			
Sea Crest Health Care MGT LLC	D	407 877-2394	
Winter Garden *(G-19594)*			
Sea Crest Health Care MGT LLC	C	352 331-3470	
Gainesville *(G-4993)*			
Sea Crest Health Care MGT LLC	D	850 689-3146	
Crestview *(G-2331)*			
Sea Crest Health Care MGT LLC	C	941 761-3499	
Bradenton *(G-1177)*			
Sea Crest Health Care MGT LLC	C	352 597-5100	
Brooksville *(G-1309)*			
Sea Crest Health Care MGT LLC	D	850 863-9494	
Fort Walton Beach *(G-4803)*			
Sea Crest Health Care MGT LLC	D	727 391-2200	
Seminole *(G-16458)*			
Sea Crest Health Care MGT LLC	D	239 334-1091	
Fort Myers *(G-4586)*			
Sea Crest Health Care MGT LLC	D	863 815-0488	
Lakeland *(G-7964)*			
Sea Crest Health Care MGT LLC	D	727 393-8279	
Largo *(G-8148)*			
Sea Crest Health Care MGT LLC	D	813 265-1600	
Tampa *(G-18256)*			
Sea Crest Health Care MGT LLC	C	941 474-9371	
Englewood *(G-3432)*			
Sea Crest Health Care MGT LLC	C	941 484-0425	
Venice *(G-18804)*			
Sea Crest Health Care MGT LLC	C	813 876-5141	
Tampa *(G-18257)*			
Sea Crest Health Care MGT LLC	D	352 383-4161	
Mount Dora *(G-10962)*			
Sea Crest Health Care MGT LLC	D	386 362-7860	
Live Oak *(G-8317)*			
Sea Crest Health Care MGT LLC	D	850 474-0570	
Pensacola *(G-14430)*			
Sea Crest Health Care MGT LLC	C	407 298-9335	
Orlando *(G-13172)*			
Sea Crest Health Care MGT LLC	C	850 877-2177	
Tallahassee *(G-17095)*			
Sea Crest Health Care MGT LLC	C	321 269-2200	
Titusville *(G-18703)*			
Sea Crest Health Care MGT LLC	C	352 746-6611	
Lecanto *(G-8225)*			

Sea Crest Health Care MGT LLC	C	904 739-0877	
Jacksonville *(G-6704)*			
Sea Crest Health Care MGT LLC	D	239 772-4600	
Cape Coral *(G-1424)*			
Sea Crest Health Care MGT LLC	C	727 784-2848	
Palm Harbor *(G-13880)*			
Sea Crest Health Care MGT LLC	C	850 877-4115	
Tallahassee *(G-17096)*			
Sea Crest Health Care MGT LLC	C	954 981-6300	
Hollywood *(G-5513)*			
Sea Crest Health Care MGT LLC	D	863 983-5123	
Clewiston *(G-1909)*			
Sea Crest Health Care MGT LLC	D	386 767-4831	
South Daytona *(G-16494)*			
Sea Crest Health Care MGT LLC	D	772 464-5262	
Fort Pierce *(G-4739)*			
Sea Crest Health Care MGT LLC	C	352 240-6402	
Gainesville *(G-4994)*			
Sea Crest Health Care MGT LLC	C	813 681-4220	
Brandon *(G-1254)*			
Sea Crest Health Care MGT LLC	D	407 931-3336	
Kissimmee *(G-7382)*			
Sea Crest Health Care MGT LLC	D	407 846-3568	
Kissimmee *(G-7383)*			
Sea Crest Health Care MGT LLC	C	850 654-4588	
Destin *(G-3077)*			
Sea Crest Health Care MGT LLC	C	954 943-5100	
Pompano Beach *(G-14891)*			
Senior Hlth - Winter Haven LLC	E	863 293-3103	
Winter Haven *(G-19659)*			
Signature Healthcare LLC	C	305 949-2626	
Miami *(G-10271)*			
Some Place Like Home Inc	E	904 744-8580	
Jacksonville *(G-6743)*			
South Broward Hospital Dst	C	954 276-6200	
Pembroke Pines *(G-14188)*			
South Tmpa Hlth Rhbltation Ctr	C	813 839-5311	
Tampa *(G-18306)*			
Sovereign Healthcare LLC	D	772 288-0060	
Palm City *(G-13801)*			
Specity Phrm Nrsing Ntwrk Inc	D	941 366-7330	
Sarasota *(G-16327)*			
St Andrews Hlth Rhbltation Ctr	E	850 763-0446	
Panama City *(G-14076)*			
Sunnyside Prpts Sarasota Inc	C	941 371-2729	
Sarasota *(G-16339)*			
Sunrise Community Inc	C	954 434-8167	
Tallahassee *(G-17123)*			
Sunrise Community Inc	C	954 434-8167	
Cooper City *(G-2014)*			
Sv/Holly Point Properties Inc	C	813 839-5311	
Tampa *(G-18353)*			
Traditions Senior MGT Inc	E	727 224-7675	
Safety Harbor *(G-15414)*			
Wesley Manor Inc	D	407 839-5050	
Orlando *(G-13417)*			
West Jacksonville Health	C	904 786-8668	
Jacksonville *(G-6929)*			
WoodInds Care Ctr Alchua Cnty	E	352 333-0558	
Gainesville *(G-5033)*			

8062 General Medical & Surgical Hospitals

Ace Medical LLC	D	904 475-2039	
Jacksonville *(G-5727)*			
Advanced Medical Specialties	D	305 595-2141	
Miami *(G-9092)*			
Adventhealth Altamonte Springs	A	407 303-5700	
Altamonte Springs *(G-16)*			
Adventhealth Polk South Inc	E	866 997-3627	
Lake Wales *(G-7673)*			
Adventist Health System/Sunbel	C	407 303-6733	
Orlando *(G-12066)*			
Adventist Health System/Sunbel	A	407 646-7000	
Winter Park *(G-19681)*			
Adventist Health System/Sunbel	D	407 303-2200	
Altamonte Springs *(G-17)*			
Adventist Health System/Sunbel	A	407 942-1500	
Lake Mary *(G-7564)*			
Adventist Health System/Sunbel	C	407 303-4000	
Winter Garden *(G-19553)*			
Adventist Health System/West	E	407 894-1465	
Orlando *(G-12067)*			
Adventist Hlth Systm/Snbelt In	A	407 357-1000	
Altamonte Springs *(G-18)*			
Adventist Hlth Systm/Snbelt In	B	407 884-3220	
Apopka *(G-148)*			
Adventist Hlth Systm/Snbelt In	A	407 846-4343	
Kissimmee *(G-7264)*			
Adventist Hlth Systm/Snbelt In	C	407 357-1000	
Altamonte Springs *(G-19)*			

Adventist Hlth Systm/Snbelt In.............B....... 407 609-7000
Apopka ***(G-149)***
Adventist Hlth Systm/Snbelt In.............C....... 941 639-3131
Punta Gorda ***(G-15189)***
Adventist Hlth Systm/Snbelt In.............B....... 407 764-4000
Kissimmee ***(G-7265)***
Adventist Hlth Systm/Snbelt In.............A....... 407 889-1000
Apopka ***(G-150)***
Adventist Hlth Systm/Snbelt In.............B....... 863 465-3777
Lake Placid ***(G-7663)***
Adventist Hlth Systm/Snbelt In.............C....... 863 773-3101
Wauchula ***(G-18956)***
Adventist Hlth Systm/Snbelt In.............D....... 386 943-4522
Deland ***(G-2842)***
Adventist Hlth Systm/Snbelt In.............A....... 407 896-6611
Orlando ***(G-12071)***
Adventist Hlth Systm/Snbelt In.............D....... 863 385-1400
Sebring ***(G-16387)***
Adventist Hlth Systm/Snbelt In.............C....... 352 253-3333
Tavares ***(G-18599)***
Adventist Hlth Systm/Snbelt In.............D....... 407 944-5200
Kissimmee ***(G-7267)***
Adventist Hlth Systm/Snbelt In.............D....... 407 200-2511
Altamonte Springs ***(G-21)***
Adventist Hlth Systm/Snbelt In.............D....... 407 357-1000
Orlando ***(G-12070)***
Adventist Hlth Systm/West Corp...........B....... 407 206-0098
Altamonte Springs ***(G-22)***
Ahs/Central Texas Inc..........................B....... 407 357-1000
Altamonte Springs ***(G-23)***
Ahs/Central Texas Inc..........................A....... 407 303-6830
Orlando ***(G-12082)***
Amisub (North Ridge Hospital).............A....... 954 776-6000
Fort Lauderdale ***(G-3606)***
Anc Healthcare Inc................................A....... 828 213-1111
Winter Park ***(G-19686)***
Anchor Health Centers PA....................E....... 239 498-9114
Bonita Springs ***(G-895)***
Aux In Memorial Hosp Jcksnvlle...........D....... 904 399-6111
Jacksonville ***(G-5826)***
Aventus Health LLC...............................D....... 407 547-3546
Orlando ***(G-12159)***
Baker County Medical Svcs Inc.............C....... 904 259-7815
Macclenny ***(G-8474)***
Baptist Health Care Corp......................A....... 850 434-4080
Pensacola ***(G-14225)***
Baptist Health Care Corp......................A....... 850 469-2338
Pensacola ***(G-14226)***
Baptist Health South Fla Inc.................A....... 786 662-7000
South Miami ***(G-16498)***
Baptist Health South Fla Inc.................A....... 786 596-1960
Miami ***(G-9212)***
Baptist Health South Fla Inc.................B....... 305 274-2030
Miami ***(G-9213)***
Baptist Health South Fla Inc.................E....... 786 235-3750
Miami ***(G-9214)***
Baptist Health South Fla Inc.................C....... 786 596-2000
Miami ***(G-9215)***
Baptist Health South Fla Inc.................D....... 786 594-6688
Miami ***(G-9216)***
▲ **Baptist Health South Fla Inc**.............C....... 305 596-1960
South Miami ***(G-16500)***
Baptist Health South Fla Inc.................B....... 786 662-4000
South Miami ***(G-16499)***
Baptist Health System Inc.....................B....... 305 667-6352
Coral Gables ***(G-2044)***
Baptist Health System Inc.....................C....... 904 321-3500
Fernandina Beach ***(G-3523)***
Baptist Health System Inc.....................A....... 904 202-4900
Jacksonville ***(G-5834)***
Baptist Health System Inc.....................A....... 904 202-2000
Jacksonville ***(G-5835)***
Baptist Hlth Care Fndation Inc.............E....... 850 469-2338
Pensacola ***(G-14227)***
▲ **Baptist Hospital Inc**..........................A....... 850 434-4011
Pensacola ***(G-14228)***
Baptist Hospital Dev Corp.....................C....... 305 271-8950
Miami ***(G-9217)***
Baptist Hospital Miami Inc....................A....... 786 596-1960
Miami ***(G-9218)***
Baptist Hospital Miami Inc....................B....... 305 598-5990
Miami ***(G-9219)***
Baptist Hospital Miami Inc....................B....... 305 596-1960
Miami ***(G-9220)***
Baptist Hospital Miami Inc....................C....... 786 302-4498
Coral Gables ***(G-2045)***
Baptist Med Ctr of Beaches Inc.............A....... 904 247-2900
Jacksonville ***(G-5839)***
Baptist Med Pk Surgery Ctr LLC...........E....... 850 939-4888
Gulf Breeze ***(G-5108)***

Bartow Regional Med Ctr Inc.................B....... 863 533-8111
Bartow ***(G-312)***
Bay County Health System LLC...........A....... 850 769-1511
Panama City ***(G-13961)***
Bay Hospital Inc.....................................C....... 850 747-7100
Panama City ***(G-13965)***
Baycare Health System Inc...................A....... 727 820-8200
Tampa ***(G-17351)***
Baycare Health System Inc...................A....... 727 519-1200
Clearwater ***(G-1541)***
Bayfront Health Spring Hill....................C....... 352 688-8200
Brooksville ***(G-1273)***
Bayfront HMA Medical Ctr LLC..............A....... 727 823-1234
Saint Petersburg ***(G-15594)***
Bethesda Health Inc..............................E....... 561 336-7000
Boynton Beach ***(G-965)***
Bethesda Hospital Inc...........................D....... 561 374-5469
Boynton Beach ***(G-966)***
Bethesda Hospital Inc...........................C....... 561 737-7733
Boynton Beach ***(G-967)***
Board of Governors State Univе...........B....... 352 512-0886
Ocala ***(G-11642)***
Boca Community Hospital.....................C....... 561 750-4730
Boca Raton ***(G-459)***
Boca Raton Orthpd Assoc LLC.............E....... 561 241-8668
Boca Raton ***(G-466)***
Boca Raton Regional Hosp Inc..............A....... 561 395-7100
Boca Raton ***(G-468)***
Bon Scurs - Vnice Hlthcare Cor.............A....... 941 485-7711
Venice ***(G-18767)***
Brandon Health Care Assoc LLC...........A....... 813 655-0404
Brandon ***(G-1219)***
Brooksvlle Prprty Rsources Inc.............C....... 352 596-4306
Brooksville ***(G-1275)***
Broward General Medical Center...........B....... 954 355-4400
Fort Lauderdale ***(G-3654)***
Brrh Corporation....................................A....... 561 395-7100
Boca Raton ***(G-484)***
Cac-Florida Medical Ctrs LLC................E....... 407 522-2082
Orlando ***(G-12225)***
Cac-Florida Medical Ctrs LLC................D....... 305 949-2000
North Miami Beach ***(G-11519)***
Calhoun-Liberty Hosp Assn Inc............D....... 850 674-5411
Blountstown ***(G-381)***
Cape Canaveral Hospital Inc.................A....... 321 434-4335
Cocoa Beach ***(G-1964)***
Cape Canaveral Hospital Inc.................A....... 321 868-8313
Merritt Island ***(G-9019)***
Cape Memorial Hospital Inc..................E....... 239 424-2000
Cape Coral ***(G-1381)***
Cardilogy Assoc of Fort Ldrdal.............D....... 954 772-2136
Fort Lauderdale ***(G-3668)***
Cardiology Consultants PA....................E....... 850 484-6500
Pensacola ***(G-14245)***
Carespot of Austin LLC..........................C....... 904 757-2008
Jacksonville ***(G-5903)***
Cedars Healthcare Group Ltd................D....... 305 689-5511
Miami ***(G-9341)***
Centennial Healthcare Corp..................C....... 850 653-8853
Apalachicola ***(G-126)***
Center For Gstrntnstnal Endsco...........E....... 561 327-7492
West Palm Beach ***(G-19080)***
Central Fla Regional Hosp Inc...............A....... 407 321-4500
Sanford ***(G-15931)***
Central Florida Health Inc.....................A....... 352 323-5000
Leesburg ***(G-8237)***
Children & Families Fla Dept.................C....... 352 955-5000
Gainesville ***(G-4855)***
Childrens Dgnstc Trtmnt Ctr In.............A....... 954 728-8080
Fort Lauderdale ***(G-3690)***
Citrus Hma LLC......................................B....... 352 563-5488
Crystal River ***(G-2343)***
Cleveland Clinic Foundation..................E....... 561 898-5100
Wellington ***(G-18977)***
Cleveland Clinic Foundation..................E....... 954 689-5000
Weston ***(G-19448)***
Cleveland Clinic Foundation..................E....... 561 804-0200
West Palm Beach ***(G-19094)***
Cleveland Clinic Foundation..................B....... 954 659-5124
Weston ***(G-19449)***
Cleveland Clnic Fla Foundation............B....... 954 659-5000
Weston ***(G-19450)***
Cleveland Clnic Fla Foundation............B....... 954 689-5000
Weston ***(G-19451)***
Cleveland Clnic Wston Hosp Nnp.........A....... 954 659-5000
Weston ***(G-19452)***
Collier Anesthesia..................................E....... 239 261-1158
Naples ***(G-11063)***
Columbia Hosp Corp S Broward............A....... 954 473-6600
Plantation ***(G-14620)***

Columbia Hospital Corp - Smm.............C....... 305 271-8415
Miami ***(G-9390)***
Columbia Hospital Palm Beaches.........A....... 561 842-6141
West Palm Beach ***(G-19098)***
Community Health Corporation.............B....... 941 917-4950
Sarasota ***(G-16127)***
Crestview Hospital Corporation............A....... 850 423-1000
Crestview ***(G-2317)***
District Hospital Holdings Inc................B....... 561 996-6571
Belle Glade ***(G-356)***
Dmh Real Estate Holdings Inc.............B....... 863 494-8401
Arcadia ***(G-229)***
Doctor P Phillips Hos.............................D....... 407 351-8533
Orlando ***(G-12436)***
Doctors Hospital Inc..............................A....... 305 666-2111
Coral Gables ***(G-2094)***
Doctors Memorial Hospital Inc..............B....... 850 584-0800
Perry ***(G-14489)***
Doctors Ostopathic Med Ctr Inc............A....... 239 768-5000
Fort Myers ***(G-4346)***
East Florida Sup Chain Svc Ctr.............C....... 954 689-4600
Miramar ***(G-10855)***
Edward White Hospital Inc.....................B....... 727 323-1111
Saint Petersburg ***(G-15659)***
Empath Health Inc.................................D....... 727 586-4432
Clearwater ***(G-1619)***
Englewood Community Hosp Inc..........B....... 941 475-6571
Englewood ***(G-3436)***
Fawcett Memorial Hospital Inc.............A....... 941 629-1181
Port Charlotte ***(G-15034)***
Flagler Hospital Inc................................A....... 904 819-5155
Saint Augustine ***(G-15440)***
Florida Cncer Spclsts RES Inst.............D....... 727 216-1143
Saint Petersburg ***(G-15675)***
▲ **Florida Hlth Sciences Ctr Inc**............B....... 813 844-7000
Tampa ***(G-17684)***
Florida Hlth Sciences Ctr Inc.................A....... 813 254-0344
Tampa ***(G-17685)***
Florida Hlth Sciences Ctr Inc.................A....... 813 236-5100
Tampa ***(G-17687)***
Florida Hosp Fla Hosp Orlndo M...........D....... 407 303-5600
Orlando ***(G-12525)***
Florida Hosp Zephyrhills Inc..................D....... 813 909-2368
Lutz ***(G-8442)***
Florida Hosp Zephyrhills Inc..................A....... 813 788-0411
Zephyrhills ***(G-19833)***
Florida Hospital......................................E....... 352 750-0608
Lady Lake ***(G-7433)***
Florida Hospital......................................E....... 352 383-6479
Mount Dora ***(G-10951)***
Florida Hospital Dade City Inc...............A....... 352 521-1100
Dade City ***(G-2386)***
Florida Hospital Mem HM Hlth..............A....... 386 446-9367
Daytona Beach ***(G-2595)***
Florida Hospital Waterman Inc..............A....... 352 253-3333
Tavares ***(G-18606)***
Florida Medical Center Inc....................B....... 305 735-6000
Lauderdale Lakes ***(G-8172)***
Florida Ste...B....... 352 375-8484
Gainesville ***(G-4897)***
Fort Walton Beach Med Ctr Inc.............A....... 850 862-1111
Fort Walton Beach ***(G-4771)***
▼ **Foundation Resolution Corp**.............A....... 352 726-1551
Inverness ***(G-5694)***
Friends of Wllngton Rgnal Med............D....... 561 798-8500
Wellington ***(G-18980)***
Galencare Inc...A....... 813 681-5551
Brandon ***(G-1233)***
Gulf Coast Medical Center.....................A....... 850 769-8341
Panama City ***(G-14022)***
Gulf Coast Medical Centre Ltd...............B....... 239 343-1000
Fort Myers ***(G-4428)***
Gulf Coast Treatment Ctr Inc................D....... 850 520-4642
Defuniak Springs ***(G-2832)***
Halifax Hlth Care Systems Inc..............A....... 386 425-3900
Daytona Beach ***(G-2609)***
Halifax Hlth Care Systems Inc..............B....... 386 254-4107
Daytona Beach ***(G-2610)***
▲ **Hc Hialeah Holdings Inc**...................A....... 305 693-6100
Hialeah ***(G-5272)***
HCA Flrida Univ Hosp Med Staff...........E....... 954 475-4400
Davie ***(G-2487)***
HCA Health Services Fla Inc.................A....... 352 596-6632
Brooksville ***(G-1288)***
HCA Health Services Fla Inc.................A....... 772 335-4000
Port Saint Lucie ***(G-15139)***
HCA Health Services Fla Inc.................C....... 941 792-6611
Bradenton ***(G-1117)***
HCA Health Services Fla Inc.................B....... 407 423-0573
Orlando ***(G-12623)***

S
I
C

HCA Holdings Inc ....D 813 888-7060
Tampa (G-17799)
Health First Inc ....E 321 434-1972
Melbourne (G-8900)
Health First Shared Svcs Inc ....C 321 434-8400
Palm Bay (G-13624)
Health First Shared Svcs Inc ....A 321 434-4300
Rockledge (G-15350)
Health Management Assoc Inc ......A 239 354-6000
Naples (G-11160)
Health Management Assoc Inc ......B 386 292-8000
Lake City (G-7531)
Health Management Assoc Inc ......B 239 348-4400
Naples (G-11159)
Healthmark of Walton Inc ....C 850 892-5171
Defuniak Springs (G-2834)
Hendry Regional Medical Center ...C 863 983-9121
Clewiston (G-1903)
Hernando Healthcare Inc ....B 352 796-5111
Brooksville (G-1290)
Hernando Hma LLC ....B 352 796-5111
Brooksville (G-1291)
Holmes County Hospital Corp ....C 850 547-8000
Bonifay (G-888)
Holmes Regional Hospice Inc ....B 321 952-0494
Melbourne (G-8908)
Holmes Regional Med Ctr Inc ....A 321 434-7000
Melbourne (G-8909)
Holy Cross Health Inc ....D 561 479-3623
Boca Raton (G-630)
Holy Cross Hospital Inc ....A 954 771-8000
Fort Lauderdale (G-3868)
Homestead Hospital Inc ....B 786 243-8000
Homestead (G-5581)
In Opportunity To Participate ....E 941 706-0339
Sarasota (G-16191)
Indian River Memorial Hosp Inc ....A 772 567-4311
Vero Beach (G-18877)
Jackson County Hospital Dst ....B 850 526-2200
Marianna (G-8680)
Jackson Health System ....E 305 585-5938
Miami (G-9780)
Jackson North Medical Center ......A 305 585-7273
Miami (G-9782)
Jackson South Community Hosp .....E 305 251-2500
Palmetto Bay (G-13945)
JFK Medical Center - N Campus .....E 561 842-6141
West Palm Beach (G-19215)
Johns Hpkins All Chld Hosp Inc .....E 727 224-0849
Saint Petersburg (G-15736)
Johns Hpkins All Chld Hosp Inc .....E 813 436-5900
Brandon (G-1241)
Johns Hpkins All Chld Hosp Inc .....A 727 898-7451
Saint Petersburg (G-15734)
Johns Hpkins All Chld Hosp Inc .....E 727 767-8831
Saint Petersburg (G-15737)
Jupiter Med Ctr Pavilion Inc ....C 561 263-4444
Jupiter (G-7097)
Jupiter Medical Center Inc ....C 561 263-7010
Jupiter (G-7098)
Jupiter Medical Center Inc ....A 561 747-2234
Jupiter (G-7099)
Jupiter Medical Center Inc ....C 561 575-2000
Jupiter (G-7100)
Jupiter Medical Center Inc ....C 561 744-4411
Jupiter (G-7102)
Kendall Healthcare Group Ltd ....B 305 227-5500
Miami (G-9817)
Kindred Healthcare LLC ....D 561 495-3188
Delray Beach (G-2974)
Kindred Hospitals East LLC ....A 954 764-8900
Fort Lauderdale (G-3921)
Kindred Hospitals East LLC ....A 727 894-8719
Saint Petersburg (G-15741)
Kindred Hospitals East LLC ....A 305 448-1585
Coral Gables (G-2133)
Kindred Hospitals East LLC ....A 954 920-9000
Hollywood (G-5464)
Kindred Hospitals East LLC ....A 813 839-6341
Tampa (G-17926)
Kindred Hospitals East LLC ....A 352 369-0513
Ocala (G-11704)
Kissimmee Surgicare Ltd ....E 407 870-0573
Kissimmee (G-7339)
Lake Wales Medical Centers Inc ....A 863 676-1433
Lake Wales (G-7690)
Lakeland Regional Med Ctr Inc ......A 863 687-1100
Lakeland (G-7904)
Lakewood Ranch Medical Center ....D 941 782-2100
Lakewood Ranch (G-8022)

▲ Largo Medical Center Inc ....A 727 588-5200
Largo (G-8127)
Larkin Community Hospital Inc ......A 305 757-5707
South Miami (G-16507)
Larkin Community Hospital Inc ......A 305 558-2500
Hialeah (G-5289)
Lawnwood Medical Center Inc ......A 772 461-4000
Fort Pierce (G-4717)
Lee Memorial Health System ....D 239 343-9555
Fort Myers (G-4479)
Lee Memorial Health System ....C 239 424-1600
Cape Coral (G-1406)
Lee Memorial Health System ....D 239 343-5000
Fort Myers (G-4481)
Lee Memorial Health System ....C 239 343-9700
Fort Myers (G-4482)
Lee Memorial Health System ....C 239 275-2050
Fort Myers (G-4484)
Lee Memorial Health System ....C 239 561-5060
Fort Myers (G-4485)
Lee Memorial Health System ....A 239 424-3625
Cape Coral (G-1407)
Lee Memorial Health System ....D 239 343-7811
Fort Myers (G-4488)
Lee Memorial Health System ....C 239 343-6410
Fort Myers (G-4489)
Lee Memorial Health System ....D 239 482-5399
Fort Myers (G-4490)
Lee Memorial Health System ....A 239 343-2000
Fort Myers (G-4480)
Lee Memorial Home Hlth Systems ..D 239 343-2000
Fort Myers (G-4491)
Lee Memorial Hospital Inc ....A 239 343-2000
Fort Myers (G-4492)
Leesburg Regional Med Ctr Inc .....A 352 323-5762
Leesburg (G-8255)
Leesburg Regional Med Ctr Inc .....C 352 323-5160
Leesburg (G-8256)
Leesburg Regional Med Ctr Inc .....C 352 323-5610
Leesburg (G-8257)
Lehigh HMA LLC ....D 239 369-2101
Lehigh Acres (G-8287)
Lifeline ....E 941 917-7416
Sarasota (G-16221)
Lifemark Hospitals Florida Inc ......A 305 823-5000
Hialeah (G-5291)
Lower Fla Keys Hlth Sys Inc ....B 305 294-5531
Key West (G-7225)
Lynn Regional Cancer Group Ctr ....D 561 955-7100
Boca Raton (G-680)
Madison Cnty Hosp Hlth Systems ...C 850 973-2271
Madison (G-8488)
Manatee Memorial Hospital LP ......A 941 746-5111
Bradenton (G-1135)
Manatee Memorial Hospital LP ......E 941 782-2100
Sarasota (G-16225)
Manatee Memorial Hospital LP ......E 941 792-0088
Bradenton (G-1136)
Manatee Memorial Hospital LP ......E 561 640-7505
West Palm Beach (G-19249)
Manatee Memorial Hospital LP ......E 941 747-7966
Bradenton (G-1137)
Manatee Palms Youth Services ......D 941 746-1388
Bradenton (G-1138)
Manor Care Delray Beach FL LLC ....A 561 638-0000
Delray Beach (G-2988)
Marathon HMA LLC ....A 305 743-5533
Marathon (G-8624)
Margate Medical Staff Inc ....B 954 974-0400
Margate (G-8656)
Mariners Hospital Inc ....C 305 852-4418
Tavernier (G-18625)
Marion Community Hospital Inc .....A 352 401-1000
Ocala (G-11717)
Marion Community Hospital Inc .....C 352 401-1013
Ocala (G-11718)
Marion West Community Hospital ...A 352 291-3000
Ocala (G-11727)
Martin Mem Hlth Systems Inc ....A 772 287-5200
Stuart (G-16640)
Martin Memorial Med Ctr Inc ....A 772 345-8100
Port Saint Lucie (G-15151)
Martin Memorial Med Ctr Inc ....C 772 287-5200
Stuart (G-16641)
Mayo Clinic ....E 904 953-7030
Jacksonville (G-6471)
▲ Mayo Clnic Jcksnvlle A Nnprfit .....A 904 953-2000
Jacksonville (G-6472)
Mdvip LLC ....D 866 404-8637
Boca Raton (G-685)

Medical Staff of The Med Ctr T ......C 727 834-4000
Trinity (G-18728)
Medlink Management Svcs Inc ....D 386 496-2323
Lake Butler (G-7506)
Memorial Health Systems Inc ....A 386 231-6000
Daytona Beach (G-2633)
Memorial Health Systems Inc ....A 954 987-2000
Hollywood (G-5475)
Memorial Healthcare Group Inc ......A 904 399-6111
Jacksonville (G-6492)
Memorial Healthcare System ....D 954 276-5500
Miramar (G-10876)
Memorial Hosp - W Volusia Inc .....B 386 943-4522
Deland (G-2870)
Memorial Hospital Flagler Inc ....D 407 776-5135
Altamonte Springs (G-75)
Memorial Hospital Flagler Inc ....C 386 586-2000
Palm Coast (G-13836)
Memorial Hospital Tampa LP ....C 866 463-7272
Largo (G-8134)
Memorial Hospital Tampa LP ....D 813 873-6400
Tampa (G-18024)
Memorial Rgonal Hosp S Aux Inc ....C 954 966-4500
Hollywood (G-5476)
Miami Bch Healthcare Group Ltd ....A 305 682-7000
Miami. (G-9954)
Miami Childrens Health Sys Inc ......E 305 666-6511
Miami (G-9958)
Miami Childrens Hosp Prpg LLC .....C 305 666-6511
Miami (G-9959)
Mid-Florida Medical Svcs Inc ....C 863 297-1702
Lakeland (G-7921)
Mid-Florida Medical Svcs Inc ....A 863 297-1895
Winter Haven (G-19646)
Moorings Incorporated ....A 239 261-1616
Naples (G-11218)
Morton Plant Hospital Assn Inc ......E 727 842-8468
New Port Richey (G-11394)
Morton Plant Hospital Assn Inc ......A 727 462-7000
Clearwater (G-1724)
Mount Sinai Med Ctr Fla Inc ....D 305 558-8700
Hialeah (G-5300)
Mount Sinai Med Ctr Fla Inc ....D 305 682-7000
Miami (G-10020)
Mount Sinai Med Ctr Fla Inc ....D 305 441-0910
Coral Gables (G-2153)
Mount Sinai Med Ctr Fla Inc ....D 305 674-2121
Miami Beach (G-10630)
Mount Sinai Med Ctr Fla Inc ....D 305 674-2599
Key Biscayne (G-7167)
Mount Sinai Med Ctr Fla Inc ....D 305 674-2307
Miami (G-10022)
Naples Community Hospital Inc ......C 239 775-2300
Marco Island (G-8636)
Naples Community Hospital Inc ......A 239 436-5000
Naples (G-11225)
Naples Community Hospital Inc ......B 239 436-6770
Naples (G-11226)
Naples Community Hospital Inc ......C 239 513-7111
Naples (G-11227)
Naples Community Hospital Inc ......B 239 455-6300
Naples (G-11228)
NAVY UNITED STATES DEPARTMENT ..D 850 505-6017
Pensacola (G-14378)
NCH Healthcare System Inc ....A 239 624-5000
Naples (G-11247)
Nemours Foundation ....C 407 567-4000
Orlando (G-12904)
North Brevard County Hospital ....A 321 268-6333
Titusville (G-18698)
North Broward Hospital Dst ....C 954 941-8300
Deerfield Beach (G-2777)
North Broward Hospital Dst ....B 954 473-7010
Fort Lauderdale (G-4002)
North Broward Medical Center ....C 954 786-6400
Deerfield Beach (G-2778)
North Brward Hosp Dst Chrtble ......C 954 728-8080
Fort Lauderdale (G-4003)
North Brward Hosp Dst Chrtble ......C 954 355-4527
Fort Lauderdale (G-4004)
North Brward Hosp Dst Chrtble ......B 954 767-5566
Fort Lauderdale (G-4005)
North Brward Hosp Dst Chrtble ......E 954 462-8323
Fort Lauderdale (G-4006)
North Brward Hosp Dst Chrtble ......D 954 491-8676
Fort Lauderdale (G-4007)
North Brward Hosp Dst Chrtble ......D 954 712-3976
Fort Lauderdale (G-4008)
North Brward Hosp Dst Chrtble ......D 954 522-3355
Fort Lauderdale (G-4010)

North Brward Hosp Dst Chrtble	C	954 355-4400	Fort Lauderdale (G-4011)
North Brward Hosp Dst Chrtble	D	954 217-5000	Weston (G-19470)
North Brward Hosp Dst Chrtble	D	954 355-4975	Fort Lauderdale (G-4012)
North Brward Hosp Dst Chrtble	A	954 344-3000	Coral Springs (G-2276)
North Brward Hosp Dst Chrtble	A	954 776-8500	Fort Lauderdale (G-4013)
North Brward Hosp Dst Chrtble	E	954 467-2140	Fort Lauderdale (G-4014)
North Brward Hosp Dst Chrtble	E	954 847-4064	Fort Lauderdale (G-4015)
North Brward Hosp Dst Chrtble	D	954 463-7313	Fort Lauderdale (G-4016)
North Brward Hosp Dst Chrtble	D	954 786-5901	Pompano Beach (G-14869)
North Brward Hosp Dst Chrtble	E	954 832-0332	Fort Lauderdale (G-4017)
North Brward Hosp Dst Chrtble	D	954 355-4400	Fort Lauderdale (G-4018)
North Brward Hosp Dst Chrtble	C	954 847-4315	Fort Lauderdale (G-4019)
North Brward Hosp Dst Chrtble	D	954 467-3006	Fort Lauderdale (G-4020)
North Fla Regional Med Ctr Inc	D	352 375-1999	Gainesville (G-4961)
North Fla Regional Med Ctr Inc	A	352 333-4100	Gainesville (G-4963)
North Oklosa Hlth Care Assoc L	D	850 689-3146	Crestview (G-2328)
Northwest Fla Surgery Ctr Ltd	D	850 747-0400	Panama City (G-14049)
Northwest Florida Cmnty Hosp	C	850 638-1610	Chipley (G-1493)
Northwest Medical Center Inc	C	954 978-4001	Margate (G-8661)
Notami Hospitals Florida Inc	B	386 719-9000	Lake City (G-7540)
Nsmc Holdings Inc	C	954 730-2860	Lauderdale Lakes (G-8179)
▼ Nsmc Holdings Inc	A	305 835-6000	Miami (G-10056)
Okeechobee Hospital Inc	B	863 763-2151	Okeechobee (G-11876)
Orlando Health Inc	C	321 841-7856	Orlando (G-12949)
Orlando Health Inc	C	407 354-1202	Orlando (G-12950)
Orlando Health Inc	C	321 841-3040	Orlando (G-12951)
Orlando Health Inc	A	407 767-1200	Longwood (G-8389)
Orlando Health Inc	A	321 841-5111	Orlando (G-12953)
Orlando Health Inc	D	407 767-8500	Altamonte Springs (G-84)
Orlando Health Inc	B	321 841-5970	Orlando (G-12954)
Orlando Health Inc	D	407 351-8587	Orlando (G-12956)
Orlando Health Inc	D	352 323-5762	Leesburg (G-8265)
▲ Orlando Health Inc	A	407 841-5111	Orlando (G-12958)
Orlando Health Inc	C	321 842-1270	Kissimmee (G-7365)
Orlando Health Inc	A	407 649-6884	Orlando (G-12959)
Orlando Health Inc	A	407 892-2135	Saint Cloud (G-15531)
Orlando Health Inc	A	407 351-8500	Orlando (G-12960)
Orlando Health Inc	C	407 841-5139	Orlando (G-12961)
Orlando Health Inc	C	321 843-1208	Orlando (G-12964)
Orlando Health Inc	C	407 649-6888	Orlando (G-12965)
Orlando Health Inc	B	407 649-6111	Orlando (G-12966)
Orlando Health Inc	C	407 898-6588	Orlando (G-12967)
Orlando Health Inc	A	407 649-9111	Orlando (G-12962)
Orlando Health Central Inc	B	407 296-1000	Ocoee (G-11820)
Orlando Health Central Inc	A	407 407-0000	Winter Garden (G-19586)

Orlando Health Foundation Inc	E	407 841-5194	Orlando (G-12968)
Osceola Regional Hospital Inc	A	407 518-3826	Kissimmee (G-7369)
Osceola Regional Hospital Inc	A	407 846-2266	Kissimmee (G-7370)
Palm Bay Community Hosp Inc	D	321 434-8000	Palm Bay (G-13632)
Palm Bay Hospital Inc	B	321 434-8000	Palm Bay (G-13634)
▲ Palm Bch Grdns Cmnty Hosp Inc	B	561 622-1411	Palm Beach Gardens (G-13760)
▲ Palm Springs General Hosp Inc	A	305 558-2500	Hialeah (G-5307)
Palmetto General Hospital Inc	C	305 823-5000	Hialeah (G-5308)
Palms West Hospital Ltd Partnr	A	561 798-3300	Loxahatchee (G-8427)
Park Place Hospital	E	407 846-0023	Kissimmee (G-7373)
Pasco-Pnllas Hllsbrugh Cmnty H	C	813 909-5490	Wesley Chapel (G-19004)
Physical Mdcine Spcialists Inc	D	904 858-7300	Jacksonville (G-6600)
Plantation General Hospital LP	A	954 587-5010	Davie (G-2506)
Port Charlotte Hma LLC	A	941 766-4122	Port Charlotte (G-15054)
Primary Care Medical Assoc	D	561 964-3003	Lake Worth (G-7748)
Professonal Anesthesia Svc Inc	E	330 253-9145	Palm Beach Gardens (G-13767)
Promise Hospital Dade Inc	D	786 609-9200	Miami Lakes (G-10755)
Public Health Tr Dade Cnty Fla	E	904 805-1171	Miami (G-10158)
Public Hlth Tr Miami Dade Cnty	A	786 256-5523	Opa Locka (G-11953)
Public Hlth Tr Miami Dade Cnty	A	786 466-4000	Miami (G-10159)
Public Hlth Tr Miami Dade Cnty	B	305 585-1111	Palmetto Bay (G-13948)
Public Hlth Tr Miami Dade Cnty	B	305 585-1111	Miami (G-10161)
Public Hlth Tr Miami Dade Cnty	B	786 466-3500	Cutler Bay (G-2376)
Public Hlth Tr Miami Dade Cnty	A	305 585-6081	Miami (G-10162)
Public Hlth Trust of Mm-Dade C	A	786 466-6900	South Miami (G-16511)
Public Hlth Trust of Mm-Dade C	A	305 355-7000	Miami (G-10164)
Public Hlth Trust of Mm-Dade C	B	305 585-1111	Miami (G-10165)
▲ Punta Gorda Hma Inc	A	941 639-3131	Punta Gorda (G-15217)
Putnam Cmnty Med Ctr N Fla LLC	B	386 328-5711	Palatka (G-13597)
Raulerson Memorial Aux Inc	D	863 763-2151	Okeechobee (G-11878)
Regional Med Ctr Bynet Pt Vlnt	D	727 869-5414	Hudson (G-5647)
Rehablttion Svcs At Dctors Hos	E	941 342-4470	Sarasota (G-16282)
Rgonal S Orlando Seminole Hosp	D	407 767-1200	Longwood (G-8396)
River Oaks Management Company	C	239 598-3051	Naples (G-11284)
Rockledge Hma LLC	C	321 636-2211	Rockledge (G-15364)
Rural Health Care Incorporated	E	386 328-0108	Palatka (G-13599)
Sacred Heart Health System Inc	C	850 229-5600	Port Saint Joe (G-15118)
▲ Sacred Heart Health System Inc	A	850 416-1600	Pensacola (G-14425)
Saint Jhns Rhbltion Hosp Nrsin	D	954 486-9676	Lauderdale Lakes (G-8183)
Santa Rosa HMA Urgent Care LLC	C	850 994-4301	Naples (G-11293)
Santa Rosa Medical Center Inc	C	850 626-7762	Milton (G-10824)
Sarasota County Pub Hosp Dst	C	941 917-4500	Lakewood Ranch (G-8028)
Sarasota County Pub Hosp Dst	C	941 917-7760	Sarasota (G-16298)
Sarasota County Pub Hosp Dst	C	941 917-7730	Sarasota (G-16299)
Sarasota County Pub Hosp Dst	A	941 917-9000	Sarasota (G-16300)

Sarasota County Pub Hosp Dst	C	941 917-1383	Sarasota (G-16301)
Sarasota County Pub Hosp Dst	C	941 917-4041	Sarasota (G-16302)
Sarasota Doctors Hospital Inc	A	941 342-1100	Sarasota (G-16303)
Sarasota Memorial Home Care	A	941 917-7730	Sarasota (G-16306)
Sebring Health Services LLC	B	863 385-6101	Sebring (G-16416)
Select Spclty Hosp - Gnsvlle I	E	352 337-3240	Gainesville (G-4995)
Select Spclty Hosp - Orlndo In	D	407 303-7869	Orlando (G-13183)
Select Specialty Hospital	C	850 473-4800	Pensacola (G-14432)
Seven Hlls Hlth Rehabilitation	E	850 877-4115	Tallahassee (G-17098)
Shands Jcksnvlle Halthcare Inc	E	904 244-0411	Jacksonville (G-6716)
▲ Shands Jcksonville Med Ctr Inc	A	904 244-0411	Jacksonville (G-6717)
▲ Shriners Hspitals For Children	C	813 972-2250	Tampa (G-18279)
Shriners Hspitals For Children	C	813 972-2250	Tampa (G-18280)
SMH Services Inc	C	941 917-9000	Sarasota (G-16322)
South Broward Hospital Dst	D	954 265-6939	Hollywood (G-5522)
South Broward Hospital Dst	C	954 987-2000	Hollywood (G-5523)
South Broward Hospital Dst	D	954 987-2000	Hollywood (G-5524)
South Broward Hospital Dst	D	954 987-2000	Pembroke Pines (G-14185)
South Broward Hospital Dst	D	954 265-9500	Hollywood (G-5525)
South Broward Hospital Dst	A	954 538-5000	Miramar (G-10897)
South Broward Hospital Dst	A	954 962-9650	Pembroke Pines (G-14186)
South Broward Hospital Dst	A	954 436-5000	Pembroke Pines (G-14187)
South Broward Hospital Dst	C	954 966-4500	Hollywood (G-5526)
South Broward Hospital Dst	D	954 458-5222	Hallandale Beach (G-5183)
South Broward Hospital Dst	D	954 276-6600	Miramar (G-10898)
South Broward Hospital Dst	B	954 987-2000	Hollywood (G-5527)
South Broward Hospital Dst	C	954 987-2000	Hollywood (G-5530)
South Broward Hospital Dst	D	954 457-0500	Hallandale Beach (G-5184)
South Broward Hospital Dst	D	954 265-3449	Hollywood (G-5529)
South Florida Baptist Hosp Inc	B	813 757-1200	Plant City (G-14581)
South Lake Hospital Inc	A	352 394-4071	Clermont (G-1889)
South Lake Hospital Inc	E	352 241-4585	Clermont (G-1890)
▲ South Miami Hospital Inc	B	786 662-4000	South Miami (G-16515)
South Miami Hospital Inc	A	305 662-8101	South Miami (G-16517)
Southast Vlsia Healthcare Corp	E	386 424-5181	New Smyrna Beach (G-11423)
Southast Vlsia Healthcare Corp	E	386 424-5040	New Smyrna Beach (G-11424)
Southast Vlsia Healthcare Corp	A	386 424-5000	New Smyrna Beach (G-11425)
Southast Vlsia Healthcare Corp	E	386 424-9421	Edgewater (G-3414)
Southern Baptist Hosp Fla Inc	A	904 399-5620	Jacksonville (G-6757)
Southwest Vlsia Halthcare Corp	C	386 917-5000	Altamonte Springs (G-100)
Southwest Vlsia Halthcare Corp	B	386 917-5000	Orange City (G-11971)
Specilty Hsptal- Tllhassee Inc	C	850 219-6800	Tallahassee (G-17110)
St Anthonys Hospital Inc	A	727 825-1100	Saint Petersburg (G-15854)
St Cloud Regional Medical Ctr	D	407 892-2135	Saint Cloud (G-15537)
St Josephs Hospital Inc	C	813 554-8500	Tampa (G-18325)

S I C

St Josephs Hospital-North......B....813 443-7000
Lutz *(G-8459)*

St Lucie Medical Ctr Aux Inc......A....772 335-4000
Port Saint Lucie *(G-15168)*

St Lukes Hospital Association......A....904 296-3700
Jacksonville *(G-6773)*

▲ St Marys Medical Center Inc......A....561 844-6300
Mangonia Park *(G-8612)*

St Vincents Health System Inc......A....904 384-7370
Jacksonville *(G-6776)*

St Vincents Health System Inc......A....904 727-5151
Jacksonville *(G-6777)*

St Vincents Health System Inc......A....904 400-6500
Jacksonville *(G-6778)*

St Vincents Health System Inc......A....904 777-0616
Jacksonville *(G-6779)*

St Vincents Medical Center......B....904 308-7300
Jacksonville *(G-6781)*

St Vincents Medical Center......A....904 296-3700
Jacksonville *(G-6782)*

St Vincents Medical Center......A....904 308-7300
Jacksonville *(G-6783)*

Starke Family Medical Ctr Inc......E....904 964-1875
Starke *(G-16583)*

Starke Hma LLC......B....904 386-2300
Lake City *(G-7548)*

Steward Melbourne Hospital Inc......B....321 752-1200
Melbourne *(G-8982)*

Steward Rockledge Hospital Inc......A....321 636-2211
Rockledge *(G-15371)*

Steward Rockledge Hospital Inc......C....321 636-2621
Cocoa *(G-1956)*

Steward Sebastian River......B....772 589-3186
Sebastian *(G-16383)*

Sun City Hospital Inc......B....813 634-3301
Sun City Center *(G-16709)*

Sunhill Medical Center......D....813 634-6704
Sun City Center *(G-16710)*

Sunsystem Development Corp......C....407 303-2784
Orlando *(G-13250)*

Surgical Ctr of The Trsure Cas......E....772 398-9898
Port Saint Lucie *(G-15170)*

Tallahassee Medical Center Inc......A....850 325-5000
Tallahassee *(G-17128)*

Tallahassee Mem Healthcare Inc......C....850 431-2255
Tallahassee *(G-17129)*

Tallahassee Mem Healthcare Inc......C....850 431-5001
Tallahassee *(G-17130)*

Tallahassee Mem Healthcare Inc......C....850 431-4226
Tallahassee *(G-17131)*

Tallahassee Mem Healthcare Inc......C....850 431-5190
Tallahassee *(G-17132)*

Tallahassee Mem Healthcare Inc......C....850 431-3867
Tallahassee *(G-17133)*

Tallahassee Mem Healthcare Inc......C....850 431-5281
Tallahassee *(G-17134)*

Tallahassee Mem Healthcare Inc......C....850 431-5440
Tallahassee *(G-17135)*

Tallahassee Mem Healthcare Inc......A....850 431-1155
Tallahassee *(G-17136)*

Tallahassee Mem Healthcare Inc......C....850 431-3867
Tallahassee *(G-17137)*

Tallahassee Mem Healthcare Inc......C....850 431-5403
Tallahassee *(G-17138)*

Tallahassee Mem Healthcare Inc......C....850 674-4524
Blountstown *(G-388)*

Tallahassee Mem Healthcare Inc......C....850 431-6800
Tallahassee *(G-17140)*

Tallahassee Mem Healthcare Inc......B....850 431-5430
Tallahassee *(G-17141)*

Tallahassee Memorial......E....850 926-7105
Crawfordville *(G-2305)*

Tallahssee Otptent Surgery Ctr......D....850 210-0550
Tallahassee *(G-17150)*

Tampa General Hosp Corp Ctr......E....813 844-7000
Tampa *(G-18382)*

Tarpon Sprng Hosp Fndation Inc......A....727 942-5000
Tarpon Springs *(G-18595)*

▼ Tenet Good Samaritan Hospital......A....561 655-5511
West Palm Beach *(G-19383)*

Tenet Healthsystem Medical Inc......B....561 988-4631
Boca Raton *(G-836)*

Tenet Healthsystem Medical Inc......E....407 859-1880
Orlando *(G-13281)*

Tenet Healthsystem Medical Inc......C....305 461-3908
Coral Gables *(G-2195)*

Tenet Healthsystem Medical Inc......C....561 883-7044
Boca Raton *(G-837)*

Tenet Healthsystem Medical Inc......D....305 940-6545
North Miami Beach *(G-11534)*

Tenet Healthsystem Medical Inc......D....352 795-8487
Crystal River *(G-2353)*

Tenet Healthsystem Medical Inc......D....954 509-3600
Coral Springs *(G-2291)*

Tenet Healthsystem Medical Inc......E....727 570-3600
Saint Petersburg *(G-15873)*

Tenet Healthsystem Medical Inc......D....469 893-2200
Mangonia Park *(G-8613)*

Tenet Healthsystem Medical Inc......D....561 495-0400
Delray Beach *(G-3025)*

Transtonal Hospitals Tampa LLC......A....813 874-7575
Tampa *(G-18438)*

Trustees Mease Hospital Inc......C....727 461-8527
Safety Harbor *(G-15415)*

Trustees Mease Hospital Inc......C....727 733-6111
Dunedin *(G-3393)*

Trustees Mease Hospital Inc......A....727 733-1111
Dunedin *(G-3394)*

Universal Hospital Svcs Inc......E....651 454-6311
Palm City *(G-13809)*

University Community Hosp Inc......D....813 909-2368
Land O Lakes *(G-8055)*

University Community Hosp Inc......A....813 903-3700
Land O Lakes *(G-8056)*

University Community Hosp Inc......C....386 740-7124
Deland *(G-2886)*

University Community Hosp Inc......D....813 783-1237
Zephyrhills *(G-19854)*

▼ University Community Hosp Inc......A....813 971-6000
Tampa *(G-18470)*

▲ University Community Hosp Inc......C....407 865-9143
Altamonte Springs *(G-111)*

University Community Hosp Inc......D....813 702-4944
Zephyrhills *(G-19855)*

University Community Hosp Inc......A....813 971-6000
Tampa *(G-18472)*

University Community Hosp Inc......D....813 615-7201
Tampa *(G-18473)*

University Community Hosp Inc......B....813 932-2222
Tampa *(G-18474)*

University Community Hosp Inc......A....813 615-7880
Tampa *(G-18475)*

University Hospital Ltd......A....954 721-2200
Tamarac *(G-17205)*

University of Miami......C....305 243-4200
Miami *(G-10446)*

University of Miami......A....305 325-5511
Miami *(G-10447)*

US Dept of the Air Force......B....850 883-8600
Eglin Afb *(G-3422)*

Variety Childrens Hospital......A....305 666-6511
Miami *(G-10459)*

Variety Childrens Hospital......E....305 666-2889
Miami *(G-10460)*

Venice Regional Hospital......D....941 486-6038
Venice *(G-18817)*

Veterans Affairs US Dept......E....813 972-2000
Tampa *(G-18504)*

Veterans Health Administration......A....813 972-2000
Tampa *(G-18505)*

Veterans Health Administration......D....407 631-1000
Cocoa *(G-1960)*

Villages Regional Medical Ctr......E....352 753-6900
Lady Lake *(G-7443)*

Villages Tr-County Med Ctr Inc......C....352 751-8000
The Villages *(G-18652)*

West Boca Medical Center Inc......A....561 488-8000
Boca Raton *(G-871)*

West Fla Regional Med Ctr Inc......A....850 494-4000
Pensacola *(G-14470)*

West Florida - Pph LLC......C....727 341-7575
South Pasadena *(G-16526)*

West Florida Physcn Netwrk LLC......E....941 752-2700
Bradenton *(G-1204)*

West Kendall Baptist Hosp Inc......B....786 467-2000
Miami *(G-10499)*

West Orange Healthcare Dst Inc......E....407 296-1000
Ocoee *(G-11829)*

West Orange Mem Hosp Tax Dst......A....407 656-3555
Ocoee *(G-11830)*

West Palm Otptent Srgery Lser......D....561 615-0110
West Palm Beach *(G-19421)*

Westchester General Hosp Inc......A....305 264-5252
Miami *(G-10501)*

Winnie Plmer Hosp For Wmen Bbi......A....321 843-1110
Orlando *(G-13441)*

▲ Winter Haven Hospital Inc......B....863 293-1121
Winter Haven *(G-19675)*

Winter Haven Hospital Inc......A....863 292-4060
Winter Haven *(G-19676)*

Winter Haven Hospital Inc......C....863 292-4060
Winter Haven *(G-19677)*

Winter Haven Hospital Inc......B....863 294-7010
Winter Haven *(G-19678)*

Winter Pk Healthcare Group Ltd......A....407 646-7000
Winter Park *(G-19792)*

Wolfson Childrens Hospital......E....386 758-1811
Lake City *(G-7553)*

Zachariah Zachariah P MD PA......E....954 229-7950
Fort Lauderdale *(G-4238)*

8063 Psychiatric Hospitals

Apalachee Center Inc......D....850 523-3333
Tallahassee *(G-16880)*

Apalachee Center Inc......E....850 973-5124
Madison *(G-8483)*

Baycare Behavioral Health Inc......D....727 848-2583
New Port Richey *(G-11366)*

Centers Inc......C....352 291-5555
Ocala *(G-11654)*

Centerstone of Florida Inc......E....941 782-4299
Bradenton *(G-1076)*

Centerstone of Florida Inc......C....941 782-4860
Bradenton *(G-1077)*

Centerstone of Florida Inc......C....941 782-4840
Bradenton *(G-1079)*

Central Fla Bhvral Hlth Ntwrk......D....813 740-4811
Tampa *(G-17446)*

Children & Families Fla Dept......A....850 663-7536
Chattahoochee *(G-1480)*

Circles of Care Inc......C....321 722-5200
Melbourne *(G-8844)*

Comprhnsive Alchlism Rhblttion......C....561 844-6400
West Palm Beach *(G-19101)*

David Lwrnce Mntal Hlth Ctr In......D....239 455-8500
Naples *(G-11089)*

Fort Lauderdale Hospital Inc......C....954 463-4321
Oakland Park *(G-11596)*

Gulf Coast Treatment Ctr Inc......E....850 863-4160
Fort Walton Beach *(G-4776)*

Hollywood Hlls Rhblttion Ctr L......E....954 981-5511
Lighthouse Point *(G-8295)*

La Amistad Residential......D....407 647-0660
Maitland *(G-8551)*

Lawnwood Medical Center Inc......C....772 467-3900
Fort Pierce *(G-4716)*

Lawnwood Medical Center Inc......A....772 461-4000
Fort Pierce *(G-4717)*

Life MGT Ctr NW Fla Inc......C....850 769-9481
Panama City *(G-14035)*

Lifestream Behavioral Ctr Inc......D....352 360-6575
Leesburg *(G-8259)*

Manatee Palms Youth Services......E....941 792-2222
Bradenton *(G-1139)*

Mental Health Resource Ctr Inc......C....904 642-9100
Jacksonville *(G-6494)*

New Hrzons of Trsure Coast Inc......D....772 468-3909
Fort Pierce *(G-4726)*

North Brward Hosp Dst Chrtble......D....954 355-5856
Fort Lauderdale *(G-4009)*

Northside Bhvoral Hlth Ctr Inc......B....813 977-8700
Tampa *(G-18090)*

Psychtric Hsptals Hrnndo Cnty......E....352 596-4306
Brooksville *(G-1305)*

▲ Punta Gorda Hma Inc......A....941 639-3131
Punta Gorda *(G-15217)*

SMA Healthcare Inc......D....386 236-3200
Daytona Beach *(G-2664)*

Sp Behavioral LLC......C....561 744-0211
Jupiter *(G-7139)*

Ten Broeck Hospitals Inc......C....407 876-2700
Windermere *(G-19550)*

Umc / Ocala Inc......B....352 671-3130
Ocala *(G-11791)*

University Behavioral LLC......B....407 281-7000
Orlando *(G-13353)*

▲ University Psychiatric Center......A....954 722-1703
Tamarac *(G-17206)*

Venice Regional Medical Center......C....941 485-7711
Venice *(G-18819)*

Wekiva Springs Center LLC......B....904 296-3533
Jacksonville *(G-6927)*

West Fla Regional Med Ctr Inc......A....850 494-4000
Pensacola *(G-14470)*

▼ Willough Healthcare Inc......C....239 775-4500
Naples *(G-11345)*

Windmoor Hlthcare Pnllas Pk In......C....727 541-2646
Clearwater *(G-1841)*

8069 Specialty Hospitals, Except Psychiatric

Adventist Hlth Sys Snbelt Hlth ....A....... 407 303-5437
Orlando *(G-12068)*
Agency For Cmnty Trtmnt Svcs I ....E....... 813 879-4173
Tampa *(G-17246)*
Agency For Cmnty Trtmnt Svcs I ....E....... 813 246-4899
Tampa *(G-17247)*
Agency For Cmnty Trtmnt Svcs I ....E....... 813 626-7250
Tampa *(G-17248)*
Agency For Cmnty Trtmnt Svcs I ....E....... 813 237-4907
Tampa *(G-17249)*
American Health Care Inc ....D....... 727 849-6939
New Port Richey *(G-11361)*
American Oncology Network LLC........E....... 866 266-0555
Fort Myers *(G-4274)*
Atlantic Shores Hospital LLC ....B....... 954 771-2711
Fort Lauderdale *(G-3617)*
Banyan Inc..E....... 305 477-3001
Doral *(G-3132)*
Banyan RES Innovation Ctr Inc ....E....... 305 757-0602
Miami *(G-9211)*
Banyan Trtmnt & Recovery LLC ....D....... 954 210-7502
Pompano Beach *(G-14749)*
Baycare Behavioral Health Inc ....D....... 352 540-9335
Brooksville *(G-1271)*
Bridgeway Center Inc ....D....... 850 833-3975
Fort Walton Beach *(G-4757)*
Cancer Care North Florida PA ....E....... 386 755-1655
Lake City *(G-7516)*
Cancer Treatment Ctrs Amer Inc ....C....... 918 286-5315
Boca Raton *(G-493)*
Cancer Trtmnt Ctrs Amer Globl ....A....... 561 923-3100
Boca Raton *(G-494)*
Caron of Florida Inc..............................D....... 561 241-7977
Boca Raton *(G-499)*
Center For DRG Free Living Inc ....D....... 407 245-0012
Orlando *(G-12257)*
Centers Inc...C....... 352 291-5555
Ocala *(G-11654)*
Central Fla Bhvral Hlth Ntwrk ....D....... 813 740-4811
Tampa *(G-17446)*
Cgh Gp Inc..D....... 305 445-8461
Coral Gables *(G-2065)*
Chapters Health System Inc ....D....... 813 969-2049
Tampa *(G-17457)*
Chapters Health System Inc ....D....... 813 877-2200
Tampa *(G-17459)*
Chemical Addctons Rcvery Effor ....D....... 850 769-1633
Panama City *(G-13980)*
Childrens Health Services Inc ....B....... 305 666-6511
Miami *(G-9362)*
CL Aviation Inc......................................C....... 800 615-3055
Boca Raton *(G-516)*
Community Hospice of Northeast.........E....... 904 272-7433
Orange Park *(G-11983)*
Comprhensive Wellness Ctrs LLC ....E....... 561 619-5858
Lantana *(G-8061)*
Comprhnsive Alchlism Rhblttion ....C....... 561 844-6400
West Palm Beach *(G-19101)*
Comprhnsive Humn Resources Inc ......E....... 305 892-8440
Miami *(G-9399)*
David Lwrnce Mntal Hlth Ctr In.............D....... 239 455-8500
Naples *(G-11089)*
Detox of South Florida Inc ....E....... 863 623-4923
Okeechobee *(G-11864)*
Drug Abuse Fndtion Palm Bch CN........C....... 561 732-0800
Delray Beach *(G-2947)*
Encompass Hlth Rhblttion Hosp ....C....... 941 921-8600
Sarasota *(G-16149)*
Escambia County School Dst................E....... 850 202-0387
Pensacola *(G-14292)*
Escambia County School Dst................C....... 850 595-1330
Pensacola *(G-14295)*
Escambia County School Dst................E....... 850 432-1222
Pensacola *(G-14298)*
First Step of Sarasota Inc......................E....... 941 753-1823
Sarasota *(G-16033)*
First Step of Sarasota Inc......................E....... 941 497-7742
Venice *(G-18780)*
Florida Cancer Specialists Pl.................D....... 561 366-4100
Wellington *(G-18978)*
▲ **Florida Cncer Spclsts RES Inst** ....D....... 239 274-8200
Fort Myers *(G-4380)*
Florida Cncer Spclsts RES Inst ....D....... 941 377-9993
Sarasota *(G-16166)*
Fort Lauderdale Hospital Inc ....C....... 954 463-4321
Oakland Park *(G-11596)*
Genesis Health Inc................................B....... 904 858-7600
Jacksonville *(G-6226)*
Goodwill Inds Broward Cnty Inc............E....... 954 486-1600
Fort Lauderdale *(G-3826)*
Health First Shared Svcs Inc ....A....... 321 434-4300
Rockledge *(G-15350)*
Healthsuth Rhblttion Hosp Lrgo............C....... 727 586-2999
Largo *(G-8115)*
Healthsuth Rhblttion Hosp Tllh ....C....... 850 325-6277
Tallahassee *(G-16995)*
Holtz Childrens Hospital ....C....... 305 585-5437
Miami *(G-9712)*
Hope Destination Inc ....D....... 954 771-2091
Fort Lauderdale *(G-3871)*
Hospice Palm Beach County Inc............B....... 561 265-6000
Delray Beach *(G-2967)*
Johns Hpkins All Chld Hosp Inc............E....... 727 834-5411
New Port Richey *(G-11390)*
Johns Hpkins All Chld Hosp Inc............D....... 727 898-7451
Saint Petersburg *(G-15733)*
Johns Hpkins All Chld Hosp Inc............A....... 727 898-7451
Saint Petersburg *(G-15734)*
Johns Hpkins All Chld Hosp Inc............E....... 727 767-8834
Saint Petersburg *(G-15735)*
Johns Hpkins All Chld Hosp Inc............E....... 813 631-5000
Tampa *(G-17899)*
Johns Hpkins All Chld Hosp Inc............E....... 727 767-8831
Saint Petersburg *(G-15737)*
Johns Hpkins All Chld Hosp Inc............E....... 941 927-8805
Sarasota *(G-16206)*
Kindred Hospitals East LLC..................A....... 904 284-9230
Green Cove Springs *(G-5057)*
Lakeview Center Inc ....C....... 850 432-1222
Pensacola *(G-14340)*
Lawnwood Medical Center Inc.............C....... 772 467-3900
Fort Pierce *(G-4716)*
Lawnwood Medical Center Inc.............A....... 772 461-4000
Fort Pierce *(G-4717)*
Lee Memorial Health System ....A....... 239 343-2000
Fort Myers *(G-4480)*
Mch Pediatric Cardiology LLC..............A....... 305 666-6511
Miami *(G-9922)*
Medical Center Clinic PA.......................D....... 850 474-8000
Pensacola *(G-14360)*
Miami Childrens Hosp RES Inst ....B....... 305 666-6511
Miami *(G-9960)*
Morton Plant Hospital Assn Inc.............E....... 727 462-7600
Belleair *(G-369)*
Nemours Foundation.............................A....... 904 697-4100
Jacksonville *(G-6534)*
North Brward Hosp Dst Chrtble.............A....... 954 344-3000
Coral Springs *(G-2276)*
North Fla Regional Med Ctr Inc ....D....... 352 375-1999
Gainesville *(G-4961)*
North Fla Regional Med Ctr Inc ....A....... 352 333-4100
Gainesville *(G-4963)*
Orlando Health Inc................................C....... 407 648-3800
Orlando *(G-12957)*
Orlando Health Inc................................A....... 407 892-2135
Saint Cloud *(G-15531)*
Orlando Health Inc................................A....... 407 649-9111
Orlando *(G-12962)*
Orlando Health Inc................................B....... 407 649-6111
Orlando *(G-12966)*
▲ **Orlando Health Inc** ....A....... 407 841-5111
Orlando *(G-12958)*
Phoenix House Foundation Inc ....E....... 727 822-7729
Saint Petersburg *(G-15797)*
Pinellas Medical Associates PA............E....... 727 528-6100
Saint Petersburg *(G-15800)*
Renaissance Inst of Palm Bch...............E....... 561 241-7977
Boca Raton *(G-769)*
Sea Crest Health Care MGT LLC ....D....... 813 265-1600
Tampa *(G-18256)*
Select Spclty Hosp - Mami Lkes ....E....... 786 609-9200
Miami Lakes *(G-10760)*
Shands Tching Hosp Clinics Inc ....D....... 352 338-0093
Gainesville *(G-4999)*
Shriners Hspitals For Children.............C....... 813 972-2250
Tampa *(G-18280)*
Shriners Hspitals For Children.............C....... 813 281-0300
Tampa *(G-18281)*
Sober Investments LLC.........................D....... 609 202-5669
Pompano Beach *(G-14901)*
South Broward Hospital Dst..................A....... 954 436-5000
Pembroke Pines *(G-14187)*
Spring Hill Welness LLC ....E....... 352 484-1999
Spring Hill *(G-16549)*
Tenet Healthsystem Medical Inc............D....... 561 495-0400
Delray Beach *(G-3025)*
Tenet Healthsystem Medical Inc............C....... 954 749-0300
Sunrise *(G-16837)*
Tri-County Human Services Inc.............E....... 863 299-7003
Winter Haven *(G-19667)*
Tri-County Human Services Inc.............E....... 863 533-4139
Bartow *(G-342)*
Turning Point of Tampa Inc...................D....... 813 882-3003
Tampa *(G-18453)*
University of Miami................................C....... 305 326-6111
Miami *(G-10445)*
Watershed Trtmnt Programs Inc ....C....... 561 807-7970
Boca Raton *(G-869)*
Westcare Gulfcoast - Fla Inc..................D....... 727 490-6767
Saint Petersburg *(G-15895)*

8071 Medical Laboratories

Access Medical Labs Inc........................D....... 561 745-1233
Jupiter *(G-7044)*
Adams Bros Cabinetry Inc ....D....... 941 639-7188
North Port *(G-11562)*
Advanced Envmtl Labs Inc ....E....... 850 219-6274
Tallahassee *(G-16870)*
American Health Associates Inc ....B....... 954 919-5005
Davie *(G-2455)*
◆ **Ameripath Inc**...................................D....... 561 712-6200
Palm Beach Gardens *(G-13684)*
Ameripath Inc...E....... 407 587-4221
Orlando *(G-12118)*
App-Pbp LLC..D....... 561 659-0770
West Palm Beach *(G-19037)*
Belt Enterprises Inc ....E....... 727 441-8723
Clearwater *(G-1546)*
Cblpath Inc ....C....... 352 732-9990
Ocala *(G-11652)*
◆ **Cell Science Systems Corp** ....D....... 954 426-2304
Deerfield Beach *(G-2721)*
Central Fla Fmly Hlth Ctr Inc.................C....... 407 322-8645
Sanford *(G-15930)*
Charles Stark Draper Lab Inc.................D....... 321 853-9574
Cape Canaveral *(G-1360)*
Clinical Pathology Labs SE....................E....... 407 674-2200
Orlando *(G-12321)*
Clinical Pthlogy Labs Sthast I................E....... 321 445-6600
Orlando *(G-12322)*
Cognoscenti Health Inst LLC.................E....... 321 445-6600
Orlando *(G-12340)*
Creative Testing Solutions.....................D....... 888 568-5992
Saint Petersburg *(G-15650)*
Diagnostic Ctrs Amer - Fla Inc..............D....... 561 727-2300
West Palm Beach *(G-19122)*
Diagnostic Services Inc.........................D....... 239 368-3031
Lehigh Acres *(G-8280)*
Diagnostic Services Inc.........................C....... 239 561-8200
Fort Myers *(G-4343)*
Ecco Lab Inc...E....... 813 932-9525
Tampa *(G-17612)*
Englewood Community Hosp Inc..........B....... 941 475-6571
Englewood *(G-3436)*
Finlay Clinical Laboratory......................D....... 305 643-2702
Miami *(G-9555)*
Florida Institute of Health......................B....... 954 484-7030
Lauderdale Lakes *(G-8171)*
Florida LLC Imaging Partners................E....... 561 543-6252
Margate *(G-8648)*
Florida Med Plz Condo Assn Inc ....D....... 407 303-5600
Orlando *(G-12531)*
Florida Open Imaging Inc.......................E....... 561 540-8100
Lake Worth *(G-7729)*
Global Pathology Laboratory.................E....... 305 825-4422
Miami Lakes *(G-10734)*
Halifax Hlth Care Systems Inc ....B....... 386 947-4655
Port Orange *(G-15076)*
▼ **Hayes Clinical Laboratory Inc**...........E....... 561 752-5550
Boynton Beach *(G-996)*
Health First Shared Svcs Inc ....D....... 321 434-5840
Merritt Island *(G-9031)*
Healthcare Amer Med Group Inc ....E....... 941 752-2700
Bradenton *(G-1118)*
Heartcare Imaging Inc ....E....... 561 746-6125
Tequesta *(G-18649)*
Immuno Laboratories Inc......................E....... 954 691-2500
Fort Lauderdale *(G-3889)*
Innovative Gx Florida Inc ....C....... 954 633-3580
Boca Raton *(G-641)*
Integrated Regional Labs.......................C....... 954 777-0139
Fort Lauderdale *(G-3896)*
Integrated Regional Labs.......................C....... 954 777-0018
West Palm Beach *(G-19204)*
International Medical Lab Inc................D....... 941 756-0000
Sarasota *(G-16038)*
Jupiter Medical Center Inc ....D....... 561 748-4100
Jupiter *(G-7101)*

S I C

Ketchum WD & Burgert Chartered ....D 850 877-0599
Tallahassee **(G-17019)**

Laboratory Corporation America ....B 786 417-3832
Hollywood **(G-5467)**

Laboratory Corporation America ....E 239 939-5274
Fort Myers **(G-4467)**

Mease Hospitals ....A 727 734-6354
Dunedin **(G-3387)**

Medical Technology Labs ....C 727 576-6311
Saint Petersburg **(G-15759)**

Miami Dade Community Svcs Inc ....E 305 631-8931
Miami **(G-9969)**

Mkr Clinical Research ....D 561 733-8315
Boynton Beach **(G-1016)**

Mri Eqpment Inv Acqisition LLC ....E 888 400-3979
Pompano Beach **(G-14860)**

Myonsite Healthcare LLC ....C 941 271-0701
Sarasota **(G-16242)**

Neogenomics Inc ....C 239 768-0600
Fort Myers **(G-4522)**

Nms Management Services Inc ....D 561 967-8884
Palm Springs **(G-13895)**

Oakridge Outpatient Center Inc ....E 954 958-0606
Fort Lauderdale **(G-4024)**

▲ Oglesby Plants Intl Inc ....C 850 762-3229
Altha **(G-116)**

P A Sarasota Pathology ....D 941 362-8900
Sarasota **(G-16254)**

Pathnet Inc ....D 561 659-0770
West Palm Beach **(G-19320)**

Presgar Medical Imaging Inc ....D 813 977-8756
Lutz **(G-8455)**

Primary Care Specialists LLC ....C 407 275-9014
Orlando **(G-13056)**

Quest Dgnstics Clncal Labs Inc ....D 352 666-7901
Spring Hill **(G-16544)**

Quest Dgnstics Clncal Labs Inc ....D 239 936-4855
Fort Myers **(G-4558)**

Quest Dgnstics Clncal Labs Inc ....D 239 561-0001
Fort Myers **(G-4559)**

Quest Dgnstics Clncal Labs Inc ....D 941 423-1531
North Port **(G-11576)**

Quest Dgnstics Clncal Labs Inc ....D 954 378-5000
Miramar **(G-10888)**

Quest Diagnostics Incorporated ....D 954 433-8730
Miramar **(G-10889)**

Quest Diagnostics Incorporated ....C 813 972-7100
Tampa **(G-18191)**

South Miami Hospital Inc ....A 305 662-8101
South Miami **(G-16517)**

Space Cast Hlth Foundation Inc ....B 321 752-1200
Melbourne **(G-8976)**

St Josephs-Baptist Hlth Care ....D 813 870-4000
Tampa **(G-18326)**

Total Renal Laboratories Inc ....C 386 738-1809
Deland **(G-2882)**

US Laboratories Inc ....D 954 236-8100
Clearwater **(G-1829)**

Vista Clinical Diagnostics LLC ....D 352 536-9270
Clermont **(G-1896)**

▲ White Wilson Medical Center PA ....B 850 863-8100
Fort Walton Beach **(G-4811)**

8072 Dental Laboratories

Cerec Dental Lab LLC ....D 786 479-6806
Miami **(G-9351)**

Crosslins Crative Ceramics Inc ....E 561 899-0606
West Palm Beach **(G-19113)**

▲ DDS Lab LLC ....D 877 337-7800
Tampa **(G-17578)**

Knight Dental Group Inc ....B 813 854-3333
Oldsmar **(G-11910)**

National Dentex LLC ....E 800 678-4140
Jupiter **(G-7118)**

National Dentex LLC ....C 561 537-8300
Jupiter **(G-7119)**

National Dentex LLC ....D 407 781-4725
Orlando **(G-12898)**

National Dentex LLC ....D 504 837-6622
Jupiter **(G-7120)**

Technics Dental Laboratory Inc ....E 954 972-2512
Margate **(G-8667)**

8082 Home Health Care Svcs

A Familiar Face Home Health ....E 941 355-9474
Sarasota **(G-16017)**

Absolute Home Health Care Inc ....E 407 870-9336
Kissimmee **(G-7262)**

Abundant Lf Nrsing Spprtive Sv ....D 352 250-2748
Mount Dora **(G-10944)**

Accu-Care Nursing Service Inc ....C 239 263-3011
Naples **(G-10997)**

Actell Elderly Care Inc ....D 321 676-8987
Melbourne **(G-8809)**

Actikare Inc ....E 888 451-5273
Tampa **(G-17231)**

Acts Rtrmnt-Life Cmmnities Inc ....C 561 362-7885
Boca Raton **(G-396)**

Advanced Homecare MGT Inc ....E 407 846-2252
Orlando **(G-12055)**

Adventist Health System/Sunbel ....C 407 303-4000
Winter Garden **(G-19553)**

Adventist Health System/Sunbel ....D 941 255-9500
Port Charlotte **(G-15017)**

Adventist Hlth Systm/Snbelt In ....C 386 671-2138
Ormond Beach **(G-13474)**

Adventist Hlth Systm/Snbelt In ....B 407 357-1000
Altamonte Springs **(G-19)**

Adventist Hlth Systm/Snbelt In ....D 407 200-2511
Altamonte Springs **(G-21)**

Advocate Health LLC ....D 800 709-5513
Venice **(G-18761)**

Affinity Care Network Inc ....E 954 782-3741
Pompano Beach **(G-14735)**

Ahcglobal Inc ....E 954 341-5600
Coral Springs **(G-2220)**

Ahs/Central Texas Inc ....A 407 691-8206
Orlando **(G-12081)**

Aicc Inc ....D 904 261-5518
Fernandina Beach **(G-3518)**

Al Ventures LLC ....D 561 396-2368
Boynton Beach **(G-959)**

All Powered Mobility LLC ....E 941 625-0103
Port Charlotte **(G-15018)**

All-Most Family Inc ....E 561 242-0150
West Palm Beach **(G-19026)**

Allegiance Senior Care LLC ....E 407 699-5002
Casselberry **(G-1441)**

Almost Family PC SW Fla LLC ....C 941 924-9540
Sarasota **(G-16083)**

Alphanet Inc ....D 305 442-1776
Coral Gables **(G-2028)**

Alternative Homemaking ....E 941 629-1161
Port Charlotte **(G-15019)**

Always There HM Care Svcs Inc ....D 727 547-2500
Pinellas Park **(G-14504)**

Always There HM Hlth Care Inc ....E 239 389-0170
Marco Island **(G-8625)**

Amada Senior Care ....E 904 512-7747
Jacksonville **(G-5772)**

American Nursing Care Inc ....D 863 421-5500
Haines City **(G-5144)**

American Providers Inc ....D 305 591-9975
Doral **(G-3119)**

Americare Home Therapy Inc ....E 386 325-4567
Palatka **(G-13584)**

Americare Home Therapy Inc ....E 386 274-3199
Daytona Beach **(G-2544)**

Amerivita Home Care Inc ....E 407 462-7670
Orlando **(G-12121)**

Arcadia Health Services Inc ....E 727 579-9414
Saint Petersburg **(G-15572)**

At Home Care Solutions Inc ....C 407 250-6989
Orlando **(G-12145)**

At Home Infusion Services LLC ....E 561 353-4663
Boca Raton **(G-432)**

Automted Hlthcare Slutions LLC ....C 888 788-4771
Sunrise **(G-16741)**

B and B Homecare Broward LLC ....D 954 370-3131
Boca Raton **(G-439)**

▲ Baptist Health South Fla Inc ....D 305 596-1960
South Miami **(G-16500)**

Bayada Home Health Care Inc ....D 904 202-4300
Jacksonville **(G-5844)**

Bayada Home Health Care Inc ....C 727 530-1201
Saint Petersburg **(G-15592)**

Baycare Health System Inc ....D 727 519-1200
Clearwater **(G-1540)**

Baycare Home Care Inc ....E 727 447-1146
Clearwater **(G-1542)**

Baycare Home Care Inc ....D 727 535-8362
Largo **(G-8081)**

Baycare Home Care Inc ....D 941 917-7730
Sarasota **(G-16099)**

Baycare Home Care Inc ....D 863 665-8866
Lakeland **(G-7814)**

Baycare Home Care Inc ....B 727 394-6461
Largo **(G-8082)**

Baycare Home Care Inc ....C 352 686-7771
Weeki Wachee **(G-18967)**

Baycare Home Care Inc ....D 727 848-2311
New Port Richey **(G-11367)**

Baycare Home Care Inc ....C 727 734-6635
Dunedin **(G-3378)**

Baycare Home Care Inc ....C 813 806-0700
Tampa **(G-17352)**

Baycare Home Care Inc ....C 352 622-2757
Ocala **(G-11638)**

Baycare Home Care Inc ....C 941 727-9880
Bradenton **(G-1056)**

Baycare Pasco Inc ....E 540 229-0602
Wesley Chapel **(G-18994)**

Big Bend Hospice Inc ....D 850 878-5310
Tallahassee **(G-16892)**

Bioplus Specialty Phrm Svcs Inc ....E 407 830-8820
Altamonte Springs **(G-30)**

Bonita Community Health Center ....D 239 949-1050
Estero **(G-3445)**

Brevard Health Alliance Inc ....D 321 848-0716
Rockledge **(G-15336)**

Brevard Health Alliance Inc ....D 321 268-0267
Titusville **(G-18678)**

Brewster Group Inc ....E 305 770-4650
Miami Lakes **(G-10713)**

Brrh Corporation ....D 561 955-4200
Boca Raton **(G-485)**

Brrh Corporation ....A 561 395-7100
Boca Raton **(G-484)**

Brrh Home Health Services Inc ....A 561 955-4040
Boca Raton **(G-486)**

Cahsah Foundation ....E 561 200-3321
Boca Raton **(G-490)**

Capri Home Care Inc ....E 727 723-1800
Palm Harbor **(G-13852)**

Care Centers of Nassau LLC ....C 904 261-5518
Fernandina Beach **(G-3524)**

Care Health Services Inc ....E 561 433-8800
Lake Worth **(G-7716)**

Care Management Services Inc ....E 407 896-2010
Orlando **(G-12236)**

Carecentrix Inc ....D 813 901-2485
Tampa **(G-17419)**

Caregiver Services Inc ....D 877 227-3448
Medley **(G-8712)**

Careservices of Bethesda LLC ....E 561 735-7900
Boynton Beach **(G-969)**

Caretenders Jacksonville LLC ....C 904 272-7607
Fleming Island **(G-3552)**

Caretenders Jacksonville LLC ....D 904 425-4202
Jacksonville **(G-5904)**

Caretenders Visiting Svcs of P ....C 727 546-8080
Pinellas Park **(G-14511)**

Caretnders Vsting Svcs Dst 6 L ....C 941 360-6974
Bradenton **(G-1072)**

Caretnders Vsting Svcs Dst 6 L ....C 941 764-7555
Port Charlotte **(G-15025)**

Caretnders Vsting Svcs Dst 7 L ....A 321 308-0321
Palm Bay **(G-13611)**

Caretnders Vsting Svcs Gnsvlle ....E 352 379-6217
Gainesville **(G-4852)**

Caretnders Vsting Svcs Hrnndo ....D 352 592-1424
Brooksville **(G-1278)**

Caretnders Vsting Svcs Ocala L ....B 352 694-8100
Ocala **(G-11651)**

Caretnders Vsting Svcs St Agst ....D 386 615-2053
Ormond Beach **(G-13481)**

Carty Healthcare Services LLC ....E 646 281-9957
Wellington **(G-18974)**

Castle Healthcare Services Inc ....E 239 676-1635
Bonita Springs **(G-901)**

Catholic Hospice Inc ....C 786 260-6462
Miami **(G-9335)**

Catholic Hospice Inc ....D 305 822-2380
Miami Lakes **(G-10714)**

Cc-Aventura Inc ....D 305 692-4700
Aventura **(G-266)**

Chapters Health System Inc ....D 813 877-2200
Tampa **(G-17459)**

Choice Mtters HM Hlthcare Inc ....E 904 680-1256
Jacksonville **(G-5946)**

CK Franchising Inc ....D 352 331-7760
Gainesville **(G-4864)**

Ckctb Inc ....E 239 590-8999
Fort Myers **(G-4313)**

CMS Home Care LLC ....C 787 620-2900
Miami Lakes **(G-10716)**

Community Aging Rtrment Svcs I ....E 727 862-9291
Hudson **(G-5634)**

Community Home Health Inc ....D 954 973-9400
Fort Lauderdale **(G-3708)**

Community Home Health Inc..........C....... 561 641-3141
Palm Springs ***(G-13890)***
Community Home Services Inc..........D....... 239 436-5777
Naples ***(G-11073)***
Community Hspice Nrthast Fla I..........C....... 904 268-5200
Jacksonville ***(G-5988)***
Compassnate HM Care Prtners LL..........E....... 863 271-7776
Lakeland ***(G-7843)***
Complete HM Care Brward Cnty L..........D....... 954 480-9519
Fort Lauderdale ***(G-3710)***
Coram Hlthcare Corp Sthern Fla..........B....... 954 431-3335
Miramar ***(G-10848)***
Cornerstone Hspice Plltive Car..........C....... 352 343-1341
Tavares ***(G-18604)***
County of Broward..........A....... 954 357-7000
Fort Lauderdale ***(G-3722)***
County of Hillsborough..........E....... 813 272-6630
Tampa ***(G-17539)***
County of Suwannee..........E....... 386 362-2708
Live Oak ***(G-8310)***
Covenant Home Health Care LLC..........B....... 850 682-5500
Crestview ***(G-2315)***
Covenant Hospice Inc..........D....... 850 433-2155
Pensacola ***(G-14273)***
Covenant Hospice Inc..........D....... 850 202-5930
Pensacola ***(G-14274)***
Covenant Hospice Inc..........E....... 850 484-3529
Pensacola ***(G-14275)***
Covenant Hospice Inc..........E....... 850 913-3236
Panama City ***(G-13988)***
Csi Ctlnos Nurses Registry Inc..........D....... 305 821-1262
Medley ***(G-8717)***
Datalink LLC..........D....... 813 903-1091
Tampa ***(G-17573)***
Dial-A-Nurse Inc..........D....... 239 434-8000
Naples ***(G-11094)***
Dick Hwser Ctr For Crbral Plsy..........E....... 850 893-6596
Tallahassee ***(G-16933)***
Doctors Choice Home Care LLC..........E....... 941 351-0199
University Park ***(G-18741)***
E Medical Group Florida Inc..........B....... 727 791-7951
Clearwater ***(G-1613)***
E Medical Group Florida Inc..........B....... 813 968-1542
Tampa ***(G-17608)***
Elder Care Options Inc..........C....... 305 854-3234
Coral Gables ***(G-2101)***
Elder Care Services Inc..........E....... 850 921-5554
Tallahassee ***(G-16940)***
Elder Services Central Fla Inc..........D....... 863 701-9100
Sebring ***(G-16394)***
Elder Services Central Fla Inc..........C....... 863 701-9100
Lakeland ***(G-7855)***
Elite Care At Home Inc..........D....... 305 231-0555
Miami Lakes ***(G-10726)***
Ellis Helen Home Care..........B....... 727 944-4300
Tarpon Springs ***(G-18583)***
Empath Health Inc..........D....... 727 586-4432
Clearwater ***(G-1619)***
Encompass Home Health..........D....... 850 785-6706
Panama City ***(G-14000)***
Etairos Health Inc..........A....... 727 614-8300
Largo ***(G-8102)***
Evangelcal Lthran Good Smrtan S..........D....... 407 870-1783
Kissimmee ***(G-7303)***
Executive Hlthcare Sltions LLC..........E....... 239 992-4779
Bonita Springs ***(G-911)***
Faith Telehealth Care LLC..........D....... 305 928-9727
Aventura ***(G-271)***
Family First Homecare LLC..........E....... 941 444-2432
Sarasota ***(G-16155)***
Family First Homecare LLC..........E....... 904 204-2273
Jacksonville ***(G-6144)***
Family Life Care Inc..........D....... 352 692-2899
Gainesville ***(G-4883)***
First-In-Care HM Hlth Agcy Inc..........D....... 941 746-8400
Bradenton ***(G-1100)***
Florida Concerned Care LLC..........B....... 727 400-4700
Clearwater ***(G-1641)***
Florida Hosp Hm Care Svc Ctr..........E....... 407 691-8202
Orlando ***(G-12526)***
Flourish In Place LLC..........E....... 407 845-9797
Orlando ***(G-12537)***
Forallkids LLC..........A....... 727 898-7451
Saint Petersburg ***(G-15679)***
Foundcare Inc..........D....... 561 432-7902
West Palm Beach ***(G-19153)***
▲ **Friends of Ctrus Nture Cast In**..........C....... 352 527-2020
Beverly Hills ***(G-378)***
Gentiva Health Services Inc..........C....... 850 769-3398
Panama City ***(G-14018)***
Gentiva Health Services Inc..........D....... 386 364-4593
Live Oak ***(G-8312)***
Gentiva Health Services Inc..........D....... 850 862-3240
Fort Walton Beach ***(G-4774)***
Gentiva Health Services Inc..........C....... 386 758-3490
Lake City ***(G-7527)***
Gentiva Health Services Inc..........E....... 813 961-8446
Tampa ***(G-17729)***
Gentiva Health Services Inc..........D....... 386 736-9224
Deland ***(G-2862)***
Gentiva Health Services Inc..........D....... 386 328-0202
Palatka ***(G-13588)***
Gentiva Health Services Inc..........D....... 888 999-2422
Tampa ***(G-17730)***
Gentiva Health Services Inc..........D....... 352 787-2780
Leesburg ***(G-8245)***
Gentiva Health Services Inc..........D....... 352 683-6858
Spring Hill ***(G-16538)***
Gentiva Health Services Inc..........D....... 321 255-9995
Melbourne ***(G-8891)***
Gentiva Health Services Inc..........C....... 904 731-3515
Orange Park ***(G-11992)***
Gentiva Health Services Inc..........D....... 407 935-1235
Kissimmee ***(G-7316)***
Gentiva Health Services Inc..........D....... 863 648-9118
Lakeland ***(G-7874)***
Gentiva Health Services Inc..........D....... 321 725-4799
Palm Bay ***(G-13620)***
Gentiva Health Services Inc..........D....... 850 526-3577
Marianna ***(G-8676)***
Gentiva Health Services Inc..........D....... 850 862-1069
Fort Walton Beach ***(G-4775)***
Gentiva Health Services Inc..........D....... 850 526-1932
Marianna ***(G-8677)***
Gentiva Health Services Inc..........D....... 813 886-5866
Tampa ***(G-17731)***
Gentiva Health Services Inc..........D....... 352 746-5010
Lecanto ***(G-8219)***
Gentiva Health Services Inc..........C....... 941 343-0509
Sarasota ***(G-16174)***
Gentiva Health Services Inc..........C....... 352 402-0660
Ocala ***(G-11695)***
Gentiva Health Services Inc..........D....... 407 935-1235
Kissimmee ***(G-7317)***
Gold Coast Home Hlth Svcs Inc..........A....... 954 785-2990
Fort Lauderdale ***(G-3824)***
Grayson United Associate LLC..........E....... 407 346-4818
Apopka ***(G-185)***
Greystone Healthcare MGT Corp..........B....... 941 764-8266
Port Charlotte ***(G-15038)***
Gsh Health Inc..........C....... 863 551-3900
Auburndale ***(G-254)***
Guardian Care Services Inc..........D....... 954 438-0005
Miami Lakes ***(G-10735)***
Guidewell-Sanitas I LLC..........C....... 786 408-8502
Lauderdale Lakes ***(G-8173)***
Guidewell-Sanitas I LLC..........C....... 786 408-8502
Coral Springs ***(G-2258)***
Gulfside Healthcare Svcs Inc..........E....... 800 561-4883
Land O Lakes ***(G-8048)***
Gulfside Hospice Inc..........D....... 800 561-4883
Land O Lakes ***(G-8049)***
Gulfside Hospice Inc..........C....... 727 845-5707
New Port Richey ***(G-11380)***
Halifax Home Health..........D....... 386 322-4700
Port Orange ***(G-15077)***
Harden Healthcare Services LLC..........B....... 727 538-2027
Clearwater ***(G-1661)***
Hawkins Roniesha..........D....... 754 246-5432
Coral Springs ***(G-2260)***
Health Care Mgt Consulting..........D....... 904 259-3111
Jacksonville ***(G-6268)***
Health Care Mgt Consulting..........E....... 904 725-7100
Jacksonville ***(G-6269)***
Health Care Mgt Consulting..........D....... 904 277-8330
Fernandina Beach ***(G-3530)***
Health Care Slutions At HM Inc..........E....... 727 530-7700
Clearwater ***(G-1663)***
Health First Inc..........B....... 321 434-4335
Rockledge ***(G-15346)***
Health First Shared Svcs Inc..........A....... 321 434-4300
Rockledge ***(G-15350)***
Healthaxis Group LLC..........D....... 888 974-2947
Tampa ***(G-17806)***
Healthcare Interventions Inc..........E....... 561 921-0550
Delray Beach ***(G-2964)***
Heart To Hart HM Care Svcs LLC..........D....... 561 717-2997
Boca Raton ***(G-626)***
Heart To Heart Group LLC..........E....... 863 949-6682
Orlando ***(G-12633)***
Hernando-Pasco Hospice Inc..........D....... 352 596-0433
Brooksville ***(G-1293)***
Hernando-Pasco Hospice Inc..........D....... 813 780-6797
Zephyrhills ***(G-19838)***
Home Care Connect LLC..........D....... 855 223-2228
Winter Park ***(G-19733)***
Home Care of Tampa Bay LLC..........E....... 941 479-7800
Palmetto ***(G-13916)***
Home Health Agcy - Collier LLC..........E....... 941 379-0801
Sarasota ***(G-16186)***
Home Health Corp America Inc..........D....... 727 942-9000
New Port Richey ***(G-11386)***
Home Health Services S Fla Inc..........E....... 954 485-7233
Plantation ***(G-14655)***
Home Health Services S Fla Inc..........E....... 954 735-7332
Plantation ***(G-14656)***
Home Hlth Agcy - Hllsbrugh LLC..........C....... 941 794-2200
Bradenton ***(G-1121)***
Home Hlth Agcy - Pinellas LLC..........C....... 727 844-3615
New Port Richey ***(G-11387)***
Home Instead Senior Care..........E....... 904 215-8520
Orange Park ***(G-11996)***
Home Instead Senior Care..........D....... 352 502-4864
Ocala ***(G-11700)***
Home Instead Senior Care..........E....... 239 226-0007
Fort Myers ***(G-4441)***
Hope Hospice & Cmnty Svcs Inc..........E....... 239 985-6400
Port Charlotte ***(G-15041)***
Hope Hospice & Cmnty Svcs Inc..........E....... 239 444-4168
Bonita Springs ***(G-922)***
Hope Hospice & Cmnty Svcs Inc..........C....... 239 482-4673
Fort Myers ***(G-4443)***
Hope Hospice & Cmnty Svcs Inc..........D....... 239 574-4888
Cape Coral ***(G-1401)***
Hopewell Alachua County LLC..........D....... 352 415-2511
Gainesville ***(G-4918)***
Hospice By Sea Inc..........A....... 561 395-5031
West Palm Beach ***(G-19185)***
Hospice Care Southeast Florida..........C....... 954 467-7423
Plantation ***(G-14658)***
Hospice of Comforter Inc..........B....... 407 682-0808
Altamonte Springs ***(G-62)***
Hospice of The Fla Sncoast Inc..........B....... 727 549-4900
Pinellas Park ***(G-14523)***
Hospice of Treasure Coast Inc..........E....... 772 403-4500
Fort Pierce ***(G-4712)***
Integrity Home Care Inc..........E....... 321 221-7099
Melbourne ***(G-8912)***
Interim Health Care of N Fla..........D....... 850 243-1152
Fort Walton Beach ***(G-4782)***
Interim Health Care of N Fla..........D....... 850 474-0767
Pensacola ***(G-14330)***
Interim Healthcare Inc..........C....... 800 338-7786
Sunrise ***(G-16787)***
Interim Home Healthcare Co..........C....... 904 448-1133
Jacksonville ***(G-6326)***
JC Home Care Inc..........E....... 904 448-9827
Jacksonville ***(G-6380)***
Jewish Family Home Care Inc..........E....... 954 908-5677
Davie ***(G-2494)***
John Knox Home Health Agcy Inc..........C....... 954 783-4009
Pompano Beach ***(G-14833)***
K & D Home Health Care Corp..........E....... 954 583-7077
Tamarac ***(G-17196)***
Kindred Healthcare LLC..........E....... 850 267-0354
Miramar Beach ***(G-10922)***
Kindred Healthcare LLC..........E....... 813 961-8446
Tampa ***(G-17925)***
Kindred Healthcare LLC..........E....... 239 277-1003
Fort Myers ***(G-4463)***
Kindred Healthcare LLC..........E....... 813 783-8145
Wesley Chapel ***(G-19001)***
Kindred Hospital Palm Bch LLC..........B....... 561 840-0754
Riviera Beach ***(G-15304)***
Lee County Care Services Inc..........E....... 239 347-9187
Cape Coral ***(G-1405)***
Lee Memorial Health System..........C....... 239 481-4111
Fort Myers ***(G-4483)***
Lee Memorial Health System..........A....... 239 343-2000
Fort Myers ***(G-4480)***
Liberator Medical Holdings Inc..........B....... 772 287-2414
Stuart ***(G-16635)***
Life & Health Alternatives Inc..........D....... 305 420-6661
Miami ***(G-9869)***
Life Care Home Hlth Svcs Corp..........B....... 561 272-5866
Delray Beach ***(G-2978)***
Lincare Holdings Inc..........C....... 800 284-2006
Clearwater ***(G-1698)***
Lincare Inc..........E....... 561 266-1011
Delray Beach ***(G-2983)***

S I C

Lincare Inc	E	863 297-8220
Lakeland *(G-7909)*		
Lincare Inc	E	352 629-8880
Ocala *(G-11713)*		
Lincare Inc	B	727 530-7700
Clearwater *(G-1699)*		
Looking Upward Inc	D	561 688-1823
Palm Beach *(G-13662)*		
Madison Cnty Hosp Hlth Systems	C	850 973-2271
Madison *(G-8488)*		
Maxim Healthcare Services Inc	C	561 733-3130
Boynton Beach *(G-1011)*		
Maxim Healthcare Services Inc	C	904 396-2199
Jacksonville *(G-6470)*		
McNa Health Care Holdings LLC	E	800 494-6262
Fort Lauderdale *(G-3965)*		
Mease Life Inc	B	727 738-3000
Dunedin *(G-3388)*		
Mederi Inc	D	352 253-0168
Eustis *(G-3498)*		
Mederi Cretenders Vs SE FL LLC	C	772 794-9777
Vero Beach *(G-18892)*		
Mederi Cretenders Vs Tampa LLC	E	813 282-8520
Tampa *(G-18017)*		
Mederi Crtnders Vs Broward LLC	D	954 484-4837
Fort Lauderdale *(G-3966)*		
Medhok Inc	D	877 692-0471
Tampa *(G-18018)*		
Medical Ctr Hm Hlth Care Svcs	A	850 431-6868
Tallahassee *(G-17040)*		
Medical Imging Prtnrshp-Jax1 L	E	904 996-8100
Fleming Island *(G-3554)*		
Miami VA Healthcare System	D	305 575-3179
Miami *(G-9983)*		
Mid-Florida Medical Svcs Inc	D	863 297-1895
Winter Haven *(G-19646)*		
Miramar Home Care Llc	D	561 829-3080
West Palm Beach *(G-19269)*		
Mission Home Care Inc	E	813 355-4804
Zephyrhills *(G-19842)*		
Mobile Medical Industries LLC	D	904 296-1913
Jacksonville *(G-6510)*		
Monte Nido Holdings LLC	D	310 457-9958
South Miami *(G-16509)*		
Morton Plant Mase Hlth Care In	A	813 788-1566
Zephyrhills *(G-19845)*		
Mrb Acquisition Corp	D	866 387-2668
Daytona Beach *(G-2639)*		
Msk RE Holdings LLC	D	386 233-9009
Orange City *(G-11969)*		
Msn Incorporated	D	954 714-6064
Oakland Park *(G-11607)*		
MTI America Inc	D	800 553-2155
Pompano Beach *(G-14861)*		
Myonsite Healthcare LLC	C	941 271-0701
Sarasota *(G-16242)*		
National Health Infusion Inc	E	941 484-5626
Nokomis *(G-11464)*		
Neighborhood HM Hlth Svcs Inc	E	786 693-9600
Miami *(G-10036)*		
North Broward Hospital Dst	C	954 785-2990
Pompano Beach *(G-14868)*		
North Fla Regional Med Ctr Inc	A	352 333-4100
Gainesville *(G-4963)*		
Nurse Care Inc	B	786 507-4321
Miami Lakes *(G-10750)*		
Nursecore Management Svcs LLC	B	941 951-6080
Sarasota *(G-16248)*		
Omni Home Health - Dst 1 LLC	C	850 505-7777
Pensacola *(G-14393)*		
Omni Home Health Services LLC	C	941 953-9494
Sarasota *(G-16252)*		
Omni Home Health Services LLC	C	352 384-9240
Gainesville *(G-4971)*		
Omni Home Hlth - Hernando LLC	C	352 628-4900
Crystal River *(G-2349)*		
One Homecare Solutions LLC	B	855 441-6900
Miramar *(G-10885)*		
Optreum LLC	E	754 216-1921
Deerfield Beach *(G-2780)*		
Palm Beach Cancer Institute	E	561 840-6181
Mangonia Park *(G-8610)*		
Partners In Care LLC	E	386 255-0645
Daytona Beach *(G-2650)*		
Pediatria Healthcare LLC	D	813 982-3695
Brandon *(G-1247)*		
Pediatria Healthcare LLC	D	850 701-3920
Tallahassee *(G-17066)*		
Pediatric Services America Inc	D	904 730-2200
Jacksonville *(G-6595)*		

▲ Pharmerica Long-Term Care LLC	B	877 874-2768
Tampa *(G-18143)*		
Philippians Management Co	D	407 628-4357
Winter Park *(G-19761)*		
Pinnacle HM Care Jcksnvlle LLC	E	813 814-6000
Oldsmar *(G-11921)*		
Pinnacle Home Care Inc	D	727 846-1919
New Port Richey *(G-11399)*		
Plan Life Care LLC	E	386 383-5120
South Daytona *(G-16492)*		
Plymouth Harbor Incorporated	B	941 365-2600
Sarasota *(G-16270)*		
Powell Supportive Services Inc	D	813 335-4891
Land O Lakes *(G-8053)*		
Precise Home Care LLC	D	904 448-8670
Jacksonville *(G-6612)*		
Preferred Care At Home	E	561 455-2627
Delray Beach *(G-3009)*		
Preferred Medical Group Inc	D	239 597-2010
Naples *(G-11267)*		
Preferred Touch Home Care Inc	E	813 803-5888
Aventura *(G-281)*		
Premier Home Healthcare Inc	D	407 373-7224
Orlando *(G-13050)*		
Prescrbed Pdtric Extnded Care	E	813 880-0320
Tampa *(G-18164)*		
Prime Care Health Agency Inc	B	305 591-7774
Miami *(G-10143)*		
Prism Healthcare Partners Ltd	E	954 200-7000
Fort Lauderdale *(G-4061)*		
Pro Med Healthcare Svcs LLC	D	727 209-0639
Saint Petersburg *(G-15810)*		
Professnal Sltons HM Hlth Agcy	C	305 262-8220
Doral *(G-3296)*		
Progressus Therapy Inc	D	813 288-8131
Tampa *(G-18177)*		
Psa Healthcare	A	321 254-4254
Melbourne *(G-8961)*		
Quali-Care Home Hlth Agcy Inc	D	305 232-3979
Palmetto Bay *(G-13950)*		
Quality Care Home Health LLC	C	941 923-6371
Sarasota *(G-16277)*		
Quality Care Home Health LLC	C	321 752-4495
Melbourne *(G-8962)*		
Quality Care Home Health LLC	C	386 756-1418
Daytona Beach *(G-2655)*		
Quality of Life Corp	E	954 608-4067
Margate *(G-8664)*		
Rauland-Borg Corp Florida	E	407 830-6175
Altamonte Springs *(G-96)*		
Reed Healthcare Services Corp	D	904 329-4975
Jacksonville *(G-6644)*		
RES-Care Inc	D	407 629-5969
Winter Park *(G-19769)*		
RES-Care Inc	E	386 257-7070
Daytona Beach *(G-2658)*		
RES-Care Inc	E	772 245-7021
Port Saint Lucie *(G-15160)*		
RES-Care Inc	D	239 936-8292
Fort Myers *(G-4568)*		
RES-Care Inc	D	321 676-5088
Melbourne *(G-8968)*		
RES-Care Inc	D	561 440-5296
Lake Worth *(G-7749)*		
RES-Care Inc	E	239 390-0824
Bonita Springs *(G-939)*		
RES-Care Inc	E	813 286-1445
Tampa *(G-18216)*		
RES-Care Inc	D	904 964-8082
Starke *(G-16581)*		
RES-Care Inc	D	904 296-5800
Jacksonville *(G-6659)*		
RES-Care Inc	D	954 677-2593
Fort Lauderdale *(G-4085)*		
RES-Care Inc	D	850 629-7072
Panama City *(G-14061)*		
RES-Care Inc	C	305 626-7800
Opa Locka *(G-11954)*		
RES-Care Inc	D	727 734-7400
Dunedin *(G-3390)*		
RES-Care Inc	D	386 248-0051
Daytona Beach *(G-2659)*		
RES-Care Inc	E	813 286-0144
Tampa *(G-18217)*		
Responsive Home Health Inc	E	954 486-6440
Fort Lauderdale *(G-4088)*		
Responsive Home Health Inc	E	954 933-2376
Fort Lauderdale *(G-4089)*		
Right Intentions Inc	D	941 739-3050
Bradenton *(G-1170)*		

Rx Home Health Services Inc	E	305 865-2244
Bay Harbor Islands *(G-349)*		
S & G Entps Middleburg LLC	E	904 779-5515
Orange Park *(G-12016)*		
Sandcastle Care Inc	B	407 454-4892
Maitland *(G-8575)*		
Sandcastle Care II LLC	B	386 457-3519
Deland *(G-2879)*		
Sarasota County Pub Hosp Dst	C	941 917-7730
Sarasota *(G-16299)*		
Schf Health Services Inc	B	321 637-2673
Rockledge *(G-15366)*		
Sea Crest Health Care MGT LLC	C	941 761-3499
Bradenton *(G-1177)*		
Senior Healthcare Services	D	954 776-4776
Fort Lauderdale *(G-4116)*		
Senior Healthcare Services	E	561 361-7561
Boca Raton *(G-793)*		
Senior Home Care	C	954 366-1621
Tamarac *(G-17204)*		
Senior Home Care Inc	D	863 682-6182
Lakeland *(G-7967)*		
Senior Home Care Inc	D	727 815-3690
New Port Richey *(G-11404)*		
Senior Home Care Inc	D	727 531-0300
Clearwater *(G-1786)*		
Senior Home Care Inc	D	904 730-4640
Jacksonville *(G-6709)*		
Senior Home Care Inc	D	352 596-5946
Spring Hill *(G-16547)*		
Senior Home Care Inc	E	352 360-1725
Leesburg *(G-8272)*		
Seniorbrdge Fmly Cmpnies NY In	D	239 430-8300
Naples *(G-11296)*		
Seniorbridge Family	D	305 529-0224
Coral Gables *(G-2184)*		
Sensicare Services Inc	D	904 265-0752
Saint Johns *(G-15548)*		
Sheridan Chld Hlthcare Svcs VA	B	954 838-2371
Sunrise *(G-16826)*		
Sheridan Healthcare Inc	E	954 389-2700
Pembroke Pines *(G-14183)*		
SMH Health Care Inc	D	941 917-8010
Sarasota *(G-16321)*		
Solantic Corporation	E	904 743-2466
Jacksonville *(G-6739)*		
South Fla Pdatric Homecare Inc	E	954 967-1900
Hollywood *(G-5531)*		
South Florida Baptist Hospital	B	813 757-1200
Plant City *(G-14582)*		
Southern Healthcare MGT II LLC	E	407 830-5309
Casselberry *(G-1459)*		
Southwest Florida Home Care	D	239 275-5233
Fort Myers *(G-4601)*		
Space Cast Hlth Foundation Inc	A	321 636-2211
Rockledge *(G-15369)*		
Space Cast Hlth Foundation Inc	B	321 752-1200
Melbourne *(G-8976)*		
Spang Inc	C	352 620-8484
Ocala *(G-11781)*		
Specilty Phrm Nrsing Ntwrk Inc	D	941 366-7330
Sarasota *(G-16327)*		
Star Multi Care Services Inc	D	954 962-0926
Pembroke Pines *(G-14191)*		
Steward Rockledge Hospital Inc	C	321 253-2200
Melbourne *(G-8983)*		
Sunbelt Home Health Care Inc	D	941 255-9500
Port Charlotte *(G-15063)*		
Sunrise Connecticut Ave Assn	A	727 863-5808
Port Richey *(G-15113)*		
Sunshine Caregivers	C	305 278-2301
Pinecrest *(G-14501)*		
Synergy Inc	B	225 201-1235
Clearwater *(G-1811)*		
Synergy HM Cr-Northwestern Reg	E	727 533-9700
Clearwater *(G-1813)*		
T E H C LLC	D	904 722-1112
Jacksonville *(G-6827)*		
T E H C LLC	D	904 722-1112
Jacksonville *(G-6828)*		
T E H C LLC	D	321 453-5535
Rockledge *(G-15374)*		
T E H C LLC	D	407 628-1114
Orlando *(G-13265)*		
Take Care of Sarasota Inc	C	941 484-8844
Venice *(G-18810)*		
Take Care of Sarasota Inc	C	941 484-8844
Sarasota *(G-16345)*		
Talgood Enterprises LLC	E	561 842-1932
North Palm Beach *(G-11558)*		

Tampa Bay Cares LLC ....E 863 686-7333
Valrico *(G-18757)*

Tarpon Helpers LLC ....E 727 210-1414
Clearwater *(G-1817)*

Tenet Healthsystem Medical Inc ....E 813 875-8888
Tampa *(G-18416)*

Tidewell Hospice Inc..........................D 941 782-4900
Bradenton *(G-1193)*

Tidewell Hospice Inc..........................D 941 548-2300
Port Charlotte *(G-15064)*

Tidewell Hospice Inc..........................D 941 441-2000
Venice *(G-18811)*

Tidewell Hospice Inc..........................D 941 845-3000
Palmetto *(G-13933)*

Tidewell Hospice Inc..........................D 941 552-5900
Lakewood Ranch *(G-8033)*

Tidewell Hospice Inc..........................D 941 979-4300
Port Charlotte *(G-15065)*

Total Home Health Inc ....E 954 962-2133
Hollywood *(G-5539)*

Towers HM Care Rehabilitation ....C 407 425-2707
Orlando *(G-13299)*

Traditional Home Care Inc....................E 954 973-9400
Fort Lauderdale *(G-4180)*

Tri County Home Care Florida ....E 954 923-0695
Hollywood *(G-5541)*

Trinity Health Care Svcs Inc..................D 954 986-1754
Miramar *(G-10906)*

United Home Care Services Inc.............C 866 585-9646
Doral *(G-3341)*

United Nursing Services Inc ....C 239 596-6003
Naples *(G-11332)*

University Community Hosp Inc ....D 813 615-7700
Tampa *(G-18471)*

Uplift Homecare LLC ....E 813 261-0130
Plant City *(G-14590)*

Urban Jacksonville Inc ....C 904 807-1203
Jacksonville *(G-6896)*

Utopia Home Care Inc.........................D 941 343-4416
Sarasota *(G-16356)*

Utopia Home Care Inc.........................C 407 385-1685
Orlando *(G-13365)*

Utopia Home Care Inc.........................D 727 841-9050
New Port Richey *(G-11409)*

Utopia Home Care Inc.........................C 727 821-3332
Largo *(G-8160)*

Villa Maria Hlth Care Svcs Inc..............E 305 891-8850
North Miami *(G-11512)*

Visiting Care Florida Inc ....C 561 433-8800
Lake Worth *(G-7759)*

Visiting Nrse Assn Hspice Fndt..............B 772 567-5551
Vero Beach *(G-18941)*

Visiting Nrse Assn of Trsure C ....D 772 567-5551
Vero Beach *(G-18942)*

Visiting Nrses Assn of S W Fla ....E 239 337-4848
Fort Myers *(G-4644)*

Visiting Nurse Assn Fla Inc...................D 727 845-8099
Trinity *(G-18732)*

Visiting Nurse Assn Fla Inc...................C 772 286-1844
Stuart *(G-16676)*

Visiting Nurse Assn Fla Inc...................D 772 286-1844
Bradenton *(G-1200)*

Visiting Nurse Assn Fla Inc...................D 863 357-2197
Okeechobee *(G-11882)*

Visiting Nurse Assn Fla Inc...................D 352 592-9800
Weeki Wachee *(G-18970)*

Visiting Nurse Assn Fla Inc...................D 772 286-8157
Stuart *(G-16677)*

Visiting Nurse Assn Fla Inc...................D 561 799-3411
West Palm Beach *(G-19410)*

Visiting Nurses Assn & Hospice...........B 772 567-5551
Vero Beach *(G-18943)*

Vitacare Home Care LLC ....D 941 999-1960
Bradenton *(G-1201)*

Vitas Healthcare Corporation ....E 386 530-4600
Palatka *(G-13604)*

Vitas Healthcare Corporation ....E 386 320-5501
Gainesville *(G-5025)*

Vitas Healthcare Corporation ....E 863 314-9333
Sebring *(G-16420)*

▲ Vitas Healthcare Corporation............B 305 374-4143
Miami *(G-10480)*

Vitas Healthcare Corporation ....D 352 527-2020
Lecanto *(G-8227)*

Vitas Healthcare Corporation ....D 407 846-8667
Kissimmee *(G-7406)*

Vitas Healthcare Corporation ....E 877 848-2720
Jacksonville *(G-6911)*

Vitas Healthcare Corporation ....E 561 496-2378
Delray Beach *(G-3032)*

Vna Hspice Indian Rver Cnty In ....D 772 567-5551
Vero Beach *(G-18944)*

Vna Respite Care ....D 407 644-2433
Orlando *(G-13388)*

Wellbox Inc ....E 866 730-6893
Jacksonville *(G-6928)*

Wellmed Medical Management Inc ....E 772 466-6855
Port Saint Lucie *(G-15175)*

Youthful Aging Home Health Inc ....E 941 925-9532
Sarasota *(G-16369)*

8092 Kidney Dialysis Centers

Americare Renal Center LLC ....C 305 448-6261
Miami *(G-9145)*

Ara-Sebring Dialysis LLC ....D 863 382-9443
Sebring *(G-16389)*

Artesia Dialysis LLC ....E 850 297-0435
Tallahassee *(G-16884)*

Bio-Mdcal Applications Fla Inc ....D 352 335-1751
Gainesville *(G-4843)*

Bio-Mdcal Applications Fla Inc ....D 904 964-8822
Starke *(G-16574)*

Bio-Mdcal Applications Fla Inc ....D 305 246-5043
Homestead *(G-5558)*

Bio-Mdcal Applications Fla Inc ....D 386 719-0217
Lake City *(G-7513)*

Bio-Mdcal Applications Fla Inc ....D 863 551-3159
Auburndale *(G-249)*

Bio-Mdcal Applications Fla Inc ....D 727 733-1112
Dunedin *(G-3380)*

Bio-Mdcal Applications Fla Inc ....E 386 758-2202
Lake City *(G-7514)*

Bio-Mdcal Applications Fla Inc ....D 321 768-9801
Middleburg *(G-10792)*

Bio-Mdcal Applications Fla Inc ....D 850 944-8997
Pensacola *(G-14236)*

Bio-Mdcal Applications Fla Inc ....D 941 924-0003
Sarasota *(G-16103)*

Bio-Mdcal Applications Fla Inc ....D 786 538-3617
Key West *(G-7194)*

Bio-Mdcal Applications Fla Inc ....E 954 367-6489
Pembroke Pines *(G-14134)*

Bio-Mdcal Applications Fla Inc ....D 772 230-6366
Stuart *(G-16593)*

Bio-Mdcal Applications Fla Inc ....D 904 515-0103
Jacksonville *(G-5861)*

Bio-Mdcal Applications Fla Inc ....D 727 848-0106
Trinity *(G-18721)*

Bio-Mdcal Applications Fla Inc ....D 850 558-6090
Tallahassee *(G-16893)*

Bio-Mdcal Applications Fla Inc ....D 727 862-0603
Hudson *(G-5632)*

Bio-Mdcal Applications Fla Inc ....D 352 463-2008
Trenton *(G-18717)*

Bio-Mdcal Applications Fla Inc ....D 850 522-5407
Panama City *(G-13971)*

Bio-Mdcal Applications Fla Inc ....D 941 351-1641
University Park *(G-18738)*

Central Fla Kidney Ctrs Inc ....D 407 843-6110
Orlando *(G-12269)*

Dialysis Clinic Inc ....E 904 764-6381
Jacksonville *(G-6066)*

Dialysis Clinic Inc ....D 904 354-0409
Jacksonville *(G-6067)*

DSI South Tampa LLC ....D 813 661-7474
Brandon *(G-1225)*

Fresenius Med Care Apllo Bch L............E 813 419-6230
Ruskin *(G-15401)*

Fresenius Med Care Csslbrry LL............E 407 551-1601
Casselberry *(G-1449)*

Fresenius Med Care E Vnice LLC...........D 941 236-9000
Venice *(G-18782)*

Fresenius Med Care Four Crners ....D 352 394-3003
Clermont *(G-1872)*

Fresenius Med Care Prkland LLC...........D 754 240-4610
Parkland *(G-14108)*

Fresenius Med Care W ATL LLC ....D 561 403-5201
Delray Beach *(G-2950)*

Fresenius Medical Care North ....C 954 629-4632
Hollywood *(G-5440)*

Fresenius Vascular Care Inc ....E 850 466-3843
Pensacola *(G-14314)*

Melbourne Kidney Center Inc ....D 321 724-0431
Melbourne *(G-8936)*

Mobil Dialysis Inc...............................D 407 324-4023
Sanford *(G-15965)*

Nephrology Assoc Centl Fla PA ....C 407 894-4693
Winter Park *(G-19753)*

Orion Medical Enterprises Inc ....E 305 651-3261
Miami *(G-10080)*

Plantation Dialysis Center LLC..............D 954 382-0151
Plantation *(G-14695)*

Renal Crepartners At Mem W LLC ....C 954 362-5010
Pembroke Pines *(G-14180)*

Renal Life Link Inc ....E 863 419-7408
Davenport *(G-2448)*

Renal Trtmnt Ctrs - Stheast LP ....E 352 508-3007
Tavares *(G-18617)*

Renal Trtmnt Ctrs - Stheast LP ....D 850 785-1233
Panama City *(G-14060)*

Southwest Jcksnvlle Dlysis Ctr ....E 904 781-7272
Jacksonville *(G-6767)*

Starks Dialysis LLC ....E 813 876-7023
Tampa *(G-18331)*

Talimena Dialysis LLC ....E 305 621-3732
Miami *(G-10361)*

Watson Clinic LLP ....E 863 680-7560
Lakeland *(G-8001)*

West Ornge Mtland Dlysis Ctr L ....D 321 418-3593
Orlando *(G-13418)*

West Ornge Orlndo Dlysis Ctr L ....E 321 710-4362
Orlando *(G-13419)*

West Ornge Wnter Grdn Dlysis C ....E 407 378-5955
Winter Garden *(G-19600)*

West Palm Dialysis LLC ....C 561 833-5355
West Palm Beach *(G-19420)*

Western Community Dialysis Ctr ....C 561 791-2252
Royal Palm Beach *(G-15392)*

8093 Specialty Outpatient Facilities, NEC

26health Inc ....E 321 800-2874
Orlando *(G-12027)*

A Plus Therapy Inc ....E 954 474-3223
Plantation *(G-14595)*

Access Medical Group Miami Inc ....E 305 635-7712
Miami *(G-9071)*

Achieve Pediatric Therapy Inc...............E 407 277-5400
Orlando *(G-12047)*

Adventist Hlth Systm/Snbelt In ....E 407 303-7600
Orlando *(G-12072)*

Agency For Cmnty Trtmnt Svcs I ....E 813 246-4899
Tampa *(G-17247)*

Agency For Cmnty Trtmnt Svcs I ....E 813 626-7250
Tampa *(G-17248)*

Allegro Senior Living LLC.....................E 561 253-8161
Jupiter *(G-7047)*

Alternate Family Care Inc ....C 954 963-0991
Hollywood *(G-5391)*

American Health Care Inc ....D 352 796-6701
Brooksville *(G-1268)*

Amethyst Recovery Center LLC ....C 954 665-3826
Port Saint Lucie *(G-15121)*

Amin Radiology Inc ....D 352 795-9200
Crystal River *(G-2340)*

Apalachee Center Inc ....D 850 875-2422
Quincy *(G-15226)*

Apalachee Center Inc ....E 850 997-3958
Monticello *(G-10930)*

Apalachee Center Inc ....D 850 523-3333
Tallahassee *(G-16880)*

Apalachee Center Inc ....E 850 973-5124
Madison *(G-8483)*

Arcadia Healthcare LLC ....C 863 676-1512
Lake Wales *(G-7674)*

Archways Inc ....C 954 763-2030
Fort Lauderdale *(G-3613)*

Aspire Health Partners Inc ....B 407 875-3700
Orlando *(G-12136)*

Aspire Health Partners Inc ....C 407 293-2123
Orlando *(G-12137)*

Aspire Health Partners Inc ....B 407 875-3700
Orlando *(G-12138)*

Aspire Health Partners Inc ....C 407 291-6335
Orlando *(G-12139)*

Aspire Health Partners Inc ....C 407 875-3700
Orlando *(G-12140)*

Aspire Health Partners Inc ....B 407 875-3700
Orlando *(G-12141)*

Atlantic Mntal Hlth Prgram Inc..............E 305 248-3488
Homestead *(G-5556)*

Banyan RES Innovation Ctr Inc ....D 954 941-9828
Pompano Beach *(G-14748)*

Banyan RES Innovation Ctr Inc ....E 305 757-0602
Miami *(G-9211)*

Banyan Trtmnt & Recovery LLC............D 954 210-7502
Pompano Beach *(G-14749)*

Bay County Health System LLC ....D 850 769-1511
Panama City *(G-13960)*

Bay County Health System LLC ....D 850 914-9844
Panama City *(G-13962)*

Company		Phone	Location	ID

Baycare Behavioral Health Inc ....D 727 841-4200
New Port Richey (G-11365)

Baycare Behavioral Health Inc ....E 727 519-1200
Clearwater (G-1536)

Baycare Behavioral Health Inc ....D 352 540-9335
Brooksville (G-1271)

Baycare Behavioral Health Inc ....D 727 841-4430
Clearwater (G-1537)

Baycare Behavioral Health Inc ....D 727 841-4430
Brooksville (G-1272)

Baycare Behavioral Health Inc ....D 727 848-2583
New Port Richey (G-11366)

Bayview Ctr For Mntal Hlth Inc ....D 305 892-4600
North Miami Beach (G-11517)

Beach House Treatment Ctr LLC ....D 561 337-3200
Juno Beach (G-7027)

Beachway Therapy Center LLC ....E 855 975-2495
West Palm Beach (G-19049)

Beckman & Associates ....D 407 647-4740
Maitland (G-8505)

Behavioral Health MGT Svcs Inc ....C 727 462-7930
Clearwater (G-1544)

Boca Raton Rehabilitation Ctr ....E 561 391-5200
Boca Raton (G-469)

Borinquen Health Care Ctr Inc ....D 305 576-6611
Miami (G-9270)

Bridgeway Center Inc ....D 850 833-3975
Fort Walton Beach (G-4757)

Brooks Skilled Nursng Facility ....C 904 528-3500
Jacksonville (G-5883)

Bws Recovery LLC ....E 303 489-0420
Jupiter (G-7053)

Can Community Health Inc ....C 941 366-0461
Sarasota (G-16115)

Carlton Manor Inc ....D 727 343-3662
Saint Petersburg (G-15613)

Centennial Healthcare Corp ....C 850 674-4311
Blountstown (G-382)

Centers Inc ....D 352 628-5020
Lecanto (G-8213)

Centers Inc ....C 352 291-5555
Ocala (G-11654)

Centerstone of Florida Inc ....C 941 721-7670
Bradenton (G-1078)

Centerstone of Florida Inc ....C 941 782-4840
Bradenton (G-1079)

Centerstone of Florida Inc ....E 941 782-4299
Bradenton (G-1076)

Central Christian Univ Inc ....D 407 290-1609
Orlando (G-12260)

Chapters Health System Inc ....D 352 746-5700
Lecanto (G-8214)

Charltte Bhvoral Hlth Care Inc ....D 941 639-8300
Punta Gorda (G-15198)

Chemical Addctons Rcvery Effor ....D 850 769-1633
Panama City (G-13980)

Children & Families Fla Dept ....C 352 330-2177
Wildwood (G-19491)

Childrens Home Society of Fla ....D 321 397-3000
Gainesville (G-4856)

Citrus Health Network Inc ....B 305 558-0151
Hialeah (G-5237)

Clay Behavioral Health Ctr Inc ....E 904 291-5561
Middleburg (G-10794)

Cleanslate Centers Inc ....D 904 527-3622
Jacksonville (G-5965)

Coastal Bhvoral Healthcare Inc ....E 941 927-8900
Sarasota (G-16124)

Community Health South Fla Inc ....B 305 246-1666
Homestead (G-5566)

Community Health South Fla Inc ....C 305 253-5100
Cutler Bay (G-2361)

Community Rehab Associates Inc ....C 877 268-4329
Saint Petersburg (G-15638)

Community Rhbilitation Ctr Inc ....E 904 358-1211
Jacksonville (G-5989)

Compass Inc ....E 561 533-9699
Lake Worth (G-7719)

Comprhensive Wellness Ctrs LLC ....E 561 619-5858
Lantana (G-8061)

Comprhnsive Alchlism Rhblttion ....C 561 844-6400
West Palm Beach (G-19101)

Comprhnsive Humn Resources Inc ....E 305 892-8440
Miami (G-9399)

Concept Health Systems Inc ....D 305 751-6501
Miami (G-9400)

Consulate Management Co LLC ....C 407 527-1550
Tallahassee (G-16923)

◆ Continucare Corporation ....D 305 350-7515
Miami (G-9410)

County of Orange ....C 407 836-8990
Orlando (G-12375)

Cove Behavioral Health Inc ....C 813 384-4202
Tampa (G-17543)

Cove Behavioral Health Inc ....D 813 984-0909
Tampa (G-17544)

D & D Rehab Center Inc ....E 305 827-7344
Hialeah (G-5249)

David Lwrnce Mntal Hlth Ctr In ....D 239 657-4434
Immokalee (G-5655)

David Lwrnce Mntal Hlth Ctr In ....D 239 455-8500
Naples (G-11089)

Deerfeld Bch Otptent Srgcal CT ....E 954 418-7222
Deerfield Beach (G-2734)

Delphi Bhvioral Hlth Group LLC ....E 954 487-1224
Fort Lauderdale (G-3758)

Devereux Foundation ....D 321 255-3988
Melbourne (G-8869)

Devereux Foundation ....E 863 595-0167
Winter Haven (G-19621)

Devereux Foundation ....E 407 362-9210
Orlando (G-12416)

Devereux Foundation ....D 407 362-9210
Melbourne (G-8870)

Directions For Mental Hlth Inc ....D 727 456-0600
Largo (G-8097)

Directions For Mental Hlth Inc ....D 727 524-4464
Clearwater (G-1608)

Disc Village Inc ....D 850 575-4388
Tallahassee (G-16934)

Discovery Point Retreat Inc ....D 786 923-3305
Miami (G-9478)

Dna Cmprhnsive Thrapy Svcs LLC ....E 239 223-2751
Fort Myers (G-4344)

Douglas Grdns Cmnty Mntal Hlth ....D 305 531-5341
Miami Beach (G-10585)

Drew Medical Inc ....E 407 788-2888
Altamonte Springs (G-45)

Drug Abuse Fndtion Palm Bch CN ....C 561 732-0800
Delray Beach (G-2947)

Dunklin Memorial Church Inc ....D 772 597-2841
Okeechobee (G-11865)

Eckerd Youth Alternatives Inc ....D 727 461-2990
Brooksville (G-1283)

Encompass Health Corporation ....D 772 324-3500
Stuart (G-16617)

Encompass Health Corporation ....D 352 592-4250
Brooksville (G-1285)

Encompass Health Corporation ....D 561 367-6090
Boca Raton (G-565)

Encompass Health Corporation ....E 850 863-7887
Fort Walton Beach (G-4767)

Encompass Hlth Rhblttion Hosp ....C 352 592-4284
Brooksville (G-1286)

Encompass Hlth Rhblttion Hosp ....E 813 607-3600
Lutz (G-8440)

Encompass Hlth Rhblttion Hosp ....E 941 921-8600
Sarasota (G-16149)

Encore Rehabilitation Svcs LLC ....C 888 974-7878
Oldsmar (G-11900)

Escambia County School Dst ....C 850 595-1330
Pensacola (G-14295)

Fairwinds Properties Inc ....D 727 449-0300
Clearwater (G-1630)

Family Frst Adlescent Svcs LLC ....E 561 617-8563
Palm Beach Gardens (G-13729)

Family Recovery Specialists PA ....C 305 595-7378
Miami (G-9544)

First Step of Sarasota Inc ....E 941 497-7742
Venice (G-18780)

First Step of Sarasota Inc ....E 941 753-1823
Sarasota (G-16033)

FL HUD Bayside LLC ....C 850 430-3300
Pensacola (G-14307)

Florida Cmnty Hlth Ctrs Inc ....D 863 983-7813
Clewiston (G-1901)

Florida Hospital Assn Inc ....D 407 303-1169
Orlando (G-12527)

Florida Hospital Ocala Inc ....C 352 368-7099
Ocala (G-11691)

Florida School Massage Inc ....E 352 378-7891
Gainesville (G-4896)

For Florida Institute ....C 863 773-2857
Wauchula (G-18961)

Fort Lauderdale Hospital Inc ....C 954 463-4321
Oakland Park (G-11596)

Gateway Community Services Inc ....E 904 387-4661
Jacksonville (G-6218)

Gateway Community Services Inc ....C 904 387-4661
Jacksonville (G-6219)

Gateway Community Services Inc ....E 904 781-0838
Jacksonville (G-6220)

Genesis Rhabilitation Hosp Inc ....E 904 858-7600
Jacksonville (G-6227)

Global Med Behavioral Hlth Cor ....E 863 353-9322
Davenport (G-2440)

Goodwill Indstres-Suncoast Inc ....C 727 523-1512
Saint Petersburg (G-15691)

Guidance/Care Center Inc ....C 305 434-7660
Key Largo (G-7178)

Hanley Center Inc ....E 561 841-1000
Mangonia Park (G-8609)

Harbor Village Inc ....E 305 691-0086
Miami (G-9682)

Harm Reduction Center LLC ....E 561 602-5224
Boynton Beach (G-995)

HBA Corporation ....E 954 587-3296
Plantation (G-14653)

HBA Corporation ....E 954 597-3311
Tamarac (G-17192)

HCA Health Services Fla Inc ....A 772 335-4000
Port Saint Lucie (G-15139)

Healogics Inc ....B 904 446-3400
Jacksonville (G-6267)

Health Care Ctr For Hmless Inc ....E 407 428-5751
Orlando (G-12626)

HealthSouth Corporation ....E 407 587-8600
Altamonte Springs (G-58)

HealthSouth Treasure Coast Inc ....E 772 778-2100
Vero Beach (G-18869)

Healthsuth Med Prtners Srgery ....D 205 970-4869
Orlando (G-12631)

Healthsuth Rhblttion Hosp Tllh ....C 850 325-6277
Tallahassee (G-16995)

Healthsuth Sea Pnes Ltd Partnr ....B 321 984-4600
Melbourne (G-8903)

Healthsuth Snrise Rhblttion Ho ....B 954 749-0300
Sunrise (G-16784)

Henderson Behavioral Hlth Inc ....E 954 486-4005
Fort Lauderdale (G-3855)

Henderson Behavioral Hlth Inc ....E 954 485-8888
Lauderdale Lakes (G-8174)

Henderson Behavioral Hlth Inc ....E 954 486-4005
Lauderdale Lakes (G-8175)

Henderson Behavioral Hlth Inc ....D 954 463-0911
Lauderdale Lakes (G-8176)

Henderson Behavioral Hlth Inc ....E 954 730-7284
Lauderdale Lakes (G-8177)

Henderson Behavioral Hlth Inc ....D 954 921-2600
Hollywood (G-5448)

Henderson Behavioral Hlth Inc ....D 954 731-1000
Fort Lauderdale (G-3856)

Henderson Behavioral Hlth Inc ....D 954 677-3113
Fort Lauderdale (G-3857)

Henderson Behavioral Hlth Inc ....E 954 731-2835
Lauderhill (G-8200)

Henderson Behavioral Hlth Inc ....E 954 731-5100
Tamarac (G-17193)

Holistix By Sea LLC ....E 954 491-3413
Margate (G-8652)

Hope Haven Association Inc ....D 904 346-5100
Jacksonville (G-6296)

Housing Partnership Inc ....E 561 841-3500
Riviera Beach (G-15299)

IM Slzbcher Ctr For Hmless I ....E 904 359-0457
Jacksonville (G-6310)

Impower Inc ....C 407 215-0095
Longwood (G-8366)

Institute For Child Fmly Hlth ....C 305 685-0381
Miami (G-9751)

Institute For Child Fmly Hlth ....D 305 685-0381
Miami (G-9752)

Institute For Child Fmly Hlth ....E 305 558-2480
Miami (G-9753)

Integrcare Rhbltation Agcy Inc ....E 954 531-1472
Delray Beach (G-2971)

J Cusaac Inc ....E 561 542-7795
Lake Worth (G-7736)

▲ Jessie Trice Cmnty Hlth Sys In ....E 305 805-1700
Miami (G-9788)

Jessie Trice Cmnty Hlth Sys In ....E 305 693-1213
Miami (G-9789)

Jessie Trice Cmnty Hlth Sys In ....E 305 887-0004
Hialeah (G-5283)

Jobworks Inc ....E 727 523-1512
Saint Petersburg (G-15732)

Kendall Spech Language Ctr Inc ....E 305 274-7883
Miami (G-9820)

Kessler Rehabilitation of Fla ....E 863 688-6931
Lakeland (G-7896)

Kidscare Therapy Center Inc ....E 305 231-3371
Hialeah (G-5287)
Kindred Hospitals East LLC ....A 904 284-9230
Green Cove Springs (G-5057)
La Amistad Foundation Inc ....E 407 331-7226
Fern Park (G-3513)
La Amistad Residential ....D 407 647-0660
Maitland (G-8551)
Lake Wales Healthcare LLC ....D 863 676-1512
Lake Wales (G-7689)
Lake Worth Enterprise LLC ....E 561 586-7404
Lake Worth (G-7739)
Lakeview Center Inc ....C 850 432-1222
Pensacola (G-14340)
Lakeview Health Systems LLC ....C 954 979-6027
Deerfield Beach (G-2764)
Leesburg Regional Med Ctr Inc ....C 352 323-5160
Leesburg (G-8256)
Lehigh Acres NH LLC ....D 239 369-2194
Lehigh Acres (G-8286)
Life Care Centers America Inc ....C 863 318-8646
Winter Haven (G-19643)
Life Concepts Inc ....D 407 298-8121
Orlando (G-12766)
Life MGT Ctr NW Fla Inc ....C 850 769-9481
Panama City (G-14035)
Life MGT Ctr NW Fla Inc ....E 850 547-5114
Bonifay (G-889)
Lifespace Communities Inc ....B 561 454-2000
Delray Beach (G-2979)
Lincare Holdings Inc ....C 800 284-2006
Clearwater (G-1698)
Lock Twns Cmnty Mntal Hlth Ctr ....D 305 628-8981
Miami Gardens (G-10690)
Mariner Health Care Inc ....D 850 386-4054
Tallahassee (G-17031)
Meditationlive Inc ....E 415 484-6018
Miami Beach (G-10616)
Mental Health ....E 850 892-8035
Defuniak Springs (G-2837)
Mental Health Care Inc ....B 813 239-8083
Tampa (G-18026)
Mental Health Care Inc ....D 813 239-8526
Wesley Chapel (G-19003)
Mental Health Resource Ctr Inc ....C 904 642-9100
Jacksonville (G-6494)
Mental Hlth Care Ctr of The Lw ....D 305 292-6843
Key West (G-7229)
▼ Mental Hlth Ctr of Jcksonville ....D 904 743-1883
Jacksonville (G-6495)
Meridian Bhvral Healthcare Inc ....C 352 374-5600
Gainesville (G-4940)
Meridian Bhvral Healthcare Inc ....D 386 496-2347
Lake Butler (G-7508)
Meridian Bhvral Healthcare Inc ....D 352 374-5600
Gainesville (G-4941)
▼ Miami Behavioral Hlth Ctr Inc ....D 305 398-6100
Miami (G-9956)
Miami Behavioral Hlth Ctr Inc ....B 305 774-3600
Coral Gables (G-2147)
Morning Star Rehab Inc ....E 954 834-2222
Fort Lauderdale (G-3977)
Morton Plant Hospital Assn Inc ....E 727 372-4000
Trinity (G-18729)
Morton Plant Hospital Assn Inc ....E 727 461-8866
Clearwater (G-1723)
Mount Sinai Med Ctr Fla Inc ....C 305 674-9100
Miami Beach (G-10629)
Mount Sinai Med Ctr Fla Inc ....D 305 535-3333
Miami (G-10021)
Mv Mental Solutions Inc ....E 786 229-6636
Hialeah (G-5302)
Naples Community Hospital Inc ....B 239 436-6770
Naples (G-11226)
▲ Naples Surgical Investors Ltd ....E 239 417-0085
Naples (G-11240)
National Sourcing Inc ....C 813 281-0013
Tampa (G-18068)
Nemours Foundation ....A 904 697-4100
Jacksonville (G-6534)
Neuropsychiatric Institute LLC ....E 813 636-8811
Tampa (G-18073)
Neurospa Tms LLC ....E 813 605-1122
Tampa (G-18074)
New Horizons Cmnty Mental Hlth ....C 305 635-0366
Miami (G-10042)
New Hrzons of Trsure Coast Inc ....D 772 468-3909
Fort Pierce (G-4726)
New Hrzons of Trsure Coast Inc ....C 772 221-4088
Stuart (G-16650)

Newington Rpid Rcvery Rhab Ctr ....D 727 742-8650
Clearwater (G-1737)
North Bay Hospital ....E 727 842-8468
New Port Richey (G-11397)
North Fla Regional Med Ctr Inc ....A 352 333-4100
Gainesville (G-4963)
Northside Bhvoral Hlth Ctr Inc ....B 813 977-8700
Tampa (G-18090)
Novavision Therapy Inc ....D 561 558-2000
Boca Raton (G-723)
Oakridge Outpatient Center Inc ....E 954 958-0606
Fort Lauderdale (G-4024)
Oglethorpe of Orlando Inc ....D 321 805-5090
Saint Cloud (G-15529)
Operation Par Inc ....D 727 545-7564
Pinellas Park (G-14530)
Options Medical Opco LLC ....D 813 995-5244
Saint Petersburg (G-15783)
Orthopedic Specialists SW Fla ....D 239 334-7000
Fort Myers (G-4529)
Osceola Mental Health Inc ....E 407 846-8029
Kissimmee (G-7367)
Palm Beach Institute Inc ....E 855 960-5456
West Palm Beach (G-19313)
Palm Beach Recovery LLC ....E 855 960-5456
West Palm Beach (G-19317)
Park Place Hospital ....E 407 846-0023
Kissimmee (G-7373)
Passagway Rsdnce Dade Cnty Inc ......E 305 635-9106
Miami (G-10098)
Pavilion At Healthpark LLC ....C 239 985-2700
Fort Myers (G-4538)
Peace River Center For Per Dev ....D 863 248-3300
Lakeland (G-7936)
Pediatric Therapy Services Inc ....D 813 662-1060
Brandon (G-1248)
Peninsula Rehabilitation Ctr ....E 386 676-4222
Ormond Beach (G-13515)
Pensacola Care Incorporated ....C 850 453-2323
Pensacola (G-14407)
Personal Enrichment Thrugh Mnta ....B 727 545-6477
Pinellas Park (G-14531)
Physicians Day Surgery Ctr LLC ....D 239 596-2557
Naples (G-11263)
Pinnacle Fertility Inc ....E 727 638-1296
Tampa (G-18154)
Positive Behavior Support ....D 772 324-8022
Stuart (G-16659)
Prescrbed Pdtric Extnded Care ....E 813 880-0320
Tampa (G-18164)
Project Health Inc ....D 352 569-2941
Sumterville (G-16696)
Psych-Scial Rhbltation Ctr Inc ....C 305 667-1036
South Miami (G-16510)
Raypar Inc ....C 863 299-2636
Winter Haven (G-19652)
Recovery By Sea LLC ....E 772 934-6542
Jensen Beach (G-7021)
Recovery First Inc ....E 954 374-4800
Hollywood (G-5504)
Recovery Village ....E 352 669-8000
Umatilla (G-18735)
Refuge A Healing Place LLC ....D 352 288-3333
Ocklawaha (G-11803)
Renaissnce Bhvral Hlth Systems ....E 904 996-0194
Jacksonville (G-6655)
Renaissnce Halthcare Group LLC ....E 407 246-5250
Orlando (G-13099)
Resources For Human Dev Inc ....E 850 951-0037
Defuniak Springs (G-2840)
Richmond Health Care Inc ....B 954 577-3600
Sunrise (G-16815)
Riverpoint Behavioral Health ....D 904 724-9202
Jacksonville (G-6669)
Rural Health Care Incorporated ....E 386 328-0108
Palatka (G-13599)
Scribeamerica LLC ....B 954 908-8600
Fort Lauderdale (G-4103)
Sea Crest Health Care MGT LLC ....D 863 815-0488
Lakeland (G-7964)
Seminole Community Mental Heal ....E 407 323-2036
Fern Park (G-3516)
SMA Healthcare Inc ....D 386 236-3200
Daytona Beach (G-2664)
Smith Community Mental Health ....E 954 321-2296
Plantation (G-14708)
Solantic Corporation ....E 904 693-0866
Jacksonville (G-6740)
South Broward Hospital Dst ....D 954 430-1700
Pembroke Pines (G-14189)

South Cnty Mental Hlth Ctr Inc ....D 561 495-0522
Delray Beach (G-3019)
Southeastern Urological Ctr PA ....D 850 309-0400
Tallahassee (G-17105)
Spectrum Programs Inc ....D 305 756-0414
Miami (G-10314)
St Andrew Bay Center Inc ....E 850 265-2951
Lynn Haven (G-8471)
St Lukes Surgical Center Inc ....B 727 938-2020
Tarpon Springs (G-18593)
Steward Rockledge Hospital Inc ....C 321 752-1000
Melbourne (G-8984)
Stewart Marchman Act ....E 386 236-3200
Daytona Beach (G-2667)
Suncoast Center Inc ....D 727 327-7656
Saint Petersburg (G-15862)
Suncoast Center Inc ....C 727 323-2528
Saint Petersburg (G-15863)
Sunrise Community Inc ....C 305 246-0425
Homestead (G-5609)
Sunrise Community Inc ....C 239 574-0039
Cape Coral (G-1428)
Surgery Ctr of Fort Lauderdale ....E 954 735-0096
Lauderdale Lakes (G-8186)
Tallahssee Dgnstc Imging Ctr A ....E 850 656-2261
Tallahassee (G-17146)
Tampa Day School ....D 813 269-2100
Tampa (G-18373)
Tenet Healthsystem Medical Inc ....D 305 364-2199
Hialeah (G-5332)
Tenet Healthsystem Medical Inc ....E 850 656-4800
Tallahassee (G-17154)
Toledo Clinic LLC ....E 772 281-2626
Port Saint Lucie (G-15172)
Transitions Rehabilitation LLC ....D 813 341-2726
Tampa (G-18435)
Treatment Ctr of The Palm Bche ....D 561 253-6790
Lake Worth (G-7756)
Treatment Partners America Inc ....D 561 218-4342
Boca Raton (G-847)
Treatment Solution So Fla Inc ....E 866 319-6126
Pompano Beach (G-14927)
Turning Point of Tampa Inc ....D 813 882-3003
Tampa (G-18453)
Watershed Trtmnt Programs Inc ....D 561 278-1440
Delray Beach (G-3033)
Watson Clinic Foundation Inc ....D 863 680-7700
Lakeland (G-7998)
West Fla Regional Med Ctr Inc ....A 850 494-4000
Pensacola (G-14470)
Winter Haven Hospital Inc ....C 863 292-4060
Winter Haven (G-19677)

8099 Health & Allied Svcs, NEC

5615292283 ....E 561 529-2283
Jupiter (G-7043)
Access Med Group Tampa III Inc ....D 786 322-7333
Miami (G-9070)
Access Medical Group Tampa Inc ....D 813 906-1411
Miami (G-9072)
Active Community Health Center ....E 954 333-8787
Sunrise (G-16731)
Adventist Health System/Sunbel ....E 352 253-3900
Tavares (G-18598)
Advisewell Inc ....D 813 397-1800
Tampa (G-17242)
Alliance Rapid Testing Lab LLC ....C 844 678-0055
Miami (G-9122)
Armor Crrctional Hlth Svcs Inc ....A 850 983-1136
Milton (G-10809)
Armor Crrctional Hlth Svcs Inc ....E 305 662-8522
Miami (G-9172)
Baptist Diagnostics Imaging ....E 904 202-2222
Fleming Island (G-3551)
Bay Area Home Health Care ....D 813 654-6690
Largo (G-8079)
Baycare Behavioral Health Inc ....D 813 428-6100
Lutz (G-8431)
Baycare Health System Inc ....E 863 421-9801
Haines City (G-5145)
Baycare Health System Inc ....C 727 394-6748
Saint Petersburg (G-15593)
Beaches Open Mri Trsure Cast L ....E 772 878-5858
Stuart (G-16592)
Bendcare LLC ....E 844 337-2363
Vero Beach (G-18840)
Biomatrix Specialty Phrm LLC ....E 954 385-7322
Plantation (G-14608)
Biotest Pharmaceuticals Corp ....E 954 987-6240
Hollywood (G-5407)

Bodylogicmd Inc	E	561 982-8620	
Boca Raton (G-477)			
Boley Centers Inc	E	727 824-5745	
Saint Petersburg (G-15601)			
Brentwood Mdow Hlth Care Assoc	C	352 746-6611	
Lecanto (G-8212)			
Brevard Health Alliance Inc	D	321 877-2740	
Cocoa (G-1920)			
Brevard Health Alliance Inc	E	321 241-6857	
Melbourne (G-8832)			
Brevard Health Alliance Inc	D	321 241-6800	
Palm Bay (G-13608)			
Broadspire Services Inc	A	954 452-4000	
Sunrise (G-16752)			
Brrh Corporation	A	561 395-7100	
Boca Raton (G-484)			
Caremax Medical Group LLC	D	786 252-8269	
Miami (G-9315)			
Carespot of Austin LLC	C	904 213-0600	
Orange Park (G-11978)			
Carisk Behavioral Health Inc	D	305 514-5300	
Miami (G-9323)			
Central Fla Inptent Mdcine LLC	C	407 647-2346	
Lake Mary (G-7575)			
Central Florida Hlth Care Inc	E	863 292-4280	
Winter Haven (G-19616)			
Children & Families Fla Dept	E	850 892-8097	
Defuniak Springs (G-2826)			
Children & Families Fla Dept	E	904 209-3250	
Saint Augustine (G-15434)			
Childrens Home Society of Fla	E	561 868-4300	
West Palm Beach (G-19084)			
Cleary Enterprise Holdings	E	813 461-2239	
Odessa (G-11836)			
Community Care Hlth Netwrk LLC	B	855 628-7497	
Seminole (G-16442)			
Community Health South Fla Inc	C	305 253-5100	
Cutler Bay (G-2361)			
Community Hlth Sltons Amer Inc	D	800 514-7621	
Clearwater (G-1585)			
Conifer Health Solutions LLC	A	727 570-3612	
Saint Petersburg (G-15642)			
Consulate Management Co LLC	C	407 865-8000	
Altamonte Springs (G-40)			
Continental Blood Components	E	305 634-9728	
Miami (G-9406)			
Conviva Care Solutions LLC	E	305 662-5200	
Miami (G-9411)			
County of Hillsborough	D	813 272-5900	
Tampa (G-17533)			
County of Volusia	D	386 258-4060	
Daytona Beach (G-2569)			
▲ Cryo-Cell International Inc	D	813 749-2100	
Oldsmar (G-11898)			
Defense Health Agency	D	850 234-4177	
Panama City Beach (G-14093)			
Defense Health Agency	D	813 827-2273	
Tampa (G-17584)			
Document Storage Systems Inc	C	813 985-1900	
Tampa (G-17598)			
Emergncy Mdcine Prfssionals PA	E	386 274-7800	
Ormond Beach (G-13488)			
Empath Health Services LLC	C	727 586-4432	
Clearwater (G-1620)			
Encompass Home Health	D	850 785-6706	
Panama City (G-14000)			
Engagent Health LLC	C	305 692-0850	
Winter Park (G-19720)			
Excite It Partners LLC	C	813 898-5800	
Tampa (G-17640)			
Falcon Consulting Group LLC	D	312 751-8900	
Miami (G-9541)			
Firefghters Emplyee Bneft Fund	E	561 969-6663	
West Palm Beach (G-19140)			
Florida Deptartment of Health	A	561 671-4081	
West Palm Beach (G-19147)			
Florida Eye Center	E	813 972-4444	
Tampa (G-17680)			
Florida Health Care Plan Inc	D	386 760-5483	
Edgewater (G-3410)			
Florida Health Care Plan Inc	D	386 238-3200	
Daytona Beach (G-2594)			
Florida Hosp Zephyrhills Inc	D	813 991-5900	
Wesley Chapel (G-18998)			
Florida Hospital Ocala Inc	C	352 620-8600	
Ocala (G-11688)			
Florida North Multispecialty	E	904 770-4803	
Jacksonville (G-6195)			
Greystone Healthcare MGT Corp	B	321 752-1000	
Viera (G-18950)			

Halifax Health Services LLC	E	386 252-4701	
Daytona Beach (G-2608)			
Health Choice Network Inc	D	305 599-1015	
Doral (G-3223)			
Health Management Assoc Inc	D	321 637-7690	
Rockledge (G-15351)			
Health Svcs Advsory Group Fla	D	813 289-6200	
Tampa (G-17804)			
Healthsuth Rhblttion Hosp Lrgo	C	727 586-2999	
Largo (G-8115)			
Hebrew Homes Health Network	E	305 347-3380	
North Miami Beach (G-11526)			
Hillcour Inc	B	863 825-4171	
Tampa (G-17825)			
▲ Hippocrates Health Inst Inc	E	561 471-8876	
West Palm Beach (G-19179)			
Hospital Investigative Servi	E	954 714-4400	
Fort Lauderdale (G-3873)			
Industrial Medicine Assoc PC	E	941 365-8833	
Sarasota (G-16193)			
Industrial Medicine Assoc PC	E	727 521-9137	
Saint Petersburg (G-15719)			
Informed Medical Decisions Inc	D	800 975-4819	
Saint Petersburg (G-15721)			
Internal Medicine Group	E	561 966-1000	
West Palm Beach (G-19205)			
▲ It Works Marketing Inc	C	952 540-5699	
Palmetto (G-13918)			
Johns Hpkins All Chld Hosp Inc	E	941 927-8805	
Sarasota (G-16206)			
Journey Hlthcare Solutions LLC	E	855 777-1160	
Coral Springs (G-2263)			
Kedplasma LLC	E	850 476-7999	
Pensacola (G-14337)			
La Mer NH LLC	C	786 533-7400	
Miami (G-9841)			
Lee Memorial Womens Health Pro	C	239 343-9734	
Fort Myers (G-4493)			
Leon County School Board	C	850 488-1206	
Tallahassee (G-17024)			
Lifelink Foundation Inc	C	813 253-2640	
Tampa (G-17949)			
Lifelink Foundation Inc	C	813 251-8017	
Tampa (G-17950)			
Lifelink Foundation Inc	E	813 253-2640	
Tampa (G-17951)			
Lifesouth Cmnty Blood Ctrs Inc	C	352 224-1600	
Gainesville (G-4935)			
Lifesouth Cmnty Blood Ctrs Inc	E	352 334-1000	
Gainesville (G-4936)			
Lifesouth Cmnty Blood Ctrs Inc	D	352 622-3544	
Ocala (G-11711)			
Lions Eye Inst For Trnsplant R	D	813 289-1200	
Tampa (G-17957)			
Mdlive Inc	C	800 400-6354	
Miramar (G-10875)			
Medicaid Done Right	D	727 498-5507	
Clearwater (G-1712)			
Medical Imaging Inc	D	352 372-2345	
Gainesville (G-4939)			
Medicus LLC	E	855 462-6334	
Tampa (G-18020)			
Metro Health Inc	D	407 382-4217	
Orlando (G-12865)			
Miami Chld Hosp Foundation Inc	E	305 666-2889	
Miami (G-9962)			
Mid-Florida Medical Svcs Inc	C	863 679-9644	
Lake Wales (G-7693)			
Mid-Florida Medical Svcs Inc	C	863 297-1840	
Winter Haven (G-19647)			
Modernzing Mdcine Gstrntrlogy	C	561 880-2998	
Boca Raton (G-698)			
Morris Center	E	352 332-2629	
Ocala (G-11740)			
Morrison MGT Specialists Inc	E	954 202-4909	
Oakland Park (G-11606)			
Morton Plant Mease Health Care	A	727 462-7052	
Clearwater (G-1727)			
Nations Best Fmly Hlth Care Pl	E	850 481-1101	
Panama City (G-14046)			
Navy Medical Operational	D	850 452-9528	
Pensacola (G-14377)			
Northbrook Hlth and Rehab Ctr	C	352 544-0749	
Brooksville (G-1303)			
Oneblood Inc	D	954 735-9600	
Fort Lauderdale (G-4028)			
Oneblood Inc	C	321 443-1886	
Orlando (G-12930)			
Oneblood Inc	B	407 455-7551	
Orlando (G-12931)			

Oneblood Inc	E	904 353-8263	
Jacksonville (G-6563)			
Oneblood Inc	D	561 540-6662	
Pompano Beach (G-14873)			
Oneblood Inc	E	813 964-1354	
Tampa (G-18101)			
Oneblood Foundation Inc	D	407 248-5480	
Orlando (G-12932)			
Orlando Health Inc	B	321 843-5092	
Orlando (G-12952)			
Orlando Health Inc	A	407 296-1600	
Winter Garden (G-19585)			
Orlando Health Inc	E	352 326-6011	
Leesburg (G-8264)			
Over Ridge LLC	E	813 431-2768	
Tampa (G-18114)			
Payerfusion Holdings LLC	E	305 760-8739	
Coral Gables (G-2167)			
Peace River Center For Per Dev	E	863 686-2300	
Lakeland (G-7935)			
Plasma Biolife Services L P	E	904 248-3972	
Jacksonville (G-6605)			
Reliance Healthcare Netwrk LLC	D	863 866-8052	
Lakeland (G-7952)			
Scribeamerica LLC	C	786 279-1057	
Fort Lauderdale (G-4104)			
Secon Inc	E	561 893-0101	
Boca Raton (G-790)			
Skybridge Healthcare LLC	E	813 579-1221	
Tampa (G-18293)			
Solantic Corporation	E	954 889-5823	
Pembroke Pines (G-14184)			
South Florida Blood Banks Inc	E	561 845-2323	
Palm Beach Gardens (G-13773)			
South Miami Hospital Inc	A	954 837-1300	
Pembroke Pines (G-14190)			
▼ Southstern Cmnty Blood Ctr Inc	C	850 877-7181	
Tallahassee (G-17108)			
State of Florida	B	904 529-3784	
Green Cove Springs (G-5064)			
Step Up Suncoast Inc	C	941 827-2887	
Sarasota (G-16058)			
Stewart Marchman Act	E	386 236-3200	
Daytona Beach (G-2667)			
Sunbelt Staffing LLC	B	813 471-0152	
Oldsmar (G-11926)			
Suncoast Center Inc	C	727 637-5170	
Clearwater (G-1804)			
Suncoast Cmmnties Blood Bnk In	E	941 954-1600	
Bradenton (G-1184)			
Sunshine State Health Plan Inc	A	904 296-6635	
Jacksonville (G-6812)			
Symx Infrastructure LLC	C	305 442-8577	
Coral Gables (G-2192)			
Team Health Inc	D	813 612-9405	
Riverview (G-15274)			
Techhealth Inc	C	866 697-2680	
Jacksonville (G-6844)			
Telespecialists LLC	D	239 208-2206	
Fort Myers (G-4624)			
Transitional Hlth Solutions LLC	E	305 403-5273	
Miami (G-10404)			
Tutogen Medical United States	C	386 418-8888	
Alachua (G-14)			
Uf Health Jacksonville	E	904 383-1040	
Jacksonville (G-6881)			
US Preventive Medicine Inc	E	866 713-1167	
Jacksonville (G-6898)			
USF Hlth Prfssons Cnfrncing Co	E	813 224-7860	
Tampa (G-18490)			
Vault Medical Services PA	D	212 880-5494	
Coral Gables (G-2205)			
Vohra Wound Physicians FL LLC	E	877 866-7123	
Miramar (G-10913)			
Wellcare of Nebraska Inc	C	813 290-6200	
Tampa (G-18540)			
West Jacksonville Health	C	904 786-8668	
Jacksonville (G-6929)			

81 LEGAL SERVICES

8111 Legal Svcs

101 E College Ave LLC	E	850 222-6891	
Tallahassee (G-16863)			
A Accident Attorney	D	352 629-6464	
Ocala (G-11623)			
A Accident Attorney	E	352 493-2200	
Gainesville (G-4826)			
Akerman LLP	C	305 374-5600	
Miami (G-9110)			

Akerman LLP ....D..... 850 224-9634	**Bush Graziano & Rice PA** ....D... 813 228-7000	**Debeabien Knght Smmons Mntzris** .....D... 407 422-2454
Tallahassee *(G-16873)*	Tampa *(G-17403)*	Orlando *(G-12409)*
Akerman LLP ....D..... 813 223-7333	**Butler Pappas Weihmuller Katz** ....C... 813 281-1900	**Debeaubien Knight Simmons** ....E... 850 201-3655
Tampa *(G-17260)*	Tampa *(G-17404)*	Tallahassee *(G-16932)*
Akerman LLP ....B..... 561 653-5000	**Carlton Fields PA** ....C... 813 895-3141	**Dell Graham PA** ....E... 352 372-4384
West Palm Beach *(G-19024)*	Tampa *(G-17424)*	Gainesville *(G-4875)*
Alan B Garfinkel PA ....E..... 407 667-2100	**Carlton Fields PA** ....D... 305 530-0050	**Dell P A Allen** ....E... 813 223-5351
Maitland *(G-8501)*	Miami *(G-9326)*	Tampa *(G-17586)*
Aldridge Pite LLP ....D..... 561 392-6391	**Carlton Fields Jorden Burt PA** ....D... 813 223-7000	**Diaz Anselmo & Associates PA** ....E... 954 564-0071
Boca Raton *(G-408)*	Tampa *(G-17425)*	Plantation *(G-14632)*
Aldridge Pite LLP ....C..... 561 278-5521	**Casey Ciklin Lubitz Martens** ....D... 561 832-5900	**Dickinson & Gibbons PA** ....E... 941 366-4680
Delray Beach *(G-2901)*	West Palm Beach *(G-19077)*	Sarasota *(G-16139)*
Alex Hanna Law ....D..... 305 883-7272	**Cechman Goldstein Buckley** ....E... 239 334-1146	**Dla Piper LLP (us)** ....D... 305 423-8500
Miami *(G-9115)*	Fort Myers *(G-4303)*	Miami *(G-9483)*
Alexander B Ramey PA ....E..... 305 598-4490	**Cheffy Passidomo** ....E... 239 261-9300	**Duane Morris LLP** ....E... 561 962-2100
Hialeah *(G-5214)*	Naples *(G-11051)*	Boca Raton *(G-558)*
Allen Dyer Dppelt Gilchrist PA ....E..... 407 841-2330	**Choice Legal Group Pa** ....E... 954 453-0365	**Duane Morris LLP** ....E... 305 960-2200
Orlando *(G-12096)*	Coral Springs *(G-2237)*	Miami *(G-9491)*
Alley Maass Rogers Lindsay PA ....E..... 561 659-1770	**City Miami Beach City Clerk** ....E... 305 604-2489	**Emmanuel Sheppard & Condon PA** ....D... 850 433-6581
Palm Beach *(G-13645)*	Miami Beach *(G-10568)*	Pensacola *(G-14289)*
Alvarez Wnthrop Thmpson Storey ...E..... 407 210-2796	**City of Coral Springs** ....B... 954 344-5906	**Farah & Farah PA** ....E... 904 396-5555
Orlando *(G-12103)*	Coral Springs *(G-2238)*	Jacksonville *(G-6149)*
Andreu Palma Lavin Solis Pllc ....E..... 305 631-0175	**City of Fort Lauderdale** ....C... 954 828-5700	**Farr Farr Emerich Sifrit** ....E... 941 460-9334
Miami *(G-9154)*	Fort Lauderdale *(G-3694)*	Punta Gorda *(G-15202)*
Anidjar & Levine PA ....E..... 239 417-0050	**City of West Palm Beach** ....C... 561 822-1464	**Federated Law Group Pllc** ....D... 561 354-9600
Fort Lauderdale *(G-3611)*	West Palm Beach *(G-19088)*	Juno Beach *(G-7031)*
Astigrraga Dvis Mllins Grssman ...E..... 305 372-8282	**Clark Fountain La Vista PRA** ....E... 561 899-2107	**Ferrell Law PA** ....D... 305 390-0570
Miami *(G-9182)*	West Palm Beach *(G-19091)*	Miami *(G-9552)*
Ausley & McMullen PA ....C..... 850 224-9115	**Clark & Washington PC** ....C... 407 219-5670	**First City Bank of Florida** ....E... 850 244-5151
Tallahassee *(G-16887)*	Orlando *(G-12310)*	Fort Walton Beach *(G-4768)*
Aylstock Wtkin Kreis Ovrhltz P ....D..... 850 202-1010	**Clark and Silverglate PA** ....C... 305 377-0700	**Fisher & Phillips LLP** ....E... 813 769-7500
Pensacola *(G-14224)*	Miami *(G-9376)*	Tampa *(G-17667)*
Baker & Hostetler LLP ....B..... 407 649-4000	**Clark Partington Hart Hart PA** ....D... 850 434-9200	**Fisher & Sauls PA** ....E... 727 822-2033
Orlando *(G-12168)*	Pensacola *(G-14259)*	Saint Petersburg *(G-15672)*
Baker & McKenzie LLP ....E..... 305 789-8999	**Clayton & McCulloh** ....E... 407 875-2655	**Fisher Rshmer Wrrnrath Dckson** ......D... 407 843-2111
Miami *(G-9201)*	Maitland *(G-8517)*	Orlando *(G-12514)*
Baker Dnlson Brman Cldwell Brk ...E..... 407 422-6600	**Cobb & Cole** ....D... 386 255-8171	**Fisher Tousey Leas & Ball PA** ....E... 904 356-2600
Orlando *(G-12171)*	Daytona Beach *(G-2561)*	Jacksonville *(G-6180)*
Barnett Bolt Krkwood Long Kche ...D..... 813 258-3148	**Cohen Law Group-Florida PA** ....D... 407 478-4878	**Fisher Tousey Leas & Ball PA** ....E... 904 356-2600
Tampa *(G-17338)*	Maitland *(G-8518)*	Ponte Vedra Beach *(G-14982)*
Bartlett Loeb Hnds Thompson PA ...D..... 813 223-3888	**Cohen Mlstein Sllers Toll Pllc** ....E... 561 515-1400	**Florida Foreclosure Attys Pllc** ....E... 727 446-4826
Tampa *(G-17340)*	Palm Beach Gardens *(G-13709)*	Boca Raton *(G-581)*
Battaglia Ross Dicus Wein P A .....D..... 727 381-2300	**Cole Scott & Kissane PA** ....D... 305 350-5300	**Foley & Lardner LLP** ....D... 813 229-2300
Saint Petersburg *(G-15589)*	Miami *(G-9386)*	Tampa *(G-17704)*
Bay Area Legal Services Inc ....E..... 813 232-1343	**Cole Scott & Kissane PA** ....D... 321 972-0000	**Ford & Harrison LLP** ....E... 404 888-3800
Tampa *(G-17344)*	Orlando *(G-12341)*	Orlando *(G-12539)*
Becker & Poliakoff PA ....C..... 954 985-4122	**Cole Scott & Kissane PA** ....D... 954 473-1112	**Foreman Friedman PA** ....E... 305 358-6555
Fort Lauderdale *(G-3633)*	Plantation *(G-14619)*	Miami *(G-9595)*
Beggs & Lane ....D..... 850 432-2451	**Colling Glbert Wrght Crter Pll** ....E... 407 712-7300	▲ **Fowler White Burnett PA** ....C... 305 789-9200
Pensacola *(G-14232)*	Orlando *(G-12345)*	Miami *(G-9606)*
Bercow Radell & Fernandez PA .....D..... 305 374-5300	**Colodny Fass PLLC** ....E... 954 492-4010	**Frank Weinberg and Black Pl** ....E... 954 474-8000
Miami *(G-9242)*	Sunrise *(G-16758)*	Plantation *(G-14647)*
Berger Singerman LLP ....E..... 954 525-9900	**Colson Hicks Eidson Matthew** ....E... 305 476-7400	**Friedman Law Associates PL** ....D... 813 221-9500
Fort Lauderdale *(G-3636)*	Coral Gables *(G-2076)*	Tampa *(G-17715)*
Berlin Patten Ebling Pllc ....D..... 941 954-9991	**Conrad & Scherer** ....E... 954 462-5500	**Fulmer Lroy Albee Bmann GL PLC** ....D... 813 739-7130
Sarasota *(G-16102)*	Fort Lauderdale *(G-3713)*	Saint Petersburg *(G-15682)*
Berman Law Group ....D..... 800 375-5555	**Conroy Simberg PA** ....C... 305 940-4821	**Furr and Cohen PA** ....E... 561 395-0500
Boca Raton *(G-448)*	Hollywood *(G-5417)*	Boca Raton *(G-592)*
Berman Rnnert Vogel Mandler PA ...D..... 305 577-4177	**Conroy Simberg PA** ....E... 850 436-6605	**Gary Wllams Prnti Wtson Gary** ....D... 772 283-8260
Miami *(G-9245)*	Pensacola *(G-14265)*	Stuart *(G-16625)*
Bilzin Smberg Bena Price Axlro ....C..... 305 374-7580	**Conroy Simberg PA** ....E... 239 337-1101	**Ged Lawyers LLP** ....E... 561 995-1966
Miami *(G-9257)*	Fort Myers *(G-4322)*	Boca Raton *(G-598)*
Blalock Walters PA ....C..... 941 748-0100	**County of Brevard** ....E... 321 264-5326	**Genovese Joblove & Battista PA** ......E... 305 349-2300
Bradenton *(G-1059)*	Titusville *(G-18684)*	Miami *(G-9615)*
Bogin Munns & Munns PA ....E..... 407 578-1334	**County of Broward** ....C... 954 831-8650	**Gerson Prston Rbnson Klein Lip** ......E... 305 868-3600
Orlando *(G-12193)*	Fort Lauderdale *(G-3734)*	Miami *(G-9628)*
Bond Schoeneck & King LLP ....E..... 239 262-8000	**County of Broward** ....C... 954 831-8650	**Ghiotto and Associates Inc** ....E... 904 886-0071
Naples *(G-11037)*	Fort Lauderdale *(G-3735)*	Jacksonville *(G-6230)*
Boss Arrighi & Hoag Pl ....E..... 727 471-0039	**County of Collier** ....A... 239 774-4434	**Glantz & Glantz PA** ....E... 800 654-1945
Saint Petersburg *(G-15604)*	Naples *(G-11080)*	Plantation *(G-14648)*
Brian Tague PA ....E..... 305 536-8480	**County of Pinellas** ....D... 727 464-6516	**Gordon & Doner PA** ....E... 561 799-5070
Miami *(G-9277)*	Clearwater *(G-1590)*	Palm Beach Gardens *(G-13736)*
Brinkl-Mcner-Morg-solo & Tatum ...D..... 954 522-2714	**County of Volusia** ....E... 386 822-5770	**Gould Cooksey Fennell PA** ....E... 772 231-1100
Fort Lauderdale *(G-3650)*	Deland *(G-2852)*	Vero Beach *(G-18860)*
Brinkley Morgan Attys At Law ......E..... 954 522-2200	**Coventbridge (usa) Inc** ....C... 904 641-7300	**Gray Robinson Pa** ....E... 954 761-8112
Fort Lauderdale *(G-3651)*	Jacksonville *(G-6004)*	Fort Lauderdale *(G-3832)*
Bruce L Scheiner & Associates .....D..... 239 939-2900	**Cummings & Lockwood LLC** ....E... 239 262-8311	**Greenberg Traurig LLP** ....D... 305 579-0500
Fort Myers *(G-4297)*	Naples *(G-11085)*	Miami *(G-9663)*
▲ **Bryant Miller Olive PA** ....E..... 850 222-8611	**Dade County Bar Association** ....E... 305 579-5733	**Greenberg Traurig PA** ....B... 305 579-0500
Tallahassee *(G-16897)*	Miami *(G-9449)*	Miami *(G-9664)*
Buchanan Ingersoll & Rooney PC ...D..... 239 334-7892	**Daniel J Newlin PA** ....D... 407 888-8000	**Greenberg Traurig PA** ....C... 305 418-6200
Tampa *(G-17397)*	Orlando *(G-12399)*	Doral *(G-3216)*
Buchanan Ingersoll & Rooney PC ...C..... 813 228-7411	**Daniels Kashtan Downs & Oramas** ...E... 305 448-7988	**Greenberg Traurig PA** ....C... 407 420-1000
Tampa *(G-17398)*	Coral Gables *(G-2088)*	Orlando *(G-12598)*
Buchanan P A Crary ....E..... 772 287-2600	**Day Pitney LLP** ....D... 561 272-1225	**Greene & Associates LLC** ....D... 941 916-9652
Stuart *(G-16597)*	Boca Raton *(G-546)*	Punta Gorda *(G-15206)*
Buntz McCumber Daniels ....E..... 813 287-2822	**Day Pitney LLP** ....C... 561 803-3500	**Greenspoon Marder LLP** ....C... 954 491-1120
Tampa *(G-17400)*	West Palm Beach *(G-19119)*	Fort Lauderdale *(G-3838)*
Burman Critton Luttier Coleman ....E..... 561 842-2820	**Dean Mead Egrton Bldwrth Cpan** ...D... 407 841-1200	**Grower & Ketchum Rutherford** ....D... 407 423-9545
West Palm Beach *(G-19069)*	Orlando *(G-12408)*	Maitland *(G-8538)*

Gunster Yoakley & Stewart ....E 904 353-1980
Jacksonville (G-6250)

Gunster Yoakley & Stewart PA ....C 561 655-1980
West Palm Beach (G-19169)

Gunster Yoakley & Stewart PA ....D 904 350-5947
Jacksonville (G-6251)

Haliczer Pettis & Schwamm PA ....E 954 523-9922
Fort Lauderdale (G-3846)

Hamilton Miller Birthisel LLP ....E 954 769-9111
Miami (G-9677)

▲ Harrell & Harrell PA ....D 904 296-9400
Jacksonville (G-6260)

Harris Barrett Mann & Dew ....D 727 892-3100
Saint Petersburg (G-15703)

Hartz George PA ....D 302 662-4800
Coral Gables (G-2118)

Hayt Hayt & Landau LLP ....E 305 661-6660
Miami (G-9686)

Henderson Frnklin Strnes Holt ....E 239 344-1100
Fort Myers (G-4436)

Hiday & Ricke PA ....E 904 363-2769
Jacksonville (G-6278)

Hill Adams Hall Scheffelin PA ....E 407 628-4848
Winter Park (G-19731)

Hill Ward Henderson Prof Assn ....C 813 221-3900
Tampa (G-17824)

Hinshaw & Culbertson LLP ....E 954 467-7900
Fort Lauderdale (G-3862)

Hinshaw & Culbertson LLP ....E 813 276-1662
Tampa (G-17830)

Hinshaw & Culbertson LLP ....D 305 358-7747
Coral Gables (G-2125)

Hogan Lawfirm LLC ....E 352 799-8423
Brooksville (G-1294)

Holland & Knight LLP ....D 305 374-8500
Miami (G-9711)

Holland & Knight LLP ....B 813 901-4200
Brandon (G-1236)

Holland & Knight LLP ....C 813 534-0562
Tampa (G-17832)

Homer Bonner Jacobs PA ....D 305 350-5100
Miami (G-9716)

Hornerxpress Inc ....B 904 730-9555
Jacksonville (G-6299)

Horr Novak & Skipp PA ....D 305 670-2525
Miami (G-9719)

Huey Guilday & Tucker PA ....E 850 701-4348
Tallahassee (G-16999)

Hughes Hubbard & Reed LLP ....D 305 379-7242
Miami (G-9731)

Hunton Andrews Kurth LLP ....D 305 810-2500
Miami (G-9733)

Hunton Andrews Kurth LLP ....D 305 536-2729
Miami (G-9734)

Hurley Rogner Miller ....D 407 571-7400
Winter Park (G-19736)

Icard Mrrill Cllis Timm Fren G ....D 941 366-8100
Sarasota (G-16190)

Immigration Experts and Svcs ....E 844 373-9635
West Palm Beach (G-19197)

Jacksnville Area Legal Aid Inc ....E 904 356-8371
Jacksonville (G-6339)

Jacobs & Goodman PA ....D 407 788-2949
Altamonte Springs (G-67)

James T Terrell ....E 904 632-2424
Jacksonville (G-6373)

▲ Johnson Pope Bkor Rppel Brns L .....D 727 461-1818
Clearwater (G-1685)

Jones Hurley & Hand PA ....E 407 895-8001
Maitland (G-8547)

Jones Fster Johnston Stubbs PA ....D 561 659-3000
West Palm Beach (G-19219)

Jorden Burt LLP ....D 305 371-2600
Miami (G-9802)

K Michelle Jessell ....E 561 483-7000
Boca Raton (G-658)

K&L Gates LLP ....D 305 539-3300
Miami (G-9808)

Kahane & Associates PA ....B 954 382-3486
Plantation (G-14661)

Kass Shuler PA ....D 813 229-0900
Tampa (G-17909)

Katz Brron Frdberg English Al ....D 305 856-2444
Miami (G-9812)

Kelley Kronenberg PA ....E 954 370-9970
Davie (G-2495)

Kenny Nachwalter PA ....E 305 373-1000
Miami (G-9822)

Klein Park & Lowe PI ....D 954 462-4602
Miami (G-9831)

Kluger Kplan Slvrman Ktzen LVl ....E 305 379-9000
Miami (G-9833)

Kozyak Tropin Throckmorton PA ....D 305 372-1800
Coral Gables (G-2134)

Krupnick Cmpbll Malne Bser SLM ....D 954 763-8181
Fort Lauderdale (G-3925)

Kubicki Draper A Prof Assn ....C 305 374-1212
Miami (G-9836)

Lancaster & Eure ....D 941 365-7575
Sarasota (G-16215)

Law Ofcs of Ron Sholes ....E 386 366-9161
Palatka (G-13592)

Law Offces Kanner Pintaluga PA ....E 561 424-0032
Boca Raton (G-667)

Law Offces of Ptrick L Crdero ....D 305 445-4855
Miami (G-9850)

Law Offices Daniel C Consuegra ....E 813 915-8660
Tampa (G-17935)

Law Offices Popkin Rosaler PA ....E 954 360-9030
Deerfield Beach (G-2766)

Leg Aid Soc Orge Cty Bar ....E 407 841-8310
Orlando (G-12760)

Legal Affairs Florida Dept ....B 850 414-3300
Tallahassee (G-17022)

Legal Aid Service of Broward ....E 954 765-8950
Plantation (G-14666)

Legal Aid Soc Palm Bch Cnty In ....E 561 655-8944
West Palm Beach (G-19231)

Legal Svcs Greater Miami Inc ....D 305 232-9680
Coral Gables (G-2135)

Levin Ppntnio Thmas Mtchell Rf ....C 850 435-7000
Pensacola (G-14345)

Lewis Brsbois Bsgard Smith LLP ....D 813 739-1900
Tampa (G-17942)

Lewis Brsbois Bsgard Smith LLP ....D 954 728-1280
Fort Lauderdale (G-3935)

Linebrger Gggan Blair Smpson L ....D 786 316-0070
Miami (G-9875)

Lisa R Carrasco Atty ....E 904 598-6106
Jacksonville (G-6440)

Litigation Svcs & Tech Fla LLC ....E 772 563-0227
Vero Beach (G-18888)

Lotane & Associates P A ....D 321 636-4861
Cocoa (G-1942)

Lowndes Drosdick Doster ....D 407 843-4600
Orlando (G-12784)

Lowndes Drsdick Dster Kntor RE ....C 407 843-4600
Orlando (G-12785)

Lucas M & D L Frm PLLC ....E 727 849-5353
New Port Richey (G-11393)

Luks and Santaniello LLC ....E 954 761-9225
Fort Lauderdale (G-3950)

Lytal Rter Smith Ivey Frnrath ....D 561 655-1990
West Palm Beach (G-19244)

Macfarlane Frguson McMullen PA ....D 813 273-4200
Tampa (G-17973)

Maher Law Firm The A Prof Corp ....E 407 839-0866
Winter Park (G-19745)

Marin Eljiek Lopez Martinez Pl ....E 305 444-5969
Miami (G-9900)

Marks Gray PA ....E 904 398-0900
Jacksonville (G-6468)

Marlow Connell Val Abr & Ad ....D 305 441-9242
Coral Gables (G-2137)

Marshall Dnnhey Wrner Clman Gg ....C 904 358-4200
Jacksonville (G-6469)

Mateer & Harbert PA ....E 407 425-9044
Orlando (G-12831)

Mc Connghhay Dffy Cnrad Pope W ....D 850 385-1246
Tallahassee (G-17037)

McCalla Raymer LLC ....D 407 674-1850
Orlando (G-12837)

McEwan Martinez & Dukes PA ....D 407 423-8571
Orlando (G-12842)

McGlinchey Stafford Pllc ....E 904 224-4449
Jacksonville (G-6482)

McGuirewoods LLP ....D 904 798-3200
Jacksonville (G-6483)

McIntosh Sawran Peltz PA ....E 954 765-1001
Fort Lauderdale (G-3964)

McIntyre Pnzrla Thnsdes Hof ....E 813 899-6059
Tampa (G-18010)

Mkrs Law PL ....E 305 446-5228
Coral Gables (G-2151)

Moody Jones & Montefusco PA ....E 954 634-1570
Plantation (G-14677)

Morgan & Morgan PA ....E 407 931-4819
Kissimmee (G-7358)

Morgan & Morgan PA ....E 239 344-9404
Naples (G-11221)

Morgan & Morgan PA ....E 561 619-2359
West Palm Beach (G-19272)

Morgan & Morgan PA ....E 941 312-6425
Sarasota (G-16238)

Morgan & Morgan PA ....E 813 229-4030
Tampa (G-18050)

Morgan & Morgan PA ....E 321 327-6936
Melbourne (G-8942)

Morgan & Morgan PA ....E 850 329-6895
Tallahassee (G-17050)

Morgan & Morgan PA ....E 850 316-9100
Pensacola (G-14368)

Morgan & Morgan PA ....E 386 281-6800
Deland (G-2873)

Morgan & Morgan PA ....E 954 318-0268
Plantation (G-14678)

Morgan & Morgan PA ....E 863 513-1310
Lakeland (G-7926)

Morgan & Morgan PA ....E 863 680-1411
Lakeland (G-7927)

Morgan & Morgan PA ....E 305 929-1900
Miami (G-10014)

Morgan & Morgan PA ....E 352 644-2000
Ocala (G-11739)

Morgan & Morgan PA ....E 904 417-4170
Saint Augustine (G-15470)

Morgan & Morgan PA ....E 727 318-6344
Saint Petersburg (G-15769)

Morgan & Morgan PA ....E 407 394-7374
Panama City (G-14044)

Morgan & Morgan PA ....E 407 849-2203
Orlando (G-12879)

Morgan & Morgan PA ....E 239 433-6880
Fort Myers (G-4518)

Morgan & Morgan PA ....E 904 398-2722
Jacksonville (G-6515)

Morgan & Morgan PA ....E 813 223-5505
Tampa (G-18051)

Morgan & Morgan PA ....E 352 343-0263
Tavares (G-18614)

Moseley Prichard Parrish ....E 904 356-1306
Jacksonville (G-6517)

Moye Obrien Orrke Pckard Mrtin ....E 407 622-5250
Maitland (G-8560)

Moyle Flngan Katz Rymond Shhan ....E 561 822-0304
North Palm Beach (G-11553)

Musca Law Offices PA ....C 954 302-5391
Fort Lauderdale (G-3983)

Musca Law Offices PA ....C 352 397-9915
Gainesville (G-4952)

Nation Law Firm PA ....E 407 339-1104
Longwood (G-8385)

Nelson Mllins Rley Scrbrugh LL ....E 561 483-7000
Boca Raton (G-711)

Nelson Mullins Riley & Sca ....B 407 839-4200
Orlando (G-12903)

Newsome Melton PA ....E 407 648-5977
Orlando (G-12912)

Office of Crmnal Cnflict Cvil ....E 561 837-5156
West Palm Beach (G-19290)

Office of Public Defender 2nd ....E 850 606-1000
Tallahassee (G-17062)

Office of State Attrney -16th ....E 305 292-3400
Key West (G-7234)

Ogden & Sullivan ....E 813 223-5111
Tampa (G-18095)

P A Abercrombie ....D 407 951-8960
Winter Park (G-19758)

P A Adams/Coogler ....E 561 478-4500
West Palm Beach (G-19302)

P A Grayrobinson ....C 407 843-8880
Orlando (G-13001)

P A Grayrobinson ....E 904 598-9929
Jacksonville (G-6574)

P A Grayrobinson ....E 321 727-8100
Melbourne (G-8955)

P A South Milhausen ....E 407 539-1638
Orlando (G-13002)

Pajcic & Pajcic PA ....D 904 261-6335
Jacksonville (G-6576)

Panza Maurer & Maynard PA ....E 954 390-0100
Fort Lauderdale (G-4041)

Pavese Grner Hvrfeld Dlton Hrs ....E 239 336-6243
Fort Myers (G-4536)

Pavese Law Firm ....D 239 334-2195
Fort Myers (G-4537)

Peckar & Abramson A Prof Corp ....E 305 358-2600
Miami (G-10107)

Perenich Clfeld Avril Noyes PA ....E 727 796-8282
Clearwater (G-1757)

Perry Young Attorney At Law PA..........E......850 215-7777
Panama City *(G-14056)*

Peterson & Bernard PA..........E......954 763-3200
Fort Lauderdale *(G-4049)*

Podhurst & Orseck PA..........E......305 358-2800
Miami *(G-10131)*

Pollack and Rosen PA..........D......305 448-0006
Coral Gables *(G-2170)*

Porges Hamlin Knowles Hawk PA..........E......941 748-3770
Bradenton *(G-1163)*

Proskauer Rose LLP..........D......561 241-7400
Boca Raton *(G-759)*

Provest LLC..........C......813 877-2844
Tampa *(G-18181)*

Quarles & Brady LLP..........E......239 262-5959
Naples *(G-11277)*

Quarles & Brady LLP..........E......813 387-0300
Tampa *(G-18190)*

Quintairos Prieto WD Boyer PA..........E......305 670-1101
Miami *(G-10176)*

Reed Smith LLP..........E......786 747-0200
Miami *(G-10190)*

Ringer Hnry Buckley Seacord PA..........E......407 841-3800
Orlando *(G-13112)*

Rissman Brrett Hurt Dnhue McLa..........C......407 839-0120
Orlando *(G-13115)*

Robert Bowling..........D......305 892-8699
North Miami *(G-11508)*

Robert J Fenstersheib PA..........E......954 456-2488
Hallandale Beach *(G-5180)*

Robert W Bleakley PA..........E......813 221-3759
Tampa *(G-18232)*

▲ Rodante Swope PA..........E......813 228-6250
Tampa *(G-18234)*

Roetzel Andress A Lgal Prof As..........E......239 649-2703
Naples *(G-11286)*

Rosenberg & Rosenberg PA..........E......954 963-0444
Hollywood *(G-5509)*

Rosenthal Levy & Simon PA..........E......561 478-2500
West Palm Beach *(G-19346)*

Ross Bush PA..........D......813 224-9255
Tampa *(G-18236)*

Rossway Swan Trney Brry Lcey O..........D......772 231-4440
Vero Beach *(G-18911)*

Rue & Ziffra PA..........E......386 788-7700
Port Orange *(G-15087)*

▲ Rumberger Kirk Cldwell Prof As..........C......407 872-7300
Orlando *(G-13148)*

Rumberger Kirk Cldwell Prof As..........D......305 358-5577
Miami *(G-10226)*

Rumberger Kirk Cldwell Prof As..........E......407 872-7300
Tallahassee *(G-17089)*

Rumberger Kirk Cldwell Prof As..........E......813 223-4253
Tampa *(G-18240)*

Rush Marshall Jones & Kelly PA..........E......407 425-5500
Orlando *(G-13150)*

Saalfield Shad PA..........E......904 355-4401
Jacksonville *(G-6684)*

Sage Law Offices..........E......954 835-0302
Sunrise *(G-16820)*

Saliwnchik Lloyd Esnschenk A P..........D......352 375-8100
Gainesville *(G-4989)*

Salter Fber Mrphy Htson Mnet P..........E......352 376-8201
Gainesville *(G-4990)*

Sandler Travis & Rosenberg PA..........D......305 267-9200
Miami *(G-10237)*

Schlesinger Construction Inc..........D......850 653-2277
Apalachicola *(G-129)*

Schwed Law PA..........D......561 694-6079
Palm Beach Gardens *(G-13770)*

Scott Tripp PA..........D......954 525-7500
Fort Lauderdale *(G-4102)*

Searcy Dnney Scrola Brnhart Sh..........C......561 686-6300
West Palm Beach *(G-19356)*

Shapiro Blasi & Wasserman PA..........D......561 477-7800
Boca Raton *(G-796)*

Sharit Bunn Chilton PA..........E......863 293-5000
Winter Haven *(G-19660)*

Sheldon J Schlesinger..........E......954 467-8800
Fort Lauderdale *(G-4119)*

Shook Hardy & Bacon LLP..........C......305 358-5171
Miami *(G-10269)*

Shook Hardy & Bacon LLP..........C......816 474-6550
Tampa *(G-18278)*

Shuffield Lowman & Wilson PA..........D......407 581-9800
Orlando *(G-13194)*

Shumaker Loop & Kendrick LLP..........D......813 225-3407
Tampa *(G-18282)*

Shutts & Bowen LLP..........E......954 524-5505
Fort Lauderdale *(G-4126)*

Shutts & Bowen LLP..........E......954 524-5505
Fort Lauderdale *(G-4127)*

Shutts & Bowen LLP..........C......305 358-6300
Miami *(G-10270)*

Shutts & Bowen LLP..........E......561 650-8510
West Palm Beach *(G-19362)*

Shutts & Bowen LLP..........E......813 229-8900
Tampa *(G-18283)*

Shutts & Bowen LLP..........E......904 647-6476
Jacksonville *(G-6723)*

Siegfried Rivera Hyman Lern..........E......305 442-3334
Coral Gables *(G-2186)*

Smith Currie & Hancock LLP..........E......850 878-3700
Fort Lauderdale *(G-4134)*

Smith Hood Prkns Loucks Stout..........D......386 254-6875
Daytona Beach *(G-2665)*

Smith Hulsey & Busey..........E......904 359-7700
Jacksonville *(G-6735)*

Sprechman & Fisher PA..........E......305 931-0100
Miami *(G-10316)*

Squire Patton Boggs (us) LLP..........E......561 650-7200
Miami *(G-10319)*

St Johns Law Group PA..........E......904 495-0400
Saint Augustine *(G-15503)*

Stabinski & Funt PA..........E......954 228-6936
Miami *(G-10322)*

Stanton & Gasdick PA..........E......407 843-1529
Orlando *(G-13234)*

State Attrney 18th Jdcial Crcu..........E......321 617-7510
Viera *(G-18951)*

Stearns Wver Mller Wssler Alhd..........C......305 789-3200
Miami *(G-10329)*

Stearns Wvr Mlr Wslr Alhdf & S..........E......954 767-2151
Fort Lauderdale *(G-4152)*

Stephens Lynn Klein Lacava..........D......305 670-3700
Miami *(G-10332)*

Stephens Lynn Klein La Cava Hf..........E......813 209-9611
Tampa *(G-18335)*

Stroock & Stroock & Lavan LLP..........E......305 358-9900
Miami *(G-10335)*

Taylor & Carls PA..........E......407 660-1040
Orlando *(G-13270)*

Taylor Day PA..........D......904 356-0700
Jacksonville *(G-6836)*

Thacker Robinson Zinz Lpa..........D......239 591-6685
Naples *(G-11319)*

Thompson Goodis Thompson..........E......727 823-0540
Saint Petersburg *(G-15875)*

Thornton Davis & Fein PA..........D......305 446-2646
Miami *(G-10387)*

Three Rivers Legal Svcs Inc..........E......352 372-0519
Gainesville *(G-5015)*

Timeshare Closing Services LLC..........C......407 370-2373
Orlando *(G-13289)*

Timothy D Padgett PA..........E......850 422-2520
Tallahassee *(G-17158)*

Todd S Aidman Atty..........E......813 261-7800
Tampa *(G-18425)*

Trenam Kemker Scharf Bark..........C......813 223-7474
Tampa *(G-18442)*

Troutman Wil Irvn Gr..........E......407 647-2277
Winter Park *(G-19780)*

Unisource Discovery Inc..........E......305 757-5739
Miami *(G-10434)*

Van Horn Law Group PA..........E......954 637-0000
Fort Lauderdale *(G-4209)*

Ver Ploeg & Marino PA..........E......305 577-3996
Miami *(G-10463)*

Vinson Law PA..........E......813 839-5708
Tampa *(G-18508)*

Visaplace..........D......561 203-8811
Boca Raton *(G-862)*

Wadley Yanchuck Berman..........E......727 937-3171
Tarpon Springs *(G-19356)*

Walton Lntaf Schrder Crson LLP..........D......305 671-1300
Miami *(G-10489)*

Weinberg Whler Hdgins Gunn Dia..........C......404 876-2700
Miami *(G-10492)*

White & Case LLP..........B......813 871-5385
Tampa *(G-18552)*

White & Case LLP..........C......305 371-2700
Miami *(G-10502)*

Whww..........E......407 423-4246
Orlando *(G-13432)*

▲ Wicker Smith Ohara McCoy Ford..........D......305 448-3939
Coral Gables *(G-2211)*

Williams Leininger & Cosby PA..........E......561 615-5666
North Palm Beach *(G-11561)*

Williams Prker Hrrson Detz Gtz..........C......941 329-6630
Sarasota *(G-16365)*

Winderwdle Hnes Ward Wdman P A..........E......407 423-4246
Winter Park *(G-19787)*

Woodward Pires & Lombardo PA..........E......239 649-6555
Naples *(G-11347)*

Wooten Kmbrugh Dmaso Dennis PA..........E......407 843-7060
Orlando *(G-13446)*

Yoss LLP..........C......305 460-1000
Coral Gables *(G-2213)*

Zakheim Law Group PA..........E......954 735-4455
Plantation *(G-14724)*

Zimmerman Kiser & Sutcliffe PA..........C......407 425-7010
Orlando *(G-13471)*

Zwicker & Associates PC..........D......978 686-2255
Jacksonville *(G-6967)*

Zwicker & Associates PC..........E......954 481-0851
Deerfield Beach *(G-2825)*

83 SOCIAL SERVICES

8322 Individual & Family Social Svcs

1501 SE 24th Road LLC..........C......352 629-8900
Ocala *(G-11620)*

1990 N McMullen Booth Road LLC..........D......727 260-2826
Clearwater *(G-1505)*

211 Palm Bch/Trasure Coast Inc..........E......561 547-8637
Lantana *(G-8057)*

211 Tampa Bay Cares Inc..........E......727 888-5211
Clearwater *(G-1506)*

2826 Clvland Ave Oprations LLC..........E......239 334-1091
Fort Myers *(G-4243)*

4kids of South Florida Inc..........E......954 979-7911
Fort Lauderdale *(G-3569)*

6 Continents Travel Netwrk LLC..........C......888 508-4805
Pembroke Pines *(G-14128)*

A & Associates Inc..........E......561 533-5303
West Palm Beach *(G-19018)*

A Reliable Transit Service..........D......813 504-3972
Tampa *(G-17217)*

Acorn Health LLC..........D......844 244-1818
Coral Gables *(G-2023)*

Adventist Hlth Systm/Snbelt In..........D......407 200-2900
Oviedo *(G-13538)*

Adventist Hlth Systm/Snbelt In..........A......407 357-1000
Altamonte Springs *(G-18)*

Advocate Program Inc..........E......305 704-0120
Miami *(G-9095)*

Agape Network Inc..........D......305 235-2616
Miami *(G-9103)*

Agency For Cmnty Trtmnt Svcs I..........E......813 246-4899
Tampa *(G-17247)*

Agency For Cmnty Trtmnt Svcs I..........E......813 626-7250
Tampa *(G-17248)*

Agency For Prsons With Dsbltie..........C......850 488-4257
Tallahassee *(G-16871)*

Agenda Cuba International Inc..........E......305 821-4815
Hialeah *(G-5213)*

Aid To Victims Dom Abuse Inc..........E......561 265-3797
Delray Beach *(G-2900)*

All Faiths Food Bank Inc..........D......941 371-0582
Sarasota *(G-16082)*

Alliance For Aging Inc..........E......305 670-6500
Miami *(G-9121)*

Alliance For Independence Inc..........D......863 665-3846
Lakeland *(G-7792)*

Alterntive Hmmking With A Hart..........D......941 488-2248
Venice *(G-18763)*

Alzheimers Community Care Inc..........C......561 683-2700
West Palm Beach *(G-19029)*

Amadeus North America Inc..........B......305 499-6613
Doral *(G-3116)*

Amavida Lakes Park LLC..........E......239 237-0501
Miami Beach *(G-10547)*

American National Red Cross..........E......772 878-7077
Fort Pierce *(G-4679)*

American National Red Cross..........E......850 682-3356
Pensacola *(G-14214)*

American National Red Cross..........E......407 894-4141
Orlando *(G-12112)*

American National Red Cross..........E......239 278-3401
Fort Myers *(G-4273)*

American National Red Cross..........E......561 996-4291
Belle Glade *(G-354)*

American National Red Cross..........E......407 644-9300
Orlando *(G-12113)*

American National Red Cross..........D......561 833-7711
West Palm Beach *(G-19034)*

American National Red Cross..........D......904 358-8091
Jacksonville *(G-5789)*

American National Red Cross..........E......904 249-9141
Jacksonville Beach *(G-6975)*

Employee Codes: A=Over 500 employees, B=251-500
C=101-250, D=51-100, E=20-50, F=10-19, G=4-9

2022 Harris Florida
Manufacturers Directory

831

S I C

American National Red Cross ... E ... 863 763-2488
Okeechobee *(G-11862)*
American National Red Cross ... D ... 954 797-3800
Fort Lauderdale *(G-3603)*
American National Red Cross ... E ... 305 326-8888
Miami *(G-9140)*
American National Red Cross ... D ... 305 644-1200
Miami *(G-9141)*
American Therapeutic Corp ... C ... 305 371-5777
Miami *(G-9144)*
Anthem Lakes LLC ... D ... 904 583-5399
Jacksonville *(G-5798)*
ARC Big Bend Inc ... E ... 850 973-4614
Madison *(G-8484)*
ARC Broward Inc ... C ... 954 746-9400
Sunrise *(G-16737)*
ARC Jacksonville Inc ... E ... 904 355-0155
Jacksonville *(G-5804)*
ARC Nature Coast Inc ... D ... 352 544-2322
Brooksville *(G-1269)*
ARC of Bradford County Inc ... E ... 904 964-7699
Starke *(G-16573)*
ARC of Indian River County Inc ... D ... 772 562-6854
Vero Beach *(G-18833)*
ARC of Palm Beach County Inc ... C ... 561 842-3213
Riviera Beach *(G-15279)*
ARC of South Florida Inc ... D ... 305 759-8500
Miami Lakes *(G-10706)*
ARC Sunrise of Central Florida ... E ... 352 787-3079
Clermont *(G-1857)*
ARC Tampa Bay Inc ... C ... 727 799-3330
Clearwater *(G-1524)*
Area Agcy On Aging Cntl Fla In ... E ... 407 514-1830
Orlando *(G-12132)*
Area Agcy On Aging For Sthwest ... E ... 239 652-6900
Fort Myers *(G-4280)*
Area Agcy On Aging Palm Bch/Tr ... E ... 561 684-5885
West Palm Beach *(G-19039)*
Arnette House Inc ... E ... 352 622-4432
Ocala *(G-11634)*
Aspire Health Partners Inc ... B ... 407 875-3700
Orlando *(G-12136)*
Aspire Health Partners Inc ... B ... 407 875-3700
Orlando *(G-12138)*
Assoction For Dev of The Excpt ... D ... 786 363-3100
Miami *(G-9179)*
Assoction For Rtrded Ctzens of ... C ... 386 325-2249
Palatka *(G-13585)*
▲ Atlantic Healthcare ... D ... 772 567-2552
Vero Beach *(G-18836)*
▼ AVI-Spl Global LLC ... A ... 813 884-7168
Tampa *(G-17324)*
Baker Cnty Cuncil On Aging Inc ... E ... 904 259-2223
Macclenny *(G-8473)*
Bannum Incorporated ... C ... 727 588-2594
Odessa *(G-11832)*
Baptist Hlth Sys Fundation Inc ... D ... 904 202-2919
Jacksonville *(G-5838)*
Baycare Behavioral Health Inc ... D ... 727 848-2583
New Port Richey *(G-11366)*
Baycare Behavioral Health Inc ... D ... 352 540-9335
Brooksville *(G-1271)*
Beaches Recovery Services LLC ... D ... 904 280-1250
Ponte Vedra *(G-14961)*
Bernard H Stern MD P A ... E ... 850 785-0108
Panama City *(G-13970)*
Big Bend Hmeless Coalition Inc ... E ... 850 576-5566
Tallahassee *(G-16891)*
Big Brthers Big Ssters Amer Co ... D ... 813 720-8778
Tampa *(G-17362)*
Big Brthers Big Ssters Mami In ... C ... 305 644-0066
Miami *(G-9253)*
Big Brthers Big Ssters Tmpa Ba ... E ... 813 769-3600
Tampa *(G-17363)*
Big Brthrs/Big Ssters Brward I ... E ... 954 584-9990
Fort Lauderdale *(G-3643)*
Boys & Girls Clubs of ... D ... 772 464-6634
Fort Pierce *(G-4686)*
Boys & Girls Clubs of ... D ... 772 398-0028
Port Saint Lucie *(G-15124)*
Boys Girls Clubs Centl Fla Inc ... D ... 407 295-1100
Orlando *(G-12198)*
Boys Girls Clubs Centl Fla Inc ... D ... 407 298-0680
Orlando *(G-12197)*
Boys Grls Clubs Palm Bch Cnty ... E ... 561 992-5399
Belle Glade *(G-355)*
Boys Grls Clubs Palm Bch Cnty ... E ... 561 881-9565
West Palm Beach *(G-19058)*
Boys Grls Clubs Palm Bch Cnty ... E ... 561 683-3392
West Palm Beach *(G-19059)*
Boys Grls Clubs Palm Bch Cnty ... E ... 561 279-0251
Delray Beach *(G-2919)*
Boys Grls Clubs Srsota Dsoto C ... E ... 941 366-7940
Sarasota *(G-16109)*
Boys Grls Clubs Srsota Dsoto C ... E ... 941 423-4405
North Port *(G-11566)*
Boys Grls Clubs Srsota Dsoto C ... E ... 941 953-9549
Sarasota *(G-16110)*
Boys Grls Clubs Srsota Dsoto C ... E ... 407 330-2456
Sanford *(G-15926)*
Branches Inc ... E ... 305 688-3551
Miami *(G-9273)*
Brandon Regional Hospital ... E ... 813 653-2770
Brandon *(G-1220)*
Bridge Senior Living LLC ... E ... 800 914-4870
Orlando *(G-12203)*
Brothers of The Good Shpherd F ... D ... 305 374-1065
Miami *(G-9288)*
Broward House Inc ... D ... 954 522-4749
Fort Lauderdale *(G-3655)*
Broward Prtnr For Homeless Inc ... D ... 954 779-3990
Fort Lauderdale *(G-3657)*
Cabbage Patch Holdings Inc ... C ... 813 514-6275
Saint Petersburg *(G-15607)*
Cabbage Patch Holdings Inc ... D ... 863 666-3010
Lakeland *(G-7823)*
Camillus House Inc ... C ... 305 374-1065
Miami *(G-9307)*
Capital City Youth Svcs Inc ... D ... 850 576-6000
Tallahassee *(G-16904)*
Capstone Adaptive ... E ... 850 432-1596
Pensacola *(G-14243)*
▲ Cardinal Florida Inc ... C ... 863 686-3784
Lakeland *(G-7824)*
Care Rsrce Cmnty Hlth Ctrs Inc ... E ... 305 576-1234
Miami *(G-9314)*
Caring Responders LLC ... C ... 866 993-0661
Clearwater *(G-1557)*
Catholic Charities Diocese ... D ... 941 359-3909
Sarasota *(G-16118)*
Catholic Chrties Centl Fla Inc ... E ... 407 677-9962
Orlando *(G-12248)*
Catholic Chrties Dcese St Ptrs ... C ... 727 893-1314
Saint Petersburg *(G-15616)*
Catholic Chrties of The Dcese ... D ... 561 775-9577
Palm Beach Gardens *(G-13701)*
Catholic Hospice Inc ... C ... 786 260-6462
Miami *(G-9335)*
Catholic Hospice Inc ... D ... 305 822-2380
Miami Lakes *(G-10714)*
Cdac Behavioral Healthcare Inc ... D ... 850 434-2724
Pensacola *(G-14252)*
Center For DRG Free Living Inc ... D ... 407 245-0010
Orlando *(G-12256)*
Center For DRG Free Living Inc ... E ... 321 264-4033
Titusville *(G-18680)*
Center For Ind Lving In Cntl F ... E ... 407 623-1070
Winter Park *(G-19697)*
Centers Inc ... C ... 352 291-5555
Ocala *(G-11654)*
Central Fla Yung MNS Chrstn As ... C ... 407 299-4358
Orlando *(G-12275)*
Central Fla Yung MNS Chrstn As ... E ... 352 536-6140
Clermont *(G-1859)*
Central Fla Yung MNS Chrstn As ... B ... 407 644-1509
Winter Park *(G-19700)*
Central Fla Yung MNS Chrstn As ... C ... 407 855-2430
Orlando *(G-12277)*
Central Fla Yung MNS Chrstn As ... B ... 407 351-9417
Orlando *(G-12278)*
Central Fla Yung MNS Chrstn As ... C ... 352 867-1441
Ocala *(G-11655)*
Central Fla Yung MNS Chrstn As ... C ... 407 381-8000
Orlando *(G-12280)*
Central Fla Yung MNS Chrstn As ... C ... 407 644-3606
Winter Park *(G-19699)*
Central Fla Yung MNS Chrstn As ... C ... 407 679-9622
Winter Park *(G-19698)*
Central Fla Yung MNS Chrstn As ... C ... 321 433-7770
Cocoa *(G-1922)*
Central Fla Yung MNS Chrstn As ... C ... 407 847-7413
Kissimmee *(G-7281)*
Central Fla Yung MNS Chrstn As ... C ... 352 343-1144
Tavares *(G-18601)*
Central Florida Group Home ... D ... 407 469-2991
Montverde *(G-10939)*
Champions For Children Inc ... E ... 813 673-4646
Tampa *(G-17455)*
Changing Homelessness Inc ... D ... 904 354-1100
Jacksonville *(G-5936)*
Childnet Inc ... B ... 561 352-2500
West Palm Beach *(G-19083)*
Childnet Inc ... D ... 954 414-6000
Fort Lauderdale *(G-3689)*
Children & Families Fla Dept ... C ... 800 962-2873
Miami *(G-9361)*
Children & Families Fla Dept ... E ... 904 723-2000
Jacksonville *(G-5944)*
Children & Families Fla Dept ... E ... 850 488-1225
Tallahassee *(G-16912)*
Children & Families Fla Dept ... D ... 866 732-2237
Naples *(G-11052)*
Children & Families Fla Dept ... E ... 407 245-0400
Orlando *(G-12296)*
Childrens Cmprhensive Svcs Inc ... D ... 850 643-4600
Bristol *(G-1260)*
Childrens Forum Inc ... E ... 850 681-7002
Tallahassee *(G-16914)*
Childrens Home Inc ... D ... 813 855-4435
Tampa *(G-17468)*
Childrens Home Society of Fla ... E ... 407 846-5220
Kissimmee *(G-7283)*
Childrens Home Society of Fla ... D ... 772 344-4020
Vero Beach *(G-18845)*
Childrens Home Society of Fla ... D ... 321 397-3000
Orlando *(G-12299)*
Childrens Home Society of Fla ... C ... 305 755-6500
Miami *(G-9363)*
Childrens Home Society of Fla ... D ... 239 334-0222
Fort Myers *(G-4309)*
Childrens Home Society of Fla ... C ... 386 304-7600
Daytona Beach *(G-2558)*
Childrens Home Society of Fla ... D ... 813 949-8946
Tampa *(G-17469)*
Childrens Home Society of Fla ... D ... 305 254-9759
Miami *(G-9364)*
Childrens Home Society of Fla ... B ... 904 493-7744
Jacksonville *(G-5945)*
Childrens Home Society of Fla ... E ... 813 949-8946
Lakeland *(G-7832)*
Childrens Home Society of Fla ... D ... 321 397-3000
Gainesville *(G-4856)*
Childrens Home Society of Fla ... E ... 321 397-3000
Deland *(G-2848)*
Childrens Home Society of Fla ... C ... 561 868-4300
West Palm Beach *(G-19084)*
Childrens Place At HM Safe Inc ... D ... 561 832-6185
West Palm Beach *(G-19085)*
Childrens Place At HM Safe Inc ... D ... 561 383-9800
Lake Worth *(G-7717)*
Childrens Svcs Cncil Brwrd CN ... D ... 954 377-1000
Tamarac *(G-17183)*
Christian Care Center Inc ... D ... 352 314-8733
Leesburg *(G-8238)*
Christian Care Center Inc ... D ... 352 787-2448
Leesburg *(G-8239)*
Citrus Cnty Assn For Rtrded CT ... C ... 352 795-5541
Lecanto *(G-8215)*
City of Boca Raton ... D ... 561 393-7807
Boca Raton *(G-512)*
City of Boca Raton ... C ... 561 338-1234
Boca Raton *(G-514)*
City of Gainesville ... D ... 352 334-3366
Gainesville *(G-4859)*
City of Maitland ... E ... 407 539-6251
Maitland *(G-8515)*
City of Miami Beach ... E ... 305 861-3616
Miami Beach *(G-10569)*
City of Orlando ... E ... 407 246-3707
Orlando *(G-12306)*
City of Palm Bay ... D ... 321 952-3443
Palm Bay *(G-13613)*
City of Pembroke Pines ... D ... 954 450-6888
Pembroke Pines *(G-14142)*
City of Saint Petersburg ... D ... 727 892-5024
Saint Petersburg *(G-15625)*
Ckctb Inc ... E ... 239 590-8999
Fort Myers *(G-4313)*
Clara White Mission Inc ... E ... 904 354-4162
Jacksonville *(G-5963)*
Claremedica Hlth Partners LLC ... D ... 786 485-1005
Hialeah *(G-5242)*
Coalition For The Hmless Cntl ... D ... 407 426-1254
Orlando *(G-12333)*
Columbus Medical Services LLC ... E ... 813 908-6773
Altamonte Springs *(G-37)*
Community Action Stops Abuse I ... D ... 727 895-4912
Saint Petersburg *(G-15636)*
Community Aging Rtrment Svcs I ... E ... 727 862-9291
Hudson *(G-5634)*

Community Aging Rtrment Svcs I.........E....... 727 847-1290
Elfers (G-3423)
Community Bsed Care Brvard Inc.........D....... 321 752-4650
Rockledge (G-15340)
Community Coop Ministries ....E....... 239 332-7687
Fort Myers (G-4320)
Community Crdnted Care For Chl.........C....... 407 522-2252
Orlando (G-12352)
Community Prtnr For Chldren In.........C....... 386 944-4709
Daytona Beach (G-2562)
Community Svcs Cncil Brvard CN.........E....... 321 639-6652
Cocoa (G-1927)
Community Svcs Cncil Brvard CN.........E....... 321 639-8770
Cocoa (G-1928)
Community Svcs Cncil Brvard CN.........E....... 321 636-9901
Cocoa (G-1929)
Communties In Schols Jcksnvlle.........B....... 904 366-6350
Jacksonville (G-5991)
Compass Inc.........E....... 561 533-9699
Lake Worth (G-7719)
Corrections Florida Department.........C....... 863 494-3727
Arcadia (G-226)
Corrections Florida Department.........D....... 850 627-8436
Quincy (G-15228)
Corrections Florida Department.........D....... 386 947-3520
Daytona Beach (G-2564)
Corrections Florida Department.........D....... 407 846-5215
Kissimmee (G-7289)
Corrections Florida Department.........D....... 954 924-3800
Hollywood (G-5420)
Corrections Florida Department.........D....... 561 804-6894
West Palm Beach (G-19108)
Corrections Florida Department.........D....... 850 674-3062
Blountstown (G-383)
Corrections Florida Department.........D....... 850 892-8075
Defuniak Springs (G-2828)
Corrections Florida Department.........D....... 386 754-1000
Lake City (G-7523)
Corrections Florida Department.........D....... 305 292-6742
Key West (G-7200)
Corrections Florida Department.........D....... 850 482-9526
Marianna (G-8673)
Corrections Florida Department.........D....... 813 987-6846
Tampa (G-17523)
Corrections Florida Department.........D....... 850 875-9644
Quincy (G-15229)
Corrections Florida Department.........D....... 305 246-6326
Florida City (G-3560)
Corrections Florida Department.........D....... 863 386-6018
Sebring (G-16392)
Corrections Florida Department.........D....... 772 221-4010
Stuart (G-16609)
Corrections Florida Department.........D....... 954 786-5466
Lauderdale Lakes (G-8170)
Corrections Florida Department.........D....... 813 233-2572
Tampa (G-17524)
Corrections Florida Department.........D....... 352 333-3640
Gainesville (G-4870)
Corrections Florida Department.........D....... 352 521-1214
Dade City (G-2384)
Council On Aging Mrtin Cnty In.........C....... 772 223-7800
Stuart (G-16610)
Council On Aging St Lucie Inc ....D....... 772 336-8608
Port Saint Lucie (G-15131)
Council On Aging West Florida ....E....... 850 432-1475
Pensacola (G-14269)
County of Brevard.........D....... 321 633-1874
Cocoa (G-1930)
County of Brevard.........E....... 321 986-8988
Merritt Island (G-9022)
County of Broward.........C....... 954 831-0482
Hollywood (G-5421)
County of Broward.........B....... 954 831-7019
Fort Lauderdale (G-3721)
County of Broward.........C....... 954 746-2055
Lauderhill (G-8191)
County of Broward.........A....... 954 357-5900
Fort Lauderdale (G-3726)
County of Broward.........C....... 954 357-6622
Fort Lauderdale (G-3728)
County of Broward.........C....... 954 831-1280
Fort Lauderdale (G-3732)
County of Broward.........B....... 954 357-7940
Coral Springs (G-2244)
County of Hillsborough.........E....... 813 276-8539
Tampa (G-17529)
County of Hillsborough.........E....... 813 272-5160
Tampa (G-17531)
County of Hillsborough.........E....... 813 272-6261
Tampa (G-17534)
County of Hillsborough.........E....... 813 307-3664
Tampa (G-17536)
County of Hillsborough.........E....... 813 272-6606
Tampa (G-17538)
County of Hillsborough.........E....... 813 272-6630
Tampa (G-17539)
County of Miami-Dade.........D....... 305 636-2290
Miami (G-9427)
County of Miami-Dade.........E....... 305 255-1433
Cutler Bay (G-2362)
Court Assist Inc.........D....... 954 587-1008
Sunrise (G-16760)
Covenant House Florida Inc.........C....... 954 561-5559
Fort Lauderdale (G-3736)
Crisis Center of Tampa Bay Inc.........C....... 813 964-1964
Tampa (G-17551)
Crosswinds Youth Services Inc.........E....... 321 394-0345
Cocoa (G-1935)
Csmn Operations LLC.........C....... 561 563-8407
Delray Beach (G-2936)
D & D Rehab Center Inc.........E....... 305 827-7344
Hialeah (G-5249)
Daniel Foundation Inc.........E....... 904 296-1055
Jacksonville (G-6042)
Daniel Memorial Inc.........C....... 904 296-1055
Jacksonville (G-6043)
Dave Mary Alper Jwish Cmnty CT.........C....... 305 271-9000
Miami (G-9460)
Dick Hwser Ctr For Crbral Plsy.........E....... 850 893-6596
Tallahassee (G-16933)
Directions For Mental Hlth Inc.........D....... 727 524-4464
Clearwater (G-1608)
Doodie Calls Inc.........E....... 813 800-7667
Osprey (G-13532)
Dr Stnley Parl Gdman Jfs Brwa.........E....... 954 370-2140
Davie (G-2476)
Drug Abuse Fndtion Palm Bch CN.........C....... 561 732-0800
Delray Beach (G-2947)
Drug Prvntion Resource Ctr Inc.........E....... 863 802-0777
Lakeland (G-7851)
Easter Seals Florida Inc.........D....... 772 380-9972
Port Saint Lucie (G-15132)
Easter Seals Florida Inc.........D....... 321 723-4474
Palm Bay (G-13619)
Easter Seals Florida Inc.........D....... 561 471-1688
West Palm Beach (G-19126)
Easter Seals South Florida Inc.........B....... 305 325-0470
Miami (G-9495)
Easter Seals Southwest Fla Inc.........C....... 941 355-7637
Sarasota (G-16032)
Eastersals Nrthast Cntl Fla In.........C....... 386 255-4568
Daytona Beach (G-2585)
Eat Right Meal Plans LLC.........D....... 813 355-8849
Tampa (G-17611)
Eckerd Youth Alternatives Inc.........D....... 352 799-5621
Brooksville (G-1284)
Economic Opprtnties Council In.........D....... 772 589-8008
Vero Beach (G-18852)
Elder Care Alachua County Inc.........D....... 352 265-9040
Gainesville (G-4879)
Elder Care Options Inc.........C....... 305 854-3234
Coral Gables (G-2101)
Elder Care Services Inc.........E....... 850 921-5554
Tallahassee (G-16940)
Embrace Families Inc.........D....... 321 441-2060
Maitland (G-8527)
Escambia County School Dst.........E....... 850 469-3996
Pensacola (G-14294)
Family Allies Inc.........D....... 321 752-4650
Rockledge (G-15344)
Family Central Inc.........B....... 954 724-4070
Wilton Manors (G-19522)
Family Chrstn Assn of Amer Inc.........E....... 305 685-4881
Miami (G-9543)
▲ Family Resource Ctr S Fla Inc.........E....... 305 374-6006
Miami (G-9545)
Family Resources Inc.........C....... 727 521-5200
Pinellas Park (G-14518)
Family Service Centers Inc.........E....... 727 531-0482
Clearwater (G-1631)
Family Support Svcs N Fla Inc.........D....... 904 421-5800
Jacksonville (G-6146)
Ferd Gldys Alpert Jwish Fmly C.........C....... 561 684-1991
West Palm Beach (G-19138)
Fi-Bay Pointe LLC.........C....... 727 867-1104
Saint Petersburg (G-15667)
Fi-Palm Beaches LLC.........C....... 561 712-1717
West Palm Beach (G-19139)
First Step of Sarasota Inc.........E....... 941 753-1823
Sarasota (G-16033)
Florida Cltion Agnst Dom Vlnce.........E....... 202 641-5592
Tallahassee (G-16962)
Florida Comm On Offnder Review.........C....... 850 922-0000
Tallahassee (G-16964)
Florida Department Corrections.........D....... 352 955-2023
Gainesville (G-4888)
Florida Department Corrections.........D....... 904 825-5038
Saint Augustine (G-15441)
Florida Department Corrections.........D....... 352 560-6000
Inverness (G-5692)
Florida Department Corrections.........D....... 407 262-7400
Casselberry (G-1448)
Florida Department Corrections.........D....... 561 434-3960
Palm Springs (G-13892)
Florida Department Corrections.........D....... 772 468-4064
Fort Pierce (G-4700)
Florida Department Corrections.........D....... 813 975-6511
Tampa (G-17678)
Florida Department Corrections.........D....... 813 975-6524
Tampa (G-17679)
Florida Department Corrections.........D....... 407 297-2000
Orlando (G-12523)
Florida Department Corrections.........D....... 904 213-2930
Green Cove Springs (G-5052)
Florida Department Corrections.........D....... 727 861-5200
New Port Richey (G-11378)
Florida Department Corrections.........D....... 904 693-5000
Jacksonville (G-6189)
Florida Department Corrections.........D....... 305 377-5270
Miami (G-9572)
Florida Department Corrections.........D....... 850 488-3596
Tallahassee (G-16965)
Florida Department Corrections.........C....... 561 992-9505
South Bay (G-16478)
Florida International Univ.........E....... 305 919-5620
North Miami (G-11491)
Florida Keys Childrens Shelter.........E....... 305 852-4246
Tavernier (G-18623)
Florida Mentor.........E....... 850 471-1417
Pensacola (G-14309)
Florida Ntwrk Yuth Fmly Svcs I.........D....... 850 922-4324
Tallahassee (G-16976)
Florida Revenue Department.........B....... 850 921-1386
Tallahassee (G-16979)
Florida Shrffs Yuth Rnches Inc.........D....... 386 842-5501
Live Oak (G-8311)
Friends Children Families Inc.........E....... 407 273-8444
Orlando (G-12550)
G & G Holistic Addiction Treat.........D....... 305 945-8384
North Miami Beach (G-11523)
Give Kids World Inc.........C....... 407 396-1114
Kissimmee (G-7318)
Golden Sands Facility Svcs LLC.........E....... 305 633-3336
Coral Gables (G-2113)
Grace Pl For Chldren Fmlies In.........D....... 239 234-2400
Naples (G-11139)
Greater Daytona Bch Area YMCA.........D....... 386 255-8773
Deland (G-2863)
Greater Dytona Bch Area Yung M.........D....... 386 532-9622
Deltona (G-3039)
Guardian Ad Litem.........E....... 904 255-8440
Jacksonville (G-6245)
Guardian Ad Litem.........E....... 727 464-6528
Clearwater (G-1658)
Guardian Ad Litem.........E....... 386 239-7803
Daytona Beach (G-2605)
Guardian Ad Litem.........C....... 813 272-5110
Tampa (G-17767)
Guardnship Prgram Dade Cnty In.........E....... 305 592-7642
Miami (G-9669)
Gulf Cast Jwish Fmly Cmnty Svc.........C....... 727 479-1800
Clearwater (G-1659)
Gulf Coast Treatment Ctr Inc.........E....... 850 863-4160
Fort Walton Beach (G-4776)
Habilitative Svcs N Fla Inc.........D....... 850 482-5391
Marianna (G-8678)
Habilitative Svcs N Fla Inc.........E....... 850 482-5391
Marianna (G-8679)
Habitat For Hmnity Grter Orlnd.........D....... 407 648-4567
Orlando (G-12611)
Harbor House Central Fla Inc.........D....... 407 886-2856
Orlando (G-12617)
Harry Chpin Fd Bnk Sthwest Fla.........D....... 239 334-7007
Fort Myers (G-4433)
Harvest Time International Inc.........D....... 407 328-9900
Sanford (G-15949)
Health Integrated Inc.........C....... 877 267-7577
Tampa (G-17803)
Healthy Mthrs-Hlthy Bbies Clti.........E....... 954 765-0550
Lauderhill (G-8199)

S I C

Healthy Start Cltion Mm-Dade I ....E 305 541-0210 Miami *(G-9691)*	**Lehigh Acres NH LLC** ....D 239 369-2194 Lehigh Acres *(G-8286)*	**New Heights Northeast Fla Inc** ....D 904 396-1462 Jacksonville *(G-6538)*
Heart Florida United Way Inc ....D 407 835-0900 Orlando *(G-12632)*	**Life Concepts Inc** ....D 407 218-4300 Orlando *(G-12765)*	**New Hrzons of Trsure Coast Inc** ....C 772 221-4088 Stuart *(G-16650)*
Help Achild Inc ....D 727 544-3900 Pinellas Park *(G-14521)*	**Life MGT Ctr NW Fla Inc** ....E 850 547-5114 Bonifay *(G-889)*	**Nextgen Alliance Inc** ....E 813 471-0747 Tampa *(G-18081)*
Help Now of Osceola Inc ....E 407 847-3286 Kissimmee *(G-7321)*	**Lighthouse Central Florida Inc** ....E 407 898-2483 Orlando *(G-12768)*	**Northast Fla Area Agcy On Agin** ....E 904 391-6600 Jacksonville *(G-6550)*
Helping Absed Nglcted Dsdvntge ....E 954 522-2911 Fort Lauderdale *(G-3854)*	**Lighthouse of Pinellas Inc** ....E 727 544-4433 Largo *(G-8131)*	**Northeast FL Comm Action Agenc** ....D 904 398-7472 Jacksonville *(G-6552)*
Henderson Behavioral Hlth Inc ....E 954 888-7999 Davie *(G-2488)*	**Little Hvana Actvties Ntrtn CT** ....D 305 858-0887 Miami *(G-9876)*	**Northwest Sstnble Lving Cncpts** ....C 800 760-5894 Orlando *(G-12918)*
Highlnds Cnty Gnlgical Soc Inc ....E 863 471-2734 Sebring *(G-16401)*	**Little Hvana Actvties Ntrtn CT** ....D 305 532-4377 Miami Beach *(G-10607)*	**NW FL Comp Svcs For Children** ....D 850 474-3696 Pensacola *(G-14391)*
His House Inc ....B 305 430-0085 Miami Gardens *(G-10686)*	**Little Steps Rhblttion Clnic I** ....D 954 801-2530 Pembroke Pines *(G-14163)*	**Oic of Broward County Inc** ....D 954 563-3535 Fort Lauderdale *(G-4025)*
Home Instead Senior Care ....E 904 215-8520 Orange Park *(G-11996)*	**Long & Associates** ....E 904 296-9770 Jacksonville *(G-6446)*	**Operation Par Inc** ....E 727 545-7564 Pinellas Park *(G-14530)*
Homeless Emergency Project Inc ....D 727 442-9041 Clearwater *(G-1669)*	**Lutheran Scial Svcs Nrthast FL** ....D 904 448-5995 Jacksonville *(G-6452)*	**Osceola Cnty Cncil On Aging In** ....C 407 846-8532 Kissimmee *(G-7366)*
Hope Womens Center ....E 954 452-9459 Davie *(G-2491)*	**Lutheran Services Florida Inc** ....D 813 868-4438 Tampa *(G-17967)*	**Our Kids Miami-Dade/Monroe Inc** ....D 305 455-6000 Miami *(G-10083)*
Housing Partnership Inc ....D 561 841-3500 Riviera Beach *(G-15299)*	**Lutheran Services Florida Inc** ....D 941 358-6330 Sarasota *(G-16224)*	**Palms West Hospital Ltd Partnr** ....D 561 798-4900 Loxahatchee *(G-8426)*
Hps Hlping People Succeed Inc ....D 772 320-0770 Jensen Beach *(G-7016)*	**Lutheran Services Florida Inc** ....D 850 453-2772 Pensacola *(G-14351)*	**Papa Inc** ....B 800 348-7951 Miami *(G-10093)*
Hubbard House Inc ....E 904 400-6333 Jacksonville *(G-6304)*	**Luthern Ministrey of Florida** ....E 850 457-1090 Pensacola *(G-14352)*	**Parc Inc** ....E 727 345-9111 Saint Petersburg *(G-15790)*
Human Development Center Inc ....E 813 623-3370 Seffner *(G-16426)*	**Madonna Villa Inc** ....E 561 842-2406 West Palm Beach *(G-19246)*	**Parent To Parent Miami Inc** ....E 305 271-9797 Miami *(G-10096)*
IM Slzbcher Ctr For Hmless I ....E 904 359-0457 Jacksonville *(G-6310)*	**Madonna Villa Inc** ....E 772 770-2900 Vero Beach *(G-18890)*	**Parent-Child Center Inc** ....E 561 841-3500 Riviera Beach *(G-15311)*
Impower Inc ....C 407 215-0095 Longwood *(G-8366)*	**Mae Volen Senior Center Inc** ....D 561 395-8920 Boca Raton *(G-682)*	**Patriot Response Group LLC** ....E 772 794-8010 Vero Beach *(G-18904)*
Incharge Debt Solutions ....D 407 291-7770 Orlando *(G-12678)*	**Manatee Childrens Services Inc** ....E 941 345-1200 Bradenton *(G-1132)*	**Personal Enrchment Thrugh Mnta** ....B 727 545-6477 Pinellas Park *(G-14531)*
Incharge Institute America Inc ....C 407 291-7770 Orlando *(G-12679)*	**Manatee Cnty Fmly Yung MNS CHR** ....B 941 792-7484 Bradenton *(G-1133)*	**Persons With Dsblties Fla Agcy** ....C 850 488-4877 Tallahassee *(G-17068)*
Island Doctors ....D 904 794-2711 Saint Augustine *(G-15456)*	**Mandel Jwish Cmnty Ctr of Palm** ....E 561 712-5200 Palm Beach Gardens *(G-13751)*	**Php-Fern Park LLC** ....E 407 331-7231 Fern Park *(G-3515)*
J B Coxwell Contracting Inc ....C 904 786-1120 Jacksonville *(G-6336)*	**Mandel Jwish Cmnty Ctr of Palm** ....E 561 740-9000 Boynton Beach *(G-1010)*	**Place of Hope Inc** ....E 561 775-7195 West Palm Beach *(G-19327)*
Jack Lee Rsen Jwish Cmnty Ctr ....D 407 387-5330 Orlando *(G-12696)*	**Marion Senior Services Inc** ....D 352 620-3501 Ocala *(G-11726)*	**Planned Parenthood Ne FL Inc** ....E 904 249-2378 Jacksonville *(G-6604)*
Jcc Charitable Project Inc ....D 813 264-9000 Tampa *(G-17892)*	**Meals On Wheels Etc Inc** ....E 407 333-8877 Sanford *(G-15964)*	**Pride Integrated Services** ....E 561 684-2370 West Palm Beach *(G-19331)*
Jewish Adption Fster Care Opto ....D 954 749-7230 Sunrise *(G-16792)*	**Meals On Whels Plus Mnatee Inc** ....D 941 747-4655 Bradenton *(G-1144)*	**Prison Rhblttive Inds Dvrsfd E** ....D 813 324-8700 Brandon *(G-1250)*
Jewish Cmnty Ctr Grter Orlndo ....E 407 869-8865 Orlando *(G-12705)*	**Menorah Manor Inc** ....C 727 345-2775 Saint Petersburg *(G-15761)*	**Probation-Core Program** ....D 772 465-9204 Fort Pierce *(G-4731)*
Jewish Cmnty Ctr Grter Orlndo ....D 407 645-5933 Maitland *(G-8546)*	**Mental Health Care Inc** ....D 813 272-2244 Tampa *(G-18025)*	**Psychological Affiliates Inc** ....E 407 740-6838 Winter Park *(G-19764)*
Jewish Cmnty Ctr of Tampa Inc ....D 813 264-9000 Tampa *(G-17894)*	**Metropolitan Charities Inc** ....E 727 321-3854 Saint Petersburg *(G-15765)*	**Psychological Associates PA** ....E 850 432-1480 Pensacola *(G-14417)*
Jewish Cmnty Ctrs S Brward Inc ....C 954 434-0499 Davie *(G-2493)*	**Metropolitan Ministries Inc** ....E 813 209-1000 Tampa *(G-18031)*	**Purpose Bilt Fmlies Fndtion In** ....E 954 554-3306 Fort Lauderdale *(G-4067)*
Jewish Cmnty Svcs S Fla Inc ....D 305 403-6500 North Miami *(G-11498)*	**Miami Bch Jewish Cmnty Ctr Inc** ....C 305 534-3206 Miami Beach *(G-10619)*	**Rebuilt Meals LLC** ....E 813 775-7104 Tampa *(G-18204)*
Jewish Community Svc of S Fla ....D 305 576-6550 North Miami *(G-11499)*	**Miami Brdge Yuth Fmly Svcs Inc** ....D 305 635-8953 Miami *(G-9957)*	**Reedy Creek Improvement Dst** ....D 407 939-3230 Lake Buena Vista *(G-7472)*
Jewish Community Svc of S Fla ....D 305 933-9820 Miami *(G-9793)*	**Miami Crbral Plsy Rsdntial Svc** ....D 305 408-4309 Miami *(G-9966)*	**Rehablttion Ctr For Chldren Ad** ....D 561 655-7266 Palm Beach *(G-13667)*
Jewish Community Svc of S Fla ....E 305 670-1911 South Miami *(G-16506)*	**Miami Crbral Plsy Rsdntial Svc** ....D 305 274-5014 Miami *(G-9967)*	**Rehablttion Ctr of St Ptrsburg** ....C 727 822-1871 Saint Petersburg *(G-15827)*
Jewish Family & Cmnty Svcs Inc ....D 904 448-1933 Jacksonville *(G-6385)*	**Miami Crbral Plsy Rsdntial Svc** ....D 305 220-9599 Miami *(G-9968)*	**Renaissance Inst of Palm Bch** ....E 561 241-7977 Boca Raton *(G-769)*
Jewish Fmly Chld Svc of Sncast ....E 941 366-2224 Sarasota *(G-16204)*	**Miami-Dade Cnty Pub Schols-158** ....C 305 443-4871 Coral Gables *(G-2148)*	**Renaissnce Bhvral Hlth Systems** ....E 904 996-0194 Jacksonville *(G-6655)*
Johns Hpkins All Chld Hosp Inc ....E 941 927-8805 Sarasota *(G-16206)*	**Mid Florida Community Svcs Inc** ....E 352 799-5177 Brooksville *(G-1302)*	**Rocky Creek Rtrement Prpts Inc** ....C 813 884-3388 Tampa *(G-18233)*
Junior Achvment of Palm Bches ....E 561 242-9468 West Palm Beach *(G-19223)*	**Mid Florida Community Svcs Inc** ....D 352 527-3809 Lecanto *(G-8222)*	**Rodriguez Chi Chi Yuth Fndtion** ....E 727 723-0516 Clearwater *(G-1777)*
Jupiter Medical Center Inc ....C 561 745-5775 Jupiter *(G-7103)*	**Mid Florida Community Svcs Inc** ....D 352 326-3540 Leesburg *(G-8262)*	**Ronald McDnald Hse Chrties of** ....E 407 206-0957 Orlando *(G-13124)*
Juvenile Wlfare Bd Pnllas Cnty ....D 727 453-5600 Clearwater *(G-1691)*	**Mid-Flrida Area Agcy On Aging** ....E 352 378-6649 Gainesville *(G-4945)*	**Safe Children Coalition Inc** ....E 941 371-4799 Sarasota *(G-16288)*
Jv Multiservice Plumbing Corp ....D 305 509-0328 Fort Lauderdale *(G-3914)*	**Middle Flint Area Cncil On Agi** ....E 850 520-4199 Defuniak Springs *(G-2838)*	**Safe Children Coalition Inc** ....B 941 955-8194 Sarasota *(G-16290)*
Kids Central Inc ....E 352 873-6332 Wildwood *(G-19498)*	**Mosaic** ....E 863 491-1003 Arcadia *(G-231)*	**Safe PI & Rape Crisis Ctr Inc** ....E 941 365-1976 Sarasota *(G-16291)*
Kids In Distress Inc ....D 954 390-7654 Wilton Manors *(G-19527)*	**Ms HUD Dixie LLC** ....D 321 723-1321 Melbourne *(G-8944)*	**Safespace Inc** ....E 772 223-2399 Stuart *(G-16664)*
Kids In Dstress Foundation Inc ....B 954 390-7654 Wilton Manors *(G-19528)*	**Naples Community Hospital Inc** ....B 239 436-6770 Naples *(G-11226)*	**Safety Shlter St Jhns Cnty Inc** ....D 904 808-8544 Saint Augustine *(G-15488)*
Lake Wales Care Center Inc ....E 863 676-6678 Lake Wales *(G-7688)*	**Nassau County Council On Aging** ....E 904 845-3331 Fernandina Beach *(G-3538)*	**Salvation Army** ....E 904 356-8641 Jacksonville *(G-6690)*
Le Jardin Community Center Inc ....E 305 248-7113 Homestead *(G-5588)*	**National Mentor Holdings Inc** ....B 561 752-8824 Boynton Beach *(G-1020)*	**Salvation Army** ....E 352 376-1743 Gainesville *(G-4991)*
Learning Empowered Inc ....E 727 442-6881 Saint Petersburg *(G-15744)*	**Neighborhood Ctr W Volusia Inc** ....D 386 734-8120 Deland *(G-2875)*	**Samuel M Hlene Sref Jwish Cmnt** ....D 954 792-6700 Plantation *(G-14703)*

Sea Crest Health Care MGT LLC ....D 352 331-3470
  Gainesville **(G-4993)**
Sea Crest Health Care MGT LLC ....C 352 597-5100
  Brooksville **(G-1309)**
Sea Crest Health Care MGT LLC ....D 850 863-9494
  Fort Walton Beach **(G-4803)**
Sea Crest Health Care MGT LLC ....C 954 981-6300
  Hollywood **(G-5513)**
Second Hrvest Fd Bnk Cntl Fla ....D 407 295-1066
  Orlando **(G-13181)**
Seminole Community Mental Heal ......E 407 323-2036
  Fern Park **(G-3516)**
Senior Connection Center Inc ....E 813 740-3888
  Tampa **(G-18267)**
Senior Friendship Centers Inc ....D 941 955-2122
  Sarasota **(G-16315)**
Senior Lifestyle Corporation..........E 813 251-6333
  Tampa **(G-18269)**
Senior Resource Assn Inc ....C 772 569-0760
  Vero Beach **(G-18918)**
Seniorbridge Family ....D 305 529-0224
  Coral Gables **(G-2184)**
Seniors First Inc ....D 407 292-0177
  Orlando **(G-13187)**
Seniors First Inc ....D 863 534-5320
  Bartow **(G-338)**
Sequel Academy Holdings LLC..........E 515 438-3494
  Pinellas Park **(G-14535)**
Serving Chldren Rching Fmlies..........E 321 236-1540
  Kissimmee **(G-7384)**
Shelter For Absed Wmen Chldren ....D 239 775-3862
  Immokalee **(G-5661)**
Smith Community Mental Health ....E 954 321-2296
  Plantation **(G-14708)**
SOS Childrens Village Fla Inc ....E 954 420-5030
  Coconut Creek **(G-2004)**
South Cnty Cmmunities Cert Inc..........D 813 458-9874
  Sun City Center **(G-16706)**
South Miami Hospital Inc ....A 786 662-5080
  South Miami **(G-16516)**
Southern Baptist Hosp Fla Inc..........B 904 202-2000
  Jacksonville **(G-6759)**
Soverign Halthcare Palm Cy LLC..........D 772 288-0060
  Palm City **(G-13802)**
St Jhns Cnty Cncil On Aging I ....C 904 209-3700
  Saint Augustine **(G-15498)**
St Jhns Cnty Wlfare Fderation ....C 904 829-6514
  Saint Augustine **(G-15499)**
Suncoast Pace Inc ....B 727 586-4432
  Clearwater **(G-1805)**
Sundari Foundation Inc ....E 305 576-4780
  Miami **(G-10342)**
Sunrise Childrens Services Inc ....E 305 273-3013
  Miami **(G-10343)**
Sunrise Community Inc..........C 813 830-7823
  Tampa **(G-18345)**
Sunrise Community Inc..........C 727 576-0492
  Saint Petersburg **(G-15866)**
Sunrise Community Inc..........B 305 275-3365
  Miami **(G-10345)**
Sunrise Northeast Inc..........C 305 596-9040
  Miami **(G-10347)**
Sunshine Babysitting Inc..........D 888 609-8979
  Maitland **(G-8584)**
Tampa Hillsboro County Lib Sys..........E 813 273-3652
  Tampa **(G-18383)**
Tampa Jcc/Federation Inc ....E 813 264-9000
  Tampa **(G-18390)**
Tampa Lighthouse For Blind Inc ....E 813 251-2407
  Tampa **(G-18391)**
Tampa Metropolitan Area YMCA..........C 813 684-1371
  Valrico **(G-18759)**
Tampa Mtro Area Yung MNS Chrst..........C 813 866-9622
  Tampa **(G-18395)**
Tampa Mtro Area Yung MNS Chrst..........D 813 224-9622
  Tampa **(G-18396)**
Tampa Mtro Area Yung MNS Chrst..........C 352 521-0484
  Dade City **(G-2397)**
Tampa Mtro Area Yung MNS Chrst..........E 813 222-1334
  Tampa **(G-18397)**
Tampa Mtro Area Yung MNS Chrst..........D 813 229-9622
  Tampa **(G-18399)**
Tampa Mtro Area Yung MNS Chrst..........D 813 780-9622
  Zephyrhills **(G-19852)**
Transition House Inc..........D 407 892-5700
  Jacksonville **(G-6873)**
Truecore Bhvoral Solutions LLC ....D 863 537-8986
  Bartow **(G-343)**
Truecore Bhvoral Solutions LLC ....D 239 210-0940
  Fort Myers **(G-4631)**

Twloha Inc..........E 321 499-3901
  Melbourne **(G-8996)**
Tykes and Teens Inc ....E 772 220-3439
  Palm City **(G-13808)**
U Empower Incorporated ....D 786 318-2337
  Miami **(G-10425)**
United Crbral Plsy Assn Mami I ....D 305 325-1080
  Miami **(G-10436)**
United Crbral Plsy Cntl Fla In ....E 407 852-3303
  Orlando **(G-13333)**
United Crbral Plsy of Srsota M ....E 941 957-3599
  Sarasota **(G-16352)**
United Crbral Plsy of Tllhssee ....E 850 878-0892
  Tallahassee **(G-17162)**
United Way Brevard County Inc ....E 321 631-2740
  Rockledge **(G-15378)**
United Way Miami Inc ....D 305 646-7000
  Miami **(G-10442)**
United Way Northeast Fla Inc ....D 904 390-3210
  Jacksonville **(G-6889)**
United Way Palm Beach Cnty Inc ....E 561 375-6600
  West Palm Beach **(G-19400)**
United Way Suncoast Inc ....E 813 274-0900
  Tampa **(G-18464)**
Unity Behavioral Health LLC..........E 561 815-2649
  North Palm Beach **(G-11559)**
University Area Cmnty Dev Corp ....D 813 558-5212
  Tampa **(G-18468)**
Urban Jacksonville Inc ....C 904 807-1203
  Jacksonville **(G-6896)**
Urban Leag of Grater Miami Inc..........D 305 696-4450
  Miami **(G-10450)**
Urban League Broward Cnty Inc ....D 954 584-0777
  Fort Lauderdale **(G-4202)**
Vitacare Prescription Svcs Inc ....B 800 350-3819
  Boca Raton **(G-866)**
Wakulla Snior Citizens Council ....E 850 926-7146
  Crawfordville **(G-2306)**
Washington County School Dst ....E 863 763-2174
  Okeechobee **(G-11885)**
Watercrest Group LLC..........D 772 766-0206
  Vero Beach **(G-18947)**
Watson Clinic Foundation Inc ....E 863 680-7700
  Lakeland **(G-7998)**
Wegmann Usa Inc ....E 407 456-0405
  Lake Mary **(G-7653)**
Wellington Group LLC..........D 850 864-4600
  Fort Walton Beach **(G-4810)**
Wellington Retreat Inc ....E 561 296-5288
  Lantana **(G-8071)**
Witt OBriens LLC ....E 954 523-2200
  Fort Lauderdale **(G-4229)**
Women In Dstress Brward Cnty I ....E 954 760-9800
  Fort Lauderdale **(G-4230)**
Women In Dstress Brward Cnty I ....D 954 760-9800
  Deerfield Beach **(G-2820)**
Womens Center Jacksonville Inc ....D 904 722-3000
  Jacksonville **(G-6939)**
YMCA of Collier County Inc ....D 239 597-3148
  Naples **(G-11349)**
YMCA of Palm Beachs ....E 561 967-3573
  Palm Springs **(G-13901)**
YMCA of Treasure Coast ....E 772 221-9622
  Stuart **(G-16683)**
YMCA Southwest Florida Inc ....D 941 475-1234
  Englewood **(G-3442)**
Young MNS Christn Assn NW Fla..........E 850 432-8327
  Pensacola **(G-14479)**
Young MNS Chrstn Assn of Flrda..........C 904 355-1436
  Jacksonville **(G-6957)**
Young MNS Chrstn Assn of Flrda..........D 904 259-0898
  Macclenny **(G-8480)**
Young MNS Chrstn Assn of Flrda..........C 904 471-9622
  Saint Augustine **(G-15515)**
Young MNS Chrstn Assn of Flrda..........C 904 464-3901
  Jacksonville **(G-6960)**
Young MNS Chrstn Assn of Flrda..........C 904 296-3220
  Fernandina Beach **(G-3546)**
Young MNS Chrstn Assn of Mrtin..........C 772 286-4444
  Stuart **(G-16684)**
Young MNS Chrstn Assn of Sncas........D 312 932-1200
  Clearwater **(G-1844)**
Young MNS Chrstn Assn of Sncas........C 727 394-9622
  Seminole **(G-16465)**
Young MNS Chrstn Assn of Sncas........D 727 787-9622
  Palm Harbor **(G-13887)**
Young MNS Chrstn Assn of Sncas........C 352 688-9622
  Spring Hill **(G-16556)**
Young MNS Chrstn Assn of Sncas........D 727 461-9622
  Clearwater **(G-1845)**

Young MNS Chrstn Assn of Sncas........D 727 772-9622
  Palm Harbor **(G-13888)**
Young MNS Chrstn Assn of Sncas........D 727 844-0332
  New Port Richey **(G-11411)**
Young MNS Chrstn Assn S Fla In ....E 305 643-2626
  Miami **(G-10524)**
Young MNS Chrstn Assn S Fla In ....D 305 635-9622
  Miami **(G-10525)**
Young MNS Chrstn Assn S Fla In ....E 305 248-5189
  Homestead **(G-5613)**
Youth & Fmly Alternatives Inc ....E 727 835-4166
  New Port Richey **(G-11412)**
Youth & Fmly Alternatives Inc ....C 863 533-6832
  Bartow **(G-344)**
▲ Youth Co-Op Inc ....E 305 643-6730
  Miami **(G-10526)**
Youth Crisis Center Inc ....D 904 720-0002
  Jacksonville **(G-6961)**
Youth Villages Inc ....E 863 513-1780
  Lakeland **(G-8013)**

8331 Job Training & Vocational Rehabilitation Svcs

9line LLC..........D 813 422-4616
  Tampa **(G-17216)**
A & Associates Inc ....E 561 533-5303
  West Palm Beach **(G-19018)**
ARC Broward Inc ....C 954 746-9400
  Sunrise **(G-16737)**
ARC of Alachua County Inc ....E 352 334-4060
  Gainesville **(G-4838)**
Archways Inc..........C 954 763-2030
  Fort Lauderdale **(G-3613)**
▼ Boeing US Trng Ad Flgt Svcs LL......B 786 265-4741
  Virginia Gardens **(G-18953)**
Boeing US Trning Flght Svcs LL ....A 786 265-4702
  Virginia Gardens **(G-18954)**
Brevard Achievement Center Inc ....B 321 632-8610
  Rockledge **(G-15335)**
Careersource Broward ....D 954 202-3830
  Fort Lauderdale **(G-3669)**
Challenge Entps N Fla Inc..........B 904 284-9859
  Green Cove Springs **(G-5048)**
Dynetech Corporation ....E 407 206-6500
  Maitland **(G-8526)**
Early Education and Care Inc ....E 850 818-9003
  Panama City **(G-13992)**
Easter Seals South Florida Inc ....B 305 325-0470
  Miami **(G-9495)**
Florida Lons Cnklin Ctrs For B ....E 386 256-4787
  Daytona Beach **(G-2596)**
Goodwill Cntl Southern Ind Inc ....E 850 877-6840
  Tallahassee **(G-16990)**
Goodwill Inds Broward Cnty Inc..........E 954 486-1600
  Fort Lauderdale **(G-3826)**
Goodwill Inds Centl Fla Inc..........C 407 857-0659
  Orlando **(G-12583)**
Goodwill Indstres-Big Bend Inc..........D 850 576-7145
  Tallahassee **(G-16991)**
Goodwill Industries N Fla Inc..........E 904 384-1361
  Jacksonville **(G-6235)**
Goodwill Industries S Fla Inc..........C 954 316-9484
  Lauderhill **(G-8198)**
Goodwill Industries S Fla Inc..........C 305 940-3252
  Miami **(G-9650)**
Goodwill Industries S Fla Inc..........C 305 248-0063
  Homestead **(G-5576)**
Gulfstream Goodwill Inds Inc ....C 561 848-7200
  Mangonia Park **(G-8608)**
Habilition Ctr For Hndcpped In ....E 561 483-4200
  Boca Raton **(G-614)**
HBA Corporation..........C 954 597-3311
  Tamarac **(G-17192)**
Hii Mission ....D 407 249-7200
  Orlando **(G-12642)**
Insite Managed Solutions LLC..........E 239 234-2700
  Cape Coral **(G-1402)**
Jewish Cmnty Svcs S Fla Inc..........B 305 899-1587
  Miami **(G-9792)**
Junior Achvement Centl Fla Inc ....E 407 898-2121
  Orlando **(G-12715)**
Kratos Training Solutions ....E 407 384-5660
  Orlando **(G-12740)**
Larc Inc ....D 239 334-6285
  Fort Myers **(G-4470)**
Life Concepts Inc..........E 407 218-4300
  Orlando **(G-12767)**
Logistic Services Intl Inc..........B 904 771-2100
  Jacksonville **(G-6445)**

Louise Grham Rgnration Ctr Inc ....E 727 327-9444
Saint Petersburg (G-15750)

Lunsford Air Consulting Inc ....E 386 586-6098
Palm Coast (G-13834)

Martin County School District ....E 772 597-3848
Indiantown (G-5680)

Omnia Group Inc ....D 813 254-9449
Tampa (G-18099)

▲ Palm Bch Habilitation Ctr Inc ....D 561 965-8500
Lake Worth (G-7742)

Prison Rhblttive Inds Dvrsfd E ....D 813 324-8700
Brandon (G-1250)

Public Hlth Tr Miami Dade Cnty ....A 305 585-6081
Miami (G-10162)

Purpose Bilt Fmlies Fndtion In ....E 954 554-3306
Fort Lauderdale (G-4067)

Right 2 Work Corporation ....E 904 232-6300
Jacksonville (G-6601)

Seagull Inds For Disabled Inc ....D 561 842-5814
Riviera Beach (G-15318)

Ser-Jobs For Progress Inc ....E 305 871-2820
Miami (G-10262)

SMA Healthcare Inc ....D 386 236-3200
Daytona Beach (G-2664)

Suncoast Workforce Board Inc ....E 941 358-4080
Bradenton (G-1185)

Suncoast Workforce Board Inc ....D 941 747-2355
Bradenton (G-1186)

Sunrise Childrens Services Inc ....E 305 273-3013
Miami (G-10343)

Sunrise Cmnty Nrtheast Fla Inc ....E 305 596-9040
Miami (G-10344)

Sunrise Community Inc ....B 305 275-3365
Miami (G-10345)

Victor 12 Inc ....D 352 843-7157
Winter Park (G-19784)

Workforce Escarosa Inc ....E 850 607-8752
Pensacola (G-14477)

Workfrce Dev Bd Flgler Vlsia C ....D 386 323-7074
Daytona Beach (G-2691)

8351 Child Day Care Svcs

All Aboard Day Care Inc ....D 239 574-5220
Cape Coral (G-1373)

Angels Aloha Childrens Ctr Inc ....E 239 461-5437
Cape Coral (G-1375)

Angels Guarding Inc ....E 954 778-5700
Deerfield Beach (G-2708)

Apopka Child Dev Ctr Inc ....E 407 889-3026
Apopka (G-153)

Appl LLC ....E 754 333-0789
Miramar (G-10838)

Army & Air Force Exchange Svc ....D 850 882-3861
Eglin A F B (G-3417)

Arr Investments Inc ....B 954 474-0750
Plantation (G-14603)

Arr Investments Inc ....C 954 432-0311
Pembroke Pines (G-14132)

Association For Retarded Citiz ....E 561 842-3213
Riviera Beach (G-15280)

Atlantis Academy Inc ....E 305 271-9771
Miami (G-9189)

Ayuda ....E 305 865-3207
Miami Beach (G-10552)

Bartram Academy Inc ....E 904 217-7630
Saint Johns (G-15543)

Bay District Schools ....E 850 767-5500
Panama City (G-13964)

Beach United Methodist Ch Inc ....E 904 249-2343
Jacksonville Beach (G-6978)

Beacon Hill Center Inc ....D 305 621-3604
Opa Locka (G-11942)

Bell Shals Bptst Ch Brndon Inc ....C 813 689-4229
Brandon (G-1215)

Biltmore School ....E 305 266-4666
Miami (G-9256)

Brentwood School Inc ....E 352 373-3222
Gainesville (G-4848)

Bridges Montessori School ....E 772 221-9490
Stuart (G-16595)

Broward Childrens Center Inc ....C 954 783-1267
Pompano Beach (G-14758)

Broward County Public Schools ....E 754 321-1400
Lauderhill (G-8189)

Calvary Assmbly of God Orlndo ....D 407 644-1199
Winter Park (G-19693)

Cambridge Academy Inc ....E 954 217-8566
Weston (G-19446)

Cambridge Schools ....E 561 791-0013
West Palm Beach (G-19071)

Candyland Boutique LLC ....E 305 979-1581
Sunny Isles Beach (G-16713)

Care 4 Kids Daycare Inc ....E 352 483-8300
Davenport (G-2437)

Center For Erly Chldhood Edcat ....E 941 753-4987
Bradenton (G-1075)

Center For Fmly Child Enrchmen ....E 305 620-6919
Miami Gardens (G-10680)

Central Fla YMCA Chldcare Svcs ....E 407 896-9220
Orlando (G-12273)

Central Fla Yung MNS Chrstn As ....C 407 679-9622
Winter Park (G-19698)

Central Fla Yung MNS Chrstn As ....C 321 433-7770
Cocoa (G-1922)

Central Fla Yung MNS Chrstn As ....C 407 847-7413
Kissimmee (G-7281)

Central Fla Yung MNS Chrstn As ....C 352 343-1144
Tavares (G-18601)

Central Fla Yung MNS Chrstn As ....C 407 644-3606
Winter Park (G-19699)

Champions For Children Inc ....E 813 673-4646
Tampa (G-17455)

Chappell ....E 904 646-2225
Jacksonville (G-5937)

Chappell Schools LLC ....E 904 739-1279
Jacksonville (G-5938)

Child Care Assn Brvard Cnty In ....E 321 634-3500
Cocoa (G-1924)

Child Care Southwest Fla Inc ....C 239 278-1002
Fort Myers (G-4308)

Child Dscvry Ctr of Frst Pres ....E 850 433-2463
Pensacola (G-14258)

Childerns Nest ....E 813 949-1494
Lutz (G-8434)

Childhood Development Svcs Inc ....C 352 629-0055
Ocala (G-11659)

Children of America Inc ....E 561 999-0710
Delray Beach (G-2927)

Childrens Care Campus Inc ....E 407 513-3000
Orlando (G-12297)

Childrens Choice Lrng Ctrs Inc ....D 813 844-2273
Tampa (G-17467)

Childrens Hse of The Windsors ....D 941 462-1349
Sarasota (G-16028)

Christ Epscpal Ch Pnte Vdra Bc ....E 904 285-6127
Ponte Vedra Beach (G-14979)

Christian Hritg Acdemy of Jcks ....E 904 733-4722
Jacksonville (G-5947)

Cinderella Nursery Inc ....E 305 885-8556
Hialeah (G-5236)

Coastline Associates Inc ....E 904 733-5797
Jacksonville (G-5973)

Collier Health Services Inc ....E 239 657-6363
Immokalee (G-5652)

Community Action Prgram Cmmtte ....C 850 438-4003
Pensacola (G-14264)

Community Baptist Church Inc ....E 941 756-8748
Bradenton (G-1084)

Congrgtion Bnai Israel Boca Rt ....D 561 241-8118
Boca Raton (G-526)

Creative Child Learning Center ....E 954 452-3346
Davie (G-2471)

Creative Insprtion Jrney Schl ....D 407 637-2711
Winter Springs (G-19801)

Creative World School Inc ....E 239 947-6177
Bonita Springs (G-906)

David Lwrnce Mntal Hlth Ctr In ....D 239 353-4144
Naples (G-11090)

Deermeadows Baptist Church Inc ....D 904 642-2200
Jacksonville (G-6054)

Dick Hwser Ctr For Crbral Plsy ....E 850 893-6596
Tallahassee (G-16933)

Diocese St Augustine Inc ....E 904 721-2144
Jacksonville (G-6070)

Dixie School District ....E 352 498-0002
Cross City (G-2338)

Dreamland Academy Corp ....E 312 282-0048
Orlando (G-12440)

Early Education and Care Inc ....E 850 818-9003
Panama City (G-13992)

Early Imprssions Midtown Inc ....E 904 206-4170
Yulee (G-19816)

Early Lrng Cltion Flrdas Hrtla ....E 941 255-1650
Port Charlotte (G-15031)

Early Lrng Cltion Manatee Cnty ....E 941 757-2900
Palmetto (G-13911)

Early Lrng Cltion Mm-Dd/Mnroe ....C 305 646-7220
Coral Gables (G-2098)

Easter Seals South Florida Inc ....B 305 325-0470
Miami (G-9495)

Easter Seals Southwest Fla Inc ....C 941 355-7637
Sarasota (G-16032)

▲ Episcopal Childrens Svcs Inc ....A 904 726-1500
Jacksonville (G-6126)

Equipcare Corp ....D 561 969-1543
Lake Worth (G-7725)

Escambia County School Dst ....E 850 479-7814
Pensacola (G-14297)

Faith Lthran Ch N Palm Bch-Mss ....E 561 848-4737
North Palm Beach (G-11546)

Family Chrstn Assn of Amer Inc ....E 305 685-4881
Miami (G-9543)

First Assmbly of God Inc Ocala ....E 352 351-1913
Ocala (G-11682)

First Baptist Ch of Temple Ter ....D 813 988-1138
Temple Terrace (G-18634)

First Baptist Ch W Hollywood ....E 954 322-4332
Hollywood (G-5434)

First Baptist Ch Windermere ....E 407 876-2234
Windermere (G-19540)

First Baptst Ch W Palm Bch Fla ....D 561 650-7400
West Palm Beach (G-19141)

First Presbt Ch Orlando Inc ....D 407 423-3441
Orlando (G-12513)

First United Methodist Church ....E 863 683-9049
Lakeland (G-7866)

First Untd Methdst Ch Brandon ....E 813 689-4161
Brandon (G-1229)

First Untd Mthdst Ch Cral Gble ....D 305 445-2578
Coral Gables (G-2107)

Florence Fller Child Dev Ctrs ....E 561 391-7274
Boca Raton (G-577)

Florence Fller Child Dev Ctrs ....E 561 391-7274
Boca Raton (G-578)

Florida United Methdst Chld HM ....C 386 668-6771
Enterprise (G-3443)

Gingerbread School Inc ....D 727 392-4870
Saint Petersburg (G-15688)

Glades Day School Inc ....D 561 996-4140
Belle Glade (G-358)

Gladeview Baptist Ch Miami Inc ....E 305 551-6143
Miami (G-9632)

Greater Daytona Bch Area YMCA ....D 386 255-8773
Deland (G-2863)

Greater Dytona Bch Area Yung M ....D 386 532-9622
Deltona (G-3039)

Growing Room ....E 239 466-6646
Fort Myers (G-4425)

Gulliver Schools Inc ....D 305 665-3593
Coral Gables (G-2115)

Happy Acres Ranch Inc ....D 904 725-1410
Jacksonville (G-6258)

Happy House Inc ....E 386 752-4736
Lake City (G-7530)

Hatch Partners Inc ....C 561 212-5064
Boca Raton (G-620)

Head Start Child Dev Fmly Svcs ....E 727 547-5979
Largo (G-8114)

Hendrcks Mem Untd Mthdst Ctr I ....E 904 720-0398
Jacksonville (G-6274)

Hershrin Schiff Day Schols Tmr ....D 941 552-2770
Sarasota (G-16183)

Highpoint Academy Inc ....E 305 552-0202
Miami (G-9704)

Hillel Community Day Schl Inc ....C 305 931-2831
Miami (G-9705)

Hispanic Humn Rsrces Cncil Inc ....E 561 434-7005
West Palm Beach (G-19180)

Hobe Sound Child Care Ctr Inc ....E 772 546-5462
Hobe Sound (G-5365)

Honey Bears Daycare Inc ....D 904 786-2128
Jacksonville (G-6295)

Indian Rver Cy Untd Mthdst Ch ....E 321 267-7922
Titusville (G-18688)

Interamerican Community Ch Inc ....E 305 262-0006
Miami (G-9756)

Island Prep LLC ....E 904 471-1100
Saint Augustine (G-15457)

Itsy Bitsy Kids Inc ....E 561 239-2625
Lauderhill (G-8203)

Jack & Jill Childrens Center ....E 954 463-8772
Fort Lauderdale (G-3902)

Jewish Cmnty Ctr Grter Orlndo ....D 407 645-5933
Maitland (G-8546)

Jewish Cmnty Ctrs S Brward Inc ....C 954 434-0499
Davie (G-2493)

Jewish Federation of South ....D 561 852-5009
Boca Raton (G-651)

Kalex Educational Company Inc ....E 305 824-0303
Hialeah (G-5285)

Kidco Creative Learning Inc ....D...... 305 576-6990
Hialeah (G-5286)

Kiddie College of South Miami ....E...... 305 552-6047
Miami (G-9828)

Kids Discovery Intl Inc ....E...... 850 623-4800
Milton (G-10818)

Kindercare Learning Ctrs LLC ....E...... 321 268-3891
Titusville (G-18690)

Kindercare Learning Ctrs LLC ....E...... 813 754-5264
Plant City (G-14566)

Kindercare Learning Ctrs LLC ....E...... 386 252-7193
Daytona Beach (G-2623)

Kinneys Kids Incorporated ....E...... 941 727-9990
Lakewood Ranch (G-8020)

Ksm School III LLC ....E...... 904 992-9002
Jacksonville (G-6410)

Ladybird Coral Springs LLC ....E...... 407 829-8530
Lake Mary (G-7606)

Ladybird Lake Mary LLC ....E...... 407 268-9081
Lake Mary (G-7607)

Ladybird Lake Nona LLC ....E...... 407 273-4331
Orlando (G-12748)

Leaps and Bounds LLC ....E...... 352 748-1242
Wildwood (G-19500)

Learning Centers of America ....E...... 727 392-3123
Seminole (G-16453)

Learning Experience Corp ....E...... 888 865-7775
Deerfield Beach (G-2767)

Levico Group Inc ....E...... 561 964-2800
West Palm Beach (G-19232)

Lincoln-Marti Cmnty Agcy Inc ....D...... 305 643-4888
Miami (G-9873)

Little Flower Catholic School ....D...... 850 456-5218
Pensacola (G-14349)

Little Hvana Actvties Ntrtn CT ....D...... 305 858-0887
Miami (G-9876)

Llirrafo Inc ....D...... 305 264-3232
Miami (G-9878)

Lovaas Center For Autism ....D...... 954 239-8517
Pembroke Pines (G-14165)

Lutz Learning Center Inc ....E...... 813 949-3484
Lutz (G-8445)

McGregor Baptist Church Inc ....C...... 239 936-5015
Fort Myers (G-4506)

Miami-Dade Cnty Pub Schols-158 ....E...... 305 531-0451
Miami Beach (G-10623)

Michal-Ann Rssell Jwish Cmnty ....C...... 305 932-4200
Miami (G-10001)

Mid Florida Community Svcs Inc ....D...... 386 736-1325
Deland (G-2871)

Millenia Kidz Inc ....E...... 508 614-5763
Orlando (G-12867)

Millhopper Montessori School ....D...... 352 375-6773
Gainesville (G-4947)

Monroe County School District ....E...... 305 852-3482
Islamorada (G-5707)

Montessori Schools Pensacola ....E...... 850 469-8138
Pensacola (G-14367)

Montessori World Inc ....D...... 407 239-6024
Orlando (G-12876)

Mount Sinai Med Ctr Fla Inc ....D...... 305 674-2307
Miami (G-10022)

Neptune Baptist Church Inc ....D...... 904 249-2307
Neptune Beach (G-11357)

Netsmart New York Inc ....C...... 888 249-1517
Saint Petersburg (G-15775)

New Heights Northeast Fla Inc ....D...... 904 396-1462
Jacksonville (G-6538)

Nicaea Acdemy Suthwest Fla Inc ....E...... 239 353-9099
Naples (G-11250)

Nobel Education Dynamics ....C...... 954 436-9911
Hollywood (G-5483)

North Lauderdale Eductl Ctrs ....E...... 954 720-9034
North Lauderdale (G-11482)

Oakcrest Day Care Center Inc ....E...... 352 622-8488
Ocala (G-11745)

Oakhurst Child Care Center Inc ....E...... 727 596-3411
Largo (G-8140)

One School of Arts LLC ....E...... 407 774-0168
Longwood (G-8388)

Palm Beach State College ....D...... 561 379-3004
Lake Worth (G-7747)

Pasadena Community Church ....E...... 727 381-2499
Saint Petersburg (G-15791)

Paxen Group Inc ....E...... 321 735-4931
Cocoa (G-1946)

Preschool Vntures of Hollywood ....C...... 954 485-0800
Oakland Park (G-11609)

Primrose School of Oviedo ....E...... 407 359-5200
Chuluota (G-1499)

Professional Learning Center ....D...... 561 487-1230
Boca Raton (G-757)

RClub Child Care Inc ....E...... 727 526-8154
Saint Petersburg (G-15823)

RClub Child Care Inc ....D...... 727 578-5437
Saint Petersburg (G-15824)

RClub Child Care Inc ....E...... 727 535-0387
Clearwater (G-1773)

Redlands Chrstn Mgrant Assn In ....B...... 239 658-3560
Immokalee (G-5659)

Safe Children Coalition Inc ....E...... 941 371-4799
Sarasota (G-16288)

Safe Children Coalition Inc ....D...... 941 955-8194
Sarasota (G-16290)

Sarasota Baptist Church Inc ....E...... 941 922-1449
Sarasota (G-16295)

Scholastic Opportunities Inc ....E...... 850 668-9072
Tallahassee (G-17094)

Second Bptst Ch Rchmond Hts In ....E...... 305 232-0499
Miami (G-10254)

Shining Stars Childcare Inc ....E...... 813 643-7247
Brandon (G-1256)

South Miami Hospital Inc ....A...... 786 662-5080
South Miami (G-16516)

Space Coast Discovery Inc ....D...... 321 729-6858
Melbourne (G-8978)

Speedy Car Wash Inc ....E...... 850 785-9274
Panama City (G-14075)

St Lkes Untd Mthdst Ch At Wnd ....D...... 407 876-4991
Orlando (G-13232)

St Paul Evang Lthran Ch Lklan ....C...... 863 644-7710
Lakeland (G-7976)

Stars of World Inc ....E...... 305 827-0014
Hialeah (G-5325)

Step Up Suncoast Inc ....C...... 941 827-2887
Sarasota (G-16058)

Sumter County School District ....E...... 352 259-2300
Lady Lake (G-7446)

Sun Grove Montessori Schl Inc ....E...... 772 464-5436
Fort Pierce (G-4741)

Sunbelt Health Care Centers ....A...... 407 975-3000
Maitland (G-8583)

Suncoast Cthdral Frst Assmbly ....C...... 727 522-2171
Saint Petersburg (G-15864)

Sunshine Babysitting Inc ....D...... 888 609-8979
Maitland (G-8584)

Tampa Metropolitan Area YMCA ....D...... 813 684-1371
Valrico (G-18759)

Tampa Mtro Area Yung MNS Chrst ....C...... 813 866-9622
Tampa (G-18395)

Tampa Mtro Area Yung MNS Chrst ....D...... 813 224-9622
Tampa (G-18396)

Tampa Mtro Area Yung MNS Chrst ....E...... 352 521-0484
Dade City (G-2397)

Tampa Mtro Area Yung MNS Chrst ....E...... 813 222-1334
Tampa (G-18397)

Tampa Mtro Area Yung MNS Chrst ....D...... 813 229-9622
Tampa (G-18399)

Tampa Mtro Area Yung MNS Chrst ....D...... 813 780-9622
Zephyrhills (G-19852)

Temple Beth Emet Inc ....E...... 954 680-1882
Cooper City (G-2016)

Temple Kol AMI Emanu-El Inc ....E...... 954 472-8700
Plantation (G-14713)

Three Bears House Inc ....D...... 352 332-7783
Gainesville (G-5013)

Three Bears House Inc ....D...... 352 332-9032
Gainesville (G-5014)

Tiny Dancer Incorporated ....E...... 941 504-8330
Sarasota (G-16349)

True School Inc ....D...... 727 447-6385
Clearwater (G-1825)

Turtle River Montessori Inc ....E...... 561 745-1995
Jupiter (G-7149)

United Crbral Plsy Cntl Fla In ....E...... 407 852-3303
Orlando (G-13333)

United Crbral Plsy of Brward P ....D...... 954 584-7178
Fort Lauderdale (G-4193)

Van Dyke United Methdst Ch Inc ....E...... 813 960-1694
Lutz (G-8463)

Victory Baptist Church Inc ....E...... 904 764-7781
Jacksonville (G-6909)

Village Pines School Inc ....E...... 305 235-6621
Miami (G-10473)

Village View Chrstn Acdemy Inc ....E...... 352 307-2100
Summerfield (G-16692)

Wayside Baptist Ch Kendall Inc ....E...... 305 595-6550
Miami (G-10491)

Winter Park Day Nursery Inc ....D...... 407 647-0505
Winter Park (G-19788)

Wiselynn Investment Group LLC ....E...... 407 891-0595
Saint Cloud (G-15539)

Wish Upon A Star Prschool Dyca ....E...... 321 726-1580
Palm Bay (G-13644)

YMCA of Palm Beachs.....................D...... 561 967-3573
Palm Springs (G-13901)

YMCA of Treasure Coast ....E...... 772 221-9622
Stuart (G-16683)

YMCA Southwest Florida Inc ....D...... 941 475-1234
Englewood (G-3442)

Young MNS Christn Assn NW Fla ....E...... 850 432-8327
Pensacola (G-14479)

Young MNS Chrstn Assn of Flrda ....C...... 904 272-4304
Orange Park (G-12026)

Young MNS Chrstn Assn of Flrda ....C...... 904 355-1436
Jacksonville (G-6957)

Young MNS Chrstn Assn of Flrda ....C...... 904 259-0898
Macclenny (G-8480)

Young MNS Chrstn Assn of Flrda ....C...... 904 471-9622
Saint Augustine (G-15515)

Young MNS Chrstn Assn of Flrda ....C...... 904 464-3901
Jacksonville (G-6960)

Young MNS Chrstn Assn of Flrda ....C...... 904 296-3220
Fernandina Beach (G-3546)

Young MNS Chrstn Assn of Flrda ....C...... 904 731-2006
Jacksonville (G-6959)

Young MNS Chrstn Assn of Grter ....D...... 727 895-9622
Saint Petersburg (G-15904)

Young MNS Chrstn Assn of Mrtin ....C...... 772 286-4444
Stuart (G-16684)

Young MNS Chrstn Assn of Sncas ....C...... 312 932-1200
Clearwater (G-1844)

Young MNS Chrstn Assn of Sncas ....C...... 727 394-9622
Seminole (G-16465)

Young MNS Chrstn Assn of Sncas ....D...... 727 787-9622
Palm Harbor (G-13887)

Young MNS Chrstn Assn of Sncas ....C...... 352 688-9622
Spring Hill (G-16556)

Young MNS Chrstn Assn of Sncas ....D...... 727 461-9622
Clearwater (G-1845)

Young MNS Chrstn Assn of Sncas ....D...... 727 772-9622
Palm Harbor (G-13888)

Young MNS Chrstn Assn of Sncas ....D...... 727 844-0332
New Port Richey (G-11411)

Young MNS Chrstn Assn S Fla In ....D...... 305 248-5189
Homestead (G-5612)

Young MNS Chrstn Assn S Fla In ....E...... 305 643-2626
Miami (G-10524)

Young MNS Chrstn Assn S Fla In ....D...... 305 635-9622
Miami (G-10525)

Young MNS Chrstn Assn S Fla In ....E...... 305 248-5189
Homestead (G-5613)

Zion Evangelical Lutheran Ch ....C...... 954 421-3146
Deerfield Beach (G-2824)

8361 Residential Care

2826 Clvland Ave Oprations LLC ....E...... 239 334-1091
Fort Myers (G-4243)

Acts Rtrmnt-Life Cmmnties Inc ....C...... 561 391-6305
Boca Raton (G-400)

Acts Rtrmnt-Life Cmmnties Inc ....B...... 772 562-7400
Vero Beach (G-18829)

AG Holdings Inc ....E...... 954 741-6700
Miami (G-9102)

Allegro Senior Living LLC ....E...... 561 253-8161
Jupiter (G-7047)

Allegro Senior Living LLC ....E...... 904 417-8902
Saint Augustine (G-15423)

Alternative Living Inc ....E...... 850 833-9165
Fort Walton Beach (G-4752)

Alternative Senior Care LLC ....E...... 407 322-2207
Sanford (G-15916)

American Retirement Corp ....D...... 386 677-0782
Ormond Beach (G-13476)

Anchorage Chld HM Bay Cnty Inc ....E...... 850 763-7102
Panama City (G-13954)

Andies Inc ....E...... 954 920-1988
Dania (G-2403)

Arbor Oaks At Greenacres ....D...... 561 432-4700
Greenacres (G-5069)

ARC Jacksonville Inc ....E...... 904 355-0155
Jacksonville (G-5803)

ARC Sunrise of Central Florida ....E...... 352 787-0899
Leesburg (G-8230)

Archways Inc ....C...... 954 763-2030
Fort Lauderdale (G-3613)

Arlington Garden LLC ....E...... 727 541-4239
Pinellas Park (G-14505)

Aspire Health Partners Inc ....C...... 407 291-6335
Orlando (G-12139)

Assisted 2 Live Inc	D	941 629-4417	
North Port (G-11564)			
Association For Retarded Citiz	E	561 842-3213	
Riviera Beach (G-15280)			
Balmoral Asssted Lving Ste LLC	E	863 465-4169	
Lake Placid (G-7664)			
Bay Point Schools Inc	D	305 215-3112	
Cutler Bay (G-2359)			
Baycare Behavioral Health Inc	E	727 519-1200	
Clearwater (G-1536)			
Bef Inc	D	727 445-4700	
Clearwater (G-1543)			
Bella Terra One LLC	E	813 388-2121	
Land O Lakes (G-8043)			
Bethamy Living Ctr Ltd Partnr	C	727 461-6613	
Clearwater (G-1547)			
Better Way of Miami Inc	E	305 779-0650	
Miami (G-9251)			
Boley Centers Inc	D	727 821-4819	
Saint Petersburg (G-15600)			
Boley Centers Inc	E	727 821-4819	
Pinellas Park (G-14507)			
Bon Secours Mercy Health Inc	D	727 563-9733	
Saint Petersburg (G-15602)			
Bridges Btc Inc	C	321 633-1000	
Rockledge (G-15337)			
Brookdale Lake Orienta	E	407 260-2345	
Altamonte Springs (G-32)			
Broward Childrens Center Inc	D	954 943-7336	
Pompano Beach (G-14757)			
Broward Childrens Center Inc	C	954 783-1267	
Pompano Beach (G-14758)			
Cabot Reserve On The Green	E	941 377-3231	
Sarasota (G-16113)			
Camelot Chateau	E	352 629-6077	
Ocala (G-11649)			
Capstone Adpttive Lrng Thrapy C	E	850 432-1596	
Pensacola (G-14244)			
Carlton Manor Inc	D	727 343-3662	
Saint Petersburg (G-15613)			
Carpenters Home Estates Inc	B	863 858-3847	
Lakeland (G-7827)			
Center For DRG Free Living Inc	D	407 245-0010	
Orlando (G-12256)			
Central Florida Communities	D	407 645-3211	
Winter Park (G-19701)			
Century Oaks Serenity LLC	D	321 722-4440	
Melbourne (G-8841)			
Charlee of Dade County Inc	D	305 779-9600	
Miami (G-9356)			
Chatswrth At Wllington Green LL	B	561 795-3360	
Wellington (G-18975)			
Childrens Home Inc	D	813 855-4435	
Tampa (G-17468)			
Childrens Home Society of Fla	D	321 397-3000	
Ocala (G-11660)			
Childrens Home Society of Fla	D	321 397-3000	
Orlando (G-12299)			
Childrens Home Society of Fla	C	305 755-6500	
Miami (G-9363)			
Childrens Home Society of Fla	D	239 334-0222	
Fort Myers (G-4309)			
Childrens Home Society of Fla	C	561 868-4300	
West Palm Beach (G-19084)			
Christian Care Center Inc	D	352 787-2448	
Leesburg (G-8239)			
Christian Home and Bb Schl Inc	D	352 383-9906	
Mount Dora (G-10947)			
City of Boca Raton	C	561 347-8833	
Boca Raton (G-513)			
Clearwater Snf LLC	E	727 210-2600	
Clearwater (G-1576)			
Concept Health Systems Inc	D	305 751-6501	
Miami (G-9400)			
Concordia of Florida Inc	B	813 977-4950	
Tampa (G-17511)			
Covenant House Florida Inc	D	954 561-5559	
Fort Lauderdale (G-3736)			
Covenant Living Florida Inc	C	954 472-2860	
Plantation (G-14625)			
Crosswinds Youth Services Inc	E	321 394-0345	
Cocoa (G-1935)			
Cypress Cove Retirement Cmnty	D	239 415-5100	
Fort Myers (G-4337)			
David Lwrnce Mntal Hlth Ctr In	D	239 455-8500	
Naples (G-11089)			
Devereux Foundation	E	407 671-7060	
Winter Park (G-19712)			
Devereux Foundation	D	407 294-5048	
Orlando (G-12417)			

Diamond Assisted Living Fcilty	E	904 863-3000	
Green Cove Springs (G-5051)			
Douglas Grdns Cmnty Mntal Hlth	D	305 531-5341	
Miami Beach (G-10585)			
Douglas T Jcbson State Vtrans	C	941 613-0919	
Port Charlotte (G-15030)			
Drug Abuse Fndtion Palm Bch CN	C	561 732-0800	
Delray Beach (G-2947)			
Duvall Homes Inc	C	386 734-2874	
Deland (G-2856)			
Eckerd Youth Alternatives Inc	D	727 461-2990	
Brooksville (G-1283)			
Eckerd Youth Alternatives Inc	D	352 799-5621	
Brooksville (G-1284)			
Eckerd Youth Alternatives Inc	D	727 461-2990	
Clearwater (G-1616)			
Eckerd Youth Alternatives Inc	D	863 763-2174	
Okeechobee (G-11866)			
Edgewood Childrens Ranch Inc	E	407 295-2464	
Orlando (G-12453)			
Episcopal Childrens Svcs Inc	D	904 674-6200	
Jacksonville (G-6125)			
▼ Epworth Village Inc	C	786 363-6948	
Hialeah (G-5257)			
Erickson Living Management LLC	B	561 227-2400	
Palm Beach Gardens (G-13725)			
Erickson Living Management LLC	A	561 227-3200	
Palm Beach Gardens (G-13726)			
Fair Havens Center LLC	B	305 887-1565	
Miami Springs (G-10782)			
Fannie E Tylor HM For The Aged	C	904 731-8230	
Jacksonville (G-6148)			
Father Flanagans Boys Home	D	407 366-3667	
Oviedo (G-13549)			
Florida Brookwood Inc	E	727 822-4789	
Saint Petersburg (G-15674)			
Florida School For The Deaf	A	904 827-2356	
Saint Augustine (G-15443)			
Florida Shrffs Yuth Rnches Inc	D	386 842-5501	
Live Oak (G-8311)			
Florida Shrffs Yuth Rnches Inc	E	352 447-2259	
Inglis (G-5684)			
Florida United Methdst Chld HM	C	386 668-6771	
Enterprise (G-3443)			
Fountains At Bayview LLC	E	786 208-5140	
Punta Gorda (G-15205)			
▲ Friends of Ctrus Nture Cast In	C	352 527-2020	
Beverly Hills (G-378)			
Gainesvlle Rhbltttion Nrsing CT	E	352 376-2461	
Gainesville (G-4907)			
Glenridge On Palmer Ranch Inc	B	941 552-5300	
Sarasota (G-16176)			
Global Med Behavioral Hlth Cor	E	863 353-9322	
Davenport (G-2440)			
Grand Villa	E	727 586-0108	
Largo (G-8113)			
Gulf Coast Treatment Ctr Inc	D	850 689-1984	
Crestview (G-2323)			
Gulf Coast Treatment Ctr Inc	E	850 863-4160	
Fort Walton Beach (G-4776)			
Hampton Manor Corporate Office	C	352 387-1830	
Ocala (G-11697)			
Hanna Oaks Retirement Cmnty	E	813 238-3053	
Tampa (G-17788)			
Harbor Retirement Assoc LLC	D	772 778-7727	
Vero Beach (G-18864)			
Harbor Retirement Assoc LLC	D	352 350-5310	
Lady Lake (G-7434)			
Harbor Retirement Assoc LLC	D	904 821-8030	
Jacksonville (G-6259)			
Harbor Retirement Assoc LLC	D	407 984-4530	
Orlando (G-12618)			
Harbor Retirement Assoc LLC	D	850 531-0404	
Havana (G-5194)			
Harbor Retirement Assoc LLC	D	772 492-5002	
Vero Beach (G-18865)			
Harbor Retirement Assoc LLC	D	352 332-4505	
Gainesville (G-4912)			
Harbor Retirement Assoc LLC	D	727 781-8686	
Palm Harbor (G-13865)			
Harbor Retirement Assoc LLC	D	954 255-5557	
Coral Springs (G-2259)			
Harbor Retirement Assoc LLC	D	239 566-8077	
Naples (G-11155)			
Hearthstone Snior Cmmnties Inc	D	863 533-0578	
Bartow (G-320)			
Hibiscus Court	D	321 951-1050	
Melbourne (G-8905)			
Holly Hill Rhf Housing Inc	C	386 226-9000	
Holly Hill (G-5381)			

Human Development Center Inc	E	813 623-3370	
Seffner (G-16426)			
Jacaranda Trace Commercial LLC	D	941 408-2000	
Venice (G-18788)			
Jewish Adpation Fster Care Opto	D	954 749-7230	
Sunrise (G-16792)			
John Knox Vlg Centl Fla Inc	B	386 775-3840	
Orange City (G-11967)			
Lake Region Homes Inc	E	352 315-7500	
Leesburg (G-8252)			
Lake Wales Healthcare LLC	D	863 676-1512	
Lake Wales (G-7689)			
Lakehouse West LLP	D	941 923-7525	
Sarasota (G-16214)			
LArche Jacksonville Inc	E	904 721-5992	
Jacksonville (G-6421)			
LCI II Inc	A	850 892-8045	
Defuniak Springs (G-2835)			
Life Care Community St Johns	C	904 342-0064	
Saint Augustine (G-15463)			
Life Care Ponte Vedra Inc	C	904 273-1700	
Ponte Vedra Beach (G-14987)			
Life Concepts Inc	E	813 623-1908	
Brandon (G-1242)			
Life Concepts Inc	E	813 972-2608	
Tampa (G-17947)			
Lifespace Communities Inc	E	561 454-2000	
Delray Beach (G-2979)			
Lifespace Communities Inc	B	561 272-9600	
Delray Beach (G-2980)			
Lifestream Behavioral Ctr Inc	D	352 360-6575	
Leesburg (G-8259)			
Macdonald Training Center Inc	D	813 870-1300	
Tampa (G-17972)			
Macdonald Training Center Inc	D	813 752-6508	
Plant City (G-14571)			
Mactown Inc	E	561 200-4786	
Boynton Beach (G-1009)			
Mactown Inc	D	305 758-4485	
Miami (G-9890)			
Madonna Villa Inc	E	772 770-2900	
Vero Beach (G-18890)			
Mandic Group Inc	E	904 797-5027	
Saint Augustine (G-15464)			
Marianna Sunland Facility	D	850 482-9484	
Marianna (G-8683)			
Marrinson Group Inc	B	954 566-8353	
Wilton Manors (G-19530)			
Miami Chld Hosp Foundation Inc	E	305 666-2889	
Miami (G-9962)			
Millenium Ventures Ltd	D	352 683-9009	
Spring Hill (G-16543)			
Mink of Lee Cnty Inc DBA Wdlnd	C	239 574-8789	
Cape Coral (G-1415)			
Moorings Park Foundation Inc	B	239 643-9111	
Naples (G-11220)			
Morton Plant Hospital Assn Inc	E	727 462-7600	
Belleair (G-369)			
New Horizons Northwest Fla Inc	D	850 474-0667	
Pensacola (G-14384)			
Nextgen Alliance Inc	E	813 471-0747	
Tampa (G-18081)			
North Oklosa Hlth Care Assoc L	D	850 689-3146	
Crestview (G-2328)			
Northport Retirement Center	E	941 426-9175	
North Port (G-11574)			
Oaks of Clearwater Inc	C	727 445-4700	
Clearwater (G-1742)			
Osprey Lodge LLC	E	352 253-5100	
Tavares (G-18615)			
Palm Cottage Operator LLC	D	321 633-1819	
Rockledge (G-15358)			
Penney Retirement Cmnty Inc	C	904 284-8200	
Penney Farms (G-14206)			
Pensacola Care Incorporated	D	813 971-3490	
Tampa (G-18134)			
Pensacola Care Incorporated	C	850 453-2323	
Pensacola (G-14407)			
Pensacola Care Incorporated	C	850 575-0619	
Tallahassee (G-17067)			
Phoenix House Foundation Inc	E	727 822-7729	
Saint Petersburg (G-15797)			
Presbyterian Retirement	B	850 878-1136	
Tallahassee (G-17075)			
Presbytrian Rtrment Cmmnties I	C	407 841-1310	
Orlando (G-13052)			
Presbytrian Rtrment Cmmnties I	D	407 839-5050	
Orlando (G-13053)			
Presbytrian Rtrment Cmmnties I	D	877 452-2588	
Orlando (G-13054)			

Presbytrian Rtrment Cmmnties I ....B 904 287-7300
Jacksonville *(G-6970)*

Presbytrian Rtrment Cmmnties I ....C 407 647-4083
Winter Park *(G-19763)*

Presbytrian Rtrment Cmmnties I ....C 941 747-1881
Bradenton *(G-1166)*

Presidential Place ....E 954 894-0059
Hollywood *(G-5495)*

Prime Care One LLC ....D 941 484-8801
Venice *(G-18798)*

Pt Richey Alf Inc ....D 727 845-0527
Port Richey *(G-15109)*

RES-Care Inc ....C 352 694-1114
Ocala *(G-11767)*

RES-Care Inc ....C 352 372-0130
Gainesville *(G-4988)*

Residential Crf Inc ....E 850 872-1742
Panama City *(G-14062)*

Residential Crf Inc ....E 850 785-0605
Panama City *(G-14063)*

Ridgecrest Nh LLC ....E 386 469-1235
Deland *(G-2878)*

Sarasota Bay Club LLC ....D 941 366-7667
Sarasota *(G-16296)*

Sarast-Mntee Jwish Hsing Cncil ....C 941 225-8369
Sarasota *(G-16312)*

Sea Crest Health Care MGT LLC ....C 954 981-6300
Hollywood *(G-5513)*

Senior Lifestyle Corporation ....E 941 893-1940
Sarasota *(G-16316)*

Senior Lifestyle Corporation ....E 941 748-1700
Bradenton *(G-1178)*

Senior Living Centers Inc ....D 727 864-5000
Saint Petersburg *(G-15844)*

Senior Lving Prpts Bynton Bch ....B 813 643-6767
Brandon *(G-1255)*

Seniorbrdge Fmly Cmpnies NY In ....D 239 430-8300
Naples *(G-11296)*

Sequelcare of Florida LLC ....D 904 777-0100
Jacksonville *(G-6711)*

Sequelcare of Florida LLC ....D 772 337-8164
Port Saint Lucie *(G-15165)*

Sequelcare of Florida LLC ....D 904 829-8850
Saint Augustine *(G-15491)*

Sequelcare of Florida LLC ....D 561 333-0664
West Palm Beach *(G-19357)*

Sequelcare of Florida LLC ....D 352 872-5152
Gainesville *(G-4996)*

Sheridan House Inc ....D 954 583-1552
Davie *(G-2516)*

Solaris Healthcare Lake Cy LLC ....C 386 758-4777
Lake City *(G-7547)*

Solaris Healthcare Osceola LLC ....D 239 919-1142
Saint Cloud *(G-15534)*

Solaris Hlthcare Ccnut Creek L ....D 239 919-1142
Coconut Creek *(G-2003)*

Solaris Snior Lving Mrritt Isl ....D 321 454-2363
Merritt Island *(G-9047)*

Spring Haven Retirement LLC ....C 863 293-0072
Winter Haven *(G-19663)*

St Mark Village Inc ....B 727 785-2576
Palm Harbor *(G-13882)*

Sugarmill Manor Inc ....D 352 382-2531
Homosassa *(G-5619)*

Summerfeld Rtrment Rsdence Ltd ....E 941 751-7200
Bradenton *(G-1182)*

Summerville Senior Living Inc ....E 352 241-0844
Clermont *(G-1891)*

Sun City Center Associates LP ....B 813 634-3347
Sun City Center *(G-16707)*

Sunnyside Prpts Sarasota Inc ....C 941 371-2729
Sarasota *(G-16339)*

Sunrise Community Inc ....C 954 744-1126
Davie *(G-2526)*

Sunrise Community Inc ....C 863 533-0837
Bartow *(G-340)*

Sunrise Community Inc ....C 239 283-3666
Cape Coral *(G-1427)*

Sunrise Community Inc ....C 850 878-0808
Tallahassee *(G-17122)*

Sunrise Senior Living LLC ....E 561 392-5940
Boca Raton *(G-831)*

Sunrise Senior Living LLC ....D 727 787-1500
Palm Harbor *(G-13883)*

Sunrise Senior Living LLC ....E 800 646-1409
Parkland *(G-14111)*

Sunrise Senior Living LLC ....D 727 381-5411
South Pasadena *(G-16524)*

Sunrise Senior Living LLC ....D 904 332-0774
Jacksonville *(G-6811)*

Sunshine Christian Home Inc ....D 727 934-8052
Holiday *(G-5376)*

Suwannee County School Dst ....D 386 842-5555
Live Oak *(G-8318)*

Terracina Grand ....E 239 455-1459
Naples *(G-11318)*

Tri-County Human Services Inc ....D 863 709-9392
Bartow *(G-341)*

Tri-County Human Services Inc ....E 863 299-7003
Winter Haven *(G-19667)*

Tri-County Human Services Inc ....E 863 533-4139
Bartow *(G-342)*

Twin Oaks Juvenile Dev Inc ....E 850 643-1090
Tallahassee *(G-17160)*

Villages Inc ....E 352 753-6655
The Villages *(G-18666)*

Visionquest Nonprofit Corp ....C 863 824-0921
Okeechobee *(G-11881)*

Volusia Flagler Family ....E 386 736-6000
Deland *(G-2891)*

Waterman Communities Inc ....E 352 383-0051
Mount Dora *(G-10965)*

Waterman Communities Inc ....E 352 383-0051
Mount Dora *(G-10966)*

▼ Willough Healthcare Inc ....E 239 775-4500
Naples *(G-11345)*

Womens Center Jacksonville Inc ....E 904 722-3000
Jacksonville *(G-6939)*

Woodhouse Inc ....E 954 786-0344
Pompano Beach *(G-14942)*

Youth & Fmly Alternatives Inc ....C 863 533-6832
Bartow *(G-344)*

Youthtrack Inc ....C 904 630-6746
Jacksonville *(G-6962)*

8399 Social Services, NEC

211 Tampa Bay Cares Inc ....E 727 888-5211
Clearwater *(G-1506)*

Adheris LLC ....D 727 579-5000
Saint Petersburg *(G-15557)*

Alliance For Met Clay Arts Wrl ....D 860 263-9029
Orlando *(G-12097)*

Americans For Immgrant Jstice ....E 305 573-1106
Virginia Gardens *(G-18952)*

Assistance Fund Inc ....E 407 801-6918
Orlando *(G-12142)*

Availity LLC ....C 904 470-4900
Jacksonville *(G-5827)*

Awp Inc ....D 407 482-3348
Orlando *(G-12163)*

Baptist Hlth S Fla Fndtion Inc ....D 786 467-5400
South Miami *(G-16501)*

Bay County Pub Lib Foundation ....E 850 522-2100
Panama City *(G-13963)*

Baycare ....E 813 632-2393
Tampa *(G-17349)*

Boys Girls Clubs Centl Fla Inc ....D 407 298-0680
Orlando *(G-12197)*

Broward Childrens Center Inc ....D 954 943-7336
Pompano Beach *(G-14757)*

Cac-Florida Medical Ctrs LLC ....D 305 324-2000
Miami *(G-9304)*

Care Rsrce Cmnty Hlth Ctrs Inc ....E 954 567-7141
Oakland Park *(G-11588)*

Care Rsrce Cmnty Hlth Ctrs Inc ....E 305 576-1234
Miami *(G-9314)*

Childrens Services Council ....E 561 740-7000
Boynton Beach *(G-973)*

Clic Inc ....D 954 591-8071
Pembroke Pines *(G-14143)*

Community Svcs Cncil Brvard CN ....E 321 636-9901
Cocoa *(G-1929)*

Compass Inc ....E 561 533-9699
Lake Worth *(G-7719)*

Compr Aids Prog of Palm Beac C ....E 561 472-9160
West Palm Beach *(G-19100)*

Cornerstone Fmly Mnistries Inc ....E 813 253-3853
Tampa *(G-17522)*

County of Broward ....C 954 497-3610
Lauderhill *(G-8192)*

County of Hillsborough ....D 813 307-8000
Tampa *(G-17530)*

Epilepsy Foundation America ....D 301 459-3700
Brandon *(G-1227)*

Florida A & M Univ Foundation ....E 850 599-3860
Tallahassee *(G-16956)*

Florida Department of Health ....B 850 245-4512
Tallahassee *(G-16966)*

Florida Equality Institute Inc ....E 813 870-3735
Saint Petersburg *(G-15677)*

Goodwill Industries S Fla Inc ....C 305 258-1068
Princeton *(G-15186)*

Habitat For Hmnity Jcksnvlle I ....E 904 798-4529
Jacksonville *(G-6254)*

Habitat For Hmnity Lee Hndry C ....D 239 652-0434
North Fort Myers *(G-11474)*

Habitat For Hmnity Mrtin Cnty ....E 772 223-8991
Stuart *(G-16629)*

Habitat For Hmnity of S Brvard ....E 321 728-4009
Palm Bay *(G-13622)*

Habitat For Hmnity Palm Bch CN ....E 561 202-1630
Greenacres *(G-5073)*

Habitat For Hmnity Palm Bch CN ....E 561 253-2080
West Palm Beach *(G-19170)*

Helping Hnds Superior Care LLC ....E 866 521-7606
New Port Richey *(G-11382)*

Hispanic Unity Florida Inc ....E 954 342-0403
Hollywood *(G-5449)*

Hospice of The Fla Sncoast Inc ....D 727 586-4432
Largo *(G-8118)*

Hospice of The Fla Sncoast Inc ....B 727 586-4432
Clearwater *(G-1672)*

Hospice of The Fla Sncoast Inc ....E 727 328-3260
Saint Petersburg *(G-15711)*

Hospice of The Fla Sncoast Inc ....B 727 586-4432
Palm Harbor *(G-13867)*

Housing Partnership Inc ....E 561 841-3500
Riviera Beach *(G-15299)*

Institute of Intrnal Adtors In ....E 407 937-1111
Lake Mary *(G-7600)*

Lady Lake Nh LLC ....D 352 259-0121
Lady Lake *(G-7437)*

Lake Community Action Agcy Inc ....E 352 357-3497
Eustis *(G-3494)*

Lake Community Action Agcy Inc ....E 352 589-2606
Eustis *(G-3495)*

Lake Wales Care Center Inc ....E 863 676-6678
Lake Wales *(G-7688)*

Levy Cnty Schols Fundation Inc ....E 352 493-6056
Chiefland *(G-1484)*

Manatee Cnty Fmly Yung MNS CHR ....B 941 792-7484
Bradenton *(G-1133)*

National Mltiple Sclerosis Soc ....E 954 731-4224
Fort Lauderdale *(G-3992)*

New Road To Learning Inc ....E 850 432-2273
Pensacola *(G-14385)*

New York Life Insurance Co ....B 813 288-5500
Tampa *(G-18076)*

Northeast FL Comm Action Agenc ....D 904 398-7472
Jacksonville *(G-6552)*

Northeast Fla Safety Council ....D 904 399-3119
Jacksonville *(G-6553)*

Pensacola Hbtat For Hmnity Inc ....E 850 476-0001
Pensacola *(G-14410)*

Powell Supportive Services Inc ....E 813 335-4891
Land O Lakes *(G-8053)*

Purpose Bilt Fmlies Fndtion In ....E 954 554-3306
Fort Lauderdale *(G-4067)*

Renaissnce Bhvral Hlth Systems ....E 904 996-0194
Jacksonville *(G-6655)*

Rocky Mtn Support Svcs Inc ....D 904 854-8100
Jacksonville *(G-6674)*

▼ Salvadran Amrcn Hmntrian Fndti ....E 305 860-0300
Coral Gables *(G-2181)*

Salvation Army ....C 813 383-5656
Lutz *(G-8456)*

Society St Vncent De Paul S Pn ....D 727 823-2516
Saint Petersburg *(G-15848)*

Space Cast Hlth Foundation Inc ....C 321 241-6600
Rockledge *(G-15370)*

Treasure Cast Hlth Council Inc ....E 561 844-4220
Palm Beach Gardens *(G-13778)*

Trinity Health Care Svcs Inc ....D 954 986-1754
Miramar *(G-10906)*

Ucf Foundation Inc ....E 407 882-1220
Orlando *(G-13324)*

United Jwish Cmnty of Brward C ....E 954 252-6900
Davie *(G-2533)*

United Way Broward County Inc ....E 954 462-4850
Fort Lauderdale *(G-4195)*

University Fla Foundation Inc ....C 352 846-2324
Gainesville *(G-5022)*

University Fla Foundation Inc ....C 352 392-1691
Gainesville *(G-5023)*

University of Miami ....E 305 284-6699
Coral Gables *(G-2201)*

Voices For Chldren Fndtion Inc ....D 305 324-5678
Miami *(G-10483)*

West Fla Regional Plg Council ....E 850 332-7976
Pensacola *(G-14471)*

S
I
C

84 MUSEUMS, ART GALLERIES, AND BOTANICAL AND ZOOLOGICAL GARDENS

8412 Museums & Art Galleries

Appleton Cultural Center Inc ....E 352 291-4455
Ocala (G-11631)
▲ Artis-Naples Inc ....B 239 597-1111
Naples (G-11017)
Bishop Mseum Scence Nature Inc ....E 941 746-4131
Bradenton (G-1058)
◆ Britto Central Inc ....E 305 531-8821
Miami (G-9287)
Bronze Kingdom Museum Inc ....E 407 203-8864
Orlando (G-12209)
Childrens Museum Tampa Inc ....E 813 443-3830
Tampa (G-17470)
County of Hillsborough ....C 813 987-6300
Tampa (G-17528)
Cox Science Center & Aqar Inc ....E 561 832-1988
West Palm Beach (G-19112)
Deette Hlden Cmmer Mseum Fndti ......E 904 356-6857
Jacksonville (G-6057)
EFC Holdings Inc ....B 305 860-0116
Miami (G-9510)
Fairchild Trpcl Btnic Grdn Inc ....D 305 667-1651
Coral Gables (G-2103)
▲ Friends of Bass Museum Inc ....E 305 673-7530
Miami Beach (G-10596)
Friends of The Mseum Fla Hstor ....E 850 245-6413
Tallahassee (G-16984)
Golisano Chld Mseum of Nples I ....E 239 514-0084
Naples (G-11138)
Great Explorations Inc ....E 727 821-8992
Saint Petersburg (G-15695)
Henry Morrison Flagler Museum ....E 561 655-2833
Palm Beach (G-13657)
High Sprng Historical Soc Inc ....D 352 514-4204
High Springs (G-5354)
Historcal Assn Suthern Fla Inc ....E 305 375-1492
Miami (G-9706)
Hollywood Art Culture Ctr Inc ....E 954 921-3274
Hollywood (G-5450)
▲ Jorge M Prez Art Mseum Mm-Dade ..D 305 375-3000
Miami (G-9803)
Key West Museum Art & History ....E 305 295-6616
Key West (G-7222)
Marion Cultural Alliance Inc ....C 352 237-3747
Ocala (G-11721)
▲ Miami Childrens Museum Inc ....E 305 373-5437
Miami (G-9961)
Museum Cntmprary Art Jcksnvlle ....E 904 366-6911
Jacksonville (G-6522)
Museum Discovery & Science Inc ....D 954 713-0914
Fort Lauderdale (G-3984)
▲ Museum of Art Inc ....E 954 525-5500
Fort Lauderdale (G-3985)
Museum of Science and Industry ....E 813 987-6000
Tampa (G-18063)
Museum of Scnce Hstory Jcksnvl ....E 904 396-7062
Jacksonville (G-6523)
▲ Norton Museum of Art Inc ....D 561 832-5196
West Palm Beach (G-19279)
Orlando Science Center Inc ....D 407 514-2000
Orlando (G-12983)
Phillip Ptrcia Frost Mseum Scn ....D 305 434-9541
Miami (G-10116)
Ramos Masters Collection Inc ....E 305 389-8437
Miami (G-10182)
◆ Ripley Entertainment Inc ....E 407 345-8010
Orlando (G-13113)
Ripley Entertainment Inc ....D 407 345-0501
Orlando (G-13114)
Saint Agstine Lghthouse Museum ....E 904 829-0745
Saint Augustine (G-15489)
▲ Salvador Dali Museum Inc ....D 727 823-3767
Saint Petersburg (G-15837)
Society of The Four Arts Inc ....E 561 655-7227
Palm Beach (G-13670)
Southstern Archlogical RES Inc ....C 407 236-7711
Orlando (G-13221)
Tallahssee Mseum Hstory Ntral ....D 850 575-8684
Tallahassee (G-17147)
▲ Tampa Museum of Art Inc ....E 813 274-8130
Tampa (G-18400)
Vero Beach Museum Art Inc ....E 772 231-0707
Vero Beach (G-18935)

8422 Arboreta, Botanical & Zoological Gardens

Bishop Mseum Scence Nature Inc ....E 941 746-4131
Bradenton (G-1058)
Bok Tower Grdns Foundation Inc ....D 863 676-1408
Lake Wales (G-7675)
Central Fla Zoological Soc Inc ....D 407 323-4450
Sanford (G-15932)
City of Miami Beach ....C 305 673-7256
Miami Beach (G-10571)
Deette Hlden Cmmer Mseum Fndti ......E 904 356-6857
Jacksonville (G-6057)
Fairchild Trpcl Btnic Grdn Inc ....D 305 667-1651
Coral Gables (G-2103)
Flamingo Gardens Inc ....D 954 473-2955
Davie (G-2481)
Florida Aquarium Inc ....D 813 273-4000
Tampa (G-17671)
Gulfarium Care Foundation Inc ....D 850 243-9046
Fort Walton Beach (G-4778)
Jacksnville Zoological Soc Inc ....C 904 757-4463
Jacksonville (G-6341)
Oceans Reefs & Aquariums LLC ....D 772 468-7008
Fort Pierce (G-4727)
Selby Mrie Botanical Grdns Inc ....E 941 366-5731
Sarasota (G-16314)
▲ Tropical Shell & Gifts Inc ....D 305 296-4557
Key West (G-7254)
Zoologcal Soc of The Palm Bche ....D 561 547-9453
West Palm Beach (G-19428)

86 MEMBERSHIP ORGANIZATIONS

8611 Business Associations

Academy Prep Foundation Inc ....E 727 322-0800
Saint Petersburg (G-15556)
ACC All Contractors Inc ....E 305 842-6338
Doral (G-3100)
Agriclture Cnsmr Svcs Fla Dept ....D 850 638-6250
Chipley (G-1488)
▼ American Welding Society Inc ....D 305 443-9353
Doral (G-3120)
Brightline Trains Florida LLC ....D 305 521-4800
Miami (G-9285)
Building Trades Assn Inc ....E 561 241-0513
Boca Raton (G-488)
Central Fla Chpter Assod Bldrs ....E 407 628-2070
Orlando (G-12262)
Downtown Visions Inc ....D 904 634-0303
Jacksonville (G-6280)
Duke Contractors LLC ....D 305 588-2054
Sweetwater (G-16860)
◆ Dundee Citrus Growers Assn ....C 863 439-1574
Dundee (G-3372)
E S I Geothermal Inc ....D 561 691-7171
Juno Beach (G-7029)
Enterprise Florida Inc ....D 407 648-2463
Orlando (G-12470)
Ferry Pass Volunteer Fire Dept ....E 850 477-1747
Pensacola (G-14304)
Florida Assn Insur Agents Inc ....E 850 893-4155
Tallahassee (G-16958)
Florida Chamber Commerce Inc ....E 850 521-1200
Tallahassee (G-16960)
Florida Health Care Assn ....D 850 224-3907
Tallahassee (G-16971)
Florida Rest & Lodging Assn ....E 850 224-2250
Tallahassee (G-16977)
Florida Rlblity Crdnting Cncl ....E 813 289-5644
Tampa (G-17696)
Florida West Coast Lsmith Assn ....D 813 757-0000
Tampa (G-17701)
◆ Global Shippers Assn Inc ....E 239 985-3006
Fort Myers (G-4420)
Greater Srsota Chmber Commerce ....E 941 955-8187
Sarasota (G-16179)
Greater Tmpa Assn of Rltors In ....E 813 879-7010
Tampa (G-17749)
Greater Tmpa Chmber Cmmrce Inc ....E 813 228-7777
Tampa (G-17750)
Hideaway Beach Association Inc ....E 239 642-6300
Marco Island (G-8630)
Horizon Bay Management LLC ....A 727 723-7110
Clearwater (G-1670)
Horizon Bay Management LLC ....D 813 287-3900
Tampa (G-17841)
Interntional SEC MGT Group Inc ....C 813 932-7814
Tampa (G-17872)

Jacksnvlle Chamber of Commerce ....C 904 366-6631
Jacksonville (G-6342)
Jacksnville Chmber Fndation Inc ....E 904 366-6600
Jacksonville (G-6343)
Jacksnvlle Rgnal Chmber Cmmrce ....E 904 366-6600
Jacksonville (G-6348)
Lakeland Area Chamber Commerce .....C 863 688-8551
Lakeland (G-7898)
League Sthastern Cr Unions Inc ....D 866 231-0545
Tallahassee (G-17021)
Northeast Florida Bldrs Assn ....E 904 725-4355
Jacksonville (G-6554)
Oswines Trade LLC ....E 850 487-1395
Doral (G-3284)
Pacific Agricultural RES Corp ....E 813 986-5599
Thonotosassa (G-18675)
Raytheon Technologies Corp ....A 860 565-4321
Jupiter (G-7130)
◆ S E Inc ....E 407 859-9317
Orlando (G-13154)
Salvation Army ....E 352 376-1743
Gainesville (G-4991)
SC Commerce Inc ....E 954 349-3197
Weston (G-19478)
Tri-County Cmnty Council Inc ....C 850 547-2444
Bonifay (G-890)
Unity of Delray Beach Inc ....D 561 276-5796
Delray Beach (G-3027)

8621 Professional Membership Organizations

Aacsb Intl - The Assn To Advnc ....D 813 769-6500
Tampa (G-17220)
AB Closing Corporation ....D 407 243-6006
Orlando (G-12041)
Access Hlth Care Physcians LLC ....E 352 796-6721
Brooksville (G-1263)
American Meetings LLC ....E 954 553-2870
Fort Lauderdale (G-3602)
Assoction For Dev of The Excpt ....D 786 363-3100
Miami (G-9179)
Assoction Pblc-Sfty-Cmmnctons ....E 386 322-2500
Daytona Beach (G-2547)
Atp Tour Inc ....E 904 285-9886
Ponte Vedra Beach (G-14974)
Broward Rgnal Hlth Plg Cncl I ....D 954 561-9681
Hollywood (G-5410)
Concord III LLC ....D 305 947-2224
North Miami Beach (G-11521)
Corsair Engineering Inc ....E 407 207-3550
Orlando (G-12370)
Dental Whale LLC ....E 404 537-5211
Sunrise (G-16763)
Early Lrng Cltion of Flgler VI ....E 386 323-2400
Daytona Beach (G-2584)
Education & Empowerment Inc ....D 863 709-4848
Winter Haven (G-19625)
Florida Assn Crt Clerks Inc ....D 850 921-0808
Tallahassee (G-16957)
Florida Assn Mrtg Brks Inc ....E 850 942-6411
Tallahassee (G-16959)
Florida Bar ....C 305 377-4445
Miami (G-9567)
Florida Bar ....C 954 835-0233
Sunrise (G-16770)
Florida Edcatn Assn Hldg Corp ....B 850 201-2800
Tallahassee (G-16967)
Florida Education Association ....E 850 224-7818
Tallahassee (G-16968)
Florida Inst of Crtif Pub Accn ....D 850 224-2727
Orlando (G-12529)
Florida Justice Association ....E 850 224-9403
Tallahassee (G-16974)
Guadalupe Center Inc ....E 239 658-1999
Immokalee (G-5658)
Guidewell Emer Doctors LLC ....E 407 801-8400
Winter Park (G-19727)
Hlb Gravier LLP ....E 305 446-3022
Coral Gables (G-2126)
Home Association Inc ....E 813 229-6901
Tampa (G-17835)
Institute of Fncl Oprtions Inc ....E 407 351-3322
Orlando (G-12685)
Internal Audit Foundation ....C 407 937-1100
Lake Mary (G-7604)
Interntnal Soc For Phrm Engrg ....E 813 960-2105
Tampa (G-17873)
Jewish Assn For Rsdntial Care ....D 561 558-2550
Boca Raton (G-650)

Marielas Choice LLC ....E 408 413-0027
Orlando *(G-12809)*

National Assn Phtshop Prfssnal ....D 813 433-5000
Oldsmar *(G-11914)*

Palm Bch Cnty Plice Bnvlent As ....D 561 304-0041
Greenacres *(G-5075)*

Parkinsons Support Group ....E 321 725-4011
Palm Bay *(G-13636)*

Saluscare Inc ....C 239 275-3222
Fort Myers *(G-4579)*

Senior Resource Assn Inc ....D 772 569-0760
Vero Beach *(G-18917)*

Soffer Heart Institute PA ....E 305 792-0555
Miami *(G-10289)*

Spherion Staffing LLC ....E 321 255-0222
Melbourne *(G-8980)*

United Teachers of Dade ....E 305 854-0220
Miami Springs *(G-10789)*

University Med Svc Assn Inc ....B 813 974-2201
Tampa *(G-18477)*

Velcon Engrg & Surveying LLC ....E 772 879-0477
Port St Lucie *(G-15183)*

8631 Labor Unions & Similar Organizations

Amateur Athletic Un of US Inc ....E 407 934-7200
Lake Buena Vista *(G-7453)*

Broward Teachers Un Local 1975 ....E 954 718-2233
Tamarac *(G-17182)*

Florida Fdrtion Clrgrds Crcuit ....D 904 477-0375
Orange Park *(G-11991)*

International Union United Au ....C 407 855-2880
Orlando *(G-12686)*

Screen Actors Gild - Amrcn Fdr ....D 305 670-7677
Doral *(G-3304)*

United Teachers of Dade ....E 305 854-0220
Miami Springs *(G-10789)*

Vero Beach Firefighters Assn ....C 772 562-2028
Vero Beach *(G-18934)*

8641 Civic, Social & Fraternal Associations

7 Heaven For Kids LLC ....D 786 701-8113
Miami *(G-9059)*

Addison Reserve Master ....A 561 637-7870
Delray Beach *(G-2899)*

Akam On-Site Inc ....D 305 673-5537
Miami Beach *(G-10544)*

Akam On-Site Inc ....D 954 843-2526
Dania *(G-2401)*

Artemis Lifestyle Services Inc ....C 407 705-2190
Kissimmee *(G-7270)*

Assistance Fund Inc ....E 407 801-6918
Orlando *(G-12142)*

Astronaut Schlrship Fndtion In ....E 407 362-7900
Orlando *(G-12144)*

Bal Hrbour Plice Bnvlent Assn ....D 305 866-4633
Surfside *(G-16851)*

Ballenisles Community Assn Inc ....E 561 625-5724
Palm Beach Gardens *(G-13688)*

Balmoral Condominium Assn Inc ....D 305 866-7792
Miami *(G-9202)*

Bankers Club Inc ....E 305 374-1448
Miami *(G-9209)*

Bay Colony Community Assn Inc ....D 239 591-2202
Naples *(G-11024)*

Bay Pines Foundation Inc ....D 727 398-6661
Bay Pines *(G-350)*

Beach-Chu Hallandale LLC ....E 954 271-3222
Hallandale Beach *(G-5166)*

Bel Canto Singers Inc ....E 386 492-1940
Port Orange *(G-15070)*

Bellamare At Wllams Island Cnd ....E 305 749-3240
Aventura *(G-265)*

Best Buddies ....E 901 207-4266
Miami *(G-9247)*

BNai Brith Yuth Orgnztion Inc ....D 954 252-1912
Davie *(G-2462)*

Boca Grnde Homeowners Assn Inc ......D 941 964-2211
Boca Grande *(G-389)*

Boca Vista Condominums ....E 727 397-6099
Madeira Beach *(G-8481)*

Boca West Master Assn Inc ....D 561 488-1598
Boca Raton *(G-473)*

Boxy Charm Inc ....C 954 329-4793
Pembroke Pines *(G-14135)*

Boy Scouts of America ....A 305 664-5612
Islamorada *(G-5702)*

Boys Girls Clubs Bay Cnty Inc ....E 850 832-9167
Panama City *(G-13973)*

Boys Girls Clubs Centl Fla Inc ....E 407 332-8668
Altamonte Springs *(G-31)*

Boys Girls Clubs Centl Fla Inc ....E 407 841-6855
Orlando *(G-12196)*

Boys Girls Clubs Centl Fla Inc ....D 407 298-0680
Orlando *(G-12197)*

Boys Girls Clubs Centl Fla Inc ....D 407 295-1100
Orlando *(G-12198)*

Boys Girls Clubs Centl Fla Inc ....D 321 242-0041
Melbourne *(G-8831)*

Boys Grls CLB Cllier Cnty Fla ....D 239 325-1700
Naples *(G-11039)*

Boys Grls CLB N Centl Fla Inc ....E 850 838-2471
Perry *(G-14486)*

Boys Grls Clubs Nrthast Fla I ....E 352 373-6639
Gainesville *(G-4847)*

Boys Town Central Florida Inc ....C 407 588-2170
Oviedo *(G-13543)*

Breakers of Fort Wlton Bch Cnd ....D 850 244-9127
Fort Walton Beach *(G-4756)*

Brickell Key One Cndo Assn Inc ....D 305 358-8080
Miami *(G-9281)*

Brickell Pl Phase II Assn Inc ....E 305 858-3891
Miami *(G-9282)*

Brickell Place Condo Assn Inc ....E 305 854-5343
Miami *(G-9283)*

Central Fla Cncil Boy Scuts AM ....E 407 889-4403
Apopka *(G-163)*

Central Fla Yung MNS Chrstn As ....C 407 679-9622
Winter Park *(G-19698)*

Central Fla Yung MNS Chrstn As ....C 407 299-4350
Orlando *(G-12274)*

Central Fla Yung MNS Chrstn As ....C 321 433-7770
Cocoa *(G-1922)*

Central Fla Yung MNS Chrstn As ....C 407 299-4358
Orlando *(G-12275)*

Central Fla Yung MNS Chrstn As ....D 407 396-3001
Kissimmee *(G-7280)*

Central Fla Yung MNS Chrstn As ....E 352 536-6140
Clermont *(G-1859)*

Central Fla Yung MNS Chrstn As ....C 407 644-3606
Winter Park *(G-19699)*

Central Fla Yung MNS Chrstn As ....B 407 644-1509
Winter Park *(G-19700)*

Central Fla Yung MNS Chrstn As ....C 407 896-9220
Orlando *(G-12276)*

Central Fla Yung MNS Chrstn As ....C 407 855-2430
Orlando *(G-12277)*

Central Fla Yung MNS Chrstn As ....B 407 351-9417
Orlando *(G-12278)*

Central Fla Yung MNS Chrstn As ....C 407 852-3520
Orlando *(G-12279)*

Central Fla Yung MNS Chrstn As ....C 407 847-7413
Kissimmee *(G-7281)*

Central Fla Yung MNS Chrstn As ....C 352 867-1441
Ocala *(G-11655)*

Central Fla Yung MNS Chrstn As ....C 407 381-8000
Orlando *(G-12280)*

Central Fla Yung MNS Chrstn As ....C 352 343-1144
Tavares *(G-18601)*

▼ Clean World Foundation Inc ....E 407 574-8353
Orlando *(G-12315)*

Coast Guard Auxiliary Assn Inc ....C 321 480-5323
Merritt Island *(G-9020)*

Community Svcs Cncil Brvard CN ....E 321 639-8770
Cocoa *(G-1928)*

Continental Utility Inc ....E 352 748-3293
Wildwood *(G-19492)*

Coronado Condo Owners Assn ....D 239 437-4306
Fort Myers *(G-4327)*

Countryside Master Assn Inc ....E 239 353-1780
Naples *(G-11079)*

County of Brevard ....E 321 455-1380
Merritt Island *(G-9021)*

County of Hillsborough ....E 813 635-3500
Riverview *(G-15252)*

Crossings Homeowners Assn ....D 305 387-0436
Miami *(G-9440)*

Development Consultants Inc ....E 954 922-3514
Hollywood *(G-5427)*

Discovery Bch Rsort Tnnis CLB ....E 321 868-7777
Cocoa Beach *(G-1970)*

Early Lrng Coalition Duval Inc ....E 904 208-2044
Jacksonville *(G-6100)*

Fairways At Tger Pt E Hmwners ....D 850 291-5610
Gulf Breeze *(G-5114)*

Family Chrstn Assn of Amer Inc ....E 305 685-4881
Miami *(G-9543)*

Fau Foundation Inc ....E 561 297-2891
Boca Raton *(G-573)*

Ferdinandsen Enterprises Inc ....E 407 770-1748
Kissimmee *(G-7306)*

First Call For Help of Broward ....E 954 537-0211
Fort Lauderdale *(G-3786)*

Fisher Island Club Inc ....B 305 535-6000
Miami *(G-9563)*

Fisher Island Cmnty Assn Inc ....D 305 535-6000
Miami Beach *(G-10594)*

Florida ATL Univ Almni Assn In ....D 561 297-3011
Boca Raton *(G-579)*

Florida High Schl Athc Assn In ....E 352 372-9551
Gainesville *(G-4892)*

For Pete Sake Foundation Inc ....E 586 413-7810
Hallandale Beach *(G-5169)*

Four Ambassadors Assn Inc ....E 305 374-6270
Miami *(G-9602)*

Foxfire Cmnty Assn Cllier Cnty ....D 239 643-3139
Naples *(G-11126)*

Fraternal Order Plice Trsure C ....D 772 971-7943
Fort Pierce *(G-4704)*

Gift of Life Marrow Registry ....E 561 982-2900
Boca Raton *(G-607)*

Girl Scout Cncil Trpcl Fla Inc ....E 305 253-4841
Miami *(G-9630)*

Girl Scouts Citrus Council Inc ....E 407 896-4475
Orlando *(G-12571)*

Girl Scouts Southeast Fla Inc ....D 561 427-0177
Lake Worth *(G-7732)*

Girl Scouts West Centl Fla Inc ....E 813 281-4475
Tampa *(G-17734)*

Girls Inc of Pinellas ....D 727 544-6230
Pinellas Park *(G-14519)*

Glades Golf and Cntry CLB Inc ....E 239 774-6899
Naples *(G-11132)*

Grand Seas Rsort Owners Assn I ....E 386 677-7880
Daytona Beach *(G-2603)*

Greater Daytona Bch Area YMCA ....D 386 255-8773
Deland *(G-2863)*

Greater Dytona Bch Area Yung M ....D 386 673-9622
Ormond Beach *(G-13497)*

Greater Dytona Bch Area Yung M ....D 386 532-9622
Deltona *(G-3039)*

Grove Isle Association Inc ....D 305 858-1207
Miami *(G-9668)*

Gulf Cast Cncil of Boy Scuts A ....E 850 333-7966
Defuniak Springs *(G-2831)*

Hamptons West Condo Assn Inc ....D 305 932-3210
Miami *(G-9680)*

Heritage Pines Cmnty Assn Inc ....D 727 861-7784
Hudson *(G-5642)*

Hideaway Beach Association Inc ....E 239 394-5555
Marco Island *(G-8629)*

Hillsboro Lghthuse Prsrvtion S ....A 954 942-2102
Pompano Beach *(G-14821)*

Hollywood Concessions Inc ....B 248 352-2010
Hallandale Beach *(G-5173)*

Hunters Creek Cmnty Assn Inc ....E 407 240-6000
Orlando *(G-12671)*

Integrated Mission Support Ser ....C 321 338-2955
Merritt Island *(G-9033)*

Jafco Childrens Foundation Inc ....D 954 749-7230
Sunrise *(G-16789)*

Jetty East Condo Assn Inc ....E 850 837-2141
Destin *(G-3065)*

John S Jmes L Knght Fndtion In ....E 305 358-1061
Miami *(G-9799)*

Johns Hpkins All Chld Hosp Inc ....E 813 631-5000
Tampa *(G-17899)*

Johns Island Prprty Owners As ....D 772 231-1666
Vero Beach *(G-18883)*

Kellsmont Owners Assoc In ....E 863 647-4698
Lakeland *(G-7895)*

Kiwonnongo Foundation Inc ....E 917 543-7474
Deltona *(G-3041)*

Knights of Columbus Inc ....E 386 734-9783
Deland *(G-2866)*

Lost Tree Yacht Club Inc ....E 561 626-3110
North Palm Beach *(G-11551)*

Maple Leaf Esttes Hmwners Corp ....E 941 629-1666
Port Charlotte *(G-15046)*

Mar-A-Lago Club LLC ....D 561 832-2600
Palm Beach *(G-13663)*

Miami-Dade Blavatsky Lodge Inc ....D 305 271-7740
Miami *(G-9988)*

Miromar Lakes LLC ....E 239 390-7700
Estero *(G-3470)*

Mission Bay Community Assn ....E 561 479-1900
Boca Raton *(G-695)*

Moonspinner Condo Assn Inc ....E 850 234-8900
Panama City *(G-14043)*

Motopara Foundation Inc ....D 813 530-6006
Tampa *(G-18057)*

SIC

Mount Sinai Med Ctr Fla Inc.................E......305 949-9656
  Sunny Isles Beach (G-16725)

National Fndtion For Advncment ....E......305 377-1140
  Miami (G-10028)

National Golf Foundation Inc.................E......561 744-6006
  Jupiter (G-7121)

Nettles Island Inc..................................E......772 229-1650
  Jensen Beach (G-7020)

North Central Florida YMCA Inc ....C......352 374-9622
  Gainesville (G-4960)

North Fla Cncil Inc Boy Scuts.................E......904 388-0591
  Jacksonville (G-6547)

Oakwood Villas......................................D......941 751-9394
  Bradenton (G-1154)

Ocean East Resort Club ....E......386 677-8111
  Ormond Beach (G-13511)

Ocean Reef Community Assn ....E......305 367-3067
  Key Largo (G-7187)

One Tquesta Pt Condominum Assn.......E......305 358-6868
  Miami (G-10073)

Palace Condominium Assn Inc ....E......305 858-1151
  Miami (G-10085)

Palm Bch Cnty Plice Bnvlent As ....D......561 304-0041
  Greenacres (G-5075)

Palm Bch Cnty Vlntr Fr-Rscue A ....D......561 616-7000
  West Palm Beach (G-19306)

Pelican Bay of Nples Fundation ....D......239 597-8081
  Naples (G-11257)

Pelican Cove Condo Assn Inc ....D......941 966-3489
  Sarasota (G-16261)

Pelican Cove Resort Condo Assn ....D......305 664-4435
  Islamorada (G-5708)

Pelican Landing Community Assn ....E......239 947-5977
  Bonita Springs (G-931)

Peridia Prprty Owners Assn Inc...........E......941 758-2582
  Bradenton (G-1160)

Pinnacle Port Community Assn ....E......850 234-7163
  Panama City Beach (G-14101)

Pinnacles Association MGT ....E......772 871-0004
  Port Saint Lucie (G-15158)

Plaza of The Palm Bches Cndo A ....E......561 655-2555
  West Palm Beach (G-19328)

Plum At Boca Point.................................D......561 395-2744
  Boca Raton (G-753)

Police Athc Leag Jcksnvlle Inc...........E......904 854-6555
  Jacksonville (G-6606)

Ponte Vedra High Schl Pto Inc...........C......904 547-7350
  Ponte Vedra (G-14970)

Pto LLC...C......863 688-1188
  Lakeland (G-7943)

Quantum On Bay Master Assn Inc ....D......786 314-7459
  Miami (G-10172)

Riviera Isles Master Assn Inc ....C......954 322-5284
  Fort Lauderdale (G-4092)

Safe Children Coalition Inc ....B......941 955-5596
  Sarasota (G-16289)

Safe Children Coalition Inc ....B......941 955-8194
  Sarasota (G-16290)

Safe Children Coalition Inc ....E......941 371-4799
  Sarasota (G-16288)

Sailfish Point Security Inc.....................E......772 225-1000
  Stuart (G-16666)

Sandpiper Cove Condo Assn ....D......850 837-9121
  Destin (G-3076)

Sea Ranch Club of Bo ....D......561 395-0447
  Boca Raton (G-787)

Seminole Boosters Inc ....E......850 644-3484
  Tallahassee (G-17097)

South Fla Cncil Inc Boy Scuts ....E......305 364-0020
  Miami Lakes (G-10764)

Specialty MGT Co Centl Fla ....E......407 647-2622
  Altamonte Springs (G-101)

Stovall House Club LLC ....C......813 287-2231
  Tampa (G-18340)

Summit Owners Association Inc ....E......850 235-8799
  Panama City Beach (G-14105)

Sun City Center Cmnty Assn Inc...........E......813 633-3500
  Sun City Center (G-16708)

Tall Timbers Research Inc ....E......850 893-4153
  Tallahassee (G-17126)

Tampa Metropolitan Area YMCA...........D......813 684-1371
  Valrico (G-18758)

Tampa Metropolitan Area YMCA...........C......813 684-1371
  Valrico (G-18759)

Tampa Mtro Area Yung MNS Chrst.......D......813 757-6677
  Plant City (G-14588)

Tampa Mtro Area Yung MNS Chrst.......B......813 962-3220
  Tampa (G-18393)

Tampa Mtro Area Yung MNS Chrst.......C......813 224-9622
  Tampa (G-18394)

Tampa Mtro Area Yung MNS Chrst.......C......813 866-9622
  Tampa (G-18395)

Tampa Mtro Area Yung MNS Chrst.......D......813 224-9622
  Tampa (G-18396)

Tampa Mtro Area Yung MNS Chrst.......C......352 521-0484
  Dade City (G-2397)

Tampa Mtro Area Yung MNS Chrst.......C......813 222-1334
  Tampa (G-18397)

Tampa Mtro Area Yung MNS Chrst.......C......813 839-0210
  Tampa (G-18398)

Tampa Mtro Area Yung MNS Chrst.......C......813 229-9622
  Tampa (G-18399)

Tampa Mtro Area Yung MNS Chrst.......D......813 780-9622
  Zephyrhills (G-19852)

Techtrueup LLC......................................C......813 393-9393
  Naples (G-11317)

Temple Ter Prof Firefighters ....E......813 416-0679
  Tampa (G-18415)

The Nature Conservancy........................E......407 682-3664
  Maitland (G-8587)

Tidelands Condominium Assn Inc ....D......386 597-4441
  Palm Coast (G-13842)

Timber Pines Cmnty Assn Inc ....D......352 666-2300
  Spring Hill (G-16551)

Tower Club ....D......954 764-8550
  Fort Lauderdale (G-4178)

Towerhouse Condominium Inc ....E......305 865-8677
  Miami Beach (G-10668)

Towers of Key Biscayne Inc ....D......305 361-9114
  Key Biscayne (G-7170)

Turnberry Towers Condo Assn ....E......305 935-3000
  Miami (G-10420)

University Club of Tampa........................E......813 223-3737
  Tampa (G-18469)

University Cntl Fla Fndtion In ....E......407 882-1220
  Orlando (G-13354)

University Fla Foundation Inc.................C......352 392-1691
  Gainesville (G-5023)

US Committee For Refugees An ....E......703 310-1130
  Lake Worth (G-7758)

Ventura Cntry CLB Cmnty Hmwner.......D......407 275-7002
  Orlando (G-13371)

Venture Out At Cdjoe Cay Inc C ....D......305 745-3233
  Cudjoe Key (G-2357)

Vesta Property Services Inc ....A......904 355-1831
  Jacksonville (G-6907)

Volus/Flgler Fmly Yung MNS CHR...........C......386 490-9801
  Deland (G-2889)

Waterside Community Assn Inc ....E......813 280-2952
  Tampa (G-18526)

Whittier Oaks Hmwners Assn Inc...........E......954 426-0151
  Boca Raton (G-875)

Williams Island Property Owner ....C......305 935-5555
  Miami (G-10506)

Winter Park Racquet Club Inc.................D......407 644-2226
  Winter Park (G-19790)

Wycliffe Golf & Cntry CLB Inc ....C......561 964-9200
  Wellington (G-18991)

Wynmoor Community Council Inc ....C......954 978-2600
  Coconut Creek (G-2010)

Yacht Rcquet CLB of Boca Rton ....E......561 368-8032
  Boca Raton (G-881)

YMCA of Palm Beachs.............................D......561 967-3573
  Palm Springs (G-13901)

YMCA of Treasure Coast ....E......772 221-9622
  Stuart (G-16683)

YMCA Southwest Florida Inc ....D......239 221-7560
  Bonita Springs (G-951)

YMCA Southwest Florida Inc ....D......941 475-1234
  Englewood (G-3442)

YMCA Southwest Florida Inc ....D......239 221-7560
  Venice (G-18824)

Young Mens Christian ....D......352 637-0132
  Beverly Hills (G-379)

Young Mens Christian ....C......904 854-2000
  Jacksonville (G-6955)

Young MNS Christn Assn NW Fla...........E......850 432-8327
  Pensacola (G-14479)

Young MNS Chrstn Assn of Flrda...........C......904 768-7112
  Jacksonville (G-6956)

Young MNS Chrstn Assn of Flrda...........C......904 355-1436
  Jacksonville (G-6957)

Young MNS Chrstn Assn of Flrda...........E......904 296-3220
  Jacksonville (G-6958)

Young MNS Chrstn Assn of Flrda...........C......904 731-2006
  Jacksonville (G-6959)

Young MNS Chrstn Assn of Flrda...........C......904 259-0898
  Macclenny (G-8480)

Young MNS Chrstn Assn of Flrda...........C......904 471-9622
  Saint Augustine (G-15515)

Young MNS Chrstn Assn of Flrda...........C......904 464-3901
  Jacksonville (G-6960)

Young MNS Chrstn Assn of Flrda...........C......904 296-3220
  Fernandina Beach (G-3546)

Young MNS Chrstn Assn of Grter...........D......727 328-9622
  Saint Petersburg (G-15903)

Young MNS Chrstn Assn of Mrtin...........C......772 286-4444
  Stuart (G-16684)

Young MNS Chrstn Assn of Mrtin...........E......772 287-8324
  Stuart (G-16685)

Young MNS Chrstn Assn of Sncas...........D......727 441-2166
  Clearwater (G-1843)

Young MNS Chrstn Assn of Sncas...........D......312 932-1200
  Clearwater (G-1844)

Young MNS Chrstn Assn of Sncas...........C......352 686-9622
  Spring Hill (G-16555)

Young MNS Chrstn Assn of Sncas...........C......727 394-9622
  Seminole (G-16465)

Young MNS Chrstn Assn of Sncas...........C......727 787-9622
  Palm Harbor (G-13887)

Young MNS Chrstn Assn of Sncas...........C......352 688-9622
  Spring Hill (G-16556)

Young MNS Chrstn Assn of Sncas...........C......727 461-9622
  Clearwater (G-1845)

Young MNS Chrstn Assn of Sncas...........C......727 772-9622
  Palm Harbor (G-13888)

Young MNS Chrstn Assn of Sncas...........C......727 844-0332
  New Port Richey (G-11411)

Young MNS Chrstn Assn S Fla In ....E......305 643-2626
  Miami (G-10524)

Young MNS Chrstn Assn S Fla In ....D......305 635-9622
  Miami (G-10525)

Young MNS Chrstn Assn S Fla In ....E......305 248-5189
  Homestead (G-5613)

Young MNS Chrstn Assn S Palm B...........C......561 738-9622
  Boynton Beach (G-1045)

Young MNS Chrstn Assn S Palm B...........C......561 395-9622
  Boca Raton (G-882)

YWCA South Florida Inc ....D......305 377-9922
  Miami (G-10528)

YWCA South Florida Inc ....D......305 349-6020
  Miami (G-10529)

8651 Political Organizations

A&A Coordinators America LLC...........E......954 674-3747
  Miami (G-9062)

▲ Republican Party of Florida ....D......850 222-7920
  Tallahassee (G-17085)

8699 Membership Organizations, NEC

Adecco Group US Charities Inc...........D......904 360-2000
  Jacksonville (G-5734)

◆ American Automobile Assn Inc ....A......407 444-7000
  Heathrow (G-5201)

American Traveler Mtr CLB Inc..............C......941 952-5522
  Sarasota (G-16089)

Americans For Immgrant Jstice ....E......305 573-1106
  Virginia Gardens (G-18952)

Archbshop Edward A McCrthy Hig........D......954 434-8820
  Southwest Ranches (G-16527)

Aspire Health Partners Inc ....B......407 875-3700
  Orlando (G-12136)

Auto Club Group ....A......813 289-5000
  Tampa (G-17321)

Auto Knight Motor Club Inc ....C......760 969-4300
  Jacksonville (G-5825)

Banyan Cmnty Hlth Fndation Inc ....A......305 757-0602
  Miami (G-9210)

Baycare Health System Inc ....A......727 820-8200
  Clearwater (G-1539)

Big Bend Cares Inc ....E......850 656-2437
  Tallahassee (G-16890)

Boys Town Central Florida Inc ....C......407 588-2170
  Oviedo (G-13543)

Brickell Fncl Svcs Mtr CLB Inc..............B......305 392-4300
  Miami (G-9280)

Caddie Master Enterprises Inc ....A......904 339-0475
  Ponte Vedra Beach (G-14978)

Cahsah Foundation ....E......561 200-3321
  Boca Raton (G-490)

Charity Slb Corporation ....E......561 578-0202
  Jupiter (G-7058)

City of Naples...E......239 213-1820
  Naples (G-11055)

Compass Inc ....E......561 533-9699
  Lake Worth (G-7719)

Conservancy Southwest Fla Inc...........E......239 262-0304
  Naples (G-11076)

Cornerstone Hspice Plltive Car...........C......352 343-1341
  Tavares (G-18604)

County of Brevard ....E 321 259-0601
Melbourne (G-8855)

County of Brevard ....C 321 636-3343
Cocoa (G-1933)

County of Broward ....C 954 359-1313
Fort Lauderdale (G-3729)

County of Martin ....D 772 283-2525
Stuart (G-16611)

Covenant Presbyterian Church ....E 850 769-9354
Panama City (G-13989)

Creative Learning Academy ....D 850 432-1768
Pensacola (G-14276)

Easter Seals Florida Inc ....D 561 471-1688
West Palm Beach (G-19126)

El Prado Xvi Condo Assn Inc ....E 305 643-9847
Miami (G-9512)

Escambia County School Dst ....E 850 453-1910
Pensacola (G-14293)

Evergrene Master Assn Inc ....D 561 626-1981
Palm Beach Gardens (G-13728)

Financial Industry Reg Auth ....C 561 416-0277
Boca Raton (G-574)

Florida Farm Bur Gen Insur Co ....A 727 466-6390
Saint Petersburg (G-15678)

Florida League Cities Inc ....D 850 222-9684
Tallahassee (G-16975)

▲ Florida Nat Parks Assn Inc ....E 305 247-1216
Homestead (G-5573)

◆ Food For Poor Inc ....B 954 427-2222
Coconut Creek (G-1988)

Friends Children Families Inc ....E 407 273-8444
Orlando (G-12550)

Gfwc Sisters of Service Inc ....D 850 738-2996
Tallahassee (G-16987)

Greater Melbourne Police ....D 321 984-7272
Melbourne (G-8896)

Greater Melbourne Police ....C 321 953-6251
Melbourne (G-8897)

▲ Hard Rock Heals Foundation Inc ....C 954 585-5703
Davie (G-2486)

Harry Chpin Fd Bnk Sthwest Fla ....D 239 334-7007
Fort Myers (G-4433)

Hospice Palm Bch Cnty Fndation ....D 561 494-6888
West Palm Beach (G-19186)

Humane Soc Vero Bch Indian Rve ......E 772 388-3331
Vero Beach (G-18872)

Humane Society of Broward Cnty ....D 954 989-3977
Fort Lauderdale (G-3882)

Humane Society of N Pinellas ....E 727 797-7722
Clearwater (G-1675)

Humane Society Tampa Bay Inc ....E 813 876-7138
Tampa (G-17845)

Ilg LLC ....D 305 666-1861
South Miami (G-16503)

Indian Nrses Assn Centl Fla In ....D 813 654-2838
Valrico (G-18753)

Interval Holding Company Inc ....A 305 666-1861
South Miami (G-16504)

Interval International Inc ....E 305 666-1861
South Miami (G-16505)

Jacksonville Humane Soc Inc ....E 904 493-4577
Jacksonville (G-6361)

Jacksonville University ....C 904 256-7846
Jacksonville (G-6370)

Jade Tactical Disaster Relief ....C 850 270-4077
Tampa (G-17887)

Jewish Fdrtion Palm Bch Cnty I ....D 561 478-0700
West Palm Beach (G-19214)

Kaufman Rossin Co A Prof Assn ....D 954 568-6590
Fort Lauderdale (G-3916)

Ladies Professional Golf Assn ....D 386 274-6200
Daytona Beach (G-2624)

LAMA Miami 305 Chapter ....D 305 699-4255
Tamarac (G-17197)

Luthern Ministrey of Florida ....E 850 457-1090
Pensacola (G-14352)

Martin Organization Inc ....E 850 687-4382
Destin (G-3068)

Miami Lghthuse For The Blind V ....D 305 856-9100
Miami (G-9976)

Moosehaven Inc ....C 904 278-1200
Orange Park (G-12004)

Multiple Sclrsis Fundation Inc ....D 954 776-6805
Fort Lauderdale (G-3981)

Nation Motor Club LLC ....C 800 338-2680
Boca Raton (G-707)

National Assn of Prof Bsbal Lg ....E 727 822-6937
Saint Petersburg (G-15773)

Nemours Fundation Pension Plan ....C 407 737-7500
Orlando (G-12905)

Oca Opprtnity Cmnty Ablity Inc ....E 407 808-7837
Orlando (G-12923)

▲ One Hope United - Fla Reg Inc ....D 786 712-0492
Cutler Bay (G-2372)

Osprey Cove Master Assn Inc ....E 239 489-4890
Fort Myers (G-4530)

Pacific Agricultural RES Corp ....E 813 986-5599
Thonotosassa (G-18675)

Pet Allnce Greater Orlando Inc ....D 407 351-7722
Orlando (G-13024)

Purpose Bilt Fmlies Fndtion In ....D 954 554-3306
Fort Lauderdale (G-4067)

Safe Children Coalition Inc ....E 941 371-4799
Sarasota (G-16288)

Salvation Army ....C 727 725-9777
Clearwater (G-1781)

Salvation Army ....E 239 278-1551
Fort Myers (G-4580)

Salvation Army ....D 407 423-8581
Orlando (G-13163)

Salvation Army ....E 321 632-6060
Cocoa (G-1950)

Salvation Army ....D 772 978-0265
Vero Beach (G-18913)

Salvation Army ....D 305 573-4200
Miami (G-10236)

Salvation Army ....D 305 637-6700
Hialeah (G-5320)

Salvation Army ....D 954 524-6991
Fort Lauderdale (G-4099)

Salvation Army ....D 561 391-1344
West Palm Beach (G-19352)

Salvation Army ....D 813 972-4777
Tampa (G-18244)

Salvation Army ....C 813 383-5656
Lutz (G-8456)

Salvation Army ....E 727 541-7781
Saint Petersburg (G-15838)

Salvation Army ....D 863 294-7493
Winter Haven (G-19658)

Salvation Army ....E 239 334-3745
Fort Myers (G-4581)

Salvation Army ....E 941 629-3170
Port Charlotte (G-15057)

Salvation Army ....E 941 484-6227
Venice (G-18801)

Salvation Army ....E 352 732-8326
Ocala (G-11774)

Salvation Army ....E 352 796-1186
Brooksville (G-1308)

Salvation Army ....E 608 782-6126
Milton (G-10822)

Salvation Army ....C 239 417-2315
Naples (G-11292)

Sarahs Kit of Trsure Coast Inc ....B 772 834-2818
Port St Lucie (G-15181)

Someone Cares Jacksonville ....E 404 750-2378
Jacksonville (G-6744)

South Florida Wildlife Center ....E 954 524-4302
Fort Lauderdale (G-4140)

Treviso Bay Golf Club Inc ....D 239 302-5738
Naples (G-11328)

Universal SEC Guard Assn Inc ....D 954 882-3374
Sunrise (G-16842)

University Athletic Assn Inc ....C 352 375-4683
Gainesville (G-5020)

University Cntl Fla Fndtion In ....E 407 882-1220
Orlando (G-13354)

87 ENGINEERING, ACCOUNTING, RESEARCH, MANAGEMENT, AND RELATED SERVICES

8711 Engineering Services

300 Engineering Group LLC ....E 305 763-9829
Coral Gables (G-2018)

A & K Energy Conservation Inc ....C 352 567-1999
Dade City (G-2379)

▲ A & P Cnsltng Trnsp Engners C ......E 305 592-7283
Doral (G-3095)

A & P Consulting Transporta ....E 786 332-3681
Medley (G-8698)

Aacg Inc ....E 352 467-7000
Dade City (G-2380)

AB Closing Corporation ....D 407 243-6006
Orlando (G-12041)

Abacus Industries Inc ....E 800 701-8152
Naples (G-10996)

Abb Inc-Coral Springs Relays ....B 919 856-2360
Coral Springs (G-2215)

ABB Inc ....D 954 450-9544
Miramar (G-10832)

Above Group Jpa Jint Ventr LLC ....E 321 345-9026
Melbourne (G-8805)

Acm Aviation Staffing LLC ....E 520 661-6154
Coral Gables (G-2022)

Adsync Technologies Inc ....D 850 497-6969
Pensacola (G-14212)

Advanced Concepts Entps Inc ....D 850 613-6170
Shalimar (G-16467)

Advanced Systems Tech Inc ....D 407 277-8069
Orlando (G-12059)

Ae Engineering Inc ....D 904 337-6324
Jacksonville (G-5746)

Aecom Technical Services Inc ....D 305 592-4800
Doral (G-3103)

Aercap Inc ....D 954 760-7777
Fort Lauderdale (G-3582)

Aerodyne Industries LLC ....C 321 613-2948
Cape Canaveral (G-1348)

Aerospace Corporation ....D 321 853-6666
Canaveral As (G-1330)

Affiliated Engineers Se Inc ....E 352 376-5500
Newberry (G-11429)

Affordable Engrg Svcs Inc ....D 407 492-0221
Orlando (G-12074)

Agilis Engineering Inc ....C 561 626-8900
Palm Beach Gardens (G-13681)

Agilis Group Inc ....C 561 626-8900
Palm Beach Gardens (G-13682)

Aim Engineering Surveying Inc ....C 239 332-4569
Fort Myers (G-4254)

Alion - Bmh Corporation ....E 407 737-3599
Orlando (G-12095)

Allen & Company Inc ....E 407 654-5355
Winter Garden (G-19554)

American Civil Construction ....E 386 847-3079
Bunnell (G-1321)

American Cnsltng Engners Fla ....D 813 435-2600
Wesley Chapel (G-18993)

American Cnsltng Prfessionals ....E 561 253-9550
West Palm Beach (G-19031)

American Compliance Tech Inc ....D 863 533-2000
Bartow (G-307)

American Engrg & Dev Corp ....C 305 825-9800
Hialeah (G-5217)

Americaribe LLC ....D 305 374-5383
Miami (G-9146)

Andromeda Systems Incorporated ......D 904 637-2020
Jacksonville (G-5797)

Andromeda Systems Incorporated ......E 757 340-9070
Orange Park (G-11974)

Aneko LLC ....E 786 220-3384
Miami Beach (G-10549)

▼ Apg Electric Inc ....C 727 530-0077
Clearwater (G-1523)

Applied Research Assoc Inc ....D 407 823-9121
Orlando (G-12125)

Applied Visual Technology Inc ....D 407 381-5311
Orlando (G-12126)

Aptim Coastal Plg & Engrg LLC ....A 561 391-8102
Boca Raton (G-425)

Aptim Corp ....E 407 287-3200
Winter Garden (G-19555)

Aptim Government Solutions LLC ....D 305 818-1888
Miami Lakes (G-10704)

Aquarius Building Inc ....C 305 824-1324
Miami Lakes (G-10705)

ARC Acquisition Corp ....E 386 626-0005
Deland (G-2844)

◆ Ardaman & Associates Inc ....C 407 855-3860
Orlando (G-12131)

Ardaman & Associates Inc ....E 239 768-6600
Fort Myers (G-4279)

Ardurra Group Inc ....D 813 880-8881
Tampa (G-17305)

Ash Group Inc ....E 813 290-8899
Tampa (G-17311)

Astrotech Space Operations LLC ....D 321 268-3830
Titusville (G-18677)

Atkins North America Inc ....D 813 282-7275
Tampa (G-17316)

Atkins North America Inc ....E 407 532-3999
Ocoee (G-11804)

Atkins North America Inc ....C 813 282-7275
Tampa (G-17317)

Atkins North America Inc ....D 813 282-7275
Fort Lauderdale (G-3615)

S
I
C

Atkins North America Inc .... C 850 575-1800
Tallahassee *(G-16886)*
Atkins North America Inc .... E 305 592-7275
Miami *(G-9184)*
Atkins North America Inc .... E 321 242-4942
Melbourne *(G-8818)*
Atkins North America Inc .... E 863 533-7000
Bartow *(G-309)*
Atkins North America Inc .... E 850 638-2288
Chipley *(G-1489)*
Atkins North America Inc .... E 850 478-9844
Pensacola *(G-14222)*
Avcon Inc .... D 407 599-1122
Orlando *(G-12158)*
Avionica LLC .... D 786 544-1100
Miami *(G-9196)*
Aw Solutions Inc .... D 407 260-0231
Longwood *(G-8345)*
Bae Systems Tech Sltons Svcs I .... C 850 344-0819
Fort Walton Beach *(G-4754)*
Barkley Cnslting Engineers Inc .... E 850 297-0440
Tallahassee *(G-16888)*
Baslee Engrg Solutions Bes Inc .... E 813 985-7800
Tampa *(G-17341)*
Bcbe Construction LLC .... E 239 643-3343
Naples *(G-11026)*
Bcc Engineering LLC .... D 305 670-2350
Miami *(G-9231)*
BEI Engineering Group Inc .... E 239 939-5490
Fort Myers *(G-4289)*
Belcan Engineering Group LLC .... B 561 799-0625
West Palm Beach *(G-19051)*
Belcan Engineering Group LLC .... D 850 934-1098
Gulf Breeze *(G-5109)*
Belcan Engineering Group LLC .... D 561 799-0625
Palm Beach Gardens *(G-13691)*
Belcan Engineering Group LLC .... D 561 799-0625
Palm Beach Gardens *(G-13692)*
Benderson Development Co LLC .... B 941 359-8303
University Park *(G-18736)*
Bermello Ajamil & Partners Inc .... D 305 859-2050
Coral Gables *(G-2051)*
Besch & Smith Civil Group Inc .... E 904 260-6393
Saint Augustine *(G-15430)*
Bionetics Corporation .... C 321 261-3780
Merritt Island *(G-9017)*
Bowman Consulting Group Ltd .... E 772 283-1413
Stuart *(G-16594)*
Bowman Consulting Group Ltd .... E 321 255-5434
Melbourne *(G-8829)*
Bracken Engineering Inc .... D 813 243-4251
Tampa *(G-17384)*
Brown and Caldwell .... E 407 661-9500
Maitland *(G-8508)*
Brph Architects Engineers Inc .... C 321 254-7666
Melbourne *(G-8835)*
Bureau Veritas Holdings Inc .... D 954 236-8100
Sunrise *(G-16753)*
Burgess & Niple Inc .... D 813 962-8689
Tampa *(G-17401)*
Burgess Civil LLC .... D 813 985-8201
Tampa *(G-17402)*
◆ Cae USA Inc .... A 813 885-7481
Tampa *(G-17408)*
Cae USA Mission Solutions Inc .... E 813 885-7481
Tampa *(G-17409)*
Calvin Giordano & Assoc Inc .... E 954 921-7781
Fort Lauderdale *(G-3665)*
CAP Government Inc .... D 954 888-9533
Fort Lauderdale *(G-3667)*
CAP Government Inc .... D 305 448-1711
Coral Gables *(G-2060)*
Cardno Inc .... D 727 531-3505
Clearwater *(G-1556)*
Carlson Environmental Cons PC .... D 863 634-7185
West Palm Beach *(G-19074)*
Carlson Environmental Cons PC .... D 817 521-4759
Jupiter *(G-7055)*
Caulfield & Wheeler Inc .... E 561 392-1991
Boca Raton *(G-500)*
Causseaux Hewett & Walpole Inc .... E 352 331-1976
Alachua *(G-4)*
CB&i Government Solutions Inc .... E 561 627-4000
Palm Beach Gardens *(G-13702)*
CDM Federal Services Inc .... D 850 386-9500
Tallahassee *(G-16908)*
CDM SMITH INC .... D 407 660-2552
Maitland *(G-8512)*
Cedarville Engrg Group LLC .... E 610 705-4500
Pensacola *(G-14253)*

Celtic Manufacturing LLC .... E 407 909-8995
Windermere *(G-19536)*
Centerline Systems Corp .... D 813 805-2714
Tampa *(G-17442)*
▲ Central Fla Eqp Rentals Inc .... C 305 883-7518
Medley *(G-8713)*
Central Florida Testing Labs .... E 727 572-9797
Clearwater *(G-1563)*
Chastain-Skillman Inc .... D 863 646-1402
Lakeland *(G-7831)*
Chen Moore and Associates Inc .... D 954 730-0707
Fort Lauderdale *(G-3686)*
Cherokee Enterprises Inc .... E 305 828-3353
Medley *(G-8714)*
City of Kissimmee .... D 407 518-2506
Kissimmee *(G-7284)*
Coastal Engineering Assoc Inc .... E 352 796-9423
Brooksville *(G-1281)*
Cole Engineering Services Inc .... C 407 674-8300
Orlando *(G-12342)*
Colliers Engrg & Design Inc .... D 813 207-1061
Tampa *(G-17495)*
Colliers Engrg & Design Inc .... D 305 597-9701
Miami *(G-9388)*
Colwill Engrg Design Build Inc .... E 813 241-2525
Tampa *(G-17499)*
Consor Engineers LLC .... E 352 226-8447
Gainesville *(G-4869)*
Consor Engineers LLC .... E 407 829-7818
Lake Mary *(G-7579)*
Consul-Tech/Gsac Corp .... E 954 438-4300
Miramar *(G-10846)*
Corradino Group Inc .... D 800 887-5551
Doral *(G-3166)*
Corradino Group Inc .... D 305 594-0735
Doral *(G-3167)*
County of Broward .... D 954 831-0903
Pompano Beach *(G-14785)*
County of Escambia .... E 850 595-3434
Pensacola *(G-14270)*
Craig A Smith & Associates Inc .... E 561 314-4445
Boca Raton *(G-536)*
Craig Technical Consulting Inc .... E 321 613-5620
Merritt Island *(G-9024)*
Craig Technical Consulting Inc .... B 321 613-5620
Merritt Island *(G-9023)*
Craven Thompson & Assoc Inc .... D 954 739-6400
Fort Lauderdale *(G-3739)*
Crestview Aerospace LLC .... A 850 682-2746
Crestview *(G-2316)*
Cribb Philbeck Weaver Group Inc .... E 813 361-2644
Tampa *(G-17550)*
Critigen LLC .... D 407 423-0030
Orlando *(G-12385)*
Critigen LLC .... D 352 335-7991
Gainesville *(G-4872)*
Csa Ocean Sciences Inc .... D 772 219-3000
Stuart *(G-16613)*
Csi International Inc .... A 954 308-4300
Fort Lauderdale *(G-3745)*
Culpepper & Terpening Inc .... E 772 464-3537
Fort Pierce *(G-4693)*
Cumbey and Fair Inc .... E 727 797-8982
Clearwater *(G-1599)*
Cummings Aerospace Inc .... E 256 704-6300
Largo *(G-8093)*
Custom Mfg & Engrg Inc .... D 727 548-0522
Pinellas Park *(G-14513)*
D & A Construction Group Inc .... E 407 960-4032
Altamonte Springs *(G-43)*
Dade Contracting Inc .... D 305 885-8851
Medley *(G-8718)*
Dalpar Corporation .... E 850 362-6426
Fort Walton Beach *(G-4761)*
David Plummer & Associates Inc .... E 305 447-0900
Coral Gables *(G-2090)*
Davis Broward & Associates .... E 850 877-5900
Tallahassee *(G-16931)*
Dcr Engineering Services Inc .... E 863 428-8080
Mulberry *(G-10976)*
DCS Corporation .... E 850 609-4200
Niceville *(G-11444)*
Dei Services Corporation .... D 407 382-0519
Orlando *(G-12411)*
Delta Consulting Engineer Inc .... E 305 667-4772
Miami *(G-9470)*
Deployment Technologies Inc .... C 603 622-3924
Cedar Key *(G-1464)*
Devore Design LLC .... E 407 500-7427
Clermont *(G-1865)*

Diversitech Inc .... E 513 772-4447
Orlando *(G-12431)*
Dlr Group Inc .... D 407 648-1331
Orlando *(G-12435)*
Dmk Associates Inc .... E 941 412-1293
Venice *(G-18779)*
Donald W McIntosh Associates .... C 407 644-4068
Winter Park *(G-19714)*
Downrite Engineering Corp .... B 305 232-2340
Miami *(G-9487)*
Draftpros LLC .... C 786 641-5131
Miami Lakes *(G-10723)*
Drmp Inc .... C 407 896-0594
Orlando *(G-12442)*
Dudek .... B 442 245-1886
Lake Worth *(G-7723)*
E C Driver & Associates Inc .... E 850 893-6148
Tallahassee *(G-16938)*
EAC Consulting Inc .... D 305 264-2557
Miami *(G-9493)*
▲ Earthbalance Corporation .... D 941 426-7878
North Port *(G-11568)*
EC Fennell PA .... C 561 471-4029
West Palm Beach *(G-19128)*
Eisman & Russo Inc .... E 904 733-1478
Jacksonville *(G-6106)*
Electric Pwr Systems Intl Inc .... D 314 890-9999
Sanford *(G-15937)*
Electro Design Engineering Inc .... C 813 621-0121
Riverview *(G-15256)*
Elite American Group Inc .... E 305 998-8999
Hallandale Beach *(G-5168)*
Ellis & Associates Inc .... D 904 880-0960
Jacksonville *(G-6108)*
Emr Inc .... E 850 897-0210
Niceville *(G-11446)*
Engineering and Info Tech Inc .... D 609 272-1515
Coral Springs *(G-2249)*
Engineering Matrix Inc .... E 727 573-4656
Saint Petersburg *(G-15661)*
Enginring Spport Personnel Inc .... C 904 778-0735
Jacksonville *(G-6118)*
England Thims & Miller Inc .... C 904 642-8990
Jacksonville *(G-6119)*
Enodis Technology Center Inc .... E 727 376-8600
Trinity *(G-18725)*
Epsilon Systems Solutions Inc .... D 904 580-5921
Jacksonville *(G-6128)*
Es NY Engineering PA .... C 954 938-9389
Fort Lauderdale *(G-3775)*
Es NY Engineering PA .... C 727 531-3505
Clearwater *(G-1627)*
Exp US Services Inc .... C 407 660-0088
Maitland *(G-8530)*
Eyp Inc .... C 407 208-0925
Orlando *(G-12484)*
F & E Aviation Holdings Inc .... C 305 871-3758
Miami Springs *(G-10781)*
Fairfax Imaging Inc .... D 703 802-1220
Tampa *(G-17643)*
Faller Davis and Assoc Inc .... D 813 261-5136
Tampa *(G-17646)*
Figg Bridge Engineers Inc .... D 850 224-7400
Tallahassee *(G-16946)*
Figg Bridge Inspection Inc .... D 850 224-7400
Tallahassee *(G-16947)*
Figg Group Inc .... E 850 224-7400
Tallahassee *(G-16948)*
▲ Fj Turbine Power Inc .... D 305 820-8494
Hialeah *(G-5261)*
Florida Design Consultants Inc .... D 727 849-7588
Land O Lakes *(G-8047)*
Florida Drawbridge Services .... C 954 788-0969
Pompano Beach *(G-14809)*
Florida Engineers Mgt Corp .... E 850 521-0500
Tallahassee *(G-16969)*
Fluor Corporation .... E 904 778-9907
Jacksonville *(G-6206)*
Fluor Federal Solutions LLC .... D 850 283-4457
Panama City *(G-14013)*
Forefront Archtcts Engners LLC .... E 352 241-4389
Clermont *(G-1871)*
FR Aleman and Associates Inc .... E 305 591-8777
Doral *(G-3205)*
Franklin Surveying & Mapping .... D 407 410-8624
Kissimmee *(G-7313)*
Freese and Nichols Inc .... D 813 467-9180
Tampa *(G-17712)*
Ftt America LLC .... C 561 427-6400
Jupiter *(G-7075)*

Company	Code	Phone
Fusion Electric & Engrg LLC	E	239 494-4881
Bonita Springs (G-914)		
G-A-I Consultants Inc	C	407 423-8398
Orlando (G-12556)		
G-A-I Consultants Inc	D	904 363-1110
Jacksonville (G-6213)		
Gas Turbine Efficiency LLC	E	407 304-5200
Orlando (G-12560)		
Gaudet Associates Inc	E	561 748-3040
Jupiter (G-7081)		
Gem Technology Intl Corp	C	305 447-1344
Miami (G-9622)		
Genesis C E & I Services LLC	E	813 620-4500
Tampa (G-17727)		
Genterra Consultants Inc	D	904 574-4484
Jacksonville (G-6228)		
George F Young Inc	D	727 822-4317
Saint Petersburg (G-15686)		
Geosyntec Consultants Inc	D	561 995-0900
Boca Raton (G-606)		
Geotech Consultants Intl Inc	E	407 331-6332
Longwood (G-8362)		
Geotechnical & Envmtl Cons Inc	E	407 898-1818
Orlando (G-12568)		
Gfa International Inc	E	561 347-0070
Delray Beach (G-2955)		
Ghd Consulting Services Inc	C	813 971-3882
Tampa (G-17733)		
Gle Associates Inc	E	813 241-8350
Tampa (G-17735)		
GM Selby & Associates Inc	D	305 666-5775
Miami (G-9642)		
Goodrich Corporation	C	904 757-3660
Jacksonville (G-6234)		
Gossamer Crossing Inc	D	916 335-8018
Vero Beach (G-18859)		
Greenman-Pedersen Inc	E	813 632-7676
Tampa (G-17753)		
Greenman-Pedersen Inc	E	813 632-7676
Tampa (G-17754)		
Gustin Cothern & Tucker Inc	E	850 678-5141
Niceville (G-11450)		
Halff Associates Inc	E	813 620-4500
Tampa (G-17785)		
Halff Associates Inc	E	352 343-8481
Tavares (G-18608)		
Hamilton Engrg & Surveying	D	813 872-4812
Tampa (G-17786)		
Harris Corporation	B	321 494-7032
Patrick Afb (G-14120)		
Harris-Mcburney Company	C	813 626-7171
Tampa (G-17794)		
Hazen and Sawyer DPC	E	813 630-4498
Tampa (G-17798)		
Hazen and Sawyer DPC	E	561 997-8070
Boca Raton (G-621)		
Hazmed Inc	E	202 742-6521
Palm Coast (G-13830)		
HDR Construction Control Corp	E	813 282-2300
Tampa (G-17801)		
HDR Engineering Inc	D	904 598-8900
Jacksonville (G-6266)		
High Wire Networks Inc	B	407 512-9102
Boca Raton (G-628)		
Hii Unmanned Systems Inc	D	850 234-8817
Panama City (G-14028)		
Hills & Associates Inc	E	813 887-3130
Tampa (G-17826)		
Hntb Corporation	D	813 402-4150
Tampa (G-17831)		
Hntb Corporation	C	305 551-8100
Miami (G-9708)		
Hntb Corporation	D	863 804-3080
Bartow (G-321)		
Hntb Corporation	D	954 903-1785
Fort Lauderdale (G-3866)		
Hntb Corporation	C	407 805-0355
Lake Mary (G-7598)		
Hok Group Inc	C	713 407-7700
Miami (G-9709)		
Hole Montes Inc	D	239 254-2000
Naples (G-11164)		
Hole Montes Inc	E	239 985-1200
Fort Myers (G-4440)		
◆ Holtec International	D	561 745-7772
Jupiter (G-7086)		
▲ I-Con Systems Inc	D	407 365-6241
Oviedo (G-13552)		
Iap Global Services LLC	D	321 784-7100
Cape Canaveral (G-1366)		

Company	Code	Phone
Ibi Group Prof Svcs USA Inc	D	954 974-2200
Boca Raton (G-637)		
Indyne Inc	C	321 867-8561
Kennedy Space Center (G-7156)		
Infinity Engineering Group LLC	D	813 434-4770
Tampa (G-17864)		
Integrated Sol For Sys Inc	D	256 489-9723
Niceville (G-11453)		
Integrted Sltons For Systems I	E	407 399-5102
Winter Park (G-19738)		
Interplan LLC	D	407 645-5008
Altamonte Springs (G-64)		
Inwood Cnsulting Engineers Inc	D	407 971-8850
Oviedo (G-13554)		
ITI Engineering LLC	E	866 245-9356
Winter Springs (G-19805)		
J H Ham Engineering Inc	E	863 646-1448
Lakeland (G-7890)		
J2 Engineering Inc	E	256 565-1604
Saint Cloud (G-15526)		
Jacobs Civil Inc	C	813 977-3434
Tampa (G-17884)		
Jacobs Engineering Group Inc	D	813 746-3416
Tampa (G-17885)		
Jacobs Government Services Co	C	352 384-7057
Gainesville (G-4926)		
Jacobs Technology Inc	D	813 282-3500
Tampa (G-17886)		
Jacobs Technology Inc	B	321 861-6255
Kennedy Space Center (G-7157)		
Jardon & Howard Tech Inc	D	407 381-7797
Orlando (G-12700)		
Jetappster Inc	E	561 345-0669
Fort Lauderdale (G-3905)		
Joe Dereuil Associates LLC	E	850 429-1951
Pensacola (G-14335)		
John F Kennedy Space Center	A	321 861-3853
Kennedy Space Center (G-7158)		
Johnson Engineering Inc	D	239 334-0046
Fort Myers (G-4454)		
Johnson Lvnson Rgan Davila Inc	D	561 689-2303
West Palm Beach (G-19218)		
Jones Edmunds & Associates Inc	C	352 377-5821
Gainesville (G-4929)		
Jordan Jones and Goulding Inc	E	561 799-3855
North Palm Beach (G-11549)		
Jorgensen Contract Svcs LLC	B	904 268-0410
Jacksonville (G-6390)		
Jva Engineering Contractor	E	305 696-7902
Miami (G-9807)		
Keith and Associates Inc	D	954 788-3400
Pompano Beach (G-14837)		
Keith and Schnars PA	D	954 776-1616
Fort Lauderdale (G-3917)		
Keller North America Inc	D	813 884-3441
Tampa (G-17913)		
Kenyon & Partners Inc	D	813 241-6568
Tampa (G-17915)		
Kiewit Infrastructure South Co	C	407 396-8211
Kissimmee (G-7337)		
Kimley-Horn and Associates Inc	D	941 379-7600
West Palm Beach (G-19226)		
Kimley-Horn and Associates Inc	E	407 898-1511
Orlando (G-12729)		
Kimley-Horn and Associates Inc	D	561 845-0665
West Palm Beach (G-19227)		
Kimley-Horn and Associates Inc	E	772 794-4100
Vero Beach (G-18884)		
◆ Kimre Inc	E	305 233-4249
Homestead (G-5587)		
Kisinger Campo & Assoc Corp	C	813 871-5331
Tampa (G-17928)		
Kratos Tech Trning Sltions Inc	D	407 678-3388
Orlando (G-12739)		
Kratos Training Solutions	E	407 384-5660
Orlando (G-12740)		
L C Radise International	E	561 841-0103
Riviera Beach (G-15306)		
L&S Diversified LLC	D	407 681-3836
Casselberry (G-1451)		
L-3 Cmmnctns Ntronix Holdings	D	212 697-1111
Melbourne (G-8918)		
L3 Technologies Inc	D	321 868-5550
Milton (G-10819)		
LLC Golden Wolf	D	240 672-7995
Lithia (G-8301)		
Lochrane Engineering Inc	E	407 896-3317
Orlando (G-12777)		
Ltm Inc	E	904 317-1874
Jacksonville (G-6450)		

Company	Code	Phone
Macaulay-Brown Inc	C	937 426-3421
Tampa (G-17971)		
Madrid Engineering Group Inc	C	863 533-9007
Bartow (G-326)		
Mantech Systems Engrg Corp	D	850 235-2876
Panama City (G-14039)		
Mantech Systems Engrg Corp	C	954 925-0200
Hollywood (G-5471)		
Mark Two Engineering Inc	D	305 889-3280
Miami Lakes (G-10740)		
Mastec North America Inc	E	407 265-2398
Longwood (G-8380)		
Matern Professional Engrg Inc	E	407 740-5020
Maitland (G-8554)		
Matthews Design Group LLC	E	904 826-1334
Saint Augustine (G-15466)		
McSwain Engineering Inc	D	850 484-0506
Pensacola (G-14358)		
Mehta and Associates Inc	E	407 657-6662
Winter Park (G-19749)		
Meridium Group Inc	E	850 567-9949
Tallahassee (G-17043)		
Mes Simulation & Training	D	407 568-1112
Christmas (G-1497)		
Metric Civil Constructors LLC	E	904 329-3506
Jacksonville (G-6500)		
Metric Engineering Inc	D	305 235-5098
Miami (G-9944)		
◆ Mgl Engineering Inc	E	863 648-0320
Lakeland (G-7920)		
Michael Baker Intl Inc	D	813 466-6000
Tampa (G-18037)		
Michael Baker Intl Inc	E	904 380-2500
Jacksonville (G-6503)		
Michael Baker Intl Inc	E	850 205-0460
Tallahassee (G-17046)		
Michael Baker Intl Inc	E	850 269-7241
Miramar Beach (G-10923)		
Miller Legg & Associates Inc	D	954 436-7000
Fort Lauderdale (G-3973)		
Mnemonics Inc	C	321 254-7300
Melbourne (G-8940)		
Mora Engineering Contrs Inc	D	954 752-8065
Casselberry (G-1452)		
Mortensen Engineering Inc	E	813 908-5555
Tampa (G-18052)		
Mott Macdonald Florida LLC	D	850 484-6011
Pensacola (G-14370)		
Mscw Inc	C	407 678-0466
Orlando (G-12885)		
N Atkins Amer Holdings Corp	B	813 282-7275
Tampa (G-18064)		
NAVY UNITED STATES DEPARTMENT	A	850 452-6132
Pensacola (G-14381)		
Neptune Tech Services Inc	E	904 646-2700
Jacksonville (G-6535)		
Nhwl Engineering Inc	E	850 893-7722
Tallahassee (G-17057)		
◆ Noble International LLC	E	888 933-5646
Orlando (G-12915)		
◆ Nodarse & Associates Inc	D	407 740-6110
Winter Park (G-19754)		
Nova Engineering & Envmtl LLC	E	954 424-2520
Davie (G-2502)		
Nova Tech An Emplyee Owned Eng	D	850 914-0002
Tallahassee (G-17061)		
Nutting Engineers of Florida	E	561 736-4900
Boynton Beach (G-1021)		
Nv5 Inc	D	954 495-2112
Hollywood (G-5485)		
Nv5 Global Inc	C	954 495-2112
Hollywood (G-5486)		
On-Point Defense Tech LLC	E	850 226-7798
Fort Walton Beach (G-4795)		
Ops Tech Alliance LLC	B	443 223-6115
Clearwater (G-1748)		
▲ Osgood Industries LLC	C	813 448-9041
Oldsmar (G-11919)		
P A Atkins	D	813 282-7275
Tampa (G-18116)		
▼ Parametric Solutions Inc	B	561 747-6107
Jupiter (G-7123)		
Passero Associates LLC	C	904 209-0870
Saint Augustine (G-15479)		
Pegasus Technologies Inc	C	904 284-2490
Green Cove Springs (G-5060)		
Pegasus Tsi Inc	D	813 876-2424
Tampa (G-18132)		
Penn Pro Inc	E	863 648-9990
Lakeland (G-7938)		

Pevida Highway Designers LLC ....E 786 228-5666
Doral (G-3289)
Picsolve Inc ....D 407 482-3131
Orlando (G-13029)
Pike Engineering Inc ....E 813 849-4147
Land O Lakes (G-8052)
Pontchartrain Partners LLC ....D 504 872-3199
Cocoa (G-1948)
Poulos & Bennett LLC ....D 407 487-2594
Orlando (G-13044)
Power & Ctrl Installations Inc ....E 904 762-1522
Jacksonville (G-6609)
◆ Power Systems Mfg LLC ....B 561 354-1100
Jupiter (G-7124)
Powerserve Technologies Inc ....D 561 840-1441
Jupiter (G-7125)
Precision Contracting Svcs Inc ....E 407 877-1900
Winter Garden (G-19589)
Prime Technological Svcs LLC ....D 850 539-2500
Havana (G-5199)
Pro Net Group Inc ....E 407 790-4165
Maitland (G-8570)
▲ Pro Sound Inc ....E 305 891-1000
North Miami (G-11507)
Professional Engineering Cons ....D 407 422-8062
Hollywood (G-5498)
Program Controls Inc ....D 786 229-4416
Miami (G-10151)
Project Support Services Inc ....C 352 288-0216
Summerfield (G-16689)
Prosser Inc ....D 904 739-3655
Jacksonville (G-6619)
Protean Design Group Inc ....E 407 246-0044
Orlando (G-13071)
◆ Pulau Corporation ....C 407 380-9191
Orlando (G-13072)
Q Grady Minor & Associates ....E 239 947-1144
Bonita Springs (G-934)
Qualus LLC ....B 321 244-0170
Lake Mary (G-7627)
Qualus Services LLC ....D 800 434-0415
Lake Mary (G-7628)
Quantem Aviation Services LLC ....D 904 741-6881
Jacksonville (G-6626)
Quantum Marine Stabilizers ....D 954 587-4205
Fort Lauderdale (G-4074)
Range Generation Next LLC ....D 310 647-9438
Patrick Afb (G-14123)
Raydon 2 LLC ....D 386 267-2936
Port Orange (G-15086)
Reliance Test & Technology LLC ....B 703 903-6952
Eglin Afb (G-3421)
Rev 1 Power Services Inc ....D 813 657-2404
Tampa (G-18222)
Rgd & Associates Inc ....E 561 743-0165
Jupiter (G-7134)
Rnd Automation & Engrg LLC ....E 941 870-5400
Bradenton (G-1173)
▼ Robbins Engineering Inc ....E 813 972-1135
Tampa (G-18230)
Rogers Lovelock & Fritz Inc ....D 407 730-8600
Orlando (G-13123)
Rone Engineering ....C 214 630-9745
Hialeah (G-5317)
RS&h Inc ....D 407 893-5800
Orlando (G-13143)
RS&h Inc ....E 321 453-0212
Merritt Island (G-9042)
RS&h Inc ....E 954 474-3005
Fort Lauderdale (G-4095)
RS&h Inc ....B 904 256-2500
Jacksonville (G-6679)
RS&h Inc ....E 813 289-5550
Tampa (G-18238)
Russell Engineering Inc ....C 941 757-0080
Bradenton (G-1174)
S&Me Inc ....E 407 797-1273
Orlando (G-13156)
◆ Safbon Water Technology Inc ....E 813 549-0182
Tampa (G-18243)
Salas OBrien Engineers Inc ....E 321 449-1128
Merritt Island (G-9043)
Schwebke-Shiskin & Associates ....E 954 435-7010
Miramar (G-10893)
Science and MGT Resources Inc ....D 850 473-9010
Pensacola (G-14429)
Sdii Global Corporation ....E 813 496-9634
Tampa (G-18255)
◆ Serf Inc ....E 850 476-8203
Cantonment (G-1342)
Six Points LLC ....D 321 735-8630
Merritt Island (G-9045)
Smith and Gillespie Engineers ....E 904 743-6950
Jacksonville (G-6734)
Southern Dev & Cnstr Inc ....C 407 977-9898
Oviedo (G-13571)
State-Line Products S Fla Inc ....E 954 971-0791
Pompano Beach (G-14910)
Stearns Cnrad Schmidt Cnslting ....D 813 621-0080
Tampa (G-18334)
Stellar Companies Inc ....C 904 899-9393
Jacksonville (G-6788)
◆ Stellar Group Incorporated ....C 904 260-2900
Jacksonville (G-6791)
Steven Feller PE Pl ....E 954 467-1402
Fort Lauderdale (G-4155)
Strom Engineering Florida Inc ....D 813 960-3900
Wesley Chapel (G-19007)
Structral Engrg Inspctions Inc ....E 813 849-5769
Lutz (G-8460)
STS Aviation Group LLC ....D 800 800-2400
Jensen Beach (G-7022)
STS Federal LLC ....C 407 965-2596
Oviedo (G-13572)
Summit Technologies Inc ....C 407 645-2326
Navarre (G-11354)
Support Systems Associates Inc ....E 877 234-7724
Melbourne (G-8990)
Symx Infrastructure LLC ....C 305 442-8577
Coral Gables (G-2192)
System Service & Engrg Inc ....E 850 441-3458
Lynn Haven (G-8472)
Systems & Technology RES LLC ....D 844 204-0963
Palm Bay (G-13640)
T Y Lin International ....E 305 567-1888
Coral Gables (G-2193)
Tactical Air Support Inc ....C 229 563-7502
Jacksonville (G-6829)
Tandel Systems Inc ....E 727 530-1110
Oldsmar (G-11929)
Taylor Engineering Inc ....E 904 731-7040
Jacksonville (G-6837)
Tbe Caribe Inc ....E 727 531-3505
Clearwater (G-1818)
TCS Aerospace LLC ....D 478 328-8537
Crestview (G-2335)
Techncal Systems Intgrtion Inc ....E 757 424-5793
Orlando (G-13276)
Tecom Group Inc ....D 321 308-0232
Melbourne (G-8992)
Telecom Engineering Cons ....D 305 592-4328
Doral (G-3331)
Terracon Consultants Inc ....E 904 900-6494
Jacksonville (G-6847)
Terracon Consultants Inc ....E 407 740-6110
Winter Park (G-19777)
Tesinc LLC ....C 813 623-1233
Tampa (G-18417)
▲ Thales Avionics Inc ....D 407 812-2600
Orlando (G-13284)
Tierra Inc ....D 407 877-1354
Winter Garden (G-19596)
Tigerbrain/Cyntergy AEC ....E 407 365-7225
Oviedo (G-13576)
TLC Engineering Solutions Inc ....E 813 637-0110
Tampa (G-18423)
TLC Engineering Solutions Inc ....C 407 841-9050
Orlando (G-13295)
Tompkins Associates Inc ....E 800 789-1257
Orlando (G-13296)
▲ Toptech Systems Inc ....C 407 332-1774
Longwood (G-8410)
Torch Technologies Inc ....C 850 613-6997
Shalimar (G-16473)
Trajectory Inc ....E 239 217-6281
Naples (G-11327)
Trans Florida Development Corp ....D 305 378-2323
Miami (G-10400)
Trans-Market Sales LLC ....E 800 282-8808
Tampa (G-18433)
Transportation Florida Dept ....D 386 961-7050
Lake City (G-7550)
Tri-Tech Electronics Inc ....D 407 277-2131
Orlando (G-13308)
Triangle Associates Inc ....E 305 817-8443
Davie (G-2531)
Tsm Corporation ....D 901 373-0300
Orlando (G-13318)
Underwater Engrg Svcs Inc ....D 772 337-3116
Fort Pierce (G-4746)
Universal Engrg Sciences LLC ....E 407 423-0504
Orlando (G-13348)
Universal Engrg Sciences LLC ....C 561 540-6200
Delray Beach (G-3028)
Upham Inc ....D 386 672-9515
Ormond Beach (G-13530)
URS Corporation Southern ....B 813 286-1711
Tampa (G-18481)
URS Group Inc ....C 813 286-1711
Tampa (G-18482)
URS Group Inc ....B 407 425-7010
Orlando (G-13357)
URS Group Inc ....D 850 233-7000
Panama City (G-14083)
URS Group Inc ....C 850 574-3197
Tallahassee (G-17168)
USA Engineering Inc ....D 941 955-7106
Sarasota (G-16067)
Valiant Global Def Svcs Inc ....C 904 542-5318
Jacksonville (G-6901)
Vanasse Hangen Brustlin Inc ....D 407 422-3330
Orlando (G-13368)
Vectrus Mission Solutions Corp ....C 850 642-1292
Freeport (G-4817)
Venergy Group LLC ....D 772 468-0053
Fort Pierce (G-4748)
Veraxx Engineering Corporation ....E 407 382-9552
Oviedo (G-13577)
◆ Verifone Inc ....C 800 837-4366
Coral Springs (G-2296)
Vertek LLC ....E 608 495-1109
Boca Raton (G-860)
Vertex Solutions LLC ....D 888 225-9398
Niceville (G-11458)
▼ Veterans Trading Company Inc ....E 352 438-0084
Ocala (G-11794)
Volkert Inc ....D 407 965-4211
Maitland (G-8598)
Volkert Inc ....D 251 342-1070
Tampa (G-18511)
Voltair Cnslting Engineers LLC ....E 813 867-4899
Tampa (G-18512)
Vos Utility LLC ....E 305 522-5137
Miami (G-10484)
Waldrop Engineering LLC ....E 239 405-7777
Bonita Springs (G-949)
Walter Hanson & Associates Inc ....E 407 518-1034
Kissimmee (G-7410)
Wgi Inc ....D 561 687-2220
West Palm Beach (G-19424)
Wgi Inc ....D 269 381-2222
West Palm Beach (G-19425)
Williams Earth Sciences Inc ....E 727 541-3444
Largo (G-8163)
Wilson & Girgenti PA ....D 813 281-2277
Tampa (G-18559)
▲ Wingerter Laboratories Inc ....E 305 944-3401
North Miami (G-11513)
Wood Envmt Infrstrcture Sltons ....E 904 396-5173
Jacksonville (G-6940)
Wood Envmt Infrstrcture Sltons ....D 352 332-3318
Newberry (G-11435)
Woolpert Inc ....D 937 461-5660
Miami (G-10512)
Worley Field Services Inc ....D 407 903-5001
Orlando (G-13450)
WW Gay Mechanical Contr Inc ....C 352 372-3963
Gainesville (G-5034)
Xorail Inc ....C 904 443-0083
Jacksonville (G-6949)
Yang Enterprises Inc ....B 407 365-7374
Oviedo (G-13578)

8712 Architectural Services

161 Corp ....D 305 443-5206
Coral Gables (G-2017)
AB Design Group Inc ....D 407 774-6078
Longwood (G-8334)
Architectureplus Intl Inc ....D 813 281-9299
Tampa (G-17302)
Arquitectonica Intl Corp ....D 305 372-1812
Miami (G-9173)
Associated Space Design Inc ....D 813 223-2293
Tampa (G-17315)
Baker Barrios Architects Inc ....D 407 926-3000
Orlando (G-12169)
Bdg Architects LLP ....E 813 323-9233
Tampa (G-17355)
Bermello Ajamil & Partners Inc ....D 305 859-2050
Coral Gables (G-2051)

Bessolo Design Group Inc ....D 727 894-4453
Saint Petersburg (G-15597)

Best Western-Ocala Park Centre ....E 352 237-4848
Ocala (G-11639)

Bilkey/Llinas Design Assoc Inc ....E 561 253-0088
West Palm Beach (G-19053)

Brph Architects Engineers Inc ....C 321 254-7666
Melbourne (G-8835)

Brph Construction Services Inc ....E 321 259-8345
Melbourne (G-8836)

Bullock Tice Associates Inc ....E 850 434-5444
Pensacola (G-14241)

Burgess & Niple Inc ....D 813 962-8689
Tampa (G-17401)

Cdr Maguire Inc ....D 786 235-8534
Doral (G-3148)

Commons Medical Dev Inc ....E 407 425-8454
Orlando (G-12349)

Corradino Group Inc ....D 800 887-5551
Doral (G-3166)

Cuhaci Ptrson Archtcts Engnrs ....C 407 661-9100
Maitland (G-8522)

Curts Gnes Hall Archt Planners ....E 813 228-0479
Tampa (G-17558)

Dlr Group Inc ....D 407 648-1331
Orlando (G-12435)

Exp US Services Inc ....C 407 660-0088
Maitland (G-8530)

Eyp Inc ....C 407 208-0925
Orlando (G-12484)

Florida Archtctral Precast Inc ....E 772 489-0920
Fort Pierce (G-4699)

Foam By Design Inc ....E 727 561-7479
Clearwater (G-1644)

Forefront Archtcts Engnrs LLC ....E 352 241-4389
Clermont (G-1871)

Fusion Electric & Engrg LLC ....E 239 494-4881
Bonita Springs (G-914)

Gbi Investors Inc ....E 561 227-0300
North Palm Beach (G-11548)

George F Young Inc ....D 727 822-4317
Saint Petersburg (G-15686)

Gle Associates Inc ....E 813 241-8350
Tampa (G-17735)

Group 4 Design Inc ....E 904 353-5900
Jacksonville (G-6244)

Harvard Jolly Inc ....E 727 896-4611
Saint Petersburg (G-15704)

Haskell Company Inc ....B 904 791-4500
Jacksonville (G-6262)

Hhcp Architects Inc ....E 407 644-2656
Orlando (G-12637)

Hhcp Design International Inc ....D 407 644-2656
Orlando (G-12638)

Hntb Corporation ....C 407 805-0355
Lake Mary (G-7598)

Hntb Corporation ....D 954 903-1785
Fort Lauderdale (G-3866)

Hok Group Inc ....C 713 407-7700
Miami (G-9709)

Huitt - Zollars Inc ....E 407 839-0414
Orlando (G-12670)

Hunton Brady Architects PA ....D 407 839-0886
Orlando (G-12672)

Icon Design Group Inc ....E 561 305-4477
Mount Dora (G-10953)

Interplan LLC ....D 407 645-5008
Altamonte Springs (G-64)

J V Scg-Cems LLC ....E 850 438-0050
Pensacola (G-14332)

Jacobs Civil Inc ....C 813 977-3434
Tampa (G-17884)

Karp Kobi Archtcts Intr Dsgns ....E 305 573-1818
Miami (G-9811)

Keesee and Associates Inc ....E 407 880-2333
Maitland (G-8550)

Leo A Daly Company ....E 305 461-9480
Miami (G-9861)

Little Dvrsfd Archtctral Cnslt ....E 407 218-8282
Orlando (G-12773)

Manhattan Construction Fla Inc ....E 239 643-6000
Naples (G-11203)

Mehta and Associates Inc ....E 407 657-6662
Winter Park (G-19749)

Mge Architects LLC ....E 305 444-0413
Coral Gables (G-2146)

Miller Legg & Associates Inc ....D 954 436-7000
Fort Lauderdale (G-3973)

Moretrench Environmental Lsg ....C 407 897-8562
Orlando (G-12878)

Mott Macdonald Florida LLC ....D 850 484-6011
Pensacola (G-14370)

N Atkins Amer Holdings Corp ....B 813 282-7275
Tampa (G-18064)

▼ Nichols Architects Inc ....D 305 443-5206
Coral Gables (G-2159)

Nicklaus Companies LLC ....E 561 227-0300
Palm Beach Gardens (G-13757)

Passero Associates LLC ....C 904 209-0870
Saint Augustine (G-15479)

Prosser Inc ....D 904 739-3655
Jacksonville (G-6619)

RE Chisholm Architects Inc ....E 305 661-2070
Miami (G-10185)

Refurbishing Works LLC ....E 407 281-1135
Orlando (G-13094)

Rogers Lovelock & Fritz Inc ....E 407 730-8600
Orlando (G-13123)

RS&h Inc ....E 813 289-5550
Tampa (G-18238)

RS&h Inc ....D 407 893-5800
Orlando (G-13143)

RS&h Inc ....E 954 474-3005
Fort Lauderdale (G-4095)

RS&h Inc ....B 904 256-2500
Jacksonville (G-6679)

Song & Associates Inc ....D 561 655-2423
West Palm Beach (G-19367)

Stantec Architecture Inc ....E 301 220-1861
Orlando (G-13233)

Stantec Architecture Inc ....E 813 223-9500
Tampa (G-18330)

Stantec Architecture Inc ....C 904 247-0787
Jacksonville (G-6784)

Studioplus LLC ....E 239 476-8888
Fort Myers (G-4609)

Symx Infrastructure LLC ....C 305 442-8577
Coral Gables (G-2192)

Triangle Associates Inc ....E 305 817-8443
Davie (G-2531)

URS Group Inc ....C 813 286-1711
Tampa (G-18482)

Will Perkins Inc ....D 305 569-1333
Coral Gables (G-2212)

Zyscovich Inc ....D 305 372-5222
Miami (G-10532)

8713 Surveying Services

All-American Surveyors Fla Inc ....E 904 279-0088
Jacksonville (G-5768)

Allen & Company Inc ....E 407 654-5355
Winter Garden (G-19554)

American Surveying Mapping Inc ....C 407 426-7979
Orlando (G-12116)

Atkins North America Inc ....D 813 282-7275
Tampa (G-17316)

Atkins North America Inc ....D 813 282-7275
Fort Lauderdale (G-3615)

Avirom and Associates Inc ....E 561 392-2594
Boca Raton (G-437)

Bowman Consulting Group Ltd ....E 772 283-1413
Stuart (G-16594)

Bowman Consulting Group Ltd ....E 321 255-5434
Melbourne (G-8829)

Caulfield & Wheeler Inc ....E 561 392-1991
Boca Raton (G-500)

Causseaux Hewett & Walpole Inc ....E 352 331-1976
Alachua (G-4)

Clary & Associates Inc ....E 904 260-2703
Jacksonville (G-5964)

Colliers Engrg & Design Inc ....D 813 207-1061
Tampa (G-17495)

Colliers Engrg & Design Inc ....D 305 597-9701
Miami (G-9388)

Consul-Tech/Gsac Corp ....E 954 438-4300
Miramar (G-10846)

County of Hillsborough ....E 813 307-4755
Tampa (G-17532)

Craig A Smith & Associates Inc ....E 561 314-4445
Boca Raton (G-536)

Craven Thompson & Assoc Inc ....D 954 739-6400
Fort Lauderdale (G-3739)

Culpepper & Terpening Inc ....E 772 464-3537
Fort Pierce (G-4693)

Cumbey and Fair Inc ....E 727 797-8982
Clearwater (G-1599)

Davis Broward & Associates ....E 850 877-5900
Tallahassee (G-16931)

Donald W McIntosh Associates ....C 407 644-4068
Winter Park (G-19714)

Drmp Inc ....C 407 896-0594
Orlando (G-12442)

Drs Training Ctrl Systems LLC ....E 850 302-3000
Fort Walton Beach (G-4762)

Echezabal & Associates Inc ....E 813 933-2505
Tampa (G-17613)

ETM Surveying & Mapping Inc ....E 904 642-8550
Jacksonville (G-6135)

First Choice Surveying Inc ....E 407 951-3425
Sanford (G-15940)

FR Aleman and Associates Inc ....E 305 591-8777
Doral (G-3205)

George F Young Inc ....D 727 822-4317
Saint Petersburg (G-15686)

Ghiotto and Associates Inc ....E 904 886-0071
Jacksonville (G-6230)

Gossamer Crossing Inc ....D 916 335-8018
Vero Beach (G-18859)

Gsp Marketing Technologies Inc ....C 727 532-0647
Clearwater (G-1656)

Gustin Cothern & Tucker Inc ....E 850 678-5141
Niceville (G-11450)

Johnson Engineering Inc ....D 239 334-0046
Fort Myers (G-4454)

Keith and Associates Inc ....D 954 788-3400
Pompano Beach (G-14837)

Keith and Schnars PA ....D 954 776-1616
Fort Lauderdale (G-3917)

L&S Diversified LLC ....E 407 681-3836
Casselberry (G-1451)

Lochrane Engineering Inc ....E 407 896-3317
Orlando (G-12777)

Miller Legg & Associates Inc ....D 954 436-7000
Fort Lauderdale (G-3973)

Nexgen Surveying LLC ....E 561 508-6272
West Palm Beach (G-19276)

Professional Engineering Cons ....D 407 422-8062
Hollywood (G-5498)

Q Grady Minor & Associates ....E 239 947-1144
Bonita Springs (G-934)

Quantum Spatial Inc ....F 920 457-3631
Saint Petersburg (G-15813)

Republic National Inc ....D 407 862-4200
Longwood (G-8394)

RM Barrineau & Assoc Inc ....E 352 622-3133
Ocala (G-11770)

Schwebke-Shiskin & Associates ....E 954 435-7010
Miramar (G-10893)

Southstern Srvying Mpping Corp ....D 407 292-8580
Orlando (G-13222)

Star Data Systems Inc ....E 561 743-7500
North Palm Beach (G-11557)

Surveying and Mapping LLC ....E 850 857-7725
Pensacola (G-14454)

Surveying and Mapping LLC ....E 850 385-1179
Tallahassee (G-17125)

Survtech Solutions Inc ....D 813 621-4929
Tampa (G-18351)

Upham Inc ....D 386 672-9515
Ormond Beach (G-13530)

Usic Locating Services LLC ....C 904 296-7754
Jacksonville (G-6900)

Walter Hanson & Associates Inc ....E 407 518-1034
Kissimmee (G-7410)

8721 Accounting, Auditing & Bookkeeping Svcs

A-Lign Compliance and SEC Inc ....E 888 702-5446
Tampa (G-17218)

Adventist Hlth Systm/Snbelt In ....B 844 259-3977
Altamonte Springs (G-20)

Advisory Services Corporation ....E 561 694-0110
Palm Beach Gardens (G-13679)

Ahearn Jasco & Company PA ....E 954 781-8800
Pompano Beach (G-14736)

American Metering Services Inc ....E 941 358-1253
Sarasota (G-16021)

Arnold Porter Kaye Scholer LLP ....C 850 807-3700
Tallahassee (G-16883)

Associated Billing Svcs Inc ....E 407 886-8164
Apopka (G-156)

B and B Management Services ....C 305 863-8860
Coral Gables (G-2039)

Bastion Capital Investment ....E 305 431-8531
Miami (G-9227)

Bdo Usa LLP ....B 305 373-5500
Miami (G-9234)

Becher Nall Brydon Spahn & Co ....E 305 512-0444
Miami Lakes (G-10712)

▲ Berkowitz Pllack Brant Advsors ....D 305 379-7000
Miami *(G-9244)*
Berman Hpkins Wrght Lham Cpas ....D 321 757-2020
Melbourne *(G-8826)*
Beyer-Brown & Associates LP ....E 407 232-9046
Orlando *(G-12186)*
Billing Masters Inc ....E 954 752-4944
Parkland *(G-14106)*
Birmingham Hospitality Corp ....E 850 934-3609
Gulf Breeze *(G-5110)*
Brimmer Burek Keelan LLP ....E 813 282-3400
Tampa *(G-17389)*
Brown Thornton Pacenta & Co PA ....E 850 434-3146
Pensacola *(G-14240)*
Capstone Corporation ....E 813 885-7766
Tampa *(G-17416)*
Carr Riggs & Ingram LLC ....D 904 471-3445
Jacksonville *(G-5910)*
Carr Riggs & Ingram LLC ....D 941 747-0500
Sarasota *(G-16116)*
Carr Riggs & Ingram LLC ....E 321 255-0088
Melbourne *(G-8838)*
Carr Riggs & Ingram LLC ....D 772 283-2356
Stuart *(G-16601)*
Carr Riggs & Ingram LLC ....E 850 785-6153
Panama City *(G-13977)*
Carr Riggs & Ingram LLC ....E 850 897-4333
Niceville *(G-11442)*
Carr Riggs & Ingram LLC ....C 407 644-7455
Winter Park *(G-19696)*
Carr Riggs & Ingram LLC ....D 850 244-8395
Destin *(G-3085)*
Carr Riggs & Ingram LLC ....C 727 446-0504
Clearwater *(G-1559)*
Carr Riggs & Ingram LLC ....E 850 878-8777
Tallahassee *(G-16906)*
Cbiz Accnting Tax Advsory Mmph ....D 305 503-4200
Miami *(G-9337)*
Cbiz Mhm LLC ....D 813 594-1400
Tampa *(G-17431)*
Cherry Bekaert LLP ....E 954 556-1720
Fort Lauderdale *(G-3687)*
Cherry Bekaert LLP ....E 786 693-6300
Coral Gables *(G-2067)*
Cherry Bekaert LLP ....E 813 251-1010
Tampa *(G-17466)*
Cherry Bekaert LLP ....E 407 423-7911
Orlando *(G-12295)*
Christopher Smith Leonard CPA ....D 941 954-4040
Sarasota *(G-16122)*
City of Jacksonville ....C 904 630-2935
Jacksonville *(G-5960)*
Client Business Services Inc ....E 239 275-2700
Fort Myers *(G-4314)*
Cliftonlarsonallen LLP ....D 239 561-1110
Fort Myers *(G-4315)*
Cliftonlarsonallen LLP ....E 813 384-2700
Tampa *(G-17488)*
Cliftonlarsonallen LLP ....E 407 802-1200
Orlando *(G-12319)*
Coadvantage Resources Inc ....D 407 422-8448
Orlando *(G-12331)*
Company Combo LLC ....D 866 428-2030
Orlando *(G-12354)*
Countrywide Payroll & Hr ....E 877 257-6662
Orlando *(G-12373)*
Daszkal Bolton LLP ....D 561 367-1040
Boca Raton *(G-544)*
Deloitte & Touche LLP ....C 904 665-1400
Jacksonville *(G-6058)*
Deloitte & Touche LLP ....D 813 273-8300
Tampa *(G-17587)*
Deloitte & Touche LLP ....D 617 960-8170
Lake Mary *(G-7584)*
Deloitte & Touche LLP ....D 561 962-7700
Boca Raton *(G-550)*
Deloitte Tax LLP ....C 617 960-8170
Miami *(G-9469)*
Dermatology Billing Assoc Inc ....E 407 678-8937
Fern Park *(G-3512)*
Diagnstic Clinic Med Group Inc ....D 727 585-7061
Largo *(G-8095)*
Divine Bllock Mrtin Sllari Pro ....E 561 686-1110
West Palm Beach *(G-19124)*
Duggan Joiner & Co ....E 352 732-0171
Ocala *(G-11675)*
E F Alvarez & Company PA ....E 305 444-6503
Coral Gables *(G-2097)*
Edward P Schmitzer CPA PA ....E 904 396-5831
Jacksonville *(G-6104)*
Eisneramper LLP ....C 305 371-6200
Miami *(G-9511)*
Ernst & Young LLP ....D 904 358-2000
Jacksonville *(G-6131)*
Ernst & Young LLP ....D 305 358-4111
Miami *(G-9531)*
Ernst & Young LLP ....D 813 225-4800
Tampa *(G-17638)*
First National Bank of Mt Dora ....E 352 383-2111
Mount Dora *(G-10950)*
First Service Corporation ....B 850 769-8981
Panama City *(G-14006)*
Forvis LLP ....D 727 223-6242
Tampa *(G-17706)*
Frazier & Deeter LLC ....D 813 874-1280
Tampa *(G-17710)*
Fuoco Group LLP ....E 561 626-0400
North Palm Beach *(G-11547)*
▲ Gamo Outdoor Usa Inc ....E 479 636-1200
Davie *(G-2483)*
Garcia Espnosa Myres Rdrguez T ....D 305 529-5440
Coral Gables *(G-2111)*
Geller Rgans Jmes Oppnhmer Cre ....E 407 425-4636
Orlando *(G-12565)*
Gevity Hr Inc ....A 941 741-4300
Lakewood Ranch *(G-8017)*
Grant Thornton LLP ....C 954 768-9900
Fort Lauderdale *(G-3831)*
Griggs Group Cpas ....E 904 280-2053
Ponte Vedra Beach *(G-14983)*
Happy Tax Franchising LLC ....C 844 426-1040
Miami Beach *(G-10599)*
Healthcare Billing Systems LLC ....C 386 274-7800
Ormond Beach *(G-13503)*
Hernando-Pasco Hospice Inc ....D 352 596-0433
Brooksville *(G-1293)*
Hoch Frey & Zugman ....E 561 393-0411
Boca Raton *(G-629)*
Hole Montes Inc ....D 239 254-2000
Naples *(G-11164)*
Hollywell Partners LLC ....E 813 394-4304
Tampa *(G-17834)*
Holyfield & Thomas LLC ....E 561 689-6000
West Palm Beach *(G-19181)*
Hurd Hwkins Myers Rdsevich PA ....E 727 501-1111
Largo *(G-8120)*
Indelible Solutions LLP ....D 850 321-5168
Jacksonville *(G-6316)*
Interval Holding Company Inc ....A 305 666-1861
South Miami *(G-16504)*
James Moore & Co PL ....D 352 378-1331
Gainesville *(G-4928)*
Joseph L Rley Anesthesia Assoc ....D 407 687-0444
Maitland *(G-8549)*
Kaufman Rossin Co A Prof Assn ....C 305 858-5600
Miami *(G-9813)*
Kavaliro Payroll Services Corp ....E 407 243-6006
Orlando *(G-12720)*
Kerkering Barberio & Co PA ....D 941 365-3745
Sarasota *(G-16211)*
Kpmg LLP ....C 305 358-2300
Miami *(G-9835)*
Kpmg LLP ....D 407 423-3426
Orlando *(G-12738)*
Leon County School Board ....C 850 487-2140
Tallahassee *(G-17025)*
Marcum LLP ....D 954 320-8000
Fort Lauderdale *(G-3956)*
Marcum LLP ....D 561 653-7300
West Palm Beach *(G-19251)*
Markham Nrton Mstller Wrght PA ....E 239 433-5554
Fort Myers *(G-4501)*
Mazars USA LLP ....E 561 422-1104
West Palm Beach *(G-19256)*
Mc Clain Groves Corporation ....E 305 503-4200
Miami *(G-9914)*
Medical Accounts Systems LLC ....E 305 373-0120
Miami *(G-9930)*
Medical Ansthsia Pain MGT Cons ....E 239 332-5344
Fort Myers *(G-4509)*
Medical Business Service Inc ....D 305 446-2378
Coral Gables *(G-2144)*
Medics Ambulance Service Inc ....E 954 763-1776
Pompano Beach *(G-14854)*
Mfp Inc ....C 727 446-0018
Sarasota *(G-16231)*
Mgsi LLC ....E 813 890-8004
Tampa *(G-18033)*
Morton Plant Mase Hlth Care In ....B 727 462-7777
Clearwater *(G-1726)*
MSL PA ....E 407 740-5400
Orlando *(G-12887)*
NAVY UNITED STATES DEPARTMENT ....B 850 452-2734
Pensacola *(G-14380)*
Nutritious Lifestyles LLC ....E 407 894-1444
Orlando *(G-12921)*
Oak Run Associates Ltd ....C 352 414-4309
Ocala *(G-11744)*
Parses Inc ....E 813 936-1090
Tampa *(G-18123)*
Payday of America LLC ....E 904 398-3374
Jacksonville *(G-6593)*
Pdr Certified Pub Accountant ....E 727 785-4447
Clearwater *(G-1755)*
Physicians Ind MGT Svcs Inc ....E 813 886-8334
Tampa *(G-18149)*
Pricewaterhousecoopers LLP ....B 813 229-0221
Tampa *(G-18166)*
Pricewaterhousecoopers LLP ....B 813 348-7000
Tampa *(G-18167)*
Pricewtrhscpers It Svcs US LLC ....E 813 348-7000
Tampa *(G-18169)*
Purvis Gray & Co ....E 352 732-3872
Gainesville *(G-4982)*
Pw Finacial Solutions LLC ....D 813 348-7725
Tampa *(G-18184)*
Rehmann Robson LLC ....D 239 254-5057
Bonita Springs *(G-936)*
Rehmann Robson LLC ....E 561 912-2300
Stuart *(G-16661)*
Rovete Inc ....E 561 659-3000
West Palm Beach *(G-19348)*
RSM US LLP ....E 727 821-6161
Saint Petersburg *(G-15833)*
RSM US LLP ....D 407 898-2727
Orlando *(G-13145)*
S Davis & Associates PA Inc ....E 954 927-5900
Hollywood *(G-5511)*
S2 Hr Solutions 1a LLC ....A 888 780-8807
Saint Petersburg *(G-15834)*
Saltmarsh Cleaveland & Gund PA ....D 850 435-8300
Pensacola *(G-14427)*
Sanson Kline Jacomino and Co ....E 305 269-8633
Miami *(G-10239)*
Sbf LLC ....D 727 343-7166
Saint Petersburg *(G-15839)*
SC&h Group Inc ....E 813 769-3555
Tampa *(G-18250)*
Schellman & Company LLC ....C 866 254-0000
Tampa *(G-18251)*
Schulman Lobel Wolfson ....E 954 840-8867
Coral Springs *(G-2283)*
Sharff Wttmer Kurtz Jackson PA ....D 305 666-7229
Coral Gables *(G-2185)*
Siegelaub Roseberg Golding & ....E 954 753-2222
Boca Raton *(G-801)*
Smyth & Hauck PA CPAs ....E 561 848-9300
North Palm Beach *(G-11556)*
Southeastern Funeral Dirs Svc ....E 904 726-5533
Jacksonville *(G-6754)*
Synergy Billing LLC ....C 386 675-4709
Daytona Beach *(G-2670)*
Tallahassee Mem Healthcare Inc ....D 850 431-1155
Tallahassee *(G-17139)*
Templeton & Company LLP ....E 561 798-9988
West Palm Beach *(G-19382)*
Thomas Howell Ferguson PA Inc ....D 850 668-8100
Tallahassee *(G-17157)*
University of Miami ....D 305 284-4877
Coral Gables *(G-2202)*
Warren Averett Companies LLC ....D 850 435-7400
Pensacola *(G-14466)*
Warren Averett Companies LLC ....E 850 244-5121
Fort Walton Beach *(G-4809)*
Withumsmith+brown PC ....D 407 849-1569
Orlando *(G-13443)*
Ww Lbv Inc ....E 407 396-8806
Kissimmee *(G-7413)*

8731 Commercial Physical & Biological Research

Advanced Concepts Entps Inc ....D 850 613-6170
Shalimar *(G-16467)*
Advanced Pier Technology LLC ....D 352 796-3847
Brooksville *(G-1265)*
Advanced Software Pdts Group ....E 239 649-1548
Naples *(G-11001)*
Aerospace Corporation ....D 321 853-6666
Canaveral As *(G-1330)*

▲ Agri-Starts Micros Inc.............E.......407 889-8055
Apopka (G-152)
Agricultural Research Service..............C....352 374-5860
Gainesville (G-4830)
Algenol Biotech LLC.................E....239 498-2000
Fort Myers (G-4259)
Applied Genetic Tech Corp..........D.....386 462-2204
Alachua (G-2)
Applied Research Assoc Inc.............E....850 678-5222
Niceville (G-11438)
Applied Research Assoc Inc...........C....850 914-3188
Panama City (G-13956)
Applied Research Assoc Inc...........D....407 823-9121
Orlando (G-12125)
Azure Summit Technology Inc.........D....321 215-2070
Melbourne (G-8822)
Barr Systems Inc....................E....352 491-3100
Gainesville (G-4842)
Battelle Memorial Institute...........A....614 424-7806
Melbourne (G-8824)
Beacon Phrm Jupiter LLC...............E....212 991-8988
Jupiter (G-7048)
Bioteknica Inc......................E....305 445-2080
Coral Gables (G-2055)
Bpc Plasma Inc......................E....561 569-3100
Boca Raton (G-479)
Brammer Bio LLC....................B....386 418-1482
Alachua (G-3)
Cardone Training Technologies.............E....305 865-5261
Miami (G-9313)
Celmark Laboratories LLC...........D....407 859-7701
Orlando (G-12252)
Compass Research LLC................E....321 202-2723
Melbourne (G-8848)
Compass Research LLC................E....407 426-9299
Orlando (G-12355)
Compass Research LLC................E....407 426-9299
Windermere (G-19537)
Conservancy Southwest Fla Inc......E....239 262-0304
Naples (G-11076)
Craig Technical Consulting Inc.............E....321 613-5620
Merritt Island (G-9024)
Design Interactive Inc................D....407 706-0977
Orlando (G-12412)
▲ Diamedix Corporation...............D....305 324-2300
Miami Lakes (G-10721)
Diversitech Inc......................E....513 772-4447
Orlando (G-12431)
Environmental Services Inc............C....386 566-2733
Ormond Beach (G-13489)
Esi Sky River Inc....................B....561 691-7171
Juno Beach (G-7030)
Fla Dpt Envirnmntal Prtection..........C....321 638-1000
Cocoa (G-1936)
Florida Max Planck Corporation...........C....561 972-9000
Jupiter (G-7070)
General Dynmics Ots Ncvlle Inc.........D....850 897-9700
Niceville (G-11449)
Goodwin Biotechnology Inc ....D....954 327-9645
Plantation (G-14650)
Guardian Fueling Technologies..........E....239 210-2053
Fort Myers (G-4426)
Harvest Croo LLC....................E....813 752-5111
Plant City (G-14561)
Hesperos Inc........................E....407 900-5915
Orlando (G-12636)
Hill Top Research Incorporated.........D....727 344-7602
Saint Petersburg (G-15707)
Imec USA Nnlctrnics Dsign Ctr ....E....407 749-7817
Kissimmee (G-7325)
Interactive Communications Inc..........B....305 807-3500
Doral (G-3241)
Issues & Answers Network Inc..........D....727 233-1879
New Port Richey (G-11389)
K9s For Warriors Research Inst ....D....904 686-1956
Ponte Vedra (G-14967)
Kbr Wyle Services LLC.................E....850 678-2126
Niceville (G-11454)
Kimera Labs Inc.....................E....305 454-7836
Miramar (G-10872)
Knights Manufacturing Company ....D....321 607-9900
Titusville (G-18691)
Leidos Inc..........................D....703 676-5590
Saint Petersburg (G-15745)
M2gen Corp.........................C....813 745-4261
Hudson (G-5644)
Mimedx Inc.........................E....813 866-0000
Tampa (G-18041)
Modis Inc..........................C....954 759-0070
Fort Lauderdale (G-3976)

Mriglobal..........................E.......321 722-1556
Palm Bay (G-13629)
Nanocap Technologies LLC............E....941 383-4536
Longboat Key (G-8308)
◆ Noble International LLC.............E....888 933-5646
Orlando (G-12915)
Northrop Grumman Systems Corp.......D....850 863-8000
Fort Walton Beach (G-4794)
▲ Oglesby Plants Intl Inc ....C....850 762-3229
Altha (G-116)
Opko Health Inc.....................C....305 575-4100
Miami (G-10076)
Ops Tech Alliance LLC................B....443 223-6115
Clearwater (G-1748)
Oxbow Corporation..................D....561 907-5400
West Palm Beach (G-19300)
Pax Technology Inc..................A....904 551-3939
Jacksonville (G-6591)
Pax Technology Inc..................E....206 234-3219
Jacksonville (G-6592)
Resilience Government Svcs Inc ....D....386 462-9663
Alachua (G-12)
▲ Sancilio & Company Inc ....D....561 847-2302
Riviera Beach (G-15317)
Sancilio & Company Inc ....D....561 847-2302
Riviera Beach (G-15316)
Sanofi Pasteur Vaxdesign Corp.........D....407 243-5600
Orlando (G-13166)
Science Applications Intl Corp ....E....703 676-4300
Panama City Beach (G-14103)
Sfbc Ft Myers Inc....................C....239 277-0730
Fort Myers (G-4591)
South Florida Kinetics Inc ....B....305 341-0423
Miami (G-10303)
Sun Health Corporation..............C....310 268-3648
Sarasota (G-16059)
▲ Synquest Laboratories Inc...........E....386 462-0788
Alachua (G-13)
Tampa Medical Group PA ....E....813 879-5485
Tampa (G-18392)
Teledyne Flir LLC....................D....407 816-0091
Orlando (G-13278)
Testamerica Laboratories Inc ....D....850 878-3994
Tallahassee (G-17156)
Tissuetech Inc......................E....786 817-6990
Miami (G-10394)
Universal Systems & Tech Inc ....E....407 219-5340
Orlando (G-13352)
Visual Awareness Technologies..........D....813 207-5055
Saint Petersburg (G-15888)

8732 Commercial Economic, Sociological & Educational Research

20/20 Research Inc..................E.......786 594-3740
Doral (G-3092)
Across Oceans Group Inc..............C....561 325-9522
Palm Beach Gardens (G-13678)
American Drctons RES Group Inc.........C....863 602-0662
Lakeland (G-7796)
American Drctons RES Group Inc.........C....863 709-0553
Lakeland (G-7797)
Avcon Inc...........................D....407 599-1122
Orlando (G-12158)
Brp US Inc..........................E....321 726-2000
Palm Bay (G-13609)
Capture Inc.........................E....772 223-5400
Stuart (G-16599)
Carbonview Research Inc ....A....561 277-6144
Jupiter (G-7054)
Center For The Advncment Scnce ....E....321 253-5107
Melbourne (G-8840)
Central Marketing Inc ....B....727 819-2217
Port Richey (G-15100)
Control Systems Research Inc ....E....850 678-7015
Shalimar (G-16469)
Cunningham Field & RES Svc Inc ....E....386 226-1461
Daytona Beach (G-2570)
Cunningham Field & RES Svc Inc ....E....386 673-1181
Ormond Beach (G-13482)
Cunningham Field & RES Svc Inc ....E....386 677-5644
Ormond Beach (G-13483)
Dart Container Sales Co LLC...........C....954 698-6556
Fort Lauderdale (G-3750)
Demarac Assocs Inc ....E....561 994-2771
Boca Raton (G-551)
Dolphins Plus Inc....................E....305 451-1993
Key Largo (G-7175)
Downs & St Germain RES Inc............D....850 906-3111
Tallahassee (G-16936)

Dtw Marketing Research Group ....E....904 491-1110
Fernandina Beach (G-3525)
Economic Research Services Inc ....E....850 562-1211
Tallahassee (G-16939)
Gartner Inc.........................D....239 561-4000
Fort Myers (G-4408)
Highpoint Solutions LLC..............D....813 414-5150
Tampa (G-17821)
Issues & Answers Network Inc..........D....727 233-1879
New Port Richey (G-11389)
Meclabs Institute LLC................D....904 813-7000
Jacksonville (G-6488)
Mriglobal..........................E....321 722-1556
Palm Bay (G-13629)
Mvl Group Inc......................A....561 748-0931
Jupiter (G-7117)
Newfold Digital Inc..................E....866 897-5421
Jacksonville (G-6540)
Nielsen Company (us) LLC.............C....813 366-3000
Oldsmar (G-11917)
Nielsen Company (us) LLC.............E....954 753-6043
Coral Springs (G-2274)
Nors Surveys Inc....................D....305 553-8585
Miami (G-10052)
▼ Original Impressions LLC...........C....305 233-1322
Weston (G-19472)
Parnters & Jh Schorr Center of ....E....561 983-4949
Greenacres (G-5076)
Pharmacy Management Svcs Inc ....A....813 626-7788
Tampa (G-18142)
Professional Survey Inc................D....727 373-7499
Fort Lauderdale (G-4064)
Quantum Research Intl Inc ....D....850 613-6680
Shalimar (G-16471)
Responsivmr Inc.....................D....561 965-8300
Greenacres (G-5080)
Review Trackers Inc..................D....866 854-7670
Green Cove Springs (G-5062)
Sales and Marketing Tech Inc ....E....407 682-2222
Longwood (G-8398)
Schlesinger Associates NY Inc ....E....407 660-1808
Maitland (G-8576)
Simmons Market RES Bur Inc ....E....800 551-6425
Deerfield Beach (G-2796)
Simmons Research LLC................D....954 246-8314
Deerfield Beach (G-2797)
Southstern Archlogical RES Inc ....C....407 236-7711
Orlando (G-13221)
Suncoast Nuroscience Assoc Inc ....C....727 824-7135
Saint Petersburg (G-15865)
United Systems and Sftwr Inc ....E....407 875-2120
Lake Mary (G-7651)

8733 Noncommercial Research Organizations

Acrc-Cardiology LLC.................E.......561 966-8815
Boynton Beach (G-957)
Advanced Concepts Entps Inc ....D....850 613-6170
Shalimar (G-16467)
Aerospace Corporation...............D....321 853-6666
Canaveral As (G-1330)
American Cancer Society Inc ....D....407 843-8680
Orlando (G-12106)
American Cancer Society Inc ....D....904 398-0537
Jacksonville (G-5776)
American Ht Ldging Eductl Inst ....D....407 999-8100
Orlando (G-12109)
Ameripath Inc......................E....407 587-4221
Orlando (G-12118)
Archbold Expeditions Inc.............E....863 465-2571
Venus (G-18825)
Buonicnti Fund To Cure Prlysis ....B....305 243-6001
Miami (G-9295)
Cognitive Research Corporation ....E....727 897-9000
Saint Petersburg (G-15630)
Craig Technical Consulting Inc ....B....321 613-5620
Merritt Island (G-9023)
Derma Care Research Labs LLC ....D....386 871-0812
Daytona Beach (G-2582)
Dolphin Research Center Inc ....D....305 289-1121
Marathon (G-8617)
Environmental Protection Agcy ....D....850 934-9208
Gulf Breeze (G-5113)
Epilepsy Foundation America ....D....301 459-3700
Brandon (G-1227)
Florida Inst For Humn Mch Cgnt ....D....850 202-4400
Pensacola (G-14308)
Florida Max Planck Corporation ....C....561 972-9000
Jupiter (G-7070)

S
I
C

▲ Florida Prton Therapy Inst Inc ....E 904 588-1239
  Jacksonville *(G-6199)*

Florida Wellcare Alliance ....E 352 746-5111
  Hernando *(G-5207)*

▲ Harbo Branc Ocean Instit Inc ....C 772 465-2400
  Fort Pierce *(G-4709)*

LD Pnkey Dntl Foundation Inc ....D 305 428-5544
  Key Biscayne *(G-7166)*

Life Extension Foundation Inc ....B 954 766-8433
  Fort Lauderdale *(G-3941)*

Mannheimer Foundation Inc ....D 305 245-1551
  Homestead *(G-5590)*

Mote Marine Laboratory Inc ....C 941 388-4441
  Sarasota *(G-16239)*

One Call Medical Inc ....D 973 257-1000
  Jacksonville *(G-6560)*

Oregon Hlth Scnce Univ Vgti FL ....D 772 345-8484
  Port Saint Lucie *(G-15157)*

Orlando Clinical RES Ctr Inc ....D 689 255-9280
  Orlando *(G-12945)*

Quantum Tech Sciences Inc ....A 321 868-0288
  Melbourne *(G-8963)*

Roskamp Institute Inc ....E 941 752-2949
  Sarasota *(G-16049)*

Sandhill Research LLC ....E 386 785-2396
  Lake Mary *(G-7636)*

Seacamp Association Inc ....C 305 872-2331
  Big Pine Key *(G-380)*

Sirion Therapeutics Inc ....E 813 496-7325
  Tampa *(G-18288)*

Skeletal Dynamics Inc ....D 305 596-7585
  Miami *(G-10280)*

South Fla Vtrans Affirs Fndtio ....D 305 575-3179
  Miami *(G-10300)*

Southstern Archlogical RES Inc ....C 407 236-7711
  Orlando *(G-13221)*

Stein Gerontological Inst Inc ....D 305 751-8626
  Miami *(G-10331)*

Sun Health Corporation ....C 310 268-3648
  Sarasota *(G-16059)*

University Clncal Rsrch-Dland ....E 386 740-0770
  Deland *(G-2885)*

University of South Florida ....E 813 974-2897
  Tampa *(G-18479)*

8734 Testing Laboratories

ABC Research Corporation ....D 352 335-5130
  Gainesville *(G-4829)*

Advanced Envmtl Labs Inc ....D 904 363-9350
  Jacksonville *(G-5742)*

Advanced Envmtl Labs Inc ....E 850 219-6274
  Tallahassee *(G-16870)*

American Compliance Tech Inc ....D 863 533-2000
  Bartow *(G-307)*

Aml Diagnostics Inc ....E 561 392-7702
  Boca Raton *(G-419)*

Applied Research Labs Inc ....E 305 624-4800
  Miami Lakes *(G-10703)*

Aventus Health LLC ....D 407 547-3546
  Orlando *(G-12159)*

Central Fla Hlth Aliance Inc ....A 352 430-1488
  Lady Lake *(G-7445)*

Central Florida Testing Labs ....E 727 572-9797
  Clearwater *(G-1563)*

Charles Stark Draper Lab Inc ....C 727 374-5959
  Saint Petersburg *(G-15623)*

Crisis Center of Tampa Bay Inc ....E 813 964-1964
  Tampa *(G-17551)*

Dna Diagnostics Center Inc ....E 954 476-4646
  Plantation *(G-14633)*

Dna Labs International Inc ....E 954 426-5163
  Deerfield Beach *(G-2736)*

Ecco Lab Inc ....E 813 932-9525
  Tampa *(G-17612)*

Elab Inc ....D 386 672-5668
  Ormond Beach *(G-13486)*

Element Mtls Tech Jupiter LLC ....E 321 327-8985
  Jupiter *(G-7064)*

Ellis & Associates Inc ....D 904 880-0960
  Jacksonville *(G-6108)*

Eurofins Envmt Tstg Sthast LLC ....D 850 474-1001
  Pensacola *(G-14300)*

Evans ....D 954 676-3887
  Doral *(G-3192)*

Fla Dept Agriclture Cnsmr Svcs ....D 850 617-7830
  Tallahassee *(G-16953)*

Fla Dpt Envirnmntal Prtection ....C 321 638-1000
  Cocoa *(G-1936)*

Florida Cncer Spclsts RES Inst ....D 352 596-1926
  Spring Hill *(G-16536)*

Florida International Univ ....E 727 395-2511
  Largo *(G-8109)*

Genesis Reference Laboratories ....D 407 232-7130
  Orlando *(G-12566)*

Genome LLC ....E 888 436-6638
  Hollywood *(G-5442)*

Indoor Air Quality Assn Inc ....E 407 562-1625
  Lake Mary *(G-7599)*

ITEL Laboratories Inc ....D 904 363-0196
  Jacksonville *(G-6335)*

Kbr Wyle Services LLC ....E 850 678-2126
  Niceville *(G-11454)*

Knights Manufacturing Company ....D 321 607-9900
  Titusville *(G-18691)*

Lab 24 LLC ....E 800 641-0133
  Boca Raton *(G-663)*

Leak Testing Specialists Inc ....E 407 737-6415
  Merritt Island *(G-9038)*

National Food Lab Inc ....E 608 395-3777
  Naples *(G-11245)*

National Frnsic Scnce Tech Ctr ....E 727 395-2511
  Largo *(G-8137)*

Neogenomics Inc ....C 239 768-0600
  Fort Myers *(G-4522)*

◆ Q-Panel Lab Products Corp ....E 440 835-8700
  Homestead *(G-5597)*

Regenative Labs LLC ....E 601 954-4517
  Pensacola *(G-14420)*

SGS North America Inc ....E 407 425-6700
  Orlando *(G-13188)*

SGS North America Inc ....E 201 508-3000
  Miami *(G-10267)*

Spectrum Analytical Inc ....E 813 888-9507
  Tampa *(G-18320)*

Sugarleaf Labs Inc ....E 704 325-0746
  Jupiter *(G-7141)*

Sun Nuclear Corp ....C 321 259-6862
  Melbourne *(G-8987)*

Testamerica Laboratories Inc ....D 850 878-3994
  Tallahassee *(G-17156)*

Testamerica Laboratories Inc ....D 407 851-2560
  Orlando *(G-13283)*

Thornton Labs Tstg Insptn Svcs ....E 813 223-9702
  Tampa *(G-18421)*

▲ Wingerter Laboratories Inc ....E 305 944-3401
  North Miami *(G-11513)*

8741 Management Services

1st Chice Facilities Svcs Corp ....D 941 758-1915
  Sarasota *(G-16016)*

21st Century Management Corp ....C 786 746-9069
  Miami *(G-9054)*

24/7 Pediatric Care Ctrs Inc ....D 904 249-3373
  Jacksonville Beach *(G-6973)*

7g Envrnmntal Cmplance MGT LLC ....E 850 304-2610
  Tallahassee *(G-16866)*

A I M Investment Corp ....D 305 538-8533
  Miami Beach *(G-10540)*

AB Closing Corporation ....D 407 243-6006
  Orlando *(G-12041)*

Abb-Diversified Holding Corp ....E 800 852-8089
  Coral Springs *(G-2216)*

Abb/Con-Cise Optical Group LLC ....B 303 506-1836
  Coral Springs *(G-2217)*

Acqualina Management LLC ....D 305 918-8000
  Sunny Isles Beach *(G-16712)*

Across Oceans Group Inc ....C 561 325-9522
  Palm Beach Gardens *(G-13678)*

Acts Rtrmnt-Life Cmmnities Inc ....E 561 362-8377
  Boca Raton *(G-398)*

Advanced Dermatology MGT Inc ....D 305 623-5595
  Miami *(G-9091)*

Advanced Dermatology MGT Inc ....E 727 344-6851
  Saint Petersburg *(G-15558)*

Advanced Dermatology MGT Inc ....E 954 447-3200
  Miramar *(G-10835)*

Advanced Dermatology MGT Inc ....E 904 503-6999
  Jacksonville *(G-5740)*

Advanced Dermatology MGT Inc ....E 321 594-5555
  Maitland *(G-8496)*

Adventist Health System/Sunbel ....D 407 200-2700
  Maitland *(G-8497)*

Advisory Services Corporation ....E 561 694-0110
  Palm Beach Gardens *(G-13679)*

AG Holdings Inc ....E 321 723-3215
  Melbourne *(G-8812)*

Agewell Living LLC ....E 561 625-0030
  Palm Beach Gardens *(G-13680)*

Alexton Incorporated ....E 703 901-4512
  Orlando *(G-12092)*

Alpha Envmtl Mnagementcorp LLC ....C 407 542-0300
  Winter Springs *(G-19797)*

Alvaco Trading Company ....D 800 852-8089
  Coral Springs *(G-2226)*

◆ America Central Corp ....D 305 871-1587
  Miami *(G-9134)*

American Meetings LLC ....E 954 553-2870
  Fort Lauderdale *(G-3602)*

Amerijet Holdings Inc ....D 800 927-6059
  Miami Springs *(G-10777)*

Annco Services LLC ....B 561 638-2540
  Delray Beach *(G-2907)*

Anthology Inc ....C 561 923-2500
  Boca Raton *(G-423)*

◆ Apollo Export Warehouse Inc ....C 305 592-8790
  Miami *(G-9161)*

Aqua Venture Holdings LLC ....A 813 855-8636
  Tampa *(G-17298)*

Archive America Limited ....D 305 633-8587
  Miami *(G-9166)*

Armstrong International Inc ....D 772 286-7175
  Stuart *(G-16590)*

Associated Property Management ....E 561 588-7210
  Lake Worth *(G-7711)*

Autonation Corporate MGT LLC ....E 954 763-6370
  Fort Lauderdale *(G-3620)*

Avcon Inc ....D 407 599-1122
  Orlando *(G-12158)*

Axios Construction Svcs LLC ....E 321 352-6829
  Fern Park *(G-3510)*

B & B Holding Enterprises Inc ....C 305 863-8860
  Coral Gables *(G-2038)*

B and B Management Services ....C 305 863-8860
  Coral Gables *(G-2039)*

B&J Services of Sebring LLC ....E 863 414-2063
  Valrico *(G-18748)*

Baptist Health Care Corp ....A 850 469-2338
  Pensacola *(G-14226)*

Baptist Health South Fla Inc ....B 786 662-4000
  South Miami *(G-16499)*

Baptist Health System Inc ....A 904 202-4900
  Jacksonville *(G-5834)*

Baptist Health System Inc ....A 904 202-2000
  Jacksonville *(G-5835)*

Baxter Business Group LLC ....E 239 776-0984
  Bonita Springs *(G-896)*

Baycare Health System Inc ....E 813 757-8354
  Plant City *(G-14545)*

Beattie Development Corp ....E 239 257-3295
  Cape Coral *(G-1378)*

Beep Inc ....D 800 640-0316
  Orlando *(G-12177)*

◆ Bernard Egan & Company ....D 772 465-7555
  Fort Pierce *(G-4682)*

Bh Management Svcs Iowa Inc ....C 954 429-9500
  Deerfield Beach *(G-2715)*

Big M Network Solutions LLC ....D 845 288-0114
  Ocoee *(G-11805)*

Bmv Debt Management Corp ....E 561 488-3109
  Boca Raton *(G-458)*

Boucher Bros Volusia Cnty LLC ....E 305 535-8177
  Miami Beach *(G-10561)*

Boucher Brothers MGT Inc ....D 305 535-8177
  Miami Beach *(G-10562)*

Boucher Brothers Miami Bch LLC ....D 305 674-6878
  Miami Beach *(G-10563)*

Box Trotter Inc ....D 352 895-1744
  Ocala *(G-11645)*

Boynton Banana Boat Inc ....E 561 278-0356
  Boynton Beach *(G-968)*

Bridges of America Inc ....C 407 291-1500
  Orlando *(G-12204)*

Buccaneer Motel Corporation ....D 239 261-1148
  Naples *(G-11042)*

Cag Logistics MGT Svcs LLC ....B 813 860-4558
  Tampa *(G-17410)*

Cape Leisure Corporation ....D 321 799-4020
  Cape Canaveral *(G-1358)*

Caremedic Systems Inc ....D 952 936-1179
  Tampa *(G-17420)*

Carlo John Inc ....D 239 481-1643
  Fort Myers *(G-4301)*

Carrick Contracting Corp ....E 561 840-1246
  West Palm Beach *(G-19076)*

Castle Management LLC ....A 954 792-6000
  Plantation *(G-14612)*

Centennial Healthcare Corp ....C 386 752-7900
  Lake City *(G-7518)*

Centennial Healthcare Corp ....C 850 674-4311
  Blountstown *(G-382)*

Centennial Healthcare Corp....C.... 407 872-9393
Orlando *(G-12254)*
Center For Spcial Neds Tr Admi....E.... 727 471-1850
Clearwater *(G-1562)*
CFI Resorts Management Inc....C.... 407 355-2463
Ocoee *(G-11810)*
CFI Resorts Management Inc....C.... 407 351-3350
Orlando *(G-12287)*
Cgi Management Inc....C.... 786 409-7000
Miami *(G-9354)*
Change Healthcare MGT Co LLC....C.... 813 854-2003
Oldsmar *(G-11896)*
Chcs Services Inc....B.... 850 432-1700
Pensacola *(G-14257)*
Civigenics Inc....D.... 561 893-0101
Boca Raton *(G-515)*
CLC Resort Management LLC....C.... 321 244-2542
Kissimmee *(G-7286)*
Cliff Drysdale Management Inc....D.... 786 483-7626
Coral Gables *(G-2069)*
Clk Multi-Family MGT LLC....C.... 407 381-9400
Orlando *(G-12323)*
◆ Club Med Sales Inc....C.... 305 925-9000
Miami *(G-9379)*
CM Management Inc....B.... 716 681-8080
Bonita Springs *(G-902)*
CMC Group Inc....E.... 305 372-0550
Miami *(G-9382)*
Coastal Marina Management LLC....E.... 850 233-1633
Panama City *(G-13983)*
Cochhbha Enterprises Inc....D.... 954 572-6802
Sunrise *(G-16757)*
Commercial Foods Inc....D.... 954 564-2910
Fort Lauderdale *(G-3706)*
Compass Management Group....E.... 239 593-1233
Naples *(G-11074)*
Concord Management Ltd....C.... 941 795-8651
Bradenton *(G-1085)*
Configuration Management Inc....D.... 732 450-1100
West Palm Beach *(G-19105)*
Copper Rver Infrstrcture Svcs....E.... 703 234-9000
Panama City *(G-13986)*
Corvel Corporation....E.... 407 547-3900
Lake Mary *(G-7581)*
Corvel Corporation....E.... 813 288-3540
Tampa *(G-17526)*
Cox Target Media Inc....A.... 727 399-3000
Saint Petersburg *(G-15648)*
CRC Holdings Inc....B.... 305 445-4229
Miami *(G-9435)*
Creighton Cnstr & MGT LLC....D.... 239 210-0455
Fort Myers *(G-4331)*
Crg Management LLC....A.... 813 517-1653
Tampa *(G-17548)*
Csi 1100 Biscayne MGT LLC....E.... 786 577-9700
Miami *(G-9445)*
Csn Power and MGT Firm LLC....D.... 813 252-5515
Wesley Chapel *(G-18995)*
CTI Resource Management Svcs....C.... 904 722-6500
Jacksonville *(G-6035)*
D3 Air & Space Operations Inc....D.... 904 217-3887
Saint Augustine *(G-15437)*
Dalpar Corporation....E.... 850 362-6426
Fort Walton Beach *(G-4761)*
Darden Corporation....D.... 407 245-4000
Orlando *(G-12401)*
Davis-Wick Talent MGT LLC....E.... 407 369-1614
Margate *(G-8644)*
Dd & S Management LLC....D.... 786 633-9924
Pembroke Pines *(G-14146)*
Dimar Management Corp....E.... 305 944-1424
North Miami Beach *(G-11522)*
Diverse Holdings LLC....E.... 561 805-1500
Boca Raton *(G-555)*
Diversified MGT Group LLC....E.... 305 772-3612
Macclenny *(G-8475)*
DMor Inc....E.... 904 693-1188
Jacksonville *(G-6074)*
Dothan Security Inc....C.... 305 470-0188
Doral *(G-3183)*
E-Transport Group LLC....D.... 888 301-7718
Jacksonville *(G-6096)*
▲ Earthbalance Corporation....D.... 941 426-7878
North Port *(G-11568)*
Elm Resources Inc....E.... 866 524-8198
Tampa *(G-17624)*
Encompass Management Group....D.... 845 778-2171
Miami Beach *(G-10590)*
Equiva Services LLC....E.... 561 575-1239
Jupiter *(G-7065)*

Evergreen Construction MGT....D.... 352 227-1460
Mount Dora *(G-10949)*
Evergreen Lifestyles MGT....E.... 321 558-6502
Winter Garden *(G-19567)*
Exela Enterprise Solutions Inc....E.... 850 549-3748
Pensacola *(G-14302)*
Exela Enterprise Solutions Inc....E.... 850 942-1308
Tallahassee *(G-16943)*
Express Dental Care LLC....A.... 813 281-0810
Tampa *(G-17642)*
F A C Hotel Ltd Partnership....E.... 239 948-0699
Bonita Springs *(G-912)*
Falcon Consulting Group LLC....D.... 312 751-8900
Miami *(G-9541)*
Fidelity Nat Title Insur Co....C.... 888 934-3354
Jacksonville *(G-6160)*
Fidelity National MGT Svcs LLC....D.... 888 934-3354
Jacksonville *(G-6163)*
Financial Hlthcare Rsurces Inc....E.... 407 678-5886
Orlando *(G-12511)*
First Service Corporation....B.... 850 769-8981
Panama City *(G-14006)*
Firstgroup America Inc....A.... 954 497-3665
Fort Lauderdale *(G-3789)*
Florida Concorde Inc....E.... 954 917-8079
Pompano Beach *(G-14808)*
Florida Dental Solutions MGT....E.... 754 242-2470
Plantation *(G-14643)*
Florida Engineers Mgt Corp....E.... 850 521-0500
Tallahassee *(G-16969)*
Florida Resort Management Ltd....C.... 305 534-0505
Miami *(G-9590)*
Florida Valenti Management Inc....A.... 813 935-8777
Tampa *(G-17699)*
Formaxx LLC....E.... 248 454-1977
Naples *(G-11124)*
Galaxy MGT Solutions LLC....D.... 404 433-8317
Port Saint Lucie *(G-15137)*
Gale Healthcare Solutions LLC....D.... 727 321-5877
Tampa *(G-17725)*
Genesis Health Inc....B.... 904 858-7600
Jacksonville *(G-6226)*
Geo Care LLC....C.... 561 893-0101
Boca Raton *(G-599)*
Gideon Toal MGT Svcs LLC....C.... 817 673-0682
Orlando *(G-12569)*
Global Jet Charters LLC....E.... 954 771-1795
Fort Lauderdale *(G-3820)*
Global Tpa LLC....C.... 813 506-6000
Tampa *(G-17738)*
Goodwill Inds Centl Fla Inc....C.... 407 857-0659
Orlando *(G-12583)*
Goodwill Industries S Fla Inc....C.... 305 258-1068
Princeton *(G-15186)*
Goodwill Industries S Fla Inc....C.... 305 940-3252
Miami *(G-9650)*
Goodwill Industries S Fla Inc....C.... 305 248-0063
Homestead *(G-5576)*
Gottlieb Temp LLC....D.... 904 346-3088
Jacksonville *(G-6237)*
Gottlieb Temp LLC....C.... 904 596-2732
Jacksonville *(G-6238)*
Greyhound Lines Inc....E.... 407 292-3422
Orlando *(G-12603)*
Greystone Healthcare MGT Corp....C.... 352 378-1558
Gainesville *(G-4910)*
Greystone Healthcare MGT Corp....C.... 813 635-9500
Tampa *(G-17759)*
Greystone Healthcare MGT Corp....C.... 727 544-1444
Kenneth City *(G-7163)*
Guggenheim Prtners Ltin Amer I....E.... 305 373-8033
Miami *(G-9670)*
Health Diagnostics LLC....C.... 305 461-6005
Miami *(G-9687)*
Health Management Systems Inc....E.... 863 519-1413
Bartow *(G-319)*
Healthchoice Inc....A.... 407 481-7100
Orlando *(G-12630)*
Healthplan Services Inc....A.... 813 289-1000
Tampa *(G-17809)*
Highland Manor Catering LLC....E.... 407 650-0100
Orlando *(G-12640)*
Hotel Management Group LLC....E.... 352 624-9530
Ocala *(G-11701)*
Hs1 Medical Management Inc....E.... 954 335-6000
Fort Lauderdale *(G-3876)*
Hss Systems LLC....D.... 727 533-3400
Largo *(G-8119)*
Indian River County....E.... 772 226-3490
Vero Beach *(G-18874)*

Indian River County....C.... 772 567-8000
Vero Beach *(G-18875)*
Inframark LLC....E.... 407 566-1935
Kissimmee *(G-7420)*
Inphynet Hospital Services....D.... 954 475-1300
Tamarac *(G-17194)*
Intermodal Support Svcs Inc....D.... 904 858-1587
Jacksonville *(G-6327)*
▲ International Lease Fin Corp....E.... 310 788-1999
Miami *(G-9766)*
Interntional Support Group LLC....D.... 954 900-1095
Pembroke Pines *(G-14155)*
Interstate Hotels Resorts Inc....D.... 407 351-1000
Orlando *(G-12688)*
Intuition LLC....C.... 904 421-7100
Jacksonville *(G-6332)*
Island Hospitality MGT LLC....E.... 561 832-6132
West Palm Beach *(G-19209)*
J2 Solutions Inc....E.... 941 492-3266
Venice *(G-18787)*
Jae Florida LLC....E.... 561 997-6002
Pompano Beach *(G-14831)*
JD ASG Management Company....E.... 904 249-4771
Jacksonville *(G-6381)*
JJ Morley Enterprises Inc....E.... 561 843-6484
West Palm Beach *(G-19216)*
John F Kennedy Space Center....A.... 855 433-4210
Merritt Island *(G-9036)*
Johns Island Prprty Owners As....D.... 772 231-1666
Vero Beach *(G-18883)*
Jomar Development & Cnstr Inc....E.... 727 584-6405
Clearwater *(G-1687)*
Joseph L Rley Anesthesia Assoc....D.... 407 687-0444
Maitland *(G-8549)*
Keith and Associates Inc....D.... 954 788-3400
Pompano Beach *(G-14837)*
Kenpat (central Florida) LLC....D.... 407 464-7070
Apopka *(G-192)*
Ker Inc....E.... 727 535-2939
Largo *(G-8123)*
▲ Kessler Enterprise Inc....E.... 407 996-9999
Orlando *(G-12725)*
Keville Enterprises Inc....C.... 617 482-3888
Jacksonville *(G-6405)*
Key Parking Services Inc....B.... 305 948-7773
Miami *(G-9825)*
Kisco Senior Living LLC....D.... 321 473-9474
Melbourne *(G-8916)*
Kr Management LLC....A.... 727 489-0857
Largo *(G-8124)*
Kynetic F LLC....B.... 904 412-7876
Jacksonville *(G-6412)*
Lake County Schools....E.... 352 324-3088
Howey In The Hills *(G-5622)*
Landmark Management Svcs Inc....E.... 954 392-6000
Pembroke Pines *(G-14160)*
▲ Laney & Duke Terminal Whse Inc....E.... 904 798-3500
Jacksonville *(G-6420)*
Lee Memorial Health System....A.... 239 343-2000
Fort Myers *(G-4480)*
Legacy MGT & Inv Group LLC....D.... 239 261-4191
Naples *(G-11194)*
Leland Management Inc....D.... 321 549-0953
Rockledge *(G-15355)*
Leland Management Inc....D.... 352 364-4620
Ocala *(G-11708)*
Leland Management Inc....D.... 352 653-2028
Gainesville *(G-4933)*
Leland Management Inc....D.... 904 223-7224
Jacksonville *(G-6426)*
Leon Management Intl Inc....D.... 305 642-5366
Miami *(G-9863)*
Levy R & H Limited Partnership....C.... 407 828-8985
Orlando *(G-12763)*
Lifeshare Management Group LLC....B.... 239 257-1504
Cape Coral *(G-1409)*
Lifeshare Management Group LLC....B.... 863 937-9650
Tampa *(G-17952)*
Lincare Procurement Inc....E.... 727 530-7700
Clearwater *(G-1700)*
Liquor Management LLC....E.... 954 358-9463
Fort Lauderdale *(G-3945)*
Livetrends Design Group LLC....D.... 352 735-2252
Mount Dora *(G-10955)*
Lloyds Register Americas Inc....E.... 754 715-6842
Plantation *(G-14667)*
Lodging Resources Inc....D.... 800 772-3359
Fernandina Beach *(G-3534)*
Logsdon Development Corp....E.... 239 431-7492
Naples *(G-11198)*

M D I Inc ....E.... 305 893-9955
North Miami *(G-11502)*
Macneill Group Inc ....C.... 954 331-4800
Sunrise *(G-16794)*
Manhattan Construction Fla Inc ....E.... 239 643-6000
Naples *(G-11203)*
Marathon Health LLC ....C.... 802 857-0400
West Melbourne *(G-19011)*
Martin Mem Hlth Systems Inc ....A.... 772 287-5200
Stuart *(G-16640)*
Martin Memorial Med Ctr Inc ....A.... 772 345-8100
Port Saint Lucie *(G-15151)*
Maruti Fleet & Mgmt LLC ....A.... 561 841-5052
West Palm Beach *(G-19254)*
▲ **Mastec Inc** ....C.... 305 599-1800
Coral Gables *(G-2138)*
Matrix Healthcare Services Inc ....C.... 813 247-2077
Tampa *(G-18002)*
Mbf Healthcare Management LLC ....D.... 954 359-8339
Opa Locka *(G-11950)*
McNeill Labor Management Inc ....D.... 561 996-1148
Belle Glade *(G-360)*
▲ **Meadowbrook Golf Group Inc** ....D.... 407 589-7200
Lakeland *(G-7917)*
Medex Ambulance Services Inc ....D.... 954 763-1776
Pompano Beach *(G-14853)*
▼ **Merchspin Inc** ....E.... 877 306-3651
Orlando *(G-12857)*
Metro Corral Partners Inc ....D.... 407 297-1920
Orlando *(G-12864)*
Metro Corral Partners Inc ....D.... 407 352-6606
Orlando *(G-12863)*
Metropolitan Hlth Networks Inc ....E.... 386 676-9690
Ormond Beach *(G-13509)*
Mid-Florida Medical Svcs Inc ....A.... 863 297-1895
Winter Haven *(G-19646)*
Millenium Management Corp ....E.... 407 996-4647
Orlando *(G-12868)*
Millennium Physician Group LLC ....C.... 239 217-4636
North Fort Myers *(G-11475)*
Moorecars LLC ....E.... 678 472-9114
Boynton Beach *(G-1018)*
Mora Wealth Management LLC ....D.... 800 657-8622
West Palm Beach *(G-19271)*
Morton Plant Mase Hlth Care In ....B.... 727 462-7777
Clearwater *(G-1726)*
Mosaic Company ....C.... 813 500-6828
Tampa *(G-18054)*
Mount Sinai Med Ctr Fla Inc ....A.... 305 674-2121
Miami Beach *(G-10630)*
MSE Branded Food Systems Inc ....E.... 770 287-0320
Miami Beach *(G-10631)*
Mstc LLC ....D.... 904 396-2220
Jacksonville *(G-6520)*
Muck Rack LLC ....C.... 212 500-1883
Miami Beach *(G-10633)*
Muvico Theaters Inc ....E.... 954 564-6550
Fort Lauderdale *(G-3987)*
National Sourcing Inc ....C.... 813 281-0013
Tampa *(G-18068)*
National State Pk Cncssons Inc ....D.... 772 595-6429
Fort Pierce *(G-4723)*
Ncb Management Services Inc ....D.... 904 737-2485
Jacksonville *(G-6532)*
Neptune Management Corporation ....E.... 954 556-9400
Plantation *(G-14683)*
New World Venture NW Florida ....D.... 850 434-7736
Pensacola *(G-14386)*
Nexogy Inc ....D.... 305 358-8952
Coral Gables *(G-2158)*
Nigella Industries Inc ....D.... 727 873-3894
Saint Petersburg *(G-15778)*
Noble Hse Hotels & Resorts Ltd ....C.... 305 295-7012
Key West *(G-7232)*
Nuco2 Management LLC ....D.... 772 221-1754
Stuart *(G-16652)*
▲ **Onespaworld US Inc** ....E.... 305 358-9002
Coral Gables *(G-2163)*
Open Text Inc ....E.... 321 951-9503
Melbourne *(G-8953)*
Orion Administration Inc ....E.... 754 307-1546
Margate *(G-8662)*
Orix USA Corporation ....A.... 214 237-2000
Oakland Park *(G-11608)*
▲ **Orlando Health Inc** ....A.... 407 841-5111
Orlando *(G-12958)*
Ormond Re Group Inc ....E.... 386 677-4453
Ormond Beach *(G-13514)*
Palace Management Group LLC ....A.... 305 445-7444
Coral Gables *(G-2164)*

Park & Eleazer Cnstr LLC ....E.... 727 216-6591
Clearwater *(G-1753)*
Parkway Maintenance & Mgt Co ....E.... 727 799-3270
Clearwater *(G-1754)*
Parkway Maintenance & Mgt Co ....E.... 352 873-0848
Ocala *(G-11759)*
Parrish McCall Constructors ....D.... 352 378-1571
Gainesville *(G-4974)*
Pasteur Medical Management LLC ....C.... 786 422-6821
Miami Lakes *(G-10752)*
Pinnacle An American MGT Svcs ....C.... 407 949-0800
Maitland *(G-8567)*
Pinnacle Hotel MGT Co LLC ....E.... 561 242-9066
Royal Palm Beach *(G-15389)*
Pinnacle Hotel MGT Co LLC ....A.... 561 622-8888
West Palm Beach *(G-19325)*
Policy Studies Inc ....D.... 850 656-3343
Tallahassee *(G-17070)*
Port Charlotte Hma LLC ....A.... 941 766-4122
Port Charlotte *(G-15054)*
Port Saint Lucie MGT LLC ....C.... 772 337-1333
Port Saint Lucie *(G-15159)*
Power Resources Fincl Svcs Inc ....E.... 954 281-5590
Pembroke Pines *(G-14176)*
Prc LLC ....A.... 786 293-4000
Cutler Bay *(G-2375)*
Prc LLC ....C.... 954 693-3700
Plantation *(G-14697)*
Prc LLC ....A.... 813 952-1010
Tampa *(G-18161)*
Prc LLC ....E.... 407 682-1556
Longwood *(G-8391)*
Preferred Medical Group Inc ....D.... 239 597-2010
Naples *(G-11267)*
Premier Corp Prof Svcs LLC ....C.... 352 324-2001
Howey In The Hills *(G-5625)*
Prime Therapeutics LLC ....A.... 877 627-6337
Orlando *(G-13058)*
Progressive Employer MGT Co Xx ....D.... 888 925-2990
Sarasota *(G-16044)*
Prosser Inc ....D.... 904 739-3655
Jacksonville *(G-6619)*
Pyg Dental Management LLC ....E.... 954 367-5671
Hollywood *(G-5499)*
Rainbow Enterprises Group Inc ....E.... 305 335-0119
Miami Lakes *(G-10756)*
Raymond James & Associates Inc ....A.... 727 567-1000
Saint Petersburg *(G-15816)*
RE Michaelson Group LLC ....C.... 904 880-0000
Jacksonville *(G-6639)*
Regal Palms Resort Spa MGT LLC ....E.... 863 354-6360
Davenport *(G-2447)*
Regal Senior Care MGT LLC ....D.... 954 613-2300
Hollywood *(G-5506)*
Resortquest RE Fla LLC ....A.... 850 837-3700
Destin *(G-3074)*
Resorts Advantage Ltd Inc ....E.... 305 670-8405
Miami *(G-10205)*
▲ **Restaurant Services Inc** ....D.... 305 529-3400
Miami *(G-10208)*
Rlh Construction LLC ....E.... 407 384-1908
Oviedo *(G-13568)*
Rlp Wealth Advisors LLC ....E.... 561 899-0808
Boca Raton *(G-776)*
Rock Management LLC ....C.... 619 831-1890
Orlando *(G-13122)*
▼ **Row Management Ltd Inc** ....E.... 954 538-8400
Sunrise *(G-16818)*
S & S Golf Management Inc ....C.... 407 384-6888
Orlando *(G-13153)*
Sagamore Partners Ltd ....C.... 305 535-8088
Miami Beach *(G-10652)*
Santafe Healthcare Inc ....E.... 352 372-8400
Gainesville *(G-4992)*
Sarasota Bay Club Lllp ....E.... 941 552-3282
Sarasota *(G-16297)*
Seacrest Services Inc ....C.... 561 697-4990
Coconut Creek *(G-2000)*
Seacrest Services Inc ....C.... 561 697-4990
West Palm Beach *(G-19354)*
Sedgwick Claims MGT Svcs Inc ....D.... 561 995-0048
Boca Raton *(G-791)*
Select Hotels Group LLC ....D.... 863 413-1122
Lakeland *(G-7966)*
Servicelink Holdings LLC ....A.... 904 854-8100
Jacksonville *(G-6713)*
Sheridan Healthcorp Inc ....A.... 954 963-6363
Hollywood *(G-5518)*
Sheridan Healthcorp Inc ....B.... 954 939-5000
Fort Lauderdale *(G-4122)*

Sky Resort Management LLC ....C.... 407 581-2151
Orlando *(G-13205)*
Smg Holdings LLC ....E.... 904 630-3900
Jacksonville *(G-6732)*
Smg Holdings LLC ....D.... 904 633-6000
Jacksonville *(G-6733)*
Smithco West Palm Beach Inc ....E.... 561 833-3793
West Palm Beach *(G-19363)*
Southern Cnstr & Design Inc ....D.... 305 971-0102
Miami *(G-10308)*
Southern Management Corp ....C.... 850 983-5262
Milton *(G-10825)*
Sports and Entrmt MGT LLC ....D.... 800 337-8403
Davie *(G-2519)*
Spottswood Management Inc ....C.... 305 294-6100
Key West *(G-7247)*
SRI Management Llc ....A.... 352 686-3831
Tallahassee *(G-17112)*
St Vincents Health System Inc ....B.... 904 273-6900
Ponte Vedra Beach *(G-15008)*
Stallion Medical MGT LLC ....C.... 954 383-0715
Weston *(G-19480)*
Strongcore Group LLC ....D.... 305 539-0680
South Miami *(G-16519)*
STS Federal LLC ....C.... 407 965-2596
Oviedo *(G-13572)*
Sunrise Hsptlity Pnscola Bch L ....E.... 850 932-5331
Gulf Breeze *(G-5135)*
Swbg Orlando Corporate Opertns ....D.... 407 226-5030
Orlando *(G-13254)*
Syniverse Communications Inc ....E.... 813 637-5000
Tampa *(G-18357)*
T J W Management Company Inc ....E.... 386 788-4546
Daytona Beach *(G-2672)*
Targeted Case MGT of Fla ....D.... 305 952-3125
Miami Lakes *(G-10766)*
Telecom Service Bureau Inc ....C.... 352 233-2700
Ocala *(G-11784)*
Terremark Construction Svcs ....E.... 786 333-4151
Miami *(G-10379)*
Titan Resources International ....E.... 877 999-4900
Kissimmee *(G-7398)*
Traffic MGT Solutions Inc ....C.... 772 460-6585
West Palm Beach *(G-19390)*
Trajectory Inc ....E.... 239 217-6281
Naples *(G-11327)*
Travel + Leisure Co ....C.... 407 626-5200
Orlando *(G-13305)*
Triumph Housing Management LLC ....E.... 786 641-5313
Miami *(G-10408)*
Truecore Bhvoral Solutions LLC ....B.... 904 547-7689
Tampa *(G-18451)*
Truecore Bhvoral Solutions LLC ....C.... 561 924-6586
Pahokee *(G-13583)*
Tullahoma HMA Physcn MGT Inc ....D.... 615 449-2065
Naples *(G-11330)*
▲ **Turnberry Residential MGT LP** ....D.... 305 937-6262
Aventura *(G-283)*
Turningpint Hlthcare Sltons LL ....C.... 407 314-7167
Lake Mary *(G-7648)*
Unifi Management LLC ....D.... 813 514-2797
Tampa *(G-18458)*
Unified Womens Healthcare LP ....D.... 561 300-2410
Boca Raton *(G-852)*
Unimac Management LLC ....C.... 407 489-8084
Orlando *(G-13330)*
◆ **Unique Vacations Inc** ....E.... 305 284-1300
Miami *(G-10433)*
University of South Flori ....E.... 813 974-2201
Tampa *(G-18478)*
University S Fla Med Svcs Sppo ....A.... 813 974-3374
Tampa *(G-18480)*
Urban Retail Properties LLC ....E.... 386 253-6783
Daytona Beach *(G-2685)*
URS Group Inc ....C.... 813 286-1711
Tampa *(G-18482)*
US Remodelers Inc ....C.... 561 994-6081
Boca Raton *(G-856)*
Value Store It Management Inc ....E.... 305 819-8850
Fort Lauderdale *(G-4208)*
▲ **Vas Aero Services LLC** ....C.... 561 998-9330
Boca Raton *(G-859)*
Verdex Construction LLC ....E.... 561 440-1600
West Palm Beach *(G-19407)*
Vesta Property Services Inc ....A.... 904 355-1831
Jacksonville *(G-6907)*
Veterans Health Administration ....C.... 305 324-4455
Miami *(G-10468)*
Virtual Resource MGT Corp ....C.... 239 948-1147
Estero *(G-3487)*

Virtuous Management Group LLC	C	850 598-0770	Miramar Beach (G-10927)
Vulcan Construction Mtls LLC	E	386 252-8581	Daytona Beach (G-2687)
W D T Inc	C	601 693-1304	Pensacola (G-14465)
Wal-Mark Contracting Group LLC	E	407 294-5051	Orlando (G-13390)
Wecare Tlc LLC	D	407 562-1212	Altamonte Springs (G-112)
Wellington Hsptality Group LLC	D	561 202-4739	West Palm Beach (G-19417)
Westminster Services Inc	D	407 839-5050	Orlando (G-13426)
Windsor Jet Management	D	954 938-9508	Fort Lauderdale (G-4227)
Wound Technology Network Inc	E	954 923-7440	Hollywood (G-5550)
Wyndham Management Corporation	D	866 932-6991	Orlando (G-13455)
Wynns Extended Care Inc	E	305 266-5665	Miami (G-10519)
Xbk Management LLC	E	954 491-6265	Fort Lauderdale (G-4235)
Young Mens Christian	C	904 854-2000	Jacksonville (G-6955)
Young MNS Chrstn Assn of Flrda	C	904 259-0898	Macclenny (G-8480)
Young MNS Chrstn Assn of Flrda	C	904 272-4304	Orange Park (G-12026)
Young MNS Chrstn Assn of Flrda	C	904 731-2006	Jacksonville (G-6959)
Young MNS Chrstn Assn of Flrda	C	904 471-9622	Saint Augustine (G-15515)
Young MNS Chrstn Assn of Flrda	C	904 464-3901	Jacksonville (G-6960)
Young MNS Chrstn Assn of Flrda	C	904 296-3220	Fernandina Beach (G-3546)
Yuengling Center	E	813 974-3111	Tampa (G-18575)
Zenith American Solutions Inc	C	813 666-6900	Tampa (G-18576)

8742 Management Consulting Services

212 Accord Corp	B	689 248-5623	Winter Park (G-19680)
25 N Market Level Office LLC	D	312 283-3683	Jacksonville (G-5713)
3gimbals LLC	E	703 957-7269	Miami Beach (G-10538)
A&A Coordinators America LLC	E	954 674-3747	Miami (G-9062)
Aacg Inc	E	352 467-7000	Dade City (G-2380)
Aba Technologies Inc	D	321 674-8540	Melbourne (G-8803)
Abacus Rx Inc	E	305 220-0400	Miami (G-9067)
ACC All Contractors Inc	E	305 842-6338	Doral (G-3100)
Accenture Federal Services LLC	C	904 899-0290	Jacksonville (G-5725)
Accenture LLP	D	786 425-7000	Coral Gables (G-2020)
Acclaris Inc	D	813 873-2020	Tampa (G-17227)
Accudata Integrated Mktg Inc	D	239 425-4400	Fort Myers (G-4247)
Ace Digital Marketing Inc	C	786 358-6347	Miami (G-9073)
Acordis International Corp	E	954 620-0072	Miramar (G-10833)
Acosta Remainco Inc	B	904 281-9800	Jacksonville (G-5729)
Across Oceans Group Inc	C	561 325-9522	Palm Beach Gardens (G-13678)
▲ **Adecco Usa Inc**	C	904 360-2000	Jacksonville (G-5735)
Adelson Arshli	E	561 564-3397	North Miami Beach (G-11515)
ADP Totalsource De IV Inc	B	305 630-1494	Miami (G-9080)
ADP Totalsource FL Xvii Inc	B	305 630-1494	Miami (G-9081)
ADP Totalsource FL Xxix Inc	B	305 630-1494	Miami (G-9082)
ADP Totalsource Group Inc	C	305 630-1000	Miami (G-9083)
ADP Totalsource I Inc	B	305 630-1494	Miami (G-9084)

ADP Totalsource III Inc	B	305 630-1494	Miami (G-9086)
ADP Totalsource MI Vi LLC	B	305 630-1494	Miami (G-9087)
ADP Totalsource MI Vii LLC	B	305 630-1000	Miami (G-9088)
Advanced Cmmncations Group Inc	E	561 375-3100	Boynton Beach (G-958)
Advanced Info Systems Group In	E	407 581-2929	Orlando (G-12056)
Advanced Pharmaceutical Cons	D	305 751-7798	Miami (G-9093)
Advanced Retail Merchandising	E	863 648-5708	Lakeland (G-7784)
Advanced Systems Tech Inc	D	407 277-8069	Orlando (G-12059)
Adventhealth Orlando	D	407 303-8110	Orlando (G-12064)
Adventist Health System/Sunbel	A	863 314-4466	Sebring (G-16386)
Affinity Insurance Services	E	954 688-5000	Coral Springs (G-2219)
Aim Engineering Surveying Inc	C	239 332-4569	Fort Myers (G-4254)
Ajg Solutions Inc	E	954 548-3011	Fort Lauderdale (G-3586)
Akimeka LLC	D	210 824-8477	Maitland (G-8499)
Alexton Incorporated	E	703 901-4512	Orlando (G-12092)
Alight (us) LLC	E	407 471-4100	Orlando (G-12093)
Alight Solutions LLC	A	407 471-4100	Orlando (G-12094)
Alignnetworks Inc	E	904 998-0211	Jacksonville (G-5764)
Allen Group	E	407 788-8822	Longwood (G-8337)
Alliance Financial Group	E	239 425-1084	Fort Myers (G-4267)
Alliancebernstein LP	C	813 314-3300	Tampa (G-17266)
▲ **Allyn International Svcs Inc**	D	239 267-4261	Fort Myers (G-4269)
American Leads Unlimited Inc	C	727 230-0038	New Port Richey (G-11362)
American Management Svcs Inc	D	800 743-0402	Orlando (G-12110)
Amicis Catered Cusine Inc	B	813 855-1100	Oldsmar (G-11892)
Amone Corp	E	954 315-5900	Plantation (G-14601)
Andco Consulting	E	844 442-6326	Winter Park (G-19687)
Antone Hope LLC	E	727 902-1517	Saint Petersburg (G-15571)
Anzu Partners LLC	E	941 773-1615	Tampa (G-17292)
Applied Concepts LLC	E	407 333-7300	Lake Mary (G-7568)
Ardurra Group Inc	D	813 880-8881	Tampa (G-17305)
Arka Technologies Inc	E	305 814-7024	Miami (G-9170)
Arma Global Corporation	D	866 554-9333	Tampa (G-17306)
Asset Acceptance LLC	C	813 569-0400	Riverview (G-15243)
Atkins North America Inc	D	813 282-7275	Tampa (G-17316)
Auxis Managed Solutions LLC	E	954 236-4000	Plantation (G-14605)
Avairpros Inc	E	239 262-0010	Naples (G-11019)
Avairpros Services Inc	D	239 262-0010	Naples (G-11020)
Avatar Communities Inc	D	305 442-7000	Kissimmee (G-7418)
Aviv Villages LLC	D	352 488-2848	The Villages (G-18653)
B3 Solutions LLC	D	571 384-1400	Port Charlotte (G-15022)
Bastion Capital Investment	E	305 431-8531	Miami (G-9227)
Bear Atlantic Group LLC	D	305 507-5545	Miami (G-9235)
Beeline Acquisition Corp	D	904 527-5700	Jacksonville (G-5852)
Beelinecom Inc	D	866 352-5463	Jacksonville (G-5853)

Bermello Ajamil & Partners Inc	D	305 859-2050	Coral Gables (G-2051)
Better Healthcare Intl	E	954 473-4082	Sunrise (G-16745)
Beyer-Brown & Associates LP	E	407 232-9046	Orlando (G-12186)
Beytin McLaughlin Ohara	D	407 622-6725	Altamonte Springs (G-29)
Bhm Healthcare Solutions Inc	D	314 422-8016	Tampa (G-17361)
Bidtellect Inc	E	561 634-7323	Delray Beach (G-2915)
◆ **Big O Tires LLC**	D	561 383-3000	Palm Beach Gardens (G-13694)
Bjce Inc	D	561 265-0255	Delray Beach (G-2916)
Blanchard Training and Dev Inc	E	386 445-0034	Palm Coast (G-13813)
Boley-Par Inc	D	727 545-7564	Pinellas Park (G-14508)
Booz Allen Hamilton Inc	E	813 281-4900	Tampa (G-17378)
Booz Allen Hamilton Inc	C	850 636-3300	Panama City (G-13972)
▼ **Brand Institute Inc**	D	305 374-2500	Miami (G-9274)
Brightfractal Inc	D	844 337-2285	Delray Beach (G-2920)
Britepool Inc	D	310 699-8346	Winter Park (G-19689)
Brooks Group Inc	C	561 214-8800	West Palm Beach (G-19066)
Bureau Veritas Holdings Inc	D	954 236-8100	Sunrise (G-16753)
Burgos Group LLC	D	888 256-7953	Orange Park (G-11977)
Business Info Tech Sltnscom In	E	407 363-0024	Orlando (G-12221)
Businessisus	E	863 916-7919	Longwood (G-8348)
C2c Innovative Solutions Inc	B	512 334-1622	Jacksonville (G-5891)
C4 Planning Solutions LLC	E	706 993-8597	Doral (G-3143)
Cag Logistics MGT Svcs LLC	B	813 860-4558	Tampa (G-17410)
Calhoun International LLC	E	813 222-8400	Tampa (G-17412)
Calls 4 Free Inc	E	727 697-7317	Saint Petersburg (G-15608)
▲ **Cambrdge Intgrted Svcs Group I**	E	954 966-4772	Hollywood (G-5413)
Capitale Engrg Cmpt Tech Peo F	E	866 228-3107	Panama City Beach (G-14092)
▲ **Cardinal Florida Inc**	C	863 686-3784	Lakeland (G-7824)
Cargo Transportation Svcs Inc	E	954 718-5555	Sunrise (G-16755)
Carley Corporation	C	407 894-5575	Orlando (G-12241)
Caulfield & Wheeler Inc	E	561 392-1991	Boca Raton (G-500)
Ce Broker Inc	D	877 434-6323	Jacksonville (G-5919)
Cell Staff LLC	E	855 561-1715	Tampa (G-17437)
Chameleon Collectve Consultng	D	800 914-0245	Davie (G-2469)
Chatter Buzz Media LLC	E	321 236-2899	Orlando (G-12291)
Chenega Logistics LLC	D	904 861-0400	Jacksonville (G-5940)
Chugach Support Services Inc	C	850 283-4242	Panama City (G-13981)
Clayton Services LLC	E	203 926-5600	Riverview (G-15249)
Client Support Team LLC	E	954 621-1905	Pompano Beach (G-14775)
Cliftonlarsonallen LLP	E	407 802-1200	Orlando (G-12319)
Coadvantage Corporation	E	941 925-2990	Bradenton (G-1081)
Coadvantage Resources 24 Inc	B	813 935-2000	Tampa (G-17491)
Coadvantage Resources IV Inc	D	704 483-9800	Bradenton (G-1082)
Coadvntage Payroll Tax Svc Inc	D	407 422-8448	Orlando (G-12332)
Coastal Cloud LLC	D	800 237-9574	Palm Coast (G-13817)

SIC

Codina Partners LLC	C	305 529-1300	
Coral Gables (G-2074)			
Colliers Engrg & Design Inc	D	305 597-9701	
Miami (G-9388)			
Colliers Engrg & Design Inc	D	813 207-1061	
Tampa (G-17495)			
Commonwealth Bpo Services LLC	B	888 355-0145	
Saint Petersburg (G-15635)			
Compass Consulting Group Inc	E	904 281-2222	
Jacksonville (G-5994)			
Compass Group Usa Inc	A	407 862-0800	
Altamonte Springs (G-38)			
▼ Complyright Inc	D	954 970-5500	
Pompano Beach (G-14780)			
Condata Global Inc	E	239 690-8361	
Fort Myers (G-4321)			
Conduction Labs Inc	E	315 569-4013	
Boca Raton (G-525)			
Consult Pr Inc	E	561 444-7265	
West Palm Beach (G-19106)			
Consumer Education Svcs Inc	E	954 377-9218	
Fort Lauderdale (G-3714)			
Consumer Sales Solutions LLC	C	727 733-8700	
Seminole (G-16443)			
Copc Intl Holdings LLC	E	407 304-9032	
Winter Park (G-19709)			
Corporate Creations Netwrk Inc	E	561 694-8107	
North Palm Beach (G-11541)			
Cosmic Concepts Ltd	C	407 757-0099	
Orlando (G-12371)			
County of Hillsborough	E	813 272-5769	
Tampa (G-17527)			
Cox Target Media Inc	A	727 399-3000	
Saint Petersburg (G-15648)			
CPM Technical Solutions Inc	E	239 495-9442	
Bonita Springs (G-905)			
CPS Graphics Inc	C	954 975-2220	
Fort Lauderdale (G-3738)			
Cronin Enterprises Inc	D	239 443-3900	
Fort Myers (G-4333)			
Crown Golf Properties LP	E	727 399-1000	
Largo (G-8092)			
Cyndx Networks LLC	E	561 489-6390	
West Palm Beach (G-19114)			
D3 Air & Space Operations Inc	D	904 217-3887	
Saint Augustine (G-15437)			
Dadata Inc	D	727 791-6440	
Palm Harbor (G-13858)			
Dart Container Sales Co LLC	C	954 698-6556	
Fort Lauderdale (G-3750)			
David Lewis & Associates Inc	D	321 872-2016	
Melbourne (G-8865)			
Dcr Workforce Inc	D	561 998-3737	
Boca Raton (G-548)			
De Sol Property Management Inc	E	786 347-2758	
Miami (G-9464)			
◆ Del Valle Brands Inc	E	305 592-8865	
Medley (G-8720)			
Deloitte Consulting LLP	E	407 710-4500	
Lake Mary (G-7585)			
Deloitte Consulting LLP	E	214 840-1464	
Miami (G-9468)			
Dermatology Billing Assoc Inc	E	407 678-8937	
Fern Park (G-3512)			
Diaz Fontanez & Associates LLC	E	800 201-0406	
Miami (G-9476)			
Digital Target Marketing LLC	E	561 202-1405	
West Palm Beach (G-19123)			
Discus International Inc	C	561 694-8107	
Palm Beach Gardens (G-13718)			
DMor Inc	E	904 693-1188	
Jacksonville (G-6074)			
Dos Health Management Inc	C	305 891-1710	
North Miami (G-11488)			
Dosl Inc	E	941 952-5522	
Sarasota (G-16142)			
Doxy Enterprises LLC	A	954 383-0049	
Miramar (G-10854)			
Drivers Alert LLC	E	800 741-5454	
Deerfield Beach (G-2737)			
Earl Enterprises Holdings Inc	D	407 903-5500	
Orlando (G-12447)			
Ecls Global LLC	E	386 248-7025	
Winter Haven (G-19624)			
Economic Research Services Inc	E	850 562-1211	
Tallahassee (G-16939)			
El Dorado Financial Inc	C	800 707-8065	
Vero Beach (G-18854)			
Ernst & Young LLP	D	904 358-2000	
Jacksonville (G-6131)			
Ernst & Young LLP	D	305 358-4111	
Miami (G-9531)			
Ernst & Young LLP	D	813 225-4800	
Tampa (G-17638)			
Eternal Bliss Amour-Propre LLC	E	321 341-5565	
Orlando (G-12477)			
Evelyns 4 Enterprise LLC	E	863 617-5889	
Lakeland (G-7857)			
Everymundo LLC	D	305 375-0045	
Miami (G-9535)			
Evolution Insight Incorporated	D	321 282-1999	
Windermere (G-19539)			
Exploratus LLC	E	786 360-1669	
Miami (G-9537)			
Fabian Innovation LLC	E	904 579-1204	
Orlando (G-12485)			
Far Ridgeline Engagements Inc	C	910 977-0910	
Tampa (G-17650)			
Fasha Corporation	E	505 991-9115	
Orlando (G-12494)			
Fbmc Benefits Management Inc	D	386 239-5710	
Daytona Beach (G-2588)			
Fbmc Benefits Management Inc	E	850 425-6200	
Ormond Beach (G-13490)			
Fbmc Benefits Management Inc	E	850 425-6200	
Tallahassee (G-16945)			
Federal Express Corporation	C	954 497-2700	
Fort Lauderdale (G-3784)			
Fedwel Inc	E	407 888-4482	
Orlando (G-12503)			
Fircosoft Inc	C	813 975-7227	
Tampa (G-17661)			
First Coast Svc Options Inc	A	904 791-8000	
Jacksonville (G-6173)			
First Marketing Company	E	954 979-0700	
Pompano Beach (G-14804)			
Firstgroup America Inc	A	954 497-3665	
Fort Lauderdale (G-3789)			
Florida Health Care Plan Inc	D	321 567-7500	
Titusville (G-18685)			
Florida International Univ	E	727 395-2511	
Largo (G-8109)			
Florida MGT Solutions Inc	C	352 872-5901	
Gainesville (G-4894)			
Florida Nr Associates	E	561 345-2065	
Greenacres (G-5072)			
Florida Trism Indust Mktg Corp	D	850 728-5878	
Tallahassee (G-16982)			
Florida Trnsp Svcs Inc	D	954 462-9159	
Fort Lauderdale (G-3798)			
Floridamakes Inc	E	240 344-7155	
Orlando (G-12535)			
Fmp Media Group Inc	D	863 207-6818	
Lake Alfred (G-7450)			
Focus Wealth Strategies LLC	E	813 305-0411	
Brandon (G-1232)			
Force Legion LLC	E	305 423-3339	
Miami (G-9593)			
Foundry Commercial LLC	D	407 540-7700	
Orlando (G-12542)			
Fountain Group LLC	A	813 356-0033	
Tampa (G-17707)			
Frankcrum 9 Inc	D	727 799-1229	
Clearwater (G-1648)			
Frontier Florida LLC	A	813 620-2518	
Tampa (G-17717)			
Fudpuckers Properties LLC	E	850 243-3833	
Fort Walton Beach (G-4772)			
G & G Dental Associates PA	E	305 274-2499	
Miami (G-9614)			
G4s Holding One Inc	B	561 622-5656	
Jupiter (G-7076)			
G4s Secure Solutions USA Inc	B	561 622-5656	
Jupiter (G-7079)			
Gb Instruments Inc	E	954 596-5000	
Deerfield Beach (G-2743)			
Gelrad LLC	E	315 853-7531	
Longboat Key (G-8325)			
Gem Technology Intl Corp	C	305 447-1344	
Miami (G-9622)			
Gevity Hr Inc	A	941 741-4300	
Lakewood Ranch (G-8017)			
Global Envmtl Indus Rspnse LLC	D	866 456-2368	
Tampa (G-17736)			
Global Halthcare Resources Inc	E	561 791-2000	
Palm Beach Gardens (G-13735)			
Global Radar Acquisition LLC	E	239 274-0048	
Fort Myers (G-4419)			
Glue Iq LLC	D	305 239-9440	
Miami (G-9641)			
Go To Market Inc	D	305 670-4645	
Miami (G-9644)			
Gorman Health Group LLC	D	202 364-8283	
Fort Lauderdale (G-3827)			
Gottlieb Temp LLC	D	904 346-3088	
Jacksonville (G-6237)			
Graphic Masters Inc	D	800 230-3873	
Miami (G-9659)			
Greenbacks Partnerships LLC	E	813 586-0167	
Tampa (G-17752)			
Gubagoo Inc	E	855 359-2574	
Boca Raton (G-613)			
Gunnstruction Inc	E	321 455-6498	
Merritt Island (G-9030)			
Gut Agency LLC	C	305 742-4469	
Coral Gables (G-2116)			
Hackett Group Inc	E	305 375-8005	
Miami (G-9675)			
Hamlin & Associates Inc	E	386 672-4113	
Ormond Beach (G-13502)			
Happyornot Americas Inc	E	408 472-3248	
Delray Beach (G-2961)			
HCC C LLc	D	321 388-6262	
Orlando (G-12624)			
Hcm Marketing Corporation	D	239 301-7000	
Estero (G-3459)			
HDR Engineering Inc	D	904 598-8900	
Jacksonville (G-6266)			
Health Care Mgt Consulting	D	904 259-3111	
Jacksonville (G-6268)			
Health Care Mgt Consulting	E	904 725-7100	
Jacksonville (G-6269)			
Health Choice Network Fla Inc	C	305 599-1015	
Doral (G-3224)			
Healthcare Appraisers Inc	E	561 330-3488	
Boca Raton (G-624)			
◆ Healthtex Distributors Inc	D	305 633-7900	
Miami (G-9690)			
Heartcare Imaging Inc	E	561 746-6125	
Tequesta (G-18649)			
HIG Capital Inc	E	305 379-2322	
Miami (G-9700)			
▲ Hig Capital Management Inc	E	305 379-2322	
Miami (G-9702)			
Hill Robinson Intl Inc	E	954 792-6112	
Fort Lauderdale (G-3859)			
Hok Group Inc	C	713 407-7700	
Miami (G-9709)			
Holland Financial Inc	D	386 671-1245	
Ormond Beach (G-13504)			
Hollywood Concessions Inc	B	248 352-2010	
Hallandale Beach (G-5173)			
Home Care For 21st Century LLC	E	833 432-2273	
Bradenton (G-1120)			
Homes Media Solutions LLC	E	877 363-4442	
Boca Raton (G-631)			
Hrq Inc	E	303 455-1118	
Pensacola (G-14325)			
Human Capital Management Inc	E	954 318-2400	
Fort Lauderdale (G-3880)			
Icbd Holdings LLC	C	833 575-2500	
West Palm Beach (G-19195)			
Image Web Design Inc	E	941 564-9323	
North Port (G-11571)			
Indelible Business Solutions	D	850 321-5168	
Jacksonville (G-6315)			
Indelible Solutions LLP	D	850 321-5168	
Jacksonville (G-6316)			
Indian Trail Improvement Dst	E	561 793-0874	
West Palm Beach (G-19199)			
Inetico Inc	E	813 258-2200	
Temple Terrace (G-18637)			
Infinity Foods LLC	E	305 333-4244	
Hialeah (G-5280)			
Informa Support Services Inc	D	941 365-4471	
Sarasota (G-16194)			
▲ Informa Usa Inc	A	561 361-6017	
Sarasota (G-16195)			
Infrastructure Co Amer LLC	E	813 635-9696	
Tampa (G-17866)			
Innovative Events LLC	D	305 670-4501	
Miami (G-9749)			
Inomax LLC	A	561 868-6060	
West Palm Beach (G-19201)			
Insite Managed Solutions LLC	E	239 234-2700	
Cape Coral (G-1402)			
Institute For Intrgvrnmntal RE	C	850 385-0600	
Tallahassee (G-17006)			
Integrated Dermatology LLC	E	561 448-9517	
Boca Raton (G-643)			

Company	Code	Phone
Integrated Solutions MGT Inc	E	813 855-3710
Tampa (G-17869)		
▲ Intercoastal Financial Group	E	800 916-0065
Fort Pierce (G-4713)		
Intermodal Support Svcs Inc	D	904 858-1587
Jacksonville (G-6327)		
International Sales Group LLC	D	305 931-6511
Miami (G-9770)		
Irelaunch LLC	E	617 512-0816
Palm Beach Gardens (G-13743)		
Isc Inc	E	727 785-0189
Clearwater (G-1679)		
◆ ISO Group Inc	E	877 330-1580
Palm Bay (G-13625)		
Jasper Steward LLC	E	754 600-9127
Pembroke Pines (G-14157)		
Jmt Charitable Foundation	C	954 475-3199
Plantation (G-14660)		
John Q Hammons Hotels MGT LLC	A	904 940-2000
Saint Augustine (G-15459)		
Joy Rockwell Enterprises Inc	C	727 442-6440
Clearwater (G-1690)		
Jsm & Associates LLC	C	352 383-2600
Tavares (G-18611)		
K Parks Consulting Inc	E	321 795-1908
Melbourne (G-8914)		
Kaneca LLC	D	904 786-2333
Jacksonville (G-6395)		
Keith and Associates Inc	D	954 788-3400
Pompano Beach (G-14837)		
Kent White and Associates Inc	A	727 515-3004
Tampa (G-17914)		
Kesaria Marketing Inc	E	856 313-7067
Tampa (G-17916)		
Key Hr LLC	E	800 922-4133
Orlando (G-12727)		
Kimble Partnership LLC	E	561 746-7920
Jupiter (G-7109)		
Knight Images Inc	E	407 206-1011
Orlando (G-12736)		
Landrum Humn Rsrce Cmpnies Inc	E	850 476-5100
Pensacola (G-14342)		
Landscape Rsrces Winter Pk LLC	E	407 672-0816
Winter Park (G-19744)		
Lannan Technologies LLC	D	321 271-8273
Saint Augustine (G-15462)		
Lee Hecht Harrison LLC	E	407 618-2200
Altamonte Springs (G-70)		
Legion Systems LLC	E	813 390-8185
Valrico (G-18755)		
Lexicon Relocation LLC	D	800 387-8242
Jacksonville (G-6430)		
Lien Solutions LLC	E	844 905-4300
Miami (G-9868)		
Little Hvana Actvties Ntrtn CT	D	305 858-0887
Miami (G-9876)		
Live Design Inc	E	786 513-9807
Coral Springs (G-2267)		
LLC Golden Wolf	C	240 672-7995
Lithia (G-8301)		
Lodging Resources Inc	D	800 772-3359
Fernandina Beach (G-3534)		
Loiseau Estates LLC	E	800 273-3817
Miami (G-9880)		
Loud and Live Wza LLC	E	305 773-0551
Doral (G-3264)		
Lukos LLC	E	813 999-0972
Tampa (G-17965)		
Lyndee Press Inc	D	407 297-8484
Orlando (G-12795)		
Lynx Services LLC	B	800 806-2573
Fort Myers (G-4498)		
Major American Mktg Intl Co	E	866 729-1274
Miami (G-9895)		
Management Hlth Solutions Inc	B	888 647-4621
Tampa (G-17980)		
Market Traders Inst Fincl Inc	C	407 740-0900
Orlando (G-12811)		
Marketlauncher Inc	E	407 774-0444
Longwood (G-8379)		
Marpai Administrators LLC	E	855 389-7330
Tampa (G-17993)		
Matthews Design Group LLC	E	904 826-1334
Saint Augustine (G-15466)		
Max Trading & Supplies LLC	E	786 247-1148
Orlando (G-12835)		
McKesson Mdcl-Srgcal Sup Chain	D	904 332-3000
Jacksonville (G-6485)		
McKinsey & Company Inc	D	727 561-2829
Saint Petersburg (G-15756)		

Company	Code	Phone
McKinsey & Company Inc	D	212 446-7000
Miramar (G-10874)		
▲ Meadowbrook Golf Group Inc	D	407 589-7200
Lakeland (G-7917)		
Media Invest LLC	E	954 869-0009
Pembroke Pines (G-14170)		
Mediagistic Inc	D	813 909-7770
Lutz (G-8448)		
Medlink Management Svcs Inc	E	386 496-2461
Lake Butler (G-7507)		
Medmetry Inc	D	833 339-0093
Aventura (G-274)		
Medwatch Inc	D	407 333-8166
Lake Mary (G-7610)		
Men of Honor Foundation Inc	D	904 425-7355
Jacksonville (G-6493)		
Merrill Lynch Prce Fnner Smith	D	561 393-4500
Boca Raton (G-689)		
Merrill Lynch Prce Fnner Smith	C	850 434-7083
Pensacola (G-14362)		
Mesirow Financial Inc	D	561 862-5300
Boca Raton (G-690)		
Messangi Corporation	E	305 731-2003
South Miami (G-16508)		
Mettler-Toledo Hi-Speed Inc	D	800 836-0836
Lutz (G-8449)		
Mge Management Experts Inc	E	727 530-4277
Saint Petersburg (G-15766)		
Midamrica ADM Rtrment Sltons L	D	863 688-4500
Lakeland (G-7924)		
▼ Miles Partnership Lllp	D	941 342-2300
Sarasota (G-16233)		
Mission 1st Group Inc	D	786 647-7466
Tampa (G-18043)		
Mission Critical Group LLC	D	904 422-9731
Jacksonville (G-6507)		
Modern Business Associates Inc	D	727 563-1500
Saint Petersburg (G-15768)		
Moten Tate Incorporated	E	407 843-3277
Windermere (G-19546)		
MT Causley Inc	D	305 246-0696
Homestead (G-5592)		
Naples Community Hospital Inc	B	239 436-6770
Naples (G-11226)		
◆ Nassal Company	D	407 648-0400
Orlando (G-12894)		
National Frnsic Scnce Tech Ctr	E	727 395-2511
Largo (G-8137)		
National Medsales Assoc LLC	E	904 458-4334
Saint Augustine (G-15471)		
National Service Source Inc	C	321 328-1032
Melbourne (G-8947)		
Nationsbenefits LLC	B	877 439-2665
Plantation (G-14681)		
Netpique LLC	C	386 264-3149
Palm Coast (G-13837)		
Neuroscience Associates Inc	D	305 296-2212
Key West (G-7230)		
Newbold Advisors LLC	E	727 535-2102
Clearwater (G-1736)		
Newlink Cmmnications Group LLC	E	305 532-7950
Miami (G-10043)		
Nms Management Services Inc	D	561 967-8884
Palm Springs (G-13895)		
◆ Noble International LLC	E	888 933-5646
Orlando (G-12915)		
North Highland Company LLC	D	404 233-1015
Tallahassee (G-17060)		
Northast Fla Hlthy Start Cltio	E	904 723-5422
Jacksonville (G-6551)		
Okaloosa County School Dst	E	850 301-3020
Niceville (G-11456)		
Old Time Pottery LLC	D	321 757-3600
Melbourne (G-8952)		
Omega Whitespace Health LLC	E	888 794-2266
Boca Raton (G-729)		
Omnia Group Inc	D	813 254-9449
Tampa (G-18099)		
▼ One Call Medical Inc	B	904 646-0199
Jacksonville (G-6561)		
Onsite Safety Inc	D	407 671-7363
Oviedo (G-13563)		
Optime Consulting Inc	E	954 217-7085
Weston (G-19471)		
Optimum Healthcare It LLC	C	904 373-0831
Jacksonville Beach (G-6998)		
Orion Solutions LLC	E	904 394-0934
Jacksonville (G-6569)		
Ovations Food Services LP	E	904 633-6150
Jacksonville (G-6571)		

Company	Code	Phone
Over Ridge LLC	E	813 431-2768
Tampa (G-18114)		
P&L Corporate Solutions LLC	D	561 618-7408
Lake Worth (G-7741)		
Pal-Med Health Services	E	305 702-9200
Hialeah (G-5306)		
Palacci Group Ltd	D	305 392-9547
Doral (G-3285)		
Palmer Kent Associates Inc	E	561 451-8440
Boca Raton (G-739)		
Palmer Prprty Preservation LLC	E	954 932-3209
Fort Lauderdale (G-4039)		
Paradigm Learning Inc	E	727 471-3170
Saint Petersburg (G-15789)		
Partsbase Inc	C	561 953-0700
Boca Raton (G-745)		
Payday Inc III	E	850 912-8884
Pensacola (G-14404)		
Pdp Group LLC	D	407 869-9300
Altamonte Springs (G-89)		
Pegasus Transtech LLC	D	813 386-6000
Tampa (G-18131)		
Peninsula Lifestyle Capital	D	239 494-8633
Naples (G-11260)		
People Inc	D	813 258-0293
Tampa (G-18135)		
Percepta LLC	C	321 435-1000
Melbourne (G-8957)		
Perform CB LLC	E	866 867-6333
Sarasota (G-16262)		
Physicians Dialysis MGT LLC	D	305 651-3261
Miami (G-10119)		
Pink Frog Company Inc	D	689 258-6031
Lake Mary (G-7623)		
Pipeline Contractors Inc	E	904 964-2019
Starke (G-16580)		
Pipers Landing Inc	D	772 283-7000
Palm City (G-13797)		
Plusone Solutions Inc	E	407 359-5929
Orlando (G-13038)		
Poulos & Bennett LLC	D	407 487-2594
Orlando (G-13044)		
Power Resources Fincl Svcs Inc	E	954 281-5590
Pembroke Pines (G-14176)		
Practicewise LLC	C	321 426-4109
Satellite Beach (G-16373)		
Prc LLC	A	786 293-4000
Cutler Bay (G-2375)		
Premier Physician MGT Svcs LLC	D	941 373-3850
Lakewood Ranch (G-8040)		
Premier Worldwide Mktg LLC	E	305 445-1077
Miami (G-10137)		
Pricewaterhousecoopers LLP	B	813 229-0221
Tampa (G-18166)		
Pricewterhousecoopers Svcs LLC	E	813 877-5083
Tampa (G-18168)		
Priority Care Solutions LLC	D	866 932-5779
Tampa (G-18172)		
Project Resources Group Inc	E	239 362-0861
Fort Myers (G-4554)		
Prosser Inc	D	904 739-3655
Jacksonville (G-6619)		
Providence Tech Solutions LLC	E	904 337-6304
Jacksonville (G-6621)		
Pure Leverage Intl Inc	E	904 701-8699
Orange Park (G-12013)		
Quality Built LLC	E	954 358-3500
Fort Lauderdale (G-4072)		
Quality Transport Services Inc	D	954 791-2505
Fort Lauderdale (G-4073)		
Quiet Professionals LLC	D	813 902-3557
Tampa (G-18192)		
Quikfillrx LLC	C	904 265-5476
Jacksonville (G-6627)		
Radius Gge Inc	D	239 948-9820
Fort Myers (G-4564)		
Ratp Dev Usa Inc	D	352 401-6958
Ocala (G-11765)		
Redchip Companies Inc	E	407 644-4256
Maitland (G-8573)		
Reef Global Inc	D	888 695-7275
Miami (G-10191)		
Regis Hr Group 2 LLC	D	786 272-5305
Miami (G-10197)		
Reimbrsment Rcvery Rsurces LLC	E	866 840-6052
Lake Mary (G-7634)		
Relation Insur Svcs Fla Inc	E	772 287-7650
Jacksonville (G-6652)		
Relation Insur Svcs Fla Inc	E	800 431-2221
Stuart (G-16662)		

S I C

Reliable Rders Trnsp Lgstics L ....E 888 639-0132
Fort Lauderdale *(G-4083)*

Republica Havas LLC ....D 786 347-4720
Coral Gables *(G-2175)*

Resource Evaluation Inc ....E 305 375-8005
Miami *(G-10207)*

Resource Solutions Tampa Inc ....E 813 855-3000
Oldsmar *(G-11923)*

Revcontent LLC ....E 941 483-4188
Sarasota *(G-16283)*

◆ Rizzani De Eccher (usa) Inc ....C 305 866-9917
Bay Harbor Islands *(G-348)*

RMC 2021 LLC ....D 850 974-2566
Destin *(G-3075)*

Rme LLC ....C 813 885-8200
Tampa *(G-18229)*

Rrml Cpitl Resources Ltd Lblty ....E 888 270-3582
Boca Raton *(G-779)*

SC&h Group Inc ....E 813 769-3555
Tampa *(G-18250)*

Seitlin & Company ....D 305 591-0090
Fort Lauderdale *(G-4112)*

Senior Resource Assn Inc ....D 772 388-5827
Sebastian *(G-16382)*

Services Ira LLC Advanta ....D 727 581-9853
Largo *(G-8151)*

Seven-One-Seven Prkg Svcs Inc ....A 813 228-7722
Tampa *(G-18273)*

Sha Associates II Ltd ....A 203 869-0900
Spring Hill *(G-16548)*

▲ Shaws Ssthern Blle Frz Fods In ....D 904 768-1591
Jacksonville *(G-6720)*

▲ Signature Consultants LLC ....E 954 677-1020
Fort Lauderdale *(G-4129)*

Silver Hill Funding LLC ....D 844 641-1035
Coral Gables *(G-2188)*

Site Ready LLC ....E 813 517-1700
Tampa *(G-18289)*

Skybridge Americas Inc ....E 763 477-7600
Miami *(G-10282)*

Skylight Inc ....E 919 271-4123
Sarasota *(G-16320)*

Smartstart Emplyment Screening ....B 813 377-4343
Clearwater *(G-1789)*

Software Quality Engrg Inc ....E 904 278-0524
Jacksonville *(G-6738)*

Solaris Employee Solutions LLC ....A 239 919-1142
Bonita Springs *(G-940)*

South Estrn Hlth MGT Assoc Inc ....D 305 863-8860
Hialeah *(G-5322)*

South Fla Bhvral Hlth Ntwrk In ....D 305 858-3335
Miami *(G-10299)*

South Florida Media Group LLC ....E 954 509-7740
Coral Springs *(G-2288)*

South Seaside Enterprises LLC ....D 954 656-2153
Fort Lauderdale *(G-4141)*

Southeastern Funeral Dirs Svc ....E 904 726-5533
Jacksonville *(G-6754)*

Spielman Company Inc ....E 561 445-1400
Delray Beach *(G-3020)*

Springleaf Fincl Holdings LLC ....B 863 293-5615
Lake Wales *(G-7700)*

Sraddha Software Solutions ....E 669 301-8146
Davie *(G-2523)*

SSS Evergreen Opco LLC ....D 239 561-9184
Naples *(G-11303)*

Staffing Concepts Inc ....E 813 258-0293
Tampa *(G-18327)*

Starguard Elite LLC ....E 407 675-4130
Orlando *(G-13236)*

Starmark International Inc ....E 954 874-9000
Fort Lauderdale *(G-4151)*

Stein Gerontological Inst Inc ....D 305 751-8626
Miami *(G-10331)*

Stewart Property Holding Ltd ....E 772 781-7614
Palm City *(G-13803)*

▼ Storm Smart Bldg Systems LLC ....D 239 938-1000
Fort Myers *(G-4608)*

Strategies Now Inc ....E 707 495-2019
Maitland *(G-8580)*

Studer Group LLC ....D 850 439-5869
Pensacola *(G-14448)*

Summit Holding Corporation ....B 863 665-6060
Lakeland *(G-7982)*

Summit Naturals Inc ....D 425 280-1696
Orlando *(G-13247)*

Sunshine Project MGT LLC ....D 407 636-2982
Maitland *(G-8585)*

Sunshine State On-Call Fla Inc ....E 386 575-2000
Debary *(G-2706)*

Superbeo LLC ....E 614 256-7047
Miami *(G-10349)*

Swbg Orlando Corporate Opertns ....D 407 226-5030
Orlando *(G-13254)*

Sylint Group Inc ....E 941 951-6015
Sarasota *(G-16343)*

Synergy Billing LLC ....C 386 675-4709
Daytona Beach *(G-2670)*

Talk2rep Inc ....E 954 933-0660
Fort Lauderdale *(G-4166)*

Taylor Consultants Inc ....E 772 210-5644
Palm City *(G-13807)*

▲ Taylor Made Systems Brdnton In ....E 941 747-1900
Oviedo *(G-13575)*

TBA Management Consulting LLC ....E 786 276-2345
Miami Beach *(G-10665)*

Team Enterprises LLC ....B 954 862-2400
Fort Lauderdale *(G-4169)*

Techtrueup LLC ....C 813 393-9393
Naples *(G-11317)*

Templeton Worldwide Inc ....A 954 527-7500
Fort Lauderdale *(G-4173)*

Templeton/Franklin Inv Svcs ....D 954 761-9357
Fort Lauderdale *(G-4174)*

▲ Terremark Worldwide Inc ....D 305 961-3200
Miami *(G-10380)*

Thompson Consulting Svcs LLC ....C 407 792-0018
Maitland *(G-8588)*

Tinsley Advertising & Mktg Inc ....D 305 856-6060
Miami *(G-10391)*

Tishman Realty Corp Florida ....C 407 934-1873
Lake Buena Vista *(G-7476)*

Tlg Consultants Inc ....E 888 230-3832
Miami *(G-10395)*

◆ Tom Zosel Associates Inc ....D 847 828-5856
Naples *(G-11325)*

Toy Tech Motors Corporation ....D 305 248-6330
Homestead *(G-5610)*

Trifecta Marketing Group LLC ....E 855 548-2624
Palm Harbor *(G-13884)*

Tropic Supply Inc ....D 386 258-8337
Daytona Beach *(G-2679)*

Truecore Bhvoral Solutions LLC ....B 904 547-7689
Tampa *(G-18451)*

Truecore Bhvoral Solutions LLC ....C 561 924-6586
Pahokee *(G-13583)*

Unifi Management LLC ....D 813 514-2797
Tampa *(G-18458)*

Uphealth Inc ....A 312 618-1322
Delray Beach *(G-3029)*

Urban Resource/Group Inc ....D 772 778-3300
Vero Beach *(G-18930)*

US Utility Suppliers Corp ....D 850 290-5456
Pompano Beach *(G-14936)*

US Water Conservation LLC ....D 954 592-0528
Fort Lauderdale *(G-4205)*

V2 Strategic Advisors LLC ....D 877 848-8272
Delray Beach *(G-3030)*

▲ Velocity Solutions LLC ....E 954 847-5800
Fort Lauderdale *(G-4211)*

Vert Nature Inc ....D 561 993-0252
Belle Glade *(G-366)*

Vertek LLC ....D 608 495-1109
Boca Raton *(G-860)*

Vertex Solutions LLC ....D 888 225-9398
Niceville *(G-11458)*

Visionamics Inc ....E 561 405-6894
Boca Raton *(G-863)*

Visual Awrness Tchnlgies Cnslt ....E 813 207-5055
Tampa *(G-18509)*

Vitas Healthcare Corporation ....E 561 496-2378
Delray Beach *(G-3032)*

Whites Site Development Inc ....D 407 302-1549
Sanford *(G-15994)*

Willis North America Inc ....E 813 281-2095
Oldsmar *(G-11936)*

Winn Technology Group Inc ....D 727 789-0006
Palm Harbor *(G-13886)*

Wise US Inc ....D 813 573-8880
Tampa *(G-18563)*

Workshop LLC ....D 305 573-4141
Miami *(G-10514)*

Worksite Communications Inc ....E 850 521-0112
Tallahassee *(G-17178)*

Wpi Services LLC ....E 877 864-3613
Juno Beach *(G-7042)*

▼ Young & Son Inc ....D 850 729-1321
Niceville *(G-11460)*

Yulista Tactical Services LLC ....E 256 319-1653
Jacksonville *(G-6963)*

Zom Inc ....D 407 644-6300
Orlando *(G-13472)*

8743 Public Relations Svcs

Ace Digital Marketing Inc ....C 786 358-6347
Miami *(G-9073)*

American Select Insurance Mgt ....E 727 772-7800
Palm Harbor *(G-13850)*

Bill Bard Associates Inc ....D 305 531-8844
Miami Beach *(G-10558)*

CBS Broadcasting Inc ....D 305 591-4444
Miami *(G-9338)*

Eventnet Usa Inc ....E 954 467-9898
Fort Lauderdale *(G-3778)*

Florida Trism Indust Mktg Corp ....D 850 728-5878
Tallahassee *(G-16982)*

Global-5 Inc ....E 407 571-6789
Longwood *(G-8363)*

Hill & Knowlton / Samcor LLC ....E 305 443-5454
Coral Gables *(G-2124)*

Jacksonville Trnsp Auth ....D 904 633-8503
Jacksonville *(G-6367)*

▲ JM Field Marketing Inc ....E 954 523-1957
Fort Lauderdale *(G-3909)*

Newlink Cmmnications Group LLC ....E 305 532-7950
Miami *(G-10043)*

▲ Premiums Prmotions Imports Inc ....E 888 451-3905
Daytona Beach *(G-2654)*

Quest Corporation America Inc ....E 813 239-7725
Land O Lakes *(G-8054)*

Republica ....E 305 442-0977
Miami *(G-10202)*

Riskwatch International LLC ....D 941 500-4525
Sarasota *(G-16284)*

Robin Shepherd Studios Inc ....E 904 359-0981
Jacksonville *(G-6673)*

Rumberger Kirk Cldwell Prof As ....E 407 872-7300
Tallahassee *(G-17089)*

Star Group Communications Inc ....D 561 807-8828
Boca Raton *(G-818)*

Starmark International Inc ....E 954 874-9000
Fort Lauderdale *(G-4151)*

Universal Cy Dev Partners Ltd ....D 407 224-4233
Orlando *(G-13345)*

Vistra Communications LLC ....E 813 961-4700
Lutz *(G-8466)*

▼ Zimmerman Agency LLC ....D 850 877-8896
Tallahassee *(G-17180)*

8744 Facilities Support Mgmt Svcs

Advanced Envmtl Labs Inc ....E 850 219-6274
Tallahassee *(G-16870)*

Alpha Envmtl Mnagementcorp LLC ....C 407 542-0300
Winter Springs *(G-19797)*

Astrotech Space Operations LLC ....D 321 268-3830
Titusville *(G-18677)*

Batallan Enterprises Inc ....D 561 805-8687
West Palm Beach *(G-19048)*

Cag Logistics MGT Svcs LLC ....B 813 860-4558
Tampa *(G-17410)*

Cec Parent Holdings LLC ....E 561 893-0101
Boca Raton *(G-501)*

Challenge Entps N Fla Inc ....B 904 284-9859
Green Cove Springs *(G-5048)*

Choice Environmental Svcs Inc ....C 239 368-2300
Lehigh Acres *(G-8277)*

Community Education Ctrs Inc ....E 561 893-0101
Boca Raton *(G-522)*

Corecivic Inc ....E 615 263-3000
Lake City *(G-7522)*

▲ Cornell Companies Inc ....D 561 893-0101
Boca Raton *(G-529)*

Cornell Corrections MGT LLC ....A 561 893-0101
Boca Raton *(G-530)*

Correctional Services Corp LLC ....D 941 953-9199
Sarasota *(G-16132)*

▲ Correctional Services Corp LLC ....D 561 893-0101
Boca Raton *(G-532)*

Corrections Florida Department ....D 904 782-2000
Lawtey *(G-8209)*

Cyprexx Services LLC ....B 813 661-5800
Brandon *(G-1223)*

Diversitech Inc ....E 513 772-4447
Orlando *(G-12431)*

Eagle Cnstr & Envmtl Svcs LLC ....B 254 442-1553
Panama City Beach *(G-14094)*

Efco USA Inc ....E 305 876-0026
Doral *(G-3187)*

ESA South Inc ....E 850 937-8505
Cantonment *(G-1339)*

Company	Code	Phone
Exlog Global LLC	E	540 295-8851
Jacksonville (G-6139)		
Florida Department Corrections	C	352 793-2525
Bushnell (G-1327)		
Florida Department Corrections	C	863 453-3174
Avon Park (G-291)		
Florida Department Corrections	C	386 719-4500
Sanderson (G-15912)		
Florida Department Corrections	C	850 237-6500
Blountstown (G-384)		
Florida Department Corrections	C	850 769-1455
Panama City (G-14010)		
Fluor Federal Solutions LLC	E	850 452-5051
Pensacola (G-14313)		
Fti-USA Inc	E	727 826-7235
Largo (G-8111)		
G4s Holding One Inc	B	561 622-5656
Jupiter (G-7076)		
G4s Secure Solutions USA Inc	B	561 622-5656
Jupiter (G-7079)		
Gcs Enrgy Rcovery Pinellas Inc	D	727 564-5000
Hudson (G-5640)		
GE Medcal Systems Info Tech In	D	561 575-5000
Jupiter (G-7082)		
Geo Design Services Inc	D	561 893-0101
Boca Raton (G-600)		
Geo Group Inc	E	954 973-4485
Pompano Beach (G-14815)		
Geo Group Inc	B	561 893-0101
Boca Raton (G-601)		
Geo Reentry Services LLC	E	561 893-0101
Boca Raton (G-603)		
Gle Associates Inc	E	813 241-8350
Tampa (G-17735)		
Government Contg Resources Inc	D	850 235-2659
Panama City Beach (G-14095)		
Hes Facilities LLC	A	865 263-1905
Jacksonville (G-6277)		
Hvide Marine Services Inc	B	954 523-2200
Fort Lauderdale (G-3883)		
Iap World Services Inc	E	321 784-7100
Cape Canaveral (G-1367)		
Indyne Inc	D	850 882-3586
Eglin Afb (G-3419)		
Indyne Inc	E	850 678-7441
Eglin Afb (G-3420)		
Indyne Inc	C	321 867-8561
Kennedy Space Center (G-7156)		
Indyne Inc	B	321 853-5811
Patrick Afb (G-14121)		
Interntional Support Group LLC	D	954 900-1095
Pembroke Pines (G-14155)		
Intracoastal Environmental LLC	E	904 249-8004
Jacksonville (G-6331)		
Lcs Corrections Services Inc	A	337 234-1533
Clearwater (G-1696)		
Mettler-Toledo Hi-Speed Inc	D	800 836-0836
Lutz (G-8449)		
Mfm Services LLC	E	904 240-1345
Jacksonville (G-6502)		
Okaloosa County School Dst	E	850 833-5801
Niceville (G-11455)		
Pacific Scientific Company	E	305 477-4711
Medley (G-8767)		
Pae Applied Technologies LLC	C	561 832-8566
West Palm Beach (G-19304)		
Re-Engneered Bus Solutions Inc	C	321 305-6984
Cocoa (G-1949)		
Regency Cnstr Palm Bch Cnty Co	D	586 741-8000
West Palm Beach (G-19341)		
Restorations Unlimited LLC	D	954 418-3000
Hollywood (G-5507)		
Rockhill Group Inc	C	850 754-0400
Molino (G-10929)		
TI Services Inc	E	813 641-2730
Ruskin (G-15404)		
Trinity Services Group Inc	D	386 792-0749
Jasper (G-7009)		
Trinity Services Group Inc	D	850 951-0358
Defuniak Springs (G-2841)		
US Facility Solutions LLC	D	888 904-7900
Sunrise (G-16843)		
Wolf Creek Federal Svcs Inc	A	321 494-5122
Patrick Afb (G-14124)		

8748 Business Consulting Svcs, NEC

Company	Code	Phone
15 Lightyears Inc	E	855 438-1515
Longwood (G-8333)		
3d3 Enterprise LLC	E	863 419-6452
Davenport (G-2433)		
3gimbals LLC	E	703 957-7269
Miami Beach (G-10538)		
7 G Solutions LLC	E	813 763-5053
Brandon (G-1210)		
A & K Energy Conservation Inc	C	352 567-1999
Dade City (G-2379)		
A&A Coordinators America LLC	E	954 674-3747
Miami (G-9062)		
Accelirate Inc	D	908 229-1167
Sunrise (G-16730)		
Adsync Technologies Inc	D	850 497-6969
Pensacola (G-14212)		
Advanced C4 Solutions Inc	E	813 282-3031
Tampa (G-17239)		
Advanced Info Systems Group In	E	407 581-2929
Orlando (G-12056)		
Aerostar Envmtl Svcs Inc	E	251 432-2664
Jacksonville (G-5747)		
Aerostar SES LLC	E	904 565-2820
Jacksonville (G-5748)		
Affinity Consulting Group LLC	D	727 544-5400
Seminole (G-16437)		
Afl Inc	E	844 410-1631
Fort Lauderdale (G-3583)		
Afx Group LLC	E	703 884-2222
Brandon (G-1212)		
Aircraft Dev Flght Arways Corp	E	305 233-6648
Miami (G-9106)		
Ally Facility Solutions Inc	E	941 536-4443
Saint Petersburg (G-15564)		
Alpha Envmtl Mnagementcorp LLC	E	407 542-0300
Winter Springs (G-19797)		
Amcom Group LLC	E	516 244-6777
Palm Beach Gardens (G-13683)		
Ampy Enterprises Inc	C	305 827-9070
Miami (G-9150)		
Anastsia Msqito Ctrl Dst St Jh	E	904 471-3107
Saint Augustine (G-15424)		
Anser Advisory Consulting LLC	E	541 948-0733
Longwood (G-8340)		
Aoh Services Inc	E	561 582-6260
Lake Worth (G-7709)		
Apb Security Services Inc	E	954 420-2250
Deerfield Beach (G-2709)		
Applied Aquatic Management Inc	D	863 533-8882
Bartow (G-308)		
Applied Research Assoc Inc	E	850 678-5222
Niceville (G-11438)		
Applied Research Assoc Inc	C	850 914-3188
Panama City (G-13956)		
Applied Technical Systems Inc	E	337 280-5447
Panama City (G-13957)		
Aptim Government Solutions LLC	D	305 818-1888
Miami Lakes (G-10704)		
Archbold Expeditions Inc	E	863 465-2571
Venus (G-18825)		
Arma Global Corporation	D	866 554-9333
Tampa (G-17306)		
Ase Telecom & Data Inc	D	305 471-9888
Doral (G-3125)		
Atms	E	321 373-4274
Melbourne (G-8819)		
Auritasllc	E	407 834-8324
Sanford (G-15919)		
Austral Education Group LLC	E	877 871-3932
Miami (G-9192)		
Avesi Inc	E	618 795-1619
Panama City Beach (G-14088)		
Bayforce Tech Solutions Inc	C	813 386-0663
Tampa (G-17353)		
Berkley Group Inc	D	954 563-2444
Fort Lauderdale (G-3639)		
Best-TEC Asb Abatement Inc	E	904 695-9900
Boynton Beach (G-964)		
Beymark Inc	E	302 559-6323
Temple Terrace (G-18630)		
Bio-Tech Consulting Inc	E	561 898-0835
Orlando (G-12188)		
Bore Tech Utilities & Maint	D	305 297-8162
Miami (G-9269)		
Bowden Road Housing Ltd	A	203 869-0900
Jacksonville (G-5875)		
BTS Group Inc	E	305 358-5850
Miami (G-9292)		
Bunch and Associates Inc	C	863 669-0861
Lakeland (G-7820)		
Bureau Veritas Holdings Inc	D	954 236-8100
Sunrise (G-16753)		
Capital Frmtion Counselors Inc	E	727 581-8702
Belleair Bluffs (G-370)		

Company	Code	Phone
Castalia Systems LLC	D	813 748-2283
Tampa (G-17429)		
Castlebridge Consulting LLC	E	813 489-9777
Tampa (G-17430)		
▼ Celestar Corporation	D	813 627-9069
Tampa (G-17436)		
Centralbdc LLC	E	561 213-1187
Boca Raton (G-504)		
Certified Cllctibles Group LLC	C	941 360-3994
Lakewood Ranch (G-8036)		
CFI Resorts Management Inc	C	407 355-2463
Ocoee (G-11810)		
Cherokee Enterprises Inc	E	305 828-3353
Medley (G-8714)		
Children & Families Fla Dept	C	352 375-8484
Gainesville (G-4854)		
City of Gainesville	D	352 393-8528
Gainesville (G-4863)		
City of Naples	E	239 213-5020
Naples (G-11054)		
Clayton Corp	E	754 422-0532
Hollywood (G-5415)		
Clean Harbors Envmtl Svcs Inc	E	863 533-6111
Bartow (G-315)		
Coastal Cloud LLC	D	800 237-9574
Palm Coast (G-13817)		
Coastal Systems Intl Inc	D	305 661-3655
Coral Gables (G-2072)		
▲ Cogistics Inc	D	863 647-9389
Lakeland (G-7840)		
◆ Comanco Environmental Corp	D	813 988-8829
Plant City (G-14550)		
▼ Complyright Inc	D	954 970-5500
Pompano Beach (G-14780)		
Consult Pr Inc	E	561 444-7265
West Palm Beach (G-19106)		
Continuum Health It LLC	D	904 994-7929
Ponte Vedra Beach (G-14980)		
Coral Springs Water Improvemen	D	954 753-0380
Coral Springs (G-2243)		
Corvus Consulting LLC	D	571 722-3198
Saint Petersburg (G-15645)		
County of Hillsborough	D	813 744-5519
Seffner (G-16424)		
Csa Ocean Sciences Inc	D	772 219-3000
Stuart (G-16613)		
Cv Technology Inc	E	561 694-9588
Jupiter (G-7061)		
Cybervision Inc	E	201 585-9809
Sunny Isles Beach (G-16715)		
▼ D P C General Contractors Inc	E	305 325-0447
Miami (G-9448)		
Dalpar Corporation	E	850 362-6426
Fort Walton Beach (G-4761)		
◆ Datamax System Solutions Inc	E	561 994-1250
Boca Raton (G-545)		
De Lima Consultants Group Inc	E	561 634-0223
Coral Springs (G-2247)		
Dedicated It LLC	E	561 491-5750
Lake Park (G-7659)		
Digisat International Inc	E	321 676-5250
Melbourne (G-8871)		
Digital Risk LLC	E	561 208-7489
Boca Raton (G-553)		
Digital Risk LLC	A	407 215-2900
Maitland (G-8524)		
Dobler Consulting Inc	E	813 322-3240
Tampa (G-17597)		
◆ Domital Corporation	E	305 594-0873
Fort Lauderdale (G-3762)		
Draftpros LLC	C	786 641-5131
Miami Lakes (G-10723)		
Dudek	B	442 245-1886
Lake Worth (G-7723)		
E D & F Man Services Inc	D	305 707-8761
Boca Raton (G-560)		
▲ Earthbalance Corporation	D	941 426-7878
North Port (G-11568)		
Easy Solutions Inc	C	866 524-4782
Doral (G-3186)		
Eden Group Inc	E	904 751-3723
Jacksonville (G-6103)		
EE&g Construction & Elec LLC	E	305 374-8300
Miami Lakes (G-10725)		
Efiie Consulting Group LLC	D	786 233-8515
Coral Gables (G-2100)		
Ekkonet Telecom LLC	E	201 424-2694
Madeira Beach (G-8482)		
Embanet-Compass Knowledge	D	877 303-2340
Orlando (G-12459)		

S I C

Emergency Response & Trnng............E...... 440 349-2700
  Jacksonville **(G-6111)**

Enadava LLC............................B...... 425 454-2686
  Sarasota **(G-16148)**

Envirnmntal Cnsulting Tech Inc............E...... 352 332-0444
  Gainesville **(G-4881)**

Environmental Services Inc............D...... 904 470-2200
  Jacksonville **(G-6123)**

Environmental Services Inc............C...... 386 566-2733
  Ormond Beach **(G-13489)**

Envisage International Corp............E...... 904 247-1387
  Neptune Beach **(G-11356)**

Equitus Corporation............E...... 888 722-8755
  Clearwater **(G-1626)**

Evans Envir Geo SCI MGM LLC............E...... 305 374-8300
  Miami Lakes **(G-10727)**

Evolution Insight Incorporated............D...... 321 282-1999
  Windermere **(G-19539)**

Florida Chapter Int Assoc Asse............D...... 850 606-6200
  Tallahassee **(G-16961)**

Florida Comm Concepts Inc............E...... 561 718-4081
  Wellington **(G-18979)**

Florida International Univ............E...... 727 395-2511
  Largo **(G-8109)**

Florida Sugar Distributors............D...... 561 366-5287
  South Bay **(G-16479)**

Frs Envrnmntal Remediation Inc............E...... 813 623-1557
  Tampa **(G-17719)**

◆ Future Energy Solutions LLC............E...... 954 714-0300
  Fort Lauderdale **(G-3810)**

G4s Holding One Inc............B...... 561 622-5656
  Jupiter **(G-7076)**

G4s Secure Solutions USA Inc............B...... 561 622-5656
  Jupiter **(G-7079)**

Gara Group Inc............E...... 833 468-4272
  Davie **(G-2484)**

GCI Consultants Holding Co LLC............E...... 561 689-0055
  West Palm Beach **(G-19162)**

Geo Group Inc............D...... 561 622-5656
  West Palm Beach **(G-19163)**

Geo Management Services Inc............C..... 561 893-0101
  Boca Raton **(G-602)**

Girard Environmental Svcs Inc............D...... 561 232-3673
  West Palm Beach **(G-19164)**

Gle Associates Inc............E...... 813 241-8350
  Tampa **(G-17735)**

▲ Global Diversified Products............E...... 727 209-0854
  Pinellas Park **(G-14520)**

Global Media Business Group............D...... 877 457-4624
  Miami **(G-9636)**

Grant Consulting Inc............E...... 561 599-4138
  Boca Raton **(G-610)**

Grupo Ngn Inc............C...... 954 800-8586
  Coral Springs **(G-2257)**

Guidewell Inc............E...... 904 363-4855
  Jacksonville **(G-6248)**

Hamlin & Associates Inc............E...... 386 672-4113
  Ormond Beach **(G-13502)**

Hazmed Inc............E...... 202 742-6521
  Palm Coast **(G-13830)**

HDR Construction Control Corp............E...... 813 282-2300
  Tampa **(G-17801)**

Health Care Dst Palm Bch Cnty............D...... 561 659-1270
  West Palm Beach **(G-19174)**

Hlg Capital Partners III LP............A...... 305 379-2322
  Miami **(G-9703)**

Hire Velocity LLC............E...... 813 286-7240
  Lutz **(G-8444)**

Homeland Intelligence Tech............E...... 727 776-7424
  Largo **(G-8117)**

Horizo Inc............D...... 904 425-7355
  Jacksonville **(G-6297)**

▲ Hotwire Communications LLC............C...... 800 355-5668
  Fort Lauderdale **(G-3875)**

Idmworks LLC............E...... 888 687-0436
  Coral Gables **(G-2129)**

Innovative Prof Solutions Inc............C...... 850 819-1691
  Panama City Beach **(G-14097)**

Insite Managed Solutions LLC............E...... 239 234-2700
  Cape Coral **(G-1402)**

Inspired Tech N Fla Inc............D...... 850 402-3700
  Tallahassee **(G-17005)**

Intergncy Rdness Solutions LLC............C...... 904 824-8273
  Saint Augustine **(G-15455)**

Intermodal Support Svcs Inc............D...... 904 858-1587
  Jacksonville **(G-6327)**

Interntional Sls Team Amer Inc............E...... 786 200-3429
  Sunny Isles Beach **(G-16721)**

Intervisual Technology Inc............E...... 954 438-1740
  Hollywood **(G-5460)**

Intuitive It Solutions LLC............D...... 877 889-1011
  Celebration **(G-1466)**

▲ Iqor Global Services LLC............B...... 727 369-0100
  Saint Petersburg **(G-15725)**

Jcg Technologies Inc............B...... 727 461-3776
  Clearwater **(G-1682)**

Jeffrey Group LLC............D...... 305 860-1000
  Miami **(G-9787)**

Jetsmarter Inc............D...... 888 984-7538
  Fort Lauderdale **(G-3906)**

Jht Inc............E...... 407 381-7797
  Orlando **(G-12707)**

Josef Silny & Associates Inc............E...... 305 273-1616
  Miami **(G-9804)**

JSOL Group Inc............E...... 954 932-2448
  Fort Lauderdale **(G-3912)**

Karia Group LLC............E...... 954 558-5157
  Hollywood **(G-5463)**

Keith and Associates Inc............E...... 954 788-3400
  Pompano Beach **(G-14837)**

Kii Telecommunications LLC............E...... 973 630-2440
  Boca Raton **(G-660)**

Krane Development Inc............D...... 813 875-4600
  Tampa **(G-17931)**

Lambic Telcom Inc............D...... 727 785-4435
  Palm Harbor **(G-13868)**

Leading Solutions LLC............D...... 407 201-5727
  Kissimmee **(G-7346)**

Leanswift Solutions Inc............E...... 321 474-3760
  Cocoa Beach **(G-1973)**

Learning House Incorporated............E...... 502 589-9878
  Maitland **(G-8553)**

Level 4 Consulting LLC............D...... 407 808-7428
  Windermere **(G-19545)**

Lexisnexis Risk Solutions Inc............C...... 800 543-6862
  Boca Raton **(G-669)**

Life of South............E...... 904 350-9660
  Jacksonville **(G-6434)**

Lincoln-Marti Schools LLC............C...... 305 642-3918
  Miami **(G-9874)**

Lumen Solutions Group Inc............D...... 703 881-9119
  Parkland **(G-14109)**

Lykins-Signtek & Dev Spc............D...... 239 594-8494
  Naples **(G-11201)**

Magnit Quick LLC............E...... 407 770-6161
  Orlando **(G-12802)**

Marketlauncher Inc............E...... 407 774-0444
  Longwood **(G-8379)**

Mes-Cmta Sb Jv LLC............D...... 813 289-4700
  Tampa **(G-18029)**

Meteor Education LLC............C...... 800 699-7516
  Gainesville **(G-4944)**

Mobile Medical Industries LLC............D...... 561 893-0163
  Boynton Beach **(G-1017)**

Modern Air Solutions LLC............E...... 850 200-5026
  Panama City Beach **(G-14099)**

Moziah Corporation............D...... 407 476-1356
  Orlando **(G-12883)**

Muscato Corporation............E...... 407 551-1300
  Altamonte Springs **(G-80)**

Naglreiter Consulting LLC............D...... 954 507-3830
  Miramar **(G-10879)**

National Frnsic Scnce Tech Ctr............E...... 727 395-2511
  Largo **(G-8137)**

National Proc Aliance Inc............E...... 954 320-4070
  Fort Lauderdale **(G-3994)**

Navis Corporation............C...... 510 267-5000
  Miami **(G-10033)**

NAVY UNITED STATES DEPARTMENT............D...... 850 234-4201
  Panama City **(G-14047)**

Newbold Advisors LLC............E...... 727 535-2102
  Clearwater **(G-1736)**

Newlink Cmmnications Group LLC............E...... 305 532-7950
  Miami **(G-10043)**

Next Level Business Svcs Inc............A...... 904 267-0528
  Seminole **(G-16456)**

Northast Fla Eductl Consortium............D...... 386 329-3800
  Palatka **(G-13596)**

Nv5 Global Inc............C...... 954 495-2112
  Hollywood **(G-5486)**

Onsite Safety Inc............D...... 407 671-7363
  Oviedo **(G-13563)**

Ops Tech Alliance LLC............B...... 443 223-6115
  Clearwater **(G-1748)**

Optimus Bus Transformation LLC............E...... 305 407-2428
  Doral **(G-3283)**

Orion Waste Solutions LLC............E...... 727 561-0360
  Clearwater **(G-1750)**

P&L Corporate Solutions LLC............D...... 561 618-7408
  Lake Worth **(G-7741)**

Palmer Prprty Preservation LLC............E...... 954 932-3209
  Fort Lauderdale **(G-4039)**

Peninsula Lifestyle Capital............D...... 239 494-8633
  Naples **(G-11260)**

Percepta LLC............C...... 321 435-1000
  Melbourne **(G-8957)**

Petrotech Southeast Inc............E...... 407 656-8114
  Astatula **(G-238)**

Pointtrade Services Inc............E...... 850 522-4102
  Panama City **(G-14057)**

Pragma Edge Inc............,C...... 224 804-0690
  Jacksonville **(G-6611)**

Priority One Financial Svcs............E...... 727 822-7171
  Saint Petersburg **(G-15808)**

Property Rgstrtion Chmpons LLC............E...... 321 405-2633
  Melbourne **(G-8960)**

Public Sfety Strtgies Group LL............D...... 612 386-8523
  Lakeland **(G-7944)**

Quintero & Partners LLC............C...... 786 953-8958
  Miami **(G-10177)**

Ramcotek Consulting LLC............E...... 850 391-5265
  Tallahassee **(G-17080)**

Rat Pack Wrldwide SEC Cnslt In............E...... 888 575-7225
  Tampa **(G-18201)**

Reedy Creek Improvement Dst............D...... 407 828-2241
  Orlando **(G-13092)**

Reedy Creek Improvement Dst............D...... 407 824-7301
  Lake Buena Vista **(G-7470)**

Revolution Technologies LLC............C...... 407 275-7575
  Orlando **(G-13105)**

Rone Engineering............C...... 214 630-9745
  Hialeah **(G-5317)**

Roundtower Technologies LLC............E...... 513 247-7900
  West Palm Beach **(G-19347)**

Rt Management Services Inc............C...... 305 556-9322
  Miami Lakes **(G-10758)**

Sahban Enterprises Inc............E...... 813 409-4414
  Valrico **(G-18756)**

SAlt Payroll Consultants Inc............D...... 727 906-4900
  Saint Petersburg **(G-15836)**

Savis Inc............E...... 847 797-8857
  Clearwater Beach **(G-1854)**

Seacamp Association Inc............C...... 305 872-2331
  Big Pine Key **(G-380)**

◆ Seacor Holdings Inc............E...... 954 523-2200
  Fort Lauderdale **(G-4109)**

Serdi-LLC............D...... 240 353-9656
  Saint Cloud **(G-15533)**

Shaycore Enterprises Inc............D...... 904 536-3732
  Jacksonville **(G-6721)**

Shr Communications LLC............D...... 786 420-7631
  Doral **(G-3309)**

Skiltrek LLC............E...... 866 620-2612
  Jacksonville Beach **(G-7003)**

Skyetec Envmtl Dgnstc Svcs Inc............E...... 904 482-4260
  Jacksonville **(G-6731)**

Smartstart Emplyment Screening............B...... 813 377-4343
  Clearwater **(G-1789)**

Solid Waste Auth Palm Bch Cnty............E...... 561 640-4000
  West Palm Beach **(G-19365)**

Solution Construction Inc............E...... 786 621-8550
  Medley **(G-8785)**

Southern Aero LLC............E...... 786 925-5043
  Homestead **(G-5608)**

Southside Development Group............C...... 941 955-9856
  Sarasota **(G-16324)**

Soyring Consulting Inc............A...... 727 822-8774
  Saint Petersburg **(G-15850)**

Special Applications Group LLC............D...... 813 254-9050
  Tampa **(G-18317)**

Spencer Trails Property............E...... 904 282-4358
  Middleburg **(G-10799)**

Star Freight LLC............E...... 904 781-4788
  Jacksonville **(G-6786)**

▲ Star2star Communications LLC............C...... 941 234-0001
  Sarasota **(G-16330)**

Stc Inc............E...... 813 737-4201
  Lithia **(G-8305)**

Success Projects Inc............C...... 407 354-3399
  Orlando **(G-13242)**

Sun Land Group Corporation............E...... 954 362-7813
  Pembroke Pines **(G-14194)**

Suncoast Safety Council Inc............E...... 727 373-7233
  Clearwater **(G-1806)**

Sykes Acquisition LLC............D...... 863 802-3000
  Lakeland **(G-7985)**

▲ Syniverse Technologies LLC............A...... 813 637-5000
  Tampa **(G-18358)**

System Soft Technologies Inc............D...... 727 723-0801
  Tampa **(G-18359)**

T T A S Inc ....E 305 444-4779
  Miami *(G-10359)*

Tandel Systems Inc ....E....... 727 530-1110
  Oldsmar *(G-11929)*

TCS Group Inc ....E 954 846-8787
  Coral Springs *(G-2290)*

Tektron Electrical Systems ....E....... 561 615-3111
  West Palm Beach *(G-19380)*

Templeton Worldwide Inc ....A 954 527-7500
  Fort Lauderdale *(G-4173)*

Templeton/Franklin Inv Svcs ....D 954 761-9357
  Fort Lauderdale *(G-4174)*

Testamerica Laboratories Inc ....D 850 878-3994
  Tallahassee *(G-17156)*

Thales Avionics Inc ....E 321 308-3900
  Melbourne *(G-8994)*

Thales Avionics Inc ....E....... 407 812-2600
  Miami *(G-10383)*

Thales Avionics Inc ....E 407 812-2600
  Orlando *(G-13285)*

The Gensight Group Inc ....D 215 489-9424
  Naples *(G-11321)*

Tides Center ....C 904 535-0055
  Atlantic Beach *(G-246)*

Total Solutions Group Inc ....D 321 972-0491
  Maitland *(G-8589)*

Tpusa - Fhcs Inc ....C 772 398-2000
  Port Saint Lucie *(G-15173)*

Traffic Safety Consultants Inc ....C 407 629-9551
  Longwood *(G-8411)*

Trajector Holdings LLC ....E 352 363-6722
  Newberry *(G-11433)*

Trident Tchnical Solutions LLC ....C 813 243-3030
  Tampa *(G-18446)*

Troc LLC ....A 305 539-3810
  Coral Gables *(G-2200)*

Tsg Enterprises LLC ....D 407 657-4169
  Casselberry *(G-1462)*

UI LLC ....C 561 615-2622
  West Palm Beach *(G-19396)*

United Nations Group LLC ....C 800 472-0948
  Miami Beach *(G-10669)*

United Safety Council Inc ....D....... 407 897-4443
  Orlando *(G-13340)*

Universal Engrg Sciences LLC ....E 407 423-0504
  Orlando *(G-13348)*

◆ USA Environmental Inc ....C 813 343-6336
  Oldsmar *(G-11933)*

Venergy Group LLC ....D 772 468-0053
  Fort Pierce *(G-4748)*

Vengroff Williams Inc ....B 941 363-5200
  Sarasota *(G-16357)*

Verizon Business Global LLC ....E 407 244-3001
  Orlando *(G-13373)*

Vertek LLC ....E 608 495-1109
  Boca Raton *(G-860)*

Village Center Cmnty Dev Dst ....C 952 205-8280
  The Villages *(G-18663)*

Village Center Cmnty Dev Dst ....E....... 352 751-6700
  The Villages *(G-18664)*

Village Center Cmnty Dev Dst ....C 352 750-0000
  The Villages *(G-18665)*

Vistra Communications LLC ....E....... 813 961-4700
  Lutz *(G-8466)*

Washington County School Dst ....D....... 850 638-6131
  Chipley *(G-1496)*

Water & Air Research Inc ....D....... 352 372-1500
  Gainesville *(G-5028)*

We Know Waste Inc ....E....... 904 246-1520
  Atlantic Beach *(G-247)*

Whitney Bradley and Brown Inc ....D....... 703 448-6081
  Niceville *(G-11459)*

Worldnet Services Corp ....E....... 954 389-5400
  Weston *(G-19488)*

Yes Him Consulting Inc ....E 727 536-0102
  Largo *(G-8165)*

Zyscovich Inc ....D....... 305 372-5222
  Miami *(G-10532)*

89 SERVICES, NOT ELSEWHERE CLASSIFIED

8999 Services Not Elsewhere Classified

626 Nrth Tyndall Pkwy Oprtons ....D 850 871-6363
  Panama City *(G-13952)*

A & P Consulting Transporta ....E 786 332-3681
  Medley *(G-8698)*

American Cnslting Prfessionals ....E 561 253-9550
  West Palm Beach *(G-19031)*

American Compliance Tech Inc ....D 863 533-2000
  Bartow *(G-307)*

Ang Kusinang Pilipino ....E 850 691-2148
  Panama City *(G-13955)*

Ash Group Inc ....E 813 290-8899
  Tampa *(G-17311)*

Aw Solutions Inc ....D 407 260-0231
  Longwood *(G-8345)*

Bestbet- Jacksonville ....B 904 646-0001
  Jacksonville *(G-5858)*

Chatter Buzz Media LLC ....E 321 236-2899
  Orlando *(G-12291)*

Chem-Tel LLC ....D 813 248-0573
  Tampa *(G-17463)*

County of Orange ....C 407 345-9800
  Orlando *(G-12378)*

County of Seminole ....E 407 321-2419
  Lake Mary *(G-7582)*

Dotjam Services Inc ....E 321 689-6020
  Oakland *(G-11582)*

Dynamac Corporation ....E 321 867-4188
  Kennedy Space Center *(G-7155)*

Ecs Federal LLC ....A 407 745-3022
  Orlando *(G-12451)*

Edd Helms Group Inc ....E 305 653-2520
  Sunrise *(G-16767)*

Elan Business Services Corp ....E 954 257-8350
  Weston *(G-19458)*

Faro Services Inc ....E 904 288-6700
  Jacksonville *(G-6150)*

First Cast Infctous Dsase Cons ....E 904 264-7132
  Orange Park *(G-11989)*

Foundation Resolution Corp ....C 352 344-9755
  Inverness *(G-5693)*

Gem Technology Intl Corp ....C 305 447-1344
  Miami *(G-9622)*

L C Graycom ....E 305 491-0464
  Miami *(G-9839)*

Mears Destination Services Inc ....A 407 422-4561
  Orlando *(G-12849)*

Overon America LLC ....D 305 357-5891
  Medley *(G-8766)*

Precision Contracting Svcs Inc ....E 239 768-0300
  Fort Myers *(G-4547)*

Red Coats Inc ....D 352 351-5335
  Ocala *(G-11766)*

Relogistics Services LLC ....E 352 796-5430
  Brooksville *(G-1306)*

Senlex Environmental LLC ....E 800 284-0394
  Miami *(G-10259)*

Service Champ Inc ....E 813 968-6791
  Tampa *(G-18272)*

Service Experts LLC ....D 904 641-2333
  Jacksonville *(G-6712)*

Sistema Universitario Ana G M ....A 954 885-5595
  Miramar *(G-10896)*

Southstern Archlogical RES Inc ....C 407 236-7711
  Orlando *(G-13221)*

State of Florida ....C 850 653-8298
  Apalachicola *(G-130)*

Telefonica International Inc ....D 305 577-8880
  Miami *(G-10372)*

Uam Agent Services Corp ....C 407 995-8000
  Lake Mary *(G-7649)*

Universal Engrg Sciences LLC ....E 407 423-0504
  Orlando *(G-13348)*

Vertical Bridge Holdings LLC ....E 561 948-6367
  Boca Raton *(G-861)*

Woodham & Associates Fla LLC ....A 866 966-3426
  Tequesta *(G-18650)*

S
I
C

ALPHABETIC SECTION

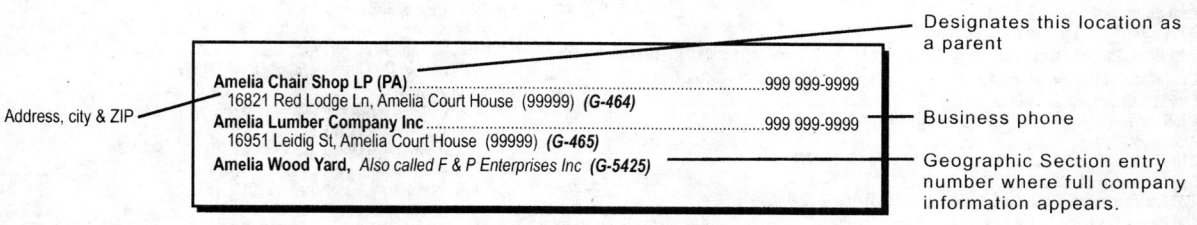

Designates this location as a parent

Address, city & ZIP →

Amelia Chair Shop LP (PA) 999 999-9999
16821 Red Lodge Ln, Amelia Court House (99999) *(G-464)*

Amelia Lumber Company Inc 999 999-9999
16951 Leidig St, Amelia Court House (99999) *(G-465)*

Amelia Wood Yard, *Also called F & P Enterprises Inc (G-5425)*

Business phone

Geographic Section entry number where full company information appears.

See footnotes for symbols and codes identification.

* Companies listed alphabetically.

* Complete physical or mailing address.

0energy Lighting Inc 855 955-1055
1110 Sligh Blvd Orlando (32806) *(G-11848)*

100 Feet Deep, Pensacola *Also called Localtoolbox Inc (G-13538)*

10858 Opco LLC 949 697-6737
10858 Se County Road 221 Starke (32091) *(G-16094)*

10x Vegan LLC 954 256-4094
1612 S Cypress Rd Pompano Beach (33060) *(G-13904)*

12 Volt USA, Kissimmee *Also called Techtronics LLC (G-6964)*

123 Diet LLC 954 643-2522
10 Fairway Dr Ste 225 Deerfield Beach (33441) *(G-2647)*

123 Dollar Plus Inc 305 456-4561
7181 Sw 8th St Miami (33144) *(G-8605)*

1425 N Washington Street LLC 904 680-6600
12808 Gran Bay Pkwy W Jacksonville (32258) *(G-5839)*

1506 N Florida LLC 813 229-0900
1505 N Florida Ave Tampa (33602) *(G-16545)*

1565 Woodworks LLC 904 347-7664
17 Linda Mar Dr Saint Augustine (32080) *(G-14803)*

1600 Lenox LLC 786 360-2553
7350 Biscayne Blvd Miami (33138) *(G-8606)*

1800flowerscom 954 683-1246
5350 Nw 35th Ter Fort Lauderdale (33309) *(G-3614)*

180bytwo 202 403-7097
600 Cleveland St Clearwater (33755) *(G-1469)*

1842 Daily Grind & Mercantile 352 543-5004
598 2nd St Cedar Key (32625) *(G-1437)*

1concier, Medley *Also called Harbor Linen LLC (G-8251)*

1source Biotechnology LLC 305 668-5888
4300 Sw 73rd Ave Miami (33155) *(G-8607)*

1st Chice Hrrcane Prtction LLC 239 325-3400
25241 Bernwood Dr Ste 6 Bonita Springs (34135) *(G-778)*

1st Choice Windows and Doors, Bonita Springs *Also called 1st Chice Hrrcane Prtction LLC (G-778)*

1st Enviro-Safety Inc 239 283-1222
10200 Betsy Pkwy Saint James City (33956) *(G-14943)*

1st Vertical Blind Company 352 343-3363
207 E Burleigh Blvd Tavares (32778) *(G-17501)*

1st Vertical Blind Factory, Tavares *Also called 1st Vertical Blind Company (G-17501)*

2 Guys Company 786 970-9275
9315 Sw 77th Ave Apt 228 Miami (33156) *(G-8608)*

20-100 Delicious Seasoning LLC 954 687-5124
6438a Pembroke Rd Miramar (33023) *(G-10454)*

2020 EMBROIDERY, Longwood *Also called Briesa Inc (G-7877)*

21st Century Chemical Inc (PA) 954 689-7111
2960 Sw 23rd Ter Ste 108 Fort Lauderdale (33312) *(G-3615)*

2204 Avenue X LLC 407 619-1410
1275 Us Highway 1 Unit 2 Vero Beach (32960) *(G-17730)*

24-7 Complete Restoration, Tampa *Also called Element Solutions LLC (G-16801)*

24/7 Software Inc 954 514-8988
12411 Nw 35th St Coral Springs (33065) *(G-2122)*

24hour Printing Inc 954 247-9575
7431 Nw 57th St Lauderhill (33319) *(G-7723)*

2951 SE Dominica Holding LLC 772 220-0038
2979 Se Monroe St Stuart (34997) *(G-16107)*

2g - Cenergy, Saint Augustine *Also called 2g Cenrgy Pwr Systems Tech Inc (G-14804)*

2g Cenrgy Pwr Systems Tech Inc (HQ) 904 342-5988
205 Commercial Dr Saint Augustine (32092) *(G-14804)*

2jcp LLC 904 834-3818
101 Marketside Ave Ponte Vedra (32081) *(G-14253)*

2leaf Press Inc 646 801-4227
1200 S Pine Island Rd Plantation (33324) *(G-13816)*

3 Cool Cats LLC 646 334-6229
429 Lenox Ave Miami Beach (33139) *(G-10159)*

3 Daughters Brewing LLC (PA) 727 495-6002
222 22nd St S Saint Petersburg (33712) *(G-14948)*

3 Miracles Corporation 407 796-9292
6843 Conway Rd Ste 120 Orlando (32812) *(G-11849)*

3 Stars Kitchen Cabinets Corp 786 285-7147
529 W 28th St Hialeah (33010) *(G-5013)*

3-Dimension Graphics Inc 305 599-3277
8031 Nw 14th St Doral (33126) *(G-3084)*

300 Technologies Inc 954 234-0018
4905 Ne 12th Ave Oakland Park (33334) *(G-11231)*

305 Media Solutions, Hollywood *Also called Mas Editorial Corp (G-5621)*

33 Wraps, Boynton Beach *Also called Clear Copy Inc (G-851)*

35 Technologies Group Inc 407 402-2119
2280 N Ronald Reagan Blvd Longwood (32750) *(G-7861)*

352ink Corp 352 373-7547
327 Nw 23rd Ave Ste 1-4 Gainesville (32609) *(G-4643)*

360 Energy Solutions LLC 786 348-2156
7650 Nw 50th St Miami (33166) *(G-8609)*

360 O and P Inc 813 985-5000
5311 E Fletcher Ave Temple Terrace (33617) *(G-17534)*

365 Sun LLC 208 357-8062
225 Nippino Trl E Nokomis (34275) *(G-11041)*

386 Nanotech Inc 727 252-9580
6860 Gulfport Blvd S South Pasadena (33707) *(G-16050)*

3a Products LLC 754 263-2968
2737 N Commerce Pkwy Miramar (33025) *(G-10455)*

3b Global LLC (PA) 813 350-7872
1202 Race Track Rd Tampa (33626) *(G-16546)*

3d Machining, Riviera Beach *Also called 3d Medical Manufacturing Inc (G-14584)*

3d Medical Manufacturing Inc 561 842-7175
2001 N Congress Ave Ste F Riviera Beach (33404) *(G-14584)*

3d Nano Batteries LLC 212 220-9300
12544 Sw Gray Fox Ln Port Saint Lucie (34987) *(G-14393)*

3d Perception Inc 321 235-7999
12605 Challenger Pkwy # 1 Orlando (32826) *(G-11850)*

3d Printing Solutions 850 443-4200
243 Cross Branch Dr Ponte Vedra (32081) *(G-14254)*

3dfx Inc 407 237-6249
279 N Texas Ave Orlando (32805) *(G-11851)*

3dmt, Daytona Beach *Also called ARC Transition LLC (G-2513)*

3dmt, Daytona Beach *Also called Aerojet Rocketdyne Inc (G-2507)*

3fdm Inc 727 877-3336
10600 Endeavour Way Largo (33777) *(G-7518)*

3g Enterprises Inc 754 366-7643
1530 Via De Pepi Boynton Beach (33426) *(G-834)*

3g Grpahics Design & Printing, Boynton Beach *Also called 3g Enterprises Inc (G-834)*

3i Implant Innovations, Palm Beach Gardens *Also called Biomet 3i LLC (G-12951)*

3lmetals Inc 305 497-4038
12987 Sw 19th Ter Miami (33175) *(G-8610)*

3M Resident Monitoring Inc 813 749-5453
1838 Gunn Hwy Odessa (33556) *(G-11531)*

3miracles, Orlando *Also called 3 Miracles Corporation (G-11849)*

3n2 LLC 407 862-3622
111 Atlantic Annex Pt # 1 Maitland (32751) *(G-8048)*

3n2 Sports, Maitland *Also called 3n2 LLC (G-8048)*

3nstar Inc 786 233-7011
10813 Nw 30th St Ste 100 Doral (33172) *(G-3085)*

3tissue LLC 904 540-4335
8286 Wstn Way Cir C9 C10 Jacksonville (32256) *(G-5840)*

4 C Timber Inc 386 937-0806
130 Odom Rd Palatka (32177) *(G-12861)*

4 Power International Stones 407 286-4677
2704 Hazelhurst Ave Orlando (32804) *(G-11852)*

4303 Silverwood LLC 904 900-1702
4401 San Jose Ln Jacksonville (32207) *(G-5841)*

4elementum LLC 305 989-1106
9149 Sw 157th Ct Miami (33196) *(G-8611)*

4ever Music LLC 407 490-0977
8201 Holmstrom Way Orlando (32827) *(G-11853)*

4f Contracting, Baker *Also called 4f Mobile Welding LLC (G-290)*

A
L
P
H
A
B
E
T
I
C

4f Mobile Welding LLC ...850 537-2290
6289 Holloway Rd Baker (32531) ***(G-290)***
4front Solutions LLC ...814 464-2000
3045 Tech Pkwy Deland (32724) ***(G-2846)***
4th St Print Shack, Saint Petersburg *Also called M Victoria Enterprises Inc* ***(G-15116)***
5 Cents T-Shirt Design, Doral *Also called Baru Agency Incorporated* ***(G-3129)***
5 Star Blinds and Shades LLC ...850 463-4155
4306 Seventh Ave Milton (32571) ***(G-10415)***
5 Star Builders Inc ...561 795-1282
3180 Frlane Frms Rd Ste 2 Wellington (33414) ***(G-17841)***
5 Star Coatings LLc ...850 628-3743
126 Escanaba Ave Panama City Beach (32413) ***(G-13324)***
50 50 Parmley Envmtl Svcs LLC ...407 593-1165
913 Robinson Ave Saint Cloud (34769) ***(G-14918)***
50 Hwy 17 S Inc ...904 225-1077
850822 Us Highway 17 Yulee (32097) ***(G-18584)***
5301 Realty LLC ...305 633-9779
950 Se 8th St Hialeah (33010) ***(G-5014)***
55 Group LLC (PA) ...954 427-8405
3220 Sw 15th St Deerfield Beach (33442) ***(G-2648)***
55 Industries LLC ...954 955-0212
3220 Sw 15th St Deerfield Beach (33442) ***(G-2649)***
55 Manufacturing Inc ...954 332-2921
3220 Sw 15th St Deerfield Beach (33442) ***(G-2650)***
5571 Halifax Inc ...239 454-4999
5571 Halifax Ave Fort Myers (33912) ***(G-4152)***
5d Bio Gold LLC ...561 756-8291
1725 Avenida Del Sol Boca Raton (33432) ***(G-382)***
5dt Inc ...407 734-5377
12249 Science Dr Ste 135 Orlando (32826) ***(G-11854)***
5hp Investments LLC ...561 655-5355
2822 S Dixie Hwy West Palm Beach (33405) ***(G-17905)***
5nine Software Inc ...561 898-1100
1555 Palm Bch Lkes Blvd S West Palm Beach (33401) ***(G-17906)***
5th Element Inc ...321 331-7028
3848 Shoreview Dr Kissimmee (34744) ***(G-6890)***
5thelement Indian Cuisine LLC ...386 302-0202
101 Palm Harbor Pkwy Palm Coast (32137) ***(G-13066)***
6 Ports LLC ...561 743-8696
250 S Central Blvd # 207 Jupiter (33458) ***(G-6673)***
7 Holdings Group LLC ...754 200-1365
10450 Nw 29th Ter Doral (33172) ***(G-3086)***
7 Plastics Inc ...407 321-5441
1680 Timocuan Way Longwood (32750) ***(G-7862)***
7 Up Snapple Southeast ...407 839-1706
1181 Tradeport Dr Orlando (32824) ***(G-11855)***
808 Island Treats, Spring Hill *Also called Romeo Ohana LLC* ***(G-16077)***
850 Screen Printing LLC ...850 549-7861
698 E Heinberg St Ste 101 Pensacola (32502) ***(G-13427)***
88 South Atlantic LLC ...386 253-0105
835 N Beach St Daytona Beach (32114) ***(G-2504)***
90-Minute Books LLC ...863 318-0464
302 Martinique Dr Winter Haven (33884) ***(G-18410)***
904 Sweet Treatz Street LLC ...800 889-3298
7643 Gate Pkwy Ste 104 Jacksonville (32256) ***(G-5842)***
905 East Hillsboro LLC ...954 480-2600
905 E Hillsboro Blvd Deerfield Beach (33441) ***(G-2651)***
911 Equipment Inc (PA) ...954 217-1745
2645 Executive Park Dr Weston (33331) ***(G-18217)***
925 Nuevos Cubanos Inc ...954 806-8375
925 N Andrews Ave Fort Lauderdale (33311) ***(G-3616)***
954 Savings Magazine ...954 900-4649
405 Sailboat Cir Weston (33326) ***(G-18218)***
9t Technology LLC ...904 703-9214
3125 Double Oaks Dr Jacksonville (32226) ***(G-5843)***
A & A Central Florida ...407 648-5666
540 N State Road 434 # 53 Altamonte Springs (32714) ***(G-26)***
A & A Electric Mtrs & Pump Svc ...407 843-5005
1320 W Central Blvd Orlando (32805) ***(G-11856)***
A & A Orthopedics Mfg ...305 256-8119
12250 Sw 129th Ct Ste 101 Miami (33186) ***(G-8612)***
A & A Publishing Corp ...561 982-8960
950 Peninsula Corporate C Boca Raton (33487) ***(G-383)***
A & A Sheetmetal Contr Corp ...305 592-2217
3067 Nw 107th Ave Doral (33172) ***(G-3087)***
A & B of Tarpon Corporation ...727 940-5333
40200 Us Highway 19 N Tarpon Springs (34689) ***(G-17456)***
A & C Concrete Products Inc ...305 232-1631
9741 Sw 168th Ter Miami (33157) ***(G-8613)***
A & E Machine Inc ...321 636-3110
1445 Lake Dr Cocoa (32922) ***(G-1896)***
A & F Paving LLC ...352 359-2282
4802 Sw 44th Cir Ocala (34474) ***(G-11313)***
A & J Aerospace Corp ...786 564-9986
8356 Nw 66th St Miami (33166) ***(G-8614)***
A & J Boatworks, Stuart *Also called Arthur Cox* ***(G-16118)***
A & J Commercial Seating Inc ...352 288-2022
10485 Se 158th Pl Summerfield (34491) ***(G-16255)***
A & J Mugs, Pensacola *Also called Martin Leonard Corporation* ***(G-13543)***
A & J Ready Mix Inc ...863 228-7154
Even Rnge 300 398 W El Clewiston (33440) ***(G-1885)***
A & K Machine & Fab Shop Inc ...904 388-7772
3451 W Beaver St Jacksonville (32254) ***(G-5844)***
A & L Septic Tank Products Inc ...407 273-2149
9304 E Colonial Dr Orlando (32817) ***(G-11857)***
A & N Corporation ...352 528-4100
707 Sw 19th Ave Williston (32696) ***(G-18327)***
A & R Kitchen Cabinet Corp ...305 338-3326
19100 Sw 106th Ave Unit 5 Cutler Bay (33157) ***(G-2281)***
A & R Material Handling Inc ...904 879-6957
540439 Us Highway 1 Callahan (32011) ***(G-1250)***
A & S Entertainment LLC ...305 627-3456
250 Ne 183rd St Miami (33179) ***(G-8615)***
A & S Equipment Co ...305 436-8207
1900 Nw 95th Ave Doral (33172) ***(G-3088)***
A & V Refrigeration Corp ...305 883-0733
997 Se 12th St Hialeah (33010) ***(G-5015)***
A 1 A Signs & Service Inc ...305 757-6950
8965 Ne 10th Ave Miami (33138) ***(G-8616)***
A 1 Fabrications Inc ...352 410-0752
12440 Charlton Dr Weeki Wachee (34614) ***(G-17834)***
A 1a Displays, Miami *Also called A 1 A Signs & Service Inc* ***(G-8616)***
A 2 Z of Lake City Inc ...386 755-0235
628 Se Allison Ct Lake City (32025) ***(G-7007)***
A A A Able Air Conditioning, Fort Lauderdale *Also called AAA Able Appliance Service Inc* ***(G-3617)***
A A A Architectural Materials, Palmetto *Also called AAA Architectural Elements* ***(G-13151)***
A A A Cabinets ...850 438-8337
6435 Ard Rd Pensacola (32526) ***(G-13428)***
A A A Signs Inc ...813 949-8397
1911 Passero Ave Lutz (33559) ***(G-7978)***
A A Sheet Metal Corp ...305 592-2217
3067 Nw 107th Ave Doral (33172) ***(G-3089)***
A Albrtini Cstm Win Treatments ...941 925-2556
4023 Sawyer Rd Ofc Sarasota (34233) ***(G-15581)***
A Albrtini Cstm Wndows Trtmnts, Sarasota *Also called A Albrtini Cstm Win Treatments* ***(G-15581)***
A and A Concrete Block Inc ...305 986-5128
4410 Sw 115th Ave Miami (33165) ***(G-8617)***
A and A Orthopedics Inc ...305 256-8119
12250 Sw 129th Ct Ste 101 Miami (33186) ***(G-8618)***
A and H Logging Inc ...352 528-3868
333 Se 4th Ave Williston (32696) ***(G-18328)***
A and J Sheet Metal Inc ...561 746-4048
1567 Cypress Dr Jupiter (33469) ***(G-6674)***
A B & B Manufacturing Inc ...904 378-3350
2141 Lane Ave N Jacksonville (32254) ***(G-5845)***
A B B Automation Technolgy Div, Coral Springs *Also called ABB Enterprise Software Inc* ***(G-2124)***
A B B Power Technolgies Div, Miami *Also called ABB Inc* ***(G-8634)***
A B G, Melbourne *Also called Aerobase Group Inc* ***(G-8356)***
A B Survey Supply Entps Inc ...772 464-9500
2603 Industrial Avenue 2 Fort Pierce (34946) ***(G-4457)***
A Bar Code Business Inc ...352 750-0077
505 Sunbelt Rd Ste 8 The Villages (32159) ***(G-17552)***
A Beka Book Inc (PA) ...850 478-8933
240 Waveland St Ste B Pensacola (32503) ***(G-13429)***
A Better Choice Marine LLC ...941 264-5019
8050 N Tamiami Trl Sarasota (34243) ***(G-15435)***
A Better Kitchen Cabinets Inc ...786 234-1897
28501 Sw 152nd Ave Lot 21 Homestead (33033) ***(G-5695)***
A C I, Bradenton *Also called Advance Controls Inc* ***(G-933)***
A C Master Motors & Controls, Miami *Also called AC Industrial Service Inc* ***(G-8639)***
A C Repairs Inc ...813 909-0809
1519 Camphor Cove Dr Lutz (33549) ***(G-7979)***
A Cappela Publishing Inc (PA) ...941 351-2050
913 Tennessee Ln Sarasota (34234) ***(G-15582)***
A Certified Screen Service ...386 673-0054
560 S Yonge St Ormond Beach (32174) ***(G-12738)***
A Cheaper Shot LLC ...727 221-3237
4604 49th St N Saint Petersburg (33709) ***(G-14949)***
A Clean Finish Inc ...407 516-1311
8848 Quail Roost Ct Jacksonville (32220) ***(G-5846)***
A Complete Sign Service Inc ...407 328-7714
2530 S Snford Ave Ste 106 Sanford (32773) ***(G-15256)***
A Crown Molding Specialist ...954 665-5640
9714 Nw 24th Ct Pembroke Pines (33024) ***(G-13367)***
A Custom Fabrication, Lake Worth *Also called J A Custom Fabricators Inc* ***(G-7208)***
A D Coaches Corner Inc ...786 242-2229
13365 Sw 135th Ave # 102 Miami (33186) ***(G-8619)***
A E T, Clearwater *Also called Advanced Engine Tech LLC* ***(G-1475)***
A F T, Miami *Also called Azex Flow Technologies Inc* ***(G-8785)***
A Fine Print of Miami LLC ...305 441-5263
2420 Sw 27th Ave Miami (33145) ***(G-8620)***
A G A Electronics Corp ...305 592-1860
7209 Nw 41st St Miami (33166) ***(G-8621)***

A Gs Mica and Custom Wdwrk LLC..................................561 351-5429
5307 East Ave West Palm Beach (33407) *(G-17907)*

A H Woodcrafter..................................305 885-2136
7313 Nw 56th St Miami (33166) *(G-8622)*

A J Giammanco & Associates..................................386 328-1254
115 Rachel Rd Palatka (32177) *(G-12862)*

A J Trophies & Awards Inc (PA)..................................850 878-7187
1387 E Lafayette St Tallahassee (32301) *(G-16404)*

A JS Pro Percussion Center..................................813 361-4939
4340 W Hillsborough Ave # 208 Tampa (33614) *(G-16547)*

A L Baxley & Sons Inc..................................352 629-5137
1542 E Highway 329 Citra (32113) *(G-1466)*

A L Custom Wood Corp..................................305 557-2434
950 W 22nd St Hialeah (33010) *(G-5016)*

A Living Testimony LLC..................................352 406-0249
2119 Bates Ave Eustis (32726) *(G-3551)*

A M Coplan Associates..................................904 737-6996
4251 University Blvd S # 201 Jacksonville (32216) *(G-5847)*

A M P, Orlando *Also called Agri Machinery & Parts Inc (G-11878)*

A M Rayonier Products Inc..................................904 261-3611
1 Rayonier Way Yulee (32097) *(G-18585)*

A M Tool & Engineering Company..................................727 375-5002
2343 Destiny Way Odessa (33556) *(G-11532)*

A Materials Group Inc..................................352 463-1254
8191 Nw 160th St Fanning Springs (32693) *(G-3571)*

A Materials Group Inc (PA)..................................386 758-3164
871 Nw Guerdon St Lake City (32055) *(G-7008)*

A Means To A Vend Inc..................................954 533-8330
4700 N Dixie Hwy Oakland Park (33334) *(G-11232)*

A Mil Air..................................813 417-9114
920 Essex Rd Brandon (33510) *(G-1081)*

A Mining Group LLC..................................386 752-7585
871 Nw Guerdon St Lake City (32055) *(G-7009)*

A Mobile Tech Llc..................................561 631-4563
9363 Whippoorwill Trl Jupiter (33478) *(G-6675)*

A Morris Industries LLC..................................239 308-2199
3824 23rd St W Lehigh Acres (33971) *(G-7803)*

A P E, Key Largo *Also called Automated Production Eqp Ape (G-6842)*

A Pallet Co Inc..................................561 798-1564
9750 Galleon Dr West Palm Beach (33411) *(G-17908)*

A Perfect View Window Tint..................................954 937-0400
1031 Cornwall B Boca Raton (33434) *(G-384)*

A Plus Construction Svcs Inc..................................904 612-0597
165 Oakhill St Jacksonville (32227) *(G-5848)*

A Plus Lamination & Finshg Inc..................................305 636-9888
5559 Nw 36th Ave Miami (33142) *(G-8623)*

A Plus Lumber Corp..................................786 899-0535
356 Palmetto Dr A Miami Springs (33166) *(G-10385)*

A Plus Marine Supply Inc (PA)..................................850 934-3890
212 Mcclure Dr Gulf Breeze (32561) *(G-4874)*

A Quallity Pallet Company..................................239 245-0900
5896 Enterprise Pkwy Fort Myers (33905) *(G-4153)*

A R Components Corp..................................786 703-8456
8544 Nw 66th St Miami (33166) *(G-8624)*

A S I, Fort Pierce *Also called Automated Services Inc (G-4468)*

A Sanborn Corporation..................................727 397-3073
15019 Madeira Way Madeira Beach (33708) *(G-8039)*

A Sign..................................321 264-0077
3670 S Hopkins Ave Titusville (32780) *(G-17565)*

A Sotolongo Polishing Marble C..................................305 271-7957
5435 Sw 99th Ct Miami (33165) *(G-8625)*

A Step Above Stairs Rails LLC..................................561 714-0646
12254 Colony Preserve Dr Boynton Beach (33436) *(G-835)*

A Superior Garage Door Company..................................305 556-6624
12195 Nw 98th Ave Hialeah (33018) *(G-5017)*

A T B Systems, Pensacola *Also called Water Technology Pensacola Inc (G-13623)*

A T C, Pompano Beach *Also called Adhesives Technology Corp (G-13910)*

A T M, Clearwater *Also called American Technical Molding Inc (G-1492)*

A T S, Fort Myers *Also called American Traction Systems Inc (G-4172)*

A Tek Steel Industries Inc..................................561 745-2858
3 Turtle Creek Dr Jupiter (33469) *(G-6676)*

A To Z Concrete Products Inc..................................727 321-6000
4451 8th Ave S Saint Petersburg (33711) *(G-14950)*

A W C, Plant City *Also called American Water Chemicals Inc (G-13738)*

A W R Cabinets Inc..................................407 323-1415
4155 Saint Johns Pkwy # 1800 Sanford (32771) *(G-15257)*

A W S C O, Santa Rosa Beach *Also called American Woodwork Specialty Co (G-15421)*

A Ward Design, Winter Haven *Also called KR Ward Inc (G-18448)*

A World of Wipes, Boca Raton *Also called Unico International Trdg Corp (G-733)*

A Wsco..................................937 263-1053
1411 Driftwood Point Rd Santa Rosa Beach (32459) *(G-15420)*

A Z Printing Delray..................................561 330-4154
645 E Atlantic Ave Delray Beach (33483) *(G-2922)*

A&C Microscopes LLC..................................786 514-3967
7925 Nw 12th St Ste 112 Doral (33126) *(G-3090)*

A&C Signs Solutions Corp..................................786 953-5600
1745 W 37th St Hialeah (33012) *(G-5018)*

A&D Woodwork Florida LLC..................................561 465-2863
7595 San Mateo Dr E Boca Raton (33433) *(G-385)*

A&H Logging Inc..................................352 528-3868
2752 Se 174th Ct Morriston (32668) *(G-10593)*

A&J Manufacturing Inc..................................912 638-4724
5001 W Cypress St Tampa (33607) *(G-16548)*

A&L Hall Investments Inc..................................904 781-5080
1384 Cortez Rd Bryceville (32009) *(G-1225)*

A&M Cleaning Solutions LLC..................................786 559-7093
4400 N Terrace Dr West Palm Beach (33407) *(G-17909)*

A&W Brick Pavers of North Fla..................................904 672-7112
7901 Baymeadows Cir E # 502 Jacksonville (32256) *(G-5849)*

A' Nue Miami, Miami *Also called ANue Ligne Inc (G-8733)*

A-1 Block Corporation..................................407 422-3768
1617 S Division Ave Orlando (32805) *(G-11858)*

A-1 City Wide Sewer Svc Inc..................................352 236-4456
6342 E Highway 326 Silver Springs (34488) *(G-16004)*

A-1 Cleaning Concepts Inc..................................772 288-7214
173 Se Norfolk Blvd Stuart (34997) *(G-16108)*

A-1 Custom Mica Inc..................................954 893-0063
5805 Plunkett St Hollywood (33023) *(G-5519)*

A-1 Door Systems Inc..................................904 327-7206
11555 Central Pkwy # 804 Jacksonville (32224) *(G-5850)*

A-1 Industries Florida Inc (PA)..................................270 316-9409
11555 Heron Bay Blvd # 2 Coral Springs (33076) *(G-2123)*

A-1 Roof Trusses Ltd Company..................................772 409-1010
4451 Saint Lucie Blvd Fort Pierce (34946) *(G-4458)*

A-1 Sportswear Inc..................................305 773-7028
18820 Nw 84th Ave Hialeah (33015) *(G-5019)*

A-Fabco Inc..................................813 677-8790
11550 S Us Highway 41 Gibsonton (33534) *(G-4792)*

A-Mari-Mix LLC..................................305 603-9134
9700 Sw 24th St Miami (33165) *(G-8626)*

A-N-L Home Solutions LLC..................................954 648-2623
1000 Ne 196th St Miami (33179) *(G-8627)*

A-Plus Prtg & Graphic Ctr Inc..................................954 327-7315
6561 Nw 18th Ct Plantation (33313) *(G-13817)*

A.M. Metal Finishing, Orlando *Also called Elite Metal Finishing East LLC (G-12122)*

A/C Cages..................................407 446-9259
890 Merrimac St Deltona (32725) *(G-3039)*

A1 Balers and Compators LLC..................................561 792-3399
13476 Orange Blvd West Palm Beach (33412) *(G-17910)*

A1 Building Components, Fort Pierce *Also called A-1 Roof Trusses Ltd Company (G-4458)*

A1 Elevators LLC..................................954 773-4443
8185 S Coral Cir North Lauderdale (33068) *(G-11074)*

A1 Pallets LLC..................................813 598-9165
11802 N Us Highway 301 Thonotosassa (33592) *(G-17560)*

A1a Electric Signs & Neon Inc..................................305 757-6950
1640 W 32nd Pl Hialeah (33012) *(G-5020)*

A1a Raw LLC..................................321 777-2526
2372 N Hwy A1a Indialantic (32903) *(G-5800)*

A1a Signs & Svc., Hialeah *Also called A1a Electric Signs & Neon Inc (G-5020)*

A1a Sportbike LLC..................................321 806-3995
1500 Shepard Dr Titusville (32780) *(G-17566)*

A1cm Shades and Blind Inc..................................305 726-3139
5521 Nw 7th Ave Miami (33127) *(G-8628)*

A2f LLC..................................305 984-9205
2010 Nw Miami Ct Unit A Miami (33127) *(G-8629)*

A2z Uniforms Inc..................................941 254-3194
999 Cattlemen Rd Unit G Sarasota (34232) *(G-15583)*

AA Casey Company..................................813 234-8831
5124 N Nebraska Ave Tampa (33603) *(G-16549)*

AA Fiberglass Inc..................................904 355-5511
9378 Arlington Expy 358 Jacksonville (32225) *(G-5851)*

AA Fiberglass Inc..................................904 355-5511
521 Copeland St Jacksonville (32204) *(G-5852)*

AA Oldco Inc (PA)..................................215 659-5300
1625 S Congress Ave # 400 Delray Beach (33445) *(G-2923)*

AA Performance..................................772 672-1164
955 13th Ln Vero Beach (32960) *(G-17731)*

AAA Able Appliance Service Inc..................................954 791-5222
430 N Andrews Ave Fort Lauderdale (33301) *(G-3617)*

AAA Architectural Elements..................................941 722-1910
1751 12th St E Palmetto (34221) *(G-13151)*

AAA Cast Stone Inc..................................941 721-8092
1470 12th St E Palmetto (34221) *(G-13152)*

AAA Custom Cabinets, Pensacola *Also called A A A Cabinets (G-13428)*

AAA Event Services LLC..................................386 454-0929
25370 Nw 8th Ln Newberry (32669) *(G-11015)*

AAA Index Tabs LLC..................................954 457-7777
201 Ansin Blvd Hallandale Beach (33009) *(G-4932)*

AAA Monterey Discount Vacuum..................................772 288-5233
514 Se Monterey Rd Stuart (34994) *(G-16109)*

AAA Porta Serve, Newberry *Also called AAA Event Services LLC (G-11015)*

AAA Security Depot Corp..................................305 652-8567
12815 Nw 45th Ave Ste 2 Opa Locka (33054) *(G-11710)*

AAA Steel Fabricators Inc..................................954 570-7211
1669 Sw 45th Way Deerfield Beach (33442) *(G-2652)*

Aaa-Affordable Pallets & Reels..................................813 740-8009
2811 N 76th St Tampa (33619) *(G-16550)*

Aabc Inc..................................727 434-4444
12722 62nd St Ste 206 Largo (33773) *(G-7519)*

Aacecorp Inc 904 353-7878
245 Riverside Ave Ste 200 Jacksonville (32202) *(G-5853)*

Aadi Inc 407 957-4557
190 E 12th St Saint Cloud (34769) *(G-14919)*

Aafw-Kimco, Tampa *Also called Dwm-2021 Inc* *(G-16789)*

Aamg, Hialeah *Also called American Archtctral Mtls GL LL* *(G-5044)*

Aap Industrial Inc 941 377-4373
1634 Barber Rd Sarasota (34240) *(G-15584)*

Aap Pump and Motor Works, Sarasota *Also called Aap Industrial Inc* *(G-15584)*

AAR Airlift Group, Palm Bay *Also called Aviation Worldwide Svcs LLC* *(G-12888)*

AAR Airlift Group Inc (HQ) 321 837-2345
2301 Commerce Park Dr Ne # 11 Palm Bay (32905) *(G-12885)*

AAR Composites, Clearwater *Also called AAR Manufacturing Inc* *(G-1470)*

AAR Corp 904 629-2810
Naval A Stn Of Jcksnvlle Jacksonville (32212) *(G-5854)*

AAR Defense Systems Logistics, Jacksonville *Also called AAR Government Services Inc (G-5855)*

AAR Government Services Inc 904 693-7260
8001 Westside Indus Dr Jacksonville (32219) *(G-5855)*

AAR Government Services Inc 321 361-3461
Aar Way Ste 101 Rockledge (32955) *(G-14687)*

AAR Hngar Jcksnvlle Nval A Stn, Jacksonville *Also called AAR Corp* *(G-5854)*

AAR Landing Gear LLC 305 883-1511
9371 Nw 100th St Medley (33178) *(G-8191)*

AAR Landing Gear Services, Medley *Also called AAR Landing Gear LLC* *(G-8191)*

AAR Manufacturing Inc 727 539-8585
14201 Myerlake Cir Clearwater (33760) *(G-1470)*

AAR Wass, Rockledge *Also called AAR Government Services Inc* *(G-14687)*

Aara Industries 954 342-9526
13165 Sw 24th St Miramar (33027) *(G-10456)*

Aardvark Sgns Prperty Svcs LLC 407 348-7446
304 W Oak St Kissimmee (34741) *(G-6891)*

Aarg Stairs & Raillings Corp 786 545-6465
2384 W 80th St Ste 7 Hialeah (33016) *(G-5021)*

Aaron Best Pita, Opa Locka *Also called Universal Bakery LLC* *(G-11797)*

Aaron Medical Industries Inc 727 384-2323
7100 30th Ave N Saint Petersburg (33710) *(G-14951)*

Aaron Rice 813 752-3820
5203 Downing St Dover (33527) *(G-3425)*

Aaron Tool Inc 941 758-9369
2819 62nd Ave E Bradenton (34203) *(G-930)*

Aaron's Welding & Repair, Callahan *Also called Aarons Equipment Repair Inc* *(G-1251)*

Aarons Equipment Repair Inc 904 879-3249
45417 Zidell Rd Callahan (32011) *(G-1251)*

Aarons Pallets 813 627-3225
5006 S 50th St Tampa (33619) *(G-16551)*

Aas, Miami Lakes *Also called American Automtn Systems Inc* *(G-10281)*

Aat Omega LLC 352 473-6673
6670 Spring Lake Rd Keystone Heights (32656) *(G-6883)*

Aaw Products Inc 305 330-6863
825 Brckhllday Dr Ste 246 Miami (33130) *(G-8630)*

Aaxon Laundry Systems LLC 954 772-7100
6100 Powerline Rd Fort Lauderdale (33309) *(G-3618)*

AB Ampere Industrial Panels 904 379-4168
96266 Dowling Dr Yulee (32097) *(G-18586)*

AB Electric Motors & Pumps 954 322-6900
6013 Johnson St Hollywood (33024) *(G-5520)*

AB Enzymes Inc 954 278-3975
150 S Pine Island Rd # 270 Plantation (33324) *(G-13818)*

AB Fire Sprinklers LLC 954 973-8054
2759 Nw 19th St Pompano Beach (33069) *(G-13905)*

AB Transportation, Medley *Also called Arte Bronce Monuments Inc* *(G-8200)*

AB Used Pallets Inc 305 594-2776
6350 Nw 72nd Ave Miami (33166) *(G-8631)*

AB Vista Inc (HQ) 954 278-3965
150 S Pine Island Rd Plantation (33324) *(G-13819)*

AB Wood Work Inc 786 701-3611
13365 Sw 135th Ave Ste 10 Miami (33186) *(G-8632)*

Aba Engineering & Mfg Inc 386 672-9665
5 Aviator Way Ormond Beach (32174) *(G-12739)*

Aba-Con Inc 321 567-4967
11 S Brown Ave Titusville (32796) *(G-17567)*

Abakan Inc (PA) 786 206-5368
2665 S Byshr Dr Ste 450 Miami (33133) *(G-8633)*

Abalux Inc 305 698-9192
8000 W 26th Ave Hialeah (33016) *(G-5022)*

Abam Export, Doral *Also called Jers Group* *(G-3268)*

Abawi Fit LLC 813 215-1833
1327 E 7th Ave Ste 204 Tampa (33605) *(G-16552)*

Abaxial Elevator, Fort Myers *Also called Jonathan Mariotti Entps LLC* *(G-4301)*

ABB Enterprise Software Inc 954 752-6700
4300 Coral Ridge Dr Coral Springs (33065) *(G-2124)*

ABB Inc 407 732-2000
680 Century Pt Lake Mary (32746) *(G-7056)*

ABB Inc 305 471-0844
8785 Sw 165th Ave Ste 302 Miami (33193) *(G-8634)*

ABB Inc 954 450-9544
10004 Premier Pkwy Miramar (33025) *(G-10457)*

ABB Installation Products Inc 386 677-9110
12 Southland Rd Ormond Beach (32174) *(G-12740)*

ABB Partners LLC 917 843-4430
340 Royal Poinciana Way # 3 Palm Beach (33480) *(G-12928)*

ABB Power Distribution, Lake Mary *Also called ABB Inc* *(G-7056)*

Abbco, Cape Canaveral *Also called American Boom and Barrier Inc* *(G-1276)*

Abbey Rogers 813 645-1400
10150 Highland Manor Dr Tampa (33610) *(G-16553)*

Abbot Hill LLC 239 260-5246
5880 Shirley St Ste 201 Naples (34109) *(G-10648)*

Abbott Citrus Ladders Inc 863 773-6322
4060 State Road 62 Bowling Green (33834) *(G-828)*

Abbott Communications Group, Maitland *Also called Abbott Printing Co* *(G-8049)*

Abbott Labs US Sbsdries Alere (HQ) 877 441-7440
30 S Keller Rd Ste 100 Orlando (32810) *(G-11859)*

Abbott Printing Co 407 831-2999
110 Atlantic Dr Ste 110 # 110 Maitland (32751) *(G-8049)*

Abbott Rapid Diagnostics, Orlando *Also called Abbott Rapid Dx North Amer LLC* *(G-11861)*

Abbott Rapid Diagnostics 877 441-7440
30 S Keller Rd Ste 100 Orlando (32810) *(G-11860)*

Abbott Rapid Dx North Amer LLC, Orlando *Also called Abbott Labs US Sbsdries Alere* *(G-11859)*

Abbott Rapid Dx North Amer LLC 877 441-7440
30 S Keller Rd Ste 100 Orlando (32810) *(G-11861)*

Abby Press Inc 407 847-5565
929 W Oak St Kissimmee (34741) *(G-6892)*

ABc Awning & Canvas Co Inc 321 253-1960
244 Avenue L Delray Beach (33483) *(G-2924)*

ABC Book Publishers Inc 904 230-0737
4940 Blackhawk Dr Jacksonville (32259) *(G-6624)*

ABC Components Inc 954 249-6286
8963 Stirling Rd Ste 5 Cooper City (33328) *(G-2015)*

ABC Enterprises 407 656-6503
16274 Lake Johns Cir Oakland (34787) *(G-11226)*

ABC Fence Systems Inc (PA) 850 638-8876
963 Industrial Dr Chipley (32428) *(G-1452)*

ABC Hammers 708 343-9900
7216 21st St E Sarasota (34243) *(G-15436)*

ABC Imaging of Washington 954 759-2037
714 N Federal Hwy Fort Lauderdale (33304) *(G-3619)*

ABC Intercargo LLC 954 908-5200
2700 Glades Cir Ste 124 Weston (33327) *(G-18219)*

ABC Printing Company, Vero Beach *Also called Linden-Beals Corp* *(G-17773)*

ABC Recyclers Collier Cnty Inc 239 643-2302
4930 21st Pl Sw Naples (34116) *(G-10649)*

ABC Screen Masters Inc 239 772-7336
1110 Ne Pine Island Rd # 23 Cape Coral (33909) *(G-1295)*

ABC Shutters Protection Corp 785 547-9527
7420 Sw 38th St Miami (33155) *(G-8635)*

Abco Graphics & Printing, Odessa *Also called Kmg Marketing LLC* *(G-11563)*

Abco Industries LLC 813 605-5900
5604 W Linebaugh Ave Tampa (33624) *(G-16554)*

Abco Products Inc 888 694-2226
6800 Nw 36th Ave Miami (33147) *(G-8636)*

Abdiversified LLC 954 791-6050
6825 W Sunrise Blvd Plantation (33313) *(G-13820)*

Abe Paints, Tampa *Also called Gulf Coast Paint & Supplies* *(G-16896)*

Abeka Print Shop Inc 850 478-8496
118 Saint John St Pensacola (32503) *(G-13430)*

Abele Sheetmetal Works Inc 561 471-1134
1964 W 9th St Ste 3 Riviera Beach (33404) *(G-14585)*

Abhai LLC 215 579-1842
194 Inlet Dr Saint Augustine (32080) *(G-14805)*

Able Railing & Welding LLC 850 243-5444
170 Park Dr Fort Walton Beach (32548) *(G-4558)*

About Face Cabinetry & Refacin 813 777-4088
110 Crenshaw Lake Rd Lutz (33548) *(G-7980)*

Above LLC 850 469-9028
140 Industrial Blvd Pensacola (32505) *(G-13431)*

Above Ground Level Aerospace 305 713-2629
13420 Sw 131st St Miami (33186) *(G-8637)*

Above Property LLC 239 263-7406
3555 Kraft Rd Unit 400 Naples (34105) *(G-10650)*

Abraaham Rosa Seasonings Inc 386 453-4827
813a Flight Line Blvd Deland (32724) *(G-2847)*

Abracol North America Corp 305 431-5596
5220 Nw 72nd Ave Ste 22 Miami (33166) *(G-8638)*

Abrasive Dynamics Inc 860 291-0664
1531 Se 24th Ter Pompano Beach (33062) *(G-13906)*

ABS Structural Corp 321 768-2067
700 E Melbourne Ave Melbourne (32901) *(G-8353)*

Absen Inc (HQ) 407 203-8870
7120 Lake Ellenor Dr Orlando (32809) *(G-11862)*

Absolute Aluminum Inc 941 497-7777
1220 Ogden Rd Venice (34285) *(G-17671)*

Absolute Aluminum & Cnstr, Venice *Also called Absolute Aluminum Inc* *(G-17671)*

Absolute Automation & Security 321 505-9989
3815 N Highway 1 Ste 101 Cocoa (32926) *(G-1897)*

Absolute Graphics Inc 954 792-3488
3721 Sw 47th Ave Ste 302 Davie (33314) ***(G-2374)***
Absolute Home Svcs Group Inc 727 275-0020
7830 38th Ave N Ste 9 Saint Petersburg (33710) ***(G-14952)***
Absolute Plastic Solutions Inc 239 313-7779
2178 Andrea Ln Fort Myers (33912) ***(G-4154)***
Absolute Powder Coating Inc 954 917-2715
1254 Nw 21st St Pompano Beach (33069) ***(G-13907)***
Absolute Technologies Inc 954 868-9045
6320 Nw 61st Ave Parkland (33067) ***(G-13342)***
Absolute Window and Door Inc 941 485-7774
177 Center Rd Venice (34285) ***(G-17672)***
Absolute Wood Creations LLC 954 251-2202
200 S Dixie Hwy Hallandale Beach (33009) ***(G-4933)***
Absolutely Amazing Ebooks, Key West *Also called Whiz Bang LLC* ***(G-6882)***
ABT Trusses Inc 352 221-4867
1310 Sw 32nd Pl Bell (32619) ***(G-334)***
Abyde, Clearwater *Also called Note Bin Inc* ***(G-1720)***
Abz Marketing Solutions Corp 305 340-1887
9716 Nw 29th St Doral (33172) ***(G-3091)***
AC Dob Led, Doral *Also called Wbn LLC* ***(G-3418)***
AC Graphics Inc 305 691-3778
1056 E 24th St Hialeah (33013) ***(G-5023)***
AC Industrial Service Inc 305 887-5541
14291 Sw 120th St Miami (33186) ***(G-8639)***
AC Pharma Corp 954 773-9735
3241 Holiday Springs Blvd Margate (33063) ***(G-8115)***
AC Plastics LLC 305 826-6333
1627 W 31st Pl Hialeah (33012) ***(G-5024)***
AC Signs LLC 407 857-5565
11100 Astronaut Blvd Orlando (32837) ***(G-11863)***
Acacia Inc 813 253-2789
904 N Rome Ave Tampa (33606) ***(G-16555)***
Academic Publication Svcs Inc 941 925-4474
3131 Clark Rd Ste 102 Sarasota (34231) ***(G-15585)***
Academy Publishing Inc 407 736-0100
210 S Semoran Blvd Orlando (32807) ***(G-11864)***
Acai Investments Llc 305 821-8872
7803 W 25th Ct Hialeah (33016) ***(G-5025)***
Acai To Go, Key Biscayne *Also called Organic Amazon Corp* ***(G-6838)***
Acasi Machinery Inc 305 805-8533
7085 Nw 46th St Miami (33166) ***(G-8640)***
ACC Fuels Operation LLC 305 246-8214
1498 N Homestead Blvd Homestead (33030) ***(G-5696)***
ACC Holdco Inc 863 578-1206
4800 State Road 60 E Mulberry (33860) ***(G-10618)***
Accar Ltd Inc 305 375-0620
56 Ne 1st St Miami (33132) ***(G-8641)***
Accelus, Palm Beach Gardens *Also called Integrity Implants Inc* ***(G-12978)***
Accendo Tobacco LLC 305 407-2222
7575 Nw 70th St Miami (33166) ***(G-8642)***
Accent Casting, Punta Gorda *Also called Accent Jewelry Inc* ***(G-14490)***
Accent Closets Inc 954 561-8800
3700 Ne 3rd Ave Deerfield Beach (33064) ***(G-2653)***
Accent Jewelry Inc 941 391-6687
2373 Talbrook Ter Punta Gorda (33983) ***(G-14490)***
Accent Neon & Sign Company (PA) 727 784-8414
1179 Ridgecrest Ct Palm Harbor (34683) ***(G-13095)***
Accent Signs, Niceville *Also called Pope Enterprises Inc* ***(G-11035)***
Accent Woodworking Inc 727 522-2700
2233 34th Way Largo (33771) ***(G-7520)***
Accentia Biopharmaceuticals (PA) 813 864-2554
324 S Hyde Park Ave # 350 Tampa (33606) ***(G-16556)***
Access Tools, Miami *Also called Merit International Entps Inc* ***(G-9535)***
Access Wrless Data Sltions LLC 813 751-2039
21756 State Road 54 # 101 Lutz (33549) ***(G-7981)***
Access-Able Technologies Inc 407 834-2999
360 Old Sanford Oviedo Rd Winter Springs (32708) ***(G-18557)***
Accommodating Services Inc 863 528-3231
19456 State Road 60 E Lake Wales (33898) ***(G-7151)***
Accon Marine Inc 727 572-9202
13665 Automobile Blvd Clearwater (33762) ***(G-1471)***
Accord Industries LLC (HQ) 407 671-6989
4001 Forsyth Rd Winter Park (32792) ***(G-18480)***
Accordance Bible Software, Altamonte Springs *Also called Oaktree Software Inc* ***(G-60)***
Accounting & Computer Systems 407 353-1570
810 Alameda St Orlando (32804) ***(G-11865)***
Accu Metal 850 912-4855
3987 N W St Ste 13 Pensacola (32505) ***(G-13432)***
Accu Right Inc 561 586-5368
1012 7th Ave S Ste 1 Lake Worth (33460) ***(G-7180)***
Accu Tech LLC 407 446-6676
1506 Max Hooks Rd Ste E Groveland (34736) ***(G-4857)***
Accu-Span Truss Co 407 321-1440
1891 High St Longwood (32750) ***(G-7863)***
Accudock, Pompano Beach *Also called Jmh Marine Inc* ***(G-14067)***
Accuform Global Inc 800 237-1001
16228 Flight Path Dr Brooksville (34604) ***(G-1128)***
Accuform Manufacturing Inc 352 799-5434
16228 Flight Path Dr Brooksville (34604) ***(G-1129)***
Accuform Signs, Brooksville *Also called Accuform Manufacturing Inc* ***(G-1129)***
Accuform Signs 800 237-1001
11119 Holbrook St Spring Hill (34609) ***(G-16060)***
Accuplace, Plantation *Also called Automatic Mfg Systems Inc* ***(G-13829)***
Accuprint Corporation 954 973-9369
1061 Sw 30th Ave Deerfield Beach (33442) ***(G-2654)***
Accuprint My Print Shop 954 973-9369
1061 Sw 30th Ave Deerfield Beach (33442) ***(G-2655)***
Accurate Metal Fabricators 407 933-2666
3718 Grissom Ln Kissimmee (34741) ***(G-6893)***
Accurate Metal Finishing Fla, Rockledge *Also called Accurate Metal Finshg Fla Inc* ***(G-14688)***
Accurate Metal Finshg Fla Inc (PA) 321 636-4900
500 Gus Hipp Blvd Rockledge (32955) ***(G-14688)***
Accurate Metal Finshg Fla Inc 321 636-4900
500 Gus Hipp Blvd Rockledge (32955) ***(G-14689)***
Accurate Metals Spinning Inc 305 885-9988
9001 Nw 97th Ter Ste K Medley (33178) ***(G-8192)***
Accurate Powder Coating Inc 321 269-6972
1417 Chaffee Dr Ste 10 Titusville (32780) ***(G-17568)***
Accurate Reproductions Inc 407 814-1622
2060 Apopka Blvd Apopka (32703) ***(G-98)***
Accurate Wldg Fabrication LLC 727 483-3125
11029 Clay Pit Rd Tampa (33610) ***(G-16557)***
Accuware Inc 305 894-6874
235 Lincoln Rd Ste 306 Miami Beach (33139) ***(G-10160)***
Acdm - Pms Inc 305 258-0347
25331 Sw 142nd Ave Homestead (33032) ***(G-5697)***
Ace Blueprinting Inc 954 771-0104
1770 Nw 64th St Ste 500 Fort Lauderdale (33309) ***(G-3620)***
Ace Boat Lifts LLC (PA) 941 493-8100
2211 S Tamiami Trl Venice (34293) ***(G-17673)***
Ace Construction Management 407 704-7803
801 N Pine Hills Rd Orlando (32808) ***(G-11866)***
Ace Custom Signs of Winter Pk 407 257-6475
922 Orange Ave Winter Park (32789) ***(G-18481)***
Ace Door Co, Port Charlotte *Also called American Cnstr Entps Inc* ***(G-14285)***
Ace Fabricators Inc 904 355-3724
1705 E 30th St Jacksonville (32206) ***(G-5856)***
Ace High Printing LLC 727 542-3897
3801 16th St N Ste B Saint Petersburg (33703) ***(G-14953)***
Ace Industries, Miami *Also called Ace Printing Inc* ***(G-8643)***
Ace Marking Devices Corp 561 833-4073
3308 S Dixie Hwy West Palm Beach (33405) ***(G-17911)***
Ace Mechanical Inc 727 304-6277
14455 Myerlake Cir Clearwater (33760) ***(G-1472)***
Ace Metalworks & Mfg Inc 239 666-1103
11821 Palm Beach Blvd Fort Myers (33905) ***(G-4155)***
Ace Mirror & Glass Works Inc 561 792-7478
14083 85th Rd N Loxahatchee (33470) ***(G-7964)***
Ace Overhead Doors, Pensacola *Also called Specialty Products Inc* ***(G-13608)***
Ace Press Inc 239 334-1118
2133 Broadway Fort Myers (33901) ***(G-4156)***
Ace Printing Inc 305 358-2572
2846 Nw 79th Ave Miami (33122) ***(G-8643)***
Ace Restoration Services LLC 786 487-1870
11921 Sw 130th St Ste 402 Miami (33186) ***(G-8644)***
Ace Rubber Stamp, West Palm Beach *Also called Ace Marking Devices Corp* ***(G-17911)***
Ace Sales Corp 305 835-0310
8085 Nw 68th St Miami (33166) ***(G-8645)***
Ace Tools 386 302-5152
17 Lee Dr Palm Coast (32137) ***(G-13067)***
Ace Window & Door, Loxahatchee *Also called Ace Mirror & Glass Works Inc* ***(G-7964)***
Ace-Pipe Welding LLC 561 727-6345
305 Camellia St Palm Beach Gardens (33410) ***(G-12944)***
Acec, Jacksonville *Also called American Commodity Exch Corp* ***(G-5883)***
Acek9.com, Stuart *Also called Radiotronics Inc* ***(G-16204)***
Acer Latin America Inc 305 392-7000
3750 Nw 87th Ave Ste 450 Doral (33178) ***(G-3092)***
Acet Joint Venture (ajv) LLC 240 509-1360
891 Sweetgrass St Loxahatchee (33470) ***(G-7965)***
Acg Materials 405 366-9500
5160 Vermont Rd Marianna (32448) ***(G-8161)***
Ach Solution USA Inc 941 355-9488
1165 Commerce Blvd N Sarasota (34243) ***(G-15437)***
Achei USA Newspaper, Deerfield Beach *Also called Brazilian Clssfied ADS-Chei In* ***(G-2680)***
Achievia Direct Inc 386 615-8708
1440 N Nova Rd Unit 311 Daytona Beach (32117) ***(G-2505)***
Achievia Optical Solutions, Daytona Beach *Also called Achievia Direct Inc* ***(G-2505)***
Aci, Aventura *Also called Action Controls Inc* ***(G-250)***
Aci Worldwide Inc (PA) 305 894-2200
2811 Ponce De Leon Blvd Coral Gables (33134) ***(G-2024)***
Acic Pharmaceuticals Inc 954 341-0795
11772 W Sample Rd Ste 103 Coral Springs (33065) ***(G-2125)***
Acm Screen Printing Inc 305 547-1552
2106 Nw 22nd Ct Miami (33142) ***(G-8646)***

ALPHABETIC

Acme, Brooksville *Also called Med-Nap LLC (G-1179)*

Acme Barricades LC (PA) 904 781-1950
9800 Normandy Blvd Jacksonville (32221) *(G-5857)*

Acme Brick Company 850 531-0725
660 Capital Cir Ne Tallahassee (32301) *(G-16405)*

Acme Cap & Branding, Sanford *Also called Acme Cap & Clothing Inc (G-15258)*

Acme Cap & Clothing Inc 407 321-5100
221 Bellagio Cir Sanford (32771) *(G-15258)*

Acme Dynamics Inc (PA) 813 752-3137
545 Avenue K Se Winter Haven (33880) *(G-18411)*

Acme Miami, Miami *Also called Acme Service Corp (G-8647)*

Acme Service Corp 305 836-4800
1290 Nw 74th St Miami (33147) *(G-8647)*

Acmt South LLC 860 645-0592
1006 Arthur Dr Lynn Haven (32444) *(G-8023)*

Acne Seal Coating and Paving, Cape Coral *Also called Homewood Holdings LLC (G-1356)*

Acolite Claude Untd Sign Inc (PA) 305 362-3333
2555 Nw 102nd Ave Ste 216 Doral (33172) *(G-3093)*

Acolite Sign Company Inc 305 362-3333
2555 Nw 102nd Ave Ste 216 Doral (33172) *(G-3094)*

Acore Shelving & Products 904 964-4320
1460 Ne State Road 16 Starke (32091) *(G-16095)*

Acoustic Communications LLC (PA) 305 463-9485
5049 Nw 114th Ct Doral (33178) *(G-3095)*

ACR Custom Trailer Products, Ocala *Also called Liles Custom Trailers (G-11429)*

ACR Electronics Inc (HQ) 954 981-3333
5757 Ravenswood Rd Fort Lauderdale (33312) *(G-3621)*

ACR Family Components LLC 352 243-0307
19900 Independence Blvd Groveland (34736) *(G-4858)*

Acrocrete Inc (HQ) 954 917-4114
1259 Nw 21st St Pompano Beach (33069) *(G-13908)*

Acroturn Industries Usa LLC 754 205-7178
4640 Lake Industrial Blvd Tavares (32778) *(G-17502)*

Acryfin Coatings LLC 772 631-3899
901 Nw New Providence Rd Stuart (34994) *(G-16110)*

Acrylic Fabrication, Oakland Park *Also called Steven R Durante (G-11299)*

Acrylic Images Inc 954 484-6633
2011 Nw 29th St Oakland Park (33311) *(G-11233)*

Acrylico Inc 561 304-2921
2633 Lantana Rd Ste 6 Lake Worth (33462) *(G-7181)*

Acrylux Paint Mfg Co Inc 954 772-0300
6010 Powerline Rd Fort Lauderdale (33309) *(G-3622)*

Acryplex Inc 305 633-7636
2380 Nw 21st Ter Unit A Miami (33142) *(G-8648)*

ACS, Orlando *Also called Conduent Image Solutions Inc (G-12041)*

ACS of West Palm Beach Inc 561 844-5790
1300 N Florida Mango Rd # 14 West Palm Beach (33409) *(G-17912)*

Act, Melbourne *Also called Alternative Cnstr Tech Inc (G-8363)*

Act USA Int'l, Melbourne *Also called ACt USA International LLC (G-8354)*

ACt USA International LLC 321 725-4200
3962 W Eau Gallie Blvd C Melbourne (32934) *(G-8354)*

Actavis Laboratories FI Inc (HQ) 954 585-1400
4955 Orange Dr Davie (33314) *(G-2375)*

Actavis Laboratories FL Inc 954 358-6100
2945 W Corp Lks Blvd Weston (33331) *(G-18220)*

Actavis Laboratories FL Inc 954 585-1400
4955 Orange Dr Davie (33314) *(G-2376)*

Actigraph LLC 850 332-7900
102 E Garden St Pensacola (32502) *(G-13433)*

Actigraph LLC 850 332-7900
49 E Chase St Pensacola (32502) *(G-13434)*

Action Controls Inc 253 243-7703
3701 N Country Club Dr # 201 Aventura (33180) *(G-250)*

Action Craft, Cape Coral *Also called Flatsmaster Marine LLC (G-1343)*

Action Craft Boats, Cape Coral *Also called CK Prime Investments Inc (G-1324)*

Action Label, Sanford *Also called J & J International Corp (G-15341)*

Action Manufacturing & Sup Inc (PA) 239 574-3443
2602 Ne 9th Ave Cape Coral (33909) *(G-1296)*

Action Mfg & Sup WPB LLC 239 574-3443
2711 Vista Pkwy Ste B5 West Palm Beach (33411) *(G-17913)*

Action Plastics Inc 352 342-4122
11665 Se Us Highway 301 Belleview (34420) *(G-357)*

Action Plating Corp 305 685-6313
1220 Ali Baba Ave Opa Locka (33054) *(G-11711)*

Action Printers Inc 772 567-4377
2571 Stockbridge Sq Sw Vero Beach (32962) *(G-17732)*

Action Printing Inc 305 592-4646
612 Nw 134th Ave Miami (33182) *(G-8649)*

Action Signs & Graphics Inc 386 752-0121
4180 S Us Highway 441 Lake City (32025) *(G-7010)*

Action Weekly Corp 561 586-8699
3708 Georgia Ave West Palm Beach (33405) *(G-17914)*

Actionable Quality Assurance 352 562-0005
747 Sw 2nd Ave Ste 170 Gainesville (32601) *(G-4644)*

Active Line Corp 786 766-1944
915 W 18th St Hialeah (33010) *(G-5026)*

Active Radiator Supply Company, Lakeland *Also called M P N Inc (G-7386)*

Active Sole 941 923-4840
4070 Sawyer Ct Sarasota (34233) *(G-15586)*

Active Thunderboats, Pompano Beach *Also called Custom Marine Concepts Inc (G-13986)*

Activedata, Naples *Also called Montague Enterprises Inc (G-10823)*

Actron Engineering, Clearwater *Also called Actron Entities Inc (G-1473)*

Actron Entities Inc 727 531-5871
13089 60th St N Clearwater (33760) *(G-1473)*

Actual Woodworking Inc 305 606-7849
668 104th Ave N Naples (34108) *(G-10651)*

Acu-Grind Tool Works Inc 941 758-6963
2118 58th Ave E Bradenton (34203) *(G-931)*

Acucall LLC 855 799-7905
1475 Park Ln S Ste 5 Jupiter (33458) *(G-6677)*

Acuderm Inc 954 733-6935
6555 Powerline Rd Ste 114 Fort Lauderdale (33309) *(G-3623)*

Acuity Technologies, Tampa *Also called Telephony Partners LLC (G-17346)*

Acusigns, Doral *Also called Acolite Claude Untd Sign Inc (G-3093)*

Ad America 904 781-5900
8679 W Beaver St Jacksonville (32220) *(G-5858)*

Ad Investment Group LLC 954 784-6900
11500 Miramar Pkwy # 300 Miramar (33025) *(G-10458)*

Ad-Co Printing, Tampa *Also called Disbrow Corporation (G-16779)*

Ad-Tar 561 732-2055
26 Bristol Ln Boynton Beach (33436) *(G-836)*

Adamas Instrument Corporation 727 540-0033
13247 38th St N Ste B Clearwater (33762) *(G-1474)*

Adams Arms Holdings LLC 727 853-0550
21228 Powell Rd Brooksville (34604) *(G-1130)*

Adams Bros Cabinetry Inc 941 639-7188
2221 Murphy Ct North Port (34289) *(G-11186)*

Adams Bros Cabinetry Inc 863 993-0501
9300 Sw Ft Winder St Arcadia (34269) *(G-187)*

Adams Glass Co 816 842-8686
116 Melbourne Ave Indialantic (32903) *(G-5801)*

Adams Group, North Port *Also called Adams Bros Cabinetry Inc (G-11186)*

Adams Hurricane Protection Inc 850 434-2336
2302 Whaley Ave Pensacola (32503) *(G-13435)*

Adaptive Insights Inc 800 303-6346
1401 Town Plaza Ct Winter Springs (32708) *(G-18558)*

Adapto Storage Products 305 887-9563
625 E 10th Ave Hialeah (33010) *(G-5027)*

Adatif Medical Incorporated (HQ) 561 840-0395
3660 Interstate Park Way Riviera Beach (33404) *(G-14586)*

Adcon Telemetry Inc (PA) 561 989-5309
1001 Nw 51st St Ste 305 Boca Raton (33431) *(G-386)*

Add Helium 239 300-0913
3590 Nw 54th St Ste 1 Fort Lauderdale (33309) *(G-3624)*

Add Some Pop, Plantation *Also called Shasta Beverages Intl Inc (G-13886)*

Add-V LLC 305 496-2445
1801 Nw 38th Ave Ste H Lauderhill (33311) *(G-7724)*

Addco Industries, Riviera Beach *Also called Addco Manufacturing Company (G-14587)*

Addco Manufacturing Company 828 733-1560
131 Riviera Dr Riviera Beach (33404) *(G-14587)*

Addison Hvac LLC 407 292-4400
7050 Overland Rd Orlando (32810) *(G-11867)*

Addison Metal Additions Inc 305 245-9860
20231 Sw 321st St Homestead (33030) *(G-5698)*

Additec, Palm City *Also called Additive Technologies LLC (G-13021)*

Additive Technologies LLC 702 686-5190
4413 Sw Cargo Way Palm City (34990) *(G-13021)*

Address-O-Lite, Pensacola *Also called Digecon Plastics International (G-13489)*

Addtad Partners Inc 727 863-0847
9704 Katy Dr Ste 2 Hudson (34667) *(G-5761)*

Adec Metal Fabrication Inc 305 401-5073
455 W 28th St Hialeah (33010) *(G-5028)*

Adelheidis Commercial Inc 239 384-8642
3847 Tamiami Trl E Naples (34112) *(G-10652)*

Adelman Steel Corp 305 691-7740
12040 Sw 113th Ave Miami (33176) *(G-8650)*

Ademero Inc 863 937-0272
4685 E County Road 540a Lakeland (33813) *(G-7265)*

Adeptus Industries Inc 941 756-7636
6224 17th St E Bradenton (34203) *(G-932)*

Aderant North America Inc 850 224-2200
1760 Summit Lake Dr 105 Tallahassee (32317) *(G-16406)*

Adf Group, Pompano Beach *Also called Adf International Inc (G-13909)*

Adf International Inc 954 931-5150
1925 Nw 15th St Ste A Pompano Beach (33069) *(G-13909)*

Adhesive Manufacturers Inc 305 495-8018
1572 Nw 182nd Way Pembroke Pines (33029) *(G-13368)*

Adhesive Technologies Fla LLC 941 228-0295
411 Pheasant Way Sarasota (34236) *(G-15587)*

Adhesives Technology Corp 754 399-1684
450 E Copans Rd Pompano Beach (33064) *(G-13910)*

ADI, Deerfield Beach *Also called Air Dimensions Inc (G-2661)*

Adidas North America Inc 321 677-0078
8200 Vineland Ave Ste 350 Orlando (32821) *(G-11868)*

Adidas Outlet Store Orlando, Orlando *Also called Adidas North America Inc (G-11868)*

Adir Scooters Inc...305 532-0019
739 5th St Miami Beach (33139) *(G-10161)*

Adjust-A-Brush, Clearwater Also called Boden Co Inc *(G-1522)*

Adler Anb Inc...954 581-2572
3721 Sw 47th Ave Ste 306 Davie (33314) *(G-2377)*

ADM Il Exhibits & Displays Inc............................813 887-1960
5690 W Crenshaw St Tampa (33634) *(G-16558)*

Adma...561 989-5800
5800 Pk Of Commerce Blvd Boca Raton (33487) *(G-387)*

Adma Biologics Inc..561 989-5800
5800 Pk Of Cmmrce Blvd Nw Boca Raton (33487) *(G-388)*

Adma Biomanufacturing LLC...............................201 478-5552
5800 Pk Of Commerce Blvd Boca Raton (33487) *(G-389)*

Admask Inc..954 962-2040
6531 Nw 13th Ct Plantation (33313) *(G-13821)*

Admiral..305 493-4355
1690 Ne 205th Ter Miami (33179) *(G-8651)*

Admiral Printing Inc...727 938-9589
5412 Provost Dr Unit 12 Holiday (34690) *(G-5487)*

Adnan Enterprises...305 430-9752
4699 Nw 183rd St Miami Gardens (33055) *(G-10248)*

Adonel Block Mfg Corp..561 615-9500
2101 Nw 110th Ave Miami (33172) *(G-8652)*

Adonel Con Pmpg Fnshg S Fla In (PA)................305 392-5416
2101 Nw 110th Ave Miami (33172) *(G-8653)*

Adorgraf Corp...786 752-1680
7770 Nw 64th St Miami (33166) *(G-8654)*

Adr Power Systems Inc (PA)................................813 241-6999
6545 125th Ave Largo (33773) *(G-7521)*

Adrenaline Productions LLC.................................305 697-6445
1200 Brickell Ave # 1950 Miami (33131) *(G-8655)*

Adrian Lucas Aluminum, Ocala Also called Luv Enterprises Inc *(G-11433)*

Adriana Hoyos, Miami Gardens Also called Ahus Inc *(G-10249)*

Adriano Gb Brick Pavers LLC...............................407 497-1517
9851 Cypress Park Dr Orlando (32824) *(G-11869)*

Adrick Marine Group Inc.....................................321 631-0776
581 Cidco Rd Cocoa (32926) *(G-1898)*

ADS-TEC Energy Inc..941 358-7445
5343 Paylor Ln Ste 200 Lakewood Ranch (34240) *(G-7481)*

Adsevero LLC..813 508-0616
8875 Hdden Rver Pkwy Ste Tampa (33637) *(G-16559)*

Adsil Inc..386 274-1382
1901 Mason Ave Ste 101 Daytona Beach (32117) *(G-2506)*

Adtec Digital, Jacksonville Also called Adtec Productions Incorporated *(G-5859)*

Adtec Productions Incorporated...........................904 720-2003
2231 Corporate Sq Blvd Jacksonville (32216) *(G-5859)*

Adultfriendfinder, Delray Beach Also called Medleycom Incorporated *(G-2986)*

Adv1, Miami Also called Advance One Wheels Inc *(G-8656)*

Adva-Lite Inc...727 369-5319
8285 Bryan Dairy Rd Seminole (33777) *(G-15967)*

Advak Techologies, Hialeah Gardens Also called Jtf Ventures LLC *(G-5439)*

Advance Controls Inc (PA)...................................941 746-3221
4505 18th St E Bradenton (34203) *(G-933)*

Advance Ctrl Mfg Jean Annette............................941 697-0846
9161 Cherry Dr Englewood (34224) *(G-3515)*

Advance Driveline, Orlando Also called Central Florida Driveshaft *(G-11997)*

Advance Green Energy Inc....................................352 765-3850
523 S Us Highway 41 Inverness (34450) *(G-5821)*

Advance One Wheels Inc......................................305 238-5833
14397 Sw 143rd Ct Ste 105 Miami (33186) *(G-8656)*

Advance Plastics Unlimited..................................305 885-6266
905 W 19th St Hialeah (33010) *(G-5029)*

Advance Solder Technology Inc...........................321 633-4777
315 Gus Hipp Blvd Rockledge (32955) *(G-14690)*

Advance Tool Company Inc..................................727 726-8907
940 Harbor Lake Ct Safety Harbor (34695) *(G-14782)*

Advanced Air International Inc.............................561 845-8212
6461 Garden Rd Ste 103 Riviera Beach (33404) *(G-14588)*

Advanced Air West Palm Bch Inc.........................561 845-8289
6461 Garden Rd Ste 102 Riviera Beach (33404) *(G-14589)*

Advanced Alum Centl Fla Inc...............................321 639-1451
155 N Range Rd Ste 13 Cocoa (32926) *(G-1899)*

Advanced Alum Polk Cnty Inc..............................863 648-5787
2941 Parkway St Lakeland (33811) *(G-7266)*

Advanced Automotive Designs.............................561 499-8812
6685 Dana Point Cv Delray Beach (33446) *(G-2925)*

Advanced Awning & Design LLC...........................904 724-5567
2155 Corp Sq Blvd Ste 100 Jacksonville (32216) *(G-5860)*

Advanced Bioprocess LLC....................................305 927-3661
3200 Nw 67th Ave Bldg 3 Miami (33166) *(G-8657)*

Advanced Bioservices LLC...................................850 476-7999
5401 Corp Wds Dr Ste 500 Pensacola (32504) *(G-13436)*

Advanced Cabinetry Inventions............................305 866-1160
7601 E Treasure Dr # 2120 North Bay Village (33141) *(G-11057)*

Advanced Cabinetry Systems, Port Charlotte Also called Woods Distinctive Designs Inc *(G-14325)*

Advanced Cable Communications, Coral Springs Also called Advanced Cmmncations Holdg Inc *(G-2126)*

Advanced Cell Engineering Inc.............................772 382-9191
819 Sw Federal Hwy # 205 Stuart (34994) *(G-16111)*

Advanced Cmmncations Holdg Inc (HQ).............954 753-0100
12409 Nw 35th St Coral Springs (33065) *(G-2126)*

Advanced Cmmnications Tech Inc........................954 444-4119
108 Nw 20th St Boca Raton (33431) *(G-390)*

Advanced Cnc Machining Inc...............................954 478-8369
6135 Nw 20th Ct Margate (33063) *(G-8116)*

Advanced Cnc Manufacturing Inc........................727 372-8222
2313 Destiny Way Odessa (33556) *(G-11533)*

Advanced Color Graphics Group, Hollywood Also called R R H Inc *(G-5651)*

Advanced Components Solutions..........................813 884-1600
22652 Laureldale Dr Lutz (33549) *(G-7982)*

Advanced Composite Systems..............................904 765-6502
10615 New Kings Rd Jacksonville (32219) *(G-5861)*

Advanced Dagnstc Solutions Inc..........................352 293-2810
3633 Little Rd Ste 103 Trinity (34655) *(G-17632)*

Advanced Design & Packg Inc..............................904 356-6063
2212 N Pearl St Jacksonville (32206) *(G-5862)*

Advanced Door Concepts, Sebring Also called Hucke Manufacturing Inc *(G-15927)*

Advanced Drainage Systems Inc..........................407 654-3989
115 N West Crown Point Rd Winter Garden (34787) *(G-18372)*

Advanced Dsign Tech Systems In.........................850 462-2868
1300 E Olive Rd Pensacola (32514) *(G-13437)*

Advanced Elctronic Diagnostics, Royal Palm Beach Also called Nilsson Nils *(G-14771)*

Advanced Electronics Labs Inc.............................305 255-6401
7375 Sw 114th St Pinecrest (33156) *(G-13661)*

Advanced Engine Tech LLC..................................727 744-2935
3087 Cherry Ln Clearwater (33759) *(G-1475)*

Advanced Equipment and Svcs, Coral Springs Also called Aesinc Advanced Eqp & Svcs *(G-2128)*

Advanced Furniture Svcs Inc................................850 390-3442
8631 Match St Pensacola (32514) *(G-13438)*

Advanced Hair Products Inc.................................561 347-2799
1287 E Nwport Ctr Dr Ste Deerfield Beach (33442) *(G-2656)*

Advanced Hermetics Inc......................................407 464-0539
2052 Platinum Rd Apopka (32703) *(G-99)*

Advanced Household MGT Inc..............................941 322-9638
6408 Parkland Dr Ste 103 Sarasota (34243) *(G-15438)*

Advanced Hurricane Protection............................772 220-1200
4517 Se Commerce Ave Stuart (34997) *(G-16112)*

Advanced Impact Tech Inc...................................727 287-4620
2310 Starkey Rd Largo (33771) *(G-7522)*

Advanced In Home Prosthetics, Tampa Also called Advanced Prosthetics Amer Inc *(G-16560)*

Advanced Infrstrcture Tech Inc............................239 992-1700
25110 Bernwood Dr # 101 Bonita Springs (34135) *(G-779)*

Advanced Intelligence Group................................904 565-1004
4195 Southside Blvd Jacksonville (32216) *(G-5863)*

Advanced Laser Systems, Orlando Also called L3 Technologies Inc *(G-12300)*

Advanced Living Quarters Inc..............................954 684-9392
426 Sw 191st Ter Pembroke Pines (33029) *(G-13369)*

Advanced Lser Systems Tech Div, Orlando Also called L-3 Cmmnctons Advnced Lser Sys *(G-12299)*

Advanced Machine and Tool Inc...........................772 465-6546
3900 Selvitz Rd Fort Pierce (34981) *(G-4459)*

Advanced Machining Inc......................................386 424-7333
1500 Airway Cir New Smyrna Beach (32168) *(G-10993)*

Advanced Magnet Lab Inc...................................321 728-7543
1604 S Hbr Cy Blvd Ste 10 Melbourne (32901) *(G-8355)*

Advanced Manufacturing Inc...............................727 573-3300
12205 28th St N Saint Petersburg (33716) *(G-14954)*

Advanced Manufacturing & Engrg........................352 629-1494
3220 Ne 24th St Ocala (34470) *(G-11314)*

Advanced Mdular Structures Inc..........................954 960-1550
1911 Nw 15th St Pompano Beach (33069) *(G-13911)*

Advanced Mechanical Entps Inc..........................954 764-2678
217 Sw 28th St Fort Lauderdale (33315) *(G-3625)*

Advanced Metal Fab Inc......................................305 557-2008
2247 W 77th St Hialeah (33016) *(G-5030)*

Advanced Metal Works Inc..................................727 449-9353
1780 Calumet St Clearwater (33765) *(G-1476)*

Advanced Metals LLC..352 494-2476
158 Hour Glass Cir Hawthorne (32640) *(G-5005)*

Advanced Mfg & Pwr Systems Inc.......................386 822-5565
1965 Bennett Ave Deland (32724) *(G-2848)*

Advanced Micro Devices Inc................................407 541-6800
3501 Quadrangle Blvd # 375 Orlando (32817) *(G-11870)*

Advanced Millwork Inc..407 294-1927
2645 Regent Ave Orlando (32804) *(G-11871)*

Advanced Modular Systems, Pompano Beach Also called Advanced Mdular Structures Inc *(G-13911)*

Advanced Outdoor Concepts Inc..........................954 429-1428
3840 W Hillsboro Blvd Deerfield Beach (33442) *(G-2657)*

Advanced Overhead Systems Inc.........................863 667-3757
3510 Craftsman Blvd Lakeland (33803) *(G-7267)*

Advanced Pallets Inc...954 785-1215
2151 N State Road 7 Margate (33063) *(G-8117)*

Advanced Pharma Research Inc...........................786 234-3709
10700 Caribbean Blvd # 30 Cutler Bay (33189) *(G-2282)*

Advanced Pharmaceutical Inc.............................866 259-7122
1065 Ne 125th St Ste 211 North Miami (33161) *(G-11087)*

Advanced Powder Coating Fla, Longwood *Also called Allstar Lighting & Sound Inc* *(G-7865)*

Advanced Prcsion Machining Inc...........................561 243-4567
1035 Nw 17th Ave Ste 3 Delray Beach (33445) *(G-2926)*

Advanced Precision Mch US Inc............................239 332-2841
3791 Edison Ave Fort Myers (33916) *(G-4157)*

Advanced Printing Finshg Inc...............................305 836-8581
1061 E 32nd St Hialeah (33013) *(G-5031)*

Advanced Prosthetics Amer Inc (HQ).....................352 383-0396
601 Mount Homer Rd Eustis (32726) *(G-3552)*

Advanced Prosthetics Amer Inc.............................813 631-9400
15043 Bruce B Downs Blvd Tampa (33647) *(G-16560)*

Advanced Prosthetics Amer Inc.............................904 269-4993
4611 Us Highway 17 Ste 4 Orange Park (32003) *(G-11811)*

Advanced Prosthetics America, Eustis *Also called Advanced Prosthetics Amer Inc* *(G-3552)*

Advanced Public Safety LLC.................................954 354-3000
400 Fairway Dr Ste 101 Deerfield Beach (33441) *(G-2658)*

Advanced Services Intl Inc...................................954 889-1366
3600 Caldwell Rd Ste 406 Miramar (33027) *(G-10459)*

Advanced Sewing...954 484-2100
3619 Nw 19th St Fort Lauderdale (33311) *(G-3626)*

Advanced Sheet Metal & Welding..........................239 430-1155
4443 Arnold Ave Naples (34104) *(G-10653)*

Advanced Software Inc..215 369-7800
1902 2nd Ave N Jacksonville Beach (32250) *(G-6627)*

Advanced Tech & Tstg Labs Inc.............................352 871-3802
17952 Cachet Isle Dr Tampa (33647) *(G-16561)*

Advanced Thermal Tech Inc (HQ)...........................561 791-5000
1400 Corporate Center Way Wellington (33414) *(G-17842)*

Advanced Truck Equipment Inc.............................561 424-0442
1315 Neptune Dr Boynton Beach (33426) *(G-837)*

Advanced Vacuum Systems LLC............................941 378-4565
2025d Porter Lake Dr Sarasota (34240) *(G-15588)*

Advanced Wldg Fbrction Dsign L...........................352 237-9800
13540 Se 31st Ave Summerfield (34491) *(G-16256)*

Advanced Xrgrphics Imging Syst...........................407 351-0232
6851 Tpc Dr Ofc Ofc Orlando (32822) *(G-11872)*

Advanta Asphalt Inc..386 362-5580
1400 Howard St E Live Oak (32064) *(G-7841)*

Advantage Airline Parts Inc (PA)............................770 521-1107
17735 Boniello Rd Boca Raton (33496) *(G-391)*

Advantage Earth Products Inc...............................904 329-1430
317 Vicki Towers Dr Saint Augustine (32092) *(G-14806)*

Advantage Medical Elec LLC (HQ)..........................954 345-9800
11705 Nw 39th St Coral Springs (33065) *(G-2127)*

Advantage Plastics, Winter Haven *Also called Salva Enterprises Inc* *(G-18467)*

Advantage Prtg Lminating Signs, Jacksonville *Also called Advantage Prtg Lmnting Fla Inc* *(G-5864)*

Advantage Prtg Lmnting Fla Inc.............................904 737-1613
4618 Sunbeam Rd Jacksonville (32257) *(G-5864)*

Advantage Software Inc......................................772 288-3266
925 Se Central Pkwy Stuart (34994) *(G-16113)*

Advantagecare Inc...407 345-8877
7081 Grand National Dr # 113 Orlando (32819) *(G-11873)*

Advantor Systems Corporation............................407 859-3350
12612 Challenger Pkwy # 3 Orlando (32826) *(G-11874)*

Advatech Corporation..732 803-8000
250 S Australian Ave # 1504 West Palm Beach (33401) *(G-17915)*

Advent Aerospace Inc (PA)...................................727 549-9600
11221 69th St Largo (33773) *(G-7523)*

Advent Glass Works Inc......................................386 497-2050
242 Sw George Gln Fort White (32038) *(G-4618)*

Adventry Corp..305 582-2977
8190 Commerce Way Miami Lakes (33016) *(G-10279)*

Adventurous Entertainment LLC...........................407 483-4057
6424 Milner Blvd 4 Orlando (32809) *(G-11875)*

Adver-T Screen Printing Inc.................................727 443-5525
408 S Saturn Ave Clearwater (33755) *(G-1477)*

Advermarket Corp..239 541-1144
954 Country Club Blvd Cape Coral (33990) *(G-1297)*

Advermarket Corp..239 542-1020
4720 Se 15th Ave Ste 205 Cape Coral (33904) *(G-1298)*

Advertisers Press..305 879-3227
4135 Sw 108th Ct Miami (33165) *(G-8658)*

Advocate House, Sarasota *Also called A Cappela Publishing Inc* *(G-15582)*

Advtravl Inc...978 549-5013
116 S Magnolia Ave Ste 2 Ocala (34471) *(G-11315)*

Ae Tent LLC...305 691-0191
2995 Nw 75th St Miami (33147) *(G-8659)*

Aeb Technologies Inc..352 417-0009
9619 W Yulee Dr Homosassa (34448) *(G-5742)*

Aei International Corp..904 724-9771
7709 Alton Ave Jacksonville (32211) *(G-5865)*

Aenova Doral Manufacturing Inc (HQ).....................305 463-2270
10400 Nw 29th Ter Doral (33172) *(G-3096)*

Aenova Doral Manufacturing Inc...........................305 463-2263
10655 Nw 29th Ter Doral (33172) *(G-3097)*

Aenova North America Inc...................................786 345-5505
14193 Sw 119th Ave Miami (33186) *(G-8660)*

AEP Group, Saint Augustine *Also called Advantage Earth Products Inc* *(G-14806)*

Aer-Flo Canvas Products Inc................................941 747-4151
4455 18th St E Bradenton (34203) *(G-934)*

Aercap Inc...954 760-7777
100 Ne 3rd Ave Ste 800 Fort Lauderdale (33301) *(G-3627)*

Aercap Group Services Inc (HQ)............................954 760-7777
100 Ne 3rd Ave Ste 800 Fort Lauderdale (33301) *(G-3628)*

Aercap Leasing USA I LLC..................................425 237-4000
801 Brickell Ave Ste 1500 Miami (33131) *(G-8661)*

Aercon Florida LLC...863 422-6360
3701 State Road 544 E Haines City (33844) *(G-4901)*

Aerial Banners Inc...954 893-0099
601 Sw 77th Way Pembroke Pines (33023) *(G-13370)*

Aerial Flags, Pinellas Park *Also called Custom Grafix Industries Inc* *(G-13678)*

Aerial Products Corporation................................800 973-9110
11653 Central Pkwy # 209 Jacksonville (32224) *(G-5866)*

Aerialife Inc..561 990-9299
1319 S L St Fl 334 Lake Worth (33460) *(G-7182)*

Aerion Corp (PA)...775 337-6682
500 Nw 62nd St Ste 400 Fort Lauderdale (33309) *(G-3629)*

Aero Door International LLC.................................407 654-0591
2770 Dillard Rd Eustis (32726) *(G-3553)*

Aero Electronics Systems Inc..............................321 269-0478
411 S Park Ave Titusville (32796) *(G-17569)*

Aero Fuel LLC..352 728-2018
9595 Silver Lake Dr Leesburg (34788) *(G-7756)*

Aero Precision Holdings LP (PA)............................925 455-9900
15501 Sw 29th St Ste 101 Miramar (33027) *(G-10460)*

Aero Precision Products Inc................................305 688-2565
14000 Nw 19th Ave Opa Locka (33054) *(G-11712)*

Aero Seating Technologies LLC............................321 264-5600
1600 Armstrong Dr Titusville (32780) *(G-17570)*

Aero Shade Technologies Inc..............................772 562-2243
3106 Industrial Avenue 3 Fort Pierce (34946) *(G-4460)*

Aero Simulation Inc...813 628-4447
8720 E Sligh Ave Tampa (33610) *(G-16562)*

Aero Supply USA, Clearwater *Also called Supliaereos USA LLC* *(G-1805)*

Aero Tech Service Assoc Inc...............................850 286-1378
1311 Florida Ave Tyndall Afb (32403) *(G-17643)*

Aero Technology Mfg Inc....................................305 345-7747
7735 Nw 64th St Ste 1 Miami (33166) *(G-8662)*

Aero Uno Llc...561 767-5597
2403 Antigua Cir Apt B1 Coconut Creek (33066) *(G-1975)*

Aero-Flex Corp...561 745-2534
3147 Jupiter Park Cir # 2 Jupiter (33458) *(G-6678)*

Aero-Hose Corp..904 215-9638
1845 Town Center Blvd # 140 Orange Park (32003) *(G-11812)*

Aero-Mach TCO Manufacturing.............................239 936-7570
604 Danley Dr Fort Myers (33907) *(G-4158)*

Aero-Marine Technologies Inc.............................941 205-5420
2800 Placida Rd Ste 103 Englewood (34224) *(G-3516)*

Aero-News Network Inc......................................863 299-8680
1335 Kingsley Ave # 831 Orange Park (32067) *(G-11813)*

Aero-Tel Wire Harness Corp................................407 445-1722
4650 Old Winter Garden Rd Orlando (32811) *(G-11876)*

Aero-Trim Control Systems Inc............................954 321-1936
4680 Sw 61st Ave Davie (33314) *(G-2378)*

Aerobase Group Inc (PA)....................................321 802-5889
145 East Dr Ste B Melbourne (32904) *(G-8356)*

Aerodyne Research LLC.....................................813 891-6300
1725 Lexington Ave Deland (32724) *(G-2849)*

Aeroessentials LLC..239 263-9915
2335 Tamiami Trl N # 407 Naples (34103) *(G-10654)*

Aerojet Rcktdyne Clman Arspc I...........................407 354-0047
7675 Municipal Dr Orlando (32819) *(G-11877)*

Aerojet Rocketdyne Inc......................................561 796-2000
15270 Endeavor Dr Jupiter (33478) *(G-6679)*

Aerojet Rocketdyne Inc......................................386 626-0001
790 Fentress Blvd Daytona Beach (32114) *(G-2507)*

Aerojet Rocketdyne De Inc..................................561 882-5150
17900 Bee Line Hwy Jupiter (33478) *(G-6680)*

Aeronate Inc..954 358-7145
20851 Johnson St Ste 109 Pembroke Pines (33029) *(G-13371)*

Aeronautical Systems Engrg Inc...........................727 375-2520
2448 Destiny Way Odessa (33556) *(G-11534)*

Aerontics Customer Support Ctr, Lakeland *Also called Lockheed Martin Corporation* *(G-7384)*

Aerosapien Technologies LLC..............................386 361-3838
601 Innovation Way Daytona Beach (32114) *(G-2508)*

Aerosmart Enterprise LLC...................................310 499-8878
7901 4th St N Ste 300 Saint Petersburg (33702) *(G-14955)*

Aerosonic LLC..727 461-3000
1212 N Hercules Ave Clearwater (33765) *(G-1478)*

Aerospace Automation LLC.................................954 260-2844
830 Sw 174th Ter Pembroke Pines (33029) *(G-13372)*

Aerospace Components Inc.................................727 347-9915
2625 75th St N Saint Petersburg (33710) *(G-14956)*

Aerospace Manufacturing, Lynn Haven *Also called Acmt South LLC* *(G-8023)*

(G-0000) Company's Geographic Section entry number

Aerospace Rotables Inc......954 452-0056
5151 Nw 109th Ave Sunrise (33351) *(G-16285)*
Aerospace Tech Group Inc......561 244-7400
620 Nw 35th St Boca Raton (33431) *(G-392)*
Aerospc/Dfense Coatings GA Inc......407 843-1140
378 Centerpointe Cir # 1272 Altamonte Springs (32701) *(G-27)*
Aerosync Engrg Consulting Inc......316 208-3367
5848 Moors Oaks Dr Milton (32583) *(G-10416)*
Aerosync Support, Milton *Also called Aerosync Engrg Consulting Inc (G-10416)*
Aerotec Aluminium Inc......407 324-5400
1696 N Beardall Ave Sanford (32771) *(G-15259)*
Aerotools Connection, Miami *Also called Forward Express One Llc (G-9168)*
Aerotools Connection LLC......305 234-3034
12625 Sw 134th Ct Ste 208 Miami (33186) *(G-8663)*
Aerowest Mfg Corp......786 367-6948
8835 Nw 117th St Hialeah (33018) *(G-5032)*
Aerox AVI Oxgn Systems LLC (HQ)......239 405-6106
12871 Trade Way Dr Ste 8 Bonita Springs (34135) *(G-780)*
Aersale 23440 LLC......305 764-3200
255 Alhambra Cir Ste 435 Coral Gables (33134) *(G-2025)*
Aersale 26346 LLC......305 764-3200
255 Alhambra Cir Ste 435 Coral Gables (33134) *(G-2026)*
Aersale Component Solutions, Miami *Also called Avborne Accessory Group Inc (G-8775)*
AES, Plant City *Also called American Engineering Svcs Inc (G-13737)*
AES Services Inc......941 237-1446
575 Bluebell Rd Venice (34293) *(G-17674)*
Aesinc Advanced Eqp & Svcs (PA)......954 857-1895
12070 Nw 40th St Ste 2 Coral Springs (33065) *(G-2128)*
Aesthetic MBL Laser Svcs Inc......954 480-2600
905 E Hillsboro Blvd Deerfield Beach (33441) *(G-2659)*
Aesthetic Mobile Laser Svcs, Deerfield Beach *Also called 905 East Hillsboro LLC (G-2651)*
Aesthetic Print & Design Inc......352 278-3714
2618 Ne 18th Ter Gainesville (32609) *(G-4645)*
Aether Media USA Inc......863 647-5500
4175 S Pipkin Rd Ste 108 Lakeland (33811) *(G-7268)*
Aetiquetas Araragua, Miami *Also called Eti-Label Inc (G-9113)*
Afab Enterprises, Eustis *Also called James O Corbett Inc (G-3560)*
Afc Cable Systems Inc......813 539-0588
2000 Tall Pines Dr Largo (33771) *(G-7524)*
Affineon Lighting......407 448-3434
16709 Amber Lk Weston (33331) *(G-18221)*
Affinity Chemical Woodbine LLC......973 873-4070
4532 W Swann Ave Tampa (33609) *(G-16563)*
Affordable At Home Has Inc......786 200-0484
8870 Sw 40th St Ste 7 Miami (33165) *(G-8664)*
Affordable Boat Cushions Inc......877 350-2628
6515 Riverview Dr Riverview (33578) *(G-14556)*
Affordable Displays, Clearwater *Also called Nauset Enterprises Inc (G-1713)*
Affordable Granite Concepts......407 332-0057
1025 Miller Dr Ste 139 Altamonte Springs (32701) *(G-28)*
Affordable Med Scrubs LLC (PA)......419 222-1088
888 Brickell Ave Ste 100 Miami (33131) *(G-8665)*
Affordable Metal Inc......305 691-8082
3522 E 10th Ct Hialeah (33013) *(G-5033)*
Affordable Scree Enclosure LLC......800 900-8586
1425 Sw 1st Ct Ste 25 Pompano Beach (33069) *(G-13912)*
Affordble Screen Enclosure LLC......561 900-8868
5480 Palm Ridge Blvd Delray Beach (33484) *(G-2927)*
Afi, Saint Petersburg *Also called American Fibertek Inc (G-14961)*
Afina Systems Inc (HQ)......305 261-1433
3350 Sw 148th Ave Ste 401 Miramar (33027) *(G-10461)*
AFL Industries Inc......561 848-1826
1101 W 13th St Riviera Beach (33404) *(G-14590)*
Aflg Invstmnts-Industrials LLC (PA)......813 443-8203
701 Suth Hward Ave 106 Tampa (33606) *(G-16564)*
Aflg Invstmnts-Industrials LLC......813 443-8203
5000 Calienta St Hernando Beach (34607) *(G-5011)*
Afrikin LLC (PA)......646 296-3613
2408 Florida St West Palm Beach (33406) *(G-17916)*
AG Parts Corporation......305 670-6227
10375 Nw 30th Ter Doral (33172) *(G-3098)*
AG Signs Plus Inc (PA)......954 709-8422
9139 Sw 20th St Apt F Boca Raton (33428) *(G-393)*
AGA, Miami *Also called A G A Electronics Corp (G-8621)*
AGA Machine Shop Inc......954 522-1108
277 Sw 33rd St Fort Lauderdale (33315) *(G-3630)*
Agape Graphics & Printing Inc......305 252-9147
14255 Sw 119th Ave Miami (33186) *(G-8666)*
Agarose Unlimited Inc......800 850-0659
707 Nw 13th St Gainesville (32601) *(G-4646)*
Agent Advantage, Tallahassee *Also called Homes Media Solutions LLC (G-16462)*
Agg International, Hollywood *Also called Snappy Structures Inc (G-5658)*
Agg Trading-W Ft Pierce Term, Fort Pierce *Also called Cemex Cnstr Mtls Fla LLC (G-4474)*
Aggressive Box Inc......813 901-9600
5444 Pioneer Park Blvd A Tampa (33634) *(G-16565)*
Agi-Vr/Wesson Inc......239 573-5132
2673 Ne 9th Ave Cape Coral (33909) *(G-1299)*
Agile Cargo Transportation LLC......407 747-0812
1601-1 N Main St Jacksonville (32206) *(G-5867)*
Agile Risk Management LLC......800 317-5497
3333 W Kennedy Blvd # 201 Tampa (33609) *(G-16566)*
Agility Press Inc......904 731-8989
3060 Mercury Rd Jacksonville (32207) *(G-5868)*
AGIsupreme Llc......818 232-6699
2252 Hayes St Hollywood (33020) *(G-5521)*
Agl Aerospace, Miami *Also called Above Ground Level Aerospace (G-8637)*
AGM Industries Inc......954 486-1112
1560 Nw 23rd Ave Fort Lauderdale (33311) *(G-3631)*
AGM Kitchen & Bath LLC......239 300-4739
4384 Progress Ave Naples (34104) *(G-10655)*
AGM Orlando Inc......407 865-9522
223 Altamonte Commerce Bl Altamonte Springs (32714) *(G-29)*
AGM Publishing Inc......727 934-9993
3049 Coldwell Dr Holiday (34691) *(G-5488)*
Agner Timber Services Inc......850 251-6615
2450 W Fair Rd Perry (32347) *(G-13629)*
Agnet Media Inc......352 671-1909
27206 Sw 22nd Pl Newberry (32669) *(G-11016)*
Agnus Distributors, Miami *Also called Dextrum Laboratories Inc (G-9025)*
Agora Leather Products, Clearwater *Also called Agora Sales Inc (G-1479)*
Agora Leather Products, Saint Petersburg *Also called Agora Sales Inc (G-14957)*
Agora Sales Inc......727 490-0499
4215 E Bay Dr Apt 802 Clearwater (33764) *(G-1479)*
Agora Sales Inc (PA)......727 321-0707
2101 28th St N Saint Petersburg (33713) *(G-14957)*
Agp Holding Corp (PA)......850 668-0006
2935 Kerry Forest Pkwy Tallahassee (32309) *(G-16407)*
Agpb LLC......561 935-4147
800 W Indiantown Rd Jupiter (33458) *(G-6681)*
AGR Fabricators Inc......904 733-9393
4879 Clydo Rd S Ste 1 Jacksonville (32207) *(G-5869)*
AGR of Florida Inc......904 733-9393
4879 Clydo Rd S Jacksonville (32207) *(G-5870)*
Agra Chem Sales Co Inc......863 453-6450
959 S Angelo Lake Rd Avon Park (33825) *(G-278)*
Agri - Source Inc......352 351-2700
4001 Ne 35th St Ocala (34479) *(G-11316)*
Agri Machinery & Parts Inc......407 299-1592
3489 All American Blvd Orlando (32810) *(G-11878)*
Agri Metal Supply Inc......386 294-1720
232 Se Indus Pk Cir Ste C Mayo (32066) *(G-8182)*
Agri-Products Inc (HQ)......850 668-0006
3015 N Shnnon Lkes Dr Ste Tallahassee (32309) *(G-16408)*
Agri-Source Fuels LLC......352 521-3460
120 E Main St Ste A Pensacola (32502) *(G-13439)*
Agrifleet Leasing Corporation......239 293-3976
100 Thornhill Rd Auburndale (33823) *(G-218)*
Agrium Advanced Tech US Inc......407 302-2024
2451 Old Lake Mary Rd Sanford (32771) *(G-15260)*
Agro & Cnstr Solutions Inc......305 593-7011
3630 Nw 115th Ave Doral (33178) *(G-3099)*
Agrosource Inc......908 251-3500
166 Beacon Ln Jupiter (33469) *(G-6682)*
Agrotek Services Incorporated......305 599-3818
6414 Nw 82nd Ave Miami (33166) *(G-8667)*
AGS Electronics Inc......850 471-1551
4400 Bayou Blvd Ste 53b Pensacola (32503) *(G-13440)*
AGS Enterprises Inc......305 716-7660
10305 Nw 41st St Ste 210 Doral (33178) *(G-3100)*
Agteck Inc......321 305-5930
150 N Wilson Ave Ste 101 Cocoa (32922) *(G-1900)*
Agua Bucha, Saint Petersburg *Also called Mother Kombucha LLC (G-15131)*
Agustin Reyes Inc......305 558-8870
2307 W 77th St Hialeah (33016) *(G-5034)*
Ahc Ventures Corp......954 978-9290
5415 Nw 24th St Ste 103 Margate (33063) *(G-8118)*
Ahus Inc......305 572-9052
3361 Nw 168th St Miami Gardens (33056) *(G-10249)*
Ai Thomas LLC......904 553-6202
220 Pnte Vdra Pk Dr Ste 1 Ponte Vedra Beach (32082) *(G-14260)*
Ai-R.com Got-Leads.com, Boca Raton *Also called Significant Solutions Corp (G-674)*
Ai2 Inc......407 645-3234
1400 Bonnie Burn Cir Winter Park (32789) *(G-18482)*
Aicon Yachts Americas LLC......910 583-5299
1801 West Ave Miami Beach (33139) *(G-10162)*
AIG Technologies Inc......954 433-0618
5001 Nw 13th Ave Ste B Deerfield Beach (33064) *(G-2660)*
Aigean Networks......754 223-2240
3496 Ne 12th Ter Oakland Park (33334) *(G-11234)*
Aim, Jacksonville *Also called R & K Marketing Inc (G-6401)*
Aim Immunotech Inc (PA)......352 448-7797
2117 Sw Highway 484 Ocala (34473) *(G-11317)*
Aim Shutters......954 861-6666
5054 N Hiatus Rd Sunrise (33351) *(G-16286)*
AIN Plastics of Florida Inc......813 242-6400
6317 Pelican Creek Cir Riverview (33578) *(G-14557)*

A L P H A B E T I C

Aiolos Group Inc............305 496-7674
2529 Nw 74th Ave Miami (33122) ***(G-8668)***
Air & Power Solutions Inc............954 427-0019
6810 Lyons Tech Pkwy # 125 Coconut Creek (33073) ***(G-1976)***
Air Alliance Inc............305 735-4864
13369 Overseas Hwy Marathon (33050) ***(G-8105)***
Air Authorities of Tampa Inc............727 525-1575
4810 110th Ave N Ste 1a Clearwater (33762) ***(G-1480)***
Air Balance Corp............305 401-8780
1789 Canova St Se Ste B Palm Bay (32909) ***(G-12886)***
Air Burners Inc............772 220-7303
4390 Sw Cargo Way Palm City (34990) ***(G-13022)***
Air Dimensions Inc............954 428-7333
1371 W Newport Center Dr # 101 Deerfield Beach (33442) ***(G-2661)***
Air Distributors Inc............352 522-0006
2541 W Dunnellon Rd Dunnellon (34433) ***(G-3461)***
Air Doctor of Swfl LLC............239 285-8774
1020 Jackson Ave Lehigh Acres (33972) ***(G-7804)***
Air Duct Systems Inc............407 839-3313
2106 W Central Blvd Orlando (32805) ***(G-11879)***
Air Esscentials Inc............305 446-1670
7055 Sw 47th St Miami (33155) ***(G-8669)***
Air Essentials, Miami *Also called Air Esscentials Inc* ***(G-8669)***
Air Flow Specialists............954 727-9507
5400 S University Dr 206a Davie (33328) ***(G-2379)***
Air Infinity Inc............941 423-1355
2616 Tusket Ave North Port (34286) ***(G-11187)***
Air Lion Incorp............386 748-9296
2609 Old Church Pl Deland (32720) ***(G-2850)***
Air Liquide America LP............407 855-8286
6675 W Wood Blvd Ste 330 Orlando (32821) ***(G-11880)***
Air Liquide Large Inds US LP............321 452-2214
7007 N Courtenay Pkwy Merritt Island (32953) ***(G-8572)***
Air Marshall Inc............954 843-0991
2870 Stirling Rd Ste 110 Hollywood (33020) ***(G-5522)***
Air Operations............305 871-5449
4000 Nw 28th St Miami (33142) ***(G-8670)***
Air Products and Chemicals Inc............407 859-5141
8300 Exchange Dr Orlando (32809) ***(G-11881)***
Air Purifying Systems Inc............954 962-0450
3750 Nw 28th St Unit 206 Miami (33142) ***(G-8671)***
Air Shelters USA LLC (PA)............215 957-6128
650 Sw 16th Ter Pompano Beach (33069) ***(G-13913)***
Air Source 1 LLC............772 626-7604
585 Nw Merc Pl Ste 103 Port St Lucie (34986) ***(G-14469)***
Air Sponge Filter Company Inc............954 752-1836
4224 Nw 120th Ave Coral Springs (33065) ***(G-2129)***
Air Supply of Future Inc............954 977-0877
1950 Nw 15th St Ste A Pompano Beach (33069) ***(G-13914)***
Air Support Tecks............386 986-5301
14 Bird Haven Pl Palm Coast (32137) ***(G-13068)***
Air Technical LLC............305 837-3274
7901 4th St N Ste 4612 Saint Petersburg (33702) ***(G-14958)***
Air Temp of America Inc............850 340-3017
423 E 16th St Panama City (32405) ***(G-13225)***
Air Turbine Technology Inc............561 994-0500
1225 Broken Sound Pkwy Nw D Boca Raton (33487) ***(G-394)***
Air-Flite Containers Inc............407 679-1200
2699 N Forsyth Rd Ste 101 Orlando (32807) ***(G-11882)***
Air-Flo/Erwood Heating and A/C, Seminole *Also called Miles of Smiles Rides Inc* ***(G-15983)***
Air-O-Matic Corp............786 364-6960
1992 Nw 95th Ave Doral (33172) ***(G-3101)***
Air-Tech of Pensacola Inc............850 433-6443
2317 Town St Pensacola (32505) ***(G-13441)***
Air-Trac, Gainesville *Also called R & J Mfg of Gainesville* ***(G-4754)***
Air2 G2 Machine, Jacksonville *Also called Foley Air LLC* ***(G-6117)***
Airam Stone Designs Inc............305 477-8009
8900 Sw 104th St Miami (33176) ***(G-8672)***
Airbus Oneweb Satellites LLC (PA)............321 522-6645
8301 Newspace Dr Merritt Island (32953) ***(G-8573)***
Airbus Onweb Stlltes N Amer LL (HQ)............321 522-6645
8301 Newspace Dr Merritt Island (32953) ***(G-8574)***
Airbus Onweb Stlltes N Amer LL............321 522-6645
8301 Newspace Dr Merritt Island (32953) ***(G-8575)***
Aircel LLC............865 681-7066
3033 Riviera Dr Ste 101 Naples (34103) ***(G-10656)***
Airco Plating Company Inc............305 633-2476
3650 Nw 46th St Miami (33142) ***(G-8673)***
Aircon Fleet Management Corp............305 234-8174
12334 Sw 131st Ave Miami (33186) ***(G-8674)***
Aircraft Electric Motors Inc............305 885-9476
5800 Nw 163rd St Miami Lakes (33014) ***(G-10280)***
Aircraft Engrg Instllion Svcs............407 438-4436
101 W Landstreet Rd Orlando (32824) ***(G-11883)***
Aircraft Systems Group Inc............727 376-9292
11528 Perpetual Dr Odessa (33556) ***(G-11535)***
Aircraft Tbular Components Inc............321 757-9020
3939 Dow Rd Melbourne (32934) ***(G-8357)***
Aircraft Technology Inc............954 744-7602
3000 Taft St Hollywood (33021) ***(G-5523)***
Airdyne Aerospace Inc............352 593-4163
3160 Premier Dr Brooksville (34604) ***(G-1131)***
Aire-Tech Rotorcraft Svcs LLC............305 696-8001
6270 Nw 37th Ave Miami (33147) ***(G-8675)***
Airehealth Inc (PA)............407 280-4107
1511 E State Road 434 # 2 Winter Springs (32708) ***(G-18559)***
Airflowbalance LLC............386 871-8136
4273 Regal Town Ln Lake Mary (32746) ***(G-7057)***
Airframe International Inc............218 461-9305
3150 Airmans Dr Fort Pierce (34946) ***(G-4461)***
Airfree USA LLC............305 772-6577
25 Se 2nd Ave Ste 1235 Miami (33131) ***(G-8676)***
Airgas Puritan Medical, Orlando *Also called Airgas Usa LLC* ***(G-11884)***
Airgas Usa LLC............407 293-6630
3100 Silver Star Rd Orlando (32808) ***(G-11884)***
Airgroup Inc............561 279-0680
9858 Glades Rd Boca Raton (33434) ***(G-395)***
Airguide Manufacturing LLC............305 888-1631
795 W 20th St Hialeah (33010) ***(G-5035)***
Airind Incorporated............954 252-0900
6511 Melaleuca Rd Southwest Ranches (33330) ***(G-16052)***
Airite Air Conditioning Inc............813 886-0235
5321 W Crenshaw St Tampa (33634) ***(G-16567)***
Airline Support Group Inc............954 971-4567
2700 W Cypress Creek Rd Fort Lauderdale (33309) ***(G-3632)***
Airlock USA LLC............305 888-6454
145 Curtiss Pkwy Miami Springs (33166) ***(G-10386)***
Airmark Components Inc............954 522-5370
2701 Sw 2nd Ave Fort Lauderdale (33315) ***(G-3633)***
Airmark Engines, Inc., Fort Lauderdale *Also called Airmark Overhaul Inc* ***(G-3634)***
Airmark Overhaul Inc............954 970-3200
6001 Nw 29th Ave Fort Lauderdale (33309) ***(G-3634)***
Airo Industries Inc............239 229-5273
2837 Fowler St Fort Myers (33901) ***(G-4159)***
Airon Corporation............321 821-9433
751 North Dr Ste 6 Melbourne (32934) ***(G-8358)***
Airplane Services Inc............850 675-1252
1817 Mineral Springs Rd Jay (32565) ***(G-6647)***
Airpro Diagnostics LLC............904 717-1711
6873 Phillips Ind Blvd Jacksonville (32256) ***(G-5871)***
Airspan Networks Inc (PA)............561 893-8670
777 W Yamato Rd Ste 310 Boca Raton (33431) ***(G-396)***
Airstar America Inc (HQ)............407 851-7830
9603 Satellite Blvd # 150 Orlando (32837) ***(G-11885)***
Airstar Orlando, Orlando *Also called Airstar America Inc* ***(G-11885)***
Airstox Inc............954 618-6573
13680 Nw 5th St Ste 140 Sunrise (33325) ***(G-16287)***
Aishwarya Tari Apparels, Mount Dora *Also called Ata Group of Companies Inc* ***(G-10597)***
Ait Environmental Technology, Ponte Vedra Beach *Also called Ai Thomas LLC* ***(G-14260)***
Ait Group, Largo *Also called Advanced Impact Tech Inc* ***(G-7522)***
Ait USA Corp............786 953-5918
8485 Nw 74th St Miami (33166) ***(G-8677)***
AJ Assoc Mfg & Engrg Co Inc............727 258-0994
5300 115th Ave N Clearwater (33760) ***(G-1481)***
Aj Associates, Clearwater *Also called AJ Assoc Mfg & Engrg Co Inc* ***(G-1481)***
Aj Associates............727 258-0994
11346 53rd St N Clearwater (33760) ***(G-1482)***
AJ AZ Woodwork Inc............561 859-4963
1917 Mears Pkwy Margate (33063) ***(G-8119)***
Aj Chem Enterprises LLC............754 203-6714
14261 Sw 120th St Miami (33186) ***(G-8678)***
Aj Originals Inc............954 563-9911
1710 Ne 63rd Ct Fort Lauderdale (33334) ***(G-3635)***
Ajax Paving Industries Fla LLC............727 584-3329
1550 Starkey Rd Largo (33771) ***(G-7525)***
Ajc Tiling Solutions LLC............863 274-1962
607 Evergreen Pl Sw Winter Haven (33880) ***(G-18412)***
Ajenat Pharmaceuticals LLC............727 471-0850
203 N Marion St Tampa (33602) ***(G-16568)***
AJF Sheet Metals Inc............305 970-6359
7495 Nw 7th St Ste 10 North Miami (33181) ***(G-11088)***
AJs Aluminum Inc............352 688-7631
5441 Spring Hill Dr Spring Hill (34606) ***(G-16061)***
Ajs Fabrication Llc............863 514-9630
5754 State Road 542 W # 2 Winter Haven (33880) ***(G-18413)***
AK Industries LLC............954 662-7038
3530 Sw 47th Ave West Park (33023) ***(G-18210)***
AK U TEC Machine & Tool Inc............727 573-5211
13191 Automobile Blvd Clearwater (33762) ***(G-1483)***
Aker Data LLC............385 394-2537
124 N Nova Rd Ormond Beach (32174) ***(G-12741)***
Akers Media Group Inc............352 787-4112
108 S 5th St Ste 201 Leesburg (34748) ***(G-7757)***
Akiknav Inc............561 842-8091
6667 42nd Ter N Ste 3 Riviera Beach (33407) ***(G-14591)***
Akira Wood Inc............352 375-0691
619 S Main St Ste A Gainesville (32601) ***(G-4647)***
Akj Industries Inc (PA)............239 939-1696
10175 6 Mile Cypress Pkwy Fort Myers (33966) ***(G-4160)***

870 2022 Harris Florida Manufacturers Directory (G-0000) Company's Geographic Section entry number

Akman Inc 407 948-0562
  2023 N Atl Ave Ste 201 Cocoa Beach (32931) *(G-1964)*

Aksa's Generator, Doral *Also called Jat Power LLC* *(G-3266)*

Akt, Orlando *Also called Playlist Live Inc* *(G-12491)*

Akt Enterprises, Orlando *Also called Merchspin Inc* *(G-12372)*

Akua Rage Entertainment Inc 904 627-5312
  10960 Beach Blvd Lot 494 Jacksonville (32246) *(G-5872)*

Akuwa Solutions Group Inc (PA) 941 343-9947
  6431 Porter Rd Ste 1 Sarasota (34240) *(G-15589)*

Al & Sons Millwork Inc 352 245-9191
  6323 Se 113th St Belleview (34420) *(G-358)*

AL Covell Electric Inc 352 544-0680
  600 S Main St Brooksville (34601) *(G-1132)*

AL Garey & Associates Inc 954 975-7992
  4300 Coral Ridge Dr Coral Springs (33065) *(G-2130)*

Al Stein Industries LLC 727 329-8755
  6911 Bryan Dairy Rd # 280 Largo (33777) *(G-7526)*

Al-FA Cabinets Inc 813 876-4205
  4803 N Grady Ave Tampa (33614) *(G-16569)*

Al-Mar Metals Inc 386 734-3377
  1725 Arredondo Grant Rd De Leon Springs (32130) *(G-2621)*

Al-Rite Fruits and Syrups Inc 305 652-2540
  18524 Ne 2nd Ave Miami (33179) *(G-8679)*

Alabama Marble Co Inc 305 718-8000
  3435 Nw 79th Ave Doral (33122) *(G-3102)*

Alabama Metal Industries Corp 863 688-9256
  1033 Pine Chase Ave Lakeland (33815) *(G-7269)*

Alachua Today Inc 386 462-3355
  14804 Main St Alachua (32615) *(G-1)*

Alacriant Holdings LLC 330 233-0523
  1051 Sand Pond Rd Ste 101 Lake Mary (32746) *(G-7058)*

Aladdin Equipment Company 941 371-3732
  900 Sarasota Center Blvd Sarasota (34240) *(G-15590)*

Alakai Defense Systems Inc 727 541-1600
  8285 Bryan Dairy Rd # 125 Largo (33777) *(G-7527)*

Alamo USA Inc 954 774-3747
  1117 Ne 10th St Hallandale Beach (33009) *(G-4934)*

Alaris Aerospace Systems LLC 954 596-8736
  1721 Blount Rd Ste 1 Pompano Beach (33069) *(G-13915)*

Alaska Inc 954 792-0545
  317 S State Road 7 Plantation (33317) *(G-13822)*

Albasol LLC 830 334-3280
  325 S Biscayne Blvd Miami (33131) *(G-8680)*

Alber Corp 954 377-7101
  7775 W Oakland Park Blvd Sunrise (33351) *(G-16288)*

Albert J Angel 954 718-3000
  1895 Ne 214th Ter Miami (33179) *(G-8681)*

Albertos On Fifth 239 430-1060
  868 5th Ave S Naples (34102) *(G-10657)*

Albireo Energy, Tampa *Also called Quality Buidixie Controls Inc* *(G-17199)*

Albrecht Consulting Inc 941 377-7755
  1350 Global Ct Sarasota (34240) *(G-15591)*

ALC Controls of Florida, Orlando *Also called Automted Lgic Corp Kennesaw GA* *(G-11935)*

Alcas USA Corp 305 591-3325
  5347 Nw 35th Ave Fort Lauderdale (33309) *(G-3636)*

Alcee Industries Inc 407 468-4573
  1701 Acme St 32805 Orlando (32805) *(G-11886)*

Alchemist Holdings LLC 772 340-7774
  8283 S Us Highway 1 Port Saint Lucie (34952) *(G-14394)*

Alchemist Holdings LLC (PA) 772 343-1111
  10482 Sw Tibre Ct Port Saint Lucie (34987) *(G-14395)*

Alchiba Inc 561 832-9292
  505 S Flagler Dr Ste 900 West Palm Beach (33401) *(G-17917)*

Alco Advanced Technologies 305 333-0831
  10773 Nw 58th St Ste 3707 Doral (33178) *(G-3103)*

Alco Services Inc 954 538-2189
  15501 Sw 29th St Miramar (33027) *(G-10462)*

Alcohol Cntrmasure Systems Inc 407 207-3337
  5776 Hoffner Ave Ste 303 Orlando (32822) *(G-11887)*

Alcolock FL Inc 407 207-3337
  5776 Hoffner Ave Ste 303 Orlando (32822) *(G-11888)*

Alcolock USA, Orlando *Also called Alcohol Cntrmasure Systems Inc* *(G-11887)*

Aldali Inc 877 384-9494
  4821 N Hale Ave Tampa (33614) *(G-16570)*

Aldana Laser Miami Inc 786 681-7752
  10201 Nw 58th St Ste 308 Doral (33178) *(G-3104)*

Aldanas Pavers Inc 305 970-5339
  3281 Nw 18th St Miami (33125) *(G-8682)*

Aldora Aluminum & GL Pdts Inc (PA) 954 441-5057
  7350 Nw 37th Ave Miami (33147) *(G-8683)*

Aleavia Brands LLC 407 289-2632
  3025 Middlesex Rd Orlando (32803) *(G-11889)*

Alectron Inc 786 397-6827
  8810 Nw 24th Ter Doral (33172) *(G-3105)*

Alegro Industries Inc 702 943-0978
  7880 N University Dr # 200 Tamarac (33321) *(G-16523)*

Alenac & Associates, Palm Springs *Also called Alenac Metals Corp* *(G-13141)*

Alenac Metals Corp 561 877-4109
  2180 S Congress Ave Ste 1 Palm Springs (33406) *(G-13141)*

Aleph Graphics Inc 305 994-9933
  1723 Nw 82nd Ave Doral (33126) *(G-3106)*

Alere Inc 813 898-5709
  1120 E Kennedy Blvd Tampa (33602) *(G-16571)*

Alert Manufacturing, West Palm Beach *Also called Alert Towing Inc* *(G-17918)*

Alert Towing Inc 561 586-5504
  8166 140th Ave N West Palm Beach (33412) *(G-17918)*

Alertgy Inc 321 914-3199
  2401 S Harbor City Blvd Melbourne (32901) *(G-8359)*

Alessi Bakery, Tampa *Also called Phils Cake Box Bakeries Inc* *(G-17164)*

Alevo Automotive Inc 954 593-4215
  301 Ne 51st St Ste 1240 Boca Raton (33431) *(G-397)*

Alex Robert Silversmith Inc 727 442-7333
  625 Pinellas St Unit C Clearwater (33756) *(G-1484)*

Alexander Industries Inc 305 888-9840
  905 W 23rd St Hialeah (33010) *(G-5036)*

Alexander Publications LLC 727 596-4544
  10322 Barry Dr Largo (33774) *(G-7528)*

Alexis Welding Express Corp 786 626-4090
  12900 Nw 30th Ave Opa Locka (33054) *(G-11713)*

Alfa Laval Aalborg Inc (HQ) 954 435-5999
  3118 Commerce Pkwy Miramar (33025) *(G-10463)*

Alfa Laval Inc 941 727-1900
  2359 Trailmate Dr Sarasota (34243) *(G-15439)*

Alfa Manufacturing LLC 305 436-8150
  4701 Nw 77th Ave Miami (33166) *(G-8684)*

Alfa Manufacturing Group LLC 305 979-7344
  17401 Nw 2nd Ave Ste 7 Miami Gardens (33169) *(G-10250)*

Alfaparf Milano, Tampa *Also called Pure-Chlor Systems Florida Inc* *(G-17194)*

Alfred Angelo Bridals, Delray Beach *Also called AA Oldco Inc* *(G-2923)*

Alfredo Welding Service LLC 954 770-8744
  5599 Commercial Blvd Winter Haven (33880) *(G-18414)*

Alfresco Air 786 275-5111
  690 Sw 1st Ct Unit Cui Miami (33130) *(G-8685)*

Algoma Hardwoods Inc 865 471-6300
  7630 Currency Dr Orlando (32809) *(G-11890)*

Algy Dance Costumes, Miami *Also called Algy Trimmings Co Inc* *(G-8686)*

Algy Trimmings Co Inc 954 457-8100
  7478 Nw 54th St Miami (33166) *(G-8686)*

Alh Systems Inc 727 787-6306
  1862 Eagle Ridge Blvd Palm Harbor (34685) *(G-13096)*

Ali Kamakhi 850 405-8591
  5663 Tecumseh Dr Tallahassee (32312) *(G-16409)*

Ali Tamposi Publishing Inc 561 306-6597
  2106 Chagall Cir West Palm Beach (33409) *(G-17919)*

Alicia Diagnostic Inc 407 365-8498
  150 W 11th St Chuluota (32766) *(G-1463)*

Alicia Studio, Hialeah *Also called Mac D&D Inc* *(G-5233)*

Alico Lighting Group Inc 305 542-2648
  140 S Dixie Hwy Unit 101 Hollywood (33020) *(G-5524)*

Alico Metal Fabricators LLC 239 454-4766
  16750 Link Ct Ste 205 Fort Myers (33912) *(G-4161)*

Alienware Corp 786 260-9625
  13462 Sw 131st St Miami (33186) *(G-8687)*

Align Optics Inc 954 748-1715
  4700 N Hiatus Rd Ste 144a Sunrise (33351) *(G-16289)*

Alive By Nature Inc 800 810-1935
  130 Corridor Rd Ste 3333 Ponte Vedra Beach (32082) *(G-14261)*

All About Her 954 559-5175
  12401 Orange Dr Davie (33330) *(G-2380)*

All About Screens, Bonita Springs *Also called Brian Schatzman* *(G-786)*

All Amercian Hot Dog Cart Co, Miami Beach *Also called Louis Di Rmndo Wrldwide Invstm* *(G-10209)*

All American Amputee 352 383-0396
  601 Mount Homer Rd Eustis (32726) *(G-3554)*

All American Barricades 305 685-6124
  2300 Sw 41st Ave Fort Lauderdale (33317) *(G-3637)*

All American Building Products 786 718-7300
  401 Se 10th St Dania (33004) *(G-2326)*

All American Lube 561 432-0476
  5865 S State Road 7 Lake Worth (33449) *(G-7183)*

All American Pet Company Inc 561 337-5340
  3801 Pga Blvd Ste 600 Palm Beach Gardens (33410) *(G-12945)*

All American Sealcoating LLC 305 961-1655
  1200 Brickell Ave # 1950 Miami (33131) *(G-8688)*

All Amrcan Bldg Strctres Cntr 407 466-4959
  401 E Cleveland St Apopka (32703) *(G-100)*

All Amrcan Trlr Connection Inc 561 582-1800
  3531 Lake Worth Rd Palm Springs (33461) *(G-13142)*

All Because LLC 407 884-6700
  2098 Sprint Blvd Apopka (32703) *(G-101)*

All Binders & Indexes Inc 305 889-9983
  860 W 20th St Hialeah (33010) *(G-5037)*

All Brght Electropolishing Inc 727 449-9353
  5100 Ulmerton Rd Ste 7 Clearwater (33760) *(G-1485)*

All Coast Manufacturing Inc 813 626-2264
  2433 S 86th St Ste F Tampa (33619) *(G-16572)*

All County Sheet Metal Inc 561 588-0099
  1930 7th Ct N Lake Worth Beach (33461) *(G-7246)*

ALPHABETIC C

All Craft Marine LLC.....813 236-8879
40047 County Road 54 Zephyrhills (33540) *(G-18601)*
All Cut Inc No Selection.....239 789-1748
2910 Hunter St Fort Myers (33916) *(G-4162)*
All Elements Mechanical Corp (PA).....866 306-0359
776 Bennett Dr Unit 101 Longwood (32750) *(G-7864)*
All Florida Engraving.....352 213-4572
17728 S County Road 325 Hawthorne (32640) *(G-5006)*
All Florida Marketing.....813 281-4641
3001 N Rocky Point Dr E Rocky Point (33607) *(G-14756)*
All Glass & Mirror LLC.....561 914-5277
4100 N Powerline Rd Ste A Pompano Beach (33073) *(G-13916)*
All Golf.....954 441-1333
950 N Flamingo Rd Pembroke Pines (33028) *(G-13373)*
All Granite & Marble Corp.....508 248-9393
1909 N Washington Blvd Sarasota (34234) *(G-15592)*
All Green Recycling Inc.....754 204-3707
811 Se 16th St Ste 105 Hollywood (33024) *(G-5525)*
All In One Cmplete Hndyman Svc.....954 708-3463
177 Sw 5th Ct Deerfield Beach (33441) *(G-2662)*
All In One Drect Mktg Slutions, Miami *Also called All In One Mail Shop Inc (G-8689)*
All In One Mail Shop Inc.....305 233-6100
11950 Sw 128th St Miami (33186) *(G-8689)*
All Liquid Envmtl Svcs LLC.....800 767-9594
4600 Powerline Rd Fort Lauderdale (33309) *(G-3638)*
All Metal Fab Inc.....904 570-9772
2021 Dennis St Jacksonville (32204) *(G-5873)*
All Metal Fabrication.....305 666-3312
9621 S Dixie Hwy Pinecrest (33156) *(G-13662)*
All Metal Roofing, Panama City *Also called Coastal Acquisitions Fla LLC (G-13244)*
All Metals Custom Inc.....727 709-4297
7200 59th St N Pinellas Park (33781) *(G-13671)*
All Metals Fabrication LLC.....904 862-6885
4235 Saint Augustine Rd Jacksonville (32207) *(G-5874)*
All Miami Signs Inc.....305 406-2420
7508 Nw 55th St Miami (33166) *(G-8690)*
All Modular Service Inc.....352 429-0868
861 W Myers Blvd Mascotte (34753) *(G-8181)*
All Moldings Inc.....305 556-6171
7950 W 26th Ave Hialeah (33016) *(G-5038)*
All Naturals Direct.....813 792-3777
12191 W Linebaugh Ave Tampa (33626) *(G-16573)*
All Phase Construction USA LLC.....754 227-5605
590 Goolsby Blvd Deerfield Beach (33442) *(G-2663)*
All Phase Custom Mill Shop Inc.....941 474-0903
7471 Sawyer Cir Port Charlotte (33981) *(G-14284)*
All Phase Welding LLC.....772 834-2980
8356 E 98th Ave Vero Beach (32967) *(G-17733)*
All Points Boats Inc.....954 767-8255
900 Sw 21st Ter Fort Lauderdale (33312) *(G-3639)*
All Polishing Solutions.....954 505-4041
3056 S State Road 7 Miramar (33023) *(G-10464)*
All Power Pro Inc.....904 310-3069
995 Egans Creek Ln Fernandina Beach (32034) *(G-3580)*
All Pro Chelo Corp.....786 317-3914
11750 Nw 87th Pl Hialeah (33018) *(G-5039)*
All Pro Ink LLC.....305 252-7644
10878 Sw 188th St Cutler Bay (33157) *(G-2283)*
All Pro Pavers Hardscapes Inc.....954 300-6281
430 S Dixie Hwy E Pompano Beach (33060) *(G-13917)*
All Purpose Prtg Graphics Inc.....904 346-0999
3521 Saint Augustine Rd Jacksonville (32207) *(G-5875)*
All Service Graphics Inc.....321 259-8957
1020 W Eau Gallie Blvd I Melbourne (32935) *(G-8360)*
All Southern Fabricators Inc.....727 573-4846
5010 126th Ave N Clearwater (33760) *(G-1486)*
All Spring Manufacturing Inds, Hollywood *Also called Carlo Morelli (G-5548)*
All Star Graphix Inc.....954 772-1972
5055 Ne 12th Ave Oakland Park (33334) *(G-11235)*
All Star Materials LLC.....352 598-7590
6760 Nw 27th Avenue Rd Ocala (34475) *(G-11318)*
All Star Printing Intl.....954 974-0333
2001 W Sample Rd Ste 100 Deerfield Beach (33064) *(G-2664)*
All Star Pvc Products, Cooper City *Also called South Florida Fabricators LLC (G-2023)*
All State Pallets, Orlando *Also called Floor Tech LLC (G-12157)*
All State Pallets Company LLC.....407 855-8087
9801 Recycle Center Rd Orlando (32824) *(G-11891)*
All Steel Bldngs Cmponents Inc.....813 671-8044
10159 S Us Highway 41 Gibsonton (33534) *(G-4793)*
All Tank Services LLC.....954 260-9443
1903 W Mcnab Rd B Pompano Beach (33069) *(G-13918)*
All Tennis LLC.....561 842-0070
1434 10th St Lake Park (33403) *(G-7121)*
All Things Digital Inc.....305 887-9464
7213 Nw 54th St Miami (33166) *(G-8691)*
All US Mold Rmval Jcksnvlle FL, Jacksonville *Also called Mold Remediation Services Inc (G-6312)*
All Venue Graphics and Signs.....954 399-7446
1700 Nw 15th Ave Ste 360 Pompano Beach (33069) *(G-13919)*
All Weld Inc.....239 348-9550
4416 18th Pl Sw Naples (34116) *(G-10658)*
All Wood Cabinetry LLC.....866 367-2516
210 Century Blvd Bartow (33830) *(G-297)*
All-American Signs Inc.....863 665-7161
206 N Eastside Dr Lakeland (33801) *(G-7270)*
All-Bright Signs, Lecanto *Also called Jwn Family Partners LP Ltd (G-7753)*
All-Jer Construction Usa Inc.....305 257-0225
12225 Sw 217th St Miami (33170) *(G-8692)*
All-Pro Accnting Bkkeeping LLC.....561 212-8418
1947 10th Ave N Lake Worth Beach (33461) *(G-7247)*
All-Pro Equipment & Rental Inc.....850 656-0208
2800 Mahan Dr Tallahassee (32308) *(G-16410)*
All-Star Sales Inc.....904 396-1653
5921 Richard St Jacksonville (32216) *(G-5876)*
All-Tag Corporation (PA).....561 998-9983
1155 Broken Sound Pkwy Nw E Boca Raton (33487) *(G-398)*
All-Tag Security Americas, Boca Raton *Also called All-Tag Corporation (G-398)*
Allan Industries.....407 875-0897
1901 Summit Tower Blvd Orlando (32810) *(G-11892)*
Allapattah Electric Motor Repr.....305 325-0330
1746 Nw 21st Ter Miami (33142) *(G-8693)*
Allapattah Industries Inc.....305 324-5900
1035 Nw 21st Ter Miami (33127) *(G-8694)*
Allay Pharmaceutical LLC (PA).....954 336-1136
16600 Nw 54th Ave Unit 23 Hialeah (33014) *(G-5040)*
Allcases Reekstin & Assoc Inc.....813 891-1313
300 Mears Blvd Oldsmar (34677) *(G-11624)*
Allclear Aerospace & Def Inc (HQ).....954 239-7844
15501 Sw 29th St Ste 101 Miramar (33027) *(G-10465)*
Allcoffee, Opa Locka *Also called Coffee Unlimited LLC (G-11732)*
Allcoffee LLC.....305 685-6856
12815 Nw 45th Ave Ste 6b Opa Locka (33054) *(G-11714)*
Allegra Direct - South Inc.....586 226-1400
2420 Lakemont Ave Orlando (32814) *(G-11893)*
Allegra Fort Myers.....239 275-5797
12140 Metro Pkwy Ste C Fort Myers (33966) *(G-4163)*
Allegra Gainesville, Gainesville *Also called 352ink Corp (G-4643)*
Allegra Marketing.....813 664-1129
2705 N Falkenburg Rd Tampa (33619) *(G-16574)*
Allegra Naples, Naples *Also called Pk Group Inc (G-10860)*
Allegra Print & Imaging, Orlando *Also called Csmc Inc (G-12060)*
Allegra Print & Imaging Center, Tampa *Also called Manci Graphics Corp (G-17035)*
Allegra Print Imging Dwntwn Tm, Tampa *Also called Output Printing Corp (G-17134)*
Allegra Print Signs Mail.....954 963-3886
5846 Stirling Rd Hollywood (33021) *(G-5526)*
Allegro Nutrition Inc.....732 364-3777
6111 Horse Mill Pl Palmetto (34221) *(G-13153)*
Allen Industries Inc.....727 573-3076
11351 49th St N Clearwater (33762) *(G-1487)*
Allen Shuffleboard LLC.....727 399-8877
6595 Seminole Blvd Seminole (33772) *(G-15968)*
Allendale Hunting Management, Leesburg *Also called Dura-Stress Inc (G-7769)*
Allensteel Inc.....239 454-1331
16281 Pine Ridge Rd Fort Myers (33908) *(G-4164)*
Allergan Sales LLC.....787 406-1203
13800 Nw 2nd St Ste 190 Sunrise (33325) *(G-16290)*
ALLEZ LLC.....205 216-6330
5171 Sw 17th Ct Plantation (33317) *(G-13823)*
Allez Partnership, Fort Myers *Also called Gulf Coast Printing (G-4277)*
Allgeo & Yerkes Entps Inc.....321 255-9030
397 Pineda Ct Melbourne (32940) *(G-8361)*
Allgolf, Pembroke Pines *Also called All Golf (G-13373)*
Alli Cats Inc.....239 274-0744
12211 S Cleveland Ave Fort Myers (33907) *(G-4165)*
Alliance Cabinets & Millwork.....407 802-9921
3231 Sw 3rd St Deerfield Beach (33442) *(G-2665)*
Alliance Commercial Eqp Inc.....772 232-8149
2460 Nw 17th Ln Ste 1 Pompano Beach (33064) *(G-13920)*
Alliance Contractors Supply, Tampa *Also called Tampa Contractors Supply Inc (G-17331)*
Alliance Metals LLC.....305 343-9536
1111 Kane Concourse # 518 Bay Harbor Islands (33154) *(G-330)*
Alliance Rsrvations Netwrk LLC (HQ).....602 889-5505
7380 W Sand Lake Rd # 360 Orlando (32819) *(G-11894)*
Alliant Tchsystems Oprtons LLC.....561 776-9876
348 Hiatt Dr Ste 100 Palm Beach Gardens (33418) *(G-12946)*
Allied Aerofoam Products LLC.....731 660-2705
1883 W State Road 84 # 106 Fort Lauderdale (33315) *(G-3640)*
Allied Aerofoam Products LLC (HQ).....813 626-0090
1883 W State Road 84 # 106 Fort Lauderdale (33315) *(G-3641)*
Allied Aerospace Inc.....786 616-8484
2223 Nw 79th Ave Doral (33122) *(G-3107)*
Allied Aerospace International.....954 429-8600
1022 E Newport Center Dr Deerfield Beach (33442) *(G-2666)*
Allied Binders, Fort Lauderdale *Also called Allied Decals-Fla Inc (G-3642)*
Allied Business Service, Clearwater *Also called Coeur De Lion Inc (G-1545)*
Allied Circuits LLC.....239 970-2299
18018 Royal Tree Pkwy Naples (34114) *(G-10659)*

Allied Decals-Fla Inc 800 940-2233
   5225 Nw 35th Ave Fort Lauderdale (33309) *(G-3642)*

Allied Foam Fabricators LLC (PA) 813 626-0090
   216 Kelsey Ln Tampa (33619) *(G-16575)*

Allied General Engrv & Plas 305 626-6585
   3485 Nw 167th St Opa Locka (33056) *(G-11715)*

Allied Graphics, Jacksonville *Also called Allied Printing Inc (G-5878)*

Allied Group, The, Deerfield Beach *Also called George Wash Cpitl Partners LLC (G-2725)*

Allied Insulated Panels Inc 800 599-3905
   6451 N Federal Hwy # 1204 Fort Lauderdale (33308) *(G-3643)*

Allied Manufacturing Inc (PA) 813 502-0300
   203 Kelsey Ln Ste G Tampa (33619) *(G-16576)*

Allied Molded Products LLC 941 723-3072
   1145 13th Ave E Palmetto (34221) *(G-13154)*

Allied Pharmacy Products Inc 516 374-8862
   2905 S Congress Ave Ste A Delray Beach (33445) *(G-2928)*

Allied Plastics Co Inc 904 359-0386
   2001 Walnut St Jacksonville (32206) *(G-5877)*

Allied Precast Products Co Inc 407 745-5605
   5640 Carder Rd Orlando (32810) *(G-11895)*

Allied Printing Inc 800 749-7683
   7403 Philips Hwy Jacksonville (32256) *(G-5878)*

Allied Steel Buildings Inc 800 508-2718
   6451 N Federal Hwy # 1202 Fort Lauderdale (33308) *(G-3644)*

Allied Telecommunications Ltd 954 370-9900
   1500 Nw 65th Ave Plantation (33313) *(G-13824)*

Allied Tube & Conduit 813 623-2681
   5128 W Hanna Ave Tampa (33634) *(G-16577)*

Allied USA Incorporated 305 235-3950
   2824 Sw 138th Path Miami (33175) *(G-8695)*

Allied-360 LLC 954 590-4940
   101 Ne 3rd Ave Ste 300 Fort Lauderdale (33301) *(G-3645)*

Allliance Precious Mtls Group 954 480-8676
   6820 Lyons Tech Pkwy Coconut Creek (33073) *(G-1977)*

Alloy Cladding 561 625-4550
   15850 Guild Ct Jupiter (33478) *(G-6683)*

Alloy Cladding Company LLC 561 625-4550
   16170 Old Us 41 Fort Myers (33912) *(G-4166)*

Allpro Fbricators Erectors Inc 954 797-7300
   3595 Burris Rd Davie (33314) *(G-2381)*

Allstair 239 313-5574
   7800 Drew Cir Ste 15 Fort Myers (33967) *(G-4167)*

Allstar Lighting & Sound Inc 407 767-0111
   754 Fleet Fin Ct Ste 102 Longwood (32750) *(G-7865)*

Allstar Printing International, Deerfield Beach *Also called All Star Printing Intl (G-2664)*

Allstar Screen Enclosures & St 954 266-9757
   9460 Poinciana Pl Apt 308 Davie (33324) *(G-2382)*

Allstate Lghtning Prtction LLC 813 240-2736
   7201 Sheldon Rd Tampa (33615) *(G-16578)*

Allsteel Processing LC 954 587-1900
   1250 Nw 23rd Ave Fort Lauderdale (33311) *(G-3646)*

Allstone Casting 305 528-1677
   6900 Nw 77th Ter Medley (33166) *(G-8193)*

Allure Shades Inc 954 543-6259
   3714 Nw 16th St Lauderhill (33311) *(G-7725)*

Alluring Group Inc 800 731-2280
   7451 Riviera Blvd Ste 112 Miramar (33023) *(G-10466)*

Alm Global LLC 305 347-6650
   1 Se 3rd Ave Ste 1750 Miami (33131) *(G-8696)*

Alm Global LLC 954 468-2600
   633 S Andrews Ave Ste 100 Fort Lauderdale (33301) *(G-3647)*

Alm Technologies Inc 904 849-7212
   850816 Us Highway 17 Yulee (32097) *(G-18587)*

Almaco Group Inc 561 558-1600
   7900 Glades Rd Ste 630 Boca Raton (33434) *(G-399)*

Almanac LLC 305 570-4311
   2223 Sw 22nd Ter Miami (33145) *(G-8697)*

Almar Industries Inc 305 385-8284
   6301 Sw 157th Pl Miami (33193) *(G-8698)*

Almi Intl Plastic Inds Inc 954 920-6836
   2227 N Federal Hwy Hollywood (33020) *(G-5527)*

Alnitak Corporation 941 727-1122
   6791 Whitfield Indus Ave Sarasota (34243) *(G-15440)*

Alnoor Import Inc 954 683-9897
   6851 W Sunrise Blvd Plantation (33313) *(G-13825)*

Aloha Screen Printing Inc 850 934-4716
   2635 Gulf Breeze Pkwy Gulf Breeze (32563) *(G-4875)*

Alonso Defense Group LLC 305 989-0927
   5076 Nw 74th Ave Miami (33166) *(G-8699)*

Aloqua Gms Inc 786 673-6838
   400 Sw 107th Ave Fl 5 Miami (33174) *(G-8700)*

Alp Industries Inc 786 845-8617
   1828 Nw 82nd Ave Doral (33126) *(G-3108)*

Alpha Advantage America LLC 305 671-3990
   323 Sunny Isles Blvd Fl 7 Sunny Isles Beach (33160) *(G-16268)*

Alpha Card Compact Media LLC 407 698-3592
   941 W Morse Blvd Ste 100 Winter Park (32789) *(G-18483)*

Alpha Coatings Inc 850 324-9454
   3040 Ashfield Estates Rd Cantonment (32533) *(G-1263)*

Alpha Commercial Printing 561 841-1415
   838 Northlake Blvd North Palm Beach (33408) *(G-11173)*

Alpha General Services Inc 863 382-1544
   1578 Alpha Rd E Sebring (33870) *(G-15913)*

Alpha Hydraulics LLC 561 355-0318
   999 W 17th St Ste 5 Riviera Beach (33404) *(G-14592)*

Alpha Industries Inc 727 443-2673
   701 N Mlk Jr Ave Clearwater (33755) *(G-1488)*

Alpha Kitchen Design LLC 941 351-1659
   4141 S Tamiami Trl Ste 9 Sarasota (34231) *(G-15593)*

Alpha Omega Commercial Limited (PA) 407 925-7913
   5820 Nature View Dr Windermere (34786) *(G-18347)*

Alpha Omega MBL Wldg Svcs Inc 813 629-5777
   2421 Mcintosh Rd Dover (33527) *(G-3426)*

Alpha Press Inc 407 299-2121
   4333 Silver Star Rd # 19 Orlando (32808) *(G-11896)*

Alpha Technology USA Corp 407 571-2060
   5401 Penn Ave Sanford (32773) *(G-15261)*

Alpha To Omega, Ormond Beach *Also called Edgewell Personal Care Company (G-12761)*

Alpha Woodwork Inc 954 347-6251
   2840 Ne 9th Ter Pompano Beach (33064) *(G-13921)*

AlphaGraphics, Orlando *Also called Kindorf Enterprises Inc (G-12287)*

AlphaGraphics, Boca Raton *Also called W H L Business Communications (G-750)*

AlphaGraphics, Lake Mary *Also called Jjaz Enterprises Inc (G-7087)*

AlphaGraphics, Tampa *Also called Reimink Printing Inc (G-17214)*

AlphaGraphics, Jupiter *Also called Agpb LLC (G-6681)*

AlphaGraphics, Fort Lauderdale *Also called South Florida Graphics Corp (G-4057)*

AlphaGraphics Us658 ....813 689-7788
   105 N Falkenburg Rd Ste D Tampa (33619) *(G-16579)*

Alphatec Communications 518 580-0520
   10570 Nw 27th St Ste 102 Doral (33172) *(G-3109)*

Alphatron Industries Inc 954 581-1418
   3411 Sw 49th Way Ste 3 Davie (33314) *(G-2383)*

Alpine Enginereed Products 954 781-3333
   1200 Park Central Blvd S Pompano Beach (33064) *(G-13922)*

Alpine Industries Corporation 941 749-1900
   2908 29th Ave E Ste A Bradenton (34208) *(G-935)*

Alpine Systems Associates Inc 305 262-3263
   11725 Nw 100th Rd Ste 1 Medley (33178) *(G-8194)*

Alpine Tool Inc 727 587-0407
   13070 90th St Largo (33773) *(G-7529)*

Alps Orthotics, Saint Petersburg *Also called Alps South LLC (G-14959)*

Alps South LLC 727 528-8566
   2895 42nd Ave N Saint Petersburg (33714) *(G-14959)*

Alq Business Development, Pembroke Pines *Also called Advanced Living Quarters Inc (G-13369)*

Alse Industries LLC 305 688-8778
   16201 Nw 49th Ave Miami Gardens (33014) *(G-10251)*

Alstom Signaling Operation LLC 781 740-8111
   1990 W Nasa Blvd Melbourne (32904) *(G-8362)*

Alt Thuyan 407 302-3655
   2025 Wp Ball Blvd Sanford (32771) *(G-15262)*

Alta Graphics, Miami *Also called Butler Graphics Inc (G-8865)*

Alta Labs, New Port Richey *Also called Ocean Global Inc (G-10976)*

Alta Pharma LLC 727 942-7645
   1245 N Florida Ave Tarpon Springs (34689) *(G-17457)*

Alta Systems Inc 352 372-2534
   6825 Nw 18th Dr Gainesville (32653) *(G-4648)*

Alta Technologies Inc 609 538-9500
   285 Plantation Cir S Ponte Vedra Beach (32082) *(G-14262)*

Altadis USA, Fort Lauderdale *Also called Itg Cigars Inc (G-3887)*

Altamonte Office Supply Inc 407 339-6911
   1983 Corporate Sq # 101 Longwood (32750) *(G-7866)*

Altanet Corporation 786 228-5758
   7950 Nw 53rd St Ste 337 Miami (33166) *(G-8701)*

Altec Inc 813 372-0058
   1041 S 86th St Tampa (33619) *(G-16580)*

Altec Industries Inc 904 647-5219
   2750 Imeson Rd Jacksonville (32220) *(G-5879)*

Altec Industries Inc 561 686-8550
   3755 Interstate Park Rd W Riviera Beach (33404) *(G-14593)*

Altec Service Center, Tampa *Also called Altec Inc (G-16580)*

Altelix LLC 561 660-9434
   1201 Clint Moore Rd Boca Raton (33487) *(G-400)*

Altered Media Inc 813 397-3892
   100 S Ashley Dr Ste 600 Tampa (33602) *(G-16581)*

Alterna Power Inc 407 287-9148
   390 N Orange Ave Orlando (32801) *(G-11897)*

Alternative Cnstr Tech Inc (PA) 321 421-6601
   2910 Bush Dr Melbourne (32935) *(G-8363)*

Alternative Coatings of SW Fla 239 537-6153
   3411 1st Ave Nw Naples (34120) *(G-10660)*

Alternative Daily 561 628-4711
   400 Clematis St Ste 203 West Palm Beach (33401) *(G-17920)*

Alternative Laboratories LLC (PA) 239 692-9160
   4740 S Cleveland Ave Fort Myers (33907) *(G-4168)*

Alternative Laboratories LLC 239 732-5337
   2190 Kirkwood Ave Naples (34112) *(G-10661)*

ALPHABETIC

Alternative Medical Entps LLC 941 702-9955
6944 N Us Highway 41 Apollo Beach (33572) *(G-90)*
Alternative Sign Group Inc 561 722-9272
8955 120th Ave N West Palm Beach (33412) *(G-17921)*
Alterntive Repr McHning Svcs L 904 861-3040
6555 Trade Center Dr Jacksonville (32254) *(G-5880)*
Alti-2 Inc 386 943-9333
1200 Flight Line Blvd # 5 Deland (32724) *(G-2851)*
Altima Technology Devices, Doral *Also called Rover Aerospace Inc* *(G-3352)*
Altira Inc 305 687-8074
3225 Nw 112th St Miami (33167) *(G-8702)*
Altis Aju Kingwood LLC 305 338-5232
175 Sw 7th St Ste 1106 Miami (33130) *(G-8703)*
Altium Packaging LLC 813 782-2695
4330 20th St Zephyrhills (33542) *(G-18602)*
Altium Packaging LLC 813 248-4300
4961 Distribution Dr Tampa (33605) *(G-16582)*
Altium Packaging LLC 386 246-4000
71 Hargrove Grade Palm Coast (32137) *(G-13069)*
Altmed Enterprises, Apollo Beach *Also called Alternative Medical Entps LLC* *(G-90)*
Alto Recycling LLC 813 962-0140
5701 W Linebaugh Ave Tampa (33624) *(G-16583)*
Alton Manufacturing Inc 305 821-0701
9511 Fontnbleau Blvd # 402 Miami (33172) *(G-8704)*
Alttec Corporation 727 547-1622
4260 114th Ter N Clearwater (33762) *(G-1489)*
Altum Aerospace, Sunrise *Also called Equs Logistics LLC* *(G-16317)*
Altum Aerospace 954 618-6573
13680 Nw 5th St Ste 140 Sunrise (33325) *(G-16291)*
Aludisc LLC 910 299-0911
2127 Nw 53rd St Boca Raton (33496) *(G-401)*
Aluma Craft Products, Miami *Also called Style-View Products Inc* *(G-9962)*
Aluma TEC Aluminun 352 732-7362
4412 Ne 2nd St Ocala (34470) *(G-11319)*
Aluma Tower Company Inc (HQ) 772 567-3423
1639 Old Dixie Hwy Vero Beach (32960) *(G-17734)*
Aluma Tower Company Inc 772 567-3423
926 Old Dixie Hwy Vero Beach (32960) *(G-17735)*
Alumacart Inc 772 675-2158
19100 Sw Warfield Blvd Indiantown (34956) *(G-5811)*
Alumatech Manufacturing Inc 941 748-8880
6063 17th St E Bradenton (34203) *(G-936)*
Alumco, Clearwater *Also called Spectra Metal Sales Inc* *(G-1795)*
Alumflo Inc 727 527-8494
2445 51st Ave N Saint Petersburg (33714) *(G-14960)*
Alumi Tech Inc 407 826-5373
5104 S Orange Ave Orlando (32809) *(G-11898)*
Alumi-Guard, Brooksville *Also called Barrette Outdoor Living Inc* *(G-1139)*
Alumicenter Inc 954 674-2631
3160 Sw 176th Way Miramar (33029) *(G-10467)*
Aluminium Design Products LLC 561 894-8775
1055 Sw 15th Ave Ste 1 Delray Beach (33444) *(G-2929)*
Aluminum Creations 386 451-0113
155 Dawson Brown Rd De Leon Springs (32130) *(G-2622)*
Aluminum Designs LLC 239 289-3388
3573 Entp Ave Ste 75 Naples (34104) *(G-10662)*
Aluminum Express Inc 954 868-2628
2745 W 78th St Hialeah (33016) *(G-5041)*
Aluminum Powder Coating 305 628-4155
16200 Nw 49th Ave Hialeah (33014) *(G-5042)*
Aluminum Powder Coating Lc 305 628-4155
16200 Nw 49th Ave Hialeah (33014) *(G-5043)*
Aluminum Products 904 829-9995
1701 Lakeside Ave Unit 12 Saint Augustine (32084) *(G-14807)*
Aluminum Products Whl Inc 904 268-4895
6963 Bus Pk Blvd N Ste 2 Jacksonville (32256) *(G-5881)*
Aluminum Tank Industries Inc 863 401-9474
36 Spirit Lake Rd Winter Haven (33880) *(G-18415)*
Alumne Manufacturing Inc 352 748-3229
801 Industrial Dr Wildwood (34785) *(G-18308)*
Alutech Corporation 305 593-2080
8548 Nw 64th St Miami (33166) *(G-8705)*
Alvean Americas Inc 305 606-0770
2525 Ponce De Leon Blvd Coral Gables (33134) *(G-2027)*
Alvis Industries Inc 941 377-7800
3300 Linden Dr Sarasota (34232) *(G-15594)*
Alvita Pharma Usa Inc 305 961-1623
8180 Nw 36th St Ste 100 Doral (33166) *(G-3110)*
Always Flowers Inc 305 572-1122
6955 Nw 52nd St Miami (33166) *(G-8706)*
Always Fun Inc 954 258-4377
5660 Sw 99th Ln Cooper City (33328) *(G-2016)*
Aly Fabrication Inc 724 898-2990
31 N Saint Augustine Blvd Saint Augustine (32080) *(G-14808)*
AM Cabinets LLC 321 663-4319
628 Alpine St Altamonte Springs (32701) *(G-30)*
AM Pavers Inc 954 275-1590
19722 Black Olive Ln Boca Raton (33498) *(G-402)*
Am2f Energy Inc 407 505-1127
501 N Orlando Ave 313-256 Winter Park (32789) *(G-18484)*
AMA Waters LLC 786 400-1630
6701 Nw 7th St Ste 175 Miami (33126) *(G-8707)*
Amado Wheel Finishing 786 732-6249
15050 Sw 137th St Miami (33196) *(G-8708)*
Amag Technology Inc 407 549-3882
858 Bright Meadow Dr Lake Mary (32746) *(G-7059)*
Amalie Oil Company (PA) 813 248-1988
1601 Mcclosky Blvd Tampa (33605) *(G-16584)*
Amami United Flavours of World 305 397-8577
224 Espanola Way Miami Beach (33139) *(G-10163)*
Amani, Tampa *Also called Elite Wheel Distributors Inc* *(G-16804)*
Amaranth Lf Sciences Phrm Inc 561 756-8291
1731 Avenida Del Sol Boca Raton (33432) *(G-403)*
Amascott LLC 352 683-4895
4142 Mariner Blvd Spring Hill (34609) *(G-16062)*
Amax Welding & Fabrication 352 544-8484
19496 Fort Dade Ave Brooksville (34601) *(G-1133)*
Amaya Solutions Inc (PA) 813 246-5448
1802 Corporate Center Ln Plant City (33563) *(G-13736)*
Amazon Cleaning & More Inc 239 594-1733
2015 Morning Sun Ln Naples (34119) *(G-10663)*
Amazon Hose & Rubber, Miami *Also called Ghx Industrial LLC* *(G-9212)*
Amazon Hose & Rubber, Tampa *Also called Ghx Industrial LLC* *(G-16879)*
Amazon Hose & Rubber, Orlando *Also called Ghx Industrial LLC* *(G-12195)*
Amazon Metal Fabricators Inc 321 631-7574
600 Cox Rd Ste C Cocoa (32926) *(G-1901)*
Amazon Origins Inc 239 404-1818
5911 Livermore Ln Naples (34119) *(G-10664)*
Amazon Printers, Miami *Also called Amazon Services Inc* *(G-8709)*
Amazon Services Inc 305 663-0585
7186 Sw 47th St Miami (33155) *(G-8709)*
Amazon Sheds and Gazebos Inc (PA) 239 498-5558
17300 Jean St Fort Myers (33967) *(G-4169)*
Amazonia Beverages, Miami *Also called AMA Waters LLC* *(G-8707)*
Amazonia Marine Products, Orlando *Also called Highvac Co LLC* *(G-12218)*
Amb Trucks, Medley *Also called Armor Supply Metals LLC* *(G-8199)*
Amba Ham Company Inc 305 754-0001
6863 Ne 3rd Ave Miami (33138) *(G-8710)*
Ambassador Marketing Group, Delray Beach *Also called Ambassador Printing Company* *(G-2930)*
Ambassador Printing Company 561 330-3668
1025 Nw 17th Ave Ste C Delray Beach (33445) *(G-2930)*
Amber Jewelers Corp 305 373-8089
36 Ne 1st St Ste 1002 Miami (33132) *(G-8711)*
Ambiance Interiors Mfg Corp 305 668-4995
7456 Sw 48th St Miami (33155) *(G-8712)*
Ambo Foods LLC 941 485-4400
727 Commerce Dr Unit C Venice (34292) *(G-17675)*
Ambo Health LLC 866 414-0188
727 Commerce Dr Venice (34292) *(G-17676)*
AMC, Coral Springs *Also called Advantage Medical Elec LLC* *(G-2127)*
AMC Development Group LLC 305 597-8641
10825 Nw 33rd St Doral (33172) *(G-3111)*
AMC Pharma Usa LLC 813 508-0160
201 E Kennedy Blvd Tampa (33602) *(G-16585)*
Amci Technologies Inc 561 596-6288
9772 El Clair Ranch Rd Boynton Beach (33437) *(G-838)*
Amco Polymers, Orlando *Also called Ravago Americas LLC* *(G-12531)*
Amcor Flexibles LLC 954 499-4800
2801 Sw 149th Ave Fl 3 Miramar (33027) *(G-10468)*
Amcor Rigid Packaging Usa LLC 407 859-7560
10260 Ringhaver Dr Orlando (32824) *(G-11899)*
Amcor Rigid Packg Latin Amer, Miramar *Also called Amcor Flexibles LLC* *(G-10468)*
AMD Aero Inc 239 561-8622
14230 Jetport Loop W Fort Myers (33913) *(G-4170)*
AMD Ornamental Inc 239 458-7437
918 Se 9th Ln Unit A Cape Coral (33990) *(G-1300)*
AME, Ocala *Also called Advanced Manufacturing & Engrg* *(G-11314)*
AME International, Brooksville *Also called AME Triton LLC* *(G-1134)*
AME Triton LLC 352 799-1111
2347 Circuit Way Brooksville (34604) *(G-1134)*
Amee Bay LLC 904 553-9873
1701 Mayport Rd Atlantic Beach (32233) *(G-203)*
Amega Sciences Inc 863 937-9792
6550 New Tampa Hwy Ste A Lakeland (33815) *(G-7271)*
Amelia Island Graphics 904 261-0740
2244 S 8th St Fernandina Beach (32034) *(G-3581)*
Amend Surgical Inc 844 281-3169
14000 Nw 126th Ter Alachua (32615) *(G-2)*
Amer-Con Corp 786 293-8004
18001 Old Cutler Rd # 401 Palmetto Bay (33157) *(G-13207)*
Amera Trail Inc 407 892-1100
4840 E I Bronson Memrl Saint Cloud (34771) *(G-14920)*
Ameracat Inc 772 882-9186
3340 N Us Highway 1 Ste 1 Fort Pierce (34946) *(G-4462)*
Amerada Stores, Saint Cloud *Also called Hess Station 09307* *(G-14928)*
Amercn Cabinets Granite Floors 727 303-0678
32140 Us Highway 19 N Palm Harbor (34684) *(G-13097)*

Ameri Food & Fuel Inc 727 584-0120
790 East Bay Dr Largo (33770) *(G-7530)*

Ameri Produ Produ Compa of Pin 813 925-0144
12157 W Linebaugh Ave # 335 Tampa (33626) *(G-16586)*

Ameri-Fax, Hialeah *Also called Amerifax Acquisition Corp (G-5052)*

Ameribuilt Stl Structures LLC 407 340-9401
1016 Moccasin Run Rd Oviedo (32765) *(G-12803)*

America Energy Inc 954 762-7763
20861 Johnson St Ste 116 Pembroke Pines (33029) *(G-13374)*

America Marine & Fuel Inc 239 261-3715
895 10th St S Ste 100 Naples (34102) *(G-10665)*

America Mia, Cooper City *Also called Always Fun Inc (G-2016)*

America Trading Inc 305 256-0101
9355 Sw 144th St Miami (33176) *(G-8713)*

American Accounting Assn 941 921-7747
9009 Town Center Pkwy # 104 Lakewood Ranch (34202) *(G-7475)*

American Acrylic Adhesives LLC 877 422-4583
2020 Wild Acres Rd Unit D Largo (33771) *(G-7531)*

American Adhesives LLC 877 422-4583
12350 Belcher Rd S 1b Largo (33773) *(G-7532)*

American Aggregates LLC 813 352-2124
9040 Kimberly Blvd Ste 61 Boca Raton (33434) *(G-404)*

American All 561 401-0885
16079 70th St N Loxahatchee (33470) *(G-7966)*

American All Scure Gtes Fnce L 407 423-4962
1316 29th St Orlando (32805) *(G-11900)*

American Aluminum ACC Inc 850 277-0869
3291 S Us Highway 19 Perry (32348) *(G-13630)*

American Architectural Mtls GL, Miami Gardens *Also called Alse Industries LLC (G-10251)*

American Archtctral Mtls GL LL 305 688-8778
16201 Nw 49th Ave Hialeah (33014) *(G-5044)*

American Archtctural Mllwk LLC 844 307-9571
248 James St Venice (34285) *(G-17677)*

American Assn Clncal Endcrnlgs, Jacksonville *Also called Aacecorp Inc (G-5853)*

American Athletic Uniforms Inc 850 729-1205
90 Eastview Ave Valparaiso (32580) *(G-17654)*

American Atlas Corp 904 273-6090
2309 Sawgrass Village Dr Ponte Vedra Beach (32082) *(G-14263)*

American Auto / Mar Wirg Inc 954 782-0193
1414 Sw 13th Ct Pompano Beach (33069) *(G-13923)*

American Automtn Systems Inc 305 620-0077
5471 Nw 159th St Miami Lakes (33014) *(G-10281)*

American Awning Company Inc 561 832-7123
537 Pine Ter West Palm Beach (33405) *(G-17922)*

American Bhvioral RES Inst LLC 888 353-1205
1515 N Federal Hwy # 300 Boca Raton (33432) *(G-405)*

American Bidet Company 954 981-1111
10821 Nw 50th St Sunrise (33351) *(G-16292)*

American Blind Corporation 305 262-2009
4232 Sw 75th Ave Miami (33155) *(G-8714)*

American Boom and Barrier Inc 321 784-2110
720 Mullet Rd Ste M Cape Canaveral (32920) *(G-1276)*

American Bottling Company 813 806-2931
5266 Eagle Trail Dr Tampa (33634) *(G-16587)*

American Bottling Company 561 732-7395
4895 Park Ridge Blvd Boynton Beach (33426) *(G-839)*

American Bottling Company 772 461-3383
3700 Avenue F Fort Pierce (34947) *(G-4463)*

American Bottling Company 941 758-7010
2919 62nd Ave E Bradenton (34203) *(G-937)*

American Bottling Company 863 665-6128
3520 Waterfield Rd Lakeland (33803) *(G-7272)*

American Bottling Company 239 489-0838
2236 Hemingway Dr Fort Myers (33912) *(G-4171)*

American Bottling Company 850 763-9069
3333 Highway 77 Panama City (32405) *(G-13226)*

American Bottling Company 904 739-1000
6001 Bowdendale Ave Jacksonville (32216) *(G-5882)*

American Bottling Company 321 433-3622
1313 W King St Cocoa (32922) *(G-1902)*

American Bronze Foundry Inc (PA) 407 328-8090
1650 E Lake Mary Blvd Sanford (32773) *(G-15263)*

American Business Cards Inc 314 739-0800
16475 Seneca Way Naples (34110) *(G-10666)*

American Cab Connection LLC 561 676-5875
16107 74th Ave N West Palm Beach (33418) *(G-17923)*

American Cabinet Mill & Supply, Merritt Island *Also called Trasport John (G-8600)*

American Carbons Inc 850 265-4214
104 New York Ave Lynn Haven (32444) *(G-8024)*

American Changer Corp 954 917-3009
1400 Nw 65th Pl Fort Lauderdale (33309) *(G-3648)*

American Chiropractor 305 434-8865
8619 Nw 68th St Ste C0138 Miami (33166) *(G-8715)*

American City Bus Journals Inc 813 873-8225
4890 W Kennedy Blvd # 85 Tampa (33609) *(G-16588)*

American Classifieds 850 747-1155
1522 Chestnut Ave Panama City (32405) *(G-13227)*

American Cmmerce Solutions Inc (PA) 863 533-0326
1400 Chamber Dr Bartow (33830) *(G-298)*

American Cnstr Entps Inc 941 629-2070
1232 Market Cir Unit 2b Port Charlotte (33953) *(G-14285)*

American Coatings Corporation 954 970-7820
1457 Banks Rd Margate (33063) *(G-8120)*

American Commodity Exch Corp (HQ) 904 687-0588
7825 Baymeadows Way No Jacksonville (32256) *(G-5883)*

American Composites Engrg 352 528-5007
20751 Ne Highway 27 Williston (32696) *(G-18329)*

American Computer & Tech Corp 786 738-3220
1775 Washington Ave 3f Miami Beach (33139) *(G-10164)*

American Concrete Inds Inc 772 464-1187
350 N Rock Rd Fort Pierce (34945) *(G-4464)*

American Container Conc 631 737-6300
5274 Bowline Ct Oxford (34484) *(G-12853)*

American Diamond Blades Corp 561 571-2166
433 Plaza Real Ste 275 Boca Raton (33432) *(G-406)*

American Diamond Distributors 954 485-7808
3600 W Coml Blvd Ste 101 Fort Lauderdale (33309) *(G-3649)*

American Diesel and Gas Inc 561 447-8500
1911 Nw 40th Ct Deerfield Beach (33064) *(G-2667)*

American Elastic & Tape Inc 305 888-0303
1675 E 11th Ave Hialeah (33010) *(G-5045)*

American Engineering Svcs Inc (PA) 813 621-3932
1802 Corporate Center Ln Plant City (33563) *(G-13737)*

American Enrgy Innovations LLC 772 221-9100
6800 Sw Jack James Dr Stuart (34997) *(G-16114)*

American Epoxy Coatings LLC 954 850-1169
1340 Stirling Rd Ste 1a Dania Beach (33004) *(G-2348)*

American Fence Shop LLC 305 681-3511
4790 E 11th Ave Hialeah (33013) *(G-5046)*

American Fibertek Inc 732 302-0660
745 43rd St S Saint Petersburg (33711) *(G-14961)*

American Fine Woodwork LLC 954 261-9793
35 Seville Cir Davie (33324) *(G-2384)*

American Foods Intl LLC 877 894-7675
2875 Ne 191st St Ph 1 Aventura (33180) *(G-251)*

American Force Wheels Inc 786 345-6301
2310 W 76th St Hialeah (33016) *(G-5047)*

American Frame Furniture Inc 305 548-3018
1857 Nw 21st Ter Miami (33142) *(G-8716)*

American Generator Svcs LLC 954 965-1210
14820 Sw 21st St Davie (33326) *(G-2385)*

American Girl Brands LLC 407 852-9771
8001 S Orange Blossom Trl # 1460 Orlando (32809) *(G-11901)*

American Heritage Press, Winter Park *Also called T Beattie Enterprises (G-18542)*

American Household Inc (HQ) 561 912-4100
2381 Nw Executive Ctr Dr Boca Raton (33431) *(G-407)*

American Hygenic Laboratories 305 891-9518
1800 Ne 114th St Ste J Miami (33181) *(G-8717)*

American Impact Media Corp 954 457-9003
413 Se 1st Ave Hallandale Beach (33009) *(G-4935)*

American Incinerators Corp 321 282-7357
2814 Silver Star Rd 201d Orlando (32808) *(G-11902)*

American Industrial Group Inc 703 757-7683
3363 Ne 163rd St Ste 611 North Miami Beach (33160) *(G-11130)*

American Injectables Inc 813 435-6014
15261 Telcom Dr Brooksville (34604) *(G-1135)*

American International Mtr Svc 727 573-9501
5150 Ulmerton Rd Ste 5 Clearwater (33760) *(G-1490)*

American Lab Test & Engrg, Coral Gables *Also called Ecosan LLC (G-2050)*

American Label Group Inc 386 274-5234
705 Fentress Blvd Daytona Beach (32114) *(G-2509)*

American Led Display Solutions 561 227-8048
8060 Nw 71st St Miami (33166) *(G-8718)*

American Led Technology, Naples *Also called Tesco of Swfl Inc (G-10923)*

American Led Technology Inc 850 863-8777
1210 Wildwood Lakes Blvd # 202 Naples (34104) *(G-10667)*

American Lifting Products, Doral *Also called Alp Industries Inc (G-3108)*

American Louvered Products Co. 813 884-1441
4910 W Knollwood St Tampa (33634) *(G-16589)*

American Lw & Promo Prods LLC 954 946-5252
100 Sw 5th St Pompano Beach (33060) *(G-13924)*

American Made Awnings, Hollywood *Also called Awnings of Hollywood Inc (G-5535)*

American Maglev Tech Fla Inc 404 386-4036
8030 Frst Cast Hwy Apt 10 Amelia Island (32034) *(G-85)*

American Marine Coverings Inc 305 889-5355
1065 Se 9th Ct Hialeah (33010) *(G-5048)*

American Marine Mfg Inc 305 497-7723
2637 W 76th St Hialeah (33016) *(G-5049)*

American MBL Restoration Inc 561 502-0764
43 Barbados Dr Palm Springs (33461) *(G-13143)*

American Mentality Inc 407 599-7255
210 E Palmetto Ave Longwood (32750) *(G-7867)*

American Metal Fab of Ctrl Fl 813 653-2788
1018 W Brandon Blvd 11b Brandon (33511) *(G-1082)*

American Metal Fabrication LLC 954 736-9819
5476 Nw 59th Pl Tamarac (33319) *(G-16524)*

American Metal Fabricators Inc 561 790-5799
1501 53rd St Mangonia Park (33407) *(G-8087)*

American Metal Gate Corp 516 659-7952
  9901 E Bay Harbor Dr Bay Harbor Islands (33154) *(G-331)*

American Metal Processors Inc 386 754-9367
  186 Se Newell Dr Lake City (32025) *(G-7011)*

American Metal Products Inc 407 293-0090
  4026 Silver Star Rd Ste A Orlando (32808) *(G-11903)*

American Mfg & Mch Inc 352 728-2222
  27137 County Road 33 Okahumpka (34762) *(G-11594)*

American Mold Detectives Inc 954 729-0640
  8201 Nw 100th Ter Tamarac (33321) *(G-16525)*

American Mold Removal Inc 561 575-7757
  17462 37th Pl N Loxahatchee (33470) *(G-7967)*

American Molding & Plas LLC 561 734-4194
  3302 Karen Dr Delray Beach (33483) *(G-2931)*

American Molding and Plas LLC 561 676-1987
  870 W Industrial Ave # 8 Boynton Beach (33426) *(G-840)*

American Moulding Corporation 321 676-8929
  710 Atlantis Rd Melbourne (32904) *(G-8364)*

American Name Plate, Pompano Beach Also called American Trophy Co *(G-13928)*

American Natural Pdts Lab Inc 305 261-5152
  7350 Nw 7th St Ste 101 Miami (33126) *(G-8719)*

American Optimal Decisions Inc 352 278-2034
  4014 Sw 98th Ter Gainesville (32608) *(G-4649)*

American Panel Corporation 352 245-7055
  5800 Se 78th St Ocala (34472) *(G-11320)*

American Pavers Consultants 954 418-0000
  1251 Ne 48th St Pompano Beach (33064) *(G-13925)*

American Pavers Manufacturing, Pompano Beach Also called American Pavers
Consultants *(G-13925)*

American Pavers Manufacturing (PA) 954 418-0000
  1251 Ne 48th St Pompano Beach (33064) *(G-13926)*

American Payment Systems 407 856-8524
  11500 S Ornge Blossom Trl Orlando (32837) *(G-11904)*

American Payment Systems 954 968-6920
  1655 S State Road 7 North Lauderdale (33068) *(G-11075)*

American Pharmaceutical Svcs 407 704-5937
  6001 Silver Star Rd Ste 2 Orlando (32808) *(G-11905)*

American Photonics, Sarasota Also called Laser Lens Tek Inc *(G-15510)*

American Pipes and Tubes Co, Sunny Isles Beach Also called Inox LLC *(G-16277)*

American Plastic Sup & Mfg Inc (PA) 727 573-0636
  11601 56th Ct N Clearwater (33760) *(G-1491)*

American Polylactide Inds 352 653-5963
  3666 Ne 25th St Ocala (34470) *(G-11321)*

American Polymer Company 786 877-4690
  2201 Nw 16th St Pompano Beach (33069) *(G-13927)*

American Powder Coating, Fort Lauderdale Also called American Prtective Coating
Inc *(G-3650)*

American Pressure Systems Inc 321 914-0827
  7608 Emerald Dr West Melbourne (32904) *(G-17892)*

American Prjcts Crprts Stl Bld, Jacksonville Also called American Projects Brokers
Inc *(G-5884)*

American Products Inc 813 925-0144
  13909 Lynmar Blvd Tampa (33626) *(G-16590)*

American Professional Ir Work 305 556-9522
  8320 Nw 103rd St Hialeah Gardens (33016) *(G-5430)*

American Projects Brokers Inc 904 343-5424
  5610 Fort Caroline Rd # 7 Jacksonville (32277) *(G-5884)*

American Prtective Coating Inc 954 561-0999
  6795 Nw 17th Ave Fort Lauderdale (33309) *(G-3650)*

American Quality Embroidery 239 772-8687
  1830 Del Prado Blvd S # 1 Cape Coral (33990) *(G-1301)*

American Quality Mfg Inc 321 636-3434
  310 Shearer Blvd Cocoa (32922) *(G-1903)*

American Recycling Systems Inc 772 225-8072
  1125 Ne Savannah Oaks Way Jensen Beach (34957) *(G-6651)*

American Refrigerants, Bradenton Also called Fireside Holdings Inc *(G-979)*

American Respiratory Solutions (PA) 386 698-4446
  1125 N Summit St Ste C Crescent City (32112) *(G-2234)*

American Roofing Services LLC 305 250-7115
  95 Merrick Way Ste 514 Coral Gables (33134) *(G-2028)*

American S-Shore Plting Sttchi 305 978-9934
  1085 E 31st St Hialeah (33013) *(G-5050)*

American Sani Partition Corp 407 656-0611
  300 Enterprise St Ocoee (34761) *(G-11520)*

American Screen Print Inc 904 443-0071
  4122 Spring Park Rd Jacksonville (32207) *(G-5885)*

American Shipper, Jacksonville Also called Howard Publications Inc *(G-6185)*

American Sign, Sebastian Also called Expert Promotions LLC *(G-15891)*

American Sign Letters 772 643-4012
  8140 Evernia St Unit 1 Sebastian (32976) *(G-15886)*

American Silica Holdings LLC 352 796-8855
  24060 Deer Run Rd Brooksville (34601) *(G-1136)*

American Specialty Sales Corp 305 947-9700
  14286 Biscayne Blvd North Miami (33181) *(G-11089)*

American Speedy Printing, Pompano Beach Also called Lmb Consultants Inc *(G-14080)*

American Sperior Compounds Inc 716 873-1209
  17409 Chelsea Downs Cir Lithia (33547) *(G-7830)*

American Stainless & Alum Pdts 423 472-4832
  315 Industrial Way Kissimmee (34746) *(G-6894)*

American Stainless Mfrs (PA) 786 275-4458
  8390 Nw 68th St Miami (33166) *(G-8720)*

American Stairs, Stuart Also called Cedrus Inc *(G-16126)*

American Standards Inc 904 683-2189
  4744 Kingsbury St Jacksonville (32205) *(G-5886)*

American Stock LLC 904 641-2055
  3225 Anniston Rd Jacksonville (32246) *(G-5887)*

American Surgical Mask Co, Tampa Also called American Surgical Mask LLC *(G-16591)*

American Surgical Mask LLC 813 606-4510
  5508 N 50th St Ste 1000 Tampa (33610) *(G-16591)*

American Tchncal Crmics Fla In, Jacksonville Also called Kyocera AVX Cmpnnts
Jcksnvlle *(G-6252)*

American Tech Netwrk Corp (PA) 800 910-2862
  2400 Nw 95th Ave Doral (33172) *(G-3112)*

American Technical Furn LLC 866 239-4204
  831 Carswell Ave Holly Hill (32117) *(G-5509)*

American Technical Molding, Clearwater Also called American Tool & Mold Inc *(G-1493)*

American Technical Molding Inc 727 447-7377
  1700 Sunshine Dr Clearwater (33765) *(G-1492)*

American Technologies Network, Doral Also called American Tech Netwrk Corp *(G-3112)*

American Technology Pdts Inc 407 960-1722
  211 Northstar Ct Sanford (32771) *(G-15264)*

American Thrmplastic Extrusion 305 769-9566
  4851 Nw 128th Street Rd Opa Locka (33054) *(G-11716)*

American Tool & Mold Inc 727 447-7377
  1700 Sunshine Dr Clearwater (33765) *(G-1493)*

American Torch Tip Company (PA) 941 753-7557
  6212 29th St E Bradenton (34203) *(G-938)*

American Traction Systems Inc 239 768-0757
  10030 Amberwood Rd Ste 1 Fort Myers (33913) *(G-4172)*

American Trffic Sfety Mtls Inc 904 284-0284
  1272 Harbor Rd Green Cove Springs (32043) *(G-4814)*

American Trophy Co 954 782-2250
  831 W Mcnab Rd Pompano Beach (33060) *(G-13928)*

American Truss 352 493-9700
  6760 Nw 138th Pl Chiefland (32626) *(G-1443)*

American Truss Chiefland LL 352 493-9700
  6750 Nw 138th Pl Chiefland (32626) *(G-1444)*

American Vet Sciences LLC 727 471-0850
  6911 Bryan Dairy Rd Largo (33777) *(G-7533)*

American Vinyl Company (PA) 305 687-1863
  600 W 83rd St Hialeah (33014) *(G-5051)*

American Vinyl Company 813 663-0157
  6715 N 53rd St Tampa (33610) *(G-16592)*

American Vly Avnics Clbrtion L 904 644-8630
  137 Industrial Loop W Orange Park (32073) *(G-11814)*

American Vulkan Corporation (HQ) 863 324-2424
  2525 Dundee Rd Winter Haven (33884) *(G-18416)*

American Water Chemicals, Plant City Also called Amaya Solutions Inc *(G-13736)*

American Water Chemicals Inc 813 246-5448
  1802 Corporate Center Ln Plant City (33563) *(G-13738)*

American Welding Society Inc (PA) 305 443-9353
  8669 Nw 36th St Ste 130 Doral (33166) *(G-3113)*

American Windows Shutters Inc 239 278-3066
  11600 Adelmo Ln Fort Myers (33966) *(G-4173)*

American Wire Group LLC (PA) 954 455-3050
  2980 Ne 207th St Ste 901 Aventura (33180) *(G-252)*

American Wldg & Installation 786 391-4800
  4851 Nw 36th Ave Miami (33142) *(G-8721)*

American Woodwork Specialty Co 937 263-1053
  1411 Driftwood Point Rd Santa Rosa Beach (32459) *(G-15421)*

American-Marsh Pumps LLC 863 646-5689
  2805 Badger Rd Lakeland (33811) *(G-7273)*

Americanlite, Hollywood Also called DK International Group Corp *(G-5568)*

Americans Gbc Corp 407 371-9584
  2484 San Tecla St # 205 Orlando (32835) *(G-11906)*

Americas Atm LLC 954 414-0341
  8751 W Broward Blvd # 30 Plantation (33324) *(G-13826)*

Americast Precast Generator 772 971-1958
  3204 Ohio Ave Fort Pierce (34947) *(G-4465)*

Americoat Corporation 863 667-1035
  2935 Barneys Pumps Pl Lakeland (33812) *(G-7274)*

Americraft Cookware LLC 352 483-7600
  152 E 3rd Ave Mount Dora (32757) *(G-10596)*

Americraft Enterprises Inc 386 756-1100
  2800 S Nova Rd Ste H3 Daytona Beach (32119) *(G-2510)*

Americut of Florida Inc 800 692-2187
  1941 Custom Dr Fort Myers (33907) *(G-4174)*

Amerifax Acquisition Corp 305 828-1701
  7290 W 18th Ln Hialeah (33014) *(G-5052)*

Amerifood Corp 305 305-5951
  1717 Nw 22nd St 6 Miami (33142) *(G-8722)*

Ameriglass Engineering Inc 305 558-6227
  2246 W 79th St Hialeah (33016) *(G-5053)*

Amerikan, Sebring Also called The Hc Companies Inc *(G-15947)*

Amerikan LLC 863 314-9417
  2006 Fortune Blvd Sebring (33870) *(G-15914)*

2022 Harris Florida
Manufacturers Directory

(G-0000) Company's Geographic Section entry number

Amerikooler LLC..305 884-8384
575 E 10th Ave Hialeah (33010) *(G-5054)*

Ameriseam, Tampa *Also called J W L Trading Company Inc (G-16960)*

Amerisigns...407 492-5644
1718 Acme St Orlando (32805) *(G-11907)*

Ameritech Die & Mold & South, Ormond Beach *Also called Ameritech Die & Mold South Inc (G-12742)*

Ameritech Die & Mold South Inc........................386 677-1770
1 E Tower Cir Ormond Beach (32174) *(G-12742)*

Ameritech Energy Corporation............................610 730-1733
1115 Enterprise Ct Ste L Holly Hill (32117) *(G-5510)*

Ameritech Powder Coating Inc............................239 274-8000
502 South Rd Unit D Fort Myers (33907) *(G-4175)*

Ameritek U.S.A., Coral Gables *Also called Chuxco Inc (G-2039)*

Amerx Health Care Corp....................................727 443-0530
164 Douglas Rd E Oldsmar (34677) *(G-11625)*

Ames Companies Inc..352 401-6370
13485 Veterans Way # 200 Orlando (32827) *(G-11908)*

Ametek Inc..800 527-9999
8600 Somerset Dr Largo (33773) *(G-7534)*

Ametek Power Instrument Inc.............................954 344-9822
4050 Nw 121st Ave Coral Springs (33065) *(G-2131)*

Ametrine LLC..786 300-7946
127 Barrington Dr Brandon (33511) *(G-1083)*

Amets Woodworks Corp......................................786 537-5982
1312 Nw 29th Ter Miami (33142) *(G-8723)*

AMF Building Products, Mangonia Park *Also called American Metal Fabricators Inc (G-8087)*

AMG Printing Solutions Corp..............................954 235-8007
2454 Nw 78th St Miami (33147) *(G-8724)*

Amglo Halogen, Largo *Also called Vision Engineering Labs (G-7704)*

Amglo Kemlite Laboratories, Largo *Also called Vision Engineering Labs (G-7705)*

AMI, Boca Raton *Also called Worldwide Media Svcs Group Inc (G-757)*

AMI Celebrity Publications LLC..........................561 997-7733
1000 American Media Way Boca Raton (33464) *(G-408)*

AMI Digital Inc..561 997-7733
1000 American Media Way Boca Raton (33464) *(G-409)*

AMI Graphics Inc..352 629-4455
1302 Sw 42nd Ave Ocala (34474) *(G-11322)*

Amick Cstm Woodcraft & Design........................407 324-8525
1450 Kastner Pl Ste 112 Sanford (32771) *(G-15265)*

Amigo Pallets Inc...305 631-2452
7650 Nw 69th Ave Medley (33166) *(G-8195)*

Amigo Pallets Inc...305 302-9751
10251 Sw 109th St Miami (33176) *(G-8725)*

Amino Cell Inc..352 291-0200
5640 Sw 6th Pl Ste 500 Ocala (34474) *(G-11323)*

Aminsa Corp...954 865-1289
612 Bald Cypress Rd Weston (33327) *(G-18222)*

Amj DOT LLC..646 249-0273
22304 Calibre Ct Apt 1304 Boca Raton (33433) *(G-410)*

Amk Plastics LLC..305 470-9088
7120 Nw 51st St Miami (33166) *(G-8726)*

Aml Extreme Powdercoating................................904 794-4313
7750 Us Highway 1 S Saint Augustine (32086) *(G-14809)*

Ammann America Inc..954 907-5776
1125 Sw 101st Rd Davie (33324) *(G-2386)*

Ammcon Corp...904 863-3196
1503 County Road 315 # 204 Green Cove Springs (32043) *(G-4815)*

Ammo-Up, Jacksonville *Also called Bag-A-Nut LLC (G-5919)*

Amorim Cork Composites Inc.............................800 558-3206
6708 Harney Rd Tampa (33610) *(G-16593)*

AMP Aero Services LLC.....................................833 267-2376
12901 Sw 122nd Ave # 105 Miami (33186) *(G-8727)*

Ampco, Lake City *Also called American Metal Processors Inc (G-7011)*

Amper Usa LLC..305 717-3101
4447 Nw 98th Ave Doral (33178) *(G-3114)*

Ampersand Graphics Inc....................................772 283-1359
553 Se Monterey Rd Stuart (34994) *(G-16115)*

Ampersand Shirt Shack.......................................772 600-8743
553 Se Monterey Rd Stuart (34994) *(G-16116)*

Amphenol Custom Cable Inc (HQ).....................813 623-2232
3221 Cherry Palm Dr Tampa (33619) *(G-16594)*

Amphenol Custom Cable Inc..............................407 393-3886
7461 Currency Dr Orlando (32809) *(G-11909)*

Amps, Deland *Also called Advanced Mfg & Pwr Systems Inc (G-2848)*

Amrad, Palm Coast *Also called Vladmir Ltd (G-13092)*

Amrav Inc...407 831-1550
1026 Miller Dr Altamonte Springs (32701) *(G-31)*

Amrob Inc...813 238-6041
4719 N Thatcher Ave Tampa (33614) *(G-16595)*

AMS, Merritt Island *Also called Tua Systems Inc (G-8602)*

AMS Fabrications Inc..813 420-0784
2816 Nw 30th Ave Oakland Park (33311) *(G-11236)*

AMS Global Suppliers Group LLC......................305 714-9441
200 S Biscayne Blvd Miami (33131) *(G-8728)*

AMS Uniforms, Miami *Also called Affordable Med Scrubs LLC (G-8665)*

Amswfl Inc..239 334-7433
4700 Laredo Ave Fort Myers (33905) *(G-4176)*

Amtec Less Lethal Systems Inc..........................850 223-4066
4700 Providence Rd Perry (32347) *(G-13631)*

Amtec Sales Inc...800 994-3318
1594 Nw 159th St Miami (33169) *(G-8729)*

Amteco Machine & Manufacturing.......................727 573-0993
4652 107th Cir N Clearwater (33762) *(G-1494)*

Amtel Security Systems Inc................................305 591-8200
1691 Nw 107th Ave Doral (33172) *(G-3115)*

Amtex-Nms Holdings Inc (PA)............................352 728-2930
2500 Industrial St Leesburg (34748) *(G-7758)*

Amware Logistics Services Inc...........................970 337-7000
2203 Sw 3rd St Pompano Beach (33069) *(G-13929)*

Amxs Corp..904 568-1416
524 Patricia Ln Jacksonville Beach (32250) *(G-6628)*

Amy Cabinetry..561 842-8091
6667 42nd Ter N Riviera Beach (33407) *(G-14594)*

Anacom Electronica, Winter Garden *Also called Edashop Inc (G-18384)*

Analili Analili, Miami *Also called Olian Inc (G-9643)*

Analog Modules Inc..407 339-4355
126 Baywood Ave Longwood (32750) *(G-7868)*

Analytical Research Systems..............................352 466-0051
12109 Highway 441 S Micanopy (32667) *(G-10395)*

Anarchy Offroad LLC (PA)..................................239 919-6681
2430 Vanderbilt Beach Rd Naples (34109) *(G-10668)*

Anavini, Miami *Also called La Providencia Express Co (G-9412)*

ANC Shutters LLC..561 966-8336
3386 Pony Run Lake Worth (33449) *(G-7184)*

Anchor & Docking Inc..239 770-2030
830 Ne 24th Ln Unit G Cape Coral (33909) *(G-1302)*

Anchor Aluminum Products South.......................305 293-7965
2807 Staples Ave Key West (33040) *(G-6853)*

Anchor Coatings Leesburg Inc...........................352 728-0777
2280 Talley Rd Leesburg (34748) *(G-7759)*

Anchor Glass Container Corp..............................904 786-1010
2121 Huron St Jacksonville (32254) *(G-5888)*

Anchor Glass Container Corp (PA)......................813 884-0000
3001 N Rocky Point Dr E # 300 Tampa (33607) *(G-16596)*

Anchor Machine & Fabricating............................813 247-3099
3905 E 7th Ave Tampa (33605) *(G-16597)*

Anchor Screen Printing LLC...............................850 243-4200
808 South Dr Fort Walton Beach (32547) *(G-4559)*

Ancient Mosaic Studios LLC..............................772 460-3145
4106 Mariah Cir Fort Pierce (34947) *(G-4466)*

Anco Precision Inc...954 429-3703
3191 Sw 11th St Ste 200 Deerfield Beach (33442) *(G-2668)*

Ancorp, Williston *Also called A & N Corporation (G-18327)*

and Services..850 805-6455
410 Racetrack Rd Ne Fort Walton Beach (32547) *(G-4560)*

and-Dell Corporation..954 523-6478
245 Sw 33rd St Fort Lauderdale (33315) *(G-3651)*

Andersen Custom Cabinetry LLC.......................407 702-4891
3071 N Orange Blossom Trl Orlando (32804) *(G-11910)*

Anderson Advanta Asphalt, Live Oak *Also called Advanta Asphalt Inc (G-7841)*

Anderson Columbia Co Inc.................................352 463-6342
8191 Nw 160th St Chiefland (32626) *(G-1445)*

Anderson Materials, Chiefland *Also called Anderson Columbia Co Inc (G-1445)*

Anderson Mfg & Upholstery Inc..........................321 267-7028
1427 Chaffee Dr Ste 4 Titusville (32780) *(G-17571)*

Anderson Mining Corporation (HQ).....................352 542-7942
624 Ne Highway 349 Old Town (32680) *(G-11621)*

Anderson Printing Services Inc..........................727 545-9000
7245 Bryan Dairy Rd Seminole (33777) *(G-15969)*

Anderson Truss LLC...386 752-3103
1730 Nw Oakland Ave Lake City (32055) *(G-7012)*

Andersons Can Line Fbrction Eq........................407 889-4665
2208 Stillwater Ave Apopka (32703) *(G-102)*

Andirali Corporation...305 542-5374
1221 Brickell Ave Ste 900 Miami (33131) *(G-8730)*

Andrade Professional Pavers..............................904 504-3257
10275 Old St Augustne 9 Jacksonville (32257) *(G-5889)*

Andre T Jean..305 647-8744
2306 Ali Baba Ave Opa Locka (33054) *(G-11717)*

Andrew Martin Swift..321 409-0509
620 Atlantis Rd Ste A Melbourne (32904) *(G-8365)*

Andrew Mj Inc..561 575-6032
10152 Indiantown Rd Jupiter (33478) *(G-6684)*

Andrew Pratt Stucco & Plst Inc..........................407 501-2609
8048 Bridgestone Dr Orlando (32835) *(G-11911)*

Andrews 1st Choice Trckg LLC...........................205 703-5717
4532 Lane Ave S Jacksonville (32210) *(G-5890)*

Andrews Cabinets Inc...850 994-0836
4025 Bell Ln Milton (32571) *(G-10417)*

Andrews Filter and Supply Corp (PA)..................407 423-3310
2309 Coolidge Ave Orlando (32804) *(G-11912)*

Andrews Sales Agency Manufactu.......................813 254-4959
3104 W San Rafael St Tampa (33629) *(G-16598)*

Andrews Warehouse Partnership.........................954 524-3330
1512 E Broward Blvd Fort Lauderdale (33301) *(G-3652)*

Andriali, Miami *Also called Andirali Corporation (G-8730)*

Andritz Iggesund Tools Inc (HQ)....813 855-6902
220 Scarlet Blvd Oldsmar (34677) ***(G-11626)***
Andros Boatworks Inc....941 351-9702
202 Industrial Blvd Sarasota (34234) ***(G-15595)***
Andrx Corporation....954 217-4500
2915 Weston Rd Weston (33331) ***(G-18223)***
Andrx Corporation....954 585-1770
13900 Nw 2nd St Ste 100 Sunrise (33325) ***(G-16293)***
Andrx Corporation (HQ)....954 585-1400
4955 Orange Dr Davie (33314) ***(G-2387)***
Andys Welding Services Inc....239 478-4907
1321 Carson Rd Immokalee (34142) ***(G-5795)***
Anesthesia Service & Equipment, Jacksonville *Also called Eagle-Eye Anesthesia Inc* ***(G-6056)***
Anew Inc....386 668-7785
32 Cunningham Rd Debary (32713) ***(G-2630)***
Anew International Corporation....386 668-7785
32 Cunningham Rd Debary (32713) ***(G-2631)***
Angle Truss Co Inc....352 343-7477
29652 State Road 19 Tavares (32778) ***(G-17503)***
Anglo Silver Liner Co....508 943-1440
7019 Indus Valley Cir Parrish (34219) ***(G-13356)***
Animal Air Service Inc....305 218-1759
1952 Nw 93rd Ave Doral (33172) ***(G-3116)***
Animal Business Concepts LLC....727 641-6176
2135 13th Ave N Saint Petersburg (33713) ***(G-14962)***
Anjon Inc....904 730-9373
4801 Dawin Rd Jacksonville (32207) ***(G-5891)***
Anko Products Inc....941 748-2307
6012 33rd St E Bradenton (34203) ***(G-939)***
Anmapec Corporation....786 897-5389
5210 Nw 5th St Miami (33126) ***(G-8731)***
Ann More, Miami *Also called Jay More Corporation* ***(G-9356)***
Anna Andres....239 335-0233
2442 Dr M L King Blvd Martin Fort Myers (33901) ***(G-4177)***
Anna Florer....352 424-2210
20426 Peachtree Ln Dade City (33523) ***(G-2313)***
Annat Inc....239 262-4639
6203 Janes Ln Ste D Naples (34109) ***(G-10669)***
Annette M Wellington-Hall Inc....954 437-9880
5830 Sheridan St Hollywood (33021) ***(G-5528)***
Annona Biosciences Inc....888 204-4980
2401 Pga Blvd Ste 196 Palm Beach Gardens (33410) ***(G-12947)***
Antebellum Manufacturing LLC....352 877-3888
1120 N Magnolia Ave Ocala (34475) ***(G-11324)***
Antennas For Cmmnctons Ocala F....352 687-4121
2499 Sw 60th Ave Ocala (34474) ***(G-11325)***
Antennas.us, Margate *Also called Myers Engineering Intl Inc* ***(G-8144)***
Anthem South LLC....973 779-1982
9710 Nw 110th Ave Unit 10 Medley (33178) ***(G-8196)***
Anthony Spagna Svc & Maint Inc....352 796-2109
3335 Mustang Dr Brooksville (34604) ***(G-1137)***
Anthony Wright Welding....850 544-1831
311 Ross Rd Tallahassee (32305) ***(G-16411)***
Anti-Ging Asthtic Lser Ctr Inc....786 539-4901
4401 Collins Ave Miami Beach (33140) ***(G-10165)***
Antifaz Woodwork Inc....786 306-7740
13365 Sw 135th Ave Miami (33186) ***(G-8732)***
Antique & Modern Cabinets Inc....904 393-9055
2384 Vans Ave Jacksonville (32207) ***(G-5892)***
Antique Automobile Radio Inc....727 785-8733
700 Tampa Rd Palm Harbor (34683) ***(G-13098)***
Antique Crystal Glass & Prcln....352 220-2666
126 Ne 2nd St Crystal River (34429) ***(G-2266)***
Antiquo Stone By F T F, Fellsmere *Also called F T F Construction Company* ***(G-3576)***
Anton Paar Quantatec Inc....561 731-4999
1900 Corporate Dr Boynton Beach (33426) ***(G-841)***
Antonyo Denard Llc....904 290-1579
1408 San Marco Blvd Jacksonville (32207) ***(G-5893)***
Antwon Publishing Company Inc....863 508-0825
806 Ware Ave Ne Winter Haven (33881) ***(G-18417)***
ANue Ligne Inc....305 638-7979
3300 Nw 41st St Miami (33142) ***(G-8733)***
Anuva Manufacturing Svcs Inc....321 821-4900
7801 Ellis Rd Ste 101 Melbourne (32904) ***(G-8366)***
Anuvia Plant City LLC....407 719-7798
660 E County Line Rd Plant City (33565) ***(G-13739)***
Anuvia Plant Ntrnts Hldngs LLC....352 720-7070
6751 W Jones Ave Zellwood (32798) ***(G-18595)***
Anuvia Plant Nutrients Corp....689 407-3430
113 S Boyd St Winter Garden (34787) ***(G-18373)***
Anvil Iron Works Inc....727 375-2884
11607 Perpetual Dr Odessa (33556) ***(G-11536)***
Anvil Paints & Coatings Inc....727 535-1411
1255 Starkey Rd Ste A Largo (33771) ***(G-7535)***
Anvil Paints and Coating, Largo *Also called Anvil Paints & Coatings Inc* ***(G-7535)***
Anything Display....239 433-9738
6225 Presidential Ct Fort Myers (33919) ***(G-4178)***
Anytime Waste, Vero Beach *Also called B & F Waste Solutions Llc* ***(G-17739)***
Anywhere Gps LLC....949 468-6842
43 Sierras Loop Saint Augustine (32086) ***(G-14810)***
Anzio Ironworks Corp....727 895-2019
14605 49th St N Ste 8 Clearwater (33762) ***(G-1495)***
Ao Precision Manufacturing LLC....386 274-5882
1870 Mason Ave Daytona Beach (32117) ***(G-2511)***
AOC Technologies Inc....727 577-9749
10560 Dr Martin L Kng Jr Saint Petersburg (33716) ***(G-14963)***
Aoclsc Inc (HQ)....813 248-1988
1601 Mcclosky Blvd Tampa (33605) ***(G-16599)***
Aocusa, Tampa *Also called Aoclsc Inc* ***(G-16599)***
Aog Detailing Services Inc....727 742-7321
6798 Crosswinds Dr N B203 Saint Petersburg (33710) ***(G-14964)***
Aonea....561 989-0067
5400 N Dixie Hwy Boca Raton (33487) ***(G-411)***
AP Buck Inc....407 851-8602
7101 Presidents Dr # 110 Orlando (32809) ***(G-11913)***
AP Lifesciences LLC....954 300-7469
12085 Research Dr Ste 155 Alachua (32615) ***(G-3)***
AP Richter Holding Co LLC....239 732-9440
1617 Gulfstar Dr S Naples (34112) ***(G-10670)***
APA Wireless Technologies Inc....954 563-8833
4066 Ne 5th Ave Oakland Park (33334) ***(G-11237)***
Apache Sheet Metal....954 214-4468
631 Stanton Ln Weston (33326) ***(G-18224)***
Apakus Inc....305 403-2603
75 Valencia Ave Ste 701 Coral Gables (33134) ***(G-2029)***
Apalachee Pole Company Inc (PA)....850 263-4457
1820 Highway 2 Graceville (32440) ***(G-4807)***
Apalachee Pole Company Inc....850 643-2121
18601 Nw County Road 379a Bristol (32321) ***(G-1116)***
Apara Productions, Miami *Also called Armadillo Sounds Inc* ***(G-8748)***
Apartment Guide, Orlando *Also called Consumer Source Inc* ***(G-12044)***
Ape South, Key Largo *Also called Automated Production Eqp Ape* ***(G-6843)***
Apellix, Jacksonville *Also called Working Drones Inc* ***(G-6619)***
Apex Aviation Group LLC....305 789-6695
801 Brickell Ave Ste 900 Miami (33131) ***(G-8734)***
Apex Color, Jacksonville *Also called Arlington Prtg Stationers Inc* ***(G-5901)***
Apex Fabrication Inc....904 259-4666
710 Griffin Ct Macclenny (32063) ***(G-8035)***
Apex Flood Fire Mold Clnup Inc....305 975-1710
1340 Sw 19th Ave Boca Raton (33486) ***(G-412)***
Apex Grinding Inc....386 624-7350
817 Swift St Ste 100 Daytona Beach (32114) ***(G-2512)***
Apex Machine Company (PA)....954 563-0209
3000 Ne 12th Ter Oakland Park (33334) ***(G-11238)***
Apex Metal Fabrication Inc....386 328-2564
4204 Duval Dr Jacksonville Beach (32250) ***(G-6629)***
Apexbuilt, Fort Myers *Also called Playa Perfection Inc* ***(G-4363)***
Apexeon Biomedical LLC....850 878-2150
3075 Hawks Landing Dr Tallahassee (32309) ***(G-16412)***
API, Tampa *Also called American Products Inc* ***(G-16590)***
API Tech North America Inc....929 255-1231
941 W Morse Blvd Ste 100 Winter Park (32789) ***(G-18485)***
Apical Pharmaceutical Corp....786 331-7200
10460 Nw 37th Ter Doral (33178) ***(G-3117)***
Apis Cor Inc....347 404-1481
3060 Venture Ln Ste 101 Melbourne (32934) ***(G-8367)***
Apogee Services Inc....561 441-5354
703 Sw 24th Ave Boynton Beach (33435) ***(G-842)***
Apollo Energy Systems Inc (PA)....954 969-7755
4100 N Powerline Rd D3 Pompano Beach (33073) ***(G-13930)***
Apollo Metro Solutions Inc....239 444-6934
2975 Horseshoe Dr S # 500 Naples (34104) ***(G-10671)***
Apollo Renal Therapeutics LLC....202 413-0963
2811 Ne 14th St Ocala (34470) ***(G-11326)***
Apollo Retail Specialists LLC (HQ)....813 712-2525
4450 E Adamo Dr Ste 501 Tampa (33605) ***(G-16600)***
Apollo Sunguard Systems Inc....941 925-3000
4487 Ashton Rd Sarasota (34233) ***(G-15596)***
Apollo Worldwide Inc....561 585-3865
158 Las Brisas Cir Hypoluxo (33462) ***(G-5794)***
Apopka Chief, The, Apopka *Also called Foliage Enterprises Inc* ***(G-134)***
Apotex Corp (HQ)....954 384-8007
2400 N Commerce Pkwy # 400 Weston (33326) ***(G-18225)***
Apparel Expressions LLC....850 314-0100
209b Lang Rd Fort Walton Beach (32547) ***(G-4561)***
Apparel Imports Inc....800 428-6849
10893 Nw 17th St Unit 126 Miami (33172) ***(G-8735)***
Apparel Machinery Services Inc....772 335-5350
1545 Se S Niemeyer Cir Port Saint Lucie (34952) ***(G-14396)***
Apparel Printers....352 463-8850
13201 Rachael Blvd Alachua (32615) ***(G-4)***
Appel 26 Corp....305 672-8645
4101 Pine Tree Dr Apt 111 Miami Beach (33140) ***(G-10166)***
Apperals Custom Finish Wdwrk....754 264-2296
22446 Sw 66th Ave Boca Raton (33428) ***(G-413)***
Appgate Inc (HQ)....866 524-4782
2 Alhambra Plz Ste Ph-1b Coral Gables (33134) ***(G-2030)***

Appi, Opa Locka *Also called Aero Precision Products Inc (G-11712)*

Appi, Miami Lakes *Also called Assocated Prtg Productions Inc (G-10282)*

Appiskey, Orlando *Also called PNC Solutions Inc (G-12492)*

Apple Machine & Supply Co 772 466-9353
5900 Orange Ave Fort Pierce (34947) *(G-4467)*

Apple Printing & Advg Spc Inc 954 524-0493
5055 Nw 10th Ter Fort Lauderdale (33309) *(G-3653)*

Apple Rush Company Inc (PA) 888 741-3777
1419 Chaffee Dr Ste 4 Titusville (32780) *(G-17572)*

Apple Sign & Awning LLC 813 948-2220
1635 Dale Mabry Hwy Ste 7 Lutz (33548) *(G-7983)*

Appliances To Go Usa Llc 239 278-0811
741 Del Prado Blvd N # 160 Cape Coral (33909) *(G-1303)*

Applied Cooling Technology LLC 239 217-5080
75 Mid Cape Ter 23 Cape Coral (33991) *(G-1304)*

Applied Design & Fabrication 954 524-6619
3525 Northern Blvd Lake Placid (33852) *(G-7137)*

Applied Fiber Concepts Inc 754 581-2744
2425 W 8th Ln Hialeah (33010) *(G-5055)*

Applied Fiber Holdings LLC 850 539-7720
25 Garrett Dr Havana (32333) *(G-4990)*

Applied Fiber Mfg LLC 850 539-7720
25 Garrett Dr Havana (32333) *(G-4991)*

Applied Genetic Tech Corp 386 462-2204
14193 Nw 119th Ter Ste 10 Alachua (32615) *(G-5)*

Applied Software Inc 215 297-9441
737 Sandy Point Ln West Palm Beach (33410) *(G-17924)*

Applied Systems Integrator Inc 321 259-6106
746 North Dr Ste B Melbourne (32934) *(G-8368)*

Applied Technologies Group Inc 813 413-7025
333 N Falkenburg Rd B227 Tampa (33619) *(G-16601)*

Applus Laboratories USA Inc (HQ) 941 205-5700
27256 Mooney Ave Bldg 10 Punta Gorda (33982) *(G-14491)*

Appo Group Inc 410 992-5500
7000 Island Blvd Apt 2309 Aventura (33160) *(G-253)*

Appointment Team Inc 561 314-5471
1530 W Boynton Beach Blvd Boynton Beach (33436) *(G-843)*

Approved Performance Tooling 305 592-7775
8405 Nw 66th St Miami (33166) *(G-8736)*

Approved Turbo Components Inc 559 627-3600
663 2nd Ln Vero Beach (32962) *(G-17736)*

Apps 47 Inc 413 200-7533
1118 Catherine St Key West (33040) *(G-6854)*

APRU LLC 888 741-3777
3125 Lake George Cove Dr Orlando (32812) *(G-11914)*

APS Promotional Solutions Inc 904 721-4977
7121 Beach Blvd Jacksonville (32216) *(G-5894)*

APT, Miami *Also called Approved Performance Tooling (G-8736)*

Aptum Technologies (usa) Inc 877 504-0091
2300 Nw 89th Pl Doral (33172) *(G-3118)*

Apure Distribution LLC 305 351-1025
5555 Biscayne Blvd Fl 3 Miami (33137) *(G-8737)*

Apw 850 332-7023
911 N 63rd Ave Pensacola (32506) *(G-13442)*

Apw Wholesale, Jacksonville *Also called Aluminum Products Whl Inc (G-5881)*

Apyelen Curves LLC 904 328-3390
614 Pecan Park Rd Jacksonville (32218) *(G-5895)*

Apyx Medical Corporation (PA) 727 384-2323
5115 Ulmerton Rd Clearwater (33760) *(G-1496)*

Aqua Engineering & Eqp Inc 407 599-2123
7206 Aloma Ave Winter Park (32792) *(G-18486)*

Aqua Finishing Solutions, Fort Pierce *Also called Faux Effects International Inc (G-4486)*

Aqua Float Co 320 524-2782
37100 Geiger Rd Zephyrhills (33542) *(G-18603)*

Aqua Pure LLC 407 521-3055
6541 N Orange Blossom Trl Orlando (32810) *(G-11915)*

Aqua Pure of SW Florida Lc, Naples *Also called Keith Dennis Markham (G-10796)*

Aqua Solutions, West Palm Beach *Also called Fovico Inc (G-18010)*

Aqua Technologies 305 246-2125
815 N Homestead Blvd Homestead (33030) *(G-5699)*

Aqua Wholesale Inc 941 341-0847
1155 Cattlemen Rd Ste B Sarasota (34232) *(G-15597)*

Aqua-Air Manufacturing, Fort Lauderdale *Also called James D Nall Co Inc (G-3891)*

Aquaback Technologies Inc 978 863-1000
9300 Scarborough Ct Port Saint Lucie (34986) *(G-14397)*

Aquacal (PA) 727 898-2412
2730 24th St N Saint Petersburg (33713) *(G-14965)*

Aquacal Autopilot Inc 727 823-5642
2737 24th St N Saint Petersburg (33713) *(G-14966)*

Aquacomfort Solutions LLC 407 831-1941
601 N Congress Ave # 311 Delray Beach (33445) *(G-2932)*

Aquaflex Printing LLC 727 914-4922
3349 118th Ave N Saint Petersburg (33716) *(G-14967)*

Aqualogix Inc (PA) 858 442-4550
4440 Pga Blvd Ste 600 Palm Beach Gardens (33410) *(G-12948)*

Aqualuma LLC 954 234-2512
3251 Sw 13th Dr Ste A Deerfield Beach (33442) *(G-2669)*

Aquarian Bath Inc 310 919-0220
46 High Ridge Rd Holly Hill (32117) *(G-5511)*

Aquarius Press Inc 305 688-0066
13795 Nw 19th Ave Opa Locka (33054) *(G-11718)*

Aquarius Silk Screen Inc 941 377-3059
5931 Palmer Blvd Sarasota (34232) *(G-15598)*

Aquatec Solutions LLC 561 717-6933
140 Nw 11th St Boca Raton (33432) *(G-414)*

Aquatech LLC 727 559-8084
3448 Avocado Rd Largo (33770) *(G-7536)*

Aquatech Manufacturing LLC 813 664-0300
7455 E Adamo Dr Tampa (33619) *(G-16602)*

Aquatectonica LLC 941 592-3071
809 Tallgrass Ln Bradenton (34212) *(G-940)*

Aquateko International LLC 904 273-7200
140 Deer Haven Dr Ponte Vedra Beach (32082) *(G-14264)*

Aquatherm Heat Pumps, Fort Myers *Also called Calorex USA LLC (G-4199)*

Aquathin Corp 800 462-7634
950 S Andrews Ave Pompano Beach (33069) *(G-13931)*

Aquatic Fabricators of S Fla 954 458-0400
2930 Sw 30th Ave Ste A Hallandale (33009) *(G-4919)*

Aquatic Technologies Inc 772 225-4389
1820 Ne Jensen Beach Blvd Jensen Beach (34957) *(G-6652)*

Aquatic Wetsuits, Hallandale *Also called Aquatic Fabricators of S Fla (G-4919)*

Aquaworx, Inc., Saint Petersburg *Also called Big Slide Enterprises Inc (G-14982)*

Aquinas Inc 727 842-2254
4936 Us Highway 19 New Port Richey (34652) *(G-10961)*

Aquino Trucks Center Corp 239 327-9708
31 Nw 13th Ave Cape Coral (33993) *(G-1305)*

Ar2 Products LLC 800 667-1263
1820 State Road 13 Ste 11 Saint Johns (32259) *(G-14944)*

ARA Food Corporation 305 592-5558
8001 Nw 60th St Miami (33166) *(G-8738)*

Araya Inc 305 229-6868
9582 Sw 40th St Ste 5 Miami (33165) *(G-8739)*

Arban & Associates Inc 850 836-4362
1464 Line Rd Ponce De Leon (32455) *(G-14248)*

Arborossa Leather, Royal Palm Beach *Also called Wellington Leather LLC (G-14773)*

ARC Acquisition Corp (PA) 386 626-0005
810 Flight Line Blvd Deland (32724) *(G-2852)*

ARC Creative Inc 904 996-7773
2683 St Jhns Bluff Rd S S Jacksonville (32246) *(G-5896)*

ARC Dimensions Inc 727 524-6139
7545 124th Ave Unit Stef Largo (33773) *(G-7537)*

ARC Electric Inc 954 583-9800
3328 Burris Rd Davie (33314) *(G-2388)*

ARC Group Worldwide, Deland *Also called ARC Acquisition Corp (G-2852)*

ARC Group Worldwide Inc (PA) 303 467-5236
810 Flight Line Blvd Deland (32724) *(G-2853)*

ARC Stone III LLC 561 478-8805
1800 4th Ave N Unit A Lake Worth Beach (33461) *(G-7248)*

ARC Transition LLC (HQ) 386 626-0001
790 Fentress Blvd Daytona Beach (32114) *(G-2513)*

ARC United Electric Motor, Tampa *Also called United Electric Motor Inc (G-17391)*

ARC-Rite Inc 386 325-3523
569 Edgewood Ave S Jacksonville (32205) *(G-5897)*

Arca LLC 305 470-1430
1220 Nw 7th St Miami (33125) *(G-8740)*

Arca Knitting Inc (PA) 305 836-0155
1060 E 23rd St Hialeah (33013) *(G-5056)*

Arca Pro Retractables LLC 407 844-5013
366 Loyd Ln Oviedo (32765) *(G-12804)*

Arcadia Aerospace Inds LLC (HQ) 941 205-5700
27256 Mooney Ave Bldg 110 Punta Gorda (33982) *(G-14492)*

Arcadia Thrift LLC 863 993-2004
129 S Mills Ave Arcadia (34266) *(G-188)*

Arcana Tileworks 407 492-0668
1226 Wntr Gdn Vnlnd Rd # 100 Winter Garden (34787) *(G-18374)*

Arcco Inc 954 564-0827
939 Nw 35th Ct Oakland Park (33309) *(G-11239)*

Arch Mirror North, Tamarac *Also called Florida A&G Co Inc (G-16531)*

Archer Ellison Inc 800 449-4095
7025 County Road 46a # 1071 Lake Mary (32746) *(G-7060)*

Archer Pharmaceuticals Inc 941 752-2949
2040 Whitfield Ave Sarasota (34243) *(G-15441)*

Archimaze Logistics Inc 954 615-7485
1776 Nw 38th Ave Fort Lauderdale (33311) *(G-3654)*

Architctral Designs Metalworks 954 532-1331
1773 Blount Rd Ste 307 Pompano Beach (33069) *(G-13932)*

Architctral Mlding Mllwrks Inc 305 638-8900
3545 Nw 50th St Miami (33142) *(G-8741)*

Architctral Mllwk Slutions Inc 727 441-1409
13090 Starkey Rd Largo (33773) *(G-7538)*

Architctral Mtal Flashings LLC 239 221-0123
2659 Ne 9th Ave Cape Coral (33909) *(G-1306)*

Architctral Sgnage Systems Inc 813 996-6777
6812 Land O Lakes Blvd Land O Lakes (34638) *(G-7488)*

Architctral Shtmtl Fbrctors In 407 672-9086
2720 Forsyth Rd Ste 200 Winter Park (32792) *(G-18487)*

Architctral WD Wkg Mlding Div 727 527-7400
3291 40th Ave N Saint Petersburg (33714) *(G-14968)*

Architctral Wdwkg Concepts Inc 239 434-0549
3863 Entp Ave Unit 2 Naples (34104) *(G-10672)*

Architctral Wdwrks Cbnetry Inc 561 848-8595
219 Coral Cay Ter Palm Beach Gardens (33418) *(G-12949)*

Architctural MBL Importers Inc 941 365-3552
2560 12th St Sarasota (34237) *(G-15599)*

Architctural WD Pdts of Naples 239 260-7156
2154 J And C Blvd Naples (34109) *(G-10673)*

Architechtural Foam Systems, Bradenton *Also called Pmh Homes Inc (G-1030)*

Architectural and Woodworking, Saint Petersburg *Also called William Leupold Sr (G-15233)*

Architectural Detail & Wdwkg 561 835-4005
2617 Pinewood Ave West Palm Beach (33407) *(G-17925)*

Architectural Foam Supply Inc 954 943-6949
100 Sw 12th Ave Pompano Beach (33069) *(G-13933)*

Architectural Fountains Inc 727 323-6068
2010 28th St N Saint Petersburg (33713) *(G-14969)*

Architectural Graphics Inc 757 427-1900
5500 Rio Vista Dr Clearwater (33760) *(G-1497)*

Architectural Masters LLC 239 290-2250
2319 Griffin Rd Leesburg (34748) *(G-7760)*

Architectural Metal Systems 407 277-1364
4881 Distribution Ct Orlando (32822) *(G-11916)*

Architectural Metal Works, Tarpon Springs *Also called Imagine That Inc (G-17478)*

Architectural Metal Works, Tarpon Springs *Also called Casco Services Inc (G-17461)*

Architectural Metals S W FL 239 334-7433
4700 Laredo Ave Fort Myers (33905) *(G-4179)*

Architectural Moulding Corp 305 638-8900
3545 Nw 50th St Miami (33142) *(G-8742)*

Architectural Openings Inc 407 260-7110
1975 Corporate Sq Longwood (32750) *(G-7869)*

Architectural Signcrafters 772 600-5032
3195 Se Gran Park Way Stuart (34997) *(G-16117)*

Architectural Spc Trdg Co 850 435-2507
310 Hickory St Pensacola (32505) *(G-13443)*

Architecture Wood Products, Naples *Also called Architctural WD Pdts of Naples (G-10673)*

Arco Automotive Products, Pensacola *Also called Arco Marine Inc (G-13444)*

Arco Computer Products LLC 954 925-2688
3100 N 29th Ct Ste 100 Hollywood (33020) *(G-5529)*

Arco Globas International, De Leon Springs *Also called Arco Globas Trading LLC (G-2623)*

Arco Globas Trading LLC 305 707-7702
6111 Lake Winona Rd De Leon Springs (32130) *(G-2623)*

Arco Marine Inc 850 455-5476
3921 W Navy Blvd Pensacola (32507) *(G-13444)*

Arcoat Coatings Corporation 561 422-9900
2351 Vista Pkwy Ste 500 West Palm Beach (33411) *(G-17926)*

Arcosa Trffic Ltg Strctres LLC 352 748-4258
1749 Cr 525e Sumterville (33585) *(G-16262)*

Arcpoint of Tallahassee Inc (PA) 850 201-2500
3520 N Monroe St Tallahassee (32303) *(G-16413)*

Arctic Industries LLC 305 883-5581
9731 Nw 114th Way Medley (33178) *(G-8197)*

Arctic Rays Llc 321 223-5780
600 Jackson Ct Satellite Beach (32937) *(G-15883)*

Arctic-Temp Ice Makers, Longwood *Also called Holiday Ice Inc (G-7901)*

Ard Printing Solutions LL 305 785-7200
14016 Sw 140th St Miami (33186) *(G-8743)*

Arde Apparel Inc 305 326-0861
1852 Nw 21st St Miami (33142) *(G-8744)*

Arden Photonics LLC 727 478-2651
4500 140th Ave N Ste 101 Clearwater (33762) *(G-1498)*

Ardmore Farms LLC 386 734-4634
1915 N Woodland Blvd Deland (32720) *(G-2854)*

Ards Awning & Upholstery Inc 863 293-2442
503 5th St Sw Winter Haven (33880) *(G-18418)*

Area Litho Inc 863 687-4656
238 N Wabash Ave Lakeland (33815) *(G-7275)*

Area Rugs Mfg Inc 904 398-5481
2068 Gamewell Rd Jacksonville (32211) *(G-5898)*

Ares Distributors Inc 305 858-0163
2601 S Bayshore Dr # 1150 Miami (33133) *(G-8745)*

Aresco Manufacturing & Safety, Palm City *Also called Cameron Textiles Inc (G-13026)*

Aressco Technologies LLC 305 245-5854
15600 Sw 288th St Ste 307 Homestead (33033) *(G-5700)*

Arete Industries, Odessa *Also called D G Morrison Inc (G-11546)*

Areweonlinecom Llc 561 572-0233
1101 N Congress Ave # 202 Boynton Beach (33426) *(G-844)*

Arfona Printing LLC 312 339-0215
1121 Bel Air Dr Apt 4 Highland Beach (33487) *(G-5459)*

Argen Foods 305 884-0037
9220 Nw 102nd St Medley (33178) *(G-8198)*

Argenal Cabinets Inc 863 670-7973
911 Hammock Shade Dr Lakeland (33809) *(G-7276)*

Argo Crates & Containers 786 487-4607
10461 Nw 26th St Doral (33172) *(G-3119)*

Argonide Corporation 407 322-2500
291 Power Ct Sanford (32771) *(G-15266)*

Argos 678 368-4300
700 Palmetto St Jacksonville (32202) *(G-5899)*

Argos 305 592-3501
12201 Nw 25th St Miami (33182) *(G-8746)*

Argos 352 376-6491
924 S Main St Gainesville (32601) *(G-4650)*

Argos Cement LLC 813 247-4831
2001 Maritime Blvd Tampa (33605) *(G-16603)*

Argos Global Partner Svcs LLC (PA) 305 365-1096
240 Crandon Blvd Ste 230 Key Biscayne (33149) *(G-6833)*

Argos Nautic Manufacturing LLC (PA) 305 856-7586
2600 Sw 3rd Ave Ste 800 Miami (33129) *(G-8747)*

Argos Ready Mix 941 629-7713
580 Prineville St Port Charlotte (33954) *(G-14286)*

Argos USA 863 687-1898
2300 Mershon St Lakeland (33815) *(G-7277)*

Argos USA LLC 850 872-1209
1601 Maple Ave Panama City (32405) *(G-13228)*

Argos USA LLC 850 235-9600
17800 Ashley Dr Panama City Beach (32413) *(G-13325)*

Argos USA LLC 850 576-4141
1005 Kissimmee St Tallahassee (32310) *(G-16414)*

Argos USA LLC 407 299-9924
2858 Sidney Ave Orlando (32810) *(G-11917)*

Argos USA LLC 352 472-4722
4000 Nw County Road 235 Th Newberry (32669) *(G-11017)*

Argos USA LLC 866 322-4547
6000 Deacon Pl Sarasota (34238) *(G-15600)*

Argos USA LLC 813 962-3213
5609 N 50th St Tampa (33610) *(G-16604)*

Argos-US LLC 407 298-1900
5109 Carder Rd Orlando (32810) *(G-11918)*

Argosy Group International LLC 888 350-7643
2405 W Princeton St Ste 9 Orlando (32804) *(G-11919)*

Argotec Inc (PA) 954 491-6550
2432 Ne 27th Ave Fort Lauderdale (33305) *(G-3655)*

Argotec Inc 407 331-9372
225 Pineda St Unit 103 Longwood (32750) *(G-7870)*

Argus International Inc 305 888-4881
318 Indian Trce Weston (33326) *(G-18226)*

Arhob LLC 727 216-6318
927 Broadway Ste A Dunedin (34698) *(G-3439)*

ARI Specialties LLC 321 269-2244
3660 Us Highway 1 Mims (32754) *(G-10446)*

Aristcrete Coating Experts LLC 386 882-3660
1264 Riverbreeze Blvd Ormond Beach (32176) *(G-12743)*

Arizona Beverage Company LLC 516 812-0303
8350 Parkline Blvd Ste 14 Orlando (32809) *(G-11920)*

Arizona Beverage Company LLC 516 812-0303
1909 N Us Highway 301 # 130 Tampa (33619) *(G-16605)*

Arizona Beverage Company LLC 516 812-0303
12721 Gran Bay Pkwy W Jacksonville (32258) *(G-5900)*

Arizona Beverage Company LLC 516 812-0303
1685 Target Ct Ste 18 Fort Myers (33905) *(G-4180)*

Arizona Chemical, Jacksonville *Also called Kraton Chemical LLC (G-6250)*

Arj Art Inc 727 535-8633
517 35th Ave N Saint Petersburg (33704) *(G-14970)*

Arj Medical Inc 813 855-1557
209 State St E Oldsmar (34677) *(G-11627)*

Arjay Printing Company Inc 904 764-6070
131 Burbank Rd Oldsmar (34677) *(G-11628)*

Ark Natural Product For Pets, Tampa *Also called S&J 34102 Inc (G-17240)*

Arkay Distributing Inc 954 536-8413
401 E Las Olas Blvd # 1400 Fort Lauderdale (33301) *(G-3656)*

Arkup Llc 786 448-8635
2100 Park Ave Apt 211s Miami Beach (33139) *(G-10167)*

Arlington Prtg Stationers Inc 904 358-2928
200 N Lee St Jacksonville (32204) *(G-5901)*

Arm Almnum Rling Mnfctures LLC 813 626-2264
2433 S 86th St Ste F Tampa (33619) *(G-16606)*

Arma Holdings Inc 813 402-0667
3030 N Rocky Point Dr W # 800 Tampa (33607) *(G-16607)*

Armada Systems Inc (PA) 850 664-5197
508 Mountain Dr Destin (32541) *(G-3058)*

Armadillo Sounds Inc 305 801-7906
4246 Nw 37th Ave Miami (33142) *(G-8748)*

Armalaser Inc 800 680-5020
5200 Nw 43rd St Gainesville (32606) *(G-4651)*

Armalaser Inc 954 937-6054
4699 N Federal Hwy # 110 Pompano Beach (33064) *(G-13934)*

Armando Grcia Cstm Cbinets Inc 305 775-5674
220 Sw 30th Rd Miami (33129) *(G-8749)*

Armbrust Aviation Group Inc 561 355-8488
8895 N Military Trl # 201 West Palm Beach (33410) *(G-17927)*

Armen Co Inc 305 206-1601
12140 Nw 12th St Plantation (33323) *(G-13827)*

Armor Accessories Inc 904 741-1717
13386 International Pkwy Jacksonville (32218) *(G-5902)*

Armor Holdings Forensics LLC 904 485-1836
13386 International Pkwy Jacksonville (32218) *(G-5903)*

Armor Oil Products LLC 813 248-1988
1601 Mcclosky Blvd Tampa (33605) *(G-16608)*

(G-0000) Company's Geographic Section entry number

Armor Products Mfg Inc.....813 764-8844
2610 Airport Rd Plant City (33563) *(G-13740)*
Armor Supply Metals LLC.....305 640-9901
12690 Nw South River Dr Medley (33178) *(G-8199)*
Armored Frog Inc.....850 418-2048
12 E Belmont St Pensacola (32501) *(G-13445)*
Armorit Precision LLC.....941 751-1292
2280 Trailmate Dr Ste 103 Sarasota (34243) *(G-15442)*
Armorit Precison.....941 751-6635
6423 Parkland Dr Sarasota (34243) *(G-15443)*
Armour Group Inc.....954 767-2030
6700 Powerline Rd Fort Lauderdale (33309) *(G-3657)*
Armoury Property & Mold Inspec.....813 503-9765
18682 Fort Smith Cir Port Charlotte (33948) *(G-14287)*
Arms, Jacksonville *Also called Alterntive Repr McHning Svcs L (G-5880)*
Arms East LLC.....561 293-2915
2335 63rd Ave E Ste M Bradenton (34203) *(G-941)*
Armstrong Power Systems LLC (PA).....305 470-0058
5100 Nw 72nd Ave Miami (33166) *(G-8750)*
Armstrong Press Inc.....561 247-1071
2680 Sw Fair Isle Rd Port Saint Lucie (34987) *(G-14398)*
Armstrong World Industries Inc.....850 433-8321
300 Myrick St Pensacola (32505) *(G-13446)*
Armstrongs Prtg & Graphics Inc (PA).....850 243-6923
30 Walter Martin Rd Ne Fort Walton Beach (32548) *(G-4562)*
Arnet Pharmaceutical Corp.....954 236-9053
2525 Davie Rd Ste 330 Davie (33317) *(G-2389)*
Arno Belo Inc.....800 734-2356
221 W Hllndale Bch Blvd P Hallandale Beach (33009) *(G-4936)*
Arnold Industries South Inc.....352 867-0190
1601 Ne 6th Ave Ocala (34470) *(G-11327)*
Arnold Lumber Company Inc.....850 547-5733
3185 Thomas Dr Bonifay (32425) *(G-766)*
Arnold Manufacturing Inc.....850 470-9200
2300 Town St Pensacola (32505) *(G-13447)*
Arnold Mnfacturing-A M C Trlrs, Pensacola *Also called Arnold Manufacturing Inc (G-13447)*
Aroma Chemicals, Jacksonville *Also called Symrise Inc (G-6526)*
Aroma Chimie Inc.....305 930-5667
1001 Brickell Bay Dr Miami (33131) *(G-8751)*
Aroma Coffee Service Inc.....239 481-7262
2168 Andrea Ln Fort Myers (33912) *(G-4181)*
AROMAR, Miami *Also called Mar Company Distributors LLC (G-9507)*
Aromatech Flavorings Inc.....407 277-5727
7001 Mccoy Rd Ste 200 Orlando (32822) *(G-11921)*
Aromavalue Inc.....866 223-7561
720 Brooker Creek Blvd # 210 Oldsmar (34677) *(G-11629)*
Arons Towing & Recovery Inc.....772 220-1151
12872 Se Suzanne Dr Hobe Sound (33455) *(G-5479)*
Around and About Inc.....954 584-1954
450 N State Road 7 Plantation (33317) *(G-13828)*
Around House Publishing Inc.....561 969-7412
3760 Country Vista Way Lake Worth (33467) *(G-7185)*
Arpi International Corporation.....305 984-9056
16275 Sw 208th Ter Miami (33187) *(G-8752)*
Arr-Maz Custom Chemicals, Mulberry *Also called Arrmaz Products Inc (G-10619)*
Arriaga Originals.....850 231-0084
10343 E County Highway 30 # 112 Panama City (32461) *(G-13323)*
Arribas Bindery Services Inc.....954 978-8886
6701 Nw 15th Way B Fort Lauderdale (33309) *(G-3658)*
Arrive Alive Traffic Ctrl LLC.....407 578-5431
3165 N John Young Pkwy Orlando (32804) *(G-11922)*
Arrmaz Products Inc (HQ).....863 578-1206
4800 State Road 60 E Mulberry (33860) *(G-10619)*
Arrow Embroidery.....850 626-1796
6434 Open Rose Dr Milton (32570) *(G-10418)*
Arrow Sheet Metal Works Inc.....813 247-2179
2710 N 36th St Tampa (33605) *(G-16609)*
Arrowhead Global LLC.....727 497-7340
22033 Us Highway 19 N Clearwater (33765) *(G-1499)*
ARS, Micanopy *Also called Analytical Research Systems (G-10395)*
Arsenal Democracy LLC.....850 296-2122
48 Commerce Ln Ste 7 Freeport (32439) *(G-4621)*
Arsenal Industries LLC.....407 506-2698
750 S Orlando Ave Ste 200 Winter Park (32789) *(G-18488)*
Arsenal Venture Partners Fla.....407 838-1400
750 S Orlando Ave Ste 200 Winter Park (32789) *(G-18489)*
Arso Enterprises Inc.....305 681-2020
4101 Nw 132nd St Opa Locka (33054) *(G-11719)*
Art & Frame Direct Inc (PA).....407 857-6000
11423 Satellite Blvd Orlando (32837) *(G-11923)*
Art & Frame Drct/Timeless Inds.....407 857-6000
11423 Satellite Blvd Orlando (32837) *(G-11924)*
Art & Frame Source Inc (PA).....727 329-6502
4251 34th St N Saint Petersburg (33714) *(G-14971)*
Art and Orchid Gallery, The, Jupiter *Also called Inter Cell Technologies Inc (G-6747)*
Art Connection Usa LLC.....954 781-0125
2860 Center Port Cir Pompano Beach (33064) *(G-13935)*
Art Craft Metals Inc.....954 946-4620
1630 Sw 13th Ct Pompano Beach (33069) *(G-13936)*
Art Edibles Inc.....407 603-4043
428 Wilmington Cir Oviedo (32765) *(G-12805)*
Art In Print Inc (PA).....561 877-0995
8640 Valhalla Dr Delray Beach (33446) *(G-2933)*
Art In Spotlight.....904 853-6661
1578 Linkside Dr Atlantic Beach (32233) *(G-204)*
Art of Iron Inc.....850 819-1500
311 W 35th Ct Panama City (32405) *(G-13229)*
Art of Printing Inc.....561 640-7344
1500 N Fl Mango Rd Ste 4 West Palm Beach (33409) *(G-17928)*
Art Sign & Neon, Fort Lauderdale *Also called Art Sign Co Inc (G-3659)*
Art Sign Co Inc.....954 763-4410
835 Nw 6th Ave Fort Lauderdale (33311) *(G-3659)*
Art Signs The, Orlando *Also called Delivery Signs LLC (G-12082)*
Art Staircase & Woodwork Llc.....239 440-6591
4229 Sw 14th Pl Cape Coral (33914) *(G-1307)*
Art Wood Cabinets Corp.....754 367-0742
1533 Sw 1st Way Deerfield Beach (33441) *(G-2670)*
Art-Crete Products Inc.....386 252-5118
1231 S Ridgewood Ave Daytona Beach (32114) *(G-2514)*
Art-Kraft Sign Co Inc.....321 727-7324
2675 Kirby Cir Ne Palm Bay (32905) *(G-12887)*
Artco Group Inc.....305 638-1785
5851 Nw 35th Ave Miami (33142) *(G-8753)*
Artcraft Engraving & Prtg Inc.....305 557-9449
7921 W 26th Ave Hialeah (33016) *(G-5057)*
Arte Bronce Monuments Inc.....305 477-0813
8600 Nw S Rver Dr Ste 109 Medley (33166) *(G-8200)*
Artec Manufacturing LLC.....305 888-4375
699 W 17th St Hialeah (33010) *(G-5058)*
Artec Metal Fabrication Inc.....305 888-4375
699 W 17th St Hialeah (33010) *(G-5059)*
Artech.....813 929-0754
5323 Swallow Dr Land O Lakes (34639) *(G-7489)*
Artech Systems Inc.....954 304-0430
333 Ne 21st Ave Deerfield Beach (33441) *(G-2671)*
Arteche USA Inc.....954 438-9499
3401 Sw 160th Ave Ste 430 Miramar (33027) *(G-10469)*
Artemis Holdings Llc (HQ).....904 284-5611
4630 County Road 209 S Green Cove Springs (32043) *(G-4816)*
Artemis Plastics, Ocala *Also called Apollo Renal Therapeutics LLC (G-11326)*
Artemisa Escobar Brothers Inc.....786 286-1493
10147 Nw 87th Ave Medley (33178) *(G-8201)*
Artex Computer Llc.....407 844-2253
4737 Nw 72nd Ave Miami (33166) *(G-8754)*
Artex Publishing Inc.....727 944-4117
3130 Westridge Dr Holiday (34691) *(G-5489)*
Artful Arnautic Assemblies LLC.....727 522-0055
2877 47th Ave N Saint Petersburg (33714) *(G-14972)*
Artful Canvas Design Inc.....727 521-0212
2877 47th Ave N Saint Petersburg (33714) *(G-14973)*
Arthrex Inc (PA).....239 643-5553
1370 Creekside Blvd Naples (34108) *(G-10674)*
Arthrex California Inc.....239 643-5553
1370 Creekside Blvd Naples (34108) *(G-10675)*
Arthrex Manufacturing Inc.....239 643-5553
1370 Creekside Blvd Naples (34108) *(G-10676)*
Arthrex Trauma Inc.....239 643-5553
1370 Creekside Blvd Naples (34108) *(G-10677)*
Arthur Cox.....772 286-5339
4800 Se Anchor Ave Stuart (34997) *(G-16118)*
Arthur Printing, Cape Coral *Also called Detailed Services Inc (G-1332)*
Artios, Orlando *Also called Richard Bryan Ingram LLC (G-12553)*
Artisan Arms Inc.....321 299-4053
2516 Jmt Industrial Dr # 105 Apopka (32703) *(G-103)*
Artisan Wood Works Inc.....239 321-9122
701 Grove Dr Naples (34120) *(G-10678)*
Artisanis Guild.....239 591-3203
1510 Rail Head Blvd Naples (34110) *(G-10679)*
Artistic Adventures Inc.....407 297-0557
2517 Shader Rd Unit 2 Orlando (32804) *(G-11925)*
Artistic Columns Inc.....954 530-5537
533 Ne 33rd St Oakland Park (33334) *(G-11240)*
Artistic Doors Inc.....561 582-0348
2223 2nd Ave N Lake Worth Beach (33461) *(G-7249)*
Artistic Elements Inc.....561 750-1554
400 E Palmetto Park Rd Boca Raton (33432) *(G-415)*
Artistic Fence Corporation.....305 805-1976
1070 Se 9th Ter Ste B Hialeah (33010) *(G-5060)*
Artistic Gate Railing.....954 348-9752
5100 Ne 12th Ave Oakland Park (33334) *(G-11241)*
Artistic Label Company Inc.....401 737-0666
20050 Sgrove St Unit 1703 Estero (33928) *(G-3540)*
Artistic Paver Mfg Inc.....305 653-7283
120 Ne 179th St Ste 1 Miami (33162) *(G-8755)*
Artistic Pavers LLC.....727 573-0918
12700 Automobile Blvd Clearwater (33762) *(G-1500)*
Artistic Statuary Inc.....954 975-9533
1490 N Powerline Rd Pompano Beach (33069) *(G-13937)*
Artistic Stoneworks, Fort Walton Beach *Also called Grevan Artistic Ventures Inc (G-4588)*

Artistic Welding Inc 954 563-3098
802 Ne 40th Ct Oakland Park (33334) ***(G-11242)***
Artnexus Online Inc 305 891-7270
12500 Ne 8th Ave North Miami (33161) ***(G-11090)***
Arts Work Unlimited Inc 305 247-9257
22150 Sw 154th Ave Miami (33170) ***(G-8756)***
Artvint Corp 727 856-3565
10441 Frierson Lake Dr Hudson (34669) ***(G-5762)***
Artworks International 561 833-9165
420 6th St West Palm Beach (33401) ***(G-17929)***
Artworks Printing Entps Inc 954 893-7984
5922 Liberty St Hollywood (33021) ***(G-5530)***
Arty-Sun LLC 561 705-2222
9045 La Fontana Blvd Boca Raton (33434) ***(G-416)***
Aruki Services LLC 850 364-5206
102 Sw 3rd St Havana (32333) ***(G-4992)***
Arvin's Engineered Solutions, Orlando *Also called Aero-Tel Wire Harness Corp* ***(G-11876)***
Arxada LLC 813 286-0404
4910 Savarese Cir Tampa (33634) ***(G-16610)***
Arya Group LLC 561 792-9992
11858 Forest Hill Blvd Wellington (33414) ***(G-17843)***
ASAP Brick Pavers and More 850 522-7123
2320 N East Ave Panama City (32405) ***(G-13230)***
ASAP Magazine & Newspaper 813 238-0184
106 W Haya St Tampa (33603) ***(G-16611)***
ASAP Screen Printing Inc 352 505-7574
4641 Nw 6th St Ste A Gainesville (32609) ***(G-4652)***
ASAP Signs & Graphics of Fla 727 443-4878
509 D St Clearwater (33756) ***(G-1501)***
Asb Sports Group LLC 305 775-4689
801 Brickell Bay Dr Miami (33131) ***(G-8757)***
Asbury Manufacturing Co LLC 954 202-7419
3355 Entp Ave Ste 160 Fort Lauderdale (33331) ***(G-3660)***
Ascend Performance Mtls Inc 850 968-7000
3000 Old Chemstrand Rd Cantonment (32533) ***(G-1264)***
Ascend Prfmce Mtls Oprtons LLC 734 819-0656
200 Pensacola Beach Rd B3 Gulf Breeze (32561) ***(G-4876)***
Ascend Prfmce Mtls Oprtons LLC 850 968-7000
3000 Old Chemstrand Rd Cantonment (32533) ***(G-1265)***
Ascendants Publishing LLC 813 391-2745
626 Se 2nd Pl Apt 3 Gainesville (32601) ***(G-4653)***
Ascent Precision Gear Corp 386 792-3215
12180 Se County Road 137 Jasper (32052) ***(G-6645)***
Asco Power Technologies LP 727 450-2730
14550 58th St N Clearwater (33760) ***(G-1502)***
Asd Surfaces LLC 561 845-5009
531 Us Highway 1 North Palm Beach (33408) ***(G-11174)***
Asecure America Inc 352 347-7951
10080 Se 67th Ter Belleview (34420) ***(G-359)***
Asemblu Inc 800 827-4419
18520 Nw 67th Ave 208 Hialeah (33015) ***(G-5061)***
Asencoex LLC 305 433-7260
10400 Nw 69th Ter Doral (33178) ***(G-3120)***
ASG Aerospace LLC 305 253-0802
12906 Sw 139th Ave Miami (33186) ***(G-8758)***
ASG Corp 718 641-4500
5235 N Bay Rd Miami Beach (33140) ***(G-10168)***
ASG Federal Inc 239 435-2200
708 Goodlette-Frank Rd N Naples (34102) ***(G-10680)***
Ash Grove, Sumterville *Also called Suwannee American Cem Co LLC* ***(G-16264)***
Ash Signs Inc 904 724-7446
2141 St Johns Bluff Rd S Jacksonville (32246) ***(G-5904)***
Ashberry Acquisition Company (PA) 813 248-0055
5409 S West Shore Blvd Tampa (33611) ***(G-16612)***
Ashberry Water Conditioning, Tampa *Also called Ashberry Acquisition Company* ***(G-16612)***
Ashley Bryan International Inc 954 351-1199
1432 E Nwport Ctr Dr Ste Deerfield Beach (33442) ***(G-2672)***
Ashley F Ward Inc 904 284-2848
3525 Enterprise Way Green Cove Springs (32043) ***(G-4817)***
Ashley Ward, Green Cove Springs *Also called Ashley F Ward Inc* ***(G-4817)***
Ashtin Inc 352 867-1900
1800 Sw College Rd Ocala (34471) ***(G-11328)***
Ashton Manufacturing LLC 941 351-5529
1633 Northgate Blvd Sarasota (34234) ***(G-15601)***
Asi, Destin *Also called Armada Systems Inc* ***(G-3058)***
Asi Chemical Inc 863 678-1814
1901 State Road 60 W Lake Wales (33859) ***(G-7152)***
Asi Global 786 703-7155
240 Crandon Blvd Ste 242 Key Biscayne (33149) ***(G-6834)***
Asian Food Solutions, Oviedo *Also called International Fd Solutions Inc* ***(G-12829)***
Asian Food Solutions Inc 888 499-6888
5600 Elmhurst Cir Oviedo (32765) ***(G-12806)***
Asieei, Largo *Also called Al Stein Industries LLC* ***(G-7526)***
Aska Communication Corp 954 708-2387
2020 Nw 129th Ave Ste 205 Miami (33182) ***(G-8759)***
Asmf, Winter Park *Also called Architctral Shtmtl Fbrctors In* ***(G-18487)***
Aso Corporation (HQ) 941 378-6600
300 Sarasota Center Blvd Sarasota (34240) ***(G-15602)***
Asottu Inc 626 627-6021
1317 Edgewater Dr # 3455 Orlando (32804) ***(G-11926)***
Asp Alarm & Elec Sups Inc 305 556-9047
7535 W 20th Ave Hialeah (33014) ***(G-5062)***
Aspen Electronics Inc 305 863-2151
7288 Nw 54th St Miami (33166) ***(G-8760)***
Aspen Products Inc 904 579-4366
1857 Inlet Cove Ct Fleming Island (32003) ***(G-3607)***
Asphericon Inc 941 564-0890
2601 Cattlemen Rd Ste 301 Sarasota (34232) ***(G-15603)***
Aspirations Winery, Clearwater *Also called Tampa Wines LLC* ***(G-1814)***
Asrc Aerospace Corp 321 867-1462
Bldg M6-744 Kennedy Space Center (32899) ***(G-6830)***
Assa Abloy Hospitality Inc 954 920-0772
5601 Powerline Rd Ste 305 Fort Lauderdale (33309) ***(G-3661)***
Asset Guardian Inc 727 942-2246
2706 Alt 19 Ste 254 Palm Harbor (34683) ***(G-13099)***
Assis Master Paint Corp 786 797-6106
511 Sw 62nd Ter Margate (33068) ***(G-8121)***
Assistrx Inc (PA) 855 421-4607
4700 Millenia Blvd # 500 Orlando (32839) ***(G-11927)***
Assistrx Inc 855 382-2533
2400 Sand Lake Rd Ste 200 Orlando (32809) ***(G-11928)***
Assocate Cbinetmakers Palm Bch 561 743-9566
134 Toney Penna Dr Jupiter (33458) ***(G-6685)***
Assocated Prtg Productions Inc 305 623-7600
13925 Nw 60th Ave Miami Lakes (33014) ***(G-10282)***
Associated Carbonic Inds LLC 786 464-1260
8610 Sw 109th St Miami (33156) ***(G-8761)***
Associated Intr Desgr Svc Inc 561 655-4926
4300 Georgia Ave West Palm Beach (33405) ***(G-17930)***
Associated Machine Company Inc 305 836-6163
6540 Nw 35th Ave Miami (33147) ***(G-8762)***
Associated Materials LLC 813 621-7058
933 Chad Ln Tampa (33619) ***(G-16613)***
Associated Paint Inc 305 885-1964
10160 Nw South River Dr Medley (33178) ***(G-8202)***
Associated Steel & Alum Co Inc 954 974-7890
3017 Nw 25th Ave Pompano Beach (33069) ***(G-13938)***
Associated Steel & Alum Ltd 954 974-7890
3017 Nw 25th Ave Pompano Beach (33069) ***(G-13939)***
Assoction Hspnic Hritg Fstival 305 885-5613
3430 E 1st Ave Hialeah (33013) ***(G-5063)***
Assura Windows and Doors LLC (PA) 954 781-4430
1543 N Powerline Rd Pompano Beach (33069) ***(G-13940)***
AST, Fort Pierce *Also called Aero Shade Technologies Inc* ***(G-4460)***
Astec, Rockledge *Also called Advance Solder Technology Inc* ***(G-14690)***
Astellas Pharma Us Inc 386 935-1220
9159 220th St O Brien (32071) ***(G-11223)***
Asterion Beverages Inc 866 335-2672
3357 Nw 97th Ave Doral (33172) ***(G-3121)***
Astor Explorations Corp 561 241-3621
5030 Champion Blvd G6162 Boca Raton (33496) ***(G-417)***
Astra Products Co Inc Tampa 813 855-3021
3675 Tampa Rd Oldsmar (34677) ***(G-11630)***
Astro Pure Incorporated 954 422-8966
2121 Ne 29th St Lighthouse Point (33064) ***(G-7825)***
Astro-Pure Water Purifiers, Lighthouse Point *Also called Astro Pure Incorporated* ***(G-7825)***
Astronics Test Systems Inc 407 381-6062
12889 Ingenuity Dr Orlando (32826) ***(G-11929)***
Astroted Inc 786 220-5898
3320 Nw 67th Ave Unit 980 Doral (33122) ***(G-3122)***
Astrumsat Communications LLC 954 368-9980
1919 W 1st St Sanford (32771) ***(G-15267)***
Asysco Inc 850 383-2522
1424 Piedmont Dr E # 100 Tallahassee (32308) ***(G-16415)***
Ata Group of Companies Inc 352 735-1588
8020 Arcadian Ct Mount Dora (32757) ***(G-10597)***
Ataly Inc 813 880-9142
5828 Johns Rd Tampa (33634) ***(G-16614)***
Ataly Graphics, Tampa *Also called Ataly Inc* ***(G-16614)***
Atco Rubber Products Inc 813 754-6678
2407 Police Center Dr Plant City (33566) ***(G-13741)***
Atdsat, Miami *Also called All Things Digital Inc* ***(G-8691)***
Ateco, Opa Locka *Also called American Thrmplastic Extrusion* ***(G-11716)***
Ateei International Corp (PA) 305 597-6408
8284 Nw 56th St Doral (33166) ***(G-3123)***
Atelier Woodworking 561 386-0811
587 105th Ave N Unit 28 Royal Palm Beach (33411) ***(G-14759)***
Atenea Maintenance and Repair, Hialeah *Also called Ediciones Atenea Inc* ***(G-5135)***
Atg, Boca Raton *Also called Aerospace Tech Group Inc* ***(G-392)***
Atg Specialty Products Corp 888 455-5499
1725 Nw 97th Ave Doral (33172) ***(G-3124)***
Athco Inc (PA) 941 351-1600
1009 Tallevast Rd Sarasota (34243) ***(G-15444)***
Athletic Guide Publishing 386 439-2250
509 S Central Ave Flagler Beach (32136) ***(G-3601)***
ATI, Hollywood *Also called Aircraft Technology Inc* ***(G-5523)***
ATI, North Port *Also called Monroe Cable LLC* ***(G-11201)***

ATI Accurate Technology 239 206-1240
1180 8th Ave W Palmetto (34221) *(G-13155)*
ATI Agency Inc 954 895-7909
123 Nw 13th St Ste 305b Boca Raton (33432) *(G-418)*
ATI By Sea Co 954 483-0526
11251 Rockinghorse Rd Hollywood (33026) *(G-5531)*
Ati2 Inc 904 396-3766
10448 Atlantic Blvd Jacksonville (32225) *(G-5905)*
Atitlan Enterprises LLC 813 362-1909
16116 Lake Magdalene Blvd Tampa (33613) *(G-16615)*
Atk Sales Corp 954 701-0465
121 S 61st Ter Ste B Hollywood (33023) *(G-5532)*
Atkins Technical Inc 860 349-3473
6911 Nw 22nd St Ste B Gainesville (32653) *(G-4654)*
Atkinson Marine Inc 954 763-1652
235 Sw 32nd Ct Fort Lauderdale (33315) *(G-3662)*
Atkore International Inc 800 882-5543
1 Town Center Rd Boca Raton (33486) *(G-419)*
Atkore Plastic Pipe Corp 813 884-2525
5128 W Hanna Ave Tampa (33634) *(G-16616)*
Atlantech Process Technology 352 751-4286
1953 Lake Miona Dr Lady Lake (32162) *(G-6994)*
Atlantic Bev Group USA Inc 239 334-3016
2711 1st St Apt 102 Fort Myers (33916) *(G-4182)*
Atlantic Book Bindery, Jacksonville *Also called Knopf & Sons Bindery Inc (G-6246)*
Atlantic Candy Company 904 429-7250
115 Whetstone Pl Saint Augustine (32086) *(G-14811)*
Atlantic Cast Prcast S Fla LLC 954 564-6245
533 Ne 33rd St Oakland Park (33334) *(G-11243)*
Atlantic Central Entps Inc 386 255-6227
336 Lpga Blvd Daytona Beach (32117) *(G-2515)*
Atlantic Coast Asphalt Co 904 268-0274
10382 Florida Min Blvd E Jacksonville (32257) *(G-5906)*
Atlantic Coast Roofing & Metal 321 449-9494
350 Myrtice Ave Ste 201 Merritt Island (32953) *(G-8576)*
Atlantic Coastal Bakery, Opa Locka *Also called Kellys Bakery Corp (G-11759)*
Atlantic Concrete Products Inc 941 355-2988
1701 Myrtle St Sarasota (34234) *(G-15604)*
Atlantic Custom Woodcraft Corp 727 645-6905
11146 Challenger Ave # 101 Odessa (33556) *(G-11537)*
Atlantic Drinking Water Systms 252 255-1110
2700 Parker Ave Fort Myers (33905) *(G-4183)*
Atlantic Dry Dock 904 251-1545
8500 Heckscher Dr Jacksonville (32226) *(G-5907)*
Atlantic Dry Ice Corportion 305 592-7000
6950 Nw 12th St Miami (33126) *(G-8763)*
Atlantic Earth Materials 321 631-0600
2185 W King St Cocoa (32926) *(G-1904)*
Atlantic Gas Services LLC 386 957-3668
2948 Meleto Blvd New Smyrna Beach (32168) *(G-10994)*
Atlantic Insulation Inc 904 354-2217
325 Dennard Ave Jacksonville (32254) *(G-5908)*
Atlantic Island Trading, Miami *Also called Ait USA Corp (G-8677)*
Atlantic Jet Center Inc 321 255-7111
1401 Gen Avi Dr Melbourne (32935) *(G-8369)*
Atlantic Jet Support Inc 954 360-7549
4801 Johnson Rd Ste 11 Coconut Creek (33073) *(G-1978)*
Atlantic Marble Company Inc 904 262-6262
11303 Bus Pk Blvd Ste 100 Jacksonville (32256) *(G-5909)*
Atlantic Marine Inc 904 251-1580
8500 Heckscher Dr Jacksonville (32226) *(G-5910)*
Atlantic MBL Imaging Svcs Inc 386 239-8271
1400 Hand Ave Ste A Ormond Beach (32174) *(G-12744)*
Atlantic Medical Products LLC 727 535-0022
9843 18th St N Ste 160 Saint Petersburg (33716) *(G-14974)*
Atlantic Models Inc 305 883-2012
10631 Nw 123rd Street Rd Medley (33178) *(G-8203)*
Atlantic Molding Inc (PA) 954 781-9340
2750 Ne 4th Ave Pompano Beach (33064) *(G-13941)*
Atlantic Multi Family I LLC 301 233-1261
9045 Vista Way Parkland (33076) *(G-13343)*
Atlantic Precision Inc 772 466-1011
1461 Commerce Centre Dr A Port Saint Lucie (34986) *(G-14399)*
Atlantic Printing Ink Company, Tampa *Also called Amrob Inc (G-16595)*
Atlantic Pro-Nutrients, Orlando *Also called Xymogen Inc (G-12725)*
Atlantic Publishing Group Inc (PA) 352 622-6220
1396 Ne 20th Ave Ste 300 Ocala (34470) *(G-11329)*
Atlantic Sails Makers 305 567-1773
2801 Sw 31st Ave Ste 2a Miami (33133) *(G-8764)*
Atlantic Ship Supply Inc 954 961-8885
2050 Sw 31st Ave Hallandale (33009) *(G-4920)*
Atlantic Steel Inc 407 599-3822
131 Sheridan Ct Longwood (32750) *(G-7871)*
Atlantic Steel Cnstr LLC 419 236-2200
18851 Ne 29th Ave Ste 700 Miami (33180) *(G-8765)*
Atlantic Steel Fabricators, Sarasota *Also called Atlantic Concrete Products Inc (G-15604)*
Atlantic Sugar Association 561 996-6541
26400 County Rd 880 Belle Glade (33430) *(G-338)*
Atlantic Tng LLC 941 355-2988
1701 Myrtle St Sarasota (34234) *(G-15605)*
Atlantic Tool & Mfg Corp S 727 546-2250
12600 Belcher Rd S # 10 Largo (33773) *(G-7539)*
Atlantic Vending Inc (PA) 954 605-6046
224 Nw 6th Ave Hallandale Beach (33009) *(G-4937)*
Atlantic West Molding & Mllwk 239 261-2874
4530 Arnold Ave Ste 3 Naples (34104) *(G-10681)*
Atlantic Wire and Rigging Inc 321 633-1552
330 Williams Point Blvd A Cocoa (32927) *(G-1905)*
Atlantis Porcelain Art Corp 305 582-8663
4241 Sw 154th Ct Miami (33185) *(G-8766)*
Atlas Boat Works Inc 239 574-2628
2404 Andalusia Blvd Cape Coral (33909) *(G-1308)*
Atlas Concrete Products Inc 407 277-0841
6452 E Colonial Dr Orlando (32807) *(G-11930)*
Atlas Copco Compressors LLC 813 247-7231
1100 N 50th St Ste 4e Tampa (33619) *(G-16617)*
Atlas Embroidery LLC 954 625-2411
2300 Sw 34th St Fort Lauderdale (33312) *(G-3663)*
Atlas Embroidery & Screen Prtg, Fort Lauderdale *Also called Atlas Embroidery LLC (G-3663)*
Atlas Industrial Scales Inc 352 610-9989
3715 Commercial Way Spring Hill (34606) *(G-16063)*
Atlas Innovative Services Inc 617 259-4529
220 Shreve St Punta Gorda (33950) *(G-14493)*
Atlas Marine Systems Inc 954 735-6767
1801 S Perimeter Rd # 150 Fort Lauderdale (33309) *(G-3664)*
Atlas Metal Industries Inc 305 625-2451
1135 Nw 159th Dr Miami (33169) *(G-8767)*
Atlas Orgnics Indian River LLC 772 563-9336
925 74th Ave Sw Vero Beach (32968) *(G-17737)*
Atlas Paper Mills LLC (HQ) 800 562-2860
3301 Nw 107th St Miami (33167) *(G-8768)*
Atlas Paper Mills LLC 305 835-8046
3725 E 10th Ct Hialeah (33013) *(G-5064)*
Atlas Peat & Soil Inc (PA) 561 734-7300
9621 S State Road 7 Boynton Beach (33472) *(G-845)*
Atlas Polymers Corp 786 312-2131
1809 Micanopy Ave Miami (33133) *(G-8769)*
Atlas Renewable Energy USA LLC 786 358-5614
1221 Brickell Ave # 1200 Miami (33131) *(G-8770)*
Atlas Screen Printing, Gainesville *Also called Paul Wales Inc (G-4746)*
Atlas Sign Industries Fla LLC 561 863-6659
1077 W Blue Heron Blvd Riviera Beach (33404) *(G-14595)*
Atlas Southeast Papers Inc 407 330-9118
3401 Saint Johns Pkwy Sanford (32771) *(G-15268)*
Atlas Tissue A Resolute Bus, Miami *Also called Resolute Tissue LLC (G-9799)*
Atlas Walls LLC 800 951-9201
10500 Rocket Ct Orlando (32824) *(G-11931)*
Atm Pavers Inc 239 322-7010
2710 Del Prado Blvd S Cape Coral (33904) *(G-1309)*
Atm Vault Corp 561 441-9294
2151 Nw Boca Raton Blvd Boca Raton (33431) *(G-420)*
Atmcentral 727 345-8460
6468 5th Ave S Saint Petersburg (33707) *(G-14975)*
Atmfla Inc (PA) 407 425-7708
4601 Sw 34th St Ste 100 Orlando (32811) *(G-11932)*
Atmospheric Wtr Solutions Inc 954 306-6763
12260 Sw 53rd St Ste 603 Cooper City (33330) *(G-2017)*
Atomic Machine & Edm Inc 239 353-9100
1236 Industrial Blvd Naples (34104) *(G-10682)*
Atria Industry 786 334-6621
1866 Nw 82nd Ave Doral (33126) *(G-3125)*
Atris Technology LLC 352 331-3100
3417 Nw 97th Blvd Ste 30 Gainesville (32606) *(G-4655)*
Atsg Logistic Support Service 904 479-3808
9526 Argyle Frest Blvd Un Jacksonville (32222) *(G-5911)*
Attack Communications Inc 954 300-2716
1314 E Las Olas Blvd Fort Lauderdale (33301) *(G-3665)*
Attenti Us Inc (PA) 813 749-5454
1838 Gunn Hwy Odessa (33556) *(G-11538)*
Attesa Holdings Group LLC 305 777-3567
2949 Coconut Ave Unit 20 Miami (33133) *(G-8771)*
Atticus Screen Printing T 407 365-9911
159 N Central Ave Ste I Oviedo (32765) *(G-12807)*
Attitude Drinks Incorporated (PA) 561 227-2727
712 Us Highway 1 Ste 200 North Palm Beach (33408) *(G-11175)*
Aubrey Organics, Tampa *Also called Nutraceutical Corporation (G-17113)*
Audacity Audio, Fort Lauderdale *Also called Audio Storage Technologies (G-3666)*
Audina Hearing Instruments Inc 407 331-0077
165 E Wildmere Ave Longwood (32750) *(G-7872)*
Audio Excellence (PA) 407 277-8790
477 N Semoran Blvd Orlando (32807) *(G-11933)*
Audio Intelligence Devices 954 418-1400
637 Jim Moran Blvd Deerfield Beach (33442) *(G-2673)*
Audio Storage Technologies 954 229-5050
1540 Ne 60th St Fort Lauderdale (33334) *(G-3666)*
Audio Video Imagineering Inc 305 947-6991
11853 Griffing Blvd Biscayne Park (33161) *(G-374)*
Audioshark Inc 954 591-9252
2635 Sherman St Hollywood (33020) *(G-5533)*

ALPHABETIC

Audrey Morris Cosmt Intl LLC..................954 332-2000
  1601 Green Rd Ste A Deerfield Beach (33064) *(G-2674)*

Aurafin-Oroamerica, Tamarac *Also called Richline Group Inc* *(G-16540)*

Aurel Partners LLC..................203 300-7470
  7025 County Road 46a # 1071380 Lake Mary (32746) *(G-7061)*

Aurora Semiconductor LLC..................727 235-6500
  9900 16th St N Saint Petersburg (33716) *(G-14976)*

Aurora Stone & Gravel LLC..................321 253-4808
  2699 Aurora Rd Melbourne (32935) *(G-8370)*

Aurum Chemicals Corp..................305 412-4141
  9485 Sw 72nd St Ste A190 Miami (33173) *(G-8772)*

Aus Manufacturing, Bonifay *Also called Park Central Inc* *(G-775)*

Aus Manufacturing, Bonifay *Also called Parts Central Inc* *(G-776)*

Aussie Boomerang Bar On Ave In..................561 436-9741
  249 N Country Club Dr Lake Worth (33462) *(G-7186)*

Austin Powder Company..................352 690-7060
  5299 Ne 97th Street Rd Anthony (32617) *(G-86)*

Austin Powder Company..................863 674-0504
  6051 Fort Denaud Rd Fort Denaud (33935) *(G-3613)*

Autek Spray Booths, Palm Harbor *Also called Tk - Autek Inc* *(G-13136)*

Autek Spray Booths..................727 709-4373
  6145 126th Ave Unit E Largo (33773) *(G-7540)*

Authentic Pavers LLC..................850 687-1678
  709 Elise Ln Destin (32541) *(G-3059)*

Authentic Trading Inc..................347 866-7241
  11107 Sw 15th Mnr Davie (33324) *(G-2390)*

Authority Software LLC..................877 603-9653
  7154 N University Dr # 211 Tamarac (33321) *(G-16526)*

Autisan International Inc..................941 349-7029
  612 Lotus Ln Sarasota (34242) *(G-15606)*

Auto Gard Qmi Inc..................727 847-5441
  5318 Lemon St New Port Richey (34652) *(G-10962)*

Auto Kare, Zellwood *Also called Goho Enterprises Inc* *(G-18598)*

Auto Labe, Fort Pierce *Also called Booth Manufacturing Company* *(G-4471)*

Auto Shopper, Lakeland *Also called Showcase Publications Inc* *(G-7434)*

Auto Tag of America Inc (PA)..................941 739-8841
  6015 31st St E Bradenton (34203) *(G-942)*

Autocraft Manufacturing Co..................321 453-1850
  810 Kemp St Merritt Island (32952) *(G-8577)*

Automated Accounting Assoc Inc..................512 669-1000
  1665 Governors Dr Pensacola (32514) *(G-13448)*

Automated Buildings Inc..................407 857-0140
  5520 Hansel Ave Orlando (32809) *(G-11934)*

Automated Integration, Tampa *Also called Applied Technologies Group Inc* *(G-16601)*

Automated Machine Products Inc..................715 256-9575
  109 Acadia Ter Kissimmee (34747) *(G-6895)*

Automated Metal Products Inc..................863 638-4404
  16070 Hwy 27 Lake Wales (33859) *(G-7153)*

Automated Mfg Systems Inc..................561 833-9898
  5700 Columbia Cir Mangonia Park (33407) *(G-8088)*

Automated Paper Converters..................954 925-0721
  400 S Dixie Hwy Hollywood (33020) *(G-5534)*

Automated Parking Corporation..................754 200-8441
  6555 Nw 9th Ave Ste 106 Fort Lauderdale (33309) *(G-3667)*

Automated Printing Services..................904 731-3244
  7124 Glendyne Dr N Jacksonville (32216) *(G-5912)*

Automated Production Eqp Ape..................631 654-1197
  2 N Blackwater Ln Key Largo (33037) *(G-6842)*

Automated Production Eqp Ape..................305 451-4722
  2 N Blackwater Ln Key Largo (33037) *(G-6843)*

Automated Services Inc..................772 461-3388
  2700 Industrial Avenue 3 Fort Pierce (34946) *(G-4468)*

Automated Sonix Corporation..................941 964-1361
  5800 Gasparilla Rd Boca Grande (33921) *(G-380)*

Automated Vacuum Systems Inc..................941 378-4565
  2228b Industrial Blvd Sarasota (34234) *(G-15607)*

Automatic Business Products Co..................888 742-7639
  4480 Eastport Park Way Port Orange (32127) *(G-14326)*

Automatic Coax and Cable Inc..................407 322-7622
  4060 Saint Johns Pkwy Sanford (32771) *(G-15269)*

Automatic Mfg Systems Inc..................954 791-1500
  1800 Nw 69th Ave Ste 102 Plantation (33313) *(G-13829)*

Automation Consulting Inc..................850 477-6477
  7100 Plantation Rd Ste 17 Pensacola (32504) *(G-13449)*

Automotive Advertising Assoc..................954 389-6500
  13024 Spring Lake Dr Cooper City (33330) *(G-2018)*

Automotive Armor Mfg Inc..................941 721-3335
  1150 13th Ave E Palmetto (34221) *(G-13156)*

Automotive Mfg & Indus PDT, Ormond Beach *Also called Florida Production Engrg Inc* *(G-12765)*

Automted Lgic Corp Kennesaw GA..................877 866-1226
  7305 Greenbriar Pkwy Orlando (32819) *(G-11935)*

Automundo Magazine, Coral Gables *Also called Automundo Productions Inc* *(G-2031)*

Automundo Productions Inc..................305 541-4198
  2520 Coral Way Ste 2 Coral Gables (33145) *(G-2031)*

Autopax Inc..................772 563-0131
  6602 Liberty Pl Vero Beach (32966) *(G-17738)*

AV Byte..................239 262-1290
  4520 Tamiami Trl N Naples (34103) *(G-10683)*

Avacs, Orange Park *Also called American Vly Avnics Clbrtion L* *(G-11814)*

Avalanche Corporation..................800 708-0087
  17109 Old Ayers Rd Brooksville (34604) *(G-1138)*

Avalex Technologies LLC..................850 470-8464
  2665 Gulf Breeze Pkwy Gulf Breeze (32563) *(G-4877)*

Avalon Aviation Inc..................954 655-0256
  1323 Se 17th St Unit 344 Fort Lauderdale (33316) *(G-3668)*

Avanti Nutritional Labs LLC (PA)..................305 822-3880
  14101 Commerce Way Miami Lakes (33016) *(G-10283)*

Avasar Corp..................321 723-3456
  435 West Dr Melbourne (32904) *(G-8371)*

Avatar Packaging Inc..................813 888-9141
  5110 W Idlewild Ave Tampa (33634) *(G-16618)*

Avaya Inc..................239 498-2737
  25798 Old Gaslight Dr Bonita Springs (34135) *(G-781)*

Avaya Inc..................305 264-7021
  1000 Nw 57th Ct Ste 100 Miami (33126) *(G-8773)*

Avborne Accesory Group LLC (HQ)..................305 593-6038
  7500 Nw 26th St Miami (33122) *(G-8774)*

Avborne Accessory Group Inc (HQ)..................305 593-6038
  7600 Nw 26th St Miami (33122) *(G-8775)*

Avc Plastics, Hialeah *Also called American Vinyl Company* *(G-5051)*

AVCO MARINE CONSTRUCTION, Hudson *Also called Avco Materials and Svcs Inc* *(G-5763)*

Avco Materials and Svcs Inc..................727 233-2043
  7032 Clark St Hudson (34667) *(G-5763)*

Avema Pharma Solutions, Miami *Also called PLD Acquisitions LLC* *(G-9722)*

Aventura Cookies Inc..................954 447-4525
  1868 Nw 140th Ter Pembroke Pines (33028) *(G-13375)*

Aventura Custom Woodwork..................305 891-9093
  1450 Ne 130th St North Miami (33161) *(G-11091)*

Aventura Magazine, Miami *Also called Stern Bloom Media Inc* *(G-9951)*

Aveoengineering LLC..................631 747-6671
  1200 Cinnamon Beach Way # 1122 Palm Coast (32137) *(G-13070)*

Aveotech International, Palm Coast *Also called Aveoengineering LLC* *(G-13070)*

Averett Septic Tank Co Inc..................863 665-1748
  2610 Longhorn Ave Lakeland (33801) *(G-7278)*

Avery Dennison Corporation..................305 228-8740
  5200 Blue Lagoon Dr # 130 Miami (33126) *(G-8776)*

Avery Dennison Corporation..................727 787-1651
  720 Sandy Hook Rd Palm Harbor (34683) *(G-13100)*

Avery Dennison Corporation..................727 785-6995
  2706 Altmate 19 N Ste 314 Palm Harbor (34683) *(G-13101)*

Aveva Drug Dlvry Systems Inc..................954 430-3340
  3280 Executive Way Miramar (33025) *(G-10470)*

Aveva Drug Dlvry Systems Inc (HQ)..................954 430-3340
  3250 Commerce Pkwy Miramar (33025) *(G-10471)*

AVI-Spl Holdings Inc (PA)..................866 708-5034
  6301 Benjamin Rd Ste 101 Tampa (33634) *(G-16619)*

AVI-Spl LLC (HQ)..................813 884-7168
  6301 Benjamin Rd Ste 101 Tampa (33634) *(G-16620)*

Aviacol Usa Corp..................786 701-2152
  2299 Nw 108th Ave Miami (33172) *(G-8777)*

Avian Inventory Management LLC..................407 787-9100
  8649 Transport Dr Ste 100 Orlando (32832) *(G-11936)*

Aviation Instrument Tech Inc (PA)..................813 783-3361
  39520 Aviation Ave Zephyrhills (33542) *(G-18604)*

Aviation Parts & Trade Corp..................954 944-2828
  12331 Nw 7th St Plantation (33325) *(G-13830)*

Aviation Trning Foundation LLC..................844 746-4968
  835 Brimfield Ct Port Orange (32127) *(G-14327)*

Aviation Worldwide Svcs LLC (HQ)..................321 837-2345
  2301 Commerce Park Dr Ne Palm Bay (32905) *(G-12888)*

Avidyne Corporation (PA)..................321 751-8520
  710 North Dr Melbourne (32934) *(G-8372)*

Avionics Support Group Inc..................305 378-9786
  13155 Sw 132nd Ave # 200 Miami (33186) *(G-8778)*

AVK Industries Inc..................904 998-8400
  2052 St Johns Bluff Rd S Jacksonville (32246) *(G-5913)*

Avl Systems Inc..................352 854-1170
  5540 Sw 6th Pl Ocala (34474) *(G-11330)*

Avon Assoc..................561 391-7188
  4101 N Ocean Blvd Boca Raton (33431) *(G-421)*

Avon Cabinet Corporation..................941 755-2866
  5821 24th St E Bradenton (34203) *(G-943)*

Avon Corrugated/Florida Corp..................305 770-3439
  15600 Nw 15th Ave Miami (33169) *(G-8779)*

Avprinting Solutions LLC..................866 207-6295
  6100 Hollywood Blvd Pembroke Pines (33024) *(G-13376)*

Avra Medical Robotics Inc..................407 956-2250
  3259 Progress Dr Ste 112a Orlando (32826) *(G-11937)*

Avro Arms, Bradenton *Also called Arms East LLC* *(G-941)*

Avrora Inc..................386 246-9112
  7 Richfield Pl Palm Coast (32164) *(G-13071)*

Avstar Fuel Systems Inc..................561 575-1560
  1365 Park Ln S Jupiter (33458) *(G-6686)*

Avstar Systems LLC..................239 793-5511
  4025 Skyway Dr Naples (34112) *(G-10684)*

Avt Technology Solutions LLC..................727 539-7429
  5350 Tech Data Dr Clearwater (33760) *(G-1503)*

AVw Inc...954 972-3338
   541 S State Road 7 Ste 2 Margate (33068) *(G-8122)*

Avym LLC...407 970-7746
   639 Oak Hollow Way Altamonte Springs (32714) *(G-32)*

AW Gates Inc...954 341-2180
   11285 Sw 1st St Coral Springs (33071) *(G-2132)*

Aw Publishing..305 856-7000
   3135 Sw 3rd Ave Miami (33129) *(G-8780)*

Aw-Tronics LLC..786 228-7835
   100 Biscayne Blvd # 1315 Miami (33132) *(G-8781)*

Awab LLC..954 763-3003
   245 Sw 32nd St Fort Lauderdale (33315) *(G-3669)*

Awards 4u, Tallahassee *Also called A J Trophies & Awards Inc* *(G-16404)*

Awareness Technology Inc (PA)........................772 283-6540
   2325 Sw Martin Hwy Palm City (34990) *(G-13023)*

Awareness Technology Inc................................772 283-6540
   1935 Sw Martin Hwy Palm City (34990) *(G-13024)*

Awe Diagnostics LLC...786 285-0755
   3401 N Miami Ave Ste 230 Miami (33127) *(G-8782)*

Awl Manufacturing Inc.......................................239 643-5780
   4406 Exchange Ave Ste 109 Naples (34104) *(G-10685)*

Awnings By Coversol...813 251-4774
   5211 W Hillsborough Ave Tampa (33634) *(G-16621)*

Awnings of Hollywood Inc..................................954 963-7717
   5828 Washington St Hollywood (33023) *(G-5535)*

Awnit Corporation
   820 S Parrott Ave Okeechobee (34974) *(G-11598)*

Aws, Doral *Also called American Welding Society Inc* *(G-3113)*

Axi International (PA)..239 690-9589
   5400 Division Dr Ste 1 Fort Myers (33905) *(G-4184)*

Axiom Diagnostics Inc..813 902-9888
   4309 W Tyson Ave Tampa (33611) *(G-16622)*

Axiom International, Clearwater *Also called Axiom Services Inc* *(G-1504)*

Axiom Manufacturing Inc....................................321 223-3394
   962 Hailey St West Melbourne (32904) *(G-17893)*

Axiom Services Inc (PA).....................................727 442-7774
   1805 Drew St Clearwater (33765) *(G-1504)*

Axion Signs Inc...954 274-1146
   1027 Ne 44th St Oakland Park (33334) *(G-11244)*

Axis, Orlando *Also called Advanced Xrgrphics Imging Syst* *(G-11872)*

Axis Group...954 580-6000
   4701 N Federal Hwy # 440 Pompano Beach (33064) *(G-13942)*

Axis Phrm Partners LLC......................................407 936-2949
   550 Technology Park Lake Mary (32746) *(G-7062)*

Axley Brothers Saw Mill Inc................................727 531-8724
   6350 123rd Ave Largo (33773) *(G-7541)*

Axogen Inc (PA)..386 462-6800
   13631 Progress Blvd # 400 Alachua (32615) *(G-6)*

Axogen Corporation...386 462-6800
   13631 Progress Blvd # 400 Alachua (32615) *(G-7)*

Axon Circuit Inc...407 265-7980
   155 National Pl Unit 105 Longwood (32750) *(G-7873)*

Axon Circuit Inc (PA)...407 265-7980
   424 S Ware Blvd Ste A Tampa (33619) *(G-16623)*

Axop Industries Inc..239 273-0911
   5091 Cherry Wood Dr Naples (34119) *(G-10686)*

Axrdham Corp...813 653-9588
   2134 Ridgemore Dr Valrico (33594) *(G-17662)*

Axtonne Inc..510 755-7480
   350 Se 1st St Delray Beach (33483) *(G-2934)*

Axxionflex, Coral Gables *Also called Ibd Industrial LLC* *(G-2069)*

Axxium Engineering LLC.....................................786 573-9808
   14032 Sw 140th St 16 Miami (33186) *(G-8783)*

Axzes LLC...786 626-1611
   3401 Nw 82nd Ave Ste 370 Doral (33122) *(G-3126)*

Ayam Beautycare LLC...305 318-2598
   19495 Biscayne Blvd # 608 Aventura (33180) *(G-254)*

Ayanna Plastics & Engrg Inc...............................727 561-4329
   4701 110th Ave N Clearwater (33762) *(G-1505)*

Ayers Office Supply, Trenton *Also called Ayers Publishing Inc* *(G-17629)*

Ayers Publishing Inc..352 463-7135
   207 N Main St Trenton (32693) *(G-17629)*

Aylynn Maritime LLC (PA)...................................954 564-6134
   400 Ocean Trail Way Jupiter (33477) *(G-6687)*

Ayon Cybersecurity Inc.......................................321 953-3033
   5155 King St Cocoa (32926) *(G-1906)*

Ayurdevas Natural Products LLC..........................786 322-0909
   2076 Nw 21st St Miami (33142) *(G-8784)*

AZ Chem Holdings LP...800 526-5294
   4600 Touchton Rd E # 1200 Jacksonville (32246) *(G-5914)*

Azar & Company, Jacksonville *Also called Azar Industries Inc* *(G-5915)*

Azar Industries Inc..904 358-2354
   719 E Union St Jacksonville (32206) *(G-5915)*

Azcue Pumps USA Inc..954 597-7602
   10308 W Mcnab Rd Tamarac (33321) *(G-16527)*

Azex Flow Technologies Inc.................................305 393-8037
   13431 Nw 19th Ln Miami (33182) *(G-8785)*

Azimuth Communications Corp.............................727 573-5735
   12770 44th St N Clearwater (33762) *(G-1506)*

Azopharma Inc..954 536-4738
   6137 Sw 19th St Miramar (33023) *(G-10472)*

Azt Technology LLC..239 352-0600
   10130 Market St Ste 7 Naples (34112) *(G-10687)*

Aztlan Foods Corp...786 202-8301
   9110 Nw 106th St Medley (33178) *(G-8204)*

Azul Stone LLC...561 655-9385
   920 Fern St West Palm Beach (33401) *(G-17931)*

Azure Computing Inc..407 359-8787
   5700 Dot Com Ct Ste 1010 Oviedo (32765) *(G-12808)*

Azurrx, Boca Raton *Also called First Wave Biopharma Inc* *(G-515)*

Azz Powder Coating - Tampa LLC (HQ)..................813 390-2802
   4901 Distribution Dr Tampa (33605) *(G-16624)*

B & A Manufacturing Co......................................561 848-8648
   3665 E Industrial Way Riviera Beach (33404) *(G-14596)*

B & B Industries Orlando Inc...............................407 366-1800
   3008 Kananwood Ct Ste 124 Oviedo (32765) *(G-12809)*

B & B of Saint Augustine Inc...............................904 829-6855
   2875 Us Highway 1 S Saint Augustine (32086) *(G-14812)*

B & B Signs & Awnings Inc..................................727 507-0600
   12305 62nd St Unit B Largo (33773) *(G-7542)*

B & B Timber Company..904 284-5541
   4880 Highway 17 S Green Cove Springs (32043) *(G-4818)*

B & B Trailers and Accessories, Saint Augustine *Also called B & B of Saint Augustine Inc* *(G-14812)*

B & B Trailers and Accessories............................904 829-6855
   2875 Us Highway 1 S Saint Augustine (32086) *(G-14813)*

B & C Sheet Metal Duct Corp...............................305 316-9212
   1025 Sw 82nd Ave Miami (33144) *(G-8786)*

B & D Machine and Tool Inc................................321 727-0098
   1720 Main St Ne Ste 3 Palm Bay (32905) *(G-12889)*

B & D Precision Tools Inc....................................305 885-1583
   2367 W 8th Ln Hialeah (33010) *(G-5065)*

B & E Rv Service & Repair LLC.............................352 401-7930
   6028 Ne 26th Ave Ocala (34479) *(G-11331)*

B & F Waste Solutions Llc...................................772 336-1113
   4901 Bethel Creek Dr F Vero Beach (32963) *(G-17739)*

B & G Instruments Inc..305 871-4445
   5000 Nw 36th St Bldg 875 Miami (33166) *(G-8787)*

B & J Atlantic Inc..904 338-0088
   5164 Shawland Rd Jacksonville (32254) *(G-5916)*

B & K Discount Cabinets LLC (PA)........................321 254-2322
   280 N Wickham Rd Melbourne (32935) *(G-8373)*

B & K Installations Inc..305 245-6968
   246 Sw 4th Ave Homestead (33030) *(G-5701)*

B & L Cremation Systems Inc..............................727 541-4666
   7205 114th Ave Ste A Largo (33773) *(G-7543)*

B & M Industries Inc..813 754-9960
   2401 Airport Rd Unit C Plant City (33563) *(G-13742)*

B & M Precision Inc...813 645-1188
   1225 4th St Sw Ruskin (33570) *(G-14774)*

B & N Wldg & Fabrication Inc...............................813 719-3956
   4200 National Guard Dr Plant City (33563) *(G-13743)*

B & P Motor Heads Inc..305 769-3183
   1815 Opa Locka Blvd Opa Locka (33054) *(G-11720)*

B & P Motors Inc...305 687-7337
   1815 Opa Locka Blvd Opa Locka (33054) *(G-11721)*

B & R Products Inc (PA)......................................305 238-1592
   18721 Sw 104th Ave Cutler Bay (33157) *(G-2284)*

B & R Profiles LLC (PA).......................................305 479-8308
   216 Homeland Cemetery Rd Bartow (33830) *(G-299)*

B & R Sales Corporation.....................................727 571-2231
   11551 43rd St N Clearwater (33762) *(G-1507)*

B & S Rigging Inc..727 532-9466
   112 Spring Time St Spring Hill (34608) *(G-16064)*

B & T Metalworks Inc...352 236-6000
   4630 Ne 35th St Ocala (34479) *(G-11332)*

B and B Roof and Floor Trusses..........................850 265-4119
   1808 Tennessee Ave Lynn Haven (32444) *(G-8025)*

B and M Sugar Products LLC...............................305 897-8427
   936 Sw 1st Ave 345 Miami (33130) *(G-8788)*

B B J Environmental Solutions, Tampa *Also called Bbj Environmental LLC* *(G-16634)*

B Braun Medical Inc...386 274-1837
   1341 N Clyde Morris Blvd Daytona Beach (32117) *(G-2516)*

B Braun Medical Inc...386 888-2000
   1845 Mason Ave Daytona Beach (32117) *(G-2517)*

B Braun Medical Inc...866 388-5120
   1830 Holsonback Dr Daytona Beach (32117) *(G-2518)*

B C Cabinetry...561 393-8937
   10625 Mendocino Ln Boca Raton (33428) *(G-422)*

B C T, Fort Lauderdale *Also called BCT International Inc* *(G-3680)*

B E Aerospace..305 459-7000
   9100 Nw 105th Cir Medley (33178) *(G-8205)*

B E Pressure Supply Inc......................................561 688-9246
   5483 Leaper Dr West Palm Beach (33407) *(G-17932)*

B F E, Jacksonville *Also called Brake-Funderburk Entps Inc* *(G-5951)*

B F Industries Inc..561 368-6662
   4201 Oak Cir Ste 29 Boca Raton (33431) *(G-423)*

B Finch Logging, Wausau *Also called Bernice I Finch* *(G-17831)*

B G Instrument Corp.....941 485-7700
112 Morse Ct North Venice (34275) ***(G-11207)***
B G Service Company Inc.....561 659-1471
1400 Alabama Ave Ste 15 West Palm Beach (33401) ***(G-17933)***
B H Bunn Company.....863 647-1555
2730 Drane Field Rd Lakeland (33811) ***(G-7279)***
B H C P Inc.....850 444-9300
4109 N Davis Hwy Pensacola (32503) ***(G-13450)***
B H Med Supplies, Miami *Also called Frozen Wheels LLC* ***(G-9177)***
B J and ME Inc.....561 368-5470
2284 N Dixie Hwy Fl 1 Boca Raton (33431) ***(G-424)***
B Line Apparel Inc.....305 953-8300
4671 E 11th Ave Hialeah (33013) ***(G-5066)***
B M H Concrete Inc.....561 615-0011
6811 Belvedere Rd West Palm Beach (33413) ***(G-17934)***
B M I Properties, Jacksonville *Also called Florida Floats Inc* ***(G-6105)***
B P I, Miami *Also called Brain Power Incorporated* ***(G-8851)***
B R Q Grossmans Inc.....954 971-1077
2087 N Powerline Rd Ste 1 Pompano Beach (33069) ***(G-13943)***
B R Signs Inc.....954 973-7700
1301 W Copans Rd Ste B6 Pompano Beach (33064) ***(G-13944)***
B Squared of Chiefland LLC.....352 507-2195
710 Nw 17th Ave Chiefland (32626) ***(G-1446)***
B T G, Alachua *Also called Back To Godhead Inc* ***(G-8)***
B T I, West Palm Beach *Also called Setty Enterprises Inc* ***(G-18149)***
B V M, Winter Springs *Also called Bob Violett Models Inc* ***(G-18561)***
B&B Custom Sheet Metal Inc.....727 938-8083
770 N Grosse Ave Ste B Tarpon Springs (34689) ***(G-17458)***
B&C Publishing Inc.....305 385-8216
13010 N Calusa Club Dr Miami (33186) ***(G-8789)***
B&C Signs.....386 426-2373
2525 Guava Dr Edgewater (32141) ***(G-3479)***
B&K Country Feeds LLC.....561 701-1852
912 Jamaican Dr West Palm Beach (33415) ***(G-17935)***
B&M, Miami *Also called B and M Sugar Products LLC* ***(G-8788)***
B&M Logging Inc.....386 397-1145
10616 Se County Road 135 White Springs (32096) ***(G-18304)***
B&M RC Racing.....313 518-3999
4336 Shadow Wood Way Winter Haven (33880) ***(G-18419)***
B&Sdelicious DESserts&cupcakes.....954 557-8350
865 Nw 27th Ter Fort Lauderdale (33311) ***(G-3670)***
B-N-J Powder Coatings LLC.....407 999-8448
111 W Pineloch Ave Ste 2 Orlando (32806) ***(G-11938)***
B-Scada Inc (PA).....352 564-9610
9030 W Fort Island Trl 9a Crystal River (34429) ***(G-2267)***
B-Token USA Inc.....305 735-2065
1111 Lincoln Rd Ste 400 Miami Beach (33139) ***(G-10169)***
B/E Aerospace Inc (HQ).....410 266-2048
1400 Corporate Center Way Wellington (33414) ***(G-17844)***
B/E Aerospace Inc.....786 337-8144
6303 Blue Lagoon Dr Miami (33126) ***(G-8790)***
B/E Aerospace Inc.....305 471-8800
9835 Nw 14th St Doral (33172) ***(G-3127)***
B224 USA Co.....786 598-8805
2508 Baywood Dr Holiday (34690) ***(G-5490)***
B2b Sign Resource.....813 855-7446
13359 W Hillsborough Ave # 104 Tampa (33635) ***(G-16625)***
B4 Enterprises Inc.....352 529-1114
241 S Main St Williston (32696) ***(G-18330)***
B4c Technologies Inc.....772 463-1557
4306 Sw Cargo Way Palm City (34990) ***(G-13025)***
Ba Precision Products Corp.....561 859-3400
2920 Nw 2nd Ave Ste 3 Boca Raton (33431) ***(G-425)***
Baa LLC.....954 292-9449
16482 Sw 18th St Miramar (33027) ***(G-10473)***
Babbala LLC.....844 869-5747
2901 Clint Moore Rd Boca Raton (33496) ***(G-426)***
Babcock & Wilcox Company.....561 478-3800
6501 N Jog Rd West Palm Beach (33412) ***(G-17936)***
Baby Abuelita Productions LLC.....305 662-7320
6619 S Dixie Hwy Ste 139 Miami (33143) ***(G-8791)***
Baby Beef USA, Miami *Also called Latin Amercn Meats & Foods USA* ***(G-9434)***
Baby Food Chef LLC.....305 335-5990
2905 W Aviary Dr Hollywood (33026) ***(G-5536)***
Baby Guard Inc.....954 741-6351
11947 W Sample Rd Coral Springs (33065) ***(G-2133)***
Baby Guard Pool Fence Co, Coral Springs *Also called Baby Guard Inc* ***(G-2133)***
Babys Coffee LLC.....305 744-9866
3178 Us Highway 1 Key West (33040) ***(G-6855)***
Bacardi Bottling Corporation.....904 757-1290
12200 N Main St Jacksonville (32218) ***(G-5917)***
Bacc Coatings LLC.....239 424-8843
926 Se 9th St Cape Coral (33990) ***(G-1310)***
Bach Diamonds.....954 921-4069
2910 Oakwood Blvd Hollywood (33020) ***(G-5537)***
Bachiller Iron Works Inc.....305 751-7773
295 Ne 71st St Miami (33138) ***(G-8792)***
Baci By Remcraft, Opa Locka *Also called Remcraft Lighting Products Inc* ***(G-11784)***
Back Lory Lee.....850 638-5430
403 Cutchins Mill Rd Chipley (32428) ***(G-1453)***
Back To Godhead Inc.....386 462-0481
13921 Nw 146th Ave Alachua (32615) ***(G-8)***
Backbone Interconnect LLC.....954 800-4749
10501 Nw 50th St 104-3 Sunrise (33351) ***(G-16294)***
Backoff Products, Fort Lauderdale *Also called Signal Dynamics Corporation* ***(G-4046)***
Backtocad Technologies LLC.....727 303-0383
601 Cleveland St Ste 310 Clearwater (33755) ***(G-1508)***
Backwoods Crossing Llc.....850 765-3753
6725 Mahan Dr Tallahassee (32308) ***(G-16416)***
Backyard Canvas & Signs Inc.....813 672-2660
11225 Restwood Dr Gibsonton (33534) ***(G-4794)***
Backyard Feed LLC.....813 846-5995
6400 County Road 214 Saint Augustine (32092) ***(G-14814)***
Badaro Group, Clearwater *Also called Pelican International Inc* ***(G-1737)***
Bader Prosthetics & Orthotics.....813 962-6100
5513 W Sligh Ave Tampa (33634) ***(G-16626)***
Badger Corporation.....954 942-5277
3450 Ne 6th Ter Pompano Beach (33064) ***(G-13945)***
Badger Welding Orlando LLC.....407 648-1100
806 W Landstreet Rd Orlando (32824) ***(G-11939)***
Badger Woodworks LLC.....386 860-9600
3800 Entp Way Ste 1160 Sanford (32771) ***(G-15270)***
Bae Systems Sthast Shpyrds Amh (HQ).....904 251-3111
8500 Heckscher Dr Jacksonville (32226) ***(G-5918)***
Bae Systems Tech Sltons Svcs I.....850 664-6070
557 Mary Esther Cut Off N Fort Walton Beach (32548) ***(G-4563)***
Bae Systems Tech Sltons Svcs I.....850 244-6433
715 Hollywood Blvd Nw Fort Walton Beach (32548) ***(G-4564)***
Bae Systems Tech Sltons Svcs I.....850 344-0832
70 Ready Ave Nw Fort Walton Beach (32548) ***(G-4565)***
Baez Enterprises Corp.....813 317-7277
6315 Morning Star Dr Seffner (33584) ***(G-15952)***
Bag Lady Dolls Inc.....305 265-0081
4392 Sw 74th Ave Miami (33155) ***(G-8793)***
Bag of Ice, Lake City *Also called Optima Associates Inc* ***(G-7036)***
Bag-A-Nut LLC.....904 641-3934
10601 Theresa Dr Jacksonville (32246) ***(G-5919)***
Bageland, Pompano Beach *Also called OPelle Enterprises Inc* ***(G-14111)***
Bagindd Prints.....954 971-9000
1843 Nw 83rd Dr Coral Springs (33071) ***(G-2134)***
Bags Express Inc.....305 500-9849
1555 Nw 97th Ave Doral (33172) ***(G-3128)***
Bahama Boat Works LLC.....561 882-4069
5490 Dexter Way Mangonia Park (33407) ***(G-8089)***
Bahamas Uphl & Mar Canvas Inc.....305 992-4346
4548 Sw 75th Ave Miami (33155) ***(G-8794)***
Bahri Industries Inc.....904 744-4472
3551 University Blvd N Jacksonville (32277) ***(G-5920)***
Baila Con Micho Inc.....786 953-8566
7911 Nw 72nd Ave Medley (33166) ***(G-8206)***
Bailey Industries Inc (PA).....352 326-2898
1107 Thomas Ave Leesburg (34748) ***(G-7761)***
Bailey Timber Co Inc.....850 674-2080
19872 State Road 20 W # 2 Blountstown (32424) ***(G-375)***
Bailey-Sigler Inc.....386 428-5566
1050 Fremont St New Smyrna Beach (32168) ***(G-10995)***
Baird, West Palm Beach *Also called Thermo Arl US Inc* ***(G-18177)***
Bajio Inc.....630 461-0915
1674 Tionia Rd New Smyrna Beach (32168) ***(G-10996)***
Baju Professional Brick Pavers.....727 234-5300
5511 110th Ave N Pinellas Park (33782) ***(G-13672)***
Baker County Press Inc.....904 259-2400
104 S 5th St Macclenny (32063) ***(G-8036)***
Baker Metal Works & Supply LLC (PA).....850 537-2010
5846 Highway 189 N Baker (32531) ***(G-291)***
Baker Metalworks and Sup Inc.....850 537-2010
5846 Highway 189 N Baker (32531) ***(G-292)***
Baker Norton US Inc.....305 575-6000
74 Nw 176th St Miami (33169) ***(G-8795)***
Baker's Sporting Goods, Jacksonville *Also called Bakers Sports Inc* ***(G-5921)***
Baker-Hill Industries Inc.....954 752-3090
3850 Nw 118th Ave Coral Springs (33065) ***(G-2135)***
Bakerly LLC (HQ).....786 539-5888
2600 S Douglas Rd Ste 410 Coral Gables (33134) ***(G-2032)***
Bakers Element, Fort Lauderdale *Also called Bay State Milling Company* ***(G-3677)***
Bakers Sports Inc (PA).....904 388-8126
3600 Beachwood Ct Jacksonville (32224) ***(G-5921)***
Balimoy Manufacturing, Mulberry *Also called Dse Inc* ***(G-10624)***
Balistic 2400 LLC.....407 955-0065
2338 Immokalee Rd Ste 177 Naples (34110) ***(G-10688)***
Ball Busines Products, Port Saint Lucie *Also called Discount Distributors Inc* ***(G-14407)***
Ball Metal Beverage Cont Corp.....813 980-6073
4700 Whiteway Dr Tampa (33617) ***(G-16627)***
Ballard Printing Inc.....904 783-4430
1233 Lane Ave S Ste 11 Jacksonville (32205) ***(G-5922)***
Ballista Tactical Systems.....954 260-0765
2881 E Oakland Park Blvd Fort Lauderdale (33306) ***(G-3671)***

Ballistic Recovery Systems Inc................651 457-7491
1543 N Powerline Rd # 3 Pompano Beach (33069) *(G-13946)*

Balls Rod & Kustom LLC................888 446-2191
5118 Nw 24th Dr Gainesville (32605) *(G-4656)*

Balm Tattoo, North Miami *Also called Delab Care USA LLC* *(G-11102)*

Balpack Incorporated................941 371-7323
5438 Ashton Ct Sarasota (34233) *(G-15608)*

Balpro Powder Coating Inc................954 797-0520
1624 Nw 38th Ave Fort Lauderdale (33311) *(G-3672)*

Balsys Technology Group Inc................407 656-3719
930 Carter Rd Ste 228 Winter Garden (34787) *(G-18375)*

Baltic Marble Inc................561 436-3774
4180 Brook Cir W West Palm Beach (33417) *(G-17937)*

Balzarano John................239 455-1231
781 14th St Se Naples (34117) *(G-10689)*

Bam Building and More, Lake City *Also called Grays Portable Buildings Inc* *(G-7020)*

Bam Enterprises Inc................850 469-8872
2906 N Davis Hwy Pensacola (32503) *(G-13451)*

Bama Printing LLC................561 855-7641
2257 Vista Pkwy Ste 11 West Palm Beach (33411) *(G-17938)*

Bamco Inc................303 886-5992
13799 Park Blvd Ste 274 Seminole (33776) *(G-15970)*

Bamcore, Ocala *Also called Global Bamboo Technologies Inc* *(G-11399)*

Bamm Manufacturing Inc................239 277-0776
1222 Hemingway Dr Fort Myers (33912) *(G-4185)*

Banaghan Wood Products Inc................386 788-6114
741 Tarry Town Trl Port Orange (32127) *(G-14328)*

Banaszak Concrete Corp................954 476-1004
2401 College Ave Davie (33317) *(G-2391)*

Bandart Enterprises Inc................954 564-1224
5303 Nw 35th Ter Fort Lauderdale (33309) *(G-3673)*

Bang Energy LLC................954 641-0570
1600 N Park Dr Weston (33326) *(G-18227)*

Banker Steel South LLC................407 293-0120
6635 Edgewater Dr Orlando (32810) *(G-11940)*

Bankingly Inc................734 201-0007
1942 Ne 148th St North Miami (33181) *(G-11092)*

Banks Airconditioning & Rfrgn................813 917-8685
5001 Miley Rd Plant City (33565) *(G-13744)*

Banks Lumber Co Inc................863 687-6068
105 Progress Rd Auburndale (33823) *(G-219)*

Banks Sign Systems Inc................954 979-0055
1791 Blount Rd Ste 1001 Pompano Beach (33069) *(G-13947)*

Banks, Roy Sign Systems, Pompano Beach *Also called Banks Sign Systems Inc* *(G-13947)*

Banners & Signs, Orange Park *Also called Banners-N-Signs Etc Inc* *(G-11815)*

Banners-N-Signs Etc Inc................904 272-3395
1970 Solomon St Orange Park (32073) *(G-11815)*

Banyan Gaming LLC................954 951-7094
245 Ne 21st Ave Ste 300 Deerfield Beach (33441) *(G-2675)*

Banyan Hill................561 455-9045
98 Se 6th Ave Ste 2 Delray Beach (33483) *(G-2935)*

Banyan Printing, Lake Worth *Also called Midds Inc* *(G-7217)*

Banyan Printing, Lake Worth Beach *Also called Midds Inc* *(G-7258)*

Baptist Communications Mission (HQ)................954 981-2271
3400 Raleigh St Hollywood (33021) *(G-5538)*

Baptist Mid-Missions Inc................863 382-6350
3417 Kenilworth Blvd Sebring (33870) *(G-15915)*

Bar Beverage Ctrl Systems Fla................239 213-3301
3427 Exchange Ave Ste 7 Naples (34104) *(G-10690)*

Bar Maid Corporation (PA)................954 960-1468
2950 Nw 22nd Ter Pompano Beach (33069) *(G-13948)*

Barbecue Superstore................305 635-4427
3800 Nw 59th St Miami (33142) *(G-8796)*

Barber Fertilizer Company................850 263-6324
5221 Highway 231 Campbellton (32426) *(G-1259)*

Barbes Publishing Inc................904 992-9945
13500 Sutton Park Dr S # 105 Jacksonville (32224) *(G-5923)*

Barco LLC................305 677-9600
475 Brickell Ave Miami (33131) *(G-8797)*

Barco Sales & Mfg Inc................954 563-3922
4201 Ne 6th Ave Oakland Park (33334) *(G-11245)*

Barcode Automation Inc................407 327-2177
207 N Moss Rd Ste 105 Winter Springs (32708) *(G-18560)*

Barcode Distributor, Miami *Also called Logiscenter LLC* *(G-9471)*

Bard Sports Corp (PA)................305 233-2200
14516 Sw 119th Ave Miami (33186) *(G-8798)*

Bare Arii LLC................352 701-6625
10610 N 30th St Apt 13g Tampa (33612) *(G-16628)*

Bare Board Group Inc (PA)................727 549-2200
8565 Somerset Dr Ste B Largo (33773) *(G-7544)*

Bare Board Group Intl LLC................727 549-2200
8565 Somerset Dr Ste B Largo (33773) *(G-7545)*

Bari Associates Inc................941 342-9385
1805 Apex Rd Sarasota (34240) *(G-15609)*

Bari Millwork & Supply LLC................954 969-9440
1975 Nw 18th St Ste C Pompano Beach (33069) *(G-13949)*

Barjo Printing and Sign................786 332-2661
7911 Nw 72nd Ave Medley (33166) *(G-8207)*

Barnacle King LLC................954 952-9140
1701 Ne 14th Ave Unit 2 Fort Lauderdale (33305) *(G-3674)*

Barnard Nut Company Inc................305 836-9999
2801 Nw 125th St Miami (33167) *(G-8799)*

Barnes & Sons Wood Producers................386 935-2229
105 Suwannee Ave Nw Branford (32008) *(G-1111)*

Barnett & Pugliano................727 826-6075
200 2nd Ave S Saint Petersburg (33701) *(G-14977)*

Baro Granite Inc................786 663-2514
2775 W 79th St Unit 6 Hialeah (33016) *(G-5067)*

Baron LLC................239 691-5783
4784 Skates Cir Fort Myers (33905) *(G-4186)*

Baron International LLC................800 531-9558
17180 Innovation Dr Jupiter (33478) *(G-6688)*

Baron Manufacturing, Pompano Beach *Also called N & N Investment Corporation* *(G-14106)*

Baron Pavers Corp................786 389-2894
3281 Nw 18th St Miami (33125) *(G-8800)*

Baron Sign Manufacturing, Jupiter *Also called Baron International LLC* *(G-6688)*

Barr Systems LLC................352 491-3100
4961 Nw 8th Ave Ste B Gainesville (32605) *(G-4657)*

Barrau & Coirin Inc................305 571-5051
6214 Ne 4th Ct Miami (33138) *(G-8801)*

Barreiro Concrete Mtls Inc................305 805-0095
25440 Sw 140th Ave Princeton (33032) *(G-14486)*

Barrett & Company................305 293-4501
3201 Flagler Ave Ste 501 Key West (33040) *(G-6856)*

Barrett Custom Designs LLC................321 242-2002
6430 Anderson Way Ste A Melbourne (32940) *(G-8374)*

Barrette Outdoor Living Inc................352 754-8555
2401 Corporate Blvd Brooksville (34604) *(G-1139)*

Barrier-1 Inc................877 224-5850
640 Garden Commerce Pkwy Winter Garden (34787) *(G-18376)*

Barron Boyz Auto................229 403-2656
1324 Fairway Village Dr Fleming Island (32003) *(G-3608)*

Barrows Aluminum Inc................386 767-3445
630 Oak Pl Ste H Port Orange (32127) *(G-14329)*

Barrs Equipment Service Inc................407 999-5214
2506 Taylor Ave Orlando (32806) *(G-11941)*

Barry Resnick................407 296-9999
480 27th St Orlando (32806) *(G-11942)*

Barstool Comforts LLC................610 737-5856
623 Front St Apt 5305 Kissimmee (34747) *(G-6896)*

Barth Industries................727 787-6392
1701 Hickory Gate Dr S Dunedin (34698) *(G-3440)*

Bartman Enterprises Inc................321 259-4898
2735 Center Pl Ste 101 Melbourne (32940) *(G-8375)*

Barton & Guestier Usa Inc................305 895-9757
4700 Biscayne Blvd # 503 Miami (33137) *(G-8802)*

Bartow Ethanol Florida LC................863 533-2498
1705 E Mann Rd Bartow (33830) *(G-300)*

Bartow Machine Works Inc................863 533-6361
441 W Vine St Bartow (33830) *(G-301)*

Baru Agency Incorporated................305 259-8800
8400 Nw 36th St Ste 450 Doral (33166) *(G-3129)*

Bas Plastics Inc................954 202-9080
1000 Nw 56th St Fort Lauderdale (33309) *(G-3675)*

Baseball Digest, Orlando *Also called Grandstand Publishing LLC* *(G-12199)*

Basecrete Technologies LLC................941 312-5142
8255 Consumer Ct Sarasota (34240) *(G-15610)*

Basewest Inc................727 573-2700
4240 116th Ter N Clearwater (33762) *(G-1509)*

BASF Corporation................850 627-7688
1101 N Madison St Quincy (32352) *(G-14541)*

Bashert Diamonds Inc................305 466-1881
3201 Ne 183rd St Apt 408 Aventura (33160) *(G-255)*

Basic Fun Inc (PA)................561 997-8901
301 E Yamato Rd Ste 4200 Boca Raton (33431) *(G-427)*

Bask, Miami *Also called Zap Mosquito Solutions Inc* *(G-10155)*

Bass Auto Industries LLC................727 446-4051
2084 Range Rd Clearwater (33765) *(G-1510)*

Bass Bulletin and Directory, Hialeah *Also called Bass Industries Inc* *(G-5068)*

Bass Industries Inc................305 751-2716
604 W 18th St Hialeah (33010) *(G-5068)*

Bastech Inc................904 737-1722
3211 Powers Ave Jacksonville (32207) *(G-5924)*

Bastech Inc................904 737-1722
3035 Powers Ave Ste 3 Jacksonville (32207) *(G-5925)*

Bastinelli Creations LLC................407 572-8073
109 Hangar Rd Kissimmee (34741) *(G-6897)*

Batech Inc................321 784-4838
760 Mullet Rd Cape Canaveral (32920) *(G-1277)*

Bath Junkie of Gainesville................352 331-3012
7529 Nw 136th St Gainesville (32653) *(G-4658)*

Bathroom World Manufacturing................954 566-0451
4160 Ne 6th Ave Oakland Park (33334) *(G-11246)*

Batter To Platter LLC................203 309-7632
2660 Jewett Ln Sanford (32771) *(G-15271)*

Batteries Plus, Lake Park *Also called Palm Beach Btry Ventures LLC* *(G-7132)*

Batteries Plus, Tampa *Also called Future Plus of Florida* *(G-16865)*

Battery Assemblers, Sanford *Also called Mathews Associates Inc* *(G-15354)*

Battery On The Go, Coconut Creek *Also called JW Marketing and Consulting* *(G-1995)*

Battery Power Solutions Inc 727 446-8400
936 Cleveland St Ste A Clearwater (33755) *(G-1511)*

Battery Savers, Riviera Beach *Also called David S Stoyka* *(G-14615)*

Battery Usa Inc (PA) 863 665-6317
1840 S Combee Rd Lakeland (33801) *(G-7280)*

Battery Usa Inc 863 665-5401
1930 S Combee Rd Lakeland (33801) *(G-7281)*

Bauducco Manufacturing Inc 305 477-9270
1705 Nw 133rd Ave Ste 101 Miami (33182) *(G-8803)*

Bauducco USA Holding Company (HQ) 305 477-9270
1705 Nw 133rd Ave Ste 101 Miami (33182) *(G-8804)*

Bauer Small Arms Trning Ctr In 850 862-1811
5615 Bauer Rd Pensacola (32507) *(G-13452)*

Bauformat South-East LLC 201 693-6635
1413 Nw 5th Ave Fort Lauderdale (33311) *(G-3676)*

Bausch & Lomb Incorporated 813 975-7700
8500 Hidden River Pkwy Tampa (33637) *(G-16629)*

Bausch & Lomb Incorporated 727 724-6600
21 N Park Place Blvd Clearwater (33759) *(G-1512)*

Bausch American Towers LLC 772 283-2771
6800 Sw Jack James Dr # 3 Stuart (34997) *(G-16119)*

Bausch Enterprises Inc 772 220-6652
3171 Se Waaler St Stuart (34997) *(G-16120)*

Bausch Lomb Surgical Inc 727 724-6600
21 N Park Place Blvd Clearwater (33759) *(G-1513)*

Bava Inc 850 893-4799
1403 Maclay Commerce Dr Tallahassee (32312) *(G-16417)*

Bavaria Corp International, Apopka *Also called Bavaria Corporation* *(G-104)*

Bavaria Corporation 407 880-0322
515 Cooper Commerce Dr # 10 Apopka (32703) *(G-104)*

Baxley Services Inc 850 675-4459
13451 Highway 89 Jay (32565) *(G-6648)*

Baxter Custom Fabrication Inc 863 289-9819
133 Browning Cir Winter Haven (33884) *(G-18420)*

Baxter Healthcare Corporation 727 544-5050
7511 114th Ave Largo (33773) *(G-7546)*

Bay Area Graphics 813 247-2400
4040 E Adamo Dr Tampa (33605) *(G-16630)*

Bay Area Prosthetics, Clearwater *Also called Baycare Home Care Inc* *(G-1514)*

Bay Area Security Shred 877 974-7337
301 Bear Ridge Cir Palm Harbor (34683) *(G-13102)*

Bay Area Signs Inc 813 677-0237
3858 E Knights Griffin Rd Plant City (33565) *(G-13745)*

Bay Armature and Supply, Tampa *Also called Electrcal Systems Cmmnications* *(G-16799)*

Bay Cabinets and Millworks 850 215-1485
20679 Panama Cy Bch Pkwy Panama City Beach (32413) *(G-13326)*

Bay City Window Company 727 323-5443
3220 Bennett St N Ste A Saint Petersburg (33713) *(G-14978)*

Bay City X-Press Signs & Prtg, Tampa *Also called Ljk & TS Partners Inc* *(G-17018)*

Bay Cnc Machine LLC 813 362-9626
305 Scarlet Blvd Oldsmar (34677) *(G-11631)*

Bay Design Marine Group Inc 239 825-8094
2319 J And C Blvd Ste 1 Naples (34109) *(G-10691)*

Bay Diecutting, Oldsmar *Also called Digital Direct Corporation* *(G-11642)*

Bay Eight Studios, North Miami Beach *Also called Palm Pheon Music Pubg LLC* *(G-11154)*

Bay Harbor Sheet Metal Inc 813 740-8662
7909 Professional Pl Tampa (33637) *(G-16631)*

Bay Meadow Architectural Mllwk 407 332-7992
400 Bay Meadow Rd Longwood (32750) *(G-7874)*

Bay Networks Inc 813 249-8103
6601 Memorial Hwy 200 Tampa (33615) *(G-16632)*

Bay State Milling Company 630 427-3400
3270 Sw 11th Ave Fort Lauderdale (33315) *(G-3677)*

Bay State Milling Company 772 597-2056
19150 Sw Warfield Blvd Indiantown (34956) *(G-5812)*

Bay Tech Industries Inc 813 854-1774
13275 Byrd Dr Odessa (33556) *(G-11539)*

Baycare Home Care Inc 727 461-5878
1237 S Myrtle Ave Clearwater (33756) *(G-1514)*

Bayfront Printing Company 727 823-1965
2235 16th Ave N Saint Petersburg (33713) *(G-14979)*

Baylee & Company LLC 305 333-6464
605 W 17th St Hialeah (33010) *(G-5069)*

Baylee Nasco, Hialeah *Also called Baylee & Company LLC* *(G-5069)*

Bayou Outdoor Equipment 850 729-2711
489 Valparaiso Pkwy Valparaiso (32580) *(G-17655)*

Bayou Printing Inc 850 678-5444
113 S John Sims Pkwy Valparaiso (32580) *(G-17656)*

Bayshore Con Prdcts/Chspake In 757 331-2300
2600 Mtland Ctr Pkwy Ste Maitland (32751) *(G-8050)*

Bayshore Concrete & Ldscp Mtls, Fort Myers *Also called Bayshore Precast Concrete Inc* *(G-4187)*

Bayshore Concrete Pdts Corp (HQ) 757 331-2300
2600 Mtland Ctr Pkwy Ste Maitland (32751) *(G-8051)*

Bayshore Precast Concrete Inc 239 543-3001
8100 Bayshore Rd Fort Myers (33917) *(G-4187)*

Bayshore Professional LLC 941 787-3023
22655 Bayshore Rd Ste 110 Punta Gorda (33980) *(G-14494)*

Bayside Cnvas Ycht Intrors Inc 954 792-8535
2830 W State Road 84 # 11 Fort Lauderdale (33312) *(G-3678)*

Bayside Small Cap Senior Loan 305 381-4100
1450 Brickell Ave Fl 31 Miami (33131) *(G-8805)*

Baytronics Manufacturing Inc 813 434-0401
620 E Twiggs St Ste 110 Tampa (33602) *(G-16633)*

Bb & T, Miami *Also called Van Teal Inc* *(G-10093)*

BBA Aviation Group, Orlando *Also called Signature AVI US Holdings Inc* *(G-12604)*

BBH General Partnership 863 425-5626
610 N Industrial Park Rd Mulberry (33860) *(G-10620)*

Bbj Environmental LLC 813 622-8550
9416 E Broadway Ave Tampa (33619) *(G-16634)*

Bbpoco, Boca Raton *Also called Brownbag Popcorn Company LLC* *(G-451)*

Bbts Logging LLC 850 997-2436
2182 S Jefferson Hwy Monticello (32344) *(G-10580)*

Bbull Usa Inc 813 855-1400
260 Scarlet Blvd Oldsmar (34677) *(G-11632)*

Bbx Sweet Holdings LLC (HQ) 954 940-4000
401 E Las Olas Blvd # 800 Fort Lauderdale (33301) *(G-3679)*

Bc Quincy, Quincy *Also called BASF Corporation* *(G-14541)*

Bc Sales 941 708-2727
3003 29th Ave E Bradenton (34208) *(G-944)*

Bca Technologies Inc 407 659-0653
1051 Winderley Pl Ste 310 Maitland (32751) *(G-8052)*

Bcc-Bgle Cmmnctons Crp-Clrin L 305 270-3333
8900 Sw 107th Ave Ste 30 Miami (33176) *(G-8806)*

Bcdirect Corp 305 623-3838
15625 Nw 15th Ave Miami (33169) *(G-8807)*

BCI, Miami *Also called Beverage Canners International* *(G-8822)*

BCT, Longwood *Also called Four G Enterprises Inc* *(G-7898)*

BCT International Inc (HQ) 305 563-1224
2810 E Oklnd Prk Blvd # 308 Fort Lauderdale (33306) *(G-3680)*

Bd Xtreme Holdings LLC 850 703-1793
2460 Development Cir Bonifay (32425) *(G-767)*

Bdc Florida LLC 561 249-0900
1300 N Florida Mango Rd # 30 West Palm Beach (33409) *(G-17939)*

Bdc Shell & Aggregate LLC 941 875-6615
2000 State Road 31 Punta Gorda (33982) *(G-14495)*

Bdd International Corp 305 573-2416
203 Nw 36th St Ste 2 Miami (33127) *(G-8808)*

Bdjl Enterprises LLC 407 678-9960
2591 Clark St Ste 208 Apopka (32703) *(G-105)*

Bdnz Associates Inc 305 379-7993
9481 Sw 134th St Miami (33176) *(G-8809)*

Bdt Concepts Inc 904 730-2590
5105 Philips Hwy Ste 205 Jacksonville (32207) *(G-5926)*

Be Aerospace, Wellington *Also called Advanced Thermal Tech Inc* *(G-17842)*

Be Merry 772 324-8289
320 Se Denver Ave Stuart (34994) *(G-16121)*

Be Power Tech Inc 954 543-5370
1500 S Powerline Rd Ste A Deerfield Beach (33442) *(G-2676)*

Be Pressure Supply, West Palm Beach *Also called B E Pressure Supply Inc* *(G-17932)*

Be The Solution Inc 850 545-2043
1400 Village Square Blvd Tallahassee (32312) *(G-16418)*

Be Whole Nutrition LLC 813 420-3057
5840 Highway 60 E Plant City (33567) *(G-13746)*

Bea Sue Vineyards Inc 352 446-5204
11025 Se Highway 42 Summerfield (34491) *(G-16257)*

Beach Access, Pinecrest *Also called Nrz Inc* *(G-13667)*

Beach Beacon 727 397-5563
9911 Seminole Blvd Seminole (33772) *(G-15971)*

Beach Embroidery & Screen Ptg 386 478-3931
806 E 3rd Ave New Smyrna Beach (32169) *(G-10997)*

Beach House Engineering 941 727-4488
1625 50th Avenue Dr E Bradenton (34203) *(G-945)*

Beach King, Orlando *Also called Alcee Industries Inc* *(G-11886)*

Beach Neon & Sign Co, Atlantic Beach *Also called General Signs and Service Inc* *(G-209)*

Beach Pharmaceuticals, Tampa *Also called Beach Products Inc* *(G-16635)*

Beach Products Inc 813 839-6565
3010 W De Leon St Ste 100 Tampa (33609) *(G-16635)*

Beachchip Technologies LLC 727 643-8106
2655 Ulmerton Rd Clearwater (33762) *(G-1515)*

Beachcomber Fibrgls Tech Inc 772 283-0200
3355 Se Lionel Ter Stuart (34997) *(G-16122)*

Beaches Woodcraft Inc 904 249-0785
14 Dutton Island Rd E Atlantic Beach (32233) *(G-205)*

Beacon Phrm Jupiter LLC 212 991-8988
210 Military Trl Jupiter (33458) *(G-6689)*

Beacon Publishing Inc 888 618-5253
631 Us Highway 1 Ste 201 North Palm Beach (33408) *(G-11176)*

Beam Associates LLC (PA) 813 855-5695
301 Commerce Blvd Ste 2 Oldsmar (34677) *(G-11633)*

Beano Publishing LLC 954 689-8339
1575 N Park Dr Ste 100 Weston (33326) *(G-18228)*

Bear Archery Inc 352 376-2327
4600 Sw 41st Blvd Gainesville (32608) *(G-4659)*

(G-0000) Company's Geographic Section entry number

Bearing Specialist Inc 305 796-3415
  1908 Nw 94th Ave Doral (33172) *(G-3130)*
Bears Metal Works Inc 863 537-5644
  320 S 1st Ave Bartow (33830) *(G-302)*
Beast Row Inc 727 787-2710
  3430 E Lake Rd Ste 1 Palm Harbor (34685) *(G-13103)*
Beautiful Cabinets Corp 813 486-9034
  1903 W Skagway Ave Tampa (33604) *(G-16636)*
Beautiful Homes Inc 800 403-1480
  471 Mariner Blvd Spring Hill (34609) *(G-16065)*
Beautiful Mailbox Co 305 403-4820
  2360 W 76th St Hialeah (33016) *(G-5070)*
Beautiko, Hialeah *Also called Niefeld Group LLC (G-5279)*
Beauty Cosmetica 305 406-1022
  3406 Nw 151st Ter Opa Locka (33054) *(G-11722)*
Beauty Lab Inc 305 687-0071
  2360 Nw 150th St Opa Locka (33054) *(G-11723)*
Beauty Pavers LLC 941 720-3655
  3600 Lk Byshore Dr Unit 1 Bradenton (34205) *(G-946)*
Beautyge Brands Usa Inc 904 693-1200
  5344 Overmyer Dr Jacksonville (32254) *(G-5927)*
Beavertail Skiffs Inc 941 705-2090
  4601 15th St E Bradenton (34203) *(G-947)*
Becarro International Corp (PA) 561 737-5585
  917 S Military Trl Ste C3 West Palm Beach (33415) *(G-17940)*
Beck Graphics, Saint Petersburg *Also called Colorgraphx Inc (G-15009)*
Beck Graphics Inc 727 443-3803
  1114 Florida Ave Ste B Palm Harbor (34683) *(G-13104)*
Becker Avionics Inc 954 450-3137
  10376 Usa Today Way Miramar (33025) *(G-10474)*
Becker Designs Inc 386 760-2280
  4188 Dairy Ct Ste C Port Orange (32127) *(G-14330)*
Becker Microbial Products Inc 954 345-9321
  11146 Nw 69th Pl Parkland (33076) *(G-13344)*
Becker USA, Miramar *Also called Becker Avionics Inc (G-10474)*
Beckman Coulter Inc 305 380-2175
  11800 Sw 147th Ave Miami (33196) *(G-8810)*
Beckman Coulter Inc 305 380-3800
  11800 Sw 147th Ave Miami (33196) *(G-8811)*
Beckman Coulter Inc 954 432-4336
  1 Sw 129th Ave Ste 201 Pembroke Pines (33027) *(G-13377)*
Bedbug Supply, Coral Springs *Also called Levita LLC (G-2178)*
Bedding Acquisition LLC (PA) 561 997-6900
  901 W Yamato Rd Ste 250 Boca Raton (33431) *(G-428)*
Bedeschi America Inc 954 602-2175
  20170 Pines Blvd Ste 301 Pembroke Pines (33029) *(G-13378)*
Bedeschi America Inc (HQ) 954 602-2175
  2600 N Military Trl # 245 Boca Raton (33431) *(G-429)*
Bedrock Industries Inc 407 859-1300
  10500 Rocket Ct Orlando (32824) *(G-11943)*
Bedrock Resources LLC 352 369-8600
  2441 E Fort King St 202 Ocala (34471) *(G-11333)*
Bee Access Products, West Palm Beach *Also called Bee Welding Inc (G-17941)*
Bee Electronics Inc 772 468-7477
  2733 Peters Rd Fort Pierce (34945) *(G-4469)*
Bee Welding Inc 561 616-9003
  2145 Indian Rd West Palm Beach (33409) *(G-17941)*
Beer Bread Company, Boca Raton *Also called Big L Brands Inc (G-431)*
Bees Brothers LLC 305 529-5789
  2990 Ponce De Leon Blvd # 202 Coral Gables (33134) *(G-2033)*
Bees Vita Plus, West Palm Beach *Also called Beesfree Inc (G-17942)*
Beesfree Inc 561 939-4860
  2101 Vista Pkwy Ste 122 West Palm Beach (33411) *(G-17942)*
Before Wind Blows LLC 407 977-4833
  282 Osprey Lakes Cir Chuluota (32766) *(G-1464)*
Behrs, Orlando *Also called P B C Central (G-12460)*
Behrs Chocolates By Design 407 648-2020
  3450 Vineland Rd Ste B Orlando (32811) *(G-11944)*
Belac LLC 813 749-3200
  420 Commerce Blvd Oldsmar (34677) *(G-11634)*
Belamour Logistics LLC 813 540-2199
  9727 Cypress Harbor Dr Gibsonton (33534) *(G-4795)*
Belatrix Software Inc 801 673-8331
  9128 Strada Pl Ste 10115 Naples (34108) *(G-10692)*
Belcher Gear Manufacturing, Tampa *Also called Lubov Manufacturing Inc (G-17023)*
Belcher Holdings Inc (PA) 727 530-1585
  12393 Belcher Rd S # 420 Largo (33773) *(G-7547)*
Belcher Holdings Inc 727 471-0850
  6911 Bryan Dairy Rd Largo (33777) *(G-7548)*
Belcher Pharm Acquisition, Largo *Also called Belcher Holdings Inc (G-7547)*
Belcher Pharmaceuticals LLC 727 471-0850
  6911 Bryan Dairy Rd # 210 Largo (33777) *(G-7549)*
Belgium Co Inc 407 957-1886
  1100 Grape Ave Ste 1 Saint Cloud (34769) *(G-14921)*
Bell Brothers Electric LLC 954 496-0632
  5222 Nw 110th Ave Coral Springs (33076) *(G-2136)*
Bell Composites Inc (PA) 561 575-9175
  23 Oak Ridge Ln Jupiter (33469) *(G-6690)*

Bell Composites Inc 561 714-9045
  8376 Garden Rd Riviera Beach (33404) *(G-14597)*
Bell Concrete Products Inc (PA) 352 463-6103
  2480 N Us Highway 129 Bell (32619) *(G-335)*
Bell Hearing Instruments Inc (PA) 813 814-2355
  700 Stevens Ave Ste B Oldsmar (34677) *(G-11635)*
Bell Performance Inc 407 831-5021
  1340 Bennett Dr Longwood (32750) *(G-7875)*
Bell Steel Company (PA) 850 432-1545
  530 S C St Pensacola (32502) *(G-13453)*
Bell Steel Company 850 479-2980
  8788 Paul Starr Dr Pensacola (32514) *(G-13454)*
Bella Blsmic Pressed Olive Inc (PA) 941 249-3571
  1200 W Retta Esplanade Punta Gorda (33950) *(G-14496)*
Bella Luna Inc 305 696-0310
  3650 E 10th Ct Hialeah (33013) *(G-5071)*
Bella Slata Spclty Drssngs Sce, Rockledge *Also called Cranco Industries Inc (G-14697)*
Bella Vista Bakery Inc 954 759-1920
  2220 Nw 82nd Ave Doral (33122) *(G-3131)*
Belladonna Hair Bar, Miramar *Also called Alluring Group Inc (G-10466)*
Bellak Color Corporation 305 854-8525
  9730 Nw 25th St Doral (33172) *(G-3132)*
Bellatrix Trade LLC 786 536-2905
  20225 Ne 16th Pl Fl 2 Miami (33179) *(G-8812)*
Belle Glade Electric Motor Svc 561 996-3333
  900 Nw 13th St Belle Glade (33430) *(G-339)*
Belle Glade FL Block, Belle Glade *Also called Cemex Cnstr Mtls Fla LLC (G-340)*
Belle Isle Furniture LLC (PA) 407 408-1266
  7210 Seminole Dr Apt 1 Belle Isle (32812) *(G-348)*
Bellini Systems Inc 813 264-9252
  4925 Indpdnc Pkwy Ste 400 Tampa (33634) *(G-16637)*
Bellowstech LLC 386 615-7530
  115 Business Center Dr Ormond Beach (32174) *(G-12745)*
BellSouth, Melbourne *Also called Yp Advrtising Pubg LLC Not LLC (G-8565)*
Beloved Inc 404 643-5177
  14040 Biscayne Blvd # 516 North Miami Beach (33181) *(G-11131)*
Belquette Inc 727 329-9483
  3634 131st Ave N Clearwater (33762) *(G-1516)*
Belsnickel Enterprises Inc 386 256-5367
  901 Valencia Rd South Daytona (32119) *(G-16018)*
Belt Corp 954 505-7400
  4032 N 29th Ave Hollywood (33020) *(G-5539)*
Belt Maintenance Group Inc (PA) 813 907-9316
  27658 Cashford Cir # 102 Wesley Chapel (33544) *(G-17870)*
Beltran Construction, Fort Pierce *Also called LAS & JB Inc (G-4500)*
Belvoir Media Group, Sarasota *Also called Belvoir Publications Inc (G-15611)*
Belvoir Publications Inc 941 929-1720
  7820 Holiday Dr Sarasota (34231) *(G-15611)*
Belzona Inc 305 512-3200
  2000 Nw 88th Ct Doral (33172) *(G-3133)*
Belzona Inc (HQ) 305 594-4994
  2000 Nw 88th Ct Doral (33172) *(G-3134)*
Bema Inc 954 761-1919
  2301 S Andrews Ave Fort Lauderdale (33316) *(G-3681)*
Bematech, Orlando *Also called Logic Controls Inc (G-12350)*
Bemeals, Hallandale Beach *Also called Qsrr Corporation (G-4967)*
Ben Hill Griffin Inc (PA) 863 635-2281
  700 S Scenic Hwy Fl 33843 Frostproof (33843) *(G-4633)*
Ben Hill Griffin Inc 863 635-2281
  72 North Ave Frostproof (33843) *(G-4634)*
Ben Kaufman Sales Co Inc 305 688-2144
  10025 Nw 116th Way Ste 14 Medley (33178) *(G-8208)*
Benada Extrusions LLC 407 323-3300
  2540 Jewett Ln Sanford (32771) *(G-15272)*
Benchmark Blueprinting, Sarasota *Also called Maki Printing LLC (G-15736)*
Benchmark Connector Corp 954 746-9929
  4501 Nw 103rd Ave Sunrise (33351) *(G-16295)*
Benchmark Contract Furniture, Jacksonville Beach *Also called Benchmark Design Group Inc (G-6630)*
Benchmark Design Group Inc (PA) 904 246-5060
  456 Osceola Ave Jacksonville Beach (32250) *(G-6630)*
Benchmark Entertainment LC 561 588-5200
  2201 4th Ave N Lake Worth Beach (33461) *(G-7250)*
Benchmark Games, Lake Worth Beach *Also called Benchmark Entertainment LC (G-7250)*
Benchmark Games Intl LLC 561 588-5200
  2201 4th Ave N Lake Worth Beach (33461) *(G-7251)*
Benchmark Metals Inc 239 699-0802
  1003 Se 12th Ave Unit 2 Cape Coral (33990) *(G-1311)*
Benchmark of Florida, Sanford *Also called Waterfall Industries Inc (G-15406)*
Benchmark of Palm Beach (PA) 706 258-3553
  205 Worth Ave Ste 315 Palm Beach (33480) *(G-12929)*
Benchmark Quality Gutters Inc 904 759-9800
  9526 Argyle Frest Blvd St Jacksonville (32222) *(G-5928)*
Benfresh LLC 786 403-5046
  7337 Nw 37th Ave Unit 3/4 Miami (33147) *(G-8813)*
Bengal Industries, Odessa *Also called Coast Wcp (G-11543)*
Bengis Signs Inc 305 592-3860
  9821 Nw 80th Ave Unit 5t Hialeah Gardens (33016) *(G-5431)*

A
L
P
H
A
B
E
T
I
C

Benitez Forklift Corp 786 307-3872
18820 Nw 57th Ave Apt 301 Hialeah (33015) ***(G-5072)***
Benjamin Moore Authorized Ret, Sunrise *Also called Suncoast Coatings* ***(G-16376)***
Benjamin Moore Authorized Ret, Panama City Beach *Also called Panhandle Paint & Dctg LLC* ***(G-13335)***
Benjamin Moore Authorized Ret, Navarre *Also called Consolidated Ace Hdwr Sup Inc* ***(G-10947)***
Benner China and Glwr of Fla 904 733-4620
5215 Philips Hwy Ste 1-3 Jacksonville (32207) ***(G-5929)***
Bennett Company, Gainesville *Also called Fabco-Air Inc* ***(G-4689)***
Bennetts Custom Cabinets Inc 904 751-1455
9897 Sisson Dr Jacksonville (32218) ***(G-5930)***
Benton Machine Works Inc 904 768-9161
740 Carlton St Jacksonville (32208) ***(G-5931)***
Benz Research and Dev LLC 941 758-8256
6447 Parkland Dr Sarasota (34243) ***(G-15445)***
Berco, Cape Coral *Also called Beverage Equipment Repair Co* ***(G-1313)***
Berg Europipe Holding Corp (HQ) 850 769-2273
5315 W 19th St Panama City (32401) ***(G-13231)***
Berg LLC 786 201-2625
3201 Ne 183rd St Apt 704 Aventura (33160) ***(G-256)***
Berg Pipe Panama City Corp (HQ) 850 769-2273
5315 W 19th St Panama City (32401) ***(G-13232)***
Bergan Tank Control, Pensacola *Also called Ian-Conrad Bergan LLC* ***(G-13522)***
Bergeron Properties & Inv, Fort Lauderdale *Also called Bergeron Sand & Rock Min Inc* ***(G-3682)***
Bergeron Sand & Rock Min Inc (PA) 954 680-6100
19612 Sw 69th Pl Fort Lauderdale (33332) ***(G-3682)***
Berkant Corp 305 771-5578
6370 Nw 82nd Ave Miami (33166) ***(G-8814)***
Berkshire Managment Associates 305 883-3277
12841 Sw 117th St Miami (33186) ***(G-8815)***
Berman Products LLC 561 743-5197
19558 Red Gum Trl Jupiter (33458) ***(G-6691)***
Bermont Excavating LLC 866 367-9557
37390 Bermont Rd Punta Gorda (33982) ***(G-14497)***
Bernard Cap LLC 305 822-4800
620 W 27th St Hialeah (33010) ***(G-5073)***
Bernice I Finch 850 638-0082
1867 6th Ave Wausau (32463) ***(G-17831)***
Berry Global Inc 727 447-8845
2940 Bay Meadow Ct Clearwater (33761) ***(G-1517)***
Berry Global Inc 941 355-7166
7350 26th Ct E Sarasota (34243) ***(G-15446)***
Berry Global Inc 305 887-2040
9016 Nw 105th Way Medley (33178) ***(G-8209)***
Berry Signs Inc 321 631-6150
1740 Huntington Ln Rockledge (32955) ***(G-14691)***
Bertram Yachts LLC (HQ) 813 527-9899
5250 W Tyson Ave Tampa (33611) ***(G-16638)***
Beson 4 Media Group, Jacksonville *Also called Barbes Publishing Inc* ***(G-5923)***
Bespoke Stitchery LLC 407 412-9937
2437 E Landstreet Rd Orlando (32824) ***(G-11945)***
Bessie Barnie, Doral *Also called Miami Tbr LLC* ***(G-3302)***
Best Bindery Corp 941 505-1779
3181 Aloe St Punta Gorda (33982) ***(G-14498)***
Best Brand Bottlers Inc 941 755-1941
6620 19th St E Unit 109 Sarasota (34243) ***(G-15447)***
Best Bubble Mailers, Hialeah *Also called Holpack Corp* ***(G-5188)***
Best Buy Awnings, Miami *Also called Business World Trading Inc* ***(G-8864)***
Best Choice Printing, Jacksonville *Also called Ballard Printing Inc* ***(G-5922)***
Best Choice Software Inc 941 747-5858
1117 30th Ave W Bradenton (34205) ***(G-948)***
Best Circuits Inc 321 425-6725
300 North Dr Ste 106 Melbourne (32934) ***(G-8376)***
Best Closures Inc 305 821-6607
9780 Nw 79th Ave Miami Lakes (33016) ***(G-10284)***
Best Community Magazine 407 571-2980
260 Maitland Ave Ste 2000 Altamonte Springs (32701) ***(G-33)***
Best Custom Tape, Miami *Also called Rela USA LLC* ***(G-9790)***
Best Door, Hialeah Gardens *Also called Best Rolling Manufacturer Inc* ***(G-5432)***
Best Engineered Surfc Tech LLC (PA) 407 932-0008
1820 Avenue A Kissimmee (34758) ***(G-6898)***
Best Fabrications Inc 863 519-6611
2145 Bravo Ave Bartow (33830) ***(G-303)***
Best Finisher 305 688-8174
2780 Nw 122nd St Miami (33167) ***(G-8816)***
Best Global Source, Apopka *Also called Oum LLC* ***(G-160)***
Best Industries Inc 772 460-8310
15860 W Park Ln Fort Pierce (34945) ***(G-4470)***
Best Iproductscom LLC 386 402-7800
111 N Ridgewood Ave Edgewater (32132) ***(G-3480)***
Best Lidar Corporation 321 425-6725
300 North Dr Ste 106 Melbourne (32934) ***(G-8377)***
Best Made Flags, Hollywood *Also called Keystone 75 Inc* ***(G-5608)***
Best Manufacturing Company 954 922-1443
3282 N 29th Ct Hollywood (33020) ***(G-5540)***
Best Metal Work 561 842-1960
3301 Elec Way Ste A West Palm Beach (33407) ***(G-17943)***
Best of Orlando Pntg & Stucco 407 947-4174
3000 Clarcona Rd Lot 763 Apopka (32703) ***(G-106)***
Best Pallets of Fl LLC 386 624-5575
1830 Patterson Ave Unit D Deland (32724) ***(G-2855)***
Best Pavers LLC 407 259-9020
8730 Hastings Beach Blvd Orlando (32829) ***(G-11946)***
Best Powder Coatings Inc 305 836-9460
3970 E 10th Ct Hialeah (33013) ***(G-5074)***
Best Price Digital Lenses Inc 850 361-4401
2013 W Yonge St Pensacola (32501) ***(G-13455)***
Best Price Mobility Inc 321 402-5955
941 Armstrong Blvd Ste B Kissimmee (34741) ***(G-6899)***
Best Products Mix Inc 305 512-9920
17541 Nw 89th Ct Hialeah (33018) ***(G-5075)***
Best Publishing Company 561 776-6066
631 Us Highway 1 Ste 307 North Palm Beach (33408) ***(G-11177)***
Best Quality Water Sys of Fla (PA) 407 971-2537
2200 Winter Springs Blvd # 106 Oviedo (32765) ***(G-12810)***
Best Rolling Manufacturer Inc 305 821-4276
9780 Nw 79th Ave Hialeah Gardens (33016) ***(G-5432)***
Best Supplier, Hialeah *Also called H Goicoechea Inc* ***(G-5181)***
Best Truss Company (PA) 305 667-6797
7035 Sw 44th St Miami (33155) ***(G-8817)***
Bestcanvas Inc 305 759-7800
3343 Nw 107th St Miami (33167) ***(G-8818)***
Bestest International Inc 714 974-8837
701 Market St Ste 111-201 Saint Augustine (32095) ***(G-14815)***
Bestest Medical, Saint Augustine *Also called Bestest International Inc* ***(G-14815)***
Bestprintingonlinecom LLC 239 263-2106
4408 Corporate Sq Naples (34104) ***(G-10693)***
Bestway Portable Building Inc 850 747-1984
2919 N Highway 231 Panama City (32405) ***(G-13233)***
Bet Er Mix Inc 352 799-5538
21101 Cortez Blvd Brooksville (34601) ***(G-1140)***
BET-Er Mix Holding Inc (PA) 727 868-9226
9301 Denton Ave Port Richey (34667) ***(G-14355)***
Bet-Er-Mixing 813 779-2774
38508 A Ave Zephyrhills (33542) ***(G-18605)***
Beta Max Inc 321 727-3737
1895 Rbert J Cnlan Blvd N Palm Bay (32905) ***(G-12890)***
Beta Max Hoist, Palm Bay *Also called Beta Max Inc* ***(G-12890)***
Beta Max Inc 321 914-0918
2750 Hudson Ave Ne Palm Bay (32905) ***(G-12891)***
Betablocks Company 424 353-1978
54 Bay Heights Dr Miami (33133) ***(G-8819)***
Betancourt Sports Ntrtn LLC (HQ) 305 593-9296
14700 Nw 60th Ave Miami Lakes (33014) ***(G-10285)***
Betawave LLC 954 223-8298
2968 Nw 60th St Fort Lauderdale (33309) ***(G-3683)***
Bethel Products LLC 954 636-2645
926 Se 9th St Cape Coral (33990) ***(G-1312)***
Betrock Info Systems Inc 954 981-2821
12330 Sw 53rd St Ste 712 Cooper City (33330) ***(G-2019)***
Better Air North America LLC 844 447-7624
691 Carrotwood Ter Plantation (33324) ***(G-13831)***
Better Built Group Inc 850 803-4044
66 N Holiday Rd Destin (32550) ***(G-3083)***
Better Mix 800 232-6833
9301 Denton Ave Hudson (34667) ***(G-5764)***
Better Plastics Inc 407 480-2909
780 Central Florida Pkwy Orlando (32824) ***(G-11947)***
Better Sourcing Worldwide, Hallandale Beach *Also called Miracles For Fun Usa Inc* ***(G-4961)***
Betty Engines Machine Shop Inc 305 458-1467
7120 Sw 44th St Ste A Miami (33155) ***(G-8820)***
Betwell Oil & Gas Company (PA) 305 821-8300
8083 Nw 103rd St Hialeah Gardens (33016) ***(G-5433)***
Beutlich Pharmaceuticals LLC (PA) 386 263-8860
7775 S Us Highway 1 H Bunnell (32110) ***(G-1226)***
Bev-Co Enterprises Inc (PA) 786 362-6368
2761 Nw 82nd Ave Miami (33122) ***(G-8821)***
Bev-Co Enterprises Inc 786 953-7109
9533 Nw 41st St Doral (33178) ***(G-3135)***
Bevel Express, Tampa *Also called Bevel Top Shop Express LLC* ***(G-16640)***
Bevel Express & Tops Lac 813 887-3174
6026 Benjamin Rd Tampa (33634) ***(G-16639)***
Bevel Top Shop Express LLC 813 299-1250
6022 Benjamin Rd Tampa (33634) ***(G-16640)***
Beverage Blocks Inc 813 309-8711
218 E Bearss Ave Ste 332 Tampa (33613) ***(G-16641)***
Beverage Canners International 305 714-7000
3505 Nw 107th St Miami (33167) ***(G-8822)***
Beverage Corp Intl Inc 305 714-7000
3505 Nw 107th St Miami (33167) ***(G-8823)***
Beverage Depot, Hialeah *Also called Hialeah Distribution Corp* ***(G-5184)***
Beverage Equipment Repair Co 239 573-0683
1020 Ne Pine Island Rd # 201 Cape Coral (33909) ***(G-1313)***

890 2022 Harris Florida Manufacturers Directory (G-0000) Company's Geographic Section entry number

Beverely's, Fort Lauderdale *Also called American Diamond Distributors* **(G-3649)**
Beverly Acquisitions Inc (PA) 561 746-3827
  240 W Indiantown Rd # 101 Jupiter (33458) **(G-6692)**
Bevolution Group, Frostproof *Also called Lemon-X Corporation* **(G-4638)**
Beyers Welding Inc 407 892-2834
  4950 Canoe Creek Rd Saint Cloud (34772) **(G-14922)**
Beyond White Spa LLC 866 399-8867
  6725 Nw 36th St Unit 600 Miami (33166) **(G-8824)**
Beyondclean LLC 561 799-5710
  601 Heritage Dr Ste 422 Jupiter (33458) **(G-6693)**
Bezels For Watches, Miami *Also called Accar Ltd Inc* **(G-8641)**
BF American Business LLC 561 856-7094
  22285 Sw 66th Ave Apt 200 Boca Raton (33428) **(G-430)**
BF One LLC 239 939-5251
  5661 Independence Cir Fort Myers (33912) **(G-4188)**
BF Weston LLC (PA) 561 844-5528
  105 Us Highway 1 North Palm Beach (33408) **(G-11178)**
Bg Expo Group LLC 305 428-3576
  11231 Nw 20th St Unit 140 Doral (33172) **(G-3136)**
Bgt Holdings LLC 239 643-9949
  200 Aviation Dr N Ste 5 Naples (34104) **(G-10694)**
BHd Precision Products Inc 941 753-0003
  2120 Whitfield Park Loop Sarasota (34243) **(G-15448)**
BHF Publishing Inc 727 536-2245
  14835 49th St N Clearwater (33762) **(G-1518)**
Bi-Ads Inc 954 525-1489
  545 Nw 7th Ter Fort Lauderdale (33311) **(G-3684)**
Bible Alliance Inc (PA) 941 748-3031
  12108 10th Ave E Bradenton (34212) **(G-949)**
Bic Corporation 727 536-7895
  14421 Myerlake Cir Clearwater (33760) **(G-1519)**
Bic Graphic USA, Clearwater *Also called Bic Corporation* **(G-1519)**
Bicentrics Inc 813 649-0225
  319 1st St Ne Ruskin (33570) **(G-14775)**
Bid Uniforms.com, North Miami Beach *Also called Stitch Count Inc* **(G-11162)**
Biddiscombe International LLC 727 299-9287
  11961 31st Ct N Saint Petersburg (33716) **(G-14980)**
Biddiscombe Labs Stylz Pdts, Saint Petersburg *Also called Biddiscombe International LLC* **(G-14980)**
Big Bend Fuel Inc 727 946-8727
  6912 Big Bend Rd Gibsonton (33534) **(G-4796)**
Big Bend Ice Cream Co 850 539-7778
  138 Staghorn Trl Havana (32333) **(G-4993)**
Big Bend Rebar Inc 850 875-8000
  1 Corporate Ct Quincy (32351) **(G-14542)**
Big Bend Truss Components Inc 850 539-5351
  52 Salem Rd Havana (32333) **(G-4994)**
Big Biz Direct 813 978-0584
  13922 Monroes Business Pa Tampa (33635) **(G-16642)**
Big Boy Inc 407 434-9251
  5972 Bent Pine Dr 1710 Orlando (32822) **(G-11948)**
Big Boy Restaurant, Orlando *Also called Big Boy Inc* **(G-11948)**
Big Cat H P V, Orlando *Also called Big Cat Humn Pwred Vhicles LLC* **(G-11949)**
Big Cat Humn Pwred Vhicles LLC 407 999-0200
  2016 Stanhome Way Orlando (32804) **(G-11949)**
Big Country Small Engine 850 348-9022
  5412 E Highway 22 Panama City (32404) **(G-13234)**
Big Cypress Distillery LLC 786 228-9740
  13995 Sw 144th Ave # 207 Miami (33186) **(G-8825)**
Big Digital Graphics LLC 561 844-4708
  1335 Old Dixie Hwy Unit 4 Lake Park (33403) **(G-7122)**
Big Dogs Mobile Polishing LLC 813 312-6892
  37310 Stanford Ave Zephyrhills (33541) **(G-18606)**
Big Eagle LLC 305 586-8766
  3051 W State Road 84 Fort Lauderdale (33312) **(G-3685)**
Big Fish Co Custom Creations 727 525-5010
  3128 Dr M L K Jr St N Mlk Saint Petersburg (33704) **(G-14981)**
Big Iron Intl Inc 407 222-2573
  3936 S Semoran Blvd Ste 2 Orlando (32822) **(G-11950)**
Big Kitchen 813 254-6112
  3719 Corporex Park Dr # 50 Tampa (33619) **(G-16643)**
Big L Brands Inc (PA) 888 552-9768
  7750 Ne Spanish Trail Ct Boca Raton (33487) **(G-431)**
Big League Cards, Casselberry *Also called Instant Locate Inc* **(G-1419)**
Big Man Friendly Trnsp LLC 941 229-3454
  11161 State Road 70 E # 1 Lakewood Ranch (34202) **(G-7476)**
Big O Tires, Juno Beach *Also called Tbc Retail Group Inc* **(G-6667)**
Big OS Stump Grinding 904 945-5900
  101 Baisden Rd Apt 2 Jacksonville (32218) **(G-5932)**
Big Rhino Screen Printing, Pensacola *Also called Above LLC* **(G-13431)**
Big Slide Enterprises Inc 727 329-8845
  10601 Oak St Ne Saint Petersburg (33716) **(G-14982)**
Big Star Systems LLC 954 243-7209
  2061 Nw 47th Ter Apt 200 Lauderhill (33313) **(G-7726)**
Big Sun Equine Products Inc (PA) 352 629-9645
  1883 Nw 58th Ln Ocala (34475) **(G-11334)**
Big Sun Plastics Inc 352 671-1844
  2615 Nw Old Blitchton Rd Ocala (34475) **(G-11335)**

Big Sun Products, Ocala *Also called Big Sun Equine Products Inc* **(G-11334)**
Big T Printing, Saint Petersburg *Also called Solseen LLC* **(G-15189)**
Big Top Manufacturing Inc 850 584-7786
  3255 Us Highway 19 N Perry (32347) **(G-13632)**
Big Wood Millwork Sales Inc 305 471-1155
  10842 Nw 27th St Doral (33172) **(G-3137)**
Bigbyte Software Systems Inc 917 370-1733
  2214 Nw 171st Ter Pembroke Pines (33028) **(G-13379)**
Bigg D Entertainment LLC 917 204-0292
  904 Stillwater Ct Weston (33327) **(G-18229)**
Bigg Wills Wheels LLC 352 222-6170
  125 Nw 23rd Ave Ste D Gainesville (32609) **(G-4660)**
Bigham Insulation & Sup Co Inc 954 522-2887
  2816 Sw 3rd Ave Fort Lauderdale (33315) **(G-3686)**
Bighill Corporation 786 497-1875
  1111 Lincoln Rd Fl 4 Miami Beach (33139) **(G-10170)**
Bigorre Aerospace Corp 727 525-8115
  6295 42nd St N Pinellas Park (33781) **(G-13673)**
Bijol & Spices, Miami *Also called Bijol and Spices Inc* **(G-8826)**
Bijol and Spices Inc 305 634-9030
  2154 Nw 22nd Ct Miami (33142) **(G-8826)**
Bikekeeper LLC 561 209-6863
  8461 Lake Worth Rd # 173 Lake Worth (33467) **(G-7187)**
Biking Boat Works Company, The, Saint Petersburg *Also called Snug Harbor Dinghies Inc* **(G-15188)**
Bill & Renee Enterprises Inc 321 452-2800
  275 Magnolia Ave Ste 2 Merritt Island (32952) **(G-8578)**
Bill Mitchell Products LLC 386 957-3009
  1726 Hibiscus Dr Edgewater (32132) **(G-3481)**
Billet Technology 561 582-6171
  714 S East Coast St Lake Worth (33460) **(G-7188)**
Billiards & Barstools, Tampa *Also called Robertson Billiard Sups Inc* **(G-17228)**
Bimbo Bakeries USA 941 875-5945
  2625 Commerce Pkwy # 112 North Port (34289) **(G-11188)**
Bimbo Bakeries USA 954 968-7684
  6783 Nw 17th Ave Fort Lauderdale (33309) **(G-3687)**
Binca LLC 305 698-8883
  10680 Nw 37th Ter Doral (33178) **(G-3138)**
Bindery LLC 407 647-7777
  611 N Wymore Rd Ste 100 Winter Park (32789) **(G-18490)**
Bingham On Site Portables LLC 813 659-0003
  3640 Sumner Rd Dover (33527) **(G-3427)**
Bingham On-Site Sewers Inc 813 659-0003
  3640 Sumner Rd Dover (33527) **(G-3428)**
Bingo Bakery Inc 305 545-9993
  2125 Nw 8th Ave Miami (33127) **(G-8827)**
Binick Digital Imaging LLC 786 420-2067
  6220 Nw 37th Ave Miami (33147) **(G-8828)**
Binickimaging, Miami *Also called Binick Digital Imaging LLC* **(G-8828)**
Binney Family of Florida Inc 727 376-5596
  11232 Challenger Ave Odessa (33556) **(G-11540)**
Bio Bubble Pets LLC 561 998-5350
  1400 Centrepark Blvd # 860 West Palm Beach (33401) **(G-17944)**
Bio Ceps Inc 727 669-7544
  15251 Roosevelt Blvd # 204 Clearwater (33760) **(G-1520)**
Bio Fuel Professionals 239 591-3835
  25 Mentor Dr Naples (34110) **(G-10695)**
Bio Nucleonics, Miami *Also called Bio-Nucleonics Pharma Inc* **(G-8829)**
Bio Therapeutics Inc 954 321-5553
  1850 Nw 69th Ave Ste 1 Plantation (33313) **(G-13832)**
Bio-Lab Inc 863 709-1411
  3125 Drane Field Rd # 10 Lakeland (33811) **(G-7282)**
Bio-Logic Systems, Orlando *Also called Natus Medical Incorporated* **(G-12408)**
Bio-Logic Systems Corp 847 949-0456
  12301 Lake Underhill Rd # 201 Orlando (32828) **(G-11951)**
Bio-Nucleonics Pharma Inc 305 576-0996
  1 Ne 19th St Miami (33132) **(G-8829)**
Bio-Pharm LLC 973 223-7163
  409 W Hallandale Beach Bl Hallandale Beach (33009) **(G-4938)**
Bio-Revival LLC 561 667-3990
  661 Maplewood Dr Ste 21 Jupiter (33458) **(G-6694)**
Bio-Tech Medical Software Inc 800 797-4711
  6750 N Andrews Ave # 325 Fort Lauderdale (33309) **(G-3688)**
Biobag Americas Inc 727 789-1646
  1059 Broadway Ste F Dunedin (34698) **(G-3441)**
Biobotanical LLC 239 458-4534
  889 Ne 27th Ln Cape Coral (33909) **(G-1314)**
Biochem Manufacturing Inc 561 799-1590
  15074 Pk Of Commerce Blvd Jupiter (33478) **(G-6695)**
Biochem Manufacturing Inc 786 210-1290
  7300 N Kendall Dr Ste 640 Miami (33156) **(G-8830)**
Biochemical Manufacturing Inc 561 799-1590
  15074 Pk Of Commerce Blvd Jupiter (33478) **(G-6696)**
Biochrom, Miramar *Also called Pro Lab Supply Corporation* **(G-10532)**
Biodegradable Packaging Corp 305 824-1164
  9775 Nw 80th Ave Hialeah Gardens (33016) **(G-5434)**
Bioderm Inc 727 507-7655
  12320 73rd Ct Largo (33773) **(G-7550)**

A
L
P
H
A
B
E
T
I
C

Bioenergetics Press...386 462-5155
19802 Old Bellamy Rd Alachua (32615) *(G-9)*
Bioenersource Inc...786 797-0496
2951 Nw 21st Ter Miami (33142) *(G-8831)*
Bioflex Medical Magnetics, Inc, Fort Lauderdale *Also called Medical Magnetics Inc (G-3936)*
Biofuse Medical Tech Inc...877 466-2434
200 S Hbr Cy Blvd Ste 402 Melbourne (32901) *(G-8378)*
Bioivt LLC...516 876-7902
7500 Nw 5th St Plantation (33317) *(G-13833)*
Biolife LLC...941 360-1300
8163 25th Ct E Sarasota (34243) *(G-15449)*
Biomar Products LLC...800 216-2080
9441 Nw 47th Ter Doral (33178) *(G-3139)*
Biomech Golf Equipment LLC...401 932-0479
711 5th Ave S Ste 212 Naples (34102) *(G-10696)*
Biomedtech Laboratories Inc (PA)...813 558-2000
3802 Spectrum Blvd # 154 Tampa (33612) *(G-16644)*
Biomet Inc...561 385-8405
4555 Riverside Dr Palm Beach Gardens (33410) *(G-12950)*
Biomet 3i LLC...561 775-9928
4555 Riverside Dr Palm Beach Gardens (33410) *(G-12951)*
Biomet Microfixation, LLC, Jacksonville *Also called Zimmer Biomet CMF Thoracic LLC (G-6623)*
Bionebicine Corp...401 648-0695
125 Estado Way Ne Saint Petersburg (33704) *(G-14983)*
Bionitrogen Holdings Corp (PA)...561 600-9550
1400 Centrepark Blvd # 860 West Palm Beach (33401) *(G-17945)*
Bioquem USA, Pompano Beach *Also called W & B Scientific Inc (G-14239)*
Biorep Technologies Inc...305 330-4449
15804 Nw 57th Ave Miami Lakes (33014) *(G-10286)*
Bioresource Technology LLC...954 792-5222
1800 N Commerce Pkwy # 1 Weston (33326) *(G-18230)*
Biosafe Supplies LLC...407 281-6658
9436 Southridge Park Ct # 400 Orlando (32819) *(G-11952)*
Biosculptor Corporation...305 823-8300
2480 W 82nd St Unit 1 Hialeah (33016) *(G-5076)*
Biosculpture Technology Inc (PA)...561 651-7816
1701 S Flagler Dr Apt 607 West Palm Beach (33401) *(G-17946)*
Bioseb, Pinellas Park *Also called Forceleader Inc (G-13687)*
Biostem Technologies Inc...954 380-8342
2836 Center Port Cir Pompano Beach (33064) *(G-13950)*
Biotech, Palm Beach *Also called Exosis Inc (G-12933)*
Biotest Plasma Center, Boca Raton *Also called Bpc Plasma Inc (G-446)*
Biotoxins Inc...407 892-6905
5705 E I Bronson Memrl Saint Cloud (34771) *(G-14923)*
Biotrackthc, Fort Lauderdale *Also called Bio-Tech Medical Software Inc (G-3688)*
Biozone Scientific Intl Inc (PA)...407 876-2000
7616 Southland Blvd # 114 Orlando (32809) *(G-11953)*
Birchwood Best, Tampa *Also called Masonite Corporation (G-17046)*
Birchwood Best, Tampa *Also called Masonite Corporation (G-17047)*
Birdie Publishing LLC...561 332-1826
701 Se 6th Ave Ste 102 Delray Beach (33483) *(G-2936)*
Birdiebox LLC...786 762-2975
2129 Nw 86th Ave Miami (33122) *(G-8832)*
Birdsall Marine Design Inc...561 832-7879
530 Nottingham Blvd West Palm Beach (33405) *(G-17947)*
Biscayne Awning & Shade Co...305 638-7933
2333 Nw 8th Ave Miami (33127) *(G-8833)*
Biscayne Bedding Intl LLC...305 633-4634
3925 E 10th Ct Hialeah (33013) *(G-5077)*
Biscayne Electric Motor & Pump...305 681-8171
830 Nw 144th St Miami (33168) *(G-8834)*
Biscayne Tennis LLC...786 231-8372
19021 Biscayne Blvd Miami (33180) *(G-8835)*
Bischoff Aero Llc...305 883-4410
8130 Nw 58th St Doral (33166) *(G-3140)*
Biscotti Gourment Bakery, Miami *Also called La Mansion Latina LLC (G-9409)*
Bisi Fasteners LLC...850 913-0101
2009 Poplar Pl 302 Panama City (32405) *(G-13235)*
Bisk Education Inc (PA)...813 621-6200
9417 Princess Palm Ave # 400 Tampa (33619) *(G-16645)*
Bisk Publishing Company, Tampa *Also called Bisk Education Inc (G-16645)*
BIW, Miami *Also called Bachiller Iron Works Inc (G-8792)*
Bizcard Xpress, Orange City *Also called MRM Creative LLC (G-11807)*
Bizcard Xpress Sanford LLC...407 688-8902
1744 Rinehart Rd Sanford (32771) *(G-15273)*
Bizzspot, Wesley Chapel *Also called Local Biz Spot Inc (G-17881)*
BJ Burns Incorporated...305 572-9500
1411 Sawgrs Corp Pkwy Sunrise (33323) *(G-16296)*
Bjb Marine Welding & Svcs Inc...954 909-4967
2700 Sw 25th Ter Fort Lauderdale (33312) *(G-3689)*
Bjm Enterprises Inc...941 746-4171
1500 15th Avenue Dr E # 104 Palmetto (34221) *(G-13157)*
Bk Cabinets, Melbourne *Also called B & K Discount Cabinets LLC (G-8373)*
Bk Plastics Industry Inc...813 920-3628
13414 Byrd Dr Odessa (33556) *(G-11541)*
Bk Technologies, Melbourne *Also called Relm Communications Inc (G-8510)*
Bk Technologies Inc (HQ)...321 984-1414
7100 Technology Dr West Melbourne (32904) *(G-17894)*
Bk Technologies Corporation (PA)...321 984-1414
7100 Technology Dr West Melbourne (32904) *(G-17895)*
Bkbl Holdings Ltd...954 920-6772
5031 N Hiatus Rd Sunrise (33351) *(G-16297)*
Bkn International Inc...301 518-7153
1610 Euclid Ave Apt B202 Miami Beach (33139) *(G-10171)*
Bks Bakery Inc...386 216-0540
2531 Dumas Dr Deltona (32738) *(G-3040)*
Bl Acquisition, Hialeah *Also called Bullet Line LLC (G-5083)*
Bl Bio Lab LLC...727 900-2707
2021 Sunnydale Blvd # 14 Clearwater (33765) *(G-1521)*
Bl Brandhouse LLC...305 600-7181
8375 Nw 30th Ter Doral (33122) *(G-3141)*
Bla Software Inc...407 355-0800
10424 Sparkle Ct Orlando (32836) *(G-11954)*
Black Aces Tactical, Longwood *Also called Eric Lemoine (G-7890)*
Black Aces Tactical, Longwood *Also called Ttc Performance Products Inc (G-7955)*
Black Bart International LLC...561 842-4045
155 E Blue Heron Blvd R2 Riviera Beach (33404) *(G-14598)*
Black Bee Aromatherapy LLC...866 399-4233
7726 Winegard Rd Orlando (32809) *(G-11955)*
Black College Monthly Inc...352 335-5771
901 Se 18th Ter Gainesville (32641) *(G-4661)*
Black College Today Inc...954 344-4469
4973 Nw 115th Ter Coral Springs (33076) *(G-2137)*
Black Coral Rum LLC (PA)...561 766-2493
1231 W 13th St Bldg 15 Riviera Beach (33404) *(G-14599)*
Black Creek Logging...904 591-9681
4159 County Road 218 Middleburg (32068) *(G-10400)*
Black Damnd Drill Grinders Inc...978 465-3799
8776 Danforth Dr Windermere (34786) *(G-18348)*
Black Diamond Coatings Inc...800 270-4050
6036 Nature Coast Blvd Brooksville (34602) *(G-1141)*
Black Diamond Systems Corp (PA)...917 539-7309
1305 Cape Pointe Cir Vero Beach (32963) *(G-17740)*
Black Ice Software LLC (PA)...561 757-4107
950 Peninsula Corporate C Boca Raton (33487) *(G-432)*
Black Knight Inc (PA)...904 854-5100
601 Riverside Ave Jacksonville (32204) *(G-5933)*
Black Knight Fincl Svcs Inc (HQ)...904 854-5100
601 Riverside Ave Jacksonville (32204) *(G-5934)*
Black Mountain, Seminole *Also called Harlan J Newman (G-15977)*
Black Oak Industries Inc...863 307-1566
9518 Waterford Oaks Blvd Winter Haven (33884) *(G-18421)*
Black Widow Custom Cases...321 327-8058
1720 Main St Ne Palm Bay (32905) *(G-12892)*
Black-Tie Publishing Inc...954 472-6003
10131 Nw 14th St Plantation (33322) *(G-13834)*
Blackbox Gps, Fort Lauderdale *Also called Embrace Telecom Inc (G-3792)*
Blackcloak Inc...833 882-5625
7025 Cty Rd 46a Ste 1071 46 A Lake Mary (32746) *(G-7063)*
Blackfin Manufacturing LLC (PA)...314 482-2766
1660 Barrett Dr Unit B Rockledge (32955) *(G-14692)*
Blackfist Magazine LLC (PA)...904 864-8695
382 Ne 191st St Ste 73388 Miami (33179) *(G-8836)*
Blackhawk Construction Co Inc (PA)...321 258-4957
3060 Airport West Dr Vero Beach (32960) *(G-17741)*
Blackhawk Quarry Co of Fla, Vero Beach *Also called Blackhawk Construction Co Inc (G-17741)*
Blacklidge Emulsions Inc...954 275-7225
2501 Wiles Rd Pompano Beach (33073) *(G-13951)*
Blacklidge Emulsions Inc...850 432-3496
4375 Mccoy Dr Pensacola (32503) *(G-13456)*
Blacklidge Emulsions Inc...813 247-5699
2701 E 2nd Ave Tampa (33605) *(G-16646)*
Blackstone Legal Supplies Inc (PA)...305 945-3450
3732 Nw 16th St Lauderhill (33311) *(G-7727)*
Blackstone Legal Supply, Lauderhill *Also called Blackstone Legal Supplies Inc (G-7727)*
Blackton Flooring Inc...407 898-2661
1714 Alden Rd Orlando (32803) *(G-11956)*
Blackwater Folk Art Inc...850 623-3470
4917 Glover Ln Milton (32570) *(G-10419)*
Blackwater Truss Systems LLC...850 623-1414
6603 Old Bagdad Hwy Milton (32583) *(G-10420)*
Blackwell Family Corporation...941 639-0200
1869 Manzana Ave Punta Gorda (33950) *(G-14499)*
Blades Direct LLC...855 225-2337
5645 Coral Ridge Dr Coral Springs (33076) *(G-2138)*
Bladorn Investments Inc...941 627-0014
1264 Market Cir Unit 6 Port Charlotte (33953) *(G-14288)*
Blair Machine & Tool Inc...904 731-4377
1301 Riverplace Blvd # 800 Jacksonville (32207) *(G-5935)*
Blair Machine and Tool LLC...904 731-4377
8665 Philips Hwy Jacksonville (32256) *(G-5936)*
Blair Propeller MA...772 283-1453
3009 Se Monroe St Stuart (34997) *(G-16123)*

ALPHABETIC SECTION BMW & Associates Inc

Blanco Gomez Maldonado LLC 305 380-1114
15588 Sw 72nd St Miami (33193) ***(G-8837)***
Blane E Taylor Welding Inc 386 931-1242
75 County Road 125 Bunnell (32110) ***(G-1227)***
Blane E Taylor Welding Inc 386 931-1240
1760 N Us Highway 1 Ormond Beach (32174) ***(G-12746)***
Blaq Luxury Collection LLC 407 496-7517
2164 Platinum Rd Ste D Apopka (32703) ***(G-107)***
Blaq Luxury Realty, Apopka *Also called Blaq Luxury Collection LLC* ***(G-107)***
Blast Ctings Powdercoating LLC 561 635-7605
1847 Aragon Ave Unit 2 Lake Worth Beach (33461) ***(G-7252)***
Blast Ctings Powdercoating LLC (PA) 561 301-9538
1745 Sawgrass Cir Greenacres (33413) ***(G-4844)***
Blast Off Equipment Inc 561 964-6199
2350 S Military Trl West Palm Beach (33415) ***(G-17948)***
Blasters Ready Jet Inc 813 985-4500
7815 Professional Pl Tampa (33637) ***(G-16647)***
Blazedpath, Fort Lauderdale *Also called Low Code Ip Holding LLC* ***(G-3922)***
Blazer Boats Inc 321 307-4761
12001 Res Pkwy Ste 236 Orlando (32826) ***(G-11957)***
Blevins Inc 904 562-7428
6740 Broadway Ave Ste H Jacksonville (32254) ***(G-5937)***
Blind Depot 954 588-4580
10794 Nw 53rd St Sunrise (33351) ***(G-16298)***
Blinds 321 Inc 305 336-9221
12335 Nw 7th St Miami (33182) ***(G-8838)***
Blinds By Randy LLC 305 300-1147
3274 Nw 181st St Miami Gardens (33056) ***(G-10252)***
Blinds R Us Corp 305 303-2072
5946 Sw 162nd Path Miami (33193) ***(G-8839)***
Blinds Side 888 610-8366
5801 N Atlantic Ave Cape Canaveral (32920) ***(G-1278)***
Blindsource LLC 954 455-1965
100 Davie Blvd Fort Lauderdale (33315) ***(G-3690)***
Blingka Inc 800 485-6793
3911 Americana Dr Tampa (33634) ***(G-16648)***
Blitz Micro Turning Inc 727 725-5005
945 Harbor Lake Ct Safety Harbor (34695) ***(G-14783)***
Blix Corporate Image LLC 305 572-9001
1352 Nw 78th Ave Doral (33126) ***(G-3142)***
Blix Graphics, Doral *Also called Blix Corporate Image LLC* ***(G-3142)***
Block Engineering Incorporated (PA) 508 251-3100
308 Lady Palm Ter Vero Beach (32963) ***(G-17742)***
Bloem LLC 407 889-5533
3000 Orange Ave Apopka (32703) ***(G-108)***
Blow Off, Margate *Also called AVw Inc* ***(G-8122)***
Blp Racing Products LLC 407 422-0394
1015 W Church St Orlando (32805) ***(G-11958)***
Blu Sense 786 616-8628
7855 Nw 29th St Doral (33122) ***(G-3143)***
Blu Sleep Products LLC (PA) 866 973-7614
1501 Green Rd Ste B Deerfield Beach (33064) ***(G-2677)***
Bluazu LLC 386 697-3743
101 Se 2nd Pl Ste 201b Gainesville (32601) ***(G-4662)***
Blue Biofuels Inc 561 693-1943
3710 Buckeye St Ste 120 Palm Beach Gardens (33410) ***(G-12952)***
Blue Butterfly Hair Extensions, Sunrise *Also called Italian Hair Extension Inc* ***(G-16325)***
Blue Chip Group LLC 305 863-9094
3400 Nw 113th Ct Doral (33178) ***(G-3144)***
Blue Chip Servicing Inc 844 607-2029
515 E Las Olas Blvd Ste 1 Fort Lauderdale (33301) ***(G-3691)***
Blue Chip Srvcing Fster Fnding, Fort Lauderdale *Also called Blue Chip Servicing Inc* ***(G-3691)***
Blue Coast Bakers LLC 386 944-0800
1899 N Us Highway 1 Ormond Beach (32174) ***(G-12747)***
Blue Diamond Orthopedic LLC 407 613-2001
6439 Milner Blvd Ste 4 Orlando (32809) ***(G-11959)***
Blue Eagle Alliance Inc 904 322-8067
4651 Salisbury Rd # 4028 Jacksonville (32256) ***(G-5938)***
Blue Earth Solutions Inc 352 729-0150
13511 Granville Ave Clermont (34711) ***(G-1861)***
Blue Gardenia LLC 727 560-0040
661 Central Ave Saint Petersburg (33701) ***(G-14984)***
Blue Hawaiian Fiberglass Pools, Largo *Also called Blue Hawaiian Products Inc* ***(G-7551)***
Blue Hawaiian Products Inc (PA) 727 535-5677
2055 Blue Hawaiian Dr Largo (33771) ***(G-7551)***
Blue Hippo LLC 407 325-4090
1090 Gills Dr Ste 100 Orlando (32824) ***(G-11960)***
Blue Hole Helicopters Inc 561 723-0378
3161 Se Chandelle Rd Jupiter (33478) ***(G-6697)***
Blue Horseshoe RES Group LLC 561 429-2030
9348 Via Elegante Wellington (33411) ***(G-17845)***
Blue Leaf Hospitality Inc 305 668-3000
2332 Galiano St 2 Coral Gables (33134) ***(G-2034)***
Blue Light USA Corp 954 766-4308
4625 Nw 103rd Ave Sunrise (33351) ***(G-16299)***
Blue Marlin Towers Inc 954 530-9140
3100 W State Road 84 # 20 Fort Lauderdale (33312) ***(G-3692)***
Blue Native of Fla Keys Inc 305 345-5305
197 Industrial Rd Big Pine Key (33043) ***(G-371)***
Blue Ocean Press Inc 954 973-1819
6299 Nw 27th Way Fort Lauderdale (33309) ***(G-3693)***
Blue Origin Florida LLC (HQ) 253 437-9300
8082 Space Commerce Way Merritt Island (32953) ***(G-8579)***
Blue Planet Envmtl Systems Inc 321 255-1931
2600 Kingswood Dr Ne Palm Bay (32905) ***(G-12893)***
Blue Planet Holdings LLC (PA) 863 559-1236
1738 Clarendon Pl Lakeland (33803) ***(G-7283)***
Blue Point Fabrication Inc 321 269-0073
3340 Lillian Blvd Titusville (32780) ***(G-17573)***
Blue Ribbon Tag & Label Corp (PA) 954 922-9292
4035 N 29th Ave Hollywood (33020) ***(G-5541)***
Blue Ribbon Tag & Label of PR 787 858-5300
4035 N 29th Ave Hollywood (33020) ***(G-5542)***
Blue Rock Inc (PA) 850 584-4324
4010 Olan Davis Rd Perry (32347) ***(G-13633)***
Blue Siren Inc 321 242-0300
3030 Venture Ln Ste 103 Melbourne (32934) ***(G-8379)***
Blue Sky Die Company, Tavares *Also called Kirtech Enterprises Inc* ***(G-17515)***
Blue Sky Labs LLC 901 268-6988
3811 University Blvd W # 4 Jacksonville (32217) ***(G-5939)***
Blue Stone Usa LLC 305 494-1141
1172 S Dixie Hwy 301 Coral Gables (33146) ***(G-2035)***
Blue Summit Wind LLC (HQ) 561 691-7171
700 Universe Blvd Juno Beach (33408) ***(G-6660)***
Blue Sun International, Doral *Also called Kayva Distribution LLC* ***(G-3271)***
Blue Tarpon Construction LLC 251 223-3630
119 W Garden St Pensacola (32502) ***(G-13457)***
Blue Water Dynamics LLC 386 957-5464
308 S Old County Rd Edgewater (32132) ***(G-3482)***
Blue Water Industries - FL LLC, Jacksonville *Also called Blue Water Industries LLC* ***(G-5940)***
Blue Water Industries LLC (PA) 904 512-7706
200 W Forsyth St Ste 1200 Jacksonville (32202) ***(G-5940)***
Blue Water Spa Covers, Apopka *Also called Bdjl Enterprises LLC* ***(G-105)***
Bluedrop USA Inc 800 563-3638
3275 Progress Dr Ste D Orlando (32826) ***(G-11961)***
Bluegate Inc 305 628-8391
16409 Nw 8th Ave Miami Gardens (33169) ***(G-10253)***
Bluegator Ground Protection, Ocala *Also called Donarra Extrusions LLC* ***(G-11370)***
Bluegrass Materials Co LLC (HQ) 919 781-4550
200 W Forsyth St Ste 1200 Jacksonville (32202) ***(G-5941)***
Blueocean Marine Services LLC 954 583-9888
340 Sw 21st Ter Fort Lauderdale (33312) ***(G-3694)***
Blues Design Group LLC 305 586-3630
3724 Nw 43rd St Miami (33142) ***(G-8840)***
Bluesky Innovations, Largo *Also called Bluesky Mast Inc* ***(G-7552)***
Bluesky Mast Inc 877 411-6278
2080 Wild Acres Rd Largo (33771) ***(G-7552)***
Bluestar Latin America Inc 954 485-1931
3561 Enterprise Way Miramar (33025) ***(G-10475)***
Bluetoad Inc 407 992-8744
2225 Lake Nally Woods Dr Gotha (34734) ***(G-4806)***
Bluewater Chairs Inc 954 318-0840
240 Sw 33rd Ct Fort Lauderdale (33315) ***(G-3695)***
Bluewater Finishing LLC 772 460-9457
1913 Sw South Macedo Blvd Port Saint Lucie (34984) ***(G-14400)***
Bluewater Marine Systems Inc 619 499-7507
360 Central Ave Ste 800 Saint Petersburg (33701) ***(G-14985)***
Blum & Company Inc 941 922-3239
5531 Cannes Cir Apt 503 Sarasota (34231) ***(G-15612)***
Blum & Fink Inc 212 695-2606
1200 N Federal Hwy # 200 Boca Raton (33432) ***(G-433)***
Blumer & Stanton Entps Inc (PA) 561 585-2525
5112 Georgia Ave West Palm Beach (33405) ***(G-17949)***
Blumer & Stanton Inc 561 585-2525
5112 Georgia Ave West Palm Beach (33405) ***(G-17950)***
Blums Woodworking LLC 850 449-7729
6708 Chelsea St Pensacola (32506) ***(G-13458)***
Blutec Glass Fabrication LLC 941 232-1600
5342 Clark Rd Unit 125 Sarasota (34233) ***(G-15613)***
Bluum Lab LLC 877 341-3339
470 Ansin Blvd Ste Aa Hallandale Beach (33009) ***(G-4939)***
Bluworld Innovations LLC 888 499-5433
635 W Michigan St Orlando (32805) ***(G-11962)***
Bluworld of Water LLC 407 426-7674
3093 Caruso Ct Ste 40-A Orlando (32806) ***(G-11963)***
BMC Services Inc 954 587-6337
2351 Sw 34th St Fort Lauderdale (33312) ***(G-3696)***
BMC Software Inc 813 227-4500
401 E Jackson St Ste 3300 Tampa (33602) ***(G-16649)***
Bmg Aerospace 786 725-4959
245 Ne 14th St Apt 3701 Miami (33132) ***(G-8841)***
Bmp Usa Inc 813 443-0757
8105 Anderson Rd Tampa (33634) ***(G-16650)***
Bms International Inc 813 247-7040
8802 E Broadway Ave Tampa (33619) ***(G-16651)***
BMW & Associates Inc 352 694-2300
4380 Se 53rd Ave Ocala (34480) ***(G-11336)***

ALPHABETIC

BMW Window Coverings, Ocala Also called BMW & Associates Inc (G-11336)

Bnj Noble Inc...........954 987-1040
5408 Stirling Rd Davie (33314) (G-2392)

Boair Inc...........954 426-9226
210 S Military Trl Deerfield Beach (33442) (G-2678)

Board Certified Media, Miami Also called Consultcanvas LLC (G-8958)

Board Shark Pcb Inc...........352 759-2100
53717 Rivertrace Rd Astor (32102) (G-202)

Boardwalk Designs Inc...........850 265-0988
1312 Louisiana Ave Lynn Haven (32444) (G-8026)

Boat Doctor, The, Tampa Also called Sheaffer Marine Inc (G-17257)

Boat Energy LLC...........954 501-2628
714 Nw 57th St Fort Lauderdale (33309) (G-3697)

Boat International Media Inc...........954 522-2628
1800 Se 10th Ave Ste 340 Fort Lauderdale (33316) (G-3698)

Boat Lift Pros of SW Fla Inc...........239 339-7080
2559 4th St Fort Myers (33901) (G-4189)

Boat Lifts By Synergy LLC...........641 676-4785
15864 Brothers Ct Ste B Fort Myers (33912) (G-4190)

Boat Master Aluminum Trailers...........239 768-2224
11950 Amedicus Ln Unit 2 Fort Myers (33907) (G-4191)

Boat Steering Solutions LLC...........727 400-4746
1070 Endeavor Ct North Venice (34275) (G-11208)

Boat Works...........904 389-0090
1282 Belmont Ter Jacksonville (32207) (G-5942)

Boatmaster/J D C I Enterprises, Fort Myers Also called Jdci Enterprises Inc (G-4297)

Boatrax Corp...........855 727-5647
1901 Brickell Ave B201 Miami (33129) (G-8842)

Boatswains Locker Inc...........904 388-0231
4565 Lakeside Dr Jacksonville (32210) (G-5943)

Bob & Lees Cabinets...........352 748-3553
4386 Warm Springs Ave Wildwood (34785) (G-18309)

Bob Kline Quality Metal Inc...........561 659-4245
2511 Division Ave West Palm Beach (33407) (G-17951)

Bob Laferriere Aircraft Inc...........727 709-2704
2769 Saint Andrews Blvd Tarpon Springs (34688) (G-17459)

Bob S Busy Bee Printing, Tampa Also called Printers Pride Inc (G-17184)

Bob Violett Models Inc...........407 327-6333
3481 State Road 419 Winter Springs (32708) (G-18561)

Bob's Machine Shop, Tampa Also called Bms International Inc (G-16651)

Bob's Printing, Boynton Beach Also called Bobs Quick Prtg & Copy Ctr (G-846)

Bob's Top End, Fort Myers Also called DNE Pot Sbob Inc (G-4237)

Bobbie Weiner Enterprises LLC...........817 615-8610
12355 Ne 13th Ave Unit 40 North Miami (33161) (G-11093)

Bobcat of Wiregrass Inc (PA)...........334 792-5121
127 Griffin Blvd Panama City Beach (32413) (G-13327)

Bobs Backflow & Plumbing Co...........904 268-8009
4640 Sub Chaser Ct # 113 Jacksonville (32244) (G-5944)

Bobs Barricades Inc...........813 886-0518
5018 24th Ave S Tampa (33619) (G-16652)

Bobs Barricades Inc...........239 656-1183
8031 Mainline Pkwy Fort Myers (33912) (G-4192)

Bobs Quick Prtg & Copy Ctr...........561 278-0203
812 Chapel Hill Blvd Boynton Beach (33435) (G-846)

Bobs Space Racers Inc...........386 677-0761
427 Whac A Mole Way Daytona Beach (32117) (G-2519)

Bobs Wldg Fbrcation Maint Inc...........863 665-0135
542 S Combee Rd Lakeland (33801) (G-7284)

Boca Beacon Co, Boca Grande Also called Hopkins & Daughter Inc (G-381)

Boca Coatings Inc...........561 400-8183
6135 Belleza Ln Boca Raton (33433) (G-434)

Boca Color Graphics Inc...........561 391-2229
139 Nw 3rd St Boca Raton (33432) (G-435)

Boca Dental Supply LLC...........800 768-5691
3401 N Federal Hwy # 211 Boca Raton (33431) (G-436)

Boca Raton Magazine, Boca Raton Also called Jes Publishing Corp (G-560)

Boca Raton Observer Magazine, Boca Raton Also called A & A Publishing Corp (G-383)

Boca Raton Printing Co...........561 395-8404
1000 Clint Moore Rd # 205 Boca Raton (33487) (G-437)

Boca Semiconductor Corporation...........561 226-8500
4260 Nw 1st Ave Ste 50 Boca Raton (33431) (G-438)

Boca Signworks...........561 393-6010
174 Glades Rd Boca Raton (33432) (G-439)

Boca Stone Design Inc...........561 362-2085
3601 N Dixie Hwy Ste 5 Boca Raton (33431) (G-440)

Boca Systems Inc...........561 998-9600
1065 S Rogers Cir Boca Raton (33487) (G-441)

Boca Terry LLC...........954 312-4400
3000 Sw 15th St Ste G Deerfield Beach (33442) (G-2679)

Bocadelray Life Magazine...........954 421-9797
4611 Johnson Rd Coconut Creek (33073) (G-1979)

Bocatech Inc...........954 397-7070
4101 Ravenswood Rd # 219 Fort Lauderdale (33312) (G-3699)

Boden Co Inc...........727 571-1234
10445 49th St N Ste B Clearwater (33762) (G-1522)

Bodhi Tree Woodwork Inc...........904 540-2655
60 N Saint Augustine Blvd Saint Augustine (32080) (G-14816)

Bodman Oil & Gas LLC...........239 430-8545
3007 Rum Row Naples (34102) (G-10697)

Bodolay Packaging Machine Div, Plant City Also called B & M Industries Inc (G-13742)

Bodree Printing Company Inc...........850 455-8511
3310 N W St Pensacola (32505) (G-13459)

Body Action Products, Land O Lakes Also called Product Max Group Inc (G-7500)

Body LLC...........850 888-2639
2950 47th Ave N Saint Petersburg (33714) (G-14986)

Body Nutrition, Saint Petersburg Also called Body LLC (G-14986)

Bodylastics International Inc (PA)...........561 254-0475
23026 Clear Echo Dr Boca Raton (33433) (G-442)

Bodylastics International Inc...........561 562-4745
3500 Nw 2nd Ave Ste 606 Boca Raton (33431) (G-443)

Bodylogicmd Franchise Corp...........561 972-9580
5000 T Rex Ave Boca Raton (33431) (G-444)

Boeing...........850 301-6635
20 Hill Ave Nw Fort Walton Beach (32548) (G-4566)

Boeing Arospc Operations Inc...........850 682-2746
5486 Fairchild Rd Hngr 3 Crestview (32539) (G-2240)

Boeing Company...........407 306-8782
13501 Ingenuity Dr # 204 Orlando (32826) (G-11964)

Boeing Company...........321 867-7380
Nasa Cswy Kennedy Space Center (32815) (G-6831)

Boeing Company...........562 797-9131
14100 Roosevelt Blvd Clearwater (33762) (G-1523)

Boeing Company...........904 317-2490
6211 Aviation Ave Jacksonville (32221) (G-5945)

Boeing Company...........321 853-6647
Hanger Rd Bldg A-0 Cape Canaveral (32920) (G-1279)

Boeing Company...........312 544-2000
100 Boeing Way Titusville (32780) (G-17574)

Bogantec Corp...........954 217-0023
1300 Stirling Rd Dania Beach (33004) (G-2349)

Bogue Executive Enterprises...........561 842-5336
1501 53rd St Mangonia Park (33407) (G-8090)

Bohemia Intrctive Smltions Inc...........407 608-7000
3050 Tech Pkwy Ste 110 Orlando (32826) (G-11965)

Bohnert Sheet Metal & Roofg Co...........305 696-6851
2225 Nw 76th St Miami (33147) (G-8843)

Boiler Inspection Services, Jacksonville Also called Whertec Inc (G-6608)

Boise Cascade Company...........800 359-6432
8007 Fl Ga Hwy Havana (32333) (G-4995)

Boland Production Supply Inc...........863 324-7784
507 Burns Ln Winter Haven (33884) (G-18422)

Boland Timber Company Inc...........850 997-5270
3616 S Byron Butler Pkwy Perry (32348) (G-13634)

Bolbox, Miami Also called Worldbox Corporation (G-10145)

Bold City Braves LLC...........904 545-3480
3385 Intl Vlg Dr W Jacksonville (32277) (G-5946)

Bold Look Inc...........305 687-8725
6721 Nw 36th Ave Miami (33147) (G-8844)

Bolidt Cruise Control Corp...........305 607-4172
14501 Nw 57th Ave Ste 111 Opa Locka (33054) (G-11724)

Bolivian Pavers LLC...........813 952-0608
4801 E Hillsborough Ave Tampa (33610) (G-16653)

Bollou Transportation LLC...........800 548-1768
11626 Ne 2nd Ave Miami (33161) (G-8845)

Bolt Lightning Protection, Clearwater Also called Lightning Master Corporation (G-1673)

Bolt Signs & Marketing LLC...........407 865-7446
2660 Bent Hickory Cir Longwood (32779) (G-7876)

Bolt Systems Inc...........407 425-0012
1700 Silver Star Rd Orlando (32804) (G-11966)

Bolton Medical Inc...........954 838-9699
799 International Pkwy Sunrise (33325) (G-16300)

Bombardier Aircraft Services, Fort Lauderdale Also called Bombardiier (G-3700)

Bombardier Trnsp Hldngs USA In...........407 450-4855
801 Sunrail Dr Sanford (32771) (G-15274)

Bombardiier...........954 622-1200
4100 Sw 11th Ter Fort Lauderdale (33315) (G-3700)

Bombastic Group Inc...........754 232-2932
2029 Tyler St Hollywood (33020) (G-5543)

Bon Appetit French Bakery, Fort Walton Beach Also called Palanjian Enterprises Inc (G-4600)

Bon Brands Inc...........800 590-7911
10299 Sthrn Blvd Unit 21 Royal Palm Beach (33411) (G-14760)

Bon Vivant Custom Woodworking, Opa Locka Also called Bon Vivant Interiors Inc (G-11725)

Bon Vivant Interiors Inc...........305 576-8066
4400 Nw 135th St Opa Locka (33054) (G-11725)

Bona Enterprises Inc (PA)...........954 927-4889
255 E Dania Beach Blvd Dania (33004) (G-2327)

Bonadeo Boat Works LLC...........772 341-9820
4431 Se Commerce Ave Stuart (34997) (G-16124)

Bonato & Pires LLC...........727 581-1220
13091 92nd St Unit 502 Largo (33773) (G-7553)

Bond Medical Group Inc...........813 264-5951
3837 Northdale Blvd # 36 Tampa (33624) (G-16654)

Bond-Pro Inc...........888 789-4985
1501 E 2nd Ave Tampa (33605) (G-16655)

Bond-Pro LLC...........813 413-7576
1501 E 2nd Ave Tampa (33605) (G-16656)

Bongiovi Aviation LLC 772 879-0578
649 Sw Whitmore Dr Port Saint Lucie (34984) *(G-14401)*

Bonita Boats Inc 321 978-1376
2900 Dusa Dr Melbourne (32934) *(G-8380)*

Bonita Daily News 239 213-6060
4415 Metro Pkwy Ste 300 Fort Myers (33916) *(G-4193)*

Bonita Grande Aggregates, Bonita Springs *Also called Bonita Grande Mining LLC (G-782)*

Bonita Grande Mining LLC 239 947-6402
25501 Bonita Grande Dr Bonita Springs (34135) *(G-782)*

Bonita Print Shop, Bonita Springs *Also called Bonita Printshop Inc (G-783)*

Bonita Print Shop, Bonita Springs *Also called I-Partner Group Inc (G-803)*

Bonita Printshop Inc 239 992-8522
28210 Old 41 Rd Unit 305 Bonita Springs (34135) *(G-783)*

Bonne Sante Group, Miami *Also called Smart For Life Inc (G-9906)*

Bonne Sante Natural Mfg Inc 305 594-4990
10575 Nw 37th Ter Doral (33178) *(G-3145)*

Bonnier Corporation 954 830-4460
705 Sw 16th St Fort Lauderdale (33315) *(G-3701)*

Bonnier Corporation (HQ) 407 628-4802
480 N Orlando Ave Ste 236 Winter Park (32789) *(G-18491)*

Bonsai American, Pensacola *Also called Bonsal American Inc (G-13460)*

Bonsal American, Pompano Beach *Also called Oldcastle Retail Inc (G-14110)*

Bonsal American Inc 813 621-2427
5455 N 59th St Tampa (33610) *(G-16657)*

Bonsal American Inc 904 783-0605
6659 Highway Ave Jacksonville (32254) *(G-5947)*

Bonsal American Inc 850 476-4223
150 E Olive Rd Pensacola (32514) *(G-13460)*

Bonus Aerospace Inc 305 887-6778
8545 Nw 79th Ave Medley (33166) *(G-8210)*

Bonus Tech Inc 786 251-4232
8575 Nw 79th Ave Ste 4d Medley (33166) *(G-8211)*

Books-A-Million Inc 813 571-2062
839 Brandon Town Ctr Mall Brandon (33511) *(G-1084)*

Boomer Times & Senior Life, Boca Raton *Also called Senior Lf Cmmnctions Group Inc (G-665)*

Boone Bait Co Inc 407 975-8775
1501 Minnesota Ave Winter Park (32789) *(G-18492)*

Boone Welding, Gainesville *Also called MPH Industries Inc (G-4735)*

Boost Lab Inc 813 443-0531
31050 Chatterly Dr Wesley Chapel (33543) *(G-17871)*

Boostan Inc 305 223-5981
8300 W Flagler St Ste 155 Miami (33144) *(G-8846)*

Boostane LLC 239 908-1615
10981 Harmony Park Dr # 5 Bonita Springs (34135) *(G-784)*

Booth Manufacturing Company 772 465-4441
3101 Industrial Ave Ste 2 Fort Pierce (34946) *(G-4471)*

Borden Dairy Company Fla LLC 863 298-9742
1000 6th St Sw Winter Haven (33880) *(G-18423)*

Borden, Ben Talent Assessment, Jacksonville *Also called Talent Assessment Inc (G-6530)*

Borders & Accents Inc 305 947-6200
1890 Ne 144th St North Miami (33181) *(G-11094)*

Bore Tech Inc 904 262-0752
5333 Skylark Ct Jacksonville (32257) *(G-5948)*

Borgesfs Inc 786 210-0327
14920 Sw 137th St Unit 2 Miami (33196) *(G-8847)*

Borgzinner Inc 561 848-2538
1160 W 13th St Ste 10 Riviera Beach (33404) *(G-14600)*

Boris Skateboards Mfg Inc 305 519-3544
695 Ne 77th St Miami (33138) *(G-8848)*

Born To Ride 813 661-9402
1051 E Brandon Blvd Brandon (33511) *(G-1085)*

Bornt Enterprises Inc 813 623-1492
9824 Currie Davis Dr Tampa (33619) *(G-16658)*

Boss Laser LLC 407 878-0880
608 Trestle Pt Sanford (32771) *(G-15275)*

Bossy Princess LLC 786 285-4435
18117 Biscayne Blvd # 1194 Aventura (33160) *(G-257)*

Bostic Steel Inc 305 592-7276
7740 Nw 34th St Doral (33122) *(G-3146)*

Boston Ntrceutical Science LLC 617 848-4560
801 Brickell Ave Miami (33131) *(G-8849)*

Boston Whaler Inc 386 428-0057
100 Whaler Way Edgewater (32141) *(G-3483)*

Boswell JM & Associates Inc 239 949-2311
270 3rd St Bonita Springs (34134) *(G-785)*

Bot International Inc 407 366-6547
1320 Tall Maple Loop Oviedo (32765) *(G-12811)*

Botanica Odomiwale Corp 305 381-5834
1301 Palm Ave Hialeah (33010) *(G-5078)*

Botanical Innovations Inc 407 332-8733
100 Candace Dr Unit 120 Maitland (32751) *(G-8053)*

Botanical Scents Nature Entps, Miami Lakes *Also called Scents Nature Enterprises Corp (G-10350)*

Bote LLC 888 855-4450
12598 Emerald Coast Pkwy Miramar Beach (32550) *(G-10568)*

Bote Boards, Miramar Beach *Also called Bote LLC (G-10568)*

Bote Boards 850 855-4046
630 Anchors St Nw Fort Walton Beach (32548) *(G-4567)*

Bote Paddle Boards 850 460-2250
383 Harbor Blvd Destin (32541) *(G-3060)*

Boulder Blimp Company Inc 303 664-1122
13350 Sw 131st St # 106 Miami (33186) *(G-8850)*

Bounce Back MBL Detailing LLC 561 336-4626
200 Knuth Rd Ste 103 Boynton Beach (33436) *(G-847)*

Bowen Medical Services Inc 386 362-1345
709 Industrial Ave Sw Live Oak (32064) *(G-7842)*

Bowman Analytics Inc 847 781-3523
5824 Bee Ridge Rd Sarasota (34233) *(G-15614)*

Box Seat Clothing Company 800 787-7792
5555 W 1st St Jacksonville (32254) *(G-5949)*

Boxrus.com, Hialeah *Also called Advanced Printing Finshg Inc (G-5031)*

Boyce Engineering Inc 727 572-6318
11861 31st Ct N Saint Petersburg (33716) *(G-14987)*

Boyd Industries Inc 727 561-9292
12900 44th St N Clearwater (33762) *(G-1524)*

Boyd Welding LLC 352 447-2405
802 Nw 27th Ave Ocala (34475) *(G-11337)*

Boyett Timber Inc 352 583-2138
45260 Lcchee Clay Sink Rd Webster (33597) *(G-17832)*

Boyle Publications Inc 941 255-0187
1039 Tamiami Trl Port Charlotte (33953) *(G-14289)*

BP International Inc 386 943-6222
510 W Arizona Ave Deland (32720) *(G-2856)*

Bpc Plasma Inc 407 207-1932
2501 Discovery Dr Orlando (32826) *(G-11967)*

Bpc Plasma Inc 561 989-5800
901 W Yamato Rd Ste 101 Boca Raton (33431) *(G-445)*

Bpc Plasma Inc (HQ) 561 569-3100
901 W Yamato Rd Ste 101 Boca Raton (33431) *(G-446)*

Bpg, Altamonte Springs *Also called Builders Publishing Group LLC (G-36)*

Bpi Labs LLC 727 471-0850
12393 Belcher Rd S # 450 Largo (33773) *(G-7554)*

Bpj International LLC 305 507-8971
11091 Nw 27th St Ste 204 Doral (33172) *(G-3147)*

BR Signs International In 954 464-7999
5944 Coral Ridge Dr Coral Springs (33076) *(G-2139)*

Brace Integrated Services Inc 813 248-6248
8205 E Adamo Dr Tampa (33619) *(G-16659)*

Braddck Mtllgl Arsp Ser Inc 561 622-2200
507 Industrial Way Boynton Beach (33426) *(G-848)*

Braddock Metallurgical Inc (HQ) 386 267-0955
14600 Duval Pl W Jacksonville (32218) *(G-5950)*

Braddock Metallurgical GA Inc 386 267-0955
400 Fentress Blvd Daytona Beach (32114) *(G-2520)*

Braddock Metallurgical MGT LLC 386 267-0955
400 Fentress Blvd Daytona Beach (32114) *(G-2521)*

Braddock Mtllrgcal - Dytona In 386 267-0955
400 Fentress Blvd Daytona Beach (32114) *(G-2522)*

Braddock Mtllurgical Holdg Inc (PA) 386 323-1500
400 Fentress Blvd Daytona Beach (32114) *(G-2523)*

Braden & Son Construction Inc 239 694-8600
6730 Circle Dr Fort Myers (33905) *(G-4194)*

Braden Kitchens Inc 321 636-4700
515 Industry Rd S Cocoa (32926) *(G-1907)*

Bradford County Telegraph Inc (PA) 904 964-6305
135 W Call St Starke (32091) *(G-16096)*

Bradford Septic Tank Company, Riviera Beach *Also called Pilot Corp of Palm Beaches (G-14661)*

Bradford Yacht Limited Inc 954 791-3800
3051 W State Road 84 Fort Lauderdale (33312) *(G-3702)*

Bradley Indus Textiles Inc 850 678-6111
101 S John Sims Pkwy Valparaiso (32580) *(G-17657)*

Brady Builders, Melbourne *Also called Brady Built Technologies Inc (G-8381)*

Brady Built Technologies Inc 270 692-6866
3661 Waynesboro Way Melbourne (32934) *(G-8381)*

Braid Sales and Marketing Inc (PA) 321 752-8180
320 North Dr Melbourne (32934) *(G-8382)*

Brain Power Incorporated 305 264-4465
4470 Sw 74th Ave Miami (33155) *(G-8851)*

Brainchild Corp 239 263-0100
3050 Horseshoe Dr N # 210 Naples (34104) *(G-10698)*

Brainchild Nutritionals, Miami *Also called Maxam Group LLC (G-9521)*

Brake-Funderburk Entps Inc 904 730-6788
8383 Baycenter Rd Jacksonville (32256) *(G-5951)*

Brambier's Windows & Walls, Port Orange *Also called Drapery Control Systems Inc (G-14333)*

Brambier's Windows & Walls, Fort Lauderdale *Also called Drapery Control Systems Inc (G-3773)*

Brammer Bio LLC 386 418-8199
13859 Progress Blvd Alachua (32615) *(G-10)*

Branch Properties Inc (PA) 352 732-4143
335 Ne Watula Ave Ocala (34470) *(G-11338)*

Brand Builders Rx LLC 727 576-4013
9843 18th St N Ste 150 Saint Petersburg (33716) *(G-14988)*

A L P H A B E T I C

Brand Label Inc 904 737-6433
8295 Western Way Cir Jacksonville (32256) *(G-5952)*

Brand Labs USA 954 532-5390
325 Sw 15th Ave Pompano Beach (33069) *(G-13952)*

Brand You Waters LLC 786 312-0840
2402 Bay Dr Pompano Beach (33062) *(G-13953)*

Brandano Displays Inc (PA) 954 956-7266
1473 Banks Rd Margate (33063) *(G-8123)*

Brandcomet, Maitland *Also called Grand Cypress Group Inc (G-8061)*

Brandfx LLC 321 632-2063
605 Townsend Rd Cocoa (32926) *(G-1908)*

Brandine Woodcraft Inc 561 266-9360
601 N Congress Ave # 203 Delray Beach (33445) *(G-2937)*

Brandon Alan Chapman 863 651-9189
114 Deen Blvd Auburndale (33823) *(G-220)*

Brandon Brown Newsom, Ponce De Leon *Also called U-Load Dumpsters LLC (G-14250)*

Brandon Crookes 954 563-8584
1034 Ne 44th Ct Oakland Park (33334) *(G-11247)*

Brandon Lock & Safe Inc 813 655-4200
4630 Eagle Falls Pl Tampa (33619) *(G-16660)*

Brantley Machine & Fabrication 904 359-0554
4003 N Canal St Jacksonville (32209) *(G-5953)*

Braswell Custom Cabinets 850 436-2645
9 Clarinda Ln Pensacola (32505) *(G-13461)*

Bravo Inc 239 471-8127
1811 Se 5th Ave Cape Coral (33990) *(G-1315)*

Bravo Construction Materials, Cape Coral *Also called Bravo Inc (G-1315)*

Brawley Distributing Co Inc 727 539-8500
7162 123rd Cir Largo (33773) *(G-7555)*

Bray Welding Inc 352 622-7780
1120 N Magnolia Ave Ocala (34475) *(G-11339)*

Brazilian Brickpavers Inc 850 699-7833
200 Racetrack Rd Ne Fort Walton Beach (32547) *(G-4568)*

Brazilian Clssfied ADS-Chei In 954 570-7568
2001 W Sample Rd Ste 422 Deerfield Beach (33064) *(G-2680)*

Brazilian Smoothie Inc 305 233-5543
13255 Sw 83rd Ave Pinecrest (33156) *(G-13663)*

BRC Sports Llc 904 388-8126
3600 Beachwood Ct Jacksonville (32224) *(G-5954)*

Break-Free Inc 800 347-1200
13386 International Pkwy Jacksonville (32218) *(G-5955)*

Breakthrough Clean Tech, Doral *Also called Atg Specialty Products Corp (G-3124)*

Breath Life Music Publishing 407 350-4669
142 White Birch Dr Kissimmee (34743) *(G-6900)*

Breathing Systems Inc 850 477-2324
8800 Grow Dr Pensacola (32514) *(G-13462)*

Breeden Pulpwood Inc 352 528-5243
Off Hwy 41 Williston (32696) *(G-18331)*

Breeze Boat Lifts, Fort Walton Beach *Also called Rocky Bayou Enterprises Inc (G-4606)*

Breeze Corporation (HQ) 239 574-1110
2510 Del Prado Blvd S Cape Coral (33904) *(G-1316)*

Breeze Newspapers 239 574-1116
14051 Jetport Loop Fort Myers (33913) *(G-4195)*

Breeze Newspapers 239 574-1110
2510 Del Prado Blvd S Cape Coral (33904) *(G-1317)*

Breeze Products Inc 727 521-4482
7207 114th Ave Ste B Largo (33773) *(G-7556)*

Breezemaker Fan Company Inc 813 248-5552
1608 N 24th St Tampa (33605) *(G-16661)*

Brefaros Nobile Food LLC 305 621-0074
5340 Nw 163rd St Miami Lakes (33014) *(G-10287)*

Breiner Machine Co Inc 352 544-0463
15373 Flight Path Dr Brooksville (34604) *(G-1142)*

Breitburn Operating LP 850 675-1704
5415 Oil Plant Rd Jay (32565) *(G-6649)*

Bremer Group Company Inc 904 645-0004
11243-5 Saint Johns Jacksonville (32246) *(G-5956)*

Bren Tuck Inc 727 561-7697
12929 44th St N Clearwater (33762) *(G-1525)*

Brenda Naused 352 344-4729
2043 S Atlantic Ave Daytona Beach (32118) *(G-2524)*

Bresee Woodwork Inc 941 355-2591
1795 Desoto Rd Sarasota (34234) *(G-15615)*

Breton USA Customers Svc Corp 941 360-2700
1753 Northgate Blvd Sarasota (34234) *(G-15616)*

Brevard Achievement Center Inc 321 632-8610
1845 Cogswell St Rockledge (32955) *(G-14693)*

Brevard Aluminum Cnstr Co 321 383-9255
4655 Calle Corto Titusville (32780) *(G-17575)*

Brevard Business News 321 951-7777
4300 Fortune Pl Ste D Melbourne (32904) *(G-8383)*

Brevard Robotics 321 637-0367
1485 Cox Rd Cocoa (32926) *(G-1909)*

Brevard Softball Magazine Inc 321 453-3711
400 Nora Ave Merritt Island (32952) *(G-8580)*

Brew Hub LLC 863 698-7600
3900 Frontage Rd S Lakeland (33815) *(G-7285)*

Brew Hub, The, Lakeland *Also called Brew Hub LLC (G-7285)*

Brewer International Inc 772 562-0555
605 90th Ave Vero Beach (32968) *(G-17743)*

Brewfab LLC 727 823-8333
2300 31st St N Saint Petersburg (33713) *(G-14989)*

Brian Belitz 407 924-5543
3130 Winding Trl Kissimmee (34746) *(G-6901)*

Brian Reck Valenzuela 386 801-5096
2885 W Huron Dr Deltona (32738) *(G-3041)*

Brian Schatzman 239 398-1798
10111 Sunshine Dr Bonita Springs (34135) *(G-786)*

Brian Slater & Associates LLC 561 886-7705
5301 N Federal Hwy # 195 Boca Raton (33487) *(G-447)*

Brianas Salad LLC 954 608-0953
5400 N Dixie Hwy Ste 7 Boca Raton (33487) *(G-448)*

Brick Markers USA Inc 561 842-1338
4430 W Tiffany Dr Ste 2 Mangonia Park (33407) *(G-8091)*

Brick Pavers By Mendoza Inc (PA) 772 925-1666
1235 S Us Highway 1 Vero Beach (32962) *(G-17744)*

Brick Pavers By Mendoza Inc. 772 408-2005
1986 21st St Sw Vero Beach (32962) *(G-17745)*

Brick Pvers Drveway Big Pavers 407 928-1217
6111 Metrowest Blvd Orlando (32835) *(G-11968)*

BrickIser Engrv Monuments Corp 786 806-0672
7964 Nw 14th St Doral (33126) *(G-3148)*

Brickmed LLC 305 774-0081
1800 Sw 27th Ave Ste 505 Miami (33145) *(G-8852)*

Bridge Chemicals Inc 954 545-9459
2455 Se 7th Dr Pompano Beach (33062) *(G-13954)*

Bridgestone Americas Inc 941 235-0445
24040 Beatrix Blvd Port Charlotte (33954) *(G-14290)*

Bridgestone Hosepower LLC (HQ) 904 264-1267
50 Industrial Loop N Orange Park (32073) *(G-11816)*

Briemad Inc 561 626-4377
2401 Pga Blvd Ste 136 Palm Beach Gardens (33410) *(G-12953)*

Briesa Inc 407 830-5307
1335 Bennett Dr Unit 173 Longwood (32750) *(G-7877)*

Bright Manufacturing LLC (PA) 954 603-4950
2933 W Cypress Creek Rd # 202 Fort Lauderdale (33309) *(G-3703)*

Brightfish Label LLC 727 521-7900
8222 118th Ave Ste 615 Largo (33773) *(G-7557)*

Brightsky LLC 239 919-8551
1004 Collier Center Way # 2 Naples (34110) *(G-10699)*

Brightwatts Inc 954 513-3352
1967 Nw 22nd St Oakland Park (33311) *(G-11248)*

Brigiz Inc 404 400-5399
7024 Hawks Nest Ter Riviera Beach (33407) *(G-14601)*

Brijot Imaging Systems Inc 407 641-4370
951 W Yamato Rd Ste 205 Boca Raton (33431) *(G-449)*

Brill Hygienic Products Inc 561 278-5600
601 N Congress Ave Delray Beach (33445) *(G-2938)*

Brinsea Products Inc. 321 267-7009
704 N Dixie Ave Titusville (32796) *(G-17576)*

Bristol Venture Service LLC 407 844-8629
16121 Bristol Lake Cir Orlando (32828) *(G-11969)*

Bristol-Myers Squibb Company 212 546-4000
11854 Skylake Pl Temple Terrace (33617) *(G-17535)*

Bristol-Myers Squibb Company 813 881-7000
4931 George Rd Tampa (33634) *(G-16662)*

Brite Lite Service Company 904 398-5305
5300 Shad Rd Jacksonville (32257) *(G-5957)*

Brite Lite Signs, Jacksonville *Also called Brite Lite Service Company (G-5957)*

Brite Lite Tribe 561 250-6824
840 Jupiter Park Dr Jupiter (33458) *(G-6698)*

Brite Shot Inc 954 418-7125
600 W Hillsboro Blvd Deerfield Beach (33441) *(G-2681)*

British Boys & Associates 305 278-1790
14480 Sw 151st Ter Miami (33186) *(G-8853)*

Brito Brick & Pavers Corp 727 214-8760
6262 142nd Ave N Clearwater (33760) *(G-1526)*

Britvic North America LLC 786 641-5041
360 Nw 27th St Miami (33127) *(G-8854)*

Broadband Fibers & Supplies 786 258-5746
10225 Collins Ave Bal Harbour (33154) *(G-293)*

Broadband International Inc (PA) 305 882-0505
11650 Nw 102nd Rd Medley (33178) *(G-8212)*

Broadcast Tech Inc (PA) 786 351-4227
10100 Nw 116th Way Ste 6 Medley (33178) *(G-8213)*

Broadsword Solutions Corp 248 341-3367
2020 Manor Ln Marathon (33050) *(G-8106)*

Broit Builders Inc 239 300-6900
1588 Vizcaya Ln Naples (34113) *(G-10700)*

Broit Lifting, Naples *Also called Broit Builders Inc (G-10700)*

Brokerage MGT Solutions Inc 561 766-0409
1095 Broken Sound Pkwy Nw # 200 Boca Raton (33487) *(G-450)*

Bromide Mining LLC 786 477-6229
2335 Nw 107th Ave Ste 127 Doral (33172) *(G-3149)*

Bromma Conquip 786 501-7130
6161 Blue Lagoon Dr Miami (33126) *(G-8855)*

Bronzart Foundry Inc 941 922-9106
5415 Ashton Ct Unit H Sarasota (34233) *(G-15617)*

Brookhaven Beverage Company, Saint Petersburg *Also called St Petersburg Dist Co LLC (G-15197)*

Brooking Industries Inc 954 533-0765
104 Liberty Center Pl Saint Augustine (32092) *(G-14817)*
Brooklands New Media LLC 305 370-3867
1000 5th St Ste 200 Miami Beach (33139) *(G-10172)*
Brooklink Green Fuels Inc 561 514-1725
7 Amherst Ct Apt B Royal Palm Beach (33411) *(G-14761)*
Brooklyn Stitch Inc 786 280-1730
20213 Ne 16th Pl Miami (33179) *(G-8856)*
Brooklyn Water Enterprises Inc 877 224-3580
1615 S Congress Ave # 103 Delray Beach (33445) *(G-2939)*
Brooks Concrete Service, Panacea *Also called Brooks Welding & Concrete Shop (G-13224)*
Brooks Welding & Concrete Shop 850 984-5279
1532 Coastal Hwy Panacea (32346) *(G-13224)*
Brooksville Printing Inc 352 848-0016
712 S Main St Brooksville (34601) *(G-1143)*
Brooksville Terminal Us11, Brooksville *Also called Lhoist North America Ala LLC (G-1174)*
Bros Williams Printing 305 769-9925
4716 E 10th Ct Hialeah (33013) *(G-5079)*
Bros Williams Printing Inc 305 769-9925
4716 E 10th Ct Hialeah (33013) *(G-5080)*
Broski Ciderworks LLC 954 657-8947
1465 Sw 6th Ct Pompano Beach (33069) *(G-13955)*
Broth Bomb LLC 813 278-1912
25778 Us Highway 19 N Clearwater (33763) *(G-1527)*
Brothers Pallets 863 944-5278
2410 Mcjunkin Rd Lakeland (33803) *(G-7286)*
Brothers Powder Coating Inc 727 846-0717
7721 Rutillio Ct Ste D New Port Richey (34653) *(G-10963)*
Brothers Wholesale Inc 631 831-8484
534 Nw Mercantile Pl Port St Lucie (34986) *(G-14470)*
Broward Armature and Generator, Fort Lauderdale *Also called Blueocean Marine Services LLC (G-3694)*
Broward Casting Foundry Inc 954 584-6400
2240 Sw 34th St Fort Lauderdale (33312) *(G-3704)*
Broward Custom Woodwork LLC 352 376-4732
401 Jim Moran Blvd Deerfield Beach (33442) *(G-2682)*
Broward Machine LLC 954 920-8004
2070 Tigertail Blvd Ste D Dania (33004) *(G-2328)*
Broward Marine, Dania *Also called Broward Yard & Marine LLC (G-2329)*
Broward Power Train Co Inc 954 772-0881
5300 Nw 12th Ave Ste 3 Fort Lauderdale (33309) *(G-3705)*
Broward Signs 954 320-9903
1901 S Federal Hwy Fort Lauderdale (33316) *(G-3706)*
Broward Yard & Marine LLC 954 927-4119
750 Ne 7th Ave Dania (33004) *(G-2329)*
Brown (usa) Inc 305 593-9228
2245 Nw 72nd Ave Miami (33122) *(G-8857)*
Brown Enterprises, Jacksonville *Also called Solar Enterprises Inc (G-6478)*
Brown International Corp LLC 863 299-2111
333 Avenue M Nw Winter Haven (33881) *(G-18424)*
Brown Jordan Company LLC (HQ) 904 495-0717
475 W Town Pl Ste 200 Saint Augustine (32092) *(G-14818)*
Brown's Septics, Silver Springs *Also called A-1 City Wide Sewer Svc Inc (G-16004)*
Brownbag Popcorn Company LLC 561 212-5664
900 Ne 4th St Apt A Boca Raton (33432) *(G-451)*
Brownies Marine Group Inc (PA) 954 462-5570
3001 Nw 25th Ave Ste 1 Pompano Beach (33069) *(G-13956)*
Browning Communications, Debary *Also called Hoffman Brothers Inc (G-2636)*
Brownlee Lighting Inc 407 297-3677
4600 Dardanelle Dr Orlando (32808) *(G-11970)*
Brownsville Orna Ir Works Inc 850 433-0521
3520 Mobile Hwy Pensacola (32505) *(G-13463)*
Brownsville Welding, Pensacola *Also called Brownsville Orna Ir Works Inc (G-13463)*
Brrh Corporation 954 427-9665
3313 W Hillsboro Blvd # 101 Deerfield Beach (33442) *(G-2683)*
BRT Oakleaf Pet Inc 904 563-1212
1619 Leon Rd Jacksonville (32246) *(G-5958)*
Bru Bottling Inc 561 324-5053
1507 Villa Juno Dr N Juno Beach (33408) *(G-6661)*
Bruce Component Systems Inc 352 628-0522
3409 W Pennington Ct Lecanto (34461) *(G-7748)*
Bruce R Ely Enterprise Inc 727 573-1643
12880 Auto Blvd Ste G Clearwater (33762) *(G-1528)*
Brunken Manufacturing Co Inc 850 438-2478
4205 W Jackson St Pensacola (32505) *(G-13464)*
Bruno Danger Custom Cabinets 754 366-1302
761 S Easy St Sebastian (32958) *(G-15888)*
Bruns Mfg Homes 863 294-4949
10 Spirit Lake Rd Winter Haven (33880) *(G-18425)*
Brunsteel Corp 305 251-7607
14065 Sw 142nd St Miami (33186) *(G-8858)*
Brunswick Commercial & 386 423-2900
100 Whaler Way Edgewater (32141) *(G-3484)*
Brunswick Corporation 850 769-1011
11 College Ave Panama City (32401) *(G-13236)*
Brunswick Corporation 954 744-3500
15351 Sw 29th St Ste 800 Miramar (33027) *(G-10476)*
Bruss Company 904 693-0688
5441 W 5th St Jacksonville (32254) *(G-5959)*

Brut Printing Co Inc 904 354-5055
503 Parker St Jacksonville (32202) *(G-5960)*
Bryan Ashley Inc 954 351-1199
1432 E Newport Center Dr Deerfield Beach (33442) *(G-2684)*
Bryan Nelco Inc 727 533-8282
15251 Roosevelt Blvd # 202 Clearwater (33760) *(G-1529)*
Bryant Machine Shop, Vero Beach *Also called Bryants Precision M F G Corp (G-17746)*
Bryants Precision M F G Corp 772 569-2319
1803 Wilbur Ave Vero Beach (32960) *(G-17746)*
Bryce Foster Inc 800 371-0395
215 Rollingwood Trl Altamonte Springs (32714) *(G-34)*
Brycoat Inc 727 490-1000
207 Vollmer Ave Oldsmar (34677) *(G-11636)*
Bryson of Brevard Inc 321 636-5116
580 Gus Hipp Blvd Rockledge (32955) *(G-14694)*
BSC Ventures, Gainesville *Also called Double Envelope Corporation (G-4679)*
BSK USA LLC 786 328-5395
201 Alhambra Cir Ste 603 Coral Gables (33134) *(G-2036)*
BT Glass & Mirror Inc 561 841-7676
3748 Prospect Ave Ste 4 West Palm Beach (33404) *(G-17952)*
Btb Refining LLC 561 999-9916
925 S Federal Hwy Ste 375 Boca Raton (33432) *(G-452)*
BTR Logging Inc 386 397-0730
10249 Se 161st Ave White Springs (32096) *(G-18305)*
Btu Reps LLC (PA) 727 235-3591
185 23rd Ave N Saint Petersburg (33704) *(G-14990)*
Bubba Foods LLC (PA) 904 482-1900
4339 Roosevelt Blvd # 400 Jacksonville (32210) *(G-5961)*
Bubba Rope LLC 877 499-8494
998 Explorer Cv Ste 130 Altamonte Springs (32701) *(G-35)*
Bubble Bath Detailing Car Wash, Opa Locka *Also called Andre T Jean (G-11717)*
Bubblemac Industries Inc 352 396-8043
11932 156th St Mc Alpin (32062) *(G-8187)*
Bubbles Body Wear, Miami *Also called Sweet and Vicious LLC (G-9981)*
Buchanan Sign & Flag, Jacksonville *Also called Buchanan Signs Screen Process (G-5962)*
Buchanan Signs Screen Process 904 725-5500
6755 Beach Blvd Jacksonville (32216) *(G-5962)*
Buchelli Glass Inc 954 695-8067
5417 Nw 50th Ct Coconut Creek (33073) *(G-1980)*
Buck Pile Inc 772 492-1056
2801 Ocean Dr Ste 101 Vero Beach (32963) *(G-17747)*
Buckeye Office Intrors Instllt, Largo *Also called Buckeye Used Office Furn Inc (G-7558)*
Buckeye Used Office Furn Inc 727 457-5287
6166 126th Ave Largo (33773) *(G-7558)*
Buckley Pallets 727 415-4497
2409 Laurelwood Dr Clearwater (33763) *(G-1530)*
Buckley Pallets LLC 727 415-4497
14550 62nd St N 2 Clearwater (33760) *(G-1531)*
Bucks Corporation Inc 850 894-2400
1920 N Monroe St Tallahassee (32303) *(G-16419)*
Buddy Bridge Inc (PA) 941 488-0799
350 Sorrento Ranches Dr Nokomis (34275) *(G-11042)*
Buddy Bridge Inc 941 586-8281
751 Us Highway 41 Byp S Venice (34285) *(G-17678)*
Buddy Custard Inc 561 715-3785
1451 W Cypress Creek Rd Fort Lauderdale (33309) *(G-3707)*
Buddy Pauls Inc 561 578-9813
301 Clematis St Ste 300 West Palm Beach (33401) *(G-17953)*
Buddy Ward & Sons Seafood 850 653-8522
3022 C 30 13 Mile Rd Apalachicola (32320) *(G-88)*
Buddy Ward Sons Seafood Trckg, Apalachicola *Also called Buddy Ward & Sons Seafood (G-88)*
Buddy's Pizza, Venice *Also called Richard Meer Investments Inc (G-17713)*
Budget Print Center, Ocala *Also called Keithco Inc (G-11419)*
Budget Printing Center LLC 561 848-5700
7241 Hvrhill Bus Pkwy # 110 Riviera Beach (33407) *(G-14602)*
Budget Signs Inc 954 941-5710
1820 Sw 7th Ave Pompano Beach (33060) *(G-13957)*
Buena Cepa Wines LLC 310 621-2566
951 Crandon Blvd Key Biscayne (33149) *(G-6835)*
Buena Vista Construction Co 407 828-2104
3291 Wed Way Lake Buena Vista (32830) *(G-6998)*
Buenavida Imports LLC 305 988-5992
3508 Nw 114th Ave Ste 205 Doral (33178) *(G-3150)*
Bufalinda USA LLC 305 979-9258
2000 Bay Dr Miami Beach (33141) *(G-10173)*
Buffalo Machine Manufacturing 727 321-1905
3140 39th Ave N Saint Petersburg (33714) *(G-14991)*
Buffalo Rock Company 850 857-3774
8801 Grow Dr Pensacola (32514) *(G-13465)*
Buffalo Wheelchair Inc 941 921-6331
4130 S Tamiami Trl Sarasota (34231) *(G-15618)*
Buggy Bagg Inc 386 758-5836
248 Sw Webbs Gln Lake City (32024) *(G-7013)*
Buggy Guard, West Palm Beach *Also called Nikiani Inc (G-18092)*
Builders Automtn McHy Co LLC 727 538-2180
12775 Starkey Rd Ste B Largo (33773) *(G-7559)*
Builders Door and Supply Inc 941 955-2311
2022 12th St Sarasota (34237) *(G-15619)*

ALPHABETIC

Builders Notice Corporation................954 764-1322
  708 S Andrews Ave Fort Lauderdale (33316) *(G-3708)*

Builders Publishing Group LLC................407 539-2938
  815 Orienta Ave Ste 1050 Altamonte Springs (32701) *(G-36)*

Building Blocks Gfrc LLC................312 243-9960
  1150 Joelson Rd Kissimmee (34744) *(G-6902)*

Building Blocks Management Inc................214 289-9737
  1150 Joelson Rd Kissimmee (34744) *(G-6903)*

Building Envelope Systems Inc................305 693-0683
  3121 E 11th Ave Hialeah (33013) *(G-5081)*

Building Management Group................305 440-9101
  2451 Nw 109th Ave Unit 5 Doral (33172) *(G-3151)*

Built LLC................813 512-6250
  602 N Newport Ave Tampa (33606) *(G-16663)*

Built Rght Ktchens of Palm Cas................386 437-7077
  7755 S Us Highway 1 Bunnell (32110) *(G-1228)*

Built Right Installers Intl................305 362-6010
  7930 W 26th Ave Unit 2 Hialeah (33016) *(G-5082)*

Built Right Pool Heaters LLC................941 505-1600
  28110 Challenger Blvd Punta Gorda (33982) *(G-14500)*

Built Story LLC................305 671-3890
  1581 Brickell Ave # 2207 Miami (33129) *(G-8859)*

Built-Rite Cabinets Inc................352 447-2238
  18290 Se Highway 19 Inglis (34449) *(G-5816)*

Bukkehave Inc................954 525-9788
  6750 N Andrews Ave # 200 Fort Lauderdale (33309) *(G-3709)*

Bulk Food Grocers, Saint Petersburg *Also called Great Amercn Natural Pdts Inc* *(G-15066)*

Bulk Manufacturing Florida Inc................813 757-2313
  3106 Central Dr Plant City (33566) *(G-13747)*

Bulk Resources Inc (PA)................813 764-8420
  1507 S Alexander St # 102 Plant City (33563) *(G-13748)*

Bulldog Neon Sign Company Inc................786 277-6366
  5728 Ne 4th Ave Miami (33137) *(G-8860)*

Bullet Line LLC (HQ)................305 623-9223
  6301 E 10th Ave Ste 110 Hialeah (33013) *(G-5083)*

Bulletin Net Inc................941 468-2569
  6000 S Tamiami Trl Sarasota (34231) *(G-15620)*

Bulletproof Hitches LLC................941 251-8110
  3145 Lakewood Ranch Blvd # 106 Bradenton (34211) *(G-950)*

Bullion International Inc................321 773-2727
  4100 N Riverside Dr Indian Harbour Beach (32937) *(G-5804)*

Bumper Doctor................850 341-1771
  95 Airport Blvd Pensacola (32503) *(G-13466)*

Bundy Signs LLC................954 296-0784
  4556 N Hiatus Rd Sunrise (33351) *(G-16301)*

Bunkys Raw Bar, Indialantic *Also called A1a Raw LLC* *(G-5800)*

Burbank Sport Nets, Jacksonville *Also called Burbank Trawl Makers Inc* *(G-5963)*

Burbank Sports Nets, Jacksonville *Also called BRC Sports Llc* *(G-5954)*

Burbank Trawl Makers Inc................904 321-0976
  13913 Duval Rd Ste 100 Jacksonville (32218) *(G-5963)*

Burch Welding & Fabrication................904 353-6513
  2324 Phoenix Ave Jacksonville (32206) *(G-5964)*

Burke Brands LLC................305 249-5628
  521 Ne 189th St Miami (33179) *(G-8861)*

Burkhart Roentgen Intl Inc................727 327-6950
  3232 Bennett St N Saint Petersburg (33713) *(G-14992)*

Burlakoff Manufacturing Co................972 889-2502
  826 Se 9th Ter Ocala (34471) *(G-11340)*

Burma Spice Inc................863 254-0960
  31 Georgetown Fort Myers (33919) *(G-4196)*

Burn By Rocky Patel................239 653-9013
  9110 Strada Pl Ste 6160 Naples (34108) *(G-10701)*

Burn Proof Gear LLC................786 634-7406
  7121 N Miami Ave Miami (33150) *(G-8862)*

Burnett Industrial Sales, Saint Augustine *Also called St Agustine Elc Mtr Works Inc* *(G-14897)*

Burnham Woods Untd Civic Group................954 532-2675
  8211 Sw 19th St North Lauderdale (33068) *(G-11076)*

Burr Printing Co Inc................863 294-3166
  4212 Hammond Dr Winter Haven (33881) *(G-18426)*

Burris Investment Group Inc................850 623-3845
  10648 Mac Gregor Dr Pensacola (32514) *(G-13467)*

Burton JC Companies Inc................239 992-2377
  24241 Production Cir Bonita Springs (34135) *(G-787)*

Buscar Inc................813 877-7272
  3403 W Morrison Ave Tampa (33629) *(G-16664)*

Busch Canvas................561 881-1605
  2428 Broadway Riviera Beach (33404) *(G-14603)*

Busch Canvas & Interiors Inc................561 881-1605
  2428 Broadway Riviera Beach (33404) *(G-14604)*

Bush Brothers Provision Co................561 832-6666
  1931 N Dixie Hwy West Palm Beach (33407) *(G-17954)*

Bushhog N Blade Work................904 669-2764
  2846 Usina Road Ext Saint Augustine (32084) *(G-14819)*

Bushnell Sawmill Inc................352 793-2740
  5178 W C 48 Bushnell (33513) *(G-1240)*

Bushnell Truss Enterprises LLC................352 793-6090
  5240 W C 476 Bushnell (33513) *(G-1241)*

Bushwacker Spirits LLC................941 200-0818
  3135 Southgate Cir Sarasota (34239) *(G-15621)*

Business Card Ex Tampa Bay, Clearwater *Also called Formica Print Solutions LLC* *(G-1606)*

Business Card Ex Tampa Bay Inc................727 535-7768
  14000 63rd Way N Clearwater (33760) *(G-1532)*

Business Center & Printshop................786 547-6681
  815 Nw 119th St Miami (33168) *(G-8863)*

Business Clinic Inc................786 473-4573
  1475 W Okeechobee Rd # 3 Hialeah (33010) *(G-5084)*

Business Forward Inc................954 967-6730
  3286 N 29th Ct Hollywood (33020) *(G-5544)*

Business Jrnl Publications Inc (HQ)................813 342-2472
  4350 W Cypress St Ste 800 Tampa (33607) *(G-16665)*

Business Report of N Cntrl FL................352 275-9469
  1314 S Main St Gainesville (32601) *(G-4663)*

Business World Trading Inc................305 238-0724
  13275 Sw 136th St Unit 22 Miami (33186) *(G-8864)*

Bust Out Promotions LLC................561 305-8313
  1375 Sw 12th Ave Pompano Beach (33069) *(G-13958)*

Busy Bee Cabinets Inc................941 628-2025
  2845 Commerce Pkwy North Port (34289) *(G-11189)*

Butler Graphics Inc................305 477-1344
  5055 Nw 74th Ave Unit 5 Miami (33166) *(G-8865)*

Butler Pavers Inc................941 423-3977
  6862 Van Camp St North Port (34291) *(G-11190)*

Buttercream Cpcakes Cof Sp Inc................305 669-8181
  1411 Sunset Dr Coral Gables (33143) *(G-2037)*

Butterkrust Bakeries, Lakeland *Also called Southern Bakeries Inc* *(G-7443)*

Buvin Jewelry Florida Inc................305 358-0170
  36 Ne 1st St Ste 217 Miami (33132) *(G-8866)*

Buy Golf Grips 4 Less................352 256-7577
  11244 Redgate St Spring Hill (34609) *(G-16066)*

Buzz Pop Cocktails Corporation (PA)................727 275-9848
  4407 Buena Vista Ln Holiday (34691) *(G-5491)*

Bxd Enterprises Inc................727 937-4100
  4148 Louis Ave Holiday (34691) *(G-5492)*

By Dancers For Dancers, Miami *Also called Lan Designs Inc* *(G-9419)*

Byblos Group Inc................305 662-6666
  7175 Sw 47th St Ste 210 Miami (33155) *(G-8867)*

Byerly Custom Design Inc................941 371-7498
  743 Gantt Ave Sarasota (34232) *(G-15622)*

Byomed LLC................305 634-6763
  1555 Ne 123rd St North Miami (33161) *(G-11095)*

Byrd Technologies Inc................954 957-8333
  3100 Sw 10th St Pompano Beach (33069) *(G-13959)*

Bytio Inc................445 888-9999
  2202 N West Shore Blvd # 2 Tampa (33607) *(G-16666)*

C & C Diversified Services LLC................772 597-1022
  7954 Sw Jack James Dr Stuart (34997) *(G-16125)*

C & C Multiservices Corp................305 200-5851
  2849 Nw 7th St Miami (33125) *(G-8868)*

C & C Services of Tampa Inc................813 477-8559
  1007 Robinson Rd Plant City (33563) *(G-13749)*

C & C Tool & Mold................863 699-5337
  3417 Paso Fino Dr Lake Placid (33852) *(G-7138)*

C & D Industrial Maint LLC................833 776-5833
  2208 58th Ave E Bradenton (34203) *(G-951)*

C & D Printing Company................727 572-9999
  12150 28th St N Saint Petersburg (33716) *(G-14993)*

C & E Cabinets Design LLC................386 410-4281
  137 W Marion Ave Edgewater (32132) *(G-3485)*

C & E Innovative MGT LLC................727 408-5146
  2454 N Mcmullen Booth Rd Clearwater (33759) *(G-1533)*

C & G Timber Harvesters Inc................850 643-1340
  10213 Nw Dan Jacobs Ln Bristol (32321) *(G-1117)*

C & H Baseball Inc (PA)................941 727-1533
  10615 Tech Ter Ste 100 Bradenton (34211) *(G-952)*

C & H Printing Inc................904 620-8444
  11315-1 St Jhns Indus Pkw Jacksonville (32246) *(G-5965)*

C & H Sign Enterprises Inc................407 826-0155
  9900 Universal Blvd # 114 Orlando (32819) *(G-11971)*

C & J Industries Inc................386 589-4907
  105 John Anderson Dr Ormond Beach (32176) *(G-12748)*

C & M Manufacturing LLC................407 673-9601
  4212 Metric Dr Winter Park (32792) *(G-18493)*

C & M Millwork Inc................352 588-5050
  30450 Commerce Dr San Antonio (33576) *(G-15246)*

C & R Designs Inc................321 383-2255
  1227 Garden St Titusville (32796) *(G-17577)*

C & R Designs Printing LLC................321 383-2255
  415 Main St Titusville (32796) *(G-17578)*

C & S Graphics Inc................813 251-4411
  1335 W North B St Tampa (33606) *(G-16667)*

C & S GRAPHICS, INC. DBA ELECTRIC SIGN COMPANY, Tampa *Also called C & S Graphics Inc* *(G-16667)*

C & S Plastics, Winter Haven *Also called Precision Plastics Group Inc* *(G-18459)*

C & S Plastics................863 294-5628
  1550 5th St Sw Winter Haven (33880) *(G-18427)*

C & S Press Inc................407 841-3000
  405 27th St Orlando (32806) *(G-11972)*

C & S Signs Inc................850 983-9540
  8895 S Lynn Rd Milton (32583) *(G-10421)*

C B Precious Metals LLC 407 790-1585
1237 Bella Vista Cir Longwood (32779) ***(G-7878)***
C C 1 Limited Partnership 305 599-2337
3201 Nw 72nd Ave Miami (33122) ***(G-8869)***
C C Calhoun Inc 863 292-9511
3750 W Lake Hamilton Dr Winter Haven (33881) ***(G-18428)***
C C Lead Inc 863 465-6458
127 Ranier Dr Lake Placid (33852) ***(G-7139)***
C Dyer Development Group LLC 727 423-6169
1125 Lake St Tarpon Springs (34689) ***(G-17460)***
C E M, Port St Lucie *Also called Composite Essential Mtls LLC* ***(G-14475)***
C E S Wireless Tech Corp 407 681-0869
931 S Semoran Blvd # 200 Winter Park (32792) ***(G-18494)***
C F Print Ltd Inc 631 567-2110
3174 Dressendorfer Dr The Villages (32163) ***(G-17553)***
C F Webb and Sons Logging LLC 850 971-5565
625 Se Old Logging Trl Lee (32059) ***(G-7755)***
C I G, Sarasota *Also called Commercial Insulating Glass Co* ***(G-15638)***
C K S, Orlando *Also called Charles K Sewell* ***(G-12005)***
C L F Enterprises 305 643-3222
111 Sw 17th Ave Miami (33135) ***(G-8870)***
C L Industries Inc 800 333-2660
8188 S Orange Ave Orlando (32809) ***(G-11973)***
C M C Steel Fabricators Inc 239 337-3480
2665 Prince St Fort Myers (33916) ***(G-4197)***
C M E, Pinellas Park *Also called Custom Mfg & Engrg Inc* ***(G-13680)***
C M I Enterprises Inc (PA) 305 622-6410
13145 Nw 45th Ave Opa Locka (33054) ***(G-11726)***
C M P G, Orlando *Also called Commercial Metal Photography* ***(G-12033)***
C M W, Lithia *Also called Central Maintenance & Wldg Inc* ***(G-7831)***
C Mike Roach Inc 864 882-1101
4847 Se Longleaf Pl Hobe Sound (33455) ***(G-5480)***
C P Enterprises of Apopka Inc 407 886-3321
3351 Laughlin Rd Mount Dora (32757) ***(G-10598)***
C P T, Cocoa Beach *Also called Cathodic Prtection Tech of Fla* ***(G-1966)***
C P Vegetable Oil Inc 954 584-0420
601 Sw 21st Ter Ste 1 Fort Lauderdale (33312) ***(G-3710)***
C Products Defense Inc 941 727-0009
4555 18th St E Bradenton (34203) ***(G-953)***
C Q M, Tampa *Also called Custom Quality Mfg Inc* ***(G-16756)***
C Q Molding Inc 786 314-1312
2081 Bahama Dr Miramar (33023) ***(G-10477)***
C Speed LLC 321 336-7939
6855 Tico Rd Ste 103 Titusville (32780) ***(G-17579)***
C W Machining Inc 352 732-5824
2820 Nw 8th Pl Ocala (34475) ***(G-11341)***
C W Products International 407 831-4966
1340 Bennett Dr Longwood (32750) ***(G-7879)***
C Y A Powder Coating LLC 727 299-9832
12099 44th St N Clearwater (33762) ***(G-1534)***
C&A Boatworks Inc 754 366-5549
1711 N Powerline Rd Pompano Beach (33069) ***(G-13960)***
C&A Lozaro Inc 407 671-8809
3000 N Goldenrod Rd Winter Park (32792) ***(G-18495)***
C&C Brick Pavers Inc 813 716-8291
8513 N Otis Ave Tampa (33604) ***(G-16668)***
C&C Company, Zellwood *Also called CC Welding & Construction LLC* ***(G-18596)***
C&C Industries, Doral *Also called Cosmetics & Cleaners Intl LLC* ***(G-3175)***
C&D Canvas Inc 954 924-3433
6110 W Falcons Lea Dr Davie (33331) ***(G-2393)***
C&D Purveyors Inc 305 562-8541
8242 Nw 70th St Miami (33166) ***(G-8871)***
C&D Sign and Lighting Svcs LLC 863 937-9323
2175 E Edgewood Dr Lakeland (33803) ***(G-7287)***
C&L Technologies, Port Saint Lucie *Also called Savage Ventures Inc* ***(G-14444)***
C&S Ostomy Pouch Covers Inc 941 423-8542
2214 Cloras St North Port (34287) ***(G-11191)***
C-Horse Software Inc 321 952-0692
1510 Charles Blvd Ne Palm Bay (32907) ***(G-12894)***
C-Mix Corp 954 670-0208
5600 Nw 12th Ave Ste 306 Fort Lauderdale (33309) ***(G-3711)***
C-Note Solutions Inc 321 952-2490
334 4th Ave Indialantic (32903) ***(G-5802)***
C-Worthy Corp 954 784-7370
241 Sw 5th Ct Pompano Beach (33060) ***(G-13961)***
C-Worthy Custom Yacht Canvas, Pompano Beach *Also called C-Worthy Corp* ***(G-13961)***
C.A.c Custom Artisan Cabinetry, Boca Raton *Also called Integral WD Cstm Cabinetry LLC* ***(G-546)***
C1 Aerospace LLC 786 712-9949
14519 Sw 138th Pl Miami (33186) ***(G-8872)***
C2 Powder Coating LLC 941 404-2671
6060 28th St E Ste 1 Bradenton (34203) ***(G-954)***
C2c Innovated Technology LLC 251 382-2277
3371 Highway 90 Bonifay (32425) ***(G-768)***
C4 Advnced Tctical Systems LLC 407 206-3886
243 Wetherbee Rd Orlando (32824) ***(G-11974)***
C4 Group LLC 850 230-4541
7551 Holley Cir Panama City (32408) ***(G-13237)***
C4ats, Orlando *Also called C4 Advnced Tctical Systems LLC* ***(G-11974)***
Ca Inc 305 559-4640
15298 Sw 17th Ter Miami (33185) ***(G-8873)***
Ca Inc 305 347-5140
1221 Brickell Ave 907 Miami (33131) ***(G-8874)***
CA Pipeline Inc 305 969-4655
15621 Sw 209th Ave Miami (33187) ***(G-8875)***
Caamacosta Inc 954 987-5895
5400 N 35th St Hollywood (33021) ***(G-5545)***
Caballero Metals Corp 305 266-9085
7315 Sw 45th St Miami (33155) ***(G-8876)***
Caballero Metals Corp 305 266-9085
7315 Sw 45th St Ste 4 Miami (33155) ***(G-8877)***
Cabinet and Stone, Tampa *Also called Kitchen and Bath Universe Inc* ***(G-16990)***
Cabinet Cnnction of Trsure Cas (PA) 772 621-4882
740 Nw Enterprise Dr Port Saint Lucie (34986) ***(G-14402)***
Cabinet Collection Inc 239 478-0359
24830 S Tamiami Trl Bonita Springs (34134) ***(G-788)***
Cabinet Design and Cnstr LLC 850 393-9724
101 S Pace Blvd Pensacola (32502) ***(G-13468)***
Cabinet Designs of Central Fla 321 636-1101
596 International Pl Rockledge (32955) ***(G-14695)***
Cabinet Designs Sarasota Inc 941 739-1607
6208 B 17th St E Bradenton (34203) ***(G-955)***
Cabinet Dreams & Things Inc 727 514-0847
13954 Sand Oak Ct Hudson (34669) ***(G-5765)***
Cabinet Factory Outlet 386 323-0778
1595 N Nova Rd Ste A Daytona Beach (32117) ***(G-2525)***
Cabinet Genies 239 458-8563
815 Se 47th Ter Cape Coral (33904) ***(G-1318)***
Cabinet Guy 2012 Inc 305 796-5242
14721 Sw 21st St Davie (33325) ***(G-2394)***
Cabinet Guy of Englewood Inc 941 475-9454
150 S Mccall Rd Englewood (34223) ***(G-3526)***
Cabinet Kings LLC 239 288-6740
11595 Kelly Rd Ste 322 Fort Myers (33908) ***(G-4198)***
Cabinet Masters Inc 727 535-0020
7168 123rd Cir Largo (33773) ***(G-7560)***
Cabinet Options Inc 904 434-1564
1170 Executive Cove Dr Saint Johns (32259) ***(G-14945)***
Cabinet Startup LLC 352 795-2655
7170 N Ira Martin Ave Crystal River (34428) ***(G-2268)***
Cabinet Systems Centl Fla Inc 407 678-0994
2716 Forsyth Rd Ste 114 Winter Park (32792) ***(G-18496)***
Cabinet Wholesale LLC 954 751-7200
1301 W Copans Rd E1-4 Pompano Beach (33064) ***(G-13962)***
Cabinetree Collection Inc 772 569-4761
860 35th Ct Sw Vero Beach (32968) ***(G-17748)***
Cabinetry Masters LLC 954 549-8646
4193 Oldfield Crossing Dr Jacksonville (32223) ***(G-5966)***
Cabinets -N- More Inc 321 355-9548
6023 Elgin Rd Cocoa (32927) ***(G-1910)***
Cabinets By Marylin Inc 954 729-3995
696 Sw 15th St Pompano Beach (33060) ***(G-13963)***
Cabinets By Wfc Inc 941 355-2703
6092 Clark Center Ave Sarasota (34238) ***(G-15623)***
Cabinets Direct USA 862 704-6138
16107 Via Monteverde Delray Beach (33446) ***(G-2940)***
Cabinets Extraordinaire, Sarasota *Also called Location 3 Holdings LLC* ***(G-15726)***
Cabinets Extraordinaire Inc (PA) 941 961-8453
7350 S Tamiami Trl Sarasota (34231) ***(G-15624)***
Cabinets Extraordinaire Inc 618 925-0515
6150 State Road 70 E # 31 Bradenton (34203) ***(G-956)***
Cabinets Moreunlimited Inc 813 789-4203
11802 Spanish Lake Dr Tampa (33635) ***(G-16669)***
Cabinets One LLC 407 227-1147
4502 Old Winter Garden Rd Orlando (32811) ***(G-11975)***
Cabinets Plus Inc 239 574-7020
1056 Ne Pine Island Rd G Cape Coral (33909) ***(G-1319)***
Cabinets Plus of America Inc 813 408-0433
3853 S Lake Dr Unit 164 Tampa (33614) ***(G-16670)***
Cabinets Unlimited, Bradenton *Also called Manatee Cabinets Inc* ***(G-1010)***
Cabinetsplusfl.com, Cape Coral *Also called Cabinets Plus Inc* ***(G-1319)***
Cable USA, Naples *Also called Marmon Aerospace & Defense LLC* ***(G-10814)***
Cables and Sensors LLC (PA) 866 373-6767
5874 S Semoran Blvd Orlando (32822) ***(G-11976)***
Cableware Technology Division, Naples *Also called Loos & Co Inc* ***(G-10807)***
Cabreras Spanish Sausages LLC 305 882-1040
765 W 27th St Hialeah (33010) ***(G-5085)***
Cabus USA Inc 305 681-0872
12300 Nw 7th Ave North Miami (33168) ***(G-11096)***
Cacao Fruit Company 954 449-8704
1500 Weston Rd Ste 200 Weston (33326) ***(G-18231)***
Cadcam Software Co 727 450-6440
28200 Us Highway 19 N E Clearwater (33761) ***(G-1535)***
Caddie Company Inc 267 332-0976
4104 Causeway Vista Dr Tampa (33615) ***(G-16671)***
Cadence Keen Innovations Inc 561 249-2219
1655 Palm Bch Lkes Blvd S West Palm Beach (33401) ***(G-17955)***

ALPHABETIC

Cadillac Graphics Inc.....954 772-2440
4521 Ne 5th Ter Oakland Park (33334) ***(G-11249)***
Cadre Holdings Inc (PA).....904 741-5400
13386 International Pkwy Jacksonville (32218) ***(G-5967)***
Caduceus International Pubg.....866 280-2900
100 Sw 75th St Ste 206 Gainesville (32607) ***(G-4664)***
Cae Healthcare Inc (HQ).....941 377-5562
6300 Edgelake Dr Sarasota (34240) ***(G-15625)***
Cae Healthcare USA Inc.....941 377-5562
6300 Edgelake Dr Sarasota (34240) ***(G-15626)***
Cae USA Inc (HQ).....813 885-7481
4908 Tampa West Blvd Tampa (33634) ***(G-16672)***
Cae USA Products, Tampa *Also called Cae USA Inc* ***(G-16672)***
CAF USA Inc.....305 753-5371
9400 Nw 37th Ave Miami (33147) ***(G-8878)***
Cafco LLC.....240 848-5574
3370 Ne 190th St Apt 2206 Miami (33180) ***(G-8879)***
Cafe Don Pablo, Miami *Also called Burke Brands LLC* ***(G-8861)***
Cafm.....407 658-6531
2023 N Atlantic Ave 223 Cocoa Beach (32931) ***(G-1965)***
Cage Works.....239 707-0847
1801 Commercial Dr Naples (34112) ***(G-10702)***
Cahill Construction Services.....239 369-9290
212 Lake Dr Lehigh Acres (33936) ***(G-7805)***
Cairo JM Car Parts Inc.....305 688-4044
12780 Cairo Ln Opa Locka (33054) ***(G-11727)***
Cal Air Forwarding.....305 871-4552
3000 Nw 74th Ave Miami (33122) ***(G-8880)***
Calcium Silicate Corp Inc.....863 902-0217
601 Watson Farm Rd Lake Harbor (33459) ***(G-7054)***
Calev Systems Inc (PA).....305 672-2900
5575 Nw 36th St Miami Springs (33166) ***(G-10387)***
Caliber Coating Inc.....813 928-1461
39615 Dawson Chase Dr Zephyrhills (33540) ***(G-18607)***
Caliber Elements LLC.....352 697-1415
9020 W Veterans Dr Homosassa (34448) ***(G-5743)***
Caliber Sales Engineering Inc (PA).....954 430-6234
5373 N Hiatus Rd Sunrise (33351) ***(G-16302)***
Calibrated Controls LLC.....904 718-0541
1931 Choctaw Trl Middleburg (32068) ***(G-10401)***
California Greens Corporation.....630 423-5760
301 N Ocean Blvd Pompano Beach (33062) ***(G-13964)***
California Shutters Inc.....305 827-9333
16350 Nw 48th Ave Miami Lakes (33014) ***(G-10288)***
Californo Corp.....855 553-6766
217 Nw 2nd Ave Hallandale Beach (33009) ***(G-4940)***
Caligiuri Corporation.....407 324-4441
518 Central Park Dr Sanford (32771) ***(G-15276)***
Calle Ocho News, Miami *Also called Pressnet Corp* ***(G-9738)***
Calloway Barge Lines Inc.....904 284-0503
967 Bulkhead Rd Pier 5 Green Cove Springs (32043) ***(G-4819)***
Calmac Corporation.....813 493-8700
1801 E Fowler Ave Tampa (33612) ***(G-16673)***
Calnat International Inc.....239 839-2581
2118 Se 1st St Cape Coral (33990) ***(G-1320)***
Calorex USA LLC.....239 482-0606
2213 Andrea Ln Ste 110 Fort Myers (33912) ***(G-4199)***
Calti Cabinets Inc.....727 744-7844
11950 67th Way Unit C Largo (33773) ***(G-7561)***
Calvert Manufacturing Inc.....407 331-5522
228 Colombo Dr Casselberry (32707) ***(G-1411)***
Calvert Solutions, Casselberry *Also called Calvert Manufacturing Inc* ***(G-1411)***
CAM Broc Sports Inc.....407 933-6524
3726 Grissom Ln Kissimmee (34741) ***(G-6904)***
Camara Industries LLC.....407 879-2549
9927 Dean Cove Ln Orlando (32825) ***(G-11977)***
Cambria, Fort Myers *Also called Cianos Tile & Marble Inc* ***(G-4208)***
Cambridge Diagnostic Pdts Inc.....954 971-4040
6880 Nw 17th Ave Fort Lauderdale (33309) ***(G-3712)***
Cambroc Sports, Kissimmee *Also called CAM Broc Sports Inc* ***(G-6904)***
Camco Chemical.....239 992-4100
3635 Bonita Beach Rd # 3 Bonita Springs (34134) ***(G-789)***
Camco Corp.....561 427-0433
1829 Park Ln S Ste 9 Jupiter (33458) ***(G-6699)***
Camcorp Industries Inc.....941 488-5000
170 Rich St Venice (34292) ***(G-17679)***
Came Americas Automation LLC.....305 433-3307
5863 Nw 159th St Miami Lakes (33014) ***(G-10289)***
Camel Enterprises Corp.....954 234-2559
2120 Ne 203rd Ter Miami (33179) ***(G-8881)***
Camel Power Drinks, Miami *Also called Camel Enterprises Corp* ***(G-8881)***
Camelot Cabinets Inc.....813 876-9150
6903 Conaty Dr Tampa (33634) ***(G-16674)***
Camera2canvas LLC.....850 276-6990
2500 Minnesota Ave Lynn Haven (32444) ***(G-8027)***
Cameron Textiles Inc.....954 454-6482
2740 Sw Martin Downs Blvd Palm City (34990) ***(G-13026)***
Camilo Muebles, Miami *Also called Camilo Office Furniture Inc* ***(G-8882)***
Camilo Office Furniture Inc (PA).....305 261-5366
7344 Sw 48th St Ste 202 Miami (33155) ***(G-8882)***
Camilo Office Furniture Inc.....305 261-5366
18360 Sw 224th St Miami (33170) ***(G-8883)***
Camp Aircraft Inc.....727 397-6076
5300 95th St N Saint Petersburg (33708) ***(G-14994)***
Camp Company St Petersburg.....727 397-6076
5300 95th St N Saint Petersburg (33708) ***(G-14995)***
Campbell Cnon Crrage Works Inc.....305 304-8528
431 Federal Point Rd East Palatka (32131) ***(G-3471)***
Campbells Ornamental & Con, Cape Coral *Also called Campbells Ornamental Concrete* ***(G-1321)***
Campbells Ornamental Concrete.....239 458-0800
1930 Ne Pine Island Rd Cape Coral (33909) ***(G-1321)***
Campbellton Farm Service, Campbellton *Also called Barber Fertilizer Company* ***(G-1259)***
Campen Companies.....904 388-6000
2160 Park St Jacksonville (32204) ***(G-5968)***
Campeones Marina Corp.....305 491-5738
600 Nw 7th Ave Miami (33136) ***(G-8884)***
Camper & Nicholsons Usa Inc (PA).....561 655-2121
450 Royal Palm Way # 100 Palm Beach (33480) ***(G-12930)***
Camphor Technologies Inc.....941 360-0025
1584 Independence Blvd Sarasota (34234) ***(G-15627)***
Campos Chemicals.....727 412-2774
3244 44th Ave N Saint Petersburg (33714) ***(G-14996)***
Campus Communications Inc.....352 376-4482
1105 W University Ave Gainesville (32601) ***(G-4665)***
Campus Publications Inc.....941 780-1326
2975 Bee Ridge Rd Ste D Sarasota (34239) ***(G-15628)***
Can Can Concealment LLC.....727 841-6930
2521b Success Dr Odessa (33556) ***(G-11542)***
Can-America, Tampa *Also called Vigo Importing Company* ***(G-17417)***
Canac Kitchens Northwest Fla, Santa Rosa Beach *Also called Emerald Coast Cabinets Inc* ***(G-15424)***
Canada Dry of Florida, Fort Pierce *Also called American Bottling Company* ***(G-4463)***
Canam Electric.....305 534-7903
4835 Collins Ave Miami Beach (33140) ***(G-10174)***
Canam Steel Corporation.....904 781-0898
140 Ellis Rd S Jacksonville (32254) ***(G-5969)***
Canarchy Craft.....813 348-6363
3924 W Spruce St Tampa (33607) ***(G-16675)***
Canaveral Custom Boats Inc.....321 783-3536
774 Mullet Rd Cape Canaveral (32920) ***(G-1280)***
Candela Controls Inc.....407 654-2420
751 Business Park Blvd # 101 Winter Garden (34787) ***(G-18377)***
Candies and Beyond Inc.....954 828-2255
14100 Nw 60th Ave Miami Lakes (33014) ***(G-10290)***
Candleworks, Melbourne *Also called Cem Ltd* ***(G-8384)***
Cane Proof LLC.....386 445-2290
5 Ethel Ln Palm Coast (32164) ***(G-13072)***
Cane Proof Window and Doors, Palm Coast *Also called Cane Proof LLC* ***(G-13072)***
Canine Chronicle, The, Ocala *Also called Endeavor Publications Inc* ***(G-11378)***
Cannon Industries Inc.....727 320-5040
5349 Seafoam Dr New Port Richey (34652) ***(G-10964)***
Cannon T4 Inc.....347 583-0477
188 Price St Naples (34113) ***(G-10703)***
Cannons of Jack LLC.....904 733-3524
6150 Richard St Jacksonville (32216) ***(G-5970)***
Canopy Specialist LLC.....813 703-6844
3301 State Road 574 Plant City (33563) ***(G-13750)***
Cansortium Charities Inc.....305 902-2720
82 Ne 26th St Miami (33137) ***(G-8885)***
Cantex Inc.....863 967-4161
101 Gandy Rd Auburndale (33823) ***(G-221)***
Cantor Design On Granite.....407 230-1568
4180 Player Cir Orlando (32808) ***(G-11978)***
Cantor Granite & Marble, Orlando *Also called Cantor Design On Granite* ***(G-11978)***
Cantwell Misc Fabricators Inc.....850 438-2912
100 E Roberts Rd Pensacola (32534) ***(G-13469)***
Canvas.....727 317-5572
1535 4th St N Saint Petersburg (33704) ***(G-14997)***
Canvas Clinical Research.....561 229-0002
8227 Kelso Dr Palm Beach Gardens (33418) ***(G-12954)***
Canvas Clinical Research (PA).....561 229-0002
3898 Via Poinciana Lake Worth (33467) ***(G-7189)***
Canvas Designers Inc.....561 881-7663
1500 Australian Ave Ste 1 Riviera Beach (33404) ***(G-14605)***
Canvas Foods Corp.....786 529-8041
19266 Seneca Ave Weston (33332) ***(G-18232)***
Canvas Freaks LLC.....407 978-6224
11300 Space Blvd Ste 4 Orlando (32837) ***(G-11979)***
Canvas Land Surveying LLC.....321 689-5330
1650 Oak Valley Dr Longwood (32750) ***(G-7880)***
Canvas Shop Inc.....407 898-6001
635 Wilmer Ave Orlando (32808) ***(G-11980)***
Canvas Spc Cstm Mar Fbrction I.....850 664-6200
18 Hollywood Blvd Sw Fort Walton Beach (32548) ***(G-4569)***

Canvas Specialties & Uphl, Fort Walton Beach *Also called Canvas Spc Cstm Mar Fbrction I (G-4569)*

Canvas West Inc 941 355-0780
1470 12th St Sarasota (34236) *(G-15629)*

Capacitor and Components LLC 954 798-8943
11841 Nw 38th Pl Sunrise (33323) *(G-16303)*

Capacity Inc 855 440-7825
2240 72nd Ave E Sarasota (34243) *(G-15450)*

Cape Britt Corp Inc 305 593-5027
2960 Nw 72nd Ave Miami (33122) *(G-8886)*

Cape Canvas Inc 239 772-0300
1036 Ne Pine Island Rd # 10 Cape Coral (33909) *(G-1322)*

Cape Coral Homes Magazine, Clearwater *Also called Kulaga William John (G-1666)*

Cape Horn Boats, Orlando *Also called Fabbro Marine Group Inc (G-12143)*

Cape Spirits Inc 239 242-5244
131 Sw 3rd Pl Cape Coral (33991) *(G-1323)*

Capital Contracting & Design (PA) 908 561-8411
817 Sw 10th St Fort Lauderdale (33315) *(G-3713)*

Capital Outlook Newspaper, Tallahassee *Also called Syndicated Programming Inc (G-16508)*

Capital Publishing Inc 813 286-8444
7341 Spring Hill Dr Spring Hill (34606) *(G-16067)*

Capital Signs, Apopka *Also called Guy Wingo Signs (G-138)*

Capital Steel Inc 352 628-1700
6260 S Tex Pt Homosassa (34448) *(G-5744)*

Capital Steel Structures, Miami *Also called Capitol Rental Bldg Eqp Inc (G-8887)*

Capital Technology Solutions 850 562-3321
3920 Monterey Pines Trl Tallahassee (32309) *(G-16420)*

Capitol Conveyors Inc 727 314-7474
1429 Warrington Way Trinity (34655) *(G-17633)*

Capitol Furniture Mfg LLC 954 485-5000
850 Broken Sound Pkwy Nw Boca Raton (33487) *(G-453)*

Capitol Rental Bldg Eqp Inc 305 633-5008
2188 Nw 25th Ave. Miami (33142) *(G-8887)*

Capra Graphics Inc 305 418-4582
1625 Nw 79th Ave Doral (33126) *(G-3152)*

Capri Kitchens Inc 813 623-1424
9507 E Us Highway 92 Tampa (33610) *(G-16676)*

Capris Furniture Inds Inc 352 629-8889
1401 Nw 27th Ave Ocala (34475) *(G-11342)*

Capsmith Inc (PA) 407 328-7660
2240 Old Lake Mary Rd Sanford (32771) *(G-15277)*

Capstone Cg LLC 941 371-3321
6348 17th Street Cir E Sarasota (34243) *(G-15451)*

Capstone Industries Inc 954 570-8889
431 Fairway Dr Ste 200 Deerfield Beach (33441) *(G-2685)*

Capstorm LLC 314 403-2143
3906 Us Highway 98 W # 1159 Santa Rosa Beach (32459) *(G-15422)*

Capt Latham LLC 904 483-6118
967 Bulkhead Rd Green Cove Springs (32043) *(G-4820)*

Captain Cabinets LLC 813 685-7179
6705 Pemberton View Dr Seffner (33584) *(G-15953)*

Captain Foods Inc 386 428-5833
207 Sapphire Rd New Smyrna Beach (32169) *(G-10998)*

Captain Rustys 813 244-2799
1958 Us Highway 98 Lorida (33857) *(G-7963)*

Captain Rustys Smoked Fish Dip, Lorida *Also called Captain Rustys (G-7963)*

Captain Zoom Products Inc 561 989-9119
10653 Stable Ln Apt 204 Wellington (33414) *(G-17846)*

Captains Fasteners Corp 954 533-9259
3706 Sw 30th Ave Fort Lauderdale (33312) *(G-3714)*

Captel Inc 407 730-3397
2602 Challenger Tech Ct Orlando (32826) *(G-11981)*

Captiva Containers LLC 800 861-3868
75 95 Ne 179th St Miami (33162) *(G-8888)*

Captiva Current Inc 239 574-1110
2340 Periwinkle Way Sanibel (33957) *(G-15413)*

Captive-Aire Systems Inc 813 448-7884
4519 George Rd Ste 150 Tampa (33634) *(G-16677)*

Capzerpharma Manufacturing LLC 561 493-4000
3677 23rd Ave S Ste B107 Lake Worth Beach (33461) *(G-7253)*

Caq International LLC 305 744-1472
900 Biscayne Blvd # 4906 Miami (33132) *(G-8889)*

Car City Engine and Machine, Pensacola *Also called Santa Rosa Auto Parts Inc (G-13600)*

Car Wash, Boynton Beach *Also called Bounce Back MBL Detailing LLC (G-847)*

Car Wash Solutions Florida Inc 941 323-8817
3310 Sw 7th St Unit 2 Ocala (34474) *(G-11343)*

Caraustar Indus Cnsmr Pdts Gro 386 328-8335
188 Comfort Rd Palatka (32177) *(G-12863)*

Caravaggio Cabinetry Inc 561 609-3355
119 S H St Lake Worth (33460) *(G-7190)*

Carbel LLC 305 599-0832
2323 Nw 82nd Ave Doral (33122) *(G-3153)*

Carbon Mine Supply LLC 606 437-9905
11023 Gatewood Dr Ste 103 Bradenton (34211) *(G-957)*

Carbon Press LLC 239 689-4406
1635 Hendry St Fort Myers (33901) *(G-4200)*

Carbon Resources Inc 941 746-8089
5206 Paylor Ln Lakewood Ranch (34240) *(G-7482)*

Carbonara Labs Inc 321 952-1303
4550 S Us Highway 1 Grant (32949) *(G-4811)*

Carbonxt Inc 352 378-4950
3951 Nw 48th Ter Ste 111 Gainesville (32606) *(G-4666)*

Card Quest Inc 813 288-0004
7902 W Waters Ave Ste C Tampa (33615) *(G-16678)*

Card Usa Inc 954 862-1300
201 N Ocean Dr Ste 200 Hollywood (33019) *(G-5546)*

Cardboard Only Inc 352 345-5060
11080 Wdlnd Waters Blvd Weeki Wachee (34613) *(G-17835)*

Cardenas Roberto Blinds of Fla 315 807-6878
13301 Sw 132nd Ave Unit 2 Miami (33186) *(G-8890)*

Cardinal Health 414 LLC 813 972-1351
3016 Usf Hawthorn Dr Tampa (33612) *(G-16679)*

Cardinal Lg Company 352 237-4410
1300 Sw 44th Ave Ocala (34474) *(G-11344)*

Cardinal Signs Inc 352 376-8494
6342 Nw 18th Dr Ste 1 Gainesville (32653) *(G-4667)*

Cardinal Straws, Jacksonville *Also called CU Holdings LLC (G-6017)*

Cardiovasular Innovation Inc 512 517-7761
4000 Hollywood Blvd Ste 5 Hollywood (33021) *(G-5547)*

Care-Metix Products Inc 813 628-8801
121 Kelsey Ln Ste F Tampa (33619) *(G-16680)*

Care.ai, Orlando *Also called Vuaant Inc (G-12709)*

Carefree Group Inc (PA) 866 800-1007
1029 5th St Miami Beach (33139) *(G-10175)*

Caregivercom Inc 954 893-0550
1871e W Oakland Park Blvd Oakland Park (33311) *(G-11250)*

Carey-Dunn Inc 561 840-1694
2001 Broadway Ste 301 Riviera Beach (33404) *(G-14606)*

Carfore Ltd 239 415-2275
11650 Chitwood Dr Fort Myers (33908) *(G-4201)*

Cargill Incorporated 407 846-4169
1845 Avenue A Kissimmee (34758) *(G-6905)*

Cargill Incorporated 813 241-4847
2120 Maritime Blvd Tampa (33605) *(G-16681)*

Cargill Food Distribution, Hialeah *Also called Cargill Meat Solutions Corp (G-5086)*

Cargill Meat Solutions Corp 305 826-3699
4220 W 91st Pl Unit 100 Hialeah (33018) *(G-5086)*

Carib Energy (usa) LLC 904 727-2559
9487 Regency Square Blvd Jacksonville (32225) *(G-5971)*

Carib Sea Inc 772 461-1113
3434 Industrial 31st St Fort Pierce (34946) *(G-4472)*

Caribbean Basin Industries Inc 941 726-7272
2407 Casey Key Rd Nokomis (34275) *(G-11043)*

Caribbean Box Company 305 667-4900
3123 Nw 73rd St Miami (33147) *(G-8891)*

Caribbean Breeze Inc 904 261-7831
1438 E Oak St Fernandina Beach (32034) *(G-3582)*

Caribbean Canvas and Mari 786 972-6377
7296 Sw 42nd Ter Miami (33155) *(G-8892)*

Caribbean Distillers LLC 863 508-1175
2200 3rd St Nw Winter Haven (33881) *(G-18429)*

Caribbean Emblems 305 593-8183
3555 Nw 79th Ave Doral (33122) *(G-3154)*

Caribbean Embroidery Designs, Doral *Also called Vyp Services LLC (G-3417)*

Caribbean Fiberglass Products 305 888-0774
5445 Nw 72nd Ave Miami (33166) *(G-8893)*

Caribbean Foam Products Inc 786 431-5024
480 W 84th St Ste 109 Hialeah (33014) *(G-5087)*

Caribbean Fuels Inc 305 233-3016
15001 Sw 141st Ter Miami (33196) *(G-8894)*

Caribbean Global Group Corp 786 449-2767
5475 Nw Saint James Dr Port St Lucie (34983) *(G-14471)*

Caribbean Interior Design Ctr, Boynton Beach *Also called Ceco Inc (G-850)*

Caribbean Paint Company Inc 305 594-4500
5295 Nw 79th Ave Doral (33166) *(G-3155)*

Caribbean Publishing Service, Palmetto Bay *Also called Caribbean Today News Magazine (G-13208)*

Caribbean Today News Magazine 305 238-2868
9020 Sw 152nd St Palmetto Bay (33157) *(G-13208)*

Caribbean Trailers Corp 305 256-1505
12240 Sw 130th St Miami (33186) *(G-8895)*

Caribe Express Associates Inc 305 222-9057
7320 Nw 12th St Ste 111 Miami (33126) *(G-8896)*

Carl Zeiss Vision Inc 727 528-8873
5600 115th Ave N Ste B Clearwater (33760) *(G-1536)*

Carlaron Inc 386 258-1183
421 Ridgewood Ave Daytona Beach (32117) *(G-2526)*

Carlees Creations Inc 786 232-0050
12275 Sw 129th Ct Miami (33186) *(G-8897)*

Carley Nigel Holdings LLC 407 212-9341
1041 Cascade Cir Apt 103 Rockledge (32955) *(G-14696)*

Carling Technologies Inc 561 745-0405
120 Intracoastal Cir # 100 Jupiter (33469) *(G-6700)*

Carlisle Interconnect Tech, Saint Augustine *Also called Tensolite LLC (G-14905)*

Carlo Morelli 954 241-1426
1926 Hollywood Blvd Hollywood (33020) *(G-5548)*

Carlos Velez Cabinets & Instal 407 929-3402
  5314 Ira St Orlando (32807) *(G-11982)*

Carlton Funeral Service, Mulberry *Also called Hicks Industries Inc (G-10627)*

Carlton Mfg Inc (PA) 352 465-2153
  20093 E Penn Ave Ste 3 Dunnellon (34432) *(G-3463)*

Carlton Mfg Associates, Dunnellon *Also called Carlton Mfg Inc (G-3463)*

Carmacks Quality Aluminum Inc 727 846-0305
  8052 Leo Kidd Ave Ste 1 Port Richey (34668) *(G-14356)*

Carman Cabinets 561 202-9871
  7800 Coral St Lantana (33462) *(G-7508)*

Carne Asada Tortilleria Nica 305 221-7001
  10404 W Flagler St Ste 5 Miami (33174) *(G-8898)*

Carol City Opa Locka News 305 669-7355
  6796 Sw 62nd Ave South Miami (33143) *(G-16031)*

Carolina Clubs Inc 561 753-6948
  11064 68th St N West Palm Beach (33412) *(G-17956)*

Carolina Company USA LLC (PA) 401 487-2749
  1019 Nell Way Lady Lake (32159) *(G-6989)*

Carolina Woodworks Inc 954 692-4662
  714 Nw 44th Ter Apt 203 Deerfield Beach (33442) *(G-2686)*

Carotex, Estero *Also called Imported Yarns LLC (G-3546)*

Carpe Diem Ice Cream Key West, Key West *Also called Carpe Diem Ice Cream LLC (G-6857)*

Carpe Diem Ice Cream LLC 305 504-4469
  300 Front St Key West (33040) *(G-6857)*

Carpe Diem Sales & Mktg Inc (PA) 407 682-1400
  4560 36th St Orlando (32811) *(G-11983)*

Carpediem LLC 229 230-1453
  618 Gulf Shore Dr Destin (32541) *(G-3061)*

Carpenter Co 863 687-9494
  5100 Frontage Rd S Lakeland (33815) *(G-7288)*

Carpenters Roofg & Shtmtl Inc 561 833-0341
  1701 W 10th St Riviera Beach (33404) *(G-14607)*

Carpentree Creation 904 300-4008
  11058 Percheron Dr Jacksonville (32257) *(G-5972)*

Carpet Clinic LLC 850 232-1170
  6927 Kelvin Ter Pensacola (32503) *(G-13470)*

Carport Solution LLC 352 789-1149
  8975 Sw Highway 200 Ocala (34481) *(G-11345)*

Carports Anywhere Inc 352 468-1116
  10858 Se County Road 221 Starke (32091) *(G-16097)*

Carrabelle Beach An Rvc 850 697-8813
  1843 Highway 98 W Carrabelle (32322) *(G-1409)*

Carrier & Tech Solutions LLC, Fort Lauderdale *Also called Guardia LLC (G-3852)*

Carrier Corporation (HQ) 800 379-6484
  13995 Pasteur Blvd Palm Beach Gardens (33418) *(G-12955)*

Carrier Global Corporation (PA) 561 365-2000
  13995 Pasteur Blvd Palm Beach Gardens (33418) *(G-12956)*

Carrier Transicold, Palm Beach Gardens *Also called Carrier Corporation (G-12955)*

Carriers Direct Inc 941 776-2979
  2623 Little Country Rd Parrish (34219) *(G-13357)*

Carrollwood Creamery 813 926-2023
  13168 N Dale Mabry Hwy Tampa (33618) *(G-16682)*

Carson Innovation Inc 727 348-0000
  46th St N Pinellas Park (33781) *(G-13674)*

Carsons Cabinetry & Design Inc 352 373-8292
  13411 Sw County Road 346 Archer (32618) *(G-196)*

Carter Day Holding Inc (PA) 239 280-0361
  27 Casa Mar Ln Naples (34103) *(G-10704)*

Carter Signs Inc 239 543-4004
  6350 Slater Mill Way Fort Myers (33917) *(G-4202)*

Carter Signs Scott, Fort Myers *Also called Carter Signs Inc (G-4202)*

Carter-Health Disposables LLC 407 296-6689
  4201 Vinelnd Rd I-13 Orlando (32811) *(G-11984)*

Carters Cabinetry Inc 386 677-4192
  4 Aviator Way Ormond Beach (32174) *(G-12749)*

Carvalho Naturals LLC 813 833-8229
  5806 Cay Cove Ct Tampa (33615) *(G-16683)*

Carvizion Inc 772 807-0307
  881 Sw Harvard Rd Port St Lucie (34953) *(G-14472)*

Cary's Kitchen Cabinets, Hialeah *Also called Jam Cabinets & Investments LLC (G-5202)*

Cas Industries LLC 813 986-2694
  2914 Appling Woods Pl Plant City (33565) *(G-13751)*

Casa Cabinets LLC (PA) 850 459-3403
  10770 S Us Highway 1 Port St Lucie (34952) *(G-14473)*

Casa De Rprsntcones Jmw CA LLC 754 707-1689
  12486 Sw 54th St Miramar (33027) *(G-10478)*

Casa Del Marinero Corp 305 374-5386
  288 Ne 2nd St Miami (33132) *(G-8899)*

Casablanca Polo Co 832 668-6804
  3500 Frlane Frms Rd Ste 5 Wellington (33414) *(G-17847)*

Casale Design Source Inc 813 873-3653
  4002 W State St Ste 100 Tampa (33609) *(G-16684)*

Casco Services Inc 727 942-1888
  153 E Oakwood St Tarpon Springs (34689) *(G-17461)*

Casebriefs LLC 646 240-4401
  2234 N Federal Hwy 413 Boca Raton (33431) *(G-454)*

Cases2go, Clearwater *Also called Root International Inc (G-1772)*

Casey Research LLC 561 455-9043
  55 Ne 5th Ave Ste 300 Delray Beach (33483) *(G-2941)*

Casino Bakery Inc 813 242-0311
  2726 N 36th St Tampa (33605) *(G-16685)*

Casmin Inc 352 253-5000
  2255 Crescent Dr Mount Dora (32757) *(G-10599)*

Casons Quality Care Svcs LLC 386 365-1016
  226 Se Lee Dr Lulu (32061) *(G-7977)*

Casper Engineering Corp 305 666-4046
  7695 Sw 133rd St Pinecrest (33156) *(G-13664)*

Cast Art International Corp 727 807-3395
  762 Marjon Ave Dunedin (34698) *(G-3442)*

Cast Crete Tampa, Seffner *Also called Florida Engineered Constru (G-15958)*

Cast Systems LLC 941 625-3474
  19400 Peachland Blvd Port Charlotte (33948) *(G-14291)*

Cast-Crete, Palm Bay *Also called Florida Engineered Constru (G-12901)*

Cast-Crete Usa LLC 813 621-4641
  6324 County Road 579 Seffner (33584) *(G-15954)*

Cast-One, Doral *Also called Castone Creations Inc (G-3156)*

Cast-Stone International Corp 561 625-0333
  11555 Us Highway 1 Palm Beach Gardens (33408) *(G-12957)*

Castcrete, Hudson *Also called Florida Engineered Constru (G-5773)*

Caste Crete 407 295-1959
  515 Ferguson Dr Ste A Orlando (32805) *(G-11985)*

Castillo's Farm Equipment, Miami *Also called Castillos Farms Inc (G-8900)*

Castillos Farms Inc 305 232-0771
  19744 Sw 177th Ave Miami (33187) *(G-8900)*

Castle Distributing Inds Inc 305 336-0855
  6506 Sw 19th St Miramar (33023) *(G-10479)*

Castle Software Inc 800 345-7606
  626 Layport Dr Sebastian (32958) *(G-15889)*

Castone Creations Inc 305 599-3367
  8309 Nw 70th St Doral (33166) *(G-3156)*

Castor Inc 813 254-1171
  1701 W Green St Tampa (33607) *(G-16686)*

Casual Tone Inc 941 722-5643
  509 9th St W Palmetto (34221) *(G-13158)*

Casualcraft, Palmetto *Also called Casual Tone Inc (G-13158)*

Cat 5 Hurricane Products LLC 941 752-4692
  6112 33rd St E Unit 105 Bradenton (34203) *(G-958)*

Cat5hp, Bradenton *Also called Cat 5 Hurricane Products LLC (G-958)*

Catalent Inc 727 803-2832
  2725 Scherer Dr N Saint Petersburg (33716) *(G-14998)*

Catalent Pharma Solutions Inc 727 572-4000
  2725 Scherer Dr N Saint Petersburg (33716) *(G-14999)*

Catalent St Petersburg, Saint Petersburg *Also called Catalent Inc (G-14998)*

Catalina Finer Food Corp 813 872-6359
  4709 N Lauber Way Tampa (33614) *(G-16687)*

Catalina Finer Foods, Tampa *Also called Catalina Finer Meat Corp (G-16688)*

Catalina Finer Meat Corp 813 876-3910
  4710 W Cayuga St Tampa (33614) *(G-16688)*

Catalina Yachts Inc 727 544-6681
  7200 Bryan Dairy Rd Largo (33777) *(G-7562)*

Catalyst Fabric Solutions LLC 850 396-4325
  3595 Industrial Park Dr Marianna (32446) *(G-8162)*

Catalyst Orthoscience Inc (PA) 239 325-9976
  14710 Tamiami Trl N # 102 Naples (34110) *(G-10705)*

Catalyst Orthoscience Inc 317 625-7548
  14700 Tamiami Trl N # 26 Naples (34110) *(G-10706)*

Catalyst Pharmaceuticals Inc (PA) 305 420-3200
  355 Alhambra Cir Ste 801 Coral Gables (33134) *(G-2038)*

Catamont Machine Works, Plant City *Also called Paj Innovative Concepts Inc (G-13788)*

Catamount Machine Works LLC 813 659-0505
  2804 Sydney Rd Plant City (33566) *(G-13752)*

Catapult 13 Crtive Studios LLC 305 788-6948
  5 Nw 39th St Street1 Miami (33127) *(G-8901)*

Catapult Lakeland Inc 863 687-3788
  226 N Kentucky Ave Lakeland (33801) *(G-7289)*

Catapult Learning LL 561 573-6025
  501 Nw 8th Ave Delray Beach (33444) *(G-2942)*

Catapult Print and Packg LLC (HQ) 407 717-4323
  5945 Hazeltine Nat Dr Orlando (32822) *(G-11986)*

Catch One Comm 772 221-0225
  1850 Sw Fountainview Blvd # 103 Port Saint Lucie (34986) *(G-14403)*

Category 5 Design, Key West *Also called Local Enterprises Inc (G-6873)*

Category 5 Manufacturing Inc 561 777-2491
  7150 Seacrest Blvd Lantana (33462) *(G-7509)*

Caterpillar Authorized Dealer, Fort Lauderdale *Also called Pantropic Power Inc (G-3973)*

Cathodic Prtection Tech of Fla 321 799-0046
  2023 N Atl Ave Ste 251 Cocoa Beach (32931) *(G-1966)*

Cathy Minh Lee 626 827-3214
  463 Patricia Ave Dunedin (34698) *(G-3443)*

Cato Steel Co 407 671-3333
  3928 Forsyth Rd Winter Park (32792) *(G-18497)*

Catskill Express LLC 954 784-5151
  1249 Hammondville Rd Pompano Beach (33069) *(G-13965)*

Causey Machine Works Inc 407 277-7570
  12131 Science Dr Orlando (32826) *(G-11987)*

Cavadas Ruben & Trisha Wagner 407 248-2659
  3125 Crystal Creek Blvd Orlando (32837) *(G-11988)*

Cavaform Inc (PA) 727 384-3676
2700 72nd St N Saint Petersburg (33710) (G-15000)

Cavaform International LLC 727 384-3676
2700 72nd St N Saint Petersburg (33710) (G-15001)

Cavallo Estate Winery LLC 352 500-9463
8123 S Lecanto Hwy Lecanto (34461) (G-7749)

Cavastone By Connie Davalos, Boca Raton Also called Cavastone LLC (G-455)

Cavastone LLC 561 994-9100
506 Nw 77th St Boca Raton (33487) (G-455)

Cavo Development Inc 305 255-7465
16380 Sw 137th Ave Miami (33177) (G-8902)

Cavok Capital LLC 727 789-0951
855 Virginia Ave Palm Harbor (34683) (G-13105)

Cawy Bottling Co Inc 305 634-8669
2440 Nw 21st Ter Miami (33142) (G-8903)

Caxton Newspapers Inc 305 538-9700
1688 Meridian Ave Ste 404 Miami Beach (33139) (G-10176)

Cayago Americas Inc 754 216-4600
1881 W State Road 84 # 104 Fort Lauderdale (33315) (G-3715)

Caylex, Orlando Also called Lexington Dsign + Fbrction E L (G-12324)

Cayman Manufacturing Inc 954 421-1170
1301 Sw 34th Ave Deerfield Beach (33442) (G-2687)

Cayman Nat Mfg Instllation Inc 954 421-1170
1301 Sw 34th Ave Deerfield Beach (33442) (G-2688)

Cayo Hueso Enterprises Inc 305 747-0020
5750 2nd Ave Key West (33040) (G-6858)

CB Parent Holdco GP LLC 727 827-0046
9620 Exec Ctr Dr N Ste 20 Saint Petersburg (33702) (G-15002)

Cbd LLC 305 615-1194
3531 Griffin Rd Ste 100 Fort Lauderdale (33312) (G-3716)

Cbd Biocare 813 380-4376
7381 114th Ave Ste 406 Largo (33773) (G-7563)

Cbd Brands Inc 561 325-0482
725 N Highway A1a C106 Jupiter (33477) (G-6701)

Cbd Life Florida Inc 352 483-8333
3109 Kurt St Eustis (32726) (G-3555)

Cbg Biotech Ltd Co (PA) 239 514-1148
100 Glenview Pl Apt 1003 Naples (34108) (G-10707)

CBI Industries Inc 305 796-9346
13225 Sw 95th Ave Miami (33176) (G-8904)

Cbm Printing Worldwide Inc 786 531-1834
1061 E 23rd St Hialeah (33013) (G-5088)

Cbm Trading Inc 954 252-7460
10620 Griffin Rd Ste 104 Davie (33328) (G-2395)

CC Control Corp 561 293-3975
5760 Corporate Way West Palm Beach (33407) (G-17957)

CC Lighting Inc 805 302-5321
11138 Green Lake Dr Boynton Beach (33437) (G-849)

CC Machine Inc (PA) 888 577-0144
618 Ridgewood Ave Ste B Holly Hill (32117) (G-5512)

CC Sportswear Inc 941 351-4205
2331 Whtfeld Indus Way Un Sarasota (34243) (G-15452)

CC Welding & Construction LLC 407 884-7474
5960 W Jone Ave Zellwood (32798) (G-18596)

CCA Industries Inc 813 601-6238
13010 Us Highway 301 Dade City (33525) (G-2314)

Ccbcc Operations LLC 850 785-6171
300 W 5th St Panama City (32401) (G-13238)

Ccf Holdco LLC 800 714-9215
1528 Sw Highway 17 Arcadia (34266) (G-189)

CCM Clllar Cnnection Miami Inc 305 406-1656
1825 Nw 79th Ave Doral (33126) (G-3157)

Ccp Bayou Printing, Valparaiso Also called Bayou Printing Inc (G-17656)

Ccp of Miami Inc 305 233-6534
13601 Sw 143rd Ct Miami (33186) (G-8905)

CCT, Hialeah Also called Custom Controls Technology Inc (G-5103)

CCT Software LLC 305 747-5682
1801 Ne 123rd St Ste 314 North Miami (33181) (G-11097)

CD Greeting LLC 954 530-1301
3260 Ne 32nd St Fort Lauderdale (33308) (G-3717)

Cda Group, Miami Beach Also called Cda Ventures Inc (G-10177)

Cda Ventures Inc 305 428-2857
270 N Shore Dr Miami Beach (33141) (G-10177)

Cdc Woodworking, Pensacola Also called Cabinet Design and Cnstr LLC (G-13468)

Cds Manufacturing Inc 850 875-4651
106 Charles Hayes Sr Dr Gretna (32332) (G-4856)

Ce Hooton Sales LLC 305 255-9722
1901 Whitfield Park Loop Sarasota (34243) (G-15453)

CE Safes and SEC Pdts Inc 239 561-1260
5650 Zip Dr Fort Myers (33905) (G-4203)

Ceautamed Worldwide LLC 866 409-6262
1289 Clint Moore Rd Boca Raton (33487) (G-456)

Cebev LLC 918 830-4417
2424 N Federal Hwy # 101 Boca Raton (33431) (G-457)

Ceco & Associates Inc 727 528-0075
6508 S 78th St Riverview (33578) (G-14558)

Ceco Coated Fasteners, Riverview Also called Ceco & Associates Inc (G-14558)

Ceco Inc 561 265-1111
2951 Sw 14th Pl Ste 39 Boynton Beach (33426) (G-850)

Cedar Creek Logging Inc 850 832-0133
4138 Harry Wells Rd Panama City (32409) (G-13239)

Cedar Fresh Home Products LLC (PA) 305 975-8524
4207 University Dr Miami (33146) (G-8906)

Cedars Bakery Group Inc 407 476-6593
4704 L B Mcleod Rd Orlando (32811) (G-11989)

Cedars Food Inc 321 724-2624
2110 Dairy Rd Ste 101 West Melbourne (32904) (G-17896)

Cedrick McDonald 813 279-1442
4205 N Florida Ave Tampa (33603) (G-16689)

Cedrus Inc 772 286-2082
9011 Sw Old Kansas Ave Stuart (34997) (G-16126)

Ceeco, Okeechobee Also called Communication Eqp & Engrg Co (G-11601)

Cei Liquidation 281 541-2444
3495 S Us Highway 1 Ste A Fort Pierce (34982) (G-4473)

Celeb Luxury LLC 954 763-0333
6545 Nova Dr Ste 201 Davie (33317) (G-2396)

Celebration Cup, Sanford Also called Compak Companies LLC (G-15288)

Celios Corporation 833 235-4671
1228 E 7th Ave Ste 313 Tampa (33605) (G-16690)

Cellec Games Inc 407 476-3590
2736 Candlewood Ct Apopka (32703) (G-109)

Cellmic LLC 310 443-2070
34266 Us Highway 19 N Palm Harbor (34684) (G-13106)

Cellofoam North America Inc 407 888-4667
11237 Astronaut Blvd Orlando (32837) (G-11990)

Cellphone Parts Express LLC 954 635-5525
2633 Park Ln Hallandale Beach (33009) (G-4941)

Celltronix 407 610-7852
2305 S Orange Ave Orlando (32806) (G-11991)

Cellular Masters Inc 305 592-7906
10900 Nw 21st St Ste 210 Miami (33172) (G-8907)

Celmark International, Orlando Also called Cemi International Inc (G-11992)

Celsius Inc 561 276-2239
2424 N Federal Hwy # 208 Boca Raton (33431) (G-458)

Celsius Holdings Inc (PA) 561 276-2239
2424 N Federal Hwy # 208 Boca Raton (33431) (G-459)

Celtic Airspares LLC 727 431-0482
28870 Us Highway 19 N # 328 Clearwater (33761) (G-1537)

Cem Ltd 321 253-1160
7331 Office Park Pl Melbourne (32940) (G-8384)

Cement Industries Inc 239 332-1440
2925 Hanson St Fort Myers (33916) (G-4204)

Cement Miami Terminal 305 221-2502
1200 Nw 137th Ave Miami (33182) (G-8908)

Cement Plant, Newberry Also called Argos USA LLC (G-11017)

Cement Precast Products Inc 352 372-0953
2033 Ne 27th Ave Gainesville (32609) (G-4668)

Cement Products Inc 727 868-9226
9301 Denton Ave Port Richey (34667) (G-14357)

Cement-It Inc 954 565-7875
2455 E Sunrise Blvd # 11 Fort Lauderdale (33304) (G-3718)

Cemex 813 995-0396
11121 Ehren Cutoff Land O Lakes (34639) (G-7490)

Cemex Inc 813 663-9712
5503 E Diana St Tampa (33610) (G-16691)

Cemex Cement Inc 904 296-2400
340 Corporate Way Ste 100 Orange Park (32073) (G-11817)

Cemex Cement Inc 352 867-5794
619 Sw 17th Loop Ocala (34471) (G-11346)

Cemex Cement Inc 850 942-4582
3440 Weems Rd Tallahassee (32317) (G-16421)

Cemex Cement Inc 727 327-5730
601 24th St S Saint Petersburg (33712) (G-15003)

Cemex Cement Inc 407 877-9623
201 Hennis Rd Winter Garden (34787) (G-18378)

Cemex Cnstr Mtls ATL LLC (HQ) 561 833-5555
1501 Belvedere Rd West Palm Beach (33406) (G-17958)

Cemex Cnstr Mtls Fla LLC 305 247-3011
15900 Sw 408th St Homestead (33034) (G-5702)

Cemex Cnstr Mtls Fla LLC 321 636-5121
209 George King Blvd Cape Canaveral (32920) (G-1281)

Cemex Cnstr Mtls Fla LLC 904 880-4958
14770 Old St Augustine Rd Jacksonville (32258) (G-5973)

Cemex Cnstr Mtls Fla LLC 800 992-3639
1290 Foxmoor St Moore Haven (33471) (G-10589)

Cemex Cnstr Mtls Fla LLC 855 292-8453
3728 Prospect Ave Naples (34104) (G-10708)

Cemex Cnstr Mtls Fla LLC 800 992-3639
Glades Cut Off Rd Fort Pierce (34981) (G-4474)

Cemex Cnstr Mtls Fla LLC 954 977-9222
1150 Nw 24th St Pompano Beach (33064) (G-13966)

Cemex Cnstr Mtls Fla LLC 561 996-5249
State Rd 80 & Fec Rr Belle Glade (33430) (G-340)

Cemex Cnstr Mtls Fla LLC 352 330-1115
4270 County Road 124a Wildwood (34785) (G-18310)

Cemex Cnstr Mtls Fla LLC 352 746-0136
2975 S Lecanto Hwy Lecanto (34461) (G-7750)

Cemex Cnstr Mtls Fla LLC 813 621-5575
9609 Palm River Rd Tampa (33619) (G-16692)

A L P H A B E T I C

Cemex Cnstr Mtls Fla LLC.....561 832-6646
1021 N Railroad Ave West Palm Beach (33401) *(G-17959)*
Cemex Cnstr Mtls Fla LLC.....800 992-3639
501 Douglas Rd E Oldsmar (34677) *(G-11637)*
Cemex Cnstr Mtls Fla LLC.....561 745-5240
1557 Jupiter Park Dr # 1 Jupiter (33458) *(G-6702)*
Cemex Cnstr Mtls Fla LLC.....800 992-3639
4807 Collins Rd Orange Park (32073) *(G-11818)*
Cemex Cnstr Mtls Fla LLC.....904 213-8860
340 Corporate Way Ste 100 Orange Park (32073) *(G-11819)*
Cemex Cnstr Mtls Fla LLC.....904 827-0369
233 Industry Pl Saint Augustine (32095) *(G-14820)*
Cemex Cnstr Mtls Fla LLC (HQ).....561 833-5555
1501 Belvedere Rd West Palm Beach (33406) *(G-17960)*
Cemex Cnstr Mtls Fla LLC.....800 992-3639
622 Cattlemen Rd Sarasota (34232) *(G-15630)*
Cemex Cnstr Mtls Fla LLC.....772 461-7102
514 S 3rd St Fort Pierce (34950) *(G-4475)*
Cemex Cnstr Mtls Fla LLC.....863 419-2875
100 Lem Carnes Rd Davenport (33837) *(G-2362)*
Cemex Cnstr Mtls PCF LLC (HQ).....561 833-5555
1501 Belvedere Rd West Palm Beach (33406) *(G-17961)*
Cemex Concrete Company.....305 558-0255
11100 Nw 138th St Medley (33178) *(G-8214)*
Cemex Materials LLC.....386 775-0790
2170 State Road 472 Deland (32724) *(G-2857)*
Cemex Materials LLC (HQ).....561 833-5555
1720 Centrepark Dr E # 100 West Palm Beach (33401) *(G-17962)*
Cemex Materials LLC.....305 223-6934
1200 Nw 137th Ave Miami (33182) *(G-8909)*
Cemex Materials LLC.....321 636-5121
3365 E Industry Rd Cocoa (32926) *(G-1911)*
Cemex Materials LLC.....305 821-5661
13292 Nw 118th Ave Medley (33178) *(G-8215)*
Cemex Materials LLC.....561 746-4556
282 Old Dixie Hwy Jupiter (33469) *(G-6703)*
Cemex Materials LLC.....772 287-0502
1232 Se Dixie Cutoff Rd Stuart (34994) *(G-16127)*
Cemex Materials LLC.....305 818-4941
13292 Nw 118th Ave Medley (33178) *(G-8216)*
Cemex Materials LLC.....904 296-2400
4807 Collins Rd Jacksonville (32244) *(G-5974)*
Cemex Materials LLC.....941 722-4578
600 9th St W Palmetto (34221) *(G-13159)*
Cemex Materials LLC.....954 523-9978
29 Sw 33rd St Fort Lauderdale (33315) *(G-3719)*
Cemex Materials LLC.....407 322-8862
2210 W 25th St Sanford (32771) *(G-15278)*
Cemex Materials LLC.....850 769-2243
714 Transmitter Rd Panama City (32401) *(G-13240)*
Cemex Materials LLC.....321 636-5121
511 Garden St Titusville (32796) *(G-17580)*
Cemex Materials LLC.....863 688-2306
801 Mccue Rd Lakeland (33815) *(G-7290)*
Cemex Materials LLC.....954 431-7655
17301 Pines Blvd Pembroke Pines (33029) *(G-13380)*
Cemex Materials LLC.....352 435-0783
27111 County Road 33 Okahumpka (34762) *(G-11595)*
Cemex Materials LLC.....813 620-3760
6302 N 56th St Tampa (33610) *(G-16693)*
Cemex Materials LLC.....305 558-0315
2201 Nw 38th Ct Miami (33142) *(G-8910)*
Cemex Materials LLC.....561 793-1442
9111 Southern Blvd West Palm Beach (33411) *(G-17963)*
Cemex Materials LLC.....561 743-4039
1001 Jupiter Park Dr # 108 Jupiter (33458) *(G-6704)*
Cemex Materials LLC.....239 332-0135
2040 Ortiz Ave Fort Myers (33905) *(G-4205)*
Cemex Materials LLC.....561 881-4472
501 Avenue S Riviera Beach (33404) *(G-14608)*
Cemex Materials LLC.....863 678-3945
534 Story Rd Lake Wales (33898) *(G-7154)*
Cemex Pacific Holdings LLC.....239 992-1400
25061 Old 41 Rd Bonita Springs (34135) *(G-790)*
Cemi International Inc.....407 859-7701
2600 Titan Row Orlando (32809) *(G-11992)*
Censys Technologies Corp.....386 314-3599
1808 Concept Ct Ste 200 Daytona Beach (32114) *(G-2527)*
Center For Business Ownership.....239 455-9393
956 Glen Lake Cir Naples (34119) *(G-10709)*
Center For Vital Living DBA.....239 213-2222
2132 Tamiami Trl N Naples (34102) *(G-10710)*
Center Sand Mine.....800 366-7263
16375 Hartwood Marsh Rd Clermont (34711) *(G-1862)*
Center Seal Inc.....863 965-7124
2714 K Ville Ave Auburndale (33823) *(G-222)*
Center Technologies, Saint Petersburg *Also called Millimeter Wave Products Inc (G-15126)*
Centered Memories LLC.....915 308-3224
2001 N Federal Hwy G209 Pompano Beach (33062) *(G-13967)*
Centerline Brackets, Saint Augustine *Also called Centerline Steel LLC (G-14821)*
Centerline Drctnal Drlg Srvcin, Labelle *Also called Centerline Drctnal Drlg Svc In (G-6980)*
Centerline Drctnal Drlg Svc In.....863 674-0913
900 S Elm St Labelle (33935) *(G-6980)*
Centerline Steel LLC.....904 217-4186
208 W Davis Industrial Dr Saint Augustine (32084) *(G-14821)*
Centerline Tool & Engrg Inc.....941 749-5519
3107 29th Ave E Ste A Bradenton (34208) *(G-959)*
Centerpoint Meats and Prov, Saint Petersburg *Also called Pinellas Provision Corporation (G-15150)*
Central Beef Ind LLC.....352 793-3671
571 W Kings Hwy Center Hill (33514) *(G-1440)*
Central Concrete Supermix Inc.....954 480-9333
1817 S Powerline Rd Deerfield Beach (33442) *(G-2689)*
Central Electric Motor Svc Inc.....863 422-4721
313 N 12th St Haines City (33844) *(G-4902)*
Central Fla Attrnsfsonists Inc.....321 299-6019
1005 Hart Branch Dr Oviedo (32765) *(G-12812)*
Central Fla Bus Solutions Inc.....863 297-9293
150 3rd St Sw Winter Haven (33880) *(G-18430)*
Central Fla Kit Bath Srfces In.....352 307-2333
2800 Se 62nd St Ocala (34480) *(G-11347)*
Central Fla Prtg Graphics LLC.....321 752-8753
772 Washburn Rd Ste A Melbourne (32934) *(G-8385)*
Central Fla Remanufacturing.....407 299-9011
2526 W Washington St Orlando (32805) *(G-11993)*
Central Fla Stl Bldg & Sup LLC.....352 266-6795
4750 S Pine Ave Ocala (34480) *(G-11348)*
Central Florida Box Corp.....407 936-1277
2950 Lake Emma Rd # 1000 Lake Mary (32746) *(G-7064)*
Central Florida Central Fla.....407 674-2626
4157 Seaboard Rd Orlando (32808) *(G-11994)*
Central Florida Cnstr Walls.....407 448-2350
5923 Bamboo Dr Orlando (32807) *(G-11995)*
Central Florida Cstm Trlrs Inc (PA).....407 851-1144
2136 4th St Orlando (32824) *(G-11996)*
Central Florida Driveshaft.....407 299-1100
5512 Carder Rd Orlando (32810) *(G-11997)*
Central Florida Ice Services.....407 779-0161
410 27th St Orlando (32806) *(G-11998)*
Central Florida Lbr & Sup Co.....407 298-5600
2721 Regent Ave Orlando (32804) *(G-11999)*
Central Florida Plating Inc.....321 452-7234
675 Cypress Dr Merritt Island (32952) *(G-8581)*
Central Florida Precast Inc.....941 730-2158
1910 1st Ave E Bradenton (34208) *(G-960)*
Central Florida Publishing Inc (PA).....407 323-5204
700 W Fulton St Sanford (32771) *(G-15279)*
Central Florida Remanufactory, Orlando *Also called Central Fla Remanufacturing (G-11993)*
Central Florida Sales & Svc.....863 967-6678
307 Mckean St Auburndale (33823) *(G-223)*
Central Florida Truss Inc (PA).....863 533-0821
1500 Us Highway 17 N Bartow (33830) *(G-304)*
Central Ink International.....786 747-8411
8107 Nw 33rd St Doral (33122) *(G-3158)*
Central Maintenance & Wldg Inc (PA).....813 229-0012
2620 E Keysville Rd Lithia (33547) *(G-7831)*
Central Maintenance & Wldg Inc.....352 795-2817
6040 N Suncoast Blvd Crystal River (34428) *(G-2269)*
Central Metal Fabricators Inc.....305 261-6262
900 Sw 70th Ave Miami (33144) *(G-8911)*
Central Printers Inc.....727 527-5879
4101 35th St N Saint Petersburg (33714) *(G-15004)*
Central Processing Corp.....352 787-3004
304 Richey Rd Leesburg (34748) *(G-7762)*
Central Sand Inc.....321 632-0308
6855 Tico Rd Unit 8 Titusville (32780) *(G-17581)*
Central Signs LLC.....386 322-7446
517 Mason Ave Ste 101 Daytona Beach (32117) *(G-2528)*
Central Signs Volusia Cnty Inc.....386 341-4842
497 Buchanan Way South Daytona (32119) *(G-16019)*
Central State Aggregates LLC.....813 788-0454
41150 Yonkers Blvd Zephyrhills (33541) *(G-18608)*
Central Steel Fabricators LLC.....904 503-1660
2144 Soutel Dr Jacksonville (32208) *(G-5975)*
Central Turbos Corp (PA).....305 406-3933
1951 Nw 97th Ave Doral (33172) *(G-3159)*
Central Wire Industries LLC.....850 983-9926
5881 Commerce Rd Milton (32583) *(G-10422)*
Centralsquare Technologies, Lake Mary *Also called Superion LLC (G-7109)*
Centralsquare Technologies, Deerfield Beach *Also called Advanced Public Safety LLC (G-2658)*
Centrex Powdercoating Inc.....813 390-2802
4901 Distribution Dr Tampa (33605) *(G-16694)*
Centrifugal Rebabbitting Inc.....954 522-3003
234 Sw 29th St Fort Lauderdale (33315) *(G-3720)*
Centro Ddgnstico Y Tratamiento, Sanford *Also called Centro De Diagnostico (G-15280)*
Centro De Diagnostico.....407 865-7020
253 Bellagio Cir Sanford (32771) *(G-15280)*

Centroid Products Inc 386 423-3574
2104 Hibiscus Dr Edgewater (32141) *(G-3486)*

Centrys LLC 407 476-4786
750 Monroe Rd Sanford (32771) *(G-15281)*

Centurion Armoring Intl Inc 813 426-3385
3911 W Eden Roc Cir Tampa (33634) *(G-16695)*

Centurion Holdings I LLC 636 349-5425
324 N Dale Mabry Hwy Tampa (33609) *(G-16696)*

Centurion Residential Inds 561 574-1483
3819 Heath Cir N West Palm Beach (33407) *(G-17964)*

Centurion Technologies, Tampa *Also called Centurion Holdings I LLC (G-16696)*

Century Boats, Zephyrhills *Also called All Craft Marine LLC (G-18601)*

Century Graphics & Metals Inc 407 262-8290
350 Northlake Blvd # 100 Altamonte Springs (32701) *(G-37)*

Century Metal Products Inc 407 293-8871
3108 Friendly Ave Orlando (32808) *(G-12000)*

Century Millworks 850 256-2565
6082 Industrial Blvd Century (32535) *(G-1442)*

Cepero Remodeling Inc 305 265-1888
6972 Sw 4th St Miami (33144) *(G-8912)*

Cepods LLC 786 520-1412
1348 Washington Ave # 257 Miami Beach (33139) *(G-10178)*

Ceramica Verea USA Corp 305 665-3923
7035 Sw 44th St Miami (33155) *(G-8913)*

Ceramlock Coatings Inc 772 781-2141
3912 Sw Bruner Ter Palm City (34990) *(G-13027)*

Cerberus Craft Distillery LLC 813 789-1556
6608 Anderson Rd Tampa (33634) *(G-16697)*

Cerenovas Inc (HQ) 800 255-2500
6303 Blue Lagoon Dr # 21 Miami (33126) *(G-8914)*

Cerenovus, Miami *Also called Depuy Synthes Products Inc (G-9018)*

Cerex Advanced Fabrics Inc 850 968-0100
610 Chemstrand Rd Cantonment (32533) *(G-1266)*

Cerno Pharmaceuticals LLC 786 763-2766
6714 Nw 72nd Ave Miami (33166) *(G-8915)*

Certainteed Corporation (HQ) 863 294-3206
101 Hatfield Rd Winter Haven (33880) *(G-18431)*

Certainteed Machine Works, Winter Haven *Also called Certainteed Corporation (G-18431)*

Certanteed Gyps Ciling Mfg Inc (HQ) 813 286-3900
4300 W Cypress St Ste 500 Tampa (33607) *(G-16698)*

Certapro Painters Centl Miami, Doral *Also called Sdkc Corp (G-3358)*

Certek Software Designs Inc 727 738-8188
507 S Paula Dr Dunedin (34698) *(G-3444)*

Certified Clean Cuts - LLC 954 903-1733
7210 Southgate Blvd North Lauderdale (33068) *(G-11077)*

Certified Metal Finishing Inc 954 979-0707
1420 Sw 28th Ave Pompano Beach (33069) *(G-13968)*

Certified Mold Free Corp 954 614-7100
2881 W Lake Vista Cir Davie (33328) *(G-2397)*

Certified Mold Treatment LLC 305 879-1839
17277 Allamanda Dr Summerland Key (33042) *(G-16261)*

Certified Whl Exterior Pdts 407 654-7170
902 Carter Rd Ste 300 Winter Garden (34787) *(G-18379)*

Cesar E Rodriguez 561 305-1312
4371 N Dixie Hwy Deerfield Beach (33064) *(G-2690)*

Cesaroni Aerospace Inc 941 400-1421
2280 Commerce Ct Bowling Green (33834) *(G-829)*

Cesibon 239 682-5028
8807 Tamiami Trl N Naples (34108) *(G-10711)*

Cessna Orlndo Citation Svc Ctr, Orlando *Also called Textron Aviation Inc (G-12653)*

Cew LLC 305 232-8892
14008 Sw 140th St Miami (33186) *(G-8916)*

Cew Technologies Inc 305 232-8892
14008 Sw 140th St Miami (33186) *(G-8917)*

CF Boatworks Inc 954 325-6007
3340 Sw 2nd Ave Fort Lauderdale (33315) *(G-3721)*

CF Industries Inc 813 782-1591
2501 Bonnie Mine Rd Bartow (33830) *(G-305)*

CF Industries Inc 813 782-1591
10608 Paul Buchman Hwy Plant City (33565) *(G-13753)*

CF Motion Inc 727 458-7092
4625 E Bay Dr Ste 306 Clearwater (33764) *(G-1538)*

CF Sign and Stamp Company, Panama City *Also called Finlayson Enterprises Inc (G-13262)*

CF Terminal, Bartow *Also called CF Industries Inc (G-305)*

Cfb Display Group, Lake Mary *Also called Central Florida Box Corp (G-7064)*

CFM&d LLC 772 220-8938
2550 Se Willoughby Blvd Stuart (34994) *(G-16128)*

CFS Inc 850 386-2902
2151 Delta Blvd Ste 101 Tallahassee (32303) *(G-16422)*

Cfu Plating 386 795-5198
7575 S Us Highway 441 # 118 Ocala (34480) *(G-11349)*

Cg Burgers (PA) 954 618-6450
1732 N Federal Hwy Fort Lauderdale (33305) *(G-3722)*

CG Quality Woodworks Inc 305 231-3480
7530 W 19th Ct Hialeah (33014) *(G-5089)*

Cg Roxane LLC 407 241-1640
2224 Hazelhurst Ave Orlando (32804) *(G-12001)*

Cg Solutionsgroup, Apopka *Also called Cellec Games Inc (G-109)*

Cgc Industries Inc 954 923-2428
200 N Dixie Hwy Hollywood (33020) *(G-5549)*

Chacho Customs 239 369-4664
2401 Gretchen Ave S F Lehigh Acres (33973) *(G-7806)*

Chad 727 433-0404
817 S Macdill Ave Tampa (33609) *(G-16699)*

Chae Dupont PA 305 697-7771
7765 Sw 87th Ave Ste 102 Miami (33173) *(G-8918)*

Chainbridge Distillery LLC 440 212-4992
3500 Ne 11th Ave Oakland Park (33334) *(G-11251)*

Chalet Suzanne Rest Cntry Inn, Lake Wales *Also called Suzanne Chalet Foods Inc (G-7176)*

Chambers Body Works Inc 352 588-3072
16556 Old Johnston Rd Dade City (33523) *(G-2315)*

Chambers Truss Inc (PA) 772 465-2012
3105 Oleander Ave Fort Pierce (34982) *(G-4476)*

Champion Coatings Inc 561 512-5985
102 Ne 60th Ave Okeechobee (34974) *(G-11599)*

Champion Controls Inc (PA) 954 318-3090
811 Nw 57th Pl Fort Lauderdale (33309) *(G-3723)*

Champion Nutrition Inc 954 233-3300
1301 Sawgrs Corp Pkwy Sunrise (33323) *(G-16304)*

Champion Performance Products, Sunrise *Also called Champion Nutrition Inc (G-16304)*

Champion Shtmtl Fabrication 407 509-7439
6450 University Blvd B2 Winter Park (32792) *(G-18498)*

Champion Welding Services LLC 786 262-5727
5608 Nw 161st St Miami Lakes (33014) *(G-10291)*

Chance Aluminum Corp 407 789-1606
11616 Landstar Blvd Orlando (32824) *(G-12002)*

Chancey Metal Products Inc 904 260-6880
5130 Sunbeam Rd Jacksonville (32257) *(G-5976)*

Change This World 407 900-8840
6790 Edgwter Cmmerce Pkwy Orlando (32810) *(G-12003)*

Channel Industries Inc 561 214-0637
511 29th St West Palm Beach (33407) *(G-17965)*

Channel Investments LLC 727 599-1360
4221 W Boy Scout Blvd # 300 Tampa (33607) *(G-16700)*

Channel Letter Network Corp 305 594-3360
7204 Nw 31st St Miami (33122) *(G-8919)*

Channel Letter USA, Delray Beach *Also called Royal Atlantic Ventures LLC (G-3013)*

Channel Letter USA Corp 561 243-9699
2275 S Federal Hwy # 350 Delray Beach (33483) *(G-2943)*

Channel Logistics LLC 856 614-5441
888 Biscayne Blvd Ste 505 Miami (33132) *(G-8920)*

Channel Microwave, Tampa *Also called Smiths Interconnect Inc (G-17277)*

Charcoal Chef Usa LLC 786 273-6511
554 Nw 41st St Miami (33127) *(G-8921)*

Chardonnay Boat Works LLC 703 981-6339
411 Walnut St Green Cove Springs (32043) *(G-4821)*

Chargers and Cases LLC 352 587-2539
5310 Alpha Dr Orlando (32810) *(G-12004)*

Chargex LLC 855 242-7439
4020 W Kennedy Blvd # 10 Tampa (33609) *(G-16701)*

Chargriller, Tampa *Also called A&J Manufacturing Inc (G-16548)*

Charian Machine & Mfg Inc 727 561-0150
4652 107th Cir N Clearwater (33762) *(G-1539)*

Chariot Eagle Inc (PA) 623 936-7545
931 Nw 37th Ave Ocala (34475) *(G-11350)*

Charisma Media 407 333-0600
1051 Sand Pond Rd Lake Mary (32746) *(G-7065)*

Charity Homes LLC 352 274-0306
12830 Sw 58th Cir Ocala (34473) *(G-11351)*

Charles & Co LLC 404 592-1190
909 Nw 10th Ter Fort Lauderdale (33311) *(G-3724)*

Charles Bryant Enterprises 850 785-3604
2700 Whisperwood Ln Panama City (32405) *(G-13241)*

Charles Composites LLC 863 357-2500
1252 Ne 12th St Okeechobee (34972) *(G-11600)*

Charles Gable Inc 239 300-0220
18511 Royal Hammock Blvd Naples (34114) *(G-10712)*

Charles Industries, Okeechobee *Also called Charles Composites LLC (G-11600)*

Charles K Sewell 407 423-1870
333 W Michigan St Orlando (32806) *(G-12005)*

Charles Machine Works Inc 813 704-4865
506 E Park Rd Plant City (33563) *(G-13754)*

Charles Screening & Alum LLC 239 369-0551
848 Theodore Vail St E Lehigh Acres (33974) *(G-7807)*

Charles Thaggard Inc 239 936-8059
1951 Collier Ave Ste A Fort Myers (33901) *(G-4206)*

Charleston Aluminum LLC 305 628-4014
1150 Nw 159th Dr Hialeah (33016) *(G-5090)*

Charlotte County Min & Mtl Inc 239 567-1800
16070 Tamiami Trl Punta Gorda (33955) *(G-14501)*

Charuvil Oil Inc DBA Valero 772 871-9050
815 E Prima Vista Blvd Port Saint Lucie (34952) *(G-14404)*

Chasco Machine & Manufacturing 727 815-3510
5071 Cedar Ridge Dr Brooksville (34601) *(G-1144)*

Chasco Machine & Mfg Inc 352 678-4188
5071 Cedar Ridge Dr Brooksville (34601) *(G-1145)*

Chase Aerospace Inc 407 812-4545
5342 Greenside Ct Orlando (32819) *(G-12006)*

Chase Metals Inc 352 669-1254
38051 State Road 19 Umatilla (32784) *(G-17644)*
Chassis King, Clearwater *Also called Interglobal Capital Inc* *(G-1645)*
Chassis King LLC 727 585-1500
1016 Pnc De Leon Blvd Clearwater (33756) *(G-1540)*
Chautuqua Vineyards Winery Inc (PA) 850 892-5887
364 Hugh Adams Rd Defuniak Springs (32435) *(G-2837)*
Checkpoint Card Group Inc 954 426-1331
1801 Green Rd Deerfield Beach (33064) *(G-2691)*
Checks Your Way Inc 386 362-4044
621 Ohio Ave N Live Oak (32064) *(G-7843)*
Checksum Software LLC 786 375-8091
7979 Nw 21st St Doral (33122) *(G-3160)*
Cheesecake Etc Desserts, Miami Springs *Also called Obem Foods Inc* *(G-10392)*
Cheesecake, Etc, Miami Springs *Also called T & W Inc* *(G-10394)*
Chef Distilled LLC 305 747-8236
107 Simonton St Key West (33040) *(G-6859)*
Chef Philippe, Hollywood *Also called Gourmet Parisien Inc* *(G-5582)*
Chefs Commissary LLC 321 303-2947
6929 Narcoossee Rd # 509 Orlando (32822) *(G-12007)*
Chelly Cosmetics Manufacturing 305 471-9608
7172 Sw 30th Rd Miami (33155) *(G-8922)*
Cheltec Inc 941 355-1045
2215 Industrial Blvd Sarasota (34234) *(G-15631)*
Chem Guard Inc 407 402-2798
3964 Buglers Rest Pl Casselberry (32707) *(G-1412)*
Chem TEC, Deerfield Beach *Also called Chem-TEC Equipment Co* *(G-2692)*
Chem-Free System Inc 954 258-5415
7168 Cataluna Cir Delray Beach (33446) *(G-2944)*
Chem-TEC Equipment Co 954 428-8259
3077 Sw 13th Dr Deerfield Beach (33442) *(G-2692)*
Chem-Tek Metal Finishing Corp 321 722-2227
636 Atlantis Rd Melbourne (32904) *(G-8386)*
Chem-Tek Plating Industries, Melbourne *Also called Chem-Tek Metal Finishing Corp* *(G-8386)*
Chemclad LLC 863 967-1156
1701 Hobbs Rd Auburndale (33823) *(G-224)*
Chemco Corp 305 623-4445
4920 Nw 165th St Miami Lakes (33014) *(G-10292)*
Chemical Dynamics Inc 813 752-4950
4206 Business Ln Plant City (33566) *(G-13755)*
Chemical Manufacturers, Boca Raton *Also called Dovo Inc* *(G-493)*
Chemical Systems of Florida, Zellwood *Also called Chemical Systems Orlando Inc* *(G-18597)*
Chemical Systems Orlando Inc 407 886-2329
6429 W Jones Ave Zellwood (32798) *(G-18597)*
Chemko Technical Services Inc 954 783-7673
1000 E Atl Blvd Ste 115 Pompano Beach (33060) *(G-13969)*
Chemline Inc 407 847-4181
1662 Broad St Kissimmee (34746) *(G-6906)*
Chemline Products Inc 727 573-2436
3813 126th Ave N Ste 7 Clearwater (33762) *(G-1541)*
Chemours Company Fc LLC 904 964-1230
Florida Plant Starke (32091) *(G-16098)*
Chemours Company Fc LLC 904 964-1200
5222 Treat Rd Starke (32091) *(G-16099)*
Chemplex Industries Inc 772 283-2700
2820 Sw 42nd Ave Palm City (34990) *(G-13028)*
Chemseal Inc 305 433-8362
7891 W 25th Ct Hialeah (33016) *(G-5091)*
Chen Technology Inc 305 621-0023
1000 Park Centre Blvd # 100 Miami Gardens (33169) *(G-10254)*
Chen, Chao Ming Company, Jacksonville *Also called Sunshine Packing & Noodle Co* *(G-6520)*
Chenega Manufacturing Svcs LLC 850 763-6013
1509 Saint Andrews Blvd Panama City (32405) *(G-13242)*
Cheney Ofs Inc 407 292-3223
3875 Bengert St Orlando (32808) *(G-12008)*
Chernin Beef Industries, Center Hill *Also called Central Beef Ind LLC* *(G-1440)*
Chervo USA Inc 561 510-2458
1201 Us Highway 1 Ste 435 North Palm Beach (33408) *(G-11179)*
Cheval Country Club 813 279-5122
545 Frederica Ln Dunedin (34698) *(G-3445)*
Chez Industries LLC 386 698-4414
2167 S Us Highway 17 Crescent City (32112) *(G-2235)*
Chhaya Corporation 407 348-9400
1988 E Osceola Pkwy Kissimmee (34743) *(G-6907)*
Chiantis 407 484-6510
685 Towne Center Blvd Sanford (32771) *(G-15282)*
Chicago Electronic Distrs Inc 312 985-6175
17097 Glenview Ave Port Charlotte (33954) *(G-14292)*
Chicago Soft Ltd 863 940-2066
1820 E Edgewood Dr # 105 Lakeland (33803) *(G-7291)*
Chick N Portions Inc 305 687-0000
12725 Nw 38th Ave Opa Locka (33054) *(G-11728)*
Chickasha Manufacturing Co Inc 405 224-0229
277 Saratoga Ct Osprey (34229) *(G-12801)*
Chicos Pallets Corp 904 236-3607
7917 W Beaver St Jacksonville (32220) *(G-5977)*
Chief Cabinets LLC 850 545-5055
4329 W Pensacola St Ste 3 Tallahassee (32304) *(G-16423)*
Chiefland Crab Company Inc 352 493-4887
1606 Sw 4th Pl Chiefland (32626) *(G-1447)*
Chikitas LLC 561 401-5033
2269 S Military Trl West Palm Beach (33415) *(G-17966)*
Chili Produkt Kft 954 655-4111
9850 Scribner Ln Wellington (33414) *(G-17848)*
Chiliprint LLC 863 547-6930
28597 Hwy 27 Dundee (33838) *(G-3434)*
Chiller Medic Inc 904 814-9446
8933 Western Way Ste 18 Jacksonville (32256) *(G-5978)*
Chilly Willys Heating & A Inc 904 772-1164
8006 Renault Dr Jacksonville (32244) *(G-5979)*
Chilton Signs & Designs LLC 863 438-0880
549 Pope Ave Nw Winter Haven (33881) *(G-18432)*
Chin & Chin Enterprises Inc 407 478-8726
3580 Aloma Ave Ste 5 Winter Park (32792) *(G-18499)*
China Public Security Tech Inc 866 821-9004
4033 12th St Ne Saint Petersburg (33703) *(G-15005)*
Chip Supply Inc (HQ) 407 298-7100
1810 S Orange Blossom Trl Apopka (32703) *(G-110)*
Chipico South, Palmetto *Also called Vienna Beef Ltd* *(G-13203)*
Chipley Newspapers Inc 850 638-0212
112 E Virginia Ave Bonifay (32425) *(G-769)*
Chiptech Inc (PA) 954 454-3554
2885 Sw 30th Ave Hallandale (33009) *(G-4921)*
Chiptronics, Miami *Also called Sonobrands LLC* *(G-9918)*
Chism Manufacturing Svcs LLC 941 896-9671
6416 Parkland Dr Sarasota (34243) *(G-15454)*
Chittum Yachts LLC (PA) 386 589-7224
4577 Sw Cargo Way Palm City (34990) *(G-13029)*
Chittum Yachts LLC 386 589-7224
4953 Se Pine Knoll Way Stuart (34997) *(G-16129)*
Chlorinators Inc 772 288-4854
1044 Se Dixie Cutoff Rd Stuart (34994) *(G-16130)*
Chocolate Compass LLC 407 600-0145
5899 Pearl Estates Ln Sanford (32771) *(G-15283)*
Choctaw Trading Co Inc 407 905-9917
99 W Plant St Winter Garden (34787) *(G-18380)*
Choctaw Willy, Winter Garden *Also called Choctaw Trading Co Inc* *(G-18380)*
Choice ADS, Deerfield Beach *Also called Forum Publishing Group Inc* *(G-2721)*
Choice Cabinets & Counters 407 670-8944
11139 Sunup Ln Orlando (32825) *(G-12009)*
Choice Products Inc 386 426-6450
143 W Palm Way Edgewater (32132) *(G-3487)*
Choice Tool & Mold LLC 941 371-6767
901 Sarasota Center Blvd Sarasota (34240) *(G-15632)*
Cholados Y Mas 813 935-9262
6729 N Armenia Ave Tampa (33604) *(G-16702)*
Chris Craft Corporation 941 351-4900
8161 15th St E Sarasota (34243) *(G-15455)*
Chris Industries Corp 941 729-7600
1118 8th Ave W Palmetto (34221) *(G-13160)*
Chris-Craft, Sarasota *Also called Chris Craft Corporation* *(G-15455)*
Chrisalen Cabinets Inc 954 682-9390
8701 Johnson St Pembroke Pines (33024) *(G-13381)*
Christian L International Inc 305 947-1722
2297 Ne 164th St Miami (33160) *(G-8923)*
Christian Workshop LLC 321 676-2396
405 West Dr Ste C Melbourne (32904) *(G-8387)*
Christie Lites Entps USA LLC (PA) 407 856-0016
6990 Lake Ellenor Dr Orlando (32809) *(G-12010)*
Christie Lites Orlando LLC (HQ) 206 223-7200
2479 Eunice Ave Orlando (32808) *(G-12011)*
Christopher R Shuman 561 800-8541
176 E 21st St Riviera Beach (33404) *(G-14609)*
Christy Lewis Sheek LLC 786 512-2999
8761 Forest Hills Blvd Coral Springs (33065) *(G-2140)*
Chrom Industries LLC 954 400-5135
3131 Sw 42nd St Fort Lauderdale (33312) *(G-3725)*
Chromalloy Castings Tampa Corp (HQ) 561 935-3571
3999 Rca Blvd Palm Beach Gardens (33410) *(G-12958)*
Chromalloy Component Svcs Inc 954 378-1999
3600 Nw 54th St Fort Lauderdale (33309) *(G-3726)*
Chromalloy Gas Turbine LLC (HQ) 561 935-3571
4100 Rca Blvd Palm Beach Gardens (33410) *(G-12959)*
Chromalloy Mtl Solutions LLC 954 378-1999
3600 Nw 54th St Fort Lauderdale (33309) *(G-3727)*
Chromatech Digital Inc 727 528-4711
4301 31st St N Saint Petersburg (33714) *(G-15006)*
Chromatech Printing, Saint Petersburg *Also called Chromatech Digital Inc* *(G-15006)*
Chrome Connection Corp 305 947-9191
15405 W Dixie Hwy North Miami Beach (33162) *(G-11132)*
Chuculu LLC 305 595-4577
9455 Sw 78th St Miami (33173) *(G-8924)*
Chunky Plates LLC 321 746-3346
2550 W Colonial Dr Orlando (32804) *(G-12012)*

Churrico Factory LLC..239 989-7616
4125 Cleveland Ave # 1370 Fort Myers (33901) *(G-4207)*

Chuxco Inc..305 470-9595
1 Alhambra Plz Ste Ph Coral Gables (33134) *(G-2039)*

Cianos Tile & Marble Inc.................................239 267-8453
5680 Halifax Ave Fort Myers (33912) *(G-4208)*

Ciao Group Inc (PA)..347 560-5040
951 W Yamato Rd Ste 101 Boca Raton (33431) *(G-460)*

CIC Conveyors, Palmetto *Also called Chris Industries Corp (G-13160)*

Ciega Inc..727 526-9048
4410 35th St N Saint Petersburg (33714) *(G-15007)*

Cielo Enterprise Solutions LLC.......................786 292-4111
12457 Sw 130th St Miami (33186) *(G-8925)*

Cienfuegos Pallets Corp..................................786 703-3686
7781 Nw 73rd Ct Medley (33166) *(G-8217)*

Cigar City Brewing, Tampa *Also called Canarchy Craft (G-16675)*

Cigar City Brewpub LLC (PA)...........................813 348-6363
3924 W Spruce St Tampa (33607) *(G-16703)*

Cigar City Printing...813 843-2751
14143 Fennsbury Dr Tampa (33624) *(G-16704)*

Cigar City Smoked Salsa LLC.........................813 421-3340
5106 N 30th St Tampa (33610) *(G-16705)*

Cigarette Racing Team LLC..............................305 769-4350
4355 Nw 128th St Opa Locka (33054) *(G-11729)*

Cim USA Inc...305 369-1040
10813 Nw 30th St Ste 108 Doral (33172) *(G-3161)*

Cincinnati Printing Service..............................239 455-0960
174 Via Perignon Naples (34119) *(G-10713)*

Cind-Al Inc...863 401-8700
13518 Granville Ave Clermont (34711) *(G-1863)*

Cinega Cstm Frmng & Design Inc....................904 686-5654
3513 Pebble Stone Ct Orange Park (32065) *(G-11820)*

Cinema Crafters Inc.......................................305 891-6121
12564 Ne 14th Ave North Miami (33161) *(G-11098)*

Cinidyne Sales Inc...941 473-3914
1811 Englewood Rd Englewood (34223) *(G-3527)*

Cintas Corporation...813 874-1401
3601 W Swann Ave Ste 107 Tampa (33609) *(G-16706)*

Cintas Corporation...239 693-8722
12771 Westlinks Dr Ste 1 Fort Myers (33913) *(G-4209)*

Cintas Fire Protection, Fort Myers *Also called Cintas Corporation (G-4209)*

Cioreview, Fort Lauderdale *Also called Valleymedia Inc (G-4115)*

Circle C Timber Inc..863 735-0383
2086 Fish Branch Rd Zolfo Springs (33890) *(G-18639)*

Circle Press...561 213-5831
5749 Camino Del Sol Boca Raton (33433) *(G-461)*

Circle Redmont Inc..321 259-7374
407 Saint Georges Ct Satellite Beach (32937) *(G-15884)*

Circle S Manufacturing Co Inc........................352 236-3580
13650 Ne 110th St Fort Mc Coy (32134) *(G-4148)*

Circor, Temple Terrace *Also called Leslie Controls Inc (G-17539)*

Circor International Inc...................................813 978-1000
12501 Telecom Dr Temple Terrace (33637) *(G-17536)*

Circuit Works Co..727 544-5336
6405 49th St N Ste B Pinellas Park (33781) *(G-13675)*

Circuitronics LLC...407 322-8300
223 Hickman Dr Ste 101 Sanford (32771) *(G-15284)*

Circuitronix LLC (PA)......................................786 364-4458
3131 Sw 42nd St Fort Lauderdale (33312) *(G-3728)*

Cirkul Inc...941 518-8596
9210 E Columbus Dr # 110 Tampa (33619) *(G-16707)*

Cirkul Inc...513 889-6708
4545 Madison Indus Ln Tampa (33619) *(G-16708)*

Ciro Manufacturing Corporation......................561 988-2139
692 S Military Trl Deerfield Beach (33442) *(G-2693)*

Ciron Custom Welding Inc...............................786 259-7589
2954 W 84th St Hialeah (33018) *(G-5092)*

Cirven Usa LLC..305 815-2545
9681 Nw 45th Ln Doral (33178) *(G-3162)*

Cisam LLC..813 404-4180
32789 Eiland Blvd Zephyrhills (33545) *(G-18609)*

Cisco Systems Inc..305 718-2600
8200 Nw 41st St Ste 400 Doral (33166) *(G-3163)*

Citadinos Corp...954 435-7529
18483 Sw 7th St Pembroke Pines (33029) *(G-13382)*

Citel America Inc..954 430-6310
10108 Usa Today Way Miramar (33025) *(G-10480)*

Citilube Inc..305 681-6064
3300 Nw 112th St Miami (33167) *(G-8926)*

Citory Solutions LLC.......................................407 766-6533
10524 Moss Park Rd # 204 Orlando (32832) *(G-12013)*

Citrix Systems Inc (PA)...................................954 267-3000
851 W Cypress Creek Rd Fort Lauderdale (33309) *(G-3729)*

Citrus County Chronicle, The, Crystal River *Also called Citrus Publishing LLC (G-2271)*

Citrus Extracts LLC..772 464-9800
3495 S Us Highway 1 Ste A Fort Pierce (34982) *(G-4477)*

Citrus Industry Magazine, Newberry *Also called Agnet Media Inc (G-11016)*

Citrus Motorsports..352 564-2453
7800 W Gulf & Lake Hwy Crystal River (34429) *(G-2270)*

Citrus Publishing LLC (HQ).............................352 563-6363
1624 N Meadowcrest Blvd Crystal River (34429) *(G-2271)*

Citrus Times Edition, Inverness *Also called Times Publishing Company (G-5835)*

Citrus World Inc (PA)......................................863 676-1411
20205 Hwy 27 Lake Wales (33853) *(G-7155)*

Citrus World Services Inc................................863 676-1411
20205 Hwy 27 Lake Wales (33853) *(G-7156)*

City Clors Dgital Prtg Ctr Inc...........................305 471-0816
1470 Nw 79th Ave Doral (33126) *(G-3164)*

City Debate Publishing Company......................305 868-1161
6538 Collins Ave Miami Beach (33141) *(G-10179)*

City Electric Supply Company..........................772 878-4944
660 Nw Peacock Blvd Port St Lucie (34986) *(G-14474)*

City Electric Supply Company..........................772 879-7440
660 Nw Peacock Blvd Port Saint Lucie (34986) *(G-14405)*

City Elevator Service Corp..............................305 345-1951
15107 Sw 138th Pl Miami (33186) *(G-8927)*

City Fashion, The, Boca Raton *Also called Amj DOT LLC (G-410)*

City News Publishing LLC................................305 332-9101
12364 Clearfalls Dr Boca Raton (33428) *(G-462)*

City of Bradenton...941 727-6360
5600 Natalie Way E Bradenton (34203) *(G-961)*

City of Cocoa Beach.......................................321 868-3342
1600 Minutemen Cswy Cocoa Beach (32931) *(G-1967)*

City of Hollywood...954 967-4230
3441 Hollywood Blvd Fl 2 Hollywood (33021) *(G-5550)*

City of Lakeland...863 834-6780
1140 E Parker St Lakeland (33801) *(G-7292)*

City of Largo, Clearwater *Also called Environmental Services (G-1587)*

City of Ocala..352 622-6803
1307 Nw 4th Ave Ocala (34475) *(G-11352)*

City Prints LLC...407 409-0509
200 E Colonial Dr Orlando (32801) *(G-12014)*

City Publications South FL..............................305 495-3311
6501 Nw 36th St Ste 300 Virginia Gardens (33166) *(G-17820)*

Citypavers, Pembroke Pines *Also called Yolo Consulting LLC (G-13426)*

CJ Labs Inc..305 234-9644
12245 Sw 128th St Unit 30 Miami (33186) *(G-8928)*

CJ Publishers Inc...727 521-6277
4940 72nd Ave N Ste 200 Pinellas Park (33781) *(G-13676)*

Cjb Industries Inc...941 552-8397
23 N Blvd Of Presidents Sarasota (34236) *(G-15633)*

CJL Bricks & Pavers Inc.................................305 527-4240
9301 Nw 33rd Ct Miami (33147) *(G-8929)*

CK Dockside Services Inc...............................954 254-0263
6141 Nw 80th Ter Parkland (33067) *(G-13345)*

CK Prime Investments Inc...............................239 574-7800
830 Ne 24th Ln Unit C Cape Coral (33909) *(G-1324)*

Ckc Industries Inc (PA)...................................813 888-9468
4908 Savarese Cir Tampa (33634) *(G-16709)*

Cki Solutions, West Palm Beach *Also called Cadence Keen Innovations Inc (G-17955)*

CKS Packaging Inc...407 423-0333
333 W Michigan St Orlando (32806) *(G-12015)*

CKS Packaging Inc...407 420-9529
7400 S Orange Ave Orlando (32809) *(G-12016)*

CKS Packaging Inc...954 925-9049
4020 N 29th Ter Hollywood (33020) *(G-5551)*

CL Gardens LLC...561 567-0504
3101 Pga Blvd Palm Beach Gardens (33410) *(G-12960)*

CL Waterside Naples LLC................................239 734-8534
5455 Tamiami Trl N Naples (34108) *(G-10714)*

Claddah Corp...407 834-8881
207 Reece Way Ste 1625 Casselberry (32707) *(G-1413)*

Cladding Systems Inc.....................................813 250-0786
3218 E 4th Ave Tampa (33605) *(G-16710)*

Claims Pages, Deltona *Also called Nationwide Publishing Company (G-3049)*

Clairson Plastics, Ocala *Also called Nanotechnovation Corporation (G-11449)*

Clare Instruments (us) Inc..............................813 886-2775
6304 Benjamin Rd Ste 506 Tampa (33634) *(G-16711)*

Clari Solutions LLC...813 679-4848
2020 W Brandon Blvd # 17 Brandon (33511) *(G-1086)*

Clariant, Gainesville *Also called Sivance LLC (G-4765)*

Clarios LLC..305 805-5600
10801 Nw 97th St Ste 21 Medley (33178) *(G-8218)*

Clarios LLC..407 850-0147
4127 Seaboard Rd Orlando (32808) *(G-12017)*

Clarios LLC..321 253-4000
1060 Aurora Rd Melbourne (32935) *(G-8388)*

Clarios LLC..866 866-0886
2900 Horseshoe Dr S # 130 Naples (34104) *(G-10715)*

Clarios LLC..904 786-9161
6973 Highway Ave Ste 301 Jacksonville (32254) *(G-5980)*

Clarios LLC..727 541-3531
8575 Largo Lakes Dr Largo (33773) *(G-7564)*

Clarity Diagnostics, Boca Raton *Also called Diagnostic Test Group LLC (G-483)*

Clark Craig Enterprises (PA)...........................813 287-0110
3901 W Kennedy Blvd Tampa (33609) *(G-16712)*

Clarks Electrical Signs & Svcs........................561 248-5932
108 W Cypress Rd Lake Worth (33467) *(G-7191)*

A
L
P
H
A
B
E
T
I
C

Clarkwestern Dietrich Building 800 693-3018
331 Sw 57th Ave Ocala (34474) *(G-11353)*

Clarkwstern Dtrich Bldg System 954 772-6300
1001 Nw 58th Ct Fort Lauderdale (33309) *(G-3730)*

Clarkwstern Dtrich Bldg System 800 543-7140
38020 Pulp Dr Dade City (33523) *(G-2316)*

Clasic Fishing Products, Clermont *Also called Cind-Al Inc (G-1863)*

Class 1, Ocala *Also called Hale Products Inc (G-11407)*

Class A Printing LLC 386 447-0520
11 Industry Dr Palm Coast (32137) *(G-13073)*

Classb.com, Tampa *Also called Shirts & Caps Inc (G-17262)*

Classic Architecutal, Oakland Park *Also called Cadillac Graphics Inc (G-11249)*

Classic Auto A Mnfactoring Inc 813 251-2356
4901 W Rio Vista Ave A Tampa (33634) *(G-16713)*

Classic Canvas & Upholstery 954 850-4994
1934 Cleveland St Hollywood (33020) *(G-5552)*

Classic Design and Mfg 850 433-4981
909 N Tarragona St Pensacola (32501) *(G-13471)*

Classic Fishing Products Inc (PA) 407 656-6133
13518 Granville Ave Clermont (34711) *(G-1864)*

Classic Hardwood Design 850 232-6473
3895 Highway 97 Molino (32577) *(G-10577)*

Classic Industries Inc 561 855-4609
3111 Fortune Way Wellington (33414) *(G-17849)*

Classic Installations LLC 954 966-1148
2401 Sw 32nd Ave Pembroke Park (33023) *(G-13362)*

Classic Iron Decor Inc 904 241-5022
1004 10th Ave S Jacksonville Beach (32250) *(G-6631)*

Classic Kitchens Brevard Inc 321 327-5972
670 S Wickham Rd Melbourne (32904) *(G-8389)*

Classic Mail Corp 386 290-0309
247 Brookline Ave Daytona Beach (32118) *(G-2529)*

Classic Metal Fabrication Inc 561 305-9532
121 Nw 11th St Boca Raton (33432) *(G-463)*

Classic Motor Sport, Holly Hill *Also called Motorsport Marketing Inc (G-5516)*

Classic Pizza Crusts Inc 954 570-8383
841 Mockingbird Ln Plantation (33324) *(G-13835)*

Classic Screen 407 699-2473
1021 Chesterfield Cir Winter Springs (32708) *(G-18562)*

Classic Screen Prtg Design Inc 407 850-0112
1353 Pine Ave Orlando (32824) *(G-12018)*

Classic Shirts Inc 850 875-2200
110 Zeta St Quincy (32351) *(G-14543)*

Classic Sign & Mirror, Pensacola *Also called Classic Design and Mfg (G-13471)*

Classic Stars Inc 305 871-6767
2355 Nw 35th Ave Miami (33142) *(G-8930)*

Classic Stucco & Stone LLC 850 892-1045
3148 Rock Hill Rd Defuniak Springs (32435) *(G-2838)*

Classic Trim Wtp Inc 305 258-3090
25400 Sw 141st Ave Ste B Princeton (33032) *(G-14487)*

Classic Uniforms, Hialeah *Also called Fashion Connection Miami Inc (G-5151)*

Classic Yacht Refinishing Inc 954 760-9626
1881 W State Road 84 # 10 Fort Lauderdale (33315) *(G-3731)*

Classica & Telecard Corp 239 354-3727
12355 Collier Blvd Ste C Naples (34116) *(G-10716)*

Classica TIcard Comm Srervices, Naples *Also called Classica & Telecard Corp (G-10716)*

Classics Reborn Publishing LLC 727 232-6739
9954 Sweet Bay Ct New Port Richey (34654) *(G-10965)*

Classique Style Inc 561 995-7557
6590 W Rogers Cir Ste 8 Boca Raton (33487) *(G-464)*

Clawson Custom Cues Inc (PA) 904 448-8748
7255 Salisbury Rd Ste 1 Jacksonvi le (32256) *(G-5981)*

Clayton Industries, Lake City *Also called Linman Inc (G-7028)*

CLC, Orlando *Also called Control Laser Corporation (G-12045)*

Clean & Shine Auto Marine 239 261-6563
4451 Gulf Shore Blvd N Naples (34103) *(G-10717)*

Clean Cut Intl LLC 866 599-7066
14255 Us Highway 1 Juno Beach (33408) *(G-6662)*

Clean Energy ESb Inc 202 905-6726
600 Biltmore Way Apt 508 Coral Gables (33134) *(G-2040)*

Clean Pack Products, Tampa *Also called Cleanpak Products LLC (G-16714)*

Clean Skin Club, Delray Beach *Also called Clean Skin LLC (G-2945)*

Clean Skin LLC 203 997-2491
1240 Tangelo Ter Ste B11 Delray Beach (33444) *(G-2945)*

Cleancor Eqp Solutions LLC (HQ) 954 523-2200
2200 Eller Dr Fort Lauderdale (33316) *(G-3732)*

Cleanpak Products LLC 813 740-8611
221 Hobbs St Ste 108 Tampa (33619) *(G-16714)*

Clear Choice Inc 407 830-6968
1045 Miller Dr Altamonte Springs (32701) *(G-38)*

Clear Copy Inc 561 369-3900
1304 N Federal Hwy Boynton Beach (33435) *(G-851)*

Clear Distribution Inc 904 330-5624
6611 Sthpint Pkwy Ste C30 Jacksconville (32216) *(G-5982)*

Clear Horizon Ventures Company 727 372-1100
9410 Eden Ave Hudson (34667) *(G-5766)*

Clear View Coatings LLC 850 210-0155
4514 Deslin Ct Tallahassee (32305) *(G-16424)*

Clear View Glass & Glazing 561 441-7675
509 Eldorado Ln Delray Beach (33444) *(G-2946)*

Clear Vision Signs and Systems, Wesley Chapel *Also called Graphics Pdts Excellence Inc (G-17878)*

Clear-Vue Inc (PA) 727 726-5386
905 Delaware St Safety Harbor (34695) *(G-14784)*

Clearant Inc (PA) 407 876-3134
6001 Lexington Park Orlando (32819) *(G-12019)*

Clearly Derm LLC (PA) 561 353-3376
7050 W Palmetto Park Rd # 30 Boca Raton (33433) *(G-465)*

Clearwater Engineering Inc 727 573-2210
14605 49th St N Ste 19 Clearwater (33762) *(G-1542)*

Clearwater Enviro Tech Inc 727 209-6400
8767 115th Ave Largo (33773) *(G-7565)*

Clearwater Manufacturing Co 813 818-0959
203 Tower Dr Oldsmar (34677) *(G-11638)*

Clero Enterprises Inc 305 681-4877
3881 Nw 125th St Opa Locka (33054) *(G-11730)*

Cleva Power, Boca Raton *Also called Cleva Technologies LLC (G-466)*

Cleva Technologies LLC 561 654-5279
1951 Nw 19th St Ste 101 Boca Raton (33431) *(G-466)*

Cleveland Diabetes Care Inc (PA) 904 394-2620
10752 Deerwood Park Blvd Jacksonville (32256) *(G-5983)*

Clever Cabinetry LLC 813 992-0020
10513 Anglecrest Dr Riverview (33569) *(G-14559)*

Clever Covers Inc 407 423-5959
524 W Winter Park St Orlando (32804) *(G-12020)*

Clever Pavers Inc 239 633-7048
2727 Clnl Blvd Apt 204 Fort Myers (33907) *(G-4210)*

Clewiston News, Okeechobee *Also called Independent Newsmedia Inc USA (G-11609)*

Clewiston Water Btlg Co LLC 863 902-1317
615 Commerce Ct Clewiston (33440) *(G-1886)*

Clifton Studio Inc 813 240-0286
4710 Eisenhower Blvd D Tampa (33634) *(G-16715)*

Climax Inc 786 264-6082
10401 Nw 28th St Doral (33172) *(G-3165)*

Climb Your Mountain Inc 571 571-8623
11345 Nw 122nd St Medley (33178) *(G-8219)*

Cline Aluminum Doors Inc 941 746-4104
112 32nd Ave W Bradenton (34205) *(G-962)*

Cline Group, Palm Beach Gardens *Also called Cline Resource and Dev Co (G-12961)*

Cline Resource and Dev Co (PA) 561 626-4999
3825 Pga Blvd Ste 1101 Palm Beach Gardens (33410) *(G-12961)*

Clinical Chmstry Spclists Corp 919 554-1424
6901 Okeechobee Blvd D5-L3 West Palm Beach (33411) *(G-17967)*

Clinical Dagnstc Solutions Inc 954 791-1773
1800 Nw 65th Ave Plantation (33313) *(G-13836)*

Clinical Refractions Perfected, Fort Myers *Also called Clinicon Corporation (G-4211)*

Clinicon Corporation 239 939-1345
3949 Evans Ave Ste 107 Fort Myers (33901) *(G-4211)*

CLJ Industries Inc 562 688-0508
6015 Chester Cir Ste 213 Jacksonville (32217) *(G-5984)*

Cljp Inc 850 678-8819
200 Hart St Niceville (32578) *(G-11028)*

Clock Spring Company Inc 561 683-6992
3875 Fiscal Ct Riviera Beach (33404) *(G-14610)*

Clondalkin LLC 866 545-8703
10950 Belcher Rd S Largo (33777) *(G-7566)*

Clonts Groves Inc 407 359-4103
285 Howard Ave Oviedo (32765) *(G-12813)*

Clorox Healthcare Holdings LLC 904 996-7758
3611 Saint Johns Ave 1 Jacksonville (32205) *(G-5985)*

Closet Rodz LLC (PA) 386 212-8188
215 Greenwood Ave Ormond Beach (32174) *(G-12750)*

Closet Systems, Clearwater *Also called Wall Bed Systems Inc (G-1848)*

Closetmaid LLC (HQ) 352 401-6000
13485 Veterans Way Orlando (32827) *(G-12021)*

Closetmaid LLC 352 351-6100
720 Sw 17th Pl Ocala (34471) *(G-11354)*

Closets By Design, Fort Lauderdale *Also called Riverstone Snctary - Cbd - Inc (G-4020)*

Clothesline Inc 850 877-9171
1369 E Lafayette St Ste A Tallahassee (32301) *(G-16425)*

Clothing, Sunrise *Also called Kikisteescom LLC (G-16333)*

Cloud Industries 816 213-2730
8275 Shadow Pine Way Sarasota (34238) *(G-15634)*

Cloud Veneer LLC 305 230-7379
1001 Brickell Bay Dr # 2700 Miami (33131) *(G-8931)*

Cloudfactors LLC 407 768-3160
7380 W Sand Lake Rd # 500 Orlando (32819) *(G-12022)*

Cloudkiss Beverages Inc 407 324-8500
3031 S Mellonville Ave Sanford (32773) *(G-15285)*

Clover Interior Systems Inc 941 484-1300
505 Lyons Bay Rd Nokomis (34275) *(G-11044)*

Clr Roasters LLC 305 591-0040
2131 Nw 72nd Ave Miami (33122) *(G-8932)*

Clrs Solutions LLC 612 481-9244
1723 Winsloe Dr Trinity (34655) *(G-17634)*

Cls Holdings Usa Inc (PA) 888 438-9132
11767 S Dixie Hwy Ste 115 Pinecrest (33156) *(G-13665)*

(G-0000) Company's Geographic Section entry number

Club Information Systems, Tampa *Also called Technolgy Training Associates* *(G-17344)*
Clupper LLC 386 956-6396
  2386 Pavillion Ter Deltona (32738) *(G-3042)*
Clutch House, Fort Lauderdale *Also called Warden Enterprises Inc* *(G-4121)*
Clx Engineering, Sanford *Also called Contrologix LLC* *(G-15292)*
Cm2 Industries Inc 305 685-4812
  1769 Opa Locka Blvd Opa Locka (33054) *(G-11731)*
CMA Interactive Corporation 954 336-6403
  5011 Neptune Ln Fort Lauderdale (33312) *(G-3733)*
CMC Bakery LLC 978 682-2382
  4100 N Powerline Rd M2 Pompano Beach (33073) *(G-13970)*
CMC Steel Fabricators, Jacksonville *Also called Commercial Metals Company* *(G-5995)*
CMC Steel Florida, Jacksonville *Also called CMC Steel Us LLC* *(G-5986)*
CMC Steel Us LLC 904 266-4261
  16770 Rebar Rd Jacksonville (32234) *(G-5986)*
Cme Arma Inc 305 633-1524
  4500 Nw 36th Ave Miami (33142) *(G-8933)*
CMF, Pompano Beach *Also called Certified Metal Finishing Inc* *(G-13968)*
CMF Medicon Surgical Inc 904 642-7500
  11200 St Jhns Indus Pkwy Jacksonville (32246) *(G-5987)*
CMF Truss Inc 352 796-5805
  13521 Ponce De Leon Blvd Brooksville (34601) *(G-1146)*
CMI, Opa Locka *Also called C M I Enterprises Inc* *(G-11726)*
CMI, Leesburg *Also called Consolidated Minerals Inc* *(G-7764)*
CMI International, Sanford *Also called Gator Dock & Marine LLC* *(G-15324)*
CMI Microclimates, Inverness *Also called Custom Manufacturing Inc* *(G-5824)*
CMI Microclimates Inc 607 569-2738
  1720 S Tranquil Ave Inverness (34450) *(G-5822)*
Cmk, Roseland *Also called Gypsy Mining Inc* *(G-14757)*
Cmn Steel Fabricators Inc 305 592-5466
  7993 Nw 60th St Miami (33166) *(G-8934)*
CMS, Sarasota *Also called Chism Manufacturing Svcs LLC* *(G-15454)*
Cmsi, Weston *Also called Contract Mfg Solutions Inc* *(G-18234)*
Cmz Industries LLC 727 726-1443
  27232 Us Highway 19 N Clearwater (33761) *(G-1543)*
Cnc Aircraft Inc 305 657-1230
  7901 4th St N Ste 4616 Saint Petersburg (33702) *(G-15008)*
Cnc Cabinet Components Inc 321 956-3470
  560 Distribution Dr Melbourne (32904) *(G-8390)*
Cnc Works Service Inc 813 777-8642
  13584 49th St N Ste 5 Clearwater (33762) *(G-1544)*
Cnc-Precision Machining Corp 786 452-9575
  1055 E 26th St Hialeah (33013) *(G-5093)*
Cnd Express Scooters LLC 407 633-1079
  721 Pincon Ln Kissimmee (34759) *(G-6975)*
Cngas Group, Hollywood *Also called Greengood Energy Corp* *(G-5585)*
Cnh Industrial America LLC 954 389-9779
  3265 Meridian Pkwy # 124 Weston (33331) *(G-18233)*
Cnr Precision Tool Inc 954 426-9650
  8480 Nw 29th Ct Coral Springs (33065) *(G-2141)*
Cns Signs Inc 904 733-4806
  3539 W Beaver St Jacksonville (32254) *(G-5988)*
Co2meter Inc 386 310-4933
  131 Business Center Dr A3 Ormond Beach (32174) *(G-12751)*
Co2meter.com, Ormond Beach *Also called Co2meter Inc* *(G-12751)*
Coale Industries, Miami *Also called TNT Packaging Inc* *(G-10016)*
Coast Controls Inc 941 355-7555
  7500 Commerce Ct Sarasota (34243) *(G-15456)*
Coast Laser Center, Sarasota *Also called Family of Smith Inc* *(G-15476)*
Coast Products LLC 850 235-2090
  169 Griffin Blvd Unit 106 Panama City Beach (32413) *(G-13328)*
Coast To Coast Designs, Miami *Also called One World Resource LLC* *(G-9653)*
Coast To Coast Solar Inc 813 406-6501
  19209 N Us Highway 41 Lutz (33549) *(G-7984)*
Coast Wcp 727 572-4249
  1806 Gunn Hwy Odessa (33556) *(G-11543)*
Coastal, Palm Beach Gardens *Also called Oldcastle Apg South Inc* *(G-12995)*
Coastal Acquisitions Fla LLC (PA) 850 769-9423
  2120 E Business 98 Panama City (32401) *(G-13243)*
Coastal Acquisitions Fla LLC 850 769-9423
  2120 E 5th St Panama City (32401) *(G-13244)*
Coastal Aircraft Parts LLC 954 980-6929
  2999 Nw 115th Ter Sunrise (33323) *(G-16305)*
Coastal and Mainland Cabinets, Fort Myers *Also called Mobius Business Group Inc (G-4327)*
Coastal Awngs Hrrcane Prtction 407 923-9482
  14438 Avalon Reserve Blvd Orlando (32828) *(G-12023)*
Coastal Cabinets & Countertops 850 424-3940
  12889 Us Highway 98 W 109a Miramar Beach (32550) *(G-10569)*
Coastal Canvas and Awning Co 239 433-1114
  5761 Independence Cir # 1 Fort Myers (33912) *(G-4212)*
Coastal Communications Corp 561 989-0600
  2500 N Military Trl # 283 Boca Raton (33431) *(G-467)*
Coastal Concrete Products LLC 239 208-4079
  7742 Alico Rd Fort Myers (33912) *(G-4213)*
Coastal Craftsmen Aluminum Inc (PA) 727 868-8802
  15046 Labor Pl Hudson (34667) *(G-5767)*

Coastal Crane and Rigging Inc 850 460-1766
  54 Pisces Dr Santa Rosa Beach (32459) *(G-15423)*
Coastal Dewatering, Clearwater *Also called Portable Pumping Systems Inc* *(G-1744)*
Coastal Directory Company 321 777-7076
  1900 S Hbr Cy Blvd Ste 30 Melbourne (32901) *(G-8391)*
Coastal Door & Mllwk Svcs LLC 561 266-3716
  1300 Sw 10th St Delray Beach (33444) *(G-2947)*
Coastal Electric 239 245-7396
  5760 Youngquist Rd Ste 9 Fort Myers (33912) *(G-4214)*
Coastal Films of Florida 904 786-2031
  627 Lane Ave N Jacksonville (32254) *(G-5989)*
Coastal Foam Systems LLC 850 470-9827
  3276 W Scott St Pensacola (32505) *(G-13472)*
Coastal Forest Resources Co (PA) 850 539-6432
  8007 Fl Ga Hwy Havana (32333) *(G-4996)*
Coastal Fuels Mktg Inc 941 722-7753
  804 N Dock St Palmetto (34221) *(G-13161)*
Coastal Hurricane Film LLC 941 268-9693
  807 Thornton Ave Nw Port Charlotte (33948) *(G-14293)*
Coastal Industries Inc (PA) 904 642-3970
  3700 St Jhns Indus Pkwy W Jacksonville (32246) *(G-5990)*
Coastal Kitchen Interiors, Naples *Also called Jfaure LLC* *(G-10790)*
Coastal Logging Inc 850 832-0133
  4138 Harry Wells Rd Panama City (32409) *(G-13245)*
Coastal Machine LLC 850 769-6117
  7424 Coastal Dr Panama City (32404) *(G-13246)*
Coastal Marine Power Inc 941 322-8182
  30710 Saddlebag Trl Myakka City (34251) *(G-10644)*
Coastal Mfg & Fabrication Inc 352 799-8706
  16208 Cortez Blvd Brooksville (34601) *(G-1147)*
Coastal Millworks Inc 561 881-7755
  3810 Consumer St Ste 2 West Palm Beach (33404) *(G-17968)*
Coastal Millworx LLC 850 250-6672
  1714 Wolfrun Ln Panama City (32405) *(G-13247)*
Coastal Observer, Lake Worth *Also called Lake Worth Herald Press Inc* *(G-7214)*
Coastal Paddle Co LLC 850 916-1600
  848 Gulf Breeze Pkwy Gulf Breeze (32561) *(G-4878)*
Coastal Plywood LLC 800 359-6432
  8007 Fl Ga Hwy Havana (32333) *(G-4997)*
Coastal Plywood Company, Havana *Also called Coastal Plywood LLC* *(G-4997)*
Coastal Powder Coatings Inc 772 283-5311
  2049 Sw Poma Dr Palm City (34990) *(G-13030)*
Coastal Printing Inc Sarasota 941 351-1515
  4391 Independence Ct Sarasota (34234) *(G-15635)*
Coastal Promotions Inc 850 460-2270
  128 Indian Bayou Dr Destin (32541) *(G-3062)*
Coastal RE-Manufacturing Inc 727 869-4808
  7620 Valencia Ave Port Richey (34668) *(G-14358)*
Coastal Scents, Bonita Springs *Also called K-Plex LLC* *(G-808)*
Coastal Screen & Rail LLC 321 917-4605
  1127 Poinsettia Dr Delray Beach (33444) *(G-2948)*
Coastal Sheet Mtalof S Fla LLC 561 718-6044
  8927 Hypoluxo Rd Ste A4 Lake Worth (33467) *(G-7192)*
Coastal Site Development, Fort Myers *Also called Coastal Concrete Products LLC* *(G-4213)*
Coastal Timberlands, Havana *Also called Coastal Forest Resources Co* *(G-4996)*
Coastal Treated Products LLC 850 539-6432
  8007 Fl Ga Hwy Havana (32333) *(G-4998)*
Coastal Wipers Inc (PA) 813 628-4464
  5705 E Hanna Ave Tampa (33610) *(G-16716)*
Coastal Wldg Fabrications Inc 954 938-7933
  740 Ne 45th St Oakland Park (33334) *(G-11252)*
Coastal Woodwork Inc 561 218-3353
  380 Sw 12th Ave Pompano Beach (33069) *(G-13971)*
Coastland Specialties LLC 239 910-5401
  28340 Trails Edge Blvd Bonita Springs (34134) *(G-791)*
Coastline Cbntry Cstm Mllwk LL 239 208-2876
  6440 Metro Plantation Rd Fort Myers (33966) *(G-4215)*
Coastline Marine, Pompano Beach *Also called US Recreational Alliance Inc* *(G-14232)*
Coastline Whl Sgns Led Disp LL 386 238-6200
  532 N Segrave St Daytona Beach (32114) *(G-2530)*
Coastline Whl Signs Svcs Ltd 386 238-6200
  532 N Segrave St Daytona Beach (32114) *(G-2531)*
Coating Application Tech Inc 781 850-5080
  1851 67th Ave E Sarasota (34243) *(G-15457)*
Coating Heaven, Orlando *Also called Nejat Arslaner* *(G-12410)*
Coating Laminating Converting, Green Cove Springs *Also called Tape Technologies Inc (G-4838)*
Coating Technology Inc 813 854-3674
  360 Scarlet Blvd Oldsmar (34677) *(G-11639)*
Coatings Smples Sltons Etc LLC 863 398-8513
  5515 Summerland Hills Dr Lakeland (33812) *(G-7293)*
Cob Industries Inc 321 723-3200
  6909 Vickie Cir West Melbourne (32904) *(G-17897)*
Cobalt Laboratories Inc 239 390-0245
  24840 S Tamiami Trl Ste 1 Bonita Springs (34134) *(G-792)*
Cobalt Laser 407 855-2833
  965 W Taft Vineland Rd # 107 Orlando (32824) *(G-12024)*
Cobb America, Deerfield Beach *Also called Advanced Outdoor Concepts Inc* *(G-2657)*

Cobex Recorders Inc 954 425-0003
6601 Lyons Rd Ste F8 Coconut Creek (33073) *(G-1981)*

Cobham Mission System Corp 850 226-6717
706 Anchors St Nw Fort Walton Beach (32548) *(G-4570)*

Cobham Satcom 407 650-9054
1538 Tropic Park Dr Sanford (32773) *(G-15286)*

Cobra Power Corporation 305 893-5018
13353 Ne 17th Ave North Miami (33181) *(G-11099)*

Coca Cola Bottling Co 813 569-3030
599 Lake Kathy Dr Brandon (33510) *(G-1087)*

Coca-Cola, Panama City *Also called Ccbcc Operations LLC* *(G-13238)*

Coca-Cola, Miami *Also called C C 1 Limited Partnership* *(G-8869)*

Coca-Cola Beverages Fla LLC 813 612-6631
4409 Madison Indus Ln Tampa (33619) *(G-16717)*

Coca-Cola Beverages Fla LLC 813 623-5411
9102 Sabal Indus Blvd Tampa (33619) *(G-16718)*

Coca-Cola Beverages Fla LLC 863 499-6300
1770 Interstate Dr Lakeland (33805) *(G-7294)*

Coca-Cola Beverages Fla LLC 941 953-3151
2150 47th St Sarasota (34234) *(G-15636)*

Coca-Cola Beverages Fla LLC 954 985-5000
3350 Pembroke Rd Hollywood (33021) *(G-5553)*

Coca-Cola Beverages Fla LLC (PA) 800 438-2653
10117 Princess Palm Ave Tampa (33610) *(G-16719)*

Coca-Cola Beverages Fla LLC 407 295-9290
2900 Mercy Dr Orlando (32808) *(G-12025)*

Coca-Cola Beverages Fla LLC 904 786-2720
1411 Huron St Jacksonville (32254) *(G-5991)*

Coca-Cola Beverages Fla LLC 386 239-3100
222 Fentress Blvd Daytona Beach (32114) *(G-2532)*

Coca-Cola Beverages Fla LLC 305 872-9715
30801 Avenue A Big Pine Key (33043) *(G-372)*

Coca-Cola Beverages Fla LLC 305 378-1073
16569 Sw 117th Ave Miami (33177) *(G-8935)*

Coca-Cola Bottling Co 305 378-1073
16569 Sw 117th Ave Miami (33177) *(G-8936)*

Coca-Cola Bottling Co Untd Inc 850 785-0697
2825 Forester Trl Panama City (32405) *(G-13248)*

Coca-Cola Bottling Co Untd Inc 850 678-9370
647 Valparaiso Pkwy Valparaiso (32580) *(G-17658)*

Coca-Cola Bottling Co Untd Inc 850 478-4800
7330 N Davis Hwy Pensacola (32504) *(G-13473)*

Coca-Cola Bottling Co Untd Inc 850 575-6122
2050 Maryland Cir Tallahassee (32303) *(G-16426)*

Coca-Cola Btlg Centl Fla LLC 832 260-0462
235 W Brandon Blvd Brandon (33511) *(G-1088)*

Coca-Cola Company 407 886-1568
2659 Orange Ave Apopka (32703) *(G-111)*

Coca-Cola Company 954 985-5000
3350 Pembroke Rd Hollywood (33021) *(G-5554)*

Coca-Cola Company 404 676-2121
2651 Orange Ave Apopka (32703) *(G-112)*

Coca-Cola Company 407 565-2465
2651 Orange Ave Apopka (32703) *(G-113)*

Coca-Cola Company 727 736-7101
427 San Christopher Dr Dunedin (34698) *(G-3446)*

Coca-Cola Company 407 295-9290
2900 Mercy Dr Orlando (32808) *(G-12026)*

Coca-Cola Company 407 358-6758
2501 Orange Ave Apopka (32703) *(G-114)*

Coca-Cola Company Distribution 407 814-1327
1451 Ocoee Apopka Rd Apopka (32703) *(G-115)*

Coca-Cola Refreshments USA Inc 863 551-3700
705 Main St Auburndale (33823) *(G-225)*

Coco Cosmetics Inc 305 622-3488
20325 Ne 15th Ct Miami (33179) *(G-8937)*

Coco Gelato Corp (PA) 786 621-2444
3514 Nw 36th St Miami (33142) *(G-8938)*

Coco Lopez Inc (PA) 954 450-3100
3401 Sw 160th Ave Ste 350 Miramar (33027) *(G-10481)*

Cocoa Bch Wtr Reclamation Dept, Cocoa Beach *Also called City of Cocoa Beach* *(G-1967)*

Cocoa Customs RC, Cocoa *Also called Cutting Edge Mch Fbrcation LLC* *(G-1913)*

Coconut Tree Btq & Gallery, Seminole *Also called Preferred Custom Printing LLC* *(G-15987)*

Cocrystal Discovery Inc 425 750-7208
4400 Biscayne Blvd # 101 Miami (33137) *(G-8939)*

Cocrystal Pharma Inc 877 262-7123
4400 Biscayne Blvd Miami (33137) *(G-8940)*

Coda Octopus Group Inc (PA) 407 735-2402
3300 S Hiawassee Rd # 104 Orlando (32835) *(G-12027)*

Code 1 Inc 786 347-7755
14048 Prater Ct Jacksonville (32224) *(G-5992)*

Codsworth Industries Inc 203 622-5151
12864 Biscayne Blvd Ste 3 North Miami (33181) *(G-11100)*

Coeur De Lion Inc 727 442-4808
1610 N Myrtle Ave Clearwater (33755) *(G-1545)*

Coffee Candy Store, The, Miami Lakes *Also called Candies and Beyond Inc* *(G-10290)*

Coffee Clloid Productions LLC 305 424-8900
12240 Sw 132nd Ct Miami (33186) *(G-8941)*

Coffee Unlimited LLC 305 685-6366
12815 Nw 45th Ave Ste 6b Opa Locka (33054) *(G-11732)*

Coffin Cabinetry & Trim Michae 352 217-3729
91 S Pine Ave Umatilla (32784) *(G-17645)*

Coffman Systems Inc 813 891-1300
300 Stevens Ave Oldsmar (34677) *(G-11640)*

Cofran International Corp 305 592-2644
1540 Nw 94th Ave Doral (33172) *(G-3166)*

Cogswell Innovations Inc 954 245-8877
2000 E Oklnd Prk Blvd # 106 Fort Lauderdale (33306) *(G-3734)*

Cohagan Engineering Inc 561 842-7779
5307 East Ave Ste 6 West Palm Beach (33407) *(G-17969)*

Cohen Capital LLC 954 661-8270
3020 E Commercial Blvd Fort Lauderdale (33308) *(G-3735)*

Coin-O-Matic Inc 305 635-4141
3950 Nw 31st Ave Miami (33142) *(G-8942)*

Coinweek LLC 407 786-5555
306 N Swetwater Cove Blvd Longwood (32779) *(G-7881)*

Cojali Usa Inc 305 960-7651
2200 Nw 102nd Ave Ste 4b Doral (33172) *(G-3167)*

Cola Group Riverside LLC 305 940-0277
16047 Collins Ave # 2103 Sunny Isles Beach (33160) *(G-16269)*

Colaianni Italian Flr Tile Mfg 954 321-8244
700 Sw 21st Ter Fort Lauderdale (33312) *(G-3736)*

Cold Fire Direct, Miami Beach *Also called Stuntwear LLC* *(G-10237)*

Cold Stone Creamery-Parkland 954 341-8033
6230 Coral Ridge Dr # 110 Coral Springs (33076) *(G-2142)*

Cold Storage Engineering Co (PA) 305 448-0099
703 Nw 62nd Ave Ste 650 Miami (33126) *(G-8943)*

Coldflo Inc 305 324-8555
1050 Nw 21st St Miami (33127) *(G-8944)*

Cole Enterprises Inc 727 441-4101
436 E Shore Dr Clearwater (33767) *(G-1546)*

Cole Machine LLC 239 571-4364
5740 Shirley St Naples (34109) *(G-10718)*

Cole Machine Naples, Naples *Also called Cole Machine LLC* *(G-10718)*

Cole-Parmer Instrument Co LLC 352 854-8080
5350 Sw 1st Ln Ocala (34474) *(G-11355)*

Coleman Aerospace 407 354-0047
5950 Lakehurst Dr Orlando (32819) *(G-12028)*

Coleo LLC 215 436-0902
1198 Champions Dr Daytona Beach (32124) *(G-2533)*

Colitz Mining Co Inc 352 795-2409
7040 N Suncoast Blvd Crystal River (34428) *(G-2272)*

Coll Builders Supply Inc 407 745-4641
6663 Narcoossee Rd # 178 Orlando (32822) *(G-12029)*

Collaborative Sftwr Solutions 954 753-2025
4721 Nw 115th Ave Coral Springs (33076) *(G-2143)*

Collectibles of SW Florida 239 332-2344
1502 Ne 11th Ter Cape Coral (33909) *(G-1325)*

Collective, The, Miami *Also called Watchfacts Inc* *(G-10124)*

Collegefrog Inc 850 696-1500
418 W Garden St Pensacola (32502) *(G-13474)*

Collfix Inc 754 264-0959
365 Sw 16th St Boca Raton (33432) *(G-468)*

Collidecom LLC 407 903-5626
4700 Mllnia Blvdn Ste 400 Orlando (32839) *(G-12030)*

Collier Business Systems 239 649-5554
2280 Linwood Ave Naples (34112) *(G-10719)*

Collins Aerospace (PA) 704 423-7000
777 S Flagler Dr Ste 1800 West Palm Beach (33401) *(G-17970)*

Collins Media & Advg LLC 954 688-9758
5453 Nw 24th St Ste 2 Margate (33063) *(G-8124)*

Collins Mfg Inc 407 889-9669
672 Johns Rd Apopka (32703) *(G-116)*

Collins Research Inc 321 401-6060
6790 Edgwter Cmmerce Pkwy Orlando (32810) *(G-12031)*

Colloidal Dynamics LLC 904 686-1536
5150 Palm Valley Rd # 303 Ponte Vedra Beach (32082) *(G-14265)*

Colonial Industries Centl Fla 407 484-5239
462 Mohave Ter Lake Mary (32746) *(G-7066)*

Colonial Press Intl Inc 305 633-1581
3690 Nw 50th St Miami (33142) *(G-8945)*

Colonial Ready Mix LLC 941 698-4022
5250 Linwood Rd Placida (33946) *(G-13734)*

Colonna Shipyard 904 246-1183
1701 Mayport Rd Atlantic Beach (32233) *(G-206)*

Color Concepts Prtg Design Co 813 623-2921
2602 Tampa East Blvd Tampa (33619) *(G-16720)*

Color Express Inc 305 558-2061
7990 W 25th Ct Hialeah (33016) *(G-5094)*

Color K Graphics, Miami *Also called K Color Corp* *(G-9382)*

Color Mstr Pressure Washer Inc 561 366-7747
7800 Springfield Lake Dr Lake Worth (33467) *(G-7193)*

Color Press Corp 786 621-8491
1835 Nw 112th Ave Ste 184 Miami (33172) *(G-8946)*

Color Press Print Inc 850 763-9884
3430 Highway 77 Ste D Panama City (32405) *(G-13249)*

Color Touch Inc 954 444-1999
3701 Nw 16th St Lauderhill (33311) *(G-7728)*

Color-Chrome Technologies Inc 954 335-0127
2345 Sw 34th St Fort Lauderdale (33312) *(G-3737)*

(G-0000) Company's Geographic Section entry number

Coloramax Printing Inc 305 541-0322
3215 Nw 7th St Miami (33125) *(G-8947)*
Colorbyte Software, Lutz *Also called Colorproof Software Inc (G-7985)*
Colorfast Coml Prtg Grphics Sv, Clearwater *Also called Colorfast Printing & Graphics (G-1547)*
Colorfast Printing & Graphics 727 531-9506
14114 63rd Way N Clearwater (33760) *(G-1547)*
Colorgraphx Inc 727 572-6364
1551 102nd Ave N Ste A Saint Petersburg (33716) *(G-15009)*
Colormet Foods LLC 888 775-3966
3610 Ne 1st Ave Miami (33137) *(G-8948)*
Colorprint Design 305 229-8880
1220 Sw 78th Ct Miami (33144) *(G-8949)*
Colorproof Software Inc 813 963-0241
234 Crystal Grove Blvd Lutz (33548) *(G-7985)*
Colortone Inc 954 455-0200
6531 Nw 18th Ct Plantation (33313) *(G-13837)*
Colossus Pavers LLC 239 601-5230
2118 Sw 39th St Cape Coral (33914) *(G-1326)*
Columbia Care Florida, Arcadia *Also called Ccf Holdco LLC (G-189)*
Columbia Films Inc 800 531-3238
43 S Pompano Pkwy Ste 461 Pompano Beach (33069) *(G-13972)*
Columbia Parcar Corp 352 753-0244
2505 Industrial St Leesburg (34748) *(G-7763)*
Columbia Ready Mix Concrete (PA) 386 755-2458
516 Nw Waldo St Lake City (32055) *(G-7014)*
Com Pac Filtration Inc 904 356-4003
2020 W Beaver St Jacksonville (32209) *(G-5993)*
Com-Ten Industries, Saint Petersburg *Also called Giebner Enterprises Inc (G-15061)*
Coma Cast Corp 305 667-6797
4383 Sw 70th Ct Miami (33155) *(G-8950)*
Combat Systems Mssion Radiness, Orlando *Also called Northrop Grumman Systems Corp (G-12422)*
Comcept Solutions LLC 727 535-1900
13799 Park Blvd Ste 307 Seminole (33776) *(G-15972)*
Comdial Real Estate Co Inc 941 564-9208
106 Cattlemen Rd Sarasota (34232) *(G-15637)*
Come Taste The Love Malaysia, Miami *Also called Wynot International LLC (G-10148)*
Comerint Inc 813 443-2466
5125 W Rio Vista Ave Tampa (33634) *(G-16721)*
Comex Systems Inc 908 881-6301
9380 Nastrand Cir Port Charlotte (33981) *(G-14294)*
Comfort Brace LLC 954 899-1563
1971 Ne 31st St Lighthouse Point (33064) *(G-7826)*
Comida Vida Inc 855 720-7663
5600 Elmhurst Cir Oviedo (32765) *(G-12814)*
Comlabs, Melbourne *Also called Communications Labs Inc (G-8392)*
Comm Dots LLC Connecting 305 505-6009
3890 Coco Grove Ave Miami (33133) *(G-8951)*
Command Medical Products Inc 386 677-7775
15 Signal Ave Ormond Beach (32174) *(G-12752)*
Commercial Acoustics, Tampa *Also called Residential Acoustics LLC (G-17216)*
Commercial Cabinetry LLC 407 440-4601
6135 Cyril Ave Orlando (32809) *(G-12032)*
Commercial Concrete Pdts Inc 813 659-3707
2705 Sammonds Rd Plant City (33563) *(G-13756)*
Commercial Division, Jacksonville *Also called Fluidra Usa LLC (G-6115)*
Commercial Door Systems Fla LL 850 466-5906
612 W Romana St Pensacola (32502) *(G-13475)*
Commercial Duct Systems LLC 877 237-3828
9707 Williams Rd Thonotosassa (33592) *(G-17561)*
Commercial Energy Services 904 589-1059
1528 Virgils Way Ste 14 Green Cove Springs (32043) *(G-4822)*
Commercial Gates and Elc LLC 386 454-2329
27317 Nw 78th Ave High Springs (32643) *(G-5454)*
Commercial Instllation Systems 727 525-2372
6175 Wdrow Wilson Blvd Ne Saint Petersburg (33703) *(G-15010)*
Commercial Insulating Glass Co (PA) 941 378-9100
6200 Porter Rd Sarasota (34240) *(G-15638)*
Commercial Metal Photography 407 295-8182
1934a Silver Star Rd Orlando (32804) *(G-12033)*
Commercial Metals Company 954 921-2500
2025 Tigertail Blvd Dania (33004) *(G-2330)*
Commercial Metals Company 904 262-9770
9625 E Florida Min Blvd Jacksonville (32257) *(G-5994)*
Commercial Metals Company 904 781-4780
10483 General Ave Jacksonville (32220) *(G-5995)*
Commercial Millworks Inc 407 648-2787
1120 S Hughey Ave Ste A Orlando (32806) *(G-12034)*
Commercial Printer Phrm Prtr, Doral *Also called Vista Color Corporation (G-3415)*
Commercial Printers Inc (PA) 954 781-3737
6600 Nw 15th Ave Fort Lauderdale (33309) *(G-3738)*
Commercial Printing, Tallahassee *Also called Bava Inc (G-16417)*
Commercial Rfrg Door Co Inc 941 371-8110
6200 Porter Rd Sarasota (34240) *(G-15639)*
Commercial Signage, Sanford *Also called Onsight Industries LLC (G-15367)*
Commercial Stone Cab Fbrctors 727 209-1141
3120 46th Ave N Saint Petersburg (33714) *(G-15011)*
Commercial Stone Fbrcators Inc 727 209-1141
3120 46th Ave N Saint Petersburg (33714) *(G-15012)*
Commercial Wood Designs Inc 407 302-9063
257 Power Ct Sanford (32771) *(G-15287)*
Common Sense Publishing LLC 561 510-1713
55 Ne 5th Ave Ste 100 Delray Beach (33483) *(G-2949)*
Commonwealth Brands Inc (HQ) 800 481-5814
5900 N Andrews Ave Ste 11 Fort Lauderdale (33309) *(G-3739)*
Commscope Technologies LLC 407 944-9116
11310 Satellite Blvd Orlando (32837) *(G-12035)*
Commski LLC 813 501-0111
13342 Whitmarsh St Spring Hill (34609) *(G-16068)*
Commstructures Inc 850 968-9293
101 E Roberts Rd Pensacola (32534) *(G-13476)*
Communcations Surveillance Inc 305 377-1211
4000 Ponce De Leon Blvd Coral Gables (33146) *(G-2041)*
Communicate 360, Orlando *Also called Open Market Enterprises LLC (G-12440)*
Communication Eqp & Engrg Co 863 357-0798
519 Sw Park St Okeechobee (34972) *(G-11601)*
Communications Labs Inc 321 701-9000
4005 Opportunity Dr Melbourne (32934) *(G-8392)*
Community MGT Systems LLC 561 214-4780
701 Nrthpint Pkwy Ste 150 West Palm Beach (33407) *(G-17971)*
Community News Papers Inc 386 752-1293
180 E Duval St Lake City (32055) *(G-7015)*
Community News Publications, Land O Lakes *Also called Manatee Media Inc (G-7498)*
Community News Publications 813 909-2800
3632 Land O Lkes Blvd Ste Lutz (33549) *(G-7986)*
Community Pharmacy Svcs LLC 727 431-8261
19387 Us Highway 19 N Clearwater (33764) *(G-1548)*
Comoderm Corp 561 756-2929
2175 N Andrews Ave Ste 4 Pompano Beach (33069) *(G-13973)*
Comp U Netcom Inc 407 539-1800
331 N Maitland Ave D10 Maitland (32751) *(G-8054)*
Compact Container Systems LLC 561 392-6910
2500 N Military Trl # 400 Boca Raton (33431) *(G-469)*
Compact Contract Inc 352 817-8058
1822 Sw 34th Ct Ocala (34474) *(G-11356)*
Compak Companies LLC 321 249-9590
751 Cornwall Rd Sanford (32773) *(G-15288)*
Compass Banners & Printing LLC 727 522-7414
5502 Haines Rd N Saint Petersburg (33714) *(G-15013)*
Compass Printing and Marketing 954 856-8331
5218 Nw 15th St Margate (33063) *(G-8125)*
Compass Publishing LLC 407 328-0970
671 Progress Way Sanford (32771) *(G-15289)*
Competition Specialties Inc 386 776-1476
16936 County Road 252 Mc Alpin (32062) *(G-8188)*
Competitor Group Inc 858 450-6510
3407 W Dr Ml King Jr 10 Tampa (33607) *(G-16722)*
Complementary Coatings Corp 386 428-6461
9592 Parksouth Ct Orlando (32837) *(G-12036)*
Complete Access Ctrl Centl Fla 407 498-0067
2013 Jaffa Dr Saint Cloud (34771) *(G-14924)*
Complete Instrmnttion Cntrls I 813 340-8545
11524 Hammock Oaks Ct Lithia (33547) *(G-7832)*
Complete Metal Solutions Intl 954 560-0583
107 Nw 5th Ave Fort Lauderdale (33311) *(G-3740)*
Complete Mold Remediators Inc 305 903-8885
31800 Sw 195th Ave Homestead (33030) *(G-5703)*
Complete Printing Solutions, Jacksonville *Also called WJS Printing Partners Inc (G-6616)*
Compliance Meds Tech LLC 786 319-9826
20855 Ne 16th Ave Ste C13 Miami (33179) *(G-8952)*
Compliancesigns LLC 800 578-1245
16228 Flight Path Dr Brooksville (34604) *(G-1148)*
Component General Inc 727 376-6655
2445 Success Dr Odessa (33556) *(G-11544)*
Componexx Corp 954 236-6569
789 Shotgun Rd Sunrise (33326) *(G-16306)*
Composite Essential Mtls LLC 772 344-0034
315 Nw Peacock Blvd Port St Lucie (34986) *(G-14475)*
Composite Holdings Inc (PA) 321 268-9625
805 Marina Rd Titusville (32796) *(G-17582)*
Composite-Fx Sales LLC 352 538-1624
9069 Se County Road 319 Trenton (32693) *(G-17630)*
Compost Jax, Jacksonville *Also called Sunshine Organics Compost LLC (G-6519)*
COMPOUND MIAMI THE, Miami *Also called A2f LLC (G-8629)*
Comprehensive Grants MGT, Lutz *Also called Gibbons Industries Inc (G-7990)*
Comprhnsive Sleep Disorder Ctr 407 834-1023
851 Douglas Ave Ste 148 Altamonte Springs (32714) *(G-39)*
Compro Solution 407 733-4130
1670 Tropic Park Dr Sanford (32773) *(G-15290)*
Compsys Inc 321 255-0399
4255 Dow Rd Melbourne (32934) *(G-8393)*
Compuclamp, Vero Beach *Also called Theft Protection Com Corp (G-17806)*
Compulink Corporation (HQ) 727 579-1500
1205 Gandy Blvd N Saint Petersburg (33702) *(G-15014)*
Computational Systems Inc 954 846-5030
1300 Concord Ter Ste 400 Sunrise (33323) *(G-16307)*

ALPHABETIC

Computational Systems Inc 863 648-9044
5030 Gateway Blvd Ste 11 Lakeland (33811) ***(G-7295)***
Computech Llc....................786 605-0012
1840 Coral Way Ste 306 Miami (33145) ***(G-8953)***
Computer Center of Sanford, Sanford *Also called Ellis & Associates of Sanford* ***(G-15312)***
Computer Forms & Supplies....................727 535-0422
1198 Hickory Dr Largo (33770) ***(G-7567)***
Computer Technician Inc....................941 479-0242
829 8th Ave W Palmetto (34221) ***(G-13162)***
Computers At Work Inc....................239 571-1050
3033 Winkler Ave Ste 210 Fort Myers (33916) ***(G-4216)***
Comres Industries, Tampa *Also called Metpar Corp* ***(G-17069)***
Comtech Antenna Systems Inc....................407 854-1950
212 Outlook Point Dr # 100 Orlando (32809) ***(G-12037)***
Comtech Systems Inc....................407 854-1950
212 Outlook Point Dr # 100 Orlando (32809) ***(G-12038)***
Comten Industries Inc....................727 520-1200
6405 49th St N Ste A Pinellas Park (33781) ***(G-13677)***
Comtronix US, Fort Myers *Also called Industrial Technology LLC* ***(G-4290)***
Con Serv Manufacturing, Lakeland *Also called Gkwf Inc* ***(G-7337)***
Con-Air Industries Inc....................407 298-5733
4157 Seaboard Rd Orlando (32808) ***(G-12039)***
Conali Express Corp....................954 531-9573
3281 Nw 65th St Fort Lauderdale (33309) ***(G-3741)***
Conc-Steel Inc....................516 882-5551
250 Palm Coast Pkwy Ne Palm Coast (32137) ***(G-13074)***
Concealment Express LLC....................888 904-2722
10066 103rd St Ste 103 Jacksonville (32210) ***(G-5996)***
Concentrated Aloe Corp....................386 673-7566
20 W Tower Cir Ormond Beach (32174) ***(G-12753)***
Concept 2 Market Inc....................954 974-0022
3000 Nw 25th Ave Ste 11 Pompano Beach (33069) ***(G-13974)***
Concept Boats Inc....................305 635-8712
2410 Nw 147th St Opa Locka (33054) ***(G-11733)***
Concept Design and Printing....................813 516-9798
7402 N 56th St Ste 810 Tampa (33617) ***(G-16723)***
Concept Elevator Group LLC (PA)....................786 845-8955
8027 Nw 71st St Miami (33166) ***(G-8954)***
Concept Group LLC....................856 767-5506
350 Hiatt Dr Ste 120 Palm Beach Gardens (33418) ***(G-12962)***
Concept One Custom Cabine....................954 829-3505
5807 Dawson St Hollywood (33023) ***(G-5555)***
Concept Software Inc....................321 250-6670
1319 Green Frest Ct Ste 4 Winter Garden (34787) ***(G-18381)***
Conchita Foods Inc (PA)....................305 888-9703
10051 Nw 99th Ave Ste 3 Medley (33178) ***(G-8220)***
Concord Print Shops, Ocala *Also called Ocala Print Quick Inc* ***(G-11458)***
Concordia Pharmaceuticals Inc....................786 304-2083
2600 Sw 3rd Ave Ste 950 Miami (33129) ***(G-8955)***
Concraft Inc (PA)....................561 689-0149
353 Swain Blvd Greenacres (33463) ***(G-4845)***
Concraft Patio Products, Greenacres *Also called Concraft Inc* ***(G-4845)***
Concrete Edge Company....................407 658-2788
1952 Saturn Blvd Orlando (32837) ***(G-12040)***
Concrete Group, Jacksonville *Also called Florida Rock Industries* ***(G-6109)***
Concrete Pdts of Palm Bches In....................561 842-2743
460 Avenue S Riviera Beach (33404) ***(G-14611)***
Concrete Products-Division, Winter Park *Also called Accord Industries LLC* ***(G-18480)***
Concrete Structures Inc....................305 597-9393
12100 Nw 58th St Miami (33010) ***(G-8956)***
Concrete Systems, Port Richey *Also called D Maxwell Company Inc* ***(G-14360)***
Concurrent Mfg Solutions LLC (HQ)....................512 637-2540
10773 Nw 58th St Ste 100 Doral (33178) ***(G-3168)***
Conde Nast Americas (HQ)....................305 371-9393
800 S Douglas Rd Ste 835 Coral Gables (33134) ***(G-2042)***
Condition Culture LLC....................786 433-8279
123 Harbors Way Boynton Beach (33435) ***(G-852)***
Condo Electric Motor Repr Corp....................305 691-5400
3615 E 10th Ct Hialeah (33013) ***(G-5095)***
Conduent Image Solutions Inc....................407 849-0279
4209 Vineland Rd Ste J2 Orlando (32811) ***(G-12041)***
Conduit Space Rcvery Systems L....................330 416-0887
5204 Lena Rd Bradenton (34211) ***(G-963)***
Coneheads Frozen Custards....................772 600-7730
43 Sw Flagler Ave Stuart (34994) ***(G-16131)***
Conexus Technologies Inc....................513 779-5448
1145 Horizon View Dr Sarasota (34242) ***(G-15640)***
Confederated Specialty Assoc I....................904 751-4754
3043 Faye Rd Jacksonville (32226) ***(G-5997)***
Conglobal Industries, Jacksonville *Also called Its Technologies Logistics LLC* ***(G-6209)***
Conibear Equipment Co Inc (PA)....................863 858-4414
8910 Us Highway 98 N Lakeland (33809) ***(G-7296)***
Conibear Recreational Vehicles, Lakeland *Also called Conibear Equipment Co Inc* ***(G-7296)***
Conklin Metal Industries Inc....................407 688-0900
3060 Pennington Dr Orlando (32804) ***(G-12042)***
Conmed Corporation (PA)....................727 392-6464
11311 Concept Blvd Largo (33773) ***(G-7568)***
Conmed Linvatec, Largo *Also called Linvatec Corporation* ***(G-7633)***
Connect Slutions Worldwide LLC....................407 492-9370
1602 Indian Bay Dr Vero Beach (32963) ***(G-17749)***
Connected Life Solutions LLC....................214 507-9331
153 Dahlia Dr Altamonte Springs (32714) ***(G-40)***
Connectpress Ltd....................505 629-0695
2015 S Tuttle Ave Ste A Sarasota (34239) ***(G-15641)***
Connectronics US Inc....................954 534-3335
101 Bradley Pl Ste 202 Palm Beach (33480) ***(G-12931)***
Connectsure, Leesburg *Also called Top Line Installation Inc* ***(G-7798)***
Connectyx Technologies Corp....................772 221-8240
850 Nw Federal Hwy # 411 Stuart (34994) ***(G-16132)***
Conquest Engineering LLC....................407 731-0519
7901 Kingspointe Pkwy # 17 Orlando (32819) ***(G-12043)***
Conquest Financial Management....................305 630-8950
11451 Nw 36th Ave Miami (33167) ***(G-8957)***
Conquest Manufacturing Fla LLC....................954 655-0139
1121 Nw 31st Ave Pompano Beach (33069) ***(G-13975)***
Conrad Markle Bldr & Cbnt....................904 744-4569
1120 Romney St Jacksonville (32211) ***(G-5998)***
Conrad Pickel Studio Inc....................772 567-1710
7777 20th St Vero Beach (32966) ***(G-17750)***
Conrad Plastics LLC....................954 391-9515
1904 S Ocean Dr Apt 1703 Hallandale Beach (33009) ***(G-4942)***
Conrad Yelvington Distrs Inc....................352 336-5049
7605 Nw 13th St Gainesville (32653) ***(G-4669)***
Conric Holdings LLC....................239 690-9840
8770 Paseo De Valencia St Fort Myers (33908) ***(G-4217)***
Conric PR & Marketing, Fort Myers *Also called Conric Holdings LLC* ***(G-4217)***
Consoldted Mch Tl Holdings LLC (PA)....................888 317-9990
712 S Ocean Shore Blvd Flagler Beach (32136) ***(G-3602)***
Consoldted Rsurce Recovery Inc....................813 262-8404
1502 N 50th St Tampa (33619) ***(G-16724)***
Consolidated Ace Hdwr Sup Inc....................850 939-9800
8188 Navarre Pkwy Navarre (32566) ***(G-10947)***
Consolidated Box, Fort Lauderdale *Also called Mas Entrprses of Ft Lauderdale* ***(G-3933)***
Consolidated Cigr Holdings Inc....................954 772-9000
5900 N Andrews Ave Ste 11 Fort Lauderdale (33309) ***(G-3742)***
Consolidated Cordage Corp....................561 347-7247
7849 Sw Ellipse Way Stuart (34997) ***(G-16133)***
Consolidated Forest Pdts Inc....................407 830-7723
320 Millinor Rd Perry (32347) ***(G-13635)***
Consolidated Forest Pdts Inc (PA)....................407 830-7723
375 Commerce Way Longwood (32750) ***(G-7882)***
Consolidated Label Co....................407 339-2626
2001 E Lake Mary Blvd Sanford (32773) ***(G-15291)***
Consolidated Metal Products....................850 576-2167
3416 Garber Dr Tallahassee (32303) ***(G-16427)***
Consolidated Minerals Inc (PA)....................352 365-6522
8500 Us Highway 441 Leesburg (34788) ***(G-7764)***
Consolidated Parking Equipment, Miami *Also called Lcn Incorporated* ***(G-9440)***
Consolidated Polymer Tech....................727 531-4191
4451 110th Ave N Clearwater (33762) ***(G-1549)***
Consolidated Tech Solutions, Pensacola *Also called Smartcop Inc* ***(G-13604)***
Construccion-Pan Americana, Miami *Also called International Cnstr Pubg* ***(G-9326)***
Constructconnect Inc....................772 770-6003
2001 9th Ave Ste 204 Vero Beach (32960) ***(G-17751)***
Construction, Jacksonville *Also called Eco Restore LLC* ***(G-6062)***
Construction, Saint Cloud *Also called Renovation Team Services LLC* ***(G-14937)***
Construction and Elec Pdts Inc....................954 972-9787
1800 Nw 15th Ave Ste 155 Pompano Beach (33069) ***(G-13976)***
Construction Bulletin Inc....................904 388-0336
7033 Commwl Ave Ste 1 Jacksonville (32220) ***(G-5999)***
Construction Collections, Fort Lauderdale *Also called Builders Notice Corporation* ***(G-3708)***
Construction Software Inc....................888 801-0675
515 E Las Olas Blvd Ste 1 Fort Lauderdale (33301) ***(G-3743)***
Construmining Inc....................786 217-3146
10885 Nw 89th Ter Unit 20 Doral (33178) ***(G-3169)***
Consultant - Med Rview Offcer, Orlando *Also called Advantagecare Inc* ***(G-11873)***
Consultant MGT Group LLC....................352 344-4001
200 W Main St Inverness (34450) ***(G-5823)***
Consultcanvas LLC....................863 214-3115
1951 Nw S Rver Dr Apt 170 Miami (33125) ***(G-8958)***
Consulting, Altamonte Springs *Also called Connected Life Solutions LLC* ***(G-40)***
Consumer Engineering Inc....................321 984-8550
1240 Clearmont St Ne # 1 Palm Bay (32905) ***(G-12895)***
Consumer Information Bur Inc....................954 971-5079
2301 W Sample Rd Ste 4-2a Pompano Beach (33073) ***(G-13977)***
Consumer Source Inc....................407 888-0745
8026 Sunport Dr Ste 304 Orlando (32809) ***(G-12044)***
Contact Center Solutions Inc....................305 499-0163
66 W Flagler St Miami (33130) ***(G-8959)***
Contact Enterprises Inc....................561 900-5134
3170 N Federal Hwy # 100 Pompano Beach (33064) ***(G-13978)***
Container Handling Solutions....................941 359-2095
1349 W University Pkwy Sarasota (34243) ***(G-15458)***
Container Mfg Solutions....................888 805-8785
10460 Sw 186th St Cutler Bay (33157) ***(G-2285)***
Container of America LLC....................954 772-5519
6278 N Federal Hwy # 615 Fort Lauderdale (33308) ***(G-3744)***

Contec Americas Inc 321 728-0172
3991 Sarno Rd Melbourne (32934) *(G-8394)*

Contech Engnered Solutions LLC 561 582-2558
7765 Sw 75th Ave Miami (33143) *(G-8960)*

Contemporary Cabinets Gulf CST 941 758-3060
2245 Whitfield Indus Way Sarasota (34243) *(G-15459)*

Contemporary Carbide Tech 386 734-0080
1730 Patterson Ave Unit B Deland (32724) *(G-2858)*

Contemporary Design Concepts 305 253-2044
12491 Sw 130th St Ste C Miami (33186) *(G-8961)*

Contemporary Interiors Inc 352 620-8686
2626 Nw 35th St Ocala (34475) *(G-11357)*

Contemprary McHnrey Engrg Svcs 386 439-0937
551 Roberts Rd Flagler Beach (32136) *(G-3603)*

Contender Boats Inc 305 230-1600
1820 Se 38th Ave Homestead (33035) *(G-5704)*

Continental Belt & Tie, Miami *Also called Continental Belt Corp* *(G-8962)*

Continental Belt Corp 305 573-8871
2267 Nw 20th St Miami (33142) *(G-8962)*

Continental Blood Bank, Miami *Also called Continental Services Group Inc* *(G-8963)*

Continental Concrete, Miami *Also called Supermix Concrete* *(G-9973)*

Continental Concrete Materials, Davie *Also called Lehigh Cement Company LLC* *(G-2433)*

Continental Concrete Products 904 388-1390
2251 Urban Rd Jacksonville (32210) *(G-6000)*

Continental Marketing Group, Miami *Also called GBIG Corporation* *(G-9194)*

Continental Palatka LLC 703 480-3800
886 N Highway 17 Palatka (32177) *(G-12864)*

Continental Printing 904 731-8989
3060 Mercury Rd Jacksonville (32207) *(G-6001)*

Continental Printing Svcs Inc 904 743-6718
4929 Toproyal Ln Jacksonville (32277) *(G-6002)*

Continental Services Group Inc (PA) 305 633-7700
1300 Nw 36th St Miami (33142) *(G-8963)*

Continental Services Group Inc 954 327-0809
2901 W Broward Blvd Fort Lauderdale (33312) *(G-3745)*

Continuity Unlimited Inc 561 358-8171
1750 W Broadway St # 112 Oviedo (32765) *(G-12815)*

Contours Rx LLC 727 827-7321
200 2nd Ave S Ste 701 Saint Petersburg (33701) *(G-15015)*

Contract Mfg Solutions Inc 954 424-9813
1880 N Commerce Pkwy # 1 Weston (33326) *(G-18234)*

Contracting Cnc Machining Inc 561 494-0703
8360 Currency Dr Ste 7 West Palm Beach (33404) *(G-17972)*

Contractors Cabinet Company 786 492-7118
5512 W Sample Rd Margate (33073) *(G-8126)*

Control and Automtn Cons Inc 305 823-8670
11300 Nw 87th Ct Ste 125 Hialeah (33018) *(G-5096)*

Control Investments Inc (PA) 954 491-6660
6001 Ne 14th Ave Fort Lauderdale (33334) *(G-3746)*

Control Laser Corporation 407 926-3500
8251 Presidents Dr # 1688 Orlando (32809) *(G-12045)*

Control Micro Systems Inc 407 679-9716
4420 Metric Dr Ste A Winter Park (32792) *(G-18500)*

Control Solutions Inc 813 247-2136
1406 N 16th St Tampa (33605) *(G-16725)*

Control Southern Inc 904 353-0004
4133 N Canal St Jacksonville (32209) *(G-6003)*

Contrologix LLC 407 878-2774
361 S White Cedar Rd Sanford (32771) *(G-15292)*

Controls On Demand Llc 321 362-5485
3834 S Hopkins Ave Titusville (32780) *(G-17583)*

Convergent Engineering Inc 352 378-4899
100 Sw 75th St Ste 106 Gainesville (32607) *(G-4670)*

Convergent Marketing LLC 561 270-7081
701 Nw 2nd Ave Delray Beach (33444) *(G-2950)*

Convergent Technologies 407 482-4381
14764 Sapodilla Dr Orlando (32828) *(G-12046)*

Converlogic Americas, Doral *Also called Converlogic Inter LLC* *(G-3170)*

Converlogic Inter LLC (PA) 786 623-4747
2254 Nw 93rd Ave Doral (33172) *(G-3170)*

Converpack Inc 786 304-1680
6891 Nw 74th St Medley (33166) *(G-8221)*

Conveyor Concepts Corporation 941 751-1200
2323 Whitfield Park Ave Sarasota (34243) *(G-15460)*

Conveyor Consulting & Rbr Corp 813 385-1254
2511 Destiny Way Odessa (33556) *(G-11545)*

Convicted Printing LLC 813 431-6286
4719 N Thatcher Ave Tampa (33614) *(G-16726)*

Convivium Press Inc 305 889-0489
7661 Nw 68th St Unit 108 Miami (33166) *(G-8964)*

Conway Bldg Cstm Woodworks LLC 407 738-9266
3001 Viscount Cir Kissimmee (34747) *(G-6908)*

Cook Manufacturing Group Inc 863 546-6183
100 E 7th St Frostproof (33843) *(G-4635)*

Cook Spring Co 941 377-5766
233 Sarasota Center Blvd Sarasota (34240) *(G-15642)*

Cooke Communications Fla LLC (PA) 305 292-7777
3140 Flagler Ave Key West (33040) *(G-6860)*

Cookie App LLC 305 330-5099
2 S Biscayne Blvd # 2680 Miami (33131) *(G-8965)*

Cool Components Inc 813 322-3814
904 E Chelsea St Tampa (33603) *(G-16727)*

Cool Flex, Palm Coast *Also called Total Performance Inc* *(G-13091)*

Cool Ocean LLC 954 848-4060
9810 Sw 4th St Plantation (33324) *(G-13838)*

Cool Pet Holistics, Saint Petersburg *Also called Animal Business Concepts LLC* *(G-14962)*

Cool Treat 407 248-0743
7001 International Dr Orlando (32819) *(G-12047)*

Coolcraft Inc 954 946-0070
1700 Nw 15th Ave Ste 330 Pompano Beach (33069) *(G-13979)*

Coolhead Helmet LLC 786 292-4829
999 Brickell Bay Dr Miami (33131) *(G-8966)*

Cooltech Holding Corp (HQ) 786 675-5236
2100 Nw 84th Ave Doral (33122) *(G-3171)*

Cooper, Sanibel *Also called CT Hydraulics Inc* *(G-15414)*

Cooper Bussmann LLC 561 998-4100
1225 Broken Sound Pkwy Nw S Boca Raton (33487) *(G-470)*

Cooper Bussmann-Automotive, Boca Raton *Also called Cooper Bussmann LLC* *(G-470)*

Cooper Notification Inc 941 487-2300
7246 16th St E Unit 105 Sarasota (34243) *(G-15461)*

Cooper Timber Harvesting Inc 863 494-0240
2056 Ne Newberry Dr Arcadia (34266) *(G-190)*

Cooper-Standard Automotive Inc 321 233-5563
3551 W 1st St Sanford (32771) *(G-15293)*

Cooper-Standard Automotive Inc 407 330-3323
501 Cornwall Rd Ste 2773 Sanford (32773) *(G-15294)*

Cooppa News Reporter 954 437-8864
13550 Sw 10th St Pembroke Pines (33027) *(G-13383)*

Coosa LLC 904 268-1187
12811 Helm Dr Jacksonville (32258) *(G-6004)*

Copaco Inc 407 333-3041
366 E Graves Ave Ste B Orange City (32763) *(G-11804)*

Copalo Inc 941 753-7828
6510 19th St E Sarasota (34243) *(G-15462)*

Copans Marketing and Advg, Pompano Beach *Also called B R Q Grossmans Inc* *(G-13943)*

Copeland Welding & Muffler Sp 904 355-6383
484 Lime St Jacksonville (32204) *(G-6005)*

Coplan Composition Service, Jacksonville *Also called A M Coplan Associates* *(G-5847)*

Copper Bottom Craft Distillery, Apollo Beach *Also called Four Seas Distilling Co LLC* *(G-92)*

Coppercom Inc 561 322-4000
3600 Fau Blvd Ste 100 Boca Raton (33431) *(G-471)*

Coppercom, A Heico, Boca Raton *Also called Coppercom Inc* *(G-471)*

Copy Cat Printing LLC 850 438-5566
3636 N L St Ste D-A Pensacola (32505) *(G-13477)*

Copy Right Bgmd Inc 904 680-0343
5569 Bowden Rd Ste 6 Jacksonville (32216) *(G-6006)*

Copy Right Printing, Bradenton *Also called W D H Enterprises Inc* *(G-1073)*

Copy Van of Florida Inc 407 366-7126
2224 Andrew Ln Oviedo (32765) *(G-12816)*

Copy Van Printing, Oviedo *Also called Copy Van of Florida Inc* *(G-12816)*

Copy Well Inc 850 222-9777
927 N Monroe St Tallahassee (32303) *(G-16428)*

Copy-Flow Inc 305 592-0930
4727 Orange Dr Davie (33314) *(G-2398)*

Coqui Pharma, Doral *Also called Coqui Rdo Pharmaceuticals Corp* *(G-3172)*

Coqui Rdo Pharmaceuticals Corp 787 685-5046
3125 Nw 84th Ave Doral (33122) *(G-3172)*

Cor International (not Inc) 850 766-2866
3204 Hastie Rd Tallahassee (32305) *(G-16429)*

Cor Label Inc 407 402-6633
901 S Chrles Rchard Ball Debary (32713) *(G-2632)*

Coral Cabinet Inc 305 484-8702
14378 Sw 98th Ter Miami (33186) *(G-8967)*

Coral Club Tee Shirts Inc 305 828-6939
3192 W 81st St Hialeah (33018) *(G-5097)*

Coral Gables Custom Design Inc 305 591-7575
4038 Nw 32nd Ave Miami (33142) *(G-8968)*

Coral Gables Living 786 552-6464
400 University Dr Fl 2 Coral Gables (33134) *(G-2043)*

Coral Reef Cast Stone Inc 561 586-1900
6100 Georgia Ave West Palm Beach (33405) *(G-17973)*

Coraldom Usa LLC 305 716-0200
4434 Nw 74th Ave Miami (33166) *(G-8969)*

Corbin Sand and Clay Inc 850 638-8462
1177 Jackson Ave Chipley (32428) *(G-1454)*

Cordaroys Wholesale Inc (PA) 352 332-1837
3421 W University Ave Gainesville (32607) *(G-4671)*

Cordell International Inc 352 694-1800
1056 Ne 16th St Ocala (34470) *(G-11358)*

Cordis Corporation (HQ) 786 313-2000
14201 Nw 60th Ave Miami Lakes (33014) *(G-10293)*

Cordoba Foods LLC 305 733-4768
4477 E 11th Ave Hialeah (33013) *(G-5098)*

Core Enterprises Incorporated 954 227-0781
3650 Coral Ridge Dr # 101 Coral Springs (33065) *(G-2144)*

Core Kites USA 321 302-0693
235 W Cocoa Beach Cswy Cocoa Beach (32931) *(G-1968)*

Core Label LLC 772 287-2141
4313 Sw Port Way Palm City (34990) *(G-13031)*

Core Moto, Titusville *Also called A1a Sportbike LLC* ***(G-17566)***
Core Oncology Inc (PA)....206 236-2100
1101 Brickell Ave 503s Miami (33131) ***(G-8970)***
Core Outdoors Inc....904 215-6866
134 Poole Blvd Saint Augustine (32095) ***(G-14822)***
Corelite Inc (PA)....305 921-4292
1060 E 30th St Hialeah (33013) ***(G-5099)***
Corellium Inc....561 502-2420
10 Se 1st Ave Ste B Delray Beach (33444) ***(G-2951)***
Corerx Inc....727 259-6950
5733 Myerlake Cir Clearwater (33760) ***(G-1550)***
Corerx Inc (PA)....727 259-6950
14205 Myerlake Cir Clearwater (33760) ***(G-1551)***
Corerx Pharmaceuticals Inc....727 259-6950
14205 Myerlake Cir Clearwater (33760) ***(G-1552)***
Coresential Energy & Lighting....919 602-0849
1201 N 50th St Tampa (33619) ***(G-16728)***
Coreslab Strctures Orlando Inc....407 855-3191
2720 County Road 470 Okahumpka (34762) ***(G-11596)***
Coreslab Structures Miami Inc....305 823-8950
10501 Nw 121st Way Medley (33178) ***(G-8222)***
Coreslab Structures Tampa Inc....602 237-3875
6301 N 56th St Tampa (33610) ***(G-16729)***
Coresystems Software USA Inc....786 497-4477
801 Brickell Ave Ste 1400 Miami (33131) ***(G-8971)***
Coresystems USA, Miami *Also called Coresystems Software USA Inc* ***(G-8971)***
Coreyco LLC....813 469-1203
6253 Candlewood Dr Wesley Chapel (33544) ***(G-17872)***
Corin USA Limited Inc (HQ)....813 977-4469
12750 Citrus Park Ln # 120 Tampa (33625) ***(G-16730)***
Corinthian Catamarans LLC....813 334-1029
4338 Auston Way Palm Harbor (34685) ***(G-13107)***
Cork Industries Inc....904 695-2400
5555 W Beaver St Jacksonville (32254) ***(G-6007)***
Corkcicle LLC....866 780-0007
1300 Brookhaven Dr Ste 2 Orlando (32803) ***(G-12048)***
Corn-E-Lee Woodcrafts....239 574-2414
1201 Se 9th Ter Cape Coral (33990) ***(G-1327)***
Cornelius Welding Inc....863 635-3668
221 N Scenic Hwy Frostproof (33843) ***(G-4636)***
Cornerstone Builders S W Fla, Fort Myers *Also called Cornerstone Kitchens Inc* ***(G-4218)***
Cornerstone Fabrication LLC....386 310-1110
291 Sprngview Commerce Dr Debary (32713) ***(G-2633)***
Cornerstone Interlocking Inc....863 944-1609
5915 Walt Loop Rd Lakeland (33809) ***(G-7297)***
Cornerstone Kitchens Inc....239 332-3020
3150 Old Metro Pkwy Fort Myers (33916) ***(G-4218)***
Cornwell, Palm Bay *Also called Walters Tools LLC* ***(G-12927)***
Corona Brushes Inc....813 885-2525
5065 Savarese Cir Tampa (33634) ***(G-16731)***
Corona Printing Company Inc....754 263-2914
1833 Sw 31st Ave Hallandale (33009) ***(G-4922)***
Coronado Paint Co Inc....386 428-6461
9592 Parksouth Ct Orlando (32837) ***(G-12049)***
Coronet Industries Inc....813 752-1161
4082 Coronet Rd Plant City (33566) ***(G-13757)***
Corp Comfort Finisher Mr....786 332-3655
2501 W 80th St Unit 1 Hialeah (33016) ***(G-5100)***
Corpdesign....866 323-6055
6695 Nw 36th Ave Miami (33147) ***(G-8972)***
Corporate & Incentive Travel, Boca Raton *Also called Coastal Communications Corp* ***(G-467)***
Corporate It, Deerfield Beach *Also called Hoerbiger America Holding Inc* ***(G-2736)***
Corporate One Hundred Inc....352 335-0901
605 Nw 53rd Ave Ste A17 Gainesville (32609) ***(G-4672)***
Corporate Printing & Advg Inc....305 273-6000
13515 Sw 99th St Miami (33186) ***(G-8973)***
Corporate Printing Svcs Inc....305 273-6000
13288 Sw 114th Ter Miami (33186) ***(G-8974)***
Corporate Signs Inc....305 500-9313
1375 Nw 97th Ave Ste 12 Doral (33172) ***(G-3173)***
Corporate Signs Inc....305 500-9313
5960 Nw 99th Ave Unit 8 Doral (33178) ***(G-3174)***
Corporate Sports & Entrtmt, Tampa *Also called Total Spcalty Publications LLC* ***(G-17362)***
Corporcion Intrncnal De Jyas V....772 343-1721
2868 Sw Port St Lcie Blvd Port Saint Lucie (34953) ***(G-14406)***
Corrocoat Usa Inc....904 268-4559
6525 Greenland Rd Jacksonville (32258) ***(G-6008)***
Corrugated Creations By Alan....904 683-4347
12807 Jordan Blair Ct Jacksonville (32225) ***(G-6009)***
Corrugated Industries Fla Inc....813 623-6606
1920 N Us Highway 301 Tampa (33619) ***(G-16732)***
Corrugating Division, Dundee *Also called Pratt Industries Inc* ***(G-3437)***
Corry Cabinet Company Inc....850 539-6455
811 N Main St Havana (32333) ***(G-4999)***
Corsicana Bedding LLC....863 534-3450
450 Polk St Bartow (33830) ***(G-306)***
Corsicana Mattress Company, Bartow *Also called Corsicana Bedding LLC* ***(G-306)***
Corvatsch Corp....305 775-2831
1894 Bay Rd Miami Beach (33139) ***(G-10180)***
Cosmesis Skincare Inc....954 963-5090
3816 Hollywood Blvd Hollywood (33021) ***(G-5556)***
Cosmetic Corp of America Inc....305 883-8434
9750 Nw 91st Ct Medley (33178) ***(G-8223)***
Cosmetic Creations Inc....904 261-7831
1438 E Oak St Fernandina Beach (32034) ***(G-3583)***
Cosmetic Solutions LLC (PA)....561 226-8600
6101 Pk Of Commerce Blvd Boca Raton (33487) ***(G-472)***
Cosmetics, Weston *Also called Kookie Kllection Kosmetics LLC* ***(G-18262)***
Cosmetics & Cleaners Intl LLC....305 592-5504
6000 Nw 97th Ave Unit 9 Doral (33178) ***(G-3175)***
Cosmo International Corp (PA)....954 798-4500
1341 W Newport Center Dr Deerfield Beach (33442) ***(G-2694)***
Cosmo International Corp....954 798-4500
1341 W Newport Center Dr Deerfield Beach (33442) ***(G-2695)***
Cosmo International Fragrances, Deerfield Beach *Also called Cosmo International Corp* ***(G-2694)***
Cosmo International Fragrances, Deerfield Beach *Also called Cosmo International Corp* ***(G-2695)***
Cosmo Leather Co, Miami *Also called Mario Kenny* ***(G-9512)***
Cosmos Ice Cream, Rockledge *Also called Mercy D LLC* ***(G-14732)***
Cosner Manufacturing LLC....863 676-2579
511 N Scenic Hwy Lake Wales (33853) ***(G-7157)***
Cost Cast Inc....863 422-5617
1301 W Commerce Ave Haines City (33844) ***(G-4903)***
Cost Cast Aluminum Corp....863 422-5617
1301 W Commerce Ave Haines City (33844) ***(G-4904)***
Costa Brick Pavers Inc....904 535-5009
12368 Brady Rd Jacksonville (32223) ***(G-6010)***
Costa Broom Works Inc....813 248-3397
3606 E 4th Ave Tampa (33605) ***(G-16733)***
Costa Del Mar, Daytona Beach *Also called Costa Inc* ***(G-2534)***
Costa Inc (HQ)....386 274-4000
2361 Mason Ave Ste 100 Daytona Beach (32117) ***(G-2534)***
Costech Lab LLC....407 476-3488
2100 Consulate Dr Ste 100 Orlando (32837) ***(G-12050)***
Costex Corporation (PA)....305 592-9769
5800 Nw 74th Ave Miami (33166) ***(G-8975)***
Costex Tractor Parts, Miami *Also called Costex Corporation* ***(G-8975)***
Coterie Care Inc....850 325-0422
701 Ferguson Dr Fort Walton Beach (32547) ***(G-4571)***
Cotton Images, Doral *Also called Cottonimagescom Inc* ***(G-3176)***
Cotton Pickin Shirts Plus....850 435-3133
2211 N Pace Blvd Pensacola (32505) ***(G-13478)***
Cottonimagescom Inc....305 251-2560
10481 Nw 28th St Doral (33172) ***(G-3176)***
Couch Ready Mix Usa Inc....850 236-9042
3008 S Highway 95a Cantonment (32533) ***(G-1267)***
Couchman Printing Company....386 756-3052
1634 S Ridgewood Ave South Daytona (32119) ***(G-16020)***
Coughlan Products Corp....973 904-1500
3043 Perdue Ter Punta Gorda (33983) ***(G-14502)***
Counter....239 566-0644
9110 Strada Pl Ste 6130 Naples (34108) ***(G-10720)***
Counter Active Inc....813 626-0022
87 Sanchez Dr E Ponte Vedra (32082) ***(G-14255)***
Counter Impressions LLC....352 589-4966
12 S Bay St Eustis (32726) ***(G-3556)***
Counter Productions Inc....386 673-6500
1052 N Beach St Daytona Beach (32117) ***(G-2535)***
Countertop Solutions Inc....239 961-0663
3930 Domestic Ave Ste B Naples (34104) ***(G-10721)***
Countrkraft Solid Surfaces Inc....321 456-5928
3390 N Courtenay Pkwy P Merritt Island (32953) ***(G-8582)***
Country Cabinets....850 547-5477
1915 Adolph Whitaker Rd Bonifay (32425) ***(G-770)***
Country Club Concierge Mag Inc....904 223-0204
830-13 A1a N Ste 496 Ponte Vedra Beach (32082) ***(G-14266)***
Country Frits Juices Nurs Corp....786 302-8487
12100 Sw 177th Ave Miami (33196) ***(G-8976)***
Country Malt Group, Plant City *Also called Great Western Malting Co* ***(G-13774)***
Country Prime Meats USA Inc....250 396-4111
9695 W Broward Blvd Plantation (33324) ***(G-13839)***
Country Pure Foods Inc....904 734-4634
1915 N Woodland Blvd Deland (32720) ***(G-2859)***
Country Store Interiors, Sarasota *Also called Dwa Inc* ***(G-15663)***
Country Tees, Jupiter *Also called Southeast Marketing Concepts* ***(G-6802)***
Countryside Locks LLC....631 561-5006
20020 Barletta Ln # 514 Estero (33928) ***(G-3541)***
Countryside Publishing Co Inc....813 925-0195
477 Commerce Blvd Oldsmar (34677) ***(G-11641)***
Countwise Llc (PA)....954 846-7011
1149 Sawgrs Corp Pkwy Sunrise (33323) ***(G-16308)***
County Cardboard LLC....772 546-1983
8970 Se Bridge Rd Hobe Sound (33455) ***(G-5481)***
County of Hernando....352 754-4042
238 Howell Ave Brooksville (34601) ***(G-1149)***

County of Orange..407 649-0076
  400 E South St Orlando (32801) *(G-12051)*

County of Sumter...352 689-4460
  910 N Main St Ste 308 Bushnell (33513) *(G-1242)*

County Plastics Corp..954 971-9205
  1801 Nw 22nd St Pompano Beach (33069) *(G-13980)*

Courtney Allen Enterprises LLC...........................571 314-4290
  1236 16th St Sarasota (34236) *(G-15643)*

Covalent Industries Inc......................................727 381-2739
  10300 49th St N Ste 434 Clearwater (33762) *(G-1553)*

Cover Style, Doral *Also called Earth & Sea Wear LLC (G-3202)*

Coverall Aluminum Inc..321 377-7874
  1980 Dolgner Pl Ste 1068 Sanford (32771) *(G-15295)*

Coverall Interiors...813 961-8261
  5102 W Linebaugh Ave Tampa (33624) *(G-16734)*

Covert Armor LLC..561 459-8077
  1101 Clare Ave Ste 2 West Palm Beach (33401) *(G-17974)*

Covington Plastics Inc......................................321 632-6775
  427 Shearer Blvd Cocoa (32922) *(G-1912)*

Covocup LLC...855 204-5106
  6621 19th St E Sarasota (34243) *(G-15463)*

Cows USA, Cutler Bay *Also called Container Mfg Solutions (G-2285)*

Cox Designer Windows Inc..................................727 847-1046
  6810 Commerce Ave Port Richey (34668) *(G-14359)*

Coyote Acquisition Co (HQ).................................941 480-1600
  1070 Technology Dr North Venice (34275) *(G-11209)*

Cozy Bar...305 532-2699
  500 S Pointe Dr Miami Beach (33139) *(G-10181)*

CP Logging Inc..850 379-8698
  20688 Ne Burlington Rd Hosford (32334) *(G-5754)*

CP Royalties LLC..888 694-9265
  301 W Platt St Tampa (33606) *(G-16735)*

CP Vegetable Oil, Fort Lauderdale *Also called C P Vegetable Oil Inc (G-3710)*

Cpc-Cryolab, Temple Terrace *Also called Circor International Inc (G-17536)*

CPD BOTTLING CLOSURE, Boca Raton *Also called New Sentry Marketing Inc (G-613)*

CPS Products Inc (HQ)...305 687-4121
  3600 Enterprise Way Miramar (33025) *(G-10482)*

Crabil Manufacturing Inc...................................727 209-8368
  9600 18th St N Saint Petersburg (33716) *(G-15016)*

Cracker Machining Inc..386 497-1335
  340 Sw Murdock Ct Fort White (32038) *(G-4619)*

Craemer US Corporation.....................................727 312-8859
  2927 Pinewood Run Palm Harbor (34684) *(G-13108)*

Craig Armstrong..786 319-6514
  1770 Normandy Dr Apt 2 Miami Beach (33141) *(G-10182)*

Craig Catamaran Corporation.............................407 290-8778
  4333 Silver Star Rd # 1 Orlando (32808) *(G-12052)*

Crain Ventures Inc...407 933-1820
  2775 Old Dixie Hwy Ste C Kissimmee (34744) *(G-6909)*

Crains Precious Metals LLC.................................954 536-8334
  11607 Palmetto Way Hollywood (33026) *(G-5557)*

Cramco Inc...305 634-7500
  5600 Nw 36th Ave Miami (33142) *(G-8977)*

Cranco Industries Inc..321 690-2695
  1710 Baldwin St Rockledge (32955) *(G-14697)*

Crandon Electric Co, Ocala *Also called Crandon Enterprises Inc (G-11359)*

Crandon Enterprises Inc.....................................352 873-8400
  255 Sw 96th Ln Ocala (34476) *(G-11359)*

Crane Co..941 480-9101
  730 Commerce Dr Venice (34292) *(G-17680)*

Crane Electronics Inc...850 244-0043
  84 Hill Ave Nw Fort Walton Beach (32548) *(G-4572)*

Crane Environmental Inc...................................941 480-9101
  730 Commerce Dr Venice (34292) *(G-17681)*

Crane Environmental Products, Venice *Also called Crane Environmental Inc (G-17681)*

Crane Pro Services, Lakeland *Also called Konecranes Inc (G-7371)*

Crankshaft Rebuilders Inc...................................407 323-4870
  1200 Albright Rd Sanford (32771) *(G-15296)*

Crawford Glass Door Co......................................954 480-6820
  3301 Sw 13th Dr Ste B Deerfield Beach (33442) *(G-2696)*

Crawford Manufacturing Company.......................513 548-6890
  8875 Hdden Rver Pkwy Ste Tampa (33637) *(G-16736)*

Crawfords Custom Woodwork..............................904 782-1375
  21535 Us Highway 301 N Lawtey (32058) *(G-7745)*

Crazy 4 Signs LLC...813 239-3085
  4819 Allen Rd Zephyrhills (33541) *(G-18610)*

CRC Press LLC (HQ)...561 994-0555
  6000 Broken Sound Pkwy Nw # 300 Boca Raton (33487) *(G-473)*

CRC Press LLC...561 361-6000
  3848 Fau Blvd Ste 310 Boca Raton (33431) *(G-474)*

Creaction Industry Llc.......................................305 779-4851
  8710 Nw 100th St Medley (33178) *(G-8224)*

Creaction Organize, Medley *Also called Creaction Industry Llc (G-8224)*

Creamer Corp...850 265-2700
  338 W Highway 388 Panama City (32409) *(G-13250)*

Create and Company Inc.....................................813 393-8778
  1023 E Columbus Dr Tampa (33605) *(G-16737)*

Createch Machine & Design, Lakeland *Also called High Performance Holdings Ltd (G-7344)*

Createco, Tampa *Also called Create and Company Inc (G-16737)*

Creating Tech Solutions LLC (PA)........................727 914-3001
  5250 140th Ave N Clearwater (33760) *(G-1554)*

Creating Tech Solutions LLC...............................727 914-3001
  5250 140th Ave N Clearwater (33760) *(G-1555)*

Creating Tech Solutions LLC...............................727 914-3001
  5250 140th Ave N Clearwater (33760) *(G-1556)*

Creations In Cabinetry Inc...................................386 237-3082
  2 Market Pl Palm Coast (32137) *(G-13075)*

Creative Archtctral Resin Pdts............................239 939-0034
  3080 Warehouse Rd Fort Myers (33916) *(G-4219)*

Creative Auto Boutique Llc................................407 654-7300
  17949 W Colonial Dr Oakland (34787) *(G-11227)*

Creative Biz Center Inc.......................................954 918-7322
  7860 W Commercial Blvd Lauderhill (33351) *(G-7729)*

Creative Builder Services Inc..............................813 818-7100
  6422 Harney Rd Ste F Tampa (33610) *(G-16738)*

Creative Cabinet Concepts Inc............................239 939-1313
  7947 Drew Cir Fort Myers (33967) *(G-4220)*

Creative Canvas Centl Fla Inc.............................407 661-1211
  436 Wekiva Rapids Dr Altamonte Springs (32714) *(G-41)*

Creative Carbide Inc (PA)....................................239 567-0041
  7880 Interstate Ct Unit A Fort Myers (33917) *(G-4221)*

Creative Color Printing Inc................................954 701-6763
  3721 Sw 47th Ave Ste 302 Davie (33314) *(G-2399)*

Creative Colors International, Brandon *Also called Patrick German Industries Inc (G-1101)*

Creative Colors International...............................239 573-8883
  1221 Se 9th Ter Cape Coral (33990) *(G-1328)*

Creative Concepts Ncj LLC (PA)..........................352 302-8100
  4203 S Purslane Dr Homosassa (34448) *(G-5745)*

Creative Concepts Ncj LLC.................................352 302-8100
  7397 S Suncoast Blvd Homosassa (34446) *(G-5746)*

Creative Concepts Orlando Inc............................407 260-1435
  1650 Forest Ave Ste 100 Longwood (32750) *(G-7883)*

Creative Counters, Jacksonville *Also called Creative Countertops Inc (G-6011)*

Creative Countertops Inc....................................904 387-2800
  4768 Highway Ave Jacksonville (32254) *(G-6011)*

Creative Curbing...352 347-3329
  15340 Se 73rd Ave Summerfield (34491) *(G-16258)*

Creative Custom Stairs.......................................941 505-0336
  3857 Acline Rd Unit 104 Punta Gorda (33950) *(G-14503)*

Creative Data Solutions Inc...............................407 333-4770
  1540 Intl Pkwy Ste 2000 Lake Mary (32746) *(G-7067)*

Creative Energies Inc...352 351-9448
  1805 Ne 19th Ave Ocala (34470) *(G-11360)*

Creative Events and Exhibits (PA).......................407 851-4754
  405 Fairlane Ave Orlando (32809) *(G-12053)*

Creative Glassworks...904 860-0865
  2062 Saint Martins Dr W Jacksonville (32246) *(G-6012)*

Creative Home and Kitchen LLC..........................786 233-8621
  2000 Nw 97th Ave Ste 112 Doral (33172) *(G-3177)*

Creative Images Embroidery................................904 730-5660
  2989 Philips Hwy Jacksonville (32207) *(G-6013)*

Creative Lighting & Power LLC............................407 967-0957
  330 Winston Creek Pkwy G Lakeland (33810) *(G-7298)*

Creative Lighting & Solar, Lakeland *Also called Creative Lighting & Power LLC (G-7298)*

Creative Loafing Inc (HQ)...................................813 739-4800
  1911 N 13th St Ste W200 Tampa (33605) *(G-16739)*

Creative Loafing Sarasota, Tampa *Also called Weekly Planet of Sarasota Inc (G-17424)*

Creative Mailbox Designs, Tampa *Also called Creative Builder Services Inc (G-16738)*

Creative Mailbox Sign Designs, Tampa *Also called Creative Sign Designs LLC (G-16740)*

Creative Marine...239 437-1010
  6261 Arc Way Fort Myers (33966) *(G-4222)*

Creative Metal Products, Boynton Beach *Also called Natural Beauty Wood Products (G-894)*

Creative Metal Studio Inc (PA)...........................321 206-6112
  849 Monroe Ave Apopka (32703) *(G-117)*

Creative Metal Works, Holt *Also called Preston Works Inc (G-5693)*

Creative Millwork Inc...305 885-5474
  7635 W 28th Ave Bay 3 Hialeah (33016) *(G-5101)*

Creative Molding Corp..786 251-4241
  2949 Nw 97th Ct Doral (33172) *(G-3178)*

Creative Monogramming, Clearwater *Also called John & Betsy Hovland (G-1654)*

Creative Printing, Sebring *Also called Creative Svcs Centl Fla Inc (G-15916)*

Creative Printing, Pompano Beach *Also called FGA Printing (G-14019)*

Creative Printing & Publishing, Sanford *Also called Paragon Products Inc (G-15369)*

Creative Printing Bay Cnty Inc............................850 784-1645
  1328 Harrison Ave Panama City (32401) *(G-13251)*

Creative Promotional Products............................407 383-7114
  1325 E Harding St Orlando (32806) *(G-12054)*

Creative Prtg & Graphics Inc...............................954 242-2562
  4402 Nw 51st Ct Coconut Creek (33073) *(G-1982)*

Creative Prtg & Screen Designs, Panama City *Also called Creative Printing Bay Cnty Inc (G-13251)*

Creative Prtg Grphic Dsign Inc............................407 855-0202
  1009 Pine St Orlando (32824) *(G-12055)*

Creative Shirts Intl Inc.......................................954 351-0909
  5214 Ne 12th Ave Oakland Park (33334) *(G-11253)*

Creative Sign Designs LLC (PA)..........................800 804-4809
  12801 Commodity Pl Tampa (33626) *(G-16740)*

Creative Signs Inc 407 293-9393
  2301 N Hiawassee Rd Apopka (32703) *(G-118)*

Creative Solid Surfacing, Fort Myers *Also called Creative Cabinet Concepts Inc* *(G-4220)*

Creative Svcs Centl Fla Inc 863 385-8383
  2023 Us Highway 27 N Sebring (33870) *(G-15916)*

Creative Tech Sarasota Inc 941 371-2743
  5959 Palmer Blvd Sarasota (34232) *(G-15644)*

Creative Vtran Productions LLC 407 656-2743
  2400 Mtland Ctr Pkwy Ste Maitland (32751) *(G-8055)*

Creative Wdwkg Concepts Inc 727 937-4165
  905 Rivo Pl Tarpon Springs (34689) *(G-17462)*

Creative Wood Graphics, Safety Harbor *Also called Signature Signs Inc* *(G-14796)*

Creative Woodwork Miami Inc 305 634-3100
  6001 Nw 37th Ave Miami (33142) *(G-8978)*

Crenshaw Die & Manufacturing 949 475-5505
  100 Zaharias Cir Daytona Beach (32124) *(G-2536)*

Crescent Garden, Miami *Also called Dotchi LLC* *(G-9046)*

Crescent Garden, Hollywood *Also called Darnel Inc* *(G-5561)*

Crespo Doors Distribution 305 244-9130
  2513 Nw 74th Ave Miami (33122) *(G-8979)*

Cress Chemical & Eqp Co Inc 407 425-2846
  519 19th St Orlando (32805) *(G-12056)*

Crestview Ready Mix, Fort Walton Beach *Also called Fort Walton Concrete Co* *(G-4583)*

Crestview Ready Mix Inc 850 682-6117
  1070 Farmer St Crestview (32539) *(G-2241)*

Creta Granite & Marble Inc 954 956-9993
  1900 Nw 33rd St Ste 10 Pompano Beach (33064) *(G-13981)*

Crevalle Boats, Wildwood *Also called Littoral Marine LLC* *(G-18315)*

Crf Group Inc 954 428-7446
  4716 N Powerline Rd Pompano Beach (33073) *(G-13982)*

Crh Americas Inc 843 672-5553
  500 S Florida Ave Ste 240 Lakeland (33801) *(G-7299)*

Crichlow Data Sciences Inc 863 616-1222
  2500 Drane Feld Rd Ste 10 Lakeland (33811) *(G-7300)*

Cricket Mini Golf Carts Inc 386 220-3536
  1575 Avi Ctr Pkwy Ste 432 Daytona Beach (32114) *(G-2537)*

Critical Disposables Inc 407 330-1154
  700 Martin L King Jr Blvd Sanford (32771) *(G-15297)*

Critical Review Journals, Crj, Boca Raton *Also called CRC Press LLC* *(G-473)*

Croci North America, Fort Myers *Also called American Windows Shutters Inc* *(G-4173)*

Croft Publishing Inc 352 473-3159
  5006 County Road 214 Keystone Heights (32656) *(G-6884)*

Crofton & Sons, Tampa *Also called Uncle Johns Pride LLC* *(G-17387)*

Crom Corporation (PA) 352 372-3436
  250 Sw 36th Ter Gainesville (32607) *(G-4673)*

Crom Corporation of America, Gainesville *Also called Crom Corporation* *(G-4673)*

Cromer International Press, Haines City *Also called Cromer Printing Inc* *(G-4905)*

Cromer Printing Inc 863 422-8651
  24 N 6th St Haines City (33844) *(G-4905)*

Crompco Inc 954 584-8488
  6531 Nw 13th Ct Plantation (33313) *(G-13840)*

Cronus Litho LLC 239 325-4846
  9010 Strada Stell Ct # 103 Naples (34109) *(G-10722)*

Crop LLC 941 923-8640
  2320 Gulf Gate Dr Sarasota (34231) *(G-15645)*

Cross Atlantic Commodities Inc (PA) 954 678-0698
  4581 Weston Rd Ste 273 Weston (33331) *(G-18235)*

Cross City Lumber LLC 352 578-8078
  59 Ne 132nd Ave Cross City (32628) *(G-2258)*

Cross City Veneer Company Inc 352 498-3226
  106 Ne 180th St Cross City (32628) *(G-2259)*

Cross Construction Svcs Inc 813 907-1013
  25221 Wesley Chapel Blvd Lutz (33559) *(G-7987)*

Cross Key Marine Canvas Inc 305 451-1302
  103761 Overseas Hwy Key Largo (33037) *(G-6844)*

Cross Match Technologies Inc (HQ) 561 622-1650
  3950 Rca Blvd Ste 5001 Palm Beach Gardens (33410) *(G-12963)*

Crosstac Corporation 406 522-9300
  12605 Nw 115th Ave B-104 Medley (33178) *(G-8225)*

Crowder Custom Rods Inc 772 220-8108
  3040 Se Dominica Ter Stuart (34997) *(G-16134)*

Crowder Rods, Stuart *Also called Crowder Custom Rods Inc* *(G-16134)*

Crowe Manufacturing 813 334-1921
  5203 S Lois Ave Tampa (33611) *(G-16741)*

Crowell Companies, Tampa *Also called Crowell Marine Inc* *(G-16742)*

Crowell Marine Inc 813 236-3625
  7305 N Florida Ave Tampa (33604) *(G-16742)*

Crown Building Pdts Fla LLC 863 993-4004
  6018 Sw Highway 72 Arcadia (34266) *(G-191)*

Crown Building Systems, Jacksonville *Also called Crown Products Company Inc* *(G-6016)*

Crown Equipment Corporation 954 786-8889
  2971 Center Port Cir Pompano Beach (33064) *(G-13983)*

Crown Equipment Corporation 407 438-5401
  404 Sunport Ln Ste 150 Orlando (32809) *(G-12057)*

Crown Equipment Corporation 813 628-5500
  4683 Oak Fair Blvd Tampa (33610) *(G-16743)*

Crown Industries of Florida 321 432-0014
  827 W Yale St Orlando (32804) *(G-12058)*

Crown Leao Industries Inc 561 866-1218
  150 E Palmetto Park Rd # 80 Boca Raton (33432) *(G-475)*

Crown Lift Trucks, Pompano Beach *Also called Crown Equipment Corporation* *(G-13983)*

Crown Lift Trucks, Orlando *Also called Crown Equipment Corporation* *(G-12057)*

Crown Lift Trucks, Tampa *Also called Crown Equipment Corporation* *(G-16743)*

Crown Plating Inc 904 783-6640
  5285 Ramona Blvd Jacksonville (32205) *(G-6014)*

Crown Printing Inc 863 682-4881
  1303 E Main St Lakeland (33801) *(G-7301)*

Crown Products LLC (PA) 954 917-1118
  935 Nw 31st Ave Ste 4 Pompano Beach (33069) *(G-13984)*

Crown Products Company Inc (PA) 904 737-7144
  6390 Philips Hwy Jacksonville (32216) *(G-6015)*

Crown Products Company Inc 904 924-8340
  3545 New Kings Rd Jacksonville (32209) *(G-6016)*

Crown Roof Tiles, Arcadia *Also called Crown Building Pdts Fla LLC* *(G-191)*

Crown Seamless Gutters Inc 561 748-9919
  7880 Coconut Blvd West Palm Beach (33412) *(G-17975)*

Crown Welding & Fabg Inc 941 737-6844
  6030 Wauchula Rd Myakka City (34251) *(G-10645)*

Crows Nest Industries Inc 740 466-2926
  2708 Lexington Dr Orange Park (32073) *(G-11821)*

Crp Machine Shop Inc 305 824-7450
  11294 Nw South River Dr Medley (33178) *(G-8226)*

Crucial Cllsion Prductions LLC 321 501-1722
  3334 Henry St Melbourne (32901) *(G-8395)*

Cruise Car Inc 941 929-1630
  1227 Hardin Ave Sarasota (34243) *(G-15464)*

Cruising Gide Publications Inc 727 733-5322
  2418 Summerwood Ct Dunedin (34698) *(G-3447)*

Crumbliss Manufacturing Co 239 693-8588
  5812 Enterprise Pkwy Fort Myers (33905) *(G-4223)*

Crumbliss Test Equipment, Fort Myers *Also called Crumbliss Manufacturing Co* *(G-4223)*

Crumpton Welding Sup & Eqp Inc 863 965-8423
  601 Charlotte Rd Auburndale (33823) *(G-226)*

Crunchi LLC 772 600-8082
  7671 Sw Ellipse Way Stuart (34997) *(G-16135)*

Crusellas & Co Inc 305 261-9580
  7014 Sw 4th St Miami (33144) *(G-8980)*

Crustys Bread Bakery 727 937-9041
  438 Athens St Tarpon Springs (34689) *(G-17463)*

Cryntel Enterprises Ltd Inc 954 577-7844
  10412 W State Road 84 # 1 Davie (33324) *(G-2400)*

Cryoderm, Margate *Also called Ahc Ventures Corp* *(G-8118)*

Cryothrapy Pain Rlief Pdts Inc 954 364-8192
  3460 Laurel Oaks Ln Hollywood (33021) *(G-5558)*

Crypto Cpitl Precious Mtls Inc 727 200-2108
  10460 Roosevelt Blvd N Saint Petersburg (33716) *(G-15017)*

Crystal Communications Inc 954 474-3072
  5600 Nw 102nd Ave Ste M Sunrise (33351) *(G-16309)*

Crystal Geyser, Orlando *Also called Cg Roxane LLC* *(G-12001)*

Crystal Panepinto Inc 941 475-9235
  667 Palomino Trl Englewood (34223) *(G-3528)*

Crystal Photonics Inc (PA) 407 328-9111
  5525 Benchmark Ln Sanford (32773) *(G-15298)*

Crystal Pool Service Inc 954 444-8282
  10718 Nw 53rd St Sunrise (33351) *(G-16310)*

Crystal River Quarries, Crystal River *Also called Colitz Mining Co Inc* *(G-2272)*

Crystal River Quarries Inc 352 795-2828
  7040 N Suncoast Blvd Crystal River (34428) *(G-2273)*

Crystek Crystals Corporation 239 561-3311
  16850 Oriole Rd Ste 3 Fort Myers (33912) *(G-4224)*

Csa International Inc 561 746-7946
  759 Parkway Jupiter (33477) *(G-6705)*

Csba Digital Printing 813 482-1608
  3601 Bay Heights Way Tampa (33611) *(G-16744)*

CSC Racing Corporation 248 548-5727
  15819 Guild Ct B Jupiter (33478) *(G-6706)*

CSC Textron 813 554-9723
  2450 N West Shore Blvd Tampa (33607) *(G-16745)*

Csg, Orlando *Also called Ddci Inc* *(G-12080)*

Csi Aerospace Inc 954 961-9800
  3000 Taft St Hollywood (33021) *(G-5559)*

Csi Home Decor Inc 754 301-2147
  5365 N Hiatus Rd Sunrise (33351) *(G-16311)*

Csl of America Inc 407 849-7070
  1900 S Orange Blossom Trl Orlando (32805) *(G-12059)*

Csmc Inc 407 246-1567
  4498 Vineland Rd Orlando (32811) *(G-12060)*

Cso Systems Inc 941 355-5653
  4139 N Washington Blvd Sarasota (34234) *(G-15646)*

CSR Enterprise Ltd 954 624-2284
  370 Nw 123rd St North Miami (33168) *(G-11101)*

Csr Performance Products, Mc Alpin *Also called Competition Specialties Inc* *(G-8188)*

CST USA Inc 404 695-2249
  20533 Biscayne Blvd # 565 Miami (33180) *(G-8981)*

CT Hydraulics Inc 724 342-3089
  1845 Ardsley Way Sanibel (33957) *(G-15414)*

2022 Harris Florida
Manufacturers Directory

(G-0000) Company's Geographic Section entry number

CT Natural 813 996-6443
2908 W Arch St Tampa (33607) *(G-16746)*

Ctm Biomedical LLC 561 650-4027
78 Sw 7th St Ste 500 Miami (33130) *(G-8982)*

Ctr Industries 321 264-1458
3980 Hammock Rd Mims (32754) *(G-10447)*

CU Holdings LLC 904 483-5700
5515 W 5th St Jacksonville (32254) *(G-6017)*

Cubco Inc 386 254-2706
605 Commercial Dr Daytona Beach (32117) *(G-2538)*

Cubic Advnced Lrng Sltions Inc 407 859-7410
2001 W Oak Ridge Rd Orlando (32809) *(G-12061)*

Cubic Corporation 407 859-7410
3862 Quadrangle Blvd # 100 Orlando (32817) *(G-12062)*

Cubic Simulation Systems Inc 407 641-2037
2001 W Oak Ridge Rd # 100 Orlando (32809) *(G-12063)*

Cubic Transportation Systems, Orlando *Also called Cubic Simulation Systems Inc (G-12063)*

Cubos LLC 786 299-2671
13832 Sw 142nd Ave Miami (33186) *(G-8983)*

Cue & Case, Jacksonville *Also called Lucas 5135 Inc (G-6265)*

Cug LLC 786 858-0499
950 S Pine Island Rd Plantation (33324) *(G-13841)*

Culinary Concepts Inc 407 228-0069
2215 Tradeport Dr Orlando (32824) *(G-12064)*

Cummins Power Generation Inc 239 337-1211
2671 Edison Ave Fort Myers (33916) *(G-4225)*

Cummins-Wagner-Florida LLC (HQ) 813 630-2220
9834 Currie Davis Dr Tampa (33619) *(G-16747)*

Cup Plus USA 321 972-1968
4440 Metric Dr Winter Park (32792) *(G-18501)*

Cupcake Inc 407 644-7800
105 Candace Dr Unit 109 Maitland (32751) *(G-8056)*

Cupcake Girls Dessert Company 904 372-4579
1516 3rd St N Jacksonville Beach (32250) *(G-6632)*

Cupcake Heaven 352 610-4433
2721 Forest Rd Spring Hill (34606) *(G-16069)*

Cupcakes Frsting Sprinkles LLC 305 769-3393
2301 Nw 155th St Opa Locka (33054) *(G-11734)*

Curallux LLC 786 888-1875
1715 Nw 82nd Ave Doral (33126) *(G-3179)*

Current 954 262-8455
3301 College Ave Asa105 Davie (33314) *(G-2401)*

Current Products Company LLC 850 435-4994
1995 Hollywood Ave Pensacola (32505) *(G-13479)*

Currin Graphics 850 505-0955
2821 Copter Rd Ste 700 Pensacola (32514) *(G-13480)*

Curry & Sons Inc 305 296-8781
3201 Flagler Ave Ste 504 Key West (33040) *(G-6861)*

Curry & Sons Prtg & Off Sup, Key West *Also called Curry & Sons Inc (G-6861)*

Curry Cabinetry Inc 813 321-3650
4831 E Broadway Ave Tampa (33605) *(G-16748)*

Curtis K Foulks 239 454-9663
2240 Hemingway Dr Ste J Fort Myers (33912) *(G-4226)*

Curv-A-Tech Corp 305 888-9631
930 W 23rd St Hialeah (33010) *(G-5102)*

Curvco Steel Structures Corp 800 956-6341
14545 S Military Trl H Delray Beach (33484) *(G-2952)*

Cusano's Baking Co., Orlando *Also called Cusanos Italian Bakery Inc (G-12065)*

Cusanos Italian Bakery Inc 786 506-4281
1904 Premier Row Orlando (32809) *(G-12065)*

Cushion Solutions Incorporated 813 253-2131
802 N Rome Ave Tampa (33606) *(G-16749)*

Cushybeds, Pompano Beach *Also called Cyber Group USA LLC (G-13987)*

Custom Aerospace Machine, Palm Bay *Also called Group E Holdings Inc (G-12903)*

Custom Agronomics Inc 772 223-0775
2300 Sw Poma Dr Palm City (34990) *(G-13032)*

Custom Atmated Prosthetics LLC 781 279-2771
1155 Ne Cleveland St Clearwater (33755) *(G-1557)*

Custom Beach Huts LLC 305 439-3991
800 S Douglas Rd Ste 300 Coral Gables (33134) *(G-2044)*

Custom Biologicals Inc 561 998-1699
1239 E Nwport Ctr Dr Ste Deerfield Beach (33442) *(G-2697)*

Custom Building Products LLC 305 885-3444
8850 Nw 79th Ave Medley (33166) *(G-8227)*

Custom Built Screen Enclosures 239 242-0224
765 Ne 19th Pl Unit 2 Cape Coral (33909) *(G-1329)*

Custom Button Company, Melbourne *Also called Promo Daddy LLC (G-8502)*

Custom Cab Doors & More Inc 954 318-1881
1538 Nw 23rd Ave Fort Lauderdale (33311) *(G-3747)*

Custom Cabinet Designs Inc 561 781-3251
128 Timber Ln Jupiter (33458) *(G-6707)*

Custom Cabinets 727 392-1676
11060 70th Ave Seminole (33772) *(G-15973)*

Custom Cabinets By Jensen LLC 813 250-0286
1704 W Fig St Tampa (33606) *(G-16750)*

Custom Cabinets Design Inc 561 210-3423
5000 Nw 3rd Ave Deerfield Beach (33064) *(G-2698)*

Custom Cabinets Inc 941 366-0428
7350 Deer Crossing Ct Sarasota (34240) *(G-15647)*

Custom Cabinets SW Florida LLC 239 415-3350
5929 Youngquist Rd Fort Myers (33912) *(G-4227)*

Custom Cable Crafters, Palm Coast *Also called Managed Data Assoc Inc (G-13082)*

Custom Cable Industries, Tampa *Also called Amphenol Custom Cable Inc (G-16594)*

Custom Canvas and Cushions, Riviera Beach *Also called Christopher R Shuman (G-14609)*

Custom Carpentry Plus LLC 305 972-3735
9801 Bel Aire Dr Cutler Bay (33157) *(G-2286)*

Custom Carts of Lakewood Ranch, Bradenton *Also called Custom Carts of Sarasota LLC (G-964)*

Custom Carts of Sarasota LLC 941 953-4445
4515 15th St E Bradenton (34203) *(G-964)*

Custom Cft Windows & Doors Inc 407 834-5400
1436 Northern Way Winter Springs (32708) *(G-18563)*

Custom Clors Powdercoating Inc 941 953-7997
1930 21st St Sarasota (34234) *(G-15648)*

Custom Comfort Medtek LLC 407 332-0062
3939 Forsyth Rd Ste A Winter Park (32792) *(G-18502)*

Custom Control Solutions Inc 850 937-8902
1520 Power Blvd Cantonment (32533) *(G-1268)*

Custom Controls Technology Inc 305 805-3700
2230 W 77th St Hialeah (33016) *(G-5103)*

Custom Cornhole Boards Inc 407 203-6886
6169 Cyril Ave Orlando (32809) *(G-12066)*

Custom Craft Laminates Inc 813 877-7100
4705 N Manhattan Ave Tampa (33614) *(G-16751)*

Custom Crafters 954 792-6119
170 Sw 5th St Pompano Beach (33060) *(G-13985)*

Custom Crate & Logistics Co 954 527-5742
280 Sw 33rd St Fort Lauderdale (33315) *(G-3748)*

Custom Design Golf LLC 770 926-4653
38 Sand Dollar Dr Ormond Beach (32176) *(G-12754)*

Custom Door Direct Llc 813 248-5757
1100 N 50th St Bldg 2 Tampa (33619) *(G-16752)*

Custom Doors & Specialties Inc 954 763-4214
2637 N Andrews Ave Wilton Manors (33311) *(G-18337)*

Custom Engraving Company, Melbourne *Also called Imprint Promotions LLC (G-8441)*

Custom Exotic Welding, Auburndale *Also called Brandon Alan Chapman (G-220)*

Custom Fab Inc (HQ) 407 859-3954
109 5th St Orlando (32824) *(G-12067)*

Custom Fabrication Inc 813 754-7571
2604 E Us Highway 92 Plant City (33566) *(G-13758)*

Custom Fbrcations Freeport Inc 850 729-0500
479 Old Florida Sr 10 Rd Valparaiso (32580) *(G-17659)*

Custom Flange Pipe LLC 863 353-6602
3700 W Lake Hamilton Dr Winter Haven (33881) *(G-18433)*

Custom Grafix Industries Inc 727 530-7300
5639 70th Ave N Pinellas Park (33781) *(G-13678)*

Custom Graphics & Sign Design 904 264-7667
99 Industrial Loop N Orange Park (32073) *(G-11822)*

Custom Graphics and Plates Inc 407 696-5448
782 Big Tree Dr Unit 100 Longwood (32750) *(G-7884)*

Custom Graphics Inc 954 563-6756
1801 Green Rd Ste B Deerfield Beach (33064) *(G-2699)*

Custom Illusionz 386 330-5245
319 Howard St E Live Oak (32064) *(G-7844)*

Custom Install Solutions Inc 916 601-1190
3632 Nw 5th Ter Boca Raton (33431) *(G-476)*

Custom Instruments LLC 561 735-9971
711 N Railroad Ave Unit 3 Boynton Beach (33435) *(G-853)*

Custom Klosets & Cabinets Inc 813 246-4806
6403 N 50th St Tampa (33610) *(G-16753)*

Custom Manufacturing Corp 305 863-1001
9324 Nw 102nd St Medley (33178) *(G-8228)*

Custom Manufacturing Inc 607 569-2738
1720 S Tranquil Ave Inverness (34450) *(G-5824)*

Custom Marble Works Inc 813 620-0475
1905 N 43rd St Tampa (33605) *(G-16754)*

Custom Marine Components Inc 904 221-6412
13755 Atlantic Blvd Jacksonville (32225) *(G-6018)*

Custom Marine Concepts Inc (PA) 954 782-1111
2500 Ne 5th Ave Pompano Beach (33064) *(G-13986)*

Custom Marine Joinery Inc 954 822-6057
4032 Ne 5th Ter Oakland Park (33334) *(G-11254)*

Custom Masters Inc 407 331-4634
401 Lake Bennett Ct Longwood (32750) *(G-7885)*

Custom Medical Products Inc 407 865-7211
3909 E Semrn Blvd Ste 599 Apopka (32703) *(G-119)*

Custom Medical Systems Inc 941 722-3434
404 10th Ave W Palmetto (34221) *(G-13163)*

Custom Metal Building Products, Tampa *Also called Corrugated Industries Fla Inc (G-16732)*

Custom Metal Creations LLC 772 807-0000
3106 S Brocksmith Rd Fort Pierce (34945) *(G-4478)*

Custom Metal Designs Inc 407 656-7771
921 W Oakland Ave Oakland (34760) *(G-11228)*

Custom Metal Fabricators Inc 407 841-8551
1415 Long St Orlando (32805) *(G-12068)*

A
L
P
H
A
B
E
T
I
C

Custom Metal Specialties Inc 727 522-3986
  3921 69th Ave N Pinellas Park (33781) *(G-13679)*

Custom Mfg & Engrg Inc 727 548-0522
  3845 Gateway Centre Blvd # 360 Pinellas Park (33782) *(G-13680)*

Custom Mica Furniture Inc 305 888-8480
  575 W 28th St Hialeah (33010) *(G-5104)*

Custom Molding & Casework Inc 407 709-7377
  1650 Travers Ln Deltona (32738) *(G-3043)*

Custom Mosaics Inc 954 610-9436
  11110 W Oakland Park Blvd Sunrise (33351) *(G-16312)*

Custom Plastic Card Company 954 426-1331
  1801 Green Rd Ste A Deerfield Beach (33064) *(G-2700)*

Custom Plastic Developments 407 847-3054
  2710 N John Young Pkwy Kissimmee (34741) *(G-6910)*

Custom Plastic Fabricators 813 884-5200
  6201 Johns Rd Ste 8 Tampa (33634) *(G-16755)*

Custom Powder Coating LLC 386 758-3973
  1129 Se Ormond Witt Rd Lake City (32025) *(G-7016)*

Custom Production, Crestview *Also called Strive Development Corporation (G-2255)*

Custom Quality Mfg Inc 813 290-0805
  5015 Tampa West Blvd Tampa (33634) *(G-16756)*

Custom Screen Printing Florida, Opa Locka *Also called John M Caldwell Distrg Co Inc (G-11758)*

Custom Sign & Awning 727 210-0941
  4502 107th Cir N Ste D Clearwater (33762) *(G-1558)*

Custom Stainless Stl Eqp Inc 305 627-6049
  16215 Nw 15th Ave Miami (33169) *(G-8984)*

Custom Stucco Inc 941 650-5649
  1921 Michigan Ave Englewood (34224) *(G-3517)*

Custom Teak Marine Woodwork 727 768-6065
  4105 8th Ave S Saint Petersburg (33711) *(G-15018)*

Custom Trade Printing.com, Auburndale *Also called Di Jam Holdings Inc (G-229)*

Custom Truss LLC 561 266-3451
  510 Industrial Ave Boynton Beach (33426) *(G-854)*

Custom Tube Products Inc 386 426-0670
  317 Base Leg Dr Edgewater (32132) *(G-3488)*

Custom Wall Systems Inc 772 408-3006
  9495 22nd St Vero Beach (32966) *(G-17752)*

Custom Watersports Eqp Inc 941 753-9949
  1218 50th Avenue Plz W Bradenton (34207) *(G-965)*

Custom WD Architectural Mllwk 786 290-5412
  13119 Sw 122nd Ave Miami (33186) *(G-8985)*

Custom WD Designs of Pensacola 850 476-9663
  3335 Addison Dr Pensacola (32514) *(G-13481)*

Custom Wheel, Holly Hill *Also called CC Machine Inc (G-5512)*

Custom Window Systems, Ocala *Also called Cws Holding Company LLC (G-11362)*

Custom Window Systems Inc 352 368-6922
  1900 Sw 44th Ave Ocala (34474) *(G-11361)*

Custom Wldg & Fabrication Inc 863 967-1000
  364 Recker Hwy Auburndale (33823) *(G-227)*

Custom Wood Products Inc 904 737-6906
  3811 University Blvd W # 10 Jacksonville (32217) *(G-6019)*

Customer 1st LLC 941 585-5123
  6413 Taneytown St North Port (34291) *(G-11192)*

Customer First Inc Naples 239 949-8518
  10940 Harmony Park Dr Bonita Springs (34135) *(G-793)*

Customer Success LLC 386 265-4882
  1892 Clubhouse Dr Port Orange (32128) *(G-14331)*

Customfab Inc 786 339-9158
  23601 Sw 133rd Ave Homestead (33032) *(G-5705)*

Cut Services LLC 305 560-0905
  8264 Nw 58th St Doral (33166) *(G-3180)*

Cutler Hammer, Tampa *Also called Eaton Corporation (G-16795)*

Cutoutz.com, Riviera Beach *Also called D I H Corporation (G-14613)*

Cutrale Citrus Juices, Auburndale *Also called Cutrale Farms Inc (G-228)*

Cutrale Citrus Juices USA Inc 352 728-7800
  11 Cloud St Leesburg (34748) *(G-7765)*

Cutrale Farms Inc 863 965-5000
  602 Mckean St Auburndale (33823) *(G-228)*

Cutting Edge Archtctral Mldngs, Sarasota *Also called Cutting Edge Moldings LLC (G-15465)*

Cutting Edge Archtctral Mldngs 941 727-1111
  7282 55th Ave E Pmb 176 Bradenton (34203) *(G-966)*

Cutting Edge Mch Fbrcation Inc 321 626-0588
  534 Saint Johns St Bldg C Cocoa (32922) *(G-1913)*

Cutting Edge Moldings LLC 734 649-1500
  7116 24th Ct E Sarasota (34243) *(G-15465)*

Cutting Edge Sgns Grphics of P 727 546-3700
  12795 49th St N Clearwater (33762) *(G-1559)*

Cv Technology Inc 561 694-9588
  15852 Mercantile Ct # 100 Jupiter (33478) *(G-6708)*

Cve Reporter Inc 954 421-5566
  3501 West Dr Deerfield Beach (33442) *(G-2701)*

Cvg Aerospace LLC 786 293-9923
  13500 Sw 134th Ave Ste 6 Miami (33186) *(G-8986)*

Cvista LLC 813 405-3000
  4333 Garden Vista Dr Riverview (33578) *(G-14560)*

Cw21 Inc 813 754-1760
  3404 E Us Highway 92 Plant City (33566) *(G-13759)*

Cwi Industrial Services, Frostproof *Also called Cornelius Welding Inc (G-4636)*

Cwp Sheet Metal Inc 407 349-0926
  1661 Bandit Way Geneva (32732) *(G-4786)*

Cws Holding Company LLC 352 368-6922
  1900 Sw 44th Ave Ocala (34474) *(G-11362)*

Cx1 Miami Mobile Mix, Homestead *Also called Cemex Cnstr Mtls Fla LLC (G-5702)*

Cxac, Weston *Also called Cross Atlantic Commodities Inc (G-18235)*

Cyalume Tech Holdings Inc (HQ) 954 315-4939
  910 Se 17th St Ste 300 Fort Lauderdale (33316) *(G-3749)*

Cyber Fuels Inc 866 771-3580
  2401 Pga Blvd Ste 196 Palm Beach Gardens (33410) *(G-12964)*

Cyber Group USA LLC 888 574-9555
  3770 Park Central Blvd N Pompano Beach (33064) *(G-13987)*

Cyber Manufacturing Inc 786 457-1973
  14440 Sw 110th St Miami (33186) *(G-8987)*

Cyber Security Solutions, Tampa *Also called Willsonet Inc (G-17432)*

Cybortrack Solutions Inc 805 904-5677
  657 Florida Central Pkwy Longwood (32750) *(G-7886)*

Cyclelogic Products, Stuart *Also called Wmr Cycle Performance Inc (G-16253)*

Cycling Quarterly LLC 786 367-2497
  1007 N Federal Hwy 383 Fort Lauderdale (33304) *(G-3750)*

Cyclo Industries, Jupiter *Also called Niteo Products LLC (G-6771)*

Cyclone Belt Washer, Clearwater *Also called Douglas Machines Corp (G-1568)*

Cyclone Power Technologies Inc (PA) 954 943-8721
  601 Ne 26th Ct Pompano Beach (33064) *(G-13988)*

Cygnus Aerospace Incorporated 850 612-1618
  1001 Industrial Dr Crestview (32539) *(G-2242)*

Cyipcom Inc 954 727-2500
  300 E Oakland Park Blvd # 358 Oakland Park (33334) *(G-11255)*

Cymed, Sarasota *Also called Nkem Inc (G-15762)*

Cypress & Grove Brewing Co LLC 352 376-4993
  1001 Nw 4th St Gainesville (32601) *(G-4674)*

Cypress Folding Cartons Inc 813 884-5418
  6025 Jet Port Indus Blvd Tampa (33634) *(G-16757)*

Cypress Pensacola LLC 850 724-1124
  1124 W Garden St Pensacola (32502) *(G-13482)*

Cypress Signs, Winter Haven *Also called Superior Unlimited Entps Inc (G-18472)*

Cyto Dyncorp Inc 813 527-6969
  110 Crenshaw Lake Rd Lutz (33548) *(G-7988)*

Czarnikow Group Ltd 786 476-0000
  333 Se 2nd Ave Ste 3410 Miami (33131) *(G-8988)*

D & A Machine Inc 407 275-5770
  7220 Old Cheney Hwy Orlando (32807) *(G-12069)*

D & B Bookbinders, Hialeah *Also called Dobbs & Brodeur Bookbinders (G-5121)*

D & B Machine Inc 941 355-8002
  1855 61st St Sarasota (34243) *(G-15466)*

D & D Building Contractors Inc 954 791-2075
  3380 Sw 50th Ave Davie (33314) *(G-2402)*

D & D Machine & Hydraulics Inc 239 275-7177
  10945 Metro Pkwy Fort Myers (33966) *(G-4228)*

D & D Manufacturing LLC (PA) 321 652-4509
  2655 Cherrywood Ln Titusville (32780) *(G-17584)*

D & D MBL Wldg Fabrication Inc (PA) 954 791-3385
  222 Sw 21st Ter Fort Lauderdale (33312) *(G-3751)*

D & D MBL Wldg Fabrication Inc 772 489-7900
  5300 Steel Blvd Fort Pierce (34946) *(G-4479)*

D & D Millwork Distributors, Davie *Also called D & D Building Contractors Inc (G-2402)*

D & D Plastering & Lath Inc 561 312-7256
  1707 Katherine Ct Lake Worth (33461) *(G-7194)*

D & D Welding, Fort Lauderdale *Also called D & D MBL Wldg Fabrication Inc (G-3751)*

D & D Welding, Fort Pierce *Also called D & D MBL Wldg Fabrication Inc (G-4479)*

D & D Welding Inc 850 438-9011
  2715 N W St Pensacola (32505) *(G-13483)*

D & D Wldg & Fabrication LLC (PA) 954 791-3385
  222 Sw 21st Ter Fort Lauderdale (33312) *(G-3752)*

D & G Custom Cabinetry Inc 954 561-8822
  5712 Coco Palm Dr Tamarac (33319) *(G-16528)*

D & G Millwork & Cabinetry LLC 305 830-3000
  2618 Ne 191st St Miami (33180) *(G-8989)*

D & I Carbide Tool Co Inc 727 848-3356
  12104 Parkwood St Hudson (34669) *(G-5768)*

D & J Logos, Tampa *Also called Image Depot (G-16932)*

D & J Machinery Inc 863 983-3171
  728 E Trinidad Ave Clewiston (33440) *(G-1887)*

D & L Auto & Marine Supplies 305 593-0560
  5601 Nw 79th Ave Doral (33166) *(G-3181)*

D & M Truss Co 850 944-4864
  2620 W Michigan Ave Pensacola (32526) *(G-13484)*

D & N Cabinetry Inc 863 471-1500
  2920 Kenilworth Blvd Sebring (33870) *(G-15917)*

D & R Delivery Services of Pb 561 602-6427
  312 Canterbury Dr W Riviera Beach (33407) *(G-14612)*

D & R Signs Inc 386 252-2777
  133 Thomasson Ave Daytona Beach (32117) *(G-2539)*

D & S Hauling, Clearwater *Also called D & S Pallets Inc (G-1560)*

D & S Logging Inc 850 638-5500
  261 Highway 273 Chipley (32428) *(G-1455)*

D & S Pallet Recycle Center 352 351-0070
  2640 Nw 35th St Ocala (34475) *(G-11363)*

D & S Pallets Inc 727 540-0061
12195 46th St N Clearwater (33762) *(G-1560)*
D & S Steel 352 489-8791
19450 Sw 5th Pl Dunnellon (34431) *(G-3464)*
D A B Constructors Inc 352 797-3537
3300 Northeast Pkwy Brooksville (34609) *(G-1150)*
D and I Trucking Express Inc 786 443-3320
21009 Nw 14th Pl Apt 353 Miami (33169) *(G-8990)*
D and S Superior Coatings Inc 360 388-6099
6150 Metro Plantation Rd Fort Myers (33966) *(G-4229)*
D C Inc Prtble Wldg Fbrication 863 533-4483
3971 Mammoth Grove Rd Frostproof (33843) *(G-4637)*
D C S, Fort Lauderdale *Also called Dons Custom Service Inc (G-3772)*
D D B Corporation 305 721-9506
7340 Nw 35th Ave Miami (33147) *(G-8991)*
D D Welding 732 998-1100
13153 Fish Cove Dr Spring Hill (34609) *(G-16070)*
D E E Custom Fabricators Inc 863 667-1850
3545 Waterfield Pkwy Lakeland (33803) *(G-7302)*
D F S, Melbourne *Also called Data Flow Systems Inc (G-8397)*
D G, Fort Lauderdale *Also called Dayton-Granger Inc (G-3758)*
D G Morrison Inc (PA) 813 865-0208
13209 Byrd Dr Odessa (33556) *(G-11546)*
D G Steel Rule Die Mfg, Miami Lakes *Also called Maq Investments Group Inc (G-10316)*
D G Yuengling and Son Inc 813 972-8500
11111 N 30th St Tampa (33612) *(G-16758)*
D Group North America LLC 646 809-0859
12486 W Atlantic Blvd Coral Springs (33071) *(G-2145)*
D I H Corporation 561 881-8705
1750 Australian Ave Ste 3 Riviera Beach (33404) *(G-14613)*
D I R Inc 863 661-5360
3430 Flightline Dr Lakeland (33811) *(G-7303)*
D J Camco Corporation 904 355-5995
2426 Dennis St Jacksonville (32204) *(G-6020)*
D J Trusses Unlimited Inc 863 687-4796
3125 Reynolds Rd Lakeland (33803) *(G-7304)*
D L S Electronics, Miami *Also called Digital Lighting Systems Inc (G-9032)*
D M P, Ocala *Also called Dixie Metal Products Inc (G-11368)*
D M S I, North Venice *Also called Diversfied Mtl Specialists Inc (G-11211)*
D M T Inc 321 267-3931
817 N Cocoa Blvd Cocoa (32922) *(G-1914)*
D Mahan Cabinets, Cutler Bay *Also called Mahan Cabinets (G-2295)*
D Maxwell Company Inc 727 868-9151
8323 Arcola Ave Port Richey (34667) *(G-14360)*
D N L Performance Inc 786 295-8831
1797 Opa Locka Blvd Opa Locka (33054) *(G-11735)*
D R C Industries Inc 954 971-0699
4100 N Powerline Rd Z1 Pompano Beach (33073) *(G-13989)*
D R Nickelson & Company Inc 386 755-6565
229 Nw Wilks Ln Ste 1 Lake City (32055) *(G-7017)*
D R P, Boca Raton *Also called Direct Response Publication (G-487)*
D R S Optronics Inc 321 309-1500
100 N Babcock St Melbourne (32935) *(G-8396)*
D T Woodcrafters Corp 305 556-3771
1677 W 31st Pl Hialeah (33012) *(G-5105)*
D Turin & Company Inc 305 825-2004
8045 W 26th Ct Hialeah (33016) *(G-5106)*
D V M Pharmaceuticals Inc 305 575-6950
3040 Universal Blvd Weston (33331) *(G-18236)*
D W Allen Marine Svcs Inc 904 358-1933
1841 Wambolt St Jacksonville (32202) *(G-6021)*
D& R Printing LLC 941 378-3311
6569 Tarawa Dr Sarasota (34241) *(G-15649)*
D&D Wood Working Inc 407 427-0106
8622 Brackenwood Dr Orlando (32829) *(G-12070)*
D&W Fine Pack LLC 305 592-4329
7740 Nw 55th St Doral (33166) *(G-3182)*
D' Lanerg, Miami *Also called American Hygenic Laboratories (G-8717)*
D-Lux Printing Inc 850 457-8494
3320 N W St Pensacola (32505) *(G-13485)*
D-R Media and Investments LLC 941 207-1602
300 Tamiami Trl S Venice (34285) *(G-17682)*
D-Rep Plastics Inc 407 240-4154
11345 53rd St N Clearwater (33760) *(G-1561)*
D1 Locker LLC 305 446-9041
4880 Nw 4th St Miami (33126) *(G-8992)*
Da Vinci Cabinetry LLC 239 633-7957
25241 Bernwood Dr Ste 7 Bonita Springs (34135) *(G-794)*
Da Vinci Systems Inc 954 688-5600
124 Th Ave Coral Springs (33065) *(G-2146)*
Daby Products Carisen 305 559-3018
5757 Sw 8th St West Miami (33144) *(G-17904)*
Dac Wood Work Inc 954 729-9232
428 Se 11th St Apt 202a Deerfield Beach (33441) *(G-2702)*
DAccord Shirts & Guayaberas 305 576-0926
7320 Nw 12th St Miami (33126) *(G-8993)*
Dackor Inc 407 654-5013
310 E Crown Point Rd Winter Garden (34787) *(G-18382)*
Dackor 3d Laminates, Winter Garden *Also called Dackor Inc (G-18382)*
Dade Doors Inc 305 556-8980
1707 W 32nd Pl Hialeah (33012) *(G-5107)*
Dade Engineering Corp 305 885-2766
6855 Edgewater Dr Apt 1e Coral Gables (33133) *(G-2045)*
Dade Engineering Group LLC 305 885-2766
7700 Nw 37th Ave Miami (33147) *(G-8994)*
Dade Equipment 305 717-9901
8260 Nw 70th St Miami (33166) *(G-8995)*
Dade Made 305 846-9482
478 W 28th St Hialeah (33010) *(G-5108)*
Dade Pump & Supply Co 305 235-5000
14261 S Dixie Hwy Miami (33176) *(G-8996)*
Dade Truss Company Inc 305 592-8245
6401 Nw 74th Ave Miami (33166) *(G-8997)*
Dads Powder Coating 813 715-6561
40420 Free Fall Ave Zephyrhills (33542) *(G-18611)*
Daeco, Coral Gables *Also called Dade Engineering Corp (G-2045)*
Dagher & Sons Inc 904 998-0911
11775 Marco Beach Dr Jacksonville (32224) *(G-6022)*
DAGHER PRINTING, Jacksonville *Also called Dagher & Sons Inc (G-6022)*
Daher Inc (PA) 954 893-1400
601 Ne 10th St Pompano Beach (33060) *(G-13990)*
Dahlquist Enterprises Inc 407 896-2294
1315 N Mills Ave Orlando (32803) *(G-12071)*
Dahlquists Printing & Graphics, Orlando *Also called Dahlquist Enterprises Inc (G-12071)*
Daigle Tool & Die Inc 954 785-9989
764 Ne 42nd St Deerfield Beach (33064) *(G-2703)*
Daikin Comfort Tech Mfg LP 904 355-4520
1934 W Beaver St Jacksonville (32209) *(G-6023)*
Daily Business Review, Miami *Also called Alm Global LLC (G-8696)*
Daily Buzz 407 673-5400
3260 University Blvd Winter Park (32792) *(G-18503)*
Daily Commercial, Leesburg *Also called Harborpoint Media LLC (G-7780)*
Daily Green 352 226-8288
436 Se 2nd St Gainesville (32601) *(G-4675)*
Daily Melt 305 519-2585
3401 N Miami Ave Miami (33127) *(G-8998)*
Daily News Inc 386 312-5200
1825 Saint Johns Ave Palatka (32177) *(G-12865)*
Daily Racing Enterprises Inc 772 287-9106
10922 Sw Hawkview Cir Stuart (34997) *(G-16136)*
Daily Room 754 200-5153
1000 S Pine Island Rd # 160 Plantation (33324) *(G-13842)*
Daily Therapy Services Inc 954 649-3620
8040 Nw 54th St Lauderhill (33351) *(G-7730)*
Dailys 904 448-0562
9143 Baymeadows Rd Jacksonville (32256) *(G-6024)*
Dailys 904 880-4784
13800 Old St Augustine Rd Jacksonville (32258) *(G-6025)*
Dailys 1113 Shell 904 608-0219
40 Settlement Dr Ponte Vedra (32081) *(G-14256)*
Dain M Bayer 407 647-0679
2333 Chantilly Ave Winter Park (32789) *(G-18504)*
Dairy Fairy LLC 305 865-1506
9457 Harding Ave Surfside (33154) *(G-16395)*
Dairy Feeds Inc (PA) 863 763-0258
1901 Nw 9th St Okeechobee (34972) *(G-11602)*
Dairy-Mix Inc 813 621-8098
9314 Princess Palm Ave Tampa (33619) *(G-16759)*
Dais Corp 727 375-8484
11552 Prosperous Dr Odessa (33556) *(G-11547)*
Daisy Crazy Inc 305 300-5144
3902 Estepona Ave Doral (33178) *(G-3183)*
Daje Industries Inc 305 592-7711
6020 Nw 99th Ave Doral (33178) *(G-3184)*
Dakim Inc 561 790-0884
11420 Okeechobee Blvd D Royal Palm Beach (33411) *(G-14762)*
Dakota Plumbing Products LLC (PA) 954 987-3430
800 Nw 65th St Ste B Fort Lauderdale (33309) *(G-3753)*
Dalane Machining Inc 813 854-5905
13530 Wright Cir Tampa (33626) *(G-16760)*
Dale Mabry Heating & Metal Co 813 877-1574
4313 W South Ave Tampa (33614) *(G-16761)*
Dale Photo and Digital Inc 954 925-0103
2960 Simms St Hollywood (33020) *(G-5560)*
Dalian Platinum Chem Ltd Corp 954 501-0564
263 Fan Palm Rd Boca Raton (33432) *(G-477)*
Dalimar Corp 727 525-8115
6295 42nd St N Pinellas Park (33781) *(G-13681)*
Dalpro Commercial Rfrgn, Tampa *Also called Allied Manufacturing Inc (G-16576)*
Dan Boudreau Inc 407 491-7611
3325 Red Ash Cir Oviedo (32766) *(G-12817)*
Dan Frame & Trim Inc 352 726-4567
7770 E Rustic Trl Inverness (34453) *(G-5825)*
Dan Lipman and Associates 561 245-8672
15852 Corintha Ter Delray Beach (33446) *(G-2953)*
Dana Andrews Woodworking 561 882-0444
1748 Australian Ave Riviera Beach (33404) *(G-14614)*
Danam Electronics, Miami Lakes *Also called Drew Scientific Inc (G-10297)*

ALPHABETIC

Danas Safty Supply Inc....305 639-6024
1622 Nw 82nd Ave Doral (33126) **(G-3185)**
Danco Machine Inc....727 501-0460
13131 92nd St Ste 608a Largo (33773) **(G-7569)**
Dandee Foods, Lakeland *Also called ME Thompson Inc* **(G-7393)**
Dandee Sandwich, Jacksonville *Also called ME Thompson Inc* **(G-6287)**
Dandy Media Corporation....954 616-6800
2031 Sw 31st Ave Hallandale (33009) **(G-4923)**
Dandyprint.com, Hallandale *Also called Dandy Media Corporation* **(G-4923)**
Danfoss LLC....850 504-4800
1769 E Paul Dirac Dr Tallahassee (32310) **(G-16430)**
Danfoss Turbocor Compressors, Tallahassee *Also called Danfoss LLC* **(G-16430)**
Dania Cut Holdings Inc....954 923-9545
760 Ne 7th Ave Dania Beach (33004) **(G-2350)**
Dania Cut Super Yacht Repair, Dania Beach *Also called Dania Cut Holdings Inc* **(G-2350)**
Danibella Inc....561 307-9274
7040 Seminole Pratt Whitn Loxahatchee (33470) **(G-7968)**
Daniel Bustamante....305 779-7777
1210 Placetas Ave Coral Gables (33146) **(G-2046)**
Daniel Lampert Communications....407 327-7000
101 Brookshire Ct Winter Springs (32708) **(G-18564)**
Danielle Fence Mfg Co Inc....863 425-3182
4855 State Road 60 W Mulberry (33860) **(G-10621)**
Daniels Manufacturing Corp....407 855-6161
526 Thorpe Rd Orlando (32824) **(G-12072)**
Daniels Offset Printing Inc....305 261-3263
8541 Franjo Rd Cutler Bay (33189) **(G-2287)**
Daniels Whl Sign & Plas Inc....386 736-4918
5224 W State Road 46 Sanford (32771) **(G-15299)**
Danifer Printing Inc....727 849-5883
7117 Us Highway 19 New Port Richey (34652) **(G-10966)**
Danker Laboratories Inc....941 758-7711
1144 Tallevast Rd Ste 106 Sarasota (34243) **(G-15467)**
Danker Labs, Sarasota *Also called Danker Laboratories Inc* **(G-15467)**
Danly Corporation (PA)....305 285-0111
3121 Commodore Plz Ph 5 Miami (33133) **(G-8999)**
Dannys Prtg Svc Sups & Eqp Inc....305 757-2282
7233 Biscayne Blvd Miami (33138) **(G-9000)**
Dannys Welding Services Inc....786 436-8087
702 Sw 32nd Ave Miami (33135) **(G-9001)**
Dans Custom Sheet Metal Inc....239 594-0530
5700 Washington St Naples (34109) **(G-10723)**
Dapp Embroidery Inc....407 260-1600
1075 Fla Cntl Pkwy Ste 25 Longwood (32750) **(G-7887)**
Dark Horse Signs and Prtg LLC....850 684-3833
6476 Starfish Cv Gulf Breeze (32563) **(G-4879)**
Dark Lake Software Inc....407 602-8046
1229 Wading Waters Cir Winter Park (32792) **(G-18505)**
Dark Lake Systems, Winter Park *Also called Dark Lake Software Inc* **(G-18505)**
Dark Storm Manufacturing LLC....516 983-3473
3390 N Courtenay Pkwy Merritt Island (32953) **(G-8583)**
Darkhorse Inc (PA)....954 849-4440
5470 Nw 10th Ter Fort Lauderdale (33309) **(G-3754)**
Darland Bakery Inc....407 894-1061
42 Cardamon Dr Orlando (32825) **(G-12073)**
Darling Ingredients Inc....904 964-8083
11313 Se 52nd Ave Starke (32091) **(G-16100)**
Darling Ingredients Inc....863 425-0065
1001 Orient Rd Tampa (33619) **(G-16762)**
Darly Filtration Inc....727 318-7064
4537 22nd St N Saint Petersburg (33714) **(G-15019)**
Darmar Cabinets Inc....786 556-5784
5273 Nw 161st St Miami Lakes (33014) **(G-10294)**
Darmerica LLC....321 219-9111
198 Wilshire Blvd Casselberry (32707) **(G-1414)**
Darmiven Inc....305 871-1157
6355 Nw 36th St Ste 506 Virginia Gardens (33166) **(G-17821)**
Darnel Inc....954 929-0085
2331 Thomas St Hollywood (33020) **(G-5561)**
Darren Thomas Glass Co Inc....863 655-9500
251 Commercial Ct Sebring (33876) **(G-15918)**
Dart Container Company Fla LLC....813 752-1990
4610 Airport Rd Plant City (33563) **(G-13760)**
Dart Container Corp Florida....941 358-1202
1952 Field Rd Ste B3 Sarasota (34231) **(G-15650)**
Dart Industries Inc (HQ)....407 826-5050
14901 S Ornge Blssom Trl Orlando (32837) **(G-12074)**
Dasan Zhone Solutions Inc....305 789-6680
801 Brickell Ave Fl 9 Miami (33131) **(G-9002)**
Dashclicks LLC....866 600-3369
2901 Stirling Rd Ste 210 Fort Lauderdale (33312) **(G-3755)**
Dashcovers Plus Depot Distrs....954 961-7774
18304 Oak Way Dr Hudson (34667) **(G-5769)**
Dasops Inc....386 258-6230
2425 Dodge Dr Daytona Beach (32118) **(G-2540)**
Dass Logistics Inc....954 837-8339
6601 Lyons Rd Ste H1 Coconut Creek (33073) **(G-1983)**
Dat Software Inc....305 266-5150
560 Nw 59th Ave Miami (33126) **(G-9003)**
Data Access International Inc....305 238-0012
14000 Sw 119th Ave Miami (33186) **(G-9004)**
Data Buoy Instrumentation LLC....239 849-7063
75 Mid Cape Ter Ste 8 Cape Coral (33991) **(G-1330)**
Data Cooling Tech Canada LLC....813 865-4701
5110 W Clifton St Tampa (33634) **(G-16763)**
Data Flow Systems Inc....321 259-5009
605 N John Rodes Blvd Melbourne (32934) **(G-8397)**
Data Graphics Inc....352 589-1312
3800 Progress Blvd Mount Dora (32757) **(G-10600)**
Data Image, Winter Park *Also called DMC Components Intl LLC* **(G-18508)**
Data Line, Sun City Center *Also called Pss Communications Inc* **(G-16266)**
Data Phone Wire & Cable Corp....954 761-7171
3420 Sw 14th St Fort Lauderdale (33312) **(G-3756)**
Data Protection Solutions, Hollywood *Also called Arco Computer Products LLC* **(G-5529)**
Data Publishers Inc....954 752-2332
9602 Nw 36th Mnr Coral Springs (33065) **(G-2147)**
Datacore Software Corporation (PA)....954 377-6000
1901 W Cypress Creek Rd # 200 Fort Lauderdale (33309) **(G-3757)**
Datagrid Inc....352 371-7608
4111 Nw 6th St Ste D Gainesville (32609) **(G-4676)**
Datamax International Corp (HQ)....407 578-8007
4501 Pkwy Commerce Blvd Orlando (32808) **(G-12075)**
Datamax-Oneil Corporation (HQ)....800 816-9649
4501 Pkwy Commerce Blvd Orlando (32808) **(G-12076)**
Datamentors LLC (PA)....813 960-7800
2319 Oak Myrtle Ln # 101 Wesley Chapel (33544) **(G-17873)**
Datum Metal Products, Mangonia Park *Also called Hoover Canvas Products Co* **(G-8092)**
Dauer Manufacturing Corp....800 883-2590
10100 Nw 116th Way Ste 1 Medley (33178) **(G-8229)**
Dauntless Usa Inc....904 996-8800
9995 Gate Pkwy N Ste 400 Jacksonville (32246) **(G-6026)**
Dave Siler Transport....239 348-3283
111 14th St Se Naples (34117) **(G-10724)**
Davenport -Block Manufacturing, Davenport *Also called Cemex Cnstr Mtls Fla LLC* **(G-2362)**
David Chittum....386 754-6127
1800 Bonita Way S Saint Petersburg (33712) **(G-15020)**
David Delights LLC....407 648-2020
4677 L B Mcleod Rd Ste J Orlando (32811) **(G-12077)**
David Dobbs Enterprises Inc (PA)....904 824-6171
4600 Us 1 N Saint Augustine (32095) **(G-14823)**
David E Ashe Sawmill....904 377-4800
5440 State Road 13 N Saint Augustine (32092) **(G-14824)**
David Gill Enterprises....863 422-5711
110 Hwy 17 92 Davenport (33837) **(G-2363)**
David Jacobs Pubg Group LLC....813 321-4119
14497 N D Mabry Hwy 135 Tampa (33618) **(G-16764)**
David Perkins Enterprises Inc....850 234-0002
7538 Mcelvey Rd Panama City Beach (32408) **(G-13329)**
David R Case....727 808-9330
18519 Floralton Dr Spring Hill (34610) **(G-16084)**
David R Nassivera Inc....352 351-1176
2250 Ne 70th St Ocala (34479) **(G-11364)**
David Russell Anodizing....407 302-4041
2501 Mccracken Rd Sanford (32771) **(G-15300)**
David S Stoyka....561 848-2599
8125 Monetary Dr Ste H6 Riviera Beach (33404) **(G-14615)**
David Sayne Masonry Inc....386 873-4696
1010 Geryl Way Deland (32724) **(G-2860)**
David Viera LLC....305 218-3401
7828 W 29th Ln Apt 101 Hialeah (33018) **(G-5109)**
David's Novelties, Pensacola *Also called Kenneth S Jarrell Inc* **(G-13534)**
Davie Embroidme....954 452-0600
2471 S University Dr Davie (33324) **(G-2403)**
Davila Woodworking Inc....954 458-0460
214 Nw 1st Ave Hallandale Beach (33009) **(G-4943)**
Davis Concrete Inc (PA)....727 733-3141
1670 Sunshine Dr Clearwater (33765) **(G-1562)**
Davis Franklin Printing Co....813 259-2500
520 N Willow Ave Tampa (33606) **(G-16765)**
Davis Kwik Kerb LLC....386 690-0058
656 S State Road 415 New Smyrna Beach (32168) **(G-10999)**
Davis Mail Services Inc....904 477-7970
13464 Grover Rd Jacksonville (32226) **(G-6027)**
Davis-Wick Talent MGT LLC....407 369-1614
5400 Nw 27th Ct Margate (33063) **(G-8127)**
Davit Master Corp....727 573-4414
5560 Ulmerton Rd Clearwater (33760) **(G-1563)**
Dax Copying and Printing Inc....954 236-3000
1868 N University Dr # 106 Plantation (33322) **(G-13843)**
Day Metal Products LLC....352 799-9258
119 E Dr M L King Jr Blvd Brooksville (34601) **(G-1151)**
Day Shopping LLC....321 616-4504
10738 Pleasant Knoll Dr Tampa (33647) **(G-16766)**
Dayoris Doors....954 374-8538
1945 Hayes St Hollywood (33020) **(G-5562)**
Daystar International Inc....813 281-0200
917 Terra Mar Dr Tampa (33613) **(G-16767)**
Dayton Industrial Corporation....941 351-4454
2237 Industrial Blvd Sarasota (34234) **(G-15651)**

Dayton Superior Corporation 407 859-4541
7415 Emerald Dunes Dr # 1200 Orlando (32822) *(G-12078)*

Dayton-Granger Inc 954 463-3451
3299 Sw 9th Ave Fort Lauderdale (33315) *(G-3758)*

Daytona Beach Jet Center, Daytona Beach *Also called Sheltair Daytona Beach LLC (G-2597)*

Daytona Cooling Systems, Doral *Also called Daytona Rubber Company Inc (G-3186)*

Daytona Dock & Seawall Service 386 255-7909
862 Terrace Ave Daytona Beach (32114) *(G-2541)*

Daytona Glass Works LLC 386 274-2550
843 Bill France Blvd Daytona Beach (32117) *(G-2542)*

Daytona Helmets International, Daytona Beach *Also called Jay Squared LLC (G-2564)*

Daytona Magic Inc 386 252-6767
136 S Beach St Daytona Beach (32114) *(G-2543)*

Daytona Parts Company 386 427-7108
1191 Turnbull Bay Rd New Smyrna Beach (32168) *(G-11000)*

Daytona Rubber Company Inc 305 513-4105
10460 Nw 29th Ter Doral (33172) *(G-3186)*

Daytona Trophy Inc 386 253-2806
2413 Bellevue Ave Daytona Beach (32114) *(G-2544)*

Daytona Welding & Fabrication 386 562-0093
837 Pinewood St Daytona Beach (32117) *(G-2545)*

Dazmed Inc 561 571-2020
508 Nw 77th St Boca Raton (33487) *(G-478)*

Dazmed Pharmaceuticals, Boca Raton *Also called Dazmed Inc (G-478)*

Db Doors Inc 561 798-6684
346 Pike Rd Ste 6 West Palm Beach (33411) *(G-17976)*

Db Motoring Group Inc 305 685-0707
8075 W 20th Ave Hialeah (33014) *(G-5110)*

Db Tucker LLC 561 301-4974
126 S Village Way Jupiter (33458) *(G-6709)*

Dbi Services LLC 239 218-5204
5893 Entp Pkwy Ste A Fort Myers (33905) *(G-4230)*

Dbn Investment LLC 407 917-2525
3300 S Hiawassee Rd # 107 Orlando (32835) *(G-12079)*

Dbt Marine Products, Largo *Also called Discount Boat Tops Inc (G-7571)*

DC Apparel Inc 863 325-9273
3260 Dundee Rd Winter Haven (33884) *(G-18434)*

DC Kerckhoff Company 239 597-7218
1901 Elsa St Naples (34109) *(G-10725)*

Dcg Enterprises LLC 813 931-4303
2702 N 35th St Tampa (33605) *(G-16768)*

DCI Counter Tops, Crystal River *Also called Deem Cabinets Inc (G-2274)*

Dcp Holdings 863 644-0030
3502 Dmg Dr Ste 102 Lakeland (33811) *(G-7305)*

Dcr Fabrication Inc 863 709-1121
4101 Holden Rd Lakeland (33811) *(G-7306)*

Dcsm, Naples *Also called Dans Custom Sheet Metal Inc (G-10723)*

Dcwfab LLC 941 320-6095
3374 Howell Pl Sarasota (34232) *(G-15652)*

Ddci Inc 407 814-0225
995 W Kennedy Blvd Ste 35 Orlando (32810) *(G-12080)*

Ddi System LLC (PA) 203 364-1200
1900 Main St Sarasota (34236) *(G-15653)*

Ddp Holdings LLC (HQ) 813 712-2515
4450 E Adamo Dr Ste 501 Tampa (33605) *(G-16769)*

DDy Martinez LLC 786 263-2672
3105 Nw 107th Ave Ste 400 Doral (33172) *(G-3187)*

De Funiak Springs Yard, Defuniak Springs *Also called Legacy Vulcan LLC (G-2840)*

De La Rosa, Lauderdale Lakes *Also called Delarosa Real Foods LLC (G-7712)*

De Lima Consultants Group Inc (PA) 954 933-7030
4216 Nw 120th Ave Coral Springs (33065) *(G-2148)*

De Loach Industries, Sarasota *Also called Wes Holdings Corp (G-15871)*

De Luna Coffee Intl Inc 850 478-6371
1014 Underwood Ave Ste D Pensacola (32504) *(G-13486)*

De Ruiter Electric Motor, Miami *Also called Dade Pump & Supply Co (G-8996)*

De Todos Tortillas Inc 305 248-4402
820 N Krome Ave Homestead (33030) *(G-5706)*

De Vinco Company 941 722-1100
435 Canning Plant Rd Seffner (33584) *(G-15955)*

Deako Coating & Chemical Inc 305 634-5162
2540 Nw 29th Ave Ste 105 Miami (33142) *(G-9005)*

Deako Coatings Chemical 305 323-9914
10459 Sw 185th Ter Cutler Bay (33157) *(G-2288)*

Deal To Win Inc 718 609-1165
4050 Ne 9th Ave Oakland Park (33334) *(G-11256)*

Dealer It Group LLC 904 518-3379
5220 Belfort Rd Ste 400 Jacksonville (32256) *(G-6028)*

Dealer Printing Service, Tampa *Also called Ed Vance Printing Company Inc (G-16797)*

Dealerups Inc 407 557-5368
4185 W Lake Mary Blvd # 2 Lake Mary (32746) *(G-7068)*

Dean Dairy Holdings LLC 239 334-1114
3579 Work Dr Fort Myers (33916) *(G-4231)*

Dean Steel Buildings Inc (PA) 239 334-1051
2929 Industrial Ave Fort Myers (33901) *(G-4232)*

Deans Cstm Shtmtl Fbrction In 813 757-6270
5106 Varnadore Ln Dover (33527) *(G-3429)*

DEb Printing & Graphics Inc 954 968-0060
6500 Nw 15th Ave Ste 100 Fort Lauderdale (33309) *(G-3759)*

Debanie Inc 239 254-1222
6631 Sable Ridge Ln Naples (34109) *(G-10726)*

Debruyne Enterprise Inc 850 562-0491
5186 Woodlane Cir Tallahassee (32303) *(G-16431)*

Debut Development LLC 863 448-9081
897 S 6th Ave Ste 1 Wauchula (33873) *(G-17825)*

Debway Corporation 305 818-6353
2343 W 76th St Hialeah (33016) *(G-5111)*

Dec Metals, Lakeland *Also called DEC Sheet Metal Inc (G-7307)*

DEC Sheet Metal Inc 863 669-0707
3015 Waterfield Cir Lakeland (33803) *(G-7307)*

Decamil, Orlando *Also called AC Signs LLC (G-11863)*

Decimal, LLC 407 330-3300
121 Central Park Pl Sanford (32771) *(G-15301)*

Decimal Engineering, Coral Springs *Also called AL Garey & Associates Inc (G-2130)*

Deco Abrusci International LLC 305 406-3401
8485 Nw 29th St Doral (33122) *(G-3188)*

Deco Boat Lifts, Safety Harbor *Also called Deco Power Lift Inc (G-14785)*

Deco Lav Inc (PA) 561 274-2110
4920 Bocaire Blvd Boca Raton (33487) *(G-479)*

Deco Power Lift Inc 727 736-4529
1041 Harbor Lake Dr Safety Harbor (34695) *(G-14785)*

Deco Shades Solutions Inc 305 558-9800
3155 W Okeechobee Rd Hialeah (33012) *(G-5112)*

Deco Truss Company Inc 305 257-1910
13980 Sw 252nd St Homestead (33032) *(G-5707)*

Deco Wraps, Doral *Also called Hammer Head Group Inc (G-3243)*

Decocandles, Miami *Also called Kaluz LLC (G-9383)*

Decon USA 440 610-5009
15 Central Ct Tarpon Springs (34689) *(G-17464)*

Decoral System USA Corporation 954 755-6021
12477 Nw 44th St Coral Springs (33065) *(G-2149)*

Decorative Precast LLC 239 566-9503
420 Sharwood Dr Naples (34110) *(G-10727)*

Decorators Resource Centl Fla, Sanford *Also called American Bronze Foundry Inc (G-15263)*

Decortive Electro Coatings Inc 386 255-7878
501 Kingston Ave Daytona Beach (32114) *(G-2546)*

Decowall 813 886-5226
6001 Johns Rd Ste 342 Tampa (33634) *(G-16770)*

Decoy Inc 305 633-6384
2480 Nw 20th St Unit D Miami (33142) *(G-9006)*

Decoy Next Level In Apparel, Miami *Also called Decoy Inc (G-9006)*

Deeja Foods Inc 321 402-8300
1770 Business Center Ln Kissimmee (34758) *(G-6911)*

Deem Cabinets Inc 352 795-1402
6843 N Citrus Ave Unit A Crystal River (34428) *(G-2274)*

Deep Ocean Woodworks Inc 407 687-2773
6289 Bordeaux Cir Sanford (32771) *(G-15302)*

Deep Planet Research LLC 517 740-1526
2412 Irwin St Melbourne (32901) *(G-8398)*

Deepstream Designs Inc 305 857-0466
2699 Tigertail Ave Apt 54 Miami (33133) *(G-9007)*

Deers Holdings Inc 805 323-6899
1108 Kane Cncurse Ste 206 Bay Harbor Islands (33154) *(G-332)*

Defend Coatings LLC 954 612-5593
9200 Nw 14th Ct Plantation (33322) *(G-13844)*

Defend-X, Boca Raton *Also called Defenstech International Inc (G-480)*

Defender Screens Intl LLC 866 802-0400
7839 Fruitville Rd Sarasota (34240) *(G-15654)*

Defense Flight Aerospace LLC 321 442-7255
5448 Hoffner Ave Ste 105 Orlando (32812) *(G-12081)*

Defense Stampings & Engrg Inc 850 438-6105
3911 Mobile Hwy Pensacola (32505) *(G-13487)*

Defense Systems Sector, Saint Augustine *Also called Northrop Grumman Systems Corp (G-14863)*

Defense Technology Systems, Loxahatchee *Also called Acet Joint Venture (ajv) LLC (G-7965)*

Defenshield Inc 904 679-3942
7000 Us Highway 1 N # 401 Saint Augustine (32095) *(G-14825)*

Defenstech International Inc 202 688-1988
2790 N Federal Hwy # 400 Boca Raton (33431) *(G-480)*

Definitive Design, Yulee *Also called Alm Technologies Inc (G-18587)*

Defrancisci Machine Co LLC 321 952-6600
2681 Aurora Rd Melbourne (32935) *(G-8399)*

Deggy Corp 305 377-2233
15485 Eagle Nest Ln # 100 Miami Lakes (33014) *(G-10295)*

Dekoron Unitherm LLC (HQ) 800 633-5015
1531 Commerce Creek Blvd Cape Coral (33909) *(G-1331)*

Dekscape 239 278-3325
17051 Alico Commerce Ct # 3 Fort Myers (33967) *(G-4233)*

Del Air Electric Co 407 531-1173
201 Tech Dr Sanford (32771) *(G-15303)*

Del Monte Fresh Produce NA Inc (HQ) 305 520-8400
241 Sevilla Ave Coral Gables (33134) *(G-2047)*

Del Monte Fresh Production Inc 863 844-5836
  5050 State Rte 60w Mulberry (33860) *(G-10622)*

Del Prado Fire and Water, Hollywood *Also called Del Prado Holdings LLC* *(G-5563)*

Del Prado Holdings LLC 305 680-7425
  4000 Hollywood Blvd # 55 Hollywood (33021) *(G-5563)*

Del Rosario Enterprises Inc 786 547-6812
  7339 Nw 79th Ter Medley (33166) *(G-8230)*

Delab Care USA LLC 754 317-5678
  2321 Laguna Cir North Miami (33181) *(G-11102)*

Delacom Detection Systems LLC 941 544-6636
  7463 Roxye Ln Sarasota (34240) *(G-15655)*

Delamere Industries Inc 813 929-0841
  19370 Oliver St Brooksville (34601) *(G-1152)*

Deland Beacon Newspaper, Deland *Also called West Bolusia Beacon* *(G-2920)*

Deland Metal Craft Company 386 734-0828
  300 W Beresford Ave Deland (32720) *(G-2861)*

Delaney Resources Inc 863 670-5924
  8831 Janmar Rd Dade City (33525) *(G-2317)*

Delarosa Real Foods LLC 718 333-0333
  2648 Nw 31st Ave Lauderdale Lakes (33311) *(G-7712)*

Delaware Chassis Works 302 378-3013
  3513 Se Gran Park Way Stuart (34997) *(G-16137)*

Delconte Packaging Inc 305 885-2800
  757 W 26th St Hialeah (33010) *(G-5113)*

Delet Doors Inc 786 250-4506
  9250 Sw 117th Ter Miami (33176) *(G-9008)*

Delevoes Lobby LLC 305 906-0475
  10850 Fl Ga Hwy Havana (32333) *(G-5000)*

Deli Fresh Foods Inc 305 652-2848
  18630 Ne 2nd Ave Miami (33179) *(G-9009)*

Delicae Gourmet LLC 727 942-2502
  1310 E Lake Dr Tarpon Springs (34688) *(G-17465)*

Delicate Designs Event Plg Inc 305 833-8725
  12080 Ne 16th Ave Apt 201 Miami (33161) *(G-9010)*

Deliciosa Food Group Inc 954 492-6131
  1177 Nw 81st St Miami (33150) *(G-9011)*

Delivery Signs LLC 407 362-7896
  40 W Crystal Lake St # 100 Orlando (32806) *(G-12082)*

Dell USA LP 512 728-8391
  14591 Sw 120th St Miami (33186) *(G-9012)*

Delphi of Florida Inc 727 561-9553
  12425 28th S N Ste 100 Saint Petersburg (33716) *(G-15021)*

Delran Business Products, Hialeah *Also called All Binders & Indexes Inc* *(G-5037)*

Delray Awning Inc 561 276-5381
  80 N Congress Ave Delray Beach (33445) *(G-2954)*

Delray Pin Factory Intl Inc 561 994-1680
  1009 Howell Harbor Dr Casselberry (32707) *(G-1415)*

Delray Tropic Holdings Inc 561 342-1501
  335 E Linton Blvd Delray Beach (33483) *(G-2955)*

Delray's Screens, Boynton Beach *Also called Plotkowski Inc* *(G-896)*

Delta Doors, Medley *Also called Vidco Industries Inc* *(G-8349)*

Delta Fountains, Jacksonville *Also called Johnston Archtctral Systems In* *(G-6231)*

Delta Group Elec Inc Fla, Rockledge *Also called Delta Group Electronics Inc* *(G-14698)*

Delta Group Electronics Inc 321 631-0799
  395 Gus Hipp Blvd Rockledge (32955) *(G-14698)*

Delta Industries, Fort Walton Beach *Also called John R Caito* *(G-4593)*

Delta International Inc 305 665-6573
  4856 Sw 72nd Ave Miami (33155) *(G-9013)*

Delta Machine LLC 386 738-2204
  1501 Lexington Ave Deland (32724) *(G-2862)*

Delta Machine & Tool Inc 386 738-2204
  1212 N Mcdonald Ave Deland (32724) *(G-2863)*

Delta Metal Finishing Inc 954 953-9898
  101 Ne 3rd Ave Ste 1500 Fort Lauderdale (33301) *(G-3760)*

Delta Mg 561 840-0577
  4440 S Tiffany Dr Ste 8 West Palm Beach (33407) *(G-17977)*

Delta Oil 813 323-3113
  823 Bayou Dr Brandon (33510) *(G-1089)*

Delta P Systems Inc 386 236-0950
  3 E Tower Cir Ormond Beach (32174) *(G-12755)*

Delta Regis Tools Inc 772 465-4302
  7370 Commercial Cir Fort Pierce (34951) *(G-4480)*

Deltana Enterprises Inc 305 592-8188
  10820 Nw 29th St Doral (33172) *(G-3189)*

Delure Publishing LLC 407 866-5448
  1021 Santa Barbara Rd Orlando (32808) *(G-12083)*

Deluxe Cars LLC 407 982-7978
  6302 Old Cheney Hwy Orlando (32807) *(G-12084)*

Deluxe Clsets Cabinets Stn LLC 786 879-3371
  15290 Sw 36th Ter Miami (33185) *(G-9014)*

Deluxe Equipment Co 941 753-4184
  7817 Alhambra Dr Bradenton (34209) *(G-967)*

Deluxe Gems LLC 407 513-2004
  13506 Summerport Vlg Pkwy Windermere (34786) *(G-18349)*

Deluxe Shades Inc 786 355-0086
  8314 Nw 56th St Doral (33166) *(G-3190)*

Deluxe Stone Inc 561 236-2322
  6129 Country Fair Cir Boynton Beach (33437) *(G-855)*

Delzotto Products Florida Inc 352 351-3834
  4575 W Highway 40 Ocala (34482) *(G-11365)*

Demaco, Melbourne *Also called Defrancisci Machine Co LLC* *(G-8399)*

Demaco LLC 321 952-6600
  121 Sw 109th Ave Apt M2 Miami (33174) *(G-9015)*

Demelle Biopharma LLC 908 240-8939
  1245 N Florida Ave Tarpon Springs (34689) *(G-17466)*

Demerx Inc 954 607-3670
  1951 Nw 7th Ave Ste 300 Miami (33136) *(G-9016)*

Demetech Corporation (PA) 305 824-1048
  5980 Miami Lakes Dr Miami Lakes (33014) *(G-10296)*

Deming Designs Inc 850 478-5765
  1090 Cobblestone Dr Pensacola (32514) *(G-13488)*

Demoss Cabinetry LLC 863 738-0080
  3003 Brooks St Ste 1 Lakeland (33803) *(G-7308)*

Denali Investments Inc 386 364-2979
  140 Palm St Ne Live Oak (32064) *(G-7845)*

Denim Lily LLC 754 264-9331
  2785 Se 11th St Pompano Beach (33062) *(G-13991)*

Denise Marie, Miami *Also called Arde Apparel Inc* *(G-8744)*

Denke Laboratories Inc 941 721-0568
  12285 Us Highway 41 N Palmetto (34221) *(G-13164)*

Denke Labratories, Palmetto *Also called Hascall Engineering and Mfg Co* *(G-13173)*

Dennis Boatworks Inc 954 260-6855
  2207 Nw 29th St Oakland Park (33311) *(G-11257)*

Dennys Electronics Inc 941 485-5400
  1044 Endeavor Ct North Venice (34275) *(G-11210)*

Dennys Welding Service Corp 321 494-2608
  1533 Tina Ln Kissimmee (34744) *(G-6912)*

Dentate Porcelain Inc 917 359-7696
  2722 Ne 1st St Ste 1 Pompano Beach (33062) *(G-13992)*

Denterprise International Inc 386 672-0450
  100 E Granada Blvd # 219 Ormond Beach (32176) *(G-12756)*

Dentsply Raintree Glenroe, Sarasota *Also called Dentsply Sirona Inc* *(G-15469)*

Dentsply Sirona Inc 262 752-4040
  7290 26th Ct E Sarasota (34243) *(G-15468)*

Dentsply Sirona Inc 941 527-4450
  7290 26th Ct E Sarasota (34243) *(G-15469)*

Dentz Design Screen Prtg LLC 609 303-0827
  56 S Dixie Hwy Ste 3 Saint Augustine (32084) *(G-14826)*

Denver Elevator Systems Inc 800 633-9788
  7073 N Atlantic Ave Cape Canaveral (32920) *(G-1282)*

Depend-O-Drain Inc 941 756-1710
  6012 33rd St E Bradenton (34203) *(G-968)*

Dependable Shutter & Glass, Davie *Also called Dependable Shutter Service Inc* *(G-2404)*

Dependable Shutter Service Inc 954 583-1411
  4741 Orange Dr Davie (33314) *(G-2404)*

Depuy Inc 305 412-8010
  6303 Blue Lagoon Dr Miami (33126) *(G-9017)*

Depuy Synthes Products Inc 305 265-6842
  6303 Blue Lagoon Dr Miami (33126) *(G-9018)*

Derecktor of Florida, Dania Beach *Also called Florida Derecktor Inc* *(G-2351)*

Derecktor Ship Yard 772 595-9326
  101 Port Ave Fort Pierce (34950) *(G-4481)*

Derm-Buro Inc 305 953-4025
  4675 E 10th Ct Hialeah (33013) *(G-5114)*

Dermaccina Dossier, Miami *Also called Nac USA Corporation* *(G-9603)*

Dermatonus 305 229-3923
  5262 Sw 158th Ave Miramar (33027) *(G-10483)*

Dermazone Solutions Inc 727 446-6882
  2440 30th Ave N Saint Petersburg (33713) *(G-15022)*

Desapro Inc 321 674-6804
  435 Gus Hipp Blvd Rockledge (32955) *(G-14699)*

Desco 941 284-1160
  1832 Bayonne St Sarasota (34231) *(G-15656)*

Desco Industries 305 255-7744
  13937 Sw 119th Ave Miami (33186) *(G-9019)*

Desco Industries Inc 305 255-7744
  13937 Sw 119th Ave Miami (33186) *(G-9020)*

Desco Machine Company LLC 954 565-2739
  3000 Ne 12th Ter Oakland Park (33334) *(G-11258)*

Desco Manufacturing Inc 941 925-7029
  4561 Samuel St Sarasota (34233) *(G-15657)*

Desert Micro, Jacksonville *Also called Western Microsystems Inc* *(G-6603)*

Desh-Videsh Media Group Inc 954 784-8100
  10088 W Mcnab Rd Tamarac (33321) *(G-16529)*

Design & Print 561 361-8299
  199 W Palmetto Park Rd Boca Raton (33432) *(G-481)*

Design & Print Solutions Inc 407 703-7861
  553 Sheeler Ave Apopka (32703) *(G-120)*

Design By Yogi LLC 954 428-9797
  3413 Sw 14th St Deerfield Beach (33442) *(G-2704)*

Design Cncepts/Marine Concepts, Sarasota *Also called Patrick Industries Inc* *(G-15533)*

Design Cncpts By Amrcn Plitics, Clearwater *Also called American Plastic Sup & Mfg Inc* *(G-1491)*

Design Communications Ltd 407 856-9661
  10611 Satellite Blvd Orlando (32837) *(G-12085)*

Design Containers Inc 904 764-6541
  2913 Westside Blvd Jacksonville (32209) *(G-6029)*

(G-0000) Company's Geographic Section entry number

Design Cores and Tubes, Jacksonville *Also called Design Containers Inc* ***(G-6029)***
Design Custom Millwork Inc....407 878-1267
130 Tech Dr Sanford (32771) ***(G-15304)***
Design Furnishings Inc....407 294-0507
3647 All American Blvd Orlando (32810) ***(G-12086)***
Design It Wraps & Graphics LLC....904 310-6032
2873 Jamestown Rd Fernandina Beach (32034) ***(G-3584)***
Design Litho Inc....813 238-7494
5205 N Florida Ave Tampa (33603) ***(G-16771)***
Design NS Leather Furniture, Boca Raton *Also called Nordic Line Inc* ***(G-620)***
Design Pro Screens Inc....407 831-6541
1287 S Oleander St Longwood (32750) ***(G-7888)***
Design Services Inc....813 949-4748
2200 Knight Rd Land O Lakes (34639) ***(G-7491)***
Design Works By Tech Pdts Inc (HQ)....941 355-2703
4500 Carmichael Ave Sarasota (34234) ***(G-15658)***
Design Your Kit Clset More Inc....786 227-6412
13400 Sw 134th Ave Ste 5 Miami (33186) ***(G-9021)***
Design-A-Rug Inc (PA)....954 943-7487
200 N Federal Hwy Deerfield Beach (33441) ***(G-2705)***
Designated Diver, Saint Augustine *Also called Designated Sports Inc* ***(G-14827)***
Designated Sports Inc....904 797-9469
3545 Us 1 S Ste A9 Saint Augustine (32086) ***(G-14827)***
Designer Films Inc....305 828-0605
7485 W 19th Ct Hialeah (33014) ***(G-5115)***
Designer Lifestyles LLC....904 631-8954
619 Cassat Ave Jacksonville (32205) ***(G-6030)***
Designer Sign Systems Inc....954 972-0707
3540 Nw 56th St Ste 201 Fort Lauderdale (33309) ***(G-3761)***
Designer Speciality Millwork, Miami *Also called Designers Specialty Cab Co Inc* ***(G-9022)***
Designer Svcs of Trsure Cast I....772 286-0855
4515 Se Commerce Ave Stuart (34997) ***(G-16138)***
Designer's Choice Cabinetry, Rockledge *Also called Designers Choice Cabinetry Inc* ***(G-14701)***
Designer's Specialty Millwork, Fort Lauderdale *Also called Designers Specialty Cab Co Inc* ***(G-3762)***
Designers Choice Cabinetry....321 632-0772
285 Barnes Blvd Rockledge (32955) ***(G-14700)***
Designers Choice Cabinetry Inc (HQ)....321 632-0772
100 Tgk Cir Rockledge (32955) ***(G-14701)***
Designers Mfg Ctr Inc....954 530-7622
4131 Ne 6th Ave Oakland Park (33334) ***(G-11259)***
Designers Plastics, Clearwater *Also called Bruce R Ely Enterprise Inc* ***(G-1528)***
Designers Plumbing Studio Inc....954 920-5997
3040 N 29th Ave Ste F Hollywood (33020) ***(G-5564)***
Designers Press Inc....407 843-3141
6305 Chancellor Dr Orlando (32809) ***(G-12087)***
Designers Specialty Cab Co Inc....954 776-4500
1730 Biscayne Blvd 201g Miami (33132) ***(G-9022)***
Designers Specialty Cab Co Inc (PA)....954 868-3440
1320 Nw 65th Pl Fort Lauderdale (33309) ***(G-3762)***
Designers Top Shop Inc....863 453-3855
12 N Anoka Ave Avon Park (33825) ***(G-279)***
Designers Tops Inc....305 599-9973
4725 Nw 36th Ave Miami (33142) ***(G-9023)***
Designers Whl Workroom Inc....239 434-7633
1035 Industrial Blvd Naples (34104) ***(G-10728)***
Designs In Rugs, Lutz *Also called Hanteri Enterprises Corp* ***(G-7993)***
Designs To Shine Inc....727 525-4297
1033 34th St N Saint Petersburg (33713) ***(G-15023)***
Designstogo Inc....561 432-1313
4317 10th Ave N Palm Springs (33461) ***(G-13144)***
Desind Industries Corp....212 729-0192
150 E Robinson St # 1009 Orlando (32801) ***(G-12088)***
Desire Fragrances Inc....646 832-3051
848 Brickell Ave Ste 1225 Miami (33131) ***(G-9024)***
Desirous Candles Inc....347 622-6987
10240 Nw 3rd St Pembroke Pines (33026) ***(G-13384)***
Deskrafters, Sanford *Also called TOS Manufacturing Inc* ***(G-15400)***
Desoto Sun, Punta Gorda *Also called Sun Coast Media Group Inc* ***(G-14534)***
Desperado Leather, Edgewater *Also called Leon Leather Company Inc* ***(G-3496)***
Destin Engraving, Destin *Also called Infinite Lasers LLC* ***(G-3071)***
Destin Machine Inc....850 837-7114
600 Fourth St Destin (32541) ***(G-3063)***
Destination Athlete Broward FL, Pompano Beach *Also called Lion Press Inc* ***(G-14078)***
Destination Bvi II Inc....850 699-9551
36120 Emerald Coast Pkwy Destin (32541) ***(G-3064)***
Destination Pavers LLC....850 319-6551
2827 Cynthia Ct Panama City (32405) ***(G-13252)***
Destiny & Light Inc....813 476-8386
5911 Sheldon Rd Tampa (33615) ***(G-16772)***
Detailed Services Inc....239 542-2452
1518 Se 46th Ln Cape Coral (33904) ***(G-1332)***
Detect Inc (HQ)....850 763-7200
2817 Highway 77 Panama City (32405) ***(G-13253)***
Deux Mains, Lake Worth *Also called Rebuild Globally Inc* ***(G-7231)***
Devatis Inc....954 316-4844
2800 W State Road 84 # 11 Fort Lauderdale (33312) ***(G-3763)***
Devclan Inc....407 933-8212
808 N Main St Kissimmee (34744) ***(G-6913)***
Devcon International Corp (HQ)....954 926-5200
595 S Federal Hwy Ste 500 Boca Raton (33432) ***(G-482)***
Devcon Security Services Corp....813 386-3849
2801 Gateway Dr Pompano Beach (33069) ***(G-13993)***
Development Flight Center, Jupiter *Also called Sikorsky Aircraft Corporation* ***(G-6799)***
Devise Solutions LLC....813 760-6393
1217 Oakhill St Seffner (33584) ***(G-15956)***
Devon Chase & Company....407 438-6466
2814 Silver Star Rd # 5 Orlando (32808) ***(G-12089)***
Devon-Aire Inc....813 884-9544
8505 Sunstate St Tampa (33634) ***(G-16773)***
Devscape Software LLC....904 625-6510
5870 Wind Cave Ln Jacksonville (32258) ***(G-6031)***
Dexter Tool 94, Mangonia Park *Also called Bogue Executive Enterprises* ***(G-8090)***
Dextrum Laboratories Inc....305 594-4020
6993 Nw 82nd Ave Ste 20 Miami (33166) ***(G-9025)***
Df Multi Services LLC....407 683-2223
845 N Garland Ave Orlando (32801) ***(G-12090)***
Dfa Dairy Brands Fluid LLC....352 754-1750
16235 Aviation Loop Dr Brooksville (34604) ***(G-1153)***
Dfa Dairy Brands Fluid LLC....386 775-6700
11231 Phillips Ind Blvd E Jacksonville (32256) ***(G-6032)***
Dfa Dairy Brands Fluid LLC....386 775-6700
650 S Wickham Rd Melbourne (32904) ***(G-8400)***
Dfa Dairy Brands Fluid LLC....352 622-4666
2205 N Pine Ave Ocala (34475) ***(G-11366)***
Dfa Dairy Brands Fluid LLC....813 621-7805
4219 E 19th Ave Tampa (33605) ***(G-16774)***
Dfd Loaders Inc....954 283-8839
11820 Nw 37th St Coral Springs (33065) ***(G-2150)***
Dg Design and Print Co LLC....321 446-6435
4290 Us Highway 1 Ste A Rockledge (32955) ***(G-14702)***
Dg Promotions, Mount Dora *Also called Data Graphics Inc* ***(G-10600)***
Dgs Retail LLC....727 388-4975
4400 34th St N Ste L Saint Petersburg (33714) ***(G-15024)***
Dgs Retail LLC....727 388-4975
307044th Avenuen N Saint Petersburg (33714) ***(G-15025)***
Dgw Technologies LLC....407 930-4437
1000 Ocoee Apopka Rd # 4 Apopka (32703) ***(G-121)***
Dhb Armor Group Inc (PA)....800 413-5155
2102 Sw 2nd St Pompano Beach (33069) ***(G-13994)***
Dhf Marketing Inc....305 884-8077
685 W 25th St Hialeah (33010) ***(G-5116)***
Dhl Express (usa) Inc....305 526-1112
5945 Nw 18th St Miami (33126) ***(G-9026)***
Dhs Enterprises Inc....727 572-9470
5150 Ulmerton Rd Ste 14 Clearwater (33760) ***(G-1564)***
Dhs Equiptment, Pompano Beach *Also called Dhs Unlimited Inc* ***(G-13995)***
Dhs Power Corp....305 599-1022
8061 Nw 67th St Miami (33166) ***(G-9027)***
Dhs Unlimited Inc....954 532-2142
4100 N Powerline Rd G3 Pompano Beach (33073) ***(G-13995)***
Dhss LLC....305 830-0327
2035 Harding St Ste 200 Hollywood (33020) ***(G-5565)***
Dhss LLC....305 405-4001
16830 Ne 19th Ave North Miami Beach (33162) ***(G-11133)***
Di Jam Holdings Inc....863 967-6949
123 Main St Auburndale (33823) ***(G-229)***
Diabetex Care....954 427-9510
1525 Nw 3rd St Deerfield Beach (33442) ***(G-2706)***
Diabetic Care Rx LLC (PA)....866 348-0441
3890 Park Central Blvd N Pompano Beach (33064) ***(G-13996)***
Diadem Sports LLC (PA)....844 434-2336
200 Park Central Blvd S Pompano Beach (33064) ***(G-13997)***
Diageo North America Inc....305 476-7761
396 Alhambra Cir Coral Gables (33134) ***(G-2048)***
Diagnostic Test Group LLC....561 347-5760
1060 Holland Dr Ste A Boca Raton (33487) ***(G-483)***
Diamond Advertising & Mktg....561 833-5129
1200 S Flagler Dr Apt 106 West Palm Beach (33401) ***(G-17978)***
Diamond Aircraft Logisctics....305 456-8400
11003 Nw 33rd St Doral (33172) ***(G-3191)***
Diamond Cabinets & Service....321 689-8289
1411 Edgewater Dr Ste 200 Orlando (32804) ***(G-12091)***
Diamond Cbd, Fort Lauderdale *Also called Cbd LLC* ***(G-3716)***
Diamond Moba Americas Inc....954 384-5828
2731 Executive Park Dr # 4 Weston (33331) ***(G-18237)***
Diamond Mt Inc....321 339-3377
4200 Dow Rd Ste Cd Melbourne (32934) ***(G-8401)***
Diamond Precision Machine Inc....321 729-8453
2300 Commerce Park Dr Ne Palm Bay (32905) ***(G-12896)***
Diamond R Fertilizer, Fort Pierce *Also called Pioneer Ag-Chem Inc* ***(G-4519)***
Diamond R Fertilizer Co Inc....863 763-2158
710 Ne 5th Ave Okeechobee (34972) ***(G-11603)***
Diamond Wellness Holdings Inc (PA)....800 433-0127
3531 Griffin Rd Fort Lauderdale (33312) ***(G-3764)***
Diamond-Mt, Melbourne *Also called Diamond Mt Inc* ***(G-8401)***

ALPHABETIC

Diamondback Airboats, Cocoa *Also called Diamondback Manufacturing LLC* ***(G-1919)***
Diamondback America, Cocoa *Also called Diamondback Cnc LLC* ***(G-1916)***
Diamondback Barrels LLC....321 305-5995
4135 Pine Tree Pl Cocoa (32926) ***(G-1915)***
Diamondback Cnc LLC....321 305-5995
3400 Grissom Pkwy Cocoa (32926) ***(G-1916)***
Diamondback Firearms LLC....321 305-5995
3400 Grissom Pkwy Cocoa (32926) ***(G-1917)***
Diamondback Manufacturing LLC....321 305-5995
1060 Cox Rd Bldg A Cocoa (32926) ***(G-1918)***
Diamondback Manufacturing LLC (PA)....321 633-5624
1060 Cox Rd Cocoa (32926) ***(G-1919)***
Diamondback Towers LLC....800 424-5624
1060 Cox Rd Bldg B Cocoa (32926) ***(G-1920)***
Diana Food Group, Pompano Beach *Also called Prima Food Corp* ***(G-14145)***
Diane Dal Lago Limited Company....813 374-2473
5915 Memorial Hwy Ste 115 Tampa (33615) ***(G-16775)***
Dianthus Miami Inc (PA)....786 800-8365
7635 Nw 27th Ave Miami (33147) ***(G-9028)***
Diapulse Corporation America....516 466-3030
250 N Dixie Hwy Unit 9 Hollywood (33020) ***(G-5566)***
Diario Las Americas, Miami *Also called Las Amrcas Mltimedia Group LLC* ***(G-9427)***
Diatomite Corp of America....305 466-0075
19925 Ne 39th Pl Miami (33180) ***(G-9029)***
Diaz Brothers Corp....305 364-4911
7750 W 24th Ave Hialeah (33016) ***(G-5117)***
Diaz Go Green Inc....407 501-2724
413 Brailiff Ct Orlando (32824) ***(G-12092)***
Dictaphone Corporation....321 255-8668
3984 Pepsi Cola Dr Melbourne (32934) ***(G-8402)***
Didi Designs Inc....305 836-0266
13376 Nw 42nd Ave Opa Locka (33054) ***(G-11736)***
Didna Inc....239 851-0966
206 Hillcrest St Orlando (32801) ***(G-12093)***
Die Verse Tool & Manufacturing, Palmetto *Also called JSB Enterprises Inc* ***(G-13177)***
Diebold Nixdorf Incorporated....407 549-2000
735 Primera Blvd Ste 215 Lake Mary (32746) ***(G-7069)***
Diemech Turbine Solution Inc....386 804-0179
1200 Flight Line Blvd # 1 Deland (32724) ***(G-2864)***
Diemold Machine Company Inc....239 482-1400
2350 Bruner Ln Fort Myers (33912) ***(G-4234)***
Diesel Machinery Intl USA....305 551-4424
4121 Sw 90th Ct Miami (33165) ***(G-9030)***
Diesel Pro Power Inc....305 545-5588
760 Nw 4th St Ste 100 Miami (33128) ***(G-9031)***
Diesel Pro Power USA, Miami *Also called Diesel Pro Power Inc* ***(G-9031)***
Dieselsite Inc....888 414-3457
7400 W Industrial Ln # 6 Homosassa (34448) ***(G-5747)***
Dietzgen Corporation (PA)....813 286-4767
121 Kelsey Ln Ste G Tampa (33619) ***(G-16776)***
Dievac Plastics, Hialeah *Also called Acai Investments Llc* ***(G-5025)***
Dig In Anchors LLC....386 308-7745
535 Hardenoak Blvd Lakeland (33813) ***(G-7309)***
Digecon Plastics International....850 477-5483
3255 Potter St Pensacola (32514) ***(G-13489)***
Digi-Net Technologies Inc (PA)....352 505-7450
4420 Nw 36th Ave Ste A Gainesville (32606) ***(G-4677)***
Digicare Biomedical Tech Inc....561 689-0408
107 Commerce Rd Boynton Beach (33426) ***(G-856)***
Digichat, Gainesville *Also called Digi-Net Technologies Inc* ***(G-4677)***
Digicrib LLC....833 932-8800
34990 Emerald Coast Pkwy Destin (32541) ***(G-3065)***
Digiportal Software Inc....407 333-2488
5224 W State Road 46 Sanford (32771) ***(G-15305)***
Digiprint & Design Corp....786 464-1770
1460 Nw 107th Ave Ste R Sweetwater (33172) ***(G-16401)***
Digital Antenna Inc....954 747-7022
5325 Nw 108th Ave Sunrise (33351) ***(G-16313)***
Digital Antomy Smltons For HLT....937 623-7377
1720 S Orange Ave Ste 300 Orlando (32806) ***(G-12094)***
Digital Asset MGT Group LLC....877 507-5777
1645 Palm Bch Lkes Blvd S West Palm Beach (33401) ***(G-17979)***
Digital Compositing Systems....954 432-4988
3309 Onyx Rd Miramar (33025) ***(G-10484)***
Digital Control Company, Clearwater *Also called Alltec Corporation* ***(G-1489)***
Digital Direct Corporation....813 448-9071
131 Burbank Rd Oldsmar (34677) ***(G-11642)***
Digital Graphics, Orlando *Also called Linographics Inc* ***(G-12331)***
Digital Lighting Systems Inc....305 264-8391
7588 Nw 8th St Fl 2 Miami (33126) ***(G-9032)***
Digital Lightwave, Largo *Also called Florida Veex Inc* ***(G-7588)***
Digital Living....407 332-9998
4303 Vineland Rd Altamonte Springs (32714) ***(G-42)***
Digital Monarch Inc....407 259-2901
1317 Edgewater Dr # 2032 Orlando (32804) ***(G-12095)***
Digital Outdoor LLC....305 944-7945
8405 Nw 29th St Doral (33122) ***(G-3192)***
Digital Pixel Displays LLC (PA)....321 948-3751
111 N Orange Ave Orlando (32801) ***(G-12096)***
Digital Printing Solutions Inc....407 671-8715
6438 University Blvd # 12 Winter Park (32792) ***(G-18506)***
Digital Propaganda Inc....407 644-8444
997 W Kennedy Blvd A12 Orlando (32810) ***(G-12097)***
Digital Publishing LLC....813 749-8640
131 Burbank Rd Oldsmar (34677) ***(G-11643)***
Digital Tech of Lakeland Inc....863 668-8770
3020 Winter Lake Rd Lakeland (33803) ***(G-7310)***
Digital Watchdog, Tampa *Also called Kaltec Electronics Inc* ***(G-16975)***
Digitech Graphics Group, Lakeland *Also called Digital Tech of Lakeland Inc* ***(G-7310)***
Digitrax Inc....850 872-9890
2443 Transmitter Rd Panama City (32404) ***(G-13254)***
Dignitas Software Development....727 392-2004
6677 Augusta Blvd Seminole (33777) ***(G-15974)***
Diji Integrated Press, Tampa *Also called Jak Corporate Holdings Inc* ***(G-16962)***
Dilan Enterprises Inc....305 887-3051
2339 W 9th Ct Hialeah (33010) ***(G-5118)***
Diligent Wldg Fabrication LLC (HQ)....561 620-4900
3500 Nw Boca Raton Blvd Boca Raton (33431) ***(G-484)***
Dillco Inc....386 734-7510
1842 Patterson Ave Deland (32724) ***(G-2865)***
Dillon Yarn Corporation (PA)....973 684-1600
3250 W Coml Blvd Ste 320 Fort Lauderdale (33309) ***(G-3765)***
Dills Enterprises LLC....941 493-1993
301 Seaboard Ave Venice (34285) ***(G-17683)***
Diloren Inc....786 618-9671
8800 Nw 13th Ter Doral (33172) ***(G-3193)***
Dilution Solutions Inc....800 451-6628
2090 Sunnydale Blvd Clearwater (33765) ***(G-1565)***
Dimar Usa Inc (PA)....954 590-8573
1332 W Mcnab Rd Fort Lauderdale (33309) ***(G-3766)***
Dimension Machine Engrg LLC....586 948-3600
5201 Sw 28th Pl Cape Coral (33914) ***(G-1333)***
Dimension Machine Tool Inc....586 948-3600
5201 Sw 28th Pl Cape Coral (33914) ***(G-1334)***
Dimension Photo Engrv Co Inc....813 251-0244
1507 W Cass St Tampa (33606) ***(G-16777)***
Dimension Printing, Tampa *Also called Dimensnal Imprssion Hldngs Inc* ***(G-16778)***
Dimensional Americas Inc....786 417-9370
10411 Nw 28th St Ste C103 Doral (33172) ***(G-3194)***
Dimensnal Imprssion Hldngs Inc....813 251-0244
1507 W Cass St Tampa (33606) ***(G-16778)***
Dimeq Process Solutions, Saint Petersburg *Also called Brewfab LLC* ***(G-14989)***
Dion Atelier Inc....305 389-9711
224 8th St Miami Beach (33139) ***(G-10183)***
Dion Fuels LLC (PA)....305 296-2000
5300 Overseas Hwy 2 Key West (33040) ***(G-6862)***
Dion Money Management LLC....413 458-4700
3101 Green Dolphin Ln Naples (34102) ***(G-10729)***
Dioxide Materials Inc....217 239-1400
1100 Holland Dr Boca Raton (33487) ***(G-485)***
Dioxyme, Fort Myers *Also called Taylor L Max L C* ***(G-4419)***
Dip-A-Dee Donuts....352 460-4266
1376 W North Blvd Leesburg (34748) ***(G-7766)***
Direcly, Coral Gables *Also called Merkari Group Inc* ***(G-2085)***
Direct Impressions Inc....239 549-4484
1335 Miramar St Cape Coral (33904) ***(G-1335)***
Direct Mail Velocity LLC....561 393-4722
1200 S Rogers Cir Ste 8 Boca Raton (33487) ***(G-486)***
Direct Optical Research Co....727 319-9000
8725 115th Ave Largo (33773) ***(G-7570)***
Direct Response Publication....561 620-3010
315 Se Mizner Blvd # 208 Boca Raton (33432) ***(G-487)***
Direct Sales and Design Inc....954 522-5477
1140 Ne 7th Ave Unit 3 Fort Lauderdale (33304) ***(G-3767)***
Dirtbag Choppers Inc....904 725-7600
27 W 11th St Atlantic Beach (32233) ***(G-207)***
Dirtrbags Chopper....904 725-7600
2426 Mayport Rd Ste 5 Jacksonville (32233) ***(G-6033)***
Disbrow Corporation (PA)....813 621-9444
8412 Sabal Indus Blvd Tampa (33619) ***(G-16779)***
Discipline Marketing Inc....305 793-7358
21230 Sw 246th St Homestead (33031) ***(G-5708)***
Discos Y Empanadas Argentina....305 326-9300
2181 Nw 10th Ave Miami (33127) ***(G-9033)***
Discount Awnings Inc....941 753-5700
6620 19th St E Unit 111 Sarasota (34243) ***(G-15470)***
Discount Boat Tops Inc....727 536-4412
14000 66th St Ste A Largo (33771) ***(G-7571)***
Discount Distributors Inc....772 336-0092
725 Se Port St Lucie Blvd # 106 Port Saint Lucie (34984) ***(G-14407)***
Discount Metal Mart, Plant City *Also called Metal Systems Inc* ***(G-13785)***
Discount Printing, Fort Lauderdale *Also called V P Press Inc* ***(G-4114)***
Discount Welds LLC....305 637-3939
2745 Nw 21st St Miami (33142) ***(G-9034)***
Discovery Canvas East Coast Co....786 487-8897
1386 Nw 54th St Miami (33142) ***(G-9035)***
Discovery Tank Testing Inc....561 840-1666
1209 Gateway Rd Ste 203 West Palm Beach (33403) ***(G-17980)***

924 2022 Harris Florida Manufacturers Directory (G-0000) Company's Geographic Section entry number

Discovery Technology Intl Inc (HQ) 941 907-4444
6700 Professional Pkwy Lakewood Ranch (34240) *(G-7483)*

Disruptor Manufacturing 407 900-2868
311 Specialty Pt Sanford (32771) *(G-15306)*

Distant Shores Media, Orlando *Also called Unfoldingword Corporation* *(G-12686)*

Distillery Deerfield LLC 954 531-6813
7277 Oxford Ct Palm Beach Gardens (33418) *(G-12965)*

Distinct Dsgns Cstm Coml Case 727 530-0119
1135 Starkey Rd Largo (33771) *(G-7572)*

Distinct.ink, Orlando *Also called Chargers and Cases LLC* *(G-12004)*

Distinctive Cabinet Designs 239 641-5165
5556 Yahl St Ste A Naples (34109) *(G-10730)*

Distinctive Creat Intr Wkshp I 954 921-1861
2126 Pierce St Hollywood (33020) *(G-5567)*

Distingshed Gntlman MBL Dtling 321 200-4331
7512 Dr Phillips Blvd 50-1 Orlando (32819) *(G-12098)*

Distribuidora Continental SA 305 374-4474
6355 Nw 36th St Ste 506 Virginia Gardens (33166) *(G-17822)*

Distribuidora Giorgio Usa LLC 305 685-6366
12815 Nw 45th Ave Opa Locka (33054) *(G-11737)*

District 95 Wood Working Inc 888 400-3136
1040 Sw 10th Ave Ste 4 Pompano Beach (33069) *(G-13998)*

Distrivalto USA Inc 305 715-0366
2020 Ponce De Leon Blvd # 1004 Coral Gables (33134) *(G-2049)*

Ditas Corp 305 558-5766
10322 Sw 27th St Miami (33165) *(G-9036)*

Ditch Central & South Florida, Plant City *Also called Charles Machine Works Inc* *(G-13754)*

Dittmer Architectural Aluminum, Winter Springs *Also called Walt Dittmer and Sons Inc* *(G-18581)*

Diva Stuff 386 256-2521
1368 N Us Highway 1 # 406 Ormond Beach (32174) *(G-12757)*

Divas Fashion 786 717-7039
8382 Bird Rd Miami (33155) *(G-9037)*

Divatti & Co LLC 786 354-1888
1050 E 17th St Miramar (33027) *(G-10485)*

Dive Rite, Lake City *Also called Lamartek Inc* *(G-7027)*

Divers Den, Panama City *Also called Gigli Enterprises Inc* *(G-13267)*

Diverse Co 863 425-4251
1950 Industrial Park Rd Mulberry (33860) *(G-10623)*

Diverse Transport Systems, Mulberry *Also called Diverse Co* *(G-10623)*

Diversfied Lifting Systems Inc 813 248-2299
6905 Parke East Blvd Tampa (33610) *(G-16780)*

Diversfied Mtl Specialists Inc 941 244-0935
105 Triple Dmd Blvd Ste 1 North Venice (34275) *(G-11211)*

Diversified Graphics Inc 407 425-9443
720 Franklin Ln Orlando (32801) *(G-12099)*

Diversified Mining Inc 407 923-3194
2178 Crandon Ave Winter Park (32789) *(G-18507)*

Diversified Pallets Inc 904 491-6800
1894 S 14th St Ste 2 Fernandina Beach (32034) *(G-3585)*

Diversified Performance System 904 765-7181
6800 N Main St Jacksonville (32208) *(G-6034)*

Diversified Products Mfg, Jacksonville *Also called Paw Inc* *(G-6358)*

Diversified Pubg & Design 239 598-4826
975 Imperl Golf Cours Bld Naples (34110) *(G-10731)*

Diversified Sales Company, Oldsmar *Also called DSC Sales of SC Inc* *(G-11644)*

Diversified Welding Inc 561 996-9398
20368 Ponce De Leon Rd Perry (32348) *(G-13636)*

Diversified Yacht Services Inc 239 765-8700
751 Fishermans Wharf Fort Myers Beach (33931) *(G-4453)*

Diversity Best Practices, Winter Park *Also called Working Mother Media Inc* *(G-18553)*

Diversityinc Media LLC 973 494-0539
111 Reef Rd Palm Beach (33480) *(G-12932)*

Diversitypro Corp 305 691-2348
6632 Sw 64th Ave South Miami (33143) *(G-16032)*

Divine Coffee Roasters, Sarasota *Also called Neat Print Inc* *(G-15760)*

Divine Dovetail 561 245-7601
1050 Nw 1st Ave Ste 7 Boca Raton (33432) *(G-488)*

Divinitas Displays LLC 407 660-6625
7598 Currency Dr Orlando (32809) *(G-12100)*

Division 5 Florida Inc 904 964-4513
417 E Weldon St Starke (32091) *(G-16101)*

Division 5 Steel, Starke *Also called Division 5 Florida Inc* *(G-16101)*

Divitae Inc 786 585-5556
570 E 65th St Hialeah (33013) *(G-5119)*

Diwi Jewelry, Oakland Park *Also called International Jwly Designs Inc* *(G-11273)*

Dixie County Advocate 352 498-3312
174 Ne Highway 351 Cross City (32628) *(G-2260)*

Dixie Lime Andstone Co 352 512-0180
2441 E Fort King St Ocala (34471) *(G-11367)*

Dixie Metal Products Inc (PA) 352 873-2554
442 Sw 54th Ct Ocala (34474) *(G-11368)*

Dixie Metalcraft Incorporated 239 337-4299
3050 Warehouse Rd Fort Myers (33916) *(G-4235)*

Dixie Restorations LLC 813 785-2159
2212 Hilda Ann Rd Zephyrhills (33540) *(G-18612)*

Dixie Signs Inc 863 644-3521
2930 Drane Field Rd Lakeland (33811) *(G-7311)*

Dixie Southern, Duette *Also called Southstern Indus Fbrcators LLC* *(G-3433)*

Dixie Sptic Tank Orange Cy LLC 386 775-3051
1200 S Leavitt Ave Orange City (32763) *(G-11805)*

Dixie Structures & Maintenance (PA) 205 274-4525
1216 Hopedale Dr Fort Myers (33919) *(G-4236)*

Dixie Tank Company 904 781-9500
5349 Highway Ave Jacksonville (32254) *(G-6035)*

Dixie Workshop Inc 352 629-4699
2350 Nw 42nd St Ocala (34475) *(G-11369)*

Dixie-Southern Arkansas LLC 479 751-9183
9135 58th Dr E Bradenton (34202) *(G-969)*

Dixon Screen Printing LLC 850 476-3924
312 W Detroit Blvd Pensacola (32534) *(G-13490)*

Dixon Ticonderoga Company (HQ) 407 829-9000
615 Crscent Exec Ct Ste 5 Lake Mary (32746) *(G-7070)*

Diy Blinds Inc 305 692-8877
19515 Presidential Way North Miami Beach (33179) *(G-11134)*

Dizenzo Manufacturing Intl Inc 954 978-4624
4400 Nw 19th Ave Ste J Deerfield Beach (33064) *(G-2707)*

Dj Cabinet Factory Inc 786 483-8868
2552 W 3rd Ct Hialeah (33010) *(G-5120)*

Dj Live Productions LLC 407 383-1740
999 Douglas Ave Altamonte Springs (32714) *(G-43)*

Dj Plastics Inc 407 656-6677
946 Century Ln Apopka (32703) *(G-122)*

Dj Roof and Solar Supply LLC 954 557-1992
2009 Admirals Way Fort Lauderdale (33316) *(G-3768)*

Dj/Pj Inc 813 907-6359
13215 38th St N Clearwater (33762) *(G-1566)*

Djfs LLC 727 551-1391
4604 49th St N Ste 1279 Saint Petersburg (33709) *(G-15026)*

DK International Assoc Inc 954 828-1256
1417 Sw 1st Ave Fort Lauderdale (33315) *(G-3769)*

DK International Group Corp 954 391-8969
1930 Harrison St Ste 307 Hollywood (33020) *(G-5568)*

Dka Distributing LLC 800 275-4352
5010 Tampa West Blvd Tampa (33634) *(G-16781)*

Dkia, Fort Lauderdale *Also called DK International Assoc Inc* *(G-3769)*

Dkm Machine Manufacturing 904 733-0103
3811 University Blvd W # 26 Jacksonville (32217) *(G-6036)*

Dl Cabinetry Orlando LLC 504 669-7847
7025 W Colonial Dr Orlando (32818) *(G-12101)*

Dl Myers Corp 609 698-8800
5500 Military Trl Ste 22 Jupiter (33458) *(G-6710)*

Dla Document Services 813 828-4646
2617 Florida Keys Ave # 25 Tampa (33621) *(G-16782)*

Dlc, Winter Springs *Also called Daniel Lampert Communications* *(G-18564)*

Dlp Industries, Miramar *Also called Press-Rite Inc* *(G-10529)*

Dlux Printing & Publishing, Pensacola *Also called D-Lux Printing Inc* *(G-13485)*

Dlz Holdings South Inc (PA) 352 344-8741
956 S Us Highway 41 Inverness (34450) *(G-5826)*

DM Oil Corp 954 835-5468
1450 Ne 26th St Wilton Manors (33305) *(G-18338)*

Dma Cabinets Inc 352 249-8147
1653b W Gulf To Lake Hwy Lecanto (34461) *(G-7751)*

DMC, Oakland Park *Also called Designers Mfg Ctr Inc* *(G-11259)*

DMC Components Intl LLC 407 478-4064
4202 Metric Dr Winter Park (32792) *(G-18508)*

DMC Industries Inc 352 620-9322
13530 N Jacksonville Rd Sparr (32192) *(G-16059)*

Dmoney365 Logistic Inc 954 529-8202
1331 S State Road 7 North Lauderdale (33068) *(G-11078)*

Dmr Creative Marketing LLC 954 725-3750
321 Goolsby Blvd Deerfield Beach (33442) *(G-2708)*

Dmso Store Inc 954 616-5699
3580 Sw 30th Ave Fort Lauderdale (33312) *(G-3770)*

Dna Surface Concepts Inc 561 328-7302
1980 Avenue L Riviera Beach (33404) *(G-14616)*

DNE Pot Sbob Inc 239 936-8880
11000 Metro Pkwy Ste 10 Fort Myers (33966) *(G-4237)*

Dnt Software Corp 407 323-0987
1710 Beacon Dr Sanford (32771) *(G-15307)*

Do You Remember Inc 305 987-9111
36 Island Ave Apt 45 Miami Beach (33139) *(G-10184)*

Dobbs & Brodeur Bookbinders 305 885-5215
1030 E 14th St Hialeah (33010) *(G-5121)*

Dobros Inc 386 279-0003
803 W New York Ave Deland (32720) *(G-2866)*

Doch LLC 571 491-7578
14630 Grenadine Dr Apt 7 Tampa (33613) *(G-16783)*

Dock Builders Supply, Gibsonton *Also called W R Williams Enterprises Inc* *(G-4803)*

Dockside At Horseshoe Beach L 352 377-4616
6809 Nw 48th Ln Gainesville (32653) *(G-4678)*

Doctor Easy Medical Pdts LLC 904 276-7200
1029 Blanding Blvd # 701 Orange Park (32065) *(G-11823)*

Doctor Granite and Cabinets 321 368-1779
3532 Chica Cir West Melbourne (32904) *(G-17898)*

Doctor Pickle LLC 772 985-5919
1279 W Palmetto Park Rd Boca Raton (33427) *(G-489)*

Doctor Scientific Organica, Riviera Beach *Also called Lavi Enterprises LLC* **(G-14642)**
Doctors Scentific Organica LLC (HQ) 888 455-9031
  1210 W 13th St Riviera Beach (33404) **(G-14617)**
Doctorxs Allergy Formula 904 758-2088
  2375 St Johns Bluff Rd S Jacksonville (32246) **(G-6037)**
Docuprint Corporation 305 639-8618
  7950 Nw 53rd St Ste 337 Miami (33166) **(G-9038)**
Docuvision Incorporated 954 791-0091
  3650 Hacienda Blvd Ste F Davie (33314) **(G-2405)**
DOE & Ingalls Florida Oper LLC 813 347-4741
  9940 Currie Davis Dr # 13 Tampa (33619) **(G-16784)**
Doerfler Manufacturing Inc 763 772-3728
  235 N Central Ave Umatilla (32784) **(G-17646)**
Doerrs Cstm Cabinets Trim LLC 904 540-7024
  1300 Wildwood Dr Saint Augustine (32086) **(G-14828)**
Doerrs Custom Cabinets & Trim 904 540-7024
  1761 Dobbs Rd Saint Augustine (32084) **(G-14829)**
Doglips Logistics LLC 407 704-0097
  471 Kestrel Dr Groveland (34736) **(G-4859)**
Dok Solution Inc (PA) 727 209-1313
  12253 62nd St Ste B Largo (33773) **(G-7573)**
Dolci Peccati LLC 954 632-8551
  1900 N Bayshore Dr Miami (33132) **(G-9039)**
Dole 305 925-7900
  10055 Nw 12th St Doral (33172) **(G-3195)**
Doll Maker LLC 800 851-5183
  11330 Tamiami Trl E Naples (34113) **(G-10732)**
Doll Maker, The, Naples *Also called Doll Maker LLC* **(G-10732)**
Doll Marine Metal Fabrica 954 941-5093
  6800 Nw 15th Way Fort Lauderdale (33309) **(G-3771)**
Doll Marine Metal Fabrication 954 941-5093
  250 S Dixie Hwy E Pompano Beach (33060) **(G-13999)**
Dolmar Foods Inc 262 303-6026
  5920 Se Hames Rd Belleview (34420) **(G-360)**
Dolomite Inc 850 482-4962
  1321 Highway 71 Marianna (32448) **(G-8163)**
Dolph Map Company Inc 954 763-4732
  1600 E Commercial Blvd Oakland Park (33334) **(G-11260)**
Dolphin Boat Lifts Inc 239 936-1782
  6440 Topaz Ct Fort Myers (33966) **(G-4238)**
Dolphin Boats, Princeton *Also called Kz Manufacturing LLC* **(G-14488)**
Dolphin Kitchen & Bath 305 482-9486
  2051 Nw 112th Ave Ste 123 Miami (33172) **(G-9040)**
Dolphin Paddlesports Inc 941 924-2785
  6018 S Tamiami Trl Sarasota (34231) **(G-15659)**
Dolphin Publishing, Miami Springs *Also called Dolphin/Curtis Publishing Co* **(G-10388)**
Dolphin Sheet Metal Inc 561 744-0242
  142 Jupiter St Jupiter (33458) **(G-6711)**
Dolphin/Curtis Publishing Co (PA) 305 594-0508
  53 Curtiss Pkwy Miami Springs (33166) **(G-10388)**
Dolphine Jewelry Contracting 561 488-0355
  9064 Villa Portofino Cir Boca Raton (33496) **(G-490)**
Domestic Custom Metals Company 239 643-2422
  4275 Progress Ave Naples (34104) **(G-10733)**
Domestic Metals, Naples *Also called Domestic Custom Metals Company* **(G-10733)**
Dominion Printers Inc 757 340-1300
  5393 Kennel St Port Charlotte (33981) **(G-14295)**
Domrey Cigar Ltd Company 941 360-8200
  3001 Gateway Ctr Pkwy N Pinellas Park (33782) **(G-13682)**
Don Bell Signs LLC 800 824-0080
  365 Oak Pl Port Orange (32127) **(G-14332)**
Don Industrial Group LLC 305 290-4237
  7760 W 20th Ave Ste 7 Hialeah (33016) **(G-5122)**
Don Schick LLC 954 491-9042
  4741 Ne 13th Ave Oakland Park (33334) **(G-11261)**
Don Signs Inc (PA) 407 344-9444
  766 Camel Ct Kissimmee (34759) **(G-6976)**
Donald Art Company Inc 407 831-2525
  713 Industry Rd Longwood (32750) **(G-7889)**
Donald Ross Gas Inc 561 776-1324
  225 Skylark Pt Jupiter (33458) **(G-6712)**
Donald Smith Logging Inc 850 697-3975
  127 Cora Mae Rd Carrabelle (32322) **(G-1410)**
Donaldson Enterprises 850 934-5030
  5041 Lantana Dr Gulf Breeze (32563) **(G-4880)**
Donarra Extrusions LLC 352 369-5552
  1811 Sw 42nd Ave Ocala (34474) **(G-11370)**
Donau Carbon US Lcc 352 465-5959
  551 N Us Highway 41 Dunnellon (34432) **(G-3465)**
Done Right Fire Gear Repr Inc 727 848-9019
  7621 Maryland Ave Hudson (34667) **(G-5770)**
Done Rite Pumps 305 953-3380
  4240 Nw 133rd St Opa Locka (33054) **(G-11738)**
Dongili Investment Group Inc 941 927-3003
  5563 Marquesas Cir Sarasota (34233) **(G-15660)**
Donica International Inc 954 217-7616
  7500 Nw 52nd St Miami (33166) **(G-9041)**
Donna Lynn Enterprises Inc 772 286-2812
  10358 Rverside Dr Ste 130 Palm Beach Gardens (33410) **(G-12966)**

Donna M Walker PA 561 289-0437
  11137 Harbour Springs Cir Boca Raton (33428) **(G-491)**
Donnelley Financial LLC 305 371-3900
  200 S Biscayne Blvd # 1750 Miami (33131) **(G-9042)**
Donoso Printing Corp 786 508-9426
  9811 Nw 80th Ave Hialeah Gardens (33016) **(G-5435)**
Donovan Home Services LLC 813 644-9488
  3390 Gandy Blvd N Saint Petersburg (33702) **(G-15027)**
Dons Cabinets and Woodworking 727 863-3404
  15801 Archer St Hudson (34667) **(G-5771)**
Dons Custom Service Inc 954 491-4043
  900 Ne 3rd Ave Fort Lauderdale (33304) **(G-3772)**
Dontech Industries Inc 847 682-1776
  9 Jefferson Ct S Saint Petersburg (33711) **(G-15028)**
Donut King of Leesburg LLC 352 250-8487
  708 S 14th St Leesburg (34748) **(G-7767)**
Donzi Yachts, Fort Lauderdale *Also called Roscioli International Inc* **(G-4026)**
Donzi Yachts By Roscioli, Bradenton *Also called Roscioli International Inc* **(G-1037)**
Door Shop, The, Hollywood *Also called Trebor USA Corp* **(G-5673)**
Door Styles Inc 305 653-4447
  1178 Nw 163rd Dr Miami (33169) **(G-9043)**
Doorknob Discount Center LLC 813 963-3104
  18404 Bittern Ave Lutz (33558) **(G-7989)**
Doormark Inc 954 418-4700
  430 Goolsby Blvd Deerfield Beach (33442) **(G-2709)**
Doors 4 U Inc 786 400-2298
  7322 Nw 79th Ter Medley (33166) **(G-8231)**
Doors and Hardware Tampa Bay, Largo *Also called Architctral Mllwk Slutions Inc* **(G-7538)**
Doors Molding and More 727 498-8552
  2894 22nd Ave N Saint Petersburg (33713) **(G-15029)**
Doorway Projects Inc 561 523-2040
  6484 Kirsten Way Lake Worth (33467) **(G-7195)**
Dor-A-Lum Corporation 305 884-3922
  7040 Nw 77th Ter Medley (33166) **(G-8232)**
Dorado Custom Boats LLC 727 786-3800
  1400 L And R Indus Blvd Tarpon Springs (34689) **(G-17467)**
Dorado Marine Inc 727 786-3800
  270 Hedden Ct Ozona (34660) **(G-12856)**
Doral Building Supply Corp 305 471-9797
  5095 Nw 79th Ave Doral (33166) **(G-3196)**
Doral Dgtal Reprographics Corp 305 704-3194
  5701 Nw 79th Ave Doral (33166) **(G-3197)**
Doral Family Journal Inc 305 300-4594
  10773 Nw 58th St Ste 96 Doral (33178) **(G-3198)**
Doral Imaging Institute LLC 305 594-2881
  2760 Sw 97th Ave Apt 101 Miami (33165) **(G-9044)**
Doralum, Medley *Also called Dor-A-Lum Corporation* **(G-8232)**
Doran Manufacturing Corp Fla 904 731-3313
  6261 Powers Ave Jacksonville (32217) **(G-6038)**
Dorward Energy Corporation 727 490-1778
  447 3rd Ave N Ste 400 Saint Petersburg (33701) **(G-15030)**
Dos Amigos Boat Works LLC 904 764-6541
  2913 Westside Blvd Jacksonville (32209) **(G-6039)**
Dosal Tobacco Corporation (PA) 305 685-2949
  4775 Nw 132nd St Opa Locka (33054) **(G-11739)**
DOT Blue Trading Inc 954 646-0448
  3100 Nw 72nd Ave Ste 126 Miami (33122) **(G-9045)**
DOT Green Energy Inc 717 505-8686
  100 Hampton Rd Lot 84 Clearwater (33759) **(G-1567)**
Dotamed LLC 786 594-0144
  6332 Nw 99th Ave Doral (33178) **(G-3199)**
Dotchi LLC 305 477-0024
  6807 Biscayne Blvd Miami (33138) **(G-9046)**
Dotrailings.com, Cocoa *Also called Amazon Metal Fabricators Inc* **(G-1901)**
Double Down Boat Works Inc 305 984-3000
  8204 Sw 103rd Ave Miami (33173) **(G-9047)**
Double DS Tobaccco 561 901-9145
  700 W Boynton Beach Blvd Boynton Beach (33426) **(G-857)**
Double Envelope Corporation 352 375-0738
  2500 Ne 39th Ave Gainesville (32609) **(G-4679)**
Double H Enterprises Inc 972 562-8588
  170 Bear Foot Trl Ormond Beach (32174) **(G-12758)**
Double Header Fish Charter 772 388-5741
  706 S Easy St Sebastian (32958) **(G-15890)**
Double J of Broward Inc (PA) 954 659-8880
  1800 N Commerce Pkwy # 2 Weston (33326) **(G-18238)**
Double R Manufacturing 352 878-4009
  15505 Nw 100th Avenue Rd Reddick (32686) **(G-14552)**
Double R Mfg Ocala Inc 352 873-1441
  5529 Sw 1st Ln Ocala (34474) **(G-11371)**
Double R Publishing 305 525-3573
  621 Nw 10th Ct Boynton Beach (33426) **(G-858)**
Doug Bloodworth Enterprises 407 247-9728
  3211 Lake Griffin Rd Lady Lake (32159) **(G-6990)**
Doug Specialties LLC 954 675-6866
  5223 Sapphire Vly Boca Raton (33486) **(G-492)**
Dougherty Manufacturing, Edgewater *Also called Blue Water Dynamics LLC* **(G-3482)**
Douglas A Fisher Inc 941 951-0189
  957 N Lime Ave Sarasota (34237) **(G-15661)**

Douglas Abbott 407 422-3597
3708 S John Young Pkwy Orlando (32839) *(G-12102)*

Douglas Fuel II Inc 305 620-0707
3701 Nw 167th St Miami Gardens (33055) *(G-10255)*

Douglas Machines Corp 727 461-3477
4500 110th Ave N Clearwater (33762) *(G-1568)*

Douglas Marine, Hollywood Also called Spa Cover Inc *(G-5662)*

Douglass Screen Printers Inc 863 687-8545
2710 New Tampa Hwy Lakeland (33815) *(G-7312)*

Dover Cylinder Head Inc (PA) 850 785-6569
2704 W 15th St 98 Panama City (32401) *(G-13255)*

Dover Cylinder Head of Jackson ....
80 Industrial Loop N A Orange Park (32073) *(G-11824)*

Dovetails A Precision 561 818-6323
5325 Georgia Ave West Palm Beach (33405) *(G-17981)*

Dovo Inc 754 244-5120
11898 Cove Pl Boca Raton (33428) *(G-493)*

Dowe Gallagher Aerospace 941 256-2179
7425 16th St E Sarasota (34243) *(G-15471)*

Dowels Pins & Shafts Inc 727 461-1255
1975 Calumet St Clearwater (33765) *(G-1569)*

Dowling Graphics Inc 727 573-5997
12920 Automobile Blvd Clearwater (33762) *(G-1570)*

Down From Hven Silk Screen Prt, Lantana Also called Wildas Jean-Joseph *(G-7517)*

Downes Trading Co 813 855-7122
5730 Stag Thicket Ln Palm Harbor (34685) *(G-13109)*

Downey Group LLC 954 972-0026
1100 Nw 15th Ave Pompano Beach (33069) *(G-14000)*

Downtown Projects I LLC 352 226-8288
702 Nw 12th Ave Gainesville (32601) *(G-4680)*

Doyle Ploch Sailmakers, Saint Petersburg Also called Southern Interest Co Inc *(G-15191)*

Doyle Sailmakers Inc 772 219-4024
900 Se Ocean Blvd Stuart (34994) *(G-16139)*

DP EMB & Screen Prints Inc 954 245-5902
3485 N Hiatus Rd Sunrise (33351) *(G-16314)*

Dp Enterprises, Panama City Beach Also called David Perkins Enterprises Inc *(G-13329)*

Dp Pet Products Inc 407 888-4627
5340 Young Pine Rd 8 Orlando (32829) *(G-12103)*

Dpdm Inc 561 327-4150
10444 White Pinto Ct Lake Worth (33449) *(G-7196)*

Dpi Information Inc 813 258-8004
8402 Laurel Fair Cir # 209 Tampa (33610) *(G-16785)*

Dpr Print & Promotional, Deerfield Beach Also called Print Basics Inc *(G-2787)*

Dprint, Lakeland Also called Douglass Screen Printers Inc *(G-7312)*

Dps Powder Coating Inc 727 573-2797
4980 110th Ave N Clearwater (33760) *(G-1571)*

Dr Jills Foot Pads Inc 954 573-6557
384 S Military Trl Deerfield Beach (33442) *(G-2710)*

Dr Lips LLC 352 203-3182
11 Plaza Real S Apt 304 Boca Raton (33432) *(G-494)*

Dr Pepper Bottling Co 407 354-5800
1700 Directors Row Orlando (32809) *(G-12104)*

Dr Pepper/Seven Up Inc 321 433-3622
1313 W King St Cocoa (32922) *(G-1921)*

Dr Pepper/Seven Up Inc 352 732-9777
3337 Sw 7th St Ocala (34474) *(G-11372)*

Dr Pepper/Seven Up Inc 561 995-6260
7251 W Plmtt Prk Rd Ste 3 Boca Raton (33433) *(G-495)*

Dr Spirits Company LLC 561 349-5005
604 Lake Ave Lake Worth (33460) *(G-7197)*

Dr Xies Jing-Tang Herbal Inc 352 591-2141
4815 Nw 8th St Ocala (34482) *(G-11373)*

Dr. Botanicals, Fort Lauderdale Also called F&J USA LLC *(G-3808)*

Dr. Pepper Snapple, Boca Raton Also called Dr Pepper/Seven Up Inc *(G-495)*

Drab To Fab 941 475-7700
136 S Mccall Rd Englewood (34223) *(G-3529)*

Draggin Trailers Inc 352 351-8790
3100 Se 50th Pl Ocala (34480) *(G-11374)*

Dragon Flower Winery, Summerfield Also called Bea Sue Vineyards Inc *(G-16257)*

Dragonfire Industries Inc 407 999-2215
4065 L B Mcleod Rd Ste G1 Orlando (32811) *(G-12105)*

Dragonfly Graphics 772 879-9800
861 Sw Lakehurst Dr Ste B Port Saint Lucie (34983) *(G-14408)*

Dragonfly Graphics Inc 352 375-2144
319 Sw 3rd Ave Gainesville (32601) *(G-4681)*

Dragons Miracle LLC 561 670-5546
160 W Camino Real Ste 154 Boca Raton (33432) *(G-496)*

Drake Inc 239 590-9199
2920 Rockfill Rd Fort Myers (33916) *(G-4239)*

Drake Ready Mix Inc 239 590-9199
2920 Rockfill Rd Fort Myers (33916) *(G-4240)*

Drake Tool Co Inc 407 859-4221
10211 General Dr Orlando (32824) *(G-12106)*

Draken International LLC 863 644-1832
3330 Flightline Dr Lakeland (33811) *(G-7313)*

Drakon Coatings Industries Inc 810 875-3874
167 Progress Cir Venice (34285) *(G-17684)*

Drapery Control Systems Inc 386 756-0101
3817 S Nova Rd Ste 104 Port Orange (32127) *(G-14333)*

Drapery Control Systems Inc (PA) 305 653-1712
5545 Nw 35th Ave D Fort Lauderdale (33309) *(G-3773)*

Drazcanna Inc (PA) 786 618-1472
6340 Sunset Dr Miami (33143) *(G-9048)*

Drb Packaging LLC 321 877-2802
386 Commerce Pkwy Rockledge (32955) *(G-14703)*

Drb Packaging LLC 321 877-2802
386 Commerce Pkwy Rockledge (32955) *(G-14704)*

Dream Cuizine 727 943-8289
4952 Ridgemoor Blvd Palm Harbor (34685) *(G-13110)*

Dreamline Aerospace 954 544-2365
7649 Pines Blvd Pembroke Pines (33024) *(G-13385)*

Dreamspinner Press LLC 800 970-3759
10800 Kilcrease Way Tallahassee (32305) *(G-16432)*

Dresser Inc 318 640-2250
12970 Normandy Blvd Jacksonville (32221) *(G-6040)*

Dresser LLC 904 781-7071
12970 Normandy Blvd Jacksonville (32221) *(G-6041)*

Drew Estate LLC (PA) 786 581-1800
12415 Sw 136th Ave Ste 7 Miami (33186) *(G-9049)*

Drew Scientific Inc (HQ) 305 418-2320
14050 Nw 57th Ct Miami Lakes (33014) *(G-10297)*

Drewlu Enterprises Inc 407 478-7872
3500 Aloma Ave Ste D9 Winter Park (32792) *(G-18509)*

Drexel Metals Inc 727 572-7900
8641 Elm Fair Blvd Tampa (33610) *(G-16786)*

Drezo Manufacturing Inc 305 864-9814
5956 Pine Tree Dr Miami Beach (33140) *(G-10185)*

Drinkable Air Inc 954 533-6415
2944 Nw 27th St Bldg 14 Lauderdale Lakes (33311) *(G-7713)*

Drinks On ME 305 LLC 786 488-2356
6118 Nw 7th Ave Miami (33127) *(G-9050)*

Drip Communication LLC 407 730-5519
6831 Edgwter Cmmerce Pkwy Orlando (32810) *(G-12107)*

Driscoll Industries LLC 407 848-7127
522 S Hunt Club Blvd # 570 Apopka (32703) *(G-123)*

Drivers World Corp 561 852-5545
20606 Carousel Cir W Boca Raton (33434) *(G-497)*

Driveshaft Power Inc 561 433-0022
10101 Lantana Rd Ste K Lake Worth (33449) *(G-7198)*

Drone Aviation, Jacksonville Also called Lighter Than Air Systems Corp *(G-6258)*

Drone Imaging Services LLC 407 620-5258
8540 Summerville Pl Orlando (32819) *(G-12108)*

Drone Pics and Vids Corp 786 558-4027
13237 Sw 45th Ln Miami (33175) *(G-9051)*

Drones Shop LLC 772 224-8118
4406 Se Graham Dr Stuart (34997) *(G-16140)*

Drs Advanced Isr LLC 321 622-1202
100 N Babcock St Melbourne (32935) *(G-8403)*

Drs Advanced Isr LLC 850 226-4888
654 Anchors St Nw Ste 1 Fort Walton Beach (32548) *(G-4573)*

Drs Allergy, Jacksonville Also called Doctorxs Allergy Formula *(G-6037)*

Drs C3 Systems Inc 850 302-3909
645 Anchors St Nw Fort Walton Beach (32548) *(G-4574)*

Drs Cengen Llc (HQ) 321 622-1500
100 Babcock St Melbourne (32935) *(G-8404)*

Drs Consolidated Controls 850 302-3000
645 Anchors St Nw Fort Walton Beach (32548) *(G-4575)*

Drs Land Electronics 321 622-1435
100 N Babcock St Melbourne (32935) *(G-8405)*

Drs Laurel Technologies (HQ) 727 541-6681
6200 118th Ave Largo (33773) *(G-7574)*

Drs Leonardo Inc 850 302-3000
645 Anchors St Nw Fort Walton Beach (32548) *(G-4576)*

Drs Leonardo Inc 850 302-3514
640 Lovejoy Rd Nw Fort Walton Beach (32548) *(G-4577)*

Drs Ntwork Imaging Systems LLC 321 309-1500
3520 Dixie Hwy Ne Palm Bay (32905) *(G-12897)*

Drs Ntwork Imaging Systems LLC (HQ) 321 309-1500
100 N Babcock St Melbourne (32935) *(G-8406)*

Drs S and T Optronics Div 321 309-1500
100 N Babcock St Melbourne (32935) *(G-8407)*

Drs Sensors Targeting Systems 321 309-1500
100 N Babcock St Melbourne (32935) *(G-8408)*

Drs Soneticom Inc 321 733-0400
100 N Babcock St Melbourne (32935) *(G-8409)*

Drs Systems Inc 973 451-3525
100 N Babcock St Melbourne (32935) *(G-8410)*

Drs Tactical Systems Inc 321 727-3672
100 N Babcock St Melbourne (32935) *(G-8411)*

Drs Technologies, Fort Walton Beach Also called Drs Training Ctrl Systems LLC *(G-4578)*

Drs Technology, Melbourne Also called Drs Soneticom Inc *(G-8409)*

Drs Training Ctrl Systems LLC (HQ) 850 302-3000
645 Anchors St Nw Fort Walton Beach (32548) *(G-4578)*

Drsingh Technologies Inc 352 334-7270
1912 Nw 67th Pl Gainesville (32653) *(G-4682)*

Drt Express Inc 305 827-5005
7855 W 2nd Ct Ste 4 Hialeah (33014) *(G-5123)*

Drt Services 321 549-1431
861 Young Ave Nw Palm Bay (32907) *(G-12898)*

A
L
P
H
A
B
E
T
I
C

Drum Circle Distilling LLC 941 358-1900
2212 Industrial Blvd Sarasota (34234) *(G-15662)*

Drummond Press Inc (PA) 904 354-2818
2472 Dennis St Jacksonville (32204) *(G-6042)*

Dry Color USA LLC 407 856-7788
8701 S Ct Skinner Orlando (32824) *(G-12109)*

Dryer Vent Wizard of Pb 561 901-3464
22 Las Flores Boynton Beach (33426) *(G-859)*

Drywall Elements 407 454-7293
1700 35th St Ste 110 Orlando (32839) *(G-12110)*

Ds Coatings Inc 321 848-4719
18 S Butler Ave Avon Park (33825) *(G-280)*

Ds Healthcare Group Inc (HQ) 888 829-4212
1850 Nw 84th Ave Ste 108 Doral (33126) *(G-3200)*

Ds Healthcare Group Inc 888 404-7770
1395 Brickell Ave Ste 800 Miami (33131) *(G-9052)*

Ds Laboratories, Doral *Also called Ds Healthcare Group Inc (G-3200)*

Ds Laboratories, Miami *Also called Ds Healthcare Group Inc (G-9052)*

Ds Powder Coating Inc 561 660-7835
1800 4th Ave N Unit B Lake Worth Beach (33461) *(G-7254)*

Ds18, Miami Gardens *Also called Spirit LLC (G-10274)*

Dsas Air Inc 954 673-5385
4509 Nw 39th St Lauderdale Lakes (33319) *(G-7714)*

DSC Sales of SC Inc (PA) 813 854-3131
455 Commerce Blvd Oldsmar (34677) *(G-11644)*

Dse Inc 863 425-1745
2701 State Rd 37 S Mulberry (33860) *(G-10624)*

Dse Inc (PA) 813 443-4809
10401 Frog Pond Dr Riverview (33569) *(G-14561)*

Dsg Clearwater Laboratory 727 530-9444
14333 58th St N Clearwater (33760) *(G-1572)*

DSign Solutions Inc 786 447-4165
1173 Nw 123rd Pl Miami (33182) *(G-9053)*

Dsx Products Inc 904 744-3400
4430 Palmetto Inlt W Jacksonville (32277) *(G-6043)*

Dtc Stairs, Miami *Also called Dade Truss Company Inc (G-8997)*

DTF Woodworks LLC 954 317-6443
5101 Sw 167th Ave Southwest Ranches (33331) *(G-16053)*

Dtg ASAP, Thonotosassa *Also called Hitmaster Graphics LLC (G-17562)*

Dti Design Trend Inc 954 680-8370
496 W 18th St Hialeah (33010) *(G-5124)*

Dtsystems Inc 813 994-0030
4834 W Gandy Blvd Tampa (33611) *(G-16787)*

Dubhouse Inc 954 524-3658
404 Se 15th St Fort Lauderdale (33316) *(G-3774)*

Duck In Truck Puppets Inc 772 334-3022
1649 Ne Sunview Ter Jensen Beach (34957) *(G-6653)*

Duck Walk, Fort Lauderdale *Also called Boat International Media Inc (G-3698)*

Ducksteins Services 352 449-5678
3 Morgan Ave Leesburg (34748) *(G-7768)*

Duckworth Steel Boats Inc 727 934-2550
1051 Island Ave Tarpon Springs (34689) *(G-17468)*

Duct Design Corporation 305 827-0110
7850 W 22nd Ave Unit 1 Hialeah (33016) *(G-5125)*

Duenas Mobile Applications LLC (PA) 305 851-3397
15600 Sw 288th St Ste 402 Homestead (33033) *(G-5709)*

Dujon Inc 813 770-3179
2480 25th St N Saint Petersburg (33713) *(G-15031)*

Dukane Seacom Inc 941 739-3200
7135 16th St E Ste 101 Sarasota (34243) *(G-15472)*

Duke Custom Fabrication LLC 954 707-1722
5846 S Flamingo Rd Cooper City (33330) *(G-2020)*

Dukeman Custom Woodwork, Jacksonville *Also called Dukemans Custom Wdwkg Inc (G-6044)*

Dukemans Custom Wdwkg Inc 904 355-5188
141 N Myrtle Ave Fl 2 Jacksonville (32204) *(G-6044)*

Dukes Brewhouse Inc 813 758-9309
1808 James L Redman Pkwy Plant City (33563) *(G-13761)*

Duley Truss Inc 352 465-0964
2591 W Dunnellon Rd 488 Dunnellon (34433) *(G-3462)*

Dulond Tool & Engineering Inc 941 758-4489
2306 Whitfield Park Loop Sarasota (34243) *(G-15473)*

Dumpster Company, Fort Myers *Also called Majic Wheels Corp (G-4316)*

Dumpstermaxx 805 552-6299
5265 University Pkwy # 101 University Park (34201) *(G-17653)*

Dumpsterme LLC 904 647-1945
13255 Lanier Rd Jacksonville (32226) *(G-6045)*

Duncan and Sons Cnstr Eqp Inc 305 216-3115
2750 Nw 209th Ter Miami Gardens (33056) *(G-10256)*

Duncanson Dynasty Inc 561 288-1349
801 Northpoint Pkwy # 97 West Palm Beach (33407) *(G-17982)*

Dunco Materials, Plant City *Also called Dunco Rock & Gravel Inc (G-13762)*

Dunco Rock & Gravel Inc 813 752-5622
3115 Sammonds Rd Plant City (33563) *(G-13762)*

Dunedin House of Beer, Dunedin *Also called Arhob LLC (G-3439)*

Dunnellon Discount Drugs, Dunnellon *Also called Kashiben Say LLC (G-3466)*

Dunrite Metal Fabricators Inc 727 299-9242
12099 44th St N Clearwater (33762) *(G-1573)*

Duos Technologies Inc (PA) 904 652-1601
6622 Sthpint Dr S Ste 310 Jacksonville (32216) *(G-6046)*

Duos Technologies Group Inc (PA) 904 652-1601
6622 Sthpint Dr S Ste 310 Jacksonville (32216) *(G-6047)*

DUOSTECH, Jacksonville *Also called Duos Technologies Group Inc (G-6047)*

Dupont, The Villages *Also called E I Du Pont De Nemours & Co (G-17554)*

Dupont Publishing Inc (PA) 727 573-9339
4707 140th Ave N Ste 302 Clearwater (33762) *(G-1574)*

Dupont Registry, Clearwater *Also called Dupont Publishing Inc (G-1574)*

Dupuy Silo Facility LLC (PA) 904 899-7200
1520 Edgewood Ave N Jacksonville (32254) *(G-6048)*

Dura-Cast Products Inc 863 638-3200
16160 Hwy 27 Lake Wales (33859) *(G-7158)*

Dura-Stress Inc (PA) 352 787-1422
11325 County Road 44 Leesburg (34788) *(G-7769)*

Dura-Weld Inc 561 586-0180
3599 23rd Ave S Ste 9 Lake Worth Beach (33461) *(G-7255)*

Durabody Usa LLC 954 357-2333
11800 Miramar Pkwy Miramar (33025) *(G-10486)*

Duracell Company 561 494-7550
515 N Flagler Dr Ste 1600 West Palm Beach (33401) *(G-17983)*

Duraguard Products, Tampa *Also called Pacific Die Cast Inc (G-17137)*

Duraline, Deland *Also called J B Nottingham & Co Inc (G-2877)*

Duramaster, Tampa *Also called Greenco Manufacturing Corp (G-16892)*

Duramaster Cylinders 813 882-0040
5688 W Crenshaw St Tampa (33634) *(G-16788)*

Durapoly Industries Inc 352 622-3455
191 N Highway 314a Silver Springs (34488) *(G-16005)*

Durbal Inc 727 531-3040
14115 63rd Way N Ste A Clearwater (33760) *(G-1575)*

Durisan, Sarasota *Also called Sanit Technologies LLC (G-15550)*

Durlach Holdings Inc 941 751-1672
6008 28th St E Ste A Bradenton (34203) *(G-970)*

Durra Quick Print 850 681-2900
1334 N Monroe St Tallahassee (32303) *(G-16433)*

Durra-Print Inc 850 222-4768
3044 W Tharpe St Tallahassee (32303) *(G-16434)*

Dusobox Corporation 407 855-5120
2501 Investors Row # 500 Orlando (32837) *(G-12111)*

Dusobox Creative Packg Group, Orlando *Also called Dusobox Corporation (G-12111)*

Duststop Air Filters, Jacksonville *Also called Duststop Filters Inc (G-6049)*

Duststop Filters Inc 904 725-1001
1843 Blue Ridge Dr Jacksonville (32246) *(G-6049)*

Dutch Packing Co Inc 305 871-3640
74 Sw Coral Ter Ste 101 Miami (33155) *(G-9054)*

Dutchy Enterprises LLC 321 877-0700
600 Cox Rd Ste A Cocoa (32926) *(G-1922)*

Duval Bakery Products Inc 904 354-7878
985 Cobblestone Dr Orange Park (32065) *(G-11825)*

Duval Fixtures Inc 904 757-3964
3600 Saint Augustine Rd Jacksonville (32207) *(G-6050)*

Duy Drugs Inc 305 594-3667
1730 Nw 79th Ave Doral (33126) *(G-3201)*

Dvc Signs LLC 727 524-8543
12350 Belcher Rd S 14b Largo (33773) *(G-7575)*

Dvh Macleod Corp 850 224-6760
1100 N Monroe St Ste A Tallahassee (32303) *(G-16435)*

Dwa Inc (PA) 941 444-1134
5401 Palmer Blvd Sarasota (34232) *(G-15663)*

Dwi Inc 321 508-9833
1960 Howell Ln Malabar (32950) *(G-8081)*

Dwm-2021 Inc 813 443-0791
7810 Professional Pl Tampa (33637) *(G-16789)*

Dwyer Precision Products Inc 904 249-3545
266 20th St N Jacksonville (32250) *(G-6051)*

Dxm Marketing Group LLC 904 332-6490
9485 Rgncy Sq Blvd # 460 Jacksonville (32225) *(G-6052)*

Dyadic Industries Intl, Jupiter *Also called Dyadic International USA Inc (G-6714)*

Dyadic International Inc (PA) 561 743-8333
140 Intrcostal Pt Dr # 404 Jupiter (33477) *(G-6713)*

Dyadic International USA Inc (HQ) 561 743-8333
140 Intrcostal Pt Dr # 404 Jupiter (33477) *(G-6714)*

Dyco Ventures LLC 863 491-7211
2692 Ne Nat Ave Arcadia (34266) *(G-192)*

Dyebar Express Ltd 954 298-5171
3390 Sw 15th St Deerfield Beach (33442) *(G-2711)*

Dyn-O-Mat Inc 561 747-2301
1201 Jupiter Park Dr # 1 Jupiter (33458) *(G-6715)*

Dynabilt Technologies Corp 305 919-9800
180 W 22nd St Hialeah (33010) *(G-5126)*

Dynacolor Graphics Inc 305 625-5388
950 Se 8th St Hialeah (33010) *(G-5127)*

Dynalco Controls Corporation (HQ) 323 589-6181
5450 Nw 33rd Ave Ste 104 Fort Lauderdale (33309) *(G-3775)*

Dynamic Alloy 352 728-7600
1018 W North Blvd Ste A Leesburg (34748) *(G-7770)*

Dynamic Aspects Inc 407 322-1923
108 Fox Chase Ct Debary (32713) *(G-2634)*

Dynamic Cabinets Inc 813 891-0667
304 Marlborough St Oldsmar (34677) *(G-11645)*

Dynamic Color Inc 954 462-0261
200 Park Central Blvd S Pompano Beach (33064) *(G-14001)*

Dynamic Engrg Innovations Inc 386 445-6000
32 Hargrove Grade Palm Coast (32137) *(G-13076)*

Dynamic Glucose Hlth Ctrs LLC 800 610-6422
515 E Las Olas Blvd Ste 1 Fort Lauderdale (33301) *(G-3776)*

Dynamic Material Systems LLC 407 353-6885
269 Aulin Ave Ste 1003 Oviedo (32765) *(G-12818)*

Dynamic Metals LLC 561 629-7304
340 Pike Rd West Palm Beach (33411) *(G-17984)*

Dynamic Precision Group Inc (PA) 772 287-7770
3651 Se Commerce Ave Stuart (34997) *(G-16141)*

Dynamic Printing of Brandon 813 664-6880
6014 Tealside Ct Lithia (33547) *(G-7833)*

Dynamic Visions Inc 941 497-1984
355 Center Ct Venice (34285) *(G-17685)*

Dynamis Epoxy LLC 941 488-3999
415 E Venice Ave Venice (34285) *(G-17686)*

Dynamis Inc 941 488-3999
415 E Venice Ave Venice (34285) *(G-17687)*

Dynamo Shredder Company, Palm Harbor *Also called New Market Enterprises Ltd (G-13121)*

Dynasel Incorporated 972 733-4447
114 Grantham A Deerfield Beach (33442) *(G-2712)*

Dynastic Investments Inc 513 570-7153
808 Ne 214th Ln Miami (33179) *(G-9055)*

Dynasty Apparel Corp (PA) 305 685-3490
13000 Nw 42nd Ave Opa Locka (33054) *(G-11740)*

Dynasystems LLC 410 343-7759
3445 Spring Branch Trl # 360 Melbourne (32935) *(G-8412)*

Dyno LLC (PA) 954 971-2910
1571 W Copans Rd Ste 105 Pompano Beach (33064) *(G-14002)*

Dyno Merchandise, Pompano Beach *Also called Dyno LLC (G-14002)*

Dynofresh, Davie *Also called Hac International Inc (G-2421)*

Dynomat Inc 561 747-2301
1201 Jupiter Park Dr Jupiter (33458) *(G-6716)*

Dynotec Plastic Inc 813 248-5335
2211 N 38th St Ste A Tampa (33605) *(G-16790)*

Dynotune Inc 941 753-8899
515 27th St E Ste 4 Bradenton (34208) *(G-971)*

E & A Industries Inc 954 278-2428
16 Ne 4th St Ste 110e Fort Lauderdale (33301) *(G-3777)*

E & D Kitchen Cabinet Inc 786 343-8558
6790 W 6th Ct Hialeah (33012) *(G-5128)*

E & E Woodcraft Corp 305 556-1443
1619 W 33rd Pl Hialeah (33012) *(G-5129)*

E & M Recycling Inc 561 718-1092
630 S Palmway Lake Worth (33460) *(G-7199)*

E & P Printing Corp 305 715-9545
7882 Nw 64th St Miami (33166) *(G-9056)*

E 3 Maintenance 904 708-7208
13720 Old St Agstine Rd S Jacksonville (32258) *(G-6053)*

E A S I, Tampa *Also called Engineered Air Systems Inc (G-16814)*

E B Custom Cabinets LLC 407 927-2346
2756 Michigan Ave Kissimmee (34744) *(G-6914)*

E Benton Grimsley Inc 850 863-4064
909 Mar Walt Dr Fort Walton Beach (32547) *(G-4579)*

E C I, Tamarac *Also called Electrical Controls Inc (G-16530)*

E C I, Hialeah *Also called Environmental Contractors Inc (G-5146)*

E G Coatings LLC 407 624-2615
1751 Covey Ct Kissimmee (34744) *(G-6915)*

E G Controls, Jacksonville *Also called E G Pump Controls Inc (G-6054)*

E G Pump Controls Inc 904 292-0110
11790 Philips Hwy Jacksonville (32256) *(G-6054)*

E I Du Pont De Nemours & Co 352 205-8103
2555 Flintshire Ave The Villages (32162) *(G-17554)*

E J M Gutter, Orlando *Also called EJM Copper Inc (G-12118)*

E L I T E Intergroup, Miami *Also called ELite Intl Group LLC (G-9086)*

E M Chadbourne Inds LLC 850 429-1797
192 Hewitt St Pensacola (32503) *(G-13491)*

E M P Inc 772 286-7343
4340 Se Commerce Ave Stuart (34997) *(G-16142)*

E M S, Odessa *Also called Electro Mech Solutions Inc (G-11549)*

E M S, Melbourne *Also called Envirnmental Mfg Solutions LLC (G-8421)*

E S A I, Orlando *Also called Enterprise System Assoc Inc (G-12130)*

E T C R Inc 305 637-0999
3181 Nw 36th Ave Miami (33142) *(G-9057)*

E T I Incorporated 727 546-6472
10610 75th St Largo (33777) *(G-7576)*

E T Plastering Inc 305 874-7082
3831 Nw 58th Ct Virginia Gardens (33166) *(G-17823)*

E&M Innovative Forager LLC (PA) 954 923-0056
736 S Military Trl Deerfield Beach (33442) *(G-2713)*

E&P Solutions and Services Inc 305 715-9545
7884 Nw 64th St Miami (33166) *(G-9058)*

E&T Horizons Ltd Liability Co 321 704-1244
2623 Chapel Bridge Ln Melbourne (32940) *(G-8413)*

E-Commerce, Saint Augustine *Also called Til Valhalla Project LLC (G-14906)*

E-Commerce, Destin *Also called Digicrib LLC (G-3065)*

E-Liquids Investment Group LLC 954 507-6060
6500 Nw 16th St Ste 1 Plantation (33313) *(G-13845)*

E-One Inc (HQ) 352 237-1122
1601 Sw 37th Ave Ocala (34474) *(G-11375)*

E-One Inc 352 237-1122
1701 Sw 37th Ave Ocala (34474) *(G-11376)*

E-One Parts Central, Ocala *Also called E-One Inc (G-11375)*

E-Sea Rider LLC 727 863-3333
4054 Louis Ave Holiday (34691) *(G-5493)*

E-Sea Rider Marine Bean Bags, Holiday *Also called E-Sea Rider LLC (G-5493)*

E-Stone USA Corp 863 655-1273
8041 Haywood Taylor Blvd Sebring (33870) *(G-15919)*

E-Stone USA Corporation 954 266-6793
472 Webster Turn Dr Sebring (33870) *(G-15920)*

E-Stone USA Corporation (HQ) 863 214-8281
1565 Nw 36th St Miami (33142) *(G-9059)*

E-Tag, Boca Raton *Also called Telsec Corporation (G-710)*

E-Z Anchor Puller Mfg Co LLC 800 800-1640
8955 Us Highway 301 N Parrish (34219) *(G-13358)*

E-Z Fastening Solutions Inc 813 854-3937
640 Brooker Creek Blvd # 425 Oldsmar (34677) *(G-11646)*

E-Z Metals Inc 239 936-7887
6133 Idlewild St Fort Myers (33966) *(G-4241)*

E-Z Weld Inc 561 844-0241
1661 Pres Barack Obama Hw Riviera Beach (33404) *(G-14618)*

E1w Games LLC 561 255-7370
14545 S Military Trl J Delray Beach (33484) *(G-2956)*

E2 Walls Inc 813 374-2010
5692 W Crenshaw St Tampa (33634) *(G-16791)*

E2g Partners LLC 813 855-2251
11200 Dr Mrtn Lther King Saint Petersburg (33716) *(G-15032)*

E3 Fluid Recovery Eng (PA) 727 754-9792
13517 65th St Largo (33771) *(G-7577)*

E3 Graphics Inc 954 510-1302
9868 W Sample Rd Coral Springs (33065) *(G-2151)*

Eag-Led LLC (PA) 813 463-2420
12918 Commodity Pl Tampa (33626) *(G-16792)*

Eagle Artistic Printing Inc 973 476-6301
10277 Shireoaks Ln Boca Raton (33498) *(G-498)*

Eagle Athletic Wear Inc (PA) 727 937-6147
720 E Tarpon Ave Tarpon Springs (34689) *(G-17469)*

Eagle Athletica LLC 305 209-7002
1000 Brickell Ave Ste 715 Miami (33131) *(G-9060)*

Eagle Aviation Maintenance, Defuniak Springs *Also called Onvoi AVI Supp and Inspect Ser (G-2841)*

Eagle Engrg & Land Dev Inc 913 948-4320
302 Sw 3rd Ave Boynton Beach (33435) *(G-860)*

Eagle I Tech Inc 772 221-8188
4529 Sw Cargo Way Palm City (34990) *(G-13033)*

Eagle Insulation Fabrication, Jacksonville *Also called Atlantic Insulation Inc (G-5908)*

Eagle Labs Incorporated (PA) 727 548-1816
5000 Park St N Ste 1202 Saint Petersburg (33709) *(G-15033)*

Eagle Manufacturing Group, Hialeah *Also called U S Holdings Inc (G-5389)*

Eagle Metal Distributors Inc 407 367-0688
603 W Landstreet Rd Ste B Orlando (32824) *(G-12112)*

Eagle Metal Products Inc 561 964-4192
100 N Country Club Blvd Lake Worth (33462) *(G-7200)*

Eagle Painting, Sunrise *Also called J & J Inc (G-16326)*

Eagle Pavers Inc 954 822-1137
51 Nw 45th Ave Deerfield Beach (33442) *(G-2714)*

Eagle Pneumatic Inc 863 644-4870
3902 Industry Blvd Lakeland (33811) *(G-7314)*

Eagle Prof Flrg Removal 813 520-3027
11548 Bay Gardens Loop Riverview (33569) *(G-14562)*

Eagle Quality Components LLC 352 516-4838
280 Hummer Way Tavares (32778) *(G-17504)*

Eagle Ready Mix 239 732-9333
9210 Collier Blvd Naples (34114) *(G-10734)*

Eagle Ready Mix LLC 239 693-1500
16576 Gator Rd Fort Myers (33912) *(G-4242)*

Eagle View Windows Inc 904 647-8221
13340 International Pkwy Jacksonville (32218) *(G-6055)*

Eagle-Eye Anesthesia Inc 817 999-9830
11233 St Jhns Indus Pkwy Jacksonville (32246) *(G-6056)*

Eagled Global Lights, Tampa *Also called Eag-Led LLC (G-16792)*

Eam Worldwide, Miami *Also called Eastern Aero Marine Inc (G-9061)*

Ear-Tronics Inc (PA) 239 275-7655
7181 College Pkwy Ste 14 Fort Myers (33907) *(G-4243)*

Earl Parker Yacht Refinishing 954 791-1811
1915 Sw 21st Ave Fort Lauderdale (33312) *(G-3778)*

Earnest Metal Fabrication, Sanford *Also called Earnest Products Inc (G-15308)*

Earnest Products Inc 407 831-1588
2000 E Lake Mary Blvd Sanford (32773) *(G-15308)*

ALPHABETIC

Eartech Inc 941 747-8193
3904 9th Ave W Bradenton (34205) *(G-972)*

Earth & Sea Wear LLC 786 332-2236
8785 Nw 13th Ter Doral (33172) *(G-3202)*

Earth Group Inc 954 979-8444
2200 N Andrews Ave Pompano Beach (33069) *(G-14003)*

Earth Vets Inc 352 332-9991
96093 Marsh Lakes Dr Fernandina Beach (32034) *(G-3586)*

Earthcore Industries LLC (PA) 904 363-3417
6899 Phillips Ind Blvd Jacksonville (32256) *(G-6057)*

Earthmover Cnstr Eqp LLC 407 401-8956
2325 Clark St Apopka (32703) *(G-124)*

Earthtnes In Hrmony With Nture, Stuart *Also called Ronald M Hart Inc (G-16209)*

Easi 360 Corp 305 213-6346
10975 Nw 65th St Doral (33178) *(G-3203)*

East 46th Auto Sales Inc 407 322-3100
3710 E State Road 46 Sanford (32771) *(G-15309)*

East 46th Trailer Sales, Sanford *Also called East 46th Auto Sales Inc (G-15309)*

East Bay Manufacturers Inc 813 524-9344
100 S Ashley Dr Ste 600 Tampa (33602) *(G-16793)*

East Coast Cabinet Co 321 392-4686
100 Eyster Blvd Rockledge (32955) *(G-14705)*

East Coast Cooling Tower Inc 904 551-5527
9850 Interstate Center Dr Jacksonville (32218) *(G-6058)*

East Coast Custom Coatings Inc 954 914-6711
2920 Nw 106th Ave Coral Springs (33065) *(G-2152)*

East Coast Door Inc 954 868-4700
1297 Se 5th Ave Pompano Beach (33060) *(G-14004)*

East Coast Fix & Mllwk Co Inc 904 733-9711
4880 Clydo Rd S Jacksonville (32207) *(G-6059)*

East Coast Floats LLC 407 203-5628
4832 New Broad St Orlando (32814) *(G-12113)*

East Coast Foam Supply Inc 321 433-8231
392 Richard Rd Rockledge (32955) *(G-14706)*

East Coast Machine Inc 321 632-4817
3022 Oxbow Cir Cocoa (32926) *(G-1923)*

East Coast Medal 561 619-6753
860 N 8th St Lantana (33462) *(G-7510)*

East Coast Metal Decks Inc 561 433-8259
620 Whitney Ave Lantana (33462) *(G-7511)*

East Coast Metals Inc 305 885-9991
7905 W 20th Ave Hialeah (33014) *(G-5130)*

East Coast Metalworks LLC 321 698-0624
6615 Bethel St Cocoa (32927) *(G-1924)*

East Coast Ornamental Wldg Inc 386 672-4340
1794 State Ave Daytona Beach (32117) *(G-2547)*

East Coast Steel Inc 386 233-1385
1084 Landers St Ormond Beach (32174) *(G-12759)*

East Coast Truss, Fort Pierce *Also called Martinez Builders Supply LLC (G-4503)*

East Ft. Pierce FL Readymix, Fort Pierce *Also called Cemex Cnstr Mtls Fla LLC (G-4475)*

Eastburn Woodworks Inc 850 456-8090
2620 Hollywood Ave Pensacola (32505) *(G-13492)*

Eastern Aero Marine Inc 305 871-4050
5502 Nw 37th Ave Miami (33142) *(G-9061)*

Eastern Irrigation Supply 352 472-3323
5328 Nw State Road 45 Newberry (32669) *(G-11018)*

Eastern Metal Supply Inc 863 682-6660
4675 Drane Field Rd Lakeland (33811) *(G-7315)*

Eastern Metal Supply NC Inc 800 432-2204
4268 Westroads Dr West Palm Beach (33407) *(G-17985)*

Eastern Ribbon & Roll Corp (PA) 813 676-8600
1920 Gunn Hwy Odessa (33556) *(G-11548)*

Eastern Shipbuilding Group Inc (PA) 850 763-1900
2200 Nelson Ave Panama City (32401) *(G-13256)*

Eastern Shipbuilding Group Inc 850 522-7400
13300 Allanton Rd Panama City (32404) *(G-13257)*

Eastern Shipyards Inc 850 763-1900
2200 Nelson Ave Panama City (32401) *(G-13258)*

Eastern Shores Printing (PA) 305 685-8976
4476 Nw 128th St Opa Locka (33054) *(G-11741)*

Eastern Shres Prtg Woven Label, Opa Locka *Also called Eastern Shores Printing (G-11741)*

Eastern Signs LLC 305 542-8274
13408 Nw 38th Ct Hialeah (33014) *(G-5131)*

Eastern Wire Products Inc 904 781-6775
5301 W 5th St Jacksonville (32254) *(G-6060)*

Eastgate Publishing Inc 772 286-0101
9015 Se Athena St Hobe Sound (33455) *(G-5482)*

Eastman Chemical Company 305 671-2800
9155 S Ddland Blvd 1116 Miami (33156) *(G-9062)*

Eastman Kodak Company 813 908-7910
5364 Ehrlich Rd Tampa (33624) *(G-16794)*

Eastman Performance Films LLC 954 920-2001
5553 Ravenswood Rd # 104 Fort Lauderdale (33312) *(G-3779)*

Easy Digital Corp 305 940-1001
16585 Nw 2nd Ave Ste 100 Miami (33169) *(G-9063)*

Easy Foam Inc 970 927-0209
4 Calendula Ct W Homosassa (34446) *(G-5748)*

Easy Foods Inc 321 300-1104
1965 Avenue A Kissimmee (34758) *(G-6916)*

Easy Foods Inc (PA) 305 599-0357
1728 Coral Way Ste 900 Miami (33145) *(G-9064)*

Easy Pavers Corp 407 967-0511
334 Windford Ct Winter Garden (34787) *(G-18383)*

Easy Picker Golf Products Inc 239 368-6600
415 Leonard Blvd N Lehigh Acres (33971) *(G-7808)*

Easy Rent Inc 904 443-7446
8535 Baymeadows Rd Ste 7 Jacksonville (32256) *(G-6061)*

Easy Signs Inc 954 673-0118
4860 N Dixie Hwy Oakland Park (33334) *(G-11262)*

Easydrift LLC 352 318-3683
13100 Nw 50th Ave Gainesville (32606) *(G-4683)*

Easylife Tech, Medley *Also called Famatel USA LLC (G-8240)*

Easylift N Bansbach Amer Inc 321 253-1999
50 West Dr Melbourne (32904) *(G-8414)*

Easyturf Inc 941 753-3312
3203 Us Highway 301 N Ellenton (34222) *(G-3510)*

EASYVISTA USA, Coral Gables *Also called Goverlan LLC (G-2064)*

Eat Fresco, Tampa *Also called Fresco Foods Inc (G-16861)*

Eaton & Wolk 305 249-1640
2665 S Byshr Dr Ste 609 Miami (33133) *(G-9065)*

Eaton Corporation 813 281-8069
1511 N West Shore Blvd # 1111 Tampa (33607) *(G-16795)*

Eaton Law 813 264-4800
14812 N Florida Ave Tampa (33613) *(G-16796)*

Ebco Envmtl Bins & Cntrs Inc 954 967-9999
2101 Sw 56th Ter West Park (33023) *(G-18211)*

Ebella Magazine 239 431-7231
5647 Naples Blvd Naples (34109) *(G-10735)*

Eberjey Intimates 305 260-0030
7400 Nw 7th St Ste 102 Miami (33126) *(G-9066)*

Ebs Quality Service Inc 305 595-4048
13210 Sw 132nd Ave Ste 1 Miami (33186) *(G-9067)*

Ebway LLC 954 971-4911
6600 Nw 21st Ave Ste A Fort Lauderdale (33309) *(G-3780)*

Ebway LLC 954 971-4911
6601 Nw 20th Ave Fort Lauderdale (33309) *(G-3781)*

EC Cabinets Inc 305 887-2091
1511 E 11th Ave Hialeah (33010) *(G-5132)*

ECB Publishing, Monticello *Also called Monticello News (G-10584)*

Ecc, Saint Petersburg *Also called Evolving Coal Corp (G-15039)*

Ecco Doors LLC 561 392-3533
505 Industrial Way Boynton Beach (33426) *(G-861)*

Ecco Doors Manufacturing LLC 561 721-6660
505 Industrial Way Boynton Beach (33426) *(G-862)*

Echo Plastic Systems 305 655-1300
1801 Green Rd Ste B Deerfield Beach (33064) *(G-2715)*

Echodog Industries Inc 407 909-1636
9350 Bentley Park Cir Orlando (32819) *(G-12114)*

Eci Pharmaceuticals LLC (PA) 954 486-8181
5311 Nw 35th Ter Fort Lauderdale (33309) *(G-3782)*

Eci Telecom Inc (HQ) 954 772-3070
5100 Nw 33rd Ave Ste 150 Fort Lauderdale (33309) *(G-3783)*

Ecleris, Medley *Also called Eusa Global LLC (G-8238)*

Eclipse Development LLC 520 370-7358
170 Lakeview Dr Apt 204 Weston (33326) *(G-18239)*

Eclipse Ehr Solutions LLC 352 488-0081
11242 Commercial Way Weeki Wachee (34614) *(G-17836)*

Eclipse Products, Weston *Also called Eclipse Development LLC (G-18239)*

Eclipse Screen and Shutters 305 216-4716
3120 Sw 114th Ave Miami (33165) *(G-9068)*

Eco Concepts Inc 954 920-9700
3607 N 29th Ave Hollywood (33020) *(G-5569)*

Eco Cups International Corp 407 308-1764
2814 Silver Star Rd Apt 4 Orlando (32808) *(G-12115)*

Eco Custom Filters Inc 786 536-6764
7725 Nw 75th Ave Medley (33166) *(G-8233)*

Eco Informativo 786 362-6789
1901 Brickell Ave B201 Miami (33129) *(G-9069)*

Eco Print Inc 305 248-1478
20450 Sw 248th St Homestead (33031) *(G-5710)*

Eco Restore LLC 904 226-9265
7563 Philips Hwy Ste 305 Jacksonville (32256) *(G-6062)*

Eco Solar Technology 904 219-0807
12334 Hidden Hills Ln Jacksonville (32225) *(G-6063)*

Eco Window Systems LLC 305 885-5299
8502 Nw 80th St Unit 103 Medley (33166) *(G-8234)*

Eco Woodwork and Design Inc 954 326-8806
3761 Ne 4th Ave Oakland Park (33334) *(G-11263)*

Eco World Water Corp 954 599-3672
150 N Federal Hwy Ste 200 Fort Lauderdale (33301) *(G-3784)*

Ecoatm LLC 858 766-7250
27001 Us Highway 19 N # 100 Clearwater (33761) *(G-1576)*

Ecolab Inc 800 931-8911
1201 Jupiter Park Dr # 1 Jupiter (33458) *(G-6717)*

Ecological Laboratories Inc 239 573-6650
2525 Ne 9th Ave Cape Coral (33909) *(G-1336)*

Ecombustible Products LLC 786 565-8610
16690 Collins Ave # 1102 Sunny Isles Beach (33160) *(G-16270)*

Ecomkbiz LLC 786 477-1865
16850 Collins Ave Ste 112 Sunny Isles Beach (33160) *(G-16271)*

Econo-Blast, Saint Petersburg Also called Maxi-Blast of Florida Inc *(G-15122)*

Econochannel Inc 305 255-2113
213 Se 10th Ave Hialeah (33010) *(G-5133)*

Economy Dntres Jcksonville LLC 904 696-6767
1680 Dunn Ave Ste 6 Jacksonville (32218) *(G-6064)*

Economy Printing Co 904 786-4070
14413 Christen Dr S Jacksonville (32218) *(G-6065)*

Economy Tent International, Miami Also called Ae Tent LLC *(G-8659)*

Economy Tent International Inc 305 691-0191
2995 Nw 75th St Miami (33147) *(G-9070)*

Ecopod, Miami Also called Sltons Envirnmntal Group Assoc *(G-9905)*

Ecoprintq Inc 305 681-7445
14261 Commerce Way # 101 Miami Lakes (33016) *(G-10298)*

Ecosan LLC 954 446-5929
2520 Coral Way Ste 2 Coral Gables (33145) *(G-2050)*

Ecosmart 561 328-6488
1313 S Killian Dr Lake Park (33403) *(G-7123)*

Ecosmart Surface & Coating TEC 402 319-1607
1313 S Killian Dr West Palm Beach (33403) *(G-17986)*

Ecosoulife USA Dist LLC 754 212-5456
3651 Fau Blvd Ste 400 Boca Raton (33431) *(G-499)*

Ecosphere Technologies Inc (PA) 772 287-4846
3491 Se Gran Park Way Stuart (34997) *(G-16143)*

Ecotec Manufacturing Inc 863 357-4500
312 Sw 7th Ave Okeechobee (34974) *(G-11604)*

Ecotech Water LLC 877 341-9500
7121 Gulf Blvd St Pete Beach (33706) *(G-16089)*

Ecs America LLC 305 798-3825
3555 Nw 79th Ave Doral (33122) *(G-3204)*

Ed Allen Inc 941 743-2646
1312 Market Cir Unit 9 Port Charlotte (33953) *(G-14296)*

ED Publications Inc 727 726-3592
2431 Estancia Blvd Bldg B Clearwater (33761) *(G-1577)*

Ed Steel Fabricator Inc 305 926-4904
4807 E 10th Ln Hialeah (33013) *(G-5134)*

Ed Vance Printing Company Inc 813 882-8888
6107 Memorial Hwy Ste E7 Tampa (33615) *(G-16797)*

Ed-Gar Leasing Company Inc 904 284-1900
1306 Idlewild Ave Green Cove Springs (32043) *(G-4823)*

Edafa Industries Inc 954 946-0830
1460 Sw 3rd St Ste 6 Pompano Beach (33069) *(G-14005)*

Edak Inc (HQ) 321 674-6804
630 Distribution Dr Melbourne (32904) *(G-8415)*

Edashop Inc 786 565-9197
15388 Arcadia Bluff Loop Winter Garden (34787) *(G-18384)*

Edc Corporation 386 951-4075
1701 Lexington Ave Deland (32724) *(G-2867)*

Edca Bakery Corporation 305 448-7843
5236 W Flagler St Coral Gables (33134) *(G-2051)*

Eddy Floor Scraper Inc 954 981-0715
1806 Sw 31st Ave Hallandale (33009) *(G-4924)*

Eddy Storm Protection 386 248-1631
1000 N Nova Rd Daytona Beach (32117) *(G-2548)*

Eden Fast Frozen Dessert LLC 787 375-0826
107 Broadway Kissimmee (34741) *(G-6917)*

Edge Aerodynamix Inc 850 238-8610
8317 Front Beach Rd # 21 Panama City Beach (32407) *(G-13330)*

Edge Power Solutions Inc 321 499-1919
5131 Industry Dr Ste 107 Melbourne (32940) *(G-8416)*

Edgeline Industries LLC (PA) 954 727-5272
1319 E Hillsboro Blvd # 514 Deerfield Beach (33441) *(G-2716)*

Edgeone LLC 561 995-7767
1141 Holland Dr Ste 1 Boca Raton (33487) *(G-500)*

Edgetech, Boca Raton Also called Edgeone LLC *(G-500)*

Edgewater Power Boats LLC 386 426-5457
211 Dale St Edgewater (32132) *(G-3489)*

Edgewater Technologies Inc 954 565-9898
1200 Ne 7th Ave Ste 4 Fort Lauderdale (33304) *(G-3785)*

Edgewell Per Care Brands LLC 386 677-9559
1190 N Rte 1 Ormond Beach (32174) *(G-12760)*

Edgewell Personal Care Company 386 673-2024
1190 N Us Highway 1 Ormond Beach (32174) *(G-12761)*

Edible Flair Inc 954 321-3608
220 Florida Ave Fort Lauderdale (33312) *(G-3786)*

Ediciones Atenea Inc 305 984-5483
15476 Nw 77th Ct Ste 601 Hialeah (33016) *(G-5135)*

Edigitalprintingcom Inc 305 378-2325
11950 Sw 128th St Miami (33186) *(G-9071)*

Edison Chouest Offshore 813 241-2165
1130 Mcclosky Blvd Tampa (33605) *(G-16798)*

Edisonecoenergycom Corporation 954 417-5326
528 Sw 5th Ave Apt 3 Fort Lauderdale (33315) *(G-3787)*

Editcar Printing Corp 305 324-5252
1929 Nw 22nd St Miami (33142) *(G-9072)*

Editorial Bautista Independent, Sebring Also called Baptist Mid-Missions Inc *(G-15915)*

Editorial Televisa Publishing, Virginia Gardens Also called Et Publishing International *(G-17824)*

Editorial Unilit, Medley Also called Spanish House Inc *(G-8324)*

Edmund C Miga 941 628-5951
23040 Bradford Ave Port Charlotte (33952) *(G-14297)*

Edmund Optics Inc 813 855-1900
141 Burbank Rd Oldsmar (34677) *(G-11647)*

Edmund Optics Florida, Oldsmar Also called Edmund Optics Inc *(G-11647)*

Edmunds Metal Works Inc 941 755-4725
6111 15th St E Ste A Bradenton (34203) *(G-973)*

Eds Aluminum Buildings Inc (PA) 850 476-2169
9555 Pensacola Blvd Pensacola (32534) *(G-13493)*

Eds Aluminum Buildings Inc 850 476-2169
Hwy 29 Molino (32577) *(G-10578)*

Eds Delight LLC 305 632-3051
2080 Ne 186th Dr North Miami Beach (33179) *(G-11135)*

Edsun Lighting Fixtures Mfg 305 888-8849
569 W 17th St Hialeah (33010) *(G-5136)*

Educational Networks Inc 866 526-0200
901 Ponce De Leon Blvd Coral Gables (33134) *(G-2052)*

Edumatics Inc 407 656-0661
7649 W Clnl Dr Ste 120 Orlando (32818) *(G-12116)*

Edward Thomas Company 561 746-1441
185 E Indiantown Rd # 114 Jupiter (33477) *(G-6718)*

Edwards Co 215 343-2133
188 Camelot Dr Nokomis (34275) *(G-11045)*

Edwards Manufacturing, Tampa Also called EMI Industries LLC *(G-16808)*

Edwards Ornamental Iron Inc 904 354-4282
1252 W Beaver St Jacksonville (32204) *(G-6066)*

Edwin B Stimpson Company Inc (PA) 954 946-3500
1515 Sw 13th Ct Pompano Beach (33069) *(G-14006)*

Edymar Design Carpentry LLC 954 822-0687
2641 W 76th St Hialeah (33016) *(G-5137)*

Eei Manufacturing Services, Clearwater Also called Englander Enterprises Inc *(G-1586)*

Eem Technologies Corp (PA) 786 606-5993
9590 Nw 40th Street Rd Doral (33178) *(G-3205)*

Eep 407 380-2828
3307 Trentwood Blvd Belle Isle (32812) *(G-349)*

Ees Design LLC 954 541-2660
2801 Nw 55th Ct Ste 5e Fort Lauderdale (33309) *(G-3788)*

Ef Enterprises of North Fla 904 739-5995
4381 Gadsden Ct Jacksonville (32207) *(G-6067)*

Effearredi Usa Inc 786 725-4948
123 Nw 23rd St Miami (33127) *(G-9073)*

Egd Euro Gourmet Deli Inc 305 937-1515
18650 Ne 28th Ct Aventura (33180) *(G-258)*

Egea Food LLC 833 353-6637
4313 Sw 75th Ave Miami (33155) *(G-9074)*

Egg Roll Skins Inc 305 836-0571
3251 E 11th Ave Hialeah (33013) *(G-5138)*

Eggplant and Dough, Brooksville Also called Mr GS Foods *(G-1184)*

Eglin Aero Club, Eglin Afb Also called James Taylor *(G-3506)*

Eglin Air Force Base 850 882-5422
205 W D Ave Ste 433 Eglin Afb (32542) *(G-3504)*

Eglin Air Force Base (PA) 850 882-3315
207 W D Ave Ste 125 Eglin Afb (32542) *(G-3505)*

Egm Manufacturing Corp 954 440-0445
10301 Nw 50th St Ste 102 Sunrise (33351) *(G-16315)*

Egmont Press, Boca Raton Also called Spett Printing Co Inc *(G-691)*

Egrs, Tampa Also called Enviro Gold Ref Systems LLC *(G-16817)*

Ehud Industries Inc 904 803-0873
9782 Nimitz Ct S Jacksonville (32246) *(G-6068)*

Ei Global Group Llc 561 999-8989
1515 N Federal Hwy # 200 Boca Raton (33432) *(G-501)*

Ei Interactive LLC 407 579-0993
121 S Orange Ave Ste 1400 Orlando (32801) *(G-12117)*

Eidolon Analytics Inc 239 288-6951
2487 N Airport Rd Fort Myers (33907) *(G-4244)*

Eidschun Engineering Inc 727 647-2300
2899 Heron Pl Clearwater (33762) *(G-1578)*

Eighteen Degrees Eighteen 904 686-1892
3787 Palm Valley Rd # 101 Ponte Vedra Beach (32082) *(G-14267)*

Eileen Kramer Inc 315 395-3831
19955 Ne 38th Ct Apt 504 Aventura (33180) *(G-259)*

Eiq Mobility Inc 561 691-7171
700 Universe Blvd Juno Beach (33408) *(G-6663)*

Eizo Rugged Solutions Inc 407 262-7100
442 Northlake Blvd # 1008 Altamonte Springs (32701) *(G-44)*

Ejco Inc 352 375-0797
927 Nw 13th St Gainesville (32601) *(G-4684)*

Ejcon, Jacksonville Also called Medway Hall Dev Group Inc *(G-6295)*

EJM Copper Inc 407 447-0074
1911 Ellman St Orlando (32804) *(G-12118)*

Ejuice Depo, Doral Also called Hmd Investment Group LLC *(G-3250)*

El American LLC 305 902-8051
420 S Dixie Hwy Coral Gables (33146) *(G-2053)*

El Clarin, Miami Also called Bcc-Bgle Cmmnctons Crp-Clrin L *(G-8806)*

El Colusa News 786 845-6868
2550 Nw 72nd Ave Ste 308 Miami (33122) *(G-9075)*

El Custom Wood Creations Inc 786 337-0014
2004 Tigertail Blvd Dania (33004) *(G-2331)*

ALPHABETIC

El Equisteo Sabor, Hialeah *Also called Miami Foods Distrs USA Inc* *(G-5250)*

EL Harley Inc...561 841-9887
2885 S Congress Ave Ste F Delray Beach (33445) *(G-2957)*

El Hispano..772 878-6488
102 Nw Airoso Blvd Port Saint Lucie (34983) *(G-14409)*

El Jaliciense Inc...850 481-1232
232 S Tyndall Pkwy Panama City (32404) *(G-13259)*

El Jefe Stucco Lath Inc...................................352 399-4837
8903 Franklin Rd Plant City (33565) *(G-13763)*

El Mira Sol Inc (PA)...813 754-5857
4008 Airport Rd Plant City (33563) *(G-13764)*

El Molino Coffee, Tampa *Also called Naviera Coffee Mills Inc* *(G-17104)*

El Quijote, Miami *Also called Elore Holdings Inc* *(G-9091)*

El Sabor Spices Inc...305 691-2300
3501 Nw 67th St Miami (33147) *(G-9076)*

El Teide North Industries................................786 830-7506
7763 Nw 64th St Ste 4 Miami (33166) *(G-9077)*

El Toro Meat Packing Corp.............................305 836-4461
738 Nw 72nd St Miami (33150) *(G-9078)*

El Trigal International......................................305 594-6610
10740 Nw 74th St Doral (33178) *(G-3206)*

Elaine Smith Inc..561 863-3333
7740 Byron Dr Riviera Beach (33404) *(G-14619)*

Elana Kattan, Opa Locka *Also called Didi Designs Inc* *(G-11736)*

Elanco Animal Health, Miami *Also called Eli Lilly and Company* *(G-9083)*

Elastec Inc..618 382-2525
401 Shearer Blvd Cocoa (32922) *(G-1925)*

Elc Security Products, Doral *Also called Starlock Inc* *(G-3375)*

Elder & Jenks LLC...727 538-5545
12595 71st Ct Largo (33773) *(G-7578)*

Eldorado Miranda Mfg Co Inc........................727 586-0707
1744 12th St Se Ofc Ofc Largo (33771) *(G-7579)*

Eldorado Stone, Fort Lauderdale *Also called Florida Silica Sand Company* *(G-3825)*

Electra Automotive Corp................................941 623-5563
1001 N 21st Ave Hollywood (33020) *(G-5570)*

Electraled Inc...727 561-7610
10990 49th St N Clearwater (33762) *(G-1579)*

Electrcal Systems Cmmnications...................813 248-4275
1601 N 43rd St Tampa (33605) *(G-16799)*

Electric Motors Lift Stn Svcs.........................727 538-4778
4480 126th Ave N Pinellas Park (33782) *(G-13683)*

Electric Pcture Dsplay Systems.....................321 757-8484
6425 Anderson Way Melbourne (32940) *(G-8417)*

Electrical Controls Inc....................................954 801-6846
9510 Bradshaw Ln Tamarac (33321) *(G-16530)*

Electriduct Inc...954 867-9100
1650 Nw 18th St Unit 801 Pompano Beach (33069) *(G-14007)*

Electrnic Shtmtal Crftsmen Fla......................321 727-0633
3675 W New Haven Ave Melbourne (32904) *(G-8418)*

Electrnic Systems Sutheast LLC....................561 955-9006
5840 Halifax Ave Fort Myers (33912) *(G-4245)*

Electro Lab Inc...813 818-7605
369 Douglas Rd E Oldsmar (34677) *(G-11648)*

Electro Mech Solutions Inc............................813 792-0400
1555 Gunn Hwy Odessa (33556) *(G-11549)*

Electro Mechanical South Inc........................941 342-9111
8203 Planters Knoll Ter Bradenton (34201) *(G-974)*

Electro Technik Industries Inc (PA)................727 530-9555
5410 115th Ave N Clearwater (33760) *(G-1580)*

Electro-Comp Services Inc.............................727 532-4262
11437 43rd St N Clearwater (33762) *(G-1581)*

Electro-Optical Imaging, Orlando *Also called Moog Inc* *(G-12389)*

Electro-Optix Inc...954 973-2800
2181 N Powerline Rd Ste 1 Pompano Beach (33069) *(G-14008)*

Electrodes Inc...727 698-7498
10350 62nd Ter Seminole (33772) *(G-15975)*

Electrolux Professional LLC...........................954 327-6778
3225 Sw 42nd St Fort Lauderdale (33312) *(G-3789)*

Electrolytic Tech Svcs LLC............................305 655-2755
19501 Ne 10th Ave Ste 203 North Miami Beach (33179) *(G-11136)*

Electrolytic Technologies Corp.......................305 655-2755
19597 Ne 10th Ave Ste G Miami (33179) *(G-9079)*

Electron Beam Development..........................772 219-4600
3591 Sw Deggeller Ct Palm City (34990) *(G-13034)*

Electronic Arts Inc..407 838-8000
515 W Amelia St Orlando (32801) *(G-12119)*

Electronic Components Fas Inc.......................407 328-8111
1305 Hstric Gldsboro Blvd Sanford (32771) *(G-15310)*

Electronic Manufacturing Co, Tampa *Also called Mdco Inc* *(G-17061)*

Electronic Monitoring, Odessa *Also called Attenti Us Inc* *(G-11538)*

Electronic Sign Supply Corp..........................305 477-0555
12601 Nw 115th Ave 106a Medley (33178) *(G-8235)*

Electrosource Inc..954 723-0840
11785 Nw 5th St Plantation (33325) *(G-13846)*

Electrostatic Industrial Pntg...........................305 696-4556
6801 Nw 25th Ave Miami (33147) *(G-9080)*

Electrotek Inc..321 231-6846
201 Steeplechase Cir Sanford (32771) *(G-15311)*

Electus Global Educatn Co Inc.......................813 885-4122
2601 E 7th Ave Tampa (33605) *(G-16800)*

Elega Fam FL More Drect Axic, Minneola *Also called Treadway Industries LLC* *(G-10453)*

Elegant House Intl LLC....................................954 457-8836
1960 Sw 30th Ave Hallandale (33009) *(G-4925)*

Element 26 LLC...413 519-1146
1810 S Ocean Dr Fort Pierce (34949) *(G-4482)*

Element Aircraft Sales LLC............................954 494-2242
1001 Sw 20th St Boca Raton (33486) *(G-502)*

Element E-Liquid, Miramar *Also called Element Eliquid LLC* *(G-10487)*

Element Eliquid LLC..754 260-5500
11411 Interchange Cir S Miramar (33025) *(G-10487)*

Element Inc Co..786 208-5693
6606 Sw 52nd Ter Miami (33155) *(G-9081)*

Element International Dist Inc.........................305 239-9228
2815 Evans St Hollywood (33020) *(G-5571)*

Element Melbourne, West Melbourne *Also called Element Mtls Tech Jupiter LLC* *(G-17899)*

Element Mtls Tech Jupiter LLC.......................321 327-8985
7780 Technology Dr West Melbourne (32904) *(G-17899)*

Element Outdoors LLC....................................888 589-9589
5412 Covered Bridge Ln Pace (32571) *(G-12857)*

Element Solutions LLC....................................352 279-3310
13014 N Dale Mbry Hwy Tampa (33618) *(G-16801)*

Element Solutions Inc (PA).............................561 207-9600
500 E Broward Blvd # 1860 Fort Lauderdale (33394) *(G-3790)*

Element Studios..407 968-2192
3328 Wax Berry Ct Windermere (34786) *(G-18350)*

Element-M LLC..954 288-8683
9835 Nw 5th Pl Plantation (33324) *(G-13847)*

Elemental Mobile Services LLC......................904 768-9840
3435 Japonica Rd N Jacksonville (32209) *(G-6069)*

Elements Accounting Inc................................305 662-4448
7344 Sw 48th St Ste 301 Miami (33155) *(G-9082)*

Elements of Space Inc....................................407 718-9690
10142 Pink Carnation Ct Orlando (32825) *(G-12120)*

Elements of Stylez..813 575-8416
30040 State Road 54 Wesley Chapel (33543) *(G-17874)*

Elements Restoration Inc................................813 330-2035
401 N Ashley Dr Tampa (33602) *(G-16802)*

Elementus Minerals LLC.................................561 815-2617
2400 E Coml Blvd Ste 810 Fort Lauderdale (33308) *(G-3791)*

Elevated Dumpsters LLC................................813 732-6338
37550 Phelps Rd Zephyrhills (33541) *(G-18613)*

Eli Lilly and Company......................................305 987-7000
8251 Sw 92nd Ave Miami (33173) *(G-9083)*

Elibro Corporation..305 466-0155
16699 Collins Ave # 1002 Sunny Isles Beach (33160) *(G-16272)*

Elicar Printing...305 324-5252
1929 Nw 22nd St Miami (33142) *(G-9084)*

Eligius Metal Works, Jacksonville *Also called Henley Metal LLC* *(G-6173)*

Elipter Corp...305 593-8355
3900 Nw 79th Ave Ste 482 Doral (33166) *(G-3207)*

Elirpa Corporation..813 986-8790
17932 Cachet Isle Dr Tampa (33647) *(G-16803)*

Elisa Technologies Inc....................................352 337-3929
2501 Nw 66th Ct Gainesville (32653) *(G-4685)*

Elite Aero LLC...727 244-3382
4828 Queen Palm Ter Ne Saint Petersburg (33703) *(G-15034)*

Elite Aluminum Corporation...........................954 949-3200
4650 Lyons Tech Pkwy Coconut Creek (33073) *(G-1984)*

Elite Awnings, Altamonte Springs *Also called A & A Central Florida* *(G-26)*

Elite Cabinet Coatings....................................352 795-2655
7170 N Ira Martin Ave Crystal River (34428) *(G-2275)*

Elite Cabinetry Inc..239 262-1144
5435 Jaeger Rd Ste 100 Naples (34109) *(G-10736)*

Elite Cast Stone Inc..305 904-3032
3805 Gaviota Dr Sun City Center (33573) *(G-16265)*

Elite Cnc Machining Inc..................................727 531-8447
6399 142nd Ave N Ste 122 Clearwater (33760) *(G-1582)*

Elite Distributors LLC.....................................407 601-6665
1716 Premier Row A Orlando (32809) *(G-12121)*

Elite Enclosures...352 323-6005
2505 Industrial St Leesburg (34748) *(G-7771)*

Elite Fire Protection Inc..................................352 639-4119
4145 County Road 561 Tavares (32778) *(G-17505)*

Elite Fitforever LLC...305 902-2358
4302 Alton Rd Ste 300 Miami Beach (33140) *(G-10186)*

Elite Flower Services Inc................................305 436-7400
6755 Nw 36th St Unit 180 Miami (33166) *(G-9085)*

ELite Intl Group LLC.......................................305 901-5005
7950 Nw 53rd St Ste 337 Miami (33166) *(G-9086)*

Elite Manufacturing US LLC...........................904 516-4796
1860 Indian River Dr Fleming Island (32003) *(G-3609)*

Elite Metal Finishing East LLC.......................407 843-0182
7594 Chancellor Dr Orlando (32809) *(G-12122)*

Elite Metal Manufacturing LLC.......................386 364-0777
10121 88th Trce Live Oak (32060) *(G-7846)*

Elite Outdoor Buildings LLC...........................386 364-1364
2008 Ohio Ave N Live Oak (32064) *(G-7847)*

Elite Panel Products, Coconut Creek *Also called Elite Aluminum Corporation* *(G-1984)*

(G-0000) Company's Geographic Section entry number

Elite Powder Coating		786 616-8084
8298 Nw 64th St Miami (33166) *(G-9087)*		
Elite Power Prtg Solutions Inc		786 387-7164
10103 Sw 166th Ct Miami (33196) *(G-9088)*		
Elite Printing & Marketing Inc		850 474-0894
3636 N L St Ste D-A Pensacola (32505) *(G-13494)*		
Elite Simulation Solutions, Oviedo *Also called Azure Computing Inc (G-12808)*		
Elite Wheel Distributors Inc (PA)		813 673-8393
3901 Riga Blvd Tampa (33619) *(G-16804)*		
Elite Woodwork, Sarasota *Also called Bresee Woodwork Inc (G-15615)*		
Elk Creek Wine		561 529-2822
4392 Nicole Cir Jupiter (33469) *(G-6719)*		
Elliot Technologies Inc		203 548-0069
4100 Ne 2nd Ave Ste 302 Miami (33137) *(G-9089)*		
Elliott Diamond Tool Inc		727 585-3839
1835 Bough Ave Unit 1 Clearwater (33760) *(G-1583)*		
Ellipsis Brewing		407 556-3241
7500 Tpc Blvd Ste 8 Orlando (32822) *(G-12123)*		
Ellis & Associates of Sanford		407 322-1128
915 W 1st St Ste B Sanford (32771) *(G-15312)*		
Ellis Family Holdings Inc		503 785-7400
6301 E 10th Ave Ste 110 Hialeah (33013) *(G-5139)*		
Ellis Trap and Cage Mfg Inc		850 969-1302
9601 N Palafox St Ste 6b Pensacola (32534) *(G-13495)*		
Ellison Graphics Corp		561 746-9256
1400 W Indiantown Rd Jupiter (33458) *(G-6720)*		
Ellison Rbm Inc		863 679-5283
4865 State Road 60 E Lake Wales (33898) *(G-7159)*		
Ellisons Premier Mar Svcs LLC		561 570-9807
1508 Cypress Dr Jupiter (33469) *(G-6721)*		
Elmridge Protection Pdts LLC		561 244-8337
1200 Clint Moore Rd Ste 1 Boca Raton (33487) *(G-503)*		
Elogic Learning LLC		813 901-8600
14934 N Florida Ave Tampa (33613) *(G-16805)*		
Elore Enterprises LLC		305 477-1650
1055 Nw 159th Dr Miami (33169) *(G-9090)*		
Elore Holdings Inc (HQ)		305 477-1650
1055 Nw 159th Dr Miami (33169) *(G-9091)*		
Elreha Printed Circuits		727 244-0130
7522 Plantation Cir Bradenton (34201) *(G-975)*		
Elro Manufacturing LLC		407 410-6006
516 Cooper Commerce Dr Apopka (32703) *(G-125)*		
Elsevier Inc		813 579-3866
8808 57th St N Pinellas Park (33782) *(G-13684)*		
Elster Amco Water LLC		352 369-6500
10 Sw 49th Ave Ste 101 Ocala (34474) *(G-11377)*		
Elster Amco Wtr Mtring Systems, Ocala *Also called Elster Amco Water LLC (G-11377)*		
Elstons Inc		727 527-7929
703 Islebay Dr Apollo Beach (33572) *(G-91)*		
Elstons Lmnted Toil Partitions, Apollo Beach *Also called Elstons Inc (G-91)*		
Eltec Instruments Inc (PA)		386 252-0411
350 Fentress Blvd Daytona Beach (32114) *(G-2549)*		
Elton Foil Embossing Inc		904 399-1510
3414 Galilee Rd Jacksonville (32207) *(G-6070)*		
Elyse Installations LLC		904 322-4754
1848 Ector Rd Jacksonville (32211) *(G-6071)*		
EM Adams Inc		772 468-6550
7496 Commercial Cir Fort Pierce (34951) *(G-4483)*		
Emac Inc (PA)		850 526-4111
4518 Lafayette St Marianna (32446) *(G-8164)*		
EMB Supplies, Tampa *Also called Pantograms Mfg Co Inc (G-17145)*		
Embrace Telecom Inc		866 933-8986
333 Las Olas Way Cu1 Fort Lauderdale (33301) *(G-3792)*		
Embraer, Boca Raton *Also called Veserca Group Ltd Inc (G-747)*		
Embraer Aero Seating Tech, Titusville *Also called Aero Seating Technologies LLC (G-17570)*		
Embraer Defense and SEC Inc		954 359-3700
2110 Cole Flyer Rd Jacksonville (32218) *(G-6072)*		
Embraer Executive Aircraft (HQ)		321 751-5050
1111 General Aviation Dr Melbourne (32935) *(G-8419)*		
Embraer Executive Jets, Melbourne *Also called Embraer Executive Aircraft Inc (G-8419)*		
Embraer Services Inc		954 359-3700
276 Sw 34th St Fort Lauderdale (33315) *(G-3793)*		
Embroidery Chimp LLC		561 775-9195
3954 Northlake Blvd Palm Beach Gardens (33403) *(G-12967)*		
Embroidery Plus		561 439-8943
824 W Lantana Rd Lantana (33462) *(G-7512)*		
Embroidery Solutions Inc		407 438-8188
6001 S Orange Ave Orlando (32809) *(G-12124)*		
Embroidery USA Inc		305 477-9973
6900 Nw 50th St Miami (33166) *(G-9092)*		
Embroidmecom Inc		813 878-2400
3909 W Kennedy Blvd Tampa (33609) *(G-16806)*		
Embroservice Inc		305 267-2323
7003 N Waterway Dr # 222 Miami (33155) *(G-9093)*		
EMC Aerospace Inc		954 316-6015
570 Ne 185th St North Miami Beach (33179) *(G-11137)*		
EMC Quality Group Corp		786 501-5891
6625 Mami Lkes Dr E Ste 2 Miami Lakes (33014) *(G-10299)*		
EMC Representations Corp		305 305-1776
1198 W 23rd St Hialeah (33010) *(G-5140)*		
EMC Respiratory Care Inc		305 829-5744
19341 Nw 82nd Ct Hialeah (33015) *(G-5141)*		
EMC Roofing LLC		786 597-6604
6405 Nikki Ln Tampa (33625) *(G-16807)*		
EMC South Florida LLC		786 352-9327
6075 Sunset Dr Ste 201 South Miami (33143) *(G-16033)*		
EMC Test Design LLC		508 292-1833
5390 Anthony Ln Sarasota (34233) *(G-15664)*		
Emc2 Improvement Corporation		786 564-9683
1720 Sw 99th Ct Miami (33165) *(G-9094)*		
Emcee Electronics Inc (PA)		941 485-1515
520 Cypress Ave Venice (34285) *(G-17688)*		
Emcee Electronics Inc		941 485-1515
223 Warfield Ave Venice (34285) *(G-17689)*		
Emcyte Corp		239 481-7725
4331 Veronica S Shoemaker Fort Myers (33916) *(G-4246)*		
EMD Serono Research & Dev Inst		978 715-1804
801 Brickell Ave Miami (33131) *(G-9095)*		
Emerald Coast Cabinets Inc		850 267-2290
5597 Us Highway 98 W # 101 Santa Rosa Beach (32459) *(G-15424)*		
Emerald Coast Coatings LLC		850 424-5244
705 Anchors St Nw Fort Walton Beach (32548) *(G-4580)*		
Emerald Coast Fabricators		850 554-6172
2120 W Wright St Pensacola (32505) *(G-13496)*		
Emerald Coast Media & Mktg		850 267-4555
790 N County Highway 393 Santa Rosa Beach (32459) *(G-15425)*		
Emerald Coast Mfg LLC		850 469-1133
4121 Warehouse Ln Pensacola (32505) *(G-13497)*		
Emerald Coast Signs		850 398-1712
4563 Rainbird Rise Rd Crestview (32539) *(G-2243)*		
Emerald Coast Truss LLC		850 623-1967
5817 Commerce Rd Milton (32583) *(G-10423)*		
Emerald Coast Wine Cellars, Defuniak Springs *Also called Chautuqua Vineyards Winery Inc (G-2837)*		
Emerald Prints LLC		850 460-5532
1169 John Sims Pkwy E Niceville (32578) *(G-11029)*		
Emerald Sails		850 240-4777
100 Old Ferry Rd Shalimar (32579) *(G-16001)*		
Emerald Technologies Corp		773 244-0092
3807 Belle Vista Dr E St Pete Beach (33706) *(G-16090)*		
Emerald Transformer, Defuniak Springs *Also called Florida Transformer Inc (G-2839)*		
Emerge Interactive Inc (PA)		772 563-0570
5375 Sol Rue Cir Vero Beach (32967) *(G-17753)*		
Emerge Nutraceuticals Inc		888 352-1683
721 S Rossiter St Mount Dora (32757) *(G-10601)*		
Emergency Standby Power LLC		850 259-2304
17 Duval St Fort Walton Beach (32547) *(G-4581)*		
Emergency Vehicle Sup Co LLC		954 428-5201
2251 Hammondville Rd Pompano Beach (33069) *(G-14009)*		
Emergency Vehicles Inc (PA)		561 848-6652
705 13th St Lake Park (33403) *(G-7124)*		
Emerging Mfg Tech Inc		407 341-3476
108 Commerce St Ste 102 Lake Mary (32746) *(G-7071)*		
Emerson Electric Co		904 741-6800
13350 International Pkwy # 102 Jacksonville (32218) *(G-6073)*		
Emerson Instr & Valve Svcs, Jacksonville *Also called Instrument & Valve Services Co (G-6201)*		
Emerson Latin America, Sunrise *Also called Computational Systems Inc (G-16307)*		
Emerson Prcess MGT Pwr Wtr Slt		941 748-8100
1401 Manatee Ave W # 400 Bradenton (34205) *(G-976)*		
Emerson Process Management, Jacksonville *Also called Emerson Electric Co (G-6073)*		
Emf Inc		321 453-3670
124 Imperial St Merritt Island (32952) *(G-8584)*		
Emhart Glass Manufacturing Inc		727 535-5502
9875 18th St N Saint Petersburg (33716) *(G-15035)*		
Emhart Inex, Saint Petersburg *Also called Emhart Glass Manufacturing Inc (G-15035)*		
EMI Filter Company, Clearwater *Also called Nordquist Dielectrics Inc (G-1718)*		
EMI Industries LLC (PA)		813 626-3166
1316 Tech Blvd Tampa (33619) *(G-16808)*		
Emilio Craig Footwear LLC		954 999-8302
16637 Magnolia Ter Montverde (34756) *(G-10588)*		
Eminel Corporation Inc		407 900-0190
8600 Com Cir Unit 148 Orlando (32819) *(G-12125)*		
Eminent Technology Inc		850 575-5655
225 E Palmer Ave Tallahassee (32301) *(G-16436)*		
EMJ Pharma Inc		973 600-9087
133 Playa Rienta Way Palm Beach Gardens (33418) *(G-12968)*		
Emjac Industries Inc		305 883-2194
1075 Hialeah Dr Hialeah (33010) *(G-5142)*		
EMK Brick Pavers LLC		813 500-9663
6505 Secrest Ct Tampa (33625) *(G-16809)*		
Emmanuel Holdings Inc		305 558-3088
2190 Nw 46th St Miami (33142) *(G-9096)*		
Emmeti USA LLC		813 490-6252
202 10th Ave N Ste A Safety Harbor (34695) *(G-14786)*		
Empanada Lady Co		786 271-6460
6732 Ne 4th Ave Miami (33138) *(G-9097)*		

Emphasys Cmpt Solutions Inc...........................305 599-2531
1200 Sw 145th Ave Ste 310 Pembroke Pines (33027) *(G-13386)*

Emphasys Software, Pembroke Pines *Also called Emphasys Cmpt Solutions Inc (G-13386)*

Empire Central, Tampa *Also called Empire Scientific (G-16810)*

Empire Corp Kit of.......................................800 432-3028
2846 Nw 79th Ave Doral (33122) *(G-3208)*

Empire Enterprises.....................................786 373-8003
2980 W 84th St Unit 11 Hialeah (33018) *(G-5143)*

Empire Scientific, Tampa *Also called TAe Trans Atlantic Elec (G-17322)*

Empire Scientific.......................................630 510-8636
4504 E Hillsborough Ave Tampa (33610) *(G-16810)*

Empire Stone and Cabinets.............................305 885-7092
720 W 27th St Hialeah (33010) *(G-5144)*

Empire Trnspt Solutions Corp..........................305 439-5677
228 W 18th St Hialeah (33010) *(G-5145)*

Empower Sftwr Sltions A Kronos, Orlando *Also called Empower Software Solutions Inc (G-12126)*

Empower Software Solutions Inc........................407 233-2000
315 E Robinson St Ste 350 Orlando (32801) *(G-12126)*

Empowered Diagnostics LLC............................206 228-5990
3341 W Mcnab Rd Pompano Beach (33069) *(G-14010)*

Empress Sissi, Sanford *Also called Caligiuri Corporation (G-15276)*

Empyre Music Publishing LLC...........................813 873-7700
1101 N Himes Ave Ste B Tampa (33607) *(G-16811)*

Ems Technologies NA LLC..............................321 259-5979
121 S Orange Ave Ste 1500 Orlando (32801) *(G-12127)*

En-Vision America Inc.................................309 452-3088
825 4th St W Palmetto (34221) *(G-13165)*

Enablesoft Inc..407 233-2626
11825 High Tech Ave # 100 Orlando (32817) *(G-12128)*

Encell Technology Inc.................................386 462-2643
12887 Nw Us Highway 441 Alachua (32615) *(G-11)*

Enchanting Creations....................................305 978-2828
210 Ne 98th St Miami Shores (33138) *(G-10382)*

Encore Analytics LLC....................................866 890-4331
86 Shirah St Destin (32541) *(G-3066)*

Encore Brandz Company.................................813 282-7073
8815 N 15th St Tampa (33604) *(G-16812)*

Encore Inc..941 359-3599
6487 Parkland Dr Ste 111 Sarasota (34243) *(G-15474)*

Encore Stone Products LLC.............................352 428-1542
711 Commercial Dr Holly Hill (32117) *(G-5513)*

Endangered Species Designs LLC........................954 613-2111
3469 W Boyntn Bch Blvd Boynton Beach (33436) *(G-863)*

Endeavor Manufacturing Inc............................954 752-6828
510 Goolsby Blvd Deerfield Beach (33442) *(G-2717)*

Endeavor Publications Inc..............................352 369-1104
4727 Nw 80th Ave Ocala (34482) *(G-11378)*

Endeavour Catamaran Corp.............................727 573-5377
3703 131st Ave N Clearwater (33762) *(G-1584)*

Endflex LLC..305 622-4070
4760 Nw 128th St Opa Locka (33054) *(G-11742)*

Endless Oceans LLC....................................561 274-1990
3125 S Federal Hwy Delray Beach (33483) *(G-2958)*

Endo-Gear LLC..305 710-6662
4390 Sw 74th Ave Miami (33155) *(G-9098)*

Endo-Therapeutics Inc.................................727 538-9570
15251 Roosevelt Blvd # 204 Clearwater (33760) *(G-1585)*

Endorphin Farms Inc...................................904 824-2006
3255 Parker Dr Saint Augustine (32084) *(G-14830)*

Endoscopy Rplacement Parts Inc........................352 472-5120
25430 Nw 8th Ln Newberry (32669) *(G-11019)*

Endurance Lasers LLC..................................239 302-0053
8285 Ibis Club Dr 81 Naples (34104) *(G-10737)*

Enduris Extrusions Inc (PA)...........................904 421-3304
7167 Old Kings Rd Jacksonville (32219) *(G-6074)*

Enduris Extrusions Inc................................321 914-0897
605 Distribution Dr Ste 1 Melbourne (32904) *(G-8420)*

Energenics Corporation.................................239 643-1711
1470 Don St Naples (34104) *(G-10738)*

Energetico Inc..213 550-5211
2260 Ne 123rd St North Miami (33181) *(G-11103)*

Energy Control Tech Inc................................954 739-8400
10220 W State Road 84 # 9 Davie (33324) *(G-2406)*

Energy Harness Corporation (PA).......................239 790-3300
71 Mid Cape Ter Ste 8 Cape Coral (33991) *(G-1337)*

Energy Harness Led Lighting, Cape Coral *Also called Energy Harness Corporation (G-1337)*

Energy Management Products LLC (PA)...................410 320-0200
6118 Riverview Blvd Bradenton (34209) *(G-977)*

Energy Services Providers Inc (HQ).....................305 947-7880
3700 Lakeside Dr 6 Miramar (33027) *(G-10488)*

Energy Sving Solutions USA LLC........................305 735-2878
1031 Ives Dairy Rd # 228 Miami (33179) *(G-9099)*

Energy Task Force LLC (HQ)............................407 523-3770
2501 Clark St Ste 101 Apopka (32703) *(G-126)*

Energybionics LLC......................................561 229-4985
519 Sw Glen Crest Way Stuart (34997) *(G-16144)*

Energycontrol.com, Davie *Also called Energy Control Tech Inc (G-2406)*

Energyware LLC...540 809-5902
17120 Reserve Ct Davie (33331) *(G-2407)*

Enersys...863 577-3900
4740 Lklnd Comrce Pkwy # 8 Lakeland (33805) *(G-7316)*

Enersys Advanced Systems Inc..........................610 208-1934
5430 70th Ave N Pinellas Park (33781) *(G-13685)*

Enforcement One Inc...................................727 816-9833
381 Roberts Rd Oldsmar (34677) *(G-11649)*

Enforty, Boca Raton *Also called Mark Benton (G-584)*

Eng Group LLC..954 323-2024
5309 Sw 34th Ave Fort Lauderdale (33312) *(G-3794)*

Eng Group LLC Teg , The, Fort Lauderdale *Also called Eng Group LLC (G-3794)*

ENG Manufacturing Inc................................727 942-3868
773 Wesley Ave Tarpon Springs (34689) *(G-17470)*

Engage Surgical, Orlando *Also called Engage UNI LLC (G-12129)*

Engage Surgical Knee LLC..............................614 915-2960
201 Wood Lake Dr Maitland (32751) *(G-8057)*

Engage UNI LLC..833 364-2432
3505 Lake Lynda Dr Orlando (32817) *(G-12129)*

Engead Gb Design & Prtg Inc...........................954 783-5161
414 E Sample Rd Pompano Beach (33064) *(G-14011)*

Engedi Specialities Inc...............................386 497-1010
429 Sw Greenwood Ter Fort White (32038) *(G-4620)*

Engine Armour Products, Tampa *Also called Armor Oil Products LLC (G-16608)*

Engine Lab of Tampa Inc...............................813 630-2422
201 S 78th St Tampa (33619) *(G-16813)*

Engineer Service Corporation...........................904 268-0482
2950 Halcyon Ln Ste 601 Jacksonville (32223) *(G-6075)*

Engineered Air Systems Inc.............................813 881-9555
6605 Walton Way Tampa (33610) *(G-16814)*

Engineered Equipment Corp.............................561 839-4008
777 S Flagler Dr Ste 800 West Palm Beach (33401) *(G-17987)*

Engineered Plastic Specialists, Orlando *Also called Mid-Florida Plastics Inc (G-12379)*

Engineered Yacht Solutions Inc.........................954 993-6989
2025 Sw 20th St Fort Lauderdale (33315) *(G-3795)*

Engineerica Systems Inc................................407 542-4982
7250 Red Bug Lake Rd # 1036 Oviedo (32765) *(G-12819)*

Engineering, Longwood *Also called Servos and Simulation Inc (G-7947)*

Engineering & Met Fabrication, Merritt Island *Also called Emf Inc (G-8584)*

Enginesaver..813 493-3861
123 Castillo Rd Ruskin (33570) *(G-14776)*

Engitork Industries Llc................................239 877-8499
222 Industrial Blvd # 13 Naples (34104) *(G-10739)*

England Trading Company LLC..........................888 969-4190
4660 Pow Mia Mem Pkwy Ste Jacksonville (32221) *(G-6076)*

Englander Enterprises Inc.............................727 461-4755
703 Grand Central St Clearwater (33756) *(G-1586)*

Englert Arts Inc.......................................561 241-9924
1021 S Rogers Cir Ste 18 Boca Raton (33487) *(G-504)*

Englewood Sun Herald, Englewood *Also called Sun Coast Media Group Inc (G-3538)*

English Ironworks Inc..................................941 364-9120
1960 21st St Sarasota (34234) *(G-15665)*

Enhancell Inc..469 363-2038
910 West Ave Apt 824 Miami Beach (33139) *(G-10187)*

Enki Group Inc...305 773-3502
11555 Sw 82nd Avenue Rd Coral Gables (33156) *(G-2054)*

Enodis Holdings Inc (HQ)...............................727 375-7010
2227 Welbilt Blvd Trinity (34655) *(G-17635)*

Enolgas Usa Inc..754 205-7902
2530 N Powerline Rd # 401 Pompano Beach (33069) *(G-14012)*

Enozo Technologies Inc...............................512 944-7772
8470 Enterprise Cir Lakewood Ranch (34202) *(G-7477)*

Enstar Holdings (us) LLC (HQ)..........................727 217-2900
150 2nd Ave N Fl 3 Saint Petersburg (33701) *(G-15036)*

Entech Controls Corp...................................954 613-2971
1031 Ives Dairy Rd Bldg 4 Miami (33179) *(G-9100)*

Entech Onsite Services LLC............................407 956-8980
280 Gus Hipp Blvd Rockledge (32955) *(G-14707)*

Entegra Roof Tile, Okeechobee *Also called Roof Tile Inc (G-11615)*

Enterprise System Assoc Inc (PA).......................407 275-0220
3259 Progress Dr Orlando (32826) *(G-12130)*

Enterprise Tech Partners LLC...........................918 851-3285
37 N Orange Ave Ste 616 Orlando (32801) *(G-12131)*

Enterra Inc...813 514-0531
2801 W Busch Blvd Tampa (33618) *(G-16815)*

Entertainment Metals Inc...............................800 817-2683
13351 Saddle Rd Ste 205 Fort Myers (33913) *(G-4247)*

Entertainment Mfg Group, Fort Myers *Also called Entertainment Metals Inc (G-4247)*

Entire Select Inc......................................954 674-2368
10857 Nw 50th St Sunrise (33351) *(G-16316)*

Entree Magazine Florida LLC..........................239 354-1245
15275 Collier Blvd # 201 Naples (34119) *(G-10740)*

Enviralum Industries Inc..............................305 752-4411
5100 Nw 72nd Ave Unit C Miami (33166) *(G-9101)*

Envirnmental Mfg Solutions LLC (PA)....................321 837-0050
7705 Progress Cir Melbourne (32904) *(G-8421)*

Enviro Focus Technology...............................813 744-5000
6505 Jewel Ave Tampa (33619) *(G-16816)*

Enviro Gold Ref Systems LLC..........813 390-7043
1430 Hobbs St Tampa (33619) *(G-16817)*

Enviro Petroleum Inc..........713 896-6996
10072 S Ocean Dr Apt 7n Jensen Beach (34957) *(G-6654)*

Enviro Water Solutions LLC..........877 842-1635
3060 Prfmce Cir Ste 2 Deland (32724) *(G-2868)*

Enviro-USA American Mfr LLC..........321 222-9551
151 Center St Ste 101 Cape Canaveral (32920) *(G-1283)*

Envirofocus Technologies LLC..........813 620-3260
1901 N 66th St Tampa (33619) *(G-16818)*

Environmental Aborbent Pdts, Jupiter *Also called Dynomat Inc (G-6716)*

Environmental Contractors Inc..........305 556-6942
2648 W 78th St Hialeah (33016) *(G-5146)*

Environmental Graphics, Odessa *Also called Binney Family of Florida Inc (G-11540)*

Environmental Mfg & Supply Inc..........850 547-5287
3255 Highway 90 Bonifay (32425) *(G-771)*

Environmental Recovery Systems..........727 344-3301
7001 Mango Ave S Saint Petersburg (33707) *(G-15037)*

Environmental Services..........727 518-3080
5100 150th Ave N Clearwater (33760) *(G-1587)*

Environmental Tectonics Corp..........407 282-3378
2100 N Alafaya Trl # 900 Orlando (32826) *(G-12132)*

Envirosafe Technologies Inc..........904 646-3456
11201 St Johns Indstrl Pk Jacksonville (32246) *(G-6077)*

Enviroseal Corporation..........772 335-8225
1019 Se Hlbrook Ct 1021 Port Saint Lucie (34952) *(G-14410)*

Envirovault LLC..........904 354-1858
1727 Bennett St Jacksonville (32206) *(G-6078)*

Enviroworks Inc..........407 889-5533
3000 Orange Ave Apopka (32703) *(G-127)*

Envision Graphics Inc..........305 470-0083
7335 Nw 35th St Miami (33122) *(G-9102)*

Enviva Pellets Cottondale LLC..........850 557-7357
2500 Green Circle Pkwy Cottondale (32431) *(G-2228)*

Envoy Therapeutics Inc..........561 210-7705
555 Heritage Dr Ste 150 Jupiter (33458) *(G-6722)*

Enzymedica Inc (PA)..........941 505-5565
771 Commerce Dr Ste 3 Venice (34292) *(G-17690)*

EO Painter Printing Company..........386 985-4877
4900 Us Highway 17 De Leon Springs (32130) *(G-2624)*

Ep Clothing LLC..........786 827-9187
13275 Sw 136th St Miami (33186) *(G-9103)*

Ep6 Group Inc..........772 332-9100
1150 Bell Ave Fort Pierce (34982) *(G-4484)*

Epare LLC..........347 682-5121
117 Ne 1st Ave Miami (33132) *(G-9104)*

EPC Inc..........636 443-1999
3629 Queen Palm Dr Tampa (33619) *(G-16819)*

Epic Elements LLC..........305 388-1384
8348 Nw 74th Ave Medley (33166) *(G-8236)*

Epic Extrusion Inc..........941 378-0835
8141 Blaikie Ct Ste 3 Sarasota (34240) *(G-15666)*

Epic Harvests LLC..........904 503-5143
5215 Philips Hwy Ste 3 Jacksonville (32207) *(G-6079)*

Epic Metals Corporation..........863 533-7404
1930 State Road 60 W Bartow (33830) *(G-307)*

Epic Promos LLC..........561 479-8055
6451 E Rogers Cir Ste 3 Boca Raton (33487) *(G-505)*

Epigenetix Inc..........561 543-7569
1004 Brooks Ln Delray Beach (33483) *(G-2959)*

Epitomi Inc..........305 971-5370
12201 Sw 128th Ct Ste 108 Miami (33186) *(G-9105)*

Epower 360 LLC (PA)..........305 330-6684
7780 Sw 71st Ave Miami (33143) *(G-9106)*

Epoxy Experts LLC..........941 565-3785
819 Lillian Ln Sarasota (34243) *(G-15475)*

Epoxy2u of Florida Inc..........239 772-0899
922 Se 14th Pl Cape Coral (33990) *(G-1338)*

Epperson & Company..........813 626-6125
5202 Shadowlawn Ave Tampa (33610) *(G-16820)*

Eps Metal Finishing..........954 782-3073
640 Ne 26th Ct Pompano Beach (33064) *(G-14013)*

Equigraph Trading Corp..........786 237-5665
13331 Sw 132nd Ave Miami (33186) *(G-9107)*

Equipment Fabricators Inc..........321 632-0990
655 Cidco Rd Cocoa (32926) *(G-1926)*

Equipment Sales & Service Inc (HQ)..........727 572-9197
12707 44th St N Clearwater (33762) *(G-1588)*

Equiservisa USA Corp..........773 530-6964
13544 Sw 124th Avenue Rd Miami (33186) *(G-9108)*

Equity Group Usa Inc..........407 421-6464
1129 Citrus Oaks Run Winter Springs (32708) *(G-18565)*

Equs Logistics LLC..........954 618-6573
13680 Nw 5th St Ste 140 Sunrise (33325) *(G-16317)*

ER Jahna Industries Inc..........863 675-3942
Highway 78 E La Belle (33935) *(G-6979)*

ER Jahna Industries Inc..........863 424-0730
4949 Sand Mine Rd Davenport (33897) *(G-2364)*

ER Jahna Industries Inc..........863 422-7617
4910 State Road 544 E Haines City (33844) *(G-4906)*

ER Precision Optical Corp..........407 292-5395
1676 E Semoran Blvd Apopka (32703) *(G-128)*

ERA Organics Inc..........800 579-9817
33 N Garden Ave Ste 120 Clearwater (33755) *(G-1589)*

Eran Group Inc..........561 289-5021
3500 Nw 2nd Ave Boca Raton (33431) *(G-506)*

Erapsco..........386 740-5335
C 0 5612 Johnson Lake Rd De Leon Springs (32130) *(G-2625)*

Erb Roberts Tillage LLC..........352 376-4888
401 E Las Olas Blvd Ste 1 Fort Lauderdale (33301) *(G-3796)*

Erba Diagnostics Inc (HQ)..........305 324-2300
14100 Nw 57th Ct Miami Lakes (33014) *(G-10300)*

Erchonia Corporation LLC..........321 473-1251
650 Atlantis Rd Melbourne (32904) *(G-8422)*

Eric Lemoine..........407 919-9783
1355 Bennett Dr Unit 129 Longwood (32750) *(G-7890)*

Erickson International LLC..........702 853-4800
161 Commerce Rd Ste 2 Boynton Beach (33426) *(G-864)*

Ericsson Inc..........856 230-6268
360 S Lake Destiny Dr Orlando (32810) *(G-12133)*

Erie Manufacturing Inc..........863 534-3743
1520 Centennial Blvd Bartow (33830) *(G-308)*

Erimark Electric Sign Co Inc..........954 423-1364
14851 Nw 27th Ave Opa Locka (33054) *(G-11743)*

Ernies Metal Fabricating..........813 679-0816
406 E Windhorst Rd Brandon (33510) *(G-1090)*

Ernies Signs..........239 992-0800
3901 Bonita Beach Rd Bonita Springs (34134) *(G-795)*

Erratic Oaks Vineyard Inc..........206 233-0683
6222 Zirkels Cir Brooksville (34604) *(G-1154)*

Erwad Real Estate, Hollywood *Also called Volvox Inc Hollywood (G-5682)*

Erwin Inc..........813 933-3323
201 N Franklin St # 2200 Tampa (33602) *(G-16821)*

ES Investments LLC (PA)..........727 536-8822
14055 Us Highway 19 N Clearwater (33764) *(G-1590)*

Es Manufacturing Inc..........727 323-4040
4590 62nd Ave N Pinellas Park (33781) *(G-13686)*

Es Tudios Corp..........305 300-9262
5483 Nw 72nd Ave Miami (33166) *(G-9109)*

Escambia Welding and Fab Inc..........850 477-3901
2474 W Nine Mile Rd B Pensacola (32534) *(G-13498)*

Esco Equipment Supply Co, Brooksville *Also called Shirley L Jordan Company Inc (G-1199)*

Esco Industries Inc..........863 666-3696
2001 Lasso Ln Lakeland (33801) *(G-7317)*

Escue Energy LLC..........561 762-1486
11903 Southern Blvd Royal Palm Beach (33411) *(G-14763)*

Esd Waste2water Inc..........800 277-3279
495 Oak Rd Ocala (34472) *(G-11379)*

Ese & Assoc Inc..........718 767-2367
11939 Sw 75th St Miami (33183) *(G-9110)*

Espace Inc..........802 735-7546
135 S River Rd Stuart (34996) *(G-16145)*

Esperanto Inc..........305 513-8980
8725 Nw 18th Ter Ste 312 Doral (33172) *(G-3209)*

Espresso Disposition Corp 1 (HQ)..........305 594-9062
6262 Bird Rd Ste 2i Miami (33155) *(G-9111)*

Esquadro Inc..........754 367-3098
217 Se 1st Ter Deerfield Beach (33441) *(G-2718)*

Esse Sales Inc..........954 368-3900
2725 Nw 30th Ave Oakland Park (33311) *(G-11264)*

Essential Oil University LLC..........502 498-8804
6150 Manasota Key Rd Englewood (34223) *(G-3530)*

Essential Publishing Group LLC (PA)..........410 440-5777
1140 Holland Dr Ste 21 Boca Raton (33487) *(G-507)*

Essential Publishing Group LLC..........561 570-7165
5319 Lake Worth Rd Greenacres (33463) *(G-4846)*

Essentialnet Solutions, Rockledge *Also called Networked Solutions Inc (G-14735)*

Essentials..........386 677-7444
150a W Granada Blvd Ormond Beach (32174) *(G-12762)*

Essex Plastics Midwest LLC Lc..........954 956-1100
1531 Nw 12th Ave Pompano Beach (33069) *(G-14014)*

Estal Usa Inc..........305 728-3272
150 Se 2nd Ave Miami (33131) *(G-9112)*

Esteemed Brands Inc..........954 442-3923
3450 Lakeside Dr Ste 120 Miramar (33027) *(G-10489)*

Esterel Technologies Inc..........724 746-3304
1082 N Alsaya Trl Ste 124 Orlando (32826) *(G-12134)*

Estero FL..........239 289-9511
23191 Fashion Dr Unit 309 Estero (33928) *(G-3542)*

Estetika Skin & Laser Spe..........262 646-9222
1463 Tangier Way Sarasota (34239) *(G-15667)*

Estradas Fiberglass Mfg Corp..........954 924-8778
16900 N Bay Rd Apt 803 Sunny Isles Beach (33160) *(G-16273)*

Estumkeda Ltd..........954 966-6300
6300 Stirling Rd Hollywood (33024) *(G-5572)*

Et Publishing International (PA)..........305 871-6400
6355 Nw 36th St Virginia Gardens (33166) *(G-17824)*

Etc Palm Beach LLC..........561 881-8118
1800 Okeechobee Rd # 100 West Palm Beach (33409) *(G-17988)*

Etchart LLC 321 504-4060
  3732 N Highway 1 Ste 5 Cocoa (32926) *(G-1927)*

Etco Automotive Products Div, Bradenton *Also called Etco Incorporated (G-978)*

Etco Incorporated 941 756-8426
  3004 62nd Ave E Bradenton (34203) *(G-978)*

Etectrx Inc 352 262-8054
  747 Sw 2nd Ave Ste 365t Gainesville (32601) *(G-4686)*

Eterna Urn Co Inc 386 258-6491
  126 Carswell Ave Daytona Beach (32117) *(G-2550)*

Eternal Elements LLC 407 830-6968
  1045 Miller Dr Altamonte Springs (32701) *(G-45)*

Eternal Smoke Inc 407 984-5090
  1321 Edgewater Dr Ste 1 Orlando (32804) *(G-12135)*

Eternity Cabinets 239 482-7172
  17000 Alico Commerce Ct Fort Myers (33967) *(G-4248)*

Etf West LLC 407 523-3770
  2501 Clark St Apopka (32703) *(G-129)*

Ethnergy International Inc 954 499-1582
  1524 Sw 59 Ln Pembroke Pines (33027) *(G-13387)*

Eti-Label Inc 305 716-0094
  6961 Nw 82nd Ave Miami (33166) *(G-9113)*

Etronics4u Inc 786 303-8429
  16850 Collins Ave 112-166 Sunny Isles Beach (33160) *(G-16274)*

Euclid Chemical Company 813 886-8811
  19215 Redwood Rd Odessa (33556) *(G-11550)*

Euramerica Gas and Oil Corp 954 858-5714
  1333 S University Dr # 202 Plantation (33324) *(G-13848)*

Euro Gear (usa) Inc (PA) 518 578-1775
  1395 Brickell Ave Ste 800 Miami (33131) *(G-9114)*

Euro Trim Inc 239 574-6646
  17200 Primavera Cir Cape Coral (33909) *(G-1339)*

Euro-Wall Systems LLC 941 979-5316
  2200 Murphy Ct North Port (34289) *(G-11193)*

Euroasia Products Inc 321 221-9398
  3956 W Town Center Blvd # 166 Orlando (32837) *(G-12136)*

Eurocraft Cabinets Inc 561 948-3034
  1217 Clint Moore Rd Boca Raton (33487) *(G-508)*

Eurogan-Usa Inc 321 356-5248
  502 Sunport Ln Ste 350 Orlando (32809) *(G-12137)*

Euroinsoles Incorporated 786 206-6117
  75 Valencia Ave Ste 201 Coral Gables (33134) *(G-2055)*

Euromotion Inc 954 612-0354
  7194 Skyline Dr Delray Beach (33446) *(G-2960)*

Europa Manufacturing Inc 954 426-2965
  4900 Lyons Tech Pkwy # 7 Coconut Creek (33073) *(G-1985)*

Europe Coating Industries LLC 786 535-4143
  8213 Nw 74th Ave Medley (33166) *(G-8237)*

European Cabinets & Design LLC 561 684-1440
  4050 Westgate Ave West Palm Beach (33409) *(G-17989)*

European Custom Casework Inc 401 356-0400
  3063 Se Gran Park Way Stuart (34997) *(G-16146)*

Europrint Inc 407 869-9955
  620 Douglas Ave Ste 1308 Altamonte Springs (32714) *(G-46)*

Eurosign Metalwerke Inc 954 717-4426
  5301 Nw 35th Ave Fort Lauderdale (33309) *(G-3797)*

Eurospa 904 242-8200
  1487 Atlantic Blvd Neptune Beach (32266) *(G-10958)*

Euroteam Wax Center, Fort Lauderdale *Also called Ft Lauderdale Wax (G-3833)*

Eusa Global LLC 786 483-7490
  11801 Nw 100th Rd Ste 17 Medley (33178) *(G-8238)*

Ev Pilotcar Inc 239 243-8023
  16121 Lee Rd Ste 107 Fort Myers (33912) *(G-4249)*

Ev Rider LLC 239 278-5054
  6410 Arc Way Ste A Fort Myers (33966) *(G-4250)*

Evamped LLC 614 205-4467
  13751 Luna Dr Naples (34109) *(G-10741)*

Evan Lloyd Designs 772 286-7723
  3576 Se Dixie Hwy Stuart (34997) *(G-16147)*

Evanios LLC 617 233-4986
  2875 S Orange Ave 500-8 Orlando (32806) *(G-12138)*

Evans Custom Cabinetry LLC 904 829-1973
  3595 Fortner Rd Saint Augustine (32084) *(G-14831)*

Eve Uam LLC 954 359-3700
  276 Sw 34th St Fort Lauderdale (33315) *(G-3798)*

Eventtracker Security LLC 410 953-6776
  100 W Cypress Creek Rd Fort Lauderdale (33309) *(G-3799)*

Everaxis Usa Inc (HQ) 239 263-3102
  3030 Horseshoe Dr S Naples (34104) *(G-10742)*

Everaxis Usa Inc 239 263-3102
  3030 Horseshoe Dr S Naples (34104) *(G-10743)*

Everest Air Corp 407 319-6204
  3830 Golden Feather Way Kissimmee (34746) *(G-6918)*

Everest Cabinets Inc 407 790-7819
  6100 Hanging Moss Rd # 5 Orlando (32807) *(G-12139)*

Everest Ice and Water Systems, Apopka *Also called Dgw Technologies LLC (G-121)*

Everest Industries LLC 786 210-0662
  9600 Nw 25th St Ste 4e Doral (33172) *(G-3210)*

Everett-Morrison Motorcars, Odessa *Also called Nu Trek Inc (G-11568)*

Everfresh Juice Co Inc 954 581-0922
  8100 Sw 10th St Ste 4000 Plantation (33324) *(G-13849)*

Everglades Boats, Edgewater *Also called R J Dougherty Associates LLC (G-3499)*

Everglades Creations Inc 305 822-3344
  2335 Nw 149th St Opa Locka (33054) *(G-11744)*

Everglades Envelope Co Inc 954 783-7920
  6650 Nw 15th Ave Fort Lauderdale (33309) *(G-3800)*

Everglades Foods Inc 863 655-2214
  6120 State Road 66 Sebring (33875) *(G-15921)*

Everglades Machine Inc 863 983-0133
  1816 Red Rd Clewiston (33440) *(G-1888)*

Evergreen Rush Industries Inc 954 825-9291
  473 Sw 126th Ave Davie (33325) *(G-2408)*

Evergreen Sweeteners Inc 305 835-6907
  3601 Nw 62nd St Miami (33147) *(G-9115)*

Evergreen Sweeteners Inc (PA) 954 381-7776
  1936 Hollywood Blvd # 20 Hollywood (33020) *(G-5573)*

Evergreen Sweeteners Inc 407 323-4250
  2200 Country Club Rd Sanford (32771) *(G-15313)*

Everlast Industries Corp 239 689-3837
  7981 Mainline Pkwy Fort Myers (33912) *(G-4251)*

Everlast Marine Products Co., Fort Myers *Also called Everlast Industries Corp (G-4251)*

Eversafe, Sarasota *Also called Matrix24 Laboratories LLC (G-15514)*

Everslim LLC 813 265-2100
  1429 Oakfield Dr Brandon (33511) *(G-1091)*

Every Thing Aluminum 561 202-9900
  615 Whitney Ave Ste 15 Lantana (33462) *(G-7513)*

Everybodywinco 954 214-4172
  66 W Flagler St Ste 900 Miami (33130) *(G-9116)*

Everyday Feminism LLC 202 643-1001
  75 N Woodward Ave Tallahassee (32313) *(G-16437)*

Everything Blockchain Inc 904 454-2111
  12574 Flagler Center Blvd Jacksonville (32258) *(G-6080)*

Everything Communicates Inc 407 578-6616
  1740 State Road 436 # 104 Winter Park (32792) *(G-18510)*

Everything Printing Inc 239 541-2679
  202 Se 44th St Cape Coral (33904) *(G-1340)*

Evies Golf Center 941 377-2399
  4735 Bee Ridge Rd Sarasota (34233) *(G-15668)*

Evm Woodwork Corp 954 970-4352
  971 Sw 70th Way North Lauderdale (33068) *(G-11079)*

Evm Woodworks Corp 954 655-6414
  7542 W Mcnab Rd North Lauderdale (33068) *(G-11080)*

Evo Motors LLC 813 621-7799
  11809 E Us Highway 92 Seffner (33584) *(G-15957)*

Evolis Inc (HQ) 954 777-9262
  3201 W Coml Blvd Ste 110 Fort Lauderdale (33309) *(G-3801)*

Evolution Intrcnnect Systems I 954 217-6223
  11870 W State Road 84 C Davie (33325) *(G-2409)*

Evolution Lighting LLC (PA) 305 558-4777
  880 Sw 145th Ave Ste 100 Pembroke Pines (33027) *(G-13388)*

Evolution Liners Inc 407 839-6213
  40 W Illiana St Orlando (32806) *(G-12140)*

Evolution Metals Corp 561 531-2314
  516 S Dixie Hwy West Palm Beach (33401) *(G-17990)*

Evolution Orthotics Inc 407 688-2860
  156 Harston Ct Lake Mary (32746) *(G-7072)*

Evolution Signs and Print Inc 904 634-5666
  11672 Philips Hwy Ste 3 Jacksonville (32256) *(G-6081)*

Evolution Voice Inc 407 204-1614
  5728 Major Blvd Ste 720 Orlando (32819) *(G-12141)*

Evolution Wldngs Fbrcation LLC 786 702-4703
  2095 Nw 141st St Opa Locka (33054) *(G-11745)*

Evolution Woodworking 407 221-5031
  670 Coffee Trl Geneva (32732) *(G-4787)*

Evolutionary Screen Printing L 863 248-2692
  3521 Waterfield Pkwy Lakeland (33803) *(G-7318)*

Evolutions - Graphics Designs-, Miami *Also called Pacheco Creative Group Inc (G-9674)*

Evolve E-Learning Solutions, Marco Island *Also called Evolve Technologies Inc (G-8111)*

Evolve Technologies Inc 239 963-8037
  950 N Collier Blvd # 400 Marco Island (34145) *(G-8111)*

Evolvegene LLC 727 623-4052
  12105 28th St N Ste A Saint Petersburg (33716) *(G-15038)*

Evolving Coal Corp 813 944-3100
  200 2nd Ave S Ste 733 Saint Petersburg (33701) *(G-15039)*

Evoqua Water Technologies LLC 813 620-0900
  4711 Oak Fair Blvd Tampa (33610) *(G-16822)*

Evora Enterprises Inc 305 261-4522
  2608 Nw 6th St Ocala (34475) *(G-11380)*

Evren Technologies Inc 352 494-0950
  404 Sw 140th Ter Ste 50 Newberry (32669) *(G-11020)*

Ew Publishing LLC 305 358-1100
  2820 Ne 30th St Apt 10 Fort Lauderdale (33306) *(G-3802)*

EW Scripps Company 772 408-5300
  1939 Se Federal Hwy Port Saint Lucie (34986) *(G-14411)*

Ewhite LLC 954 530-3382
  2633 Bayview Dr Fort Lauderdale (33306) *(G-3803)*

Exact Inc 904 783-6640
  5285 Ramona Blvd Jacksonville (32205) *(G-6082)*

Exactech Inc (HQ) 352 377-1140
  2320 Nw 66th Ct Gainesville (32653) *(G-4687)*

Exactus Pharmacy Solutions Inc 888 314-3874
8715 Henderson Rd Tampa (33634) *(G-16823)*

Exalos Inc 215 669-4488
824 Se 12th St Fort Lauderdale (33316) *(G-3804)*

Excalibur Aircraft 863 385-9486
6439 Tractor Rd Sebring (33876) *(G-15922)*

Excalibur Cabinetry LLC 248 697-6158
19709 W Eldorado Dr # 32 Eustis (32736) *(G-3557)*

Excalibur Coach Svc & Sls LLC 407 302-9139
1830 Bobby Lee Pt Sanford (32771) *(G-15314)*

Excalibur Manufacturing Corp (PA) 352 544-0055
16186 Flight Path Dr Brooksville (34604) *(G-1155)*

Excel Converting Inc 786 318-2222
6950 Nw 37th Ct Miami (33147) *(G-9117)*

Excel Fuel Inc 727 547-5511
6201 54th Ave N Saint Petersburg (33709) *(G-15040)*

Excel Handbags Co Inc 305 836-8800
3651 Nw 81st St Miami (33147) *(G-9118)*

Excel Millwork & Moulding Inc 850 576-7228
7001 Fortune Blvd Midway (32343) *(G-10412)*

Excel Palm Beach Llc 616 864-6650
351 N Jog Rd West Palm Beach (33413) *(G-17991)*

Excelag Corp (PA) 305 670-0145
7300 N Kendall Dr Ste 640 Miami (33156) *(G-9119)*

Excell Cabinet Corp 561 628-9059
8233 Gator Ln West Palm Beach (33411) *(G-17992)*

Excell Coatings Inc 321 868-7968
745 Scallop Dr Cape Canaveral (32920) *(G-1284)*

Excell Solutions LLC 407 615-9330
5115 N Socrum Loop Rd Lakeland (33809) *(G-7319)*

Excell Woodwork Corp 954 461-0465
1917 Mears Pkwy Margate (33063) *(G-8128)*

Excellent Performance Inc 561 296-0776
4650 Dyer Blvd Riviera Beach (33407) *(G-14620)*

Excelor LLC 321 300-3315
7380 W Sand Lake Rd # 500 Orlando (32819) *(G-12142)*

Exces International LLC 561 880-8920
3460 Frlane Frms Rd Ste 1 Wellington (33414) *(G-17850)*

Excess Liquidator LLC 407 247-9105
3012 Kananwood Ct Ste 132 Oviedo (32765) *(G-12820)*

Exclusive Apparel LLC 800 859-6260
2598 E Sunrise Blvd # 2104 Fort Lauderdale (33304) *(G-3805)*

Exclusive Bats LLC 305 450-3858
10930 Nw 138th St Unit 1 Hialeah (33018) *(G-5147)*

Exec Technology Corp 305 394-8132
7224 Nw 56th St Miami (33166) *(G-9120)*

Executive Label Inc 954 978-6983
5447 Nw 24th St Ste 5 Margate (33063) *(G-8129)*

Executive Printers of Florida, Medley *Also called Hobby Press Inc (G-8253)*

Executive Prtg & Mailing Svcs, Pompano Beach *Also called Leila K Moavero (G-14076)*

Exelan Pharmaceuticals Inc 561 287-6631
370 W Cmino Grdns Blvd St Boca Raton (33432) *(G-509)*

Exhaust Technologies Inc 561 744-9500
851 Jupiter Park Ln Jupiter (33458) *(G-6723)*

Exide Battery 904 783-1224
600 Suemac Rd Ste 1 Jacksonville (32254) *(G-6083)*

Exist Inc 954 739-7030
1650 Nw 23rd Ave Ste A Fort Lauderdale (33311) *(G-3806)*

Exist Clothing & Embroidery, Fort Lauderdale *Also called Exist Inc (G-3806)*

Exit Ten Inc 407 574-2433
100 Highline Dr Unit 116 Longwood (32750) *(G-7891)*

Exodus Aviation, Fort Lauderdale *Also called Exodus Management LLC (G-3807)*

Exodus Management LLC 954 995-4407
6750 N Andrews Ave Ste 20 Fort Lauderdale (33309) *(G-3807)*

Exosis Inc 240 417-4477
109 Everglade Ave Palm Beach (33480) *(G-12933)*

Exotic Countertop Inc 954 979-8188
2160 Nw 22nd St Pompano Beach (33069) *(G-14015)*

Exotic Interiors, Lauderdale Lakes *Also called Tropic Shield Inc (G-7721)*

Exotic Marble Polishing Inc 786 318-6568
12325 Ne 9th Ave Apt 4 North Miami (33161) *(G-11104)*

Exotics By Cedrick, Tampa *Also called Cedrick McDonald (G-16689)*

Exotics Car Wraps 786 768-6798
245 Ne 183rd St Ste 3a Miami (33179) *(G-9121)*

Expandothane, Yulee *Also called Soythane Technologies Inc (G-18594)*

Expert Mold Removal Inc 407 925-6443
14929 Lenze Dr Tavares (32778) *(G-17506)*

Expert Printing and Graphics, Palmetto Bay *Also called Inkpressions Inc (G-13213)*

Expert Promotions LLC 772 643-4012
434 Georgia Blvd Sebastian (32958) *(G-15891)*

Expert Shutter Services Inc 772 871-1915
668 Sw Whitmore Dr Port Saint Lucie (34984) *(G-14412)*

Expert TS of Jacksonville 904 387-2500
711 Cassat Ave Jacksonville (32205) *(G-6084)*

Exploration Resources Intn Geo 601 747-0726
1130 Business Center Dr Lake Mary (32746) *(G-7073)*

Exploration Services LLC 352 505-3578
4440 Ne 41st Ter Gainesville (32609) *(G-4688)*

Explotrain LLC 850 862-5344
26 Eglin Pkwy Se Ste 2 Fort Walton Beach (32548) *(G-4582)*

Export Diesel LLC (PA) 305 396-1943
1835 Nw 112th Ave Ste 173 Miami (33172) *(G-9122)*

Expose Yourself USA, Weston *Also called Tigo Inc (G-18292)*

Express, Tarpon Springs *Also called Marrakech Inc (G-17482)*

Express Badging Services Inc 321 784-5925
1980 N Atl Ave Ste 525 Cocoa Beach (32931) *(G-1969)*

Express Brake International 352 304-6263
4376 Ne 35th St Ocala (34479) *(G-11381)*

Express Ironing Inc 305 261-1072
4707 Sw 75th Ave Miami (33155) *(G-9123)*

Express Ironing of Miami, Miami *Also called Express Ironing Inc (G-9123)*

Express Label Co Inc 407 332-4774
1955 Corp Sq Ste 1001 Longwood (32750) *(G-7892)*

Express Paper Company Inc 305 685-4929
5590 Nw 163rd St Miami Lakes (33014) *(G-10301)*

Express Press Inc 813 884-3310
107 N Jefferson St Tampa (33602) *(G-16824)*

Express Printing, Tallahassee *Also called Copy Well Inc (G-16428)*

Express Printing & Office Sups 904 765-9696
9840 Interstate Center Dr Jacksonville (32218) *(G-6085)*

Express Printing Center Inc 813 909-1085
2355 Raden Dr Land O Lakes (34639) *(G-7492)*

Express Prtg Winter Haven Inc 863 294-3286
757 Cypress Gardens Blvd Winter Haven (33880) *(G-18435)*

Express Signs & Graphics Inc 407 889-4433
547 Garden Heights Dr Winter Garden (34787) *(G-18385)*

Express Tools Inc 954 663-4333
14521 Sw 21st St Davie (33325) *(G-2410)*

Express Vision Care Inc 786 587-7404
1550 W 84th St Ste 15 Hialeah (33014) *(G-5148)*

Expressions In Wood 954 956-0005
4270 Nw 19th Ave Ste A Pompano Beach (33064) *(G-14016)*

Expressway Oil Corp 786 302-9534
7391 Nw 78th St Medley (33166) *(G-8239)*

Exquisite Wood Works By Al 321 634-5398
5565 Schenck Ave Ste 5 Rockledge (32955) *(G-14708)*

Extant Aerospace, Melbourne *Also called Symetrics Industries LLC (G-8543)*

Extant Aerospace, Melbourne *Also called Extant Cmpnnts Group Hldngs In (G-8423)*

Extant Cmpnnts Group Hldngs In 321 254-1500
1615 W Nasa Blvd Melbourne (32901) *(G-8423)*

Extra Time Solutions 407 625-2198
3695 Peaceful Valley Dr Clermont (34711) *(G-1865)*

Extreme Brake Integration Inc 352 342-9596
5817 Nw 44th Ave Ocala (34482) *(G-11382)*

Extreme Brake Integration Inc 888 844-7734
1909 Ne 25th Ave Ocala (34470) *(G-11383)*

Extreme Care Inc 239 898-3709
11997 Princess Grace Ct Cape Coral (33991) *(G-1341)*

Extreme Coatings, Saint Petersburg *Also called Surface Engrg & Alloy Co Inc (G-15205)*

Extreme Coatings 727 528-7998
2895 46th Ave N Saint Petersburg (33714) *(G-15041)*

Extreme Crafts LLC 561 989-7400
999 Nw 51st St Ste 100 Boca Raton (33431) *(G-510)*

Extreme H2o, Sarasota *Also called Hydrogel Vision Corporation (G-15496)*

Extreme Manufacturing LLC 888 844-7734
1909 Ne 25th Ave Ocala (34470) *(G-11384)*

Extreme Wood Works S Fla Inc 305 463-8614
1520 Nw 79th Ave Doral (33126) *(G-3211)*

Exxelia Usa Inc (HQ) 407 695-6562
1221 N Us Highway 17 92 Longwood (32750) *(G-7893)*

Eye Specialists Mid Florida PA 863 937-4515
2004 E County Road 540a Lakeland (33813) *(G-7320)*

Eye Wall Industries Inc 850 607-2288
3920 W Navy Blvd Pensacola (32507) *(G-13499)*

Eye-Dye, Pensacola *Also called Bam Enterprises Inc (G-13451)*

Eyedose Inc 786 853-6194
66 W Flagler St Ste 900 Miami (33130) *(G-9124)*

Eyes Med Billing & Consulting 618 308-7016
785 Oaklf Plntn Pkwy Orange Park (32065) *(G-11826)*

Eyeson Dgtal Srvllnce MGT Syst 305 808-3344
64 Ne 1st St Miami (33132) *(G-9125)*

EZ Boatworks Inc 772 475-8721
10602 Sw Corey Pl Palm City (34990) *(G-13035)*

EZ Loder Adjstble Boat Trlrs S 800 323-8190
1462 Commerce Centre Dr Port Saint Lucie (34986) *(G-14413)*

EZ Neon Inc 561 262-7813
12179 179th Ct N Jupiter (33478) *(G-6724)*

EZ Truck Services Inc 239 728-3022
19595 N River Rd Alva (33920) *(G-80)*

EZ Turn Signal Kits, Fernandina Beach *Also called Pops Turn LLC (G-3596)*

Ezassi, Ponte Vedra Beach *Also called Zassi Holdings Inc (G-14283)*

Ezell Precision Tool Co 727 573-3575
4733 122nd Ave N Clearwater (33762) *(G-1591)*

Ezproducts International Inc 863 735-0813
612 N Florida Ave Wauchula (33873) *(G-17826)*

Ezverify & Validate LLC 855 398-3981
1401 Nw 136th Ave Ste 400 Sunrise (33323) *(G-16318)*

Ezy Wrap, Defuniak Springs *Also called Professional Products Inc* *(G-2842)*

Ezy-Glide Inc 850 638-4403
715 7th St Chipley (32428) *(G-1456)*

Ezywipe of America, Miami *Also called Beyond White Spa LLC* *(G-8824)*

F & J Specialty Products Inc 352 680-1177
404 Cypress Rd Ocala (34472) *(G-11385)*

F & R General Interiors Corp 305 635-4747
480 W 20th St Hialeah (33010) *(G-5149)*

F & S Cabinets Inc 386 822-9525
1307 Yorktown St Deland (32724) *(G-2869)*

F & S Mill Works 407 349-9948
522 Cemetery Rd Geneva (32732) *(G-4788)*

F C Machine Corporation 407 673-9601
4212 Metric Dr Winter Park (32792) *(G-18511)*

F D Signworks LLC 561 248-6323
941 S Military Trl F5 West Palm Beach (33415) *(G-17993)*

F I B US Corp 239 262-6070
3966 Arnold Ave Naples (34104) *(G-10744)*

F I M C O, Tampa *Also called Florida Ink Mfg Co Inc* *(G-16846)*

F K Instrument, Clearwater *Also called F K Instrument Co Inc* *(G-1592)*

F K Instrument Co Inc 727 461-6060
2134 Sunnydale Blvd Clearwater (33765) *(G-1592)*

F L F Corp 561 747-7077
810 Saturn St Ste 28 Jupiter (33477) *(G-6725)*

F M E, West Palm Beach *Also called Florida Microelectronics LLC* *(G-18005)*

F O F Plastics Inc 727 937-2144
1614 Tallahassee Dr Tarpon Springs (34689) *(G-17471)*

F P G, Fort Lauderdale *Also called Florida Packg & Graphics Inc* *(G-3823)*

F S View Fla Flambeau Newsppr 850 561-6653
277 N Magnolia Dr Tallahassee (32301) *(G-16438)*

F T F Construction Company 772 571-1850
25 N Myrtle St Fellsmere (32948) *(G-3576)*

F W I Inc 407 509-9739
1388 S Ronald Reagan Blvd Longwood (32750) *(G-7894)*

F&J USA LLC (PA) 800 406-6190
601 Sw 21st Ter Fort Lauderdale (33312) *(G-3808)*

F-Response, Tampa *Also called Agile Risk Management LLC* *(G-16566)*

F2f Inc 561 833-9661
10800 Avenida Del Rio Delray Beach (33446) *(G-2961)*

Faac International Inc (HQ) 904 448-8952
3160 Murrell Rd Rockledge (32955) *(G-14709)*

Fab Defense Inc 386 263-3054
873 Hull Rd Unit 5 Ormond Beach (32174) *(G-12763)*

Fab Rite Inc 561 848-8181
4636 Dyer Blvd Riviera Beach (33407) *(G-14621)*

Faba Cabinets & Such LLC 813 871-1529
7029 W Hillsborough Ave Tampa (33634) *(G-16825)*

Fabbro Marine Group Inc 321 701-8141
100 E Pine St Ste 110 Orlando (32801) *(G-12143)*

Fabco Metal Products LLC 386 252-3730
1490 Frances Dr Daytona Beach (32124) *(G-2551)*

Fabco-Air Inc 352 373-3578
3716 Ne 49th Ave Gainesville (32609) *(G-4689)*

Fabis Group Corporation 305 718-3638
8025 Nw 68th St Miami (33166) *(G-9126)*

Fabmaster Inc 727 216-6750
2100 Palmetto St Ste A Clearwater (33765) *(G-1593)*

Fabric Innovations Inc 305 860-5757
7318 Sw 48th St Miami (33155) *(G-9127)*

Fabricatd Componnts Inc 321 784-3688
106 Aucila Rd Cocoa Beach (32931) *(G-1970)*

Fabricated Products Tampa Inc 813 247-4001
1100 S 56th St Tampa (33619) *(G-16826)*

Fabricated Wire Products Inc 813 802-8463
401 Lutie Dr Valrico (33594) *(G-17663)*

Fabricating Technologies LLC 352 473-6673
6670 Spring Lake Rd Keystone Heights (32656) *(G-6885)*

Fabrication Florida Ventr LLC 954 388-5014
1201 Nw 65th Pl Fort Lauderdale (33309) *(G-3809)*

Fabrico Inc 386 736-7373
1700 E Intl Speedway Blvd Deland (32724) *(G-2870)*

Fabrox LLC 904 342-4048
2 Sunshine Blvd Ormond Beach (32174) *(G-12764)*

Fabsouth LLC (HQ) 954 938-5800
721 Ne 44th St Oakland Park (33334) *(G-11265)*

Fabtech Supply, Jacksonville *Also called Ft Acquisition Company Llc* *(G-6123)*

Fabworx LLC 239 573-9353
848 Se 9th St Cape Coral (33990) *(G-1342)*

Facelove Cosmetics Inc (PA) 786 346-7357
18202 Homestead Ave Miami (33157) *(G-9128)*

Factorfox Software LLC 305 671-9526
14221 Sw 120th St Miami (33186) *(G-9129)*

Factory Direct Cab Refacing 954 445-6635
1060 Scarlet Oak St Hollywood (33019) *(G-5574)*

Factorymart Inc 561 202-9820
3875 Fiscal Ct Ste 400 West Palm Beach (33404) *(G-17994)*

Facts Engineering LLC 727 375-8888
8049 Photonics Dr Trinity (34655) *(G-17636)*

Faes Srt Inc 941 960-6742
7619 Trillium Blvd Sarasota (34241) *(G-15669)*

Faf Distribution LLC 561 717-3353
2200 Nw Corp Blvd Ste 407 Boca Raton (33431) *(G-511)*

Fagerberg Industries LLC 352 318-2254
100 Sw 75th St Ste 206 Gainesville (32607) *(G-4690)*

Fairbanks and Fairbanks Inc 850 293-1184
405 S K St Pensacola (32502) *(G-13500)*

Fairing Xchange LLC 904 589-5253
144 Industrial Loop E Orange Park (32073) *(G-11827)*

Faithful Heart Froyo LLC 407 325-3052
2405 Whitehall Cir Winter Park (32792) *(G-18512)*

Falco Industries Inc 407 956-0045
1550 Dixon Rd Longwood (32779) *(G-7895)*

Falcon Commercial Aviation LLC 786 340-9464
13500 Sw 134th Ave Ste 3 Miami (33186) *(G-9130)*

Falconpro Industries Inc 305 556-4456
1690 W 40th St Hialeah (33012) *(G-5150)*

Falfas Cabinet & Stone LLC 941 960-2065
1705 Cattlemen Rd Sarasota (34232) *(G-15670)*

Falken Design Corporation 765 688-0809
1200 Brickell Bay Dr # 2715 Miami (33131) *(G-9131)*

Fam Industries Inc 281 779-0650
7039 Mirabelle Dr Jacksonville (32258) *(G-6086)*

Famatel USA LLC 754 217-4841
9800 Nw 100th Rd 1 Medley (33178) *(G-8240)*

Family Magazines, Sarasota *Also called Florida Family Magazine Inc* *(G-15676)*

Family of Smith Inc (PA) 941 726-0873
5899 Whitfield Ave # 104 Sarasota (34243) *(G-15476)*

Family System Solution Whl Inc 954 431-5254
8409 Sheraton Dr Miramar (33025) *(G-10490)*

Family Vision Center 321 454-3002
228 S Courtenay Pkwy # 5 Merritt Island (32952) *(G-8585)*

Famous MBL Car Wash Prssure CL 786 720-1326
8255 Nw 22nd Ave Miami (33147) *(G-9132)*

Fan America Inc 941 955-9788
2235 6th St Sarasota (34237) *(G-15671)*

Fanam Inc 941 955-9788
2043 Global Ct Sarasota (34240) *(G-15672)*

Fanatics Mounted Memories Inc 866 578-9115
8100 Nations Way Jacksonville (32256) *(G-6087)*

Fantasy Brewmasters LLC 239 206-3247
950 Commercial Blvd Naples (34104) *(G-10745)*

Fantasy Chocolates Inc 561 276-9007
1815 Cypress Lake Dr Orlando (32837) *(G-12144)*

Fantasy Escapes, Holiday *Also called Admiral Printing Inc* *(G-5487)*

Fantasy Marble & Granite Inc 954 788-0433
400 Sw 12th Ave Ste 4/5 Pompano Beach (33069) *(G-14017)*

Fanto Group LLC (PA) 407 857-5101
9550 Satellite Blvd # 170 Orlando (32837) *(G-12145)*

Faour Glass Technologies, Tampa *Also called Faours Mirror Corp* *(G-16827)*

Faours Mirror Corp 813 884-3297
5119 W Knox St Ste A Tampa (33634) *(G-16827)*

Far Chemical, Palm Bay *Also called Far Research Inc* *(G-12899)*

Far Research Inc 321 723-6160
2210 Wilhelmina Ct Ne Palm Bay (32905) *(G-12899)*

Faraday Inc 813 536-6104
802 E Whiting St Tampa (33602) *(G-16828)*

Farartis LLC 305 594-5704
12050 Nw 28th Ave Miami (33167) *(G-9133)*

Farm Cut LLC 813 754-3321
3508 Sydney Rd Plant City (33566) *(G-13765)*

Farma International Inc 305 670-4416
9400 S Ddland Blvd Ste 60 Miami (33156) *(G-9134)*

Farmco Manufacturers Inc 813 645-0611
1110 4th St Sw Ruskin (33570) *(G-14777)*

Farmer Mold and Mch Works Inc 727 522-0515
2904 44th Ave N Saint Petersburg (33714) *(G-15042)*

Farmers Cooperative Inc (PA) 386 362-1459
1841 Howard St W Live Oak (32064) *(G-7848)*

Faro Technologies Inc 800 736-0234
125 Technology Park Lake Mary (32746) *(G-7074)*

Faro Technologies Inc (PA) 407 333-9911
250 Technology Park Lake Mary (32746) *(G-7075)*

Fasco Epoxies Inc 772 464-0808
2550 N Us Highway 1 Fort Pierce (34946) *(G-4485)*

Fashion Connection Miami Inc 305 882-0782
900 W 19th St Hialeah (33010) *(G-5151)*

Fashion Pool USA Inc 970 367-4797
6111 Linton St Jupiter (33458) *(G-6726)*

Fashion Store, Jacksonville *Also called Apyelen Curves LLC* *(G-5895)*

Fashionable Canes 727 547-8866
7381 114th Ave Ste 402b Largo (33773) *(G-7580)*

Fassi Equipment Inc 954 385-6555
2800 Glades Cir Ste 127 Weston (33327) *(G-18240)*

Fassidigitalcom Inc 954 385-6555
2800 Gldes Crcles Ste 127 Weston (33327) *(G-18241)*

Fassiequipment.com, Weston *Also called Fassi Equipment Inc* *(G-18240)*

Fassmer Service America LLC (HQ) 305 557-8875
3650 Nw 15th St Lauderhill (33311) *(G-7731)*

2022 Harris Florida
Manufacturers Directory

(G-0000) Company's Geographic Section entry number

Fast Frontier Printing 407 538-5621
  7360 Ulmerton Rd Apt 19d Largo (33771) *(G-7581)*

Fast Fuel Corp 786 251-0373
  2274 W 80th St Unit 4 Hialeah (33016) *(G-5152)*

Fast Labels 904 626-0508
  8680 Bandera Cir S Jacksonville (32244) *(G-6088)*

Fast Lane Autoshop LLC 954 835-5728
  813 Nw 1st St Fort Lauderdale (33311) *(G-3810)*

Fast Signs 813 999-4981
  14618 N Dale Mabry Hwy Tampa (33618) *(G-16829)*

Fast Signs 239 498-7200
  28440 Old 41 Rd Bonita Springs (34135) *(G-796)*

Fast Signs of Brandon 813 655-9036
  2020 Brandon Crossing Cir Brandon (33511) *(G-1092)*

Fastener Specialties Mfg Co, West Palm Beach *Also called Sockets & Specials Inc (G-18156)*

Fastener Specialty Corp 631 903-4453
  24100 Tiseo Blvd Unit 14 Port Charlotte (33980) *(G-14298)*

Fastglas 904 765-2222
  12819 Fenwick Island Ct E Jacksonville (32224) *(G-6089)*

Fastkit Corp. 305 599-0839
  11250 Nw 25th St Ste 100 Doral (33172) *(G-3212)*

Fastkit Corp. 754 227-8234
  11250 Nw 25th St Ste 100 Sweetwater (33172) *(G-16402)*

Fastsigns, Brandon *Also called Fast Signs of Brandon (G-1092)*

Fastsigns, Fernandina Beach *Also called Island Life Graphics Inc (G-3588)*

Fastsigns, Tallahassee *Also called Bucks Corporation Inc (G-16419)*

Fastsigns, Saint Petersburg *Also called Lucke Group Inc (G-15114)*

Fastsigns, Oldsmar *Also called Hunt RDS Inc (G-11657)*

Fastsigns, Fernandina Beach *Also called Island Life Graphics Inc (G-3589)*

Fastsigns, Deerfield Beach *Also called Hermes 7 Communications LLC (G-2733)*

Fastsigns, Pembroke Pines *Also called Mwr Sign Enterprises Inc (G-13407)*

Fastsigns, Tampa *Also called Fast Signs (G-16829)*

Fastsigns, Jacksonville *Also called Easy Rent Inc (G-6061)*

Fastsigns, Bonita Springs *Also called Fast Signs (G-796)*

Fastsigns, Miami *Also called Signs 2 U Inc (G-9888)*

Fastsigns, Orlando *Also called MGM Cargo LLC (G-12377)*

Fastsigns, Brandon *Also called Clari Solutions LLC (G-1086)*

Fastsigns, Fort Myers *Also called Alli Cats Inc (G-4165)*

Fastsigns, Orlando *Also called R & A Power Graphics Inc (G-12523)*

Fastsigns, Tampa *Also called Calmac Corporation (G-16673)*

Fastsigns, Miami *Also called Bdnz Associates Inc (G-8809)*

Fastsigns, Orlando *Also called C & H Sign Enterprises Inc (G-11971)*

Fastsigns, Sarasota *Also called Sarasota Signs and Visuals (G-15816)*

Fastsigns, Casselberry *Also called T & C Godby Enterprises Inc (G-1434)*

Fastsigns, Jacksonville *Also called Ash Signs Inc (G-5904)*

Fastsigns, Miami *Also called Sign Development Corporation (G-9884)*

Fastsigns, Davie *Also called Windstone Development Intl Lc (G-2499)*

Fastsigns, Oakland Park *Also called Sebco Industries Inc (G-11292)*

Fastsigns, Clearwater *Also called Lucke Enterprises Inc (G-1676)*

Fastsigns, Apopka *Also called Quick Advertising Inc (G-166)*

Fastsigns, Tampa *Also called Clark Craig Enterprises (G-16712)*

Fastsigns 305 628-3278
  15925 Nw 57th Ave Miami Lakes (33014) *(G-10302)*

Fastsigns 727 341-0084
  4058 Park St N Saint Petersburg (33709) *(G-15043)*

Fastsigns 305 747-7115
  146 Madeira Ave Coral Gables (33134) *(G-2056)*

Fastsigns 305 945-4700
  15405 W Dixie Hwy North Miami Beach (33162) *(G-11138)*

Fastsigns 954 404-8341
  3328 Griffin Rd Fort Lauderdale (33312) *(G-3811)*

Fastsigns 954 416-3434
  2841 Hollywood Blvd Hollywood (33020) *(G-5575)*

Fastsigns 407 542-1234
  2200 Winter Springs Blvd # 118 Oviedo (32765) *(G-12821)*

Fastsigns 850 477-9744
  6060 Tippin Ave Pensacola (32504) *(G-13501)*

Fastsigns 176101 .... 321 307-2400
  7640 N Wickham Rd Melbourne (32940) *(G-8424)*

Fastsigns 176501, Saint Augustine *Also called FDA Signs LLC (G-14832)*

Fastsigns2043 .... 305 988-5264
  2401 N Federal Hwy Boca Raton (33431) *(G-512)*

Fasulo Granite & Marble Inc 561 371-5410
  368 River Edge Rd Jupiter (33477) *(G-6727)*

Fat and Weird Cookie Co LLC 850 832-9150
  2540 Jenks Ave Panama City (32405) *(G-13260)*

Father & Son Fence Supply LLC 352 848-3180
  16300 Wiscon Rd Brooksville (34601) *(G-1156)*

Father's Table, The, Sanford *Also called Fathers Table LLC (G-15315)*

Fathers Table LLC (PA) 407 324-1200
  2100 Country Club Rd Sanford (32771) *(G-15315)*

Fathym Inc 303 905-4402
  2303 14th St W Palmetto (34221) *(G-13166)*

Fatovich Technologies LLC 772 597-1326
  2159 Sw Cameron Ln Palm City (34990) *(G-13036)*

Faulkner Inc of Miami 305 885-4731
  7275 W 20th Ave Hialeah (33014) *(G-5153)*

Faulkner Media LLC 855 393-3393
  3324 W University Ave Gainesville (32607) *(G-4691)*

Faulkner Plastics, Hialeah *Also called Faulkner Inc of Miami (G-5153)*

Faulkner Press, Gainesville *Also called Faulkner Media LLC (G-4691)*

Faux Effects International Inc 800 270-8871
  2701 Industrial Avenue 2 Fort Pierce (34946) *(G-4486)*

Faver Inc 305 448-6060
  3430 Main Hwy Miami (33133) *(G-9135)*

FB Beer Company, Naples *Also called Fantasy Brewmasters LLC (G-10745)*

FBI Industries Inc 239 462-1176
  11020 Yellow Poplar Dr Fort Myers (33913) *(G-4252)*

Fbo Key Largo LLC 305 451-3018
  14 Rainbow Dr Key Largo (33037) *(G-6845)*

Fbr 1804 Inc 305 340-3114
  18320 Ne 21st Ct North Miami Beach (33179) *(G-11139)*

Fbs Fortified & Ballistic SEC 561 409-6300
  3350 Nw Boca Raton Blvd Boca Raton (33431) *(G-513)*

FCA North America Holdings LLC 305 597-2222
  9975 Nw 12th St Doral (33172) *(G-3213)*

FCA North America Holdings LLC 407 826-7021
  10300 Boggy Creek Rd # 1 Orlando (32824) *(G-12146)*

Fcbn LLC 408 505-1324
  2637 E Atl Blvd 22868 Pompano Beach (33062) *(G-14018)*

Fcm, Odessa *Also called Florida Custom Mold Inc (G-11552)*

Fcs Holdings Inc 352 793-5151
  530 W Kings Hwy Center Hill (33514) *(G-1441)*

Fcs Holdings Inc (PA) 352 787-0608
  8500 Us Highway 441 Leesburg (34788) *(G-7772)*

Fcs Industries Corp 407 947-3127
  406 Anessa Rose Loop Ocoee (34761) *(G-11521)*

Fcs Industries Corp 407 412-5642
  6996 Piazza Grande Ave # 314 Orlando (32835) *(G-12147)*

Fct-Combustion Inc 610 725-8840
  5049 Sw 35th Ter Tce Fort Lauderdale (33312) *(G-3812)*

FDA Signs LLC 904 800-1776
  2303 N Ponce De Leon Blvd A Saint Augustine (32084) *(G-14832)*

Fdc Print LLC 305 885-8707
  950 Se 8th St Hialeah (33010) *(G-5154)*

Fdc Vitamins, LLC, Miami Lakes *Also called Vitamin Shoppe Florida LLC (G-10377)*

FDM of Clearwater Inc 727 544-8801
  10850 75th St Largo (33777) *(G-7582)*

Fea Inc 407 330-3535
  5333 Pen Ave Sanford (32773) *(G-15316)*

Feagle Logging LLC 386 365-2689
  805 Ne Indigo Dr Lake City (32055) *(G-7018)*

Featherlite Exhibits 800 229-5533
  1715 E Sewaha St Tampa (33612) *(G-16830)*

Featherlocks, Boynton Beach *Also called Condition Culture LLC (G-852)*

Fedan Corp 305 885-5415
  2280 W 1st Ave Hialeah (33010) *(G-5155)*

Fedan Tire Co, Hialeah *Also called Fedan Corp (G-5155)*

Federal Eastern Intl Inc 954 533-4506
  3516 W Broward Blvd Fort Lauderdale (33312) *(G-3813)*

Federal Heath Sign Company LLC 817 685-9075
  1128 Beville Rd Ste E Daytona Beach (32114) *(G-2552)*

Federal Millwork Corp 954 522-0653
  3300 Se 6th Ave Fort Lauderdale (33316) *(G-3814)*

Federal Suppliers Guide, Oldsmar *Also called Countryside Publishing Co Inc (G-11641)*

Feds Apparel 954 932-0685
  2230 Sw 70th Ave Ste 1 Davie (33317) *(G-2411)*

Feick Corporation 305 271-8550
  8869 Sw 131st St Miami (33176) *(G-9136)*

Fekel Stucco Plastering Inc 239 571-5464
  3780 29th Ave Sw Naples (34117) *(G-10746)*

Fekkai Brands LLC 954 791-6050
  6825 W Sunrise Blvd Plantation (33313) *(G-13850)*

Fekkai Retail LLC (PA) 866 514-8048
  6825 W Sunrise Blvd Plantation (33313) *(G-13851)*

Feldenkreis' Holdings LLC (PA) 305 592-2830
  3000 Nw 107th Ave Doral (33172) *(G-3214)*

Felix Reynoso 954 497-2330
  3062 Nw 23rd Ter Oakland Park (33311) *(G-11266)*

Fellowship Enterprises Inc 727 726-5997
  995 Harbor Lake Dr Ste 10 Safety Harbor (34695) *(G-14787)*

Fencing - Retail, Brooksville *Also called Father & Son Fence Supply LLC (G-1156)*

Fenix Wester Corp 305 324-9105
  2006 Nw 20th St Miami (33142) *(G-9137)*

Fenwall LLC (PA) 813 343-5979
  12850 Commodity Pl Tampa (33626) *(G-16831)*

Feria De Artesania Para TI 407 545-0909
  5425 Calla Lily Ct Kissimmee (34758) *(G-6919)*

Fermatex Enterprises Inc 407 332-8320
  685 S Rnald Reagan Blvd Orlando (32808) *(G-12148)*

Fernandina Observer Inc 904 261-4372
  205 Lighthouse Cir Fernandina Beach (32034) *(G-3587)*

ALPHABETIC

Ferrari Express Inc 305 374-5003
36 Ne 1st St Ste 1049 Miami (33132) *(G-9138)*

Ferrera Embroidery & Prtg Ser 786 667-2680
21709 Hobby Horse Ln Christmas (32709) *(G-1462)*

Ferrera Tooling Inc 863 646-8500
3960 Air Park Dr Lakeland (33811) *(G-7321)*

Ferrin Signs Inc 561 802-4242
945 26th St West Palm Beach (33407) *(G-17995)*

Ferris Stahl-Meyers Packing, Madison *Also called Prg Packing Corp (G-8046)*

Fertec Inc 850 478-6480
141 Terry Dr Pensacola (32503) *(G-13502)*

Fetco, Clearwater *Also called Magnatronix Corporation Inc (G-1680)*

Fewtek Inc 727 736-0533
2539 Gary Cir Apt 201 Dunedin (34698) *(G-3448)*

Ff Systems Inc 239 288-4255
2840 Hunter St Fort Myers (33916) *(G-4253)*

Ffo Leesburg LLC 352 315-0783
9917 Us Highway 441 Leesburg (34788) *(G-7773)*

Ffutter Fetti, Largo *Also called Parti Line International Inc (G-7655)*

FGA Printing 954 763-1122
2550 N Powerline Rd # 105 Pompano Beach (33069) *(G-14019)*

Fgmg International 305 988-7436
2820 Lightwood St Deltona (32738) *(G-3044)*

Fgt Cabinetry LLC 321 800-2036
1031 Crews Comm Dr Ste 13 Orlando (32837) *(G-12149)*

Fhs Enterprises LLC 754 214-9379
2875 S Congress Ave Ste D Delray Beach (33445) *(G-2962)*

Fi Aerospace Solutions Inc 786 395-3289
7938 Nw 66th St Miami (33166) *(G-9139)*

Fi Foil Co, Auburndale *Also called Fi-Foil Company Inc (G-230)*

Fi-Foil Company Inc 863 965-1846
612 W Bridgers Ave Auburndale (33823) *(G-230)*

Fiberbuilt Umbrellas Inc 954 484-9139
2201 W Atlantic Blvd Pompano Beach (33069) *(G-14020)*

Fiberflon Usa Inc 786 953-7329
1835 Nw 112th Ave Miami (33172) *(G-9140)*

Fiberglass Fabrication, Cocoa *Also called Fun Marine Inc (G-1930)*

Fiberoptic Engineering Corp 850 763-2289
6541 Bayline Dr Panama City (32404) *(G-13261)*

Fibertronics Inc 321 473-8933
2900 Dusa Dr Melbourne (32934) *(G-8425)*

Fibre Tech Inc 727 539-0844
2323 34th Way Largo (33771) *(G-7583)*

Ficap 407 302-3316
705 Remington Oak Dr Lake Mary (32746) *(G-7076)*

Fidelity Manufacturing LLC 352 414-4700
1900 Ne 25th Ave Ocala (34470) *(G-11386)*

Fidelity Printing Corporation 727 522-9557
3662 Morris St N Saint Petersburg (33713) *(G-15044)*

Field Forensics Inc 727 490-3609
1601 3rd St S Saint Petersburg (33701) *(G-15045)*

Field Office, Tampa *Also called Viasat Inc (G-17414)*

Field Service Office, Lake Buena Vista *Also called Jfh Technologies LLC (G-6999)*

Fiero Enterprises Inc 954 454-5004
203 Nw 5th Ave Hallandale Beach (33009) *(G-4944)*

Fiesta Marine Products Inc 727 856-6900
11016 State Road 52 Hudson (34669) *(G-5772)*

Fiesta Pontoon Boats, Hudson *Also called Fiesta Marine Products Inc (G-5772)*

Fifo Wireless, Miami *Also called Cellular Masters Inc (G-8907)*

Fiik Skateboards LLC 561 405-9541
5300 Powerline Rd Ste 209 Fort Lauderdale (33309) *(G-3815)*

Fiik Skateboards LLC (PA) 561 316-8234
7050 W Palmetto Park Rd Boca Raton (33433) *(G-514)*

Fill Tech Solutions Inc 200 .... 727 572-8550
11401 Belcher Rd S # 230 Largo (33773) *(G-7584)*

Filmfastener LLC 813 926-8721
12052 49th St N C Clearwater (33762) *(G-1594)*

Filorga Americas Inc 786 266-7429
429 Lenox Ave Miami Beach (33139) *(G-10188)*

Filta Group Inc (PA) 407 996-5550
7075 Kingspointe Pkwy # 1 Orlando (32819) *(G-12150)*

Filter King LLC 877 570-9755
200 Se 1st St Ste 502 Miami (33131) *(G-9141)*

Filter Research Corporation 321 802-3444
1270 Clearmont St Ne # 15 Palm Bay (32905) *(G-12900)*

Filter Specialists Inc 516 801-9944
1750 Filter Dr Deland (32724) *(G-2871)*

Filters Plus Inc 813 232-2000
6708 Benjamin Rd Ste 200 Tampa (33634) *(G-16832)*

Filthy Food LLC 786 916-5556
16500 Nw 15th Ave Miami (33169) *(G-9142)*

Filthy Rich of Jacksonville 904 342-5092
41b King St Saint Augustine (32084) *(G-14833)*

Fimco Manufacturing Inc 561 624-3308
15795 Corporate Rd N Jupiter (33478) *(G-6728)*

Final Touch Molding Cabinetry 239 948-7856
25070 Bernwood Dr Bonita Springs (34135) *(G-797)*

Final Tuch Mlding Cbinetry Inc 239 298-0980
25070 Bernwood Dr Bonita Springs (34135) *(G-798)*

Finastra USA Corporation 800 989-9009
744 Primera Blvd Ste 2000 Lake Mary (32746) *(G-7077)*

Finastra USA Corporation 800 394-8778
8010 Sunport Dr Ste 101 Orlando (32809) *(G-12151)*

Fincantieri Marine Repair LLC 904 990-5869
9485 Rgncy Sq Blvd # 101 Jacksonville (32225) *(G-6090)*

Findexcom Inc (PA) 561 328-6488
1097 Jupiter Park Ln Jupiter (33458) *(G-6729)*

Fine Archtctral Mllwk Shutters 954 491-2055
800 Nw 57th Pl Fort Lauderdale (33309) *(G-3816)*

Fine Art Connoisseur, Boca Raton *Also called Stream Line Publishing Inc (G-698)*

Fine Art Lamps, Hialeah *Also called Gq Investments LLC (G-5176)*

Fine D-Zign Signs, Saint Cloud *Also called Zeeeees Corporation (G-14942)*

Fine Line Custom Millwork LLC 941 628-9611
1683 Ne Bishop St Arcadia (34266) *(G-193)*

Fine Line Pavers Inc 561 389-9819
6480 Bischoff Rd West Palm Beach (33413) *(G-17996)*

Fine Line Printing & Graphics, Titusville *Also called Integrity Business Svcs Inc (G-17592)*

Fine Surfaces and More Inc 305 691-5752
8850 Nw 15th St Doral (33172) *(G-3215)*

Fine Things, Miami *Also called Mia Consulting & Trading Inc (G-9542)*

Fine Wood Design Inc 727 531-8000
12087 62nd St Unit 8 Largo (33773) *(G-7585)*

Fine Wood Work, Pensacola *Also called Southern Woodworks Fine Wdwkg (G-13607)*

Fine Woodworks 954 448-9206
15145 Se 175th St Weirsdale (32195) *(G-17839)*

Finecraft Cabinetry, Bradenton *Also called Sarasota Kitchens Closets Inc (G-1041)*

Finecraft Custom Cabinetry 941 378-1901
6209 Clarity Ct Sarasota (34240) *(G-15673)*

Finest Global Products. Com, Sarasota *Also called S and S Morris LLC (G-15804)*

Finesta Inc 786 439-1647
12650 Nw 25th St Ste 112 Miami (33182) *(G-9143)*

Finfrock Design Inc 407 293-4000
2400 Apopka Blvd Apopka (32703) *(G-130)*

Finfrock Industries Inc 407 293-4000
2400 Apopka Blvd Apopka (32703) *(G-131)*

Finger Lakes Custom Mfg LLC 315 283-4849
1211 Ne 17th Rd Ocala (34470) *(G-11387)*

Finger Mate Inc 954 458-2700
2500 E Hallandale Beach B Hallandale Beach (33009) *(G-4945)*

Finishing Group Florida Inc 954 981-2171
3997 Pembroke Rd Hollywood (33021) *(G-5576)*

Finlayson Enterprises Inc 850 785-7953
1802 Beck Ave Panama City (32405) *(G-13262)*

Finns Brass and Silver Polsg 904 387-1165
2025 Hamilton St Jacksonville (32210) *(G-6091)*

Finotex USA Corp (PA) 305 593-1102
6942 Nw 50th St Miami (33166) *(G-9144)*

Finyl Products Inc 352 351-4033
8657 Nw 80th Ave Ocala (34482) *(G-11388)*

Fiori Bruna Pasta Products, Miami Lakes *Also called Brefaros Nobile Food LLC (G-10287)*

Fiplex Communications Inc (PA) 305 884-8991
2101 Nw 79th Ave Doral (33122) *(G-3216)*

Fire Brands LLC 877 800-4398
1688 Meridian Ave Ste 600 Miami Beach (33139) *(G-10189)*

Fire Fly Fuels Inc 941 404-6820
1550 Global Ct Sarasota (34240) *(G-15674)*

Fire Technologies Corp 305 592-1914
2302 Lucaya Ln Apt D1 Coconut Creek (33066) *(G-1986)*

Firebird Scrubs and More LLC 904 258-7514
805 Glendale Ln Orange Park (32065) *(G-11828)*

Firedrake Inc 813 713-8902
39309 Air Park Rd Zephyrhills (33542) *(G-18614)*

Firefly Aircraft Parts Inc 954 870-7833
150 S Pine Island Rd Plantation (33324) *(G-13852)*

Firehouse Promotions Inc 407 990-1600
2450 Maitland Center Pkwy Maitland (32751) *(G-8058)*

Fireside Holdings Inc 941 371-0300
2053 58th Avenue Cir E Bradenton (34203) *(G-979)*

Firestone Complete Auto Care, Port Charlotte *Also called Bridgestone Americas Inc (G-14290)*

Firetainment Inc 888 552-7897
2415 N John Young Pkwy Orlando (32804) *(G-12152)*

Firmenich Incorporated 863 292-7456
4330 Drane Field Rd Lakeland (33811) *(G-7322)*

Firmenich Incorporated 863 646-0165
4300 Drane Field Rd Lakeland (33811) *(G-7323)*

Firmenich Incorporated 863 646-0165
3919 Kidron Rd Lakeland (33811) *(G-7324)*

Firmenich Lakeland 863 646-0165
3919 Kidron Rd Lakeland (33811) *(G-7325)*

First America Products 904 683-1253
153 Industrial Loop S Orange Park (32073) *(G-11829)*

First America Products LLC 904 215-8075
9710 E Indigo St Ste 203 Miami (33157) *(G-9145)*

First Block LLC 727 462-2526
615 Drew St Clearwater (33755) *(G-1595)*

First Case Cash LLC 954 200-5374
225 Holiday Dr Hallandale Beach (33009) *(G-4946)*

2022 Harris Florida
Manufacturers Directory

(G-0000) Company's Geographic Section entry number

First Cast Strpping MBL Sndbls 904 733-5915
4846 Philips Hwy Jacksonville (32207) *(G-6092)*

First Check Diagnostics LLC 858 805-2425
30 S Keller Rd Ste 100 Orlando (32810) *(G-12153)*

First Class Liaisons LLC 954 882-8634
2470 Wellington Green Dr Wellington (33414) *(G-17851)*

First Class Media Inc 561 719-3433
1003 Jupiter Park Ln # 5 Jupiter (33458) *(G-6730)*

First Coast Cargo Inc 844 774-7711
7643 Gate Pkwy Ste 104-31 Jacksonville (32256) *(G-6093)*

First Coast Concrete Pumping 904 262-6488
6115 Earline Cir N Jacksonville (32258) *(G-6094)*

First Coast Continuous Forms, Orange Park Also called Zilla Inc *(G-11847)*

First Coast Fabrication Inc 904 849-7426
96144 Nassau Pl Yulee (32097) *(G-18588)*

First Coast Granite & MBL Inc 904 388-1217
6860 Phillips Ind Blvd Jacksonville (32256) *(G-6095)*

First Coast Pavers Corp 904 410-0278
204 Blairmore Blvd Orange Park (32073) *(G-11830)*

First Coast Tee Shirt Co Inc 904 737-1985
5971 Powers Ave Ste 104 Jacksonville (32217) *(G-6096)*

First Communications Inc 850 668-7990
2910 Krry Frest Pkwy Ste Tallahassee (32309) *(G-16439)*

First Edition Design Inc 941 921-2607
5202 Old Ashwood Dr Sarasota (34233) *(G-15675)*

First Edition Design Pubg, Sarasota Also called First Edition Design Inc *(G-15675)*

First Grade Food Corporation 813 886-6118
5134 W Hanna Ave Tampa (33634) *(G-16833)*

First Impression Design MGT, North Miami Also called Cinema Crafters Inc *(G-11098)*

First Impression Doors & More, West Palm Beach Also called Db Doors Inc *(G-17976)*

First Impression Graphic Svcs, Fort Lauderdale Also called Walruss Enterprises Inc *(G-4120)*

First Impressions Industries, North Miami Also called J M Interiors Inc *(G-11107)*

First Impressions Printing 352 237-6141
1847 Sw 27th Ave Ocala (34471) *(G-11389)*

First Imprseesion South Flo 954 525-0342
1509 Sw 1st Ave Fort Lauderdale (33315) *(G-3817)*

First Imprssion Doors More Inc 561 798-6684
346 Pike Rd Ste 6 West Palm Beach (33411) *(G-17997)*

First Imprssons Prtg Cmmnctons 407 831-6100
851 E State Road 434 Longwood (32750) *(G-7896)*

First Look Display Group, Tampa Also called Caddie Company Inc *(G-16671)*

First Look Inc 954 240-0530
757 Se 17th St 986 Fort Lauderdale (33316) *(G-3818)*

First Marketing Company (PA) 954 979-0700
3300 Gateway Dr Pompano Beach (33069) *(G-14021)*

First Mate Inc 954 475-2750
11950 Nw 27th St Plantation (33323) *(G-13853)*

First Shot Mold and Tool 321 269-0031
1125 White Dr Titusville (32780) *(G-17585)*

First Sign Corp 954 972-7222
2085 N Powerline Rd Ste 1 Pompano Beach (33069) *(G-14022)*

First Tee Miami Daga 305 633-4583
1802 Nw 37th Ave Miami (33125) *(G-9146)*

First Wave Biopharma Inc 561 589-7020
777 W Yamato Rd Ste 502 Boca Raton (33431) *(G-515)*

First Windows Incorporated 813 508-9388
27524 Cashford Cir Wesley Chapel (33544) *(G-17875)*

Firstcut 786 740-3683
3030 Virginia St Miami (33133) *(G-9147)*

Firstline Products Inc 401 219-0378
7036 Twin Hills Ter Lakewood Ranch (34202) *(G-7478)*

Firstpath Laboratory Svcs LLC 954 977-6977
3141 W Mcnab Rd Pompano Beach (33069) *(G-14023)*

Fis Avantgard LLC (HQ) 484 582-2000
347 Riverside Ave Jacksonville (32202) *(G-6097)*

Fis Group Inc 786 622-3308
3820 Nw 125th St Opa Locka (33054) *(G-11746)*

Fis Kiodex LLC 904 438-6000
601 Riverside Ave Jacksonville (32204) *(G-6098)*

Fischer Panda Generators Inc 954 462-2800
351 S Andrews Ave Pompano Beach (33069) *(G-14024)*

Fischer Panda Generators LLC 954 462-2800
351 S Andrews Ave Pompano Beach (33069) *(G-14025)*

Fisher Cabinet Company LLC 850 944-4171
3900 N Palafox St Pensacola (32505) *(G-13503)*

Fisher Electric Technology Inc 727 345-9122
2801 72nd St N Saint Petersburg (33710) *(G-15046)*

Fishermans Center Inc 561 844-5150
56 E Blue Heron Blvd Riviera Beach (33404) *(G-14622)*

Fishers of Keys Inc 305 296-8671
5700 4th Ave Key West (33040) *(G-6863)*

Fishgum (PA) 256 394-2761
2040 Jamaica Dr Navarre (32566) *(G-10948)*

Fishgum 256 394-2760
1830 Cowen Rd Gulf Breeze (32563) *(G-4881)*

Fiskars Brands Inc 407 889-5533
3000 Orange Ave Apopka (32703) *(G-132)*

Fit Canvas Inc 954 258-9352
870 Sw 50th Ave Margate (33068) *(G-8130)*

Fit Like Foots, Clearwater Also called C & E Innovative MGT LLC *(G-1533)*

Fitletic Sports LLC 305 907-6663
1049 Nw 1st Ct Hallandale Beach (33009) *(G-4947)*

Fitteam Global LLC 586 260-1487
4440 Pga Blvd Ste 600 Palm Beach Gardens (33410) *(G-12969)*

Fitusa Manufacturing, Ormond Beach Also called Fabrox LLC *(G-12764)*

Fitzlord Inc 904 731-2041
650 E 27th St Jacksonville (32206) *(G-6099)*

Five Oceans Florida Inc 772 221-8188
4529 Sw Cargo Way Palm City (34990) *(G-13037)*

Five Sports Inc 727 209-1750
11880 28th St N Ste 100 Saint Petersburg (33716) *(G-15047)*

Five Star Bakery 954 983-6133
6847 Miramar Pkwy Miramar (33023) *(G-10491)*

Five Star Builders W Palm Bch, Wellington Also called 5 Star Builders Inc *(G-17841)*

Five Star Feld Svcs Applchia L 347 446-6816
3539 S Federal Hwy Apt L Boynton Beach (33435) *(G-865)*

Five Star Gurmet Foods Fla Inc 239 280-0336
3600 Shaw Blvd Naples (34117) *(G-10747)*

Five Star Marble and Stone 904 887-4736
117 Taylor Ridge Ave Ponte Vedra (32081) *(G-14257)*

Five Star Measurement, Boynton Beach Also called Five Star Feld Svcs Applchia L *(G-865)*

Five Star Millwork Inc 954 956-7665
4100 N Powerline Rd Y4 Pompano Beach (33073) *(G-14026)*

Five Star Quality Mfg Corp 954 972-4772
2200 Ne 62nd Ct Fort Lauderdale (33308) *(G-3819)*

Five Star Screening LLC 800 788-8315
1615 Broad Winged Hawk Dr Ruskin (33570) *(G-14778)*

Five Star Shutters, Fort Lauderdale Also called Five Star Quality Mfg Corp *(G-3819)*

Five Star Sports Tickets 440 899-2000
1755 E Hallandale Bch Hallandale Beach (33009) *(G-4948)*

Five Stones Mine LLC (PA) 813 967-2123
18500 Us Highway 441 Canal Point (33438) *(G-1260)*

Fix n Fly Drones LLC 321 474-2291
2105 N Jamaica St Tampa (33607) *(G-16834)*

Fizgig LLC 754 423-0349
1174 Sw 121st Ave Pembroke Pines (33025) *(G-13389)*

Fjh Music Company Inc 954 382-6061
2525 Davie Rd Ste 360 Davie (33317) *(G-2412)*

FK Instrument Co LLC 727 472-2003
2134 Sunnydale Blvd Clearwater (33765) *(G-1596)*

Fk Irons Inc 855 354-7667
1771 Nw 79th Ave Doral (33126) *(G-3217)*

Fka Enroute Emergency Systems, Tampa Also called Infor Public Sector Inc *(G-16943)*

Fka Racing Inc 386 938-4211
3994 Nw 36th Loop Jennings (32053) *(G-6650)*

Fkp 561 493-0076
2950 Commerce Park Dr # 6 Boynton Beach (33426) *(G-866)*

FL Central Cnstr & Rmdlg 863 701-3548
8120 Timberidge Loop W Lakeland (33809) *(G-7326)*

FL Industries Inc 954 422-3766
2930 Ne 8th Ave Pompano Beach (33064) *(G-14027)*

FL Precast LLC 321 356-9673
12679 Maribou Cir Orlando (32828) *(G-12154)*

Fla Property Holdings Inc 813 888-8796
13980 Nw 58th Ct Miami Lakes (33014) *(G-10303)*

Flagship Marine Inc 772 781-4242
3211 Se Gran Park Way Stuart (34997) *(G-16148)*

Flagshipmd LLC 904 302-6160
7800 Belfort Pkwy Ste 230 Jacksonville (32256) *(G-6100)*

Flagstone Pavers, Brooksville Also called Fsp-Ges Inc *(G-1158)*

Flagstone Pavers South 239 225-5646
1251 Ne 48th St Pompano Beach (33064) *(G-14028)*

Flaire Corporation 352 237-1220
4647 Sw 40th Ave Ocala (34474) *(G-11390)*

Flame Boss, Orlando Also called Collins Research Inc *(G-12031)*

Flamingo Crossing, Key West Also called McConnell Corp *(G-6875)*

Flamingo Graphics, Opa Locka Also called Pasa Services Inc *(G-11780)*

Flamingo Pavers Inc 850 974-0094
289 Tropical Way Freeport (32439) *(G-4622)*

Flamingo Printing Brevard Inc 321 723-2771
1785 Waverly Pl Melbourne (32901) *(G-8426)*

Flamingo Travel, Saint Augustine Also called Jls of St Augustine Inc *(G-14849)*

Flamm Industries Inc 904 356-2876
1313 Haines St Jacksonville (32206) *(G-6101)*

Flanders Corp 727 822-4411
2399 26th Ave N Saint Petersburg (33713) *(G-15048)*

Flare Clothing Inc 863 859-1800
3800 Us Highway 98 N # 746 Lakeland (33809) *(G-7327)*

Flash Prints LLC 786 422-3195
19401 Nw 23rd Ave Miami Gardens (33056) *(G-10257)*

Flash Roofing and Shtmtl LLC 786 237-9440
17425 Sw 109th Ct Miami (33157) *(G-9148)*

Flash Sales Inc 954 914-2689
4401 Nw 167th St Miami Gardens (33055) *(G-10258)*

Flat Glass Distributors LLC 904 354-5413
5355 Shawland Rd Jacksonville (32254) *(G-6102)*

A
L
P
H
A
B
E
T
I
C

Flat Island Boatworks LLC...850 434-8295
700 Myrick St Pensacola (32505) *(G-13504)*
Flatsmaster Marine LLC...239 574-7800
830 Ne 24th Ln Unit C Cape Coral (33909) *(G-1343)*
Flatwoods Forest Products Inc...352 787-1161
240 State Road 44 Leesburg (34748) *(G-7774)*
Flavana LLC...561 285-7034
1480 S Dixie Hwy E Pompano Beach (33060) *(G-14029)*
Flavcity Corp...413 221-0041
3050 Sw 14th Pl Ste 14 Boynton Beach (33426) *(G-867)*
Flavor Right Foods SE, Tampa *Also called Southeast Dairy Processors Inc (G-17284)*
Flavorworks Inc...561 588-8246
10130 Northlake Blvd West Palm Beach (33412) *(G-17998)*
Flayco Products Inc...813 879-1356
4821 N Hale Ave Tampa (33614) *(G-16835)*
Flc Machines Inc...352 728-2303
8010 Us Highway 441 Leesburg (34788) *(G-7775)*
Fleabusters, Fort Lauderdale *Also called Rx For Fleas Inc (G-4034)*
Fleaworld Div, Orlando *Also called United Trophy Manufacturing (G-12690)*
Fleda Pharmaceuticals Corp...813 920-9882
13231 Byrd Legg Dr Odessa (33556) *(G-11551)*
Fleet Spc An Enforcement One, Oldsmar *Also called Enforcement One Inc (G-11649)*
Fleetboss Globl Pstning Sltons...407 265-9559
241 Obrien Rd Fern Park (32730) *(G-3578)*
Fleetistics, Wesley Chapel *Also called Iler Group Inc (G-17879)*
Fleetmatics...727 483-9016
4211 W Boy Scout Blvd # 4 Tampa (33607) *(G-16836)*
Fleurette, Boca Raton *Also called Blum & Fink Inc (G-433)*
Fleurissima Inc (PA)...305 572-0203
4242 Ne 2nd Ave Miami (33137) *(G-9149)*
Flex Beauty Labs LLC...646 302-8542
7512 Dr Phillips Blvd Orlando (32819) *(G-12155)*
Flex Innovations LLC...866 310-3539
313 Seaboard Ave Unit B Venice (34285) *(G-17691)*
Flex Pack USA LLC...407 704-0800
1205 Pine Ave Orlando (32824) *(G-12156)*
Flexfield Express, Orlando *Also called Sage Implementations LLC (G-12567)*
Flexible Prtg Solutions LLC...727 446-3014
2070 Weaver Park Dr Clearwater (33765) *(G-1597)*
Flexiinternational Sftwr Inc...239 298-5700
856 3rd Ave S Ste 200 Naples (34102) *(G-10748)*
Flexiteek Americas Inc...954 973-4335
3109 Nw 25th Ave Pompano Beach (33069) *(G-14030)*
Flexo Concepts Manufacturing...305 233-7075
13552 Sw 129th St Miami (33186) *(G-9150)*
Flexofferscom Inc...305 999-9940
990 Biscayne Blvd Miami (33132) *(G-9151)*
Flexshopper LLC...561 922-6609
2700 N Military Trl # 200 Boca Raton (33431) *(G-516)*
Flexsol Holding Corp (PA)...954 941-6333
1531 Nw 12th Ave Pompano Beach (33069) *(G-14031)*
Flexstake Inc...239 481-3539
2150 Andrea Ln Fort Myers (33912) *(G-4254)*
Flickdirect Inc...561 330-2987
7495 Atl Ave Ste 200-347 Delray Beach (33446) *(G-2963)*
Flight Aerotech LLC...305 901-6001
7241 Nw 54th St Miami (33166) *(G-9152)*
Flight Source LLC...954 249-8449
2011 S Perimeter Rd Fort Lauderdale (33309) *(G-3820)*
Flight Velocity...866 937-9371
279 Old Moody Blvd Palm Coast (32164) *(G-13077)*
Flint LLC...813 622-8899
1212 Maydell Dr Tampa (33619) *(G-16837)*
Flints Wrecker Service Inc...863 676-1318
6442 State Road 60 E Lake Wales (33898) *(G-7160)*
Flite Rite Industries, Fort Lauderdale *Also called Florida Funeral Shipping Cntrs (G-3821)*
Flite Technology Inc...321 631-2050
2511 Friday Rd Cocoa (32926) *(G-1928)*
Flo King Filter Systems, Longwood *Also called Custom Masters Inc (G-7885)*
Flo Sun Land Corporation...561 655-6303
340 Royal Poinciana Way # 316 Palm Beach (33480) *(G-12934)*
Float-On Corporation...772 569-4440
1925 98th Ave Vero Beach (32966) *(G-17754)*
Floor and Bath Solutions...954 368-6698
2718 N Dixie Hwy Wilton Manors (33334) *(G-18339)*
Floor Tech LLC...407 855-8087
9801 Recycle Center Rd Orlando (32824) *(G-12157)*
Floors Inc...813 879-5720
6205 Johns Rd Ste 1 Tampa (33634) *(G-16838)*
Floral City Airboat Co Inc (PA)...352 637-4390
5098 S Florida Ave Inverness (34450) *(G-5827)*
Floribbean Inc...844 282-8459
6800 Bird Rd Miami (33155) *(G-9153)*
Florical Systems Inc (PA)...352 372-8326
4500 Nw 27th Ave Ste B1 Gainesville (32606) *(G-4692)*
Florida A&G Co Inc...800 432-8132
10200 Nw 67th St Tamarac (33321) *(G-16531)*
Florida AA Pallets Inc...305 805-1522
7611 Nw 74th Ave Medley (33166) *(G-8241)*
Florida Aero Precision Inc (HQ)...561 848-6248
120 Reed Rd Lake Park (33403) *(G-7125)*
Florida Air Cleaning Inc...727 573-5281
13584 49th St N Ste 17 Clearwater (33762) *(G-1598)*
Florida Airboat Propeller...863 324-1653
602 Burns Ln Winter Haven (33884) *(G-18436)*
Florida Aluminum and Steel Inc...863 967-4191
100 Thornhill Rd Auburndale (33823) *(G-231)*
Florida Amico...863 688-9256
1033 Pine Chase Ave Lakeland (33815) *(G-7328)*
Florida Applied Films, Lakeland *Also called SMc Diversified Services Inc (G-7436)*
Florida Best Hearing...863 402-0094
4739 N Congress Ave Boynton Beach (33426) *(G-868)*
Florida Bid Reporting Service...850 539-7522
313 Williams St Ste 11 Tallahassee (32303) *(G-16440)*
Florida Block, Medley *Also called McMaster Concrete Products LLC (G-8275)*
Florida Block & Ready Mix LLC...813 623-3700
5208 36th Ave S Tampa (33619) *(G-16839)*
Florida Boat Lift...813 873-1614
4821 N Manhattan Ave Tampa (33614) *(G-16840)*
Florida Brewery Inc...863 965-1825
202 Gandy Rd Auburndale (33823) *(G-232)*
Florida Brick and Clay Co Inc...813 754-1521
1708 Turkey Creek Rd Plant City (33566) *(G-13766)*
Florida Bus Unlimited Inc...407 656-1175
1925 W Princeton St Orlando (32804) *(G-12158)*
Florida Can Manufacturing LLC...863 356-5260
100 Florida Can Way Winter Haven (33880) *(G-18437)*
Florida Candy Buffets LLC...407 529-5880
3279 Safe Harbor Ln Lake Mary (32746) *(G-7078)*
Florida Candy Factory Inc...727 446-0024
721 Lakeview Rd Clearwater (33756) *(G-1599)*
Florida Cane Distillery, The, Tampa *Also called Florida Distillery LLC (G-16842)*
Florida Caribbean Distillers, Auburndale *Also called Florida Distillers Co (G-233)*
Florida Catholic Media Inc...407 373-0075
50 E Robinson St Orlando (32801) *(G-12159)*
Florida Cental Logging Inc...863 272-5364
7328 Us Highway 98 N Lakeland (33809) *(G-7329)*
Florida Central Extrusion Inc...863 324-2541
3700 Dundee Rd Unit 9 Winter Haven (33884) *(G-18438)*
Florida CMC Rebar...407 518-5101
1395 Chaffee Rd S 2 Jacksonville (32221) *(G-6103)*
Florida Coast Lighting Systems, Miami *Also called Municipal Lighting Systems Inc (G-9601)*
Florida Coca-Cola Bottling Co...561 848-0055
6553 Garden Rd Riviera Beach (33404) *(G-14623)*
Florida Coca-Cola Bottling Co (HQ)...813 569-2600
521 Lake Kathy Dr Brandon (33510) *(G-1093)*
Florida Coca-Cola Bottling Co...772 461-3636
3939 Saint Lucie Blvd Fort Pierce (34946) *(G-4487)*
Florida Columns, Safety Harbor *Also called Spaulding Craft Inc (G-14798)*
Florida Concrete Pipe Corp...352 742-2232
25750 C R 561 Astatula (34705) *(G-199)*
Florida Concrete Recycling Inc...352 495-2044
18515 Sw Archer Rd Archer (32618) *(G-197)*
Florida Container Depot, Brooksville *Also called GOTG LLC (G-1159)*
Florida Container Services...407 302-2197
3795 S Sanford Ave Sanford (32773) *(G-15317)*
Florida Cool Ring Company...863 858-2211
2220 Gator Creek Ranch Rd Lakeland (33809) *(G-7330)*
Florida Copier Connections...407 844-9690
8022 Office Ct Ste 100 Orlando (32809) *(G-12160)*
Florida Craft Distributors LLC...813 528-7902
2650 Jewett Ln Sanford (32771) *(G-15318)*
Florida Crushed Stone Co...352 799-7460
3919 Cr 673 Bushnell (33513) *(G-1243)*
Florida Crystal Refinery Inc (HQ)...561 366-5200
1 N Clematis St Ste 200 West Palm Beach (33401) *(G-17999)*
Florida Crystals, Palm Beach *Also called Flo Sun Land Corporation (G-12934)*
Florida Crystals, West Palm Beach *Also called Okeelanta Corporation (G-18097)*
Florida Crystals Corporation (HQ)...561 655-6303
1 N Clematis St Ste 200 West Palm Beach (33401) *(G-18000)*
Florida Crystals Corporation...561 366-5000
626 N Dixie Hwy West Palm Beach (33401) *(G-18001)*
Florida Crystals Corporation...561 992-5635
8501 S Us Hwy 27 Ave South Bay (33493) *(G-16015)*
Florida Crystals Corporation...561 515-8080
1 N Clematis St Ste 400 West Palm Beach (33401) *(G-18002)*
Florida Crystals Food, South Bay *Also called Florida Crystals Corporation (G-16015)*
Florida Crystals Food Corp...561 366-5100
1 N Clematis St Ste 200 West Palm Beach (33401) *(G-18003)*
Florida Custom Cabinets Inc...850 769-4781
3536 E Orlando Rd Panama City (32404) *(G-13263)*
Florida Custom Fabricators Inc...407 892-8538
2315 Tyson Rd Saint Cloud (34771) *(G-14925)*
Florida Custom Mold Inc (PA)...813 343-5080
1806 Gunn Hwy Odessa (33556) *(G-11552)*
Florida Cypress & Fence Co...561 392-3011
3922 Sw Saint Lucie Ln Palm City (34990) *(G-13038)*

Florida Dacco/Detroit Inc 813 879-4131
  3611 W Chestnut St Tampa (33607) *(G-16841)*

Florida Derecktor Inc (PA) 954 920-5756
  775 Taylor Ln Dania Beach (33004) *(G-2351)*

Florida Design Inc 561 997-1660
  621 Nw 53rd St Ste 370 Boca Raton (33487) *(G-517)*

Florida Design Mfg Assoc Inc 561 533-0733
  7430 Pine Tree Ln West Palm Beach (33406) *(G-18004)*

Florida Designer Cabinets Inc 352 793-8555
  1034 S Us 301 Sumterville (33585) *(G-16263)*

Florida Discharge Machine, Largo Also called FDM of Clearwater Inc *(G-7582)*

Florida Distillers Co 863 967-4481
  425 Recker Hwy Auburndale (33823) *(G-233)*

Florida Distillery LLC 813 892-5431
  1625 Emerald Hill Way Valrico (33594) *(G-17664)*

Florida Distillery LLC 813 347-6565
  501 S Falkenburg Rd C5 Tampa (33619) *(G-16842)*

Florida Dragline Operation 305 824-9755
  3163 W 81st St Hialeah (33018) *(G-5156)*

Florida Dragline Operations, Miami Also called North American Coal Corp *(G-9628)*

Florida Dredge and Dock LLC 727 942-7888
  1040 Island Ave Tarpon Springs (34689) *(G-17472)*

Florida E Coast Holdings Corp 904 279-3152
  6140 Philips Hwy Jacksonville (32216) *(G-6104)*

Florida East Coast Railway, Jacksonville Also called Florida E Coast Holdings Corp *(G-6104)*

Florida Elc Mtr Co Miami Inc 305 759-3835
  6350 Ne 4th Ct Miami (33138) *(G-9154)*

Florida Elreha Corporation 727 327-6236
  2510 Terminal Dr S Saint Petersburg (33712) *(G-15049)*

Florida Embroidered Patch & 561 748-9356
  1095 Jupiter Park Dr # 8 Jupiter (33458) *(G-6731)*

Florida Emrgncy Eqp Upfitters, Hialeah Also called South Florida Tech Svcs Inc *(G-5356)*

Florida Engine Rebuilders Corp 305 232-8784
  12500 Sw 130th St Ste 13 Miami (33186) *(G-9155)*

Florida Engineered Constru (PA) 813 621-4641
  6324 County Road 579 Seffner (33584) *(G-15958)*

Florida Engineered Constru 727 863-7451
  16835 Us Highway 19 Hudson (34667) *(G-5773)*

Florida Engineered Constru 321 953-5161
  2590 Kirby Cir Ne Palm Bay (32905) *(G-12901)*

Florida Enviromental Cons 407 402-2828
  9734 Crenshaw Cir Clermont (34711) *(G-1866)*

Florida Eqine Publications Inc 352 732-8686
  801 Sw 60th Ave Ocala (34474) *(G-11391)*

Florida Extracts, Tavares Also called Palmate LLC *(G-17520)*

Florida Extruders Intl Inc 407 323-3300
  2540 Jewett Ln Sanford (32771) *(G-15319)*

Florida Fabrication Inc 407 212-0105
  800 Johns Rd Apopka (32703) *(G-133)*

Florida Family Magazine Inc 941 922-5437
  4851 Hoyer Dr Sarasota (34241) *(G-15676)*

Florida Fence Post Co Inc (PA) 863 735-1361
  5251 State Road 64 W Ona (33865) *(G-11709)*

Florida Finisher Inc 941 722-5643
  509 9th St W Palmetto (34221) *(G-13167)*

Florida Fishing Products 239 938-4612
  205 W Ohio Ave Tampa (33603) *(G-16843)*

Florida Flexible 305 512-2222
  2681 W 81st St Hialeah (33016) *(G-5157)*

Florida Floats Inc (HQ) 904 358-3362
  1813 Dennis St Jacksonville (32204) *(G-6105)*

Florida Flvors Cncentrates Inc 561 775-5714
  205 Sedona Way Palm Beach Gardens (33418) *(G-12970)*

Florida Food Products LLC (PA) 352 357-4141
  2231 W County Road 44 # 1 Eustis (32726) *(G-3558)*

Florida Forest Products LLC 727 585-2067
  700 Beach Dr Ne Apt 803 Saint Petersburg (33701) *(G-15050)*

Florida Frames Inc 727 572-4064
  12880 Auto Blvd Ste B Clearwater (33762) *(G-1600)*

Florida Fresh Seafood Corp 305 694-1733
  7337 Nw 37th Ave Unit 7 Miami (33147) *(G-9156)*

Florida Freshner Corp 954 349-0348
  1138 Sunflower Cir Weston (33327) *(G-18242)*

Florida Froyo Inc 407 977-4911
  725 Primera Blvd Lake Mary (32746) *(G-7079)*

Florida Funeral Shipping Cntrs 954 957-9259
  1321c Nw 65th Pl Ste C Fort Lauderdale (33309) *(G-3821)*

Florida General Trading Inc (PA) 813 391-2149
  6195 N Us Highway 441 Ocala (34475) *(G-11392)*

Florida Generators, West Palm Beach Also called Frank Theodore Johanson *(G-18012)*

Florida Georgia Welding Supply, Jacksonville Also called Southstern Stnless Fbrctors In *(G-6496)*

Florida Glass of Tampa Bay 813 925-1330
  13929 Lynmar Blvd Tampa (33626) *(G-16844)*

Florida Glsd Holdings Inc 321 633-4644
  851 Greensboro Rd Cocoa (32926) *(G-1929)*

Florida Gold Foods LLC 347 595-1983
  1770 Business Center Ln Kissimmee (34758) *(G-6920)*

Florida Graphic Printing Inc 386 253-4532
  503 Mason Ave Daytona Beach (32117) *(G-2553)*

Florida Handrail & Fabrication, Gainesville Also called Gainesville Wldg & Fabrication *(G-4702)*

Florida Harbor Homes Inc 941 284-8363
  850 Bayshore Dr Englewood (34223) *(G-3531)*

Florida Health Care News Inc 813 989-1330
  215 Bullard Pkwy Temple Terrace (33617) *(G-17537)*

Florida Heritage Wdwkg LLC 941 705-9980
  2237 Industrial Blvd Sarasota (34234) *(G-15677)*

Florida Homes & Lifestyle, Sarasota Also called Florida Homes Magazine LLC *(G-15679)*

Florida Homes Magazine 941 227-7331
  1900 Main St Ste 312 Sarasota (34236) *(G-15678)*

Florida Homes Magazine LLC 941 549-5960
  2345 Bee Ridge Rd Ste 3 Sarasota (34239) *(G-15679)*

Florida Hose & Hydraulics Inc 305 887-9577
  7128 Nw 72nd Ave Ste 336 Miami (33166) *(G-9157)*

Florida Hospital Assn MGT Corp 407 841-6230
  827 Highland Ave Orlando (32803) *(G-12161)*

Florida Hydro Power & Light Co 386 328-2470
  171 Comfort Rd Palatka (32177) *(G-12866)*

Florida Hytorc 813 990-9470
  22131 Hwy Us19 Clearwater (33765) *(G-1601)*

Florida Ice Corporation 305 685-9377
  13401 Nw 38th Ct Opa Locka (33054) *(G-11747)*

Florida Indus Solutions LLC 833 746-7347
  13773 N Nebraska Ave Tampa (33613) *(G-16845)*

Florida Ink Mfg Co Inc 813 247-2911
  1715 Temple St Tampa (33619) *(G-16846)*

Florida Jacksonville Forklift 904 674-6898
  1063 Haines St Jacksonville (32206) *(G-6106)*

Florida Keys Keylime Products 305 853-0378
  95231 Overseas Hwy Key Largo (33037) *(G-6846)*

Florida Keys Keynoter, Marathon Also called Keynoter Publishing Co Inc *(G-8108)*

Florida Kit Cbnets Amercn Corp 305 828-2830
  9325 W Okeechobee Rd Hialeah (33016) *(G-5158)*

Florida Knife Co 941 371-2104
  1735 Apex Rd Sarasota (34240) *(G-15680)*

Florida Kolmiami Corporation 305 582-0114
  6491 Cow Pen Rd Apt H102 Miami Lakes (33014) *(G-10304)*

Florida Laminated Tempered GL, Miami Also called US Global Glass LLC *(G-10080)*

Florida Laminating & Uv Svcs, Saint Petersburg Also called Florida Print Solutions Inc *(G-15051)*

Florida Law Weekly, Tallahassee Also called Judicial & ADM RES Assoc *(G-16464)*

Florida Level & Transit Co Inc 813 623-3307
  5468 56th Cmmrce Pk Blvd Tampa (33610) *(G-16847)*

Florida Lift Stations Corp 305 887-8485
  9498 Nw South River Dr Medley (33166) *(G-8242)*

Florida Lift Systems, Tampa Also called Southern States Toyota Lift *(G-17290)*

Florida Living LLC 352 556-9691
  7410 Dent St Brooksville (34601) *(G-1157)*

Florida Machine & Casting Co 561 655-3771
  8011 Monetary Dr Ste A6 Riviera Beach (33404) *(G-14624)*

Florida Machining Center, Clearwater Also called Riva Industries Inc *(G-1768)*

Florida Made Door Co (PA) 352 742-1000
  1 N Dale Mabry Hwy # 950 Tampa (33609) *(G-16848)*

Florida Marine, Riviera Beach Also called Carey-Dunn Inc *(G-14606)*

Florida Marine Joiner Svc Inc 813 514-1125
  4917 Hartford St Tampa (33619) *(G-16849)*

Florida Marine Products Inc 813 248-2283
  2001 E 5th Ave Tampa (33605) *(G-16850)*

Florida Marking Products LLC 407 834-3000
  1205 Sarah Ave Ste 171 Longwood (32750) *(G-7897)*

Florida Mattress Wholesale 941 244-2139
  527 Us Highway 41 Byp N Venice (34285) *(G-17692)*

Florida Mch Works Ltd Partnr 904 225-2090
  86412 Gene Lassere Blvd Yulee (32097) *(G-18589)*

Florida Media Inc 407 816-9596
  1268 Bent Oak Trl Altamonte Springs (32714) *(G-47)*

Florida Metal Services Inc 727 541-6441
  6951 108th Ave Largo (33777) *(G-7586)*

Florida Metal-Craft Inc 407 656-1100
  47 S Dillard St Winter Garden (34787) *(G-18386)*

Florida Metallizing Svc Inc 863 425-1143
  1810 State Road 37 S Mulberry (33860) *(G-10625)*

Florida Micro Devices Inc 954 973-7200
  4676 Nw 60th Ln Coral Springs (33067) *(G-2153)*

Florida Microelectronics LLC 561 845-8455
  1601 Hill Ave Ste E West Palm Beach (33407) *(G-18005)*

Florida Mining Enterprises LLC 904 270-2646
  2207 Alicia Ln Atlantic Beach (32233) *(G-208)*

Florida Mkb Holdings LLC 407 281-7909
  16212 Sr 50 Clermont (34711) *(G-1867)*

Florida Mold Stoppers Inc 954 445-5560
  5520 S University Dr Davie (33328) *(G-2413)*

Florida Monthly, Altamonte Springs Also called Florida Media Inc *(G-47)*

Florida Motors Inc 786 524-9001
  1515 Nw 167th St Ste 300 Miami (33169) *(G-9158)*

Florida Natural Flavors Inc 407 834-5979
170 Lyman Rd Casselberry (32707) ***(G-1416)***
Florida Nbty Manufacturing 561 922-4800
901 Broken Sound Pkwy Nw Boca Raton (33487) ***(G-518)***
Florida Nonwovens Inc 407 241-2701
1111 Central Florida Pkwy Orlando (32837) ***(G-12162)***
Florida North Inc 352 606-2408
10294 Maybird Ave Weeki Wachee (34613) ***(G-17837)***
Florida North Emulsions Inc 386 328-1733
701 N Moody Rd Ste 151 Palatka (32177) ***(G-12867)***
Florida North Hearing Solution 386 466-0902
2228 Nw 44th Pl Gainesville (32605) ***(G-4693)***
Florida North Lumber Co Inc 850 643-2238
Hwy 12 S Bristol (32321) ***(G-1118)***
Florida North Lumber Inc 850 263-4457
18601 Nw County Road 12 Bristol (32321) ***(G-1119)***
Florida Nutri Labs LLC 863 607-6708
2715 Badger Rd Lakeland (33811) ***(G-7331)***
Florida Oil Service Inc 813 655-4753
16220 Ternglade Dr Lithia (33547) ***(G-7834)***
Florida Orange Groves Inc 727 347-4025
1500 Pasadena Ave S South Pasadena (33707) ***(G-16051)***
Florida Orange Groves Winery, South Pasadena *Also called Florida Orange Groves Inc* ***(G-16051)***
Florida Ordnance Corporation 954 493-8691
4740 Nw 15th Ave Fort Lauderdale (33309) ***(G-3822)***
Florida Packg & Graphics Inc 954 781-1440
6680 Nw 16th Ter Fort Lauderdale (33309) ***(G-3823)***
Florida Pillow Company 407 648-9121
1012 Sligh Blvd Orlando (32806) ***(G-12163)***
Florida Playground & Steel Co 813 247-2812
4701 S 50th St Tampa (33619) ***(G-16851)***
Florida Plntn Shutters LLC 386 788-7766
1725 S Nova Rd Ste A1 South Daytona (32119) ***(G-16021)***
Florida Plywoods Inc 850 948-2211
1228 Nw Us 221 Greenville (32331) ***(G-4854)***
Florida Pole Settlers & Crane 772 283-6820
4157 Sw Moore St Palm City (34990) ***(G-13039)***
Florida Polsg & Restoration 305 688-2988
2163 Opa Locka Blvd Opa Locka (33054) ***(G-11748)***
Florida Pool Products Inc 727 531-8913
14550 62nd St N Clearwater (33760) ***(G-1602)***
Florida Power Systems, Jacksonville *Also called V-Blox Corporation* ***(G-6584)***
Florida Pre-Fab Inc 813 247-3934
2907 Sagasta St Tampa (33619) ***(G-16852)***
Florida Precast Industries Inc 239 390-2868
9210 Estero Pk Cmmons Blv Estero (33928) ***(G-3543)***
Florida Precision Mch Met Work 813 486-5050
5904 Lynn Rd Tampa (33624) ***(G-16853)***
Florida Precision Tool, Clearwater *Also called James Reese Enterprises Inc* ***(G-1652)***
Florida Print Finishers Inc 850 877-8503
1621 Capital Cir Ne Ste F Tallahassee (32308) ***(G-16441)***
Florida Print Solutions Inc (PA) 727 327-5500
432 31st St N Saint Petersburg (33713) ***(G-15051)***
Florida Printing Group Inc 954 956-8570
1850 S Ocean Blvd Apt 904 Pompano Beach (33062) ***(G-14032)***
Florida Probe Corporation 352 372-1142
3700 Nw 91st St Ste C100 Gainesville (32606) ***(G-4694)***
Florida Production Engrg Inc (HQ) 386 677-2566
2 E Tower Cir Ormond Beach (32174) ***(G-12765)***
Florida Prsthtics Orthtics Inc 305 553-1217
9981 Sw 12th St Miami (33174) ***(G-9159)***
Florida Prtctive Ctngs Cons In 407 322-1243
482 Cardinal Oaks Ct Lake Mary (32746) ***(G-7080)***
Florida Pwdr Cting Shtters Inc 561 588-2410
854 N Dixie Hwy Lantana (33462) ***(G-7514)***
Florida Q-Railing Co 407 450-1808
3734 Mercy Star Ct # 130 Orlando (32808) ***(G-12164)***
Florida Quality Truss Inc 954 975-3384
3635 Park Central Blvd N Pompano Beach (33064) ***(G-14033)***
Florida Quality Truss Inds Inc (PA) 954 971-3167
3635 Park Central Blvd N Pompano Beach (33064) ***(G-14034)***
Florida Rdway Grdrail Sgns Inc 561 719-7478
1137 Silver Beach Rd Lake Park (33403) ***(G-7126)***
Florida Refresco Inc 863 665-5515
2090 Bartow Rd Lakeland (33801) ***(G-7332)***
Florida Research, Clearwater *Also called Cole Enterprises Inc* ***(G-1546)***
Florida Roadway Signs Inc 561 722-4067
1137 Silver Beach Rd Lake Park (33403) ***(G-7127)***
Florida Rock 941 625-1244
580 Prineville St Port Charlotte (33954) ***(G-14299)***
Florida Rock 352 472-4722
4000 Nw County Road 235 Newberry (32669) ***(G-11021)***
Florida Rock Concrete 407 877-6180
15150 Pine Valley Blvd Clermont (34711) ***(G-1868)***
Florida Rock Concrete Inc 904 355-1781
700 Palmetto St Jacksonville (32202) ***(G-6107)***
Florida Rock Industries (HQ) 904 355-1781
4707 Gordon St Jacksonville (32216) ***(G-6108)***
Florida Rock Industries 305 592-4100
5920 W Linebaugh Ave Tampa (33624) ***(G-16854)***
Florida Rock Industries 239 454-2831
14341 Alico Rd Fort Myers (33913) ***(G-4255)***
Florida Rock Industries 407 847-6457
49 Neptune Rd Kissimmee (34744) ***(G-6921)***
Florida Rock Industries 407 299-7494
2858 Sidney Ave Orlando (32810) ***(G-12165)***
Florida Rock Industries 904 355-1781
10151 Deerwood Park Blvd # 10 Jacksonville (32256) ***(G-6109)***
Florida Roofing & Shtmtl LLC 561 517-9675
17975 89th Pl N Loxahatchee (33470) ***(G-7969)***
Florida Rs Technology, Palm City *Also called Five Oceans Florida Inc* ***(G-13037)***
Florida Rs Technology, Palm City *Also called Eagle I Tech Inc* ***(G-13033)***
Florida Sales & Marketing 239 274-3103
11840 Metro Pkwy Fort Myers (33966) ***(G-4256)***
Florida Salt Scrubs, Delray Beach *Also called Fhs Enterprises LLC* ***(G-2962)***
Florida Screen Enterprise, Opa Locka *Also called Yale Ogron Mfg Co Inc* ***(G-11802)***
Florida Screen Services Inc 407 316-0466
805 W Central Blvd Orlando (32805) ***(G-12166)***
Florida Sentinel Bulletin, Tampa *Also called Florida Sentinel Publishing Co* ***(G-16855)***
Florida Sentinel Publishing Co 813 248-1921
2207 E 21st Ave Tampa (33605) ***(G-16855)***
Florida Septic Inc 352 481-2455
5757 Se 211th St Hawthorne (32640) ***(G-5007)***
Florida Shed Company Inc (PA) 727 524-9191
3865 Tyrone Blvd N Saint Petersburg (33709) ***(G-15052)***
Florida Sheet Metal, Melbourne *Also called Singer Holdings Inc* ***(G-8523)***
Florida Shutter Factory Inc 954 687-4793
3069 Nw 26th St Fort Lauderdale (33311) ***(G-3824)***
Florida Shutters Inc 772 569-2200
1055 Commerce Ave Vero Beach (32960) ***(G-17755)***
Florida Sign Source 407 316-0466
505 W Robinson St Orlando (32801) ***(G-12167)***
Florida Silica Sand Company 954 923-8323
2962 Trivium Cir Ste 105 Fort Lauderdale (33312) ***(G-3825)***
Florida Sncast Helicopters LLC 941 355-1525
8191 N Tamiami Trl # 104 Sarasota (34243) ***(G-15477)***
Florida Sncast Trism Prmtons I 727 544-1212
10750 75th St Largo (33777) ***(G-7587)***
Florida Southern Environmental, Pensacola *Also called Southern Environmental Inc* ***(G-13605)***
Florida Spcialty Coatings Corp 727 224-6883
3270 Suntree Blvd Ste 214 Melbourne (32940) ***(G-8427)***
Florida Sprayers Inc (PA) 813 989-0500
8808 Venture Cv Ste 101 Temple Terrace (33637) ***(G-17538)***
Florida Stainless Steel ACC 727 207-2575
5601 Cactus Cir Spring Hill (34606) ***(G-16071)***
Florida Star & News, Jacksonville *Also called Florida Star Inc* ***(G-6110)***
Florida Star Inc 904 766-8834
1257 Edgewood Ave W Jacksonville (32208) ***(G-6110)***
Florida State Graphics Inc 727 328-0733
2828 20th Ave N Saint Petersburg (33713) ***(G-15053)***
Florida Steam Services Inc 407 247-8250
349 Whitcomb Dr Geneva (32732) ***(G-4789)***
Florida Stl Frame Truss Mfg LL 813 460-0006
2312 Cypress Cv Ste 101 Wesley Chapel (33544) ***(G-17876)***
Florida Storm Panels Inc 305 685-9000
14475 Nw 26th Ave Opa Locka (33054) ***(G-11749)***
Florida Stucco Corp 561 487-1301
21195 Boca Rio Rd Boca Raton (33433) ***(G-519)***
Florida Style Aluminum Inc 239 689-8662
15481 Old Wedgewood Ct Fort Myers (33908) ***(G-4257)***
Florida Sugar Distributors (HQ) 561 655-6303
1 N Clematis St Ste 310 West Palm Beach (33401) ***(G-18006)***
Florida Sugar Farmers 863 983-7276
111 Ponce De Leon Ave Clewiston (33440) ***(G-1889)***
Florida Sun Printing, Callahan *Also called Southern Company Entp Inc* ***(G-1258)***
Florida Sunshine Stucco LLC 407 947-2088
9484 Boggy Creek Rd Orlando (32824) ***(G-12168)***
Florida SW Drones LLC 239 785-8337
1425 Sw 43rd Ter Cape Coral (33914) ***(G-1344)***
Florida Tape & Labels Inc 941 921-5788
5717b Lawton Dr Sarasota (34233) ***(G-15681)***
Florida Tees, Tallahassee *Also called Florida Print Finishers Inc* ***(G-16441)***
Florida Thread & Trimming 954 240-2474
7395 W 18th Ln Hialeah (33014) ***(G-5159)***
Florida Trading Company, Tavares *Also called Florida Trident Trading LLC* ***(G-17507)***
Florida Trailer Ranch LLC 904 289-7710
14770 Normandy Blvd Jacksonville (32234) ***(G-6111)***
Florida Transformer Inc (HQ) 850 892-2711
4509 St Hwy 83 N Defuniak Springs (32433) ***(G-2839)***
Florida Trend Magazine, Saint Petersburg *Also called Trend Magazines Inc* ***(G-15216)***
Florida Trident Trading LLC 352 253-1400
3801 State Road 19 Tavares (32778) ***(G-17507)***
Florida Truck Parts 786 251-8614
13115 W Okeechobee Rd # 101 Hialeah Gardens (33018) ***(G-5436)***

Florida Truss Corporation 407 438-2553
1302 Abberton Dr Orlando (32837) **(G-12169)**
Florida Turbine Tech Inc (HQ) 561 427-6400
1701 Military Trl Ste 110 Jupiter (33458) **(G-6732)**
Florida Vault Service Inc 727 527-4992
3007 47th Ave N Saint Petersburg (33714) **(G-15054)**
Florida Veex Inc 727 442-6677
2100 Tall Pines Dr Largo (33771) **(G-7588)**
Florida Weekly 239 333-2135
2891 Center Pointe Dr # 300 Fort Myers (33916) **(G-4258)**
Florida West Poggenpohl 239 948-9005
10800 Corkscrew Rd # 105 Estero (33928) **(G-3544)**
Florida Wilbert Inc (PA) 904 765-2641
5050 New Kings Rd Jacksonville (32209) **(G-6112)**
Florida Wilbert Inc 352 728-3531
27439 Hayward Worm Frm Rd Okahumpka (34762) **(G-11597)**
Florida Wire & Rigging Sup Inc 407 422-6218
4524 36th St Orlando (32811) **(G-12170)**
Florida Wire and Rigging Works, Miami *Also called Miami Cordage LLC* **(G-9549)**
Florida Wood, Longwood *Also called F W I Inc* **(G-7894)**
Florida Wood Creations Inc 239 561-5411
42881 Lake Babcock Dr # 200 Punta Gorda (33982) **(G-14504)**
Florida's Natural Growers, Lake Wales *Also called Citrus World Inc* **(G-7155)**
Floridahorse, The, Ocala *Also called Florida Eqine Publications Inc* **(G-11391)**
Floridas Best Inc 407 682-9570
839 Sunshine Ln Altamonte Springs (32714) **(G-48)**
Floridas Finest Industries 239 333-1777
5294 Summerlin Fort Myers (33907) **(G-4259)**
Floridas Hotspots Publishing 954 928-1862
5090 Ne 12th Ave Oakland Park (33334) **(G-11267)**
Floridas Natural Food Svc Inc 888 657-6600
20205 Hwy 27 Lake Wales (33853) **(G-7161)**
Floridian Blinds Llc 786 250-4697
10735 Sw 216th St Unit 40 Miami (33170) **(G-9160)**
Floridian Title Group Inc 305 792-4911
20801 Biscayne Blvd # 306 Miami (33180) **(G-9161)**
Flospine LLC 561 705-3080
3651 Fau Blvd Ste 400 Boca Raton (33431) **(G-520)**
Flotech LLC (HQ) 904 358-1849
136 Eastport Rd Jacksonville (32218) **(G-6113)**
Flowers Bakeries LLC 850 875-4997
321 W Jefferson St Quincy (32351) **(G-14544)**
Flowers Bakery, Sarasota *Also called Flowers Bkg Co Bradenton LLC* **(G-15478)**
Flowers Baking, Pensacola *Also called Franklin Baking Company LLC* **(G-13511)**
Flowers Baking Co LLC 850 763-2541
2133 Transmitter Rd Panama City (32404) **(G-13264)**
Flowers Baking Co Miami LLC 305 599-8457
2681 Nw 104th Ct Doral (33172) **(G-3218)**
Flowers Baking Co Miami LLC (HQ) 305 652-3416
17800 Nw Miami Ct Miami (33169) **(G-9162)**
Flowers Baking Company, Quincy *Also called Flowers Bakeries LLC* **(G-14544)**
Flowers Baking Company, Lakeland *Also called Flowers Bkg Co Bradenton LLC* **(G-7333)**
Flowers Baking Company, Avon Park *Also called Flowers Bkg Co Bradenton LLC* **(G-281)**
Flowers Baking Company, Orlando *Also called Flowers Bkg Co Bradenton LLC* **(G-12171)**
Flowers Baking Company, Hudson *Also called Flowers Bkg Co Bradenton LLC* **(G-5774)**
Flowers Baking Company, Kissimmee *Also called Flowers Bkg Co Bradenton LLC* **(G-6922)**
Flowers Baking Company, Bonita Springs *Also called Flowers Bkg Co Bradenton LLC* **(G-799)**
Flowers Baking Company, Bradenton *Also called Flowers Bkg Co Bradenton LLC* **(G-980)**
Flowers Bkg Co Bradenton LLC 941 627-0752
23240 Bayshore Rd Port Charlotte (33980) **(G-14300)**
Flowers Bkg Co Bradenton LLC 941 758-5656
2610 Mine And Mill Rd 4-9 Lakeland (33801) **(G-7333)**
Flowers Bkg Co Bradenton LLC 941 758-5656
1202 State Road 64 W Avon Park (33825) **(G-281)**
Flowers Bkg Co Bradenton LLC 941 758-5656
4301 N Pine Hills Rd Orlando (32808) **(G-12171)**
Flowers Bkg Co Bradenton LLC 941 758-5656
16721 Us Highway 19 Hudson (34667) **(G-5774)**
Flowers Bkg Co Bradenton LLC 941 758-5656
4990 S Orange Blossom Trl Kissimmee (34758) **(G-6922)**
Flowers Bkg Co Bradenton LLC 941 758-5656
26240 Old 41 Rd Bonita Springs (34135) **(G-799)**
Flowers Bkg Co Bradenton LLC 941 758-5656
720 9th St E Bradenton (34208) **(G-980)**
Flowers Bkg Co Bradenton LLC (HQ) 941 758-5656
6490 Parkland Dr Sarasota (34243) **(G-15478)**
Flowers Bkg Co Thomasville LLC 229 226-5331
3385 S Monroe St Tallahassee (32301) **(G-16442)**
Flowers Bkg Jacksonville LLC (HQ) 904 354-3771
2261 W 30th St Jacksonville (32209) **(G-6114)**
Flowers Logging Co Inc 850 639-2856
5644 Sw Odeen Flowers Rd Kinard (32449) **(G-6889)**
Flowhance Inc 305 690-0784
1951 Nw 7th Ave Miami (33136) **(G-9163)**
Flowmaster Inc 561 249-1145
14231 83rd Ln N Loxahatchee (33470) **(G-7970)**
Flowmatic, Dunnellon *Also called Watts Water Technologies Inc* **(G-3470)**
Floyd Fabrication LLC 330 289-7351
2821 Sanderling St Haines City (33844) **(G-4907)**
Floyd Publications Inc 813 707-8783
702 W Dr Mrtn Lther King Plant City (33563) **(G-13767)**
Flt Geosystems, Tampa *Also called Florida Level & Transit Co Inc* **(G-16847)**
Fluenz Inc 305 209-1695
1000 5th St Ste 200 Miami Beach (33139) **(G-10190)**
Fluid Handling Support Corp 786 623-2105
6030 Nw 99th Ave Unit 409 Doral (33178) **(G-3219)**
Fluid Metalworks Inc 850 332-0103
55 S A St Pensacola (32502) **(G-13505)**
Fluid Metalworks Inc -105 ....850 332-0103
55 S A St Pensacola (32502) **(G-13506)**
Fluid Routing Solutions LLC 352 732-0222
3100 Se Maricamp Rd Ocala (34471) **(G-11393)**
Fluidra Usa LLC 904 378-4486
8525 Mallory Rd Jacksonville (32220) **(G-6115)**
Flushing Amusement Inc 813 780-7900
40423 Air Time Ave Zephyrhills (33542) **(G-18615)**
Fluxxer, Pompano Beach *Also called Lubrexx Specialty Products LLC* **(G-14082)**
Flyer Studios Inc 786 402-9596
13740 Sw 33rd Ct Davie (33330) **(G-2414)**
Flying Colors Air Parts 352 728-1900
2727 W Main St Leesburg (34748) **(G-7776)**
Flying W Plastics Fl Inc 904 800-2451
109 Stevens St Jacksonville (32254) **(G-6116)**
Flyrite Banner Makers Inc 352 873-7501
3459 Sw 74th Ave Ste 100 Ocala (34474) **(G-11394)**
Flyteone Inc 813 421-1410
2687 Westchester Dr N Clearwater (33761) **(G-1603)**
FM Meat Products Ltd Partnr 352 546-3000
19798 Ne Highway 315 Fort Mc Coy (32134) **(G-4149)**
FM Publications Enterprise Inc 561 670-7205
6742 Forest Hill Blvd Greenacres (33413) **(G-4847)**
FMC Power Inc 786 353-2379
450 Alton Rd Miami Beach (33139) **(G-10191)**
FMC/Rhyno LLC 813 838-2264
5115 W Knox St Tampa (33634) **(G-16856)**
Fng Express Inc 863 471-9669
4343 Schumacher Rd Sebring (33872) **(G-15923)**
Foam & Psp Inc 954 816-5648
3325 Griffin Rd Ste 208 Fort Lauderdale (33312) **(G-3826)**
Foam By Design Inc 727 561-7479
10606 49th St N Clearwater (33762) **(G-1604)**
Foam Decoration Inc 786 293-8813
13800 Sw 142nd Ave Miami (33186) **(G-9164)**
Foam Factory Inc 954 485-6700
10137 Spyglass Way Boca Raton (33498) **(G-521)**
Foam Masters Inc 239 403-0755
4506 Mercantile Ave Naples (34104) **(G-10749)**
Foam Molding LLC 813 434-7044
3211 W Beach St Tampa (33607) **(G-16857)**
Focal Point Publishing LLC 877 469-9530
4131 Nw 13th St Ste 200 Gainesville (32609) **(G-4695)**
Focus Community Publications 407 892-0019
980 Orange Ave Saint Cloud (34769) **(G-14926)**
Focus On Water Inc 239 275-1880
10160 Mcgregor Blvd Fort Myers (33919) **(G-4260)**
Fogmaster Corporation (PA) 954 481-9975
1051 Sw 30th Ave Deerfield Beach (33442) **(G-2719)**
Foh Inc 305 757-7940
7630 Biscayne Blvd Miami (33138) **(G-9165)**
Foil Inc 442 233-3645
201 E Wright St Pensacola (32501) **(G-13507)**
Foilmania, Doral *Also called Bellak Color Corporation* **(G-3132)**
Folders Tabs Et Cetera 813 884-3651
4906 Savarese Cir Tampa (33634) **(G-16858)**
Foley Air LLC 904 379-2243
136 Ellis Rd N Jacksonville (32254) **(G-6117)**
Foley Cellulose LLC 850 584-1121
3510 Contractors Rd Perry (32348) **(G-13637)**
Foliage Enterprises Inc 407 886-2777
400 N Park Ave Apopka (32712) **(G-134)**
Fonon Technologies Inc (PA) 407 477-5618
1101 N Keller Rd Ste G Orlando (32810) **(G-12172)**
Food Marketing Consultants Inc 954 322-2668
2805 N Commerce Pkwy Miramar (33025) **(G-10492)**
Food Partners Inc 863 298-8771
340 W Central Ave Ste 200 Winter Haven (33880) **(G-18439)**
Food Spot 59, Miami *Also called Millenium Oil & Gas Distrs Inc* **(G-9570)**
Food Supply & Wine, Miami Beach *Also called Stripping Alpaca LLC* **(G-10236)**
Foods Div, Leesburg *Also called Cutrale Citrus Juices USA Inc* **(G-7765)**
Foot Function Lab Inc 954 753-2500
11540 Wiles Rd Ste 1 Coral Springs (33076) **(G-2154)**
Foot Print To Sccess Clbhuse I 954 657-8010
3521 W Broward Blvd # 10 Lauderhill (33312) **(G-7732)**
Foot-In-Your-mouth Inc 850 438-0876
9721 Fowler Ave Pensacola (32534) **(G-13508)**
Foote Woodworking Inc 941 923-6553
8347 Midnight Pass Rd Sarasota (34242) **(G-15682)**

ALPHABETIC

For Eyes Optcal Ccnut Grove In (HQ) 305 557-9004
  3601 Sw 160th Ave Ste 400 Miramar (33027) *(G-10493)*

For-A Latin America Inc 305 261-2345
  5200 Blue Lagoon Dr # 130 Miami (33126) *(G-9166)*

Force Enterprises Coatings LLC 561 480-7298
  1130 Quaye Lake Cir # 106 West Palm Beach (33411) *(G-18007)*

Force Imaging Group LLC 888 406-2120
  1936 Bruce B Downs Blvd Wesley Chapel (33544) *(G-17877)*

Forceleader Inc 727 521-1808
  6405 49th St N Ste A Pinellas Park (33781) *(G-13687)*

Forcon Precision Products LLC 239 574-4543
  1110 Ne Pine Island Rd Cape Coral (33909) *(G-1345)*

Ford Press Inc 352 787-4650
  305 S Canal St Leesburg (34748) *(G-7777)*

Ford Wire and Cable Corp 772 388-3660
  7756 130th St Sebastian (32958) *(G-15892)*

Forecast Products, Fort Lauderdale Also called Forecast Trading Corporation *(G-3827)*

Forecast Trading Corporation 954 979-1120
  2760 Nw 63rd Ct Fort Lauderdale (33309) *(G-3827)*

Foremost Chemicals Inc 727 522-8518
  6543 46th St N Ste 1102 Pinellas Park (33781) *(G-13688)*

Foresight Reserves LP 561 626-4999
  3801 Pga Blvd Ste 903 Palm Beach Gardens (33410) *(G-12971)*

Forest Research Institute Inc 631 436-4600
  2915 Weston Rd Weston (33331) *(G-18243)*

Forest Research Institute Inc 954 622-5600
  13800 Nw 2nd St Ste 190 Sunrise (33325) *(G-16319)*

Forestry Resources LLC (PA) 239 332-3966
  4325 Michigan Link Fort Myers (33905) *(G-4261)*

Forever Current Studios LLC 561 544-7303
  1161 Holland Dr Boca Raton (33487) *(G-522)*

Forever Signs Inc 305 885-3411
  2400 W 3rd Ct Hialeah (33010) *(G-5160)*

Forever Yung Altrntive Hlthcar, South Miami Also called EMC South Florida LLC *(G-16033)*

Forewarn LLC 561 757-4550
  2650 N Military Trl # 300 Boca Raton (33431) *(G-523)*

Forge Unlimited Co 727 900-7600
  10880 49th St N Clearwater (33762) *(G-1605)*

Foris Inc 904 394-2618
  1111 Brickell Ave Miami (33131) *(G-9167)*

Forklifts, Palm Beach Gardens Also called Infinite Handling Services LLC *(G-12976)*

Form Script - Form Print LLC 954 345-3727
  9101 W Sample Rd Apt 101 Coral Springs (33065) *(G-2155)*

Form-Co Inc 800 745-3700
  2487 Tradeport Dr Ste 200 Orlando (32824) *(G-12173)*

Formal Wear International, Miami Also called Apparel Imports Inc *(G-8735)*

Formica Print Solutions LLC 800 669-5601
  14000 63rd Way N Clearwater (33760) *(G-1606)*

Formsystems Inc 850 479-0800
  3700 Creighton Rd Ste 3 Pensacola (32504) *(G-13509)*

Formulated Solutions LLC (PA) 727 373-3970
  11775 Starkey Rd Largo (33773) *(G-7589)*

Formulated Solutions LLC 727 456-0302
  1776 11th Ave N Saint Petersburg (33713) *(G-15055)*

Formweld Fitting Inc 850 626-4888
  8118 Progress Dr Milton (32583) *(G-10424)*

Forno De Minas Usa Inc 954 840-6533
  242 Sw 12th Ave Deerfield Beach (33442) *(G-2720)*

Fort Dearborn Company 772 600-2756
  4313 Sw Port Way Palm City (34990) *(G-13040)*

Fort Lauderdale Molding, Delray Beach Also called Plastimold Products Inc *(G-2998)*

Fort Lauderdale Wdwkg Inc 954 935-0366
  3001 Sw 10th St Pompano Beach (33069) *(G-14035)*

Fort Meyers Beach Bulletin, Cape Coral Also called Breeze Corporation *(G-1316)*

Fort Myers Asphalt Plant, Fort Myers Also called S T Wooten Corporation *(G-4389)*

Fort Myers Digital LLC 239 482-3086
  6381 Corp Pk Cir Ste 2 Fort Myers (33966) *(G-4262)*

Fort Walton Co, Crestview Also called Crestview Ready Mix Inc *(G-2241)*

Fort Walton Concrete Co 850 243-8114
  26 Industrial St Nw Fort Walton Beach (32548) *(G-4583)*

Fort Walton Machining Inc 800 223-0881
  635 Anchors St Nw Fort Walton Beach (32548) *(G-4584)*

Fort Walton Machining Inc (PA) 850 244-9095
  43 Jet Dr Nw Fort Walton Beach (32548) *(G-4585)*

Forterra Pipe & Precast LLC 863 401-6800
  1285 Lucerne Loop Rd Ne Winter Haven (33881) *(G-18440)*

Forterra Pipe & Precast LLC 386 734-6228
  840 West Ave Deland (32720) *(G-2872)*

Forterra Pressure Pipe Inc 386 328-8841
  245 Comfort Rd Palatka (32177) *(G-12868)*

Fortified Building Pdts Inc 850 432-2485
  2001 W Government St Pensacola (32502) *(G-13510)*

Fortified Shutters, Pensacola Also called Fortified Building Pdts Inc *(G-13510)*

Fortress Impact Wndows Dors LL 954 621-2395
  6788 Nw 17th Ave Fort Lauderdale (33309) *(G-3828)*

Fortress Marine Anchors, Fort Lauderdale Also called Nav-X LLC *(G-3956)*

Forts Services LLC 786 942-4389
  4650 Lyons Tech Pkwy Coconut Creek (33073) *(G-1987)*

Fortune Media Group Inc 954 379-4321
  6250 Coral Ridge Dr # 100 Coral Springs (33076) *(G-2156)*

Forum Publishing Group Inc (HQ) 954 698-6397
  1701 Green Rd Ste B Deerfield Beach (33064) *(G-2721)*

Forum Publishing Group Inc 954 596-5650
  333 Sw 12th Ave Deerfield Beach (33442) *(G-2722)*

Forward Express One Llc 305 234-3034
  12625 Sw 134th Ct Ste 208 Miami (33186) *(G-9168)*

Forward Inertia LLC 617 794-8877
  1010 Brickell Ave # 4004 Miami (33131) *(G-9169)*

Forza X1 Inc 772 202-8039
  3101 S Us Highway 1 Fort Pierce (34982) *(G-4488)*

Fossco Inc 850 983-1330
  3948 Garcon Point Rd Milton (32583) *(G-10425)*

Foster & Foster Worldwide LLC 352 362-9102
  635 Lexington Pkwy Apopka (32712) *(G-135)*

Foulks Forest, Fort Myers Also called Curtis K Foulks *(G-4226)*

Foundation Art Services, Fort Lauderdale Also called Frametastic Inc *(G-3830)*

Foundry 904 257-5020
  1384 N Nova Rd Daytona Beach (32117) *(G-2554)*

Foundry-Mill Ltd 954 467-0287
  425 N Andrews Ave Ste 1 Fort Lauderdale (33301) *(G-3829)*

Fountain Youth Bathrooms Inc 772 626-9626
  2559 Sw Kenilworth St Port Saint Lucie (34953) *(G-14414)*

Four G Enterprises Inc 407 834-4143
  1150 Florida Central Pkwy Longwood (32750) *(G-7898)*

Four Purls 863 293-6261
  1226 7th St Nw Winter Haven (33881) *(G-18441)*

Four Seas Distilling Co LLC 813 645-0057
  915 Bunker View Dr Apollo Beach (33572) *(G-92)*

Four WD Consulting & Pubg LLC 561 969-7412
  2721 Vista Pkwy West Palm Beach (33411) *(G-18008)*

Four X Four Organics 561 687-1514
  5331 Ruth Dr West Palm Beach (33415) *(G-18009)*

Fournies Associates 561 445-5102
  1226 Nw 19th Ter Delray Beach (33445) *(G-2964)*

Fovico Inc 561 624-5400
  15908 77th Trl N West Palm Beach (33418) *(G-18010)*

Fowlers Sheet Metal Inc 561 659-3309
  4716 Georgia Ave West Palm Beach (33405) *(G-18011)*

Fox Equipment LLC (PA) 904 531-3150
  965 Bunker Ave Green Cove Springs (32043) *(G-4824)*

Fox Furniture, Daytona Beach Also called Rex Fox Enterprises Inc *(G-2590)*

Fox Industries of Swfl Inc 239 732-6199
  5701 Houchin St Ste 7 Naples (34109) *(G-10750)*

Fox Manufacturing LLC 904 531-3150
  965 Bunker Ave Green Cove Springs (32043) *(G-4825)*

Foxhound, Boynton Beach Also called Maxord LLC *(G-890)*

Fpc Printing Inc 813 626-9430
  201 Kelsey Ln Tampa (33619) *(G-16859)*

Fragrance Expresscom LLC 800 372-4726
  1221 Nw 165th St Miami (33169) *(G-9170)*

Fragrance Health and Buty Aids, Miami Also called Fragrance Expresscom LLC *(G-9170)*

Frako Concrete Services Inc 305 551-8196
  10312 Sw 3rd St Miami (33174) *(G-9171)*

Frame Tech of Orlando, Altamonte Springs Also called Amrav Inc *(G-31)*

Frametastic Inc 954 567-2800
  5470 Nw 10th Ter Fort Lauderdale (33309) *(G-3830)*

Framors Trading Inc 305 382-8782
  14951 Sw 70th St Miami (33193) *(G-9172)*

Franczak Roofing, Casselberry Also called Mf Industries LLC *(G-1425)*

Franja Corp 954 659-1950
  1515 Veracruz Ln Weston (33327) *(G-18244)*

Frank Murray & Sons Inc 561 845-1366
  1515 Se 16th St Fort Lauderdale (33316) *(G-3831)*

Frank Theodore Johanson 800 607-0690
  1317 S Killian Dr West Palm Beach (33403) *(G-18012)*

Franklin Baking Company LLC 850 478-8360
  9201 N Davis Hwy Pensacola (32514) *(G-13511)*

Franklin Dodd Communications, Hialeah Also called Fdc Print LLC *(G-5154)*

Franklin Equipment, Hilliard Also called Greg Franklin Enterprises Inc *(G-5465)*

Franklin Trade Graphics, Hialeah Also called 5301 Realty LLC *(G-5014)*

Franz A Ullrich Jr 863 773-4653
  514 N Florida Ave Wauchula (33873) *(G-17827)*

Frascold USA Corporation 855 547-5600
  5343 Bowden Rd 2 Jacksonville (32216) *(G-6118)*

Fraser Millworks Inc 904 768-7710
  9424 Sisson Dr Jacksonville (32218) *(G-6119)*

Fraser West 850 601-2560
  1509 S Byron Butler Pkwy Perry (32348) *(G-13638)*

Fraser West Inc 904 289-7261
  6640 County Road 218 Jacksonville (32234) *(G-6120)*

Fraser West Inc 904 290-6460
  9022 Se 186th Pl Lake Butler (32054) *(G-7000)*

Frattle Stairs & Rails Inc 904 384-3495
  465 Tresca Rd Jacksonville (32225) *(G-6121)*

Fraziers Fbrication Prfmce LLC 813 928-1449
  4730 Durant Rd Dover (33527) *(G-3430)*

Frc Electrical Industries Inc (PA) 321 676-3300
1260 Clearmont St Ne Palm Bay (32905) *(G-12902)*
Fred International LLC 786 539-1600
3350 Sw 148th Ave Ste 120 Miramar (33027) *(G-10494)*
Frederic Thomas USA Inc 239 593-8000
5621 Strand Blvd Ste 301 Naples (34110) *(G-10751)*
Free Press Publishing Company 813 254-5888
1010 W Cass St Tampa (33606) *(G-16860)*
Freedom Brick Pavers LLC 863 224-6008
2625 Shiner Dr Lake Wales (33898) *(G-7162)*
Freedom Enterprise & Associate, Sanford *Also called Fea Inc (G-15316)*
Freedom Fabrication Inc 850 539-4194
815 N Main St Ste B Havana (32333) *(G-5001)*
Freedom Metal Finishing Inc 727 573-2464
5095 113th Ave N Clearwater (33760) *(G-1607)*
Freedom Steel Building Corp 561 330-0447
1883 W State Road 84 # 106 Fort Lauderdale (33315) *(G-3832)*
Freeman S Magic LLC 786 286-8197
12420 Sw 18th Ter Miami (33175) *(G-9173)*
Freeman Electric Co Inc 850 785-7448
534 Oak Ave Panama City (32401) *(G-13265)*
Freeman Pallets Inc 352 328-9326
3530 Se Hawthorne Rd Gainesville (32641) *(G-4696)*
Freeport Fountains LLC 407 330-1150
1510 Kastner Pl Ste 3 Sanford (32771) *(G-15320)*
Freeport Truss Company Inc 850 835-4541
16676 Us Highway 331 S Freeport (32439) *(G-4623)*
Freewing Flight Tech Inc 813 752-8552
607 S Alexander St Ste Plant City (33563) *(G-13768)*
Freezetone Products LLC 305 961-1116
7986 Nw 14th St Doral (33126) *(G-3220)*
Freight Train Trucking Corp 407 509-0611
2503 Bross Dr Saint Cloud (34771) *(G-14927)*
Freon & Fabric, Deltona *Also called Brian Reck Valenzuela (G-3041)*
Fresco Foods Inc (PA) 813 551-2100
9410 E Broadway Ave Tampa (33619) *(G-16861)*
Fresco Group Inc 239 936-8055
13300 S Clevlnd Ave Ste 5 Fort Myers (33907) *(G-4263)*
Fresenius Kabi Usa LLC 847 550-2300
1733 Nw 79th Ave Doral (33191) *(G-3221)*
Fresh 561 330-4345
4801 Linton Blvd Delray Beach (33445) *(G-2965)*
Fresh Blends North America Inc 531 665-8200
955 Nw 17th Ave Ste J Delray Beach (33445) *(G-2966)*
Fresh Brandz LLC 813 880-7110
6201 Johns Rd Ste 11 Tampa (33634) *(G-16862)*
Fresh Choice MA Rket 407 448-8956
10249 S John Young Pkwy Orlando (32837) *(G-12174)*
Fresh Ink Print LLC 407 412-5905
4729 Patch Rd Ste 200 Orlando (32822) *(G-12175)*
Fresh Ink Signs & Graphics, Orlando *Also called Fresh Ink Print LLC (G-12175)*
Fresh Mark Corporation 352 394-7746
12518 El Viento Rd Clermont (34711) *(G-1869)*
Fresh On Fifth 305 234-5678
448 Ocean Dr Ste 2 Miami Beach (33139) *(G-10192)*
Fresh Press 305 942-8571
15334 W Dixie Hwy North Miami Beach (33162) *(G-11140)*
Fresh Start Beverage Company (PA) 561 757-6541
4001 N Ocean Blvd Apt B30 Boca Raton (33431) *(G-524)*
Fresh Thread Llc 904 677-9505
2823 State Road A1a Jacksonville (32233) *(G-6122)*
Freshco Ltd 772 287-2111
7929 Sw Jack James Dr Stuart (34997) *(G-16149)*
Freshetech LLC 516 519-3453
1211 Pine Ave Orlando (32824) *(G-12176)*
Fretto Prints Inc 904 687-1985
255 Se Us Highway 19 # 1 Crystal River (34429) *(G-2276)*
Frida's Bakery and Cafe, Largo *Also called Rouzbeh Inc (G-7672)*
Friedman & Greenberg PA 954 370-4774
8181 W Broward Blvd # 300 Plantation (33324) *(G-13854)*
Friedman Bros Dcrtive Arts Inc 800 327-1065
9015 Nw 105th Way Medley (33178) *(G-8243)*
Friendfinder.com, Delray Beach *Also called Various Inc (G-3032)*
Friendly Welding Inc 786 953-8413
4600 E 10th Ln Hialeah (33013) *(G-5161)*
Friends Professional Sty 561 734-4660
1521 Neptune Dr Boynton Beach (33426) *(G-869)*
Frieze, The, Miami Beach *Also called Worlds Greatest Ice Cream Inc (G-10247)*
Frio Distributors Inc 813 567-1493
1406 Mercantile Ct Plant City (33563) *(G-13769)*
Fritanga Y Tortilla Modra 305 649-9377
1885 W Flagler St Miami (33135) *(G-9174)*
Frito-Lay North America Inc 407 295-1810
2800 Silver Star Rd Orlando (32808) *(G-12177)*
Fritz Commercial Printing Inc 561 585-6869
5401 S Dixie Hwy West Palm Beach (33405) *(G-18013)*
Frog Publications Inc 352 588-2082
11820 Uradco Pl Ste 105 San Antonio (33576) *(G-15247)*
Fromkin Energy LLC 954 683-2509
4630 N University Dr Coral Springs (33067) *(G-2157)*
Front of House Inc 305 757-7940
7630 Biscayne Blvd # 105 Miami (33138) *(G-9175)*
Front of House Rm 360 By Foh, Miami *Also called Foh Inc (G-9165)*
Frontier Communications, Micanopy *Also called Frontier Electronics (G-10396)*
Frontier Electronics 954 255-0911
255 W Smith Ave Micanopy (32667) *(G-10396)*
Frontier Ready Mix Inc 727 544-1000
8311 63rd Way N Pinellas Park (33781) *(G-13689)*
Frostbite Nitrogen Ice Cream 305 933-5482
2305 Ne 197th St Miami (33180) *(G-9176)*
Frosting 772 234-2915
2915 Cardinal Dr Vero Beach (32963) *(G-17756)*
Frozen Wheels LLC 305 799-2258
16565 Nw 15th Ave Miami (33169) *(G-9177)*
Fruit Dynamics LLC 239 643-7373
4206 Mercantile Ave Naples (34104) *(G-10752)*
Fruitful International, Hialeah Gardens *Also called Fruitful LLC (G-5437)*
Fruitful LLC 954 534-9828
10030 Nw 79th Ave Hleahg Hialeah Gardens (33016) *(G-5437)*
Fruselva Usa LLC 949 798-0061
801 Brickell Ave Ste 800 Miami (33131) *(G-9178)*
Frz Marine 941 322-2631
3152 Lena Ln Sarasota (34240) *(G-15683)*
Fsbc, Boca Raton *Also called Fresh Start Beverage Company (G-524)*
Fsf Manufacturing Inc 407 971-8280
575 Econ River Pl Oviedo (32765) *(G-12822)*
Fshs Inc 941 625-5929
4210 Whidden Blvd Port Charlotte (33980) *(G-14301)*
FSI Group, Pensacola *Also called Formsystems Inc (G-13509)*
Fsp-Ges Inc 352 799-7933
9070 Old Cobb Rd Brooksville (34601) *(G-1158)*
Ft Acquisition Company Llc 904 367-0095
6600 Suemac Pl 2 Jacksonville (32254) *(G-6123)*
Ft Lauderdale Wax 954 256-9291
1912 N Sederal Hwy Fort Lauderdale (33305) *(G-3833)*
Fuel Air Spark Technology 901 260-3278
160 10th St N Naples (34102) *(G-10753)*
Fuel Cell Inc 954 776-7555
7841 Nw 56th St Doral (33166) *(G-3222)*
Fuel Connection 305 354-8115
14290 W Dixie Hwy North Miami (33161) *(G-11105)*
Fuel Medics, North Miami Beach *Also called Fuel Solutions Distrs LLC (G-11141)*
Fuel N Go LLC 239 656-1072
10351 Corkscrew Rd Estero (33928) *(G-3545)*
Fuel Productions LLC 904 342-7826
1960 Us Highway 1 S 199 Saint Augustine (32086) *(G-14834)*
Fuel Solutions LLC 813 969-2506
14213 Banbury Way Tampa (33624) *(G-16863)*
Fuel Solutions Distrs LLC 305 528-3758
3777 Ne 163rd St Pmb 148 North Miami Beach (33160) *(G-11141)*
Fuel Tanks To Go LLC 865 604-4726
13 Cypress Road Pass Ocala (34472) *(G-11395)*
Fuel U Fast Inc 561 654-0212
5660 Wind Drift Ln Boca Raton (33433) *(G-525)*
Fuelmatics Corp 305 807-4923
17641 Sw 87th Ave Palmetto Bay (33157) *(G-13209)*
Fuelmyschool 407 952-1030
4344 Indian Deer Rd Windermere (34786) *(G-18351)*
Fuels Unlimited Inc 407 302-3193
509 S French Ave Sanford (32771) *(G-15321)*
Fueltec Systems LLC 828 212-1141
11388 Okeechobee Blvd Royal Palm Beach (33411) *(G-14764)*
Fuentes Custom Woodwork LLC 941 232-0635
1490 Blvd Of The Arts Sarasota (34236) *(G-15684)*
Fuji International LLC 941 961-5472
6259 Sturbridge Ct Sarasota (34238) *(G-15685)*
Full Bore Directional Inc 727 327-7784
4921 15th Ave S Gulfport (33707) *(G-4897)*
Full Circle Directional Inc 352 568-0639
2161 Sw 83rd Pl Bushnell (33513) *(G-1244)*
Full Circle Integration LLC 504 615-5501
127b N John Sims Pkwy Valparaiso (32580) *(G-17660)*
Full Cut Tabs LLC 941 316-1510
2153 10th St Sarasota (34237) *(G-15686)*
Full House, Melbourne *Also called Braid Sales and Marketing Inc (G-8382)*
Full Lf Natural Hlth Pdts LLC 954 889-4019
1932 Hollywood Blvd Hollywood (33020) *(G-5577)*
Full Life Direct LLC 800 305-3043
1932 Hollywood Blvd Hollywood (33020) *(G-5578)*
Full Press Apparel Inc 850 222-1003
3445 Garber Dr Tallahassee (32303) *(G-16443)*
Fuller Amusements 352 629-2792
2250 Se 52nd St Ocala (34480) *(G-11396)*
Fullerton 799 Inc 727 572-7040
5300 115th Ave N Clearwater (33760) *(G-1608)*
Fully Promoted, Tampa *Also called Embroidmecom Inc (G-16806)*
Fully Promoted 561 615-8655
1369 N Military Trl West Palm Beach (33409) *(G-18014)*

ALPHABETIC

Fun Electronics Inc ... 305 933-4646
2999 Ne 191st St Ph 2 Miami (33180) *(G-9179)*
Fun Marine Inc ... 321 576-1100
682 Industry Rd S Cocoa (32926) *(G-1930)*
Function Please LLC (PA) ... 305 792-7900
2001 Tyler St Ste 5 Hollywood (33020) *(G-5579)*
Fundamental Micro LP ... 239 434-7434
9130 Galleria Ct Fl 3 Naples (34109) *(G-10754)*
Funsparks, Clearwater *Also called System Enterprises LLC (G-1808)*
Fuqua Sawmill Inc ... 352 236-3456
1751 Nw 33rd Ave Ocala (34475) *(G-11397)*
Furniture Concepts 2000 Inc ... 954 946-0310
454 Ne 28th St Pompano Beach (33064) *(G-14036)*
Furniture Concepts Inc ... 727 535-0093
2180 34th Way Ste D Largo (33771) *(G-7590)*
Furniture Design Gallery, Sanford *Also called Furniture Design of Centl Fla (G-15322)*
Furniture Design of Centl Fla ... 407 330-4430
219 Hickman Dr Sanford (32771) *(G-15322)*
Furnival Cabinetry LLC ... 321 638-1223
7235 Camilo Rd Cocoa (32927) *(G-1931)*
Furnival Construction LLC ... 321 638-1223
7235 Camilo Rd Cocoa (32927) *(G-1932)*
Furrytails LLC ... 407 654-1465
555 Winderley Pl Ste 300 Maitland (32751) *(G-8059)*
Furst-Mcness Company ... 386 755-5605
3830 Nw Brown Rd Lake City (32055) *(G-7019)*
Fury Surf Shack ... 305 747-0799
201 Front St Ste 109 Key West (33040) *(G-6864)*
Fuse Builds LLC ... 617 602-4001
4480 Eagle Falls Pl Tampa (33619) *(G-16864)*
Fuse Fabrication Llc ... 863 225-5698
1935 Industrial Park Rd Mulberry (33860) *(G-10626)*
Fusion Energy Solutions LLC ... 941 366-9936
5506 Independence Ct B Punta Gorda (33982) *(G-14505)*
Fusion Industries ... 239 592-7070
1998 Trade Center Way Naples (34109) *(G-10755)*
Fusion Industries LLC ... 239 415-7554
16710 Gator Rd Fort Myers (33912) *(G-4264)*
Fusion Industries Intl LLC ... 239 415-7554
16710 Gator Rd Fort Myers (33912) *(G-4265)*
Fusion Welding ... 239 288-6530
15865 Brothers Ct Fort Myers (33912) *(G-4266)*
Fussion International Inc ... 305 662-4848
446 Loretto Ave Coral Gables (33146) *(G-2057)*
Futch Printing & Mailing Inc ... 904 388-3995
4606 Shirley Ave Jacksonville (32210) *(G-6124)*
Futura International, Clearwater *Also called Opie Choice LLC (G-1728)*
Future Designs By Lahijani, Miami *Also called Lux Unlimited Inc (G-9488)*
Future Foam Inc ... 407 857-2510
1351 Gemini Blvd Orlando (32837) *(G-12178)*
Future Foods LLC ... 786 390-5226
1005 Lake Ave Lake Worth (33460) *(G-7201)*
Future House ... 904 683-9177
11201 Ponset Rd Jacksonville (32218) *(G-6125)*
Future Modes Inc ... 305 654-9995
1910 Ne 206th St Miami (33179) *(G-9180)*
Future Plus of Florida ... 612 240-7275
138 S Dale Mabry Hwy Tampa (33609) *(G-16865)*
Futurecow, Sanford *Also called Alpha Technology USA Corp (G-15261)*
Futurescape Inc ... 386 679-4120
6119 Del Mar Dr Port Orange (32127) *(G-14334)*
Fuzion Digital Signs ... 844 529-0505
4409 N Clark Ave Tampa (33614) *(G-16866)*
Fuzion Prfmce Coatings LLC ... 561 364-2474
6790 N Ocean Blvd Ocean Ridge (33435) *(G-11517)*
Fw Shoring Company ... 813 248-2495
7532 Malta Ln Tampa (33637) *(G-16867)*
Fw Shoring Company ... 517 676-8800
11128 Boggy Creek Rd Orlando (32824) *(G-12179)*
Fws Distributors LLC (PA) ... 407 543-6291
14501 Nw 57th Ave Ste 113 Miami (33014) *(G-9181)*
Fyi Software Inc ... 239 272-6016
4850 Tamiami Trl N # 301 Naples (34103) *(G-10756)*
G & A Manufacturing Inc ... 352 473-6882
6045 State Road 21 Keystone Heights (32656) *(G-6886)*
G & B Trading Imports, Miami *Also called Valentina Signa Inc (G-10090)*
G & F Manufacturing Inc ... 239 939-7446
7902 Interstate Ct Fort Myers (33917) *(G-4267)*
G & G Latin Business Inc ... 954 385-8085
16668 Saddle Club Rd Weston (33326) *(G-18245)*
G & G Pressure Washers Inc ... 786 376-1800
7331 Branch St Hollywood (33024) *(G-5580)*
G & K Aluminum Inc ... 772 283-1297
3110 Se Slater St Stuart (34997) *(G-16150)*
G & R Machine Inc ... 407 324-1600
701 Cornwall Rd Ste A Sanford (32773) *(G-15323)*
G & S Boats Inc ... 850 835-7700
143 Yacht Dr Freeport (32439) *(G-4624)*
G & S Machine Shop Corp ... 305 863-7866
7715 Nw 74th Ave Medley (33166) *(G-8244)*
G A C Inc/Gulf Associates, Deerfield Beach *Also called Gulf Associates Control Inc (G-2728)*
G A Food Services, Fort Lauderdale *Also called GA Fd Svcs Pinellas Cnty LLC (G-3835)*
G and W Craftsman LLC ... 440 453-2770
2249 Kirkwood Ave Naples (34112) *(G-10757)*
G B Welding & Fabrication LLC ... 954 967-2573
2397 College Ave Davie (33317) *(G-2415)*
G Black Logging LLC ... 850 379-8747
15698 Ne Moore St Hosford (32334) *(G-5755)*
G D Pallets LLC ... 772 713-8251
695 S Us 1 Vero Beach (32962) *(G-17757)*
G E Generators, Pensacola *Also called GE Renewables North Amer LLC (G-13512)*
G F C, Belle Glade *Also called Glades Formulating Corporation (G-341)*
G F E Inc ... 954 583-7005
3030 Burris Rd Davie (33314) *(G-2416)*
G G Millwork Contractor Inc ... 305 522-6333
26008 Gaspar Ct Howey In The Hills (34737) *(G-5758)*
G G Millwork Contractor Inc (PA) ... 305 852-1718
300 Atlantic Dr Unit 7 Key Largo (33037) *(G-6847)*
G G Schmitt & Sons Inc ... 717 394-3701
7230 15th St E Sarasota (34243) *(G-15479)*
G Haddock Rowland Inc ... 904 845-2725
376488 Kings Ferry Rd Hilliard (32046) *(G-5463)*
G J Embroidery Inc ... 407 284-8036
6839 Narcoossee Rd Ste 33 Orlando (32822) *(G-12180)*
G J Sheet Metal Corp ... 954 709-9011
4710 Ne 2nd Way Deerfield Beach (33064) *(G-2723)*
G K Woodworks ... 941 232-3910
5365 Matthew Ct Sarasota (34231) *(G-15687)*
G M F, Lakeland *Also called GMF Industries Inc (G-7338)*
G M R, Tampa *Also called Gulf Marine Repair Corporation (G-16898)*
G Metal Industries Inc ... 305 633-0300
3670 Nw 49th St Miami (33142) *(G-9182)*
G Phillips and Sons LLC ... 248 705-5873
8987 Wildlife Loop Sarasota (34238) *(G-15688)*
G Print Inc ... 305 316-2266
2392 W 80th St Ste 1 Hialeah (33016) *(G-5162)*
G S C, Hialeah *Also called General Stair Corporation (G-5170)*
G S Printers Inc ... 305 931-2755
1239 N Flagler Dr Fort Lauderdale (33304) *(G-3834)*
G S Servicore Corp ... 305 888-0189
3630 E 10th Ct Hialeah (33013) *(G-5163)*
G&F Mnfctring Mfr Glfstream He, Fort Myers *Also called G & F Manufacturing Inc (G-4267)*
G-Car Inc (PA) ... 305 883-8223
235 W 75th Pl Hialeah (33014) *(G-5164)*
G-Forces Div, Hialeah *Also called Derm-Buro Inc (G-5114)*
G.A. Foods, Saint Petersburg *Also called GA Fd Svcs Pinellas Cnty LLC (G-15057)*
G2 Harness LLC ... 915 892-2494
12000 28th St Nnull Saint Petersburg (33716) *(G-15056)*
G2c Enterprises Inc ... 850 398-5368
695 Sioux Cir Crestview (32536) *(G-2244)*
G2c Enterprises Inc ... 850 585-4166
695 Sioux Cir Crestview (32536) *(G-2245)*
G2pn.com, Saint Petersburg *Also called Go 2 Print Now Inc (G-15063)*
G6 Embroidery LLC ... 904 729-1191
6001 Argyle Frest Blvd St Jacksonville (32244) *(G-6126)*
GA Fd Svcs Pinellas Cnty LLC (PA) ... 727 573-2211
12200 32nd Ct N Saint Petersburg (33716) *(G-15057)*
GA Fd Svcs Pinellas Cnty LLC ... 954 972-8884
1750 W Mcnab Rd Fort Lauderdale (33309) *(G-3835)*
GA Fd Svcs Pinellas Cnty LLC ... 239 693-5090
5501 Division Dr Fort Myers (33905) *(G-4268)*
Ga-MA & Associates Inc (PA) ... 352 687-8840
404 Cypress Rd Ocala (34472) *(G-11398)*
Gaab Locks LLC ... 305 788-8515
21014 Sheridan St Fort Lauderdale (33332) *(G-3836)*
Gable Enterprises ... 727 455-5576
1008 Lenna Ave Seffner (33584) *(G-15959)*
Gables Engineering Inc ... 305 774-4400
247 Greco Ave Coral Gables (33146) *(G-2058)*
Gabol Screen Printing Co ... 305 681-3882
12815 Nw 45th Ave Opa Locka (33054) *(G-11750)*
Gabrielas Memoirs Inc ... 305 666-9991
5750 Sw 45th Ter Miami (33155) *(G-9183)*
Gadal Laboratories Inc ... 786 732-2571
12178 Sw 128th St Miami (33186) *(G-9184)*
Gadgetcat LLC ... 802 238-3671
465 North Shore Dr Cocoa Beach (32931) *(G-1971)*
Gadsden County Shopping Guide, Quincy *Also called Gadsden County Times Inc (G-14545)*
Gadsden County Times Inc ... 850 627-7649
9 W King St Quincy (32351) *(G-14545)*
Gaemmerler (us) Corporation ... 941 465-4400
2906 Corporate Way Palmetto (34221) *(G-13168)*
GAF Materials, Tampa *Also called Standard Industries Inc (G-17298)*
Gain Solar LLC ... 305 933-1060
18205 Biscayne Blvd Aventura (33160) *(G-260)*
Gainesville ... 352 339-0294
8039 Sw 67th Rd Gainesville (32608) *(G-4697)*

Gainesville Ice Company 352 378-2604
508 Se 11th Ave Gainesville (32601) *(G-4698)*
Gainesville Iron Works Inc 352 373-4004
2341 Nw 66th Ct Gainesville (32653) *(G-4699)*
Gainesville Ironworks, Gainesville *Also called Gainesville Iron Works Inc (G-4699)*
Gainesville Sun 352 374-5000
2700 Sw 13th St Gainesville (32608) *(G-4700)*
Gainesville Sun Publishing Co (HQ) 352 378-1411
2700 Sw 13th St Gainesville (32608) *(G-4701)*
Gainesville Wldg & Fabrication 352 373-0384
2327 Ne 19th Dr Gainesville (32609) *(G-4702)*
Gainesville/Ocala Business, Ocala *Also called Ocala Magazine (G-11454)*
Galactic News Service 239 431-7470
6809 Wellington Dr Naples (34109) *(G-10758)*
Galan Express Inc 305 438-8738
1150 Sw 154th Ave Miami (33194) *(G-9185)*
Galaxy America Inc 941 697-0324
7431 Sawyer Cir Port Charlotte (33981) *(G-14302)*
Galaxy Custom Granite Inc 352 220-2822
5388 E Jasmine Ln Inverness (34453) *(G-5828)*
Galaxy Medals Inc 321 269-0840
1125 White Dr Titusville (32780) *(G-17586)*
Galaxy Screenprinting Inc 407 862-2224
925 Sunshine Ln Altamonte Springs (32714) *(G-49)*
Galea Corporation 305 663-0244
4679 Sw 72nd Ave Miami (33155) *(G-9186)*
Galileo, Homestead *Also called Discipline Marketing Inc (G-5708)*
Galix Bmedical Instrumentation 305 534-5905
8205 Nw 30th Ter Doral (33122) *(G-3223)*
Gallant Inc 800 330-1343
1267 Wntr Gdn Vnlnd Rd # 230 Winter Garden (34787) *(G-18387)*
Galleon Decals & Die Cuts, Altamonte Springs *Also called Galleon Industries Inc (G-50)*
Galleon Industries Inc 708 478-5444
279 Douglas Ave Ste 1112 Altamonte Springs (32714) *(G-50)*
Gallery Industries, Hollywood *Also called Stanley Industries of S Fla (G-5664)*
Galletas La Unica, Miami *Also called Star Bakery Inc (G-9946)*
Galletas Yeya, Miami *Also called Tuly Corporation (G-10045)*
Galley Maid Marine Pdts Inc 863 467-6070
60 Ne 110th St Okeechobee (34972) *(G-11605)*
Gallop Group Inc 813 251-6242
2402 S Ardson Pl Tampa (33629) *(G-16868)*
Galtronics Telemetry Inc 386 202-2055
1 Hargrove Grade Ste 5 Palm Coast (32137) *(G-13078)*
Gam Laser Inc (PA) 407 851-8999
7100 Tpc Dr Ste 200 Orlando (32822) *(G-12181)*
Gama TEC Corporation 305 362-0456
2208 W 79th St Hialeah (33016) *(G-5165)*
Gambler Bass Boats, Groveland *Also called Maritec Industries Inc (G-4866)*
Game Fisherman Inc 772 220-4850
1384 Nw Coconut Point Ln Stuart (34994) *(G-16151)*
Gamma Insulators Corp (PA) 585 302-0878
2121 Ponce De Leon Blvd Coral Gables (33134) *(G-2059)*
Gammerler US, Bradenton *Also called Gammerlertech Corporation (G-981)*
Gammerlertech Corporation 941 803-0150
3135 Lakewood Ranch Blvd # 107 Bradenton (34211) *(G-981)*
Gand Inc 240 575-0622
1000 5th St Ste 200 Miami Beach (33139) *(G-10193)*
Gandy Printers Inc 850 222-5847
1800 S Monroe St Tallahassee (32301) *(G-16444)*
Gannet Technologies LLC 941 870-3444
7135 16th St E Ste 115 Sarasota (34243) *(G-15480)*
Gap Antenna Products Inc 772 571-9922
99 N Willow St Fellsmere (32948) *(G-3577)*
GAp Imaging Intl LLC 407 268-9746
2558 Dwyer Ln Lake Mary (32746) *(G-7081)*
Gapv 786 257-1681
7800 Sw 57th Ave Ste 219c South Miami (33143) *(G-16034)*
Gar Business Group LLC 321 632-5133
386 Commerce Pkwy Rockledge (32955) *(G-14710)*
Gar Industries Corp 954 456-8088
10426 Bermuda Dr Hollywood (33026) *(G-5581)*
Gar International 954 704-9590
3315 Commerce Pkwy Miramar (33025) *(G-10495)*
Gar-P Industries Inc 305 888-7252
10890 Nw South River Dr Medley (33178) *(G-8245)*
Garbo Sport International Inc 305 599-8797
11231 Nw 20th St Unit 122 Miami (33172) *(G-9187)*
Garcia Custom Cabinetry 864 420-3882
1000 Nw 1st Ave Miami (33136) *(G-9188)*
Garcia Deluxe Services Corp 786 291-4329
1240 W 34th St Hialeah (33012) *(G-5166)*
Garcia Door & Window Inc 305 635-0644
2787 Nw 34th St Miami (33142) *(G-9189)*
Garcia Iron Works 305 888-0080
365 W 21st St Hialeah (33010) *(G-5167)*
Garcia Mining Company LLC (PA) 863 902-9777
6605 Garcia Dr Clewiston (33440) *(G-1890)*
Garcia Woodwork Entps Inc 954 226-3906
1961 Nw 29th St Oakland Park (33311) *(G-11268)*
Garco Manufacturing Co Inc 321 868-3778
1400 S Orlando Ave Cocoa Beach (32931) *(G-1972)*
Gardber-Gibson, Tampa *Also called Gardner Asphalt Corporation (G-16870)*
Gardner Asphalt Corporation (HQ) 813 248-2101
4161 E 7th Ave Tampa (33605) *(G-16869)*
Gardner Asphalt Corporation 813 248-2101
4001 E 7th Ave Tampa (33605) *(G-16870)*
Gardner-Gibson Mfg Inc (HQ) 813 248-2101
4161 E 7th Ave Tampa (33605) *(G-16871)*
Gardner-Watson Decking Inc 813 891-9849
305 Scarlet Blvd Ste A Oldsmar (34677) *(G-11650)*
Gardners Screen Enclosures 813 843-8527
1113 Lake Shore Ranch Dr Seffner (33584) *(G-15960)*
Garelick Mfg Co 727 545-4571
7151 114th Ave Largo (33773) *(G-7591)*
Garlington Landeweer Mar Inc 772 283-7124
3370 Se Slater St Stuart (34997) *(G-16152)*
Garment Corporation of America 305 531-4040
801 Arthur Godfrey Rd # 3 Miami Beach (33140) *(G-10194)*
Garment Gear Inc 850 215-2121
1522 Degama Ave Panama City (32405) *(G-13266)*
Garmin International Inc 305 674-7701
513 Lincoln Rd Miami Beach (33139) *(G-10195)*
Garrett Tin & Brother Inc 727 236-5434
2536 Palesta Dr Trinity (34655) *(G-17637)*
Garrison Lickle Aircraft 561 833-7111
400 S Ocean Blvd Ofc Palm Beach (33480) *(G-12935)*
Garvin Management Company Inc (PA) 850 893-4719
4042 Sawgrass Cir Tallahassee (32309) *(G-16445)*
Garware Fulflex USA Inc (PA) 305 436-8915
1695 Nw 110th Ave Ste 301 Miami (33172) *(G-9190)*
Gas Light Services Inc 941 232-8668
4545 Mariotti Ct Unit L Sarasota (34233) *(G-15689)*
Gas Turbine Efficiency Inc 407 304-5200
300 Sunport Ln Ste 100 Orlando (32809) *(G-12182)*
Gas Turbine Efficiency LLC 407 304-5200
300 Sunport Ln Ste 100 Orlando (32809) *(G-12183)*
Gas Turbine Support Inc 786 242-4513
13901 Sw 119th Ave Miami (33186) *(G-9191)*
Gaseous Fuel Systems Corp 954 693-9475
3360 Entp Ave Ste 180 Weston (33331) *(G-18246)*
Gaspari Nutrition, Palmetto *Also called Allegro Nutrition Inc (G-13153)*
Gatchell Violins Company Inc 321 733-1499
1377 W New Haven Ave West Melbourne (32904) *(G-17900)*
Gate Access Systems, Jacksonville *Also called Edwards Ornamental Iron Inc (G-6066)*
Gate Cfv Solutions Inc 772 388-3387
100 Sebastian Indus Pl Sebastian (32958) *(G-15893)*
Gate Petroleum Company 904 998-7126
11040 Mccormick Rd Jacksonville (32225) *(G-6127)*
Gate Petroleum Company 904 396-0517
4100 Heckscher Dr Jacksonville (32226) *(G-6128)*
Gate Precast Company 904 520-5795
402 Zoo Pkwy Jacksonville (32226) *(G-6129)*
Gate Precast Company (HQ) 904 732-7668
9540 San Jose Blvd Jacksonville (32257) *(G-6130)*
Gate Precast Company 407 847-5285
1018 Sawdust Trl Kissimmee (34744) *(G-6923)*
Gate Precast Concrete, Kissimmee *Also called Gate Precast Company (G-6923)*
Gate Precast Erection Co 904 737-7220
9540 San Jose Blvd Jacksonville (32257) *(G-6131)*
Gatecrafterscom 800 537-4283
13100 State Road 54 Odessa (33556) *(G-11553)*
Gatehouse Media LLC 863 401-6900
455 6th St Nw Winter Haven (33881) *(G-18442)*
Gaterman Products LLC 386 253-1899
114 Meadowbrook Cir Daytona Beach (32114) *(G-2555)*
Gates Corporation 954 926-7823
15751 Sw 41st St Ste 100 Davie (33331) *(G-2417)*
Gateway Wreless Communications 561 732-6444
3600 S Congress Ave Boynton Beach (33426) *(G-870)*
Gator Dock & Marine LLC 407 323-0190
2880 S Mellonville Ave Sanford (32773) *(G-15324)*
Gator Door East Inc 904 824-2827
2150 Dobbs Rd Saint Augustine (32086) *(G-14835)*
Gator Drain Cleaning Equipment 954 584-4441
5411 Orange Dr Davie (33314) *(G-2418)*
Gator Fabrications LLC 352 245-7227
3450 Se 132nd Ln Belleview (34420) *(G-361)*
Gator Feed Co Inc 863 763-3337
1205 Us Highway 98 N Okeechobee (34972) *(G-11606)*
Gator Freds, Wesley Chapel *Also called Transport PC USA Inc (G-17888)*
Gator Polymers LLC 866 292-7306
3302 Se 22nd Ave Cape Coral (33904) *(G-1346)*
Gator Shack 863 381-2222
4651 Us Highway 98 Sebring (33876) *(G-15924)*
Gator Stampings Intl Inc 941 753-9598
6610 33rd St E Sarasota (34243) *(G-15481)*
Gator Telecom, Pompano Beach *Also called Devcon Security Services Corp (G-13993)*
Gator Welding Inc 561 746-0049
4597 Se Marie Way Stuart (34997) *(G-16153)*

ALPHABETIC

Gatsby Spas Inc 813 754-4122
  4408 Airport Rd Plant City (33563) *(G-13770)*

Gattas Corp 727 733-5886
  745 Main St Ste B Dunedin (34698) *(G-3449)*

Gattas Marine Services, Dunedin *Also called Gattas Corp (G-3449)*

Gatto Furniture, Fort Lauderdale *Also called Broward Casting Foundry Inc (G-3704)*

Gaukaupa Raceway 904 483-3473
  8405 Beach Blvd Jacksonville (32216) *(G-6132)*

Gaumard Scientific Company Inc 305 971-3790
  14700 Sw 136th St Miami (33196) *(G-9192)*

Gause Built Marine Inc 727 937-9113
  728 Wesley Ave Ste 10 Tarpon Springs (34689) *(G-17473)*

Gautier Fabrication Inc 941 485-2464
  1049 Endeavor Ct North Venice (34275) *(G-11212)*

Gaynor Group Inc 954 749-1228
  5030 N Hiatus Rd Sunrise (33351) *(G-16320)*

Gb Airlink Inc 561 593-7284
  2524 Se Wtham Feld Dr Uni Stuart (34996) *(G-16154)*

Gb Brick Pavers Inc 407 453-5505
  4409 S Kirkman Rd Apt 303 Orlando (32811) *(G-12184)*

Gb Cabinets Incorporated 863 446-0676
  3907 Palazzo St Sebring (33872) *(G-15925)*

Gb Energy Management LLC 305 792-4650
  2875 Ne 191st St Ste 901 Miami (33180) *(G-9193)*

Gb Energy Tech 561 450-6047
  2875 S Congress Ave Ste B Delray Beach (33445) *(G-2967)*

Gb Printing 954 941-3778
  414 E Sample Rd Pompano Beach (33064) *(G-14037)*

Gbc By Glen Bergquist LLC 352 348-7957
  2101 Edgewood Ave Leesburg (34748) *(G-7778)*

Gbc Interiors LLC 386 624-8294
  958 Roberts Blvd Deltona (32725) *(G-3045)*

Gbc Solutions LLC 904 705-2415
  6982 Roundleaf Dr Jacksonville (32258) *(G-6133)*

Gbi Intralogistics Solutions 954 596-5000
  1143 W Newport Center Dr Deerfield Beach (33442) *(G-2724)*

GBIG Corporation 866 998-8466
  8744 Sw 133rd St Miami (33176) *(G-9194)*

GBS, Pembroke Pines *Also called Gypsum Bd Specialists USA Corp (G-13394)*

Gc Cabinet Express Inc 561 662-0369
  1335 Old Dixie Hwy # 20 Lake Park (33403) *(G-7128)*

Gcato 1959 Enterprises LLC 954 937-6282
  2750 Nw 11th St Pompano Beach (33069) *(G-14038)*

Gce, Clearwater *Also called Skinny Mixes LLC (G-1785)*

Gcn Media Services, Pompano Beach *Also called Gcn Publishing Inc (G-14039)*

Gcn Publishing Inc 203 665-6211
  49 N Federal Hwy 338 Pompano Beach (33062) *(G-14039)*

Gdp Consulting Inc (PA) 561 401-9195
  15074 Park Of Commerce Bl Jupiter (33478) *(G-6733)*

GE 904 570-3151
  12079 Normandy Blvd Jacksonville (32221) *(G-6134)*

GE Aviation Systems LLC 727 532-6370
  14100 Roosevelt Blvd Clearwater (33762) *(G-1609)*

GE Aviation Systems LLC 727 531-7781
  14200 Roosevelt Blvd Clearwater (33762) *(G-1610)*

GE Aviation Systems LLC 727 539-1631
  14200 Roosevelt Blvd Clearwater (33762) *(G-1611)*

GE Consumer Corporation 904 696-9775
  600 Whittaker Rd Jacksonville (32218) *(G-6135)*

GE Consumer Distribution, Jacksonville *Also called GE Consumer Corporation (G-6135)*

GE Glass Inc 305 599-7725
  4455 Nw 73rd Ave Miami (33166) *(G-9195)*

GE Medcal Systems Info Tech In 561 575-5000
  100 Marquette Dr Jupiter (33458) *(G-6734)*

GE Renewables North Amer LLC (HQ) 850 474-4011
  8301 Scenic Hwy Pensacola (32514) *(G-13512)*

Gear Dynamics Inc 305 691-0151
  3685 Nw 106th St Miami (33147) *(G-9196)*

Geat Lakes Water Cond Systems, Naples *Also called Great Lakes Wtr Trtmnt Systems (G-10766)*

Geddis Inc 800 844-6792
  2221 Paddock Cir Dunedin (34698) *(G-3450)*

Geekshive Inc 888 797-4335
  9100 S Ddland Blvd Ste 15 Miami (33156) *(G-9197)*

Geiger Logging Inc 904 845-7534
  28714 Yellow Rose Ln Hilliard (32046) *(G-5464)*

Gelander Industries Inc 352 343-3100
  611 Southridge Indl Dr Tavares (32778) *(G-17508)*

Gelateria Milani LLC 305 532-8562
  436 Espanola Way Miami Beach (33139) *(G-10196)*

Gelato Petrini LLC 561 600-4088
  1205 Sw 4th Ave Delray Beach (33444) *(G-2968)*

Geltech Inc 407 382-4003
  2603 Challenger Tech Ct # 100 Orlando (32826) *(G-12185)*

Geltech Solutions Inc 561 427-6144
  1460 Park Ln S Ste 1 Jupiter (33458) *(G-6735)*

Gem Aerospace 786 464-5900
  10300 Nw 19th St Doral (33172) *(G-3224)*

Gem Asset Acquisition LLC 904 268-6063
  9556 Historic Kings Rd S Jacksonville (32257) *(G-6136)*

Gem Asset Acquisition LLC 407 888-2080
  6441 Pinecastle Blvd Orlando (32809) *(G-12186)*

Gem Asset Acquisition LLC 813 630-1695
  5050 Denver St Tampa (33619) *(G-16872)*

Gem Freshco LLC 772 595-0070
  3586 Oleander Ave Fort Pierce (34982) *(G-4489)*

Gem Inc of Capri, Naples *Also called Gem Remotes Inc (G-10759)*

Gem Industries, Sunrise *Also called Gaynor Group Inc (G-16320)*

Gem Industries Inc 321 302-8985
  370 Cox Rd Cocoa (32926) *(G-1933)*

Gem Paver Systems Inc (PA) 305 805-0000
  9845 Nw 118th Way Medley (33178) *(G-8246)*

Gem Remotes Inc 239 642-0873
  3527 Plover Ave Unit 2 Naples (34117) *(G-10759)*

Gemini Group USA Inc 305 338-1066
  16371 Sw 56th Ter Miami (33193) *(G-9198)*

Gemco Division, Palm Beach Gardens *Also called Chromalloy Gas Turbine LLC (G-12959)*

Gemseal Pavement Products 305 328-9159
  5050 Denver St Tampa (33619) *(G-16873)*

Gemseal Pavements Pdts - Tampa, Tampa *Also called Gem Asset Acquisition LLC (G-16872)*

Gemseal Pvments Pdts - Jackson, Jacksonville *Also called Gem Asset Acquisition LLC (G-6136)*

Gemseal Pvments Pdts - Orlando, Orlando *Also called Gem Asset Acquisition LLC (G-12186)*

Gemstone Cabinetry LLC 941 426-5656
  2845 Commerce Pkwy North Port (34289) *(G-11194)*

Gen-Prodics Inc 772 221-8464
  2029 Sw Oak Ridge Rd Palm City (34990) *(G-13041)*

Genca Corp 727 524-3622
  13805 58th St N Clearwater (33760) *(G-1612)*

Gencor Industries Inc (PA) 407 290-6000
  5201 N Orange Blossom Trl Orlando (32810) *(G-12187)*

Genecell International LLC 305 382-6737
  2664 Nw 97th Ave Doral (33172) *(G-3225)*

Genel/Landec Inc 305 591-9990
  10845 Nw 29th St Doral (33172) *(G-3226)*

Genensys LLC 407 701-4158
  7269 Winding Lake Cir Oviedo (32765) *(G-12823)*

General & Duplicating Services 305 541-2116
  3150 Ponce De Leon Blvd Coral Gables (33134) *(G-2060)*

General Asphalt Co Inc 305 592-6005
  4850 Nw 72nd Ave Miami (33166) *(G-9199)*

General Business Services 904 260-1099
  12412 San Jose Blvd # 101 Jacksonville (32223) *(G-6137)*

General Cabinets Inc 727 863-3404
  15801 Archer St Port Richey (34667) *(G-14361)*

General Cabinets Pasco County, Hudson *Also called Dons Cabinets and Woodworking (G-5771)*

General Capacitor LLC 510 371-2700
  132-1 Hamilton Park Dr Tallahassee (32304) *(G-16446)*

General Clamp Industries Inc 407 859-6000
  1155 Central Florida Pkwy Orlando (32837) *(G-12188)*

General Defense Corporation 954 444-0155
  4960 Sw 52nd St Ste 413 Davie (33314) *(G-2419)*

General Dynamics Corporation 407 380-9384
  3275 Progress Dr Orlando (32826) *(G-12189)*

General Dynamics Corporation 850 897-9700
  115 Hart St Niceville (32578) *(G-11030)*

General Dynamics-Ots Inc (HQ) 727 578-8100
  100 Carillon Pkwy Ste 100 # 100 Saint Petersburg (33716) *(G-15058)*

General Dynmics Land Systems I 850 574-4700
  2930 Commonwealth Blvd Tallahassee (32303) *(G-16447)*

General Dynmics Mssion Systems 407 823-7000
  12001 Res Pkwy Ste 500 Orlando (32826) *(G-12190)*

General Dynmics Nassco Mayport, Jacksonville *Also called Metro Machine Corp (G-6302)*

General Dynmics Ord Tctcal Sys 727 578-8243
  3340 Scherer Dr N Ste E Saint Petersburg (33716) *(G-15059)*

General Dynmics Ord Tctcal Sys (HQ) 727 578-8100
  100 Carillon Pkwy Saint Petersburg (33716) *(G-15060)*

General Electric Company 203 796-1000
  12854 Kenan Dr Ste 201 Jacksonville (32258) *(G-6138)*

General Floors, Doral *Also called Genfloor LLC (G-3230)*

General Hydraulic Solutions Inc 727 561-0719
  10601 47th St N Clearwater (33762) *(G-1613)*

General Impact GL Windows Corp 305 558-8103
  290 W 78th Rd Hialeah (33014) *(G-5168)*

General Machine Company Inc 941 756-2815
  5207 Malaga Ave Sarasota (34235) *(G-15690)*

General Metal Intl Inc 305 628-2052
  13580 Sw 51st St Miramar (33027) *(G-10496)*

General Metals & Plastics Inc 904 354-8224
  2727 Waller St Jacksonville (32205) *(G-6139)*

General Mills Inc 305 591-1771
  8400 Nw 36th St Ste 310 Doral (33166) *(G-3227)*

General Mro Aerospace Inc 305 482-9903
  10990 Nw 92nd Ter Medley (33178) *(G-8247)*

General Oceanics Inc 305 621-2882
  1295 Nw 163rd St Miami (33169) *(G-9200)*

General Pillows & Fiber Inc 305 884-8300
605 W 17th St Hialeah (33010) *(G-5169)*
General Pneumatics Inflation 941 216-3500
2236 72nd Ave E Sarasota (34243) *(G-15482)*
General Power Limited Inc 800 763-0359
9930 Nw 21st St Fl 1 Doral (33172) *(G-3228)*
General Rubber Corporation 941 412-0001
405 Commercial Ct Ste C Venice (34292) *(G-17693)*
General Saw Company 813 231-3167
2902 E Sligh Ave Tampa (33610) *(G-16874)*
General Screen Service Co 305 226-0741
5033 Sw 151st Pl Miami (33185) *(G-9201)*
General Sign, Miami Also called C L F Enterprises *(G-8870)*
General Sign Service Inc 904 355-5630
1940 Spearing St Jacksonville (32206) *(G-6140)*
General Signs and Service Inc 904 372-4238
20 Donner Rd Atlantic Beach (32233) *(G-209)*
General Stair Corporation 305 769-9900
690 W 83rd St Hialeah (33014) *(G-5170)*
General Welding Svc Entps Inc 305 592-9483
8115 Nw 56th St Doral (33166) *(G-3229)*
Generations Metier Inc 239 458-8127
883 Ne 27th Ln Cape Coral (33909) *(G-1347)*
Generex Laboratories LLC 239 592-7255
1915 Trade Center Way Naples (34109) *(G-10760)*
Generex Labs, Naples Also called Generex Laboratories LLC *(G-10760)*
Genesis Caribbean Cuisine LLC 718 503-4308
304 E Pine St Lakeland (33801) *(G-7334)*
Genesis Electric Motors Inc 727 572-1414
6330 118th Ave Unit A Largo (33773) *(G-7592)*
Genesis Health Institute Inc 954 561-3175
1001 Ne 26th St Wilton Manors (33305) *(G-18340)*
Genesis II Systems Inc 954 489-1124
2425 E Coml Blvd Ste 101 Fort Lauderdale (33308) *(G-3837)*
Genesis Reference Laboratories 407 232-7130
7924 Forest Cy Rd Ste 210 Orlando (32810) *(G-12191)*
Genesis Systems LLC 417 499-3301
3108 N Boundary Blvd # 9 Tampa (33621) *(G-16875)*
Genesys Band 347 701-5670
2036 Torrey Dr Orlando (32818) *(G-12192)*
Geneva Foods LLC (PA) 407 302-4751
2664 Jewett Ln Sanford (32771) *(G-15325)*
Geneva Systems Inc 352 235-2990
712 Simmons Trl Green Cove Springs (32043) *(G-4826)*
Genfloor LLC 305 477-1557
6312 Nw 99th Ave Doral (33178) *(G-3230)*
Genh2 Inc 321 223-5950
1325 White Dr Titusville (32780) *(G-17587)*
Genh2 Corp 530 654-3642
1325 White Dr Titusville (32780) *(G-17588)*
Genicon Inc 407 657-4851
2455 Ridgemoor Dr Orlando (32828) *(G-12193)*
Genie Cap Inc 941 355-5730
4410 Independence Ct Sarasota (34234) *(G-15691)*
Genie Publishing 863 937-7769
5111 Fernbrook Ln Lakeland (33811) *(G-7335)*
Genie Shelf 305 213-4382
10935 Sw 138th Ct Miami (33186) *(G-9202)*
Genius Central Systems Inc 800 360-2231
2025 Lakewood Ranch Blvd # 202 Bradenton (34211) *(G-982)*
Genos Construction Inc 234 303-3427
12421 Us Highway 301 # 228 Dade City (33525) *(G-2318)*
Genpak LLC 863 243-1068
55 Pine Ridge Dr Lake Placid (33852) *(G-7140)*
Gensco Laboratories LLC 754 263-2898
8550 Nw 33rd St Ste 200 Doral (33122) *(G-3231)*
Gensco Pharma, Doral Also called Gensco Laboratories LLC *(G-3231)*
Genteel Coatings LLC 772 708-1781
10151 Se 195th St Inglis (34449) *(G-5817)*
Gentry Printing Company LLC 727 441-1914
2070 Gentry St Clearwater (33765) *(G-1614)*
Genuine Ad Inc 786 399-6484
17600 N Bay Rd Apt 406 Sunny Isles Beach (33160) *(G-16275)*
Genuine Denim 305 491-1326
851 Ne 182nd Ter North Miami Beach (33162) *(G-11142)*
Genzyme Corporation 800 245-4363
1031 Ives Dairy Rd # 228 Miami (33179) *(G-9203)*
Genzyme Genetics, Miami Also called Genzyme Corporation *(G-9203)*
Geo Environmental, Miami Also called General Oceanics Inc *(G-9200)*
Geocommand Inc 561 347-9215
3700 Airport Rd Ste 410 Boca Raton (33431) *(G-526)*
Geodetic Services Inc 321 724-6831
1511 Riverview Dr Melbourne (32901) *(G-8428)*
Geonova Gaming LLC 908 414-5874
2989 Siesta View Dr Kissimmee (34744) *(G-6924)*
Georg Fischer LLC (HQ) 305 418-9150
10540 Nw 26th St Doral (33172) *(G-3232)*
George & Company LLC 239 949-3650
28771 S Diesel Dr Ste 3 Bonita Springs (34135) *(G-800)*

George Birney Jr 407 851-5604
6714 Bouganvillea Cres Dr Orlando (32809) *(G-12194)*
George Gillespie LLC 561 744-6191
15611 78th Dr N West Palm Beach (33418) *(G-18015)*
George Wash Cpitl Partners LLC (PA) 786 910-1778
1022 E Newport Center Dr Deerfield Beach (33442) *(G-2725)*
George's Metal Fab, Medley Also called Georges Welding Services Inc *(G-8248)*
Georges Welding Services Inc 305 822-2445
11400 Nw 134th St Medley (33178) *(G-8248)*
Georgesoft Inc 850 329-5517
207 W Park Ave Ste B Tallahassee (32301) *(G-16448)*
Georgia Mktg & Sign Co LLC 800 286-8671
2121 Vista Pkwy West Palm Beach (33411) *(G-18016)*
Georgia-Florida Bark and Mulch, Monticello Also called Randy Wheeler *(G-10585)*
Georgia-Pacific LLC 850 584-1121
1 Buckeye Dr Perry (32348) *(G-13639)*
Georgia-Pacific LLC 386 328-8826
155 Country Ct Palatka (32177) *(G-12869)*
Georgia-Pacific LLC 850 379-4000
12995 Ne State Road 65 Hosford (32334) *(G-5756)*
Georgia-Pacific LLC 386 328-8826
County Rd 216 E Palatka (32177) *(G-12870)*
Georgia-Pacific LLC 404 652-4000
5240 Ne 64th Ave Silver Springs (34488) *(G-16006)*
Georgian American Alloys Inc (PA) 305 375-7560
200 Suth Bscyne Blvd Ste Miami (33131) *(G-9204)*
Geotechnical & Materials Inc 813 814-0671
530 Lafayette Blvd Oldsmar (34677) *(G-11651)*
Gerber Coburn Optical Inc 305 592-4705
2585 Nw 74th Ave Miami (33122) *(G-9205)*
Gerdau Ameristeel, Tampa Also called Sheffield Steel Corporation *(G-17258)*
Gerdau Ameristeel Corp (HQ) 813 286-8383
4221 W Boy Scout Blvd # 600 Tampa (33607) *(G-16876)*
Gerdau Ameristeel US Inc (HQ) 813 286-8383
4221 W Boy Scout Blvd # 600 Tampa (33607) *(G-16877)*
Gerdau Ameristeel US Inc 813 752-7550
4006 Paul Buchman Hwy Plant City (33565) *(G-13771)*
Gerdau Ameristeel US Inc 813 752-7550
2100 Joe Mcintosh Rd Plant City (33565) *(G-13772)*
Gerdau Long Steel America, Tampa Also called Gerdau USA Inc *(G-16878)*
Gerdau Long Steel North Amer, Tampa Also called Gerdau Ameristeel US Inc *(G-16877)*
Gerdau USA Inc (HQ) 813 286-8383
4221 W Boy Scout Blvd Tampa (33607) *(G-16878)*
Germain Awning Center, Miami Also called Germain Canvas & Awning Co *(G-9206)*
Germain Canvas & Awning Co 305 751-4963
921 Belle Meade Island Dr Miami (33138) *(G-9206)*
Germfree Laboratories Inc 386 265-4300
4 Sunshine Blvd Ormond Beach (32174) *(G-12766)*
Germkleen LLC 954 947-5602
1160 N Federal Hwy # 916 Fort Lauderdale (33304) *(G-3838)*
Gerogari Dsplay Mnfacture Corp 305 888-0993
5517 Nw 72nd Ave Miami (33166) *(G-9207)*
Gesco Ice Cream Vending Corp (PA) 718 782-3232
17555 Collins Ave # 2903 Sunny Isles Beach (33160) *(G-16276)*
Gess Technologies LLC 305 231-6322
7292 W 20th Ave Hialeah (33016) *(G-5171)*
Get Hams Inc 850 386-7123
3396 Lakeshore Dr Tallahassee (32312) *(G-16449)*
Getabstract Inc 305 936-2626
20900 Ne 30th Ave Ste 315 Miami (33180) *(G-9208)*
Getfpv LLC 941 444-0021
1060 Goodrich Ave Sarasota (34236) *(G-15692)*
Getitcleaned 239 331-2891
3520 6th Ave Ne Naples (34120) *(G-10761)*
Gevas Pckg Converting Tech Ltd 561 202-0800
3553 High Ridge Rd Boynton Beach (33426) *(G-871)*
Gex, Palm City Also called Intelligent Operating Tech Inc *(G-13045)*
Gexa Energy California LLC 561 691-7171
700 Universe Blvd Juno Beach (33408) *(G-6664)*
GF & Associate Group LLC 954 593-4788
7750 Okeechobee Blvd West Palm Beach (33411) *(G-18017)*
GF Piping Systems, Doral Also called Georg Fischer LLC *(G-3232)*
GF Woodworks 407 716-3712
1306 Pressview Ave Altamonte Springs (32701) *(G-51)*
Gfoodz LLC 561 703-4505
10356 Willow Oaks Trl Boynton Beach (33473) *(G-872)*
GFS, Weston Also called Gaseous Fuel Systems Corp *(G-18246)*
Gfs Corp 954 693-9657
3360 Entp Ave Ste 180 Weston (33331) *(G-18247)*
Gfsf Inc 727 478-7284
2404 Merchant Ave Odessa (33556) *(G-11554)*
Gfx Inc (PA) 305 499-9789
4810 Nw 74th Ave Miami (33166) *(G-9209)*
Gg Professional Painting Corp 786 716-8972
2001 Ludlam Rd Apt 317 Miami (33155) *(G-9210)*
Ggb1 LLC 305 387-5334
9828 Sw 146th Pl Miami (33186) *(G-9211)*
Ggs Snacks & Things Inc 954 297-9375
10010 Sw 11th St Pembroke Pines (33025) *(G-13390)*

Ghx Industrial LLC 305 620-4313
1001 Nw 159th Dr Miami (33169) *(G-9212)*

Ghx Industrial LLC 813 223-7554
1103 N 50th St Tampa (33619) *(G-16879)*

Ghx Industrial LLC 407 843-8190
4105 Seaboard Rd Orlando (32808) *(G-12195)*

GI, Gainesville *Also called Gainesville Ice Company (G-4698)*

Gibbons Industries Inc 352 330-0294
1927 Passero Ave Lutz (33559) *(G-7990)*

Gibson Wldg Shetmetal Vent Inc 850 837-6141
335 Mountain Dr Destin (32541) *(G-3067)*

Giebner Enterprises Inc 727 520-1200
4760 Brittany Dr S Apt 20 Saint Petersburg (33715) *(G-15061)*

Gifting Goodies, Jacksonville *Also called William Marie LLC (G-6612)*

Giggle Magazine, Gainesville *Also called Irving Publications LLC (G-4715)*

Gigli Enterprises Inc (PA) 850 871-4777
4833 E Business Hwy 98 Panama City (32404) *(G-13267)*

Gigliola Inc 954 564-7871
3341 E Oakland Park Blvd Fort Lauderdale (33308) *(G-3839)*

Gilbane Boatworks LLC 561 744-2223
19137 Se Federal Hwy # 1 Tequesta (33469) *(G-17550)*

Gilco Spring of Florida Inc 813 855-4631
3991 Tampa Rd Oldsmar (34677) *(G-11652)*

Gild Corporation 305 378-6982
15411 Sw 160th St Miami (33187) *(G-9213)*

Gilda Industries Inc 305 887-8286
2525 W 4th Ave Hialeah (33010) *(G-5172)*

Giliberti Inc 772 597-1870
16015 Sw Farm Rd Indiantown (34956) *(G-5813)*

Gill Manufacturing Inc 863 422-5711
110 S Hwy 17 92 Davenport (33837) *(G-2365)*

Gilla Inc (PA) 416 843-2881
475 Fentress Blvd Ste L Daytona Beach (32114) *(G-2556)*

Gillette Sign & Lighting Inc 352 256-2225
1609 Warbler St Zephyrhills (33540) *(G-18616)*

Gilman Building Products, Jacksonville *Also called Maxville LLC (G-6281)*

Gilman Building Products LLC 904 548-1000
581705 White Oak Rd Yulee (32097) *(G-18590)*

Gilman's Cabinets, Lecanto *Also called Gilmans Custom Furn & Cabinets (G-7752)*

Gilmans Custom Furn & Cabinets 352 746-3532
4625 W Homosassa Trl Lecanto (34461) *(G-7752)*

Gilson Inc 904 725-7612
730 Trinidad Rd Jacksonville (32216) *(G-6141)*

Gioia Sails South LLC 386 597-2876
14 Commerce Blvd Palm Coast (32164) *(G-13079)*

Giovanni Art In Cstm Furn Inc 954 698-1008
1478 Sw 1st Way Deerfield Beach (33441) *(G-2726)*

Giovannis Bakery Inc 727 536-2253
299 Keene Rd Largo (33771) *(G-7593)*

Giraldo & Donalisio Corp 239 567-2206
3909 Ne 19th Ave Cape Coral (33909) *(G-1348)*

Girgis Auto Brothers, Orlando *Also called Deluxe Cars LLC (G-12084)*

Givaudan Fragrances Corp 863 667-0821
4705 Us Highway 92 E Lakeland (33801) *(G-7336)*

Givaudan Roure Flavors, Lakeland *Also called Givaudan Fragrances Corp (G-7336)*

Givr Packaging LLC 321 345-6875
2428 Irwin St Melbourne (32901) *(G-8429)*

Giz Studio Inc 305 416-5001
601 Nw 11th St Miami (33136) *(G-9214)*

Gizmos Lion Sheet Metal Inc 561 684-8480
1648 Donna Rd West Palm Beach (33409) *(G-18018)*

Gj Francos Stair Co Inc 727 510-4102
1079 Woodbrook Dr S Largo (33770) *(G-7594)*

Gjcb Signs Graphics Inc 352 429-0803
136 S Main Ave Groveland (34736) *(G-4860)*

Gk Inc (PA) 215 223-7207
2724 Ne 35th Dr Fort Lauderdale (33308) *(G-3840)*

GK Hair, Fort Lauderdale *Also called Van Tibolli Beauty Corp (G-4116)*

GK Window Treatments Inc 954 786-2927
231 Sw 5th St Pompano Beach (33060) *(G-14040)*

GKN Aerospace Florida LLC 314 412-8311
6051 Ventr Crossings Blvd Panama City (32409) *(G-13268)*

Gkwf Inc 863 644-6925
520 W Brannen Rd Lakeland (33813) *(G-7337)*

Glades Formulating Corporation 561 996-4200
909 Nw 13th St Belle Glade (33430) *(G-341)*

Glades Sugar House, Belle Glade *Also called Sugar Cane Growers Coop Fla (G-343)*

Glamer Medspa LLC 305 744-6908
2114 N Flamingo Rd Pembroke Pines (33028) *(G-13391)*

Glamour Goddess Jewelry, Boca Raton *Also called Trine Industries Inc (G-724)*

Glasfloss Industries Inc 904 741-9922
1310 Tradeport Dr Jacksonville (32218) *(G-6142)*

Glaspro 941 488-4586
101 Pond Cypress Rd Venice (34292) *(G-17694)*

Glasrite Inc 863 967-8151
627 W Bridgers Ave Auburndale (33823) *(G-234)*

Glass Pros of Tampa, Tampa *Also called Johnson & Jackson GL Pdts Inc (G-16968)*

Glass Tech Corp 305 633-6491
3103 Nw 20th St Miami (33142) *(G-9215)*

Glass Works, Chuluota *Also called Jsl Enterprises of Orlando (G-1465)*

Glass Works of Largo Inc 727 535-9808
2020 Wild Acres Rd Unit D Largo (33771) *(G-7595)*

Glassarium LLC 786 631-7080
444 Ne 30th St Unit 804 Miami (33137) *(G-9216)*

Glasser Boat Works Inc 321 626-0061
1670 Barrett Dr Rockledge (32955) *(G-14711)*

Glassflake International Inc 904 268-4000
6525 Greenland Rd Jacksonville (32258) *(G-6143)*

Glasslam, Pompano Beach *Also called Nebula Glass International Inc (G-14107)*

GLC 3 & Rental Corp 954 916-1551
11490 Nw 20th Ct Plantation (33323) *(G-13855)*

GLC 3 Concrete, Plantation *Also called GLC 3 & Rental Corp (G-13855)*

Gle Holdings Inc 305 295-7585
3255 Flagler Ave Ste 301 Key West (33040) *(G-6865)*

Gleim Publications Inc 352 375-0772
4201 Nw 95th Blvd Gainesville (32606) *(G-4703)*

Gleman Sons Cstm Woodworks LLC 407 314-9638
110 Tech Dr Sanford (32771) *(G-15326)*

Glennmar Supply LLC 727 536-1955
6265 118th Ave Largo (33773) *(G-7596)*

Glenny Stone Works Inc 786 502-3918
3000 Nw 77th Ct Doral (33122) *(G-3233)*

Glenroe Technologies Inc 941 554-5262
7290 26th Ct E Sarasota (34243) *(G-15483)*

Glidden Professional Paint Ctr, Tampa *Also called PPG Architectural Finishes Inc (G-17171)*

Glider Printing LLC 813 601-8907
13377 W Hillsborough Ave Uni Tampa (33635) *(G-16880)*

GLM Publishing LLC 561 409-7696
2165 Nw 30th Rd Boca Raton (33431) *(G-527)*

GLo Consumer Svcs & Prtg Co 954 977-5450
6223 Nw 15th Ct Margate (33063) *(G-8131)*

Global Agriculture Tech Engrg, Sebastian *Also called Gate Cfv Solutions Inc (G-15893)*

Global Aliment Inc 786 536-5261
7791 Nw 46th St Ste 308 Doral (33166) *(G-3234)*

Global Bamboo Technologies Inc 707 730-0288
310 Cypress Rd Ocala (34472) *(G-11399)*

Global Biometric, Tampa *Also called Secure Biometric Corporation (G-17249)*

Global Cabinet Distributors 305 625-9814
16355 Nw 48th Ave Miami Lakes (33014) *(G-10305)*

Global Composite USA Inc 813 898-7987
6608 S West Shore Blvd Tampa (33616) *(G-16881)*

Global Directories Inc 954 571-8283
450 Fairway Dr Ste 204 Deerfield Beach (33441) *(G-2727)*

Global Diversified Products 727 209-0854
5195 102nd Ave N Pinellas Park (33782) *(G-13690)*

Global Equipment & Mfg LLC 800 436-1932
7650 Nw 50th St Miami (33166) *(G-9217)*

Global Force Enterprises LLC 786 317-8197
2331 W Lake Miramar Cir Miramar (33025) *(G-10497)*

Global Friction Products Inc 813 241-2700
2003 S 50th St Tampa (33619) *(G-16882)*

Global Galan Logistics Inc 754 263-2708
3132 Sw 173rd Ter Miramar (33029) *(G-10498)*

Global GI Lc 863 551-1079
343 Hamilton Shores Dr Ne Winter Haven (33881) *(G-18443)*

Global Holdings and Dev LLC 949 500-4997
3850 Oaks Clubhouse Dr Pompano Beach (33069) *(G-14041)*

Global Impressions Inc 727 531-1290
1299 Starkey Rd Ste 103 Largo (33771) *(G-7597)*

Global Intl Investments LLC 305 825-2288
6175 Nw 167th St Ste G32 Hialeah (33015) *(G-5173)*

Global Intrcnnect Slutions LLC 239 254-0326
4522 Executive Dr Ste 103 Naples (34119) *(G-10762)*

Global Life Technologies Corp 301 337-2059
300 Aragon Ave Ste 214 Coral Gables (33134) *(G-2061)*

Global Manufacturing Tech Inc 239 657-3720
160 Airpark Blvd Unit 101 Immokalee (34142) *(G-5796)*

Global Marketing Corp 973 426-1088
3752 Summerwind Cir Bradenton (34209) *(G-983)*

Global Materials Company 800 797-3736
2051 W Blue Heron Blvd Riviera Beach (33404) *(G-14625)*

Global Media Press Corp 813 857-5898
6723 N Armenia Ave Tampa (33604) *(G-16883)*

Global Mind USA LLC 305 402-2190
250 Nw 23rd St Unit 212 Miami (33127) *(G-9218)*

Global Ordnance LLC (PA) 941 549-8388
2150 Whitfield Ave Sarasota (34243) *(G-15484)*

Global Performance Windows Inc 954 942-3322
1881 Sw 3rd St Pompano Beach (33069) *(G-14042)*

Global Pharma Analytics LLC 701 491-7770
225 Chimney Corner Ln # 30 Jupiter (33458) *(G-6736)*

Global Porte 305 416-5001
601 Nw 11th St Miami (33136) *(G-9219)*

Global Prime Wood LLC 770 292-9200
2875 Ne 191st St Ste 500 Aventura (33180) *(G-261)*

Global Printing Services Inc 305 446-7628
3150 Ponce De Leon Blvd Coral Gables (33134) *(G-2062)*

Global Printing Solutions Inc 727 458-3483
2569 25th Ave N Saint Petersburg (33713) *(G-15062)*

Global Products Group LLC (PA) 866 320-4367
13760 Reptron Blvd Tampa (33626) (G-16884)

Global Publishing Inc 904 262-0491
9799 Old St Augustine Rd Jacksonville (32257) (G-6144)

Global Reach Rx Pbf LLC 786 703-1988
10560 Nw 27th St Ste 101a Doral (33172) (G-3235)

Global Recash LLC 818 297-4437
3191 Coral Way Coral Gables (33145) (G-2063)

Global Satellite Prpts LLC 954 459-3000
1901 S Andrews Ave Fort Lauderdale (33316) (G-3841)

Global Seashell Industries LLC 813 677-6674
4930 Distribution Dr Tampa (33605) (G-16885)

Global Seven Inc 973 664-1900
1936 Grove St Sarasota (34239) (G-15693)

Global Stone Collection LLC 772 467-1924
1800 N Us Highway 1 Fort Pierce (34946) (G-4490)

Global Stone Collection LLC (PA) 772 467-1924
1405 N Us Highway 1 Fort Pierce (34950) (G-4491)

Global Stone Corp 786 601-2459
10780 Sw 188th St Cutler Bay (33157) (G-2289)

Global Stone Project Entp, Saint Petersburg Also called Commercial Stone Fbrcators
Inc (G-15012)

Global Supply Solutions LLC 757 227-6757
1988 Lewis Turner Blvd # 1 Fort Walton Beach (32547) (G-4586)

Global Tech Led LLC 877 748-5533
1883 W State Road 84 # 106 Fort Lauderdale (33315) (G-3842)

Global Tire Rcycl of Smter CNT 352 330-2213
1201 Industrial Dr Wildwood (34785) (G-18311)

Global Tire Recycling Inc (PA) 352 330-2213
1201 Industrial Dr Wildwood (34785) (G-18312)

Global Tissue Group Jax, Jacksonville Also called Gtg-Jax LLC (G-6159)

Global Trading Inc (PA) 305 471-4455
7500 Nw 25th St Unit 12 Miami (33122) (G-9220)

Global Turbine Services Inc 786 476-2166
9374 Nw 102nd St Medley (33178) (G-8249)

Global Windows, Pompano Beach Also called Global Performance Windows Inc (G-14042)

Global Wrless Sltions Tech Inc 941 744-2511
101 Riverfront Blvd # 400 Bradenton (34205) (G-984)

Globalink Mfg Solutions 239 455-5166
3893 Mannix Dr Ste 514 Naples (34114) (G-10763)

Globaltek Art & Design, Sweetwater Also called Globaltek Office Supply Inc (G-16403)

Globaltek Office Supply Inc 305 477-2988
11200 Nw 25th St Ste 123 Sweetwater (33172) (G-16403)

Globaltel, Boca Raton Also called Interactive Media Tech Inc (G-547)

Globe Boyz International LLC 305 308-8160
1365 Nw 84th Ter Miami (33147) (G-9221)

Globe Specialty Metals Inc (HQ) 786 509-6900
600 Brickell Ave Ste 3100 Miami (33131) (G-9222)

Globe Trailers Florida Inc 941 753-6425
3101 59th Avenue Dr E Bradenton (34203) (G-985)

Glodea Kitchens, Jacksonville Also called Glodea Store Corp (G-6145)

Glodea Store Corp 888 400-4937
521 Copeland St Jacksonville (32204) (G-6145)

Glomaster Signs Inc 772 464-0718
4141 Bandy Blvd Fort Pierce (34981) (G-4492)

Glory Company, Orlando Also called Glory Sandblasting Inc (G-12196)

Glory Sandblasting Inc 407 422-0078
2922 38th St Orlando (32839) (G-12196)

Gloval Displays Inc 800 972-0353
1100 Nw 159th Dr Miami Gardens (33169) (G-10259)

Gloves USA Corp 786 536-2905
6842 Nw 77th Ct Ste W301 Miami (33166) (G-9223)

Glow Bench Systems Intl (PA) 954 315-4615
1580 Sawgrs Corp Pkwy # 13 Sunrise (33323) (G-16321)

Glu, Miami Beach Also called Craig Armstrong (G-10182)

Glucorell Inc 407 384-3388
130 White Oak Cir Maitland (32751) (G-8060)

Gma-Food LLC 646 469-8599
24756 State Road 54 Lutz (33559) (G-7991)

Gmed, Boca Raton Also called Modernzing Mdcine Gstrntrlogy (G-604)

GMF Industries Inc 863 646-5081
4600 Drane Field Rd Lakeland (33811) (G-7338)

Gml Coatings LLC 941 755-2176
10315 Technology Ter Bradenton (34211) (G-986)

Gml Industries LLC 352 671-7619
5542 Sw 6th Pl Ocala (34474) (G-11400)

Gms Sheet Metal & AC Inc 772 221-0585
3377 Sw 42nd Ave Ste D Palm City (34990) (G-13042)

Gmx Technologies LLC 917 697-0211
1111 Russell Dr Apt A Highland Beach (33487) (G-5460)

Gnekow Family Winery LLC 209 463-0697
132 Ne 21st Ct Wilton Manors (33305) (G-18341)

Gnj Manufacturing Inc 305 651-8644
5811 Hallandale Bch Blvd West Park (33023) (G-18212)

Gnr Orthopedic Designs, Ocala Also called Great Northen Rehab PC (G-11403)

Gns Embroidery 850 775-1147
1713 Moylan Rd Panama City Beach (32407) (G-13331)

Gns Technologies LLC 561 367-3774
5612 Pacific Blvd Apt 704 Boca Raton (33433) (G-528)

Go 2 Print Now Inc 800 500-4276
2390 26th Ave N Saint Petersburg (33713) (G-15063)

Go Latinos Magazine LLC 786 601-7693
13345 Sw 264th Ter Homestead (33032) (G-5711)

Go Lighting Service, Weston Also called Itelecom USA Inc (G-18257)

Go Mobile Signs 239 245-7803
13468 Palm Beach Blvd C Fort Myers (33905) (G-4269)

Go Puck, Sarasota Also called Capacity Inc (G-15450)

Gobczynskis Printery Inc 941 758-5734
6452 Parkland Dr Sarasota (34243) (G-15485)

Godatafeed, Plantation Also called Method Merchant Inc (G-13868)

Godawa Septic Tank Service, Daytona Beach Also called P & L Creech Inc (G-2579)

Godwin and Singer Inc 727 896-8631
1415 Burlington Ave N Saint Petersburg (33705) (G-15064)

Goen3 Corporation (PA) 407 601-6000
6555 Sanger Rd Ste 100 Orlando (32827) (G-12197)

Goengineer Inc 800 688-3234
9100 Wndermere Rd Ste 208 Windermere (34786) (G-18352)

Goforit Inc 727 785-7616
34034 Us Highway 19 N Palm Harbor (34684) (G-13111)

Gogps USA Inc 941 751-2363
7152 15th St E Sarasota (34243) (G-15486)

Goho Enterprises Inc 407 884-0770
3351 Laughlan Rd Zellwood (32798) (G-18598)

Goizper USA, Sarasota Also called Torque Technologies Products (G-15570)

Gold Banner USA Inc 305 576-2215
2660 Nw 3rd Ave Miami (33127) (G-9224)

Gold Bond Building Pdts LLC 813 672-8269
12949 S Us Highway 41 Gibsonton (33534) (G-4797)

Gold Buyers of America LLC 877 721-8033
2001 20th Ln Greenacres (33463) (G-4848)

Gold Coast Aero Accessories 561 965-7767
2633 Lantana Rd Ste 23 Lake Worth (33462) (G-7202)

Gold Coast Plst & Stucco Inc 954 275-9132
1815 Nw 64th Way Margate (33063) (G-8132)

Gold Coast Printing Inc 813 853-2219
401 E Jackson St Ste 2340 Tampa (33602) (G-16886)

Gold Coffee Roasters Inc 561 746-8110
1425 Park Ln S Jupiter (33458) (G-6737)

Gold Eagle, Miami Also called Bard Sports Corp (G-8798)

Gold Effects Inc 727 573-1990
13130 56th Ct Ste 609 Clearwater (33760) (G-1615)

Gold Granite & Marble 863 439-9794
930 Robert Rd Unit 47 Lake Hamilton (33851) (G-7050)

Gold Network of Miami Inc 305 343-7355
17620 Nw 63rd Ct Hialeah (33015) (G-5174)

Gold Plating Specialties 239 851-9323
17560 Allentown Rd Fort Myers (33967) (G-4270)

Gold Seal Cutlery, Saint Petersburg Also called Southern Supply and Mfg Co (G-15193)

Gold Shine LLC 561 419-3253
3301 N University Dr # 100 Coral Springs (33065) (G-2158)

Gold Star Printers, Fort Lauderdale Also called G S Printers Inc (G-3834)

Gold-Rep Corporation 954 892-5868
750 Heritage Dr Weston (33326) (G-18248)

Goldberg Systems LLC 843 513-5277
575 24th Ave Se Saint Petersburg (33705) (G-15065)

Golden Aluminum Extrusion LLC 330 372-2300
1650 Alumax Cir Plant City (33566) (G-13773)

Golden Boar Product Corp 305 500-9392
7224 Nw 25th St Miami (33122) (G-9225)

Golden Boatlifts, North Fort Myers Also called Golden Manufacturing Inc (G-11061)

Golden Century Inc 954 933-2911
1935 Banks Rd Margate (33063) (G-8133)

Golden Glades Raceway LLC 305 321-9627
17021 Nw 27th Ave Miami Gardens (33056) (G-10260)

Golden Global Corp 954 695-7025
21573 San Germain Ave Boca Raton (33433) (G-529)

Golden Hands Welding Inc 786 728-6838
9161 Sw 181st Ter Palmetto Bay (33157) (G-13210)

Golden Manufacturing Inc 239 337-4141
17611 East St Unit B North Fort Myers (33917) (G-11061)

Golden Print Inc 561 833-9661
2701 Sw 6th St Boynton Beach (33435) (G-873)

Golden Ribbon Corporation 727 545-4499
10321 72nd St Largo (33777) (G-7598)

Golden Wood Works LLC 239 677-8540
2529 Sw 26th Pl Cape Coral (33914) (G-1349)

Goldfaden Skincare, Hollywood Also called Cosmesis Skincare Inc (G-5556)

Goldfield Cnsld Mines Co (HQ) 321 724-1700
100 Rialto Pl Ste 500 Melbourne (32901) (G-8430)

Goldys Box Co 954 648-1623
3267 Trussler Ter The Villages (32163) (G-17555)

Golf Agronomics Sand & Hlg Inc 800 626-1359
2165 17th St Sarasota (34234) (G-15694)

Golf America Southwest Fla Inc 904 688-0280
2049 Crown Dr Saint Augustine (32092) (G-14836)

Golf Shaft Deals Inc 321 591-7824
529 Franklyn Ave Indialantic (32903) (G-5803)

Golfweek, Orlando Also called Turnstile Publishing Company (G-12682)

A
L
P
H
A
B
E
T
I
C

Goloso Food Llc 321 277-2055
  1700 35th St Ste 107 Orlando (32839) **(G-12198)**

Gondia Machine Shop, Medley *Also called Medley Machine Shop Inc* **(G-8277)**

Gondia Machine Shop Inc 305 763-7494
  9452 Nw 109th St Medley (33178) **(G-8250)**

Gontech Custom Wood Corp 305 323-0765
  2005 Sw 129th Ct Miami (33175) **(G-9226)**

Gonzalez Aerospace Services 561 227-1575
  1035 S State Road 7 # 313 Wellington (33414) **(G-17852)**

Good 4 Tklc Inc 321 632-4340
  5020 Nova Ave Rockledge (32955) **(G-14712)**

Good Catch Inc 305 757-7700
  6713 Ne 3rd Ave Miami (33138) **(G-9227)**

Good Chance Inc 754 263-2792
  20851 Johnson St Ste 107 Pembroke Pines (33029) **(G-13392)**

Good Chance Textile Inc 754 263-2792
  20851 Johnson St Ste 107 Pembroke Pines (33029) **(G-13393)**

Good Feet, Orlando *Also called Rlcjc Inc* **(G-12557)**

Good Gal Storage G.G.s, Fort Lauderdale *Also called Kron Designs LLC* **(G-3908)**

Good Jams LLC 702 379-5551
  6450 N Federal Hwy Boca Raton (33487) **(G-530)**

Good Neighbor Pharmacy, Largo *Also called St Mary Pharmacy LLC* **(G-7690)**

Good Rep Inc 407 869-6531
  100 Bay Hammock Ln Longwood (32779) **(G-7899)**

Good Time Outdoors Inc 352 401-9070
  4600 W Highway 326 Ocala (34482) **(G-11401)**

Good Times Sports Bar and Gril 239 369-7000
  700 Leeland Hts Blvd W Lehigh Acres (33936) **(G-7809)**

Goodcat LLC 239 254-8288
  1440 Rail Head Blvd Ste 5 Naples (34110) **(G-10764)**

Goodpress Publishing LLC 561 865-8101
  4731 W Atlantic Ave Ste 5 Delray Beach (33445) **(G-2969)**

Goodrich Corporation 305 622-4500
  3201 Nw 167th St Miami Gardens (33056) **(G-10261)**

Goodrich Corporation 904 757-3660
  6061 Goodrich Blvd Jacksonville (32226) **(G-6146)**

Goodrich Lighting Systems Inc 813 891-7100
  129 Fairfield St Oldsmar (34677) **(G-11653)**

Goodtime Printing Inc 352 629-8838
  1522 E Silver Sprng Blvd Ocala (34470) **(G-11402)**

Goodwater Albemarle Co, Delray Beach *Also called Worrell Water Technologies LLC* **(G-3038)**

Goodwill Industries S Fla Inc 941 745-8459
  2563 Lakewood Ranch Blvd Bradenton (34211) **(G-987)**

Goodwin Heart Pine Company, Micanopy *Also called Goodwin Lumber Company Inc* **(G-10397)**

Goodwin Lumber Company Inc 352 466-0339
  106 Sw 109th Pl Micanopy (32667) **(G-10397)**

Goodyear Belts, Miami Lakes *Also called Adventry Corp* **(G-10279)**

Gooee LLC 727 510-0663
  1444 S Belcher Rd Clearwater (33764) **(G-1616)**

Gopi Glass Sales & Svcs Corp 305 592-2089
  7450 Nw 41st St Miami (33166) **(G-9228)**

Gopole, Saint Johns *Also called Ar2 Products LLC* **(G-14944)**

Gorilla Bats LLC 813 285-9409
  11223 Saint Andrews Ct Riverview (33579) **(G-14563)**

Gorilla Boost, Fort Lauderdale *Also called Two Brothers Cultivation LLC* **(G-4102)**

Goruck LLC (HQ) 904 708-2081
  415 Pablo Ave Ste 140 Jacksonville Beach (32250) **(G-6633)**

Goruck Holdings LLC (PA) 904 708-2081
  415 Pablo Ave Ste 140 Jacksonville Beach (32250) **(G-6634)**

Gosan Usa Inc 904 356-4181
  1926 Spearing St Jacksonville (32206) **(G-6147)**

Gosimplyconnect, Fort Lauderdale *Also called Simply45 LLC* **(G-4049)**

Goss Inc 386 423-0311
  1419 Industrial Dr New Smyrna Beach (32168) **(G-11001)**

Got It Inc 954 899-0001
  107 E Palmetto Park Rd Boca Raton (33432) **(G-531)**

GOTG LLC 800 381-4684
  19182 Powell Rd 1 Brooksville (34604) **(G-1159)**

Gotobilling LLC 800 305-1534
  218 E Bearss Ave Ste 368 Tampa (33613) **(G-16887)**

Gotrg, Miami *Also called Recon Group LLP* **(G-9786)**

Gould Signs Inc 772 221-1218
  3035 Se Waaler St Stuart (34997) **(G-16155)**

Gourmet 3005 Inc 786 334-6250
  2315 W 77th St Hialeah (33016) **(G-5175)**

Gourmet Cup, Valrico *Also called Rae Launo Corporation* **(G-17669)**

Gourmet Food Solutions LLC 413 687-3285
  19950 W Country Club Dr # 101 Aventura (33180) **(G-262)**

Gourmet Parisien Inc 305 778-0756
  1943 Sherman St Hollywood (33020) **(G-5582)**

Goverlan LLC 888 330-4188
  2655 S Le Jeune Rd # 1001 Coral Gables (33134) **(G-2064)**

Govpay Network LLC 866 893-9678
  12855 Sw 132nd St Ste 204 Miami (33186) **(G-9229)**

Goyard Miami LLC 305 894-9235
  9700 Collins Ave Ste 118 Bal Harbour (33154) **(G-294)**

GPM Fab & Supply LLC 813 689-7107
  1504 Lenna Ave Seffner (33584) **(G-15961)**

Gps Education LLC 386 756-7575
  2463 Old Samsula Rd Port Orange (32128) **(G-14335)**

Gpt Media Group Corporation 954 315-0990
  140 Park Central Blvd S Pompano Beach (33064) **(G-14043)**

Gq Investments LLC 305 821-3850
  3840 W 104th St Unit 20 Hialeah (33018) **(G-5176)**

Gr Dynamics LLC 850 897-9700
  115 Hart St Niceville (32578) **(G-11031)**

Grabber Construction Pdts Inc 813 249-2281
  5835 Barry Rd Ste 107 Tampa (33634) **(G-16888)**

Graber Cabinets, Sarasota *Also called Morning Star of Sarasota Inc* **(G-15751)**

Graber Cabinets, Bradenton *Also called Woodtech Global Inc* **(G-1079)**

Grace Bible Church 850 623-4671
  6331 Chestnut St Milton (32570) **(G-10426)**

Grace Prsthtic Fabrication Inc 727 842-2265
  7928 Rutillio Ct New Port Richey (34653) **(G-10967)**

Graduate Plastics Inc (PA) 305 687-0405
  15800 Nw 15th Ave Miami (33169) **(G-9230)**

Grafix, Clearwater *Also called Labelpro Inc* **(G-1670)**

Graflex Inc 561 691-5959
  15855 Assembly Loop # 100 Jupiter (33478) **(G-6738)**

Grafton Cosmetics, Boynton Beach *Also called Grafton Products Corp* **(G-874)**

Grafton Furniture Company 305 696-3811
  3401 Nw 71st St Miami (33147) **(G-9231)**

Grafton Products Corp 561 738-2886
  1801 Corporate Dr Boynton Beach (33426) **(G-874)**

Graham & Company LLC 904 281-0003
  9440 Philips Hwy Ste 1 Jacksonville (32256) **(G-6148)**

Grahams Welding Fabrication 850 865-0899
  622 Fairway Ave Ne Fort Walton Beach (32547) **(G-4587)**

Grain Machinery Mfg Corp 305 620-2525
  1130 Nw 163rd Dr Miami (33169) **(G-9232)**

Grainman, Miami *Also called Grain Machinery Mfg Corp* **(G-9232)**

Grampus Enterprises Inc 305 491-9827
  2800 Glades Cir Ste 109 Weston (33327) **(G-18249)**

Grampus Tech, Weston *Also called Grampus Enterprises Inc* **(G-18249)**

Gran Savana USA, Orlando *Also called Goloso Food Llc* **(G-12198)**

Granada Art Service, Miami *Also called Granada Prtg & Graphics Corp* **(G-9233)**

Granada Prtg & Graphics Corp 305 593-5266
  8693 Nw 66th St Miami (33166) **(G-9233)**

Grand Band, Hollywood *Also called J Lea LLC* **(G-5602)**

Grand Buffet 941 752-3388
  4848 14th St W Bradenton (34207) **(G-988)**

Grand Cypress Group Inc 407 622-1993
  151 N Maitland Ave Maitland (32751) **(G-8061)**

Grand Havana Inc 305 297-2207
  407 Lincoln Rd Ste 2a Miami Beach (33139) **(G-10197)**

Grand Western, Orlando *Also called Cheney Ofs Inc* **(G-12008)**

Grand Woodworking Llc 239 594-9663
  663 Hickory Rd Naples (34108) **(G-10765)**

Grandstand Publishing LLC 847 491-6440
  390 N Orange Ave Ste 2300 Orlando (32801) **(G-12199)**

Granite Imports Inc 732 500-2549
  1500 Gateway Blvd Ste 250 Boynton Beach (33426) **(G-875)**

Granite Services Intl Inc 813 242-7400
  201 N Franklin St # 1000 Tampa (33602) **(G-16889)**

Granite Tampa Bay, Odessa *Also called International Gran & Stone LLC* **(G-11559)**

Granite World Inc 813 243-6556
  7024 Benjamin Rd Tampa (33634) **(G-16890)**

Grannys Cheesecake & More Inc 210 343-9610
  13106 Barth Pl Riverview (33579) **(G-14564)**

Grannys Cheesecake & More Inc 561 847-6599
  17003 Nw 32nd Ave Okeechobee (34972) **(G-11607)**

Grant Printing, Fort Lauderdale *Also called Jrg Systems Inc* **(G-3898)**

Grapevine Usa Inc 786 510-9122
  333 Las Olas Way Fort Lauderdale (33301) **(G-3843)**

Graph-Plex Corp 772 766-3866
  5240 95th St Sebastian (32958) **(G-15894)**

Graph-Plex Inc 954 920-0905
  2830 N 28th Ter Hollywood (33020) **(G-5583)**

Graphic and Printing Svcs Corp 954 486-8868
  5035 Nw 37th Ave Tamarac (33309) **(G-16532)**

Graphic Banner LLP 954 491-9441
  1330 E Commercial Blvd Oakland Park (33334) **(G-11269)**

Graphic Center Group Corp 305 961-1649
  2150 Coral Way Fl 1 Coral Gables (33145) **(G-2065)**

Graphic Data Inc 954 493-8003
  7378 W Atlantic Blvd Margate (33063) **(G-8134)**

Graphic Designs Intl Inc 772 287-0000
  3161 Se Slater St Stuart (34997) **(G-16156)**

Graphic Difference Inc A 954 748-6990
  7362 W Commercial Blvd Lauderhill (33319) **(G-7733)**

Graphic Dynamics Inc 954 728-8452
  735 Nw 7th Ter Fort Lauderdale (33311) **(G-3844)**

Graphic Images Inc 954 984-0015
  2301 Nw 33rd Ct Ste 105 Pompano Beach (33069) **(G-14044)**

Graphic Installers Inc 863 646-5543
4403 Holden Rd Lakeland (33811) ***(G-7339)***
Graphic Masters Inc 800 230-3873
801 Brickell Ave Ste 300 Miami (33131) ***(G-9234)***
Graphic Press, Titusville *Also called Graphic Reproductions Inc* ***(G-17589)***
Graphic Press Corporation 850 562-2262
5123a Woodlane Cir Ste A Tallahassee (32303) ***(G-16450)***
Graphic Printing Corp 561 994-3586
751 Park Of Commerce Dr Boca Raton (33487) ***(G-532)***
Graphic Reproductions Inc 321 267-1111
2214 Garden St Ste B Titusville (32796) ***(G-17589)***
Graphic Sign Dsign Cntl Fla LL 386 547-4569
529 Ridgewood Ave Daytona Beach (32117) ***(G-2557)***
Graphica Services Inc 305 232-5333
12943 Sw 133rd Ct Miami (33186) ***(G-9235)***
Graphics Arts Bindery Inc 352 394-4077
3023 Pinnacle Ct Clermont (34711) ***(G-1870)***
Graphics Designer Inc 561 687-7993
2353 N Military Trl C West Palm Beach (33409) ***(G-18019)***
Graphics Pdts Excellence Inc 813 884-1578
5335 Emory Dr Wesley Chapel (33543) ***(G-17878)***
Graphics Screen Printing & EMB, Tarpon Springs *Also called Eagle Athletic Wear Inc* ***(G-17469)***
Graphics Type Color Entps Inc 305 591-7600
2300 Nw 7th Ave Miami (33127) ***(G-9236)***
Graphink Incorporated 305 468-9463
8850 Nw 13th Ter Unit 103 Doral (33172) ***(G-3236)***
Graphix By Fran Inc 239 939-3125
12541 Metro Pkwy Ste 10 Fort Myers (33966) ***(G-4271)***
Graphix Solutions of America 727 898-6744
12015 Major Turner Run Parrish (34219) ***(G-13359)***
Grass Choppers 305 253-1217
11861 Sw 180th St Miami (33177) ***(G-9237)***
Grass Pro Shops Inc 813 381-3890
303 S Falkenburg Rd Tampa (33619) ***(G-16891)***
Grate Fireplace & Stone Shoppe 239 939-7187
16611 S Tamiami Trl Fort Myers (33908) ***(G-4272)***
Grate Ideas of America LLC 844 292-6044
1417 Sw 1st Ave Fort Lauderdale (33315) ***(G-3845)***
Graves Company, Pompano Beach *Also called Vee Enterprises Inc* ***(G-14235)***
Gravity Ink & Stitch Inc 954 558-0119
2910 Nw 130th Ave Apt 112 Sunrise (33323) ***(G-16322)***
Gravity Produce LLC 269 471-9463
4401 Bay Beach Ln Apt 844 Fort Myers Beach (33931) ***(G-4454)***
Gravitystorm Inc 772 519-3009
7402 Fort Walton Ave Fort Pierce (34951) ***(G-4493)***
Gray Information Solutions Inc 352 684-6655
12812 Coronado Dr Spring Hill (34609) ***(G-16072)***
Gray Logging LLC 850 973-3863
811 Ne Oats Ave Madison (32340) ***(G-8042)***
Gray Logging LLC 850 973-3863
665 Sw Harvey Greene Dr Madison (32340) ***(G-8043)***
Gray Seismic Monitoring LLC 904 728-3299
2220 County Road 210 W # 10 Jacksonville (32259) ***(G-6625)***
Grays Portable Buildings Inc 386 755-6449
792 Sw Bascom Norris Dr Lake City (32025) ***(G-7020)***
Grazed LLC 786 534-3975
9399 Nw 13th St Doral (33172) ***(G-3237)***
Grease TEC Holding LLC 352 742-2440
28615 Lake Indus Blvd Tavares (32778) ***(G-17509)***
Greased Lightning, Winter Haven *Also called Global Gl Lc* ***(G-18443)***
Great Amercn Natural Pdts Inc 727 521-4372
4121 16th St N Saint Petersburg (33703) ***(G-15066)***
Great American Imports Llc 786 524-4120
3758 Nw 54th St Miami (33142) ***(G-9238)***
Great American Woodworks Inc 727 375-1212
11445 Pyramid Dr Odessa (33556) ***(G-11555)***
Great Atlantic Outfitters 904 722-0196
803 North St Jacksonville (32211) ***(G-6149)***
Great Bay Distributors Inc 727 584-8626
2310 Starkey Rd Holiday (34690) ***(G-5494)***
Great Bay Fabrication Inc 727 536-1924
2111 34th Way Largo (33771) ***(G-7599)***
Great Bay Signs Inc 727 437-1091
19106 Gulf Blvd Unit 302 Indian Shores (33785) ***(G-5810)***
Great Cir Vntures Holdings LLC (PA) 305 638-2650
2105 Nw 86th Ave Doral (33122) ***(G-3238)***
Great Escape Publishing 561 860-8266
101 Se 6th Ave Ste A Delray Beach (33483) ***(G-2970)***
Great Hse Mdia Group of Pbls I 407 779-3846
4449 Riverton Dr Orlando (32817) ***(G-12200)***
Great Lakes Wtr Trtmnt Systems 269 381-0210
1000 Wiggins Pass Rd Naples (34110) ***(G-10766)***
Great Locations Inc (PA) 954 943-1188
2745 E Atl Blvd Ste 305 Pompano Beach (33062) ***(G-14045)***
Great Northern Corporation 920 739-3671
1420 Vantage Way S # 100 Jacksonville (32218) ***(G-6150)***
Great Northern Rehab PC (PA) 352 732-8868
2620 Se Merrycamp Rd Ocala (34471) ***(G-11403)***
Great Northern Rehab PC 352 732-8868
2620 Se Maricamp Rd Ocala (34471) ***(G-11404)***
Great South Timber & Lbr Inc 386 752-3774
1135 Se State Road 100 Lake City (32025) ***(G-7021)***
Great South Timber & Lbr Inc (PA) 386 755-3046
517 Se Baya Dr Lake City (32025) ***(G-7022)***
Great Southern Wood Prsv Inc 352 793-9410
194 Cr 527a Lake Panasoffkee (33538) ***(G-7119)***
Great Virtualworks LLC 800 606-6518
4100 Sw 28th Way Fort Lauderdale (33312) ***(G-3846)***
Great Western Malting Co 360 991-0888
225 S County Line Rd Plant City (33566) ***(G-13774)***
Greater 7th Digital Press Inc 305 681-2412
14627 Nw 7th Ave Miami (33168) ***(G-9239)***
Greater Miami Elks Lodge Inc 305 754-5899
5150 Nw 2nd Ave Miami (33127) ***(G-9240)***
Greathouse Signs LLC 407 247-2668
156 Holly St Apopka (32712) ***(G-136)***
Grecian & Company Inc 386 344-1967
2988 Nw Us Highway 41 Lake City (32055) ***(G-7023)***
Greco Alum Railings USA Inc 727 372-4545
9410 Eden Ave Hudson (34667) ***(G-5775)***
Greek Island Spice Inc 954 761-7161
2905 Sw 2nd Ave Fort Lauderdale (33315) ***(G-3847)***
Green Air Controls, Freeport *Also called Green Air Group LLC* ***(G-4625)***
Green Air Group LLC 850 608-3065
902 State Highway 20 E # 104 Freeport (32439) ***(G-4625)***
Green Applications LLC 954 900-2290
3233 Sw 2nd Ave Ste 200 Fort Lauderdale (33315) ***(G-3848)***
Green Biofuels LLC 305 639-3030
3123 Nw 73rd St Miami (33147) ***(G-9241)***
Green Biofuels Miami LLC 305 639-3030
3123 Nw 73rd St Ste A-C Miami (33147) ***(G-9242)***
Green Bull Products Inc 386 402-0409
310 Washington St New Smyrna (32168) ***(G-10992)***
Green Bullion Fincl Svcs LLC 954 960-7000
3613 N 29th Ave Hollywood (33020) ***(G-5584)***
Green Creative LLC 866 774-5433
519 Codisco Way Sanford (32771) ***(G-15327)***
Green Energy Enterprises Inc 904 207-6503
9300 Normandy Blvd # 502 Jacksonville (32221) ***(G-6151)***
Green Energy Enterprises Inc (PA) 904 309-8993
9300 Normandy Blvd # 511 Jacksonville (32221) ***(G-6152)***
Green Essentials LLC 786 584-4377
7480 Bird Rd Ste 810 Miami (33155) ***(G-9243)***
Green Forest Industries Inc 941 721-0504
1365 12th St E Palmetto (34221) ***(G-13169)***
Green Forest Products LLC 352 341-5500
105 N Apopka Ave Inverness (34450) ***(G-5829)***
Green Fuel Systems LLC 352 483-5005
24745 Lester Way Eustis (32736) ***(G-3559)***
Green Global Energy Systems 305 253-3413
18868 Sw 80th Ct Cutler Bay (33157) ***(G-2290)***
Green Holness, Orlando *Also called Florida Copier Connections* ***(G-12160)***
Green Leaf Foods LLC 305 308-9167
4050 Sw 145th Ter Miramar (33027) ***(G-10499)***
Green Light Printing Inc 305 576-5858
151 Nw 36th St Miami (33127) ***(G-9244)***
Green Marine Fuels Inc 305 775-3546
3220 S Dixie Hwy Miami (33133) ***(G-9245)***
Green Mountain Specialties 386 469-0057
2004 Brunswick Ln 5 Deland (32724) ***(G-2873)***
Green Papers Inc 305 956-3535
15660 W Dixie Hwy North Miami Beach (33162) ***(G-11143)***
Green Plant LLC 305 397-9394
3600 Nw 59th St Miami (33142) ***(G-9246)***
Green Power Systems LLC 904 545-1311
4155 Lakeside Dr Jacksonville (32210) ***(G-6153)***
Green Rhino Enrgy Slutions LLC (PA) 407 925-5868
1451 Ocoee Apopka Rd Apopka (32703) ***(G-137)***
Green Roads of Florida 954 626-0574
5150 Sw 48th Way Davie (33314) ***(G-2420)***
Green Shades Software Inc 904 807-0160
7020 A C Skinner Pkwy Jacksonville (32256) ***(G-6154)***
Green Sheet, The, Port Charlotte *Also called Sun Coast Media Group Inc* ***(G-14318)***
Green Surfaces, Miami *Also called Blues Design Group LLC* ***(G-8840)***
Green Toad Printers, North Miami Beach *Also called Green Papers Inc* ***(G-11143)***
Green Touch Industries Inc 561 659-5525
100 Us Highway 1 West Palm Beach (33403) ***(G-18020)***
Greenco Manufacturing Corp 813 882-4400
5688 W Crenshaw St Frnt Tampa (33634) ***(G-16892)***
Greencore LLC 727 251-9837
970 Tyrone Blvd N Saint Petersburg (33710) ***(G-15067)***
Greene Publishing Inc 850 973-6397
1695 S State Road 53 Madison (32340) ***(G-8044)***
Greenes Reserve Inc 954 304-0791
3373 Nw 10th St Bldg 200 Ocala (34475) ***(G-11405)***
Greengood Energy Corp 954 417-6117
3389 Sheridan St Ste 410 Hollywood (33021) ***(G-5585)***

ALPHABETIC

Greenie Tots Inc 888 316-6126
772 Nw 132nd Ave Plantation (33325) *(G-13856)*

Greenlam America Inc 305 640-0388
8750 Nw 36th St Ste 635 Doral (33178) *(G-3239)*

Greenlam Laminates, Doral Also called Greenlam America Inc *(G-3239)*

Greens First, Boca Raton Also called Ceautamed Worldwide LLC *(G-456)*

Greentechnologies LLC (PA) 352 379-7780
3926 Nw 34th Dr Gainesville (32605) *(G-4704)*

Greentex America LLC 305 908-8580
520 S Dixie Hwy Ofc 120 Hallandale Beach (33009) *(G-4949)*

Greentree Marketing Svcs Inc 800 557-9567
1828 Sw 24th Ave Fort Lauderdale (33312) *(G-3849)*

Greenwave Biodiesel LLC 239 682-7700
420 W Mcnab Rd Fort Lauderdale (33309) *(G-3850)*

Greenway Bridge LLC 631 901-4561
1340 Kings Estate Rd Saint Augustine (32086) *(G-14837)*

Greenwise Bankcard 954 673-0406
4400 W Sample Rd Coconut Creek (33073) *(G-1988)*

Greenwood Lake News Inc (PA) 845 477-2575
13032 Pinnacle Ln Hudson (34669) *(G-5776)*

Greenwood Lk & W Milford News, Hudson Also called Greenwood Lake News Inc *(G-5776)*

Greg Allens Inc (PA) 904 262-8912
7071 Davis Creek Rd Jacksonville (32256) *(G-6155)*

Greg Clark Welding Inc 904 226-2952
6108 Arlington Rd Jacksonville (32211) *(G-6156)*

Greg Franklin Enterprises Inc 904 675-9129
551797 Us Highway 1 Hilliard (32046) *(G-5465)*

Greg Pyle Enterprises, High Springs Also called Commercial Gates and Elc LLC *(G-5454)*

Greg Valentine LLC 239 332-0855
3590 Old Metro Pkwy Fort Myers (33916) *(G-4273)*

Greg Valley 941 739-6628
2010 Whitfield Park Loop Sarasota (34243) *(G-15487)*

Gregg Tool & Die Co Inc 305 685-6309
4725 E 10th Ct Hialeah (33013) *(G-5177)*

Gregomarc LLC 305 559-9777
9772 Sw 8th St Miami (33174) *(G-9247)*

Greif Inc 863 967-2419
211 Sandra Jackson Rd Auburndale (33823) *(G-235)*

Gremed Group Corp 305 392-5331
8040 Nw 14th St Doral (33126) *(G-3240)*

Gresso LLC 305 515-8677
495 Brickell Ave Apt 3902 Miami (33131) *(G-9248)*

Grevan Artistic Ventures Inc (PA) 850 243-8111
622 Lovejoy Rd Nw Fort Walton Beach (32548) *(G-4588)*

Greyfield Holdings Inc (PA) 407 830-8861
900 Central Park Dr Sanford (32771) *(G-15328)*

Greyfield Holdings Inc 407 927-4476
711 Ironwood Ct Winter Springs (32708) *(G-18566)*

Greylor Dynesco Co Inc 239 574-2011
2340 Andalusia Blvd Cape Coral (33909) *(G-1350)*

Greymatter Distillery 904 723-1114
1221 Mayport Rd Atlantic Beach (32233) *(G-210)*

Greyson Corp 407 830-7443
726 N Us Highway 17 92 Longwood (32750) *(G-7900)*

Grezzo Usa Llc 954 885-0331
1109 Pelican Ln Hollywood (33019) *(G-5586)*

Gribetz International, Sunrise Also called Leggett & Platt Incorporated *(G-16336)*

Griffin & Holman Inc 904 781-4531
1855 Cassat Ave Ste 8 Jacksonville (32210) *(G-6157)*

GRIFFIN FERTILIZER CO, Frostproof Also called Ben Hill Griffin Inc *(G-4633)*

Griffin Industries LLC 904 964-8083
11313 Se 52nd Ave Starke (32091) *(G-16102)*

Griffin Industries LLC 407 857-5474
408 W Landstreet Rd Orlando (32824) *(G-12201)*

Griffin Industries LLC 813 626-1135
1001 Orient Rd Tampa (33619) *(G-16893)*

Griffin Sawmill & Woodworking 863 241-5180
845 W Lake Wales Rd N Lake Wales (33859) *(G-7163)*

Griffis Timber Inc 904 275-2372
11625 Willie Griffis Rd Sanderson (32087) *(G-15253)*

Griffiths Corporation 407 851-8342
10659 Rocket Blvd Orlando (32824) *(G-12202)*

Griffon Graphics Inc 954 922-1800
2117 Hollywood Blvd Hollywood (33020) *(G-5587)*

Grille Tech Inc 305 537-0053
5101 Nw 36th Ave Miami (33142) *(G-9249)*

Grille Tech Inc 305 537-0053
3611 Nw 74th St Miami (33147) *(G-9250)*

Grimes Aerospace Company 407 276-6083
12807 Lake Drive Ext Delray Beach (33444) *(G-2971)*

Grind It LLC 813 310-9710
17002 Hanna Rd Lutz (33549) *(G-7992)*

Grinder Wear Parts Inc 503 982-0881
2062 20th Ave Se Largo (33771) *(G-7600)*

Grindhard Coatings Inc 772 221-9986
7850 Sw Ellipse Way Stuart (34997) *(G-16157)*

Grinnell Fire Prtction Systems, Boca Raton Also called Grinnell LLC *(G-533)*

Grinnell LLC (HQ) 561 988-3658
1501 Nw 51st St Boca Raton (33431) *(G-533)*

Grip Tooling Technologies LLC 813 654-6832
1202 Telfair Rd Brandon (33510) *(G-1094)*

Griswold Ready Mix Con Inc 904 751-3796
11660 Camden Rd Jacksonville (32218) *(G-6158)*

Grizzly Manufacturing Inc 386 755-0220
174 Ne Cortez Ter Lake City (32055) *(G-7024)*

Grizzly Printing Parlour LLC 786 416-2494
14244 Sw 90th Ter Miami (33186) *(G-9251)*

Grizzly Products Corp 813 545-3828
4406 W Virginia Ave Tampa (33614) *(G-16894)*

Grms Servicing LLC 850 278-1000
249 Mack Byou Loop Ste 30 Santa Rosa Beach (32459) *(G-15426)*

Grom Social Enterprises Inc (PA) 561 287-5776
2060 Nw Boca Raton Blvd Boca Raton (33431) *(G-534)*

Groovy Toys LLC 772 878-0790
585 Nw Merc Pl Ste 108 Port Saint Lucie (34986) *(G-14415)*

Grooyi, Port Saint Lucie Also called Groovy Toys LLC *(G-14415)*

Group E Holdings Inc 321 724-0127
2144 Franklin Dr Ne Palm Bay (32905) *(G-12903)*

Group Heros Inc 305 635-0219
5720 Nw 35th Ave Miami (33142) *(G-9252)*

Group III Asphalt Inc 850 983-0611
6108 Wastle Rd Milton (32583) *(G-10427)*

Group III International Inc 954 984-1607
2981 W Mcnab Rd Ste 1 Pompano Beach (33069) *(G-14046)*

Group Steel Inc (PA) 786 319-1222
3492 W 84th St Hialeah (33018) *(G-5178)*

Group Steel Inc 305 965-0614
2437 Sw 138th Ave Miami (33175) *(G-9253)*

Group Tws LLC 337 499-2928
20415 Walnut Grove Ln Tampa (33647) *(G-16895)*

Grove Medical LLC 305 903-6402
11926 Sw 8th St Miami (33184) *(G-9254)*

Grove Power Inc 305 599-2045
158 Doral (33122) *(G-3241)*

Growers Fertilizer Corporation (PA) 863 956-1101
312 N Buena Vista Dr Lake Alfred (33850) *(G-6995)*

Growhealthy Holdings LLC 863 223-8882
324 Datura St West Palm Beach (33401) *(G-18021)*

Growth Logistics Inc 800 846-2363
67 Nw 183rd St Miami Gardens (33169) *(G-10262)*

Growve, Saint Petersburg Also called Viva 5 LLC *(G-15228)*

Grub Company 347 464-9770
6 Fernwood Trl Ormond Beach (32174) *(G-12767)*

Gruenewald Mfg Co Inc 978 777-0200
9800 Se 176th Court Rd Ocklawaha (32179) *(G-11519)*

Grunenthal Services Inc 786 364-6308
1005 Sw 87th Ave Miami (33174) *(G-9255)*

Grupo De Diarios America LLC 305 577-0094
848 Brickell Ave Ste 600 Miami (33131) *(G-9256)*

Grupo Editorial Expansion 305 374-9003
2800 Ponce De Leon Blvd # 1160 Coral Gables (33134) *(G-2066)*

Grupo Phoenix Corp Svcs LLC (HQ) 954 241-0023
2980 Ne 207th St Ste 705 Miami (33180) *(G-9257)*

GS Gelato and Desserts Inc 850 243-5455
1785 Fim Blvd Fort Walton Beach (32547) *(G-4589)*

GSE America LLC (PA) 863 583-4343
3928 Anchuca Dr Ste 3 Lakeland (33811) *(G-7340)*

GSE Jetall Inc 305 688-2111
4821 Nw 128th St Opa Locka (33054) *(G-11751)*

Gsg Group Inc 954 733-8219
2918 Nw 28th St Lauderdale Lakes (33311) *(G-7715)*

GSM, Jacksonville Also called Gray Seismic Monitoring LLC *(G-6625)*

Gss Gear, Fort Walton Beach Also called Global Supply Solutions LLC *(G-4586)*

Gsw Stucco LLC 904 246-0783
827 20th St N Jacksonville Beach (32250) *(G-6635)*

Gt Grandstands Inc 813 305-1415
2810 Sydney Rd Plant City (33566) *(G-13775)*

Gt Ice LLC, Ponte Vedra Also called 2jcp LLC *(G-14253)*

GT Industries Inc 954 962-9700
3109 Stirling Rd Ste 200 Fort Lauderdale (33312) *(G-3851)*

Gt Machining 941 809-5735
1400 Commerce Blvd Ste G Sarasota (34243) *(G-15488)*

Gt Pallets LLC 786 541-6532
958 Nw 73rd St Miami (33150) *(G-9258)*

Gt Technologies Inc 850 575-8181
2919 Commonwealth Blvd Tallahassee (32303) *(G-16451)*

Gt Technologies I Inc 850 575-8181
2919 Commonwealth Blvd Tallahassee (32303) *(G-16452)*

GTC Media, Miami Also called Graphics Type Color Entps Inc *(G-9236)*

GTE, Orlando Also called Gas Turbine Efficiency LLC *(G-12183)*

GTE, Orlando Also called Gas Turbine Efficiency Inc *(G-12182)*

Gtg-Jax LLC 904 861-3290
11801 Central Pkwy Jacksonville (32224) *(G-6159)*

Gtgjfe LLC 904 800-6333
5570 Fl Min Blvd S Ste 1 Jacksonville (32257) *(G-6160)*

Gti Systems Inc (PA) 863 965-2002
1250 Hobbs Rd Auburndale (33823) *(G-236)*

GTM Manufacturing Inc 407 654-6598
 14350 Eastside St Groveland (34736) *(G-4861)*

Gto Access Systems LLC 850 575-0176
 3121 Hartsfield Rd Tallahassee (32303) *(G-16453)*

Gto Performance Air Boats, Ocala *Also called Good Time Outdoors Inc* *(G-11401)*

Gto USA Inc (PA) 727 216-6907
 805 Court St Clearwater (33756) *(G-1617)*

Guanabana & Co LLC 904 891-5256
 8802 Corporate Square Ct # 306 Jacksonville (32216) *(G-6161)*

Guanabana Artisan Ice Pops, Jacksonville *Also called Guanabana & Co LLC* *(G-6161)*

Guard Dog Valves Inc 239 793-6886
 14500 Tamiami Trl E Naples (34114) *(G-10767)*

Guardfish Enterprises LLC 850 455-4114
 3931 W Navy Blvd Pensacola (32507) *(G-13513)*

Guardia LLC (PA) 954 670-2900
 5900 N Andrews Ave Ste 10 Fort Lauderdale (33309) *(G-3852)*

Guardian Essentials LLC 817 401-0200
 137 Nw 1st Ave Delray Beach (33444) *(G-2972)*

Guardian Fire Equipment, Miami *Also called Target Manufacturing Inc* *(G-9994)*

Guardian Hurricane Protection 305 805-7050
 5729 Nw 159th St Miami Lakes (33014) *(G-10306)*

Guardian Ign Interlock Mfg Inc 321 205-1730
 2971 Oxbow Cir Ste A Cocoa (32926) *(G-1934)*

Guardian Industries Cor 954 525-3481
 3060 Sw 2nd Ave Fort Lauderdale (33315) *(G-3853)*

Guardian Manufacturing, Cocoa *Also called Guardian Ign Interlock Mfg Inc* *(G-1934)*

Guardian Solar LLC 727 504-2790
 4366 Louis Ave Ste 106 Holiday (34691) *(G-5495)*

Guerilla Technologies Inc 772 283-0500
 4203 Sw High Meadows Ave Palm City (34990) *(G-13043)*

Guerrilla Press 352 281-7420
 314 Ne 10th St Apt 201 Gainesville (32601) *(G-4705)*

Guerrilla Prtg Solutions LLC 352 394-7770
 304 Mohawk Rd Minneola (34715) *(G-10451)*

Guest Service Publications Inc 516 333-3474
 28026 Pisces Ln Bonita Springs (34135) *(G-801)*

Guided Particle Systems Inc 727 424-8790
 1000 College Blvd Bldg 11 Pensacola (32504) *(G-13514)*

Guideline Central, Lake Mary *Also called International Guidelines Ctr* *(G-7086)*

Guimar Inc 305 888-1547
 1224 E 4th Ave Hialeah (33010) *(G-5179)*

Gulf Associates Control Inc 954 426-0536
 231 Se 1st Ter Deerfield Beach (33441) *(G-2728)*

Gulf ATL Pump & Dredge LLC (PA) 386 362-2761
 954 Nw 244th Dr Newberry (32669) *(G-11022)*

Gulf Atlantic Culvert Company 850 562-2384
 5344 Gateway Dr Tallahassee (32303) *(G-16454)*

Gulf Breeze Apparel LLC 941 488-8337
 616 Cypress Ave Venice (34285) *(G-17695)*

Gulf Breeze News Inc 850 932-8986
 913 Gulf Breeze Pkwy # 35 Gulf Breeze (32561) *(G-4882)*

Gulf Cable LLC 201 720-2417
 5700 Industrial Blvd Milton (32583) *(G-10428)*

Gulf Coast Airways Inc 239 403-3020
 526 Terminal Dr Naples (34104) *(G-10768)*

Gulf Coast Aluminum, Fort Myers *Also called Tag Media Group LLC* *(G-4417)*

Gulf Coast Business Review 941 906-9386
 650 Central Ave Ste 5 Sarasota (34236) *(G-15695)*

Gulf Coast Business World Inc 850 864-1511
 3 Racetrack Rd Nw Fort Walton Beach (32547) *(G-4590)*

Gulf Coast Cabinetry Inc 850 769-3799
 22200 Panama Cy Bch Pkwy Panama City Beach (32413) *(G-13332)*

Gulf Coast Cabinets Carpentry 239 222-2994
 11824 Rosalinda Ct Fort Myers (33912) *(G-4274)*

Gulf Coast Elc Mtr Svc Inc 850 433-5134
 3810 Hopkins St Pensacola (32505) *(G-13515)*

Gulf Coast Fabricators Inc 850 584-5979
 3480 S Byron Butler Pkwy Perry (32348) *(G-13640)*

Gulf Coast Growers Florida LLC 941 981-3888
 2105 S Dock St Palmetto (34221) *(G-13170)*

Gulf Coast Hyperbarics, Panama City *Also called Gulf Coast Hyperberic Inc* *(G-13269)*

Gulf Coast Hyperberic Inc 850 271-1441
 215 Forest Park Cir Panama City (32405) *(G-13269)*

Gulf Coast Installers LLC 239 273-4663
 28720 S Diesel Dr Bonita Springs (34135) *(G-802)*

Gulf Coast Monuments, Crestview *Also called Gulf Coast Wilbert Inc* *(G-2246)*

Gulf Coast Non Emergency Trans 239 825-1350
 17531 Boat Club Dr Fort Myers (33908) *(G-4275)*

Gulf Coast Paint & Supplies 813 932-3093
 1910 N Us Highway 301 Tampa (33619) *(G-16896)*

Gulf Coast Pavers, Labelle *Also called Labelle Brick Pavers Tile LLC* *(G-6982)*

Gulf Coast Precast Inc 239 337-0021
 2506 Precast Ct Fort Myers (33916) *(G-4276)*

Gulf Coast Printing, Largo *Also called Sun Coast Paper & Envelope Inc* *(G-7692)*

Gulf Coast Printing 239 482-5555
 11000 Panther Printing Wa Fort Myers (33908) *(G-4277)*

Gulf Coast Program 727 945-1402
 3515 Alt 19 Ste B Palm Harbor (34683) *(G-13112)*

Gulf Coast Ready Mix LLC 352 621-3900
 8778 W Jump Ct Homosassa (34448) *(G-5749)*

Gulf Coast Rebar Inc 813 247-1200
 1301 E 4th Ave Tampa (33605) *(G-16897)*

Gulf Coast Shades & Blinds LLC 850 332-2100
 714 Roanoke Ct Gulf Breeze (32561) *(G-4883)*

Gulf Coast Signs Sarasota Inc 941 355-8841
 1713 Northgate Blvd Sarasota (34234) *(G-15696)*

Gulf Coast Timber Company 850 271-8818
 8206 S Holland Rd Panama City (32409) *(G-13270)*

Gulf Coast Wilbert Inc (PA) 850 682-8004
 100 Martin St Crestview (32536) *(G-2246)*

Gulf Connectors Inc 239 657-2986
 160 Airpark Blvd Unit 104 Immokalee (34142) *(G-5797)*

Gulf Contours Inc 941 639-3933
 7500 Golf Course Blvd Punta Gorda (33982) *(G-14506)*

Gulf County Ship Building Inc 850 229-9300
 1550 Old Dynamite Dock Rd Port Saint Joe (32456) *(G-14388)*

Gulf Electronics 727 595-3840
 12155 Meadowbrook Ln Largo (33774) *(G-7601)*

Gulf Fiberoptics Inc 813 891-1993
 448 Commerce Blvd Oldsmar (34677) *(G-11654)*

Gulf Glo Banners and Signs LLC 850 234-0952
 8808 Front Beach Rd Panama City (32407) *(G-13271)*

Gulf Machining, Clearwater *Also called Walkup Enterprises Inc* *(G-1847)*

Gulf Machining Inc 727 571-1244
 5040 110th Ave N Clearwater (33760) *(G-1618)*

Gulf Marine Repair Corporation (PA) 813 247-3153
 1800 Grant St Tampa (33605) *(G-16898)*

Gulf Medical Fiberoptics Inc 813 855-6618
 448 Commerce Blvd Oldsmar (34677) *(G-11655)*

Gulf Packaging Co 727 441-1117
 1756 Emerald Dr Clearwater (33756) *(G-1619)*

Gulf Photonics Inc 813 855-6618
 448 Commerce Blvd Oldsmar (34677) *(G-11656)*

Gulf Publishing Company Inc (PA) 727 596-2863
 11470 Oakhurst Rd Largo (33774) *(G-7602)*

Gulf South Distributors Inc 850 244-1522
 707 Anchors St Nw Fort Walton Beach (32548) *(G-4591)*

Gulf States Automation Inc 850 475-0724
 245 W Airport Blvd Ste B Pensacola (32505) *(G-13516)*

Gulf Stream Gear, Boca Raton *Also called Super Grafix Inc* *(G-704)*

Gulf Tool Corporation 850 456-0840
 8470 Gulf Beach Hwy Pensacola (32507) *(G-13517)*

Gulf View Plastics Inc 727 379-3072
 18816 Oak Way Dr Hudson (34667) *(G-5777)*

Gulfcoast Gabber Inc 727 321-6965
 1419 49th St S Gulfport (33707) *(G-4898)*

Gulfcoast Sailing Inc 727 823-1968
 1354 20th St N Saint Petersburg (33713) *(G-15068)*

Gulfport Grind Inc 727 343-2785
 5825 20th Ave S Gulfport (33707) *(G-4899)*

Gulfport Industries Inc 813 885-1000
 6308 Benjamin Rd Ste 714 Tampa (33634) *(G-16899)*

Gulfshore Custom Woodworks LLC 239 205-0777
 1012 Nw 36th Ave Cape Coral (33993) *(G-1351)*

Gulfshore Manufacturing Inc 352 447-1330
 131 Highway 19 N Inglis (34449) *(G-5818)*

Gulfstream Alum & Shutter Corp 772 287-6476
 1673 Se Pomeroy St Stuart (34997) *(G-16158)*

Gulfstream Goodwill Inds Inc 561 362-8662
 1662 N Federal Hwy Boca Raton (33432) *(G-535)*

Gulfstream Graphics Inc 561 276-0006
 955 S Congress Ave # 103 Delray Beach (33445) *(G-2973)*

Gulfstream Land Company LLC 772 286-3456
 200 Sw Monterey Rd Stuart (34994) *(G-16159)*

Gulfstream Media Group Inc 954 462-4488
 1401 E Broward Blvd # 206 Fort Lauderdale (33301) *(G-3854)*

Gulfstream Mses Invstmnts Grou 305 975-6186
 1535 Biarritz Dr Miami Beach (33141) *(G-10198)*

Gulfstream Natural Gas Sys LLC 941 723-7000
 4610 Buckeye Rd Palmetto (34221) *(G-13171)*

Gulfstream Shipbuilding LLC 850 835-5125
 116 Shipyard Rd Freeport (32439) *(G-4626)*

Gulfstream Unsnkable Boats LLC 813 820-6100
 5251 W Tyson Ave Tampa (33611) *(G-16900)*

Gulfstream Yachts, Tampa *Also called Gulfstream Unsnkable Boats LLC* *(G-16900)*

Gull Tool & Machine Inc 727 527-0808
 3033 47th Ave N Frnt Saint Petersburg (33714) *(G-15069)*

Gun Drilling of Florida, Largo *Also called Lundy Enterprises Inc* *(G-7635)*

Gun Vault 850 391-7651
 3305 Capital Cir Ne # 103 Tallahassee (32308) *(G-16455)*

Gunderlin Ltd Inc 305 696-6071
 3625 E 11th Ave Hialeah (33013) *(G-5180)*

Gunn Prtg & Lithography Inc 813 870-6010
 4415 W Dr Martin L King Martin Luther Tampa (33614) *(G-16901)*

Gunns Welding & Fabricating 727 393-5238
 4729 96th St N Saint Petersburg (33708) *(G-15070)*

Gunter Septic Tank Mfg 813 654-1214
 1434 E Dr Mrtn Lther King Seffner (33584) *(G-15962)*

A
L
P
H
A
B
E
T
I
C

Gurtan Designs 954 972-6100
  1048 Sw 4th Ter Pompano Beach (33060) *(G-14047)*
Gutcher's Quickprint, Tampa *Also called Mad Inc (G-17030)*
Guthman Signs LLC 941 218-0014
  4914 Lena Rd Unit 101 Bradenton (34211) *(G-989)*
Gutters Unlimited Plus, Naples *Also called Fox Industries of Swfl Inc (G-10750)*
Guy Gasket Inc 561 703-1774
  4446 Carver St Lake Worth (33461) *(G-7203)*
Guy Wingo Signs 407 578-1132
  2682 Pemberton Dr Apopka (32703) *(G-138)*
Guyton Industries LLC 772 208-3019
  14601 Sw 168th Ave Indiantown (34956) *(G-5814)*
Guyton's Custom Design, Indiantown *Also called Guyton Industries LLC (G-5814)*
Gvj Corp 786 224-2808
  15120 Sw 159th Ct Miami (33196) *(G-9259)*
Gw Creamery LLC 904 509-6202
  1458 S 6th St Macclenny (32063) *(G-8037)*
Gw Schultz Tool, Tavares *Also called Gws Tool LLC (G-17510)*
Gwa Alper, Delray Beach *Also called Delray Tropic Holdings Inc (G-2955)*
Gwb Coatings LLC 407 271-7732
  3612 Danby Ct Orlando (32812) *(G-12203)*
Gwmf Holdings LLC 305 788-1473
  16791 Royal Poinciana Dr Weston (33326) *(G-18250)*
Gws Tool LLC (HQ) 352 343-8778
  595 County Road 448 Tavares (32778) *(G-17510)*
Gws Tool Group, Tavares *Also called Gws Tool Holdings LLC (G-17511)*
Gws Tool Holdings LLC (HQ) 352 343-8778
  595 County Road 448 Tavares (32778) *(G-17511)*
Gypsum Bd Specialists USA Corp 954 348-8869
  241 Nw 217th Way Pembroke Pines (33029) *(G-13394)*
Gypsum Supply - Tampa, Tampa *Also called Cemex Cnstr Mtls Fla LLC (G-16692)*
Gypsum Supply - Wildwood, Wildwood *Also called Cemex Cnstr Mtls Fla LLC (G-18310)*
Gypsy Mining Inc 772 589-5547
  12855 79th Ave Roseland (32957) *(G-14757)*
Gyro-Gale Inc 772 283-1711
  2981 Se Dominica Ter # 4 Stuart (34997) *(G-16160)*
Gyrosolar Corp 954 554-9990
  2655 Edgewater Dr Weston (33332) *(G-18251)*
Gyrx LLC 904 641-2599
  11222 St Johns Indus Pkwy Jacksonville (32246) *(G-6162)*
H & F Industries Corp 727 271-4974
  3341 Wiltshire Dr Holiday (34691) *(G-5496)*
H & H Gypsum LLC 321 972-5571
  371 Oleander Way Ste 1325 Casselberry (32707) *(G-1417)*
H & H Printing Inc 407 422-2932
  1406 W Washington St Orlando (32805) *(G-12204)*
H & H Products Company 407 299-5410
  6600 Magnolia Homes Rd Orlando (32810) *(G-12205)*
H & H Publishing Co Inc 727 442-7760
  1231 Kapp Dr Clearwater (33765) *(G-1620)*
H & H Signs Inc 941 485-0556
  426 E Venice Ave Venice (34285) *(G-17696)*
H & J Asphalt Inc 305 635-8110
  4310 Nw 35th Ave Miami (33142) *(G-9260)*
H & M Printing Inc 407 831-8030
  104 Loren Ct Sanford (32771) *(G-15329)*
H & M Steel 904 765-3465
  9843 Evans Rd Jacksonville (32208) *(G-6163)*
H & T Global Circuit Fctry LLC 727 327-6236
  2510 Terminal Dr S Saint Petersburg (33712) *(G-15071)*
H & W Creative Colors, Cape Coral *Also called Creative Colors International (G-1328)*
H A Friend & Company Inc 847 746-1248
  1521 Neptune Dr Boynton Beach (33426) *(G-876)*
H B Sherman Traps Inc 850 575-8727
  3731 Peddie Dr Tallahassee (32303) *(G-16456)*
H B Tutun Jr Logging Inc 850 584-9324
  2930 Old Foley Rd Perry (32348) *(G-13641)*
H C A, Largo *Also called Southwest Florida Regional (G-7688)*
H D Quickprint & Disc Off Sups 407 678-1355
  7820 Wendell Rd Orlando (32807) *(G-12206)*
H D Quikprint & Disc Off Sups, Orlando *Also called H D Quickprint & Disc Off Sups (G-12206)*
H Goicoechea Inc 305 805-3333
  695 E 10th Ave Hialeah (33010) *(G-5181)*
H H Terry Co Inc 239 593-0132
  4445 Dunlin Ct Naples (34119) *(G-10769)*
H I T Lighting Corp 772 221-1155
  3399 Sw 42nd Ave Palm City (34990) *(G-13044)*
H Jones Timber LLC 386 312-0603
  546 W Peniel Rd Palatka (32177) *(G-12871)*
H Lamm Industries Inc 954 491-8929
  4425 Ne 6th Ter Oakland Park (33334) *(G-11270)*
H M D, Sanford *Also called Alt Thuyan (G-15262)*
H M J Corporation 954 229-1873
  81 Bay Colony Dr Fort Lauderdale (33308) *(G-3855)*
H Park Services LLC 844 607-2142
  200 E Robinson St Orlando (32801) *(G-12207)*

H Q Inc 941 721-7588
  210 9th Street Dr W Palmetto (34221) *(G-13172)*
H Sixto Distributors Inc 305 688-5242
  13301 Nw 38th Ct Opa Locka (33054) *(G-11752)*
H T I, Belleview *Also called Heat Treating Incorporated (G-362)*
H V Payne Mfg LLC 941 773-1112
  164 Cowpen Ln Sarasota (34240) *(G-15697)*
H&J Asphalt Plant, Miami *Also called H & J Asphalt Inc (G-9260)*
H&K Home Supplies Distrs LLC 786 308-6024
  10818 Sw 240th St Homestead (33032) *(G-5712)*
H&M Phillips Inc 727 797-4600
  12772 Burns Dr Odessa (33556) *(G-11556)*
H&R Welding Equipment Repr Inc 904 487-9829
  937 Bulkhead Rd Green Cove Springs (32043) *(G-4827)*
H&S Swanson Fmly Holdings Inc (HQ) 727 541-3575
  9000 68th St N Pinellas Park (33782) *(G-13691)*
H&T Global Circuits, Saint Petersburg *Also called H & T Global Circuit Fctry LLC (G-15071)*
H.A.L.o, Orlando *Also called Helping Adlscnts Live Optmstcl (G-12213)*
H2 Home Collection Inc 714 916-9513
  1601-1 N Main St # 3159 Jacksonville (32206) *(G-6164)*
H20logy Inc 904 829-6098
  3233 County Road 208 Saint Augustine (32092) *(G-14838)*
H2c Brands LLC (PA) 904 342-7485
  110 Cumberland Park Dr # 205 Saint Augustine (32095) *(G-14839)*
H2c Brands LLC 360 338-0449
  5831 Fleet Landing Blvd Atlantic Beach (32233) *(G-211)*
H2o International Inc 954 570-3464
  3001 Sw 15th St Ste C Deerfield Beach (33442) *(G-2729)*
H2ocean LLC (PA) 866 420-2326
  7938 Sw Jack James Dr Stuart (34997) *(G-16161)*
H2r Corp (PA) 727 541-3444
  3921 76th Ave N Pinellas Park (33781) *(G-13692)*
H317 Logistics LLC 404 307-1621
  9019 Somerset Bay Ln # 402 Vero Beach (32963) *(G-17758)*
HA Morton Corp 352 220-9790
  2930 Ne 24th St Ocala (34470) *(G-11406)*
Haas Laser Technologies Inc 954 529-7273
  1612 Eastlake Way Weston (33326) *(G-18252)*
Hac International Inc 954 584-4530
  3911 Sw 47th Ave Ste 914 Davie (33314) *(G-2421)*
Hailey Cian LLC 954 895-7143
  201 Sw 2nd St Fort Lauderdale (33301) *(G-3856)*
Haines City Mine, Haines City *Also called ER Jahna Industries Inc (G-4906)*
Hairmax Lasercomb, Boca Raton *Also called Lexington International LLC (G-578)*
Hairnet Company, The, Jacksonville *Also called Hnc Enterprises Inc (G-6178)*
Halcyon Aviation Capital LLC 305 615-1575
  8350 Nw 52nd Ter Ste 301 Doral (33166) *(G-3242)*
Halcyon Manufacturing Inc 386 454-0811
  24587 Nw 178th Pl High Springs (32643) *(G-5455)*
Hale Products Inc 352 629-5020
  607 Nw 27th Ave Ocala (34475) *(G-11407)*
Halex Corporation 239 216-4444
  2059 Trade Center Way Naples (34109) *(G-10770)*
Halifax Media Group LLC (HQ) 386 265-6700
  2339 Beville Rd Daytona Beach (32119) *(G-2558)*
Halifax Media Group LLC 941 361-4800
  1777 Main St Ste 200 Sarasota (34236) *(G-15698)*
Halifax Media Holdings LLC (PA) 386 681-2404
  901 6th St Daytona Beach (32117) *(G-2559)*
Halifax Plastic Inc 386 252-2442
  221 Fentress Blvd Daytona Beach (32114) *(G-2560)*
Halkey-Roberts Corporation (HQ) 727 471-4200
  2700 Halkey Roberts Pl N Saint Petersburg (33716) *(G-15072)*
Hall Fountains Inc 954 484-8530
  5500 Nw 22nd Ave Fort Lauderdale (33309) *(G-3857)*
Hall Industries Incorporated 239 768-0372
  11850 Regional Ln Unit 6 Fort Myers (33913) *(G-4278)*
Hall Metal Corp 772 460-0706
  4700 Magnum Dr Fort Pierce (34981) *(G-4494)*
Halldale Media Inc 407 322-5605
  4300 W Lake Mary Blvd # 1 Lake Mary (32746) *(G-7082)*
Halliday Industries LLC 321 288-3979
  7715 Ellis Rd Ste A Melbourne (32904) *(G-8431)*
Halliday Product, Orlando *Also called HP Preferred Ltd Partners (G-12229)*
Halliday Products Inc 407 298-4470
  6401 Edgewater Dr Orlando (32810) *(G-12208)*
Hallmark Emblems Inc 813 223-5427
  2401 N Tampa St Tampa (33602) *(G-16902)*
Hallmark Nameplate Inc 352 383-8142
  1717 Lincoln Ave Mount Dora (32757) *(G-10602)*
Halma Holdings Inc 973 832-2658
  8060 Bryan Dairy Rd Ste A Seminole (33777) *(G-15976)*
Halo Fishing LLC 321 373-2055
  520 Atz Rd Malabar (32950) *(G-8082)*
Haman Industries Inc 813 626-5700
  2402 S 54th St Tampa (33619) *(G-16903)*
Hamant Airboats LLc 321 259-6998
  1705 Southland Ave Melbourne (32935) *(G-8432)*

2022 Harris Florida
Manufacturers Directory

(G-0000) Company's Geographic Section entry number

Hamburg House Inc 305 557-9913
6157 Nw 167th St Ste F20 Hialeah (33015) (G-5182)

Hamilton Printing Inc 772 334-0151
779 Ne Dixie Hwy Jensen Beach (34957) (G-6655)

Hamilton Sundstrand Corp 860 654-6252
2901 Nw 27th Ave Pompano Beach (33069) (G-14048)

Hammer Haag Steel Inc 727 216-6903
12707 Us Highway 19 N Clearwater (33764) (G-1621)

Hammer Head Group Inc 305 436-5691
8900 Nw 33rd St Ste 100 Doral (33172) (G-3243)

Hammond Enterprises 386 575-2402
1460 William St Leesburg (34748) (G-7779)

Hammond Kitchens & Bath LLC 321 768-9549
7618 Silver Sands Rd Melbourne (32904) (G-8433)

Hamner Parking Lot Service 954 328-3216
2151 Ne 55th St Fort Lauderdale (33308) (G-3858)

Hampton Hexane Transfer Stn, Starke Also called Darling Ingredients Inc (G-16100)

Hamsard Usa Inc 386 761-1830
2330 S Nova Rd Ste A Daytona Beach (32119) (G-2561)

Hamworthy Inc (HQ) 305 597-7520
2900 Sw 42nd St Fort Lauderdale (33312) (G-3859)

Hanaya LLC 904 285-7575
543 Le Master Dr Ponte Vedra Beach (32082) (G-14268)

Hancor Inc 863 655-5499
115 N West Crown Point Rd Winter Garden (34787) (G-18388)

Hand 2 Hand Sanitizer, Lake Wales Also called Asi Chemical Inc (G-7152)

Hand Carved Creations 561 893-0292
5331 N Dixie Hwy Ste 3 Boca Raton (33487) (G-536)

Handal Foods LLC 954 753-0649
11822 Nw 30th Ct Coral Springs (33065) (G-2159)

Handcraft Woodworking Inc 561 241-9911
7608 Nw 6th Ave Boca Raton (33487) (G-537)

Handcraft Woodworking Inc 954 418-6356
1498 Nw 3rd St Deerfield Beach (33442) (G-2730)

Handcrafted Pewter, Fort Myers Also called Bamm Manufacturing Inc (G-4185)

Hanes-Harris Design Cons 813 237-0202
6106 N Nebraska Ave Ste A Tampa (33604) (G-16904)

Hangar Door Spclsts Design Inc 772 266-9070
7876 Sw Jack James Dr Stuart (34997) (G-16162)

Hanger Clinic, Tallahassee Also called Hanger Prsthetcs & Ortho Inc (G-16457)

Hanger Clinic, Cape Coral Also called Hanger Prsthtics Orthotics Inc (G-1352)

Hanger Clinic, Orange Park Also called Advanced Prosthetics Amer Inc (G-11811)

Hanger Prsthetcs & Ortho Inc 850 216-2392
2717 Mahan Dr Ste 2 Tallahassee (32308) (G-16457)

Hanger Prsthtics Orthotics Inc 239 772-4510
323 Del Prado Blvd S Cape Coral (33990) (G-1352)

Hankison 352 273-1220
4647 Sw 40th Ave Ocala (34474) (G-11408)

Hans-Mill Corp 904 395-2288
5406 W 1st St Jacksonville (32254) (G-6165)

Hansa Ophthalmics LLC 305 594-1789
4083 Nw 79th Ave Doral (33166) (G-3244)

Hansen Plastics Division, Clearwater Also called Tuthill Corporation (G-1836)

Hanson and Bringle Cabinets, Key West Also called Cayo Hueso Enterprises Inc (G-6858)

Hanson Lehigh Cement 800 665-6006
575 Cargo Rd Cape Canaveral (32920) (G-1285)

Hanson Pipe & Products, Deland Also called Forterra Pipe & Precast LLC (G-2872)

Hanteri Enterprises Corp 813 949-8729
1915 Vandervort Rd Lutz (33549) (G-7993)

Happy Endings of Miami Inc 305 759-4467
651 Nw 106th St Miami (33150) (G-9261)

Happy Kids For Kids Inc 954 730-7922
1380 W Mcnab Rd Fort Lauderdale (33309) (G-3860)

Happy Mix LLC 954 880-0160
8747 Stirling Rd Cooper City (33328) (G-2021)

Harberson Rv Pinellas LLC 727 937-6176
2112 Us Highway 19 Holiday (34691) (G-5497)

Harbinger, Jacksonville Also called Quality Neon Sign Company (G-6399)

Harbor Entps Ltd Lblty Co 229 403-0756
2417 Fleischmann Rd Ste 4 Tallahassee (32308) (G-16458)

Harbor Homes 941 320-2670
2624 Marlette St Sarasota (34231) (G-15699)

Harbor Imaging 941 883-8383
3430 Tamiami Trl Ste B Port Charlotte (33952) (G-14303)

Harbor Linen LLC (HQ) 305 805-8085
10800 Nw 106th St Ste 12 Medley (33178) (G-8251)

Harbor Machine Inc 727 772-9515
374 Foxcroft Dr E Palm Harbor (34683) (G-13113)

Harbor View Boat Trailers 941 916-3777
17 Callao St Punta Gorda (33983) (G-14507)

Harbor Woodworks, Safety Harbor Also called Mike C Lohmeyer (G-14792)

Harborpoint Media LLC (PA) 352 365-8200
212 E Main St Leesburg (34748) (G-7780)

Harbortech Plastics LLC 727 944-2425
3151 Grand Blvd Holiday (34690) (G-5498)

Harcourt Education, Orlando Also called Houghton Mifflin Harcourt Pubg (G-12226)

Harcros Chemicals Inc 813 247-4531
5132 Trenton St Tampa (33619) (G-16905)

Hard Chrome Enterprises Inc 561 844-2529
220 10th St Lake Park (33403) (G-7129)

Harder Prcision Components Inc 727 442-4212
1123 Seminole St Clearwater (33755) (G-1622)

Hardie Pipe, Plant City Also called James Hardie Building Pdts Inc (G-13778)

Hardrives Industries Inc 561 278-0456
2101 S Congress Ave Delray Beach (33445) (G-2974)

Hardscapecom LLC 561 998-5000
15132 Pk Of Cmmrce Blvd S Jupiter (33478) (G-6739)

Hardware Concepts Inc 305 685-1337
3758 Nw 54th St Miami (33142) (G-9262)

Hardware Online Store 954 565-5678
4343 N Andrews Ave Fort Lauderdale (33309) (G-3861)

Hardware Parts Corporation 561 994-2121
5030 Champion Blvd 6250 Boca Raton (33496) (G-538)

Hardy Logging Company Inc 850 994-1955
3901 Willard Norris Rd Pace (32571) (G-12858)

Hare Lumber & Ready Mix Inc 863 983-8725
425 E Haiti Ave Clewiston (33440) (G-1891)

Harlan J Newman 727 216-6419
10490 75th St Ste A Seminole (33777) (G-15977)

Harlen S Woodworking 850 774-2224
1709 Tennessee Ave Lynn Haven (32444) (G-8028)

Harley Boat, Bartow Also called Harley Shipbuilding Corp (G-310)

Harley Boat Corporation 863 533-2800
300 S 1st Ave Bartow (33830) (G-309)

Harley Boats, Bartow Also called Harley Boat Corporation (G-309)

Harley Shipbuilding Corp 863 533-2800
300 S 1st Ave Bartow (33830) (G-310)

Harmsco Filtration Products, Riviera Beach Also called Harmsco Inc (G-14626)

Harmsco Inc (PA) 561 848-9628
7169 49th Ter N Riviera Beach (33407) (G-14626)

Harn Ro Systems Inc 941 488-9671
310 Center Ct Venice (34285) (G-17697)

Harold Brley For Ormond Bch Cy 386 853-9000
902 Village Dr Ormond Beach (32174) (G-12768)

Harper Limbach Inc 813 207-0057
9051 Fla Min Blvd Ste 103 Tampa (33634) (G-16906)

Harper Screen Enclosures LLC 813 417-5937
11217 Rice Creek Rd Riverview (33569) (G-14565)

Harpers Manufacturing Spc 941 629-3490
24730 Sandhill Blvd # 902 Punta Gorda (33983) (G-14508)

Harrells LLC (HQ) 863 687-2774
5105 New Tampa Hwy Lakeland (33815) (G-7341)

Harrington Corporation 863 326-6130
1101 Snively Ave Winter Haven (33880) (G-18444)

Harris Aerial LLC (PA) 407 725-7886
1043 Seminola Blvd Casselberry (32707) (G-1418)

Harris Corporation, Gcsd, Melbourne Also called L3harris Technologies Inc (G-8458)

Harris Letterpress, Clearwater Also called Ironhorse Pressworks Inc (G-1649)

Harris Lighting, Jacksonville Also called Harris Manufacturing Inc (G-6166)

Harris Manufacturing Inc 877 204-7540
9143 Philips Hwy Ste 420 Jacksonville (32256) (G-6166)

Harris Woodworks LLC 561 543-3265
4078 Jonquil Cir S Palm Beach Gardens (33410) (G-12972)

Harrison Concrete Inc 321 276-0562
2021 E Grant Ave Orlando (32806) (G-12209)

Harrison Gypsum LLC 850 762-4315
5160 Vermont Rd Marianna (32448) (G-8165)

Harrison Logging 352 591-2779
17701 Nw 133rd Court Rd Williston (32696) (G-18332)

Harrison Metals Inc 352 588-2436
11640 Corporate Lake Blvd San Antonio (33576) (G-15248)

Harry Cashatt Stucco LLC 941 468-2166
310 W Cowles St Englewood (34223) (G-3532)

Harry J Honan 405 273-9315
1051 Singer Dr Riviera Beach (33404) (G-14627)

Harry Pickett 904 845-4643
37752 Kings Ferry Rd Hilliard (32046) (G-5466)

Harsco Corporation 717 506-2071
5950 Old 41a Hwy Tampa (33619) (G-16907)

Hart S Ceramic & Stone Inc 850 217-6145
981 Highway 98 E Ste 3 Destin (32541) (G-3068)

Hartco Inc 904 353-5259
25 E Beaver St Jacksonville (32202) (G-6167)

Hartco International 386 698-4668
2288 S Us Highway 17 Crescent City (32112) (G-2236)

Hartley Press Inc 904 398-5141
4250 Saint Augustine Rd Jacksonville (32207) (G-6168)

Hartman Enterprises 239 200-8998
14960 Collier Blvd Naples (34119) (G-10771)

Hartman Windows and Doors LLC 561 296-9600
2107 Blue Heron Blvd W Riviera Beach (33404) (G-14628)

Hartmans Canine Center LLC 352 978-6592
6242 Oil Well Rd Clermont (34714) (G-1871)

Hartmans Print Center Inc 941 475-2220
2828 S Mccall Rd Ste 37 Englewood (34224) (G-3518)

Harts Mobility LLC 404 769-4234
5257 Nw Torino Lakes Cir Port St Lucie (34986) (G-14476)

**A
L
P
H
A
B
E
T
I
C**

Hartsock Sawmill Inc.....352 753-3581
2939 Hartsock Sawmill Rd Lady Lake (32159) ***(G-6991)***
Harvest Moon Distributors LLC.....321 297-7942
3450 Parkway Center Ct Orlando (32808) ***(G-12210)***
Harvest Print & Bus Svcs Inc.....850 681-2488
1613 Capital Cir Ne Tallahassee (32308) ***(G-16459)***
Harvest Print Mktg Sltions LLC.....850 681-2488
1613 Capital Cir Ne Tallahassee (32308) ***(G-16460)***
Harvest Printing, Tallahassee *Also called Harvest Print Mktg Sltions LLC* ***(G-16460)***
Harvest Prtg & Copy Ctr Inc.....850 681-2488
1613 Capital Cir Ne Tallahassee (32308) ***(G-16461)***
Harvey Branker and Assoc PA.....954 966-4445
3816 Hollywood Blvd # 203 Hollywood (33021) ***(G-5588)***
Harvey Covington Thomas S Fla, Hollywood *Also called Harvey Branker and Assoc PA* ***(G-5588)***
Harwil Fixtures Inc.....904 692-1051
103 W Saint Johns Ave Hastings (32145) ***(G-4988)***
Hasbro Latin America Inc (HQ).....305 931-3180
5200 Blue Lagoon Dr Fl 10 Miami (33126) ***(G-9263)***
Hascall Engineering and Mfg Co.....941 723-2833
1608 20th Ave E Palmetto (34221) ***(G-13173)***
Hascall-Denke, Palmetto *Also called Denke Laboratories Inc* ***(G-13164)***
Hatalom Corporation.....407 567-2556
11315 Corp Blvd Ste 210 Orlando (32817) ***(G-12211)***
Hatch Enterprises Inc.....386 935-1419
8199 Us Highway 27 Branford (32008) ***(G-1112)***
HATCH LIGHTING, Tampa *Also called Hatch Transformers Inc* ***(G-16908)***
Hatch Transformers Inc.....813 288-8006
7821 Woodland Center Blvd Tampa (33614) ***(G-16908)***
Hathaspace, Tampa *Also called Atitlan Enterprises LLC* ***(G-16615)***
Haute Living Inc.....305 798-1373
999 Brickell Ave Ste 520 Miami (33131) ***(G-9264)***
Havana Dream Cigars, Miami *Also called Havana Dreams LLC* ***(G-9265)***
Havana Dreams LLC.....305 322-7599
2621 Sw 132nd Ave Miami (33175) ***(G-9265)***
Hawk Protection Incorporated.....954 980-9631
1020 Sw 98th Ave Pembroke Pines (33025) ***(G-13395)***
Hawk Racing.....941 209-1790
6060 28th St E Ste 5 Bradenton (34203) ***(G-990)***
Hawker Beechcraft Services, Tampa *Also called Textron Aviation Inc* ***(G-17350)***
Hawkhead International Inc.....904 264-4295
90 Industrial Loop N Orange Park (32073) ***(G-11831)***
Hawks Nuts Inc.....813 872-0900
4713 N Hale Ave Tampa (33614) ***(G-16909)***
Hawks Orgnal Jmbo Bled Peanuts, Tampa *Also called Hawks Nuts Inc* ***(G-16909)***
Hawthorne & Son Industries LLC.....954 980-8427
2630 W Broward Blvd # 203 Fort Lauderdale (33312) ***(G-3862)***
Hawver Aluminum Foundry Inc.....813 961-1497
9526 N Trask St Tampa (33624) ***(G-16910)***
Hay Tech.....850 592-2424
6468 Wolf Pond Rd Bascom (32423) ***(G-329)***
Hayley Carson Odom Cordrays.....850 830-8270
4508 Pottery Pl Destin (32541) ***(G-3069)***
Hayman Safe Co Inc.....407 365-5434
1291 N County Road 426 Oviedo (32765) ***(G-12824)***
Hazmat Software LLC.....407 416-5434
760 Heather Glen Cir Lake Mary (32746) ***(G-7083)***
HB Sealing Products Inc (HQ).....727 796-1300
420 Park Place Blvd # 100 Clearwater (33759) ***(G-1623)***
HB Tuten Jr Logging Inc.....850 584-9324
3870 S Byron Butler Pkwy Perry (32348) ***(G-13642)***
Hbp Pipe & Precast LLC.....904 529-8228
4210 Highway 17 S Us Green Cove Springs (32043) ***(G-4828)***
Hbt Forestry Services Inc.....850 584-9324
2930 Old Foley Rd Perry (32348) ***(G-13643)***
Hbys Enterprises LLC.....855 290-9900
1170 Tree Swallow Dr # 347 Winter Springs (32708) ***(G-18567)***
Hc Grupo Inc.....954 227-0150
2929 N University Dr # 105 Coral Springs (33065) ***(G-2160)***
Hci Books, Deerfield Beach *Also called Health Communications Inc* ***(G-2731)***
Hco Holding I Corporation.....863 533-0522
2701 State Road 60 W Bartow (33830) ***(G-311)***
Hcr Software Solutions Inc.....904 638-6177
13400 Sutton Park Dr S # 1101 Jacksonville (32224) ***(G-6169)***
HCW Biologics Inc.....954 842-2024
2929 N Commerce Pkwy Miramar (33025) ***(G-10500)***
HCW THERAPEUTICS, Miramar *Also called HCW Biologics Inc* ***(G-10500)***
Hd Kit, Hialeah Gardens *Also called IESC Diesel Corp* ***(G-5438)***
Hdd LLC.....561 346-9054
412 Clematis St West Palm Beach (33401) ***(G-18022)***
Hdh Agri Products LLC.....352 343-3484
27536 County Road 561 Tavares (32778) ***(G-17512)***
Hdl Therapeutics Inc.....772 453-2770
601 21st St Ste 300 Vero Beach (32960) ***(G-17759)***
Headhunter Inc.....954 462-5953
3380 Sw 11th Ave Fort Lauderdale (33315) ***(G-3863)***
Headhunter Spearfishing Co.....954 745-0747
1140 Ne 7th Ave Unit 6 Fort Lauderdale (33304) ***(G-3864)***
Headwaters Incorporated.....407 273-9221
5100 S Alafaya Trl Orlando (32831) ***(G-12212)***
Headwear International, Miami Lakes *Also called Ladove Inc* ***(G-10311)***
Health & Muscles.....305 225-2929
14144 Sw 8th St Miami (33184) ***(G-9266)***
Health and Beauty Mfg LLC.....727 565-0797
7205 30th Ave N Saint Petersburg (33710) ***(G-15073)***
Health Communications Inc.....954 360-0909
3201 Sw 15th St Deerfield Beach (33442) ***(G-2731)***
Health Robotics Canada LLC.....786 388-5339
6303 Blue Lagoon Dr # 310 Miami (33126) ***(G-9267)***
Health Star Inc.....321 914-6012
625 E Merritt Ave Ste I Merritt Island (32953) ***(G-8586)***
Healtheintentions Inc (PA).....954 394-8867
500 Ne 185th St Unit 8 Miami (33179) ***(G-9268)***
Healthier Choices MGT Corp (PA).....305 600-5004
3800 N 28th Way Hollywood (33020) ***(G-5589)***
Healthlight LLC.....224 231-0342
110 Front St Ste 300 Jupiter (33477) ***(G-6740)***
Healthline Medical Pdts Inc.....407 656-0704
1065 E Story Rd Winter Garden (34787) ***(G-18389)***
Healthlink, Jacksonville *Also called Clorox Healthcare Holdings LLC* ***(G-5985)***
Healthme Technology Inc.....888 994-3627
1250 Pine Ridge Rd Naples (34108) ***(G-10772)***
Healthquest Technologies LLC.....850 997-6300
1817 W Capps Hwy Monticello (32344) ***(G-10581)***
Healthy Schools LLC.....904 887-4540
3546 Saint Johns Bluff Rd Jacksonville (32224) ***(G-6170)***
Heara Inc.....305 651-5200
19595 Ne 10th Ave Ste H Miami (33179) ***(G-9269)***
Heartland Metals Inc.....863 465-7501
127 Ranier Dr Lake Placid (33852) ***(G-7141)***
Heartway USA, Fort Myers *Also called Imc-Heartway LLC* ***(G-4286)***
Heat Treating Incorporated.....352 245-8811
6740 Se 110th St Unit 508 Belleview (34420) ***(G-362)***
Heat-Pipe Technology Inc.....813 470-4250
6904 Parke East Blvd Tampa (33610) ***(G-16911)***
Heath Corporation.....863 638-1819
1303 Meyers Rd Lake Wales (33859) ***(G-7164)***
Heavy Hwy Infrastructure LLC.....407 323-8853
2210 W 25th St Sanford (32771) ***(G-15330)***
Hecht Rubber Corporation.....904 731-3401
6161 Philips Hwy Jacksonville (32216) ***(G-6171)***
Hector & Hector Inc.....305 629-8864
6790 Nw 84th Ave Miami (33166) ***(G-9270)***
Hector Corporation.....786 308-5853
2127 Nw 88th St Miami (33147) ***(G-9271)***
Hedrick Walker & Assoc Inc.....352 735-2600
3425 Lake Center Dr Ste 2 Mount Dora (32757) ***(G-10603)***
Heet, Palm Beach Gardens *Also called Pret-EE LLC* ***(G-13001)***
Heico Aerospace Corporation (HQ).....954 987-6101
3000 Taft St Hollywood (33021) ***(G-5590)***
Heico Aerospace Holdings Corp (HQ).....954 987-4000
3000 Taft St Hollywood (33021) ***(G-5591)***
Heico Aerospace Holdings Corp.....305 463-0455
7875 Nw 64th St Miami (33166) ***(G-9272)***
Heico Company, Tampa *Also called Leader Tech Inc* ***(G-17002)***
Heico Component Repair Group, Miami *Also called Northwings Accessories Corp* ***(G-9629)***
Heico Corporation.....305 374-1745
825 Brickell Bay Dr # 1643 Miami (33131) ***(G-9273)***
Heico Corporation.....305 463-0455
7900 Nw 64th St Miami (33166) ***(G-9274)***
Heico Corporation (PA).....954 987-4000
3000 Taft St Hollywood (33021) ***(G-5592)***
Heico Electronic Tech Corp (HQ).....954 987-6101
3000 Taft St Hollywood (33021) ***(G-5593)***
Heico Electronic Tech Group, Hollywood *Also called Heico Electronic Tech Corp* ***(G-5593)***
Heico Flight Support Corp (HQ).....954 987-4000
3000 Taft St Hollywood (33021) ***(G-5594)***
Heico Parts Group, Hollywood *Also called Jet Avion Corporation* ***(G-5606)***
Heights Tower Systems Inc.....850 455-1210
1529 Gulf Beach Hwy Pensacola (32507) ***(G-13518)***
Heirloom Design Group LLC.....407 735-2224
2770 Apopka Blvd Apopka (32703) ***(G-139)***
Heli Aviation Florida LLC.....941 355-1525
8191 N Tmami Trail Hngar Hangar Sarasota (34243) ***(G-15489)***
Heli-Tech Inc.....850 763-9000
4405 De Len Dr Panama City (32404) ***(G-13272)***
Helical Communication Tech Inc.....561 762-2823
634 Barnes Blvd Ste 206 Rockledge (32955) ***(G-14713)***
Helicopter Helmet LLC (PA).....843 556-0405
274 West Dr Melbourne (32904) ***(G-8434)***
Helicopter Helmets.com, Melbourne *Also called Helicopter Helmet LLC* ***(G-8434)***
Helios Technologies Inc.....941 351-6648
1155 Commerce Blvd N Sarasota (34243) ***(G-15490)***
Helios Technologies Inc (PA).....941 362-1200
7456 16th St E Sarasota (34243) ***(G-15491)***
Helios Technologies Inc.....941 328-1769
701 Tallevast Rd Sarasota (34243) ***(G-15492)***

960 2022 Harris Florida Manufacturers Directory (G-0000) Company's Geographic Section entry number

Helios Technologies Inc...941 362-1200
1500 W University Pkwy Sarasota (34243) ***(G-15493)***
Hell's Bay Boatworks, Titusville *Also called Hells Bay Marine Inc* ***(G-17591)***
Heller Cabinetry Inc...321 729-9690
415 Stan Dr Melbourne (32904) ***(G-8435)***
Hells Bay Boatworks LLC...321 383-8223
1520 Chaffee Dr Titusville (32780) ***(G-17590)***
Hells Bay Marine Inc...321 383-8223
1520 Chaffee Dr Titusville (32780) ***(G-17591)***
Helms Hauling & Materials Llc...850 218-6895
1423 Pine St Niceville (32578) ***(G-11032)***
Helms Hauling and Materials, Niceville *Also called Helms Hauling & Materials Llc* ***(G-11032)***
Helping Adlscnts Live Optmstcl...407 257-8221
4844 Cason Cove Dr # 204 Orlando (32811) ***(G-12213)***
Hemarus Llc-Jcksnvle Plsma Ctr...904 642-1005
601 Heritage Dr 118 Jupiter (33458) ***(G-6741)***
Hemco Corporation...904 993-0380
260 E Altamonte Dr Altamonte Springs (32701) ***(G-52)***
Hemco Industries Inc (PA)...305 769-0606
2500 Ne 135th St Ph 5 North Miami (33181) ***(G-11106)***
Hemingway Rum Company LLC (PA)...305 414-8754
201 Simonton St Key West (33040) ***(G-6866)***
Hemingway Rum Company LLC...863 937-8107
5300 Gateway Blvd Lakeland (33811) ***(G-7342)***
Hemp Cbd Daily Inc...904 672-7623
13724 Shady Woods St N Jacksonville (32224) ***(G-6172)***
Hemp Pantry, Inverness *Also called Jans Ventures LLC* ***(G-5830)***
Henderson Machine Inc...954 419-9789
1809 S Powerline Rd # 110 Deerfield Beach (33442) ***(G-2732)***
Henderson Prestress Con Inc...727 938-2828
822 Anclote Rd Tarpon Springs (34689) ***(G-17474)***
Hendry Corporation...813 241-9206
1800 Grant St Tampa (33605) ***(G-16912)***
Hendry Marine Industries Inc...813 241-9206
1800 Grant St Tampa (33605) ***(G-16913)***
Hendry Shipyard Joint Ventr 1...813 241-9206
1800 Grant St Tampa (33605) ***(G-16914)***
Henefelt Precision Pdts Inc...727 531-0406
8475 Ulmerton Rd Largo (33771) ***(G-7603)***
Henley Metal LLC...904 353-4770
6593 Powers Ave Ste 23 Jacksonville (32217) ***(G-6173)***
Henry W Long...352 542-7068
264 Se 752nd Ave Old Town (32680) ***(G-11622)***
Henrys Hickory House Inc...904 493-4420
249 Copeland St Jacksonville (32204) ***(G-6174)***
Henscratch Farms Inc...863 699-2060
980 Henscratch Rd Lake Placid (33852) ***(G-7142)***
Henscratch Farms Winery, Lake Placid *Also called Henscratch Farms Inc* ***(G-7142)***
Hensoldt Avionics Usa LLC...941 306-1328
2480 Fruitville Rd Ste 6 Sarasota (34237) ***(G-15700)***
Hentzen Coatings Inc...727 572-4474
5182 126th Ave N Clearwater (33760) ***(G-1624)***
Hepburn Industries Inc...305 757-6688
300 Ne 59th St Miami (33137) ***(G-9275)***
Hera Cases LLC...305 322-8960
6901 Edgewater Dr Apt 315 Coral Gables (33133) ***(G-2067)***
Herald-Advocate Publishing Co...863 773-3255
115 S 7th Ave Wauchula (33873) ***(G-17828)***
Heralpin Usa Inc...305 218-0174
10570 Nw 27th St Ste H101 Doral (33172) ***(G-3245)***
Herbert Pavers Inc...941 447-4909
3031 46th Ave E Bradenton (34203) ***(G-991)***
Herbko Inc...305 932-3572
3000 Island Blvd Ph 5 Aventura (33160) ***(G-263)***
Hercules Sealing Products, Clearwater *Also called HB Sealing Products Inc* ***(G-1623)***
Herff Jones, Winter Park *Also called Herff Jones Inc* ***(G-18513)***
Herff Jones Inc...407 647-4373
112 N Wymore Rd Winter Park (32789) ***(G-18513)***
Herff Jones LLC...904 641-4060
12086 Fort Caroline Rd # 201 Jacksonville (32225) ***(G-6175)***
Heritage Cntl Fla Jwish News I...407 834-8277
207 Obrien Rd Ste 101 Fern Park (32730) ***(G-3579)***
Heritage Manufacturing Svcs...727 906-5599
4365 22nd St N Saint Petersburg (33714) ***(G-15074)***
Heritage Medcall LLC...813 221-1000
202 E Virginia Ave Tampa (33603) ***(G-16915)***
Heritage Newspaper, Fern Park *Also called Heritage Cntl Fla Jwish News I* ***(G-3579)***
Heritage Plastics, Tampa *Also called Atkore Plastic Pipe Corp* ***(G-16616)***
Heritage Publishing Inc...904 296-1304
8130 Bymdws Cir W Ste 101 Jacksonville (32256) ***(G-6176)***
Heritage Signs...904 529-7446
1282 Energy Cove Ct Green Cove Springs (32043) ***(G-4829)***
Heritage Skin Care Inc...305 757-9264
180 Ne 99th St Miami Shores (33138) ***(G-10383)***
Herman Cabinets Inc...727 459-6730
1000 Belcher Rd S Largo (33771) ***(G-7604)***
Herman Group, Bradenton *Also called Spraying Systems Co* ***(G-1051)***
Hermes 7 Communications LLC...954 426-1998
430 W Hillsboro Blvd Deerfield Beach (33441) ***(G-2733)***
Hermes Technical Intl Inc...305 477-8993
8227 Nw 54th St Doral (33166) ***(G-3246)***
Hernandez Metal Fabricators...305 970-4145
15062 Sw 9th Way Miami (33194) ***(G-9276)***
Hernandez Mobile Welding Inc...954 347-4071
20320 Nw 258th St Okeechobee (34972) ***(G-11608)***
Hernandez Ornamental Inc...305 592-7296
1910 Nw 96th Ave Doral (33172) ***(G-3247)***
Hernandez Printing Service Inc...305 642-0483
1771 W Flagler St Miami (33135) ***(G-9277)***
Hernando Litho Printing, Brooksville *Also called Hernando Lithoprinting Inc* ***(G-1160)***
Hernando Lithoprinting Inc...352 796-4136
969 Hale Ave Brooksville (34601) ***(G-1160)***
Hernol Usa Inc...786 263-3341
201 Alhambra Cir Ste 6 Coral Gables (33134) ***(G-2068)***
Hernon Manufacturing Inc...407 322-4000
121 Tech Dr Sanford (32771) ***(G-15331)***
Heroal USA Inc...888 437-6257
7022 Tpc Dr Ste 100 Orlando (32822) ***(G-12214)***
Herpel Inc (PA)...561 585-5573
6400 Georgia Ave West Palm Beach (33405) ***(G-18023)***
Hes Products Inc...407 834-0741
87 Old Wiggins Ln Ormond Beach (32174) ***(G-12769)***
Hess Express...772 335-9975
10453 S Us Highway 1 Port Saint Lucie (34952) ***(G-14416)***
Hess Logistics Inc...954 668-7101
7508 Appalachian Ln Parkland (33067) ***(G-13346)***
Hess Station 09307...407 891-7156
4500 13th St Saint Cloud (34769) ***(G-14928)***
Hexion Inc...863 669-2565
2525 S Combee Rd Lakeland (33801) ***(G-7343)***
Hey Day...305 763-8660
1825 West Ave Miami Beach (33139) ***(G-10199)***
Hey Mama Wines Inc...479 530-3057
332 Calle Escada Santa Rosa Beach (32459) ***(G-15427)***
Hf Scientific Inc...888 203-7248
16260 Arprt Pk Dr Ste 140 Fort Myers (33913) ***(G-4279)***
Hg Brokerage Services Inc...407 294-3507
2813 S Hiawassee Rd # 301 Orlando (32835) ***(G-12215)***
HG Trading Cia Inc...305 986-5702
1055 Se 9th Ter Hialeah (33010) ***(G-5183)***
Hg2 Emergency Lighting LLC...407 426-7700
477 N Semoran Blvd Orlando (32807) ***(G-12216)***
HGP Industries, Tampa *Also called Oldcastle Buildingenvelope Inc* ***(G-17121)***
HI Tech Aviation Welding LLC...305 591-3393
8060 Nw 67th St Miami (33166) ***(G-9278)***
HI Tech Construction Svc Inc...863 968-0731
5540 Commercial Blvd Winter Haven (33880) ***(G-18445)***
HI Tech Granite and Marble...407 230-4363
11362 Space Blvd Orlando (32837) ***(G-12217)***
HI Tech Printing Systems Inc...954 933-9155
3411 Ne 6th Ter Pompano Beach (33064) ***(G-14049)***
HI Tech Welding, Miami *Also called HI Tech Aviation Welding LLC* ***(G-9278)***
Hi-TEC Laboratories Inc...850 835-6822
9646 State Highway 20 W Freeport (32439) ***(G-4627)***
Hialeah Distribution Corp...786 200-2498
270 W 25th St Hialeah (33010) ***(G-5184)***
Hialeah Plating...305 953-4143
4335 E 10th Ave Hialeah (33013) ***(G-5185)***
Hialeah Powder Coating Corp...786 275-4107
1690 W 33rd Pl Hialeah (33012) ***(G-5186)***
Hickory Springs Mfg Co...352 622-7583
5407 Nw 44th Ave Ocala (34482) ***(G-11409)***
Hicks Industries Inc (PA)...863 425-4155
2005 Industrial Park Rd Mulberry (33860) ***(G-10627)***
Hicks Industries Inc...954 226-5148
2257 Sw 66th Ter Davie (33317) ***(G-2422)***
Hid Global Corp...561 622-9013
3950 Rca Blvd Ste 5001 Palm Beach Gardens (33410) ***(G-12973)***
Hid Global Corporation...954 990-2782
600 Corporate Dr Ste 310 Fort Lauderdale (33334) ***(G-3865)***
Hidalgo Corp...305 379-0110
14 Ne 1st Ave Ste 805 Miami (33132) ***(G-9279)***
Hidalgo Jewelry, Miami *Also called Hidalgo Corp* ***(G-9279)***
Hidenet Scrities Architectures, West Palm Beach *Also called Bionitrogen Holdings Corp* ***(G-17945)***
Higgins Group Corp...305 681-4444
3198 Nw 125th St Miami (33167) ***(G-9280)***
High End Defense Solutions LLC...305 647-2597
8080 W 26th Ct Hialeah (33016) ***(G-5187)***
High Export, Doral *Also called AMC Development Group LLC* ***(G-3111)***
High Five Industries Inc...954 673-1811
2719 Hollywood Blvd Hollywood (33020) ***(G-5595)***
High Noon Holsters, Holiday *Also called High Noon Unlimited Inc* ***(G-5499)***
High Noon Unlimited Inc...727 939-2701
4339 Buena Vista Ln Holiday (34691) ***(G-5499)***
High Performance Boats & Cars, Fort Myers *Also called P B C H Incorporated* ***(G-4353)***
High Performance Holdings Ltd...815 874-9421
625 Mccue Rd Ste 1 Lakeland (33815) ***(G-7344)***

A L P H A B E T I C

High Performance Systems Inc......................863 294-5566
1201 Amercn Superior Blvd Winter Haven (33880) *(G-18446)*

High Power Services, Saint Petersburg *Also called David Chittum (G-15020)*

High Sierra Terminaling LLC......................954 764-8818
1200 Se 20th St Fort Lauderdale (33316) *(G-3866)*

High Standard Aviation Inc......................305 599-8855
5900 Nw 97th Ave Unit 3 Doral (33178) *(G-3248)*

High Tech Hoist Corp......................321 733-3387
3682 N Wickham Rd 225 Melbourne (32935) *(G-8436)*

High Tech Precision Mfg LLC......................954 302-1995
10392 W State Road 84 # 1 Davie (33324) *(G-2423)*

High Temp Industries......................215 794-0864
3808 Sw 6th Ter Cape Coral (33991) *(G-1353)*

High Top Products Corp......................305 633-3287
8187 Nw 8th St Apt 108 Miami (33126) *(G-9281)*

High Velocity, Naples *Also called Sano Associates Inc (G-10883)*

Highland Cabinet Inc......................863 385-4396
739 Glenwood Ave Sebring (33870) *(G-15926)*

Highland Cabinet Shop, Sebring *Also called Highland Cabinet Inc (G-15926)*

Highland Mint, Indian Harbour Beach *Also called Bullion International Inc (G-5804)*

Highlander Stone Corp......................786 333-1151
14105 Nw 19th Ave Opa Locka (33054) *(G-11753)*

Highlands Ethanol LLC......................813 421-1090
2202 N West Shore Blvd Tampa (33607) *(G-16916)*

Highrolla Empire LLC......................954 743-5324
7901 4th St N Ste 300 Saint Petersburg (33702) *(G-15075)*

Highroller Fishing Lure Co LLC......................352 215-2925
4630 Nw 30th St Gainesville (32605) *(G-4706)*

Highseer.com, Doral *Also called Parker Davis Hvac Intl Inc (G-3323)*

Highvac Co LLC......................407 969-0399
3842 Commerce Loop Orlando (32808) *(G-12218)*

Highway Sfety Mtr Vhcles Fla D......................561 640-6826
470 Columbia Dr Ste E200 West Palm Beach (33409) *(G-18024)*

Highway Systems Incorporated......................813 907-7512
4450 Pet Ln Lutz (33559) *(G-7994)*

Hilcraft Engraving Inc......................305 871-6100
3960 Nw 26th St Miami (33142) *(G-9282)*

Hill Dermaceuticals Inc......................407 323-1887
2650 S Mellonville Ave Sanford (32773) *(G-15332)*

Hill Donnelly Corporation (PA)......................800 525-1242
10126 Windhorst Rd Tampa (33619) *(G-16917)*

Hill Enterprises LLC......................850 478-4455
125 Terry Dr Pensacola (32503) *(G-13519)*

Hill Labs Inc......................407 323-1887
2650 S Mellonville Ave Sanford (32773) *(G-15333)*

Hill Printing Inc......................407 654-4282
1220 Wntr Gdn Vnlnd Rd # 104 Winter Garden (34787) *(G-18390)*

Hilliard Bruce Vineyards LLC......................305 979-2601
1521 Alton Rd Ste 842 Miami Beach (33139) *(G-10200)*

Hills Inc......................321 723-5560
7785 Ellis Rd Melbourne (32904) *(G-8437)*

Hilomast LLC......................386 668-6784
402 Chairman Ct Ste 100 Debary (32713) *(G-2635)*

Hilton International Inc......................941 371-2600
6055 Porter Way Sarasota (34232) *(G-15701)*

Hilton Software LLC......................954 323-2244
2730 N University Dr Coral Springs (33065) *(G-2161)*

Hiltronics Corporation......................954 341-9100
3979 Nw 126th Ave Coral Springs (33065) *(G-2162)*

Himes Signs Inc......................850 837-1159
4 Commerce Dr Ste 4 # 4 Destin (32541) *(G-3070)*

Himgc Limited......................213 443-8729
1301 Beville Rd Daytona Beach (32119) *(G-2562)*

Himmel Losungen Group Hlg LLC......................786 631-5531
4711 Nw 79th Ave Ste 12l Doral (33166) *(G-3249)*

Hinckley......................239 919-8142
535 5th Ave S Naples (34102) *(G-10773)*

Hine Automation LLC......................813 749-7519
12495 34th St N Ste B Saint Petersburg (33716) *(G-15076)*

Hines Bending Systems Inc......................239 433-2132
6441 Metro Plantation Rd Fort Myers (33966) *(G-4280)*

Hines Energy Complex......................863 519-6106
7700 County Road 555 S Bartow (33830) *(G-312)*

Hinsilblon Ltd Inc......................239 418-1133
12381 S Cleveland Ave Fort Myers (33907) *(G-4281)*

Hinsilblon Laboratories, Fort Myers *Also called Hinsilblon Ltd Inc (G-4281)*

Hipaat International Inc......................905 405-6299
340 9th St N Naples (34102) *(G-10774)*

Hippo Tampa LLC......................813 391-9152
605 Bosphorous Ave Tampa (33606) *(G-16918)*

Hire Authority......................561 477-6663
8445 Miller Dr Miami (33155) *(G-9283)*

His, Pinellas Park *Also called HIS Cabinetry Inc (G-13693)*

HIS Cabinetry Inc......................727 527-7262
6200 49th St N Pinellas Park (33781) *(G-13693)*

Hisco Pump South LLC......................904 786-4488
2664 Robert St Jacksonville (32207) *(G-6177)*

Hispacom Inc......................954 255-2622
9900 W Sample Rd Ste 200 Coral Springs (33065) *(G-2163)*

Hispanic Amercn Pubg Group Inc......................305 961-1132
1200 Brickell Ave # 1950 Miami (33131) *(G-9284)*

Hispanic Certified Foods Inc......................305 772-6815
1741 Nw 33rd St Pompano Beach (33064) *(G-14050)*

Hit Promotional Products Inc (PA)......................727 541-5561
7150 Bryan Dairy Rd Largo (33777) *(G-7605)*

Hitachi Cable America Inc......................850 476-0907
9101 Ely Rd Pensacola (32514) *(G-13520)*

Hitachi Rail STS Usa Inc......................415 397-7010
11150 Nw 122nd St Medley (33178) *(G-8252)*

Hitachi Vantara Corporation......................407 517-4532
5950 Hazeltine Nat Dr Orlando (32822) *(G-12219)*

Hitech Truss Inc......................352 797-0877
6179 Nature Coast Blvd Brooksville (34602) *(G-1161)*

Hitek Property LLC......................352 797-0877
6179 Nature Coast Blvd Brooksville (34602) *(G-1162)*

Hitek Truss, Brooksville *Also called Hitech Truss Inc (G-1161)*

Hitex Marketing Group Inc......................305 406-1150
1566 Nw 108th Ave Miami (33172) *(G-9285)*

Hitman Industries LLC......................321 735-8562
150 N Wilson Ave Cocoa (32922) *(G-1935)*

Hitmaster Graphics LLC......................267 269-8220
12206 Hazen Ave Thonotosassa (33592) *(G-17562)*

Hizer Machine Mfg Inc......................386 755-3155
12137 Se Us Highway 41 White Springs (32096) *(G-18306)*

Hj German Corner LLC......................239 672-8462
3674 Cleveland Ave Fort Myers (33901) *(G-4282)*

Hki Soundigital USA LLC......................786 600-1056
345 Bryan Rd Dania (33004) *(G-2332)*

HM Factory LLC......................305 897-0004
2952 Nw 72nd Ave Miami (33122) *(G-9286)*

HM Froyos LLC......................561 339-0603
8204 Firenze Blvd Orlando (32836) *(G-12220)*

Hmb Steel Corporation......................321 636-6511
4080 Pines Industrial Ave Rockledge (32955) *(G-14714)*

Hmd Investment Group LLC......................305 244-1290
7753 Nw 53rd St Doral (33166) *(G-3250)*

Hnc Enterprises Inc......................904 448-9387
1624 Talbot Ave Jacksonville (32205) *(G-6178)*

Hnc Machine Shop Corp......................305 299-4023
13900 Sw 139th Ct Miami (33186) *(G-9287)*

Hnm Medical LLC......................866 291-8498
20855 Ne 16th Ave Ste C15 Miami (33179) *(G-9288)*

HOB Corporation......................813 988-2272
5604 E 122nd Ave Tampa (33617) *(G-16919)*

Hobbs Trucking LLC......................904 463-5681
15616 County Road 108 Hilliard (32046) *(G-5467)*

Hobby Press Inc......................305 887-4333
8001 Nw 74th Ave Medley (33166) *(G-8253)*

Hock, John W Co, Gainesville *Also called John W Hock Company (G-4716)*

Hoerbger Auto Cmfort Systems L......................334 321-2292
1191 E Nwport Ctr Dr Ste Deerfield Beach (33442) *(G-2734)*

Hoerbger Cmprssion Tech Amer H (HQ)......................954 974-5700
3350 Gateway Dr Pompano Beach (33069) *(G-14051)*

Hoerbiger America Holding Inc (PA)......................954 422-9850
1432 E Nwport Ctr Dr Ste Deerfield Beach (33442) *(G-2735)*

Hoerbiger America Holding Inc......................954 422-9850
1191 E Newport Center Dr Deerfield Beach (33442) *(G-2736)*

Hoerbiger Compression Technolo, Pompano Beach *Also called Hoerbiger Corp America Inc (G-14052)*

Hoerbiger Corp America Inc (HQ)......................954 974-5700
3350 Gateway Dr Pompano Beach (33069) *(G-14052)*

Hoerbiger Gas Engine Systems, Deerfield Beach *Also called Hoerbiger Service Inc (G-2737)*

Hoerbiger Service Inc......................954 422-9850
1432 E Nwport Ctr Dr Ste Deerfield Beach (33442) *(G-2737)*

Hoerndler Inc......................239 643-2008
4165 Corporate Sq Naples (34104) *(G-10775)*

Hoffman Brothers Inc......................407 563-5004
275 S Chrles Rchard Ball Debary (32713) *(G-2636)*

Hoffman Commercial Group Inc (HQ)......................561 967-2213
1815 Cypress Lake Dr Orlando (32837) *(G-12221)*

Hoffman Mint, Fort Lauderdale *Also called American Changer Corp (G-3648)*

Hoffman's Chocolates, Orlando *Also called Hoffman Commercial Group Inc (G-12221)*

Hoffstetter Tool & Die Inc......................727 573-7775
4371 112th Ter N Clearwater (33762) *(G-1625)*

Hofmann & Leavy Inc......................954 698-0000
3251 Sw 13th Dr Ste 3 Deerfield Beach (33442) *(G-2738)*

Hog Technologies, Stuart *Also called Waterblasting Technologies Inc (G-16248)*

Hogan Assessment Systems Inc......................904 992-0302
13500 Sutton Park Dr S # 401 Jacksonville (32224) *(G-6179)*

Hogenkamp Research Inc......................850 677-1072
308 Plantation Hill Rd Gulf Breeze (32561) *(G-4884)*

Hohol Marine Products......................386 734-0630
2741 W New York Ave Deland (32720) *(G-2874)*

Hoipong Customs Inc......................954 684-9232
18331 Pines Blvd Pembroke Pines (33029) *(G-13396)*

Holbrook Metal Fabrication LLC......................386 937-5441
341 N Highway 17 Palatka (32177) *(G-12872)*

Holcomb Industries Flp......................................480 363-9988
2655 Ulmerton Rd 303 Clearwater (33762) *(G-1626)*

Holeshot Performance Wheels, Bunnell *Also called World Class Machining Inc* *(G-1238)*

Holeshot Raceway Inc...407 864-1095
434 Terrace Dr Oviedo (32765) *(G-12825)*

Holiday Cleaners Inc..727 842-6989
3640 Calera Dr New Port Richey (34652) *(G-10968)*

Holiday Ice Inc...407 831-2077
204 Short Ave Longwood (32750) *(G-7901)*

Holland Creative Services Inc...............................904 732-4932
2736 University Blvd W # 1 Jacksonville (32217) *(G-6180)*

Holland Pump Company (PA).................................561 697-3333
7312 Westport Pl West Palm Beach (33413) *(G-18025)*

Holland Pump Company..904 880-0010
2720 Lane Ave N Jacksonville (32254) *(G-6181)*

Holland Welding LLC..904 675-6106
7014 Abbot Ct Jacksonville (32216) *(G-6182)*

Hollander Sleep & Decor, Boca Raton *Also called Bedding Acquisition LLC* *(G-428)*

Hollow Metal Inc...813 246-4112
2803 Park Meadow Dr Valrico (33594) *(G-17665)*

Holly Sargent...954 560-6973
1000 Se 4th St Apt 315 Fort Lauderdale (33301) *(G-3867)*

Hollywood Cllctibles Group LLC............................407 985-4613
11491 Rocket Blvd Orlando (32824) *(G-12222)*

Hollywood Design & Concepts...............................954 458-4634
26534 Bloomfield Ave Yalaha (34797) *(G-18583)*

Hollywood Houndz LLC...407 614-2108
4101 Briar Gate Ln Winter Garden (34787) *(G-18391)*

Hollywood Iron Works Inc.....................................954 962-0556
2313 Sw 57th Ter West Park (33023) *(G-18213)*

Hollywood Lodging Inc...305 803-7455
2601 N 29th Ave Hollywood (33020) *(G-5596)*

Hollywood Machine Shop Inc.................................954 893-6103
5835 Rodman St Hollywood (33023) *(G-5597)*

Hollywood Water Trtmnt Plant, Hollywood *Also called City of Hollywood* *(G-5550)*

Hollywood Woodwork Inc......................................954 920-5009
2951 Pembroke Rd Hollywood (33020) *(G-5598)*

Hollywood Woodwork LLC......................................954 920-5009
2951 Pembroke Rd Hollywood (33020) *(G-5599)*

Holmes Stamp Company (PA)................................904 396-2291
2021 Saint Augustine Rd E Jacksonville (32207) *(G-6183)*

Holmes Tool & Engineering Inc.............................850 547-4417
1019 N Waukesha St Bonifay (32425) *(G-772)*

Holpack Corp..786 565-3969
3840 W 104th St Unit 7 Hialeah (33018) *(G-5188)*

Holtec International (PA)......................................561 745-7772
1001 N Us Highway 1 Jupiter (33477) *(G-6742)*

Holyland Tapestries Inc.......................................305 255-7955
14565 Sw 75th Ave Palmetto Bay (33158) *(G-13211)*

Homac Manufacturing, Ormond Beach *Also called ABB Installation Products Inc* *(G-12740)*

Home & Garden Industries Inc..............................305 634-0681
5700 Nw 32nd Ave Miami (33142) *(G-9289)*

Home Aide Diagnostics Inc...................................954 794-0212
1072 S Powerline Rd Deerfield Beach (33442) *(G-2739)*

Home and Design Magazine..................................239 598-4826
809 Walkerbilt Rd Ste 4 Naples (34110) *(G-10776)*

Home County Times Advertiser, Bonifay *Also called Chipley Newspapers Inc* *(G-769)*

Home Design Group Corp......................................305 888-5836
220 W 21st St Hialeah (33010) *(G-5189)*

Home Elments St Petersburg Inc...........................727 510-5700
790 Cordova Blvd Ne Saint Petersburg (33704) *(G-15077)*

Home Fashion Source, Chipley *Also called Westpoint Home Inc* *(G-1461)*

Home Healthcare 2000 Inc...................................954 977-4450
1290 Sw 30th Ave Pompano Beach (33069) *(G-14053)*

Home Improver Inc...239 549-6901
1732 Se 47th Ter Cape Coral (33904) *(G-1354)*

Home Imprv & Developers LLC..............................305 902-3015
11070 Sw 25th Ct Apt 1030 Miramar (33025) *(G-10501)*

Home Mag, The, Saint Augustine *Also called Old Port Group LLC* *(G-14869)*

Home Mag, The, Longwood *Also called Samjay Media Group Orlando LLC* *(G-7944)*

Home Pride Cabinets Inc.......................................813 887-3782
8503 Sunstate St Tampa (33634) *(G-16920)*

Home Protection Team, Miami *Also called Security Tech Group Inc* *(G-9863)*

Home Robot LLC..850 826-8720
53 Ferry Rd Ne Fort Walton Beach (32548) *(G-4592)*

Home Source Manufacturing Inc...........................404 663-0647
3595 Industrial Park Dr Marianna (32446) *(G-8166)*

Home Town News, South Miami *Also called Miller Publishing Co Inc* *(G-16039)*

Home Works Bay County Inc..................................850 215-7880
4902 E Highway 98 Panama City (32404) *(G-13273)*

Home-Art Corporation..352 326-3337
2408 Us Highway 441/27 Fruitland Park (34731) *(G-4641)*

Homemag Inc..239 549-6960
1732 Se 47th Ter Cape Coral (33904) *(G-1355)*

Homerun Derby Bats Only LLC..............................813 545-3887
6931 Potomac Cir Riverview (33578) *(G-14566)*

Homes & Land Magazine, Melbourne *Also called Shelton Group LLC* *(G-8520)*

Homes & Land Magazine, Bonita Springs *Also called Boswell JM & Associates Inc* *(G-785)*

Homes & Land of Emerald Coast, Niceville *Also called North Metro Media* *(G-11033)*

Homes Magazine Inc..239 334-7168
2133 Broadway Fort Myers (33901) *(G-4283)*

Homes Media Solutions LLC (HQ).........................850 350-7800
325 John Knox Rd Bldg 200 Tallahassee (32303) *(G-16462)*

Homes Real Estate Magazine, Fort Myers *Also called Homes Magazine Inc* *(G-4283)*

Homestead Diagnostic Ctr Inc..............................305 246-5600
650 Ne 22nd Ter Ste 100 Homestead (33033) *(G-5713)*

Homestead Newspapers Inc..................................305 245-2311
125 Ne 8th St Ste 2 Homestead (33030) *(G-5714)*

Hometown Foods Usa LLC.....................................305 887-5200
11800 Nw 102nd Rd Ste 6 Medley (33178) *(G-8254)*

Hometown News LC (PA)......................................772 465-5656
1102 S Us Highway 1 Fort Pierce (34950) *(G-4495)*

Homewood Holdings LLC.......................................941 740-3655
745 Ne 19th Pl Ste E Cape Coral (33909) *(G-1356)*

Homyn Enterprises Corp.......................................305 870-9720
4050 Nw 29th St Miami (33142) *(G-9290)*

Honchin Inc..305 235-3800
10397 Sw 186th St Cutler Bay (33157) *(G-2291)*

Honda Generators of Tampa, Tampa *Also called Interbay Air Compressors Inc* *(G-16948)*

Honduras Food Services Inc..................................310 940-2071
2337 Sw Archer Rd Apt 302 Gainesville (32608) *(G-4707)*

Honest Hands LLC...413 262-3892
13907 Carrollwood Vlg Run Tampa (33618) *(G-16921)*

Honeycomb Company America Inc.........................941 756-8781
1950 Limbus Ave Sarasota (34243) *(G-15494)*

Honeycommcore LLC (PA)....................................561 747-2678
15771 80th Dr N West Palm Beach (33418) *(G-18026)*

Honeywell Authorized Dealer, Jacksonville *Also called Southern Technologies* *(G-6494)*

Honeywell Authorized Dealer, Tampa *Also called Airite Air Conditioning Inc* *(G-16567)*

Honeywell Authorized Dealer, Clearwater *Also called Source 1 Solutions Inc* *(G-1787)*

Honeywell Authorized Dealer, Maitland *Also called Southern Hvac Corporation* *(G-8074)*

Honeywell Authorized Dealer, Orlando *Also called Mechanical Svcs Centl Fla Inc* *(G-12368)*

Honeywell Authorized Dealer, Orlando *Also called Innovative Svc Solutions LLC* *(G-12246)*

Honeywell Authorized Dealer, Plant City *Also called C & C Services of Tampa Inc* *(G-13749)*

Honeywell Authorized Dealer, Largo *Also called Straight Polarity Welding Inc* *(G-7691)*

Honeywell International Inc...................................727 539-5080
13350 Us Highway 19 N Clearwater (33764) *(G-1627)*

Honeywell International Inc...................................505 358-0676
13051 66th St Largo (33773) *(G-7606)*

Honeywell International Inc...................................727 531-4611
13350 Us Highway 19 N Clearwater (33764) *(G-1628)*

Honeywell International Inc...................................813 573-1166
13190 56th Ct Ste 403 Clearwater (33760) *(G-1629)*

Hontus Ltd (PA)..786 322-3022
11450 Nw 122nd St Ste 100 Medley (33178) *(G-8255)*

Hontus, Ltd., Inc., Medley *Also called Hontus Ltd* *(G-8255)*

Hood Depot International Inc.................................954 570-9860
710 S Powerline Rd Ste H Deerfield Beach (33442) *(G-2740)*

Hook International, Pinellas Park *Also called Global Diversified Products* *(G-13690)*

Hook International Inc..727 209-0855
6795 114th Ave Largo (33773) *(G-7607)*

Hooper Corp...954 382-5711
6900 Sw 21st Ct Davie (33317) *(G-2424)*

Hoosier Lightening Inc...407 290-3323
2415 N John Young Pkwy Orlando (32804) *(G-12223)*

Hoot/Wisdom Music Pubg LLC..............................561 297-3205
777 Glades Rd Boca Raton (33431) *(G-539)*

Hoover Canvas Products, Fort Lauderdale *Also called Major Canvas Products Inc* *(G-3928)*

Hoover Canvas Products Co (PA)...........................954 764-1711
844 Nw 9th Ave Fort Lauderdale (33311) *(G-3868)*

Hoover Canvas Products Co..................................954 541-9745
5107 N Australian Ave Mangonia Park (33407) *(G-8092)*

Hoover Canvas Products Co..................................561 844-4444
5107 N Australian Ave Mangonia Park (33407) *(G-8093)*

Hoover Pumping Systems Corp..............................954 971-7350
2801 N Powerline Rd Pompano Beach (33069) *(G-14054)*

Hope Technical Sales & Svcs.................................941 412-1204
692 Sawgrass Bridge Rd Venice (34292) *(G-17698)*

Hopkins & Daughter Inc.......................................941 964-2995
431 Park Ave Boca Grande (33921) *(G-381)*

Hopkins Manufacturing Co...................................620 591-8229
855 Pine St Tarpon Springs (34689) *(G-17475)*

Hoppin Pop Kettle Stop LLC (PA)..........................502 220-2372
1850 Emerson St Jacksonville (32207) *(G-6184)*

Hopscotch Technology Group Inc..........................305 846-0942
1288 Sanctuary Dr Oviedo (32766) *(G-12826)*

Horizon Duplication Inc..407 767-5000
841 Nicolet Ave Ste 5 Winter Park (32789) *(G-18514)*

Horizon Industries Inc..561 315-5439
180 Business Park Way B1 Royal Palm Beach (33411) *(G-14765)*

Horizon Media Express, Winter Park *Also called Horizon Duplication Inc* *(G-18514)*

Horizon Pharmaceuticals Inc................................561 844-7227
10180 Riveside Dr Ste 8 Palm Beach Gardens (33410) *(G-12974)*

Horizon Publications Inc......................................386 427-1000
508 Tanal St New Smyrna Beach (32168) *(G-11002)*

Hornblasters Inc 813 783-8058
6511 N 54th St Tampa (33610) *(G-16922)*

Horseshoe 863 438-6632
150 California Blvd Davenport (33897) *(G-2366)*

Horseshoe Picking Inc 305 345-5778
21400 Sw 392nd St Homestead (33034) *(G-5715)*

Horseshoe Shrimp Boat LLC 352 356-1982
77 Main St Horseshoe Beach (32648) *(G-5753)*

Hose McCann Communications, Deerfield Beach *Also called Hose-Mccann Telephone Co*
Inc (G-2741)

Hose Power USA 863 669-9333
3110 Winter Lake Rd Lakeland (33803) *(G-7345)*

Hose-Mccann Telephone Co Inc (PA) 954 429-1110
1241 W Newport Center Dr Deerfield Beach (33442) *(G-2741)*

Hoseline Inc 407 892-2599
1619 Park Commerce Ct Saint Cloud (34769) *(G-14929)*

Hoseline Inc 541 258-8984
701 Nw 37th Ave Ocala (34475) *(G-11410)*

Hot Action Sportswear Inc 386 677-5680
307 Division Ave Ormond Beach (32174) *(G-12770)*

Hot Dog Shoppe LLC 850 682-3649
1308 N Ferdon Blvd Crestview (32536) *(G-2247)*

Hot Off Press 386 238-8700
952 Big Tree Rd South Daytona (32119) *(G-16022)*

Hot Sauce Harrys Inc 941 423-7092
1077 Innovation Ave # 10 North Port (34289) *(G-11195)*

Hot Shot Welding Inc 727 585-1900
1135 Starkey Rd Ste 10 Largo (33771) *(G-7608)*

Hot Tub Parts LLC 727 573-9611
6190 45th St N Ste A Saint Petersburg (33714) *(G-15078)*

Hotspot Magazine of Florida, Wilton Manors *Also called Venice Quarters Inc (G-18344)*

Hotspray Industrial Coatings 407 658-5700
1932 N Goldenrod Rd Orlando (32807) *(G-12224)*

Hotsy Cleaning Systems, Longwood *Also called Lee Chemical Corporation (G-7917)*

Hough Industries Inc 863 634-1664
21612 N County Road 349 O Brien (32071) *(G-11224)*

Houghton Mifflin Harcourt 407 345-2000
9400 S Park Loop Orlando (32819) *(G-12225)*

Houghton Mifflin Harcourt Pubg 561 951-5518
100 Gibraltar St Royal Palm Beach (33411) *(G-14766)*

Houghton Mifflin Harcourt Pubg 407 345-2000
9400 S Park Center Loop Orlando (32819) *(G-12226)*

Houghton Mifflin Harcourt Pubg 954 975-0508
1840 Nw 16th St Pompano Beach (33069) *(G-14055)*

House Doctair Inc 239 349-7497
5438 Ferrari Ave Ave Maria (34142) *(G-248)*

House of Cabinets Ltd Inc 352 795-5300
4107 N Citrus Ave Crystal River (34428) *(G-2277)*

House of Llull Atelier LLC 305 964-7921
13850 Sw 143rd Ct Ste 19 Miami (33186) *(G-9291)*

House of Marble & Granite Inc (PA) 239 261-0099
440 Tamiami Trl N Naples (34102) *(G-10777)*

House of Metal LLC 727 540-0637
4161 114th Ter N Clearwater (33762) *(G-1630)*

House of Wood, Mangonia Park *Also called Terry D Triplett Inc (G-8102)*

House Plastics Unlimited Inc 407 843-3290
2580 S Orange Blossom Trl Orlando (32805) *(G-12227)*

Housmans Alum & Screening Inc 321 255-2778
2911 Dusa Dr Ste E Melbourne (32934) *(G-8438)*

Hoverfly Technologies Inc 407 985-4500
12151 Res Pkwy Ste 100 Orlando (32826) *(G-12228)*

Hoveround Corporation (PA) 941 739-6200
2151 Whitfield Indus Way Sarasota (34243) *(G-15495)*

Howard & Mary Glavin, Jacksonville *Also called Mtg Designs Inc (G-6626)*

Howard Imprinting Machine Co 813 884-2398
5013 Tampa West Blvd Tampa (33634) *(G-16923)*

Howard Publications Inc (HQ) 904 355-2601
501 W Bay St Ste 200 Jacksonville (32202) *(G-6185)*

Howard Scripts Inc 561 746-5111
800 W Indiantown Rd Jupiter (33458) *(G-6743)*

Howell Logging & Land Clearing 352 528-2698
20253 Ne 20th St Williston (32696) *(G-18333)*

Howies Instant Printing Inc 561 686-8699
1572 Palm Bch Lakes Blvd West Palm Beach (33401) *(G-18027)*

Howmedica Osteonics Corp 941 378-4600
8235 Blaikie Ct Sarasota (34240) *(G-15702)*

Howmedica Osteonics Corp 954 714-7933
505 Nw 65th Ct Ste 102 Fort Lauderdale (33309) *(G-3869)*

Howmedica Osteonics Corp 813 886-3450
8731 Florida Mining Blvd Tampa (33634) *(G-16924)*

Howmedica Osteonics Corp 954 791-6078
2944 Trivium Cir Fort Lauderdale (33312) *(G-3870)*

Hoya Largo 727 531-8964
12345 Starkey Rd Ste E Largo (33773) *(G-7609)*

HP Preferred Ltd Partners 407 298-4470
6401 Edgewater Dr Orlando (32810) *(G-12229)*

Hps, Miami *Also called Hernandez Printing Service Inc (G-9277)*

Hr Ease Inc 813 414-0040
2002 N Lois Ave Ste 220 Tampa (33607) *(G-16925)*

HRF Exploration & Prod LLC (PA) 561 847-4743
250 El Dorado Ln Palm Beach (33480) *(G-12936)*

Hrh Door Corp 850 474-9890
3395 Addison Dr Pensacola (32514) *(G-13521)*

Hs Stone Gallery LLC 305 200-5810
1660 Nw 82nd Ave Doral (33126) *(G-3251)*

Hsc, Jacksonville *Also called Holmes Stamp Company (G-6183)*

Ht Medical LLC 888 594-8633
111 W Jefferson St # 100 Orlando (32801) *(G-12230)*

Hte, Bonifay *Also called Holmes Tool & Engineering Inc (G-772)*

Hth Engineering Inc 727 939-8853
825 Cypress Trail Dr Tarpon Springs (34688) *(G-17476)*

Hti 941 723-4570
210 9th Street Dr W Palmetto (34221) *(G-13174)*

Hts Controls Inc 813 287-5512
4918 W Grace St Tampa (33607) *(G-16926)*

Hub Steel, Groveland *Also called Suncoast Projects LLC (G-4873)*

Hucke Manufacturing Inc 863 655-3667
222 Commercial Pl Sebring (33876) *(G-15927)*

Huckins Yacht Corporation 904 389-1125
3482 Lake Shore Blvd Jacksonville (32210) *(G-6186)*

Hudson Cabinets & Millwork LLC 239 218-0451
6261 Metro Plantation Rd Fort Myers (33966) *(G-4284)*

Hudson Do It Best Hardware, Hudson *Also called Td Tra -Dix Supply Inc (G-5788)*

Hudson Technologies, Ormond Beach *Also called Hudson Tool & Die Company*
Inc (G-12771)

Hudson Tool & Die Company Inc 386 672-2000
1327 N Us Highway 1 Ormond Beach (32174) *(G-12771)*

Hudsons Wldg & Fabrication Inc 941 355-4858
10845 Forest Run Dr Bradenton (34211) *(G-992)*

Huff Carbide Tool Inc 727 848-4001
6541 Industrial Ave Port Richey (34668) *(G-14362)*

Hugh Robinson Inc 954 484-0660
2718 Nw 31st Ave Lauderdale Lakes (33311) *(G-7716)*

Hughes Consolidated Services 904 438-5710
4712 Royal Ave Jacksonville (32205) *(G-6187)*

Hughes Corporation 954 755-7111
4000 Nw 121st Ave Coral Springs (33065) *(G-2164)*

Hughes Fabrication 239 481-1376
2304 Bruner Ln Ste 1 Fort Myers (33912) *(G-4285)*

Hughes Trim LLC 863 206-6048
7613 Currency Dr Orlando (32809) *(G-12231)*

Human Rights Defense Center, Lake Worth *Also called Prison Legal News (G-7229)*

Human Sign 239 573-4292
1830 Del Prado Blvd S Cape Coral (33990) *(G-1357)*

Humic Growth Solutions Inc (PA) 904 392-7201
709 Eastport Rd Jacksonville (32218) *(G-6188)*

Humic Growth Solutions Inc 904 329-1012
938 Hall Park Rd Green Cove Springs (32043) *(G-4830)*

Humic Growth Solutions Inc 904 329-1012
112 Badger Park Dr Saint Johns (32259) *(G-14946)*

Hummingbirds Ai Inc 305 432-2787
8140 Hawthorne Ave Miami Beach (33141) *(G-10201)*

Humo E-Liquids, Plantation *Also called E-Liquids Investment Group LLC (G-13845)*

Hunt Enterprises Inc 863 682-6187
1224 E Lime St Lakeland (33801) *(G-7346)*

Hunt RDS Inc 813 249-7551
3898 Tampa Rd Oldsmar (34677) *(G-11657)*

Hunt Ventures Inc 941 375-3699
232 Bahama St Venice (34285) *(G-17699)*

Hunter Aerospace Supply LLC 954 321-8848
3331 Nw 55th St Fort Lauderdale (33309) *(G-3871)*

Hunter Wood Products, Deland *Also called Island Shutter Co Inc (G-2876)*

Hunting Report The, Miami *Also called Oxpecker Enterprise Inc (G-9673)*

Huntley Stemwood Inc 904 237-4005
2785 Black Creek Dr Middleburg (32068) *(G-10402)*

Huntsman Properties LLC 305 653-2288
951 Nw 200th Ter Miami (33169) *(G-9292)*

Hurricane Graphics Inc 305 760-9154
3331 Nw 168th St Miami Gardens (33056) *(G-10263)*

Hurricane Marine Mfg Inc 772 260-3950
3301 Se Slater St Stuart (34997) *(G-16163)*

Hurricane Marine Mfg S Inc 305 735-4461
88665 Old Hwy Tavernier (33070) *(G-17531)*

Hurricane Medical Inc 941 753-1517
5315 Lena Rd Bradenton (34211) *(G-993)*

Hurricane Roofing & Shtmtl Inc 954 968-8155
1905 Mears Pkwy Margate (33063) *(G-8135)*

Hurricane Shtters Cntl Fla Inc 321 639-2622
3460 Us Highway 1 Rockledge (32955) *(G-14715)*

Hurricane Shutter & Plus Inc 786 287-0007
8004 Sw 149th Ave Miami (33193) *(G-9293)*

Hurst Awning Company Inc (PA) 305 693-0600
3613 N 29th Ave Hollywood (33020) *(G-5600)*

Hussmann Corporation 813 623-1199
9216 Palm River Rd # 201 Tampa (33619) *(G-16927)*

Hut Global Inc 561 571-2523
131 S Federal Hwy Apt 721 Boca Raton (33432) *(G-540)*

2022 Harris Florida
Manufacturers Directory

(G-0000) Company's Geographic Section entry number

ALPHABETIC SECTION ICI Custom Parts Inc

Hutchins Co Inc 727 442-6651
1195 Kapp Dr Clearwater (33765) **(G-1631)**

Hy-Tech Thermal Solutions LLC 321 984-9777
159 Park Hill Blvd Melbourne (32904) **(G-8439)**

Hybrid Engines Corp 954 591-5303
1001 S Riverside Dr Pompano Beach (33062) **(G-14056)**

Hybrid Impressions Inc (PA) 305 392-5029
8020 W 30th Ct Hialeah (33018) **(G-5190)**

Hybrid Sources Inc 772 563-9100
2950 43rd Ave Vero Beach (32960) **(G-17760)**

Hyco, Clearwater *Also called Hytronics Corp* **(G-1635)**

Hycomb Usa Inc 954 251-1691
311 W Ansin Blvd Hallandale Beach (33009) **(G-4950)**

Hydes Screening Inc 954 345-6743
3700 Nw 124th Ave Ste 126 Coral Springs (33065) **(G-2165)**

Hydrapower International Inc 239 642-5379
950 N Collier Blvd # 202 Marco Island (34145) **(G-8112)**

Hydraulic Net, Saint Augustine *Also called Hydraulicnet LLC* **(G-14840)**

Hydraulicnet LLC 630 543-7630
6980 Us Highway 1 N # 107 Saint Augustine (32095) **(G-14840)**

Hydrex LLC 727 443-3900
627 Pinellas St Unit C Clearwater (33756) **(G-1632)**

Hydro Extrusion Usa LLC 904 794-1500
200 Riviera Blvd Saint Augustine (32086) **(G-14841)**

Hydro Precision Tubing USA LLC (HQ) 321 636-8147
100 Gus Hipp Blvd Rockledge (32955) **(G-14716)**

Hydro Remelt 904 794-1500
200 Riviera Blvd Saint Augustine (32086) **(G-14842)**

Hydro-Dyne Engineering Inc 727 532-0777
4750 118th Ave N Oldsmar (34677) **(G-11658)**

Hydrodynamic Coatings Llc 954 344-8830
12149 Nw 77th Mnr Parkland (33076) **(G-13347)**

Hydrofoils Incorporated 561 964-6399
4151 Lake Worth Rd Lake Worth (33466) **(G-7204)**

Hydrogel Vision Corporation 941 739-1382
7575 Commerce Ct Sarasota (34243) **(G-15496)**

Hydrogen Diesel Prfmce Inc 407 847-6064
2410 Sabra Ct Kissimmee (34744) **(G-6925)**

Hydrogen Innovations Co 727 386-8805
39650 Us Highway 19 N Tarpon Springs (34689) **(G-17477)**

Hydrogen One Inc 352 361-6974
6880 Se 104th St Belleview (34420) **(G-363)**

Hydrogen Technology Corp 800 315-9554
900 West Ave Apt 501 Miami Beach (33139) **(G-10202)**

Hydrolec Inc 904 730-3766
5050 Stepp Ave Jacksonville (32216) **(G-6189)**

Hydromassage, Clearwater *Also called JTL Enterprises (delaware)* **(G-1656)**

Hydron Technologies Inc 727 342-5050
9843 18th St N Ste 150 Saint Petersburg (33716) **(G-15079)**

Hydroplus 386 341-2768
1712 Fern Palm Dr Ste 7 Edgewater (32132) **(G-3490)**

Hydroplus Inc 941 479-7473
615 Riviera Dunes Way # 207 Palmetto (34221) **(G-13175)**

Hyend Mfg Inc 727 828-0826
4711 126th Ave N Ste H Clearwater (33762) **(G-1633)**

Hygenator Pillow Service, Hialeah *Also called General Pillows & Fiber Inc* **(G-5169)**

Hygenator Pillow Service Inc 305 325-0250
10100 E Calusa Club Dr Miami (33186) **(G-9294)**

Hygreen Inc 352 327-9747
3630 Sw 47th Ave Ste 100 Gainesville (32608) **(G-4708)**

Hyland Custom Cabinetry, Naples *Also called Thomas Rley Artisans Guild Inc* **(G-10925)**

Hylton & Assoc 321 303-2862
1449 Sackett Cir Orlando (32818) **(G-12232)**

Hymeg Corporation 800 322-1953
5410 115th Ave N Clearwater (33760) **(G-1634)**

Hyper-Sub Platform Tech Inc 386 365-6021
4661 W State Road 238 Lake Butler (32054) **(G-7001)**

Hyperform Inc (HQ) 321 632-6503
5440 Schenck Ave Rockledge (32955) **(G-14717)**

Hyperion Managing LLC 904 612-3987
2751-2 Larsen Rd Jacksonville (32207) **(G-6190)**

Hyperion Munitions Inc 844 622-8339
8601 Somerset Dr Ste A Largo (33773) **(G-7610)**

Hytronics Corp 727 535-0413
5410 115th Ave N Clearwater (33760) **(G-1635)**

I ABC Corp 904 645-6000
11711 Marco Beach Dr Jacksonville (32224) **(G-6191)**

I B Furniture Inc 941 371-5764
1236 Porter Rd Unit 4 Sarasota (34240) **(G-15703)**

I Be Cakin LLC 954 707-3865
720 Nw 17th St Pompano Beach (33060) **(G-14057)**

I C Probotics Inc 407 339-8298
122 E Lake Ave Longwood (32750) **(G-7902)**

I C T S America Inc 786 307-2993
8400 Nw 36th St Ste 450 Doral (33166) **(G-3252)**

I F F, Jacksonville *Also called Interntnal Flvors Frgrnces Inc* **(G-6203)**

I F F Augusta, Jacksonville *Also called Interntnal Flvors Frgrnces Inc* **(G-6204)**

I I S, Boynton Beach *Also called Innovative Indus Solutions Inc* **(G-879)**

I J Precious Metals Inc 305 371-3009
22 Ne 1st St Miami (33132) **(G-9295)**

I M I Publishing Inc 615 957-9288
425 Cove Twr Dr Apt 1204 Naples (34110) **(G-10778)**

I M S, Ormond Beach *Also called Information Mgt Svcs Inc* **(G-12773)**

I P G, Sarasota *Also called Intertape Polymer Corp* **(G-15707)**

I P M, Naples *Also called International Packaging Mchs* **(G-10785)**

I P S, Floral City *Also called Instant Printing Services Inc* **(G-3611)**

I P Team Inc 772 398-4664
701 Nw Federal Hwy # 301 Stuart (34994) **(G-16164)**

I R Bowen & Sons, Jacksonville *Also called Skipper Wright Inc* **(G-6476)**

I S M, Orlando *Also called Industrial Smoke & Mirrors Inc* **(G-12242)**

I S T, Sarasota *Also called Industry Standard Technology* **(G-15499)**

I T Management Express Inc 954 237-6999
16140 Sw 51st St Ste 1 Miramar (33027) **(G-10502)**

I Wed Today, Miami *Also called Carlees Creations Inc* **(G-8897)**

I Wentworth Inc 561 231-7544
645 Beachland Blvd Vero Beach (32963) **(G-17761)**

I-Con Systems Inc 407 365-6241
3100 Camp Rd Oviedo (32765) **(G-12827)**

I-Partner Group Inc (PA) 239 449-4749
28200 Old 41 Rd Unit 204 Bonita Springs (34135) **(G-803)**

I-Pop Inc 561 567-9000
475 N Cleary Rd Unit 4 West Palm Beach (33413) **(G-18028)**

I.T.S. USA, Maitland *Also called US Implant Solutions LLC* **(G-8077)**

I2k Digital Solutions LLC 305 507-0707
7884 Nw 64th St Miami (33166) **(G-9296)**

I3, Naples *Also called Intellgent Instrumentation Inc* **(G-10783)**

I3 Microsystems Inc 727 235-6532
9900 16th St N Saint Petersburg (33716) **(G-15080)**

Iacono Iron LLC 561 640-1696
163 N Cleary Rd Ste C5 West Palm Beach (33413) **(G-18029)**

Iag Engine Center LLC 305 591-0643
6929 Nw 46th St Miami (33166) **(G-9297)**

Iaire LLC 407 873-2538
2100 Consulate Dr Ste 102 Orlando (32837) **(G-12233)**

Iamgold Purchasing Svcs Inc 713 671-5973
2000 Nw 97th Ave Ste 114 Doral (33172) **(G-3253)**

Ian-Conrad Bergan LLC (PA) 850 434-1286
1001 E Belmont St Pensacola (32501) **(G-13522)**

Ianorod JB LLC 954 217-3014
4579 Weston Rd Weston (33331) **(G-18253)**

Ibd Industrial LLC 786 655-7577
1825 Ponce De Leon Blvd Coral Gables (33134) **(G-2069)**

Ibi Systems Inc 954 978-9225
6842 Nw 20th Ave Fort Lauderdale (33309) **(G-3872)**

Ibiz Inc 954 781-4714
1700 Nw 15th Ave Pompano Beach (33069) **(G-14058)**

Ibiz Wrld Class Detailing Pdts, Pompano Beach *Also called Ibiz Inc* **(G-14058)**

Ibs Manufacturing LLC 352 629-9752
18 Ne 16th St Ocala (34470) **(G-11411)**

Ibs Partners Ltd (PA) 954 581-0922
1 N University Dr Ut400a Plantation (33324) **(G-13857)**

Ibtm Engineering Inc 239 246-1876
1291 Par View Dr Sanibel (33957) **(G-15415)**

Ic Industries Inc 305 696-8330
1101 E 33rd St Fl 2 Hialeah (33013) **(G-5191)**

Icare Industries Inc (PA) 727 512-3000
4399 35th St N Ste 100 Saint Petersburg (33714) **(G-15081)**

Icarecom LLC 954 768-7100
401 E Las Olas Blvd Ste 1 Fort Lauderdale (33301) **(G-3873)**

Icat Resource LLC 410 908-9369
450 S Gulfview Blvd 703s Clearwater Beach (33767) **(G-1860)**

ICC, Miami Lakes *Also called International Casting Corp* **(G-10308)**

Icco, Coral Springs *Also called Hispacom Inc* **(G-2163)**

Ice Bunker A&M Corp 786 368-0924
717 W 27th St Hialeah (33010) **(G-5192)**

Ice Cream Club Inc (PA) 561 731-3331
1580 High Ridge Rd Boynton Beach (33426) **(G-877)**

Ice Link 2018 LLC 305 988-4023
1963 10th Ave N Lake Worth Beach (33461) **(G-7256)**

Ice Magic Holdings, Orlando *Also called Ice Magic-Orlando Inc* **(G-12234)**

Ice Magic-Orlando Inc (PA) 407 816-1905
9468 American Eagle Way # 100 Orlando (32837) **(G-12234)**

Ice Pop Factory, Plant City *Also called Frio Distributors Inc* **(G-13769)**

Ice Sheet Metal LLC 850 872-2129
29 E 10th St Panama City (32401) **(G-13274)**

Iceblox Inc 717 697-1900
7436 Evesborough Ln New Port Richey (34655) **(G-10969)**

Icecold2 LLC 855 326-2665
10004 N Dale Mabry Hwy Tampa (33618) **(G-16928)**

Icecool World, Tampa *Also called Icecold2 LLC* **(G-16928)**

Icemule Company Inc 904 325-9012
601 S Ponce De Leon Blvd Saint Augustine (32084) **(G-14843)**

Ichosen1 Inc 844 403-4055
1441 Brickell Ave Ste 17 Miami (33131) **(G-9298)**

ICI Custom Parts Inc 813 888-7979
13911 Bittersweet Way Tampa (33625) **(G-16929)**

ALPHABETIC

ICM Precious Metals Inc 917 327-8171
36 Ne 1st St Miami (33132) *(G-9299)*
ICM Printing Co Inc 352 377-7468
5510 Sw 41st Blvd Ste 101 Gainesville (32608) *(G-4709)*
Icmfg & Associates Inc 727 258-4995
3734 131st Ave N Ste 11 Clearwater (33762) *(G-1636)*
ICO USA Corp 305 253-0871
15815 Sw 89th Ave Palmetto Bay (33157) *(G-13212)*
Icome2fix LLC 954 789-4102
400 Nw 26th St Miami (33127) *(G-9300)*
Icon, Saint Augustine *Also called Industrial Cnstr Svcs Dsign In (G-14846)*
Icon Aircraft Inc 813 387-6603
825 Severn Ave Tampa (33606) *(G-16930)*
Icon Embroidery Inc 407 858-0886
2833 Butler Bay Dr N Windermere (34786) *(G-18353)*
Icon Industries 352 988-3895
3015 Shady Oak Pl Groveland (34736) *(G-4862)*
Icon Welding & Fabrication LLC 941 822-8822
8145 27th St E Sarasota (34243) *(G-15497)*
Icorp-Ifoam Specialty Products 407 328-8500
250 Power Ct Sanford (32771) *(G-15334)*
Icosi Manufacturing LLC 813 854-1333
11134 Challenger Ave Odessa (33556) *(G-11530)*
Icpf Development Group LLC (PA) 727 474-9927
514 N Betty Ln Clearwater (33755) *(G-1637)*
Ics Inex Inspection Systems 727 535-5502
13075 Us Highway 19 N Clearwater (33764) *(G-1638)*
Ictc USA, Brooksville *Also called Interconnect Cable Tech Corp (G-1164)*
ID Print Inc 954 923-8374
6561 Nw 18th Ct Plantation (33313) *(G-13858)*
Ida Solutions 305 603-9835
10302 Nw S Rver Dr Ste 15 Medley (33178) *(G-8256)*
Idaho Timber LLC 386 758-8111
176 Sw Midtown Pl Ste 101 Lake City (32025) *(G-7025)*
Idd, Coconut Creek *Also called Interntnal Drectional Drlg Inc (G-1994)*
Idea Design Studio Inc 305 823-6008
8562 Nw 56th St Doral (33166) *(G-3254)*
Ideal Aluminum, Saint Augustine *Also called Ideal Deals LLC (G-14844)*
Ideal Cabinetry, Bartow *Also called All Wood Cabinetry LLC (G-297)*
Ideal Deals LLC 386 736-1700
3200 Parker Dr Saint Augustine (32084) *(G-14844)*
Ideal Fastener Corporation 201 207-6722
10800 Biscayne Blvd # 810 Miami (33161) *(G-9301)*
Ideal Gas LLC 904 417-6470
3200 Parker Dr Saint Augustine (32084) *(G-14845)*
Ideal Image Brandon 813 982-3420
1602 Oakfield Dr Ste 105 Brandon (33511) *(G-1095)*
Ideal Publishing Co Inc 727 321-0785
3063 Lown St N Saint Petersburg (33713) *(G-15082)*
Ideasphere, Boca Raton *Also called Twinlab Holdings Inc (G-729)*
Identifire Safety, West Palm Beach *Also called F D Signworks LLC (G-17993)*
Identity Holding Company LLC 941 355-5171
7525 Pennsylvania Ave # 101 Sarasota (34243) *(G-15498)*
Identity Stronghold LLC 941 475-8480
563 Paul Morris Dr Unit B Englewood (34223) *(G-3533)*
Idex International, Tampa *Also called Island Designs Outlet Inc (G-16954)*
IDI, Bradenton *Also called Innovative Designs of Sarasota (G-995)*
Idproductsource LLC 772 336-4269
651 Nw Enterprise Dr Port Saint Lucie (34986) *(G-14417)*
Ies Sales and Service LLC 305 687-9400
5050 Nw 36th Ave Miami (33142) *(G-9302)*
Ies Sales and Service LLC 305 525-6079
2233 Nw 77th Ter Miami (33147) *(G-9303)*
IESC Diesel Corp 305 470-9306
13202 Nw 107th Ave Unit 4 Hialeah Gardens (33018) *(G-5438)*
Ifco Systems Us LLC (PA) 813 463-4103
3030 N Rocky Point Dr W # 300 Tampa (33607) *(G-16931)*
Iff Chemical Holdings Inc 904 783-2180
2051 Lane Ave N Jacksonville (32254) *(G-6192)*
Igbo Network LLC 352 727-4113
5021 Nw 34th Blvd Ste D Gainesville (32605) *(G-4710)*
Igovsolutions LLC 407 574-3056
1307 S Intl Pkwy Ste 2061 Lake Mary (32746) *(G-7084)*
Iguana Graphics Inc 813 657-7800
1345 Oakfield Dr Brandon (33511) *(G-1096)*
Ii-VI Aerospace & Defense Inc 727 375-8562
6716 Industrial Ave Port Richey (34668) *(G-14363)*
Iis Incorporated 561 547-4297
3020 High Ridge Rd Boynton Beach (33426) *(G-878)*
Ijkb LLC 941 953-9046
502 N Spoonbill Dr Sarasota (34236) *(G-15704)*
Ike Behar, Miramar *Also called Regina Behar Enterprises Inc (G-10535)*
IL Mobile, Deerfield Beach *Also called Ramos Woodwork LLC (G-2795)*
IL Nuts Inc 786 366-4536
19098 W Dixie Hwy Miami (33180) *(G-9304)*
Ilab By PGT Innovations, North Venice *Also called PGT Innovations Inc (G-11217)*
Ilan Custom Woodwork LLC 727 272-5070
1630 N Hercules Ave Ste D Clearwater (33765) *(G-1639)*
Ilay Ventures LLC (PA) 786 503-5335
1688 Meridian Ave Ste 700 Miami Beach (33139) *(G-10203)*
Iler Group Inc 877 467-0326
15310 Amberly Dr Ste 250 Wesley Chapel (33544) *(G-17879)*
Ilex Organics LLC 386 566-3826
504 Pullman Rd Edgewater (32132) *(G-3491)*
Iliad Biotechnologies LLC 954 336-0777
4581 Weston Rd Ste 260 Weston (33331) *(G-18254)*
Illinois Tool Works Inc 561 422-9241
2107 W Blue Heron Blvd Riviera Beach (33404) *(G-14629)*
Illinois Tool Works Inc 941 721-1000
11001 Us Highway 41 N Palmetto (34221) *(G-13176)*
Illinois Tool Works Inc 863 665-3338
3606 Craftsman Blvd Lakeland (33803) *(G-7347)*
Illuminated Lightpanels Inc 954 484-6633
2011 Nw 29th St Oakland Park (33311) *(G-11271)*
Ils Management LLC 321 252-0100
930 S Hbr Cy Blvd Ste 505 Melbourne (32901) *(G-8440)*
Ilsc Holdings Lc 480 935-4230
12001 Science Dr Ste 160 Orlando (32826) *(G-12235)*
Image 360, Jacksonville *Also called ARC Creative Inc (G-5896)*
Image 360 561 395-0745
6560 E Rogers Cir Boca Raton (33487) *(G-541)*
Image Depot 813 685-7116
2017 E Fowler Ave Tampa (33612) *(G-16932)*
Image Experts Inc 727 488-7556
4556 36th Ave N Saint Petersburg (33713) *(G-15083)*
Image Graphics 2000 Inc 954 332-3380
2450 W Sample Rd Ste 20 Pompano Beach (33073) *(G-14059)*
Image Impressions, Tamarac *Also called Graphic and Printing Svcs Corp (G-16532)*
Image International Inc 561 793-9560
8040 Belvedere Rd Ste 1 West Palm Beach (33411) *(G-18030)*
Image One Corporation 813 888-8288
6202 Benjamin Rd Ste 103 Tampa (33634) *(G-16933)*
Image Printing & Graphics LLC 321 783-5555
8649 Villanova Dr Cape Canaveral (32920) *(G-1286)*
Image Prtg & Digital Svcs Inc 850 244-3380
315 E Hollywood Blvd # 3 Mary Esther (32569) *(G-8177)*
Image360 - Lauderhill, Lauderhill *Also called Graphic Difference Inc A (G-7733)*
Image360 South Tampa, Tampa *Also called Z & L Partners Inc (G-17454)*
Image360 St Petersburg Central, Saint Petersburg *Also called Bayfront Printing Company (G-14979)*
Imagecare Maintenance Systems 727 536-8646
14055 46th St N Ste 1108 Clearwater (33762) *(G-1640)*
Imagik International Corp 786 631-5003
8390 Nw 25th St Doral (33122) *(G-3255)*
Imagination Creations Inc 561 744-7802
2895 Jupiter Park Dr # 300 Jupiter (33458) *(G-6744)*
Imagination Enterprises LLC 504 289-9691
7616 Southland Blvd # 102 Orlando (32809) *(G-12236)*
Imagine That Inc 813 728-8324
155 E Oakwood St Tarpon Springs (34689) *(G-17478)*
Imaging Diagnostic Systems Inc 954 581-9800
1221 E Robinson St Orlando (32801) *(G-12237)*
Imaging For Life, Sarasota *Also called US Pet Imaging LLC (G-15865)*
IMC Agrico, Mulberry *Also called Mos Holdings Inc (G-10634)*
IMC Lighting Inc 305 373-4422
2915 Biscayne Blvd # 301 Miami (33137) *(G-9305)*
IMC Storage 305 418-0069
3955 Adra Ave Doral (33178) *(G-3256)*
Imc-Heartway LLC (PA) 239 275-6767
5681 Independence Cir A Fort Myers (33912) *(G-4286)*
IMD Software Inc 813 685-2138
5203 Sand Trap Pl Valrico (33596) *(G-17666)*
Imerys Perlite Usa Inc 850 875-1282
612 S Shelfer St Quincy (32351) *(G-14546)*
Imh, Jacksonville *Also called Industrial Mobile Hydraulics (G-6196)*
IMI, Pompano Beach *Also called International Medical Inds Inc (G-14063)*
IMI, Gainesville *Also called Innovative Machine Inc (G-4711)*
IMI Publishing Inc 239 529-5081
640 21st St Nw Naples (34120) *(G-10779)*
Imm Survivor Inc 239 454-7020
17030 Alico Center Rd Fort Myers (33967) *(G-4287)*
Immokalee Ranch 239 657-2000
4451 County Road 846 Immokalee (34142) *(G-5798)*
Immudyne Nutritional LLC 914 714-8901
3930 Hollywood Ave Pensacola (32505) *(G-13523)*
Immunotek Bio Centers LLC 337 500-1175
825 9th St W Bradenton (34205) *(G-994)*
Immunotek Bio Centers LLC 561 270-6712
4560 Lake Worth Rd Greenacres (33463) *(G-4849)*
Immunotek Bio Centers LLC 772 577-7194
2710 S Us Highway 1 Fort Pierce (34982) *(G-4496)*
Immunotek Bio Centers LLC 404 345-3570
1225 W King St Cocoa (32922) *(G-1936)*
Impact Design Group Inc 904 636-8989
4613 Philips Hwy Ste 207 Jacksonville (32207) *(G-6193)*
Impact Education Inc 239 482-0202
18180 Old Dominion Ct Fort Myers (33908) *(G-4288)*

Impact Kings LLC 786 842-3166
  7141 N Waterway Dr Miami (33155) *(G-9306)*
Impact Molding Clearwater LLC 847 718-9300
  2050 Sunnydale Blvd Clearwater (33765) *(G-1641)*
Impact Promotional Pubg LLC 727 736-6228
  1546 Main St Dunedin (34698) *(G-3451)*
Impact Register Inc 727 585-8572
  1870 Starkey Rd Ste 1 Largo (33771) *(G-7611)*
Impact Safe Glass Corporation 813 247-5528
  2705 N 35th St Tampa (33605) *(G-16934)*
Imperial Fabric and Decorators, Ocala *Also called Lasalle Bristol Corporation (G-11425)*
Imperial Foam & Insul Mfg Co 386 673-4177
  2360 Old Tomoka Rd W Ormond Beach (32174) *(G-12772)*
Imperial Imprinting LLC 772 633-8256
  8815 92nd Ct Vero Beach (32967) *(G-17762)*
Imperial Industries Inc (HQ) 954 917-4114
  1259 Nw 21st St Pompano Beach (33069) *(G-14060)*
Imperial Kitchens Inc 239 208-9359
  12541 Metro Pkwy Ste 14 Fort Myers (33966) *(G-4289)*
Imperial Motor Parts, Lakeland *Also called Battery Usa Inc (G-7281)*
Imperial Motor Parts-Division, Lakeland *Also called Battery Usa Inc (G-7280)*
Imperial Photoengraving 772 924-1731
  11013 Sw Redwing Dr Stuart (34997) *(G-16165)*
Imperial Privacy Systems LLC 954 782-7130
  1400 Sw 8th St Pompano Beach (33069) *(G-14061)*
Imperx Inc (PA) 561 989-0006
  6421 Congress Ave Ste 204 Boca Raton (33487) *(G-542)*
Impex, Miami *Also called MP&tr Corp (G-9594)*
Impex of Doral Inc 305 470-0041
  7850 Nw 80th St Medley (33166) *(G-8257)*
Impexpar LLC 786 238-5700
  10540 Nw 26th St Ste G302 Doral (33172) *(G-3257)*
Imported Yarns LLC 239 405-2974
  21561 Pelican Sound Dr # 101 Estero (33928) *(G-3546)*
Impremedia LLC 407 767-0070
  685 S Ronald Reagan Blvd Longwood (32750) *(G-7903)*
Impress Ink LLC (PA) 407 982-5646
  540 N Goldenrod Rd Ste A Orlando (32807) *(G-12238)*
Impress Ink LLC 561 635-6442
  1462 Bella Coola Dr Orlando (32828) *(G-12239)*
Impress Ink Screen Prtg & EMB, Orlando *Also called Impress Ink LLC (G-12238)*
Impress3d LLC 312 339-0215
  1121 Bel Air Dr Apt 4 Highland Beach (33487) *(G-5461)*
Impressions Dry Cleaners Inc 561 988-3030
  6201 N Federal Hwy Ste 1 Boca Raton (33487) *(G-543)*
Impressions of Miami Inc 305 666-0277
  6960 Sw 47th St Miami (33155) *(G-9307)*
Impressive Pavers Inc 321 508-9991
  2883 Glasbern Cir West Melbourne (32904) *(G-17901)*
Imprint 941 484-5151
  3449 Tech Dr Unit 212 Nokomis (34275) *(G-11046)*
Imprint Promotions LLC 321 622-8946
  405 N Wickham Rd Ste A Melbourne (32935) *(G-8441)*
Imprints International Inc 561 202-0105
  150 Businefl Pk Way Ste 2 Royal Palm Beach (33411) *(G-14767)*
Improved Racing Products LLC 407 705-3054
  4855 Dist Ct Ste 1 Orlando (32822) *(G-12240)*
Impulse Air Inc 904 475-1822
  2126 W 21st St Jacksonville (32209) *(G-6194)*
IMS, Cape Coral *Also called Project and Cnstr Wldg Inc (G-1376)*
IMS Publishing Inc 954 761-8777
  1850 Se 17th St Ste 107 Fort Lauderdale (33316) *(G-3874)*
In Diversified Plant Services 813 453-7025
  22528 Laureldale Dr Lutz (33549) *(G-7995)*
In Focus Interactive Magazine 954 966-1233
  3001 Sw 64th Ter Miramar (33023) *(G-10503)*
In Gear Fashions Inc (PA) 305 830-2900
  4401 Nw 167th St Miami Gardens (33055) *(G-10264)*
In Stock Printers Inc 727 447-2515
  725 Stevens Ave Oldsmar (34677) *(G-11659)*
In The Bite 561 529-3940
  342 Toney Penna Dr Jupiter (33458) *(G-6745)*
In The Loop Brewing Inc 813 857-0111
  3338 Land O Lakes Blvd Land O Lakes (34639) *(G-7493)*
In The News Inc 813 882-8886
  3706 N Ridge Ave Tampa (33603) *(G-16935)*
In Touch Electronics LLC 813 818-9990
  13944 Lynmar Blvd Bldg 2 Tampa (33626) *(G-16936)*
In-O-Vate Technologies, Jupiter *Also called 6 Ports LLC (G-6673)*
Inceptra LLC (PA) 954 442-5400
  1900 N Commerce Pkwy Weston (33326) *(G-18255)*
Incity Property Management, West Palm Beach *Also called Incity Security Inc (G-18031)*
Incity Security Inc 561 306-9228
  3560 Inv Ln Ste 102 West Palm Beach (33404) *(G-18031)*
Inclan Machine Shop Inc 305 846-9675
  4401 Sw 75th Ave Miami (33155) *(G-9308)*
Increte Systems, Odessa *Also called Euclid Chemical Company (G-11550)*
Increte Systems 813 886-8811
  1725 Gunn Hwy Odessa (33556) *(G-11557)*

Independent Florida Alligator, Gainesville *Also called Campus Communications Inc (G-4665)*
Independent Newsmedia Inc USA 863 983-9148
  107 Sw 17th St Ste D Okeechobee (34974) *(G-11609)*
Independent Printing, Daytona Beach *Also called Tiffany and Associates Inc (G-2613)*
Independent Resources Inc (PA) 813 237-0945
  5010 N Nebraska Ave Tampa (33603) *(G-16937)*
Indian River All-Fab Inc 772 778-0032
  1119 18th Pl Vero Beach (32960) *(G-17763)*
Indian River Armature Inc 772 461-2067
  120 Lakes End Dr Apt A Fort Pierce (34982) *(G-4497)*
Indian River Biodiesel LLC 321 586-7670
  1810 Okeechobee Rd Ste A West Palm Beach (33409) *(G-18032)*
Indian River Brewery Corp 321 728-4114
  200 Imperial Blvd Cape Canaveral (32920) *(G-1287)*
Indian River Select, Stuart *Also called Freshco Ltd (G-16149)*
Indian Rver Brwing C/Flrida Be, Cape Canaveral *Also called Indian River Brewery Corp (G-1287)*
Indian Rver HM Prfssionals Inc 561 906-3881
  3306 Fargo Ave Lake Worth (33467) *(G-7205)*
Indicali Inc 831 905-4780
  15310 Amberly Dr Ste 250 Tampa (33647) *(G-16938)*
Indigo Mountain Inc 239 947-0023
  4280 Mourning Dove Dr Naples (34119) *(G-10780)*
Indoor Trampoline Arena Inc 321 222-1300
  605 Hickmar Cir Sanford (32771) *(G-15335)*
Indra Systems Inc 407 567-1977
  3505 Lake Lynda Dr # 200 Orlando (32817) *(G-12241)*
Inductive Technologies Inc 727 536-7861
  5410 115th Ave N Clearwater (33760) *(G-1642)*
Inductoweld Tube Corp 646 734-7094
  3350 Ne 33rd Ave Fort Lauderdale (33308) *(G-3875)*
Industrial & Marine Maint Inc 813 622-8338
  5511 24th Ave S Tampa (33619) *(G-16939)*
Industrial Brush Corporation 863 647-5643
  4000 Drane Field Rd Lakeland (33811) *(G-7348)*
Industrial Cmpsite Systems LLC 863 646-8551
  4225 Drane Field Rd Lakeland (33811) *(G-7349)*
Industrial Cnstr Svcs Dsign In (PA) 904 827-9795
  4405 Sartillo Rd Ste A Saint Augustine (32095) *(G-14846)*
Industrial Cnveyor Systems Inc 305 255-0200
  18693 Sw 103rd Ct Cutler Bay (33157) *(G-2292)*
Industrial Coating Solutions 813 333-8988
  7307 Yardley Way Tampa (33647) *(G-16940)*
Industrial Construction & Wldg 863 644-6124
  3341 Blueberry Dr Lakeland (33811) *(G-7350)*
Industrial Filter Pump Mfg Co 708 656-7800
  2680 Us Highway 1 Mims (32754) *(G-10448)*
Industrial Galvanizers Miami, Miami *Also called Industrial Glvanizers Amer Inc (G-9310)*
Industrial Galvanizers Miami 305 681-8844
  3350 Nw 119th St Miami (33167) *(G-9309)*
Industrial Galvanizers Tampa, Tampa *Also called Industrial Glvanizers Amer Inc (G-16941)*
Industrial Glvanizers Amer Inc 813 621-8990
  9520 E Broadway Ave Tampa (33619) *(G-16941)*
Industrial Glvanizers Amer Inc 305 681-8844
  3350 Nw 119th St Miami (33167) *(G-9310)*
Industrial Glvnzers Stheastern 813 621-8990
  3350 Nw 119th St Miami (33167) *(G-9311)*
Industrial Marine Inc 904 781-4707
  7259 Old Plank Rd Jacksonville (32254) *(G-6195)*
Industrial Marking Eqp Co Inc 561 626-8520
  4152 Lazy Hammock Rd Palm Beach Gardens (33410) *(G-12975)*
Industrial Marking Svcs Inc 727 541-7622
  10830 Canal St Ste C Largo (33777) *(G-7612)*
Industrial Mobile Hydraulics 904 866-7592
  1180 Lane Ave N Jacksonville (32254) *(G-6196)*
Industrial Nanotech Inc 800 767-3998
  1415 Panther Ln Naples (34109) *(G-10781)*
Industrial Oviedo LLC 786 350-8153
  7601 E Trsore Dr Unit 121 Miami Beach (33141) *(G-10204)*
Industrial Plastic Pdts Inc 305 822-3223
  14025 Nw 58th Ct Miami Lakes (33014) *(G-10307)*
Industrial Plastic Systems, Lakeland *Also called Industrial Cmpsite Systems LLC (G-7349)*
Industrial Plastic Systems Inc 863 646-8551
  4225 Drane Field Rd Lakeland (33811) *(G-7351)*
Industrial Products Div, Fort Lauderdale *Also called Nasco Industries Inc (G-3953)*
Industrial Projects Services 813 265-2957
  4102 W Linebaugh Ave # 103 Tampa (33624) *(G-16942)*
Industrial Repair, Jacksonville *Also called Liddys Machine Shop Inc (G-6257)*
Industrial Repair Inc 239 368-7435
  551 Westgate Blvd Ste 111 Lehigh Acres (33971) *(G-7810)*
Industrial Scan Inc 407 322-3664
  223 Hickman Dr Ste 109 Sanford (32771) *(G-15336)*
Industrial Shadeports Inc 954 755-0661
  6600 Nw 12th Ave Ste 220 Fort Lauderdale (33309) *(G-3876)*
Industrial Smoke & Mirrors Inc 407 299-9400
  3024 Shader Rd Orlando (32808) *(G-12242)*
Industrial Spring Corp 954 524-2558
  3129 Peachtree Cir Davie (33328) *(G-2425)*

ALPHABETIC

Industrial Technology, Riviera Beach *Also called Tera Industries Inc* *(G-14681)*
Industrial Technology LLC................................877 224-5534
  6310 Techster Blvd Ste 3 Fort Myers (33966) *(G-4290)*
Industrial Welding & Maint................................352 799-3432
  10080 Cobb Rd Brooksville (34601) *(G-1163)*
Industrias De AsIntes Y Acero, Miami *Also called Agrotek Services Incorporated* *(G-8667)*
Industry Standard Technology................................941 355-2100
  1868 University Pkwy Sarasota (34243) *(G-15499)*
Industry Weapon Inc................................877 344-8450
  4033 Tampa Rd Ste 103 Oldsmar (34677) *(G-11660)*
Industry West, Jacksonville *Also called England Trading Company LLC* *(G-6076)*
Inen USA Corp................................305 343-6666
  12750 Cairo Ln Opa Locka (33054) *(G-11754)*
Ineos New Planet Bioenergy LLC................................772 794-7900
  925 74th Ave Sw Vero Beach (32968) *(G-17764)*
Infinite Handling Services LLC................................561 939-6336
  4440 Pga Blvd Ste 600 Palm Beach Gardens (33410) *(G-12976)*
Infinite Lasers LLC................................850 424-3759
  45 Harbor Blvd Destin (32541) *(G-3071)*
Infinite Print LLC................................727 942-2121
  1014 Us Highway 19 # 114 Holiday (34691) *(G-5500)*
Infinite Ret Design & Mfg Corp................................305 967-8339
  7320 Nw 36th Ave Miami (33147) *(G-9312)*
Infiniti Digital Equipment Inc................................305 477-6333
  10500 Nw 29th Ter Doral (33172) *(G-3258)*
Infiniti Paint & Coatings, Deerfield Beach *Also called Lapolla Industries LLC* *(G-2751)*
Infinity Embroidery, Hialeah *Also called VSF Corp* *(G-5416)*
Infinity Genome Sciences Inc................................321 327-7365
  301 Riverside Dr Melbourne Beach (32951) *(G-8566)*
Infinity Manufactured Inds................................727 532-4453
  12450 Enterprise Blvd Largo (33773) *(G-7613)*
Infinity Manufacturing LLC................................954 531-6918
  4811 Lyons Tech Pkwy Coconut Creek (33073) *(G-1989)*
Infinity Signs & Graphix LLC................................407 270-6733
  1887 Central Florida Pkwy Orlando (32837) *(G-12243)*
Inflatable Design Works Corp................................786 242-1049
  13350 Sw 131st St Unit 10 Miami (33186) *(G-9313)*
Infopia USA LLC................................321 225-3620
  7160 Bright Ave Cocoa (32927) *(G-1937)*
Infor (us) LLC................................407 916-9100
  5464 Fox Hollwo Dr Boca Raton (33486) *(G-544)*
Infor Public Sector Inc................................813 207-6911
  3501 E Frontage Rd # 350 Tampa (33607) *(G-16943)*
Informa Usa Inc................................561 361-6017
  101 Paramount Dr Ste 100 Sarasota (34232) *(G-15705)*
Information Builders Inc................................407 804-8000
  300 Primera Blvd Ste 100 Lake Mary (32746) *(G-7085)*
Information Mgt Svcs Inc................................386 677-5073
  107 Sundance Trl Ormond Beach (32176) *(G-12773)*
Informulate LLC................................866 222-2307
  7437 Winding Lake Cir Oviedo (32765) *(G-12828)*
Infrared Associates Inc................................772 223-6670
  2851 Se Monroe St Stuart (34997) *(G-16166)*
Infrared Systems Dev Corp................................407 679-5101
  7319 Sandscove Ct Ste 4 Winter Park (32792) *(G-18515)*
Infrastructure Repair Systems................................727 327-4216
  3113 Lown St N Saint Petersburg (33713) *(G-15084)*
Infupharma LLC................................305 301-3389
  6720 Tyler St Hollywood (33024) *(G-5601)*
Ing Phrmctcal Pdts Prvate Lbel, Sunrise *Also called Interntnal Ntrctcals Group Inc* *(G-16324)*
Ingeant Florida LLC................................954 868-2879
  5163 Woodfield Way Coconut Creek (33073) *(G-1990)*
Ingear, Miami Gardens *Also called In Gear Fashions Inc* *(G-10264)*
Ingelub Corp................................407 656-8800
  12935 W Colonial Dr Winter Garden (34787) *(G-18392)*
Ingenria Prcura Y Cnstrccion C................................407 639-4288
  12250 Menta St Ste 202 Orlando (32837) *(G-12244)*
Ingenus Pharmaceuticals LLC (PA)................................407 354-5365
  4901 Vineland Rd Ste 260 Orlando (32811) *(G-12245)*
Ingersoll Rand................................954 391-4500
  2884 Corporate Way Miramar (33025) *(G-10504)*
Ingersoll-Rand, Panama City *Also called Trane Technologies Company LLC* *(G-13314)*
Ingram Signalization Inc................................850 433-8267
  4522 N Davis Hwy Pensacola (32503) *(G-13524)*
Ingrams Backhoe Dumptruck Svc................................850 718-6042
  2155 Roark Rd Cottondale (32431) *(G-2229)*
Initial Marine Corporation................................407 321-1340
  650 Hickman Cir Sanford (32771) *(G-15337)*
Ink & Toner Plus................................813 783-1650
  10149 Connerly Rd Dade City (33525) *(G-2319)*
Ink Bros Printing LLC................................407 494-9585
  1372 Bennett Dr Unit 164 Longwood (32750) *(G-7904)*
Ink Master Graphics, Jacksonville *Also called Time Printing Co Inc* *(G-6552)*
Ink Publishing Corporation................................786 206-9867
  806 S Douglas Rd Ste 300 Coral Gables (33134) *(G-2070)*
Ink Publishing Corporation (HQ)................................786 482-2065
  800 Suth Dglas Rd Ste 250 Coral Gables (33134) *(G-2071)*
Ink-Trax Inc................................850 235-4849
  238 W 5th St Panama City (32401) *(G-13275)*

Inklab Signs Inc................................786 430-8100
  12324 Sw 117th Ct Miami (33186) *(G-9314)*
Inkpressions Inc................................305 261-0872
  13804 Sw 83rd Ct Palmetto Bay (33158) *(G-13213)*
Inky Fingers Printing Inc................................904 384-1900
  4613 Philips Hwy Ste 207 Jacksonville (32207) *(G-6197)*
Inline Filling Systems LLC................................941 486-8800
  216 Seaboard Ave Venice (34285) *(G-17700)*
Inman Orthodontic Labs Inc................................954 340-8477
  3953 Nw 126th Ave Coral Springs (33065) *(G-2166)*
Innergy................................941 815-8655
  315 E Olympia Ave # 251 Punta Gorda (33950) *(G-14509)*
Inneuroco Inc (PA)................................954 742-5988
  19700 Stirling Rd Unit 1 Southwest Ranches (33332) *(G-16054)*
Innevape LLC................................631 957-6500
  9718 Katy Dr Ste 2 Hudson (34667) *(G-5778)*
Innfocus Inc................................305 378-2651
  12415 Sw 136th Ave Ste 3 Miami (33186) *(G-9315)*
Innocor Foam Tech - Acp Inc................................305 685-6341
  3225 Nw 107th St Miami (33167) *(G-9316)*
Innomed Technologies Inc (HQ)................................800 200-9842
  6601 Lyons Rd Ste B1 Coconut Creek (33073) *(G-1991)*
Innova Eco Bldg Systems LLC................................305 455-7707
  3300 Nw 110th St Miami (33167) *(G-9317)*
Innova Gel, Miami *Also called Innova Softgel LLC* *(G-9318)*
Innova Home LLC................................561 855-2450
  6200 S Dixie Hwy West Palm Beach (33405) *(G-18033)*
Innova Softgel LLC................................855 536-8872
  14193 Sw 119th Ave Miami (33186) *(G-9318)*
Innovate Audio Visual Inc................................561 249-1117
  3460 Frlane Frms Rd Ste 1 Wellington (33414) *(G-17853)*
Innovated Industrial Svcs Inc................................863 701-2711
  1416 Chamber Dr Bartow (33830) *(G-313)*
Innovatier Inc................................863 688-4548
  2769 New Tampa Hwy Lakeland (33815) *(G-7352)*
Innovation Laboratories, Miami Lakes *Also called One Innovation Labs Llc* *(G-10333)*
Innovation Marine Corporation................................941 355-7852
  8011 15th St E Sarasota (34243) *(G-15500)*
Innovation Pavers Llc................................850 687-2864
  559 Kelly St Destin (32541) *(G-3072)*
Innovations By Mirart, Pompano Beach *Also called Mirart Inc* *(G-14101)*
Innovative Base Tech LLC................................727 391-9009
  5030 Seminole Blvd Saint Petersburg (33708) *(G-15085)*
Innovative Cabinet & Case Work, Clearwater *Also called Rich Maid Cabinets Inc* *(G-1766)*
Innovative Carbide Inc................................863 696-7999
  6403 Park Ln Unit 1 Lake Wales (33898) *(G-7165)*
Innovative Cnstr Group LLC (HQ)................................904 398-5690
  5216 Shad Rd Jacksonville (32257) *(G-6198)*
Innovative Contractors, Nokomis *Also called Innovative Fabricators Fla Inc* *(G-11047)*
Innovative Data Solutions, Orlando *Also called Powerdms Inc* *(G-12497)*
Innovative Designs of Sarasota................................941 752-7779
  6224 31st St E Ste 8 Bradenton (34203) *(G-995)*
Innovative Fabricators Fla Inc................................941 375-8668
  104 Palmetto Rd W Nokomis (34275) *(G-11047)*
Innovative Fasteners LLc................................561 542-2152
  6601 Lyons Rd Ste I5 Coconut Creek (33073) *(G-1992)*
Innovative Heat Concepts LLC................................305 248-4971
  127 Sw 5th Ave Homestead (33030) *(G-5716)*
Innovative Indus Solutions Inc (PA)................................561 733-1548
  3020 High Ridge Rd Boynton Beach (33426) *(G-879)*
Innovative Ink, Lakeland *Also called Parkinson Enterprises Inc* *(G-7406)*
Innovative Machine Inc................................386 418-8880
  6115 Nw 123rd Pl Gainesville (32653) *(G-4711)*
Innovative Mfg Solutions LLC................................904 647-5300
  7949 Atl Blvd Unit 209 Jacksonville (32211) *(G-6199)*
Innovative Optics LLC................................239 994-0695
  8520 Bessemer Ave North Port (34287) *(G-11196)*
Innovative PDT Solutions LLC................................407 933-2029
  2710 N John Young Pkwy Kissimmee (34741) *(G-6926)*
Innovative Powder Coating Inc................................954 537-2558
  550 Ne 33rd St Oakland Park (33334) *(G-11272)*
Innovative Power Solutions LLC................................732 544-1075
  2250 Whitfield Ave Sarasota (34243) *(G-15501)*
Innovative Signs Inc................................407 830-5155
  957 Penfield Cv Sanford (32773) *(G-15338)*
Innovative Software Tech Inc................................813 920-9435
  2802 N Howard Ave Tampa (33607) *(G-16944)*
Innovative Spine Care Inc................................813 920-3022
  8333 Gunn Hwy Tampa (33626) *(G-16945)*
Innovative Steel Tech Inc................................813 767-1746
  12620 S Us Highway 41 Gibsonton (33534) *(G-4798)*
Innovative Support Systems Inc................................407 682-7570
  1030 Sunshine Ln Ste 1000 Altamonte Springs (32714) *(G-53)*
Innovative Surfaces Inc................................305 446-9059
  3218 Ponce De Leon Blvd Coral Gables (33134) *(G-2072)*
Innovative Svc Solutions LLC................................407 296-5211
  3144 N John Young Pkwy Orlando (32804) *(G-12246)*
Innovative Tech By Design Inc................................321 676-3194
  2469 Palm Bay Rd Ne 9 Palm Bay (32905) *(G-12904)*

Innovtive Cabinets Closets Inc 904 475-2336
5772 Mining Ter Jacksonville (32257) **(G-6200)**

Innovtive Win Cncpts Doors Inc 561 493-2303
4336 Juniper Ter Boynton Beach (33436) **(G-880)**

Innquest Corporation 813 288-4900
19321 Us Highway 19 N # 407 Clearwater (33764) **(G-1643)**

Innquest Software, Clearwater *Also called Innquest Corporation* **(G-1643)**

Inovart Inc 941 751-2324
2304 58th Ave E Bradenton (34203) **(G-996)**

Inovinox Usa LLC 800 780-1017
7875 Sw 104th St Miami (33156) **(G-9319)**

Inox LLC 305 409-2764
19201 Collins Ave Ste 131 Sunny Isles Beach (33160) **(G-16277)**

Inox Stainless Specialist LLC 407 764-2456
1336 Sw 8th St Pompano Beach (33069) **(G-14062)**

Inperium Corp 305 901-5650
1111 Lincoln Rd Ste 760 Miami Beach (33139) **(G-10205)**

Inpro Corp Ike 407 342-9912
9025 Boggy Creek Rd Orlando (32824) **(G-12247)**

Inprodelca Inc 865 687-7921
702 Nw 170th Ter Pembroke Pines (33028) **(G-13397)**

Inprovit Vital Health, Orlando *Also called Vital Health Corporation* **(G-12702)**

Inquirer Newspapers Inc 772 257-6230
2046 Treasure Coast Plz Vero Beach (32960) **(G-17765)**

Insanejournalcom 561 315-9311
2372 Pinewood Ln West Palm Beach (33415) **(G-18034)**

Inseco Inc 239 939-1072
2897 South St Fort Myers (33916) **(G-4291)**

Insight Optical Mfg Co Fla Inc 787 758-9096
3601 Sw 160th Ave Ste 400 Miramar (33027) **(G-10505)**

Insight Software LLC (HQ) 305 495-0022
3265 Meridian Pkwy # 112 Weston (33331) **(G-18256)**

Insightec Inc (HQ) 786 534-3849
801 Brickell Ave Ste 1600 Miami (33131) **(G-9320)**

Insl-X Coronado Lenmar, Orlando *Also called Complementary Coatings Corp* **(G-12036)**

Inspec Solutions LLC (PA) 866 467-7320
330 Carswell Ave Holly Hill (32117) **(G-5514)**

Inspec Solutions LLC 866 467-7320
2111 Bayless Blvd Daytona Beach (32114) **(G-2563)**

Inspecs USA LC 727 771-7710
30798 Us Highway 19 N Palm Harbor (34684) **(G-13114)**

Inspectech Aeroservice Inc 954 359-6766
902 Sw 34th St Fort Lauderdale (33315) **(G-3877)**

Inspiration Foam Inc 407 498-0040
2860 Nicole Ave Kissimmee (34744) **(G-6927)**

Inspire ME Bracelets 404 644-7771
3333 Ne 16th Pl Fort Lauderdale (33305) **(G-3878)**

Inspired Closets Central FL 352 748-0770
3107 E State Road 44 Wildwood (34785) **(G-18313)**

Inspired Energy Inc 352 472-4855
25440 Nw 8th Pl Newberry (32669) **(G-11023)**

Inspired Energy LLC 352 472-4855
25440 Nw 8th Pl Newberry (32669) **(G-11024)**

Inspired Surf Boards 904 347-8879
2310 Dobbs Rd Saint Augustine (32086) **(G-14847)**

Inspired Therapeutics LLC 339 222-0847
7309 S Highway A1a Melbourne Beach (32951) **(G-8567)**

Instabook Corp 352 332-1311
12300 Nw 56th Ave Gainesville (32653) **(G-4712)**

Instacrete Mobile Concrete 813 956-3741
6253 Candlewood Dr Zephyrhills (33544) **(G-18617)**

Instanatural LLC 800 290-6932
12001 Res Pkwy Ste 244 Orlando (32826) **(G-12248)**

Instant Garden Inc 305 815-1090
7751 W 28th Ave Unit 2 Hialeah (33016) **(G-5193)**

Instant Locate Inc 800 431-0812
920 State Road 436 Casselberry (32707) **(G-1419)**

Instant Printing & Copy Center 727 849-1199
3307 Us Highway 19 Holiday (34691) **(G-5501)**

Instant Printing Services Inc 727 546-8036
8885 E Haines Ct Floral City (34436) **(G-3611)**

Instant Signs of South Florida, Miami *Also called Galea Corporation* **(G-9186)**

Instatech Industries Inc 954 415-4392
9835 Lake Worth Rd Ste 16 Lake Worth (33467) **(G-7206)**

Instazorb International Inc 561 416-7302
500 Ne Spanish River Blvd Boca Raton (33431) **(G-545)**

Insteel Wire Products Company 904 275-2100
1 Wiremill Rd Sanderson (32087) **(G-15254)**

Institute For Prosthetic Advan 850 784-0320
2315 Ruth Hentz Ave Panama City (32405) **(G-13276)**

Institutional Eye Care Inc 866 604-2931
27499 Rvrview Ctr Blvd St Bonita Springs (34134) **(G-804)**

Institutional Products Inc 305 248-4955
1011 Nw 6th St Homestead (33030) **(G-5717)**

Instorescreen Inc 646 301-4690
2338 Immokalee Rd Naples (34110) **(G-10782)**

Instrument & Valve Services Co 904 741-6800
13350 Intl Pkwy Ste 102 Jacksonville (32218) **(G-6201)**

Instrument Transformers LLC 727 229-0616
1907 Calumet St Clearwater (33765) **(G-1644)**

Insty-Prints, Tallahassee *Also called Garvin Management Company Inc* **(G-16445)**

Insty-Prints, Boca Raton *Also called B J and ME Inc* **(G-424)**

Insty-Prints, Mary Esther *Also called Image Prtg & Digital Svcs Inc* **(G-8177)**

Insulation Design & Dist LLC 850 332-7312
1879 Ziglar Rd Cantonment (32533) **(G-1269)**

Insulator Seal Incorporated (HQ) 941 751-2880
6460 Parkland Dr Sarasota (34243) **(G-15502)**

Insulow, Maitland *Also called Glucorell Inc* **(G-8060)**

Insurance Plus 904 567-1553
820 A1a N Ste W18 Ponte Vedra Beach (32082) **(G-14269)**

Intec Printing Solutions Corp 813 949-7799
16011 N Nebraska Ave Lutz (33549) **(G-7996)**

Intech Graphics, Naples *Also called Ngp Corporate Square Inc* **(G-10836)**

Intech Printing & Direct Mail, Naples *Also called Sosumi Holdings Inc* **(G-10896)**

Integra Connect LLC (PA) 800 742-3069
501 S Flagler Dr Ste 600 West Palm Beach (33401) **(G-18035)**

Integral WD Cstm Cabinetry LLC 561 361-5111
176 Glades Rd Ste A Boca Raton (33432) **(G-546)**

Integrated Cable Solutions 813 769-5740
5905 Johns Rd Ste 101 Tampa (33634) **(G-16946)**

Integrated Components Corp 305 824-0484
2592 W 78th St Hialeah (33016) **(G-5194)**

Integrated Dealer Systems Inc 800 962-7872
640 Brooker Creek Blvd Oldsmar (34677) **(G-11661)**

Integrated Diagnostics Group, Miami *Also called Sanzay Corporation* **(G-9846)**

Integrated Laser Systems Inc 954 489-8282
11383 Lakeview Dr Coral Springs (33071) **(G-2167)**

Integrated Metal Products Inc 863 687-4110
2923 Old Tampa Hwy Lakeland (33803) **(G-7353)**

Integrated Sensors LLC 419 536-3212
201 Thorntor Dr Palm Beach Gardens (33418) **(G-12977)**

Integrated Surroundings Inc 850 932-0848
4333 Gulf Breeze Pkwy Gulf Breeze (32563) **(G-4885)**

Integrated Systems & Services, Saint Petersburg *Also called Ysi Inc* **(G-15242)**

Integritrust Sclutions LLC 850 685-9801
2078 Bahama Dr Navarre (32566) **(G-10949)**

Integrity Business Svcs Inc (PA) 321 267-9294
3700 S Hopkins Ave Ste E Titusville (32780) **(G-17592)**

Integrity Engineering Corp 954 458-0500
301 W Ansin Blvd Hallandale Beach (33009) **(G-4951)**

Integrity Implants Inc 561 529-3861
354 Hiatt Dr Ste 100 Palm Beach Gardens (33418) **(G-12978)**

Integrity Marine, Hallandale Beach *Also called Integrity Engineering Corp* **(G-4951)**

Integrity Medical, Jupiter *Also called Integrity Technologies LLC* **(G-6746)**

Integrity Prsthetics Orthotics 813 416-5905
12206 Bruce B Downs Blvd Tampa (33612) **(G-16947)**

Integrity Technologies LLC 561 768-9023
5270 Pennock Point Rd Jupiter (33458) **(G-6746)**

Integrted Dsign Dev Cntl Fla I 407 268-4300
410 W 4th St Sanford (32771) **(G-15339)**

Intelbase Security Corporation 703 371-9181
400 Night Hawk Ln Saint Augustine (32080) **(G-14848)**

Intellgent Haring Systems Corp (PA) 305 668-6102
6860 Sw 81st St Miami (33143) **(G-9321)**

Intellgent Instrumentation Inc (PA) 520 573-0887
1421 Pine Ridge Rd # 120 Naples (34109) **(G-10783)**

Intelliclean Solutions LLC (PA) 615 293-2299
444 Brickell Ave Ste 800 Miami (33131) **(G-9322)**

Intelligent Heater LLC 305 248-4971
127 Sw 5th Ave Homestead (33030) **(G-5718)**

Intelligent Operating Tech Inc 303 400-9640
4437 Sw Cargo Way Palm City (34990) **(G-13045)**

Intellitec Motor Vehicles LLC (HQ) 386 738-7307
1455 Jacobs Rd Deland (32724) **(G-2875)**

Intellitech Inc 727 914-7000
11801 28th St N Ste 5 Saint Petersburg (33716) **(G-15086)**

Inteplast Engineered Films Inc 407 851-6620
7549 Brokerage Dr Orlando (32809) **(G-12249)**

Inter Cell Technologies Inc 561 575-6868
6671 W Indiantown Rd # 56439 Jupiter (33458) **(G-6747)**

Inter Gard R&D LLC 954 476-5574
15491 Sw 12th St Sunrise (33326) **(G-16323)**

Inter Ordnance, Melbourne *Also called O I Inc* **(G-8486)**

Interactive Cards Inc 863 688-4548
2787 New Tampa Hwy Lakeland (33815) **(G-7354)**

Interactive Legal, Melbourne *Also called Ils Management LLC* **(G-8440)**

Interactive Media Tech Inc (PA) 561 999-9116
7999 N Federal Hwy # 400 Boca Raton (33487) **(G-547)**

Interactyx Americas Inc 888 575-2266
3461 Bonita Bay Blvd # 2 Bonita Springs (34134) **(G-805)**

Interamericas Beverages Inc 561 881-1340
1726 Avenue L Riviera Beach (33404) **(G-14630)**

Interbay Air Compressors Inc 813 831-8213
5110 S West Shore Blvd Tampa (33611) **(G-16948)**

Interbeverage LLC 305 961-1110
3100 Nw 74th Ave Miami (33122) **(G-9323)**

Intercit Inc 863 646-0165
4330 Drane Field Rd Lakeland (33811) **(G-7355)**

Intercomp ... 407 637-9766
5910 Morningstar Cir Delray Beach (33484) ***(G-2975)***
Interconnect Cable Tech Corp ... 352 796-1716
16090 Flight Path Dr Brooksville (34604) ***(G-1164)***
Intercultural Communications ... 813 926-2617
18411 Keystone Grove Blvd Odessa (33556) ***(G-11558)***
Interface Technology Group Inc ... 321 433-1165
2107 Us Highway 1 Rockledge (32955) ***(G-14718)***
Interfries Inc (PA) ... 786 427-1427
18800 Ne 29th Ave Apt 426 Miami (33180) ***(G-9324)***
Interglobal Capital Inc ... 727 585-1500
1016 Pnc De Leon Blvd Clearwater (33756) ***(G-1645)***
Interior Design ... 646 805-0200
3651 Fau Blvd Ste 200 Boca Raton (33431) ***(G-548)***
Interior Dsign Media Group LLC ... 561 750-0151
3731 Fau Blvd Ste 1 Boca Raton (33431) ***(G-549)***
Interior Views Inc ... 727 527-8899
5625 70th Ave N Pinellas Park (33781) ***(G-13694)***
Interlachen Cabinets Inc ... 352 481-6078
2010 State Road 20 Hawthorne (32640) ***(G-5008)***
Interlake Industries Inc ... 863 688-5665
1022 County Line Rd Lakeland (33815) ***(G-7356)***
Interlake Stamping Florida Inc ... 863 688-5665
1022 County Line Rd Lakeland (33815) ***(G-7357)***
Interlink Software Inc ... 407 927-0898
8946 Leeland Archer Blvd Orlando (32836) ***(G-12250)***
Intermas Nets USA Inc ... 305 442-1416
2655 S Le Jeune Rd # 810 Coral Gables (33134) ***(G-2073)***
Intermed Group Inc (PA) ... 561 586-3667
13301 Nw Us Highway 441 Alachua (32615) ***(G-12)***
Intermedix Corporation (HQ) ... 954 308-8700
6451 N Federal Hwy # 1000 Fort Lauderdale (33308) ***(G-3879)***
Internano, Delray Beach *Also called Rave LLC* ***(G-3012)***
International Baler Corp ... 904 358-3812
5400 Rio Grande Ave Jacksonville (32254) ***(G-6202)***
International C & C Corp ... 727 249-0675
10831 Canal St Largo (33777) ***(G-7614)***
International Casting Corp ... 305 558-3515
6187 Miami Lakes Dr E Miami Lakes (33014) ***(G-10308)***
International Closet Center ... 305 883-6551
7330 Nw 79th Ter Medley (33166) ***(G-8258)***
International Clothiers Inc ... 914 715-5600
4000 Twrside Ter Ste 2412 Miami (33138) ***(G-9325)***
International Cnstr Pubg ... 305 668-4999
4913 Sw 75th Ave Miami (33155) ***(G-9326)***
International Composite ... 206 349-7468
1468 Northgate Blvd Sarasota (34234) ***(G-15706)***
International Dock Pdts Inc ... 954 964-5315
3101 Sw 25th St Ste 106 Hallandale Beach (33009) ***(G-4952)***
International Epoxies Sealers, San Antonio *Also called S & R Fastener Co Inc* ***(G-15252)***
International Fd Solutions Inc (PA) ... 888 499-6888
5600 Elmhurst Cir Oviedo (32765) ***(G-12829)***
International Finishes Inc ... 561 948-1066
7777 Glades Rd Boca Raton (33434) ***(G-550)***
International Food Eqp Inc ... 305 785-5100
1280 Partridge Ave Miami Springs (33166) ***(G-10389)***
International Gran & Stone LLC ... 813 920-6500
1842 Gunn Hwy Odessa (33556) ***(G-11559)***
International Greenscapes LLC ... 760 631-6789
20855 Ne 16th Ave Ste C4 Miami (33179) ***(G-9327)***
International Guidelines Ctr ... 407 878-7606
106 Commerce St Ste 105 Lake Mary (32746) ***(G-7086)***
International H20 Inc ... 954 854-1638
18387 Ne 4th Ct North Miami Beach (33179) ***(G-11144)***
International Imaging Mtls Inc ... 727 834-8200
2300 Destiny Way Odessa (33556) ***(G-11560)***
International Iron Works LLC (PA) ... 305 835-0190
3585 E 10th Ct Hialeah (33013) ***(G-5195)***
International Jwly Designs Inc ... 954 577-9099
4750 N Dixie Hwy Ste 3 Oakland Park (33334) ***(G-11273)***
International Keg Rental LLC ... 407 900-9992
10450 Trkey Lk Rd Unit 69 Orlando (32819) ***(G-12251)***
International Machine Shop, Miami *Also called International Mch Works Inc* ***(G-9328)***
International Mch Works Inc ... 305 635-3585
3631 Nw 48th Ter Miami (33142) ***(G-9328)***
International Mdse Sources Inc (PA) ... 239 430-9993
4551 Gulf Shore Blvd N Naples (34103) ***(G-10784)***
International Medical Inds Inc ... 954 917-9570
2981 Gateway Dr Pompano Beach (33069) ***(G-14063)***
International Ozone Svcs LLC ... 352 978-9785
320924 Sunnygo Dr Ste 210 Mount Dora (32757) ***(G-10604)***
International Packaging Mchs ... 239 643-2020
3963 Enterprise Ave Naples (34104) ***(G-10785)***
International Paint LLC ... 321 636-9722
3062 Oxbow Cir Cocoa (32926) ***(G-1938)***
International Paint LLC ... 305 620-9220
3489 Nw 167th St Opa Locka (33056) ***(G-11755)***
International Paper Company ... 407 855-2121
711 E Lancaster Rd Orlando (32809) ***(G-12252)***
International Paper Company ... 813 717-9100
2402 Police Center Dr Plant City (33566) ***(G-13776)***
International Paper Company ... 813 621-0584
6706 N 53rd St Tampa (33610) ***(G-16949)***
International Paper Company ... 850 968-2121
375 Muscogee Rd Cantonment (32533) ***(G-1270)***
International Polymer Svcs LLC ... 401 529-6855
3431 Mai Kai Dr Pensacola (32526) ***(G-13525)***
International Power USA LLC ... 305 534-7993
2091 Nw 139th St Miami (33015) ***(G-9329)***
International Printing & Copyi ... 954 295-5239
5379 Lyons Rd Coconut Creek (33073) ***(G-1993)***
International Prtg Ad Spc Inc ... 772 398-4664
701 Nw Federal Hwy # 301 Stuart (34994) ***(G-16167)***
International Quiksigns Inc ... 954 462-7446
804 Se 17th St Fort Lauderdale (33316) ***(G-3880)***
International Ship Repair & MA ... 813 247-1118
1601 Sahlman Dr Tampa (33605) ***(G-16950)***
International Shipyards Ancona ... 305 371-7722
1850 Se 17th St Ste 200 Fort Lauderdale (33316) ***(G-3881)***
International Sign Design Corp ... 727 541-5573
10831 Canal St Largo (33777) ***(G-7615)***
International Signs & Ltg Inc ... 407 332-9663
714 Commerce Cir Longwood (32750) ***(G-7905)***
International Sound Corp ... 305 556-1000
1550 W 35th Pl Hialeah (33012) ***(G-5196)***
International Specialist, Tampa *Also called Phil Lau* ***(G-17162)***
International Tool Mchs of Fla ... 386 446-0500
5 Industry Dr Palm Coast (32137) ***(G-13080)***
International Trader Company, Miami *Also called Bellatrix Trade LLC* ***(G-8812)***
International Trading Company, Opa Locka *Also called Lear Investors Inc* ***(G-11763)***
International Treescapes, Miami *Also called International Greenscapes LLC* ***(G-9327)***
International Uniform, Miami *Also called Interntnal Export Uniforms Inc* ***(G-9330)***
International Vapor Group LLC (HQ) ... 305 824-4027
14300 Commerce Way Miami Lakes (33016) ***(G-10309)***
International Vault Inc ... 941 390-4505
16227 Daysailor Trl Lakewood Ranch (34202) ***(G-7479)***
International Whl Tile LLC ... 772 223-5151
3500 Sw 42nd Ave Palm City (34990) ***(G-13046)***
Internet Marketing Press ... 850 271-4333
818 Radcliff Ave Lynn Haven (32444) ***(G-8029)***
Interni Cucine Itln Cabinetry, Fort Lauderdale *Also called Interni Cucine LLC* ***(G-3882)***
Interni Cucine LLC ... 954 486-7000
1783 Nw 38th Ave Fort Lauderdale (33311) ***(G-3882)***
Internl Sterilization Lab LLC ... 352 429-3200
217 Sampey Rd Groveland (34736) ***(G-4863)***
Interntnal Drectional Drlg Inc ... 954 890-1331
6601 Lyons Rd Ste A5 Coconut Creek (33073) ***(G-1994)***
Interntnal Export Uniforms Inc ... 305 869-9900
4000 Nw 29th St Miami (33142) ***(G-9330)***
Interntnal Flvors Frgrnces Inc ... 904 783-2180
2051 Lane Ave N Jacksonville (32254) ***(G-6203)***
Interntnal Flvors Frgrnces Inc ... 706 796-2800
2051 Lane Ave N Jacksonville (32254) ***(G-6204)***
Interntnal Ntrctcals Group Inc ... 786 518-2903
771 Shotgun Rd Sunrise (33326) ***(G-16324)***
Interntnal Pckg Athntic Cisine, Winter Springs *Also called Ipac Inc* ***(G-18568)***
Interntnal Srvillance Tech Inc (PA) ... 954 574-1100
160 Sw 12th Ave Deerfield Beach (33442) ***(G-2742)***
Interntnal Synrgy For Tchncal ... 321 305-0863
12001 Res Pkwy Ste 236 Orlando (32826) ***(G-12253)***
Interntnal Tech Sltons Sup LLC ... 305 364-5229
2636 Nw 97th Ave Doral (33172) ***(G-3259)***
Interntonal Linear Matrix Corp ... 727 549-1808
10831 Canal St Seminole (33777) ***(G-15978)***
Interprint Incorporated (HQ) ... 727 531-8957
12350 Us 19 N Clearwater (33764) ***(G-1646)***
Interprint Web Printing, Clearwater *Also called Interprint Incorporated* ***(G-1646)***
Interrail Engineering Inc ... 904 268-6411
12443 San Jose Blvd # 1103 Jacksonville (32223) ***(G-6205)***
Interrail Power Inc ... 904 268-6411
12443 San Jose Blvd Jacksonville (32223) ***(G-6206)***
Interstate Recycling Waste Inc ... 407 812-5555
5232 Laval Dr Orlando (32839) ***(G-12254)***
Interstate Signcrafters LLC ... 561 547-3760
130 Commerce Rd Boynton Beach (33426) ***(G-881)***
Interstate Wldg & Fabrication ... 727 446-1449
1939 Sherwood St Clearwater (33765) ***(G-1647)***
Intertape Polymer Corp (HQ) ... 888 898-7834
100 Paramount Dr Ste 300 Sarasota (34232) ***(G-15707)***
Intertape Polymer Corp ... 813 621-8410
9940 Currie Davis Dr Tampa (33619) ***(G-16951)***
Intertape Polymer Group, Sarasota *Also called Ipg (us) Holdings Inc* ***(G-15708)***
Intertape Polymer US Inc ... 941 727-5788
3647 Cortez Rd W Ste 102 Bradenton (34210) ***(G-997)***
Intertech Supply Inc ... 786 200-0561
13334 Sw 9th Ter Miami (33184) ***(G-9331)***
Intertech Worldwide Corp (PA) ... 561 395-5441
4400 N Federal Hwy # 125 Boca Raton (33431) ***(G-551)***

Intertek Auto-Sun-Shade, Hialeah *Also called Intertek International Corp* ***(G-5197)***
Intertek International Corp....305 883-8700
401 Se 11th Ave Hialeah (33010) ***(G-5197)***
Intertex Miami LLC....305 627-3536
50 Ne 179th St Bay 1-2 Miami (33162) ***(G-9332)***
Intouch Inc....702 572-4786
5036 Dr Phillips Blvd Orlando (32819) ***(G-12255)***
Intouch Gps LLC....877 593-2981
439 S Florida Ave 100b Lakeland (33801) ***(G-7358)***
Intradeco Apparel Inc (HQ)....305 264-8888
9500 Nw 108th Ave Medley (33178) ***(G-8259)***
Intralock International Inc....561 447-8282
6560 W Rogers Cir Ste 24 Boca Raton (33487) ***(G-552)***
Intrepid Machine Inc....352 540-9919
2305 Circuit Way Brooksville (34604) ***(G-1165)***
Intrepid Machine Inc....813 854-3825
12020 Race Track Rd Tampa (33626) ***(G-16952)***
Intrepid Powerboats Inc....954 922-7544
11700 Belcher Rd S Largo (33773) ***(G-7616)***
Intrepid Powerboats Inc (HQ)....954 324-4196
805 Ne E 3rd St Dania (33004) ***(G-2333)***
Intrinsic Interventions Inc....614 205-8465
223 Dolphin Cove Ct Bonita Springs (34134) ***(G-806)***
Intuition Ale Works, Jacksonville *Also called Rpd Management LLC* ***(G-6435)***
Intuitos LLC....727 522-2301
2300 Tall Pines Dr # 120 Largo (33771) ***(G-7617)***
Inusa Manufacturing LLC....786 451-5227
2500 Sw 32nd Ave Pembroke Park (33023) ***(G-13363)***
Invacare Corporation....800 532-8677
4457 63rd Cir N Pinellas Park (33781) ***(G-13695)***
Invacare Corporation....727 522-8677
4501 63rd Cir N Pinellas Park (33781) ***(G-13696)***
Invacare Florida Corporation....407 321-5630
2101 E Lake Mary Blvd Sanford (32773) ***(G-15340)***
Invel, Orlando *Also called Goen3 Corporation* ***(G-12197)***
Inventis North America Inc....844 683-6847
2503 S Wa Ave Ste 586 Titusville (32780) ***(G-17593)***
Inversiones Medicas SIS, Doral *Also called Ivan & Ivan LLC* ***(G-3263)***
Inversnes Wlldel Asociados Inc....305 591-0931
8250 Nw 58th St Doral (33166) ***(G-3260)***
Inversnes Wlldel Asociados Inc (PA)....305 591-0118
4700 Nw 72nd Ave Miami (33166) ***(G-9333)***
Invincible Boat Company LLC....305 685-2704
4700 Nw 132nd St Opa Locka (33054) ***(G-11756)***
Inviro Tek Inc....215 499-1209
11334 Boggy Creek Rd # 1 Orlando (32824) ***(G-12256)***
Invision Auto Systems Inc....407 956-5161
3001 Directors Row Orlando (32809) ***(G-12257)***
Invision Auto Systems Inc (HQ)....407 956-5161
2351 J Lawson Blvd Orlando (32824) ***(G-12258)***
Invision Industries Inc....407 451-8353
2351 J Lawson Blvd Orlando (32824) ***(G-12259)***
Invivo Corporation (HQ)....301 525-9683
3545 Sw 47th Ave Gainesville (32608) ***(G-4713)***
Invivo Corporation....352 336-0010
3600 Sw 47th Ave Gainesville (32608) ***(G-4714)***
Invo Bioscience Inc (PA)....978 878-9505
5582 Broadcast Ct Lakewood Ranch (34240) ***(G-7484)***
Invoinet Inc (HQ)....305 432-5366
1111 Brickell Ave # 1860 Miami (33131) ***(G-9334)***
Iomartcloud Inc....954 880-1680
601 21st St Vero Beach (32960) ***(G-17766)***
Ionemoto Inc....617 784-1401
300 Industrial Cir Sebastian (32958) ***(G-15895)***
IPA Prosthetics & Orthotics, Panama City *Also called Institute For Prosthetic Advan* ***(G-13276)***
Ipac Inc....407 699-7507
1270 Belle Ave Unit 115 Winter Springs (32708) ***(G-18568)***
IPC Company USA, Orlando *Also called Ingenria Prcura Y Cnstrccion C* ***(G-12244)***
IPC Global....727 470-2134
1062 Cephas Rd Clearwater (33765) ***(G-1648)***
Ipeg Corporation....239 963-1470
5400 Jaeger Rd Ste 2 Naples (34109) ***(G-10786)***
Ipg (us) Holdings Inc (HQ)....941 727-5788
100 Paramount Dr Ste 300 Sarasota (34232) ***(G-15708)***
Ipg (us) Inc (HQ)....941 727-5788
100 Paramount Dr Ste 300 Sarasota (34232) ***(G-15709)***
Ipg Network Corp....305 681-4001
3155 Nw 40th St Miami (33142) ***(G-9335)***
Ipline LLC....305 675-4235
18152 Sw 144th Ct Miami (33177) ***(G-9336)***
Ipq Trade Corp....786 522-2310
488 Ne 18th St Ste Cu1 Miami (33132) ***(G-9337)***
Ipro Force LLC....603 766-8716
6929 Corley Ave Windermere (34786) ***(G-18354)***
Ips, Lakeland *Also called Industrial Plastic Systems Inc* ***(G-7351)***
Ips, Sarasota *Also called Innovative Power Solutions LLC* ***(G-15501)***
Ipts Inc....561 844-8216
7221 Hvrhill Bus Pkwy # 103 Riviera Beach (33407) ***(G-14631)***
Ipvision Software LLC....813 728-3175
5905 Johns Rd Tampa (33634) ***(G-16953)***
Iq Formulations Llc....954 533-9256
10151 Nw 67th St Tamarac (33321) ***(G-16533)***
Iq Valves Co....321 729-9634
425 West Dr Melbourne (32904) ***(G-8442)***
Ir Clinical, West Palm Beach *Also called Clinical Chmstry Spclists Corp* ***(G-17967)***
Iradimed Corporation....407 677-8022
1025 Willa Springs Dr Winter Springs (32708) ***(G-18569)***
Ireco Inc....239 593-3749
853 Palm View Dr Naples (34110) ***(G-10787)***
Iris Inc....561 921-0847
955 Nw 17th Ave Ste D Delray Beach (33445) ***(G-2976)***
Iris Diagnostics, Miami *Also called Beckman Coulter Inc* ***(G-8810)***
Iris International Inc (HQ)....818 709-1244
11800 Sw 147th Ave Miami (33196) ***(G-9338)***
Irms Inc....321 631-1161
2191 Rockledge Dr Rockledge (32955) ***(G-14719)***
Iron Bridge Tools Inc....954 596-1090
101 Ne 3rd Ave Ste 1800 Fort Lauderdale (33301) ***(G-3883)***
Iron Container LLC (PA)....305 726-2150
8505 Nw 74th St Miami (33166) ***(G-9339)***
Iron Metal USA Corp....786 757-3263
8572 Nw 93rd St Medley (33166) ***(G-8260)***
Iron Strength Corp....305 226-6866
9568 Sw 40th St Miami (33165) ***(G-9340)***
Iron-Art & Fence Inc....407 699-1734
731 N Us Highway 17 92 # 201 Longwood (32750) ***(G-7906)***
Ironbeer Soft Drink, Doral *Also called Sunshine Bottling Co* ***(G-3384)***
Ironclad Impact Wndows Dors LL....954 743-4321
3701 Sw 47th Ave Ste 106 Davie (33314) ***(G-2426)***
Ironclad Welding Inc....954 925-7987
1205 Sw 4th Ave Dania (33004) ***(G-2334)***
Ironhorse Pressworks Inc....727 462-9988
406 S Jupiter Ave Clearwater (33755) ***(G-1649)***
Ironside Press....772 569-8484
1001 20th Pl Vero Beach (32960) ***(G-17767)***
Ironwifi LLC....800 963-6221
3071 N Orange Blossom Trl C Orlando (32804) ***(G-12260)***
Ironworks Inc of Orange Park....904 291-9330
1701 Blanding Blvd Middleburg (32068) ***(G-10403)***
Irving Publications LLC....352 219-4688
5745 Sw 75th St Unit 286 Gainesville (32608) ***(G-4715)***
Is4ts, Orlando *Also called Interntnal Synrgy For Tchncal* ***(G-12253)***
ISA Group Corp....305 748-1578
2665 S Byshr Dr Ste 710 Miami (33133) ***(G-9341)***
ISA Group Corp....786 201-8360
1204 Placetas Ave Coral Gables (33146) ***(G-2074)***
Iscar Ground Services Eqp, Miami Gardens *Also called Iscar GSE Corp* ***(G-10266)***
Iscar GSE Corp....305 364-8886
1182 Nw 159th Dr Miami Gardens (33169) ***(G-10265)***
Iscar GSE Corp....305 364-8886
1180 Nw 159th Dr Miami Gardens (33169) ***(G-10266)***
Ischa Products LLC....305 609-8244
23616 Sw 107th Pl Homestead (33032) ***(G-5719)***
Isl, Groveland *Also called Internl Sterilization Lab LLC* ***(G-4863)***
Isla Instruments LLC....561 603-4685
13884 71st Pl N West Palm Beach (33412) ***(G-18036)***
Islamorada Boatworks LLC....786 393-4752
4501 S Ridgewood Ave Edgewater (32141) ***(G-3492)***
Island Bottles....305 304-7673
718 Emma St Key West (33040) ***(G-6867)***
Island Designs Outlet Inc....813 855-0020
14501 Mccormick Dr Tampa (33626) ***(G-16954)***
Island Dream Itln Ice Dssrts L....904 778-6839
9501 Arlington Expy Fc4 Jacksonville (32225) ***(G-6207)***
Island Fever LLC....941 639-6400
1200 W Retta Esplanade # 19 Punta Gorda (33950) ***(G-14510)***
Island Joys....561 201-6005
3679 Nw 19th St Fort Lauderdale (33311) ***(G-3884)***
Island Life Graphics Inc (PA)....904 206-6997
3114 Egans Bluff Rd Fernandina Beach (32034) ***(G-3588)***
Island Life Graphics Inc....904 261-0340
1410 E Oak St Fernandina Beach (32034) ***(G-3589)***
Island Media Publishing LLC....904 556-3002
120 N 15th St Fernandina Beach (32034) ***(G-3590)***
Island Millwork Inc....352 694-5565
3621 Ne 36th Ave Ocala (34479) ***(G-11412)***
Island Natural Originals LLC....561 287-0095
150 Nw 16th St Boca Raton (33432) ***(G-553)***
Island Park Custom Woodworking....239 437-9670
16270 Old Us 41 Fort Myers (33912) ***(G-4292)***
Island Pcket Saward Yachts LLC....727 535-6431
1979 Wild Acres Rd Largo (33771) ***(G-7618)***
Island Print Shop....239 642-0077
3888 Mannix Dr Ste 301 Naples (34114) ***(G-10788)***
Island Shutter Co Inc....386 738-9455
1838 Patterson Ave Deland (32724) ***(G-2876)***
Island Style Homes Inc....772 464-6259
4275 Mariah Cir Fort Pierce (34947) ***(G-4498)***

ALPHABETIC

Island Sun Newspaper, Sanibel *Also called Lorken Publications Inc* ***(G-15416)***
Island Tops, Jacksonville *Also called Fastglas* ***(G-6089)***
Islander, Key Biscayne *Also called Samara Publishing* ***(G-6839)***
Islandoor Company 954 524-3667
951 Nw 9th Ave Fort Lauderdale (33311) ***(G-3885)***
ISO Panel, Medley *Also called Mr Winter Inc* ***(G-8285)***
Isoaid LLC 727 815-3262
7824 Clark Moody Blvd Port Richey (34668) ***(G-14364)***
Isobev Inc (HQ) 561 701-5385
1327 Se Dixie Hwy Stuart (34994) ***(G-16168)***
Isocialmedia Digital Marketing 561 510-1124
433 Plaza Real Ste 275 Boca Raton (33432) ***(G-554)***
Isoflex Technologies Intl LLC 561 210-5170
3434 Sw 15th St B Deerfield Beach (33442) ***(G-2743)***
Isofrut Company Inc 305 961-1681
380 Nw 24th St Miami (33127) ***(G-9342)***
Isolyser, Jacksonville *Also called Microtek Medical Inc* ***(G-6304)***
Isoprenoids LLC 813 785-6446
3802 Spectrum Blvd # 153 Tampa (33612) ***(G-16955)***
Isp Optics Corporation (HQ) 914 591-3070
2603 Challenger Tech Ct # 100 Orlando (32826) ***(G-12261)***
Ispg Inc 941 896-3999
10504 Technology Ter Bradenton (34211) ***(G-998)***
Ispy Equities LLC 813 731-0676
12309 Field Point Way Spring Hill (34610) ***(G-16085)***
It Busness Solutions Group Inc 407 260-0116
800 Waterway Pl Longwood (32750) ***(G-7907)***
It Is Finished Inc 813 598-9585
24851 Ravello St Land O Lakes (34639) ***(G-7494)***
It Labs LLC 310 490-6142
1810 Flower Dr Palm Beach Gardens (33410) ***(G-12979)***
IT Pacs Pro Software Inc 954 678-1270
5612 Pembroke Rd Ste A West Park (33023) ***(G-18214)***
It Smells Good 904 899-2818
1705 W 4th St Jacksonville (32209) ***(G-6208)***
It's A "10" Haircare, Coral Springs *Also called Its A 10 Inc* ***(G-2168)***
Ita Inc 386 301-5172
9 W Tower Cir Ste C Ormond Beach (32174) ***(G-12774)***
Italfloor Tile, Fort Lauderdale *Also called Colaianni Italian Flr Tile Mfg* ***(G-3736)***
Italian Cabinetry Inc 786 534-2742
3250 Ne 1st Ave Ste 305 Miami (33137) ***(G-9343)***
Italian Cast Stones Inc 813 902-8900
5418 W Ingraham St Tampa (33616) ***(G-16956)***
Italian Hair Extension Inc 954 839-5366
10770 Nw 53rd St Sunrise (33351) ***(G-16325)***
Italian Idea Srq LLC 941 330-0525
136 S Pineapple Ave Sarasota (34236) ***(G-15710)***
Italian Moonshiners Inc 954 687-4500
8300 Nw 53rd St Ste 350 Doral (33166) ***(G-3261)***
Italian Rose Garlic Pdts LLC (HQ) 561 863-5556
1380 W 15th St Riviera Beach (33404) ***(G-14632)***
Italkraft LLC (PA) 305 406-1301
2900 Nw 77th Ct Doral (33122) ***(G-3262)***
Itd Food Safety, Palm Bay *Also called Innovative Tech By Design Inc* ***(G-12904)***
Iteg LLC 305 399-2510
333 Las Olas Way Cu1 Fort Lauderdale (33301) ***(G-3886)***
Itelecom USA Inc 305 557-4660
1422 Canary Island Dr Weston (33327) ***(G-18257)***
Itg Cigars Inc 813 623-2262
3901 Roga Blvd Tampa (33619) ***(G-16957)***
Itg Cigars Inc (HQ) 954 772-9000
5900 N Andrews Ave Ste 11 Fort Lauderdale (33309) ***(G-3887)***
ITI Engineering LLC 866 245-9356
1081 Willa Springs Dr Winter Springs (32708) ***(G-18570)***
Itiles LLC 954 609-0984
2255 Glades Rd Ste 324a Boca Raton (33431) ***(G-555)***
ITM, Palm Coast *Also called International Tool Mchs of Fla* ***(G-13080)***
Itqlick Inc 855 487-5425
2100 E Hlnd Bch Blvd # 203 Hallandale Beach (33009) ***(G-4953)***
Its A 10 Inc 954 227-7813
4613 N University Dr # 478 Coral Springs (33067) ***(G-2168)***
Its Technologies Logistics LLC 904 751-1300
8831 Moncrief Dinsmore Rd Jacksonville (32219) ***(G-6209)***
ITT Flygt LLC, Apopka *Also called Xylem Water Solutions Fla LLC* ***(G-186)***
ITT Water & Wastewater USA Inc 407 880-2900
2152 Sprint Blvd Apopka (32703) ***(G-140)***
ITW Alpine, Fort Lauderdale *Also called ITW Blding Cmponents Group Inc* ***(G-3888)***
ITW Blding Cmponents Group Inc 863 422-8685
1950 Marley Dr 3 Haines City (33844) ***(G-4908)***
ITW Blding Cmponents Group Inc 954 781-3333
6451 N Federal Hwy # 101 Fort Lauderdale (33308) ***(G-3888)***
ITW Professional Auto Pdts, Lakeland *Also called Illinois Tool Works Inc* ***(G-7347)***
Ityx Solutions Inc 407 474-4383
2915 Musselwhite Ave Orlando (32804) ***(G-12262)***
Iva Parts Broker LLC 239 222-2604
2708 Sw 165th Ave Miramar (33027) ***(G-10506)***
Ivan & Ivan LLC 305 507-8793
1465 Nw 97th Ave Doral (33172) ***(G-3263)***
Ivax Corporation (HQ) 305 329-3795
4400 Biscayne Blvd Miami (33137) ***(G-9344)***
Ivax Pharmaceuticals LLC (HQ) 305 575-6000
74 Nw 176th St Miami (33169) ***(G-9345)***
Ivax Research Inc (HQ) 305 668-7688
4400 Biscayne Blvd Miami (33137) ***(G-9346)***
Ivax Teva 954 384-5316
2945 W Corp Lks Blvd A Weston (33331) ***(G-18258)***
Iver Services 786 329-3018
2381 Ne 135th Ter North Miami Beach (33181) ***(G-11145)***
Iverica Industrial Inc 305 691-1659
1044 E 29th St Hialeah (33013) ***(G-5198)***
Ivm Usa Inc 786 693-2755
800 Brickell Ave Ste 550 Miami (33131) ***(G-9347)***
Ivory International Inc (HQ) 305 687-2244
9500 Nw 108th Ave Medley (33178) ***(G-8261)***
Izabellas Creations Inc 786 429-3441
14252 Sw 140th St Ste 111 Miami (33186) ***(G-9348)***
Izzycue, Miami Beach *Also called Bkn International Inc* ***(G-10171)***
J & A Big Pavers LLC 321 948-0019
6214 W Robinson St Orlando (32835) ***(G-12263)***
J & A Custom Cabinetry Inc 786 255-4181
15825 Sw 285th St Homestead (33033) ***(G-5720)***
J & D Manufacturing Inc 813 854-1700
375 Mears Blvd Oldsmar (34677) ***(G-11662)***
J & D Oldja LLC 727 526-3240
4424 34th St N Saint Petersburg (33714) ***(G-15087)***
J & E Custom Cabinets Inc 727 868-2820
9926 Denton Ave Port Richey (34667) ***(G-14365)***
J & G Explosives LLC 407 883-0734
413 Idlewyld Dr Fort Lauderdale (33301) ***(G-3889)***
J & H Supply Co Inc 561 582-3346
825 N Dixie Hwy Lake Worth (33460) ***(G-7207)***
J & I Ventures Inc 561 845-0030
4390 Westroads Dr Ste 2 West Palm Beach (33407) ***(G-18037)***
J & J Inc 954 746-7300
10062 Nw 50th St Sunrise (33351) ***(G-16326)***
J & J Custom Mica Inc 239 433-2828
1361 Canterbury Dr Fort Myers (33901) ***(G-4293)***
J & J Door Manufacturing Inc 850 769-2554
2325 Transmitter Rd Panama City (32404) ***(G-13277)***
J & J International Corp 407 349-7114
240 Power Ct Ste 132 Sanford (32771) ***(G-15341)***
J & J Litho Enterprises Inc (PA) 239 433-2311
6835 Intl Ctr Blvd Ste 9 Fort Myers (33912) ***(G-4294)***
J & J Marine Service Inc 813 741-2190
2922 46th Ave N Saint Petersburg (33714) ***(G-15088)***
J & J Refregrator, Miami *Also called Coldflo Inc* ***(G-8944)***
J & J Steel Services Corp 305 878-8929
9401 Nw 109th St Unit 5 Medley (33178) ***(G-8262)***
J & J Stone Tops Inc 305 305-8993
13760 Nw 19th Ave Opa Locka (33054) ***(G-11757)***
J & J Wldg Stl Fbrction Fla In 813 754-0771
364 Recker Hwy Auburndale (33823) ***(G-237)***
J & K 8 Inc 954 984-8585
1591 N Powerline Rd Pompano Beach (33069) ***(G-14064)***
J & N Stone Inc 941 924-6200
6111 Clark Center Ave Sarasota (34238) ***(G-15711)***
J & N Stone Inc (PA) 863 422-7369
135 Bargain Barn Rd Davenport (33837) ***(G-2367)***
J & P Deerfield Inc 954 571-6665
1191 W Newport Center Dr Deerfield Beach (33442) ***(G-2744)***
J & R Metal Fabrications, Jupiter *Also called Spring Loaded Inc* ***(G-6804)***
J & S Cypress Inc 352 383-3864
28625 Cypress Mill Rd Sorrento (32776) ***(G-16010)***
J & V Cabinets & More Inc 352 390-6378
2321 Ne 43rd St Ocala (34479) ***(G-11413)***
J & V Paverscorp 786 510-4389
2614 Sw 36th Ave Miami (33133) ***(G-9349)***
J & Z Production and Pblcy Inc 786 718-8204
4045 Ne 15th St Homestead (33033) ***(G-5721)***
J A Blnds Decorations More LLC 754 422-4778
12540 Sw 37th St Miami (33175) ***(G-9350)***
J A Custom 561 615-4680
3042 Ike Rd Ste 17 West Palm Beach (33411) ***(G-18038)***
J A Custom Fabricators Inc 561 615-4680
1230 Wingfield St Lake Worth (33460) ***(G-7208)***
J and A Maintenance 754 234-0708
6220 Nw 15th St Sunrise (33313) ***(G-16327)***
J and L Artistry 904 701-3070
8166 Jamaica Rd S Jacksonville (32216) ***(G-6210)***
J B Nottingham & Co Inc 386 873-2990
1731 Patterson Ave Deland (32724) ***(G-2877)***
J Bristol LLC 407 488-6744
2715 Norris Ave Winter Park (32789) ***(G-18516)***
J C Industries Inc 863 773-9199
6105 33rd St E Bradenton (34203) ***(G-999)***
J C M I, Lakeland *Also called JC Machine Inc* ***(G-7360)***
J C Machine Shop, Miami *Also called JC Industrial Mfg Corp* ***(G-9359)***

J C Newman Cigar Co (PA) 813 248-2124
2701 N 16th St Tampa (33605) ***(G-16958)***
J C S Engineering & Dev 305 888-7911
211 W 22nd St Hialeah (33010) ***(G-5199)***
J Cube Inc 407 699-6866
180 E Trade Winds Rd Casselberry (32708) ***(G-1420)***
J D Aluminum 239 543-3558
18161 Sandy Pines Cir Fort Myers (33917) ***(G-4295)***
J D M Corp 305 947-5876
1551 Nw 93rd Ave Doral (33172) ***(G-3264)***
J F V Designs Inc 321 228-7469
220 Southridge Indus Dr Tavares (32778) ***(G-17513)***
J Herbert Corporation 407 846-0588
1751 S John Young Pkwy Kissimmee (34741) ***(G-6928)***
J I S Associates 321 777-6829
445 Cardinal Dr Satellite Beach (32937) ***(G-15885)***
J J Cabinets Appliances 786 573-0300
8833 Sw 129th St Miami (33176) ***(G-9351)***
J J M Services Inc 954 437-1880
12004 Miramar Pkwy Miramar (33025) ***(G-10507)***
J K & M Ink Corporation 813 875-3106
4714 N Thatcher Ave Tampa (33614) ***(G-16959)***
J L M Machine Co Inc 941 748-4288
2704 29th Ave E Bradenton (34208) ***(G-1000)***
J Lea LLC 954 921-1422
916 N 20th Ave Hollywood (33020) ***(G-5602)***
J M Econo-Print Inc 305 591-3620
303 Camilo Ave Coral Gables (33134) ***(G-2075)***
J M Interiors Inc 305 891-6121
12564 Ne 14th Ave North Miami (33161) ***(G-11107)***
J M Milling Inc 386 546-6826
120 Dog Branch Rd East Palatka (32131) ***(G-3472)***
J N C Investments, Coral Springs *Also called Jnc Habitat Investments Inc* ***(G-2170)***
J P Poly Bag Company 727 804-5866
1783 Marsh Wren Way Palm Harbor (34683) ***(G-13115)***
J Q Bell & Sons 904 879-1597
44247 Bell Ln Callahan (32011) ***(G-1252)***
J R C Concrete Products Inc 850 456-9665
994 S Fairfield Dr Lot 2 Pensacola (32506) ***(G-13526)***
J R Wheeler Corporation 954 585-8950
3748 Sw 30th Ave Fort Lauderdale (33312) ***(G-3890)***
J Ross Publishing Inc 954 727-9333
300 S Pine Island Rd # 305 Plantation (33324) ***(G-13859)***
J S Trading Inc 954 791-9035
6524 Nw 13th Ct Plantation (33313) ***(G-13860)***
J Schor R Inc 954 621-5279
1776 N Pine Island Rd Plantation (33322) ***(G-13861)***
J T Walker Industries Inc (PA) 727 461-0501
1310 N Hercules Ave Ste A Clearwater (33765) ***(G-1650)***
J Turner & Co, Ponte Vedra Beach *Also called Jt Enterprises Group LLC* ***(G-14270)***
J V G Inc 727 584-7136
12509 Ulmerton Rd Largo (33774) ***(G-7619)***
J W Dawson Co Inc 305 634-8618
3739 Nw 43rd St Miami (33142) ***(G-9352)***
J W Group Inc (PA) 386 423-8828
2004 Sabal Palm Dr Edgewater (32141) ***(G-3493)***
J W L Trading Company Inc 813 854-1128
13801 W Hillsborough Ave Tampa (33635) ***(G-16960)***
J&B Cmmnication Solutions Corp 786 346-7449
6555 Stirling Rd Davie (33314) ***(G-2427)***
J&C Equipment, Fort Myers *Also called Eidolon Analytics Inc* ***(G-4244)***
J&D Oil Field Intl Inc 305 436-0024
3785 Nw 82nd Ave Ste 206 Doral (33166) ***(G-3265)***
J&D Oilfield International, Doral *Also called J&D Oil Field Intl Inc* ***(G-3265)***
J&J Sheet Mtal Fabercation LLC 941 752-0569
728 Winter Garden Dr Sarasota (34243) ***(G-15503)***
J&Jh Stucco Inc 813 482-5282
12713 Lovers Ln Riverview (33579) ***(G-14567)***
J&K Kitchen, Bath and Stone, Pompano Beach *Also called J & K 8 Inc* ***(G-14064)***
J&N Keystone of Florida 305 528-1677
6900 Nw 77th Ter Medley (33166) ***(G-8263)***
J&S Inks LLC 305 999-0304
1212 Ne 176th Ter North Miami Beach (33162) ***(G-11146)***
J-Coast Woodworks LLC 561 262-6144
1312 Commerce Ln Jupiter (33458) ***(G-6748)***
J-Ko Company 561 795-7377
200 Business Park Way D Royal Palm Beach (33411) ***(G-14768)***
J-Kup Corp 352 683-5629
1260 Lori Dr Spring Hill (34606) ***(G-16073)***
J. C. Mch Sp & Met Fabrication, Miami *Also called JC Machine Works Corp* ***(G-9360)***
J.W. Appley and Son, Clearwater *Also called Dj/Pj Inc* ***(G-1566)***
J2b Industrial LLC 904 574-8919
5941 Richard St Unit 19 Jacksonville (32216) ***(G-6211)***
Ja Engineering II Corp (HQ) 954 744-7560
3000 Taft St Hollywood (33021) ***(G-5603)***
JA Uniforms Inc 305 234-1231
12323 Sw 132nd Ct Miami (33186) ***(G-9353)***
Jab-B-Inc 813 803-3995
18125 N Us Highway 41 # 104 Lutz (33549) ***(G-7997)***
Jabberwocky LLC 310 717-3343
2 S Biscayne Blvd # 2680 Miami (33131) ***(G-9354)***
Jabil Advnced Mech Sltions Inc 727 577-9749
10560 Dr M Lth Kng Jr St Martin Saint Petersburg (33716) ***(G-15089)***
Jabil Circuit 727 577-9749
9700 18th St N Saint Petersburg (33716) ***(G-15090)***
Jabil Circuit LLC (HQ) 727 577-9749
10560 Dr Mlk Jr St N Saint Petersburg (33716) ***(G-15091)***
Jabil Circuit LLC 727 577-9749
3201 34th St S Saint Petersburg (33711) ***(G-15092)***
Jabil Def & Arospc Svcs LLC (HQ) 727 577-9749
10500 Dr Mrtn Lther King Saint Petersburg (33716) ***(G-15093)***
Jabil Def & Arospc Svcs LLC (HQ) 727 577-9749
10560 Dr Mlk Jr St N Saint Petersburg (33716) ***(G-15094)***
Jabil Inc (PA) 727 577-9749
10800 Roosevelt Blvd N Saint Petersburg (33716) ***(G-15095)***
Jabil Inc 727 577-9749
10500 Dr Mlk Jr St N Dock Saint Petersburg (33716) ***(G-15096)***
Jabil Inc 727 803-3110
1300 Dr Marti Luthe King Saint Petersburg (33705) ***(G-15097)***
Jabil Inc 727 577-9749
10500 Dr Mrtn Lther King Saint Petersburg (33716) ***(G-15098)***
Jabil Luxembourg Manufacturing, Saint Petersburg *Also called Jabil Inc* ***(G-15097)***
Jabm Advisors Inc 727 458-3755
2839 Grey Oaks Blvd Tarpon Springs (34688) ***(G-17479)***
Jabs Investors Corp 561 540-2693
1815 10th Ave N Ste A Lake Worth Beach (33461) ***(G-7257)***
Jace Fabrication Inc 727 547-6873
9930 62nd St N Pinellas Park (33782) ***(G-13697)***
Jack W Dixon, Pensacola *Also called Dixon Screen Printing LLC* ***(G-13490)***
Jack's Magic, Largo *Also called Jacks Magic Products Inc* ***(G-7620)***
Jackie Z Style Co St Pete LLC 727 258-4849
113 2nd Ave N Saint Petersburg (33701) ***(G-15099)***
Jackiezstyleco, Saint Petersburg *Also called Jackie Z Style Co St Pete LLC* ***(G-15099)***
Jacks Magic Products Inc 727 536-4500
12435 73rd Ct Largo (33773) ***(G-7620)***
Jacksnvlle Advnced McHning LLC 904 292-2999
9655 Fl Min Blvd W Jacksonville (32257) ***(G-6212)***
Jacksnvlle Ornge Pk Rdymx Con, Orange Park *Also called Cemex Cnstr Mtls Fla LLC* ***(G-11818)***
Jackson County Times, Marianna *Also called Woody Hatcher* ***(G-8176)***
Jackson Equipment Inc 904 845-3696
2310 Shipwreck Cir W Jacksonville (32224) ***(G-6213)***
Jacksonville Box & Woodwork Co 904 354-1441
5011 Buffalo Ave Jacksonville (32206) ***(G-6214)***
Jacksonville Cyber Defense, Jacksonville *Also called Tier5 Technical Services* ***(G-6551)***
Jacksonville Free Press 904 634-1993
1122 Edgewood Ave W Jacksonville (32208) ***(G-6215)***
Jacksonville Magazine, Jacksonville *Also called White Publishing Co Inc* ***(G-6610)***
Jacksonville Rail Yard, Jacksonville *Also called Martin Marietta Materials Inc* ***(G-6277)***
Jacksonville Steel Pdts Inc 904 268-3364
6085 Greenland Rd Jacksonville (32258) ***(G-6216)***
Jacksonville Tire Rescue Inc 904 783-1296
7010 Lenox Ave Jacksonville (32205) ***(G-6217)***
Jacobsen Homes, Safety Harbor *Also called Jacobsen Manufacturing Inc* ***(G-14788)***
Jacobsen Manufacturing Inc (PA) 727 726-1138
600 Packard Ct Safety Harbor (34695) ***(G-14788)***
Jacore Technologies 813 860-7465
1346 Osceola Hollow Rd Odessa (33556) ***(G-11561)***
Jacqulnes Lvely Drpes Blnds LL 407 826-1566
11407 Bentry St Orlando (32824) ***(G-12264)***
Jacu Coffee, Miami *Also called Adrenaline Productions LLC* ***(G-8655)***
Jada Foods LLC 305 319-0263
3126 John P Curci Dr # 1 Hallandale Beach (33009) ***(G-4954)***
JADA Transitions LLC 561 377-8194
1201 Abaco Ln Riviera Beach (33404) ***(G-14633)***
Jade Software Corporation USA 904 677-5133
10151 Deerwood Park Blvd Jacksonville (32256) ***(G-6218)***
Jade Tactical Disaster Relief 850 270-4077
3816 W Sligh Ave Tampa (33614) ***(G-16961)***
Jadus Justice Apperal LLC 954 394-6259
1478 Avon Ln North Lauderdale (33068) ***(G-11081)***
Jafar On Fifth, Miami Beach *Also called Fresh On Fifth* ***(G-10192)***
Jaffer Wll Drllng A Div of AC 954 523-6669
1451 Se 9th Ct Hialeah (33010) ***(G-5200)***
Jag Stucco Inc 813 210-6577
4047 Marlow Loop Land O Lakes (34639) ***(G-7495)***
Jahna Concrete Inc (PA) 863 453-4353
103 County Road 17a W Avon Park (33825) ***(G-282)***
Jahna Concrete Inc 863 453-4353
104 S Railroad Ave Avon Park (33825) ***(G-283)***
Jaiba Cabinets Inc 305 364-3646
8125 W 20th Ave Hialeah (33014) ***(G-5201)***
Jain Irrigation Holdings Corp 863 422-4000
3777 State Road 544 E Haines City (33844) ***(G-4909)***
Jak Corporate Holdings Inc 813 289-1660
4920 W Cypress St Ste 100 Tampa (33607) ***(G-16962)***

ALPHABETIC

Jakobsen Tool Co Inc 727 447-1143
  805 Pierce St Clearwater (33756) **(G-1651)**

Jam Cabinets & Investments LLC 305 823-9020
  2795 W 78th St Hialeah (33016) **(G-5202)**

JAM Welding Service Inc 305 662-3787
  5818 Sw 68th St South Miami (33143) **(G-16035)**

Jamali Industries LLC 954 908-5075
  1455 Nw 126th Ln Sunrise (33323) **(G-16328)**

Jamar Cnstr Fabrication Inc 321 400-0333
  119 Commerce Way Sanford (32771) **(G-15342)**

Jambco Millwork Inc 954 977-4998
  101 S State Road 7 Margate (33068) **(G-8136)**

Jamco Industrial Inc 866 848-5400
  3800 Entp Way Ste 1110 Sanford (32771) **(G-15343)**

Jamerica Inc 561 488-6247
  11188 Jasmine Hill Cir Boca Raton (33498) **(G-556)**

James A De Flippo Co 407 851-2765
  4665 Gatlin Oaks Ln Orlando (32806) **(G-12265)**

James Caldwell Stump Grinding 813 843-1262
  1310 Whitehurst Rd Plant City (33563) **(G-13777)**

James D Nall Co Inc (PA) 305 884-8363
  1883 W State Road 84 # 106 Fort Lauderdale (33315) **(G-3891)**

James Fletcher Cnstr Inc 619 405-9316
  312 W Pennsylvania Ave Bonifay (32425) **(G-773)**

James G Dowling 407 509-9484
  1375 Palm Way Sanford (32773) **(G-15344)**

James Hardie Building Pdts Inc 813 478-1758
  809 S Woodrow Wilson St Plant City (33563) **(G-13778)**

James Hines Printing 904 398-5110
  1650 Art Museum Dr Ste 18 Jacksonville (32207) **(G-6219)**

James O Corbett Inc 352 483-1222
  2151 W County Road 44 Eustis (32726) **(G-3560)**

James Reese Enterprises Inc 727 386-5311
  1714 Misty Plateau Trl Clearwater (33765) **(G-1652)**

James Simmons Cabinets Inc 407 468-1802
  4835 Berrywood Dr Orlando (32812) **(G-12266)**

James Spear Design Inc 727 592-9600
  12253 62nd St Ste A Largo (33773) **(G-7621)**

James Taylor 850 882-5148
  200 W Escambia Rd Eglin Afb (32542) **(G-3506)**

James Testa 954 962-5840
  5621 Johnson St Hollywood (33021) **(G-5604)**

Jamestown Kitchens Inc 941 359-1166
  4050 N Washington Blvd Sarasota (34234) **(G-15712)**

Jamison Industries Inc 813 886-4888
  7710 N Ola Ave Tampa (33604) **(G-16963)**

Jamison Paints, Tampa Also called Jamison Industries Inc **(G-16963)**

Jamo Inc 305 885-3444
  8850 Nw 79th Ave Medley (33166) **(G-8264)**

Jamuna1 LLC 407 313-5927
  4654 River Gem Ave Windermere (34786) **(G-18355)**

Jan and Jean Inc 813 645-0680
  1010 E Shell Point Rd Ruskin (33570) **(G-14779)**

Jane and George Industries 727 698-4903
  4197 49th Ave S Saint Petersburg (33711) **(G-15100)**

Janine of London Inc 954 772-3593
  45 Fort Royal Is Fort Lauderdale (33308) **(G-3892)**

Janoro Fixture Mfg Corp 305 887-2524
  249 W 29th St Hialeah (33012) **(G-5203)**

Jans Ventures LLC 352 341-1710
  2044 Highway 44 W Inverness (34453) **(G-5830)**

Jansen Shutters & Spc Ltd 941 484-4700
  115 Morse Ct North Venice (34275) **(G-11213)**

Janus International Group LLC 407 859-6770
  10407 Rocket Blvd Orlando (32824) **(G-12267)**

Janusz Art Stone Inc 305 754-7171
  7025 Ne 2nd Ave Miami (33138) **(G-9355)**

Japan Fabricare Inc 407 366-9986
  9 Alafaya Woods Blvd Oviedo (32765) **(G-12830)**

Jar Joy, Sanford Also called Batter To Platter LLC **(G-15271)**

Jar-Den Llc 860 334-7539
  7400 Castanea Dr Port Richey (34668) **(G-14366)**

Jarden Plastic Solutions 864 879-8100
  2381 Nw Executive Ctr Dr Boca Raton (33431) **(G-557)**

Jareed Online Publishing LLC, Tallahassee Also called Ali Kamakhi **(G-16409)**

JAs Business Solutions Inc 954 975-0025
  200 Park Central Blvd S Pompano Beach (33064) **(G-14065)**

JAS Interconnect Solutions, Pompano Beach Also called JAs Business Solutions Inc **(G-14065)**

JAS Powder Coating LLC 954 916-7711
  219 Sw 21st Ter Fort Lauderdale (33312) **(G-3893)**

JAS Powder Coating LLC 386 410-6675
  1710 Industrial Ave Edgewater (32132) **(G-3494)**

Jasmine Purkiss 386 244-7726
  2526 Hibiscus Dr 108-08 Edgewater (32141) **(G-3495)**

Jat Power LLC 305 592-0103
  8000 Nw 29th St Doral (33122) **(G-3266)**

Javalution Coffee Company 954 568-1747
  2485 E Sunrise Blvd # 20 Fort Lauderdale (33304) **(G-3894)**

Jax Enterprises LLC 904 786-6909
  7042 Wiley Rd Jacksonville (32210) **(G-6220)**

Jax Metals LLC 904 731-4655
  6600 Suemac Pl 2 Jacksonville (32254) **(G-6221)**

Jax Tire Rescue, Jacksonville Also called Jacksonville Tire Rescue Inc **(G-6217)**

Jax Truss Inc 904 710-8198
  450526 State Road 200 Callahan (32011) **(G-1253)**

Jay Berry Signs 352 805-4050
  125 Montclair Rd Ste 1 Leesburg (34748) **(G-7781)**

Jay More Corporation 786 384-1299
  540 Nw 26th St Miami (33127) **(G-9356)**

Jay Robinson Cabinet Sales Inc 954 298-3009
  683 Ne 42nd St Oakland Park (33334) **(G-11274)**

Jay Squared LLC 386 677-7700
  1810 Mason Ave Daytona Beach (32117) **(G-2564)**

Jay Strong Lighting Inc 813 253-0490
  2007 W Dekle Ave Tampa (33606) **(G-16964)**

Jayco International LLC 407 855-8880
  7451 Brokerage Dr Orlando (32809) **(G-12268)**

Jayco Screens Inc 850 456-0673
  9131 W Highway 98 Pensacola (32506) **(G-13527)**

Jayco Signs Inc 407 339-5252
  149 Atlantic Dr Maitland (32751) **(G-8062)**

Jayco Woodworks Inc 850 814-3041
  9338 Resota Beach Rd Panama City (32409) **(G-13278)**

Jaydad LLC 407 508-6267
  2734 Dixie Ln Kissimmee (34744) **(G-6929)**

Jayshree Holdings Inc 352 429-1000
  18830 State Road 19 Groveland (34736) **(G-4864)**

Jazwares LLC (HQ) 954 845-0800
  1067 Shotgun Rd Sunrise (33326) **(G-16329)**

Jazziz Magazine Inc 561 893-6868
  2650 N Military Trl # 140 Boca Raton (33431) **(G-558)**

Jazzy Dogs Publishing LLC 941 726-0343
  204 Millet Pl Nokomis (34275) **(G-11048)**

JB Thome & Co Inc 727 642-0588
  1110 Boca Ciega Isle Dr St Pete Beach (33706) **(G-16091)**

JB Wood Werks LLC 239 314-4462
  2550 Sw 27th Ave Cape Coral (33914) **(G-1358)**

Jbjb Holdings LLC 239 267-1975
  14110 Clear Water Ln Fort Myers (33907) **(G-4296)**

Jblaze Inc 954 680-3962
  4910 Sw 172nd Ave Southwest Ranches (33331) **(G-16055)**

Jbr Exteriors Inc 772 873-0600
  1201 Sw Biltmore St Port Saint Lucie (34983) **(G-14418)**

Jbt Aerotech-Military Programs, Orlando Also called John Bean Technologies Corp **(G-12275)**

Jbt Food Tech, Lakeland Also called Jbt Foodtech Citrus Systems **(G-7359)**

Jbt Foodtech, Lakeland Also called John Bean Technologies Corp **(G-7361)**

Jbt Foodtech Citrus Systems 863 683-5411
  400 Fairway Ave Lakeland (33801) **(G-7359)**

Jbt LLC (PA) 407 463-2045
  528 W Yale St Orlando (32804) **(G-12269)**

Jbt LLC 513 238-4218
  2875 Citrus Lake Dr # 205 Naples (34109) **(G-10789)**

JC & A of South Florida Inc 305 445-6665
  3109 Grand Ave Miami (33133) **(G-9357)**

JC 323 Media Pubg Group Inc 772 940-3510
  7186 Ontario Shores Pl Lake Worth (33467) **(G-7209)**

JC Best Finish Cabinet Inc 786 216-5571
  2150 Nw 35th St Miami (33142) **(G-9358)**

JC Industrial Mfg Corp 305 634-5280
  5700 Nw 32nd Ct Miami (33142) **(G-9359)**

JC Machine Inc 863 644-2815
  3620 Airport Rd Lakeland (33811) **(G-7360)**

JC Machine Works Corp 305 634-5280
  5700 Nw 32nd Ct Miami (33142) **(G-9360)**

JC Toys Group Inc 305 592-3541
  2841 Nw 107th Ave Doral (33172) **(G-3267)**

JC Voyage LLC (PA) 603 686-0065
  2403 Nw 30th Rd Boca Raton (33431) **(G-559)**

Jci Jones Chemicals Inc 904 355-0779
  1433 Talleyrand Ave Jacksonville (32206) **(G-6222)**

Jco Metals Inc 386 734-5867
  1665 Lexington Ave # 106 Deland (32724) **(G-2878)**

JCP Signs Inc 305 790-5336
  20483 Sw 127th Pl Miami (33177) **(G-9361)**

Jcs Contracting Inc 407 348-4555
  731 Duncan Ave Kissimmee (34744) **(G-6930)**

Jcs Limited Corporation 954 822-2887
  7611 Nw 70th Ave Tamarac (33321) **(G-16534)**

JD Pavers Inc 904 245-9183
  1304 8th St N Jacksonville Beach (32250) **(G-6636)**

JD Tools LLC 407 767-5175
  786 Big Tree Dr Longwood (32750) **(G-7908)**

JD Wine Concepts LLC 407 730-3082
  1312 Wilfred Dr Orlando (32803) **(G-12270)**

JDB Dense Flow Inc 727 785-8500
  1004 Bee Pond Rd Palm Harbor (34683) **(G-13116)**

Jdci Enterprises, Fort Myers Also called Boat Master Aluminum Trailers **(G-4191)**

Jdci Enterprises Inc 239 768-2292
11950 Amedicus Ln Unit 2 Fort Myers (33907) **(G-4297)**

Jdjsis Inc 561 732-2388
8645 N Military Trl # 501 West Palm Beach (33410) **(G-18039)**

Jdl Surface Innovations Inc 239 772-0077
922 Se 14th Pl Cape Coral (33990) **(G-1359)**

JDM of Miami LLC 305 253-4650
14195 Sw 139th Ct Miami (33186) **(G-9362)**

Jdr and Associates Inc 941 926-1800
5379 Ocean Blvd Sarasota (34242) **(G-15713)**

Jds Uniforms, Groveland Also called Gjcb Signs Graphics Inc **(G-4860)**

Jdt Servicing LLC 813 909-8640
24310 Breezy Oak Ct Lutz (33559) **(G-7998)**

JEAN ARCHIBALD DBA JGA ASSOC, Grant Also called Jga Lighting LLC **(G-4812)**

Jean La Frite 305 397-8747
1520 Washington Ave Miami Beach (33139) **(G-10206)**

Jeanius Publishing LLC 239 560-5229
108 Airview Ave Lehigh Acres (33936) **(G-7811)**

Jeb Thermofoil of South Fla 305 887-6214
1065 E 16th St Hialeah (33010) **(G-5204)**

Jefco Manufacturing Inc 954 527-4220
718 Nw 1st St Fort Lauderdale (33311) **(G-3895)**

Jeffcoat Signs, Gainesville Also called Kevin Jeffers Inc **(G-4717)**

Jefferson Slnoid Vlves USA Inc 305 249-8120
20225 Ne 15th Ct Miami (33179) **(G-9363)**

Jeffrey B Gould 410 463-0796
1711 Cotswold Dr Orlando (32825) **(G-12271)**

Jeffrey Bowden Cabinets Llc 727 992-9187
12437 Banbury Ave New Port Richey (34654) **(G-10970)**

Jeld-Wen Inc 407 343-8596
1700 Avenue A Kissimmee (34758) **(G-6931)**

Jem Art Inc 954 966-7078
801 Shotgun Rd Sunrise (33326) **(G-16330)**

Jenard Fresh Incorporated 407 240-4545
1144 Mid Florida Dr Orlando (32824) **(G-12272)**

Jenasis Structures Inc 813 238-7620
6514 Grazing Ln Odessa (33556) **(G-11562)**

Jennifer Yoder Sung 352 748-6655
9235 County Road 128d Wildwood (34785) **(G-18314)**

Jennings Mobile HM Set Up LLC 863 965-0883
1048 Us Highway 92 W Auburndale (33823) **(G-238)**

Jenoptik North America Inc (HQ) 561 881-7400
16490 Innovation Dr Jupiter (33478) **(G-6749)**

Jenoptik Optical Systems LLC (HQ) 561 881-7400
16490 Innovation Dr Ste A Jupiter (33478) **(G-6750)**

Jensen Inert Products, Coral Springs Also called Jensen Scientific Products Inc **(G-2169)**

Jensen Scientific Products Inc 954 344-2006
3773 Nw 126th Ave Coral Springs (33065) **(G-2169)**

Jenzano Incorporated 386 761-4474
820 Oak St Port Orange (32127) **(G-14336)**

Jepsen Tool Company Inc 904 262-2793
6864 Phillips Pkwy Dr S Jacksonville (32256) **(G-6223)**

Jer-Air Manufacturing Inc 352 591-2674
22750 Highway 441 N Micanopy (32667) **(G-10398)**

Jerae Inc 954 989-6665
6031 Hollywood Blvd Hollywood (33024) **(G-5605)**

Jers Group 786 953-6419
8625 Nw 54th St Doral (33166) **(G-3268)**

Jes Publishing Corp 561 997-8683
1000 Clint Moore Rd # 103 Boca Raton (33487) **(G-560)**

Jessica Pavers Inc 305 970-4879
555 Ne 160th Ter Miami (33162) **(G-9364)**

Jesus Cabinets Corp 786 285-1088
1701 W 42nd Pl Hialeah (33012) **(G-5205)**

Jesus In Trenches Inc 800 865-8274
1314 E Las Olas Blvd Fort Lauderdale (33301) **(G-3896)**

Jet Avion Corporation 954 987-6101
3000 Taft St Hollywood (33021) **(G-5606)**

Jet Factory LLC (PA) 786 387-6865
1900 Nw 33rd Ct Ste 5 Pompano Beach (33064) **(G-14066)**

Jet Fuel Catering LLC 954 804-1146
1920 Nw 137th Way Pembroke Pines (33028) **(G-13398)**

Jet Graphics Inc 305 264-4333
4101 Sw 73rd Ave Miami (33155) **(G-9365)**

Jet Helseth Manufacturing Inc 407 324-9001
1730 Patterson Ave Deland (32724) **(G-2879)**

Jet Press, Cape Canaveral Also called Image Printing & Graphics LLC **(G-1286)**

Jet Research Development Inc 954 427-0404
1215 W Newport Center Dr Deerfield Beach (33442) **(G-2745)**

Jet-Set Printing Inc 407 339-1900
130 N Cypress Way Casselberry (32707) **(G-1421)**

Jetboatpilot LLC 850 960-3236
2743 Forester Trl Panama City (32405) **(G-13279)**

Jetspares International Inc 407 876-3978
10650 Chase Rd Bldg 5 Windermere (34786) **(G-18356)**

Jetstream Fabrication LLC 772 287-3338
1880 Se Federal Hwy Stuart (34994) **(G-16169)**

Jewelnet Corp 561 989-8383
72 Se 6th Ave Apt K Delray Beach (33483) **(G-2977)**

Jewelry Tray Factory, The, Sunrise Also called Jld Manufacturing Corp **(G-16331)**

Jewels Handmade LLC 407 283-9951
2648 Renegade Dr Apt 101 Orlando (32818) **(G-12273)**

Jewish Burial Society America 954 424-1899
15310 Strathearn Dr # 11505 Delray Beach (33446) **(G-2978)**

Jewish Press Group of Tmpa Bay 727 535-4400
1101 Belcher Rd S Ste H Largo (33771) **(G-7622)**

Jewish Press Group Tampa Bay, Largo Also called Jewish Press Group of Tmpa Bay **(G-7622)**

Jewm Inc 973 942-1555
4834 Exeter Estate Ln Lake Worth (33449) **(G-7210)**

Jf Aerospace Inc 786 242-6686
12242 Sw 132nd Ct Miami (33186) **(G-9366)**

Jf Flakes and Powers Inc 407 414-6467
2313 Windcrest Lake Cir Orlando (32824) **(G-12274)**

Jfaure LLC 239 631-5324
22758 J&C Blvd Naples (34109) **(G-10790)**

Jfe Compost 863 532-9629
11000 Red Barn Rd Ne Okeechobee (34974) **(G-11610)**

Jfh Technologies LLC 407 938-9336
1500 W Buena Vista Dr Lake Buena Vista (32830) **(G-6999)**

Jfliszo Industries Inc 239 215-6965
17051 Alico Commerce Ct # 3 Fort Myers (33967) **(G-4298)**

Jfr Hazardous Services Inc 716 313-2844
16609 Villalenda De Avila Tampa (33613) **(G-16965)**

Jga Lighting LLC 772 408-8224
3869 Garden Wood Cir Grant (32949) **(G-4812)**

Jglc Enterprises LLC 772 223-7393
3920 Se Commerce Ave Stuart (34997) **(G-16170)**

Jhi Technology, Pensacola Also called Joe Hearn Innovative Tech LLC **(G-13528)**

JHK LLC 786 871-0150
7950 Nw 53rd St Ste 215 Miami (33166) **(G-9367)**

Jhn North LLC 561 294-5613
3554 Lothair Ave Boynton Beach (33436) **(G-882)**

Jhr Management, West Palm Beach Also called Coral Reef Cast Stone Inc **(G-17973)**

Jibe Ltg N Amer Ltd Lblty Co 954 899-4040
9825 Marina Blvd Boca Raton (33428) **(G-561)**

Jiffi Print, Coral Springs Also called Media Systems Inc **(G-2181)**

Jim Appleys Tru-Arc Inc 727 571-3007
5140 110th Ave N Clearwater (33760) **(G-1653)**

Jim Baird Cabinets 772 569-0936
1020 11th Pl Ste 1 Vero Beach (32960) **(G-17768)**

Jim Rinaldos Cabinetry Inc 813 788-2715
37828 Sky Ridge Cir Dade City (33525) **(G-2320)**

Jim Smith Boats Inc 772 286-9049
4396 Se Commerce Ave Stuart (34997) **(G-16171)**

Jimbob Printing Inc 850 973-2633
482 Sw Range Ave Madison (32340) **(G-8045)**

Jimenez Enterprises Group 561 391-6800
5851 Holmberg Rd Apt 3723 Parkland (33067) **(G-13348)**

Jimmy & Toons Icecream Sp LLC 850 752-2291
104 E Washington St Quincy (32351) **(G-14547)**

Jireh AC & Rfrgn Inc 305 216-2774
5001 Sw 142nd Pl Miami (33175) **(G-9368)**

Jireh Woodwork Inc 954 515-8041
3821 Nw 9th Ave Deerfield Beach (33064) **(G-2746)**

Jiva Cubes Inc 305 788-1200
9264 Dickens Ave Surfside (33154) **(G-16396)**

Jj Screenprint LLC 941 587-1801
1850 Porter Lake Dr Ste 1 Sarasota (34240) **(G-15714)**

Jjaz Enterprises Inc 407 330-0245
1061 S Sun Dr Ste 1033 Lake Mary (32746) **(G-7087)**

Jjj & H Inc 904 389-1130
4237 Salisbury Rd Ste 200 Jacksonville (32216) **(G-6224)**

JK&m Ink, Tampa Also called J K & M Ink Corporation **(G-16959)**

Jk2 Scenic LLC 407 703-2977
541 Live Pine Cir Apopka (32703) **(G-141)**

Jka Pump Specialists 561 686-4455
5407 N Haverhill Rd 344-345 West Palm Beach (33407) **(G-18040)**

Jkg Group 561 866-2850
160 Nw 51st St Boca Raton (33431) **(G-562)**

JKS Industries Inc 863 425-1745
2701 Cozart Rd Mulberry (33860) **(G-10628)**

JKS Industries Inc (PA) 727 573-1305
4644 W Gandy Blvd Tampa (33611) **(G-16966)**

JKS Residual Assets LLC 904 346-3200
1431 Riverplace Blvd # 910 Jacksonville (32207) **(G-6225)**

Jl Optical Inc 386 428-6928
2908 Palma Ln New Smyrna Beach (32168) **(G-11003)**

Jl Optical Microscopes, New Smyrna Beach Also called Jl Optical Inc **(G-11003)**

JL Welding Inc 786 442-4319
6510 Sw 64th Ct South Miami (33143) **(G-16036)**

Jlb Enterprises Tampa Inc 813 545-3830
4500 Grainary Ave Tampa (33624) **(G-16967)**

Jld Manufacturing Corp 877 358-5462
4747 N Nob Hill Rd Ste 8 Sunrise (33351) **(G-16331)**

Jlg Industries Inc 786 558-8909
10974 Nw 63rd St Doral (33178) **(G-3269)**

Jls Dairy Holdings, Miami Also called Latin Dairy Foods LLC **(G-9436)**

Jls of St Augustine Inc 904 797-6098
3161 Mac Rd Saint Augustine (32086) *(G-14849)*

Jlt Custom Works Inc 863 245-3371
2239 Greenleaf Rd Wauchula (33873) *(G-17829)*

JM Cabinets Incorp 863 699-2888
1212 County Road 621 E Lake Placid (33852) *(G-7143)*

JM Coatings Inc 407 312-1115
1910 Longwood Lk Mary Rd Longwood (32750) *(G-7909)*

JM Custom Millworks Inc 561 582-5600
1113 48th St Ste 2 Mangonia Park (33407) *(G-8094)*

JM Custom Woodworking 561 582-5600
1113 48th St Ste 2 Mangonia Park (33407) *(G-8095)*

JM Ocean Mar Canvas & Uphl Inc 786 473-7143
1825 Sw 31st Ave Hallandale (33009) *(G-4926)*

Jmf Dgital Print Solutions Inc 954 362-4929
19150 Sw 16th St Pembroke Pines (33029) *(G-13399)*

Jmg Counters LLC 904 551-7006
5120 W Beaver St Jacksonville (32254) *(G-6226)*

Jmg Strategies LLC 305 606-2117
300 S Pointe Dr Apt 907 Miami Beach (33139) *(G-10207)*

Jmh Marine Inc 954 785-7557
1790 Sw 13th Ct Pompano Beach (33069) *(G-14067)*

Jmi-Dniels Pharmaceuticals Inc 727 323-5151
2517 25th Ave N Saint Petersburg (33713) *(G-15101)*

Jml Pavers LLC 239 240-0082
18657 Holly Rd Fort Myers (33967) *(G-4299)*

JMP Fashion Inc (PA) 305 633-9920
2199 Nw 20th St Unit 2 Miami (33142) *(G-9369)*

Jmp Marine LLC 305 599-0009
2000 Nw 84th Ave Ste 244 Doral (33122) *(G-3270)*

Jmp USA, Doral *Also called Jmp Marine LLC (G-3270)*

JMS Corporate Group LLC 786 219-6114
21205 Ne 37th Ave Aventura (33180) *(G-264)*

JMS Designs of Florida Inc 954 572-6100
4550 N Hiatus Rd Sunrise (33351) *(G-16332)*

Jnc Habitat Investments Inc 954 249-7469
645 Nw 112th Way Coral Springs (33071) *(G-2170)*

Jnc Welding & Fabricating Inc 954 227-9424
3769 Nw 126th Ave Coral Springs (33065) *(G-2171)*

Jng Lighting 561 707-2028
9905 Baywinds Dr Apt 2302 West Palm Beach (33411) *(G-18041)*

JNJ & Company Inc 239 489-0053
17650 Oak Creek Rd Alva (33920) *(G-81)*

Jo MO Enterprises Inc 708 599-8098
20966 Estada Ln Boca Raton (33433) *(G-563)*

Joanne James Russell 805 467-3331
2166 Blossom Way S Saint Petersburg (33712) *(G-15102)*

Job News 904 296-3006
6620 S Sthpint Dr Ste 300 Jacksonville (32256) *(G-6227)*

Jodan Technology Inc 561 515-5556
7708 Coral Colony Way Lake Worth (33467) *(G-7211)*

Jodar Inc 561 375-6277
354 Ne 5th St Boca Raton (33432) *(G-564)*

Jode Corporation 321 684-1769
9565 Riverview Dr Sebastian (32976) *(G-15887)*

Joe Hearn Innovative Tech LLC 850 898-3744
600 Univ Ofc Blvd 17c Pensacola (32504) *(G-13528)*

Joe Taylor Restoration (PA) 954 972-5390
855 Nw 17th Ave Ste C Delray Beach (33445) *(G-2979)*

Joe Taylor Restoration 888 814-1455
216 Waldo Ave Lehigh Acres (33971) *(G-7812)*

Johannsen Boat Works Inc 772 567-4612
690 4th Pl Ste D Vero Beach (32962) *(G-17769)*

John & Betsy Hovland 727 449-2032
2073 Range Rd Clearwater (33765) *(G-1654)*

John A Cruce Jr Inc 850 584-9755
311 Glenridge Rd Perry (32348) *(G-13644)*

John Andersen 407 702-4891
923 Ridgeside Ct Apopka (32712) *(G-142)*

John Bean Technologies Corp 863 683-5411
400 Fairway Ave Lakeland (33801) *(G-7361)*

John Bean Technologies Corp 407 851-3377
7300 Presidents Dr Orlando (32809) *(G-12275)*

John Deere Authorized Dealer, Fort Walton Beach *Also called Emergency Standby Power LLC (G-4581)*

John Deere Authorized Dealer, Sebring *Also called Tradewinds Power Corp (G-15948)*

John Deere Authorized Dealer, Doral *Also called Tradewinds Power Corp (G-3400)*

John Deere Authorized Dealer, Fort Myers *Also called Mwi Corporation (G-4335)*

John Franklin Mowery 202 468-8644
100 W Venice Ave Ste E Venice (34285) *(G-17701)*

John Harvey Green 850 643-2544
301 1st St Bristol (32321) *(G-1120)*

John Hurst Outdoor Svcs LLC 850 556-7459
3694 Corinth Dr Tallahassee (32308) *(G-16463)*

John L Shadd Enterprises 386 496-3989
Us Hwy 121 Lake Butler (32054) *(G-7002)*

John Lacquey Enterprises Inc 386 935-1705
8125 264th St Branford (32008) *(G-1113)*

John M Caldwell Distrg Co Inc 305 685-9822
1150 Ali Baba Ave Opa Locka (33054) *(G-11758)*

John Mader Enterprises Inc 239 731-5455
18161 N Tamiami Trl Fort Myers (33903) *(G-4300)*

John Measel Cabinets, Sarasota *Also called Midnite Son II of Sarasota (G-15746)*

John R Caito 850 612-0179
91 Ready Ave Nw Fort Walton Beach (32548) *(G-4593)*

John S Wilson Inc 410 442-2400
6222 Parkers Hammock Rd Naples (34112) *(G-10791)*

John Stewart Enterprises Inc 904 356-9392
502 N Hogan St Jacksonville (32202) *(G-6228)*

John W Hock Company 352 378-3209
7409 Nw 23rd Ave Gainesville (32606) *(G-4716)*

Johnny Devil Inc 305 634-0700
7301 Nw 36th Ct Miami (33147) *(G-9370)*

Johnny Green Logging, Bristol *Also called John Harvey Green (G-1120)*

Johnny Heaven, Miami *Also called Johnny Devil Inc (G-9370)*

Johnny Sellers Logging Inc 850 643-5214
Turkey Creek Rd Bristol (32321) *(G-1121)*

Johnny Under Pressure LLC 850 530-8763
7250 Frank Reeder Rd Pensacola (32526) *(G-13529)*

Johns & Conner Inc 904 845-4430
15924 County Road 108 Hilliard (32046) *(G-5468)*

Johns & Conner Logging Inc 904 845-4430
15924 County Road 108 Hilliard (32046) *(G-5469)*

Johns & Connor Inc 904 845-4541
28244 Pond View Cir Hilliard (32046) *(G-5470)*

Johns Manville Corporation 904 786-0298
5510 W 12th St Jacksonville (32254) *(G-6229)*

Johns Pass Winery 727 362-0008
12945 Village Blvd Madeira Beach (33708) *(G-8040)*

Johnson & Jackson GL Pdts Inc 813 630-9774
4912 N Manhattan Ave Tampa (33614) *(G-16968)*

Johnson & Johnson 954 534-1141
1024 Se 3rd Ave Apt 304 Dania Beach (33004) *(G-2352)*

Johnson & Johnson 813 972-0204
8800 Grand Oak Cir # 500 Tampa (33637) *(G-16969)*

Johnson & Johnson 305 261-3500
6303 Blue Lagoon Dr # 450 Miami (33126) *(G-9371)*

Johnson & Johnson Global Svcs, Tampa *Also called Johnson & Johnson (G-16969)*

Johnson & Johnson Services Inc 239 598-4444
5811 Pelican Bay Blvd Naples (34108) *(G-10792)*

Johnson Bros Prcsion Prcast Pd. 239 947-6734
24263 Production Cir Bonita Springs (34135) *(G-807)*

Johnson Brothers Whl Meats Inc 850 763-2828
1640 Martin Luther King J Panama City (32405) *(G-13280)*

Johnson Controls, Medley *Also called Clarios LLC (G-8218)*

Johnson Controls, Orlando *Also called Clarios LLC (G-12017)*

Johnson Controls, Melbourne *Also called Clarios LLC (G-8388)*

Johnson Controls, Naples *Also called Clarios LLC (G-10715)*

Johnson Controls, Medley *Also called York International Corporation (G-8352)*

Johnson Controls, Jacksonville *Also called Clarios LLC (G-5980)*

Johnson Controls Inc 407 291-1971
4433 Parkbreeze Ct Orlando (32808) *(G-12276)*

Johnson Controls Inc 954 233-3000
3300 Corporate Ave Weston (33331) *(G-18259)*

Johnson Controls Inc 813 623-1188
3802 Sugar Palm Dr Frc Tampa (33619) *(G-16970)*

Johnson Controls Inc 305 883-3760
9960 Nw 116th Way Ste 4 Medley (33178) *(G-8265)*

Johnson Controls Inc 772 283-1633
3101 Se Carnivale Ct Stuart (34994) *(G-16172)*

Johnson Environmental Services, Fort Lauderdale *Also called All Liquid Envmtl Svcs LLC (G-3638)*

Johnson Jhnson Vision Care Inc (HQ) 904 443-1000
7500 Centurion Pkwy Jacksonville (32256) *(G-6230)*

Johnson Printing, Palmetto *Also called Bjm Enterprises Inc (G-13157)*

Johnson Well Equipment Inc 850 453-3131
8480 Gulf Beach Hwy Pensacola (32507) *(G-13530)*

Johnson Woodworking 772 473-1404
3470 Leghorn Rd Malabar (32950) *(G-8083)*

Johnsons Management Group Inc 904 261-4044
1485 S 8th St Fernandina Beach (32034) *(G-3591)*

Johnsons Woodwork Incorporated 904 826-4100
175 Cumberland Park Dr Saint Augustine (32095) *(G-14850)*

Johnston Archtctral Systems In 904 886-9030
11494 Columbia Park Dr W Jacksonville (32258) *(G-6231)*

Joiner Land Clearing LLC 850 997-5729
1417 Government Farm Rd Monticello (32344) *(G-10582)*

Joiners Enterprises Inc 850 623-5593
4973 Joiner Cir Milton (32583) *(G-10429)*

Joint Force Enterprises, Jacksonville *Also called Gtgjfe LLC (G-6160)*

Jomar Metal Fabrication Inc 407 857-1259
1239 Spruce Ave Orlando (32824) *(G-12277)*

Jon Paul Inc 954 564-4221
3353 Galt Ocean Dr 55 Fort Lauderdale (33308) *(G-3897)*

Jon Paul Jewelers, Fort Lauderdale *Also called Jon Paul Inc (G-3897)*

Jonas Software USA Inc 800 476-0094
9295 Scenic Hwy Pensacola (32514) *(G-13531)*

(G-0000) Company's Geographic Section entry number

Jonathan Mariotti Entps LLC 855 353-8280
608 Danley Dr Unit C Fort Myers (33907) *(G-4301)*

Jonel Knitting Mills Inc 305 887-7333
7130 W 12th Ln Hialeah (33014) *(G-5206)*

Jones Awnings & Canvas Inc 954 784-6966
127 Nw 16th St Pompano Beach (33060) *(G-14068)*

Jones Communications Inc 407 448-6615
312 W 1st St Ste 503 Sanford (32771) *(G-15345)*

Jones Field Services Pamela 904 368-9777
9904 Nw County Road 229 Starke (32091) *(G-16103)*

Jones Mediaamerica Inc 305 289-4524
11399 Overseas Hwy 5sw Marathon (33050) *(G-8107)*

Joni Industries Inc 352 799-5456
16230 Aviation Loop Dr Brooksville (34604) *(G-1166)*

Jordan Brown Inc (HQ) 904 495-0717
475 W Town Pl Ste 200 Saint Augustine (32092) *(G-14851)*

Jordan Florida Group 813 219-0100
3102 W Harbor View Ave Tampa (33611) *(G-16971)*

Jordan Logistics Co LLC 813 787-7791
216 Apollo Beach Blvd Apollo Beach (33572) *(G-93)*

Jordan Norris Inc 407 846-1400
997 W Kennedy Blvd Ste A1 Orlando (32810) *(G-12278)*

Jordan Weld Fabrication 386 789-3606
3300 Sky St Deltona (32738) *(G-3046)*

Jormac Aerospace 727 549-9600
11221 69th St Largo (33773) *(G-7623)*

Jormac Aerospace Inc 727 549-9600
13130 56th Ct Ste 604 Clearwater (33760) *(G-1655)*

Joro Fashions Florida Inc 305 888-8110
6650 Sw 123rd St Pinecrest (33156) *(G-13666)*

Jose Leal Enterprises Inc 305 887-9611
705 W 20th St Hialeah (33010) *(G-5207)*

Jose Morales Hurricane Shutter 786 315-1835
13271 Sw 17th Ln Miami (33175) *(G-9372)*

Jose Polanco 305 631-1784
614 Sw 22nd Ave Miami (33135) *(G-9373)*

Jose Rodriguez Met Fabrication 305 305-6110
2451 Brickell Ave Miami (33129) *(G-9374)*

Joseph J Taylor Truss 321 482-4039
2599 Larry Ct Melbourne (32935) *(G-8443)*

Joshua Throckmorton 561 236-3349
2000 Lion Cntry Safari Rd Loxahatchee (33470) *(G-7971)*

Josper Chef USA, Miami *Also called Charcoal Chef Usa LLC (G-8921)*

Journal Housing Science, Coral Gables *Also called Ural & Associates Inc (G-2116)*

Jox Sox, Boca Raton *Also called Zokos Group Inc (G-764)*

Joy's Gourmet, Melbourne *Also called Joys International Foods Inc (G-8444)*

Joyce Telectronics Corp 727 461-3525
40421 Chancey Rd Ste 101 Zephyrhills (33542) *(G-18618)*

Joyner Inc 850 832-6326
9740 Steel Field Rd Panama City Beach (32413) *(G-13333)*

Joys International Foods Inc 321 242-6520
2600 Aurora Rd Ste Q Melbourne (32935) *(G-8444)*

Joyson Safety Systems, Lakeland *Also called Key Automotive Florida LLC (G-7366)*

JP Cosmetics Inc 305 231-4963
1687 W 32nd Pl Hialeah (33012) *(G-5208)*

JP Custom Metals Inc 786 318-2855
7200 Nw 29th Ct Miami (33147) *(G-9375)*

JP Donvan Prcsion McHining LLC 321 383-1171
201 Paint St Rockledge (32955) *(G-14720)*

Jpl Associates Inc 954 929-6024
1250 E Hallandale Beach B Hallandale Beach (33009) *(G-4955)*

Jpm Import LLC 800 753-3009
7350 Nw 1st St Apt 207 Margate (33063) *(G-8137)*

JPS Digital LLC 813 501-6040
4860 S Marsh Hawk Ter Inverness (34452) *(G-5831)*

Jpt-Tech LLC 352 219-7860
11094 Nw 188th Street Rd Micanopy (32667) *(G-10399)*

Jr Boarts Packaging, Rockledge *Also called Gar Business Group LLC (G-14710)*

Jr Electronics, Miami *Also called Iron Strength Corp (G-9340)*

Jr Embroidery Inc 305 253-6968
12321 Sw 133rd Ct Miami (33186) *(G-9376)*

Jr Plastics Corporation 352 401-0880
5111 S Pine Ave Ste G Ocala (34480) *(G-11414)*

JR Wood Works Inc 305 401-6056
7954 Ne 4th Ave Miami (33138) *(G-9377)*

Jrf Technology LLC 813 443-5273
9830 Currie Davis Dr Tampa (33619) *(G-16972)*

Jrg Systems Inc 954 962-1020
1239 N Flagler Dr Fort Lauderdale (33304) *(G-3898)*

Jrh Sport Industries Inc 904 940-3381
6550 State Road 16 Saint Augustine (32092) *(G-14852)*

Jrmetal Ornamental 954 989-2607
3725 Pembroke Rd Ste A11 Hollywood (33021) *(G-5607)*

Jrs Limb Tree & Farm LLC 407 383-4843
297 Grant Line Rd Sanford (32771) *(G-15346)*

Jrt Manufacturing LLC 321 363-4133
421 Cornwall Rd Sanford (32773) *(G-15347)*

Js2 Aerospace Corp 954 840-3620
1888 Nw 21st St Pompano Beach (33069) *(G-14069)*

JSB Enterprises Inc 941 723-2288
1650 12th St E Palmetto (34221) *(G-13177)*

Jsi Scientific Inc 732 845-1925
862 105th Ave N Ste 18 Naples (34108) *(G-10793)*

Jsl Enterprises of Orlando 386 767-9653
1434 Circle Ln Chuluota (32766) *(G-1465)*

Jsm Creations Inc 239 229-8746
16260 Saddlewood Ln Cape Coral (33991) *(G-1360)*

Jsn Blue Thunder LLC 786 398-5222
1876 Nw 7th St Miami (33125) *(G-9378)*

Jsp Manufacturing Holdings LLC 727 488-5353
6203 80th Ave N Pinellas Park (33781) *(G-13698)*

Jsr Wellness Inc 561 748-2477
5500 Village Blvd Ste 202 West Palm Beach (33407) *(G-18042)*

Jssa Inc 321 383-7798
895 Buffalo Rd Titusville (32796) *(G-17594)*

Jst Power Equipment Inc 844 631-9046
30 Skyline Dr Lake Mary (32746) *(G-7088)*

Jt Enterprises Group LLC (PA) 904 803-9338
280 Village Main St Ponte Vedra Beach (32082) *(G-14270)*

Jt Enterprises Group LLC 904 551-2680
6100 Philips Hwy Jacksonville (32216) *(G-6232)*

Jta Industries LLC (PA) 407 352-4255
9165 Phillips Grove Ter Orlando (32836) *(G-12279)*

Jta Industries LLC 321 663-4395
3391 S Kirkman Rd # 1223 Orlando (32811) *(G-12280)*

Jtac Industries LLC 813 928-0628
2509 Trkey Creek Rd Ste 1 Plant City (33566) *(G-13779)*

Jte Inc 941 925-2605
3959 Sawyer Rd Sarasota (34233) *(G-15715)*

Jtf Ventures LLC 305 556-5156
7889 Nw 98th St Hialeah Gardens (33016) *(G-5439)*

Jti Duty-Free USA Inc 305 377-3922
501 Brickell Dr Ste 402 Miami (33131) *(G-9379)*

JTL Enterprises (delaware) 727 536-5566
15395 Roosevelt Blvd Clearwater (33760) *(G-1656)*

JTS Woodworking Inc 561 272-7996
75 Nw 18th Ave Delray Beach (33444) *(G-2980)*

Juan Bermudez, Sunrise *Also called Neopod Systems LLC (G-16346)*

Juan F Montano 305 274-0512
7895 Sw 57th Ter Miami (33143) *(G-9380)*

Juan Pampanas Designs Inc 305 573-7550
32 Nw 20th St Miami (33127) *(G-9381)*

Juan Rodriguez Cabinetry Corp 305 467-3878
221 W 41st St Hialeah (33012) *(G-5209)*

Judicial & ADM RES Assoc 850 222-3171
1327 N Adams St Tallahassee (32303) *(G-16464)*

Juice Culture LLC 407 312-8079
805 S Orlando Ave Ste H Winter Park (32789) *(G-18517)*

Juiceblendz, Weston *Also called Ianorod JB LLC (G-18253)*

Juiceco, Vero Beach *Also called United Jice Companies Amer Inc (G-17811)*

Juicera, Miami *Also called Healtheintentions Inc (G-9268)*

Julio Garcia Satellite 407 414-3223
1248 S John Young Pkwy Kissimmee (34741) *(G-6932)*

Juniors Bait and Seafood Inc 321 480-5492
1500 Maple Ave Melbourne (32935) *(G-8445)*

Junk Cars Broward County, Oakland Park *Also called Raceway Towing LLC (G-11291)*

Juno Ironcraft 561 352-0471
1233 Old Dixie Hwy Lake Park (33403) *(G-7130)*

Jupiter Bach North America Inc 850 476-6304
3301 Bill Metzger Ln Pensacola (32514) *(G-13532)*

Jupiter Compass LLC 561 444-6740
600 S Entrada Way Apt 204 Palm Beach Gardens (33410) *(G-12980)*

Jupiter Courier, Jupiter *Also called Howard Scripts Inc (G-6743)*

Jupiter Courier, Stuart *Also called Stuart News (G-16230)*

Jupiter Industries LLC 239 225-9041
9373 Laredo Ave Fort Myers (33905) *(G-4302)*

Jupiter Mar Intl Holdings Inc (PA) 941 729-5000
1103 12th Ave E Palmetto (34221) *(G-13178)*

Jupiter Petroleum Inc 561 622-1276
5490 Military Trl Jupiter (33458) *(G-6751)*

Jupiter Weld & Repair, Jupiter *Also called Jupiter Welding LLC (G-6752)*

Jupiter Welding LLC 561 801-3585
1525 Cypress Dr Jupiter (33469) *(G-6752)*

Juracsik, Ted Tool & Die, Delray Beach *Also called Tibor Inc (G-3026)*

Juritis USA LLC 954 529-2168
2500 Weston Rd Ste 105 Weston (33331) *(G-18260)*

Just Counters Other Stuff Inc 941 235-1300
1489 Market Cir Bldg 309 Port Charlotte (33953) *(G-14304)*

Just Door Toolz LLC 954 448-6872
1552 Sw Abingdon Ave Port Saint Lucie (34953) *(G-14419)*

Just Engines 561 575-2681
209 Circle W Jupiter (33458) *(G-6753)*

Just For Nets, Tampa *Also called Lee Fisher International Inc (G-17004)*

Just For Nets 813 871-1133
4817 N Lois Ave Ste 104 Tampa (33614) *(G-16973)*

Just In Time Cnc Machinin 585 247-3850
4551 Nw 44th Ave Ocala (34482) *(G-11415)*

Just Now Jennings LLC 239 331-0315
　6542 Chestnut Cir Naples (34109) *(G-10794)*

Just Say Print Inc 954 254-7793
　1500 Nw 112th Way Coral Springs (33071) *(G-2172)*

Just Steel Inc 941 755-7811
　3100 Whitfield Ave Ste B Sarasota (34243) *(G-15504)*

Just-In-Time Mfg Corp 321 752-7552
　3153 Skyway Cir Ste 101 Melbourne (32934) *(G-8446)*

Justi Group Inc 813 855-5779
　305 Marlborough St Oldsmar (34677) *(G-11663)*

Justice Government Supply Inc 954 559-3038
　555 Pacific Grove Dr # 2 West Palm Beach (33401) *(G-18043)*

Justin Bell Logging Inc 904 759-9006
　44001 Bell Ln Callahan (32011) *(G-1254)*

Juvent Medical Inc 732 748-8866
　3111 Shell Mound Blvd Fort Myers Beach (33931) *(G-4455)*

JV Installations Corp 407 849-0262
　1310 W Central Blvd Orlando (32805) *(G-12281)*

JV&h Corporation 954 305-9043
　2200 N Commerce Pkwy # 20 Weston (33326) *(G-18261)*

Jvl Produce Inc 813 862-6155
　4633 Musket Dr Lakeland (33810) *(G-7362)*

JW Appley and Son Inc 727 572-4910
　13215 38th St N Clearwater (33762) *(G-1657)*

JW Austin Industries Inc 321 723-2422
　7713 Ellis Rd Melbourne (32904) *(G-8447)*

JW Machine, Orlando *Also called Praesto Enterprises LLC (G-12498)*

JW Marketing and Consulting 866 323-0001
　6574 N State Road 7 # 27 Coconut Creek (33073) *(G-1995)*

JW Performance Transm Inc 321 632-6205
　1826 Baldwin St Rockledge (32955) *(G-14721)*

Jwdi Realty LLC 561 331-2481
　8830 Lyndall Ln Palm Beach Gardens (33403) *(G-12981)*

Jwn Family Partners LP Ltd 352 628-4910
　6198 S Lecanto Hwy Lecanto (34461) *(G-7753)*

Jwo Industries Inc 352 551-6943
　510 E Alfred St Ste A Tavares (32778) *(G-17514)*

K & A Audio Inc 941 925-7648
　4604 Ashton Rd Sarasota (34233) *(G-15716)*

K & B Landscape Supplies Inc 800 330-8816
　3900 E State Road 44 Deland (32724) *(G-2880)*

K & C The Printer, North Miami *Also called American Specialty Sales Corp (G-11089)*

K & G Box Inc 904 356-6063
　2212 N Pearl St Jacksonville (32206) *(G-6233)*

K & G Creations, Delray Beach *Also called Jewelnet Corp (G-2977)*

K & I Creative Plas & WD LLC 904 923-0409
　582 Nixon St Jacksonville (32204) *(G-6234)*

K & I Plastics Inc 904 387-0438
　582 Nixon St Jacksonville (32204) *(G-6235)*

K & K Precision Manufacturing 850 769-9080
　2307 Industrial Dr Panama City (32405) *(G-13281)*

K & M Custom Cabinetry Inc 727 791-3993
　977 Withlacoochee St A Safety Harbor (34695) *(G-14789)*

K & M Truss Inc 407 880-4551
　2844 N Ornge Blssom Trl Zellwood (32798) *(G-18599)*

K & N Industries Inc 850 939-7722
　9218 Navarre Pkwy Navarre (32566) *(G-10950)*

K & T Manufacturing Inc 407 814-7700
　557 Cooper Indus Pkwy Apopka (32703) *(G-143)*

K and G Food Services LLC 954 857-9283
　9500 Sandhill Crane Dr West Palm Beach (33412) *(G-18044)*

K Bausch Mfg Corp 772 485-2426
　2813 Se Monroe St Stuart (34997) *(G-16173)*

K C I Kone Crane, Plant City *Also called Kone Crane Maintenance Svcs (G-13783)*

K C Industries LLC 863 425-1195
　2420 Old Highway 60 Mulberry (33860) *(G-10629)*

K C Screen 407 977-9636
　1705 Evans St Oviedo (32765) *(G-12831)*

K C W Electric Company Inc 850 878-2051
　4765 Shelfer Rd Tallahassee (32305) *(G-16465)*

K Color Corp 305 579-2290
　7255 Nw 68th St Ste 1 Miami (33166) *(G-9382)*

K H S Inc 941 359-4000
　5501 N Washington Blvd Sarasota (34243) *(G-15505)*

K J C O Inc (PA) 954 401-4299
　481 Ambleside Dr Titusville (32780) *(G-17595)*

K K Woodworking 321 724-1298
　2300 Kahler Ln Malabar (32950) *(G-8084)*

K L Distributing Inc 415 800-2158
　7425 Sailfish Dr Hudson (34667) *(G-5779)*

K M I International Inc 561 588-5514
　2501 Park St Lake Worth (33460) *(G-7212)*

K N M Food Store 239 334-7699
　2441 Hanson St Fort Myers (33901) *(G-4303)*

K Pro Supply Co Inc 941 758-1226
　2135 Whitfield Park Ave Sarasota (34243) *(G-15506)*

K R O Enterprises Ltd 309 797-2213
　7950 Preserve Cir Apt 816 Naples (34119) *(G-10795)*

K Rain, Riviera Beach *Also called K-Rain Manufacturing Corp (G-14635)*

K V Water Equipment & Krane Co 941 723-0707
　730 Commerce Dr Venice (34292) *(G-17702)*

K&M Power Systems LLC 866 945-9100
　7641 Central Indus Dr Riviera Beach (33404) *(G-14634)*

K&T Stoneworks Inc 561 798-8486
　101 N Benoist Farms Rd West Palm Beach (33411) *(G-18045)*

K-Kraft Cabinets Inc 321 632-8800
　1751 Cogswell St Rockledge (32955) *(G-14722)*

K-Kraft Industries Inc 321 632-8800
　1751 Cogswell St Rockledge (32955) *(G-14723)*

K-O Concepts Inc 407 296-7788
　1200 White Dr Ste D Titusville (32780) *(G-17596)*

K-Plex LLC 239 963-2280
　3960 Via Del Ray Bonita Springs (34134) *(G-808)*

K-Rain Manufacturing Corp (PA) 561 844-1002
　1640 Australian Ave Riviera Beach (33404) *(G-14635)*

K-Technologies Inc 863 940-4815
　4306 Wallace Rd Lakeland (33812) *(G-7363)*

K12 Print Inc 800 764-7600
　3875 Fiscal Ct Ste 400 West Palm Beach (33404) *(G-18046)*

K20 Oil LLC 954 421-1735
　1201 S Military Trl Deerfield Beach (33442) *(G-2747)*

Kabinets By Kinsey Inc 813 222-0460
　3815 N Florida Ave Tampa (33603) *(G-16974)*

Kabrit Repair Services LLC 407 714-1470
　9118 Panzani Pl Windermere (34786) *(G-18357)*

Kachemak Bay Flying Service 850 398-8699
　5545 John Givens Rd Crestview (32539) *(G-2248)*

Kacoo Usa LLC 727 233-8237
　4500 140th Ave N Ste 101 Clearwater (33762) *(G-1658)*

Kadassa Inc 954 684-8361
　3541 Dr Martin Luther Kin Riviera Beach (33404) *(G-14636)*

Kafe PA Nou LLC 305 953-3344
　17100 N Bay Rd Apt 1514 Sunny Isles Beach (33160) *(G-16278)*

Kai Limited 954 957-8586
　1650 W Mcnab Rd Fort Lauderdale (33309) *(G-3899)*

Kalashnikov USA, Pompano Beach *Also called Rwc Group LLC (G-14164)*

Kalitec Direct LLC 407 545-2063
　865 Oviedo Blvd Ste 1017 Oviedo (32765) *(G-12832)*

Kalitec Medical, Oviedo *Also called Kalitec Direct LLC (G-12832)*

Kaltec Electronics Inc 813 888-9555
　5436 W Crenshaw St Tampa (33634) *(G-16975)*

Kaluz LLC 786 991-2260
　7105 Nw 41st St Miami (33166) *(G-9383)*

Kam Tatonetti, Delray Beach *Also called Kc & B Custom Inc (G-2981)*

Kamaj Business Group Inc 813 863-9967
　601 N Ashley Dr Ste 1 Tampa (33602) *(G-16976)*

Kaman Aerospace Corporation 904 485-1410
　227 Gun Club Rd Jacksonville (32218) *(G-6236)*

Kaman Aerospace Corporation 904 751-5369
　9410 Parker Ave Jacksonville (32218) *(G-6237)*

Kaman Precision Products Inc (HQ) 407 282-1000
　6655 E Colonial Dr Orlando (32807) *(G-12282)*

Kamco Industries LLC 772 299-1401
　5720 Us Highway 1 Vero Beach (32967) *(G-17770)*

Kamel Software Inc 407 672-0202
　1809 E Broadway St # 134 Oviedo (32765) *(G-12833)*

Kameleon Press Inc 850 566-2522
　1925 Benjamin Chaires Rd Tallahassee (32317) *(G-16466)*

Kamsa, Doral *Also called Asterion Beverages Inc (G-3121)*

Kamtex USA Incorporated 954 733-1044
　2916 Nw 28th St Lauderdale Lakes (33311) *(G-7717)*

Kanalflakt Inc (PA) 941 359-3267
　1712 Northgate Blvd Sarasota (34234) *(G-15717)*

Kane-Miller Corp (PA) 941 346-2003
　1515 Ringling Blvd # 840 Sarasota (34236) *(G-15718)*

Kanger Wholesale USA, Tamarac *Also called Lightfire Holdings LLC (G-16535)*

Karigam Enterprises Inc 305 358-7755
　1110 Brickell Ave Ste 702 Miami (33131) *(G-9384)*

Karmanos Printing & Graphics, Tallahassee *Also called Oompha Inc (G-16486)*

Karnak Corporation 352 481-4145
　147 Pine Tree Rd East Palatka (32131) *(G-3473)*

Karnak South Inc 954 761-7606
　1010 Se 20th St Fort Lauderdale (33316) *(G-3900)*

Karob Instrument Inc 352 732-2414
　1644 Ne 22nd Ave Ocala (34470) *(G-11416)*

Karob Manufacturing Inc 352 732-2414
　1644 Ne 22nd Ave Bldg Ste Ocala (34470) *(G-11417)*

Karry Industries Inc 904 398-4007
　4007 Saint Augustine Rd Jacksonville (32207) *(G-6238)*

Kaseya US LLC (PA) 415 694-5700
　701 Brickell Ave Ste 400 Miami (33131) *(G-9385)*

Kashiben Say LLC 352 489-4960
　11150 N Williams St Dunnellon (34432) *(G-3466)*

Kasulik II LLC 786 629-8978
　1170 E Hllndale Bch Blvd Hallandale Beach (33009) *(G-4956)*

Katcheri Davis Services LLC 754 222-4464
　10365 Jolynn Ct E Jacksonville (32225) *(G-6239)*

Katherine Scures 772 589-7409
　373 Sebastian Blvd Sebastian (32958) *(G-15896)*

(G-0000) Company's Geographic Section entry number

Kationx Corp (PA)...321 338-5050
2412 Irwin St Ste 61 Melbourne (32901) ***(G-8448)***
Katmai Electronic Systems, Orlando *Also called Ilsc Holdings Lc* ***(G-12235)***
Kavi Skin Solutions Inc...415 839-5156
3520 South St Titusville (32780) ***(G-17597)***
Kawasumi Laboratories Amer Inc...813 630-5554
10002 Princess Palm Ave # 324 Tampa (33619) ***(G-16977)***
Kawneer Architectural Products, Orlando *Also called Kawneer Company Inc* ***(G-12283)***
Kawneer Company Inc...407 648-4511
4645 L B Mcleod Rd Orlando (32811) ***(G-12283)***
Kay Diamond Products LLC...561 994-5400
1080 Holland Dr Ste 2 Boca Raton (33487) ***(G-565)***
Kay Enterprises...352 732-5770
2026 Se 3rd Pl Ocala (34471) ***(G-11418)***
Kay Peak Group Inc...754 307-5400
6510 W Atlantic Blvd Margate (33063) ***(G-8138)***
Kaycha TN LLC...954 686-0610
4101 Sw 47th Ave Davie (33314) ***(G-2428)***
Kayva Distribution LLC...305 428-2816
2201 Nw 102nd Pl Ste 4a Doral (33172) ***(G-3271)***
Kazdin Industries Inc...772 223-5511
5258 Sw Anhinga Ave Palm City (34990) ***(G-13047)***
KB Aerospace Co...754 366-9194
401 E Las Olas Blvd Fort Lauderdale (33301) ***(G-3901)***
KB Electronics, Coral Springs *Also called Nidec Motor Corporation* ***(G-2197)***
Kbf Design Gallery Inc...407 830-7703
1295 S Orlando Ave Maitland (32751) ***(G-8063)***
Kbfs, Crestview *Also called Kachemak Bay Flying Service* ***(G-2248)***
Kbn Corporation...321 327-9792
4670 Lipscomb St Ne Ste 6 Palm Bay (32905) ***(G-12905)***
Kc & B Custom Inc...561 276-1887
2413 N Federal Hwy Unit A Delray Beach (33483) ***(G-2981)***
Kc Marine Services Inc...954 766-8100
213 Sw 21st St Fort Lauderdale (33315) ***(G-3902)***
Kci...352 572-2873
24 S Ponder Ave Lecanto (34461) ***(G-7754)***
KCm Mch Sp Broward Cnty Inc...954 475-8732
2394 Sw 66th Ter Davie (33317) ***(G-2429)***
KCS Professional Coatings Inc...813 850-6386
2603 E Lake Ave Tampa (33610) ***(G-16978)***
Kcw Cnc and Laser Engraving, Palm Harbor *Also called Kevins Custom Woodworking* ***(G-13117)***
Kd-Pharma Usa Inc...786 345-5500
14193 Sw 119th Ave Ste 10 Miami (33186) ***(G-9386)***
Kdavid Woodwork + Design Inc...754 205-2433
7546 W Mcnab Rd North Lauderdale (33068) ***(G-11082)***
KDD Inc (PA)...239 689-8402
16431 Domestic Ave Fort Myers (33912) ***(G-4304)***
Kea Kitchen Cabinetry Inc...954 639-6233
6310 Walk Cir Boca Raton (33433) ***(G-566)***
Keavys Corner LLC...863 658-0235
12413 Us Highway 98 Sebring (33876) ***(G-15928)***
Kee Kreative LLC...954 931-2579
3405 Nw 14th Ct Lauderhill (33311) ***(G-7734)***
Keel & Curley Winery LLC...813 752-9100
5210 Thonotosassa Rd Plant City (33565) ***(G-13780)***
Keels & Wheels, Sarasota *Also called Mio Publication Inc* ***(G-15517)***
Keene Metal Fabricators Inc...813 621-2455
5912 E Broadway Ave Tampa (33619) ***(G-16979)***
Keens Portable Buildings...850 223-1939
2320 S Byron Butler Pkwy Perry (32348) ***(G-13645)***
Keens Portable Buildings Inc...386 364-7995
620 Howard St W Live Oak (32064) ***(G-7849)***
Keepit Neat...352 867-0541
11630 Ne Jacksonville Rd Anthony (32617) ***(G-87)***
Keepmefresh...502 407-7902
614 E Highway 50 Ste 122 Clermont (34711) ***(G-1872)***
Keg Connect LLC...727 821-8752
100 2nd Ave S Ste 701 Saint Petersburg (33701) ***(G-15103)***
Keith Dennis Markham...239 353-4122
220 24th Ave Ne Naples (34120) ***(G-10796)***
Keith Eickert Power Pdts LLC...386 446-0660
11 Industry Dr Palm Coast (32137) ***(G-13081)***
Keithco Inc...352 351-4741
1519 S Pine Ave Ocala (34471) ***(G-11419)***
Keithco Enterprises, Ocala *Also called Steven Chancas* ***(G-11499)***
Kel Glo Corp...305 751-5641
54 Ne 73rd St Miami (33138) ***(G-9387)***
Kel-TEC Cnc Industries Inc...321 631-0068
1505 Cox Rd Cocoa (32926) ***(G-1939)***
Keller Industrial Inc...813 831-1871
11001 Fern Hill Dr Riverview (33578) ***(G-14568)***
Keller Manufacturing Inc...863 937-8928
4442 Holden Rd Lakeland (33811) ***(G-7364)***
Keller-Nglillis Design Mfg Inc...727 733-4111
655 San Christopher Dr Dunedin (34698) ***(G-3452)***
Kellstrom Aerospace Group Inc (HQ)...954 538-2482
2500 N Military Trl Ste 4 Boca Raton (33431) ***(G-567)***
Kellstrom Coml Arospc Inc...305 818-5400
14400 Nw 77th Ct Ste 306 Miami Lakes (33016) ***(G-10310)***
Kellstrom Defense, Miramar *Also called Allclear Aerospace & Def Inc* ***(G-10465)***
Kelly Foods...904 354-7600
2240 Dennis St Jacksonville (32204) ***(G-6240)***
Kellys Bakery Corp...305 685-4622
3990 Nw 132nd St Unit A Opa Locka (33054) ***(G-11759)***
KELSIES BLINDS, Oviedo *Also called Kelsies Blinds* ***(G-12834)***
Kelsies Blinds...407 977-0827
2464 W State Rd Ste 1028 Oviedo (32765) ***(G-12834)***
Keltec, Cocoa *Also called Kel-TEC Cnc Industries Inc* ***(G-1939)***
Kelton Company LLC...850 434-6830
220 W Garden St Ste 605 Pensacola (32502) ***(G-13533)***
Keltour US Inc...239 424-8901
71 Mid Cape Ter Unit 1/2 Cape Coral (33991) ***(G-1361)***
Kemco Industries LLC...407 322-1230
70 Keyes Ave Sanford (32773) ***(G-15348)***
Kemco Systems Co LLC (PA)...727 573-2323
11500 47th St N Clearwater (33762) ***(G-1659)***
Kemet Corporation (HQ)...954 766-2800
1 E Broward Blvd Ste 200 Fort Lauderdale (33301) ***(G-3903)***
Kemet Ventures LLC...407 403-2958
10524 Moss Park Rd Orlando (32832) ***(G-12284)***
Kemira Water Solutions Inc...863 533-5990
808 E Main St Lakeland (33801) ***(G-7365)***
Kemp, Ocala *Also called Flaire Corporation* ***(G-11390)***
Kemp, Ocala *Also called SPX Flow Technology Usa Inc* ***(G-11498)***
Kemp Signs Inc...561 840-6382
1740 Hill Ave Mangonia Park (33407) ***(G-8096)***
Kempfer Sawmill Inc...407 892-2955
6254 Kempfer Rd Saint Cloud (34773) ***(G-14930)***
Kempharm Inc (PA)...321 939-3416
1180 Celebration Blvd # 10 Celebration (34747) ***(G-1438)***
Ken Clearys Two LLC...727 573-0700
10900 47th St N Clearwater (33762) ***(G-1660)***
Ken R Avery Painting Inc...813 855-5037
3704 State Road 580 W Oldsmar (34677) ***(G-11664)***
Kenart Holdings Llc...561 863-5556
1380 W 15th St Riviera Beach (33404) ***(G-14637)***
Kenco - 2000 Inc...386 672-1590
1539 Garden Ave Daytona Beach (32117) ***(G-2565)***
Kenco Hospitality Inc...954 921-5434
1000 Nw 56th St Fort Lauderdale (33309) ***(G-3904)***
Kenco Quilting & Textiles Inc...954 921-5434
1000 Nw 56th St Fort Lauderdale (33309) ***(G-3905)***
Kenco Signs Awning LLC...386 672-1590
1538 Garden Ave Holly Hill (32117) ***(G-5515)***
Kendal Signs, Rockledge *Also called Bryson of Brevard Inc* ***(G-14694)***
Kendal Signs Inc...321 636-5116
580 Gus Hipp Blvd Rockledge (32955) ***(G-14724)***
Kendall Fuel Inc...305 270-7735
9949 N Kendall Dr Miami (33176) ***(G-9388)***
Kendall News, South Miami *Also called Your Hometown Newspaper Inc* ***(G-16049)***
Kendall Sign and Design Inc...305 595-2000
14271 Sw 120th St Ste 103 Miami (33186) ***(G-9389)***
Kendoo Technology Inc...305 592-9688
1950 Nw 94th Ave Lowr Doral (33172) ***(G-3272)***
Kenexa Learning Inc...407 562-1905
601 S Lake Destiny Rd # 30 Maitland (32751) ***(G-8064)***
Kenexa Learning Inc...407 548-0434
100 Colonial Center Pkwy # 1 Lake Mary (32746) ***(G-7089)***
Kenfar Corporation...813 443-5222
5926 Jet Port Industrial Tampa (33634) ***(G-16980)***
Kennedy Craft Cabinets Inc...239 598-1566
5790 Washington St Naples (34109) ***(G-10797)***
Kennesaw Fruit & Juice, Pompano Beach *Also called R & Z Ventures Inc* ***(G-14154)***
Kenneth A Jeffus Fine Art LLC...954 849-0553
9355 Nw 18th Pl Plantation (33322) ***(G-13862)***
Kenneth E Keller...239 649-7579
4110 Entp Ave Ste 116 Naples (34116) ***(G-10798)***
Kenneth Jake Linton...850 526-0121
4430 Magnolia Rd Marianna (32448) ***(G-8167)***
Kenneth S Jarrell Inc...334 215-7774
9859 N Palafox St Pensacola (32534) ***(G-13534)***
Kenney Communications Inc (PA)...407 859-3113
1215 Spruce Ave Orlando (32824) ***(G-12285)***
Kenny Skylights LLC...407 330-5150
5294 Tower Way Sanford (32773) ***(G-15349)***
Kenny-Ts Inc...850 575-6644
1471 Capital Cir Nw # 10 Tallahassee (32303) ***(G-16467)***
Kens Gas Piping Inc...850 897-4149
419 Adams Ave Ste A Valparaiso (32580) ***(G-17661)***
Kens Stump Grinding LLC...407 948-5031
3848 Beachman Dr Orlando (32810) ***(G-12286)***
Kent Manufacturing Venice Inc...941 485-8871
155 Toscavilla Blvd Nokomis (34275) ***(G-11049)***
Kent Mfg Fla Keys Inc...941 488-0355
248 James St Venice (34285) ***(G-17703)***

ALPHABETIC

Kenton Industries LLC...863 675-8233
1477 Forestry Division Rd Labelle (33935) ***(G-6981)***
Kentucky Leatherworks, Orange Park *Also called Old Kentucky Leather Works Inc* ***(G-11835)***
Kentucky Welding LLC...305 852-7433
100 Palm Ln Islamorada (33036) ***(G-5836)***
Keratin Cure, Opa Locka *Also called Beauty Cosmetica* ***(G-11722)***
Keratronix Inc...954 753-5741
4377 Nw 124th Ave Coral Springs (33065) ***(G-2173)***
Kericure Inc...855 888-5374
26620 Easy St Wesley Chapel (33544) ***(G-17880)***
Kerno LLC...954 261-5854
20958 Sheridan St Fort Lauderdale (33332) ***(G-3906)***
Kerry Consulting Corp...561 364-9969
30 Lawrence Lake Dr Boynton Beach (33436) ***(G-883)***
Kerry I&F Contracting Company...813 359-5182
1111 W Dr Mrtn Lther King Plant City (33563) ***(G-13781)***
Kerry Inc...813 359-5181
1111 W Dr Mrtn Lther King Plant City (33563) ***(G-13782)***
Kerry Ingredients & Flavours, Plant City *Also called Kerry Inc* ***(G-13782)***
Kesin Pharma Corporation...833 537-4679
3874 Tampa Rd Ste 100 Oldsmar (34677) ***(G-11665)***
Keter North America LLC (HQ)...765 298-6800
901 W Yamato Rd Ste 180 Boca Raton (33431) ***(G-568)***
Kevco Builders Inc...352 308-8025
2104 S Bay St Eustis (32726) ***(G-3561)***
Kevin Jeffers Inc...352 377-2322
1611 S Main St Gainesville (32601) ***(G-4717)***
Kevin M Lukasiewicz...561 588-5853
1025 W 17th St Riviera Beach (33404) ***(G-14638)***
Kevins Custom Woodworking...727 804-8422
246 Arbor Dr E Palm Harbor (34683) ***(G-13117)***
Key Automotive Florida LLC...863 668-6000
5300 Allen K Breed Hwy Lakeland (33811) ***(G-7366)***
Key Biscayne Smoothie Company...305 441-7882
249 Catalonia Ave Coral Gables (33134) ***(G-2076)***
Key Largo Canvas, Key Largo *Also called Cross Key Marine Canvas Inc* ***(G-6844)***
Key Logging...386 328-6984
229 Lynn Dr Hollister (32147) ***(G-5508)***
Key Packaging Company Inc...941 355-2728
7350 15th St E Sarasota (34243) ***(G-15507)***
Key Safety Systems Inc...863 668-6000
5300 Allen K Breed Hwy Lakeland (33811) ***(G-7367)***
Key West Citizen, Key West *Also called Cooke Communications Fla LLC* ***(G-6860)***
Key West Multihull, Key West *Also called Multihull Technologies Inc* ***(G-6877)***
Key West Printing LLC...305 517-6711
5585 2nd Ave Ste 1 Key West (33040) ***(G-6868)***
Key West Wldg Fabrication Inc...305 296-5555
5650 1st Ave Key West (33040) ***(G-6869)***
Keylon Lighting Services Inc...352 279-3249
6931 Remington Rd Brooksville (34602) ***(G-1167)***
Keymark Corporation Florida...863 858-5500
2540 Knights Station Rd Lakeland (33810) ***(G-7368)***
Keynoter Publishing Co Inc...305 743-5551
3015 Overseas Hwy Marathon (33050) ***(G-8108)***
Keyplex, Miami *Also called Morse Enterprises Limited Inc* ***(G-9589)***
Keys Blinds Inc...
1103 Truman Ave Key West (33040) ***(G-6870)***
Keys Deck & Dock Supplies Inc...305 451-8001
100151 Overseas Hwy Key Largo (33037) ***(G-6848)***
KEys International Group LLC...855 213-0399
2674 Grassmoor Loop Apopka (32712) ***(G-144)***
Keystone 75 Inc...954 430-1880
5620 Dewey St Hollywood (33023) ***(G-5608)***
Keystone Color Works Inc...813 250-1313
2411 S Hesperides St Tampa (33629) ***(G-16981)***
Keystone Development, Jacksonville *Also called Keystone Industries LLC* ***(G-6241)***
Keystone Industries LLC (PA)...239 337-7474
1915 Wigmore St Jacksonville (32206) ***(G-6241)***
Keystone Precast & Columns Cor...305 216-5375
29630 Sw 183rd Ct Homestead (33030) ***(G-5722)***
Keystone Products Inc...305 245-4716
1414 Nw 3rd Ave Homestead (33034) ***(G-5723)***
Keystone Rv Company...813 228-0625
1201 Old Hopewell Rd # 9 Tampa (33619) ***(G-16982)***
Keystone Steel Products Co...813 248-9828
3101 E 2nd Ave Tampa (33605) ***(G-16983)***
Keystone Water Company LLC...863 465-1932
200 Turner Rd Lake Placid (33852) ***(G-7144)***
Keytroller LLC...813 877-4500
3907 W Martin Luther King Tampa (33614) ***(G-16984)***
Keytroller LLC...813 877-4500
3907 W Dr Mart Luth Kng B Martin Luther King Tampa (33614) ***(G-16985)***
Kgs Agro Group, Highland Beach *Also called Gmx Technologies LLC* ***(G-5460)***
Khaled W Akkawi...321 396-3108
1349 S Orange Blossom Trl Apopka (32703) ***(G-145)***
Kibby Foods LLC...305 456-3635
2315 W 77th St Hialeah (33016) ***(G-5210)***
KID Group Inc...888 805-8851
4010 S 57th Ave Ste 104 Greenacres (33463) ***(G-4850)***
Kid-U-Not Inc...407 324-2112
1201 Central Park Dr Sanford (32771) ***(G-15350)***
Kiddidoo USA, Miami Beach *Also called Sports Structure Intl LLC* ***(G-10234)***
Kids Wood...407 332-9663
714 Commerce Cir Longwood (32750) ***(G-7910)***
Kidstance LLC...954 245-9916
2441 Nw 16th Ln Pompano Beach (33064) ***(G-14070)***
Kights Printing & Office Pdts...904 731-7990
8505-1 Baymeadows Rd Jacksonville (32256) ***(G-6242)***
Kiinde LLC...914 303-6308
6300 N Wickham Rd Ste 130 Melbourne (32940) ***(G-8449)***
Kik Custom Products, Auburndale *Also called Sewell Products Florida LLC* ***(G-244)***
Kikisteescom LLC...888 620-4110
5600 Nw 102nd Ave Sunrise (33351) ***(G-16333)***
Kimball Electronics Group LLC...813 854-2000
13750 Reptron Blvd Tampa (33626) ***(G-16986)***
Kimball Electronics Tampa Inc...813 814-5229
13750 Reptron Blvd Tampa (33626) ***(G-16987)***
Kimberlyn Investments Co...305 448-6328
2828 Coral Way Ste 309 Coral Gables (33145) ***(G-2077)***
Kimera Koffee, Coral Gables *Also called Kraken Koffee LLC* ***(G-2079)***
Kinane Corp...772 288-6580
310 Se Denver Ave Stuart (34994) ***(G-16174)***
Kincaid Plastics Inc...352 754-9979
2400 Corporate Blvd Brooksville (34604) ***(G-1168)***
Kinco Ltd (HQ)...904 355-1476
5245 Old Kings Rd Jacksonville (32254) ***(G-6243)***
Kindorf Enterprises Inc...407 858-0331
1650 Sand Lake Rd Ste 115 Orlando (32809) ***(G-12287)***
Kinematics and Controls Corp...352 796-0300
15151 Technology Dr Brooksville (34604) ***(G-1169)***
Kinetic Industries LLC...727 572-7604
10445 49th St N Ste A Clearwater (33762) ***(G-1661)***
Kinetic Research, Tampa *Also called Bader Prosthetics & Orthotics* ***(G-16626)***
Kinetic Research Inc...813 962-6300
5513 W Sligh Ave Tampa (33634) ***(G-16988)***
Kinetics Usa Inc...561 988-8826
990 S Rogers Cir Ste 5 Boca Raton (33487) ***(G-569)***
Kinetronics Corporation...941 951-2432
5316 Lena Rd Bradenton (34211) ***(G-1001)***
King & Grube Advg & Prtg LLC...727 327-6033
1211 10th St Sw Largo (33770) ***(G-7624)***
King & Grube Inc...727 327-6033
1211 10th St Sw Largo (33770) ***(G-7625)***
King Arthur's Tools, Tallahassee *Also called Round Table Tools' Inc* ***(G-16496)***
King Brands LLC...239 313-2057
9910 Bavaria Rd Fort Myers (33913) ***(G-4305)***
King Construction & Glass LLC...407 508-6286
1414 Grandview Blvd Kissimmee (34744) ***(G-6933)***
King Han Inc...860 933-8574
3725 S Access Rd Ste C Englewood (34224) ***(G-3519)***
King Kanine LLC...833 546-4738
150 S Pine Island Rd # 115 Plantation (33324) ***(G-13863)***
King Mobile Welding Andrew...386 437-1007
1645 County Road 302 Bunnell (32110) ***(G-1229)***
King of Socks...772 204-3286
2085 Se N Blackwell Dr Port St Lucie (34952) ***(G-14477)***
King Pharmaceuticals LLC...954 575-7085
2814 N University Dr Coral Springs (33065) ***(G-2174)***
King Pharmaceuticals LLC...423 989-8000
2540 26th Ave N Saint Petersburg (33713) ***(G-15104)***
King Plastic Corporation...941 423-8666
1100 N Toledo Blade Blvd North Port (34288) ***(G-11197)***
King Printing & Graphics Inc...813 681-5060
634 Oakfield Dr Brandon (33511) ***(G-1097)***
King Tech Print LLC...786 362-6249
7205 Nw 44th St Miami (33166) ***(G-9390)***
King's Office Supply & Prtg Co, Crescent City *Also called Scott Brevard Inc* ***(G-2238)***
Kingdom Coatings Inc...904 600-1424
2779 Indigo Cir Middleburg (32068) ***(G-10404)***
Kingman Cstm Stairs & Trim LLC...561 547-9888
436 Lytle St West Palm Beach (33405) ***(G-18047)***
Kings & Queens Cabinets...863 646-6972
841 Windsor St Lakeland (33803) ***(G-7369)***
Kings Creek Flowers, Miami *Also called Ebs Quality Service Inc* ***(G-9067)***
Kings Four Crners Auto Dtling...866 886-4383
940 Us Highway 27 Clermont (34714) ***(G-1873)***
Kings Han Manufacturing, Englewood *Also called King Han Inc* ***(G-3519)***
Kings Pharmacy, Coral Springs *Also called King Pharmaceuticals LLC* ***(G-2174)***
Kingspan - Asi, Deland *Also called Kingspan Insulated Panels Inc* ***(G-2881)***
Kingspan Deland Plant, Deland *Also called Kingspan Insulated Panels Inc* ***(G-2882)***
Kingspan Insulated Panels Inc (HQ)...386 626-6789
726 Summerhill Dr Deland (32724) ***(G-2881)***
Kingspan Insulated Panels Inc...386 626-6789
725 Summerhill Dr Deland (32724) ***(G-2882)***
Kingspan Insulation LLC...305 921-0100
12501 Nw 38th Ave Opa Locka (33054) ***(G-11760)***
Kingspan-Medusa Inc (HQ)...386 626-6789
726 Summerhill Dr Deland (32724) ***(G-2883)***

Kingston Automotive & Wldg LLC 727 378-4881
8039 Palatine Dr Hudson (34667) (G-5780)

Kino Sandals Inc 305 294-5044
107 Fitzpatrick St Key West (33040) (G-6871)

Kino Shoe Factory, Key West Also called Kino Sandals Inc (G-6871)

Kira Labs Inc 954 978-4549
3400 Gateway Dr Ste 100 Pompano Beach (33069) (G-14071)

Kirchman Corporation (PA) 877 384-0936
2001 Summit Park Dr # 100 Orlando (32810) (G-12288)

Kirkland Industries LLC 386 496-3491
4638 Sw 150th Rd Lake Butler (32054) (G-7003)

Kirtech Enterprises Inc 352 742-7222
28210 Lake Indus Blvd Tavares (32778) (G-17515)

Kiskeya Minerals Usa LLC 305 328-5082
8249 Nw 70th St Miami (33166) (G-9391)

Kiss Polymers LLC 813 962-2703
12515 Sugar Pine Way Tampa (33624) (G-16989)

Kissimmee Iron Works Inc 407 870-8872
2741 Old Dixie Hwy Kissimmee (34744) (G-6934)

Kissimmee Printing 407 518-2514
1230 Simpson Rd Kissimmee (34744) (G-6935)

Kit Residential Designs Inc 305 796-5940
5921 Nw 176th St Unit 2 Hialeah (33015) (G-5211)

Kitchen & Bath Center Inc (PA) 850 244-3996
20 Ready Ave Nw Fort Walton Beach (32548) (G-4594)

Kitchen and Bath Universe Inc 813 887-5658
6606 N 56th St Tampa (33610) (G-16990)

Kitchen Classics LLC 941 629-6990
4265 Tamiami Trl Unit K Punta Gorda (33980) (G-14511)

Kitchen Counter Connections 386 677-9471
123 N Orchard St Ste 3e Ormond Beach (32174) (G-12775)

Kitchen Design Center, Fort Walton Beach Also called Gulf South Distributors Inc (G-4591)

Kitchen Dsgns By Joan E Rbbins 321 727-0012
7690 Industrial Rd Melbourne (32904) (G-8450)

Kitchen Sink Express LLC 800 888-6604
1986 Brae Moor Dr Dunedin (34698) (G-3453)

Kitchen USA Inc 904 714-1970
6965 Philips Hwy Jacksonville (32216) (G-6244)

Kitchenest, Doral Also called Creative Home and Kitchen LLC (G-3177)

Kitchens By US, Pembroke Pines Also called M X Corporation (G-13401)

Kitchens By US 407 745-4923
4201 L B Mcleod Rd Orlando (32811) (G-12289)

Kitchens Crafters Inc 407 788-0560
302 Black Gum Trl Longwood (32779) (G-7911)

Kitchens Rta LLC 407 969-0902
2467 N John Young Pkwy Orlando (32804) (G-12290)

Kitchens, Baths & Closets, Boca Raton Also called Got It Inc (G-531)

Kite Technology Group LLC 407 557-0512
2642 Michigan Ave Ste C Kissimmee (34744) (G-6936)

Kiteman Productions Inc 407 943-8480
5200 Ridgeway Dr Orlando (32819) (G-12291)

Kitko Corp 786 287-8900
10773 Nw 58th St Ste 87 Doral (33178) (G-3273)

Kizable LLC 727 600-3469
1125 Ne 16th Ter Fort Lauderdale (33304) (G-3907)

Kj Collections, Ponte Vedra Beach Also called Lynn Jackson Kimberly (G-14271)

Kj Reynolds Inc 904 829-6488
3520 Ag Ctr Dr Ste 306 Saint Augustine (32092) (G-14853)

KLA Industries 727 315-4719
801 West Bay Dr Ste 203 Largo (33770) (G-7626)

Klaaventura LLC 305 931-2322
600 Sw 1st Ave Miami (33130) (G-9392)

Kleen Wheels Corporation 954 791-9112
5000 Oakes Rd Ste H Davie (33314) (G-2430)

Kleids Enterprises Inc 727 796-7900
22023 Us Highway 19 N Clearwater (33765) (G-1662)

Klimaire Products Inc 305 593-8358
2190 Nw 89th Pl Doral (33172) (G-3274)

Klinco Inc 734 949-4999
2164 Nw 22nd Ct Miami (33142) (G-9393)

Kling Fabrication Inc 727 321-7233
6563 46th St N Ste 705 Pinellas Park (33781) (G-13699)

Klocke of America Inc 239 561-5800
16260 Arprt Pk Dr Ste 125 Fort Myers (33913) (G-4306)

Klopfer Holdings Inc 727 472-2002
2134 Sunnydale Blvd Clearwater (33765) (G-1663)

Klopp Coin Counters, Oldsmar Also called Klopp International Inc (G-11666)

Klopp International Inc 813 855-6789
237 Dunbar Ct Oldsmar (34677) (G-11666)

Klopp of Florida Inc 813 855-6789
251 Dunbar Ave Oldsmar (34677) (G-11667)

Kloth Inc 954 578-5687
10111 Nw 46th St Sunrise (33351) (G-16334)

Klugman Enterprises LLC 352 318-9623
7410 Linden Ln Sarasota (34243) (G-15508)

Klyo Medical Systems Inc 305 330-5025
1464 Nw 82nd Ave Doral (33126) (G-3275)

Km Coatings Mfg Jr 602 253-1168
1111 W Newport Center Dr Deerfield Beach (33442) (G-2748)

Km Industrial Racking Inc 813 900-7457
8989 Ulmerton Rd Largo (33771) (G-7627)

Km Precast Inc 239 438-2146
7701 Gardner Dr Unit 101 Naples (34109) (G-10799)

Km Press Dental Ceramics LLC 828 299-8500
8900 Blind Pass Rd A306 Sarasota (34242) (G-15719)

Kme, Ocala Also called Kovatch Mobile Equipment Corp (G-11420)

Kme Amrica Mar Tube Ftting LLC 904 265-4001
3440 Evergreen Ave Jacksonville (32206) (G-6245)

Kmg Marketing LLC 727 376-7200
11515 Pyramid Dr Odessa (33556) (G-11563)

Kmr Concrete Inc 863 519-9077
2835 State Road 60 E Bartow (33830) (G-314)

Kms Medical LLC 305 266-3388
13755 Sw 119th Ave Miami (33186) (G-9394)

Kmss Products Inc 800 646-3005
9225 Ulmerton Rd Ste D Largo (33771) (G-7628)

Kn Machine & Tools Inc 561 748-3035
3125 Jupiter Park Cir # 4 Jupiter (33458) (G-6754)

Knb Manufacturers 407 733-0364
1817 Barksdale Dr Orlando (32822) (G-12292)

KNex Ltd Partnership Group 215 997-7722
301 E Yamato Rd Ste 4200 Boca Raton (33431) (G-570)

Knight Bacon Associates 772 388-5115
9577 Gator Dr Unit 1 Sebastian (32958) (G-15897)

Knight Fire & Security Inc 561 471-8221
7513 Central Indus Dr Riviera Beach (33404) (G-14639)

Knight Industrial Eqp Inc 863 646-2997
3701 Airfield Dr W Lakeland (33811) (G-7370)

Knight Industries 772 344-2053
1001 Sw Cornelia Ave Port Saint Lucie (34953) (G-14420)

Knight Vision Lllp 321 607-9900
701 Columbia Blvd Titusville (32780) (G-17598)

Knight Welding Supply LLC 561 889-5342
3131 Se Waaler St Stuart (34997) (G-16175)

Knight-Rddr/Miami Herald Cr Un 305 376-2181
1 Herald Plz Fl 2 Miami (33132) (G-9395)

Knights Farm Fresh Feeds Inc 352 793-2242
5376 Cr 316a Bushnell (33513) (G-1245)

Knights Manufacturing Company 321 607-9900
701 Columbia Blvd Titusville (32780) (G-17599)

Knightsbridge Steel LLC 786 532-0290
507 W 17th St Hialeah (33010) (G-5212)

Knopf & Sons Bindery Inc (PA) 904 353-5115
1817 Florida Ave Jacksonville (32206) (G-6246)

Knopf & Sons Bindery Inc 904 355-4411
1817 Florida Ave Jacksonville (32206) (G-6247)

Knothole Creations Inc 727 561-9107
13205 40th St N Clearwater (33762) (G-1664)

Knowles Plastics Inc 954 232-8756
10301 Nw 16th Ct Coral Springs (33071) (G-2175)

Knowles' Mobile Marine, Coral Springs Also called Knowles Plastics Inc (G-2175)

Knox Aluminum Inc 813 645-3529
720 4th St Sw Ste B Ruskin (33570) (G-14780)

Ko Orthotics Inc 954 570-8096
5130 Heron Ct Coconut Creek (33073) (G-1996)

Koala Tee Inc (usa) 941 954-7700
2160 17th St Sarasota (34234) (G-15720)

Kobalt Music Pubg Amer Inc 305 200-5682
2100 Ponce De Leon Blvd Coral Gables (33134) (G-2078)

Kobetron LLC 850 939-5222
1778 Sea Lark Ln Navarre (32566) (G-10951)

Kodiak Software Inc 727 599-8839
832 Narcissus Ave Clearwater (33767) (G-1665)

Kohler Sdmo, Miramar Also called Sdmo Generating Sets Inc (G-10541)

Koho Software Inc 813 390-1309
6030 Printery St Unit 103 Tampa (33616) (G-16991)

Kohtler Elevator Inds Inc (PA) 305 687-7037
4115 Nw 132nd St Unit B Opa Locka (33054) (G-11761)

Koki Interiors Furn Mfg Inc 305 558-6573
7680 W 7th Ave Hialeah (33014) (G-5213)

Kolich Electric Motor Co Inc 954 969-8605
3420 Nw 25th Ave Pompano Beach (33069) (G-14072)

Kollsman Inc 407 312-1384
12600 Challenger Pkwy Orlando (32826) (G-12293)

Kollsman Instrument Division, Palm Beach Gardens Also called Sequa
Corporation (G-13008)

Kollsut International Inc 305 438-6877
1763 Ne 162nd St North Miami Beach (33162) (G-11147)

Komatsu Mining Corp 407 491-0758
3253 Hidden Lake Dr Winter Garden (34787) (G-18393)

Komatsu Mining Corp 863 804-0131
1321 State Road 630 W Fort Meade (33841) (G-4150)

Kombucha 221b.c., Sarasota Also called Mad At SAD LLC (G-15732)

Kommander Software Inc 407 906-2121
2271 E Steven St Inverness (34453) (G-5832)

Kommercial Refrigeration Inc 863 299-3000
810 Hillside Ct N Winter Haven (33881) (G-18447)

Kona Gold LLC 844 714-2224
746 North Dr Ste A Melbourne (32934) (G-8451)

Konadocks LLC 407 909-0606
　230 Deer Island Rd　Winter Garden (34787) *(G-18394)*

Koncept Systems LLC 786 610-0122
　10755 Sw 244th Ter　Homestead (33032) *(G-5724)*

Kone Crane Maintenance Svcs 813 707-0086
　2007 Wood Ct Ste 5　Plant City (33563) *(G-13783)*

Konecranes Inc 813 707-0086
　3633 Century Blvd Ste 2　Lakeland (33811) *(G-7371)*

Konnected Inc 407 286-3138
　5718 Old Cheney Hwy　Orlando (32807) *(G-12294)*

Konus USA Corporation 305 884-7618
　7530 Nw 79th St　Medley (33166) *(G-8266)*

Kony Inc 407 730-5669
　7380 W Sand Lake Rd # 390　Orlando (32819) *(G-12295)*

Kookie Kllection Kosmetics LLC 888 811-1657
　2645 Executive Park Dr　Weston (33331) *(G-18262)*

Kool Ledz LLC 561 212-5843
　21238 Stonewood Dr　Boca Raton (33428) *(G-571)*

Koozie Group, Clearwater *Also called Scribe Opco Inc (G-1778)*

Kopy Kats Club Ormond Bch Inc 386 437-3281
　74 Bridgewater Ln　Ormond Beach (32174) *(G-12776)*

Koral Manufacturing Inc 727 548-5040
　8720 66th Ct N　Pinellas Park (33782) *(G-13700)*

Koral Precision LLC 727 548-5040
　8720 66th Ct N　Pinellas Park (33782) *(G-13701)*

Korangy Publishing Inc 786 334-5052
　6318 Biscayne Blvd　Miami (33138) *(G-9396)*

Koszegi Industries Inc 954 419-9544
　1801 Green Rd Ste E　Deerfield Beach (33064) *(G-2749)*

Kova Laboratories Inc 954 978-8730
　1711 Banks Rd　Margate (33063) *(G-8139)*

Kovatch Mobile Equipment Corp 800 235-3928
　1703 Sw 42nd Ave　Ocala (34474) *(G-11420)*

Kover Corp 305 888-0146
　1375 Nw 97th Ave Ste 12　Doral (33172) *(G-3276)*

Kozuba & Sons Distillery Inc 813 857-8197
　1960 5th Ave S　Saint Petersburg (33712) *(G-15105)*

Kpa LLC 352 671-9249
　1720 Sw 27th Pl　Ocala (34471) *(G-11421)*

KPc Southern Industries Inc 954 943-0254
　600 Ne 28th St　Pompano Beach (33064) *(G-14073)*

Kr Solutions Group US LLC 305 307-8353
　1500 Nw 89th Ct Ste 115　Doral (33172) *(G-3277)*

KR Ward Inc 863 325-9070
　1000 Hoover Rd　Winter Haven (33884) *(G-18448)*

Kraft Foods, Coral Gables *Also called Mondelez Global LLC (G-2089)*

Kraft Heinz Foods Company 904 632-3400
　735 E Bay St　Jacksonville (32202) *(G-6248)*

Kraft Heinz Foods Company 407 786-8157
　2180 W State Road 434 # 2112　Longwood (32779) *(G-7912)*

Kraft Heinz Foods Company 727 459-4527
　3901 52nd Ave N　Saint Petersburg (33714) *(G-15106)*

Kraft Heinz Foods Company 239 694-3663
　5521 Division Dr　Fort Myers (33905) *(G-4307)*

Kraft Heinz Foods Company 904 695-1300
　7500 Forshee Dr　Jacksonville (32219) *(G-6249)*

Kraken Koffee LLC 833 546-3725
　2555 Ponce De Leon Blvd　Coral Gables (33134) *(G-2079)*

Kramer Pharmacal Inc 305 226-0641
　8900 Sw 24th St　Miami (33165) *(G-9397)*

Kramski North America Inc 727 828-1500
　8222 118th Ave Ste 650　Largo (33773) *(G-7629)*

Krane Environmental, Venice *Also called K V Water Equipment & Krane Co (G-17702)*

Kraton Chemical LLC (HQ) 904 928-8700
　4600 Touchton Rd E # 1200　Jacksonville (32246) *(G-6250)*

Kraton Chemical LLC 850 785-8521
　2 S Everitt Ave　Panama City (32401) *(G-13282)*

Kratos Def & SEC Solutions Inc 866 606-5867
　8601 Transport Dr　Orlando (32832) *(G-12296)*

Krausz Usa Inc 352 509-3600
　331 Sw 57th Ave　Ocala (34474) *(G-11422)*

Kreate Printing Inc 305 542-1336
　3440 Ne 192nd St Apt 1c　Miami (33180) *(G-9398)*

Kreatech, Miami *Also called Kreate Printing Inc (G-9398)*

Kreateck International Corp 772 925-1216
　1707 20th St　Vero Beach (32960) *(G-17771)*

Kreative Ceramics Inc 321 278-9889
　2165 Twisted Pine Rd　Ocoee (34761) *(G-11522)*

Kreative Drive Inc 786 845-8605
　8953 Nw 23rd St　Doral (33172) *(G-3278)*

Kreyol Essence LLC 786 453-8287
　8325 Ne 2nd Ave Ste 117　Miami (33138) *(G-9399)*

Krieger Publishing Co Inc 321 724-9542
　1725 Krieger Ln　Malabar (32950) *(G-8085)*

Kristine Window Treatments LLC 305 623-8302
　15998 Nw 49th Ave　Hialeah (33014) *(G-5214)*

Krohn Lighting LLC 407 949-7231
　191 Varsity Cir　Altamonte Springs (32714) *(G-54)*

Krome Brewing Company LLC 786 601-9337
　17480 Sw 232nd St　Miami (33170) *(G-9400)*

Kron Designs LLC 954 941-0800
　6818 Nw 20th Ave　Fort Lauderdale (33309) *(G-3908)*

Kronos Incorporated 813 207-1987
　5405 Cypress Center Dr # 300　Tampa (33609) *(G-16992)*

Krs Global Biotechnology Inc 888 502-2050
　791 Park Of Commerce Blvd # 600　Boca Raton (33487) *(G-572)*

Krs Global Biotechnology Mfg, Boca Raton *Also called Krs Global Biotechnology Inc (G-572)*

Krs MSA LLC 727 264-7605
　1324 Seven Springs Blvd　New Port Richey (34655) *(G-10971)*

Krunchy Krisps LLC 561 309-7049
　2740 Sw Martin Downs Blvd　Palm City (34990) *(G-13048)*

Krunchy Melts, Hallandale Beach *Also called Jada Foods LLC (G-4954)*

Ksm Electronics Inc (PA) 954 642-7050
　6301 Nw 5th Way Ste 1500　Fort Lauderdale (33309) *(G-3909)*

Ksr Publishing Inc 941 388-7050
　2477 Stickney Point Rd 315b　Sarasota (34231) *(G-15721)*

Kt Properties & Dev Inc 386 253-0610
　500 Walker St　Daytona Beach (32117) *(G-2566)*

Kuando Trading Corp 786 603-3772
　1001 Brickell Bay Dr　Miami (33131) *(G-9401)*

Kulaga William John 727 536-3180
　2080 Envoy Ct　Clearwater (33764) *(G-1666)*

Kulfi LLC 855 488-4273
　1100 Holland Dr　Boca Raton (33487) *(G-573)*

Kus Usa Inc 954 463-1075
　3350 Davie Rd Ste 203　Davie (33314) *(G-2431)*

Kusser Fountainworks, Tampa *Also called Kusser Graniteworks Usa Inc (G-16993)*

Kusser Graniteworks Usa Inc 813 248-3428
　3109 E 4th Ave　Tampa (33605) *(G-16993)*

Kustom Industrial Fabricators 407 965-1940
　265 Hunt Park Cv　Longwood (32750) *(G-7913)*

Kustom Us Inc (PA) 407 965-1940
　640 E State Road 434 # 1000　Longwood (32750) *(G-7914)*

Kw Products Inc 813 855-7817
　305 Mears Blvd　Oldsmar (34677) *(G-11668)*

Kwik Kerb LLC 386 453-1004
　844 Williams Ln　Port Orange (32127) *(G-14337)*

Kwik Kopy Printing, Fort Myers *Also called J & J Litho Enterprises Inc (G-4294)*

Kwikie Dup Ctr Pinellas Pk Inc 727 544-7788
　8520 49th St N　Pinellas Park (33781) *(G-13702)*

Kwikie Printing, Pinellas Park *Also called Kwikie Dup Ctr Pinellas Pk Inc (G-13702)*

Kwikprint Manufacturing Co Inc 904 737-3755
　4868 Victor St　Jacksonville (32207) *(G-6251)*

Kyaeto Systems, Saint Petersburg *Also called Donovan Home Services LLC (G-15027)*

Kyocera AVX Cmpnnts Jcksnvlle 904 724-2000
　2201 Corporate Sq Blvd　Jacksonville (32216) *(G-6252)*

Kyocera Dcment Sltons Sthast L 772 562-0511
　480 Okeechobee Rd Ste 101　Fort Pierce (34947) *(G-4499)*

Kyp Go Inc 386 736-3770
　1551 Lakeside Dr　Deland (32720) *(G-2884)*

Kysor Industrial Corporation (HQ) 727 376-8600
　2227 Welbilt Blvd　Trinity (34655) *(G-17638)*

Kysor Warren, Trinity *Also called Kysor Industrial Corporation (G-17638)*

Kz Manufacturing LLC 305 257-2628
　24601 Packinghouse Rd # 1　Princeton (33032) *(G-14488)*

L & A Quality Products Inc 305 326-9300
　2181 Nw 10th Ave　Miami (33127) *(G-9402)*

L & C Metals LLC 407 859-2600
　711 Central Florida Pkwy　Orlando (32824) *(G-12297)*

L & D Steel USA Inc 727 538-9917
　13240 Belcher Rd S　Largo (33773) *(G-7630)*

L & H Boats Inc 772 288-2291
　3350 Se Slater St　Stuart (34997) *(G-16176)*

L & L Automotive Electric Inc 631 471-5230
　4575 Carolwood Dr　Melbourne (32934) *(G-8452)*

L & L Orna Alum Ironworks Inc 561 547-5605
　5601 Georgia Ave　West Palm Beach (33405) *(G-18048)*

L & M Pallet Services Inc 863 519-3502
　1190 Us Highway 17 S　Bartow (33830) *(G-315)*

L & N Label Company Inc 727 442-5400
　2051 Sunnydale Blvd　Clearwater (33765) *(G-1667)*

L & S Bait Co Inc 727 584-7691
　1415 E Bay Dr　Largo (33771) *(G-7631)*

L & S Design & Construction 772 220-1745
　3561 Sw Corporate Pkwy　Palm City (34990) *(G-13049)*

L A Ornamental & Rack Corp 305 696-0419
　3708 Nw 82nd St　Miami (33147) *(G-9403)*

L A R Manufacturing LLC 727 846-7860
　6828 Commerce Ave　Port Richey (34668) *(G-14367)*

L A Rust Inc 954 749-5009
　10231 Nw 53rd St　Sunrise (33351) *(G-16335)*

L and C Science and Tech Inc 305 200-3531
　2205 W 80th St Ste 1　Hialeah (33016) *(G-5215)*

L and D Logging 850 859-1013
　701 Sandspur Rd　Westville (32464) *(G-18301)*

L and TW Oodwork LLC 305 742-4362
　17420 Sw 236th St　Homestead (33031) *(G-5725)*

(G-0000) Company's Geographic Section entry number

L C Acme Barricades 813 623-2263
  2611 S 82nd St Tampa (33619) *(G-16994)*
L C Acme Barricades 863 816-5874
  8135 Tomkow Rd Lakeland (33809) *(G-7372)*
L C Acme Barricades 561 657-8222
  3705 Interstate Park Way Riviera Beach (33404) *(G-14640)*
L C Ch International Inc 305 888-1323
  7395 W 18th Ln Hialeah (33014) *(G-5216)*
L C Clark Publishing Inc 561 627-3393
  600 Sandtree Dr Ste 107 Palm Beach Gardens (33403) *(G-12982)*
L C Industries Inc 850 581-0117
  125 Bennett Ave Hurlburt Field (32544) *(G-5792)*
L C La Finestra 305 599-8093
  2790 Nw 104th Ct Doral (33172) *(G-3279)*
L C Npee 888 316-3718
  451 E 10th Ct Hialeah (33010) *(G-5217)*
L C Southwind Manufacturing 352 687-1999
  415 Cypress Rd Ocala (34472) *(G-11423)*
L D F Services 386 947-9256
  1111 State Ave Daytona Beach (32117) *(G-2567)*
L E M G Inc 727 461-5300
  1878 Drew St Clearwater (33765) *(G-1668)*
L J'S Tops & Bottoms, Boynton Beach *Also called Ljs Tops & Bottoms (G-887)*
L M Compressor LLC 352 484-0850
  5800 Sw 25th St Ste 100 Ocala (34474) *(G-11424)*
L P I, Hollywood *Also called LPI Industries Corporation (G-5615)*
L R Gator Corporation 407 578-6616
  4380 L B Mcleod Rd Orlando (32811) *(G-12298)*
L R M, Rockledge *Also called Lrm Industries Intl Inc (G-14727)*
L R P, Palm Beach Gardens *Also called Lrp Publications Inc (G-12988)*
L S I, Miami *Also called Logistic Systems Inc (G-9472)*
L W Timber Co Inc 850 592-2597
  3830 Highway 69 Greenwood (32443) *(G-4855)*
L&R Imaging 678 691-3204
  2450 W Sample Rd Ste 8 Pompano Beach (33073) *(G-14074)*
L-3 Cmmnctons Advnced Lser Sys 407 295-5878
  2500 N Orange Blossom Trl Orlando (32804) *(G-12299)*
L-3 Cmmnctons Ntronix Holdings 212 697-1111
  1025 W Nasa Blvd Melbourne (32919) *(G-8453)*
L2d Outdoors Inc 954 757-6116
  4300 Nw 120th Ave Coral Springs (33065) *(G-2176)*
L3 Aviation Products Inc 941 371-0811
  490 1st Ave S Ste 600 Saint Petersburg (33701) *(G-15107)*
L3 Crestview Aerospace 850 682-2746
  5486 Fairchild Rd Crestview (32539) *(G-2249)*
L3 Technologies, Saint Petersburg *Also called L3 Aviation Products Inc (G-15107)*
L3 Technologies Inc 321 409-6122
  1200 Woody Burke Rd Melbourne (32901) *(G-8454)*
L3 Technologies Inc 941 371-0811
  490 1st Ave S Saint Petersburg (33701) *(G-15108)*
L3 Technologies Inc 904 269-5026
  208 Industrial Loop S Orange Park (32073) *(G-11832)*
L3 Technologies Inc 407 295-5878
  2500 N Orange Blossom Trl Orlando (32804) *(G-12300)*
L3 Technologies Inc 407 354-0047
  7675 Municipal Dr Orlando (32819) *(G-12301)*
L3harris Interstate Elec Corp 321 730-0119
  Cape Cnvral Ar Bldg 54815 Cocoa Beach (32932) *(G-1973)*
L3harris Interstate Elec Corp 321 730-0119
  Air Force Sta Bldg 54815 Cape Canaveral (32920) *(G-1288)*
L3harris Technologies Inc (PA) 321 727-9100
  1025 W Nasa Blvd Melbourne (32919) *(G-8455)*
L3harris Technologies Inc 321 309-7848
  407 N John Rodes Blvd Melbourne (32934) *(G-8456)*
L3harris Technologies Inc 407 581-3782
  7022 Tpc Dr Ste 500 Orlando (32822) *(G-12302)*
L3harris Technologies Inc 260 451-6814
  5690 W Cypress St Ste B Tampa (33607) *(G-16995)*
L3harris Technologies Inc 321 768-4660
  2800 Jordan Blvd Malabar (32950) *(G-8086)*
L3harris Technologies Inc 321 727-4255
  Plant 16 Troutman Blvd Palm Bay (32905) *(G-12906)*
L3harris Technologies Inc 321 727-4660
  1000 Charles J Herbert Dr Palm Bay (32905) *(G-12907)*
L3harris Technologies Inc 321 984-0782
  150 S Wickham Rd Melbourne (32904) *(G-8457)*
L3harris Technologies Inc 321 727-4000
  1025 W Nasa Blvd Melbourne (32902) *(G-8458)*
L3harris Technologies Inc 321 727-9100
  1025 W Nasa Blvd Melbourne (32919) *(G-8459)*
L4 Design LLC (PA) 407 262-8200
  2701 Mtland Ctr Pkwy Ste Maitland (32751) *(G-8065)*
L4 Design LLC 224 612-5045
  2701 Mtland Ctr Pkwy Ste Maitland (32751) *(G-8066)*
La Autentica 786 409-3779
  2294 W 78th St Hialeah (33016) *(G-5218)*
La Autentica Foods Inc 305 888-6727
  2294 W 78th St Hialeah (33016) *(G-5219)*
La Caja China, Hialeah *Also called L C Ch International Inc (G-5216)*

La Chiquita Tortilla Mfr 407 251-8290
  6918 Presidents Dr Orlando (32809) *(G-12303)*
La Coronella Meat Processing 305 691-2630
  9566 Nw 7th Ave Miami (33150) *(G-9404)*
La Cuisine Intl Distrs Inc 305 418-0010
  2005 Nw 115th Ave Miami (33172) *(G-9405)*
La Esquina Del Le Billto 305 477-4225
  8601 Nw 58th St Unit 101 Doral (33166) *(G-3280)*
La Esquina Del Lechon, Doral *Also called La Esquina Del Le Billto (G-3280)*
La Experiencia Crankshaft 305 823-6161
  9910 Nw 80th Ave Unit 2m Hialeah Gardens (33016) *(G-5440)*
La Fabrika Retail Services LLC 786 525-4491
  6303 Blue Lagoon Dr Ste 4 Miami (33126) *(G-9406)*
La Gaceta Publishing Inc 813 248-3921
  3210 E 7th Ave Tampa (33605) *(G-16996)*
La Gaceta Tri-Lingual Weekly, Tampa *Also called La Gaceta Publishing Inc (G-16996)*
La Genomics LLC 407 909-1120
  5939 Blakeford Dr Windermere (34786) *(G-18358)*
La Glass, Miami *Also called MA Glass & Mirror LLC (G-9493)*
La Lechonera Media, Miami *Also called La Lechonera Products Inc (G-9407)*
La Lechonera Products Inc 305 635-2303
  2161 Nw 22nd Ct Miami (33142) *(G-9407)*
La Luna Ltd 305 644-0444
  1638 Sw 8th St Miami (33135) *(G-9408)*
La Mansion Latina LLC 305 406-1606
  9183 Sw 152nd Path Miami (33196) *(G-9409)*
La Mar Orlando LLC 407 423-2051
  621 Commonwealth Ave Orlando (32803) *(G-12304)*
La Montina Inc 305 324-0083
  1445 Nw 22nd St Miami (33142) *(G-9410)*
La Moti Roof & Tile Inc 305 635-2641
  1360 Nw 29th St Miami (33142) *(G-9411)*
La Parada Criolla Inc 321 207-7100
  254 W State Road 434 Longwood (32750) *(G-7915)*
La Pavers Inc 407 209-9163
  2349 Lake Debra Dr Orlando (32835) *(G-12305)*
La Perle Memorials, Inverness *Also called Perl Inc (G-5833)*
La Perlelle LLC 941 388-2458
  17 Fillmore Dr Sarasota (34236) *(G-15722)*
La Perrada Del Gordo Boca LLC 561 968-6978
  2650 S Military Trl West Palm Beach (33415) *(G-18049)*
La Physique', Eustis *Also called A Living Testimony LLC (G-3551)*
La Prensa, Longwood *Also called Impremedia LLC (G-7903)*
La Providencia Express Co 305 409-9894
  4728 Sw 74th Ave Miami (33155) *(G-9412)*
La Province Inc 305 538-2406
  2106 Nw 13th Ave Miami (33142) *(G-9413)*
La Real Foods Inc 305 232-6449
  13013 Sw 122nd Ave Miami (33186) *(G-9414)*
La Real Tortillas, Miami *Also called La Real Foods Inc (G-9414)*
La Sin Rival, Miami *Also called Gregomarc LLC (G-9247)*
La Tropical Brewing Co LLC 786 362-5429
  1825 Ponce De Leon Blvd Coral Gables (33134) *(G-2080)*
La Villarena Meat & Pork Inc (PA) 305 759-0555
  6455 Ne 3rd Ave Miami (33138) *(G-9415)*
La Voz De La Calle, Hialeah *Also called Voice Publishing Co Inc (G-5414)*
La Zero Inc 727 545-1175
  8100 Park Blvd N Ste 41 Pinellas Park (33781) *(G-13703)*
Laal Manufacturing Inc 786 859-3613
  55 Ne 1st St Ste 55 # 55 Miami (33132) *(G-9416)*
Lab Kingz LLC 561 808-4216
  514 Sw 15th Ter Delray Beach (33444) *(G-2982)*
Label Company 850 438-7334
  680 E Heinberg St Pensacola (32502) *(G-13535)*
Label Graphics Inc 561 798-8180
  11298 Roselynn Way Lake Worth (33449) *(G-7213)*
Label Printing Service 727 820-1226
  1245 N Hercules Ave Clearwater (33765) *(G-1669)*
Label Tape Systems, Sarasota *Also called Dongili Investment Group Inc (G-15660)*
Labelclick Inc 727 548-8345
  630 Brooker Creek Blvd # 340 Oldsmar (34677) *(G-11669)*
Labelflex, Miami *Also called Tradingflex Inc (G-10034)*
Labelle Brick Pavers Tile LLC 863 230-3100
  1515 Forestry Division Rd Labelle (33935) *(G-6982)*
Labelpro Inc 727 538-2149
  14409 60th St N Clearwater (33760) *(G-1670)*
Labinal Power Systems, Sarasota *Also called Safran Power Uk Ltd (G-15548)*
Lablogic Systems Inc 813 626-6848
  1911 N Us Highway 301 # 140 Tampa (33619) *(G-16997)*
Lac Inc 407 671-6610
  3580 Aloma Ave Ste 1 Winter Park (32792) *(G-18518)*
Lactalogics Inc 772 202-0407
  8883 S Us Highway 1 Port Saint Lucie (34952) *(G-14421)*
Ladiesfitcamp LLC 954 226-7034
  6876 Sw 15th St North Lauderdale (33068) *(G-11083)*
Ladove Inc 305 823-8051
  5701 Miami Lakes Dr E Miami Lakes (33014) *(G-10311)*

A
L
P
H
A
B
E
T
I
C

Ladove Industries Inc..................................305 624-2456
5701 Miami Lakes Dr E Miami Lakes (33014) *(G-10312)*

Lagaci Inc...954 929-1395
2201 Stirling Rd Ste 101 Fort Lauderdale (33312) *(G-3910)*

Lagaci Sport, Fort Lauderdale *Also called Lagaci Inc (G-3910)*

Lahia America Corp....................................305 254-6212
12401 Sw 134th Ct Miami (33186) *(G-9417)*

Laird International Corp...............................954 532-3794
2300 Nw 30th Pl Bldg 9 Pompano Beach (33069) *(G-14075)*

Lajoie Investment Corp................................954 463-3271
819 Nw 7th Ter Fort Lauderdale (33311) *(G-3911)*

Lakay Vita LLC...786 985-7552
419 N Federal Hwy Apt 209 Hallandale Beach (33009) *(G-4957)*

Lake & Bay Boats LLC.................................813 949-7300
5770 Shirley St Naples (34109) *(G-10800)*

Lake Aerospace Services, Miramar *Also called VSI & Partners Inc (G-10562)*

Lake Area Watersports LLC............................352 475-3434
829 N State Road 21 Melrose (32666) *(G-8571)*

Lake City Mediplex LLC................................386 752-2209
162 Nw Birdie Pl Lake City (32055) *(G-7026)*

Lake City Reporter, Lake City *Also called Community News Papers Inc (G-7015)*

Lake Door and Trim Inc...............................352 589-5566
1589 Pine Grove Rd Eustis (32726) *(G-3562)*

Lake News, Mount Dora *Also called Triangle Shopping Guide Inc (G-10616)*

Lake News LLC..407 251-1314
9836 Sweetleaf St Orlando (32827) *(G-12306)*

Lake Park Auto Machine Inc...........................561 848-6197
404 Foresta Ter West Palm Beach (33415) *(G-18050)*

Lake Point Restoration LLC............................561 924-9100
12012 South Shore Blvd # 10 Wellington (33414) *(G-17854)*

Lake Sentinel, Tavares *Also called Sentinel Cmmnctons News Vntres (G-17522)*

Lake Worth Herald Press Inc.........................561 585-9387
1313 Central Ter Lake Worth (33460) *(G-7214)*

Lakeland Box Spring 0026, Lakeland *Also called Leggett & Platt Incorporated (G-7378)*

Lakeland Lures Inc.....................................863 644-3127
955 Oak Ln Lakeland (33811) *(G-7373)*

Lakeland Outdoor Advertising, Coral Gables *Also called Outdoor Media Inc (G-2094)*

Lakeridge Winery & Vineyards, Clermont *Also called Seavin Inc (G-1882)*

Lakes Metal Fabrication Inc...........................954 731-2010
2350 Nw 30th Ct Oakland Park (33311) *(G-11275)*

Lakeshore Custom Wood Pdts Inc......................813 623-2790
5210 Shadowlawn Ave Tampa (33610) *(G-16998)*

Lakeside Publishing Co LLC............................847 491-6440
3180 Burgundy Dr N Palm Beach Gardens (33410) *(G-12983)*

Lakeside Recreational Inc............................863 467-1530
4074 Us Highway 441 Se Okeechobee (34974) *(G-11611)*

Lakeview Dirt Co Inc..................................904 824-2586
105 Beechers Point Dr Welaka (32193) *(G-17840)*

Lakewood Juices, Miami *Also called Allapattah Industries Inc (G-8694)*

Lakewood Manufacturing Co Inc........................443 398-5015
10696 Grande Blvd West Palm Beach (33412) *(G-18051)*

Lakewood Manufacutring, West Palm Beach *Also called Lakewood Manufacturing Co Inc (G-18051)*

Lakewood Organics LLC...............................305 324-5900
2125 Nw 10th Ct Miami (33127) *(G-9418)*

Lamartek Inc..386 752-1087
175 Nw Washington St Lake City (32055) *(G-7027)*

Lamb Tec Inc...305 798-6266
7755 Sw 193rd Ln Cutler Bay (33157) *(G-2293)*

Lambert Corporation Florida...........................407 841-2940
20 Coburn Ave Orlando (32805) *(G-12307)*

Lambs Signs Inc......................................941 792-4453
4230 26th St W Bradenton (34205) *(G-1002)*

Laminar Flow Systems Inc.............................386 253-8833
1585 Avi Ctr Pkwy Ste 605 Daytona Beach (32114) *(G-2568)*

Laminations Southeast, Jacksonville *Also called Great Northern Corporation (G-6150)*

Lamm Industries Inc...................................718 368-0181
330 188th St Sunny Isles Beach (33160) *(G-16279)*

Lampshade Direct, Deerfield Beach *Also called Lampshades of Florida Inc (G-2750)*

Lampshades of Florida Inc.............................954 491-3377
4280 Nw 5th Dr Deerfield Beach (33442) *(G-2750)*

Lan Designs Inc..305 661-7878
7169 Sw 44th St Miami (33155) *(G-9419)*

Lan Industries LLC.....................................305 889-2087
5413 Nw 74th Ave Miami (33166) *(G-9420)*

Lan Music Corp...305 722-5842
13611 S Dixie Hwy Miami (33176) *(G-9421)*

Lanai Lights LLC.......................................239 415-2561
3411 Hanson St Unit A Fort Myers (33916) *(G-4308)*

Lanco & Harris Corp....................................407 240-4000
600 Mid Florida Dr Orlando (32824) *(G-12308)*

Land Leather Inc.......................................305 594-2260
1927 Nw 135th Ave Miami (33182) *(G-9422)*

Land Marine Service Inc...............................561 626-2947
2590 W Edgewater Dr West Palm Beach (33410) *(G-18052)*

Land O Lakes Winery LLC..............................813 995-9463
3901 Land O Lakes Blvd Land O Lakes (34639) *(G-7496)*

Landing Aerospace Inc................................305 687-0100
4604 Nw 133rd St Opa Locka (33054) *(G-11762)*

Landis Service Company, Tampa *Also called Coastal Wipers Inc (G-16716)*

Landmark Aviation.....................................305 296-5422
3471 S Roosevelt Blvd Key West (33040) *(G-6872)*

Landmark Fingerprinting...............................754 205-6505
1855 N State Road 7 Margate (33063) *(G-8140)*

Landmark Precast LLC.................................305 242-8888
438 Nw 10th Ave Homestead (33030) *(G-5726)*

Landscape/Irrigation, Fort Myers *Also called One Srce Prperty Solutions Inc (G-4351)*

Landtech Data Corporation............................561 790-1265
1460 Royal Palm Bch Blvd Royal Palm Beach (33411) *(G-14769)*

Landtech Software Co., Royal Palm Beach *Also called Landtech Data Corporation (G-14769)*

Lane Care LLC...727 316-3708
3241 Fox Chase Cir N Palm Harbor (34683) *(G-13118)*

Lane Construction Corporation........................863 665-0457
3350 Reynolds Rd Lakeland (33803) *(G-7374)*

Lanfranchi North America Inc..........................813 901-5333
8401 Benjamin Rd Ste A Tampa (33634) *(G-16999)*

Langstons Utility Buildings...........................813 659-0141
4298 State Road 60 W Mulberry (33860) *(G-10630)*

Lanzas Distributor Inc.................................305 885-5966
7251 Nw 54th St Miami (33166) *(G-9423)*

Lanzas Foods, Miami *Also called Lanzas Distributor Inc (G-9423)*

Lap of Amer Lser Applctons LLC.......................561 416-9250
161 Commerce Rd Ste 3 Boynton Beach (33426) *(G-884)*

Lapel Pin & Button Company Inc (PA)..................407 677-6144
10151 University Blvd Orlando (32817) *(G-12309)*

Lapin Sheet Metal Company............................407 423-9897
3825 Gardenia Ave Orlando (32839) *(G-12310)*

Lapolla Industries LLC................................954 379-0241
720 S Military Trl Deerfield Beach (33442) *(G-2751)*

Laporte Inv Holdings Inc..............................863 294-4498
512 6th St Nw Winter Haven (33881) *(G-18449)*

Lapure Water Products Inc............................727 521-3993
6330 46th St N Ste 112 Pinellas Park (33781) *(G-13704)*

Laras...305 576-0036
3841 Ne 2nd Ave Ste 301 Miami (33137) *(G-9424)*

Largent Fuels USA LLC.................................786 431-5981
1200 Brickell Ave Ste 240 Miami (33131) *(G-9425)*

Largo Aluminum Inc....................................305 852-2390
86500 Overseas Hwy Islamorada (33036) *(G-5837)*

Larrick Group Inc......................................941 351-2700
1845 57th St Sarasota (34243) *(G-15509)*

Larry Burr Printing Co, Winter Haven *Also called Burr Printing Co Inc (G-18426)*

Larry C Cribb..904 845-2804
28145 Enterprise Dr Hilliard (32046) *(G-5471)*

Larry Johnson Inc......................................305 888-2300
701 W 25th St Hialeah (33010) *(G-5220)*

Larry Woleys Trim Cabinets LLC.......................850 526-3974
3440 Larkspur Cir Marianna (32446) *(G-8168)*

Larrys Extreme Audio Tint LLC........................941 766-8468
19360 Strathcona Ave Port Charlotte (33954) *(G-14305)*

Larrys Mobilcrete Inc..................................352 336-2525
1104 Nw 50th Ave Ste A Gainesville (32609) *(G-4718)*

Larrys Rigs...561 967-7791
2460 Sunset Dr West Palm Beach (33415) *(G-18053)*

Larsen..305 989-4043
3 Melody Ln Stuart (34996) *(G-16177)*

Larsen Cabinetmaker Co...............................305 252-1212
14374 Sw 142nd Ave Miami (33186) *(G-9426)*

Larson Industries Incorporated (PA)..................352 262-0566
409 Sw 4th Ave Gainesville (32601) *(G-4719)*

Larson-Burton Incorporated..........................815 637-9500
1010 N Nova Rd Daytona Beach (32117) *(G-2569)*

Larter & Sons..732 290-1515
83 River Dr Jupiter (33469) *(G-6755)*

LAS & JB Inc..772 672-5315
4840 S Us Highway 1 Fort Pierce (34982) *(G-4500)*

Las Amrcas Mltimedia Group LLC.......................305 633-3341
888 Brickell Ave Ste 500 Miami (33131) *(G-9427)*

Las Zirh Americas Inc.................................305 942-7597
2792 Nw 24th St Miami (33142) *(G-9428)*

Lasalle Bristol Corporation...........................352 687-2151
9798 Se Maricamp Rd Ocala (34472) *(G-11425)*

Lasalle Bristol Corporation...........................863 680-1729
5030 Great Oak Dr Lakeland (33815) *(G-7375)*

Lase, Cutler Bay *Also called Light and Sound Equipment Inc (G-2294)*

Laser, Orlando *Also called Superior Metal (G-12637)*

Laser Assault...801 374-3400
9863 Creet Cir Navarre (32566) *(G-10952)*

Laser Cnstr & Restoration.............................786 536-2065
6043 Nw 167th St Ste A8 Hialeah (33015) *(G-5221)*

Laser Creations Incorporated.........................800 771-7151
946 Century Ln Apopka (32703) *(G-146)*

Laser Interceptor Usa LLC............................352 688-0708
18260 Mason Smith Rd Brooksville (34604) *(G-1170)*

Laser Lens Tek Inc...................................941 752-5811
6621 19th St E Sarasota (34243) *(G-15510)*

Laser Light Litho Corp..........305 899-0713
1440 Ne 131st St North Miami (33161) *(G-11108)*

Laser Magic, Apopka *Also called Laser Creations Incorporated* *(G-146)*

Laser Photo-Tooling Svcs Inc..........561 393-4710
5081 N Dixie Hwy Boca Raton (33431) *(G-574)*

LASER RESTORATION, Hialeah *Also called Laser Cnstr & Restoration* *(G-5221)*

Laser Surgical Florida Inc..........954 609-7639
900 Biscayne Blvd # 2001 Miami (33132) *(G-9429)*

Laserpath Technologies LLC..........407 247-3930
2789 Wrights Rd Ste 1021 Oviedo (32765) *(G-12835)*

Lasersight Incorporated (PA)..........407 678-9900
10244 E Clnl Dr Ste 201 Orlando (32817) *(G-12311)*

Lasersight Technologies Inc..........407 678-9900
10244 E Clnl Dr Ste 201 Orlando (32817) *(G-12312)*

Laserstar Technologies Corp..........401 438-1500
2461 Orlando Central Pkwy Orlando (32809) *(G-12313)*

Laserstar Technologies Corp..........407 248-1142
2453 Orlando Central Pkwy Orlando (32809) *(G-12314)*

Lash Makers LLC..........800 989-6912
65 Ne 16th St Miami (33132) *(G-9430)*

Lastrada Furniture Inc (PA)..........954 485-6000
1785 Nw 38th Ave Fort Lauderdale (33311) *(G-3912)*

Lastrada Furniture & Interiors, Fort Lauderdale *Also called Lastrada Furniture Inc* *(G-3912)*

Lata LLC..........772 324-8170
2447 Se Dixie Hwy Stuart (34996) *(G-16178)*

Latam Group Corp..........305 793-8961
12453 Sw 124th Ter Miami (33186) *(G-9431)*

Latam Optical LLC..........786 275-3284
2585 Nw 74th Ave Miami (33122) *(G-9432)*

Latamready LLC..........786 600-2641
12550 Biscayne Blvd North Miami (33181) *(G-11109)*

LAtelier Pris Hute Design LLC..........800 792-3550
6151 Biscayne Blvd Miami (33137) *(G-9433)*

Latham Marine Inc..........954 462-3055
280 Sw 32nd Ct Fort Lauderdale (33315) *(G-3913)*

Latham Plastics Inc..........813 783-7212
40119 County Road 54 Zephyrhills (33540) *(G-18619)*

Laticrete International Inc..........561 844-4667
6769 White Dr Ste A Riviera Beach (33407) *(G-14641)*

Latin Amercn Meats & Foods USA (PA)..........305 477-2700
6939 Nw 82nd Ave Miami (33166) *(G-9434)*

Latin Amrcn Fncl Pblctions Inc (HQ)..........305 416-5261
1101 Brickell Ave # 1200 Miami (33131) *(G-9435)*

Latin Dairy Foods LLC..........305 888-1788
2175 Nw 24th Ave Miami (33142) *(G-9436)*

Latin Goddess Press Inc..........917 703-1356
872 Leopard Trl Winter Springs (32708) *(G-18571)*

Latin Press Inc..........305 285-3133
600 Sw 22nd Ave Miami (33135) *(G-9437)*

Latin Quarters LLC (PA)..........954 470-8034
5100 Sw 6th St Margate (33068) *(G-8141)*

Latinfinance, Miami *Also called Latin Amrcn Fncl Pblctions Inc* *(G-9435)*

Latino Entps La Chqita Trtilla..........407 251-8290
6918 Presidents Dr Orlando (32809) *(G-12315)*

Latitude 235 Coffee and Tea (PA)..........941 556-2600
7245 21st St E Sarasota (34243) *(G-15511)*

Latitude 27 Canvas, Vero Beach *Also called Tony William Sitko* *(G-17808)*

Latitude 29 Publishing..........904 429-7889
2104 Sandy Branch Pl Saint Augustine (32092) *(G-14854)*

Latitude Clean Tech Group Inc..........561 417-0687
190 Nw Spanish River Blvd # 101 Boca Raton (33431) *(G-575)*

Latteri & Sons Inc..........813 876-1800
305 N Glen Ave Tampa (33609) *(G-17000)*

Latteri & Sons Vault and Monu, Tampa *Also called Latteri & Sons Inc* *(G-17000)*

Lau International Inc..........305 381-9855
36 Ne 1st St Ste 438 Miami (33132) *(G-9438)*

Lauderdale Graphics Corp (PA)..........954 450-0800
1625 Sw 117th Ave Davie (33325) *(G-2432)*

Laughing Mermaid The, Melbourne *Also called Pure Wave Organics Inc* *(G-8504)*

Laundromart..........561 487-4343
23182 Sandalfoot Plaza Dr Boca Raton (33428) *(G-576)*

Laura Knit Collection Inc (PA)..........305 945-8222
3224 Ne 167th St North Miami Beach (33160) *(G-11148)*

Laurey Co, Pompano Beach *Also called Strategic Brands Inc* *(G-14203)*

Lavi Enterprises LLC..........561 721-7170
1210 W 13th St Riviera Beach (33404) *(G-14642)*

Lavish Ice Cream LLC..........561 408-1616
500 S Australian Ave # 60 West Palm Beach (33401) *(G-18054)*

Lawex Corporation (PA)..........305 259-9755
1550 Madruga Ave Ste 508 Coral Gables (33146) *(G-2081)*

Lawko Inc..........904 389-2850
5126 Ortega Blvd Jacksonville (32210) *(G-6253)*

Lawrence Commercial Systems..........850 574-8723
451 Geddie Rd Tallahassee (32304) *(G-16468)*

Lawrence Factor Inc..........305 430-9152
4790 Nw 157th St Miami Lakes (33014) *(G-10313)*

Lawson Industries Inc (PA)..........305 696-8660
8501 Nw 90th St Medley (33166) *(G-8267)*

Lawton Connect, Orlando *Also called Lawton Printers Inc* *(G-12316)*

Lawton Printers Inc..........407 260-0400
649 Triumph Ct Orlando (32805) *(G-12316)*

Laycock Systems Inc..........813 248-3555
1601 N 43rd St Tampa (33605) *(G-17001)*

Laza Iron Works Inc..........305 754-8200
7251 N Miami Ave Miami (33150) *(G-9439)*

Lc Alliances, Key Biscayne *Also called Argos Global Partner Svcs LLC* *(G-6833)*

Lcf Pavers Inc..........239 826-8177
1825 Linhart Ave Lot 25 Fort Myers (33901) *(G-4309)*

LCI, Orlando *Also called C L Industries Inc* *(G-11973)*

LCI DISTRIBUTORS, Miami *Also called La Cuisine Intl Distrs Inc* *(G-9405)*

LCI-Ieu, Hurlburt Field *Also called L C Industries Inc* *(G-5792)*

Lcn Incorporated..........305 461-2770
6949 Nw 82nd Ave Miami (33166) *(G-9440)*

Lcr Signs & Services..........772 882-5276
2862 Se Buccaneer Cir Port Saint Lucie (34952) *(G-14422)*

Ld Telecommunications Inc..........954 628-3029
2101 W Commercial Blvd Fort Lauderdale (33309) *(G-3914)*

Ldc, Welaka *Also called Lakeview Dirt Co Inc* *(G-17840)*

LDI Printing and Signs, Tampa *Also called Sand Dollar Printing Inc* *(G-17245)*

LDM Industries Inc..........305 216-1545
12904 Sw 132nd Ct Miami (33186) *(G-9441)*

LDS Vacuum Products Inc (PA)..........407 862-4643
773 Big Tree Dr Longwood (32750) *(G-7916)*

Le Atelier Paris Haute Design, Miami *Also called Officine Gullo USA LLC* *(G-9639)*

Le Labo..........786 636-6928
2621 Nw 2nd Ave Miami (33127) *(G-9442)*

Le Mundo Vino LLC..........786 369-5232
12323 Sw 130th St Miami (33186) *(G-9443)*

Le Publications Inc..........954 766-8433
3600 W Commercial Blvd Fort Lauderdale (33309) *(G-3915)*

Le Soleil De La Floride, Hollywood *Also called Griffon Graphics Inc* *(G-5587)*

LE Wood Work Inc..........786 269-4275
3325 Nw 80th St Miami (33147) *(G-9444)*

Lead 2 Design..........954 757-6116
4302 Nw 120th Ave Coral Springs (33065) *(G-2177)*

Lead Enterprises Inc..........305 635-8644
3300 Nw 29th St Miami (33142) *(G-9445)*

Leadair Inc..........407 343-7571
113 Hangar Rd Kissimmee (34741) *(G-6937)*

Leader Mulch, Miami *Also called Rubber 2 Go Llc* *(G-9827)*

Leader Tech Inc..........813 855-6921
12420 Race Track Rd Tampa (33626) *(G-17002)*

Leadex..........305 266-2028
4731 Sw 75th Ave Miami (33155) *(G-9446)*

Leading Edge Aerospace Llc..........305 608-6826
16115 Nw 52nd Ave Miami Gardens (33014) *(G-10267)*

LEAFYWELL, Plantation *Also called Nxgen Brands LLC* *(G-13875)*

Leals Tires & Wheels..........239 491-2214
1585 Gretchen Ave S # 1 Lehigh Acres (33973) *(G-7813)*

Lean Design & Mfg Inc..........727 415-3504
19412 Livingston Ave Lutz (33559) *(G-7999)*

Lean Green Enterprises LLC..........954 525-2971
2125 S Andrews Ave Fort Lauderdale (33316) *(G-3916)*

Leandro Mora Studio LLC..........786 376-9166
4038 Nw 32nd Ave Miami (33142) *(G-9447)*

Lear Investors Inc (PA)..........305 681-8582
4154 Nw 132nd St Opa Locka (33054) *(G-11763)*

Learning For Life Press LLC..........352 234-0472
165 Morning Star Rd Venice (34285) *(G-17704)*

Leather Craftsmen Inc (PA)..........631 752-9000
700 Cocoanut Ave Unit 208 Sarasota (34236) *(G-15723)*

Leather or Not..........813 972-9667
17231 Dona Michelle Dr Tampa (33647) *(G-17003)*

Leatherjacket4, Lakeland *Also called Shaikh Rizwan* *(G-7432)*

Leatherworks Inc..........305 471-4430
9631 Nw 33rd St Doral (33172) *(G-3281)*

Leblon Cachaca, Miami *Also called Leblon LLC* *(G-9448)*

Leblon LLC..........954 649-0148
2701 S Le Jeune Rd Miami (33134) *(G-9448)*

Lecanto Ready Mix Con Plant, Lecanto *Also called Cemex Cnstr Mtls Fla LLC* *(G-7750)*

Lectora, Deerfield Beach *Also called Trivantis Corporation* *(G-2828)*

Led Are US LLC (PA)..........305 823-2803
9840 Nw 77th Ave Hialeah Gardens (33016) *(G-5441)*

Led Lghting Slutions Globl LLC..........855 309-1702
6118 Riverview Blvd Bradenton (34209) *(G-1003)*

Led Lighting, Hialeah Gardens *Also called Luminoso LLC* *(G-5442)*

Led Lighting Solutions, Bradenton *Also called Energy Management Products LLC* *(G-977)*

Led Nation Corp..........888 590-1720
7859 Nw 15th St Doral (33126) *(G-3282)*

Led Pro Services, Clearwater *Also called Icpf Development Group LLC* *(G-1637)*

Led Supply, The, Kissimmee *Also called Logic Illumination LLC* *(G-6939)*

Led Surf Lighting Inc..........239 687-4458
3425 Radio Rd Ste 202 Naples (34104) *(G-10801)*

Led Technologies Incorporated..........800 337-9565
12821 Starkey Rd Ste 4900 Largo (33773) *(G-7632)*

A L P H A B E T I C

Leda Printing Inc 941 922-1563
3939 S Tamiami Trl Sarasota (34231) *(G-15724)*

Ledger (HQ) 863 802-7000
300 W Lime St Lakeland (33815) *(G-7376)*

Ledger Publishing Company, Lakeland *Also called Ledger (G-7376)*

Ledradiant LLC 305 901-1313
615 N 21st Ave Hollywood (33020) *(G-5609)*

Lee Chemical Corporation 407 843-6950
460 W State Road 434 # 128 Longwood (32750) *(G-7917)*

Lee County Fuels Inc 239 349-5322
16272 Cutters Ct Fort Myers (33908) *(G-4310)*

Lee Designs Llc 239 278-4245
3300 Palm Ave Fort Myers (33901) *(G-4311)*

Lee Fisher International Inc 813 875-6296
3922 W Osborne Ave Tampa (33614) *(G-17004)*

Lee McCullough Inc 352 796-7100
Hud Brooksville (34606) *(G-1171)*

Lee Net Services Inc 904 777-4833
8216 Cheryl Ann Ln Jacksonville (32244) *(G-6254)*

Lee Printing Inc (PA) 904 396-5715
2653 Isabella Blvd Unit 4 Jacksonville Beach (32250) *(G-6637)*

Leeder Group Inc 305 436-5030
8508 Nw 66th St Miami (33166) *(G-9449)*

Leeds Machining Co 407 671-3688
4025 Bibb Ln Orlando (32817) *(G-12317)*

Leesburg Concrete Company Inc 352 787-4177
1335 Thomas Ave Leesburg (34748) *(G-7782)*

Leesburg Printing Company 352 787-3348
3606 Parkway Blvd Leesburg (34748) *(G-7783)*

Leeward Tech 305 215-4526
815 N Homestead Blvd # 405 Homestead (33030) *(G-5727)*

Lefab Commercial LLC 305 456-1306
76 Miracle Mile Coral Gables (33134) *(G-2082)*

Legacy Cabinet Company, The, Niceville *Also called Cljp Inc (G-11028)*

Legacy Cnstr Rmdlg Clg Svcs LL 800 638-9646
500 N Federal Hwy Ste 631 Hallandale Beach (33009) *(G-4958)*

Legacy Components LLC 813 964-6805
4613 N Clark Ave Tampa (33614) *(G-17005)*

Legacy Delights LLC 321 222-9330
1317 Edgewater Dr # 5119 Orlando (32804) *(G-12318)*

Legacy Publishing Services 407 647-3787
1883 Lee Rd Winter Park (32789) *(G-18519)*

Legacy Vulcan LLC 407 855-9902
8500 Florida Rock Rd Orlando (32824) *(G-12319)*

Legacy Vulcan LLC 407 321-5323
4150 Maverick Ct Sanford (32771) *(G-15351)*

Legacy Vulcan LLC 352 796-5690
14556 Ponce De Leon Blvd Brooksville (34601) *(G-1172)*

Legacy Vulcan LLC 727 321-4667
1020 31st St S Saint Petersburg (33712) *(G-15109)*

Legacy Vulcan LLC 407 299-7494
2858 Sidney Ave Orlando (32810) *(G-12320)*

Legacy Vulcan LLC 352 376-2182
924 S Main St Gainesville (32601) *(G-4720)*

Legacy Vulcan LLC 352 394-6196
3310 Green Swamp Rd Clermont (34714) *(G-1874)*

Legacy Vulcan LLC 850 951-0562
104 Lee S Pl Defuniak Springs (32435) *(G-2840)*

Legacy Vulcan LLC 863 687-7625
2300 Mershon St Lakeland (33815) *(G-7377)*

Legacy Vulcan LLC 386 659-2477
1 Mile W On Hwy 100 Grandin (32138) *(G-4810)*

Legacy Vulcan LLC 850 997-1490
2792 Gamble Rd Lloyd (32337) *(G-7857)*

Legacy Vulcan Corp 352 742-2122
27222 County Road 561 Tavares (32778) *(G-17516)*

Legacy Wdm LLC 352 799-5434
16228 Flight Path Dr Brooksville (34604) *(G-1173)*

Legal Components, Clearwater *Also called Ezell Precision Tool Co (G-1591)*

Legar Inc 561 635-5882
303 E Woolbright Rd # 103 Boynton Beach (33435) *(G-885)*

Legend Moto LLC 863 946-2002
1100 Us Highway 27 Moore Haven (33471) *(G-10590)*

Leggett & Platt Incorporated 727 856-3154
15800 Hudson Ave Spring Hill (34610) *(G-16086)*

Leggett & Platt Incorporated 954 846-0300
13800 Nw 4th St Sunrise (33325) *(G-16336)*

Leggett & Platt Incorporated 904 786-0750
925 Lane Ave N Jacksonville (32254) *(G-6255)*

Leggett & Platt Incorporated 863 666-8999
2715 Crystal Lk Acres Dr Lakeland (33801) *(G-7378)*

Lehigh Acrs Fre Cnrl & Rscue 239 303-5300
636 Thomas Sherwin Ave S Lehigh Acres (33974) *(G-7814)*

Lehigh Cement Company LLC 813 248-4000
3920 Pendola Point Rd Tampa (33619) *(G-17006)*

Lehigh Cement Company LLC 954 581-2812
3575 Sw 49th Way Davie (33314) *(G-2433)*

Lehigh Cement Company LLC 321 323-5039
9012 Marlin St Cape Canaveral (32920) *(G-1289)*

Lehigh White Cement Co LLC (HQ) 561 812-7439
1601 Forum Pl Ste 1110 West Palm Beach (33401) *(G-18055)*

Lehigh White Cement Co LLC 561 812-7441
3920 Pendola Point Rd Tampa (33619) *(G-17007)*

Leidos SEC Dtction Automtn Inc 407 926-1900
7558 Southland Blvd # 130 Orlando (32809) *(G-12321)*

Leila K Moavero 954 978-0018
1800 Nw 15th Ave Ste 140 Pompano Beach (33069) *(G-14076)*

Leisure Activities Usa LLC 727 417-7128
2399 26th Ave N Saint Petersburg (33713) *(G-15110)*

Leisure Furniture Powder CT 239 597-4343
1076 Business Ln Ste 7 Naples (34110) *(G-10802)*

Leisurelay365, Miami *Also called Eyedose Inc (G-9124)*

Leiton Decor & Design 786 286-4776
4237 Nw 37th Ct Miami (33142) *(G-9450)*

Lek Technology Consultants Inc 407 877-6505
12788 Gillard Rd Winter Garden (34787) *(G-18395)*

Lemnature Aquafarms Usa Inc 772 207-4794
455 146th Ave Vero Beach (32968) *(G-17772)*

Lemon Bay Truss & Supply Co 941 698-0800
5300 Linwood Rd Placida (33946) *(G-13735)*

Lemon Grass Industries Inc 954 418-6110
5920 Nw 59th Ave Parkland (33067) *(G-13349)*

Lemon-X Corporation 863 635-8400
500 S Lake Reedy Blvd Frostproof (33843) *(G-4638)*

Lenco Holdings LLC 305 360-0895
1223 Sw 1st Way Deerfield Beach (33441) *(G-2752)*

Lenco Marine Solutions LLC 772 288-2662
4700 Se Municipal Ct Stuart (34997) *(G-16179)*

Lenkbar LLC 239 732-5915
2705 Corporate Flight Dr Naples (34104) *(G-10803)*

Lennox Global Ltd (HQ) 305 718-2921
2335 Nw 107th Ave Ste 132 Doral (33172) *(G-3283)*

Lennox International Inc 352 379-9630
605 Nw 53rd Ave Ste A4 Gainesville (32609) *(G-4721)*

Lennox Letts 954 630-5989
801 Nw 1st St Fort Lauderdale (33311) *(G-3917)*

Lennox Miami Corp 305 763-8655
1900 Collins Ave Miami Beach (33139) *(G-10208)*

Lennox National Account S 954 745-3482
4418 Sw 74th Ave Miami (33155) *(G-9451)*

Lenntech USA LLC 877 453-8095
5975 Sunset Dr Ste 802 South Miami (33143) *(G-16037)*

Lenoc Chemical Solutions Inc 229 499-0665
2970 Manuel Rd Bowling Green (33834) *(G-830)*

Lensar Inc 888 536-7271
2800 Discovery Dr Ste 100 Orlando (32826) *(G-12322)*

Lenstec Inc (PA) 727 571-2272
1765 Commerce Ave N Saint Petersburg (33716) *(G-15111)*

Lentus Products LLC 203 913-7600
215 Celebration Pl # 520 Kissimmee (34747) *(G-6938)*

Lenz Group LLC 305 467-5351
4925 Sw 185th Ter Miramar (33029) *(G-10508)*

Leo Fashions Inc 305 887-1032
230 W 23rd St Hialeah (33010) *(G-5222)*

Leo Manufacturing, Fort Lauderdale *Also called Lajoie Investment Corp (G-3911)*

Leon Leather Company Inc 386 304-1902
3735 Us Highway 1 Edgewater (32141) *(G-3496)*

Leon Screening & Repair Inc 850 575-2840
1223 Airport Dr Tallahassee (32304) *(G-16469)*

Leopard Brands Inc 954 794-0007
6800 E Rogers Cir Boca Raton (33487) *(G-577)*

Lerner Enterprises Inc 440 323-5529
19367 Abhenry Cir Port Charlotte (33948) *(G-14306)*

Lerness Shoe Corp 305 643-6525
2155 Sw 8th St Miami (33135) *(G-9452)*

Lesco Inc 863 655-2424
425 Haywood Taylor Blvd Sebring (33870) *(G-15929)*

Lesco Service Center, Sebring *Also called Lesco Inc (G-15929)*

Leslie Controls Inc (HQ) 813 978-1000
12501 Telecom Dr Temple Terrace (33637) *(G-17539)*

Leslie Industries Inc 850 422-0099
2454 Centerville Rd Tallahassee (32308) *(G-16470)*

Lester A Dine Inc 561 624-3009
351 Hiatt Dr Palm Beach Gardens (33418) *(G-12984)*

Lester Manufacturing LLC 305 898-0306
2131 Nw 23rd Ct Miami (33142) *(G-9453)*

Leto LLC 813 486-8049
14483 62nd St N Clearwater (33760) *(G-1671)*

Levario Coatings Intl USA 954 871-6461
4000 Island Blvd Apt 70 Aventura (33160) *(G-265)*

Levatas 561 622-4511
1250 Elizabeth Ave Ste 3 West Palm Beach (33401) *(G-18056)*

Levelblox Inc (PA) 941 907-8822
6371 Bus Blvd Ste 200 Sarasota (34240) *(G-15725)*

Levenhuk Inc (PA) 800 342-1706
6021 Catlin Dr Tampa (33647) *(G-17008)*

Levil Technology Corp 407 542-3971
1704 Kennedy Pt Ste 1124 Oviedo (32765) *(G-12836)*

Levinson Built LLC..561 712-9882
  1638 Donna Rd West Palm Beach (33409) *(G-18057)*

Levita LLC..954 227-7468
  12410 Nw 39th St Coral Springs (33065) *(G-2178)*

Levitech Services LLC..904 576-0562
  112 5th Ave S Apt 301 Jacksonville Beach (32250) *(G-6638)*

Lewis Vault & Precast Inc.......................................352 351-2992
  1731 Sw 7th Ave Ocala (34471) *(G-11426)*

Lewis-Riggs Custom Guitars Inc.............................407 538-3710
  1001 Lake Sherwood Dr Orlando (32818) *(G-12323)*

Lexington Cutter Inc...941 739-2726
  2951 63rd Ave E Bradenton (34203) *(G-1004)*

Lexington Dsign + Fbrction E L................................407 578-4720
  613 Triumph Ct Ste 1 Orlando (32805) *(G-12324)*

Lexington International LLC....................................800 973-4769
  1040 Holland Dr Boca Raton (33487) *(G-578)*

Lexmark International Inc.......................................954 345-2442
  10866 Nw 14th St Coral Springs (33071) *(G-2179)*

Lexmark International Inc..305 467-2200
  5201 Blue Lagoon Dr # 87 Miami (33126) *(G-9454)*

Lexprint LLC...305 661-2424
  4255 Sw 72nd Ave Miami (33155) *(G-9455)*

Lextm3 Systems LLC...954 888-1024
  15751 Sw 41st St Ste 300 Davie (33331) *(G-2434)*

Lf of America Corp..561 988-0303
  7700 Congress Ave # 1120 Boca Raton (33487) *(G-579)*

Lftd Partners Inc (PA)..847 915-2446
  4227 Habana Ave Jacksonville (32217) *(G-6256)*

Lg Smart Blinds Corp..305 704-0696
  8752 Sw 2nd Ter Miami (33174) *(G-9456)*

Lg-TEC Corporation..305 770-4005
  2021 Coolidge St Hollywood (33020) *(G-5610)*

Lgl Group Inc (PA)...407 298-2000
  2525 Shader Rd Orlando (32804) *(G-12325)*

Lgl Latin America Operations, Doral *Also called Lennox Global Ltd* *(G-3283)*

Lh Travis, Winter Haven *Also called Travis Lh LLC* *(G-18475)*

Lhoist North America Ala LLC..................................352 585-3488
  10245 Cement Plant Rd Brooksville (34601) *(G-1174)*

Lhoist North America Ala LLC..................................817 732-8164
  1263 Hammondville Rd Pompano Beach (33069) *(G-14077)*

Lhoist North America Tenn Inc.................................352 629-7990
  11661 Nw Gainesville Rd Ocala (34482) *(G-11427)*

Liberty Aluminum Co...239 369-3000
  5613a 6th St W Lehigh Acres (33971) *(G-7815)*

Liberty Balloons LLC...239 947-3338
  10401 Morningside Ln Bonita Springs (34135) *(G-809)*

Liberty Calhoun Journal Inc....................................850 643-3333
  11493 Nw Summers Rd Bristol (32321) *(G-1122)*

Liberty Health Sciences Inc....................................386 462-0141
  14810 Nw 94th Ave Alachua (32615) *(G-13)*

Liberty Printing, Odessa *Also called H&M Phillips Inc* *(G-11556)*

Liberty Woodworking Inc...727 642-9652
  6563 46th St N Ste 702 Pinellas Park (33781) *(G-13705)*

Lidarit Inc...407 632-2622
  7208 W Sand Lake Rd Orlando (32819) *(G-12326)*

Liddys Machine Shop Inc..904 354-0134
  7621 Holiday Rd S Jacksonville (32216) *(G-6257)*

Liebherr Cranes Inc..305 817-7500
  15101 Nw 112th Ave Hialeah (33018) *(G-5223)*

Liebherr Nenzing Crane, Hialeah *Also called Liebherr Cranes Inc* *(G-5223)*

Life All Natural, Miami *Also called Lan Industries LLC* *(G-9420)*

Life Extension, Fort Lauderdale *Also called Le Publications Inc* *(G-3915)*

Life Proteomics Inc..813 864-7646
  8875 Hidden River Pkwy Tampa (33637) *(G-17009)*

Life Spice and Ingredients LLC (PA)........................708 301-0447
  300 Cherry Ln Palm Beach (33480) *(G-12937)*

Life Wear Technologies, Pompano Beach *Also called Modular Thermal Tech LLC* *(G-14104)*

Lifecell, Hallandale Beach *Also called South Beach Skin Care Inc* *(G-4973)*

Lifeco Foods North America....................................321 348-5896
  855 E Plant St Ste 1700 Winter Garden (34787) *(G-18396)*

Lifegard Prfcation Systems LLC..............................813 875-7777
  7028 W Waters Ave Ste 228 Tampa (33634) *(G-17010)*

Lifegate Publishing LLC..561 602-0089
  1110 Parkside Green Dr Greenacres (33415) *(G-4851)*

Lifeline Software Inc...866 592-1343
  161 Commerce Rd Ste 3 Boynton Beach (33426) *(G-886)*

Lifelink Foundation Inc...407 218-8783
  1739 S Orange Ave Orlando (32806) *(G-12327)*

Lifes A Stitch..386 385-3079
  2510 Crill Ave Palatka (32177) *(G-12873)*

Lifesaving Systems Corporation.............................813 645-2748
  220 Elsberry Rd Apollo Beach (33572) *(G-94)*

Lifestyle Magazine...386 423-2772
  1210 S Riverside Dr New Smyrna Beach (32168) *(G-11004)*

Lifestyle Media Group LLC......................................954 377-9470
  3511 W Commercial Blvd Fort Lauderdale (33309) *(G-3918)*

Lifestyle Publications LLC.......................................954 217-1165
  1675 Market St Ste 203 Weston (33326) *(G-18263)*

Lifetile, Lake Wales *Also called Royal Westlake Roofing LLC* *(G-7172)*

Lifetime Environmental Designs..............................352 237-7177
  3550 Sw 74th Ave Ocala (34474) *(G-11428)*

Lifetime Shutters Inc..407 402-3365
  3005 Juneberry Ter Oviedo (32766) *(G-12837)*

Lifetime Wellness Centers Inc.................................321 693-8698
  618 Washburn Rd Ste A Melbourne (32934) *(G-8460)*

Lift Aerospace Corp...305 851-5237
  6960 Nw 50th St Miami (33166) *(G-9457)*

Lift Spectrum Technologies LLC..............................407 228-8343
  4700 Millenia Blvd # 175 Orlando (32839) *(G-12328)*

Light Age Press Inc..352 242-4530
  5660 County Road 561 Clermont (34714) *(G-1875)*

Light and Sound Equipment Inc..............................305 233-3737
  10777 Sw 188th St Cutler Bay (33157) *(G-2294)*

Light Integration Inc...407 681-0072
  477 Commerce Way Ste 105 Longwood (32750) *(G-7918)*

Light Solutions Inc...305 884-3468
  8795 Nw 100th St Medley (33178) *(G-8268)*

Light Source Business Systems...............................772 562-5046
  582 N Mercantile Pl Port Saint Lucie (34986) *(G-14423)*

Light-Tech Inc..863 385-6000
  8880 W Josephine Rd Sebring (33875) *(G-15930)*

Lightening Print, Saint Petersburg *Also called Ideal Publishing Co Inc* *(G-15082)*

Lighter Than Air Systems Corp (HQ).......................904 834-4400
  11651 Central Pkwy # 118 Jacksonville (32224) *(G-6258)*

Lightfire Holdings LLC...866 375-0541
  10601 State St Ste 5 Tamarac (33321) *(G-16535)*

Lighthouse Boatworks Inc.......................................561 667-7382
  512 N Hepburn Ave Jupiter (33458) *(G-6756)*

Lighthouse Express World Inc.................................754 210-6196
  3880 N 28th Ter Hollywood (33020) *(G-5611)*

Lighting Science Group Corp (HQ)...........................321 779-5520
  3905 W Eau Gallie Blvd # 101 Melbourne (32934) *(G-8461)*

Lighting Technologies...850 462-1790
  1810 Barrancas Ave Pensacola (32502) *(G-13536)*

Lightking Outdoor, Doral *Also called Digital Outdoor LLC* *(G-3192)*

Lightn Up Inc...954 797-7778
  10401 Nw 53rd St Sunrise (33351) *(G-16337)*

Lightnet Usa Inc...305 260-6444
  123 Nw 23rd St Miami (33127) *(G-9458)*

Lightning Connecting Rods LLC...............................727 733-2054
  1630 N Hercules Ave Ste B Clearwater (33765) *(G-1672)*

Lightning Master Corporation..................................800 749-6800
  2100 Palmetto St Ste A Clearwater (33765) *(G-1673)*

Lightning Phase II Inc...727 539-1800
  10700 76th Ct Seminole (33777) *(G-15979)*

Lightning Prtction Systems Inc................................239 643-4323
  38818 Exchange Ave Naples (34104) *(G-10804)*

Lightning Specialists Inc...727 938-3560
  11498 Prosperous Dr Odessa (33556) *(G-11564)*

Lightpath Technologies Inc (PA)..............................407 382-4003
  2603 Challenger Tech Ct Orlando (32826) *(G-12329)*

Lightsource Imaging Solutions, Port Saint Lucie *Also called Light Source Business Systems* *(G-14423)*

Lightworks Inc..305 456-3520
  7035 Sw 47th St Ste A Miami (33155) *(G-9459)*

Lignotech Florida LLC...904 577-9077
  6 Gum St Fernandina Beach (32034) *(G-3592)*

Lilas Desserts Inc...305 252-1441
  12309 Sw 130th St Miami (33186) *(G-9460)*

Liles Custom Trailers...352 368-2652
  4940 N Us Highway 441 Ocala (34475) *(G-11429)*

Liles Oil Company..407 739-2083
  201 Kraft Dr Casselberry (32707) *(G-1422)*

Lillian Bay Medical Inc...941 815-7373
  260 1st Ave S Ste 200 Saint Petersburg (33701) *(G-15112)*

Lillys Gastronomia Italiana FL, Hallandale Beach *Also called Lillys Gstrnmia Itlana Fla Inc* *(G-4959)*

Lillys Gstrnmia Itlana Fla Inc..................................305 655-2111
  370 Ansin Blvd Hallandale Beach (33009) *(G-4959)*

Limas Pavers and Services Inc................................904 314-7719
  7901 Bymdws Cir E Ste 44 Jacksonville (32256) *(G-6259)*

Limbitless Solutions Inc (PA)..................................407 494-3661
  4217 E Plaza Dr Orlando (32816) *(G-12330)*

Lime Group...941 485-0272
  416 Lime Dr Nokomis (34275) *(G-11050)*

Limited Designs LLC...305 547-9909
  382 Ne 191st St 87394 Miami (33179) *(G-9461)*

Limitless Mobile Wholesale Inc (PA)........................321 710-6936
  885 Sedalia St Ocoee (34761) *(G-11523)*

Lincoln Smith Ventures LLC....................................863 337-6670
  2058 E Edgewood Dr Lakeland (33803) *(G-7379)*

Lincoln Tactical LLC...813 419-3110
  1319 Brahma Dr Valrico (33594) *(G-17667)*

Lincoln-Marti Cmnty Agcy Inc (PA)..........................305 643-4888
  2700 Sw 8th St Miami (33135) *(G-9462)*

Lincoln-Marti Cmnty Agcy Inc.................................646 463-6120
  450 Sw 16th Ave Miami (33135) *(G-9463)*

Linde Inc...813 626-3636
  6915 E Adamo Dr Tampa (33619) *(G-17011)*

A
L
P
H
A
B
E
T
I
C

Linde Inc 321 267-2311
2801 Hammock Rd Mims (32754) *(G-10449)*

Linden-Beals Corp 772 562-0624
1547 20th St Vero Beach (32960) *(G-17773)*

Lindley Foods LLC 407 884-9433
2023 Apex Ct Apopka (32703) *(G-147)*

Lindorm Inc 305 888-0762
601 Plover Ave Miami Springs (33166) *(G-10390)*

Lindsay Precast Inc 800 669-2278
13365 Southern Precast Dr Alachua (32615) *(G-14)*

Lindsey Macke Bindery Printing 727 514-3570
11626 Prosperous Dr Odessa (33556) *(G-11565)*

Linenmaster LLC 772 212-2710
601 21st St Ste 300 Vero Beach (32960) *(G-17774)*

Linenwood Home LLC 850 607-7445
24 E Brainerd St Pensacola (32501) *(G-13537)*

Liners of Legend, Hialeah *Also called Maritime Replicas America Inc (G-5243)*

Linga Pos LLC (PA) 800 619-5931
4501 Tamiami Trl N # 400 Naples (34103) *(G-10805)*

Linkpoint LLC 305 903-9191
137 E Enid Dr Key Biscayne (33149) *(G-6836)*

Linman Inc 904 755-6800
Us Hwy 100 Lake City (32055) *(G-7028)*

Linographics Inc 407 422-8700
617 N Magnolia Ave Orlando (32801) *(G-12331)*

Linpharma Inc 888 989-3237
5401 S Kirkman Rd Ste 310 Orlando (32819) *(G-12332)*

Linpharma Inc 888 989-3237
601 S Fremont Ave Tampa (33606) *(G-17012)*

Linqs Inc 321 244-2626
1511 E State Road 434 # 2 Winter Springs (32708) *(G-18572)*

Linvatec Corporation (HQ) 727 392-6464
11311 Concept Blvd Largo (33773) *(G-7633)*

Linville Enterprises LLC 813 782-1558
38333 5th Ave Zephyrhills (33542) *(G-18620)*

Linx Defense LLC 805 233-2472
4507 Furling Ln Ste 205 Destin (32541) *(G-3073)*

Lioher Enterprise Corp 305 685-0005
13939 Nw 60th Ave Miami Lakes (33014) *(G-10314)*

Lion Ink Print Inc 561 358-8925
8091 N Military Trl Ste 7 West Palm Beach (33410) *(G-18058)*

Lion Locs LLC 704 802-2752
1002 Lucerne Ter Orlando (32806) *(G-12333)*

Lion Pool Products, Palatka *Also called A J Giammanco & Associates (G-12862)*

Lion Press Inc 954 971-6193
1913 W Copans Rd Pompano Beach (33064) *(G-14078)*

Lion Sheet Metal Inc 561 840-0540
1648 Donna Rd West Palm Beach (33409) *(G-18059)*

Lionheart Printers LLC 561 781-8300
1312 Commerce Ln Ste A15 Jupiter (33458) *(G-6757)*

Lions Gate Publishing Prod LLC 954 733-9576
1720 Nw 26th Ter Fort Lauderdale (33311) *(G-3919)*

Lions Intl MGT Group Inc 813 367-2517
8875 Hidden River Pkwy # 304 Tampa (33637) *(G-17013)*

Lip Trading Co 954 987-0306
3460 N 34th Ave Hollywood (33021) *(G-5612)*

Lippert Components Inc 267 825-0665
1900 47th Ter E Bradenton (34203) *(G-1005)*

Lipscomb and Finch, Jacksonville *Also called Lipscomb Finch Co (G-6260)*

Lipscomb Finch Co 904 415-4265
7750 Belfort Pkwy Apt 737 Jacksonville (32256) *(G-6260)*

Liqui-Box Corporation 863 676-7602
104 S Scenic Hwy Lake Wales (33853) *(G-7166)*

Liquid Bottles LLC 888 222-5232
3165 Lakewood Ranch Blvd Bradenton (34211) *(G-1006)*

Liquid Ed Inc 727 943-8616
740 Wesley Ave Tarpon Springs (34689) *(G-17480)*

Liquid Metal Products Inc 402 895-4436
901 Sw 73rd Street Rd Ocala (34476) *(G-11430)*

Liquid Packaging Systems, Lake Wales *Also called Liqui-Box Corporation (G-7166)*

Liquid Soul Dgtal Graphics LLC 407 948-6973
3628 E Esther St Orlando (32812) *(G-12334)*

Liquid Technolgy Corp 832 804-8650
340 Scarlet Blvd Oldsmar (34677) *(G-11670)*

Liquidcapsule Mfg LLC 813 431-0532
9216 Palm River Rd # 203 Tampa (33619) *(G-17014)*

Liquiguard Technologies Inc 954 566-0996
5807 N Andrews Way Fort Lauderdale (33309) *(G-3920)*

Lisa Bakery Inc 305 888-8431
2460 W 1st Ave Hialeah (33010) *(G-5224)*

Lisa Mc Call 850 265-4241
1740 Sherman Ave Panama City (32405) *(G-13283)*

Lisa Todd International LLC 305 445-2632
1441 Nw N River Dr 3a Miami (33125) *(G-9464)*

List + Beisler Corp 646 866-6960
200 Suth Bscyne Blvd Lvel Level Miami (33131) *(G-9465)*

List Distillery LLC 239 208-7214
3680 Evans Ave Fort Myers (33901) *(G-4312)*

List Industries Inc (PA) 954 429-9155
401 Jim Moran Blvd Deerfield Beach (33442) *(G-2753)*

List Manufacturing Inc 954 429-9155
401 Jim Moran Blvd Deerfield Beach (33442) *(G-2754)*

List Plymouth LLC 954 429-9155
401 Jim Moran Blvd Deerfield Beach (33442) *(G-2755)*

Lit TV Network Llc 904 274-0732
7901 Baymeadows Way Ste 8 Jacksonville (32256) *(G-6261)*

Lite Cart Corp 954 659-7671
1950 Lake Ave Se Unit A Largo (33771) *(G-7634)*

Lite Crete Insulated Concrete, Miami *Also called Litecrete Inc (G-9466)*

Litecrete Inc 305 500-9373
8095 Nw 64th St Miami (33166) *(G-9466)*

Liteworks Lighting Productions 407 888-8677
752 Palm Dr Orlando (32803) *(G-12335)*

Lithionics Battery LLC 727 726-4204
1770 Calumet St Clearwater (33765) *(G-1674)*

Lithium Battery Co Intl 813 504-0074
4912 W Knox St Ste 100 Tampa (33634) *(G-17015)*

Litho Art Inc 305 232-7098
12190 Sw 131st Ave Miami (33186) *(G-9467)*

Litho Haus Printers Inc (PA) 850 671-6600
2843 Industrial Plaza Dr A1 Tallahassee (32301) *(G-16471)*

Lithocraft Inc 386 761-3584
4460 S Ridgewood Ave Port Orange (32127) *(G-14338)*

Lithographing Art, Miami *Also called Litho Art Inc (G-9467)*

Lithohaus Printers, Tallahassee *Also called Litho Haus Printers Inc (G-16471)*

Lithotec Commercial Printing 727 541-4614
12350 Us Highway 19 N Clearwater (33764) *(G-1675)*

Litterbin LLC 772 633-7184
669 2nd Ln Vero Beach (32962) *(G-17775)*

Little River Marine 352 378-5025
250 Se 10th Ave Gainesville (32601) *(G-4722)*

Little Steps Daycare, Miami *Also called B & C Sheet Metal Duct Corp (G-8786)*

Littoral Marine LLC 352 400-4222
1520 Industrial Dr Wildwood (34785) *(G-18315)*

Live Aerospace Inc 305 910-0091
7205 Nw 68th St Ste 11 Miami (33166) *(G-9468)*

Live Oak Feed Mill, Live Oak *Also called Pilgrims Pride Corporation (G-7851)*

Live Well Cbds, Davie *Also called Michelle Ann Lillo (G-2440)*

Live Wise Naturals LLC 866 866-0075
13502 4th Plz E Bradenton (34212) *(G-1007)*

Lively Company LLC 617 737-1199
501 E Jackson St Ste 301 Tampa (33602) *(G-17016)*

Livetv 321 722-0783
1333 Gateway Dr Ste 1007 Melbourne (32901) *(G-8462)*

Livie Water, Orlando *Also called Aqua Pure LLC (G-11915)*

Liviliti Health Products Corp 888 987-0744
2140 Sw Main Blvd Lake City (32025) *(G-7029)*

Living Color Aquarium Corp 844 522-8265
740 S Porwerline Rd Ste E Deerfield Beach (33442) *(G-2756)*

Living Color Enterprises Inc 954 970-9511
720 S Powerline Rd Ste D Deerfield Beach (33442) *(G-2757)*

Living Fuel Inc 813 254-0777
1409 W Swann Ave Tampa (33606) *(G-17017)*

Living Well Spending Less Inc 941 209-1811
307 Taylor St Punta Gorda (33950) *(G-14512)*

Living With Art Kitchens and 954 561-4030
1041 Se 7th Ave Pompano Beach (33060) *(G-14079)*

Liza Gold Corp 305 885-0731
9 E 20th St Hialeah (33010) *(G-5225)*

LJ&j Lathing Inc 386 325-5040
402 N 16th St B6 Palatka (32177) *(G-12874)*

Ljk & TS Partners Inc 941 661-5675
7031 Benjamin Rd Ste E Tampa (33634) *(G-17018)*

Ljs Tops & Bottoms 561 736-7868
3050 Sw 14th Pl Ste 11 Boynton Beach (33426) *(G-887)*

Lk Industries, Jacksonville *Also called Load King Manufacturing Co (G-6263)*

LLC Best Block (PA) 239 789-3531
2858 Sidney Ave Orlando (32810) *(G-12336)*

LLC Best Block 239 789-3531
5609 N 50th St Tampa (33610) *(G-17019)*

Llc, Clondalkin, Largo *Also called Clondalkin LLC (G-7566)*

Llorens Phrm Intl Div Inc 305 716-0595
7080 Nw 37th Ct Miami (33147) *(G-9469)*

Lloyd Industries Inc 904 541-1655
138 Industrial Loop W Orange Park (32073) *(G-11833)*

Llumina Press, Fort Lauderdale *Also called Media Creations Inc (G-3934)*

Lm Industrial Inc 407 240-8911
1429 Central Florida Pkwy Orlando (32837) *(G-12337)*

Lmb Consultants Inc 954 537-9590
1280 S Powerline Rd # 17 Pompano Beach (33069) *(G-14080)*

Lmn Printing Co Inc 386 428-9928
118 N Ridgewood Ave Edgewater (32132) *(G-3497)*

LMS Manufacturing LLC 850 526-0121
4430 Magnolia Rd Marianna (32448) *(G-8169)*

Lnl Logistics LLC 386 977-9276
915 Doyle Rd Ste 303-150 Deltona (32725) *(G-3047)*

Load Banks Direct LLC 859 554-2522
309 Nassau St N Venice (34285) *(G-17705)*

(G-0000) Company's Geographic Section entry number

Load King Manufacturing 904 633-7352
14001 Atlantic Blvd Jacksonville (32225) (G-6262)

Load King Manufacturing Co (PA) 904 354-8882
1357 W Beaver St Jacksonville (32209) (G-6263)

Loadmaster Alum Boat Trlrs Inc 813 689-3096
10105 Cedar Run Tampa (33619) (G-17020)

Lobby Docs LLC 850 294-0013
3472 Weems Rd Tallahassee (32317) (G-16472)

Lobo Industries LLC 407 310-3219
14179 Amelia Island Way Orlando (32828) (G-12338)

Loboy, Fort Walton Beach Also called Magna Manufacturing Inc (G-4595)

Local Biz Spot Inc (PA) 866 446-1790
26747 Saxony Way Wesley Chapel (33544) (G-17881)

Local Enterprises Inc 305 295-0026
3201 Flagler Ave Ste 501 Key West (33040) (G-6873)

Local Woodwork LLC 954 551-1515
5491 Nw 15th St Margate (33063) (G-8142)

Localtoolbox Inc 415 250-3232
2720 Bayou Grande Blvd Pensacola (32507) (G-13538)

Location 3 Holdings LLC 941 342-3443
5686 Fruitville Rd Sarasota (34232) (G-15726)

Lockheed Martin Aeronautics, Pinellas Park Also called Lockheed Martin
Corporation (G-13706)

Lockheed Martin Corporation 407 306-6405
100 Global Innovation Cir Orlando (32825) (G-12339)

Lockheed Martin Corporation 407 306-1000
12506 Lake Underhill Rd Orlando (32825) (G-12340)

Lockheed Martin Corporation 407 517-6627
1700 Tradeport Dr Orlando (32824) (G-12341)

Lockheed Martin Corporation 863 647-0100
1040 S Pkwy Frontage Rd Lakeland (33813) (G-7380)

Lockheed Martin Corporation 407 306-4803
4504 Bridgeton Ln Orlando (32817) (G-12342)

Lockheed Martin Corporation 727 578-6940
9300 28th St N Ste A Pinellas Park (33782) (G-13706)

Lockheed Martin Corporation 321 635-7621
2900 Murrell Rd Rockledge (32955) (G-14725)

Lockheed Martin Corporation 407 356-2000
5600 W Sand Lake Rd Orlando (32819) (G-12343)

Lockheed Martin Corporation 305 599-3004
7925 Nw 12th St Doral (33126) (G-3284)

Lockheed Martin Corporation 352 687-2163
498 Oak Rd Ocala (34472) (G-11431)

Lockheed Martin Corporation 813 855-5711
3655 Tampa Rd Oldsmar (34677) (G-11671)

Lockheed Martin Corporation 321 853-5194
Pier Rd Cape Canaveral (32920) (G-1290)

Lockheed Martin Corporation 407 356-1034
8751 Lockheed Martin Blvd Orlando (32819) (G-12344)

Lockheed Martin Corporation 863 647-0100
1040 S Pkwy Frontage Rd Lakeland (33813) (G-7381)

Lockheed Martin Corporation 863 647-0558
1040 South Blvd Lakeland (33803) (G-7382)

Lockheed Martin Corporation 863 647-0100
1040 S Pkwy Frontage Rd Lakeland (33813) (G-7383)

Lockheed Martin Corporation 407 356-2000
5600 W Sand Lake Rd Mp-26 Orlando (32819) (G-12345)

Lockheed Martin Corporation 850 475-0724
5041 Bayou Blvd Ste 301 Pensacola (32503) (G-13539)

Lockheed Martin Corporation 863 647-0303
1040 S Pkwy Frontage Rd Lakeland (33813) (G-7384)

Lockheed Martin Corporation 301 897-6000
100 E 17th St Riviera Beach (33404) (G-14643)

Lockheed Martin Government, Lakeland Also called Lockheed Martin Corporation (G-7380)

Lockheed Martin Mis Fire Ctrl, Orlando Also called Lockheed Martin Corporation (G-12343)

Lockheed Martin Mis Fire Ctrl, Orlando Also called Lockheed Martin Corporation (G-12344)

Lockheed Mrtin Gyrcam Systems 407 356-6500
5600 W Sand Lake Rd Mp-265 Orlando (32819) (G-12346)

Lockheed Mrtin Intgrted System 407 356-2000
5600 W Sand Lake Rd Orlando (32819) (G-12347)

Lockheed Mrtin Mllmter Tech In 407 356-4186
5600 W Sand Lake Rd Orlando (32819) (G-12348)

Lockheed Mrtin Rtary Mssion Sy, Orlando Also called Lockheed Mrtin Trning Sltons
I (G-12349)

Lockheed Mrtin Trning Sltons I (HQ) 856 722-3317
100 Global Innovation Cir Orlando (32825) (G-12349)

Locksmith Killers, Doral Also called Ecs America LLC (G-3204)

Lockwood Aircraft Corporation 863 655-4242
1 Lockwood Ln Sebring (33870) (G-15931)

Locus Diagnostics LLC 321 727-3077
1055 S John Rodes Blvd Melbourne (32904) (G-8463)

Locus Location Systems LLC 321 727-3077
1055 S John Rodes Blvd Melbourne (32904) (G-8464)

Locus Solutions LLC 561 575-7600
7121 Fairway Dr Ste 400 Palm Beach Gardens (33418) (G-12985)

Locus Traxx Worlwide, Palm Beach Gardens Also called Locus Solutions LLC (G-12985)

Locust Usa Inc 305 889-5410
8312 Nw 74th Ave Medley (33166) (G-8269)

Locust Power, Medley Also called Locust Usa Inc (G-8269)

Locususa, Melbourne Also called Locus Diagnostics LLC (G-8463)

Lodex Enterprises Corp 954 442-3843
17048 Sw 38th Dr Miramar (33027) (G-10509)

Lofton Enterprises Trckg LLC 786 220-6053
1065 Sw 8th St Miami (33130) (G-9470)

Logan Laboratories LLC 813 316-4824
2333 W Hillsborough Ave Tampa (33603) (G-17021)

Loggerhead Distillery LLC 321 800-8566
124 W 2nd St Sanford (32771) (G-15352)

Logic Controls Inc 800 576-9647
404 Sunport Ln Ste 550 Orlando (32809) (G-12350)

Logic Illumination LLC 407 906-0126
3600 Commerce Blvd 102b Kissimmee (34741) (G-6939)

Logic Springs Technologies, Lake Mary Also called Microvision Technology Corp (G-7095)

Logical Data Solutions Inc 561 694-9229
31 Windward Isle Palm Beach Gardens (33418) (G-12986)

Logiscenter LLC 800 729-0236
5201 Blue Lagoon Dr Fl 8 Miami (33126) (G-9471)

Logistic Systems Inc (PA) 305 477-4999
2175 Nw 115th Ave Miami (33172) (G-9472)

Logoi Inc 305 232-5880
12900 Sw 128th St Ste 204 Miami (33186) (G-9473)

Logos Promote Inc 407 447-5646
3804 N John Young Pkwy Orlando (32804) (G-12351)

Logoxpress Inc 954 973-4994
2520 N Powerline Rd # 303 Pompano Beach (33069) (G-14081)

Logsdon and Associates Inc 407 292-0084
13049 Lake Roper Ct Windermere (34786) (G-18359)

Logus Manufacturing Corp 561 842-3550
1711 Longwood Rd Ste A West Palm Beach (33409) (G-18060)

Logus Microwave, West Palm Beach Also called Logus Manufacturing Corp (G-18060)

Loksak Inc 239 331-5550
6507 Marbella Dr Naples (34105) (G-10806)

Lollipop Children Center Inc 386 755-3953
416 Se Ermine Ave Lake City (32025) (G-7030)

Lollipops and Gumdrops Inc 954 389-7032
2459 Greenbrier Ct Weston (33327) (G-18264)

Lombardis Woodworking 305 439-7208
1000 Oriole Ave Miami Springs (33166) (G-10391)

Londos Fine Cabinetry LLC 727 544-2929
6901 Bryan Dairy Rd # 130 Seminole (33777) (G-15980)

Long, H W Logging, Old Town Also called Henry W Long (G-11622)

Longboat Key News Inc 941 387-2200
5370 Gulf Of Mexico Dr Longboat Key (34228) (G-7858)

Longboat Observer, Sarasota Also called Observer Group Inc (G-15765)

Longbow Marine Inc 954 616-5737
1305 Sw 1st Ave Fort Lauderdale (33315) (G-3921)

Longchamp Usa Inc 305 372-1628
1450 Brickell Ave # 2140 Miami (33131) (G-9474)

Longeveron Inc 305 909-0840
1951 Nw 7th Ave Ste 520 Miami (33136) (G-9475)

Lonza 727 608-6802
5709 Johns Rd Ste 1209 Tampa (33634) (G-17022)

Look Worldwide Inc 305 662-1287
6851 Sw 31st St Miami (33155) (G-9476)

Looper Sports Connection Inc 352 796-7974
19225 Cortez Blvd Brooksville (34601) (G-1175)

Loos & Co Inc 239 643-5667
901 Industrial Blvd Naples (34104) (G-10807)

Lopco Aviation, Miami Also called Lopez & Company Inc (G-9477)

Lopco Aviation, Doral Also called Lopez & Company Inc (G-3285)

Lopez & Company Inc (PA) 305 302-3045
2221 Ne 164th St Miami (33160) (G-9477)

Lopez & Company Inc 305 302-3045
10773 Nw 58th St Ste 250 Doral (33178) (G-3285)

Lopresti Aviation, Sebastian Also called Lopresti Speed Merchants Inc (G-15898)

Lopresti Speed Merchants Inc 772 562-4757
210 Airport Dr E Sebastian (32958) (G-15898)

Lor-Ed Enterprises LLC 352 750-1999
309 Lagrande Blvd Lady Lake (32159) (G-6992)

Lorefice Steel Corp 786 609-1593
3510 Nw 31st St Miami (33142) (G-9478)

Loren/Wtp 954 846-9800
3040 N 29th Ave Hollywood (33020) (G-5613)

Lorente International LLC 877 281-6469
6950 Bryan Dairy Rd Ste A Seminole (33777) (G-15981)

Lorenze & Associates Inc 407 682-7570
1030 Sunshine Ln Ste 1000 Altamonte Springs (32714) (G-55)

Lori Roberts Print Shop I 813 882-8456
20332 Ayers Rd Brooksville (34604) (G-1176)

Lorina Inc 305 779-3085
8750 Nw 36th St Ste 260 Doral (33178) (G-3286)

Loris 1 Inc 727 847-4499
3544 Grand Blvd New Port Richey (34652) (G-10972)

Lorken Publications Inc (PA) 239 395-1213
1640 Periwinkle Way Ste 2 Sanibel (33957) (G-15416)

Los Atntcos Sndwich Cuban Cafe 407 282-2322
7339 E Colonial Dr Ste 1 Orlando (32807) (G-12352)

A
L
P
H
A
B
E
T
I
C

Los Coquitos.....407 289-9315
1319 E Vine St Kissimmee (34744) ***(G-6940)***
Los Latinos Magazine Inc.....305 882-9074
138 Hialeah Dr Hialeah (33010) ***(G-5226)***
Los Primos Express Svcs LLC.....786 701-3297
12039 Sw 132nd Ct Miami (33186) ***(G-9479)***
Losobe LLC.....850 748-3162
943 Candlestick Ct Pensacola (32514) ***(G-13540)***
Lost Fabrication LLC.....772 971-3467
3811 Crossroads Pkwy Fort Pierce (34945) ***(G-4501)***
Lott Qa Group Inc.....201 693-2224
27499 Riverview Center Bl Bonita Springs (34134) ***(G-810)***
Lotts Concrete Products Inc.....407 656-2112
510 E Bay St Winter Garden (34787) ***(G-18397)***
Lotus Containers Inc.....786 590-1056
1000 Brickell Ave Ste 640 Miami (33131) ***(G-9480)***
Lotus Stress Relief LLC.....941 706-2778
2965 Bee Ridge Rd Sarasota (34239) ***(G-15727)***
Louis Chocolates, Jacksonville *Also called Louis Sherry Company LLC* ***(G-6264)***
Louis Di Rmndo Wrldwide Invstm.....786 536-7578
2410 N Shore Ter Miami Beach (33141) ***(G-10209)***
Louis Poulsen USA Inc.....954 349-2525
3260 Meridian Pkwy Weston (33331) ***(G-18265)***
Louis Sherry Company LLC.....904 482-1900
4339 Rosevlt Blvd Ste 400 Jacksonville (32210) ***(G-6264)***
Lov Industries Inc.....407 406-8221
742 Royal Palm Dr Kissimmee (34743) ***(G-6941)***
Love Is In The Air Corp.....305 828-8181
2284 W 77th St Hialeah (33016) ***(G-5227)***
Low Code Ip Holding LLC.....833 260-2151
401 E Las Olas Blvd Ste 1 Fort Lauderdale (33301) ***(G-3922)***
Low Vision Aids Inc (PA).....954 722-1580
2125 Sw Highway 484 Ocala (34473) ***(G-11432)***
Lowe Gear Printing.....866 714-9965
15510 N Nebraska Ave B Lutz (33549) ***(G-8000)***
Lowell Plant Usf5, Ocala *Also called Lhoist North America Tenn Inc* ***(G-11427)***
Loxahatchee Mobile Equipment R.....561 723-6378
17506 37th Pl N Loxahatchee (33470) ***(G-7972)***
Loxahatchee Shutter & Alum Inc.....561 513-9581
16758 67th Ct N Loxahatchee (33470) ***(G-7973)***
Loyalty Mechanical LLC.....718 502-0632
6619 S 78th St Riverview (33578) ***(G-14569)***
LP Auto & Home Glass.....772 335-3697
2471 Se Sapelo Ave Fort Pierce (34952) ***(G-4502)***
LP Express Services, Miami *Also called Los Primos Express Svcs LLC* ***(G-9479)***
LP Watch Group Inc.....954 985-3827
101 S State Road 7 # 201 Hollywood (33023) ***(G-5614)***
Lpi Inc.....702 403-8555
6101 45th St N Saint Petersburg (33714) ***(G-15113)***
LPI Industries Corporation.....954 987-4000
3000 Taft St Hollywood (33021) ***(G-5615)***
Lps, Boca Raton *Also called Laser Photo-Tooling Svcs Inc* ***(G-574)***
Lps Group LLC (PA).....305 668-8780
7900 Sw 57th Ave Ph 23 South Miami (33143) ***(G-16038)***
LPs Lath Plst & Stucco Inc.....954 444-3727
513 Nw 16th Ave Fort Lauderdale (33311) ***(G-3923)***
Lps Lighting Sound Video Prod, Miami Lakes *Also called Lps Production LLC* ***(G-10315)***
Lps Production LLC.....786 208-6217
15901 Nw 59th Ave Miami Lakes (33014) ***(G-10315)***
Lr Printing LLC.....407 558-0543
1060 E Industrial Dr L Orange City (32763) ***(G-11806)***
Lra Architectural WD Work Inc.....305 801-5573
915 W 72nd St Hialeah (33014) ***(G-5228)***
Lrg Solutions Inc.....321 978-1050
1950 Murrell Rd Ste 3 Rockledge (32955) ***(G-14726)***
Lrm Industries Intl Inc.....321 635-9797
135 Gus Hipp Blvd Rockledge (32955) ***(G-14727)***
Lrp Conferences LLC (HQ).....215 784-0860
360 Hiatt Dr Palm Beach Gardens (33418) ***(G-12987)***
Lrp Publications Inc (PA).....215 784-0860
360 Hiatt Dr Palm Beach Gardens (33418) ***(G-12988)***
Lrvs Barricades LLC.....305 343-6101
8461 Nw 61st St Miami (33166) ***(G-9481)***
Ls Industries LLC.....850 278-6215
31 White Heron Dr Santa Rosa Beach (32459) ***(G-15428)***
Lsj Corp.....954 920-0905
2301 N 21st Ave Hollywood (33020) ***(G-5616)***
Lst, Orlando *Also called Lift Spectrum Technologies LLC* ***(G-12328)***
Ltb Aerospace LLC.....954 251-1141
2250 Nw 102nd Pl Doral (33172) ***(G-3287)***
LTSC LLC.....863 678-0011
28 W Park Ave Lake Wales (33853) ***(G-7167)***
Lubov Manufacturing Inc.....813 873-2640
4747 N West Shore Blvd Tampa (33614) ***(G-17023)***
Lubrexx Specialty Products LLC.....561 988-7500
4100 N Powerline Rd O1 Pompano Beach (33073) ***(G-14082)***
Lubrication Global LLC.....954 239-9522
8450 Nw 56th St Doral (33166) ***(G-3288)***
Lucas 5135 Inc.....800 835-7665
8130 Bymdws Way W Ste 10 Jacksonville (32256) ***(G-6265)***
Lucas Construction Inc.....386 623-0088
5 Echo Woods Way Ormond Beach (32174) ***(G-12777)***
Lucien Piccard, Hollywood *Also called LP Watch Group Inc* ***(G-5614)***
Lucien Piccard/Arnex Watch Co.....954 241-2745
101 S State Road 7 # 201 Hollywood (33023) ***(G-5617)***
Lucke Enterprises Inc.....727 797-1177
2781 Gulf To Bay Blvd Clearwater (33759) ***(G-1676)***
Lucke Group Inc.....727 525-4949
408 33rd Ave N Ste A Saint Petersburg (33704) ***(G-15114)***
Lucky Dog Printing Inc.....407 346-1663
1404 Hamlin Ave Saint Cloud (34771) ***(G-14931)***
Lucky Dog Screen Printing Mg.....407 629-8838
2716 Forsyth Rd Ste 105 Winter Park (32792) ***(G-18520)***
Lucky Fortune Cookie, Tampa *Also called First Grade Food Corporation* ***(G-16833)***
Lucky Pig, Miami *Also called Golden Boar Product Corp* ***(G-9225)***
Lucy Print, Miami *Also called A Fine Print of Miami LLC* ***(G-8620)***
Ludlow Fibc Corp.....305 702-5000
13260 Nw 45th Ave Opa Locka (33054) ***(G-11764)***
Lufemor Inc.....305 557-2162
5392 W 16th Ave Hialeah (33012) ***(G-5229)***
Luftcar LLC.....408 905-0036
12001 Res Pkwy Ste 236 Orlando (32826) ***(G-12353)***
Lug Usa LLC.....855 584-5433
8546 Palm Pkwy Ste 305 Orlando (32836) ***(G-12354)***
Lugloc LLC.....305 961-1765
550 Nw 29th St Miami (33127) ***(G-9482)***
Lui Technical Services Inc.....954 803-7610
11821 Nw 34th Pl Sunrise (33323) ***(G-16338)***
Luis Martinez Cigar Co.....800 822-4427
2701 N 16th St Tampa (33605) ***(G-17024)***
Lujotex LLC.....954 322-1001
14359 Miramar Pkwy # 290 Miramar (33027) ***(G-10510)***
Luke's Ice Cream, Riviera Beach *Also called Kevin M Lukasiewicz* ***(G-14638)***
Lululemon.....813 973-3879
28211 Paseo Dr Ste 160 Wesley Chapel (33543) ***(G-17882)***
Lumastream Inc (PA).....727 827-2805
2201 1st Ave S Saint Petersburg (33712) ***(G-15115)***
Lumber Unlimited, Ponte Vedra Beach *Also called Trusses Unlimited Inc* ***(G-14281)***
Lumenier Holdco LLC (PA).....941 444-0021
1060 Goodrich Ave Sarasota (34236) ***(G-15728)***
Lumenier LLC.....941 444-0021
1060 Goodrich Ave Sarasota (34236) ***(G-15729)***
Lumenis Ltd.....305 508-5052
6800 Sw 40th St Ste 102 Miami (33155) ***(G-9483)***
Lumilum LLC.....305 233-2844
12400 Sw 134th Ct Ste 1 Miami (33186) ***(G-9484)***
Luminar LLC.....407 900-5259
2603 Discovery Dr Ste 100 Orlando (32826) ***(G-12355)***
Luminar Holdco, LLC, Orlando *Also called Luminar LLC* ***(G-12355)***
Luminar Technologies Inc (PA).....407 900-5259
2603 Discovery Dr Ste 100 Orlando (32826) ***(G-12356)***
Luminar Technologies Inc.....407 900-5259
12601 Research Pkwy Orlando (32826) ***(G-12357)***
Luminoso LLC.....305 364-8099
9800 Nw 78th Ave Hialeah Gardens (33016) ***(G-5442)***
Lumiron Inc.....305 652-2599
20725 Ne 16th Ave Ste A33 Miami (33179) ***(G-9485)***
Lumishore Usa LLC.....941 405-3302
7137 24th Ct E Sarasota (34243) ***(G-15512)***
Lumitec LLC.....561 272-9840
1405 Poinsettia Dr Ste 10 Delray Beach (33444) ***(G-2983)***
Lumo Print Inc.....305 246-0003
27750 S Dixie Hwy Homestead (33032) ***(G-5728)***
Lumos Diagnostics Inc.....941 556-1850
7040 Prof Pkwy Ste B Lakewood Ranch (34240) ***(G-7485)***
Luna Negra Productions Inc.....786 247-1215
3110 Sw 129th Ave Miami (33175) ***(G-9486)***
Lunasea Lighting, Homosassa *Also called Aeb Technologies Inc* ***(G-5742)***
Lunchclub, Miami *Also called Elliot Technologies Inc* ***(G-9089)***
Lundy Enterprises Inc.....727 549-1292
6951 114th Ave Largo (33773) ***(G-7635)***
LUnion Logistics LLC.....866 586-4660
4000 Hollywood Blvd 555s Hollywood (33021) ***(G-5618)***
Luong Moc III Inc.....407 478-8726
3580 Aloma Ave Ste 5 Winter Park (32792) ***(G-18521)***
Lupin Oncology Inc.....239 316-1900
5801 Pelican Bay Blvd # 5 Naples (34108) ***(G-10808)***
Lupin Research Inc.....800 466-1450
4006 Nw 124th Ave Coral Springs (33065) ***(G-2180)***
Lusa Supplier LLC.....305 885-7634
7339 Nw 66th St Miami (33166) ***(G-9487)***
Luther Industries LLC.....813 833-5652
3101 River Grove Dr Tampa (33610) ***(G-17025)***
Lutimi Nr Corp.....954 245-7986
3190 S State Road 7 # 18 Miramar (33023) ***(G-10511)***
Lutz Fuel Inc.....727 376-3013
7821 Lachlan Dr Trinity (34655) ***(G-17639)***
Lutz Radiology, Lutz *Also called Meditek-Icot Inc* ***(G-8003)***

Luv Enterprises Inc 352 867-8440
  141 Sw 71st Pl Ocala (34476) *(G-11433)*

Luvix Group, Miami *Also called Gloves USA Corp (G-9223)*

Lux Unlimited Inc 305 871-8774
  4121 Nw 27th St Miami (33142) *(G-9488)*

Luxe Brands Inc (PA) 954 791-6050
  6825 W Sunrise Blvd Plantation (33313) *(G-13864)*

Luxe Prints LLC 941 484-4500
  329 Central Ave Sarasota (34236) *(G-15730)*

Luxe Vintages LLC 561 558-7399
  14545 S Military Trl J Delray Beach (33484) *(G-2984)*

Luxebrands LLC 866 514-8048
  6825 W Sunrise Blvd Plantation (33313) *(G-13865)*

Luxurable Kitchen & Bath Llc 727 286-8927
  11601 66th St Largo (33773) *(G-7636)*

Luxury Boat Services Inc 360 451-2888
  1073 Sw Abingdon Ave Port Saint Lucie (34953) *(G-14424)*

Luxury Motor Cars LLC 407 398-6933
  420 S Orange Ave Ste 220 Orlando (32801) *(G-12358)*

Luxury Woodworking Soluti 786 398-1785
  3468 W 84th St Unit 108 Hialeah (33018) *(G-5230)*

Luxury World LLC 954 746-8776
  4667 Nw 103rd Ave Sunrise (33351) *(G-16339)*

LV Thompson Inc 813 248-3456
  5015 E Hillsborough Ave Tampa (33610) *(G-17026)*

LW Rozzo Inc 954 435-8501
  17200 Pines Blvd Pembroke Pines (33029) *(G-13400)*

Lx Hausys America Inc 813 249-7658
  1820 Massaro Blvd Ste 300 Tampa (33619) *(G-17027)*

Lx Limited LLC 888 610-0642
  1756 Pontiac Cir N Melbourne (32935) *(G-8465)*

Lykes Memorial Co Library, Brooksville *Also called County of Hernando (G-1149)*

Lyndan Inc 813 977-6683
  5402 E Hanna Ave Tampa (33610) *(G-17028)*

Lynn Electronics LLC (PA) 215 355-8200
  936 Nw 1st St Fort Lauderdale (33311) *(G-3924)*

Lynn Industrial Welding Inc 850 584-4494
  182 E Park St Perry (32348) *(G-13646)*

Lynn Jackson Kimberly 904 285-7745
  12350 Arbor Dr Ponte Vedra Beach (32082) *(G-14271)*

Lynx Products Corp Inc 941 727-9676
  2424 Manatee Ave W # 203 Bradenton (34205) *(G-1008)*

Lyons Machine Tool Co Inc 904 797-1550
  5115 Cres Technical Ct Saint Augustine (32086) *(G-14855)*

Lyric Choir Gown Company 904 725-7977
  6801 Beach Blvd Jacksonville (32216) *(G-6266)*

M & B Products Inc (PA) 813 988-2211
  8601 Harney Rd Temple Terrace (33637) *(G-17540)*

M & C Assemblies Inc 800 462-7779
  904 Live Oak St Tarpon Springs (34689) *(G-17481)*

M & E Kitchen Cabinets Inc 786 346-9987
  7237 W 29th Ln Hialeah (33018) *(G-5231)*

M & H Enterprises Inc 305 885-5945
  589 W 27th St Hialeah (33010) *(G-5232)*

M & L Timber Inc 386 437-0895
  Sr 11 Bunnell (32110) *(G-1230)*

M & M Enterprises Daytona LLC (PA) 386 672-1554
  1502 State Ave Daytona Beach (32117) *(G-2570)*

M & M Industries, Seminole *Also called Modular Molding Intl Inc (G-15984)*

M & M Plastics Inc 305 688-4335
  15800 Nw 15th Ave Miami (33169) *(G-9489)*

M & M Rehabilitation, Gainesville *Also called Orthotic Prsthtic Rhbltion As (G-4744)*

M & M Signs 904 381-7353
  524 Stockton St Jacksonville (32204) *(G-6267)*

M & M Studios Inc 561 744-2754
  1445 Jupiter Park Dr # 1 Jupiter (33458) *(G-6758)*

M & N Capital Enterprises LLC 800 865-5064
  5160 W Clifton St Tampa (33634) *(G-17029)*

M & N Plastics 863 646-0208
  5579 Summerland Hills Dr Lakeland (33812) *(G-7385)*

M & R Seafood Inc 352 498-5150
  Hwy 351a Cross City (32628) *(G-2261)*

M & R Technologies, Bartow *Also called Maintnnce Reliability Tech Inc (G-316)*

M & S Computer Products Inc 561 244-5400
  11419 Wingfoot Dr Boynton Beach (33437) *(G-888)*

M & W Electric Motors Inc 850 433-0400
  1250 Barrancas Ave Pensacola (32502) *(G-13541)*

M A K Manufacturing Inc 352 343-5881
  13742 County Road 448 Tavares (32778) *(G-17517)*

M and P Plating, Saint Petersburg *Also called Ni-Chro Plating Corp (G-15139)*

M and T Pro Coating Inc 727 272-4620
  2200 Euclid Cir N Clearwater (33764) *(G-1677)*

M Austin Forman 954 763-8111
  888 Se 3rd Ave Ste 501 Fort Lauderdale (33316) *(G-3925)*

M Bilt Enterprises Inc 352 528-5566
  1821 Sw 28th St Ocala (34471) *(G-11434)*

M C Assembly, Melbourne *Also called M C Test Service Inc (G-8466)*

M C H Journal Services Inc 352 336-4215
  8430 Sw 55th Pl Gainesville (32608) *(G-4723)*

M C Test Service Inc (HQ) 321 253-0541
  425 North Dr Melbourne (32934) *(G-8466)*

M D Mold LLC 941 214-0854
  20439 Stardust Ave Port Charlotte (33952) *(G-14307)*

M D Nutra-Luxe LLC 239 561-9699
  12801 Commwl Dr Ste 1 Fort Myers (33913) *(G-4313)*

M D R International Inc 305 944-5335
  14861 Ne 20th Ave North Miami (33181) *(G-11110)*

M E C I, Hudson *Also called Marine Engine Controls Inc (G-5782)*

M F B International Inc 305 436-6601
  8323 Nw 64th St Miami (33166) *(G-9490)*

M G I USA Inc Mastercarte, Melbourne *Also called MGI Usa Inc (G-8475)*

M J Boturla Industries Inc 386 574-0811
  1885 S Lehigh Dr Deltona (32738) *(G-3048)*

M L Solutions Inc 305 506-5113
  1395 Brckwell Ave Ste 800 Miami (33132) *(G-9491)*

M Micro Technologies Inc 954 973-6166
  2901 Gateway Dr Pompano Beach (33069) *(G-14083)*

M O Precision Molders Inc 727 573-4466
  13750 49th St N Clearwater (33762) *(G-1678)*

M P E, Apopka *Also called Motor Protection Electronics (G-155)*

M P N Inc 863 606-5999
  815 Pear St Lakeland (33815) *(G-7386)*

M Pet Group Corp 954 455-5003
  2980 Ne 207th St Ste 701 Aventura (33180) *(G-266)*

M R M S Inc 305 576-3000
  571 Nw 29th St Miami (33127) *(G-9492)*

M S Amtex-N Inc 352 326-9729
  2500 Industrial St Leesburg (34748) *(G-7784)*

M Seven Holdings LLC 888 462-7577
  11750 Metro Pkwy Ste A Fort Myers (33966) *(G-4314)*

M Vb Industries Inc 954 480-6448
  510 Goolsby Blvd 5 Deerfield Beach (33442) *(G-2758)*

M Victoria Enterprises Inc 727 576-8090
  9109 4th St N Saint Petersburg (33702) *(G-15116)*

M W M Services Inc 561 844-0955
  7655 Enterprise Dr Ste 4 Riviera Beach (33404) *(G-14644)*

M Wegener Inc 561 848-2408
  24 Springdale Cir Palm Springs (33461) *(G-13145)*

M X Corporation 305 597-9881
  1531 Nw 180th Way Pembroke Pines (33029) *(G-13401)*

M&B Steel Fabricators Inc 407 486-1774
  2536 Hansrob Rd Orlando (32804) *(G-12359)*

M&D Signs 561 296-3636
  2898 Forest Hill Blvd West Palm Beach (33406) *(G-18061)*

M&E Timber Inc 850 584-6650
  2451 E Ellison Rd Perry (32347) *(G-13647)*

M&L Cabinets Inc 941 761-8100
  7320 Manatee Ave W Bradenton (34209) *(G-1009)*

M-Biolabs Inc 239 571-0435
  1415 Panther Ln Naples (34109) *(G-10809)*

M.T.s Pavers & Pools, Deerfield Beach *Also called Martins Pavers & Pools Corp (G-2764)*

M/V Marine Inc 904 633-7992
  609 Talleyrand Ave Jacksonville (32202) *(G-6268)*

M12 Lenses Inc 407 973-4403
  350 Pinestraw Cir Altamonte Springs (32714) *(G-56)*

M3 Biopharma Inc 858 603-8296
  5437 Manchini St Sarasota (34238) *(G-15731)*

M30 Freedom Inc 813 433-1776
  4018 Stornoway Dr Land O Lakes (34638) *(G-7497)*

MA Glass & Mirror LLC 305 593-8555
  6550 Nw 82nd Ave Miami (33166) *(G-9493)*

MA Metal Fabricators Inc 786 343-0268
  937 Nw 97th Ave Apt 104 Miami (33172) *(G-9494)*

Mabel Lake Loop LLC 863 326-7144
  2503 Partridge Dr Winter Haven (33884) *(G-18450)*

Mabel's Quality Products, Hallandale Beach *Also called Mabels Place Corp (G-4960)*

Mabels Place Corp 786 355-0435
  370 Ansin Blvd 370 # 370 Hallandale Beach (33009) *(G-4960)*

Mac D&D Inc 305 821-9452
  971 W 53rd St Hialeah (33012) *(G-5233)*

Mac Directory, Miami Beach *Also called American Computer & Tech Corp (G-10164)*

MAc Entps Tampa Bay Inc 813 363-2601
  4928 Ladyfish Ct New Port Richey (34652) *(G-10973)*

Mac Gregor Smith Blueprinters 407 423-5944
  1500 S Division Ave Orlando (32805) *(G-12360)*

Mac Paper Converters LLC 800 334-7026
  8370 Philips Hwy Jacksonville (32256) *(G-6269)*

Mac Papers Envelope Converters, Jacksonville *Also called Mac Paper Converters LLC (G-6269)*

Macbonner Computer Services, Holmes Beach *Also called Macbonner Inc (G-5690)*

Macbonner Inc 941 778-7978
  315 58th St Unit J Holmes Beach (34217) *(G-5690)*

Machin Signs Inc 305 694-0464
  2530 Nw 77th St Miami (33147) *(G-9495)*

Machine Engineers Inc 904 353-8289
  651 E 8th St Jacksonville (32206) *(G-6270)*

Machine Shop, Deerfield Beach *Also called Anco Precision Inc (G-2668)*

Machine Technology Inc.....863 298-8001
108 Investment Ct Sebring (33876) ***(G-15932)***
Machine Tool Masters Inc.....850 432-2829
3947 Stoddard Rd Pensacola (32526) ***(G-13542)***
Machine Top LLC.....786 238-8926
720 Sw 4th Ct Dania (33004) ***(G-2335)***
Machitech Automation LLC.....314 756-2288
1199 W Newport Center Dr Deerfield Beach (33442) ***(G-2759)***
Macho Products Inc.....800 327-6812
10045 102nd Ter Sebastian (32958) ***(G-15899)***
Macias Gabions Inc.....850 910-8000
3801 Environ Blvd Apt 519 Lauderhill (33319) ***(G-7735)***
Mack Concrete, Astatula *Also called Mack Industries Inc* ***(G-201)***
Mack Concrete Industries Inc.....352 742-2333
23902 County Road 561 Astatula (34705) ***(G-200)***
Mack Industries Inc.....352 742-2333
23902 County Road 561 Astatula (34705) ***(G-201)***
Mack Sales Inc.....772 283-2306
3129 Se Dominica Ter Stuart (34997) ***(G-16180)***
Mack Technologies Florida Inc.....321 725-6993
7505 Technology Dr Melbourne (32904) ***(G-8467)***
Maclan Corporation Inc (PA).....863 665-4814
1808 S Combee Rd Lakeland (33801) ***(G-7387)***
Macpac Inc.....904 315-6457
830-13 A1a N 477 Ponte Vedra Beach (32082) ***(G-14272)***
Macrocap Labs Inc (PA).....321 234-6282
975 Bennett Dr Longwood (32750) ***(G-7919)***
Mactech Power Line and Cable.....954 895-9966
15120 Sw 49th St Miramar (33027) ***(G-10512)***
Mad Inc.....813 251-9334
4030 Henderson Blvd Tampa (33629) ***(G-17030)***
Mad At SAD LLC.....941 203-8854
4050 Middle Ave Sarasota (34234) ***(G-15732)***
Madan Corporation (PA).....954 925-0077
130 Sw 3rd Ave Dania Beach (33004) ***(G-2353)***
Madan Kosher Foods, Dania Beach *Also called Madan Corporation* ***(G-2353)***
Madart.....321 961-9264
3635 S Ridge Cir Titusville (32796) ***(G-17600)***
Madden Millworks.....310 514-2640
1650 Margaret St 116 Jacksonville (32204) ***(G-6271)***
Maddox Foundry & Mch Works LLC.....352 495-2121
13370 Sw 170th St Archer (32618) ***(G-198)***
Maddox Industries Inc.....561 529-2165
16401 134th Ter N Jupiter (33478) ***(G-6759)***
Maddys Print Shop LLC.....954 749-0440
5450 Nw 33rd Ave Ste 108 Fort Lauderdale (33309) ***(G-3926)***
Made Fur You Inc.....813 444-7707
12121 Little Rd Hudson (34667) ***(G-5781)***
Made To Match Clothing Company, Clearwater *Also called Kleids Enterprises Inc* ***(G-1662)***
Mader Electric Motors, Fort Myers *Also called John Mader Enterprises Inc* ***(G-4300)***
Madewell Kitchens Inc.....727 856-1014
11619 State Road 52 Port Richey (34669) ***(G-14368)***
Madico Inc (HQ).....727 327-2544
9251 Belcher Rd N Ste A Pinellas Park (33782) ***(G-13707)***
Madiera Service Group Inc.....727 323-3800
9225 Ulmerton Rd Ste 318 Largo (33771) ***(G-7637)***
Madison Avenue Furniture, Sarasota *Also called Studio 21 Lighting Inc* ***(G-15841)***
Madison Millwork & Cabinet Co.....954 966-7551
5746 Dawson St Ste A Hollywood (33023) ***(G-5619)***
Madow Group.....410 526-4780
1409 Remington Trace Dr Port Charlotte (33953) ***(G-14308)***
Madson Inc.....305 863-7390
10925 Nw South River Dr Medley (33178) ***(G-8270)***
Madson Meat, Medley *Also called Madson Inc* ***(G-8270)***
Maestroshield, Fort Myers *Also called USA Shutter Company LLC* ***(G-4436)***
Mafeks International LLC.....561 997-2080
4755 Tech Way Ste 208 Boca Raton (33431) ***(G-580)***
Mag Works Inc.....305 823-4440
7725 W 2nd Ct Hialeah (33014) ***(G-5234)***
Mag-Tags Inc.....850 294-1809
4446 Sierra Ct Tallahassee (32309) ***(G-16473)***
Magellan Aviation Group Lllp.....561 266-0845
1100 Holland Dr Boca Raton (33487) ***(G-581)***
Magellan Intl Lbrction Chem Te.....386 257-3456
317 Carswell Ave Daytona Beach (32117) ***(G-2571)***
Magellan Pharmaceuticals Inc.....813 623-6800
1202 Tech Blvd Ste 106 Tampa (33619) ***(G-17031)***
Magenav Inc.....718 551-1815
3530 Nw 53rd St Fort Lauderdale (33309) ***(G-3927)***
Maggac Corporation.....561 439-2707
7629 Santee Ter Lake Worth (33467) ***(G-7215)***
Maggard Fndtion For Blind Phys.....407 637-5302
1270 Marty Blvd Ste 101 Altamonte Springs (32714) ***(G-57)***
Magic Candle, Orlando *Also called Imagination Enterprises LLC* ***(G-12236)***
Magic Fabricators Inc.....407 332-0722
320 Commercial St Casselberry (32707) ***(G-1423)***
Magic Faucet Bidet, Miami *Also called M F B International Inc* ***(G-9490)***
Magic Print Copy Center.....239 332-4456
2133 Broadway Fort Myers (33901) ***(G-4315)***
Magic Tilt Trailer Mfg Co Inc.....727 535-5561
2161 Lions Club Rd Clearwater (33764) ***(G-1679)***
Magic Trailers, Clearwater *Also called Magic Tilt Trailer Mfg Co Inc* ***(G-1679)***
Magical Creamery LLC.....407 719-6866
965 Helmsley Ct Apt 101 Lake Mary (32746) ***(G-7090)***
Magna Manufacturing Inc.....850 243-1112
85 Hill Ave Nw Fort Walton Beach (32548) ***(G-4595)***
Magnaprint Corp.....954 376-8416
1522 E Commercial Blvd Oakland Park (33334) ***(G-11276)***
Magnatrade International Corp.....305 696-5694
745 Sw 35th Ave Ste 204 Miami (33135) ***(G-9496)***
Magnatronix Corporation Inc.....727 536-7861
5410 115th Ave N Clearwater (33760) ***(G-1680)***
Magnetic Automation Corp.....321 635-8585
3160 Murrell Rd Rockledge (32955) ***(G-14728)***
Magnetic Bookmarks, Cape Coral *Also called Collectibles of SW Florida* ***(G-1325)***
Magnetic Jewellry Inc.....954 975-5868
2900 W Sample Rd Pompano Beach (33073) ***(G-14084)***
Magneto Sports LLC.....760 593-4589
360 Nw 27th St Miami (33127) ***(G-9497)***
Magnificat Holdings LLC.....727 798-0512
1125 Eldridge St Clearwater (33755) ***(G-1681)***
Magnifying America, Ocala *Also called Low Vision Aids Inc* ***(G-11432)***
Magnolia Bakery, Ocala *Also called Magnolias Gurmet Bky Itln Deli* ***(G-11435)***
Magnolia Custom Cabinetry LLC.....941 906-8744
1830 S Osprey Ave Ste 107 Sarasota (34239) ***(G-15733)***
Magnolia Machine Company.....863 965-8201
1088 Us Highway 92 W Auburndale (33823) ***(G-239)***
Magnolia Millwork Intl Inc.....407 585-3470
231 Plaza Oval Casselberry (32707) ***(G-1424)***
Magnolia Press, Sanford *Also called H & M Printing Inc* ***(G-15329)***
Magnolias Gurmet Bky Itln Deli.....352 207-2667
1412 N Magnolia Ave Ocala (34475) ***(G-11435)***
Magnum Audio Group Inc.....813 870-2857
4504 W Spruce St Apt 112 Tampa (33607) ***(G-17032)***
Magnum Coatings Inc.....407 704-0786
802 Lumsden Reserve Dr Brandon (33511) ***(G-1098)***
Magnum Marine Corporation.....305 931-4292
2900 Ne 188th St Miami (33180) ***(G-9498)***
Magnum Pavers Corp.....754 367-1832
3261 Sw 1st St Apt A Deerfield Beach (33442) ***(G-2760)***
Magnum Venus Plastech.....727 573-2955
5148 113th Ave N Clearwater (33760) ***(G-1682)***
Magnus Hitech Industries Inc.....321 724-9731
1605 Lake St Melbourne (32901) ***(G-8468)***
Maguires Welding Services Inc.....813 382-3558
38736 Pretty Pond Rd Zephyrhills (33540) ***(G-18621)***
Mahan Cabinets.....305 255-3325
10471 Sw 184th Ter Cutler Bay (33157) ***(G-2295)***
Maher Industries Inc.....407 928-5288
5434 Osprey Isle Ln Orlando (32819) ***(G-12361)***
Mahigaming LLC.....561 504-1534
245 Ne 21st Ave Ste 200 Deerfield Beach (33441) ***(G-2761)***
Mahnkes Orthtics Prsthtics of (PA).....954 772-1299
4990 Sw 72nd Ave Ste 107 Miami (33155) ***(G-9499)***
Mailbox Publishing Inc.....772 334-2121
2081 Se Ocean Blvd Fl 4 Stuart (34996) ***(G-16181)***
Mailing & Bindery Systems Inc.....813 416-8965
3959 Van Dyke Rd Lutz (33558) ***(G-8001)***
Main & Six Brewing Company LLC.....904 673-0144
2922 Madrid Ave E Jacksonville (32217) ***(G-6272)***
Main Packaging Supply.....305 863-7176
7317 Nw 61st St Miami (33166) ***(G-9500)***
Main Tape Co Inc.....561 248-8867
521 27th St West Palm Beach (33407) ***(G-18062)***
Main USA Corp.....305 499-4994
8549 Nw 68th St Miami (33166) ***(G-9501)***
Mainstream Engineering Corp.....321 631-3550
200 Yellow Pl Rockledge (32955) ***(G-14729)***
Mainstream Fiber Networks.....941 807-6100
5124 Redbriar Ct Sarasota (34238) ***(G-15734)***
Maintnnce Reliability Tech Inc.....863 533-0300
1421 Chamber Dr Bartow (33830) ***(G-316)***
Maison Goyard, Bal Harbour *Also called Goyard Miami LLC* ***(G-294)***
Maitland Furniture Inc.....386 677-7711
1711 State Ave Daytona Beach (32117) ***(G-2572)***
Majestic Foods, Hialeah *Also called Majesty Foods LLC* ***(G-5235)***
Majestic Machine & Engrg Inc.....904 257-9115
570 Us Highway 90 E Jacksonville (32234) ***(G-6273)***
Majestic Metals Inc.....813 380-6885
1807 N Waterman Dr Valrico (33594) ***(G-17668)***
Majestic Ultimate Design Inc.....954 533-8677
4431 Ne 6th Ave Oakland Park (33334) ***(G-11277)***
Majestic Unsc Spcial Intllgnce, Ponce De Leon *Also called United Ntons Space Crps Mltary* ***(G-14251)***
Majestic Woodworks.....352 429-2520
156 Groveland Farms Rd Groveland (34736) ***(G-4865)***
Majesty Foods LLC.....305 817-1888
2740 W 81st St Hialeah (33016) ***(G-5235)***

Majic Nails, Winter Garden Also called Vicx LLC (G-18407)

Majic Stairs Inc 352 255-1390
744 Abaco Path The Villages (32163) (G-17556)

Majic Stairs Inc (PA) 352 446-6295
120 Cypress Rd Ocala (34472) (G-11436)

Majic Wheels Corp (PA) 239 313-5672
1950 Custom Dr Fort Myers (33907) (G-4316)

Major Canvas Products Inc 954 764-1711
844 Nw 9th Ave Fort Lauderdale (33311) (G-3928)

Major League Signs Inc 954 600-5505
9103 Nw 171st Ln Hialeah (33018) (G-5236)

Major Partitions Ltd Corp 813 286-8634
405 S Dale Mabry Hwy # 260 Tampa (33609) (G-17033)

Major Products Company 386 673-8381
841 Buena Vista Ave Ormond Beach (32174) (G-12778)

Mak Food Service, Miami Also called Deli Fresh Foods Inc (G-9009)

Makai Marine Industries Inc 954 425-0203
730 S Deerfield Ave Ste 8 Deerfield Beach (33441) (G-2762)

Make A Statement Gifts, Boca Raton Also called Sep Communications LLC (G-669)

Make Your Mark Promo .com, Bradenton Also called Say What Screen Prtg & EMB
Inc (G-1042)

Maki Printing LLC 941 809-7574
1173 Palmer Wood Ct Sarasota (34236) (G-15735)

Maki Printing LLC (PA) 941 925-4802
4130 Boca Pointe Dr Sarasota (34238) (G-15736)

Mako Hose & Rubber Co 561 795-6200
8331 Mc Allister Way 100a West Palm Beach (33411) (G-18063)

Mako Surgical Corp (HQ) 866 647-6256
3365 Enterprise Ave Weston (33331) (G-18266)

Malema Engineering Corporation (HQ) 561 995-0595
1060 S Rogers Cir Boca Raton (33487) (G-582)

Malema Flow Sensors, Boca Raton Also called Malema Engineering Corporation (G-582)

Maleta Import 305 592-2410
6928 Nw 12th St Miami (33126) (G-9502)

Mama Asian Noodle Bar 954 973-1670
4437 Lyons Rd Coconut Creek (33073) (G-1997)

Mama Bear Lawn Care Press 863 517-5322
30290 Josie Billie Hwy Clewiston (33440) (G-1892)

Mamalu Wood LLC 305 261-6332
7003 N Waterway Dr # 207 Miami (33155) (G-9503)

Mambi Cheese Company Inc 305 324-5282
2151 Nw 10th Ave Miami (33127) (G-9504)

Mambo LLC 305 860-2544
1800 Nw 94th Ave Doral (33172) (G-3289)

Man Capital Corporation (PA) 954 946-9092
591 Sw 13th Ter Pompano Beach (33069) (G-14085)

Man-Trans LLC 850 222-6993
4920 Woodlane Cir Tallahassee (32303) (G-16474)

Managed Data Assoc Inc 386 449-8419
80 Beechwood Ln Palm Coast (32137) (G-13082)

Management Hlth Solutions Inc 888 647-4621
5701 E Hillsborough Ave Tampa (33610) (G-17034)

Management International Inc 954 763-8811
1828 Se 1st Ave Fort Lauderdale (33316) (G-3929)

Manasota Optics Inc 941 359-1748
1743 Northgate Blvd Sarasota (34234) (G-15737)

Manasota Pallets Inc 941 360-0562
7952 Fruitville Rd Sarasota (34240) (G-15738)

Manatee Bay Enterprises Inc 407 245-3600
2234 W Taft Vnlnd Rd A Orlando (32837) (G-12362)

Manatee Cabinets Inc 941 792-8656
8700 Cortez Rd W Bradenton (34210) (G-1010)

Manatee Media Inc 813 909-2800
3632 Land O Lakes Blvd Land O Lakes (34639) (G-7498)

Manatee Printers Inc 941 746-9100
1007 30th Ave W Bradenton (34205) (G-1011)

Manatee Shirts and Graphics, Saint Petersburg Also called Arj Art Inc (G-14970)

Manatee Smoothies LLC 985 640-3088
1161 E State Road 70 Lakewood Ranch (34202) (G-7480)

Manatee Tool Inc 941 355-9252
1400 Commerce Blvd Ste Cd Sarasota (34243) (G-15513)

Manci Graphics Corp 813 664-1129
2705 N Falkenburg Rd Tampa (33619) (G-17035)

Mancini Inc 954 583-7220
1878 Nw 21st St Pompano Beach (33069) (G-14086)

Mancini Packing Company 863 735-2000
3500 Mancini Pl Zolfo Springs (33890) (G-18640)

Mandala Tool Company Inc 305 652-4575
18588 Ne 2nd Ave Miami (33179) (G-9505)

Mandrel Exhaust Systems, Cutler Bay Also called Trubendz Technology Inc (G-2309)

Mangiamo, Miami Beach Also called Bighill Corporation (G-10170)

Mango Bang, Bonita Springs Also called Winds (G-827)

Mango Bottling Inc 321 631-1005
767 Clearlake Rd Cocoa (32922) (G-1940)

Mango Publications 863 583-4773
715 S New York Ave Lakeland (33815) (G-7388)

Mancini Foods, Zolfo Springs Also called Mancini Packing Company (G-18640)

Manifest Distilling LLC 904 619-1479
960 E Forsyth St Jacksonville (32202) (G-6274)

Manley Farms Inc (PA) 239 597-6416
1040 Collier Center Way # 12 Naples (34110) (G-10810)

Manley Farms North, Naples Also called Manley Farms Inc (G-10810)

Mann+hummel Filtration Technol 305 499-5100
10505 Nw 112th Ave Ste 22 Medley (33178) (G-8271)

Manna Pro Farm Supply, Tampa Also called Manna Pro Products LLC (G-17036)

Manna Pro Products LLC 813 620-9007
7000 E Adamo Dr Ste A Tampa (33619) (G-17036)

Manning Company 954 523-9355
223 Sw 28th St Fort Lauderdale (33315) (G-3930)

Manns Diversified Inds Inc 407 310-5938
380 S State Road 434 # 10 Altamonte Springs (32714) (G-58)

Mannys Stone Depot Corp 954 744-2506
2200 W 8th Ave Hialeah (33010) (G-5237)

Manor Steel Fabricators 941 722-8077
1507 18th Avenue Dr E Palmetto (34221) (G-13179)

Manotiles LLC 954 803-3303
14364 Canalview Dr Apt A Delray Beach (33484) (G-2985)

Mansci Inc 866 763-2122
6925 Lake Ellenor Dr # 136 Orlando (32809) (G-12363)

Mansfield International Inc 954 632-3280
3561 N 55th Fort Lauderdale (33301) (G-3931)

Mantis Security Corporation 571 418-3665
1990 Main St Ste 770 Sarasota (34236) (G-15739)

Mantua Manufacturing Co 813 621-3714
8108 Krauss Blvd B Tampa (33619) (G-17037)

Manucci Winery Inc 805 239-4770
4060 Ne Breakwater Dr Jensen Beach (34957) (G-6656)

Manufacturer, Daytona Beach Also called Magellan Intl Lbrction Chem Te (G-2571)

Manufacturer, Hallandale Beach Also called Arno Belo Inc (G-4936)

Manufacturer, Melbourne Also called Edge Power Solutions Inc (G-8416)

Manufacturer, Live Oak Also called Smith Steps Inc (G-7856)

Manufacturer, Miami Lakes Also called Texene LLC (G-10364)

Manufacturer - Distributor, Eustis Also called R C D Corporation (G-3565)

Manufacturers Inv Group LLC 630 285-0800
6670 Spring Lake Rd Keystone Heights (32656) (G-6887)

Manufacturing, Holly Hill Also called North American Diagnostics LLC (G-5517)

Manufacturing, Palmetto Bay Also called Metal 2 Metal Inc (G-13214)

Manufacturing, Edgewater Also called Sapphire Exchange LLC (G-3500)

Manufacturing, Hialeah Also called East Coast Metals Inc (G-5130)

Manufacturing, Sanford Also called Quantumfly Enterprises Inc (G-15379)

Manufacturing, Fort Lauderdale Also called All Points Boats Inc (G-3639)

Manufacturing By Skema Inc 954 797-7325
3801 Sw 47th Ave Ste 501 Davie (33314) (G-2435)

Manufacturing Facility, Flagler Beach Also called Sea Ray Boats Inc (G-3605)

Manufacturing Inc Sp 305 362-0456
2200 W 77th St Hialeah (33016) (G-5238)

Manufacturing Martin LLC Kls 904 641-0421
11228 St Jhns Indus Pkwy Jacksonville (32246) (G-6275)

Manufctring Prcess Ctrl Instrs, Orlando Also called Red Meters LLC (G-12538)

Manufctring Sls Pipe Bnding Eq, Fort Myers Also called Hines Bending Systems
Inc (G-4280)

Manufacturers Metal Forming Mch, Sarasota Also called Marchant Machine
Corporation (G-15741)

Manutech Assembly Inc (PA) 305 888-2800
7901 Nw 67th St Miami (33166) (G-9506)

Map & Globe LLC (PA) 407 898-0757
113 Candace Dr Ste 3 Maitland (32751) (G-8067)

Map and Globe Store, The, Maitland Also called Map & Globe LLC (G-8067)

Mapei Corporation (HQ) 954 246-8888
1144 E Newport Center Dr Deerfield Beach (33442) (G-2763)

Mapei Corporation 954 485-8637
1851 Nw 22nd St Fort Lauderdale (33311) (G-3932)

Maq Investments Group Inc 305 691-1468
14312 Commerce Way Miami Lakes (33016) (G-10316)

Mar Company Distributors LLC 786 477-4174
6750 Nw 79th Ave Miami (33166) (G-9507)

Mar Cor Purification Inc 484 991-0220
5001 Gateway Blvd Ste 21 Lakeland (33811) (G-7389)

Mar-Co Gas Services Inc 561 745-0085
11138 161st St N Jupiter (33478) (G-6760)

Mar-Quipt, Pompano Beach Also called Byrd Technologies Inc (G-13959)

Maracom Marine, Doral Also called Marathon Technology Corp (G-3291)

Marajo Diesel Power Corp 786 212-1485
1950 Nw 93rd Ave Doral (33172) (G-3290)

Maramed Orthopedic Systems, Hialeah Also called Maramed Precision Corporation (G-5239)

Maramed Precision Corporation 305 823-8300
2480 W 82nd St Unit 1 Hialeah (33016) (G-5239)

Marathon Engineering Corp 239 303-7378
5615 2nd St W Lehigh Acres (33971) (G-7816)

Marathon Ribbon Co, Largo Also called Golden Ribbon Corporation (G-7598)

Marathon Technology Corp 305 592-1340
8280 Nw 56th St Doral (33166) (G-3291)

Marbelite International Corp 941 378-0860
1500 Global Ct Sarasota (34240) (G-15740)

Marble Bridge Inc 239 213-1411
3827 Arnold Ave Naples (34104) **(G-10811)**
Marble Club Creamery, Estero *Also called Rd Abukaf 1 Inc* **(G-3549)**
Marble Crafters, Daytona Beach *Also called Showcase Marble Inc* **(G-2598)**
Marble Designs, Naples *Also called Debanie Inc* **(G-10726)**
Marble Designs of FL Inc 321 269-6920
1975 Silver Star Rd Titusville (32796) **(G-17601)**
Marble Lite Products Corp 305 557-8766
9920 Nw 79th Ave Hialeah Gardens (33016) **(G-5443)**
Marble Works Kit & Bath Ctr, Fort Walton Beach *Also called Kitchen & Bath Center Inc* **(G-4594)**
Marblue, Dania Beach *Also called Marware Inc* **(G-2354)**
Marbon Inc 561 822-9999
10723 Ibis Reserve Cir West Palm Beach (33412) **(G-18064)**
Marcela Creations Inc 813 253-0556
1802 W Kennedy Blvd Tampa (33606) **(G-17038)**
March Inc 239 593-4074
16160 Performance Way Naples (34110) **(G-10812)**
March Performance, Naples *Also called March Inc* **(G-10812)**
Marchant Machine Corporation 301 937-4481
8713 Amaretto Ave Sarasota (34238) **(G-15741)**
Marco Polo Publications Inc 866 610-9441
360 Central Ave Ste 1260 Saint Petersburg (33701) **(G-15117)**
Marconi Line Inc 321 639-1130
1870 Huntington Ln Rockledge (32955) **(G-14730)**
Marcos Professional Cabinets C 305 962-4378
1412 W 39th Pl Hialeah (33012) **(G-5240)**
Marcus V Hall 352 490-9694
14271 Nw 66th Ave Chiefland (32626) **(G-1448)**
Marden Industries Inc 863 682-7882
26855 Airport Rd Punta Gorda (33982) **(G-14513)**
Mares Services Corp 305 752-0093
14758 Sw 56th St Miami (33185) **(G-9508)**
Marex, Plantation *Also called Maritime Executive LLC* **(G-13866)**
Marey International LLC 787 727-0277
8113 Nw 68th St Miami (33166) **(G-9509)**
Margarita International, Miami *Also called Margarita Interml Trading Inc* **(G-9510)**
Margarita Internl Trading Inc 305 688-1300
5601 Nw 72nd Ave Miami (33166) **(G-9510)**
Margo Outdoor Living Inc (HQ) 912 496-2999
2562 Cabot Commerce Dr Jacksonville (32226) **(G-6276)**
Margo State Line, Inc., Jacksonville *Also called Margo Outdoor Living Inc* **(G-6276)**
Maria Dill Inc 352 394-0418
17649 Us Highway 27 B3 Clermont (34715) **(G-1876)**
Maria E Acosta 305 231-5543
4004 W 11th Ln Hialeah (33012) **(G-5241)**
Maria Fuentes LLC 305 717-3404
10130 Sw 32nd St Miami (33165) **(G-9511)**
Marianna Lime Products Inc 850 526-3580
3333 Valley View Rd Marianna (32446) **(G-8170)**
Marianna Limestone LLC 954 581-1220
3333 Valley View Rd Marianna (32446) **(G-8171)**
Marianna Truss Inc 850 594-5420
3644 Highway 71 Marianna (32446) **(G-8172)**
Marimba Cocina Mexicana II Inc 321 268-6960
3758 S Washington Ave Titusville (32780) **(G-17602)**
Marina Medical Instruments Inc 954 924-4418
8190 W State Road 84 Davie (33324) **(G-2436)**
Marine Concepts, Sarasota *Also called Patrick Industries Inc* **(G-15534)**
Marine Concepts 239 283-0800
2443 Sw Pine Island Rd Cape Coral (33991) **(G-1362)**
Marine Customs Unlimited 772 223-8005
3355 Se Dixie Hwy Stuart (34997) **(G-16182)**
Marine Digital Integrators LLC 772 210-2403
7667 Sw Ellipse Way Stuart (34997) **(G-16183)**
Marine Electrical Engineer, Port Saint Lucie *Also called Luxury Boat Services Inc* **(G-14424)**
Marine Electronics Engine 727 459-5593
4801 96th St N Saint Petersburg (33708) **(G-15118)**
Marine Engine Controls Inc 727 518-8080
9035 Wister Ln Hudson (34669) **(G-5782)**
Marine Exhaust Systems Inc (PA) 561 848-1238
3640 Fiscal Ct Ste D Riviera Beach (33404) **(G-14645)**
Marine Hdwr Specialists Inc 561 766-1987
3570 Consumer St Ste 1 West Palm Beach (33404) **(G-18065)**
Marine Industrial Paint Co Inc 727 527-3382
4590 60th Ave N Saint Petersburg (33714) **(G-15119)**
Marine Inland Fabricators, Panama City *Also called Sisco Marine LLC* **(G-13309)**
Marine Manufacturing Inc 305 885-3493
295 W 23rd St Hialeah (33010) **(G-5242)**
Marine Metal Products Co 727 461-5575
2154 Calumet St Clearwater (33765) **(G-1683)**
Marine Pleasure Craft, Cutler Bay *Also called South Florida Marine* **(G-2304)**
Marine Spc Cstm Fabricator 813 855-0554
360 Mears Blvd Oldsmar (34677) **(G-11672)**
Mariner International Trvl Inc 954 925-4150
850 Ne 3rd St Ste 201 Dania (33004) **(G-2336)**
Mariner Publications LLC (PA) 941 426-9645
2250 Firebrand Rd North Port (34288) **(G-11198)**
Marinetek North America Inc 727 498-8741
111 2nd Ave Ne Ste 360 Saint Petersburg (33701) **(G-15120)**
Marinize Products Corp 954 989-7990
3986 Pembroke Rd Hollywood (33021) **(G-5620)**
Mario Kenny 786 274-0527
789 Ne 83rd St Miami (33138) **(G-9512)**
Marion Metal Works Inc 352 351-4221
4750 S Pine Ave Ocala (34480) **(G-11437)**
Marion Precision Tool Inc 352 867-0080
1800 Nw 10th St Ocala (34475) **(G-11438)**
Marion Rock Inc 352 687-2023
5979 Se Maricamp Rd Ocala (34472) **(G-11439)**
Marios Casting Jewelry Inc 305 374-2894
36 Ne 1st St Ste 851 Miami (33132) **(G-9513)**
Marios Metalcraft 239 649-0085
4227 Mercantile Ave Ste A Naples (34104) **(G-10813)**
Maris Mtalcraft Powdr Coating, Naples *Also called Marios Metalcraft* **(G-10813)**
Maris Worden Aerospace Inc 514 895-8075
2001 S Ridgewood Ave South Daytona (32119) **(G-16023)**
Maritec Industries Inc 352 429-8888
20150 Independence Blvd Groveland (34736) **(G-4866)**
Maritech Machine Inc 850 872-0852
1740 Sherman Ave Panama City (32405) **(G-13284)**
Maritime Custom Designs Inc 941 716-0255
170 Rich St Venice (34292) **(G-17706)**
Maritime Executive LLC 954 848-9955
7473 Nw 4th St Plantation (33317) **(G-13866)**
Maritime Replicas America Inc 305 386-1958
1275 W 47th Pl Ste 423 Hialeah (33012) **(G-5243)**
Maritime Replicas Usa LLC 305 921-9690
70 Dorset B Boca Raton (33434) **(G-583)**
Maritime SEC Strtegies Fla LLC 912 704-0300
5251 W Tyson Ave Tampa (33611) **(G-17039)**
Marjon Specialty Foods, Plant City *Also called Farm Cut LLC* **(G-13765)**
Mark 7 Reloading LLC, Fort Myers *Also called M Seven Holdings LLC* **(G-4314)**
Mark Benton 754 203-9377
900 N Federal Hwy Boca Raton (33432) **(G-584)**
Mark Housman Screen RPS Inc 321 255-2778
2911 Dusa Dr Ste E Melbourne (32934) **(G-8469)**
Mark Master Inc 813 988-6000
11111 N 46th St Tampa (33617) **(G-17040)**
Mark McManus Inc 239 454-1300
15821 Chief Ct Fort Myers (33912) **(G-4317)**
Mark Plating Co 561 655-4370
441 25th St West Palm Beach (33407) **(G-18066)**
Mark Trece, Lakeland *Also called Mark/Trece Inc* **(G-7390)**
Mark V Printing LLC 954 563-2505
140 Ne 32nd Ct Oakland Park (33334) **(G-11278)**
Mark Walters LLC 727 742-3091
1126 15th Ave N Saint Petersburg (33704) **(G-15121)**
Mark Wayne Adams Inc 407 756-5862
490 Wekiva Cove Rd Longwood (32779) **(G-7920)**
Mark Weisser Productions, Boynton Beach *Also called Mark Wsser Grphic Prdctons Inc* **(G-889)**
Mark Wsser Grphic Prdctons Inc 305 888-7445
8941 Golden Mountain Cir Boynton Beach (33473) **(G-889)**
Mark/Trece Inc 863 647-4372
5385 Gateway Blvd Lakeland (33811) **(G-7390)**
Marker Industries LLC 954 907-2647
3980 Oaks Clubhouse Dr Pompano Beach (33069) **(G-14087)**
Market Ink Usa Inc 561 502-3438
1000 S Military Trl Ste D West Palm Beach (33415) **(G-18067)**
Market Logic, Doral *Also called Esperanto Inc* **(G-3209)**
Market Ready 407 324-4273
1721 Missouri Ave Sanford (32771) **(G-15353)**
Marketing Bar, The, Pensacola *Also called Mc Squared Group Inc* **(G-13544)**
Marketshare LLC 631 273-0598
6790 E Rogers Cir Boca Raton (33487) **(G-585)**
Marko Garage Doors & Gates Inc 561 547-4001
248 Davis Rd Palm Springs (33461) **(G-13146)**
Marlin & Barrel Distillery LLC 321 230-4755
115 S 2nd St Fernandina Beach (32034) **(G-3593)**
Marlin Coatings LLC 850 224-1370
3666 Peddie Dr Tallahassee (32303) **(G-16475)**
Marlin Darlin Air LLC 727 726-1136
2819 West Bay Dr Belleair Bluffs (33770) **(G-355)**
Marlin Graphics Inc 561 743-5220
1251 Jupiter Park Dr # 7 Jupiter (33458) **(G-6761)**
Marlin Yacht Manufacturing 305 586-3586
1350 Hammondville Rd A Pompano Beach (33069) **(G-14088)**
Marlo Electronics Inc 561 477-0856
2412 Nw 35th St Boca Raton (33431) **(G-586)**
Marlon Inc 813 901-8488
8513 Sunstate St Tampa (33634) **(G-17041)**
Marlyn Steel Decks Inc 813 621-1375
6808 Harney Rd Tampa (33610) **(G-17042)**
Marlyn Steel Products Inc 813 621-1375
6808 Harney Rd Tampa (33610) **(G-17043)**

Marmon Aerospace & Defense LLC................239 643-6400
 2584 Horseshoe Dr S Naples (34104) *(G-10814)*

Marnis Dolce................407 915-7607
 2928 Rapollo Ln Apopka (32712) *(G-148)*

Marpro Marine Ways LLC................727 447-4930
 1822 N Belcher Rd Clearwater (33765) *(G-1684)*

Marquez Brothers Inc................305 888-0090
 9115 Nw 93rd St Medley (33178) *(G-8272)*

Marquis Media Group................941 255-0087
 26360 Trinilas Dr Punta Gorda (33983) *(G-14514)*

Marquis Software Dev Inc................850 877-8864
 1625 Summit Lake Dr # 105 Tallahassee (32317) *(G-16476)*

Marrakech Inc................727 942-2218
 720 Wesley Ave Ste 11 Tarpon Springs (34689) *(G-17482)*

Mars Precision Products Inc................727 846-0505
 8526 Leo Kidd Ave Port Richey (34668) *(G-14369)*

Mars Talent Agency................561 748-6566
 18406 Se Lakeside Dr Jupiter (33469) *(G-6762)*

Marsig Group Inc................813 840-3714
 23100 State Road 54 # 18 Lutz (33549) *(G-8002)*

Martell Glass................786 336-0142
 7246 Nw 25th St Miami (33122) *(G-9514)*

Marti Lincoln Community Agency, Miami *Also called Lincoln-Marti Cmnty Agcy Inc* *(G-9463)*

Martin & Vleminckx Rides LLC................407 566-0036
 31096 Us Hwy 27 N Haines City (33844) *(G-4910)*

Martin County Hometown News, Fort Pierce *Also called Hometown News LC* *(G-4495)*

Martin Leonard Corporation................850 434-2203
 24 N Palafox St Pensacola (32502) *(G-13543)*

Martin Lithograph Inc................813 254-1553
 505 N Rome Ave Tampa (33606) *(G-17044)*

Martin Marietta Materials Inc................904 596-0230
 5942 Soutel Dr Jacksonville (32219) *(G-6277)*

Martin Marietta Materials Inc................850 981-9020
 6134 Wastle Rd Milton (32583) *(G-10430)*

Martin Marietta Materials Inc................850 913-0083
 1602 B Ave Panama City (32401) *(G-13285)*

Martin Sprocket & Gear Inc................813 623-1705
 3201 Queen Palm Dr Tampa (33619) *(G-17045)*

Martin-Weston Co................727 545-8877
 10860 76th Ct Ste B Largo (33777) *(G-7638)*

Martinez Builders Supply LLC................772 466-2480
 5285 Saint Lucie Blvd Fort Pierce (34946) *(G-4503)*

Martinez Distributors Corp................305 882-8282
 3081 Nw 74th Ave Miami (33122) *(G-9515)*

Martinez Truss Company Inc................305 883-6261
 9280 Nw S River Dr Medley (33166) *(G-8273)*

Martins Pavers & Pools Corp................754 368-4413
 220 Nw 40th Ct Deerfield Beach (33064) *(G-2764)*

Martinson Mica Wood Pdts Inc................305 688-4445
 13740 Nw 19th Ave Opa Locka (33054) *(G-11765)*

Maruti Fence, Orlando *Also called Maruti Technology Inc* *(G-12364)*

Maruti Technology Inc................407 704-4775
 1775 Colton Dr Orlando (32822) *(G-12364)*

Marvelous Mushrooms, Medley *Also called Ida Solutions* *(G-8256)*

Marware Inc................954 927-6031
 1206 Stirling Rd Bay 9a-B Dania Beach (33004) *(G-2354)*

Mary Lake Life Mag Inc................407 324-2644
 881 Silversmith Cir Lake Mary (32746) *(G-7091)*

Mary Lake Life Magazine Inc................407 324-2644
 3232 W Lake Mary Blvd # 1420 Lake Mary (32746) *(G-7092)*

Mary Lame Wrought Iron & Alum................727 934-2879
 1022 Us Highway 19 Holiday (34691) *(G-5502)*

Mary Symon................813 986-4676
 13206 Emerald Acres Ave Dover (33527) *(G-3431)*

Marysol Technologies Inc................727 712-1523
 1444c S Belcher Rd 136 Clearwater (33764) *(G-1685)*

Mas Editorial Corp................305 748-0124
 1596 Trailhead Ter Hollywood (33021) *(G-5621)*

Mas Entrprses of Ft Lauderdale................904 356-9606
 1883 W State Road 84 # 10 Fort Lauderdale (33315) *(G-3933)*

Mas Hvac Inc................904 531-3140
 4010 Deerpark Blvd Elkton (32033) *(G-3507)*

Masa Trading LLC................561 729-3293
 1454 Sw 11th Ter Pompano Beach (33069) *(G-14089)*

Masaka LLC................786 800-8337
 3105 Nw 107th Ave Ste 601 Doral (33172) *(G-3292)*

Masc Aspen Partners LLC................212 545-1076
 17639 Lake Estates Dr Boca Raton (33496) *(G-587)*

Maschmeyer Concrete Co Fla................386 668-7801
 275 Benson Junction Rd Debary (32713) *(G-2637)*

Maschmeyer Concrete Co Fla................407 339-5311
 1601 S Ronald Reagan Blvd Longwood (32750) *(G-7921)*

Maschmeyer Concrete Co Fla (PA)................561 848-9112
 1142 Watertower Rd Lake Park (33403) *(G-7131)*

Maschmeyer Concrete Co Fla................863 420-6800
 4949 Sand Mine Rd Davenport (33897) *(G-2368)*

Mask Giant, Delray Beach *Also called Straw Giant Company* *(G-3022)*

Maskco Technologies Inc................877 261-6405
 1348 Washington Ave Miami Beach (33139) *(G-10210)*

Masking Systems of America................813 920-2271
 13221 Byrd Dr Odessa (33556) *(G-11566)*

Mason Vitamins Inc................800 327-6005
 15750 Nw 59th Ave Miami Lakes (33014) *(G-10317)*

Mason Ways Indstrctble Plas LL................561 478-8838
 580 Village Blvd Ste 330 West Palm Beach (33409) *(G-18068)*

Mason-Florida LLC................352 638-9003
 2415 Griffin Rd Leesburg (34748) *(G-7785)*

Masonite Corporation (HQ)................813 877-2726
 1242 E 5th Ave Tampa (33605) *(G-17046)*

Masonite Corporation................715 354-3441
 1205 E 5th Ave Tampa (33605) *(G-17047)*

Masonite Holdings Inc................813 877-2726
 201 N Franklin St Ste 300 Tampa (33602) *(G-17048)*

Masonite International, Tampa *Also called Masonite US Corporation* *(G-17052)*

Masonite International Corp................813 889-3861
 5502 Pioneer Park Blvd Tampa (33634) *(G-17049)*

Masonite International Corp (PA)................813 877-2726
 1242 E 5th Ave Tampa (33605) *(G-17050)*

Masonite International Corp................904 225-3889
 86554 Gene Lassere Blvd Yulee (32097) *(G-18591)*

Masonite International Corp................813 877-2726
 1242 E 5th Ave Tampa (33605) *(G-17051)*

Masonite US Corporation................813 877-2726
 1242 E 5th Ave Tampa (33605) *(G-17052)*

Massachusetts Bay Clam Co Inc................813 855-4599
 13605 W Hillsborough Ave Tampa (33635) *(G-17053)*

Masseys Metals................813 626-8275
 2251 Massaro Blvd Tampa (33619) *(G-17054)*

Massimo & Umberto Inc................954 993-0842
 132 Sw 3rd Ave Dania Beach (33004) *(G-2355)*

Massimo Roma LLC................561 302-5998
 1395 Brickell Ave Ste 900 Miami (33131) *(G-9516)*

Masso Estate Winery LLC (PA)................305 707-7749
 3150 Sw 38th Ave Ste 1303 Coral Gables (33146) *(G-2083)*

Master Alum & SEC Shutter Co................727 725-1744
 950 Harbor Lake Ct Safety Harbor (34695) *(G-14790)*

Master Cabinet Maker Inc................941 723-0278
 5004 Us Highway 41 N A Palmetto (34221) *(G-13180)*

Master Construction Pdts Inc (PA)................407 857-1221
 501 Thorpe Rd Orlando (32824) *(G-12365)*

Master Fabricators Inc................786 537-7440
 12101 Sw 114th Pl Miami (33176) *(G-9517)*

Master Kitchen Cabinets................239 225-9668
 12960 Commerce Lk Dr # 8 Fort Myers (33913) *(G-4318)*

Master Machine & Tool Co II................863 425-4902
 2010 Moores Ln Mulberry (33860) *(G-10631)*

Master Marine................904 329-1541
 14255 Beach Blvd Jacksonville (32250) *(G-6278)*

Master Mold Corp................941 486-0000
 123 Morse Ct North Venice (34275) *(G-11214)*

Master Nutrition Labs Inc................786 847-2000
 13165 Nw 47th Ave Opa Locka (33054) *(G-11766)*

Master Overland LLC................727 255-3764
 16214 Aviation Loop Dr Brooksville (34604) *(G-1177)*

Master Painting & Sealants LLC................305 910-5104
 480 Ne 112th St Miami (33161) *(G-9518)*

Master Screen Printing................407 625-8902
 6782 N Orng Blflm Trl D Orlando (32810) *(G-12366)*

Master Syrup Makers, Miami *Also called Al-Rite Fruits and Syrups Inc* *(G-8679)*

Master Tool Co Inc................305 557-1020
 6115 Nw 153rd St Miami Lakes (33014) *(G-10318)*

Master Universe LLC................786 246-3190
 1410 Ne 200th St Miami (33179) *(G-9519)*

Master-Kraft Cabinetry................863 661-2083
 305 Keystone Rd Auburndale (33823) *(G-240)*

Mastercraft Shtters Blinds LLC................904 379-7544
 1700 E Church St Jacksonville (32202) *(G-6279)*

Mastercut Tool Corp................727 726-5336
 965 Harbor Lake Dr Safety Harbor (34695) *(G-14791)*

Masters Block - North LLC................407 212-7704
 1037 New York Ave Saint Cloud (34769) *(G-14932)*

Mat Div-Ft Lauder Maint Shop, Pompano Beach *Also called Cemex Cnstr Mtls Fla LLC* *(G-13966)*

Mat Div-Palm Beach Maint Shop, West Palm Beach *Also called Cemex Cnstr Mtls Fla LLC* *(G-17959)*

Mat Industries LLC................847 821-9630
 1815 Griffin Rd Ste 400 Dania Beach (33004) *(G-2356)*

Mat-Vac Technology Inc................386 238-7017
 410 Arroyo Ln Daytona Beach (32114) *(G-2573)*

Matawan Tool & Mfg Co Inc................772 221-3706
 2861 Sw Brighton Way Palm City (34990) *(G-13050)*

Matchware Inc (PA)................800 880-2810
 511 W Bay St Ste 460 Tampa (33606) *(G-17055)*

Matco Tools, Davie *Also called Express Tools Inc* *(G-2410)*

Matco Transload Us06, Pompano Beach *Also called Lhoist North America Ala LLC* *(G-14077)*

Material Conveying Maint Inc................813 677-3740
 6535 Carrington Sky Dr Apollo Beach (33572) *(G-95)*

A
L
P
H
A
B
E
T
I
C

Material Conveying Maint Inc (PA)..........813 740-1111
4901 30th Ave S Tampa (33619) *(G-17056)*

Materials Div-Jacksonville ADM, Orange Park *Also called Cemex Cnstr Mtls Fla LLC (G-11819)*

Materials Div-Jupiter Lab, Jupiter *Also called Cemex Cnstr Mtls Fla LLC (G-6702)*

Matherson Organics LLC..........647 801-6977
1400 Vlg Sq Blvd 3-85899 Tallahassee (32312) *(G-16477)*

Matheson Tri-Gas Inc..........561 615-3000
18000 Bee Line Hwy Jupiter (33478) *(G-6763)*

Matheson Tri-Gas Inc..........727 572-8737
12650 49th St N Clearwater (33762) *(G-1686)*

Mathews Associates Inc..........407 323-3390
220 Power Ct Sanford (32771) *(G-15354)*

Matrix Coatings Corp..........561 848-1288
3575 Investment Ln West Palm Beach (33404) *(G-18069)*

Matrix Coatings Inc..........561 848-1288
3575 Investment Ln West Palm Beach (33404) *(G-18070)*

Matrix Composites Inc..........321 633-4480
275 Barnes Blvd Rockledge (32955) *(G-14731)*

Matrix Machining & Mfg LLC (PA)..........908 355-1900
1904 Calumet St Clearwater (33765) *(G-1687)*

Matrix Marketing Solutions Inc..........407 654-5736
13629 Lake Cawood Dr Windermere (34786) *(G-18360)*

Matrix Media LLC..........435 313-2877
989 Georgia Ave Palm Harbor (34683) *(G-13119)*

Matrix Packaging of Florida (HQ)..........305 358-9696
1001 Brickell Bay Dr Miami (33131) *(G-9520)*

Matrix24 Laboratories LLC..........941 879-3048
1453 Tallevast Rd Sarasota (34243) *(G-15514)*

Matry Group LLC..........407 461-9797
10 S Flag Dr Kissimmee (34759) *(G-6977)*

Matschel of Flagler Inc..........386 446-4595
239 Marshside Dr Saint Augustine (32080) *(G-14856)*

Matteo Graphics Inc..........239 652-1002
160 Hunter Blvd Ste A1 Cape Coral (33909) *(G-1363)*

Mattheessons..........305 296-1616
106 Duval St Key West (33040) *(G-6874)*

Matthews International Corp..........407 886-5533
2045 Sprint Blvd Apopka (32703) *(G-149)*

Mattis Aerospace..........305 910-2377
26085 S Dixie Hwy Homestead (33032) *(G-5729)*

Mattress Makers USA Inc..........904 906-2793
7660 Gainesville Ave Jacksonville (32208) *(G-6280)*

Matusalem & Company, Miami *Also called Ron Matusalem & Matusa Fla Inc (G-9823)*

Mau Mau Corporation..........305 440-5203
555 Jefferson Ave Miami Beach (33139) *(G-10211)*

Maui Holdings LLC..........904 741-5400
250 Royal Palm Way # 201 Palm Beach (33480) *(G-12938)*

Maupin House Publishing Inc..........800 524-0634
2300 Nw 71st Pl Gainesville (32653) *(G-4724)*

Maven Medical Mfg Inc..........727 518-0555
2250 Lake Ave Se Largo (33771) *(G-7639)*

Maverick Boat Group Inc..........772 465-0631
4551 Saint Lucie Blvd Fort Pierce (34946) *(G-4504)*

Maverick Boat Group Inc (HQ)..........772 465-0631
3207 Industrial 29th St Fort Pierce (34946) *(G-4505)*

Maverick Composites Inc..........561 601-3393
6105 Francis St Jupiter (33458) *(G-6764)*

Maverick Natural Resources LLC..........239 657-2171
909 County Road 846 Immokalee (34142) *(G-5799)*

Max Avw Professional LLC..........954 972-3338
441 S State Road 7 Ste 4 Margate (33068) *(G-8143)*

Max Graphix LLC..........904 408-1543
583 S 6th St Macclenny (32063) *(G-8038)*

Max Torque LLC..........863 701-8000
3360 Flightline Dr Lakeland (33811) *(G-7391)*

Max-Pak Inc (HQ)..........863 682-0123
2808 New Tampa Hwy Lakeland (33815) *(G-7392)*

Maxam Group LLC..........305 952-3227
20725 Ne 16th Ave Ste A1 Miami (33179) *(G-9521)*

Maxant Button & Supply Inc..........770 460-2227
5901 Plantation Rd Plantation (33317) *(G-13867)*

Maxant Buttons LLC..........770 460-2227
213 Florida Ave Nw Moore Haven (33471) *(G-10591)*

Maxeff Industries Inc..........941 893-5804
1251 Commerce Blvd S Sarasota (34243) *(G-15515)*

Maxi-Blast of Florida Inc..........727 572-0909
11000 Gandy Blvd N Saint Petersburg (33702) *(G-15122)*

Maxigraphics Inc..........954 978-0740
2201 W Sample Rd Ste 8-2a Pompano Beach (33073) *(G-14090)*

Maxijet Inc..........863 439-3667
8400 Lake Trask Rd Dundee (33838) *(G-3435)*

Maximilian Zenho & Co Inc..........352 875-1190
2775 Nw 49th Ave Unit 205 Ocala (34482) *(G-11440)*

Maxit Corporation..........904 998-9520
1102 A1a N Ste 206 Ponte Vedra Beach (32082) *(G-14273)*

Maxogen Group LLC..........305 814-0734
2719 Hollywood Blvd Hollywood (33020) *(G-5622)*

Maxord LLC..........405 256-2381
10849 Sunset Ridge Cir Boynton Beach (33473) *(G-890)*

Maxpak, Lakeland *Also called Max-Pak Inc (G-7392)*

Maxrodon Marble Inc..........772 562-7543
2250 Old Dixie Hwy Se Vero Beach (32962) *(G-17776)*

Maxville LLC..........904 289-7261
6640 County Road 218 Jacksonville (32234) *(G-6281)*

Maxxfi LLC..........513 289-6521
3428 Sw 25th Pl Cape Coral (33914) *(G-1364)*

Maxxim Medical Group Inc..........727 571-3717
4750 118th Ave N Clearwater (33762) *(G-1688)*

May & Well Inc..........813 333-5806
8907 Regents Park Dr # 390 Tampa (33647) *(G-17057)*

Mayaca Materials, Canal Point *Also called Five Stones Mine LLC (G-1260)*

Mayers Jwly Co Hollywood Inc (PA)..........954 921-1422
2002 Grant St Hollywood (33020) *(G-5623)*

Mayhew/Bestway LLC..........631 586-4702
2a Sunshine Blvd Ormond Beach (32174) *(G-12779)*

Maymaan Research LLC..........954 374-9376
3904 N 29th Ave Hollywood (33020) *(G-5624)*

Mayo Clinic..........904 953-2000
14225 Zumbro Dr Jacksonville (32224) *(G-6282)*

Mayo Clinic..........904 953-2000
4500 San Pablo Rd S Jacksonville (32224) *(G-6283)*

Mayo Clnic Pet Rdchmstry Fclty, Jacksonville *Also called Mayo Clinic (G-6282)*

Mayo Clnic Pet Rdchmstry Fclty, Jacksonville *Also called Mayo Clinic (G-6283)*

Mayo Plastics Mfg Inc..........386 294-1049
232 Se Indus Cir S B Mayo (32066) *(G-8183)*

Mayo Truss Co Inc..........386 294-3988
845 E Us 27 Mayo (32066) *(G-8184)*

Mayworth Showcase Works Inc..........813 251-1558
12711 N Armenia Ave Tampa (33612) *(G-17058)*

Mazi Group Inc..........786 800-2425
333 Se 2nd Ave Miami (33131) *(G-9522)*

MB Welding Inc..........727 548-0923
7360 46th Ave N Saint Petersburg (33709) *(G-15123)*

Mbf Industries Inc..........407 323-9414
210 Tech Dr Sanford (32771) *(G-15355)*

MBL, Naples *Also called M-Biolabs Inc (G-10809)*

Mc Assembly Holdings Inc (HQ)..........321 253-0541
425 North Dr Melbourne (32934) *(G-8470)*

Mc Assembly International LLC (HQ)..........321 253-0541
425 North Dr Melbourne (32934) *(G-8471)*

Mc Assembly LLC..........321 253-0541
425 North Dr Melbourne (32934) *(G-8472)*

Mc Connie Enterprises Inc..........813 247-3827
4707 30th Ave S Tampa (33619) *(G-17059)*

Mc Connie Fence, Tampa *Also called Mc Connie Enterprises Inc (G-17059)*

Mc Graphics LLC..........727 579-1527
1527 102nd Ave N Saint Petersburg (33716) *(G-15124)*

MC Intl Transportation..........305 805-8228
8321 Nw 68th St Miami (33166) *(G-9523)*

MC Johnson Co..........239 293-0901
2037 J And C Blvd Naples (34109) *(G-10815)*

MC Mieth Manufacturing Inc..........386 767-3494
665 Herbert St Port Orange (32129) *(G-14339)*

MC Miller Co Inc..........772 794-9448
11640 Us Highway 1 Sebastian (32958) *(G-15900)*

Mc Monumental Group Inc..........305 651-9113
281 Ne 168th Ter North Miami Beach (33162) *(G-11149)*

Mc Oil and Gas LLC..........239 649-7013
4301 Gulf Shore Blvd N Naples (34103) *(G-10816)*

Mc Squared Group Inc..........850 435-4600
260 S Tarragona St # 140 Pensacola (32502) *(G-13544)*

McCabinet Inc (PA)..........727 608-5929
7273 112th Ave N Largo (33773) *(G-7640)*

McCain Mills Inc..........813 752-6478
5605 Paul Buchman Hwy Plant City (33565) *(G-13784)*

McCain Sales of Florida Inc..........772 461-0665
3001 Orange Ave Fort Pierce (34947) *(G-4506)*

McCallum Cabinets Inc..........352 372-2344
3004 Ne 21st Way Gainesville (32609) *(G-4725)*

McCarthy Fabrication LLC..........407 943-4909
201 N Maple Ave Ste 2 Sanford (32771) *(G-15356)*

McClatchy Shared Services Ctr..........305 740-8800
3511 Nw 91st Ave Doral (33172) *(G-3293)*

McClellan Logging Inc..........352 468-1856
State Rd 325 Hampton (32044) *(G-4986)*

McCluneys Orthpd Prsthetic Svc..........352 373-5754
2930 Nw 16th Ave Gainesville (32605) *(G-4726)*

McCluneys Orthpd Prsthtic Srvi, Gainesville *Also called McCluneys Orthpd Prsthetis Svc (G-4726)*

McColl Display Solutions..........813 333-6613
8416 Iron Mountain Trl Windermere (34786) *(G-18361)*

McConnell Corp..........305 296-6124
1107 Duval St Key West (33040) *(G-6875)*

McCord Holding, Melbourne *Also called Fastsigns 176101 (G-8424)*

McCormick Restaurant Services..........561 706-5554
7682 Solimar Cir Boca Raton (33433) *(G-588)*

McCullough Bottled Water, Brooksville *Also called Lee McCullough Inc (G-1171)*

McDirt Industries Inc 850 944-0112
 5570 Bellview Ave Pensacola (32526) **(G-13545)**

McDs Pro LLC 954 302-3054
 2021 Sw 70th Ave Bay 15 Davie (33317) **(G-2437)**

McEs LLC 321 363-4977
 2499 Old Lake Mary Rd # 102 Sanford (32771) **(G-15357)**

McGee Enterprises Inc 904 328-3226
 8535 Baymeadows Rd Ste 28 Jacksonville (32256) **(G-6284)**

McGrail Signs & Graphics LLC 850 435-1017
 1011 N P St Pensacola (32505) **(G-13546)**

McIlpack Inc 561 988-8545
 1750 Nw 15th Ave Ste 535 Pompano Beach (33069) **(G-14091)**

McKenny Printing Entp Inc 727 420-4944
 2748 25th St N Saint Petersburg (33713) **(G-15125)**

McKenzie Marine LLC 904 770-2488
 100 Douglas Park Dr Saint Augustine (32084) **(G-14857)**

McLaren Industries Inc (PA) 310 212-1333
 9985 103rd St Jacksonville (32210) **(G-6285)**

McM Food Corp 305 885-9254
 7385 Nw 78th St Medley (33166) **(G-8274)**

McM Industries Inc 727 259-9894
 1721 Penny Ln Clearwater (33756) **(G-1689)**

McManus Superboats, Fort Myers Also called Mark McManus Inc **(G-4317)**

McMaster Concrete Products LLC 305 863-8854
 8720 Nw 91st St Medley (33178) **(G-8275)**

McMill LLC 561 279-3232
 4800 N Federal Hwy 302d Boca Raton (33431) **(G-589)**

McMillan Logging Inc 850 643-4819
 15405 Nw Pea Ridge Rd Bristol (32321) **(G-1123)**

McMullen Road LLC 813 854-3100
 12941 Memorial Hwy Tampa (33635) **(G-17060)**

McNeill Signs Inc (PA) 561 737-6304
 555 S Dixie Hwy E Pompano Beach (33060) **(G-14092)**

McNeill Signs Inc 386 586-7100
 400 Ninth St Bunnell (32110) **(G-1231)**

McNeilus Truck and Mfg Inc 954 366-4769
 1700 Nw 33rd St Pompano Beach (33064) **(G-14093)**

MCP, Orlando Also called Master Construction Pdts Inc **(G-12365)**

MCR Amrcan Pharmaceuticals Inc 352 754-8587
 16255 Aviation Loop Dr Brooksville (34604) **(G-1178)**

MCR Compression Services LLC (PA) 432 552-8720
 1261 S Haberland Blvd North Port (34288) **(G-11199)**

MCR Compression Services LLC 210 760-7650
 1158 S Haberland Blvd North Port (34288) **(G-11200)**

McT, Safety Harbor Also called Mastercut Tool Corp **(G-14791)**

McW Parts, Sunrise Also called Nippon Maciwumei Co **(G-16347)**

MD Audio Engineering Inc 305 593-8361
 6941 Nw 42nd St Miami (33166) **(G-9524)**

MDC Engineering Inc (PA) 941 358-0610
 1701 Desoto Rd Sarasota (34234) **(G-15742)**

Mdco Inc 813 855-4068
 13440 Wright Cir Tampa (33626) **(G-17061)**

Mdg Tools, Miami Also called Aaw Products Inc **(G-8630)**

Mdh Graphic Services Inc 561 533-9000
 5001 Georgia Ave West Palm Beach (33405) **(G-18071)**

Mdi Products LLC 772 228-7371
 10055 102nd Ter Sebastian (32958) **(G-15901)**

Mdintouch Us Inc 786 268-1161
 11735 Sw 103rd Ave Miami (33176) **(G-9525)**

MDK Enterpises Inc 904 288-6855
 11623 Columbia Park Dr E Jacksonville (32258) **(G-6286)**

Mdr LLC 954 845-9500
 14101 Nw 4th St Sunrise (33325) **(G-16340)**

Mdso Security Office, Palm Bay Also called L3harris Technologies Inc **(G-12906)**

Mdt Technologies Inc 305 308-2902
 10619 Nw 122nd St Medley (33178) **(G-8276)**

Mdy Services Inc 954 392-1542
 19418 Sw 27th St Miramar (33029) **(G-10513)**

ME Thompson Inc (PA) 904 356-6258
 2178 W 21st St Jacksonville (32209) **(G-6287)**

ME Thompson Inc 863 667-3732
 1840 Fairbanks St Lakeland (33805) **(G-7393)**

Meachem Steel Inc 352 735-7333
 25546 High Hampton Cir Sorrento (32776) **(G-16011)**

Meadowbrook Inc 800 338-2232
 970 Egrets Run Apt 102 Naples (34108) **(G-10817)**

Meadowbrook Press, Naples Also called Meadowbrook Inc **(G-10817)**

Meads International Inc (HQ) 407 356-8400
 5600 W Sand Lake Rd Orlando (32819) **(G-12367)**

Measurements International Inc 315 393-1323
 343 Clermont Ave Lake Mary (32746) **(G-7093)**

Mec Cryo LLC 813 644-3764
 4430 E Adamo Dr Ste 305 Tampa (33605) **(G-17062)**

Mechanical Air Concepts, Doral Also called Climax Inc **(G-3165)**

Mechanical Design Corp 772 388-8782
 100 Industrial Park Blvd Sebastian (32958) **(G-15902)**

Mechanical Dynamics Inc 863 292-0709
 1116 5th St Sw Winter Haven (33880) **(G-18451)**

Mechanical Svcs Centl Fla Inc (HQ) 407 857-3510
 9820 Satellite Blvd Orlando (32837) **(G-12368)**

Mecol Oil Tools Corp 305 638-7686
 1741 Nw 21st St Miami (33142) **(G-9526)**

Med Alert Response Inc 407 730-3571
 6239 Edgewater Dr Ste N1 Orlando (32810) **(G-12369)**

Med Dental Equipment (import) 786 417-8486
 7795 Sw 161st Ave Miami (33193) **(G-9527)**

Med X Change LLC (HQ) 941 746-0538
 417 8th St W Bradenton (34205) **(G-1012)**

Med X Change, Inc., Bradenton Also called Med X Change LLC **(G-1012)**

Med-Nap LLC 352 796-6020
 301 Marianne St Brooksville (34601) **(G-1179)**

Medaffinity Corporation 850 254-9690
 2350 Phillips Rd Apt 1110 Tallahassee (32308) **(G-16478)**

Medallion Leisure Furniture 305 626-0000
 800 Nw 166th St Miami (33169) **(G-9528)**

Medattend LLC 561 465-2735
 1200 Clint Moore Rd Ste 5 Boca Raton (33487) **(G-590)**

Medfab Corporation 813 854-2646
 210 Douglas Rd E Oldsmar (34677) **(G-11673)**

Medfare LLC 561 998-9444
 6560 W Rogers Cir Ste 13 Boca Raton (33487) **(G-591)**

Media Creations Inc 954 726-0902
 7101 W Coml Blvd Ste 4e Fort Lauderdale (33319) **(G-3934)**

Media Digittal LLC 305 506-0470
 8410 Nw 53rd Ter Ste 107 Doral (33166) **(G-3294)**

Media Edge Communications LLC 352 313-6700
 3951 Nw 48th Ter Ste 219 Gainesville (32606) **(G-4727)**

Media Edge Publishing, Gainesville Also called Media Edge Communications LLC **(G-4727)**

Media Publishing, Orlando Also called Great Hse Mdia Group of Pbls I **(G-12200)**

Media Systems Inc 954 427-4411
 3859 Nw 124th Ave Coral Springs (33065) **(G-2181)**

Media Works Inc 904 398-5518
 1451 Louisa St Jacksonville (32207) **(G-6288)**

Mediaops Inc 516 857-7409
 751 Park Of Commerce Dr # 108 Boca Raton (33487) **(G-592)**

Mediawrite LLC 239 344-9988
 6835 Intl Ctr Blvd Ste 9 Fort Myers (33912) **(G-4319)**

Medic Healthcare LLC 954 336-1776
 6750 N Andrews Ave # 200 Fort Lauderdale (33309) **(G-3935)**

Medica360 LLC 941 500-2890
 1109 Millpond Ct Osprey (34229) **(G-12802)**

Medical Concepts, Chipley Also called Back Lory Lee **(G-1453)**

Medical Defense Company Inc 954 614-3266
 1300 Nw 84th Ave Doral (33126) **(G-3295)**

Medical Developmental Research 727 793-0170
 2451 Enterprise Rd Clearwater (33763) **(G-1690)**

Medical Energy Inc 850 313-6277
 8806 Paul Starr Dr Pensacola (32514) **(G-13547)**

Medical Examiners Office Dst 1, Pensacola Also called P A Vivid Pathology **(G-13564)**

Medical ID Solutions, Orlando Also called Price Chpper Med Wrstbands Inc **(G-12505)**

Medical Magnetics Inc 954 565-8500
 5970 Sw 32nd Ter Fort Lauderdale (33312) **(G-3936)**

Medical Outfitters Inc (PA) 305 885-4045
 8062 Nw 66th St Miami (33166) **(G-9529)**

Medical Outfitters Inc 305 332-9103
 1666 J F Kennedy Cswy # 409 North Bay Village (33141) **(G-11058)**

Medical Sftwr Integrators Inc 561 570-4680
 5269 Springhill Dr Pensacola (32503) **(G-13548)**

Medical Waste Industries Inc 407 325-4832
 612 Downing St New Smyrna Beach (32168) **(G-11005)**

Medicomp Inc (PA) 321 676-0010
 600 Atlantis Rd Melbourne (32904) **(G-8473)**

Mediscope Manufacturing Inc 954 975-9997
 401 Briny Ave Apt 405 Pompano Beach (33062) **(G-14094)**

Meditek-Icot Inc 813 909-7476
 1916 Highland Oaks Blvd Lutz (33559) **(G-8003)**

Mediware BCT, Jacksonville Also called Mediware Info Systems Inc **(G-6289)**

Mediware Info Systems Inc 904 281-0467
 7800 Belfort Pkwy Ste 291 Jacksonville (32256) **(G-6289)**

Medley Machine Shop Inc 305 884-3200
 9452 Nw 109th St Medley (33178) **(G-8277)**

Medleycom Incorporated 408 745-5418
 1615 S Congress Ave # 10 Delray Beach (33445) **(G-2986)**

Medline Industries LP 863 337-4797
 1062 Old Dixie Hwy Auburndale (33823) **(G-241)**

Medmard Win Trtmnts Blinds Inc 772 344-5714
 797 Sw Sail Ter Port Saint Lucie (34953) **(G-14425)**

Medone Surgical Inc 941 359-3129
 670 Tallevast Rd Sarasota (34243) **(G-15516)**

Medrx Inc 727 584-9600
 1200 Starkey Rd Ste 105 Largo (33771) **(G-7641)**

Medstone Pharma LLC 305 777-7872
 3300 Corp Ave Ste 114 Weston (33331) **(G-18267)**

Medtek Medical Solutions LLC 786 458-8080
 6961 Nw 82nd Ave Miami (33166) **(G-9530)**

Medtel Services LLC (PA) 941 753-5000
 2511 Corporate Way Palmetto (34221) **(G-13181)**

A L P H A B E T I C

Medtrnic Sofamor Danek USA Inc............................904 645-6925
10245 Centurion Pkwy N Jacksonville (32256) *(G-6290)*

Medtronic............................305 458-7260
14420 Nw 60th Ave Miami Lakes (33014) *(G-10319)*

Medtronic (HQ)............................305 818-4100
14400 Nw 60th Ave Miami Lakes (33014) *(G-10320)*

Medtronic Inc............................904 296-9600
6743 Southpoint Dr N Jacksonville (32216) *(G-6291)*

Medtronic Usa Inc............................702 308-1302
6743 Southpoint Dr N Jacksonville (32216) *(G-6292)*

Medtronic Usa Inc............................786 709-4200
9850 Nw 41st St Ste 450 Doral (33178) *(G-3296)*

Medtronic Xomed Inc (HQ)............................904 296-9600
6743 Southpoint Dr N Jacksonville (32216) *(G-6293)*

Medtronic Xomed Inc............................904 296-9600
4102 Southpoint Blvd Jacksonville (32216) *(G-6294)*

Medway Hall Dev Group Inc (PA)............................904 786-0622
590 Beautyrest Ave Jacksonville (32254) *(G-6295)*

Medx Corporation............................352 351-2005
839 Nw 25th Ave Ocala (34475) *(G-11441)*

Meelko Co............................845 600-3379
3890 Nw 132nd St Unit F Opa Locka (33054) *(G-11767)*

Meg Systems Inc............................239 263-5833
2030 River Reach Dr # 138 Naples (34104) *(G-10818)*

Mega Book Inc............................352 378-4567
2937 Ne 19th Dr Gainesville (32609) *(G-4728)*

Mega Power............................813 855-6664
211 Violet St Ste 100 Largo (33773) *(G-7642)*

Mega Stitch Embroidery, Miami *Also called Izabellas Creations Inc* *(G-9348)*

Megabooks, Gainesville *Also called Mega Book Inc* *(G-4728)*

Megacolor Print LLC............................305 499-9395
221 Meridian Ave Apt 413 Miami Beach (33139) *(G-10212)*

Megafend Mooring Products, Fort Lauderdale *Also called Yacht 10 Inc* *(G-4139)*

Megamalls Inc............................407 891-2111
2432 13th St Saint Cloud (34769) *(G-14933)*

Megamaxmoney LLC............................561 523-4458
931 Village Blvd West Palm Beach (33409) *(G-18072)*

Megamaxmoney LLC (PA)............................561 523-4458
4843 Palmbrooke Cir West Palm Beach (33417) *(G-18073)*

Megatron Equity Partners Inc............................305 789-6688
801 Brickell Ave Ste 900 Miami (33131) *(G-9531)*

Megawattage LLC (PA)............................954 328-0232
850 Sw 21st Ter Fort Lauderdale (33312) *(G-3937)*

Megawattage.com Generators, Fort Lauderdale *Also called Megawattage LLC* *(G-3937)*

Megin Us LLC (PA)............................954 341-2965
11772 W Sample Rd Coral Springs (33065) *(G-2182)*

MEI Companies Inc............................352 361-6895
12150 Ne 7th Ave Citra (32113) *(G-1467)*

MEI Development Corporation............................954 341-3302
11772 W Sample Rd Ste 101 Coral Springs (33065) *(G-2183)*

MEI Micro Inc............................407 514-2619
4767 New Broad St Ste 337 Orlando (32814) *(G-12370)*

Mel Ray Industries, Crescent City *Also called Chez Industries LLC* *(G-2235)*

Melanie R Bush Pavers............................772 501-7295
8316 106th Ave Vero Beach (32967) *(G-17777)*

Melbourne Architectural Mllwk............................321 308-3297
325 East Dr Melbourne (32904) *(G-8474)*

Melbourne-Tillman Wtr Ctrl Dst............................321 723-7233
5990 Minton Rd Nw Palm Bay (32907) *(G-12908)*

Melitta North America (HQ)............................727 535-2111
13925 58th St N Clearwater (33760) *(G-1691)*

Melitta USA, Clearwater *Also called Melitta North America Inc* *(G-1691)*

Melitta Usa Inc (HQ)............................727 535-2111
13925 58th St N Clearwater (33760) *(G-1692)*

Melmar Cstm Met Finshg Svc Inc............................954 327-5788
5990 Sw 42nd Pl Davie (33314) *(G-2438)*

Melodon Software Inc............................407 654-1234
2813 S Hiawassee Rd # 302 Orlando (32835) *(G-12371)*

Melt-Tech Polymers Inc............................305 887-6148
7570 Nw 79th St Medley (33166) *(G-8278)*

Meltpoint Plastics Intl Inc............................305 887-8020
7570 Nw 79th St Medley (33166) *(G-8279)*

Memco Inc............................352 241-2302
1789 Ec 48 Bushnell (33513) *(G-1246)*

Memco Enviro Safe, Bushnell *Also called Memco Inc* *(G-1246)*

Memo Labs Inc............................561 842-0586
8390 Currency Dr Ste 4 West Palm Beach (33404) *(G-18074)*

Memon Industries LLC............................772 204-3131
3386 Se Cassell Ln Stuart (34997) *(G-16184)*

Memphis Metal Manufacturing Co............................901 276-6363
10811 Barbados Isle Dr Tampa (33647) *(G-17063)*

Menchies Frz Ygurt Five Points, Wilton Manors *Also called Tee-Hee Corp* *(G-18343)*

Mendez Brothers LLC............................305 685-3490
13000 Nw 42nd Ave Opa Locka (33054) *(G-11768)*

Mendez Fuel............................305 227-0470
3201 Coral Way Coral Gables (33145) *(G-2084)*

Menu Design, Saint Augustine *Also called David Dobbs Enterprises Inc* *(G-14823)*

Menu Men Inc............................305 633-7925
1301 Nw 27th Ave Miami (33125) *(G-9532)*

Meopta USA Inc............................631 436-5900
7826 Photonics Dr Trinity (34655) *(G-17640)*

Mercaereo Inc............................305 307-0672
6346 Nw 99th Ave Doral (33178) *(G-3297)*

Mercantile Two............................941 388-0059
28 S Blvd Of Presidents Sarasota (34236) *(G-15743)*

Mercaworld and CIA LLC............................786 212-5905
20871 Johnson St Ste 115 Pembroke Pines (33029) *(G-13402)*

Merced Industrial Corp............................908 309-0170
230 Nw 107th Ave Apt 106 Miami (33172) *(G-9533)*

Mercer Products Company Inc............................352 357-0057
37235 State Road 19 Umatilla (32784) *(G-17647)*

Mercers Fresh Roasted Coffees............................941 286-7054
4678 Tamiami Trl Unit 109 Punta Gorda (33980) *(G-14515)*

Merchant Central Plaza............................239 574-7166
159 Hancock Bridge Pkwy Cape Coral (33990) *(G-1365)*

Merchants Metals Inc............................813 333-5515
2835 Overpass Rd Ste 100 Tampa (33619) *(G-17064)*

Merchants Metals LLC............................904 781-3920
5918-1 Lane Cir S Jacksonville (32254) *(G-6296)*

Merchants Metals LLC............................813 980-0938
4921 Joanne Kearney Blvd Tampa (33619) *(G-17065)*

Merchants Metals LLC............................561 478-0059
1601 Hill Ave Ste B West Palm Beach (33407) *(G-18075)*

Merchspin Inc............................877 306-3651
6424 Forest City Rd Orlando (32810) *(G-12372)*

Merck Sharp & Dohme Corp............................305 512-6062
14240 Plmetto Frontage Rd Miami Lakes (33016) *(G-10321)*

Merck Sharp & Dohme LLC............................305 698-4600
13900 Nw 57th Ct Miami Lakes (33014) *(G-10322)*

Merco Frame, Miami *Also called Mercoframes Optical Corp* *(G-9534)*

Mercoframes Optical Corp............................305 882-0120
5555 Nw 74th Ave Miami (33166) *(G-9534)*

Mercury Machining Co Inc (PA)............................850 433-5017
1085 W Gimble St Pensacola (32502) *(G-13549)*

Mercury Marine, Miramar *Also called Brunswick Corporation* *(G-10476)*

Mercury Marine Power Division, Panama City *Also called Brunswick Corporation* *(G-13236)*

Mercury Printing, Sarasota *Also called Seapress Inc* *(G-15822)*

Mercury Systems Inc............................352 371-2567
800 Sw 2nd Ave Ste 300 Gainesville (32601) *(G-4729)*

Mercy D LLC............................321 212-7712
3320 Thurloe Dr Rockledge (32955) *(G-14732)*

Merenguitoscom LLC............................305 685-2709
4847 E 10th Ct Hialeah (33013) *(G-5244)*

Mergenet Medical Inc............................561 208-3770
1701 W Hillsboro Blvd # 303 Deerfield Beach (33442) *(G-2765)*

Meridian Cable LLC............................904 770-4687
141 Senora Ct Saint Augustine (32095) *(G-14858)*

Meridian Centre............................253 620-4542
6531 Park Of Commerce Blv Boca Raton (33487) *(G-593)*

Meridian Life Science Inc............................561 241-0223
1121 Holland Dr Ste 27 Boca Raton (33487) *(G-594)*

Meridian South Aviation LLC............................727 536-5387
15875 Fairchild Dr Clearwater (33762) *(G-1693)*

Merit Diamond Corporation............................954 883-3660
1900 Tyler St Fl 3 Hollywood (33020) *(G-5625)*

Merit Fastener Corporation (PA)............................407 331-4815
2510 N Ronald Reagan Blvd Longwood (32750) *(G-7922)*

Merit Fastener Corporation............................813 626-3748
5416 56th Cmmerce Pk Blvd Tampa (33610) *(G-17066)*

Merit International Entps Inc............................305 635-1011
1628 Nw 28th St Miami (33142) *(G-9535)*

Merit Investments Inc............................877 997-8335
6400 N Andrews Ave # 200 Fort Lauderdale (33309) *(G-3938)*

Merit Screw............................352 344-3744
3484 E Hartley Ct Hernando (34442) *(G-5009)*

Merit Screw Products, Hernando *Also called Merit Screw* *(G-5009)*

Merits Health Products Inc............................239 772-0579
4245 Evans Ave Fort Myers (33901) *(G-4320)*

Merkari Group Inc............................305 748-3260
2222 Ponce De Leon Blvd Coral Gables (33134) *(G-2085)*

Merkavah International Inc............................305 909-6798
201 S Biscayne Blvd Miami (33131) *(G-9536)*

Merle Harris Enterprises Inc............................386 677-7060
724 Big Tree Rd South Daytona (32119) *(G-16024)*

Merlin Industries Inc............................954 472-6891
2201 College Ave Davie (33317) *(G-2439)*

Merlola Industries LLC............................888 418-0408
7950 Nw 53rd St Ste 341 Miami (33166) *(G-9537)*

Mermaid Marine Air, Fort Myers *Also called Mermaid Mfg Southwest Fla Inc* *(G-4321)*

Mermaid Mfg Southwest Fla Inc............................239 418-0535
2651 Park Windsor Dr # 203 Fort Myers (33901) *(G-4321)*

Merrick Industries Inc............................850 265-3611
10 Arthur Dr Lynn Haven (32444) *(G-8030)*

Merrill-Stevens Dry Dock Co (PA)............................305 640-5676
1270 Nw 11th St Miami (33125) *(G-9538)*

Merrill-Stevens Yachts, Miami *Also called Merrill-Stevens Dry Dock Co* *(G-9538)*

Merritt Hollow Metal Inc............................727 656-4380
10822 124th Ave Largo (33778) *(G-7643)*

Merritt Island Plant, Merritt Island *Also called Sea Ray Boats Inc* **(G-8593)**

Merritt Mfg LLC 407 481-1074
2347 Foggy Ridge Pkwy Land O Lakes (34639) **(G-7499)**

Merritt Precision Tech Inc 321 453-2334
3425 N Courtenay Pkwy Merritt Island (32953) **(G-8587)**

Merry Mailman Inc 954 786-1146
3907 N Federal Hwy Pompano Beach (33064) **(G-14095)**

Messer LLC 925 606-2000
430 S Congress Ave Ste 7 Delray Beach (33445) **(G-2987)**

Messner Printing, Winter Haven *Also called Messner Publications Inc* **(G-18452)**

Messner Publications Inc 863 318-1595
3250 Dundee Rd Winter Haven (33884) **(G-18452)**

Mestizo Foods LLC 352 414-4900
3031 W Silver Sprng Blvd Ocala (34475) **(G-11442)**

Mestizo Peruvian Cuisine Llc 561 469-1164
511 Northwood Rd West Palm Beach (33407) **(G-18076)**

Met-Con Inc 321 632-4880
465 Canaveral Groves Blvd Cocoa (32926) **(G-1941)**

Metabolic Nutrition, Tamarac *Also called Iq Formulations Llc* **(G-16533)**

Metal 2 Metal Inc 954 253-9450
17040 Sw 87th Ct Palmetto Bay (33157) **(G-13214)**

Metal Aire, Clearwater *Also called Metal Industries Inc* **(G-1695)**

Metal Building Erection, Jacksonville *Also called Jax Enterprises LLC* **(G-6220)**

Metal Building Kings 412 522-4797
8050 N University Dr Tamarac (33321) **(G-16536)**

Metal Building Supplies LLC 407 935-9714
800 E Donegan Ave Kissimmee (34744) **(G-6942)**

Metal Container Corporation 904 695-7600
1100 Ellis Rd N Jacksonville (32254) **(G-6297)**

Metal Craft of Pensacola Inc 850 478-8333
4 E Hannah St Pensacola (32534) **(G-13550)**

Metal Creations Sarasota Llc 941 922-7096
1985 Cattlemen Rd Unit F Sarasota (34232) **(G-15744)**

Metal Culverts Inc 727 531-1431
2148 Pine Forest Dr Clearwater (33764) **(G-1694)**

Metal Essence Inc 407 478-8480
910 Waterway Pl Longwood (32750) **(G-7923)**

Metal Express LLC 786 391-0093
7216 Nw 25th St Miami (33122) **(G-9539)**

Metal Fabrication and 850 205-2300
3600 Weems Rd Ste D Tallahassee (32317) **(G-16479)**

Metal Fabricators, De Leon Springs *Also called Al-Mar Metals Inc* **(G-2621)**

Metal Fronts Inc 727 547-6700
10930 75th St Seminole (33777) **(G-15982)**

Metal Improvement Company LLC 305 592-5960
1940 Nw 70th Ave Miami (33126) **(G-9540)**

Metal Industries Inc (HQ) 727 441-2651
1985 Carroll St Clearwater (33765) **(G-1695)**

Metal Industries Inc 813 855-5695
301 Commerce Blvd Bldg 4 Oldsmar (34677) **(G-11674)**

Metal Industries Inc 352 793-8610
400 Walker Ave Bushnell (33513) **(G-1247)**

Metal Industries Inc 727 441-2651
1310 N Hercules Ave Clearwater (33765) **(G-1696)**

Metal Industries Inc 813 855-4651
301 Commerce Blvd Oldsmar (34677) **(G-11675)**

Metal Magix Inc 754 235-9996
3711 Ne 11th Ave Ste 4 Pompano Beach (33064) **(G-14096)**

Metal Mart Systems Inc 863 533-4040
255 Century Blvd Bartow (33830) **(G-317)**

Metal Processors Inc 813 654-0050
200 S Falkenburg Rd Tampa (33619) **(G-17067)**

Metal Products Company LC 850 526-5593
3787 Industrial Park Dr Marianna (32446) **(G-8173)**

Metal Rock Inc 407 886-6440
174a Semoran Commerce Pl # 103 Apopka (32703) **(G-150)**

Metal Roof Factory Inc 321 632-8300
599 Gus Hipp Blvd Rockledge (32955) **(G-14733)**

Metal Sales Manufacturing Corp 904 783-3660
7110 Stuart Ave Jacksonville (32254) **(G-6298)**

Metal Shop, The, Dunnellon *Also called Air Distributors Inc* **(G-3461)**

Metal Spray Painting Powder 954 227-2744
3701 Nw 126th Ave Ste 4 Coral Springs (33065) **(G-2184)**

Metal Supply and Machining Inc 561 276-4941
1304 Gwenzell Ave Ste B Delray Beach (33444) **(G-2988)**

Metal Systems Inc 813 752-7088
3301 Paul Buchman Hwy Plant City (33565) **(G-13785)**

Metal Technologies Group Inc 904 429-7727
1105 Registry Blvd Saint Augustine (32092) **(G-14859)**

Metal Works By Gal 407 486-7198
5650 S Sanford Ave Sanford (32773) **(G-15358)**

Metal-Tech Controls Corp 941 575-7677
3441 Saint Croix Ct Punta Gorda (33950) **(G-14516)**

Metalco Mfg Inc 305 592-0704
700 W 20th St Hialeah (33010) **(G-5245)**

Metalcraft, Pensacola *Also called Metal Craft of Pensacola Inc* **(G-13550)**

Metalcraft Industries Inc 352 680-3555
120 Cypress Rd Ocala (34472) **(G-11443)**

Metalcraft of Pensacola Inc 850 478-8333
4 E Hannah St Pensacola (32534) **(G-13551)**

Metalcraft Services Tampa Inc 813 558-8700
10706 N 46th St Tampa (33617) **(G-17068)**

Metalcrafters LLC 904 257-9036
10759 Grayson St Jacksonville (32220) **(G-6299)**

Metalex LLC 941 918-4431
3816 Cutlass Byu Nokomis (34275) **(G-11051)**

Metalfab Inc (PA) 352 588-9901
28212 Rice Rd San Antonio (33576) **(G-15249)**

Metalhouse LLC 407 270-3000
4705 S Apk Vnlnd Rd # 140 Orlando (32819) **(G-12373)**

Metalmaster Machine Shop Inc 407 423-9049
4549 L B Mcleod Rd Orlando (32811) **(G-12374)**

Metalmaster Manufacturing Svcs, Orlando *Also called Metalmaster Machine Shop Inc* **(G-12374)**

Metalplate Galvanizing LP 904 768-6330
7123 Moncrief Rd W Jacksonville (32219) **(G-6300)**

Metals & Mining, West Palm Beach *Also called Evolution Metals Corp* **(G-17990)**

Metals Supermarket, Tampa *Also called Tryana LLC* **(G-17376)**

Metalworks Engineering Corp 305 223-0011
1745 W 32nd Pl Hialeah (33012) **(G-5246)**

Metavante Banking Solutions, Orlando *Also called Kirchman Corporation* **(G-12288)**

Metavante Holdings LLC (HQ) 904 438-6000
601 Riverside Ave Jacksonville (32204) **(G-6301)**

Methapharm Inc 954 341-0795
11772 W Sample Rd Ste 101 Coral Springs (33065) **(G-2185)**

Method Merchant Inc 954 745-7998
150 S Pine Island Rd # 530 Plantation (33324) **(G-13868)**

Meticulous Detail Inc 813 310-6440
16418 N Florida Ave Lutz (33549) **(G-8004)**

Metpar Corp 813 249-0391
7211 Anderson Rd Tampa (33634) **(G-17069)**

Metpro Supply Inc 863 425-7155
5070 State Road 60 E Mulberry (33860) **(G-10632)**

Metritek Corporation (PA) 561 995-2414
849 Nw 126th Ave Coral Springs (33071) **(G-2186)**

Metritek Group LLC 561 995-2414
370 Camino Gardens Blvd Boca Raton (33432) **(G-595)**

Metro Defense Services Inc 407 285-2304
3001 Aloma Ave 227 Winter Park (32792) **(G-18522)**

Metro Door Brickell LLC 786 326-4748
2660 Ne 189th St Miami (33180) **(G-9541)**

Metro Life Media Inc 813 745-3658
3404 S Omar Ave Tampa (33629) **(G-17070)**

Metro Machine Corp 904 249-7772
599 Wonderwood Dr Jacksonville (32233) **(G-6302)**

Metro Roof Tile Inc 863 467-0042
9845 Nw 118th Way Medley (33178) **(G-8280)**

Metro Signs Inc 954 410-4343
1220 S State Road 7 Hollywood (33023) **(G-5626)**

Metronow, Orlando *Also called Milsav LLC* **(G-12382)**

Metropolis Corp 954 951-1011
2455 E Sunrise Blvd # 909 Fort Lauderdale (33304) **(G-3939)**

Metropolis Graphics Inc 407 740-5455
805 S Orlando Ave Ste D Winter Park (32789) **(G-18523)**

Metropolis Iron By Design, Fort Myers *Also called Alico Metal Fabricators LLC* **(G-4161)**

Metropolitan Mix 904 242-0743
3108 Sawgrass Village Cir Ponte Vedra Beach (32082) **(G-14274)**

Metrotech Media & Lighting Inc 844 463-8761
38 S Blue Angel Pkwy # 108 Pensacola (32506) **(G-13552)**

Mettler-Toledo Inc 407 423-3856
45 N Magnolia Ave Orlando (32801) **(G-12375)**

Mew Automation LLC 305 319-9199
12630 Nw 115th Ave Medley (33178) **(G-8281)**

Mf Industries LLC 407 457-7531
1215 Guinevere Dr Casselberry (32707) **(G-1425)**

MFA, Port Saint Joe *Also called Monumntal Fabrication Amer Inc* **(G-14389)**

Mfjr Pavers LLC 239 440-2580
1621 Red Cedar Dr Fort Myers (33907) **(G-4322)**

Mfr Empire Corp 786 558-7122
5729 Nw 151st St Miami Lakes (33014) **(G-10323)**

Mft Stamps 352 360-5797
132 E Magnolia Ave Eustis (32726) **(G-3563)**

Mfx Corp 407 429-4051
7065 Westpointe Blvd # 205 Orlando (32835) **(G-12376)**

Mg Cabinet Installers LLC 561 530-7961
3860 Miller Rd Apt B Palm Springs (33461) **(G-13147)**

Mg Coating and Sealants LLC 305 409-0915
1280 Ne 137th Ter North Miami (33161) **(G-11111)**

Mg Woodwork Inc 561 459-7552
5540 Nw 76th Pl Ste A Pompano Beach (33073) **(G-14097)**

MGI Usa Inc 321 751-6755
3143 Skyway Cir Melbourne (32934) **(G-8475)**

Mgl Engineering Inc 863 648-0320
2740 Parkway St Lakeland (33811) **(G-7394)**

MGM Blinds and Shutters Inc
145 Canal St New Smyrna Beach (32168) **(G-11006)**

MGM Cargo LLC 407 770-1500
  7154 W Colonial Dr Orlando (32818) *(G-12377)*

Mgo America, Miami *Also called Innova Eco Bldg Systems LLC (G-9317)*

Mhkap LLC 239 919-0786
  2059 Tamiami Trl E Naples (34112) *(G-10819)*

Mhms Corp 813 948-0504
  142 Whitaker Rd Ste A Lutz (33549) *(G-8005)*

MI Metals Inc (HQ) 813 855-5695
  301 Commerce Blvd Oldsmar (34677) *(G-11676)*

Mia Consulting & Trading Inc (PA) 305 640-3077
  7806 Nw 71st St Ste 209 Miami (33166) *(G-9542)*

Mia Products Company 786 479-4021
  71 W 22nd St Apt 9 Hialeah (33010) *(G-5247)*

Miacucina LLC 305 792-9494
  3650 N Miami Ave Miami (33127) *(G-9543)*

Miacucina LLC 305 444-7383
  105 Miracle Mile Coral Gables (33134) *(G-2086)*

Miami 954 874-7707
  3661 S Miami Ave Ste 407 Miami (33133) *(G-9544)*

Miami Asphalt Striping 305 386-3253
  10400 Sw 186th Ln Cutler Bay (33157) *(G-2296)*

Miami Awning, Miami *Also called Miami Beach Awning Co (G-9546)*

Miami Balloons & Signs, Miami *Also called Miami Banners & Signs Inc (G-9545)*

Miami Banners & Signs Inc 305 262-4460
  6335 Nw 74th Ave Miami (33166) *(G-9545)*

Miami Beach Awning Co 305 576-2029
  3905 Nw 31st Ave Miami (33142) *(G-9546)*

Miami Cellophane Inc 786 293-2212
  7485 W 19th Ct Hialeah (33014) *(G-5248)*

Miami Cocktail Company Inc (PA) 305 482-1974
  2750 Nw 3rd Ave Ste 14 Miami (33127) *(G-9547)*

Miami Compressor Rbldrs Inc 305 303-2251
  3230 Nw 38th St Miami (33142) *(G-9548)*

Miami Cordage LLC 305 636-3000
  2475 Nw 38th St Miami (33142) *(G-9549)*

Miami Daily Business Review, Fort Lauderdale *Also called Alm Global LLC (G-3647)*

Miami Decor Inc 800 235-2197
  7351 Nw 61st St Miami (33166) *(G-9550)*

Miami Diver, Miami *Also called SGS US East Coast LLC (G-9874)*

Miami Engrv Co-Oxford Prtg Co 305 371-9595
  54 Nw 11th St Miami (33136) *(G-9551)*

Miami Epic Tees Corp 305 224-3465
  10990 Nw 138th St Unit 16 Hialeah (33018) *(G-5249)*

Miami Eyeworks Inc 954 316-6757
  2114 N Flamingo Rd # 115 Pembroke Pines (33028) *(G-13403)*

Miami Filter LLC 772 466-1440
  7384 Commercial Cir Fort Pierce (34951) *(G-4507)*

Miami Foods Distrs USA Inc 305 512-3246
  2761 W 77th Pl Hialeah (33016) *(G-5250)*

Miami Grandstand Entrmt Corp 305 636-9665
  2330 W 79th St Hialeah (33016) *(G-5251)*

Miami Hang Gliding Corp 863 805-0440
  12655 E State Road 80 Clewiston (33440) *(G-1893)*

Miami Herald 305 269-7768
  4302 Sw 73rd Ave Miami (33155) *(G-9552)*

Miami Herald 800 843-4372
  3500 Nw 89th Ct Doral (33172) *(G-3298)*

Miami Industrial Motor Inc 305 593-2370
  8252 Nw 58th St Doral (33166) *(G-3299)*

Miami Leasing Inc 786 431-1215
  14532 Sw 129th St Miami (33186) *(G-9553)*

Miami Metal Deck, Hialeah *Also called Miami Metal Roofing LLC (G-5252)*

Miami Metal Roofing LLC 305 749-6356
  16000 Nw 49th Ave A Hialeah (33014) *(G-5252)*

Miami Metals II Inc 305 685-8505
  12900 Nw 38th Ave Opa Locka (33054) *(G-11769)*

Miami Mix Corp 954 704-9682
  15014 Sw 21st St Miramar (33027) *(G-10514)*

Miami Ndt Inc 305 599-9393
  8050 Nw 90th St Medley (33166) *(G-8282)*

Miami News 24 Inc 786 331-8141
  6874 Nw 113th Pl Doral (33178) *(G-3300)*

Miami Oliveoil & Beyond Llc 954 632-2762
  1783 Nw 79th Ave Doral (33126) *(G-3301)*

Miami Power Wheels 305 553-1888
  9500 Sw 40th St Ste 305 Miami (33165) *(G-9554)*

Miami Prestige Interiors Inc 305 685-3343
  3000 Nw 125th St Unit C Miami (33167) *(G-9555)*

Miami Quality Graphics Inc 305 634-9506
  3701 Nw 51st St Miami (33142) *(G-9556)*

Miami Quality Packg & Finshg, Miami *Also called Miami Quality Graphics Inc (G-9556)*

Miami Quality Pavers Corp 305 408-3444
  5800 Sw 177th Ave Ste 101 Miami (33193) *(G-9557)*

Miami Railing Design Corp 305 926-0062
  4401 Sw 75th Ave Ste 10 Miami (33155) *(G-9558)*

Miami Screenprint Supply Inc 305 622-7532
  5566 Nw 161st St Miami Lakes (33014) *(G-10324)*

Miami Ship Repair & Wldg Svcs 305 491-4161
  4460 Ne 16th Ave Oakland Park (33334) *(G-11279)*

Miami Sign Shop Inc 305 431-2455
  13899 Biscayne Blvd # 155 North Miami Beach (33181) *(G-11150)*

Miami Sublimation, Hialeah *Also called Active Line Corp (G-5026)*

Miami Switchgear Company 786 336-5783
  7060 Nw 52nd St Miami (33166) *(G-9559)*

Miami Tank, Fort Pierce *Also called Miami Filter LLC (G-4507)*

Miami Tape Inc 305 558-9211
  6175 Nw 167th St Ste G38 Hialeah (33015) *(G-5253)*

Miami Tbr LLC 786 275-4773
  1919 Nw 82nd Ave Doral (33126) *(G-3302)*

Miami Tech Inc (PA) 305 693-7054
  3611 Nw 74th St Miami (33147) *(G-9560)*

Miami Tech Inc 786 354-1115
  1725 W 39th Pl Hialeah (33012) *(G-5254)*

Miami Technics LLC 754 227-5459
  457 Goolsby Blvd Deerfield Beach (33442) *(G-2766)*

Miami Tees Inc 305 623-3908
  5120 Nw 165th St Ste 101 Miami Lakes (33014) *(G-10325)*

Miami Times 305 694-6210
  900 Nw 54th St Miami (33127) *(G-9561)*

Miami Transformers Corp 305 257-1491
  13935 Sw 252nd St Homestead (33032) *(G-5730)*

Miami Trucolor Offset Svc Co 954 962-5230
  2211 Sw 57th Ter West Park (33023) *(G-18215)*

Miami Wall, Hialeah *Also called Larry Johnson Inc (G-5220)*

Miami Wall Systems Inc 305 888-2300
  701 W 25th St Hialeah (33010) *(G-5255)*

Miami-Dade Truck & Eqp Svc Inc 305 691-2932
  3294 Nw 69th St Miami (33147) *(G-9562)*

Mica Craft & Design Inc 561 863-5354
  3905 Investment Ln Ste 15 West Palm Beach (33404) *(G-18077)*

Mica Pdts & WD Boca Raton Inc 561 395-4686
  150 Glades Rd Boca Raton (33432) *(G-596)*

Mica Visions Inc 727 712-3213
  2650 Enterprise Rd Ste D Clearwater (33763) *(G-1697)*

Mica Works Cabinetry, Gainesville *Also called Micaworks Cabinetry Inc (G-4730)*

Micaworks Cabinetry Inc 352 336-1707
  4440 Sw 35th Ter Gainesville (32608) *(G-4730)*

Micco Aircraft Company, Hollywood *Also called Estumkeda Ltd (G-5572)*

Michael Giordano Intl Inc (PA) 305 948-6673
  14851 Ne 20th Ave North Miami (33181) *(G-11112)*

Michael L Lariviere Inc 239 267-2738
  17537 Braddock Rd Fort Myers (33967) *(G-4323)*

Michael P Wahlquist 850 643-5139
  13036 Nw Freeman Rd Bristol (32321) *(G-1124)*

Michael Rybvich Sons Boat Wrks 561 627-9168
  2175 Idlewild Rd Palm Beach Gardens (33410) *(G-12989)*

Michael Valentines Inc 239 332-0855
  10660 Clear Lake Loop # 234 Fort Myers (33908) *(G-4324)*

Michel 1 Trucking LLC 786 297-9681
  66 W Flagler St Ste 900 Miami (33130) *(G-9563)*

Michelle Ann Lillo 954 723-0580
  12640 Sw 7th Pl Davie (33325) *(G-2440)*

Michelle Lynn Solutions Inc 786 413-0455
  1395 Brickell Ave Ste 800 Miami (33131) *(G-9564)*

Michelsons Trophies Inc 305 687-9898
  14730 Nw 7th Ave Miami (33168) *(G-9565)*

Michigan Avenue Bridge Inc 352 236-4044
  4690 Ne 35th St Ocala (34479) *(G-11444)*

Michigan Drill, Miami *Also called Republic Drill/Apt Corp (G-9797)*

Michigan Group Inc 954 328-6341
  5481 Wiles Rd Coconut Creek (33073) *(G-1998)*

Michigan Pmps Elc Mtrs Repr Co 407 841-6800
  1210 W Michigan St Orlando (32805) *(G-12378)*

Michigan St Pump & Electric, Orlando *Also called Michigan Pmps Elc Mtrs Repr Co (G-12378)*

Mickey Truck Bodies Inc 352 620-0015
  601 Nw 24th Ct Ocala (34475) *(G-11445)*

Micole Electric Sign Company 954 796-4293
  10840 Sw 1st Ct Coral Springs (33071) *(G-2187)*

Micon Packaging Inc 813 855-4651
  301 Commerce Blvd Bldg 1 Oldsmar (34677) *(G-11677)*

Micon Packaging Products, Oldsmar *Also called Metal Industries Inc (G-11675)*

Micro Audiometrics Corporation 386 888-7878
  1901 Mason Ave Ste 104 Daytona Beach (32117) *(G-2574)*

Micro Cmpt Systems Sthwest Fla (PA) 239 643-6672
  2553 Longboat Dr Naples (34104) *(G-10820)*

Micro Contacts Inc 954 973-6166
  2901 Gateway Dr Pompano Beach (33069) *(G-14098)*

Micro Control Systems Inc 239 694-0089
  5580 Enterprise Pkwy Fort Myers (33905) *(G-4325)*

Micro Crane Inc 954 755-2225
  3610 Nw 118th Ave Ste 4 Coral Springs (33065) *(G-2188)*

Micro Design International, Lake Mary *Also called Totally Storage Inc (G-7112)*

Micro Engineering Inc 407 886-4849
  1428 E Semrn Blvd Ste 120 Apopka (32703) *(G-151)*

Micro Matic Usa Inc 352 799-6331
  15111 Dispense Ln Brooksville (34604) *(G-1180)*

Micro Matic Usa Inc (HQ).....352 544-1081
2386 Simon Ct Brooksville (34604) *(G-1181)*
Micro Pneumatic Logic Inc.....954 935-6821
2901 Gateway Dr Pompano Beach (33069) *(G-14099)*
Micro Printing Inc.....954 676-5757
2571 Nw 4th Ct Fort Lauderdale (33311) *(G-3940)*
Micro Quality Corp.....954 354-5572
438 S Military Trl Deerfield Beach (33442) *(G-2767)*
Micro Systems Inc (HQ).....850 244-2332
35 Hill Ave Nw Fort Walton Beach (32548) *(G-4596)*
Micro Technology of Brevard.....321 733-1766
255 West Dr Melbourne (32904) *(G-8476)*
Micro Tool & Engineering Inc.....561 842-7381
7575 Centl Indus Dr Ste A Riviera Beach (33404) *(G-14646)*
Micro Typing Systems Inc.....954 970-9500
1295 Sw 29th Ave Pompano Beach (33069) *(G-14100)*
Micro-Ant LLC.....904 683-8394
7898 Baymeadows Way Jacksonville (32256) *(G-6303)*
Microcomputer Services.....561 988-7000
1200 S Rogers Cir Ste 8 Boca Raton (33487) *(G-597)*
Microflex Inc.....386 672-1945
1810 N Us Highway 1 Ormond Beach (32174) *(G-12780)*
Microflex Automotive, Ormond Beach *Also called Microflex Inc* *(G-12780)*
Microgerm Defense LLC.....561 309-0842
2257 Vista Pk Way Ste 22 West Palm Beach (33411) *(G-18078)*
Microjig Inc.....855 747-7233
7212 Sandscove Ct Winter Park (32792) *(G-18524)*
Microlumen Inc.....813 886-1200
1 Microlumen Way Oldsmar (34677) *(G-11678)*
Micromicr Corporation.....954 922-8044
35 Sw 12th Ave Ste 112 Dania (33004) *(G-2337)*
Micron Fiber - Tech Inc.....386 668-7895
230 Sprngview Commerce Dr Debary (32713) *(G-2638)*
Micron Pharmaworks, LLC, Odessa *Also called Pharmaworks LLC* *(G-11569)*
Microsalt Inc.....877 825-0655
515 N Flagler Dr Ste P300 West Palm Beach (33401) *(G-18079)*
Microsemi Corp.....407 965-5687
1064 Greenwood Blvd # 124 Lake Mary (32746) *(G-7094)*
Microsimulators Inc.....407 696-8722
1612 White Dove Dr Winter Springs (32708) *(G-18573)*
Microsoft Corporation.....813 281-3900
5426 Bay Center Dr # 700 Tampa (33609) *(G-17071)*
Microsoft Corporation.....425 882-8080
6750 N Andrews Ave # 400 Fort Lauderdale (33309) *(G-3941)*
Micross Components, Clearwater *Also called Micross Prmier Smcdtr Svcs LLC* *(G-1698)*
Micross Components, Apopka *Also called Chip Supply Inc* *(G-110)*
Micross Inc (PA).....407 298-7100
1810 S Orange Blossom Trl Apopka (32703) *(G-152)*
Micross Minco LLC.....512 339-3422
1810 S Orange Blossom Trl Apopka (32703) *(G-153)*
Micross Prmier Smcdtr Svcs LLC.....727 532-1777
4400 140th Ave N Ste 140 Clearwater (33762) *(G-1698)*
Microtechnologies, Pompano Beach *Also called Micro Pneumatic Logic Inc* *(G-14099)*
Microtechnologies, Pompano Beach *Also called M Micro Technologies Inc* *(G-14083)*
Microtek Medical Inc.....904 741-2964
13500 Tradeport Cir E Jacksonville (32218) *(G-6304)*
Microtex Electronics Inc.....386 426-1922
13191 Kingfisher Rd Weeki Wachee (34614) *(G-17838)*
Microtool and Instrument Inc.....786 242-8780
15203 Sw 87th Ave Palmetto Bay (33157) *(G-13215)*
Microvision Technology Corp.....407 333-2943
43 Skyline Dr Ste 3051 Lake Mary (32746) *(G-7095)*
Microwave Electronics.....561 432-8511
6314 Dornich Ln Lake Worth (33463) *(G-7216)*
Mictron Inc.....941 371-6564
8130 Fruitville Rd Sarasota (34240) *(G-15745)*
Mid Florida Signs, Leesburg *Also called Sign Design of Florida Inc* *(G-7793)*
Mid Florida Steel Corp.....321 632-8228
870 Cidco Rd Cocoa (32926) *(G-1942)*
Mid State Machine & Fabg, Lakeland *Also called Mid-State Machine & Fabg Corp* *(G-7395)*
Mid State Plastics, Ruskin *Also called Jan and Jean Inc* *(G-14779)*
Mid State Screen Graphics LLC.....727 573-2299
13183 38th St N Clearwater (33762) *(G-1699)*
Mid West Lettering Company.....850 477-6522
7800 Sears Blvd Pensacola (32514) *(G-13553)*
Mid-Florida Plastics Inc.....407 856-1805
780 Central Florida Pkwy Orlando (32824) *(G-12379)*
Mid-Florida Publications Inc (PA).....352 589-8811
4645 N Highway 19a Mount Dora (32757) *(G-10605)*
Mid-Florida Sportswear LLC.....386 258-5632
2415 Bellevue Ave Daytona Beach (32114) *(G-2575)*
Mid-Flrida Lbr Acqisitions Inc.....863 533-0155
4281 Echo Ave Bartow (33830) *(G-318)*
Mid-State Machine & Fabg Corp (PA).....863 665-6233
2730 Mine And Mill Rd Lakeland (33801) *(G-7395)*
Mid-State Machine Company LLC.....704 636-7029
4516 Longboat Ln Fort Myers (33919) *(G-4326)*
Midds Inc.....561 586-6220
128 S Dixie Hwy Lake Worth (33460) *(G-7217)*
Midds Inc.....561 586-6220
1937 10th Ave N Lake Worth Beach (33461) *(G-7258)*
Midgard Inc.....863 696-1224
6402 State Road 60 E Lake Wales (33898) *(G-7168)*
Midnight Express Pwr Boats Inc.....954 745-8284
351 Ne 185th St Miami (33179) *(G-9566)*
Midnite Son II of Sarasota.....941 377-6029
1257 Porter Rd Sarasota (34240) *(G-15746)*
Midway Labs Usa LLC.....561 571-6252
6401 Congress Ave Ste 100 Boca Raton (33487) *(G-598)*
Midwest Mtal Fbrction Cstm Rll.....317 769-6489
13331 Seaside Harbour Dr North Fort Myers (33903) *(G-11062)*
Migrandy Corp.....321 459-0044
675 Cypress Dr Merritt Island (32952) *(G-8588)*
Miguel Casa Corp.....305 887-0098
2005 W 4th Ave Hialeah (33010) *(G-5256)*
Mll Oil Holding Inc.....321 200-0039
1201 Hays St Tallahassee (32301) *(G-16480)*
Mike Blackburn Welding LLC.....850 643-8464
19983 Ne Hentz Ave Blountstown (32424) *(G-376)*
Mike C Lohmeyer.....727 669-0808
1010 Park Ct Bldg A Safety Harbor (34695) *(G-14792)*
Mike Cope Race Cars LLC.....352 585-2810
14152 63rd Way N Clearwater (33760) *(G-1700)*
Mike Pulver LLC.....386 747-8951
703 Deerfoot Rd Deland (32720) *(G-2885)*
Mikes Aluminum Products LLC.....407 855-1989
4445 Story Rd Saint Cloud (34772) *(G-14934)*
Mikes Precision Inc.....305 558-6421
1929 W 76th St Hialeah (33014) *(G-5257)*
Mikes Print Shop Inc.....407 718-4964
2118 Poinciana Rd Winter Park (32792) *(G-18525)*
Mikes Trck Prts Mch Sp Plus I.....786 534-9608
7337 Nw 54th St Miami (33166) *(G-9567)*
Mil-Sat LLC.....954 862-3613
12555 Orange Dr Davie (33330) *(G-2441)*
Mil-Spec Metal Finishing Inc.....386 426-7188
706 W Park Ave Ste A Edgewater (32132) *(G-3498)*
Mil-Tec Incorporated.....239 369-2880
5578 6th St W Lehigh Acres (33971) *(G-7817)*
Milano Worldwide Corp.....561 266-0201
222 W Yamato Rd Ste 106 Boca Raton (33431) *(G-599)*
Milans Machine Shop & Wldg Svc.....305 592-2447
8052 Nw 56th St Doral (33166) *(G-3303)*
Milbank Manufacturing Co.....813 623-2681
3214 Queen Palm Dr Tampa (33619) *(G-17072)*
Milca Bottling Company.....305 365-0044
620 Harbor Cir Key Biscayne (33149) *(G-6837)*
Milcom Services Inc.....561 907-6816
1963 10th Ave N Lake Worth Beach (33461) *(G-7259)*
Mile Marker News, Key West *Also called Overseas Radio LLC* *(G-6879)*
Milenium Publishing LLC.....786 573-9974
12742 Sw 103rd Ct Miami (33176) *(G-9568)*
Miles of Smiles Rides Inc.....727 528-1227
10530 72nd St Ste 705 Seminole (33777) *(G-15983)*
Miles of Wood Inc.....305 300-6370
5951 Sw 44th Ter Miami (33155) *(G-9569)*
Miles Partnership II LLC (PA).....941 342-2300
6751 Prof Pkwy W Ste 200 Sarasota (34240) *(G-15747)*
Mill-Rite Woodworking Co Inc.....727 527-7808
6401 47th St N Pinellas Park (33781) *(G-13708)*
Millenia Froyo LLC.....407 694-9938
9066 Harbor Isle Dr Windermere (34786) *(G-18362)*
Millenium Engine Plating Inc.....305 688-0098
600 W 84th St Hialeah (33014) *(G-5258)*
Millenium Natural Health Pdts, Doral *Also called Bonne Sante Natural Mfg Inc* *(G-3145)*
Millenium Oil & Gas Distrs Inc.....305 220-3669
12801 Sw 42nd St Miami (33175) *(G-9570)*
Millenium Wood Boxes Inc.....305 969-5510
13139 Sw 122nd Ave Miami (33186) *(G-9571)*
Millennium Glass Inc.....305 638-1785
5851 Nw 35th Ave Miami (33142) *(G-9572)*
Millennium Metals Inc.....904 358-8366
10200 Eastport Rd Jacksonville (32218) *(G-6305)*
Millennium Pharmaceuticals Inc.....866 466-7779
6509 Hazeltine Nat Dr Orlando (32822) *(G-12380)*
Miller Brothers Contractors.....941 371-4162
990 Cattlemen Rd Sarasota (34232) *(G-15748)*
Miller Creative Graphics.....904 771-5855
8725 Youngerman Ct # 101 Jacksonville (32244) *(G-6306)*
Miller Creative Works Inc.....904 504-3212
710 9th Ave N Jacksonville (32250) *(G-6307)*
Miller Leasing, Tampa *Also called Crawford Manufacturing Company* *(G-16736)*
Miller Marine Yacht Svc Inc.....850 265-6768
7141 Grassy Point Rd Panama City (32409) *(G-13286)*
Miller Publishing Co Inc.....305 669-7355
6796 Sw 62nd Ave South Miami (33143) *(G-16039)*
Miller Signs LLC.....786 395-9420
2501 N 69th Ave Hollywood (33024) *(G-5627)*

ALPHABETIC

Miller-Leaman Inc 386 248-0500
800 Orange Ave Daytona Beach (32114) **(G-2576)**

Millerknoll Inc 904 858-9918
1015 Kings Ave Jacksonville (32207) **(G-6308)**

Millerknoll Inc 305 572-2909
4141 Ne 2nd Ave Miami (33137) **(G-9573)**

Millers Custom Metals Inc 561 540-6263
1224 Pope Ln Lake Worth (33460) **(G-7218)**

Milliken & Company 352 244-2267
5002 Ne 54th Pl Gainesville (32609) **(G-4731)**

Milliken & Milliken Inc 941 474-0223
101 S Mccall Rd Englewood (34223) **(G-3534)**

Milliken Industries, Englewood Also called Milliken & Milliken Inc **(G-3534)**

Millimeter Wave Products Inc 727 563-0034
2007 Gandy Blvd N # 1310 Saint Petersburg (33702) **(G-15126)**

Mills & Murphy Sftwr Systems 727 577-1236
618 94th Ave N Saint Petersburg (33702) **(G-15127)**

Mills & Nebraska, Orlando Also called Central Florida Lbr & Sup Co **(G-11999)**

Mills & Nebraska Door & Trim 407 472-2742
2721 Regent Ave Orlando (32804) **(G-12381)**

Millwork and Design Inc 352 544-0444
22309 Rodeo Dr Brooksville (34602) **(G-1182)**

Millwork Masters LLC 727 807-6221
7013 Us Highway 19 New Port Richey (34652) **(G-10974)**

Millwork Plus Inc 352 343-2121
262 Hummer Way Tavares (32778) **(G-17518)**

Milsav LLC 407-556-5055
10542 Wittenberg Way Orlando (32832) **(G-12382)**

Miltechnologies Inc 305 817-4244
13980 Nw 58th Ct Miami Lakes (33014) **(G-10326)**

Milton Newspapers Inc 850 623-2120
6576 Caroline St Milton (32570) **(G-10431)**

Milton Truss Company, Milton Also called Emerald Coast Truss LLC **(G-10423)**

Milton Yard, Milton Also called Martin Marietta Materials Inc **(G-10430)**

Mimi's Ravioli, Hollywood Also called Termine Ravioli Manufacturing **(G-5669)**

Mims Welding Incorporated 863 612-9819
90 Evans Rd Labelle (33935) **(G-6983)**

Minco LLC 813 340-7769
2931 W Wallcraft Ave Tampa (33611) **(G-17073)**

Minder Research Inc 772 463-6522
3000 Se Waaler St Stuart (34997) **(G-16185)**

Mine Survival Inc 850 774-0025
9210 Pnama Cy Bch Pkwy St Panama City Beach (32407) **(G-13334)**

Minea Usa Llc 800 971-3216
1550 S Dixie Hwy Ste 216 Coral Gables (33146) **(G-2087)**

Mineral Development LLC 863 354-3113
4000 Sr 60 E Mulberry (33860) **(G-10633)**

Mineral Life Intl Inc 305 661-9854
6732 Sw 71st Ct Miami (33143) **(G-9574)**

Mini Circuits Lab Inc 305 558-6381
2160 W 80th St Hialeah (33016) **(G-5259)**

Mini Truckin, Tampa Also called Hornblasters Inc **(G-16922)**

Minisportsballs.com, Tampa Also called Put Your Name On It LLC **(G-17195)**

Mink Bar LLC 954 758-2085
10231 Sw 4th Ct Unit 202 Pembroke Pines (33025) **(G-13404)**

Mink Milli LLC 813 606-0416
610 E Zack St Ste 110-407 Tampa (33602) **(G-17074)**

Minute Man Press 727 791-1115
1425 Main St Ste C Dunedin (34698) **(G-3454)**

Minuteman Industries Inc 813 248-1776
1407 E 5th Ave Tampa (33605) **(G-17075)**

Minuteman Press, Coral Springs Also called E3 Graphics Inc **(G-2151)**

Minuteman Press, Boca Raton Also called Spinnaker Holding Company **(G-692)**

Minuteman Press, Hialeah Also called Semprun & Morales Corporation **(G-5345)**

Minuteman Press, Minneola Also called Guerrilla Prtg Solutions LLC **(G-10451)**

Minuteman Press, Orlando Also called Pamatian Group Inc **(G-12464)**

Minuteman Press, Jacksonville Also called Sonshine Digital Graphics Inc **(G-6479)**

Minuteman Press, Naples Also called Just Now Jennings LLC **(G-10794)**

Minuteman Press, West Palm Beach Also called 5hp Investments LLC **(G-17905)**

Minuteman Press, Orlando Also called Relion Enterprises LLC **(G-12546)**

Minuteman Press, Fort Lauderdale Also called Bema Inc **(G-3681)**

Minuteman Press, Jupiter Also called Tiba Enterprises Inc **(G-6809)**

Minuteman Press, Hollywood Also called Taie Inc **(G-5668)**

Minuteman Press, Sunrise Also called Printrust Inc **(G-16357)**

Minuteman Press, Lakeland Also called Lincoln Smith Ventures LLC **(G-7379)**

Minuteman Press, North Palm Beach Also called Universal Graphics & Prtg Inc **(G-11184)**

Minuteman Press, Dunedin Also called Minute Man Press **(G-3454)**

Minuteman Press, New Port Richey Also called Danifer Printing Inc **(G-10966)**

Minuteman Press, Miramar Also called J J M Services Inc **(G-10507)**

Minuteman Press, Stuart Also called Kinane Corp **(G-16174)**

Minuteman Press, Miami Also called Boostan Inc **(G-8846)**

Minuteman Press, Longwood Also called It Busness Solutions Group Inc **(G-7907)**

Minuteman Press, Jacksonville Also called R A Printing Inc **(G-6402)**

Minuteman Press, Vero Beach Also called Spinnaker Vero Inc **(G-17802)**

Minuteman Press, Miami Also called Orellana Investments Inc **(G-9663)**

Minuteman Press 727 535-3800
2475 E Bay Dr Ste A Largo (33771) **(G-7644)**

Minuteman Press 813 884-2476
5519 Hanley Rd Tampa (33634) **(G-17076)**

Minuteman Press 904 733-5578
1370 Marsh Harbor Dr Jacksonville (32225) **(G-6309)**

Minuteman Press 305 242-6800
22469 Sw 103rd Ave Cutler Bay (33190) **(G-2297)**

Minuteman Press 863 337-6670
2058 E Edgewood Dr Ste C Lakeland (33803) **(G-7396)**

Minuteman Press 386 255-2767
201 N Ridgewood Ave Daytona Beach (32114) **(G-2577)**

Minuteman Press 352 728-6333
1417 E Main St Leesburg (34748) **(G-7786)**

Minuteman Press 772 301-0222
6967 Hancock Dr Port Saint Lucie (34952) **(G-14426)**

Minuteman Press 727 214-2275
9600 66th St N Ste A Pinellas Park (33782) **(G-13709)**

Minuteman Press 954 804-8304
6677 Lake Worth Rd Lake Worth (33467) **(G-7219)**

Minuteman Systems & Alarms, Tampa Also called Minuteman Industries Inc **(G-17075)**

Minutemen Printing, Pompano Beach Also called United Printing Sales Inc **(G-14228)**

Mio Gourmet Products LLC 305 219-0253
616 W 27th St Hialeah (33010) **(G-5260)**

Mio Publication Inc 941 351-2411
1864 University Pkwy Sarasota (34243) **(G-15517)**

Mip-Technology Corp 239 221-3604
28100 Bonita Grande Dr # 101 Bonita Springs (34135) **(G-811)**

Mipe Corp 305 825-1195
3960 W 16th Ave Ste 208 Hialeah (33012) **(G-5261)**

Miracle Noodle, Miami Also called Strumba Media LLC **(G-9959)**

Miracle Seafood Manufacturers 850 653-2114
610 Us Highway 98 Apalachicola (32320) **(G-89)**

Miracles For Fun Usa Inc 561 702-8217
1835 E Hllndale Bch Blvd Hallandale Beach (33009) **(G-4961)**

Miraflex Corporation 786 380-4494
7950 Nw 53rd St Ste 324 Doral (33166) **(G-3304)**

Mirage & Co Inc 407 301-5850
3826 Cedar Hammock Trl Saint Cloud (34772) **(G-14935)**

Mirage Manufacturing Inc 352 377-4146
3001 Ne 20th Way Gainesville (32609) **(G-4732)**

Mirage Systems Inc 386 740-9222
1501a Lexington Ave Deland (32724) **(G-2886)**

Miramar Cosmetic Inc 305 455-5016
2301 Nw 107th Ave Ste 101 Doral (33172) **(G-3305)**

Miramar Labs, Doral Also called Miramar Cosmetic Inc **(G-3305)**

Miramar Mrmids Synchro Team LL 786 520-6678
16801 Miramar Pkwy Miramar (33027) **(G-10515)**

Miramar Publishing Inc 305 695-0639
1030 14th St Miami Beach (33139) **(G-10213)**

Mirandas Woodcraft LLC 954 306-3568
3764 Nw 16th St Lauderhill (33311) **(G-7736)**

Mirart Inc 954 974-5230
2707 Gateway Dr Pompano Beach (33069) **(G-14101)**

Mircalear, Gainesville Also called Florida North Hearing Solution **(G-4693)**

Mirocos LLC 305 674-6921
8450 Nw 68th St Miami (33166) **(G-9575)**

Mirrolure, Largo Also called L & S Bait Co Inc **(G-7631)**

Mirrors & More Inc 954 782-7272
3390 Ne 6th Ter Pompano Beach (33064) **(G-14102)**

Mirrors 2 Go, Miami Also called Italian Cabinetry Inc **(G-9343)**

Misc Metal Fabrication LLC 754 264-1026
3001 Sw 15th St Ste A Deerfield Beach (33442) **(G-2768)**

Misfit Gaming 954 347-0906
6401 Congress Ave Boca Raton (33487) **(G-600)**

Mishaal Aerospace Corporation 786 353-2685
31 Se 5th St Apt 3415 Miami (33131) **(G-9576)**

Mishas Cupcakes Inc (PA) 786 200-6153
5616 Sunset Dr Miami (33143) **(G-9577)**

Mishy Sportswear 305 819-7556
7305 W 19th Ct Hialeah (33014) **(G-5262)**

Miss BS Inc 305 981-9900
13899 Biscayne Blvd # 309 North Miami Beach (33181) **(G-11151)**

Mister Cabinet Deluxe Inc 305 205-3601
2280 W 77th St Hialeah (33016) **(G-5263)**

Mitek Inc 727 536-7891
11910 62nd St Largo (33773) **(G-7645)**

Mitek Inc 813 675-1224
1801a Massaro Blvd Tampa (33619) **(G-17077)**

Mitek USA Inc 813 906-3122
1801a Massaro Blvd Tampa (33619) **(G-17078)**

Mito Corp 786 208-3114
1488 Nw 158th Ln Pembroke Pines (33028) **(G-13405)**

Mitsubishi Power Americas Inc (HQ) 407 688-6100
400 Colonial Center Pkwy # 500 Lake Mary (32746) **(G-7096)**

Mitsubshi Htchi Pwr Systems Am, Lake Mary Also called Mitsubishi Power Americas Inc **(G-7096)**

Mitten Manufacturing 941 722-1818
1614 20th St E Unit 102 Palmetto (34221) **(G-13182)**

Mittera, Jacksonville *Also called Trend Offset Printing Svcs Inc (G-6567)*
Mitts and Merrill LP....352 343-7001
28623 Lake Indus Blvd Tavares (32778) **(G-17519)**
Mityflex, Bradenton *Also called Anko Products Inc (G-939)*
Mix It At Loop....407 201-8948
2617 W Osceola Pkwy Kissimmee (34741) **(G-6943)**
Mix It Loop Inc....407 902-9334
12517 Greco Dr Orlando (32824) **(G-12383)**
Mix Masters Inc....386 846-9239
523 Virginia Ave Unit B Port Orange (32127) **(G-14340)**
Mixers Bar & Grille, Palm Harbor *Also called Beast Row Inc (G-13103)*
Mizkan America Inc....863 956-0391
445 N Dakota Ave Lake Alfred (33850) **(G-6996)**
MJK Industries Inc....954 788-7494
201 Se 3rd Ct Pompano Beach (33060) **(G-14103)**
MJM Cabinet Inc....786 953-5000
226 W 23rd St Hialeah (33010) **(G-5264)**
MJM Manufacturing Inc....305 620-2020
5205 Nw 161st St Miami Lakes (33014) **(G-10327)**
Mjr Enterprises Inc....352 483-0735
1895 Irma Rd Eustis (32726) **(G-3564)**
Mjr Woodworks LLC....407 403-5430
552 Cooper Indus Pkwy Apopka (32703) **(G-154)**
Mk Aviation LLC....305 825-4810
9471 Nw 12th St Doral (33172) **(G-3306)**
MK Brothers Inc....407 847-9547
2790 Michigan Ave Ste 318 Kissimmee (34744) **(G-6944)**
Mk Monomers LLC....732 928-5800
905 Brickell Bay Dr # 23 Miami (33131) **(G-9578)**
Mkm Sarasota LLC....941 358-0383
2363 Industrial Blvd Sarasota (34234) **(G-15749)**
Mli Intgrted Graphic Solutions, Tampa *Also called Martin Lithograph Inc (G-17044)*
Mlxl Productions Inx....904 350-0048
2935 Dawn Rd Jacksonville (32207) **(G-6310)**
Mm Wood Designs Inc....561 602-2775
2859 Cormorant Rd Delray Beach (33444) **(G-2989)**
Mmats Inc....561 842-0600
15132 Pk Of Commerce Blvd Jupiter (33478) **(G-6765)**
Mmats Professional Audio, Jupiter *Also called Mmats Inc (G-6765)*
Mmi North America Inc....616 649-1912
344 Ponte Vedra Blvd Ponte Vedra Beach (32082) **(G-14275)**
Mmo Industries Inc....727 452-8665
4710 Eisenhower Blvd A1 Tampa (33634) **(G-17079)**
Mmp-Boca Raton LLC....561 392-8626
1609 Nw 2nd Ave Boca Raton (33432) **(G-601)**
Mmt Technologies Inc....863 619-2926
4302 Holden Rd Lakeland (33811) **(G-7397)**
Mmx Manufacturing LLC....786 456-5072
6508 Nw 77th Ct Miami (33166) **(G-9579)**
MN Trades Inc....954 455-9320
200 Leslie Dr Ofc Hallandale Beach (33009) **(G-4962)**
MO Steel Fbricator Erector Inc....305 945-4855
353 Ne 185th St Miami (33179) **(G-9580)**
Moba Corp....305 868-3700
10155 Collins Ave # 1807 Bal Harbour (33154) **(G-295)**
Mobica Center, Hialeah *Also called Mister Cabinet Deluxe Inc (G-5263)*
Mobile 1 Inc....954 283-8100
3680 W Oakland Park Blvd Lauderdale Lakes (33311) **(G-7718)**
Mobile Auto Solutions LLC....561 903-5328
1578 Quail Dr Apt 10 West Palm Beach (33409) **(G-18080)**
Mobile Home Rebuilders LLC....863 838-9547
3618 Deborah Dr Lakeland (33810) **(G-7398)**
Mobile Meals....813 907-6325
8909 Magnolia Chase Cir Tampa (33647) **(G-17080)**
Mobile Mini Inc....866 344-4092
2850 Country Club Blvd Orange Park (32073) **(G-11834)**
Mobile Mini Inc....954 745-0026
12905 Nw 32nd Ave Opa Locka (33054) **(G-11770)**
Mobile Power Generators LLC....352 365-2777
634 State Road 44 Leesburg (34748) **(G-7787)**
Mobile Rugged Tech Corp....781 771-6743
4767 New Broad St Orlando (32814) **(G-12384)**
Mobile Rving....954 870-7095
2150 Sw 10th St Ste A Deerfield Beach (33442) **(G-2769)**
Mobile Sign Service Inc....954 579-8628
4381 Nw 4th St Coconut Creek (33066) **(G-1999)**
Mobile Specialties Inc....407 878-5469
1683 N Beardall Ave # 117 Sanford (32771) **(G-15359)**
Mobile Walkways, Sanford *Also called Mobile Specialties Inc (G-15359)*
Mobile4lessusa Corp....954 706-0582
708 Sw 10th St Deerfield Beach (33441) **(G-2770)**
Mobilebits Holdings Corp (PA)....941 225-6115
5901 N Honore Ave Ste 120 Sarasota (34243) **(G-15518)**
Mobilehelp LLC (HQ)....561 347-6255
5050 Conference Way N # 125 Boca Raton (33431) **(G-602)**
Mobilepower LLC....843 706-6108
5975 Sunset Dr South Miami (33143) **(G-16040)**
Mobilite Corporation....407 321-5630
2101 E Lake Mary Blvd Sanford (32773) **(G-15360)**

Mobility Freedom Inc....407 495-1333
7260 Narcoossee Rd Orlando (32822) **(G-12385)**
Mobius Business Group Inc....239 274-8900
1961 Dana Dr Fort Myers (33907) **(G-4327)**
Mobvious Corp....786 497-6620
2100 Coral Way Ste 200 Miami (33145) **(G-9581)**
Mode Marimba Inc....561 512-5001
19960 Earlwood Dr Jupiter (33458) **(G-6766)**
Model Expo, Miami *Also called Model Shipways Inc (G-9582)*
Model Screw Products, Clearwater *Also called MSP Industries LLC (G-1706)*
Model Shipways Inc....800 222-3876
2613 Nw 20th St Miami (33142) **(G-9582)**
Modern Digital Imaging Inc....850 222-7514
519 N Monroe St Tallahassee (32301) **(G-16481)**
Modern Display, Doral *Also called J D M Corp (G-3264)*
Modern Garden Miami LLC....305 440-4200
422 Nw North River Dr Miami (33128) **(G-9583)**
Modern Graphic Arts, Saint Petersburg *Also called Sandy-Alexander Inc (G-15176)*
Modern Happy Home Llc....954 436-0055
1201 E Sunrise Blvd # 305 Fort Lauderdale (33304) **(G-3942)**
Modern Mail Print Slutions Inc....727 572-6245
14201 58th St N Clearwater (33760) **(G-1701)**
Modern Settings LLC....800 645-5585
6331 Porter Rd Unit 8 Sarasota (34240) **(G-15750)**
Modern Silicone Tech Inc....727 873-1805
10601 Us Highway 19 N Pinellas Park (33782) **(G-13710)**
Modern Tchncal Molding Dev LLC....727 343-2942
2600 72nd St N Saint Petersburg (33710) **(G-15128)**
Modern Welding Company Fla Inc....407 843-1270
1801 Atlanta Ave Orlando (32806) **(G-12386)**
Modernizing Medicine Inc (PA)....561 880-2998
4850 Network Way Ste 200 Boca Raton (33431) **(G-603)**
Moderno Porcelain Works LLC....954 607-3535
13807 Nw 4th St Sunrise (33325) **(G-16341)**
Modernzing Mdcine Gstrntrlogy....561 880-2998
4850 Network Way Ste 200 Boca Raton (33431) **(G-604)**
Modest Logistics LLC....321 314-2825
2295 S Hiawassee Rd Orlando (32835) **(G-12387)**
Modified Kids Ride On Toys, Pompano Beach *Also called Kidstance LLC (G-14070)*
Modmed, Boca Raton *Also called Modernizing Medicine Inc (G-603)*
Modpros Elevator Inc....786 863-0092
10750 Nw 53rd St Sunrise (33351) **(G-16342)**
Modular Life Solutions LLC....904 900-7965
6622 Sthpint Dr S Ste 250 Jacksonville (32216) **(G-6311)**
Modular Molding Intl Inc....727 541-1333
10521 75th St Ste B Seminole (33777) **(G-15984)**
Modular Thermal Tech LLC (PA)....954 785-1055
1520 Sw 5th Ct Pompano Beach (33069) **(G-14104)**
Modulex Miami LLC....786 424-0857
14 Ne 1st Ave Ste 707 Miami (33132) **(G-9584)**
Moduslink Corporation....305 888-8091
10990 Nw 92nd Ter Medley (33178) **(G-8283)**
Moffitt Corporation Inc (PA)....904 241-9944
1351 13th Ave S Ste 130 Jacksonville Beach (32250) **(G-6639)**
Moffitt Fan Corporation....585 768-7010
1351 13th Ave S Ste 130 Jacksonville Beach (32250) **(G-6640)**
Mohawk Industries Inc....918 272-0184
2500 Sw 32nd Ave Hollywood (33023) **(G-5628)**
Mohawk Manufacturing Company....407 849-0333
963 N Ronald Reagan Blvd Longwood (32750) **(G-7924)**
Mohnark Pharmaceuticals Inc....954 607-4559
5150 Sw 48th Way Ste 604 Davie (33314) **(G-2442)**
Moi, Sarasota *Also called Manasota Optics Inc (G-15737)*
Moisttech Corp....941 351-7870
6408 Parkland Dr Ste 104 Sarasota (34243) **(G-15519)**
Mojowax Media Inc....805 550-6013
1100 Yale Ave Bradenton (34207) **(G-1013)**
Mold Be Gone Plus....239 672-5321
14120 Carlotta St Fort Myers (33905) **(G-4328)**
Mold Busters LLC....786 360-6464
12900 Sw 80th St Miami (33183) **(G-9585)**
Mold Control Systems Inc....561 316-5412
2000 Pga Blvd Ste 4440 Palm Beach Gardens (33408) **(G-12990)**
Mold Expert....954 829-3102
2812 Nw 87th Ave Coral Springs (33065) **(G-2189)**
Mold Pros Franchising Inc....239 262-6653
3428 Runaway Ln Ste 106 Naples (34114) **(G-10821)**
Mold R US Inc....954 850-6653
6596 Taft St Hollywood (33024) **(G-5629)**
Mold Remediation Services Inc....904 574-5266
7643 Gate Pkwy 104-57 Jacksonville (32256) **(G-6312)**
Molded Container, Hialeah *Also called Ellis Family Holdings Inc (G-5139)*
Molded Moments Art....954 913-0793
1477 Running Oak Ln Royal Palm Beach (33411) **(G-14770)**
Molding Depot Inc....813 348-4837
3707 W Carmen St Tampa (33609) **(G-17081)**
Molds and Plastic McHy Inc....305 828-3456
13180 N Bayshore Dr North Miami (33181) **(G-11113)**

ALPHABETIC

Moldsbiz 352 327-2720
4579 Nw 6th St Ste B Gainesville (32609) *(G-4733)*

Molekule Inc 352 871-3803
3802 Spectrum Blvd # 143 Tampa (33612) *(G-17082)*

Molex LLC 727 521-2700
4650 62nd Ave N Pinellas Park (33781) *(G-13711)*

Molex Tampa Bay Operations, Pinellas Park Also called Molex LLC *(G-13711)*

Molly & Friends, Gainesville Also called Munro International Inc *(G-4736)*

Mollys Marine Service LLC 239 262-2628
895 10th St S Naples (34102) *(G-10822)*

Mollys Suds LLC 678 361-5456
7490 30th Ave N A Saint Petersburg (33710) *(G-15129)*

Moloney Die Company 904 388-3654
5002 Palmer Ave Jacksonville (32210) *(G-6313)*

Moloney Wire Dies, Jacksonville Also called Moloney Die Company *(G-6313)*

Momenry Inc 318 668-0888
100 S Ashley Dr Ste 600 Tampa (33602) *(G-17083)*

Momentum Comfort Gear Inc 305 653-5050
470 Ne 185th St Miami (33179) *(G-9586)*

Mommy & ME Molds LLC 727 460-0335
1359 Monterey Blvd Ne Saint Petersburg (33704) *(G-15130)*

Mon Reve, Sunrise Also called Entire Select Inc *(G-16316)*

Monar Corporation 954 650-1930
9825 W Sample Rd Ste 202 Coral Springs (33065) *(G-2190)*

Monarch Printing & Design, Port Charlotte Also called Bladorn Investments Inc *(G-14288)*

Monarch Safety Products Inc 407 442-0269
121 S Orange Ave Ste 1500 Orlando (32801) *(G-12388)*

Monarq Americas LLC 305 632-7448
55 Merrick Way Ste 202 Coral Gables (33134) *(G-2088)*

Monarq Group, Coral Gables Also called Monarq Americas LLC *(G-2088)*

Mondelez Global LLC 305 774-6273
396 Alhambra Cir Ste 1000 Coral Gables (33134) *(G-2089)*

Mondolfo LLC 954 523-1115
1145 S Federal Hwy Fort Lauderdale (33316) *(G-3943)*

Money Tree Atm Mfg LLC 850 244-5543
130 Staff Dr Ne Fort Walton Beach (32548) *(G-4597)*

Money Tree Publishing, Crestview Also called Wrongs Without Wremedies LLC *(G-2257)*

Monier Lifetile Inc 561 338-8200
135 Nw 20th St Boca Raton (33431) *(G-605)*

Monin Inc (HQ) 727 461-3033
2100 Range Rd Clearwater (33765) *(G-1702)*

Monin Gourmet Flavorings, Clearwater Also called Monin Inc *(G-1702)*

Monison Pallets Inc 904 359-0235
3160 W 45th St Jacksonville (32209) *(G-6314)*

Monison Pallets Inc (PA) 305 637-1600
5420 Nw 37th Ave Miami (33142) *(G-9587)*

Monitor Products Inc 352 544-2620
15400 Flight Path Dr Brooksville (34604) *(G-1183)*

Monkey Shack 850 234-0082
11840 Front Beach Rd A Panama City (32407) *(G-13287)*

Monogram Online, Oakland Park Also called Deal To Win Inc *(G-11256)*

Monroe Cable LLC 941 429-8484
2529 Commerce Pkwy North Port (34289) *(G-11201)*

Monroe Concrete Products Inc 305 296-5606
155 Overseas Hwy Key West (33040) *(G-6876)*

Monroy Aerospace 954 344-4936
10908 Nw 17th Mnr Coral Springs (33071) *(G-2191)*

Monsanto Company 863 673-2157
2221 Keri Rd Felda (33930) *(G-3572)*

Monsta Performance Inc 321 848-7256
691 Washburn Rd Melbourne (32934) *(G-8477)*

Monster Tech USA, Tampa Also called Monstertech Corporation *(G-17084)*

Monster Transmission & Prfmce, Brooksville Also called Avalanche Corporation *(G-1138)*

Monstertech Corporation 813 898-0405
4498 Eagle Falls Pl Tampa (33619) *(G-17084)*

Mont Everest Inc (PA) 727 209-0864
6795 114th Ave Largo (33773) *(G-7646)*

Mont Krest, Largo Also called Mont Everest Inc *(G-7646)*

Montague Enterprises Inc 239 631-5292
1004 Collier Center Way # 206 Naples (34110) *(G-10823)*

Montalvos Raceway LLC 239 289-6931
280 35th Ave Ne Naples (34120) *(G-10824)*

Montebana Fuels LLC 954 385-5374
1565 Sandpiper Cir Weston (33327) *(G-18268)*

Montedana Fuels 305 887-6754
2090 Palm Ave Hialeah (33010) *(G-5265)*

Monteocha Coatings Inc 352 367-3136
2607 Ne 56th Ter Gainesville (32609) *(G-4734)*

Montesino International Corp 954 767-6185
1816 N Dixie Hwy Fort Lauderdale (33305) *(G-3944)*

Montgomery Industries Intl 904 355-4055
2017 Thelma St Jacksonville (32206) *(G-6315)*

Monthly Media, Largo Also called Village Scribe Printing Co *(G-7703)*

Monticello Milling Co Inc 850 997-5521
500 S Jefferson St Monticello (32344) *(G-10583)*

Monticello News 850 997-3568
180 W Washington St Monticello (32344) *(G-10584)*

Montres Corum Usa LLC 954 279-1220
14050 Nw 14th St Ste 110 Sunrise (33323) *(G-16343)*

Monty Sanitation, Naples Also called Rmmj Inc *(G-10878)*

Monty Sanitation Inc 239 597-2486
5545 Shirley St Naples (34109) *(G-10825)*

Monument Pharmacy, Jacksonville Also called Shriji Swami LLC *(G-6467)*

Monumental Air Inc 954 383-9507
4333 Nw 64th Ave Coral Springs (33067) *(G-2192)*

Monumental Enterprises Inc 305 803-8493
7958 Pines Blvd Ste 242 Pembroke Pines (33024) *(G-13406)*

Monumntal Fabrication Amer Inc 850 227-9500
950 W Rutherford St Port Saint Joe (32456) *(G-14389)*

Moody Construction Svcs Inc 941 776-1542
12450 County Road 39 Duette (34219) *(G-3432)*

Moog 305 471-0444
1525 Nw 82nd Ave Doral (33126) *(G-3307)*

Moog IDS, Orlando Also called Moog Inc *(G-12390)*

Moog Inc 321 435-8722
7455 Emerald Dunes Dr # 2200 Orlando (32822) *(G-12389)*

Moog Inc 407 451-9534
7455 Emerald Dunes Dr # 2200 Orlando (32822) *(G-12390)*

Moon Express Inc 650 241-8577
100 Space Port Way Cape Canaveral (32920) *(G-1291)*

Moonex, Cape Canaveral Also called Moon Express Inc *(G-1291)*

Moore & Bode Group LLC 786 615-9389
2221 Se 27th Dr Homestead (33035) *(G-5731)*

Moore Computer Consultants, Miramar Also called Digital Compositing Systems *(G-10484)*

Moore Solutions Inc 772 337-4005
1680 Se Lyngate Dr # 202 Port St Lucie (34952) *(G-14478)*

Moores Mar of Palm Beaches Inc 561 841-2235
1410 Avenue E Riviera Beach (33404) *(G-14647)*

Mooring Yacht Brokerage, Dania Also called Mariner International Trvl Inc *(G-2336)*

Moose Tracts Inc 407 491-1412
2325 Ohio Dr Orlando (32803) *(G-12391)*

Mor EZ Clips 352 867-1879
4151 Ne 22nd Ct Ocala (34479) *(G-11446)*

MOR Printing Inc 954 377-1197
6561 Nw 18th Ct Plantation (33313) *(G-13869)*

Mor Printing & Envelopes, Plantation Also called MOR Printing Inc *(G-13869)*

Moralmar Kitchen Cabinets 305 819-8402
3130 W 15th Ave Hialeah (33012) *(G-5266)*

Moran Transport 305 824-3366
9829 Nw 129th Ter Hialeah (33018) *(G-5267)*

Morcent Import Export Inc 727 442-9735
1702 Indian Rocks Rd Belleair (33756) *(G-352)*

Morelia Paletas Gourmet, Coral Gables Also called Lefab Commercial LLC *(G-2082)*

Moreno & Sons Inc 786 402-8919
2535 Ambassador Ave Hollywood (33026) *(G-5630)*

Moretrench Enviromental Svcs, Riverview Also called Keller Industrial Inc *(G-14568)*

Morey Machining & Mfg Inc 239 693-8699
9350 Workmen Way Fort Myers (33905) *(G-4329)*

Morgan Technical Services 772 466-5757
5512 Silver Oak Dr Fort Pierce (34982) *(G-4508)*

Morganelli & Associates Inc 386 738-3669
1401 Saratoga St Deland (32724) *(G-2887)*

Morgannas Alchemy LLC 727 505-8376
10347 Palladio Dr New Port Richey (34655) *(G-10975)*

Morgans Elc Mtr & Pump Svc, Cocoa Beach Also called Morgans Elc Mtr & Pump Svc *(G-1974)*

Morgans Elc Mtr & Pump Svc 321 960-2209
157 N Orlando Ave Cocoa Beach (32931) *(G-1974)*

Mori Lee LLC (PA) 954 418-6165
3155 Sw 10th St Ste 6a1 Deerfield Beach (33442) *(G-2771)*

Morlee Lampshade Co Inc 305 500-9310
6915 Nw 43rd St Miami (33166) *(G-9588)*

Morning Glory Lawn Maint Inc 407 376-5833
4750 Nantucket Ln Orlando (32808) *(G-12392)*

Morning Star Industries Inc 800 440-6050
630 Ne Jensen Beach Blvd Jensen Beach (34957) *(G-6657)*

Morning Star of Sarasota Inc 941 371-0392
1985 Cattlemen Rd Unit A Sarasota (34232) *(G-15751)*

Morning Star Personalized AP 772 569-8412
621 2nd Ln Vero Beach (32962) *(G-17778)*

Moroccan Khlii Inc 813 699-0096
808 N Macdill Ave Tampa (33609) *(G-17085)*

Morris Mica Cabinets Inc 954 979-6838
1920 Nw 22nd Ct Pompano Beach (33069) *(G-14105)*

Morris Valves Inc 305 477-6525
5590 Nw 84th Ave Ste C Doral (33166) *(G-3308)*

Morris Visitor Publications 407 423-0618
801 N Magnolia Ave # 201 Orlando (32803) *(G-12393)*

Morrison Meat Packers, Miami Also called El Toro Meat Packing Corp *(G-9078)*

Morrissy & Co 850 934-4243
204 Fairpoint Dr Gulf Breeze (32561) *(G-4886)*

Morse Enterprises Limited Inc 407 682-6500
400 N Ny Ave Ste 200 Miami (33129) *(G-9589)*

Morten Enterprises Inc (PA) 727 531-8957
12350 Us Highway 19 N Clearwater (33764) *(G-1703)*

Morton Plant Mease Health Care................727 462-7052
430 Pinellas St Clearwater (33756) **(G-1704)**

Morton Salt Inc...................................321 868-7136
450 Cargo Rd Cape Canaveral (32920) **(G-1292)**

Mos Holdings Inc................................763 577-2700
5000 Old Highway 37 Mulberry (33860) **(G-10634)**

Mosaic..863 860-1328
5810 Deer Flag Dr Lakeland (33811) **(G-7399)**

Mosaic Company...................................813 775-2827
8817 S Us Highway 41 Riverview (33578) **(G-14570)**

Mosaic Company (PA)............................800 918-8270
101 E Kennedy Blvd # 2500 Tampa (33602) **(G-17086)**

Mosaic Company, The, Tampa *Also called Mosaic Global Sales LLC* **(G-17087)**

Mosaic Crop Nutrition LLC.....................813 500-6800
13830 Circa Crossing Dr Lithia (33547) **(G-7835)**

Mosaic Fertilizer LLC (HQ)....................813 500-6300
13830 Circa Crossing Dr Lithia (33547) **(G-7836)**

Mosaic Global Sales LLC (HQ).................763 577-2700
101 E Kennedy Blvd # 250 Tampa (33602) **(G-17087)**

Mosaics Liquidation Co Inc....................772 468-8453
901 S 3rd St Fort Pierce (34950) **(G-4509)**

Mosch International Corp.......................786 616-9108
6400 Nw 72nd Ave Miami (33166) **(G-9590)**

Moser Automotive................................561 881-5665
2391 President Barack Oba Riviera Beach (33404) **(G-14648)**

Mossberg Group Inc.............................386 274-5882
14 Broadriver Rd Ormond Beach (32174) **(G-12781)**

Most Valuable Pavers............................239 590-5217
224 Sw 22nd Pl Cape Coral (33991) **(G-1366)**

Motaz Inc...239 334-7699
2441 Hanson St Fort Myers (33901) **(G-4330)**

Mother Earth Stone LLC.......................407 878-2854
4035 Maronda Way Sanford (32771) **(G-15361)**

Mother Kombucha LLC..........................727 767-0408
4360 28th St N Saint Petersburg (33714) **(G-15131)**

Motherkin Cleaners, Oviedo *Also called Japan Fabricare* **(G-12830)**

Motionvibe Innovations LLC...................202 285-0235
4031 Caddie Dr E Bradenton (34203) **(G-1014)**

Motor City Classics Inc.........................954 473-2201
12717 W Sunrise Blvd Sunrise (33323) **(G-16344)**

Motor Coach Inds Intl Inc......................407 246-1414
1155 Elboc Way Winter Garden (34787) **(G-18398)**

Motor Magnetics Inc............................727 873-3180
2801 72nd St N Saint Petersburg (33710) **(G-15132)**

Motor Protection Electronics..................407 299-3825
2464 Vulcan Rd Apopka (32703) **(G-155)**

Motor Service Group LLC......................305 592-2440
6600 Nw 77th Ct Miami (33166) **(G-9591)**

Motor Service Inc................................305 592-2440
6600 Nw 77th Ct Miami (33166) **(G-9592)**

Motor Services Region 9, West Palm Beach *Also called Highway Sfety Mtr Vhcles Fla D* **(G-18024)**

Motorola Solutions...............................239 939-7717
13891 Jetport Loop Ste 9 Fort Myers (33913) **(G-4331)**

Motorola Solutions Inc.........................954 723-5000
8000 W Sunrise Blvd Plantation (33322) **(G-13870)**

Motors For Less, Pembroke Pines *Also called Ventilex Inc* **(G-13423)**

Motors Pumps and Accessories...............305 883-3181
7530 Nw 77th St Medley (33166) **(G-8284)**

Motorsport Games Inc (HQ)...................305 507-8799
5972 Ne 4th Ave Miami (33137) **(G-9593)**

Motorsport Marketing Inc......................386 239-0523
915 Ridgewood Ave Holly Hill (32117) **(G-5516)**

Motortronics, Clearwater *Also called Phasetronics Inc* **(G-1738)**

Motus Gi LLC.....................................954 541-8000
1301 E Broward Blvd # 31 Fort Lauderdale (33301) **(G-3945)**

Motus GI Holdings Inc (PA)...................954 541-8000
1301 E Broward Blvd Fl 3 Fort Lauderdale (33301) **(G-3946)**

Motus Gi, Inc., Fort Lauderdale *Also called Motus Gi LLC* **(G-3945)**

Moulton Publications Inc.......................772 234-8871
956 20th St Ste 101 Vero Beach (32960) **(G-17779)**

Mount Dora Olive Oil Company...............352 735-8481
351b N Donnelly St Mount Dora (32757) **(G-10606)**

Mounted Memories Inc..........................866 236-2541
15701 Sw 29th St Miramar (33027) **(G-10516)**

Moyo..352 208-2770
6027 Sw 54th St Ste 201 Ocala (34474) **(G-11447)**

Mp 93 Screen Print and EMB LLC...........407 592-3657
3330 Vineland Rd Ste C Orlando (32811) **(G-12394)**

Mp Tennis Inc (PA)..............................813 961-8844
14843 N Dale Mabry Hwy Tampa (33618) **(G-17088)**

MP&tr Corp..305 456-9292
1717 N Byshore Dr Apt 345 Miami (33132) **(G-9594)**

Mpact Sales Solutions...........................630 669-5937
622 Largovista Dr Oakland (34787) **(G-11229)**

Mpc Company Inc................................863 802-1722
4300 Steward Rd Lakeland (33815) **(G-7400)**

Mpc Containment Systems LLC (HQ)........773 927-4121
880 N Spring Garden Ave Deland (32720) **(G-2888)**

Mpc Group LLC (PA)............................773 927-4120
880 N Spring Garden Ave Deland (32720) **(G-2889)**

MPH Industries Inc..............................352 372-9533
2406 Ne 19th Dr Gainesville (32609) **(G-4735)**

Mpp Coatings Inc................................386 334-4484
3837 Long Grove Ln Port Orange (32129) **(G-14341)**

Mpr Audio System LLC.........................305 988-8524
3465 Nw 71st Ter Miami (33147) **(G-9595)**

MPS North America LLC (HQ).................407 472-1280
5728 Major Blvd Ste 528 Orlando (32819) **(G-12395)**

Mr Alex Pavers Corp............................941 726-7273
4010 Deberry Dr Sarasota (34233) **(G-15752)**

Mr Americas 2 LLC..............................407 217-2282
15771 State Road 535 K Orlando (32821) **(G-12396)**

Mr Bills Fine Foods..............................727 581-9850
1115 Ponce De Leon Blvd Clearwater (33756) **(G-1705)**

Mr Bones Stump Grinding......................941 927-0790
5590 Swift Rd Sarasota (34231) **(G-15753)**

Mr Cool Waters Inc (PA).......................305 234-6311
12009 Sw 129th Ct Unit 5 Miami (33186) **(G-9596)**

Mr Foamy, Fort Myers *Also called Mr Foamy Southwest Fl LLC* **(G-4332)**

Mr Foamy Southwest Fl LLC...................239 461-3110
3411 Hanson St Unit A Fort Myers (33916) **(G-4332)**

Mr Graphic Prtg & Signs LLC.................561 424-1724
2300 Palm Bch Lkes Blvd S West Palm Beach (33409) **(G-18081)**

Mr GS Foods.......................................352 799-1806
15402 Aviation Loop Dr Brooksville (34604) **(G-1184)**

Mr Gummy Vitamins LLC.......................855 674-8669
12845 Nw 45th Ave Opa Locka (33054) **(G-11771)**

Mr Gutter Cutter Inc............................772 286-7780
3102 Se Dixie Hwy Stuart (34997) **(G-16186)**

Mr Mica Wood Inc................................561 278-5821
1300 Sw 10th St Ste 3 Delray Beach (33444) **(G-2990)**

Mr Next Level Investment LLC.................786 718-8056
25118 Sw 108th Ct Homestead (33032) **(G-5732)**

Mr Rach, Coral Springs *Also called Foot Function Lab Inc* **(G-2154)**

Mr Shower Door, Fort Myers *Also called KDD Inc* **(G-4304)**

Mr Tango Sausages, Miami *Also called Special Americas Bbq Inc* **(G-9936)**

Mr Winter Inc.....................................800 327-3371
8800 Nw 77th Ct Medley (33166) **(G-8285)**

Mri Depot Inc.....................................407 696-9822
1075 Fla Cntl Pkwy Ste 20 Longwood (32750) **(G-7925)**

Mri Specialists....................................561 369-2144
1800 W Woolbright Rd # 100 Boynton Beach (33426) **(G-891)**

Mrl Industries, Keystone Heights *Also called Manufacturers Inv Group LLC* **(G-6887)**

MRM Creative LLC...............................386 218-5940
1209 Saxon Blvd Ste 4 Orange City (32763) **(G-11807)**

Mrn Biologics LLC...............................508 989-6090
3732 Nw 126th Ave Coral Springs (33065) **(G-2193)**

Mro Aerospace Inc..............................727 546-4820
10530 72nd St Ste 701 Largo (33777) **(G-7647)**

Mrreal Deal Barbque LLC......................561 271-8749
1050 Dotterel Rd Apt 200 Delray Beach (33444) **(G-2991)**

Mrs Traylors Plntn Style Foods, Panama City *Also called Charles Bryant Enterprises* **(G-13241)**

Mrs. Pasta, Dania Beach *Also called Massimo & Umberto Inc* **(G-2355)**

Ms Mobile Wldg & Fabrication.................904 591-1488
5314 Long Branch Rd Jacksonville (32234) **(G-6316)**

MSA Aircraft Products...........................772 562-2243
3106 Industrial Avenue 3 Fort Pierce (34946) **(G-4510)**

Msh Brick Pavers Inc............................941 822-6472
5640 Fountain Lake Cir Bradenton (34207) **(G-1015)**

Msm Outdoors, Fernandina Beach *Also called Sws Services Inc* **(G-3598)**

MSP Industries LLC..............................727 443-5764
1500 N Belcher Rd Clearwater (33765) **(G-1706)**

Msr Welding, Oakland Park *Also called Miami Ship Repair & Wldg Svcs* **(G-11279)**

Mt-Propeller Usa Inc............................386 736-7762
1180 Airport Terminal Dr Deland (32724) **(G-2890)**

Mtc Engineering LLC............................321 636-9480
428 Shearer Blvd Cocoa (32922) **(G-1943)**

Mtc Seal Coating Services Inc.................313 759-9423
4221 Drexel Ave Orlando (32808) **(G-12397)**

Mtec Trailer Supply..............................813 659-1647
3804 Sydney Rd Plant City (33566) **(G-13786)**

Mtg Designs Inc..................................904 923-1620
1249 Cunningham Creek Dr Jacksonville (32259) **(G-6626)**

MTI Aviation Inc..................................305 817-4244
13150 Nw 45th Ave Opa Locka (33054) **(G-11772)**

Mtm, Pensacola *Also called Machine Tool Masters Inc* **(G-13542)**

MTM&d, Saint Petersburg *Also called Modern Tchnncal Molding Dev LLC* **(G-15128)**

Mtn Government Services Inc..................954 538-4000
3044 N Commerce Pkwy Miramar (33025) **(G-10517)**

Mtng Usa Corp....................................305 670-0979
11334 Sw 157th Pl Miami (33196) **(G-9597)**

Mtronpti, Orlando *Also called Piezo Technology Inc* **(G-12486)**

MTS Medication Tech Inc (HQ)................727 576-6311
2003 Gandy Blvd N Ste 800 Saint Petersburg (33702) **(G-15133)**

MTS Packaging Systems Inc (PA) 727 576-6311
2003 Gandy Blvd N Ste 800 Saint Petersburg (33702) *(G-15134)*

MTS Sales & Marketing Inc 727 812-2830
12920 Automobile Blvd Clearwater (33762) *(G-1707)*

Mtservicer LLC 305 200-1254
8140 Nw 155th St Miami Lakes (33016) *(G-10328)*

Muelby Construction Services 561 376-7614
378 Northlake Blvd North Palm Beach (33408) *(G-11180)*

Mueller Industries Inc 901 753-3200
525 Okeechobee Blvd # 860 West Palm Beach (33401) *(G-18082)*

Mulberry Railcar, Mulberry *Also called Southstern Rail Svcs Mlbrry FL (G-10640)*

Mulch & Stone Emporium Inc 352 237-7870
7699 Sw Highway 200 Ocala (34476) *(G-11448)*

Mulch and Soil Company, The, Fort Myers *Also called Forestry Resources LLC (G-4261)*

Muller Fire Protection Inc 305 636-9780
2311 Sw 98th Pl Miami (33165) *(G-9598)*

Multi Parts Supply Usa Inc (PA) 561 748-1515
1649 Park Ln S Jupiter (33458) *(G-6767)*

Multi Soft II Inc 305 579-8000
4400 Biscayne Blvd Fl 10 Miami (33137) *(G-9599)*

Multi-Color Printing Inc 772 287-1676
1249 Se Dixie Cutoff Rd Stuart (34994) *(G-16187)*

Multi-Commercial Services Corp 305 235-1373
15420 Sw 136th St Unit 26 Miami (33196) *(G-9600)*

Multi-Flex LLC 941 360-6500
8046 36th Street Cir E Sarasota (34243) *(G-15520)*

Multi-Panels Corporation 800 723-8620
360 Central Ave Ste 800 Saint Petersburg (33701) *(G-15135)*

Multicore Photonics Inc 407 325-7800
5832 N Dean Rd Orlando (32817) *(G-12398)*

Multicore Photonics Inc 407 325-7800
319 N Crystal Lake Dr Orlando (32803) *(G-12399)*

Multicore Technologies LLC 407 325-7800
319 N Crystal Lake Dr Orlando (32803) *(G-12400)*

Multifix Cbd LLC 786 487-0792
3740 E 10th Ct Hialeah (33013) *(G-5268)*

Multihull Technologies Inc 305 296-2773
6811 Shrimp Rd Key West (33040) *(G-6877)*

Multimedia Effects Inc 800 367-3054
9715 W Broward Blvd Ste 3 Plantation (33324) *(G-13871)*

Multiparts, Jupiter *Also called Multi Parts Supply Usa Inc (G-6767)*

Multiple Tech Industries Inc 561 795-0759
7809 W Commercial Blvd Tamarac (33351) *(G-16537)*

Multitrode Inc 561 737-1210
6560 E Rogers Cir Boca Raton (33487) *(G-606)*

Mumford Micro Mch Works LLC 814 720-7291
1882 Porter Lake Dr # 103 Sarasota (34240) *(G-15754)*

Mundi Intl Trading Corp 305 205-0062
1971 Landing Way Weston (33326) *(G-18269)*

Municipal Code Corporation (HQ) 850 576-3171
1700 Capital Cir Sw Tallahassee (32310) *(G-16482)*

Municipal Lighting Systems Inc (PA) 305 666-4210
7035 Sw 47th St Ste A Miami (33155) *(G-9601)*

Municipal Supply & Sign, Naples *Also called Annat Inc (G-10669)*

Munro International Inc 352 337-1535
1030 Se 4th St Gainesville (32601) *(G-4736)*

Munters Corporation 239 936-1555
108 6th St Fort Myers (33907) *(G-4333)*

Murphy Bed USA Inc (PA) 954 493-9001
4330 N Federal Hwy Fort Lauderdale (33308) *(G-3947)*

Murray Products, Fort Lauderdale *Also called Frank Murray & Sons Inc (G-3831)*

Murse Properties LLC 941 966-3380
6650 S Tammy Amy Trl Sarasota (34231) *(G-15755)*

Muscle Fx LLC 305 514-0061
2221 Ne 164th St Ste 1267 North Miami Beach (33160) *(G-11152)*

Muscle LLC 772 678-6176
15 Sw Osceola St Stuart (34994) *(G-16188)*

Muscle Mixes Inc 407 872-7576
1617 Hillcrest St Orlando (32803) *(G-12401)*

Muse Gelato Inc 407 363-1443
7362 Futures Dr Ste 20 Orlando (32819) *(G-12402)*

Mustang Vacuum Systems Inc 941 377-1440
7135 16th St E Ste 115 Sarasota (34243) *(G-15521)*

Mutual Industries North Inc 239 332-2400
2940 Walpear St Unit 1 Fort Myers (33916) *(G-4334)*

Muv, Miami *Also called Wpp Group Usa Inc (G-10147)*

Mvp Group LLC 786 600-4687
3560 Nw 56th St Fort Lauderdale (33309) *(G-3948)*

Mvr Copiadoras Digitales 786 366-1842
9649 Nw 33rd St Doral (33172) *(G-3309)*

Mvs International Inc 954 727-3383
702 Willow Bend Rd Weston (33327) *(G-18270)*

Mwg Company Inc 305 232-7344
10665 Sw 185th Ter Cutler Bay (33157) *(G-2298)*

Mwi Corporation (PA) 954 426-1500
33 Nw 2nd St Deerfield Beach (33441) *(G-2772)*

Mwi Corporation 239 337-4747
4945 Kim Ln Fort Myers (33905) *(G-4335)*

Mwi Pumps, Deerfield Beach *Also called Mwi Corporation (G-2772)*

Mwr Sign Enterprises Inc 954 914-2709
9909 Pines Blvd Pembroke Pines (33024) *(G-13407)*

Mws Drapery Inc 305 794-3811
496 W 18th St Hialeah (33010) *(G-5269)*

Mxn Inc 813 654-3173
10120 Woodberry Rd Tampa (33619) *(G-17089)*

My Adventure To Fit Inc 727 200-3081
1245 N Hercules Ave Clearwater (33765) *(G-1708)*

My Clone Solution 813 442-9925
4532 W Kennedy Blvd 183 Tampa (33609) *(G-17090)*

My Drone Services, Sebastian *Also called Viper Drones LLC (G-15911)*

My Familys Seasonings LLC 863 698-7968
15301 Roosevelt Blvd # 303 Clearwater (33760) *(G-1709)*

My Favorite Things, Eustis *Also called Mft Stamps (G-3563)*

My Focus Inc 305 826-4480
3514 W 94th St Hialeah (33018) *(G-5270)*

My Passion On A Plate LLC 954 857-6382
7901 Southgate Blvd C3 North Lauderdale (33068) *(G-11084)*

My Print Shop, Deerfield Beach *Also called Accuprint Corporation (G-2654)*

My Print Shop Inc 954 973-9369
1061 Sw 30th Ave Deerfield Beach (33442) *(G-2773)*

My Reviewers LLC 813 404-9734
3802 Spectrum Blvd 8 Tampa (33612) *(G-17091)*

My Shower Door Tampa LLC (PA) 239 337-3667
16431 Domestic Ave Fort Myers (33912) *(G-4336)*

My Vision Express, Weston *Also called Insight Software LLC (G-18256)*

Myarea Network Inc 800 830-7994
500 E Kennedy Blvd # 101 Tampa (33602) *(G-17092)*

Mydor Industries Inc 954 927-1140
470 Sw 9th St Dania (33004) *(G-2338)*

Myers Cabinetry LLC 850 872-1794
3631 N Highway 231 Panama City (32404) *(G-13288)*

Myers Cstm Cabinets Furn Corp 561 602-0755
3151 Sw 14th Pl Ste 7 Boynton Beach (33426) *(G-892)*

Myers Engineering Intl Inc 954 975-2712
5425 Nw 24th St Ste 202 Margate (33063) *(G-8144)*

Myers Printing Inc 813 237-0288
5601 N Florida Ave Tampa (33604) *(G-17093)*

Myfilterking.com, Miami *Also called Filter King LLC (G-9141)*

Mymd Pharmaceuticals Fla Inc 813 864-2566
900 W Platt St Ste 200 Tampa (33606) *(G-17094)*

Myreviewers, Tampa *Also called My Reviewers LLC (G-17091)*

Myriam Interiors Inc (PA) 305 626-9898
16301 Nw 49th Ave Hialeah (33014) *(G-5271)*

Myrlen Inc 800 662-4762
3814 Nw 126th Ave Coral Springs (33065) *(G-2194)*

Mysky Aircraft Inc 386 492-6908
205 Cessna Blvd Ste 1 Port Orange (32128) *(G-14342)*

Mytek Industries 727 536-7891
11910 62nd St Largo (33773) *(G-7648)*

Myton Industries Inc 954 989-0113
1981 S Park Rd Hallandale (33009) *(G-4927)*

MZ Machine Inc 561 744-2791
3046 Jupiter Park Cir Jupiter (33458) *(G-6768)*

N & H Construction Inc 904 282-2224
1708 Nolan Rd Middleburg (32068) *(G-10405)*

N & N Investment Corporation 954 590-3800
3001 Nw 16th Ter Pompano Beach (33064) *(G-14106)*

N A Comandulli LLC 941 870-2878
6935 15th St E Units105 Sarasota (34243) *(G-15522)*

N A Whittenburg, Sarasota *Also called Design Works By Tech Pdts Inc (G-15658)*

N C A Manufacturing Inc 727 441-2651
1985 Carroll St Clearwater (33765) *(G-1710)*

N E D LLC 610 442-1017
902 Clint Moore Rd # 206 Boca Raton (33487) *(G-607)*

N Ear Pro, Tampa *Also called N-Ear Pro Inc (G-17095)*

N Media Group LLC (PA) 239 594-1322
4500 Executive Dr Ste 320 Naples (34119) *(G-10826)*

N R I, Riviera Beach *Also called Neptune Research Inc (G-14650)*

N V Texpack Group 305 358-9696
3225 Aviation Ave Ste 303 Miami (33133) *(G-9602)*

N Y I Industries Inc 561 248-6760
926 Lehto Ln Lake Worth (33461) *(G-7220)*

N-Ear Pro Inc 877 290-4599
4821 N Grady Ave Tampa (33614) *(G-17095)*

N-Viro Inc 904 781-4707
7259 Old Plank Rd Jacksonville (32254) *(G-6317)*

N23d Services LLC 754 217-3362
20974 Sheridan St Fort Lauderdale (33332) *(G-3949)*

N2w Software Inc 561 225-2483
500 S Australian Ave # 910 West Palm Beach (33401) *(G-18083)*

N3xt L3vel 2 Point 0 LLC 863 777-3778
1248 E Hillsborough Ave Tampa (33604) *(G-17096)*

N3xt Up Exotic LLC 863 777-3778
1248 E Hillsborough Ave Tampa (33604) *(G-17097)*

Nabi 561 989-5800
5800 Pk Of Commerce Blvd Boca Raton (33487) *(G-608)*

Nac USA Corporation 800 396-0149
9000 Sw 137th Ave Miami (33186) *(G-9603)*

(G-0000) Company's Geographic Section entry number

Nace Aircraft Cabinetry Inc................................754 366-5799
  1701 Nw 22nd St Fort Lauderdale (33311) *(G-3950)*

Nadco Tapes & Labels Inc.................................941 751-6693
  2240 72nd Ter E Sarasota (34243) *(G-15523)*

Nahuel Trading Corp.......................................305 999-9944
  17838 State Road 9 Miami (33162) *(G-9604)*

Nai Print Solutions LLC...................................850 637-1260
  457 Strandview Dr Pensacola (32534) *(G-13554)*

Naia Brick Pavers Inc....................................727 638-4734
  8216 43rd Way N Pinellas Park (33781) *(G-13712)*

Naiad Dynamics Us Inc....................................954 797-7566
  3750 Hacienda Blvd Ste A Davie (33314) *(G-2443)*

Naked Whey Inc..352 246-7294
  382 Ne 191st St Miami (33179) *(G-9605)*

Namro Industries Inc.....................................561 704-8063
  4336 Juniper Ter Boynton Beach (33436) *(G-893)*

Nana Foods Inc..407 363-7183
  5219 Timberview Ter Orlando (32819) *(G-12403)*

Nanas Original Stromboli Inc.............................954 771-6262
  5421 Ne 14th Ave Fort Lauderdale (33334) *(G-3951)*

Nano Dimension 3d, Sunrise *Also called Nano Dimension USA Inc* *(G-16345)*

Nano Dimension USA Inc...................................650 209-2866
  13798 Nw 4th St Ste 315 Sunrise (33325) *(G-16345)*

Nano Liquitec LLC...813 447-1742
  5627 Terrain De Golf Dr Lutz (33558) *(G-8006)*

Nano Safe Coatings Inc...................................561 747-5758
  5500 Military Trl Ste 22 Jupiter (33458) *(G-6769)*

Nanocann Research Labs LLC...............................850 630-4676
  7328 Sw 48th St Miami (33155) *(G-9606)*

Nanotech Energy Inc (PA).................................800 995-5491
  323 Sunny Isles Blvd 7thf Sunny Isles Beach (33160) *(G-16280)*

Nanotechnovation Corporation.............................352 732-3244
  2811 Ne 14th St Ocala (34470) *(G-11449)*

Napac Inc...904 766-4470
  5355 Ramona Blvd Jacksonville (32205) *(G-6318)*

Naple Daily News, The, Fort Myers *Also called Bonita Daily News* *(G-4193)*

Naples Armature Works, Naples *Also called Robert E Weissenborn Sr* *(G-10879)*

Naples C&D Recycling Facility, Naples *Also called Yahl Mulching & Recycling Inc* *(G-10945)*

Naples Hang Gliding, Clewiston *Also called Miami Hang Gliding Corp* *(G-1893)*

Naples Hma LLC...239 390-2174
  24231 Walden Center Dr # 201 Estero (34134) *(G-3547)*

Naples Hotrods & Prfmce LLC..............................239 653-9076
  6122 Janes Ln Naples (34109) *(G-10827)*

Naples Illustrated, Naples *Also called Palm Beach Media Group Inc* *(G-10846)*

Naples Illustrated, West Palm Beach *Also called Palm Beach Liquidation Company* *(G-18110)*

Naples Illustrated.......................................239 434-6966
  3066 Tamiami Trl Mre 10 Moore Ste 102 Naples (34102) *(G-10828)*

Naples Iron Works Inc....................................239 649-7265
  4551 Arnold Ave Naples (34104) *(G-10829)*

Naples Powder Coating LLC................................239 352-3500
  1141 19th St Sw Naples (34117) *(G-10830)*

Naples Printing Inc......................................239 643-2442
  1100 Coml Blvd Ste 114 Naples (34104) *(G-10831)*

Naples Stone Consulting LLC..............................239 325-8653
  1881 Trade Center Way Naples (34109) *(G-10832)*

Naples Team Sports Center, Naples *Also called Synergy Sports LLC* *(G-10918)*

Naples Woodworks Inc.....................................239 287-1632
  6080 Golden Oaks Ln Naples (34119) *(G-10833)*

Nardis Enterprises LLC...................................954 529-0691
  2831 Ne 56th Ct Fort Lauderdale (33308) *(G-3952)*

Naroh Manufacturing LLC..................................321 806-4875
  185 Gus Hipp Blvd Rockledge (32955) *(G-14734)*

Narramore Machine Shop Inc...............................863 667-1004
  2770 Industrial Park Dr Lakeland (33801) *(G-7401)*

Nasco Aerospace and Elec LLC.............................727 344-7554
  3232 44th Ave N Saint Petersburg (33714) *(G-15136)*

Nasco Industries Inc.....................................954 733-8665
  3541 Nw 53rd St Fort Lauderdale (33309) *(G-3953)*

Nassau Printing & Off Sup Inc............................904 879-2305
  542028 Us Highway 1 Callahan (32011) *(G-1255)*

Natalia Likhacheva, Nokomis *Also called 365 Sun LLC* *(G-11041)*

Natalies Orchid Island Juice, Fort Pierce *Also called Orchid Island Juice Co Inc* *(G-4514)*

National Aerospace Group Inc.............................817 226-0315
  928 36th Ct Sw Vero Beach (32968) *(G-17780)*

National Assemblers Inc..................................877 915-5505
  6586 Hypoluxo Rd Ste 145 Lake Worth (33467) *(G-7221)*

National Bedding Company LLC.............................561 840-8491
  3774 Interstate Park Rd N Riviera Beach (33404) *(G-14649)*

National Beverage Corp (PA)..............................954 581-0922
  8100 Sw 10th St Ste 4000 Plantation (33324) *(G-13872)*

National Bidet Corp......................................786 325-6593
  7150 Indian Creek Dr Miami Beach (33141) *(G-10214)*

National Carburetors Inc.................................904 636-9400
  2461 Rolac Rd Jacksonville (32207) *(G-6319)*

National Carwash Solutions Inc...........................813 973-3507
  5624 56th Cmmerce Pk Blvd Tampa (33610) *(G-17098)*

National Chemical Sply...................................800 515-9938
  4151 Sw 47th Ave Davie (33314) *(G-2444)*

National Chemical Supply Inc.............................954 683-1645
  6930 Sw 16th St Plantation (33317) *(G-13873)*

National Custom Insignia Inc.............................813 313-2561
  8875 Hdden Rver Pkwy Ste Tampa (33637) *(G-17099)*

National Custom Table Pads...............................239 596-6805
  6030 English Oaks Ln Naples (34119) *(G-10834)*

National Cylinder Head Exchang...........................813 870-6340
  4408 N Thatcher Ave Tampa (33614) *(G-17100)*

National Cylinder Services LLC (PA)......................407 299-8454
  4601 Dardanelle Dr Orlando (32808) *(G-12404)*

National Diesel Engine Inc...............................810 516-6855
  253 S 78th St Tampa (33619) *(G-17101)*

National Direct Signs LLC................................561 320-2102
  777 S Flagler Dr West Palm Beach (33401) *(G-18084)*

National Glass Pdts & Distrs.............................303 762-9768
  814 Ponce De Leon Blvd Coral Gables (33134) *(G-2090)*

National Gypsum, Gibsonton *Also called Proform Finishing Products LLC* *(G-4799)*

National Gypsum Company, Orlando *Also called Proform Finishing Products LLC* *(G-12514)*

National Health Alliance LLC.............................727 504-3915
  500 N West Shore Blvd # 640 Tampa (33609) *(G-17102)*

National Indexing Systems, Orlando *Also called Nis Print Inc* *(G-12418)*

National Intelligence Academy, Deerfield Beach *Also called Interntnal Srvillance Tech Inc* *(G-2742)*

National Jewellers, Hallandale Beach *Also called Finger Mate Inc* *(G-4945)*

National Mold Testing....................................561 626-7418
  1057 Siena Oaks Cir E West Palm Beach (33410) *(G-18085)*

National Molding LLC.....................................727 546-7470
  11311 74th St Largo (33773) *(G-7649)*

National Molding LLC (PA)................................305 823-5440
  14427 Nw 60th Ave Miami Lakes (33014) *(G-10329)*

National Multiple Listing Inc (PA).......................954 772-8880
  6511 Bay Club Dr Apt 2 Fort Lauderdale (33308) *(G-3954)*

National Newspaper Placem................................866 404-5913
  766 N Sun Dr Ste 2090 Lake Mary (32746) *(G-7097)*

National Pallets...305 324-1021
  2160 Nw 8th Ave Miami (33127) *(G-9607)*

National Pipe Welding Inc................................904 588-2589
  9473 Smokey Rd Glen Saint Mary (32040) *(G-4804)*

National Police Ammunition, Hialeah *Also called L C Npee* *(G-5217)*

National Powdr Coating Fla Inc...........................941 756-1322
  6004 31st St E Bradenton (34203) *(G-1016)*

National Print & Design, Delray Beach *Also called Art In Print Inc* *(G-2933)*

National Saw Company, Largo *Also called Brawley Distributing Co Inc* *(G-7555)*

National Sign Inc..727 572-1503
  5651 116th Ave N Clearwater (33760) *(G-1711)*

National Std Parts Assoc Inc.............................850 456-5771
  1301 E Belmont St Pensacola (32501) *(G-13555)*

National Stoneworks LLC..................................954 349-1609
  3360 Entp Ave Ste 100 Weston (33331) *(G-18271)*

National Traffic Signs Inc...............................727 446-7983
  14521 60th St N Clearwater (33760) *(G-1712)*

National Woodworks Inc...................................407 489-3572
  4122 Mercy Industrial Ct Orlando (32808) *(G-12405)*

Nationwide Coils & Coatings, Weston *Also called Northrich Florida LLC* *(G-18274)*

Nationwide Industries Inc (PA)...........................813 988-2628
  3505 Cragmont Dr Tampa (33619) *(G-17103)*

Nationwide Prtctive Cting Mfrs...........................941 753-7500
  7106 24th Ct E Sarasota (34243) *(G-15524)*

Nationwide Publishing Company (PA).......................352 253-0017
  537 Deltona Blvd Deltona (32725) *(G-3049)*

Native Outfitters, West Palm Beach *Also called Bdc Florida LLC* *(G-17939)*

Native Sun Sports, Pinellas Park *Also called Rock N Roll Custom Screened S* *(G-13727)*

Native Vanilla LLC.......................................407 724-1995
  1255 W Airport Blvd Sanford (32773) *(G-15362)*

Natura-Vigor, Davie *Also called Arnet Pharmaceutical Corp* *(G-2389)*

Natural Beauty Wood Products.............................561 732-0224
  1120 Se 1st St Boynton Beach (33435) *(G-894)*

Natural Crvings Pet Treats LLC...........................786 404-8099
  1100 Nw 7th St Homestead (33030) *(G-5733)*

Natural Fruit Corp.......................................305 887-7525
  770 W 20th St Hialeah (33010) *(G-5272)*

Natural Hats and More LLC................................954 549-0819
  5801 Wiley St Hollywood (33023) *(G-5631)*

Natural Immunogenics Corp (PA)...........................888 328-8840
  7504 Pennsylvania Ave Sarasota (34243) *(G-15525)*

Natural Light, The, Lynn Haven *Also called The Natural Light Inc* *(G-8034)*

Natural Organic Products Intl............................352 383-8252
  710 S Rossiter St Mount Dora (32757) *(G-10607)*

Natural Stone Sltons Fnest SRS (PA)......................941 954-1100
  2303 17th St Sarasota (34234) *(G-15756)*

Natural Vitamins Lab Corp................................305 265-1660
  12845 Nw 45th Ave Opa Locka (33054) *(G-11773)*

Natural Vitamins Lab Corp................................305 265-1660
  4400 Nw 133rd St Opa Locka (33054) *(G-11774)*

Natural Vitamins Labs, Opa Locka *Also called Natural Vitamins Lab Corp* *(G-11774)*

Natural Wood Works LLC...................................954 445-1493
  2382 W 77th St Hialeah (33016) *(G-5273)*

Natural4naturalz LLC 561 621-1546
561 Old Farm Pl Clewiston (33440) *(G-1894)*

Nature Coast Precision Mfg LLC 727 424-3848
16706 Wishingwell Ln Spring Hill (34610) *(G-16087)*

Nature Medrx Inc 239 215-8557
1342 Clnl Blvd Unit C20 Fort Myers (33907) *(G-4337)*

Naturecity LLC 800 593-2563
990 S Rogers Cir Ste 11 Boca Raton (33487) *(G-609)*

Natureform Hatchery Systems, Jacksonville *Also called Pas Reform North America LLC (G-6356)*

Natures Bioscience LLC 800 570-7450
5020 Clark Rd Sarasota (34233) *(G-15757)*

Natures Bounty Co 800 327-0908
1297 Clint Moore Rd Boca Raton (33487) *(G-610)*

Natures Clear LLC 561 503-1751
2328 10th Ave N Ste 501d Lake Worth (33461) *(G-7222)*

Natures Earth Products Inc 561 688-8101
2200 N Fl Mango Rd # 403 West Palm Beach (33409) *(G-18086)*

Natures Fuel Inc 407 808-4272
2254 Saw Palmetto Ln Orlando (32828) *(G-12406)*

Natures Gift Cbd 954 405-1000
320 Ne 12th Ave Apt 506 Hallandale Beach (33009) *(G-4963)*

Natures Heathy Gourmet 772 873-0180
1260 Sw Biltmore St Port St Lucie (34983) *(G-14479)*

Natures Own Pest Control Inc 941 378-3334
1899 Porter Lake Dr # 103 Sarasota (34240) *(G-15758)*

Natures Power and Energy LLC 813 907-6279
30131 Clearview Dr Wesley Chapel (33545) *(G-17883)*

Natus Medical Incorporated 321 235-8213
12301 Lake Underhill Rd # 201 Orlando (32828) *(G-12407)*

Natus Medical Incorporated 847 949-5200
12301 Lake Underhill Rd # 201 Orlando (32828) *(G-12408)*

Nauset Enterprises Inc 727 443-3469
2120 Calumet St Ste 1 Clearwater (33765) *(G-1713)*

Nautical Acquisitions Corp 727 541-6664
7301 114th Ave Largo (33773) *(G-7650)*

Nautical Flair, Riviera Beach *Also called Canvas Designers Inc (G-14605)*

Nautical Specialists Inc 954 761-7130
2841 Ne 36th St Fort Lauderdale (33308) *(G-3955)*

Nautical Structures, Largo *Also called Nautical Acquisitions Corp (G-7650)*

Nautical Structures Inds Inc (PA) 727 541-6664
7301 114th Ave Largo (33773) *(G-7651)*

Nautilus Cabinetry Inc 239 598-1011
1826 Trade Center Way I Naples (34109) *(G-10835)*

Nav-X LLC 954 978-9988
1386 W Mcnab Rd Fort Lauderdale (33309) *(G-3956)*

Nava Pets Inc 407 982-7256
400 North St Unit 184 Longwood (32750) *(G-7926)*

Navarre 3d Printing LLC (PA) 850 281-6780
300 Mary Esther Blvd # 66 Mary Esther (32569) *(G-8178)*

Navarre 3d Printing LLC 850 281-6780
8131 Country Bay Blvd Navarre (32566) *(G-10953)*

Navarre Fishing Rodeo, Navarre *Also called Sandpaper Marketing Inc (G-10956)*

Navatech Usa LLC 305 600-4458
20200 Nw 2nd Ave Ste 106 Miami (33169) *(G-9608)*

Naviera Coffee Mills Inc 813 248-2521
2012 E 7th Ave Tampa (33605) *(G-17104)*

Navigator Kitchens & Cnstr, Parrish *Also called Navigtor Kitchens Cabinets Inc (G-13360)*

Navigtor Kitchens Cabinets Inc 941 776-9482
12726 24th Street Cir E Parrish (34219) *(G-13360)*

Navinta III Inc 561 997-6959
1003 Clint Moore Rd Boca Raton (33487) *(G-611)*

Navistar Inc 305 513-2255
8600 Nw 36th St Ste 304 Doral (33166) *(G-3310)*

Navmar Applied Sciences Corp 904 423-0927
7254 Golden Wings Rd Jacksonville (32244) *(G-6320)*

Naztec International Group LLC 561 802-4110
263 N Jog Rd West Palm Beach (33413) *(G-18087)*

Naztec International Group LLC (PA) 561 802-4110
8983 Okeechobee Blvd # 202 West Palm Beach (33411) *(G-18088)*

Nb Fuel LLC 954 382-3893
10428 Laurel Rd Davie (33328) *(G-2445)*

Nb Products Inc 904 807-0140
1551 Atl Blvd Ste 105 Jacksonville (32207) *(G-6321)*

Nbk Maintenance, Saint Augustine *Also called Old City Marine LLC (G-14868)*

Nbl1 Inc 954 524-3616
280 Sw 6th St Fort Lauderdale (33301) *(G-3957)*

Nbs Prformance Fabrication Inc 727 541-1833
5649 70th Ave N Pinellas Park (33781) *(G-13713)*

NC II, Sarasota *Also called NC IV Inc (G-15759)*

NC IV Inc 941 378-9133
10687 Fruitville Rd Sarasota (34240) *(G-15759)*

Ncc Promotional, Groveland *Also called Novelty Crystal Corp (G-4867)*

Ncdi, Doral *Also called New Concepts Distrs Intl LLC (G-3311)*

Ncg Medical Systems Inc (PA) 407 788-1906
1402 Edgewater Dr Ste 101 Orlando (32804) *(G-12409)*

NCH (fl) Funding LLC 321 777-7777
525 N Harbor City Blvd Melbourne (32935) *(G-8478)*

NCH Marine LLC 754 422-4237
13325 Sw 28th St Davie (33330) *(G-2446)*

Nci 813 749-1799
11327 Countryway Blvd Tampa (33626) *(G-17105)*

Ncp Solutions LLC 205 849-5200
841 Prudential Dr # 1200 Jacksonville (32207) *(G-6322)*

Ndh Medical Inc 727 570-2293
11001 Roosevelt Blvd N # 150 Saint Petersburg (33716) *(G-15137)*

Ne Media Group Inc 954 733-8393
2880 W Oklnd Prk Blvd # 207 Oakland Park (33311) *(G-11280)*

Nearly Natural LLC 800 711-0544
3870 W 108th St Unit 20 Hialeah (33018) *(G-5274)*

Neat Clean Group Inc 727 459-6079
2523 Marina Key Ln Clearwater (33763) *(G-1714)*

Neat Print Inc 941 545-1517
2147 Porter Lake Dr Ste G Sarasota (34240) *(G-15760)*

Nebraska Printing Inc 813 870-6871
3849 W Azeele St Tampa (33609) *(G-17106)*

Nebula Glass International Inc 954 975-3233
1601 Blount Rd Pompano Beach (33069) *(G-14107)*

Nebula Led Lighting Systems of 813 907-0001
28832 Falling Leaves Way Wesley Chapel (33543) *(G-17884)*

Need A Dumpster LLC 888 407-3867
1733 Benbow Ct Ste 5 Apopka (32703) *(G-156)*

Need Printing, Pompano Beach *Also called Gb Printing (G-14037)*

Neelco Industries Inc 321 632-5303
420 Shearer Blvd Cocoa (32922) *(G-1944)*

Neglex Inc 305 551-4177
300 Sw 107th Ave Ste 114 Miami (33174) *(G-9609)*

Neighbor To Neighbor Newspaper 904 278-7256
1906 Farm Way Middleburg (32068) *(G-10406)*

Neighborhood News & Lifestyles 727 943-0551
220 S Safford Ave Tarpon Springs (34689) *(G-17483)*

Nejat Arslaner 321 300-5464
2555 N Forsyth Rd Ste E Orlando (32807) *(G-12410)*

Nelco Products Inc 727 533-8282
15251 Roosevelt Blvd # 202 Clearwater (33760) *(G-1715)*

Nelson and Affiliates Inc 352 316-5641
3324 W University Ave Gainesville (32607) *(G-4737)*

Nelson Mch Sp Wldg & Engrg Inc 305 710-5029
13990 Nw 22nd Ave Opa Locka (33054) *(G-11775)*

Nelson Plastics Inc 407 339-3570
578 North St Longwood (32750) *(G-7927)*

Nelson Raceway LLC 904 206-1625
96321 Bay View Dr Fernandina Beach (32034) *(G-3594)*

Nelsons Truck and Trlr Sls LLC 352 732-8908
4131 Nw Blitchton Rd Ocala (34482) *(G-11450)*

Nelver Airparts Inc 305 378-0072
12360 Sw 132nd Ct Ste 205 Miami (33186) *(G-9610)*

Nem, Bradenton *Also called New England Machinery Inc (G-1018)*

Nemal Electronics Intl Inc (PA) 305 899-0900
12240 Ne 14th Ave North Miami (33161) *(G-11114)*

Nemee, Riviera Beach *Also called Akiknav Inc (G-14591)*

Neocabinet Inc 310 927-1008
1623 Plunkett St Hollywood (33020) *(G-5632)*

Neocis Inc 855 963-6247
2800 Biscayne Blvd # 600 Miami (33137) *(G-9611)*

Neon Cowboys LLC 949 514-5557
2312 Clark St Ste 5 Apopka (32703) *(G-157)*

Neon Workforce Technologies 305 458-8244
2300 W 84th St Ste 601 Hialeah (33016) *(G-5275)*

Neopod Systems LLC (PA) 954 603-3100
1329 Shotgun Rd Sunrise (33326) *(G-16346)*

Neos Technologies Inc (PA) 321 242-7818
4300 Fortune Pl Ste C Melbourne (32904) *(G-8479)*

Neotech Company 954 570-5833
140 Se 7th St Apt 4 Deerfield Beach (33441) *(G-2774)*

Nephron Pharmaceuticals 407 913-3142
1162 Bella Vida Blvd Orlando (32828) *(G-12411)*

Nephron Pharmaceuticals Corp 407 999-2225
4121 Sw 34th St Orlando (32811) *(G-12412)*

Neptune Designs Inc 305 294-8131
301 Duval St Key West (33040) *(G-6878)*

Neptune Petroleum LLC 561 684-2844
3974 Okeechobee Blvd # 2 West Palm Beach (33409) *(G-18089)*

Neptune Precision Composites, Jacksonville *Also called Neptune Tech Services Inc (G-6323)*

Neptune Research Inc (PA) 561 683-6992
3875 Fiscal Ct Ste 100 Riviera Beach (33404) *(G-14650)*

Neptune Tech Services Inc (PA) 904 646-2700
11657 Central Pkwy # 405 Jacksonville (32224) *(G-6323)*

Nessmith Dye Cutting & Finshg 904 353-6317
536 E 4th St Jacksonville (32206) *(G-6324)*

Nestle Professional, Thonotosassa *Also called Nestle Usa Inc (G-17563)*

Nestle Professional Vitality, Thonotosassa *Also called Nestle Usa Inc (G-17564)*

Nestle Usa Inc 813 273-5355
11471 N Us Highway 301 # 10 Thonotosassa (33592) *(G-17563)*

Nestle Usa Inc 813 301-4638
11441 N Us Highway 301 Thonotosassa (33592) *(G-17564)*

2022 Harris Florida
Manufacturers Directory

(G-0000) Company's Geographic Section entry number

Netexpressusa Inc (PA)..888 575-1245
  8991 Daniels Center Dr # 105 Fort Myers (33912) *(G-4338)*

Nets Depot Inc..305 215-5579
  9949 Nw 89th Ave Unit 13 Medley (33178) *(G-8286)*

Netting Professionals LLC..904 432-8987
  1600 N 14th St Fernandina Beach (32034) *(G-3595)*

Network USA, Bradenton Also called Inovart Inc *(G-996)*

Networked Solutions Inc...321 259-3242
  7145 Turner Rd Ste 102 Rockledge (32955) *(G-14735)*

Networking Dynamics, Clearwater Also called Universal Software Solutions *(G-1839)*

Networks Assets LLC...954 334-1390
  3265 Meridian Pkwy # 134 Weston (33331) *(G-18272)*

Neubert Aero Corp...352 345-4828
  16110 Flight Path Dr Brooksville (34604) *(G-1185)*

Neuro Pharmalogics Inc..240 476-4491
  901 Nw 35th St Boca Raton (33431) *(G-612)*

Neuro20 Technologies Corp...813 990-7138
  3802 Spectrum Blvd # 111 Tampa (33612) *(G-17107)*

Neurotronics Inc...352 372-9955
  13800 Tech City Cir 400 Alachua (32615) *(G-15)*

Neutral Guard LLC...954 249-6600
  1401 Sw 34th Ave Fort Lauderdale (33312) *(G-3958)*

Nev International Inc...407 671-0045
  1211 State Road 436 # 141 Casselberry (32707) *(G-1426)*

Never Wrong Toys & Games LLC...................................941 371-0909
  2201 Cantu Ct Ste 100 Sarasota (34232) *(G-15761)*

New & Improved Services LLC......................................904 323-2348
  2438 Automobile Dr Jacksonville (32209) *(G-6325)*

New Age Windows & Doors Corp...................................305 889-0703
  7196 Nw 77th Ter Medley (33166) *(G-8287)*

New Best Packers Inc...386 328-5127
  1122 Bronson St Palatka (32177) *(G-12875)*

New Breed Clothing llc..941 773-7406
  1120 Magellan Dr Sarasota (34243) *(G-15526)*

New Century..305 670-3510
  7950 Sunset Dr Miami (33143) *(G-9612)*

New Choices, Boca Raton Also called Raytash Inc *(G-648)*

New Concepts Distrs Intl LLC......................................305 463-8735
  2315 Nw 107th Ave Ste 1b5 Doral (33172) *(G-3311)*

New Dairy Opco LLC...305 652-3720
  501 Ne 181st St North Miami Beach (33162) *(G-11153)*

New Dawn Coffee Company Inc....................................727 321-5155
  2336 5th Ave S Saint Petersburg (33712) *(G-15138)*

New Design Furniture Mfg, Lauderdale Lakes Also called Shorr Enterprises Inc *(G-7719)*

New Dimensions, Riviera Beach Also called Pendulum One Inc *(G-14658)*

New Energy Fuels LLC...281 205-0153
  259 Ford Ave Labelle (33935) *(G-6984)*

New England Crftsmen Bston Irn.................................727 789-1618
  4177 Corporate Ct Palm Harbor (34683) *(G-13120)*

New England Granite & Marble.....................................772 283-8667
  890 Sw Enterprise Way Stuart (34997) *(G-16189)*

New England Machinery...941 755-5550
  6204 29th St E Bradenton (34203) *(G-1017)*

New England Machinery Inc..941 755-5550
  2820 62nd Ave E Bradenton (34203) *(G-1018)*

New ERA Music Group LLC...800 454-9751
  66 W Flagler St Ste 900 Miami (33130) *(G-9613)*

New ERA Technology Corp..352 746-3569
  620 W Sunset Strip Dr Beverly Hills (34465) *(G-368)*

New Era, The, Miami Also called New ERA Music Group LLC *(G-9613)*

New Generation Aerospace Inc.....................................305 882-1410
  8004 Nw 90th St Medley (33166) *(G-8288)*

New Generation Computing Inc (HQ).............................800 690-0642
  14900 Nw 79th Ct Ste 100 Miami Lakes (33016) *(G-10330)*

New Generation Packaging LLC.....................................786 259-6670
  16542 Nw 54th Ave Miami Gardens (33014) *(G-10268)*

New Gnrtion Abndant Mssion Ch...................................772 497-5871
  2017 Sw Tropical Ter Port Saint Lucie (34953) *(G-14427)*

New Gnrtion Jews Abndant Mssio, Port Saint Lucie Also called New Gnrtion Abndant Mssion Ch *(G-14427)*

New Hope Sugar Company..561 366-5120
  1 N Clematis St West Palm Beach (33401) *(G-18090)*

New IEM Power Systems LLC..904 365-4444
  3600 Prt Jcksnvl Pkwy Jacksonville (32226) *(G-6326)*

New Image Printing Promotion.....................................904 240-1516
  9556 Historic Kings Rd S Jacksonville (32257) *(G-6327)*

New Kitchen Concepts, Daytona Beach Also called Counter Productions Inc *(G-2535)*

New Laser Tech Inc..305 450-0456
  7003 Greentree Ln Miami Lakes (33014) *(G-10331)*

New Life Publishing Inc...239 549-9152
  4103 Sw 27th Ave Cape Coral (33914) *(G-1367)*

New Line Transport LLC..305 223-9200
  9931 Old Lakeland Hwy Dade City (33525) *(G-2321)*

New Marco Foods Inc..305 836-0571
  3251 E 11th Ave Hialeah (33013) *(G-5276)*

New Market Enterprises Ltd...484 341-8004
  392 Harbor Ridge Dr Palm Harbor (34683) *(G-13121)*

New Mix Products..904 292-1920
  4465 Crooked Oak Ct Jacksonville (32257) *(G-6328)*

New Millennium Bldg Systems LLC................................386 466-1300
  1992 Nw Bascom Norris Dr Lake City (32055) *(G-7031)*

New Nautical Coatings Inc (HQ)....................................727 523-8053
  14805 49th St N Clearwater (33762) *(G-1716)*

New River Cabinet & Fix Inc..954 938-9200
  750 Nw 57th Ct Fort Lauderdale (33309) *(G-3959)*

New Sentry Marketing Inc..561 982-9599
  878 Nafa Dr Boca Raton (33487) *(G-613)*

New Smyrna Beach Plas Plant, New Smyrna Beach Also called Sonoco Products Company *(G-11012)*

New Smyrna Daily Journal, Daytona Beach Also called News-Journal Corporation *(G-2578)*

New Style Kit Cabinets Corp...305 989-9665
  2735 W 61st St Apt 104 Hialeah (33016) *(G-5277)*

New T Management Inc..954 927-4889
  255 E Dania Beach Blvd # 2 Dania (33004) *(G-2339)*

New Technology Precision Machi..................................561 624-3830
  15300 Pk Of Commerce Blvd Jupiter (33478) *(G-6770)*

New Underground RR Pubg Co.......................................305 825-1444
  14411 Commerce Way # 320 Miami Lakes (33016) *(G-10332)*

New Vbb LLC...904 631-5978
  3044 Mercury Rd S Jacksonville (32207) *(G-6329)*

New Vision Display Inc..407 480-5800
  135 W Central Blvd # 330 Orlando (32801) *(G-12413)*

New Vision Furniture Inc..305 562-9428
  4115 Nw 132nd St Unit I Opa Locka (33054) *(G-11776)*

New Vision Pharmaceuticals LLC...................................954 721-5000
  10200 Nw 67th St Tamarac (33321) *(G-16538)*

New Vision Signs Corp..786 514-6822
  15446 Sw 25th Ter Miami (33185) *(G-9614)*

New Wave Designs, Vero Beach Also called Morning Star Personalized AP *(G-17778)*

New Wave Surgical Corp..866 346-8883
  3700 Nw 124th Ave Ste 135 Coral Springs (33065) *(G-2195)*

New World Enclosures Inc..904 334-4752
  1350 Riviera Dr Green Cove Springs (32043) *(G-4831)*

New World Gold Corporation (PA)..................................561 962-4139
  350 Cmino Grdns Blvd Ste Boca Raton (33432) *(G-614)*

New World Holdings Inc..561 888-4939
  655 Se 1st St Delray Beach (33483) *(G-2992)*

New World Medicinals, Delray Beach Also called New World Holdings Inc *(G-2992)*

New World Publications Inc..904 737-6558
  1861 Cornell Rd Jacksonville (32207) *(G-6330)*

New World Trade Inc...941 205-5873
  8249 Skylane Way Ste 111 Punta Gorda (33982) *(G-14517)*

New World Welding Inc..786 423-1575
  3714 Nw 50th St Miami (33142) *(G-9615)*

New York Intl Bread Co..407 843-9744
  1500 W Church St Orlando (32805) *(G-12414)*

New York Nails...904 448-6040
  5869 University Blvd W Jacksonville (32216) *(G-6331)*

New You Media LLC..800 606-6518
  4150 Sw 28th Way Fort Lauderdale (33312) *(G-3960)*

Newbeauty Media Group LLC...561 961-7600
  3651 Nw 8th Ave Ste 400 Boca Raton (33431) *(G-615)*

Newbeauty Media Group, Lllp, Boca Raton Also called Newbeauty Media Group LLC *(G-615)*

Newbevco Inc (HQ)...954 581-0922
  8100 Sw 10th St Plantation (33324) *(G-13874)*

Newcastle Shipyards LLC...386 312-0000
  106 Dory Rd Saint Augustine (32086) *(G-14860)*

Newell Brands Inc..858 729-4138
  2381 Nw Executive Ctr Dr Boca Raton (33431) *(G-616)*

Newer Spreader, Sanford Also called Rugby Road Corp *(G-15383)*

Newflo LLC..718 795-5691
  4613 N University Dr Coral Springs (33067) *(G-2196)*

Newlink Cabling Systems Inc (PA).................................305 477-8063
  11701 Nw 102nd Rd Ste 21 Medley (33178) *(G-8289)*

Newmark International, Bartow Also called Valmont Newmark Inc *(G-328)*

Newmil Inc..954 444-4471
  2029 Sw 20th St Fort Lauderdale (33315) *(G-3961)*

Newmile Partners LLC..800 674-3474
  9030 Camden Field Pkwy Riverview (33578) *(G-14571)*

News & Sun Sentinel Company, Fort Lauderdale Also called Sun-Sentinel Company LLC *(G-4073)*

News Chief, Winter Haven Also called Gatehouse Media LLC *(G-18442)*

News Features USA Inc...305 298-5313
  6301 Collins Ave Miami Beach (33141) *(G-10215)*

News Herald..850 785-6550
  221 E 23rd St Ste B Panama City (32405) *(G-13289)*

News Leader Inc...352 242-9818
  637 8th St Clermont (34711) *(G-1877)*

News-Journal Corporation (PA).....................................386 252-1511
  901 6th St Daytona Beach (32117) *(G-2578)*

News-Journal Corporation...386 283-5664
  4984 Palm Coast Pkwy Nw # 5 Palm Coast (32137) *(G-13083)*

Newsmax Media Inc..561 686-1165
  1501 Nrthpint Pkwy Ste 10 West Palm Beach (33407) *(G-18091)*

Newspaper Printing Company.......................................727 572-7488
  12198 44th St N Clearwater (33762) *(G-1717)*

Newspaper Printing Company 813 839-0035
 5210 S Lois Ave Tampa (33611) (G-17108)
Newspaper Publishers Inc 561 793-7606
 12794 Frest Hl Blvd Ste 3 Wellington (33414) (G-17855)
Newvida Products LLC 863 781-9232
 4757 Sweetwater Rd Zolfo Springs (33890) (G-18641)
Nex Software LLC 786 200-3396
 29690 Sw 183rd Ct Homestead (33030) (G-5734)
Nex-Xos Worldwide LLC (PA) 305 433-8376
 3922 Pembroke Rd Hollywood (33021) (G-5633)
Nexgen Framing System LLC 321 508-6763
 2288 Wilhelmina Ct Ne Palm Bay (32905) (G-12909)
Nexogy Inc 305 358-8952
 2121 Ponce De Leon Blvd # 200 Coral Gables (33134) (G-2091)
Nexogy Sac, Fort Lauderdale Also called Ld Telecommunications Inc (G-3914)
Nexpub, Miramar Also called Print Factory LLC (G-10530)
Nexpub Inc 954 392-5889
 3820 Executive Way Miramar (33025) (G-10518)
Nexstar Broadcasting Inc 863 683-6531
 223 S Florida Ave Lakeland (33801) (G-7402)
Next Door Company 954 772-6666
 4005 E 10th Ct Hialeah (33013) (G-5278)
Next Gen Web Solutions, Jacksonville Also called Ngweb Solutions LLC (G-6332)
Next Generation Home Pdts Inc 727 834-9400
 701 S Howard Ave Tampa (33606) (G-17109)
Next Level, Pompano Beach Also called SC Capital Ventures Inc (G-14168)
Next Step Advertising Inc 305 371-4428
 1444 Biscayne Blvd # 208 Miami (33132) (G-9616)
Next Step Products LLC 407 857-9900
 9400 Southridge Park Ct # 200 Orlando (32819) (G-12415)
Nextera Fibernet LLC 866 787-2637
 700 Universe Blvd Juno Beach (33408) (G-6665)
Nextgen, Tampa Also called Next Generation Home Pdts Inc (G-17109)
Nextower LLC 407 907-7984
 11895 Sw 33rd Ln Gainesville (32608) (G-4738)
Nextplat Corp (PA) 305 560-5355
 18851 Ne 29th Ave Ste 700 Aventura (33180) (G-267)
Nextreef Systems, Myakka City Also called Stony Coral Investments LLC (G-10647)
Nextsource Biotechnology LLC 305 753-6360
 80 Sw 8th St Miami (33130) (G-9617)
Nexus Alliance Corp 321 945-4283
 160 Vista Oak Dr Longwood (32779) (G-7928)
Nexus Mint LLC 561 306-9898
 4440 Pga Blvd Ste 600 Palm Beach Gardens (33410) (G-12991)
Nfi Masks LLC 239 990-6546
 16140 Lee Rd Unit 120 Fort Myers (33912) (G-4339)
Nfjb Inc 954 771-1100
 60 Nw 60th St Fort Lauderdale (33309) (G-3962)
Nfk Corporation (PA) 305 378-2116
 8158 Sw 118th Pl Miami (33183) (G-9618)
Ngf Distributors Inc 407 816-7554
 3035 Turkey Ave Oviedo (32765) (G-12838)
Ngp Corporate Square Inc 239 643-3430
 4408 Corporate Sq Naples (34104) (G-10836)
Ngweb Solutions LLC 904 332-9001
 6821 Sthpint Dr N Ste 220 Jacksonville (32216) (G-6332)
Ni-Chro Plating Corp 727 327-5118
 700 37th St S Saint Petersburg (33711) (G-15139)
Niagara Industries Inc 305 876-9010
 2540 Nw 38th Ct Miami (33142) (G-9619)
Niagratech Industries Inc 305 876-9010
 2540 Nw 38th Ct Miami (33142) (G-9620)
Niba Collections, Hollywood Also called Niba Designs Inc (G-5634)
Niba Designs Inc (PA) 305 456-6230
 3609 N 29th Ave Hollywood (33020) (G-5634)
Nic4 Inc 877 455-2131
 111 Kelsey Ln Ste D Tampa (33619) (G-17110)
Nichols Truck Bodies LLC 904 781-5080
 1168 Cahoon Rd S Jacksonville (32221) (G-6333)
Nickols Cbinetry Woodworks Inc 941 485-7894
 765 U S 41 Byp S Bypass S Venice (34285) (G-17707)
Nicolette Mayer Collection Inc 561 241-6906
 3750 Ne 6th Dr Boca Raton (33431) (G-617)
Nicraf Software & Creat Inc 813 842-9648
 17413 Equestrian Trl Odessa (33556) (G-11567)
Nida Corporation (PA) 321 727-2265
 300 S John Rodes Blvd Melbourne (32904) (G-8480)
Nida-Core Corporation (HQ) 772 343-7300
 541 Nw Interpark Pl Port Saint Lucie (34986) (G-14428)
Nidec Motor Corporation 954 346-4900
 12095 Nw 39th St Coral Springs (33065) (G-2197)
Niefeld Group LLC 786 587-7423
 2420 W 80th St Unit 5 Hialeah (33016) (G-5279)
Niftys Inc 786 878-4725
 78 Sw 7th St Miami (33130) (G-9621)
Nighthawk Running LLC 407 443-8404
 1623 Wycliff Dr Orlando (32803) (G-12416)
Nighthawk Safety, Orlando Also called Nighthawk Running LLC (G-12416)

Nightingale Corp 800 363-8954
 11380 Prosperity Farms Rd Palm Beach Gardens (33410) (G-12992)
Nightmoves Magazine, Oldsmar Also called PA C Publishing Inc (G-11684)
Nightscenes Inc 813 855-9416
 12802 Commodity Pl Tampa (33626) (G-17111)
Nik Public Safety, Jacksonville Also called Armor Holdings Forensics LLC (G-5903)
Nikiani Inc 305 606-1104
 717 Maritime Way West Palm Beach (33410) (G-18092)
Nikki Beach Publishing LLC 305 538-1111
 1 Ocean Dr Miami Beach (33139) (G-10216)
Nilfisk Pressure-Pro LLC 772 672-3697
 7300 Commercial Cir Fort Pierce (34951) (G-4511)
Nillium Holdings LLC 352 720-7070
 6751 Jones Ave Mount Dora (32757) (G-10608)
Nilsson Nils 561 790-2400
 1128 Royal Palm Bch Royal Palm Beach (33411) (G-14771)
Nina Plastic Bags Inc (PA) 407 802-6828
 1903 Cypress Lake Dr Orlando (32837) (G-12417)
Nina Plastics, Orlando Also called Nina Plastic Bags Inc (G-12417)
Nine Enterprises Inc 904 998-8880
 3633 Southside Blvd Jacksonville (32216) (G-6334)
Nine Mile Raceway Inc 850 937-1845
 1281 Lear Ct Cantonment (32533) (G-1271)
Niobium Technology Group LLC 786 292-2613
 3100 Nw 72nd Ave Ste 108 Miami (33122) (G-9622)
Nippon Maciwumei Co 954 533-7747
 4500 N Hiatus Rd Ste 214 Sunrise (33351) (G-16347)
Nis Print Inc 407 423-7575
 1809 S Division Ave Orlando (32805) (G-12418)
Nissi & Jireh Inc 866 897-7657
 2413 Main St 232 Miramar (33025) (G-10519)
Nissi Elastic Corp 305 968-3812
 961 E 17th St Hialeah (33010) (G-5280)
Nite-Bright Sign Company Inc 239 466-2616
 16061 Pine Ridge Rd Fort Myers (33908) (G-4340)
Niteo Products LLC 561 745-1812
 902 S Us Highway 1 Jupiter (33477) (G-6771)
Nitesol Inc 407 557-4042
 1831 Tallokas Ave Orlando (32805) (G-12419)
Nitro Gulf, Stuart Also called Nitro Leisure Products Inc (G-16190)
Nitro Leisure Products Inc 414 272-5084
 4490 Se Cheri Ct Stuart (34997) (G-16190)
Nitrogen Jupiter LLC 561 662-2150
 6779 W Indiantown Rd Jupiter (33458) (G-6772)
Nitv Federal Services LLC 561 798-6280
 11400 Fortune Cir West Palm Beach (33414) (G-18093)
Nivcoe International Dev 321 282-3666
 2020 W Fairbanks Ave # 102 Winter Park (32789) (G-18526)
Nivel Holdings LLC (PA) 904 741-6161
 3510 Pt Jacksonville Park Jacksonville (32226) (G-6335)
Nivel Parts & Mfg Co LLC (HQ) 904 741-6161
 3510-1 Port Jcksnvlle Pkw Jacksonville (32226) (G-6336)
Nivel Parts Manufacturing, Jacksonville Also called Nivel Holdings LLC (G-6335)
Nkc Electronics Inc 954 471-8368
 2875 Kinsington Cir Weston (33332) (G-18273)
Nkem Inc 800 582-0707
 1451 Sarasota Center Blvd Sarasota (34240) (G-15762)
Nml, Boca Raton Also called Mmp-Boca Raton LLC (G-601)
No 1 Beauty Salon Furniture 954 981-0403
 4712 Ne 12th Ave Oakland Park (33334) (G-11281)
No Boundaries Transportation 850 263-1903
 3330 Highway 2 Bonifay (32425) (G-774)
No Equal Design Inc 305 971-5177
 6995 Nw 46th St A Miami (33166) (G-9623)
No Live Bait Needed LLC 305 479-8719
 12078 Miramar Pkwy Miramar (33025) (G-10520)
No No-See-Um, Fort Myers Also called Velmaxxx Enterprises Inc (G-4439)
No. 1 Bsf, Oakland Park Also called No 1 Beauty Salon Furniture (G-11281)
Noa International Inc 954 835-5258
 3066 Payson Way Wellington (33414) (G-17856)
Noahs MBL Tire Auto Solutions 904 250-1502
 2060 W 21st St Jacksonville (32209) (G-6337)
Nobel Aerospace LLC 786 210-0716
 1532 Nw 89th Ct Doral (33172) (G-3312)
Nobility Homes Inc (PA) 352 732-5157
 3741 Sw 7th St Ocala (34474) (G-11451)
Nobility Homes Inc 352 245-5126
 6432 Se 115th Ln Belleview (34420) (G-364)
Nobility Plant 8, Belleview Also called Nobility Homes Inc (G-364)
Noble Wood Works 561 702-2889
 225 Nw 16th St Pompano Beach (33060) (G-14108)
Noble Worldwide Fla Citrus Sls, Winter Haven Also called Wm G Roe & Sons Inc (G-18478)
Noble's Jockey Apparel, Davie Also called Bnj Noble Inc (G-2392)
Noell Design Group Inc 561 391-9942
 1050 Nw 1st Ave Ste 16 Boca Raton (33432) (G-618)
Noflood Inc 239 776-1671
 17061 Alico Commerce Ct # 107 Fort Myers (33967) (G-4341)
NOGHOLD, Hialeah Also called Noguera Holdings LLC (G-5281)

Noguera Holdings LLC 305 846-9144
  1635 W 32nd Pl Hialeah (33012) **(G-5281)**

Nohbo Labs LLC 321 345-5319
  1581 Robert J Conlan Blvd Palm Bay (32905) **(G-12910)**

Nomi Rubinstein Inc 305 467-7888
  267 Ne 166th St Miami (33162) **(G-9624)**

Noodle Time Inc 305 593-0770
  8685 Nw 53rd Ter Miami (33166) **(G-9625)**

Nopetro LLC 305 441-9059
  1152 Capital Cir Nw Tallahassee (32304) **(G-16483)**

Nopi, Mount Dora Also called Natural Organic Products Intl **(G-10607)**

Norco, Deland Also called Delta Machine & Tool Inc **(G-2863)**

Nordic Group LLC (PA) 561 789-8676
  2220 Sw 11th Pl Boca Raton (33486) **(G-619)**

Nordic Line Inc (PA) 561 338-5545
  1080 Nw 1st Ave Boca Raton (33432) **(G-620)**

Nordic Made Inc 954 651-6208
  3801 Sw 47th Ave Ste 503 Davie (33314) **(G-2447)**

Nordquist Dielectrics Inc 727 585-7990
  12750 59th Way N Clearwater (33760) **(G-1718)**

Nores Precision Inc 954 420-0025
  44 Se 9th St Deerfield Beach (33441) **(G-2775)**

Norman Engineering Corporation 407 425-6433
  2579 N Orange Blossom Trl Orlando (32804) **(G-12420)**

Normandin LLC 941 739-8046
  2206 72nd Dr E Sarasota (34243) **(G-15527)**

Norris Precision Mfg Inc 727 572-6330
  4680 110th Ave N Clearwater (33762) **(G-1719)**

Norseman Shipbuilding Corp 305 545-6815
  437 Nw South River Dr Miami (33128) **(G-9626)**

Nortech Engineering Inc 508 823-8520
  13001 Cedar Creek Dr Port Charlotte (33953) **(G-14309)**

Nortek Global Hvac LLC 305 592-6154
  12250 Nw 25th St Ste 100 Miami (33182) **(G-9627)**

North America Bio Fuel Corp 877 877-9279
  1767 Lakewood Ranch Blvd # 210 Bradenton (34211) **(G-1019)**

North America Wireline LLC 870 365-5401
  6057 Clay Cir Gulf Breeze (32563) **(G-4887)**

North American Coal Corp 305 824-9018
  18300 Sw 122nd St Miami (33196) **(G-9628)**

North American Diagnostics LLC 855 752-6879
  618 Ridgewood Ave Ste 100 Holly Hill (32117) **(G-5517)**

North American Mining 305 824-3181
  10025 Nw 116th Way Ste 1 Medley (33178) **(G-8290)**

North American Operations, Orlando Also called Esterel Technologies Inc **(G-12134)**

North American Signal LLC 850 462-1790
  1810 Barrancas Ave Pensacola (32502) **(G-13556)**

North Amrcn Adhesives Coatings, Deerfield Beach Also called Mapei Corporation **(G-2763)**

North Amrcn Prtection Ctrl LLC 407 788-3717
  190 N Westmonte Dr Altamonte Springs (32714) **(G-59)**

North Amrcn Signal Systems LLC 352 376-8341
  605 Nw 53rd Ave Ste A17 Gainesville (32609) **(G-4739)**

North Central Advertiser Inc 386 755-2917
  358 Nw Main Blvd Lake City (32055) **(G-7032)**

North Coast Machining Inc 954 942-6943
  2311 Ne 26th St Lighthouse Point (33064) **(G-7827)**

North Erie Electronics Inc 561 839-8127
  1001 N Us Highway 1 # 506 Jupiter (33477) **(G-6773)**

North FL Custom Coatings Inc 904 251-4462
  2896 Cortez Rd Jacksonville (32246) **(G-6338)**

North Florida AG Services Inc 352 494-3978
  3151 Sw Custom Made Cir Lake City (32024) **(G-7033)**

North Florida Brick Pavers LLC 850 255-0336
  664 E Shipwreck Rd Santa Rosa Beach (32459) **(G-15429)**

North Florida Lumber, Bristol Also called North Florida Woodlands Inc **(G-1125)**

North Florida Printing Inc 386 362-1080
  109 Tuxedo Ave Ne Live Oak (32064) **(G-7850)**

North Florida Vault LLC 386 303-2267
  561 Nw Hilton Ave Lake City (32055) **(G-7034)**

North Florida Woodlands Inc 850 643-2238
  18601 Nw County Road 12 Bristol (32321) **(G-1125)**

North Fort Myers Prescr Sp 239 599-4120
  16251 N Cleveland Ave # 13 North Fort Myers (33903) **(G-11063)**

North Metro Media 850 650-1014
  160 Baywind Dr Niceville (32578) **(G-11033)**

North Orange Avenue Properties 407 420-5000
  633 N Orange Ave Orlando (32801) **(G-12421)**

North Palm Printing Center 561 622-2839
  4588 Juniper Ln Palm Beach Gardens (33418) **(G-12993)**

North Port Pavers Inc 941 391-7557
  6099 Estates Dr North Port (34291) **(G-11202)**

North Shore Hldngs Lghthuse Pt 954 785-1055
  4130 Ne 24th Ave Lighthouse Point (33064) **(G-7828)**

North W Fla Cncl of Blind Cor 850 982-7867
  2807 Sandy Ridge Rd Gulf Breeze (32563) **(G-4888)**

Northast Wtr Rclmtion Fclities, Saint Petersburg Also called Northeast Water Reclamation **(G-15140)**

Northeast Florida Coatings 904 383-0749
  299 N Mimosa Ave Middleburg (32068) **(G-10407)**

Northeast Water Reclamation 727 893-7779
  1160 62nd Ave Ne Saint Petersburg (33702) **(G-15140)**

Northland Manufacturing Inc 850 878-5149
  3485 S Monroe St Tallahassee (32301) **(G-16484)**

Northpointe Bank 239 308-4532
  8660 College Pkwy Ste 150 Fort Myers (33919) **(G-4342)**

Northrich Florida LLC 954 678-6602
  2111 N Commerce Pkwy Weston (33326) **(G-18274)**

Northrop Grmman Feld Spport Sv (HQ) 904 810-4665
  5000 Us Highway 1 N B02-60 Saint Augustine (32095) **(G-14861)**

Northrop Grmman Mssion Systems, Orlando Also called Northrop Grumman Systems Corp **(G-12423)**

Northrop Grmman Tchncal Svcs I 321 837-7000
  1235 Evans Rd Melbourne (32904) **(G-8481)**

Northrop Grmman Tchncal Svcs I 904 825-3300
  5000 Us Highway 1 N Saint Augustine (32095) **(G-14862)**

Northrop Grumman Corporation, Melbourne Also called Northrop Grumman Systems Corp **(G-8484)**

Northrop Grumman Corporation 321 951-5000
  2000 W Nasa Blvd Melbourne (32904) **(G-8482)**

Northrop Grumman ISS Intl Inc 321 951-5695
  2000 W Nasa Blvd Melbourne (32904) **(G-8483)**

Northrop Grumman Systems Corp 904 825-3300
  5000 Us Highway 1 N Saint Augustine (32095) **(G-14863)**

Northrop Grumman Systems Corp 904 810-5957
  125 International Golf Saint Augustine (32095) **(G-14864)**

Northrop Grumman Systems Corp 850 452-7970
  130 West Ave Ste C Pensacola (32508) **(G-13557)**

Northrop Grumman Systems Corp 850 863-8000
  1992 Lewis Turner Blvd Fort Walton Beach (32547) **(G-4598)**

Northrop Grumman Systems Corp 407 295-4010
  2787 S Orange Blossom Trl Apopka (32703) **(G-158)**

Northrop Grumman Systems Corp 321 951-5000
  2000 W Nasa Blvd Melbourne (32904) **(G-8484)**

Northrop Grumman Systems Corp 321 235-3800
  2300 Discovery Dr Ste 150 Orlando (32826) **(G-12422)**

Northrop Grumman Systems Corp 904 825-3300
  5000 Us Highway 1 N Saint Augustine (32095) **(G-14865)**

Northrop Grumman Systems Corp 561 515-3651
  348 Hiatt Dr Ste 100 Palm Beach Gardens (33418) **(G-12994)**

Northrop Grumman Systems Corp 407 737-4900
  11474 Corp Blvd Ste 120 Orlando (32817) **(G-12423)**

Northside Pharmacy LLC 256 398-7500
  36474c Emerald Coast Pkwy Destin (32541) **(G-3074)**

Northside Sheet Metal Inc 850 769-1461
  2836 Transmitter Rd Panama City (32404) **(G-13290)**

Northstar Aviation USA LLC 321 600-4557
  1431 General Aviation Dr Melbourne (32935) **(G-8485)**

Northwest Florida Daily News, Panama City Also called Panama City News Herald **(G-13293)**

Northwest Florida Daily News, Fort Walton Beach Also called Panama City News Herald **(G-4601)**

Northwest Florida Daily News (HQ) 850 863-1111
  2 Eglin Pkwy Ne Fort Walton Beach (32548) **(G-4599)**

Northwings Accessories Corp (HQ) 305 463-0455
  7875 Nw 64th St Miami (33166) **(G-9629)**

Norton Manufacturing & Svc Inc 352 225-1225
  11590 Se 30th St Morriston (32668) **(G-10594)**

Norwood Promotional Products, Clearwater Also called Scribe Manufacturing Inc **(G-1777)**

Nosta Inc 305 634-1435
  1235 Nw 29th St Miami (33142) **(G-9630)**

Nosta Carpenter Shop, Miami Also called Nosta Inc **(G-9630)**

Nostalgic America Inc 561 585-1724
  102 Ne 2nd St Ste 172 Boca Raton (33432) **(G-621)**

Note Bin Inc 727 642-8530
  29399 Us 19 N Ste 360 Clearwater (33761) **(G-1720)**

Notice Four LLC 954 652-1168
  2775 Nw 62nd St Fort Lauderdale (33309) **(G-3963)**

Notions, Miami Also called Scott Slide Fasteners Inc **(G-9858)**

Noumenon Corporation 302 296-5460
  1616 Cape Coral Pkwy W Cape Coral (33914) **(G-1368)**

Nouveau Cosmetique Usa Inc 321 332-6976
  189 S Orange Ave Ste 1110 Orlando (32801) **(G-12424)**

Nova Laserlight LLC 407 226-0609
  7600 Dr Phillips Blvd Orlando (32819) **(G-12425)**

Nova Solid Surfaces Inc 239 888-0975
  12350 Crystal Commerce Lo Fort Myers (33966) **(G-4343)**

Novagroup LLC (PA) 305 471-4824
  3470 Nw 82nd Ave Ste 790 Doral (33122) **(G-3313)**

Novak Machining Inc 727 527-5473
  3921 69th Ave N Pinellas Park (33781) **(G-13714)**

Novaphos Inc 863 285-8607
  3200 County Rte 630 W Fort Meade (33841) **(G-4151)**

Noveltex Miami Inc 305 887-8191
  151 E 10th Ave Hialeah (33010) **(G-5282)**

Novelty Crystal Corp 352 429-9036
  9326 Bentley Park Cir Orlando (32819) **(G-12426)**

Novelty Crystal Corp 352 429-9036
  21005 Obrien Rd Groveland (34736) **(G-4867)**

Noven Pharmaceuticals Inc (HQ) 305 964-3393
11960 Sw 144th St Miami (33186) (G-9631)

Noven Therapeutics LLC 212 682-4420
11960 Sw 144th St Miami (33186) (G-9632)

Novena TEC LLC (PA) 407 392-1868
4767 New Broad St Orlando (32814) (G-12427)

Novicon Industries 813 854-3235
400 Roberts Rd Oldsmar (34677) (G-11679)

Novo Aero Services Llc 786 319-8637
6965 Vista Pkwy N Ste 16 West Palm Beach (33411) (G-18094)

Novurania of America Inc 772 567-9200
2105 S Us Highway 1 Vero Beach (32962) (G-17781)

Novus Clip Signs & Video Prod 239 471-5639
12771 Metro Pkwy Ste 1 Fort Myers (33966) (G-4344)

Nowvision Technologies Inc 813 943-4639
618 De Buel Rd Bldng A Lutz (33549) (G-8007)

Noxtak Corp 786 586-7927
21011 Johnson St Ste 110 Pembroke Pines (33029) (G-13408)

Npact America Inc 904 755-6259
14476 Duval Pl W Ste 109 Jacksonville (32218) (G-6339)

Npc of Tampa Inc 813 839-0035
5210 S Lois Ave Tampa (33611) (G-17112)

NPC&ug Inc 239 694-7255
22021 Luckey Lee Ln Alva (33920) (G-82)

Nphase Inc 805 750-8580
1015 Atl Blvd Pmb 328 328 Pmb Atlantic Beach (32233) (G-212)

NRG Barrriers South, Jacksonville Also called Johns Manville Corporation (G-6229)

Nrz Inc 305 345-7303
12885 Sw 82nd Ave Pinecrest (33156) (G-13667)

Nscrypt Inc 407 275-4720
12151 Res Pkwy Ste 150 Orlando (32826) (G-12428)

NSK Latin America Inc (HQ) 305 477-0605
11601 Nw 107th St Ste 200 Miami (33178) (G-9633)

Nspa, Pensacola Also called National Std Parts Assoc Inc (G-13555)

Nst Global LLC 941 748-2270
3145 Lakewood Ranch Blvd Bradenton (34211) (G-1020)

NTS Industries Inc 317 847-6675
1218 W New Hampshire St Orlando (32804) (G-12429)

Nu Earth Labs LLC 727 648-4787
150 Douglas Ave Dunedin (34698) (G-3455)

Nu Tech Coating Systems 813 448-9381
525 Lafayette Blvd Oldsmar (34677) (G-11680)

Nu Trek Inc 813 920-4348
16708 Hutchison Rd Odessa (33556) (G-11568)

Nu-Art Signs Inc 305 531-9850
3343 Nw 7th Ave Miami (33127) (G-9634)

Nu-Pac Industries, Pompano Beach Also called Ross Industries Inc (G-14162)

Nu-Vue Industries Inc 305 694-0397
1055 E 29th St Hialeah (33013) (G-5283)

Nubo Bottle Company LLC 954 283-9057
10241 Sw Visconti Way Port Saint Lucie (34986) (G-14429)

Nucor LLC 786 290-9328
8835 Harding Ave Surfside (33154) (G-16397)

Nucor Steel Florida Inc 863 546-5800
22 Nucor Dr Frostproof (33843) (G-4639)

Nucycle Energy of Tampa LLC 813 848-0509
2067 S County Line Rd Plant City (33566) (G-13787)

Nuenergy Technologies Corp 866 895-6838
601 Cleveland St Ste 501 Clearwater (33755) (G-1721)

Nuevo Mundo Company 305 207-8155
9702 Sw 40th St Miami (33165) (G-9635)

Nuflo Inc 904 265-4001
3440 Evergreen Ave Ste 1 Jacksonville (32206) (G-6340)

Nuform Cabinetry 954 532-2746
1745 N Powerline Rd Pompano Beach (33069) (G-14109)

Nulab Inc 727 446-1126
519 Cleveland St Ste 101 Clearwater (33755) (G-1722)

Nuline Sensors LLC 407 473-0765
210 Specialty Pt Sanford (32771) (G-15363)

Numerator Technologies Inc 941 807-5333
862 Freeling Dr Sarasota (34242) (G-15763)

Nunez Machine Shop Inc 786 615-4261
9809 Nw 80th Ave Hialeah Gardens (33016) (G-5444)

Nupress of Miami Inc 305 594-2100
2050 Nw 94th Ave Doral (33172) (G-3314)

Nursery Supplies Inc 407 846-9750
2050 Avenue A Kissimmee (34758) (G-6945)

Nurserymens Sure-Gro Corp 772 770-0462
4390 Us Highway 1 Vero Beach (32967) (G-17782)

Nusfc LLC 920 725-7000
8351 Nw 93rd St Medley (33166) (G-8291)

Nutop International LLC 954 909-0010
2601 E Oklnd Prk Blvd # 205 Fort Lauderdale (33306) (G-3964)

Nutra Pharma Corp 954 509-0911
4001 Nw 73rd Way Coral Springs (33065) (G-2198)

Nutra Sciences World Inc 305 302-8870
8125 W 8th Ct Hialeah (33014) (G-5284)

Nutra-Lift Skin Care, Fort Lauderdale Also called Younger You Inc (G-4142)

Nutraceutical Corporation 813 877-4186
5046 W Linebaugh Ave Tampa (33624) (G-17113)

Nutraceuticals Factory LLC 727 692-7294
11860 31st Ct N Saint Petersburg (33716) (G-15141)

Nutrakey LLC 321 234-6282
975 Bennett Dr Longwood (32750) (G-7929)

Nutramedix LLC 561 745-2917
2885 Jupiter Park Dr # 1600 Jupiter (33458) (G-6774)

Nutrasource LLC (PA) 786 427-4305
1395 Brickell Ave Ste 800 Miami (33131) (G-9636)

Nutricorp LLC 305 680-4896
671 W 18th St Hialeah (33010) (G-5285)

Nutrifusion LLC 404 240-0030
10641 Airport Rd N Ste 31 Naples (34109) (G-10837)

Nutrition Laboratories Inc 915 496-7531
2151 Logan St Clearwater (33765) (G-1723)

Nutrition Laboratories Inc 727 442-2747
2141 Logan St Clearwater (33765) (G-1724)

Nutrition World Health Market, Palm Beach Gardens Also called Briemad Inc (G-12953)

Nutritious You LLC 941 203-5203
6583 Midnight Pass Rd Sarasota (34242) (G-15764)

Nutritorch 561 777-9079
8073 Pelican Harbour Dr Lake Worth (33467) (G-7223)

Nuts About Florida, Miami Also called Barnard Nut Company Inc (G-8799)

Nutty Scoopz, Jacksonville Also called Hoppin Pop Kettle Stop LLC (G-6184)

Nuwas Deva LLC 786 859-2819
2240 N Sherman Cir # 507 Miramar (33025) (G-10521)

Nv5geospatial, Saint Petersburg Also called Quantum Spatial Inc (G-15168)

Nvaulted Enterprises Inc 305 632-0525
2080 S Ocean Dr Apt 306 Hallandale Beach (33009) (G-4964)

Nvip LLC 469 955-4427
2231 Linwood Ave Naples (34112) (G-10838)

Nvs Coating Systems Inc 239 784-3972
250 Stanhope Cir Naples (34104) (G-10839)

Nwgc, Boca Raton Also called New World Gold Corporation (G-614)

Nwh Publishing Llc 904 217-3911
659 Los Caminos St Saint Augustine (32095) (G-14866)

Nwi, Sarasota Also called Genie Cap Inc (G-15691)

Nwi Enterprises, Tampa Also called Nationwide Industries Inc (G-17103)

Nwl Inc 800 742-5695
4701 Crump Rd Lake Hamilton (33851) (G-7051)

Nwl Inc 561 848-9009
8050 Monetary Dr Riviera Beach (33404) (G-14651)

Nxgen Brands Inc (PA) 954 329-2205
2322 Se 8th St Cape Coral (33990) (G-1369)

Nxgen Brands LLC 888 315-6339
8032 Lakepointe Dr Plantation (33322) (G-13875)

Nylacarb Corp 772 569-5999
1725 98th Ave Vero Beach (32966) (G-17783)

Nypro Healthcare LLC 727 577-9749
10560 Dr Martin Luther Saint Petersburg (33716) (G-15142)

Nypro Inc 727 577-9749
10560 Dr Mlj Jr St N Martin Saint Petersburg (33716) (G-15143)

Nyrstar Us Inc 954 400-6464
350 E Las Olas Blvd # 800 Fort Lauderdale (33301) (G-3965)

O I Inc 321 212-7801
295 North Dr Ste A Melbourne (32934) (G-8486)

O Mustad & Son USA Inc 206 284-7871
2315 Nw 107th Ave Ste 88 Doral (33172) (G-3315)

O'Malley Valve Co., Saint Petersburg Also called OMalley Manufacturing Inc (G-15147)

Oai, Tampa Also called Outdoor America Images Inc (G-17133)

Oai Enterprises LLC 239 225-1350
12960 Commerce Lakes Dr Fort Myers (33913) (G-4345)

Oakbrook Sales Inc 800 773-0979
2200 Butts Rd Ste 200 Boca Raton (33431) (G-622)

Oakhurst Marketing Inc 727 532-8255
2400 31st S S Saint Petersburg (33712) (G-15144)

Oakhurst Signs, Saint Petersburg Also called Oakhurst Marketing Inc (G-15144)

Oakley Signs, Maitland Also called L4 Design LLC (G-8065)

Oakridge Globl Enrgy Sltons In 321 610-7959
3520 Dixie Hwy Ne Palm Bay (32905) (G-12911)

Oaktree Software Inc 407 339-5855
222 S Westmonte Dr # 251 Altamonte Springs (32714) (G-60)

Oase North America Inc 800 365-3880
7241 Hvrhill Bus Pkwy # 105 Riviera Beach (33407) (G-14652)

Oasis Alignment Services Inc 850 484-2994
7501 Sears Blvd Pensacola (32514) (G-13558)

Oath Corporation 407 221-7288
395 Richard Rd Ste D Rockledge (32955) (G-14736)

OB Inc (PA) 321 223-0332
5020 Scott Rd Cocoa (32926) (G-1945)

Obd Genie Inc 321 250-3650
500 Geneva Dr Oviedo (32765) (G-12839)

Obdgenie, Oviedo Also called Obd Genie LLC (G-12839)

Obem Foods Inc 305 887-0258
400 Swallow Dr Miami Springs (33166) (G-10392)

Oberon Industries Inc 321 245-7338
1900 Stanley St Orlando (32803) (G-12430)

Observer Group, Sarasota Also called Observer Media Group Inc (G-15766)

2022 Harris Florida
Manufacturers Directory

(G-0000) Company's Geographic Section entry number

Observer Group 407 654-5500
446 N Dillard St Winter Garden (34787) *(G-18399)*

Observer Group and Gulf Coast 239 263-0122
2960 Immokalee Rd Naples (34110) *(G-10840)*

Observer Group Inc 941 383-5509
1970 Main St Fl 3 Sarasota (34236) *(G-15765)*

Observer Media Group Inc (PA) 941 366-3468
1970 Main St Fl 3 Sarasota (34236) *(G-15766)*

Observer Media Group Inc 941 349-4949
5011 Ocean Blvd Ste 206 Sarasota (34242) *(G-15767)*

Observer, The, New Smyrna Beach *Also called Horizon Publications Inc (G-11002)*

Ocala Bedrock, Ocala *Also called Bedrock Resources LLC (G-11333)*

Ocala Breeders Sales Co Inc (PA) 352 237-4667
1701 Sw 60th Ave Ocala (34474) *(G-11452)*

Ocala Breeders' Feed & Supply, Ocala *Also called Ocala Breeders Sales Co Inc (G-11452)*

Ocala Concrete Services LLC 352 694-4300
3498 W Highway 326 Ocala (34475) *(G-11453)*

Ocala Engineering-Traffic Div, Ocala *Also called City of Ocala (G-11352)*

Ocala Magazine 352 622-2995
743 E Fort King St Ocala (34471) *(G-11454)*

Ocala Manufacturing 352 433-6643
10245 N Us Highway 27 Ocala (34482) *(G-11455)*

Ocala Metal Products Inc 352 861-4500
800 N Pine Ave Ocala (34475) *(G-11456)*

Ocala Pharmacy LLC 352 509-7890
8290 Sw Highway 200 Ocala (34481) *(G-11457)*

Ocala Print Quick Inc 352 629-0736
600 S Magnolia Ave Ocala (34471) *(G-11458)*

Ocala Publication Incorporated 352 732-0073
908 Se 16th St Ocala (34471) *(G-11459)*

Ocala Star Banner Corporation 352 867-4010
2700 Sw 13th St Gainesville (32608) *(G-4740)*

Ocala Style Magazine, Ocala *Also called Ocala Publication Incorporated (G-11459)*

OCC My Stone LLC 786 352-1567
10090 Nw 80th Ct Apt 1238 Hialeah Gardens (33016) *(G-5445)*

Ocean Bio-Chem LLC (HQ) 954 587-6280
4041 Sw 47th Ave Davie (33314) *(G-2448)*

Ocean Blue Graphics Inc 561 881-2022
1841 W 10th St Ste 1 Riviera Beach (33404) *(G-14653)*

Ocean Blue Graphics Design Inc 561 881-2022
1841 W 10th St Ste 1 Riviera Beach (33404) *(G-14654)*

Ocean Breeze, Stuart *Also called 2951 SE Dominica Holding LLC (G-16107)*

Ocean Dynamics USA Inc 305 770-1800
18377 Ne 4th Ct Miami (33179) *(G-9637)*

Ocean Global Inc 727 842-7544
4925 Southshore Dr New Port Richey (34652) *(G-10976)*

Ocean Insight, Orlando *Also called Ocean Optics Inc (G-12432)*

Ocean Kitchen Cabinets 352 745-7110
4445 Sw 35th Ter Ste 200 Gainesville (32608) *(G-4741)*

Ocean Master Marine Inc 561 840-0448
837 W 13th St Unit C Riviera Beach (33404) *(G-14655)*

Ocean Media, Stuart *Also called Mailbox Publishing Inc (G-16181)*

Ocean Optics Inc 407 673-0041
3500 Quadrangle Blvd Orlando (32817) *(G-12431)*

Ocean Optics Inc (HQ) 407 673-0041
3500 Quadrangle Blvd Orlando (32817) *(G-12432)*

Ocean Optics Inc 727 545-0741
3500 Quadrangle Blvd Orlando (32817) *(G-12433)*

Ocean Pharmaceuticals Inc 954 473-4717
5373 N Hiatus Rd Sunrise (33351) *(G-16348)*

Ocean Potion, Cocoa *Also called Florida Glsd Holdings Inc (G-1929)*

Ocean Tech, West Palm Beach *Also called J & I Ventures Inc (G-18037)*

Ocean Test Equipment Inc 954 474-6603
2021 Sw 70th Ave Ste B1 Davie (33317) *(G-2449)*

Ocean Waves Inc 904 372-4743
525 3rd St N Ste 105 Jacksonville Beach (32250) *(G-6641)*

Ocean Way Transport LLC 407 669-3822
4529 Piedmont St Orlando (32811) *(G-12434)*

Ocean Woodworks Inc 904 246-7178
1701 Mayport Rd Ste 1 Atlantic Beach (32233) *(G-213)*

Oceana Software LLC 813 335-6966
5202 Quarrystone Ln Tampa (33624) *(G-17114)*

Oceaneering International Inc 985 329-3282
1700 C Ave Panama City (32401) *(G-13291)*

Oceanic Electrical Mfg Co Inc 908 355-1900
1904 Calumet St Clearwater (33765) *(G-1725)*

Oceanstyle By Burgess, Miami Beach *Also called Oceanstyle LLC (G-10217)*

Oceanstyle LLC 305 672-9400
390 Alton Rd Ste 2 Miami Beach (33139) *(G-10217)*

Ocoa LLC 407 898-1961
800 N Magnolia Ave # 1400 Orlando (32803) *(G-12435)*

OCon Enterprise Inc 954 920-6700
821 N 21st Ave Hollywood (33020) *(G-5635)*

Ocoos, Ocala *Also called Advtravl Inc (G-11315)*

Ocoow LLC 805 266-7616
2340 Sopchoppy Hwy Sopchoppy (32358) *(G-16009)*

Octal Ventures Inc 727 526-9288
6544 44th St N Ste 1205 Pinellas Park (33781) *(G-13715)*

Octametro LLC 305 715-9713
8539 Nw 56th St Doral (33166) *(G-3316)*

Octex Holdings LLC (PA) 941 371-6767
901 Sarasota Center Blvd Sarasota (34240) *(G-15768)*

Oculus Surgical Inc 772 236-2622
562 Nw Merc Pl Ste 104 Port St Lucie (34986) *(G-14480)*

Odara Kanvas Cosmetics 239 785-8013
1126 Homer Ave S Lehigh Acres (33973) *(G-7818)*

Odyssey, Jacksonville *Also called Benner China and Glwr of Fla (G-5929)*

Odyssey Manufacturing Co 407 582-9051
250 Central Florida Pkwy Orlando (32824) *(G-12436)*

Odyssey Manufacturing Co (PA) 813 635-0339
1484 Massaro Blvd Tampa (33619) *(G-17115)*

Odyssey Manufacturing Co 813 635-0339
5361 Hartford St Tampa (33619) *(G-17116)*

Oerlikon USA Inc 727 577-4999
10050 16th St N Saint Petersburg (33716) *(G-15145)*

Ofab Inc 352 629-0040
1909 Ne 25th Ave Ocala (34470) *(G-11460)*

Off The Wall Screen Printing, Lynn Haven *Also called Rinehart Corp (G-8031)*

Office Express Corp 786 503-6800
1835 Nw 112th Ave Ste 174 Miami (33172) *(G-9638)*

Office Furniture By Tempo Inc 305 685-3077
4136 E 10th Ln Hialeah (33013) *(G-5286)*

Office Graphic Design, Coral Gables *Also called Graphic Center Group Corp (G-2065)*

Office of Medical Examiner 772 464-7378
2500 S 35th St Fort Pierce (34981) *(G-4512)*

Office, The, Miami *Also called A & S Entertainment LLC (G-8615)*

Official Gear Company Inc 407 721-9110
106 Deer Run Lake Dr Ormond Beach (32174) *(G-12782)*

Officine Gullo USA LLC 800 781-7125
6151 Biscayne Blvd Miami (33137) *(G-9639)*

Offshore Inland Mar Olfld Svcs 251 443-5550
640 S Barracks St Pensacola (32502) *(G-13559)*

Offshore Performance Spc Inc 239 481-2768
15881 Chief Ct Fort Myers (33912) *(G-4346)*

OGrady Tool Company 239 560-3395
7721 Hidden Pond Ln Fort Myers (33917) *(G-4347)*

Ogre Custom Fabrications LLC 321 544-2142
2495 Jen Dr Ste 10 Melbourne (32940) *(G-8487)*

OH Catering Inc 305 903-9271
3006 Sw 155th Ave Miami (33185) *(G-9640)*

Ohana Liquids LLC 888 642-6244
900 N Atlantic Ave New Smyrna Beach (32169) *(G-11007)*

OHanrahan Consultants Inc 727 531-3375
6414 125th Ave Largo (33773) *(G-7652)*

OHM Americas LLC 800 467-7275
3736 Sw 30th Ave Fort Lauderdale (33312) *(G-3966)*

OHM Power Solutions, Fort Lauderdale *Also called OHM Americas LLC (G-3966)*

Ohmac Chemical Group, Largo *Also called OHanrahan Consultants Inc (G-7652)*

Oi Distribution, Weston *Also called Original Impressions LLC (G-18276)*

Oil For Amer Exploration LLC 701 690-2407
2903 Royal Isle Dr Tallahassee (32312) *(G-16485)*

Oil Water Separator Tech LLC 561 693-3250
7020 Georgia Ave Ste A West Palm Beach (33405) *(G-18095)*

Oils R US 1 800 .... 305 681-0909
3300 Nw 112th St Miami (33167) *(G-9641)*

Ojm, Miami *Also called Lau International Inc (G-9438)*

Okay Pure Naturals, Opa Locka *Also called Xtreme Tools International Inc (G-11801)*

Okee-B Inc 561 996-3040
1125 Ne 18th St Belle Glade (33430) *(G-342)*

Okeechbee Asp Rady Mxed Con In 863 763-7373
503 Nw 9th St Okeechobee (34972) *(G-11612)*

Okeechobee Petroleum LLC 561 478-1083
6970 Okeechobee Blvd West Palm Beach (33411) *(G-18096)*

Okeelanta Corporation 561 996-9072
6 Mile S Of S Bay Hwy 27 South Bay (33493) *(G-16016)*

Okeelanta Corporation (HQ) 561 366-5100
1 N Clematis St Ste 200 West Palm Beach (33401) *(G-18097)*

Okeelanta Sugar, South Bay *Also called Okeelanta Corporation (G-16016)*

OL Products Inc 813 854-3575
100 Mount Vernon St Oldsmar (34677) *(G-11681)*

Olas Foods Specialty Mkt Inc 813 447-5127
5791 54th Ave N Kenneth City (33709) *(G-6832)*

Old & New Brick Pavers LLC 908 249-6130
5221 Alligator Flag Ln Orlando (32811) *(G-12437)*

Old 97 Company (HQ) 813 246-4180
4829 E 7th Ave Tampa (33605) *(G-17117)*

Old Castle Coastal, Gainesville *Also called Oldcastle Building Produc (G-4742)*

Old City Building 850 432-7723
201 E Government St Pensacola (32502) *(G-13560)*

Old City Gates 904 669-7938
2008 W Lymington Way Saint Augustine (32084) *(G-14867)*

Old City Marine LLC 904 252-6887
76 Dockside Dr Ste 112 Saint Augustine (32084) *(G-14868)*

Old Heritage Medcall Inc 813 221-1000
202 E Virginia Ave Tampa (33603) *(G-17118)*

Old Kentucky Leather Works Inc 904 269-1369
1532 Arena Rd Orange Park (32003) *(G-11835)*

Old Meeting House Home Made Ic................................813 254-0977
901 Sw Howard Ave Tampa (33606) *(G-17119)*

Old Oak Truss Company................................813 689-6597
1460 State Rd 574 Seffner (33584) *(G-15963)*

Old Port Group LLC................................904 819-5812
1301 Plntn Is Dr S 206b Saint Augustine (32080) *(G-14869)*

Old World Marble and Gran Inc................................239 596-4777
1998 Trade Center Way # 1 Naples (34109) *(G-10841)*

Oldcastle Apg South Inc................................813 367-9780
3801 Pga Blvd Ste 806 Palm Beach Gardens (33410) *(G-12995)*

Oldcastle Apg South Inc................................863 421-7422
1980 Marley Dr Haines City (33844) *(G-4911)*

Oldcastle Architectural Inc................................813 886-7761
5603 Anderson Rd Tampa (33614) *(G-17120)*

Oldcastle Building Produc................................352 377-1699
3302 Ne 2nd St Gainesville (32609) *(G-4742)*

Oldcastle Buildingenvelope Inc................................813 247-3184
5115 Hartford St Tampa (33619) *(G-17121)*

Oldcastle Buildingenvelope Inc................................305 651-6630
17851 Nw Miami Ct Miami (33169) *(G-9642)*

Oldcastle Buildingenvelope Inc................................813 663-0949
8655 Elm Fair Blvd Tampa (33610) *(G-17122)*

Oldcastle Coastal, Riviera Beach *Also called Paver Systems LLC (G-14657)*

Oldcastle Coastal................................813 621-2427
5455 N 59th St Tampa (33610) *(G-17123)*

Oldcastle Coastal Inc................................813 886-7761
5603 Anderson Rd Tampa (33614) *(G-17124)*

Oldcastle Coastal Inc................................813 932-1007
8910 N 12th St Tampa (33604) *(G-17125)*

Oldcastle Coastal Inc (HQ)................................813 367-9780
4630 Woodlnd Corp Blvd Tampa (33614) *(G-17126)*

Oldcastle Infrastructure Inc................................305 887-3527
7311 Nw 77th St Medley (33166) *(G-8292)*

Oldcastle Infrastructure Inc................................800 642-1540
1410 Industrial Dr Wildwood (34785) *(G-18316)*

Oldcastle Infrastructure Inc................................407 855-7580
690 W Taft Vineland Rd Orlando (32824) *(G-12438)*

Oldcastle Infrastructure Inc................................239 574-8896
2140 Pondella Rd Cape Coral (33909) *(G-1370)*

Oldcastle Lawn & Garden, Lakeland *Also called Crh Americas Inc (G-7299)*

Oldcastle Retail Inc................................954 971-1200
1200 Nw 18th St Pompano Beach (33069) *(G-14110)*

Olde Hearth Bread Company, Casselberry *Also called Claddah Corp (G-1413)*

Olde World Craftsmen Inc................................239 229-3806
15970 Lake Candlewood Dr Fort Myers (33908) *(G-4348)*

Oldja Enterprises Inc................................727 526-3240
4424 34th St N Saint Petersburg (33714) *(G-15146)*

Oldsmar Ready Mix Con Plant, Oldsmar *Also called Cemex Cnstr Mtls Fla LLC (G-11637)*

Oldsmar Service Center, Oldsmar *Also called Structall Building Systems Inc (G-11698)*

Olevin Compounds LLC................................954 993-5148
12758 Sw 47th St Miramar (33027) *(G-10522)*

Olewo USA, Sarasota *Also called Advanced Household MGT Inc (G-15438)*

Olian Inc................................305 233-9116
13011 Sw 132nd St Miami (33186) *(G-9643)*

Olive Florida Oil Company................................941 483-1865
307 W Venice Ave Ste A Venice (34285) *(G-17708)*

Olive Naples Oil Company................................239 275-5100
7101 Cypress Lake Dr Fort Myers (33907) *(G-4349)*

Olive Naples Oil Company (PA)................................239 596-3000
2368 Immokalee Rd Naples (34110) *(G-10842)*

Olive Tree II................................813 991-8781
2653 Bruce B Downs Blvd Wesley Chapel (33544) *(G-17885)*

Olive Zarzis Oil LLC................................941 284-0291
5142 Factory Shops Blvd Ellenton (34222) *(G-3511)*

Oliveira Services Corp................................772 834-4803
972 Sw Paar Dr Port Saint Lucie (34953) *(G-14430)*

Oliveri Woodworking Inc................................561 478-7233
3001 Tuxedo Ave West Palm Beach (33405) *(G-18098)*

Ollie Pippa International Inc................................888 851-6533
21733 Old Bridge Trl Boca Raton (33428) *(G-623)*

Ollo Usa LLC................................941 366-0600
1223 S Tamiami Trl Sarasota (34239) *(G-15769)*

Olmedo Printing Corp................................305 262-4666
710 Sw 73rd Ct Miami (33144) *(G-9644)*

Oly Custom Cabinets Miami Inc................................305 216-3947
13285 Sw 39th St Miami (33175) *(G-9645)*

Olympian Led Inc................................321 747-3220
3620 S Hopkins Ave Titusville (32780) *(G-17603)*

Olympic Case Co, Tampa *Also called Qps Companies Inc (G-17197)*

OMalley Manufacturing Inc................................727 327-6817
4228 8th Ave S Saint Petersburg (33711) *(G-15147)*

Omax Home Inc................................239 980-2755
1946 Dana Dr Fort Myers (33907) *(G-4350)*

Omb America, Miami *Also called Transamerica Intl Brdcstg Inc (G-10037)*

Omega Energy Usa LLC................................786 245-0642
600 Brickell Ave Ste 1530 Miami (33131) *(G-9646)*

Omega Garage Doors Inc................................352 620-8830
7751 Industrial Rd Melbourne (32904) *(G-8488)*

Omega Gas Inc................................786 277-2176
18401 Sw 115th Ave Miami (33157) *(G-9647)*

Omega Lift Corporation................................561 840-0088
6701 Garden Rd Ste 1 Riviera Beach (33404) *(G-14656)*

Omega Medical Imaging LLC................................407 323-9400
3400 Saint Johns Pkwy # 1020 Sanford (32771) *(G-15364)*

Omega One Research Inc................................561 995-9611
6458 E Rogers Cir Boca Raton (33487) *(G-624)*

Omega Power Systems Inc................................772 219-0045
4443 Se Commerce Ave Stuart (34997) *(G-16191)*

Omega Prof Brick Pavers Inc................................727 243-4659
3679 141st Ave Apt B Largo (33771) *(G-7653)*

Omega Publishing................................727 815-0402
6014 Us Highway 19 # 305 New Port Richey (34652) *(G-10977)*

Omega Sign Service Corporation................................727 505-7833
11301 Biddeford Pl New Port Richey (34654) *(G-10978)*

Omega3 Innovations, Venice *Also called Ambo Health LLC (G-17676)*

OMI of Lake City LLC................................386 288-5632
4066 Nw Wisteria Dr Lake City (32055) *(G-7035)*

Omni Displays LLC................................352 799-9997
15261 Telcom Dr Brooksville (34604) *(G-1186)*

Omni Marine Enterprises LLC................................941 474-4614
2640 S Mccall Rd Englewood (34224) *(G-3520)*

Omnia Inc................................863 619-8100
3125 Drane Feld Rd Ste 29 Lakeland (33811) *(G-7403)*

Omnia Incorporated................................863 619-8100
3125 Drane Feld Rd Ste 29 Lakeland (33811) *(G-7404)*

Omniaelectronics LLC................................631 742-5719
7945 East Dr Apt 204 North Bay Village (33141) *(G-11059)*

Omnifund, Tampa *Also called Gotobilling LLC (G-16887)*

Omnimark Enterprises LLC................................516 351-9075
6843 Narcoossee Rd Orlando (32822) *(G-12439)*

Omnisphere Corporation (PA)................................305 388-4075
9950 Sw 107th Ave Ste 100 Miami (33176) *(G-9648)*

Omnisys LLC................................800 325-2017
551 N Cattlemen Rd Sarasota (34232) *(G-15770)*

Omnivore Technologies Inc................................800 293-4058
13577 Feather Sound Dr # 390 Clearwater (33762) *(G-1726)*

Omt Inc................................772 287-3762
648 Se Monterey Rd Stuart (34994) *(G-16192)*

Omt LLC................................954 327-1447
3848 Sw 30th Ave Fort Lauderdale (33312) *(G-3967)*

Omz Industries LLC................................786 210-6763
6010 Nw 99th Ave Unit 102 Doral (33178) *(G-3317)*

On Demand Envelopes, Hallandale Beach *Also called Services On Demand Print Inc (G-4970)*

On Demand Printing, Oldsmar *Also called Ronecker Holdings LLC (G-11697)*

On Demand Spclty Envelope Corp................................305 681-5345
917 Sw 10th St Hallandale Beach (33009) *(G-4965)*

On Site AG Services................................863 382-7502
359 S Commerce Ave Sebring (33870) *(G-15933)*

On Site Svcs of Mid FL................................407 444-2951
265 Damascus Rd Deland (32724) *(G-2891)*

On The Go Food & Fuel Inc................................727 815-0823
6444 Massachusetts Ave New Port Richey (34653) *(G-10979)*

On-Board Media Inc................................305 673-0400
8400 Nw 36th St Ste 500 Doral (33166) *(G-3318)*

On-Q Software Inc................................305 553-6566
13764 Sw 11th St Miami (33184) *(G-9649)*

On-Site Lighting & Sign Svcs................................256 693-1018
5925 Flaxman St Pensacola (32506) *(G-13561)*

On-Spot Portable Machine Co................................734 525-0880
20612 Dennisport Ln North Fort Myers (33917) *(G-11064)*

Onan Gasoline Engines, Fort Myers *Also called Cummins Power Generation Inc (G-4225)*

Onan Generators & Engines................................772 334-8282
883 Ne Dixie Hwy Jensen Beach (34957) *(G-6658)*

Onaris................................305 579-0056
14 Ne 1st Ave Ste 607 Miami (33132) *(G-9650)*

Onboard Media, Doral *Also called On-Board Media Inc (G-3318)*

Onca Gear LLC................................857 253-8207
2372 W 77th St Hialeah (33016) *(G-5287)*

One Bio Corp................................305 328-8662
19950 W Country Club Dr Aventura (33180) *(G-268)*

One Biotechnology Company................................941 355-8451
1833 57th St Ste A Sarasota (34243) *(G-15528)*

One Hour Printing................................386 763-3111
661 Beville Rd Ste 109 South Daytona (32119) *(G-16025)*

One Hundred Ten Percent, Ponte Vedra Beach *Also called Recover Gear LLC (G-14280)*

One Innovation Labs Llc................................305 985-3950
14520 Nw 60th Ave Miami Lakes (33014) *(G-10333)*

One Milo Inc................................305 804-0266
1010 Brickell Ave #2709 Miami (33131) *(G-9651)*

One Nursing Care LLC................................954 441-6644
3351 Executive Way Miramar (33025) *(G-10523)*

One Price Drycleaners Tampa (PA)................................727 734-3353
1850 Main St Dunedin (34698) *(G-3456)*

One Resonance Sensors LLC................................407 637-0771
101 Gordon St Sanford (32771) *(G-15365)*

One Source Industries Inc 813 855-3440
200 Pine Ave N Ste A Oldsmar (34677) ***(G-11682)***
One Source Technology, Largo *Also called Computer Forms & Supplies* ***(G-7567)***
One Srce Prperty Solutions Inc 239 800-9771
7139 N Brentwood Rd Fort Myers (33919) ***(G-4351)***
One Step Papers LLC (PA) 305 238-2296
12105 Sw 130th St Ste 202 Miami (33186) ***(G-9652)***
One Stop Generator Shop Inc 561 840-0009
3600 Inv Ln Ste 104 West Palm Beach (33404) ***(G-18099)***
One World Resource LLC 305 445-9199
4608 Sw 74th Ave Miami (33155) ***(G-9653)***
ONeill Industries Intl Inc (PA) 850 754-0312
8 E Quintette Rd Ste B Cantonment (32533) ***(G-1272)***
Onesource Information Services, Tampa *Also called Hill Donnelly Corporation* ***(G-16917)***
Onesource of Florida Inc 904 620-0003
6720 Arlington Expy Jacksonville (32211) ***(G-6341)***
Onetown Boards 786 704-5921
580 Nw 120th St Miami (33168) ***(G-9654)***
Onezeno LLC 407 539-1665
3300 University Blvd # 218 Winter Park (32792) ***(G-18527)***
Ongoing Care Solutions Inc 727 526-0707
11721 Us Highway 19 N Clearwater (33764) ***(G-1727)***
Onicon Incorporated (HQ) 727 447-6140
11451 Belcher Rd S Largo (33773) ***(G-7654)***
Online German Publisher LLC 239 344-8953
1000 Nw 37th Pl Cape Coral (33993) ***(G-1371)***
Online Labels LLC (PA) 407 936-3900
2001 E Lake Mary Blvd Sanford (32773) ***(G-15366)***
Onlinewall 800 210-0194
169 Nw 36th St Miami (33127) ***(G-9655)***
Onnow.fm, Jacksonville Beach *Also called Levitech Services LLC* ***(G-6638)***
Onpoint Global 651 788-1274
8325 Ne 2nd Ave Ste 100 Miami (33138) ***(G-9656)***
Onsight Industries LLC 407 830-8861
900 Central Park Dr Sanford (32771) ***(G-15367)***
Onsite Rlble Forklift Svcs Inc 305 305-8638
714 E 28th St Hialeah (33013) ***(G-5288)***
Ontyte LLC 561 880-8920
3460 Fairlane Farms Rd # 15 Wellington (33414) ***(G-17857)***
Onvoi AVI Supp and Inspect Ser 805 312-3274
619 Airpark Rd Defuniak Springs (32435) ***(G-2841)***
Onyx Armor, Miami *Also called Onyx Protective Group Inc* ***(G-9657)***
Onyx Protective Group Inc 305 282-4455
7359 Nw 34th St Miami (33122) ***(G-9657)***
Oompha Inc 850 222-7210
1754 Thomasville Rd Tallahassee (32303) ***(G-16486)***
OP Yacht Services Corp 954 451-3677
2015 Sw 20th St Ste 220 Fort Lauderdale (33315) ***(G-3968)***
Opa-Locka Pallets Inc 305 681-8212
3180 Nw 131st St Opa Locka (33054) ***(G-11777)***
OPelle Enterprises Inc 954 942-7338
1471 Sw 5th Ct Pompano Beach (33069) ***(G-14111)***
Open House Magazine Inc 305 576-6011
505 Ne 30th St Apt 405 Miami (33137) ***(G-9658)***
Open International LLC 305 265-0310
13019 Mar St Coral Gables (33156) ***(G-2092)***
Open Magnetic Scanning Ltd 954 202-5097
4805 N Dixie Hwy Oakland Park (33334) ***(G-11282)***
Open Market Enterprises LLC 407 322-5434
3461 Parkway Center Ct Orlando (32808) ***(G-12440)***
Open Palm Press Inc 813 870-3839
3839 W Kennedy Blvd Tampa (33609) ***(G-17127)***
Openkm Usa LLC 407 257-2640
1715 Branchwater Trl Orlando (32825) ***(G-12441)***
Opensky Drones LLC 954 340-9125
12453 Nw 44th St Coral Springs (33065) ***(G-2199)***
Openwater Seafood LLC 407 440-0656
13435 S Orange Ave Orlando (32824) ***(G-12442)***
Operatons Prcrment Sup Chain S 954 960-5890
2501 Nw 34th Pl Ste B21b Pompano Beach (33069) ***(G-14112)***
Opie Choice LLC (PA) 352 331-3741
3870 Nw 83rd St Gainesville (32606) ***(G-4743)***
Opie Choice LLC 727 726-5157
22047 Us Highway 19 N Clearwater (33765) ***(G-1728)***
Opie Choice Network, Gainesville *Also called Opie Choice LLC* ***(G-4743)***
OPif- Our Plstic Is Fntstic 954 636-4228
698 1/2 Nw 16 Stunits E F Lauderhill (33311) ***(G-7737)***
Opinicus Textron Inc 813 792-9300
1827 Northpointe Pkwy Lutz (33558) ***(G-8008)***
Opko Curna LLC 305 575-4100
4400 Biscayne Blvd Miami (33137) ***(G-9659)***
Opko Health Inc (PA) 305 575-4100
4400 Biscayne Blvd Miami (33137) ***(G-9660)***
Opreme Beverage Corp 954 699-0669
5151 Corporate Way Jupiter (33458) ***(G-6775)***
Optek International, Largo *Also called Intuitos LLC* ***(G-7617)***
Optical Hong Kong 305 200-5522
6073 Nw 167th St Ste C20 Hialeah (33015) ***(G-5289)***
Optical Whl Opt Frmes Opt Sngl, Pembroke Pines *Also called Miami Eyeworks Inc* ***(G-13403)***
Optigrate Corporation 407 542-7704
562 S Econ Cir Oviedo (32765) ***(G-12840)***
Optima Associates Inc 877 371-1555
2469 W Us Highway 90 # 130 Lake City (32055) ***(G-7036)***
Optimal Station, Alachua *Also called Optimal Vending Systems LLC* ***(G-16)***
Optimal Vending Systems LLC 301 633-2353
22806 Nw County Road 241 Alachua (32615) ***(G-16)***
Optimum Power & Envmt Fla, Deerfield Beach *Also called Reynoso & Associates Inc* ***(G-2800)***
Optimum Spring Mfg Inc 904 567-5999
150 Hilden Rd Ste 316 Ponte Vedra (32081) ***(G-14258)***
Optimus Fleet LLC 407 590-5060
7550 Futures Dr Orlando (32819) ***(G-12443)***
Optoelectronics Inc 954 642-8997
160 W Camino Real Boca Raton (33432) ***(G-625)***
Optronic Laboratories LLC 407 422-3171
4632 36th St Orlando (32811) ***(G-12444)***
Oracle America Inc 888 595-6310
267 Harbor Blvd Port Charlotte (33954) ***(G-14310)***
Oracle America Inc 407 380-0058
3501 Quadrangle Blvd # 151 Orlando (32817) ***(G-12445)***
Oracle America Inc 407 458-1200
7453 T G Lee Blvd Orlando (32822) ***(G-12446)***
Oracle America Inc 813 287-1700
7453 T G Lee Blvd Orlando (32822) ***(G-12447)***
Oracle America Inc 305 260-7200
6505 Blue Lagoon Dr # 40 Miami (33126) ***(G-9661)***
Oracle Corporation 772 337-4141
1701 Se Hillmoor Dr D16 Port Saint Lucie (34952) ***(G-14431)***
Oracle Corporation 772 466-0704
2100 Nebraska Ave Fort Pierce (34950) ***(G-4513)***
Oracle Essence Inc 786 258-8153
1341 St Tropez Cir Weston (33326) ***(G-18275)***
Oracle Systems Corporation 407 458-1200
7453 T G Lee Blvd Orlando (32822) ***(G-12448)***
Oracle Systems Corporation 650 506-7000
2640 Golden Gate Pkwy Naples (34105) ***(G-10843)***
Oral Stericlean, Tampa *Also called 3b Global LLC* ***(G-16546)***
Oralbiolife Inc 305 401-2622
1521 Alton Rd Miami Beach (33139) ***(G-10218)***
Orange County Countertops 407 294-8677
2600 Pemberton Dr Apopka (32703) ***(G-159)***
Orange Park Machine Inc 904 269-1935
84 Industrial Loop N Orange Park (32073) ***(G-11836)***
Orange Peel Gazette Inc 407 892-5556
145 E 13th St Saint Cloud (34769) ***(G-14936)***
Orange State Steel Cnstr Inc 727 544-3398
6201 80th Ave N Pinellas Park (33781) ***(G-13716)***
Orange Sunshine Graphics Inc 954 797-7425
5051 S State Road 7 # 517 Davie (33314) ***(G-2450)***
Orbe Inc 954 534-2264
2310 Nw 30th Ct Oakland Park (33311) ***(G-11283)***
Orbeco-Hellige, Sarasota *Also called Tintometer Inc* ***(G-15568)***
Orbital Corporation of Tampa 813 782-7300
40421 Chancey Rd Ste 101 Zephyrhills (33542) ***(G-18622)***
Orbital Sciences LLC 703 406-5474
5335 N Courtenay Pkwy Merritt Island (32953) ***(G-8589)***
ORBSAT, Aventura *Also called Nextplat Corp* ***(G-267)***
Orbusneich Medical Inc 954 730-0711
5363 Nw 35th Ave Fort Lauderdale (33309) ***(G-3969)***
Orca Composites LLC 206 349-5300
1468 Northgate Blvd Sarasota (34234) ***(G-15771)***
Orchid Envy 941 485-1122
339 W Venice Ave Venice (34285) ***(G-17709)***
Orchid Island Juice Co Inc 772 465-1122
330 N Us Highway 1 Fort Pierce (34950) ***(G-4514)***
Orcom Labs Inc 321 773-0741
131 Tomahawk Dr Ste 9b Indian Harbour Beach (32937) ***(G-5805)***
Ord of Ahepa Ch 356 Daily & T 727 791-1040
2555 Enterprise Rd Ste 10 Clearwater (33763) ***(G-1729)***
Order Counter Com Point Svc S, Pensacola *Also called Ordercounter Inc* ***(G-13562)***
Ordercounter Inc 850 332-5540
9270 University Pkwy # 102 Pensacola (32514) ***(G-13562)***
Orellana Coatings Inc 305 389-4610
9447 Fontainebleau Blvd Miami (33172) ***(G-9662)***
Orellana Investments Inc 305 477-2817
2818 Nw 79th Ave Miami (33122) ***(G-9663)***
Organabio LLC 305 676-2586
7800 Sw 57th Ave Ste 225 South Miami (33143) ***(G-16041)***
Organic Amazon Corp 305 365-7811
104 Crandon Blvd Key Biscayne (33149) ***(G-6838)***
Organic Cane Company Inc 561 385-4081
923 Se Lincoln Ave Stuart (34994) ***(G-16193)***
Organizacion Marketing Mix LLC 407 924-2709
1006 Verona St Kissimmee (34741) ***(G-6946)***
Oria Lab LLC 786 302-8142
13140 Sw 134th St Ste 12 Miami (33186) ***(G-9664)***

ALPHABETIC

Oriental Packing Company Inc (PA) 305 235-1829
12221 Sw 104th Ter Miami (33186) *(G-9665)*

Oriental Red Apple LLC 646 853-1468
255 Park Blvd Miami (33126) *(G-9666)*

Oriflow 727 400-4881
2125 Range Rd Ste B Clearwater (33765) *(G-1730)*

Origin Pc LLC 305 971-1000
12400 Sw 134th Ct Ste 8 Miami (33186) *(G-9667)*

Original Impressions LLC 305 233-1322
2965 W Corp Lks Blvd Weston (33331) *(G-18276)*

Original Pnguin Direct Oprtions 305 592-2830
3000 Nw 107th Ave Doral (33172) *(G-3319)*

Original Seat Sack Company., Naples *Also called Youthful Innovations LLC* *(G-10946)*

Originates Inc 954 233-2500
20900 Ne 30th Ave Ste 707 Aventura (33180) *(G-269)*

Originclear Inc (PA) 323 939-6645
13575 58th St N Ste 200 Clearwater (33760) *(G-1731)*

Orion Dntl Sls Trning Repr LLC 888 674-6657
4721 Rockvale Dr Kissimmee (34758) *(G-6947)*

Orion Energy Systems Inc 920 892-5825
9143 Philips Hwy Ste 420 Jacksonville (32256) *(G-6342)*

Orion Engineered Systems, Jacksonville *Also called Orion Energy Systems Inc* *(G-6342)*

Orion Power Systems Inc (PA) 877 385-1654
2939 W Beaver St Jacksonville (32254) *(G-6343)*

Orion Press, Miami *Also called Print Bold Corp* *(G-9740)*

Orion Repair, Kissimmee *Also called Orion Dntl Sls Trning Repr LLC* *(G-6947)*

Orion Technologies LLC 407 476-2120
12605 Challenger Pkwy # 130 Orlando (32826) *(G-12449)*

Orion Travel Technologies Inc (PA) 407 574-6649
200 Celebration Pl # 840 Celebration (34747) *(G-1439)*

Orion Visual Group, Miami *Also called Print Pro Shop Inc* *(G-9742)*

Orka Cabinets Inc 954 907-2456
12022 Nw 47th St Coral Springs (33076) *(G-2200)*

Orkan18 ....855 675-2618
9835 Lake Worth Rd Ste 16 Lake Worth (33467) *(G-7224)*

Orlando Blinds Factory 407 697-0521
210 N Goldenrod Rd Ste 1 Orlando (32807) *(G-12450)*

Orlando Branding Agency LLC 407 692-8868
1035 Covington St Oviedo (32765) *(G-12841)*

Orlando Brewing Partners 407 843-6783
1401 W Gore St Ste 3 Orlando (32805) *(G-12451)*

Orlando Flores 305 898-2111
3841 Sw 92nd Ave Miami (33165) *(G-9668)*

Orlando Ice Cream Company, Orlando *Also called Muse Gelato Inc* *(G-12402)*

Orlando Ice Servive Corp 407 999-4940
410 27th St Orlando (32806) *(G-12452)*

Orlando Metal Fabrication Inc 407 850-4313
11516 Satellite Blvd Orlando (32837) *(G-12453)*

Orlando Metro Magazine, Tampa *Also called Metro Life Media Inc* *(G-17070)*

Orlando Mtal Bldg Erectors LLC 407 917-9762
17540 Se 294th Court Rd Umatilla (32784) *(G-17648)*

Orlando Novelty LLC (PA) 407 858-9499
1624 Premier Row Orlando (32809) *(G-12454)*

Orlando Novelty Wholesale, Orlando *Also called Orlando Novelty LLC* *(G-12454)*

Orlando Plating Co 407 843-1140
601 N Orange Blossom Trl Orlando (32805) *(G-12455)*

Orlando Post, Margate *Also called Trading Post of Central Fla* *(G-8157)*

Orlando Sentinnel Media Group, Orlando *Also called Sentinel Cmmnctons News Vntres* *(G-12584)*

Orlando Shutters Blinds & More, Lake Mary *Also called Orlando Shutters LLC* *(G-7098)*

Orlando Shutters LLC (PA) 407 495-5250
4300 W Lake Mary Blvd # 1 Lake Mary (32746) *(G-7098)*

Orlando Times Inc 407 841-3052
4403 Vineland Rd Ste B5 Orlando (32811) *(G-12456)*

Orlando Weekly, Orlando *Also called The Scranton Times L P* *(G-12655)*

Orlandos Forklift Service LLC 407 761-9104
3138 Natoma Way Orlando (32825) *(G-12457)*

Ormond Beach Clinical RES LLC 386 310-7462
1400 Hand Ave Ste L Ormond Beach (32174) *(G-12783)*

Ormond Beach Observer 386 492-2784
310 Wilmette Ave Ste 3 Ormond Beach (32174) *(G-12784)*

Ornamental Columns Statues Inc 239 482-3911
16179 S Tamiami Trl Fort Myers (33908) *(G-4352)*

Ornamntal Design Ironworks Inc 813 626-8449
4706 N Falkenburg Rd Tampa (33610) *(G-17128)*

Ornamntal Metal Specialist Inc 786 360-5727
7889 Nw 173rd St Hialeah (33015) *(G-5290)*

Ortega Custom Cabinets Inc 813 403-7101
7006 Hazelhurst Ct Tampa (33615) *(G-17129)*

Ortega Industries and Mfg 305 688-0090
13281 Nw 43rd Ave Opa Locka (33054) *(G-11778)*

Orthomerica Products Inc 407 290-6592
6333 N Orange Blossom Trl Orlando (32810) *(G-12458)*

Orthopedic Designs N Amer Inc 813 443-4905
5912 Breckenridge Pkwy F Tampa (33610) *(G-17130)*

Orthosensor Inc (HQ) 954 577-7770
1855 Griffin Rd Ste A310 Dania Beach (33004) *(G-2357)*

Orthotic Prsthtic Rhbltion As 352 331-3399
6608 Nw 9th Blvd Gainesville (32605) *(G-4744)*

Orvino Imports & Distrg Inc 954 785-3100
11927 W Sample Rd Coral Springs (33065) *(G-2201)*

Oryza Pharmaceuticals Inc 954 881-5481
4117 Nw 124th Ave Coral Springs (33065) *(G-2202)*

Osborne Metals 727 441-1703
324 S Madison Ave Clearwater (33756) *(G-1732)*

Oscar E Perez 786 442-6889
13901 Sw 26th Ter Miami (33175) *(G-9669)*

Osceola Farms Co (HQ) 561 655-6303
340 Royal Poinciana Way # 315 Palm Beach (33480) *(G-12939)*

Osceola Farms Co 561 924-7156
Us Highway 98 Hatton Hwy Pahokee (33476) *(G-12860)*

Osceola Press, Kissimmee *Also called Crain Ventures Inc* *(G-6909)*

Osceola Shopper, Kissimmee *Also called Sun Publications Florida Inc* *(G-6961)*

Osceola Shopper, Lakeland *Also called Sun Publications Florida Inc* *(G-7452)*

Osceola Star 407 933-0174
921 Emmett St Kissimmee (34741) *(G-6948)*

Osceola Woman Newspaper LLC 407 891-9771
111 E Monu Ave Unit 401 Kissimmee (34741) *(G-6949)*

Oscor Inc (HQ) 727 937-2511
3816 Desoto Blvd Palm Harbor (34683) *(G-13122)*

Osd Display, Orlando *Also called New Vision Display Inc* *(G-12413)*

OSG America LLC 813 209-0600
302 Knights Run Ave # 1200 Tampa (33602) *(G-17131)*

Osgood Industries LLC 813 448-9041
601 Burbank Rd Oldsmar (34677) *(G-11683)*

Osko Inc 305 599-7161
8085 Nw 90th St Medley (33166) *(G-8293)*

Osmi Inc (PA) 561 330-9300
7777 Glades Rd Ste 200 Boca Raton (33434) *(G-626)*

Ostara Usa LLC (PA) 813 666-8123
2720 S Falkenburg Rd Riverview (33578) *(G-14572)*

OSteen Plastic Inc 954 434-4921
17539 Sw 59th Ct Southwest Ranches (33331) *(G-16056)*

Ostrich Market Inc 954 873-1957
381 Dayton Blvd Melbourne (32904) *(G-8489)*

Otis Elevator Company 561 618-4831
5500 Village Blvd West Palm Beach (33407) *(G-18100)*

Otis Elevator Company 561 623-4594
11760 Us Highway 1 # 600 Palm Beach Gardens (33408) *(G-12996)*

Otis Elevator Company 305 816-5740
5381 Nw 33rd Ave Ste 103 Fort Lauderdale (33309) *(G-3970)*

Otoc LLC 813 265-8352
4035 Priory Cir Tampa (33618) *(G-17132)*

Ott Welding, Bonita Springs *Also called Burton JC Companies Inc* *(G-787)*

Ottica Dante Americas LLC 561 322-0186
10890 Haydn Dr Boca Raton (33498) *(G-627)*

Otus Corp Intl LLC 305 833-6078
8306 Mills Dr 222 Miami (33183) *(G-9670)*

Ouality Precast, Mulberry *Also called Quality Block & Supply Inc* *(G-10635)*

Ouhlala Gourmet Corp 305 774-7332
2655 S Le Jeune Rd # 1011 Coral Gables (33134) *(G-2093)*

Oum LLC 407 886-1511
531 Cooper Indus Pkwy Apopka (32703) *(G-160)*

Oumph, Lake Worth *Also called Future Foods LLC* *(G-7201)*

Our City Media of Florida LLC 954 306-1007
400 Swgrss Corp Pkwy 200c Sunrise (33325) *(G-16349)*

Our Seniors Guidecom Inc 904 655-2130
14286-19 Bch Blvd Ste 335 Jacksonville (32246) *(G-6344)*

Our Village Okeechobee LLC 863 467-0158
205 Ne 2nd St Okeechobee (34972) *(G-11613)*

Our Warehouse Inc 954 786-1234
2749 E Atlantic Blvd Pompano Beach (33062) *(G-14113)*

Ouro Custom Woodwork Inc 954 428-0735
12 Sw 9th St Deerfield Beach (33441) *(G-2776)*

Outback Series, The, Deland *Also called Pain Away LLC* *(G-2892)*

Outdoor America Images Inc (PA) 813 888-8796
4545 W Hillsborough Ave Tampa (33614) *(G-17133)*

Outdoor America Images Inc. 813 888-8796
13982 Nw 58th Ct Miami Lakes (33014) *(G-10334)*

Outdoor Images Central Fla Inc 407 825-9944
4061 Forrestal Ave Unit 2 Orlando (32806) *(G-12459)*

Outdoor Media Inc 305 529-1400
3195 Ponce De Leon Blvd # 300 Coral Gables (33134) *(G-2094)*

Outdoor Products LLC 352 473-0886
125 Sw 284th Ave Steinhatchee (32359) *(G-16106)*

Outform Inc (PA) 800 204-0524
82 Ne 26th St Unit 103 Miami (33137) *(G-9671)*

Outline Technologies Inc 904 858-9933
9920 Blakeford Mill Rd Jacksonville (32256) *(G-6345)*

Outlook International Electric, Sunrise *Also called BJ Burns Incorporated* *(G-16296)*

Outpost 30a LLC 850 909-0138
11 N Castle Harbour Dr F Inlet Beach (32461) *(G-5819)*

Outpost North Lake 352 669-2430
131 N Central Ave Umatilla (32784) *(G-17649)*

Output Printing Corp 813 228-8800
107 N Jefferson St Tampa (33602) *(G-17134)*

Outreach Corporation 888 938-7356
1208 E Kennedy Blvd Tampa (33602) *(G-17135)*

Outstanding Events Inc 772 463-5406
5380 Sw Landing Creek Dr Palm City (34990) *(G-13051)*

Overall-Honeycomb LLC (HQ) 941 756-8781
1950 Limbus Ave Sarasota (34243) *(G-15529)*

Overhead Door Corporation 850 474-9890
3395 Addison Dr Pensacola (32514) *(G-13563)*

Overseas Publishing Management, Virginia Gardens *Also called Distribuidora Continental SA (G-17822)*

Overseas Radio LLC 305 296-1630
3732 Flagler Ave Key West (33040) *(G-6879)*

Overstitch Inc 954 505-8567
4651 Sheridan St Ste 200 Hollywood (33021) *(G-5636)*

Overture Life Inc 323 420-6343
55 Merrick Way Ste 401 Coral Gables (33134) *(G-2095)*

Ovipost Inc 707 776-6108
635 A Rd Labelle (33935) *(G-6985)*

Owens Corning Sales LLC 863 291-3046
3327 Queens Cove Loop Winter Haven (33880) *(G-18453)*

Owens Corning Sales LLC 904 353-7361
1035 Talleyrand Ave Jacksonville (32206) *(G-6346)*

Owens Distributors Inc 407 302-8602
2850 W Airport Blvd Sanford (32771) *(G-15368)*

Own's Libby Ford, Tallahassee *Also called Pilkington North America Inc (G-16487)*

Oxbow Activated Carbon LLC, West Palm Beach *Also called Puragen LLC (G-18131)*

Oxbow Calcining LLC 580 874-2201
1601 Forum Pl Ph 2 West Palm Beach (33401) *(G-18101)*

Oxbow Calcining Usa Inc (HQ) 580 874-2201
1601 Forum Pl Ste 1400 West Palm Beach (33401) *(G-18102)*

Oxbow Carbon LLC (HQ) 561 907-5400
1601 Forum Pl Ste 1400 West Palm Beach (33401) *(G-18103)*

Oxbow Enterprises Intl LLC 561 907-5400
1601 Forum Pl Ste 1400 West Palm Beach (33401) *(G-18104)*

Oxendine Publishing Inc 352 373-6907
412 Nw 16th Ave Gainesville (32601) *(G-4745)*

Oxford Acquisition, Miami *Also called Miami Engrv Co-Oxford Prtg Co (G-9551)*

Oxigeno Nitrogeno Inc 954 659-3881
16200 Golf Club Rd Weston (33326) *(G-18277)*

Oxley Cabinet Warehouse Inc 786 377-4281
1031 Ives Dairy Rd Miami (33179) *(G-9672)*

Oxpecker Enterprise Inc 305 253-5301
12182 Sw 128th St Miami (33186) *(G-9673)*

Oxygen Development LLC (PA) 954 480-2675
1525 S Congress Ave Palm Springs (33406) *(G-13148)*

Oxygenix Mold and Odor LLC 850 926-5421
467 Parkside Cir Crawfordville (32327) *(G-2231)*

Oxzgen Inc 844 569-9436
40180 Us Highway 19 N Tarpon Springs (34689) *(G-17484)*

Oz Naturals LLC 561 602-2932
319 Clematis Ste 700 West Palm Beach (33401) *(G-18105)*

Ozinga South Florida Inc 305 594-2828
3905 Nw 107th Ave Ste 106 Doral (33178) *(G-3320)*

Ozinga South Florida Inc (PA) 786 422-4694
2401 College Ave Davie (33317) *(G-2451)*

Ozingaready Mix, Doral *Also called Ozinga South Florida Inc (G-3320)*

P & G Printing Group Inc 954 971-2511
2034 Mears Pkwy Margate (33063) *(G-8145)*

P & J Graphics Inc 813 626-3243
11407 Cerca Del Rio Pl Temple Terrace (33617) *(G-17541)*

P & L Creech Inc 386 547-4182
2960 S Nova Rd Daytona Beach (32119) *(G-2579)*

P & M Sheet Metal Corp 954 618-8513
4963 Frattina St Ave Maria (34142) *(G-249)*

P & S Logging Inc 904 845-4256
15864 County Road 108 Hilliard (32046) *(G-5472)*

P A Vivid Pathology (PA) 850 416-7780
5149 N 9th Ave Ste 122 Pensacola (32504) *(G-13564)*

P B C Central 407 648-2020
3450 Vineland Rd Ste B Orlando (32811) *(G-12460)*

P B C Cultural Counsel 561 471-2903
1555 Palm Bch Lakes Blvd West Palm Beach (33401) *(G-18106)*

P B C H Incorporated 239 567-5030
7941 Mercantile St Fort Myers (33917) *(G-4353)*

P D I S Inc 561 243-8442
2801 Rosselle St Jacksonville (32205) *(G-6347)*

P D P, Boca Raton *Also called Practical Design Products Co (G-639)*

P D Services, Oakland Park *Also called Powless Drapery Service Inc (G-11287)*

P P P, Doral *Also called Professional Pet Products Inc (G-3339)*

P S Analytical Inc 954 429-1577
1761 W Hillsboro Blvd Deerfield Beach (33442) *(G-2777)*

P S Research Corp 954 558-8727
3702 Nw 16th St Lauderhill (33311) *(G-7738)*

P S T Computers Inc 954 566-1600
2692 Sw 12th St Deerfield Beach (33442) *(G-2778)*

P T I, Miramar *Also called Propulsion Tech Intl LLC (G-10534)*

P&A Machine 407 275-5770
7220 Old Cheney Hwy Orlando (32807) *(G-12461)*

P&G Pavers Inc 561 716-5113
6671 W Indiantown Rd 50-2 Jupiter (33458) *(G-6776)*

P&L Machine & Tool Company Inc 727 863-0847
9704 Katy Dr Ste 2 Hudson (34667) *(G-5783)*

P&L Machine and Tool Co, Hudson *Also called Addtad Partners Inc (G-5761)*

P&S Industries LLC 954 975-3384
3635 Park Central Blvd N Pompano Beach (33064) *(G-14114)*

P'Kolino Studio, Miami *Also called PKolino LLC (G-9719)*

P3 Fleet LLC 904 549-5500
11950 New Kings Rd Jacksonville (32219) *(G-6348)*

P3d Creations LLC 407 801-9126
105 Candace Dr Unit 121 Maitland (32751) *(G-8068)*

PA C Publishing Inc 813 814-1505
850 Dunbar Ave Oldsmar (34677) *(G-11684)*

Paal Technologies Holdings Inc 954 368-5000
5387 N Nob Hill Rd Sunrise (33351) *(G-16350)*

Paas, Ocala *Also called Signature Brands LLC (G-11491)*

Pac Printing, Pinellas Park *Also called Process Automation Corporation (G-13724)*

Pac Seating Systems Inc 772 286-6670
3370 Sw 42nd Ave Palm City (34990) *(G-13052)*

Paca Foods LLC 813 628-8228
5212 Cone Rd Tampa (33610) *(G-17136)*

Pace Enclosures Inc 239 275-3818
12101 Crystal Condo Rd Fort Myers (33966) *(G-4354)*

Pace Machine & Tool Inc 561 747-5444
7986 Sw Jack James Dr Stuart (34997) *(G-16194)*

Pace Machine Tool Inc 248 960-9903
13564 Ingraham Blvd Port Charlotte (33981) *(G-14311)*

Pace Tech Inc 727 442-8118
2040 Calumet St Clearwater (33765) *(G-1733)*

Pacem Defense, Perry *Also called Amtec Less Lethal Systems Inc (G-13631)*

Pacemate LLC 305 322-5074
518 13th St W Bradenton (34205) *(G-1021)*

Pacer Electronics Florida Inc (PA) 941 378-5774
1555 Apex Rd Sarasota (34240) *(G-15772)*

Pacheco Creative Group Inc 305 541-1400
2164 Nw 19th Ave Miami (33142) *(G-9674)*

Pacific 305 785-9068
8526 Nw 70th St Miami (33166) *(G-9675)*

Pacific Arches Corporation 352 236-7787
1740 Se 18th St Ste 1302 Ocala (34471) *(G-11461)*

Pacific Coast Feather LLC (PA) 206 624-1057
901 W Yamato Rd Ste 250 Boca Raton (33431) *(G-628)*

Pacific Die Cast Inc (PA) 813 316-2221
12802 Commodity Pl Tampa (33626) *(G-17137)*

Pacific Limited, Miami *Also called Pacific Ltd Corp (G-9677)*

Pacific Limited International 305 358-1900
825 Brickell Bay Dr # 17 Miami (33131) *(G-9676)*

Pacific Ltd Corp 305 358-1900
825 Brickell Bay Dr # 17 Miami (33131) *(G-9677)*

Pacific Pavers Inc 941 238-7854
6326 5th Street Cir E Bradenton (34203) *(G-1022)*

Pacira Biosciences Inc (PA) 813 553-6680
5401 W Kennedy Blvd Lncln Tampa (33609) *(G-17138)*

Pacira Pharmaceuticals Inc 813 553-6680
5401 W Kennedy Blvd Lncln Lincoln Tampa (33609) *(G-17139)*

Pack4u LLC 407 857-2871
7531 Currency Dr Orlando (32809) *(G-12462)*

Packaging & Resources Inc 954 288-9678
19245 S Gardenia Ave Weston (33332) *(G-18278)*

Packaging Alternatives Corp (PA) 352 867-5050
4130 Sw 13th St Ocala (34474) *(G-11462)*

Packaging Corporation America 386 792-0810
5939 Se Us Highway 41 Jasper (32052) *(G-6646)*

Packaging Corporation America 407 299-1300
3785 Bryn Mawr St Orlando (32808) *(G-12463)*

Packaging Corporation America 813 626-7006
1450 Massaro Blvd Tampa (33619) *(G-17140)*

Packaging Corporation America 863 967-0641
2155 42nd St Nw Winter Haven (33881) *(G-18454)*

Packaging Corporation America 904 757-8140
659 Eastport Rd Jacksonville (32218) *(G-6349)*

Packaging Corporation America 305 770-3439
15600 Nw 15th Ave Ste A Miami (33169) *(G-9678)*

Packaging Corporation America 305 685-8956
3500 Nw 110th St Miami (33167) *(G-9679)*

Packaging Machines, Sarasota *Also called MDC Engineering Inc (G-15742)*

Packard & Company Inc 941 451-8201
787 Commerce Dr Venice (34292) *(G-17710)*

Pad Printing Technology Corp 941 739-8667
1835 59th Ter E Bradenton (34203) *(G-1023)*

Pad Printing Technology Group 941 739-8667
1835 59th Ter E Bradenton (34203) *(G-1024)*

Padgett Communications Inc 727 323-5800
5005 W Laurel St Ste 103 Tampa (33607) *(G-17141)*

Padgett Manufacturing Inc 941 756-8566
2915 62nd Ave E Bradenton (34203) *(G-1025)*

Padgetts Pulpwood Inc 904 282-5112
3745 Old Jennings Rd Middleburg (32068) *(G-10408)*

Page Golfs Yellow Directory 305 378-8038
7251 Sw 152nd St Palmetto Bay (33157) *(G-13216)*

Page One LLC 833 467-2431
1231 Stirling Rd Ste 107 Dania (33004) *(G-2340)*

Pageantry Magazine, Longwood *Also called Pageantry Tlent Entrmt Svcs In (G-7930)*

Pageantry Tlent Entrmt Svcs In 407 260-2262
1855 W State Road 434 Longwood (32750) *(G-7930)*

Pagnifique, Miami *Also called Farartis LLC (G-9133)*

Pagnifique USA, Miramar *Also called Panamerican Food LLC (G-10524)*

Pain Away LLC 800 215-8739
1515 Detrick Ave Deland (32724) *(G-2892)*

Painassist Inc 248 875-4222
6199 54th St S Saint Petersburg (33715) *(G-15148)*

Painting & Specialty Coatings, Bartow *Also called RSR Industrial Coatings Inc (G-324)*

Paints & Coatings Inc 239 997-6645
17660 East St North Fort Myers (33917) *(G-11065)*

Paints N Cocktails Inc 954 514-7383
14710 Ne 2nd Ct Miami (33161) *(G-9680)*

Pair ODice Brewing Co LLC 727 755-3423
4400 118th Ave N Ste 205 Clearwater (33762) *(G-1734)*

Paj Innovative Concepts Inc 813 659-0505
2804 Sydney Rd Plant City (33566) *(G-13788)*

Paksource Global, Sarasota *Also called Profile Packaging (G-15788)*

Pal-King Inc 904 334-8797
1300 W Beaver St Jacksonville (32209) *(G-6350)*

Palafox Marine Inc 850 438-9354
490 S L St Pensacola (32502) *(G-13565)*

Palanjian Enterprises Inc 850 244-2848
420 Mary Esther Cut Off N Fort Walton Beach (32548) *(G-4600)*

Palatka Daily News, Palatka *Also called Daily News Inc (G-12865)*

Palatka Tube Plant, Palatka *Also called Caraustar Indus Cnsmr Pdts Gro (G-12863)*

Palatka Welding Shop Inc 386 328-1507
1301 Madison St Palatka (32177) *(G-12876)*

Paleo Bakehouse Inc 786 253-1051
12581 Sw 134th Ct Ste 101 Miami (33186) *(G-9681)*

Paleo Simplified LLC 813 446-5969
605 S Bayshore Blvd Safety Harbor (34695) *(G-14793)*

Pall Aeropower Corporation (HQ) 727 849-9999
10540 Ridge Rd Ste 100 New Port Richey (34654) *(G-10980)*

Pall Aeropower Corporation 727 849-9999
1750 Filter Dr Deland (32724) *(G-2893)*

Pall Filtration and Sep 386 822-8000
1750 Filter Dr Deland (32724) *(G-2894)*

Palladio Beauty Group, Hollywood *Also called Pb Group LLC (G-5638)*

Palladio Beauty Group LLC 954 922-4311
3912 Pembroke Rd Hollywood (33021) *(G-5637)*

Palladium Graphics, Tampa *Also called HOB Corporation (G-16919)*

Pallet Consultants LLC (HQ) 954 946-2212
810 Nw 13th Ave Pompano Beach (33069) *(G-14115)*

Pallet Creations Inc 239 601-0606
421 18th St Ne Naples (34120) *(G-10844)*

Pallet Depot LLC 863 686-6245
6300 New Tampa Hwy Lakeland (33815) *(G-7405)*

Pallet Direct Inc 888 433-1727
5660 Cypress Hollow Way Naples (34109) *(G-10845)*

Pallet Doctor Inc 904 444-2514
221 N Hogan St Ste 371 Jacksonville (32202) *(G-6351)*

Pallet Dude LLC 941 720-1667
7952 Fruitville Rd Sarasota (34240) *(G-15773)*

Pallet Enterprises of Florida 305 836-3204
7525 Nw 37th Ave Unit D Miami (33147) *(G-9682)*

Pallet Ex Jacksonville Inc 904 781-2500
7779 Hammond Blvd Jacksonville (32220) *(G-6352)*

Pallet Exchange Inc 386 734-0133
1219 Doris St Orange City (32763) *(G-11808)*

Pallet Express Inc 813 752-1600
1503 Turkey Creek Rd Plant City (33566) *(G-13789)*

Pallet Express of Jkvl Inc 904 781-2500
7779 Hammond Blvd Jacksonville (32220) *(G-6353)*

Pallet Holdings LLC (PA) 561 367-0009
1200 N Federal Hwy # 207 Boca Raton (33432) *(G-629)*

Pallet Industries Inc (HQ) 954 935-5804
1815 S Powerline Rd Deerfield Beach (33442) *(G-2779)*

Pallet Logix Corp 407 834-2336
1655 Jackson St Longwood (32750) *(G-7931)*

Pallet One of Mobile LLC 251 960-1107
6001 Foxtrot Ave Bartow (33830) *(G-319)*

Pallet Recall Inc 941 727-1944
6755 33rd St E Sarasota (34243) *(G-15530)*

Pallet Services Inc (PA) 813 754-7719
1705 Turkey Creek Rd Plant City (33566) *(G-13790)*

Pallet Services of Plant City, Plant City *Also called Pallet Services Inc (G-13790)*

Pallet Services Plant City LLC 813 752-1600
1705 Turkey Creek Rd Plant City (33566) *(G-13791)*

Pallet Solutions Inc 305 801-8314
7525 Nw 37th Ave Unit D Miami (33147) *(G-9683)*

Palletone Inc (HQ) 800 771-1147
6001 Foxtrot Ave Bartow (33830) *(G-320)*

Palletone of Texas LP (HQ) 903 628-5695
1470 Us Highway 17 S Bartow (33830) *(G-321)*

Pallets Plus Inc 813 759-6355
2606 N Airport Rd Plant City (33563) *(G-13792)*

Pallets To Go Inc 305 654-0303
1691 Nw 23rd St Miami (33142) *(G-9684)*

Palm Bch Pssport Pblctons Mdia, West Palm Beach *Also called Passport Pblcations Media Corp (G-18113)*

Palm Beach Aggregates LLC 561 795-6550
20125 Southern Blvd Loxahatchee (33470) *(G-7974)*

Palm Beach Btry Ventures LLC (PA) 561 881-8900
1250 Northlake Blvd Lake Park (33403) *(G-7132)*

Palm Beach Cast Stone Inc 561 835-4085
809 N Railroad Ave West Palm Beach (33401) *(G-18107)*

Palm Beach Cstm Woodworks LLC 561 575-5335
1315 53rd St Ste 5 Mangonia Park (33407) *(G-8097)*

Palm Beach Daily News, West Palm Beach *Also called Palm Beach Newspapers Inc (G-18111)*

Palm Beach Embroidery USA Inc 561 506-6307
8645 N Military Trl West Palm Beach (33410) *(G-18108)*

Palm Beach Iron Works Inc 561 683-1816
7768 Belvedere Rd West Palm Beach (33411) *(G-18109)*

Palm Beach Junior Clg Prnt Shp 561 969-0122
4200 S Congress Ave Lake Worth (33461) *(G-7225)*

Palm Beach Limestone, West Palm Beach *Also called Palm Beach Cast Stone Inc (G-18107)*

Palm Beach Liquidation Company (PA) 561 659-0210
1000 N Dixie Hwy Ste C West Palm Beach (33401) *(G-18110)*

Palm Beach Media Group Inc 239 434-6966
3066 Tamiami Trl N # 102 Naples (34103) *(G-10846)*

Palm Beach Newspapers Inc 561 820-3800
2751 S Dixie Hwy West Palm Beach (33405) *(G-18111)*

Palm Beach Post, West Palm Beach *Also called Pathfnders Palm Bch-Mrtin Cnty (G-18114)*

Palm Beach Precious Metals 561 662-6025
3200 Frost Rd Palm Springs (33406) *(G-13149)*

Palm Beach Smoothies Com Inc 561 379-8647
150 N Us Highway 1 Ste 5 Tequesta (33469) *(G-17551)*

Palm Beach Trim Inc 561 588-8746
6900 W State Road 84 Davie (33317) *(G-2452)*

Palm Beach Woodwork Co Inc 561 844-8818
1101 53rd Ct S Ste B Mangonia Park (33407) *(G-8098)*

Palm Coast Observer LLC 386 447-9723
1 Florida Park Dr N # 103 Palm Coast (32137) *(G-13084)*

Palm Furniture Systems Inc 305 888-7009
8181 Nw 91st Ter Ste 2 Medley (33166) *(G-8294)*

Palm Labs Adhesives LLC 321 710-4850
3063 Enterprise Rd Ste 31 Debary (32713) *(G-2639)*

Palm Pheon Music Pubg LLC 305 705-2405
15421 W Dixie Hwy North Miami Beach (33162) *(G-11154)*

Palm Print Inc 561 833-9661
919 N Dixie Hwy West Palm Beach (33401) *(G-18112)*

Palm Printing, Lakewood Ranch *Also called Stewart-Hedrick Inc (G-7487)*

Palm Prnting/Printers Ink Corp 239 332-8600
5900 Enterprise Pkwy Fort Myers (33905) *(G-4355)*

Palm Prtg Strgc Solutions LLC 239 332-8600
2306 Dr Mrtn Luther King Fort Myers (33901) *(G-4356)*

Palm Tree Computer Systems Inc (PA) 407 359-3356
19 E Broadway St Oviedo (32765) *(G-12842)*

Palmas Printing Inc (PA) 321 984-4451
200 East Dr Melbourne (32904) *(G-8490)*

Palmate LLC 352 508-7800
200 County Road 448 Tavares (32778) *(G-17520)*

Palmer Manufacturing Co LLC 772 287-7770
3651 Se Commerce Ave Stuart (34997) *(G-16195)*

Palmetto Canning Company 941 722-1100
3601 Us Highway 41 N Palmetto (34221) *(G-13183)*

Palmetto Printing Inc 305 253-2444
3065 Ohio St Miami (33133) *(G-9685)*

Palmland Paper Co Inc 954 764-6910
708 Ne 2nd Ave Fort Lauderdale (33304) *(G-3971)*

Pamatian Group Inc (PA) 407 291-8387
997 W Kennedy Blvd Ste A1 Orlando (32810) *(G-12464)*

Pamplona Foods Inc 305 970-4120
9600 Sw 122nd Ct Miami (33186) *(G-9686)*

Pan American Chemical Co., Miami *Also called Sheila Shine Inc (G-9878)*

Pan American Cnstr Plant 305 477-5058
8000 Nw 74th St Medley (33166) *(G-8295)*

Pan American Graphic Inc 305 885-1962
9745 Nw 80th Ave Hialeah Gardens (33016) *(G-5446)*

Panama City Concrete Inc 850 851-3637
1119 Lindenwood Dr Panama City (32405) *(G-13292)*

Panama City News Herald (HQ) 850 747-5000
501 W 11th St Panama City (32401) *(G-13293)*

Panama City News Herald 850 863-1111
2 Eglin Pkwy Ne Fort Walton Beach (32548) *(G-4601)*

Panama City Pallet Inc 850 769-1040
1706 Maple Ave Panama City (32405) *(G-13294)*

Panama City Tint Center 850 640-0167
526 E 6th St Panama City (32401) *(G-13295)*

Panama City Yard, Panama City *Also called Martin Marietta Materials Inc (G-13285)*

Panama Jack Inc...407 843-8110
230 Ernestine St Orlando (32801) *(G-12465)*

Panama Pallets Co Inc..850 769-1040
1706 Maple Ave Panama City (32405) *(G-13296)*

Panamco LLC..305 856-7100
701 Nw 62nd Ave Ste 800 Miami (33126) *(G-9687)*

Panamerican Food LLC (PA)...305 594-5704
10491 N Commerce Pkwy Miramar (33025) *(G-10524)*

Panamtech Inc (PA)..954 587-3769
700 Nw 70th Ter Plantation (33317) *(G-13876)*

Panapastry LLC..305 883-1557
9001 Nw 97th Ter Ste M Medley (33178) *(G-8296)*

Panda Moni Yum Lake City LL..352 494-5193
2888 W Us Highway 90 Lake City (32055) *(G-7037)*

Panda Printing LLC...239 970-9727
16010 Old 41 N Unit 102 Naples (34110) *(G-10847)*

Pandia Press Inc..352 789-8156
312 Forest Rd Mount Dora (32757) *(G-10609)*

Pane Rustica Bakery & Cafe..813 902-8828
3225 S Macdill Ave Tampa (33629) *(G-17142)*

Panel Armor Products LLC...407 960-5946
1970 Corporate Sq Unit B Longwood (32750) *(G-7932)*

Panelfold Inc...305 688-3501
10700 Nw 36th Ave Miami (33167) *(G-9688)*

Paneltronics Incorporated...305 823-9777
11960 Nw 87th Ct Ste 1 Hialeah (33018) *(G-5291)*

Pangenex Corporation (PA)..352 346-4045
9950 Princess Palm Ave Tampa (33619) *(G-17143)*

Panhandle Paint & Dctg LLC..850 596-9248
8103 Panama City Bch Pkwy Panama City Beach (32407) *(G-13335)*

Panoff Publishing Inc..954 377-7777
6261 Nw 6th Way Ste 100 Fort Lauderdale (33309) *(G-3972)*

Panoptex Technologies Inc...407 412-0222
6555 Sanger Rd Ste 100 Orlando (32827) *(G-12466)*

Pantaleon Commodities Corp..786 542-6333
601 Brickell Key Dr # 60 Miami (33131) *(G-9689)*

Panther Printing Inc...239 936-5050
11580 Marshwood Ln Fort Myers (33908) *(G-4357)*

Panther Printing LLC (PA)...239 936-5050
5101 N Federal Hwy Pompano Beach (33064) *(G-14116)*

Panther Printing LLC...954 651-7766
551 Fairway Dr Pompano Beach (33069) *(G-14117)*

Panther Software Inc..800 856-8729
10800 Biscayne Blvd # 201 Miami (33161) *(G-9690)*

Pantograms Inc..813 839-5697
4537 S Dale Mabry Hwy Tampa (33611) *(G-17144)*

Pantograms Mfg Co Inc...813 839-5697
4537 S Dale Mabry Hwy Tampa (33611) *(G-17145)*

Pantropic Power Inc..954 797-7972
1881 W State Road 84 # 103 Fort Lauderdale (33315) *(G-3973)*

Papa Johns Peanuts Inc...904 389-2511
2555 W Beaver St Jacksonville (32254) *(G-6354)*

Papenfuss Holdings Inc...239 775-9090
11430 Tamiami Trl E Naples (34113) *(G-10848)*

Paper Bag Manufacturers Inc...305 685-1100
4131 Nw 132nd St Opa Locka (33054) *(G-11779)*

Paper Chase...561 641-5319
6626 Via Rienzo Lake Worth (33467) *(G-7226)*

Paper Converter, Odessa *Also called Eastern Ribbon & Roll Corp (G-11548)*

Paper Fish Printing Inc...239 481-3555
17251 Alico Center Rd # 5 Fort Myers (33967) *(G-4358)*

Paper Free Technology Inc..515 270-1505
10626 Windsmont Ct Lehigh Acres (33936) *(G-7819)*

Paper Machine Services Inc...608 365-8095
9010 Old Hickory Cir Fort Myers (33912) *(G-4359)*

Paper Palm LLC...407 647-3328
621 Commonwealth Ave Orlando (32803) *(G-12467)*

Paper Pushers of America Inc..386 872-7025
2430 S Atlantic Ave Ste C Daytona Beach (32118) *(G-2580)*

Papers Unlimited Plus Inc (PA).......................................215 947-1155
161 Remo Pl Palm Beach Gardens (33418) *(G-12997)*

Papila Design Inc...407 240-2992
701 W Landstreet Rd Orlando (32824) *(G-12468)*

Papous Craft Distillery LLC..813 766-9539
605 N Pinellas Ave Tarpon Springs (34689) *(G-17485)*

Par, Lutz *Also called Psychlgcal Assssment Rsrces In (G-8012)*

Para Todo Mal Mezcal LLC..786 837-3119
2100 Coral Way Ste 703 Miami (33145) *(G-9691)*

Parabel Inc...321 409-7415
1901 S Hbr Cy Blvd Ste 60 Melbourne (32901) *(G-8491)*

Parachute Laboratories, Deland *Also called Jco Metals Inc (G-2878)*

Paradigm Leaders LLC...850 441-3289
7946 Front Beach Rd Panama City Beach (32407) *(G-13336)*

Paradigm Parachute and Defense....................................928 580-9013
4040 Ashland Ave Pensacola (32534) *(G-13566)*

Paradigm Plastics, Panama City Beach *Also called Paradigm Leaders LLC (G-13336)*

Paradigm Plastics Inc...727 797-3555
912 3rd St N Ste D Safety Harbor (34695) *(G-14794)*

Paradigm Precision, Stuart *Also called Turbocombustor Technology Inc (G-16243)*

Paradigm Precision LLC..954 634-8012
2400 E Commercial Blvd Fort Lauderdale (33308) *(G-3974)*

Paradise Inc (PA)..813 752-1155
5110 W Poe Ave Tampa (33629) *(G-17146)*

Paradise Air Fresh LLC..561 972-0375
3029 Sw 42nd Ave Palm City (34990) *(G-13053)*

Paradise Archtctral Panels Stl, Miami *Also called Paradise Awnings Corporation (G-9692)*

Paradise Awnings Corporation...305 597-5714
4310 Nw 36th Ave Miami (33142) *(G-9692)*

Paradise Building Mtls LLC...407 267-3378
665 Youngstown Pkwy # 268 Altamonte Springs (32714) *(G-61)*

Paradise Cable Industries..941 488-6092
723 Commerce Dr Unit H Venice (34292) *(G-17711)*

Paradise Cstm Screening & EMB......................................954 566-9096
2180 Sw 71st Ter Davie (33317) *(G-2453)*

Paradise EMB & Silkscreen Inc...305 595-6441
8801 Sw 129th St Miami (33176) *(G-9693)*

Paradise Embroidery, Lauderdale Lakes *Also called Gsg Group Inc (G-7715)*

Paradise Label Inc..863 860-8779
4021 S Frontage Rd Plant City (33566) *(G-13793)*

Paradise Oaks Woodworking Inc.......................................863 206-0858
218 E Bearss Ave Ste 378 Tampa (33613) *(G-17147)*

Paradise Pool Care & Co LLC (PA)...................................239 338-7715
2605 27th St Sw Lehigh Acres (33976) *(G-7820)*

Paradise Wldg Cstm Fabrication......................................239 961-8864
3888 Mannix Dr Ste 310 Naples (34114) *(G-10849)*

Paradox Marine, Fort Lauderdale *Also called Edgewater Technologies Inc (G-3785)*

Paraflow Energy Solutions LLC..713 239-0336
6501 Congress Ave Ste 100 Boca Raton (33487) *(G-630)*

Paragon Globl Sup Slutions LLC.......................................813 745-9902
301 W Platt St Ste 98 Tampa (33606) *(G-17148)*

Paragon Plastics Inc...321 631-6212
1401 Armstrong Dr Titusville (32780) *(G-17604)*

Paragon Printers, Melbourne *Also called QP Consulting Inc (G-8506)*

Paragon Products Inc..407 302-9147
2300 Old Lake Mary Rd Sanford (32771) *(G-15369)*

Paragon Water Systems Inc...727 538-4704
13805 Monroe Park Tampa (33635) *(G-17149)*

Parallel Florida LLC...404 920-4890
2203 N Lois Ave Ste M275 Tampa (33607) *(G-17150)*

Paramount Depot LLC..786 275-0107
7975 Nw 56th St Doral (33166) *(G-3321)*

Paramount Digital Pubg LLC...813 489-5029
123 W Bloomingdale Ave # 3 Brandon (33511) *(G-1099)*

Paramount Electronic Mfg Co...954 781-3755
1551 Sw 6th Ter Boca Raton (33486) *(G-631)*

Paramount Industries Inc (PA)..954 781-3755
1020 Sw 10th Ave Ste 6 Pompano Beach (33069) *(G-14118)*

Paramount Marketing Inc..352 608-8801
138 Juniper Loop Cir Ocala (34480) *(G-11463)*

Paramount Mold LLC...954 772-2333
1701 W Cypress Creek Rd Fort Lauderdale (33309) *(G-3975)*

Paramount Molded Products Inc.......................................954 772-2333
1701 W Cypress Creek Rd Fort Lauderdale (33309) *(G-3976)*

Paramount Sales & Consulting, Pompano Beach *Also called Paramount Industries Inc (G-14118)*

Paramount Stoneworks, Holly Hill *Also called Encore Stone Products LLC (G-5513)*

Parasol Films Inc..954 478-8661
9503 Nw 73rd St Tamarac (33321) *(G-16539)*

Parcus Medical LLC...941 755-7965
6423 Parkland Dr Sarasota (34243) *(G-15531)*

Parinto Global Enterprises LLC..305 606-3107
5213 Nw 79th Ave Doral (33166) *(G-3322)*

Paris Ink Inc...561 990-1194
1020 Holland Dr Ste 119 Boca Raton (33487) *(G-632)*

Park Central Inc..850 547-1660
704 W Highway 90 Bonifay (32425) *(G-775)*

Park Lake Printers, Orlando *Also called Florida Hospital Assn MGT Corp (G-12161)*

Park Place Manufacturing Inc...863 382-0126
454 Park St Sebring (33870) *(G-15934)*

Park Place Truss Inc..863 382-0126
500 Park St Sebring (33870) *(G-15935)*

Park Place Truss & Design Inc..863 382-0126
206 W Center Ave Sebring (33870) *(G-15936)*

Park Plus Florida Inc...954 929-7511
1111 Old Griffin Rd Dania (33004) *(G-2341)*

Park Row Printing, Plantation *Also called Crompco Inc (G-13840)*

Parker Boatworks Inc...954 585-1059
617 Nw 7th Ave Fort Lauderdale (33311) *(G-3977)*

Parker Davis Hvac Intl Inc..305 513-4488
3250 Nw 107th Ave Doral (33172) *(G-3323)*

Parker Machinery Co Inc...904 356-5038
424 Copeland St Jacksonville (32204) *(G-6355)*

Parker Plastics, Hollywood *Also called Gar Industries Corp (G-5581)*

Parker Protective Products LLC..800 879-0329
1965 Ne 148th St North Miami (33181) *(G-11115)*

Parker Research Corporation..727 796-4066
2642 Enterprise Rd Clearwater (33763) *(G-1735)*

Parker-Hannifin Corporation 305 470-8800
7400 Nw 19th St Ste A Miami (33126) *(G-9694)*

Parker-Hannifin Corporation 239 304-1000
3580 Shaw Blvd Naples (34117) *(G-10850)*

Parkinson Enterprises Inc 863 688-7900
1840 Harden Blvd Lakeland (33803) *(G-7406)*

Parklanders, Coral Springs *Also called Data Publishers Inc* *(G-2147)*

Parkside Publishing LLC 888 386-1115
1633 W Classical Blvd Delray Beach (33445) *(G-2993)*

Parkson Corporation (HQ) 954 974-6610
1401 W Cypress Creek Rd # 100 Fort Lauderdale (33309) *(G-3978)*

Parkstone International Inc 954 205-0075
110 E Broward Blvd # 170 Fort Lauderdale (33301) *(G-3979)*

Parkway Dental Services LLC 800 257-0400
9914 State Road 52 Hudson (34669) *(G-5784)*

Parkway Printing Inc 239 936-6970
6371 Arc Way Ste 1 Fort Myers (33966) *(G-4360)*

Parodi General Group Corp 954 306-1098
5431 Nw 50th Ct Coconut Creek (33073) *(G-2000)*

Parras Plastic Inc 305 972-9537
13894 Sw 139th Ct Miami (33186) *(G-9695)*

Parrillo Inc 386 767-8011
1644 S Ridgewood Ave South Daytona (32119) *(G-16026)*

Parrish Inc 386 985-4879
5498 Aragon Ave De Leon Springs (32130) *(G-2626)*

Parthenon Prints Inc 850 769-8321
909 W 39th St Panama City (32405) *(G-13297)*

Parti Line International Inc 504 522-0300
9219 133rd Ave Unit 1e Largo (33773) *(G-7655)*

Parts Cage Inc 904 373-7800
280 Business Park Cir # 412 Saint Augustine (32095) *(G-14870)*

Parts Central Inc 850 547-1660
704 W Highway 90 Bonifay (32425) *(G-776)*

Partsvu LLC 239 643-2292
829 Airport Pulling Rd N Naples (34104) *(G-10851)*

Pas Reform North America LLC 904 358-0355
2550 Cabot Commerce Dr Jacksonville (32226) *(G-6356)*

Pasa Services Inc 305 594-8662
13015 Nw 38th Ave Opa Locka (33054) *(G-11780)*

Pasco Vision Center 813 788-7656
38038 North Ave Zephyrhills (33542) *(G-18623)*

Passion Labels & Packaging 941 312-5003
1223 Tallevast Rd Sarasota (34243) *(G-15532)*

Passport Pblcations Media Corp 561 615-3900
1555 Palm Beach Lakes Blv West Palm Beach (33401) *(G-18113)*

Passur Aerospace Inc (PA) 203 622-4086
3452 Lake Lynda Dr # 190 Orlando (32817) *(G-12469)*

Passur Aerospace Inc 631 589-6800
5750 Major Blvd Ste 530 Orlando (32819) *(G-12470)*

Pastrana Prime LLC 407 470-9339
524 Madrigal Ct Orlando (32825) *(G-12471)*

Pat Clark Custom Woodworking L 941 376-1387
5180 Island Date St Sarasota (34232) *(G-15774)*

Patco Electronics, Clearwater *Also called Creating Tech Solutions LLC* *(G-1556)*

Pathfinder Shirts 407 865-6530
865 Sunshine Ln Altamonte Springs (32714) *(G-62)*

Pathfnders Palm Bch-Mrtin Cnty 561 820-4262
2751 S Dixie Hwy West Palm Beach (33405) *(G-18114)*

Pathway Holdings LLC 813 514-7899
5002 Us Highway 41 N Palmetto (34221) *(G-13184)*

Patient Care America, Pompano Beach *Also called Diabetic Care Rx LLC* *(G-13996)*

Patient Portal Tech Inc (PA) 877 779-6627
2000 Pga Blvd Ste 4440 North Palm Beach (33408) *(G-11181)*

Patio Products Mfg LLC 813 664-0158
9706 E Us Highway 92 Tampa (33610) *(G-17151)*

Patio Products Mfg Inc 813 681-3806
509 S Larry Cir Brandon (33511) *(G-1100)*

Patlon Industries Inc 305 255-7744
13913 Sw 119th Ave Miami (33186) *(G-9696)*

Patrice Inc 941 359-2577
1747 Independence Blvd E7 Sarasota (34234) *(G-15775)*

Patrick German Industries Inc 727 251-3015
1302 Wallwood Dr Brandon (33510) *(G-1101)*

Patrick Industries Inc 941 556-6311
6805 15th St E Sarasota (34243) *(G-15533)*

Patrick Industries Inc 941 556-6311
6805 15th St E Sarasota (34243) *(G-15534)*

Patrick Industries Inc 239 283-0800
2443 Sw Pine Island Rd Cape Coral (33991) *(G-1372)*

Patriot Building & Cnstr Inc 863 634-8489
11175 Muller Rd Fort Pierce (34945) *(G-4515)*

Patriot Fire Defense Inc 321 313-2265
4451 Enterprise Ct Melbourne (32934) *(G-8492)*

Patriot Foundation Systems LLC 352 668-4842
30427 Commerce Dr San Antonio (33576) *(G-15250)*

Patriot Person Defense 813 470-8025
1604 White Dove Ct Brandon (33510) *(G-1102)*

Patriot Press Inc 407 625-7516
14141 Lake Price Dr Orlando (32826) *(G-12472)*

Patriot Stairs LLC 407 489-6248
736 Red Coach Ave Deltona (32725) *(G-3050)*

Patriot Welding Inc 954 798-8819
151 Sw 5th St W Pompano Beach (33060) *(G-14119)*

Patten Co Inc 707 826-2887
1803 Madrid Ave Lake Worth Beach (33461) *(G-7260)*

Patten Group, Lake Worth Beach *Also called Patten Co Inc* *(G-7260)*

Pattern Grading & Marker Svcs 305 495-9963
3650 Sw 141st Ave Miramar (33027) *(G-10525)*

Patterson Publishing LLC 863 701-2707
214 Traders Aly Lakeland (33801) *(G-7407)*

Patti Marine Enterprises Inc 850 453-1282
306 S Pinewood Ln Pensacola (32507) *(G-13567)*

Pattison Sign Lease (us) LLC 407 345-8010
7576 Kingspointe Pkwy # 18 Orlando (32819) *(G-12473)*

Patty King Inc 305 817-1888
2740 W 81st St Hialeah (33016) *(G-5292)*

Patty King Production Plant, Hialeah *Also called Patty King Inc* *(G-5292)*

Pattys On Main LLC 941 650-9080
1400 Main St Sarasota (34236) *(G-15776)*

Paul Himber Inc 561 586-3741
5324 Georgia Ave West Palm Beach (33405) *(G-18115)*

Paul Wales Inc 352 371-2120
131 Se 10th Ave Gainesville (32601) *(G-4746)*

Paul White Logging Inc 850 379-8651
65 South Hosford (32334) *(G-5757)*

Paul Wong 863 465-1114
1475 Jersey St Ne Lake Placid (33852) *(G-7145)*

Paulas Dves Sign TS Other Prtg 239 673-8923
1122 Se 21st Ln Cape Coral (33990) *(G-1373)*

Pauls Twing Dsptch Cntl Fla I 407 323-4446
1919 W 1st St Sanford (32771) *(G-15370)*

Pavemax 386 206-3113
1120 Enterprise Ct Daytona Beach (32117) *(G-2581)*

Pavement Marking & Signs Inc 786 431-6788
2039 Opa Locka Blvd Opa Locka (33054) *(G-11781)*

Paver Action Inc 954 868-1468
3741 Ne 18th Ave Pompano Beach (33064) *(G-14120)*

Paver Paradise LLC 561 843-3031
2468 Sw Cameo Blvd Port St Lucie (34953) *(G-14481)*

Paver Systems LLC (HQ) 561 844-5202
7167 Interpace Rd Riviera Beach (33407) *(G-14657)*

Paver Systems LLC 407 859-9117
39 E Landstreet Rd Orlando (32824) *(G-12474)*

Paver Technologies LLC 772 213-8905
2110 Captains Walk Vero Beach (32963) *(G-17784)*

Paver Way LLC 321 303-0968
160 N Spring Trl Altamonte Springs (32714) *(G-63)*

Pavers & Bricks Services Corp 305 986-2544
749 Ne 81st St Miami (33138) *(G-9697)*

Pavers By Leandro Peralta Corp 941 323-7338
2142 Dodge Ave Sarasota (34234) *(G-15777)*

Pavers Inc 352 754-3875
14497 Ponce De Leon Blvd Brooksville (34601) *(G-1187)*

Pavers Professional Inc 239 878-6989
4086 Stillwood Dr Jacksonville (32257) *(G-6357)*

Pavers Solutions Inc 754 551-1924
201 Nw 43rd St Deerfield Beach (33064) *(G-2780)*

Paverscape Inc 407 381-1022
2914 Dean Ridge Rd Orlando (32825) *(G-12475)*

Paverscape Solutions LLC 850 497-5557
21 Professional Ct Miramar Beach (32550) *(G-10570)*

Paversealingcom Corp 407 951-6437
1225 Windsor Ave Longwood (32750) *(G-7933)*

Paveway Systems Inc 386 659-1316
114 Indian Lakes Ln Florahome (32140) *(G-3610)*

Pavilion Furniture, Hialeah *Also called Tuuci Worldwide LLC* *(G-5388)*

Paw Inc 904 724-0310
8330 Atlantic Blvd Jacksonville (32211) *(G-6358)*

Paw Print Co 561 753-5588
1593 Trotter Ct West Palm Beach (33414) *(G-18116)*

Pawtitas, Miami *Also called Cafco LLC* *(G-8879)*

Pax Ctholic Communications Inc 305 638-9729
1779 Nw 28th St Miami (33142) *(G-9698)*

Paxen Publishing LLC (PA) 321 425-3030
2194 Highway A1a Ste 208 Indian Harbour Beach (32937) *(G-5806)*

Payfin Enterprises, Miramar Beach *Also called Renovation Flooring LLC* *(G-10572)*

Payless Brick Pavers LLC 904 629-7436
8719 Derry Dr Jacksonville (32244) *(G-6359)*

Paylocity Holding Corporation 407 878-6585
615 Crescent Executive Ct Lake Mary (32746) *(G-7099)*

Payo LLC 786 368-8655
12481 N Stonebrook Cir Davie (33330) *(G-2454)*

Payton America Inc 954 428-3326
1805 S Powerline Rd # 109 Deerfield Beach (33442) *(G-2781)*

Payton Group International, Deerfield Beach *Also called Payton America Inc* *(G-2781)*

Pb Group LLC 954 922-4311
3912 Pembroke Rd Hollywood (33021) *(G-5638)*

Pb Holdco LLC 772 465-6006
3901 Saint Lucie Blvd Fort Pierce (34946) *(G-4516)*

Pbc Pavers Borba Co 407 296-7727
1841 S Kirkman Rd # 1311 Orlando (32811) *(G-12476)*

Pbcw Shutters and More, Mangonia Park Also called Palm Beach Cstm Woodworks
LLC *(G-8097)*

Pbg Golf Restaurant, West Palm Beach Also called K and G Food Services LLC *(G-18044)*

Pbi/Gordon Corp 850 478-2770
8809 Ely Rd Pensacola (32514) *(G-13568)*

PC Masters Corp 305 582-5595
5951 Nw 151st St Ste 35 Miami Lakes (33014) *(G-10335)*

PC of Titusville Inc 321 267-1161
701 Columbia Blvd Titusville (32780) *(G-17605)*

PCA, Pompano Beach Also called Printing Corp of Americas Inc *(G-14147)*

PCA, Tampa Also called Packaging Corporation America *(G-17140)*

Pca/Jacksonville 336, Jacksonville Also called Packaging Corporation America *(G-6349)*

PCA/Miami Gardens 350, Miami Also called Packaging Corporation America *(G-9678)*

PCA/Supply Services 302c, Orlando Also called Packaging Corporation America *(G-12463)*

Pca/Valdosta 645a, Jasper Also called Packaging Corporation America *(G-6646)*

PCA/Winter Haven 394, Winter Haven Also called Packaging Corporation America *(G-18454)*

PCC Print Shop, Inc., Pensacola Also called Abeka Print Shop Inc *(G-13430)*

PCF, Pensacola Also called Publishers Crcltion Flfilment *(G-13587)*

PCG, Jacksonville Also called Pinnacle Cmmncations Group LLC *(G-6372)*

PCI, Rockledge Also called Precision Circuits Inc *(G-14739)*

PCI Communications Inc 941 729-5202
1202 Gary Ave Unit 113 Ellenton (34222) *(G-3512)*

Pcm and S L Plota Co LLC 727 547-6277
8016 118th Ave Largo (33773) *(G-7656)*

Pcm Products Inc 321 267-7500
1225 White Dr Titusville (32780) *(G-17606)*

Pcp Tactical LLC 772 473-3472
3895 39th Sq Vero Beach (32960) *(G-17785)*

Pcs Phosphate/White Springs, White Springs Also called White Springs AG Chem
Inc *(G-18307)*

Pcsi, Sanford Also called Pre-Cast Specialties Inc *(G-15373)*

Pd Partners, Tampa Also called Product Dev Partners LLC *(G-17188)*

PDC 386 322-2808
4480 Eastport Park Way Port Orange (32127) *(G-14343)*

PDM LLC 317 605-6656
147 Athenian Way Tarpon Springs (34689) *(G-17486)*

Pdma Corporation 813 621-6463
5909 Hampton Oaks Pkwy C Tampa (33610) *(G-17152)*

Pdr of The Gables, Fort Lauderdale Also called Relu Co *(G-4014)*

Pe Manufacturing Company Fla 727 823-8172
11400 47th St N Ste A Clearwater (33762) *(G-1736)*

Peace Millwork Co Inc 305 573-6222
3535 Nw 50th St Miami (33142) *(G-9699)*

Peak Electronics Inc 305 888-1588
7255 Nw 68th St Ste 8 Miami (33166) *(G-9700)*

Peak Nutritional Products LLC 813 884-4989
5525 Johns Rd Ste 905 Tampa (33634) *(G-17153)*

Peak Performance Nutrients Inc 561 266-1038
1505 Poinsettia Dr Ste 4 Delray Beach (33444) *(G-2994)*

Peak Sheet Metal Solutions Inc 954 775-6393
5283 Sw Leeward Ln Palm City (34990) *(G-13054)*

Peaktop Technologies Inc 561 598-6005
1727 Okeechobee Rd West Palm Beach (33409) *(G-18117)*

Pearce Logging LLC 386 365-1880
9335 Nw 148th Trl Lake Butler (32054) *(G-7004)*

Pearcey Enterprise 904 235-3096
7806 N 52nd St Tampa (33617) *(G-17154)*

Pearl Academy LLC 904 619-6419
450 Busch Dr Unit 6 Jacksonville (32218) *(G-6360)*

Pearson Group LLC 786 498-3532
3115 Nw 135th St Opa Locka (33054) *(G-11782)*

Pearsons Ready-Mix Con Inc 386 294-3637
968 S State Road 51 Mayo (32066) *(G-8185)*

Peartree Cabinets & Design LLC 941 377-7655
1635 12th St Sarasota (34236) *(G-15778)*

Peavy Enterprises Inc 863 297-6513
4204 Recker Hwy Winter Haven (33880) *(G-18455)*

Ped-Stuart Corporation 352 754-6001
15351 Flight Path Dr Brooksville (34604) *(G-1188)*

Pedano Custom Furniture Inc 904 704-9329
10617 Coleman Rd Jacksonville (32257) *(G-6361)*

Pedicraft Inc 904 348-3170
4134 Saint Augustine Rd Jacksonville (32207) *(G-6362)*

Pedronis Cast Stone Inc 904 783-1690
5169 Edgewood Ct Jacksonville (32254) *(G-6363)*

Peek Traffic Corporation 941 366-8770
6408 Parkland Dr Ste 102 Sarasota (34243) *(G-15535)*

Peekaboo Organics LLC 305 527-7162
8918 Abbott Ave Surfside (33154) *(G-16398)*

Peeks Mobile App Corp 407 931-3878
3955 Golden Finch Way Kissimmee (34746) *(G-6950)*

Peerless Instrument Co Inc 954 921-6006
2030 Coolidge St Hollywood (33020) *(G-5639)*

Peerless Wind Systems 516 249-6900
8681 Hawkwood Bay Dr Boynton Beach (33473) *(G-895)*

Pegasus Aerospace 850 376-0991
290 Vinings Way Blvd # 6103 Destin (32541) *(G-3075)*

Pegasus Clean Air Mtr Cars Inc 954 682-2000
2400 W Cypress Creek Rd Fort Lauderdale (33309) *(G-3980)*

Pegasus Laboratories Inc (HQ) 850 478-2770
8809 Ely Rd Pensacola (32514) *(G-13569)*

Pegasus Water Systems, Cape Coral Also called Action Manufacturing & Sup Inc *(G-1296)*

Pegbroad Data System, Jacksonville Also called Southeastern Peg Bd Prtrs Inc *(G-6488)*

Peggy Jennings Design, Saint Petersburg Also called PJ Designs Inc *(G-15151)*

Pei Shores Inc 407 523-2899
4100 Silver Star Rd Ste C Orlando (32808) *(G-12477)*

Peixoto, Miami Also called Rme Studio Inc *(G-9812)*

Pelican International Inc 727 388-9895
6140 Ulmerton Rd Clearwater (33760) *(G-1737)*

Pelican Press, Sarasota Also called Observer Media Group Inc *(G-15767)*

Pelican Pumps, West Palm Beach Also called Channel Industries Inc *(G-17965)*

Pelican Water Systems, Deland Also called Enviro Water Solutions LLC *(G-2868)*

Pelican Wire, Naples Also called Wire Experts Group Inc *(G-10940)*

Pelican Woodworks Inc 904 687-5759
4975 Moultrie Reserve Ct Saint Augustine (32086) *(G-14871)*

Pelliccione Builders Sup Inc 941 334-3014
17056 Wayzata Ct North Fort Myers (33917) *(G-11066)*

Pelliconi Florida LLC (HQ) 407 855-6984
2501 Principal Row Orlando (32837) *(G-12478)*

Pem-Air LLC 954 321-8726
5921 Sw 44th Ct Davie (33314) *(G-2455)*

Pem-Air Turbine Eng Svcs LLC 954 900-9956
16300 Flight Path Dr Brooksville (34604) *(G-1189)*

Pemberton Inc 407 831-6688
103 Highline Dr Longwood (32750) *(G-7934)*

Pembroke Office Industries LLC 954 589-1329
1500 S 66th Ave Hollywood (33023) *(G-5640)*

Pembroke Pines FL Readymix, Pembroke Pines Also called Cemex Materials LLC *(G-13380)*

Pemco, Clearwater Also called Pe Manufacturing Company Fla *(G-1736)*

Pemco, Boca Raton Also called Paramount Electronic Mfg Co *(G-631)*

Pemco, Hialeah Also called Petroleum Equipment and Mfg Co *(G-5294)*

Pen Power, Tampa Also called Granite Services Intl Inc *(G-16889)*

Pena General Welding Inc 786 255-2153
4788 Sw 75th Ave Miami (33155) *(G-9701)*

Pendulum One Inc 561 844-8169
6555 Garden Rd Ste 13 Riviera Beach (33404) *(G-14658)*

Penek Chemical Industries Inc 954 978-6501
4100 N Powerline Rd Z5 Pompano Beach (33073) *(G-14121)*

Penguin Door Company, Jacksonville Also called Penguin Door Holding Co LLC *(G-6364)*

Penguin Door Holding Co LLC 904 540-4450
2903 Burke St Jacksonville (32254) *(G-6364)*

Penguin Random House LLC 305 206-8715
8950 Sw 74th Ct Ste 2010 Miami (33156) *(G-9702)*

Peniel Inc 305 594-2739
11844 Sw 27th St Miramar (33025) *(G-10526)*

Peninsula Metal Finishing Inc 407 291-1023
2550 Dinneen Ave Orlando (32804) *(G-12479)*

Peninsula Steel Inc 813 473-8133
4504 Sydney Rd Plant City (33566) *(G-13794)*

Peninsula Steel Inc (HQ) 956 795-1966
4504 Sydney Rd Plant City (33566) *(G-13795)*

Peninsula Tissue Corporation 305 863-0704
2630 Nw 72nd Ave Miami (33122) *(G-9703)*

Penngear LLC 215 968-2403
1134 Old Dominion Rd Gainesville (32612) *(G-4747)*

Penny Hoarder, The, Saint Petersburg Also called Taylor Media LLC *(G-15210)*

Pensacola Orthtc & Prostetic 850 478-7676
5855 Creek Station Dr Pensacola (32504) *(G-13570)*

Pensacola Sign & Graphics Inc 850 433-7878
3711 N Palafox St Pensacola (32505) *(G-13571)*

Pensacola Voice Inc 850 434-6963
213 E Yonge St Pensacola (32503) *(G-13572)*

Pensacola Wood Treating Co 850 433-1300
1813 E Gadsden St Pensacola (32501) *(G-13573)*

Penstripe Graphics 904 726-0200
4251 University Blvd S # 402 Jacksonville (32216) *(G-6365)*

Pentacles Energy GP LLC 786 552-9931
1600 Ponce De Leon Blvd Coral Gables (33134) *(G-2096)*

Pentair Flow Technologies 904 538-0894
8952 Western Way Jacksonville (32256) *(G-6366)*

Pentair LLC 386 469-0566
3060 Prfmce Cir Ste 2 Deland (32724) *(G-2895)*

Pentair Union Engineering N.A., Daytona Beach Also called Union Engineering N Amer
LLC *(G-2615)*

Pepper Tree 941 922-2662
715 N Wa Blvd Ste B Sarasota (34236) *(G-15779)*

Peppertree Press LLC 941 922-2662
6341 Yellow Wood Pl Sarasota (34241) *(G-15780)*

Pepsi Beverages Company 407 241-4110
7701 Southland Blvd Orlando (32809) *(G-12480)*

Pepsi Bottling Group 863 452-9920
1006 W Cornell St Avon Park (33825) *(G-284)*

Pepsi Bottling Group Inc 863 687-7605
   4100 Frontage Rd S Lakeland (33815) *(G-7408)*
Pepsi St Pete 727 527-8113
   4451 34th St N Saint Petersburg (33714) *(G-15149)*
Pepsi-Cola, Lakeland Also called Pepsi Bottling Group Inc *(G-7408)*
Pepsi-Cola, Medley Also called Pepsico Inc *(G-8297)*
Pepsi-Cola Bottling Co Tampa 239 643-4642
   1171 Industrial Blvd Naples (34104) *(G-10852)*
Pepsi-Cola Bottling Co Tampa (HQ) 813 971-2550
   11315 N 30th St Tampa (33612) *(G-17155)*
Pepsi-Cola Bottling Co Tampa 941 378-1058
   7881 Fruitville Rd Sarasota (34240) *(G-15781)*
Pepsi-Cola Bottling Co Tampa 407 857-3301
   1700 Directors Row Orlando (32809) *(G-12481)*
Pepsi-Cola Bottling Co Tampa 239 337-2011
   3625 Mrtin Lther King Blv Fort Myers (33916) *(G-4361)*
Pepsi-Cola Bottling Co Tampa 727 942-3664
   5406 Whippoorwill Dr Holiday (34690) *(G-5503)*
Pepsi-Cola Bottling Co Tampa 407 826-5929
   7501 Monetary Dr Orlando (32809) *(G-12482)*
Pepsi-Cola Btlg Ft Ldrdl-Palm 561 848-1000
   7305 Garden Rd Riviera Beach (33404) *(G-14659)*
Pepsi-Cola Metro Btlg Co Inc 904 733-1627
   5829 Pepsi Pl Jacksonville (32216) *(G-6367)*
Pepsi-Cola Metro Btlg Co Inc 407 354-5800
   7380 W Sand Lake Rd # 230 Orlando (32819) *(G-12483)*
Pepsi-Cola Metro Btlg Co Inc 352 376-8276
   6335 Nw 18th Dr Gainesville (32653) *(G-4748)*
Pepsi-Cola Metro Btlg Co Inc 863 551-4500
   5023 Recker Hwy Winter Haven (33880) *(G-18456)*
Pepsi-Cola Metro Btlg Co Inc 352 629-8911
   525 Sw 16th St Ocala (34471) *(G-11464)*
Pepsi-Cola Metro Btlg Co Inc 321 242-2984
   3951 Sarno Rd Melbourne (32934) *(G-8493)*
Pepsi-Cola Metro Btlg Co Inc 772 464-6150
   3620 Crossroads Pkwy Fort Pierce (34945) *(G-4517)*
Pepsico, Jacksonville Also called Pepsi-Cola Metro Btlg Co Inc *(G-6367)*
Pepsico, Saint Petersburg Also called Pepsi St Pete *(G-15149)*
Pepsico, Naples Also called Pepsi-Cola Bottling Co Tampa *(G-10852)*
Pepsico, Avon Park Also called Pepsi Bottling Group *(G-284)*
Pepsico, Fort Pierce Also called Pepsi-Cola Metro Btlg Co Inc *(G-4517)*
Pepsico, Tallahassee Also called Refreshment Services Inc *(G-16493)*
Pepsico Inc 305 593-7500
   8701 Nw 93rd St Medley (33178) *(G-8297)*
Pepsico Inc 407 933-5542
   1650 S Poinciana Blvd Kissimmee (34758) *(G-6951)*
Pepsico Beverage Distributors 305 537-4477
   1000 Nw 57th Ct Miami (33126) *(G-9704)*
Pepsico Latin America Beverage 305 537-4477
   1000 Nw 57th Ct Ste 800 Miami (33126) *(G-9705)*
Peralta Group Inc 954 502-8100
   4566 N Hiatus Rd Sunrise (33351) *(G-16351)*
Perch Security Inc 844 500-1810
   4110 George Rd Ste 200 Tampa (33634) *(G-17156)*
Perez Industries Inc 239 992-2444
   26364 Old 41 Rd Bonita Springs (34135) *(G-812)*
Perfect Brick Pavers Inc 727 534-2506
   5626 Quist Dr Port Richey (34668) *(G-14370)*
Perfect Care, Orlando Also called Ncg Medical Systems Inc *(G-12409)*
Perfect Copy & Print Inc 727 743-0913
   6541 44th St N Ste 6002 Pinellas Park (33781) *(G-13717)*
Perfect Oil Inc 954 984-8944
   2900 W Sample Rd Pompano Beach (33073) *(G-14122)*
Perfect Pavers South Fla LLC 954 779-1855
   5809 N Andrews Way Fort Lauderdale (33309) *(G-3981)*
Perfect Reflections Inc 813 991-4361
   7708 Avocet Dr Zephyrhills (33544) *(G-18624)*
Perfectus Pet Food LLC 800 774-3296
   3300 Oakwood Blvd Hollywood (33020) *(G-5641)*
Performance Boats Inc 305 956-9549
   2050 Ne 153rd St North Miami Beach (33162) *(G-11155)*
Performance Cnc Corp 786 334-6445
   5535 Nw 161st St Miami Lakes (33014) *(G-10336)*
Performance Coatings Inc 850 733-0082
   3749 Gulf Breeze Pkwy Gulf Breeze (32563) *(G-4889)*
Performance Designs Inc 386 738-2224
   1300 E Intl Speedway Blvd Deland (32724) *(G-2896)*
Performance Machining Svcs Inc 850 469-9106
   4161 Warehouse Ln Pensacola (32505) *(G-13574)*
Performance Powder Coating 407 339-4000
   416 Commerce Way Longwood (32750) *(G-7935)*
Performance Pumps Inc 407 339-6700
   321 Oleander Way Casselberry (32707) *(G-1427)*
Performance Sales and Svc Inc 863 465-2814
   1130 Us Highway 27 N Lake Placid (33852) *(G-7146)*
Performance Technology 2000 .... 772 463-1056
   1501 Se Decker Ave # 129 Stuart (34994) *(G-16196)*
Performnce Glzing Slutions LLC 305 975-3717
   7239 Nw 54th St Miami (33166) *(G-9706)*

Perfumeland 407 354-3342
   5216 Vanguard St Orlando (32819) *(G-12484)*
Perfumery, The, Englewood Also called Essential Oil University LLC *(G-3530)*
Perii Inc 321 253-2269
   2755 N Bnana Rver Dr Ste Merritt Island (32952) *(G-8590)*
Perii Software, Merritt Island Also called Perii Inc *(G-8590)*
Peripheral Services Inc 813 854-1181
   103 Pine Ave S Oldsmar (34677) *(G-11685)*
Perkins Power, Doral Also called Southeast Power Group Inc *(G-3370)*
Perkins Power Corp 904 278-9919
   5820 Nw 84th Ave Doral (33166) *(G-3324)*
Perl Inc 352 726-2483
   5009 S Florida Ave Inverness (34450) *(G-5833)*
Perma Cap, Davie Also called Kleen Wheels Corporation *(G-2430)*
Permacraft Sign & Trophies Co, South Daytona Also called Parrillo Inc *(G-16026)*
Permasafe Prtctive Catings LLC 866 372-9622
   6855 Lyons Tech Cir Ste 1 Coconut Creek (33073) *(G-2001)*
Permasteelisa North Amer Corp 305 265-4405
   703 Nw 62nd Ave Ste 950 Miami (33126) *(G-9707)*
Permatile Roofing, Lakeland Also called Advanced Alum Polk Cnty Inc *(G-7266)*
Perpetual Marketing Assoc Inc (PA) 813 949-9385
   25126 State Road 54 Lutz (33559) *(G-8009)*
Perri Brothers and Associates 305 887-8686
   9001 Nw 97th Ter Medley (33178) *(G-8298)*
Perry Baromedical Corporation (HQ) 561 840-0395
   3750 Prospect Ave Riviera Beach (33404) *(G-14660)*
Perry Composites LLC 850 584-8400
   1290 Houck Rd Perry (32348) *(G-13648)*
Perry Ellis International Inc (HQ) 305 592-2830
   3000 Nw 107th Ave Doral (33172) *(G-3325)*
Perry Fiberglas Products Inc 321 609-9036
   5415 Village Dr Rockledge (32955) *(G-14737)*
Perry Newspapers Inc 850 584-5513
   123 S Jefferson St Perry (32347) *(G-13649)*
Perry Precast Inc 386 294-2710
   232 Se Industrial Pk Cir Mayo (32066) *(G-8186)*
Personal Brands LLC 855 426-7765
   508 Sw 12th Ave Deerfield Beach (33442) *(G-2782)*
Pestwest Usa LLC 941 358-1983
   7135 16th St E Ste 124 Sarasota (34243) *(G-15536)*
Pet & Feed Store, Jacksonville Also called BRT Oakleaf Pet Inc *(G-5958)*
Pet Doc FL LLC 407 437-6614
   1630 Sand Key Cir Oviedo (32765) *(G-12843)*
Pet Pages, Sarasota Also called T V HI Lites Penny Saver Inc *(G-15848)*
Pet Services of Florida LLC 352 746-6888
   3404 N Lecanto Hwy Beverly Hills (34465) *(G-369)*
Pete Peterson Signs Inc 352 625-2307
   11094 Ne Highway 314 Silver Springs (34488) *(G-16007)*
Peter Fogel 561 245-5252
   8108 Summer Shores Dr Delray Beach (33446) *(G-2995)*
Peter Printer Inc 305 558-0147
   1355 W 49th St Hialeah (33012) *(G-5293)*
Peter T Amann 561 848-2770
   8111 Garden Rd Ste G West Palm Beach (33404) *(G-18118)*
Peterbrooke Choclat Fctry LLC 904 273-7878
   880 State Rd A1a Ste 4 1 A Ponte Vedra Beach (32082) *(G-14276)*
Peters Structural Products 863 229-5275
   1320 Hidden Creek Ct Winter Haven (33880) *(G-18457)*
Petersen Industries Inc 863 676-1493
   4000 State Road 60 W Lake Wales (33859) *(G-7169)*
Petersen Metals, Hudson Also called Clear Horizon Ventures Company *(G-5766)*
Peterson Enterprises LLC 386 456-3400
   12502 158th Ter Mc Alpin (32062) *(G-8189)*
Peterson Manufacturing LLC 941 371-4989
   155 Cattlemen Rd Sarasota (34232) *(G-15782)*
Petes Seal Coating 857 251-1912
   2300 Ne 15th Ter Pompano Beach (33064) *(G-14123)*
Petit Custom Wood Works 954 200-3111
   3673 W Valley Green Dr Davie (33328) *(G-2456)*
Petite Beaute, Miami Also called Desire Fragrances Inc *(G-9024)*
Petlift S & B Mfg Inc 941 346-2211
   6012 31st St E Bradenton (34203) *(G-1026)*
Petnet Solutions Inc 813 627-0022
   9204 Florida Palm Dr Tampa (33619) *(G-17157)*
Petroheral, Doral Also called Heralpin Usa Inc *(G-3245)*
Petroimage, Belleview Also called Petroleum Group LLC *(G-365)*
Petroleum Containment Inc 904 358-1700
   8873 Western Way Jacksonville (32256) *(G-6368)*
Petroleum Equipment and Mfg Co 305 558-9573
   2185 W 76th St Hialeah (33016) *(G-5294)*
Petroleum Group LLC 352 304-5500
   6432 Se 115th Ln Belleview (34420) *(G-365)*
Petroleum Marine LLC 561 422-9018
   15985 Meadow Wood Dr West Palm Beach (33414) *(G-18119)*
Petrosol Processing & Refining 305 442-7400
   2655 S Le Jeune Rd # 1003 Miami (33134) *(G-9708)*
Petrotech Services Inc 813 248-0743
   1807 E 2nd Ave Tampa (33605) *(G-17158)*

Petrotech Services Inc (PA)....813 248-0743
4041 Maritime Blvd Tampa (33605) ***(G-17159)***
Petruj Chemical Corp....305 556-1271
8055 Nw 98th St Hialeah Gardens (33016) ***(G-5447)***
Petti, Vince, Hallandale Beach *Also called South Broward Brace Inc* ***(G-4974)***
Pettit Racing, Riviera Beach *Also called Excellent Performance Inc* ***(G-14620)***
Pettit Tools & Supplies Inc....954 781-2640
4391 Ne 11th Ave Pompano Beach (33064) ***(G-14124)***
Pfa Publishing....727 512-5814
6020 Shore Blvd S Gulfport (33707) ***(G-4900)***
Pfaff Engraving, Miami Lakes *Also called Pfaffco Inc* ***(G-10337)***
Pfaffco Inc....305 635-0986
14329 Commerce Way Miami Lakes (33016) ***(G-10337)***
Pfci LLC....239 435-3575
4610 Enterprise Ave Naples (34104) ***(G-10853)***
Pfi, Lake Wales *Also called Pipeline Fabricators Inc* ***(G-7170)***
Pfi Inc....407 822-4499
607 Savage Ct Longwood (32750) ***(G-7936)***
Pfmc Bayer Limited Partnership....850 244-1310
257 W Miracle Strip Pkwy Mary Esther (32569) ***(G-8179)***
Pg5 Industries LLC....786 256-0896
15604 Sw 78th Pl Palmetto Bay (33157) ***(G-13217)***
Pgh Industries Ltd....847 849-0800
1016 Bel Air Dr Highland Beach (33487) ***(G-5462)***
Pgms, Miramar *Also called Pattern Grading & Marker Svcs* ***(G-10525)***
PGT American Inc (PA)....813 962-4400
5330 Ehrlich Rd Ste 102 Tampa (33624) ***(G-17160)***
PGT Custom Windows Doors, North Venice *Also called PGT Industries Inc* ***(G-11216)***
PGT Escrow Issuer Inc....941 480-1600
1070 Technology Dr North Venice (34275) ***(G-11215)***
PGT Industries Inc (HQ)....941 480-1600
1070 Technology Dr North Venice (34275) ***(G-11216)***
PGT Innovations Inc....941 480-1600
3440 Technology Dr North Venice (34275) ***(G-11217)***
PGT Innovations Inc (PA)....941 480-1600
1070 Technology Dr North Venice (34275) ***(G-11218)***
Phantom Products Inc....321 690-6729
474 Barnes Blvd Rockledge (32955) ***(G-14738)***
Phantom Sales Group Inc....888 614-1232
1550 Centennial Blvd Bartow (33830) ***(G-322)***
Phantom Technologies Inc....407 265-2567
2280 N Ronald Reagan Blvd # 103 Longwood (32750) ***(G-7937)***
Phantom Usa LLC....863 353-5972
101 Shepard Ave Dundee (33838) ***(G-3436)***
Pharma Resources Inc....973 780-5241
380 S State Road 434 Altamonte Springs (32714) ***(G-64)***
Pharmachem, Opa Locka *Also called World Perfumes Inc* ***(G-11800)***
Pharmacy Automation Systems, Largo *Also called Q E M Inc* ***(G-7665)***
Pharmacy Automtn Systems LLC....727 544-6522
8790 66th Ct N Pinellas Park (33782) ***(G-13718)***
Pharmacy Hn Llc....786 307-0509
3501 Nw 67th St Ste B Miami (33147) ***(G-9709)***
Pharmalab Enterprises Inc (PA)....305 821-4002
14501 Nw 60th Ave Miami Lakes (33014) ***(G-10338)***
Pharmalink Inc....800 257-3527
8285 Bryan Dairy Rd # 200 Largo (33777) ***(G-7657)***
Pharmamed Global Distributors, Fort Lauderdale *Also called Pharmamed USA Inc* ***(G-3982)***
Pharmamed USA Inc....954 533-4462
3778 Sw 30th Ave Fort Lauderdale (33312) ***(G-3982)***
Pharmaseal LLC....561 840-0050
3330 Fairchild Grdns Ave Palm Beach Gardens (33420) ***(G-12998)***
Pharmatech LLC (PA)....954 581-7881
4131 Sw 47th Ave Ste 1403 Davie (33314) ***(G-2457)***
Pharmatech LLC....954 629-2444
4131 Sw 47th Ave Ste 1405 Davie (33314) ***(G-2458)***
Pharmatech Pharmatech LLC....954 583-8778
3597 Nw 19th St Fort Lauderdale (33311) ***(G-3983)***
Pharmaworks LLC....727 232-8200
2346 Success Dr Odessa (33556) ***(G-11569)***
Pharmco Laboratories Inc....321 268-1313
3520 South St Titusville (32780) ***(G-17607)***
Phase Integration LLC....877 778-8885
815 S Main St Jacksonville (32207) ***(G-6369)***
Phasetronics Inc (PA)....727 573-1819
1600 Sunshine Dr Clearwater (33765) ***(G-1738)***
Pheasant Run Wind LLC....561 691-7171
700 Universe Blvd Juno Beach (33408) ***(G-6666)***
Phelps Dodge Intl Corp (HQ)....305 648-7888
9850 Nw 41st St Ste 200 Doral (33178) ***(G-3326)***
Phelps Motorsports LLC....239 417-2042
2255 Linwood Ave Naples (34112) ***(G-10854)***
Phg Kendall LLC....954 392-8788
4651 Sheridan St Ste 480 Hollywood (33021) ***(G-5642)***
PHI CHI Foundation Inc....561 526-3401
740 Sw 50th Ter Margate (33068) ***(G-8146)***
Phidal Inc....786 288-0339
2875 Ne 191st St Ste 704 Aventura (33180) ***(G-270)***
Phil & Brenda Johnson Inc....813 623-5478
5609 E Hillsborough Ave Tampa (33610) ***(G-17161)***
Phil Lau....813 631-8643
16309 Millan De Avila Tampa (33613) ***(G-17162)***
Phil Rowe Signs Inc....561 832-8688
805 N Dixie Hwy West Palm Beach (33401) ***(G-18120)***
Philias Supreme LLC....786 865-1335
1362 Nw 100th Ter Miami (33147) ***(G-9710)***
Philip Stein, Pembroke Park *Also called Pstein Inc* ***(G-13364)***
Philips North America LLC....305 969-7447
13305 Sw 106th Ave Miami (33176) ***(G-9711)***
Phillip Roy Inc....727 593-2700
13200 106th Ave Largo (33774) ***(G-7658)***
Phillips Energy Inc (HQ)....850 682-5127
806 W James Lee Blvd Crestview (32536) ***(G-2250)***
Phillips Graphics Inc....352 622-1776
1711 Sw 17th St Ocala (34471) ***(G-11465)***
Phillips Metal Products, Boca Raton *Also called Diligent Wldg Fabrication LLC* ***(G-484)***
Phillips Printing Services LLC....941 526-6570
5103 Lena Rd Unit 107 Bradenton (34211) ***(G-1027)***
Philly Swirl, Tampa *Also called Phillys Famous Water Ice Inc* ***(G-17163)***
Phillys Famous Water Ice Inc....813 248-8644
1102 N 28th St Tampa (33605) ***(G-17163)***
Phils Cake Box Bakeries Inc....813 348-0128
4705 W Cayuga St Tampa (33614) ***(G-17164)***
Phintec LLC....321 214-2500
618 E South St Ste 500 Orlando (32801) ***(G-12485)***
Phl Pool Services, Ormond Beach *Also called Professional Holiday Lighting* ***(G-12789)***
Phlebotomists On Wheels Inc....954 873-7591
1451 W Cypress Creek Rd # 300 Fort Lauderdale (33309) ***(G-3984)***
Phlexapeel LLC....407 990-1854
100 Rialto Pl Ste 743 Melbourne (32901) ***(G-8494)***
Phocas Software....863 738-9107
235 S Maitland Ave Maitland (32751) ***(G-8069)***
Phoenix Catastrophe Svcs LLC....918 321-2100
5417 E County Highway 30a Santa Rosa Beach (32459) ***(G-15430)***
Phoenix Coating Resources, Mulberry *Also called Saint-Gobain Corporation* ***(G-10637)***
Phoenix Custom Gear LLC....561 808-7181
1730 S Federal Hwy # 242 Delray Beach (33483) ***(G-2996)***
Phoenix Defense Group LLC....941 776-8714
3013 Old Orchard Ln Parrish (34219) ***(G-13361)***
Phoenix Dewatering Inc....407 330-7015
1980 Cameron Ave Sanford (32771) ***(G-15371)***
Phoenix Enterprises Fla LLC....813 986-9000
7616 Industrial Ln Temple Terrace (33637) ***(G-17542)***
Phoenix Group Florida Inc (PA)....954 563-1224
3000 Ne 30th Pl Fl 5 Fort Lauderdale (33306) ***(G-3985)***
Phoenix Jewelry Mfg Inc....305 477-2515
1499 Nw 79th Ave Doral (33126) ***(G-3327)***
Phoenix Media Network Inc....561 994-1118
6531 Pk Of Commerce Blvd Boca Raton (33487) ***(G-633)***
Phoenix Medical Research LLC....786 762-2040
8900 Sw 24th St Ste 210 Miami (33165) ***(G-9712)***
Phoenix Metal Products Inc....772 595-6386
3000 Industrial Avenue 3 Fort Pierce (34946) ***(G-4518)***
Phoenix Mountain Inds LLC....239 348-9895
351 Burnt Pine Dr Naples (34119) ***(G-10855)***
Phoenix Navtech LLC....407 285-4536
6943 Beargrass Rd Harmony (34773) ***(G-4987)***
Phoenix Publications....954 609-7586
777 S Federal Hwy Pompano Beach (33062) ***(G-14125)***
Phoenix Tanks, Jacksonville *Also called Envirovault LLC* ***(G-6078)***
Phoenix Trans Parts, Seminole *Also called Phoenix Transmission Parts Inc* ***(G-15985)***
Phoenix Transmission Parts Inc (PA)....727 541-0269
7000 Bryan Dairy Rd A4 Seminole (33777) ***(G-15985)***
Phoenix Trinity Mfg Inc....937 619-0172
10620 Harris Loop Hudson (34667) ***(G-5785)***
Phoenix Wood Products Inc (PA)....888 304-1131
3761 Ne 36th Ave Ocala (34479) ***(G-11466)***
Phone Wave Inc....352 683-8101
178 Mariner Blvd Spring Hill (34609) ***(G-16074)***
Phoscrete Corporation (PA)....561 420-0595
1800 Nw 15th Ave Ste 130 Pompano Beach (33069) ***(G-14126)***
Photo Finishing News Inc....239 992-4421
11618 Quail Village Way Naples (34119) ***(G-10856)***
Photo Offset Inc....305 666-1067
4824 Sw 72nd Ave Miami (33155) ***(G-9713)***
Photoengraving Inc (PA)....813 253-3427
502 N Willow Ave Tampa (33606) ***(G-17165)***
Photofinishing News, Naples *Also called Photo Finishing News Inc* ***(G-10856)***
Photon Towers Inc....305 235-7337
17290 Sw 192nd St Miami (33187) ***(G-9714)***
Phototelesis LP....321 254-1500
1615 W Nasa Blvd Melbourne (32901) ***(G-8495)***
Phy-Med....305 925-0141
8905 Sw 87th Ave Ste 200 Miami (33176) ***(G-9715)***
Phylomed, Plantation *Also called Bio Therapeutics Inc* ***(G-13832)***
Physician Hearing Care....239 261-7722
11121 Health Park Blvd # 700 Naples (34110) ***(G-10857)***
Physicians Imaging LLC (PA)....352 383-3716
3615 Lake Center Dr Mount Dora (32757) ***(G-10610)***

A L P H A B E T I C

Physicians Regional - Pine, Estero *Also called Naples Hma LLC* **(G-3547)**

Physiorx LLC 407 718-5549
2706 Rew Cir Ocoee (34761) **(G-11524)**

Pica Sales and Engineering 239 992-9079
19771 Chapel Trce Estero (33928) **(G-3548)**

Picanova Inc 786 705-2120
3443 Nw 107th St Miami (33167) **(G-9716)**

Picasso Embroidery Systems 305 827-9666
11952 Miramar Pkwy Miramar (33025) **(G-10527)**

Pick-A-Load Dispatch LLC 954 907-8245
6812 Nw 4th St Margate (33063) **(G-8147)**

Picket Fence Childrens 813 713-8589
4931 Allen Rd Zephyrhills (33541) **(G-18625)**

Pickett Logging, Hilliard *Also called Harry Pickett* **(G-5466)**

Pickhardt Professional Sr 941 737-7262
4329 14th Street Cir Palmetto (34221) **(G-13185)**

Pickle Pro LLC 844 332-7069
3527 Plover Ave Unit 2 Naples (34117) **(G-10858)**

Pickled Art Inc 954 635-7370
1495 N Federal Hwy Fort Lauderdale (33304) **(G-3986)**

Pickles Plus 941 661-6139
6196 Tidwell St North Port (34291) **(G-11203)**

Pictures and Mirrors, Orlando *Also called Total Vision Design Group* **(G-12663)**

Piecemakers LLC 786 517-1829
5521 Nw 78th Ave Doral (33166) **(G-3328)**

Piecemakers Llc 786 517-1829
120 N Knights Ave Brandon (33510) **(G-1103)**

Piedmont Plastics Inc 386 274-4627
2175 Mason Ave Daytona Beach (32117) **(G-2582)**

Pier 220 Inc 321 264-2011
2 A Max Brewer Mem Pkwy Titusville (32796) **(G-17608)**

Pierce Manufacturing Inc 727 573-0400
12770 44th St N Clearwater (33762) **(G-1739)**

Pierce Manufacturing Inc 941 748-3900
1512 38th Ave E Bradenton (34208) **(G-1028)**

Piergate LLC 813 938-9170
35377 Condominium Blvd Zephyrhills (33541) **(G-18626)**

Piezo Technology Inc (HQ) 407 298-2000
2525 Shader Rd Orlando (32804) **(G-12486)**

Pigments Black Diamond 904 241-2533
1316 Barrington Cir Saint Augustine (32092) **(G-14872)**

Pikantitos LLC 305 937-4827
19500 W Dixie Hwy # 101 Aventura (33180) **(G-271)**

Pikmykid, Kidio, Tampa *Also called Sachi Tech Inc* **(G-17242)**

Pilgrims Pride Corporation 386 362-4171
1306 Howard St W Live Oak (32064) **(G-7851)**

Pilkington North America Inc 305 470-1813
8850 Nw 24th Ter Doral (33172) **(G-3329)**

Pilkington North America Inc 800 759-0940
3646 Hartsfield Rd # 110 Tallahassee (32303) **(G-16487)**

Pilkington North America Inc 407 295-8560
4500 Seaboard Rd Ste A Orlando (32808) **(G-12487)**

Pillar Inc 904 545-4993
2232 Corporate Sq Blvd Jacksonville (32216) **(G-6370)**

Pillow Plus Manufacturing Inc 305 652-2218
515 Ne 189th St Miami (33179) **(G-9717)**

Pilot Corp of Palm Beaches 561 848-2928
7117 49th Ter N Riviera Beach (33407) **(G-14661)**

Pilot Steel Inc 954 978-3615
1950 W Copans Rd Pompano Beach (33064) **(G-14127)**

Pin Creator, The, Winter Springs *Also called Hbys Enterprises LLC* **(G-18567)**

Pin King LLC 561 622-6367
11562 Winchester Dr Palm Beach Gardens (33410) **(G-12999)**

Pin-N-Win Wrestling Club Inc 904 276-8038
117 Suzanne Ave Orange Park (32073) **(G-11837)**

Pine Fuel LLC 407 345-7960
5004 Old Winter Garden Rd Orlando (32811) **(G-12488)**

Pine Top Logging LLC 386 365-0857
27687 65th Rd Branford (32008) **(G-1114)**

Pineapple Grove Woodworks Inc 561 676-1287
3740 Prospect Ave West Palm Beach (33404) **(G-18121)**

Pinecrest Tribune 305 662-2277
6796 Sw 62nd Ave South Miami (33143) **(G-16042)**

Pinellas Blind and Shutter Inc 727 481-4461
5100 Ulmerton Rd Ste 22 Clearwater (33760) **(G-1740)**

Pinellas Custom Cabinets Inc 727 864-4263
8800 126th Ave Largo (33773) **(G-7659)**

Pinellas Electric Mtr Repr Inc 727 572-0777
12990 44th St N Clearwater (33762) **(G-1741)**

Pinellas Provision Corporation 727 822-2701
201 16th St S Saint Petersburg (33705) **(G-15150)**

Pink Cupcake Inc 904 434-9599
1013 Atlantic Blvd Atlantic Beach (32233) **(G-214)**

Pinnacle Cabinets Closets LLC 850 477-5402
9900b N Palafox St Pensacola (32534) **(G-13575)**

Pinnacle Cbinets By Design Inc 239 440-2950
2550 Edison Ave Fort Myers (33901) **(G-4362)**

Pinnacle Central Company Inc (PA) 904 354-5746
103 Bryan St Jacksonville (32202) **(G-6371)**

Pinnacle Cmmncations Group LLC 904 910-0444
7949 Atl Blvd Unit 201 Jacksonville (32211) **(G-6372)**

Pinnacle Foods Inc 321 952-7926
5905 S Highway A1a Melbourne Beach (32951) **(G-8568)**

Pinocho Bakery, Coral Gables *Also called Edca Bakery Corporation* **(G-2051)**

Pinos Window Corporation 305 888-9903
6860 Nw 75th St Medley (33166) **(G-8299)**

Pinto Palma Sound LLC 877 959-1815
10665 Sw 190th St # 3103 Cutler Bay (33157) **(G-2299)**

Pinzon Caramel Syrup 305 591-2472
6937 Nw 52nd St Miami (33166) **(G-9718)**

Pioneer Aerospace Corporation 850 623-3330
8101 Opportunity Dr Milton (32583) **(G-10432)**

Pioneer Ag-Chem Inc (PA) 772 464-9300
4100 Glades Cut Off Rd Fort Pierce (34981) **(G-4519)**

Pioneer Development Entps Inc 239 592-0001
5901 Shirley St Naples (34109) **(G-10859)**

Pioneer Dredge Inc 904 732-2151
8515 Baymeadows Way # 201 Jacksonville (32256) **(G-6373)**

Pioneer Led Lighting Corp 305 620-5300
4980 Nw 165th St Unit A1 Miami Lakes (33014) **(G-10339)**

Pioneer Metals, Jacksonville *Also called Daikin Comfort Tech Mfg LP* **(G-6023)**

Pioneer Printing and Signs, Cape Coral *Also called Everything Printing Inc* **(G-1340)**

Pioneer Screen Inc 772 260-3068
2740 Sw Martin Downs Blvd Palm City (34990) **(G-13055)**

Pioneer Surgical Technology 906 225-5629
11621 Research Cir Alachua (32615) **(G-17)**

Pioneer Welding & Fabrication 407 880-4997
532 Hillend Ct Apopka (32712) **(G-161)**

PIP Marketing Signs Print 904 825-2372
248 State Road 312 Saint Augustine (32086) **(G-14873)**

PIP Printing, Port Richey *Also called Premier Printing Signs* **(G-14371)**

PIP Printing, Kissimmee *Also called Abby Press Inc* **(G-6892)**

PIP Printing, Palm Beach Gardens *Also called Donna Lynn Enterprises Inc* **(G-12966)**

PIP Printing, Fort Lauderdale *Also called Bandart Enterprises Inc* **(G-3673)**

PIP Printing, Merritt Island *Also called Bill & Renee Enterprises Inc* **(G-8578)**

PIP Printing 352 622-3224
11 Sw 1st Ave Ocala (34471) **(G-11467)**

PIP Printing 386 258-3326
133 W Intl Speedway Blvd Daytona Beach (32114) **(G-2583)**

PIP Printing 622 Inc 813 935-8113
10428 N Florida Ave Tampa (33612) **(G-17166)**

Pipco, Fort Lauderdale *Also called Wool Wholesale Plumbing Supply* **(G-4136)**

Pipe Welders Inc (PA) 954 587-8400
2965 W State Road 84 Fort Lauderdale (33312) **(G-3987)**

Pipeline Fabricators Inc 863 678-0977
733 Carlton Ave Lake Wales (33853) **(G-7170)**

Piper Aircraft Inc (PA) 772 567-4361
2926 Piper Dr Vero Beach (32960) **(G-17786)**

Pipes R US 813 661-4420
12002 E Dr M Lthr Kng Jr Martin Luther Seffner (33584) **(G-15964)**

Pipette Solutions LLC 877 974-7388
1749 Grand Rue Dr Casselberry (32707) **(G-1428)**

Pipewelders Marine Inc 954 587-8400
2965 W State Road 84 Fort Lauderdale (33312) **(G-3988)**

Piranha Boatworks LLC 619 417-3592
1210 Sarah Ave Longwood (32750) **(G-7938)**

Pitman Allen Boat Repr & Maint 727 772-9848
970 Cortland Way Palm Harbor (34683) **(G-13123)**

Pitney Bowes Inc 813 639-1110
600 N West Shore Blvd # 810 Tampa (33609) **(G-17167)**

Pitts Fabrication LLC 850 259-4548
617 James Lee Rd Fort Walton Beach (32547) **(G-4602)**

Pivotal Sign & Graphics Inc 727 462-2266
3075 Braeloch Cir W Clearwater (33761) **(G-1742)**

Pivotal Therapeutics US Inc 905 856-9797
3651 Fau Blvd Ste 400 Boca Raton (33431) **(G-634)**

Pixe International Corp 850 574-6469
2306 Domingo Dr Tallahassee (32304) **(G-16488)**

Pixeloptics Inc 954 376-1542
6750 N Andrews Ave Fort Lauderdale (33309) **(G-3989)**

Pixels On Target LLC 305 614-0890
14050 Nw 14th St Ste 170 Sunrise (33323) **(G-16352)**

Pixelteq Inc (HQ) 727 545-0741
3500 Quadrangle Blvd Orlando (32817) **(G-12489)**

Pixotine Products Inc 305 479-1335
1095 Jupiter Park Dr # 12 Jupiter (33458) **(G-6777)**

Pizza Packet, Boca Raton *Also called Pizza Spice Packet LLC* **(G-635)**

Pizza Spice Packet LLC 718 831-7036
170 Ne 2nd St Unit 491 Boca Raton (33429) **(G-635)**

Pizzaros 239 390-0349
24611 Production Cir Bonita Springs (34135) **(G-813)**

PJ Designs Inc (PA) 727 525-0599
1515 Park St N Saint Petersburg (33710) **(G-15151)**

Pjm, Doral *Also called Phoenix Jewelry Mfg Inc* **(G-3327)**

Pk Graphicz 305 534-2184
1000 W Mcnab Rd Pompano Beach (33069) **(G-14128)**

Pk Group Inc 239 643-2442
3930 Domestic Ave Ste A Naples (34104) **(G-10860)**

Pki Group, Miramar *Also called Professnal Kit Instller Group* ***(G-10533)***
PKolino LLC 888 403-8992
7300 Nw 35th Ave Miami (33147) ***(G-9719)***
Pl Smoothie LLC 954 554-0450
10234 Sw 26th St Davie (33324) ***(G-2459)***
Placetas Pallet Corp 305 633-4262
195 W 19th St Hialeah (33010) ***(G-5295)***
Plan Automation LLC 786 502-1812
350 Lincoln Rd Miami Beach (33139) ***(G-10219)***
Plan B Manufacturing Inc 904 633-7888
1636 Wambolt St Jacksonville (32202) ***(G-6374)***
Planar Energy Devices Inc 407 459-1440
653 W Michigan St Orlando (32805) ***(G-12490)***
Planet, Sunrise *Also called Kloth Inc* ***(G-16334)***
Planet Fiat of West Miami, Doral *Also called FCA North America Holdings LLC* ***(G-3213)***
Planet Inhouse Inc 321 216-2189
3000 N Wickham Rd Melbourne (32935) ***(G-8496)***
Plant 2, Havana *Also called Tms Enterprises LLC* ***(G-5003)***
Plant City Observer LLC 813 704-6850
110 E Reynolds St 100b Plant City (33563) ***(G-13796)***
Plant Foods Inc 772 567-5741
5051 41st St Vero Beach (32967) ***(G-17787)***
Plant Partners Inc 941 752-1039
6691 33rd St E Ste B3 Sarasota (34243) ***(G-15537)***
Plant Solutions Inc 305 242-3103
15901 Sw 272nd St Homestead (33031) ***(G-5735)***
Plantain Products Company 800 477-2447
2440 Nw 116th St Ste 100 Miami (33167) ***(G-9720)***
Plantation Botanicals Inc 863 675-2984
1401 County Rd Ste 830 Felda (33930) ***(G-3573)***
Plantation Journal Corporation 954 226-6170
7860 Peters Rd Ste F110 Plantation (33324) ***(G-13877)***
Plantation Medicinals Inc 863 675-2984
1401 County Rd Ste 830 Felda (33930) ***(G-3574)***
Plantation Shutters Inc 772 208-8245
1388 Commerce Ctr Dr Port Saint Lucie (34986) ***(G-14432)***
Plantfinder, Cooper City *Also called Betrock Info Systems Inc* ***(G-2019)***
Plantogen Skin Care, Boca Raton *Also called Ollie Pippa International Inc* ***(G-623)***
Plasma Biolife Services L P 407 388-1052
1385 State Road 436 Casselberry (32707) ***(G-1429)***
Plasma Creations LLC 561 324-8214
6014 14th Pl S West Palm Beach (33415) ***(G-18122)***
Plasma Cutting LLC 954 558-1371
3140 W Hllandale Bch Blvd Hallandale (33009) ***(G-4928)***
Plasma Energy Group LLC 813 760-6385
17402 Isbell Ln Odessa (33556) ***(G-11570)***
Plasma-Therm Inc 856 753-8111
1150 16th St N Saint Petersburg (33705) ***(G-15152)***
Plasma-Therm LLC (PA) 727 577-4999
10050 16th St N Saint Petersburg (33716) ***(G-15153)***
Plasmine Technology Inc (HQ) 850 438-8550
3298 Summit Blvd Ste 35 Pensacola (32503) ***(G-13576)***
Plastec Ventilation Inc 941 751-7596
2012 58th Avenue Cir E Bradenton (34203) ***(G-1029)***
Plasti-Card Corporation 305 944-2726
7901 Clay Mica Ct Delray Beach (33446) ***(G-2997)***
Plastic and Products Mktg LLC 352 867-8078
3445 Sw 6th St Ocala (34474) ***(G-11468)***
Plastic Art Sign Company Inc 850 455-4114
3931 W Navy Blvd Pensacola (32507) ***(G-13577)***
Plastic Arts Sign Co, Pensacola *Also called Guardfish Enterprises LLC* ***(G-13513)***
Plastic Coated Papers Inc 850 968-6100
1701 E Kingsfield Rd Pensacola (32534) ***(G-13578)***
Plastic Components Inc (PA) 305 885-0561
9051 Nw 97th Ter Medley (33178) ***(G-8300)***
Plastic Composites Inc 352 669-5822
630 Goodbar Ave Umatilla (32784) ***(G-17650)***
Plastic Concepts & Designs Inc 904 396-7500
880 Us Highway 301 S # 1 Jacksonville (32234) ***(G-6375)***
Plastic Concepts Ltd Inc 727 942-6684
1456 L And R Indus Blvd Tarpon Springs (34689) ***(G-17487)***
Plastic International, Medley *Also called Plastic Components Inc* ***(G-8300)***
Plastic Kingdom Inc 561 586-9300
407 N Dixie Hwy Lake Worth (33460) ***(G-7227)***
Plastic Masters International 386 312-9775
327 State Road 207 East Palatka (32131) ***(G-3474)***
Plastic Parts Inc 954 974-3051
4100 N Powerline Rd Z5 Pompano Beach (33073) ***(G-14129)***
Plastic Sealing Company Inc 954 956-9797
1940 Nw 18th St Ste 1 Pompano Beach (33069) ***(G-14130)***
Plastic Solutions Inc 727 202-6815
801 West Bay Dr Ste 308 Largo (33770) ***(G-7660)***
Plastic Solutions of Pompano 800 331-7081
4100 N Powerline Rd Z5 Pompano Beach (33073) ***(G-14131)***
Plastic Specialties Inc 239 643-0933
3573 Arnold Ave Ste B Naples (34104) ***(G-10861)***
Plastic Trading Intl Inc 863 688-1983
3612 Ventura Dr E Lakeland (33811) ***(G-7409)***
Plastics America Inc 813 620-3711
8501 E Adamo Dr Tampa (33619) ***(G-17168)***
Plastics Dynamics Inc 954 565-7122
4301 Ne 11th Ave Oakland Park (33334) ***(G-11284)***
Plastics For Mankind Inc (PA) 305 687-5917
13050 Nw 47th Ave Opa Locka (33054) ***(G-11783)***
Plastiform, Opa Locka *Also called Plastics For Mankind Inc* ***(G-11783)***
Plastimold Products Inc 561 869-0183
250 N Congress Ave Delray Beach (33445) ***(G-2998)***
Plastirex LLC 305 471-1111
1552 Sun Pure Rd Avon Park (33825) ***(G-285)***
Plastix Usa LLC 305 891-0091
900 N Federal Hwy Ste 104 Hollywood (33020) ***(G-5643)***
Platecrafters Corporation 215 997-1990
782 Big Tree Dr Longwood (32750) ***(G-7939)***
Platesmart Technologies 813 749-0892
640 Brooker Creek Blvd # 465 Oldsmar (34677) ***(G-11686)***
Plating Resources Inc 321 632-2435
2845 W King St Ste 108 Cocoa (32926) ***(G-1946)***
Plating Technologies Inc 772 220-4201
2971 Se Dominica Ter # 12 Stuart (34997) ***(G-16197)***
Platinium Rosis Inc 786 617-9973
1602 Alton Rd 602 Miami Beach (33139) ***(G-10220)***
Platinum Cbd Inc 386 756-1902
1709 Arash Cir Port Orange (32128) ***(G-14344)***
Platinum Group Usa Inc 561 274-7553
75 N Congress Ave Delray Beach (33445) ***(G-2999)***
Platinum Ltg Productions LLC 941 320-1906
8051 N Tamiami Trl D10 Sarasota (34243) ***(G-15538)***
Platinum Mfg Intl Inc 727 544-4555
10166 66th St N Pinellas Park (33782) ***(G-13719)***
Platinum Signs and Design LLC 407 971-3640
352 W Melody Ln Casselberry (32707) ***(G-1430)***
Playa Perfection Inc 440 670-8154
5686 Youngquist Rd Fort Myers (33912) ***(G-4363)***
Playbill Magazine, Miami *Also called Playbill Southern Publishing* ***(G-9721)***
Playbill Southern Publishing 305 595-1984
10001 Sw 54th St Miami (33165) ***(G-9721)***
Players Media Group Inc 509 254-4949
5267 Zenith Garden Loop Brooksville (34601) ***(G-1190)***
Playlist Live Inc 877 306-3651
6424 Forest City Rd Orlando (32810) ***(G-12491)***
Playoff Technologies LLC 407 497-2202
1430 Elizabeth Dr Winter Park (32789) ***(G-18528)***
Playtex Manufacturing Inc 386 677-9559
1190 N Us Highway 1 Ormond Beach (32174) ***(G-12785)***
Plaza Materials Corp 813 788-0454
41150 Yonkers Blvd Zephyrhills (33541) ***(G-18627)***
Plazadoor Corp 561 578-5450
4425 Sw Cargo Way Palm City (34990) ***(G-13056)***
PLC Cabinets Installed Ltd 239 641-7565
1408 Rail Head Blvd Naples (34110) ***(G-10862)***
PLD Acquisitions LLC 305 463-2270
10400 Nw 29th Ter Miami Miami (33172) ***(G-9722)***
Pleasure Interiors LLC 941 756-9969
2207 Industrial Blvd Sarasota (34234) ***(G-15783)***
Plotkowski Inc (PA) 561 740-2226
210 Se 12th Ave Ste 1 Boynton Beach (33435) ***(G-896)***
Pls Print, Clearwater *Also called Precision Litho Service Inc* ***(G-1747)***
Plumb Rite of Central Florida 407 292-0750
2850 Overland Rd Apopka (32703) ***(G-162)***
Plus Communication, Lake Mary *Also called Charisma Media* ***(G-7065)***
Plus Communications Inc (PA) 407 333-0600
600 Rinehart Rd Lake Mary (32746) ***(G-7100)***
Plus Communications Inc 407 333-0600
600 Rinehart Rd Lake Mary (32746) ***(G-7101)***
Plushbeds Inc 888 449-5738
17076 Boca Club Blvd # 4 Boca Raton (33487) ***(G-636)***
Plywood Express Inc 954 956-7576
2601 Gateway Dr Ste B Pompano Beach (33069) ***(G-14132)***
PM Craftsman 863 665-0815
3525 Craftsman Blvd Lakeland (33803) ***(G-7410)***
PM Engraving Corp 786 573-5292
18425 Sw 200th St Miami (33187) ***(G-9723)***
PM Enterprises Holdings LLC (PA) 407 846-0588
1751 S John Young Pkwy Kissimmee (34741) ***(G-6952)***
PMC Enterprises Mgmt Division 239 949-6566
11216 Tamiami Trl N Naples (34110) ***(G-10863)***
PMC North America Inc 727 530-0714
2060 34th Way Largo (33771) ***(G-7661)***
PMF Tech Corp 786 636-7021
11411 Nw 74th Ter Doral (33178) ***(G-3330)***
Pmh Homes Inc 941 234-5121
14705 21st Ave E Bradenton (34212) ***(G-1030)***
Pmr Gestion Inc 561 501-5190
1100 Sw 10th St Delray Beach (33444) ***(G-3000)***
PNC Manufacturing Leather 407 201-2069
4107 S Orange Blossom Trl Kissimmee (34746) ***(G-6953)***
PNC Solutions Inc 407 401-8275
219 N Brown Ave Orlando (32801) ***(G-12492)***

ALPHABETIC

(PA)=Parent Co (HQ)=Headquarters (DH)=Div Headquarters

Pneumatic Products Corporation 352 873-5793
4647 Sw 40th Ave Ocala (34474) *(G-11469)*

Pneumatic Scale Angelus 727 535-4100
5320 140th Ave N Clearwater (33760) *(G-1743)*

Pneumatic Scale Clearwater, Clearwater *Also called Pneumatic Scale Angelus (G-1743)*

Poblocki Sign Co Southeast LLC 407 660-3174
3851 Center Loop Orlando (32808) *(G-12493)*

Pocketec Inc 772 692-8020
50 Ne Dixie Hwy Ste E7 Stuart (34994) *(G-16198)*

Pod All Solutions Corp 805 291-2675
5203 Sw 159th Ct Miami (33185) *(G-9724)*

Podgo Printing LLC 954 874-9100
3810 N 29th Ave Hollywood (33020) *(G-5644)*

POET LLC 904 619-6901
4373 Marsh Hawk Dr S Jacksonville (32218) *(G-6376)*

Poggesi USA, Miramar *Also called Suntyx LLC (G-10550)*

Pogi Beauty LLC 305 600-1305
3800 Ne 1st Ave Miami (33137) *(G-9725)*

Pohl Custom Cabinetry Inc 239 643-5661
3601 Arnold Ave Naples (34104) *(G-10864)*

Poinciana Milling Complex Inc 407 587-5525
1770 Business Center Ln Kissimmee (34758) *(G-6954)*

Point Blank Enterprises Inc 954 846-8222
2102 Sw 2nd St Pompano Beach (33069) *(G-14133)*

Point Blank Enterprises Inc (HQ) 954 630-0900
2102 Sw 2nd St Pompano Beach (33069) *(G-14134)*

Point Blank Enterprises Inc 305 820-4270
14100 Nw 58th Ct Miami Lakes (33014) *(G-10340)*

Point Blank Intrmdate Hldg LLC 954 630-0900
2102 Sw 2nd St Pompano Beach (33069) *(G-14135)*

Point Blank Protective Apprl (PA) 954 630-0900
2102 Sw 2nd St Pompano Beach (33069) *(G-14136)*

Point Blank Scrnprnting Design 850 234-9745
116 Rusty Gans Dr Panama City (32408) *(G-13298)*

Point Distillery LLC 727 269-5588
11807 Little Rd New Port Richey (34654) *(G-10981)*

Polaris Electrical Connectors, Odessa *Also called Polaris Sales Co Inc (G-11571)*

Polaris Sales Co Inc 727 372-1703
11625 Prosperous Dr Odessa (33556) *(G-11571)*

Polaris Trading Corp 954 956-6999
2205 Nw 45th Ave Coconut Creek (33066) *(G-2002)*

Polenghi Usa Inc 954 637-4900
720 S Powerline Rd Ste C Deerfield Beach (33442) *(G-2783)*

Poli Group Intl Inc 305 468-8986
1574 Nw 108th Ave Miami (33172) *(G-9726)*

Poli Sign Supplies, Miami *Also called Poli Group Intl Inc (G-9726)*

Policrete LLC 305 552-7026
3399 Nw 72nd Ave Ste 108 Miami (33122) *(G-9727)*

Polimix Usa LLC 305 888-4752
11750 Nw South River Dr Medley (33178) *(G-8301)*

Polk Air Filter Sales Inc 863 688-4436
1851 E Gary Rd Lakeland (33801) *(G-7411)*

Polk County Democrat (PA) 863 533-4183
99 3rd St Nw Winter Haven (33881) *(G-18458)*

Pollak Industries 850 438-4651
2313 Truman Ave Pensacola (32505) *(G-13579)*

Polly Concrete Products Co 850 897-3314
1495 Cedar St Niceville (32578) *(G-11034)*

Polo Players Edition 561 968-5208
9011 Lake Worth Rd B Lake Worth (33467) *(G-7228)*

Polson Transportation LLC 614 733-9677
9032 Pomelo Rd W Fort Myers (33967) *(G-4364)*

Poly Coatings of South Inc 941 371-8555
5944 Sandphil Rd Sarasota (34232) *(G-15784)*

Poly Plastic Packaging Co Inc 561 498-9040
18800 Long Lake Dr Boca Raton (33496) *(G-637)*

Poly Systems Co, West Palm Beach *Also called Peter T Amann (G-18118)*

Poly-Chem Corp 305 593-1928
3039 Ne Quayside Ln Miami (33138) *(G-9728)*

Polyglass Roofg Watering Svcs, Deerfield Beach *Also called Polyglass USA Inc (G-2784)*

Polyglass USA Inc (HQ) 954 246-8888
1111 W Newport Center Dr Deerfield Beach (33442) *(G-2784)*

Polygon Solutions Inc 239 628-4800
6461 Metro Plantation Rd Fort Myers (33966) *(G-4365)*

Polyhistor International Inc 904 646-5666
11200 Saint Johns Jacksonville (32246) *(G-6377)*

Polymatics Plastic Processing, Clearwater *Also called Kinetic Industries LLC (G-1661)*

Polymersan LLC 305 887-3824
1181 Se 9th Ter Ste B Hialeah (33010) *(G-5296)*

Polypack Inc (PA) 727 578-5000
3301 Gateway Ctr Blvd N Pinellas Park (33782) *(G-13720)*

Polypack Limited Partnership 727 578-5000
3301 Gateway Ctr Blvd N Pinellas Park (33782) *(G-13721)*

Polyplastics, Boca Raton *Also called Poly Plastic Packaging Co Inc (G-637)*

Polytech International LLC 904 354-9355
6635 Highway Ave Jacksonville (32254) *(G-6378)*

Polyumac Inc 305 691-9093
1060 E 30th St Hialeah (33013) *(G-5297)*

Poma Corporation 561 790-5799
9040 Belvedere Rd West Palm Beach (33411) *(G-18123)*

Pompadour Products Inc 954 345-2700
1197 Nw 83rd Ave Coral Springs (33071) *(G-2203)*

Pompanette LLC 813 885-2182
7712 Cheri Ct Tampa (33634) *(G-17169)*

Pompano Precision Products Inc 954 942-5900
141 Sw 5th St Pompano Beach (33060) *(G-14137)*

Pompano Precision Products Inc (PA) 954 946-6059
1100 Sw 12th Ave Pompano Beach (33069) *(G-14138)*

Pomper Sheet Metal Inc 954 492-9717
4444 Ne 11th Ave Oakland Park (33334) *(G-11285)*

Poms Enterprises Inc 954 358-1359
5425 Nw 24th St Ste 210 Margate (33063) *(G-8148)*

Ponce De Leon Construction 786 554-3685
440 Nw 132nd Ave Miami (33182) *(G-9729)*

Pond Industries Inc 727 526-5483
1942 Iowa Ave Ne Saint Petersburg (33703) *(G-15154)*

Ponte Vedra Wns Civic Aliance 904 834-3543
359 San Juan Dr Ponte Vedra Beach (32082) *(G-14277)*

Poof Game LLC 239 245-2957
4209 9th St Sw Lehigh Acres (33976) *(G-7821)*

Pool Cleaning Service, Labelle *Also called South West Adventure Team LLC (G-6986)*

Popcorn Junkie LLC 407 634-0042
4649 Parkbreeze Ct Orlando (32808) *(G-12494)*

Pope Enterprises Inc 850 729-7446
516 John Sims Pkwy E Niceville (32578) *(G-11035)*

Pops Turn LLC 843 725-8890
4828 Frst Coast Hwy Ste 6 Fernandina Beach (32034) *(G-3596)*

Popstops Marketing Inc 800 209-4571
111 2nd Ave Ne Ste 1201 Saint Petersburg (33701) *(G-15155)*

Porath Fine Cabinetry Inc 561 616-9400
3101 Tuxedo Ave West Palm Beach (33405) *(G-18124)*

Porche Systems, Pensacola *Also called Automation Consulting Inc (G-13449)*

Pork and Shake, Cape Coral *Also called Aquino Trucks Center Corp (G-1305)*

Port Canaveral FL Canaveral Rm, Cape Canaveral *Also called Cemex Cnstr Mtls Fla LLC (G-1281)*

Port Canaveral Yard, Tampa *Also called Vgcm LLC (G-17413)*

Port Hmlton Rfinery Trnsp Lllp 305 299-0251
2555 Ponce De Leon Blvd Coral Gables (33134) *(G-2097)*

Port Manatee Ship Repair 941 417-2613
2114 Piney Point Rd Palmetto (34221) *(G-13186)*

Port Palm Cold Storage Inc 386 328-5127
1122 Bronson St Palatka (32177) *(G-12877)*

Port Printing Co 561 848-1402
3532 Broadway Riviera Beach (33404) *(G-14662)*

Port Saint Wich LLC (PA) 772 237-2000
3961 Sw Port St Lcie Blvd Port Saint Lucie (34953) *(G-14433)*

Port St Lucie News 772 287-1550
1939 Se Federal Hwy Stuart (34994) *(G-16199)*

Port St. Lucie News, Port Saint Lucie *Also called EW Scripps Company (G-14411)*

Portable Pumping Systems Inc 727 518-9191
4760 Spring Ave Clearwater (33762) *(G-1744)*

Portable-Shade USA LLC 321 704-8100
428 Shearer Blvd Cocoa (32922) *(G-1947)*

Portalp Usa Inc 800 474-3667
1030 Collier Center Way # 10 Naples (34110) *(G-10865)*

Porter Pizza Box Florida (PA) 800 626-0828
6094 Us Highway 98 S Lakeland (33812) *(G-7412)*

Poseidon Boat Manufacturing 239 362-3736
5826 Corporation Cir Fort Myers (33905) *(G-4366)*

Poseidon Industries Inc 305 812-2582
5462 Williamsburg Dr Punta Gorda (33982) *(G-14518)*

Poseidon Services Inc 786 294-8529
12685 Nw 11th Ln Miami (33182) *(G-9730)*

Poseidon Window Treatments LLC 954 920-1112
1942 Tigertail Blvd Dania Beach (33004) *(G-2358)*

Positive Energy Inc 929 220-5880
1221 Brickell Ave Ste 900 Miami (33131) *(G-9731)*

Positiveid Corporation (PA) 561 805-8000
1690 S Congress Ave # 201 Delray Beach (33445) *(G-3001)*

Positivenergy, Miami *Also called Positive Energy Inc (G-9731)*

Potenza Hrc, Miami *Also called Potenza Services Inc (G-9732)*

Potenza Services Inc 305 400-4938
10711 Sw 216th St Miami (33170) *(G-9732)*

Potter Roemer LLC 786 845-0842
8306 Nw 14th St Doral (33126) *(G-3331)*

Potters Coffee Company 850 525-1793
1727 Creighton Rd Pensacola (32504) *(G-13580)*

Pottre Gardening Products LLC 941 224-8856
1115 76th St Nw Bradenton (34209) *(G-1031)*

Poulsen Lighting, Weston *Also called Louis Poulsen USA Inc (G-18265)*

Povia Paints Inc (PA) 239 791-0011
2897 South St Fort Myers (33916) *(G-4367)*

Powder Coating Factory LLC 407 286-4550
635 Wilmer Ave Orlando (32808) *(G-12495)*

Powder Systems Inc 352 680-3558
120 Cypress Rd Ocala (34472) *(G-11470)*

Powdertech Plus Inc 904 269-1719
98 Industrial Loop N Orange Park (32073) *(G-11838)*

Powell Steel LLC 386 406-1017
603 S Center St Ormond Beach (32174) *(G-12786)*

Powell Woodworking LLC 407 883-9181
5150 Sage Cedar Pl Sanford (32771) *(G-15372)*

Power Bright Technologies, Fort Lauderdale *Also called Bright Manufacturing LLC (G-3703)*

Power Evolution Inc 305 318-8476
14163 Sapphire Bay Cir Orlando (32828) *(G-12496)*

Power Flow Systems Inc 386 253-8833
795 Fentress Blvd Ste A Daytona Beach (32114) *(G-2584)*

Power Grid Pros Inc 716 378-1419
618 Heritage Dr Weston (33326) *(G-18279)*

Power Kleen Corporation 813 854-2648
101 S Bayview Blvd Oldsmar (34677) *(G-11687)*

Power Plus Inc 386 672-7579
550 Parque Dr Ormond Beach (32174) *(G-12787)*

Power Point Graphics Inc 561 351-5599
19528 Sedgefield Ter Boca Raton (33498) *(G-638)*

Power Printing of Florida ....
4001 35th St N Saint Petersburg (33714) *(G-15156)*

Power Printing of Florida 727 823-1162
956 1st Ave N Saint Petersburg (33705) *(G-15157)*

Power Quality International, Odessa *Also called Gfsf Inc (G-11554)*

Power Quality Intl LLC 727 478-7284
2404 Merchant Ave Odessa (33556) *(G-11572)*

Power Sports Treasure Coast 772 463-6428
2212 Se Indian St Stuart (34997) *(G-16200)*

Power Suspension & Parts LLC 305 986-2235
13550 Nw 107th Ave Unit D Hialeah Gardens (33018) *(G-5448)*

Power Systems Inc 561 354-1100
1440 W Indiantown Rd # 200 Jupiter (33458) *(G-6778)*

Power Systems Mfg LLC 561 354-1100
1440 W Indiantown Rd # 200 Jupiter (33458) *(G-6779)*

Power Technology Southeast, Leesburg *Also called Mobile Power Generators LLC (G-7787)*

Power Tek LLC 904 814-7007
154 Cornell Rd Saint Augustine (32086) *(G-14874)*

Power Vac Corporation 954 491-0188
4811 Ne 12th Ave Oakland Park (33334) *(G-11286)*

Power Wthin Cnsling Cnsltn LLC 863 242-3023
280 Patterson Rd Ste 1 Haines City (33844) *(G-4912)*

Powerbees Incorporated 561 797-5927
1375 Gateway Blvd Boynton Beach (33426) *(G-897)*

Powercases Inc 239 415-3846
18281 Via Caprini Dr Miromar Lakes (33913) *(G-10575)*

Powerchord Inc (PA) 727 823-1530
360 Central Ave Fl 5 Saint Petersburg (33701) *(G-15158)*

Powerdms Inc 407 992-6000
101 S Garland Ave Ste 300 Orlando (32801) *(G-12497)*

Powerficient LLC 800 320-2535
6250 Nw 27th Way Fort Lauderdale (33309) *(G-3990)*

Powerful Foods LLC 305 637-7300
9171 S Dixie Hwy Pinecrest (33156) *(G-13668)*

Powerful Yogurt, Pinecrest *Also called Powerful Foods LLC (G-13668)*

Powerline Group Inc 631 828-1183
8406 Hawks Gully Ave Delray Beach (33446) *(G-3002)*

Powerphase LLC 561 299-3970
1001 N Us Highway 1 # 206 Jupiter (33477) *(G-6780)*

Powerpump LLC 305 514-3030
11447 Nw 34th St Doral (33178) *(G-3332)*

Powers Industries LLC 954 706-6001
3800 Galt Ocean Dr Ph 1 Fort Lauderdale (33308) *(G-3991)*

Powersports 911 Inc 813 769-2468
5911 Benjamin Center Dr Tampa (33634) *(G-17170)*

Powertech Generators, Leesburg *Also called Ptse Holding Inc (G-7789)*

Powless Drapery Service Inc 954 566-7863
4029 Ne 10th Ave Oakland Park (33334) *(G-11287)*

Pozin Enterprises Inc 800 741-1456
14493 62nd St N Clearwater (33760) *(G-1745)*

Ppa Miami Corp 305 436-0460
8620 Nw 64th St Ste 10 Miami (33166) *(G-9733)*

PPG Architectural Finishes Inc 813 877-5841
3102 W Kennedy Blvd Tampa (33609) *(G-17171)*

PPG Inc 813 831-9902
5133 W Cypress St Tampa (33607) *(G-17172)*

PPG Industries Inc 305 477-0541
1376 Nw 78th Ave Doral (33126) *(G-3333)*

Ppi, Sarasota *Also called Premier Prfmce Interiors Inc (G-15539)*

Ppi Group, Fort Lauderdale *Also called Panoff Publishing Inc (G-3972)*

Ppi International Corp 954 838-1008
1649 Nw 136th Ave Sunrise (33323) *(G-16353)*

PQ Pharmacy LLC 352 477-8977
15215 Technology Dr Brooksville (34604) *(G-1191)*

Practical Design Products Co 561 995-4023
1101 Holland Dr Boca Raton (33487) *(G-639)*

Practicepanther, Miami *Also called Panther Software Inc (G-9690)*

Pradere Manufacturing Corp 305 823-0190
7655 W 20th Ave Hialeah (33014) *(G-5298)*

Pradere Office Products, Hialeah *Also called Pradere Manufacturing Corp (G-5298)*

Praesto Enterprises LLC 407 298-9171
2525 Industrial Blvd Orlando (32804) *(G-12498)*

Pratt & Whitney 561 796-6701
15270 Endeavor Dr Jupiter (33478) *(G-6781)*

Pratt Industries Inc 863 439-4184
331 W Frederick Ave Dundee (33838) *(G-3437)*

Pratt Plastics, Titusville *Also called Richard K Pratt LLC (G-17614)*

Praxair, Tampa *Also called Linde Inc (G-17011)*

Praxis Software Inc 407 226-5691
7575 Kingspointe Pkwy # 9 Orlando (32819) *(G-12499)*

Pre-Cast Specialties Inc 954 781-4040
3850 E Lake Mary Blvd Sanford (32773) *(G-15373)*

Pre-Cast Specialties LLC (PA) 954 781-4040
3850 E Lake Mary Blvd Sanford (32773) *(G-15374)*

Pre-Mix Marble Tite Inc 954 917-7665
1259 Nw 21st St Pompano Beach (33069) *(G-14139)*

Pre-Tech Inc 863 422-5079
3052 Us Highway 17 92 N Haines City (33844) *(G-4913)*

Preble Enterprises Inc 954 480-6919
1339 Sw 1st Way Deerfield Beach (33441) *(G-2785)*

Precast and Foam Works LLC 727 657-9195
29757 66th Way N Clearwater (33761) *(G-1746)*

Precast Depot Inc 305 885-2530
11002 Nw South River Dr Medley (33178) *(G-8302)*

Precast Designs Inc 407 856-5444
10305 Rocket Ct Orlando (32824) *(G-12500)*

Precast Keystone, Naples *Also called Pfci LLC (G-10853)*

Precast Solution System Inc 813 949-7929
2045 Chesapeake Dr Ste 2 Odessa (33556) *(G-11573)*

Precast Specialties, Sanford *Also called Pre-Cast Specialties LLC (G-15374)*

Precast Technical Assistance 850 432-8446
21 S Tarragona St Ste 101 Pensacola (32502) *(G-13581)*

Precious Metal Exchange 321 727-2278
2610 Ranch Rd Melbourne (32904) *(G-8497)*

Precious Metal Group LLC 904 219-8358
5410 Blanding Blvd Jacksonville (32244) *(G-6379)*

Precious Metals Buyers LLC (PA) 813 880-9544
6201 Johns Rd Ste 5 Tampa (33634) *(G-17173)*

Precious Metals Buyers LLC 813 417-7857
7028 W Waters Ave Tampa (33634) *(G-17174)*

Precise Pavers Inc 863 528-8000
2581 Nelson St Auburndale (33823) *(G-242)*

Precise Print Florida 813 960-4958
410 W Chapman Rd Lutz (33548) *(G-8010)*

Precise Technologies Inc 727 535-5594
12395 75th St Largo (33773) *(G-7662)*

Precision Aluminum Products, Deerfield Beach *Also called Preble Enterprises Inc (G-2785)*

Precision Ammunition LLC 813 626-0077
5402 E Diana St Tampa (33610) *(G-17175)*

Precision Analog Systems Co 954 587-0668
1021 Sw 75th Ave Plantation (33317) *(G-13878)*

Precision Auto Tint Dsign Corp 727 385-8788
746 Haven Pl Tarpon Springs (34689) *(G-17488)*

Precision Brazing Inc 954 942-8971
471 Ne 28th St Pompano Beach (33064) *(G-14140)*

Precision Cabinetry LLC 386 218-3340
2240 E Old Mill Dr Deltona (32725) *(G-3051)*

Precision Ceramic & Stone Llc ....
810 33rd Ct Sw Vero Beach (32968) *(G-17788)*

Precision Ceramics Usa Inc 727 388-5060
9843 18th St N Ste 120 Saint Petersburg (33716) *(G-15159)*

Precision Circuits Inc 321 632-8629
550 Gus Hipp Blvd Rockledge (32955) *(G-14739)*

Precision Coating Rods Inc 813 855-5054
600 Mount Vernon St Oldsmar (34677) *(G-11688)*

Precision Concepts (miami) LLC 305 825-5244
7300 W 18th Ln Hialeah (33014) *(G-5299)*

Precision Directional Drlg LLC 941 320-8308
5010 60th Dr E Bradenton (34203) *(G-1032)*

Precision Econowind LLC 239 997-3860
8940 N Fork Dr North Fort Myers (33903) *(G-11067)*

Precision Equipment Co Inc 561 689-4400
197 65th Ter N West Palm Beach (33413) *(G-18125)*

Precision Ers 813 257-0900
7710 N 30th St Tampa (33610) *(G-17176)*

Precision Fabg & Clg Co Inc 321 635-2000
3975 E Railroad Ave Cocoa (32926) *(G-1948)*

Precision Fabrication Corp 941 488-2474
510 Church St Nokomis (34275) *(G-11052)*

Precision Gate & Security Inc (PA) 813 404-6278
2341 Porter Lake Dr # 205 Sarasota (34240) *(G-15785)*

Precision Infinity Systems Inc 407 490-2320
14569 Jamaica Dogwood Dr Orlando (32828) *(G-12501)*

Precision Laboratories Inc 407 774-4261
165 E Wildmere Ave Longwood (32750) *(G-7940)*

Precision Leak Detection Inc 904 996-9290
84 Autumn Springs Ct W Jacksonville (32225) *(G-6380)*

Precision Lift Industries Inc 877 770-5862
3605 N Davis Hwy Pensacola (32503) *(G-13582)*

A
L
P
H
A
B
E
T
I
C

Precision Litho Service Inc...727 573-1763
4250 118th Ave N Clearwater (33762) ***(G-1747)***
Precision Machine Tech LLC...305 594-1789
4083 Nw 79th Ave Doral (33166) ***(G-3334)***
Precision Manufacturing, Fort Myers *Also called OGrady Tool Company* ***(G-4347)***
Precision Metal Industries Inc...954 942-6303
1408 Sw 8th St Pompano Beach (33069) ***(G-14141)***
Precision Metal Parts Inc...727 526-9165
4725 28th St N Saint Petersburg (33714) ***(G-15160)***
Precision Metal Services Inc...407 843-3682
33243 Equestrian Trl Sorrento (32776) ***(G-16012)***
Precision Mold & Tool Inc...407 847-5687
2780 N John Young Pkwy Kissimmee (34741) ***(G-6955)***
Precision Mold Tech Inc...305 594-1789
4083 Nw 79th Ave Doral (33166) ***(G-3335)***
Precision Mtal Fbrications Inc...305 691-0616
3600 E 10th Ct 20 Hialeah (33013) ***(G-5300)***
Precision Paddleboards...954 616-8046
429 Seabreeze Blvd 214 Fort Lauderdale (33316) ***(G-3992)***
Precision Plastics, Delray Beach *Also called Axtonne Inc* ***(G-2934)***
Precision Plastics Group Inc...863 299-6639
1635 7th St Sw Winter Haven (33880) ***(G-18459)***
Precision Printing of Columbus...561 509-7269
11831 Fox Hill Cir Boynton Beach (33473) ***(G-898)***
Precision Qulty Machining Inc...407 831-7240
710 Golden Spike Ln Sanford (32771) ***(G-15375)***
Precision Resistor Co Inc...727 541-5771
9442 Laura Anne Dr Seminole (33776) ***(G-15986)***
Precision Resources Inc (PA)...321 635-2000
3975 E Railroad Ave Cocoa (32926) ***(G-1949)***
Precision Shaft Technology...727 442-1711
1717 Overbrook Ave Clearwater (33755) ***(G-1748)***
Precision Shapes Inc (PA)...321 269-2555
8835 Grissom Pkwy Titusville (32780) ***(G-17609)***
Precision Small Engine Company...954 974-1960
2510 Nw 16th Ln Pompano Beach (33064) ***(G-14142)***
Precision Stone, Delray Beach *Also called PSC Building Group Inc* ***(G-3008)***
Precision Svcs Jcksonville Inc...904 781-3770
5201 W Beaver St Jacksonville (32254) ***(G-6381)***
Precision Tech Aero Inc...305 603-8347
6051 Nw 153rd St Miami Lakes (33014) ***(G-10341)***
Precision Tech Machining LLC...321 693-3469
1421 Albert Dr Melbourne (32935) ***(G-8498)***
Precision Tl Engrg Gnsvlle Inc...352 376-2533
2709 Ne 20th Way Gainesville (32609) ***(G-4749)***
Precision Tool & Mold Inc...727 573-4441
12050 44th St N Clearwater (33762) ***(G-1749)***
Precision Turbines Inc (PA)...561 447-0032
11250 Aviation Blvd Ste 4 West Palm Beach (33412) ***(G-18126)***
Precision Turning Corporation...386 364-5788
715 Goldkist Blvd Sw Live Oak (32064) ***(G-7852)***
Precision Window Films, Tarpon Springs *Also called Precision Auto Tint Dsign Corp* ***(G-17488)***
Precision Woodcraft, Lake Worth *Also called Maggac Corporation* ***(G-7215)***
Precon Corporation...352 332-1200
115 Sw 140th Ter Newberry (32669) ***(G-11025)***
Predator Products, Jacksonville *Also called Clawson Custom Cues Inc* ***(G-5981)***
Preferred Custom Printing LLC...727 443-1900
7000 Bryan Dairy Rd B2 Seminole (33777) ***(G-15987)***
Preferred Materials Inc (HQ)...904 288-0244
4636 Scarborough Dr Lutz (33559) ***(G-8011)***
Preferred Metal Products Inc...407 296-4449
3614 Princeton Oaks St Orlando (32808) ***(G-12502)***
Preferred Pallets Llc...863 401-9517
4353 Fussell Ln Winter Haven (33880) ***(G-18460)***
Preferred Pcks Pblications Inc...954 377-8000
1335 Shotgun Rd Sunrise (33326) ***(G-16354)***
Preferred Printing & Graphics, West Palm Beach *Also called Sunshine Printing Inc* ***(G-18170)***
Preferred Signs Inc...954 922-0126
1906 N Dixie Hwy Hollywood (33020) ***(G-5645)***
Preferred Stitching Inc...813 737-3996
10552 Lithia Pinecrest Rd Lithia (33547) ***(G-7837)***
Preform LLC...888 826-5161
3845 Deerpark Blvd Elkton (32033) ***(G-3508)***
Prege...954 908-1535
1475 W Cypress Creek Rd Fort Lauderdale (33309) ***(G-3993)***
Prekcom LLC...877 773-5669
429 Lenox Ave Miami Beach (33139) ***(G-10221)***
Premdor Finance LLC...813 877-2726
1 N Dale Mabry Hwy # 950 Tampa (33609) ***(G-17177)***
Premier Archtctural Shtmtl Inc...727 373-8937
8501 Northton Groves Blvd Odessa (33556) ***(G-11574)***
Premier Blinds & Verticals...305 244-0598
881 Ne 1st Pl Hialeah (33010) ***(G-5301)***
Premier Brush Inc...850 271-5736
2230 Industrial Dr Panama City (32405) ***(G-13299)***
Premier Cabinets LLC...407 760-9060
3036 Kananwood Ct # 1024 Oviedo (32765) ***(G-12844)***
Premier Cabinets & Trim LLC...321 345-4923
1240 Clearmont St Ne # 10 Palm Bay (32905) ***(G-12912)***
Premier Coatings LLC...954 797-9275
450 Nw 27th Ave Fort Lauderdale (33311) ***(G-3994)***
Premier Corporate Printing...305 378-8480
3414 Galilee Rd Jacksonville (32207) ***(G-6382)***
Premier Corporate Printing LLC...305 378-8480
3414 Galilee Rd Jacksonville (32207) ***(G-6383)***
Premier Die Casting Company...732 634-3000
47 S Prospect Dr Coral Gables (33133) ***(G-2098)***
Premier Distributor of Miami...305 821-9671
1635 W 40th St Hialeah (33012) ***(G-5302)***
Premier Fabricating Llc...813 855-4633
232 Dunbar Ct Oldsmar (34677) ***(G-11689)***
Premier Fabricators LLC...772 323-2042
7413 Commercial Cir Fort Pierce (34951) ***(G-4520)***
Premier Gas and Grills, Green Cove Springs *Also called Premier Specialty Service LLC* ***(G-4832)***
Premier Global Enterprises...561 747-7303
261 Isle Way Palm Beach Gardens (33418) ***(G-13000)***
Premier Lab Supply Inc...772 873-1700
691 Nw Enterprise Dr Port Saint Lucie (34986) ***(G-14434)***
Premier Luxury Group LLC...954 358-9885
2860 W State Road 84 Ste Fort Lauderdale (33312) ***(G-3995)***
Premier Manufacturing Pdts LLC...239 542-0260
730 Ne 19th Pl Cape Coral (33909) ***(G-1374)***
Premier Pallet Recycler LLC...561 722-0457
1230 Gateway Rd Ste 1 West Palm Beach (33403) ***(G-18127)***
Premier Pallets Inc...813 986-4889
5805 Breckenridge Pkwy A Tampa (33610) ***(G-17178)***
Premier Parties Entertainment...352 375-6122
805 Nw 13th St Gainesville (32601) ***(G-4750)***
Premier Plastics LLC (PA)...305 805-3333
1500 Gateway Blvd Ste 250 Boynton Beach (33426) ***(G-899)***
Premier Plastics LLC...305 805-3333
500 S Federal Hwy # 2715 Hallandale Beach (33009) ***(G-4966)***
Premier Prfmce Interiors Inc...941 752-6271
6304 17th Street Cir E Sarasota (34243) ***(G-15539)***
Premier Printing Signs...727 849-2493
6520 Industrial Ave Ste 1 Port Richey (34668) ***(G-14371)***
Premier Printing Solutions Inc...305 490-0244
6600 Nw 15th Ave Fort Lauderdale (33309) ***(G-3996)***
Premier Services of Fl Inc...678 815-6078
2305 Garland Ct 1 Tallahassee (32303) ***(G-16489)***
Premier Sign & Service Inc...239 258-6979
7716 6th Pl Lehigh Acres (33936) ***(G-7822)***
Premier Specialty Service LLC...904 531-9315
3293 Highway 17 Green Cove Springs (32043) ***(G-4832)***
Premier Stoneworks LLC...561 330-3737
1455 Sw 4th Ave Delray Beach (33444) ***(G-3003)***
Premier Tees...941 681-2688
2780 Worth Ave Englewood (34224) ***(G-3521)***
Premier Water & Enrgy Tech Inc...904 268-1152
11481 Columbia Park Dr W Jacksonville (32258) ***(G-6384)***
Premier Water Tanks LLC...352 910-0188
425 Flatwoods Rd Leesburg (34748) ***(G-7788)***
Premiere Manufacturing Co LLC...407 747-3955
1480 Mrtin Lther King Jr Sanford (32771) ***(G-15376)***
Premiere Plastering, Jacksonville *Also called MDK Enterpises Inc* ***(G-6286)***
Premieretrade Forex LLC...407 287-4149
103 Commerce St Ste 140 Lake Mary (32746) ***(G-7102)***
Premium Absrbent Dspsables LLC...561 737-6377
3030 Sw 13th Pl Ste A Boynton Beach (33426) ***(G-900)***
Premium Coating LLC...727 270-1173
10 S Duncan Ave Clearwater (33755) ***(G-1750)***
Premium Dynamic Lens...813 891-9912
640 Brooker Creek Blvd # 435 Oldsmar (34677) ***(G-11690)***
Premium Latin Music Inc...212 873-1472
1545 Sw 14th Ter Miami (33145) ***(G-9734)***
Premium Marine Inc...786 903-0851
777 Brickell Ave Ste 500 Miami (33131) ***(G-9735)***
Premium Powder Coating...386 789-0216
1872 Sweetwater Bnd Deltona (32738) ***(G-3052)***
Premium Quality Meats Inc...239 309-4418
7979 Riviera Blvd Miramar (33023) ***(G-10528)***
Premium Rubber Bands Inc...305 321-0333
9430 Sw 136th St Miami (33176) ***(G-9736)***
Premix-Marbletite Mfg Co (HQ)...954 970-6540
1259 Nw 21st St Pompano Beach (33069) ***(G-14143)***
Premix-Marbletite Mfg Co...407 327-0830
325 Old Sanford Oviedo Rd Winter Springs (32708) ***(G-18574)***
Prepaid Solutions LLC...305 834-7422
601 Brickell Key Dr # 70 Miami (33131) ***(G-9737)***
Presage Analytics Inc...800 309-1704
27500 Rvrview Ctr Blvd St Bonita Springs (34134) ***(G-814)***
Prescient Logistics LLC...407 547-2680
576 Monroe Rd Ste 1304 Sanford (32771) ***(G-15377)***
Presidium, Lakeland *Also called Slappey Communications LLC* ***(G-7435)***
Press Ex Inc...727 532-4177
8601 Somerset Dr Largo (33773) ***(G-7663)***

Press Gourmet Sandwiches ...954 440-0422
6206 N Federal Hwy Fort Lauderdale (33308) *(G-3997)*
Press Print Graphics LLC ...850 249-3700
106 N Gulf Blvd Ste C Panama City Beach (32413) *(G-13337)*
Press Printing Company, Fort Myers *Also called Press Printing Enterprises Inc (G-4368)*
Press Printing Enterprises Inc ...239 598-1500
3601 Hanson St Fort Myers (33916) *(G-4368)*
Press Room Inc ...954 792-6729
619 Sw 159th Ter Pembroke Pines (33027) *(G-13409)*
Press-Rite Inc ...954 963-7373
2125 Sw 60th Way Miramar (33023) *(G-10529)*
Pressex Inc ...727 299-8500
12910 Automobile Blvd Clearwater (33762) *(G-1751)*
Pressnet Corp ...786 728-1369
321 Nw 63rd Ct Miami (33126) *(G-9738)*
Presstige Printing, Bonita Springs *Also called Customer First Inc Naples (G-793)*
Pressure Systems Innvtions LLC ...561 249-2708
3750 Investment Ln Ste 4 West Palm Beach (33404) *(G-18128)*
Pressure Washers USA ...561 848-7970
1440 10th Ct Bay A Lake Park (33403) *(G-7133)*
Prestige A B Ready Mix, Clermont *Also called Prestige/Ab Ready Mix LLC (G-1878)*
Prestige Aluminum Railing Inc ...904 966-2163
4778 Se 142nd Way Starke (32091) *(G-16104)*
Prestige Brands International ...914 524-6800
26811 S Bay Dr Ste 300 Bonita Springs (34134) *(G-815)*
Prestige Concrete, Melbourne *Also called Prestige/Ab Ready Mix LLC (G-8499)*
Prestige Construction Jax LLC ...904 334-4772
1114 Las Robida Dr Jacksonville (32211) *(G-6385)*
Prestige Entertainment, North Miami *Also called Codsworth Industries Inc (G-11100)*
Prestige Flrg Instllations Inc ...407 291-0609
3065 Pennington Dr Orlando (32804) *(G-12503)*
Prestige Glass Art LLC ...941 921-6758
8005 Megan Hammock Way Sarasota (34240) *(G-15786)*
Prestige Granite & Marble, Orlando *Also called Prestige Flrg Instllations Inc (G-12503)*
Prestige Machine, and Tool, Largo *Also called Bonato & Pires LLC (G-7553)*
Prestige Publication Group ...305 538-9700
1688 Meridian Ave Ste 404 Miami Beach (33139) *(G-10222)*
Prestige Service Group ...954 532-9014
2520 Nw 16th Ln Pompano Beach (33064) *(G-14144)*
Prestige Spa Covers, Pinellas Park *Also called Prestige Spas Inc (G-13722)*
Prestige Spas Inc ...727 576-8600
2875 Mci Dr N Pinellas Park (33782) *(G-13722)*
Prestige/Ab Ready Mix LLC (PA) ...561 478-9980
7228 Westport Pl Ste C West Palm Beach (33413) *(G-18129)*
Prestige/Ab Ready Mix LLC ...407 654-3330
17600 State Road 50 Clermont (34711) *(G-1878)*
Prestige/Ab Ready Mix LLC ...321 751-2566
2585 Avocado Ave Melbourne (32935) *(G-8499)*
Prestige/Ab Ready Mix LLC ...772 468-4666
4190 Selvitz Rd Fort Pierce (34981) *(G-4521)*
Preston Works Inc ...850 932-0888
599 Armistead Blvd Holt (32564) *(G-5693)*
Prestressed Systems Inc ...305 556-6699
11405 Nw 112th Ct Doral (33178) *(G-3336)*
Presys Instruments Inc ...305 495-3335
14453 Sw 84th St Miami (33183) *(G-9739)*
Pret-EE LLC ...561 839-4338
4440 Pga Blvd Ste 600 Palm Beach Gardens (33410) *(G-13001)*
Pretec Directional Drlg LLC ...786 220-7667
800 S Douglas Rd Ste 1200 Coral Gables (33134) *(G-2099)*
Pretty Vulgar LLC ...561 465-8831
17605 Circle Pond Ct Boca Raton (33496) *(G-640)*
Prevail Solutions LLC ...727 210-6600
19321 Us Highway 19 N # 605 Clearwater (33764) *(G-1752)*
Prg Packing Corp (PA) ...201 242-5500
294 Sw Harvey Greene Dr Madison (32340) *(G-8046)*
Price Brothers Company ...386 328-8841
245 Comfort Rd Palatka (32177) *(G-12878)*
Price Chopper Inc ...407 679-1600
6325 Mccoy Rd Orlando (32822) *(G-12504)*
Price Chopper Wristbands, Orlando *Also called Price Chopper Inc (G-12504)*
Price Chpper Med Wrstbands Inc ...407 505-5809
6325 Mccoy Rd Orlando (32822) *(G-12505)*
Price King 2 LLC ...786 337-8801
495 W 29th St Hialeah (33012) *(G-5303)*
Pride Florida ...813 621-9262
1913 N Us Highway 301 # 100 Tampa (33619) *(G-17179)*
Priko Corp ...305 556-3558
16500 Nw 86th Ct Miami Lakes (33016) *(G-10342)*
Prima Food Corp ...954 788-0411
4020 Ne 10th Way Pompano Beach (33064) *(G-14145)*
Prima Foods International Inc ...352 732-9148
2140 Ne 36th Ave Ocala (34470) *(G-11471)*
Primal Innovation Tech LLC ...407 558-9366
10150 Highland Manor Dr # 200 Tampa (33610) *(G-17180)*
Primary Metals Intl LLC ...800 243-1923
4637 Vincennes Blvd Ste 2 Cape Coral (33904) *(G-1375)*
Prime Custom Cabinets & Design, Pompano Beach *Also called District 95 Wood Working Inc (G-13998)*
Prime Enterprises LLC ...305 625-4929
16363 Nw 49th Ave Hialeah (33014) *(G-5304)*
Prime Global Group Inc ...386 676-2200
3 E Tower Cir Ormond Beach (32174) *(G-12788)*
Prime Hotel Group US, Hollywood *Also called Phg Kendall LLC (G-5642)*
Prime Karts, Pensacola *Also called Prime Pedal Karts LLC (G-13584)*
Prime Life Ntrtn Companyllc ...754 307-7137
1239 E Nwport Ctr Dr Ste Deerfield Beach (33442) *(G-2786)*
Prime Manufacturing Canada ...850 332-7193
9235 Roe St Pensacola (32514) *(G-13583)*
Prime Matter Labs, Hialeah *Also called Prime Enterprises LLC (G-5304)*
Prime Meridian Trading Corp ...954 727-2152
4624 N Hiatus Rd Sunrise (33351) *(G-16355)*
Prime Molding Technologies Inc ...561 721-2799
3765 Investment Ln Ste A Riviera Beach (33404) *(G-14663)*
Prime Packaging Inc ...305 625-6737
16363 Nw 49th Ave Hialeah (33014) *(G-5305)*
Prime Pavers Inc ...941 320-7878
7235 Mauna Loa Blvd Sarasota (34241) *(G-15787)*
Prime Pedal Karts LLC ...850 475-0450
9235 Roe St Pensacola (32514) *(G-13584)*
Prime Tech Coatings Inc ...561 844-2312
1135 53rd Ct N Mangonia Park (33407) *(G-8099)*
Prime Technical Coatings, Mangonia Park *Also called Prime Tech Coatings Inc (G-8099)*
Prime Technological Svcs LLC ...850 539-2500
102 Technology Way Havana (32333) *(G-5002)*
Prime Topco LLC ...305 625-4929
16363 Nw 49th Ave Hialeah (33014) *(G-5306)*
Primetime Industries LLC ...813 781-0196
32671 Natural Bridge Rd Wesley Chapel (33543) *(G-17886)*
Primo Water Corporation ...844 237-7466
4221 W Boy Scout Blvd Tampa (33607) *(G-17181)*
Primus Sterilizer Company LLC (HQ) ...402 344-4200
7936 Forest City Rd Orlando (32810) *(G-12506)*
Prince Minerals Inc ...832 241-2169
710 S Rossiter St Mount Dora (32757) *(G-10611)*
Princess Preserve Inc ...954 771-7204
1660 W Mcnab Rd Fort Lauderdale (33309) *(G-3998)*
Princeton Custom Cabinetry, Margate *Also called Princeton Industries Inc (G-8149)*
Princeton Industries Inc (PA) ...954 344-9155
1790 Mears Pkwy Margate (33063) *(G-8149)*
Princeton Machine Shop, Homestead *Also called Acdm - Pms Inc (G-5697)*
Princeton Tool South LLC ...813 600-8143
9009 King Palm Dr Tampa (33619) *(G-17182)*
Print & Post Inc ...786 603-9279
18117 Biscayne Blvd Aventura (33160) *(G-272)*
Print Administrate ...407 877-5923
1273 Winter Gdn Winter Garden (34787) *(G-18400)*
Print All Promotions LLC ...800 971-3209
18202 Sandalwood Dr 18 Wildwood (34785) *(G-18317)*
Print Art Screen Printing Inc ...386 258-5186
340 Marion St Daytona Beach (32114) *(G-2585)*
Print Avenue, Naples *Also called American Business Cards Inc (G-10666)*
Print Basics Inc ...954 354-0700
1059 Sw 30th Ave Deerfield Beach (33442) *(G-2787)*
Print Big Inc ...305 398-8898
1680 W 33rd Pl Hialeah (33012) *(G-5307)*
Print Bold Corp ...305 517-1281
13995 Sw 144th Ave Ste 20 Miami (33186) *(G-9740)*
Print Dynamics ...954 524-9294
1223 N Flagler Dr Fort Lauderdale (33304) *(G-3999)*
Print E-Solution Inc ...954 588-5454
409 Goolsby Blvd Deerfield Beach (33442) *(G-2788)*
Print Esolutions, Deerfield Beach *Also called Print E-Solution Inc (G-2788)*
Print Etc Inc ...813 972-2800
13121 Canopy Creek Dr Tampa (33625) *(G-17183)*
Print Express ...904 737-6641
1889 Southampton Rd Jacksonville (32207) *(G-6386)*
Print Factory LLC ...954 392-5889
3820 Executive Way Miramar (33025) *(G-10530)*
Print Farm Inc (PA) ...305 592-2895
3511 Nw 74th Ave Miami (33122) *(G-9741)*
Print Headquarters ...772 286-2812
10358 Rverside Dr Ste 130 Palm Beach Gardens (33410) *(G-13002)*
Print It Plus, Royal Palm Beach *Also called Dakim Inc (G-14762)*
Print Mart Inc ...727 796-0064
1430 Main St Dunedin (34698) *(G-3457)*
Print Media, Miami *Also called Amtec Sales Inc (G-8729)*
Print Motion Inc ...786 212-1817
8000 Nw 31st St Ste 4 Doral (33122) *(G-3337)*
Print Now-Business Cards Today, Pensacola *Also called Printnow Inc (G-13586)*
Print One Inc ...813 273-0240
3898 Tampa Rd Ste B Oldsmar (34677) *(G-11691)*
Print Pelican, Riviera Beach *Also called Topline Prtg & Graphics Inc (G-14683)*
Print Pro Shop Inc ...305 859-8282
660 Nw 85th St Miami (33150) *(G-9742)*
Print Production Services Inc ...321 557-4414
2435 Michigan St Melbourne (32904) *(G-8500)*

Print Resources 904 316-0373
  3728 Philips Hwy Ste 11 Jacksonville (32207) **(G-6387)**

Print Rite Co 305 757-0611
  748 Ne 79th St Miami (33138) **(G-9743)**

Print Shack 352 799-2972
  210 W Jefferson St Brooksville (34601) **(G-1192)**

Print Shop of Chiefland Inc 352 493-0322
  208 N Main St Chiefland (32626) **(G-1449)**

Print Shop, The, Fort Myers Also called Proprint of Naples Inc **(G-4370)**

Print Shop, The, Chiefland Also called Print Shop of Chiefland Inc **(G-1449)**

Print Signs & Banners 305 600-1349
  4244 Sw 73rd Ave Miami (33155) **(G-9744)**

Print Signs and Banners, Miami Also called Psb Miami Corp **(G-9755)**

Print Solution Digital LLC 305 819-7420
  6540 W 20th Ave Unit 3 Hialeah (33016) **(G-5308)**

Print Store LLC 727 656-1376
  4722 Kylemore Ct Palm Harbor (34685) **(G-13124)**

Print This and That 386 344-4420
  231 Nw Burk Ave Ste 101 Lake City (32055) **(G-7038)**

Print-It Usacom Inc 954 370-2200
  13660 W State Road 84 Davie (33325) **(G-2460)**

Print123.com, Titusville Also called C & R Designs Printing LLC **(G-17578)**

Print123.com, Titusville Also called C & R Designs Inc **(G-17577)**

Printec Inc 813 854-1075
  241 Douglas Rd E Ste 1 Oldsmar (34677) **(G-11692)**

Printed Systems Inc 904 281-0909
  1309 Saint Johns Bluff Rd Jacksonville (32225) **(G-6388)**

Printer Pix 863 273-3447
  353 Gordon St Sanford (32771) **(G-15378)**

Printerpix, Lake Mary Also called Treasured Photo Gifts LLC **(G-7113)**

Printers Edge LLC 407 294-8542
  6229 Edgewater Dr Ste 400 Orlando (32810) **(G-12507)**

Printers of Pensacola LLC 850 434-2588
  1207 W Garden St Pensacola (32502) **(G-13585)**

Printers Pride Inc 813 932-8683
  7211 N Dale Mabry Hwy Tampa (33614) **(G-17184)**

Printers Printer Inc 954 917-2773
  2681 W Mcnab Rd Pompano Beach (33069) **(G-14146)**

Printers, The, Apopka Also called All Because LLC **(G-101)**

Printery, The, Sarasota Also called Gobczynskis Printery Inc **(G-15485)**

Printex Worldwide Inc 954 518-0722
  2037 Sw 31st Ave Hallandale (33009) **(G-4929)**

Printfarm, Miami Also called Print Farm Inc **(G-9741)**

Printfast & Office Supplies, Indian Harbour Beach Also called Steven M Roessler LLC **(G-5808)**

Printhouseusacom Inc 305 231-0202
  450 W 28th St Ste 2 Hialeah (33010) **(G-5309)**

Printing and Labels Inc 954 578-4411
  5405 Nw 102nd Ave Ste 218 Sunrise (33351) **(G-16356)**

Printing Connection Too Inc 954 584-4197
  4960 Sw 52nd St Ste 409 Davie (33314) **(G-2461)**

Printing Corp of Americas Inc 954 943-6087
  620 Sw 12th Ave Pompano Beach (33069) **(G-14147)**

Printing Department LLC 386 253-7990
  176 Carswell Ave Daytona Beach (32117) **(G-2586)**

Printing Depot Inc 813 855-6758
  3898 Tampa Rd Ste B Oldsmar (34677) **(G-11693)**

Printing Edge Inc 904 399-3343
  2205 Emerson St Jacksonville (32207) **(G-6389)**

Printing Express 305 512-0900
  1608 W 68th St Hialeah (33014) **(G-5310)**

Printing For A Cause LLC 786 496-0637
  360 Central Ave Ste 800 Saint Petersburg (33701) **(G-15161)**

Printing Grphics Cnnection Inc 305 222-6144
  823 Nw 133rd Ct Miami (33182) **(G-9745)**

Printing Mart Inc 954 753-0323
  1951 W Copans Rd Ste 2 Pompano Beach (33064) **(G-14148)**

Printing Mart Inc South Fla 954 753-0323
  1951 W Copans Rd Ste 2 Pompano Beach (33064) **(G-14149)**

Printing Online, Miami Also called Tag & Label of Florida Inc **(G-9992)**

Printing Place, The, New Port Richey Also called Aquinas Inc **(G-10961)**

Printing Sensations, Miami Gardens Also called Hurricane Graphics Inc **(G-10263)**

Printing Services Plus LLC 813 279-1903
  100 S Ashley Dr Tampa (33602) **(G-17185)**

Printing Unlimited, Naples Also called K R O Enterprises Ltd **(G-10795)**

Printing USA, Winter Park Also called Drewlu Enterprises Inc **(G-18509)**

Printing Usa Inc 407 857-7468
  4732 S Orange Blossom Trl Orlando (32839) **(G-12508)**

Printing.com, Tampa Also called Suncoast Specialty Prtg Inc **(G-17315)**

Printing.com, South Daytona Also called Couchman Printing Company **(G-16020)**

Printing.com, Tallahassee Also called Modern Digital Imaging Inc **(G-16481)**

Printing.com, Jacksonville Also called Holland Creative Services Inc **(G-6180)**

Printing.com, Jacksonville Also called Media Works Inc **(G-6288)**

Printing.com, Jacksonville Also called Miller Creative Graphics **(G-6306)**

Printing.com 5point, Jacksonville Also called Wingard LLC **(G-6614)**

Printmaster Inc 954 771-6104
  5220 Ne 12th Ave Oakland Park (33334) **(G-11288)**

Printmor 954 247-9405
  3941 Nw 126th Ave Coral Springs (33065) **(G-2204)**

Printmor Large Format Printing, Coral Springs Also called Printmor **(G-2204)**

Printnow Inc 850 435-1149
  5555 N Davis Hwy Ste H Pensacola (32503) **(G-13586)**

Printrust Inc 954 572-0790
  10112 W Oakland Park Blvd Sunrise (33351) **(G-16357)**

Prints 2 Go Inc 727 725-1700
  24129 Us Highway 19 N Clearwater (33763) **(G-1753)**

Printshaqcom Inc 954 678-7286
  1654 Jackson St Hollywood (33020) **(G-5646)**

Printworks 850 681-6909
  4753 Blountstown Hwy Tallahassee (32304) **(G-16490)**

Priority 1 Signs 954 971-8689
  1911 Nw 40th Ct Deerfield Beach (33064) **(G-2789)**

Priority Abatement Remediation, Tampa Also called Jfr Hazardous Services Inc **(G-16965)**

Priority Manufacturing, Miami Also called M R M S Inc **(G-9492)**

Priority One Signs, Deerfield Beach Also called Volunteer Capital LLC **(G-2832)**

Priority Printing Inc 727 446-6605
  2125 Range Rd Ste B Clearwater (33765) **(G-1754)**

Prision Brewing Co LLC 305 487-2780
  8302 Nw 14th St Doral (33126) **(G-3338)**

Prism Venture Partners LLC 561 427-6565
  675 W Indiantown Rd # 103 Jupiter (33458) **(G-6782)**

Prisma Direct 954 638-4753
  17773 Sw 24th Ct Miramar (33029) **(G-10531)**

Prisna Latino 305 525-9292
  7455 Nw 50th St Miami (33166) **(G-9746)**

Prison Legal News 561 360-2523
  1013 Lucerne Ave Ste 206 Lake Worth (33460) **(G-7229)**

Pristine Environment LLC 727 541-5748
  6575 80th Ave N Pinellas Park (33781) **(G-13723)**

Pristine Laser Center 407 389-1200
  1180 Spring Cntre S Blvd Altamonte Springs (32714) **(G-65)**

Privacy Glass Solutions, Coral Springs Also called Vistamatic LLC **(G-2226)**

Privacy Window Design Inc 386 761-7306
  600 Oak St Ste 2b Port Orange (32127) **(G-14345)**

Private Label Express, Coral Springs Also called De Lima Consultants Group Inc **(G-2148)**

Private Label Skin Na LLC 877 516-2200
  2260 118th Ave N Saint Petersburg (33716) **(G-15162)**

Prive International Inc 888 750-5850
  19597 Ne 10th Ave Ste F North Miami Beach (33179) **(G-11156)**

Prive Porter LLC 561 479-9200
  980 N Federal Hwy Boca Raton (33432) **(G-641)**

Pro Chem Products Inc 407 425-5533
  1340 W Central Blvd Orlando (32805) **(G-12509)**

Pro Co Inc 321 422-0900
  910 Belle Ave Ste 1000 Winter Springs (32708) **(G-18575)**

Pro Color Coating LLC 941 661-4769
  244 Macarthur Dr Port Charlotte (33954) **(G-14312)**

Pro Duffers Orlando 407 641-7626
  1144 Ballyshannon Pkwy Orlando (32828) **(G-12510)**

Pro Dumpsters Inc 407 910-6341
  3864 Wood Thrush Dr Kissimmee (34744) **(G-6956)**

Pro Edge Cutlery LLC 239 304-8000
  4484 Arnold Ave Naples (34104) **(G-10866)**

Pro Edge Paper, Naples Also called Pro Edge Cutlery LLC **(G-10866)**

Pro Fuse 305 982-8457
  11231 Nw 20th St Miami (33172) **(G-9747)**

Pro Horizons Inc 813 764-8844
  2610 Airport Rd Plant City (33563) **(G-13797)**

Pro Kitchen Cabinets Corp 786 768-4291
  10675 Sw 190th St Ste 110 Cutler Bay (33157) **(G-2300)**

Pro Lab Supply Corporation 305 600-0444
  12086 Miramar Pkwy Miramar (33025) **(G-10532)**

Pro Millwork Installations 561 302-5869
  1420 Sw 30th Ave Boynton Beach (33426) **(G-901)**

Pro Pak Enterprises Inc 888 375-2275
  741 Nw 42nd Way Deerfield Beach (33442) **(G-2790)**

Pro Pet Distributors, Orlando Also called Dp Pet Products Inc **(G-12103)**

Pro Poly of America Inc 352 629-1414
  230 Ne 25th Ave Ste 300 Ocala (34470) **(G-11472)**

Pro Poly of America (PA) 352 629-1414
  1821 Nw 57th St Ocala (34475) **(G-11473)**

Pro Powder Coating Inc 941 505-8010
  5474 Williamsburg Dr Punta Gorda (33982) **(G-14519)**

Pro Stair & Trim Inc 407 415-2566
  9322 Highpoint Blvd Brooksville (34613) **(G-1193)**

Pro Street Choppers Inc 407 389-2047
  917 Suwannee Dr Apopka (32703) **(G-163)**

Pro Tech Custom Cabinet 727 863-5143
  9100 Bolton Ave Port Richey (34667) **(G-14372)**

Pro Trim of Central Florida 863 294-4646
  2456 Hartridge Point Dr W Winter Haven (33881) **(G-18461)**

Pro Water Sports, Melrose Also called Lake Area Watersports LLC **(G-8571)**

Pro Water Treatment Inc 954 650-1955
  1935 Mears Pkwy Frnt Margate (33063) **(G-8150)**

Pro Weld of South Florida Inc 954 984-0104
3101 Vista Del Mar Margate (33063) *(G-8151)*

Pro-Ad Media Inc 863 802-5043
115 Allamanda Dr Lakeland (33803) *(G-7413)*

Pro-Chemicals USA Corp 305 885-7922
7575 Nw 82nd St Medley (33166) *(G-8303)*

Pro-Copy Inc 813 988-5900
5219 E Fowler Ave Temple Terrace (33617) *(G-17543)*

Pro-Crete Material Corporation 352 748-1505
1617 S Division Ave Orlando (32805) *(G-12511)*

Pro-Lab, Weston *Also called Professional Laboratories Inc (G-18280)*

Pro-Machine Inc 407 296-5031
6150 Edgewater Dr Ste H Orlando (32810) *(G-12512)*

Pro-Mix Inc 305 556-6699
11405 Nw 138th St Medley (33178) *(G-8304)*

Pro-Publishing Inc 954 888-7726
18020 Sw 66th St Southwest Ranches (33331) *(G-16057)*

Pro-Tech Coatings Inc 813 248-1477
3201 E 3rd Ave Tampa (33605) *(G-17186)*

Pro-Tools, Temple Terrace *Also called Phoenix Enterprises Fla LLC (G-17542)*

Pro-Trim Millwork Inc 239 592-5454
3995 Upolo Ln Naples (34119) *(G-10867)*

Pro-Weld Inc 863 453-9353
222 S Forest Ave Unit 1 Avon Park (33825) *(G-286)*

Proandre Hygiene Systems Inc 305 433-3493
1200 Brickell Ave # 1950 Miami (33131) *(G-9748)*

Probag Inc 305 883-3266
9955 Nw 88th Ave Medley (33178) *(G-8305)*

Probalance Inc 727 531-8506
28059 Us Highway 19 N # 300 Clearwater (33761) *(G-1755)*

Probiora Health LLC 214 850-2519
6302 Benjamin Rd Ste 409 Tampa (33634) *(G-17187)*

Probotix 844 472-9262
628 Lovejoy Rd Nw Unit 3e Fort Walton Beach (32548) *(G-4603)*

Process Automation Corporation 727 541-6280
5260 87th Ave N Pinellas Park (33782) *(G-13724)*

Process Solutions, Palm Beach Gardens *Also called United Associates Group Inc (G-13014)*

Procorp LLC 904 477-6762
8535 Baymeadows Rd Ste 58 Jacksonville (32256) *(G-6390)*

Procraft Cabinetry Florida LLC 754 212-2277
1850 S Powerline Rd Ste A Deerfield Beach (33442) *(G-2791)*

Procyon Corporation (PA) 727 447-2998
1300 S Highland Ave Clearwater (33756) *(G-1756)*

Prodair Corporation (HQ) 850 994-5511
4575 Highway 90 Milton (32571) *(G-10433)*

Prodalim USA Inc (HQ) 407 656-1000
355 9th St Winter Garden (34787) *(G-18401)*

Prodeco Technologies LLC 954 974-6730
1601 Green Rd Deerfield Beach (33064) *(G-2792)*

Prodigy Customs 407 832-1752
527 Little Wekiva Rd Altamonte Springs (32714) *(G-66)*

Produce Business Magazine, Boca Raton *Also called Phoenix Media Network Inc (G-633)*

Product Dev Experts Inc 714 366-9000
2440 Se Federal Hwy # 101 Stuart (34994) *(G-16201)*

Product Dev Partners LLC 813 908-6775
6291 W Linebaugh Ave Tampa (33625) *(G-17188)*

Product Max Group Inc 813 949-5061
8011 Land O Lakes Blvd Land O Lakes (34638) *(G-7500)*

Production Metal Stampings Inc 850 981-8240
8133 Opportunity Dr Milton (32583) *(G-10434)*

Production System Engineering 863 299-7330
3204 E Lake Hamilton Dr Winter Haven (33881) *(G-18462)*

Productiv Elements LLC 305 283-4790
8815 Sw 96th St Miami (33176) *(G-9749)*

Productive Products Inc 904 570-5553
321 Valverde Ln Saint Augustine (32086) *(G-14875)*

Products By O2 Inc 561 392-1892
3020 High Ridge Rd # 300 Boynton Beach (33426) *(G-902)*

Profab Corporation 352 369-5010
1056 Ne 16th St Ocala (34470) *(G-11474)*

Profab Corporation (PA) 352 369-5515
4901 Nw 5th St Ocala (34482) *(G-11475)*

Profab Electronics Inc 954 917-1998
2855 W Mcnab Rd Pompano Beach (33069) *(G-14150)*

Profab Plastics, Ocala *Also called Profab Corporation (G-11475)*

Profast Corporation 305 827-7801
5854 Miami Lakes Dr E Miami Lakes (33014) *(G-10343)*

Profast Usa Inc 305 827-7801
5854 Miami Lakes Dr E Miami Lakes (33014) *(G-10344)*

Profbox of America Inc 786 454-8148
17071 W Dixie Hwy Ste 116 North Miami Beach (33160) *(G-11157)*

Professional Bindery Inc 305 633-3761
3668 Nw 48th Ter Miami (33142) *(G-9750)*

Professional Coating Systems 904 477-7138
2187 Nw 247th St Lawtey (32058) *(G-7746)*

Professional Ctr At Gardens 561 394-5200
190 Se 5th Ave Delray Beach (33483) *(G-3004)*

Professional Engrv & Trophy, North Miami *Also called Cabus USA Inc (G-11096)*

Professional Holiday Lighting 208 709-2968
181 Royal Dunes Cir Ormond Beach (32176) *(G-12789)*

Professional Kitchen Cabinets 305 888-5660
1035 E 13th St Hialeah (33010) *(G-5311)*

Professional Laboratories Inc 954 384-4446
1675 N Commerce Pkwy Weston (33326) *(G-18280)*

Professional Pet Products Inc 305 592-1992
1873 Nw 97th Ave Doral (33172) *(G-3339)*

Professional Products 323 754-1287
4949 Marbrisa Dr Apt 102 Tampa (33624) *(G-17189)*

Professional Products Inc 850 892-5731
54 Hugh Adams Rd Defuniak Springs (32435) *(G-2842)*

Professional Shoring & Supply, Tampa *Also called Fw Shoring Company (G-16867)*

Professional Shoring & Supply, Orlando *Also called Fw Shoring Company (G-12179)*

Professional Signs 305 662-5957
6460 Sw 35th St Miami (33155) *(G-9751)*

Professional Site & Trnspt Inc 386 239-6800
3728 W Intl Spwy Blvd Daytona Beach (32124) *(G-2587)*

Professnl Kit Instller Group 954 436-1513
1892 Sw 152nd Ter Miramar (33027) *(G-10533)*

Professnl Mtal Innovation Inc 786 354-3091
3492 W 84th St Unit 110 Hialeah (33018) *(G-5312)*

Professnl Reproduction of Jax 904 389-4141
7029 Commonwealth Ave Jacksonville (32220) *(G-6391)*

Professional Paver Restorations 352 797-8411
3259 Dothan Ave Spring Hill (34609) *(G-16075)*

Professor Software Company 561 691-5455
268 Barbados Dr Jupiter (33458) *(G-6783)*

Profile Packaging Inc 941 359-6678
1712 Northgate Blvd Sarasota (34234) *(G-15788)*

Profile Racing Inc 727 392-8307
4803 95th St N Saint Petersburg (33708) *(G-15163)*

Profile Tool & Gear, Saint Petersburg *Also called Profile Racing Inc (G-15163)*

Profilegorilla, Jacksonville *Also called Silvershore Partners LLC (G-6472)*

Profire Inc 305 665-5313
9621 S Dixie Hwy Pinecrest (33156) *(G-13669)*

Profitsword LLC 407 909-8822
7512 Dr Phillips Blvd Orlando (32819) *(G-12513)*

Profold Inc 772 589-0063
10300 99th Way Sebastian (32958) *(G-15903)*

Proform Finishing Products LLC 813 672-8269
12949 S Us Highway 41 Gibsonton (33534) *(G-4799)*

Proform Finishing Products LLC 407 438-3450
1650 Central Florida Pkwy Orlando (32837) *(G-12514)*

Proform Finishing Products LLC 904 284-0221
1767 Wildwood Rd Green Cove Springs (32043) *(G-4833)*

Profounda Health & Beauty 407 270-7792
10501 S Orange Ave # 124 Orlando (32824) *(G-12515)*

Program Works Inc 407 489-4140
1511 E State Road 434 # 2001 Winter Springs (32708) *(G-18576)*

Prographix Inc 863 298-8081
2614 Avenue G Nw Winter Haven (33880) *(G-18463)*

Progress Fuels Corporation (HQ) 727 824-6600
1 Progress Plz Fl 11 Saint Petersburg (33701) *(G-15164)*

Progress Rail Services Corp 352 748-8008
4198 E County Road 462 Wildwood (34785) *(G-18318)*

Progress Rail Services Corp 239 643-3013
3581 Mercantile Ave Naples (34104) *(G-10868)*

Progress Rail Services Corp 904 783-1143
420 Agmac Ave Jacksonville (32254) *(G-6392)*

Progress Wine Group, Miami *Also called Fws Distributors LLC (G-9181)*

Progressive Aerodyne Inc 352 253-0108
3801 State Road 19 Tavares (32778) *(G-17521)*

Progressive Cabinetry 941 866-6975
6404 Manatee Ave W Ste N Bradenton (34209) *(G-1033)*

Progressive Industrial Inc 941 723-0201
1412 18th Avenue Dr E Palmetto (34221) *(G-13187)*

Progressive Machine Co Inc 386 333-6850
3 E Tower Cir Ormond Beach (32174) *(G-12790)*

Progressive Power Products Inc 904 354-1819
4062 N Liberty St Jacksonville (32206) *(G-6393)*

Progressive Printing Co Inc 904 388-0746
4505 Lexington Ave Jacksonville (32210) *(G-6394)*

Progressive Printing Services, Delray Beach *Also called Progressive Printing Solutions (G-3005)*

Progressive Printing Solutions 800 370-5591
601 N Congress Ave # 208 Delray Beach (33445) *(G-3005)*

Progressive Screens, Sarasota *Also called Defender Screens Intl LLC (G-15654)*

Project and Cnstr Wldg Inc 239 772-9299
2603 Andalusia Blvd Cape Coral (33909) *(G-1376)*

Project Mold 561 213-6167
7666 Cypress Cres Boca Raton (33433) *(G-642)*

Project Pros Woodworking Inc 239 454-6800
17051 Jean St Ste 12 Fort Myers (33967) *(G-4369)*

Projstream LLC 407 476-1084
1540 Intl Pkwy 2000 Lake Mary (32746) *(G-7103)*

Prolabel Inc 305 620-2202
621 W 20th St Hialeah (33010) *(G-5313)*

Prolific Cabinetry & More Inc 904 448-6575
7660 Philips Hwy Ste 5 Jacksonville (32256) *(G-6395)*

A
L
P
H
A
B
E
T
I
C

Prolific Resource Inc 727 868-9341
12045 Cobble Stone Dr Port Richey (34667) *(G-14373)*

Proline Chemical & Plastics LL 850 835-6822
9646 State Highway 20 W Freeport (32439) *(G-4628)*

Prolink Software Corporation 860 659-5928
999 Vanderbilt Beach Rd Naples (34108) *(G-10869)*

Promed Biosciences Inc 888 655-9155
9375 Us Highway 19 N A Pinellas Park (33782) *(G-13725)*

Promedica Inc 813 854-1905
114 Douglas Rd E Oldsmar (34677) *(G-11694)*

Promex LLC 305 884-2400
1415 E 11th Ave Hialeah (33010) *(G-5314)*

Promo Daddy LLC 877 557-2336
812 N Apollo Blvd Melbourne (32935) *(G-8501)*

Promo Daddy LLC (PA) 352 390-3081
800 N Apollo Blvd Melbourne (32935) *(G-8502)*

Promo Printing Group, Tampa *Also called PPG Inc (G-17172)*

Promo Printing Group Inc 813 541-3509
3210 S Dale Mabry Hwy Tampa (33629) *(G-17190)*

Promoitalia LLC 305 347-5178
1221 Brickell Ave Miami (33131) *(G-9752)*

Promotional Concepts Team, Hallandale Beach *Also called Jpl Associates Inc (G-4955)*

Promotional Mktg Online LLC 941 347-8564
17377 Ophir Ln Punta Gorda (33955) *(G-14520)*

Promowear 561 372-0505
9547 Cinnamon Ct Parkland (33076) *(G-13350)*

Propak Software, Winter Haven *Also called Central Fla Bus Solutions Inc (G-18430)*

Propel Builders Inc 407 960-5116
111 S Maitland Ave # 200 Maitland (32751) *(G-8070)*

Property Armor, Jacksonville *Also called Rm Brands Inc (G-6431)*

Property Solutions and Cnstr, Jacksonville *Also called A Clean Finish Inc (G-5846)*

Propglide USA Corp 305 520-0150
4769 Nw 72nd Ave Miami (33166) *(G-9753)*

Proplus Products Inc 863 375-2487
149 County Line Rd E Bowling Green (33834) *(G-831)*

Proprint of Naples Inc (PA) 239 775-3553
5900 Enterprise Pkwy Fort Myers (33905) *(G-4370)*

Propulsion Tech Intl LLC 954 874-0274
15301 Sw 29th St Ste 100 Miramar (33027) *(G-10534)*

Prosegur Eas Usa LLC 561 900-2744
598 Hillsboro Tech Dr Deerfield Beach (33441) *(G-2793)*

Proserv Technologies Inc 727 265-3190
2148 Tamarron Ter Palm Harbor (34683) *(G-13125)*

Proservices Supply LLC 858 254-4415
12620 Beach Blvd Ste 3304 Jacksonville (32246) *(G-6396)*

Proshowmaker Inc 813 765-2676
2310 Foggy Ridge Pkwy Land O Lakes (34639) *(G-7501)*

Prosolus Inc (HQ) 305 514-0270
6701 Nw 7th St Ste 165 Miami (33126) *(G-9754)*

Prospect Avenue Rm, Naples *Also called Cemex Cnstr Mtls Fla LLC (G-10708)*

Prospect Plastics Inc 954 564-7282
836 Ne 44th St Oakland Park (33334) *(G-11289)*

Prospects Plastics, Oakland Park *Also called Prospect Plastics Inc (G-11289)*

Prosthetic Laboratories 305 250-9900
1270 Bird Rd Coral Gables (33146) *(G-2100)*

Prosun International LLC 727 825-0400
2442 23rd St N Saint Petersburg (33713) *(G-15165)*

Protect All Coating Inc 727 278-7454
2458 36th Ave N Saint Petersburg (33713) *(G-15166)*

Protective Enclosures Co LLC 321 441-9689
277 Douglas Ave Ste 1012 Altamonte Springs (32714) *(G-67)*

Protective Group A Point Blank, Pompano Beach *Also called Point Blank Enterprises Inc (G-14134)*

Protective Group A Pt Blank Co, Miami Lakes *Also called Point Blank Enterprises Inc (G-10340)*

Protective Group Inc 305 820-4266
14100 Nw 58th Ct Miami Lakes (33014) *(G-10345)*

Protective Products Entps, Pompano Beach *Also called Point Blank Enterprises Inc (G-14133)*

Protective Products Entps Inc 954 630-0900
2102 Sw 2nd St Pompano Beach (33069) *(G-14151)*

Protege Media LLC 310 738-9567
5945 Nw Dowell Ct Port Saint Lucie (34986) *(G-14435)*

Protek Custom Coatings LLC 850 656-7923
1320 Gateshead Cir Tallahassee (32317) *(G-16491)*

Protek Electronics Inc 941 351-4399
1781 Independence Blvd Sarasota (34234) *(G-15789)*

Protek Systems Inc 561 395-8155
1250 Wallace Dr Ste B Delray Beach (33444) *(G-3006)*

Protex Inc 727 573-4665
10500 47th St N Clearwater (33762) *(G-1757)*

Protext Mobility Inc (PA) 435 881-3611
55 Se 2nd Ave Delray Beach (33444) *(G-3007)*

Proto Corp 727 573-4665
10500 47th St N Clearwater (33762) *(G-1758)*

Proto Plus Inc 561 471-5325
350 Tall Pines Rd Ste B West Palm Beach (33413) *(G-18130)*

Prototype Plastics LLC 941 371-3380
1523 Edgar Pl Sarasota (34240) *(G-15790)*

Prototype Plstic Extrusion Inc 727 572-0803
3637 131st Ave N Clearwater (33762) *(G-1759)*

Proud Tshirts Corp 888 233-3426
1801 Ne 123rd St Ste 314 North Miami (33181) *(G-11116)*

Proven Industries Inc 813 895-4385
2310 S Dock St Ste 111 Palmetto (34221) *(G-13188)*

Provictus Inc 561 437-0232
4440 Pga Blvd Ste 635 Palm Beach Gardens (33410) *(G-13003)*

Prowin Industries Inc 954 584-5686
6120 Nw 11th St Sunrise (33313) *(G-16358)*

Proximity Mills LLC 813 251-3060
4020 W Kennedy Blvd # 10 Tampa (33609) *(G-17191)*

Prs In Vivo Holdings Inc 305 420-5935
1680 Michigan Ave Ste 722 Miami Beach (33139) *(G-10223)*

PS & QS Custom Prints LLC 352 231-3961
4024 Ne 1st Dr Gainesville (32609) *(G-4751)*

PS Cabinet Works Inc 239 850-2162
217 Jefferson Ave Lehigh Acres (33936) *(G-7823)*

Psb Miami Corp 786 870-4880
7406 Sw 48th St Miami (33155) *(G-9755)*

PSC Building Group Inc 561 756-6811
900 Sw 15th Ave Delray Beach (33444) *(G-3008)*

PSI, Oldsmar *Also called Peripheral Services Inc (G-11685)*

PSI Printing, Jacksonville *Also called Printed Systems Inc (G-6388)*

PSM, Jupiter *Also called Power Systems Mfg LLC (G-6779)*

Psp Industrial Laundry Eqp LLC 305 517-1421
2700 Gateway Dr Pompano Beach (33069) *(G-14152)*

Pss Communications Inc 408 496-3330
309 Bryce Ct Sun City Center (33573) *(G-16266)*

PST, Clearwater *Also called Precision Shaft Technology (G-1748)*

PST Computers, Deerfield Beach *Also called P S T Computers Inc (G-2778)*

Pstein Inc 305 373-0037
4350 W Hllandale Bch Blvd Pembroke Park (33023) *(G-13364)*

Psychlgcal Assssment Rsrces In (PA) 813 968-3003
16204 N Florida Ave Lutz (33549) *(G-8012)*

Pte Systems International LLC (PA) 305 863-3409
1950 W 8th Ave Hialeah (33010) *(G-5315)*

Ptse Holding Inc 800 760-0027
634 State Road 44 Leesburg (34748) *(G-7789)*

Publi Signs 954 927-4411
250 N Dixie Hwy Unit 5 Hollywood (33020) *(G-5647)*

Public Image Printing Inc 727 363-1800
5050 Gulf Blvd Ste C St Pete Beach (33706) *(G-16092)*

Publicaciones Internacional, Doral *Also called Spanish Peri & Bk Sls Inc (G-3371)*

Publify Press Inc (PA) 774 248-4056
2412 Irwin St Ste 53 Melbourne (32901) *(G-8503)*

Publishers Crcltion Flfllment 877 723-6668
3351b Mclemore Dr Pensacola (32514) *(G-13587)*

Publishers Direct Choice LLC 305 264-5998
1440 Sw 78th Ave Miami (33144) *(G-9756)*

Publishers Guild Inc 904 273-5394
2309 Sawgrass Village Dr Ponte Vedra Beach (32082) *(G-14278)*

Publishers of Seniors Today, South Daytona *Also called Merle Harris Enterprises Inc (G-16024)*

Publishing, Venice *Also called D-R Media and Investments LLC (G-17682)*

Publishing Research Inc 954 921-4026
1313 Ne 125th St North Miami (33161) *(G-11117)*

Puch Manufacturing Corporation 407 650-9926
3701 Saint Valentine Way Orlando (32811) *(G-12516)*

Pulau International Corp (PA) 407 380-9191
12633 Challenger Pkwy # 2 Orlando (32826) *(G-12517)*

Pulling Inc 305 224-2469
12797 Nw 13th St Sunrise (33323) *(G-16359)*

Pulsaderm LLC 877 474-4038
12801 Commwl Dr Ste 2 Fort Myers (33913) *(G-4371)*

Pulsafeeder Inc 941 575-2900
27101 Airport Rd Punta Gorda (33982) *(G-14521)*

Pulsafeeder Spo Inc 941 575-3800
27101 Airport Rd Punta Gorda (33982) *(G-14522)*

Pulsar Process Measurement Inc 850 279-4882
11451 Belcher Rd S Largo (33773) *(G-7664)*

Puma Aero Marine Inc 904 638-5888
622 Ne 14th Ave Apt 10 Fort Lauderdale (33304) *(G-4000)*

Puma Marble Co Inc 305 758-6461
5445 Nw 2nd Ave Miami (33127) *(G-9757)*

Punta Gorda Sun Herald, Port Charlotte *Also called Sun Coast Media Group Inc (G-14317)*

Puppet Workshop Inc (PA) 305 666-2655
295 E 10th Ct Hialeah (33010) *(G-5316)*

Puppet Workshop Inc 305 666-2655
7040 Sw 47th St Fl 2 Miami (33155) *(G-9758)*

Pura Vida Dairy Inc 305 817-1762
3130 W 84th St U1 Hialeah (33018) *(G-5317)*

Puradyn Filter Tech Inc 561 547-9499
2017 High Ridge Rd Boynton Beach (33426) *(G-903)*

Puragen LLC (HQ) 561 907-5400
1601 Forum Pl Ste 1400 West Palm Beach (33401) *(G-18131)*

Puragen LLC 760 630-5724
11300 Us Highway 1 # 203 North Palm Beach (33408) *(G-11182)*
Puraglobe Florida LLC 813 247-1754
4420 Pendola Point Rd Tampa (33619) *(G-17192)*
Purchasing Department, West Palm Beach *Also called Florida Crystals Corporation* *(G-18002)*
Pure Bright Lighting LLC 954 780-8700
711 Bayshore Dr Apt 302 Fort Lauderdale (33304) *(G-4001)*
Pure Laboratories LLC 888 425-6649
5909 Nw 18th Dr Gainesville (32653) *(G-4752)*
Pure Labs LLC 561 659-2229
240 10th St 1 West Palm Beach (33401) *(G-18132)*
Pure Lead Products, Lake Placid *Also called Heartland Metals Inc* *(G-7141)*
Pure Postcards Inc 877 446-2434
1938 Byram Dr Clearwater (33755) *(G-1760)*
Pure Solutions Inc 813 925-1098
14100 Mccormick Dr Tampa (33626) *(G-17193)*
Pure Source LLC 305 477-8111
9750 Nw 17th St Doral (33172) *(G-3340)*
Pure Source, The, Doral *Also called Pure Source LLC* *(G-3340)*
Pure Water Changes Inc 407 699-2837
7775 Maslin St Windermere (34786) *(G-18363)*
Pure Wave Organics Inc 321 368-7002
2861 Saint James Ln Melbourne (32935) *(G-8504)*
Pure-Chlor Systems Florida Inc 305 437-9937
8200 Nw 33rd St Ste 109 Tampa (33614) *(G-17194)*
Purecoat International LLC (PA) 561 844-0100
3301 Elec Way Ste B West Palm Beach (33407) *(G-18133)*
Purecycle Technologies Inc (PA) 877 648-3565
5950 Hazeltine National D Orlando (32822) *(G-12518)*
Purify Fuels Inc 949 842-6159
14113 N Cypress Cove Cir Davie (33325) *(G-2462)*
Purina Animal Nutrition LLC 863 262-4332
2815 Drane Field Rd Lakeland (33811) *(G-7414)*
Puritair LLC 954 281-5105
1320 Nw 65th Pl Ste 201 Fort Lauderdale (33309) *(G-4002)*
Puromax, Port Charlotte *Also called Fshs Inc* *(G-14301)*
Purovite Inc 305 364-5727
7347 Sw 45th St Miami (33155) *(G-9759)*
Purox Brands Corp 305 392-0738
5801 E 10th Ave Unit 108 Hialeah (33013) *(G-5318)*
Purplefly Press LLC 954 682-2726
2301 Nw 93rd Ln Sunrise (33322) *(G-16360)*
Pursuit Boats, Fort Pierce *Also called Pb Holdco LLC* *(G-4516)*
Pusateri, Thomas J MD, Zephyrhills *Also called Pasco Vision Center* *(G-18623)*
Push Designs Printing Inc 321 591-1645
1101 W Hibiscus Blvd # 204 Melbourne (32901) *(G-8505)*
Pusher Intakes Inc 772 212-9290
9100 16th Pl Vero Beach (32966) *(G-17789)*
Put Your Name On It LLC 813 972-1460
16057 Tampa Palms Blvd W # 4 Tampa (33647) *(G-17195)*
Putnam Paper & Packaging Inc 904 328-5101
109 Jax Ln Palatka (32177) *(G-12879)*
Puzzled Caterpillars Inc 904 379-9219
5230 Anisa Ct Jacksonville (32209) *(G-6397)*
Pvc Spiral Supply, Tampa *Also called Marlon Inc* *(G-17041)*
Pvc Windoors Inc 305 940-3608
1815 Ne 144th St North Miami (33181) *(G-11118)*
Pvh Corp 850 269-0482
10746 Us Highway 98 W # 158 Miramar Beach (32550) *(G-10571)*
PWS International 850 432-4222
5 Clarinda Ln Pensacola (32505) *(G-13588)*
Pylon Manufacturing Corp (HQ) 800 626-4902
600 W Hillsboro Blvd # 4 Deerfield Beach (33441) *(G-2794)*
Pyramid Imaging Inc 813 984-0125
945 E 11th Ave Tampa (33605) *(G-17196)*
Pyramid Mouldings, Green Cove Springs *Also called Artemis Holdings Llc* *(G-4816)*
Pyrotecnico of Florida LLC 352 588-5086
30435 Commerce Dr Ste 102 San Antonio (33576) *(G-15251)*
Pyure Company Inc 561 735-3701
2055 High Ridge Rd Boynton Beach (33426) *(G-904)*
Q E M Inc 727 545-8833
6513 116th Ave Largo (33773) *(G-7665)*
Q Industries Inc 954 689-2263
401 E Las Olas Blvd # 130 Fort Lauderdale (33301) *(G-4003)*
Q Plastering and Stucco Inc 239 530-1712
5422 Texas Ave Naples (34113) *(G-10870)*
Q Sea, Tampa *Also called Ultrasonics and Magnetics* *(G-17385)*
Q Squared Design LLC 212 686-8860
19064 Marquesa Dr Fort Myers (33913) *(G-4372)*
Q-Pac Systems Inc 904 863-5300
4010 Deerpark Blvd Elkton (32033) *(G-3509)*
Q2 Aerospace LLC 305 591-9469
1751 Nw 129th Ave Ste 115 Miami (33182) *(G-9760)*
Qci Britannic Inc (PA) 305 860-0102
1600 Ponce De Leon Blvd # 907 Coral Gables (33134) *(G-2101)*
Qcms, Sarasota *Also called Quality Contract Mfg Svcs LLC* *(G-15540)*
QEP Co Inc 561 994-5550
1001 Broken Sound Pkwy Nw A Boca Raton (33487) *(G-643)*

Qgiv Inc 888 855-9595
207 Bartow Rd Lakeland (33801) *(G-7415)*
Qhslab Inc 929 379-6503
901 Nrthpint Pkwy Ste 302 West Palm Beach (33407) *(G-18134)*
Qlty Alumn Boat Lifts Inc 850 434-6446
2375 W Herman Ave Pensacola (32505) *(G-13589)*
Qol Medical LLC (PA) 772 584-3640
3405 Ocean Dr Vero Beach (32963) *(G-17790)*
Qorvo Inc 407 886-8860
1818 S Orange Blossom Trl Apopka (32703) *(G-164)*
Qorvo Us Inc 407 886-8860
1818 S Orange Blossom Trl Apopka (32703) *(G-165)*
QP Consulting Inc 321 727-2442
2110 Dairy Rd Ste 102 Melbourne (32904) *(G-8506)*
Qps Companies Inc (PA) 813 246-5525
9110 King Palm Dr Ste 101 Tampa (33619) *(G-17197)*
Qsrr Corporation 305 322-9867
3126 John P Curci Dr # 4 Hallandale Beach (33009) *(G-4967)*
Qssi, Tampa *Also called Nightscenes Inc* *(G-17111)*
Qtm Inc 813 891-1300
300 Stevens Ave Oldsmar (34677) *(G-11695)*
Qtronics Inc 850 267-0102
279 Santa Rosa St Santa Rosa Beach (32459) *(G-15431)*
Quad Intl Incorporated 305 662-5959
1629 Nw 84th Ave Doral (33126) *(G-3341)*
Quad/Graphics Inc 813 837-3436
4646 S Grady Ave Tampa (33611) *(G-17198)*
Quadramed Corporation 904 355-2900
225 Water St Ste 2250 Jacksonville (32202) *(G-6398)*
Quail Height Golf Club 386 752-3339
161 Sw Quail Heights Ter Lake City (32025) *(G-7039)*
Quaker Oats Company 407 846-5926
1650 S Poinciana Blvd Kissimmee (34758) *(G-6957)*
Qualcomm Atheros Inc 407 284-7314
5955 T G Lee Blvd Ste 600 Orlando (32822) *(G-12519)*
Qualitel Inc 954 464-3991
2414 N Federal Hwy Hollywood (33020) *(G-5648)*
Qualitest USA Lc 877 884-8378
401 E Las Olas Blvd Ste 1 Fort Lauderdale (33301) *(G-4004)*
Quality 1 Appraisal Inc 786 859-4085
18831 Nw 78th Pl Hialeah (33015) *(G-5319)*
Quality Aerospace Coatings LLC 863 619-2628
3610 Airport Rd Lakeland (33811) *(G-7416)*
Quality Alum Boat Lifts Inc 850 434-6446
2375 W Herman Ave Pensacola (32505) *(G-13590)*
Quality Anodizing Inc 954 791-8711
5990 Sw 42nd Pl Davie (33314) *(G-2463)*
Quality Arts Lcp LLC 305 735-2310
7880 W 25th Ct Hialeah (33016) *(G-5320)*
Quality Bakery Products LLC (HQ) 954 779-3663
888 E Las Olas Blvd # 700 Fort Lauderdale (33301) *(G-4005)*
Quality Banner Company, Ocala *Also called AMI Graphics Inc* *(G-11322)*
Quality Beverage Services, Tampa *Also called Dcg Enterprises LLC* *(G-16768)*
Quality Block & Supply Inc 863 425-3070
1590 Industrial Park Rd Mulberry (33860) *(G-10635)*
Quality Building Controls Inc 813 885-5005
10011 Williams Rd Tampa (33624) *(G-17199)*
Quality Cabinets & Counters 239 948-5364
7869 Drew Cir Unit 1 Fort Myers (33967) *(G-4373)*
Quality Cable & Communications, Orlando *Also called Quality Cable Contractors Inc* *(G-12520)*
Quality Cable Contractors Inc 407 246-0606
1936 Premier Row Orlando (32809) *(G-12520)*
Quality Cmpnents Tampa Bay LLC 727 623-4909
6801 114th Ave Largo (33773) *(G-7666)*
Quality Cmponents Assembly Inc 954 792-5151
440 Nw 27th Ave Fort Lauderdale (33311) *(G-4006)*
Quality Contract Mfg Svcs LLC 941 355-7787
1905 72nd Dr E Sarasota (34243) *(G-15540)*
Quality Creations Inc 727 571-4332
10550 47th St N Clearwater (33762) *(G-1761)*
Quality Custom Cabinet Design 352 728-4292
2215 Griffin Rd Leesburg (34748) *(G-7790)*
Quality Custom Cabinets LLC 201 873-6607
1155 Sanddune Ln Apt 206 Melbourne (32935) *(G-8507)*
Quality Driven 941 923-3322
4023 Sawyer Rd Unit 216 Sarasota (34233) *(G-15791)*
Quality Enclosures, Sarasota *Also called Sarasota Shower Door Company* *(G-15815)*
Quality Engineered Products Co 813 885-1693
4506 Quality Ln Tampa (33634) *(G-17200)*
Quality Fabrication Mch Works, Lake City *Also called Quality Industries America Inc* *(G-7041)*
Quality Fbrction Mch Works Inc 386 755-0220
3631 E Us Highway 90 Lake City (32055) *(G-7040)*
Quality Finishers Inc 954 782-3073
640 Ne 26th Ct Pompano Beach (33064) *(G-14153)*
Quality Images, Jacksonville *Also called Impact Design Group Inc* *(G-6193)*
Quality Industrial Chem Inc 727 573-5760
3161 118th Ave N Saint Petersburg (33716) *(G-15167)*

Quality Industries America Inc (PA) 386 755-0220
   3631 E Us Highway 90 Lake City (32055) *(G-7041)*

Quality Life Publishing Co 239 513-9907
   6210 Shirley St Ste 112 Naples (34109) *(G-10871)*

Quality Machine Service Inc 610 554-3917
   2199 Fernwood St Port Charlotte (33948) *(G-14313)*

Quality Manufacturing Svcs Inc 407 531-6000
   400 Caring Dr Ste 1010 Lake Mary (32746) *(G-7104)*

Quality Metal Fabricators Inc 813 831-7320
   2610 E 5th Ave Tampa (33605) *(G-17201)*

Quality Metal Works, Plant City *Also called Telese Properties Inc (G-13809)*

Quality Metal Works, Plant City *Also called Telese Inc (G-13808)*

Quality Metal Worx LLC 863 353-6638
   1306 Melbourne Ave Haines City (33844) *(G-4914)*

Quality Mills, Lake City *Also called Grizzly Manufacturing Inc (G-7024)*

Quality Molds USA Inc 321 632-6066
   2402 Cherbourg Rd Cocoa (32926) *(G-1950)*

Quality Neon Sign Company (PA) 904 268-4681
   5300 Shad Rd Jacksonville (32257) *(G-6399)*

Quality Pavers South Fla LLC 954 881-1919
   11200 Nw 18th St Plantation (33323) *(G-13879)*

Quality Petroleum Corp 863 635-6708
   301 Hwy 630 E Frostproof (33843) *(G-4640)*

Quality Powder Coating Inc 941 378-0051
   2025 Porter Lake Dr F Sarasota (34240) *(G-15792)*

Quality Precast & Company 407 877-1000
   416 E Bay St Winter Garden (34787) *(G-18402)*

Quality Precision Pdts Co Inc 305 885-4596
   678 W 27th St Hialeah (33010) *(G-5321)*

Quality Printing Inc 386 255-1565
   705 W Intl Speedway Blvd Daytona Beach (32114) *(G-2588)*

Quality Railings Miami Corp 786 400-0462
   460 W 18th St Hialeah (33010) *(G-5322)*

Quality Ready Mix Inc (PA) 561 833-5555
   1720 Centrepark Dr E # 100 West Palm Beach (33401) *(G-18135)*

Quality Rescreening 941 625-9765
   17221 Alico Center Rd # 2 Fort Myers (33967) *(G-4374)*

Quality Screen Enclosure LLC 954 226-1980
   3800 Hillcrest Dr Apt 210 Hollywood (33021) *(G-5649)*

Quality Shavings South Florida 561 433-9955
   10191 Lantana Rd Lake Worth (33449) *(G-7230)*

Quality Socket Screw Mfg Corp 941 475-9585
   2790 Worth Ave Englewood (34224) *(G-3522)*

Quality Software LLC 561 714-2314
   55 Se 2nd Ave 1 Delray Beach (33444) *(G-3009)*

Quality Steel Fabricators Inc 813 247-7110
   4544 Hartford St Tampa (33619) *(G-17202)*

Quality Stinless Stl Works Inc 305 519-0142
   873 W 48th St Hialeah (33012) *(G-5323)*

Quality Stones R US LLC 904 551-5619
   10475 Fortune Pkwy St Jacksonville (32256) *(G-6400)*

Quality Tool Inc 386 265-1492
   659 Copeland Dr Haines City (33844) *(G-4915)*

Quality Vaults Inc (PA) 407 656-8781
   751 S Bluford Ave Ocoee (34761) *(G-11525)*

Quality Wood Machine Inc 305 221-0218
   8410 Sw 33rd Ter Miami (33155) *(G-9761)*

Qualitysat Corp 305 232-4211
   13355 Sw 135th Ave Miami (33186) *(G-9762)*

Qualtec Solutions, Ocala *Also called HA Morton Corp (G-11406)*

Quantachrome Instruments, Boynton Beach *Also called Anton Paar Quantatec Inc (G-841)*

Quantem Fbo Group Kssimmee LLC 407 846-8001
   3950 Merlin Dr Kissimmee (34741) *(G-6958)*

Quantoro Publishing, Miami *Also called Quanturo Publishing Inc (G-9767)*

Quantum Assets LLC 786 484-1187
   638 Nw 11th St Miami (33136) *(G-9763)*

Quantum Care R&D LLC 407 365-1179
   1339 Palo Alto Ct Winter Springs (32708) *(G-18577)*

Quantum Creations LLC 786 233-6769
   15705 Nw 13th Ave Miami Gardens (33169) *(G-10269)*

Quantum Envmtl Slutions St Inc 800 975-8721
   2699 Stirling Rd Ste C Fort Lauderdale (33312) *(G-4007)*

Quantum Group LLC (PA) 305 926-1036
   12769 Sw 146th Ln Miami (33186) *(G-9764)*

Quantum Leap Winery, Orlando *Also called JD Wine Concepts LLC (G-12270)*

Quantum Limit Partners LLC (PA) 954 849-3720
   1037 Se 2nd Ct Fort Lauderdale (33301) *(G-4008)*

Quantum Pharmaceuticals Llc 321 724-0625
   429 Riverview Ln Melbourne Beach (32951) *(G-8569)*

Quantum Reflex Integration Inc 352 228-0766
   716 Sw Kings Bay Dr Crystal River (34429) *(G-2278)*

Quantum Safety Services Inc 786 420-0735
   20280 Sw 190th St Miami (33187) *(G-9765)*

Quantum Servicing Corporation 305 229-6675
   790 Nw 107th Ave Ste 400 Miami (33172) *(G-9766)*

Quantum Spatial Inc (HQ) 920 457-3631
   10033 Dr Mrtn Lther King Saint Petersburg (33716) *(G-15168)*

Quantum Storage Systems, Miami *Also called Graduate Plastics Inc (G-9230)*

Quantum Technology Inc 407 333-9348
   108 Commerce St Ste 101 Lake Mary (32746) *(G-7105)*

Quantumfly Enterprises Inc 407 807-7050
   2664 Jewett Ln Sanford (32771) *(G-15379)*

Quanturo Publishing Inc 305 373-3700
   4141 Ne 2nd Ave Ste 202 Miami (33137) *(G-9767)*

Quartz Unlimited Inc 561 720-7460
   2255 Glades Rd Ste 324 Boca Raton (33431) *(G-644)*

Quartz Unlimited LLC 561 306-1243
   5030 Champion Blvd Boca Raton (33496) *(G-645)*

Quartzo LLC 888 813-3442
   5115 Shadowlawn Ave Tampa (33610) *(G-17203)*

Quasar Light Therapy, Sarasota *Also called Silver Bay LLC (G-15556)*

Queen B Hair Collection LLC 954 393-2791
   17111 Nw 10th Ct Miami (33169) *(G-9768)*

Quest Controls Inc (PA) 941 729-4799
   208 9th Street Dr W Palmetto (34221) *(G-13189)*

Quest Desk Solutions, Tampa *Also called Koho Software Inc (G-16991)*

Quest Drape, Sunrise *Also called Bkbl Holdings Ltd (G-16297)*

Quest Drape 407 888-8164
   10003 Satellite Blvd # 210 Orlando (32837) *(G-12521)*

Quest Environmental Pdts Inc 321 984-4423
   6928 Sonny Dale Dr Ste A Melbourne (32904) *(G-8508)*

Quest Manufacturing Corp 305 513-8583
   11200 Nw 138th St Medley (33178) *(G-8306)*

Queteq, Sanford *Also called Watts Technologies LLC (G-15407)*

Queuelogix LLC 404 721-3928
   1200 E Las Olas Blvd # 201 Fort Lauderdale (33301) *(G-4009)*

Quick Advertising Inc 407 774-0003
   3030 E Semrn Blvd Ste 236 Apopka (32703) *(G-166)*

Quick Cans Inc 407 415-1361
   7034 Arbor Ct Winter Park (32792) *(G-18529)*

Quick Lift Inc 305 471-0147
   8491 Nw 54th St Doral (33166) *(G-3342)*

Quick Print Center, Hialeah *Also called Lufemor Inc (G-5229)*

Quick Prints LLC 954 526-9013
   3145 Davie Blvd Fort Lauderdale (33312) *(G-4010)*

Quick Prints LLC 954 594-9415
   8201 Peters Rd Ste 1000 Plantation (33324) *(G-13880)*

Quick Protective Systems Inc 772 220-3315
   421 Sw California Ave # 101 Stuart (34994) *(G-16202)*

Quick-Med Technologies Inc 352 379-0611
   902 Nw 4th St Gainesville (32601) *(G-4753)*

Quickload Custom Built Trlrs, Saint Petersburg *Also called J & J Marine Service Inc (G-15088)*

Quickprint Business Center, Punta Gorda *Also called Blackwell Family Corporation (G-14499)*

Quickprint Line 561 740-9930
   2015 Corporate Dr Boynton Beach (33426) *(G-905)*

Quickseries Publishing Inc 954 584-1606
   5100 Nw 33rd Ave Ste 247 Fort Lauderdale (33309) *(G-4011)*

Quicksilver Prtg & Copying Inc 813 888-6811
   3816a W Sligh Ave Tampa (33614) *(G-17204)*

Quickwood LLC 866 888-5858
   13506 Summerport Vlg Pkwy Windermere (34786) *(G-18364)*

Quiet Flex 352 429-3286
   7730 American Way Groveland (34736) *(G-4868)*

Quiet Technology Aerospace Inc 305 687-9808
   4100 N 29th Ter Hollywood (33020) *(G-5650)*

Quik Shred 561 841-1822
   1070 E Indiantown Rd # 308 Jupiter (33477) *(G-6784)*

Quik Tek Inc 772 501-3471
   2046 Treasure Coast Plz Vero Beach (32960) *(G-17791)*

Quikrete Companies LLC 813 719-6612
   1902 Wood Ct Plant City (33563) *(G-13798)*

Quikrete Companies LLC 850 623-0559
   7101 Windwood Ln Milton (32583) *(G-10435)*

Quikrete Companies LLC 863 665-5127
   4230 Maine Ave Lakeland (33801) *(G-7417)*

Quikrete of Pensacola, Milton *Also called Quikrete Companies LLC (G-10435)*

Quintessential Home Svcs LLC 850 259-5064
   503 Second Ave Destin (32541) *(G-3076)*

Quirantes Orthopedics Inc 305 261-1382
   5840 W Flagler St Miami (33144) *(G-9769)*

Qwikpik Golf LLC 407 505-5546
   10096 Tavistock Rd Orlando (32827) *(G-12522)*

R & A Industries Inc 352 307-6655
   306 Aulin Ave Oviedo (32765) *(G-12845)*

R & A Performance Fuel Inc 954 237-9824
   12951 Nw 1st St Pembroke Pines (33028) *(G-13410)*

R & A Power Graphics Inc 407 898-5770
   5000 E Colonial Dr Orlando (32803) *(G-12523)*

R & C Sales & Mfg Inc 904 824-2223
   18 Hargrove Grade Ste 101 Palm Coast (32137) *(G-13085)*

R & D Sleeves Llc (PA) 407 886-9010
   520 W Orange Blossom Trl Apopka (32712) *(G-167)*

R & D Surf 321 636-4456
   488 Gus Hipp Blvd Rockledge (32955) *(G-14740)*

R & H Platting, Oakland Park *Also called Felix Reynoso (G-11266)*

R & J Custom Cabinets Inc 813 871-5779
3907 W Cayuga St Tampa (33614) (G-17205)

R & J Enterprises, Green Cove Springs Also called Shark Tooth Enterprises Inc (G-4837)

R & J Mfg of Gainesville 352 375-3130
2001 Ne 31st Ave Gainesville (32609) (G-4754)

R & K Builders, Pensacola Also called R & K Portable Buildings (G-13591)

R & K Buildings Inc 850 995-9525
4213 Avalon Blvd Milton (32583) (G-10436)

R & K Marketing Inc 904 745-0022
11657 Central Pkwy # 401 Jacksonville (32224) (G-6401)

R & K Portable Builders, Milton Also called R & K Buildings Inc (G-10436)

R & K Portable Buildings 850 857-7899
8120 Pensacola Blvd Pensacola (32534) (G-13591)

R & K Welding and Fabrication 863 422-8728
4709 Crump Rd Lake Hamilton (33851) (G-7052)

R & L Manufacturing Inc 772 770-9300
5021 41st St Unit 2 Vero Beach (32967) (G-17792)

R & M Logging Inc 904 813-4877
17313 Bell Rd Hilliard (32046) (G-5473)

R & R Designer Cabinets Inc 954 735-6435
3063 Nw 23rd Way Oakland Park (33311) (G-11290)

R & R Door and Trim Inc 561 844-5496
8111 Garden Rd Ste J West Palm Beach (33404) (G-18136)

R & R Doors Corp 305 982-8106
1660 W 33rd Pl Hialeah (33012) (G-5324)

R & R Livestock Solutions Inc 863 223-8443
7 Lincoln Ave Lake Wales (33853) (G-7171)

R & R Mica Works Inc 305 231-1887
6541 Lake Blue Dr Miami Lakes (33014) (G-10346)

R & R Stone Industries Inc 888 999-4921
7941 Nw 67th St Miami (33166) (G-9770)

R & S Marble Designs Inc 941 475-3111
505 Paul Morris Dr Englewood (34223) (G-3535)

R & S Metalworks & Co LLC 772 466-3303
5690 Carlton Rd Port Saint Lucie (34987) (G-14436)

R & S Snacks LLC 954 839-5482
1660 Sw Buttercup Ave Port Saint Lucie (34953) (G-14437)

R & Y Automotive AC Cmpsr 305 919-9232
15315 Ne 21st Ave North Miami Beach (33162) (G-11158)

R & Y Automotive AC Cmpsr (PA) 305 947-1173
15315 Ne 21st Ave North Miami Beach (33162) (G-11159)

R & Z Ventures Inc 954 532-7938
1300 Sw 1st Ct Pompano Beach (33069) (G-14154)

R A Printing Inc 904 733-5578
4185 Sunbeam Rd Ste 100 Jacksonville (32257) (G-6402)

R and R Machine Shop 941 621-8143
6601 Taylor Rd Punta Gorda (33950) (G-14523)

R and R Rebar, Winter Garden Also called Quality Precast & Company (G-18402)

R B Casting Inc 407 648-2005
637 22nd St Orlando (32805) (G-12524)

R C D Corporation 352 589-0099
2850 Dillard Rd Eustis (32726) (G-3565)

R C R Manufacturing Inc 786 499-9245
9279 Sw 38th St Miami (33165) (G-9771)

R C Specialized International 407 681-5905
1436 State Road 436 Casselberry (32707) (G-1431)

R Dorian Millworks LLC 561 863-9125
2361 Vista Pkwy Ste 7 West Palm Beach (33411) (G-18137)

R F Laboratories Inc 920 564-2700
31355 Bear Pond Dr # 46 Sorrento (32776) (G-16013)

R G Management Inc 407 889-3100
3640 Princeton Oaks St Orlando (32808) (G-12525)

R H Quality Metal LLC 407 279-2454
1324 Adair Rd Davenport (33837) (G-2369)

R Hunter Holdings Inc 407 843-0182
7594 Chancellor Dr Orlando (32809) (G-12526)

R J Dougherty Associates LLC 386 409-2202
544 Air Park Rd Edgewater (32132) (G-3499)

R J Marine Group Inc 772 232-6590
619 Nw Baker Rd Stuart (34994) (G-16203)

R J Reynolds Tobacco Company 772 873-6955
2687 Sw Domina Rd Port Saint Lucie (34953) (G-14438)

R Js Boat Lifts Inc 352 394-5666
18249 E Apshawa Rd Clermont (34715) (G-1879)

R K Constructors of Centl Fla 407 222-5376
4630 S Kirkman Rd Ste 221 Orlando (32811) (G-12527)

R K L Enterprises of Pensacola 850 432-2335
3740 N Pace Blvd Pensacola (32505) (G-13592)

R M A, Fort Myers Also called Resource Management Associates (G-4379)

R M Equipment Inc 305 477-9312
6975 Nw 43rd St Miami (33166) (G-9772)

R P Welding, Navarre Also called Real Pro Welding Inc (G-10954)

R R Donnelley & Sons Company 407 859-2030
9125 Bachman Rd Orlando (32824) (G-12528)

R R H Inc 954 966-1209
5900 Johnson St Hollywood (33021) (G-5651)

R Residual Corp 810 874-6727
59 Ponte Vedra Blvd Ponte Vedra Beach (32082) (G-14279)

R S Apparel Inc 305 599-4939
8454 Nw 58th St Doral (33166) (G-3343)

R S Design Inc 727 525-8292
6351 46th St N Pinellas Park (33781) (G-13726)

R S S Partners Inc 904 241-6144
1301 1st St S Apt 1501 Jacksonville Beach (32250) (G-6642)

R Smith Printing Inc 518 827-7700
4820 Joseph St Hastings (32145) (G-4989)

R T Industries Inc 352 427-2632
4926 N Coleus Ter Crystal River (34428) (G-2279)

R T Publishing Inc 904 886-4919
12443 San Jose Blvd # 403 Jacksonville (32223) (G-6403)

R Townsend Rescreens Inc 239 244-4759
30390 Cedar Rd Punta Gorda (33982) (G-14524)

R Y D Enterprises Inc 305 655-1045
20815 Ne 16th Ave Ste B7 Miami (33179) (G-9773)

R&D Machine LLC 813 891-9109
130 Scarlet Blvd Oldsmar (34677) (G-11696)

R&D Manufacturing Inds Inc 352 351-8800
1031 Ne 16th St Ocala (34470) (G-11476)

R&K Mehall Inc 727 781-8780
211 Whisper Lake Rd Palm Harbor (34683) (G-13126)

R&M Orthotics Inc 954 547-6722
10939 Nw 62nd Ct Parkland (33076) (G-13351)

R&R Racing Engines, Punta Gorda Also called R and R Machine Shop (G-14523)

R&S Intrnational Inv Group LLC 305 576-3000
571 Nw 29th St Miami (33127) (G-9774)

R-Da Trading LLC 954 278-6983
2893 Executive Park Dr Weston (33331) (G-18281)

R-Lines LLC 954 457-7777
201 Ansin Blvd Hallandale Beach (33009) (G-4968)

R.S.T., Coral Gables Also called Radiation Shield Tech Inc (G-2102)

R4 Integration Inc 850 226-6913
45 Beal Pkwy Ne Fort Walton Beach (32548) (G-4604)

Ra Co AMO Inc 561 626-7232
4100 Burns Rd Palm Beach Gardens (33410) (G-13004)

Raaw, Coral Gables Also called Raw Foods International Llc (G-2103)

Raber Industries Inc 239 728-5527
2190 Sebastian Ct Alva (33920) (G-83)

Rabud Inc 954 925-4199
110 N Bryan Rd Dania (33004) (G-2342)

Race Part Solutions 561 999-8911
1181 S Rogers Cir Ste 18 Boca Raton (33487) (G-646)

Race Performance Machine Shop 813 443-8225
4707 N Lois Ave Tampa (33614) (G-17206)

Racerink LLC 239 470-0872
1515 Cypress Dr Jupiter (33469) (G-6785)

Racestar Manufacturing, Altamonte Springs Also called Superlite Aluminum Pdts Inc (G-73)

Raceway 6852 .... 850 944-8212
7910 Pine Forest Rd Pensacola (32526) (G-13593)

Raceway Electric LLC 772 260-6530
208 Sw Aubudon Ave Port Saint Lucie (34984) (G-14439)

Raceway Towing LLC 754 244-9597
480 Ne 35th Ct Unit 4 Oakland Park (33334) (G-11291)

Rachel Ally 727 804-9596
9437 Debbie Ln Hudson (34669) (G-5786)

Racing Shell Covers LLC 732 236-0435
3899 Mannix Dr Ste 409 Naples (34114) (G-10872)

Racing Spirit Llc 305 373-6671
241 Ne 61st St Miami (33137) (G-9775)

RAD Wear Inc 352 727-4498
2135 Nw 40th Ter Ste A Gainesville (32605) (G-4755)

Radiaction Inc 561 351-3697
1855 Griffin Rd Ste A309 Dania Beach (33004) (G-2359)

Radial Inc 561 737-5151
1903 S Congress Ave # 460 Boynton Beach (33426) (G-906)

Radiance Radiology Inc 727 934-5500
37566 Us Highway 19 N Palm Harbor (34684) (G-13127)

Radiant Power Corp (HQ) 941 739-3200
7135 16th St E Ste 101 Sarasota (34243) (G-15541)

Radiant Power Idc LLC 760 945-0230
7135 16th St E Ste 101 Sarasota (34243) (G-15542)

Radiant Printing, Lakeland Also called William Burns (G-7474)

Radiant-Seacom Repairs Corp 941 739-3200
7135 16th St E Ste 101 Sarasota (34243) (G-15543)

Radiation Shield Tech Inc 866 733-6766
6 Aragon Ave Coral Gables (33134) (G-2102)

Radica LLC 954 383-0089
10471 Nw 36th St Doral (33178) (G-3344)

Radio OEM Inc 920 564-6622
31355 State Road 46 Sorrento (32776) (G-16014)

Radio Paz, Miami Also called Pax Ctholic Communications Inc (G-9698)

Radiotronics Inc 772 600-7574
1315 Sw Commerce Way Stuart (34997) (G-16204)

Radixx Solutions Intl Inc (HQ) 407 856-9009
20 N Orange Ave Ste 150 Orlando (32801) (G-12529)

Radwag USA LLC 305 651-3522
19599 Ne 10th Ave Ste E North Miami Beach (33179) (G-11160)

Rae Launo Corporation 813 242-4281
2606 Durant Oaks Dr Valrico (33596) (G-17669)

Rafab Spcialty Fabrication Inc 407 422-3750
2116 W Central Blvd Orlando (32805) (G-12530)

Rafael Moreaun, Miami *Also called Amber Jewelers Corp (G-8711)*

Rafaella, Doral *Also called Supreme International LLC (G-3386)*

Rafferty Holdings LLC 352 248-0906
2722 Nw 74th Pl Gainesville (32653) *(G-4756)*

Rafferty Machine and Tool, Gainesville *Also called Rafferty Holdings LLC (G-4756)*

Ragalta, Hallandale Beach *Also called Kasulik II LLC (G-4956)*

Raider Outboards Inc 321 383-9585
1885 Armstrong Dr Titusville (32780) *(G-17610)*

Rail Scale Inc 904 302-5154
111 Nature Walk Pkwy # 105 Saint Augustine (32092) *(G-14876)*

Rail Tech 407 834-6966
674 Maitland Ave Altamonte Springs (32701) *(G-68)*

Railings Plus Inc 386 437-4501
1150 State Rd 11 Ste 201 Bunnell (32110) *(G-1232)*

Railtec Constructions Company 410 795-0712
4949 N Hwy A1a Apt 182 Hutchinson Island (34949) *(G-5793)*

Railtech Construction, Hutchinson Island *Also called Railtec Constructions Company (G-5793)*

Raimonda Investment Group Inc 352 347-8899
5911 Se Hames Rd Belleview (34420) *(G-366)*

Rainbow Cabinets, Ocala *Also called Michigan Avenue Bridge Inc (G-11444)*

Rainbow Cabinets Inc 352 236-4044
4690 Ne 35th St Ocala (34479) *(G-11477)*

Rainbow Eb Buenavista 305 982-8153
8554 Sw 8th St Miami (33144) *(G-9776)*

Rainbow Ink Products Inc 954 252-6030
15640 Lancelot Ct Davie (33331) *(G-2464)*

Rainbow Lght Ntrtnal Systems I (HQ) 954 233-3300
1301 Sawgrs Corp Pkwy Sunrise (33323) *(G-16361)*

Rainbow Pool Supply Inc 407 324-9616
2920 W Airport Blvd Sanford (32771) *(G-15380)*

Rainbow Precision Mfg Corp 561 691-1658
4371 Northlake Blvd Palm Beach Gardens (33410) *(G-13005)*

Rainbow Printing Inc 561 364-9000
10699 Cambay Dr Boynton Beach (33437) *(G-907)*

Rainbow Storage 386 362-1171
7434 County Road 795 Live Oak (32060) *(G-7853)*

Rainbows End 727 733-8572
1450 Wetherington Way Palm Harbor (34683) *(G-13128)*

Rainbows End Quilt Shoppe, Palm Harbor *Also called Rainbows End (G-13128)*

Raintree Graphics, Jacksonville *Also called All-Star Sales Inc (G-5876)*

Rakiline LLC 904 800-2632
6180 Fort Caroline Rd Jacksonville (32277) *(G-6404)*

Rally Manufacturing Inc 305 628-2886
7200 Corp Ctr Dr Ste 308 Miami (33126) *(G-9777)*

Ralph & Llerena Pallets Inc 305 446-2651
495 E 47th St Hialeah (33013) *(G-5325)*

Ralph Santore & Sons Inc 386 437-2242
2546 County Road 305 Bunnell (32110) *(G-1233)*

Raltron Electronics, Doral *Also called Rami Technology USA LLC (G-3345)*

Ram Investments South Fla Inc (PA) 305 759-6419
11102 Nw South River Dr Medley (33178) *(G-8307)*

Ram Sales LLC 844 726-6382
7400 Nw 37th Ave Miami (33147) *(G-9778)*

Ram Steel Framing, Miami *Also called Ram Sales LLC (G-9778)*

Ram-Lin, Orlando *Also called Central Florida Cstm Trlrs Inc (G-11996)*

Rami Technology USA LLC 305 593-6033
10400 Nw 33rd St Ste 290 Doral (33172) *(G-3345)*

Ramirez Cbnets Blnds Gran Mr 352 606-0049
3645 Commercial Way Spring Hill (34606) *(G-16076)*

Ramos Woodwork LLC 954 861-7679
1955 Sw 15th Pl Deerfield Beach (33442) *(G-2795)*

Rampell Software 561 628-5102
122 N County Rd Palm Beach (33480) *(G-12940)*

Rampmaster Inc 305 691-9090
11098 Biscayne Blvd # 401 Miami (33161) *(G-9779)*

Ramsay Marine Services LLC 561 881-1234
999 W 17th Ste 1 Riviera Beach (33404) *(G-14664)*

Ramseys Prtg & Off Pdts Inc 850 227-7468
209 Reid Ave Port Saint Joe (32456) *(G-14390)*

Ramstar Corporation 561 499-8488
5304 Ventura Dr Delray Beach (33484) *(G-3010)*

Rancheritos 561 479-0046
8903 Glades Rd Ste A10 Boca Raton (33434) *(G-647)*

Rand Search Light Advertising 954 476-7620
11330 Sw 17th St Davie (33325) *(G-2465)*

Randal R Young 800 584-9937
876 Geneva Dr Oviedo (32765) *(G-12846)*

Randall Birge 850 373-6131
2579 Lilly Dr Bonifay (32425) *(G-777)*

Randazza Enterprises Inc 813 677-0041
8824 Van Fleet Rd Riverview (33578) *(G-14573)*

Randolph Cnstr Group Inc 954 276-2889
1191 N Federal Hwy Ste 1 Delray Beach (33483) *(G-3011)*

Randy Morris Logging Inc 850 773-9010
4259 Highway 77 Chipley (32428) *(G-1457)*

Randy Wheeler 850 997-1248
1560 Spring Hollow Dr Monticello (32344) *(G-10585)*

Ranger Associates Inc 407 869-0024
688 Florida Central Pkwy Longwood (32750) *(G-7941)*

Ranger Plastic Extrusions Inc 817 640-6067
15320 Blue Bay Cir Fort Myers (33913) *(G-4375)*

Ranger Prtg & Promotional Pdts, Longwood *Also called Ranger Associates Inc (G-7941)*

Rankine-Hinman Mfg Co 904 808-0404
6980 Us Highway 1 N # 108 Saint Augustine (32095) *(G-14877)*

Ranorex Inc 727 835-5570
28050 Us Highway 19 N # 303 Clearwater (33761) *(G-1762)*

Rap Snacks Inc 305 926-9594
150 Se 2nd Ave Ph 6 Miami (33131) *(G-9780)*

Rapid Composites LLC 941 322-6647
2216 72nd Dr E Sarasota (34243) *(G-15544)*

Rapid Graphix Inc 941 639-2043
10251 Tamiami Trl Punta Gorda (33950) *(G-14525)*

Rapid Industries Inc 772 287-0651
3100 Se Waaler St Stuart (34997) *(G-16205)*

Rapid Metal Products Inc 863 701-0058
4257 Holden Rd Lakeland (33811) *(G-7418)*

Rapid Press, Inc, Tallahassee *Also called Rapid Rater Company (G-16492)*

Rapid Print, Jacksonville *Also called Professnal Reproduction of Jax (G-6391)*

Rapid Print Southwest Fla Inc 239 590-9797
12244 Treeline Ave Ste 4 Fort Myers (33913) *(G-4376)*

Rapid Rater Company 850 893-7346
3626 Cagney Dr Tallahassee (32309) *(G-16492)*

Rapid Reproductions LLC 607 843-2221
108 Seagrape Rd Melbourne Beach (32951) *(G-8570)*

Rapid Response 407 774-9877
250 Altmnte Commerce 10 Altamonte Springs (32714) *(G-69)*

Rapid Signs and T Shirts 786 486-2804
27466 S Dixie Hwy Homestead (33032) *(G-5736)*

Rapid Switch Systems LLC 941 720-7380
4601 15th St E Bradenton (34203) *(G-1034)*

Raptor Wear Products USA Inc 786 972-0326
7842 Nw 71st St Miami (33166) *(G-9781)*

Ras Concrete Construction Inc 239 775-3709
5501 Cynthia Ln Naples (34112) *(G-10873)*

Raskin Industries LLC 561 997-6658
710 S Powerline Rd Ste G Deerfield Beach (33442) *(G-2796)*

Rass Fast Pallet Inc 786 877-2854
4214 Nw 11th Pl Miami (33127) *(G-9782)*

Rat-Trap Bait Company Inc 863 967-2148
106 Adams St Auburndale (33823) *(G-243)*

Rational Ediscovery LLC 518 489-3000
35 Ne 40th St Fl 3 Miami (33137) *(G-9783)*

Ravago Americas LLC (HQ) 407 773-7777
1900 Smmit Twr Blvd Ste 9 Orlando (32810) *(G-12531)*

Ravago Holdings America Inc (PA) 407 875-9595
1900 Smmit Twr Blvd Ste 9 Orlando (32810) *(G-12532)*

Rave LLC (HQ) 561 330-0411
430 S Congress Ave Ste 7 Delray Beach (33445) *(G-3012)*

Raven Forest Operating LLC 727 497-2727
13014 N Dale Mbry Hwy # 736 Tampa (33618) *(G-17207)*

Ravenswood Import Export Ltd L 863 800-0210
204 S Main Ave Ste 5 Lake Placid (33852) *(G-7147)*

Ravic Technologies LLC 954 237-3241
7939 Nw 84th St Ste 101 Medley (33166) *(G-8308)*

Raw Energy Materials Corp 954 270-9000
170 Se 13th St Pompano Beach (33060) *(G-14155)*

Raw Foods International Llc 305 856-1991
2600 S Douglas Rd Ste 410 Coral Gables (33134) *(G-2103)*

Ray Eaton Yacht Service Inc 954 583-8762
2311 Sw 33rd Ter Fort Lauderdale (33312) *(G-4012)*

Ray Electric Outboards Inc 239 574-1948
908 Ne 24th Ln Unit 6 Cape Coral (33909) *(G-1377)*

Ray Graphics Inc 863 325-0911
1895 Executive Rd Winter Haven (33884) *(G-18464)*

Ray Machine Inc 850 784-1116
3711 N Highway 231 Panama City (32404) *(G-13300)*

Raygraphics, Winter Haven *Also called Ray Graphics Inc (G-18464)*

Raymond Newkirk 772 359-0237
920 Angle Rd Fort Pierce (34947) *(G-4522)*

Raynetcrm LLC 813 489-9565
121 Ginger Rd Venice (34293) *(G-17712)*

Rayonier A M Products Inc (HQ) 904 357-9100
1301 Riverplace Blvd Jacksonville (32207) *(G-6405)*

Rayonier Advanced Materials, Jacksonville *Also called Rayonier AM Sales and Tech Inc (G-6407)*

Rayonier Advanced Mtls Inc (PA) 904 357-4600
1301 Riverplace Blvd # 23 Jacksonville (32207) *(G-6406)*

Rayonier Advanced Mtls Inc 904 261-3611
10 Gum St Fernandina Beach (32034) *(G-3597)*

Rayonier AM Sales and Tech Inc (HQ) 904 357-4600
1301 Riverplace Blvd # 23 Jacksonville (32207) *(G-6407)*

Rayonier Inc 904 277-1343
1 Rayonier Way Yulee (32097) *(G-18592)*

Rayovac Corp 727 393-0966
7636 91st St Largo (33777) *(G-7667)*

Rays Mobile Service LLC 754 204-5816
4846 N University Dr Lauderhill (33351) *(G-7739)*

Rays Pallets, Fort Pierce *Also called Raymond Newkirk* ***(G-4522)***
Raytash Inc (PA) 561 347-8863
1420 Sw 1st St Boca Raton (33486) ***(G-648)***
Raytheon Company 310 647-9438
7887 Bryan Dairy Rd # 110 Largo (33777) ***(G-7668)***
Raytheon Company 727 768-8468
7887 Bryan Dairy Rd # 110 Largo (33777) ***(G-7669)***
Raytheon Company 310 647-9438
7401 22nd Ave N Bldg D Saint Petersburg (33710) ***(G-15169)***
Raytheon Company 407 207-9223
12792 Research Pkwy # 100 Orlando (32826) ***(G-12533)***
Raytheon Company 321 235-1700
2603 Challenger Tech Ct Orlando (32826) ***(G-12534)***
Raytheon Technologies Corp 860 565-4321
17900 Bee Line Hwy Jupiter (33478) ***(G-6786)***
Razient LLC 855 747-5911
990 Biscayne Blvd Ste 503 Miami (33132) ***(G-9784)***
RB Cabinetry LLC 850 685-5316
408 Evergreen Dr Ste A Destin (32541) ***(G-3077)***
RB Custom Welding LLC 813 280-9860
5210 E 10th Ave Tampa (33619) ***(G-17208)***
RB Home Goods LLC 786 690-3008
218 Nw 12th Ave Apt 801 Miami (33128) ***(G-9785)***
RB Kanalflakt Inc 941 359-3267
1712 Northgate Blvd Sarasota (34234) ***(G-15793)***
Rbj Timber Inc 904 879-1597
44247 Bell Ln Callahan (32011) ***(G-1256)***
Rbs Woodwork Corp 754 214-7682
1621 Banks Rd Margate (33063) ***(G-8152)***
RC Investment Casting 305 801-9088
4570 E 11th Ave Hialeah (33013) ***(G-5326)***
Rcai, Saint Petersburg *Also called Restorative Care America Inc* ***(G-15171)***
Rcr Coffee Company Inc (PA) 813 248-6264
402 N 22nd St Tampa (33605) ***(G-17209)***
RCS Wood Crafters LLC 305 836-0120
1051 E 24th St Hialeah (33013) ***(G-5327)***
Rcs Woodcrafters, Hialeah *Also called RCS Wood Crafters LLC* ***(G-5327)***
Rd Abukaf 1 Inc 239 390-8788
8017 Plaza Del Lago Dr # 109 Estero (33928) ***(G-3549)***
Rdc Manufacturing Inc 772 286-6921
3353 Se Gran Park Way Stuart (34997) ***(G-16206)***
Rde Connectors & Cables Inc 954 746-6400
5277 Nw 108th Ave Sunrise (33351) ***(G-16362)***
RDS Industrial Inc 321 631-0121
436 Shearer Blvd Cocoa (32922) ***(G-1951)***
RDS Manufacturing Inc 850 584-6898
300 Industrial Park Dr Perry (32348) ***(G-13650)***
RDt Business Enterprises Inc 954 525-1133
3333 Se 14th Ave Fort Lauderdale (33316) ***(G-4013)***
Re-Bus LLC 772 418-7711
5015 Saint Lucie Blvd Fort Pierce (34946) ***(G-4523)***
Re-Think It Inc 407 671-6000
6770 Curtis St Orlando (32807) ***(G-12535)***
Reach Cooling Group, Hialeah *Also called Reach International Inc* ***(G-5328)***
Reach International Inc 305 863-6360
625 E 10th Ave Hialeah (33010) ***(G-5328)***
Reading Truck Body LLC 727 943-8911
1476 L And R Indus Blvd Tarpon Springs (34689) ***(G-17489)***
Reading Truck Body LLC 727 943-8911
1476 L&R Industrial Blvd Tarpon Springs (34689) ***(G-17490)***
Ready Building Products Inc 941 639-6222
7000 Progress Dr Punta Gorda (33982) ***(G-14526)***
Ready Containment LLC 941 739-9486
2300 S Dock St Ste 101 Palmetto (34221) ***(G-13190)***
Ready Machine Corp 850 479-1722
6155 Drexel Rd Pensacola (32504) ***(G-13594)***
Ready Mix Usa LLC 850 227-7677
1001 Ccil G Cstin Sr Blvd Port Saint Joe (32456) ***(G-14391)***
Readymix, Saint Augustine *Also called Cemex Cnstr Mtls Fla LLC* ***(G-14820)***
Readymix - Moore Haven Rm, Moore Haven *Also called Cemex Cnstr Mtls Fla LLC* ***(G-10589)***
Readymix - Port St Joe, Port Saint Joe *Also called Ready Mix Usa LLC* ***(G-14391)***
Reagan H Fox III Inc 850 584-9229
Woods Creek Rd Perry (32347) ***(G-13651)***
Reah Group LLC 727 423-0668
2721 W Gray St Tampa (33609) ***(G-17210)***
Real Extract Ventures Inc 561 371-3532
2200 Merriweather Way Wellington (33414) ***(G-17858)***
Real Fleet Solutions LLC 321 631-2414
605 Townsend Rd Cocoa (32926) ***(G-1952)***
Real Gold Inc 386 873-4849
1853 Patterson Ave Unit 4 Deland (32724) ***(G-2897)***
Real Ketones LLC 801 244-8610
111 2nd Ave Ne Ste 1401 Saint Petersburg (33701) ***(G-15170)***
Real Print & Ship Inc 727 787-1949
4047 Carlyle Lakes Blvd Palm Harbor (34685) ***(G-13129)***
Real Pro Welding Inc 850 939-3469
8285 East Bay Blvd Navarre (32566) ***(G-10954)***
Real Producers, Land O Lakes *Also called M30 Freedom Inc* ***(G-7497)***
Real Producers, Oviedo *Also called Orlando Branding Agency LLC* ***(G-12841)***
Real Solutions, Melbourne *Also called Alstom Signaling Operation LLC* ***(G-8362)***
Real Thread Inc 407 679-3895
1101 N Keller Rd Ste A Orlando (32810) ***(G-12536)***
Real Time Labratories, Boca Raton *Also called Kinetics Usa Inc* ***(G-569)***
Real-Time Laboratories LLC (HQ) 561 988-8826
990 S Rogers Cir Ste 5 Boca Raton (33487) ***(G-649)***
Realm Labs LLC 561 549-9099
7700 Congress Ave # 3110 Boca Raton (33487) ***(G-650)***
Realpure Bottling Inc 601 849-9910
2445 Nw 42nd St Ocala (34475) ***(G-11478)***
Realstargps, Orlando *Also called Sunrise Financial Assoc Inc* ***(G-12634)***
Realti Hub LLC 754 242-4759
18801 Nw 42nd Ave Miami Gardens (33055) ***(G-10270)***
Realty Systems Inc 386 439-0460
3165 Old Kings Rd S Flagler Beach (32136) ***(G-3604)***
Rebah Fabrication Inc 407 857-3232
12081 Stone Bark Trl Orlando (32824) ***(G-12537)***
Rebar Alchemist, Port Saint Lucie *Also called Alchemist Holdings LLC* ***(G-14395)***
Reboundersz Purchasing Dev, Sanford *Also called Indoor Trampoline Arena Inc* ***(G-15335)***
Rebuild Globally Inc 407 801-9936
810 S K St Lake Worth (33460) ***(G-7231)***
Recall Technologies Inc 321 952-4422
1651 Seabury Point Rd Nw Palm Bay (32907) ***(G-12913)***
Recommend Magazine, Miami Lakes *Also called Worth Intl Media Group* ***(G-10379)***
Recommend Travel Publications 305 826-4763
5979 Nw 151st St Ste 120 Miami Lakes (33014) ***(G-10347)***
Recon Group LLP 855 874-8741
20200 W Dixie Hwy # 1005 Miami (33180) ***(G-9786)***
Recordsone LLC 301 440-8119
10641 Airport Rd N Pullingr Naples (34109) ***(G-10874)***
Recover Gear LLC 904 280-9660
822 A1a N Ponte Vedra Beach (32082) ***(G-14280)***
Recycled Vinyl 727 434-1857
848 Myrtle St Sarasota (34234) ***(G-15794)***
Recycling Center 386 364-5865
700 Houston Ave Nw Live Oak (32064) ***(G-7854)***
Red 7 Tees LLC 850 612-7007
189 W Oakdale Ave Crestview (32536) ***(G-2251)***
Red Brick Publishing LLC 718 208-3600
6647 Conch Ct Boynton Beach (33437) ***(G-908)***
Red Giant Entertainment Inc (PA) 877 904-7334
614 E Hwy 50 Ste 235 Clermont (34711) ***(G-1880)***
Red Hot Trends Inc 305 888-6951
7911 Nw 72nd Ave Ste 107 Medley (33166) ***(G-8309)***
Red Kite Group Inc 305 665-7620
5701 Sunset Dr South Miami (33143) ***(G-16043)***
Red Level Dolomite, Crystal River *Also called Crystal River Quarries Inc* ***(G-2273)***
Red Meters LLC 407 337-0110
6520 Pinecastle Blvd Orlando (32809) ***(G-12538)***
Red Oak Software Inc (PA) 973 316-6064
528 67th St Holmes Beach (34217) ***(G-5691)***
Red Phoenix Extracts, Fort Pierce *Also called Cei Liquidation Inc* ***(G-4473)***
Red Smith Foods Inc 954 581-1996
4145 Sw 47th Ave Davie (33314) ***(G-2466)***
Redat of North America Inc 407 246-1600
120 Bonnie Loch Ct Orlando (32806) ***(G-12539)***
Redberd Printing 407 622-2292
803 S Orlando Ave Winter Park (32789) ***(G-18530)***
Redbird Printing 904 654-8371
803 S Orlando Ave Ste J Winter Park (32789) ***(G-18531)***
Redbud Enterprises Inc 386 752-5696
1435 Nw County Road 25a Lake City (32055) ***(G-7042)***
Reddi Sign Corporation 904 757-0680
107 Mott St Jacksonville (32254) ***(G-6408)***
Reddy Ice Corporation 772 461-5046
2901 Industrial Avenue 2 Fort Pierce (34946) ***(G-4524)***
Reddy Ice Corporation 850 433-2191
1511 W Government St Pensacola (32502) ***(G-13595)***
Reddy Ice Corporation 904 388-2653
5849 Commonwealth Ave Jacksonville (32254) ***(G-6409)***
Reddy Ice Corporation 850 233-0128
1225 Moylan Rd Panama City (32407) ***(G-13301)***
Reddy Ice Corporation 561 881-9501
7719 Garden Rd West Palm Beach (33404) ***(G-18138)***
Reddy Ice Inc 407 296-8300
1920 Commerce Oak Ave Orlando (32808) ***(G-12540)***
Redeag Le, Lakeland *Also called Redeagle International LLC* ***(G-7419)***
Redeagle International LLC 863 682-6698
5143 S Lakeland Dr Ste 4 Lakeland (33813) ***(G-7419)***
Rederick Metal Industries 305 396-3396
9550 Nw 12th St Ste 12 Doral (33172) ***(G-3346)***
Redington Counters Inc 954 725-6699
702 S Military Trl Deerfield Beach (33442) ***(G-2797)***
Reditek Corporation 954 781-1069
2826 Center Port Cir Pompano Beach (33064) ***(G-14156)***
Redsled DBA Bulldog Equipment 954 448-5221
2691 Sw Windship Way Stuart (34997) ***(G-16207)***

ALPHABETIC

Redstone Corporation..321 213-2135
606 Gladiola St Hngr 255 Merritt Island (32952) *(G-8591)*

Reduction International LLC................................954 905-5999
2700 Glades Cir Ste 134 Weston (33327) *(G-18282)*

Redwire Corporation (HQ)....................................650 701-7722
8226 Philips Hwy Ste 101 Jacksonville (32256) *(G-6410)*

Reed Brenan, Orlando *Also called Reed Brennan Media Associates* *(G-12541)*

Reed Brennan Media Associates..........................407 894-7300
628 Virginia Dr Orlando (32803) *(G-12541)*

Reed Minerals Division, Tampa *Also called Harsco Corporation* *(G-16907)*

Reeds Metal Manufacturing Inc............................352 498-0100
16454 Se Highway 19 Cross City (32628) *(G-2262)*

Reef Cleaners Inc...772 905-7166
2190 Nw Reserve Park Trce # 7 Port St Lucie (34986) *(G-14482)*

Reef Pavers Inc..904 471-0859
604 Barbara Ln Jacksonville Beach (32250) *(G-6643)*

Reese Corporation...305 653-1000
12140 Porto Way Parkland (33076) *(G-13352)*

Referral & Residual Exchange L...........................813 655-5000
9376 Balm Riverview Rd Riverview (33569) *(G-14574)*

Reflection Manufacturing....................................407 297-5727
10336 Pointview Ct Orlando (32836) *(G-12542)*

Reflections BEAch&resortwear.............................954 776-1230
104 Commercial Blvd Laud By Sea (33308) *(G-7711)*

Reflective Moments LLC.....................................561 716-2106
3152 Saint Annes Dr Boca Raton (33496) *(G-651)*

Reflectivity Inc...386 738-1008
320 S Spring Garden Ave Deland (32720) *(G-2898)*

Refly of Miami Inc...786 762-2748
7360 Nw 35th St Miami (33122) *(G-9787)*

Refresco Beverages US Inc..................................352 567-2200
15340 Citrus Country Dr Dade City (33523) *(G-2322)*

Refresco Beverages US Inc..................................813 241-0147
4506 Acline Dr E Tampa (33605) *(G-17211)*

Refresco Beverages US Inc (PA)...........................813 313-1800
8118 Woodland Center Blvd Tampa (33614) *(G-17212)*

Refresco US Holding Inc (HQ).............................813 313-1863
8118 Woodland Center Blvd Tampa (33614) *(G-17213)*

Refreshing Smoothie..904 549-5366
9550 Baymeadows Rd Jacksonville (32256) *(G-6411)*

Refreshment Services Inc...................................850 574-0281
3919 W Pensacola St Tallahassee (32304) *(G-16493)*

Refrigeration Panels, Miami *Also called Refrigrtion Engnred Systems In* *(G-9789)*

Refrigeration Panels Inc.....................................305 836-6900
7215 Nw 36th Ave Miami (33147) *(G-9788)*

Refrigrtion Engnred Systems In............................305 836-6900
7215 Nw 36th Ave Miami (33147) *(G-9789)*

Reftec International Inc.....................................800 214-4883
10530 Portal Xing Ste 104 Bradenton (34211) *(G-1035)*

Reftec Intl Systems LLC.....................................727 290-9830
6950 112th Cir Largo (33773) *(G-7670)*

Regal Boats, Orlando *Also called Regal Marine Industries Inc* *(G-12543)*

Regal Cabinets Inc..407 678-1003
3903 Forsyth Rd Winter Park (32792) *(G-18532)*

Regal Marine Industries Inc (PA).........................407 851-4360
2300 Jetport Dr Orlando (32809) *(G-12543)*

Regency Cap & Gown Company............................904 724-3500
7534 Atlantic Blvd Jacksonville (32211) *(G-6412)*

Regency Custom Cabinets Inc...............................239 332-7977
8207 Katanga Ct Fort Myers (33916) *(G-4377)*

Regeneration Technologies Inc.............................386 418-8888
11621 Research Cir Alachua (32615) *(G-18)*

Regenerative Proc Plant LLC................................727 781-0818
34176 Us Highway 19 N Palm Harbor (34684) *(G-13130)*

Regent Cabinetry and More Inc............................239 693-2207
5610 Zip Dr Fort Myers (33905) *(G-4378)*

Regent Labs Inc (PA)..954 426-4889
700 W Hillsboro Blvd 2-206 Deerfield Beach (33441) *(G-2798)*

Regent Labs Inc..954 426-4889
473 Goolsby Blvd Deerfield Beach (33442) *(G-2799)*

Regina Behar Enterprises Inc..............................305 557-5212
11440 Interchange Cir N Miramar (33025) *(G-10535)*

Regional Cnstr Resources Inc...............................713 789-5131
66 N Washington Dr Sarasota (34236) *(G-15795)*

Regional Trailer Repair Inc................................912 484-7729
1048 Escambia St Jacksonville (32208) *(G-6413)*

Rehrig Pacific Company.......................................407 857-3888
7452 Presidents Dr Orlando (32809) *(G-12544)*

Reich Metal Fabricators Inc................................561 585-3173
5405 Webster Ave West Palm Beach (33405) *(G-18139)*

Reiley Tool Company LLC....................................360 929-0350
3950 Equestrian Ct Middleburg (32068) *(G-10409)*

Reilly Foam Corp..561 842-8090
3896 Westroads Dr Riviera Beach (33407) *(G-14665)*

Reimink Printing Inc..813 289-4663
4209 W Kennedy Blvd Tampa (33609) *(G-17214)*

Reinecker Grinders Corp......................................954 974-6190
1700 Nw 15th Ave Ste 310 Pompano Beach (33069) *(G-14157)*

Reins Inc...904 868-3381
5357 Winrose Falls Dr Jacksonville (32258) *(G-6414)*

Rekord Services LLC..706 401-1791
11603 Waterbend Ct Wellington (33414) *(G-17859)*

Rela USA LLC..786 656-5069
8398 Nw 70th St Miami (33166) *(G-9790)*

Relaxium, Boca Raton *Also called American Bhvioral RES Inst LLC* *(G-405)*

Relcom Industries Inc..561 304-7717
3900 Woodlake Blvd # 200 Greenacres (33463) *(G-4852)*

Reliabilityweb.com, Fort Myers *Also called Netexpressusa Inc* *(G-4338)*

Reliable Business Technologies.............................386 561-9944
8497 Sw 136th Loop Ocala (34473) *(G-11479)*

Reliable Cabinet Designs.....................................941 473-3403
6900 San Casa Dr Unit 1 Englewood (34224) *(G-3523)*

Reliable Custom Imprints Corp.............................407 834-0571
448 Commerce Way Unit 100 Longwood (32750) *(G-7942)*

Reliable Finishes..321 723-3334
7730 Industrial Rd Melbourne (32904) *(G-8509)*

Reliable Pool Enclsres Screens, Orlando *Also called Reliable Pool Enclsres Screns* *(G-12545)*

Reliable Pool Enclsres Screns..............................407 731-3408
5558 Force Four Pkwy Orlando (32839) *(G-12545)*

Reliable Site Solutions LLC................................904 238-3113
55050 Bartram Trl Callahan (32011) *(G-1257)*

Reliable Tool and Machine Inc.............................561 844-8848
328 W 11th St Riviera Beach (33404) *(G-14666)*

Reliance Media Inc..505 243-1821
515 Cooper Commerce Dr # 140 Apopka (32703) *(G-168)*

Reliance Petro Holdings LLC................................352 390-8039
1820 Se 18th Ave Ste 3 Ocala (34471) *(G-11480)*

Reliance Supply Co USA LLC................................954 971-9111
1880 Nw 18th St Pompano Beach (33069) *(G-14158)*

Reliatex Inc...813 621-6021
6004 Bonacker Dr Tampa (33610) *(G-17215)*

Relion Enterprises LLC......................................321 287-4225
13526 Village Park Dr # 202 Orlando (32837) *(G-12546)*

Reliox Corporation...904 729-5097
8475 Western Way Ste 155 Jacksonville (32256) *(G-6415)*

Relm Communications Inc..................................321 953-7800
7100 Technology Dr Melbourne (32904) *(G-8510)*

Relmada Therapeutics Inc..................................646 876-3459
2222 Ponce De Leon Blvd Coral Gables (33134) *(G-2104)*

Relu Co..786 717-5665
1885 W State Road 84 # 103 Fort Lauderdale (33315) *(G-4014)*

Remas Draperies Etc Inc.....................................904 845-9300
27777 Conner Nelson Rd Hilliard (32046) *(G-5474)*

Remco Industries International.............................954 462-0000
917 Nw 8th Ave Fort Lauderdale (33311) *(G-4015)*

Remco Specialty Products Co, Fort Lauderdale *Also called Remco Industries International* *(G-4015)*

Remcoda LLC...908 239-4137
18201 Collins Ave # 4501 Sunny Isles Beach (33160) *(G-16281)*

Remcraft Lighting Products Inc............................305 687-9031
12870 Nw 45th Ave Opa Locka (33054) *(G-11784)*

Remetall USA Inc..888 212-3812
3000 Ne 190th St Apt 202 Aventura (33180) *(G-273)*

Remior Industries Inc..305 883-8722
9165 Nw 96th St Miami (33178) *(G-9791)*

Remodeling Guys, The, Lakeland *Also called Solara Industries Inc* *(G-7439)*

Renacer Bros LLC...305 935-6777
18839 Biscayne Blvd # 150 Miami (33180) *(G-9792)*

Renaissance Entp Group LLC................................941 284-7854
155 W Dearborn St Englewood (34223) *(G-3536)*

Renaissance Fabrication, Pensacola *Also called Renaissance Man Incorporated* *(G-13596)*

Renaissance Man Incorporated.............................850 432-1177
2203 N Pace Blvd Pensacola (32505) *(G-13596)*

Renaissance Steel LLC.......................................941 773-7290
6508 E Fowler Ave Temple Terrace (33617) *(G-17544)*

Renco Usa Inc..321 637-1000
5959 Blue Lagoon Dr Miami (33126) *(G-9793)*

Renesas Electronics Amer Inc..............................321 724-7000
1650 Rbert J Cnlan Blvd N Palm Bay (32905) *(G-12914)*

Renew Life Holdings Corp....................................925 368-9711
2405 College Ave Unit 105 Davie (33317) *(G-2467)*

Renewable Fuels Group LLC................................305 388-3028
15184 Sw 111th St Miami (33196) *(G-9794)*

Renick Enterprises Inc..561 863-4183
1211 W 13th St Riviera Beach (33404) *(G-14667)*

Rennak Inc..305 558-0144
6161 Miami Lakes Dr E Miami Lakes (33014) *(G-10348)*

Renova Land and Sea LLC..................................786 916-2695
4954 Sw 128th Ave Miramar (33027) *(G-10536)*

Renovaship Inc...954 342-9062
2700 S Park Rd Hallandale Beach (33009) *(G-4969)*

Renovatec Enterprise Inc....................................954 444-8694
2590 Nw 4th Ct Fort Lauderdale (33311) *(G-4016)*

Renovation Concrete, Jacksonville *Also called Outline Technologies Inc* *(G-6345)*

Renovation Flooring LLC......................................850 460-7295
11714 Us Highway 98 W Miramar Beach (32550) *(G-10572)*

Renovation Team Services LLC.............................352 696-0215
5103 Caspian St Saint Cloud (34771) *(G-14937)*

Renue Systems South East Fla, Aventura *Also called Services NS 18 LLC* *(G-275)*

Renzetti Inc 321 267-7705
 8800 Grissom Pkwy Titusville (32780) *(G-17611)*

Repair Electrical Motors Ac/DC, Opa Locka *Also called Done Rite Pumps* *(G-11738)*

Repco Equipment Leasing Inc 727 584-3329
 1550 Starkey Rd Largo (33771) *(G-7671)*

Repgas Inc 786 202-8434
 571 Nw Merc Pl Unit 102 Port Saint Lucie (34986) *(G-14440)*

Replenish Ink Inc 818 206-2424
 701 Brickell Ave Key Blvd Miami (33131) *(G-9795)*

Reporgraphics Unlimited Inc 386 253-7990
 124 Bay St Daytona Beach (32114) *(G-2589)*

Repro Plus Inc 407 843-1492
 850 S Hughey Ave Orlando (32801) *(G-12547)*

Reprographic Services Inc 305 859-8282
 1036 Sw 8th St Miami (33130) *(G-9796)*

Reprographic Solutions Inc (PA) 772 340-3430
 234 Sw Port St Lucie Blvd Port Saint Lucie (34984) *(G-14441)*

Repscrubs, Sanford *Also called Prescient Logistics LLC* *(G-15377)*

Reptile World, Saint Cloud *Also called Biotoxins Inc* *(G-14923)*

Republic Drill/Apt Corp (PA) 305 592-7777
 7840 Nw 62nd St Miami (33166) *(G-9797)*

Republic Newspapers Inc 813 782-1558
 38333 5th Ave Zephyrhills (33542) *(G-18628)*

Republic Newspapers Inc 352 394-2183
 732 W Montrose St Clermont (34711) *(G-1881)*

Republic Packaging Florida Inc 305 685-5175
 4570 Nw 128th St Opa Locka (33054) *(G-11785)*

Repwire LLC 786 486-1823
 5500 Nw 106th Ct Doral (33178) *(G-3347)*

RES-Net Microwave, Clearwater *Also called Electro Technik Industries Inc* *(G-1580)*

RES-Net Microwave Inc 727 530-9555
 5410 115th Ave N Clearwater (33760) *(G-1763)*

Resa Pwr Slutions Plant Cy LLC 813 752-6550
 1401 Mercantile Ct Plant City (33563) *(G-13799)*

Rescue Metal Framing LLC 561 660-5945
 2601 Delmar Pl Fort Lauderdale (33301) *(G-4017)*

Research II, Ormond Beach *Also called Hes Products Inc* *(G-12769)*

Resell Mfg LLC 407 478-8181
 2600 Maitland Center Pkwy Maitland (32751) *(G-8071)*

Resharp Industries 352 362-1730
 5101 Se 11th Ave Ocala (34480) *(G-11481)*

Resident Cmnty News Group Inc 904 962-6876
 1650 Margaret St 31 Jacksonville (32204) *(G-6416)*

Residential Acoustics LLC 813 922-2390
 6122 Benjamin Rd Tampa (33634) *(G-17216)*

Residual Innovations LLC 407 459-5497
 7253 Pleasant Dr Orlando (32818) *(G-12548)*

Resilient Group Inc 518 434-4414
 3114 Double Oaks Dr Jacksonville (32226) *(G-6417)*

Reso Inc 561 328-8539
 1930 Avenue L Riviera Beach (33404) *(G-14668)*

Resolute Cross City LLC 352 498-3363
 40 Sw 10th St Cross City (32628) *(G-2263)*

Resolute Cross Cy RE Hldngs LL 352 498-3363
 40 Sw 10th St Cross City (32628) *(G-2264)*

Resolute FP Florida Inc (HQ) 800 562-2860
 3301 Nw 107th St Miami (33167) *(G-9798)*

Resolute Tissue LLC 305 636-5741
 3301 Nw 107th St Miami (33167) *(G-9799)*

Resolute Tissue Sales 800 562-2860
 3725 E 10th Ct Hialeah (33013) *(G-5329)*

Resolver Group Inc 941 387-7410
 20 Lighthouse Point Dr Longboat Key (34228) *(G-7859)*

Resort Poolside Shops Inc 407 256-5853
 2912 Nela Ave Belle Isle (32809) *(G-350)*

Resort Window Treatments Inc 813 355-4877
 5157 Gall Blvd Zephyrhills (33542) *(G-18629)*

Resource Group US LLC 833 223-3266
 1510 Logue Rd Myakka City (34251) *(G-10646)*

Resource Management Associates 239 656-0818
 1675 Temple Ter Ste 2 Fort Myers (33917) *(G-4379)*

Resource Myakka, Myakka City *Also called Resource Group US LLC* *(G-10646)*

Resources In Rare Mining 954 800-5251
 800 E Broward Blvd # 700 Fort Lauderdale (33301) *(G-4018)*

Respect Foods 561 557-2832
 4731 Cadiz Cir Palm Beach Gardens (33418) *(G-13006)*

Responsive Machining Inc 321 225-4011
 1650 Chaffee Dr Titusville (32780) *(G-17612)*

Restifo Investments LLC 305 468-0013
 1424 Nw 82nd Ave Doral (33126) *(G-3348)*

Restonic/San Francisco, Boca Raton *Also called Sleeprite Industries Inc* *(G-683)*

Restoration Arts 305 953-9755
 15301 Nw 34th Ave Miami Gardens (33054) *(G-10271)*

Restoration Games LLC 954 937-1970
 12717 W Sunrise Blvd Sunrise (33323) *(G-16363)*

Restoration Medical LLC 863 272-0250
 5235 Nichols Dr E Lakeland (33812) *(G-7420)*

Restorative Care America Inc (PA) 727 573-1595
 12221 33rd St N Saint Petersburg (33716) *(G-15171)*

Restorative Products Inc 813 342-4432
 13560 Wright Cir Tampa (33626) *(G-17217)*

Retail Cloud Technologies LLC (PA) 727 210-1700
 380 Park Place Blvd # 250 Clearwater (33759) *(G-1764)*

Retail Sales/ Installations, Spring Hill *Also called Ramirez Cbnets Blnds Gran Mr* *(G-16076)*

Retreat 813 254-2014
 123 S Hyde Park Ave Tampa (33606) *(G-17218)*

Reuse Salvage Inc 772 485-3248
 40668 Se Russell Way Port Salerno (34992) *(G-14468)*

Rev Amblance Group Orlando Inc (HQ) 407 677-7777
 2737 Forsyth Rd Winter Park (32792) *(G-18533)*

Rev Old Inc 954 523-9396
 4001 Sw 47th Ave Ste 201 Davie (33314) *(G-2468)*

Rev Personal Care LLC 832 217-8585
 2905 Payson Way Wellington (33414) *(G-17860)*

Rev-Tech Mfg Solutions LLC 727 577-4999
 9900 18th St N Ste 105 Saint Petersburg (33716) *(G-15172)*

Revenge Advnced Composites LLC 727 572-1410
 12705 Daniel Dr Clearwater (33762) *(G-1765)*

Revere Manufactured Pdts Inc 904 503-9733
 323 Hwy Ave Jacksonville (32254) *(G-6418)*

Revere Survival Inc 904 503-9733
 5323 Highway Ave Jacksonville (32254) *(G-6419)*

Reverso, Davie *Also called Rev Old Inc* *(G-2468)*

Revive Light Therapy, Largo *Also called Led Technologies Incorporated* *(G-7632)*

Revlon Inc 904 693-1254
 540 Beautyrest Ave Jacksonville (32254) *(G-6420)*

Revlon Consumer Products Corp 904 378-4167
 5344 Overmyer Dr Jacksonville (32254) *(G-6421)*

Revology Cars LLC 800 974-4463
 6756 Edgwter Cmmrce Pkwy Orlando (32810) *(G-12549)*

Revolution Air Craft Services 954 747-4773
 2511 Nw 16th Ln Ste 3 Pompano Beach (33064) *(G-14159)*

Revolution Brands Intl LLC (PA) 786 571-3876
 10801 Nw 97th St Medley (33178) *(G-8310)*

Revtech 727 369-1750
 10050 16th St N Saint Petersburg (33716) *(G-15173)*

Reward Lighting Net LLC 561 832-1819
 6000 Georgia Ave Ste 10 West Palm Beach (33405) *(G-18140)*

Rex 3, Davie *Also called Rex Three Inc* *(G-2469)*

Rex Fox Enterprises Inc 386 677-3752
 1966 N Nova Rd Daytona Beach (32117) *(G-2590)*

Rex Lumber Graceville LLC (HQ) 850 263-2056
 5299 Alabama St Graceville (32440) *(G-4808)*

Rex Lumber LLC 850 643-2172
 Highway 12 S Bristol (32321) *(G-1126)*

Rex Lumber LLC (PA) 850 263-2056
 5299 Alabama St Graceville (32440) *(G-4809)*

Rex Three Inc (PA) 954 452-8301
 15431 Sw 14th St Davie (33326) *(G-2469)*

Rexpro Services 561 328-6488
 1097 Jupiter Park Ln # 8 Jupiter (33458) *(G-6787)*

Reyes Cabinets Installation 305 216-1683
 10311 Sw 45th St Miami (33165) *(G-9800)*

Reyes Granite & Marble Corp 305 599-7330
 7905 Nw 60th St Miami (33166) *(G-9801)*

Reyes Interlocking Pavers Inc 863 698-9179
 1317 E Calhoun St Plant City (33563) *(G-13800)*

Reyes Jewelers Corp 305 431-8303
 36 Ne 1st St Ste 734 Miami (33132) *(G-9802)*

Reyes Stucco Inc 321 557-1319
 1515 Peachtree St Lot 3 Cocoa (32922) *(G-1953)*

Reynolds Aluminum Recycl Div, Pensacola *Also called Wise Recycling 1 LLC* *(G-13627)*

Reynoso & Associates Inc 954 360-0601
 434 Sw 12th Ave Deerfield Beach (33442) *(G-2800)*

Rezolin LLC 386 677-8238
 131 Business Center Dr A7 Ormond Beach (32174) *(G-12791)*

Rfg Consulting Services Inc 786 498-2177
 801 Brickell Ave Ste 900 Miami (33131) *(G-9803)*

Rfg Consulting Services Inc 832 298-5696
 7214 Nw 78th Ter Medley (33166) *(G-8311)*

Rfg Petro Systems LLC (PA) 941 487-7524
 32 S Osprey Ave Ste 1 Sarasota (34236) *(G-15796)*

Rfis Security Solutions, Lake Mary *Also called Microsemi Corp* *(G-7094)*

Rfl & Figlio LLC 904 765-2222
 12819 Fenwick Island Ct E Jacksonville (32224) *(G-6422)*

RG Groundworks LLC 352 474-7949
 5915 Nw 210th St Newberry (32669) *(G-11026)*

RG Mechanical USA LLC 954 835-5287
 12660 Sw 13th St Davie (33325) *(G-2470)*

Rgf Environmental, Riviera Beach *Also called Rgf Marine Envmtl Tech Inc* *(G-14670)*

Rgf Environmental Group Inc 800 842-7771
 1101 W 13th St Riviera Beach (33404) *(G-14669)*

Rgf Marine Envmtl Tech Inc 561 848-1826
 1101 W 13th St Riviera Beach (33404) *(G-14670)*

Rgrauto Inc 305 952-5522
 20801 Biscayne Blvd Aventura (33180) *(G-274)*

Rgu Color Inc 386 252-9979
  3133 S Ridgewood Ave # 1 South Daytona (32119) *(G-16027)*

Rhinestntransfersdirectcom Inc 484 254-6410
  1821 Verde Way Orlando (32835) *(G-12550)*

Rhino Tire Usa Llc 407 777-5598
  11423 Satellite Blvd Orlando (32837) *(G-12551)*

Rhino Tools Inc 305 332-7750
  18844 Nw 89th Ct Hialeah (33018) *(G-5330)*

Rhodes Brothers Miami Inc 305 456-9682
  37 Deer Run Miami Springs (33166) *(G-10393)*

Rhonda Clanton 305 502-7050
  6133 Nw 181st Ter Cir S Hialeah (33015) *(G-5331)*

Rhyno Glass, Tampa *Also called FMC/Rhyno LLC (G-16856)*

Rhythm Healthcare LLC 877 843-6464
  3300 Tyrone Blvd N Saint Petersburg (33710) *(G-15174)*

Riani Pavers Inc 239 321-1875
  1735 Brantley Rd Apt 2015 Fort Myers (33907) *(G-4380)*

Ribbon Wholesale Corp 786 457-0555
  219 Sw 21st Ct Miami (33135) *(G-9804)*

Ribeiro Stones LLC 407 723-8802
  2207 Silver Star Rd Orlando (32804) *(G-12552)*

Rice Machinery Supply Co Inc 305 620-2274
  1130 Nw 163rd Dr Miami (33169) *(G-9805)*

Rich Haven Interiors, Davenport *Also called J & N Stone Inc (G-2367)*

Rich Ice Cream Co 561 833-7585
  2915 S Dixie Hwy West Palm Beach (33405) *(G-18141)*

Rich Maid Cabinets Inc 727 572-4857
  12706 Daniel Dr Clearwater (33762) *(G-1766)*

Rich Woodturning Inc 305 573-9142
  5626 Nw 161st St Miami Lakes (33014) *(G-10349)*

Richard Bryan Ingram LLC 407 677-7779
  2454 N Forsyth Rd Orlando (32807) *(G-12553)*

Richard C Good 321 639-6383
  1125 White Dr Titusville (32780) *(G-17613)*

Richard K Pratt LLC 321 482-9494
  1325 White Dr Titusville (32780) *(G-17614)*

Richard Lyn 954 326-1017
  7944 Forest Blvd North Lauderdale (33068) *(G-11085)*

Richard Meer Investments Inc 941 484-6551
  822 Pinebrook Rd Venice (34285) *(G-17713)*

Richard Wagner LLC 239 450-1721
  9601 Campbell Cir Naples (34109) *(G-10875)*

Richards Brazilian Sausage LLC 786 609-3554
  18503 Pines Blvd Ste 310 Pembroke Pines (33029) *(G-13411)*

Richards Mobile Welding 954 913-0487
  3541 Nw 73rd Way Coral Springs (33065) *(G-2205)*

Richards Paint Mfg Co Inc (PA) 321 636-6200
  200 Paint St Rockledge (32955) *(G-14741)*

Richardsons Cabinet Works 850 832-8298
  3724 Chandler Fenn Dr Panama City (32404) *(G-13302)*

Richland Towers Inc 813 286-4140
  400 N Ashley Dr Ste 2500 Tampa (33602) *(G-17219)*

Richline Group Inc 954 718-3200
  6701 Nob Hill Rd Tamarac (33321) *(G-16540)*

Richter Industries Inc 239 732-9440
  1617 Gulfstar Dr S Naples (34112) *(G-10876)*

Rick Ernissee Woodworks LLC 727 421-7711
  1556 Tilley Ave Clearwater (33756) *(G-1767)*

Rick's Quality Printing & Sign, Cocoa *Also called Ricks Quality Prtg & Signs (G-1954)*

Rickeys World Famous Sauce Inc 954 829-9464
  4799 Hollywood Blvd Hollywood (33021) *(G-5652)*

Ricks Pallet Co Inc 305 884-4896
  2420 W 3rd Ave Hialeah (33010) *(G-5332)*

Ricks Quality Prtg & Signs 321 504-7446
  681 Industry Rd S Ste A Cocoa (32926) *(G-1954)*

Ricoma International Corp 305 418-4421
  11555 Nw 124th St Medley (33178) *(G-8312)*

Ricordea Publishing, Miami *Also called Two Little Fishies Inc (G-10050)*

Ricos Candy Snack & Bakery, Hialeah *Also called Ricos Tostaditos Inc (G-5333)*

Ricos Tostaditos Inc 305 885-7392
  740 W 28th St Hialeah (33010) *(G-5333)*

Ridan Industries LLC 813 258-8334
  301 W Platt St Ste 339 Tampa (33606) *(G-17220)*

Rider Kitchen Cabinets Inc 786 502-6663
  5320 Nw 180th Ter Miami Gardens (33055) *(G-10272)*

Ridgeway Timber Inc 352 463-6013
  3949 Nw County Road 341 Bell (32619) *(G-336)*

Ridgway Roof Truss Company 352 376-4436
  235 Sw 11th Pl Gainesville (32601) *(G-4757)*

Riegl Usa Inc 407 248-9927
  14707 W Colonial Dr Winter Garden (34787) *(G-18403)*

Rieker LLC 407 496-1555
  5337 Foxshire Ct Orlando (32819) *(G-12554)*

Right To Bear Arms LLC 772 794-1188
  1225 S Us Highway 1 Vero Beach (32962) *(G-17793)*

Rigid Coatings & Castings Inc 352 396-8738
  2585 Clark St Apopka (32703) *(G-169)*

Rigid Machine Services Inc 352 396-8738
  3290 Overland Rd Apopka (32703) *(G-170)*

Rik Enterprises Inc 239 772-9485
  954 Ne Pine Island Rd G Cape Coral (33909) *(G-1378)*

Rika Bakeries Inc 305 691-5673
  1025 E 24th St Hialeah (33013) *(G-5334)*

Riley & Company Inc (PA) 407 265-9963
  5491 Benchmark Ln Sanford (32773) *(G-15381)*

Riley Gear Corporation (PA) 904 829-5652
  1 Precision Dr Saint Augustine (32092) *(G-14878)*

Riley Risk Inc 202 601-0500
  1301 Plntn Is Dr S Saint Augustine (32080) *(G-14879)*

Rima Cargo LLC 305 477-8002
  8375 Nw 68th St Miami (33166) *(G-9806)*

Rinaldi Printing & Packaging, Tampa *Also called Rinaldi Printing Company (G-17221)*

Rinaldi Printing Company 813 569-0033
  4514 E Adamo Dr Tampa (33605) *(G-17221)*

Rinehart Corp 850 271-5600
  1515 Ohio Ave Lynn Haven (32444) *(G-8031)*

Ring Lift, Lakeland *Also called Ring Power Corporation (G-7421)*

Ring of Fire Radio LLC 866 666-6114
  316 S Baylen St Pensacola (32502) *(G-13597)*

Ring Power Corporation 863 606-0512
  3425 Reynolds Rd Lakeland (33803) *(G-7421)*

Ring Power Corporation 904 354-1858
  1544 E 8th St Jacksonville (32206) *(G-6423)*

Rinker Materials, Lake Wales *Also called Cemex Materials LLC (G-7154)*

Rinker Materials 352 330-1115
  4270 County Road 124a Wildwood (34785) *(G-18319)*

Rinker Materials 305 345-4127
  13100 Nw 118th Ave Medley (33178) *(G-8313)*

Rinker Materials Corp 352 799-7881
  10311 Cement Plant Rd Brooksville (34601) *(G-1194)*

Rinker Materials Corp 305 386-0078
  8800 Sw 177th Ave Miami (33196) *(G-9807)*

Rinker Materials Corp 386 775-0790
  2170 State Road 472 Deland (32724) *(G-2899)*

Rinker Materials Corp Con 305 818-4952
  12155 Nw 136th St Medley (33178) *(G-8314)*

Rinker Portland Cement, Miami *Also called Cemex Materials LLC (G-8909)*

Rinseworks Inc 954 946-0070
  1700 Nw 15th Ave Ste 330 Pompano Beach (33069) *(G-14160)*

Rio Pavers Inc 321 388-6757
  7297 Mardell Ct Orlando (32835) *(G-12555)*

Rio's Concrete Equipment, Medley *Also called Rios Con Pmpg & Rentl Inc (G-8315)*

Rios Con Pmpg & Rentl Inc 305 888-7909
  8750 Nw 93rd St Medley (33178) *(G-8315)*

Ripa & Associates Inc 813 623-6777
  1409 Tech Blvd Ste 1 Tampa (33619) *(G-17222)*

Rippee Construction Inc 850 668-6805
  2107 Delta Way Tallahassee (32303) *(G-16494)*

Rising Stoners Inc 305 300-7851
  3533 Jefferson St Miami (33133) *(G-9808)*

Ritchie 904 783-0416
  8477 Graybar Dr Jacksonville (32221) *(G-6424)*

Ritchie Swimwear, Weston *Also called Double J of Broward Inc (G-18238)*

Ritco Foods LLC 954 727-3554
  1671 Nw 144th Ter Ste 107 Sunrise (33323) *(G-16364)*

Ritetest, Pompano Beach *Also called Firstpath Laboratory Svcs LLC (G-14023)*

Ritter Kit Bath & Closet LLC 239 272-4551
  4870 Tallowood Way Naples (34116) *(G-10877)*

Ritter's Printing, Fort Lauderdale *Also called Princess Preserve Inc (G-3998)*

Riva Industries Inc 813 573-1601
  4986 113th Ave N Clearwater (33760) *(G-1768)*

Rival Roof Tile Delivery Corp 786 251-2631
  103 Sw 18th Ave Apt 7 Miami (33135) *(G-9809)*

River City Advg Objectional 904 731-3452
  3514 Morton St Jacksonville (32217) *(G-6425)*

River City Powersports Inc 386 259-5724
  895 Diplomat Dr Unit E Debary (32713) *(G-2640)*

River City Stucco Inc 904 234-9526
  117 Magnolia Ave Jacksonville (32218) *(G-6426)*

River Craft LLC 407 867-0584
  2148 Orinoco Dr Ste 356 Orlando (32837) *(G-12556)*

River Printing, Jacksonville *Also called John Stewart Enterprises Inc (G-6228)*

Rivercity Custom Cabinetry Inc 904 247-0807
  1863 Mayport Rd Jacksonville (32233) *(G-6427)*

Riverhawk Fast Sea Frames LLC 912 484-3112
  5251 W Tyson Ave Tampa (33611) *(G-17223)*

Riverhead Housing Inc 630 688-6791
  3044 Sw 42nd St Fort Lauderdale (33312) *(G-4019)*

Riverland Logging Inc 904 845-4326
  25190 County Road 121 Hilliard (32046) *(G-5475)*

Riverstone Snctary - Cbd - Inc 954 473-1254
  2101 W Coml Blvd Ste 3500 Fort Lauderdale (33309) *(G-4020)*

Riverview Community News, Lutz *Also called Community News Publications (G-7986)*

Riverview Drones Inc 813 451-4744
  11326 Lake Lucaya Dr Riverview (33579) *(G-14575)*

Riverview Millworks Inc 904 764-9571
  9157 Lem Turner Rd Jacksonville (32208) *(G-6428)*

Riverwatch Marina & Boatyard, Stuart *Also called Gulfstream Land Company LLC (G-16159)*

Riviera Beach FL Warehouse Bm, Riviera Beach *Also called Cemex Materials LLC (G-14608)*

Riw of Jacksonville Inc 904 356-5635
608 Carmen St Jacksonville (32206) *(G-6429)*

Rizo Industries Inc 561 420-2548
310 Hemlock Rd West Palm Beach (33409) *(G-18142)*

Rizzo Management, Lake Worth *Also called Polo Players Edition (G-7228)*

Rj Foods 863 425-3282
104 N Church Ave Mulberry (33860) *(G-10636)*

RJ Forklift Services Inc 786 539-6613
8567 Coral Way Miami (33155) *(G-9810)*

Rj Staab Stone Co 352 377-3313
824 N Main St Williston (32696) *(G-18334)*

Rjh Technical Services Inc 813 655-7947
517 Gornto Lake Rd Brandon (33510) *(G-1104)*

Rjs Racing Equipment, Jupiter *Also called CSC Racing Corporation (G-6706)*

RL Schreiber Inc (PA) 954 972-7102
2745 W Cypress Creek Rd Fort Lauderdale (33309) *(G-4021)*

RLC Networks Inc 904 262-0587
14678 Longview Dr S Jacksonville (32223) *(G-6430)*

Rlcjc Inc 407 370-3338
4684 Millenia Plaza Way Orlando (32839) *(G-12557)*

Rls (usa) Inc 561 596-0556
7802 Woodland Center Blvd Tampa (33614) *(G-17224)*

Rm Brands Inc 904 356-0092
2910 W Beaver St Jacksonville (32254) *(G-6431)*

Rm Custom Woodcraft Inc 786 355-7387
10400 Nw 36th Ct Miami (33147) *(G-9811)*

RM Imaging Incorporated 561 361-8090
2499 Glades Rd Ste 206 Boca Raton (33431) *(G-652)*

RMC, Opa Locka *Also called Miami Metals II Inc (G-11769)*

RMC Ewell Inc 850 879-0959
16040 State Highway 20 Niceville (32578) *(G-11036)*

RMC Ewell Inc 850 863-5040
1787 F I M Rd Fort Walton Beach (32547) *(G-4605)*

RMC Ewell Inc 407 282-0984
7400 Narcoossee Rd Orlando (32822) *(G-12558)*

Rme Studio Inc 305 409-0856
7245 Ne 4th Ave Ste 102 Miami (33138) *(G-9812)*

Rmk Merrill Stevens Prpts LLC 305 324-5211
881 Nw 13th Ave Miami (33125) *(G-9813)*

Rmk Merrill-Stevens, Miami *Also called Rmk Merrill Stevens Prpts LLC (G-9813)*

Rmmj Inc 239 597-2486
5545 Shirley St Naples (34109) *(G-10878)*

RMR Distributors Inc 813 908-1141
9610 Norwood Dr Tampa (33624) *(G-17225)*

Road Block Fabrication Inc 708 417-6091
16140 Lee Rd Unit 100 Fort Myers (33912) *(G-4381)*

Road Master 561 479-6450
203 W State Road 84 Fort Lauderdale (33315) *(G-4022)*

Road Signs Inc 941 321-0695
2017 Whitfield Park Dr Sarasota (34243) *(G-15545)*

Roadsafe Traffic Systems Inc 386 755-0140
2118 Nw County Road 25a Lake City (32055) *(G-7043)*

Roan Manufacturing Inc 813 510-4929
23791 Oaks Blvd Land O Lakes (34639) *(G-7502)*

Rob Dinic Interiors, Lakeland *Also called D I R Inc (G-7303)*

Robba, Emilio, Miami *Also called Fleurissima Inc (G-9149)*

Robbins Lumber, Tampa *Also called Robbins Manufacturing Company (G-17226)*

Robbins Manufactuing Co 352 793-2443
12904 Sr 471 Webster (33597) *(G-17833)*

Robbins Manufacturing Company (PA) 813 971-3030
1003 E 131st Ave Tampa (33612) *(G-17226)*

Robbins Manufacturing Company 888 558-8199
1003 E 131st Ave Tampa (33612) *(G-17227)*

Roberlo Usa Inc 786 334-6191
8501 Nw 17th St Ste 103 Doral (33126) *(G-3349)*

Robert E Weissenborn Sr (PA) 239 262-1771
1101 5th Ave S Naples (34102) *(G-10879)*

Robert Gomes Publishing Inc 941 637-6080
8512 Alan Blvd Punta Gorda (33982) *(G-14527)*

Robert James Cstm Met Fabg LLC 772 214-0996
2900 N Canal St Jacksonville (32209) *(G-6432)*

Robert McKee Enterprises Inc 772 291-2159
7744 Sw Jack James Dr Stuart (34997) *(G-16208)*

Robert Ojeda Metalsmith Inc 561 507-5511
10151 Yeoman Ln Royal Palm Beach (33411) *(G-14772)*

Robert Petrucci Inc 954 772-2333
1701 W Cypress Creek Rd Fort Lauderdale (33309) *(G-4023)*

Robert St Croix Sculpture Stu 561 835-1753
1400 Alabama Ave Ste 6 West Palm Beach (33401) *(G-18143)*

Robert's Saw Company, Tampa *Also called RSC Industries Inc (G-17236)*

Roberto Valverde 305 324-5252
1929 Nw 22nd St Miami (33142) *(G-9814)*

Roberts Consolidated Inds, Boca Raton *Also called QEP Co Inc (G-643)*

Roberts Lumber Company Inc 850 584-4573
3655 E Us 27 Hwy Perry (32347) *(G-13652)*

Roberts Printing, Clearwater *Also called Roberts Quality Printing Inc (G-1769)*

Roberts Quality Printing Inc 727 442-4011
2049 Calumet St Clearwater (33765) *(G-1769)*

Roberts Vault Co Inc 352 567-0110
14621 Roberts Barn Rd Dade City (33523) *(G-2323)*

Robertson Billiard Sups Inc 813 229-2778
1721 N Franklin St Tampa (33602) *(G-17228)*

Robertson Transformer Co 917 603-8530
4152 Independence Ct C2 Sarasota (34234) *(G-15797)*

Robertson Worldwide, Sarasota *Also called Robertson Transformer Co (G-15797)*

Robinson Fans Inc 724 452-6121
3955 Drane Field Rd Lakeland (33811) *(G-7422)*

Robomow USA Inc 844 762-6669
9050 16th Pl Ste 1 Vero Beach (32966) *(G-17794)*

Robot-Costumes Technologies 904 535-0074
120 Cumberland Park Dr # 305 Saint Augustine (32095) *(G-14880)*

Robotic Parking Systems Inc 727 539-7275
12812 60th St N Clearwater (33760) *(G-1770)*

Robotic Security Systems Inc 850 871-9300
6530 E Highway 22 Panama City (32404) *(G-13303)*

Robotics Fabrication Inc 850 896-4987
5835 Bay Line Dr Panama City (32404) *(G-13304)*

Robotray, Miami *Also called Bcdirect Corp (G-8807)*

Robs Bageland Inc 954 640-5470
8201 W Sunrise Blvd Plantation (33322) *(G-13881)*

Robson Corporation 941 753-6935
2231 Whitfield Park Loop Sarasota (34243) *(G-15546)*

Rochester Electro-Medical Inc 813 994-7519
11711 Nw 39th St Coral Springs (33065) *(G-2206)*

Rock & Roll, Wellington *Also called Noa International Inc (G-17856)*

Rock Bottom Bottles LLC 901 237-9929
1447 Tallevast Rd Sarasota (34243) *(G-15547)*

Rock Brick Pavers Inc 407 692-6816
344 S Hart Blvd Orlando (32835) *(G-12559)*

Rock Brothers Brewing LLC 917 324-8175
1901 N 15th St Tampa (33605) *(G-17229)*

Rock Intl Distributors Inc 305 513-3314
8279 Nw 66th St Miami (33166) *(G-9815)*

Rock N Roll Custom Screened S 727 528-2111
4590 62nd Ave N Pinellas Park (33781) *(G-13727)*

Rock Ridge Materials Inc 321 268-8455
1525 White Dr Titusville (32780) *(G-17615)*

Rock River Tool Inc 941 753-6343
2953 63rd Ave E Bradenton (34203) *(G-1036)*

Rockers Stone Inc 305 447-1231
3615 Plaza St Miami (33133) *(G-9816)*

Rocket Crafters Launch LLC 321 222-0858
2941 Oxbow Cir Cocoa (32926) *(G-1955)*

Rocket International, Fort Myers *Also called Rocket Marine Inc (G-4382)*

Rocket Marine Inc 239 275-0880
2360 Crystal Rd Fort Myers (33907) *(G-4382)*

Rocket Sign Supplies LLC 239 995-4684
3587 Vrnica S Shmker Blvd Fort Myers (33916) *(G-4383)*

Rocket Towne Inc 561 478-1274
412 Tall Pines Rd West Palm Beach (33413) *(G-18144)*

Rocket Vending Inc 561 672-1373
19234 S Creekshore Ct Boca Raton (33498) *(G-653)*

Rockford Ettco Procunier Inc 863 688-0071
304 Winston Creek Pkwy Lakeland (33810) *(G-7423)*

Rockledge Phrm Mfg LLC 321 636-0717
417 Richard Rd Rockledge (32955) *(G-14742)*

Rockpack Inc 407 757-0798
2549 Clark St Apopka (32703) *(G-171)*

Rockwell Automation Inc 954 306-7900
2200 N Commerce Pkwy # 107 Weston (33326) *(G-18283)*

Rockwell Automation Inc 813 466-6400
5820 W Cypress St Ste E Tampa (33607) *(G-17230)*

Rockwell Collins, Wellington *Also called B/E Aerospace Inc (G-17844)*

Rockwell Collins Inc 321 768-7303
1100 W Hibiscus Blvd Melbourne (32901) *(G-8511)*

Rocky Bayou Enterprises Inc 850 244-4567
630 Lovejoy Rd Nw Fort Walton Beach (32548) *(G-4606)*

Rockymountain Lifenet 863 533-5168
5581 Airport Blvd Bartow (33830) *(G-323)*

Rocla Concrete Tie Inc 772 800-1855
600 S 3rd St Fort Pierce (34950) *(G-4525)*

Rod Biscayne Manufacturing 305 884-0808
425 E 9th St Hialeah (33010) *(G-5335)*

Roden International Inc (PA) 954 929-1900
3741 N Park Rd Hollywood (33021) *(G-5653)*

Rodents On The Road, East Palatka *Also called Karnak Corporation (G-3473)*

Rodes Printing Corp 305 559-5263
8369 Bird Rd Miami (33155) *(G-9817)*

Rodriguez Welding 305 856-3749
220 Sw 6th St Miami (33130) *(G-9818)*

Roebic Laboratories Inc 561 799-3380
1213 Ocean Dunes Cir Jupiter (33477) *(G-6788)*

Rogers Holster Co, Jacksonville *Also called Safariland LLC* ***(G-6445)***
Rogers Septic Tanks Inc 203 259-9947
10603 Sw Capraia Way Port Saint Lucie (34986) ***(G-14442)***
Rogers Sign Corp 352 799-1923
701 S Lemon Ave Brooksville (34601) ***(G-1195)***
Rogue Industries LLC 850 797-9228
217 Miracle Strip Pkwy Se Fort Walton Beach (32548) ***(G-4607)***
Roja Med Inc 305 381-5803
168 Se 1st St Ste 403 Miami (33131) ***(G-9819)***
Rokey Corporation 561 470-0164
18188 Blue Lake Way Boca Raton (33498) ***(G-654)***
Rolin Industries Inc 850 654-1704
94 Ready Ave Nw Unit A1 Fort Walton Beach (32548) ***(G-4608)***
Rolite Co 920 251-1006
7841 Birdie Bend Way Sarasota (34241) ***(G-15798)***
Roll A Way, Tampa *Also called Valco Group Inc* ***(G-17402)***
Roll-A-Guard, Largo *Also called Aabc Inc* ***(G-7519)***
Rolladen Inc 954 454-4114
1328 Bennett Dr Longwood (32750) ***(G-7943)***
Roller Coat Industries, Tampa *Also called Rollercoat Industries Inc* ***(G-17231)***
Roller Die + Forming 502 804-5571
4630 County Road 209 S Green Cove Springs (32043) ***(G-4834)***
Rollercoat Industries Inc 813 621-4668
10135 E Us Highway 92 Tampa (33610) ***(G-17231)***
Rollertech Corp 239 645-6698
5845 Corporation Cir Fort Myers (33905) ***(G-4384)***
Rolling Door Parts Inc 305 888-5020
8187 Nw 71st St Miami (33166) ***(G-9820)***
Rolling Greens Mobile Home Pk 352 624-0022
1899 Se 58th Ave Ocala (34480) ***(G-11482)***
Rolling Shield Incorporated 305 436-6661
9875 Nw 79th Ave Hialeah Gardens (33016) ***(G-5449)***
Rolling Shield Parts Inc 305 436-6661
9875 Nw 79th Ave Hialeah Gardens (33016) ***(G-5450)***
Rollingshield, Hialeah Gardens *Also called Rolling Shield Parts Inc* ***(G-5450)***
Rolls Axle Lc 813 764-0242
702 Hitchcock St Plant City (33563) ***(G-13801)***
Rolls Rite Trailers Inc 850 526-2290
3741 Industrial Park Dr Marianna (32446) ***(G-8174)***
Rolls Shading Systems Llc 561 955-0557
1301 W Copans Rd Pompano Beach (33064) ***(G-14161)***
Rollshield LLC 727 441-2243
1151 Kapp Dr Clearwater (33765) ***(G-1771)***
Rolltech Hurricanes Shutters, Pensacola *Also called Adams Hurricane Protection Inc* ***(G-13435)***
Rolo Gang LLC 561 538-8173
11503 Sw 26th Pl Miramar (33025) ***(G-10537)***
Rolsafe LLC 239 225-2487
12801 Commwl Dr Ste 7 Fort Myers (33913) ***(G-4385)***
Rolu Woodcraft Inc 305 685-0914
4733 E 11th Ave Hialeah (33013) ***(G-5336)***
Roma Casting Inc 305 577-0289
14 Ne 1st Ave Ste 306 Miami (33132) ***(G-9821)***
Romano Group LLC 305 255-4242
12253 Sw 130th St Miami (33186) ***(G-9822)***
Romark Laboratories LC 813 282-8544
542 Severn Ave Tampa (33606) ***(G-17232)***
Romax Industries Inc 305 773-6657
8620 Nw 190th Ter Hialeah (33015) ***(G-5337)***
Romco Fuels Inc 954 474-5392
10835 Sw 38th Dr Davie (33328) ***(G-2471)***
Rome Supply, Pompano Beach *Also called Bari Millwork & Supply LLC* ***(G-13949)***
Romeo Ohana LLC 808 500-3420
12501 Drayton Dr Spring Hill (34609) ***(G-16077)***
Romeo Roseau Ecommerce 561 633-1352
245 Ne 6th Ave Boynton Beach (33435) ***(G-909)***
Romine Reprographics Svcs, Apopka *Also called Design & Print Solutions Inc* ***(G-120)***
Ron Matusalem & Matusa Fla Inc 305 448-8255
1205 Sw 37th Ave Ste 300 Miami (33135) ***(G-9823)***
Ronaele Mustang Inc 954 319-7433
5965 Manchester Way Tamarac (33321) ***(G-16541)***
Ronald M Hart Inc 772 600-8497
43 Sw Osceola St Stuart (34994) ***(G-16209)***
Ronco Aircraft and Marine Inc (PA) 321 220-0209
1774 Plantation Cir Se Palm Bay (32909) ***(G-12915)***
Ronco Machine Inc 904 827-9795
2100 Dennis St Jacksonville (32204) ***(G-6433)***
Ronecker Holdings LLC 813 855-5559
303 Mears Blvd Oldsmar (34677) ***(G-11697)***
Ronmar Industries Inc 561 630-8035
8990 Lakes Blvd West Palm Beach (33412) ***(G-18145)***
Ronnie & Moes Italian Ice LLC 786 970-1805
7900 Nw 27th Ave Ste 602a Miami (33147) ***(G-9824)***
Ronnies Welding & Machine Inc 305 238-0972
18640 Sw 104th Ct Cutler Bay (33157) ***(G-2301)***
Rontan North America Inc 305 599-2974
7859 Nw 46th St Ste 5b Doral (33166) ***(G-3350)***
Roof Tile Administration Inc 863 467-0042
1289 Ne 9th Ave Okeechobee (34972) ***(G-11614)***
Roof Tile Inc 863 467-0042
1289 Ne 9th Ave Okeechobee (34972) ***(G-11615)***
Roof-A-Cide West LLC 877 258-8998
1640 Field Rd Sarasota (34231) ***(G-15799)***
Roomy Design Organizers LLC 407 703-9550
330 Cooper Palms Pkwy A Apopka (32703) ***(G-172)***
Roorda Buiders Inc 727 410-7776
15115 Race Track Rd Odessa (33556) ***(G-11575)***
Root International Inc 813 482-1732
237 176th Terrace Dr E Redington Shores (33708) ***(G-14554)***
Root International Inc (PA) 813 265-1808
4910 Creekside Dr Ste B Clearwater (33760) ***(G-1772)***
Rope Works Inc 954 525-6575
262 Sw 33rd St Fort Lauderdale (33315) ***(G-4024)***
Roper Industrial Pdts Inv Co 941 556-2601
6901 Prof Pkwy E Ste 200 Sarasota (34240) ***(G-15800)***
Roper Technologies Inc (PA) 941 556-2601
6901 Prof Pkwy E Ste 200 Sarasota (34240) ***(G-15801)***
Roque Brothers Corp 305 885-6995
5646 Nw 35th Ct Miami (33142) ***(G-9825)***
Roro Inc 561 909-6220
300 S Australian Ave # 16 West Palm Beach (33401) ***(G-18146)***
Ros Holding Corporation 954 581-9200
3201 W State Road 84 Fort Lauderdale (33312) ***(G-4025)***
Roscioli International Inc (PA) 941 755-7411
3201 W State Road 84 Fort Lauderdale (33312) ***(G-4026)***
Roscioli International Inc 941 755-7411
6111 21st St E Bradenton (34203) ***(G-1037)***
Rose Poster Printing, Miami Lakes *Also called Outdoor America Images Inc* ***(G-10334)***
Rose Printing Co Inc 850 339-8093
2504 Harriman Cir Tallahassee (32308) ***(G-16495)***
Rosebel Gold Mines NV, Doral *Also called Iamgold Purchasing Svcs Inc* ***(G-3253)***
Rosier Manufacturing Company 386 409-7223
409 W Intl Speedway Blvd Daytona Beach (32114) ***(G-2591)***
Ross Industries Inc 954 752-2800
11440 W Sample Rd Pompano Beach (33065) ***(G-14162)***
Ross Slade Inc 813 250-0488
5024 W Nassau St Tampa (33607) ***(G-17233)***
Rossam Industries Inc 305 493-5111
811 Nw 57th Pl Fort Lauderdale (33309) ***(G-4027)***
Rosuca International LLC 305 332-5572
5639 Nw 113th Ct Doral (33178) ***(G-3351)***
Rotab Inc 954 447-7746
20950 Sheridan St Fort Lauderdale (33332) ***(G-4028)***
Rotary Manufacturing LLC 941 564-8038
3276 Commerce Pkwy North Port (34289) ***(G-11204)***
Rotburg Instruments Amer Inc 954 331-8046
1560 Sawgrass Corporate Sunrise (33323) ***(G-16365)***
Roth Lighting, Fort Lauderdale *Also called Roth Southeast Lighting LLC* ***(G-4029)***
Roth Southeast Lighting LLC 954 423-6640
204 Sw 21st Ter Fort Lauderdale (33312) ***(G-4029)***
Rotor Works, Sarasota *Also called Florida Sncast Helicopters LLC* ***(G-15477)***
Round Table Tools Inc 850 877-7650
3645 Hartsfield Rd Tallahassee (32303) ***(G-16496)***
Rourke Educational Media LLC 772 234-6001
2145 14th Ave Ste 2 Vero Beach (32960) ***(G-17795)***
Rourke Publishing Group, Vero Beach *Also called Rourke Ray Publishing Co Inc* ***(G-17796)***
Rourke Ray Publishing Co Inc 772 234-6001
1701 Highway A1a Ste 300 Vero Beach (32963) ***(G-17796)***
Route4me Inc 888 552-9045
1010 N Florida Ave Tampa (33602) ***(G-17234)***
Rouzbeh Inc 727 587-7077
9700 Ulmerton Rd Largo (33771) ***(G-7672)***
Rov Railway Industry LLC 305 299-8264
10135 W Sunrise Blvd # 101 Plantation (33322) ***(G-13882)***
Rover Aerospace Inc 305 594-7799
2254 Nw 94th Ave Doral (33172) ***(G-3352)***
Rowe Industries Inc 302 855-0585
2525 Sw 32nd Ave Pembroke Park (33023) ***(G-13365)***
Rowe Manufacturing LLC 407 324-5757
722 Golden Spike Ln Sanford (32771) ***(G-15382)***
Rowell Laboratories Inc 407 929-9445
174 Semoran Commerce Pl # 110 Apopka (32703) ***(G-173)***
Rowell Labs, Apopka *Also called Rowell Laboratories Inc* ***(G-173)***
Rowland Publishing Inc 850 878-0554
1932 Miccosukee Rd Tallahassee (32308) ***(G-16497)***
Rox Volleyball 877 769-2121
3520 Ag Ctr Dr Ste 310 Saint Augustine (32092) ***(G-14881)***
Roxy Lady LLC 954 706-6735
1904 Nw 16th Ct Fort Lauderdale (33311) ***(G-4030)***
Roy Smith S Screen 561 792-3381
16648 71st Ln N Loxahatchee (33470) ***(G-7975)***
Royal Ancient Superfoods 305 600-1747
10530 Nw 37th Ter Doral (33178) ***(G-3353)***
Royal Atlantic Ventures LLC 561 243-9699
1505 Poinsettia Dr H-9 Delray Beach (33444) ***(G-3013)***
Royal Baths Manufacturing Co 407 854-1740
1920 Premier Row Orlando (32809) ***(G-12560)***
Royal Canes 727 474-0792
12399 Belcher Rd S # 160 Largo (33773) ***(G-7673)***

Royal Concrete Concepts Inc (PA) 561 689-5398
1410 Park Ln S Ste 2 Jupiter (33458) **(G-6789)**

Royal Cup Inc 813 664-8902
3502 Queen Palm Dr Ste A Tampa (33619) **(G-17235)**

Royal Foam US LLC 904 345-5400
4225 James E Casey Dr Jacksonville (32219) **(G-6434)**

Royal Headwear & EMB Inc 305 889-8480
7675 Nw 80th Ter Medley (33166) **(G-8316)**

Royal Industries Inc 954 871-6807
16621 Royal Poinciana Ct Weston (33326) **(G-18284)**

Royal Manor Vineyard & Winery 386 684-6270
224 Royal Ave Interlachen (32148) **(G-5820)**

Royal Palm Press Inc 941 575-4299
25560 Technology Blvd Punta Gorda (33950) **(G-14528)**

Royal Precision Products Inc 305 685-5490
13171 Nw 43rd Ave Opa Locka (33054) **(G-11786)**

Royal Press, Orlando Also called Fermatex Enterprises Inc **(G-12148)**

Royal Prestige 813 464-9872
5221 Nw 33rd Ave Fort Lauderdale (33309) **(G-4031)**

Royal Screen Enclosures Inc 407 970-0864
18241 Sky Top Ln Groveland (34736) **(G-4869)**

Royal Tees Inc 941 366-0056
5556 Palmer Blvd Sarasota (34232) **(G-15802)**

Royal Truss Corp 786 222-1100
10900 Nw South River Dr Medley (33178) **(G-8317)**

Royal Westlake Roofing LLC 863 676-9405
200 Story Rd Lake Wales (33898) **(G-7172)**

Royaltea 407 401-9969
714 N Mills Ave Orlando (32803) **(G-12561)**

Royce, Sarasota Also called Rp International LLC **(G-15803)**

Rp High Performance Inc 561 863-2800
2391 President Barack Oba Riviera Beach (33404) **(G-14671)**

Rp International LLC (PA) 941 894-1228
3400 S Tamiami Trl # 300 Sarasota (34239) **(G-15803)**

Rpd Management LLC 904 710-8911
720 King St Jacksonville (32204) **(G-6435)**

Rpe, Fort Myers Also called Ranger Plastic Extrusions Inc **(G-4375)**

Rperf Technologies Corp 954 629-2359
6584 Nw 56th Dr Coral Springs (33067) **(G-2207)**

RPM, Rockledge Also called Rockledge Phrm Mfg LLC **(G-14742)**

RPM Co 352 542-3110
27908 Se Hwy 19 Old Town (32680) **(G-11623)**

RPM Crushers and Screens 941 769-0420
24710 Sandhill Blvd # 8 Punta Gorda (33983) **(G-14529)**

RPM Graphics Inc 239 275-3278
508 Owen Ave N Lehigh Acres (33971) **(G-7824)**

Rpp Devices 772 807-7098
625 Nw Commodity Cv Port Saint Lucie (34986) **(G-14443)**

Rq Welding Inc 786 609-3384
6011 Sw 109th Ave Miami (33173) **(G-9826)**

Rrd Commercial Print - Orlando, Orlando Also called R R Donnelley & Sons
Company **(G-12528)**

RSC Industries Inc 813 886-4711
5451 W Waters Ave Tampa (33634) **(G-17236)**

RSC Molding Inc 516 351-9871
475 N Cleary Rd Unit 4 West Palm Beach (33413) **(G-18147)**

RSR Industrial Coatings Inc 863 537-1110
1577 Centennial Blvd Bartow (33830) **(G-324)**

Rssi Barriers Llc 850 871-9300
6530 E Highway 22 Panama City (32404) **(G-13305)**

Rsvp Skinnies Inc (PA) 786 853-8032
11100 Sw 74th Ct Pinecrest (33156) **(G-13670)**

Rt22 Creations Inc 954 254-8258
5438 Nw 10th Ter Fort Lauderdale (33309) **(G-4032)**

Rta Cabinets & More LLC 321 288-3068
222 E Eau Gallie Blvd Indian Harbour Beach (32937) **(G-5807)**

RTC Solutions Inc 919 439-8680
4370 Oakes Rd Ste 700 Davie (33314) **(G-2472)**

Rti Donor Services Inc 321 431-2464
401 N Wickham Rd Ste 143 Melbourne (32935) **(G-8512)**

Rti Surgical Inc 386 418-8888
11621 Research Cir Alachua (32615) **(G-19)**

Rtj Group Inc 954 999-4060
1451 Nw 62nd St Ste 300 Fort Lauderdale (33309) **(G-4033)**

Rtp Corp 954 597-5333
2832 Center Port Cir Pompano Beach (33064) **(G-14163)**

Rubber 2 Go Llc 305 688-8566
3551 Nw 116th St Miami (33167) **(G-9827)**

Rubber B LLC 305 771-2369
605 Lincoln Rd Ste 210 Miami Beach (33139) **(G-10224)**

Rubber Designs LLC 706 383-7528
500 Sw 6th Ter Ocala (34471) **(G-11483)**

Rubens Custom Cabinets Inc 813 510-8397
1310 W Termino St Tampa (33612) **(G-17237)**

Rubin Iron Works LLC 904 356-5635
608 Carmen St Jacksonville (32206) **(G-6436)**

Rubinelli Woodwork Inc 954 445-0537
8891 Sw 16th St Boca Raton (33433) **(G-655)**

Rubingers Manufacturing Co 863 665-1599
2626 Mine And Mill Ln Lakeland (33801) **(G-7424)**

Rubix Foods LLC 904 268-8999
13203 Flagler Center Blvd Jacksonville (32258) **(G-6437)**

Ruby Vanrum 850 643-5155
12167 Nw Freeman Rd Bristol (32321) **(G-1127)**

Rubyquartz Technology LLC 305 406-0211
10400 Nw 33rd St Ste 290 Doral (33172) **(G-3354)**

Rudd & Son Welding Inc 850 476-2110
81 E Ten Mile Rd Pensacola (32534) **(G-13598)**

Rudd Welding, Pensacola Also called Rudd & Son Welding Inc **(G-13598)**

Rudolph & ME, Port Charlotte Also called Edmund C Miga **(G-14297)**

Rudys Ready Mix 305 382-9283
5800 Sw 122nd Ave Miami (33183) **(G-9828)**

Rugby Road Corp 407 328-5474
3941 Saint Johns Pkwy Sanford (32771) **(G-15383)**

Ruke Inc 239 292-2553
1226 Main St Windermere (34786) **(G-18365)**

Rulon Company of Georgia 904 584-1400
2000 Ring Way Saint Augustine (32092) **(G-14882)**

Runaware Inc 954 907-9052
5440 Nw 108th Way Coral Springs (33076) **(G-2208)**

Runn-It LLC 800 932-8052
66 W Flagler St Ste 900 Miami (33130) **(G-9829)**

Running Board Warehouse, Ocala Also called Thi E-Commerce LLC **(G-11501)**

Rupp Marine Inc 772 286-5300
4761 Se Anchor Ave Stuart (34997) **(G-16210)**

Rusco Inc 352 597-2522
13360 Chambord St Brooksville (34613) **(G-1196)**

Rush Flyers 954 332-0509
6561 Nw 18th Ct Plantation (33313) **(G-13883)**

Rush To Excellence Prtg Inc 904 367-0100
4204 Spring Park Rd Jacksonville (32207) **(G-6438)**

Russanos Express LLC 772 220-3329
2946 Sw Mapp Rd Palm City (34990) **(G-13057)**

Russell Associates Inc (HQ) 727 815-3100
10540 Ridge Rd Ste 300 New Port Richey (34654) **(G-10982)**

Russell Bindery, Saint Augustine Also called Russells Bindery Inc **(G-14883)**

Russell Bros Alum Andzing Ctin 407 323-5619
1001 Cornwall Rd Sanford (32773) **(G-15384)**

Russell Bros Alum Anodizing, Sanford Also called Russell Bros Alum Andzing
Ctin **(G-15384)**

Russell Hobbs Inc (HQ) 954 883-1000
3633 S Flamingo Rd Miramar (33027) **(G-10538)**

Russell Home Imprvmnt Ctr Inc 954 436-9186
3250 Sw 131st Ter Davie (33330) **(G-2473)**

Russells Bindery Inc 904 829-3100
90 Palmer St Saint Augustine (32084) **(G-14883)**

Rustic Steel Creations Inc 813 222-0016
3919 N Highland Ave Tampa (33603) **(G-17238)**

Rustwerks 407 399-2262
5519 Commerce Dr Orlando (32839) **(G-12562)**

Ruvos LLC (PA) 850 254-7270
2252 Klarn Ctr Blvd Tallahassee (32309) **(G-16498)**

Rv Air Inc (PA) 309 657-4300
628 Cleveland St Apt 1407 Clearwater (33755) **(G-1773)**

Rvcc of Florida 352 569-5870
2540 W C 48 Bushnell (33513) **(G-1248)**

Rvr Elettronica, Doral Also called RVR USA LLC **(G-3355)**

RVR USA LLC 305 471-9091
7782 Nw 46th St 20 Doral (33166) **(G-3355)**

Rwc Group LLC 754 222-1407
3901 Ne 12th Ave Ste 400 Pompano Beach (33064) **(G-14164)**

Rwla Enterprises LLC 772 334-1248
2810 Se Dune Dr Apt 1104 Stuart (34996) **(G-16211)**

Rx For Fleas Inc 954 351-9244
6555 Powerline Rd Ste 412 Fort Lauderdale (33309) **(G-4034)**

Rxenergy LLC 727 726-4204
2449 N Mcmullen Booth Rd Clearwater (33759) **(G-1774)**

Rxgenesys LLC 786 220-8366
175 Sw 7th St Ste 2417 Miami (33130) **(G-9830)**

Rxprinting and Graphics LLC 407 965-3039
4909 S Orange Ave Orlando (32806) **(G-12563)**

Ryan Manufacturing Inc 386 325-3644
339b State Road 207 East Palatka (32131) **(G-3475)**

Ryan Petroleum, Fort Myers Also called Ryan Tire & Petroleum Inc **(G-4386)**

Ryan Scientific LLC 904 284-6025
4035a Reynolds Blvd Green Cove Springs (32043) **(G-4835)**

Ryan Tire & Petroleum Inc 239 334-1351
2650 Edison Ave Fort Myers (33916) **(G-4386)**

Ryans Custom Coatings 863 669-3310
7096 Remington Oaks Loop Lakeland (33810) **(G-7425)**

Ryd Enterprises, Miami Also called R Y D Enterprises Inc **(G-9773)**

Ryder Orthopedics Inc (PA) 239 939-0009
1500 Royal Palm Square Bl Fort Myers (33919) **(G-4387)**

Ryder Welding Service Inc 305 685-6630
350 Ali Baba Ave Opa Locka (33054) **(G-11787)**

Ryman Hospitality Prpts Inc 904 284-2770
625 Oak St Green Cove Springs (32043) **(G-4836)**

Rytex Industries Inc 727 557-7450
12855 Belcher Rd S Largo (33773) **(G-7674)**

A L P H A B E T I C

Rz Service Group LLC...............................904 402-2313
12574 Flagler Center Blvd Jacksonville (32258) *(G-6439)*

S & B Industries Inc...............................305 367-1068
11052 Sw 162nd Ter Miami (33157) *(G-9831)*

S & B Metal Products E Fla Inc...............................386 274-0092
1811 Holsonback Dr Daytona Beach (32117) *(G-2592)*

S & B Metal Products S Fla Inc...............................941 727-3669
6012 31st St E Bradenton (34203) *(G-1038)*

S & B Metal Products S Fla Inc (PA)...............................941 727-3669
5301 Gateway Blvd Lakeland (33811) *(G-7426)*

S & J Custom Fabrication Inc...............................352 246-1462
5955 Indian Trl Keystone Heights (32656) *(G-6888)*

S & K Prfmce Machining & Fab...............................954 306-2214
11911 Nw 27th Ct Plantation (33323) *(G-13884)*

S & R Fastener Co Inc...............................352 588-0768
30241 Commerce Dr San Antonio (33576) *(G-15252)*

S & S Enterprises, Summerfield Also called Stephen Shives *(G-16260)*

S & S Metal and Plastics Inc...............................904 731-4655
6600 Suemac Pl 2 Jacksonville (32254) *(G-6440)*

S & S Performance Inc...............................305 951-9846
80460 Overseas Hwy Islamorada (33036) *(G-5838)*

S & S Precast Inc...............................239 992-8685
25095 Old 41 Rd Bonita Springs (34135) *(G-816)*

S & S Propeller Co Inc...............................718 359-3393
3040 Sw 10th St Pompano Beach (33069) *(G-14165)*

S & S Welding Inc...............................863 533-2888
2850 Us Highway 17 S Bartow (33830) *(G-325)*

S & W Nash Seafood, Apalachicola Also called Miracle Seafood Manufacturers *(G-89)*

S 3 Marketing Group LLC...............................317 491-3398
1663 Bunting Ln Sanibel (33957) *(G-15417)*

S A Feather Co Inc...............................239 693-6363
5852 Enterprise Pkwy Fort Myers (33905) *(G-4388)*

S A Florikan-E LLC...............................800 322-8666
2404 Commerce Ct Bowling Green (33834) *(G-832)*

S A Gloria Corp...............................305 575-2900
6705 S Red Rd Ste 405 South Miami (33143) *(G-16044)*

S A Microtechnologies LLC...............................954 973-6166
2901 Gateway Dr Pompano Beach (33069) *(G-14166)*

S and S Morris LLC...............................404 431-7803
1630 Assisi Dr Sarasota (34231) *(G-15804)*

S B Lighting LLC...............................850 687-1166
2889 N Highway 81 Ponce De Leon (32455) *(G-14249)*

S D Modular Displays, Fort Lauderdale Also called Sdm Acquisition Corporation *(G-4041)*

S E Inc...............................407 859-9317
6448 Pinecastle Blvd # 104 Orlando (32809) *(G-12564)*

S E S, Hialeah Also called Select Engineered Systems Inc *(G-5343)*

S F C, Medley Also called South Florida Concrete & Rdymx *(G-8321)*

S G F Inc...............................813 996-2528
3018 Joan Ct Land O Lakes (34639) *(G-7503)*

S G M, Pompano Beach Also called Southern Grouts & Mortars Inc *(G-14193)*

S Gager Industries Inc...............................904 268-6727
11436 Philips Hwy Jacksonville (32256) *(G-6441)*

S I P Corporation...............................813 884-8300
7210 Anderson Rd Ste A Tampa (33634) *(G-17239)*

S King Fulton Div, Hallandale Beach Also called International Dock Pdts Inc *(G-4952)*

S M D Research Inc...............................561 451-9895
9151 Pine Springs Dr Boca Raton (33428) *(G-656)*

S M I, Largo Also called Suncoast Molders Inc *(G-7693)*

S M I Cabinetry Inc...............................407 841-0292
2525 N Orange Blossom Trl Orlando (32804) *(G-12565)*

S N S Auto Sports LLC...............................727 546-2700
7061 49th St N Pinellas Park (33781) *(G-13728)*

S O S Printing & Office Supply, Destin Also called Weidenhamer Corporation *(G-3082)*

S P Manufacturing LLC...............................305 362-0456
2208 W 79th St Hialeah (33016) *(G-5338)*

S P Sheet Metal Co Inc...............................609 698-8800
5500 Military Trl Ste 22 Jupiter (33458) *(G-6790)*

S Printing Inc...............................305 633-3343
2207 Nw 23rd Ave Miami (33142) *(G-9832)*

S R P, Bradenton Also called Southern Reinforced Plas Inc *(G-1050)*

S S Designs Inc...............................863 965-2576
5558 Commercial Blvd Winter Haven (33880) *(G-18465)*

S T A Sales, Clearwater Also called Hutchins Co Inc *(G-1631)*

S T Wooten Corporation...............................239 337-9486
16560 Mass Ct Fort Myers (33912) *(G-4389)*

S V Bags America Inc...............................954 577-9091
1563 Sandpiper Cir Weston (33327) *(G-18285)*

S&H Arcylic Coatings Inc...............................352 232-1249
4673 Chamber Ct Spring Hill (34609) *(G-16078)*

S&J 34102 Inc...............................239 592-9388
609 E Jackson St Ste 100 Tampa (33602) *(G-17240)*

S&J Aluminum Works Inc...............................850 492-5700
5623 Bauer Rd Pensacola (32507) *(G-13599)*

S&L Cnstrction Specialists Inc...............................407 300-5080
13412 Heswall Run Orlando (32832) *(G-12566)*

S&P USA Vntilation Systems LLC...............................904 731-4711
6393 Powers Ave Jacksonville (32217) *(G-6442)*

S&S Consulting Partners LLC...............................850 803-8379
139 Bayside Dr Niceville (32578) *(G-11037)*

S&S Craftsmen Inc...............................813 247-4429
6404 E Columbus Dr Tampa (33619) *(G-17241)*

S&S Global Supply LLC...............................786 529-4799
730 W 38th Pl Hialeah (33012) *(G-5339)*

S&S Performance Marine, Islamorada Also called S & S Performance Inc *(G-5838)*

S.A. Feather Co., Inc. Florida, Fort Myers Also called S A Feather Co Inc *(G-4388)*

S3 Industries Inc...............................305 498-8364
4160 Sw 99th Ave Miami (33165) *(G-9833)*

S4j Manufacturing Services Inc...............................239 574-9400
2685 Ne 9th Ave Cape Coral (33909) *(G-1379)*

Saas Transportation Inc...............................850 650-7709
3551 Scenic Highway 98 Destin (32541) *(G-3078)*

Sab Fuels Inc...............................786 213-3399
2616 Stickney Point Rd Sarasota (34231) *(G-15805)*

Sabcon Underground LLC...............................863 268-8225
1730 Dundee Rd Winter Haven (33884) *(G-18466)*

Sabic Innovative Plastics...............................386 409-5540
703 South St New Smyrna Beach (32168) *(G-11008)*

Sabine Inc...............................386 418-2000
13301 Nw Us Highway 441 Alachua (32615) *(G-20)*

Sabrosol Laboratories LLC...............................305 290-4038
12585 Ne 7th Ave North Miami (33161) *(G-11119)*

Sachi Tech Inc...............................813 649-8028
5005 W Laurel St Ste 204 Tampa (33607) *(G-17242)*

Sacyr Environment USA LLC...............................202 361-4568
3191 Coral Way Ste 510 Miami (33145) *(G-9834)*

SAE, Orlando Also called Sky Aerospace Engineering Inc *(G-12608)*

Saf Aerospace LLC...............................813 376-0883
8006 N Highland Ave Tampa (33604) *(G-17243)*

Safari Programs Inc (PA)...............................305 621-1000
8010 Westside Indus Dr Jacksonville (32219) *(G-6443)*

Safari Sun LLC...............................407 339-7291
928 Josiane Ct Ste 1007 Altamonte Springs (32701) *(G-70)*

Safariland LLC...............................904 741-5400
3041 Faye Rd Jacksonville (32226) *(G-6444)*

Safariland LLC...............................904 646-0141
3041 Faye Rd Jacksonville (32226) *(G-6445)*

Safariland LLC (HQ)...............................904 741-5400
13386 International Pkwy Jacksonville (32218) *(G-6446)*

Safariland LLC...............................904 741-5400
4101 Bulls Bay Hwy Jacksonville (32219) *(G-6447)*

Safariland Group, Jacksonville Also called Safariland LLC *(G-6446)*

Safariland Group, The, Jacksonville Also called Cadre Holdings Inc *(G-5967)*

Safco Software...............................561 750-7879
7654 Solimar Cir Boca Raton (33433) *(G-657)*

Safe, Saint Augustine Also called Security and Fire Elec Inc *(G-14890)*

Safe Banks and Lock...............................954 762-3565
2870 Ne 55th Ct Fort Lauderdale (33308) *(G-4035)*

Safe Glass, Riviera Beach Also called Security Impact GL Hldings LLC *(G-14674)*

Safe Industries Inc...............................321 639-8646
396 Gus Hipp Blvd Ste B Rockledge (32955) *(G-14743)*

Safe Money Report, Jupiter Also called Weiss Research Inc *(G-6826)*

Safe Passage Home Inc...............................904 241-4211
9 Hopson Rd Jacksonville (32250) *(G-6448)*

Safe Pro Inc...............................954 494-5768
1650 W 33rd Pl Hialeah (33012) *(G-5340)*

Safe Stride, Largo Also called Kmss Products Inc *(G-7628)*

Safeboot Corp...............................239 298-7000
2640 Golden Gate Pkwy # 1 Naples (34105) *(G-10880)*

Safecraft Rstraint Systems Inc...............................813 758-3571
3959 Van Dyke Rd Lutz (33558) *(G-8013)*

Safeguard America Inc (PA)...............................305 859-9000
3935 Nw 26th St Miami (33142) *(G-9835)*

Safeprints LLC...............................305 960-7391
9155 S Dadeland Blvd # 1504 Miami (33156) *(G-9836)*

Safetarp Corp...............................904 824-7277
1950 State Road 16 Saint Augustine (32084) *(G-14884)*

Safetek International Inc (PA)...............................702 558-8202
6560 W Rogers Cir Boca Raton (33487) *(G-658)*

Safetogether Ltd Liability Co...............................954 227-2236
5917 Nw 63rd Way Parkland (33067) *(G-13353)*

Safety Clamps Inc...............................904 781-2809
233 Santa Barbara Ave Jacksonville (32254) *(G-6449)*

Safety Compliance Publ Inc...............................844 556-3149
3600 S State Road 7 # 204 Miramar (33023) *(G-10539)*

Safety Intl Bags & Straps Inc...............................407 830-0888
160 Lyman Rd Casselberry (32707) *(G-1432)*

Safety Zone Specialists Inc...............................863 984-1385
2318 Old Combee Rd 107 Lakeland (33805) *(G-7427)*

Safilo Inc...............................305 262-5727
703 Nw 62nd Ave Ste 100 Miami (33126) *(G-9837)*

Safran Power Uk Ltd...............................941 739-7207
2250 Whitfield Ave Sarasota (34243) *(G-15548)*

Safran Power Usa LLC...............................941 758-7726
2250 Whitfield Ave Sarasota (34243) *(G-15549)*

Saftron Manufacturing LLC...............................305 233-5511
6012 33rd St E Bradenton (34203) *(G-1039)*

Sage Implementations LLC...............................407 290-6952
7648 San Remo Pl Orlando (32835) *(G-12567)*

(G-0000) Company's Geographic Section entry number

Sage Imports Corp 305 962-0631
232 Andalusia Ave Ste 201 Coral Gables (33134) *(G-2105)*

Sagrad Inc 321 726-9400
202 West Dr Melbourne (32904) *(G-8513)*

Sahlman Holding Company Inc (PA) 813 248-5726
1601 Sahlman Dr Tampa (33605) *(G-17244)*

SAI Super Software Solutions 407 445-2520
5230 Cona Reef Ct Orlando (32810) *(G-12568)*

Saikou Optics Incorporated 407 986-4200
3259 Progress Dr Ste 128 Orlando (32826) *(G-12569)*

Sailor Made Cstm Woodworks LLC 805 587-1197
190 Wading Bird Cir Sw Palm Bay (32908) *(G-12916)*

Sailor Made Custom Woodworks L 805 587-1197
571 Haverty Ct Ste H Rockledge (32955) *(G-14744)*

Saint Augustine Cast Stone 904 794-2626
4960 Cres Technical Ct Saint Augustine (32086) *(G-14885)*

Saint George Industries LLC 786 212-1176
9130 S Dadelnd Blvd 180 Miami (33156) *(G-9838)*

Saint Gobain, Largo Also called Saint-Gobain Prfmce Plas Corp *(G-7675)*

Saint Gobain Performance Plas, Clearwater Also called Saint-Gobain Prfmce Plas Corp *(G-1775)*

Saint Judas Tadeus Foundry, Hialeah Also called St Judas Tadeus Foundry Inc *(G-5360)*

Saint Petersburg Cabinets Inc 727 327-4800
2547 24th Ave N Saint Petersburg (33713) *(G-15175)*

Saint Petersburg Times, Port Richey Also called Times Publishing Company *(G-14379)*

Saint-Gobain Corporation 863 425-3299
2377 State Road 37 S Mulberry (33860) *(G-10637)*

Saint-Gobain Prfmce Plas Corp 727 373-1299
8615 126th Ave Ste 650 Largo (33773) *(G-7675)*

Saint-Gobain Prfmce Plas Corp 727 531-4191
4451 110th Ave N Clearwater (33762) *(G-1775)*

Saint-Gobain Vetrotex Amer Inc 407 834-8968
110 Atlantic Annex Pt Maitland (32751) *(G-8072)*

Sakar Zebulun, Hollywood Also called High Five Industries Inc *(G-5595)*

Sal Aerospace Engineering LLC 305 791-0593
11990 Sw 128th St Miami (33186) *(G-9839)*

Sal Praschnik Inc 305 866-4323
1090 Kane Cncurse Ste 101 Bay Harbor Islands (33154) *(G-333)*

Salco Electric Supply LLC 305 777-0200
4000 Ponce De Leon Blvd Coral Gables (33146) *(G-2106)*

Salco Industries Inc 941 377-7717
263 Field End St Sarasota (34240) *(G-15806)*

Sales, Tampa Also called Outreach Corporation *(G-17135)*

Sales & Distribution, Davie Also called Gates Corporation *(G-2417)*

Salmi and Company Inc 443 243-8537
8328 Randall Dr Navarre (32566) *(G-10955)*

Salon By Destiny & Light, The, Tampa Also called Destiny & Light Inc *(G-16772)*

Salon Technologies Intl 407 301-3726
8810 Com Cir Ste 20-22 Orlando (32819) *(G-12570)*

Salsa Cuba Inc 305 993-9757
1275 W 49th St Hialeah (33012) *(G-5341)*

Salsa Pembroke Pines Inc 954 461-0532
601 Sw 145th Ter Pembroke Pines (33027) *(G-13412)*

Salsa Three Inc 954 990-2223
10167 W Sunrise Blvd Plantation (33322) *(G-13885)*

Salsa Tropical LLC 786 362-9034
15110 Sw 56th St Miami (33185) *(G-9840)*

Salt 1 To 1 .... 407 538-2134
11221 John Wycliffe Blvd Orlando (32832) *(G-12571)*

Salt 1to1 Inc 407 721-8107
214 N Goldenrod Rd Ste 8 Orlando (32807) *(G-12572)*

Salt International Corp 305 698-8889
2798 Sw 32nd Ave Pembroke Park (33023) *(G-13366)*

Salt Life LLC 904 595-5370
240 3rd St S Jacksonville Beach (32250) *(G-6644)*

Saltage Inc 305 462-8960
9092 Nw S River Dr Ste 61 Medley (33166) *(G-8318)*

Saltex Group Corp 305 477-3187
7509 Nw 36th St Miami (33166) *(G-9841)*

Salty Boats Rjl Inc 863 802-0543
900 Industrial Dr Wildwood (34785) *(G-18320)*

Salty Industries LLC 321 626-6331
729 Columbus Ave Unit 102 Melbourne (32901) *(G-8514)*

Salva Enterprises Inc 863 291-4407
654 Post Ave Sw Winter Haven (33880) *(G-18467)*

Salvia Tile & Stone Inc 239 643-7770
303 Airport Pulling Rd N Naples (34104) *(G-10881)*

Sam S Accrsio Sons Pkg Prod In 305 246-3455
1225 Nw 2nd St Homestead (33030) *(G-5737)*

Sam Weiss Woodworking Inc 954 975-8158
5195 Nw 15th St Margate (33063) *(G-8153)*

Samara Publishing 305 361-3333
104 Crandon Blvd Ste 301 Key Biscayne (33149) *(G-6839)*

Samarian Products LLC 212 781-2121
780 Fifth Ave S Ste 200 Naples (34102) *(G-10882)*

Sameday Printing Inc 800 411-3106
6815 Biscayne Blvd Miami (33138) *(G-9842)*

Saminco Inc (PA) 239 561-1561
10030 Amberwood Rd Ste 5 Fort Myers (33913) *(G-4390)*

Samjay Media Group Orlando LLC 407 865-7526
187 Sabal Palm Dr Ste 200 Longwood (32779) *(G-7944)*

Sampletech 727 239-7055
1953 Whitney Way Clearwater (33760) *(G-1776)*

Sams Closet Inc 954 354-8386
1717 Sw 1st Way Ste 28 Deerfield Beach (33441) *(G-2801)*

Sams Gas 386 698-1033
2680 S Us Highway 17 Crescent City (32112) *(G-2237)*

Samson & Surrey LLC 305 902-3336
8950 Sw 74th Ct Ste 1909 Miami (33156) *(G-9843)*

Samson Metal and Machine Inc 863 665-0283
3145 Us Highway 92 E Lakeland (33801) *(G-7428)*

Samteck Inc 813 210-6784
1005 Croydonwood Cir Brandon (33510) *(G-1105)*

San Bernardo Ice Cream, Miramar Also called Food Marketing Consultants Inc *(G-10492)*

San Marco Place Condo Assn 504 812-0352
1478 Riverplace Blvd Jacksonville (32207) *(G-6450)*

San Sebastian Winery, Saint Augustine Also called Seavin Inc *(G-14889)*

Sanacare, Miami Also called Ace Sales Corp *(G-8645)*

Sanbornwebdesigns.com, Madeira Beach Also called A Sanborn Corporation *(G-8039)*

Sanbur Inc 941 371-7446
4118 Bee Ridge Rd Sarasota (34233) *(G-15807)*

Sanchelima Dairy Products, Miami Also called Mambi Cheese Company Inc *(G-9504)*

Sanchelima International Inc 305 591-4343
1783 Nw 93rd Ave Doral (33172) *(G-3356)*

Sanchez Brothers Corp 561 992-0062
6500 Us Highway 27 S South Bay (33493) *(G-16017)*

Sancilio & Company Inc 561 847-2302
3874 Fiscal Ct Ste 200 Riviera Beach (33404) *(G-14672)*

Sand Dollar Charters LLC 903 734-5376
147 Middle Way New Smyrna Beach (32169) *(G-11009)*

Sand Dollar Printing Inc 813 740-1953
3910 N Us Highway 301 # 250 Tampa (33619) *(G-17245)*

Sand Hill Rock LLC 772 216-4852
7660 Ne 304th St Okeechobee (34972) *(G-11616)*

Sandar Industries Inc 904 246-4309
1545 Main St Atlantic Beach (32233) *(G-215)*

Sanderson Pipe Corporation (PA) 904 275-3289
1 Enterprise Blvd Sanderson (32087) *(G-15255)*

Sandow Media LLC 646 805-0200
3651 Fau Blvd Ste 200 Boca Raton (33431) *(G-659)*

Sandow Media LLC (PA) 561 961-7749
3651 Nw 8th Ave Ste 200 Boca Raton (33431) *(G-660)*

Sandow Media-Airport Linehaul, Boca Raton Also called Sandow Media LLC *(G-660)*

Sandpaper Marketing Inc 850 939-8040
7502 Harvest Village Ct Navarre (32566) *(G-10956)*

Sandpaper Publishing Inc 850 939-8040
7502 Harvest Village Ct Gulf Breeze (32566) *(G-4890)*

Sandpiper Turbine LLC 407 377-7220
3955 Merlin Dr Kissimmee (34741) *(G-6959)*

Sands Molding Inc 813 345-8646
23324 Gracewood Cir Land O Lakes (34639) *(G-7504)*

Sandvik Mining & Cnstr USA LLC (HQ) 386 462-4100
13500 Nw County Road 235 Alachua (32615) *(G-21)*

Sandy Finished Wood Inc 954 615-7271
3163 Sw 13th Ct Fort Lauderdale (33312) *(G-4036)*

Sandy Lender Inc 239 272-8613
2200 Nw 5th St Cape Coral (33993) *(G-1380)*

Sandy-Alexander Inc 727 579-1527
1527 102nd Ave N Saint Petersburg (33716) *(G-15176)*

Sanibel Print & Graphics 239 454-1001
15630 Mcgregor Blvd Ste 1 Fort Myers (33908) *(G-4391)*

Saniflow Corporation 305 424-2433
3325 Nw 70th Ave Miami (33122) *(G-9844)*

Sanit Technologies LLC 941 351-9114
7810 25th Ct E Unit 106 Sarasota (34243) *(G-15550)*

Sanitation Products of America, Tallahassee Also called Spa Concepts Inc *(G-16502)*

Sanitube LLC (PA) 863 606-5960
180 Contractors Way Lakeland (33801) *(G-7429)*

Sano Associates Inc 239 403-2650
3827 Progress Ave Naples (34104) *(G-10883)*

Sanofi US Services Inc 407 736-0226
2501 Discovery Dr Orlando (32826) *(G-12573)*

Sanomedics Inc (PA) 305 433-7814
7777 Glades Rd Ste 100 Boca Raton (33434) *(G-661)*

Santa Bell Capitav Group, Sanibel Also called Captiva Current Inc *(G-15413)*

Santa Fe Truss Company Inc 386 454-7711
5079 Sw 80th Ave Bell (32619) *(G-337)*

Santa Rosa Auto Parts Inc 850 477-7747
50 Industrial Blvd Pensacola (32503) *(G-13600)*

Santanas Pwrsprts Small Eng Rp 813 658-3530
7941 N Armenia Ave Tampa (33604) *(G-17246)*

Santiago Chopper LLC (PA) 813 671-9097
10935 Sonora Dr Gibsonton (33534) *(G-4800)*

Santiago of Key West Inc 305 304-6063
1301 United St Key West (33040) *(G-6880)*

Santillana USA Pubg Co Inc (HQ) 305 591-9522
8333 Nw 53rd St Ste 402 Miami (33166) *(G-9845)*

Santiva Chronicle LLC 239 472-0559
1420 Albatross Rd Sanibel (33957) *(G-15418)*

Santos Frozen Foods Inc 813 875-4901
2746 W Main St Tampa (33607) *(G-17247)*

Sanzay Corporation 305 826-9886
1080 Nw 163rd Dr Miami (33169) *(G-9846)*

Sanzogo Corporation 561 334-2138
2000 Glades Rd Ste 214 Boca Raton (33431) *(G-662)*

SANZOGO WINDOW AND WALL, Boca Raton Also called Sanzogo Corporation *(G-662)*

SAP Enterprises Inc 954 871-8688
309 Sw 77th Ave North Lauderdale (33068) *(G-11086)*

Sapa Extrsons St Augustine LLC 904 794-1500
200 Riviera Blvd Saint Augustine (32086) *(G-14886)*

Sapa Prcsion Tubing Adrian Inc 321 636-8147
100 Gus Hipp Blvd Rockledge (32955) *(G-14745)*

Saphire Disinfection Products, Lake Butler Also called Saphire Services LLC *(G-7005)*

Saphire Services LLC 386 247-1048
250 Sw 9th Ave Lake Butler (32054) *(G-7005)*

Sapore Di Vino Inc 561 818-8411
6905 Nw 51st St Miami (33166) *(G-9847)*

Sapphire Exchange LLC 407 926-8305
107 S Ridgewood Ave Edgewater (32132) *(G-3500)*

Sapphire LLC 561 346-7449
6432 Melaleuca Ln Greenacres (33463) *(G-4853)*

Saputo Dairy Foods Usa LLC 904 354-0406
2198 W Beaver St Jacksonville (32209) *(G-6451)*

Sar Wholesale Sign Factory 813 949-8397
1903 Passero Ave Lutz (33559) *(G-8014)*

Sara Glove Company Inc 866 664-7272
7935 Airprt Pulling N Ste Naples (34109) *(G-10884)*

Sarah Louise Inc 941 377-9656
8263 Blaikie Ct Sarasota (34240) *(G-15808)*

Sarasota Archtctural Wdwkg LLC 941 684-1614
6110 Clark Center Ave Sarasota (34238) *(G-15809)*

Sarasota Byfront Plg Orgnztion 941 203-5316
655 N Tamiami Trl Sarasota (34236) *(G-15810)*

Sarasota Cabinetry Inc 941 351-5588
3080 N Washington Blvd # 25 Sarasota (34234) *(G-15811)*

Sarasota Cattlemen Rm, Sarasota Also called Cemex Cnstr Mtls Fla LLC *(G-15630)*

Sarasota Cottages LLC 941 724-2245
1628 7th St Sarasota (34236) *(G-15812)*

Sarasota Herald Tribune, Sarasota Also called Halifax Media Group LLC *(G-15698)*

Sarasota Herald-Tribune 941 358-4000
1800 University Pkwy Sarasota (34243) *(G-15551)*

Sarasota Herald-Tribune 941 745-7808
8713 State Road 70 E Bradenton (34202) *(G-1040)*

Sarasota Herald-Tribune (HQ) 941 953-7755
801 S Tamiami Trl Sarasota (34236) *(G-15813)*

Sarasota Herald-Tribune 941 953-7755
1777 Main St Ste 400 Sarasota (34236) *(G-15814)*

Sarasota Kitchens Closets Inc 941 722-7505
5822 24th St E Bradenton (34203) *(G-1041)*

Sarasota Leather Gallery Inc (PA) 800 741-4336
15941 Us Highway 19 Hudson (34667) *(G-5787)*

Sarasota Precision Engrg Inc (PA) 941 727-3444
2305 72nd Ave E Sarasota (34243) *(G-15552)*

Sarasota Shower Door Company 941 378-0051
2025e Porter Lake Dr Sarasota (34240) *(G-15815)*

Sarasota Signs and Visuals 941 355-5746
4070 N Washington Blvd Sarasota (34234) *(G-15816)*

Sarasota Welding, North Venice Also called Srq Welding Inc *(G-11219)*

Sarasota-Manatee Originals Inc 941 365-2800
1215 S Tamiami Trl Sarasota (34239) *(G-15817)*

Sarasotas Finest MBL Gran Inc 941 365-9697
550 Mango Ave Sarasota (34237) *(G-15818)*

Sargeant Bulk Asphalt Inc 954 763-4796
321 E Hillsboro Blvd Deerfield Beach (33441) *(G-2802)*

Sargeant Marine Inc 561 999-9916
3020 N Military Trl # 100 Boca Raton (33431) *(G-663)*

Sargent Aerospace and Defense, Miami Also called Avborne Accesory Group LLC *(G-8774)*

Sargent Cycle Upholstery, Jacksonville Also called Sargent Seat Cover Co Inc *(G-6452)*

Sargent Seat Cover Co Inc 904 355-2529
44 E 1st St Jacksonville (32206) *(G-6452)*

Sarniya Enterprises Inc 352 347-6030
3620 Arbor Chase Dr Palm Harbor (34683) *(G-13131)*

Sas Group, Port Saint Lucie Also called Synergy Ancillary Services LLC *(G-14453)*

Sas R & D Services Inc 954 432-2345
2371 Sw 195th Ave Miramar (33029) *(G-10540)*

Sas Usa Inc 305 428-0200
6801 Nw 77th Ave Ste 302 Miami (33166) *(G-9848)*

Sasco Machining Inc 561 746-8233
904 Penn Trl Jupiter (33458) *(G-6791)*

Sasquatch Cabinet Company 941 365-4950
6841 Energy Ct Lakewood Ranch (34240) *(G-7486)*

Satchel Group, Edgewater Also called Jasmine Purkiss *(G-3495)*

Satcom Direct Government Inc (PA) 321 777-3000
1050 Satcom Ln Melbourne (32940) *(G-8515)*

Satcom Scientific Inc 407 856-1050
5644 Commerce Dr Ste G Orlando (32839) *(G-12574)*

Satellite Now Inc 239 945-0520
411 Sw 34th Ter Cape Coral (33914) *(G-1381)*

Saten Leaf Nursery Inc 305 216-5340
13822 Sw 282nd Ter Homestead (33033) *(G-5738)*

Sathyam Publications Inc 562 667-6622
400 Sw 107th Ave Miami (33174) *(G-9849)*

Satin Sensation Co 786 290-4114
16657 Sw 79th Ter Miami (33193) *(G-9850)*

Satin Soles, Dunedin Also called Cathy Minh Lee *(G-3443)*

Saugus Valley Corp 954 772-4077
8716 Nw 54th St Coral Springs (33067) *(G-2209)*

Saul Signs Inc 305 266-8484
10631 Nw 123rd Street Rd Medley (33178) *(G-8319)*

Savage Ventures Inc 772 335-5655
1702 Se Village Green Dr Port Saint Lucie (34952) *(G-14444)*

Savi Air, Stuart Also called Gb Airlink Inc *(G-16154)*

Saving For College LLC 954 770-5136
444 Brickell Ave Ste 820 Miami (33131) *(G-9851)*

Savory Life LLC 813 981-2022
6766 Waterton Dr Riverview (33578) *(G-14576)*

Savory Street 941 312-4027
411 N Orange Ave Sarasota (34236) *(G-15819)*

Savvy Associate Inc 954 941-6986
1480 Sw 3rd St Ste 5 Pompano Beach (33069) *(G-14167)*

Saw Palmetto Berries Cooperati 239 775-4286
7440 Friendship Ln Naples (34120) *(G-10885)*

Saw Palmetto Florida LLC 239 775-4286
7440 Friendship Ln Naples (34120) *(G-10886)*

Sawgrass Nutra Labs LLC 844 688-7244
7018 A C Skinner Pkwy # 230 Jacksonville (32256) *(G-6453)*

Sawstreet LLC 407 601-4907
6450 Kingspointe Pkwy # 6 Orlando (32819) *(G-12575)*

Sawyer Products Inc 727 725-1177
605 7th Ave N Safety Harbor (34695) *(G-14795)*

Say What Screen Prtg & EMB Inc 941 745-5822
10912 8th Ave E Bradenton (34212) *(G-1042)*

Sazon Inc 305 591-9785
2000 Nw 92nd Ave Doral (33172) *(G-3357)*

Sb Pallets, South Bay Also called Sanchez Brothers Corp *(G-16017)*

Sb Signs Inc 561 688-9100
1300 N Florida Mango Rd # 20 West Palm Beach (33409) *(G-18148)*

Sb Tactical, Bradenton Also called Nst Global LLC *(G-1020)*

SBC Laser, Opa Locka Also called Cm2 Industries Inc *(G-11731)*

Sbm Beauty LLC 850 567-7338
831 Sikes St Quincy (32351) *(G-14548)*

Sbr Custom Cabinets Inc 407 765-8134
4093 Floralwood Ct Orlando (32812) *(G-12576)*

SBS, Melbourne Also called SBs Precision Shtmtl Inc *(G-8516)*

SBs Precision Shtmtl Inc 321 951-7411
615 Distribution Dr Melbourne (32904) *(G-8516)*

SBS Promotional Solutions, Jacksonville Also called Shipping + Business Svcs LLC *(G-6465)*

SBT River PIP Project 919 469-5095
4400 N Alafaya Trl Orlando (32826) *(G-12577)*

SC Cabinet LLC 561 429-5369
7655 Enterprise Dr Riviera Beach (33404) *(G-14673)*

SC Capital Ventures Inc 954 657-8563
3025 Nw 25th Ave Pompano Beach (33069) *(G-14168)*

SC Edge, Port Saint Lucie Also called Catch One Comm *(G-14403)*

SC Elearning LLC 561 293-2543
400 Fairway Dr Ste 101 Deerfield Beach (33441) *(G-2803)*

SC Gastronomic Crew Inc 786 864-1212
127 Miracle Mile Coral Gables (33134) *(G-2107)*

SC Parent Corporation 703 351-0200
1450 Brickell Ave Fl 31 Miami (33131) *(G-9852)*

SC Purchaser Corporation 703 351-0200
1450 Brickell Ave Fl 31 Miami (33131) *(G-9853)*

Scalable Software Inc 239 603-7090
2060 Painted Palm Dr Naples (34119) *(G-10887)*

Scale Models Arts & Tech 305 949-1706
15455 W Dixie Hwy Ste G North Miami Beach (33162) *(G-11161)*

Scan Technology Inc (PA) 931 723-0304
10305 Nw 4th Pl Gainesville (32607) *(G-4758)*

Scanid Inc 305 607-3523
444 Brickell Ave Miami (33131) *(G-9854)*

Scar Heal, Saint Petersburg Also called Atlantic Medical Products LLC *(G-14974)*

Scarb Industries Inc 772 597-3898
15845 Sw Warfield Blvd Indiantown (34956) *(G-5815)*

Sccy Firearms, Daytona Beach Also called Sccy Industries LLC *(G-2593)*

Sccy Industries LLC 386 322-6336
1800 Concept Ct Daytona Beach (32114) *(G-2593)*

Scent Fill, Oldsmar Also called Aromavalue Inc *(G-11629)*

Scents Nature Enterprises Corp 305 547-2334
7850 Nw 98th St Miami Lakes (33016) *(G-10350)*

Scents of Nature Enterprises 305 547-2334
7850 Nw 98th St Miami Lakes (33016) *(G-10351)*

Scentsability Candles 954 234-4405
11480 W Sample Rd Coral Springs (33065) *(G-2210)*

Scentstional Soaps Candles Inc 941 485-1443
  730 Commerce Dr Venice (34292) *(G-17714)*

Scf Processing LLC 352 377-0858
  1604 Nw 8th Ave Gainesville (32603) *(G-4759)*

Schark Skinz, Sebastian *Also called Shark Skinz (G-15904)*

Scheduall Scheduall Scheduall 954 334-5400
  2719 Hollywood Blvd Hollywood (33020) *(G-5654)*

Schick LLC 718 810-3804
  20412 Ne 15th Ct Miami (33179) *(G-9855)*

Schimmbros Inc 407 796-8361
  3726 Grissom Ln Kissimmee (34741) *(G-6960)*

Schnebly Redlands Winery Inc 786 247-2060
  30205 Sw 217th Ave Homestead (33030) *(G-5739)*

Schneidder Industries LLC 850 207-0929
  1690 Dunn Ave Apt 408 Daytona Beach (32114) *(G-2594)*

Schnupp Manufacturing Co Inc 305 325-0520
  2113 Nw 17th Ave Miami (33142) *(G-9856)*

Schoen Industries Inc 305 491-5993
  4831 Calasans Ave Saint Cloud (34771) *(G-14938)*

Schoenhut LLC 904 810-1945
  6480b Us Highway 1 N Saint Augustine (32095) *(G-14887)*

Schoenhut Piano Company, Saint Augustine *Also called Schoenhut LLC (G-14887)*

School New Letter Program, Orlando *Also called Academy Publishing Inc (G-11864)*

School-On-Wheels 239 530-8522
  13520 Tamiami Trl E Naples (34114) *(G-10888)*

Schooner Prints Inc 727 397-8572
  8632 115th Ave Largo (33773) *(G-7676)*

Schott Solutions Inc 786 340-5116
  201 Sw 97th Ter Pembroke Pines (33025) *(G-13413)*

Schrappers Fine Cabinetry, Jupiter *Also called Beverly Acquisitions Inc (G-6692)*

Schrappers Fine Cabinetry Inc 561 746-3827
  240 W Indiantown Rd # 101 Jupiter (33458) *(G-6792)*

Schreiber, Fort Lauderdale *Also called Parkson Corporation (G-3978)*

Schur & Company LLC 904 353-8075
  9410 Florida Min Blvd E Jacksonville (32257) *(G-6454)*

Schurco Slurry Pumps, Jacksonville *Also called Schur & Company LLC (G-6454)*

Schurr Sails Inc 850 438-9354
  490 S L St Pensacola (32502) *(G-13601)*

Schwabs Enterprises, Valparaiso *Also called Bayou Outdoor Equipment (G-17655)*

Schwartz Electro-Optics Inc 407 297-8988
  8337 Southpark Cir Orlando (32819) *(G-12578)*

Schwarz Bros Manufacturing Co 309 342-5814
  1455 Little Creek Dr Pensacola (32506) *(G-13602)*

Schwarz Partners Packaging LLC 863 682-0123
  2808 New Tampa Hwy Lakeland (33815) *(G-7430)*

Schwarz Prtners Pckg Miami LLC 305 693-1399
  1101 E 33rd St Hialeah (33013) *(G-5342)*

Schwing Bioset 239 237-2174
  12290 Treeline Ave Fort Myers (33913) *(G-4392)*

SCI, Deerfield Beach *Also called Sustainable Casework Inds LLC (G-2818)*

SCI, Cocoa *Also called Service Corp International (G-1956)*

SCi Architectural Wdwrk Inc 954 247-9601
  2801 Nw 55th Ct Ste 1w Fort Lauderdale (33309) *(G-4037)*

SCI Materials LLC 352 878-4979
  15251 N Highway 329 Reddick (32686) *(G-14553)*

SCI Undercar Inc (PA) 727 327-2278
  2447 5th Ave S Saint Petersburg (33712) *(G-15177)*

SCI-Chem, Kissimmee *Also called Chemline Inc (G-6906)*

Science Daily LLC 239 596-2624
  4034 Roberts Point Rd Sarasota (34242) *(G-15820)*

Science First LLC 904 225-5558
  86475 Gene Lassere Blvd Yulee (32097) *(G-18593)*

Science of Water LLC 904 654-0778
  1177 Park Ave Ste 5 Orange Park (32073) *(G-11839)*

Scientific Instruments Inc 561 881-8500
  4400 W Tiffany Dr Mangonia Park (33407) *(G-8100)*

Scientific Research Products 954 971-0600
  1850 W Mcnab Rd Fort Lauderdale (33309) *(G-4038)*

Scif Solutions Inc (PA) 904 298-0631
  11518 Normandy Blvd Jacksonville (32221) *(G-6455)*

Scky Industries Inc 352 595-7782
  855 W Highway 318 Citra (32113) *(G-1468)*

Scope Worker LLC 917 855-5379
  2121 Nw 2nd Ave Ste 203 Miami (33127) *(G-9857)*

Score Group, The, Doral *Also called Quad Intl Incorporated (G-3341)*

Scorpion Equity LLC 352 512-0800
  5817 Nw 44th Ave Ocala (34482) *(G-11484)*

Scorpion Racing Products, Ocala *Also called Scorpion Equity LLC (G-11484)*

Scosta Corp (PA) 863 385-8242
  3670 Commerce Center Dr Sebring (33870) *(G-15937)*

Scosta Corp 863 385-8242
  3705 Commerce Center Dr Sebring (33870) *(G-15938)*

Scot Pump Company, Fort Lauderdale *Also called Wilo USA LLC (G-4133)*

Scott Brevard Inc 386 698-1121
  306 Central Ave Crescent City (32112) *(G-2238)*

Scott Fischer Enterprises LLC (PA) 844 749-2363
  12730 Commwl Dr Ste 2 Fort Myers (33913) *(G-4393)*

Scott Industrial Systems Inc 904 693-3318
  4130 N Canal St Jacksonville (32209) *(G-6456)*

Scott Safety LLC 239 340-8695
  13999 W Sr 78 Moore Haven (33471) *(G-10592)*

Scott Sign Systems Inc (HQ) 941 355-5171
  7525 Pennsylvania Ave C Sarasota (34243) *(G-15553)*

Scott Slide Fasteners Inc 305 576-3328
  545 Nw 26th St Miami (33127) *(G-9858)*

Scott Washer Inc 407 432-2648
  1513 Regan Ave Orlando (32807) *(G-12579)*

Scott-Clark LP 512 756-7300
  4670 Links Village Dr B10 Ponce Inlet (32127) *(G-14252)*

Scott-Clark Medical, Ponce Inlet *Also called Scott-Clark LP (G-14252)*

Scott-Douglas Design Inc 727 535-7900
  6275 147th Ave Largo (33770) *(G-7677)*

Scotties Canvas & Mar Sup LLC 239 995-7479
  2211 N Tamiami Trl North Fort Myers (33903) *(G-11068)*

Scottish Spirits Imports Inc 954 332-1116
  3101 N Federal Hwy # 301 Fort Lauderdale (33306) *(G-4039)*

Scotts Company LLC 352 429-0066
  20605 State Road 19 Groveland (34736) *(G-4870)*

Scp Commercial Printing 561 998-0870
  1100 Holland Dr Boca Raton (33487) *(G-664)*

SCR, Tampa *Also called Shafers Clssic Rprductions Inc (G-17255)*

SCR Precision Tube Bending Inc 813 622-7091
  5407 24th Ave S Tampa (33619) *(G-17248)*

Scratchoffstore, Oviedo *Also called Randal R Young (G-12846)*

Screen Enclosure Services Inc 239 334-6528
  502 South Rd Unit A Fort Myers (33907) *(G-4394)*

Screen Graphics Florida Inc (PA) 800 346-4420
  1801 N Andrews Ave Pompano Beach (33069) *(G-14169)*

Screen Machine 941 962-0395
  3312 33rd St W Bradenton (34205) *(G-1043)*

Screen Machines LLC 386 527-1368
  2422 Old Samsula Rd Port Orange (32128) *(G-14346)*

Screen Monkey Corp 352 746-7091
  5841 W Kime Ln Homosassa (34448) *(G-5750)*

Screen Printing Unlimited, Naples *Also called Westview Corp Inc (G-10937)*

Screen Process Printers Inc 904 354-8708
  101 S Myrtle Ave Jacksonville (32204) *(G-6457)*

Screen Tech 321 536-6091
  1501 Bermuda Ave Merritt Island (32952) *(G-8592)*

Screenco North Inc 561 840-3300
  11211 81st Ct N Palm Beach Gardens (33412) *(G-13007)*

Screenprint Plus Inc 239 549-7284
  1336 Se 47th St Cape Coral (33904) *(G-1382)*

Screens Fast 239 565-1211
  1435 Terra Palma Dr Fort Myers (33901) *(G-4395)*

Screenworks Usa Inc 407 426-9999
  2234 W Taft Vineland Rd Orlando (32837) *(G-12580)*

Scribe Inc 215 336-5094
  3758 Sw 30th Ave Fort Lauderdale (33312) *(G-4040)*

Scribe Manufacturing Inc (PA) 727 524-7482
  14421 Myerlake Cir Clearwater (33760) *(G-1777)*

Scribe Manufacturing Inc 727 536-7895
  3001 Tech Dr N Saint Petersburg (33716) *(G-15178)*

Scribe Opco Inc (PA) 727 536-7895
  14421 Myerlake Cir Clearwater (33760) *(G-1778)*

Script Central LLC 954 805-8581
  1680 Michigan Ave Ste 800 Miami Beach (33139) *(G-10225)*

Scs Software Inc 727 871-8366
  2840 West Bay Dr Ste 125 Belleair Bluffs (33770) *(G-356)*

Sct Software, Vero Beach *Also called Supply Chain Technologies LLC (G-17804)*

Scully Industries 941 349-5561
  314 Island Cir Sarasota (34242) *(G-15821)*

Sculpture House Inc 609 466-2986
  3804 Crossroads Pkwy Fort Pierce (34945) *(G-4526)*

Scutti America Inc 954 384-2377
  2700 Glades Cir Ste 160 Weston (33327) *(G-18286)*

Scytl, Tampa *Also called Soe Software Corporation (G-17278)*

SD Government, Melbourne *Also called Satcom Direct Government Inc (G-8515)*

Sdi Industries Inc 321 733-1128
  1216 Prospect Ave 101 Melbourne (32901) *(G-8517)*

Sdkc Corp 305 469-7578
  9624 Nw 47th Ter Doral (33178) *(G-3358)*

Sdm Acquisition Corporation 954 462-1919
  590 Sw 9th St Ste 9 Fort Lauderdale (33315) *(G-4041)*

Sdm Industries Inc 904 814-2814
  13 Hargrove Grade Palm Coast (32137) *(G-13086)*

Sdmo Generating Sets Inc 305 863-0012
  3801 Commerce Pkwy Miramar (33025) *(G-10541)*

SDr Specialties Services LLC 386 878-6771
  4511n Us Highway 17 De Leon Springs (32130) *(G-2627)*

SDS Dental Inc 954 730-3636
  1280 Sw 27th Ave Pompano Beach (33069) *(G-14170)*

SE Custom Lift Systems Inc 954 941-8090
  1801 Sw 7th Ave Pompano Beach (33060) *(G-14171)*

Sea 21-21 LLC 954 366-4677
  2211 Nw 30th Pl Pompano Beach (33069) *(G-14172)*

A
L
P
H
A
B
E
T
I
C

Sea and Shore Custom Canvas Up................954 983-3060
3629 Washington St Hollywood (33021) **(G-5655)**

Sea Breeze Marine Co................561 368-0463
1601 Sw 1st Way Ste 16 Deerfield Beach (33441) **(G-2804)**

Sea Breeze Small Engine................205 329-0759
415 Fernwood St Panama City Beach (32407) **(G-13338)**

Sea Cast Curb Adptors Crbs LLC................772 466-2400
2601 Industrial Avenue 3 Fort Pierce (34946) **(G-4527)**

Sea Creations Inc................407 857-2000
408 Bif Ct Orlando (32809) **(G-12581)**

Sea Enterprise Adventures, Medley Also called Ram Investments South Fla Inc **(G-8307)**

Sea Force Center Console LLC (PA)................941 417-7017
12277 Us Highway 41 N Palmetto (34221) **(G-13191)**

Sea Force Ix Inc................941 721-9009
1403 Pinetree Cir Wimauma (33598) **(G-18345)**

Sea Gear Corporation................321 728-9116
700 S John Rodes Blvd B1 Melbourne (32904) **(G-8518)**

Sea Hawk Boats, Sebring Also called Sea Hawk Industries Inc **(G-15939)**

Sea Hawk Industries Inc................863 385-1995
523 Pear St Sebring (33870) **(G-15939)**

Sea Hunter Inc................305 257-3344
25545 Sw 140th Ave Princeton (33032) **(G-14489)**

Sea King Canvas & Shade, Fort Myers Also called Sea King Kanvas & Shade Inc **(G-4396)**

Sea King Kanvas & Shade Inc................239 481-3535
15581 Pine Ridge Rd Ste A Fort Myers (33908) **(G-4396)**

Sea Link Holdings LLC................727 523-8660
13151 66th St Largo (33773) **(G-7678)**

Sea Link International Irb Inc (PA)................727 523-8660
13151 66th St Largo (33773) **(G-7679)**

Sea Products Inc (PA)................904 781-8200
4925 Bulls Bay Hwy Jacksonville (32219) **(G-6458)**

Sea Ray Boats Inc................386 439-3401
1958 Unsinkable St Flagler Beach (32136) **(G-3605)**

Sea Ray Boats Inc................321 459-9463
350 Sea Ray Dr Merritt Island (32953) **(G-8593)**

Sea Ray Boats Inc................321 459-2930
350 Sea Ray Dr Merritt Island (32953) **(G-8594)**

Sea Ray Boats Inc................321 452-9876
200 Sea Ray Dr Merritt Island (32953) **(G-8595)**

Sea Ray PD&e, Merritt Island Also called Sea Ray Boats Inc **(G-8595)**

Sea Side Specialties................561 276-6518
1200 S Swinton Ave Delray Beach (33444) **(G-3014)**

Sea Site Inc................305 403-3002
1180 Nw 163rd Dr Miami (33169) **(G-9859)**

Sea Suns, Miami Also called Sir Winston Garments Inc **(G-9900)**

Sea Systems Group Inc................434 374-9553
10631 Whittington Ct Largo (33773) **(G-7680)**

Seaboard Folding Box Company, Boca Raton Also called Sfbc LLC **(G-670)**

Seaboard Manufacturing LLC................727 497-3572
13214 38th St N Clearwater (33762) **(G-1779)**

Seabob, Fort Lauderdale Also called Cayago Americas Inc **(G-3715)**

Seabreeze Publication Centl FL................561 741-7770
1102 W Indiantown Rd # 5 Jupiter (33458) **(G-6793)**

Seabreeze Publications, Fort Myers Also called Seabreze Cmmncations Group Inc **(G-4397)**

Seabreeze Publications, Jupiter Also called Seabreeze Publication Centl FL **(G-6793)**

Seabreze Cmmncations Group Inc................239 278-4222
5630 Halifax Ave Fort Myers (33912) **(G-4397)**

Seacoast Air Conditioning & Sh................772 466-2400
3108 Industrial 31st St Fort Pierce (34946) **(G-4528)**

Seacor Marine LLC................954 523-2200
2200 Eller Dr Fort Lauderdale (33316) **(G-4042)**

Seacure Inc................904 353-5353
9485 Regency Square Blvd # 110 Jacksonville (32225) **(G-6459)**

Seadek, Rockledge Also called Hyperform Inc **(G-14717)**

Seagate Productions LLC................561 506-7750
1162 Rialto Dr Boynton Beach (33436) **(G-910)**

Seagear Performance Apparel, Miami Also called CBI Industries Inc **(G-8904)**

Seahill Press Inc................805 845-8636
214 N 3rd St Ste A Leesburg (34748) **(G-7791)**

Seal Outdoors Inc................877 323-7325
5900 Sw 56th Ter South Miami (33143) **(G-16045)**

Seal Shield LLC (PA)................877 325-7443
111 N Magnolia Ave # 1025 Orlando (32801) **(G-12582)**

Seal Tek, Miami Beach Also called Drezo Manufacturing Inc **(G-10185)**

Seal-Tite Plastic Packg Co Inc................305 264-9015
4655 Sw 74th Ave Miami (33155) **(G-9860)**

Sealift LLC................321 638-0301
3390 N Courtenay Pkwy A Merritt Island (32953) **(G-8596)**

Sealites, Oakland Park Also called Arcco Inc **(G-11239)**

Sealmaster of Wisconsin................954 979-5458
1831 Nw 33rd St Pompano Beach (33064) **(G-14173)**

Sealy Mattress Mfg Co LLC................407 855-8523
11220 Space Blvd Orlando (32837) **(G-12583)**

Seapress Inc................941 366-8494
4281 Clark Rd Sarasota (34233) **(G-15822)**

Seaquest Marine LLC................781 888-8850
777 Brickell Ave Miami (33131) **(G-9861)**

Searaven Glauben LLC................727 230-8840
6429 Brevard St Saint Augustine (32080) **(G-14888)**

Searobotics Corporation................772 742-3700
7765 Sw Ellipse Way Stuart (34997) **(G-16212)**

Seaside Aluminum llc................386 252-4940
230 Carswell Ave Daytona Beach (32117) **(G-2595)**

Seaside Graphics Inc................954 782-7151
100 Sw 5th St Pompano Beach (33060) **(G-14174)**

Seasucker LLC (PA)................941 586-2664
1912 44th Ave E Bradenton (34203) **(G-1044)**

Seat Savers Plus Inc................305 256-7863
12105 Sw 129th Ct Bay 10 Miami (33186) **(G-9862)**

Seatbelt Solutions Llc................855 642-3964
15835 Corporate Rd N Jupiter (33478) **(G-6794)**

Seatech Fabrication Inc................954 410-0524
101 Se 7th St Unit 5 Deerfield Beach (33441) **(G-2805)**

Seating Constructors Usa Inc................813 505-7560
2347 Circuit Way Brooksville (34604) **(G-1197)**

Seating Installation Group LLC................727 289-7652
12100 31st Ct N Saint Petersburg (33716) **(G-15179)**

Seatorque Control Systems LLC................772 220-3020
2779 Se Monroe St Stuart (34997) **(G-16213)**

Seattle Engraving Center LLC................813 330-7620
1073 E Brandon Blvd Brandon (33511) **(G-1106)**

Seavee Boats................305 705-3158
1950 Ne 135th St North Miami (33181) **(G-11120)**

Seavin Inc (PA)................352 394-8627
19239 Us Highway 27 Clermont (34715) **(G-1882)**

Seavin Inc................904 826-1594
157 King St Saint Augustine (32084) **(G-14889)**

Seaward Group USA, Tampa Also called Clare Instruments (us) Inc **(G-16711)**

Seaway Plastics Engrg LLC................352 799-3167
16186 Flight Path Dr Brooksville (34604) **(G-1198)**

Seaway Plastics Engrg LLC................727 777-6032
6041 Siesta Ln Port Richey (34668) **(G-14374)**

Seaway Plastics Engrg LLC (HQ)................727 845-3235
6006 Siesta Ln Port Richey (34668) **(G-14375)**

Sebastian Sea Products In................772 321-3997
1800 Us Highway 1 Vero Beach (32960) **(G-17797)**

Sebco Industries Inc................954 566-8500
211 E Oakland Park Blvd Oakland Park (33334) **(G-11292)**

Sebring Custom Tanning Inc................863 655-1600
429 Webster Turn Dr Sebring (33870) **(G-15940)**

Sebring Septic Tank Precast Co................863 655-2030
8037 Associate Blvd Sebring (33876) **(G-15941)**

Sebring's Precast Products, Sebring Also called Sebring Septic Tank Precast Co **(G-15941)**

SEC, Hollywood Also called Simulated Envmt Concepts Inc **(G-5657)**

Secretbandz, Sunrise Also called Syi Inc **(G-16378)**

Secure Biometric Corporation................813 832-1164
2909 W Bay Court Ave Tampa (33611) **(G-17249)**

Secure On-Site Shredding, Palm Harbor Also called Bay Area Security Shred **(G-13102)**

Secure Wrap, Miami Also called Homyn Enterprises Corp **(G-9290)**

Security and Fire Elec Inc (PA)................904 844-0964
2590 Dobbs Rd Saint Augustine (32086) **(G-14890)**

Security Hmntrian Rlief Envmtl, Tampa Also called Jade Tactical Disaster Relief **(G-16961)**

Security Impact GL Hldings LLC................561 844-3100
6555 Garden Rd Ste 1 Riviera Beach (33404) **(G-14674)**

Security Oracle Inc................352 988-5985
3614 Solana Cir Clermont (34711) **(G-1883)**

Security Plastics, Miami Lakes Also called National Molding LLC **(G-10329)**

Security Tech Group Inc................305 631-2228
9425 Sw 72nd St Ste 100 Miami (33173) **(G-9863)**

Security World Electronics................786 285-5303
19704 Nw 48th Ct Miami Gardens (33055) **(G-10273)**

Securus Brot LLC................954 532-8065
2400 Sw 132nd Ter Miramar (33027) **(G-10542)**

See Magazines, Sarasota Also called Miles Partnership II LLC **(G-15747)**

See-Ray Plumbing Inc................772 489-2474
2020 Old Dixie Hwy Se Vero Beach (32962) **(G-17798)**

Seelye Acquisitions Inc................407 656-6677
946 Century Ln Apopka (32703) **(G-174)**

Seemore Shirts & Tees LLC................954 708-1100
1829 N University Dr Coral Springs (33071) **(G-2211)**

Segers Aerospace Corporation................850 689-2198
5582 Fairchild Rd Crestview (32539) **(G-2252)**

Segutronic International Inc................305 463-8551
11042 Nw 72nd Ter Doral (33178) **(G-3359)**

Seiter Enterprises Inc................813 728-8324
155 E Oakwood St Tarpon Springs (34689) **(G-17491)**

Sel West Coast Inc................352 373-6354
817 Ne Waldo Rd Gainesville (32641) **(G-4760)**

Select Engineered Systems Inc................305 823-5410
7991 W 26th Ave Hialeah (33016) **(G-5343)**

Select Europe Inc................866 204-0899
3000 Sw 15th St Ste E Deerfield Beach (33442) **(G-2806)**

Select Machinery Inc................941 960-1970
4590 Ashton Rd Sarasota (34233) **(G-15823)**

Select Wines LLC................786 642-7445
6039 Collins Ave Apt 901 Miami Beach (33140) **(G-10226)**

Selectwo Machine Company Inc 407 788-3102
1695 Ee Williamson Rd Longwood (32779) *(G-7945)*

Self Made Dynasty LLC 754 303-3134
4811 E Pcf View Ter Fl 33 Flr 333 Fort Lauderdale (33309) *(G-4043)*

Sellink Aviation Fuel Div LLC 305 336-6627
4019 Nw 28th St Miami (33142) *(G-9864)*

Sellinkafs, Miami *Also called Sellink Aviation Fuel Div LLC (G-9864)*

Selma's Cookies, Apopka *Also called Lindley Foods LLC (G-147)*

Selmas Cookies Inc (PA) 407 884-9433
2023 Apex Ct Apopka (32703) *(G-175)*

Sembco Stl Erection Met Bldg 561 863-0606
3450 Dr Mrtn Lther King J Riviera Beach (33404) *(G-14675)*

Semenario Accion, West Palm Beach *Also called Action Weekly Corp (G-17914)*

Semg Incorporated 407 777-6860
225 Aberdeen St Davenport (33896) *(G-2370)*

Semiconductor Technology Inc 772 341-0800
3131 Se Jay St Stuart (34997) *(G-16214)*

Semilab Sdi, Temple Terrace *Also called Semilab USA LLC (G-17545)*

Semilab USA LLC (PA) 813 977-2244
12415 Telecom Dr Temple Terrace (33637) *(G-17545)*

Seminole County Public Schools 407 320-0393
1722 W Airport Blvd Sanford (32771) *(G-15385)*

Seminole Feed Division, Ocala *Also called Seminole Stores Inc (G-11485)*

Seminole Marico Fertilizer Div, Ocala *Also called Branch Properties Inc (G-11338)*

Seminole Paper & Printing Co 305 379-8481
60 Nw 3rd St Miami (33128) *(G-9865)*

Seminole Precast LLC 386 668-7745
331 Benson Junction Rd Debary (32713) *(G-2641)*

Seminole Printing Inc 305 823-7204
2310 W 78th St Hialeah (33016) *(G-5344)*

Seminole Sign Company LLC 863 623-6600
16900 Reservation Rd Ne Okeechobee (34974) *(G-11617)*

Seminole State Signs & Ltg 954 316-6030
5071 S State Road 7 # 717 Davie (33314) *(G-2474)*

Seminole Stores Inc 352 732-4143
335 Ne Watula Ave Ocala (34470) *(G-11485)*

Semplastics 407 353-6885
269 Aulin Ave Ste 1003 Oviedo (32765) *(G-12847)*

Semprun & Morales Corporation 305 698-2554
3418 W 84th St Ste 100 Hialeah (33018) *(G-5345)*

Sen-Dure Products Inc 954 973-1260
6785 Nw 17th Ave Fort Lauderdale (33309) *(G-4044)*

Sen-Pack Inc 386 763-3312
820 Rasley Rd New Smyrna Beach (32168) *(G-11010)*

Send It Sweetly LLC 239 850-5500
1309 Se 47th Ter Cape Coral (33904) *(G-1383)*

Senda De Vida Publishers 305 262-2627
14320 Sw 143rd Ct # 705 Miami (33186) *(G-9866)*

Senelco Iberia Inc 561 912-6000
500 Nw 12th Ave Deerfield Beach (33442) *(G-2807)*

Senior Lf Cmmnctions Group Inc 561 392-4550
1515 N Federal Hwy # 300 Boca Raton (33432) *(G-665)*

Senior Life of Florida 321 242-1235
7350 Shoppes Dr Ste 102 Melbourne (32940) *(G-8519)*

Senior Times Magazine, Gainesville *Also called Tower Publications Inc (G-4777)*

Senior Voice America Inc 813 444-1011
3820 Northdale Blvd 205a Tampa (33624) *(G-17250)*

Seniors Vent Mgmt Inc 305 266-0988
6100 Blue Lagoon Dr # 110 Miami (33126) *(G-9867)*

Sensatek Propulsion Tech Inc 850 321-5993
1 Aerospace Blvd Daytona Beach (32114) *(G-2596)*

Sensenich Technologies Inc 813 703-8446
2008 Wood Ct Plant City (33563) *(G-13802)*

Sensidyne LP 727 530-3602
1000 112th Cir N Ste 100 Saint Petersburg (33716) *(G-15180)*

Sensor Systems LLC 727 347-2181
2800 Anvil St N Saint Petersburg (33710) *(G-15181)*

Sensormatic 561 912-6429
1110 Sw 18th St Boca Raton (33486) *(G-666)*

Sensormatic Electronics Corp 561 989-7000
951 W Yamato Rd Boca Raton (33431) *(G-667)*

Sensus Healthcare Inc 561 922-5808
851 Broken Sound Pkwy Nw Boca Raton (33487) *(G-668)*

Sentech Eas Corporation (PA) 954 426-2965
4900 Lyons Tech Pkwy # 7 Coconut Creek (33073) *(G-2003)*

Sentinel Cmmnctons News Vntres (HQ) 407 420-5000
633 N Orange Ave Orlando (32801) *(G-12584)*

Sentinel Cmmnctons News Vntres 407 420-6229
210 Pembrook Pl Longwood (32779) *(G-7946)*

Sentinel Cmmnctons News Vntres 407 420-5291
75 E Amelia St Orlando (32801) *(G-12585)*

Sentinel Cmmnctons News Vntres 352 742-5900
2012 Classique Ln Tavares (32778) *(G-17522)*

Sentinel Direct, Orlando *Also called Sentinel Cmmnctons News Vntres (G-12585)*

Sentinel Inc 239 263-9888
3673 Exchange Ave Ste 1 Naples (34104) *(G-10889)*

Sentinel Sq Off Bldg MGT & Lsg 727 461-7700
300 S Duncan Ave Ste 291 Clearwater (33755) *(G-1780)*

Sentinel Storm Protection, Naples *Also called Sentinel Inc (G-10889)*

Sentry Food Solutions LLC 904 482-1900
4339 Roosevelt Blvd # 400 Jacksonville (32210) *(G-6460)*

Sentry Protection Technology 941 306-4949
6202 Clarity Ct Sarasota (34240) *(G-15824)*

Sep Communications LLC 561 998-0870
6001 Park Of Commerce Blv Boca Raton (33487) *(G-669)*

Sep National Logistics LLC 239 439-2239
15050 Elderberry Ln Fort Myers (33907) *(G-4398)*

Sepac Corp 305 718-3379
5201 Blue Lagoon Dr Miami (33126) *(G-9868)*

Separation Systems Inc 850 932-1433
100 Nightingale Ln A Gulf Breeze (32561) *(G-4891)*

Sepco, Stuart *Also called Solar Electric Power Company (G-16224)*

Sepronet Inc 305 463-8551
11042 Nw 72nd Ter Doral (33178) *(G-3360)*

Septic Tank Drain Fld/Nsite Sw, Sarasota *Also called Miller Brothers Contractors (G-15748)*

Sequa Corporation (HQ) 561 935-3571
3999 Rca Blvd Palm Beach Gardens (33410) *(G-13008)*

Sequel Industries Inc 850 517-6088
360 Juniper Dr Freeport (32439) *(G-4629)*

Sequoia Brands Inc 813 969-2000
13100 State Road 54 Odessa (33556) *(G-11576)*

Ser-Mat International LLC 954 525-1417
3200 Nw 27th Ave Ste 106 Pompano Beach (33069) *(G-14175)*

Serbin Printing Inc 941 366-0755
1500 N Washington Blvd Sarasota (34236) *(G-15825)*

Serenity Hair Extensions LLC 407 917-1788
1235 Providence Blvd R10 Deltona (32725) *(G-3053)*

Serf Inc 850 476-8203
3065 S Highway 29 Cantonment (32533) *(G-1273)*

Sergeant Bretts Coffee LLC 561 451-0048
1991 Nw 38th Ter Coconut Creek (33066) *(G-2004)*

Sergios Printing Inc 305 971-4112
14265 Sw 140th St Miami (33186) *(G-9869)*

Series Usa LLC 305 932-4626
20900 Ne 30th Ave Ste 901 Miami (33180) *(G-9870)*

Serigraphia Inc 850 243-9743
223 Troy St Ne Fort Walton Beach (32548) *(G-4609)*

Serigraphic Arts Inc 813 626-1070
6806 Parke East Blvd Tampa (33610) *(G-17251)*

Seronix Corporation 352 406-1698
27109 Oak Shadow Ln Mount Dora (32757) *(G-10612)*

Serv-Pak Corp 954 962-4262
5844 Dawson St Hollywood (33023) *(G-5656)*

Servdata Inc 305 269-7374
7401 Sw 163rd St Palmetto Bay (33157) *(G-13218)*

Servers 4 Networks, Boynton Beach *Also called M & S Computer Products Inc (G-888)*

Service Bindery Entps Inc 727 823-9866
3228 Morris St N Saint Petersburg (33713) *(G-15182)*

Service Bindery of Pinellas, Saint Petersburg *Also called Service Bindery Entps Inc (G-15182)*

Service Corp International 321 636-6041
Us Hwy 1 Frontenac Cocoa (32927) *(G-1956)*

Service D N D Dumpster 813 989-3867
7909 Professional Pl Tampa (33637) *(G-17252)*

Service Modern Trade LLC 708 942-9154
4108 Prima Lago Cir Lakeland (33810) *(G-7431)*

Services NS 18 LLC 786 546-3295
19900 E Country Club Dr Aventura (33180) *(G-275)*

Services On Demand Print Inc 305 681-5345
917 Sw 10th St Hallandale Beach (33009) *(G-4970)*

Servision Inc 305 900-4999
2100 E Hallandale Beach B Hallandale Beach (33009) *(G-4971)*

Servo Tech Inc 727 573-7998
4785 110th Ave N Clearwater (33762) *(G-1781)*

Servos and Simulation Inc 407 807-0208
421 Meadowridge Cv Longwood (32750) *(G-7947)*

Servotech, Clearwater *Also called Servo Tech Inc (G-1781)*

Sesame Flyers of South Florida 954 274-7233
6781 Nw 45th St Lauderhill (33319) *(G-7740)*

Sesolinc Grp Inc (PA) 772 287-9090
50 Se Ocean Blvd Ste 202 Stuart (34994) *(G-16215)*

Set Machine Inc 786 488-9788
6630 Sw 45th St Miami (33155) *(G-9871)*

Set Up Inc 239 542-4142
170 Sw 51st St Cape Coral (33914) *(G-1384)*

Setty Enterprises Inc 561 844-3711
4128 Westroads Dr # 225 West Palm Beach (33407) *(G-18149)*

Seven Defenses Corporation 786 448-5701
10550 Nw 74th St Unit 202 Doral (33178) *(G-3361)*

Seven Group USA Inc 305 392-9193
1681 Nw 79th Ave Doral (33126) *(G-3362)*

Seven Keys Co of Florida 954 946-5010
450 Sw 12th Ave Pompano Beach (33069) *(G-14176)*

Seven-Up Snapple Southeast, Tampa *Also called American Bottling Company (G-16587)*

Seven-Up Snapple Southeast, Jacksonville *Also called American Bottling Company (G-5882)*

Severstal Export Miami Corp., Doral *Also called Ssemiami Corporation (G-3374)*

Sevilla Cabinets Inc 305 888-2174
1550 W 34th Pl Hialeah (33012) *(G-5346)*

Sew Right, Pompano Beach *Also called Logoxpress Inc (G-14081)*

Sewell Products Florida LLC 863 967-4463
909 Magnolia Ave Auburndale (33823) *(G-244)*

Sextant Marketing LLC 800 691-9980
1860 N Avnida Rpblica De Tampa (33605) *(G-17253)*

Seyer - Tech Industries Inc 305 233-2672
1420 Sw 152nd Pl Miami (33194) *(G-9872)*

SF&kf Enterprises LLC 727 614-9902
13801 Walsingham Rd Ste B Largo (33774) *(G-7681)*

Sfa Systems Inc 561 585-5927
1230 Wingfield St Lake Worth (33460) *(G-7232)*

Sfada Tag Agency Inc 305 981-1077
625 Ne 124th St North Miami (33161) *(G-11121)*

Sfbc LLC 978 342-8921
7035 Queenferry Cir Boca Raton (33496) *(G-670)*

SFE Investments, Clearwater *Also called Sure-Feed Engineering Inc (G-1806)*

Sfi, West Park *Also called Shoreline Foundation Inc (G-18216)*

Sfi Inc 407 834-2258
1730 N Forsyth Rd Orlando (32807) *(G-12586)*

Sg Blocks Inc (PA) 646 240-4235
5011 Gate Pkwy Bldg 100s Jacksonville (32256) *(G-6461)*

Sg Global LLC (PA) 305 726-3439
12120 Sw 105th Ter Miami (33186) *(G-9873)*

Sgm Lighting Inc 407 440-3601
7806 Kingspointe Pkwy Orlando (32819) *(G-12587)*

Sgmc Microwave, Melbourne *Also called Andrew Martin Swift (G-8365)*

SGS Designs Inc 813 258-2691
1515 W Cypress St Tampa (33606) *(G-17254)*

SGS Pavers Inc 561 436-7276
5633 Marseilles Port Ln Boynton Beach (33472) *(G-911)*

SGS US East Coast LLC 305 571-9700
12062 Nw 27th Ave Miami (33167) *(G-9874)*

Sgt. Bretts Healthy Lifestyles, Coconut Creek *Also called Sergeant Bretts Coffee LLC (G-2004)*

Sh Shower & Tub Enclosures LLC 786 229-2529
4101 Sw 74th Ct Miami (33155) *(G-9875)*

Shade Experts USA LLC 561 422-3200
11117 Alameda Bay Ct Wellington (33414) *(G-17861)*

Shade Saver Inc 850 650-0884
3330 Nw 95th Avenue Rd Ocala (34482) *(G-11486)*

Shade Systems Inc 352 237-0135
4150 Sw 19th St Ocala (34474) *(G-11487)*

Shades By Ana Inc 305 238-4858
12240 Sw 128th St Miami (33186) *(G-9876)*

Shades To You LLC 407 889-0049
1676 E Semoran Blvd Apopka (32703) *(G-176)*

Shadow Trailers Inc 352 529-2190
951 Sw 21st Pl Williston (32696) *(G-18335)*

Shadow-Caster Led Lighting LLC 727 474-2877
2060 Calumet St Clearwater (33765) *(G-1782)*

Shadow-Caster Marine, Clearwater *Also called Shadow-Caster Led Lighting LLC (G-1782)*

Shafers Clssic Rprductions Inc 813 622-7091
5407 24th Ave S Tampa (33619) *(G-17255)*

Shaikh Rizwan 202 740-9796
316 N Canal Ave Lakeland (33801) *(G-7432)*

Shaka Energy Exploration Inc 561 279-1379
1118 Island Dr Delray Beach (33483) *(G-3015)*

Shalimar Raceway DBA Gulfcoast 850 651-7848
1183 N Eglin Pkwy Shalimar (32579) *(G-16002)*

Shalom Adventure 727 375-7502
5160 Spike Horn Dr New Port Richey (34653) *(G-10983)*

Shanker Industries Realty Inc (PA) 631 940-9889
3900 Fiscal Ct Ste 100 West Palm Beach (33404) *(G-18150)*

Shantui America Corp 786 491-9114
5201 Nw 77th Ave Ste 600 Miami (33166) *(G-9877)*

Shapes Group Ltd Co 321 837-0500
1415 Fundation Pk Blvd Se Palm Bay (32909) *(G-12917)*

Shapes Precision Manufacturing, Palm Bay *Also called Shapes Group Ltd Co (G-12917)*

Shapley, Fort Myers *Also called Carfore Ltd (G-4201)*

Shar Family Enterprises Llc 352 365-6988
2207 Aitkin Loop Leesburg (34748) *(G-7792)*

Sharing Three Inc 305 884-8384
575 E 10th Ave Hialeah (33010) *(G-5347)*

Shark Signs of Ne Fl Inc 904 766-6222
5317 Shen Ave Jacksonville (32205) *(G-6462)*

Shark Skinz 772 388-9621
300 Industrial Park Blvd # 5 Sebastian (32958) *(G-15904)*

Shark Tools, Deerfield Beach *Also called T H L Diamond Products Inc (G-2820)*

Shark Tooth Enterprises Inc 904 449-8247
981 Martin Ave Green Cove Springs (32043) *(G-4837)*

Sharp Marketing LLC 954 565-2711
655 W Prospect Rd Oakland Park (33309) *(G-11293)*

Shashi LLC 561 447-8800
6926 Royal Orchid Cir Delray Beach (33446) *(G-3016)*

Shashy Enterprises Inc 352 732-3904
1824 N Magnolia Ave Ocala (34475) *(G-11488)*

Shasta Beverages Intl Inc 954 581-0922
8100 Sw 10th St Ste 4000 Plantation (33324) *(G-13886)*

Shaver Millwork, Vero Beach *Also called Shaver Properties Inc (G-17799)*

Shaver Properties Inc 772 569-3466
6010 Old Dixie Hwy Ste K Vero Beach (32967) *(G-17799)*

Shaw Development LLC (PA) 239 405-6100
25190 Bernwood Dr Bonita Springs (34135) *(G-817)*

Shaw's Site Preparation, Perry *Also called Shaws Welding Inc (G-13653)*

Shaws Fiberglass Inc 863 425-9176
6925b State Road 60 W Mulberry (33860) *(G-10638)*

Shaws Sthern Blle Frz Fods In 904 768-1591
821 Virginia St Jacksonville (32208) *(G-6463)*

Shaws Welding Inc 850 584-7197
1530 S Dixie Hwy Perry (32348) *(G-13653)*

Sheaffer Boats Inc 813 872-7644
3916 W South Ave Tampa (33614) *(G-17256)*

Sheaffer Marine Inc 813 872-7311
3916 W South Ave Tampa (33614) *(G-17257)*

Shealy Revel B Inc 352 629-1552
606 Ne 35th St Ocala (34479) *(G-11489)*

Shear Elements LLC 954 678-8528
8741 Nw 50th St Lauderhill (33351) *(G-7741)*

Shearwater Marine Fl Inc 772 781-5553
4519 Se Commerce Ave Stuart (34997) *(G-16216)*

Sheas Salsa LLC 954 371-7781
11328 Regatta Ln Wellington (33449) *(G-17862)*

Shed4less LLC 863 660-7300
3147 Us Highway 98 S Lakeland (33803) *(G-7433)*

Sheds Galore and More LLC 386 362-1786
1410 Howard St E Live Oak (32064) *(G-7855)*

Sheds Plus Miami, Orange City *Also called Superior Sheds Inc (G-11810)*

Sheet Metal Systems Inc 727 548-1711
6482 Park Blvd N Ste A Pinellas Park (33781) *(G-13729)*

Sheet Metal Unlimited, Stuart *Also called Jglc Enterprises LLC (G-16170)*

Sheet Metal Unlimited 772 872-7440
3920 Se Commerce Ave Stuart (34997) *(G-16217)*

Sheffield Steel Corporation 918 245-1335
4221 W Boy Scout Blvd # 600 Tampa (33607) *(G-17258)*

Sheila Shine Inc 305 557-1729
1201 Nw 1st Pl Miami (33136) *(G-9878)*

Shelbie Press Inc 407 896-4600
1203 N Mills Ave Orlando (32803) *(G-12588)*

Shelf Genie, Orlando *Also called Shelfgenie-Orlando (G-12589)*

Shelfgenie 877 814-3643
16422 Carrara Way # 102 Naples (34110) *(G-10890)*

Shelfgenie-Orlando 407 808-5925
10603 Arbor View Blvd Orlando (32825) *(G-12589)*

Shell Aerospace LLC 786 400-2660
7500 Nw 25th St Unit 1a Miami (33122) *(G-9879)*

Shell Producers Corp 813 247-3153
1200 Sertoma Dr Tampa (33605) *(G-17259)*

Shelleys Cshions Umbrellas Mfg, Miami *Also called Shelleys Cushions Mfg Inc (G-9880)*

Shelleys Cushions Mfg Inc 305 633-1790
3640 Nw 52nd St Miami (33142) *(G-9880)*

Shellie Desk, Tampa *Also called Sullenberger Inc (G-17306)*

Sheltair Daytona Beach LLC 386 255-0471
561 Pearl Harbor Dr Daytona Beach (32114) *(G-2597)*

Shelton Group LLC 321 676-8981
1333 Gateway Dr Ste 1013 Melbourne (32901) *(G-8520)*

Shenk Enterprises LLC 386 753-1959
985 Harley Strcklnd Blvd Orange City (32763) *(G-11809)*

Sheps Welding Inc 352 493-1730
9791 Nw County Road 345 Chiefland (32626) *(G-1450)*

Shermans Welding & Maintence 904 731-3460
6299 Powers Ave Ste 3 Jacksonville (32217) *(G-6464)*

Sherry J Bertucelli Inc 407 760-7585
3827 E Kaley Ave Orlando (32812) *(G-12590)*

Sherry Manufacturing Co Inc 305 693-7000
3287 Nw 65th St Miami (33147) *(G-9881)*

Shgar Kane Couture Inc 407 205-8038
4900 Silver Oaks Village Orlando (32808) *(G-12591)*

Shield Products Inc 904 880-6060
6010 Nw 99th Ave Unit 110 Doral (33178) *(G-3363)*

Shifted Industries 561 302-8915
6930 Swamp Dr Groveland (34736) *(G-4871)*

Shiloh Import/Export LLC 404 514-4109
7049 Woodmont Way Tamarac (33321) *(G-16542)*

Shilpico Inc 561 306-5625
22360 Sands Point Dr Boca Raton (33433) *(G-671)*

Shima Group Corp 305 463-0288
10836 Nw 27th St Doral (33172) *(G-3364)*

Shineline Buffing & Detail 941 268-1033
11338 1st Ave Punta Gorda (33955) *(G-14530)*

Shining Tree Inc 855 688-7987
2952 Payson Way Wellington (33414) *(G-17863)*

Shiny Prints 561 200-2872
143 Juno St Jupiter (33458) *(G-6795)*

Shipping + Business Svcs LLC 904 240-1737
12627 San Jose Blvd Ste 5 Jacksonville (32223) *(G-6465)*

Shipping Depot Inc 813 347-2494
4835 W Cypress St Tampa (33607) *(G-17260)*

Shipping Dept, Naples *Also called Alternative Laboratories LLC (G-10661)*

Shipyard Dog Prints, Crystal River *Also called Fretto Prints Inc* **(G-2276)**

Shirley L Jordan Company Inc 352 754-1117
15270 Flight Path Dr Brooksville (34604) **(G-1199)**

Shirley Simon & Associates LLC 813 247-2100
4951b E Adamo Dr Ste 216 Tampa (33605) **(G-17261)**

Shirts & Caps Inc 813 788-7026
9437 Corporate Lake Dr Tampa (33634) **(G-17262)**

Shirts n Things Inc 954 434-7480
6001 Orange Dr Davie (33314) **(G-2475)**

Shiseido Americas Corporation 305 416-6021
1221 Brickell Ave Fl 26 Miami (33131) **(G-9882)**

Shl Pharma LLC 954 725-2008
588 Jim Moran Blvd Deerfield Beach (33442) **(G-2808)**

Sho ME Natural Products, Brooksville *Also called Sho ME Nutriceuticals Inc* **(G-1200)**

Sho ME Nutriceuticals Inc 352 797-9600
15431 Flight Path Dr Brooksville (34604) **(G-1200)**

Shocksocks LLC 352 258-0496
2979 Se Gran Park Way Stuart (34997) **(G-16218)**

Shop Munki, Oviedo *Also called Excess Liquidator LLC* **(G-12820)**

Shopworks LLC 561 491-6000
1101 N Olive Ave West Palm Beach (33401) **(G-18151)**

Shore Trendz LLC 954 608-7375
560 Nw 118th Ave Plantation (33325) **(G-13887)**

Shoreline Foundation Inc 954 985-0981
2781 Sw 56th Ave West Park (33023) **(G-18216)**

Shoreline Plastics LLC 904 696-2981
7167 Old Kings Rd Jacksonville (32219) **(G-6466)**

Shoreline Printing Company 954 491-0311
5100 Ne 12th Ave A Oakland Park (33334) **(G-11294)**

Shoreline Shutter Systems Inc 386 299-2219
494 Nash Ln Port Orange (32127) **(G-14347)**

Shores Global LLC 305 716-0848
2440 Nw 116th St Ste 600 Miami (33167) **(G-9883)**

Shorr Enterprises Inc 954 733-9840
3033 Nw 28th St Lauderdale Lakes (33311) **(G-7719)**

Short Stop Print Inc 941 474-4313
1101 S Mccall Rd Unit A Englewood (34223) **(G-3537)**

Showcase Marble Inc 386 253-6646
405 6th St Daytona Beach (32117) **(G-2598)**

Showcase Publications Inc 863 687-4377
1211 E Main St Lakeland (33801) **(G-7434)**

Shower Doors Unlimited Inc 561 547-0702
74 Baytree Ln Boynton Beach (33436) **(G-912)**

Showerfloss Inc 239 947-2855
20930 Persimmon Pl Estero (33928) **(G-3550)**

Shredded Tire Inc 954 970-8565
6680 Nw 17th Ave Fort Lauderdale (33309) **(G-4045)**

Shri Guru Krupa Smoothies Inc 904 461-9090
112 Sea Grove Main St Saint Augustine (32080) **(G-14891)**

Shrieve Chemical Co Chemi, Winter Haven *Also called American Vulkan Corporation* **(G-18416)**

Shriji Swami LLC 904 727-3434
1301 Monument Rd Ste 22 Jacksonville (32225) **(G-6467)**

Shukla Medical Inc 732 474-1769
8300 Sheen Dr Saint Petersburg (33709) **(G-15183)**

Shurhold Products Company 772 287-1313
3119 Sw 42nd Ave Palm City (34990) **(G-13058)**

Shutter Down Storm Protection 813 957-8936
3940 E Knights Griffin Rd Plant City (33565) **(G-13803)**

Shutter Lubrication & Service 561 745-8956
1821 W 10th St Ste 3 Jupiter (33469) **(G-6796)**

Shutter2think Inc 850 291-8301
1014 Raintree Ln Palm Beach Gardens (33410) **(G-13009)**

Shutterman Storm & Security 239 455-9166
751 4th St Ne Naples (34120) **(G-10891)**

Shutterreflections 813 351-9979
19111 Larchmont Dr Odessa (33556) **(G-11577)**

Shutters On Sale Inc 386 756-0009
1307 Crepe Myrtle Ln Port Orange (32128) **(G-14348)**

Shuttertek Inc 772 828-6149
566 Se Floresta Dr Port Saint Lucie (34983) **(G-14445)**

Shwinco Industries Inc 850 271-8900
400 Aberdeen Loop Lynn Haven (32444) **(G-8032)**

Shyft Group Inc 954 946-9955
15335 Pk Of Commerce Blvd Jupiter (33478) **(G-6797)**

Si Aerospace Group Inc 786 384-2338
10877 Nw 33rd St Doral (33172) **(G-3365)**

Sia Swimwear, Jacksonville *Also called Regency Cap & Gown Company* **(G-6412)**

Sibe Automation LLC 352 690-1741
1521 Sw 12th Ave Ste 700 Ocala (34471) **(G-11490)**

Sibex Inc (PA) 727 726-4343
430 N Suncoast Blvd Crystal River (34429) **(G-2280)**

Sibex Systems Division, Crystal River *Also called Sibex Inc* **(G-2280)**

Sibling Group Holdings, Inc., Miami *Also called Drazcanna Inc* **(G-9048)**

Sic Products LLC 904 374-2639
5130 Kristin Ct Naples (34105) **(G-10892)**

Sicamu Inc 850 270-6283
1066 Strong Rd Quincy (32351) **(G-14549)**

Sicoma North America Inc 800 921-7559
11300 47th St N Clearwater (33762) **(G-1783)**

Sid Signs, Miami *Also called Signs International Distr Corp* **(G-9891)**

Siebers Graphic, Port Richey *Also called Prolific Resource Inc* **(G-14373)**

Siemens AG 386 822-8000
1750 Filter Dr Deland (32724) **(G-2900)**

Siemens Corporation 407 736-5629
4041 Forest Island Dr Orlando (32826) **(G-12592)**

Siemens Energy Inc 407 736-1400
3850 Quadrangle Blvd Orlando (32817) **(G-12593)**

Siemens Energy Inc 407 206-5008
11842 Corporate Orlando (32817) **(G-12594)**

Siemens Energy Inc 407 736-7957
11950 Corporate Blvd Orlando (32817) **(G-12595)**

Siemens Gmesa Rnwble Enrgy Inc (HQ) 407 736-2000
11950 Corporate Blvd Orlando (32817) **(G-12596)**

Siemens Gmesa Rnwble Enrgy Inc 407 721-3273
4400 N Alafaya Trl Q2 Orlando (32826) **(G-12597)**

Siemens Industry Inc 407 650-3570
4506 L B Mcleod Rd Ste C Orlando (32811) **(G-12598)**

Siemens Industry Inc 941 355-2971
2650 Tallevast Rd Sarasota (34243) **(G-15554)**

Siemens Industry Inc 954 436-8848
2270 Nw 185th Way Pembroke Pines (33029) **(G-13414)**

Siemens Industry Software Inc 407 517-5919
2101 Park Center Dr # 290 Orlando (32835) **(G-12599)**

Sientra Inc 813 751-7576
1302 Guiles Hill Ct Brandon (33511) **(G-1107)**

Sierra Nevada Corporation 850 659-3600
1150 N Eglin Pkwy Shalimar (32579) **(G-16003)**

Sif Technology Company LLC 941 225-8363
7245 16th St E Unit 101 Sarasota (34243) **(G-15555)**

Sig, Saint Petersburg *Also called Seating Installation Group LLC* **(G-15179)**

Sighthound Inc 407 974-5694
520 N Orlando Ave Apt 1 Winter Park (32789) **(G-18534)**

Sigillu, Weston *Also called Gold-Rep Corporation* **(G-18248)**

Siglo Holdings LLC 727 369-5220
8285 Bryan Dairy Rd Largo (33777) **(G-7682)**

Sigma Marketing, Orange Park *Also called Sigma Press Inc* **(G-11840)**

Sigma Netics LLC 954 473-2106
12644 Sw 8th Ct Davie (33325) **(G-2476)**

Sigma Press Inc 904 264-6006
1543 Kingsley Ave Ste 7 Orange Park (32073) **(G-11840)**

Sign & Vehicle Wraps Inc 407 859-8631
1011 W Lancaster Rd Ste 7 Orlando (32809) **(G-12600)**

Sign A Rama 954 796-1644
10200 W Sample Rd Coral Springs (33065) **(G-2212)**

Sign A Rama 813 264-0022
3118 Belmore Rd Tampa (33618) **(G-17263)**

Sign A Rama Inc (HQ) 561 640-5570
2121 Vista Pkwy West Palm Beach (33411) **(G-18152)**

Sign A Rama Inc 904 998-8880
3633 Southside Blvd Jacksonville (32216) **(G-6468)**

Sign and Design Depot LLC 239 995-7446
960 Pondella Rd Ste C North Fort Myers (33903) **(G-11069)**

Sign Art Group, The, Tampa *Also called Hanes-Harris Design Cons* **(G-16904)**

Sign Depot Co 407 894-0090
1100 W Colonial Dr Unit 1 Orlando (32804) **(G-12601)**

Sign Design and Creations 954 724-2884
5000 Nw 17th St Ste 3 Margate (33063) **(G-8154)**

Sign Design of Florida Inc 352 787-3882
3602 Parkway Blvd Ste 2 Leesburg (34748) **(G-7793)**

Sign Development Corporation 305 227-6250
8240 W Flagler St Miami (33144) **(G-9884)**

Sign Effex, Winter Haven *Also called Laporte Inv Holdings Inc* **(G-18449)**

Sign Graphix Inc 954 571-7131
242 S Military Trl Deerfield Beach (33442) **(G-2809)**

Sign King, Longwood *Also called Greyson Corp* **(G-7900)**

Sign Man Inc 321 259-1703
4580 N Us Highway 1 Melbourne (32935) **(G-8521)**

Sign On LLC 239 800-9454
4519 Del Prado Blvd S B Cape Coral (33904) **(G-1385)**

Sign One Inc 305 888-6565
760 E 51st St Hialeah (33013) **(G-5348)**

Sign Partners Inc 561 270-6919
1181 S Rogers Cir Ste 3 Boca Raton (33487) **(G-672)**

Sign Pro America 412 908-9832
3811 University Blvd W # 37 Jacksonville (32217) **(G-6469)**

Sign Producers Inc 407 855-8864
555 W Landstreet Rd Orlando (32824) **(G-12602)**

Sign Rockers LLC 866 212-9697
12485 Sw 137th Ave # 206 Miami (33186) **(G-9885)**

Sign Savers Corp (PA) 305 909-9967
12385 Sw 129th Ct Ste 1 Miami (33186) **(G-9886)**

Sign Solutions, Plantation *Also called J Schor R Inc* **(G-13861)**

Sign Solutions of Tampa Bay 813 269-5990
3921 W Dr M Lthr Kng Jr Martin Luther Tampa (33614) **(G-17264)**

Sign Source The, Belleview *Also called Raimonda Investment Group Inc* **(G-366)**

Sign Space 786 360-2670
  2365 Nw 70th Ave Miami (33122) *(G-9887)*

Sign Stapler 800 775-3971
  1969 S Alafaya Trl Orlando (32828) *(G-12603)*

Sign Star, Tampa *Also called West Central Signs Inc (G-17427)*

Sign Systems Grphic Dsigns Inc 813 281-2400
  5031 W Grace St Tampa (33607) *(G-17265)*

Sign Tech Inc 941 575-1349
  25191 Olympia Ave Ste 1 Punta Gorda (33950) *(G-14531)*

Sign Up Now Sign Company LLC 754 224-9091
  3993 Cypress Reach Ct # 205 Pompano Beach (33069) *(G-14177)*

Sign Wizard 352 365-6922
  3195 Us Highway 441/27 Fruitland Park (34731) *(G-4642)*

Sign X-Press, Largo *Also called International C & C Corp (G-7614)*

Sign Zoo, Sarasota *Also called Zoo Holdings LLC (G-15882)*

Sign-A-Rama, Pompano Beach *Also called Crf Group Inc (G-13982)*

Sign-A-Rama, Lakeland *Also called C&D Sign and Lighting Svcs LLC (G-7287)*

Sign-A-Rama, North Fort Myers *Also called Signarama (G-11070)*

Sign-A-Rama, Lutz *Also called Signs of Tampa Bay LLC (G-8015)*

Sign-A-Rama, Coral Springs *Also called Sign A Rama (G-2212)*

Sign-A-Rama, Naples *Also called Signarama Naples (G-10893)*

Sign-A-Rama, Stuart *Also called Sp Sign LLC (G-16226)*

Sign-A-Rama, Fort Myers *Also called Jbjb Holdings LLC (G-4296)*

Sign-A-Rama, West Palm Beach *Also called Sign A Rama Inc (G-18152)*

Sign-A-Rama, North Miami Beach *Also called White Sands Dmg Inc (G-11170)*

Sign-A-Rama, Winter Park *Also called Everything Communicates Inc (G-18510)*

Sign-A-Rama, Miami *Also called Barrau & Coirin Inc (G-8801)*

Sign-A-Rama, Jacksonville *Also called Sign A Rama Inc (G-6468)*

Sign-A-Rama, West Palm Beach *Also called Graphics Designer Inc (G-18019)*

Sign-A-Rama, Delray Beach *Also called Sneids Inc (G-3019)*

Sign-A-Rama, Tampa *Also called Sign A Rama (G-17263)*

Sign-A-Rama, Miami *Also called Kendall Sign and Design Inc (G-9389)*

Sign-O-Saurus Daytona Inc 386 322-5222
  2127 S Ridgewood Ave South Daytona (32119) *(G-16028)*

Sign-O-Saurus Inc 407 677-8965
  3008 S Us Highway 17/92 Casselberry (32707) *(G-1433)*

Signage Pro LLC 813 671-4272
  9624 Birnamwood St Riverview (33569) *(G-14577)*

Signal Dynamics Corporation 904 342-4008
  6500 Nw 21st Ave Ste 1 Fort Lauderdale (33309) *(G-4046)*

Signalvault LLC 407 878-6365
  156 S Charles Richard Bea Debary (32713) *(G-2642)*

Signarama 239 997-1644
  4621 Bayshore Rd North Fort Myers (33917) *(G-11070)*

Signarama - Woodstock, West Palm Beach *Also called Georgia Mktg & Sign Co LLC (G-18016)*

Signarama Dwntwn Fort Lderdale 954 990-4749
  1422 Se 17th St Fort Lauderdale (33316) *(G-4047)*

Signarama Naples 239 330-3737
  1095 5th Ave N Naples (34102) *(G-10893)*

Signarama-Sarasota 941 554-8798
  4435 S Tamiami Trl Sarasota (34231) *(G-15826)*

Signature Athletics Inc 561 212-9284
  1025 W Indiantown Rd # 10 Jupiter (33458) *(G-6798)*

Signature AVI US Holdings Inc (HQ) 407 648-7230
  13485 Veterans Way # 600 Orlando (32827) *(G-12604)*

Signature Brands LLC (PA) 352 622-3134
  808 Sw 12th St Ocala (34471) *(G-11491)*

Signature Brands LLC 352 622-3134
  1930 Sw 38th Ave Ste 300 Ocala (34474) *(G-11492)*

Signature Brands LLC 352 622-3134
  1921 Sw 44th Ave Ocala (34474) *(G-11493)*

Signature Cabinets, Oakland Park *Also called Brandon Crookes (G-11247)*

Signature Computer Svcs Inc 954 421-0950
  7040 W Palmetto Park Rd Boca Raton (33433) *(G-673)*

Signature Granite Inc 813 443-5597
  3904 S 51st St Tampa (33619) *(G-17266)*

Signature Printing Inc 305 828-9992
  5725 Nw 151st St Miami Lakes (33014) *(G-10352)*

Signature Signs Inc 727 725-1044
  1450 10th St S Unit C Safety Harbor (34695) *(G-14796)*

Signcraft LLC 561 543-0034
  3694 Old Lighthouse Cir Wellington (33414) *(G-17864)*

Signcraft & More Inc 386 755-4754
  1554 E Duval St Lake City (32055) *(G-7044)*

Signcraft Magazine, Fort Myers *Also called Signcraft Publishing Co Inc (G-4399)*

Signcraft Publishing Co Inc 239 939-4644
  3950 Ellis Rd Fort Myers (33905) *(G-4399)*

Signcrafters of Central Fla 352 323-1862
  1134 E North Blvd Leesburg (34748) *(G-7794)*

SIGNGEEK DBA PENSACOLA SIGN & GRAPHICS, Pensacola *Also called Pensacola Sign & Graphics Inc (G-13571)*

Significant Solutions Corp 561 703-7703
  3003 W Yamato Rd Ste C8 Boca Raton (33434) *(G-674)*

Signing Off Now Inc 941 747-1000
  1101 29th Ave W Bradenton (34205) *(G-1045)*

Signingordercom LLC 904 300-0104
  410-10 Blnding Blvd Ste 1 Orange Park (32073) *(G-11841)*

Signode Industrial Group LLC 866 347-1820
  14025 Riveredge Dr Tampa (33637) *(G-17267)*

Signpost LLC 813 334-7678
  1236 Trust Ln Maitland (32751) *(G-8073)*

Signposts, Maitland *Also called Signpost LLC (G-8073)*

Signprinters, Tallahassee *Also called Mag-Tags Inc (G-16473)*

Signs 2 Sell LLC 850 277-0518
  6804 Highway 77 Panama City (32409) *(G-13306)*

Signs 2 U Inc 305 227-6250
  8240 W Flagler St Miami (33144) *(G-9888)*

Signs By Akos LLC 941 625-6845
  3212 Elkcam Blvd Port Charlotte (33952) *(G-14314)*

Signs By Design of Miami, Cutler Bay *Also called Honchin Inc (G-2291)*

Signs By Tomorrow, Fort Myers *Also called Thomas United Inc (G-4422)*

Signs By Tomorrow, West Palm Beach *Also called Sb Signs Inc (G-18148)*

Signs By Tomorrow, Sarasota *Also called Jte Inc (G-15715)*

Signs Connection Inc 305 978-5777
  600 Ne 36th St Apt 807 Miami (33137) *(G-9889)*

Signs For You Inc 305 635-6662
  7495 Nw 48th St Miami (33166) *(G-9890)*

Signs Galore Inc 850 683-8010
  111 Hammock St Crestview (32536) *(G-2253)*

Signs In One Day, Sarasota *Also called Sanbur Inc (G-15807)*

Signs International Distr Corp 305 715-0017
  8461 Nw 61st St Miami (33166) *(G-9891)*

Signs Now, Hollywood *Also called Business Forward Inc (G-5544)*

Signs Now, Bradenton *Also called Lambs Signs Inc (G-1002)*

Signs Now 386 238-5507
  1440 N Nova Rd Ste 308 Daytona Beach (32117) *(G-2599)*

Signs Now 727 524-8500
  12350 Belcher Rd S 14a Largo (33773) *(G-7683)*

Signs Now (PA) 850 383-6500
  1551 Capital Cir Se Ste 6 Tallahassee (32301) *(G-16499)*

Signs Now Inc 407 628-2410
  1003 S Orlando Ave Winter Park (32789) *(G-18535)*

Signs Now of Brandon Inc 813 684-0047
  1947 W Brandon Blvd Brandon (33511) *(G-1108)*

Signs Now St Augustine Inc 904 810-5838
  1711 Lakeside Ave Ste 1 Saint Augustine (32084) *(G-14892)*

Signs of America Tampa Corp 813 243-9243
  4025 W Waters Ave Tampa (33614) *(G-17268)*

Signs of Reilly 954 263-7829
  1121 W Mcnab Rd Pompano Beach (33069) *(G-14178)*

Signs of Tampa Bay LLC 813 526-0484
  1903 Passero Ave Lutz (33559) *(G-8015)*

Signs of Time Inc 772 240-9590
  1700 Sw Belgrave Ter Stuart (34997) *(G-16219)*

Signs Plus New IDS-New Tech In 941 378-4262
  4242 Mcintosh Ln Sarasota (34232) *(G-15827)*

Signs Supreme Inc 561 795-0111
  17224 Gulf Pine Cir Wellington (33414) *(G-17865)*

Signs Unlimited - Sea Inc 352 732-7341
  618 S Magnolia Ave Ocala (34471) *(G-11494)*

Signs Unlimited Bay County Inc 850 785-1061
  507 E 7th St Panama City (32401) *(G-13307)*

Signs Unlimited Inc 727 845-0330
  331 A1a Beach Blvd Saint Augustine (32080) *(G-14893)*

Signs Usa Inc 813 901-9333
  4123 W Hillsborough Ave Tampa (33614) *(G-17269)*

Signsations Inc 561 989-1900
  5425 N Dixie Hwy Ste 2 Boca Raton (33487) *(G-675)*

Signsharks Sign Service 904 766-6222
  7030 N Main St Jacksonville (32208) *(G-6470)*

Signsitecom Inc 386 487-0265
  162 Sw Spencer Ct Ste 106 Lake City (32024) *(G-7045)*

Signsourse USA Incorporated 954 561-1234
  2500 E Oakland Park Blvd Fort Lauderdale (33306) *(G-4048)*

Signway Inc 407 696-7446
  2964 Forsyth Rd Winter Park (32792) *(G-18536)*

Sike Usa Inc 786 331-4020
  3004 Nw 82nd Ave Doral (33122) *(G-3366)*

Sikorsky Aircraft Corp 772 210-0849
  2324 Se Liberator Ln Stuart (34996) *(G-16220)*

Sikorsky Aircraft Corporation 561 775-5142
  17900 Bee Line Hwy Jupiter (33478) *(G-6799)*

Silcar Corp 305 557-8391
  1475 W 82nd St Hialeah (33014) *(G-5349)*

Silco Software Technology Inc 813 475-4591
  16223 Ivy Lake Dr Odessa (33556) *(G-11578)*

Silent Giant Publishing Inc 305 725-7911
  20009 Ne 6th Court Cir Miami (33179) *(G-9892)*

Silent Standby Power Sup LLC 954 253-9557
  3866 Prospect Ave 5 West Palm Beach (33404) *(G-18153)*

Silestone of Tampa, Ponte Vedra *Also called Counter Active Inc (G-14255)*

Siligom USA LLC 786 406-6262
  5930 Nw 99th Ave Unit 9 Doral (33178) *(G-3367)*

Silk Safari Inc 561 689-3882
613 Madeline Dr West Palm Beach (33413) *(G-18154)*

Silkmasters Inc 904 372-8958
1911 Sw 80th Dr Gainesville (32607) *(G-4761)*

Silver Bay LLC 941 306-5812
1431 Tallevast Rd Sarasota (34243) *(G-15556)*

Silver Enterprises Assoc Inc 239 542-0068
1417 Sw 52nd Ter Cape Coral (33914) *(G-1386)*

Silver Hawk Aerospace Inc 954 301-1453
1041 Nw 31st Ave Pompano Beach (33069) *(G-14179)*

Silver Horn Jerky Inc 850 208-1433
3715 Mobile Hwy Pensacola (32505) *(G-13603)*

Silver Sheet-Florida Inc 850 230-9711
17742 Ashley Dr Panama City (32413) *(G-13308)*

Silver Springs Citrus Inc 352 324-2101
25411 N Mare Ave Howey In The Hills (34737) *(G-5759)*

Silver Springs Citrus LLC 352 324-2101
25411 N Mare Ave Howey In The Hills (34737) *(G-5760)*

Silver Star On Lime LLC 941 312-4566
2739 Aspinwall St Sarasota (34237) *(G-15828)*

Silverhorse Racing LLC 321 722-2813
700 S John Rodes Blvd Melbourne (32904) *(G-8522)*

Silverline Furniture Corp 305 663-9560
15940 Sw 60th St Miami (33193) *(G-9893)*

Silverman Fence Mfg Inc 904 730-0882
4698 Dusk Ct Jacksonville (32207) *(G-6471)*

Silvershore Partners LLC 904 562-0812
10175 Fortune Pkwy # 60 Jacksonville (32256) *(G-6472)*

Silversphere Holdings, Daytona Beach Also called Tel-Tron Technologies Corp *(G-2608)*

Sima Group, Coral Gables Also called SMR Management Inc *(G-2109)*

Simar Industries Inc 352 622-2287
805 Nw 25th Ave Ocala (34475) *(G-11495)*

Simco, Avon Park Also called Standard Injection Molding Inc *(G-289)*

Simco Machine and Tool Inc 863 452-1151
2029 State Road 64 W Avon Park (33825) *(G-287)*

Simetri Inc 321 972-9980
937 S Semoran Blvd # 100 Winter Park (32792) *(G-18537)*

Simkins Industries Inc 305 899-8184
5080 Biscayne Blvd Ste A Miami (33137) *(G-9894)*

Simmonds Precision Pdts Inc 904 757-3660
6061 Goodrich Blvd Jacksonville (32226) *(G-6473)*

Simons Hallandale Inc 561 468-1174
850 Ives Dairy Rd Ste T9 Miami (33179) *(G-9895)*

Simplepin LLC 800 727-4136
8954 Se Bridge Rd Hobe Sound (33455) *(G-5483)*

Simpleshow USA Corp 844 468-5447
7300 Biscayne Blvd # 100 Miami (33138) *(G-9896)*

Simplex Inc 352 357-2828
4085 N Highway 19a Mount Dora (32757) *(G-10613)*

Simplex Manufacturing Inc 941 378-8700
6300 Tower Ln Unit 4 Sarasota (34240) *(G-15829)*

Simplex Time Recorder Co 561 988-7200
1501 Nw 51st St Boca Raton (33431) *(G-676)*

Simplex Tool and Mold, Sarasota Also called Simplex Manufacturing Inc *(G-15829)*

Simplexgrinnell Holdings LLC (HQ) 978 731-2500
1501 Nw 51st St Boca Raton (33431) *(G-677)*

Simplicity Esports 386 479-9091
1697 N Woodland Blvd Deland (32720) *(G-2901)*

Simplicity Esports LLC 855 345-9467
7000 W Plmtt Prk Rd Ste 5 Boca Raton (33433) *(G-678)*

Simplicity Esports & Gaming Co (PA) 855 345-9467
7000 W Plmtt Prk Rd Ste 5 Boca Raton (33433) *(G-679)*

Simplified Fabricators Inc 561 335-3488
9040 Belvedere Rd West Palm Beach (33411) *(G-18155)*

Simplified Systems Inc 305 672-7676
4014 Chase Ave Ph Miami Beach (33140) *(G-10227)*

Simplify, Naples Also called Brightsky LLC *(G-10699)*

Simplimatic Automation 941 360-6500
7245 16th St E Unit 114 Sarasota (34243) *(G-15557)*

Simply Cabinets LLC 850 541-3712
630 Malaga Pl Panama City Beach (32413) *(G-13339)*

Simply Closets & Cabinets 239 994-4264
10105 Amberwood Rd Ste 6 Alva (33920) *(G-84)*

Simply Cupcakes 239 262-5184
2490 Outrigger Ln Naples (34104) *(G-10894)*

Simply Group II LLC 407 960-4690
4366 Ronald Reagan Blvd Sanford (32773) *(G-15386)*

Simply Reliable Inc 800 209-9332
10460 Roosevelt Blvd N Saint Petersburg (33716) *(G-15184)*

Simply Shutters, Port Saint Lucie Also called Plantation Shutters Inc *(G-14432)*

Simply Sweet Company Inc (PA) 386 873-6516
1431 Orange Camp Rd Deland (32724) *(G-2902)*

Simply The Best Magazine, Delray Beach Also called Goodpress Publishing LLC *(G-2969)*

Simply45 LLC 954 982-2017
3490 Sw 30th Ave Fort Lauderdale (33312) *(G-4049)*

Simplynas, Sanford Also called Simply Group II LLC *(G-15386)*

Simpson 954 804-0829
7137 Pinecreek Ln Coconut Creek (33073) *(G-2005)*

Simpson Construction and Roofg 863 443-0710
418 E Elm St Avon Park (33825) *(G-288)*

Simpson Screens Inc 904 757-1498
11458 Harlan Dr Jacksonville (32218) *(G-6474)*

Sims Machine & Controls Inc 352 799-2405
15538 Aviation Loop Dr Brooksville (34604) *(G-1201)*

Sims Promotions, Jennings Also called Fka Racing Inc *(G-6650)*

Simtec Silicone Parts LLC 954 656-4212
9658 Premier Pkwy Miramar (33025) *(G-10543)*

Simulated Envmt Concepts Inc 754 263-3184
3937 Pembroke Rd Hollywood (33021) *(G-5657)*

Sin Pin Inc 877 805-5665
600 Nw Dixie Hwy Stuart (34994) *(G-16221)*

Sincere Fuel Inc 954 433-3577
16100 Sw 51st St Miramar (33027) *(G-10544)*

Sincere Sentiments Inc 352 287-1232
8001 E Shannon Ct Inverness (34450) *(G-5834)*

Sincerus Pharmaceuticals Inc (PA) 800 604-5032
3265 W Mcnab Rd Pompano Beach (33069) *(G-14180)*

Sinclair Industries LLC (PA) 305 215-0990
101691 Overseas Hwy Key Largo (33037) *(G-6849)*

Sindoni North America LLC 786 536-9171
2665 S Bayshore Dr Miami (33133) *(G-9897)*

Sinergie Printing Inc 786 493-6167
1717 N Bayshore Dr Miami (33132) *(G-9898)*

Singer Holdings Inc 321 724-0900
3160 Skyway Cir Melbourne (32934) *(G-8523)*

Singing Machine Company Inc (PA) 954 596-1000
6301 Nw 5th Way Ste 2900 Fort Lauderdale (33309) *(G-4050)*

Singletary Systems Inc 508 865-4445
5264 62nd Ave S Saint Petersburg (33715) *(G-15185)*

Singletons AV Solutions Inc 407 404-1506
8907 Southern Breeze Dr Orlando (32836) *(G-12605)*

Singular Grape Inc 305 508-4000
7380 W Sand Lake Rd Orlando (32819) *(G-12606)*

Sinmat Commercial LLC 352 334-7270
1912 Nw 67th Pl Gainesville (32653) *(G-4762)*

Sino Eagle Usa Inc 727 259-3570
1000 Bass Blvd Dunedin (34698) *(G-3458)*

Sinobec Resources LLC 561 409-2205
1901 Green Rd Ste E Deerfield Beach (33064) *(G-2810)*

Sinocare Meditech Inc 800 342-7226
2400 Nw 55th Ct Fort Lauderdale (33309) *(G-4051)*

Sinofresh Healthcare Inc (PA) 941 270-2627
2357 S Tamiami Trl Unit 3 Venice (34293) *(G-17715)*

Sintavia LLC (PA) 954 474-7800
2500 Sw 39th St Fort Lauderdale (33312) *(G-4052)*

Sio Cnc Machining Inc 727 533-8271
14241 60th St N Clearwater (33760) *(G-1784)*

Sipp Technologies LLC 904 374-5606
5245 Old Kings Rd Jacksonville (32254) *(G-6475)*

Sippers By Design 305 371-5087
555 Ne 15th St Miami (33132) *(G-9899)*

Sipradius LLC (PA) 954 290-2434
5814 Nw 74th Ter Parkland (33067) *(G-13354)*

Sir Speedy, Orlando Also called La Mar Orlando LLC *(G-12304)*

Sir Speedy, Sarasota Also called Leda Printing Inc *(G-15724)*

Sir Speedy, West Palm Beach Also called Palm Print Inc *(G-18112)*

Sir Speedy, Miami Also called Bdd International Corp *(G-8808)*

Sir Speedy, West Palm Beach Also called Steven K Bakum Inc *(G-18164)*

Sir Speedy, Coral Gables Also called General & Duplicating Services *(G-2060)*

Sir Speedy, Orlando Also called Paper Palm LLC *(G-12467)*

Sir Speedy, Palm Harbor Also called Goforit Inc *(G-13111)*

Sir Speedy, Tallahassee Also called Dvh Macleod Corp *(G-16435)*

Sir Speedy, Coral Springs Also called Saugus Valley Corp *(G-2209)*

Sir Speedy, Seminole Also called Anderson Printing Services Inc *(G-15969)*

Sir Speedy, Longwood Also called Vmak Corp *(G-7958)*

Sir Speedy, Clearwater Also called L E M G Inc *(G-1668)*

Sir Speedy, Jacksonville Also called Hartco Inc *(G-6167)*

Sir Speedy, Largo Also called J V G Inc *(G-7619)*

Sir Speedy, Miami Lakes Also called Rennak Inc *(G-10348)*

Sir Speedy, Hollywood Also called South Broward Printing Inc *(G-5660)*

Sir Speedy, Tampa Also called Phil & Brenda Johnson Inc *(G-17161)*

Sir Speedy, Lakeland Also called Aether Media USA Inc *(G-7268)*

Sir Speedy, Palm Beach Gardens Also called Premier Global Enterprises *(G-13000)*

Sir Speedy, Hialeah Also called Guimar Inc *(G-5179)*

Sir Speedy, Coral Gables Also called Global Printing Services Inc *(G-2062)*

Sir Speedy, Saint Petersburg Also called Power Printing of Florida *(G-15157)*

Sir Speedy, Tampa Also called Mxn Inc *(G-17089)*

Sir Speedy, Spring Hill Also called J-Kup Corp *(G-16073)*

Sir Speedy Printing Center 352 683-8758
1260 Lori Dr Spring Hill (34606) *(G-16079)*

Sir Winston Garments Inc 305 499-3144
13428 Sw 131st St Miami (33186) *(G-9900)*

Sira 352 377-4947
912 Nw 13th St Gainesville (32601) *(G-4763)*

Sirs Commercial Print, Boca Raton *Also called Sirs Publishing Inc* ***(G-680)***
Sirs Publishing Inc (HQ) 800 521-0600
5201 Congress Ave Ste 250 Boca Raton (33487) ***(G-680)***
SIS Holdings LP (PA) 855 699-8372
2333 Ponce De Leon Blvd Coral Gables (33134) ***(G-2108)***
Sisco Marine LLC 850 265-1383
1725 Buchanan St Panama City (32409) ***(G-13309)***
Sitecrafters of Florida Inc 813 258-4696
3242 Henderson Blvd # 200 Tampa (33609) ***(G-17270)***
Sivance LLC (HQ) 352 376-8246
5002 Ne 54th Pl Gainesville (32609) ***(G-4764)***
Sivance LLC 352 376-8246
4404 Ne 53rd Rd Gainesville (32609) ***(G-4765)***
Siw Solutions LLC 561 274-9392
975 S Congress Ave Delray Beach (33445) ***(G-3017)***
Sixto Packaging, Opa Locka *Also called H Sixto Distributors Inc* ***(G-11752)***
Sizemore Ultimate Food Trucks, Bunnell *Also called Sizemore Welding Inc* ***(G-1234)***
Sizemore Welding Inc 386 437-4073
205 N Bay St Bunnell (32110) ***(G-1234)***
Sjg Machine Inc 352 345-3656
316 Marianne St Brooksville (34601) ***(G-1202)***
Sjostrom Electronics, Boca Raton *Also called Sjostrom Industries Inc* ***(G-681)***
Sjostrom Industries Inc 561 368-2000
1400 Nw 9th Ave Apt 1 Boca Raton (33486) ***(G-681)***
Sk Worldwide LLC (PA) 786 360-4842
9553 Harding Ave Ste 310 Surfside (33154) ***(G-16399)***
Skagfield Corporation (PA) 850 878-1144
270 Crossway Rd Tallahassee (32305) ***(G-16500)***
Skampas Performance Group 305 974-0047
19201 Collins Ave Cu-137 Sunny Isles Beach (33160) ***(G-16282)***
Skandia Window Fashions, Tallahassee *Also called Skagfield Corporation* ***(G-16500)***
Skateboard Supercross LLC 786 529-8187
725 92nd St Surfside (33154) ***(G-16400)***
Skater Socks 850 424-6764
516 Mountain Dr Ste 104 Destin (32541) ***(G-3079)***
Ski Rixen - Quiet Waters Inc 954 429-0215
401 S Powerline Rd Deerfield Beach (33442) ***(G-2811)***
Ski Rixen USA, Deerfield Beach *Also called Ski Rixen - Quiet Waters Inc* ***(G-2811)***
Skide Llc 305 537-4275
6303 Blue Lagoon Dr Miami (33126) ***(G-9901)***
Skies Limit Printing 772 340-1090
10504 S Us Highway 1 Port Saint Lucie (34952) ***(G-14446)***
Skill-Metric Machine & Tl Inc 561 454-8900
1424 Gwenzell Ave 3c Delray Beach (33444) ***(G-3018)***
Skim-A-Round Inc 631 223-5072
28282 Industrial St # 2 Bonita Springs (34135) ***(G-818)***
Skin Combat LLC 727 517-3376
5200 Seminole Blvd Saint Petersburg (33708) ***(G-15186)***
Skin Pro International Inc 305 528-9095
14345 Sunset Ln Southwest Ranches (33330) ***(G-16058)***
Skinmetics Inc 305 663-5750
4850 Sw 72nd Ave Miami (33155) ***(G-9902)***
Skinny Mixes LLC 727 826-0306
2849 Executive Dr Ste 210 Clearwater (33762) ***(G-1785)***
Skinutra Inc 813 992-1742
5136 W Clifton St Tampa (33634) ***(G-17271)***
Skip One Seafood Inc 239 463-8788
17650 San Carlos Blvd Fort Myers Beach (33931) ***(G-4456)***
Skipper Wright Inc 904 354-4381
634 Dyal St Jacksonville (32206) ***(G-6476)***
Sky Aerospace Engineering 407 251-7111
4219 Lindy Cir Orlando (32827) ***(G-12607)***
Sky Aerospace Engineering Inc (PA) 407 251-7111
9419 Tradeport Dr Orlando (32827) ***(G-12608)***
Sky Device, Miami Beach *Also called Sky Phone LLC* ***(G-10228)***
Sky Medical Inc 954 747-3188
5229 Nw 108th Ave Sunrise (33351) ***(G-16366)***
Sky Organics LLC 561 295-1890
2901 Clint Moore Rd Ste 2 Boca Raton (33496) ***(G-682)***
Sky Phone LLC (PA) 305 531-5218
1348 Washington Ave # 350 Miami Beach (33139) ***(G-10228)***
Sky Technics Aviation Sls Inc 305 885-7499
15915 Nw 59th Ave Miami Lakes (33014) ***(G-10353)***
Sky-High Sign & Lighting Inc 813 994-3954
30 Citrus Dr Palm Harbor (34684) ***(G-13132)***
Skycross, Melbourne *Also called Viatech of Delaware Inc* ***(G-8558)***
Skyhigh Accessories Inc 954 316-3936
4344 Peters Rd Plantation (33317) ***(G-13888)***
Skyline Attractions LLC 407 587-0080
5233 Alleman Dr Orlando (32809) ***(G-12609)***
Skylink Technology Inc 609 689-9200
1707 Whitney Isles Dr Windermere (34786) ***(G-18366)***
Skylite Signs & Services Inc 305 362-5015
1640 W 32nd Pl Hialeah (33012) ***(G-5350)***
Skymo LLC 305 676-6739
12260 Sw 53rd St Ste 609 Cooper City (33330) ***(G-2022)***
Skyo Industries Inc 631 586-4702
2 Sunshine Blvd Ormond Beach (32174) ***(G-12792)***
Skyways Technics Americas LLC 786 615-2443
13447 Ne 17th Ave North Miami (33181) ***(G-11122)***
Slabs Plus, Ruskin *Also called Bicentrics Inc* ***(G-14775)***
Slainte Wines Inc (PA) 954 474-4547
8958 W State Road 84 Davie (33324) ***(G-2477)***
Slappey Communications LLC 863 619-5600
624 Midflorida Dr Lakeland (33813) ***(G-7435)***
Slasher Printing Center Inc 305 835-7366
6701 Nw 22nd St Sunrise (33313) ***(G-16367)***
Slasher Printing Services, Sunrise *Also called Slasher Printing Center Inc* ***(G-16367)***
Slate Group LLC 786 484-9408
9357 Sw 77th Ave Miami (33156) ***(G-9903)***
Slate Solutions LLC 754 200-6752
7060 W State Road 84 # 12 Davie (33317) ***(G-2478)***
Slater Lighting Solutions, Boca Raton *Also called Brian Slater & Associates LLC* ***(G-447)***
Slaton & Sons Enterprises Inc 561 308-7187
7912 Plantation Lakes Dr Port Saint Lucie (34986) ***(G-14447)***
Slb1989 Inc 772 344-3609
1066 Sw Bayshore Blvd Port Saint Lucie (34983) ***(G-14448)***
Sleep Group Solutions, Hollywood *Also called Dhss LLC* ***(G-5565)***
Sleep Group Solutions, North Miami Beach *Also called Dhss LLC* ***(G-11133)***
Sleep International LLC (PA) 813 247-5337
5223 16th Ave S Tampa (33619) ***(G-17272)***
Sleep Please, Hollywood *Also called Function Please LLC* ***(G-5579)***
Sleepmed Incorporated 941 361-3035
5432 Bee Ridge Rd Ste 170 Sarasota (34233) ***(G-15830)***
Sleeprite Industries Inc 650 344-1980
7087 Mandarin Dr Boca Raton (33433) ***(G-683)***
Sleepy Dragon Studios Inc 561 714-6156
22814 Sw 88th Path Cutler Bay (33190) ***(G-2302)***
Sleuth Inc 941 745-9903
3988 E State Road 64 Bradenton (34208) ***(G-1046)***
Slg Solutions Inc 786 379-4676
12000 Sw 210th Ter Miami (33177) ***(G-9904)***
Slick Designs & AP Miami Inc 305 836-7950
3710 E 10th Ct Hialeah (33013) ***(G-5351)***
Slim and Soft Bread LLC 305 759-2126
15051 Royal Oaks Ln # 2105 North Miami (33181) ***(G-11123)***
Slipaway Ceramics Inc 727 577-1936
236 87th Ave Ne Saint Petersburg (33702) ***(G-15187)***
SLM Boats Inc 386 738-4425
1948 Sunset Ct Deland (32720) ***(G-2903)***
Sloan Health Products LLC (PA) 727 504-3915
500 N West Shore Blvd # 640 Tampa (33609) ***(G-17273)***
Slr Rifleworks LLC 855 757-7435
1232 Wntr Gdn Vnlnd Rd Winter Garden (34787) ***(G-18404)***
Sltons Envirnmntal Group Assoc 305 665-5594
2950 Sw 27th Ave Ste 2 Miami (33133) ***(G-9905)***
Slueth Bldg Sys Investigations, Bradenton *Also called Sleuth Inc* ***(G-1046)***
Slyce Inc 727 408-5272
311 Gulf Blvd Ste 2 Indian Rocks Beach (33785) ***(G-5809)***
Smart Access Inc 407 331-4724
2950 Lake Emma Rd # 1030 Lake Mary (32746) ***(G-7106)***
Smart For Life, Riviera Beach *Also called Doctors Scientific Organica LLC* ***(G-14617)***
Smart For Life Inc (PA) 786 749-1221
990 Biscayne Blvd # 1203 Miami (33132) ***(G-9906)***
Smart Glass Systems Inc 954 801-5349
8201 Peters Rd Plantation (33324) ***(G-13889)***
Smart Guard Shutters LLC 386 227-6295
79 Pritchard Dr Palm Coast (32164) ***(G-13087)***
Smart Guides 813 534-0940
20013 Outpost Point Dr Tampa (33647) ***(G-17274)***
Smart Kid USA Inc 754 366-6666
2701 Ne 23rd St Pompano Beach (33062) ***(G-14181)***
Smart Material Corp (PA) 941 870-3337
2170 Main St Ste 302 Sarasota (34237) ***(G-15831)***
Smart Shutters Inc 786 391-1100
3070 Nw 72nd Ave Miami (33122) ***(G-9907)***
Smart Signs Inc 754 701-8910
4153 Sw 47th Ave Ste 177 Davie (33314) ***(G-2479)***
Smart Snacks LLC 954 860-8833
10205 Collins Ave Apt 206 Bal Harbour (33154) ***(G-296)***
Smart Stream Inc 904 223-1511
13500 Sutton Park Dr S # 7 Jacksonville (32224) ***(G-6477)***
Smart Tracks Inc 239 938-1000
6182 Idlewild St Fort Myers (33966) ***(G-4400)***
Smartadvocate LLC (PA) 239 390-1000
27299 Riverview Center Bl Bonita Springs (34134) ***(G-819)***
Smartbear Software 954 312-0188
4611 Johnson Rd Unit 4 Coconut Creek (33073) ***(G-2006)***
Smartcart Ev LLC 727 906-7001
245 10th Ave N Safety Harbor (34695) ***(G-14797)***
Smartcolor Graphics, Jupiter *Also called Edward Thomas Company* ***(G-6718)***
Smartcop Inc 850 429-0082
1765 E Nine Mile Rd Pensacola (32514) ***(G-13604)***
Smarte Carte Inc 407 857-5841
9251 Jeff Fuqua Blvd # 1596 Orlando (32827) ***(G-12610)***
Smarthome-Products Inc (PA) 727 490-7260
1560 Faulds Rd W Clearwater (33756) ***(G-1786)***

Smartmatic Corporation (HQ)..................................561 862-0747
1001 Broken Sound Pkwy Nw D Boca Raton (33487) *(G-684)*

Smartpoll Election Solutions, West Palm Beach *Also called Naztec International Group LLC (G-18088)*

Smartsat Inc..727 535-6880
8222 118th Ave Ste 600 Largo (33773) *(G-7684)*

Smartscience Laboratories Inc.............................813 925-8454
13760 Reptron Blvd Tampa (33626) *(G-17275)*

Smartt, North Miami Beach *Also called Scale Models Arts & Tech (G-11161)*

SMc Diversified Services Inc................................863 698-9696
7120 Regent Dr Lakeland (33810) *(G-7436)*

Smdk Corp...239 444-1736
4802 Kittiwake Ct Naples (34119) *(G-10895)*

SMI Cabinetry Stone Millwork, Orlando *Also called S M I Cabinetry Inc (G-12565)*

Smilefy Inc..302 465-6606
221 W Hallandale B106 Hallandale Beach (33009) *(G-4972)*

Smith Boat Designs Inc..954 782-1000
1200 S Dixie Hwy W Pompano Beach (33060) *(G-14182)*

Smith Challenger Mfg Svcs Inc............................863 248-2624
3434 Waterfield Rd Lakeland (33803) *(G-7437)*

Smith Equipment & Supply Co..............................863 665-4904
3825 Maine Ave Lakeland (33801) *(G-7438)*

Smith Machine Services Inc..................................904 845-2002
552121 Us Highway 1 Hilliard (32046) *(G-5476)*

Smith Mountain, Miami *Also called Aldora Aluminum & GL Pdts Inc (G-8683)*

Smith Power Boats, Pompano Beach *Also called Smith Boat Designs Inc (G-14182)*

Smith Products Co Inc (PA)..................................386 325-4534
1005 Kirby St Palatka (32177) *(G-12880)*

Smith Products Kitchens, Palatka *Also called Smith Products Co Inc (G-12880)*

Smith Steps Inc..386 963-5655
6944 Us Highway 90 Live Oak (32060) *(G-7856)*

Smith Surface Prep Systems Inc..........................954 941-9744
2504 Nw 19th St Pompano Beach (33069) *(G-14183)*

Smith Surface-Prep Solutions, Pompano Beach *Also called Smith Surface Prep Systems Inc (G-14183)*

Smithbilt Industries Inc (PA)...............................321 690-0902
1061 Us Highway 92 W Auburndale (33823) *(G-245)*

Smiths Interconnect Inc (HQ)..............................813 901-7200
4726 Eisenhower Blvd Tampa (33634) *(G-17276)*

Smiths Interconnect Inc......................................813 901-7200
4726 Eisenhower Blvd Tampa (33634) *(G-17277)*

Smiths Interconnect Group Ltd.............................805 370-5580
8851 Sw Old Kansas Ave Stuart (34997) *(G-16222)*

Smiths Intrcnnect Americas Inc............................772 286-9300
8851 Sw Old Kansas Ave Stuart (34997) *(G-16223)*

Smiths Woodworks Inc..863 381-6564
3005 Waterway Dr Lake Placid (33852) *(G-7148)*

Smittys Boat Tops and Mar Eqp............................305 245-0229
23701 Sw 212th Ave Homestead (33031) *(G-5740)*

Smittys Boat Tops Sndwner Bats, Homestead *Also called Smittys Boat Tops and Mar Eqp (G-5740)*

Smittys Welding Shop..321 723-4533
2526 S Harbor City Blvd Melbourne (32901) *(G-8524)*

Smokersvaporcom Incorporated...........................727 258-4942
1129 Woodbrook Dr Largo (33770) *(G-7685)*

Smokey Mountain Cabinets Inc.............................386 325-1677
103 E Lake St Palatka (32177) *(G-12881)*

Smoothie Corp..305 588-0867
10211 Sw 137th Ct Miami (33186) *(G-9908)*

Smoothies Recharge...954 999-0332
2101 N University Dr Sunrise (33322) *(G-16368)*

SMR Management Inc (PA).....................................305 529-2488
1728 Coral Way Coral Gables (33145) *(G-2109)*

Smurfit Kappa Packaging LLC (HQ)......................954 838-9738
1301 Intl Pkwy Ste 550 Sunrise (33323) *(G-16369)*

Smurfit Kappa The America's, Sunrise *Also called Smurfit Kappa Packaging LLC (G-16369)*

Smx-US Inc...914 840-5631
80 Sw 8th St Ste 2000 Miami (33130) *(G-9909)*

Sna Software LLC (PA)..866 389-6750
1730 Santa Maria Pl Orlando (32806) *(G-12611)*

Snapple Beverages...941 758-7010
2919 62nd Ave E Bradenton (34203) *(G-1047)*

Snappy Structures Inc..954 926-6611
2324 Hayes St Hollywood (33020) *(G-5658)*

Snapspace Solutions LLC.......................................561 756-6610
626 Landshark Blvd Daytona Beach (32124) *(G-2600)*

Sneakz LLC..201 693-5695
2895 Jupiter Park Dr # 500 Jupiter (33458) *(G-6800)*

Sneakz Organic, Jupiter *Also called Sneakz LLC (G-6800)*

Sneids Inc..561 278-7446
2905 S Congress Ave Ste E Delray Beach (33445) *(G-3019)*

Snif-Snax Ltd...786 613-7007
540 Brickell Key Dr C2 Miami (33131) *(G-9910)*

Snk America Inc..407 831-7766
3551 W State Road 46 Sanford (32771) *(G-15387)*

Snookton Inc..352 429-1133
146 E Broad St Groveland (34736) *(G-4872)*

Snow-Nabstedt Power Transmissi.........................603 661-5551
3007 29th Ave E Bradenton (34208) *(G-1048)*

Snows Custom Furniture Inc..................................772 794-4430
4009 Us Highway 1 Vero Beach (32960) *(G-17800)*

Snug Harbor Dinghies Inc......................................727 578-0618
10121 Snug Harbor Rd Ne Saint Petersburg (33702) *(G-15188)*

Soapy Chef, The, Hollywood *Also called Baby Food Chef LLC (G-5536)*

Sobe Express...305 674-4454
1205 Lincoln Rd Ste 209 Miami Beach (33139) *(G-10229)*

Sobel Westex...954 942-5777
750 Nw 33rd St Ste B Pompano Beach (33064) *(G-14184)*

Sobrino Custom Cabinets Inc................................786 564-2699
2220 W 10th Ct Hialeah (33010) *(G-5352)*

Socati Corp..503 634-2378
1776 N Pine Island Rd # 309 Plantation (33322) *(G-13890)*

Socialmetrix, Miami *Also called Smx-US Inc (G-9909)*

Societees Inc..786 208-9880
3200 Collins Ave Apt 114 Miami Beach (33140) *(G-10230)*

Sockets & Specials Inc..561 582-7022
7110 Georgia Ave West Palm Beach (33405) *(G-18156)*

Socratic Solutions Inc...813 324-7018
220 W Brandon Blvd # 207 Brandon (33511) *(G-1109)*

Sod Depot & Gravel Inc..321 728-2766
1378 Malabar Rd Se Palm Bay (32907) *(G-12918)*

Soda Service of Florida LLC..................................727 595-7632
14184 Mark Dr Largo (33774) *(G-7686)*

Sodikart USA..561 493-0290
1025 Gateway Blvd Boynton Beach (33426) *(G-913)*

Soe Software Corporation......................................813 490-7150
1111 N West Shore Blvd # 300 Tampa (33607) *(G-17278)*

Sofie Co..407 321-9076
136 Commerce Way Sanford (32771) *(G-15388)*

Soft Tech America Inc (PA)....................................954 563-3198
401 E Las Olas Blvd # 1400 Fort Lauderdale (33301) *(G-4053)*

Soft Water Techs, West Palm Beach *Also called Duncanson Dynasty Inc (G-17982)*

Softech International Inc..305 233-4813
1421 Sw 107th Ave Miami (33174) *(G-9911)*

Softex Paper Inc (PA)...386 328-8488
1400 Reid St Palatka (32177) *(G-12882)*

Software, Port Saint Lucie *Also called System Data Resource (G-14454)*

Software Product Solutions LLC............................561 798-6727
12713 Westport Cir West Palm Beach (33414) *(G-18157)*

Software To Systems Inc..513 893-4367
2491 Se Gillette Ave Port Saint Lucie (34952) *(G-14449)*

Softwarekey.com, Winter Garden *Also called Concept Software Inc (G-18381)*

Softwareteacher Inc..954 593-3333
300 N Highway A1a H104 Jupiter (33477) *(G-6801)*

Sogofishing LLC..800 308-0259
1542 Nw 15th Ave Fort Lauderdale (33311) *(G-4054)*

Sohacki Industries Inc...904 826-0130
185 Cumberland Park Dr Saint Augustine (32095) *(G-14894)*

Sol Davis Printing Inc...813 353-3609
5205 N Lois Ave Tampa (33614) *(G-17279)*

Sol-A-Trol Aluminum Pdts Inc..............................305 681-2020
4101 Nw 132nd St Opa Locka (33054) *(G-11788)*

Sol-A-Trol Aluminum Products, Opa Locka *Also called Arso Enterprises Inc (G-11719)*

Sola Therapy, Melbourne *Also called Uroshape LLC (G-8555)*

Solair Group Llc...786 269-0160
10421 Sw 187th Ter Cutler Bay (33157) *(G-2303)*

Solana Repair Services LLC.................................754 281-8860
3220 Sw 15th St Deerfield Beach (33442) *(G-2812)*

Solar Electric Power Company...............................772 220-6615
1521 Se Palm Ct Stuart (34994) *(G-16224)*

Solar Energy Specialist Corp.................................863 514-9532
1130 1st St S Winter Haven (33880) *(G-18468)*

Solar Enterprises Inc..904 724-2262
8841 Corporate Square Ct Jacksonville (32216) *(G-6478)*

Solar Erectors US Inc..305 823-8950
10501 Nw 121st Way Medley (33178) *(G-8320)*

Solar Manufacturing Inc (PA)..............................954 973-8488
1888 Nw 22nd Ct Pompano Beach (33069) *(G-14185)*

Solar Manufacturing Inc.......................................954 973-8488
2195 N Andrews Ave Ste 11 Pompano Beach (33069) *(G-14186)*

Solar Packaging Corp..305 621-5551
4920 Nw 165th St Miami Lakes (33014) *(G-10354)*

Solar Shades Draperies & More.............................954 600-3419
1081 Nw 101st Way Plantation (33322) *(G-13891)*

Solar Stik Inc (PA)...800 793-4364
13 N Leonardi St Saint Augustine (32084) *(G-14895)*

Solar Tech Universal, Riviera Beach *Also called Solartech Universal LLC (G-14676)*

Solar Tint Inc...305 663-4663
5887 Sw 70th St South Miami (33143) *(G-16046)*

Solar Turbines Incorporated..................................305 476-6855
701 Nw 62nd Ave Ste 600 Miami (33126) *(G-9912)*

Solar Venetian Blinds Inc......................................305 634-4553
3639 Nw 47th St Miami (33142) *(G-9913)*

Solar X...386 673-2111
630 S Yonge St Us1 Ormond Beach (32174) *(G-12793)*

Solar-X of Daytona, Ormond Beach *Also called Solar X (G-12793)*

Solara Inc 305 592-4748
 5105 Nw 159th St Miami Lakes (33014) *(G-10355)*

Solara Industries Inc 863 688-3330
 4190 Waring Rd Lakeland (33811) *(G-7439)*

Solara Labs, Miami Lakes *Also called Solara Inc (G-10355)*

Solarbeam International Inc 305 248-8400
 15600 Sw 288th St Ste 307 Homestead (33033) *(G-5741)*

Solarenergy.com, Jacksonville *Also called Sunset Power Inc (G-6518)*

Solartech Universal LLC 561 440-8000
 1800 President Barack Oba Riviera Beach (33404) *(G-14676)*

Solartex, Apopka *Also called Enviroworks Inc (G-127)*

Sole Inc 305 513-2603
 8029 Nw 54th St Doral (33166) *(G-3368)*

Solid Print Solutions Inc 561 670-4391
 1961 10th Ave N Lake Worth Beach (33461) *(G-7261)*

Solid Start Inc 863 937-9297
 2801 Saluda Rd Lakeland (33801) *(G-7440)*

Solidar Express Coatings LLC 727 585-2192
 12912 91st St N Largo (33773) *(G-7687)*

Solidexperts Inc 954 772-1903
 2005 W Cypress Creek Rd Fort Lauderdale (33309) *(G-4055)*

Solitron Devices Inc 561 848-4311
 3301 Electronics Way C West Palm Beach (33407) *(G-18158)*

Sollunar Energy Inc 352 293-2347
 4142 Mariner Blvd Ste 510 Spring Hill (34609) *(G-16080)*

Solo Printing LLC 305 594-8699
 7860 Nw 66th St Miami (33166) *(G-9914)*

Solseen LLC 727 322-3131
 2801 16th St N Saint Petersburg (33704) *(G-15189)*

Solstice Sleep Products Inc 813 438-8830
 500 S Falkenburg Rd Tampa (33619) *(G-17280)*

Soltec Electronics LLC 321 288-5689
 1001 Pelican Ln Rockledge (32955) *(G-14746)*

Solucnes Elctrcas Intgrles LLC 305 804-4201
 2609 Ne 189th St Miami (33180) *(G-9915)*

Solunet 321 369-9719
 1571 Robert J Conlan Blvd Palm Bay (32905) *(G-12919)*

Solution Asset Management LLC 786 288-9408
 1918 Harrison St Hollywood (33020) *(G-5659)*

Solution Publishing LLC 813 291-0840
 2701 N Rocky Point Dr # 180 Tampa (33607) *(G-17281)*

Solutions Manufacturing Inc 321 848-0848
 570 Haverty Ct Rockledge (32955) *(G-14747)*

Somatics LLC 847 234-6761
 720 Commerce Dr Unit 101 Venice (34292) *(G-17716)*

Somay Manufacturing Inc (PA) 305 637-4757
 4301 Nw 35th Ave Miami (33142) *(G-9916)*

Somec, Sanford *Also called Snk America Inc (G-15387)*

Somero Enterprises Inc (PA) 906 482-7252
 14530 Global Pkwy Fort Myers (33913) *(G-4401)*

Something In A Tin Inc 305 785-6891
 2401 Ne 199th St Miami (33180) *(G-9917)*

Somfy Systems Inc 561 292-3483
 1200 Sw 35th Ave Boynton Beach (33426) *(G-914)*

Somni Specialty Sleep, Deerfield Beach *Also called Blu Sleep Products LLC (G-2677)*

Son Life Prsthtics Orthtics In (PA) 352 596-2257
 4138 Daisy Dr Hernando Beach (34607) *(G-5012)*

Sonapa LLC 407 782-0459
 3406 S Atlantic Ave New Smyrna Beach (32169) *(G-11011)*

Sondra Roberts, West Palm Beach *Also called Becarro International Corp (G-17940)*

Sonec, Miami Lakes *Also called Scents of Nature Enterprises (G-10351)*

Song-Chuan USA Inc 954 788-5889
 2841 Center Port Cir Pompano Beach (33064) *(G-14187)*

Sonia Land Inc 305 798-4912
 5536 Sw 8th St Coral Gables (33134) *(G-2110)*

Sonic Boatworks LLC 561 631-6071
 309 Angle Rd Fort Pierce (34947) *(G-4529)*

Sonnys Strings Inc 407 862-4905
 311 E Morse Blvd Apt 1-3 Winter Park (32789) *(G-18538)*

Sonobrands LLC (PA) 305 418-9367
 1970 Nw 129th Ave Ste 108 Miami (33182) *(G-9918)*

Sonoco Products Company 386 424-0970
 1601 Tionia Rd New Smyrna Beach (32168) *(G-11012)*

Sonshine Digital Graphics Inc 904 858-1000
 4613 Philips Hwy Ste 207 Jacksonville (32207) *(G-6479)*

Sonus-USA, Oldsmar *Also called Bell Hearing Instruments Inc (G-11635)*

Sony Discos 305 420-4540
 3390 Mary St Ste 220 Miami (33133) *(G-9919)*

Sony Music Publishing (us) LLC 305 532-9064
 1111 Lincoln Rd Ste 803 Miami Beach (33139) *(G-10231)*

Sophio Software Inc (PA) 323 446-2172
 6300 Ne 1st Ave Ste 201 Fort Lauderdale (33334) *(G-4056)*

Sophist Research LLC 305 763-8184
 110 Wshngton Ave Apt 1524 Miami Beach (33139) *(G-10232)*

Sophix Solutions Inc 813 837-9555
 1228 E 7th Ave Ste 225 Tampa (33605) *(G-17282)*

Soren Technologies Inc 954 236-9998
 817 S University Dr # 106 Plantation (33324) *(G-13892)*

SOS Food Lab LLC (PA) 305 594-9933
 14802 Nw 107th Ave Unit 5 Hialeah Gardens (33018) *(G-5451)*

SOs Services On Prtg Corp 305 225-6000
 2738 W 68th Pl Hialeah (33016) *(G-5353)*

SOS Sign & Lighting Services, South Daytona *Also called Sign-O-Saurus Daytona Inc (G-16028)*

SOS Software, Minneola *Also called Synergistic Office Solutions (G-10452)*

SOS Software Corp 786 237-4903
 950 Brickell Bay Dr # 53 Miami (33131) *(G-9920)*

Sosumi Holdings Inc 239 634-3430
 4408 Corporate Sq Naples (34104) *(G-10896)*

Sota Manufacturing Inc (PA) 561 368-8007
 1561 Sw 6th Ave Boca Raton (33486) *(G-685)*

Sota Manufacturing LLC 561 251-3389
 124 Ne 32nd Ct Oakland Park (33334) *(G-11295)*

Soto Industries LLC 941 830-6000
 3420 Bal Harbor Blvd Punta Gorda (33950) *(G-14532)*

Soto Metal Fabrication Inc (PA) 786 486-7125
 7025 Sw 16th Ter Miami (33155) *(G-9921)*

Soul Kass Boutique LLC 682 429-4323
 1218 Bet Raines Rd Molino (32577) *(G-10579)*

Sound Anchors Inc 321 724-1237
 2835 Kirby Cir Ne Ste 110 Palm Bay (32905) *(G-12920)*

Sound Connections Intl 813 948-2707
 611 Chancellar Dr Lutz (33548) *(G-8016)*

Source 1 Solutions Inc 727 538-4114
 4904 Creekside Dr Clearwater (33760) *(G-1787)*

Source Contract LLC 305 630-8950
 11451 Nw 36th Ave Miami (33167) *(G-9922)*

Source Outdoor, Miami *Also called Conquest Financial Management (G-8957)*

Source Sup In Plyurethanes Inc 239 573-3637
 2645 Ne 9th Ave Unit 12 Cape Coral (33909) *(G-1387)*

Sourglass Brewing 407 262-0056
 480 S Ronald Reagan Blvd Longwood (32750) *(G-7948)*

South Amercn Lbr & Timber LLC 786 280-8326
 78 Sw 7th St Ste 500 Miami (33130) *(G-9923)*

South Bay Home Services LLC 813 260-4708
 4832 Sandy Glen Way Wimauma (33598) *(G-18346)*

South Bay Hospital 813 634-3301
 4016 Sun City Center Blvd Sun City Center (33573) *(G-16267)*

South Bch Orthtics Prsthtics I 352 512-0262
 7305 Sw Gaines Ave Stuart (34997) *(G-16225)*

South Beach Brewing Company, Saint Petersburg *Also called 3 Daughters Brewing LLC (G-14948)*

South Beach Cigar Factory LLC 786 216-7475
 1059 Collins Ave Ste 108 Miami Beach (33139) *(G-10233)*

South Beach Skin Care Inc (PA) 954 606-5057
 701 N Federal Hwy Ste 400 Hallandale Beach (33009) *(G-4973)*

South Broward Brace Inc 954 458-0656
 1920 E Hallndale Bch 702 Hallandale Beach (33009) *(G-4974)*

South Broward Printing Inc 954 962-1309
 5845 Hollywood Blvd Ste C Hollywood (33021) *(G-5660)*

South Carolina Minerals Inc (PA) 352 365-6522
 8500 Us Highway 441 Leesburg (34788) *(G-7795)*

South Country Sheds LLC 863 491-8700
 1460 Sw Price Child St Arcadia (34266) *(G-194)*

South Dade News Leader, Homestead *Also called Homestead Newspapers Inc (G-5714)*

South East Fuel LLC 407 392-4668
 5600 Butler National Dr Orlando (32812) *(G-12612)*

Southm Estrn Prstressed Con Inc 561 793-1177
 860 N Benoist Farms Rd West Palm Beach (33411) *(G-18159)*

South Fla Pavement Coatings 954 979-5997
 1831 Nw 33rd St Pompano Beach (33064) *(G-14188)*

South Florida Aluminum, Lake Worth *Also called Sfa Systems Inc (G-7232)*

South Florida Con Block LLC 305 408-3444
 5800 Sw 177th Ave Ste 101 Miami (33193) *(G-9924)*

South Florida Concrete & Rdymx 305 888-0420
 9500 Nw 109th St Medley (33178) *(G-8321)*

South Florida Core Distrs 954 452-9091
 2030 Sw 71st Ter Ste C6 Davie (33317) *(G-2480)*

South Florida Cutting 305 693-6711
 3965 E 10th Ct Hialeah (33013) *(G-5354)*

South Florida Digest Inc 954 458-0635
 305 Nw 10th Ter Hallandale Beach (33009) *(G-4975)*

South Florida Fabricators LLC 954 802-6782
 4960 Sw 91st Ter Cooper City (33328) *(G-2023)*

South Florida Field Techs Inc 954 325-6548
 1598 Newhaven Point Ln West Palm Beach (33411) *(G-18160)*

South Florida Finger Printing 305 661-1636
 5900 Sw 73rd St Ste 304 South Miami (33143) *(G-16047)*

South Florida Graphics Corp 954 917-0606
 1770 Nw 64th St Ste 500 Fort Lauderdale (33309) *(G-4057)*

South Florida Institut 305 668-2853
 7600 Sw 57th Ave Ste 201 South Miami (33143) *(G-16048)*

South Florida Jazz Inc 954 474-8889
 7860 Peters Rd Ste F110 Plantation (33324) *(G-13893)*

South Florida Laboratory Llc 954 889-0335
 3395 Lake Worth Rd Palm Springs (33461) *(G-13150)*

South Florida Marine 305 232-8788
  19301 Sw 106th Ave Ste 13 Cutler Bay (33157) *(G-2304)*

South Florida Pallet Inc 305 330-7663
  224 Nw 136th Pl Miami (33182) *(G-9925)*

South Florida Pallets Dist 305 330-7663
  1951 Nw 89th Pl Ste 100 Doral (33172) *(G-3369)*

South Florida Parenting 954 747-3050
  6501 Nob Hill Rd Tamarac (33321) *(G-16543)*

South Florida Pavers Corp 786 517-9100
  18506 Nw 67th Ave Hialeah (33015) *(G-5355)*

South Florida Petro Svcs LLC 561 793-2102
  2550 Eisenhower Blvd # 11 Fort Lauderdale (33316) *(G-4058)*

South Florida Sheet Metal (PA) 954 647-6457
  2038 Nw 141st Ave Pembroke Pines (33028) *(G-13415)*

South Florida Stairs Inc 561 822-3110
  2019 Corporate Dr Boynton Beach (33426) *(G-915)*

South Florida Strip-Tees Inc 954 972-4899
  1740 Nw 22nd Ct Ste 10 Pompano Beach (33069) *(G-14189)*

South Florida Suntimes, Hallandale Beach *Also called South Florida Digest Inc* *(G-4975)*

South Florida Tech Svcs Inc 786 286-2882
  2333 W 3rd Ct Hialeah (33010) *(G-5356)*

South Florida Textile Inc 954 973-5677
  1301 W Copans Rd Ste E7 Pompano Beach (33064) *(G-14190)*

South Florida Time, West Palm Beach *Also called Diamond Advertising & Mktg* *(G-17978)*

South Florida Tissue Paper Co, Miami Lakes *Also called Express Paper Company Inc* *(G-10301)*

South Florida Trane, Miramar *Also called Trane US Inc* *(G-10554)*

South Florida Woodworkers Inc 954 868-5043
  2873 Sw 16th St Fort Lauderdale (33312) *(G-4059)*

South Jacksonville - R/M, B/M, Jacksonville *Also called Cemex Cnstr Mtls Fla LLC* *(G-5973)*

South Lake Press, Clermont *Also called Republic Newspapers Inc* *(G-1881)*

South Marion Meats 352 245-2096
  13770 S Highway 475 Summerfield (34491) *(G-16259)*

South Pacific Trading Company 352 567-2200
  15340 Citrus Country Dr Dade City (33523) *(G-2324)*

South Walton Pharmacy LLC 850 622-3313
  2050 W County Highway 30a # 106 Santa Rosa Beach (32459) *(G-15432)*

South West Adventure Team LLC 903 288-4739
  505 W Hickpochee Ave # 2001 Labelle (33935) *(G-6986)*

Southast Auto Acquisition Corp 305 885-8689
  7575 Nw 74th Ave Medley (33166) *(G-8322)*

Southast Clking Slant Svcs LLC 813 731-8778
  2426 Branchwood Rd Plant City (33567) *(G-13804)*

Southast Protein Purveyors LLC 912 354-2770
  604 Lake Elizabeth Dr Winter Haven (33884) *(G-18469)*

Southastern Specialty Coatings 904 616-9186
  33 W 55th St Jacksonville (32208) *(G-6480)*

Southcoast Marine Products, Clearwater *Also called General Hydrulic Solutions Inc* *(G-1613)*

Southcoast Marine Products Inc 727 573-4821
  12550 47th Way N Clearwater (33762) *(G-1788)*

Southeast Atlantic, Lakeland *Also called American Bottling Company* *(G-7272)*

Southeast Atlantic Bev Corp 904 731-3644
  6001 Bowdendale Ave Jacksonville (32216) *(G-6481)*

Southeast Atlantic Bevera 904 739-1000
  5900 Nw 72nd Ave Miami (33166) *(G-9926)*

Southeast Business Center, Orlando *Also called FCA North America Holdings LLC* *(G-12146)*

Southeast Carbon Works Inc 561 422-1798
  1243 Canyon Way Wellington (33414) *(G-17866)*

Southeast Clinical RES LLC 904 296-3260
  6817 Sthpint Pkwy Ste 902 Jacksonville (32216) *(G-6482)*

Southeast Compounding Phrm LLC 813 644-7700
  3906 Cragmont Dr Tampa (33619) *(G-17283)*

Southeast Corn Traders LLC 843 372-4315
  1936 Hollywood Blvd # 20 Hollywood (33020) *(G-5661)*

Southeast Dairy Processors Inc 813 620-1516
  3811 E Columbus Dr Tampa (33605) *(G-17284)*

Southeast Diesel, Doral *Also called Perkins Power Corp* *(G-3324)*

Southeast Elevator Llc 772 461-0030
  811 Edwards Rd Fort Pierce (34982) *(G-4530)*

Southeast Energy Inc 561 883-1051
  23257 State Road 7 # 107 Boca Raton (33428) *(G-686)*

Southeast Finishing Group Inc (PA) 407 299-4620
  2807 Mercy Dr Orlando (32808) *(G-12613)*

Southeast Food Service News, Naples *Also called Southeast Publishing Co Inc* *(G-10897)*

Southeast Gen Contrs Group Inc 877 407-3535
  10380 Sw Vlg Ctr Dr 232 Port St Lucie (34987) *(G-14483)*

Southeast Id LLC 954 571-6665
  5830 Nw 163rd St Miami Lakes (33014) *(G-10356)*

Southeast Intl Chem Co Inc 904 992-4007
  221 N Hogan St 230 Jacksonville (32202) *(G-6483)*

Southeast Manufacturing Inc 866 550-2511
  4921 E 7th Ave Tampa (33605) *(G-17285)*

Southeast Marketing Concepts 561 747-7010
  801 Maplewood Dr Ste 11 Jupiter (33458) *(G-6802)*

Southeast Modular Mfg, Leesburg *Also called M S Amtex-N Inc* *(G-7784)*

Southeast Offset Inc 305 623-7788
  4880 Nw 157th St Miami Lakes (33014) *(G-10357)*

Southeast Packg Sanitation LLC 904 634-7911
  2899 Powers Ave Ste 4 Jacksonville (32207) *(G-6484)*

Southeast Plastics, Daytona Beach *Also called Halifax Plastic Inc* *(G-2560)*

Southeast Power Group Inc (PA) 305 592-9745
  5820 Nw 84th Ave Doral (33166) *(G-3370)*

Southeast Print Programs Inc 813 885-3203
  5023 W Rio Vista Ave Tampa (33634) *(G-17286)*

Southeast Publications USA Inc 954 368-4686
  2150 Sw 10th St Ste A Deerfield Beach (33442) *(G-2813)*

Southeast Publishing Co Inc (PA) 239 213-1277
  2539 Avila Ln Naples (34105) *(G-10897)*

Southeast Review Inc 850 644-4230
  405 Williams Building Tallahassee (32306) *(G-16501)*

Southeast Security Products 954 786-5900
  1387 Sw 12th Ave Pompano Beach (33069) *(G-14191)*

Southeast Window Coverings 904 372-0326
  6900 Philips Hwy Ste 46 Jacksonville (32216) *(G-6485)*

Southeast Woodcrafters Inc 561 392-2929
  1566 Nw 1st Ave Boca Raton (33432) *(G-687)*

Southeast Worldwide, Medley *Also called Southast Auto Acquisition Corp* *(G-8322)*

Southeast-Atlantic, Fort Myers *Also called American Bottling Company* *(G-4171)*

Southeastern Aluminum, Jacksonville *Also called Sea Products Inc* *(G-6458)*

Southeastern Aluminum Pdts LLC 800 243-8200
  4925 Bulls Bay Hwy Jacksonville (32219) *(G-6486)*

Southeastern Door Company LLC 561 746-5493
  1505 Commerce Ln Jupiter (33458) *(G-6803)*

Southeastern Engineering Inc 321 984-2521
  1340 Clearmont St Ne # 304 Palm Bay (32905) *(G-12921)*

Southeastern Ltg Solutions 386 238-1711
  821 Fentress Ct Daytona Beach (32117) *(G-2601)*

Southeastern Marine Power LLC 727 545-2700
  7398 46th Ave N Saint Petersburg (33709) *(G-15190)*

Southeastern Mktg Assoc Inc 954 421-7388
  1522 Se 10th St Deerfield Beach (33441) *(G-2814)*

Southeastern Pallets Inc 904 783-8363
  2203 W Beaver St Jacksonville (32209) *(G-6487)*

Southeastern Paper Group Inc 864 574-0440
  7080 Havertys Way Lakeland (33805) *(G-7441)*

Southeastern Peg Bd Prtrs Inc 904 731-0357
  2750 Dawn Rd Jacksonville (32207) *(G-6488)*

Southeastern Pipe Precast Inc 850 587-7473
  2900 N Highway 95a Cantonment (32533) *(G-1274)*

Southeastern Printing Co Inc (PA) 772 287-2141
  950 Se 8th St Hialeah (33010) *(G-5357)*

Southeastern Printing Co Inc 772 287-2141
  4313 Sw Port Way Palm City (34990) *(G-13059)*

Southeastern Printing Co Inc 305 885-8707
  6001 Pk Of Cmmrce Blvd St Boca Raton (33487) *(G-688)*

Southeastern Seating Inc 813 273-9858
  903 E 17th Ave Tampa (33605) *(G-17287)*

Southeastern Truck Tops Inc 386 761-0002
  402 6th St Daytona Beach (32117) *(G-2602)*

Southern Air Comprsr Svc Inc 863 425-9111
  2260 Peerless Rd Mulberry (33860) *(G-10639)*

Southern Aluminum and Stl Inc 850 484-4700
  2501 S Highway 29 Cantonment (32533) *(G-1275)*

Southern Aluminum Inc 239 275-3367
  677 Stonecrest Ln Cape Coral (33909) *(G-1388)*

Southern Automated Systems Inc 863 815-7444
  2415 W Socrum Loop Rd Lakeland (33810) *(G-7442)*

Southern Awning Inc (PA) 561 586-0464
  313 S H St Lake Worth (33460) *(G-7233)*

Southern Bakeries Inc (HQ) 863 682-1155
  3355 W Memorial Blvd Lakeland (33815) *(G-7443)*

Southern Balloon Works, Jacksonville *Also called Aerial Products Corporation* *(G-5866)*

Southern Balloon Works Inc 727 388-8360
  11653 Central Pkwy # 209 Jacksonville (32224) *(G-6489)*

Southern Blade & Supply, Ocala *Also called Shashy Enterprises Inc* *(G-11488)*

Southern Boating & Yachting 954 522-5515
  1591 E Atl Blvd Ste 200 Pompano Beach (33060) *(G-14192)*

Southern Boating Magazine, Pompano Beach *Also called Southern Boating & Yachting* *(G-14192)*

Southern Brothers Racing LLC 850 509-2223
  443 Charlie Harris Loop Quincy (32352) *(G-14550)*

Southern Business Card Inc 305 944-2931
  7901 Clay Mica Ct Delray Beach (33446) *(G-3020)*

Southern Closet Systems Inc 813 926-9348
  13211 Byrd Dr Odessa (33556) *(G-11579)*

Southern Coating Systems Inc 863 712-9900
  880 Mandalay Ave Apt C507 Clearwater (33767) *(G-1789)*

Southern Coatings of Ts LLC 727 858-6586
  1109 Sunset Dr Tarpon Springs (34689) *(G-17492)*

Southern Company Entp Inc 904 879-2101
  54024 Cravey Rd Callahan (32011) *(G-1258)*

Southern Contracting N FL Inc 850 674-3570
  19073 Ne State Road 69 Blountstown (32424) *(G-377)*

Southern Covert, Fort Pierce *Also called Wheeler Lumber LLC* *(G-4554)*

Southern Cross Boatworks Inc 954 467-5801
  2019 Sw 20th St Ste 111 Fort Lauderdale (33315) *(G-4060)*

A L P H A B E T I C

Southern Cross Shutter Systems 941 585-2152
  21271 Dearborn Ave Port Charlotte (33954) *(G-14315)*

Southern Custom Iron & Art LLC 561 586-8400
  3787 Boutwell Rd Lake Worth Beach (33461) *(G-7262)*

Southern Die Casting Corp 305 635-6571
  3560 Nw 59th St Miami (33142) *(G-9927)*

Southern Door Technologies 386 496-3844
  9124 S County Road 231 Lake Butler (32054) *(G-7006)*

Southern Drydock Inc 904 355-9945
  8153 Six Mile Way Saint Augustine (32092) *(G-14896)*

Southern Environmental Inc 850 944-4475
  6690 W Nine Mile Rd Pensacola (32526) *(G-13605)*

Southern Exhibits Graphics Inc 407 423-2860
  4360 36th St Unit 1 Orlando (32811) *(G-12614)*

Southern Fabricating Machinery 813 966-3983
  10417 S County Road 39 Lithia (33547) *(G-7838)*

Southern Fiber Inc 786 916-3052
  4715 Nw 157th St Ste 104 Miami Lakes (33014) *(G-10358)*

Southern Fiberglass Inc 904 387-2246
  41 Spring St Jacksonville (32254) *(G-6490)*

Southern Fuel Inc 904 545-5163
  7028 E Mount Vernon St Glen Saint Mary (32040) *(G-4805)*

Southern Fuelwood Inc 352 472-4324
  28826 W Newberry Rd Newberry (32669) *(G-11027)*

Southern Gear, Miami *Also called Gear Dynamics Inc (G-9196)*

Southern Gear & Machine Inc 305 691-6300
  3685 Nw 106th St Miami (33147) *(G-9928)*

Southern Graphic Machine LLC 615 812-0778
  3441 Juniper Dr Edgewater (32141) *(G-3501)*

Southern Grdns Ctrus Hldg Corp (HQ) 863 983-8121
  111 Ponce De Leon Ave Clewiston (33440) *(G-1895)*

Southern Grouts & Mortars Inc (PA) 954 943-2288
  1502 Sw 2nd Pl Pompano Beach (33069) *(G-14193)*

Southern Hvac Corporation (HQ) 407 917-1800
  485 N Keller Rd Ste 515 Maitland (32751) *(G-8074)*

Southern Innovative Energy Inc 321 747-9205
  4373 Fletcher Ln Ste 2 Titusville (32780) *(G-17616)*

Southern Interest Co Inc 727 471-2040
  2233 3rd Ave S Saint Petersburg (33712) *(G-15191)*

Southern International Svcs 954 349-7321
  18970 Ne 4th Ct Miami (33179) *(G-9929)*

Southern Lbr & Treating Co Inc 904 695-0784
  1433 Lane Cir E Jacksonville (32254) *(G-6491)*

Southern Lights 727 849-4442
  3822 Grayton Dr New Port Richey (34652) *(G-10984)*

Southern Litho II LLC 724 394-3693
  9010 Strada Stell Ct # 103 Naples (34109) *(G-10898)*

Southern Manufacturing Inc 305 267-1943
  7064 Sw 10th St Miami (33144) *(G-9930)*

Southern Mch TI & Rbldrs Inc 941 749-0988
  2923 62nd Ave E Bradenton (34203) *(G-1049)*

Southern Mfg & Fabrication LLC 407 894-8851
  2000 E Lake Mary Blvd Sanford (32773) *(G-15389)*

Southern Mfg Tech Inc 813 888-8151
  5910 Johns Rd Tampa (33634) *(G-17288)*

Southern Mfg Upholstery Inc 727 573-1006
  3670 131st Ave N Clearwater (33762) *(G-1790)*

Southern Micro Etch Inc 954 781-5999
  610 Ne 29th St Pompano Beach (33064) *(G-14194)*

Southern Ordnance, Longwood *Also called Exit Ten Inc (G-7891)*

Southern Packaging McHy Corp 305 245-3045
  550 Nw 3rd Ave Florida City (33034) *(G-3612)*

Southern Pines Inc 239 947-1515
  26300 Southern Pines Dr Bonita Springs (34135) *(G-820)*

Southern Plastics & Rubber Co 386 672-1167
  565 Parque Dr Ormond Beach (32174) *(G-12794)*

Southern Pre Cast Structures L 352 569-1128
  4457 Cr 542h Bushnell (33513) *(G-1249)*

Southern Recreation Inc 904 387-4390
  4060 Edison Ave Jacksonville (32254) *(G-6492)*

Southern Reinforced Plas Inc 941 746-8793
  2904 29th Ave E Ste F Bradenton (34208) *(G-1050)*

Southern Softwoods Inc 863 666-1404
  2425 Lasso Ln Lakeland (33801) *(G-7444)*

SOUTHERN SPRING & STAMPING INC (PA) 941 488-2276
  401 Substation Rd Venice (34285) *(G-17717)*

Southern States Gluing Svcs 850 469-9667
  3865 N Palafox St Pensacola (32505) *(G-13606)*

Southern States Motive Pwr LLC 813 621-3338
  6601 E Adamo Dr Tampa (33619) *(G-17289)*

Southern States Toyota Lift (PA) 904 764-7662
  115 S 78th St Tampa (33619) *(G-17290)*

Southern Strl Stl Fla Inc 727 327-7123
  1000 31st St S Saint Petersburg (33712) *(G-15192)*

Southern Supply and Mfg Co 727 323-7099
  1501 22nd St N Saint Petersburg (33713) *(G-15193)*

Southern Surgical Consultants 904 296-7828
  11653 Central Pkwy # 201 Jacksonville (32224) *(G-6493)*

Southern Switch & Contacts 727 789-0951
  855 Virginia Ave Palm Harbor (34683) *(G-13133)*

Southern Tape & Label Inc 321 632-5275
  1107 Peachtree St Cocoa (32922) *(G-1957)*

Southern Technologies 904 266-2100
  270 Us Highway 90 E Jacksonville (32234) *(G-6494)*

Southern Truss Companies Inc 772 464-4160
  2590 N Kings Hwy Fort Pierce (34951) *(G-4531)*

Southern Underground Inds 954 226-3865
  5979 Nw 151st St Ste 223 Miami Lakes (33014) *(G-10359)*

Southern Welding & Mechanics 305 772-0961
  592 W 28th St Hialeah (33010) *(G-5358)*

Southern Wheel & Rim Inc 904 786-7542
  1044 Lane Ave S Jacksonville (32205) *(G-6495)*

Southern Winding Service Inc 813 621-6555
  5302 Saint Paul St Tampa (33619) *(G-17291)*

Southern Wood Services LLC 352 279-3208
  6288 California St Brooksville (34604) *(G-1203)*

Southern Woodworks Fine Wdwkg 850 456-0550
  1170 Mahogany Mill Rd Pensacola (32507) *(G-13607)*

Southern-Bartlett Intl LLC 407 374-1613
  4070 S Pipkin Rd Lakeland (33811) *(G-7445)*

Southernstone Cabinets Inc 727 538-0123
  12520 Automobile Blvd Clearwater (33762) *(G-1791)*

Southfloridagaynewscom 954 530-4970
  2520 N Dixie Hwy Wilton Manors (33305) *(G-18342)*

Southland Milling Co 850 674-8448
  21474 Se Coastal St Blountstown (32424) *(G-378)*

Southland Power & Enrgy Co LLC 800 217-6040
  5215 Nw 35th Ave Fort Lauderdale (33309) *(G-4061)*

Southland Services LLC 850 393-2444
  4828 State Highway 20 E Freeport (32439) *(G-4630)*

Southpoint Sportswear LLC 305 885-3045
  11525 Nw 124th St Medley (33178) *(G-8323)*

Southpointe Precision 239 225-1350
  12960 Commerce Lk Dr # 10 Fort Myers (33913) *(G-4402)*

Southprint Corp 813 237-8000
  6816 N River Blvd Tampa (33604) *(G-17292)*

Southridge Outdoor Storage 352 516-5598
  595 County Road 448 Tavares (32778) *(G-17523)*

Southstern Arspc Svcs Ltd Lblt 305 992-8257
  1816 Sw 7th Ave Pompano Beach (33060) *(G-14195)*

Southstern Indus Fbrcators LLC 941 776-1211
  12650 County Road 39 Duette (34219) *(G-3433)*

Southstern Rail Svcs Mlbrry FL 863 425-4986
  1200 Prairie Mine Rd Mulberry (33860) *(G-10640)*

Southstern Stnless Fbrctors In 904 354-4381
  634 Dyal St Jacksonville (32206) *(G-6496)*

Southwest Aggregates, Punta Gorda *Also called Charlotte County Min & Mtl Inc (G-14501)*

Southwest Choppers Inc 239 242-1101
  2123 Ne 3rd Ter Cape Coral (33909) *(G-1389)*

Southwest Custom Coatings Inc 239 682-9462
  4498 22nd Ave Se Naples (34117) *(G-10899)*

Southwest Eqp For Hrnando Cnty 352 596-5142
  13484 Chambord St Brooksville (34613) *(G-1204)*

Southwest Fla Newspapers Inc 239 574-9733
  308 Se 25th Ter Cape Coral (33904) *(G-1390)*

Southwest Florida Regional 615 344-9551
  12901 Starkey Rd Largo (33773) *(G-7688)*

Southwest Precision AG Inc 863 674-5799
  14960 S Sr 29 Felda (33930) *(G-3575)*

Southwest Signal Inc 813 621-4949
  1984 Georgia Ave Englewood (34224) *(G-3524)*

Southwest Steel Group Inc 239 283-8980
  3405 Yucatan Pkwy Cape Coral (33993) *(G-1391)*

Southwest Strl Systems Inc 239 693-6000
  5774 Corporation Cir Fort Myers (33905) *(G-4403)*

Southwest Turbine Inc 305 769-1765
  4550 E 10th Ct Hialeah (33013) *(G-5359)*

Southwest Woodwork Inc 239 213-0126
  429 Production Blvd Naples (34104) *(G-10900)*

Southwind Aviation Supply LLC 405 491-0500
  752 Strihal Loop Oakland (34787) *(G-11230)*

Southwings Avionics and ACC 305 825-6755
  5429 Nw 161st St Miami Lakes (33014) *(G-10360)*

Southwire Company LLC 727 535-0572
  11211 69th St Largo (33773) *(G-7689)*

Southwire Company LLC 850 423-4680
  5680 John Givens Rd Crestview (32539) *(G-2254)*

Sovita Retail Inc 888 871-2408
  1317 Edgewater Dr # 1943 Orlando (32804) *(G-12615)*

Sox LLC 561 501-0057
  950 Pnnsula Corp Cir Ste Boca Raton (33487) *(G-689)*

Sox Erosion Solutions, Boca Raton *Also called Sox LLC (G-689)*

Soythane Technologies Inc 904 225-1047
  850709 Us Highway 17 Yulee (32097) *(G-18594)*

SP Publications LLC 239 595-9040
  495 Grand Blvd Ste 206 Miramar Beach (32550) *(G-10573)*

Sp Sign LLC 772 562-0955
  2201 Se Indian St Unit E4 Stuart (34997) *(G-16226)*

SP&e, Fort Lauderdale *Also called Southland Power & Enrgy Co LLC (G-4061)*

2022 Harris Florida
Manufacturers Directory

(G-0000) Company's Geographic Section entry number

Spa Concepts Inc 850 575-0921
  3191 W Tharpe St Tallahassee (32303) *(G-16502)*

Spa Cover Inc 954 923-8801
  2310 Hayes St Hollywood (33020) *(G-5662)*

Spa World Corporation (PA) 866 588-8008
  5701 Nw 35th Ave Miami (33142) *(G-9931)*

Space Cast IntlIgent Sltons In 321 622-6858
  770 North Dr Ste B Melbourne (32934) *(G-8525)*

Space Coast Distributors 386 239-0305
  726 N Segrave St Daytona Beach (32114) *(G-2603)*

Space Coast Hydraulics Inc 321 504-6006
  1265 Us Highway 1 Rockledge (32955) *(G-14748)*

Space Coast Industries Inc 321 633-9336
  700 Cox Rd Ste 1 Cocoa (32926) *(G-1958)*

Space Coast Map LLC 321 242-4538
  1359 Richmond Dr Melbourne (32935) *(G-8526)*

Space Exploration Tech Corp 310 363-6000
  Cape Cnaveral A Force Sta Cape Canaveral (32920) *(G-1293)*

Space Flyers Inc 305 219-6990
  11115 W Okeechobee Rd # 1 Hialeah Gardens (33018) *(G-5452)*

Space Lighting, Miami Also called IMC Lighting Inc *(G-9305)*

Space Machine & Engrg Corp 727 323-2221
  2327 16th Ave N Saint Petersburg (33713) *(G-15194)*

Space Manufacturing Inc 727 532-9466
  14271 60th St N Clearwater (33760) *(G-1792)*

Space Masters 954 561-8800
  3700 Ne 3rd Ave Oakland Park (33334) *(G-11296)*

Space-Eyes, Miami Also called Channel Logistics LLC *(G-8920)*

Spacecast Pltg Met Rfnshing In 321 254-2880
  975 Aurora Rd Melbourne (32935) *(G-8527)*

Spacelabs Healthcare Inc 904 786-5113
  14476 Duval Pl W Ste 303 Jacksonville (32218) *(G-6497)*

Spacemakers Closets SW Fla Inc 239 598-0222
  2044 J And C Blvd Naples (34109) *(G-10901)*

Spacewerks Inc 727 540-9714
  13100 56th Ct Ste 711 Clearwater (33760) *(G-1793)*

Spacios Design Group Inc 305 696-1766
  7370 Nw 36th Ave Miami (33147) *(G-9932)*

Spancrete Inc 305 599-8885
  7907 Nw 53rd St 347 Miami (33166) *(G-9933)*

Spancrete of Florida LLC 863 655-1515
  400 Deer Trl E Sebring (33876) *(G-15942)*

Spancrete Southeast Inc 863 655-1515
  400 Deer Trl E Sebring (33876) *(G-15943)*

Spanglish Advertising Cor 305 244-0918
  6857 Ne 3rd Ave Miami (33138) *(G-9934)*

Spanish House Inc 305 503-1191
  8167 Nw 84th St Medley (33166) *(G-8324)*

Spanish Peri & Bk Sls Inc 305 592-3919
  2105 Nw 102nd Ave Doral (33172) *(G-3371)*

Spanish Publishers LLC 305 233-3365
  8871 Sw 129th St Miami (33176) *(G-9935)*

Spanish Trail Lumber Co LLC 850 592-8512
  6112 Old Spanish Trl Marianna (32448) *(G-8175)*

Sparkles and Suspenders FL 754 701-4528
  5405 Nw 67th Ave Lauderhill (33319) *(G-7742)*

Sparks Cabinetry 954 367-2750
  1685 S State Road 7 Hollywood (33023) *(G-5663)*

Sparton Corporation (HQ) 847 762-5800
  5612 Johnson Lake Rd De Leon Springs (32130) *(G-2628)*

Sparton Deleon Springs LLC (HQ) 386 985-4631
  5612 Johnson Lake Rd De Leon Springs (32130) *(G-2629)*

Sparton Electronics, Brooksville Also called Spartronics Brooksville LLC *(G-1206)*

Spartronics Brooksville LLC (HQ) 352 799-6520
  30167 Power Line Rd Brooksville (34602) *(G-1205)*

Spartronics Brooksville LLC 352 799-6520
  30167 Power Line Rd Brooksville (34602) *(G-1206)*

Spaulding Craft Inc 727 726-2316
  1053 Harbor Lake Dr Safety Harbor (34695) *(G-14798)*

Spec-TEC Manufacturing Inc 954 749-4204
  10794 Nw 53rd St Sunrise (33351) *(G-16370)*

Special Americas Bbq Inc 305 637-7377
  11411 Nw 107th St Ste 1 Miami (33178) *(G-9936)*

Special Coatings Inc 239 301-2714
  6210 Shirley St Ste 105 Naples (34109) *(G-10902)*

Special Editions Publishing, Altamonte Springs Also called Special
Editionspublishing *(G-71)*

Special Editionspublishing 407 862-7737
  999 Douglas Ave Ste 3317 Altamonte Springs (32714) *(G-71)*

Special Nutrients LLC 305 857-9830
  2766 Sw 37th Ave Coconut Grove (33133) *(G-2014)*

Special Publications Inc 352 622-2995
  743 Se Fort King Rd Ocala (34471) *(G-11496)*

Special Tool Solutions Inc 904 356-5671
  11699 Camden Rd Jacksonville (32218) *(G-6498)*

Speciality Wood Sales, Winter Haven Also called Peavy Enterprises Inc *(G-18455)*

Specialized Off Road Vehicles 352 735-1385
  2183 Croat St Mount Dora (32757) *(G-10614)*

Specialties Unlimited 239 482-8433
  14726 Calusa Palms Dr # 101 Fort Myers (33919) *(G-4404)*

Specialty Contractor, Lehigh Acres Also called Marathon Engineering Corp *(G-7816)*

Specialty Def Systems KY Inc 904 741-5400
  13386 International Pkwy Jacksonville (32218) *(G-6499)*

Specialty Fabrication LLC 863 683-0708
  4015 Drane Field Rd Lakeland (33811) *(G-7446)*

Specialty Fabrication Wldg Inc 352 669-9353
  680 Goodbar Ave Umatilla (32784) *(G-17651)*

Specialty Fin Consulting Corp (PA) 717 246-1661
  5541 Gulf Of Mexico Dr Longboat Key (34228) *(G-7860)*

Specialty Food Group LLC (HQ) 305 392-5000
  9835 Nw 14th St Doral (33172) *(G-3372)*

Specialty Forged Wheels Inc 786 332-5925
  12146 Sw 114th Pl Miami (33176) *(G-9937)*

Specialty Glass, Oldsmar Also called Justi Group Inc *(G-11663)*

Specialty Maintenance & Constr 863 644-8432
  4121 Drane Field Rd Lakeland (33811) *(G-7447)*

Specialty Packaging & Display, Titusville Also called Richard C Good *(G-17613)*

Specialty Pharmacy Svcs Inc 321 953-2004
  1555 W Nasa Blvd Ste B Melbourne (32901) *(G-8528)*

Specialty Powder Coating LLC 813 782-2720
  7640 Chenkin Rd Zephyrhills (33540) *(G-18630)*

Specialty Productions Inc 786 399-1393
  2476 Sw 25th Ter Miami (33133) *(G-9938)*

Specialty Products Inc 850 438-4264
  2325 W Cervantes St Pensacola (32505) *(G-13608)*

Specialty Stamp & Sign, Orlando Also called Liquid Soul Dgtal Graphics LLC *(G-12334)*

Specialty Steel Holdco Inc 305 375-7560
  200 Biscayne Blvd Miami (33132) *(G-9939)*

Specialty Structures Inc 386 668-0474
  218 Plumosa Rd Debary (32713) *(G-2643)*

Specialty Tank and Eqp Co 904 353-8761
  857 Robinson Ave Jacksonville (32209) *(G-6500)*

Specialty Wood Manufacturing, Kissimmee Also called Welshman Investment Corp *(G-6972)*

Specilty Strctres Instllations, Debary Also called Specialty Structures Inc *(G-2643)*

Spector Manufacturing Inc 860 559-6068
  22 Sw Riverway Blvd Palm City (34990) *(G-13060)*

Spectra Chrome LLC 727 573-1990
  13130 56th Ct Ste 611 Clearwater (33760) *(G-1794)*

Spectra Composites East Fla 772 461-7747
  7445 Commercial Cir Fort Pierce (34951) *(G-4532)*

Spectra Metal Sales Inc 727 530-5435
  5100 140th Ave N Clearwater (33760) *(G-1795)*

Spectra Powder Coating Inc 786 351-7448
  7242 Nw 33rd St Miami (33122) *(G-9940)*

Spectraflex Inc 850 892-3900
  83 Lancelot Rd Defuniak Springs (32433) *(G-2843)*

Spectrum Bridge Inc 407 792-1570
  110 Timberlachen Cir # 1012 Lake Mary (32746) *(G-7107)*

Spectrum Engineering & Mfg Inc 727 376-5510
  11609 Pyramid Dr Odessa (33556) *(G-11580)*

Spectrum Engineering Inc 239 277-1182
  1342 Clnl Blvd Ste D31 Fort Myers (33907) *(G-4405)*

Spectrum Packaging, Orlando Also called R G Management Inc *(G-12525)*

Spectrum Signworks LLC 239 908-0505
  2920 Leonardo Ave Naples (34119) *(G-10903)*

Spectrumit Inc 850 202-5263
  1101 N Palafox St Pensacola (32501) *(G-13609)*

Speech Bin 772 770-0006
  1965 25th Ave Vero Beach (32960) *(G-17801)*

Speed Custom Cabinet Corp 407 953-1479
  6923 Narcoossee Rd Orlando (32822) *(G-12616)*

Speed Mobile Oil Change Inc 305 763-4352
  5580 Sw 88th Pl Miami (33165) *(G-9941)*

Speed Print One Inc 305 374-5936
  8840 Sw 86th St Miami (33173) *(G-9942)*

Speed Pro Miami 954 534-9503
  11341 Interchange Cir S Miramar (33025) *(G-10545)*

Speed-D-Print, Pensacola Also called R K L Enterprises of Pensacola *(G-13592)*

Speedline Athletic Wear Inc 813 876-1375
  1804 N Habana Ave Tampa (33607) *(G-17293)*

Speedline Team Sports Inc 813 876-1375
  1804 N Habana Ave Tampa (33607) *(G-17294)*

Speedpro Imaging, Port Saint Lucie Also called Slaton & Sons Enterprises Inc *(G-14447)*

Speedpro Imaging, Boca Raton Also called Paris Ink Inc *(G-632)*

Speedpro Imaging St Petersburg, Saint Petersburg Also called McKenny Printing Entp Inc *(G-15125)*

Speedpro Imaging St Petersburg 727 266-0956
  5111 Queen Palm Ter Ne Saint Petersburg (33703) *(G-15195)*

Speedsource Inc 954 578-7071
  4 South Dr Key Largo (33037) *(G-6850)*

Speedway Press, Daytona Beach Also called Quality Printing Inc *(G-2588)*

Speedy Sign, Lake City Also called Speedysigns Com Inc *(G-7046)*

Speedysigns Com Inc 386 755-2006
  162 Sw Spencer Ct Ste 101 Lake City (32024) *(G-7046)*

Speedysignsusa.com,, Lake City Also called Signsitecom Inc *(G-7045)*

Speer Laboratories LLC 954 586-8700
  4950 W Prospect Rd Fort Lauderdale (33309) *(G-4062)*

A
L
P
H
A
B
E
T
I
C

Spencer Fabrications Inc................352 343-0014
29511 County Road 561 Tavares (32778) *(G-17524)*

Speranza Therapeutics Corp................844 477-3726
433 Plaza Real Ste 275 Boca Raton (33432) *(G-690)*

Sperry Manufacturing, Venice *Also called Sperry Marketing Group Inc (G-17718)*

Sperry Marketing Group Inc................941 483-4667
107 Corporation Way Venice (34285) *(G-17718)*

Spett Printing Co Inc................561 241-9758
4115 Georges Way Boca Raton (33434) *(G-691)*

Sphere Access Inc (PA)................336 501-6159
400 N Ashley Dr Ste 1775 Tampa (33602) *(G-17295)*

SPI, Orlando *Also called Sign Producers Inc (G-12602)*

SPI, Doral *Also called Structral Prestressed Inds Inc (G-3380)*

SPI LLC................786 907-4022
11200 Nw 107th St Ste 8 Miami (33178) *(G-9943)*

Spice Island Boat Works Inc................954 632-9453
505 Se 18th St Fort Lauderdale (33316) *(G-4063)*

Spice World, Orlando *Also called Jenard Fresh Incorporated (G-12272)*

Spice World LLC (PA)................407 851-9432
8101 Presidents Dr Orlando (32809) *(G-12617)*

Spicer Industries Inc................352 732-5300
840 Nw 24th Ct Ocala (34475) *(G-11497)*

Spiegel Pavers Inc................954 687-5797
3400 Blue Lake Dr Apt 102 Pompano Beach (33064) *(G-14196)*

Spiegel Pavers Inc................954 687-5797
7761 Nw 42nd Pl 1 Coral Springs (33065) *(G-2213)*

Spiker USA Corporation................850 710-3043
38 S Blue Angel Pkwy Pensacola (32506) *(G-13610)*

Spikes Press & Printhouse LLC................850 438-2293
1201 Barrancas Ave Pensacola (32502) *(G-13611)*

Spin Free LLC................561 775-2534
11316 Avery Rd Palm Beach Gardens (33410) *(G-13010)*

Spin Magnetics................863 676-9333
22501 Us Highway 27 Lake Wales (33859) *(G-7173)*

Spincontrol Gearing LLC................863 241-9055
4535 Tiger Creek Trl Lake Wales (33898) *(G-7174)*

Spinenet LLC................321 439-1806
1300 Minnesota Ave # 200 Winter Park (32789) *(G-18539)*

Spinnaker Holding Company................561 392-8626
1609 Nw 2nd Ave Boca Raton (33432) *(G-692)*

Spinnaker Vero Inc................772 567-4645
983 12th St Ste A Vero Beach (32960) *(G-17802)*

Spires Empire LLC................305 797-0622
1106 Grinnell St Key West (33040) *(G-6881)*

Spirit LLC................954 592-0227
1400 Nw 159th St Ste 101 Miami Gardens (33169) *(G-10274)*

Spirit Sales Corporation................850 878-0366
2818 Industrial Plaza Dr D Tallahassee (32301) *(G-16503)*

Spiritwear Today................239 676-7384
28711 N Diesel Dr Unit 9 Bonita Springs (34135) *(G-821)*

Splash of Color LLC................732 735-3090
2885 Starshire Cv Jacksonville (32257) *(G-6501)*

Spliffpuff LLC................786 493-4529
6961 Nw 111th Ave Doral (33178) *(G-3373)*

Splinter Woodworking Inc................305 731-9334
738 Dotterel Rd Delray Beach (33444) *(G-3021)*

Spmc, Florida City *Also called Southern Packaging McHy Corp (G-3612)*

Sponge Merchant International................727 919-3523
1028 Peninsula Ave Tarpon Springs (34689) *(G-17493)*

Sponsor Locker, Winter Park *Also called Playoff Technologies LLC (G-18528)*

Spoons Chilly................321 610-8966
4980 N Wickham Rd Ste 106 Melbourne (32940) *(G-8529)*

Sport America Magazine................727 391-3099
248 144th Ave Madeira Beach (33708) *(G-8041)*

Sport Products of Tampa Inc................813 630-5552
8721 Ashworth Dr Tampa (33647) *(G-17296)*

Sportailor Inc................305 754-3255
6501 Ne 2nd Ct Miami (33138) *(G-9944)*

Sports N Stuff Screen Printing................407 859-0437
3975 Forrestal Ave # 600 Orlando (32806) *(G-12618)*

Sports Radar Ltd................352 503-6825
7397 S Suncoast Blvd Homosassa (34446) *(G-5751)*

Sports Structure Intl LLC................305 777-2225
1680 Michigan Ave Ste 700 Miami Beach (33139) *(G-10234)*

Sposen Signature Homes LLC................239 244-8886
2311 Santa Barbara Blvd # 111 Cape Coral (33991) *(G-1392)*

Spot-On Wldg Met Fbrcation LLC................239 825-7452
2365 14th Ave Ne Naples (34120) *(G-10904)*

Spotlight Graphics Inc................941 929-1500
6054 Clark Center Ave Sarasota (34238) *(G-15832)*

Spray Box LLC................850 567-2724
768 Lupine Ln Tallahassee (32308) *(G-16504)*

Spray-Tech Staining Inc................407 443-4239
569 Darby Way Longwood (32779) *(G-7949)*

Spraying Systems Co................813 259-9400
5107 Lena Rd Unit 110 Bradenton (34211) *(G-1051)*

Spraymation Development Corp................954 484-9700
4180 Nw 10th Ave Fort Lauderdale (33309) *(G-4064)*

Spring Hill Bakery LLC................954 825-3419
374 Winthrop Dr Spring Hill (34609) *(G-16081)*

Spring Hill Newsletter, Hudson *Also called Tom Watson Enterprises Inc (G-5789)*

Spring Loaded Inc................561 747-8785
315 Commerce Way Ste 1 Jupiter (33458) *(G-6804)*

Spring Oaks LLC................352 592-1150
725 Desoto Ave Brooksville (34601) *(G-1207)*

Springbig Holdings Inc................800 772-9172
621 Nw 53rd St Ste 260 Boca Raton (33487) *(G-693)*

Sprint Printing Company LLC................239 947-2221
28380 Old 41 Rd Ste 4 Bonita Springs (34135) *(G-822)*

Spruce Creek Cabinetry Inc................386 756-0041
601 Lemon St Ste C Port Orange (32127) *(G-14349)*

SPS, Jacksonville *Also called Southeast Packg Sanitation LLC (G-6484)*

SPS Drilling Exploration Prod................305 777-3553
1 Alhambra Plz Ste Ph Coral Gables (33134) *(G-2111)*

SPX Corporation................863 602-9061
399 N Prairie Indus Pkwy Mulberry (33860) *(G-10641)*

SPX Flow Technology, Ocala *Also called Pneumatic Products Corporation (G-11469)*

SPX Flow Technology Usa Inc (HQ)................352 237-1220
4647 Se 40th Ave Ocala (34474) *(G-11498)*

Spyder Graphics Inc................954 561-9725
3601 Ne 5th Ave Oakland Park (33334) *(G-11297)*

Square One Armoring Svcs Co................305 477-1109
12370 Sw 130th St Miami (33186) *(G-9945)*

Squared Machine & Tool Inc A................678 988-2477
1851 Cowen Rd Unit F Gulf Breeze (32563) *(G-4892)*

Squire Industries Inc................813 523-1505
1118 Sparkman Rd Plant City (33566) *(G-13805)*

Srb Servicing LLC................850 278-1000
249 Mack Bayou Loop # 302 Santa Rosa Beach (32459) *(G-15433)*

Srm Blinds Inc................321 269-5332
4303 Kenneth Ct Titusville (32780) *(G-17617)*

Srm Concrete................850 588-7677
17803 Ashley Dr Panama City (32413) *(G-13310)*

Srm Waterproofing Sealants Inc................407 963-3619
2899 Burwood Ave Orlando (32837) *(G-12619)*

Srq Fabrications Inc................941 780-5496
6707 Avenue C Sarasota (34231) *(G-15833)*

Srq Media Group, Sarasota *Also called Trafalger Communications Inc (G-15857)*

Srq Sign Partners LLC................941 357-0319
1621 W University Pkwy Sarasota (34243) *(G-15558)*

Srq Storm Protection LLC................941 341-0334
1899 Porter Lake Dr # 105 Sarasota (34240) *(G-15834)*

Srq Welding Inc................941 484-5947
121 Triple Dmd Blvd North Venice (34275) *(G-11219)*

SRS Health Software, Tampa *Also called SRS Software LLC (G-17297)*

SRS Software LLC................201 802-1300
4221 W Boy Scout Blvd # 200 Tampa (33607) *(G-17297)*

Srt Wireless LLC................954 797-7850
1613 Nw 136th Ave Bldg C Sunrise (33323) *(G-16371)*

Ss & S Industries Inc................321 327-2500
620 Di Lido St Ne Melbourne (32907) *(G-8530)*

SS White Technologies Inc (PA)................727 626-2800
8300 Sheen Dr Saint Petersburg (33709) *(G-15196)*

SSE and Associates Inc................954 973-7144
1500 W Copans Rd Ste A9 Pompano Beach (33064) *(G-14197)*

SSE AND ASSOCIATES, INC., Pompano Beach *Also called SSE and Associates Inc (G-14197)*

SSE Publications LLC................954 835-7616
1 Panther Pkwy Sunrise (33323) *(G-16372)*

Ssemiami Corporation................305 322-1890
8350 Nw 52nd Ter Ste 408 Doral (33166) *(G-3374)*

Ssh Holding Inc................678 942-1800
10055 Seminole Blvd Seminole (33772) *(G-15988)*

Ssi Wood Products, Tampa *Also called S&S Craftsmen Inc (G-17241)*

SSP, Miami *Also called Steering & Suspension Parts (G-9948)*

Ssvm Partners Inc................239 825-6282
8293 Consumer Ct Sarasota (34240) *(G-15835)*

St Acquisitions LLC................941 753-1095
1701 Desoto Rd Sarasota (34234) *(G-15836)*

ST Action Pro Inc................321 632-4111
3815 N Highway 1 Ste 50 Cocoa (32926) *(G-1959)*

St Agustine Elc Mtr Works Inc................904 829-8211
14 Center St Saint Augustine (32084) *(G-14897)*

St Augustine Dist Co LLC................904 825-4962
112 Riberia St Saint Augustine (32084) *(G-14898)*

St Augustine Marina Inc................904 824-4394
404 Riberia St Saint Augustine (32084) *(G-14899)*

St Augustine Record................904 829-6562
1 News Pl Saint Augustine (32086) *(G-14900)*

St Augustine Shipbuilding, Saint Augustine *Also called St Augustine Trawlers Inc (G-14901)*

St Augustine Trawlers Inc................904 824-4394
404 Riberia St Saint Augustine (32084) *(G-14901)*

St Cloud Door Company, Saint Cloud *Also called Aadi Inc (G-14919)*

St Cloud Prtg Signs & Cstm AP, Saint Cloud *Also called Megamalls Inc (G-14933)*

St Cloud Wldg Fabrication Inc................407 957-2344
3724 Hickory Tree Rd Saint Cloud (34772) *(G-14939)*

St Ives Burrups................305 685-7381
13449 Nw 42nd Ave Opa Locka (33054) *(G-11789)*

St John Designs, West Palm Beach *Also called American Cab Connection LLC* *(G-17923)*
St Johns Bky & Gourmet Fd Co (PA).............................813 727-3528
  6301 Powers Ave Jacksonville (32217) *(G-6502)*
St Johns Optical Systems LLC...................................407 280-3787
  101 Gordon St Sanford (32771) *(G-15390)*
St Johns Ship Building Inc.......................................386 328-6054
  560 Stokes Landing Rd Palatka (32177) *(G-12883)*
St Johns Turf Care LLC...352 258-3314
  1040 Hstngs Federal Pt Rd East Palatka (32131) *(G-3476)*
St Judas Tadeus Foundry Inc.....................................305 512-3612
  2160 W 10th Ct Hialeah (33010) *(G-5360)*
St Lucie Bakery, Port Saint Lucie *Also called Slb1989 Inc* *(G-14448)*
St Lucie Signs LLC...772 971-6363
  1147 Hernando St Fort Pierce (34949) *(G-4533)*
St Marks Powder Inc..850 577-2824
  7121 Coastal Hwy Crawfordville (32327) *(G-2232)*
St Mary Pharmacy Inc...727 585-1333
  1290 West Bay Dr Largo (33770) *(G-7690)*
St Marys Cabinetry Inc...239 331-1030
  4660 22nd Ave Se Naples (34117) *(G-10905)*
St Pete Auto Aids, Saint Petersburg *Also called Quality Industrial Chem Inc* *(G-15167)*
St Pete Paper Company..727 572-9868
  2324 20th St E Palmetto (34221) *(G-13192)*
St Petersburg Dist Co LLC..727 581-1544
  800 31st St S Saint Petersburg (33712) *(G-15197)*
St. Cloud Wldg & Fabrication, Saint Cloud *Also called St Cloud Wldg Fabrication Inc (G-14939)*
STA Cabinet Depot...719 502-5454
  320 State Road 16 Saint Augustine (32084) *(G-14902)*
STA-Con Incorporated (PA)..407 298-5940
  2525 S Orange Blossom Trl Apopka (32703) *(G-177)*
Stabil Concrete Pavers LLC.......................................941 739-7823
  7080 28th Street Ct E Sarasota (34243) *(G-15559)*
Stabil Concrete Products LLC....................................727 321-6000
  4451 8th Ave S Saint Petersburg (33711) *(G-15198)*
Stable Concrete Product, Saint Petersburg *Also called A To Z Concrete Products Inc (G-14950)*
Stacy Lee Montgomery..863 662-3163
  6320 Cypress Gardens Blvd Winter Haven (33884) *(G-18470)*
Stacy's Printing, Winter Haven *Also called Stacy Lee Montgomery (G-18470)*
Stadium 1 Software LLC..561 498-8356
  7115 Rue Notre Dame Miami Beach (33141) *(G-10235)*
Stadson Technology Corporation.................................561 372-2648
  3651 Fau Blvd Ste 400 Boca Raton (33431) *(G-694)*
Stainless Fabricators Inc...813 926-7113
  11107 Challenger Ave Odessa (33556) *(G-11581)*
Stainless Marine Inc...305 681-7893
  13800 Nw 19th Ave Opa Locka (33054) *(G-11790)*
Stainless Steel Kitchens Corp....................................305 999-1543
  7601 E Treasure Dr # 2120 North Bay Village (33141) *(G-11060)*
Stainless Stl Fbrction Svcs Fl, Palmetto *Also called Westcoast Metalworks Inc (G-13205)*
Stal Creations, Boca Raton *Also called Dolphine Jewelry Contracting (G-490)*
Stall Master Company (PA)..352 279-0089
  4377 Commercial Way Spring Hill (34606) *(G-16082)*
Stallion King LLC...321 503-7368
  7901 4th St N Ste 4691 Saint Petersburg (33702) *(G-15199)*
Stamas Yacht Inc...727 937-4118
  300 Pampas Ave Tarpon Springs (34689) *(G-17494)*
Stamm Manufacturing, Fort Pierce *Also called World Industrial Equipment Inc (G-4557)*
Stamp Concrete & Pavers Inc.....................................561 880-1527
  230 Cherry Ave Merritt Island (32953) *(G-8597)*
Stampco Inc..904 737-6144
  2930 Mercury Rd Jacksonville (32207) *(G-6503)*
Stan Weaver and Company...407 581-6940
  3663 All American Blvd Orlando (32810) *(G-12620)*
Stand Vertical Inc...407 474-0456
  983 Bennett Rd Apt 103 Orlando (32814) *(G-12621)*
Standard Carbon LLC..352 465-5959
  551 N Us Highway 41 Dunnellon (34432) *(G-3467)*
Standard Clay Mines...609 466-2986
  3804 Crossroads Pkwy Fort Pierce (34945) *(G-4534)*
Standard Industries Inc...813 248-7000
  5138 Madison Ave Tampa (33619) *(G-17298)*
Standard Injection Molding Inc...................................863 452-9090
  2027 State Road 64 W Avon Park (33825) *(G-289)*
Standard Kegs & Equipment, Medley *Also called Standard Kegs LLC (G-8325)*
Standard Kegs LLC..305 454-9721
  9106 Nw 106th St Medley (33178) *(G-8325)*
Standard Precast Inc..904 268-0466
  12300 Presidents Ct Jacksonville (32220) *(G-6504)*
Standard Printing & Copy Ctr, Saint Augustine *Also called Kj Reynolds Inc (G-14853)*
Standard Purification, Dunnellon *Also called Standard Carbon LLC (G-3467)*
Standard Register Inc...954 492-9986
  4710 Nw 15th Ave Fort Lauderdale (33309) *(G-4065)*
Standard Rivet Company Inc.....................................386 872-6477
  1640 S Segrave St South Daytona (32119) *(G-16029)*
Standard Sand & Silica Company (PA)............................863 422-7100
  1850 Us Highway 17 92 N Davenport (33837) *(G-2371)*

Standard Sand & Silica Company.................................352 625-2385
  15450 Ne 14th Street Rd Silver Springs (34488) *(G-16008)*
Standard Sand & Silica Company.................................863 419-9673
  2 Us Highway 17 92 N Haines City (33844) *(G-4916)*
Standard Technology Inc...386 671-7406
  1230 N Us Highway 1 # 18 Ormond Beach (32174) *(G-12795)*
Standard Truss & Roof Sup Inc...................................863 422-8293
  608 N 12th St Haines City (33844) *(G-4917)*
Stanley Chair Company Inc.......................................813 884-1436
  5110 W Hanna Ave Tampa (33634) *(G-17299)*
Stanley Industries of S Fla (PA)..................................954 929-8770
  3001 S Ocean Dr Apt 1423 Hollywood (33019) *(G-5664)*
Stanron Corporation...954 974-8050
  2770 Nw 63rd Ct Fort Lauderdale (33309) *(G-4066)*
Stanron Steel Specialties Div, Fort Lauderdale *Also called Stanron Corporation (G-4066)*
Stans Septic Svc Con Pdts Inc....................................941 639-3976
  5287 Duncan Rd Punta Gorda (33982) *(G-14533)*
Star Bakery Inc..305 633-4284
  3914 Nw 32nd Ave Miami (33142) *(G-9946)*
Star Bedding Mfg Corp..305 887-5209
  1053 E 14th St Hialeah (33010) *(G-5361)*
Star Brite, Davie *Also called Star-Brite Distributing Inc (G-2481)*
Star Envirotech Inc...714 427-1244
  1010 E 31st St Hialeah (33013) *(G-5362)*
Star Fabricators...904 899-6569
  989 Imeson Park Blvd Jacksonville (32218) *(G-6505)*
Star Led, Fort Lauderdale *Also called Green Applications LLC (G-3848)*
Star Pharmaceuticals LLC..800 845-7827
  2881 E Oakland Park Blvd # 221 Fort Lauderdale (33306) *(G-4067)*
Star Products...407 929-6969
  1632 Brook Hollow Dr Orlando (32824) *(G-12622)*
Star Quality Inc..813 875-9955
  4006 W Crest Ave Tampa (33614) *(G-17300)*
Star Sight Innovations..307 786-2911
  107 Tangelo Ter Crescent City (32112) *(G-2239)*
Star-Brite Distributing Inc.......................................954 587-6280
  4041 Sw 47th Ave Davie (33314) *(G-2481)*
Star-Seal of Florida Inc..954 484-8402
  2740 Nw 55th Ct Fort Lauderdale (33309) *(G-4068)*
Starboard Consulting LLC..407 622-6414
  2170 W State Road 434 Longwood (32779) *(G-7950)*
Starbridge Networks, Weston *Also called Networks Assets LLC (G-18272)*
Stark Enterprises Inc...941 341-0319
  1964 Barber Rd Sarasota (34240) *(G-15837)*
Starke Waste Wtr Trtmnt Plant....................................904 964-7999
  602 Edwards Rd Starke (32091) *(G-16105)*
Starkey Products Inc...386 479-3908
  425 Fox Run Debary (32713) *(G-2644)*
Starline Education Inc..808 631-1818
  414 Garden St Titusville (32796) *(G-17618)*
Starlite Inc..727 392-2929
  10861 91st Ter Seminole (33772) *(G-15989)*
Starlock Inc..305 477-2303
  8252 Nw 30th Ter Doral (33122) *(G-3375)*
Starmakers Rising Inc (PA).......................................561 989-8999
  17239 Boca Club Blvd # 6 Boca Raton (33487) *(G-695)*
Starmark, Safety Harbor *Also called Vanlympia Inc (G-14800)*
Starr Wheel Group Inc..954 935-5536
  3659 Nw 124th Ave Coral Springs (33065) *(G-2214)*
Start Stop.com, Tarpon Springs *Also called Hth Engineering Inc (G-17476)*
Startech Lake City Inc..386 466-1969
  109 Nw Spring Hill Ct Lake City (32055) *(G-7047)*
Stat Biomedical LLC...210 365-1495
  2865 Night Heron Dr Mims (32754) *(G-10450)*
Statcorp Medical, Jacksonville *Also called Spacelabs Healthcare Inc (G-6497)*
State Lighting Co Inc...561 371-9529
  405 4th Way West Palm Beach (33407) *(G-18161)*
State of Florida..850 488-1234
  250 Marriott Dr Tallahassee (32301) *(G-16505)*
Statement Marine LLC...727 525-5235
  12011 49th St N Clearwater (33762) *(G-1796)*
Statements 2000 LLC...561 249-1587
  1374 N Killian Dr Ste A West Palm Beach (33403) *(G-18162)*
Stateside Indus Solutions LLC....................................305 301-4052
  14900 Sw 30th St # 278663 Miramar (33027) *(G-10546)*
Statewide Blnds Shtters More I....................................813 480-8638
  3030 Starkey Blvd New Port Richey (34655) *(G-10985)*
Statewide Cstm Cbinets Fla Inc...................................813 788-3856
  38535 Palm Grove Dr Zephyrhills (33542) *(G-18631)*
Statewide Materials, Titusville *Also called Rock Ridge Materials Inc (G-17615)*
Statgear, Fort Lauderdale *Also called Magenav Inc (G-3927)*
Stature Software LLC...888 782-8881
  620 Palencia Club Dr # 104 Saint Augustine (32095) *(G-14903)*
Stay Smart Care LLC...321 682-7113
  941 W Morse Blvd Winter Park (32789) *(G-18540)*
Stayfilm Inc..786 961-1007
  2234 Sw 8th St Miami (33135) *(G-9947)*
Steadfast Woodworking Inc.......................................386 748-1744
  680 Cumberland Rd Deland (32724) *(G-2904)*

Stedi Press, Doral *Also called Capra Graphics Inc (G-3152)*

Steeda Engineering and Mfg LLC 954 960-0774
1351 Nw Steeda Way Pompano Beach (33069) *(G-14198)*

Steel City Inc 850 785-9596
749 E 15th St Panama City (32405) *(G-13311)*

Steel Cnstr Systems Holdg Co 407 438-1664
11250 Astronaut Blvd Orlando (32837) *(G-12623)*

Steel Components Inc 954 427-6820
4701 Johnson Rd Ste 1 Coconut Creek (33073) *(G-2007)*

Steel Fabricators LLC (HQ) 954 772-0440
721 Ne 44th St Oakland Park (33334) *(G-11298)*

Steel Plus Service Center Inc 407 328-7169
2525 Magnolia Ave Sanford (32773) *(G-15391)*

Steel Products Inc 941 351-8128
1821 Myrtle St Sarasota (34234) *(G-15838)*

Steel Systems, Pensacola *Also called Bell Steel Company (G-13454)*

Steel Technology & Design 863 665-2525
401 Howard Ave Apt C Lakeland (33815) *(G-7448)*

Steele Industries Inc 800 674-7302
10510 Portal Xing Ste 101 Bradenton (34211) *(G-1052)*

Steen Aero Lab LLC 321 725-4160
1451 Clearmont St Ne Palm Bay (32905) *(G-12922)*

Steering & Suspension Parts 786 523-3726
2740 Nw 35th St Miami (33142) *(G-9948)*

Steevie Stash LLC 954 860-3138
1733 Nw 112th Ter Miami (33167) *(G-9949)*

Steiner-Atlantic LLC 305 754-4551
1714 Nw 215th St Miami Gardens (33056) *(G-10275)*

Stellar Group of South Florida 305 715-7246
5574 Nw 79th Ave Doral (33166) *(G-3376)*

Stellar On-Site Llc 904 945-1908
27167 Betina Dr Hilliard (32046) *(G-5477)*

Stellar Sign and Design LLC 407 660-3174
3851 Center Loop Orlando (32808) *(G-12624)*

Stellar Signs Grap 561 721-6060
5401 N Haverhill Rd West Palm Beach (33407) *(G-18163)*

Stellarnet Inc 813 855-8687
14390 Carlson Cir Tampa (33626) *(G-17301)*

Stem Holdings Inc (PA) 561 948-5410
2201 Nw Corp Blvd Ste 205 Boca Raton (33431) *(G-696)*

Stem Holdings Florida Inc 561 948-5410
2201 Nw Corp Blvd Ste 205 Boca Raton (33431) *(G-697)*

Stemler Corporation 727 577-1216
1873 64th Ave N Saint Petersburg (33702) *(G-15200)*

Stemtech Healthsciences Corp 954 715-6000
10370 Usa Today Way Miramar (33025) *(G-10547)*

Stemworks LLC 407 595-8451
12301 Lake Underhill Rd Orlando (32828) *(G-12625)*

Stenner Pump Company Inc (PA) 904 641-1666
3174 Desalvo Rd Jacksonville (32246) *(G-6506)*

Step Zone LLC 850 983-3758
6674 Elva St Milton (32570) *(G-10437)*

Stephen Gould Corporation 813 886-8460
5132 Tampa West Blvd A Tampa (33634) *(G-17302)*

Stephen Shives 352 454-6522
14628 Se 95th Ct Summerfield (34491) *(G-16260)*

Stephens Advertising Inc 904 354-7004
7029 Commwl Ave Ste 9 Jacksonville (32220) *(G-6507)*

Stephens Group 941 623-9689
20101 Peachland Blvd # 2 Port Charlotte (33954) *(G-14316)*

Stephs Woodworking LLC 772 571-2661
6065 21st St Sw Vero Beach (32968) *(G-17803)*

Stepincorp Auto Solutions LLC 786 864-3222
12480 Nw 25th St Ste 115 Miami (33182) *(G-9950)*

Steriline North America I 941 405-2039
872 62nd Street Cir E Bradenton (34208) *(G-1053)*

Steripack (usa) Limited LLC 863 648-2333
4255 S Pipkin Rd Lakeland (33811) *(G-7449)*

Steris Corporation 813 852-8002
3903 Northdale Blvd 120e Tampa (33624) *(G-17303)*

Steritool Inc 904 388-3672
2376 Lake Shore Blvd Jacksonville (32210) *(G-6508)*

Sterling Eqp Mfg Cntl Fla Inc 352 669-3255
803 Line St Umatilla (32784) *(G-17652)*

Sterling Facility Services LLC 772 871-2161
523 Nw Peacock Blvd Port Saint Lucie (34986) *(G-14450)*

Sterling Fibers Inc 850 994-5311
5005 Sterling Way Milton (32571) *(G-10438)*

Sterling Industry LLC 561 845-2440
834 W 13th Ct Riviera Beach (33404) *(G-14677)*

Sterling Manufacturing, Sarasota *Also called Ssvm Partners Inc (G-15835)*

Sterling Mdr Inc 954 725-2777
741 Nw 42nd Way Deerfield Beach (33442) *(G-2815)*

Sterling Steel Fabrications 561 366-8600
1139 53rd Ct N Mangonia Park (33407) *(G-8101)*

Sterling Stl Cstm Alum Fbrcton 561 386-7166
837 W 13th St Riviera Beach (33404) *(G-14678)*

Stern Bloom Media Inc 954 454-8522
20454 Ne 34th Ct Miami (33180) *(G-9951)*

Stern Brands Inc 321 622-8584
3153 Skyway Cir Melbourne (32934) *(G-8531)*

Steve Baie Enterprises Inc 407 822-3997
2456 Clark St Apopka (32703) *(G-178)*

Steve Printer Inc 941 375-8657
601 Cypress Ave Venice (34285) *(G-17719)*

Steve Unser Cabinetry Inc 239 631-2951
5550 Shirley St Naples (34109) *(G-10906)*

Steven Chancas 352 629-5016
1519 S Pine Ave Ocala (34471) *(G-11499)*

Steven K Bakum Inc 561 804-9110
4634 S Dixie Hwy West Palm Beach (33405) *(G-18164)*

Steven M Roessler LLC 321 773-2300
1859 South Patrick Dr Indian Harbour Beach (32937) *(G-5808)*

Steven R Durante 954 564-9913
1056 Ne 44th Pl Oakland Park (33334) *(G-11299)*

Stewart Materials Inc 561 972-4517
2875 Jupiter Park Dr # 1100 Jupiter (33458) *(G-6805)*

Stewart-Hedrick Inc 941 907-0090
6001 Business Blvd Lakewood Ranch (34240) *(G-7487)*

Stewarts Elc Mtr Works Inc 407 859-1837
8951 Trussway Blvd Orlando (32824) *(G-12626)*

Stick With US Delivery Svc LLC 561 425-4910
1481 7th St West Palm Beach (33401) *(G-18165)*

Stiebel Eltron Inc 800 826-5537
2060 Whitfield Park Ave Sarasota (34243) *(G-15560)*

Still Water Industries Inc 561 845-6033
8400 Garden Rd Ste A West Palm Beach (33404) *(G-18166)*

Stilldragon North America LLC 561 845-8009
7788 Centl Indus Dr Ste 6 Riviera Beach (33404) *(G-14679)*

Stimwave LLC 800 965-5134
1310 Park Central Blvd S Pompano Beach (33064) *(G-14199)*

Stimwave Technologies Inc (PA) 800 965-5134
1310 Park Central Blvd S Pompano Beach (33064) *(G-14200)*

Stinger Fiberglass Designs Inc 321 268-1118
1525 Armstrong Dr Titusville (32780) *(G-17619)*

Stirling Winery 727 734-4025
461 Main St Dunedin (34698) *(G-3459)*

Stitch By Stitch 305 979-2275
1675 W 49th St Hialeah (33012) *(G-5363)*

Stitch Count Inc 609 929-9019
20404 Ne 16th Pl North Miami Beach (33179) *(G-11162)*

Stitch Ink Inc 954 203-0868
2684 Nw 31st Ave Lauderdale Lakes (33311) *(G-7720)*

Stitch Logo Inc 727 446-0228
2165 Sunnydale Blvd Ste H Clearwater (33765) *(G-1797)*

Stitched National Harbor LLC 786 483-8740
701 S Miami Ave Unit 177c Miami (33130) *(G-9952)*

Stitchez LLC 904 221-9148
13714 Longs Landing Rd W Jacksonville (32225) *(G-6509)*

Stitching Around Inc 305 665-1600
4862 Sw 72nd Ave Miami (33155) *(G-9953)*

Stitching Heart LLC 904 379-7990
8174 Lexington Dr Jacksonville (32208) *(G-6510)*

Stm Industries LLC 813 854-3544
9524 N Trask St Tampa (33624) *(G-17304)*

Stockdale Technologies Inc 407 323-5121
104 Commerce St Lake Mary (32746) *(G-7108)*

Stocking Factory 305 745-2681
30554 5th Ave Big Pine Key (33043) *(G-373)*

Stoller Chemical Co of Florida 352 357-3173
1451 Pine Grove Rd Eustis (32726) *(G-3566)*

Stoltz Industries Inc 954 792-3270
9704 E Tree Tops Ct Davie (33328) *(G-2482)*

Stone and Equipment Inc 305 665-0002
4681 Sw 72nd Ave Ste 104 Miami (33155) *(G-9954)*

Stone Brick Pavers Inc 407 844-1455
1699 Cambridge Village Ct Ocoee (34761) *(G-11526)*

Stone Center Inc 863 669-0292
2205 E Edgewood Dr Lakeland (33803) *(G-7450)*

Stone Central of Central Fla 352 689-0075
3200 Ne 37th Pl Wildwood (34785) *(G-18321)*

Stone Craft Masters LLC 786 401-7060
7975 Nw 54th St Doral (33166) *(G-3377)*

Stone Design By Santos LLC 954 366-1919
1440 Nw 14th Ave Pompano Beach (33069) *(G-14201)*

Stone Harbor Homes LLC 239 672-7687
5225 Sw 22nd Pl Cape Coral (33914) *(G-1393)*

Stone Metals LLC 813 605-7363
4021 S Frontage Rd Plant City (33566) *(G-13806)*

Stone Mosaics 321 773-3635
1735 Biltz Ave Ne Palm Bay (32905) *(G-12923)*

Stone Palace 407 896-0872
1901 N Orange Ave Orlando (32804) *(G-12627)*

Stone Systems South Fla LLC 954 584-4058
3501 Nw 16th St Lauderhill (33311) *(G-7743)*

Stone Trend International Inc 941 927-9113
6244 Clark Center Ave # 3 Sarasota (34238) *(G-15839)*

Stonecrfters Archtctral Prcast (PA) 727 544-1210
10820 75th St Ste A Seminole (33777) *(G-15990)*

Stonehardscapes Intl Inc......................................954 989-4050
   5755 Powerline Rd Fort Lauderdale (33309) (G-4069)
Stonehenge Architectural Corp.............................954 325-6729
   308 Se 5th St Dania (33004) (G-2343)
Stonehenge Gems, Pompano Beach Also called Our Warehouse Inc (G-14113)
Stonelight LLC...239 514-3272
   4775 Aston Gardens Way # 205 Naples (34109) (G-10907)
Stoneworks Inc..305 666-6676
   6840 Sw 81st Ter Miami (33143) (G-9955)
Stoneworks of Art, Miami Also called Stoneworks Inc (G-9955)
Stonexchange Inc...305 513-9795
   9605 Nw 13th St Doral (33172) (G-3378)
Stony Coral Investments LLC..............................941 704-5391
   23410 78th Ave E Myakka City (34251) (G-10647)
Stony Creek Sand & Gravel LLC (PA)....................804 229-0015
   2103 N Riverside Dr Pompano Beach (33062) (G-14202)
Storage and Canopy Inc.......................................863 840-4005
   990 Us Highway 27 S Venus (33960) (G-17729)
Storage Building Company LLC.............................863 738-1319
   429 10th Ave W Ste B Palmetto (34221) (G-13193)
Storage Heaven, Plantation Also called Multimedia Effects Inc (G-13871)
Store It Cold LLC...720 456-1178
   9731 Nw 114th Way Medley (33178) (G-8326)
Storm Depot Palm Beach LLC..............................561 721-9800
   1202 S Congress Ave Ste A West Palm Beach (33406) (G-18167)
Stormforce Jacksonville LLC...............................904 288-6639
   6111 Gazebo Park Pl N # 21 Jacksonville (32257) (G-6511)
Stormquant Inc...408 840-2003
   1431 Chaffee Dr Ste 1 Titusville (32780) (G-17620)
Storngerrx, Miami Also called Asb Sports Group LLC (G-8757)
Storopack Inc...305 805-9696
   11825 Nw 100th Rd Ste 5 Medley (33178) (G-8327)
Storterchilds Printing Co Inc...............................352 376-2658
   1540 Ne Waldo Rd Gainesville (32641) (G-4766)
Story Citrus Inc..863 638-1619
   20205 Hwy 27 Lake Wales (33853) (G-7175)
Stout Defense PA..352 665-9266
   5215 Sw 91st Ter Gainesville (32608) (G-4767)
Stover Manufacturing LLC..................................386 238-3775
   825 Ballough Rd Daytona Beach (32114) (G-2604)
Stover Manufacturing LLC....................................386 235-7060
   919 Alexander Ave Port Orange (32129) (G-14350)
Straight Line Mllwk & Sup Inc..............................561 422-0444
   1315 N Jog Rd Ste 101 West Palm Beach (33413) (G-18168)
Straight Polarity Welding Inc...............................727 530-7224
   12855 Belcher Rd S Ste 19 Largo (33773) (G-7691)
Strand Core, Milton Also called Central Wire Industries LLC (G-10422)
Strands Inc (PA)...415 398-4333
   3390 Mary St Ste 116 Miami (33133) (G-9956)
Strang Communications, Lake Mary Also called Plus Communications Inc (G-7100)
Strasse Forged LLC...786 701-3649
   13979 Sw 140th St Miami (33186) (G-9957)
Strasser Enterprises..386 677-5163
   1504 State Ave Daytona Beach (32117) (G-2605)
Strata Analytics Holdg US LLC..............................954 349-4630
   1560 Sawgrs Corp Pkwy Sunrise (33323) (G-16373)
Stratco Pharmaceuticals LLC...............................813 403-5060
   2600 Lakepointe Pkwy Odessa (33556) (G-11582)
Strategic Brands Inc..516 745-6100
   2810 Center Port Cir Pompano Beach (33064) (G-14203)
Strategic Products Inc...321 752-0441
   5100 Laguna Vista Dr Melbourne (32934) (G-8532)
Strategy Marketing Group, Fort Myers Also called Panther Printing Inc (G-4357)
Stratford Care Usa Inc (HQ)...............................877 498-2002
   2600 Lakepointe Pkwy Odessa (33556) (G-11583)
Stratford Corporation..727 443-1573
   1555 Sunshine Dr Clearwater (33765) (G-1798)
Stratonet Inc (PA)...863 382-8503
   935 Mall Ring Rd Sebring (33870) (G-15944)
Stratos Airparts Corp..772 266-9157
   7897 Sw Jack James Dr Stuart (34997) (G-16227)
Stratos Light Wave Inc..321 308-4100
   1333 Gateway Dr Ste 1007 Melbourne (32901) (G-8533)
Stratos Optical, Melbourne Also called Stratos Light Wave Inc (G-8533)
Stratton Home Decor, Sunrise Also called Jem Art Inc (G-16330)
Stratton Inc Dm...904 268-6052
   7653 Bayard Blvd Jacksonville (32256) (G-6512)
Stratus Pharmaceuticals Inc...............................305 254-6793
   12379 Sw 130th St Miami (33186) (G-9958)
Straw Giant Company..561 430-0729
   10290 W Atlantic Ave Delray Beach (33448) (G-3022)
Straw Life Inc..386 935-2850
   25434 87th Dr O Brien (32071) (G-11225)
Stream Line Publishing Inc...................................561 655-8778
   331 Se Mizner Blvd Boca Raton (33432) (G-698)
Stream2sea LLC..866 960-9513
   2498 Commerce Ct Bowling Green (33834) (G-833)
Streaming Store, The, Jacksonville Also called Videolinq Streaming Svcs LLC (G-6591)

Streamline Aluminum Inc......................................239 561-7200
   12651 Metro Pkwy Ste 1 Fort Myers (33966) (G-4406)
Streamline Extrusion Inc.....................................727 796-4277
   3105 Ashwood Ln Safety Harbor (34695) (G-14799)
Streamline Numerics Inc.....................................352 271-8841
   3221 Nw 13th St Ste A Gainesville (32609) (G-4768)
Streamline Performance Boats C.............................305 393-8848
   7711 W 22nd Ave Hialeah (33016) (G-5364)
Streamline Publishing Inc.....................................561 655-8778
   331 Se Mizner Blvd Boca Raton (33432) (G-699)
Streamline Technologies Inc................................407 679-1696
   1900 Town Plaza Ct Winter Springs (32708) (G-18578)
Street Elements Magazine Inc..............................813 935-5894
   3902 E Powhatan Ave Tampa (33610) (G-17305)
Street Lighting Equipment Corp.............................954 961-9140
   2601 W Abiaca Cir Davie (33328) (G-2483)
Street Signs USA Inc...561 848-1411
   1137 Silver Beach Rd Lake Park (33403) (G-7134)
Streetrod Productions Inc....................................352 751-3953
   11962 County Road 101 The Villages (32162) (G-17557)
Streetrod Productions Florida, The Villages Also called Streetrod Productions Inc (G-17557)
Streetwise Maps Inc (HQ)....................................941 358-1956
   4376 Independence Ct A Sarasota (34234) (G-15840)
Strena Medical LLC...305 406-3931
   3016 Nw 82nd Ave Doral (33122) (G-3379)
Stretch Blow Systems LLC...................................239 275-2207
   5237 Smmrlin Commons Blvd Fort Myers (33907) (G-4407)
Strictly Ecommerce...352 672-6566
   5210 Ne 49th Ter Gainesville (32609) (G-4769)
Strictly Toolboxes..352 672-6566
   4820 Ne 49th Rd Gainesville (32609) (G-4770)
Striker Orthopedic, Sarasota Also called Howmedica Osteonics Corp (G-15702)
Stripping Alpaca LLC...207 208-9687
   2301 Collins Ave Apt 1143 Miami Beach (33139) (G-10236)
Strive Development Corporation.............................850 689-2124
   3100 Adora Teal Way Crestview (32539) (G-2255)
Strong Enterprises, Orlando Also called S E Inc (G-12564)
Strong Publications LLC..813 362-8224
   3809 Tristram Loop Land O Lakes (34638) (G-7505)
Strong Tower Vineyard...352 799-7612
   17810 Forge Dr Spring Hill (34610) (G-16088)
Strongbridge International LLC...............................904 278-7499
   154 Industrial Loop S Orange Park (32073) (G-11842)
Stronghaven, Jacksonville Also called K & G Box Inc (G-6233)
Structall Building Systems Inc (PA)........................813 855-2627
   350 Burbank Rd Oldsmar (34677) (G-11698)
Structral Prestressed Inds Inc...............................305 556-6699
   11405 Nw 112th Ct Doral (33178) (G-3380)
Structural Cnstr Orlando Inc.................................407 383-9719
   2200 Winter Springs Blvd Oviedo (32765) (G-12848)
Structural Composites Inc...................................321 951-9464
   360 East Dr Melbourne (32904) (G-8534)
Structural Steel of Brevard...................................321 726-0271
   6951 Vickie Cir Ste A Melbourne (32904) (G-8535)
Structure Glass Solutions LLC...............................954 499-9450
   13202 Nw 107th Ave Unit 8 Hialeah (33018) (G-5365)
Structure Medical LLC (HQ)................................239 262-5551
   9935 Business Cir Naples (34112) (G-10908)
Structurz Exhibits & Graphics, Fort Lauderdale Also called J R Wheeler
Corporation (G-3890)
Strumba Media LLC (PA)......................................800 948-4205
   382 Ne 191st St Ste 6920 Miami (33179) (G-9959)
Stryker Mako, Weston Also called Mako Surgical Corp (G-18266)
Stryker Orthopaedics, Tampa Also called Howmedica Osteonics Corp (G-16924)
Stryker Orthopedics..904 296-6000
   7014 A C Skinner Pkwy Jacksonville (32256) (G-6513)
Stryker Spine, Fort Lauderdale Also called Howmedica Osteonics Corp (G-3870)
STS Air-Pro, Miramar Also called STS Distribution Solutions LLC (G-10548)
STS Apparel Corp...305 628-4000
   325 W 74th Pl Hialeah (33014) (G-5366)
STS Distribution Solutions LLC..............................844 359-4673
   11650 Miramar Pkwy # 500 Miramar (33025) (G-10548)
Stuart Boatworks Inc...772 600-7121
   3515 Se Lionel Ter Stuart (34997) (G-16228)
Stuart Building Products LLC...............................239 461-3100
   3601 Work Dr Fort Myers (33916) (G-4408)
Stuart Composites LLC.......................................772 266-4285
   6900 Nw 77th Ct Miami (33166) (G-9960)
Stuart Industries Inc...305 651-3474
   526 Ne 190th St Miami (33179) (G-9961)
Stuart Magazine...954 332-3214
   1401 E Broward Blvd # 206 Fort Lauderdale (33301) (G-4070)
Stuart News, Stuart Also called Port St Lucie News (G-16199)
Stuart News (HQ)...772 287-1550
   1939 Se Federal Hwy Stuart (34994) (G-16229)
Stuart News..772 287-1550
   1939 Se Federal Hwy Stuart (34994) (G-16230)
Stuart Pro Green...772 286-0510
   3121 Se Slater St Stuart (34997) (G-16231)

A
L
P
H
A
B
E
T
I
C

Stuart Promotional Products, Brooksville *Also called Ped-Stuart Corporation* ***(G-1188)***
Stuart Propeller & Marine, Stuart *Also called E M P Inc* ***(G-16142)***
Stuart Stair & Furniture Mfg 772 287-4097
3220 Se Dominica Ter Stuart (34997) ***(G-16232)***
Stuart Web Inc 772 287-8022
5675 Se Grouper Ave Stuart (34997) ***(G-16233)***
Stuart Yacht Builders 561 747-1947
450 Sw Salerno Rd Stuart (34997) ***(G-16234)***
Stuart-Dean Co Inc 305 652-9595
2279 Nw 102nd Pl Doral (33172) ***(G-3381)***
Studio 21 Lighting Inc 941 355-2677
1507 Mango Ave Sarasota (34237) ***(G-15841)***
Studio Becker Florida LLC 305 514-0400
4216 Ponce De Leon Blvd Coral Gables (33146) ***(G-2112)***
Studio Luxe Cstm Cabinetry LLC 941 371-4010
2035 Constitution Blvd Sarasota (34231) ***(G-15842)***
Studio M LLC 954 918-8528
225 Nw 79th Ter Margate (33063) ***(G-8155)***
Stump Industries LLC 239 940-5754
1300 Lee St Fort Myers (33901) ***(G-4409)***
Stuntwear LLC 305 842-2115
6538 Collins Ave Unit 414 Miami Beach (33141) ***(G-10237)***
Stush AP USA/Stush Style LLC 404 940-3445
2500 N University Dr Sunrise (33322) ***(G-16374)***
Style Crest Products 863 709-8735
5001 Gateway Blvd Ste 14 Lakeland (33811) ***(G-7451)***
Style-View Products Inc 305 634-9688
1800 N Byshore Dr Apt 400 Miami (33132) ***(G-9962)***
Stylecraft Cabinets Mfg Inc 941 474-4824
2780 Ivy St Unit 1 Englewood (34224) ***(G-3525)***
Stylecraft Fine Cabinetry, Stuart *Also called Omt Inc* ***(G-16192)***
Styleline Doors, Sarasota *Also called Commercial Rfrg Door Co Inc* ***(G-15639)***
Stylepoint Us LLC 954 990-6778
1401 Ne 9th St Apt 39 Fort Lauderdale (33304) ***(G-4071)***
Styleview Industries, Fort Myers *Also called Fresco Group Inc* ***(G-4263)***
Stylors Inc 904 765-4453
640 W 41st St Jacksonville (32206) ***(G-6514)***
Sublimation Station Inc 407 605-5300
1656 N Goldenrod Rd Orlando (32807) ***(G-12628)***
Submersible Systems LLC 714 842-6566
3425 Bannerman Rd 105-4 Tallahassee (32312) ***(G-16506)***
Sugar Cane Growers Coop Fla (PA) 561 996-5556
1500 George Wedgworth Way Belle Glade (33430) ***(G-343)***
Sugar Fancies LLC 786 558-9087
1091 Sw 134th Ct Miami (33184) ***(G-9963)***
Sugar Works Distillery LLC 386 463-0120
1714 State Road 44 New Smyrna Beach (32168) ***(G-11013)***
Sugart, Lauderhill *Also called Add-V LLC* ***(G-7724)***
Suinpla LLC 786 747-4829
12605 Nw 115th Ave # 106 Medley (33178) ***(G-8328)***
Suits Stlttos Lpstick Fndtion 954 903-9426
1995 E Oklnd Prk Blvd Fort Lauderdale (33306) ***(G-4072)***
Sukalde Inc (PA) 786 399-0087
5271 Sw 8th St Apt 213 Coral Gables (33134) ***(G-2113)***
Sullenberger Inc 813 988-4525
8949 Maislin Dr Tampa (33637) ***(G-17306)***
Sullivan Penny Woodworking 561 860-1163
2 Abbey Ln Apt 104 Delray Beach (33446) ***(G-3023)***
Sulzer Ems Inc 407 858-9447
7200 Lake Ellenor Dr Orlando (32809) ***(G-12629)***
Sumiflex LLC 954 578-6998
773 Shotgun Rd Sunrise (33326) ***(G-16375)***
Summation Research Inc 321 254-2580
305 East Dr Ste D Melbourne (32904) ***(G-8536)***
Summit Aerospace Inc 305 871-5449
4000 Nw 28th St Miami (33142) ***(G-9964)***
Summit ATL Productions LLC 407 930-5488
3320 Vineland Rd Ste A Orlando (32811) ***(G-12630)***
Summit Dental Systems, Pompano Beach *Also called SDS Dental Inc* ***(G-14170)***
Summit Holsters LLC 386 383-4090
843 Superior St Deltona (32725) ***(G-3054)***
Summit Orthopedic Tech Inc 239 919-8081
2975 Horseshoe Dr S # 100 Naples (34104) ***(G-10909)***
Sumter Planning Department, Bushnell *Also called County of Sumter* ***(G-1242)***
Sun & Earth Microbiology Llc 786 354-8894
20205 Sw 79th Ct Cutler Bay (33189) ***(G-2305)***
Sun 3d Corporation 954 210-6010
1951 W Copans Rd Ste 8 Pompano Beach (33064) ***(G-14204)***
Sun Barrier Products Inc 407 830-9085
159 Baywood Ave Longwood (32750) ***(G-7951)***
Sun Belt Graphics Inc 954 424-3139
15431 Sw 14th St Davie (33326) ***(G-2484)***
Sun Business Systems Inc (PA) 727 547-6540
10900 47th St N Clearwater (33762) ***(G-1799)***
Sun Catalina Holdings LLC 305 558-4777
16200 Nw 59th Ave Ste 101 Miami Lakes (33014) ***(G-10361)***
Sun City Blinds LLC (PA) 727 522-6695
2426 63rd Ter E Ellenton (34222) ***(G-3513)***
Sun Coast Converters Inc 850 864-2361
631 Anchors St Nw Fort Walton Beach (32548) ***(G-4610)***
Sun Coast Industries LLC 941 355-7166
7350 26th Ct E Sarasota (34243) ***(G-15561)***
Sun Coast Media Group Inc (HQ) 941 206-1300
23170 Harborview Rd Port Charlotte (33980) ***(G-14317)***
Sun Coast Media Group Inc 941 207-1000
200 E Venice Ave Fl 1 Venice (34285) ***(G-17720)***
Sun Coast Media Group Inc 863 494-7600
23170 Harborview Rd Punta Gorda (33980) ***(G-14534)***
Sun Coast Media Group Inc 941 681-3000
120 W Dearborn St Englewood (34223) ***(G-3538)***
Sun Coast Media Group Inc 941 206-1900
2726 Tamiami Trl Ste B Port Charlotte (33952) ***(G-14318)***
Sun Coast Orthotics Assn, Miami *Also called Mahnkes Orthtics Prsthtics of* ***(G-9499)***
Sun Coast Paper & Envelope Inc 727 545-9566
2050 Tall Pines Dr Ste A Largo (33771) ***(G-7692)***
Sun Coast Pavers, Brooksville *Also called Pavers Inc* ***(G-1187)***
Sun Coast Surgical & Med Sup 813 881-0065
2711 N 58th St Tampa (33619) ***(G-17307)***
Sun Coatings LLC 727 531-4100
4701 E 7th Ave Tampa (33605) ***(G-17308)***
Sun Coatings, Inc., Tampa *Also called Sun Coatings LLC* ***(G-17308)***
Sun Electronic Systems Inc 321 383-9400
1845 Shepard Dr Titusville (32780) ***(G-17621)***
Sun Graphic Technologies Inc 941 753-7541
2310 Whitfield Park Ave Sarasota (34243) ***(G-15562)***
Sun Gro Horticulture Dist Inc 407 291-1676
6021 Beggs Rd Orlando (32810) ***(G-12631)***
Sun Hydraulics Corporation 941 362-1300
803 Tallevast Rd Sarasota (34243) ***(G-15563)***
Sun Indalex LLC 561 394-0550
5200 Town Center Cir # 470 Boca Raton (33486) ***(G-700)***
Sun Krafts of Volusia County 386 441-1961
217 Royal Dunes Cir Ormond Beach (32176) ***(G-12796)***
Sun Light Products, Miramar *Also called General Metal Intl Inc* ***(G-10496)***
Sun Mackie LLC 561 394-0550
5200 Town Center Cir # 470 Boca Raton (33486) ***(G-701)***
Sun Metals Systems Inc 813 889-0718
5008 Tampa West Blvd Tampa (33634) ***(G-17309)***
Sun Microstamping Technologies, Clearwater *Also called ES Investments LLC* ***(G-1590)***
Sun Microsystems, Port Charlotte *Also called Oracle America Inc* ***(G-14310)***
Sun Microsystems, Orlando *Also called Oracle America Inc* ***(G-12445)***
Sun Nation Corp 954 822-5460
2861 Nw 22nd Ter Pompano Beach (33069) ***(G-14205)***
Sun Nuclear Corp 321 259-6862
425 Pineda Ct Ste A Melbourne (32940) ***(G-8537)***
Sun Nuclear Corp (HQ) 321 259-6862
3275 Suntree Blvd Melbourne (32940) ***(G-8538)***
Sun Orchard LLC 863 422-5062
1200 S 30th St Haines City (33844) ***(G-4918)***
Sun Orchard LLC (PA) 786 646-9200
8600 Nw 36th St Ste 250 Doral (33166) ***(G-3382)***
Sun Paper Company 305 887-0040
7925 Nw 12th St Ste 321 Doral (33126) ***(G-3383)***
Sun Pipe and Valves LLC 772 408-5530
710 Nw Enterprise Dr Port Saint Lucie (34986) ***(G-14451)***
Sun Print Management LLC 727 945-0255
5441 Provost Dr Holiday (34690) ***(G-5504)***
Sun Publication of Florida, Clermont *Also called News Leader Inc* ***(G-1877)***
Sun Publications Florida Inc 321 402-0257
108 Church St Kissimmee (34741) ***(G-6961)***
Sun Publications Florida Inc (HQ) 863 583-1202
7060 Havertys Way Lakeland (33805) ***(G-7452)***
Sun Screen Print Inc 904 674-0520
4849 Dawin Rd Ste 3 Jacksonville (32207) ***(G-6515)***
Sun Screenprinting Lindycal, Sarasota *Also called Sun Graphic Technologies Inc* ***(G-15562)***
Sun Shell Blinds & Shades Corp 678 975-1082
17649 Sw 54th St Miramar (33029) ***(G-10549)***
Sun State Systems Inc 904 269-2544
140 Industrial Loop W Orange Park (32073) ***(G-11843)***
Sun Valley Tech Solutions Inc 480 463-4101
31437 Heatherstone Dr Wesley Chapel (33543) ***(G-17887)***
Sun Works Plastics Inc 727 573-2343
15373 Roosevelt Blvd # 202 Clearwater (33760) ***(G-1800)***
Sun-Art Designs Inc 954 929-6622
2806 N 29th Ave Ste 2 Hollywood (33020) ***(G-5665)***
Sun-Glo Plating Co, Clearwater *Also called Pozin Enterprises Inc* ***(G-1745)***
Sun-Pac Manufacturing Inc 813 925-8787
14201 Mccormick Dr Tampa (33626) ***(G-17310)***
Sun-Rock Inc 727 938-0013
904 Anclote Rd Tarpon Springs (34689) ***(G-17495)***
Sun-Sentinel Company LLC (HQ) 954 356-4000
500 E Broward Blvd # 800 Fort Lauderdale (33394) ***(G-4073)***
Sun-Sentinel Company LLC 954 356-4000
333 Sw 12th Ave Deerfield Beach (33442) ***(G-2816)***
Sun-Sentinel Company Inc 954 735-6414
3585 Nw 54th St Fort Lauderdale (33309) ***(G-4074)***

1064 2022 Harris Florida Manufacturers Directory (G-0000) Company's Geographic Section entry number

ALPHABETIC SECTION
Sunshine Lighters

Sun-Tek Manufacturing Inc 407 859-2117
10303 General Dr Orlando (32824) ***(G-12632)***
Sun-Tek Skylights, Orlando *Also called Sun-Tek Manufacturing Inc* ***(G-12632)***
Sunbeam Americas Holdings LLC 561 912-4100
2381 Nw Executive Ctr Dr Boca Raton (33431) ***(G-702)***
Sunbeam Bread, Jacksonville *Also called Flowers Bkg Jacksonville LLC* ***(G-6114)***
Sunbeam Outdoor Products, Boca Raton *Also called American Household Inc* ***(G-407)***
Sunbeam Products Inc (HQ) 561 912-4100
2381 Nw Executive Ctr Dr Boca Raton (33431) ***(G-703)***
Sunbelt Forest Ventures LLC 863 496-3054
6001 Foxtrot Ave Bartow (33830) ***(G-326)***
Sunbelt Lettering, Pensacola *Also called Mid West Lettering Company* ***(G-13553)***
Sunbelt Metals & Mfg Inc 407 889-8960
920 S Bradshaw Rd Apopka (32703) ***(G-179)***
Sunbelt Transformer Ltd 305 517-3657
2063 Blount Rd Pompano Beach (33069) ***(G-14206)***
Sunbelt Usa Inc 239 353-5519
132 Vista Ln Naples (34119) ***(G-10910)***
Sunciti Industries Inc 407 877-8081
3402 Rex Dr Winter Garden (34787) ***(G-18405)***
Sunco Plastics Inc 305 238-2864
8501 Nw 90th St Miami (33166) ***(G-9965)***
Suncoast Accrdted Gmlgical Lab 941 756-8787
4016 Cortez Rd W Ste 1201 Bradenton (34210) ***(G-1054)***
Suncoast Aluminum Furn Inc 239 267-8300
6291 Thomas Rd Fort Myers (33912) ***(G-4410)***
Suncoast Assemblers LLC 407 947-8835
2114 Belle Isle Ave Belle Isle (32809) ***(G-351)***
Suncoast Cartons & Crating LLC 813 242-8477
5601 Airport Blvd Tampa (33634) ***(G-17311)***
Suncoast Coatings 954 306-2149
10101 Nw 46th St Sunrise (33351) ***(G-16376)***
Suncoast Diesel, Fort Walton Beach *Also called Sun Coast Converters Inc* ***(G-4610)***
Suncoast Electric Mtr Svc Inc 813 247-4104
2502 E 5th Ave Tampa (33605) ***(G-17312)***
Suncoast Fabrics Inc 239 566-3313
5400 Yahl St Ste A Naples (34109) ***(G-10911)***
Suncoast Heat Treat Inc 386 267-0955
400 Fentress Blvd Daytona Beach (32114) ***(G-2606)***
Suncoast Heat Treat Inc (PA) 561 776-7763
507 Industrial Way Boynton Beach (33426) ***(G-916)***
Suncoast Identification Tech 239 277-9922
13300 S Clevlnd Ave Ste 5 Fort Myers (33907) ***(G-4411)***
Suncoast Idntfction Sltons LLC 239 277-9922
618 Danley Dr Fort Myers (33907) ***(G-4412)***
Suncoast Industries of Florida, Fort Myers *Also called E-Z Metals Inc* ***(G-4241)***
Suncoast Investmens of PA 941 722-5391
1511 20th Ave E Palmetto (34221) ***(G-13194)***
Suncoast Led Displays LLC 727 683-2777
2366 Knoll Ave S Palm Harbor (34683) ***(G-13134)***
Suncoast Lmntion Idntification, Fort Myers *Also called Suncoast Identification Tech* ***(G-4411)***
Suncoast Molders Inc 727 546-0041
10760 76th Ct Largo (33777) ***(G-7693)***
Suncoast News 727 815-1023
11321 Us Highway 19 Port Richey (34668) ***(G-14376)***
Suncoast Pallets Inc 813 988-1623
11506 Cerca Del Rio Pl Temple Terrace (33617) ***(G-17546)***
Suncoast Post-Tension Ltd 305 592-5075
7223 Nw 46th St 29 Miami (33166) ***(G-9966)***
Suncoast Projects LLC 407 581-0665
7500 Republic Dr Groveland (34736) ***(G-4873)***
Suncoast Rebuild Center Inc 813 238-3433
2717 N 58th St Tampa (33619) ***(G-17313)***
Suncoast Research Labs Inc 727 344-7627
2901 Anvil St N Saint Petersburg (33710) ***(G-15201)***
Suncoast Sign Shop Inc 941 448-5835
8466 Cookwood Rdg Sarasota (34231) ***(G-15843)***
Suncoast Signs Inc 813 664-0699
9601 E Us Highway 92 Tampa (33610) ***(G-17314)***
Suncoast Specialty Prtg Inc 813 951-0899
6401 N River Blvd Tampa (33604) ***(G-17315)***
Suncoast Stone Inc 561 364-2061
151 Nw 18th Ave Delray Beach (33444) ***(G-3024)***
Suncoast Toner Cartridge Inc 727 945-0255
5441 Provost Dr Holiday (34690) ***(G-5505)***
Suncoast Tool & Gage Inds Inc 727 572-8000
11625 54th St N Clearwater (33760) ***(G-1801)***
Suncoast Trends Inc 727 321-4948
2860 21st Ave N Saint Petersburg (33713) ***(G-15202)***
Suncoast Window Fashion, Naples *Also called Suncoast Fabrics Inc* ***(G-10911)***
Suncrest Sheds Inc (PA) 863 675-8600
1451 Commerce Dr Labelle (33935) ***(G-6987)***
Suncrest Sheds of South Fla 305 231-1990
9600 Nw 77th Ave Miami Lakes (33016) ***(G-10362)***
Sundog Education, Merritt Island *Also called Sundog Software LLC* ***(G-8598)***
Sundog Software LLC 425 635-8683
4022 Tradewinds Trl Merritt Island (32953) ***(G-8598)***
Sundown Lighting 561 254-3738
417 Se Atlantic Dr Lantana (33462) ***(G-7515)***
Sundown Manufacturing Inc 727 828-0826
4505 131st Ave N Ste 26 Clearwater (33762) ***(G-1802)***
Sundrinks, Miami *Also called D D B Corporation* ***(G-8991)***
Sunflex Wall Systems LP 239 220-1570
1494 Pacaya Cv Naples (34119) ***(G-10912)***
Sungard, Jacksonville *Also called Fis Avantgard LLC* ***(G-6097)***
Sungard Asset MGT Systems Inc 561 656-2007
100 Village Square Xing Palm Beach Gardens (33410) ***(G-13011)***
Sunglo Paint, Clearwater *Also called Leto LLC* ***(G-1671)***
Sungraf Inc 954 456-8500
325 W Ansin Blvd Hallandale Beach (33009) ***(G-4976)***
Suniland Press Inc 305 235-8811
7379 Nw 31st St Miami (33122) ***(G-9967)***
Sunluver Smoothies Inc 239 331-5431
160 12th Ave Nw Naples (34120) ***(G-10913)***
Sunmaster of Naples Inc 239 261-3581
900 Industrial Blvd Naples (34104) ***(G-10914)***
Sunnibunni 941 554-8744
1916 Bay Rd Sarasota (34239) ***(G-15844)***
Sunnman Inc 305 505-6615
2475 W 8th Ln Hialeah (33010) ***(G-5367)***
Sunny Hill International Inc 386 736-5757
901 W New York Ave Deland (32720) ***(G-2905)***
Sunny Skies Enterprises Inc 954 316-6015
570 Ne 185th St North Miami Beach (33179) ***(G-11163)***
Sunnyland Usa Inc 772 293-0293
600 Citrus Ave Ste 200 Fort Pierce (34950) ***(G-4535)***
Sunnypics LLC 407 992-6210
618 E South St Ste 500 Orlando (32801) ***(G-12633)***
Sunoptic Technologies LLC (PA) 877 677-2832
6018 Bowdendale Ave Jacksonville (32216) ***(G-6516)***
Sunpack of Pensacola Inc 850 476-9838
8500 Fowler Ave Pensacola (32534) ***(G-13612)***
Sunpost, Miami Beach *Also called Caxton Newspapers Inc* ***(G-10176)***
Sunpost Newspaper Group, Miami Beach *Also called Prestige Publication Group* ***(G-10222)***
Sunray Reflections Inc 305 305-6350
956 Harrison St Hollywood (33019) ***(G-5666)***
Sunrise 386 627-5029
26 N Village Dr Palm Coast (32137) ***(G-13088)***
Sunrise Fiberglass Inc 305 636-4111
15750 Sw 92nd Ave Unit 32 Palmetto Bay (33157) ***(G-13219)***
Sunrise Financial Assoc Inc 321 439-9797
14004 Chcora Crssing Blvd Orlando (32828) ***(G-12634)***
Sunrise Foods LLC 904 613-4756
4520 Swilcan Bridge Ln N Jacksonville (32224) ***(G-6517)***
Sunrise Manufacturing Intl Inc 813 780-7369
4035 Correia Dr Zephyrhills (33542) ***(G-18632)***
Sunrise Printing & Signs 321 284-3803
1218 Dyer Blvd Kissimmee (34741) ***(G-6962)***
Sunrise Trampolines and Nets 727 526-9288
6544 44th St N Ste 1205 Pinellas Park (33781) ***(G-13730)***
Sunrise Yacht Products, Pinellas Park *Also called Octal Ventures Inc* ***(G-13715)***
Sunrise Yacht Products, Pinellas Park *Also called Sunrise Trampolines and Nets* ***(G-13730)***
Sunrui Ttnium Prcsion Pdts Inc 727 953-7101
1058 Cephas Rd Clearwater (33765) ***(G-1803)***
Suns Eye Inc 407 519-4904
2098 Tall Pine Trl Geneva (32732) ***(G-4790)***
Suns Up of Swf LLC 301 470-2678
191 Lee Rd Venice (34292) ***(G-17721)***
Sunset Cadillac of Sarasota 941 922-1571
2200 Bee Ridge Rd Sarasota (34239) ***(G-15845)***
Sunset Metal Fabrication Inc 386 215-4520
1211 Porter Rd Unit 7 Sarasota (34240) ***(G-15846)***
Sunset Pavers Inc 239 208-7293
8210 Katanga Ct Fort Myers (33916) ***(G-4413)***
Sunset Power Inc 866 485-2757
5191 Shawland Rd Jacksonville (32254) ***(G-6518)***
Sunset Publications Inc 321 727-8500
630 S Wickham Rd Ste 107 Melbourne (32904) ***(G-8539)***
Sunshine Alance Cabinets Mllwk 954 621-7444
712 S Military Trl Deerfield Beach (33442) ***(G-2817)***
Sunshine Avionics LLC 954 517-1294
963 W 81st Pl Hialeah (33014) ***(G-5368)***
Sunshine Bottling Co 305 592-4366
8447 Nw 54th St Doral (33166) ***(G-3384)***
Sunshine Canvas Inc 352 787-4436
240 State Road 44 Leesburg (34748) ***(G-7796)***
Sunshine Cap Company 863 688-8147
1142 W Main St Lakeland (33815) ***(G-7453)***
Sunshine Cordage Corporation 305 592-3750
7190 Nw 12th St Miami (33126) ***(G-9968)***
Sunshine Driveways Inc 954 394-7373
7750 Nw 35th St Hollywood (33024) ***(G-5667)***
Sunshine Filters Pinellas Inc 727 530-3884
12415 73rd Ct Largo (33773) ***(G-7694)***
Sunshine Health Products Inc 954 493-5469
6245 Powerline Rd Ste 106 Fort Lauderdale (33309) ***(G-4075)***
Sunshine Lighters 386 322-1300
730 Glades Ct Port Orange (32127) ***(G-14351)***

ALPHABETIC

Sunshine Ltd Tape & Label Spc 561 832-9656
516 24th St West Palm Beach (33407) ***(G-18169)***
Sunshine Marine Tanks Inc 305 805-9898
8045 Nw 90th St Medley (33166) ***(G-8329)***
Sunshine Metal Products Inc 407 331-1300
195 Magnolia St Altamonte Springs (32701) ***(G-72)***
Sunshine Nylon Products Inc 352 754-9932
16101 Flight Path Dr Brooksville (34604) ***(G-1208)***
Sunshine Oil and Gas Inc (PA) 305 367-3100
13230 Sw 132nd Ave Ste 22 Miami (33186) ***(G-9969)***
Sunshine Oil and Gas Fla Inc, Miami *Also called Sunshine Oil and Gas Inc* ***(G-9969)***
Sunshine Organics Compost LLC 904 900-3072
6478 Buffalo Ave Jacksonville (32208) ***(G-6519)***
Sunshine Packaging Inc 305 887-8141
880 W 19th St Hialeah (33010) ***(G-5369)***
Sunshine Packing & Noodle Co 904 355-7561
57 Cantee St Jacksonville (32204) ***(G-6520)***
Sunshine Peanut Company (PA) 813 988-6987
7405 Temple Terrace Hwy A Temple Terrace (33637) ***(G-17547)***
Sunshine Piping Inc 850 763-4834
6513 Bayline Dr Panama City (32404) ***(G-13312)***
Sunshine Printing Inc (PA) 561 478-2602
2605 Old Okeechobee Rd West Palm Beach (33409) ***(G-18170)***
Sunshine Provisions, Deerfield Beach *Also called E&M Innovative Forager LLC* ***(G-2713)***
Sunshine Spray Foam Insulation 239 221-8704
10923 K Nine Dr Bonita Springs (34135) ***(G-823)***
Sunshine Supplements Inc (PA) 407 751-4299
120 E Marks St Ste 250 Orlando (32803) ***(G-12635)***
Sunshine Tape & Label, West Palm Beach *Also called Sunshine Ltd Tape & Label Spc* ***(G-18169)***
Sunshine Tool LLC 941 351-6330
7245 16th St E Unit 114 Sarasota (34243) ***(G-15564)***
Sunshine Welding, Cape Canaveral *Also called Batech Inc* ***(G-1277)***
Sunshine Windows Mfg Inc 305 364-9952
1785 W 33rd Pl Hialeah (33012) ***(G-5370)***
Sunsof Inc (PA) 305 691-1875
5821 E 10th Ave Hialeah (33013) ***(G-5371)***
Sunstate Awng Grphic Dsign Inc 407 260-6118
50 Keyes Ave Sanford (32773) ***(G-15392)***
Sunstate Uav LLC 904 580-4828
1093 A1a Beach Blvd # 170 Saint Augustine (32080) ***(G-14904)***
Suntech Doors, Sarasota *Also called Ashton Manufacturing LLC* ***(G-15601)***
Suntek Window Films, Fort Lauderdale *Also called Eastman Performance Films LLC* ***(G-3779)***
Suntree Diagnostic Center 321 259-8800
7970 N Wickham Rd Ste 102 Melbourne (32940) ***(G-8540)***
Suntree Technologies Inc 321 637-7552
798 Clearlake Rd Ste 2 Cocoa (32922) ***(G-1960)***
Suntyx LLC 786 558-2233
11550 Interchange Cir N Miramar (33025) ***(G-10550)***
Sunybell LLC 727 301-2832
4344 Cold Harbor Dr New Port Richey (34653) ***(G-10986)***
Super Brite Screw Corp 305 822-6560
16 Sw 1st Ave Miami (33130) ***(G-9970)***
Super Cleaning Woman Services 954 670-7527
1528 N Andrews Ave Fort Lauderdale (33311) ***(G-4076)***
Super Color Inc 954 964-4656
5905 Sw 58th Ct Davie (33314) ***(G-2485)***
Super Color Digital LLC 407 240-1660
3450 Vineland Rd Ste 200 Orlando (32811) ***(G-12636)***
Super Grafix Inc 561 585-1519
2889 Nw 24th Ter Boca Raton (33431) ***(G-704)***
Super Stone Inc (PA) 305 681-3561
1251 Burlington St Opa Locka (33054) ***(G-11791)***
Super Swim Corp 239 275-7600
10711 Deer Run Farms Rd Fort Myers (33966) ***(G-4414)***
Super Tool Inc 941 751-9677
2951 63rd Ave E Bradenton (34203) ***(G-1055)***
Super-Pufft Snacks Usa Inc 905 564-1180
700 Super Pufft St Perry (32348) ***(G-13654)***
Superchips Inc 407 585-7000
1790 E Airport Blvd Sanford (32773) ***(G-15393)***
Superflow Inc 786 238-8253
1400 Lincoln Rd Apt 604 Miami Beach (33139) ***(G-10238)***
Superformance Mfg Inc 305 420-6034
2637 W 76th St Hialeah (33016) ***(G-5372)***
Superheat Fgh Services Inc 519 396-1324
895 E Lemon St Bartow (33830) ***(G-327)***
Superion LLC 407 304-3235
1000 Business Center Dr Lake Mary (32746) ***(G-7109)***
Superior Asphalt Inc 941 755-2850
4703 15th St E Bradenton (34203) ***(G-1056)***
Superior Avionics Inc 954 917-9194
2700 W Cypress Creek Rd Fort Lauderdale (33309) ***(G-4077)***
Superior Cast Stone LLC 863 634-4771
6344 Se 30th Pkwy Okeechobee (34974) ***(G-11618)***
Superior Chrome Plating Inc 832 659-0873
861 101st Ave N Naples (34108) ***(G-10915)***
Superior Dash LLC 386 761-1265
1960 S Segrave St South Daytona (32119) ***(G-16030)***
Superior Dental & Surgical Mfg 772 335-5200
1501 Se Village Green Dr Port Saint Lucie (34952) ***(G-14452)***
Superior Design Products, Tampa *Also called Bornt Enterprises Inc* ***(G-16658)***
Superior Electronics 941 355-9500
7519 Pennsylvania Ave # 102 Sarasota (34243) ***(G-15565)***
Superior Electronics Inc 727 733-0700
1140 Kapp Dr Clearwater (33765) ***(G-1804)***
Superior Fabrication Inc 941 639-2966
5524 Independence Ct Punta Gorda (33982) ***(G-14535)***
Superior Fabrics Inc 954 975-8122
7901 S Woodridge Dr Parkland (33067) ***(G-13355)***
Superior Fire & Lf Safety Inc 850 572-0265
1709 Sw 15th Ave Cape Coral (33991) ***(G-1394)***
Superior Frameless Showers, Pompano Beach *Also called All Glass & Mirror LLC* ***(G-13916)***
Superior Group Companies Inc (PA) 727 397-9611
10055 Seminole Blvd Seminole (33772) ***(G-15991)***
Superior Group Companies Inc 727 397-9611
10055 Seminole Blvd Seminole (33772) ***(G-15992)***
Superior Kitchens Inc (PA) 772 286-6801
2680 Se Federal Hwy Stuart (34994) ***(G-16235)***
Superior Leaf Inc 561 480-2464
523 Ogston St Ste A West Palm Beach (33405) ***(G-18171)***
Superior Metal 407 522-8100
2409 N John Young Pkwy Orlando (32804) ***(G-12637)***
Superior Metal Fabricators Inc 407 295-5772
2411 N John Young Pkwy Orlando (32804) ***(G-12638)***
Superior Millwork Company Inc 904 355-5676
501 E 27th St Jacksonville (32206) ***(G-6521)***
Superior Oil 2016 Inc 305 851-5140
5477 Nw 72nd Ave Miami (33166) ***(G-9971)***
Superior Pallets Llc 863 875-4041
4353 Fussell Ln Winter Haven (33880) ***(G-18471)***
Superior Pavers and Stone LLC 904 887-7831
731 Duval Station Rd # 107 Jacksonville (32218) ***(G-6522)***
Superior Printers, Plantation *Also called Admask Inc* ***(G-13821)***
Superior Printers Inc 407 644-3344
1884 W Fairbanks Ave Winter Park (32789) ***(G-18541)***
Superior Quality Contractors 786 371-7991
17240 Nw 64th Ave Apt 206 Hialeah (33015) ***(G-5373)***
Superior Quick Print, Winter Park *Also called Superior Printers Inc* ***(G-18541)***
Superior Redi-Mix 850 575-1532
61 Commerce Ln Midway (32343) ***(G-10413)***
Superior Roof Tile Mfg 850 892-2299
50 Hugh Adams Rd Defuniak Springs (32435) ***(G-2844)***
Superior Shade & Blind Co Inc 954 975-8122
11100 Nw 24th St Coral Springs (33065) ***(G-2215)***
Superior Sheds Inc (PA) 386 774-9861
2323 S Volusia Ave Orange City (32763) ***(G-11810)***
Superior Shutters, Sarasota *Also called Greg Valley* ***(G-15487)***
Superior Signs and Prints 954 780-6351
1800 Nw 15th Ave Pompano Beach (33069) ***(G-14207)***
Superior Signs Inc 407 601-7964
3975 Forrestal Ave # 600 Orlando (32806) ***(G-12639)***
Superior Sleep Technology Inc 305 888-0953
705 E 10th Ave Hialeah (33010) ***(G-5374)***
Superior Solid Surface Inc 727 842-9947
8609 Squib Dr Port Richey (34668) ***(G-14377)***
Superior Storm Solutions 305 638-8420
1501 Nw 79th St Miami (33147) ***(G-9972)***
Superior Surgical Mfg Co 800 727-8643
10055 Seminole Blvd Seminole (33772) ***(G-15993)***
Superior Trim & Door Inc (PA) 407 408-7624
615 Sprior Cmmrce Blvd St Apopka (32703) ***(G-180)***
Superior Truss Systems Inc 305 591-9918
8500 Nw 58th St Doral (33166) ***(G-3385)***
Superior Unlimited Entps Inc 863 294-1683
160 Spirit Lake Rd Winter Haven (33880) ***(G-18472)***
Superior Waterway Services Inc 561 799-5852
6701 Garden Rd Ste 1 Riviera Beach (33404) ***(G-14680)***
Superiorlaser, Orlando *Also called Superior Metal Fabricators Inc* ***(G-12638)***
Superleaf, West Palm Beach *Also called Superior Leaf Inc* ***(G-18171)***
Superlite Aluminum Pdts Inc 407 682-2121
1090 Rainer Dr Altamonte Springs (32714) ***(G-73)***
Supermarket Services Inc 954 525-0439
4100 Sw 47th Ave Davie (33314) ***(G-2486)***
Supermedia LLC 813 402-3753
5102 W Laurel St Tampa (33607) ***(G-17316)***
Supermedia LLC 727 576-1300
10200 Mrtn Lther King St Saint Petersburg (33716) ***(G-15203)***
Supermedia LLC 972 453-7000
9620 Exec Ctr Dr N Ste 10 Saint Petersburg (33702) ***(G-15204)***
Supermix Concrete (PA) 954 858-0780
4300 Sw 74th Ave Miami (33155) ***(G-9973)***
Supermix Concrete 305 265-4465
4550 Glades Cut Off Rd Fort Pierce (34981) ***(G-4536)***
Supersonic Imagine Inc 954 660-3528
2625 Weston Rd Weston (33331) ***(G-18287)***

1066 2022 Harris Florida Manufacturers Directory (G-0000) Company's Geographic Section entry number

Supersweet Frog LLC 863 386-4917
2932 Us Highway 27 N Sebring (33870) *(G-15945)*

Supertrak Inc 941 505-7800
26855 Airport Rd Punta Gorda (33982) *(G-14536)*

Supliaereos USA LLC 727 754-4915
21941 Us Highway 19 N Clearwater (33765) *(G-1805)*

Supper On Wheels Inc 305 205-8999
2423 Sw 147th Ave Miami (33185) *(G-9974)*

Supply Chain Technologies LLC 732 282-1000
601 21st St Ste 300 Vero Beach (32960) *(G-17804)*

Supply Expediters Intl Inc 305 805-4255
911 Nw 209th Ave Ste 103 Pembroke Pines (33029) *(G-13416)*

Supply Network Inc 954 791-2287
3436 Sw 22nd St Fort Lauderdale (33312) *(G-4078)*

Support Aircraft Parts Inc 305 975-3767
13058 Sw 133rd Ct Miami (33186) *(G-9975)*

Support Systems Associates Inc 321 724-5566
700 S John Rodes Blvd Melbourne (32904) *(G-8541)*

Supreme International LLC (HQ) 305 592-2830
3000 Nw 107th Ave Doral (33172) *(G-3386)*

Supreme Seat Covers, Miami *Also called Seat Savers Plus Inc (G-9862)*

Sure Torque, Sarasota *Also called St Acquisitions LLC (G-15836)*

Sure-Feed Engineering Inc 727 571-3330
12050 49th St N Clearwater (33762) *(G-1806)*

Surefire Strgc Solutions LLC 305 720-7118
9611 Sw 130th St Miami (33176) *(G-9976)*

Surepods LLC 407 859-7034
2300 Principal Row # 101 Orlando (32837) *(G-12640)*

Sureshade, Bradenton *Also called Lippert Components Inc (G-1005)*

Sureweld Welding Inc 813 918-1857
3050 W Socrum Loop Rd Lakeland (33810) *(G-7454)*

Surf Lighting Inc 305 888-7851
210 W 24th St Hialeah (33010) *(G-5375)*

Surf Outfitter 813 489-4587
1413 S Howard Ave Ste 104 Tampa (33606) *(G-17317)*

Surface Engrg & Alloy Co Inc (PA) 727 528-3734
2895 46th Ave N Saint Petersburg (33714) *(G-15205)*

Surface Finishing Tech Inc 727 577-7777
12200 34th St N Ste A Clearwater (33762) *(G-1807)*

Surgentec LLC 561 990-7882
911 Clint Moore Rd Boca Raton (33487) *(G-705)*

Surgimed Corporation 912 674-7660
9900 W Sample Rd Coral Springs (33065) *(G-2216)*

Suriparts Corp 954 639-7700
21020 Sheridan St Fort Lauderdale (33332) *(G-4079)*

Survey Supplies Inc 305 477-1555
1779 Nw 79th Ave Doral (33126) *(G-3387)*

Survitec Survivor Cft Mar Inc 954 374-4276
9640 Premier Pkwy Miramar (33025) *(G-10551)*

Survival Armor Inc 239 210-0891
12621 Corp Lakes Dr Ste 8 Fort Myers (33913) *(G-4415)*

Survival Products Inc 954 966-7329
1655 Nw 136th Ave M Sunrise (33323) *(G-16377)*

Survivor Industries Inc 805 385-5560
9399 Nw 13th St Doral (33172) *(G-3388)*

Sustainable Casework Inds LLC 954 980-6506
720 S Deerfield Ave Ste 1 Deerfield Beach (33441) *(G-2818)*

Sutton Draperies Inc 305 653-7738
1762 Ne 205th Ter Miami (33179) *(G-9977)*

Suviche International LLC 305 777-3530
2175 Nw 24th Ave Miami (33142) *(G-9978)*

Suvillaga Construction MGT LLC 305 323-8380
11411 Nw 7th St Apt 206 Miami (33172) *(G-9979)*

Suwannee American Cem Co LLC (HQ) 352 569-5393
4750 E C 470 Sumterville (33585) *(G-16264)*

Suwannee River Shellfish, Cross City *Also called M & R Seafood Inc (G-2261)*

Suzanne Chalet Foods Inc 863 676-6011
3800 Chalet Suzanne Dr Lake Wales (33859) *(G-7176)*

Suzano Pulp & Paper 954 772-7716
550 W Cypress Creek Rd # 420 Fort Lauderdale (33309) *(G-4080)*

Sv Microwave Inc 561 840-1800
2400 Cntre Pk W Dr Ste 10 West Palm Beach (33409) *(G-18172)*

SW, Miami *Also called Spa World Corporation (G-9931)*

SW Premier Products LLC 941 275-6677
28100 Challenger Blvd # 1 Punta Gorda (33982) *(G-14537)*

Swami Foods LLC 888 697-9264
1617 Kersley Cir Lake Mary (32746) *(G-7110)*

Swans Feed Mill 813 782-6969
8916 Fort King Rd Zephyrhills (33541) *(G-18633)*

Swapper 850 973-6653
115 Se Madison St Madison (32340) *(G-8047)*

Swatch Group Caribbean 877 839-5224
5301 Blue Lagoon Dr # 620 Miami (33126) *(G-9980)*

Sweepy Group Products LLC 305 556-3450
14501 Nw 60th Ave Unit 37 Miami Lakes (33014) *(G-10363)*

Sweet Additions LLC (PA) 561 472-0178
4440 Pga Blvd Ste 600 Palm Beach Gardens (33410) *(G-13012)*

Sweet and Vicious LLC (PA) 305 576-0012
111 Ne 21st St Miami (33137) *(G-9981)*

Sweet and Vicious LLC 772 907-3030
1512 N Lakeside Dr Lake Worth (33460) *(G-7234)*

Sweet Creations By L S Young 772 584-7206
953 Old Dixie Hwy Ste B11 Vero Beach (32960) *(G-17805)*

Sweet Mix LLC 561 227-8332
2644 Starwood Cir West Palm Beach (33406) *(G-18173)*

Sweet Tooth Inc 305 682-1400
18435 Ne 19th Ave North Miami Beach (33179) *(G-11164)*

Sweet Treats 239 598-3311
7935 Airprt Plng Rd N 1 Ste 11 Naples (34109) *(G-10916)*

Sweetlight Systems 239 245-8159
1506 Alhambra Dr Fort Myers (33901) *(G-4416)*

Sweetreats of Naples Inc 239 598-3311
7935 Airport Pulling Rd N Naples (34109) *(G-10917)*

Sweetsies 386 566-6762
26 Ullman Pl Palm Coast (32164) *(G-13089)*

Sweetwater Today Inc 305 456-4724
35 Sw 114th Ave Miami (33174) *(G-9982)*

Swf Bonita Beach Inc 239 466-6600
3540 Bonita Beach Rd Bonita Springs (34134) *(G-824)*

Swfl Hurricane Shutters Inc 239 454-4944
422 Sw 2nd Ter Ste 214 Cape Coral (33991) *(G-1395)*

Swi Publishing Inc 352 538-1438
116 Sw 40th Ter Gainesville (32607) *(G-4771)*

Swift Print Service Inc 239 458-2212
1431 Se 10th St Unit B Cape Coral (33990) *(G-1396)*

Swim Buoy 305 953-4101
2596 Ali Baba Ave Opa Locka (33054) *(G-11792)*

Swim By Chuck Handy Inc 305 519-4946
15415 Ne 21st Ave North Miami Beach (33162) *(G-11165)*

Swipe K12 School Solutions, Saint Augustine *Also called Webidcard Inc (G-14912)*

Swire Pacific Holdings Inc 305 371-3877
98 Se 7th St Ste 610 Miami (33131) *(G-9983)*

Swisher International (HQ) 904 353-4311
459 E 16th St Jacksonville (32206) *(G-6523)*

Swisher Intl Group Inc 904 353-4311
14425 Duval Rd Jacksonville (32218) *(G-6524)*

Swiss Components Inc 321 723-6729
405 West Dr Ste A Melbourne (32904) *(G-8542)*

Swisscosmet Corp 727 842-9419
5540 Rowan Rd New Port Richey (34653) *(G-10987)*

Swisstech Machinery LLC 407 416-2383
8815 Conroy Windermere Rd Orlando (32835) *(G-12641)*

Switchgear Unlimited, Plant City *Also called Resa Pwr Slutions Plant Cy LLC (G-13799)*

Swoogo LLC (PA) 212 655-9810
4646 Ashton Rd Sarasota (34233) *(G-15847)*

Sws Services Inc 904 802-2120
1453 S 8th St Fernandina Beach (32034) *(G-3598)*

Sy-Klone Company LLC 904 448-6563
4390 Imeson Rd Jacksonville (32219) *(G-6525)*

Sy-Klone International, Jacksonville *Also called Sy-Klone Company LLC (G-6525)*

Syana Enterprises Inc 305 582-4708
1880 Sw 24th St Miami (33145) *(G-9984)*

Syft, Tampa *Also called Management Hlth Solutions Inc (G-17034)*

Syi Inc 954 323-2483
10152 Nw 50th St Sunrise (33351) *(G-16378)*

Sylios Corp (PA) 727 821-6200
735 Arlington Ave N # 308 Saint Petersburg (33701) *(G-15206)*

Symbee/Symbee Connect, Vero Beach *Also called Connect Slutions Worldwide LLC (G-17749)*

Symbol Mattress Florida Inc 407 343-4626
5000 Mercantile Ln Kissimmee (34758) *(G-6963)*

Symetrics Industries LLC 321 254-1500
1615 W Nasa Blvd Melbourne (32901) *(G-8543)*

Symetrics Technology Group LLC 321 254-1500
1615 W Nasa Blvd Melbourne (32901) *(G-8544)*

Symme3d LLC 321 220-1584
1 S Orange Ave Ste 502 Orlando (32801) *(G-12642)*

Symmetrical Stair Inc 561 228-4800
2115 Sw 2nd St Pompano Beach (33069) *(G-14208)*

Symmetry Pavers Inc 813 340-0724
2407 Vandervort Rd Lutz (33549) *(G-8017)*

Symrise Inc 904 768-5800
601 Crestwood St Jacksonville (32208) *(G-6526)*

Symrna Ready Mix 352 330-1001
8302 Ne 44th Dr Wildwood (34785) *(G-18322)*

Syn-Tech Systems Inc (PA) 850 878-2558
100 Four Points Way Tallahassee (32305) *(G-16507)*

Syncron Ems LLC 321 409-0025
2330 Commerce Park Dr Ne # 6 Palm Bay (32905) *(G-12924)*

Syndaver Labs Inc (PA) 813 600-5530
8506 Benjamin Rd Ste C Tampa (33634) *(G-17318)*

Syndesis Inc 954 483-9548
392 Sw 159th Dr Pembroke Pines (33027) *(G-13417)*

Syndicated Programming Inc 850 877-0105
1363 Mahan Dr Tallahassee (32308) *(G-16508)*

Synergistic Office Solutions 352 242-9100
11350 Tuscarora Ln Minneola (34715) *(G-10452)*

Synergy Ancillary Services LLC 561 249-7238
11350 Sw Village Pkwy Port Saint Lucie (34987) *(G-14453)*

Synergy Biologics LLC...850 656-4277
2849 Pablo Ave Tallahassee (32308) **(G-16509)**
Synergy Communication MGT LLC (PA)...800 749-3160
400 Imperial Blvd Cape Canaveral (32920) **(G-1294)**
Synergy Custom Fixtures Corp...305 693-0055
215 Se 10th Ave Hialeah (33010) **(G-5376)**
Synergy Labs Inc...954 525-1133
888 Se 3rd Ave Ste 301 Fort Lauderdale (33316) **(G-4081)**
Synergy Metal Finishing, Titusville *Also called Jssa Inc* **(G-17594)**
Synergy Rehab Technologies Inc...407 943-7500
1404 Hamlin Ave Unit B Saint Cloud (34771) **(G-14940)**
Synergy Sports LLC...239 593-9374
6300 Taylor Rd Naples (34109) **(G-10918)**
Synergy Thermal Foils Inc...954 420-9553
12175 Nw 39th St Coral Springs (33065) **(G-2217)**
Synergylabs LLC...954 525-1133
888 Se 3rd Ave Ste 301 Fort Lauderdale (33316) **(G-4082)**
Synkt Games Inc...305 779-5611
1820 Micanopy Ave Miami (33133) **(G-9985)**
Synnova Health Inc...305 253-5433
18001 Old Cutler Rd # 42 Palmetto Bay (33157) **(G-13220)**
Synold LLC...305 266-3388
13755 Sw 119th Ave Miami (33186) **(G-9986)**
SYNTECH, Tallahassee *Also called Syn-Tech Systems Inc* **(G-16507)**
Syntheon, Miami *Also called Synold LLC* **(G-9986)**
Synthes3d USA Inc...321 946-1303
1800 Pembrook Dr Orlando (32810) **(G-12643)**
Sypris Electronics LLC (HQ)...813 972-6000
10421 University Ctr Dr Tampa (33612) **(G-17319)**
Syrac Ordnance Inc...727 612-6090
6626 Osteen Rd Ste 331 New Port Richey (34653) **(G-10988)**
System 48 Plus Inc...561 844-5305
3866 Prospect Ave Ste 1 West Palm Beach (33404) **(G-18174)**
System Data Resource...954 213-8008
11422 Sw Hillcrest Cir Port Saint Lucie (34987) **(G-14454)**
System Enterprises LLC...888 898-3600
319 Windward Is Clearwater (33767) **(G-1808)**
Systematix Inc...850 983-2213
5953 Commerce Rd Milton (32583) **(G-10439)**
Systemone Technologies Inc (PA)...305 593-8015
8305 Nw 27th St Ste 107 Doral (33122) **(G-3389)**
Systems Engrg RES & Facilities, Cantonment *Also called Serf Inc* **(G-1273)**
Syxa Enterprise, North Bay Village *Also called Omniaelectronics LLC* **(G-11059)**
Szabo Pos Displays Inc...941 778-0192
1501 63rd St W Bradenton (34209) **(G-1057)**
T & C Creations, Lakeland *Also called PM Craftsman* **(G-7410)**
T & C Godby Enterprises Inc...407 831-6334
915 State Road 436 Casselberry (32707) **(G-1434)**
T & D Screen Enclosures, Wildwood *Also called Jennifer Yoder Sung* **(G-18314)**
T & E Pavers Inc...239 243-6229
1319 Sw 10th Pl Cape Coral (33991) **(G-1397)**
T & M Atlantic Inc...786 332-4773
436 Sw 8th St Miami (33130) **(G-9987)**
T & M Industries Inc...954 778-2238
1106 Se 14th Dr Deerfield Beach (33441) **(G-2819)**
T & R Marine Corp...850 584-4261
3309 E Us 27 Hwy Perry (32347) **(G-13655)**
T & R Store Fixtures Inc...305 751-0377
2700 N Miami Ave Miami (33127) **(G-9988)**
T & T Concrete Specialties, Orlando *Also called Precast Designs Inc* **(G-12500)**
T & W Inc...305 887-0258
400 Swallow Dr Miami Springs (33166) **(G-10394)**
T & Y Cabinets Inc...305 512-0802
7380 W 20th Ave Ste 102 Hialeah (33016) **(G-5377)**
T A C Armatures & Pumps Corp...305 835-8845
800 Nw 73rd St Miami (33150) **(G-9989)**
T and C Sales Inc...321 632-0920
1950 Murrell Rd Ste 10 Rockledge (32955) **(G-14749)**
T and M Woodworking Inc...352 748-6655
3321 Ne 37th Pl Wildwood (34785) **(G-18323)**
T B A, Tampa *Also called Tampa Brass and Aluminum Corp* **(G-17330)**
T Beattie Enterprises...407 679-2000
7208 Aloma Ave Ste 300 Winter Park (32792) **(G-18542)**
T Bower Enterprises Inc...863 984-3050
1824 Pearce Rd Polk City (33868) **(G-13903)**
T C B Products Inc...941 723-9820
1507 17th St E Palmetto (34221) **(G-13195)**
T C Deliveries...813 881-1830
7002 Parke East Blvd Tampa (33610) **(G-17320)**
T D C S, Davie *Also called Technical Drive Ctrl Svcs Inc* **(G-2487)**
T D R Inc...941 505-0800
30436 Holly Rd Punta Gorda (33982) **(G-14538)**
T Disney Trucking & Grading...813 443-6258
9250 Bay Plaza Blvd # 311 Tampa (33619) **(G-17321)**
T E M Inc...352 371-3898
8930 Nw 13th St Gainesville (32653) **(G-4772)**
T E S S Electrical Sales & Svc, Fort Lauderdale *Also called TESS LLC* **(G-4087)**
T H L Diamond Products Inc...954 596-5012
312 S Powerline Rd Deerfield Beach (33442) **(G-2820)**
T H Stone...561 361-3966
4521 N Dixie Hwy Boca Raton (33431) **(G-706)**
T J Sales Associates Inc...407 328-0777
4355 Saint Johns Pkwy Sanford (32771) **(G-15394)**
T L Fahringer, Tampa *Also called TL Fahringer Co Inc* **(G-17356)**
T M Building Products Ltd...954 781-4430
601 Nw 12th Ave Pompano Beach (33069) **(G-14209)**
T M Tooling Inc...561 712-0903
7341 Westport Pl Ste B West Palm Beach (33413) **(G-18175)**
T R C, Clearwater *Also called Technology Research LLC* **(G-1822)**
T R S...407 298-5490
6330 Silver Star Rd Orlando (32818) **(G-12644)**
T S E Industries Inc (PA)...727 573-7676
5180 113th Ave N Clearwater (33760) **(G-1809)**
T S E Industries Inc...727 540-1368
5260 113th Ave N Clearwater (33760) **(G-1810)**
T S F, Tarpon Springs *Also called Tarpon Stnless Fabricators Inc* **(G-17496)**
T Sals Shirt Co...850 916-9229
1161 Oriole Beach Rd Gulf Breeze (32563) **(G-4893)**
T Shirt Center Inc...305 655-1955
19900 Ne 15th Ct Miami (33179) **(G-9990)**
T T Publications Inc...407 327-4817
203 W State Road 434 A Winter Springs (32708) **(G-18579)**
T V Hl Lites Penny Saver Inc...941 378-5353
6950 Webber Rd Sarasota (34240) **(G-15848)**
T V Log, Orlando *Also called Tribune Media Services Inc* **(G-12671)**
T V Trac Ltd...516 371-1111
7 Island Dr Boynton Beach (33436) **(G-917)**
T&S Kitchen and Bbq LLC...863 608-6223
4798 S Florida Ave 235 Lakeland (33813) **(G-7455)**
T&T Sons Inc...859 576-3316
1999 N County Road 426 Oviedo (32765) **(G-12849)**
T-Brand Fertilizer Inc...386 437-2970
801 N Bay St Bunnell (32110) **(G-1235)**
T-Formation Inc Tallahassee...850 574-0122
864 Commerce Blvd Midway (32343) **(G-10414)**
T-Shirt Express...904 448-3761
8286 Western Way Cir Jacksonville (32256) **(G-6527)**
T-Shirt Florida, Miami *Also called Jose Polanco* **(G-9373)**
T-Shirts Plus Color Inc...305 267-7664
4156 Sw 74th Ct Miami (33155) **(G-9991)**
T-Wiz Prtg & EMB Designs LLC...954 280-8949
464 W Melrose Cir Fort Lauderdale (33312) **(G-4083)**
Taber Incorporated...401 245-2800
9624 Sw Nuova Way Port St Lucie (34986) **(G-14484)**
Table Golf Llc...813 435-6111
667 W Lumsden Rd Brandon (33511) **(G-1110)**
Tablecloth Co, Lake Worth *Also called Jewm Inc* **(G-7210)**
Tables Designs, Odessa *Also called Great American Woodworks Inc* **(G-11555)**
Taco Marine, Miramar *Also called Taco Metals LLC* **(G-10552)**
Taco Marine, Seminole *Also called Taco Metals LLC* **(G-15994)**
Taco Metals LLC (HQ)...305 652-8566
3020 N Commerce Pkwy Miramar (33025) **(G-10552)**
Taco Metals LLC...727 224-4282
6950 Bryan Dairy Rd Ste A Seminole (33777) **(G-15994)**
Taco Mix Corp...239 498-9448
1740 Wilson Blvd N Naples (34120) **(G-10919)**
Taco Time, Perry *Also called Perry Newspapers Inc* **(G-13649)**
Tactical Air Support Inc...229 563-7502
13401 Aerospace Way # 945 Jacksonville (32221) **(G-6528)**
Tactical Phaser Corp...321 262-4140
2993 Moore Dr Oviedo (32765) **(G-12850)**
Tactical Prchute Dlvry Systems...813 782-7482
4035 Correia Dr Zephyrhills (33542) **(G-18634)**
Tactical Products Group LLC...561 265-4066
1914 Corporate Dr Boynton Beach (33426) **(G-918)**
TAe Trans Atlantic Elec Inc (PA)...631 595-9206
4504 E Hillsborough Ave Tampa (33610) **(G-17322)**
Tag & Label of Florida Inc...305 255-1050
13375 Sw 128th St Ste 106 Miami (33186) **(G-9992)**
Tag Media Group LLC...239 288-0499
16751 Link Ct Fort Myers (33912) **(G-4417)**
Tagalong Inc...561 585-7400
5485 Old Spanish Trl Lantana (33462) **(G-7516)**
Tags & Labels Printing Inc...954 455-2867
520 Ne 1st Ave Hallandale Beach (33009) **(G-4977)**
Tagua Gun Leather, Miami *Also called Zen Distributors Group II LLC* **(G-10156)**
Tagua Leather Corporation...305 637-3014
2047 Nw 24th Ave Miami (33142) **(G-9993)**
Taie Inc (PA)...954 966-0233
4171 N State Road 7 Hollywood (33021) **(G-5668)**
Taika Logistics LLC...813 945-2911
401 E Jackson St Tampa (33602) **(G-17323)**
Tail Activewear, Doral *Also called Great Cir Vntures Holdings LLC* **(G-3238)**
Tailored Living, Fort Lauderdale *Also called Premier Coatings LLC* **(G-3994)**
Tak Paper Corp...786 287-8900
10773 Nw 58th St Ste 651 Doral (33178) **(G-3390)**

1068
2022 Harris Florida
Manufacturers Directory
(G-0000) Company's Geographic Section entry number

Taken For Granite 727 235-1559
4481 Pompano Dr Se Saint Petersburg (33705) *(G-15207)*
Takeria Mix Inc 904 338-9157
6680 Powers Ave Ste 108 Jacksonville (32217) *(G-6529)*
Talaria Company LLC 239 261-2870
3450 Westview Dr Unit 11 Naples (34104) *(G-10920)*
Talaria Company LLC 772 403-5387
4550 Se Boatyard Ave Stuart (34997) *(G-16236)*
Talent Assessment Inc 904 260-4102
6838 Phillips Pkwy Dr S Jacksonville (32256) *(G-6530)*
Tallahassee Democrat 850 599-2100
277 N Magnolia Dr Tallahassee (32301) *(G-16510)*
Tallahassee Magazine, Tallahassee *Also called Rowland Publishing Inc (G-16497)*
Tallahassee Powder Coating, Tallahassee *Also called Tallahassee Welding & Mch Sp (G-16511)*
Tallahassee Welding & Mch Sp 850 576-9596
1220 Lake Bradford Rd Tallahassee (32304) *(G-16511)*
Talon Industries, Odessa *Also called International Imaging Mtls Inc (G-11560)*
Talon Industries Inc 727 517-0052
111 8th St Belleair Beach (33786) *(G-354)*
Talon Marine 941 753-7400
1968 Whitfield Park Ave Sarasota (34243) *(G-15566)*
Tamco, Tampa *Also called LV Thompson Inc (G-17026)*
Tamco Group, Port St Lucie *Also called City Electric Supply Company (G-14474)*
Tamilite Lighting, Port Saint Lucie *Also called City Electric Supply Company (G-14405)*
Tamlite 772 878-4944
660 Nw Peacock Blvd Port St Lucie (34986) *(G-14485)*
Tamlite Lighting - New Whse 772 879-7440
660 Nw Peacock Blvd Port Saint Lucie (34986) *(G-14455)*
Tampa Amalgamated Steel Corp 813 621-0550
5215 Saint Paul St Tampa (33619) *(G-17324)*
Tampa Armature Works Inc 904 757-7790
10520 Busch Dr N Jacksonville (32218) *(G-6531)*
Tampa Armature Works Inc 813 612-2600
440 S 78th St Tampa (33619) *(G-17325)*
Tampa Bay Business Journal, Tampa *Also called American City Bus Journals Inc (G-16588)*
Tampa Bay Cabinets Inc 813 781-9468
6509 Santiago Ct Apollo Beach (33572) *(G-96)*
Tampa Bay Coatings Inc 727 823-9866
3228 Morris St N Saint Petersburg (33713) *(G-15208)*
Tampa Bay Copack, Dade City *Also called South Pacific Trading Company (G-2324)*
Tampa Bay Grand Prix (PA) 727 527-8464
12350 Automobile Blvd Clearwater (33762) *(G-1811)*
Tampa Bay Machining Inc 813 855-8456
13601 Mccormick Dr Tampa (33626) *(G-17326)*
Tampa Bay Magazine, Clearwater *Also called Tampa Bay Publications Inc (G-1812)*
Tampa Bay Newspapers Inc 727 397-5563
9911 Seminole Blvd Seminole (33772) *(G-15995)*
Tampa Bay Powder Coating Inc 813 964-5667
9601 Norwood Dr Ste B Tampa (33624) *(G-17327)*
Tampa Bay Powersports LLC 813 968-7888
13521 N Florida Ave Tampa (33613) *(G-17328)*
Tampa Bay Press Inc 813 886-1415
4710 Eisenhower Blvd B12 Tampa (33634) *(G-17329)*
Tampa Bay Print Shop LLC 813 321-8790
2904 S Falkenburg Rd Riverview (33578) *(G-14578)*
Tampa Bay Publications Inc 727 791-4800
2531 Landmark Dr Ste 101 Clearwater (33761) *(G-1812)*
Tampa Bay Sports Entrmt LLC (PA) 727 893-8111
490 1st Ave S Saint Petersburg (33701) *(G-15209)*
Tampa Bay Times, Clearwater *Also called Times Holding Co (G-1831)*
Tampa Bay Times 352 754-6100
13045 Cortez Blvd Brooksville (34613) *(G-1209)*
Tampa Bay Times Storefront, Saint Petersburg *Also called Times Holding Co (G-15212)*
Tampa Brass and Aluminum Corp 813 885-6064
8511 Florida Mining Blvd Tampa (33634) *(G-17330)*
Tampa Contractors Supply Inc 813 418-7284
5017 N Coolidge Ave Tampa (33614) *(G-17331)*
Tampa Fiberglass Inc 813 248-6828
4209 Raleigh St Tampa (33619) *(G-17332)*
Tampa Fork Lift Inc 904 674-6899
7033 Commonwealth Ave Jacksonville (32220) *(G-6532)*
Tampa Machine Products Inc 813 854-3332
151 Vollmer Ave Oldsmar (34677) *(G-11699)*
Tampa Media Group Inc 813 259-7711
202 S Parker St Tampa (33606) *(G-17333)*
Tampa Media Group Inc (PA) 813 259-7711
202 S Parker St Tampa (33606) *(G-17334)*
Tampa Media Group LLC 813 259-7100
202 S Parker St Tampa (33606) *(G-17335)*
Tampa Metal Works Inc 813 628-9223
6601 N 50th St Tampa (33610) *(G-17336)*
Tampa Microwave, Saint Petersburg *Also called E2g Partners LLC (G-15032)*
Tampa Microwave LLC 813 855-2251
16255 Bay Vista Dr # 100 Clearwater (33760) *(G-1813)*
Tampa Pallet Co, Tampa *Also called Haman Industries Inc (G-16903)*
Tampa Pool Company, Tampa *Also called Jlb Enterprises Tampa Inc (G-16967)*
Tampa Printing Company 813 612-7746
4907 N Florida Ave Tampa (33603) *(G-17337)*
Tampa Printing Solutions, Tampa *Also called Printing Services Plus LLC (G-17185)*
Tampa Sheet Metal Company 813 251-1845
1402 W Kennedy Blvd Tampa (33606) *(G-17338)*
Tampa Ship LLC 813 248-9310
1130 Mcclosky Blvd Tampa (33605) *(G-17339)*
TAMPA STEEL & SUPPLY, Tampa *Also called Urban Metals LLC (G-17396)*
Tampa Steel Erecting Company 813 677-7184
5127 Bloomingdale Ave Tampa (33619) *(G-17340)*
Tampa Tank & Welding Inc 813 241-0123
12781 S Us Highway 41 Gibsonton (33534) *(G-4801)*
Tampa Tribune, Lakeland *Also called Nexstar Broadcasting Inc (G-7402)*
Tampa Tribune Company, The, Tampa *Also called Tampa Media Group Inc (G-17333)*
Tampa Tribune, The, Tampa *Also called Tampa Media Group Inc (G-17334)*
Tampa Wines LLC 727 799-9463
22041 Us Highway 19 N Clearwater (33765) *(G-1814)*
Tampa Yacht Manufacturing LLC 813 792-2114
3671 131st Ave N Clearwater (33762) *(G-1815)*
Tampa Yard, Tampa *Also called Vgcm LLC (G-17412)*
Tan Printing Inc 954 986-9869
2211 John P Lyons Ln Hallandale Beach (33009) *(G-4978)*
Tangle Corporation 904 712-0042
1535 Blair Rd Jacksonville (32221) *(G-6533)*
Tannehill Intl Inds Inc (PA) 850 265-3611
10 Arthur Dr Lynn Haven (32444) *(G-8033)*
Tanning Research Labs LLC (HQ) 386 677-9559
1190 N Us Highway 1 Ormond Beach (32174) *(G-12797)*
Tannous Innovations LLC 754 220-6645
2157 Nw 22nd St Pompano Beach (33069) *(G-14210)*
Tantasia 239 274-5455
5100 S Cleveland Ave # 312 Fort Myers (33907) *(G-4418)*
Tap Express Inc 305 468-0038
9625 Nw 33rd St Doral (33172) *(G-3391)*
Tape Technologies Inc 904 284-0284
1272 Harbor Rd Green Cove Springs (32043) *(G-4838)*
Tapesouth Inc 904 642-1800
1626 Nw 55th Pl Gainesville (32653) *(G-4773)*
Tapinfluence Inc 720 726-4071
480 N Orlando Ave Ste 200 Winter Park (32789) *(G-18543)*
Tapioca Fit 954 842-3924
156 N University Dr Pembroke Pines (33024) *(G-13418)*
Tar Building LLC 407 896-7252
1155 N Orange Ave Orlando (32804) *(G-12645)*
Target Copy Gainesville Inc 352 372-1171
3422 Sw Archer Rd Gainesville (32608) *(G-4774)*
Target Graphics Inc 941 365-8809
2053 13th St Sarasota (34237) *(G-15849)*
Target Manufacturing Inc 305 633-0361
3430 Nw 38th St Miami (33142) *(G-9994)*
Target Marine Inc 863 293-3592
125 Bomber Rd Winter Haven (33880) *(G-18473)*
Target Marine Manufacturers, Winter Haven *Also called Target Marine Inc (G-18473)*
Target Print & Mail 850 671-6600
2843 Industrial Plaza Dr A1 Tallahassee (32301) *(G-16512)*
Tarin Services LLC 803 526-9643
5404 24th Ave S Tampa (33619) *(G-17341)*
Tarmac America, Orlando *Also called Paver Systems LLC (G-12474)*
Tarmac America Inc 386 427-0438
200 N Flagler Ave Edgewater (32132) *(G-3502)*
Tarmac Florida, Jacksonville *Also called Titan America LLC (G-6556)*
Tarmac Florida Inc 954 481-2800
455 Fairway Dr Deerfield Beach (33441) *(G-2821)*
Tarmac Standard Concrete, Deerfield Beach *Also called Titan America LLC (G-2826)*
Taronis Fuels Inc 727 934-3448
12707 44th St N Clearwater (33762) *(G-1816)*
Tarpon Springs Distillery, Tarpon Springs *Also called Papous Craft Distillery LLC (G-17485)*
Tarpon Stnless Fabricators Inc 727 942-1821
911 Rivo Pl Ste B Tarpon Springs (34689) *(G-17496)*
Tarps and Beyond, Ocala *Also called Evora Enterprises Inc (G-11380)*
Tarvin Mobile Home Service 727 734-3400
329 Archimedes St Palm Harbor (34683) *(G-13135)*
Tassel Depot, Deerfield Beach *Also called Hofmann & Leavy Inc (G-2738)*
Taste Advantage LLC 863 619-8101
3135 Drane Feld Rd Ste 22 Lakeland (33811) *(G-7456)*
Taste of Thai LLC 850 581-3340
3475 Gulf Breeze Pkwy Gulf Breeze (32563) *(G-4894)*
Tasteful Delight LLC 305 879-6487
1919 W 10th St Apt 43 Lakeland (33805) *(G-7457)*
Tastyz LLC 772 480-5741
1120 Sunset Strip Sunrise (33313) *(G-16379)*
Tata Tea Extractions Inc 813 754-2602
1001 W Dr Mlk Jr Blvd Martin Luther Plant City (33563) *(G-13807)*
Tattoo Factory Inc (PA) 941 923-4110
2828 Proctor Rd Ste 2 Sarasota (34231) *(G-15850)*
Tattoo Promotion Factory, Sarasota *Also called Tattoo Factory Inc (G-15850)*
Tatum Brothers Lumber Co Inc 904 782-3690
22796 Nw County Road 200a Lawtey (32058) *(G-7747)*

ALPHABETIC

Taurus Chutes Inc 954 445-0146
3030 Nw 23rd Ave Oakland Park (33311) *(G-11300)*

Tavarez Sporting Goods Inc 347 441-9690
1840 Coral Way Miami (33145) *(G-9995)*

Taw Jacksonville Service Ctr, Jacksonville *Also called Tampa Armature Works Inc* *(G-6531)*

Taw Payroll Inc 813 621-5661
440 S 78th St Tampa (33619) *(G-17342)*

Taw Tampa Service Center, Tampa *Also called Tampa Armature Works Inc* *(G-17325)*

Taylor & Francis Group LLC 800 516-0186
1990 Main St Ste 750 Sarasota (34236) *(G-15851)*

Taylor & Francis Group LLC (HQ) 561 994-0555
6000 Broken Sound Pkwy Nw # 300 Boca Raton (33487) *(G-707)*

Taylor Building Elements LLC 863 287-2228
116 Van Fleet Ct Auburndale (33823) *(G-246)*

Taylor Communications Inc 813 689-5099
12003 Embarcadero Dr Seffner (33584) *(G-15965)*

Taylor Communications Inc 813 886-5511
5131 Tampa West Blvd Tampa (33634) *(G-17343)*

Taylor Communications Inc 954 632-6501
1551 Sawgrs Corp Pkwy 1 Sunrise (33323) *(G-16380)*

Taylor Concrete Inc 941 737-7225
503 10th St E Palmetto (34221) *(G-13196)*

Taylor Electronics Inc 941 925-3605
7061b S Tamiami Trl Sarasota (34231) *(G-15852)*

Taylor Farms Florida Inc 407 859-3373
7492 Chancellor Dr Orlando (32809) *(G-12646)*

Taylor L Max L C 833 346-9963
12751 S Cleveland Ave Fort Myers (33907) *(G-4419)*

Taylor Made Plastics Inc 941 926-0200
1561 Global Ct Ste A Sarasota (34240) *(G-15853)*

Taylor Made Scrub Hats LLC 615 348-7802
10044 Creek Bluff Dr Riverview (33578) *(G-14579)*

Taylor Made Systems Brdnton In (PA) 941 747-1900
2750 Kansas St Oviedo (32765) *(G-12851)*

Taylor Media LLC 727 317-5800
490 1st Ave S Ste 800 Saint Petersburg (33701) *(G-15210)*

Taylor Sign & Design Inc 904 396-4652
4162 Saint Augustine Rd Jacksonville (32207) *(G-6534)*

Taylor-Cotton-Ridley Inc 904 733-8373
4873 Victor St Jacksonville (32207) *(G-6535)*

Taylors Indus Coatings Inc 800 932-3049
108 Drive J A Wltshire Av Lake Wales (33853) *(G-7177)*

Tbc Retail Group Inc 702 395-2100
823 Donald Ross Rd Juno Beach (33408) *(G-6667)*

Tbo, Tampa *Also called Tampa Media Group LLC* *(G-17335)*

TCH, Boca Raton *Also called Twinlab Cnsld Holdings Inc* *(G-726)*

Tcm Imagineering Inc 407 323-6494
1835 Bennett Ave Deland (32724) *(G-2906)*

TCS Electrical Co 844 827-1040
302 Sudduth Cir Ne Fort Walton Beach (32548) *(G-4611)*

Tct Manufacturing 352 735-5070
21911 Us Highway 441 Mount Dora (32757) *(G-10615)*

Td Coating Inc 786 325-4211
12420 Nw 5th Ave North Miami (33168) *(G-11124)*

Td Tra -Dix Supply Inc 727 869-8662
14196 Us Highway 19 Hudson (34667) *(G-5788)*

Tdk Electronics Inc 561 509-7771
6530 N Ocean Blvd Ocean Ridge (33435) *(G-11518)*

Tdse Inc 352 399-6413
3151 Ne 37th Pl Wildwood (34785) *(G-18324)*

Tdt Manufacturing LLC (PA) 239 573-7498
2137 Se 19th Pl Cape Coral (33990) *(G-1398)*

Te Olde Foundry Shoppe Inc 239 261-3911
4573 Exchange Ave Ste 7 Naples (34104) *(G-10921)*

Teak Isle Inc 407 656-8885
401 Capitol Ct Ocoee (34761) *(G-11527)*

Teak Isle Manufacturing, Ocoee *Also called Teak Isle Inc* *(G-11527)*

Teakdecking Systems Inc 941 756-0600
7061 15th St E Sarasota (34243) *(G-15567)*

Team Cymru Inc 847 378-3300
901 Intrntl Pkwy Ste 30 Lake Mary (32746) *(G-7111)*

Team Edition Apparel Inc 941 744-2041
4208 19th Street Ct E Bradenton (34208) *(G-1058)*

Team Hammer Screen Printing 863 666-1108
2328 E Main St Lakeland (33801) *(G-7458)*

Team Inkjet 954 554-3250
1440 Coral Ridge Dr 339 Coral Springs (33071) *(G-2218)*

Team Ip, Stuart *Also called International Prtg Ad Spc Inc* *(G-16167)*

Team Ip Sports LLC 772 398-4664
850 Nw Federal Hwy 229 Stuart (34994) *(G-16237)*

Team Plastics Inc 386 740-9555
2025 Eidson Dr Deland (32724) *(G-2907)*

TEam Service Corp New York 410 365-1574
1040 Coronado Ct Marco Island (34145) *(G-8113)*

Team Solutions Dental LLC 407 542-1552
2675 S Design Ct Sanford (32773) *(G-15395)*

Teamwork Commerce, Clearwater *Also called Retail Cloud Technologies LLC* *(G-1764)*

Teaposh Naturals LLC 904 683-2099
9501 Arlington Expy # 135 Jacksonville (32225) *(G-6536)*

Tearepair Inc 813 948-6898
2223 Knight Rd Land O Lakes (34639) *(G-7506)*

TEC Air Inc 772 335-8220
2195 N Kings Hwy Fort Pierce (34951) *(G-4537)*

TEC Composites Inc 904 765-6502
10615 New Kings Rd Jacksonville (32219) *(G-6537)*

Tech Comm Inc 954 712-7777
511 Se 32nd Ct Fort Lauderdale (33316) *(G-4084)*

Tech Data Education Inc 727 539-7429
5350 Tech Data Dr Clearwater (33760) *(G-1817)*

Tech Data Resources LLC 727 539-7429
5350 Tech Data Dr Clearwater (33760) *(G-1818)*

Tech Data Tennessee Inc 727 539-7429
5350 Tech Data Dr Clearwater (33760) *(G-1819)*

Tech To Site 813 253-9381
41 Cypress Blvd W Homosassa (34446) *(G-5752)*

Techcrete Archtectural Precast, Miami *Also called Berkshire Managment Associates* *(G-8815)*

Technamold Inc 727 561-0030
5190 110th Ave N Clearwater (33760) *(G-1820)*

Techncal Pntg Jacksonville Inc 904 652-1129
1401 Wheels Rd Bldg 3 Jacksonville (32218) *(G-6538)*

Technet Corp 305 582-5369
10595 Nw 43rd Ter Doral (33178) *(G-3392)*

Technetics Group Daytona Inc (HQ) 386 253-0628
305 Fentress Blvd Daytona Beach (32114) *(G-2607)*

Technetics Group Deland, De Land *Also called Technetics Group LLC* *(G-2620)*

Technetics Group LLC 386 736-7373
1700 E Intl Speedway Blvd Deland (32724) *(G-2908)*

Technetics Group LLC 386 736-7373
1700 E Intl Speedway Blvd De Land (32724) *(G-2620)*

Technical Components Inc (PA) 863 646-3253
3901 Industry Blvd Ste 6 Lakeland (33811) *(G-7459)*

Technical Drive Ctrl Svcs Inc 954 471-6521
5081 S State Road 7 Davie (33314) *(G-2487)*

Technical International Corp 305 374-1054
1000 Brickell Ave Ste 625 Miami (33131) *(G-9996)*

Technical Ord Solutions LLC (PA) 850 223-2393
9495 Puckett Rd Perry (32348) *(G-13656)*

Technical Sales & Engineering, Venice *Also called General Rubber Corporation* *(G-17693)*

Technical Service Labs Inc 850 243-3722
95 Ready Ave Nw Fort Walton Beach (32548) *(G-4612)*

Technico 561 588-8300
507 S G St Lake Worth (33460) *(G-7235)*

Technicraft Plastics Inc 954 927-2575
1253 Stirling Rd Dania (33004) *(G-2344)*

Technicuff Corp 352 326-2833
2525 Industrial St Leesburg (34748) *(G-7797)*

Technifinish Inc 727 576-5955
5095 113th Ave N Clearwater (33760) *(G-1821)*

Techniflex LLC 561 235-0844
4400 N Federal Hwy Ste 51 Boca Raton (33431) *(G-708)*

Technipower LLC 954 346-2442
210 N University Dr # 700 Coral Springs (33071) *(G-2219)*

Technisys LLC 305 728-5372
701 Brickell Ave Ste 1550 Miami (33131) *(G-9997)*

Technlogy Integration Svcs LLC 904 565-4050
4600 Touchton Rd E # 1150 Jacksonville (32246) *(G-6539)*

Techno Aerospace, North Miami *Also called Techno-Coatings Inc* *(G-11125)*

Techno Cabinets Inc 305 910-9929
1681 Nw 97th Ave Doral (33172) *(G-3393)*

Techno Solis USA, Saint Petersburg *Also called Techno-Solis Inc* *(G-15211)*

Techno Trading Manufacturing (PA) 689 777-0755
1730 Langley Ave Ste B Deland (32724) *(G-2909)*

Techno-Coatings Inc 305 945-2220
1865 Ne 144th St North Miami (33181) *(G-11125)*

Techno-Solis Inc 727 823-6766
301 20th St S Saint Petersburg (33712) *(G-15211)*

Technolgy Training Associates 813 249-0303
1412 Tech Blvd Tampa (33619) *(G-17344)*

Technologies Drs Unmanned Inc 850 302-3909
645 Anchors St Nw Fort Walton Beach (32548) *(G-4613)*

Technologies For Tomorrow Inc 850 478-5222
1106 N 9th Ave Pensacola (32501) *(G-13613)*

Technology Products Design Inc 321 432-3537
3806 Hield Rd Nw Palm Bay (32907) *(G-12925)*

Technology RES A Southwire Co, Largo *Also called Southwire Company LLC* *(G-7689)*

Technology Research, Clearwater *Also called Creating Tech Solutions LLC* *(G-1555)*

Technology Research LLC (HQ) 727 535-0572
4525 140th Ave N Ste 900 Clearwater (33762) *(G-1822)*

Technomarine Usa Inc 305 438-0880
7600 Corp Ctr Dr Ste 4 Miami (33126) *(G-9998)*

Techtrade 201 706-8130
6900 Tvstock Lkes Blvd St Orlando (32827) *(G-12647)*

Techtran Lenses Inc 561 623-5490
601 Heritage Dr Ste 118 Jupiter (33458) *(G-6806)*

Techtron Corporation 239 513-0800
1400 Rail Head Blvd Naples (34110) *(G-10922)*

2022 Harris Florida
Manufacturers Directory

(G-0000) Company's Geographic Section entry number

Techtronics LLC 407 738-4680
2450 Smith St Ste A Kissimmee (34744) ***(G-6964)***
Teckno Corp 305 677-3487
8640 Nw 101st Pl Doral (33178) ***(G-3394)***
Tecnam US Inc 863 655-2400
29536 Flying Fortress Ln Sebring (33870) ***(G-15946)***
Tecnico Corporation 904 853-6118
490 Levy Rd Atlantic Beach (32233) ***(G-216)***
Tecnografic Inc 954 928-1714
1010 Nw 51st Pl Fort Lauderdale (33309) ***(G-4085)***
Tecnometales Onis Cnc LLC 786 637-8316
21011 Johnson St Ste 110 Pembroke Pines (33029) ***(G-13419)***
Teco Diversified Inc (HQ) 813 228-4111
702 N Franklin St Tampa (33602) ***(G-17345)***
Tecore Government Services LLC 410 872-6000
295 North Dr Ste G Melbourne (32934) ***(G-8545)***
Tecport Optics Inc 407 855-1212
6457 Hazeltine National D Orlando (32822) ***(G-12648)***
Tectron 904 355-5512
546 Ellis Rd S Jacksonville (32254) ***(G-6540)***
Tectron Engineering Company (PA) 904 394-0683
5820 Commonwealth Ave Jacksonville (32254) ***(G-6541)***
Tectron Metal Detection, Jacksonville *Also called Tectron Engineering Company* ***(G-6541)***
Tecvalco USA Inc 866 427-3444
270 Barnes Blvd Rockledge (32955) ***(G-14750)***
Ted Cases Inc 561 809-1030
2385 Nw Executive Ctr Boca Raton (33431) ***(G-709)***
Teddy Mountain LLC (PA) 877 480-2327
1901 S John Young Pkwy # 104 Kissimmee (34741) ***(G-6965)***
Teds Sheds of Tampa 239 344-2900
10311 Bonita Beach Rd Se Bonita Springs (34135) ***(G-825)***
Tee Line Corp 786 350-9526
11883 62nd Ln N West Palm Beach (33412) ***(G-18176)***
Tee-Hee Corp 754 200-4962
2607 N Dixie Hwy Wilton Manors (33334) ***(G-18343)***
Teeko Graphics Inc 386 754-5600
2018 Sw Main Blvd Lake City (32025) ***(G-7048)***
Tees By Bo Inc 305 382-8551
13220 Sw 66th St Miami (33183) ***(G-9999)***
Tees Please Inc 857 472-3391
9278 Se Sharon St Hobe Sound (33455) ***(G-5484)***
Teething Egg, The, Boca Raton *Also called Babbala LLC* ***(G-426)***
Teeze International Inc 727 726-3592
2431 Estancia Blvd Clearwater (33761) ***(G-1823)***
Tehgol Industries LLC 904 439-5623
25 N Market St Ste 121 Jacksonville (32202) ***(G-6542)***
Tejeda Sheet Metal & Aluminum 305 609-5477
651 W 43rd Pl Hialeah (33012) ***(G-5378)***
Tek-Lite Inc 410 775-7123
1279 Tipperary Dr Melbourne (32940) ***(G-8546)***
Tekk Supply Inc 954 444-5782
290 Sw 14th Ave Pompano Beach (33069) ***(G-14211)***
Tekmatic Corp 305 972-1300
7522 Sw 143rd Ave Miami (33183) ***(G-10000)***
Tekna Manufacturing LLC 813 782-6700
39248 South Ave Zephyrhills (33542) ***(G-18635)***
Teknatool Usa Inc 727 954-3433
4499 126th Ave N Clearwater (33762) ***(G-1824)***
Teknifab Industries Inc 321 722-1922
179 Park Hill Blvd Melbourne (32904) ***(G-8547)***
Teknocraft Inc 321 729-9634
425 West Dr Melbourne (32904) ***(G-8548)***
Tektrol Inc 305 305-0937
11013 Nw 30th St Doral (33172) ***(G-3395)***
Tektronix Inc 407 660-2727
151 Southhall Ln Ste 170 Maitland (32751) ***(G-8075)***
Tel Test, Gainesville *Also called Corporate One Hundred Inc* ***(G-4672)***
Tel-Tron Technologies Corp (PA) 386 523-1070
2570 W Intl Spwy Blvd # 200 Daytona Beach (32114) ***(G-2608)***
Teledyne Flir LLC 407 816-0091
8210 Presidents Dr Orlando (32809) ***(G-12649)***
Teledyne Flir LLC 850 678-4503
701 John Sims Pkwy E Niceville (32578) ***(G-11038)***
Teledyne Impulse, Daytona Beach *Also called Teledyne Instruments Inc* ***(G-2610)***
Teledyne Instruments Inc 386 236-0780
1026 N Williamson Blvd Daytona Beach (32114) ***(G-2609)***
Teledyne Instruments Inc 386 888-0880
1026 N Williamson Blvd Daytona Beach (32114) ***(G-2610)***
Teledyne Odi, Daytona Beach *Also called Teledyne Instruments Inc* ***(G-2609)***
Teledyne Technologies Inc 805 373-4545
1026 N Williamson Blvd Daytona Beach (32114) ***(G-2611)***
Teleios Manufacturing Inc 904 490-0600
8940 Western Way Ste 15 Jacksonville (32256) ***(G-6543)***
Telelect East, Wildwood *Also called Terex Corporation* ***(G-18325)***
Telematic Systems Inc 239 217-0629
2029 Club House Rd North Fort Myers (33917) ***(G-11071)***
Telephony Partners LLC 813 769-4690
5215 W Laurel St Ste 210 Tampa (33607) ***(G-17346)***
Telese Inc 813 752-6015
1207 Wood Ct Plant City (33563) ***(G-13808)***
Telese Properties Inc 813 752-6015
1207 Wood Ct Plant City (33563) ***(G-13809)***
Telesis Technology Corporation 941 795-7441
1611 12th St E Palmetto (34221) ***(G-13197)***
Teleview Racing Patrol, Hialeah *Also called International Sound Corp* ***(G-5196)***
Telexpress La Musica Inc 813 879-1914
6310 N Armenia Ave Ste A Tampa (33604) ***(G-17347)***
Teligentems, Havana *Also called Prime Technological Svcs LLC* ***(G-5002)***
Tellabs International Inc 954 492-0120
1000 Corporate Dr Ste 300 Fort Lauderdale (33334) ***(G-4086)***
Tellus Products LLC (HQ) 561 996-5556
1500 George Wedgworth Way Belle Glade (33430) ***(G-344)***
Telsec Corporation 561 998-9983
1155 Broken Sound Pkwy Nw E Boca Raton (33487) ***(G-710)***
Tempered Glass Industries Inc 727 499-0284
11116 47th St N Ste B Clearwater (33762) ***(G-1825)***
Temple Terrace Industries Inc 813 752-7546
4208 Business Ln Plant City (33566) ***(G-13810)***
Temsa North America Inc 407 807-6950
404 Zell Dr Orlando (32824) ***(G-12650)***
Ten In Motion LLC 407 226-0204
8544 Commodity Cir Orlando (32819) ***(G-12651)***
Ten Star Promotions, Tampa *Also called Ten Star Supply Co Inc* ***(G-17348)***
Ten Star Supply Co Inc 813 254-6921
7902 Hopi Pl Tampa (33634) ***(G-17348)***
Ten4 Solutions LLC 302 544-1120
2342 Laurel Rd E # 7308 Nokomis (34275) ***(G-11053)***
Tend Skin International Inc 954 382-0800
2090 Sw 71st Ter Ste G9 Davie (33317) ***(G-2488)***
Tendonease LLC 888 224-0319
1738 Sw Foxpoint Trl Palm City (34990) ***(G-13061)***
Tennessee Tool and Fixture LLC 931 954-5316
1750 Barcelona Way Winter Park (32789) ***(G-18544)***
Tennier Industries Inc (PA) 561 999-9710
950 Pnnsula Corp Cir Ste Boca Raton (33487) ***(G-711)***
Tensik Inc 954 937-9505
3955 W Lake Hamilton Dr Winter Haven (33881) ***(G-18474)***
Tensolite LLC 904 829-5600
100 Tensolite Dr Saint Augustine (32092) ***(G-14905)***
Tent Renters Supply, Tampa *Also called M & N Capital Enterprises LLC* ***(G-17029)***
Tentech Corporation 305 938-0389
7330 Nw 66th St Miami (33166) ***(G-10001)***
Tep Manufacturing Co 321 632-1417
1950 Murrell Rd Ste 5 Rockledge (32955) ***(G-14751)***
Tequesta Community Health Ctr 561 713-0798
470 Tequesta Dr Jupiter (33469) ***(G-6807)***
Tera Industries Inc 561 848-7272
7634 Central Indus Dr Riviera Beach (33404) ***(G-14681)***
Teranex Systems Inc 407 888-4300
2602 Challenger Tech Ct # 240 Orlando (32826) ***(G-12652)***
Terex Corporation 352 330-4044
3400 Ne 37th Pl Wildwood (34785) ***(G-18325)***
Terfa Litter USA Inc 416 358-4495
17720 N Bay Rd Apt 5a Sunny Isles Beach (33160) ***(G-16283)***
Terlyn Industries Inc 727 592-0772
4906 Creekside Dr Ste D Clearwater (33760) ***(G-1826)***
Terminal Service Company 850 739-5702
2778 W Tharpe St Tallahassee (32303) ***(G-16513)***
Termine Ravioli Manufacturing (PA) 954 983-3711
5714 Johnson St Hollywood (33021) ***(G-5669)***
Terra Beauty Bars, Deerfield Beach *Also called Terra Beauty Products Inc* ***(G-2822)***
Terra Beauty Products Inc 561 674-2136
440 S Military Trl Deerfield Beach (33442) ***(G-2822)***
Terra Nova Pvers Hrdscape Slto 904 662-2999
7095 Stonelion Cir Jacksonville (32256) ***(G-6544)***
Terracassa LLC 786 581-7741
950 Nw 72nd St Unit 102 Miami (33150) ***(G-10002)***
Terrades Custom Woodworks Inc 305 316-2908
219 W 27th St Hialeah (33010) ***(G-5379)***
Terraferma USA Corporation 305 994-7892
2201 Nw 93rd Ave Doral (33172) ***(G-3396)***
Terrafuse USA Inc 904 207-9564
14476 Duval Pl W Ste 206 Jacksonville (32218) ***(G-6545)***
Terran Orbital Corporation, Boca Raton *Also called Terran Orbital Operating Corp* ***(G-713)***
Terran Orbital Corporation (PA) 561 988-1704
6800 Broken Sound Pkwy Nw Boca Raton (33487) ***(G-712)***
Terran Orbital Operating Corp (HQ) 561 988-1704
6800 Broken Sound Pkwy Nw S Boca Raton (33487) ***(G-713)***
Terrastone Inc 305 234-8384
8747 Sw 134th St Miami (33176) ***(G-10003)***
Terry Boca Inc 561 893-0333
512 Hillsboro Tech Dr Deerfield Beach (33441) ***(G-2823)***
Terry D Triplett Inc 561 251-3641
1103 53rd Ct S Ste B Mangonia Park (33407) ***(G-8102)***
Terry Laboratories LLC 321 259-1630
7005 Technology Dr Melbourne (32904) ***(G-8549)***
Terumo Aortic, Sunrise *Also called Bolton Medical Inc* ***(G-16300)***
Tervis Tumbler Company (PA) 941 966-2114
201 Triple Diamond Blvd North Venice (34275) ***(G-11220)***

Tesco Equipment LLC...954 752-7994
3661 Nw 126th Ave Coral Springs (33065) *(G-2220)*
Tesco of Swfl Inc...239 234-6490
3992 Prospect Ave Ste C Naples (34104) *(G-10923)*
TESS LLC (HQ)...954 583-6262
2900 Sw 2nd Ave Fort Lauderdale (33315) *(G-4087)*
Tess Enterprises Inc...727 573-9701
13150 38th St N Clearwater (33762) *(G-1827)*
Tesseract Sensors LLC...407 385-2498
101 Gordon St Sanford (32771) *(G-15396)*
Testa & Sons Signs, Hollywood *Also called James Testa (G-5604)*
Testmaxx Services Corporation...954 946-7100
6330 N Andrews Ave 312 Fort Lauderdale (33309) *(G-4088)*
Tetra Process Technology...813 886-9331
5415 W Sligh Ave Ste 102 Tampa (33634) *(G-17349)*
Teva Pharmaceuticals...954 382-7729
13900 Nw 2nd St Sunrise (33325) *(G-16381)*
Teva Pharmaceuticals Usa Inc...305 575-6000
74 Nw 176th St Miami (33169) *(G-10004)*
Tex Medical, Weston *Also called Oxigeno Nitrogeno Inc (G-18277)*
Tex Z-E Corp...305 769-0202
12815 Nw 45th Ave Opa Locka (33054) *(G-11793)*
Tex-Cote LLC (HQ)...800 454-0340
2422 E 15th St Panama City (32405) *(G-13313)*
Texene LLC...305 200-5001
5860 Miami Lakes Dr E Miami Lakes (33014) *(G-10364)*
Textron Aviation Inc...813 878-4500
2450 N West Shore Blvd # 2 Tampa (33607) *(G-17350)*
Textron Aviation Inc...407 859-1245
4134 Bear Rd Orlando (32827) *(G-12653)*
Textron Ground Support Eqp Inc...954 359-5730
1800 Sw 34th St Fort Lauderdale (33315) *(G-4089)*
Textured Coatings...850 360-1451
169 Griffin Blvd Panama City Beach (32413) *(G-13340)*
Tf Defense LLC...321 961-7596
147 Toluca Dr Kissimmee (34743) *(G-6966)*
Tfl of Orlando...407 936-1553
2586 N Orange Blossom Trl Orlando (32804) *(G-12654)*
Tg Express Services LLC...862 218-7752
160 Nw 176th St Miami Gardens (33169) *(G-10276)*
Tg Oil Services...407 576-9571
14520 Sw 21st St Davie (33325) *(G-2489)*
Tg United Inc...888 627-9139
16255 Aviation Loop Dr Brooksville (34604) *(G-1210)*
TGI, Miami *Also called Tridor Group Inc (G-10040)*
Thaler's Printing Cetner, Lauderhill *Also called Thalers Printing Center Inc (G-7744)*
Thalers Printing Center Inc...954 741-6522
4970 N University Dr Lauderhill (33351) *(G-7744)*
Thales Dis Cpl Usa Inc...954 888-6200
900 S Pine Island Rd Plantation (33324) *(G-13894)*
Thales Esecurity Inc...954 888-6200
900 S Pine Island Rd Plantation (33324) *(G-13895)*
Thalo Assist LLC...786 340-6892
2893 Executive Park Dr # 203 Weston (33331) *(G-18288)*
That Software Guy Inc...727 533-8109
12825 Pineforest Way W Largo (33773) *(G-7695)*
Thatcher Chemical Company, Deland *Also called Thatcher Chemical Florida Inc (G-2910)*
Thatcher Chemical Florida Inc (HQ)...386 734-3966
245 Hazen Rd Deland (32720) *(G-2910)*
Thayer Citrus, Dundee *Also called Thayer Industries Inc (G-3438)*
Thayer Industries Inc (PA)...813 719-6597
5600 Lake Trask Rd Dundee (33838) *(G-3438)*
The Caldwell Manufacturing Co...386 418-3525
11600 Nw 173rd St Ste 110 Alachua (32615) *(G-22)*
The Forklift Company Inc...863 595-8156
290 W Harbord St Lake Alfred (33850) *(G-6997)*
The Hc Companies Inc...863 314-9417
2006 Fortune Blvd Sebring (33870) *(G-15947)*
The Nanosteel Company LLC (HQ)...407 838-1427
485 N Keller Rd Ste 100 Maitland (32751) *(G-8076)*
The Natural Light Inc...850 265-0800
1020 Arthur Dr Lynn Haven (32444) *(G-8034)*
The Press Gazette, Milton *Also called Milton Newspapers Inc (G-10431)*
The Scranton Times L P...407 377-0400
16 W Pine St Orlando (32801) *(G-12655)*
The Sobe Group Inc...305 884-4008
8125 Nw 74th Ave Unit 3 Medley (33166) *(G-8330)*
Theater Ears Inc...561 305-0519
20423 State Road 7 Ste F1 Boca Raton (33498) *(G-714)*
Theclipcom Inc...305 599-3871
91766 Overseas Hwy Tavernier (33070) *(G-17532)*
Theft Protection Com Corp...772 231-6677
656 Broadway St Vero Beach (32960) *(G-17806)*
Theissen Training Systems Inc...352 490-8020
3705 Sw 42nd Ave Ste 2 Gainesville (32608) *(G-4775)*
Themeworks Incorporated...386 454-7500
17594 High Sprng Main St High Springs (32643) *(G-5456)*
Therapeuticsmd Inc (PA)...561 961-1900
951 W Yamato Rd Ste 220 Boca Raton (33431) *(G-715)*
Theretbicom Inc...917 796-1443
725 Tanglewood Cir Weston (33327) *(G-18289)*
Thermaband Inc...248 497-1665
2502 Eagle Watch Ln Weston (33327) *(G-18290)*
Thermacon, West Palm Beach *Also called Vertarib Inc (G-18195)*
Thermal Braze Inc...561 746-6640
231 Venus St Jupiter (33458) *(G-6808)*
Thermal Conversion Tech Inc...904 358-3720
101 Copeland St Jacksonville (32204) *(G-6546)*
Thermal Matrix Intl LLC...813 222-3274
101 E Kennedy Blvd # 322 Tampa (33602) *(G-17351)*
Thermal Scanning Inc...407 617-2927
5121 Contoura Dr Orlando (32810) *(G-12656)*
Thermalroll.com, Wesley Chapel *Also called Force Imaging Group LLC (G-17877)*
Thermo Arl US Inc (PA)...800 532-4752
1400 Northpoint Pkwy # 50 West Palm Beach (33407) *(G-18177)*
Thermo Compaction Systems Inc...863 370-3799
5001 Gateway Blvd Ste 22 Lakeland (33811) *(G-7460)*
Thermo Electron North Amer LLC (HQ)...561 688-8700
1400 Nrthpint Pkwy Ste 10 West Palm Beach (33407) *(G-18178)*
Thermo Fisher Scientific Inc...561 688-8700
1400 Nrthpint Pkwy Ste 10 West Palm Beach (33407) *(G-18179)*
Thermo King of Ocala Inc...352 867-7700
6015 Nw 44th Ave Ocala (34482) *(G-11500)*
Thermocarbon Inc (PA)...407 834-7800
391 W Melody Ln Casselberry (32707) *(G-1435)*
Thermodyne Powder Coating, Pensacola *Also called Foot-In-Your-mouth Inc (G-13508)*
Thermoval Solenoid Valves Usa...954 835-5523
4651 Sw 51st St Ste 808 Davie (33314) *(G-2490)*
Thetradebaycom LLC...954 607-2405
451 Conservation Dr Weston (33327) *(G-18291)*
Thi E-Commerce LLC...352 327-4058
4414 Sw College Rd # 14 Ocala (34474) *(G-11501)*
Thida Thai Jewelry...561 455-4249
47 E Flagler St Miami (33131) *(G-10005)*
Thinglobal LLC...561 923-8559
7700 Congress Ave # 1122 Boca Raton (33487) *(G-716)*
Think Education Solutions LLC...954 345-7839
5411 N University Dr # 203 Coral Springs (33067) *(G-2221)*
Think Outloud Printing...239 800-3219
613 Sw Pine Island Rd Cape Coral (33991) *(G-1399)*
Think Print, Pompano Beach *Also called Tko Print Solutions Inc (G-14214)*
Thinking Foods Inc...305 433-8287
123 Nw 23rd St Miami (33127) *(G-10006)*
Thinkprint, Pompano Beach *Also called Gpt Media Group Corporation (G-14043)*
Thinktech Corporation...954 501-3034
1840 Vista Way Margate (33063) *(G-8156)*
Thomas A Glassman LLC...239 822-2219
3840 7th Ave Nw Naples (34120) *(G-10924)*
Thomas C Gibbs Custom Cabinets...239 872-6279
12141 Clover Dr Fort Myers (33905) *(G-4420)*
Thomas Mix Kitchens Baths Inc...239 229-4323
18070 S Tamiami Trl # 13 Fort Myers (33908) *(G-4421)*
Thomas Products LLC...563 639-9099
503 Pecan Ln Bradenton (34212) *(G-1059)*
Thomas Rley Artisans Guild Inc (PA)...239 591-3203
1510 Rail Head Blvd Naples (34110) *(G-10925)*
Thomas Sign and Awning Co Inc...727 573-7757
4590 118th Ave N Clearwater (33762) *(G-1828)*
Thomas Smith & Company Inc...863 858-2199
3828 Knights Station Rd Lakeland (33810) *(G-7461)*
Thomas United Inc...239 561-7446
12700 Metro Pkwy Ste 3 Fort Myers (33966) *(G-4422)*
Thomas White LLC...813 704-4406
1302 N Orange St Plant City (33563) *(G-13811)*
Thompson Awning & Shutter Co...904 355-1616
2036 Evergreen Ave Jacksonville (32206) *(G-6547)*
Thompson Manufacturing Inc...239 332-0446
2700 Evans Ave Unit 1 Fort Myers (33901) *(G-4423)*
Thompson Repairs Inc...904 384-5175
4857 Dignan St Jacksonville (32254) *(G-6548)*
Thompson Sales Group Inc...239 332-0446
2700 Evans Ave Unit 1 Fort Myers (33901) *(G-4424)*
Thompsons Arprt Hnger Svcs LLC...239 825-7466
11622 Laertes Ln Naples (34114) *(G-10926)*
Thor Guard Inc (PA)...954 835-0900
1193 Sawgrs Corp Pkwy Sunrise (33323) *(G-16382)*
Thor Guard Weather, Sunrise *Also called Thor Guard Inc (G-16382)*
Thor Manufacturing Inc...866 955-8467
7050 W Plmtt Prk Rd Ste 1 Boca Raton (33433) *(G-717)*
Those Cabinet Guys Inc...703 927-2460
8 Market Place Ct Palm Coast (32137) *(G-13090)*
Thread Graphics Embroidery...407 688-7026
1731 Timber Hills Dr Deland (32724) *(G-2911)*
Thread Pit Inc...352 505-0065
2708 Ne Waldo Rd Gainesville (32609) *(G-4776)*
Threadbird LLC...407 545-6506
7550 Brokerage Dr Orlando (32809) *(G-12657)*
Threattrack Security Inc (HQ)...855 885-5566
311 Park Place Blvd # 300 Clearwater (33759) *(G-1829)*

1072 2022 Harris Florida Manufacturers Directory (G-0000) Company's Geographic Section entry number

Three Brothers Boards 386 310-4927
212 S Beach St Ste 100 Daytona Beach (32114) *(G-2612)*

Three Cay G LLC 904 930-4554
5121 Bowden Rd Ste 107 Jacksonville (32216) *(G-6549)*

Three D Products Corp 954 971-6511
6889 Nw 28th Way Fort Lauderdale (33309) *(G-4090)*

Three60printing LLC 954 271-2701
3350 Sw 148th Ave Ste 110 Miramar (33027) *(G-10553)*

Threez Company LLC (PA) 904 422-9224
1225 W Beaver St Ste 123 Jacksonville (32204) *(G-6550)*

Thrifty Nickle Want ADS, Panama City *Also called American Classifieds (G-13227)*

Thrifty Nickle, The, Panama City *Also called Want ADS of Hot Springs Inc (G-13319)*

Thriv Industries LLC 404 436-3230
402 W Atlantic Ave 65 Delray Beach (33444) *(G-3025)*

Throw Raft LLC 954 366-8004
1202 Ne 8th Ave Fort Lauderdale (33304) *(G-4091)*

Thule Inc 850 584-3448
606 Industrial Park Dr Perry (32348) *(G-13657)*

Thule North America, Perry *Also called Thule Inc (G-13657)*

Thunder Bay Enterprises Inc 352 796-9551
5130 Broad St Brooksville (34601) *(G-1211)*

Thunder Bay Foods Corporation 727 943-0606
13182 38th St N Clearwater (33762) *(G-1830)*

Thunder Energies Corporation (PA) 786 855-6190
8570 Stirling Rd Ste 102 Hollywood (33024) *(G-5670)*

Thunderbird Press Inc 321 269-7616
205 N Mantor Ave Titusville (32796) *(G-17622)*

Thunderforce Inc 315 403-8026
9920 Eagles Point Cir # 3 Port Richey (34668) *(G-14378)*

Ti-Pagos Usa Inc 786 310-7423
20200 W Dixie Hwy Ste 603 Miami (33180) *(G-10007)*

Tias Milkshakes and More 954 391-8753
6768 Stirling Rd Hollywood (33024) *(G-5671)*

Tiba Enterprises Inc 561 575-3037
1601 Commerce Ln Ste 102 Jupiter (33458) *(G-6809)*

Tibor Inc 561 272-0770
255 N Congress Ave Delray Beach (33445) *(G-3026)*

Tic Light Electrical Corp 305 712-3499
11519 Sw 172nd Ter Miami (33157) *(G-10008)*

Tic Logistics, Miami *Also called Tobruk International Corp (G-10017)*

Ticket Drop Traffic Defense 305 332-3186
20137 Ne 16th Pl Miami (33179) *(G-10009)*

Ticks-N-All LLC 321 445-9497
4503 Winderwood Cir Orlando (32835) *(G-12658)*

Tidal Wave Tanks Fabrications 863 425-7795
3275 Mulford Rd Mulberry (33860) *(G-10642)*

Tides Marine Inc 954 420-0949
3251 Sw 13th Dr Ste A Deerfield Beach (33442) *(G-2824)*

Tidewater Incentives Group Ltd 410 734-0691
5292 Layton Dr Venice (34293) *(G-17722)*

Tidewater Promotions, Venice *Also called Tidewater Incentives Group Ltd (G-17722)*

Tidwells Orthotics and Prosthe 954 346-5402
4450 Nw 126th Ave Ste 106 Coral Springs (33065) *(G-2222)*

Tie Collection LLC 305 323-1420
8071 Westfield Cir Vero Beach (32966) *(G-17807)*

Tiempo LLC 941 780-9900
1250 S Tamiami Trl Sarasota (34239) *(G-15854)*

Tienda Maya 561 965-0900
6082 S Congress Ave Lake Worth (33462) *(G-7236)*

Tier5 Technical Services 904 435-3484
16167 Kayla Cove Ct Jacksonville (32218) *(G-6551)*

Tiffany and Associates Inc 386 252-7351
500 Mason Ave Daytona Beach (32117) *(G-2613)*

Tiffany Quilting & Drapery 407 834-6386
206 E Palmetto Ave Longwood (32750) *(G-7952)*

Tig Technologies Inc 561 691-3633
4250 Bandy Blvd Fort Pierce (34981) *(G-4538)*

Tigart Welding LLC 407 371-1820
1468 Auburn Green Loop Winter Park (32792) *(G-18545)*

Tiger Business Forms Inc 305 888-3528
7765 W 20th Ave Hialeah (33014) *(G-5380)*

Tiger Composites Inc 386 334-0941
1531 Airway Cir New Smyrna Beach (32168) *(G-11014)*

Tiger Custom Cabinets Inc 813 748-7286
6032 Crestridge Rd Tampa (33634) *(G-17352)*

Tiger Meat & Provisions, Miami *Also called La Montina Inc (G-9410)*

Tiger/Southland, Hialeah *Also called Tiger Business Forms Inc (G-5380)*

Tightails, Sebastian *Also called Ionemoto Inc (G-15895)*

Tightline Publications Inc 954 570-7174
2795 Sw 11th Pl Deerfield Beach (33442) *(G-2825)*

Tigo Inc 954 935-5990
16522 Ruby Lk Weston (33331) *(G-18292)*

Tikal Pavers Inc 850 892-2207
5991 Coy Burgess Loop Defuniak Springs (32435) *(G-2845)*

Tiki Water Sports Inc 305 852-9298
94.5 Ocean Side Key Largo (33037) *(G-6851)*

Tikore Industries LLC 954 616-5902
14397 Sw 143rd Ct Ste 106 Miami (33186) *(G-10010)*

Til Valhalla Project LLC 904 579-3414
3400 Agricultural Ctr Dr Saint Augustine (32092) *(G-14906)*

Tiles of Pompano Inc 954 642-1993
119 S Federal Hwy Pompano Beach (33062) *(G-14212)*

Timber Creek Distilling Llc 408 439-0973
146 Country Club Dr W Destin (32541) *(G-3080)*

Timbercraft of Naples Inc 239 566-2559
802 Tallow Tree Ct Naples (34108) *(G-10927)*

Timberland Door LLC 727 539-8600
12555 Entp Blvd Ste 102 Largo (33773) *(G-7696)*

Timberwolf Organics Ltd Lblty 407 877-8779
13506 Summerport Vlg Pkwy Windermere (34786) *(G-18367)*

Time Adjusters Conference Inc 386 274-4210
5807 Spruce Creek Wods Dr Port Orange (32127) *(G-14352)*

Time Finance Adjusters, Port Orange *Also called Time Adjusters Conference Inc (G-14352)*

Time Industries Inc 321 676-2080
709 Silver Palm Ave Ste J Melbourne (32901) *(G-8550)*

Time Is Money Campaign LLC 352 255-5273
16750 Abbey Hill Ct Clermont (34711) *(G-1884)*

Time Printing Co Inc 904 396-9967
3504 Saint Augustine Rd Jacksonville (32207) *(G-6552)*

Timeless Reflections, Orlando *Also called Art & Frame Direct Inc (G-11923)*

Timeless Treasures Doll Club 813 854-6208
12020 Steppingstone Blvd Tampa (33635) *(G-17353)*

Times Holding Co 727 445-4249
1130 Cleveland St Ste 100 Clearwater (33755) *(G-1831)*

Times Holding Co (HQ) 727 893-8111
490 1st Ave S Saint Petersburg (33701) *(G-15212)*

Times Holding Co 813 226-3300
1000 N Ashley Dr Ste 700 Tampa (33602) *(G-17354)*

Times Media Services Inc 727 893-8111
490 1st Ave S Saint Petersburg (33701) *(G-15213)*

Times Microwave Systems Inc 203 949-8400
2400 Cntre Pk W Dr Ste 10 West Palm Beach (33409) *(G-18180)*

Times Publishing Company (HQ) 727 893-8111
490 1st Ave S Saint Petersburg (33701) *(G-15214)*

Times Publishing Company 727 849-6397
11321 Us Highway 19 Port Richey (34668) *(G-14379)*

Times Publishing Company 352 567-6660
301 W Main St Inverness (34450) *(G-5835)*

Timilon Corporation 239 330-9650
24301 Walden Center Dr # 101 Bonita Springs (34134) *(G-826)*

Timus Inc 904 614-4342
8131 Baymeadows Cir Jacksonville (32256) *(G-6553)*

Tin Cup Catering, Ocala *Also called Ashtin Inc (G-11328)*

Tin Man Co 305 365-1926
2828 Coral Way Ste 207 Coral Gables (33145) *(G-2114)*

Tin-Rez Corp Inc 561 654-3133
6615 Boynton Beach Blvd Boynton Beach (33437) *(G-919)*

Tinfoil Hats LLC 407 844-0578
11858 Sw 100th Ter Miami (33186) *(G-10011)*

Tintometer Inc (HQ) 941 756-6410
6456 Parkland Dr Sarasota (34243) *(G-15568)*

Tip Top Canvas and Uphl Inc 954 524-6214
6501 E Tropical Way Plantation (33317) *(G-13896)*

Tip Top Prtg of Volusia Cnty 386 760-7701
1325 Beville Rd Daytona Beach (32119) *(G-2614)*

Tip Tops of America Inc 352 357-9559
100 S Bay St Eustis (32726) *(G-3567)*

Tiptops Inc 352 357-9559
100 S Bay St Eustis (32726) *(G-3568)*

Tire Experts LLC 305 663-3508
10903 Nw 122nd St Medley (33178) *(G-8331)*

Tiregraficx, Orlando *Also called Eminel Corporation Inc (G-12125)*

Tita Itln Import & Export LLC 305 608-4258
1408 Nw 23rd St Miami (33142) *(G-10012)*

Titan America LLC 800 520-2083
6557 Greenland Rd Jacksonville (32258) *(G-6554)*

Titan America LLC 954 523-9790
2500 Sw 2nd Ave Fort Lauderdale (33315) *(G-4092)*

Titan America LLC 904 296-0609
1220 Eastport Rd Jacksonville (32218) *(G-6555)*

Titan America LLC 321 259-0490
2575 Avocado Ave Melbourne (32935) *(G-8551)*

Titan America LLC 305 667-2522
7355 Sw 48th St Miami (33155) *(G-10013)*

Titan America LLC 561 842-5309
1453 53rd St Mangonia Park (33407) *(G-8103)*

Titan America LLC 305 761-1944
11955 Nw 102nd Rd Medley (33178) *(G-8332)*

Titan America LLC 800 396-3434
1300 S Swinton Ave Delray Beach (33444) *(G-3027)*

Titan America LLC 954 481-2800
10100 Nw 121st Way Medley (33178) *(G-8333)*

Titan America LLC 904 296-0609
7330 Philips Hwy Jacksonville (32256) *(G-6556)*

Titan America LLC 954 426-8407
455 Fairway Dr Ste 200 Deerfield Beach (33441) *(G-2826)*

Titan America LLC 772 467-2101
4199 Selvitz Rd Fort Pierce (34981) *(G-4539)*

Titan America LLC 407 240-9824
339 Thorpe Rd Ofc Orlando (32824) *(G-12659)*

Titan America LLC 800 396-3434
9151 Weisman Way West Palm Beach (33411) *(G-18181)*

Titan America LLC 941 486-2220
515 Gene Green Rd Nokomis (34275) *(G-11054)*

Titan America LLC 305 364-2200
10100 Nw 121st Way Medley (33178) *(G-8334)*

Titan America Tarmac 941 484-2276
500 Gene Green Rd Nokomis (34275) *(G-11055)*

Titan Dealer Services LLC 813 839-7406
2911 W Bay Court Ave Tampa (33611) *(G-17355)*

Titan Florida, Medley *Also called Titan America LLC (G-8334)*

Titan Florida LLC 800 588-3939
10100 Nw 121st Way Medley (33178) *(G-8335)*

Titan Mfg Inc 239 939-5152
6381 Metro Plantation Rd Fort Myers (33966) *(G-4425)*

Titan Natural Focus Corp 305 778-7005
2701 Vista Pkwy West Palm Beach (33411) *(G-18182)*

Titan Oil Tools LLC 941 356-3010
8466 Lockwood Ridge Rd Sarasota (34243) *(G-15569)*

Titan Service Industry Llc 678 313-4707
2044 Anchor Ave Deland (32720) *(G-2912)*

Titan Specialty Cnstr Inc 850 916-7660
8188 Armstrong Rd Milton (32583) *(G-10440)*

Titan Sunrooms, Milton *Also called Titan Specialty Cnstr Inc (G-10440)*

Titan Tools LLC 818 984-1001
2622 Flournoy Cir S # 23 Clearwater (33764) *(G-1832)*

Titan Trailers LLC 813 298-8597
2406 E State Road 60 Valrico (33595) *(G-17670)*

Titanic Brewing Company Inc 305 668-1742
5813 Ponce De Leon Blvd Coral Gables (33146) *(G-2115)*

Titanic Restaurant & Brewery, Coral Gables *Also called Titanic Brewing Company Inc (G-2115)*

Titanium Development LLC 407 844-8664
3209 Prkchster Sq Blvd Ap Orlando (32835) *(G-12660)*

Titanium Gynmastics & Cheer 813 689-2200
7017 Lithia Pinecrest Rd Lithia (33547) *(G-7839)*

Titanium Integration LLC 561 775-1898
11211 Prosperity Farms Rd Palm Beach Gardens (33410) *(G-13013)*

Titanium Pavers, Orlando *Also called Titanium Development LLC (G-12660)*

Titanium Performance LLC 407 712-5770
1233 Valley Creek Run Winter Park (32792) *(G-18546)*

Titanium Prof Hyraulics 917 929-5044
1982 Avenue L Ste A Riviera Beach (33404) *(G-14682)*

Titanium Real Estate LLC 863 808-0445
1543 Lakeland Hills Blvd Lakeland (33805) *(G-7462)*

Titans Protective Coatings LLC 561 370-2085
150 Evernia St Jupiter (33458) *(G-6810)*

Titans USA Ltd 727 290-9897
4371 112th Ter N Clearwater (33762) *(G-1833)*

Titanus Technologies LLC 888 378-2673
2876 S Park Rd Hallandale Beach (33009) *(G-4979)*

Tite-Dri Industries, Boynton Beach *Also called Premium Absrbent Dspsables LLC (G-900)*

Tizzoni Cucine Inc 305 698-8889
2798 Sw 32nd Ave Hollywood (33023) *(G-5672)*

TJ Cabinetry Inc 407 886-8294
4333 Silver Star Rd # 14 Orlando (32808) *(G-12661)*

Tk - Autek Inc 727 572-7473
270 Foxcroft Dr E Palm Harbor (34683) *(G-13136)*

Tk Cabinets 386 325-6906
500 N Pine St Palatka (32177) *(G-12884)*

Tk Custom Canvas & Upholstery 954 609-3477
1849 S Dixie Hwy Pompano Beach (33060) *(G-14213)*

TK Tires & Wheels Inc 321 473-8945
2400 S Harbor City Blvd Melbourne (32901) *(G-8552)*

Tko Print Solutions Inc 954 315-0990
140 Park Central Blvd S Pompano Beach (33064) *(G-14214)*

Tks Printing & Promo Products 904 469-0968
3107 Spring Glen Rd Ste 2 Jacksonville (32207) *(G-6557)*

TL Fahringer Co Inc 813 681-2373
10103 Cedar Run Tampa (33619) *(G-17356)*

TL Sheet Metal Inc 813 871-3780
4203 N Lauber Way Ste 8 Tampa (33614) *(G-17357)*

TLC Food Truck LLC 305 879-2488
8602 Nw 22nd Ave Miami (33147) *(G-10014)*

TLC Recovery Center S Fla LLC 954 533-0783
465 Sw 20th Ave Fort Lauderdale (33312) *(G-4093)*

Tld LLC 813 927-7554
14512 N Nebraska Ave Tampa (33613) *(G-17358)*

Tm Cabinetry LLC 954 639-1725
313 Ansin Blvd Hallandale Beach (33009) *(G-4980)*

Tm Marketing Group LLC 954 848-9955
3200 S Andrews Ave # 100 Fort Lauderdale (33316) *(G-4094)*

Tm USA Inc 954 801-4649
1628 Nw 82nd Ave Doral (33126) *(G-3397)*

Tmarketing Products, Tampa *Also called Tropical Enterprises Intl Inc (G-17371)*

TMC, Fort Lauderdale *Also called Manning Company (G-3930)*

Tmf Plastic Solutions LLC 941 748-2946
4690 19th Street Ct E Bradenton (34203) *(G-1060)*

Tmg Manufacturing Corp 813 464-2299
5517 W Sligh Ave Ste 100 Tampa (33634) *(G-17359)*

TMI, Jacksonville *Also called Too Many Ideas Inc (G-6559)*

TMMR Holdings LLC (PA) 407 295-5200
301 Enterprise St Unit A Ocoee (34761) *(G-11528)*

Tms Enterprises LLC 850 539-2500
102 Technology Way Havana (32333) *(G-5003)*

Tmt Printing & Mailing, Gulf Breeze *Also called Town Street Print Shop Inc (G-4895)*

TN Cruz, Miami *Also called Whole Coffee Company LLC (G-10131)*

Tnr Technical Inc (PA) 407 321-3011
301 Central Park Dr Sanford (32771) *(G-15397)*

TNT, Tampa *Also called Shirley Simon & Associates LLC (G-17261)*

TNT Custom Cabinetry Inc 561 662-0964
11093 49th St N West Palm Beach (33411) *(G-18183)*

TNT Custom Marine Inc (PA) 305 931-3157
3030 Ne 188th St Miami (33180) *(G-10015)*

TNT Packaging Inc 305 769-0616
17375 Ne 7th Ave Miami (33162) *(G-10016)*

TNT Supplements, Leesburg *Also called Total Nutrition Technology LLC (G-7799)*

TNT Transfer Inc 561 594-0123
7833 Sw Ellipse Way Stuart (34997) *(G-16238)*

Tobruk International Corp 305 406-0263
6970 Nw 50th St Miami (33166) *(G-10017)*

Tockwogh LLC 813 920-3413
15406 Patterson Rd Odessa (33556) *(G-11584)*

Today Magazines Group, Ocala *Also called Special Publications Inc (G-11496)*

Todays Frozen Desserts Inc 305 994-9940
7156 Nw 50th St Miami (33166) *(G-10018)*

Todays Restaurant News Inc 561 620-8888
6165 Old Court Rd Apt 224 Boca Raton (33433) *(G-718)*

Todo En Uno 305 263-6934
6601 W Flagler St Miami (33144) *(G-10019)*

Toledo Doors Inc 305 633-4352
4710 Nw 37th Ave Miami (33142) *(G-10020)*

Toledo Iron Works, Miami *Also called Toledo Doors Inc (G-10020)*

Toledo Sales Inc 305 389-3441
835 Nw 7th Street Rd Miami (33136) *(G-10021)*

Tolliver Aluminum Service Inc 561 582-8939
6810 Georgia Ave West Palm Beach (33405) *(G-18184)*

Tolliver Powder Coating, West Palm Beach *Also called Tolliver Aluminum Service Inc (G-18184)*

Tom Burke Services 863 940-4504
6244 Troi Ln Lakeland (33813) *(G-7463)*

Tom George Yacht Group 727 734-8707
17166 Us Highway 19 N Clearwater (33764) *(G-1834)*

Tom Haggetts Pressure Cleaning 407 932-0140
3781 Sierra Dr Merritt Island (32953) *(G-8599)*

Tom Sweet 727 515-9015
6310 103rd Ave N Pinellas Park (33782) *(G-13731)*

Tom Watson Enterprises Inc 352 683-5097
9629 Amilia Dr Ste 4 Hudson (34667) *(G-5789)*

Tom's Instant Printing, Jacksonville *Also called Toms Instant Printing Inc (G-6558)*

Tomasa Healthy Passion, Hialeah *Also called Sunsof Inc (G-5371)*

Tomatoes & Olive Oil LLC 941 822-9709
1055 Us Highway 41 Byp S Venice (34285) *(G-17723)*

TOMI Aircraft Inc 863 446-3001
1310 Flight Line Blvd Deland (32724) *(G-2913)*

Tommy & Giordy Buy/Sell 786 797-6973
15060 Nw 22nd Ave Opa Locka (33054) *(G-11794)*

Toms Instant Printing Inc 904 396-0686
3100 Beach Blvd Jacksonville (32207) *(G-6558)*

Tomsons Inc (PA) 248 646-0677
6520 Manasota Key Rd Englewood (34223) *(G-3539)*

Tonbo Imaging Inc 814 441-0475
1351 Sawgrs Corp Pkwy # 104 Sunrise (33323) *(G-16383)*

Tone Printing LLC (PA) 855 505-8663
1221 Brickell Ave Fl 9 Miami (33131) *(G-10022)*

Toner Cartridge Recharge Inc 305 968-1045
7923 Nw 163rd Ter Miami Lakes (33016) *(G-10365)*

Toner City Corp 954 945-5392
4137 Stirling Rd Apt 103 Davie (33314) *(G-2491)*

Toner Technologies Inc 561 547-9710
2900 Commerce Park Dr # 11 Boynton Beach (33426) *(G-920)*

Tonertype Inc 813 915-1300
5100 W Cypress St Tampa (33607) *(G-17360)*

Tony Doukas Racing, Punta Gorda *Also called T D R Inc (G-14538)*

Tony William Sitko 772 321-6361
2306 7th Ave Vero Beach (32960) *(G-17808)*

Too Many Ideas Inc 904 396-9245
1716 Hendricks Ave Jacksonville (32207) *(G-6559)*

Toogle Industries LLC 863 688-8975
127 N Lake Parker Ave Lakeland (33801) *(G-7464)*

Tools & More, Brooksville *Also called Woodcrafts By Angel Inc (G-1223)*

Tooter Lingo Liquer, Cocoa *Also called Mango Bottling Inc (G-1940)*

Top 10 Floors, Tampa *Also called Proximity Mills LLC (G-17191)*

Top Choice Cabinets and Tops 786 389-4590
  785 Nw 126th Ct Miami (33182) *(G-10023)*

Top Drawer Inc 305 620-1102
  5190 Nw 165th St Miami Lakes (33014) *(G-10366)*

Top Drawer Printers Inc 305 620-1102
  5190 Nw 165th St Miami Lakes (33014) *(G-10367)*

Top Drinks USA Corp 305 407-3514
  3550 Biscayne Blvd # 507 Miami (33137) *(G-10024)*

Top End, Pinellas Park *Also called Invacare Corporation* *(G-13695)*

Top End Wheelchair Sports, Pinellas Park *Also called Invacare Corporation* *(G-13696)*

Top Flite Manufacturing Inc 800 219-2601
  14262 Sw 140th St Ste 108 Miami (33186) *(G-10025)*

Top Hat Food Services LLC 630 825-2800
  11799 Granite Woods Loop Venice (34292) *(G-17724)*

Top Kitchen Cabinets 305 392-9938
  12650 Nw 107th Ave Medley (33178) *(G-8336)*

Top Line Installation Inc 352 636-4192
  2134 Aitkin Loop Leesburg (34748) *(G-7798)*

Top Notch Diecutting Foil STA 904 346-3511
  4246 Saint Augustine Rd Jacksonville (32207) *(G-6560)*

Top Notch Wood Works Inc 954 445-7861
  526 Nw 43rd Pl Miami (33126) *(G-10026)*

Top of The Line Coating Inc 407 485-8546
  13209 Briar Forest Ct Orlando (32828) *(G-12662)*

Top Optical Lab 305 662-2893
  4444 Sw 71st Ave Ste 111 Miami (33155) *(G-10027)*

Top Quality Yacht Refinishing 954 522-5232
  1513 Sw 18th Ave Fort Lauderdale (33312) *(G-4095)*

Top Sales Co 561 852-4311
  17047 Boca Club Blvd 141b Boca Raton (33487) *(G-719)*

Top Spec US Inc 904 345-0814
  1650 Margaret St Jacksonville (32204) *(G-6561)*

Top Trtment Cstomes Accesories 239 936-4600
  50 Mildred Dr Unit A Fort Myers (33901) *(G-4426)*

Top Wines Import LLC (PA) 305 917-3600
  80 Sw 8th St Ste 2000 Miami (33130) *(G-10028)*

Topflite Components, Miami *Also called Top Flite Manufacturing Inc (G-10025)*

Topgolf International Inc 813 298-1811
  10690 Palm River Rd Tampa (33619) *(G-17361)*

Tophet-Blyth LLC 239 594-5477
  1415 Panther Ln Ste 402 Naples (34109) *(G-10928)*

Topline Hy-Lift Johnson Inc (PA) 352 799-4668
  2251 Topline Way Brooksville (34604) *(G-1212)*

Topline Prtg & Graphics Inc 561 881-2267
  1401 W 13th St Ste 104 Riviera Beach (33404) *(G-14683)*

Tops Kitchen Cabinet LLC 954 933-9988
  1900 Nw 18th St Pompano Beach (33069) *(G-14215)*

Tops Software 813 960-8300
  2495 Entp Rd Ste 201 Clearwater (33763) *(G-1835)*

Toro Company 407 321-2901
  3000 S Mellonville Ave # 422 Sanford (32773) *(G-15398)*

Torque Technologies Products 630 462-1188
  1623 W University Pkwy Sarasota (34243) *(G-15570)*

Torrington Brush Works Inc (PA) 941 355-1499
  4377 Independence Ct Sarasota (34234) *(G-15855)*

Torro Foods LLC 305 558-3212
  6725 Main St Miami Lakes (33014) *(G-10368)*

Tortilla Bay 941 778-3663
  5318 Marina Dr Holmes Beach (34217) *(G-5692)*

Tortilleria America Inc 239 462-2175
  2853 Work Dr Ste 1-2 Fort Myers (33916) *(G-4427)*

Tortilleria Dona Chela 941 953-4045
  1155 N Washington Blvd Sarasota (34236) *(G-15856)*

Tortilleria Gallo De Oro LLC 561 818-7829
  3511 Se Dixie Hwy Stuart (34997) *(G-16239)*

Tortilleria La Rancherita 941 747-7949
  3010 14th St W Bradenton (34205) *(G-1061)*

Tortilleria Lamexicana 7 Inc 407 324-3100
  2715 S Orlando Dr Sanford (32773) *(G-15399)*

Tortilleria Santa Rosa 239 839-0832
  18067 Constitution Cir Fort Myers (33967) *(G-4428)*

TOS Manufacturing Inc 407 330-3880
  4280 Saint Johns Pkwy Sanford (32771) *(G-15400)*

Total Ntrtn & Therapeutics PA 352 259-5190
  809 Highway 466 Ste 202c Lady Lake (32159) *(G-6993)*

Total Nutrition Technology LLC 352 435-0050
  154 Park Center St Ste A Leesburg (34748) *(G-7799)*

Total of Florida 239 768-9400
  12881 Metro Pkwy Fort Myers (33966) *(G-4429)*

Total Pavers Corp 561 902-7665
  2529 Sw Grotto Cir Port Saint Lucie (34953) *(G-14456)*

Total Performance Inc 203 265-5667
  75 N Lakewalk Dr Palm Coast (32137) *(G-13091)*

Total Print Inc 772 589-9658
  1132 Us Highway 1 Sebastian (32958) *(G-15905)*

Total Sign Solutions 561 264-2551
  7655 Enterprise Dr Ste A8 Riviera Beach (33404) *(G-14684)*

Total Spcalty Publications LLC (PA) 813 405-2610
  1715 N West Shore Blvd # 266 Tampa (33607) *(G-17362)*

Total Vision Design Group 407 438-6933
  7552 10th Chancellor Dr Orlando (32809) *(G-12663)*

Total Window Inc 954 921-0109
  1249 Stirling Rd Ste 15 Dania (33004) *(G-2345)*

Totally Bananas LLC 954 674-9421
  5081 S State Road 7 # 803 Davie (33314) *(G-2492)*

Totally Glass & Blinds Llc 561 929-6125
  1027 Egremont Dr West Palm Beach (33406) *(G-18185)*

Totally Products LLC 786 942-9218
  1101 S Rogers Cir Ste 10 Boca Raton (33487) *(G-720)*

Totally Storage Inc 407 472-6000
  59 Skyline Dr Ste 1550 Lake Mary (32746) *(G-7112)*

Totalprint USA 855 915-1300
  5100 W Cypress St Tampa (33607) *(G-17363)*

Toteum All Trckg Trnsprting L 888 506-5890
  5401 S Kirkman Rd Ste 310 Orlando (32819) *(G-12664)*

Toti Media Inc 239 472-0205
  2422 Palm Ridge Rd # 103 Sanibel (33957) *(G-15419)*

Toucan Industries Inc 954 590-2222
  1857 Sw 3rd St Pompano Beach (33069) *(G-14216)*

Toucanvas, Fort Myers *Also called Nite-Bright Sign Company Inc (G-4340)*

Touch Dynamic Inc 888 508-6824
  5525 N Nob Hill Rd Sunrise (33351) *(G-16384)*

Touche Software LLC 786 241-9907
  15616 Sw 62nd St Miami (33193) *(G-10029)*

Touchless Cover LLC 407 679-2217
  10150 Central Port Dr Orlando (32824) *(G-12665)*

Touchpoint Medical Inc (PA) 813 854-1905
  2200 Touchpoint Dr Odessa (33556) *(G-11585)*

Tough Seal, Wesley Chapel *Also called Kericure Inc (G-17880)*

Tow Times, Winter Springs *Also called T T Publications Inc (G-18579)*

Tower Optical Corporation 561 740-2525
  3600 S Congress Ave Ste J Boynton Beach (33426) *(G-921)*

Tower Publications Inc 352 372-5468
  4400 Nw 36th Ave Gainesville (32606) *(G-4777)*

Town Country Industries 727 862-5483
  16748 Scheer Blvd Hudson (34667) *(G-5790)*

Town Crier Newspaper, Wellington *Also called Newspaper Publishers Inc (G-17855)*

Town Street Print Shop Inc 850 432-8300
  1142 Bayview Ln Gulf Breeze (32563) *(G-4895)*

Townley Engineering & Mfg Co, Candler *Also called Townley Engrg & Mfg Co Inc (G-1261)*

Townley Engrg & Mfg Co Inc (PA) 352 687-3001
  10551 Se 110th St Rd Candler (32111) *(G-1261)*

Townley Foundry & Mch Co Inc 352 687-3001
  10551 Se 110th St Rd Candler (32111) *(G-1262)*

Townsend Ceramics & Glass Inc 321 269-5671
  3535 South St Titusville (32780) *(G-17623)*

Townsend Signs Inc 386 255-1955
  515 Lpga Blvd Holly Hill (32117) *(G-5518)*

Townsend's, Titusville *Also called Townsend Ceramics & Glass Inc (G-17623)*

Tox Manufacturing Group LLC 310 909-4937
  2145 Sanford Ct Vero Beach (32963) *(G-17809)*

Toyops, Pensacola *Also called Triops Inc (G-13615)*

Toys For Boys Miami LLC 786 464-0160
  1924 N Miami Ave Miami (33136) *(G-10030)*

TP Aerospace Technics LLC (HQ) 407 730-9988
  6470 Narcoossee Rd Ste A Orlando (32822) *(G-12666)*

Tpi Aluminum 239 332-3900
  5612 6th Ave Fort Myers (33907) *(G-4430)*

TPL Manufacturing Inc 954 783-3400
  8854 Pinion Dr Lake Worth (33467) *(G-7237)*

Tpr Systems Inc 850 983-8600
  8100 Armstrong Rd Milton (32583) *(G-10441)*

Tqmuch, Doral *Also called Bella Vista Bakery Inc (G-3131)*

Tra Publishing LLP 305 424-6468
  245 Ne 37th St Miami (33137) *(G-10031)*

Trac Ecological America Inc 954 583-4922
  3400 Sw 26th Ter Ste A3 Fort Lauderdale (33312) *(G-4096)*

Tracking Solutions Corp 877 477-2922
  7791 Nw 46th St Ste 306 Doral (33166) *(G-3398)*

Tracto Parts Corp 305 972-1357
  7401 Nw 68th St Ste 122 Miami (33166) *(G-10032)*

Trademark Components Inc 813 948-2233
  21432 Keating Way Lutz (33549) *(G-8018)*

Trademark Signs LLC 954 859-6220
  2051 Green Rd Ste E Deerfield Beach (33064) *(G-2827)*

Tradepak Inc 305 871-2247
  4041 Nw 25th St A Miami (33142) *(G-10033)*

Tradestation Technologies Inc (HQ) 954 652-7000
  8050 Sw 10th St Ste 2000 Plantation (33324) *(G-13897)*

Tradewind Custom Cabinetry LLC 239 257-3295
  1213 Cape Coral Pkwy E Cape Coral (33904) *(G-1400)*

Tradewinds Climate System LLC 855 452-0005
  10300 Nw 19th St Ste 105 Doral (33172) *(G-3399)*

Tradewinds Power Corp 863 382-2166
  2717 Alt Us Hwy 27 S Sebring (33870) *(G-15948)*

Tradewinds Power Corp (HQ) 305 592-9745
  5820 Nw 84th Ave Doral (33166) *(G-3400)*

Trading Company, The, Largo *Also called Ttc-The Trading Company Inc (G-7699)*

A
L
P
H
A
B
E
T
I
C

Trading Post of Central Fla 954 675-2149
7626 Nw 25th St Margate (33063) *(G-8157)*

Tradingflex Inc 877 522-3535
1395 Brickell Ave Ste 800 Miami (33131) *(G-10034)*

Trafalger Communications Inc 941 365-7702
331 S Pineapple Ave Sarasota (34236) *(G-15857)*

Traffic Control Pdts Fla Inc 813 621-8484
4020 Edison Ave Fort Myers (33916) *(G-4431)*

Traffic Control Pdts Fla Inc 407 521-6777
249 N Ivey Ln Ste A Orlando (32811) *(G-12667)*

Traffic Control Pdts Fla Inc 352 372-7088
5639 Witten Rd Jacksonville (32254) *(G-6562)*

Traffipax LLC 561 881-7400
16490 Innovation Dr Jupiter (33478) *(G-6811)*

Trailblazerai Inc 727 859-2732
10460 Rsvelt Blvd N 298 Saint Petersburg (33716) *(G-15215)*

Trailer 1, Port Saint Lucie *Also called Sterling Facility Services LLC (G-14450)*

Trailer Source, The, Ocala *Also called U-Dump Trailers LLC (G-11505)*

Trailmate Inc 941 739-5743
6620 Suemac Pl Jacksonville (32254) *(G-6563)*

Trainor Metal Products Inc 561 395-5520
171 Nw 16th St Boca Raton (33432) *(G-721)*

Trak Engineering Incorporated 850 878-4585
2901 Crescent Dr Tallahassee (32301) *(G-16514)*

Trakka USA LLC 505 345-0270
4725 Lena Rd Unit 103 Bradenton (34211) *(G-1062)*

Traklite Wheels, Hialeah *Also called Db Motoring Group Inc (G-5110)*

Trane Central America Inc 305 592-8646
7650 Nw 19th St Ste 270 Miami (33126) *(G-10035)*

Trane Inc 352 237-0136
4500 Sw 40th Ave Ocala (34474) *(G-11502)*

Trane Inc 772 621-3200
400 Nw Enterprise Dr Port Saint Lucie (34986) *(G-14457)*

Trane Inc 954 421-7133
2103 Sw 3rd St Pompano Beach (33069) *(G-14217)*

Trane Technologies Company LLC 305 592-0672
2660 Nw 89th Ct Doral (33172) *(G-3401)*

Trane Technologies Company LLC 850 873-8200
200 Aberdeen Loop Panama City (32405) *(G-13314)*

Trane US Inc 813 877-8251
902 N Himes Ave Tampa (33609) *(G-17364)*

Trane US Inc 239 277-0344
14241 Jtport Loop W Ste 1 Fort Myers (33913) *(G-4432)*

Trane US Inc 904 538-8600
8929 Western Way Ste 1 Jacksonville (32256) *(G-6564)*

Trane US Inc 954 499-6900
2884 Corporate Way Miramar (33025) *(G-10554)*

Trane US Inc 561 683-1521
6965 Vista Pkwy N Ste 11 West Palm Beach (33411) *(G-18186)*

Trane US Inc 850 574-1726
104-1 Hamilton Park Dr Tallahassee (32304) *(G-16515)*

Trane US Inc 813 877-8253
4720 E Adamo Dr Tampa (33605) *(G-17365)*

Trane US Inc 305 592-8646
7600 Nw 19th St Ste 105 Miami (33126) *(G-10036)*

Trann Technologies Inc 888 668-6700
12526 Us Hwy 90 Mossy Head (32434) *(G-10595)*

Trans - Cem Dade City, Dade City *Also called New Line Transport LLC (G-2321)*

Trans-Resources LLC 305 933-8301
17780 Collins Ave Sunny Isles Beach (33160) *(G-16284)*

Transamerica Intl Brdcstg Inc 305 477-0973
3100 Nw 72nd Ave Ste 112 Miami (33122) *(G-10037)*

Transand, Crestview *Also called G2c Enterprises Inc (G-2245)*

Transdermal Technologies Inc 561 848-2345
521 Northlake Blvd Ste B North Palm Beach (33408) *(G-11183)*

Transition of Slc Inc 772 461-4486
7300 Commercial Cir Fort Pierce (34951) *(G-4540)*

Transitions Lenses, Pinellas Park *Also called Transitions Optical Inc (G-13732)*

Transitions Optical Inc 727 545-0400
9251 Belcher Rd N Ste B Pinellas Park (33782) *(G-13732)*

Transmotion Medical, Ocala *Also called Winco Mfg LLC (G-11513)*

Transport A/C Inc 954 254-4822
91 S Madison Dr Pensacola (32505) *(G-13614)*

Transport PC USA Inc 813 264-1700
1423 Baythorn Dr Wesley Chapel (33543) *(G-17888)*

Transportation, Callahan *Also called Reliable Site Solutions LLC (G-1257)*

Transprtation Ctrl Systems Inc 813 630-2800
1030 S 86th St Tampa (33619) *(G-17366)*

Transtat Equipment Inc 407 857-2040
510 Thorpe Rd Orlando (32824) *(G-12668)*

Trap World LLC 305 517-5676
2125 Biscayne Blvd # 400 Miami (33137) *(G-10038)*

Trash Express SW Inc 239 340-5291
3040 Oasis Grand Blvd # 2104 Fort Myers (33916) *(G-4433)*

Trasport John 321 452-6789
645 S Plumosa St Ste 5 Merritt Island (32952) *(G-8600)*

Trauma Tattoos, Winter Park *Also called Simetri Inc (G-18537)*

Traumaone Helicopter Base 386 755-9294
3792 E Us Highway 90 Lake City (32055) *(G-7049)*

Traveling Canvas Corporation 305 259-2001
15400 Sw 67th Ct Palmetto Bay (33157) *(G-13221)*

Travis Lh LLC 863 967-0628
1800 42nd St Nw Winter Haven (33881) *(G-18475)*

Treace Medical Concepts Inc 904 373-5940
203 Fort Wade Rd Unit 150 Ponte Vedra (32081) *(G-14259)*

Treadmill Parts Zone 305 336-5600
11401 Nw 122nd St Medley (33178) *(G-8337)*

Treadstone Performance 305 972-9600
10340 Sw 187th St Cutler Bay (33157) *(G-2306)*

Treadstone Prfmce Engrg Inc 888 789-4586
9486 Sw 222nd Ln Cutler Bay (33190) *(G-2307)*

Treadway Industries LLC 352 326-3313
410 Virginia St Minneola (34715) *(G-10453)*

Treasure Cast Prenting Mag Inc 772 672-8588
2162 Nw Reserve Park Trce Port Saint Lucie (34986) *(G-14458)*

Treasure Chest of Sweetwater 407 788-0020
2901 W State Road 434 # 121 Longwood (32779) *(G-7953)*

Treasure Coast Canvas 772 210-2588
6538 Se Federal Hwy Stuart (34997) *(G-16240)*

Treasure Coast Machines Inc 772 283-2024
3081 Se Slater St Stuart (34997) *(G-16241)*

Treasure Coast Seadoo Yamaha, Stuart *Also called Power Sports Treasure Coast (G-16200)*

Treasure Coast Sealing Co 772 834-5014
8949 Se Bridge Rd Hobe Sound (33455) *(G-5485)*

Treasure Coastline, Fort Lauderdale *Also called Gulfstream Media Group Inc (G-3854)*

Treasure Cove II Inc 941 966-2004
8927 S Tamiami Trl Sarasota (34238) *(G-15858)*

Treasure CST Curb & Therm Plas 772 287-0391
2580 Sw Hidden Pond Way Palm City (34990) *(G-13062)*

Treasured Photo Gifts LLC 407 324-4816
107 Commerce St Lake Mary (32746) *(G-7113)*

Trebor USA Corp 954 922-1620
3901 N 29th Ave Hollywood (33020) *(G-5673)*

Tree Innovations, Maitland *Also called Botanical Innovations Inc (G-8053)*

Treetop Industries LLC 904 471-4412
219 Marshside Dr Saint Augustine (32080) *(G-14907)*

Tremron Inc (HQ) 305 825-9000
11321 Nw 138th St Medley (33178) *(G-8338)*

Tremron LLC (PA) 904 359-5900
2885 Saint Clair St Jacksonville (32254) *(G-6565)*

Tremron LLC 904 886-1970
9440 Philips Hwy Jacksonville (32256) *(G-6566)*

Tremron LLC 863 491-0990
3144 Ne Highway 17 Arcadia (34266) *(G-195)*

Tremron Group, Jacksonville *Also called Tremron LLC (G-6565)*

Tremron Group, Arcadia *Also called Tremron LLC (G-195)*

Trend At LLC 786 300-2550
2627 S Bayshore Dr Miami (33133) *(G-10039)*

Trend Magazines Inc (HQ) 727 821-5800
490 1st Ave S Ste 800 Saint Petersburg (33701) *(G-15216)*

Trend Offset Printing Svcs Inc 562 598-2446
10301 Busch Dr N Jacksonville (32218) *(G-6567)*

Trendy Entertainment Inc 814 384-7123
4910 Sw 78th Ln Gainesville (32608) *(G-4778)*

Trenwa Inc 863 666-1680
1920 Longhorn Ave Lakeland (33801) *(G-7465)*

Trepko Inc 813 443-0794
4893 W Waters Ave Ste C-F Tampa (33634) *(G-17367)*

Tres Leches Factory & Beyond, Doral *Also called Parinto Global Enterprises LLC (G-3322)*

Trese Inc 321 632-7272
2040 Murrell Rd Rockledge (32955) *(G-14752)*

Trese Printing, Rockledge *Also called Trese Inc (G-14752)*

Tri Inc 813 267-1201
107 S Willow Ave Tampa (33606) *(G-17368)*

Tri C Petroleum Inc 941 756-3370
6442 Shoal Creek St Cir Bradenton (34202) *(G-1063)*

Tri County Metals 850 574-4001
3708 Nw Passage Tallahassee (32303) *(G-16516)*

Tri County Printing Co In 561 477-8487
9070 Kimberly Blvd Boca Raton (33434) *(G-722)*

Tri Gas 05, Clearwater *Also called Matheson Tri-Gas Inc (G-1686)*

Tri Tech Metal Inc 727 946-1229
6925 Daubon Ct New Port Richey (34655) *(G-10989)*

Tri-County Aerospace Inc 305 639-3356
2080 Nw 96th Ave Doral (33172) *(G-3402)*

Tri-County Cabinetry Wdwrk LLC 850 238-6226
16050 Nw Ashley Shiver Rd Altha (32421) *(G-78)*

Tri-County Chemical Co 407 682-3550
2578 Park St Unit 5 Apopka (32712) *(G-181)*

Tri-County Woodworking LLC 954 850-2222
3001 Sw 10th St Pompano Beach (33069) *(G-14218)*

Tri-Deck LLC (PA) 386 748-3239
3402 Black Willow Trl Deland (32724) *(G-2914)*

Tri-Edge Industries LLC 561 703-5961
6586 Hypoluxo Rd Lake Worth (33467) *(G-7238)*

Tri-Fecta Solutions LLC 954 908-1669
3900 W Commercial Blvd Fort Lauderdale (33309) *(G-4097)*

Tri-H Metal Products Inc....941 753-7311
5815 21st St E Bradenton (34203) ***(G-1064)***
Tri-State Demolition LLC....850 597-8722
5272 Crawfordville Rd Tallahassee (32305) ***(G-16517)***
Tri-Tech Electronics Inc....407 277-2131
9480 E Colonial Dr Orlando (32817) ***(G-12669)***
Tri-Tech of Florida Inc....727 544-8836
5151 Park St N Saint Petersburg (33709) ***(G-15217)***
Tria Beauty, Tampa *Also called Channel Investments LLC* ***(G-16700)***
Triach Industries, Hollywood *Also called Triarch International Inc* ***(G-5674)***
Triad Edm Inc....352 489-5336
14872 Sw 111th St Dunnellon (34432) ***(G-3468)***
Triad Electric Vehicles, Boca Raton *Also called Valiant Transport Group LLC* ***(G-741)***
Triad Isotopes Inc (PA)....407 455-6700
4205 Vineland Rd Ste L13 Orlando (32811) ***(G-12670)***
Trial Exhibits Inc (PA)....813 258-6153
1177 W Cass St Tampa (33606) ***(G-17369)***
Trialworks, Coral Gables *Also called Lawex Corporation* ***(G-2081)***
Triangle Reprogressives, Orlando *Also called Repro Plus Inc* ***(G-12547)***
Triangle Shopping Guide, Mount Dora *Also called Mid-Florida Publications Inc* ***(G-10605)***
Triangle Shopping Guide Inc....352 589-8811
4645 N Highway 19a Mount Dora (32757) ***(G-10616)***
Triarch International Inc....305 622-3400
4811 Sarazen Dr Hollywood (33021) ***(G-5674)***
Triatomic Environmental Inc....561 748-4864
1838 Park Ln S Jupiter (33458) ***(G-6812)***
Tribune Media Services Inc....407 420-6200
64 E Concord St Orlando (32801) ***(G-12671)***
Tribute Baking Company, Medley *Also called Hometown Foods Usa LLC* ***(G-8254)***
Tricen Technologies Fla LLC (PA)....866 620-9407
500 Farmers Market Rd # 6 Fort Pierce (34982) ***(G-4541)***
Trident Building Systems Inc....941 755-7073
2812 Tallevast Rd Sarasota (34243) ***(G-15571)***
Trident Pontoons Inc....352 253-1400
28240 Lake Indus Blvd Tavares (32778) ***(G-17525)***
Tridor Group Inc....786 707-2241
10118 W Flagler St Miami (33174) ***(G-10040)***
Trifecta Phrmceuticals USA LLC (PA)....888 296-9067
4100 N Powerline Rd J4 Pompano Beach (33073) ***(G-14219)***
Trifecta Publishing....863 676-6311
3900 Chalet Suzanne Dr Lake Wales (33859) ***(G-7178)***
Trigeant Ep Ltd....561 999-9916
3020 N Military Trl # 100 Boca Raton (33431) ***(G-723)***
Trikaroo....800 679-3415
5525 Commerce Dr Ste 1 Orlando (32839) ***(G-12672)***
Trilectron....941 721-1000
11001 Us Highway 41 N Palmetto (34221) ***(G-13198)***
Trim Rite Trimmings and Lace, Hialeah *Also called American S-Shore Plting Sttchi* ***(G-5050)***
Trim Spot, Eustis *Also called Kevco Builders Inc* ***(G-3561)***
Trim-Line of Miami Inc....305 556-6210
2755 W 81st St Hialeah (33016) ***(G-5381)***
Trim-Pak Corporation (PA)....407 851-8900
8700 S Orange Ave Orlando (32824) ***(G-12673)***
Trine Industries Inc....561 995-1995
2901 Clint Moore Rd Boca Raton (33496) ***(G-724)***
Trinetics Group, Melbourne *Also called Stern Brands Inc* ***(G-8531)***
Trinity Creamery Inc....813 926-2023
14167 Wadsworth Dr Odessa (33556) ***(G-11586)***
Trinity Exterior Solutions LLC....850 393-9682
4292 Sundance Way Holt (32564) ***(G-5694)***
Trinity Fabricators Inc....904 284-9657
825 Corporate Sq Green Cove Springs (32043) ***(G-4839)***
Trinity Graphic Usa Inc....941 355-2636
885 Tallevast Rd Ste D Sarasota (34243) ***(G-15572)***
Trinity Manufacturing Corp....941 727-9595
6205 31st St E Ste A Bradenton (34203) ***(G-1065)***
Trinity Materials, Fanning Springs *Also called A Materials Group Inc* ***(G-3571)***
Trinity Mobility Inc....727 389-1438
8343 Royal Hart Dr New Port Richey (34653) ***(G-10990)***
Trinu Powder Coating LLC....727 316-6700
7915 Congress St Port Richey (34668) ***(G-14380)***
Trio Envmtl Solutions LLC....850 543-9125
301 Friar Tuck Rd Mary Esther (32569) ***(G-8180)***
Triops Inc....850 479-4415
3330 Mclemore Dr Ste B Pensacola (32514) ***(G-13615)***
Triple Crown Printing....561 939-6440
5801 Congress Ave Boca Raton (33487) ***(G-725)***
Triple J Marketing LLC....813 247-6999
301 W Platt St Tampa (33606) ***(G-17370)***
Triple Play Cmmunications Corp....321 327-8997
250 East Dr Ste F Melbourne (32904) ***(G-8553)***
Triple Seven Home LLC....321 652-5151
3385 Grant Rd Grant (32949) ***(G-4813)***
Tripp Electric Motors Inc....561 996-3333
1233 Nw Avenue L Belle Glade (33430) ***(G-345)***
Tritech Industries LLC....954 383-3545
5204 Ne 12th Ave Oakland Park (33334) ***(G-11301)***
Triton Seafood Co....305 888-8999
7301 Nw 77th St Medley (33166) ***(G-8339)***
Triton Stone Holdings LLC (PA)....219 669-4890
800 Nw 65th St Fort Lauderdale (33309) ***(G-4098)***
Triton Submarines LLC....772 770-1995
10055 102nd Ter Sebastian (32958) ***(G-15906)***
Triumph Arstrctres - Vght Coml, Stuart *Also called Triumph Group Inc* ***(G-16242)***
Triumph Group Inc....772 220-5000
1845 Se Airport Rd Stuart (34996) ***(G-16242)***
Triumph Group Consulting....352 213-3007
1720 Nw 122nd St Gainesville (32606) ***(G-4779)***
Triumph Hosiery Corp....954 929-6021
4624 Hollywood Blvd # 205 Hollywood (33021) ***(G-5675)***
Triumph Transport Inc....863 226-7276
1104 Bartow Rd Apt 173 Lakeland (33801) ***(G-7466)***
Triumphant Magazine LLC....407 549-5443
2651 Arcadia St Deltona (32738) ***(G-3055)***
Triumvirate Environmental....407 859-4441
10100 Rocket Blvd Orlando (32824) ***(G-12674)***
Trivantis, Deerfield Beach *Also called SC Elearning LLC* ***(G-2803)***
Trivantis Corporation (HQ)....513 929-0188
400 Fairway Dr Ste 101 Deerfield Beach (33441) ***(G-2828)***
Trivecta Pharmaceuticals Inc....561 856-0842
1 E Broward Blvd Ste 700 Fort Lauderdale (33301) ***(G-4099)***
Trividia Meditech LLC....954 677-9201
2400 Nw 55th Ct Fort Lauderdale (33309) ***(G-4100)***
Troika Group Inc....561 313-1119
12300 South Shore Blvd # 20 Wellington (33414) ***(G-17867)***
Trojan Fla Powdr Coating Inc....941 351-0500
1300 Hardin Ave Sarasota (34243) ***(G-15573)***
Trolley Boats....727 588-1100
9470 Ulmerton Rd Ste 6b Largo (33771) ***(G-7697)***
Tromtech, Pompano Beach *Also called Savvy Associate Inc* ***(G-14167)***
Trophy Animal Health Care, Pensacola *Also called Pegasus Laboratories Inc* ***(G-13569)***
Tropic Guard Industries LLC....813 447-3938
6727 Clair Shore Dr Apollo Beach (33572) ***(G-97)***
Tropic Isles Co-Op Inc....941 721-8888
1503 28th Ave W Palmetto (34221) ***(G-13199)***
Tropic Manufacturing Inc....863 673-3179
1451 Commerce Dr Labelle (33935) ***(G-6988)***
Tropic Seal Industries Inc....239 543-8069
1745 Coral Way Fort Myers (33917) ***(G-4434)***
Tropic Shield Inc....954 731-5553
3031 Nw 28th St Lauderdale Lakes (33311) ***(G-7721)***
Tropic Shirts, Tarpon Springs *Also called Tropic Signs Inc* ***(G-17497)***
Tropic Signs Inc....727 942-4129
716 Wesley Ave Ste 5 Tarpon Springs (34689) ***(G-17497)***
Tropical Asphalt LLC....954 983-3434
1904 Sw 31st Ave Hallandale (33009) ***(G-4930)***
Tropical Assemblies Inc....954 396-9999
4066 Ne 5th Ave Oakland Park (33334) ***(G-11302)***
Tropical Awning Florida Inc....561 276-1144
335 Se 1st Ave Ste A Delray Beach (33444) ***(G-3028)***
Tropical Custom Coatings....941 475-3663
11354 Zola Ave Port Charlotte (33981) ***(G-14319)***
Tropical Designs, Melbourne *Also called Allgeo & Yerkes Entps Inc* ***(G-8361)***
Tropical Dvrsons Mrina MGT Inc....954 922-0387
3200 N 29th Ave Hollywood (33020) ***(G-5676)***
Tropical Enterprises Intl Inc (PA)....813 837-9800
8625 Florida Mining Blvd Tampa (33634) ***(G-17371)***
Tropical MBC LLC....727 498-6511
250 Corey Ave St Pete Beach (33706) ***(G-16093)***
Tropical Mfg Inc....305 394-6280
783 W 18th St Hialeah (33010) ***(G-5382)***
Tropical Paper Box....305 592-5520
1401 Nw 78th Ave Doral (33126) ***(G-3403)***
Tropical Paver Sealing....727 786-4011
4834 Windingbrook Trl Wesley Chapel (33544) ***(G-17889)***
Tropical Pcb Design Svcs Inc....561 784-9536
7960 Banyan Blvd Loxahatchee (33470) ***(G-7976)***
Tropical Prints Inc A Corp....305 261-9926
4401 Sw 75th Ave Ste 2 Miami (33155) ***(G-10041)***
Tropical Sands....786 573-3094
16000 Sw 200th St Miami (33187) ***(G-10042)***
Tropical Showers Inc....954 260-5196
1433 Ne 28th St Pompano Beach (33064) ***(G-14220)***
Tropical Signs & Graphics....321 458-7742
425 Deb Ln Merritt Island (32952) ***(G-8601)***
Tropical Skoops Llc....954 440-8736
11635 Red Rd Miramar (33025) ***(G-10555)***
Tropical Stencil Pcb Inc....561 972-5133
1530 Cypress Dr Ste E Jupiter (33469) ***(G-6813)***
Tropical Textiles Intl Inc....305 364-4595
6073 Nw 167th St Ste C17 Hialeah (33015) ***(G-5383)***
Tropicana Manufacturing Co Inc....800 237-7799
1001 13th Ave E Bradenton (34208) ***(G-1066)***
Tropicana Products Inc (HQ)....941 747-4461
1001 13th Ave E Bradenton (34208) ***(G-1067)***
Tropicana Products Inc....772 465-2030
6500 Glades Cut Off Rd Fort Pierce (34981) ***(G-4542)***
Tropichem Research Labs LLC....561 804-7603
15335 Pk Of Cmmrce Blvd S Jupiter (33478) ***(G-6814)***

ALPHABETIC

Tropichem Research Labs LLC (PA)............................314 686-4614
  15843 Guild Ct Jupiter (33478) (G-6815)

Tropicolor Display Graphics, Miami Beach Also called Tropicolor Photo Service
Inc (G-10239)

Tropicolor Photo Service Inc.....................................305 672-3720
  1442 Alton Rd Miami Beach (33139) (G-10239)

Tropix Marble Company..239 334-2371
  17121 Primavera Cir Cape Coral (33909) (G-1401)

Troxel Aerospace Inds Inc..720 626-0454
  2023 Ne 55th Blvd Gainesville (32641) (G-4780)

Troy Industries Inc..305 324-1742
  2100 Nw 102nd Pl Doral (33172) (G-3404)

Troy Thompson Inc...813 716-1598
  20255 Denny Dr Brooksville (34601) (G-1213)

Trs, Orlando Also called T R S (G-12644)

Trs Industries Inc...561 880-0031
  6845 Finamore Cir Lake Worth (33467) (G-7239)

Trs Wireless Inc...407 447-7333
  1711 S Division Ave Orlando (32805) (G-12675)

Tru Cane Sugar Corp...561 833-1731
  1 N Clematis St Ste 200 West Palm Beach (33401) (G-18187)

Tru Craft Woodworks LLC...561 441-2742
  1865 Sw 4th Ave Ste D9 Delray Beach (33444) (G-3029)

Tru Dimensions Printing Inc......................................407 339-3410
  2100 N R Reagan Blvd 10 Longwood (32750) (G-7954)

Tru Mension Mfg Solutions.......................................321 255-4665
  3900 Dow Rd Ste C Melbourne (32934) (G-8554)

Tru Simulation + Training Inc.....................................813 792-9300
  1551 Gunn Hwy Odessa (33556) (G-11587)

Tru-Flo Corp...561 996-5850
  924 Nw 13th St Belle Glade (33430) (G-346)

Trubendz Technology Inc..305 378-9337
  18495 S Dixie Hwy Ste 213 Cutler Bay (33157) (G-2308)

Trubendz Technology Inc (PA)...................................305 378-9337
  19101 Sw 108th Ave # 19 Cutler Bay (33157) (G-2309)

Trucraft Specialties Inc..561 441-2742
  1503 Hummingbird Dr Delray Beach (33444) (G-3030)

True Back, Belleair Also called Morcent Import Export Inc (G-352)

True Bloods Colonial Printing, Lakeland Also called Hunt Enterprises Inc (G-7346)

True Grit Abrasives Inc...813 247-5219
  7015 E 14th Ave Tampa (33619) (G-17372)

True House Inc..386 325-9085
  150 State Road 207 East Palatka (32131) (G-3477)

True House Inc (PA)..904 757-7500
  4745 Sutton Park Ct # 501 Jacksonville (32224) (G-6568)

True Line Industries Inc..561 745-4828
  13841 151st Ln N Jupiter (33478) (G-6816)

True Loaf, Miami Beach Also called Corvatsch Corp (G-10180)

True Plumbing Svc Inc...941 296-5123
  11729 Meadowgate Pl Bradenton (34211) (G-1068)

True Stone Corp..772 334-9797
  7324 Commercial Cir Fort Pierce (34951) (G-4543)

True Stone Masonry LLC...772 334-9797
  7324 Commercial Cir Fort Pierce (34951) (G-4544)

True Truss, Jacksonville Also called True House Inc (G-6568)

Truear Inc...352 314-8805
  18997 Us Highway 441 Mount Dora (32757) (G-10617)

Truecare24 Inc...240 434-0963
  8270 Woodland Center Blvd Tampa (33614) (G-17373)

Truenorth Iq Inc...678 849-5000
  1193 Se Port St Lcie Blvd Port Saint Lucie (34952) (G-14459)

Truesouth Marine Corp..813 286-0716
  4810 Culbreath Isles Rd Tampa (33629) (G-17374)

Truffles Coffee House & Bakery, Jacksonville Also called St Johns Bky & Gourmet Fd
Co (G-6502)

Trugard, Doral Also called Interntnal Tech Sltons Sup LLC (G-3259)

Trugreen Products LLC..954 629-5794
  1010 S Ocean Blvd Apt 408 Pompano Beach (33062) (G-14221)

Trujillo Oil Plant Inc...305 696-8701
  3325 Nw 62nd St Miami (33147) (G-10043)

Trulieve Cannabis Corp (HQ)....................................844 878-5438
  6749 Ben Bostic Rd Quincy (32351) (G-14551)

Trumeter Company Inc (HQ).....................................954 725-6699
  6601 Lyons Rd Ste H7 Coconut Creek (33073) (G-2008)

Truplate, Tampa Also called Photoengraving Inc (G-17165)

Trusco Manufacturing Company.................................352 237-0311
  545 Nw 68th Ave Ocala (34482) (G-11503)

Truss Systems of Vlsia Flgler....................................386 255-3009
  3615 S Us Highway 1 Bunnell (32110) (G-1236)

Truss William...954 438-4710
  17800 Nw 14th St Pembroke Pines (33029) (G-13420)

Trusscorp International Inc..305 882-8826
  9590 Nw 89th Ave Medley (33178) (G-8340)

Trusses Unlimited Inc (PA)......................................904 355-6611
  320 San Juan Dr Ponte Vedra Beach (32082) (G-14281)

Trussway Manufacturing Inc......................................407 857-2777
  8850 Trussway Blvd Orlando (32824) (G-12676)

Trusswood Inc..321 383-0366
  3620 Bobbi Ln Titusville (32780) (G-17624)

Truth Nutrition LLC...754 400-0382
  4302 Hollywood Blvd # 16 Hollywood (33021) (G-5677)

Truvoice Telecom Inc...888 448-5556
  3102 Cherry Palm Dr # 145 Tampa (33619) (G-17375)

Trx Integration Inc...727 797-4707
  401 Corbett St Ste 470 Belleair (33756) (G-353)

Trxade Inc...727 230-1915
  3840 Land O Lakes Blvd Land O Lakes (34639) (G-7507)

Try Wine Inc..727 898-9463
  11812 143rd St Largo (33774) (G-7698)

Tryana LLC..813 467-9916
  4901 W Rio Vista Ave A Tampa (33634) (G-17376)

TSA Rewinds Florida Inc...305 681-2030
  13050 Nw 47th Ave Opa Locka (33054) (G-11795)

Tsb Emulsions LLC..904 249-5115
  1306 Big Tree Rd Neptune Beach (32266) (G-10959)

TSC, Fort Walton Beach Also called Northrop Grumman Systems Corp (G-4598)

Tsd Group Corp...954 940-2111
  306 International Pkwy B Sunrise (33325) (G-16385)

Tsl-Reico, Fort Walton Beach Also called Technical Service Labs Inc (G-4612)

Tsm Champ LLC...615 806-7900
  2359 Trailmate Dr Sarasota (34243) (G-15574)

Tsn Manufacturing...813 740-1876
  4011 E 21st Ave Tampa (33605) (G-17377)

Tsn Manufacturing Inc..727 709-9802
  807 Hickory Fork Dr Seffner (33584) (G-15966)

TSO Mobile, Doral Also called Tracking Solutions Corp (G-3398)

TST Industries LLC..386 868-2011
  623 Pleasant St Lake Helen (32744) (G-7055)

Ttc Performance Products Inc...................................407 630-9359
  1355 Bennett Dr Unit 129 Longwood (32750) (G-7955)

Ttc-The Trading Company Inc (PA)..............................503 982-0880
  2062 20th Ave Se Largo (33771) (G-7699)

TTI Holdings Inc (PA)..813 623-2675
  2710 E 5th Ave Tampa (33605) (G-17378)

Tts Food LLC...305 622-2726
  15990 Nw 49th Ave Hialeah (33014) (G-5384)

Tua Systems Inc...321 453-3200
  3645 N Courtenay Pkwy Merritt Island (32953) (G-8602)

Tua Systems of Florida Inc..321 341-4944
  3645 N Courtenay Pkwy Merritt Island (32953) (G-8603)

Tube Services-Division, Jacksonville Also called Flotech LLC (G-6113)

Tubos Inc..727 504-0633
  718 4th Ave Ne Largo (33770) (G-7700)

Tucker Lithographic Co...904 276-0568
  661 Blanding Blvd Ste 103 Orange Park (32073) (G-11844)

Tucker Trckg Log Jhnny E Tcker..................................850 258-1982
  2371 County Road 381 Wewahitchka (32465) (G-18302)

Tucker-Davis Technologies Inc...................................386 462-9622
  11930 Research Cir Alachua (32615) (G-23)

Tuckers Machine & Stl Svc Inc...................................352 787-3157
  400 County Road 468 Leesburg (34748) (G-7800)

Tuf Top Coatings...727 527-3382
  4590 60th Ave N Saint Petersburg (33714) (G-15218)

Tuflex Manufacturing Co...954 781-0605
  8421 Sw 28th St Davie (33328) (G-2493)

Tuka Imports LLC...305 640-8336
  3729 Nw 71st St Miami (33147) (G-10044)

Tulipan Bakery Inc (PA)...561 832-6107
  740 Belvedere Rd West Palm Beach (33405) (G-18188)

Tuly Corporation...305 633-0710
  3820 Nw 32nd Ave Miami (33142) (G-10045)

Tumbling Pines Inc..386 437-2668
  10987 State Road 11 Bunnell (32110) (G-1237)

Tupperware Brands Corporation (PA)...........................407 826-5050
  14901 S Ornge Blossom Trl Orlando (32837) (G-12677)

Tupperware Intl Holdings Corp (HQ)............................407 826-5050
  14901 S Ornge Blossom Trl Orlando (32837) (G-12678)

Tupperware Products Inc...407 826-5050
  14901 S Ornge Blossom Trl Orlando (32837) (G-12679)

Tupperware Turkey Inc..407 826-5050
  14901 S Orange Blossom Tr Orlando (32837) (G-12680)

Tupperware US Inc (HQ)..407 826-5050
  14901 S Ornge Blossom Trl Orlando (32837) (G-12681)

Turbine Broach Company..352 795-1163
  521 E Overdrive Cir Hernando (34442) (G-5010)

Turbine Controls LLC..954 517-1706
  3501 Enterprise Way Miramar (33025) (G-10556)

Turbine Generator Maint Inc (PA)................................239 573-1233
  125 Sw 3rd Pl Ste 300 Cape Coral (33991) (G-1402)

Turbine Kinetics Inc...954 744-7526
  3000 Taft St Hollywood (33021) (G-5678)

Turbine Parts Repair Inc...850 983-8600
  8100 Armstrong Rd Milton (32583) (G-10442)

Turbine Resources Intl LLC......................................850 377-0449
  2595a Dog Track Rd Pensacola (32506) (G-13616)

Turbine Solution Group, Deland Also called Diemech Turbine Solution Inc (G-2864)

Turbine Weld Industries LLC.......................................941 485-5113
  402 Substation Rd Venice (34285) (G-17725)

Turbo Parts LLC 352 351-4510
  810 Nw 25th Ave Ste 102 Ocala (34475) *(G-11504)*

Turbo Rotating Spare US, Miami *Also called Multi-Commercial Services Corp (G-9600)*

Turbo Vacuum, Orlando *Also called Walden Consulting LLC (G-12710)*

Turbocombustor Technology Inc (HQ) 772 287-7770
  3651 Se Commerce Ave Stuart (34997) *(G-16243)*

Turbousa Inc 954 767-8631
  1867 Ne 33rd St Oakland Park (33306) *(G-11303)*

Turf Care Supply LLC 863 655-0700
  422 Webster Turn Dr Sebring (33870) *(G-15949)*

Turin Em Inc 305 825-2004
  8045 W 26th Ct Hialeah (33016) *(G-5385)*

Turn Key Industries 813 671-3446
  9901 Alafia River Ln Gibsonton (33534) *(G-4802)*

Turner Envirologic Inc 954 422-9566
  1140 Sw 34th Ave Deerfield Beach (33442) *(G-2829)*

Turner Machine & Supply Co 772 464-4550
  5000 Orange Ave Fort Pierce (34947) *(G-4545)*

Turning Point Propellers Inc 904 900-7739
  11762 Marco Beach Dr # 2 Jacksonville (32224) *(G-6569)*

Turnstile Publishing Company (HQ) 407 563-7000
  1500 Park Center Dr Orlando (32835) *(G-12682)*

Turtle Publishing Co 904 568-1484
  1034 Hendricks Ave Jacksonville (32207) *(G-6570)*

Tuscola Wind II LLC 561 691-7171
  700 Universe Blvd Juno Beach (33408) *(G-6668)*

Tutela Monitoring Systems LLC 941 462-1067
  485 Mariner Blvd Spring Hill (34609) *(G-16083)*

Tuthill Corporation 727 446-8593
  2050 Sunnydale Blvd Clearwater (33765) *(G-1836)*

Tutogen Medical Inc (HQ) 386 418-8888
  11621 Research Cir Alachua (32615) *(G-24)*

Tutti Hogar International LLC 305 705-4735
  19472 Diplomat Dr Miami (33179) *(G-10046)*

Tuuci, Hialeah *Also called Ultimate Umbrella Company Inc (G-5390)*

Tuuci LLC 305 634-5116
  1000 Se 8th St Ste A Hialeah (33010) *(G-5386)*

Tuuci Worldwide 305 634-5116
  1000 Se 8th St Hialeah (33010) *(G-5387)*

Tuuci Worldwide LLC 305 823-3480
  16200 Nw 49th Ave Hialeah (33014) *(G-5388)*

Tuuci Worldwide LLC (PA) 305 634-5116
  2900 Nw 35th St Miami (33142) *(G-10047)*

TV Film International Inc 305 671-3265
  2600 Sw 3rd Ave Ste 850 Miami (33129) *(G-10048)*

TV Shield, The, Altamonte Springs *Also called Protective Enclosures Co LLC (G-67)*

TW Byrds Sons Inc 386 935-1544
  11860 E Us 27 Branford (32008) *(G-1115)*

Twin Upholstery & Furn Mfg 954 791-0744
  1868 Nw 38th Ave 3 Fort Lauderdale (33311) *(G-4101)*

Twin Vee Catamarans Inc 772 429-2525
  3101 S Us Highway 1 Fort Pierce (34982) *(G-4546)*

Twinlab Cnsld Holdings Inc (PA) 561 443-4301
  4800 T Rex Ave Ste 305 Boca Raton (33431) *(G-726)*

Twinlab Consolidation Corp 800 645-5626
  4800 T Rex Ave Ste 350 Boca Raton (33431) *(G-727)*

Twinlab Corporation 800 645-5626
  4800 T Rex Ave Ste 305 Boca Raton (33431) *(G-728)*

Twinlab Holdings Inc (PA) 800 645-5626
  4800 T Rex Ave Ste 305 Boca Raton (33431) *(G-729)*

Twinlab Holdings Inc 800 645-5626
  2255 Glades Rd Ste 342w Boca Raton (33431) *(G-730)*

Twinoxide-Usa Inc 321 207-8524
  3700 N Courtenay Pkwy Merritt Island (32953) *(G-8604)*

Twins & Martin Equipment Corp 954 802-0345
  80 Sw 8th St Ste 2056 Miami (33130) *(G-10049)*

Twinstar Optics & Coatings Inc 727 847-2300
  6741 Commerce Ave Port Richey (34668) *(G-14381)*

Twinstar Optics Ctngs Cyrstals, Port Richey *Also called Twinstar Optics & Coatings Inc (G-14381)*

Twisted Coffee Canyon Roasters, Pensacola *Also called De Luna Coffee Intl Inc (G-13486)*

Two B Printing Inc 954 566-4886
  625 Ne 42nd St Oakland Park (33334) *(G-11304)*

Two Brothers Cultivation LLC 954 478-2402
  817 Se 2nd Ave Apt 518 Fort Lauderdale (33316) *(G-4102)*

Two Guys Plumbing Supply LLc 321 263-0021
  1030 Sunshine Ln Ste 1020 Altamonte Springs (32714) *(G-74)*

Two Little Fishies Inc 305 623-7695
  15801 Nw 15th Ave Miami (33169) *(G-10050)*

Two Mermaids Swim & Resort Wr, The Villages *Also called Two Mermaids Villages LLC (G-17558)*

Two Mermaids Villages LLC (PA) 352 259-4722
  1039 Canal St The Villages (32162) *(G-17558)*

Two Paper Chasers LLC 813 251-5090
  3214 W San Miguel St Tampa (33629) *(G-17379)*

Two Roads Consulting LLC 305 395-8821
  469 Limewood Ave Dunedin (34698) *(G-3460)*

Two Scents LLC DBA Vinevida 888 527-6805
  14935 Nw 27th Ave Opa Locka (33054) *(G-11796)*

Two Tree Inc 352 284-1763
  24 Nw 33rd Ct Ste A Gainesville (32607) *(G-4781)*

Two Way Radio Gear Inc 800 984-1534
  3245 Okeechobee Rd Fort Pierce (34947) *(G-4547)*

Tws Cabinets LLC 863 614-4693
  2947 Vermont Ave Lakeland (33803) *(G-7467)*

Tws Fabricators 954 983-9749
  2001 N Us Highway 27 Pembroke Pines (33029) *(G-13421)*

TX Trading Inc 786 303-9950
  20355 Ne 34th Ct Apt 427 Miami (33180) *(G-10051)*

Tyco Machine Inc 352 544-0210
  1400 Ponce De Leon Blvd Brooksville (34601) *(G-1214)*

Tycoon Tutti Inc 305 624-7811
  1361 Nw 155th Dr Miami (33169) *(G-10052)*

Tyler Fabricators, Delray Beach *Also called Sea Side Specialties (G-3014)*

Tyrex Ore & Minerals Company 305 333-5288
  8950 Sw 74th Ct Fl 22 Miami (33156) *(G-10053)*

Tyrolit Company, Trinity *Also called Meopta USA Inc (G-17640)*

Tys Variety Co 813 643-1515
  8330 N Florida Ave Tampa (33604) *(G-17380)*

Tyson Petroleum Contrs LLC 850 727-0082
  5311 Tallapoosa Rd Tallahassee (32303) *(G-16518)*

U B Corp 813 884-1463
  9829 Wilsky Blvd Tampa (33615) *(G-17381)*

U C Cabinet Inc 407 322-0968
  222 Hickman Dr Sanford (32771) *(G-15401)*

U C Fab of Florida LLC 407 614-4210
  301 Enterprise St Unit C Ocoee (34761) *(G-11529)*

U D T Inc 850 784-0537
  2304 Grant Ave Panama City (32405) *(G-13315)*

U Got Recovery Inc 407 343-9919
  3406 W Vine St Kissimmee (34741) *(G-6967)*

U M P 305 740-4996
  6262 Bird Rd Miami (33155) *(G-10054)*

U S A Coatings Inc 904 477-0916
  2361 Edwards Ave Jacksonville (32254) *(G-6571)*

U S Awning, Sarasota *Also called United States Awning Company (G-15864)*

U S Composites Inc 561 588-1001
  5101 Georgia Ave West Palm Beach (33405) *(G-18189)*

U S Hardware Supply Inc 407 657-1551
  4675 Metric Dr Winter Park (32792) *(G-18547)*

U S Holdings Inc (PA) 305 885-0301
  3200 W 84th St Hialeah (33018) *(G-5389)*

U S Sign and Mill, Fort Myers *Also called US Sign and Mill Inc (G-4435)*

U Tech, Brooksville *Also called Unbridled Technologies LLC (G-1215)*

U-Dump Trailers LLC 352 351-8510
  2610 Nw 10th St Ocala (34475) *(G-11505)*

U-Load Dumpsters LLC 352 318-3045
  1450 Mitchell Rd Ponce De Leon (32455) *(G-14250)*

U2 Cloud LLC 888 370-5433
  1300 Cooks Ln Green Cove Springs (32043) *(G-4840)*

UAS Drone Corp (PA) 561 693-1424
  420 Royal Palm Way # 100 Palm Beach (33480) *(G-12941)*

UCI Paints, Fort Lauderdale *Also called Union Chemical Industries Corp (G-4105)*

Uct Coatings Inc (PA) 772 872-7110
  3300 Sw 42nd Ave Palm City (34990) *(G-13063)*

Uct Defense, Palm City *Also called Uct Coatings Inc (G-13063)*

Uct2, Miami *Also called Unique Custom Truck & Trlr LLC (G-10063)*

UDC Usa Inc (PA) 813 281-0200
  100 S Ashley Dr Ste 1620 Tampa (33602) *(G-17382)*

Ufg Group Inc (PA) 561 425-6829
  2121 Vista Pkwy West Palm Beach (33411) *(G-18190)*

Uflex Usa Inc 941 351-2628
  6442 Parkland Dr Sarasota (34243) *(G-15575)*

Ufp Orlando LLC 407 982-3312
  7205 Rose Ave Orlando (32810) *(G-12683)*

Ufp Palm Bch LLC DBA Ufp Mami 786 837-0552
  11400 Nw 32nd Ave Miami (33167) *(G-10055)*

Ufp Tampa LLC 813 971-3030
  1003 E 131st Ave Tampa (33612) *(G-17383)*

Ufp Technologies Inc 407 933-4880
  2175 Partin Settlement Rd Kissimmee (34744) *(G-6968)*

Ugp, Longwood *Also called American Mentality Inc (G-7867)*

Uip International Inc (PA) 954 785-3539
  1350 S Dixie Hwy E Pompano Beach (33060) *(G-14222)*

Uk Sailmakers Inc (PA) 941 365-7245
  324 Bernard Ave Sarasota (34243) *(G-15576)*

Uk Sailmakers Sarasota, Sarasota *Also called Uk Sailmakers Inc (G-15576)*

Uk Sails Makers, Miami *Also called Atlantic Sails Makers (G-8764)*

Ukg Inc 954 331-7000
  1485 N Park Dr Weston (33326) *(G-18293)*

Ukg Inc 954 331-7000
  2000 Ultimate Way Weston (33326) *(G-18294)*

Ullman Sails Florida, Sarasota *Also called Douglas A Fisher Inc (G-15661)*

Ullrich's, Wauchula *Also called Franz A Ullrich Jr (G-17827)*

Ultima Design South Fla Inc 305 477-9300
  11305 Nw 128th St Medley (33178) *(G-8341)*

Ultimate Cargo Services LLC.....................954 251-1680
10752 Deerwood Park Blvd Jacksonville (32256) *(G-6572)*

Ultimate Compressor LLC.........................305 720-3079
400 S Hollybrook Dr Apt 1 Pembroke Pines (33025) *(G-13422)*

Ultimate Containers Pro LLC......................786 241-4306
355 Nw 171st St Miami Gardens (33169) *(G-10277)*

Ultimate Door Palm Beach Inc....................561 642-2828
2800 2nd Ave N Lake Worth (33461) *(G-7240)*

Ultimate Kronos Group, Weston *Also called Ukg Inc (G-18294)*

Ultimate Machining Corporation..................954 749-9810
4741 Nw 103rd Ave Sunrise (33351) *(G-16386)*

Ultimate Marine Centl Fla LLC....................407 849-1100
3419 Wd Judge Dr Ste 150 Orlando (32808) *(G-12684)*

Ultimate Overstock LLC...........................407 851-1017
4967 Intl Dr Ste 3a27 Orlando (32819) *(G-12685)*

Ultimate Swimwear Inc...........................386 668-8900
247 N Westmonte Dr Altamonte Springs (32714) *(G-75)*

Ultimate Tool Inc................................954 489-9996
5105 Ne 12th Ave Oakland Park (33334) *(G-11305)*

Ultimate Umbrella Company Inc (PA).............305 634-5116
1000 Se 8th St Ste A Hialeah (33010) *(G-5390)*

Ultimaxx Inc....................................877 300-3424
3651 Fau Blvd Ste 400 Boca Raton (33431) *(G-731)*

Ultimaxx Health, Boca Raton *Also called Ultimaxx Inc (G-731)*

Ultimaxx Health LLC.............................877 300-3424
3651 Fau Blvd Ste 400 Boca Raton (33431) *(G-732)*

Ultra Aerospace Inc.............................305 728-6361
12235 Sw 128th St Miami (33186) *(G-10056)*

Ultra Airconditioning Inc........................877 333-0189
801 Nrthpint Pkwy Ste 106 West Palm Beach (33407) *(G-18191)*

Ultra Base Systems, Saint Petersburg *Also called Innovative Base Tech LLC (G-15085)*

Ultra Clean Systems Inc.........................813 925-1003
110 Douglas Rd E Oldsmar (34677) *(G-11700)*

Ultra Defense, Tampa *Also called UDC Usa Inc (G-17382)*

Ultra Graphics Corp.............................305 593-0202
132 Sw 96th Ave Miami (33174) *(G-10057)*

Ultra Pharma LLC...............................954 532-7539
3131 W Mcnab Rd Pompano Beach (33069) *(G-14223)*

Ultra Prcsion McHning Grnding..................321 725-9655
2870 Kirby Cir Ne Ste 6 Palm Bay (32905) *(G-12926)*

Ultra Tuff Manufacturing Inc....................970 252-9457
8845 Se Robwyn St Hobe Sound (33455) *(G-5486)*

Ultra-Max LLC...................................850 728-8442
3115 Gallimore Dr Tallahassee (32305) *(G-16519)*

Ultra-Pure Bottled Water Inc....................813 835-7873
5202 S Lois Ave Tampa (33611) *(G-17384)*

Ultrabox Inc....................................941 371-0000
5827 17th St E Bradenton (34203) *(G-1069)*

Ultraclenz LLC..................................800 931-8911
1201 Jupiter Park Dr # 1 Jupiter (33458) *(G-6817)*

Ultrafast Systems LLC...........................941 360-2161
8330 Consumer Ct Sarasota (34240) *(G-15859)*

Ultraflex Systems Florida Inc (PA)................973 664-6739
6333 Pelican Creek Cir Riverview (33578) *(G-14580)*

Ultrapanel Marine Inc...........................772 285-4258
2665 S Byshr Dr Ste 220 Miami (33133) *(G-10058)*

Ultrasonic Technologies Inc......................813 973-1702
27247 Breakers Dr Wesley Chapel (33544) *(G-17890)*

Ultrasonics and Magnetics.......................813 740-1800
5275 Causeway Blvd Ste 2 Tampa (33619) *(G-17385)*

Ultratech International Inc (PA)...................904 292-9019
11542 Davis Creek Ct Jacksonville (32256) *(G-6573)*

Ultroid Technologies Inc.........................877 858-0555
3140 W Kennedy Blvd Tampa (33609) *(G-17386)*

Um Kitchen Cabinets Inc.........................772 224-5445
965 Sw North Globe Ave Port Saint Lucie (34953) *(G-14460)*

Uma Holdings Inc...............................786 587-1349
601 S 21st Ave Hollywood (33020) *(G-5679)*

Umbrella Buses Inc..............................754 457-4004
9800 Us 192 Davenport (33897) *(G-2372)*

Umbusa, Davenport *Also called Umbrella Buses Inc (G-2372)*

Umg Recordings Inc.............................305 532-4754
404 Wshington Ave Ste 800 Miami Beach (33139) *(G-10240)*

Unaflex LLC (PA)................................954 943-5002
1350 S Dixie Hwy E Pompano Beach (33060) *(G-14224)*

Unbridled Technologies LLC......................888 334-8402
21125 Cortez Blvd Brooksville (34601) *(G-1215)*

Uncle Carlos Gelatos............................810 523-8506
141 Melody Ln Fort Pierce (34950) *(G-4548)*

Uncle Johns Pride LLC...........................813 685-7745
10250 Woodberry Rd Tampa (33619) *(G-17387)*

Unconventional Marine, Orlando *Also called Summit ATL Productions LLC (G-12630)*

Undersea Breathing Systems.....................561 588-7698
2565 N Dixie Hwy Lake Worth (33460) *(G-7241)*

Underwater Lights Usa Inc.......................954 760-4447
3406 Sw 26th Ter Ste 5 Fort Lauderdale (33312) *(G-4103)*

Underwood Butcher Block Co Inc.................904 338-2348
51 Nitram St Ste 500 Jacksonville (32211) *(G-6574)*

Underwter Fish Light Ltd Lblty...................941 391-5846
20400 Veterans Blvd Port Charlotte (33954) *(G-14320)*

Unfoldingword Corporation.......................407 900-3005
10524 Moss Park Rd # 204 Orlando (32832) *(G-12686)*

UNI Glide Trailer, Venice *Also called Dills Enterprises LLC (G-17683)*

UNI-Box Inc.....................................954 733-3550
1700 Nw 27th St Oakland Park (33311) *(G-11306)*

UNI-Pak Corp....................................407 830-9300
1015 N Ronald Reagan Blvd Longwood (32750) *(G-7956)*

Unibeast Sports LLC.............................813 255-2827
14218 Poke Ridge Dr Riverview (33579) *(G-14581)*

Unico International Trdg Corp.....................561 338-3338
5499 N Federal Hwy Ste P Boca Raton (33487) *(G-733)*

Unicomp Corp of America........................954 755-1710
10101 W Sample Rd Stop 1 Coral Springs (33065) *(G-2223)*

Unicornio Bakery LLC............................786 665-1602
8255 Lake Dr Doral (33166) *(G-3405)*

Unicraft Corp....................................305 633-4945
3640 Nw 52nd St Miami (33142) *(G-10059)*

Unidad Editorial.................................305 371-4428
1444 Biscayne Blvd Miami (33132) *(G-10060)*

Unifab Co, Oakland Park *Also called UNI-Box Inc (G-11306)*

Unifi Aviation LLC................................954 377-2724
50 Terminal Dr Fort Lauderdale (33315) *(G-4104)*

Uniform Authority, The, Miami *Also called International Clothiers Inc (G-9325)*

Uniform Nametape Company Inc..................813 839-6737
5701 S Dale Mabry Hwy Tampa (33611) *(G-17388)*

Unilens Corp USA...............................727 544-2531
21 N Park Place Blvd Clearwater (33759) *(G-1837)*

Unilever..904 378-0298
12200 Presidents Ct Jacksonville (32220) *(G-6575)*

Unimat Industries LLC...........................305 716-0358
6980 Nw 43rd St Miami (33166) *(G-10061)*

Unimed Surgical Products Inc....................727 546-1900
10401 Belcher Rd S Seminole (33777) *(G-15996)*

Uninsred Untd Prchute Tech LLC.................386 736-7589
1645 Lexington Ave Deland (32724) *(G-2915)*

Uninsured Relative Workshop.....................386 736-7589
1645 Lexington Ave Deland (32724) *(G-2916)*

Union Chemical Industries Corp..................954 581-6060
1320 Nw 23rd Ave Fort Lauderdale (33311) *(G-4105)*

Union County Times, Starke *Also called Bradford County Telegraph Inc (G-16096)*

Union Engineering N Amer LLC...................386 445-4200
2361 Mason Ave Ste 100 Daytona Beach (32117) *(G-2615)*

Union Pvc Industries Inc.........................305 883-1640
295 W 27th St Hialeah (33010) *(G-5391)*

Unipower, Coral Springs *Also called Technipower LLC (G-2219)*

Unipress Corporation............................813 623-3731
3501 Queen Palm Dr Tampa (33619) *(G-17389)*

Unique Custom Cabinet Inc......................786 247-4196
6900 Nw 77th Ct Miami (33166) *(G-10062)*

Unique Custom Truck & Trlr LLC.................305 403-7042
7248 Sw 42nd Ter Miami (33155) *(G-10063)*

Unique Designs & Finishes Inc...................772 335-4884
1443 Se Huffman Rd Port Saint Lucie (34952) *(G-14461)*

Unique Electronics Inc (PA)......................407 422-3051
1320 26th St Orlando (32805) *(G-12687)*

Unique Led Products LLC........................440 520-4959
408 Madonna North Port (34287) *(G-11205)*

Unique Marble Inc...............................772 766-4432
780 8th Ct Vero Beach (32962) *(G-17810)*

Unique Marble Polishing Inc......................305 969-1554
18093 Sw 135th Ave Miami (33177) *(G-10064)*

Unique Originals Inc.............................305 634-2274
19205 Sw 66th St Fort Lauderdale (33332) *(G-4106)*

Unique Rabbit Studios Inc........................954 691-1390
1631 S Dixie Hwy Ste B1 Pompano Beach (33060) *(G-14225)*

Unique Recording Software Inc...................917 854-5403
21218 Saint Andrews Blvd Boca Raton (33433) *(G-734)*

Unique Technology Inc...........................941 358-5410
1523 Edgar Pl Sarasota (34240) *(G-15860)*

Unique Technology Inds LLC......................941 358-5410
1523 Edgar Pl Sarasota (34240) *(G-15861)*

Unique Tool & Die LLC...........................772 464-5006
3343 S Us Highway 1 Ste 4 Fort Pierce (34982) *(G-4549)*

Uniroyal Engineered Pdts LLC (HQ)...............941 906-8580
1800 2nd St Ste 970 Sarasota (34236) *(G-15862)*

Uniroyal Globl Engnred Pdts In (PA)..............941 906-8580
1800 2nd St Ste 970 Sarasota (34236) *(G-15863)*

Uniscan LLC....................................305 322-7669
10913 Nw 30th St Ste 101 Doral (33172) *(G-3406)*

Unisigns Usa Inc................................305 509-5232
5526 Nw 79th Ave Doral (33166) *(G-3407)*

Unison Industries LLC (HQ)......................904 739-4000
7575 Baymeadows Way Jacksonville (32256) *(G-6576)*

Unisource Stone LLC............................561 493-0660
2575 Se Federal Hwy # 101 Stuart (34994) *(G-16244)*

Unite Parent Corp (PA)..........................800 432-1729
2000 Ultimate Way Weston (33326) *(G-18295)*

United Abrasives Inc............................239 300-0033
3551 Westview Dr Naples (34104) *(G-10929)*

United Adhesive Products Inc................................863 698-9484
  4202 Hammond Dr Winter Haven (33881) *(G-18476)*

United Advantage Signs Inc................................813 855-3300
  206 Tower Dr Oldsmar (34677) *(G-11701)*

United Advg Publications................................954 730-9700
  3313 W Coml Blvd Ste 130 Fort Lauderdale (33309) *(G-4107)*

United Aerospace Corporation................................954 364-0085
  9800 Premier Pkwy Miramar (33025) *(G-10557)*

United AG Svcs Amer Inc................................352 793-1682
  534 Cr Ste 529a Lake Panasoffkee (33538) *(G-7120)*

United American Machinery LLC................................727 442-1711
  1717 Overbrook Ave Clearwater (33755) *(G-1838)*

United Armour Products LLC................................813 767-9624
  1601 N 39th St Tampa (33605) *(G-17390)*

United Associates Group Inc................................561 840-0050
  3330 Frchild Gdns Ave Palm Beach Gardens (33410) *(G-13014)*

United Beddings Corp................................786 333-4795
  421 W 28th St Hialeah (33010) *(G-5392)*

United Biosource LLC (ubc)................................877 599-7748
  680 Century Pt Lake Mary (32746) *(G-7114)*

United Cabinets Corp................................305 887-5050
  867 W 30th St Hialeah (33012) *(G-5393)*

United Chair Industries LLC................................386 333-0800
  16442 Ivy Lake Dr Odessa (33556) *(G-11588)*

United Circuits Inc................................954 971-6860
  1410 Sw 29th Ave Ste 300 Pompano Beach (33069) *(G-14226)*

United Concrete Products LLC (HQ)................................786 402-3536
  8351 Nw 93rd St Medley (33166) *(G-8342)*

United Drones LLC................................305 978-1480
  9146 Quartz Ln Naples (34120) *(G-10930)*

United Electric Motor Inc................................813 238-7872
  905 E Ida St Tampa (33603) *(G-17391)*

United Electronics Corporation................................954 888-1024
  1 Se 3rd Ave Ste 158 Miami (33131) *(G-10065)*

United Express Intl Corp................................305 591-3292
  7302 Nw 34th St Miami (33122) *(G-10066)*

United Fabrication & Maint................................863 295-9000
  622 Snively Ave Eloise (33880) *(G-3514)*

United Franchise Group, West Palm Beach *Also called Ufg Group Inc (G-18190)*

United Granite Inc................................813 391-4323
  3906 S 51st St Tampa (33619) *(G-17392)*

United Jice Companies Amer Inc................................772 562-5442
  505 66th Ave Sw Vero Beach (32968) *(G-17811)*

United Machining Service Inc................................407 422-7710
  2410 Coolidge Ave Orlando (32804) *(G-12688)*

United Manufacturing Svcs LLC................................941 224-1692
  2908 29th Ave E Bradenton (34208) *(G-1070)*

United Metal Fabrications Inc................................305 962-1608
  1635 Ne 133rd St North Miami (33181) *(G-11126)*

United Metro Media, Jacksonville *Also called Job News (G-6227)*

United Ntons Space Crps Mltary (PA)................................702 373-2351
  10310 County Highway 3280 Ponce De Leon (32455) *(G-14251)*

United Oil Company, Miami *Also called United Oil Packers Inc (G-10067)*

United Oil Packers Inc................................305 687-6457
  3200 Nw 125th St Stop 4 Miami (33167) *(G-10067)*

United Ophthalmics, Doral *Also called Hansa Ophthalmics LLC (G-3244)*

United Pillow Mfg Inc................................305 636-9747
  5646 Nw 35th Ct Miami (33142) *(G-10068)*

United Plastic Fabricating Inc................................352 291-2477
  5000 Nw 5th St Ocala (34482) *(G-11506)*

United Printing LLC................................954 554-7969
  2323 Ne 26th Ave Pompano Beach (33062) *(G-14227)*

United Printing Sales Inc................................954 942-4300
  51 N Federal Hwy Pompano Beach (33062) *(G-14228)*

United Rail Inc................................904 503-9757
  13500 Sutton Park Dr S # 601 Jacksonville (32224) *(G-6577)*

United Seal & Tag Label Corp................................941 625-6799
  19237 Pine Bluff Ct Port Charlotte (33948) *(G-14321)*

United Ship Service Corp (PA)................................954 583-4588
  1341 Sw 21st Ter Fort Lauderdale (33312) *(G-4108)*

United Sierra Group Corp (PA)................................305 297-5835
  8218 Commerce Way Miami Lakes (33016) *(G-10369)*

United Sierra Group Corp................................305 297-5835
  8200 Commerce Way Miami Lakes (33016) *(G-10370)*

United Signs Systems, Oldsmar *Also called United Advantage Signs Inc (G-11701)*

United Space Alliance................................321 853-3417
  5530 Gross Ct Orlando (32810) *(G-12689)*

United Space Coast Cables Inc................................321 952-1040
  7703 Tech Dr Ste 100 West Melbourne (32904) *(G-17902)*

United State Foam & Coatings................................954 972-5005
  2303 W Mcnab Rd Ste 16 Pompano Beach (33069) *(G-14229)*

United State Postal Service................................904 783-7145
  1815 Silver St Jacksonville (32206) *(G-6578)*

United States Awning Company................................941 955-7010
  1935 18th St Sarasota (34234) *(G-15864)*

United States Concrete Pipe, Pompano Beach *Also called Mancini Inc (G-14086)*

United States Crene, Orlando *Also called General Clamp Industries Inc (G-12188)*

United States Filter Corp................................772 466-5955
  7374 Commercial Cir Fort Pierce (34951) *(G-4550)*

United States Fndry & Mfg Corp, Medley *Also called US Manufacturing Company (G-8346)*

United States Green Enrgy Corp................................540 295-4843
  1074 Windchime Way Pensacola (32503) *(G-13617)*

United States Gypsum Company................................904 768-2501
  6825 Evergreen Ave Jacksonville (32208) *(G-6579)*

United States Gypsum Company................................305 688-8744
  3301 Nw 125th St Miami Shores (33167) *(G-10384)*

United Strings Intl LLC................................561 790-4191
  352 Tall Pines Rd Ste G West Palm Beach (33413) *(G-18192)*

United Tool Corporation................................305 884-3068
  16258 Nw 78th Pl Miami Lakes (33016) *(G-10371)*

United Trophy Manufacturing (PA)................................407 841-2525
  610 N Parramore Ave Orlando (32801) *(G-12690)*

United Vertical Blinds LLC................................786 348-8000
  1261 Nw 175th St Miami (33169) *(G-10069)*

United Visual Branding LLC................................813 855-3300
  206 Tower Dr Oldsmar (34677) *(G-11702)*

United Wireless Tech Inc................................561 302-9350
  300 Se 5th Ave Apt 8180 Boca Raton (33432) *(G-735)*

Unitron Prcision Machining Inc................................407 299-4180
  2482 Clark St Apopka (32703) *(G-182)*

Unity Marine Inc................................954 321-1727
  2860 W State Road 84 # 118 Fort Lauderdale (33312) *(G-4109)*

Universal 3d Innovation Inc................................516 837-9423
  3891 Commerce Pkwy Miramar (33025) *(G-10558)*

Universal Alum Windows & Doors................................305 825-7900
  1675 W 31st Pl Hialeah (33012) *(G-5394)*

Universal Bakery LLC................................786 566-3303
  1050 Ali Baba Ave Opa Locka (33054) *(G-11797)*

Universal Brass Fabrication................................561 691-5445
  109 Palm Point Cir Palm Beach Gardens (33418) *(G-13015)*

Universal Cntact Lenses of Fla................................904 731-3410
  3840 Williamsburg Pk Blvd Jacksonville (32257) *(G-6580)*

Universal Con & Rdymx Corp................................305 512-3400
  10505 W Okeechobee Rd # 10 Hialeah (33018) *(G-5395)*

Universal Concrete & Ready Mix................................305 888-4101
  11790 Nw South River Dr Medley (33178) *(G-8343)*

Universal Crgo Doors & Svc LLC................................305 594-9175
  8490 Nw 68th St Miami (33166) *(G-10070)*

Universal Die Services Inc................................863 665-6092
  2646 Lasso Ln Lakeland (33801) *(G-7468)*

Universal Erectors Inc................................813 621-8111
  5668 Fshhawk Crssing Blvd Lithia (33547) *(G-7840)*

Universal Forest Products, Tampa *Also called Ufp Tampa LLC (G-17383)*

Universal Gear, Tampa *Also called S I P Corporation (G-17239)*

Universal Graphics & Prtg Inc................................561 845-6404
  120 Us Highway 1 Ste 1 North Palm Beach (33408) *(G-11184)*

Universal HM Hlth Indus Sups I................................813 493-7904
  7320 E Fletcher Ave Tampa (33637) *(G-17393)*

Universal Kit Cabinets Closets................................305 406-9096
  2905 Welcome Cir Kissimmee (34746) *(G-6969)*

Universal Labeling Systems Inc (PA)................................727 327-2123
  3501 8th Ave S Saint Petersburg (33711) *(G-15219)*

Universal Metal Works Inc................................904 765-2600
  14600 Duval Pl W Ste 52 Jacksonville (32218) *(G-6581)*

Universal Microwave Corp (PA)................................352 754-2200
  6036 Nature Coast Blvd Brooksville (34602) *(G-1216)*

Universal Networking Svcs Co................................281 825-9790
  200 2nd Ave S Ste 432 Saint Petersburg (33701) *(G-15220)*

Universal Packaging Co, Medley *Also called Universal Transactions Inc (G-8344)*

Universal PC Organization Inc................................321 285-9206
  8082 Wellsmere Cir Orlando (32835) *(G-12691)*

Universal Polishing Systems................................407 227-9516
  4333 Silver Star Rd # 175 Orlando (32808) *(G-12692)*

Universal Precision Inds Inc................................727 581-7097
  1876 Lake Ave Se Ste A Largo (33771) *(G-7701)*

Universal Printing Company................................305 592-5387
  3100 Nw 74th Ave Miami (33122) *(G-10071)*

Universal Prof Coatings Inc................................954 294-5236
  2125 Candlewood Ct Middleburg (32068) *(G-10410)*

Universal Recording, Miami Beach *Also called Umg Recordings Inc (G-10240)*

Universal Ribbon Corporation................................305 471-0828
  8111 Nw 68th St Miami (33166) *(G-10072)*

Universal School Products Inc................................904 273-8590
  2309 Sawgrass Village Dr Ponte Vedra Beach (32082) *(G-14282)*

Universal Screen Graphics Inc................................813 623-5335
  4897 W Waters Ave Ste H Tampa (33634) *(G-17394)*

Universal Seat Cvers Auto ACC (PA)................................305 262-3955
  2370 Ludlam Rd Miami (33155) *(G-10073)*

Universal Signs................................954 366-1535
  6045 Nw 31st Ave Fort Lauderdale (33309) *(G-4110)*

Universal Signs & Accessories, Fort Pierce *Also called McCain Sales of Florida Inc (G-4506)*

Universal Software Solutions................................727 298-8877
  912 Drew St Ste 104 Clearwater (33755) *(G-1839)*

Universal Stncling Mkg Systems................................727 894-3027
  205 15th Ave Se Saint Petersburg (33701) *(G-15221)*

Universal Surgical Appliance................................305 652-0810
  400 Ne 191st St Miami (33179) *(G-10074)*

A
L
P
H
A
B
E
T
I
C

Universal Tech Inc 786 220-8032
3042 Nw 72nd Ave Miami (33122) (G-10075)

Universal Training Sftwr Inc 561 981-6421
301 Ne 51st St Ste 1240 Boca Raton (33431) (G-736)

Universal Transactions Inc 305 887-4677
12870 Nw South River Dr Medley (33178) (G-8344)

Universal Welding Service Co 305 898-9130
9921 Nw 80th Ave Unit 1u Hialeah Gardens (33016) (G-5453)

Universal Wood Design 772 569-5389
1708 Old Dixie Hwy # 102 Vero Beach (32960) (G-17812)

Uniware Houseware Corp 305 952-4958
5275 Nw 163rd St Miami Lakes (33014) (G-10372)

Uniweld Products Inc (PA) 954 584-2000
2850 Ravenswood Rd Fort Lauderdale (33312) (G-4111)

Unlimited Cabinet Designs Inc 954 923-3269
1798 Sw 31st Ave Hallandale (33009) (G-4931)

Unlimited Impressions, Doral Also called Restifo Investments LLC (G-3348)

Unlimited Marine Mfg, Hialeah Also called Superformance Mfg Inc (G-5372)

Unlimited Marine Mfg Inc 305 420-6034
2637 W 76th St Hialeah (33016) (G-5396)

Unlimited Printing & Copying, Oldsmar Also called Print One Inc (G-11691)

Unlimited Welding Inc 407 327-3333
235 Old Sanford Oviedo Rd Winter Springs (32708) (G-18580)

Unno Tekno LLC 786 536-5992
6451 Nw 102nd Ave Unit 4 Doral (33178) (G-3408)

Up - N - Atom 904 716-5431
3443 Maiden Voyage Cir S Jacksonville (32257) (G-6582)

Up2speed Printing Inc 850 508-2620
8081 W 28th Ave Hialeah (33016) (G-5397)

Upaya Holdings Inc 850 261-9203
350 Grapetree Dr Apt 405 Key Biscayne (33149) (G-6840)

Upexi Inc (PA) 701 353-5425
17129 Us Highway 19 N Clearwater (33764) (G-1840)

Upper Keys Snacks Llc 305 298-6109
2841 Sw 175th Ave Miramar (33029) (G-10559)

Upright Aluminum Inc 239 731-6644
7908 Interstate Ct North Fort Myers (33917) (G-11072)

Uproxx Media Inc 917 603-2374
1602 Alton Rd Ste 447 Miami Beach (33139) (G-10241)

UPS Store 4332, The, Miramar Also called Lujotex LLC (G-10510)

Upstream Installation Inc 904 829-3507
1835 Us Highway 1 S # 119 Saint Augustine (32084) (G-14908)

Upt Vector, Deland Also called Uninsred Untd Prchute Tech LLC (G-2915)

Upton House Cooler Corporation 305 633-2531
2490 Nw 7th Ave Miami (33127) (G-10076)

Uptown Cstm Cabinets of Naples 239 825-8432
6260 Shirley St Ste 603 Naples (34109) (G-10931)

Ur Cabinets 813 434-6454
4042 W Kennedy Blvd Tampa (33609) (G-17395)

Ural & Associates Inc 305 446-9462
3608 Anderson Rd Coral Gables (33134) (G-2116)

Urano Publishing Inc 305 233-3365
8871 Sw 129th Ter Miami (33176) (G-10077)

Urban Charge LLC 305 809-6625
1330 West Ave Apt 1411 Miami Beach (33139) (G-10242)

Urban Extreme LLC 954 248-9007
4303 Hayes St Hollywood (33021) (G-5680)

Urban Metals LLC 813 241-2801
1301 N 26th St Tampa (33605) (G-17396)

Urban Stone Works 305 754-7171
7025 Ne 2nd Ave Miami (33138) (G-10078)

Urbaprint LLC 786 502-3223
649 Conservation Dr Weston (33327) (G-18296)

Urecon Systems Inc 321 638-2364
4046 N Goldenrod Rd 162 Winter Park (32792) (G-18548)

Urecon Systems Inc 904 695-3332
7136 Smallow Run Winter Park (32792) (G-18549)

Uren North America LLC 410 924-3478
2990 Ponce De Leon Blvd Coral Gables (33134) (G-2117)

Uroshape LLC 321 960-2484
1130 S Harbor City Blvd Melbourne (32901) (G-8555)

US 1 Truck Sales LLC 904 545-1233
10126 New Kings Rd Jacksonville (32219) (G-6583)

US Aire, Bushnell Also called Metal Industries Inc (G-1247)

US American Plastic Corp 305 200-3683
2164 Nw 22nd Ct Miami (33142) (G-10079)

US Applied Phys Ics Group 321 567-7270
1650 Chaffee Dr Titusville (32780) (G-17625)

US Applied Physics Group LLC 321 607-9023
7065 Challenger Ave Titusville (32780) (G-17626)

US Barcodes Inc 727 849-1196
6740 Commerce Ave Port Richey (34668) (G-14382)

US Bindery Inc 305 622-7070
5330 Nw 161st St Miami Lakes (33014) (G-10373)

US Blanks LLC 321 253-3626
282 N Wickham Rd Melbourne (32935) (G-8556)

US Blinds, South Daytona Also called Florida Plntn Shutters LLC (G-16021)

US Body Source, Jacksonville Also called Rfl & Figlio LLC (G-6422)

US Building Systems Corp 954 281-2100
401 Fairway Dr Ste 100 Deerfield Beach (33441) (G-2830)

US Bullnosing 954 567-0404
216 Ne 33rd St Oakland Park (33334) (G-11307)

US China Mining Group Inc 813 514-2873
15310 Amberly Dr Ste 250 Tampa (33647) (G-17397)

US Chutes Corp 860 567-4000
751 Park Of Commerce Dr # 108 Boca Raton (33487) (G-737)

US Communications Industries (PA) 772 468-7477
2733 Peters Rd Fort Pierce (34945) (G-4551)

US Composites 561 588-1001
6670 White Dr Riviera Beach (33407) (G-14685)

US Concrete Products Corp 954 973-0368
1878 Nw 21st St Pompano Beach (33069) (G-14230)

US Conveyor Solutions Inc 352 343-0085
3714 County Road 561 Tavares (32778) (G-17526)

US Cremation Equipment, Orlando Also called American Incinerators Corp (G-11902)

US Custom Fabrication Inc 954 917-6161
1858 Nw 21st St Pompano Beach (33069) (G-14231)

US Defib Medical Tech LLC 305 887-7552
7831 Nw 72nd Ave Medley (33166) (G-8345)

US Diagnostics Inc 866 216-5308
6600 Nw 16th St Ste 1 Plantation (33313) (G-13898)

US Foundry, Hialeah Also called US Manufacturing Company (G-5398)

US Foundry, Medley Also called Nusfc LLC (G-8291)

US Fuels Inc 254 559-1212
928 Rotonda Cir Rotonda West (33947) (G-14758)

US Generator Inc 772 778-0131
725 Commerce Center Dr J Sebastian (32958) (G-15907)

US Global Glass LLC 305 651-6630
220 Ne 187th St Miami (33179) (G-10080)

US Golf Liquidators Inc 407 677-1118
6955 Hanging Moss Rd Orlando (32807) (G-12693)

US Granite and Quartz, Weston Also called National Stoneworks LLC (G-18271)

US Hemp and Oil LLC 352 817-2455
1010 Ne 16th St Ocala (34470) (G-11507)

US Implant Solutions LLC 407 971-8054
1778 N Park Ave Ste 200 Maitland (32751) (G-8077)

US Iron LLC 765 210-4111
755 Grand Blvd Ste 105b Miramar Beach (32550) (G-10574)

US Ironworks Company 850 588-5995
328 Wahoo Rd Panama City (32408) (G-13316)

US Manufacturing Company (HQ) 305 885-0301
8351 Nw 93rd St Medley (33166) (G-8346)

US Manufacturing Company 305 556-1661
3200 W 84th St Hialeah (33018) (G-5398)

US Marine Supply, Dania Beach Also called US Metal Fabricators Inc (G-2360)

US Metal Fabricators Inc 954 921-0800
800 Old Griffin Rd Dania Beach (33004) (G-2360)

US Mold Inc 561 748-2223
612 N Orange Ave Ste A4 Jupiter (33458) (G-6818)

US Natural Gas Corp 727 482-1505
735 Arlington Ave N # 308 Saint Petersburg (33701) (G-15222)

US Nutraceuticals Inc 352 357-2004
2751 Nutra Ln Eustis (32726) (G-3569)

US Orthotics Inc 813 621-7797
8605 Palm River Rd Tampa (33619) (G-17398)

US Pack Group LLC 954 556-1840
5011 N Hiatus Rd Sunrise (33351) (G-16387)

US Patriot Industries Inc 954 802-7402
100 Golden Isles Dr Hallandale Beach (33009) (G-4981)

US Paver Co 954 292-4373
22809 Horse Shoe Way Boca Raton (33428) (G-738)

US Paverscape Inc 772 223-7287
1735 Se Federal Hwy Stuart (34994) (G-16245)

US Pet Imaging LLC (PA) 941 921-0383
3830 Bee Ridge Rd Ste 100 Sarasota (34233) (G-15865)

US Pipe Fabrication LLC 860 769-6097
109 5th St Orlando (32824) (G-12694)

US Precast Corp 305 364-8253
3200 W 84th St Hialeah (33018) (G-5399)

US Precast Corporation 305 885-8471
8351 Nw 93rd St Medley (33166) (G-8347)

US Precious Metals Inc 786 814-5804
1825 Ponce De Leon Blvd Coral Gables (33134) (G-2118)

US Recreational Alliance Inc 954 782-7279
820 Sw 14th Ct Pompano Beach (33060) (G-14232)

US Sample Corp 954 495-4525
10386 Stonebridge Blvd Boca Raton (33498) (G-739)

US Security Defense Corp 407 979-1478
1181 E Alfred St Tavares (32778) (G-17527)

US Sheet Metal Inc 305 884-7705
7333 Nw 66th St Miami (33166) (G-10081)

US Sign and Mill Inc 239 936-9154
7981 Mainline Pkwy Fort Myers (33912) (G-4435)

US Signs Inc 727 862-7933
16631 Scheer Blvd Port Richey (34667) (G-14383)

US Spars Inc 386 462-3760
6320 Nw 123rd Pl Gainesville (32653) (G-4782)

US Submarines Inc (PA) 208 687-9057
  9015 Pl Vero Beach (32966) *(G-17813)*

US Thrillrides LLC 407 909-8898
  11536 Lake Butler Blvd Windermere (34786) *(G-18368)*

US Truss Inc 561 686-4000
  3400 45th St West Palm Beach (33407) *(G-18193)*

USA Aluminum 305 303-9121
  1880 S Ocean Dr Hallandale Beach (33009) *(G-4982)*

USA and International RES Inc 786 558-5115
  1200 Nw 78th Ave Ste 112 Doral (33126) *(G-3409)*

USA Express Pallets Corp 786 251-9543
  4655 Nw 36th Ave Miami (33142) *(G-10082)*

USA Hemp Solutions, Hialeah *Also called V P R A R T LLC (G-5405)*

USA Marine Engines 954 614-4810
  2600 Sw 3rd Ave Fort Lauderdale (33315) *(G-4112)*

USA Maritime Enterprises Inc 954 764-8360
  2600 Esnhwer Blvd Lhigh C Lehigh Cement Fort Lauderdale (33308) *(G-4113)*

USA Plastic Industry, Miami *Also called Emmanuel Holdings Inc (G-9096)*

USA Printing LLC 754 275-5048
  26 Se 3rd Ave Hallandale Beach (33009) *(G-4983)*

USA Rare Earth LLC (PA) 813 867-6155
  1001 Water St Ste 600 Tampa (33602) *(G-17399)*

USA Recmar Corp. 786 554-3505
  918 Nw 106th Avenue Cir Miami (33172) *(G-10083)*

USA Scientific Inc (HQ) 352 237-6288
  346 Sw 57th Ave Ocala (34474) *(G-11508)*

USA Sheet Metal Inc 786 517-3482
  650 W 18th St Hialeah (33010) *(G-5400)*

USA Shutter Company LLC 239 596-8883
  2141 Flint Dr Fort Myers (33916) *(G-4436)*

USA Signs Inc 305 470-2333
  7230 Nw 46th St Miami (33166) *(G-10084)*

USA Today, Fort Myers *Also called Anna Andres (G-4177)*

USA Vigil 386 736-8464
  1400 Flight Line Blvd Deland (32724) *(G-2917)*

Usacompressors.com, Miami *Also called Miami Compressor Rbldrs Inc (G-9548)*

Usaxray, Saint Petersburg *Also called Burkhart Roentgen Intl Inc (G-14992)*

USB Plastics 727 375-8840
  11805 State Road 54 Odessa (33556) *(G-11589)*

Usbev Plastics LLC 813 855-0700
  3874 Tampa Rd Oldsmar (34677) *(G-11703)*

Usbev Products Inc 727 375-8840
  11805 State Road 54 Odessa (33556) *(G-11590)*

Usdirectorycom LLC 561 989-7400
  999 Nw 51st St Ste 100 Boca Raton (33431) *(G-740)*

USF Fabrication Inc (PA) 305 556-1661
  3200 W 84th St Hialeah (33018) *(G-5401)*

USG International Ltd 305 688-8744
  3001 Nw 125th St Miami (33167) *(G-10085)*

Usher Land & Timber Inc 352 493-4221
  6551 Nw 100th St Chiefland (32626) *(G-1451)*

Usmi Pallets Inc 813 765-4309
  3301 Sam Allen Oaks Cir Plant City (33565) *(G-13812)*

USP Structural Connectors, Largo *Also called Mitek Inc (G-7645)*

Uspharma Ltd 954 817-4418
  13900 Nw 57th Ct Miami Lakes (33014) *(G-10374)*

Ussi LLC 941 244-2408
  752 Commerce Dr Ste 15 Venice (34292) *(G-17726)*

Usvi Pharmaceuticals LLC 305 643-8841
  1301 Nw 84th Ave Ste 101 Doral (33126) *(G-3410)*

UTC Aerospace Systems, Miami Gardens *Also called Goodrich Corporation (G-10261)*

UTC Aerospace Systems, Jacksonville *Also called Simmonds Precision Pdts Inc (G-6473)*

UTC Aerospace Systems, Pompano Beach *Also called Hamilton Sundstrand Corp (G-14048)*

UTC Aerospace Systems 954 538-8971
  3601 S Flamingo Rd Miramar (33027) *(G-10560)*

Utilis Usa LLC 850 226-7043
  36 Tupelo Ave Se Fort Walton Beach (32548) *(G-4614)*

Utilitech Inc 863 767-0600
  130 W Main St Wauchula (33873) *(G-17830)*

Utilities Structures Inc 239 334-7757
  2700 Evans Ave Unit 2 Fort Myers (33901) *(G-4437)*

Utility Services Authority LLC 772 344-9339
  275 W Coker Rd Fort Pierce (34945) *(G-4552)*

Utility Vault, Wildwood *Also called Oldcastle Infrastructure Inc (G-18316)*

Utilytech Company 813 778-6952
  630 Baldwin Dr Kissimmee (34758) *(G-6970)*

Utopia Grilling LLC 727 488-1355
  3511 Cockatoo Dr New Port Richey (34652) *(G-10991)*

Utopic Software LLC (PA) 813 444-2231
  1213 E 6th Ave Tampa (33605) *(G-17400)*

Uts Systems LLC 850 226-4301
  36 Tupelo Ave Se Ste A Fort Walton Beach (32548) *(G-4615)*

Uvisors 813 716-1113
  4919 W Bartlett Dr Tampa (33603) *(G-17401)*

Uvirx Therapeutics Inc 813 309-1976
  640 Brooker Creek Blvd Oldsmar (34677) *(G-11704)*

Uzzi Amphibious Gear LLC 954 777-9595
  205 Ansin Blvd Hallandale Beach (33009) *(G-4984)*

V & C Supply Ornamental Corp 305 634-9040
  6400 Nw 72nd Ave Miami (33166) *(G-10086)*

V & F Air Conditioning Sup LLC 305 477-1040
  7320 Nw 12th St Ste 107 Miami (33126) *(G-10087)*

V & G Industries Inc 786 853-1265
  4965 E 10th Ct Hialeah (33013) *(G-5402)*

V A Electrical Motors Ctr Inc 305 825-3327
  4011 W 18th Ave Hialeah (33012) *(G-5403)*

V and N Advanced Auto Sys LLC 321 504-6440
  415 Gus Hipp Blvd Rockledge (32955) *(G-14753)*

V G Carpentry LLC 786 531-7824
  4855 E 10th Ct Hialeah (33013) *(G-5404)*

V G I, Largo *Also called Vgi Medical LLC (G-7702)*

V I P Printing 386 258-3326
  133 W Intl Speedway Blvd Daytona Beach (32114) *(G-2616)*

V J Pro Fabrics, Mount Dora *Also called C P Enterprises of Apopka Inc (G-10598)*

V L Pavers Corp 954 605-0061
  3055 Palm Pl Margate (33063) *(G-8158)*

V M P, Boca Raton *Also called Vehicle Maint Program Inc (G-744)*

V M Visual Mdsg Dctr Group Inc 305 759-9910
  600 Nw 62nd St Miami (33150) *(G-10088)*

V P I, Lake Worth *Also called Vertex Precision Inc (G-7242)*

V P Press Inc 954 581-7531
  3934 Davie Blvd Fort Lauderdale (33312) *(G-4114)*

V P R A R T LLC 786 205-4526
  2630 W 81st St Hialeah (33016) *(G-5405)*

V-Blox Corporation 904 425-4908
  3653 Regent Blvd Ste 408 Jacksonville (32224) *(G-6584)*

V-Bro Products LLC 352 267-6235
  28114 County Road 561 Tavares (32778) *(G-17528)*

V-Lumber LLC 305 510-4458
  15201 Nw 34th Ave Opa Locka (33054) *(G-11798)*

V12 Data, Wesley Chapel *Also called Datamentors LLC (G-17873)*

V2 Cigs (PA) 305 517-1149
  1521 Alton Rd Ste 275 Miami Beach (33139) *(G-10243)*

V2 Cigs 305 240-6387
  3050 Biscayne Blvd # 700 Miami (33137) *(G-10089)*

Vac Cubes Inc 727 944-3337
  536 E Tarpon Ave Ste 5 Tarpon Springs (34689) *(G-17498)*

Vac-Con Inc (HQ) 904 284-4200
  969 Hall Park Rd Green Cove Springs (32043) *(G-4841)*

Vac-Tron Equipment, Okahumpka *Also called American Mfg & Mch Inc (G-11594)*

Vacation Vault, Doral *Also called Blue Chip Group LLC (G-3144)*

Val DOr Apparel LLC (PA) 954 363-7340
  6820 Lyons Tech Cir # 220 Coconut Creek (33073) *(G-2009)*

Valco Group Inc 813 870-0482
  2203 N Lois Ave Ste 937 Tampa (33607) *(G-17402)*

Valdor Apparel, Coconut Creek *Also called Val DOr Apparel LLC (G-2009)*

Valensa International, Eustis *Also called US Nutraceuticals Inc (G-3569)*

Valentina Signa Inc 305 264-0673
  7343 Nw 56th St Miami (33166) *(G-10090)*

Valentines Glass & Metal, Fort Myers *Also called Greg Valentine LLC (G-4273)*

Valentini Italian Spc Co 305 638-0822
  4290 Nw 37th Ct Miami (33142) *(G-10091)*

Valiant Products Inc 863 688-7998
  939 Quincy St Lakeland (33815) *(G-7469)*

Valiant Transport Group LLC 855 648-7423
  5030 Chmpn Blvd Ste G11 Boca Raton (33496) *(G-741)*

Validsoft 813 334-9745
  19103 Centre Rose Blvd Lutz (33558) *(G-8019)*

Valintech 941 366-8885
  2260 Whitfield Park Ave Sarasota (34243) *(G-15577)*

Valley Forge Textiles LLC 954 971-1776
  1390 Sw 30th Ave Pompano Beach (33069) *(G-14233)*

Valley Proteins (de) Inc 704 718-6568
  6142 Old Soutel Ct Jacksonville (32219) *(G-6585)*

Valley Proteins (de) Inc 910 282-7900
  465 Caboose Pl Mulberry (33860) *(G-10643)*

Valley Surgical Inc 954 768-9886
  1000 W Mcnab Rd Pompano Beach (33069) *(G-14234)*

Valleymedia Inc 510 565-7559
  600 S Andrews Ave Ste 405 Fort Lauderdale (33301) *(G-4115)*

Valmont Newmark Inc 863 533-6465
  4131 Us Highway 17 S Bartow (33830) *(G-328)*

Valmont Stheastern Galvanizing, Miami *Also called Industrial Glvnzers Stheastern (G-9311)*

Valor Latin Group Inc 305 791-5255
  8320 Nw 14th St Doral (33126) *(G-3411)*

Value Providers LLC 321 567-0919
  2441 Bellevue Ave Daytona Beach (32114) *(G-2617)*

Valuesafes Inc 877 629-6214
  24128 Peachland Blvd Port Charlotte (33954) *(G-14322)*

Valve Research & Mfg Co, Deerfield Beach *Also called Jet Research Development Inc (G-2745)*

Vampa Tires Supplies Inc 305 888-1001
  7243 Nw 54th St Miami (33166) *(G-10092)*

Vampire Wire, Lutz *Also called Sound Connections Intl (G-8016)*

Van Aernam Logging & Trucking 352 498-5809
  County Rd 351 A Cross City (32628) *(G-2265)*

Van Aernam Timber Management, Cross City *Also called Van Aernam Logging & Trucking* ***(G-2265)***
Van Charles Inc....954 394-3242
4794 Ne 11th Ave Oakland Park (33334) ***(G-11308)***
Van Gogh Signs & Displays....813 849-7446
5020 N Florida Ave Tampa (33603) ***(G-17403)***
Van Heusen, Miramar Beach *Also called Pvh Corp* ***(G-10571)***
Van Linda Iron Works Inc....561 586-8400
3787 Boutwell Rd Lake Worth Beach (33461) ***(G-7263)***
Van Nevel Aerospace LLC....337 936-2504
1932 Holley Timber Rd Cottondale (32431) ***(G-2230)***
Van Teal Inc....305 751-6767
7240 Ne 4th Ave Miami (33138) ***(G-10093)***
Van Tibolli Beauty Corp....305 390-0044
4800 Nw 15th Ave Unit E Fort Lauderdale (33309) ***(G-4116)***
Van Zant Timber Incorporated....904 845-4661
373120 Kings Ferry Rd Hilliard (32046) ***(G-5478)***
Van-Ess Manufacturing Inc....352 799-1015
15311 Flight Path Dr Brooksville (34604) ***(G-1217)***
Vanavac Inc....813 752-1391
1309 Joe Mcintosh Rd Plant City (33565) ***(G-13813)***
Vanbert Corporation....561 945-5856
1855 Sw 4th Ave Ste B3 Delray Beach (33444) ***(G-3031)***
Vandalay Inds Manatee Cnty LLC....941 756-6028
6832 14th St W Bradenton (34207) ***(G-1071)***
Vandalize Boat Works....305 450-2014
3480 Nw 21st St Miami (33142) ***(G-10094)***
Vanguard Products Group Inc....813 855-9639
720 Brooker Creek Blvd Oldsmar (34677) ***(G-11705)***
Vanguard Protex Global, Oldsmar *Also called Vanguard Products Group Inc* ***(G-11705)***
Vanguard Systems Corp....727 528-0121
10460 Roosevelt Blvd N Saint Petersburg (33716) ***(G-15223)***
Vanguardistas LLC....386 868-2919
564 S Yonge St Ormond Beach (32174) ***(G-12798)***
Vanity Fair Brands LP....904 538-0288
10300 Southside Blvd Jacksonville (32256) ***(G-6586)***
Vanity Furs of Avondale LLC....904 387-9900
4555 Saint Johns Ave # 6 Jacksonville (32210) ***(G-6587)***
Vanlex Clothing Inc....305 431-4669
5850 Miami Lakes Dr E Miami Lakes (33014) ***(G-10375)***
Vanlympia Inc....727 725-5055
605 7th Ave N Safety Harbor (34695) ***(G-14800)***
Vapeworld, Boca Raton *Also called Warehouse Goods LLC* ***(G-753)***
Vapex Environmental Tech Inc....407 277-0900
2971 Oxbow Cir Ste A Cocoa (32926) ***(G-1961)***
Vapor Group Inc (PA)....954 792-8450
20725 Ne 16th Ave Ste A4 Miami (33179) ***(G-10095)***
Vapor Group Inc (PA)....954 792-8450
20200 W Dixie Hwy Ste 906 Miami (33180) ***(G-10096)***
Vaporbrands International Inc....352 573-6130
40 Easthampton B West Palm Beach (33417) ***(G-18194)***
Vaprzone LLC....941 882-4841
448 Us Highway 41 Byp N Venice (34285) ***(G-17727)***
Vargas Enterprises Inc....561 989-0908
2518 Nw 64th Blvd Boca Raton (33496) ***(G-742)***
Varibelt Incorporated....305 775-1568
13216 Sw 45th Ln Miami (33175) ***(G-10097)***
Various Inc (PA)....561 900-3691
1615 S Congress Ave # 103 Delray Beach (33445) ***(G-3032)***
Varnums Rest Home, Bristol *Also called Ruby Vanrum* ***(G-1127)***
Vasco Winds LLC....561 691-7171
700 Universe Blvd Juno Beach (33408) ***(G-6669)***
Vass Holdings Inc (PA)....863 295-5664
146 Avenue B Nw Winter Haven (33881) ***(G-18477)***
Vault Structures Inc....239 332-3270
3640 Work Dr Fort Myers (33916) ***(G-4438)***
Vaya Space, Cocoa *Also called Rocket Crafters Launch LLC* ***(G-1955)***
Vazko LLC....786 521-0808
10957 Nw 123rd St Medley (33178) ***(G-8348)***
Vazkor Technologies S Fla Inc....561 357-9029
605 E Boynton Beach Blvd Boynton Beach (33435) ***(G-922)***
Vb-S1 Issuer LLC....561 948-6367
750 Park Of Cmn Boca Raton (33487) ***(G-743)***
Vc Atlantic Woodwork....305 219-9411
14322 Sw 117th Ter Miami (33186) ***(G-10098)***
Vc Displays Inc....352 796-0060
15250 Flight Path Dr Brooksville (34604) ***(G-1218)***
Vc Technology, Brooksville *Also called Vc Displays Inc* ***(G-1218)***
Vdc Display Systems, Cocoa *Also called Video Display Corporation* ***(G-1963)***
Veatic....888 474-2999
2450 Smith St Ste P Kissimmee (34744) ***(G-6971)***
Vecellio & Grogan Inc....305 822-5322
18300 Nw 122nd Ave Hialeah (33018) ***(G-5406)***
Vecellio Management Svcs Inc....561 793-2102
450 Royal Palm Way Fl 2 Palm Beach (33480) ***(G-12942)***
Vecom Usa LLC....813 901-5300
4803 George Rd Ste 300 Tampa (33634) ***(G-17404)***
Vector Engineering & Mfg Corp....708 474-3900
16320 Burniston Dr Tampa (33647) ***(G-17405)***
Vector Group Ltd (PA)....305 579-8000
4400 Biscayne Blvd Miami (33137) ***(G-10099)***
Vector Solutions, Tampa *Also called Vector-Solutionscom Inc* ***(G-17406)***
Vector-Solutionscom Inc (PA)....813 207-0012
4890 W Kennedy Blvd # 30 Tampa (33609) ***(G-17406)***
Vedic Origins Inc....407 712-5614
478 E Altamonte Dr # 108 Altamonte Springs (32701) ***(G-76)***
Vee Enterprises Inc....954 960-0300
4100 N Powerline Rd I5 Pompano Beach (33073) ***(G-14235)***
Vee Industries Inc....561 732-1083
211 Se 9th Ave Boynton Beach (33435) ***(G-923)***
Veeam Software Corporation....614 339-8200
15137 Sw 36th St Davie (33331) ***(G-2494)***
Veethree Electronics & Mar LLC....941 538-7775
2050 47th Ter E Bradenton (34203) ***(G-1072)***
Veethree Instruments, Bradenton *Also called Veethree Electronics & Mar LLC* ***(G-1072)***
Vega....239 574-1798
447 Ne 8th Ter Cape Coral (33909) ***(G-1403)***
Vegan Suckers LLC....904 265-5263
11111 San Jose Blvd Ste 5 Jacksonville (32223) ***(G-6588)***
Veggiespetit Pois Inc....305 826-7867
2202 W 78th St Hialeah (33016) ***(G-5407)***
Vehicle Maint Program Inc....561 362-6080
3595 N Dixie Hwy Ste 7 Boca Raton (33431) ***(G-744)***
Vela Research LP....727 507-5300
13577 Feather Sound Dr # 550 Clearwater (33762) ***(G-1841)***
Velcorp Gems Vels, Green Cove Springs *Also called Virginia Electronic & Ltg Corp* ***(G-4842)***
Velez Custom Cabinetry Corp....772 418-9565
5810 Nw Gillespie Ave Port Saint Lucie (34986) ***(G-14462)***
Velgen Wheels, Miami *Also called Sg Global LLC* ***(G-9873)***
Velmaxxx Enterprises Inc....239 689-4343
10941 Gladiolus Dr Unit 9 Fort Myers (33908) ***(G-4439)***
Velocity Inc....772 589-1860
200 Airport Dr W Sebastian (32958) ***(G-15908)***
Velocity Aerospace - Nmb Inc....214 396-9030
570 Ne 185th St North Miami Beach (33179) ***(G-11166)***
Velocity Aircraft Inc....772 589-1860
200 Airport Dr W Sebastian (32958) ***(G-15909)***
Velocity Machine Works LLC....850 727-5066
364 Marpan Ln Tallahassee (32305) ***(G-16520)***
Venair Inc....305 362-8920
16713 Park Centre Blvd Miami Gardens (33169) ***(G-10278)***
Venchi US Inc....646 448-8663
1111 Brickell Ave # 2650 Miami (33131) ***(G-10100)***
Venco Marine Inc....954 923-0036
2012 Hayes St Hollywood (33020) ***(G-5681)***
Vendapin LLC (PA)....352 796-2693
16381 Cherokee Rd Brooksville (34601) ***(G-1219)***
Vending Company, Boca Raton *Also called Rocket Vending Inc* ***(G-653)***
Veneer Source, Tavares *Also called J F V Designs Inc* ***(G-17513)***
Veneta Cucine Inc....305 949-5223
2020 Ne 163rd St Ste 100 North Miami Beach (33162) ***(G-11167)***
Venfood Disrtibutors, Hialeah *Also called Tts Food LLC* ***(G-5384)***
Venga LLC....561 665-8200
955 Nw 17th Ave Delray Beach (33445) ***(G-3033)***
Venice Custom Cabinets Inc....941 488-5000
510 Colonia Ln E Nokomis (34275) ***(G-11056)***
Venice Granit & Marble Inc....941 483-4363
159 Progress Cir Venice (34285) ***(G-17728)***
Venice Herald Tribune....941 486-3000
1777 Main St Sarasota (34236) ***(G-15866)***
Venice Quarters Inc....954 318-3483
2435 N Dixie Hwy Wilton Manors (33305) ***(G-18344)***
Venkata SAI Corporation....352 746-7076
3502 N Lecanto Hwy Beverly Hills (34465) ***(G-370)***
Venom Allstars LLC....407 575-3484
1205 Crown Park Cir Winter Garden (34787) ***(G-18406)***
Vensoft Corp....786 991-2080
2530 Ne 208th Ter Miami (33180) ***(G-10101)***
Ventex Technology Inc (PA)....561 354-6300
1201 Jupiter Park Dr Jupiter (33458) ***(G-6819)***
Venti Group LLC....949 264-3185
1521 Alton Rd Ste 697 Miami Beach (33139) ***(G-10244)***
Ventilation Air Inc....954 975-9501
901 Ne 4th St Pompano Beach (33060) ***(G-14236)***
Ventilex Inc....954 433-1321
20871 Jhnson St Units 103 Pembroke Pines (33029) ***(G-13423)***
Ventum LLC....786 838-1113
1100 14th St Miami Beach (33139) ***(G-10245)***
Ventura Cleaners, Kissimmee *Also called Chhaya Corporation* ***(G-6907)***
Ventura Foods LLC....772 878-1400
485 Nw Enterprise Dr Port Saint Lucie (34986) ***(G-14463)***
Venture Circle Enterprises LLC....407 678-7489
140 Maritime Dr Sanford (32771) ***(G-15402)***
Venture Circle Intl LLC....407 677-6004
140 Maritime Dr Sanford (32771) ***(G-15403)***
Venue Advertising Inc....561 844-1778
815 S Us Highway 1 # 103 Jupiter (33477) ***(G-6820)***
Venue Marketing Group, Jupiter *Also called Venue Advertising Inc* ***(G-6820)***

1084 2022 Harris Florida Manufacturers Directory (G-0000) Company's Geographic Section entry number

Venus Manufacturing Co Inc 904 645-3187
 11711 Marco Beach Dr Jacksonville (32224) **(G-6589)**

Ver-Val Enterprises Inc 850 244-7931
 646 Anchors St Nw Ste 8 Fort Walton Beach (32548) **(G-4616)**

Vera Custom Woodworking I 941 726-8831
 1468 12th St E Palmetto (34221) **(G-13200)**

Vera Custom Woodworking Inc 321 355-0161
 9113 49th Ave E Palmetto (34221) **(G-13201)**

Veracity Tech Solutions LLC 402 658-4113
 8245 Mccarty St Pensacola (32534) **(G-13618)**

Vercipia Biofuels, Tampa Also called Highlands Ethanol LLC **(G-16916)**

Verde GSE Inc 888 837-5221
 12291 Us Highway 41 N Palmetto (34221) **(G-13202)**

Verde Speed Machine Shop Corp 305 233-3299
 10780 Sw 190th St Cutler Bay (33157) **(G-2310)**

Verdu-Us LLC 407 776-3017
 741 Caribbean Dr Davenport (33897) **(G-2373)**

Verhi Inc 850 477-4880
 824 Creighton Rd Ste A Pensacola (32504) **(G-13619)**

Veridien Corporation (PA) 727 576-1600
 1100 4th St N Ste 202 Saint Petersburg (33701) **(G-15224)**

Verified Label & Print Inc 813 290-7721
 7905 Hopi Pl Tampa (33634) **(G-17407)**

Verifone Inc (HQ) 800 837-4366
 2744 N University Dr Coral Springs (33065) **(G-2224)**

Verifone Inc 727 953-4000
 300 Park Place Blvd # 100 Clearwater (33759) **(G-1842)**

Verifone Inc 727 535-9200
 12501 B 562nd St N Clearwater (33755) **(G-1843)**

Verifone Systems Inc (PA) 408 232-7800
 2744 N University Dr Coral Springs (33065) **(G-2225)**

Veritas Farms Inc (PA) 561 288-6603
 1512 E Broward Blvd # 300 Fort Lauderdale (33301) **(G-4117)**

Veriteq Acquisition Corp 561 805-8007
 220 Congress Park Dr # 200 Delray Beach (33445) **(G-3034)**

Verizon, Saint Petersburg Also called Supermedia LLC **(G-15203)**

Vero Beach Magazine, Vero Beach Also called Moulton Publications Inc **(G-17779)**

Vero Beach Printing Inc 772 562-4267
 3280 Quay Dock Rd Vero Beach (32967) **(G-17814)**

Vero News 772 234-5727
 1240 Olde Doubloon Dr Vero Beach (32963) **(G-17815)**

Veroch LLC 954 990-7544
 10573 Nw 53rd St Sunrise (33351) **(G-16388)**

Veronica Knits Inc 305 887-7333
 490 W 18th St Hialeah (33010) **(G-5408)**

Veronicas Health Crunch LLC 352 409-1124
 88 Fanny Ann Way Freeport (32439) **(G-4631)**

Versachem, Riviera Beach Also called Illinois Tool Works Inc **(G-14629)**

Versacomp Inc 954 561-8778
 4021 Ne 5th Ter Oakland Park (33334) **(G-11309)**

Versailles Lighting Inc 561 945-5744
 1305 Poinsettia Dr Ste 6 Delray Beach (33444) **(G-3035)**

Versatile Manufacturing Inc (PA) 954 561-8083
 4021 Ne 5th Ter Oakland Park (33334) **(G-11310)**

Versatile Manufacturing Inc 954 561-8083
 4020 Ne 5th Ter Oakland Park (33334) **(G-11311)**

Versatile Packagers LLC 813 664-1171
 933 Chad Ln Ste C Tampa (33619) **(G-17408)**

Versatile Water Jet, Oakland Park Also called Versatile Manufacturing Inc **(G-11310)**

Versatus Hpc Inc 561 544-8862
 4700 Nw 2nd Ave Boca Raton (33431) **(G-745)**

Versea Diagnostics LLC 800 397-0670
 1000 N Florida Ave Tampa (33602) **(G-17409)**

Versea Holdings Inc 800 397-0670
 1000 N Florida Ave Tampa (33602) **(G-17410)**

Vertaeon LLC 404 823-6232
 747 Sw 2nd Ave Ste 349 Gainesville (32601) **(G-4783)**

Vertaloc, Plantation Also called US Diagnostics Inc **(G-13898)**

Vertarib Inc (PA) 877 815-8610
 9005 Southern Blvd West Palm Beach (33411) **(G-18195)**

Vertec Inc 850 478-6480
 141 Terry Dr Pensacola (32503) **(G-13620)**

Vertex Precision Inc 561 582-6171
 714 S East Coast St Lake Worth (33460) **(G-7242)**

Vertical Assesment Assoc LLC 850 210-0401
 17752 Ne Charlie Johns St Blountstown (32424) **(G-379)**

Vertical Aviation Tech Inc 407 322-9488
 1609 Hangar Rd Bldg 332 Sanford (32773) **(G-15404)**

Vertical Bridge Towers LLC 561 948-6367
 750 Park Of Commerce Boca Raton (33487) **(G-746)**

Vertical Cable, Hallandale Also called Chiptech Inc **(G-4921)**

Vertical Flight Technology Inc 407 687-3126
 3385 Shady Run Rd Melbourne (32934) **(G-8557)**

Vertical Land Inc (PA) 850 819-2535
 7950 Front Beach Rd Panama City (32407) **(G-13317)**

Vertical Land Inc 850 244-5263
 621 Mckenzie Ave Panama City (32401) **(G-13318)**

Vertical Reality Inc 305 238-4522
 17511 Sw 99th Rd Palmetto Bay (33157) **(G-13222)**

Vertical Reality Mfg Inc 305 238-4522
 17511 Sw 99th Rd Palmetto Bay (33157) **(G-13223)**

Vertical Systems Inspctons Inc 954 775-6023
 899 E Country Club Cir Plantation (33317) **(G-13899)**

Vertical Village Inc 772 340-0400
 10658 S Us Highway 1 Port Saint Lucie (34952) **(G-14464)**

Verticals Unlimited, Ocoee Also called TMMR Holdings LLC **(G-11528)**

Vertimax LLC 800 699-5867
 8108 Benjamin Rd Ste 201 Tampa (33634) **(G-17411)**

Vertiv, Sunrise Also called Alber Corp **(G-16288)**

Vertiv Corporation 954 377-7101
 7775 W Oakland Park Blvd Sunrise (33351) **(G-16389)**

Vertiv It Systems Inc 954 746-9000
 550 W Cypress Creek Rd # 200 Fort Lauderdale (33309) **(G-4118)**

Vertpac LLC 407 886-9010
 520 W Orange Blossom Trl Apopka (32712) **(G-183)**

Veru Healthcare, Miami Also called Veru Inc **(G-10102)**

Veru Inc (PA) 305 509-6897
 2916 N Miami Ave Ste 1000 Miami (33127) **(G-10102)**

Very Tasty LLC 305 636-4140
 2177 Nw 24th Ct Miami (33142) **(G-10103)**

Veserca Group Ltd Inc 561 210-7400
 20694 Nw 27th Ave Boca Raton (33434) **(G-747)**

Vesta T Hetherington 561 588-9933
 5411 S Olive Ave West Palm Beach (33405) **(G-18196)**

Vesta's, West Palm Beach Also called Vesta T Hetherington **(G-18196)**

Vestagen Tchnical Textiles Inc 407 781-2570
 1301 W Colonial Dr Orlando (32804) **(G-12695)**

Vested Metals Intl LLC 904 495-7278
 7000 Us Highway 1 N # 503 Saint Augustine (32095) **(G-14909)**

Vesten Woodworks LLC 407 780-9295
 200 Colorado Springs Way Saint Augustine (32092) **(G-14910)**

Vestex, Orlando Also called Vestagen Tchnical Textiles Inc **(G-12695)**

Vet Sonic Inc 305 681-4486
 1099 E 47th St Hialeah (33013) **(G-5409)**

Vet-Equip Inc 239 537-3402
 999 Vanderbilt Beach Rd # 200 Naples (34108) **(G-10932)**

Vetbiotek Inc 727 308-2030
 640 Douglas Rd E Ste A Oldsmar (34677) **(G-11706)**

Veterans Metal LLC (PA) 727 572-9470
 5150 Ulmerton Rd Ste 14 Clearwater (33760) **(G-1844)**

Vetio Animal Health, Jupiter Also called Tropichem Research Labs LLC **(G-6815)**

Vetio Dev't & Mfg Plant, Jupiter Also called Tropichem Research Labs LLC **(G-6814)**

Vette Brakes & Products Inc 727 345-5292
 7490 30th Ave N Saint Petersburg (33710) **(G-15225)**

Vf, Riverview Also called Workwear Outfitters LLC **(G-14583)**

Vf, Tampa Also called Workwear Outfitters LLC **(G-17437)**

Vfinity Inc 239 244-2555
 837 5th Ave S Ste 200 Naples (34102) **(G-10933)**

Vfm Aerosystems LLC 786 567-2348
 10050 Nw 44th Ter Apt 301 Doral (33178) **(G-3412)**

Vgcm LLC 813 247-7625
 3510 Pendola Point Rd Tampa (33619) **(G-17412)**

Vgcm LLC 813 620-4889
 2001 Maritime Blvd Tampa (33605) **(G-17413)**

Vgi Medical LLC 727 565-1235
 11651 87th St Largo (33773) **(G-7702)**

Vgr Holding LLC (HQ) 305 579-8000
 4400 S Biscayne Blvd # 10 Miami (33131) **(G-10104)**

Via Cabinets Corp 407 633-1915
 3113 Willie Mays Pkwy Orlando (32811) **(G-12696)**

Via Optronics LLC 407 745-5031
 6220 Hzltine Nat Dr Ste 1 Orlando (32822) **(G-12697)**

Vianny Corporation 239 888-4536
 6860 Daniels Pkwy Fort Myers (33912) **(G-4440)**

Viasat Inc 813 880-5000
 4211 W Boy Scout Blvd # 550 Tampa (33607) **(G-17414)**

Viatech of Delaware Inc 321 308-6600
 7341 Office Park Pl # 102 Melbourne (32940) **(G-8558)**

Viatek Consumer Pdts Group Inc (PA) 423 402-9010
 2081 Se Ocean Blvd Ste 3a Stuart (34996) **(G-16246)**

Viatek Products, Stuart Also called Viatek Consumer Pdts Group Inc **(G-16246)**

Vicbag LLC 305 423-7042
 80 Sw 8th St Ste 2000 Miami (33130) **(G-10105)**

Viccarbe Inc 305 670-0979
 8950 Sw 74th Ct Ste 1406 Miami (33156) **(G-10106)**

Vicente Gandia Pla 310 699-8559
 7300 N Kendall Dr Ste 470 Miami (33156) **(G-10107)**

Vicente Gandia USA, Miami Also called Vicente Gandia Pla **(G-10107)**

Vicente Gandia Usa Inc 310 699-8559
 7300 N Kendall Dr Ste 470 Miami (33156) **(G-10108)**

Vick Houston, Fort Lauderdale Also called Attack Communications Inc **(G-3665)**

Vickery and Company 813 987-2100
 7911 Professional Pl Tampa (33637) **(G-17415)**

Victores Machine Shop, Miami Also called Group Heros Inc **(G-9252)**

Victoriano Pantoja, Orlando Also called Causey Machine Works Inc **(G-11987)**

Victors Cstm Qlting Bdspread I 305 362-1990
 2765 W 78th St Hialeah (33016) **(G-5410)**

(PA)=Parent Co (HQ)=Headquarters (DH)=Div Headquarters

Victors Die Cutting Inc 305 599-0255
 1385 Se 9th Ave Hialeah (33010) (G-5411)
Victors Trim Molding Crown Bas 727 403-6057
 6142 38th Ave N Saint Petersburg (33710) (G-15226)
Victory Coatings Inc 954 708-4388
 4742 Lago Vista Dr Coconut Creek (33073) (G-2010)
Victory Custom Cabinetry 727 937-2284
 2623 Grand Blvd Holiday (34690) (G-5506)
Victory Tailgate LLC 407 704-8775
 8673 Transport Dr Orlando (32832) (G-12698)
Victory Valet Services LLC 904 521-6517
 5549 Fort Caroline Rd # 107 Jacksonville (32277) (G-6590)
Victus LLC (PA) 305 663-2129
 4918 Sw 74th Ct Miami (33155) (G-10109)
Victus Capital Enterprises Inc (PA) 727 442-6677
 1780 102nd Ave N Ste 500 Saint Petersburg (33716) (G-15227)
Vicx LLC 407 674-2073
 1273 Wntr Gdn Vnlnd Rd Winter Garden (34787) (G-18407)
Vidacann LLC 772 672-1178
 4844 Race Track Rd Saint Johns (32259) (G-14947)
Vidco Industries Inc 305 888-0077
 7500 Nw 69th Ave Frnt Ste Medley (33166) (G-8349)
Video Display Corporation (PA) 800 241-5005
 5155 King St Cocoa (32926) (G-1962)
Video Display Corporation 813 854-2259
 13948 Lynmar Blvd Tampa (33626) (G-17416)
Video Display Corporation 321 784-4427
 5155 King St Cocoa (32926) (G-1963)
Videoling Streaming Svcs LLC 904 330-1026
 4651 Salisbury Rd Jacksonville (32256) (G-6591)
Vidrepur of America LLC 305 468-9008
 2301 Nw 84th Ave Miami (33122) (G-10110)
Vienna Beauty Products Co (PA) 937 228-7109
 222 Harbour Dr Apt 100 Naples (34103) (G-10934)
Vienna Beef Ltd 941 723-7234
 2650 Corporate Way Palmetto (34221) (G-13203)
Viesel Fuel LLC 772 781-4300
 1000 Se Monterey Cmns # 206 Stuart (34996) (G-16247)
Viewpoint Systems LLC 850 450-0681
 730 W Garden St Pensacola Pensacola (32502) (G-13621)
Vigo Importing Company 813 884-3491
 4701 Tony Alessi Sr Ave Tampa (33614) (G-17417)
Viking Aircraft Engines LLC 386 416-8383
 735 Air Park Rd 3c Edgewater (32132) (G-3503)
Viking Cases, Saint Petersburg Also called Stemler Corporation (G-15200)
Viking Kabinets Inc 305 238-9025
 10445 Sw 186th Ln Cutler Bay (33157) (G-2311)
Viking Woodworking 352 237-5050
 13401 W Highway 328 Ocala (34482) (G-11509)
Vilano Interiors Inc 904 824-3439
 112 Oak Ave Saint Augustine (32084) (G-14911)
Village Bread & Bagells, Jacksonville Also called New Vbb LLC (G-6329)
Village Scribe Printing Co 727 585-7388
 1548 Shirley Pl Largo (33770) (G-7703)
Villagran Printing Corp 786 230-6638
 765 Nw 34th St Miami (33127) (G-10111)
Villar Stone & Paver Works LLC 860 209-2907
 1140 Seaside Dr Sarasota (34242) (G-15867)
Vin-Dotco Inc 727 217-9200
 2875 Mci Dr N Unit B Pinellas Park (33782) (G-13733)
Vinavil Americas Corporation 954 246-8888
 1144 E Newport Center Dr Deerfield Beach (33442) (G-2831)
Vince & Sons Pasta Co, Boca Raton Also called Jo MO Enterprises Inc (G-563)
Vine & Grind, Treasure Island Also called Vine and Grind LLC (G-17628)
Vine and Grind LLC 727 420-3122
 111 107th Ave Ste 1 Treasure Island (33706) (G-17628)
Vineyard 101 LLC 727 819-5300
 12930 Us Highway 19 Hudson (34667) (G-5791)
Vingcard, Fort Lauderdale Also called Assa Abloy Hospitality Inc (G-3661)
Vinland Corporation 954 475-9093
 11600 Nw 20th St Plantation (33323) (G-13900)
Vinland International Inc 954 316-2007
 1700 Nw 65th Ave Ste 12 Plantation (33313) (G-13901)
Vinland Marketing Inc 954 602-2177
 1152 N University Dr # 304 Pembroke Pines (33024) (G-13424)
Vintage Art and Sign LLC 770 815-7887
 1419 29th St 3 Niceville (32578) (G-11039)
Vintage Ironworks LLC 407 339-2555
 671 Newburyport Ave Altamonte Springs (32701) (G-77)
Vinyl Bros 850 396-5977
 5668 Gulf Breeze Pkwy # 4 Gulf Breeze (32563) (G-4896)
Vinyl Corp (HQ) 305 477-6464
 8000 Nw 79th Pl Ste 4 Miami (33166) (G-10112)
Vinyl Etchings Inc 727 845-5300
 6641 Industrial Ave Port Richey (34668) (G-14384)
Vinyl Lettering and Signs 239 537-7355
 1315 Wildwood Lakes Blvd # 8 Naples (34104) (G-10935)
Vinylize Creation LLC 954 478-3172
 2201 Sw 84th Ter Miramar (33025) (G-10561)

Vinylot of Florida Inc 954 978-8424
 2048 Mears Pkwy Margate (33063) (G-8159)
Vinylot Signs & Graphics, Margate Also called Vinylot of Florida Inc (G-8159)
Violet Defense LLC 407 433-1104
 189 S Orange Ave Ste 1400 Orlando (32801) (G-12699)
VIP 2000 Tv Inc 305 373-2400
 1200 Brickell Ave # 1575 Miami (33131) (G-10113)
Vlp Prtg Night CLB Sups LLC 561 603-2846
 1000 Holland Dr Ste 1 Boca Raton (33487) (G-748)
VIP Scooter Rental, Miami Beach Also called Adir Scooters Inc (G-10151)
VIP Software Corporation 813 837-4347
 6000 S Florida Ave # 6832 Lakeland (33807) (G-7470)
VIP Sports Idrive, Orlando Also called Ultimate Overstock LLC (G-12685)
Viper 4x4 .... 305 468-9818
 11924 Perspective Dr Windermere (34786) (G-18369)
Viper Communication Systems (HQ) 352 694-7030
 4211 Sw 13th St Ocala (34474) (G-11510)
Viper Drones Inc 321 427-5837
 214 Briarcliff Cir Sebastian (32958) (G-15910)
Viper Drones LLC 205 677-3700
 214 Briarcliff Cir Sebastian (32958) (G-15911)
Vipre, Clearwater Also called Threattrack Security Inc (G-1829)
Virag Biosciences, West Palm Beach Also called Virag Distribution LLC (G-18197)
Virag Distribution LLC 844 448-4724
 700 S Rosemary Ave # 204 West Palm Beach (33401) (G-18197)
Virginia Electronic & Ltg Corp (PA) 904 230-2840
 1293 Energy Cove Ct Green Cove Springs (32043) (G-4842)
Virgo Aerospace LLC 954 816-3455
 6180 Royal Birkdale Dr Lake Worth (33463) (G-7243)
Vishay Americas Inc 407 804-2567
 735 Primera Blvd Lake Mary (32746) (G-7115)
Visible Results USA Inc 913 706-8248
 1550 Corolla Ct 1 Reunion (34747) (G-14555)
Vision Analytical Inc (PA) 305 801-7140
 4444 Sw 71st Ave Ste 112 Miami (33155) (G-10114)
Vision Blocks Inc 321 254-7478
 1634 Cypress Ave Melbourne (32935) (G-8559)
Vision Candles Inc 305 836-8650
 7363 Nw 36th Ave Miami (33147) (G-10115)
Vision Concepts Ink Inc 305 463-8003
 8953 Nw 23rd St Doral (33172) (G-3413)
Vision Conveyor Inc 352 343-3300
 32834 Lakeshore Dr Tavares (32778) (G-17529)
Vision Engineering Labs 727 812-2000
 8787 Enterprise Blvd Largo (33773) (G-7704)
Vision Engineering Labs 727 812-2035
 8787 Enterprise Blvd Largo (33773) (G-7705)
Vision Manufacturing Tech Inc 904 579-5272
 137 Industrial Loop W Orange Park (32073) (G-11845)
Vision Mt, Orange Park Also called Vision Manufacturing Tech Inc (G-11845)
Vision Solution Technology LL 305 477-4480
 10367 Nw 41st St Doral (33178) (G-3414)
Vision Source Inc 407 435-9958
 9262 Bent Arrow Cv Apopka (32703) (G-184)
Vision Systems North Amer Inc 321 265-5110
 1801 Penn St Ste 104 Melbourne (32901) (G-8560)
Vision Web Offset LLC 305 433-6188
 13930 Nw 60th Ave Miami Lakes (33014) (G-10376)
Visionare LLC 305 989-7271
 12251 Towne Lake Dr Fort Myers (33913) (G-4441)
Visions Millwork Inc 239 390-0811
 15674 Spring Line Ln Fort Myers (33905) (G-4442)
Visions Sky Corp 888 788-8609
 18154 Cadence St Orlando (32820) (G-12700)
Visiontech Components LLC 727 547-5466
 5120 110th Ave N Clearwater (33760) (G-1845)
Vista Color Corporation 305 635-2000
 1401 Nw 78th Ave Ste 201 Doral (33126) (G-3415)
Vista Magazine, Miami Beach Also called Vista Publishing Corporation (G-10246)
Vista Products Inc (HQ) 904 725-2242
 8801 Corporate Square Ct Jacksonville (32216) (G-6592)
Vista Publishing Corporation 305 416-4644
 6538 Collins Ave Miami Beach (33141) (G-10246)
Vista Serv Corp 239 275-1973
 2346 Winkler Ave Fort Myers (33901) (G-4443)
Vista System LLC 941 365-4646
 1800 N East Ave Ste 102 Sarasota (34234) (G-15868)
Vista-Pro Automotive LLC 352 867-7272
 2410 Nw 8th Pl Ocala (34475) (G-11511)
Vistakon, Jacksonville Also called Johnson Jhnson Vision Care Inc (G-6230)
Vistakon Pharmaceuticals LLC 904 443-1000
 7500 Centurion Pkwy # 100 Jacksonville (32256) (G-6593)
Vistamatic LLC 866 466-9525
 11713 Nw 39th St Coral Springs (33065) (G-2226)
Vistapharm Inc 727 530-1633
 7265 Ulmerton Rd Largo (33771) (G-7706)
Vistapharm Inc 727 530-1633
 13707 66th St Largo (33771) (G-7707)

2022 Harris Florida
Manufacturers Directory

(G-0000) Company's Geographic Section entry number

Visual Acoustics LLC......786 390-6128
591 Nw 35th St Miami (33127) ***(G-10116)***
Visual Comm Specialists Inc......407 936-7300
707 Platinum Pt Ste 2001 Lake Mary (32746) ***(G-7116)***
Visual Signs LLC......407 693-0200
7041 Grand National Dr Orlando (32819) ***(G-12701)***
Vital Graphics and Signs Inc......305 557-8181
2131 W 60th St Hialeah (33016) ***(G-5412)***
Vital Health Corporation (HQ)......407 522-1125
6000 Metrowest Blvd # 200 Orlando (32835) ***(G-12702)***
Vital Imging Diagnstc Ctrs LLC......305 569-9992
7101 Sw 99th Ave Ste 109 Miami (33173) ***(G-10117)***
Vital Pharma Research Inc......786 666-0592
2300 W 84th St Ste 303 Hialeah (33016) ***(G-5413)***
Vital Printing Corporation......561 659-2367
1983 10th Ave N Lake Worth Beach (33461) ***(G-7264)***
Vital Signs of Orlando Inc......407 297-0680
2111 S Division Ave Ste A Orlando (32805) ***(G-12703)***
Vital Solutions LLC......561 848-1717
3755 Fiscal Ct Ste 2 West Palm Beach (33404) ***(G-18198)***
Vital Usa Inc......561 282-6074
525 S Flagler Dr Ste 301 West Palm Beach (33401) ***(G-18199)***
Vitalleo Health, Neptune Beach *Also called Vitalleo LLC* ***(G-10960)***
Vitalleo LLC......904 474-5330
2300 Marsh Point Rd 302c Neptune Beach (32266) ***(G-10960)***
Vitamin Shoppe Florida LLC (HQ)......305 468-1600
14620 Nw 60th Ave Miami Lakes (33014) ***(G-10377)***
Vitaminmed LLC......727 443-7008
300 S Duncan Ave Ste 263 Clearwater (33755) ***(G-1846)***
Vitapak LLC......954 661-0390
21070 Sheridan St Fort Lauderdale (33332) ***(G-4119)***
Viterra Affordable Shutters......239 738-6364
1104 Se 46th Ln Ste 2 Cape Coral (33904) ***(G-1404)***
Vitsur Industries Inc......561 744-1290
130 Evernia St Ste 3 Jupiter (33458) ***(G-6821)***
Viva 5 LLC (HQ)......561 239-2239
239 2nd Ave S Ste 200 Saint Petersburg (33701) ***(G-15228)***
Viva Led LLC......786 491-9290
2944 Nw 72nd Ave Miami (33122) ***(G-10118)***
Vivid Images USA Inc......904 620-0303
240 Talleyrand Ave A Jacksonville (32202) ***(G-6594)***
Vivid Sportwear, Miami *Also called T Shirt Center Inc* ***(G-9990)***
Vividus LLC......954 326-1954
3265 W Mcnab Rd Pompano Beach (33069) ***(G-14237)***
Vivonex LLC......210 695-9244
24 Dockside Ln Key Largo (33037) ***(G-6852)***
Vizcom Enterprises Llc......407 324-8338
1265 Upsala Rd Ste 1133 Sanford (32771) ***(G-15405)***
Vizergy, Jacksonville *Also called Jjj & H Inc* ***(G-6224)***
Viztek Inc......904 448-9936
6491 Powers Ave Jacksonville (32217) ***(G-6595)***
Vj Publications Inc......407 461-0707
1551 W Marvin St Longwood (32750) ***(G-7957)***
Vladmir Ltd......386 445-6000
32 Hargrove Grade Palm Coast (32137) ***(G-13092)***
Vlex 1450 LLC......954 218-5443
1199 Hidden Valley Way Weston (33327) ***(G-18297)***
Vlex LLC......800 335-6202
1200 Brickell Ave # 1800 Miami (33131) ***(G-10119)***
Vloc Incorporated......727 375-8562
6716 Industrial Ave Port Richey (34668) ***(G-14385)***
Vm, Jacksonville *Also called Venus Manufacturing Co Inc* ***(G-6589)***
Vm Jewelry, Port Saint Lucie *Also called Corporcion Intrncnal De Jyas V* ***(G-14406)***
Vmak Corp......407 260-1199
131 Applewood Dr Longwood (32750) ***(G-7958)***
Vmax Vision Inc......321 972-1823
2600 Mtland Ctr Pkwy Ste Maitland (32751) ***(G-8078)***
Vmoviles Inc......954 609-2510
17111 Biscayne Blvd Aventura (33160) ***(G-276)***
Vmoviles Power Solar Energy, Aventura *Also called Vmoviles Inc* ***(G-276)***
VMS Usa Inc......727 434-1577
8060 Cypress Garden Ct Seminole (33777) ***(G-15997)***
Voda Technologies LLC......727 645-6030
3909 Mimosa Pl Palm Harbor (34685) ***(G-13137)***
Voda USA, Miami *Also called Main USA Corp* ***(G-9501)***
Vogue Aerospace & Defense Inc......321 289-0872
1712 Commercial Dr Naples (34112) ***(G-10936)***
Vogue Latinoamerica, Coral Gables *Also called Conde Nast Americas* ***(G-2042)***
Voice of South Marion......352 245-3161
5513 Se 113th St Belleview (34420) ***(G-367)***
Voice Publishing Co Inc......305 687-5555
4696 E 10th Ct Hialeah (33013) ***(G-5414)***
Voicetech, Sarasota *Also called Omnisys LLC* ***(G-15770)***
Volac Inc......800 759-7569
4132 Castle Gate Dr Pace (32571) ***(G-12859)***
Volaero Drones, Sunrise *Also called Volaero Uav Drnes Hldings Corp* ***(G-16390)***
Volaero Uav Drnes Hldings Corp......954 261-3105
5375 N Hiatus Rd Sunrise (33351) ***(G-16390)***
Volcano Industries Inc......770 300-0041
1125 Commerce Blvd N Sarasota (34243) ***(G-15578)***
Volpino Corp......904 264-8808
1551 Pine Hammock Trl Orange Park (32003) ***(G-11846)***
Volt Lighting......813 978-3700
16011 N Nebraska Ave # 102 Lutz (33549) ***(G-8020)***
Volt Resistance, Saint Augustine *Also called H2c Brands LLC* ***(G-14839)***
Volume Cases, Boca Raton *Also called Hut Global Inc* ***(G-540)***
Volunteer Capital LLC......954 366-6659
1911 Nw 40th Ct Deerfield Beach (33064) ***(G-2832)***
Volusia Waste Inc......386 878-3322
1455 Brayton Cir Deltona (32725) ***(G-3056)***
Volvox Inc Hollywood......954 961-4942
537 N Rainbow Dr Hollywood (33021) ***(G-5682)***
Vonn Lighting, North Miami Beach *Also called Vonn LLC* ***(G-11168)***
Vonn LLC......888 604-8666
3323 Ne 163rd St Ph 706 North Miami Beach (33160) ***(G-11168)***
Vos Systems LLC......352 317-2954
304 W University Ave Gainesville (32601) ***(G-4784)***
Voss Bindery Inc......904 396-3330
2565 Philips Hwy Jacksonville (32207) ***(G-6596)***
Vossen Wheels Inc......305 463-7778
1598 Nw 82nd Ave Doral (33126) ***(G-3416)***
Vowells Downtown Inc......850 432-5175
1233 Barrancas Ave Pensacola (32502) ***(G-13622)***
Vowells Printing, Pensacola *Also called Vowells Downtown Inc* ***(G-13622)***
Voxx Automotive Corp (HQ)......631 231-7750
2351 J Lawson Blvd Orlando (32824) ***(G-12704)***
Voxx Automotive Corporation......407 842-7000
2351 J Lawson Blvd Orlando (32824) ***(G-12705)***
Voxx Electronics, Orlando *Also called Voxxhirschmann Corporation* ***(G-12707)***
Voxx International Corporation (PA)......800 645-7750
2351 J Lawson Blvd Orlando (32824) ***(G-12706)***
Voxxhirschmann Corporation......866 869-7888
2351 J Lawson Blvd Orlando (32824) ***(G-12707)***
Voyager Offroad LLC......941 235-7225
1602 Market Cir Unit 8 Port Charlotte (33953) ***(G-14323)***
Voyomotive LLC......888 321-4633
1058 N Tamiami Trl # 108 Sarasota (34236) ***(G-15869)***
VP Cast Stone Corp......305 691-9306
879 E 25th St 899 Hialeah (33013) ***(G-5415)***
Vp Castone, Hialeah *Also called VP Cast Stone Corp* ***(G-5415)***
Vplenish Nutritionals Inc......954 304-4000
101 Plaza Real S Apt 306 Boca Raton (33432) ***(G-749)***
Vpr 4x4......305 468-9818
1870 Saturn Blvd Orlando (32837) ***(G-12708)***
Vpr Brands LP (PA)......954 715-7001
1141 Sawgrs Corp Pkwy Sunrise (33323) ***(G-16391)***
Vr Preserve Development LLC......561 370-3617
1804 N Dixie Hwy Ste A West Palm Beach (33407) ***(G-18200)***
Vreeland Woodworking LLC......727 365-0241
1407 Tampa Rd Palm Harbor (34683) ***(G-13138)***
Vs Carbonics Inc......305 903-6501
3491 Nw 79th St Miami (33147) ***(G-10120)***
Vs Coatings LLC......305 677-6224
3491 Nw 79th St Miami (33147) ***(G-10121)***
VSF Corp......305 769-2202
4241 W 108th St Unit 1 Hialeah (33018) ***(G-5416)***
VSI, Fort Myers *Also called Vault Structures Inc* ***(G-4438)***
VSI & Partners Inc......954 205-8653
14501 Sw 39th St Miramar (33027) ***(G-10562)***
Vso, Orlando *Also called Vital Signs of Orlando Inc* ***(G-12703)***
Vtech Io, Fort Myers *Also called Computers At Work Inc* ***(G-4216)***
Vtronix LLC......305 471-7600
7900 Nw 68th St Miami (33166) ***(G-10122)***
Vuaant Inc (PA)......407 701-6975
7300 Sandlake Commons Blv Orlando (32819) ***(G-12709)***
Vuessence Inc......813 792-7123
17633 Gunn Hwy Ste 107 Odessa (33556) ***(G-11591)***
Vuflow Filters Co Inc......352 597-2607
13370 Chambord St Brooksville (34613) ***(G-1220)***
Vulcan Construction Mtls LLC......386 252-8581
405 Madison Ave Daytona Beach (32114) ***(G-2618)***
Vulcan Machine Inc......813 664-0032
4201 Byshore Blvd Unit 18 Tampa (33611) ***(G-17418)***
Vulcan Machine -2020, Tampa *Also called Vulcan Machine Inc* ***(G-17418)***
Vulcan Materials, Tavares *Also called Legacy Vulcan Corp* ***(G-17516)***
Vulcan Materials Company, Fort Myers *Also called Florida Rock Industries* ***(G-4255)***
Vulcan Materials Company......205 298-3000
2001 Maritime Blvd Tampa (33605) ***(G-17419)***
Vulcan Mtls Co Vestavia Al, Jacksonville *Also called Florida Rock Industries* ***(G-6108)***
Vulcan Steel, Jacksonville *Also called Fitzlord Inc* ***(G-6099)***
Vulcan Steel......561 945-1259
326 Jupiter Lakes Blvd # 2 Jupiter (33458) ***(G-6822)***
Vuram Inc......813 421-8000
12802 Tampa Oaks Blvd # 241 Temple Terrace (33637) ***(G-17548)***
Vurb LLC......561 441-8870
2450 W Sample Rd Ste 14 Pompano Beach (33073) ***(G-14238)***

ALPHABETIC

Vutec Corporation 954 545-9000
4420 Old Dixie Hwy Vero Beach (32967) *(G-17816)*

Vuziq, Homestead Also called Duenas Mobile Applications LLC *(G-5709)*

Vve, Fort Walton Beach Also called Ver-Val Enterprises Inc *(G-4616)*

Vx Technologies 608 774-5221
2541 Southridge Rd Delray Beach (33444) *(G-3036)*

Vxpass, Delray Beach Also called Vx Technologies *(G-3036)*

Vy Spine LLC 866 489-7746
2236 Capital Cir Ne # 103 Tallahassee (32308) *(G-16521)*

Vyp Services LLC 305 593-8183
3555 Nw 79th Ave Doral (33122) *(G-3417)*

W & B Scientific Inc 954 607-1500
1301 W Copans Rd Ste G1 Pompano Beach (33064) *(G-14239)*

W & W Manufacturing Co 516 942-0011
4504 E Hillsborough Ave Tampa (33610) *(G-17420)*

W C Edge Jewelry Co Division, Hollywood Also called Mayers Jwly Co Hollywood Inc *(G-5623)*

W C H Enterprises Inc 239 267-7549
17640 Holly Oak Ave Fort Myers (33967) *(G-4444)*

W D H Enterprises Inc 941 758-6500
4230 26th St W Bradenton (34205) *(G-1073)*

W D Wilson Inc (PA) 813 626-6989
3005 S 54th St Tampa (33619) *(G-17421)*

W E Connery Boat Builders 239 549-8014
5787 Sw 9th Ct Cape Coral (33914) *(G-1405)*

W E W Enterprises Inc 941 751-6610
6103 28th St E Ste A Bradenton (34203) *(G-1074)*

W H L Business Communications 561 361-9202
2880 N Federal Hwy Boca Raton (33431) *(G-750)*

W Kost Inc 772 286-3700
4175 Sw Martin Hwy Palm City (34990) *(G-13064)*

W R Bonsal Plant 44, Tampa Also called Bonsal American Inc *(G-16657)*

W R Grace & Co - Conn 561 982-7776
6001 Broken Sound Pkwy # 600 Boca Raton (33487) *(G-751)*

W R Williams Enterprises Inc 813 677-2000
6202 Powell Rd Gibsonton (33534) *(G-4803)*

W&I Properties LLC 786 985-1642
3400 Davie Rd Apt 515 Davie (33314) *(G-2495)*

W&W Engineering Company, Palm Harbor Also called Westlund Engineering Inc *(G-13139)*

W.L. Installers, Hollywood Also called William Laroque Installers Inc *(G-5684)*

W.S.I., Margate Also called Willson & Son Industry Inc *(G-8160)*

W2e International Corp 561 362-9595
2200 Nw Corp Blvd Ste 210 Boca Raton (33431) *(G-752)*

Wafer World Inc 561 842-4441
1100 Tech Pl Ste 104 West Palm Beach (33407) *(G-18201)*

Wagner Pavers Contractor 321 633-5131
403 Hawk St Ste A Rockledge (32955) *(G-14754)*

Wai Corporate - USA, Miramar Also called Wetherill Associates Inc *(G-10564)*

Wake Up Beautiful 941 792-6500
6646 Cortez Rd W Bradenton (34210) *(G-1075)*

Wakulla News 850 926-7102
3119a Crawfordville Hwy Crawfordville (32327) *(G-2233)*

Walden Consulting LLC 407 563-3620
1021 E Robinson St Ste A Orlando (32801) *(G-12710)*

Walden Timber Harvesting Inc 850 674-4884
13851 Nw Sand Cut Trl Altha (32421) *(G-79)*

Walin Tools LLC 850 226-8632
642a Anchors St Nw Fort Walton Beach (32548) *(G-4617)*

Walker Electric Inc 941 729-5015
9945 Sw 194th Ct Dunnellon (34432) *(G-3469)*

Walker Graphics Inc 954 964-1688
2039 Coolidge St B Hollywood (33020) *(G-5683)*

Walker Products 941 723-9820
1507 17th St E Palmetto (34221) *(G-13204)*

Walker Stainless Eqp Co LLC 352 343-2606
27620 County Road 561 Tavares (32778) *(G-17530)*

Walker Wood Products Inc 904 448-5202
6112 Quattlebaum Rd Jacksonville (32217) *(G-6597)*

Walkup Enterprises Inc 727 571-1244
5040 110th Ave N Clearwater (33760) *(G-1847)*

Wall Bed Systems Inc 419 738-5207
5040 140th Ave N Clearwater (33760) *(G-1848)*

Wall Sculpture By Grutan, Pompano Beach Also called Gurtan Designs *(G-14047)*

Wall Way Corporation 305 484-7600
9001 Nw 97th Ter Ste F Medley (33178) *(G-8350)*

Wall Way USA of Florida, Medley Also called Wall Way Corporation *(G-8350)*

Wallace Industries Inc 561 833-8554
316 Valencia Rd West Palm Beach (33401) *(G-18202)*

Wallace Industries Inc 561 301-0811
906 N Dixie Hwy Lake Worth (33460) *(G-7244)*

Walling Crate Company 352 787-5211
507 N 14th St Leesburg (34748) *(G-7801)*

Wallpaper For Windows, Cocoa Also called Etchart LLC *(G-1927)*

Walruss Enterprises Inc 954 525-0342
1509 Sw 1st Ave Fort Lauderdale (33315) *(G-4120)*

Walt Dittmer and Sons Inc 407 699-1755
1006 Shepard Rd Winter Springs (32708) *(G-18581)*

Walter Green Inc 850 227-7946
252 Marina Dr Port Saint Joe (32456) *(G-14392)*

Walter Haas Graphics Inc 305 883-2257
123 W 23rd St Hialeah (33010) *(G-5417)*

Walters Tools LLC 321 537-4788
2998 Hester Ave Se Palm Bay (32909) *(G-12927)*

Walton Son Newspapers, Santa Rosa Beach Also called Emerald Coast Media & Mktg *(G-15425)*

Waltzing Waters Inc 239 574-5181
1410 Se 10th St Cape Coral (33990) *(G-1406)*

Want ADS of Hot Springs Inc (PA) 501 623-4404
713 E 12th St Panama City (32401) *(G-13319)*

Wanted Dead or Alive Inc 239 633-5080
1011 April Ln North Fort Myers (33903) *(G-11073)*

War Chest River LLC 954 736-7704
675 Nw 97th St Miami (33150) *(G-10123)*

Warbird Marine Holdings LLC (PA) 844 341-2504
4700 Nw 132nd St Opa Locka (33054) *(G-11799)*

Warden Enterprises Inc (PA) 954 463-4404
807 Nw 7th St Fort Lauderdale (33311) *(G-4121)*

Warehouse Goods LLC 877 865-2260
1095 Broken Sound Pkwy Nw # 300 Boca Raton (33487) *(G-753)*

Warensford Well Drilling Inc 386 738-3257
329 S Blue Lake Ave Deland (32724) *(G-2918)*

Warfighter Fcsed Logistics Inc 740 513-4692
936 Nw 1st St Fort Lauderdale (33311) *(G-4122)*

Warren Equipment Inc 813 752-5126
2299 Us Highway 92 E Plant City (33563) *(G-13814)*

Warren Heim Corp 772 466-8265
3107 Industrial 25th St Fort Pierce (34946) *(G-4553)*

Warren Manufacturing, Hialeah Also called Warren Technology Inc *(G-5418)*

Warren Technology Inc 305 556-6933
2050 W 73rd St Hialeah (33016) *(G-5418)*

Warwick Logging 386 328-9358
119 Putnam County Blvd East Palatka (32131) *(G-3478)*

Warwick, Blane, East Palatka Also called Warwick Logging *(G-3478)*

Washers-R-Us Inc 850 573-0221
2205 Park Rd Alford (32420) *(G-25)*

Washington CL Inc 813 739-4800
810 N Howard Ave Tampa (33606) *(G-17422)*

Washington County News (HQ) 850 638-4242
1364 N Railroad Ave Chipley (32428) *(G-1458)*

Washington Free Weekly, Tampa Also called Washington CL Inc *(G-17422)*

Washington Shores Element 407 250-6260
944 W Lake Mann Dr Orlando (32805) *(G-12711)*

Waste Advantage Corporation 800 358-2873
230 Tresana Blvd Unit 64 Jupiter (33478) *(G-6823)*

Waste Advantage Magazine, Jupiter Also called Waste Advantage Corporation *(G-6823)*

Waste Management Inc Florida 954 984-2000
5400 Rex Dr Winter Garden (34787) *(G-18408)*

Waste Petro Recover 305 345-4199
4680 W 13th Ln Apt 316 Hialeah (33012) *(G-5419)*

Wastequip Manufacturing Co LLC 704 900-4654
2624 Mine And Mill Ln Lakeland (33801) *(G-7471)*

Watchfacts Inc 786 797-5705
14 Ne 1st Ave Ste 1102 Miami (33132) *(G-10124)*

Water Bagel Boca East LIlp 347 661-7171
201 N Us Highway 1 Ste C5 Jupiter (33477) *(G-6824)*

Water Boy Inc 239 461-0860
1520 Lee St Fort Myers (33901) *(G-4445)*

Water Technology Pensacola Inc 850 477-4789
3000 W Nine Mile Rd Pensacola (32534) *(G-13623)*

Water Works Tech Group LLC 954 979-2480
4100 N Powerline Rd Q3 Pompano Beach (33073) *(G-14240)*

Waterblasting Technologies Inc (PA) 772 223-7393
3920 Se Commerce Ave Stuart (34997) *(G-16248)*

Waterbox Aquariums, Longwood Also called Waterbox Usa LLC *(G-7959)*

Waterbox Usa LLC (PA) 800 674-2608
320 W Sabal Palm Pl # 10 Longwood (32779) *(G-7959)*

Waterboyz-Wbz Inc 850 433-2929
380 N 9th Ave Pensacola (32502) *(G-13624)*

Waterbrick International Inc 877 420-9283
13506 Smmrport Vlg Pkwy S Windermere (34786) *(G-18370)*

Waterfall Industries Inc 407 330-2003
915 Cornwall Rd Sanford (32773) *(G-15406)*

Waterfilterusa 386 469-0138
3060 Prfmce Cir Ste 2 Deland (32724) *(G-2919)*

Waterford Press, Safety Harbor Also called Waterford Publishing Group LLC *(G-14802)*

Waterford Press Inc 727 812-0140
1040 Harbor Lake Dr Safety Harbor (34695) *(G-14801)*

Waterford Publishing Group LLC 727 812-0140
1040 Harbor Lake Dr Safety Harbor (34695) *(G-14802)*

Waterheaterdepot.com, Sunrise Also called Peralta Group Inc *(G-16351)*

Waterhouse Press LLC 781 975-6191
4481 Legendary Dr Ste 200 Destin (32541) *(G-3081)*

Waterhuse Archtctral Wdwrk LLC 786 534-4943
4261 Nw 36th Ave Miami (33142) *(G-10125)*

Waterjet Robotics USA LLC 772 403-2192
86 Cayman Pl Palm Beach Gardens (33418) *(G-13016)*

2022 Harris Florida
Manufacturers Directory

(G-0000) Company's Geographic Section entry number

Watermakers Inc 954 467-8920
2233 S Andrews Ave Fort Lauderdale (33316) *(G-4123)*

Waterproof Charters Inc 941 639-7626
320 Cross St Punta Gorda (33950) *(G-14539)*

Watson Steel Products 716 853-2233
8067 Nw 66th St Miami (33166) *(G-10126)*

Watson Therapeutics Inc 954 266-1000
3400 Enterprise Way Miramar (33025) *(G-10563)*

Wattcore Inc 571 482-6777
4 Commerce Blvd Palm Coast (32164) *(G-13093)*

Wattera LLC 954 400-5135
3131 Sw 42nd St Fort Lauderdale (33312) *(G-4124)*

Watts Juicery 904 372-0693
1013 Atlantic Blvd Atlantic Beach (32233) *(G-217)*

Watts One LLC 305 606-1816
13670 Doubletree Trl Wellington (33414) *(G-17868)*

Watts Technologies 407 512-5750
2647 N Design Ct Sanford (32773) *(G-15407)*

Watts Water Technologies Inc 352 465-2000
11611 Sw 147th Ct Dunnellon (34432) *(G-3470)*

Watts Welding Inc 863 978-3371
18400 County Road 630 Lake Wales (33898) *(G-7179)*

Wau USA Corp 305 361-6110
240 Crandon Blvd Ste 278 Key Biscayne (33149) *(G-6841)*

Wave Tech Plus Corp 813 855-7007
11940 Race Track Rd Tampa (33626) *(G-17423)*

Way Beyond Bagels Inc 561 638-1320
16850 S Jog Rd Ste 108 Delray Beach (33446) *(G-3037)*

Way Bright Sign Systems 615 480-4602
93 Dune Lakes Cir E305 Santa Rosa Beach (32459) *(G-15434)*

Wayloo Inc 954 914-3192
2700 W Cypress Creek Rd Fort Lauderdale (33309) *(G-4125)*

Wayloomoto LLC 954 636-1510
7060 W State Road 84 # 8 Davie (33317) *(G-2496)*

Wayne Dixon LLC 352 279-6886
27340 Popiel Rd Brooksville (34602) *(G-1221)*

Wayne Metal Products Inc 407 321-7168
5461 Benchmark Ln Sanford (32773) *(G-15408)*

Wb Medical Transport LLC 561 827-8877
177 Sw Hawthorne Cir Port Saint Lucie (34953) *(G-14465)*

Wbn LLC 786 870-4172
1630 Nw 82nd Ave Doral (33126) *(G-3418)*

Wbt Apparel Inc 305 891-1107
1175 Ne 125th St Ste 102 North Miami (33161) *(G-11127)*

Wbz Boarding House, Pensacola *Also called Waterboyz-Wbz Inc (G-13624)*

Wcm Group Inc 516 238-4261
1516 N Daytona Ave Flagler Beach (32136) *(G-3606)*

Wco Enterprises, Jacksonville *Also called Flamm Industries Inc (G-6101)*

Wd-40 Company 305 463-9158
2151 S Le Jeune Rd # 308 Miami (33134) *(G-10127)*

Wdc Miami Inc 305 884-2800
9721 Nw 114th Way Medley (33178) *(G-8351)*

We Bronze Wholesale LLC 954 922-8826
2736 N Federal Hwy Fort Lauderdale (33306) *(G-4126)*

We Love Tec LLC 305 433-4453
2032 Ne 155th St North Miami Beach (33162) *(G-11169)*

We Make Vitamins LLC 863 607-6708
2715 Badger Rd Lakeland (33811) *(G-7472)*

We Mix You Match Inc 561 615-0253
6524 Patricia Dr West Palm Beach (33413) *(G-18203)*

We RE Organized 407 323-5133
1441 Kastner Pl Unit 111 Sanford (32771) *(G-15409)*

We Sign It Inc 561 310-2542
17 Nuevo Leon Port Saint Lucie (34952) *(G-14466)*

We Sign It Inc 772 800-7373
889 E Prima Vista Blvd Port Saint Lucie (34952) *(G-14467)*

Weapons Systems, Palm Beach Gardens *Also called Northrop Grumman Systems Corp (G-12994)*

Wear Fund LLC 239 313-3907
93 Mildred Dr Ste B Fort Myers (33901) *(G-4446)*

Wearable Nalia LLC 561 629-5804
5081 Palo Verde Pl Haverhill (33415) *(G-5004)*

Web Offset Printing Co Inc 727 572-7488
12198 44th St N Clearwater (33762) *(G-1849)*

Webb-Mason Inc 727 531-1112
12397 Belcher Rd S # 240 Largo (33773) *(G-7708)*

Webcom Group Inc (HQ) 904 680-6600
5335 Gate Pkwy Ste 200 Jacksonville (32256) *(G-6598)*

Webelectric Products Inc 440 389-5647
333 Colony Blvd The Villages (32162) *(G-17559)*

Weber Manufacturing, North Venice *Also called Weber Mfg & Supplies Inc (G-11221)*

Weber Mfg & Supplies Inc 941 488-5185
3430 Technology Dr North Venice (34275) *(G-11221)*

Weber South Fl LLC 239 543-7240
40800 Cook Brown Rd Punta Gorda (33982) *(G-14540)*

Webidcard Inc 443 280-1577
89 Mitad Cir Saint Augustine (32095) *(G-14912)*

Webvoip Inc 305 793-2061
6400 N Andrews Ave # 490 Fort Lauderdale (33309) *(G-4127)*

Wecando Print LLC 754 222-9144
424 Sw 12th Ave Deerfield Beach (33442) *(G-2833)*

Wedding Bells, Parkland *Also called Reese Corporation (G-13352)*

Weddings By Tina 904 235-3740
4720 Salisbury Rd Jacksonville (32256) *(G-6599)*

Wedgworth Farms Inc 561 996-2076
2607 Sammonds Rd Plant City (33563) *(G-13815)*

Wedgworths Inc (PA) 561 996-2076
651 Nw 9th St Belle Glade (33430) *(G-347)*

Wedgworths Inc 561 996-2076
211 Sr 70 W Lake Placid (33852) *(G-7149)*

Weehoo Inc 720 477-3700
803 Whitcomb Blvd Tarpon Springs (34689) *(G-17499)*

Weekly Challenger Newspaper 727 896-2922
2500 Dr Mrtn Lther King J Saint Petersburg (33705) *(G-15229)*

Weekly Newspaper 305 743-0844
9709 Overseas Hwy Marathon (33050) *(G-8109)*

Weekly Planet, Tampa *Also called Creative Loafing Inc (G-16739)*

Weekly Planet of Sarasota Inc 813 739-4800
810 N Howard Ave Tampa (33606) *(G-17424)*

Weekly Schulte Valdes 813 221-1154
1635 N Tampa St Ste 100 Tampa (33602) *(G-17425)*

Weeks Gas Hme of The Brbc Sprs, Miami *Also called Barbecue Superstore (G-8796)*

Weibel Equipment Inc 571 278-1989
7801 Mainsail Ln Sarasota (34240) *(G-15870)*

Weidenhamer Corporation 850 837-3190
808 Wild Oak Ave Destin (32541) *(G-3082)*

Weider Publications LLC 561 998-7424
1000 American Media Way Boca Raton (33464) *(G-754)*

Weightech USA LLC 954 666-0877
10384 W State Road 84 # 6 Davie (33324) *(G-2497)*

Weigle's Equipment Repair, Apopka *Also called Rockpack Inc (G-171)*

Weimer Mechanical Services Inc 813 645-2258
1701 E Shell Point Rd Ruskin (33570) *(G-14781)*

Weimer Services, Ruskin *Also called Weimer Mechanical Services Inc (G-14781)*

Weiss Group LLC (PA) 561 627-3300
15430 Endeavor Dr Ste 101 Jupiter (33478) *(G-6825)*

Weiss Research Inc 561 627-3300
15430 Endeavor Dr Ste 101 Jupiter (33478) *(G-6826)*

Welbilt Inc (HQ) 727 375-7010
2227 Welbilt Blvd Trinity (34655) *(G-17641)*

Welch Allyn Inc 305 669-9003
2500 Nw 107th Ave Ste 300 Doral (33172) *(G-3419)*

Weldcorp Industries 561 339-7713
15188 Pk Of Cmmrce Blvd S Jupiter (33478) *(G-6827)*

Welding Anything Anywhere LLC 561 762-1404
6231 Pga Blvd Palm Beach Gardens (33418) *(G-13017)*

Welding Around 772 342-3233
5205b Sw 69th St Palm City (34990) *(G-13065)*

Well Bilt Industries, Ocala *Also called M Bilt Enterprises Inc (G-11434)*

Well Bilt Industries Usa LLC 352 528-5566
3001 Sw 67th Avenue Rd # 100 Ocala (34474) *(G-11512)*

Well Made Bus Solutions LLC 754 227-7268
5671 Nw 40th Ter Coconut Creek (33073) *(G-2011)*

Wellington Forum, Deerfield Beach *Also called Forum Publishing Group Inc (G-2722)*

Wellington Leather LLC 561 790-0034
320 Business Park Way Royal Palm Beach (33411) *(G-14773)*

Wells & Drew Companies, The, Jacksonville *Also called Wells Legal Supply Inc (G-6600)*

Wells Legal Supply Inc 904 399-1510
3414 Galilee Rd Jacksonville (32207) *(G-6600)*

Wellstream International Ltd 850 636-4800
6521 Bayline Dr Panama City (32404) *(G-13320)*

Welshman Investment Corp 407 933-4444
1570 Kelley Ave Ste 2 Kissimmee (34744) *(G-6972)*

Wemerge Inc 561 305-2070
3620 W Hillsboro Blvd Coconut Creek (33073) *(G-2012)*

Wemi Sports 305 446-5178
156 Giralda Ave Coral Gables (33134) *(G-2119)*

Wennerwear, Edgewater *Also called J W Group Inc (G-3493)*

Wep Sourcing, Miami *Also called World Event Promotions LLC (G-10143)*

Weplenish LLC 954 909-4183
150 S Pine Island Rd Plantation (33324) *(G-13902)*

Were In Stitches 813 264-4804
14807 N Florida Ave Tampa (33613) *(G-17426)*

Werever Products Inc 813 241-9701
6120 Pelican Creek Cir Riverview (33578) *(G-14582)*

Werever Waterproof Cabinetry, Riverview *Also called Werever Products Inc (G-14582)*

Wes Holdings Corp 941 371-4995
818 Cattlemen Rd Sarasota (34232) *(G-15871)*

Wes Industries Inc (PA) 941 371-7617
6389 Tower Ln Sarasota (34240) *(G-15872)*

Weschler Instruments, Coral Springs *Also called Hughes Corporation (G-2164)*

Wesco Partners Inc 941 484-8224
1125 Commerce Blvd N Sarasota (34243) *(G-15579)*

Wesley Chapel Fuel Inc 813 907-9994
27616 Wesley Chapel Blvd Wesley Chapel (33544) *(G-17891)*

Wesol Distribution LLC 407 921-9248
1486 Seminola Blvd Unit 1 Casselberry (32707) *(G-1436)*

West Bay Door, Tampa *Also called Florida Made Door Co* *(G-16848)*
West Bolusia Beacon 386 734-4622
  110 W New York Ave Deland (32720) *(G-2920)*
West Central Signs Inc 813 980-6763
  3502 Queen Palm Dr Ste C Tampa (33619) *(G-17427)*
West Coast Brace & Limb, Temple Terrace *Also called Westcoast Brace & Limb Inc* *(G-17549)*
West Coast Castings Inc 941 753-2969
  1211 44th Ave E Bradenton (34203) *(G-1076)*
West Coast Shutters Sunburst 727 894-0044
  128 19th St S Ste B Saint Petersburg (33712) *(G-15230)*
West Coast Signs 941 755-5686
  2310 Whitfield Indus Way Sarasota (34243) *(G-15580)*
West Coast Signs Inc 941 755-5686
  2071 58th Avenue Cir E Bradenton (34203) *(G-1077)*
West End 407 322-7475
  202 Sanford Ave Sanford (32771) *(G-15410)*
West Florida Precision Mch LLC 727 939-0030
  728 Anclote Rd Tarpon Springs (34689) *(G-17500)*
West Fraser Inc 904 786-4155
  109 Halsema Rd S Jacksonville (32220) *(G-6601)*
West Fraser Inc 850 587-1000
  401 Champion Mc David (32568) *(G-8190)*
West Harbour Woodworking LLC 954 822-7543
  2543 Nw 49th Ave Apt 203 Lauderdale Lakes (33313) *(G-7722)*
West Orange Times, Winter Garden *Also called Winter Garden Times Inc* *(G-18409)*
West Palm Beach Service Center, Riviera Beach *Also called Altec Industries Inc* *(G-14593)*
West Palm Installers Inc 305 406-3575
  5141 Nw 79th Ave Unit 1 Doral (33166) *(G-3420)*
West Palm Machining & Welding 561 841-2725
  4650 Dyer Blvd Riviera Beach (33407) *(G-14686)*
West Pharmaceutical Svcs Inc 727 546-2402
  5280 118th Ave N Clearwater (33760) *(G-1850)*
West Phrm Svcs Fla Inc 727 546-2402
  5111 Park St N Saint Petersburg (33709) *(G-15231)*
West Point Industries Inc 561 848-8381
  1300 Old Dixie Hwy # 101 Lake Park (33403) *(G-7135)*
West Point Stevens 850 638-9421
  1414 Main St Chipley (32428) *(G-1459)*
West Side Gazette, Fort Lauderdale *Also called Bi-Ads Inc* *(G-3684)*
West Texas Protein Inc 806 250-5959
  601 Riverside Ave Jacksonville (32204) *(G-6602)*
West Wood Manufacturing, Bradenton *Also called Cabinet Designs Sarasota Inc* *(G-955)*
Westchster Gold Fbricators Inc 941 625-0666
  4200 Tamiami Trl Ste F Port Charlotte (33952) *(G-14324)*
Westcoast Brace & Limb Inc (PA) 813 985-5000
  5311 E Fletcher Ave Temple Terrace (33617) *(G-17549)*
Westcoast Brace & Limb Inc 407 502-0024
  341 N Maitland Ave # 210 Maitland (32751) *(G-8079)*
Westcoast Metalworks Inc 941 920-3201
  3308 39th St E Palmetto (34221) *(G-13205)*
Westech Development Group Inc 954 505-5090
  3010 N Andrews Avenue Ext Pompano Beach (33064) *(G-14241)*
Westech Industries, Pompano Beach *Also called Westech Development Group Inc* *(G-14241)*
Western Fabricating LLC 239 676-5382
  17061 Alico Commerce Ct Fort Myers (33967) *(G-4447)*
Western Graphite Inc (PA) 850 270-2808
  1045 E Washington St Monticello (32344) *(G-10586)*
Western Intl Gas Cylinders Inc 813 635-9321
  1502 Orient Rd Tampa (33619) *(G-17428)*
Western Microsystems Inc (PA) 800 547-7082
  4230 Pablo Pro Ct Ste 200 Jacksonville (32224) *(G-6603)*
Western Reserve Tool Machine, Jupiter *Also called North Erie Electronics Inc* *(G-6773)*
Westlund Engineering Inc 727 572-4343
  3116 Roxmere Dr Palm Harbor (34685) *(G-13139)*
Westpoint Home Inc 850 415-4100
  1056 Commerce Ave Chipley (32428) *(G-1460)*
Westpoint Home Inc 850 415-4100
  1414 Main St Chipley (32428) *(G-1461)*
Westran Corporation 727 375-7010
  2227 Welbilt Blvd Trinity (34655) *(G-17642)*
Westrock Cp LLC 904 261-5551
  600 N 8th St Fernandina Beach (32034) *(G-3599)*
Westrock Cp LLC 904 356-5611
  2002 E 18th St Jacksonville (32206) *(G-6604)*
Westrock Cp LLC 850 785-4311
  1 S Everitt Ave Panama City (32401) *(G-13321)*
Westrock Cp LLC 904 714-7151
  9469 Eastport Rd Jacksonville (32218) *(G-6605)*
Westrock Cp LLC 407 843-1300
  4364 Sw 34th St Orlando (32811) *(G-12712)*
Westrock CP LLC 407 859-9701
  375 W 7th St Orlando (32824) *(G-12713)*
Westrock Lake Mary 407 936-1277
  2950 Lake Emma Rd Lake Mary (32746) *(G-7117)*
Westrock Rkt LLC 904 714-1643
  1660 Prudential Dr # 202 Jacksonville (32207) *(G-6606)*

Westrom Software 866 480-1879
  903 7th Ave Vero Beach (32960) *(G-17817)*
Westview Corp Inc 239 643-5699
  3419 Westview Dr Naples (34104) *(G-10937)*
Wetherill Associates Inc (PA) 800 877-3340
  3300 Corporate Way Miramar (33025) *(G-10564)*
Wf Brick Pavers Inc 813 506-1941
  12704 Tar Flower Dr Tampa (33626) *(G-17429)*
Wf Fuel 941 706-4953
  300 N Washington Blvd Sarasota (34236) *(G-15873)*
Wgentv, Doral *Also called Mambo LLC* *(G-3289)*
Wharton Pepper Co 850 997-4359
  2873a St Augustine Rd Monticello (32344) *(G-10587)*
What To Drink B4 You Drink, Orlando *Also called Sunshine Supplements Inc* *(G-12635)*
Whatever Lo Que Sea LLC 786 429-3462
  2087 Nw 135th Ave Miami (33182) *(G-10128)*
Whats Wrong Publishing Co 904 388-3494
  2641 Park St Jacksonville (32204) *(G-6607)*
Wheel Systems Intl Inc 920 235-9888
  7645 Tralee Way Bradenton (34202) *(G-1078)*
Wheel Wright 850 626-2662
  6899 Deception Rd Milton (32583) *(G-10443)*
Wheelblast Inc 813 715-7117
  3951 Copeland Dr Zephyrhills (33542) *(G-18636)*
Wheeled Coach Industries, Winter Park *Also called Rev Amblance Group Orlando Inc* *(G-18533)*
Wheeler Lumber LLC 772 464-4400
  1031 Digiorgio Rd Fort Pierce (34982) *(G-4554)*
Wheeler Trading Inc 305 430-7100
  5851 Nw 159th St Miami Lakes (33014) *(G-10378)*
Wheelhouse Direct LLC 239 246-8788
  17595 S Tamiami Trl # 125 Fort Myers (33908) *(G-4448)*
Wheels A Million 754 444-2869
  1100 Nw 54th St Fort Lauderdale (33309) *(G-4128)*
Wheels For You Inc 772 485-0162
  5701 Pinetree Dr Fort Pierce (34982) *(G-4555)*
Whelen Aerospace Tech LLC 800 859-4757
  210 Airport Dr E Sebastian (32958) *(G-15912)*
Wherrell Machine LLC 863 357-0900
  107 Sw 2nd St Okeechobee (34974) *(G-11619)*
Whertec Inc (HQ) 904 278-6503
  5409 Highway Ave Jacksonville (32254) *(G-6608)*
Whertec Technologies Inc 866 207-6503
  5409 Highway Ave Jacksonville (32254) *(G-6609)*
Whetstone Chocolate Factory, Saint Augustine *Also called Whetstone Industries Inc* *(G-14913)*
Whetstone Industries Inc 904 824-0888
  100 Whetstone Pl Ste 100 # 100 Saint Augustine (32086) *(G-14913)*
Whigham Citrus Packing House 772 569-7190
  10525 State Road 60 Vero Beach (32966) *(G-17818)*
Whigham Citrus Pkg Hse McHy, Vero Beach *Also called Whigham Citrus Packing House* *(G-17818)*
Whip-It Inventions Inc (PA) 850 626-6300
  5946 Commerce Rd Milton (32583) *(G-10444)*
Whirlpool Corporation 407 438-5899
  13201 S Orange Ave Orlando (32824) *(G-12714)*
Whispering Oaks Winery 352 748-0449
  10934 County Road 475 Oxford (34484) *(G-12854)*
White Aluminum Fabrication Inc 772 219-3245
  3195 Se Lionel Ter Stuart (34997) *(G-16249)*
White Cardboard Corp 786 260-4692
  3671 Nw 81st St Miami (33147) *(G-10129)*
White Cliff, Miami *Also called Kiskeya Minerals Usa LLC* *(G-9391)*
White County Stone LLC 415 516-0849
  135 Churchill Rd West Palm Beach (33405) *(G-18204)*
White Cross Supply Co, Naples *Also called Vienna Beauty Products Co* *(G-10934)*
White Horse Fashion Cuisine 561 847-4549
  14440 Pierson Rd Wellington (33414) *(G-17869)*
White Mop Wringer Company 813 971-2223
  10702 N 46th St Tampa (33617) *(G-17430)*
White Oak Energy Backleverage (HQ) 561 691-7171
  700 Universe Blvd Juno Beach (33408) *(G-6670)*
White Oak Energy Holdings LLC 561 691-7171
  700 Universe Blvd Juno Beach (33408) *(G-6671)*
White Publishing Co Inc 904 389-3622
  1531 Osceola St Jacksonville (32204) *(G-6610)*
White Rose Installation 772 562-6698
  1266 14th Ave Sw Vero Beach (32962) *(G-17819)*
White Sands Dmg Inc 305 947-7731
  1798 Ne 163rd St North Miami Beach (33162) *(G-11170)*
White Sign Company LLC 407 342-7887
  909 S Charles Richard Bea Debary (32713) *(G-2645)*
White Springs AG Chem Inc 386 397-8101
  15843 Se 78th St White Springs (32096) *(G-18307)*
White Square Chemical Inc 302 212-4555
  91760 Overseas Hwy Tavernier (33070) *(G-17533)*
Whitecap Promotions LLC 813 960-4918
  2523 Cozumel Dr Tampa (33618) *(G-17431)*

Whitehouse Custom Scrn PR 727 321-7398
7183 30th Ave N Saint Petersburg (33710) *(G-15232)*

Whites Holdings Inc Centl Fla 727 863-6072
9301 Denton Ave Port Richey (34667) *(G-14386)*

Whitewater Boat Corp 305 756-9191
280 Nw 73rd St Miami (33150) *(G-10130)*

Whitewave Foods, Jacksonville Also called Wwf Operating Company LLC *(G-6620)*

Whitfield Timber Company Inc (PA) 850 639-5556
101 N Highway 71 Wewahitchka (32465) *(G-18303)*

Whiticar Boat Works Inc (PA) 772 287-2883
3636 Se Old St Lucie Blvd Stuart (34996) *(G-16250)*

Whitley Welding Company L 904 576-3410
4280 Chokeberry Rd Middleburg (32068) *(G-10411)*

Whitman Industries LLC 239 216-6171
1825 Dogwood Dr Marco Island (34145) *(G-8114)*

Whittington Energy Co 321 984-2128
730 E Strwbrdge Ave Ste 2 Melbourne (32901) *(G-8561)*

Whiz Bang LLC 305 296-0160
926 Truman Ave Key West (33040) *(G-6882)*

Whk Biosystems LLC 727 209-8402
11345 53rd St N Clearwater (33760) *(G-1851)*

Whole 9 Golf & Cigars 407 814-9994
1710 Stefan Cole Ln Apopka (32703) *(G-185)*

Whole Coffee Company LLC 786 364-4444
1130 Nw 159th Dr Miami (33169) *(G-10131)*

Whole Enchlada Fresh Mxcan Gri 954 561-4040
4115 N Federal Hwy Fort Lauderdale (33308) *(G-4129)*

Whole Tomato Software Inc 408 323-1590
1990 Main St Ste 750 Sarasota (34236) *(G-15874)*

Whole Trade, Lake Worth Also called Bikekeeper LLC *(G-7187)*

Wholesale Cornhole Bags, Orlando Also called Custom Cornhole Boards Inc *(G-12066)*

Wholesale Foreign Products Brk, Coconut Creek Also called Polaris Trading Corp *(G-2002)*

Wholesale Screen Prtg Nples In 239 263-7061
3584 Mercantile Ave Ste B Naples (34104) *(G-10938)*

Wholesale Sign Superstore Inc 321 212-8458
580 Gus Hipp Blvd Rockledge (32955) *(G-14755)*

Wholesale Trade, Naples Also called ABC Recyclers Collier Cnty Inc *(G-10649)*

Wholesalers, Hialeah Also called Love Is In The Air Corp *(G-5227)*

Whr Holdings LLC (PA) 954 342-4342
3402 Sw 26th Ter Ste 10 Fort Lauderdale (33312) *(G-4130)*

Wialan Technologies LLC (PA) 954 749-3481
10271 Nw 46th St Sunrise (33351) *(G-16392)*

Wicked Dolphin Distillery 239 565-7947
131 Sw 3rd Pl Cape Coral (33991) *(G-1407)*

Wicked Polishing Inc 561 255-7554
11254 67th Pl N West Palm Beach (33412) *(G-18205)*

Wicked Woodworks Inc 352 455-8402
25245 Mcbrady Ln Eustis (32736) *(G-3570)*

Wicked Woodworks Inc (PA) 305 714-2209
1314 Sw 1st Ave Ste 4 Fort Lauderdale (33315) *(G-4131)*

Wicks Unlimited Inc 631 472-2010
1515 Sw 13th Ct Pompano Beach (33069) *(G-14242)*

Wide Open Armory LLC 727 202-5980
8200 113th St Ste 104 Seminole (33772) *(G-15998)*

Widell Industries Inc (PA) 800 237-5963
6622 Industrial Ave Port Richey (34668) *(G-14387)*

Wilaen, Miami Also called Wireless Latin Entrmt Inc *(G-10137)*

Wilcox Steel Company LLC 727 443-0461
1101 Kapp Dr Clearwater (33765) *(G-1852)*

Wild Coyote Winery, Jensen Beach Also called Manucci Winery Inc *(G-6656)*

Wild Diamond Vineyards LLC 305 892-8699
1680 Ne 135th St North Miami (33181) *(G-11128)*

Wild Prints LLC 561 800-6536
12415 76th Rd N West Palm Beach (33412) *(G-18206)*

Wildas Jean-Joseph 561 929-1907
701 Miner Rd Lantana (33462) *(G-7517)*

Wildner Sign & Paint Co 239 997-5155
17 Nicholas Pkwy W Cape Coral (33991) *(G-1408)*

Wilkenson Hi-Rise, Fort Lauderdale Also called Whr Holdings LLC *(G-4130)*

Wilkerson Instrument Co Inc 863 647-2000
2915 Parkway St Lakeland (33811) *(G-7473)*

Wilkinson Hi-Rise LLC 954 342-4400
3402 Sw 26th Ter Ste 10 Fort Lauderdale (33312) *(G-4132)*

Wilkinson Steel Supply LLC 904 757-1522
3210 Faye Rd Jacksonville (32226) *(G-6611)*

Will & Mia Corp 617 943-6914
1250 Ne 207th Ter Miami (33179) *(G-10132)*

Will Garrett Towers, Plantation Also called Tip Top Canvas and Uphl Inc *(G-13896)*

Will Shutter U Inc 772 285-3600
2087 Nw Marsh Rabbit Ln Jensen Beach (34957) *(G-6659)*

Will-Rite Industries Inc 305 253-1985
10853 Sw 188th St Cutler Bay (33157) *(G-2312)*

Willett Prcision Machining Inc 727 573-9299
11339 43rd St N Clearwater (33762) *(G-1853)*

William B Rudow Inc 941 957-4200
1122 Goodrich Ave Sarasota (34236) *(G-15875)*

William Burns 877 462-5872
1800 Via Lago Dr Lakeland (33810) *(G-7474)*

William Laroque Installers Inc 305 769-1717
5820 Sheridan St Hollywood (33021) *(G-5684)*

William Leupold Sr 727 527-7400
3291 40th Ave N Saint Petersburg (33714) *(G-15233)*

William Marie LLC 904 536-9542
8271 Haverhill St Jacksonville (32211) *(G-6612)*

Williams & Bennett, Orlando Also called Fantasy Chocolates Inc *(G-12144)*

Williams Communications Inc 850 689-6651
701 Ashley Dr Crestview (32536) *(G-2256)*

Williams Industrial Svcs LLC 904 696-9994
11380 Island Dr 1 Jacksonville (32226) *(G-6613)*

Williams Jewelry and Mfg Co 727 823-7676
3152 Morris St N Saint Petersburg (33713) *(G-15234)*

Williams Minerals Co Inc 304 897-6003
168 Seville Chase Dr Winter Springs (32708) *(G-18582)*

Williams Orthtc-Prosthetic Inc 850 385-6655
2360 Centerville Rd Tallahassee (32308) *(G-16522)*

Williams Specialties, Hialeah Also called Bros Williams Printing Inc *(G-5080)*

Williams Specialties Inc 305 769-9925
4716 E 10th Ct Hialeah (33013) *(G-5420)*

Williams Tenders Usa Inc 954 648-6560
451 S Federal Hwy Pompano Beach (33062) *(G-14243)*

Williams Timber Inc 850 584-2760
215 Sunset Ln Perry (32348) *(G-13658)*

Willie Maes Pies LLC 407 655-9360
843 Cypress Pkwy 253 Kissimmee (34759) *(G-6978)*

Willis Aeronautical Svcs Inc 561 272-5402
3151 Nw 27th Ave Ste 101 Pompano Beach (33069) *(G-14244)*

Willis Custom Yachts LLC 772 221-9100
6800 Sw Jack James Dr # 1 Stuart (34997) *(G-16251)*

Willis Industries Inc 954 830-6163
5064 S University Dr Davie (33328) *(G-2498)*

Willis Marine Inc 772 283-7189
4361 Se Commerce Ave Stuart (34997) *(G-16252)*

Williston Timber Co Inc 352 528-2699
4351 Ne 176th Ave Williston (32696) *(G-18336)*

Wills Prestress Inc 239 417-9117
680 31st St Sw Naples (34117) *(G-10939)*

Willson & Son Industry Inc 954 972-5073
2000 Banks Rd Ste H1 Margate (33063) *(G-8160)*

Willsonet Inc 813 336-8175
2502 N Rocky Point Dr # 820 Tampa (33607) *(G-17432)*

Willy Walt Inc 727 209-2872
2390 26th Ave N Saint Petersburg (33713) *(G-15235)*

Wilma Schumann Skin Care Pdts, Miami Also called Skinmetics Inc *(G-9902)*

Wilo USA LLC 954 524-6776
3001 Sw 3rd Ave Ste 7 Fort Lauderdale (33315) *(G-4133)*

Wilson Custom Cabinets 954 296-1095
810 Nw 45th St Fort Lauderdale (33309) *(G-4134)*

Wilson Manifolds Inc 954 771-6216
4700 Ne 11th Ave Oakland Park (33334) *(G-11312)*

Wilson Mch & Wldg Works Inc 904 829-3737
5760 Us Highway 1 N Saint Augustine (32095) *(G-14914)*

Wilson Msclineous Fabrications, Tampa Also called W D Wilson Inc *(G-17421)*

Wilson Printing USA LLC 727 536-4173
1085 Cephas Rd Clearwater (33765) *(G-1854)*

Wilsons Machine Products Inc 407 644-2020
1844 Kentucky Ave Winter Park (32789) *(G-18550)*

Wiltcher Industries Inc 704 907-9838
1034 Sudbury Ln Ormond Beach (32174) *(G-12799)*

Wilton Wind II LLC 561 691-7171
700 Universe Blvd Juno Beach (33408) *(G-6672)*

Wilwoodman Inc 386 334-7929
3 Market Pl Ste C Palm Coast (32137) *(G-13094)*

Winans Electric Motors LLC 863 875-5710
1150 Us Highway 92 W Auburndale (33823) *(G-247)*

Winatic Corporation 727 538-8917
5410 115th Ave N Clearwater (33760) *(G-1855)*

Winchster Interconnect Rf Corp 800 881-9689
3950 Dow Rd Melbourne (32934) *(G-8562)*

Winchster Intrcnnect Hrmtics L (HQ) 321 254-4067
3950 Dow Rd Melbourne (32934) *(G-8563)*

Winco Mfg LLC (PA) 352 854-2929
5516 Sw 1st Ln Ocala (34474) *(G-11513)*

Wind Blue Technology LLC 850 218-9398
7502 Sears Blvd Pensacola (32514) *(G-13625)*

Wind River Systems Inc 321 726-9463
100 Rialto Pl Ste 525 Melbourne (32901) *(G-8564)*

Windbrella Products Corp 561 734-5222
2114 Corporate Dr Boynton Beach (33426) *(G-924)*

Windermere Nannies LLC 407 782-2057
6526 Old Brick Rd Ste 120 Windermere (34786) *(G-18371)*

Windoor Incorporated 407 481-8400
1070 Technology Dr North Venice (34275) *(G-11222)*

Window Craftsmen Inc 941 922-1844
6031 Clark Center Ave Sarasota (34238) *(G-15876)*

Windows Doors Etc, Saint Petersburg Also called Bay City Window Company *(G-14978)*

Windowware Pro 904 584-9191
2085 A1a S Ste 201 Saint Augustine (32080) *(G-14915)*

A
L
P
H
A
B
E
T
I
C

Winds 239 948-0777
4555 Bonita Beach Rd Bonita Springs (34134) *(G-827)*

Windsor & York Inc 561 687-8424
7233 Southern Blvd West Palm Beach (33413) *(G-18207)*

Windsor Imaging, Oakland Park *Also called Open Magnetic Scanning Ltd (G-11282)*

Windsor Metal Finishing, Kissimmee *Also called Best Engineered Surfc Tech LLC (G-6898)*

Windsor Window Company 321 385-3880
1450 Shepard Dr Titusville (32780) *(G-17627)*

Windstar Express Inc 786 252-1569
19499 Ne 10th Ave Miami (33179) *(G-10133)*

Windstone Development Intl Lc 954 370-7201
7080 W State Road 84 Davie (33317) *(G-2499)*

Windward Associates Corp 954 336-8085
265 Bryan Rd Dania (33004) *(G-2346)*

Windward Communications Inc 727 584-7191
2401 West Bay Dr Ste 414 Largo (33770) *(G-7709)*

Windy City Apparel, Sarasota *Also called CC Sportswear Inc (G-15452)*

Wine and Canvas Dev LLC 239 980-9138
6351 Emerald Bay Ct Fort Myers (33908) *(G-4449)*

Wine Plum Inc 844 856-7586
11 Sw 12th Ave Ste 104 Dania Beach (33004) *(G-2361)*

Wine World Inc 786 348-8780
12650 Nw 25th St Ste 112 Miami (33182) *(G-10134)*

Wingard LLC 904 387-2570
76 S Laura St Ste 1501 Jacksonville (32202) *(G-6614)*

Wings Aircraft Finance, Fort Lauderdale *Also called Aercap Group Services Inc (G-3628)*

Wings Things Monogramming Inc 850 455-3081
3815 W Navy Blvd Pensacola (32507) *(G-13626)*

Winner Group, Sebring *Also called Winntel USA (G-15950)*

Winntel USA 863 451-1789
4014 Vilabella Dr Sebring (33872) *(G-15950)*

Winrise Enterprises LLC 786 621-6705
15701 Sw 29th St 100 Miramar (33027) *(G-10565)*

Winslow Life Raft Co, Lake Suzy *Also called Winslow Marine Products Corp (G-7150)*

Winslow Marine Products Corp 941 613-6666
11700 Sw Winslow Dr Lake Suzy (34269) *(G-7150)*

Winslow Microplastics Corp 305 493-3501
20257 Ne 15th Ct Miami (33179) *(G-10135)*

Winsted Thermographers Inc 305 944-7862
917 Sw 10th St Hallandale Beach (33009) *(G-4985)*

Winston & Sons Inc 954 562-1984
9735 Nw 76th St Tamarac (33321) *(G-16544)*

Winston Furniture Company Ala, Saint Augustine *Also called Jordan Brown Inc (G-14851)*

Winston Manufacturing, Opa Locka *Also called Everglades Creations Inc (G-11744)*

Winston Manufacturing Corp 305 822-3344
1745 W 32nd Pl Ste 55 Hialeah (33012) *(G-5421)*

Winsulator Corporation 941 365-7901
3350 S Osprey Ave Sarasota (34239) *(G-15877)*

Wintel 407 834-1188
1051 Bennett Dr Ste 101 Longwood (32750) *(G-7960)*

Winter Garden Times Inc 407 656-2121
661 Garden Commerce Pkwy Winter Garden (34787) *(G-18409)*

Winter Park Distilling Co LLC 407 801-2714
1288 Orange Ave Winter Park (32789) *(G-18551)*

Winter Park Publishing Co LLC 941 320-6627
201 W Canton Ave Ste 125b Winter Park (32789) *(G-18552)*

Winwood Print 786 615-3188
591 Nw 29th St Miami (33127) *(G-10136)*

Wire Experts Group Inc (PA) 239 597-8555
3650 Shaw Blvd Naples (34117) *(G-10940)*

Wire Mesh Corp 706 922-5179
4034 Faye Rd Jacksonville (32226) *(G-6615)*

Wire Products Inc of Florida (PA) 954 772-1477
4300 Nw 10th Ave Fort Lauderdale (33309) *(G-4135)*

Wired Rite Systems Inc 707 838-1122
1748 Independence Blvd C5 Sarasota (34234) *(G-15878)*

Wireless Latin Entrmt Inc 305 858-7740
5301 Blue Lagoon Dr # 180 Miami (33126) *(G-10137)*

Wiremaid Products Division, Vero Beach *Also called Vutec Corporation (G-17816)*

Wiremil Division, Sanderson *Also called Insteel Wire Products Company (G-15254)*

Wiretec Ignition Inc 407 578-4569
1901 4th St W Palmetto (34221) *(G-13206)*

Wireworld By David Salz Inc 954 474-4464
6545 Nova Dr Ste 204 Davie (33317) *(G-2500)*

Wireworld Cable Technology, Davie *Also called Wireworld By David Salz Inc (G-2500)*

Wise Gas Fuel Card LLC 954 636-4291
1058 Bluewood Ter Weston (33327) *(G-18298)*

Wise Recycling 1 LLC 850 477-5273
601 W Hope Dr Pensacola (32534) *(G-13627)*

Wish Inc 305 653-9474
33 Nw 168th St North Miami Beach (33169) *(G-11171)*

Wishbone Woodworking Inc 239 262-7230
121 Pinehurst Cir Naples (34113) *(G-10941)*

Wittman Pharma Inc (PA) 352 799-9813
16206 Flight Path Dr Brooksville (34604) *(G-1222)*

Wiztel USA Inc 416 457-5513
18281 Via Caprini Dr Miromar Lakes (33913) *(G-10576)*

Wj Bergin Cabinetry LLC 407 271-8982
1228 28th St Orlando (32805) *(G-12715)*

WJS Printing Partners Inc 904 731-0357
2750 Dawn Rd Jacksonville (32207) *(G-6616)*

Wlc Wood Works Inc 305 896-6460
1340 Nw 48th Pl Deerfield Beach (33064) *(G-2834)*

Wm G Roe & Sons Inc 863 294-3577
500 Avenue R Sw Winter Haven (33880) *(G-18478)*

Wmr Cycle Performance Inc 772 426-3000
7749 Sw Ellipse Way Stuart (34997) *(G-16253)*

Wohlers Publishing Inc 305 289-1644
10701 6th Avenue Gulf Marathon (33050) *(G-8110)*

Wolf Americas LLC 407 704-2051
3113 Willie Mays Pkwy Orlando (32811) *(G-12716)*

Wolf Rock Drills, Orlando *Also called Wolf Americas LLC (G-12716)*

Wonder Emporium Millwork Fab 407 850-3131
10779 Satellite Blvd Orlando (32837) *(G-12717)*

Wonder Holdings Acquisition 305 379-2322
1450 Brickell Ave # 3100 Miami (33131) *(G-10138)*

Wonderland Products Inc 904 786-0144
5772 Lenox Ave Jacksonville (32205) *(G-6617)*

Wonderworld 100 LLC 407 618-3207
2209 S Fern Creek Ave Orlando (32806) *(G-12718)*

Wood Arts of India, Sanford *Also called Deep Ocean Woodworks Inc (G-15302)*

Wood Aspects 321 800-8875
1384 Saratoga St Deland (32724) *(G-2921)*

Wood Dimensions, Tallahassee *Also called Debruyne Enterprise Inc (G-16431)*

Wood Drams Inc of Palm Beaches 561 842-9814
1137 Silver Beach Rd Lake Park (33403) *(G-7136)*

Wood Machine Corp 407 851-8714
491 Thorpe Rd Orlando (32824) *(G-12719)*

Wood One LLC 727 639-5620
2416 52nd Ave N Saint Petersburg (33714) *(G-15236)*

Wood Product Services Inc 813 248-2221
2417 N 70th St Tampa (33619) *(G-17433)*

Wood Scapes Interiors 386 454-1540
26509 W Us Highway 27 High Springs (32643) *(G-5457)*

Wood Splinter Corp 305 721-7215
15451 Sw 60th St Miami (33193) *(G-10139)*

Wood Stile Inc 561 329-4671
644 Marbella Ln North Palm Beach (33403) *(G-11185)*

Wood U Envision 561 601-1973
4252 Westroads Dr West Palm Beach (33407) *(G-18208)*

Wood Zone Inc 305 971-5550
13751 Sw 147th Ave Miami (33196) *(G-10140)*

Woodcraft LLC 850 217-7757
2218 Avenida De Sol Navarre (32566) *(G-10957)*

Woodcrafters, The, Bradenton *Also called W E W Enterprises Inc (G-1074)*

Woodcrafts By Angel Inc 352 754-9335
15400 Shady St Brooksville (34604) *(G-1223)*

Woodfield Pharmaceutical LLC 281 530-3077
66 W Flagler St Ste 1000 Miami (33130) *(G-10141)*

Woodies Inc 305 266-9209
2041 Sw 82nd Pl Miami (33155) *(G-10142)*

Woods Distinctive Designs Inc 941 698-7535
7450 Sawyer Cir Port Charlotte (33981) *(G-14325)*

Woods n Water Magazine Inc 850 584-3824
3427 Puckett Rd Perry (32348) *(G-13659)*

Woods Printing Ocala Inc 352 629-1665
1740 Ne 23rd Ter Ocala (34470) *(G-11514)*

Woodshed Woodworks LLC 904 540-0354
55 Florida Ave Saint Augustine (32084) *(G-14916)*

Woodtech Global Inc 941 371-0392
5822 24th St E Bradenton (34203) *(G-1079)*

Woodwards Cabinets Inc 850 835-0071
17921 Us Highway 331 S Freeport (32439) *(G-4632)*

Woodwards Custom Cabinets, Freeport *Also called Woodwards Cabinets Inc (G-4632)*

Woodwork Unlimited Inc 352 267-4051
4075 County Road 106 Oxford (34484) *(G-12855)*

Woodworkers Cabinet Inc 239 593-1718
6189 Taylor Rd Ste 2 Naples (34109) *(G-10942)*

Woodworkers Cabinet Naples Inc 239 593-1718
6189 Taylor Rd Naples (34109) *(G-10943)*

Woodworks Cabinetry Inc 904 924-5300
4541 Saint Augustine Rd Jacksonville (32207) *(G-6618)*

Woodworks Kit & Bath Designs 813 926-0570
8717 Gunn Hwy Odessa (33556) *(G-11592)*

Woodworks of Tampa Bay LLC 813 330-5836
333 N Falkenburg Rd B209 Tampa (33619) *(G-17434)*

Woodworkx Unlimited Inc 772 882-4197
103 N 13th St Fort Pierce (34950) *(G-4556)*

Woody Hatcher 850 526-1501
2866 Madison St Marianna (32448) *(G-8176)*

Woodys Acres LLC 352 345-8145
4000 Crum Rd Brooksville (34604) *(G-1224)*

Woodys Enterprises LLC 407 892-1900
1110b Quotation Ct Saint Cloud (34772) *(G-14941)*

Woodys Heating & AC LLC 651 829-4570
14250 A And W Bulb Rd Fort Myers (33908) *(G-4450)*

Woodys Hedging LLC 863 557-4525
225 Water Tank Rd Lake Hamilton (33851) *(G-7053)*

2022 Harris Florida
Manufacturers Directory

(G-0000) Company's Geographic Section entry number

Wool Wholesale Plumbing Supply 954 763-3632
1321 Ne 12th Ave Fort Lauderdale (33304) *(G-4136)*

Woovfu Inc 719 301-1661
7901 4th St N Ste 300 Saint Petersburg (33702) *(G-15237)*

Wop's Hops Brewing Company, Geneva *Also called Wops Hops Brewing Llc (G-4791)*

Wops Hops Brewing Llc (PA) 407 927-8929
510 S Cochran Rd Geneva (32732) *(G-4791)*

Workep Inc 787 634-1115
11930 N Bayshore Dr North Miami (33181) *(G-11129)*

Workforce Audio Inc 866 360-6416
4821 N Grady Ave Tampa (33614) *(G-17435)*

Working Cow Homemade Inc 727 572-7251
4711 34th St N Unit F Saint Petersburg (33714) *(G-15238)*

Working Drones Inc 904 647-4511
2180 Emerson St Jacksonville (32207) *(G-6619)*

Working Mother Media Inc 212 351-6400
480 N Orlando Ave Ste 236 Winter Park (32789) *(G-18553)*

Workwear Outfitters Inc 336 424-6000
4408 W Linebaugh Ave Tampa (33624) *(G-17436)*

Workwear Outfitters LLC 813 671-2986
8221 Eagle Palm Dr Riverview (33578) *(G-14583)*

Workwear Outfitters LLC 813 969-6481
6422 Harney Rd Ste F Tampa (33610) *(G-17437)*

World Boat Manufacturing Inc 863 824-0015
8040 Nw 144th Trl Okeechobee (34972) *(G-11620)*

World City, Coral Gables *Also called Worldcity Inc (G-2120)*

World Class Awards, Seminole *Also called Lorente International LLC (G-15981)*

World Class Machining Inc 386 437-7036
6650 S Us Highway 1 Bunnell (32110) *(G-1238)*

World Container Services LLC 305 400-4850
3341 Nw 82nd Ave Doral (33122) *(G-3421)*

World Electronics Inc 954 318-1044
10794 Nw 53rd St Sunrise (33351) *(G-16393)*

World Emblem International Inc (PA) 305 899-9006
4601 Sheridan St Ste 300 Hollywood (33021) *(G-5685)*

World Event Promotions LLC 800 214-3408
4302 Sw 73rd Ave Miami (33155) *(G-10143)*

World Foods & Flavors USA LLC 561 619-3655
4245 E Main St Jupiter (33458) *(G-6828)*

World Frost Inc 786 439-4445
14853 Sw 152nd Ter Miami (33187) *(G-10144)*

World Fuel Cx LLC 305 428-8000
9800 Nw 41st St Ste 400 Doral (33178) *(G-3422)*

World Golf Collection, Saint Augustine *Also called Golf America Southwest Fla Inc (G-14836)*

World Hlth Enrgy Holdings Inc (PA) 561 870-0440
1825 Nw Corp Blvd Ste 110 Boca Raton (33431) *(G-755)*

World Indus Resources Corp (HQ) 727 572-9991
13100 56th Ct Ste 710 Clearwater (33760) *(G-1856)*

World Industrial Equipment Inc 772 461-6056
4850 Orange Ave Fort Pierce (34947) *(G-4557)*

World Jet Fuel Report, West Palm Beach *Also called Armbrust Aviation Group Inc (G-17927)*

World of Awnings Inc 305 884-6699
151 W 21st St Hialeah (33010) *(G-5422)*

World of Brigadeiro LLC 954 488-4597
4240 Oak Cir Boca Raton (33431) *(G-756)*

World of Window Coverings, Palm Beach Gardens *Also called L C Clark Publishing Inc (G-12982)*

World Perfumes Inc 305 822-0004
2360 Nw 150th St Opa Locka (33054) *(G-11800)*

World Plate 386 597-7832
2323 N State St Unit 55 Bunnell (32110) *(G-1239)*

World Politics Review LLC 202 903-8398
825 S Orleans Ave Tampa (33606) *(G-17438)*

World Precision Instrs LLC (PA) 941 371-1003
175 Sarasota Center Blvd Sarasota (34240) *(G-15879)*

World Product Solution, Saint Petersburg *Also called Wps Skincare LLC (G-15239)*

World Product Solutions, Saint Petersburg *Also called Private Label Skin Na LLC (G-15162)*

World Publications Inc 407 628-4802
460 N Orlando Ave Ste 200 Winter Park (32789) *(G-18554)*

World Stone and Design LLC 850 235-0399
19709 Panama Cy Bch Pkwy Panama City (32413) *(G-13322)*

World Wide Export Management, Coral Gables *Also called Wemi Sports (G-2119)*

World Wide Frozen Foods LLC 954 266-8500
800 W Cypress Creek Rd Fort Lauderdale (33309) *(G-4137)*

World Wide Hardware, Tampa *Also called Worldwide Door Components Inc (G-17440)*

Worldbox Corporation 305 253-8800
8333 Nw 66th St Miami (33166) *(G-10145)*

Worldcity Inc 305 441-2244
251 Valencia Ave Coral Gables (33134) *(G-2120)*

Worldglass Corporation 813 609-2453
5600 Airport Blvd Ste C Tampa (33634) *(G-17439)*

Worlds Columbian Exonumis 561 734-4433
802 North Rd Boynton Beach (33435) *(G-925)*

Worlds Greatest Ice Cream Inc 305 538-0207
1626 Michigan Ave Miami Beach (33139) *(G-10247)*

Worldwide Auto Systems Corp 954 439-6332
900 Tallwood Ave Apt 307 Hollywood (33021) *(G-5686)*

Worldwide Building Intl Inc 786 744-7076
1840 Coral Way Miami (33145) *(G-10146)*

Worldwide Challenge Magazine 407 826-2390
100 Lake Hart Dr Ste 1600 Orlando (32832) *(G-12720)*

Worldwide Door Components Inc (PA) 813 870-0003
5017 N Coolidge Ave Tampa (33614) *(G-17440)*

Worldwide Draperies West LLC 305 887-9611
705 W 20th St Hialeah (33010) *(G-5423)*

Worldwide Embroidery Inc 386 761-2688
4471 Eastport Park Way Port Orange (32127) *(G-14353)*

Worldwide Intl Trade LLC 305 414-9774
601 S 21st Ave Hollywood (33020) *(G-5687)*

Worldwide Media Svcs Group Inc 212 545-4800
1000 American Media Way Boca Raton (33464) *(G-757)*

Worldwide Media Svcs Group Inc 561 989-1342
1000 American Media Way Boca Raton (33464) *(G-758)*

Worldwide Pallet LLC 205 671-5210
686 Polar Bear Rd Naples (34113) *(G-10944)*

Worldwide Sportswear Inc 386 761-2688
4471 Eastport Park Way Port Orange (32127) *(G-14354)*

Worldwide Technology Inc (PA) 813 855-2443
141 Stevens Ave Ste 10 Oldsmar (34677) *(G-11707)*

Worldwide Ticketcraft, Boynton Beach *Also called Worldwide Tickets & Labels Inc (G-926)*

Worldwide Tickets & Labels Inc 877 426-5754
3606 Quantum Blvd Boynton Beach (33426) *(G-926)*

Worrell Water Technologies LLC 434 973-6365
14 S Swinton Ave Delray Beach (33444) *(G-3038)*

Worth Intl Media Group (PA) 305 826-4763
5979 Nw 151st St Ste 120 Miami Lakes (33014) *(G-10379)*

Worth Metals Inc 904 626-1434
4135 Highway 17 S Green Cove Springs (32043) *(G-4843)*

Worthington Industries LLC 813 979-1000
17501 Preserve Walk Ln Tampa (33647) *(G-17441)*

Worthington Millwork LLC 800 872-1608
17842 Ashley Dr C Panama City Beach (32413) *(G-13341)*

Wow Business 813 301-2620
400 N Tampa St Ste 1000 Tampa (33602) *(G-17442)*

Wow Innovations, Fort Lauderdale *Also called Color-Chrome Technologies Inc (G-3737)*

Wpp Group Usa Inc 305 341-8132
601 Brickell Key Dr # 700 Miami (33131) *(G-10147)*

Wpr Inc 850 626-7713
4175 Briarglen Rd Milton (32583) *(G-10445)*

Wps Skincare LLC 877 516-2200
2260 118th Ave N Saint Petersburg (33716) *(G-15239)*

WR Kershaw Inc 386 673-0602
12 Aviator Way Ormond Beach (32174) *(G-12800)*

Wrap Installers Inc 407 404-2914
915 Diplomat Dr Ste 104 Debary (32713) *(G-2646)*

Wrap-Art Inc 954 428-1819
712 S Military Trl Deerfield Beach (33442) *(G-2835)*

Wrapfink, Hollywood *Also called Metro Signs Inc (G-5626)*

Wrico Stamping Co of Florida, Orlando *Also called Griffiths Corporation (G-12202)*

Wright Printery Inc 386 252-6571
735 N Ridgewood Ave Daytona Beach (32114) *(G-2619)*

Wristband Specialty, Deerfield Beach *Also called Wristband Supply LLC (G-2836)*

Wristband Supply LLC 954 571-3993
3000 Sw 15th St Ste F Deerfield Beach (33442) *(G-2836)*

Write Stuff Enterprises LLC 954 462-6657
1001 S Andrews Ave # 120 Fort Lauderdale (33316) *(G-4138)*

Wrobel Industries Inc 727 560-6850
1004 Us Highway 19 # 202 Holiday (34691) *(G-5507)*

Wrongs Without Wremedies LLC 850 423-0828
6256 Bullet Dr Crestview (32536) *(G-2257)*

WSa Engineered Systems Inc 414 481-4120
3000 W Nine Mile Rd Ste A Pensacola (32534) *(G-13628)*

Wurth Wood Group Inc 800 432-1149
5102 W Hanna Ave Tampa (33634) *(G-17443)*

WW Timber LLC 352 584-4550
8999 Us Highway 19 S Perry (32348) *(G-13660)*

Wwf Operating Company LLC 904 354-0406
2198 W Beaver St Jacksonville (32209) *(G-6620)*

Wwgso, Rockledge *Also called Good 4 Tklc Inc (G-14712)*

Wws Contracting LLC 813 868-3100
142 W Platt St Tampa (33606) *(G-17444)*

Wwsa Solids LLC 561 588-9299
2921 Commerce Park Dr Boynton Beach (33426) *(G-927)*

Www Tcpalm Company 772 287-1550
1939 S Federal Hwy Stuart (34994) *(G-16254)*

Www.alephgraphics.com, Doral *Also called Aleph Graphics Inc (G-3106)*

Www.royalfoam.us, Jacksonville *Also called Royal Foam US LLC (G-6434)*

Www.tpgus.com, Delray Beach *Also called Platinum Group Usa Inc (G-2999)*

Wyla Inc (PA) 904 886-4338
6920 Phillips Ind Blvd Jacksonville (32256) *(G-6621)*

Wyla Laces, Jacksonville *Also called Wyla Inc (G-6621)*

Wylde Woodworking Co 954 942-7630
4031 Ne 12th Ave Pompano Beach (33064) *(G-14245)*

A
L
P
H
A
B
E
T
I
C

Wynot International LLC.....305 218-8794
230 Ne 4th St Apt 1012 Miami (33132) ***(G-10148)***
X Metal Industrie, Oldsmar *Also called Metal Industries Inc* ***(G-11674)***
Xcape Solutions Inc (PA).....813 369-5261
207 Crystal Grove Blvd # 101 Lutz (33548) ***(G-8021)***
Xcelience LLC.....813 286-0404
5415 W Laurel St Tampa (33607) ***(G-17445)***
Xcelience LLC (HQ).....813 286-0404
4910 Savarese Cir Tampa (33634) ***(G-17446)***
Xcelience Holdings LLC.....813 286-0404
4910 Savarese Cir Tampa (33634) ***(G-17447)***
Xcessive Inc.....866 919-9527
8714 Nw 153rd Ter Miami Lakes (33018) ***(G-10380)***
Xcessive Engines, Miami Lakes *Also called Xcessive Inc* ***(G-10380)***
Xe Global Polsg Systems LLC.....941 685-9788
5651 Creekwood Cir Sarasota (34233) ***(G-15880)***
Xeleum Lighting LLC (HQ).....954 617-8170
751 Park Of Commerce Dr # 100 Boca Raton (33487) ***(G-759)***
Xenix Medical, Orlando *Also called Ht Medical LLC* ***(G-12230)***
Xerographic Copy Center, Gainesville *Also called Ejco Inc* ***(G-4684)***
Xerox Business Services LLC.....407 926-4228
2290 Premier Row Orlando (32809) ***(G-12721)***
Xhale Inc (PA).....352 371-8488
3630 Sw 47th Ave Ste 100 Gainesville (32608) ***(G-4785)***
Xikar Inc.....816 474-7555
3350 Entp Ave Ste 120 Weston (33331) ***(G-18299)***
Xilinx Inc.....407 365-8644
3518 Buckingham Ct Oviedo (32765) ***(G-12852)***
Xl Carts Inc.....904 277-7111
474415 E State Road 200 Fernandina Beach (32034) ***(G-3600)***
Xmre, Hollywood *Also called Nex-Xos Worldwide LLC* ***(G-5633)***
Xothermic Inc.....407 951-8008
311 Riverbend Blvd Longwood (32779) ***(G-7961)***
Xperient LLC.....407 265-8000
250 W Church Ave Ste 100 Longwood (32750) ***(G-7962)***
Xpondr Corporation.....727 541-4149
10751 75th St Seminole (33777) ***(G-15999)***
Xpress Finance Inc (PA).....407 629-0095
807 S Orlando Ave Ste B Deltona (32738) ***(G-3057)***
Xpress Materials LLC.....352 748-2200
8302 Ne 44th Dr Wildwood (34785) ***(G-18326)***
Xpress Precision Products Inc.....305 685-2127
4432 E 10th Ct Hialeah (33013) ***(G-5424)***
Xscream Inc.....727 449-9353
1780 Calumet St Clearwater (33765) ***(G-1857)***
Xtreme Boats, Bonifay *Also called Bd Xtreme Holdings LLC* ***(G-767)***
Xtreme Dumpster Services Corp.....407 272-8899
6142 Buford St Orlando (32835) ***(G-12722)***
Xtreme Electronic Designs Inc.....561 557-3667
1432 S Lakeside Dr Apt 9 Lake Worth (33460) ***(G-7245)***
Xtreme Pallets Inc.....954 302-8915
5440 Nw 55th Blvd Apt 108 Coconut Creek (33073) ***(G-2013)***
Xtreme Powder Coating Inc.....352 219-3807
5679 Sw County Road 341 Trenton (32693) ***(G-17631)***
Xtreme Signs & Printing Inc.....321 438-3954
4401 Vineland Rd Ste A9 Orlando (32811) ***(G-12723)***
Xtreme Tools International Inc.....305 622-7474
15400 Nw 34th Ave Opa Locka (33054) ***(G-11801)***
Xts Corp.....305 863-7779
8870 Nw 18th Ter Doral (33172) ***(G-3423)***
Xue Wu Inc.....727 532-4571
4445 E Bay Dr Ste 302 Clearwater (33764) ***(G-1858)***
Xx Press One Inc.....407 287-2673
3257 S Chickasaw Trl Orlando (32829) ***(G-12724)***
Xylem Water Solutions Fla LLC.....561 848-1200
2152 Sprint Blvd Apopka (32703) ***(G-186)***
Xylem Water Solutions USA Inc.....407 880-2900
455 Harvest Time Dr Sanford (32771) ***(G-15411)***
Xymogen Inc (PA).....407 445-0203
6900 Kingspointe Pkwy Orlando (32819) ***(G-12725)***
Xymogen Manufacturing LLC.....800 647-6100
6900 Kingspointe Pkwy Orlando (32819) ***(G-12726)***
Xymoprint LLC.....407 504-2170
6900 Kingspointe Pkwy Orlando (32819) ***(G-12727)***
XYZ Manufacturing Inc.....941 426-5656
3455 Bobcat Vlg Ctr Rd North Port (34288) ***(G-11206)***
Y F Leung Inc (PA).....305 651-6851
1155 Ne 177th Ter North Miami Beach (33162) ***(G-11172)***
Y F Yachts, Sarasota *Also called Copalo Inc* ***(G-15462)***
Y&D Machine Shop Inc.....786 717-6356
748 E 51st St Hialeah (33013) ***(G-5425)***
Y3k LLC.....561 835-0404
44 Cocoanut Row Ste T1 Palm Beach (33480) ***(G-12943)***
Yaadie Fiesta Group Inc.....562 766-8033
1293 N University Dr Coral Springs (33071) ***(G-2227)***
Yacht 10 Inc.....954 759-9929
3001 Sw 3rd Ave Ste 1 Fort Lauderdale (33315) ***(G-4139)***
Yacht Furn By Eclipse LLC.....954 792-7339
7050 W State Road 84 Davie (33317) ***(G-2501)***
Yacht International Magazine, Fort Lauderdale *Also called IMS Publishing Inc* ***(G-3874)***
Yacht-Mate Products Inc.....954 527-0112
3200 S Andrews Ave Ste 10 Fort Lauderdale (33316) ***(G-4140)***
Yahl Mulching & Recycling Inc.....239 352-7888
2250 Washburn Ave Naples (34117) ***(G-10945)***
Yale Ogron Mfg Co Inc (PA).....305 687-0424
15201 Nw 34th Ave Opa Locka (33054) ***(G-11802)***
Yale Ogron Mfg Co Inc.....305 687-0424
15201 Nw 34th Ave Opa Locka (33054) ***(G-11803)***
Yam Machine Shop and Iron Work.....786 246-4174
3710 Nw 50th St Miami (33142) ***(G-10149)***
Yandles Quality Roof Trusses.....352 732-3000
834 N Magnolia Ave Ocala (34475) ***(G-11515)***
Yarbrough Tire Svc Inc.....863 385-1574
1532 Sebring Pkwy Sebring (33870) ***(G-15951)***
Yard House Hallandale Bch LLC.....561 691-6901
11701 Lk Vctr Grdn Ave Palm Beach Gardens (33410) ***(G-13018)***
Yarey Inc.....954 520-6015
18840 Mariner Inlet Dr Boca Raton (33498) ***(G-760)***
Yatfl Inc.....786 643-8660
19425 Sw 188th St Miami (33187) ***(G-10150)***
Yauchler Properties LLC.....863 662-5570
119 Avenue D Se Winter Haven (33880) ***(G-18479)***
Yeager Manufacturing Tech LLC.....407 573-7033
7005 Stapoint Ct Winter Park (32792) ***(G-18555)***
Yellow Green Aerospace Inc.....954 599-4161
2525 Ponce De Leon Blvd # 300 Coral Gables (33134) ***(G-2121)***
Yellow Pages, Deerfield Beach *Also called Global Directories Inc* ***(G-2727)***
Yes Ink Solutions, Ocala *Also called Yes Solutions Gallery LLC* ***(G-11516)***
Yes Solutions Gallery LLC.....352 622-7937
4901 E Slver Sprng Blvd Ocala (34470) ***(G-11516)***
Yesco Orlando South.....407 922-5856
929 W Oak St Kissimmee (34741) ***(G-6973)***
Yesco Sign and Lighting.....407 321-3577
1940 Dolgner Pl Sanford (32771) ***(G-15412)***
Yesil Inc.....516 858-0244
23400 Milano Ct Boca Raton (33433) ***(G-761)***
Yfan LLC.....786 453-3724
5340 Nw 163rd St Miami Lakes (33014) ***(G-10381)***
Ygaero, Coral Gables *Also called Yellow Green Aerospace Inc* ***(G-2121)***
Yield - St. Augustine, Saint Augustine *Also called Yield Design* ***(G-14917)***
Yield Design.....402 321-2196
25 Palmer St Saint Augustine (32084) ***(G-14917)***
Yieldx Inc.....646 328-9803
2980 Ne 207th St Ste 504 Aventura (33180) ***(G-277)***
Yippy Inc (PA).....877 947-7901
999 Brickell Ave Ste 610 Miami (33131) ***(G-10151)***
YKK AP America Inc.....561 736-7808
8846 Andy Ct Apt C Boynton Beach (33436) ***(G-928)***
YKK AP America Inc.....407 856-0660
7608 Currency Dr Orlando (32809) ***(G-12728)***
Ymg Iron Work & Metal Design.....305 343-2537
21650 Nw 3rd Pl Pembroke Pines (33029) ***(G-13425)***
Yo Mama's Foods, Clearwater *Also called Magnificat Holdings LLC* ***(G-1681)***
Yogurico, Hialeah *Also called Pura Vida Dairy Inc* ***(G-5317)***
Yogurt Breeze LLC.....407 412-5939
10727 Narcoossee Rd B4 Orlando (32832) ***(G-12729)***
Yogurtology.....727 895-1393
3043 4th St N Saint Petersburg (33704) ***(G-15240)***
Yogurtology.....813 839-4200
3017 W Gandy Blvd Tampa (33611) ***(G-17448)***
Yogurtology.....813 969-2500
12400 N Dale Mabry Hwy B Tampa (33618) ***(G-17449)***
Yogurtology.....813 926-9090
7889 Gunn Hwy Tampa (33626) ***(G-17450)***
Yolo Consulting LLC.....954 993-4517
2364 Nw 159th Ave Pembroke Pines (33028) ***(G-13426)***
Yolo Las Olas LLC.....954 522-3002
200 Sw 2nd St Fort Lauderdale (33301) ***(G-4141)***
Yoly Munoz Corp.....305 860-3839
102 Se 1st St Miami (33131) ***(G-10152)***
Yonder Woodworks Inc.....561 547-5777
4901 Georgia Ave West Palm Beach (33405) ***(G-18209)***
York Bridge Concepts Inc.....813 482-0613
2423 Brunello Trce Lutz (33558) ***(G-8022)***
York International Corporation.....407 850-0147
10003 Satellite Blvd Orlando (32837) ***(G-12730)***
York International Corporation.....813 663-9332
8633 Elm Fair Blvd Tampa (33610) ***(G-17451)***
York International Corporation.....305 805-5600
10801 Nw 97th St Ste 21 Medley (33178) ***(G-8352)***
Yos Bottling LLC.....863 258-6820
15240 Citrus Country Dr Dade City (33523) ***(G-2325)***
Yosniel Finishing Inc.....305 890-3287
1171 W 28th St Apt 8 Hialeah (33010) ***(G-5426)***
Youmop LLC.....248 343-2013
1220 Sw 35th Ave Boynton Beach (33426) ***(G-929)***
Young Boats, Inglis *Also called Gulfshore Manufacturing Inc* ***(G-5818)***

1094 2022 Harris Florida Manufacturers Directory (G-0000) Company's Geographic Section entry number

Young Guns Embroidery Inc 813 814-9172
143 Scarlet Blvd Oldsmar (34677) *(G-11708)*

Younger You Inc (PA) 954 924-4462
5961 Bayview Dr Fort Lauderdale (33308) *(G-4142)*

Youngquist Brothers Rock Inc 239 267-6000
15401 Alico Rd Fort Myers (33913) *(G-4451)*

Your Cabinet Source Inc 352 728-3806
2606 South St Ste 4 Leesburg (34748) *(G-7802)*

Your Dreams Cabinets Corp 305 305-3729
7635 W 28th Ave Hialeah (33016) *(G-5427)*

Your Hometown Newspaper Inc 305 669-7355
6796 Sw 62nd Ave South Miami (33143) *(G-16049)*

Your ID Guard 904 354-8989
4811 Beach Blvd Ste 433 Jacksonville (32207) *(G-6622)*

Your Name Printing 813 621-2400
6502 N 54th St Tampa (33610) *(G-17452)*

Your Name Prtg Envlope Mfg Inc 813 621-2408
6502 N 54th St Tampa (33610) *(G-17453)*

Your Performance Solutions 305 278-2762
14417 Sw 143rd Ct Miami (33186) *(G-10153)*

Your Vizion By Chance, Riviera Beach *Also called JADA Transitions LLC (G-14633)*

Yourmembershipcom Inc (PA) 727 827-0046
9620 Exec Ctr Dr N Ste 20 Saint Petersburg (33702) *(G-15241)*

Youthful Innovations LLC 239 596-2200
3066 Tamiami Trl N # 101 Naples (34103) *(G-10946)*

Yovino Printing, Margate *Also called P & G Printing Group Inc (G-8145)*

Yp Advrtising Pubg LLC Not LLC 321 956-5400
100 Rialto Pl Ste 300 Melbourne (32901) *(G-8565)*

Yp General Work & Cabinets 786 317-0973
600 Nw 111th St Miami (33168) *(G-10154)*

Ysi Inc (HQ) 727 565-2201
9843 18th St N Ste 1200 Saint Petersburg (33716) *(G-15242)*

Ysl Graphics LLC 954 916-7255
4642 N Hiatus Rd Sunrise (33351) *(G-16394)*

Yudkin Fuel Co 561 487-0418
7544 Rexford Rd Boca Raton (33434) *(G-762)*

Yummy Foods Inc 305 681-8437
10408 W State Road 84 # 102 Davie (33324) *(G-2502)*

Yung Payper Chasers Entrmt LLC 727 239-2880
695 Central Ave Saint Petersburg (33701) *(G-15243)*

Yvel Usa Inc 561 391-5119
6000 Glades Rd Ste 1153 Boca Raton (33431) *(G-763)*

Z & L Partners Inc 813 639-0066
4920 W Cypress St Ste 100 Tampa (33607) *(G-17454)*

Z & N Manufacturing Corp 407 518-1114
1732 Kelley Ave Kissimmee (34744) *(G-6974)*

Z Cans LLC 941 748-6688
1111 Brambling Ct Bradenton (34212) *(G-1080)*

Z Spars, Gainesville *Also called US Spars Inc (G-4782)*

Zachey Design Marble Inc 754 367-6261
1649 Moffett St 4 Hollywood (33020) *(G-5688)*

Zag Medical, Miami *Also called Endo-Gear LLC (G-9098)*

Zahbuilt, Melbourne *Also called Melbourne Architectural Mllwk (G-8474)*

Zahn Builders Inc 718 885-2202
4628 N Federal Hwy Lighthouse Point (33064) *(G-7829)*

Zaho Global Enterprises LLC 321 239-0653
2275 Hillshire Dr Orlando (32828) *(G-12731)*

Zaniboni Lighting LLC 727 213-0410
101 N Garden Ave Ste 230 Clearwater (33755) *(G-1859)*

Zap Mosquito Solutions Inc 786 732-0772
13442 Sw 131st St Miami (33186) *(G-10155)*

Zap Skim'ers, Venice *Also called Glaspro (G-17694)*

Zassi Holdings Inc (PA) 904 432-8315
822 A1a N Ste 104 Ponte Vedra Beach (32082) *(G-14283)*

Zayas Fashions Inc (PA) 305 823-1438
665 W 33rd St Hialeah (33012) *(G-5428)*

Zbc Cabinetry 239 332-2940
3593 Vrnica S Shmker Blvd Fort Myers (33916) *(G-4452)*

Zd Realty LLC 866 672-1212
2135 13th Ave N Saint Petersburg (33713) *(G-15244)*

Zebra Stripes Inc 561 685-0654
915 Nw 7th St Dania (33004) *(G-2347)*

Zebra Technologies Corporation 305 716-2200
3100 Sw 145th Ave Ste 350 Miramar (33027) *(G-10566)*

Zed Promo's, Fort Lauderdale *Also called Zedora Inc (G-4143)*

Zedora Inc 954 332-3322
110 E Broward Blvd Fort Lauderdale (33301) *(G-4143)*

Zeeeees Corporation 407 624-3796
6164 Blue Pond Way Saint Cloud (34771) *(G-14942)*

Zefon International, Ocala *Also called Cole-Parmer Instrument Co LLC (G-11355)*

Zel Custom Manufacturing LLC 303 880-8701
11419 Challenger Ave Odessa (33556) *(G-11593)*

Zel Tech Trining Solutions LLC 757 722-5565
7123 University Blvd Winter Park (32792) *(G-18556)*

Zellermayer Supply Corp (PA) 561 848-0057
1231 52nd St Ste B Mangonia Park (33407) *(G-8104)*

Zellwin Farms Company (PA) 407 886-9241
6052 Jones Ave Zellwood (32798) *(G-18600)*

Zen Distributors Group II LLC 305 637-3014
2047 Nw 24th Ave Miami (33142) *(G-10156)*

Zenit Service LLC 407 878-7840
309 Grand Valley Dr Lake Mary (32746) *(G-7118)*

Zenith Rollers Llc 954 493-6484
764 Nw 57th Ct Fort Lauderdale (33309) *(G-4144)*

Zenithtech Industries Inc 386 454-7630
27124 Nw 203rd Pl High Springs (32643) *(G-5458)*

Zennergy LLC 813 382-3460
3918 N Highland Ave Tampa (33603) *(G-17455)*

Zeno Furniture & Mat Mfg Co 954 764-1212
671 Nw 4th Ave Fort Lauderdale (33311) *(G-4145)*

Zeno Mattress and Furn Mfg Co, Fort Lauderdale *Also called Zeno Furniture & Mat Mfg Co (G-4145)*

Zep-Pro, Fort Lauderdale *Also called Zeppelin Products Inc (G-4146)*

Zephyr Feed Company Inc 813 782-1578
40140 Lynbrook Dr Zephyrhills (33540) *(G-18637)*

Zephyrhills Corp 813 778-0595
4330 20th St Zephyrhills (33542) *(G-18638)*

Zephyrhills Water, Zephyrhills *Also called Zephyrhills Corp (G-18638)*

Zeppelin Products Inc 954 989-8808
3744 Sw 30th Ave Fort Lauderdale (33312) *(G-4146)*

Zepsa Industries 754 307-2173
41 Sw 6th St Pompano Beach (33060) *(G-14246)*

Zerion Group LLC 877 872-1726
235 S Maitland Ave # 100 Maitland (32751) *(G-8080)*

Zeroc Inc 561 283-1480
4425 Military Trl Ste 209 Jupiter (33458) *(G-6829)*

Zeroll Co (HQ) 772 461-3811
3355 Entp Ave Ste 160 Weston (33331) *(G-18300)*

Zerons Metal Designers Inc 305 688-2240
115 117 W 24th St Hialeah (33010) *(G-5429)*

Zesty Brands LLC 954 348-2827
2160 Premier Row Orlando (32809) *(G-12732)*

Zesty Paws LLC 407 358-6601
12124 High Tech Ave Ste 2 Orlando (32817) *(G-12733)*

Zeta Kitchen & Bath Inc 786 552-2322
6905 Nw 82nd Ave Miami (33166) *(G-10157)*

Zeus Industries 727 530-4373
12545 Creekside Dr Largo (33773) *(G-7710)*

Zhone Technologies Inc 510 777-7151
7340 Bryan Dairy Rd # 150 Seminole (33777) *(G-16000)*

Zhyno Inc 844 313-1900
3898 Pembroke Rd Hollywood (33021) *(G-5689)*

Ziehm Imaging Inc 407 615-8560
6280 Hzltine Nat Dr 100 Orlando (32822) *(G-12734)*

Zilla Inc 904 610-1436
4265 Eldridge Loop Orange Park (32073) *(G-11847)*

Zimmer Biomet CMF Thoracic LLC 574 267-6639
1520 Tradeport Dr Jacksonville (32218) *(G-6623)*

Zimmer Dental Inc 561 776-6700
4555 Riverside Dr Palm Beach Gardens (33410) *(G-13019)*

Zinc Guy Inc (PA) 954 907-2752
3811 Sw 47th Ave Ste 617 Davie (33314) *(G-2503)*

Ziptek LLC 941 953-5509
1250 S Tamiami Trl # 303 Sarasota (34239) *(G-15881)*

Zitec Inc 850 678-9747
1031 Partin Dr N Niceville (32578) *(G-11040)*

Zk Cabinets Inc 407 421-7307
5509 Commerce Dr Orlando (32839) *(G-12735)*

Zoag LLC 862 591-2969
102 Alegria Way Palm Beach Gardens (33418) *(G-13020)*

Zoe Express Logistics LLC 407 967-8762
4530 S Orange Blossom Trl U Orlando (32839) *(G-12736)*

Zoho Stone LLC 727 230-6956
34318 Us Highway 19 N Palm Harbor (34684) *(G-13140)*

Zokos Group Inc 888 756-9769
6800 E Rogers Cir Boca Raton (33487) *(G-764)*

Zollan, Miami Lakes *Also called Pioneer Led Lighting Corp (G-10339)*

Zom Monterra LP 407 644-6300
2001 Summit Park Dr # 300 Orlando (32810) *(G-12737)*

Zoo Holdings LLC 941 355-5653
4139 N Wa Blvd Sarasota (34234) *(G-15882)*

Zoya Inc 954 523-6531
641 Sw 3rd Ave Fort Lauderdale (33315) *(G-4147)*

Zpacks Corp 321 215-5658
7703 Technology Dr West Melbourne (32904) *(G-17903)*

Zsno Ft Lauderdale 954 792-2223
3801 Commerce Pkwy Miramar (33025) *(G-10567)*

Zulkifal Kiani LLC 765 291-4529
7901 4th St N Saint Petersburg (33702) *(G-15245)*

Zumex Usa Inc 305 591-0061
1573 Nw 82nd Ave Doral (33126) *(G-3424)*

Zumro Manufacturing Inc 954 782-7779
650 Sw 16th Ter Pompano Beach (33069) *(G-14247)*

Zurigo Trading Inc 305 244-4681
5077 Nw 7th St Apt 1118 Miami (33126) *(G-10158)*

Zweifel International, Orlando *Also called Creative Events and Exhibits (G-12053)*

Zyloware Corporation 561 479-4640
21214 Via Ventura Boca Raton (33433) *(G-765)*

A
L
P
H
A
B
E
T
I
C

PRODUCT INDEX

• Product categories are listed in alphabetical order.

A

ABRASIVE SAND MINING
ABRASIVES
ABRASIVES: Aluminum Oxide Fused
ABRASIVES: sandpaper
ACCELERATION INDICATORS & SYSTEM COMPONENTS: Aerospace
ACCELERATORS: Electrostatic Particle
ACCELERATORS: Linear
ACCELEROMETERS
ACCOUNTING MACHINES & CASH REGISTERS
ACCOUNTING MACHINES WHOLESALERS
ACCOUNTING SVCS, NEC
ACID RESIST: Etching
ACOUSTICAL BOARD & TILE
ACRYLIC RESINS
ACTOR
ADDITIVE BASED PLASTIC MATERIALS: Plasticizers
ADHESIVES
ADHESIVES & SEALANTS
ADHESIVES & SEALANTS WHOLESALERS
ADHESIVES: Adhesives, plastic
ADHESIVES: Epoxy
ADRENAL DERIVATIVES
ADVERTISING AGENCIES
ADVERTISING AGENCIES: Consultants
ADVERTISING COPY WRITING SVCS
ADVERTISING DISPLAY PRDTS
ADVERTISING MATERIAL DISTRIBUTION
ADVERTISING REPRESENTATIVES: Electronic Media
ADVERTISING REPRESENTATIVES: Magazine
ADVERTISING REPRESENTATIVES: Newspaper
ADVERTISING REPRESENTATIVES: Printed Media
ADVERTISING SPECIALTIES, WHOLESALE
ADVERTISING SVCS: Direct Mail
ADVERTISING SVCS: Display
ADVERTISING SVCS: Outdoor
ADVERTISING SVCS: Poster, Exc Outdoor
ADVERTISING SVCS: Poster, Outdoor
AEROSOLS
AGENTS, BROKERS & BUREAUS: Personal Service
AGRICULTURAL CHEMICALS: Trace Elements
AGRICULTURAL DISINFECTANTS
AGRICULTURAL EQPT: BARN, SILO, POULTRY, DAIRY/LIVESTOCK MACH
AGRICULTURAL EQPT: Barn Stanchions & Standards
AGRICULTURAL EQPT: Fertilizing Machinery
AGRICULTURAL EQPT: Fertilizng, Sprayng, Dustng/Irrigatn Mach
AGRICULTURAL EQPT: Grade, Clean & Sort Machines, Fruit/Veg
AGRICULTURAL EQPT: Harvesters, Fruit, Vegetable, Tobacco
AGRICULTURAL EQPT: Irrigation Eqpt, Self-Propelled
AGRICULTURAL EQPT: Soil Preparation Mach, Exc Turf & Grounds
AGRICULTURAL EQPT: Spreaders, Fertilizer
AGRICULTURAL EQPT: Trailers & Wagons, Farm
AGRICULTURAL LIMESTONE: Ground
AGRICULTURAL MACHINERY & EQPT REPAIR
AIR CLEANING SYSTEMS
AIR CONDITIONERS: Motor Vehicle
AIR CONDITIONING & VENTILATION EQPT & SPLYS: Wholesales
AIR CONDITIONING EQPT
AIR CONDITIONING REPAIR SVCS
AIR CONDITIONING UNITS: Complete, Domestic Or Indl
AIR MATTRESSES: Plastic
AIR PURIFICATION EQPT
AIR, WATER & SOLID WASTE PROGRAMS ADMINISTRATION SVCS
AIRCRAFT & AEROSPACE FLIGHT INSTRUMENTS & GUIDANCE SYSTEMS
AIRCRAFT & HEAVY EQPT REPAIR SVCS
AIRCRAFT ASSEMBLY PLANTS
AIRCRAFT CONTROL SYSTEMS:
AIRCRAFT CONTROL SYSTEMS: Electronic Totalizing Counters

AIRCRAFT DEALERS
AIRCRAFT ENGINES & ENGINE PARTS: Airfoils
AIRCRAFT ENGINES & ENGINE PARTS: Mount Parts
AIRCRAFT ENGINES & ENGINE PARTS: Research & Development, Mfr
AIRCRAFT ENGINES & PARTS
AIRCRAFT EQPT & SPLYS WHOLESALERS
AIRCRAFT FLIGHT INSTRUMENTS
AIRCRAFT FUELING SVCS
AIRCRAFT LIGHTING
AIRCRAFT MAINTENANCE & REPAIR SVCS
AIRCRAFT PARTS & AUX EQPT: Panel Assy/Hydro Prop Test Stands
AIRCRAFT PARTS & AUXILIARY EQPT: Accumulators, Propeller
AIRCRAFT PARTS & AUXILIARY EQPT: Ailerons
AIRCRAFT PARTS & AUXILIARY EQPT: Aircraft Training Eqpt
AIRCRAFT PARTS & AUXILIARY EQPT: Assys, Subassemblies/Parts
AIRCRAFT PARTS & AUXILIARY EQPT: Bodies
AIRCRAFT PARTS & AUXILIARY EQPT: Body & Wing Assys & Parts
AIRCRAFT PARTS & AUXILIARY EQPT: Body Assemblies & Parts
AIRCRAFT PARTS & AUXILIARY EQPT: Gears, Power Transmission
AIRCRAFT PARTS & AUXILIARY EQPT: Military Eqpt & Armament
AIRCRAFT PARTS & AUXILIARY EQPT: Oxygen Systems
AIRCRAFT PARTS & AUXILIARY EQPT: Refueling Eqpt, In Flight
AIRCRAFT PARTS & AUXILIARY EQPT: Research & Development, Mfr
AIRCRAFT PARTS & AUXILIARY EQPT: Rotor Blades, Helicopter
AIRCRAFT PARTS & EQPT, NEC
AIRCRAFT PARTS WHOLESALERS
AIRCRAFT SEATS
AIRCRAFT SERVICING & REPAIRING
AIRCRAFT: Airplanes, Fixed Or Rotary Wing
AIRCRAFT: Autogiros
AIRCRAFT: Motorized
AIRCRAFT: Research & Development, Manufacturer
AIRFRAME ASSEMBLIES: Guided Missiles
AIRLINE TRAINING
AIRLOCKS
AIRPORT TERMINAL SVCS
AIRPORTS, FLYING FIELDS & SVCS
ALARM SYSTEMS WHOLESALERS
ALARMS: Burglar
ALARMS: Fire
ALCOHOL: Ethyl & Ethanol
ALKALIES & CHLORINE
ALKALOIDS & OTHER BOTANICAL BASED PRDTS
ALLOYS: Additive, Exc Copper Or Made In Blast Furnaces
ALTERNATORS & GENERATORS: Battery Charging
ALTERNATORS: Automotive
ALUMINUM
ALUMINUM PRDTS
ALUMINUM: Coil & Sheet
ALUMINUM: Ingots & Slabs
ALUMINUM: Pigs
ALUMINUM: Rolling & Drawing
AMMONIA & AMMONIUM SALTS
AMMUNITION
AMMUNITION: Components
AMMUNITION: Mines & Parts, Ordnance
AMMUNITION: Paper Shells, Empty, Blank/Loaded, 30mm & Below
AMMUNITION: Rockets
AMMUNITION: Shot, Steel
AMMUNITION: Small Arms
AMPLIFIERS
AMPLIFIERS: Pulse Amplifiers
AMPLIFIERS: RF & IF Power
AMUSEMENT & REC SVCS: Attractions, Concessions & Rides

AMUSEMENT & RECREATION SVCS: Gambling & Lottery Svcs
AMUSEMENT & RECREATION SVCS: Night Club, Exc Alcoholic Bev
AMUSEMENT & RECREATION SVCS: Swimming Pool, Non-Membership
AMUSEMENT & RECREATION SVCS: Theme Park
AMUSEMENT & RECREATION SVCS: Tourist Attraction, Commercial
AMUSEMENT MACHINES: Coin Operated
AMUSEMENT PARK DEVICES & RIDES
AMUSEMENT PARK DEVICES & RIDES: Carnival Mach & Eqpt, NEC
AMUSEMENT PARKS
ANALGESICS
ANALYZERS: Network
ANALYZERS: Petroleum Prdts
ANALYZERS: Respiratory
ANESTHESIA EQPT
ANIMAL BASED MEDICINAL CHEMICAL PRDTS
ANIMAL FEED & SUPPLEMENTS: Livestock & Poultry
ANIMAL FOOD & SUPPLEMENTS: Chicken Feeds, Prepared
ANIMAL FOOD & SUPPLEMENTS: Citrus Seed Meal
ANIMAL FOOD & SUPPLEMENTS: Dog
ANIMAL FOOD & SUPPLEMENTS: Dog & Cat
ANIMAL FOOD & SUPPLEMENTS: Feed Premixes
ANIMAL FOOD & SUPPLEMENTS: Feed Supplements
ANIMAL FOOD & SUPPLEMENTS: Hay, Cubed
ANIMAL FOOD & SUPPLEMENTS: Livestock
ANIMAL FOOD & SUPPLEMENTS: Mineral feed supplements
ANIMAL FOOD & SUPPLEMENTS: Pet, Exc Dog & Cat, Dry
ANIMAL FOOD & SUPPLEMENTS: Pet, Exc Dog & Cat, Frozen
ANIMAL FOOD & SUPPLEMENTS: Rolled Oats
ANIMAL FOOD & SUPPLEMENTS: Specialty, Mice & Other Pets
ANODIZING EQPT
ANODIZING SVC
ANTENNAS: Radar Or Communications
ANTENNAS: Receiving
ANTENNAS: Satellite, Household Use
ANTIFREEZE
ANTIQUE SHOPS
APARTMENT LOCATING SVCS
APPAREL ACCESS STORES
APPAREL DESIGNERS: Commercial
APPAREL PRESSING SVCS
APPAREL: Hand Woven
APPLIANCE PARTS: Porcelain Enameled
APPLIANCE REPAIR
APPLIANCES, HOUSEHOLD: Drycleaning Machines, Incl Coin-Op
APPLIANCES, HOUSEHOLD: Kitchen, Major, Exc Refrigs & Stoves
APPLIANCES: Household, NEC
APPLIANCES: Household, Refrigerators & Freezers
APPLIANCES: Major, Cooking
APPLIANCES: Small, Electric
APPLICATIONS SOFTWARE PROGRAMMING
AQUARIUM ACCESS, METAL
AQUARIUM DESIGN & MAINTENANCE SVCS
AQUARIUMS & ACCESS: Glass
AQUARIUMS & ACCESS: Plastic
ARCHITECTURAL SVCS
ARMATURE REPAIRING & REWINDING SVC
ARMATURES: Automotive
ARMOR PLATES
AROMATIC CHEMICAL PRDTS
ART & ORNAMENTAL WARE: Pottery
ART DEALERS & GALLERIES
ART DESIGN SVCS
ART MARBLE: Concrete
ART SPLY STORES
ARTIFICIAL FLOWERS & TREES
ARTISTS' EQPT
ARTISTS' MATERIALS: Clay, Modeling
ARTISTS' MATERIALS: Frames, Artists' Canvases
ARTISTS' MATERIALS: Pencils & Leads

ARTWORK: Framed
ASBESTOS PRDTS: Pipe Covering, Heat Insulatng Matl, Exc Felt
ASBESTOS PRODUCTS
ASBESTOS REMOVAL EQPT
ASPHALT & ASPHALT PRDTS
ASPHALT COATINGS & SEALERS
ASPHALT MINING & BITUMINOUS STONE QUARRYING SVCS
ASPHALT PLANTS INCLUDING GRAVEL MIX TYPE
ASSEMBLIES: Exciter, Motor Or Generator Parts
ASSEMBLING SVC: Clocks
ASSEMBLING SVC: Plumbing Fixture Fittings, Plastic
ASSOCIATIONS: Business
ASSOCIATIONS: Manufacturers'
ASSOCIATIONS: Trade
ATHLETIC CLUB & GYMNASIUMS, MEMBERSHIP
ATLASES
ATOMIZERS
AUCTIONEERS: Fee Basis
AUDIO & VIDEO EQPT, EXC COMMERCIAL
AUDIO COMPONENTS
AUDIO ELECTRONIC SYSTEMS
AUDIO-VISUAL PROGRAM PRODUCTION SVCS
AUDIOLOGICAL EQPT: Electronic
AUDIOLOGISTS' OFFICES
AUTO & HOME SUPPLY STORES: Auto & Truck Eqpt & Parts
AUTO & HOME SUPPLY STORES: Auto Air Cond Eqpt, Sell/Install
AUTO & HOME SUPPLY STORES: Automotive Access
AUTO & HOME SUPPLY STORES: Automotive parts
AUTO & HOME SUPPLY STORES: Batteries, Automotive & Truck
AUTOCLAVES: Laboratory
AUTOMATED TELLER MACHINE NETWORK
AUTOMATIC REGULATING CNTRLS: Flame Safety, Furnaces & Boiler
AUTOMATIC REGULATING CNTRLS: Liq Lvl, Residential/Comm Heat
AUTOMATIC REGULATING CONTROL: Building Svcs Monitoring, Auto
AUTOMATIC REGULATING CONTROLS: AC & Refrigeration
AUTOMATIC TELLER MACHINES
AUTOMOBILES: Off-Highway, Electric
AUTOMOTIVE & TRUCK GENERAL REPAIR SVC
AUTOMOTIVE BATTERIES WHOLESALERS
AUTOMOTIVE BODY, PAINT & INTERIOR REPAIR & MAINTENANCE SVC
AUTOMOTIVE GLASS REPLACEMENT SHOPS
AUTOMOTIVE LETTERING & PAINTING SVCS
AUTOMOTIVE LETTERING SVCS
AUTOMOTIVE PARTS, ACCESS & SPLYS
AUTOMOTIVE PARTS: Plastic
AUTOMOTIVE PRDTS: Rubber
AUTOMOTIVE REPAIR SHOPS: Electrical Svcs
AUTOMOTIVE REPAIR SHOPS: Engine Rebuilding
AUTOMOTIVE REPAIR SHOPS: Engine Repair, Exc Diesel
AUTOMOTIVE REPAIR SHOPS: Machine Shop
AUTOMOTIVE REPAIR SHOPS: Powertrain Components Repair Svcs
AUTOMOTIVE REPAIR SHOPS: Sound System Svc & Installation
AUTOMOTIVE REPAIR SHOPS: Tire Repair Shop
AUTOMOTIVE REPAIR SHOPS: Torque Converter Repair
AUTOMOTIVE REPAIR SHOPS: Trailer Repair
AUTOMOTIVE REPAIR SVC
AUTOMOTIVE SPLYS & PARTS, NEW, WHOLESALE: Alternators
AUTOMOTIVE SPLYS & PARTS, NEW, WHOLESALE: Engines/Eng Parts
AUTOMOTIVE SPLYS & PARTS, NEW, WHOLESALE: Pumps, Oil & Gas
AUTOMOTIVE SPLYS & PARTS, NEW, WHOLESALE: Splys
AUTOMOTIVE SPLYS & PARTS, USED, WHOLESALE
AUTOMOTIVE SPLYS & PARTS, USED, WHOLESALE: Access, NEC
AUTOMOTIVE SPLYS & PARTS, WHOLESALE, NEC
AUTOMOTIVE SPLYS/PART, NEW, WHOL: Spring, Shock Absorb/Strut
AUTOMOTIVE SVCS
AUTOMOTIVE SVCS, EXC REPAIR & CARWASHES: Maintenance
AUTOMOTIVE SVCS, EXC RPR/CARWASHES: High Perf Auto Rpr/Svc
AUTOMOTIVE TOWING & WRECKING SVC

AUTOMOTIVE TOWING SVCS
AUTOMOTIVE TRANSMISSION REPAIR SVC
AUTOMOTIVE WELDING SVCS
AUTOMOTIVE: Bodies
AUTOMOTIVE: Seating
AUTOTRANSFORMERS: Electric
AVIATION PROPELLER & BLADE REPAIR SVCS
AVIATION SCHOOL
AWNINGS & CANOPIES
AWNINGS & CANOPIES: Awnings, Fabric, From Purchased Matls
AWNINGS & CANOPIES: Canopies, Fabric, From Purchased Matls
AWNINGS & CANOPIES: Fabric
AWNINGS: Fiberglass
AWNINGS: Metal

B

BACKHOES
BADGES: Identification & Insignia
BAGS & CONTAINERS: Textile, Exc Sleeping
BAGS & SACKS: Shipping & Shopping
BAGS: Canvas
BAGS: Cellophane
BAGS: Cement, Made From Purchased Materials
BAGS: Duffle, Canvas, Made From Purchased Materials
BAGS: Food Storage & Frozen Food, Plastic
BAGS: Food Storage & Trash, Plastic
BAGS: Garment Storage Exc Paper Or Plastic Film
BAGS: Laundry, From Purchased Materials
BAGS: Laundry, Garment & Storage
BAGS: Paper
BAGS: Paper, Made From Purchased Materials
BAGS: Plastic
BAGS: Plastic & Pliofilm
BAGS: Plastic, Made From Purchased Materials
BAGS: Rubber Or Rubberized Fabric
BAGS: Textile
BAGS: Trash, Plastic Film, Made From Purchased Materials
BAGS: Vacuum cleaner, Made From Purchased Materials
BAGS: Wardrobe, Closet Access, Made From Purchased Materials
BAKERIES, COMMERCIAL: On Premises Baking Only
BAKERIES: On Premises Baking & Consumption
BAKERY FOR HOME SVC DELIVERY
BAKERY MACHINERY
BAKERY PRDTS, FROZEN: Wholesalers
BAKERY PRDTS: Bagels, Fresh Or Frozen
BAKERY PRDTS: Bakery Prdts, Partially Cooked, Exc frozen
BAKERY PRDTS: Biscuits, Baked, Baking Powder & Raised
BAKERY PRDTS: Bread, All Types, Fresh Or Frozen
BAKERY PRDTS: Cakes, Bakery, Exc Frozen
BAKERY PRDTS: Cakes, Bakery, Frozen
BAKERY PRDTS: Cones, Ice Cream
BAKERY PRDTS: Cookies
BAKERY PRDTS: Cookies & crackers
BAKERY PRDTS: Crackers
BAKERY PRDTS: Doughnuts, Exc Frozen
BAKERY PRDTS: Dry
BAKERY PRDTS: Frozen
BAKERY PRDTS: Pastries, Danish, Frozen
BAKERY PRDTS: Pastries, Exc Frozen
BAKERY PRDTS: Pies, Exc Frozen
BAKERY PRDTS: Rolls, Bread Type, Fresh Or Frozen
BAKERY PRDTS: Wholesalers
BAKERY PRDTS: Yeast Goods, Sweet, Exc Frozen
BAKERY: Wholesale Or Wholesale & Retail Combined
BALCONIES: Metal
BALLOONS: Toy & Advertising, Rubber
BANDAGES
BANDS: Plastic
BANKING SCHOOLS, TRAINING
BANNERS: Fabric
BAR JOISTS & CONCRETE REINFORCING BARS: Fabricated
BARBECUE EQPT
BARGES BUILDING & REPAIR
BARRELS: Shipping, Metal
BARRICADES: Metal
BARS & BAR SHAPES: Steel, Cold-Finished, Own Hot-Rolled
BARS & BAR SHAPES: Steel, Hot-Rolled
BARS, COLD FINISHED: Steel, From Purchased Hot-Rolled
BARS: Cargo, Stabilizing, Metal
BARS: Concrete Reinforcing, Fabricated Steel
BASES, BEVERAGE

BATCHING PLANTS: Cement Silos
BATHING SUIT STORES
BATHROOM ACCESS & FITTINGS: Vitreous China & Earthenware
BATHROOM FIXTURES: Plastic
BATHTUBS: Concrete
BATTERIES, EXC AUTOMOTIVE: Wholesalers
BATTERIES: Alkaline, Cell Storage
BATTERIES: Dry
BATTERIES: Rechargeable
BATTERIES: Storage
BATTERIES: Wet
BATTERY CHARGERS
BATTERY CHARGERS: Storage, Motor & Engine Generator Type
BATTERY REPAIR & SVCS
BEARINGS & PARTS Ball
BEARINGS: Ball & Roller
BEAUTY & BARBER SHOP EQPT
BEAUTY & BARBER SHOP EQPT & SPLYS WHOLESALERS
BEAUTY SALONS
BEDDING, BEDSPREADS, BLANKETS & SHEETS
BEDDING, BEDSPREADS, BLANKETS & SHEETS: Bedspread, Lace
BEDDING, FROM SILK OR MANMADE FIBER
BEDS: Hospital
BEDSPREADS & BED SETS, FROM PURCHASED MATERIALS
BEDSPREADS, COTTON
BEEKEEPERS' SPLYS
BEEKEEPERS' SPLYS: Honeycomb Foundations
BEER & ALE WHOLESALERS
BEER, WINE & LIQUOR STORES
BELLOWS
BELLS: Electric
BELTING: Fabric
BELTING: Rubber
BELTS: Conveyor, Made From Purchased Wire
BELTS: Seat, Automotive & Aircraft
BEVERAGE BASES & SYRUPS
BEVERAGE PRDTS: Brewers' Grain
BEVERAGE PRDTS: Brewers' Rice
BEVERAGE STORES
BEVERAGE, NONALCOHOLIC: Iced Tea/Fruit Drink, Bottled/Canned
BEVERAGES, ALCOHOLIC: Beer
BEVERAGES, ALCOHOLIC: Beer & Ale
BEVERAGES, ALCOHOLIC: Bourbon Whiskey
BEVERAGES, ALCOHOLIC: Cocktails
BEVERAGES, ALCOHOLIC: Cordials & Premixed Cocktails
BEVERAGES, ALCOHOLIC: Distilled Liquors
BEVERAGES, ALCOHOLIC: Gin
BEVERAGES, ALCOHOLIC: Liquors, Malt
BEVERAGES, ALCOHOLIC: Rum
BEVERAGES, ALCOHOLIC: Scotch Whiskey
BEVERAGES, ALCOHOLIC: Vodka
BEVERAGES, ALCOHOLIC: Wine Coolers
BEVERAGES, ALCOHOLIC: Wines
BEVERAGES, MALT
BEVERAGES, MILK BASED
BEVERAGES, NONALCOHOLIC: Bottled & canned soft drinks
BEVERAGES, NONALCOHOLIC: Carbonated
BEVERAGES, NONALCOHOLIC: Carbonated, Canned & Bottled, Etc
BEVERAGES, NONALCOHOLIC: Cider
BEVERAGES, NONALCOHOLIC: Flavoring extracts & syrups, nec
BEVERAGES, NONALCOHOLIC: Fruit Drnks, Under 100% Juice, Can
BEVERAGES, NONALCOHOLIC: Fruit Juices, Concentrtd, Fountain
BEVERAGES, NONALCOHOLIC: Lemonade, Bottled & Canned, Etc
BEVERAGES, NONALCOHOLIC: Soft Drinks, Canned & Bottled, Etc
BEVERAGES, NONALCOHOLIC: Tea, Iced, Bottled & Canned, Etc
BEVERAGES, WINE & DISTILLED ALCOHOLIC, WHOLESALE: Wine
BEVERAGES, WINE/DISTILLED ALCOHOLIC, WHOL: Bttlg Wine/Liquor
BICYCLE ASSEMBLY SVCS
BICYCLES, PARTS & ACCESS
BIDETS: Vitreous China

BILLFOLD INSERTS: Plastic
BILLIARD & POOL TABLES & SPLYS
BILLIARD EQPT & SPLYS WHOLESALERS
BILLING & BOOKKEEPING SVCS
BINDING SVC: Books & Manuals
BINDING SVC: Magazines
BINDING SVC: Trade
BINOCULARS
BINS: Prefabricated, Metal Plate
BIOLOGICAL PRDTS: Antitoxins
BIOLOGICAL PRDTS: Bacteriological Media
BIOLOGICAL PRDTS: Blood Derivatives
BIOLOGICAL PRDTS: Exc Diagnostic
BIOLOGICAL PRDTS: Extracts
BIOLOGICAL PRDTS: Serums
BIOLOGICAL PRDTS: Vaccines
BIOLOGICAL PRDTS: Vaccines & Immunizing
BIOLOGICAL PRDTS: Venoms
BIOLOGICAL PRDTS: Veterinary
BIRTH CONTROL DEVICES: Rubber
BITUMINOUS & LIGNITE COAL LOADING & PREPARATION
BLADES: Saw, Hand Or Power
BLANKBOOKS & LOOSELEAF BINDERS
BLANKBOOKS: Account
BLANKBOOKS: Albums, Record
BLANKBOOKS: Scrapbooks
BLANKETS: Horse
BLAST SAND MINING
BLASTING SVC: Sand, Metal Parts
BLINDS & SHADES: Vertical
BLINDS : Window
BLINDS, WOOD
BLOCKS & BRICKS: Concrete
BLOCKS: Acoustical, Concrete
BLOCKS: Drystack Interlocking, Concrete
BLOCKS: Insulating, Concrete
BLOCKS: Landscape Or Retaining Wall, Concrete
BLOCKS: Paving
BLOCKS: Paving, Asphalt, Not From Refineries
BLOCKS: Paving, Concrete
BLOCKS: Paving, Cut Stone
BLOCKS: Standard, Concrete Or Cinder
BLOOD RELATED HEALTH SVCS
BLOWERS & FANS
BLOWERS & FANS
BLUEPRINTING SVCS
BLUING
BOAT & BARGE COMPONENTS: Metal, Prefabricated
BOAT BUILDING & REPAIR
BOAT BUILDING & REPAIRING: Fiberglass
BOAT BUILDING & REPAIRING: Hydrofoil
BOAT BUILDING & REPAIRING: Kits, Not Models
BOAT BUILDING & REPAIRING: Lifeboats
BOAT BUILDING & REPAIRING: Motorboats, Inboard Or Out-
board
BOAT BUILDING & REPAIRING: Motorized
BOAT BUILDING & REPAIRING: Pontoons, Exc Aircraft & In-
flat
BOAT BUILDING & REPAIRING: Rigid, Plastic
BOAT BUILDING & REPAIRING: Tenders, Small Motor Craft
BOAT BUILDING & REPAIRING: Yachts
BOAT BUILDING & RPRG: Fishing, Small, Lobster, Crab,
Oyster
BOAT DEALERS
BOAT DEALERS: Canoe & Kayak
BOAT DEALERS: Marine Splys & Eqpt
BOAT DEALERS: Outboard
BOAT LIFTS
BOAT REPAIR SVCS
BOAT YARD: Boat yards, storage & incidental repair
BOATS & OTHER MARINE EQPT: Plastic
BOATS: Plastic, Nonrigid
BODIES: Truck & Bus
BODY PARTS: Automobile, Stamped Metal
BOILER REPAIR SHOP
BOILERS: Low-Pressure Heating, Steam Or Hot Water
BOLTS: Handle, Wooden, Hewn
BOLTS: Metal
BONDS, RAIL: Electric, Propulsion & Signal Circuit Uses
BOOK STORES
BOOKS, WHOLESALE
BOOTHS: Spray, Sheet Metal, Prefabricated
BOOTS: Men's
BOOTS: Women's
BORING MILL

BOTTLE CAPS & RESEALERS: Plastic
BOTTLED GAS DEALERS: Propane
BOTTLED WATER DELIVERY
BOTTLES: Plastic
BOULDER: Crushed & Broken
BOUTIQUE STORES
BOXES & CRATES: Rectangular, Wood
BOXES & SHOOK: Nailed Wood
BOXES, GARBAGE: Concrete
BOXES: Corrugated
BOXES: Mail Or Post Office, Collection/Storage, Sheet Metal
BOXES: Packing & Shipping, Metal
BOXES: Paperboard, Folding
BOXES: Paperboard, Set-Up
BOXES: Plastic
BOXES: Stamped Metal
BRAKES & BRAKE PARTS
BRASS GOODS, WHOLESALE
BRAZING SVCS
BRICK, STONE & RELATED PRDTS WHOLESALERS
BRICKS & BLOCKS: Structural
BRICKS : Ceramic Glazed, Clay
BRICKS : Paving, Clay
BRICKS: Concrete
BROADCASTING & COMMS EQPT: Antennas,
Transmitting/Comms
BROADCASTING & COMMS EQPT: Rcvr-Transmitter Unt,
Transceiver
BROADCASTING & COMMS EQPT: Trnsmttng TV Anten-
nas/Grndng Eqpt
BROADCASTING & COMMUNICATION EQPT: Transmit-Re-
ceiver, Radio
BROADCASTING & COMMUNICATIONS EQPT: Cellular
Radio Telephone
BROADCASTING & COMMUNICATIONS EQPT: Studio Eqpt,
Radio & TV
BROADCASTING & COMMUNICATIONS EQPT: Transmitting,
Radio/TV
BROKERS & DEALERS: Securities
BROKERS' SVCS
BROKERS: Automotive
BROKERS: Contract Basis
BROKERS: Food
BROKERS: Mortgage, Arranging For Loans
BROKERS: Printing
BROKERS: Yacht
BRONZE FOUNDRY, NEC
BROOMS & BRUSHES
BROOMS & BRUSHES: Household Or Indl
BROOMS & BRUSHES: Paint & Varnish
BROOMS & BRUSHES: Paint Rollers
BROOMS & BRUSHES: Paintbrushes
BRUCITE MINING
BRUSHES
BRUSHES: Rubber
BUFFING FOR THE TRADE
BUILDING & STRUCTURAL WOOD MBRS: Timbers, Struct,
Lam Lumber
BUILDING & STRUCTURAL WOOD MEMBERS
BUILDING BOARD & WALLBOARD, EXC GYPSUM
BUILDING BOARD: Gypsum
BUILDING CLEANING & MAINTENANCE SVCS
BUILDING CLEANING SVCS
BUILDING COMPONENTS: Structural Steel
BUILDING ITEM REPAIR SVCS, MISCELLANEOUS
BUILDING PRDTS & MATERIALS DEALERS
BUILDING PRDTS: Concrete
BUILDING PRDTS: Stone
BUILDING STONE, ARTIFICIAL: Concrete
BUILDINGS & COMPONENTS: Prefabricated Metal
BUILDINGS: Farm & Utility
BUILDINGS: Mobile, For Commercial Use
BUILDINGS: Portable
BUILDINGS: Prefabricated, Metal
BUILDINGS: Prefabricated, Plastic
BUILDINGS: Prefabricated, Wood
BUILDINGS: Prefabricated, Wood
BULLETPROOF VESTS
BUMPERS: Motor Vehicle
BURGLAR ALARM MAINTENANCE & MONITORING SVCS
BURIAL VAULTS: Concrete Or Precast Terrazzo
BURIAL VAULTS: Stone
BURNERS: Gas, Indl
BURNERS: Gas-Oil, Combination
BUSHINGS: Cast Steel, Exc Investment

BUSHINGS: Rubber
BUSINESS ACTIVITIES: Non-Commercial Site
BUSINESS FORMS WHOLESALERS
BUSINESS FORMS: Printed, Continuous
BUSINESS FORMS: Printed, Manifold
BUSINESS FORMS: Strip, Manifold
BUSINESS FORMS: Unit Sets, Manifold
BUSINESS SUPPORT SVCS
BUSINESS TRAINING SVCS
BUTTONS

C

CABINETS & CASES: Show, Display & Storage, Exc Wood
CABINETS: Bathroom Vanities, Wood
CABINETS: Entertainment
CABINETS: Entertainment Units, Household, Wood
CABINETS: Factory
CABINETS: Filing, Wood
CABINETS: Kitchen, Metal
CABINETS: Kitchen, Wood
CABINETS: Office, Wood
CABINETS: Show, Display, Etc, Wood, Exc Refrigerated
CABLE TELEVISION PRDTS
CABLE: Fiber
CABLE: Fiber Optic
CABLE: Ropes & Fiber
CABLE: Steel, Insulated Or Armored
CABS: Indl Trucks & Tractors
CAFETERIAS
CAGES: Wire
CALCULATING & ACCOUNTING EQPT
CAMERA & PHOTOGRAPHIC SPLYS STORES
CAMERA & PHOTOGRAPHIC SPLYS STORES: Cameras
CAMERAS & RELATED EQPT: Photographic
CANDLE SHOPS
CANDLES
CANDLES: Wholesalers
CANDY & CONFECTIONS: Cake Ornaments
CANDY & CONFECTIONS: Candy Bars, Including Chocolate
Covered
CANDY & CONFECTIONS: Chocolate Candy, Exc Solid
Chocolate
CANDY & CONFECTIONS: Fruit & Fruit Peel
CANDY & CONFECTIONS: Nuts, Candy Covered
CANDY & CONFECTIONS: Popcorn Balls/Other Trtd Popcorn
Prdts
CANDY, NUT & CONFECTIONERY STORES: Candy
CANDY, NUT & CONFECTIONERY STORES: Produced For
Direct Sale
CANDY: Chocolate From Cacao Beans
CANDY: Hard
CANES & TRIMMINGS, EXC PRECIOUS METAL
CANNED SPECIALTIES
CANOPIES: Sheet Metal
CANS: Aluminum
CANS: Composite Foil-Fiber, Made From Purchased Materials
CANS: Metal
CANVAS PRDTS
CANVAS PRDTS, WHOLESALE
CANVAS PRDTS: Boat Seats
CANVAS PRDTS: Convertible Tops, Car/Boat, Fm Purchased
Mtrl
CANVAS PRDTS: Shades, Made From Purchased Materials
CAPACITORS & CONDENSERS
CAPACITORS: NEC
CAPACITORS: Series
CAPS: Plastic
CAR WASH EQPT
CAR WASH EQPT & SPLYS WHOLESALERS
CARBIDES
CARBON REMOVING SOLVENT
CARBURETORS
CARDIOVASCULAR SYSTEM DRUGS, EXC DIAGNOSTIC
CARDS, PLASTIC, UNPRINTED, WHOLESALE
CARDS: Greeting
CARDS: Identification
CARDS: Playing
CARNIVAL SPLYS, WHOLESALE
CARPET & UPHOLSTERY CLEANING SVCS
CARPET & UPHOLSTERY CLEANING SVCS: Carpet/Furni-
ture, On Loc
CARPETS & RUGS: Tufted
CARPETS, RUGS & FLOOR COVERING
CARPETS: Hand & Machine Made
CARRIER EQPT: Telephone Or Telegraph

INDEX

CARRYING CASES, WHOLESALE
CARS: Electric
CARTS: Grocery
CASES, WOOD
CASES: Carrying
CASES: Carrying, Clothing & Apparel
CASES: Jewelry
CASES: Packing, Nailed Or Lock Corner, Wood
CASES: Plastic
CASES: Shipping, Nailed Or Lock Corner, Wood
CASES: Shipping, Wood, Wirebound
CASH REGISTERS WHOLESALERS
CASINGS: Storage, Missile & Missile Components
CASKETS & ACCESS
CAST STONE: Concrete
CASTERS
CASTINGS GRINDING: For The Trade
CASTINGS: Aerospace Investment, Ferrous
CASTINGS: Aerospace, Aluminum
CASTINGS: Aerospace, Nonferrous, Exc Aluminum
CASTINGS: Aluminum
CASTINGS: Bronze, NEC, Exc Die
CASTINGS: Commercial Investment, Ferrous
CASTINGS: Die, Aluminum
CASTINGS: Die, Magnesium & Magnesium-Base Alloy
CASTINGS: Die, Nonferrous
CASTINGS: Die, Zinc
CASTINGS: Gray Iron
CASTINGS: Lead
CASTINGS: Machinery, Aluminum
CASTINGS: Machinery, Brass
CASTINGS: Machinery, Nonferrous, Exc Die or Aluminum
  Copper
CASTINGS: Precision
CASTINGS: Zinc
CAT BOX FILLER
CATALOG & MAIL-ORDER HOUSES
CATALOG SALES
CATALYSTS: Chemical
CATAPULTS
CATCH BASIN CLEANING SVC
CATCH BASIN COVERS: Concrete
CATERERS
CEILING SYSTEMS: Luminous, Commercial
CELLULOID PRDTS
CELLULOSE DERIVATIVE MATERIALS
CEMENT, EXC LINOLEUM & TILE
CEMENT: Hydraulic
CEMENT: Masonry
CEMENT: Natural
CEMETERY MEMORIAL DEALERS
CERAMIC FIBER
CERAMIC FLOOR & WALL TILE WHOLESALERS
CHAIN: Tire, Made From Purchased Wire
CHAINS: Power Transmission
CHAMBERS: Space Simulation, Metal Plate
CHANGE MAKING MACHINES
CHARCOAL: Activated
CHASING SVC: Metal
CHASSIS: Automobile Trailer
CHASSIS: Motor Vehicle
CHEESE WHOLESALERS
CHEMICAL ELEMENTS
CHEMICAL PROCESSING MACHINERY & EQPT
CHEMICALS & ALLIED PRDTS WHOLESALERS, NEC
CHEMICALS & ALLIED PRDTS, WHOL: Chemical, Organic,
  Synthetic
CHEMICALS & ALLIED PRDTS, WHOLESALE: Chemicals,
  Indl
CHEMICALS & ALLIED PRDTS, WHOLESALE: Chemicals,
  Indl & Heavy
CHEMICALS & ALLIED PRDTS, WHOLESALE: Compressed
  Gas
CHEMICALS & ALLIED PRDTS, WHOLESALE: Detergents
CHEMICALS & ALLIED PRDTS, WHOLESALE: Dry Ice
CHEMICALS & ALLIED PRDTS, WHOLESALE: Essential Oils
CHEMICALS & ALLIED PRDTS, WHOLESALE: Indl Gases
CHEMICALS & ALLIED PRDTS, WHOLESALE: Oil Additives
CHEMICALS & ALLIED PRDTS, WHOLESALE: Plastics Ma-
  terials, NEC
CHEMICALS & ALLIED PRDTS, WHOLESALE: Plastics
  Prdts, NEC
CHEMICALS & ALLIED PRDTS, WHOLESALE: Plastics
  Sheets & Rods
CHEMICALS & ALLIED PRDTS, WHOLESALE: Resins

CHEMICALS & ALLIED PRDTS, WHOLESALE: Resins, Plas-
  tics
CHEMICALS & ALLIED PRDTS, WHOLESALE: Spec
  Clean/Sanitation
CHEMICALS & OTHER PRDTS DERIVED FROM COKING
CHEMICALS, AGRICULTURE: Wholesalers
CHEMICALS/ALLIED PRDTS, WHOL: Coal Tar Prdts,
  Prim/Intermdt
CHEMICALS: Agricultural
CHEMICALS: Alcohols
CHEMICALS: Aluminum Compounds
CHEMICALS: Brine
CHEMICALS: Fire Retardant
CHEMICALS: Fluorine, Elemental
CHEMICALS: Fuel Tank Or Engine Cleaning
CHEMICALS: High Purity Grade, Organic
CHEMICALS: High Purity, Refined From Technical Grade
CHEMICALS: Inorganic, NEC
CHEMICALS: Iodine, Elemental
CHEMICALS: Medicinal
CHEMICALS: Medicinal, Inorganic, Uncompounded, Bulk
CHEMICALS: Medicinal, Organic, Uncompounded, Bulk
CHEMICALS: Muriate Of Potash, Not From Mines
CHEMICALS: NEC
CHEMICALS: Organic, NEC
CHEMICALS: Reagent Grade, Refined From Technical Grade
CHEMICALS: Water Treatment
CHESTS: Bank, Metal
CHILD DAY CARE SVCS
CHILDBIRTH PREPARATION CLINIC
CHILDREN'S & INFANTS' CLOTHING STORES
CHINA & GLASS: Decalcomania Work
CHLORINE
CHLOROPRENE RUBBER: Neoprene
CHOCOLATE, EXC CANDY FROM BEANS: Chips, Powder,
  Block, Syrup
CHOCOLATE, EXC CANDY FROM PURCH CHOC: Chips,
  Powder, Block
CHURCHES
CHUTES: Metal Plate
CIGAR & CIGARETTE HOLDERS
CIGARETTE & CIGAR PRDTS & ACCESS
CIRCUIT BOARD REPAIR SVCS
CIRCUIT BOARDS, PRINTED: Television & Radio
CIRCUIT BOARDS: Wiring
CIRCUIT BREAKERS
CIRCUITS, INTEGRATED: Hybrid
CIRCUITS: Electronic
CLAMPS: Metal
CLAY PRDTS: Architectural
CLAYS, EXC KAOLIN & BALL
CLEANERS: Boiler Tube
CLEANING EQPT: Blast, Dustless
CLEANING EQPT: Commercial
CLEANING EQPT: Dirt Sweeping Units, Indl
CLEANING EQPT: Floor Washing & Polishing, Commercial
CLEANING EQPT: High Pressure
CLEANING OR POLISHING PREPARATIONS, NEC
CLEANING PRDTS: Automobile Polish
CLEANING PRDTS: Bleaches, Household, Dry Or Liquid
CLEANING PRDTS: Degreasing Solvent
CLEANING PRDTS: Deodorants, Nonpersonal
CLEANING PRDTS: Disinfectants, Household Or Indl Plant
CLEANING PRDTS: Drain Pipe Solvents Or Cleaners
CLEANING PRDTS: Drycleaning Preparations
CLEANING PRDTS: Indl Plant Disinfectants Or Deodorants
CLEANING PRDTS: Laundry Preparations
CLEANING PRDTS: Polishing Preparations & Related Prdts
CLEANING PRDTS: Sanitation Preparations
CLEANING PRDTS: Sanitation Preps, Disinfectants/Deodor-
  ants
CLEANING PRDTS: Specialty
CLEANING SVCS: Industrial Or Commercial
CLOSURES: Plastic
CLOTHING & ACCESS STORES
CLOTHING & ACCESS, WOMEN, CHILD & INFANT,
  WHOLESALE: Under
CLOTHING & ACCESS, WOMEN, CHILD & INFANT, WHSLE:
  Sportswear
CLOTHING & ACCESS, WOMEN, CHILDREN & INFANT,
  WHOL: Handbags
CLOTHING & ACCESS, WOMEN, CHILDREN & INFANT,
  WHOL: Uniforms
CLOTHING & ACCESS, WOMEN, CHILDREN/INFANT,
  WHOL: Outerwear

CLOTHING & ACCESS, WOMEN, CHILDREN/INFANT,
  WHOL: Swimsuits
CLOTHING & ACCESS, WOMENS, CHILDREN & INFANTS,
  WHOL: Hats
CLOTHING & ACCESS: Arm bands, Elastic
CLOTHING & ACCESS: Costumes, Lodge
CLOTHING & ACCESS: Costumes, Theatrical
CLOTHING & ACCESS: Footlets
CLOTHING & ACCESS: Garters
CLOTHING & ACCESS: Handicapped
CLOTHING & ACCESS: Hospital Gowns
CLOTHING & ACCESS: Men's Miscellaneous Access
CLOTHING & ACCESS: Suspenders
CLOTHING & APPAREL STORES: Custom
CLOTHING & FURNISHINGS, MEN'S & BOYS', WHOLE-
  SALE: Hats
CLOTHING & FURNISHINGS, MEN'S & BOYS', WHOLE-
  SALE: Outerwear
CLOTHING & FURNISHINGS, MEN'S & BOYS', WHOLE-
  SALE: Shirts
CLOTHING & FURNISHINGS, MEN'S & BOYS', WHOLE-
  SALE: Uniforms
CLOTHING & FURNISHINGS, MENS & BOYS, WHOL:
  Sportswear/Work
CLOTHING & FURNISHINGS, MENS & BOYS, WHOLE-
  SALE: Apprl Belts
CLOTHING STORES: Formal Wear
CLOTHING STORES: Jeans
CLOTHING STORES: Shirts, Custom Made
CLOTHING STORES: T-Shirts, Printed, Custom
CLOTHING STORES: Uniforms & Work
CLOTHING STORES: Unisex
CLOTHING STORES: Work
CLOTHING, WOMEN & CHILD, WHLSE: Dress, Suit, Skirt &
  Blouse
CLOTHING: Academic Vestments
CLOTHING: Access
CLOTHING: Access, Women's & Misses'
CLOTHING: Aprons, Harness
CLOTHING: Aprons, Work, Exc Rubberized & Plastic, Men's
CLOTHING: Athletic & Sportswear, Men's & Boys'
CLOTHING: Athletic & Sportswear, Women's & Girls'
CLOTHING: Baker, Barber, Lab/Svc Ind Apparel, Washable,
  Men
CLOTHING: Bathing Suits & Swimwear, Girls, Children & In-
  fant
CLOTHING: Bathing Suits & Swimwear, Knit
CLOTHING: Bathrobes, Mens & Womens, From Purchased
  Materials
CLOTHING: Beachwear, Knit
CLOTHING: Belts
CLOTHING: Blouses & Shirts, Girls' & Children's
CLOTHING: Blouses, Women's & Girls'
CLOTHING: Blouses, Womens & Juniors, From Purchased
  Mtrls
CLOTHING: Brassieres
CLOTHING: Bridal Gowns
CLOTHING: Children's, Girls'
CLOTHING: Coats & Jackets, Leather & Sheep-Lined
CLOTHING: Coats & Suits, Men's & Boys'
CLOTHING: Costumes
CLOTHING: Disposable
CLOTHING: Dresses
CLOTHING: Formal Jackets, Mens & Youth, From Purchased
  Matls
CLOTHING: Girdles & Other Foundation Garments, Knit
CLOTHING: Gowns & Dresses, Wedding
CLOTHING: Hats & Caps, NEC
CLOTHING: Hats & Caps, Uniform
CLOTHING: Hats, Harvest, Straw
CLOTHING: Helmets, Jungle Cloth, Wool Lined
CLOTHING: Hosiery, Men's & Boys'
CLOTHING: Hosiery, Pantyhose & Knee Length, Sheer
CLOTHING: Hospital, Men's
CLOTHING: Jackets, Knit
CLOTHING: Knit Underwear & Nightwear
CLOTHING: Leather
CLOTHING: Leather & sheep-lined clothing
CLOTHING: Lounge, Bed & Leisurewear
CLOTHING: Maternity
CLOTHING: Men's & boy's clothing, nec
CLOTHING: Men's & boy's underwear & nightwear
CLOTHING: Neckwear
CLOTHING: Outerwear, Knit

CLOTHING: Outerwear, Lthr, Wool/Down-Filled, Men, Youth/Boy
CLOTHING: Outerwear, Women's & Misses' NEC
CLOTHING: Robes & Dressing Gowns
CLOTHING: Service Apparel, Women's
CLOTHING: Shirts
CLOTHING: Shirts & T-Shirts, Knit
CLOTHING: Shirts, Dress, Men's & Boys'
CLOTHING: Shirts, Sports & Polo, Men's & Boys'
CLOTHING: Shirts, Uniform, From Purchased Materials
CLOTHING: Shirts, Women's & Juniors', From Purchased Mtrls
CLOTHING: Skirts, Knit
CLOTHING: Socks
CLOTHING: Sportswear, Women's
CLOTHING: Suits, Men's & Boys', From Purchased Materials
CLOTHING: Swimwear, Men's & Boys'
CLOTHING: Swimwear, Women's & Misses'
CLOTHING: T-Shirts & Tops, Knit
CLOTHING: T-Shirts & Tops, Women's & Girls'
CLOTHING: Trousers & Slacks, Men's & Boys'
CLOTHING: Underwear, Knit
CLOTHING: Underwear, Women's & Children's
CLOTHING: Uniforms & Vestments
CLOTHING: Uniforms, Ex Athletic, Women's, Misses' & Juniors'
CLOTHING: Uniforms, Men's & Boys'
CLOTHING: Uniforms, Military, Men/Youth, Purchased Materials
CLOTHING: Uniforms, Policemen's, From Purchased Materials
CLOTHING: Uniforms, Team Athletic
CLOTHING: Uniforms, Work
CLOTHING: Vests
CLOTHING: Warm Weather Knit Outerwear, Including Beachwear
CLOTHING: Waterproof Outerwear
CLOTHING: Work Apparel, Exc Uniforms
CLOTHING: Work, Men's
CLOTHS: Polishing, Plain
COAL MINING EXPLORATION & TEST BORING SVC
COAL MINING SERVICES
COAL MINING: Bituminous Coal & Lignite-Surface Mining
COAL PREPARATION PLANT: Bituminous or Lignite
COAL, MINERALS & ORES, WHOLESALE: Coal
COAL, MINERALS & ORES, WHOLESALE: Gold Ore
COATING COMPOUNDS: Tar
COATING SVC
COATING SVC: Aluminum, Metal Prdts
COATING SVC: Metals & Formed Prdts
COATING SVC: Rust Preventative
COATING SVC: Silicon
COATINGS: Epoxy
COATINGS: Polyurethane
COFFEE MAKERS: Electric
COFFEE SVCS
COILS & TRANSFORMERS
COILS: Pipe
COIN COUNTERS
COINS & TOKENS: Non-Currency
COKE: Calcined Petroleum, Made From Purchased Materials
COKE: Petroleum & Coal Derivative
COKE: Petroleum, Not From Refineries
COLOR PIGMENTS
COLOR SEPARATION: Photographic & Movie Film
COLORING & FINISHING SVC: Aluminum Or Formed Prdts
COLORS: Pigments, Inorganic
COLORS: Pigments, Organic
COLUMNS: Concrete
COLUMNS: Paper-Mache Or Plaster Of Paris
COMMERCIAL & OFFICE BUILDINGS RENOVATION & REPAIR
COMMERCIAL ART & GRAPHIC DESIGN SVCS
COMMERCIAL CONTAINERS WHOLESALERS
COMMERCIAL EQPT WHOLESALERS, NEC
COMMERCIAL EQPT, WHOLESALE: Mannequins
COMMERCIAL EQPT, WHOLESALE: Neon Signs
COMMERCIAL EQPT, WHOLESALE: Restaurant, NEC
COMMERCIAL LAUNDRY EQPT
COMMERCIAL PRINTING & NEWSPAPER PUBLISHING COMBINED
COMMODITY CONTRACT TRADING COMPANIES
COMMON SAND MINING
COMMUNICATION HEADGEAR: Telephone
COMMUNICATIONS EQPT & SYSTEMS, NEC

COMMUNICATIONS EQPT: Microwave
COMMUNICATIONS SVCS: Cellular
COMMUNICATIONS SVCS: Data
COMMUNICATIONS SVCS: Internet Connectivity Svcs
COMMUNICATIONS SVCS: Internet Host Svcs
COMMUNICATIONS SVCS: Online Svc Providers
COMMUNICATIONS SVCS: Proprietary Online Svcs Networks
COMMUNICATIONS SVCS: Satellite Earth Stations
COMMUNICATIONS SVCS: Telephone, Data
COMMUNITY SVCS EMPLOYMENT TRAINING PROGRAM
COMPACT LASER DISCS: Prerecorded
COMPACTORS: Trash & Garbage, Residential
COMPOSITION STONE: Plastic
COMPOST
COMPRESSORS: Air & Gas
COMPRESSORS: Air & Gas, Including Vacuum Pumps
COMPRESSORS: Refrigeration & Air Conditioning Eqpt
COMPRESSORS: Repairing
COMPUTER & COMPUTER SOFTWARE STORES
COMPUTER & COMPUTER SOFTWARE STORES: Peripheral Eqpt
COMPUTER & COMPUTER SOFTWARE STORES: Personal Computers
COMPUTER & COMPUTER SOFTWARE STORES: Printers & Plotters
COMPUTER & COMPUTER SOFTWARE STORES: Software & Access
COMPUTER & COMPUTER SOFTWARE STORES: Software, Bus/Non-Game
COMPUTER & COMPUTER SOFTWARE STORES: Software, Computer Game
COMPUTER & COMPUTER SOFTWARE STORES: Word Process Eqpt/Splys
COMPUTER & DATA PROCESSING EQPT REPAIR & MAINTENANCE
COMPUTER & OFFICE MACHINE MAINTENANCE & REPAIR
COMPUTER & SFTWR STORE: Modem, Monitor, Terminal/Disk Drive
COMPUTER DISKETTES WHOLESALERS
COMPUTER FACILITIES MANAGEMENT SVCS
COMPUTER FORMS
COMPUTER GRAPHICS SVCS
COMPUTER INTERFACE EQPT: Indl Process
COMPUTER PAPER WHOLESALERS
COMPUTER PERIPHERAL EQPT, NEC
COMPUTER PERIPHERAL EQPT, WHOLESALE
COMPUTER PERIPHERAL EQPT: Decoders
COMPUTER PERIPHERAL EQPT: Encoders
COMPUTER PERIPHERAL EQPT: Graphic Displays, Exc Terminals
COMPUTER PERIPHERAL EQPT: Input Or Output
COMPUTER PROGRAMMING SVCS
COMPUTER RELATED MAINTENANCE SVCS
COMPUTER SOFTWARE DEVELOPMENT
COMPUTER SOFTWARE DEVELOPMENT & APPLICATIONS
COMPUTER SOFTWARE SYSTEMS ANALYSIS & DESIGN: Custom
COMPUTER STORAGE DEVICES, NEC
COMPUTER STORAGE UNITS: Auxiliary
COMPUTER SYSTEMS ANALYSIS & DESIGN
COMPUTER TERMINALS
COMPUTER-AIDED MANUFACTURING SYSTEMS SVCS
COMPUTERS, NEC
COMPUTERS, NEC, WHOLESALE
COMPUTERS, PERIPHERALS & SOFTWARE, WHOLESALE: Printers
COMPUTERS, PERIPHERALS & SOFTWARE, WHOLESALE: Software
COMPUTERS: Mini
COMPUTERS: Personal
CONCENTRATES, DRINK
CONCRETE BUGGIES: Powered
CONCRETE MIXERS
CONCRETE PLANTS
CONCRETE PRDTS
CONCRETE PRDTS, PRECAST, NEC
CONCRETE REINFORCING MATERIAL
CONCRETE: Asphaltic, Not From Refineries
CONCRETE: Dry Mixture
CONCRETE: Ready-Mixed
CONDENSERS & CONDENSING UNITS: Air Conditioner
CONDENSERS: Heat Transfer Eqpt, Evaporative

CONDENSERS: Motors Or Generators
CONDUITS & FITTINGS: Electric
CONFECTIONS & CANDY
CONFETTI: Made From Purchased Materials
CONNECTORS & TERMINALS: Electrical Device Uses
CONNECTORS: Electrical
CONNECTORS: Electronic
CONNECTORS: Power, Electric
CONSTRUCTION & MINING MACHINERY WHOLESALERS
CONSTRUCTION EQPT: Airport
CONSTRUCTION EQPT: Attachments
CONSTRUCTION EQPT: Attachments, Backhoe Mounted, Hyd Pwrd
CONSTRUCTION EQPT: Backhoes, Tractors, Cranes & Similar Eqpt
CONSTRUCTION EQPT: Cranes
CONSTRUCTION EQPT: Graders, Road
CONSTRUCTION EQPT: Ladder Ditchers, Vertical Boom Or Wheel
CONSTRUCTION EQPT: Roofing Eqpt
CONSTRUCTION EQPT: Trucks, Off-Highway
CONSTRUCTION EQPT: Wellpoint Systems
CONSTRUCTION EQPT: Wrecker Hoists, Automobile
CONSTRUCTION MATERIALS, WHOL: Concrete/Cinder Bldg Prdts
CONSTRUCTION MATERIALS, WHOLESALE: Aggregate
CONSTRUCTION MATERIALS, WHOLESALE: Air Ducts, Sheet Metal
CONSTRUCTION MATERIALS, WHOLESALE: Awnings
CONSTRUCTION MATERIALS, WHOLESALE: Block, Concrete & Cinder
CONSTRUCTION MATERIALS, WHOLESALE: Blocks, Building, NEC
CONSTRUCTION MATERIALS, WHOLESALE: Brick, Exc Refractory
CONSTRUCTION MATERIALS, WHOLESALE: Building Stone, Granite
CONSTRUCTION MATERIALS, WHOLESALE: Building Stone, Marble
CONSTRUCTION MATERIALS, WHOLESALE: Building, Exterior
CONSTRUCTION MATERIALS, WHOLESALE: Building, Interior
CONSTRUCTION MATERIALS, WHOLESALE: Cement
CONSTRUCTION MATERIALS, WHOLESALE: Ceramic, Exc Refractory
CONSTRUCTION MATERIALS, WHOLESALE: Concrete Mixtures
CONSTRUCTION MATERIALS, WHOLESALE: Door Frames
CONSTRUCTION MATERIALS, WHOLESALE: Drywall Materials
CONSTRUCTION MATERIALS, WHOLESALE: Glass
CONSTRUCTION MATERIALS, WHOLESALE: Gravel
CONSTRUCTION MATERIALS, WHOLESALE: Joists
CONSTRUCTION MATERIALS, WHOLESALE: Limestone
CONSTRUCTION MATERIALS, WHOLESALE: Millwork
CONSTRUCTION MATERIALS, WHOLESALE: Mobile Offices/Comm Units
CONSTRUCTION MATERIALS, WHOLESALE: Molding, All Materials
CONSTRUCTION MATERIALS, WHOLESALE: Pallets, Wood
CONSTRUCTION MATERIALS, WHOLESALE: Paving Materials
CONSTRUCTION MATERIALS, WHOLESALE: Prefabricated Structures
CONSTRUCTION MATERIALS, WHOLESALE: Roof, Asphalt/Sheet Metal
CONSTRUCTION MATERIALS, WHOLESALE: Roofing & Siding Material
CONSTRUCTION MATERIALS, WHOLESALE: Sand
CONSTRUCTION MATERIALS, WHOLESALE: Septic Tanks
CONSTRUCTION MATERIALS, WHOLESALE: Skylights, All Materials
CONSTRUCTION MATERIALS, WHOLESALE: Stone, Crushed Or Broken
CONSTRUCTION MATERIALS, WHOLESALE: Stucco
CONSTRUCTION MATERIALS, WHOLESALE: Tile & Clay Prdts
CONSTRUCTION MATERIALS, WHOLESALE: Tile, Clay/Other Ceramic
CONSTRUCTION MATERIALS, WHOLESALE: Windows
CONSTRUCTION MATLS, WHOL: Doors, Combination, Screen-Storm
CONSTRUCTION MATLS, WHOLESALE: Struct Assy, Prefab, NonWood

CONSTRUCTION MTRLS, WHOL: Exterior Flat Glass, Plate/Window
CONSTRUCTION SAND MINING
CONSTRUCTION SITE PREPARATION SVCS
CONSTRUCTION: Airport Runway
CONSTRUCTION: Bridge
CONSTRUCTION: Commercial & Institutional Building
CONSTRUCTION: Commercial & Office Building, New
CONSTRUCTION: Dams, Waterways, Docks & Other Marine
CONSTRUCTION: Dock
CONSTRUCTION: Drainage System
CONSTRUCTION: Foundation & Retaining Wall
CONSTRUCTION: Heavy Highway & Street
CONSTRUCTION: Indl Building & Warehouse
CONSTRUCTION: Indl Buildings, New, NEC
CONSTRUCTION: Marine
CONSTRUCTION: Nonresidential Buildings, Custom
CONSTRUCTION: Oil & Gas Pipeline Construction
CONSTRUCTION: Parking Lot
CONSTRUCTION: Power & Communication Transmission Tower
CONSTRUCTION: Pumping Station
CONSTRUCTION: Residential, Nec
CONSTRUCTION: Single-Family Housing
CONSTRUCTION: Steel Buildings
CONSTRUCTION: Swimming Pools
CONSTRUCTION: Tennis Court
CONSTRUCTION: Utility Line
CONSTRUCTION: Waste Water & Sewage Treatment Plant
CONSTRUCTION: Water Main
CONSULTING SVC: Business, NEC
CONSULTING SVC: Chemical
CONSULTING SVC: Computer
CONSULTING SVC: Data Processing
CONSULTING SVC: Engineering
CONSULTING SVC: Financial Management
CONSULTING SVC: Management
CONSULTING SVC: Marketing Management
CONSULTING SVC: Online Technology
CONSULTING SVC: Sales Management
CONSULTING SVC: Telecommunications
CONSULTING SVCS, BUSINESS: Communications
CONSULTING SVCS, BUSINESS: Environmental
CONSULTING SVCS, BUSINESS: Lighting
CONSULTING SVCS, BUSINESS: Sys Engnrg, Exc Computer/Prof
CONSULTING SVCS, BUSINESS: Systems Analysis & Engineering
CONSULTING SVCS, BUSINESS: Systems Analysis Or Design
CONSULTING SVCS, BUSINESS: Test Development & Evaluation
CONSULTING SVCS: Oil
CONSULTING SVCS: Scientific
CONTACT LENSES
CONTACTS: Electrical
CONTAINERS, GLASS: Milk Bottles
CONTAINERS, GLASS: Water Bottles
CONTAINERS: Air Cargo, Metal
CONTAINERS: Cargo, Wood
CONTAINERS: Cargo, Wood & Metal Combination
CONTAINERS: Cargo, Wood & Wood With Metal
CONTAINERS: Corrugated
CONTAINERS: Foil, Bakery Goods & Frozen Foods
CONTAINERS: Food & Beverage
CONTAINERS: Food, Folding, Made From Purchased Materials
CONTAINERS: Frozen Food, Made From Purchased Materials
CONTAINERS: Glass
CONTAINERS: Ice Cream, Made From Purchased Materials
CONTAINERS: Liquid Tight Fiber, From Purchased Materials
CONTAINERS: Metal
CONTAINERS: Plastic
CONTAINERS: Sanitary, Food
CONTAINERS: Shipping & Mailing, Fiber
CONTAINERS: Shipping, Wood
CONTAINERS: Wood
CONTRACT FOOD SVCS
CONTRACTOR: Rigging & Scaffolding
CONTRACTORS: Access Control System Eqpt
CONTRACTORS: Access Flooring System Installation
CONTRACTORS: Acoustical & Insulation Work
CONTRACTORS: Appliance Installation
CONTRACTORS: Artificial Turf Installation

CONTRACTORS: Asphalt
CONTRACTORS: Awning Installation
CONTRACTORS: Banking Machine Installation & Svc
CONTRACTORS: Building Eqpt & Machinery Installation
CONTRACTORS: Building Sign Installation & Mntnce
CONTRACTORS: Cable Laying
CONTRACTORS: Cable Splicing Svcs
CONTRACTORS: Carpentry Work
CONTRACTORS: Carpentry, Cabinet & Finish Work
CONTRACTORS: Carpentry, Cabinet Building & Installation
CONTRACTORS: Carpentry, Finish & Trim Work
CONTRACTORS: Ceramic Floor Tile Installation
CONTRACTORS: Commercial & Office Building
CONTRACTORS: Computer Installation
CONTRACTORS: Computer Power Conditioning Svcs
CONTRACTORS: Computerized Controls Installation
CONTRACTORS: Concrete
CONTRACTORS: Concrete Pumping
CONTRACTORS: Concrete Reinforcement Placing
CONTRACTORS: Concrete Repair
CONTRACTORS: Construction Site Cleanup
CONTRACTORS: Countertop Installation
CONTRACTORS: Directional Oil & Gas Well Drilling Svc
CONTRACTORS: Dock Eqpt Installation, Indl
CONTRACTORS: Electric Power Systems
CONTRACTORS: Electrical
CONTRACTORS: Electronic Controls Installation
CONTRACTORS: Energy Management Control
CONTRACTORS: Excavating
CONTRACTORS: Exterior Concrete Stucco
CONTRACTORS: Exterior Insulation & Finish Application
CONTRACTORS: Fence Construction
CONTRACTORS: Fiber Optic Cable Installation
CONTRACTORS: Fiberglass Work
CONTRACTORS: Fire Detection & Burglar Alarm Systems
CONTRACTORS: Floor Laying & Other Floor Work
CONTRACTORS: Flooring
CONTRACTORS: Foundation & Footing
CONTRACTORS: Garage Doors
CONTRACTORS: Gas Detection & Analysis Svcs
CONTRACTORS: Gas Field Svcs, NEC
CONTRACTORS: General Electric
CONTRACTORS: Glass Tinting, Architectural & Automotive
CONTRACTORS: Glass, Glazing & Tinting
CONTRACTORS: Gutters & Downspouts
CONTRACTORS: Heating & Air Conditioning
CONTRACTORS: Highway & Street Construction, General
CONTRACTORS: Highway Sign & Guardrail Construction & Install
CONTRACTORS: Home & Office Intrs Finish, Furnish/Remodel
CONTRACTORS: Hydraulic Eqpt Installation & Svcs
CONTRACTORS: Hydraulic Well Fracturing Svcs
CONTRACTORS: Indl Building Renovation, Remodeling & Repair
CONTRACTORS: Kitchen & Bathroom Remodeling
CONTRACTORS: Kitchen Cabinet Installation
CONTRACTORS: Machinery Installation
CONTRACTORS: Marble Installation, Interior
CONTRACTORS: Masonry & Stonework
CONTRACTORS: Mechanical
CONTRACTORS: Millwrights
CONTRACTORS: Multi-Family Home Remodeling
CONTRACTORS: Nonresidential Building Design & Construction
CONTRACTORS: Office Furniture Installation
CONTRACTORS: Oil & Gas Aerial Geophysical Exploration Svcs
CONTRACTORS: Oil & Gas Building, Repairing & Dismantling Svc
CONTRACTORS: Oil & Gas Field Salt Water Impound/Storing Svc
CONTRACTORS: Oil & Gas Well Casing Cement Svcs
CONTRACTORS: Oil & Gas Well Drilling Svc
CONTRACTORS: Oil & Gas Well Flow Rate Measurement Svcs
CONTRACTORS: Oil & Gas Well Redrilling
CONTRACTORS: Oil & Gas Wells Svcs
CONTRACTORS: Oil Field Haulage Svcs
CONTRACTORS: Oil Field Lease Tanks: Erectg, Clng/Rprg Svcs
CONTRACTORS: Oil Field Pipe Testing Svcs
CONTRACTORS: Oil/Gas Field Casing,Tube/Rod Running,Cut/Pull

CONTRACTORS: Oil/Gas Well Construction, Rpr/Dismantling Svcs
CONTRACTORS: On-Site Welding
CONTRACTORS: Ornamental Metal Work
CONTRACTORS: Painting & Wall Covering
CONTRACTORS: Painting, Commercial, Exterior
CONTRACTORS: Painting, Commercial, Interior
CONTRACTORS: Painting, Indl
CONTRACTORS: Painting, Residential
CONTRACTORS: Parking Lot Maintenance
CONTRACTORS: Patio & Deck Construction & Repair
CONTRACTORS: Pile Driving
CONTRACTORS: Playground Construction & Eqpt Installation
CONTRACTORS: Pole Cutting
CONTRACTORS: Post Disaster Renovations
CONTRACTORS: Precast Concrete Struct Framing & Panel Placing
CONTRACTORS: Prefabricated Window & Door Installation
CONTRACTORS: Pulpwood, Engaged In Cutting
CONTRACTORS: Refrigeration
CONTRACTORS: Roofing
CONTRACTORS: Roofing & Gutter Work
CONTRACTORS: Roustabout Svcs
CONTRACTORS: Safety & Security Eqpt
CONTRACTORS: Sandblasting Svc, Building Exteriors
CONTRACTORS: Screening, Window & Door
CONTRACTORS: Septic System
CONTRACTORS: Sheet Metal Work, NEC
CONTRACTORS: Single-family Home General Remodeling
CONTRACTORS: Solar Energy Eqpt
CONTRACTORS: Special Trades, NEC
CONTRACTORS: Store Front Construction
CONTRACTORS: Structural Steel Erection
CONTRACTORS: Stucco, Interior
CONTRACTORS: Svc Well Drilling Svcs
CONTRACTORS: Textile Warping
CONTRACTORS: Tile Installation, Ceramic
CONTRACTORS: Underground Utilities
CONTRACTORS: Unit Paver Installation
CONTRACTORS: Warm Air Heating & Air Conditioning
CONTRACTORS: Water Well Drilling
CONTRACTORS: Water Well Servicing
CONTRACTORS: Window Treatment Installation
CONTRACTORS: Windows & Doors
CONTRACTORS: Wood Floor Installation & Refinishing
CONTRACTORS: Wrecking & Demolition
CONTROL CIRCUIT DEVICES
CONTROL EQPT: Electric
CONTROL EQPT: Electric Buses & Locomotives
CONTROL PANELS: Electrical
CONTROLS & ACCESS: Indl, Electric
CONTROLS & ACCESS: Motor
CONTROLS: Air Flow, Refrigeration
CONTROLS: Automatic Temperature
CONTROLS: Electric Motor
CONTROLS: Environmental
CONTROLS: Marine & Navy, Auxiliary
CONTROLS: Relay & Ind
CONTROLS: Remote, Boat
CONTROLS: Thermostats
CONTROLS: Thermostats, Exc Built-in
CONTROLS: Truck, Indl Battery
CONTROLS: Water Heater
CONVERTERS: Data
CONVERTERS: Frequency
CONVERTERS: Power, AC to DC
CONVEYOR SYSTEMS
CONVEYOR SYSTEMS: Pneumatic Tube
CONVEYOR SYSTEMS: Robotic
CONVEYORS & CONVEYING EQPT
COOKING & FOOD WARMING EQPT: Commercial
COOKING & FOODWARMING EQPT: Coffee Brewing
COOKING & FOODWARMING EQPT: Commercial
COOKING & FOODWARMING EQPT: Microwave Ovens, Commercial
COOKING EQPT, HOUSEHOLD: Convection Ovens, Incldg Portable
COOKING EQPT, HOUSEHOLD: Ranges, Electric
COOKWARE: Fine Earthenware
COOLERS & ICE CHESTS: Polystyrene Foam
COOLING TOWERS: Wood
COPPER ORE MINING
COPPER ORES
COPPER: Rolling & Drawing
CORD & TWINE

CORK & CORK PRDTS
CORK & CORK PRDTS: Tiles
CORRUGATED PRDTS: Boxes, Partition, Display Items, Sheet/Pad
COSMETIC PREPARATIONS
COSMETICS & TOILETRIES
COSMETICS WHOLESALERS
COSMETOLOGY & PERSONAL HYGIENE SALONS
COSTUME JEWELRY & NOVELTIES: Apparel, Exc Precious Metals
COSTUME JEWELRY & NOVELTIES: Bracelets, Exc Precious Metals
COSTUME JEWELRY & NOVELTIES: Exc Semi & Precious
COSTUME JEWELRY & NOVELTIES: Pins, Exc Precious Metals
COUGH MEDICINES
COUNTER & SINK TOPS
COUNTERS & COUNTING DEVICES
COUNTERS OR COUNTER DISPLAY CASES, EXC WOOD
COUNTERS OR COUNTER DISPLAY CASES, WOOD
COUNTING DEVICES: Gauges, Press Temp Corrections Computing
COUNTING DEVICES: Production
COUNTING DEVICES: Tally
COUPLINGS: Hose & Tube, Hydraulic Or Pneumatic
COURIER SVCS, AIR: Package Delivery, Private
COVERS: Automobile Seat
COVERS: Automotive, Exc Seat & Tire
COVERS: Canvas
COVERS: Hot Tub & Spa
CRADLES: Boat
CRANE & AERIAL LIFT SVCS
CRANES & MONORAIL SYSTEMS
CRANES: Indl Plant
CRANES: Overhead
CRANKSHAFTS & CAMSHAFTS: Machining
CRANKSHAFTS: Motor Vehicle
CRATES: Fruit, Wood Wirebound
CRUDE PETROLEUM & NATURAL GAS PRODUCTION
CRUDE PETROLEUM & NATURAL GAS PRODUCTION
CRUDE PETROLEUM PRODUCTION
CRYSTALS
CRYSTALS & CRYSTAL ASSEMBLIES: Radio
CUBICLES: Electric Switchboard Eqpt
CULTURE MEDIA
CULVERTS: Sheet Metal
CUPS & PLATES: Foamed Plastics
CUPS: Plastic Exc Polystyrene Foam
CURBING: Granite Or Stone
CURLING FEATHERS
CURTAIN & DRAPERY FIXTURES: Poles, Rods & Rollers
CURTAIN WALLS: Building, Steel
CUSHIONS & PILLOWS
CUSHIONS & PILLOWS: Bed, From Purchased Materials
CUSHIONS & PILLOWS: Boat
CUSHIONS: Carpet & Rug, Foamed Plastics
CUSHIONS: Textile, Exc Spring & Carpet
CUT STONE & STONE PRODUCTS
CUTLERY
CUTLERY, STAINLESS STEEL
CYLINDER & ACTUATORS: Fluid Power

D

DAIRY PRDTS STORE: Ice Cream, Packaged
DAIRY PRDTS WHOLESALERS: Fresh
DAIRY PRDTS: Butter
DAIRY PRDTS: Cheese
DAIRY PRDTS: Cream Substitutes
DAIRY PRDTS: Custard, Frozen
DAIRY PRDTS: Dairy Based Desserts, Frozen
DAIRY PRDTS: Dietary Supplements, Dairy & Non-Dairy Based
DAIRY PRDTS: Dried & Powdered Milk & Milk Prdts
DAIRY PRDTS: Fermented & Cultured Milk Prdts
DAIRY PRDTS: Frozen Desserts & Novelties
DAIRY PRDTS: Ice Cream & Ice Milk
DAIRY PRDTS: Ice Cream, Bulk
DAIRY PRDTS: Ice Cream, Packaged, Molded, On Sticks, Etc.
DAIRY PRDTS: Milk, Chocolate
DAIRY PRDTS: Milk, Condensed & Evaporated
DAIRY PRDTS: Milk, Fluid
DAIRY PRDTS: Milk, Processed, Pasteurized, Homogenized/Btld
DAIRY PRDTS: Natural Cheese

DAIRY PRDTS: Processed Cheese
DAIRY PRDTS: Spreads, Cheese
DAIRY PRDTS: Whey, Powdered
DAIRY PRDTS: Yogurt, Exc Frozen
DAIRY PRDTS: Yogurt, Frozen
DATA PROCESSING & PREPARATION SVCS
DATA PROCESSING SVCS
DAVITS
DECORATIVE WOOD & WOODWORK
DEFENSE SYSTEMS & EQPT
DEGREASING MACHINES
DEHYDRATION EQPT
DENTAL EQPT
DENTAL EQPT & SPLYS
DENTAL EQPT & SPLYS WHOLESALERS
DENTAL EQPT & SPLYS: Autoclaves
DENTAL EQPT & SPLYS: Dental Materials
DENTAL EQPT & SPLYS: Enamels
DENTAL EQPT & SPLYS: Impression Materials
DENTAL EQPT & SPLYS: Laboratory
DENTAL EQPT & SPLYS: Metal
DENTAL EQPT & SPLYS: Orthodontic Appliances
DENTAL EQPT & SPLYS: Sterilizers
DENTAL EQPT & SPLYS: Tools, NEC
DENTAL INSTRUMENT REPAIR SVCS
DEPARTMENT STORES: Army-Navy Goods
DERMATOLOGICALS
DERRICKS
DESIGN SVCS, NEC
DESIGN SVCS: Commercial & Indl
DESIGN SVCS: Computer Integrated Systems
DETECTION APPARATUS: Electronic/Magnetic Field, Light/Heat
DETECTION EQPT: Aeronautical Electronic Field
DETECTIVE & ARMORED CAR SERVICES
DETECTORS: Water Leak
DIAGNOSTIC SUBSTANCES
DIAGNOSTIC SUBSTANCES OR AGENTS: Enzyme & Isoenzyme
DIAGNOSTIC SUBSTANCES OR AGENTS: Hematology
DIAGNOSTIC SUBSTANCES OR AGENTS: In Vitro
DIAGNOSTIC SUBSTANCES OR AGENTS: In Vivo
DIAGNOSTIC SUBSTANCES OR AGENTS: Microbiology & Virology
DIAGNOSTIC SUBSTANCES OR AGENTS: Radioactive
DIAMONDS: Cutting & Polishing
DIAPERS: Disposable
DIATOMACEOUS EARTH: Ground Or Treated
DICE & DICE CUPS
DIE CUTTING SVC: Paper
DIE SETS: Presses, Metal Stamping
DIES & TOOLS: Special
DIES: Cutting, Exc Metal
DIES: Steel Rule
DIETICIANS' OFFICES
DIMENSION STONE: Buildings
DIODES: Light Emitting
DIODES: Solid State, Germanium, Silicon, Etc
DIRECT SELLING ESTABLISHMENTS, NEC
DIRECT SELLING ESTABLISHMENTS: Bakery Goods, House-To-House
DIRECT SELLING ESTABLISHMENTS: Encyclopedias & Publications
DIRECT SELLING ESTABLISHMENTS: Food Svcs
DIRECT SELLING ESTABLISHMENTS: Snacks
DISCS & TAPE: Optical, Blank
DISHWASHING EQPT: Commercial
DISK DRIVES: Computer
DISPENSERS, TISSUE: Plastic
DISPENSERS: Soap
DISPENSING EQPT & PARTS, BEVERAGE: Coolers, Milk/Water, Elec
DISPENSING EQPT & PARTS, BEVERAGE: Fountain/Other Beverage
DISPLAY FIXTURES: Wood
DISPLAY ITEMS: Corrugated, Made From Purchased Materials
DISPLAY LETTERING SVCS
DISPLAY STANDS: Merchandise, Exc Wood
DISTANCE MEASURING EQPT OR DME: Aeronautical
DISTILLATION PRDTS: Wood
DISTILLERS DRIED GRAIN & SOLUBLES
DISTRIBUTORS: Motor Vehicle Engine
DIVING EQPT STORES
DOCK EQPT & SPLYS, INDL

DOCKS: Floating, Wood
DOCKS: Prefabricated Metal
DOCUMENT DESTRUCTION SVC
DOCUMENT EMBOSSING SVCS
DOLOMITE: Crushed & Broken
DOLOMITE: Dimension
DOOR & WINDOW REPAIR SVCS
DOOR FRAMES: Wood
DOOR MATS: Rubber
DOOR OPERATING SYSTEMS: Electric
DOOR PARTS: Sashes, Wood
DOORS & WINDOWS WHOLESALERS: All Materials
DOORS & WINDOWS: Screen & Storm
DOORS & WINDOWS: Storm, Metal
DOORS: Fiberglass
DOORS: Fire, Metal
DOORS: Garage, Overhead, Metal
DOORS: Garage, Overhead, Wood
DOORS: Glass
DOORS: Hangar, Metal
DOORS: Rolling, Indl Building Or Warehouse, Metal
DOORS: Screen, Metal
DOORS: Wooden
DRAINAGE PRDTS: Concrete
DRAPERIES & CURTAINS
DRAPERIES & DRAPERY FABRICS, COTTON
DRAPERIES: Plastic & Textile, From Purchased Materials
DRAPERY & UPHOLSTERY STORES: Draperies
DRAPES & DRAPERY FABRICS, FROM MANMADE FIBER
DRILL BITS
DRILLING MACHINERY & EQPT: Oil & Gas
DRILLING MACHINERY & EQPT: Water Well
DRILLS & DRILLING EQPT: Mining
DRILLS: Core
DRINK MIXES, NONALCOHOLIC: Cocktail
DRINKING PLACES: Bars & Lounges
DRINKING PLACES: Wine Bar
DRIVE SHAFTS
DRIVES: High Speed Indl, Exc Hydrostatic
DRUG STORES
DRUG TESTING KITS: Blood & Urine
DRUGS & DRUG PROPRIETARIES, WHOLESALE: Bandages
DRUGS & DRUG PROPRIETARIES, WHOLESALE: Medicinals/Botanicals
DRUGS & DRUG PROPRIETARIES, WHOLESALE: Pharmaceuticals
DRUGS & DRUG PROPRIETARIES, WHOLESALE: Vitamins & Minerals
DRUGS: Parasitic & Infective Disease Affecting
DRUMS: Brake
DRUMS: Fiber
DRYCLEANING & LAUNDRY SVCS: Commercial & Family
DRYCLEANING EQPT & SPLYS WHOLESALERS
DRYCLEANING EQPT & SPLYS: Commercial
DRYERS & REDRYERS: Indl
DUCTS: Sheet Metal
DUMPSTERS: Garbage
DYES & PIGMENTS: Organic
DYES & TINTS: Household
DYES OR COLORS: Food, Synthetic

E

EATING PLACES
EDUCATIONAL SVCS
ELASTOMERS
ELECTRIC MOTOR REPAIR SVCS
ELECTRIC POWER DISTRIBUTION TO CONSUMERS
ELECTRIC SERVICES
ELECTRIC WATER HEATERS WHOLESALERS
ELECTRICAL APPARATUS & EQPT WHOLESALERS
ELECTRICAL APPLIANCES, TELEVISIONS & RADIOS WHOLESALERS
ELECTRICAL CURRENT CARRYING WIRING DEVICES
ELECTRICAL DISCHARGE MACHINING, EDM
ELECTRICAL EQPT & SPLYS
ELECTRICAL EQPT FOR ENGINES
ELECTRICAL EQPT REPAIR & MAINTENANCE
ELECTRICAL EQPT REPAIR SVCS
ELECTRICAL EQPT: Automotive, NEC
ELECTRICAL EQPT: Household
ELECTRICAL GOODS, WHOLESALE: Answering Machines, Telephone
ELECTRICAL GOODS, WHOLESALE: Boxes & Fittings
ELECTRICAL GOODS, WHOLESALE: Cable Conduit

ELECTRICAL GOODS, WHOLESALE: Capacitors
ELECTRICAL GOODS, WHOLESALE: Connectors
ELECTRICAL GOODS, WHOLESALE: Electrical Appliances, Major
ELECTRICAL GOODS, WHOLESALE: Electronic Parts
ELECTRICAL GOODS, WHOLESALE: Fire Alarm Systems
ELECTRICAL GOODS, WHOLESALE: Fittings & Construction Mat
ELECTRICAL GOODS, WHOLESALE: Flashlights
ELECTRICAL GOODS, WHOLESALE: Garbage Disposals
ELECTRICAL GOODS, WHOLESALE: Generators
ELECTRICAL GOODS, WHOLESALE: Household Appliances, NEC
ELECTRICAL GOODS, WHOLESALE: Light Bulbs & Related Splys
ELECTRICAL GOODS, WHOLESALE: Lighting Fixtures, Comm & Indl
ELECTRICAL GOODS, WHOLESALE: Lugs & Connectors
ELECTRICAL GOODS, WHOLESALE: Mobile telephone Eqpt
ELECTRICAL GOODS, WHOLESALE: Motor Ctrls, Starters & Relays
ELECTRICAL GOODS, WHOLESALE: Motors
ELECTRICAL GOODS, WHOLESALE: Panelboards
ELECTRICAL GOODS, WHOLESALE: Radio & TV Or TV Eqpt & Parts
ELECTRICAL GOODS, WHOLESALE: Security Control Eqpt & Systems
ELECTRICAL GOODS, WHOLESALE: Semiconductor Devices
ELECTRICAL GOODS, WHOLESALE: Switchboards
ELECTRICAL GOODS, WHOLESALE: Switchgear
ELECTRICAL GOODS, WHOLESALE: Telephone & Telegraphic Eqpt
ELECTRICAL GOODS, WHOLESALE: Telephone Eqpt
ELECTRICAL GOODS, WHOLESALE: Transformer & Transmission Eqpt
ELECTRICAL GOODS, WHOLESALE: Transformers
ELECTRICAL GOODS, WHOLESALE: Tubes, Rcvg & Txmtg Or Indl
ELECTRICAL GOODS, WHOLESALE: Video Eqpt
ELECTRICAL GOODS, WHOLESALE: Wire & Cable
ELECTRICAL GOODS, WHOLESALE: Wire/Cable, Telephone/Telegraph
ELECTRICAL INDL APPARATUS, NEC
ELECTRICAL MEASURING INSTRUMENT REPAIR & CALIBRATION SVCS
ELECTRICAL SPLYS
ELECTRICAL SUPPLIES: Porcelain
ELECTROMEDICAL EQPT
ELECTROMETALLURGICAL PRDTS
ELECTRON BEAM: Cutting, Forming, Welding
ELECTRON TUBES
ELECTRON TUBES: Cathode Ray
ELECTRONIC COMPONENTS
ELECTRONIC DETECTION SYSTEMS: Aeronautical
ELECTRONIC DEVICES: Solid State, NEC
ELECTRONIC EQPT REPAIR SVCS
ELECTRONIC LOADS & POWER SPLYS
ELECTRONIC PARTS & EQPT WHOLESALERS
ELECTRONIC SECRETARIES
ELECTRONIC SHOPPING
ELECTRONIC TRAINING DEVICES
ELECTROPLATING & PLATING SVC
ELEMENTARY & SECONDARY MILITARY ACADEMIES
ELEMENTARY & SECONDARY SCHOOLS, PUBLIC
ELEMENTARY & SECONDARY SCHOOLS, SPECIAL EDUCATION
ELEVATORS & EQPT
ELEVATORS: Automobile
ELEVATORS: Stair, Motor Powered
EMBALMING FLUID
EMBLEMS: Embroidered
EMBOSSING SVC: Paper
EMBROIDERING & ART NEEDLEWORK FOR THE TRADE
EMBROIDERING SVC
EMBROIDERING SVC: Schiffli Machine
EMBROIDERY ADVERTISING SVCS
EMBROIDERY KITS
EMERGENCY ALARMS
EMERGENCY SHELTERS
EMPLOYMENT AGENCY SVCS
EMPLOYMENT SVCS: Labor Contractors
ENAMELS
ENCLOSURES: Electronic
ENCLOSURES: Screen

ENGINE PARTS & ACCESS: Internal Combustion
ENGINE REBUILDING: Diesel
ENGINE REBUILDING: Gas
ENGINEERING SVCS
ENGINEERING SVCS: Acoustical
ENGINEERING SVCS: Aviation Or Aeronautical
ENGINEERING SVCS: Chemical
ENGINEERING SVCS: Electrical Or Electronic
ENGINEERING SVCS: Energy conservation
ENGINEERING SVCS: Industrial
ENGINEERING SVCS: Marine
ENGINEERING SVCS: Mechanical
ENGINEERING SVCS: Petroleum
ENGINEERING SVCS: Professional
ENGINEERING SVCS: Sanitary
ENGINES & ENGINE PARTS: Guided Missile
ENGINES: Diesel & Semi-Diesel Or Duel Fuel
ENGINES: Gasoline, NEC
ENGINES: Internal Combustion, NEC
ENGINES: Jet Propulsion
ENGINES: Marine
ENGRAVING SVC, NEC
ENGRAVING SVC: Jewelry & Personal Goods
ENGRAVING SVCS
ENGRAVING: Currency
ENGRAVINGS: Plastic
ENTERTAINERS & ENTERTAINMENT GROUPS
ENTERTAINMENT GROUP
ENTERTAINMENT PROMOTION SVCS
ENVELOPES
ENZYMES
EPOXY RESINS
EQUIPMENT: Pedestrian Traffic Control
EQUIPMENT: Rental & Leasing, NEC
ETCHING & ENGRAVING SVC
ETCHING SVC: Metal
ETCHING SVC: Photochemical
ETHERS
ETHYLENE-PROPYLENE RUBBERS: EPDM Polymers
EXCAVATING EQPT
EXHAUST SYSTEMS: Eqpt & Parts
EXPLOSIVES
EXPLOSIVES: Secondary High
EXTENSION CORDS
EXTRACTS, FLAVORING
EYEGLASSES
EYEGLASSES: Sunglasses
EYELASHES, ARTIFICIAL

F

FABRIC SOFTENERS
FABRICATED METAL PRODUCTS, NEC
FABRICS: Apparel & Outerwear, Broadwoven
FABRICS: Apparel & Outerwear, Cotton
FABRICS: Apparel & Outerwear, From Manmade Fiber Or Silk
FABRICS: Awning Stripes, Cotton
FABRICS: Bags & Bagging, Cotton
FABRICS: Balloon Cloth, Cotton
FABRICS: Broadwoven, Cotton
FABRICS: Broadwoven, Synthetic Manmade Fiber & Silk
FABRICS: Broadwoven, Wool
FABRICS: Canvas
FABRICS: Chemically Coated & Treated
FABRICS: Coated Or Treated
FABRICS: Cotton, Narrow
FABRICS: Decorative Trim & Specialty, Including Twist Weave
FABRICS: Denims
FABRICS: Felts, Blanketing & Upholstery, Wool
FABRICS: Fiberglass, Broadwoven
FABRICS: Furniture Denim
FABRICS: Gauze
FABRICS: Ginghams
FABRICS: Glass & Fiberglass, Broadwoven
FABRICS: Hand Woven
FABRICS: Jean
FABRICS: Lace & Lace Prdts
FABRICS: Lace, Knit, NEC
FABRICS: Laminated
FABRICS: Lawns, Cotton
FABRICS: Metallized
FABRICS: Nonwoven
FABRICS: Nylon, Broadwoven
FABRICS: Polyethylene, Broadwoven
FABRICS: Print, Cotton
FABRICS: Resin Or Plastic Coated

FABRICS: Sail Cloth
FABRICS: Satin
FABRICS: Scrub Cloths
FABRICS: Shirting, From Manmade Fiber Or Silk
FABRICS: Specialty Including Twisted Weaves, Broadwoven
FABRICS: Tapestry, Cotton
FABRICS: Trimmings
FABRICS: Trimmings, Textile
FABRICS: Umbrella Cloth, Cotton
FABRICS: Upholstery, Cotton
FABRICS: Varnished Glass & Coated Fiberglass
FABRICS: Woven, Narrow Cotton, Wool, Silk
FACIAL SALONS
FACILITIES SUPPORT SVCS
FAMILY CLOTHING STORES
FANS, BLOWING: Indl Or Commercial
FANS, VENTILATING: Indl Or Commercial
FANS: Ceiling
FARM MACHINERY REPAIR SVCS
FARM SPLY STORES
FARM SPLYS WHOLESALERS
FARM SPLYS, WHOLESALE: Feed
FARM SPLYS, WHOLESALE: Fertilizers & Agricultural Chemicals
FARM SPLYS, WHOLESALE: Garden Splys
FASTENERS WHOLESALERS
FASTENERS: Metal
FASTENERS: Notions, NEC
FASTENERS: Notions, Zippers
FASTENERS: Wire, Made From Purchased Wire
FATTY ACID ESTERS & AMINOS
FAUCETS & SPIGOTS: Metal & Plastic
FEATHERS & FEATHER PRODUCTS
FELT: Acoustic
FENCE POSTS: Iron & Steel
FENCES & FENCING MATERIALS
FENCES OR POSTS: Ornamental Iron Or Steel
FENCING DEALERS
FENCING MADE IN WIREDRAWING PLANTS
FENCING MATERIALS: Docks & Other Outdoor Prdts, Wood
FENCING MATERIALS: Plastic
FENCING MATERIALS: Wood
FERROSILICON, EXC MADE IN BLAST FURNACES
FERTILIZER MINERAL MINING
FERTILIZERS: NEC
FERTILIZERS: Nitrogen Solutions
FERTILIZERS: Nitrogenous
FERTILIZERS: Phosphatic
FIBER & FIBER PRDTS: Acrylic
FIBER & FIBER PRDTS: Organic, Noncellulose
FIBER & FIBER PRDTS: Protein
FIBER & FIBER PRDTS: Synthetic Cellulosic
FIBER & FIBER PRDTS: Vinyl
FIBER OPTICS
FIBER PRDTS: Pressed, Wood Pulp, From Purchased Materials
FIBERS: Carbon & Graphite
FILLERS & SEALERS: Putty
FILM & SHEET: Unsupported Plastic
FILM: Motion Picture
FILTERS
FILTERS & SOFTENERS: Water, Household
FILTERS & STRAINERS: Pipeline
FILTERS: Air
FILTERS: Air Intake, Internal Combustion Engine, Exc Auto
FILTERS: Gasoline, Internal Combustion Engine, Exc Auto
FILTERS: General Line, Indl
FILTERS: Motor Vehicle
FILTRATION DEVICES: Electronic
FINANCIAL INVESTMENT ADVICE
FINDINGS & TRIMMINGS: Apparel
FINDINGS & TRIMMINGS: Fabric
FINGERNAILS, ARTIFICIAL
FINGERPRINT EQPT
FINISHING AGENTS
FINISHING AGENTS: Textile
FIRE ARMS, SMALL: Guns Or Gun Parts, 30 mm & Below
FIRE ARMS, SMALL: Machine Guns & Grenade Launchers
FIRE CONTROL EQPT REPAIR SVCS, MILITARY
FIRE CONTROL OR BOMBING EQPT: Electronic
FIRE DETECTION SYSTEMS
FIRE OR BURGLARY RESISTIVE PRDTS
FIRE PROTECTION EQPT
FIREARMS & AMMUNITION, EXC SPORTING, WHOLESALE
FIREARMS: Large, Greater Than 30mm

INDEX

FOUNDRIES: Steel Investment
FOUNDRY MACHINERY & EQPT
FOUNTAINS, METAL, EXC DRINKING
FOUNTAINS: Concrete
FOUNTAINS: Plaster Of Paris
FRACTIONATION PRDTS OF CRUDE PETROLEUM, HY-
   DROCARBONS, NEC
FRAMES & FRAMING WHOLESALE
FRANCHISES, SELLING OR LICENSING
FREIGHT FORWARDING ARRANGEMENTS
FREIGHT FORWARDING ARRANGEMENTS: Foreign
FREIGHT TRANSPORTATION ARRANGEMENTS
FREON
FRICTION MATERIAL, MADE FROM POWDERED METAL
FRITS
FRUITS & VEGETABLES WHOLESALERS: Fresh
FUEL ADDITIVES
FUEL TREATING
FUEL: Rocket Engine, Organic
FUELS: Diesel
FUELS: Ethanol
FUELS: Gas, Liquefied
FUELS: Jet
FUELS: Oil
FUNGICIDES OR HERBICIDES
FUR: Apparel
FURNACES & OVENS: Indl
FURNITURE & CABINET STORES: Cabinets, Custom Work
FURNITURE & CABINET STORES: Custom
FURNITURE & FIXTURES Factory
FURNITURE COMPONENTS: Porcelain Enameled
FURNITURE PARTS: Metal
FURNITURE STOCK & PARTS: Carvings, Wood
FURNITURE STOCK & PARTS: Chair Seats, Hardwood
FURNITURE STOCK & PARTS: Dimension Stock, Hardwood
FURNITURE STOCK & PARTS: Frames, Upholstered Furni-
   ture, Wood
FURNITURE STOCK & PARTS: Hardwood
FURNITURE STORES
FURNITURE STORES: Cabinets, Kitchen, Exc Custom Made
FURNITURE STORES: Custom Made, Exc Cabinets
FURNITURE STORES: Office
FURNITURE STORES: Outdoor & Garden
FURNITURE UPHOLSTERY REPAIR SVCS
FURNITURE WHOLESALERS
FURNITURE, BARBER & BEAUTY SHOP
FURNITURE, CHURCH: Concrete
FURNITURE, HOUSEHOLD: Wholesalers
FURNITURE, OUTDOOR & LAWN: Wholesalers
FURNITURE, WHOLESALE: Chairs
FURNITURE, WHOLESALE: Lockers
FURNITURE, WHOLESALE: Restaurant, NEC
FURNITURE, WHOLESALE: Waterbeds
FURNITURE: Assembly Hall
FURNITURE: Backs & Seats, Metal Household
FURNITURE: Bar furniture
FURNITURE: Bean Bag Chairs
FURNITURE: Bed Frames & Headboards, Wood
FURNITURE: Bedroom, Wood
FURNITURE: Beds, Household, Incl Folding & Cabinet, Metal
FURNITURE: Box Springs, Assembled
FURNITURE: Buffets
FURNITURE: Cabinets & Filing Drawers, Office, Exc Wood
FURNITURE: Cabinets & Vanities, Medicine, Metal
FURNITURE: Chairs & Couches, Wood, Upholstered
FURNITURE: Chairs, Dental
FURNITURE: Chairs, Household Upholstered
FURNITURE: Chairs, Household Wood
FURNITURE: Chairs, Office Exc Wood
FURNITURE: Chairs, Office Wood
FURNITURE: Chests, Cedar
FURNITURE: Desks, Wood
FURNITURE: Fiberglass & Plastic
FURNITURE: Frames, Box Springs Or Bedsprings, Metal
FURNITURE: Garden, Exc Wood, Metal, Stone Or Concrete
FURNITURE: Hospital
FURNITURE: Hotel
FURNITURE: Household, Metal
FURNITURE: Household, Upholstered On Metal Frames
FURNITURE: Household, Upholstered, Exc Wood Or Metal
FURNITURE: Household, Wood
FURNITURE: Hydraulic Barber & Beauty Shop Chairs
FURNITURE: Institutional, Exc Wood
FURNITURE: Kitchen & Dining Room
FURNITURE: Kitchen & Dining Room, Metal

FURNITURE: Lawn & Garden, Except Wood & Metal
FURNITURE: Lawn & Garden, Metal
FURNITURE: Lawn, Metal
FURNITURE: Lawn, Wood
FURNITURE: Living Room, Upholstered On Wood Frames
FURNITURE: Mattresses & Foundations
FURNITURE: Mattresses, Box & Bedsprings
FURNITURE: Mattresses, Innerspring Or Box Spring
FURNITURE: NEC
FURNITURE: Novelty, Wood
FURNITURE: Office Panel Systems, Exc Wood
FURNITURE: Office Panel Systems, Wood
FURNITURE: Office, Exc Wood
FURNITURE: Office, Wood
FURNITURE: Rattan
FURNITURE: Restaurant
FURNITURE: School
FURNITURE: Ship
FURNITURE: Sleep
FURNITURE: Stadium
FURNITURE: Stools, Household, Wood
FURNITURE: Storage Chests, Household, Wood
FURNITURE: Table Tops, Marble
FURNITURE: Tables & Table Tops, Wood
FURNITURE: Theater
FURNITURE: Unfinished, Wood
FURNITURE: Upholstered
FURNITURE: Vanity Dressers, Wood
FURNITURE: Wicker & Rattan
FUSES: Electric
Furs

G

GAMES & TOYS: Automobiles, Children's, Pedal Driven
GAMES & TOYS: Banks
GAMES & TOYS: Board Games, Children's & Adults'
GAMES & TOYS: Craft & Hobby Kits & Sets
GAMES & TOYS: Dolls & Doll Clothing
GAMES & TOYS: Dolls, Exc Stuffed Toy Animals
GAMES & TOYS: Electronic
GAMES & TOYS: Game Machines, Exc Coin-Operated
GAMES & TOYS: Go-Carts, Children's
GAMES & TOYS: Hobby Horses
GAMES & TOYS: Kits, Science, Incl Microscopes/Chemistry
   Sets
GAMES & TOYS: Miniature Dolls, Collectors'
GAMES & TOYS: Models, Airplane, Toy & Hobby
GAMES & TOYS: Models, Boat & Ship, Toy & Hobby
GAMES & TOYS: Musical Instruments
GAMES & TOYS: Puzzles
GAMES & TOYS: Scooters, Children's
GAMES & TOYS: Strollers, Baby, Vehicle
GARAGES: Portable, Prefabricated Metal
GARBAGE CONTAINERS: Plastic
GARBAGE DISPOSERS & COMPACTORS: Commercial
GAS & OIL FIELD EXPLORATION SVCS
GAS & OIL FIELD SVCS, NEC
GAS FIELD MACHINERY & EQPT
GAS STATIONS
GAS STATIONS WITH CONVENIENCE STORES
GAS: Refinery
GASES & LIQUIFIED PETROLEUM GASES
GASES: Flourinated Hydrocarbon
GASES: Helium
GASES: Hydrogen
GASES: Indl
GASES: Neon
GASES: Nitrogen
GASES: Oxygen
GASKETS & SEALING DEVICES
GASOLINE BLENDING PLANT
GATES: Dam, Metal Plate
GATES: Ornamental Metal
GAUGES
GAUGES: Pressure
GEARS
GEARS & GEAR UNITS: Reduction, Exc Auto
GEARS: Power Transmission, Exc Auto
GELATIN CAPSULES
GEM STONES MINING, NEC: Natural
GEMSTONE & INDL DIAMOND MINING SVCS
GENERAL MERCHANDISE, NONDURABLE, WHOLESALE
GENERATING APPARATUS & PARTS: Electrical
GENERATION EQPT: Electronic
GENERATOR REPAIR SVCS

GENERATORS SETS: Steam
GENERATORS: Automotive & Aircraft
GENERATORS: Electric
GENERATORS: Electrochemical, Fuel Cell
GENERATORS: Gas
GENERATORS: Storage Battery Chargers
GENERATORS: Thermo-Electric
GIFT SHOP
GIFT WRAP: Paper, Made From Purchased Materials
GIFT, NOVELTY & SOUVENIR STORES: Gifts & Novelties
GIFTS & NOVELTIES: Wholesalers
GLASS & GLASS CERAMIC PRDTS, PRESSED OR
   BLOWN: Tableware
GLASS FABRICATORS
GLASS PRDTS, FROM PURCHASED GLASS: Enameled
GLASS PRDTS, FROM PURCHASED GLASS: Glass Beads,
   Reflecting
GLASS PRDTS, FROM PURCHASED GLASS: Glassware
GLASS PRDTS, FROM PURCHASED GLASS: Insulating
GLASS PRDTS, FROM PURCHASED GLASS: Mirrored
GLASS PRDTS, FROM PURCHASED GLASS: Mirrors,
   Framed
GLASS PRDTS, PRESSED OR BLOWN: Barware
GLASS PRDTS, PRESSED OR BLOWN: Bowls
GLASS PRDTS, PRESSED OR BLOWN: Bulbs, Electric
   Lights
GLASS PRDTS, PRESSED OR BLOWN: Glass Fibers, Textile
GLASS PRDTS, PRESSED OR BLOWN: Glassware, Art Or
   Decorative
GLASS PRDTS, PRESSED OR BLOWN: Ophthalmic, Exc
   Flat
GLASS PRDTS, PRESSED OR BLOWN: Optical
GLASS PRDTS, PRESSED OR BLOWN: Ornaments, Christ-
   mas Tree
GLASS PRDTS, PRESSED OR BLOWN: Tubing
GLASS PRDTS, PRESSED/BLOWN: Glassware, Art,
   Decor/Novelty
GLASS PRDTS, PURCHASED GLASS: Glassware, Scien-
   tific/Tech
GLASS PRDTS, PURCHASED GLASS: Insulating, Multiple-
   Glazed
GLASS PRDTS, PURCHD GLASS: Furniture Top, Cut,
   Beveld/Polshd
GLASS PRDTS, PURCHSD GLASS: Ornamental, Cut, En-
   graved/Décor
GLASS STORE: Leaded Or Stained
GLASS STORES
GLASS: Broadwoven Fabrics
GLASS: Fiber
GLASS: Flat
GLASS: Indl Prdts
GLASS: Insulating
GLASS: Pressed & Blown, NEC
GLASS: Safety
GLASS: Stained
GLASS: Structural
GLASS: Tempered
GLASSWARE WHOLESALERS
GLASSWARE: Cut & Engraved
GLOBAL POSITIONING SYSTEMS & EQPT
GLOVES: Fabric
GLOVES: Leather, Work
GLOVES: Safety
GLOVES: Welders'
GLOVES: Work
GLUE
GLYCERIN
GLYCOL ETHERS
GOLD BULLION PRODUCTION
GOLD ORE MINING
GOLD ORES
GOLD ORES PROCESSING
GOLF CARTS: Powered
GOLF CARTS: Wholesalers
GOLF EQPT
GOURMET FOOD STORES
GOVERNMENT, EXECUTIVE OFFICES: Mayors'
GRANITE: Crushed & Broken
GRANITE: Cut & Shaped
GRANITE: Dimension
GRAPHIC ARTS & RELATED DESIGN SVCS
GRAPHITE MINING SVCS
GRASSES: Artificial & Preserved
GRAVEL & PEBBLE MINING
GRAVEL MINING

GRAVEL: Painted
GREASES & INEDIBLE FATS, RENDERED
GREASES: Lubricating
GREENHOUSES: Prefabricated Metal
GREETING CARDS WHOLESALERS
GRILLS & GRILLWORK: Woven Wire, Made From Purchased Wire
GRITS: Crushed & Broken
GROCERIES WHOLESALERS, NEC
GROCERIES, GENERAL LINE WHOLESALERS
GUARD PROTECTIVE SVCS
GUARDRAILS
GUIDANCE SYSTEMS & EQPT: Space Vehicle
GUIDED MISSILES & SPACE VEHICLES
GUIDED MISSILES & SPACE VEHICLES: Research & Development
GUIDED MISSILES/SPACE VEHICLE PARTS/AUX EQPT: Research/Devel
GUM & WOOD CHEMICALS
GUN PARTS MADE TO INDIVIDUAL ORDER
GUN SIGHTS: Optical
GUTTERS
GUTTERS: Sheet Metal
GYPSUM & CALCITE MINING SVCS
GYPSUM BOARD
GYPSUM MINING
GYPSUM PRDTS

H

HAIR & HAIR BASED PRDTS
HAIR CARE PRDTS
HAIR CARE PRDTS: Hair Coloring Preparations
HAIR CARE PRDTS: Home Permanent Kits
HAIR CARE PRDTS: Tonics
HAIR CURLERS: Beauty Shop
HAIR DRESSING, FOR THE TRADE
HAND TOOLS, NEC: Wholesalers
HANDBAG STORES
HANDBAGS
HANDBAGS: Men's
HANDBAGS: Women's
HANDLES: Wood
HANDYMAN SVCS
HANG GLIDERS
HARDWARE
HARDWARE & BUILDING PRDTS: Plastic
HARDWARE STORES
HARDWARE STORES: Builders'
HARDWARE STORES: Door Locks & Lock Sets
HARDWARE STORES: Pumps & Pumping Eqpt
HARDWARE STORES: Tools
HARDWARE WHOLESALERS
HARDWARE, WHOLESALE: Builders', NEC
HARDWARE: Aircraft
HARDWARE: Aircraft & Marine, Incl Pulleys & Similar Items
HARDWARE: Builders'
HARDWARE: Cabinet
HARDWARE: Door Opening & Closing Devices, Exc Electrical
HARDWARE: Furniture
HARDWARE: Furniture, Builders' & Other Household
HARDWARE: Parachute
HARDWARE: Rubber
HARNESS ASSEMBLIES: Cable & Wire
HARNESSES, HALTERS, SADDLERY & STRAPS
HEADPHONES: Radio
HEALTH AIDS: Exercise Eqpt
HEALTH AIDS: Vaporizers
HEALTH FOOD & SUPPLEMENT STORES
HEARING AIDS
HEARING TESTING SVCS
HEAT EXCHANGERS
HEAT TREATING: Metal
HEATERS: Swimming Pool, Electric
HEATERS: Swimming Pool, Oil Or Gas
HEATING & AIR CONDITIONING UNITS, COMBINATION
HEATING APPARATUS: Steam
HEATING EQPT & SPLYS
HEATING EQPT: Complete
HEATING UNITS & DEVICES: Indl, Electric
HELICOPTERS
HELMETS: Athletic
HELMETS: Steel
HELP SUPPLY SERVICES
HIDES & SKINS
HIGH ENERGY PARTICLE PHYSICS EQPT

HITCHES: Trailer
HOBBY, TOY & GAME STORES: Hobbies, NEC
HOISTS
HOLDING COMPANIES, NEC
HOLDING COMPANIES: Investment, Exc Banks
HOME ENTERTAINMENT EQPT: Electronic, NEC
HOME ENTERTAINMENT REPAIR SVCS
HOME FURNISHINGS WHOLESALERS
HOME IMPROVEMENT & RENOVATION CONTRACTOR AGENCY
HOME MOVIES DEVELOPING & PROCESSING
HOMEFURNISHING STORES: Barbeque Grills
HOMEFURNISHING STORES: Beddings & Linens
HOMEFURNISHING STORES: Brushes
HOMEFURNISHING STORES: Lighting Fixtures
HOMEFURNISHING STORES: Vertical Blinds
HOMEFURNISHING STORES: Window Shades, NEC
HOMEFURNISHINGS & SPLYS, WHOLESALE: Decorative
HOMEFURNISHINGS, WHOLESALE: Blinds, Venetian
HOMEFURNISHINGS, WHOLESALE: Blinds, Vertical
HOMEFURNISHINGS, WHOLESALE: Decorating Splys
HOMEFURNISHINGS, WHOLESALE: Draperies
HOMEFURNISHINGS, WHOLESALE: Kitchenware
HOMEFURNISHINGS, WHOLESALE: Mirrors/Pictures, Framed/Unframd
HOMEFURNISHINGS, WHOLESALE: Pillowcases
HOMEFURNISHINGS, WHOLESALE: Pottery
HOMEFURNISHINGS, WHOLESALE: Sheets, Textile
HOMEFURNISHINGS, WHOLESALE: Window Covering Parts & Access
HOMEFURNISHINGS, WHOLESALE: Wood Flooring
HOMES, MODULAR: Wooden
HONES
HONEYCOMB CORE & BOARD: Made From Purchased Materials
HORMONES OR DERIVATIVES
HORSE & PET ACCESSORIES: Textile
HORSE ACCESS: Harnesses & Riding Crops, Etc, Exc Leather
HORSESHOES
HOSE: Automobile, Rubber
HOSE: Flexible Metal
HOSE: Plastic
HOSE: Pneumatic, Rubber Or Rubberized Fabric, NEC
HOSE: Rubber
HOSES & BELTING: Rubber & Plastic
HOSPITAL EQPT REPAIR SVCS
HOT TUBS
HOT TUBS: Plastic & Fiberglass
HOUSEHOLD APPLIANCE STORES
HOUSEHOLD APPLIANCE STORES: Appliance Parts
HOUSEHOLD ARTICLES, EXC FURNITURE: Cut Stone
HOUSEHOLD ARTICLES: Metal
HOUSEHOLD FURNISHINGS, NEC
HOUSEWARES, ELECTRIC, EXC COOKING APPLIANCES & UTENSILS
HOUSEWARES, ELECTRIC: Air Purifiers, Portable
HOUSEWARES, ELECTRIC: Appliances, Personal
HOUSEWARES, ELECTRIC: Broilers
HOUSEWARES, ELECTRIC: Cooking Appliances
HOUSEWARES, ELECTRIC: Curlers, Hair
HOUSEWARES, ELECTRIC: Dryers, Hand & Face
HOUSEWARES, ELECTRIC: Fans, Exhaust & Ventilating
HOUSEWARES, ELECTRIC: Heaters, Immersion
HOUSEWARES, ELECTRIC: Heating, Bsbrd/Wall, Radiant Heat
HOUSEWARES, ELECTRIC: Lighters, Cigarette
HOUSEWARES, ELECTRIC: Massage Machines, Exc Beauty/Barber
HOUSEWARES: Dishes, Earthenware
HOUSEWARES: Dishes, Plastic
HOUSEWARES: Toothpicks, Wood
HUB CAPS: Automobile, Stamped Metal
HYDRAULIC EQPT REPAIR SVC
HYDRAULIC FLUIDS: Synthetic Based
HYDROELECTRIC POWER GENERATION
Hard Rubber & Molded Rubber Prdts

I

ICE
ICE CREAM & ICES WHOLESALERS
ICE: Dry
IDENTIFICATION PLATES
IGNITION APPARATUS & DISTRIBUTORS
IGNITION COILS: Automotive

IGNITION SYSTEMS: Internal Combustion Engine
INCENSE
INCINERATORS
INCINERATORS: Concrete
INCUBATORS & BROODERS: Farm
INDICATORS: Cabin Environment
INDL & PERSONAL SVC PAPER WHOLESALERS
INDL & PERSONAL SVC PAPER, WHOL: Bags, Paper/Disp Plastic
INDL & PERSONAL SVC PAPER, WHOL: Boxes, Corrugtd/Solid Fiber
INDL & PERSONAL SVC PAPER, WHOL: Container, Paper/Plastic
INDL EQPT SVCS
INDL GASES WHOLESALERS
INDL HELP SVCS
INDL MACHINERY & EQPT WHOLESALERS
INDL MACHINERY REPAIR & MAINTENANCE
INDL PATTERNS: Foundry Patternmaking
INDL PROCESS INSTR: Transmit, Process Variables
INDL PROCESS INSTRUMENTS: Chromatographs
INDL PROCESS INSTRUMENTS: Control
INDL PROCESS INSTRUMENTS: Controllers, Process Variables
INDL PROCESS INSTRUMENTS: Digital Display, Process Variables
INDL PROCESS INSTRUMENTS: Elements, Primary
INDL PROCESS INSTRUMENTS: Fluidic Devices, Circuit & Systems
INDL PROCESS INSTRUMENTS: Temperature
INDL PROCESS INSTRUMENTS: Water Quality Monitoring/Cntrl Sys
INDL SPLYS WHOLESALERS
INDL SPLYS, WHOL: Fasteners, Incl Nuts, Bolts, Screws, Etc
INDL SPLYS, WHOLESALE: Abrasives
INDL SPLYS, WHOLESALE: Bearings
INDL SPLYS, WHOLESALE: Brushes, Indl
INDL SPLYS, WHOLESALE: Cans, Fruits & Vegetables
INDL SPLYS, WHOLESALE: Fasteners & Fastening Eqpt
INDL SPLYS, WHOLESALE: Gaskets
INDL SPLYS, WHOLESALE: Hydraulic & Pneumatic Pistons/Valves
INDL SPLYS, WHOLESALE: Mill Splys
INDL SPLYS, WHOLESALE: Power Transmission, Eqpt & Apparatus
INDL SPLYS, WHOLESALE: Seals
INDL SPLYS, WHOLESALE: Signmaker Eqpt & Splys
INDL SPLYS, WHOLESALE: Tools
INDL SPLYS, WHOLESALE: Valves & Fittings
INDL TRUCK REPAIR SVCS
INDUCTORS
INDUSTRIAL & COMMERCIAL EQPT INSPECTION SVCS
INFORMATION RETRIEVAL SERVICES
INFRARED OBJECT DETECTION EQPT
INK OR WRITING FLUIDS
INK: Letterpress Or Offset
INK: Lithographic
INK: Printing
INK: Screen process
INNER TUBES: Airplane
INSECTICIDES
INSECTICIDES & PESTICIDES
INSPECTION & TESTING SVCS
INSTALLATION OF CITIZENS BAND ANTENNAS
INSTRUMENTS & ACCESSORIES: Surveying
INSTRUMENTS & METERS: Measuring, Electric
INSTRUMENTS, LAB: Spectroscopic/Optical Properties Measuring
INSTRUMENTS, LABORATORY: Gas Chromatographic
INSTRUMENTS, LABORATORY: Photometers
INSTRUMENTS, LABORATORY: Photomicrographic
INSTRUMENTS, LABORATORY: Spectrometers
INSTRUMENTS, MEASURING & CNTRL: Geophysical/Meteorological
INSTRUMENTS, MEASURING & CNTRL: Radiation & Testing, Nuclear
INSTRUMENTS, MEASURING & CNTRL: Testing, Abrasion, Etc
INSTRUMENTS, MEASURING & CNTRLG: Aircraft & Motor Vehicle
INSTRUMENTS, MEASURING & CNTRLG: Fatigue Test, Indl, Mech
INSTRUMENTS, MEASURING & CNTRLG: Thermometers/Temp Sensors

INSTRUMENTS, MEASURING & CNTRLNG: Press & Vac Ind, Acft Eng
INSTRUMENTS, MEASURING & CONTROLLING: Breathalyzers
INSTRUMENTS, MEASURING & CONTROLLING: Fuel System, Aircraft
INSTRUMENTS, MEASURING & CONTROLLING: Gas Detectors
INSTRUMENTS, MEASURING & CONTROLLING: Gauges, Rain
INSTRUMENTS, MEASURING & CONTROLLING: Leak Detection, Liquid
INSTRUMENTS, MEASURING & CONTROLLING: Photogrammetrical
INSTRUMENTS, MEASURING & CONTROLLING: Polygraph
INSTRUMENTS, MEASURING & CONTROLLING: Ultrasonic Testing
INSTRUMENTS, MEASURING/CNTRLG: Fare Registers, St Cars/Buses
INSTRUMENTS, MEASURING/CNTRLNG: Med Diagnostic Sys, Nuclear
INSTRUMENTS, OPTICAL: Aiming Circles, Fire Control
INSTRUMENTS, OPTICAL: Elements & Assemblies, Exc Ophthalmic
INSTRUMENTS, OPTICAL: Lenses, All Types Exc Ophthalmic
INSTRUMENTS, OPTICAL: Magnifying, NEC
INSTRUMENTS, OPTICAL: Test & Inspection
INSTRUMENTS, SURGICAL & MED: Cleaning Eqpt, Ultrasonic Med
INSTRUMENTS, SURGICAL & MED: Fixation Appliances, Internal
INSTRUMENTS, SURGICAL & MED: Gastroscopes, Exc Electromedcal
INSTRUMENTS, SURGICAL & MEDICAL: Biopsy
INSTRUMENTS, SURGICAL & MEDICAL: Blood & Bone Work
INSTRUMENTS, SURGICAL & MEDICAL: Blood Pressure
INSTRUMENTS, SURGICAL & MEDICAL: Catheters
INSTRUMENTS, SURGICAL & MEDICAL: Clamps
INSTRUMENTS, SURGICAL & MEDICAL: Inhalation Therapy
INSTRUMENTS, SURGICAL & MEDICAL: Inhalators
INSTRUMENTS, SURGICAL & MEDICAL: Lasers, Surgical
INSTRUMENTS, SURGICAL & MEDICAL: Needles, Suture
INSTRUMENTS, SURGICAL & MEDICAL: Ophthalmic
INSTRUMENTS, SURGICAL & MEDICAL: Plates & Screws, Bone
INSTRUMENTS, SURGICAL & MEDICAL: Skin Grafting
INSTRUMENTS, SURGICAL/MED: Microsurgical, Exc Electromedical
INSTRUMENTS: Analytical
INSTRUMENTS: Analyzers, Internal Combustion Eng, Electronic
INSTRUMENTS: Analyzers, Spectrum
INSTRUMENTS: Combustion Control, Indl
INSTRUMENTS: Digital Panel Meters, Electricity Measuring
INSTRUMENTS: Endoscopic Eqpt, Electromedical
INSTRUMENTS: Eye Examination
INSTRUMENTS: Frequency Meters, Electrical, Mech & Electronic
INSTRUMENTS: Indl Process Control
INSTRUMENTS: Infrared, Indl Process
INSTRUMENTS: Instrument Relays, All Types
INSTRUMENTS: Laser, Scientific & Engineering
INSTRUMENTS: Liquid Level, Indl Process
INSTRUMENTS: Measurement, Indl Process
INSTRUMENTS: Measuring & Controlling
INSTRUMENTS: Measuring Electricity
INSTRUMENTS: Measuring, Electrical Energy
INSTRUMENTS: Measuring, Electrical Power
INSTRUMENTS: Medical & Surgical
INSTRUMENTS: Nautical
INSTRUMENTS: Power Measuring, Electrical
INSTRUMENTS: Radio Frequency Measuring
INSTRUMENTS: Standards & Calibration, Electrical Measuring
INSTRUMENTS: Temperature Measurement, Indl
INSTRUMENTS: Test, Digital, Electronic & Electrical Circuits
INSTRUMENTS: Test, Electrical, Engine
INSTRUMENTS: Test, Electronic & Electric Measurement
INSTRUMENTS: Test, Electronic & Electrical Circuits
INSTRUMENTS: Vibration
INSULATING BOARD, CELLULAR FIBER
INSULATING COMPOUNDS
INSULATION & CUSHIONING FOAM: Polystyrene
INSULATION & ROOFING MATERIALS: Wood, Reconstituted

INSULATION: Fiberglass
INSULATORS & INSULATION MATERIALS: Electrical
INSULATORS, PORCELAIN: Electrical
INTEGRATED CIRCUITS, SEMICONDUCTOR NETWORKS, ETC
INTERCOMMUNICATIONS SYSTEMS: Electric
INTERIOR DECORATING SVCS
INTERIOR DESIGN SVCS, NEC
INVERTERS: Nonrotating Electrical
INVERTERS: Rotating Electrical
INVESTMENT ADVISORY SVCS
IRON & STEEL PRDTS: Hot-Rolled
IRON ORE MINING
IRON ORE PELLETIZING
IRON ORES
IRRIGATION EQPT WHOLESALERS
IRRIGATION SYSTEMS, NEC Water Distribution Or Sply Systems

J

JACKS: Hydraulic
JANITORIAL EQPT & SPLYS WHOLESALERS
JARS: Plastic
JEWELERS' FINDINGS & MATERIALS
JEWELERS' FINDINGS & MATERIALS: Castings
JEWELERS' FINDINGS & MTLS: Jewel Prep, Instr, Tools, Watches
JEWELRY & PRECIOUS STONES WHOLESALERS
JEWELRY APPAREL
JEWELRY FINDINGS & LAPIDARY WORK
JEWELRY REPAIR SVCS
JEWELRY STORES
JEWELRY STORES: Clocks
JEWELRY STORES: Precious Stones & Precious Metals
JEWELRY STORES: Watches
JEWELRY, PRECIOUS METAL: Bracelets
JEWELRY, PRECIOUS METAL: Cigar & Cigarette Access
JEWELRY, PRECIOUS METAL: Cigarette Lighters
JEWELRY, PRECIOUS METAL: Medals, Precious Or Semiprecious
JEWELRY, PRECIOUS METAL: Necklaces
JEWELRY, PRECIOUS METAL: Settings & Mountings
JEWELRY, WHOLESALE
JEWELRY: Decorative, Fashion & Costume
JEWELRY: Precious Metal
JOB PRINTING & NEWSPAPER PUBLISHING COMBINED
JOB TRAINING & VOCATIONAL REHABILITATION SVCS
JOB TRAINING SVCS
JOINTS: Expansion
JOINTS: Expansion, Pipe
JOISTS: Concrete
JOISTS: Long-Span Series, Open Web Steel
JUICE, FROZEN: Wholesalers

K

KEYBOARDS: Computer Or Office Machine
KEYS, KEY BLANKS
KITCHEN CABINET STORES, EXC CUSTOM
KITCHEN CABINETS WHOLESALERS
KITCHEN TOOLS & UTENSILS WHOLESALERS
KITCHEN UTENSILS: Food Handling & Processing Prdts, Wood
KITCHEN UTENSILS: Wooden
KITCHENWARE: Plastic
KITS: Plastic
KNIT OUTERWEAR DYEING & FINISHING, EXC HOSIERY & GLOVE
KNIVES: Agricultural Or indl

L

LABELS: Cotton, Printed
LABELS: Paper, Made From Purchased Materials
LABELS: Woven
LABORATORIES, TESTING: Food
LABORATORIES: Biological Research
LABORATORIES: Biotechnology
LABORATORIES: Commercial Nonphysical Research
LABORATORIES: Dental
LABORATORIES: Dental, Artificial Teeth Production
LABORATORIES: Environmental Research
LABORATORIES: Medical
LABORATORIES: Noncommercial Research
LABORATORIES: Physical Research, Commercial
LABORATORIES: Testing

LABORATORIES: Testing
LABORATORY APPARATUS & FURNITURE
LABORATORY APPARATUS & FURNITURE: Worktables
LABORATORY APPARATUS, EXC HEATING & MEASURING
LABORATORY APPARATUS: Laser Beam Alignment Device
LABORATORY APPARATUS: Particle Size Reduction
LABORATORY APPARATUS: Sample Preparation Apparatus
LABORATORY CHEMICALS: Organic
LABORATORY EQPT: Chemical
LABORATORY EQPT: Clinical Instruments Exc Medical
LABORATORY EQPT: Incubators
LADDERS: Metal
LADDERS: Permanent Installation, Metal
LADDERS: Wood
LAMINATED PLASTICS: Plate, Sheet, Rod & Tubes
LAMINATING SVCS
LAMP & LIGHT BULBS & TUBES
LAMP BULBS & TUBES, ELECTRIC: For Specialized Applications
LAMP BULBS & TUBES, ELECTRIC: Health, Infrared/Ultraviolet
LAMP BULBS & TUBES, ELECTRIC: Light, Complete
LAMP SHADES: Plastic
LAMPS: Arc Units, Electrotherapeutic
LAMPS: Desk, Commercial
LAMPS: Floor, Residential
LAMPS: Table, Residential
LAMPS: Ultraviolet
LAMPS: Wall, Residential
LAND SUBDIVISION & DEVELOPMENT
LAPIDARY WORK: Contract Or Other
LAPIDARY WORK: Jewel Cut, Drill, Polish, Recut/Setting
LASER SYSTEMS & EQPT
LASERS: Welding, Drilling & Cutting Eqpt
LATH: Woven Wire, Made From Purchased Wire
LATHES
LAUNDRIES, EXC POWER & COIN-OPERATED
LAUNDRY & DRYCLEANER AGENTS
LAUNDRY EQPT: Commercial
LAWN & GARDEN EQPT
LAWN & GARDEN EQPT STORES
LAWN & GARDEN EQPT: Blowers & Vacuums
LAWN & GARDEN EQPT: Grass Catchers, Lawn Mower
LAWN & GARDEN EQPT: Lawnmowers, Residential, Hand Or Power
LAWN & GARDEN EQPT: Tractors & Eqpt
LAWN & GARDEN EQPT: Trimmers
LAWN MOWER REPAIR SHOP
LEAD & ZINC
LEAD & ZINC ORES
LEAD PENCILS & ART GOODS
LEASING & RENTAL SVCS: Cranes & Aerial Lift Eqpt
LEASING & RENTAL: Construction & Mining Eqpt
LEASING & RENTAL: Medical Machinery & Eqpt
LEASING & RENTAL: Office Machines & Eqpt
LEASING & RENTAL: Utility Trailers & RV's
LEATHER GOODS, EXC FOOTWEAR, GLOVES, LUGGAGE/BELTING, WHOL
LEATHER GOODS: Aprons, Welders', Blacksmiths', Etc
LEATHER GOODS: Boxes
LEATHER GOODS: Card Cases
LEATHER GOODS: Desk Sets
LEATHER GOODS: Harnesses Or Harness Parts
LEATHER GOODS: Holsters
LEATHER GOODS: NEC
LEATHER GOODS: Personal
LEATHER GOODS: Sewing Cases
LEATHER GOODS: Stirrups, Wood Or Metal
LEATHER GOODS: Wallets
LEATHER TANNING & FINISHING
LEATHER: Artificial
LEATHER: Handbag
LEATHER: Shoe
LEATHER: Upholstery
LEGAL OFFICES & SVCS
LEGAL PROCESS SERVERS
LENSES: Plastic, Exc Optical
LICENSE TAGS: Automobile, Stamped Metal
LIFE RAFTS: Rubber
LIFE SAVING & SURVIVAL EQPT REPAIR SVCS, NON-MEDICAL
LIFESAVING & SURVIVAL EQPT, EXC MEDICAL, WHOLESALE
LIGHT SENSITIVE DEVICES
LIGHTING EQPT: Area & Sports Luminaries

MACHINERY: Brewery & Malting
MACHINERY: Centrifugal
MACHINERY: Coin Wrapping
MACHINERY: Concrete Prdts
MACHINERY: Construction
MACHINERY: Cryogenic, Industrial
MACHINERY: Custom
MACHINERY: Dredging
MACHINERY: Electronic Component Making
MACHINERY: Electronic Teaching Aids
MACHINERY: Engraving
MACHINERY: Extruding
MACHINERY: Fiber Optics Strand Coating
MACHINERY: Folding
MACHINERY: Gas Producers
MACHINERY: General, Industrial, NEC
MACHINERY: Ice Cream
MACHINERY: Ice Making
MACHINERY: Industrial, NEC
MACHINERY: Jewelers
MACHINERY: Labeling
MACHINERY: Logging Eqpt
MACHINERY: Marking, Metalworking
MACHINERY: Metalworking
MACHINERY: Milling
MACHINERY: Mining
MACHINERY: Optical Lens
MACHINERY: Ozone
MACHINERY: Packaging
MACHINERY: Paper Industry Miscellaneous
MACHINERY: Pharmaciutical
MACHINERY: Photoengraving
MACHINERY: Photographic Reproduction
MACHINERY: Plastic Working
MACHINERY: Polishing & Buffing
MACHINERY: Printing Presses
MACHINERY: Recycling
MACHINERY: Riveting
MACHINERY: Robots, Molding & Forming Plastics
MACHINERY: Rubber Working
MACHINERY: Screening Eqpt, Electric
MACHINERY: Semiconductor Manufacturing
MACHINERY: Service Industry, NEC
MACHINERY: Sheet Metal Working
MACHINERY: Specialty
MACHINERY: Stone Working
MACHINERY: Tapping
MACHINERY: Textile
MACHINERY: Tire Retreading
MACHINERY: Tire Shredding
MACHINERY: Voting
MACHINERY: Woodworking
MACHINES: Forming, Sheet Metal
MACHINISTS' TOOLS: Measuring, Precision
MACHINISTS' TOOLS: Precision
MACHINISTS' TOOLS: Scales, Measuring, Precision
MAGAZINES, WHOLESALE
MAGNETIC INK & OPTICAL SCANNING EQPT
MAGNETIC INK RECOGNITION DEVICES
MAGNETIC RESONANCE IMAGING DEVICES: Nonmedical
MAGNETIC SHIELDS, METAL
MAGNETIC TAPE, AUDIO: Prerecorded
MAGNETOHYDRODYNAMIC DEVICES OR MHD
MAGNETS: Ceramic
MAGNIFIERS
MAIL-ORDER BOOK CLUBS
MAIL-ORDER HOUSE, NEC
MAIL-ORDER HOUSES: Collectibles & Antiques
MAIL-ORDER HOUSES: Computer Eqpt & Electronics
MAIL-ORDER HOUSES: Cosmetics & Perfumes
MAIL-ORDER HOUSES: Fitness & Sporting Goods
MAIL-ORDER HOUSES: General Merchandise
MAIL-ORDER HOUSES: Gift Items
MAIL-ORDER HOUSES: Magazines
MAIL-ORDER HOUSES: Order Taking Office Only
MAIL-ORDER HOUSES: Tools & Hardware
MAILING SVCS, NEC
MALLETS: Rubber
MANAGEMENT CONSULTING SVCS: Automation & Robotics
MANAGEMENT CONSULTING SVCS: Business
MANAGEMENT CONSULTING SVCS: Business Planning & Organizing
MANAGEMENT CONSULTING SVCS: Corporate Objectives & Policies

MANAGEMENT CONSULTING SVCS: Incentive Or Award Program
MANAGEMENT CONSULTING SVCS: Industrial
MANAGEMENT CONSULTING SVCS: Industrial & Labor
MANAGEMENT CONSULTING SVCS: Industry Specialist
MANAGEMENT CONSULTING SVCS: Information Systems
MANAGEMENT CONSULTING SVCS: Manufacturing
MANAGEMENT CONSULTING SVCS: Restaurant & Food
MANAGEMENT CONSULTING SVCS: Retail Trade Consultant
MANAGEMENT CONSULTING SVCS: Transportation
MANAGEMENT SERVICES
MANAGEMENT SVCS, FACILITIES SUPPORT: Environ Remediation
MANAGEMENT SVCS: Administrative
MANAGEMENT SVCS: Business
MANAGEMENT SVCS: Personnel
MANAGEMENT SVCS: Restaurant
MANGANESE ORES MINING
MANHOLES & COVERS: Metal
MANHOLES COVERS: Concrete
MANICURE PREPARATIONS
MANNEQUINS
MANUFACTURED & MOBILE HOME DEALERS
MANUFACTURING INDUSTRIES, NEC
MAPS
MARBLE BOARD
MARBLE, BUILDING: Cut & Shaped
MARINAS
MARINE APPAREL STORES
MARINE ENGINE REPAIR SVCS
MARINE HARDWARE
MARINE RELATED EQPT
MARINE RELATED EQPT: Cranes, Ship
MARINE SPLY DEALERS
MARINE SPLYS WHOLESALERS
MARINE SVC STATIONS
MARKERS
MARKING DEVICES
MARKING DEVICES: Canceling Stamps, Hand, Rubber Or Metal
MARKING DEVICES: Embossing Seals & Hand Stamps
MARKING DEVICES: Irons, Marking Or Branding
MARKING DEVICES: Screens, Textile Printing
MARKING DEVICES: Seal Presses, Notary & Hand
MARKING DEVICES: Stencil Machines
MASSAGE MACHINES, ELECTRIC: Barber & Beauty Shops
MASSAGE PARLORS
MASTS: Cast Aluminum
MATERIAL GRINDING & PULVERIZING SVCS NEC
MATERIALS HANDLING EQPT WHOLESALERS
MATS & MATTING, MADE FROM PURCHASED WIRE
MATS OR MATTING, NEC: Rubber
MATS, MATTING & PADS: Auto, Floor, Exc Rubber Or Plastic
MATS, MATTING & PADS: Door, Paper, Grass, Reed, Coir, Etc
MATS: Blasting, Rope
MATTRESS PROTECTORS: Rubber
MATTRESS STORES
MEAL DELIVERY PROGRAMS
MEAT & MEAT PRDTS WHOLESALERS
MEAT CUTTING & PACKING
MEAT MARKETS
MEAT PRDTS: Bacon, Slab & Sliced, From Slaughtered Meat
MEAT PRDTS: Calf's Foot Jelly, From Purchased Meat
MEAT PRDTS: Canned
MEAT PRDTS: Dried Beef, From Purchased Meat
MEAT PRDTS: Frozen
MEAT PRDTS: Ham, Boiled, From Purchased Meat
MEAT PRDTS: Ham, Boneless, From Purchased Meat
MEAT PRDTS: Ham, Canned, From Purchased Meat
MEAT PRDTS: Lamb, From Slaughtered Meat
MEAT PRDTS: Pork, From Slaughtered Meat
MEAT PRDTS: Prepared Beef Prdts From Purchased Beef
MEAT PRDTS: Prepared Pork Prdts, From Purchased Meat
MEAT PRDTS: Sausages, From Purchased Meat
MEAT PRDTS: Smoked
MEAT PRDTS: Snack Sticks, Incl Jerky, From Purchased Meat
MEAT PRDTS: Variety, Fresh Edible Organs
MEAT PROCESSED FROM PURCHASED CARCASSES
MEATS, PACKAGED FROZEN: Wholesalers
MECHANICAL INSTRUMENT REPAIR SVCS
MEDICAL & HOSPITAL EQPT WHOLESALERS

MEDICAL & HOSPITAL SPLYS: Radiation Shielding Garments
MEDICAL & SURGICAL SPLYS: Abdominal Support, Braces/Trusses
MEDICAL & SURGICAL SPLYS: Belts, Linemen's Safety
MEDICAL & SURGICAL SPLYS: Braces, Elastic
MEDICAL & SURGICAL SPLYS: Braces, Orthopedic
MEDICAL & SURGICAL SPLYS: Canes, Orthopedic
MEDICAL & SURGICAL SPLYS: Clothing, Fire Resistant & Protect
MEDICAL & SURGICAL SPLYS: Cosmetic Restorations
MEDICAL & SURGICAL SPLYS: Cotton & Cotton Applicators
MEDICAL & SURGICAL SPLYS: Cotton, Incl Cotton Balls
MEDICAL & SURGICAL SPLYS: Dressings, Surgical
MEDICAL & SURGICAL SPLYS: Foot Appliances, Orthopedic
MEDICAL & SURGICAL SPLYS: Limbs, Artificial
MEDICAL & SURGICAL SPLYS: Models, Anatomical
MEDICAL & SURGICAL SPLYS: Orthopedic Appliances
MEDICAL & SURGICAL SPLYS: Personal Safety Eqpt
MEDICAL & SURGICAL SPLYS: Prosthetic Appliances
MEDICAL & SURGICAL SPLYS: Sponges
MEDICAL & SURGICAL SPLYS: Stretchers
MEDICAL & SURGICAL SPLYS: Sutures, Non & Absorbable
MEDICAL & SURGICAL SPLYS: Traction Apparatus
MEDICAL & SURGICAL SPLYS: Walkers
MEDICAL & SURGICAL SPLYS: Welders' Hoods
MEDICAL EQPT: Cardiographs
MEDICAL EQPT: Defibrillators
MEDICAL EQPT: Diagnostic
MEDICAL EQPT: Electromedical Apparatus
MEDICAL EQPT: Electrotherapeutic Apparatus
MEDICAL EQPT: Laser Systems
MEDICAL EQPT: MRI/Magnetic Resonance Imaging Devs, Nuclear
MEDICAL EQPT: Patient Monitoring
MEDICAL EQPT: Sterilizers
MEDICAL EQPT: Ultrasonic Scanning Devices
MEDICAL EQPT: X-Ray Apparatus & Tubes, Therapeutic
MEDICAL HELP SVCS
MEDICAL SUNDRIES: Rubber
MEDICAL SVCS ORGANIZATION
MEDICAL, DENTAL & HOSPITAL EQPT, WHOL: Hospital Eqpt & Splys
MEDICAL, DENTAL & HOSPITAL EQPT, WHOL: Hosptl Eqpt/Furniture
MEDICAL, DENTAL & HOSPITAL EQPT, WHOL: Surgical Eqpt & Splys
MEDICAL, DENTAL & HOSPITAL EQPT, WHOLESALE: Hearing Aids
MEDICAL, DENTAL & HOSPITAL EQPT, WHOLESALE: Med Eqpt & Splys
MEDICAL, DENTAL & HOSPITAL EQPT, WHOLESALE: Orthopedic
MEDICAL, DENTAL & HOSPITAL EQPT, WHOLESALE: Oxygen Therapy
MEDICAL, DENTAL & HOSPITAL EQPT, WHOLESALE: Safety
MEMBERSHIP ORGANIZATIONS, NEC: Charitable
MEMBERSHIP ORGANIZATIONS, PROFESSIONAL: Accounting Assoc
MEMBERSHIP ORGANIZATIONS, RELIGIOUS: Pentecostal Church
MEN'S & BOYS' CLOTHING STORES
MEN'S & BOYS' CLOTHING WHOLESALERS, NEC
MEN'S & BOYS' SPORTSWEAR CLOTHING STORES
MEN'S & BOYS' SPORTSWEAR WHOLESALERS
MESSAGE CONCENTRATORS
METAL & STEEL PRDTS: Abrasive
METAL COMPONENTS: Prefabricated
METAL DETECTORS
METAL FABRICATORS: Architechtural
METAL FABRICATORS: Plate
METAL FABRICATORS: Sheet
METAL FABRICATORS: Structural, Ship
METAL FINISHING SVCS
METAL MINING SVCS
METAL SERVICE CENTERS & OFFICES
METAL SPINNING FOR THE TRADE
METAL STAMPING, FOR THE TRADE
METAL STAMPINGS: Ornamental
METAL: Heavy, Perforated
METALS SVC CENTERS & WHOL: Structural Shapes, Iron Or Steel
METALS SVC CENTERS & WHOLESALERS: Cable, Wire

METALS SVC CENTERS & WHOLESALERS: Iron & Steel Prdt, Ferrous
METALS SVC CENTERS & WHOLESALERS: Rails & Access
METALS SVC CENTERS & WHOLESALERS: Reinforcement Mesh, Wire
METALS SVC CENTERS & WHOLESALERS: Steel
METALS SVC CTRS & WHOLESALERS: Aluminum Bars, Rods, Etc
METALS: Honeycombed
METALS: Precious NEC
METALS: Primary Nonferrous, NEC
METALWORK: Miscellaneous
METALWORK: Ornamental
METALWORKING MACHINERY WHOLESALERS
METEOROLOGIC TRACKING SYSTEMS
METERING DEVICES: Gas Meters, Domestic & Large Cap, Indl
METERING DEVICES: Measuring, Mechanical
METERING DEVICES: Water Quality Monitoring & Control Systems
METERS: Altimeters
METERS: Liquid
METERS: Power Factor & Phase Angle
MGMT CONSULTING SVCS: Matls, Incl Purch, Handle & Invntry
MICA PRDTS
MICROCIRCUITS, INTEGRATED: Semiconductor
MICROFILM EQPT
MICROMETERS
MICROPHONES
MICROPROCESSORS
MICROSCOPES
MICROSCOPES: Electron & Proton
MICROWAVE COMPONENTS
MICROWAVE OVENS: Household
MILITARY GOODS & REGALIA STORES
MILK, FLUID: Wholesalers
MILLING: Cereal Flour, Exc Rice
MILLING: Chemical
MILLING: Grains, Exc Rice
MILLWORK
MIMEOGRAPHING SVCS
MINE & QUARRY SVCS: Nonmetallic Minerals
MINE DEVELOPMENT SVCS: Nonmetallic Minerals
MINE EXPLORATION SVCS: Nonmetallic Minerals
MINERAL ABRASIVES MINING SVCS
MINERAL MINING: Nonmetallic
MINERAL WOOL
MINERAL WOOL INSULATION PRDTS
MINERALS: Ground or Treated
MINING EQPT: Locomotives & Parts
MINING EXPLORATION & DEVELOPMENT SVCS
MINING MACHINES & EQPT: Concentration, Metallurgical/Mining
MINING MACHINES & EQPT: Washers, Aggregate & Sand
MINING SVCS, NEC: Lignite
MISSILES: Ballistic, Complete
MISSILES: Guided
MIXING EQPT
MIXTURES & BLOCKS: Asphalt Paving
MOBILE COMMUNICATIONS EQPT
MOBILE HOMES
MOBILE HOMES, EXC RECREATIONAL
MOBILE HOMES: Indl Or Commercial Use
MOBILE HOMES: Personal Or Private Use
MODELS: Airplane, Exc Toy
MODELS: Boat, Exc Toy
MODELS: General, Exc Toy
MODULES: Computer Logic
MODULES: Solid State
MOLDED RUBBER PRDTS
MOLDING COMPOUNDS
MOLDING SAND MINING
MOLDINGS & TRIM: Metal, Exc Automobile
MOLDINGS OR TRIM: Automobile, Stamped Metal
MOLDINGS, ARCHITECTURAL: Plaster Of Paris
MOLDINGS: Picture Frame
MOLDS: Indl
MONUMENTS & GRAVE MARKERS, EXC TERRAZZO
MOPS: Floor & Dust
MOTION PICTURE & VIDEO PRODUCTION SVCS
MOTION PICTURE & VIDEO PRODUCTION SVCS: Educational, TV
MOTION PICTURE EQPT
MOTION PICTURE PRODUCTION ALLIED SVCS

MOTOR & GENERATOR PARTS: Electric
MOTOR REBUILDING SVCS, EXC AUTOMOTIVE
MOTOR REPAIR SVCS
MOTOR SCOOTERS & PARTS
MOTOR VEHICLE ASSEMBLY, COMPLETE: Ambulances
MOTOR VEHICLE ASSEMBLY, COMPLETE: Autos, Incl Specialty
MOTOR VEHICLE ASSEMBLY, COMPLETE: Bus/Large Spclty Vehicles
MOTOR VEHICLE ASSEMBLY, COMPLETE: Buses, All Types
MOTOR VEHICLE ASSEMBLY, COMPLETE: Cars, Armored
MOTOR VEHICLE ASSEMBLY, COMPLETE: Fire Department Vehicles
MOTOR VEHICLE ASSEMBLY, COMPLETE: Military Motor Vehicle
MOTOR VEHICLE ASSEMBLY, COMPLETE: Patrol Wagons
MOTOR VEHICLE ASSEMBLY, COMPLETE: Personnel Carriers
MOTOR VEHICLE ASSEMBLY, COMPLETE: Truck & Tractor Trucks
MOTOR VEHICLE ASSEMBLY, COMPLETE: Truck Tractors, Highway
MOTOR VEHICLE ASSEMBLY, COMPLETE: Wreckers, Tow Truck
MOTOR VEHICLE DEALERS: Cars, Used Only
MOTOR VEHICLE DEALERS: Trucks, Tractors/Trailers, New & Used
MOTOR VEHICLE PARTS & ACCESS: Acceleration Eqpt
MOTOR VEHICLE PARTS & ACCESS: Air Conditioner Parts
MOTOR VEHICLE PARTS & ACCESS: Body Components & Frames
MOTOR VEHICLE PARTS & ACCESS: Booster Cables, Jump-Start
MOTOR VEHICLE PARTS & ACCESS: Cleaners, air
MOTOR VEHICLE PARTS & ACCESS: Clutches
MOTOR VEHICLE PARTS & ACCESS: Cylinder Heads
MOTOR VEHICLE PARTS & ACCESS: Electrical Eqpt
MOTOR VEHICLE PARTS & ACCESS: Engines & Parts
MOTOR VEHICLE PARTS & ACCESS: Engs & Trans,Factory, Rebuilt
MOTOR VEHICLE PARTS & ACCESS: Frames
MOTOR VEHICLE PARTS & ACCESS: Fuel Pumps
MOTOR VEHICLE PARTS & ACCESS: Fuel Systems & Parts
MOTOR VEHICLE PARTS & ACCESS: Gears
MOTOR VEHICLE PARTS & ACCESS: Horns
MOTOR VEHICLE PARTS & ACCESS: Lubrication Systems & Parts
MOTOR VEHICLE PARTS & ACCESS: Manifolds
MOTOR VEHICLE PARTS & ACCESS: PCV Valves
MOTOR VEHICLE PARTS & ACCESS: Pumps, Hydraulic Fluid Power
MOTOR VEHICLE PARTS & ACCESS: Trailer Hitches
MOTOR VEHICLE PARTS & ACCESS: Transmission Housings Or Parts
MOTOR VEHICLE PARTS & ACCESS: Transmissions
MOTOR VEHICLE PARTS & ACCESS: Water Pumps
MOTOR VEHICLE PARTS & ACCESS: Wipers, Windshield
MOTOR VEHICLE PARTS & ACCESS: Wiring Harness Sets
MOTOR VEHICLE SPLYS & PARTS WHOLESALERS: New
MOTOR VEHICLE SPLYS & PARTS WHOLESALERS: Used
MOTOR VEHICLE: Hardware
MOTOR VEHICLE: Radiators
MOTOR VEHICLE: Steering Mechanisms
MOTOR VEHICLE: Wheels
MOTOR VEHICLES & CAR BODIES
MOTOR VEHICLES, WHOLESALE: Motor scooters
MOTOR VEHICLES, WHOLESALE: Truck bodies
MOTOR VEHICLES, WHOLESALE: Truck tractors
MOTOR VEHICLES, WHOLESALE: Trucks, commercial
MOTORCYCLE & BICYCLE PARTS: Saddles & Seat Posts
MOTORCYCLE ACCESS
MOTORCYCLE DEALERS
MOTORCYCLE DEALERS: All-Terrain Vehicle Parts & Access
MOTORCYCLE DEALERS: Motor Scooters
MOTORCYCLE PARTS & ACCESS DEALERS
MOTORCYCLES & RELATED PARTS
MOTORCYCLES: Wholesalers
MOTORS: Electric
MOTORS: Generators
MOTORS: Pneumatic
MOUNTING SVC: Display
MOUTHWASHES
MOVING SVC: Local
MUSIC BOXES
MUSIC DISTRIBUTION APPARATUS

MUSIC VIDEO PRODUCTION SVCS
MUSICAL INSTRUMENTS & ACCESS: NEC
MUSICAL INSTRUMENTS & PARTS: String
MUSICAL INSTRUMENTS WHOLESALERS
MUSICAL INSTRUMENTS: Bells
MUSICAL INSTRUMENTS: Electric & Electronic
MUSICAL INSTRUMENTS: Guitars & Parts, Electric & Acoustic
MUSICAL INSTRUMENTS: Marimbas
MUSICAL INSTRUMENTS: Mouthpieces
MUSICAL INSTRUMENTS: Strings, Instrument
MUSICAL INSTRUMENTS: Violins & Parts

N

NAME PLATES: Engraved Or Etched
NAMEPLATES
NATIONAL SECURITY FORCES
NATIONAL SECURITY, GOVERNMENT: Air Force
NATURAL ETHANE PRODUCTION
NATURAL GAS COMPRESSING SVC, On-Site
NATURAL GAS LIQUIDS PRODUCTION
NATURAL GAS PRODUCTION
NATURAL PROPANE PRODUCTION
NAUTICAL REPAIR SVCS
NAVIGATIONAL SYSTEMS & INSTRUMENTS
NET & NETTING PRDTS
NETS: Laundry
NETTING: Plastic
NETTING: Rope
NETTING: Woven Wire, Made From Purchased Wire
NEW & USED CAR DEALERS
NEWSPAPERS & PERIODICALS NEWS REPORTING SVCS
NEWSSTAND
NICKEL ALLOY
NONCURRENT CARRYING WIRING DEVICES
NONDURABLE GOODS WHOLESALERS, NEC
NONFERROUS: Rolling & Drawing, NEC
NONMETALLIC MINERALS: Support Activities, Exc Fuels
NOTARIES PUBLIC
NOTIONS: Hooks, Crochet
NOVELTIES
NOVELTIES, DURABLE, WHOLESALE
NOVELTIES: Plastic
NOZZLES & SPRINKLERS Lawn Hose
NOZZLES: Spray, Aerosol, Paint Or Insecticide
NUCLEAR FUELS SCRAP REPROCESSING
NUCLEAR REACTORS: Military Or Indl
NUCLEAR SHIELDING: Metal Plate
NURSERIES & LAWN & GARDEN SPLY STORES, RETAIL
NURSERIES & LAWN & GARDEN SPLY STORES, RETAIL: Fertilizer
NURSERIES & LAWN & GARDEN SPLY STORES, RETAIL: Sod
NURSERIES/LAWN/GARDEN SPLY STORES, RET: Hydroponic Eqpt/Sply
NURSERIES/LAWN/GRDN SPLY STORE, RET: Nursery Stck, Seed/Bulb
NURSERY STOCK, WHOLESALE
NUTRITION SVCS
NUTS: Metal
NYLON FIBERS

O

OFFICE EQPT WHOLESALERS
OFFICE EQPT, WHOLESALE: Blueprinting
OFFICE EQPT, WHOLESALE: Dictating Machines
OFFICE EQPT, WHOLESALE: Photocopy Machines
OFFICE FIXTURES: Wood
OFFICE FURNITURE REPAIR & MAINTENANCE SVCS
OFFICE MACHINES, NEC
OFFICE SPLY & STATIONERY STORES
OFFICE SPLY & STATIONERY STORES: Office Forms & Splys
OFFICE SPLYS, NEC, WHOLESALE
OFFICES & CLINICS OF DRS OF MED: Em Med Ctr, Freestanding
OFFICES & CLINICS OF HEALTH PRACTITIONERS: Physical Therapy
OFFICES & CLINICS OF OPTOMETRISTS: Specialist, Optometrists
OIL & GAS FIELD MACHINERY
OIL FIELD MACHINERY & EQPT
OIL FIELD SVCS, NEC
OILS & ESSENTIAL OILS
OILS & GREASES: Blended & Compounded

OILS & GREASES: Lubricating
OILS, ANIMAL OR VEGETABLE, WHOLESALE
OILS: Lubricating
OILS: Lubricating
OINTMENTS
OLEFINS
OPEN PIT COPPER ORE MINING
OPERATOR TRAINING, COMPUTER
OPHTHALMIC GOODS
OPHTHALMIC GOODS WHOLESALERS
OPHTHALMIC GOODS, NEC, WHOLESALE: Contact Lenses
OPHTHALMIC GOODS: Eyewear, Protective
OPHTHALMIC GOODS: Frames & Parts, Eyeglass & Spectacle
OPHTHALMIC GOODS: Frames, Lenses & Parts, Eyeglasses
OPHTHALMIC GOODS: Lenses, Ophthalmic
OPTICAL GOODS STORES
OPTICAL GOODS STORES: Contact Lenses, Prescription
OPTICAL GOODS STORES: Eyeglasses, Prescription
OPTICAL GOODS STORES: Opticians
OPTICAL INSTRUMENTS & APPARATUS
OPTICAL INSTRUMENTS & LENSES
OPTOMETRIC EQPT & SPLYS WHOLESALERS
ORAL PREPARATIONS
ORDNANCE
ORDNANCE: Smoke Generators
ORGANIZATIONS: Bacteriological Research
ORGANIZATIONS: Civic & Social
ORGANIZATIONS: Medical Research
ORGANIZATIONS: Professional
ORGANIZATIONS: Religious
ORGANIZERS, CLOSET & DRAWER Plastic
ORNAMENTS: Christmas Tree, Exc Electrical & Glass
OSCILLATORS
OSCILLATORS
OUTBOARD MOTORS & PARTS
OUTLETS: Electric, Convenience
OUTREACH PROGRAM
OVENS: Cremating
OVERBURDEN REMOVAL SVCS: Nonmetallic Minerals

P

PACKAGE DESIGN SVCS
PACKAGED FROZEN FOODS WHOLESALERS, NEC
PACKAGING & LABELING SVCS
PACKAGING MATERIALS, INDL: Wholesalers
PACKAGING MATERIALS, WHOLESALE
PACKAGING MATERIALS: Paper
PACKAGING MATERIALS: Paper, Coated Or Laminated
PACKAGING MATERIALS: Paperboard Backs For Blister/Skin Pkgs
PACKAGING MATERIALS: Plastic Film, Coated Or Laminated
PACKAGING MATERIALS: Polystyrene Foam
PACKAGING: Blister Or Bubble Formed, Plastic
PACKING & CRATING SVC
PACKING MATERIALS: Mechanical
PADS: Mattress
PAGERS: One-way
PAINT & PAINTING SPLYS STORE: Brushes, Rollers, Sprayers
PAINT STORE
PAINTING SVC: Metal Prdts
PAINTS & ADDITIVES
PAINTS & ALLIED PRODUCTS
PAINTS, VARNISHES & SPLYS WHOLESALERS
PAINTS, VARNISHES & SPLYS, WHOLESALE: Paints
PAINTS: Asphalt Or Bituminous
PAINTS: Marine
PAINTS: Oil Or Alkyd Vehicle Or Water Thinned
PAINTS: Waterproof
PALLET REPAIR SVCS
PALLETS
PALLETS & SKIDS: Wood
PALLETS: Plastic
PALLETS: Wooden
PANEL & DISTRIBUTION BOARDS & OTHER RELATED APPARATUS
PANEL & DISTRIBUTION BOARDS: Electric
PANELS, FLAT: Plastic
PANELS: Building, Metal
PANELS: Building, Plastic, NEC
PANELS: Building, Wood
PAPER & BOARD: Die-cut
PAPER CONVERTING
PAPER MANUFACTURERS: Exc Newsprint

PAPER PRDTS
PAPER PRDTS: Book Covers
PAPER PRDTS: Cleansing Tissues, Made From Purchased Material
PAPER PRDTS: Feminine Hygiene Prdts
PAPER PRDTS: Infant & Baby Prdts
PAPER PRDTS: Napkin Stock
PAPER PRDTS: Napkins, Made From Purchased Materials
PAPER PRDTS: Pin Tickets, Made From Purchased Paper
PAPER PRDTS: Sanitary
PAPER PRDTS: Toilet Tissue, Stock
PAPER PRDTS: Towels, Napkins/Tissue Paper, From Purchd Mtrls
PAPER PRDTS: Wrappers, Blank, Made From Purchased Materials
PAPER, WHOLESALE: Printing
PAPER: Adhesive
PAPER: Art
PAPER: Bag
PAPER: Book
PAPER: Business Form
PAPER: Cardboard
PAPER: Cloth, Lined, Made From Purchased Materials
PAPER: Coated & Laminated, NEC
PAPER: Gift Wrap
PAPER: Kraft
PAPER: Magazine
PAPER: Packaging
PAPER: Specialty
PAPER: Tissue
PAPER: Transfer, Gold Or Silver, From Purchased Materials
PAPER: Waxed, Made From Purchased Materials
PAPER: Wrapping
PAPER: Wrapping & Packaging
PAPERBOARD
PAPERBOARD PRDTS: Container Board
PAPERBOARD PRDTS: Tagboard
PAPERBOARD: Corrugated
PARACHUTES
PARKING STRUCTURE
PARTICLEBOARD
PARTICLEBOARD: Laminated, Plastic
PARTITIONS & FIXTURES: Except Wood
PARTITIONS: Nonwood, Floor Attached
PARTITIONS: Wood & Fixtures
PARTITIONS: Wood, Floor Attached
PARTS: Metal
PARTY & SPECIAL EVENT PLANNING SVCS
PATENT OWNERS & LESSORS
PATIENT MONITORING EQPT WHOLESALERS
PATROL SVCS: Electric Transmission Or Gas Lines
PATTERNS: Indl
PAVERS
PAVING MATERIALS: Coal Tar, Not From Refineries
PAWN SHOPS
PAY TELEPHONE NETWORK
PEAT GRINDING SVCS
PEDESTALS: Marble
PENCILS & PARTS: Mechanical
PENS & PENCILS: Mechanical, NEC
PERFUME: Concentrated
PERFUME: Perfumes, Natural Or Synthetic
PERFUMES
PERLITE: Processed
PERMANENT WAVE EQPT & MACHINES
PERSONAL CREDIT INSTITUTIONS: Consumer Finance Companies
PEST CONTROL IN STRUCTURES SVCS
PEST CONTROL SVCS
PESTICIDES
PESTICIDES WHOLESALERS
PET ACCESS: Collars, Leashes, Etc, Exc Leather
PET COLLARS, LEASHES, MUZZLES & HARNESSES: Leather
PET SPLYS
PET SPLYS WHOLESALERS
PETROLEUM PRDTS WHOLESALERS
PEWTER WARE
PHARMACEUTICAL PREPARATIONS: Adrenal
PHARMACEUTICAL PREPARATIONS: Druggists' Preparations
PHARMACEUTICAL PREPARATIONS: Medicines, Capsule Or Ampule
PHARMACEUTICAL PREPARATIONS: Pills
PHARMACEUTICAL PREPARATIONS: Powders

PHARMACEUTICAL PREPARATIONS: Proprietary Drug PRDTS
PHARMACEUTICAL PREPARATIONS: Solutions
PHARMACEUTICAL PREPARATIONS: Tablets
PHARMACEUTICAL PREPARATIONS: Tranquilizers Or Mental Drug
PHARMACEUTICALS
PHARMACEUTICALS: Medicinal & Botanical Prdts
PHONOGRAPH RECORDS: Prerecorded
PHOSPHATE ROCK MINING
PHOSPHATES
PHOTO RECONNAISSANCE SYSTEMS
PHOTOCOPY MACHINE REPAIR SVCS
PHOTOCOPY MACHINES
PHOTOCOPY SPLYS WHOLESALERS
PHOTOCOPYING & DUPLICATING SVCS
PHOTOGRAPHIC EQPT & SPLYS
PHOTOGRAPHIC EQPT & SPLYS WHOLESALERS
PHOTOGRAPHIC EQPT & SPLYS, WHOLESALE: Project, Motion/Slide
PHOTOGRAPHIC EQPT & SPLYS: Cameras, Aerial
PHOTOGRAPHIC EQPT & SPLYS: Develpg Mach/Eqpt, Still/Motion
PHOTOGRAPHIC EQPT & SPLYS: Film, Sensitized
PHOTOGRAPHIC EQPT & SPLYS: Plates, Sensitized
PHOTOGRAPHIC EQPT & SPLYS: Printing Eqpt
PHOTOGRAPHIC EQPT & SPLYS: Printing Frames
PHOTOGRAPHIC EQPT & SPLYS: Reels, Film
PHOTOGRAPHIC EQPT & SPLYS: Toners, Prprd, Not Chem Plnts
PHOTOGRAPHY SVCS: Passport
PHOTOVOLTAIC Solid State
PHYSICIANS' OFFICES & CLINICS: Medical doctors
PICTURE FRAMES: Metal
PICTURE FRAMES: Wood
PIECE GOODS & NOTIONS WHOLESALERS
PIECE GOODS, NOTIONS & DRY GOODS, WHOL: Textiles, Woven
PIECE GOODS, NOTIONS & DRY GOODS, WHOLESALE: Fabrics
PIECE GOODS, NOTIONS & DRY GOODS, WHOLESALE: Fabrics, Knit
PIECE GOODS, NOTIONS & OTHER DRY GOODS, WHOLESALE: Buttons
PIECE GOODS, NOTIONS & OTHER DRY GOODS, WHOLESALE: Notions
PIECE GOODS, NOTIONS & OTHER DRY GOODS, WHOLESALE: Ribbons
PIECE GOODS, NOTIONS/DRY GOODS, WHOL: Drapery Mtrl, Woven
PIECE GOODS, NOTIONS/DRY GOODS, WHOL: Fabrics, Synthetic
PIGMENTS, INORGANIC: Black
PILING: Prefabricated, Concrete
PILOT SVCS: Aviation
PINS
PINS: Dowel
PIPE & FITTING: Fabrication
PIPE & FITTINGS: Cast Iron
PIPE & FITTINGS: Pressure, Cast Iron
PIPE & TUBES: Copper & Copper Alloy
PIPE JOINT COMPOUNDS
PIPE, CULVERT: Concrete
PIPE, CYLINDER: Concrete, Prestressed Or Pretensioned
PIPE: Concrete
PIPE: Irrigation, Sheet Metal
PIPE: Plastic
PIPE: Seamless Steel
PIPE: Sheet Metal
PIPES & FITTINGS: Fiber, Made From Purchased Materials
PIPES & TUBES
PIPES & TUBES: Steel
PIPES & TUBES: Welded
PIPES: Steel & Iron
PIPES: Tobacco
PLANING MILL, NEC
PLANING MILLS: Millwork
PLANTERS: Plastic
PLAQUES: Picture, Laminated
PLASMAS
PLASTER WORK: Ornamental & Architectural
PLASTIC PRDTS
PLASTICS FILM & SHEET
PLASTICS FILM & SHEET: Polyethylene
PLASTICS FILM & SHEET: Vinyl

PLASTICS FINISHED PRDTS: Laminated
PLASTICS MATERIAL & RESINS
PLASTICS MATERIALS, BASIC FORMS & SHAPES WHOLESALERS
PLASTICS PROCESSING
PLASTICS SHEET: Packing Materials
PLASTICS: Blow Molded
PLASTICS: Carbohydrate
PLASTICS: Cast
PLASTICS: Extruded
PLASTICS: Finished Injection Molded
PLASTICS: Injection Molded
PLASTICS: Molded
PLASTICS: Polystyrene Foam
PLASTICS: Thermoformed
PLATEMAKING SVC: Color Separations, For The Printing Trade
PLATES
PLATES: Steel
PLATES: Truss, Metal
PLATING & FINISHING SVC: Decorative, Formed Prdts
PLATING & POLISHING SVC
PLATING SVC: Chromium, Metals Or Formed Prdts
PLATING SVC: Electro
PLATING SVC: NEC
PLAYGROUND EQPT
PLEATING & STITCHING SVC
PLUGS: Electric
PLUMBING & HEATING EQPT & SPLY, WHOLESALE: Hydronic Htg Eqpt
PLUMBING & HEATING EQPT & SPLYS WHOLESALERS
PLUMBING & HEATING EQPT & SPLYS, WHOL: Pipe/Fitting, Plastic
PLUMBING & HEATING EQPT & SPLYS, WHOL: Plumbing Fitting/Sply
PLUMBING & HEATING EQPT & SPLYS, WHOL: Water Purif Eqpt
PLUMBING FIXTURES
PLUMBING FIXTURES: Plastic
PLUMBING FIXTURES: Vitreous
PLUMBING FIXTURES: Vitreous China
POINT OF SALE DEVICES
POKER CHIPS
POLES & POSTS: Concrete
POLICE PROTECTION: Bureau Of Criminal Investigation, Govt
POLISHING SVC: Metals Or Formed Prdts
POLYCARBONATE RESINS
POLYESTERS
POLYETHYLENE RESINS
POLYPROPYLENE RESINS
POLYSTYRENE RESINS
POLYURETHANE RESINS
POLYVINYL CHLORIDE RESINS
POPCORN & SUPPLIES WHOLESALERS
PORCELAIN ENAMELED PRDTS & UTENSILS
POSTAL EQPT: Locker Boxes, Exc Wood
POSTERS
POTTERY
POTTING SOILS
POULTRY & POULTRY PRDTS WHOLESALERS
POULTRY & SMALL GAME SLAUGHTERING & PROCESSING
POWDER: Metal
POWDER: Silver
POWER GENERATORS
POWER OUTLETS & SOCKETS
POWER SUPPLIES: All Types, Static
POWER TOOLS, HAND: Drills & Drilling Tools
POWER TOOLS, HAND: Grinders, Portable, Electric Or Pneumatic
POWER TRANSMISSION EQPT: Aircraft
POWER TRANSMISSION EQPT: Mechanical
POWER TRANSMISSION EQPT: Vehicle
POWERED GOLF CART DEALERS
PRECAST TERRAZZO OR CONCRETE PRDTS
PRECIOUS METALS
PREFABRICATED BUILDING DEALERS
PRERECORDED TAPE, CD & RECORD STORE: Record, Disc/Tape
PRERECORDED TAPE, CD/RECORD STORES: Audio Tapes, Prerecorded
PRERECORDED TAPE, COMPACT DISC & RECORD STORES: Compact Disc
PRESS CLIPPING SVC

PRESSED & MOLDED PULP PRDTS, NEC: From Purchased Materials
PRESTRESSED CONCRETE PRDTS
PRIMARY METAL PRODUCTS
PRINT CARTRIDGES: Laser & Other Computer Printers
PRINTED CIRCUIT BOARDS
PRINTERS & PLOTTERS
PRINTERS' SVCS: Folding, Collating, Etc
PRINTERS: Computer
PRINTERS: Magnetic Ink, Bar Code
PRINTING & BINDING: Books
PRINTING & BINDING: Pamphlets
PRINTING & EMBOSSING: Plastic Fabric Articles
PRINTING & ENGRAVING: Card, Exc Greeting
PRINTING & ENGRAVING: Invitation & Stationery
PRINTING & STAMPING: Fabric Articles
PRINTING MACHINERY
PRINTING MACHINERY, EQPT & SPLYS: Wholesalers
PRINTING TRADES MACHINERY & EQPT REPAIR SVCS
PRINTING, COMMERCIAL Newspapers, NEC
PRINTING, COMMERCIAL: Announcements, NEC
PRINTING, COMMERCIAL: Bags, Plastic, NEC
PRINTING, COMMERCIAL: Business Forms, NEC
PRINTING, COMMERCIAL: Cards, Playing, NEC
PRINTING, COMMERCIAL: Cards, Visiting, Incl Business, NEC
PRINTING, COMMERCIAL: Certificates, Security, NEC
PRINTING, COMMERCIAL: Decals, NEC
PRINTING, COMMERCIAL: Directories, Telephone, NEC
PRINTING, COMMERCIAL: Envelopes, NEC
PRINTING, COMMERCIAL: Fashion Plates, NEC
PRINTING, COMMERCIAL: Imprinting
PRINTING, COMMERCIAL: Invitations, NEC
PRINTING, COMMERCIAL: Labels & Seals, NEC
PRINTING, COMMERCIAL: Letterpress & Screen
PRINTING, COMMERCIAL: Literature, Advertising, NEC
PRINTING, COMMERCIAL: Magazines, NEC
PRINTING, COMMERCIAL: Maps, NEC
PRINTING, COMMERCIAL: Menus, NEC
PRINTING, COMMERCIAL: Promotional
PRINTING, COMMERCIAL: Publications
PRINTING, COMMERCIAL: Schedules, Transportation, NEC
PRINTING, COMMERCIAL: Screen
PRINTING, COMMERCIAL: Stationery, NEC
PRINTING, COMMERCIAL: Tags, NEC
PRINTING, LITHOGRAPHIC: Advertising Posters
PRINTING, LITHOGRAPHIC: Calendars & Cards
PRINTING, LITHOGRAPHIC: Color
PRINTING, LITHOGRAPHIC: Decals
PRINTING, LITHOGRAPHIC: Forms & Cards, Business
PRINTING, LITHOGRAPHIC: Letters, Circular Or Form
PRINTING, LITHOGRAPHIC: Menus
PRINTING, LITHOGRAPHIC: Newspapers
PRINTING, LITHOGRAPHIC: Offset & photolithographic printing
PRINTING, LITHOGRAPHIC: On Metal
PRINTING, LITHOGRAPHIC: Post Cards, Picture
PRINTING, LITHOGRAPHIC: Promotional
PRINTING, LITHOGRAPHIC: Publications
PRINTING, LITHOGRAPHIC: Tags
PRINTING, LITHOGRAPHIC: Trading Stamps
PRINTING, LITHOGRAPHIC: Transfers, Decalcomania Or Dry
PRINTING: Books
PRINTING: Books
PRINTING: Commercial, NEC
PRINTING: Engraving & Plate
PRINTING: Fabric, Narrow
PRINTING: Flexographic
PRINTING: Gravure, Business Form & Card
PRINTING: Gravure, Color
PRINTING: Gravure, Envelopes
PRINTING: Gravure, Forms, Business
PRINTING: Gravure, Job
PRINTING: Gravure, Labels
PRINTING: Gravure, Rotogravure
PRINTING: Gravure, Seals
PRINTING: Gravure, Stationery & Invitation
PRINTING: Gravure, Visiting Cards
PRINTING: Laser
PRINTING: Letterpress
PRINTING: Lithographic
PRINTING: Offset
PRINTING: Pamphlets
PRINTING: Photolithographic
PRINTING: Roller, Broadwoven Fabrics, Cotton

PRINTING: Screen, Broadwoven Fabrics, Cotton
PRINTING: Screen, Fabric
PRINTING: Screen, Manmade Fiber & Silk, Broadwoven Fabric
PRINTING: Thermography
PRODUCT STERILIZATION SVCS
PRODUCTS: Petroleum & coal, NEC
PROFESSIONAL EQPT & SPLYS, WHOLESALE: Bank
PROFESSIONAL EQPT & SPLYS, WHOLESALE: Engineers', NEC
PROFESSIONAL EQPT & SPLYS, WHOLESALE: Optical Goods
PROFESSIONAL EQPT & SPLYS, WHOLESALE: Scientific & Engineerg
PROFESSIONAL EQPT & SPLYS, WHOLESALE: Theatrical
PROFESSIONAL INSTRUMENT REPAIR SVCS
PROFILE SHAPES: Unsupported Plastics
PROMOTION SVCS
PROPELLERS: Boat & Ship, Cast
PROPELLERS: Boat & Ship, Machined
PROPELLERS: Ship, Nec
PROPULSION UNITS: Guided Missiles & Space Vehicles
PROTECTION EQPT: Lightning
PROTECTIVE FOOTWEAR: Rubber Or Plastic
PUBLIC RELATIONS SVCS
PUBLISHERS: Art Copy & Poster
PUBLISHERS: Book
PUBLISHERS: Book Clubs, No Printing
PUBLISHERS: Books, No Printing
PUBLISHERS: Catalogs
PUBLISHERS: Directories, NEC
PUBLISHERS: Guides
PUBLISHERS: Magazines, No Printing
PUBLISHERS: Maps
PUBLISHERS: Miscellaneous
PUBLISHERS: Music Book & Sheet Music
PUBLISHERS: Newsletter
PUBLISHERS: Newspaper
PUBLISHERS: Newspapers, No Printing
PUBLISHERS: Pamphlets, No Printing
PUBLISHERS: Periodical Statistical Reports, No Printing
PUBLISHERS: Periodical, With Printing
PUBLISHERS: Periodicals, Magazines
PUBLISHERS: Periodicals, No Printing
PUBLISHERS: Technical Manuals
PUBLISHERS: Technical Manuals & Papers
PUBLISHERS: Telephone & Other Directory
PUBLISHERS: Textbooks, No Printing
PUBLISHERS: Trade journals, No Printing
PUBLISHING & BROADCASTING: Internet Only
PUBLISHING & PRINTING: Art Copy
PUBLISHING & PRINTING: Book Music
PUBLISHING & PRINTING: Books
PUBLISHING & PRINTING: Catalogs
PUBLISHING & PRINTING: Directories, NEC
PUBLISHING & PRINTING: Guides
PUBLISHING & PRINTING: Magazines: publishing & printing
PUBLISHING & PRINTING: Music, Book
PUBLISHING & PRINTING: Newsletters, Business Svc
PUBLISHING & PRINTING: Newspapers
PUBLISHING & PRINTING: Pamphlets
PUBLISHING & PRINTING: Posters
PUBLISHING & PRINTING: Shopping News
PUBLISHING & PRINTING: Technical Manuals
PUBLISHING & PRINTING: Textbooks
PUBLISHING & PRINTING: Trade Journals
PULP MILLS
PULP MILLS: Mechanical & Recycling Processing
PULSE FORMING NETWORKS
PUMP JACKS & OTHER PUMPING EQPT: Indl
PUMPS
PUMPS & PARTS: Indl
PUMPS & PUMPING EQPT REPAIR SVCS
PUMPS & PUMPING EQPT WHOLESALERS
PUMPS, HEAT: Electric
PUMPS: Aircraft, Hydraulic
PUMPS: Domestic, Water Or Sump
PUMPS: Fluid Power
PUMPS: Hydraulic Power Transfer
PUMPS: Measuring & Dispensing
PUMPS: Oil Well & Field
PUMPS: Vacuum, Exc Laboratory
PUPPETS & MARIONETTES
PURIFICATION & DUST COLLECTION EQPT
PUSHCARTS

INDEX

Q

QUARTZ CRYSTALS: Electronic
QUILTING SVC & SPLYS, FOR THE TRADE

R

RACEWAYS
RACKS: Bicycle, Automotive
RACKS: Display
RACKS: Pallet, Exc Wood
RACKS: Railroad Car, Vehicle Transportation, Steel
RADAR SYSTEMS & EQPT
RADIO & TELEVISION COMMUNICATIONS EQUIPMENT
RADIO & TELEVISION REPAIR
RADIO BROADCASTING & COMMUNICATIONS EQPT
RADIO COMMUNICATIONS: Airborne Eqpt
RADIO EQPT: Citizens Band
RADIO MAGNETIC INSTRUMENTATION
RADIO PRODUCERS
RADIO RECEIVER NETWORKS
RADIO, TELEVISION & CONSUMER ELECTRONICS
  STORES: Eqpt, NEC
RADIOS WHOLESALERS
RAIL & STRUCTURAL SHAPES: Aluminum rail & structural
  shapes
RAILINGS: Prefabricated, Metal
RAILROAD CARGO LOADING & UNLOADING SVCS
RAILROAD EQPT
RAILROAD EQPT: Cars & Eqpt, Dining
RAILROAD EQPT: Cars & Eqpt, Train, Freight Or Passenger
RAILROAD EQPT: Cars, Maintenance
RAILROAD EQPT: Cars, Rebuilt
RAILROAD RELATED EQPT: Railway Track
RAILROAD TIES: Concrete
RAILROADS: Long Haul
RAILS: Rails, rolled & drawn, aluminum
RAILS: Steel Or Iron
RAMPS: Prefabricated Metal
REAL ESTATE AGENCIES: Residential
REAL ESTATE AGENTS & MANAGERS
REAL ESTATE APPRAISERS
REAL ESTATE INVESTMENT TRUSTS
REAL ESTATE OPERATORS, EXC DEVELOPERS: Commer-
  cial/Indl Bldg
REAL ESTATE OPERATORS, EXC DEVELOPERS: Property,
  Retail
RECEIVERS: Radio Communications
RECORDING TAPE: Video, Blank
RECORDS & TAPES: Prerecorded
RECOVERY SVC: Iron Ore, From Open Hearth Slag
RECOVERY SVCS: Solvents
RECREATIONAL VEHICLE DEALERS
RECREATIONAL VEHICLE PARTS & ACCESS STORES
RECYCLING: Paper
REELS: Wood
REFINERS & SMELTERS: Aluminum
REFINERS & SMELTERS: Copper
REFINERS & SMELTERS: Nonferrous Metal
REFINERS & SMELTERS: Silicon, Primary, Over 99% Pure
REFINING: Petroleum
REFRACTORIES: Brick
REFRACTORIES: Cement, nonclay
REFRACTORIES: Clay
REFRACTORIES: Nonclay
REFRACTORIES: Tile & Brick, Exc Plastic
REFRIGERATION & HEATING EQUIPMENT
REFRIGERATION EQPT: Complete
REFRIGERATION REPAIR SVCS
REFRIGERATION SVC & REPAIR
REFRIGERATORS & FREEZERS WHOLESALERS
REFUSE SYSTEMS
REGULATION & ADMIN, GOVT: Public Svc Commission, Exc
  Transp
REGULATORS: Power
REGULATORS: Transmission & Distribution Voltage
RELAYS & SWITCHES: Indl, Electric
REMOVERS & CLEANERS
RENTAL CENTERS: General
RENTAL SVCS: Aircraft
RENTAL SVCS: Business Machine & Electronic Eqpt
RENTAL SVCS: Eqpt & Prop, Motion Picture Production
RENTAL SVCS: Floor Maintenance Eqpt
RENTAL SVCS: Sound & Lighting Eqpt
RENTAL SVCS: Work Zone Traffic Eqpt, Flags, Cones, Etc
RENTAL: Passenger Car

RENTAL: Portable Toilet
RESEARCH, DEVELOPMENT & TEST SVCS, COMM: Cmptr
  Hardware Dev
RESEARCH, DEVELOPMENT & TEST SVCS, COMM: Re-
  search, Exc Lab
RESEARCH, DEVELOPMENT & TESTING SVCS, COMM:
  Research Lab
RESEARCH, DEVELOPMENT & TESTING SVCS, COMMER-
  CIAL: Business
RESEARCH, DEVELOPMENT & TESTING SVCS, COMMER-
  CIAL: Energy
RESEARCH, DEVELOPMENT & TESTING SVCS, COMMER-
  CIAL: Medical
RESEARCH, DVLPT & TEST SVCS, COMM: Mkt Analysis or
  Research
RESIDUES
RESINS: Custom Compound Purchased
RESISTORS
RESISTORS & RESISTOR UNITS
RESOLVERS
RESORT HOTELS
RESPIRATORY SYSTEM DRUGS
RESTAURANT EQPT: Carts
RESTAURANT EQPT: Food Wagons
RESTAURANT EQPT: Sheet Metal
RESTAURANTS: Fast Food
RESTAURANTS:Full Svc, Cajun
RESTAURANTS:Full Svc, Chinese
RESTAURANTS:Full Svc, Ethnic Food
RESTAURANTS:Full Svc, Family, Independent
RESTAURANTS:Full Svc, Italian
RESTAURANTS:Full Svc, Mexican
RESTAURANTS:Limited Svc, Coffee Shop
RESTAURANTS:Limited Svc, Fast-Food, Chain
RESTAURANTS:Limited Svc, Frozen Yogurt Stand
RESTAURANTS:Limited Svc, Ice Cream Stands Or Dairy
  Bars
RESTAURANTS:Limited Svc, Pizza
RESTRAINTS
RESTROOM CLEANING SVCS
RETAIL BAKERY: Cakes
RETAIL BAKERY: Cookies
RETAIL BAKERY: Doughnuts
RETAIL FIREPLACE STORES
RETAIL LUMBER YARDS
RETAIL STORES, NEC
RETAIL STORES: Alcoholic Beverage Making Eqpt & Splys
RETAIL STORES: Aquarium Splys
RETAIL STORES: Artificial Limbs
RETAIL STORES: Audio-Visual Eqpt & Splys
RETAIL STORES: Autograph Splys
RETAIL STORES: Awnings
RETAIL STORES: Baby Carriages & Strollers
RETAIL STORES: Banners
RETAIL STORES: Binoculars & Telescopes
RETAIL STORES: Business Machines & Eqpt
RETAIL STORES: Cake Decorating Splys
RETAIL STORES: Canvas Prdts
RETAIL STORES: Cleaning Eqpt & Splys
RETAIL STORES: Concrete Prdts, Precast
RETAIL STORES: Cosmetics
RETAIL STORES: Educational Aids & Electronic Training Mat
RETAIL STORES: Electronic Parts & Eqpt
RETAIL STORES: Farm Eqpt & Splys
RETAIL STORES: Fiberglass Materials, Exc Insulation
RETAIL STORES: Flags
RETAIL STORES: Hair Care Prdts
RETAIL STORES: Hearing Aids
RETAIL STORES: Hospital Eqpt & Splys
RETAIL STORES: Ice
RETAIL STORES: Maps & Charts
RETAIL STORES: Medical Apparatus & Splys
RETAIL STORES: Mobile Telephones & Eqpt
RETAIL STORES: Monuments, Finished To Custom Order
RETAIL STORES: Motors, Electric
RETAIL STORES: Orthopedic & Prosthesis Applications
RETAIL STORES: Pet Splys
RETAIL STORES: Photocopy Machines
RETAIL STORES: Police Splys
RETAIL STORES: Rubber Stamps
RETAIL STORES: Safety Splys & Eqpt
RETAIL STORES: Sunglasses
RETAIL STORES: Telephone & Communication Eqpt
RETAIL STORES: Water Purification Eqpt
RETREADING MATERIALS: Tire

REUPHOLSTERY & FURNITURE REPAIR
REUPHOLSTERY SVCS
REWINDING SVCS
RIBBONS: Machine, Inked Or Carbon
RIPRAP QUARRYING
RIVETS: Metal
ROAD MATERIALS: Bituminous
ROAD MATERIALS: Bituminous, Not From Refineries
ROBOTS: Assembly Line
ROCKETS: Space & Military
ROD & BAR: Aluminum
RODS: Plastic
RODS: Steel & Iron, Made In Steel Mills
RODS: Welding
ROLLERS & FITTINGS: Window Shade
ROLLING MILL EQPT: Galvanizing Lines
ROLLING MILL MACHINERY
ROOF DECKS
ROOFING MATERIALS: Asphalt
ROOFING MATERIALS: Sheet Metal
ROOFING MEMBRANE: Rubber
ROOM COOLERS: Portable
ROPE
RUBBER
RUBBER BANDS
RUBBER PRDTS
RUBBER PRDTS: Automotive, Mechanical
RUBBER PRDTS: Mechanical
RUBBER PRDTS: Oil & Gas Field Machinery, Mechanical
RUBBER PRDTS: Reclaimed
RUBBER PRDTS: Sheeting
RUBBER PRDTS: Silicone
RUBBER PRDTS: Sponge
RUBBER PRDTS: Wet Suits
RUG BINDING
RUGS : Hand & Machine Made
RUST REMOVERS

S

SAFES & VAULTS: Metal
SAFETY EQPT & SPLYS WHOLESALERS
SAFETY INSPECTION SVCS
SAILBOAT BUILDING & REPAIR
SAILS
SALES PROMOTION SVCS
SALT
SAMPLE BOOKS
SAND & GRAVEL
SAND MINING
SAND: Hygrade
SAND: Silica
SANDBLASTING EQPT
SANDBLASTING SVC: Building Exterior
SANITARY SVC, NEC
SANITARY SVCS: Environmental Cleanup
SANITARY SVCS: Liquid Waste Collection & Disposal
SANITARY SVCS: Sanitary Landfill, Operation Of
SANITARY SVCS: Waste Materials, Recycling
SANITARY WARE: Metal
SANITATION CHEMICALS & CLEANING AGENTS
SASHES: Door Or Window, Metal
SATCHELS
SATELLITE COMMUNICATIONS EQPT
SATELLITES: Communications
SAUNA ROOMS: Prefabricated
SAW BLADES
SAWDUST & SHAVINGS
SAWING & PLANING MILLS
SAWING & PLANING MILLS: Custom
SAWS & SAWING EQPT
SCALES & BALANCES, EXC LABORATORY
SCALES: Indl
SCALES: Truck
SCANNING DEVICES: Optical
SCHOOL BUS SVC
SCHOOLS & EDUCATIONAL SVCS, NEC
SCIENTIFIC INSTRUMENTS WHOLESALERS
SCREENS: Door, Metal Covered Wood
SCREENS: Door, Wood Frame
SCREENS: Projection
SCREENS: Window, Metal
SCREENS: Window, Wood Framed
SCREENS: Woven Wire
SCREW MACHINE PRDTS
SCREW MACHINES

SCREWS: Metal
SEALANTS
SEALS: Hermetic
SEALS: Oil, Rubber
SEARCH & DETECTION SYSTEMS, EXC RADAR
SEARCH & NAVIGATION SYSTEMS
SEARCH & RESCUE SVCS
SEASHELLS, WHOLESALE
SEAT BELTS: Automobile & Aircraft
SEATING: Bleacher, Portable
SEATING: Chairs, Table & Arm
SEATING: Stadium
SECRETARIAL & COURT REPORTING
SECRETARIAL SVCS
SECURITY CONTROL EQPT & SYSTEMS
SECURITY DEVICES
SECURITY EQPT STORES
SECURITY PROTECTIVE DEVICES MAINTENANCE & MONITORING SVCS
SECURITY SYSTEMS SERVICES
SELF-PROPELLED AIRCRAFT DEALER
SEMICONDUCTOR CIRCUIT NETWORKS
SEMICONDUCTOR DEVICES: Wafers
SEMICONDUCTORS & RELATED DEVICES
SENSORS: Infrared, Solid State
SENSORS: Radiation
SENSORS: Temperature, Exc Indl Process
SEPTIC TANK CLEANING SVCS
SEPTIC TANKS: Concrete
SEPTIC TANKS: Plastic
SEWAGE & WATER TREATMENT EQPT
SEWAGE FACILITIES
SEWAGE TREATMENT SYSTEMS & EQPT
SEWER CLEANING EQPT: Power
SEWING CONTRACTORS
SEWING KITS: Novelty
SEWING MACHINES & PARTS: Indl
SEWING, NEEDLEWORK & PIECE GOODS STORES: Sewing & Needlework
SEXTANTS
SHADES: Lamp & Light, Residential
SHADES: Lamp Or Candle
SHADES: Window
SHAFTS: Flexible
SHAPES & PILINGS, STRUCTURAL: Steel
SHAPES: Extruded, Aluminum, NEC
SHEARS
SHEET METAL SPECIALTIES, EXC STAMPED
SHEETING: Window, Plastic
SHELL MINING
SHELLAC
SHELVING, MADE FROM PURCHASED WIRE
SHELVING: Office & Store, Exc Wood
SHIP BUILDING & REPAIRING: Cargo Vessels
SHIP BUILDING & REPAIRING: Cargo, Commercial
SHIP BUILDING & REPAIRING: Dredges
SHIP BUILDING & REPAIRING: Ferryboats
SHIP BUILDING & REPAIRING: Landing
SHIP BUILDING & REPAIRING: Lighters, Marine
SHIP BUILDING & REPAIRING: Lighthouse Tenders
SHIP BUILDING & REPAIRING: Patrol Boats
SHIP BUILDING & REPAIRING: Rigging, Marine
SHIP BUILDING & REPAIRING: Tugboats
SHIP COMPONENTS: Metal, Prefabricated
SHIPBUILDING & REPAIR
SHIPPING AGENTS
SHOCK ABSORBERS: Indl
SHOE & BOOT ACCESS
SHOE MATERIALS: Counters
SHOE MATERIALS: Heel Parts
SHOE MATERIALS: Plastic
SHOE MATERIALS: Quarters
SHOE MATERIALS: Rands
SHOE STORES: Orthopedic
SHOE STORES: Women's
SHOES: Canvas, Rubber Soled
SHOES: Men's
SHOES: Men's, Sandals
SHOES: Plastic Or Rubber
SHOES: Sandals, Rubber
SHOES: Women's
SHOES: Women's, Dress
SHOES: Women's, Sandals
SHOT PEENING SVC
SHOWCASES & DISPLAY FIXTURES: Office & Store

SHOWER STALLS: Metal
SHOWER STALLS: Plastic & Fiberglass
SHREDDERS: Indl & Commercial
SHUTTERS, DOOR & WINDOW: Metal
SHUTTERS, DOOR & WINDOW: Plastic
SHUTTERS: Door, Wood
SHUTTERS: Window, Wood
SIDING & STRUCTURAL MATERIALS: Wood
SIDING MATERIALS
SIDING: Precast Stone
SIDING: Sheet Metal
SIGN LETTERING & PAINTING SVCS
SIGN PAINTING & LETTERING SHOP
SIGNALING APPARATUS: Electric
SIGNALS: Railroad, Electric
SIGNALS: Traffic Control, Electric
SIGNALS: Transportation
SIGNS & ADVERTISING SPECIALTIES
SIGNS & ADVERTISING SPECIALTIES: Novelties
SIGNS & ADVERTISING SPECIALTIES: Signs
SIGNS & ADVERTSG SPECIALTIES: Displays/Cutouts Window/Lobby
SIGNS, EXC ELECTRIC, WHOLESALE
SIGNS: Electrical
SIGNS: Neon
SILICONE RESINS
SILICONES
SILK SCREEN DESIGN SVCS
SILLS, WINDOW: Cast Stone
SILO STAVES: Concrete Or Cast Stone
SILVER ORE MINING
SILVER ORES
SIMULATORS: Electronic Countermeasure
SIMULATORS: Flight
SIRENS: Vehicle, Marine, Indl & Warning
SIZES
SKILL TRAINING CENTER
SKIN CARE PRDTS: Suntan Lotions & Oils
SKYLIGHTS
SLAB & TILE, ROOFING: Concrete
SLAB & TILE: Precast Concrete, Floor
SLAG PRDTS
SLAG: Crushed Or Ground
SLAUGHTERING & MEAT PACKING
SLIDES & EXHIBITS: Prepared
SLINGS: Rope
SLIPPERS: House
SLOT MACHINES
SLUGS: Slugs, aluminum
SOAPS & DETERGENTS
SOFT DRINKS WHOLESALERS
SOFTWARE PUBLISHERS: Application
SOFTWARE PUBLISHERS: Business & Professional
SOFTWARE PUBLISHERS: Computer Utilities
SOFTWARE PUBLISHERS: Education
SOFTWARE PUBLISHERS: Home Entertainment
SOFTWARE PUBLISHERS: NEC
SOFTWARE PUBLISHERS: Operating Systems
SOFTWARE PUBLISHERS: Publisher's
SOFTWARE PUBLISHERS: Word Processing
SOFTWARE TRAINING, COMPUTER
SOIL CONDITIONERS
SOLAR CELLS
SOLAR HEATING EQPT
SOLVENTS
SOLVENTS: Organic
SONAR SYSTEMS & EQPT
SOUND EQPT: Electric
SOUND EQPT: Underwater
SOUVENIRS, WHOLESALE
SOYBEAN PRDTS
SPACE FLIGHT OPERATIONS, EXC GOVERNMENT
SPACE PROPULSION UNITS & PARTS
SPACE RESEARCH & TECHNOLOGY PROGRAMS ADMINISTRATION
SPACE VEHICLE EQPT
SPACE VEHICLES
SPARK PLUGS: Internal Combustion Engines
SPEAKER SYSTEMS
SPECIALTY FOOD STORES: Coffee
SPECIALTY FOOD STORES: Dietetic Foods
SPECIALTY FOOD STORES: Health & Dietetic Food
SPECIALTY FOOD STORES: Juices, Fruit Or Vegetable
SPECIALTY FOOD STORES: Tea
SPECIALTY FOOD STORES: Vitamin

SPECIALTY SAWMILL PRDTS
SPECULATIVE BUILDERS: Single-Family Housing
SPICE & HERB STORES
SPIKES: Steel, Wire Or Cut
SPINDLES: Textile
SPORTING & ATHLETIC GOODS: Arrows, Archery
SPORTING & ATHLETIC GOODS: Balls, Baseball, Football, Etc
SPORTING & ATHLETIC GOODS: Boomerangs
SPORTING & ATHLETIC GOODS: Bowling Alleys & Access
SPORTING & ATHLETIC GOODS: Bows, Archery
SPORTING & ATHLETIC GOODS: Bridges, Billiard & Pool
SPORTING & ATHLETIC GOODS: Buckets, Fish & Bait
SPORTING & ATHLETIC GOODS: Driving Ranges, Golf, Electronic
SPORTING & ATHLETIC GOODS: Fishing Eqpt
SPORTING & ATHLETIC GOODS: Fishing Tackle, General
SPORTING & ATHLETIC GOODS: Gymnasium Eqpt
SPORTING & ATHLETIC GOODS: Hooks, Fishing
SPORTING & ATHLETIC GOODS: Hunting Eqpt
SPORTING & ATHLETIC GOODS: Ping-Pong Tables
SPORTING & ATHLETIC GOODS: Pools, Swimming, Exc Plastic
SPORTING & ATHLETIC GOODS: Pools, Swimming, Plastic
SPORTING & ATHLETIC GOODS: Protective Sporting Eqpt
SPORTING & ATHLETIC GOODS: Racket Sports Eqpt
SPORTING & ATHLETIC GOODS: Rackets/Frames, Tennis, Etc
SPORTING & ATHLETIC GOODS: Reels, Fishing
SPORTING & ATHLETIC GOODS: Rods & Rod Parts, Fishing
SPORTING & ATHLETIC GOODS: Shafts, Golf Club
SPORTING & ATHLETIC GOODS: Shooting Eqpt & Splys, General
SPORTING & ATHLETIC GOODS: Shuffleboards & Shuffleboard Eqpt
SPORTING & ATHLETIC GOODS: Skateboards
SPORTING & ATHLETIC GOODS: Skates & Parts, Roller
SPORTING & ATHLETIC GOODS: Team Sports Eqpt
SPORTING & ATHLETIC GOODS: Tennis Eqpt & Splys
SPORTING & ATHLETIC GOODS: Trampolines & Eqpt
SPORTING & ATHLETIC GOODS: Water Skis
SPORTING & ATHLETIC GOODS: Water Sports Eqpt
SPORTING & REC GOODS, WHOLESALE: Boats, Canoes, Etc/Eqpt
SPORTING & RECREATIONAL GOODS & SPLYS WHOLESALERS
SPORTING & RECREATIONAL GOODS, WHOLESALE: Boat Access & Part
SPORTING & RECREATIONAL GOODS, WHOLESALE: Diving
SPORTING & RECREATIONAL GOODS, WHOLESALE: Golf
SPORTING & RECREATIONAL GOODS, WHOLESALE: Gymnasium
SPORTING & RECREATIONAL GOODS, WHOLESALE: Watersports
SPORTING GOODS
SPORTING GOODS STORES, NEC
SPORTING GOODS STORES: Firearms
SPORTING GOODS STORES: Fishing Eqpt
SPORTING GOODS STORES: Pool & Billiard Tables
SPORTING GOODS STORES: Surfing Eqpt & Splys
SPORTING GOODS STORES: Team sports Eqpt
SPORTING GOODS: Fishing Nets
SPORTING GOODS: Skin Diving Eqpt
SPORTING GOODS: Surfboards
SPORTS APPAREL STORES
SPOUTING: Plastic & Fiberglass Reinforced
SPRAYING & DUSTING EQPT
SPRAYING EQPT: Agricultural
SPRINGS: Automobile
SPRINGS: Clock, Precision
SPRINGS: Gun, Precision
SPRINGS: Mechanical, Precision
SPRINGS: Precision
SPRINGS: Steel
SPRINGS: Wire
SPRINKLER SYSTEMS: Field
SPRINKLING SYSTEMS: Fire Control
SPROCKETS: Power Transmission
STAGE LIGHTING SYSTEMS
STAINLESS STEEL
STAINLESS STEEL WARE
STAINS: Biological
STAIRCASES & STAIRS, WOOD
STAMPED ART GOODS FOR EMBROIDERING

INDEX

STAMPINGS: Metal
STAPLES
STAPLES: Steel, Wire Or Cut
STARTERS: Electric Motor
STARTERS: Motor
STATIC ELIMINATORS: Ind
STATIONARY & OFFICE SPLYS, WHOLESALE: Laser Printer Splys
STATIONERY & OFFICE SPLYS WHOLESALERS
STATIONERY PRDTS
STATORS REWINDING SVCS
STATUARY & OTHER DECORATIVE PRDTS: Nonmetallic
STATUARY GOODS, EXC RELIGIOUS: Wholesalers
STEEL & ALLOYS: Tool & Die
STEEL FABRICATORS
STEEL MILLS
STEEL: Cold-Rolled
STEEL: Laminated
STENCILS
STENCILS & LETTERING MATERIALS: Die-Cut
STERILIZERS, BARBER & BEAUTY SHOP
STOCK CAR RACING
STOKERS: Mechanical, Domestic Or Indl
STONE: Cast Concrete
STONE: Dimension, NEC
STONE: Quarrying & Processing, Own Stone Prdts
STONEWARE PRDTS: Pottery
STOOLS: Factory
STORE FIXTURES: Wood
STORE FRONTS: Prefabricated, Metal
STORES: Auto & Home Supply
STORES: Drapery & Upholstery
STRAPPING
STRAW GOODS
STRAWS: Drinking, Made From Purchased Materials
STRUCTURAL SUPPORT & BUILDING MATERIAL: Concrete
STUCCO
STUDIOS: Artist
STUDS & JOISTS: Sheet Metal
SUBMARINE BUILDING & REPAIR
SUNDRIES & RELATED PRDTS: Medical & Laboratory, Rubber
SUNROOMS: Prefabricated Metal
SUPERMARKETS & OTHER GROCERY STORES
SURFACE ACTIVE AGENTS
SURFACE ACTIVE AGENTS: Oils & Greases
SURFACERS: Concrete Grinding
SURGICAL & MEDICAL INSTRUMENTS WHOLESALERS
SURGICAL APPLIANCES & SPLYS
SURGICAL APPLIANCES & SPLYS
SURGICAL EQPT: See Also Instruments
SURGICAL IMPLANTS
SURVEYING & MAPPING: Land Parcels
SURVEYING SVCS: Aerial Digital Imaging
SVC ESTABLISH EQPT, WHOLESALE: Carpet/Rug Clean Eqpt & Sply
SVC ESTABLISHMENT EQPT & SPLYS WHOLESALERS
SVC ESTABLISHMENT EQPT, WHOL: Cleaning & Maint Eqpt & Splys
SVC ESTABLISHMENT EQPT, WHOL: Liquor Dispensing Eqpt/Sys
SVC ESTABLISHMENT EQPT, WHOLESALE: Beauty Parlor Eqpt & Sply
SVC ESTABLISHMENT EQPT, WHOLESALE: Vending Machines & Splys
SWIMMING POOL & HOT TUB CLEANING & MAINTE-NANCE SVCS
SWIMMING POOL EQPT: Filters & Water Conditioning Systems
SWIMMING POOL SPLY STORES
SWIMMING POOLS, EQPT & SPLYS: Wholesalers
SWITCHBOARD APPARATUS, EXC INSTRUMENTS
SWITCHES
SWITCHES: Electric Power
SWITCHES: Electric Power, Exc Snap, Push Button, Etc
SWITCHES: Electronic
SWITCHES: Electronic Applications
SWITCHES: Flow Actuated, Electrical
SWITCHES: Solenoid
SWITCHES: Time, Electrical Switchgear Apparatus
SWITCHGEAR & SWITCHBOARD APPARATUS
SYNCHROS
SYNTHETIC RESIN FINISHED PRDTS, NEC
SYRUPS, FLAVORING, EXC DRINK
SYSTEMS ENGINEERING: Computer Related

SYSTEMS INTEGRATION SVCS
SYSTEMS INTEGRATION SVCS: Local Area Network
SYSTEMS SOFTWARE DEVELOPMENT SVCS

T

TABLE OR COUNTERTOPS, PLASTIC LAMINATED
TABLE TOPS: Porcelain Enameled
TABLECLOTHS & SETTINGS
TABLETS & PADS
TABLETS & PADS: Book & Writing, Made From Purchased Material
TAGS & LABELS: Paper
TAGS: Paper, Blank, Made From Purchased Paper
TALLOW: Animal
TANK COMPONENTS: Military, Specialized
TANK TOWERS: Metal Plate
TANKS & OTHER TRACKED VEHICLE CMPNTS
TANKS: Concrete
TANKS: Fuel, Including Oil & Gas, Metal Plate
TANKS: Lined, Metal
TANKS: Plastic & Fiberglass
TANKS: Standard Or Custom Fabricated, Metal Plate
TANKS: Storage, Farm, Metal Plate
TANKS: Water, Metal Plate
TANNERIES: Leather
TAPE DRIVES
TAPES, ADHESIVE: MedicaL
TAPES: Coated Fiberglass, Pipe Sealing Or Insulating
TAPES: Fabric
TAPES: Pressure Sensitive
TAPES: Pressure Sensitive, Rubber
TAPES: Tie, Woven Or Braided
TAPES: Zipper
TAPS
TAR
TARGET DRONES
TARPAULINS
TEETHING RINGS: Rubber
TELECOMMUNICATION EQPT REPAIR SVCS, EXC TELE-PHONES
TELECOMMUNICATION SYSTEMS & EQPT
TELECOMMUNICATIONS CARRIERS & SVCS: Wired
TELECOMMUNICATIONS CARRIERS & SVCS: Wireless
TELEGRAPH EQPT WHOLESALERS
TELEMARKETING BUREAUS
TELEMETERING EQPT
TELEPHONE ANSWERING SVCS
TELEPHONE CENTRAL OFFICE EQPT: Dial Or Manual
TELEPHONE EQPT INSTALLATION
TELEPHONE EQPT: Modems
TELEPHONE EQPT: NEC
TELEPHONE STATION EQPT & PARTS: Wire
TELEPHONE SVCS
TELEPHONE: Fiber Optic Systems
TELEPHONE: Headsets
TELEPHONE: Sets, Exc Cellular Radio
TELEPHONES: Sound Powered, Without Battery
TELEVISION BROADCASTING & COMMUNICATIONS EQPT
TELEVISION: Closed Circuit Eqpt
TELEVISION: Monitors
TEMPERING: Metal
TEMPORARY RELIEF SVCS
TENTS: All Materials
TERMINAL BOARDS
TEST BORING, METAL MINING
TESTERS: Battery
TESTERS: Environmental
TESTERS: Physical Property
TESTERS: Spark Plug
TESTERS: Water, Exc Indl Process
TESTING SVCS
TEXTILE & APPAREL SVCS
TEXTILE FABRICATORS
TEXTILE FINISHING: Chemical Coating Or Treating, Narrow
TEXTILE FINISHING: Dyeing, Broadwoven, Cotton
TEXTILE: Finishing, Cotton Broadwoven
TEXTILE: Finishing, Raw Stock NEC
TEXTILE: Goods, NEC
TEXTILES: Jute & Flax Prdts
TEXTILES: Linen Fabrics
TEXTILES: Recovering Textile Fibers From Clippings & Rags
THEATRICAL SCENERY
THERMOMETERS: Medical, Digital
THERMOPLASTIC MATERIALS
THERMOSETTING MATERIALS

THREAD & YARN, RUBBER: Fabric Covered
THREAD: Embroidery
THREAD: Thread, From Manmade Fiber
TIE SHOPS
TILE: Brick & Structural, Clay
TILE: Clay, Drain & Structural
TILE: Clay, Roof
TILE: Concrete, Drain
TILE: Mosaic, Ceramic
TILE: Quarry, Clay
TILE: Stamped Metal, Floor Or Wall
TILE: Terrazzo Or Concrete, Precast
TILE: Wall & Floor, Ceramic
TILE: Wall, Ceramic
TIN
TIRE & INNER TUBE MATERIALS & RELATED PRDTS
TIRE DEALERS
TIRE RECAPPING & RETREADING
TIRES & INNER TUBES
TIRES & TUBES WHOLESALERS
TIRES & TUBES, WHOLESALE: Truck
TIRES: Auto
TIRES: Motorcycle, Pneumatic
TIRES: Plastic
TITANIUM MILL PRDTS
TOBACCO & PRDTS, WHOLESALE: Cigarettes
TOBACCO & PRDTS, WHOLESALE: Cigars
TOBACCO & TOBACCO PRDTS WHOLESALERS
TOBACCO: Chewing & Snuff
TOBACCO: Cigarettes
TOBACCO: Cigars
TOBACCO: Smoking
TOILET PREPARATIONS
TOILETRIES, COSMETICS & PERFUME STORES
TOILETRIES, WHOLESALE: Toilet Preparations
TOILETRIES, WHOLESALE: Toiletries
TOILETS: Metal
TOILETS: Portable Chemical, Plastics
TOMBSTONES: Terrazzo Or Concrete, Precast
TOOL & DIE STEEL
TOOLS & EQPT: Used With Sporting Arms
TOOLS: Carpenters', Including Levels & Chisels, Exc Saws
TOOLS: Hand
TOOLS: Hand, Carpet Layers
TOOLS: Hand, Engravers'
TOOLS: Hand, Jewelers'
TOOLS: Hand, Masons'
TOOLS: Hand, Mechanics
TOOLS: Hand, Power
TOOTHBRUSHES: Exc Electric
TOOTHPASTES, GELS & TOOTHPOWDERS
TOPS, DISPENSER OR SHAKER, ETC: Plastic
TOWELETTES: Premoistened
TOWELS: Fabric & Nonwoven, Made From Purchased Materials
TOWELS: Indl
TOWERS, SECTIONS: Transmission, Radio & Television
TOWERS: Bubble, Cooling, Fractionating, Metal Plate
TOWING BARS & SYSTEMS
TOYS
TOYS & HOBBY GOODS & SPLYS, WHOLESALE: Amusement Goods
TOYS & HOBBY GOODS & SPLYS, WHOLESALE: Toys & Games
TOYS, HOBBY GOODS & SPLYS WHOLESALERS
TOYS: Dolls, Stuffed Animals & Parts
TOYS: Kites
TOYS: Video Game Machines
TRADE SHOW ARRANGEMENT SVCS
TRAFFIC CONTROL FLAGGING SVCS
TRAILER COACHES: Automobile
TRAILERS & PARTS: Boat
TRAILERS & PARTS: Horse
TRAILERS & PARTS: Truck & Semi's
TRAILERS & TRAILER EQPT
TRAILERS OR VANS: Horse Transportation, Fifth-Wheel Type
TRAILERS: Bodies
TRAILERS: Demountable Cargo Containers
TRAILERS: House, Exc Permanent Dwellings
TRAILERS: Semitrailers, Missile Transportation
TRAILERS: Semitrailers, Truck Tractors
TRAILERS: Truck, Chassis
TRANSFORMERS: Control
TRANSFORMERS: Distribution
TRANSFORMERS: Electric

INDEX

Product category ──→ **BOXES: Folding**

Edgar & Son Paperboard ....G....... 999 999-9999
Yourtown **(G-11480)**

Ready Box Co..E....... 999 999-9999
Anytown **(G-7097)**

City ──→

Indicates approximate employment figure
A = Over 500 employees, B = 251-500
C = 101-250, D = 51-100, E = 20-50
F = 10-19, G = 4-9

Business phone

Geographic Section entry number where full
company information appears.

See footnotes for symbols and codes identification.

• Refer to the Industrial Product Index preceding this section to locate product headings.

ABRASIVE SAND MINING

Standard Sand & Silica Company ....G....... 863 419-9673
Haines City **(G-4916)**

ABRASIVES

Abrasive Dynamics Inc...........................F....... 860 291-0664
Pompano Beach **(G-13906)**
All Polishing Solutions.......................G....... 954 505-4041
Miramar **(G-10464)**
Bobs Barricades Inc ....E....... 813 886-0518
Tampa **(G-16652)**
Harsco Corporation ....F....... 717 506-2071
Tampa **(G-16907)**
Kay Diamond Products LLC ....F....... 561 994-5400
Boca Raton **(G-565)**
Maxi-Blast of Florida Inc ....G....... 727 572-0909
Saint Petersburg **(G-15122)**
Microtool and Instrument Inc ....E....... 786 242-8780
Palmetto Bay **(G-13215)**
Sheila Shine Inc ....E....... 305 557-1729
Miami **(G-9878)**
True Grit Abrasives Inc........................F....... 813 247-5219
Tampa **(G-17372)**
United Abrasives Inc ....F....... 239 300-0033
Naples **(G-10929)**
Wwsa Solids LLC ....F....... 561 588-9299
Boynton Beach **(G-927)**

ABRASIVES: Aluminum Oxide Fused

Abracol North America Corp ....G....... 305 431-5596
Miami **(G-8638)**

ABRASIVES: sandpaper

Sandpaper Marketing Inc ....G....... 850 939-8040
Navarre **(G-10956)**

ACCELERATION INDICATORS & SYSTEM COMPONENTS: Aerospace

Praesto Enterprises LLC ....G....... 407 298-9171
Orlando **(G-12498)**
Rover Aerospace Inc ....G....... 305 594-7799
Doral **(G-3352)**
Russell Associates Inc ....G....... 727 815-3100
New Port Richey **(G-10982)**
Troxel Aerospace Inds Inc ....F....... 720 626-0454
Gainesville **(G-4780)**

ACCELERATORS: Linear

Interntonal Linear Matrix Corp.............F....... 727 549-1808
Seminole **(G-15978)**

ACCELEROMETERS

Impact Register Inc...............................G....... 727 585-8572
Largo **(G-7611)**

ACCOUNTING MACHINES & CASH REGISTERS

Logic Controls Inc ....E....... 800 576-9647
Orlando **(G-12350)**
Shade Saver Inc ....G....... 850 650-0884
Ocala **(G-11486)**

ACCOUNTING MACHINES WHOLESALERS

Southeastern Peg Bd Prtrs Inc ....G....... 904 731-0357
Jacksonville **(G-6488)**

ACCOUNTING SVCS, NEC

Copy Van of Florida Inc ....G....... 407 366-7126
Oviedo **(G-12816)**
Excelor LLC ....F....... 321 300-3315
Orlando **(G-12142)**

ACID RESIST: Etching

ACC Holdco Inc....................................C....... 863 578-1206
Mulberry **(G-10618)**

ACRYLIC RESINS

Acrocrete Inc..G....... 954 917-4114
Pompano Beach **(G-13908)**
Falken Design Corporation ....G....... 765 688-0809
Miami **(G-9131)**
Idea Design Studio Inc ....F....... 305 823-6008
Doral **(G-3254)**

ACTOR

Survival Products Inc ....G....... 954 966-7329
Sunrise **(G-16377)**

ADDITIVE BASED PLASTIC MATERIALS: Plasticizers

Rehrig Pacific Company.......................F....... 407 857-3888
Orlando **(G-12544)**

ADHESIVES

Adhesive Manufacturers Inc................G....... 305 495-8018
Pembroke Pines **(G-13368)**
Adhesive Technologies Fla LLC...........G....... 941 228-0295
Sarasota **(G-15587)**
Adhesives Technology Corp.................D....... 754 399-1684
Pompano Beach **(G-13910)**
American Acrylic Adhesives LLC..........G....... 877 422-4583
Largo **(G-7531)**
American Adhesives LLC ....G....... 877 422-4583
Largo **(G-7532)**
Mapei Corporation ....C....... 954 246-8888
Deerfield Beach **(G-2763)**
Mapei Corporation ....D....... 954 485-8637
Fort Lauderdale **(G-3932)**
Palm Labs Adhesives LLC ....F....... 321 710-4850
Debary **(G-2639)**
PPG Architectural Finishes Inc ....G....... 813 877-5841
Tampa **(G-17171)**
Southern Grouts & Mortars Inc ....D....... 954 943-2288
Pompano Beach **(G-14193)**
T S E Industries Inc..............................D....... 727 573-7676
Clearwater **(G-1809)**
United Adhesive Products Inc ....G....... 863 698-9484
Winter Haven **(G-18476)**

ADHESIVES & SEALANTS

Anchor Coatings Leesburg Inc............E....... 352 728-0777
Leesburg **(G-7759)**
Gardner-Gibson Mfg Inc.......................F....... 813 248-2101
Tampa **(G-16871)**
Illinois Tool Works Inc ....F....... 561 422-9241
Riviera Beach **(G-14629)**
Jamo Inc ....D....... 305 885-3444
Medley **(G-8264)**
Lambert Corporation Florida ....E....... 407 841-2940
Orlando **(G-12307)**
Lapolla Industries LLC ....F....... 954 379-0241
Deerfield Beach **(G-2751)**
Lehigh White Cement Co LLC ....C....... 561 812-7441
Tampa **(G-17007)**

Masking Systems of America

Masking Systems of America ....F....... 813 920-2271
Odessa **(G-11566)**
Ocoow LLC ....G....... 805 266-7616
Sopchoppy **(G-16009)**
P S Research Corp................................G....... 954 558-8727
Lauderhill **(G-7738)**
Quality Industrial Chem Inc ....F....... 727 573-5760
Saint Petersburg **(G-15167)**
R C D Corporation.................................G....... 352 589-0099
Eustis **(G-3565)**
Syana Enterprises Inc ....G....... 305 582-4708
Miami **(G-9984)**

ADHESIVES & SEALANTS WHOLESALERS

Nebula Glass International Inc ....E....... 954 975-3233
Pompano Beach **(G-14107)**

ADHESIVES: Adhesives, paste

Laticrete International Inc ....E....... 561 844-4667
Riviera Beach **(G-14641)**

ADHESIVES: Epoxy

Dynamis Epoxy LLC ....G....... 941 488-3999
Venice **(G-17686)**
Fasco Epoxies Inc.................................F....... 772 464-0808
Fort Pierce **(G-4485)**
Hernon Manufacturing Inc ....D....... 407 322-4000
Sanford **(G-15331)**
S & R Fastener Co Inc ....F....... 352 588-0768
San Antonio **(G-15252)**

ADRENAL DERIVATIVES

Xymogen Inc...C....... 407 445-0203
Orlando **(G-12725)**

ADVERTISING AGENCIES

Comcept Solutions LLC ....E....... 727 535-1900
Seminole **(G-15972)**
Conric Holdings LLC ....F....... 239 690-9840
Fort Myers **(G-4217)**
Flexofferscom Inc ....G....... 305 999-9940
Miami **(G-9151)**
Jpl Associates Inc................................F....... 954 929-6024
Hallandale Beach **(G-4955)**
King & Grube Inc...................................F....... 727 327-6033
Largo **(G-7625)**
Media Digittal LLC.................................G....... 305 506-0470
Doral **(G-3294)**
Passport Pblcations Media Corp..........E....... 561 615-3900
West Palm Beach **(G-18113)**
Premier Parties Entertainment ....E....... 352 375-6122
Gainesville **(G-4750)**
Special Publications Inc.......................F....... 352 622-2995
Ocala **(G-11496)**
Venue Advertising Inc ....E....... 561 844-1778
Jupiter **(G-6820)**
Wpp Group Usa Inc...............................F....... 305 341-8132
Miami **(G-10147)**

ADVERTISING AGENCIES: Consultants

Carlaron Inc..G....... 386 258-1183
Daytona Beach **(G-2526)**
Charisma Media ....D....... 407 333-0600
Lake Mary **(G-7065)**
Mc Squared Group Inc..........................G....... 850 435-4600
Pensacola **(G-13544)**
Reed Brennan Media Associates ....E....... 407 894-7300
Orlando **(G-12541)**

ADVERTISING COPY WRITING SVCS

Las Amrcas Mltimedia Group LLC ....F 305 633-3341
Miami *(G-9427)*

Pensacola Voice Inc ....G 850 434-6963
Pensacola *(G-13572)*

ADVERTISING DISPLAY PRDTS

Brandano Displays Inc ....E 954 956-7266
Margate *(G-8123)*

Brevard Achievement Center Inc ....B 321 632-8610
Rockledge *(G-14693)*

Creative Events and Exhibits ....G 407 851-4754
Orlando *(G-12053)*

Look Worldwide Inc ....G 305 662-1287
Miami *(G-9476)*

Mediawrite LLC ....G 239 344-9988
Fort Myers *(G-4319)*

ADVERTISING MATERIAL DISTRIBUTION

Gdp Consulting Inc ....G 561 401-9195
Jupiter *(G-6733)*

Kenney Communications Inc ....F 407 859-3113
Orlando *(G-12285)*

Wayloo Inc ....G 954 914-3192
Fort Lauderdale *(G-4125)*

ADVERTISING REPRESENTATIVES: Electronic Media

Media Digittal LLC ....G 305 506-0470
Doral *(G-3294)*

ADVERTISING REPRESENTATIVES: Magazine

Rowland Publishing Inc ....E 850 878-0554
Tallahassee *(G-16497)*

ADVERTISING REPRESENTATIVES: Media

Supermedia LLC ....D 727 576-1300
Saint Petersburg *(G-15203)*

ADVERTISING REPRESENTATIVES: Newspaper

Nexstar Broadcasting Inc ....F 863 683-6531
Lakeland *(G-7402)*

Orange Peel Gazette Inc ....G 407 892-5556
Saint Cloud *(G-14936)*

Sarasota Herald-Tribune ....E 941 953-7755
Sarasota *(G-15814)*

West Bolusia Beacon ....F 386 734-4622
Deland *(G-2920)*

ADVERTISING REPRESENTATIVES: Printed Media

Collins Media & Advg LLC ....F 954 688-9758
Margate *(G-8124)*

Mc Squared Group Inc ....G 850 435-4600
Pensacola *(G-13544)*

MGM Cargo LLC ....G 407 770-1500
Orlando *(G-12377)*

Shipping + Business Svcs LLC ....G 904 240-1737
Jacksonville *(G-6465)*

Showcase Publications Inc ....E 863 687-4377
Lakeland *(G-7434)*

ADVERTISING SPECIALTIES, WHOLESALE

Above LLC ....F 850 469-9028
Pensacola *(G-13431)*

Ampersand Graphics Inc ....F 772 283-1359
Stuart *(G-16115)*

Apparel Printers ....G 352 463-8850
Alachua *(G-4)*

Artworks Printing Entps Inc ....G 954 893-7984
Hollywood *(G-5530)*

Bros Williams Printing ....G 305 769-9925
Hialeah *(G-5079)*

Eagle Athletic Wear Inc ....F 727 937-6147
Tarpon Springs *(G-17469)*

Express Signs & Graphics Inc ....F 407 889-4433
Winter Garden *(G-18385)*

Gdp Consulting Inc ....G 561 401-9195
Jupiter *(G-6733)*

Independent Resources Inc ....E 813 237-0945
Tampa *(G-16937)*

Izabellas Creations Inc ....G 786 429-3441
Miami *(G-9348)*

Koala Tee Inc (usa) ....E 941 954-7700
Sarasota *(G-15720)*

Laser Creations Incorporated ....E 800 771-7151
Apopka *(G-146)*

M & H Enterprises Inc ....G 305 885-5945
Hialeah *(G-5232)*

Metropolis Graphics Inc ....G 407 740-5455
Winter Park *(G-18523)*

Paints N Cocktails Inc ....F 954 514-7383
Miami *(G-9680)*

Put Your Name On It LLC ....G 813 972-1460
Tampa *(G-17195)*

Serigraphic Arts Inc ....F 813 626-1070
Tampa *(G-17251)*

Three60printing LLC ....F 954 271-2701
Miramar *(G-10553)*

Tidewater Incentives Group Ltd ....F 410 734-0691
Venice *(G-17722)*

Tip Top Prtg of Volusia Cnty ....G 386 760-7701
Daytona Beach *(G-2614)*

Tru Dimensions Printing Inc ....G 407 339-3410
Longwood *(G-7954)*

Verified Label & Print Inc ....F 813 290-7721
Tampa *(G-17407)*

ADVERTISING SVCS: Direct Mail

Customer First Inc Naples ....E 239 949-8518
Bonita Springs *(G-793)*

Direct Impressions Inc ....E 239 549-4484
Cape Coral *(G-1335)*

Dxm Marketing Group LLC ....F 904 332-6490
Jacksonville *(G-6052)*

Futch Printing & Mailing Inc ....F 904 388-3995
Jacksonville *(G-6124)*

Hill Donnelly Corporation ....E 800 525-1242
Tampa *(G-16917)*

Microcomputer Services ....G 561 988-7000
Boca Raton *(G-597)*

Ncp Solutions LLC ....D 205 849-5200
Jacksonville *(G-6322)*

Original Impressions LLC ....C 305 233-1322
Weston *(G-18276)*

Tip Top Prtg of Volusia Cnty ....G 386 760-7701
Daytona Beach *(G-2614)*

W D H Enterprises Inc ....G 941 758-6500
Bradenton *(G-1073)*

ADVERTISING SVCS: Display

A W R Cabinets Inc ....F 407 323-1415
Sanford *(G-15257)*

Fastsigns ....G 850 477-9744
Pensacola *(G-13501)*

La Fabrika Retail Services LLC ....G 786 525-4491
Miami *(G-9406)*

Sarasota Herald-Tribune ....E 941 953-7755
Sarasota *(G-15814)*

Sarasota Signs and Visuals ....G 941 355-5746
Sarasota *(G-15816)*

ADVERTISING SVCS: Outdoor

Fast Signs ....G 239 498-7200
Bonita Springs *(G-796)*

ADVERTISING SVCS: Poster, Exc Outdoor

Shipping + Business Svcs LLC ....G 904 240-1737
Jacksonville *(G-6465)*

ADVERTISING SVCS: Poster, Outdoor

Cutting Edge Sgns Grphics of P ....G 727 546-3700
Clearwater *(G-1559)*

Shipping + Business Svcs LLC ....G 904 240-1737
Jacksonville *(G-6465)*

AEROSOLS

AVw Inc ....E 954 972-3338
Margate *(G-8122)*

AGENTS, BROKERS & BUREAUS: Personal Service

Eem Technologies Corp ....G 786 606-5993
Doral *(G-3205)*

AGRICULTURAL CHEMICALS: Trace Elements

Agra Chem Sales Co Inc ....G 863 453-6450
Avon Park *(G-278)*

AGRICULTURAL DISINFECTANTS

Biochem Manufacturing Inc ....F 561 799-1590
Jupiter *(G-6695)*

Redeagle International LLC ....G 863 682-6698
Lakeland *(G-7419)*

AGRICULTURAL EQPT: BARN, SILO, POULTRY, DAIRY/LIVESTOCK MACH

Industrial Cnveyor Systems Inc ....F 305 255-0200
Cutler Bay *(G-2292)*

Sanchelima International Inc ....F 305 591-4343
Doral *(G-3356)*

AGRICULTURAL EQPT: Barn Stanchions & Standards

5 Star Builders Inc ....G 561 795-1282
Wellington *(G-17841)*

AGRICULTURAL EQPT: Fertilizing Machinery

Agrifleet Leasing Corporation ....E 239 293-3976
Auburndale *(G-218)*

Conibear Equipment Co Inc ....G 863 858-4414
Lakeland *(G-7296)*

AGRICULTURAL EQPT: Fertilizng, Sprayng, Dustng/Irrigatn Mach

Neelco Industries Inc ....F 321 632-5303
Cocoa *(G-1944)*

Toro Company ....F 407 321-2901
Sanford *(G-15398)*

AGRICULTURAL EQPT: Grade, Clean & Sort Machines, Fruit/Veg

Delaney Resources Inc ....G 863 670-5924
Dade City *(G-2317)*

AGRICULTURAL EQPT: Harvesters, Fruit, Vegetable, Tobacco

Bag-A-Nut LLC ....G 904 641-3934
Jacksonville *(G-5919)*

Okee-B Inc ....D 561 996-3040
Belle Glade *(G-342)*

AGRICULTURAL EQPT: Irrigation Eqpt, Self-Propelled

Eastern Irrigation Supply ....G 352 472-3323
Newberry *(G-11018)*

Jain Irrigation Holdings Corp ....B 863 422-4000
Haines City *(G-4909)*

K-Rain Manufacturing Corp ....E 561 844-1002
Riviera Beach *(G-14635)*

Maxijet Inc ....E 863 439-3667
Dundee *(G-3435)*

Thayer Industries Inc ....G 813 719-6597
Dundee *(G-3438)*

AGRICULTURAL EQPT: Soil Preparation Mach, Exc Turf & Grounds

Amega Sciences Inc ....G 863 937-9792
Lakeland *(G-7271)*

Fogmaster Corporation ....G 954 481-9975
Deerfield Beach *(G-2719)*

Golf Agronomics Sand & Hlg Inc ....G 800 626-1359
Sarasota *(G-15694)*

Manley Farms Inc ....G 239 597-6416
Naples *(G-10810)*

Resource Group US LLC ....G 833 223-3266
Myakka City *(G-10646)*

AGRICULTURAL EQPT: Spreaders, Fertilizer

50 50 Parmley Envmtl Svcs LLC ....G 407 593-1165
Saint Cloud *(G-14918)*

Irms Inc ....F 321 631-1161
Rockledge *(G-14719)*

Rugby Road Corp ....G...... 407 328-5474
Sanford (G-15383)

AGRICULTURAL EQPT: Trailers & Wagons, Farm

Bulk Resources Inc ....G...... 813 764-8420
Plant City (G-13748)
C P Enterprises of Apopka Inc..............G...... 407 886-3321
Mount Dora (G-10598)

AGRICULTURAL LIMESTONE: Ground

Marianna Lime Products Inc ....G...... 850 526-3580
Marianna (G-8170)
Marianna Limestone LLC ....F...... 954 581-1220
Marianna (G-8171)

AGRICULTURAL MACHINERY & EQPT REPAIR

Everglades Machine Inc ....G...... 863 983-0133
Clewiston (G-1888)
McEs LLC ....G...... 321 363-4977
Sanford (G-15357)

AGRICULTURAL MACHINERY & EQPT: Wholesalers

Argos Global Partner Svcs LLC ....G...... 305 365-1096
Key Biscayne (G-6833)

AIR CLEANING SYSTEMS

Air-O-Matic Corp ....G...... 786 364-6960
Doral (G-3101)
Atco Rubber Products Inc...................D...... 813 754-6678
Plant City (G-13741)
Chilly Willys Heating & A Inc ....G...... 904 772-1164
Jacksonville (G-5979)
Florida Air Cleaning Inc.....................G...... 727 573-5281
Clearwater (G-1598)
Rainbow Eb Buenavista ....G...... 305 982-8153
Miami (G-9776)
Triatomic Environmental Inc..............F...... 561 748-4864
Jupiter (G-6812)
Worldwide Technology Inc.................E...... 813 855-2443
Oldsmar (G-11707)

AIR CONDITIONERS: Motor Vehicle

Classic Auto A Mnfactoring Inc ....F...... 813 251-2356
Tampa (G-16713)
Hoseline Inc....................................F...... 407 892-2599
Saint Cloud (G-14929)
Re-Bus LLC ....G...... 772 418-7711
Fort Pierce (G-4523)
Transport A/C Inc ....G...... 954 254-4822
Pensacola (G-13614)

AIR CONDITIONING & VENTILATION EQPT & SPLYS: Wholesales

Parker Davis Hvac Intl Inc ....E...... 305 513-4488
Doral (G-3323)
Total of Florida ....G...... 239 768-9400
Fort Myers (G-4429)

AIR CONDITIONING EQPT

A C Repairs Inc ....G...... 813 909-0809
Lutz (G-7979)
Air Source 1 LLC ....G...... 772 626-7604
Port St Lucie (G-14469)
Baez Enterprises Corp ....F...... 813 317-7277
Seffner (G-15952)
Carrier Corporation..........................C...... 800 379-6484
Palm Beach Gardens (G-12955)
Chiller Medic Inc ....G...... 904 814-9446
Jacksonville (G-5978)
Energetico Inc ....G...... 213 550-5211
North Miami (G-11103)
Everest Air Corp ....F...... 407 319-6204
Kissimmee (G-6918)
Flagship Marine Inc ....G...... 772 781-4242
Stuart (G-16148)
Global Equipment & Mfg LLC ....E...... 800 436-1932
Miami (G-9217)
Innovative Svc Solutions LLC ....E...... 407 296-5211
Orlando (G-12246)
Klimaire Products Inc ....F...... 305 593-8358
Doral (G-3274)

Kommercial Refrigeration Inc.............G...... 863 299-3000
Winter Haven (G-18447)
Mas Hvac Inc ....F...... 904 531-3140
Elkton (G-3507)
Mito Corp ....F...... 786 208-3114
Pembroke Pines (G-13405)
Monar Corporation ....G...... 954 650-1930
Coral Springs (G-2190)
Northrich Florida LLC ....F...... 954 678-6602
Weston (G-18274)
Parker Davis Hvac Intl Inc ....E...... 305 513-4488
Doral (G-3323)
Proservices Supply LLC ....G...... 858 254-4415
Jacksonville (G-6396)
South Florida Marine ....G...... 305 232-8788
Cutler Bay (G-2304)
Total of Florida ....G...... 239 768-9400
Fort Myers (G-4429)
Trane Central America Inc.................E...... 305 592-8646
Miami (G-10035)
V & F Air Conditioning Sup LLC ....F...... 305 477-1040
Miami (G-10087)
Warren Technology Inc.....................C...... 305 556-6933
Hialeah (G-5418)

AIR CONDITIONING REPAIR SVCS

Air Doctor of Swfl LLC......................G...... 239 285-8774
Lehigh Acres (G-7804)
Chiller Medic Inc ....G...... 904 814-9446
Jacksonville (G-5978)
Con-Air Industries Inc ....D...... 407 298-5733
Orlando (G-12039)
Everest Air Corp ....F...... 407 319-6204
Kissimmee (G-6918)
Innovative Svc Solutions LLC ....E...... 407 296-5211
Orlando (G-12246)
South Florida Marine ....G...... 305 232-8788
Cutler Bay (G-2304)

AIR CONDITIONING UNITS: Complete, Domestic Or Indl

Air Doctor of Swfl LLC......................G...... 239 285-8774
Lehigh Acres (G-7804)
Aquacal Autopilot Inc ....C...... 727 823-5642
Saint Petersburg (G-14966)
Electrolux Professional LLC ....F...... 954 327-6778
Fort Lauderdale (G-3789)
First America Products ....F...... 904 683-1253
Orange Park (G-11829)
First America Products LLC ....G...... 904 215-8075
Miami (G-9145)
Innovative Support Systems Inc ....G...... 407 682-7570
Altamonte Springs (G-53)
James D Nall Co Inc.........................E...... 305 884-8363
Fort Lauderdale (G-3891)
Mermaid Mfg Southwest Fla Inc ....F...... 239 418-0535
Fort Myers (G-4321)
Southern Hvac Corporation ....G...... 407 917-1800
Maitland (G-8074)
Trane Technologies Company LLC ......A...... 850 873-8200
Panama City (G-13314)
Zenit Service LLC ....G...... 407 878-7840
Lake Mary (G-7118)

AIR MATTRESSES: Plastic

Dotchi LLC ....E...... 305 477-0024
Miami (G-9046)
Innovative PDT Solutions LLC.............F...... 407 933-2029
Kissimmee (G-6926)

AIR PURIFICATION EQPT

Advanced Tech & Tstg Labs Inc ....G...... 352 871-3802
Tampa (G-16561)
Air Purifying Systems Inc ....G...... 954 962-0450
Miami (G-8671)
Atitlan Enterprises LLC ....G...... 813 362-1909
Tampa (G-16615)
Better Air North America LLC ....G...... 844 447-7624
Plantation (G-13831)
Biozone Scientific Intl Inc ....G...... 407 876-2000
Orlando (G-11953)
Iaire LLC ....G...... 407 873-2538
Orlando (G-12233)
Timilon Corporation ....F...... 239 330-9650
Bonita Springs (G-826)
Turner Envirologic ....E...... 954 422-9566
Deerfield Beach (G-2829)

Wes Holdings Corp ....F...... 941 371-4995
Sarasota (G-15871)

AIR, WATER & SOLID WASTE PROGRAMS ADMINISTRATION SVCS

Platinium Rosis Inc ....G...... 786 617-9973
Miami Beach (G-10220)

AIRCRAFT & AEROSPACE FLIGHT INSTRUMENTS & GUIDANCE SYSTEMS

ABC Components Inc ....F...... 954 249-6286
Cooper City (G-2015)
Aerospace Automation LLC ....G...... 954 260-2844
Pembroke Pines (G-13372)
Avidyne Corporation ....D...... 321 751-8520
Melbourne (G-8372)
Dayton-Granger Inc ....C...... 954 463-3451
Fort Lauderdale (G-3758)
Deep Planet Research LLC ....G...... 517 740-1526
Melbourne (G-8398)
Gables Engineering Inc ....B...... 305 774-4400
Coral Gables (G-2058)
George Wash Cpitl Partners LLC ....G...... 786 910-1778
Deerfield Beach (G-2725)
GKN Aerospace Florida LLC ....D...... 314 412-8311
Panama City (G-13268)
Green Energy Enterprises Inc ....F...... 904 207-6503
Jacksonville (G-6151)
Green Energy Enterprises Inc ....F...... 904 309-8993
Jacksonville (G-6152)
Honeywell International Inc ....B...... 727 539-5080
Clearwater (G-1627)
Jormac Aerospace Inc......................F...... 727 549-9600
Clearwater (G-1655)
L3 Technologies Inc.........................G...... 904 269-5026
Orange Park (G-11832)
Mercaereo Inc ....G...... 305 307-0672
Doral (G-3297)
Nelver Airparts Inc ....G...... 305 378-0072
Miami (G-9610)
New Generation Aerospace Inc ....G...... 305 882-1410
Medley (G-8288)
Pratt & Whitney ....E...... 561 796-6701
Jupiter (G-6781)
Revolution Air Craft Services ....F...... 954 747-4773
Pompano Beach (G-14159)
Sota Manufacturing Inc ....G...... 561 368-8007
Boca Raton (G-685)
Supliaereos USA LLC ....G...... 727 754-4915
Clearwater (G-1805)
Tactical Air Support Inc ....C...... 229 563-7502
Jacksonville (G-6528)
Teleios Manufacturing Inc ....G...... 904 490-0600
Jacksonville (G-6543)
Willis Aeronautical Svcs Inc ....F...... 561 272-5402
Pompano Beach (G-14244)

AIRCRAFT & HEAVY EQPT REPAIR SVCS

Heico Corporation ....C...... 954 987-4000
Hollywood (G-5592)
Interntnal Synrgy For Tchncal ....G...... 321 305-0863
Orlando (G-12253)
Solana Repair Services LLC ....G...... 754 281-8860
Deerfield Beach (G-2812)
Southwest Eqp For Hrnando Cnty ......G...... 352 596-5142
Brooksville (G-1204)
Telesis Technology Corporation ....F...... 941 795-7441
Palmetto (G-13197)
Ver-Val Enterprises Inc ....F...... 850 244-7931
Fort Walton Beach (G-4616)

AIRCRAFT ASSEMBLY PLANTS

Above Ground Level Aerospace ....F...... 305 713-2629
Miami (G-8637)
Aercap Inc......................................D...... 954 760-7777
Fort Lauderdale (G-3627)
Aercap Group Services Inc ....F...... 954 760-7777
Fort Lauderdale (G-3628)
Aercap Leasing USA I LLC ....F...... 425 237-4000
Miami (G-8661)
Aerial Products Corporation...............F...... 800 973-9110
Jacksonville (G-5866)
Aerosmart Enterprise LLC ....E...... 310 499-8878
Saint Petersburg (G-14955)
Air Support Tecks ....G...... 386 986-5301
Palm Coast (G-13068)

PRODUCT

Aircraft Systems Group Inc ....G..... 727 376-9292
Odessa *(G-11535)*

Altum Aerospace ....F 954 618-6573
Sunrise *(G-16291)*

Amxs Corp ....E 904 568-1416
Jacksonville Beach *(G-6628)*

ASG Aerospace LLC ....G...... 305 253-0802
Miami *(G-8758)*

Aviation Parts & Trade Corp ....G...... 954 944-2828
Plantation *(G-13830)*

Bmg Aerospace ....G...... 786 725-4959
Miami *(G-8841)*

Bob Laferriere Aircraft Inc ....G...... 727 709-2704
Tarpon Springs *(G-17459)*

Boeing ....E 850 301-6635
Fort Walton Beach *(G-4566)*

Boeing Arospc Operations Inc ....F 850 682-2746
Crestview *(G-2240)*

Boeing Company ....C 407 306-8782
Orlando *(G-11964)*

Boeing Company ....F 321 867-7380
Kennedy Space Center *(G-6831)*

Boeing Company ....G...... 562 797-9131
Clearwater *(G-1523)*

Boeing Company ....F 904 317-2490
Jacksonville *(G-5945)*

Boeing Company ....B 321 853-6647
Cape Canaveral *(G-1279)*

Bombardier Trnsp Hldngs USA In ....E 407 450-4855
Sanford *(G-15274)*

Bombardiier ....F 954 622-1200
Fort Lauderdale *(G-3700)*

C1 Aerospace LLC ....G...... 786 712-9949
Miami *(G-8872)*

Celtic Airspares LLC ....G...... 727 431-0482
Clearwater *(G-1537)*

Coleman Aerospace ....F 407 354-0047
Orlando *(G-12028)*

CSC Textron ....G...... 813 554-9723
Tampa *(G-16745)*

Diamond Aircraft Logisctics ....G...... 305 456-8400
Doral *(G-3191)*

Diloren Inc ....G...... 786 618-9671
Doral *(G-3193)*

Dowe Gallagher Aerospace ....G...... 941 256-2179
Sarasota *(G-15471)*

Draken International LLC ....E 863 644-1832
Lakeland *(G-7313)*

Dreamline Aerospace ....G...... 954 544-2365
Pembroke Pines *(G-13385)*

ELite Intl Group LLC ....F 305 901-5005
Miami *(G-9086)*

Embraer Defense and SEC Inc ....G...... 954 359-3700
Jacksonville *(G-6072)*

Embraer Executive Aircraft Inc ....C 321 751-5050
Melbourne *(G-8419)*

Embraer Services Inc ....A 954 359-3700
Fort Lauderdale *(G-3793)*

EMC Aerospace Inc ....E 954 316-6015
North Miami Beach *(G-11137)*

Estumkeda Ltd ....F 954 966-6300
Hollywood *(G-5572)*

Excalibur Aircraft ....G...... 863 385-9486
Sebring *(G-15922)*

Full Circle Integration LLC ....F 504 615-5501
Valparaiso *(G-17660)*

Garrison Lickle Aircraft ....G 561 833-7111
Palm Beach *(G-12935)*

Gb Airlink Inc ....G...... 561 593-7284
Stuart *(G-16154)*

General Dynamics Corporation ....E 850 897-9700
Niceville *(G-11030)*

GKN Aerospace Florida LLC ....D 314 412-8311
Panama City *(G-13268)*

Gonzalez Aerospace Services ....G...... 561 227-1575
Wellington *(G-17852)*

Green Energy Enterprises Inc ....F 904 207-6503
Jacksonville *(G-6151)*

Gulf Coast Airways Inc ....G...... 239 403-3020
Naples *(G-10768)*

Gulfstream Mses Invstmnts Grou ....G...... 305 975-6186
Miami Beach *(G-10198)*

Harris Aerial LLC ....F 407 725-7886
Casselberry *(G-1418)*

High Standard Aviation Inc ....E 305 599-8855
Doral *(G-3248)*

Jade Tactical Disaster Relief ....C 850 270-4077
Tampa *(G-16961)*

Kaman Aerospace Corporation ....B 904 485-1410
Jacksonville *(G-6236)*

Kaman Aerospace Corporation ....G...... 904 751-5369
Jacksonville *(G-6237)*

KB Aerospace Co ....G...... 754 366-9194
Fort Lauderdale *(G-3901)*

L3 Technologies ....G...... 904 269-5026
Orange Park *(G-11832)*

Landmark Aviation ....G...... 305 296-5422
Key West *(G-6872)*

Lift Aerospace Corp ....E 305 851-5237
Miami *(G-9457)*

Lighter Than Air Systems Corp ....F 904 834-4400
Jacksonville *(G-6258)*

Lockheed Martin Corporation ....B 305 599-3004
Doral *(G-3284)*

Lockheed Martin Corporation ....G...... 850 475-0724
Pensacola *(G-13539)*

Lockheed Mrtin Mllmter Tech In ....F 407 356-4186
Orlando *(G-12348)*

Luftcar LLC ....F 408 905-0036
Orlando *(G-12353)*

Maris Worden Aerospace Inc ....G...... 514 895-8075
South Daytona *(G-16023)*

Max Torque LLC ....F 863 701-8000
Lakeland *(G-7391)*

Meridian South Aviation LLC ....G...... 727 536-5387
Clearwater *(G-1693)*

Micro Systems Inc ....C 850 244-2332
Fort Walton Beach *(G-4596)*

Mysky Aircraft Inc ....G...... 386 492-6908
Port Orange *(G-14342)*

Nobel Aerospace LLC ....G...... 786 210-0716
Doral *(G-3312)*

Northrop Grmman Feld Spport Sv ....D 904 810-4665
Saint Augustine *(G-14861)*

Northstar Aviation USA LLC ....E 321 600-4557
Melbourne *(G-8485)*

Onvoi AVI Supp and Inspect Ser ....F 805 312-3274
Defuniak Springs *(G-2841)*

Pegasus Aerospace ....G...... 850 376-0991
Destin *(G-3075)*

Progressive Aerodyne Inc ....G...... 352 253-0108
Tavares *(G-17521)*

Puma Aero Marine Inc ....G...... 904 638-5888
Fort Lauderdale *(G-4000)*

R4 Integration Inc ....E 850 226-6913
Fort Walton Beach *(G-4604)*

Ronco Aircraft and Marine Inc ....G...... 321 220-0209
Palm Bay *(G-12915)*

Si Aerospace Group Inc ....G...... 786 384-2338
Doral *(G-3365)*

Southstern Arspc Svcs Ltd Lblt ....G...... 305 992-8257
Pompano Beach *(G-14195)*

Southwings Avionics and ACC ....G...... 305 825-6755
Miami Lakes *(G-10360)*

Supliaereos USA LLC ....G...... 727 754-4915
Clearwater *(G-1805)*

Tactical Air Support Inc ....C 229 563-7502
Jacksonville *(G-6528)*

Tecnam US Inc ....G...... 863 655-2400
Sebring *(G-15946)*

Textron Aviation Inc ....E 813 878-4500
Tampa *(G-17350)*

Textron Aviation Inc ....C 407 859-1245
Orlando *(G-12653)*

TP Aerospace Technics LLC ....G...... 407 730-9988
Orlando *(G-12666)*

UAS Drone Corp ....G...... 561 693-1424
Palm Beach *(G-12941)*

Veserca Group Ltd Inc ....F 561 210-7400
Boca Raton *(G-747)*

Viper Drones LLC ....G...... 205 677-3700
Sebastian *(G-15911)*

Virgo Aerospace LLC ....G...... 954 816-3455
Lake Worth *(G-7243)*

Vogue Aerospace & Defense Inc ....G...... 321 289-0872
Naples *(G-10936)*

VSI & Partners Inc ....F 954 205-8653
Miramar *(G-10562)*

AIRCRAFT CONTROL SYSTEMS:

Aviation Instrument Tech Inc ....G...... 813 783-3361
Zephyrhills *(G-18604)*

Suriparts Corp ....G...... 954 639-7700
Fort Lauderdale *(G-4079)*

AIRCRAFT CONTROL SYSTEMS: *Electronic Totalizing Counters*

Avalex Technologies LLC ....C 850 470-8464
Gulf Breeze *(G-4877)*

GE Aviation Systems LLC ....G...... 727 532-6370
Clearwater *(G-1609)*

GE Aviation Systems LLC ....E 727 539-1631
Clearwater *(G-1611)*

Honeywell International Inc ....A 727 531-4611
Clearwater *(G-1628)*

Radiant Power Idc LLC ....E 760 945-0230
Sarasota *(G-15542)*

AIRCRAFT DEALERS

Veserca Group Ltd Inc ....F 561 210-7400
Boca Raton *(G-747)*

AIRCRAFT ENGINES & ENGINE PARTS: *Airfoils*

Sequa Corporation ....A 561 935-3571
Palm Beach Gardens *(G-13008)*

AIRCRAFT ENGINES & ENGINE PARTS: *Mount Parts*

Dynamic Precision Group Inc ....E 772 287-7770
Stuart *(G-16141)*

Propulsion Tech Intl LLC ....B 954 874-0274
Miramar *(G-10534)*

Simmonds Precision Pdts Inc ....F 904 757-3660
Jacksonville *(G-6473)*

Turbocombustor Technology Inc ....B 772 287-7770
Stuart *(G-16243)*

AIRCRAFT ENGINES & ENGINE PARTS: *Research & Development, Mfr*

V and N Advanced Auto Sys LLC ....G...... 321 504-6440
Rockledge *(G-14753)*

AIRCRAFT ENGINES & PARTS

Acmt South LLC ....F 860 645-0592
Lynn Haven *(G-8023)*

Advantage Airline Parts Inc ....G...... 770 521-1107
Boca Raton *(G-391)*

Aerojet Rocketdyne De Inc ....C 561 882-5150
Jupiter *(G-6680)*

Aerosapien Technologies LLC ....E 386 361-3838
Daytona Beach *(G-2508)*

Aerosync Engrg Consulting Inc ....G...... 316 208-3367
Milton *(G-10416)*

Aersale 23440 LLC ....G...... 305 764-3200
Coral Gables *(G-2025)*

Air Alliance Inc ....G...... 305 735-4864
Marathon *(G-8105)*

Air Lion Incorp ....G...... 386 748-9296
Deland *(G-2850)*

Air Marshall Inc ....F 954 843-0991
Hollywood *(G-5522)*

Aircraft Technology Inc ....E 954 744-7602
Hollywood *(G-5523)*

Airmark Overhaul Inc ....G...... 954 970-3200
Fort Lauderdale *(G-3634)*

Airstox Inc ....G...... 954 618-6573
Sunrise *(G-16287)*

Atomic Machine & Edm Inc ....G...... 239 353-9100
Naples *(G-10682)*

Avstar Fuel Systems Inc ....G...... 561 575-1560
Jupiter *(G-6686)*

Bogue Executive Enterprises ....F 561 842-5336
Mangonia Park *(G-8090)*

Bonus Aerospace Inc ....G...... 305 887-6778
Medley *(G-8210)*

Bonus Tech Inc ....F 786 251-4232
Medley *(G-8211)*

Chromalloy Component Svcs Inc ....C 954 378-1999
Fort Lauderdale *(G-3726)*

Chromalloy Gas Turbine LLC ....A 561 935-3571
Palm Beach Gardens *(G-12959)*

Csi Aerospace Inc ....F 954 961-9800
Hollywood *(G-5559)*

ELite Intl Group LLC ....F 305 901-5005
Miami *(G-9086)*

Falcon Commercial Aviation LLC ....F 786 340-9464
Miami *(G-9130)*

Flight Source LLC ....G...... 954 249-8449
Fort Lauderdale *(G-3820)*

Florida Aero Precision Inc ....E 561 848-6248
Lake Park *(G-7125)*

Florida Turbine Tech Inc ....G...... 561 427-6400
Jupiter *(G-6732)*

2022 Harris Florida
Manufacturers Directory

(G-0000) Company's Geographic Section entry number

Fossco Inc ....G..... 850 983-1330
Milton *(G-10425)*

Gas Turbine Support Inc ....G... 786 242-4513
Miami *(G-9191)*

Global Turbine Services Inc ....F 786 476-2166
Medley *(G-8249)*

Goodrich Corporation ....G... 305 622-4500
Miami Gardens *(G-10261)*

H H Terry Co Inc ....F 239 593-0132
Naples *(G-10769)*

Hamilton Sundstrand Corp ....D..... 860 654-6252
Pompano Beach *(G-14048)*

Heico Aerospace Corporation ....E 954 987-6101
Hollywood *(G-5590)*

Heico Aerospace Holdings Corp ....G...... 954 987-4000
Hollywood *(G-5591)*

Heico Aerospace Holdings Corp ....F 305 463-0455
Miami *(G-9272)*

Heico Corporation ....G... 305 374-1745
Miami *(G-9273)*

Heico Corporation ....E 305 463-0455
Miami *(G-9274)*

Heico Corporation ....C 954 987-4000
Hollywood *(G-5592)*

Heico Electronic Tech Corp ....E 954 987-6101
Hollywood *(G-5593)*

Heico Flight Support Corp ....E 954 987-4000
Hollywood *(G-5594)*

Honeywell International Inc ....G... 813 573-1166
Clearwater *(G-1629)*

Iag Engine Center LLC ....D..... 305 591-0643
Miami *(G-9297)*

Interntnal Synrgy For Tchncal ....G... 321 305-0863
Orlando *(G-12253)*

Ja Engineering II Corp ....F 954 744-7560
Hollywood *(G-5603)*

Jet Avion Corporation ....D..... 954 987-6101
Hollywood *(G-5606)*

Lopez & Company Inc ....E 305 302-3045
Doral *(G-3285)*

LPI Industries Corporation ....D..... 954 987-4000
Hollywood *(G-5615)*

Magellan Aviation Group Lllp ....D..... 561 266-0845
Boca Raton *(G-581)*

Miami Leasing Inc ....G... 786 431-1215
Miami *(G-9553)*

Miami Ndt Inc ....F 305 599-9393
Medley *(G-8282)*

Miltechnologies Inc ....G... 305 817-4244
Miami Lakes *(G-10326)*

MTI Aviation Inc ....E 305 817-4244
Opa Locka *(G-11772)*

Norris Precision Mfg Inc ....D..... 727 572-6330
Clearwater *(G-1719)*

Northwings Accessories Corp ....D..... 305 463-0455
Miami *(G-9629)*

Operatons Prcrment Sup Chain S ....G... 954 960-5890
Pompano Beach *(G-14112)*

Overall-Honeycomb LLC ....F 941 756-8781
Sarasota *(G-15529)*

Palmer Manufacturing Co LLC ....F 772 287-7770
Stuart *(G-16195)*

Parker-Hannifin Corporation ....E 239 304-1000
Naples *(G-10850)*

Precision Shapes Inc ....E 321 269-2555
Titusville *(G-17609)*

Precision Turbines Inc ....G... 561 447-0032
West Palm Beach *(G-18126)*

Radiant-Seacom Repairs Corp ....F 941 739-3200
Sarasota *(G-15543)*

Raytheon Technologies Corp ....A..... 860 565-4321
Jupiter *(G-6786)*

Saf Aerospace LLC ....G... 813 376-0883
Tampa *(G-17243)*

Skill-Metric Machine & TI Inc ....E 561 454-8900
Delray Beach *(G-3018)*

Sohacki Industries Inc ....E 904 826-0130
Saint Augustine *(G-14894)*

Solana Repair Services LLC ....G... 754 281-8860
Deerfield Beach *(G-2812)*

Sunshine Avionics LLC ....G... 954 517-1294
Hialeah *(G-5368)*

Supliaereos USA LLC ....G... 727 754-4915
Clearwater *(G-1805)*

Treasure Coast Machines Inc ....F 772 283-2024
Stuart *(G-16241)*

Turbine Kinetics Inc ....F 954 744-7526
Hollywood *(G-17243)*

Turbine Weld Industries LLC ....E 941 485-5113
Venice *(G-17725)*

Vfm Aerosystems LLC ....G... 786 567-2348
Doral *(G-3412)*

AIRCRAFT EQPT & SPLYS WHOLESALERS

Aerotools Connection LLC ....G..... 305 234-3034
Miami *(G-8663)*

M Bilt Enterprises Inc ....F 352 528-5566
Ocala *(G-11434)*

Mirage Systems Inc ....F 386 740-9222
Deland *(G-2886)*

Tobruk International Corp ....G..... 305 406-0263
Miami *(G-10017)*

AIRCRAFT FLIGHT INSTRUMENTS

Becker Avionics Inc ....F 954 450-3137
Miramar *(G-10474)*

Trilectron ....G..... 941 721-1000
Palmetto *(G-13198)*

AIRCRAFT FUELING SVCS

Atlantic Jet Center Inc ....G 321 255-7111
Melbourne *(G-8369)*

AIRCRAFT LIGHTING

B/E Aerospace Inc ....E 410 266-2048
Wellington *(G-17844)*

B/E Aerospace Inc ....E 786 337-8144
Miami *(G-8790)*

Radiant Power Corp ....D..... 941 739-3200
Sarasota *(G-15541)*

AIRCRAFT MAINTENANCE & REPAIR SVCS

Aviation Instrument Tech Inc ....G... 813 783-3361
Zephyrhills *(G-18604)*

High Standard Aviation Inc ....E 305 599-8855
Doral *(G-3248)*

Safran Power Usa LLC ....C 941 758-7726
Sarasota *(G-15549)*

AIRCRAFT PARTS & AUX EQPT: Panel Assy/Hydro Prop Test Stands

Honeycomb Company America Inc ....C 941 756-8781
Sarasota *(G-15494)*

AIRCRAFT PARTS & AUXILIARY EQPT: Accumulators, Propeller

Mt-Propeller Usa Inc ....F 386 736-7762
Deland *(G-2890)*

AIRCRAFT PARTS & AUXILIARY EQPT: Aircraft Training Eqpt

ELite Intl Group LLC ....F 305 901-5005
Miami *(G-9086)*

Heico Corporation ....C 954 987-4000
Hollywood *(G-5592)*

AIRCRAFT PARTS & AUXILIARY EQPT: Assys, Subassemblies/Parts

AAR Manufacturing Inc ....D..... 727 539-8585
Clearwater *(G-1470)*

Airplane Services Inc ....G... 850 675-1252
Jay *(G-6647)*

Donica International Inc ....F 954 217-7616
Miami *(G-9041)*

Monroy Aerospace ....G... 954 344-4936
Coral Springs *(G-2191)*

Omnia Inc ....G... 863 619-8100
Lakeland *(G-7403)*

Parker-Hannifin Corporation ....E 239 304-1000
Naples *(G-10850)*

Pioneer Aerospace Corporation ....F 850 623-3330
Milton *(G-10432)*

Simmonds Precision Pdts Inc ....F 904 757-3660
Jacksonville *(G-6473)*

Steen Aero Lab LLC ....G... 321 725-4160
Palm Bay *(G-12922)*

AIRCRAFT PARTS & AUXILIARY EQPT: Bodies

Aersale 26346 LLC ....D..... 305 764-3200
Coral Gables *(G-2026)*

AIRCRAFT PARTS & AUXILIARY EQPT: Body & Wing Assys & Parts

American Enrgy Innovations LLC ....F 772 221-9100
Stuart *(G-16114)*

AMP Aero Services LLC ....F 833 267-2376
Miami *(G-8727)*

Integritrust Solutions LLC ....G... 850 685-9801
Navarre *(G-10949)*

Precision Shapes Inc ....E 321 269-2555
Titusville *(G-17609)*

Stratos Airparts Corp ....F 772 266-9157
Stuart *(G-16227)*

Tri-Tech Electronics Inc ....D..... 407 277-2131
Orlando *(G-12669)*

AIRCRAFT PARTS & AUXILIARY EQPT: Body Assemblies & Parts

55 Industries LLC ....E 954 955-0212
Deerfield Beach *(G-2649)*

Aerospace Rotables Inc ....F 954 452-0056
Sunrise *(G-16285)*

Avalon Aviation Inc ....G... 954 655-0256
Fort Lauderdale *(G-3668)*

Cnc Aircraft Inc ....G... 305 657-1230
Saint Petersburg *(G-15008)*

Firefly Aircraft Parts Inc ....G... 954 870-7833
Plantation *(G-13852)*

Setty Enterprises Inc ....F 561 844-3711
West Palm Beach *(G-18149)*

Shark Skinz ....G... 772 388-9621
Sebastian *(G-15904)*

AIRCRAFT PARTS & AUXILIARY EQPT: Dusting & Spraying Eqpt

Stuart Pro Green ....G... 772 286-0510
Stuart *(G-16231)*

AIRCRAFT PARTS & AUXILIARY EQPT: Gears, Power Transmission

Coast Wcp ....E 727 572-4249
Odessa *(G-11543)*

Southern Gear & Machine Inc ....D..... 305 691-6300
Miami *(G-9928)*

AIRCRAFT PARTS & AUXILIARY EQPT: Military Eqpt & Armament

General Dynamics-Ots Inc ....D..... 727 578-8100
Saint Petersburg *(G-15058)*

Lopez & Company Inc ....G... 305 302-3045
Miami *(G-9477)*

Zitec Inc ....G... 850 678-9747
Niceville *(G-11040)*

AIRCRAFT PARTS & AUXILIARY EQPT: Oxygen Systems

Aerox AVI Oxgn Systems LLC ....G... 239 405-6106
Bonita Springs *(G-780)*

AIRCRAFT PARTS & AUXILIARY EQPT: Refueling Eqpt, In Flight

Smart Material Corp ....G... 941 870-3337
Sarasota *(G-15831)*

AIRCRAFT PARTS & AUXILIARY EQPT: Research & Development, Mfr

Aerosapien Technologies LLC ....E 386 361-3838
Daytona Beach *(G-2508)*

Aircon Fleet Management Corp ....E 305 234-8174
Miami *(G-8674)*

Aire-Tech Rotorcraft Svcs LLC ....F 305 696-8001
Miami *(G-8675)*

Arrowhead Global LLC ....F 727 497-7340
Clearwater *(G-1499)*

Aveoengineering LLC ....G... 631 747-6671
Palm Coast *(G-13070)*

Exodus Management LLC ....G... 954 995-4407
Fort Lauderdale *(G-3807)*

Interntnal Synrgy For Tchncal ....G... 321 305-0863
Orlando *(G-12253)*

Rolin Industries Inc ....G... 850 654-1704
Fort Walton Beach *(G-4608)*

P
R
O
D
U
C
T

Employee Codes: A=Over 500 employees, B=251-500
C=101-250, D=51-100, E=20-50, F=10-19, G=4-9   2022 Harris Florida
Manufacturers Directory   1123

AIRCRAFT PARTS & AUXILIARY EQPT: Rotor Blades, Helicopter

Acmt South LLC ....F 860 645-0592
Lynn Haven *(G-8023)*

AIRCRAFT PARTS & EQPT, NEC

A R Components Corp ....F 786 703-8456
Miami *(G-8624)*

AAR Airlift Group Inc ....E 321 837-2345
Palm Bay *(G-12885)*

AAR Corp ....G 904 629-2810
Jacksonville *(G-5854)*

AAR Government Services Inc ....F 904 693-7260
Jacksonville *(G-5855)*

AAR Government Services Inc ....F 321 361-3461
Rockledge *(G-14687)*

AAR Landing Gear LLC ....E 305 883-1511
Medley *(G-8191)*

ABC Intercargo LLC ....G 954 908-5200
Weston *(G-18219)*

Advanced Thermal Tech Inc ....E 561 791-5000
Wellington *(G-17842)*

Advent Aerospace Inc ....F 727 549-9600
Largo *(G-7523)*

Aero Precision Holdings LP ....G 925 455-9900
Miramar *(G-10460)*

Aero-Flex Corp ....E 561 745-2534
Jupiter *(G-6678)*

Aero-Hose Corp ....F 904 215-9638
Orange Park *(G-11812)*

Aerobase Group Inc ....E 321 802-5889
Melbourne *(G-8356)*

Aerojet Rocketdyne Inc ....G 386 626-0001
Daytona Beach *(G-2507)*

Aeronate Inc ....G 954 358-7145
Pembroke Pines *(G-13371)*

Aerosonic LLC ....C 727 461-3000
Clearwater *(G-1478)*

Aerotools Connection LLC ....G 305 234-3034
Miami *(G-8663)*

Aerowest Mfg Corp ....G 786 367-6948
Hialeah *(G-5032)*

Air Operations ....G 305 871-5449
Miami *(G-8670)*

Aircraft Engrg Instlltion Svcs ....E 407 438-4436
Orlando *(G-11883)*

Airdyne Aerospace Inc ....E 352 593-4163
Brooksville *(G-1131)*

Airframe International Inc ....F 218 461-9305
Fort Pierce *(G-4461)*

Airind Incorporated ....G 954 252-0900
Southwest Ranches *(G-16052)*

Airline Support Group Inc ....F 954 971-4567
Fort Lauderdale *(G-3632)*

Airmark Components Inc ....E 954 522-5370
Fort Lauderdale *(G-3633)*

AJ Assoc Mfg & Engrg Co Inc ....F 727 258-0994
Clearwater *(G-1481)*

Aj Associates ....F 727 258-0994
Clearwater *(G-1482)*

Alaris Aerospace Systems LLC ....F 954 596-8736
Pompano Beach *(G-13915)*

Alco Services Inc ....E 954 538-2189
Miramar *(G-10462)*

Allclear Aerospace & Def Inc ....F 954 239-7844
Miramar *(G-10465)*

Allied Aerospace Inc ....F 786 616-8484
Doral *(G-3107)*

Allied Aerospace International ....G 954 429-8600
Deerfield Beach *(G-2666)*

Alm Technologies Inc ....E 904 849-7212
Yulee *(G-18587)*

American Vly Avnics Clbrtion L ....F 904 644-8630
Orange Park *(G-11814)*

Apex Aviation Group LLC ....G 305 789-6695
Miami *(G-8734)*

Aqua Float Co ....G 320 524-2782
Zephyrhills *(G-18603)*

Arcadia Aerospace Inds LLC ....E 941 205-5700
Punta Gorda *(G-14492)*

Argos Global Partner Svcs LLC ....G 305 365-1096
Key Biscayne *(G-6833)*

Arma Holdings Inc ....F 813 402-0667
Tampa *(G-16607)*

Atlantic Jet Support Inc ....G 954 360-7549
Coconut Creek *(G-1978)*

Atlantic Precision Inc ....E 772 466-1011
Port Saint Lucie *(G-14399)*

Avborne Accesory Group LLC ....E 305 593-6038
Miami *(G-8774)*

Avborne Accessory Group Inc ....E 305 593-6038
Miami *(G-8775)*

Aviacol Usa Corp ....G 786 701-2152
Miami *(G-8777)*

Aviation Worldwide Svcs LLC ....F 321 837-2345
Palm Bay *(G-12888)*

Avionics Support Group Inc ....E 305 378-9786
Miami *(G-8778)*

B & J Atlantic Inc ....E 904 338-0088
Jacksonville *(G-5916)*

B E Aerospace ....G 305 459-7000
Medley *(G-8205)*

B/E Aerospace Inc ....D 305 471-8800
Doral *(G-3127)*

B/E Aerospace Inc ....E 410 266-2048
Wellington *(G-17844)*

B/E Aerospace Inc ....G 786 337-8144
Miami *(G-8776)*

Ballistic Recovery Systems Inc ....D 651 457-7491
Pompano Beach *(G-13946)*

Baron LLC ....G 239 691-5783
Fort Myers *(G-4186)*

Bigorre Aerospace Corp ....F 727 525-8115
Pinellas Park *(G-13673)*

Bischoff Aero Llc ....F 305 883-4410
Doral *(G-3140)*

Borgesfs Inc ....G 786 210-0327
Miami *(G-8847)*

Chase Aerospace Inc ....F 407 812-4545
Orlando *(G-12006)*

Choice Products Inc ....F 386 426-6450
Edgewater *(G-3487)*

Clero Enterprises Inc ....G 305 681-4877
Opa Locka *(G-11730)*

Coastal Machine LLC ....G 850 769-6117
Panama City *(G-13246)*

Collins Aerospace ....F 704 423-7000
West Palm Beach *(G-17970)*

Composite-Fx Sales LLC ....G 352 538-1624
Trenton *(G-17630)*

Crane Electronics Inc ....D 850 244-0043
Fort Walton Beach *(G-4572)*

Cvg Aerospace LLC ....G 786 293-9923
Miami *(G-8986)*

Cygnus Aerospace Incorporated ....E 850 612-1618
Crestview *(G-2242)*

Daher Inc ....G 954 893-1400
Pompano Beach *(G-13990)*

Dalimar Corp ....G 727 525-8115
Pinellas Park *(G-13681)*

Dass Logistics Inc ....F 954 837-8339
Coconut Creek *(G-1983)*

Don Industrial Group LLC ....F 305 290-4237
Hialeah *(G-5122)*

Doorway Projects Inc ....G 561 523-2040
Lake Worth *(G-7195)*

Edge Aerodynamix Inc ....F 850 238-8610
Panama City Beach *(G-13330)*

Electronic Components Fas Inc ....G 407 328-8111
Sanford *(G-15310)*

Equs Logistics LLC ....F 954 618-6573
Sunrise *(G-16317)*

Fl Aerospace Solutions Inc ....G 786 395-3289
Miami *(G-9139)*

Flight Aerotech LLC ....G 305 901-6001
Miami *(G-9152)*

Flight Velocity ....G 866 937-9371
Palm Coast *(G-13077)*

Flying Colors Air Parts ....G 352 728-1900
Leesburg *(G-7776)*

Forward Express One Llc ....F 305 234-3034
Miami *(G-9168)*

Freewing Flight Tech Inc ....G 813 752-8552
Plant City *(G-13768)*

Fuel Cell Inc ....G 954 776-7555
Doral *(G-3222)*

General Dynmics Ord Tctcal Sys ....G 727 578-8243
Saint Petersburg *(G-15059)*

General Mro Aerospace Inc ....G 305 482-9903
Medley *(G-8247)*

Gigli Enterprises Inc ....G 850 871-4777
Panama City *(G-13267)*

Global Intl Investments LLC ....G 305 825-2288
Hialeah *(G-5173)*

Gold Coast Aero Accessories ....G 561 965-7767
Lake Worth *(G-7202)*

Goodrich Corporation ....G 305 622-4500
Miami Gardens *(G-10261)*

Goodrich Lighting Systems Inc ....E 813 891-7100
Oldsmar *(G-11653)*

GSE America LLC ....G 863 583-4343
Lakeland *(G-7340)*

GSE Jetall Inc ....G 305 688-2111
Opa Locka *(G-11751)*

Halcyon Aviation Capital LLC ....G 305 615-1575
Doral *(G-3242)*

Heli-Tech Inc ....F 850 763-9000
Panama City *(G-13272)*

Hensoldt Avionics Usa LLC ....G 941 306-1328
Sarasota *(G-15700)*

Hermes Technical Intl Inc ....E 305 477-8993
Doral *(G-3246)*

High Standard Aviation Inc ....E 305 599-8855
Doral *(G-3248)*

Himmel Losungen Group Hlg LLC ....G 786 631-5531
Doral *(G-3249)*

Honeywell International Inc ....D 505 358-0676
Largo *(G-7606)*

Icon Aircraft Inc ....F 813 387-6603
Tampa *(G-16930)*

ITI Engineering LLC ....E 866 245-9356
Winter Springs *(G-18570)*

Jetspares International Inc ....G 407 876-3978
Windermere *(G-18356)*

Jf Aerospace Inc ....G 786 242-6686
Miami *(G-9366)*

Jormac Aerospace ....D 727 549-9600
Largo *(G-7623)*

Js2 Aerospace Corp ....G 954 840-3620
Pompano Beach *(G-14069)*

Kachemak Bay Flying Service ....F 850 398-8699
Crestview *(G-2248)*

Kaman Aerospace Corporation ....B 904 485-1410
Jacksonville *(G-6236)*

Kaman Aerospace Corporation ....G 904 751-5369
Jacksonville *(G-6237)*

Karob Instrument Inc ....G 352 732-2414
Ocala *(G-11416)*

Kellstrom Coml Arospc Inc ....E 305 818-5400
Miami Lakes *(G-10310)*

L3harris Technologies Inc ....E 321 727-4660
Palm Bay *(G-12907)*

Laminar Flow Systems Inc ....F 386 253-8833
Daytona Beach *(G-2568)*

Landing Aerospace Inc ....G 305 687-0100
Opa Locka *(G-11762)*

Live Aerospace Inc ....G 305 910-0091
Miami *(G-9468)*

Lockwood Aircraft Corporation ....F 863 655-4242
Sebring *(G-15931)*

Loos & Co Inc ....D 239 643-5667
Naples *(G-10807)*

Lopresti Speed Merchants Inc ....E 772 562-4757
Sebastian *(G-15898)*

Ltb Aerospace LLC ....G 954 251-1141
Doral *(G-3287)*

Mattis Aerospace ....G 305 910-2377
Homestead *(G-5729)*

Maverick Composites Inc ....G 561 601-3393
Jupiter *(G-6764)*

Miami Technics LLC ....F 754 227-5459
Deerfield Beach *(G-2766)*

Micro Systems Inc ....C 850 244-2332
Fort Walton Beach *(G-4596)*

Micro Tool & Engineering Inc ....F 561 842-7381
Riviera Beach *(G-14646)*

Mk Aviation LLC ....G 305 825-4810
Doral *(G-3306)*

Mro Aerospace Inc ....F 727 546-4820
Largo *(G-7647)*

MSA Aircraft Products ....F 772 562-2243
Fort Pierce *(G-4510)*

N23d Services LLC ....G 754 217-3362
Fort Lauderdale *(G-3949)*

Nasco Aerospace and Elec LLC ....F 727 344-7554
Saint Petersburg *(G-15136)*

National Aerospace Group Inc ....G 817 226-0315
Vero Beach *(G-17780)*

Northstar Aviation USA LLC ....E 321 600-4557
Melbourne *(G-8485)*

Novo Aero Services Llc ....G 786 319-8637
West Palm Beach *(G-18094)*

Parts Cage Inc ....F 904 373-7800
Saint Augustine *(G-14870)*

Pem-Air LLC ....F 954 321-8726
Davie *(G-2455)*

Piper Aircraft Inc ....A 772 567-4361
Vero Beach *(G-17786)*

Power Flow Systems Inc ....F 386 253-8833
  Daytona Beach **(G-2584)**

Precision Tech Aero Inc ....F 305 603-8347
  Miami Lakes **(G-10341)**

Precision TI Engrg Gnsvlle Inc ....E 352 376-2533
  Gainesville **(G-4749)**

Quiet Technology Aerospace Inc ....E 305 687-9808
  Hollywood **(G-5650)**

R4 Integration Inc ....E 850 226-6913
  Fort Walton Beach **(G-4604)**

Radiant Power Corp ....D 941 739-3200
  Sarasota **(G-15541)**

Raytheon Technologies Corp ....A 860 565-4321
  Jupiter **(G-6786)**

Redstone Corporation ....G 321 213-2135
  Merritt Island **(G-8591)**

Saf Aerospace LLC ....G 813 376-0883
  Tampa **(G-17243)**

Safran Power Uk Ltd ....G 941 739-7207
  Sarasota **(G-15548)**

Safran Power Usa LLC ....C 941 758-7726
  Sarasota **(G-15549)**

Saint-Gobain Corporation ....A 863 425-3299
  Mulberry **(G-10637)**

Sal Aerospace Engineering LLC ....F 305 791-0593
  Miami **(G-9839)**

Savvy Associate Inc ....F 954 941-6986
  Pompano Beach **(G-14167)**

Sensenich Technologies Inc ....G 813 703-8446
  Plant City **(G-13802)**

Signature AVI US Holdings Inc ....F 407 648-7230
  Orlando **(G-12604)**

Silver Hawk Aerospace Inc ....F 954 301-1453
  Pompano Beach **(G-14179)**

Sky Aerospace Engineering ....G 407 251-7111
  Orlando **(G-12607)**

Sky Aerospace Engineering Inc ....G 407 251-7111
  Orlando **(G-12608)**

Sky Technics Aviation Sls Inc ....G 305 885-7499
  Miami Lakes **(G-10353)**

Skyhigh Accessories Inc ....G 954 316-3936
  Plantation **(G-13888)**

Skyways Technics Americas LLC ....G 786 615-2443
  North Miami **(G-11122)**

Sohacki Industries Inc ....E 904 826-0130
  Saint Augustine **(G-14894)**

Solair Group Llc ....E 786 269-0160
  Cutler Bay **(G-2303)**

Southeastern Engineering Inc ....E 321 984-2521
  Palm Bay **(G-12921)**

Southern Fiberglass Inc ....F 904 387-2246
  Jacksonville **(G-6490)**

Southwind Aviation Supply LLC ....F 405 491-0500
  Oakland **(G-11230)**

Summit Aerospace Inc ....G 305 871-5449
  Miami **(G-9964)**

Sunny Skies Enterprises Inc ....E 954 316-6015
  North Miami Beach **(G-11163)**

Superior Avionics Inc ....G 954 917-9194
  Fort Lauderdale **(G-4077)**

Supliaereos USA LLC ....G 727 754-4915
  Clearwater **(G-1805)**

Support Aircraft Parts Inc ....F 305 975-3767
  Miami **(G-9975)**

Support Systems Associates Inc ....E 321 724-5566
  Melbourne **(G-8541)**

Survival Products Inc ....G 954 966-7329
  Sunrise **(G-16377)**

Tesco Equipment LLC ....E 954 752-7994
  Coral Springs **(G-2220)**

TL Fahringer Co Inc ....G 813 681-2373
  Tampa **(G-17356)**

Tobruk International Corp ....G 305 406-0263
  Miami **(G-10017)**

TOMI Aircraft Inc ....G 863 446-3001
  Deland **(G-2913)**

Tri-Tech of Florida Inc ....F 727 544-8836
  Saint Petersburg **(G-15217)**

Tritech Industries LLC ....G 954 383-3545
  Oakland Park **(G-11301)**

Triumph Group Inc ....B 772 220-5000
  Stuart **(G-16242)**

Triumph Group Consulting ....G 352 213-3007
  Gainesville **(G-4779)**

Turbine Controls LLC ....D 954 517-1706
  Miramar **(G-10556)**

Turbocombustor Technology Inc ....B 772 287-7770
  Stuart **(G-16243)**

UDC Usa Inc ....E 813 281-0200
  Tampa **(G-17382)**

Ultra Aerospace Inc ....F 305 728-6361
  Miami **(G-10056)**

Unison Industries LLC ....A 904 739-4000
  Jacksonville **(G-6576)**

United Aerospace Corporation ....E 954 364-0085
  Miramar **(G-10557)**

Universal Crgo Doors & Svc LLC ....E 305 594-9175
  Miami **(G-10070)**

UTC Aerospace Systems ....G 954 538-8971
  Miramar **(G-10560)**

Velocity Aerospace - Nmb Inc ....E 214 396-9030
  North Miami Beach **(G-11166)**

Velocity Aircraft Inc ....G 772 589-1860
  Sebastian **(G-15909)**

Ver-Val Enterprises Inc ....F 850 244-7931
  Fort Walton Beach **(G-4616)**

Viking Aircraft Engines LLC ....G 386 416-8383
  Edgewater **(G-3503)**

Viper Drones Inc ....F 321 427-5837
  Sebastian **(G-15910)**

Vision Manufacturing Tech Inc ....E 904 579-5272
  Orange Park **(G-11845)**

Vision Systems North Amer Inc ....F 321 265-5110
  Melbourne **(G-8560)**

Whelen Aerospace Tech LLC ....F 800 859-4757
  Sebastian **(G-15912)**

Willis Aeronautical Svcs Inc ....F 561 272-5402
  Pompano Beach **(G-14244)**

Yellow Green Aerospace Inc ....G 954 599-4161
  Coral Gables **(G-2121)**

AIRCRAFT PARTS WHOLESALERS

Exodus Management LLC ....G 954 995-4407
  Fort Lauderdale **(G-3807)**

Shark Skinz ....G 772 388-9621
  Sebastian **(G-15904)**

AIRCRAFT SEATS

B/E Aerospace Inc ....E 410 266-2048
  Wellington **(G-17844)**

B/E Aerospace Inc ....G 786 337-8144
  Miami **(G-8790)**

Pac Seating Systems Inc ....E 772 286-6670
  Palm City **(G-13052)**

AIRCRAFT SERVICING & REPAIRING

Chromalloy Gas Turbine LLC ....A 561 935-3571
  Palm Beach Gardens **(G-12959)**

Florida Aero Precision Inc ....E 561 848-6248
  Lake Park **(G-7125)**

Heli-Tech Inc ....F 850 763-9000
  Panama City **(G-13272)**

Vertical Aviation Tech Inc ....F 407 322-9488
  Sanford **(G-15404)**

AIRCRAFT TURBINES

Pem-Air Turbine Eng Svcs LLC ....F 954 900-9956
  Brooksville **(G-1189)**

AIRCRAFT: Airplanes, Fixed Or Rotary Wing

Aerion Corp ....G 775 337-6682
  Fort Lauderdale **(G-3629)**

Boeing Company ....F 312 544-2000
  Titusville **(G-17574)**

J Cube Inc ....F 407 699-6866
  Casselberry **(G-1420)**

Northrop Grumman Systems Corp ......A 904 825-3300
  Saint Augustine **(G-14863)**

Northrop Grumman Systems Corp ....C 904 825-3300
  Saint Augustine **(G-14865)**

Piper Aircraft Inc ....A 772 567-4361
  Vero Beach **(G-17786)**

Velocity Inc ....E 772 589-1860
  Sebastian **(G-15908)**

AIRCRAFT: Autogiros

Aero Tech Service Assoc Inc ....F 850 286-1378
  Tyndall Afb **(G-17643)**

Extreme Crafts LLC ....F 561 989-7400
  Boca Raton **(G-510)**

AIRCRAFT: Motorized

Drone Imaging Services LLC ....G 407 620-5258
  Orlando **(G-12108)**

Drone Pics and Vids Corp ....G 786 558-4027
  Miami **(G-9051)**

Fix n Fly Drones LLC ....G 321 474-2291
  Tampa **(G-16834)**

Florida SW Drones LLC ....G 239 785-8337
  Cape Coral **(G-1344)**

Lumenier Holdco LLC ....G 941 444-0021
  Sarasota **(G-15728)**

Lumenier LLC ....F 941 444-0021
  Sarasota **(G-15729)**

Navmar Applied Sciences Corp ....C 904 423-0927
  Jacksonville **(G-6320)**

Opensky Drones LLC ....G 954 340-9125
  Coral Springs **(G-2199)**

Riverview Drones Inc ....G 813 451-4744
  Riverview **(G-14575)**

Tiger Composites Inc ....F 386 334-0941
  New Smyrna Beach **(G-11014)**

Volaero Uav Drnes Hldings Corp ....F 954 261-3105
  Sunrise **(G-16390)**

AIRCRAFT: Research & Development, Manufacturer

Kiss Polymers LLC ....F 813 962-2703
  Tampa **(G-16989)**

Uts Systems LLC ....G 850 226-4301
  Fort Walton Beach **(G-4615)**

AIRFRAME ASSEMBLIES: Guided Missiles

Atsg Logistic Support Service...............E 904 479-3808
  Jacksonville **(G-5911)**

AIRLINE TRAINING

Gleim Publications Inc ....D 352 375-0772
  Gainesville **(G-4703)**

AIRLOCKS

Airlock USA LLC ....F 305 888-6454
  Miami Springs **(G-10386)**

AIRPORT TERMINAL SVCS

G S Servicore Corp ....E 305 888-0189
  Hialeah **(G-5163)**

AIRPORTS, FLYING FIELDS & SVCS

Homyn Enterprises Corp...............D 305 870-9720
  Miami **(G-9290)**

Lift Aerospace Corp...............E 305 851-5237
  Miami **(G-9457)**

ALARM SYSTEMS WHOLESALERS

Ddci Inc ....D 407 814-0225
  Orlando **(G-12080)**

Incity Security Inc ....F 561 306-9228
  West Palm Beach **(G-18031)**

ALARMS: Burglar

Ddci Inc ....D 407 814-0225
  Orlando **(G-12080)**

Keytroller LLC ....F 813 877-4500
  Tampa **(G-16984)**

Minuteman Industries Inc ....G 813 248-1776
  Tampa **(G-17075)**

Security Tech Group Inc ....G 305 631-2228
  Miami **(G-9863)**

Vanguard Products Group Inc ....D 813 855-9639
  Oldsmar **(G-11705)**

ALARMS: Fire

Superior Fire & Lf Safety Inc...............F 850 572-0265
  Cape Coral **(G-1394)**

ALCOHOL: Ethyl & Ethanol

Highlands Ethanol LLC ....G 813 421-1090
  Tampa **(G-16916)**

Omega Energy Usa LLC ....G 786 245-0642
  Miami **(G-9646)**

POET LLC ....G 904 619-6901
  Jacksonville **(G-6376)**

ALKALIES & CHLORINE

Bio-Lab Inc ....F 863 709-1411
  Lakeland **(G-7282)**

FMC Power Inc ....G 786 353-2379
  Miami Beach **(G-10191)**

PRODUCT

ALKALIES & CHLORINE

Universal Transactions Inc ....F 305 887-4677
Medley *(G-8344)*

ALKALOIDS & OTHER BOTANICAL BASED PRDTS

Liberty Health Sciences Inc ....G 386 462-0141
Alachua *(G-13)*
US Nutraceuticals Inc ....E 352 357-2004
Eustis *(G-3569)*

ALLOYS: Additive, Exc Copper Or Made In Blast Furnaces

Additive Technologies LLC ....G 702 686-5190
Palm City *(G-13021)*

ALTERNATORS & GENERATORS: Battery Charging

Cleva Technologies LLC ....F 561 654-5279
Boca Raton *(G-466)*

ALTERNATORS: Automotive

Central Fla Remanufacturing ....G 407 299-9011
Orlando *(G-11993)*
T R S ....D 407 298-5490
Orlando *(G-12644)*

ALUMINUM

Ad Investment Group LLC ....C 954 784-6900
Miramar *(G-10458)*
AJs Aluminum Inc ....G 352 688-7631
Spring Hill *(G-16061)*
All Coast Manufacturing Inc ....G 813 626-2264
Tampa *(G-16572)*
Alumacart Inc ....F 772 675-2158
Indiantown *(G-5811)*
Charleston Aluminum LLC ....F 305 628-4014
Hialeah *(G-5090)*
Eastern Metal Supply Inc ....E 863 682-6660
Lakeland *(G-7315)*
Florida Sales & Marketing ....E 239 274-3103
Fort Myers *(G-4256)*
Glassarium LLC ....E 786 631-7080
Miami *(G-9216)*
Ideal Deals LLC ....C 386 736-1700
Saint Augustine *(G-14844)*
Mary Lame Wrought Iron & Alum ....E 727 934-2879
Holiday *(G-5502)*
Monstertech Corporation ....E 813 898-0405
Tampa *(G-17084)*
Streamline Aluminum Inc ....F 239 561-7200
Fort Myers *(G-4406)*

ALUMINUM PRDTS

Absolute Aluminum Inc ....D 941 497-7777
Venice *(G-17671)*
Aldora Aluminum & GL Pdts Inc ....E 954 441-5057
Miami *(G-8683)*
Aludisc LLC ....E 910 299-0911
Boca Raton *(G-401)*
Alumacart Inc ....F 772 675-2158
Indiantown *(G-5811)*
Alumi Tech Inc ....F 407 826-5373
Orlando *(G-11898)*
Aluminum Products Whl Inc ....G 904 268-4895
Jacksonville *(G-5881)*
American Products Inc ....G 813 925-0144
Tampa *(G-16590)*
American Windows Shutters Inc ....E 239 278-3066
Fort Myers *(G-4173)*
Amswfl Inc ....F 239 334-7433
Fort Myers *(G-4176)*
Architctral Mtal Flashings LLC ....F 239 221-0123
Cape Coral *(G-1306)*
Associated Steel & Alum Co Inc ....F 954 974-7890
Pompano Beach *(G-13938)*
Benada Extrusions LLC ....F 407 323-3300
Sanford *(G-15272)*
Cline Aluminum Doors Inc ....E 941 746-4104
Bradenton *(G-962)*
Contech Engnered Solutions LLC ....F 561 582-2558
Miami *(G-8960)*
Cross Key Marine Canvas Inc ....G 305 451-1302
Key Largo *(G-6844)*
Eagle Metal Distributors Inc ....E 407 367-0688
Orlando *(G-12112)*

Expert Shutter Services Inc ....D 772 871-1915
Port Saint Lucie *(G-14412)*
Florida Extruders Intl Inc ....D 407 323-3300
Sanford *(G-15319)*
Gulf Electronics ....F 727 595-3840
Largo *(G-7601)*
Hydro Remelt ....F 904 794-1500
Saint Augustine *(G-14842)*
Jupiter Industries LLC ....G 239 225-9041
Fort Myers *(G-4302)*
Karnak South Inc ....F 954 761-7606
Fort Lauderdale *(G-3900)*
Keymark Corporation Florida ....C 863 858-5500
Lakeland *(G-7368)*
Largo Aluminum Inc ....F 305 852-2390
Islamorada *(G-5837)*
Liberty Aluminum Co ....E 239 369-3000
Lehigh Acres *(G-7815)*
Magic Tilt Trailer Mfg Co Inc ....E 727 535-5561
Clearwater *(G-1679)*
Mary Lame Wrought Iron & Alum ....E 727 934-2879
Holiday *(G-5502)*
Metal Container Corporation ....C 904 695-7600
Jacksonville *(G-6297)*
Naples Iron Works Inc ....E 239 649-7265
Naples *(G-10829)*
Nav-X LLC ....E 954 978-9988
Fort Lauderdale *(G-3956)*
RDS Manufacturing Inc ....C 850 584-6898
Perry *(G-13650)*
Rolling Shield Incorporated ....E 305 436-6661
Hialeah Gardens *(G-5449)*
Sapa Prcsion Tubing Adrian Inc ....D 321 636-8147
Rockledge *(G-14745)*
Sinobec Resources LLC ....E 561 409-2205
Deerfield Beach *(G-2810)*
Snappy Structures Inc ....F 954 926-6611
Hollywood *(G-5658)*
Style-View Products Inc ....E 305 634-9688
Miami *(G-9962)*
Superlite Aluminum Pdts Inc ....G 407 682-2121
Altamonte Springs *(G-73)*
T and C Sales Inc ....G 321 632-0920
Rockledge *(G-14749)*
Te Olde Foundry Shoppe Inc ....G 239 261-3911
Naples *(G-10921)*
Titan Specialty Cnstr Inc ....E 850 916-7660
Milton *(G-10440)*

ALUMINUM: Coil & Sheet

Polytech International LLC ....F 904 354-9355
Jacksonville *(G-6378)*

ALUMINUM: Ingots & Slabs

Gyrosolar Corp ....G 954 554-9990
Weston *(G-18251)*

ALUMINUM: Pigs

Tru Mension Mfg Solutions ....G 321 255-4665
Melbourne *(G-8554)*

ALUMINUM: Rolling & Drawing

Affordable Scree Enclosure LLC ....F 800 900-8586
Pompano Beach *(G-13912)*
Aluminium Design Products LLC ....G 561 894-8775
Delray Beach *(G-2929)*
Carmacks Quality Aluminum Inc ....G 727 846-0305
Port Richey *(G-14356)*
Spectra Metal Sales Inc ....F 727 530-5435
Clearwater *(G-1795)*

AMMUNITION

Arma Holdings Inc ....F 813 402-0667
Tampa *(G-16607)*
Dse Inc ....F 813 443-4809
Riverview *(G-14561)*
General Dynmics Ord Tctcal Sys ....C 727 578-8100
Saint Petersburg *(G-15060)*
Global Ordnance LLC ....E 941 549-8388
Sarasota *(G-15484)*
Gti Systems Inc ....E 863 965-2002
Auburndale *(G-236)*
Kaman Precision Products Inc ....C 407 282-1000
Orlando *(G-12282)*
Lockheed Martin Corporation ....E 407 356-2000
Orlando *(G-12345)*

AMMUNITION: Components

Syrac Ordnance Inc ....G 727 612-6090
New Port Richey *(G-10988)*

AMMUNITION: Mines & Parts, Ordnance

Carbon Mine Supply LLC ....G 606 437-9905
Bradenton *(G-957)*

AMMUNITION: Paper Shells, Empty, Blank/Loaded, 30mm & Below

Boland Production Supply Inc ....G 863 324-7784
Winter Haven *(G-18422)*

AMMUNITION: Rockets

Cesaroni Aerospace Inc ....E 941 400-1421
Bowling Green *(G-829)*

AMMUNITION: Shot, Steel

Hyperion Munitions Inc ....F 844 622-8339
Largo *(G-7610)*

AMMUNITION: Small Arms

Arms East LLC ....G 561 293-2915
Bradenton *(G-941)*
Dse Inc ....E 863 425-1745
Mulberry *(G-10624)*
General Dynmics Ord Tctcal Sys ....C 727 578-8100
Saint Petersburg *(G-15060)*
Global Ordnance LLC ....E 941 549-8388
Sarasota *(G-15484)*
Gti Systems Inc ....E 863 965-2002
Auburndale *(G-236)*
Jsn Blue Thunder LLC ....G 786 398-5222
Miami *(G-9378)*
L C Npee ....E 888 316-3718
Hialeah *(G-5217)*
Oath Corporation ....G 407 221-7288
Rockledge *(G-14736)*
Paul Wong ....G 863 465-1114
Lake Placid *(G-7145)*
Pcp Tactical LLC ....G 772 473-3472
Vero Beach *(G-17785)*
Precision Ammunition LLC ....G 813 626-0077
Tampa *(G-17175)*
ST Action Pro Inc ....G 321 632-4111
Cocoa *(G-1959)*
Wide Open Armory LLC ....G 727 202-5980
Seminole *(G-15998)*

AMPLIFIERS

Astra Products Co Inc Tampa ....E 813 855-3021
Oldsmar *(G-11630)*
Dj Live Productions LLC ....G 407 383-1740
Altamonte Springs *(G-43)*
Hki Soundigital USA LLC ....G 786 600-1056
Dania *(G-2332)*

AMPLIFIERS: RF & IF Power

Analog Modules Inc ....D 407 339-4355
Longwood *(G-7868)*

AMUSEMENT & REC SVCS: Attractions, Concessions & Rides

3dfx Inc ....F 407 237-6249
Orlando *(G-11851)*

AMUSEMENT & RECREATION SVCS: Gambling & Lottery Svcs

Ocala Breeders Sales Co Inc ....E 352 237-4667
Ocala *(G-11452)*

AMUSEMENT & RECREATION SVCS: Night Club, Exc Alcoholic Bev

A2f LLC ....G 305 984-9205
Miami *(G-8629)*

AMUSEMENT & RECREATION SVCS: Swimming Pool, Non-Membership

South West Adventure Team LLC ....G 903 288-4739
Labelle *(G-6986)*

AMUSEMENT & RECREATION SVCS: Theme Park

3dfx Inc ....F 407 237-6249
Orlando *(G-11851)*
US Thrillrides LLC ....G 407 909-8898
Windermere *(G-18368)*

AMUSEMENT & RECREATION SVCS: Tourist Attraction, Commercial

Biotoxins Inc ....G 407 892-6905
Saint Cloud *(G-14923)*

AMUSEMENT MACHINES: Coin Operated

Flushing Amusement Inc ....G 813 780-7900
Zephyrhills *(G-18615)*
Fuller Amusements ....G 352 629-2792
Ocala *(G-11396)*

AMUSEMENT PARK DEVICES & RIDES

3dfx Inc ....F 407 237-6249
Orlando *(G-11851)*
Bobs Space Racers Inc ....C 386 677-0761
Daytona Beach *(G-2519)*
Rfg Consulting Services Inc ....G 832 298-5696
Medley *(G-8311)*
Skyline Attractions LLC ....F 407 587-0080
Orlando *(G-12609)*
US Thrillrides LLC ....G 407 909-8898
Windermere *(G-18368)*
Vertical Reality Inc ....G 305 238-4522
Palmetto Bay *(G-13222)*
Vertical Reality Mfg Inc ....G 305 238-4522
Palmetto Bay *(G-13223)*

AMUSEMENT PARK DEVICES & RIDES: Carnival Mach & Eqpt, NEC

Entech Onsite Services LLC ....G 407 956-8980
Rockledge *(G-14707)*
Transport PC USA Inc ....G 813 264-1700
Wesley Chapel *(G-17888)*

AMUSEMENT PARKS

United Trophy Manufacturing ....E 407 841-2525
Orlando *(G-12690)*

ANALGESICS

Grunenthal Services Inc ....F 786 364-6308
Miami *(G-9255)*

ANALYZERS: Network

Akuwa Solutions Group Inc ....F 941 343-9947
Sarasota *(G-15589)*
C2c Innovated Technology LLC ....G 251 382-2277
Bonifay *(G-768)*
Gray Information Solutions Inc ....G 352 684-6655
Spring Hill *(G-16072)*
Jones Mediaamerica Inc ....C 305 289-4524
Marathon *(G-8107)*
Lee Net Services Inc ....G 904 777-4833
Jacksonville *(G-6254)*
Meg Systems Inc ....G 239 263-5833
Naples *(G-10818)*

ANALYZERS: Petroleum Prdts

Roper Technologies Inc ....E 941 556-2601
Sarasota *(G-15801)*

ANALYZERS: Respiratory

Airehealth Inc ....G 407 280-4107
Winter Springs *(G-18559)*

ANESTHESIA EQPT

Biorep Technologies Inc ....F 305 330-4449
Miami Lakes *(G-10286)*
Eagle-Eye Anesthesia Inc ....G 817 999-9830
Jacksonville *(G-6056)*

ANIMAL FEED & SUPPLEMENTS: Livestock & Poultry

AB Vista Inc ....G 954 278-3965
Plantation *(G-13819)*

B&K Country Feeds LLC ....G 561 701-1852
West Palm Beach *(G-17935)*
BRT Oakleaf Pet Inc ....G 904 563-1212
Jacksonville *(G-5958)*
Buddy Custard Inc ....G 561 715-3785
Fort Lauderdale *(G-3707)*
Cargill Incorporated ....F 813 241-4847
Tampa *(G-16681)*
Dalian Platinum Chem Ltd Corp ....G 954 501-0564
Boca Raton *(G-477)*
Furst-Mcness Company ....G 386 755-5605
Lake City *(G-7019)*
Griffin Industries LLC ....D 904 964-8083
Starke *(G-16102)*
Higgins Group Corp ....E 305 681-4444
Miami *(G-9280)*
Nulab Inc ....D 727 446-1126
Clearwater *(G-1722)*
Plantation Botanicals Inc ....E 863 675-2984
Felda *(G-3573)*
Purina Animal Nutrition LLC ....F 863 262-4332
Lakeland *(G-7414)*
Swans Feed Mill ....G 813 782-6969
Zephyrhills *(G-18633)*
Thomas Products LLC ....G 563 639-9099
Bradenton *(G-1059)*

ANIMAL FOOD & SUPPLEMENTS: Chicken Feeds, Prepared

Backyard Feed LLC ....G 813 846-5995
Saint Augustine *(G-14814)*
Zephyr Feed Company Inc ....G 813 782-1578
Zephyrhills *(G-18637)*

ANIMAL FOOD & SUPPLEMENTS: Citrus Seed Meal

Tropicana Products Inc ....A 941 747-4461
Bradenton *(G-1067)*

ANIMAL FOOD & SUPPLEMENTS: Dog

Snif-Snax Ltd ....F 786 613-7007
Miami *(G-9910)*
Synergy Labs Inc ....E 954 525-1133
Fort Lauderdale *(G-4081)*

ANIMAL FOOD & SUPPLEMENTS: Dog & Cat

All American Pet Company Inc ....F 561 337-5340
Palm Beach Gardens *(G-12945)*
Cargill Incorporated ....E 407 846-4169
Kissimmee *(G-6905)*
Grazed LLC ....D 786 534-3975
Doral *(G-3237)*
Natural Crvings Pet Treats LLC ....G 786 404-8099
Homestead *(G-5733)*
Zesty Paws LLC ....E 407 358-6601
Orlando *(G-12733)*

ANIMAL FOOD & SUPPLEMENTS: Feed Premixes

Dairy Feeds Inc ....G 863 763-0258
Okeechobee *(G-11602)*

ANIMAL FOOD & SUPPLEMENTS: Feed Supplements

Advanced Household MGT Inc ....G 941 322-9638
Sarasota *(G-15438)*
Animal Business Concepts LLC ....F 727 641-6176
Saint Petersburg *(G-14962)*
Coronet Industries Inc ....E 813 752-1161
Plant City *(G-13757)*
Mr Gummy Vitamins LLC ....G 855 674-8669
Opa Locka *(G-11771)*
Special Nutrients LLC ....F 305 857-9830
Coconut Grove *(G-2014)*

ANIMAL FOOD & SUPPLEMENTS: Hay, Cubed

Hay Tech ....G 850 592-2424
Bascom *(G-329)*

ANIMAL FOOD & SUPPLEMENTS: Livestock

Aroma Chimie Inc ....E 305 930-5667
Miami *(G-8751)*

Branch Properties Inc ....D 352 732-4143
Ocala *(G-11338)*
Gator Feed Co Inc ....F 863 763-3337
Okeechobee *(G-11606)*
Manna Pro Products LLC ....E 813 620-9007
Tampa *(G-17036)*
Monticello Milling Co Inc ....G 850 997-5521
Monticello *(G-10583)*
Ocala Breeders Sales Co Inc ....E 352 237-4667
Ocala *(G-11452)*

ANIMAL FOOD & SUPPLEMENTS: Mineral feed supplements

Stratford Care Usa Inc ....F 877 498-2002
Odessa *(G-11583)*

ANIMAL FOOD & SUPPLEMENTS: Pet, Exc Dog & Cat, Dry

Perfectus Pet Food LLC ....G 800 774-3296
Hollywood *(G-5641)*

ANIMAL FOOD & SUPPLEMENTS: Pet, Exc Dog & Cat, Frozen

Seminole Stores Inc ....F 352 732-4143
Ocala *(G-11485)*

ANIMAL FOOD & SUPPLEMENTS: Poultry

Cargill Incorporated ....E 407 846-4169
Kissimmee *(G-6905)*

ANIMAL FOOD & SUPPLEMENTS: Specialty, Mice & Other Pets

Karnak Corporation ....G 352 481-4145
East Palatka *(G-3473)*

ANODIZING EQPT

Al Stein Industries LLC ....F 727 329-8755
Largo *(G-7526)*

ANODIZING SVC

Certified Metal Finishing Inc ....E 954 979-0707
Pompano Beach *(G-13968)*
David Russell Anodizing ....G 407 302-4041
Sanford *(G-15300)*
Dhs Enterprises Inc ....G 727 572-9470
Clearwater *(G-1564)*
Elite Metal Finishing East LLC ....F 407 843-0182
Orlando *(G-12122)*
Gti Systems Inc ....E 863 965-2002
Auburndale *(G-236)*
Peninsula Metal Finishing Inc ....E 407 291-1023
Orlando *(G-12479)*
R Hunter Holdings Inc ....E 407 843-0182
Orlando *(G-12526)*
Russell Bros Alum Andzing Ctin ....F 407 323-5619
Sanford *(G-15384)*
Veterans Metal LLC ....G 727 572-9470
Clearwater *(G-1844)*

ANTENNAS: Radar Or Communications

ARC Group Worldwide Inc ....E 303 467-5236
Deland *(G-2853)*
Bluesky Mast Inc ....F 877 411-6278
Largo *(G-7552)*
Frontier Electronics ....G 954 255-0911
Micanopy *(G-10396)*
Maxxfi LLC ....F 513 289-6521
Cape Coral *(G-1364)*
Pinnacle Cmmncations Group LLC ......F 904 910-0444
Jacksonville *(G-6372)*

ANTENNAS: Receiving

Concept Group LLC ....E 856 767-5506
Palm Beach Gardens *(G-12962)*
Digital Antenna Inc ....F 954 747-7022
Sunrise *(G-16313)*
Hascall Engineering and Mfg Co ....F 941 723-2833
Palmetto *(G-13173)*
Niftys Inc ....F 786 878-4725
Miami *(G-9621)*

PRODUCT

ANTENNAS: Satellite, Household Use

All Things Digital Inc ....E 305 887-9464
Miami *(G-8691)*

Micro-Ant LLC ....D 904 683-8394
Jacksonville *(G-6303)*

ANTIFREEZE

Global Diversified Products ....E 727 209-0854
Pinellas Park *(G-13690)*

ANTIQUE SHOPS

Finns Brass and Silver Polsg ....G 904 387-1165
Jacksonville *(G-6091)*

APPAREL ACCESS STORES

Walter Green Inc ....G 850 227-7946
Port Saint Joe *(G-14392)*

Zayas Fashions Inc ....E 305 823-1438
Hialeah *(G-5428)*

APPAREL DESIGNERS: Commercial

Shgar Kane Couture Inc ....G 407 205-8038
Orlando *(G-12591)*

APPAREL PRESSING SVCS

Blue Ocean Press Inc ....E 954 973-1819
Fort Lauderdale *(G-3693)*

APPAREL: Hand Woven

Point Blank Intrmdate Hldg LLC ....E 954 630-0900
Pompano Beach *(G-14135)*

APPLIANCE PARTS: Porcelain Enameled

Boca Stone Design Inc ....G 561 362-2085
Boca Raton *(G-440)*

APPLIANCE REPAIR

Tri-Tech Electronics Inc ....D 407 277-2131
Orlando *(G-12669)*

APPLIANCES, HOUSEHOLD: Drycleaning Machines, Incl Coin-Op

Japan Fabricare Inc ....G 407 366-9986
Oviedo *(G-12830)*

APPLIANCES, HOUSEHOLD: Kitchen, Major, Exc Refrigs & Stoves

Appliances To Go Usa Llc ....G 239 278-0811
Cape Coral *(G-1303)*

Clean Cut Intl LLC ....F 866 599-7066
Juno Beach *(G-6662)*

Deers Holdings Inc ....G 805 323-6899
Bay Harbor Islands *(G-332)*

Dka Distributing LLC ....G 800 275-4352
Tampa *(G-16781)*

La Cuisine Intl Distrs Inc ....E 305 418-0010
Miami *(G-9405)*

Minea Usa Llc ....F 800 971-3216
Coral Gables *(G-2087)*

Unique Designs & Finishes Inc ....F 772 335-4884
Port Saint Lucie *(G-14461)*

APPLIANCES, HOUSEHOLD: Laundry Machines, Incl Coin-Operated

Whirlpool Corporation ....E 407 438-5899
Orlando *(G-12714)*

APPLIANCES: Household, Refrigerators & Freezers

Acme Service Corp ....F 305 836-4800
Miami *(G-8647)*

GE Consumer Corporation ....E 904 696-9775
Jacksonville *(G-6135)*

Wine Plum Inc ....F 844 856-7586
Dania Beach *(G-2361)*

APPLIANCES: Major, Cooking

Creative Home and Kitchen LLC ....F 786 233-8621
Doral *(G-3177)*

Mr Next Level Investment LLC ....F 786 718-8056
Homestead *(G-5732)*

APPLIANCES: Small, Electric

Aaron Rice ....G 813 752-3820
Dover *(G-3425)*

American Household Inc ....D 561 912-4100
Boca Raton *(G-407)*

Avstar Systems LLC ....G 239 793-5511
Naples *(G-10684)*

Clean Cut Intl LLC ....F 866 599-7066
Juno Beach *(G-6662)*

Eaton Corporation ....G 813 281-8069
Tampa *(G-16795)*

Flash Sales Inc ....G 954 914-2689
Miami Gardens *(G-10258)*

Pure Laboratories LLC ....C 888 425-6649
Gainesville *(G-4752)*

Sunbeam Americas Holdings LLC ....E 561 912-4100
Boca Raton *(G-702)*

Sunbeam Products Inc ....B 561 912-4100
Boca Raton *(G-703)*

Uniware Houseware Corp ....E 305 952-4958
Miami Lakes *(G-10372)*

Viatek Consumer Pdts Group Inc ....E 423 402-9010
Stuart *(G-16246)*

APPLICATIONS SOFTWARE PROGRAMMING

Channel Logistics LLC ....F 856 614-5441
Miami *(G-8920)*

Deep Planet Research LLC ....G 517 740-1526
Melbourne *(G-8398)*

Hummingbirds Ai Inc ....E 305 432-2787
Miami Beach *(G-10201)*

Sachi Tech Inc ....F 813 649-8028
Tampa *(G-17242)*

Sleepy Dragon Studios Inc ....G 561 714-6156
Cutler Bay *(G-2302)*

Stormquant Inc ....F 408 840-2003
Titusville *(G-17620)*

AQUARIUM ACCESS, METAL

Endless Oceans LLC ....G 561 274-1990
Delray Beach *(G-2958)*

AQUARIUM DESIGN & MAINTENANCE SVCS

Endless Oceans LLC ....G 561 274-1990
Delray Beach *(G-2958)*

AQUARIUMS & ACCESS: Glass

Carib Sea Inc ....E 772 461-1113
Fort Pierce *(G-4472)*

Endless Oceans LLC ....G 561 274-1990
Delray Beach *(G-2958)*

Living Color Enterprises Inc ....E 954 970-9511
Deerfield Beach *(G-2757)*

Shark Tooth Enterprises Inc ....F 904 449-8247
Green Cove Springs *(G-4837)*

Waterbox Usa LLC ....G 800 674-2608
Longwood *(G-7959)*

AQUARIUMS & ACCESS: Plastic

Endless Oceans LLC ....G 561 274-1990
Delray Beach *(G-2958)*

ARCHITECTURAL PANELS OR PARTS: Porcelain Enameled

Hardscapecom LLC ....G 561 998-5000
Jupiter *(G-6739)*

ARCHITECTURAL SVCS

Foam By Design Inc ....E 727 561-7479
Clearwater *(G-1604)*

J A Custom Fabricators Inc ....F 561 615-4680
Lake Worth *(G-7208)*

Lightnet Usa Inc ....E 305 260-6444
Miami *(G-9458)*

Southwest Woodwork Inc ....F 239 213-0126
Naples *(G-10900)*

ARCHITECTURAL SVCS: Engineering

Alternative Cnstr Tech Inc ....G 321 421-6601
Melbourne *(G-8363)*

ARMATURE REPAIRING & REWINDING SVC

New Generation Aerospace Inc ....G 305 882-1410
Medley *(G-8288)*

ARMOR PLATES

Automotive Armor Mfg Inc ....F 941 721-3335
Palmetto *(G-13156)*

AROMATIC CHEMICAL PRDTS

Tsd Group Corp ....F 954 940-2111
Sunrise *(G-16385)*

Two Scents LLC DBA Vinevida ....E 888 527-6805
Opa Locka *(G-11796)*

Warehouse Goods LLC ....E 877 865-2260
Boca Raton *(G-753)*

ART & ORNAMENTAL WARE: Pottery

Ronald M Hart Inc ....G 772 600-8497
Stuart *(G-16209)*

ART DEALERS & GALLERIES

Brandine Woodcraft Inc ....G 561 266-9360
Delray Beach *(G-2937)*

ART DESIGN SVCS

Doral Dgtal Reprographics Corp ......G 305 704-3194
Doral *(G-3197)*

Liteworks Lighting Productions ....F 407 888-8677
Orlando *(G-12335)*

ART MARBLE: Concrete

Kitchen & Bath Center Inc ....E 850 244-3996
Fort Walton Beach *(G-4594)*

Maxrodon Marble Inc ....G 772 562-7543
Vero Beach *(G-17776)*

ART NEEDLEWORK, MADE FROM PURCHASED MATERIALS

Izabellas Creations Inc ....G 786 429-3441
Miami *(G-9348)*

ART SPLY STORES

Art & Frame Direct Inc ....C 407 857-6000
Orlando *(G-11923)*

ARTIFICIAL FLOWERS & TREES

Botanical Innovations Inc ....G 407 332-8733
Maitland *(G-8053)*

International Greenscapes LLC ....D 760 631-6789
Miami *(G-9327)*

ARTISTS' EQPT

Sculpture House Inc ....F 609 466-2986
Fort Pierce *(G-4526)*

ARTISTS' MATERIALS: Clay, Modeling

Standard Clay Mines ....G 609 466-2986
Fort Pierce *(G-4534)*

ARTISTS' MATERIALS: Frames, Artists' Canvases

Art & Frame Direct Inc ....C 407 857-6000
Orlando *(G-11923)*

Art & Frame Source Inc ....E 727 329-6502
Saint Petersburg *(G-14971)*

M & M Studios Inc ....G 561 744-2754
Jupiter *(G-6758)*

ARTISTS' MATERIALS: Pencils & Leads

Dixon Ticonderoga Company ....D 407 829-9000
Lake Mary *(G-7070)*

ARTWORK: Framed

Inusa Manufacturing LLC ....G 786 451-5227
Pembroke Park *(G-13363)*

Ngf Distributors Inc ....F 407 816-7554
Oviedo *(G-12838)*

Onlinewall ....G 800 210-0194
Miami *(G-9655)*

ASBESTOS PRDTS: Pipe Covering, Heat Insulatng Matl, Exc Felt

Cahill Construction Services ....G...... 239 369-9290
Lehigh Acres *(G-7805)*

ASBESTOS PRODUCTS

American Coatings Corporation ....G...... 954 970-7820
Margate *(G-8120)*

ASBESTOS REMOVAL EQPT

Mold Remediation Services Inc ....G...... 904 574-5266
Jacksonville *(G-6312)*

ASPHALT & ASPHALT PRDTS

Blacklidge Emulsions Inc ....F 954 275-7225
Pompano Beach *(G-13951)*

Group III Asphalt Inc ....F 850 983-0611
Milton *(G-10427)*

ASPHALT COATINGS & SEALERS

Acryfin Coatings LLC ....G...... 772 631-3899
Stuart *(G-16110)*

All American Sealcoating LLC ....G...... 305 961-1655
Miami *(G-8688)*

Aristcrete Coating Experts LLC ....G...... 386 882-3660
Ormond Beach *(G-12743)*

C C Lead Inc ....F 863 465-6458
Lake Placid *(G-7139)*

Campen Companies ....G...... 904 388-6000
Jacksonville *(G-5968)*

Carpenters Roofg & Shtmtl Inc ....E 561 833-0341
Riviera Beach *(G-14607)*

Coatings Smples Sltons Etc LLC ....G...... 863 398-8513
Lakeland *(G-7293)*

Coma Cast Corp ....F 305 667-6797
Miami *(G-8950)*

Harsco Corporation ....F 717 506-2071
Tampa *(G-16907)*

Hco Holding I Corporation ....F 863 533-0522
Bartow *(G-311)*

High Sierra Terminaling LLC ....F 954 764-8818
Fort Lauderdale *(G-3866)*

Metro Roof Tile Inc ....F 863 467-0042
Medley *(G-8280)*

Monier Lifetile Inc ....G...... 561 338-8200
Boca Raton *(G-605)*

Owens Corning Sales LLC ....D...... 904 353-7361
Jacksonville *(G-6346)*

Royal Westlake Roofing LLC ....F 863 676-9405
Lake Wales *(G-7172)*

Sargeant Bulk Asphalt Inc ....G...... 954 763-4796
Deerfield Beach *(G-2802)*

Standard Industries Inc ....D...... 813 248-7000
Tampa *(G-17298)*

Super Stone Inc ....E 305 681-3561
Opa Locka *(G-11791)*

Tropical Asphalt LLC ....F 954 983-3434
Hallandale *(G-4930)*

ASPHALT MINING & BITUMINOUS STONE QUARRYING SVCS

Coraldom Usa LLC ....G...... 305 716-0200
Miami *(G-8969)*

ASPHALT PLANTS INCLUDING GRAVEL MIX TYPE

D A B Constructors Inc ....G...... 352 797-3537
Brooksville *(G-1150)*

Gencor Industries Inc ....C...... 407 290-6000
Orlando *(G-12187)*

Hco Holding I Corporation ....F 863 533-0522
Bartow *(G-311)*

S T Wooten Corporation ....E 239 337-9486
Fort Myers *(G-4389)*

ASSEMBLIES: Exciter, Motor Or Generator Parts

Chism Manufacturing Svcs LLC ....F 941 896-9671
Sarasota *(G-15454)*

ASSEMBLING & PACKAGING SVCS: Cosmetic Kits

Audrey Morris Cosmt Intl LLC ....E 954 332-2000
Deerfield Beach *(G-2674)*

ASSEMBLING SVC: Clocks

LP Watch Group Inc ....E 954 985-3827
Hollywood *(G-5614)*

ASSEMBLING SVC: Plumbing Fixture Fittings, Plastic

M & C Assemblies Inc ....A...... 800 462-7779
Tarpon Springs *(G-17481)*

ASSOCIATIONS: Business

Raytheon Technologies Corp ....A...... 860 565-4321
Jupiter *(G-6786)*

S E Inc ....E 407 859-9317
Orlando *(G-12564)*

ASSOCIATIONS: Trade

American Welding Society Inc ....D...... 305 443-9353
Doral *(G-3113)*

ATHLETIC CLUB & GYMNASIUMS, MEMBERSHIP

Cheval Country Club ....G...... 813 279-5122
Dunedin *(G-3445)*

ATLASES

American Atlas Corp ....G...... 904 273-6090
Ponte Vedra Beach *(G-14263)*

ATOMIZERS

All Points Boats Inc ....D...... 954 767-8255
Fort Lauderdale *(G-3639)*

Audio Excellence ....G...... 407 277-8790
Orlando *(G-11933)*

Debut Development LLC ....E 863 448-9081
Wauchula *(G-17825)*

Enduris Extrusions Inc ....D...... 321 914-0897
Melbourne *(G-8420)*

Gulfstream Goodwill Inds Inc ....E 561 362-8662
Boca Raton *(G-535)*

Horizon Industries Inc ....F 561 315-5439
Royal Palm Beach *(G-14765)*

Jta Industries LLC ....G...... 321 663-4395
Orlando *(G-12280)*

Lov Industries Inc ....F 407 406-8221
Kissimmee *(G-6941)*

Manufacturing Martin LLC Kls ....F 904 641-0421
Jacksonville *(G-6275)*

Massimo Roma LLC ....G...... 561 302-5998
Miami *(G-9516)*

Real Gold Inc ....G...... 386 873-4849
Deland *(G-2897)*

Richter Industries Inc ....G...... 239 732-9440
Naples *(G-10876)*

Riley & Company Inc ....F 407 265-9963
Sanford *(G-15381)*

Seaboard Manufacturing LLC ....G...... 727 497-3572
Clearwater *(G-1779)*

Sequel Industries Inc ....F 850 517-6088
Freeport *(G-4629)*

Strictly Ecommerce ....G...... 352 672-6566
Gainesville *(G-4769)*

Techniflex LLC ....E 561 235-0844
Boca Raton *(G-708)*

Tekna Manufacturing LLC ....G...... 813 782-6700
Zephyrhills *(G-18635)*

Thor Manufacturing Inc ....G...... 866 955-8467
Boca Raton *(G-717)*

XYZ Manufacturing Inc ....G...... 941 426-5656
North Port *(G-11206)*

Zoya Inc ....G...... 954 523-6531
Fort Lauderdale *(G-4147)*

AUCTIONEERS: Fee Basis

Ocala Breeders Sales Co Inc ....E 352 237-4667
Ocala *(G-11452)*

AUDIO & VIDEO EQPT, EXC COMMERCIAL

Andrew Mj Inc ....G...... 561 575-6032
Jupiter *(G-6684)*

Attack Communications Inc ....G...... 954 300-2716
Fort Lauderdale *(G-3665)*

Audioshark Inc ....G...... 954 591-9252
Hollywood *(G-5533)*

AVI-Spl Holdings Inc ....A...... 866 708-5034
Tampa *(G-16619)*

AVI-Spl LLC ....B...... 813 884-7168
Tampa *(G-16620)*

Da Vinci Systems Inc ....E 954 688-5600
Coral Springs *(G-2146)*

Drivers World Corp ....G...... 561 852-5545
Boca Raton *(G-497)*

Home Robot LLC ....G...... 850 826-8720
Fort Walton Beach *(G-4592)*

K & A Audio Inc ....F 941 925-7648
Sarasota *(G-15716)*

Mdt Technologies Inc ....G...... 305 308-2902
Medley *(G-8276)*

Nowvision Technologies Inc ....G...... 813 943-4639
Lutz *(G-8007)*

Padgett Communications Inc ....E 727 323-5800
Tampa *(G-17141)*

Perpetual Marketing Assoc Inc ....G...... 813 949-9385
Lutz *(G-8009)*

Philips North America LLC ....D...... 305 969-7447
Miami *(G-9711)*

Raytheon Company ....E 727 768-8468
Largo *(G-7669)*

Raytheon Company ....C...... 310 647-9438
Largo *(G-7668)*

RLC Networks Inc ....G...... 904 262-0587
Jacksonville *(G-6430)*

S N S Auto Sports LLC ....G...... 727 546-2700
Pinellas Park *(G-13728)*

SF&kf Enterprises LLC ....F 727 614-9902
Largo *(G-7681)*

Stellar Group of South Florida ....G...... 305 715-7246
Doral *(G-3376)*

Voxx International Corporation ....B...... 800 645-7750
Orlando *(G-12706)*

Wireworld By David Salz Inc ....F 954 474-4464
Davie *(G-2500)*

AUDIO COMPONENTS

Singing Machine Company Inc ....F 954 596-1000
Fort Lauderdale *(G-4050)*

Sound Anchors Inc ....G...... 321 724-1237
Palm Bay *(G-12920)*

AUDIO ELECTRONIC SYSTEMS

Audio Video Imagineering Inc ....G...... 305 947-6991
Biscayne Park *(G-374)*

Fun Electronics Inc ....F 305 933-4646
Miami *(G-9179)*

Koncept Systems LLC ....E 786 610-0122
Homestead *(G-5724)*

Lamm Industries Inc ....G...... 718 368-0181
Sunny Isles Beach *(G-16279)*

Magnum Audio Group Inc ....G...... 813 870-2857
Tampa *(G-17032)*

MD Audio Engineering Inc ....G...... 305 593-8361
Miami *(G-9524)*

Mpr Audio System LLC ....G...... 305 988-8524
Miami *(G-9595)*

Power Evolution Inc ....G...... 305 318-8476
Orlando *(G-12496)*

Sonobrands LLC ....G...... 305 418-9367
Miami *(G-9918)*

Spirit LLC ....E 954 592-0227
Miami Gardens *(G-10274)*

Sun Mackie LLC ....A...... 561 394-0550
Boca Raton *(G-701)*

AUDIO-VISUAL PROGRAM PRODUCTION SVCS

Baptist Communications Mission ....F 954 981-2271
Hollywood *(G-5538)*

AUDIOLOGICAL EQPT: Electronic

Inventis North America Inc ....G...... 844 683-6847
Titusville *(G-17593)*

Megin Us LLC ....G...... 954 341-2965
Coral Springs *(G-2182)*

Employee Codes: A=Over 500 employees, B=251-500
C=101-250, D=51-100, E=20-50, F=10-19, G=4-9

2022 Harris Florida
Manufacturers Directory

1129

PRODUCT

Micro Audiometrics Corporation .... G 386 888-7878
Daytona Beach (G-2574)

AUDIOLOGISTS' OFFICES

Ear-Tronics Inc .... G 239 275-7655
Fort Myers (G-4243)

AUTO & HOME SUPPLY STORES: Auto & Truck Eqpt & Parts

Emergency Vehicle Sup Co LLC .... E 954 428-5201
Pompano Beach (G-14009)

AUTO & HOME SUPPLY STORES: Auto Air Cond Eqpt, Sell/Install

K C W Electric Company Inc .... G 850 878-2051
Tallahassee (G-16465)

AUTO & HOME SUPPLY STORES: Automotive Access

Hornblasters Inc .... E 813 783-8058
Tampa (G-16922)
Reading Truck Body LLC .... E 727 943-8911
Tarpon Springs (G-17489)

AUTO & HOME SUPPLY STORES: Automotive parts

Dhs Power Corp .... G 305 599-1022
Miami (G-9027)
Gear Dynamics Inc .... G 305 691-0151
Miami (G-9196)
T R S .... D 407 298-5490
Orlando (G-12644)
Total Performance Inc .... F 203 265-5667
Palm Coast (G-13091)

AUTO & HOME SUPPLY STORES: Batteries, Automotive & Truck

Battery Usa Inc .... E 863 665-6317
Lakeland (G-7280)
Future Plus of Florida .... F 612 240-7275
Tampa (G-16865)
Palm Beach Btry Ventures LLC .... G 561 881-8900
Lake Park (G-7132)
Rayovac Corp .... G 727 393-0966
Largo (G-7667)

AUTOCLAVES: Laboratory

Genecell International LLC .... F 305 382-6737
Doral (G-3225)

AUTOMATED TELLER MACHINE NETWORK

Atmcentral .... G 727 345-8460
Saint Petersburg (G-14975)

AUTOMATIC REGULATING CNTRLS: Flame Safety, Furnaces & Boiler

Whertec Technologies Inc .... G 866 207-6503
Jacksonville (G-6609)

AUTOMATIC REGULATING CNTRLS: Liq Lvl, Residential/Comm Heat

Intelligent Heater LLC .... G 305 248-4971
Homestead (G-5718)

AUTOMATIC REGULATING CONTROL: Building Svcs Monitoring, Auto

Automated Buildings Inc .... F 407 857-0140
Orlando (G-11934)
Clarios LLC .... D 305 805-5600
Medley (G-8218)
Johnson Controls Inc .... F 954 233-3000
Weston (G-18259)
Maintnnce Reliability Tech Inc .... E 863 533-0300
Bartow (G-316)
Top Line Installation Inc .... G 352 636-4192
Leesburg (G-7798)

AUTOMATIC REGULATING CONTROLS: AC & Refrigeration

Air Authorities of Tampa Inc .... G 727 525-1575
Clearwater (G-1480)
C & C Services of Tampa Inc .... G 813 477-8559
Plant City (G-13749)
Dais Corp .... F 727 375-8484
Odessa (G-11547)
Dsas Air Inc .... G 954 673-5385
Lauderdale Lakes (G-7714)
Gulf States Automation Inc .... E 850 475-0724
Pensacola (G-13516)
Jireh AC & Rfrgn Inc .... F 305 216-2774
Miami (G-9368)
Nautical Specialists Inc .... G 954 761-7130
Fort Lauderdale (G-3955)

AUTOMATIC REGULATING CONTROLS: Energy Cutoff, Residtl/Comm

Easi 360 Corp .... G 305 213-6346
Doral (G-3203)

AUTOMATIC TELLER MACHINES

Adnan Enterprises .... G 305 430-9752
Miami Gardens (G-10248)
Americas Atm LLC .... F 954 414-0341
Plantation (G-13826)
Atmcentral .... G 727 345-8460
Saint Petersburg (G-14975)
Atmfla Inc .... G 407 425-7708
Orlando (G-11932)
Diebold Nixdorf Incorporated .... F 407 549-2000
Lake Mary (G-7069)
Eep .... F 407 380-2828
Belle Isle (G-349)
K N M Food Store .... G 239 334-7699
Fort Myers (G-4303)
Money Tree Atm Mfg LLC .... G 850 244-5543
Fort Walton Beach (G-4597)
Motaz Inc .... G 239 334-7699
Fort Myers (G-4330)
Sarniya Enterprises Inc .... G 352 347-6030
Palm Harbor (G-13131)

AUTOMATIC VENDING MACHINES: Mechanisms & Parts

Atlantic Vending Inc .... G 954 605-6046
Hallandale Beach (G-4937)

AUTOMOBILES & OTHER MOTOR VEHICLES WHOLESALERS

Vehicle Maint Program Inc .... F 561 362-6080
Boca Raton (G-744)

AUTOMOBILES: Off-Highway, Electric

Cruise Car Inc .... F 941 929-1630
Sarasota (G-15464)
Moran Transport .... G 305 824-3366
Hialeah (G-5267)

AUTOMOBILES: Off-Road, Exc Recreational Vehicles

Specialized Off Road Vehicles .... G 352 735-1385
Mount Dora (G-10614)

AUTOMOTIVE & TRUCK GENERAL REPAIR SVC

Fidelity Manufacturing LLC .... E 352 414-4700
Ocala (G-11386)
Harberson Rv Pinellas LLC .... G 727 937-6176
Holiday (G-5497)
Palatka Welding Shop Inc .... E 386 328-1507
Palatka (G-12876)
Tbc Retail Group Inc .... G 702 395-2100
Juno Beach (G-6667)
Transtat Equipment Inc .... F 407 857-2040
Orlando (G-12668)

AUTOMOTIVE BATTERIES WHOLESALERS

Battery Usa Inc .... E 863 665-6317
Lakeland (G-7280)

AUTOMOTIVE BODY, PAINT & INTERIOR REPAIR & MAINTENANCE SVC

Patrick German Industries Inc .... G 727 251-3015
Brandon (G-1101)
Sargent Seat Cover Co Inc .... E 904 355-2529
Jacksonville (G-6452)

AUTOMOTIVE GLASS REPLACEMENT SHOPS

Darren Thomas Glass Co Inc .... G 863 655-9500
Sebring (G-15918)

AUTOMOTIVE LETTERING & PAINTING SVCS

Doug Bloodworth Enterprises .... G 407 247-9728
Lady Lake (G-6990)

AUTOMOTIVE LETTERING SVCS

Thomas United Inc .... G 239 561-7446
Fort Myers (G-4422)

AUTOMOTIVE PARTS, ACCESS & SPLYS

300 Technologies Inc .... F 954 234-0018
Oakland Park (G-11231)
AA Performance .... G 772 672-1164
Vero Beach (G-17731)
Ach Solution USA Inc .... G 941 355-9488
Sarasota (G-15437)
Addco Manufacturing Company .... E 828 733-1560
Riviera Beach (G-14587)
Adr Power Systems Inc .... G 813 241-6999
Largo (G-7521)
Aero Seating Technologies LLC .... G 321 264-5600
Titusville (G-17570)
Air Temp of America Inc .... G 850 340-3017
Panama City (G-13225)
Autocraft Manufacturing Co .... E 321 453-1850
Merritt Island (G-8577)
Balls Rod & Kustom LLC .... G 888 446-2191
Gainesville (G-4656)
Battery Usa Inc .... E 863 665-6317
Lakeland (G-7280)
Battery Usa Inc .... G 863 665-5401
Lakeland (G-7281)
Beach House Engineering .... G 941 727-4488
Bradenton (G-945)
Bill Mitchell Products LLC .... F 386 957-3009
Edgewater (G-3481)
Billet Technology .... G 561 582-6171
Lake Worth (G-7188)
Blp Racing Products LLC .... F 407 422-0394
Orlando (G-11958)
Boat Steering Solutions LLC .... G 727 400-4746
North Venice (G-11208)
Boost Lab Inc .... F 813 443-0531
Wesley Chapel (G-17871)
Carvizion Inc .... G 772 807-0307
Port St Lucie (G-14472)
CC Machine Inc .... F 888 577-0144
Holly Hill (G-5512)
Chromalloy Castings Tampa Corp .... C 561 935-3571
Palm Beach Gardens (G-12958)
Competition Specialties Inc .... F 386 776-1476
Mc Alpin (G-8188)
Cooper-Standard Automotive Inc .... E 321 233-5563
Sanford (G-15293)
Crankshaft Rebuilders Inc .... D 407 323-4870
Sanford (G-15296)
Custom Quality Mfg Inc .... E 813 290-0805
Tampa (G-16756)
Dashcovers Plus Depot Distrs .... G 954 961-7774
Hudson (G-5769)
Delphi of Florida Inc .... F 727 561-9553
Saint Petersburg (G-15021)
Desco Machine Company LLC .... G 954 565-2739
Oakland Park (G-11258)
Diaz Go Green Inc .... G 407 501-2724
Orlando (G-12092)
Dover Cylinder Head Inc .... E 850 785-6569
Panama City (G-13255)
Dsx Products Inc .... G 904 744-3400
Jacksonville (G-6043)
Dynotune Inc .... G 941 753-8899
Bradenton (G-971)
Enforcement One Inc .... F 727 816-9833
Oldsmar (G-11649)

Eng Group LLC ....G...... 954 323-2024
Fort Lauderdale *(G-3794)*

Enstar Holdings (us) LLC ....E...... 727 217-2900
Saint Petersburg *(G-15036)*

Etco Incorporated ....C...... 941 756-8426
Bradenton *(G-978)*

Evamped LLC ....G...... 614 205-4467
Naples *(G-10741)*

Excel Palm Beach Llc ....G...... 616 864-6650
West Palm Beach *(G-17991)*

Exhaust Technologies Inc ....G...... 561 744-9500
Jupiter *(G-6723)*

Extreme Brake Integration Inc ....G...... 888 844-7734
Ocala *(G-11383)*

Extreme Manufacturing LLC ....F...... 888 844-7734
Ocala *(G-11384)*

Faes Srt Inc ....G...... 941 960-6742
Sarasota *(G-15669)*

FCA North America Holdings LLC.......G...... 305 597-2222
Doral *(G-3213)*

FCA North America Holdings LLC.......E...... 407 826-7021
Orlando *(G-12146)*

Florida Dacco/Detroit Inc ....E...... 813 879-4131
Tampa *(G-16841)*

Florida Motors Inc ....G...... 786 524-9001
Miami *(G-9158)*

Flowmaster Inc ....G...... 561 249-1145
Loxahatchee *(G-7970)*

Fluid Routing Solutions LLC ....B...... 352 732-0222
Ocala *(G-11393)*

Forecast Trading Corporation ....E...... 954 979-1120
Fort Lauderdale *(G-3827)*

Fuelmatics Corp ....G...... 305 807-4923
Palmetto Bay *(G-13209)*

Gaterman Products LLC.....................G...... 386 253-1899
Daytona Beach *(G-2555)*

Hale Products Inc ....C...... 352 629-5020
Ocala *(G-11407)*

Harry J Honan ....G...... 405 273-9315
Riviera Beach *(G-14627)*

IESC Diesel Corp...............................G...... 305 470-9306
Hialeah Gardens *(G-5438)*

Intertek International Corp ....E...... 305 883-8700
Hialeah *(G-5197)*

Ionemoto Inc.....................................G...... 617 784-1401
Sebastian *(G-15895)*

Isoflex Technologies Intl LLC ....G...... 561 210-5170
Deerfield Beach *(G-2743)*

JMS Corporate Group LLC..................G...... 786 219-6114
Aventura *(G-264)*

Jodar Inc ....F...... 561 375-6277
Boca Raton *(G-564)*

Johnsons Management Group Inc ......G...... 904 261-4044
Fernandina Beach *(G-3591)*

Key Automotive Florida LLC...............B...... 863 668-6000
Lakeland *(G-7366)*

Key Safety Systems Inc.....................C...... 863 668-6000
Lakeland *(G-7367)*

KEys International Group LLC..............G...... 855 213-0399
Apopka *(G-144)*

Lambs Signs Inc ....F...... 941 792-4453
Bradenton *(G-1002)*

Latham Marine Inc ....G...... 954 462-3055
Fort Lauderdale *(G-3913)*

Lightning Connecting Rods LLC..........G...... 727 733-2054
Clearwater *(G-1672)*

Lockheed Martin Corporation.............E...... 407 356-2000
Orlando *(G-12345)*

Luminar Technologies Inc..................E...... 407 900-5259
Orlando *(G-12356)*

Luminar Technologies Inc..................E...... 407 900-5259
Orlando *(G-12357)*

Luxury Motor Cars LLC ....F...... 407 398-6933
Orlando *(G-12358)*

M P N Inc ....F...... 863 606-5999
Lakeland *(G-7386)*

Man-Trans LLC ....F...... 850 222-6993
Tallahassee *(G-16474)*

March Inc ....E...... 239 593-4074
Naples *(G-10812)*

Minder Research Inc ....F...... 772 463-6522
Stuart *(G-16185)*

Mobilepower LLC ....G...... 843 706-6108
South Miami *(G-16040)*

Motor Coach Inds Intl Inc ....F...... 407 246-1414
Winter Garden *(G-18398)*

Partsvu LLC ....C...... 239 643-2292
Naples *(G-10851)*

Paw Inc ....E...... 904 724-0310
Jacksonville *(G-6358)*

Phoenix Transmission Parts Inc..........G...... 727 541-0269
Seminole *(G-15985)*

Pierce Manufacturing Inc ....D...... 941 748-3900
Bradenton *(G-1028)*

Power Suspension & Parts LLC ....G...... 305 986-2235
Hialeah Gardens *(G-5448)*

Precision Shaft Technology ....G...... 727 442-1711
Clearwater *(G-1748)*

Propglide USA Corp ....G...... 305 520-0150
Miami *(G-9753)*

Pusher Intakes Inc ....F...... 772 212-9290
Vero Beach *(G-17789)*

R C Specialized International...............G...... 407 681-5905
Casselberry *(G-1431)*

Race Part Solutions ....G...... 561 999-8911
Boca Raton *(G-646)*

Rally Manufacturing Inc ....C...... 305 628-2886
Miami *(G-9777)*

RDS Manufacturing Inc ....C...... 850 584-6898
Perry *(G-13650)*

Reach International Inc ....E...... 305 863-6360
Hialeah *(G-5328)*

Redat of North America Inc................F...... 407 246-1600
Orlando *(G-12539)*

Revolution Brands Intl LLC.................G...... 786 571-3876
Medley *(G-8310)*

Road Master ....G...... 561 479-6450
Fort Lauderdale *(G-4022)*

Ruke Inc ....G...... 239 292-2553
Windermere *(G-18365)*

Santa Rosa Auto Parts Inc ....E...... 850 477-7747
Pensacola *(G-13600)*

Santiago Chopper LLC.......................G...... 813 671-9097
Gibsonton *(G-4800)*

Sea Systems Group Inc ....G...... 434 374-9553
Largo *(G-7680)*

Shafers Clssic Rprductions Inc...........G...... 813 622-7091
Tampa *(G-17255)*

Shark Skinz ....G...... 772 388-9621
Sebastian *(G-15904)*

Shearwater Marine Fl Inc ....F...... 772 781-5553
Stuart *(G-16216)*

Signal Dynamics Corporation.............G...... 904 342-4008
Fort Lauderdale *(G-4046)*

Silverhorse Racing LLC ....G...... 321 722-2813
Melbourne *(G-8522)*

Sizemore Welding Inc ....E...... 386 437-4073
Bunnell *(G-1234)*

Skyo Industries Inc ....E...... 631 586-4702
Ormond Beach *(G-12792)*

SMR Management Inc ....G...... 305 529-2488
Coral Gables *(G-2109)*

Southeast Carbon Works Inc ....G...... 561 422-1798
Wellington *(G-17866)*

Southeastern Engineering Inc ....E...... 321 984-2521
Palm Bay *(G-12921)*

Square One Armoring Svcs Co ....D...... 305 477-1109
Miami *(G-9945)*

Starkey Products Inc ....F...... 386 479-3908
Debary *(G-2644)*

Steering & Suspension Parts ....G...... 786 523-3726
Miami *(G-9948)*

Strasse Forged LLC............................G...... 786 701-3649
Miami *(G-9957)*

Thi E-Commerce LLC ....D...... 352 327-4058
Ocala *(G-11501)*

Total Performance Inc ....F...... 203 265-5667
Palm Coast *(G-13091)*

Treadstone Performance ....F...... 305 972-9600
Cutler Bay *(G-2306)*

Treadstone Prfmce Engrg Inc ....F...... 888 789-4586
Cutler Bay *(G-2307)*

U S Hardware Supply Inc ....E...... 407 657-1551
Winter Park *(G-18547)*

Urban Charge LLC ....G...... 305 809-6625
Miami Beach *(G-10242)*

Vista-Pro Automotive LLC ....F...... 352 867-7272
Ocala *(G-11511)*

Voxxhirschmann Corporation..............C...... 866 869-7888
Orlando *(G-12707)*

Voyomotive LLC ....F...... 888 321-4633
Sarasota *(G-15869)*

Vpr 4x4 ....G...... 305 468-9818
Orlando *(G-12708)*

Walker Products ....D...... 941 723-9820
Palmetto *(G-13204)*

Webelectric Products Inc ....G...... 440 389-5647
The Villages *(G-17559)*

Wetherill Associates Inc ....C...... 800 877-3340
Miramar *(G-10564)*

Wheels A Million ....G...... 754 444-2869
Fort Lauderdale *(G-4128)*

Woodys Acres LLC ....G...... 352 345-8145
Brooksville *(G-1224)*

Yarbrough Tire Svc Inc ....G...... 863 385-1574
Sebring *(G-15951)*

AUTOMOTIVE PARTS: Plastic

Dixie Restorations LLC ....G...... 813 785-2159
Zephyrhills *(G-18612)*

Fuel Air Spark Technology ....F...... 901 260-3278
Naples *(G-10753)*

International Power USA LLC ....G...... 305 534-7993
Miami *(G-9329)*

Jers Group ....G...... 786 953-6419
Doral *(G-3268)*

Pcm and S L Plota Co LLC ....F...... 727 547-6277
Largo *(G-7656)*

Sea Link Holdings LLC ....G...... 727 523-8660
Largo *(G-7678)*

Southast Auto Acquisition Corp ....E...... 305 885-8689
Medley *(G-8322)*

Sunset Cadillac of Sarasota ....F...... 941 922-1571
Sarasota *(G-15845)*

Superior Dash LLC ....G...... 386 761-1265
South Daytona *(G-16030)*

United American Machinery LLC..........F...... 727 442-1711
Clearwater *(G-1838)*

AUTOMOTIVE PRDTS: Rubber

Paragon Globl Sup Slutions LLC ....F...... 813 745-9902
Tampa *(G-17148)*

Polyhistor International Inc................G...... 904 646-5666
Jacksonville *(G-6377)*

Ready Containment LLC ....F...... 941 739-9486
Palmetto *(G-13190)*

AUTOMOTIVE REPAIR SHOPS: Electrical Svcs

L & L Automotive Electric Inc ....G...... 631 471-5230
Melbourne *(G-8452)*

AUTOMOTIVE REPAIR SHOPS: Engine Rebuilding

Engine Lab of Tampa Inc....................G...... 813 630-2422
Tampa *(G-16813)*

AUTOMOTIVE REPAIR SHOPS: Engine Repair, Exc Diesel

Godwin and Singer Inc.......................G...... 727 896-8631
Saint Petersburg *(G-15064)*

AUTOMOTIVE REPAIR SHOPS: Machine Shop

Aero Technology Mfg Inc ....F...... 305 345-7747
Miami *(G-8662)*

AUTOMOTIVE REPAIR SHOPS: Powertrain Components Repair Svcs

Acme Service Corp.............................F...... 305 836-4800
Miami *(G-8647)*

AUTOMOTIVE REPAIR SHOPS: Sound System Svc & Installation

Flints Wrecker Service Inc ....G...... 863 676-1318
Lake Wales *(G-7160)*

AUTOMOTIVE REPAIR SHOPS: Tire Repair Shop

Jacksonville Tire Rescue Inc ....F...... 904 783-1296
Jacksonville *(G-6217)*

AUTOMOTIVE REPAIR SHOPS: Torque Converter Repair

Avalanche Corporation ....D...... 800 708-0087
Brooksville *(G-1138)*

AUTOMOTIVE REPAIR SHOPS: Trailer Repair

Amera Trail Inc ....E...... 407 892-1100
Saint Cloud *(G-14920)*

PRODUCT

J & J Marine Service Inc..................G...... 813 741-2190
Saint Petersburg **(G-15088)**

Steel Plus Service Center Inc...........G...... 407 328-7169
Sanford **(G-15391)**

Terminal Service Company ....C...... 850 739-5702
Tallahassee **(G-16513)**

AUTOMOTIVE REPAIR SVC

American Auto / Mar Wirg Inc ....G...... 954 782-0193
Pompano Beach **(G-13923)**

Toogle Industries LLC ....G...... 863 688-8975
Lakeland **(G-7464)**

AUTOMOTIVE SPLYS & PARTS, NEW, WHOLESALE: Alternators

T R S..D...... 407 298-5490
Orlando **(G-12644)**

AUTOMOTIVE SPLYS & PARTS, NEW, WHOLESALE: Engines/Eng Parts

Sen-Dure Products Inc ....D...... 954 973-1260
Fort Lauderdale **(G-4044)**

AUTOMOTIVE SPLYS & PARTS, NEW, WHOLESALE: Splys

Pro Chem Products Inc ....G...... 407 425-5533
Orlando **(G-12509)**

AUTOMOTIVE SPLYS & PARTS, USED, WHOLESALE

B & P Motor Heads Inc ....G...... 305 769-3183
Opa Locka **(G-11720)**

Remetall USA Inc ....F...... 888 212-3812
Aventura **(G-273)**

AUTOMOTIVE SPLYS & PARTS, USED, WHOLESALE: Access, NEC

Hornblasters Inc ....E...... 813 783-8058
Tampa **(G-16922)**

AUTOMOTIVE SPLYS & PARTS, WHOLESALE, NEC

Argos Global Partner Svcs LLC ....G...... 305 365-1096
Key Biscayne **(G-6833)**

Bukkehave Inc ....G...... 954 525-9788
Fort Lauderdale **(G-3709)**

D & L Auto & Marine Supplies ....G...... 305 593-0560
Doral **(G-3181)**

Motor Service Group LLC ....G...... 305 592-2440
Miami **(G-9591)**

Motor Service Inc ....G...... 305 592-2440
Miami **(G-9592)**

Naztec International Group LLC ....F...... 561 802-4110
West Palm Beach **(G-18088)**

Southast Auto Acquisition Corp........E...... 305 885-8689
Medley **(G-8322)**

Total Performance Inc ....F...... 203 265-5667
Palm Coast **(G-13091)**

Voxx International Corporation ....B...... 800 645-7750
Orlando **(G-12706)**

Wetherill Associates Inc ....C...... 800 877-3340
Miramar **(G-10564)**

AUTOMOTIVE SPLYS/PART, NEW, WHOL: Spring, Shock Absorb/Strut

Hornblasters Inc ....E...... 813 783-8058
Tampa **(G-16922)**

AUTOMOTIVE SVCS

Florida Oil Service Inc ....F...... 813 655-4753
Lithia **(G-7834)**

AUTOMOTIVE SVCS, EXC REPAIR & CARWASHES: Maintenance

Creative Colors International............F...... 239 573-8883
Cape Coral **(G-1328)**

K C W Electric Company Inc ....G...... 850 878-2051
Tallahassee **(G-16465)**

AUTOMOTIVE SVCS, EXC RPR/CARWASHES: High Perf Auto Rpr/Svc

Revology Cars LLC.........................F...... 800 974-4463
Orlando **(G-12549)**

AUTOMOTIVE TOWING & WRECKING SVC

Palatka Welding Shop Inc ....E...... 386 328-1507
Palatka **(G-12876)**

AUTOMOTIVE TOWING SVCS

Arons Towing & Recovery Inc ....G...... 772 220-1151
Hobe Sound **(G-5479)**

AUTOMOTIVE TRANSMISSION REPAIR SVC

Phoenix Transmission Parts Inc........G...... 727 541-0269
Seminole **(G-15985)**

AUTOMOTIVE WELDING SVCS

Bjb Marine Welding & Svcs Inc ....F...... 954 909-4967
Fort Lauderdale **(G-3689)**

H&R Welding Equipment Repr Inc ....G...... 904 487-9829
Green Cove Springs **(G-4827)**

Kingston Automotive & Wldg LLC .....G...... 727 378-4881
Hudson **(G-5780)**

Mims Welding Incorporated ....G...... 863 612-9819
Labelle **(G-6983)**

Tarin Services LLC ....G...... 803 526-9643
Tampa **(G-17341)**

AUTOMOTIVE: Bodies

Speedsource Inc ....G...... 954 578-7071
Key Largo **(G-6850)**

AUTOMOTIVE: Seating

Clarios LLC ....E...... 407 850-0147
Orlando **(G-12017)**

Clarios LLC ....D...... 321 253-4000
Melbourne **(G-8388)**

Clarios LLC ....E...... 866 866-0886
Naples **(G-10715)**

Johnson Controls Inc ....E...... 407 291-1971
Orlando **(G-12276)**

Johnson Controls Inc ....D...... 813 623-1188
Tampa **(G-16970)**

Johnson Controls Inc ....E...... 305 883-3760
Medley **(G-8265)**

Johnson Controls Inc ....F...... 772 283-1633
Stuart **(G-16172)**

AUTOTRANSFORMERS: Electric

Backbone Interconnect LLC ....E...... 954 800-4749
Sunrise **(G-16294)**

AVIATION PROPELLER & BLADE REPAIR SVCS

Willis Aeronautical Svcs Inc ....F...... 561 272-5402
Pompano Beach **(G-14244)**

AVIATION SCHOOL

3d Perception Inc ....F...... 321 235-7999
Orlando **(G-11850)**

Cae USA Inc ....A...... 813 885-7481
Tampa **(G-16672)**

ELite Intl Group LLC ....F...... 305 901-5005
Miami **(G-9086)**

Gleim Publications Inc ....D...... 352 375-0772
Gainesville **(G-4703)**

AWNINGS & CANOPIES

Coastal Awngs Hrrcane Prtction ....G...... 407 923-9482
Orlando **(G-12023)**

Emerald Sails ....G...... 850 240-4777
Shalimar **(G-16001)**

General Metals & Plastics Inc ....G...... 904 354-8224
Jacksonville **(G-6139)**

Kenco - 2000 Inc ....F...... 386 672-1590
Daytona Beach **(G-2565)**

No Equal Design Inc ....G...... 305 971-5177
Miami **(G-9623)**

Parrish Inc ....G...... 386 985-4879
De Leon Springs **(G-2626)**

AWNINGS & CANOPIES: Awnings, Fabric, From Purchased Matls

A & A Central Florida ....F...... 407 648-5666
Altamonte Springs **(G-26)**

ABc Awning & Canvas Co Inc ....F...... 321 253-1960
Delray Beach **(G-2924)**

Advanced Awning & Design LLC ....G...... 904 724-5567
Jacksonville **(G-5860)**

American Awning Company Inc ....G...... 561 832-7123
West Palm Beach **(G-17922)**

Ards Awning & Upholstery Inc ....F...... 863 293-2442
Winter Haven **(G-18418)**

Awnings By Coversol ....E...... 813 251-4774
Tampa **(G-16621)**

Biscayne Awning & Shade Co ....E...... 305 638-7933
Miami **(G-8833)**

Canvas Shop Inc ....F...... 407 898-6001
Orlando **(G-11980)**

Coastal Canvas and Awning Co ....F...... 239 433-1114
Fort Myers **(G-4212)**

Cross Key Marine Canvas Inc ....G...... 305 451-1302
Key Largo **(G-6844)**

Delray Awning Inc ....F...... 561 276-5381
Delray Beach **(G-2954)**

Discount Awnings Inc ....G...... 941 753-5700
Sarasota **(G-15470)**

Florida Shutters Inc ....E...... 772 569-2200
Vero Beach **(G-17755)**

Hoover Canvas Products Co ....E...... 954 764-1711
Fort Lauderdale **(G-3868)**

Hoover Canvas Products Co ....F...... 954 541-9745
Mangonia Park **(G-8092)**

Hoover Canvas Products Co ....F...... 561 844-4444
Mangonia Park **(G-8093)**

Jones Awnings & Canvas Inc ....E...... 954 784-6966
Pompano Beach **(G-14068)**

Major Canvas Products Inc ....F...... 954 764-1711
Fort Lauderdale **(G-3928)**

Miami Beach Awning Co ....E...... 305 576-2029
Miami **(G-9546)**

Milliken & Milliken Inc ....E...... 941 474-0223
Englewood **(G-3534)**

Paradise Awnings Corporation ....E...... 305 597-5714
Miami **(G-9692)**

Sunstate Awng Grphic Dsign Inc ....E...... 407 260-6118
Sanford **(G-15392)**

Thomas Sign and Awning Co Inc ....C...... 727 573-7757
Clearwater **(G-1828)**

Thompson Awning & Shutter Co ....F...... 904 355-1616
Jacksonville **(G-6547)**

Treasure Coast Canvas ....F...... 772 210-2588
Stuart **(G-16240)**

Tropical Awning Florida Inc ....F...... 561 276-1144
Delray Beach **(G-3028)**

United States Awning Company..........E...... 941 955-7010
Sarasota **(G-15864)**

AWNINGS & CANOPIES: Canopies, Fabric, From Purchased Matls

Apollo Sunguard Systems Inc ....F...... 941 925-3000
Sarasota **(G-15596)**

Logsdon and Associates Inc ....G...... 407 292-0084
Windermere **(G-18359)**

Mason-Florida LLC ....F...... 352 638-9003
Leesburg **(G-7785)**

Portable-Shade USA LLC ....G...... 321 704-8100
Cocoa **(G-1947)**

AWNINGS & CANOPIES: Fabric

Air Shelters USA LLC ....E...... 215 957-6128
Pompano Beach **(G-13913)**

Big Top Manufacturing Inc ....D...... 850 584-7786
Perry **(G-13632)**

Canopy Specialist LLC ....F...... 813 703-6844
Plant City **(G-13750)**

Coastal Awngs Hrrcane Prtction ....G...... 407 923-9482
Orlando **(G-12023)**

Fabis Group Corporation ....G...... 305 718-3638
Miami **(G-9126)**

Got It Inc ....G...... 954 899-0001
Boca Raton **(G-531)**

Iis Incorporated ....G...... 561 547-4297
Boynton Beach **(G-878)**

Southern Awning Inc ....E...... 561 586-0464
Lake Worth **(G-7233)**

AWNINGS: Fiberglass

Coastal Awngs Hrrcane Prtction ....G....... 407 923-9482
Orlando (G-12023)
Iis Incorporated ....G.......561 547-4297
Boynton Beach (G-878)
Safe Pro Inc ....G....... 954 494-5768
Hialeah (G-5340)

AWNINGS: Metal

Alumflo Inc ....G....... 727 527-8494
Saint Petersburg (G-14960)
Dolphin Sheet Metal Inc ....F 561 744-0242
Jupiter (G-6711)
Florida Shutters Inc ....E 772 569-2200
Vero Beach (G-17755)
Fresco Group Inc ....E 239 936-8055
Fort Myers (G-4263)
Hurst Awning Company Inc ....E 305 693-0600
Hollywood (G-5600)
Rolling Shield Incorporated ....E 305 436-6661
Hialeah Gardens (G-5449)
Rolling Shield Parts Inc ....F 305 436-6661
Hialeah Gardens (G-5450)
Style-View Products Inc ....E 305 634-9688
Miami (G-9962)
Thompson Awning & Shutter Co ....F 904 355-1616
Jacksonville (G-6547)
United States Awning Company ....E 941 955-7010
Sarasota (G-15864)

BABY PACIFIERS: Rubber

Nissi & Jireh Inc ....E 866 897-7657
Miramar (G-10519)

BACKHOES

Ingrams Backhoe Dumptruck Svc ....G....... 850 718-6042
Cottondale (G-2229)

BADGES: Identification & Insignia

Express Badging Services Inc ....F 321 784-5925
Cocoa Beach (G-1969)
Hbys Enterprises LLC ....F 855 290-9900
Winter Springs (G-18567)
One Source Industries Inc ....G....... 813 855-3440
Oldsmar (G-11682)
Ped-Stuart Corporation ....E 352 754-6001
Brooksville (G-1188)
Suncoast Idntfction Sltons LLC ....F 239 277-9922
Fort Myers (G-4412)
Superior Group Companies Inc ....C 727 397-9611
Seminole (G-15991)

BAGS & CONTAINERS: Textile, Exc Sleeping

Paper Bag Manufacturers Inc ....F 305 685-1100
Opa Locka (G-11779)
Suncoast Trends Inc ....G....... 727 321-4948
Saint Petersburg (G-15202)

BAGS & SACKS: Shipping & Shopping

Atlantic Ship Supply Inc ....G....... 954 961-8885
Hallandale (G-4920)
Bryce Foster Inc ....G....... 800 371-0395
Altamonte Springs (G-34)

BAGS: Canvas

Armor Products Mfg Inc ....F 813 764-8844
Plant City (G-13740)
Cameron Textiles Inc ....G....... 954 454-6482
Palm City (G-13026)
Safety Intl Bags & Straps Inc ....F 407 830-0888
Casselberry (G-1432)
Warren Heim Corp ....F 772 466-8265
Fort Pierce (G-4553)

BAGS: Cellophane

Cavadas Ruben & Trisha Wagner ....G....... 407 248-2659
Orlando (G-11988)
H Sixto Distributors Inc ....F 305 688-5242
Opa Locka (G-11752)

BAGS: Cement, Made From Purchased Materials

Ready Building Products Inc ....G....... 941 639-6222
Punta Gorda (G-14526)

BAGS: Duffle, Canvas, Made From Purchased Materials

Abco Industries LLC ....G....... 813 605-5900
Tampa (G-16554)

BAGS: Food Storage & Frozen Food, Plastic

Seal-Tite Plastic Packg Co Inc ....D....... 305 264-9015
Miami (G-9860)

BAGS: Food Storage & Trash, Plastic

Inteplast Engineered Films Inc ....D....... 407 851-6620
Orlando (G-12249)

BAGS: Garment Storage Exc Paper Or Plastic Film

Premier Plastics LLC ....G....... 305 805-3333
Boynton Beach (G-899)

BAGS: Laundry, From Purchased Materials

Cameron Textiles Inc ....G....... 954 454-6482
Palm City (G-13026)

BAGS: Laundry, Garment & Storage

Armor Products Mfg Inc ....F 813 764-8844
Plant City (G-13740)

BAGS: Paper

Aspen Products Inc ....B 904 579-4366
Fleming Island (G-3607)
Harmsco Inc ....D....... 561 848-9628
Riviera Beach (G-14626)
Paper Bag Manufacturers Inc ....F 305 685-1100
Opa Locka (G-11779)
Trend At LLC ....E 786 300-2550
Miami (G-10039)

BAGS: Paper, Made From Purchased Materials

J S Trading Inc ....G....... 954 791-9035
Plantation (G-13860)
Pro Pak Enterprises Inc ....F 888 375-2275
Deerfield Beach (G-2790)
S V Bags America Inc ....G....... 954 577-9091
Weston (G-18285)
Tak Paper Corp ....G....... 786 287-8900
Doral (G-3390)

BAGS: Plastic

Coastal Films of Florida ....D....... 904 786-2031
Jacksonville (G-5989)
Cosner Manufacturing LLC ....F 863 676-2579
Lake Wales (G-7157)
Diversitypro Corp ....D....... 305 691-2348
South Miami (G-16032)
H Goicoechea Inc ....F 305 805-3333
Hialeah (G-5181)
J P Poly Bag Company ....G....... 727 804-5866
Palm Harbor (G-13115)
Jan and Jean Inc ....G....... 813 645-0680
Ruskin (G-14779)
Koszegi Industries Inc ....E 954 419-9544
Deerfield Beach (G-2749)
Premium Absrbent Dspsables LLC ....E 561 737-6377
Boynton Beach (G-900)
R & D Sleeves Llc ....E 407 886-9010
Apopka (G-167)
Starlock Inc ....G....... 305 477-2303
Doral (G-3375)
Sterling Mdr Inc ....F 954 725-2777
Deerfield Beach (G-2815)
US American Plastic Corp ....F 305 200-3683
Miami (G-10079)

BAGS: Plastic & Pliofilm

Construction and Elec Pdts Inc ....F 954 972-9787
Pompano Beach (G-13976)
Flexsol Holding Corp ....E 954 941-6333
Pompano Beach (G-14031)
Jr Plastics Corporation ....D....... 352 401-0880
Ocala (G-11414)

BAGS: Plastic, Made From Purchased Materials

Bags Express Inc ....G....... 305 500-9849
Doral (G-3128)
Biobag Americas Inc ....F 727 789-1646
Dunedin (G-3441)
Buggy Bagg Inc ....G....... 386 758-5836
Lake City (G-7013)
Crown Products LLC ....G....... 954 917-1118
Pompano Beach (G-13984)
CSR Enterprise Ltd ....G....... 954 624-2284
North Miami (G-11101)
Dairy-Mix Inc ....F 813 621-8098
Tampa (G-16759)
Dynasel Incorporated ....G....... 972 733-4447
Deerfield Beach (G-2712)
J S Trading Inc ....G....... 954 791-9035
Plantation (G-13860)
Mhms Corp ....E 813 948-0504
Lutz (G-8005)
Pharmaseal LLC ....F 561 840-0050
Palm Beach Gardens (G-12998)
Plastix Usa LLC ....D....... 305 891-0091
Hollywood (G-5643)
Poly Plastic Packaging Co Inc ....E 561 498-9040
Boca Raton (G-637)
Pro Pak Enterprises Inc ....F 888 375-2275
Deerfield Beach (G-2790)

BAGS: Textile

Matteo Graphics Inc ....G....... 239 652-1002
Cape Coral (G-1363)
Wayloo Inc ....G....... 954 914-3192
Fort Lauderdale (G-4125)
Youthful Innovations LLC ....G....... 239 596-2200
Naples (G-10946)

BAGS: Trash, Plastic Film, Made From Purchased Materials

Litterbin LLC ....G....... 772 633-7184
Vero Beach (G-17775)

BAGS: Vacuum cleaner, Made From Purchased Materials

ACS of West Palm Beach Inc ....G....... 561 844-5790
West Palm Beach (G-17912)

BAGS: Wardrobe, Closet Access, Made From Purchased Materials

Sams Closet Inc ....G....... 954 354-8386
Deerfield Beach (G-2801)
Space Masters ....F 954 561-8800
Oakland Park (G-11296)

BAKERIES, COMMERCIAL: On Premises Baking Only

B&Sdelicious DESserts&cupcakes ....G....... 954 557-8350
Fort Lauderdale (G-3670)
Bauducco Manufacturing Inc ....F 305 477-9270
Miami (G-8803)
Bauducco USA Holding Company ....G....... 305 477-9270
Miami (G-8804)
Cedars Bakery Group Inc ....F 407 476-6593
Orlando (G-11989)
Corvatsch Corp ....F 305 775-2831
Miami Beach (G-10180)
Crustys Bread Bakery ....G....... 727 937-9041
Tarpon Springs (G-17463)
Cupcake Inc ....G....... 407 644-7800
Maitland (G-8056)
Cupcakes Frsting Sprinkles LLC ....G....... 305 769-3393
Opa Locka (G-11734)
Duval Bakery Products Inc ....G....... 904 354-7878
Orange Park (G-11825)
Five Star Bakery ....G....... 954 983-6133
Miramar (G-10491)
Flowers Bakeries LLC ....E 850 875-4997
Quincy (G-14544)
Flowers Baking Co LLC ....G....... 850 763-2541
Panama City (G-13264)
Flowers Bkg Co Bradenton LLC ....F 941 627-0752
Port Charlotte (G-14300)
Flowers Bkg Co Bradenton LLC ....E 941 758-5656
Lakeland (G-7333)

PRODUCT

Flowers Bkg Co Bradenton LLC .... F 941 758-5656
Avon Park (G-281)
Flowers Bkg Co Bradenton LLC .... E 941 758-5656
Orlando (G-12171)
Flowers Bkg Co Bradenton LLC .... E 941 758-5656
Hudson (G-5774)
Flowers Bkg Co Bradenton LLC .... E 941 758-5656
Kissimmee (G-6922)
Flowers Bkg Co Bradenton LLC .... E 941 758-5656
Bonita Springs (G-799)
Flowers Bkg Co Bradenton LLC .... E 941 758-5656
Bradenton (G-980)
Franklin Baking Company LLC .... G 850 478-8360
Pensacola (G-13511)
Fresh On Fifth .... G 305 234-5678
Miami Beach (G-10192)
Heara Inc .... G 305 651-5200
Miami (G-9269)
La Province Inc .... F 305 538-2406
Miami (G-9413)
Marnis Dolce .... G 407 915-7607
Apopka (G-148)
Merenguitoscom LLC .... G 305 685-2709
Hialeah (G-5244)
New Marco Foods Inc .... F 305 836-0571
Hialeah (G-5276)
Obem Foods Inc .... G 305 887-0258
Miami Springs (G-10392)
OPelle Enterprises Inc .... E 954 942-7338
Pompano Beach (G-14111)
Pink Cupcake Inc .... G 904 434-9599
Atlantic Beach (G-214)
Simply Cupcakes .... G 239 262-5184
Naples (G-10894)
Slb1989 Inc .... G 772 344-3609
Port Saint Lucie (G-14448)
Spring Hill Bakery LLC .... E 954 825-3419
Spring Hill (G-16081)
Star Bakery Inc .... F 305 633-4284
Miami (G-9946)
T & W Inc .... G 305 887-0258
Miami Springs (G-10394)

BAKERIES: On Premises Baking & Consumption

Claddah Corp .... F 407 834-8881
Casselberry (G-1413)
Edca Bakery Corporation .... F 305 448-7843
Coral Gables (G-2051)
Flowers Baking Co Miami LLC .... D 305 652-3416
Miami (G-9162)
Pane Rustica Bakery & Cafe .... F 813 902-8828
Tampa (G-17142)
Way Beyond Bagels Inc .... G 561 638-1320
Delray Beach (G-3037)

BAKERY FOR HOME SVC DELIVERY

Bks Bakery Inc .... G 386 216-0540
Deltona (G-3040)

BAKERY MACHINERY

Deluxe Equipment Co .... F 941 753-4184
Bradenton (G-967)

BAKERY PRDTS, FROZEN: Wholesalers

Bks Bakery Inc .... G 386 216-0540
Deltona (G-3040)

BAKERY PRDTS: Bagels, Fresh Or Frozen

Brothers Wholesale Inc .... E 631 831-8484
Port St Lucie (G-14470)
Hometown Foods Usa LLC .... C 305 887-5200
Medley (G-8254)

BAKERY PRDTS: Bakery Prdts, Partially Cooked, Exc frozen

Fat and Weird Cookie Co LLC .... F 850 832-9150
Panama City (G-13260)
I Be Cakin LLC .... G 954 707-3865
Pompano Beach (G-14057)
Unicornio Bakery LLC .... F 786 665-1602
Doral (G-3405)

BAKERY PRDTS: Biscuits, Baked, Baking Powder & Raised

Savory Street .... G 941 312-4027
Sarasota (G-15819)

BAKERY PRDTS: Bread, All Types, Fresh Or Frozen

Caamacosta Inc .... G 954 987-5895
Hollywood (G-5545)
Casino Bakery Inc .... F 813 242-0311
Tampa (G-16685)
Claddah Corp .... F 407 834-8881
Casselberry (G-1413)
Flowers Bkg Co Bradenton LLC .... C 941 758-5656
Sarasota (G-15478)
Flowers Bkg Co Thomasville LLC .... F 229 226-5331
Tallahassee (G-16442)
Panamerican Food LLC .... E 305 594-5704
Miramar (G-10524)
Southern Bakeries Inc .... C 863 682-1155
Lakeland (G-7443)

BAKERY PRDTS: Cakes, Bakery, Exc Frozen

Blanco Gomez Maldonado LLC .... G 305 380-1114
Miami (G-8837)
Churrico Factory LLC .... G 239 989-7616
Fort Myers (G-4207)
Cupcake Girls Dessert Company .... G 904 372-4579
Jacksonville Beach (G-6632)
Cupcake Heaven .... G 352 610-4433
Spring Hill (G-16069)
Desirous Candles Inc .... G 347 622-6987
Pembroke Pines (G-13384)
El Trigal International .... E 305 594-6610
Doral (G-3206)
Gigliola Inc .... G 954 564-7871
Fort Lauderdale (G-3839)
Gregomarc LLC .... G 305 559-9777
Miami (G-9247)
Juan F Montano .... G 305 274-0512
Miami (G-9380)
Sweetsies .... G 386 566-6762
Palm Coast (G-13089)
Todo En Uno .... G 305 263-6934
Miami (G-10019)

BAKERY PRDTS: Cakes, Bakery, Frozen

Sugar Fancies LLC .... G 786 558-9087
Miami (G-9963)

BAKERY PRDTS: Cones, Ice Cream

Carpe Diem Ice Cream LLC .... G 305 504-4469
Key West (G-6857)

BAKERY PRDTS: Cookies

Ambo Foods LLC .... G 941 485-4400
Venice (G-17675)
Aventura Cookies Inc .... G 954 447-4525
Pembroke Pines (G-13375)
First Grade Food Corporation .... E 813 886-6118
Tampa (G-16833)
Jada Foods LLC .... F 305 319-0263
Hallandale Beach (G-4954)
Lavi Enterprises LLC .... D 561 721-7170
Riviera Beach (G-14642)
Lindley Foods LLC .... G 407 884-9433
Apopka (G-147)
Selmas Cookies Inc .... E 407 884-9433
Apopka (G-175)
Smart Snacks LLC .... G 954 860-8833
Bal Harbour (G-296)

BAKERY PRDTS: Cookies & crackers

Magnolias Gurmet Bky Itln Deli .... G 352 207-2667
Ocala (G-11435)
Paleo Bakehouse Inc .... G 786 253-1051
Miami (G-9681)
Paleo Simplified LLC .... G 813 446-5969
Safety Harbor (G-14793)
Ricos Tostaditos Inc .... F 305 885-7392
Hialeah (G-5333)

BAKERY PRDTS: Crackers

Gilda Industries Inc .... G 305 887-8286
Hialeah (G-5172)

Rika Bakeries Inc .... F 305 691-5673
Hialeah (G-5334)
Tuly Corporation .... F 305 633-0710
Miami (G-10045)

BAKERY PRDTS: Doughnuts, Exc Frozen

Dip-A-Dee Donuts .... E 352 460-4266
Leesburg (G-7766)
Donut King of Leesburg LLC .... G 352 250-8487
Leesburg (G-7767)

BAKERY PRDTS: Dry

Bingo Bakery Inc .... F 305 545-9993
Miami (G-8827)
Megatron Equity Partners Inc .... F 305 789-6688
Miami (G-9531)
Sapphire Exchange LLC .... G 407 926-8305
Edgewater (G-3500)
Star Bakery Inc .... F 305 633-4284
Miami (G-9946)

BAKERY PRDTS: Frozen

Blue Coast Bakers LLC .... E 386 944-0800
Ormond Beach (G-12747)
Caligiuri Corporation .... E 407 324-4441
Sanford (G-15276)
Epic Harvests LLC .... E 904 503-5143
Jacksonville (G-6079)
Hometown Foods Usa LLC .... C 305 887-5200
Medley (G-8254)
OPelle Enterprises Inc .... E 954 942-7338
Pompano Beach (G-14111)
Sunsof Inc .... E 305 691-1875
Hialeah (G-5371)

BAKERY PRDTS: Pastries, Danish, Frozen

La Autentica .... G 786 409-3779
Hialeah (G-5218)

BAKERY PRDTS: Pastries, Exc Frozen

Bkn International Inc .... G 301 518-7153
Miami Beach (G-10171)
Panapastry LLC .... G 305 883-1557
Medley (G-8296)
Tuly Corporation .... F 305 633-0710
Miami (G-10045)

BAKERY PRDTS: Pies, Exc Frozen

Darland Bakery Inc .... F 407 894-1061
Orlando (G-12073)
Empanada Lady Co .... G 786 271-6460
Miami (G-9097)

BAKERY PRDTS: Pretzels

Polaris Trading Corp .... G 954 956-6999
Coconut Creek (G-2002)

BAKERY PRDTS: Rolls, Bread Type, Fresh Or Frozen

Egg Roll Skins Inc .... F 305 836-0571
Hialeah (G-5138)

BAKERY PRDTS: Wholesalers

Gfoodz LLC .... G 561 703-4505
Boynton Beach (G-872)
Southern Bakeries Inc .... C 863 682-1155
Lakeland (G-7443)

BAKERY: Wholesale Or Wholesale & Retail Combined

904 Sweet Treatz Street LLC .... G 800 889-3298
Jacksonville (G-5842)
Bakerly LLC .... G 786 539-5888
Coral Gables (G-2032)
Bimbo Bakeries USA .... G 941 875-5945
North Port (G-11188)
Bimbo Bakeries USA .... F 954 968-7684
Fort Lauderdale (G-3687)
Brooklyn Water Enterprises Inc .... E 877 224-3580
Delray Beach (G-2939)
Buttercream Cpcakes Cof Sp Inc .... F 305 669-8181
Coral Gables (G-2037)
Clear Distribution Inc .... G 904 330-5624
Jacksonville (G-5982)

CMC Bakery LLC......................E......978 682-2382
Pompano Beach (G-13970)

Coleo LLC.................................F......215 436-0902
Daytona Beach (G-2533)

Cusanos Italian Bakery Inc.........E......786 506-4281
Orlando (G-12065)

Ebs Quality Service Inc.............F......305 595-4048
Miami (G-9067)

Edca Bakery Corporation............F......305 448-7843
Coral Gables (G-2051)

Enchanting Creations..................G......305 978-2828
Miami Shores (G-10382)

Farartis LLC..............................G......305 594-5704
Miami (G-9133)

Flowers Baking Co Miami LLC......E......305 599-8457
Doral (G-3218)

Flowers Bkg Jacksonville LLC.......D......904 354-3771
Jacksonville (G-6114)

Frosting..................................G......772 234-2915
Vero Beach (G-17756)

Gfoodz LLC..............................G......561 703-4505
Boynton Beach (G-872)

Giovannis Bakery Inc.................F......727 536-2253
Largo (G-7593)

H&K Home Supplies Distrs LLC.......F......786 308-6024
Homestead (G-5712)

Ipq Trade Corp..........................F......786 522-2310
Miami (G-9337)

Kellys Bakery Corp.....................F......305 685-4622
Opa Locka (G-11759)

La Mansion Latina LLC...............G......305 406-1606
Miami (G-9409)

Lisa Bakery Inc.........................G......305 888-8431
Hialeah (G-5224)

Magnolias Gurmet Bky Itln Deli......G......352 207-2667
Ocala (G-11435)

Master Universe LLC..................F......786 246-3190
Miami (G-9519)

Mishas Cupcakes Inc..................F......786 200-6153
Miami (G-9577)

Mr GS Foods.............................F......352 799-1806
Brooksville (G-1184)

New Vbb LLC............................E......904 631-5978
Jacksonville (G-6329)

New York Intl Bread Co................D......407 843-9744
Orlando (G-12414)

Palanjian Enterprises Inc.............F......850 244-2848
Fort Walton Beach (G-4600)

Pane Rustica Bakery & Cafe..........F......813 902-8828
Tampa (G-17142)

Parinto Global Enterprises LLC......G......305 606-3107
Doral (G-3322)

Payo LLC..................................G......786 368-8655
Davie (G-2454)

Phils Cake Box Bakeries Inc.........D......813 348-0128
Tampa (G-17164)

RB Home Goods LLC...................F......786 690-3008
Miami (G-9785)

Rouzbeh Inc.............................F......727 587-7077
Largo (G-7672)

Sindoni North America LLC...........G......786 536-9171
Miami (G-9897)

St Johns Bky & Gourmet Fd Co.......E......813 727-3528
Jacksonville (G-6502)

Swami Foods LLC.......................F......888 697-9264
Lake Mary (G-7110)

Sweet Creations By L S Young.......G......772 584-7206
Vero Beach (G-17805)

Tulipan Bakery Inc.....................G......561 832-6107
West Palm Beach (G-18188)

Universal Bakery LLC...................G......786 566-3303
Opa Locka (G-11797)

Way Beyond Bagels Inc...............G......561 638-1320
Delray Beach (G-3037)

Willie Maes Pies LLC..................F......407 655-9360
Kissimmee (G-6978)

World of Brigadeiro LLC..............G......954 488-4597
Boca Raton (G-756)

Yummy Foods Inc......................G......305 681-8437
Davie (G-2502)

BALCONIES: Metal

Clear Horizon Ventures Company......F......727 372-1100
Hudson (G-5766)

Frattle Stairs & Rails Inc.............F......904 384-3495
Jacksonville (G-6121)

Solara Industries Inc...................E......863 688-3330
Lakeland (G-7439)

BALLOONS: Toy & Advertising, Rubber

Aerial Products Corporation..........F......800 973-9110
Jacksonville (G-5866)

Boulder Blimp Company Inc.........F......303 664-1122
Miami (G-8850)

Put Your Name On It LLC..............G......813 972-1460
Tampa (G-17195)

BANDS: Plastic

Price Chpper Med Wrstbands Inc......G......407 505-5809
Orlando (G-12505)

BANKING SCHOOLS, TRAINING

West Texas Protein Inc...............F......806 250-5959
Jacksonville (G-6602)

BANNERS: Fabric

AMI Graphics Inc.......................E......352 629-4455
Ocala (G-11322)

Boulder Blimp Company Inc.........F......303 664-1122
Miami (G-8850)

Delray Awning Inc......................F......561 276-5381
Delray Beach (G-2954)

Flyrite Banner Makers Inc............F......352 873-7501
Ocala (G-11394)

Gulf Glo Banners and Signs LLC......G......850 234-0952
Panama City (G-13271)

Imprint Promotions LLC...............G......321 622-8946
Melbourne (G-8441)

In The News Inc.........................D......813 882-8886
Tampa (G-16935)

Kiteman Productions Inc..............G......407 943-8480
Orlando (G-12291)

Outdoor America Images Inc.........E......813 888-8796
Tampa (G-17133)

BAR FIXTURES: Wood

Roomy Design Organizers LLC........F......407 703-9550
Apopka (G-172)

BAR JOISTS & CONCRETE REINFORCING BARS: Fabricated

Capstone Cg LLC.......................F......941 371-3321
Sarasota (G-15451)

BARBECUE EQPT

A&J Manufacturing Inc...............E......912 638-4724
Tampa (G-16548)

Advanced Outdoor Concepts Inc......G......954 429-1428
Deerfield Beach (G-2657)

American Household Inc..............D......561 912-4100
Boca Raton (G-407)

Dryer Vent Wizard of Pb...............F......561 901-3464
Boynton Beach (G-859)

Firetainment Inc........................G......888 552-7897
Orlando (G-12152)

L C Ch International Inc................G......305 888-1323
Hialeah (G-5216)

Premier Specialty Service LLC........G......904 531-9315
Green Cove Springs (G-4832)

Profire Inc...............................F......305 665-5313
Pinecrest (G-13669)

Sunbeam Americas Holdings LLC......E......561 912-4100
Boca Raton (G-702)

Sunbeam Products Inc................B......561 912-4100
Boca Raton (G-703)

BARGES BUILDING & REPAIR

Hendry Shipyard Joint Ventr 1........F......813 241-9206
Tampa (G-16914)

BARRELS: Shipping, Metal

Container of America LLC...............F......954 772-5519
Fort Lauderdale (G-3744)

Extreme Coatings.......................G......727 528-7998
Saint Petersburg (G-15041)

Migrandy Corp...........................G......321 459-0044
Merritt Island (G-8588)

BARRICADES: Metal

Acme Barricades LC....................E......904 781-1950
Jacksonville (G-5857)

All American Barricades................G......305 685-6124
Fort Lauderdale (G-3637)

Bobs Barricades Inc....................E......813 886-0518
Tampa (G-16652)

Bobs Barricades Inc....................F......239 656-1183
Fort Myers (G-4192)

L C Acme Barricades....................G......813 623-2263
Tampa (G-16994)

L C Acme Barricades....................G......863 816-5874
Lakeland (G-7372)

L C Acme Barricades....................G......561 657-8222
Riviera Beach (G-14640)

Lrvs Barricades LLC....................G......305 343-6101
Miami (G-9481)

Rssi Barriers Llc.........................E......850 871-9300
Panama City (G-13305)

Safety Zone Specialists Inc...........G......863 984-1385
Lakeland (G-7427)

Traffic Control Pdts Fla Inc...........G......813 621-8484
Fort Myers (G-4431)

Traffic Control Pdts Fla Inc...........F......407 521-6777
Orlando (G-12667)

Traffic Control Pdts Fla Inc...........E......352 372-7088
Jacksonville (G-6562)

BARS & BAR SHAPES: Steel, Cold-Finished, Own Hot-Rolled

Florida Stl Frame Truss Mfg LL........G......813 460-0006
Wesley Chapel (G-17876)

Sheffield Steel Corporation...........C......918 245-1335
Tampa (G-17258)

BARS & BAR SHAPES: Steel, Hot-Rolled

Urban Metals LLC......................F......813 241-2801
Tampa (G-17396)

BARS, COLD FINISHED: Steel, From Purchased Hot-Rolled

Stuart Building Products LLC........D......239 461-3100
Fort Myers (G-4408)

BARS: Cargo, Stabilizing, Metal

Gyro-Gale Inc...........................G......772 283-1711
Stuart (G-16160)

BARS: Concrete Reinforcing, Fabricated Steel

Atlantic Steel Cnstr LLC...............G......419 236-2200
Miami (G-8765)

Brunsteel Corp..........................G......305 251-7607
Miami (G-8858)

Commercial Metals Company..........E......954 921-2500
Dania (G-2330)

Gerdau Ameristeel US Inc.............B......813 286-8383
Tampa (G-16877)

Gerdau USA Inc..........................B......813 286-8383
Tampa (G-16878)

Gulf Coast Rebar Inc..................E......813 247-1200
Tampa (G-16897)

Raw Energy Materials Corp..........G......954 270-9000
Pompano Beach (G-14155)

S & S Welding Inc......................F......863 533-2888
Bartow (G-325)

BASES, BEVERAGE

Al-Rite Fruits and Syrups Inc.........G......305 652-2540
Miami (G-8679)

Bev-Co Enterprises Inc...............G......786 362-6368
Miami (G-8821)

Bev-Co Enterprises Inc...............E......786 953-7109
Doral (G-3135)

Cape Britt Corp Inc.....................G......305 593-5027
Miami (G-8886)

Celsius Inc..............................F......561 276-2239
Boca Raton (G-458)

Coastal Promotions Inc...............G......850 460-2270
Destin (G-3062)

Fresh Start Beverage Company.......G......561 757-6541
Boca Raton (G-524)

Nutrition Laboratories Inc.............E......727 442-2747
Clearwater (G-1724)

Probalance Inc.........................G......727 531-8506
Clearwater (G-1755)

Sunny Hill International Inc...........G......386 736-5757
Deland (G-2905)

Top Drinks USA Corp...................G......305 407-3514
Miami (G-10024)

Yos Bottling LLC ....F 863 258-6820
Dade City (G-2325)

BATCHING PLANTS: Cement Silos

Scutti America Inc ....G 954 384-2377
Weston (G-18286)

BATHING SUIT STORES

Double J of Broward Inc ....E 954 659-8880
Weston (G-18238)

Ultimate Swimwear Inc ....F 386 668-8900
Altamonte Springs (G-75)

BATHROOM ACCESS & FITTINGS: Vitreous China & Earthenware

Alabama Marble Co Inc ....F 305 718-8000
Doral (G-3102)

National Bidet Corp ....G 786 325-6593
Miami Beach (G-10214)

Terracassa LLC ....G 786 581-7741
Miami (G-10002)

BATHROOM FIXTURES: Plastic

See-Ray Plumbing Inc ....E 772 489-2474
Vero Beach (G-17798)

Spa World Corporation ....E 866 588-8008
Miami (G-9931)

BATHTUBS: Concrete

Hamsard Usa Inc ....C 386 761-1830
Daytona Beach (G-2561)

BATTERIES, EXC AUTOMOTIVE: Wholesalers

Exide Battery ....G 904 783-1224
Jacksonville (G-6083)

Rayovac Corp ....G 727 393-0966
Largo (G-7667)

TAe Trans Atlantic Elec Inc ....E 631 595-9206
Tampa (G-17322)

BATTERIES: Alkaline, Cell Storage

Cleva Technologies LLC ....F 561 654-5279
Boca Raton (G-466)

Inspired Energy LLC ....C 352 472-4855
Newberry (G-11024)

BATTERIES: Dry

Tnr Technical Inc ....F 407 321-3011
Sanford (G-15397)

BATTERIES: Lead Acid, Storage

Clarios LLC ....E 407 850-0147
Orlando (G-12017)

BATTERIES: Rechargeable

Creating Tech Solutions LLC ....E 727 914-3001
Clearwater (G-1554)

Kendoo Technology Inc ....G 305 592-9688
Doral (G-3272)

Mathews Associates Inc ....C 407 323-3390
Sanford (G-15354)

BATTERIES: Storage

3d Nano Batteries LLC ....G 212 220-9300
Port Saint Lucie (G-14393)

Advanced Cell Engineering Inc .....F 772 382-9191
Stuart (G-16111)

Amper Usa LLC ....G 305 717-3101
Doral (G-3114)

Authentic Trading Inc ....G 347 866-7241
Davie (G-2390)

Caliber Sales Engineering Inc ......E 954 430-6234
Sunrise (G-16302)

Chargex LLC ....G 855 242-7439
Tampa (G-16701)

Chicago Electronic Distrs Inc ....F 312 985-6175
Port Charlotte (G-14292)

Clarios LLC ....G 904 786-9161
Jacksonville (G-5980)

Creating Tech Solutions LLC ....E 727 914-3001
Clearwater (G-1556)

Duracell Company ....E 561 494-7550
West Palm Beach (G-17983)

Encell Technology Inc ....E 386 462-2643
Alachua (G-11)

Enersys Advanced Systems Inc ....D 610 208-1934
Pinellas Park (G-13685)

Es Tudios Corp ....G 305 300-9262
Miami (G-9109)

Exide Battery ....G 904 783-1224
Jacksonville (G-6083)

Inspired Energy Inc ....E 352 472-4855
Newberry (G-11023)

Lithionics Battery LLC ....F 727 726-4204
Clearwater (G-1674)

Lithium Battery Co Intl ....F 813 504-0074
Tampa (G-17015)

Nanotech Energy Inc ....E 800 995-5491
Sunny Isles Beach (G-16280)

Palm Beach Btry Ventures LLC .....G 561 881-8900
Lake Park (G-7132)

Rainbow Storage ....F 386 362-1171
Live Oak (G-7853)

Southern States Motive Pwr LLC ...F 813 621-3338
Tampa (G-17289)

Tnr Technical Inc ....F 407 321-3011
Sanford (G-15397)

W & W Manufacturing Co ....F 516 942-0011
Tampa (G-17420)

BATTERIES: Wet

Adva-Lite Inc ....C 727 369-5319
Seminole (G-15967)

Creating Tech Solutions LLC ....E 727 914-3001
Clearwater (G-1554)

Creating Tech Solutions LLC ....E 727 914-3001
Clearwater (G-1556)

Empire Scientific ....G 630 510-8636
Tampa (G-16810)

Future Plus of Florida ....F 612 240-7275
Tampa (G-16865)

JW Marketing and Consulting ....G 866 323-0001
Coconut Creek (G-1995)

Oakridge Globl Enrgy Sltons In .....E 321 610-7959
Palm Bay (G-12911)

Rayovac Corp ....G 727 393-0966
Largo (G-7667)

TAe Trans Atlantic Elec Inc ....E 631 595-9206
Tampa (G-17322)

BATTERY CHARGERS

Creating Tech Solutions LLC ....E 727 914-3001
Clearwater (G-1554)

Lithium Battery Co Intl ....F 813 504-0074
Tampa (G-17015)

BATTERY CHARGERS: Storage, Motor & Engine Generator Type

Capacity Inc ....F 855 440-7825
Sarasota (G-15450)

Positive Energy Inc ....F 929 220-5880
Miami (G-9731)

BATTERY CHARGING GENERATORS

ADS-TEC Energy Inc ....F 941 358-7445
Lakewood Ranch (G-7481)

Powerpump LLC ....E 305 514-3030
Doral (G-3332)

BATTERY REPAIR & SVCS

Ameritech Energy Corporation ......G 610 730-1733
Holly Hill (G-5510)

Battery Usa Inc ....E 863 665-6317
Lakeland (G-7280)

BEARINGS & PARTS Ball

Centrifugal Rebabbitting Inc ....F 954 522-3003
Fort Lauderdale (G-3720)

BEARINGS: Ball & Roller

Bearing Specialist Inc ....G 305 796-3415
Doral (G-3130)

Debway Corporation ....G 305 818-6353
Hialeah (G-5111)

NSK Latin America Inc ....G 305 477-0605
Miami (G-9633)

BEAUTY & BARBER SHOP EQPT

American Polylactide Inds ....G 352 653-5963
Ocala (G-11321)

Brewer International Inc ....F 772 562-0555
Vero Beach (G-17743)

Brooking Industries Inc ....G 954 533-0765
Saint Augustine (G-14817)

C & M Manufacturing LLC ....G 407 673-9601
Winter Park (G-18493)

Certified Clean Cuts - LLC ....F 954 903-1733
North Lauderdale (G-11077)

CLJ Industries Inc ....G 562 688-0508
Jacksonville (G-5984)

Cmz Industries LLC ....G 727 726-1443
Clearwater (G-1543)

Daje Industries Inc ....G 305 592-7711
Doral (G-3184)

Deal To Win Inc ....E 718 609-1165
Oakland Park (G-11256)

Desco Industries ....G 305 255-7744
Miami (G-9019)

Desind Industries Corp ....G 212 729-0192
Orlando (G-12088)

Driscoll Industries LLC ....G 407 848-7127
Apopka (G-123)

East Coast Metals Inc ....E 305 885-9991
Hialeah (G-5130)

Ecotec Manufacturing Inc ....E 863 357-4500
Okeechobee (G-11604)

Egm Manufacturing Corp ....F 954 440-0445
Sunrise (G-16315)

Elite Flower Services Inc ....E 305 436-7400
Miami (G-9085)

Fam Industries Inc ....F 281 779-0650
Jacksonville (G-6086)

Florida Rock Industries ....G 305 592-4100
Tampa (G-16854)

Florida Rock Industries ....F 239 454-2831
Fort Myers (G-4255)

Florida Rock Industries ....G 407 299-7494
Orlando (G-12165)

Gibbons Industries Inc ....G 352 330-0294
Lutz (G-7990)

Gml Industries LLC ....G 352 671-7619
Ocala (G-11400)

Goodwill Industries S Fla Inc ....C 941 745-8459
Bradenton (G-987)

Hall Industries Incorporated ....G 239 768-0372
Fort Myers (G-4278)

Ibs Manufacturing LLC ....G 352 629-9752
Ocala (G-11411)

Its Technologies Logistics LLC ......B 904 751-1300
Jacksonville (G-6209)

Jtac Industries LLC ....G 813 928-0628
Plant City (G-13779)

Keystone Rv Company ....B 813 228-0625
Tampa (G-16982)

Kirkland Industries LLC ....G 386 496-3491
Lake Butler (G-7003)

Lester Manufacturing LLC ....G 305 898-0306
Miami (G-9453)

Model Shipways Inc ....E 800 222-3876
Miami (G-9582)

No 1 Beauty Salon Furniture ....G 954 981-0403
Oakland Park (G-11281)

Omz Industries LLC ....F 786 210-6763
Doral (G-3317)

Powers Industries LLC ....F 954 706-6001
Fort Lauderdale (G-3991)

Premier Plastics LLC ....G 305 805-3333
Boynton Beach (G-899)

Premier Plastics LLC ....G 305 805-3333
Hallandale Beach (G-4966)

Prime Manufacturing Canada ....G 850 332-7193
Pensacola (G-13583)

Rederick Metal Industries ....E 305 396-3396
Doral (G-3346)

Reflection Manufacturing ....D 407 297-5727
Orlando (G-12542)

Rytex Industries Inc ....F 727 557-7450
Largo (G-7674)

S P Manufacturing LLC ....G 305 362-0456
Hialeah (G-5338)

Scarb Industries Inc ....F 772 597-3898
Indiantown (G-5815)

Sota Manufacturing LLC ....E 561 251-3389
Oakland Park (G-11295)

Sun-Art Designs Inc ....F 954 929-6622
Hollywood (G-5665)

Tactical Prchute Dlvry Systems............F......813 782-7482
 Zephyrhills (G-18634)
The Caldwell Manufacturing Co ....D......386 418-3525
 Alachua (G-22)
Wcm Group Inc ....G......516 238-4261
 Flagler Beach (G-3606)

BEAUTY SALONS

New York Nails ....G......904 448-6040
 Jacksonville (G-6331)

BED & BREAKFAST INNS

Manucci Winery Inc ....G......805 239-4770
 Jensen Beach (G-6656)

BEDDING, BEDSPREADS, BLANKETS & SHEETS

Sobel Westex ....D......954 942-5777
 Pompano Beach (G-14184)
Tuka Imports LLC ....F......305 640-8336
 Miami (G-10044)

BEDDING, BEDSPREADS, BLANKETS & SHEETS: Bedspread, Lace

Jayco International LLC ....D......407 855-8880
 Orlando (G-12268)

BEDDING, FROM SILK OR MANMADE FIBER

Bedding Acquisition LLC ....G......561 997-6900
 Boca Raton (G-428)
Solstice Sleep Products Inc ....E......813 438-8830
 Tampa (G-17280)

BEDS: Hospital

Kci ....G......352 572-2873
 Lecanto (G-7754)
Medtek Medical Solutions LLC ....F......786 458-8080
 Miami (G-9530)
Mhkap LLC ....G......239 919-0786
 Naples (G-10819)

BEDSPREADS & BED SETS, FROM PURCHASED MATERIALS

Associated Intr Desgr Svc Inc ....F......561 655-4926
 West Palm Beach (G-17930)
Distinctive Creat Intr Wkshp I.............F......954 921-1861
 Hollywood (G-5567)
Kenco Hospitality Inc ....D......954 921-5434
 Fort Lauderdale (G-3904)
Kenco Quilting & Textiles Inc ....F......954 921-5434
 Fort Lauderdale (G-3905)
Mac D&D Inc ....G......305 821-9452
 Hialeah (G-5233)
Tiffany Quilting & Drapery ....F......407 834-6386
 Longwood (G-7952)

BEDSPREADS, COTTON

Jose Leal Enterprises Inc....................D......305 887-9611
 Hialeah (G-5207)

BEEKEEPERS' SPLYS

Rev-Tech Mfg Solutions LLC ....E......727 577-4999
 Saint Petersburg (G-15172)

BEEKEEPERS' SPLYS: Honeycomb Foundations

Honeycommcore LLC...........................G......561 747-2678
 West Palm Beach (G-18026)

BEER & ALE WHOLESALERS

D G Yuengling and Son Inc ....D......813 972-8500
 Tampa (G-16758)

BEER, WINE & LIQUOR STORES

Pair ODice Brewing Co LLC.................G......727 755-3423
 Clearwater (G-1734)

BELLOWS

Bellowstech LLC ....E......386 615-7530
 Ormond Beach (G-12745)

Tectron ....F......904 355-5512
 Jacksonville (G-6540)

BELLS: Electric

Bell Brothers Electric LLC ....F......954 496-0632
 Coral Springs (G-2136)

BELTING: Fabric

Signature AVI US Holdings Inc ....F......407 648-7230
 Orlando (G-12604)

BELTING: Rubber

Adventry Corp ....F......305 582-2977
 Miami Lakes (G-10279)
Gate Petroleum Company ....G......904 998-7126
 Jacksonville (G-6127)
Gates Corporation ....D......954 926-7823
 Davie (G-2417)
Signature AVI US Holdings Inc ....F......407 648-7230
 Orlando (G-12604)

BELTS: Conveyor, Made From Purchased Wire

Belt Maintenance Group Inc ....G......813 907-9316
 Wesley Chapel (G-17870)
Roro Inc ....E......561 909-6220
 West Palm Beach (G-18146)

BELTS: Seat, Automotive & Aircraft

CSC Racing Corporation ....F......248 548-5727
 Jupiter (G-6706)
Key Safety Systems Inc.......................C......863 668-6000
 Lakeland (G-7367)
Seatbelt Solutions Llc ....E......855 642-3964
 Jupiter (G-6794)

BEVERAGE POWDERS

Flavcity Corp ....G......413 221-0041
 Boynton Beach (G-867)
Rsvp Skinnies Inc ....G......786 853-8032
 Pinecrest (G-13670)

BEVERAGE PRDTS: Brewers' Grain

Brew Hub LLC ....E......863 698-7600
 Lakeland (G-7285)

BEVERAGE PRDTS: Brewers' Rice

Hyperion Managing LLC.......................G......904 612-3987
 Jacksonville (G-6190)

BEVERAGE STORES

Babys Coffee LLC ....G......305 744-9866
 Key West (G-6855)
Ritco Foods LLC ....G......954 727-3554
 Sunrise (G-16364)

BEVERAGE, NONALCOHOLIC: Iced Tea/Fruit Drink, Bottled/Canned

Arizona Beverage Company LLC ....F......516 812-0303
 Orlando (G-11920)
Arizona Beverage Company LLC ....F......516 812-0303
 Tampa (G-16605)
Arizona Beverage Company LLC ....F......516 812-0303
 Jacksonville (G-5900)
Arizona Beverage Company LLC ....F......516 812-0303
 Fort Myers (G-4180)
Celsius Holdings Inc............................E......561 276-2239
 Boca Raton (G-459)
Fresh Start Beverage Company ....G......561 757-6541
 Boca Raton (G-524)
Polenghi Usa Inc ....F......954 637-4900
 Deerfield Beach (G-2783)

BEVERAGES, ALCOHOLIC: Beer

3 Daughters Brewing LLC ....F......727 495-6002
 Saint Petersburg (G-14948)
Arhob LLC ....F......727 216-6318
 Dunedin (G-3439)
Canarchy Craft ....C......813 348-6363
 Tampa (G-16675)
Cigar City Brewpub LLC ....G......813 348-6363
 Tampa (G-16703)

Cypress & Grove Brewing Co LLC........F......352 376-4993
 Gainesville (G-4674)
D G Yuengling and Son Inc ....D......813 972-8500
 Tampa (G-16758)
Ellipsis Brewing ....G......407 556-3241
 Orlando (G-12123)
Florida Craft Distributors LLC ....F......813 528-7902
 Sanford (G-15318)
Great Bay Distributors Inc ....C......727 584-8626
 Holiday (G-5494)
Indian River Brewery Corp...................F......321 728-4114
 Cape Canaveral (G-1287)
International Keg Rental LLC ....F......407 900-9992
 Orlando (G-12251)
Krome Brewing Company LLC ....F......786 601-9337
 Miami (G-9400)
Le Mundo Vino LLC ....F......786 369-5232
 Miami (G-9443)
Prision Brewing Co LLC.......................G......305 487-2780
 Doral (G-3338)
Rpd Management LLC ....G......904 710-8911
 Jacksonville (G-6435)
Titanic Brewing Company Inc..............F......305 668-1742
 Coral Gables (G-2115)

BEVERAGES, ALCOHOLIC: Beer & Ale

Bold City Braves LLC ....G......904 545-3480
 Jacksonville (G-5946)
Cerberus Craft Distillery LLC...............G......813 789-1556
 Tampa (G-16697)
Dukes Brewhouse Inc..........................F......813 758-9309
 Plant City (G-13761)
Fantasy Brewmasters LLC ....G......239 206-3247
 Naples (G-10745)
Florida Brewery Inc.............................E......863 965-1825
 Auburndale (G-232)
In The Loop Brewing Inc ....G......813 857-0111
 Land O Lakes (G-7493)
Keg Connect LLC ....G......727 821-8752
 Saint Petersburg (G-15103)
Main & Six Brewing Company LLC ....G......904 673-0144
 Jacksonville (G-6272)
Orlando Brewing Partners ....G......407 843-6783
 Orlando (G-12451)
Rock Brothers Brewing LLC ....E......917 324-8175
 Tampa (G-17229)
Sourglass Brewing ....G......407 262-0056
 Longwood (G-7948)
Wops Hops Brewing Llc.......................G......407 927-8929
 Geneva (G-4791)

BEVERAGES, ALCOHOLIC: Bourbon Whiskey

Samson & Surrey LLC ....F......305 902-3336
 Miami (G-9843)

BEVERAGES, ALCOHOLIC: Cocktails

Buzz Pop Cocktails Corporation ....F......727 275-9848
 Holiday (G-5491)
Miami Cocktail Company Inc ....G......305 482-1974
 Miami (G-9547)

BEVERAGES, ALCOHOLIC: Cordials & Premixed Cocktails

Arco Globas Trading LLC.....................E......305 707-7702
 De Leon Springs (G-2623)

BEVERAGES, ALCOHOLIC: Distilled Liquors

Big Cypress Distillery LLC...................G......786 228-9740
 Miami (G-8825)
Black Coral Rum LLC ....G......561 766-2493
 Riviera Beach (G-14599)
Bushwacker Spirits LLC ....F......941 200-0818
 Sarasota (G-15621)
Cape Spirits Inc...................................G......239 242-5244
 Cape Coral (G-1323)
Caribbean Distillers LLC ....E......863 508-1175
 Winter Haven (G-18429)
Chainbridge Distillery LLC...................G......440 212-4992
 Oakland Park (G-11251)
Chef Distilled LLC ....G......305 747-8236
 Key West (G-6859)
Diageo North America Inc ....E......305 476-7761
 Coral Gables (G-2048)
Distillery Deerfield LLC........................G......954 531-6813
 Palm Beach Gardens (G-12965)

PRODUCT

Dr Spirits Company LLC ....G...... 561 349-5005
Lake Worth *(G-7197)*
Florida Distillery LLC ....G....... 813 892-5431
Valrico *(G-17664)*
Four Seas Distilling Co LLC ....G....... 813 645-0057
Apollo Beach *(G-92)*
Greymatter Distillery ....G....... 904 723-1114
Atlantic Beach *(G-210)*
Hemingway Rum Company LLC ....F 863 937-8107
Lakeland *(G-7342)*
Island Joys ....G....... 561 201-6005
Fort Lauderdale *(G-3884)*
JB Thome & Co Inc ....G....... 727 642-0588
St Pete Beach *(G-16091)*
Kozuba & Sons Distillery Inc ....G....... 813 857-8197
Saint Petersburg *(G-15105)*
La Tropical Brewing Co LLC ....G....... 786 362-5429
Coral Gables *(G-2080)*
Leblon LLC ....G....... 954 649-0148
Miami *(G-9448)*
List Distillery LLC ....F 239 208-7214
Fort Myers *(G-4312)*
Loggerhead Distillery LLC ....G....... 321 800-8566
Sanford *(G-15352)*
Manifest Distilling LLC ....F 904 619-1479
Jacksonville *(G-6274)*
Marlin & Barrel Distillery LLC ....G....... 321 230-4755
Fernandina Beach *(G-3593)*
Papous Craft Distillery LLC ....G....... 813 766-9539
Tarpon Springs *(G-17485)*
Para Todo Mal Mezcal LLC ....G....... 786 837-3119
Miami *(G-9691)*
St Augustine Dist Co LLC ....E 904 825-4962
Saint Augustine *(G-14898)*
St Petersburg Dist Co LLC ....F 727 581-1544
Saint Petersburg *(G-15197)*
Stilldragon North America LLC ....G....... 561 845-8009
Riviera Beach *(G-14679)*
Sugar Works Distillery LLC ....G....... 386 463-0120
New Smyrna Beach *(G-11013)*
Timber Creek Distilling Llc ....G....... 408 439-0973
Destin *(G-3080)*
Wicked Dolphin Distillery ....G....... 239 565-7947
Cape Coral *(G-1407)*
Winter Park Distilling Co LLC ....F 407 801-2714
Winter Park *(G-18551)*
World Frost Inc ....G....... 786 439-4445
Miami *(G-10144)*

BEVERAGES, ALCOHOLIC: Gin

Incity Security Inc ....F 561 306-9228
West Palm Beach *(G-18031)*

BEVERAGES, ALCOHOLIC: Liquors, Malt

Pair ODice Brewing Co LLC ....G....... 727 755-3423
Clearwater *(G-1734)*

BEVERAGES, ALCOHOLIC: Rum

Bacardi Bottling Corporation ....C 904 757-1290
Jacksonville *(G-5917)*
Hemingway Rum Company LLC ....G....... 305 414-8754
Key West *(G-6866)*
Ron Matusalem & Matusa Fla Inc ....F 305 448-8255
Miami *(G-9823)*

BEVERAGES, ALCOHOLIC: Scotch Whiskey

Scottish Spirits Imports Inc ....F 954 332-1116
Fort Lauderdale *(G-4039)*

BEVERAGES, ALCOHOLIC: Vodka

Florida Distillery LLC ....G....... 813 347-6565
Tampa *(G-16842)*
Italian Moonshiners Inc ....G....... 954 687-4500
Doral *(G-3261)*

BEVERAGES, ALCOHOLIC: Wine Coolers

3 Cool Cats LLC ....G....... 646 334-6229
Miami Beach *(G-10159)*

BEVERAGES, ALCOHOLIC: Wines

1506 N Florida LLC ....G....... 813 229-0900
Tampa *(G-16545)*
Barton & Guestier Usa Inc ....G....... 305 895-9757
Miami *(G-8802)*
Bea Sue Vineyards Inc ....G....... 352 446-5204
Summerfield *(G-16257)*

Buena Cepa Wines LLC ....G....... 310 621-2566
Key Biscayne *(G-6835)*
Cavallo Estate Winery LLC ....G....... 352 500-9463
Lecanto *(G-7749)*
Chautuqua Vineyards Winery Inc ....F 850 892-5887
Defuniak Springs *(G-2837)*
De Vinco Company ....G....... 941 722-1100
Seffner *(G-15955)*
Elk Creek Wine ....G....... 561 529-2822
Jupiter *(G-6719)*
Erratic Oaks Vineyard Inc ....G....... 206 233-0683
Brooksville *(G-1154)*
Faraday Inc ....F 813 536-6104
Tampa *(G-16828)*
Florida Orange Groves Inc ....F 727 347-4025
South Pasadena *(G-16051)*
Fws Distributors LLC ....G....... 407 543-6291
Miami *(G-9181)*
Gnekow Family Winery LLC ....F 209 463-0697
Wilton Manors *(G-18341)*
Gravity Produce LLC ....G....... 269 471-9463
Fort Myers Beach *(G-4454)*
Henscratch Farms Inc ....G....... 863 699-2060
Lake Placid *(G-7142)*
Hey Mama Wines Inc ....G....... 479 530-3057
Santa Rosa Beach *(G-15427)*
JD Wine Concepts LLC ....G....... 407 730-3082
Orlando *(G-12270)*
Joanne James Russell ....G....... 805 467-3331
Saint Petersburg *(G-15102)*
Johns Pass Winery ....G....... 727 362-0008
Madeira Beach *(G-8040)*
Keel & Curley Winery LLC ....F 813 752-9100
Plant City *(G-13780)*
Land O Lakes Winery LLC ....G....... 813 995-9463
Land O Lakes *(G-7496)*
Manucci Winery Inc ....G....... 805 239-4770
Jensen Beach *(G-6656)*
Masso Estate Winery LLC ....G....... 305 707-7749
Coral Gables *(G-2083)*
Mirocos LLC ....G....... 305 674-6921
Miami *(G-9575)*
Orvino Imports & Distrg Inc ....F 954 785-3100
Coral Springs *(G-2201)*
Royal Manor Vineyard & Winery ....G....... 386 684-6270
Interlachen *(G-5820)*
Sapore Di Vino Inc ....G....... 561 818-8411
Miami *(G-9847)*
Schnebly Redlands Winery Inc ....E 786 247-2060
Homestead *(G-5739)*
Seavin Inc ....E 352 394-8627
Clermont *(G-1882)*
Seavin Inc ....E 904 826-1594
Saint Augustine *(G-14889)*
Select Wines LLC ....G....... 786 642-7445
Miami Beach *(G-10226)*
Slainte Wines Inc ....G....... 954 474-4547
Davie *(G-2477)*
Sonapa LLC ....G....... 407 782-0459
New Smyrna Beach *(G-11011)*
Stirling Winery ....G....... 727 734-4025
Dunedin *(G-3459)*
Strong Tower Vineyard ....G....... 352 799-7612
Spring Hill *(G-16088)*
Tampa Wines LLC ....G....... 727 799-9463
Clearwater *(G-1814)*
Tita Itln Import & Export LLC ....G....... 305 608-4258
Miami *(G-10012)*
Top Wines Import LLC ....F 305 917-3600
Miami *(G-10028)*
Vicente Gandia Pla ....C 310 699-8559
Miami *(G-10107)*
Vicente Gandia Usa Inc ....G....... 310 699-8559
Miami *(G-10108)*
Whispering Oaks Winery ....G....... 352 748-0449
Oxford *(G-12854)*
Wine World Inc ....G....... 786 348-8780
Miami *(G-10134)*

BEVERAGES, MALT

Center For Vital Living DBA ....F 239 213-2222
Naples *(G-10710)*

BEVERAGES, MILK BASED

Attitude Drinks Incorporated ....G....... 561 227-2727
North Palm Beach *(G-11175)*
Sneakz LLC ....G....... 201 693-5695
Jupiter *(G-6800)*

BEVERAGES, NONALCOHOLIC: Bottled & canned soft drinks

Al-Rite Fruits and Syrups Inc ....G....... 305 652-2540
Miami *(G-8679)*
Bacardi Bottling Corporation ....C 904 757-1290
Jacksonville *(G-5917)*
Bang Energy LLC ....F 954 641-0570
Weston *(G-18227)*
C C 1 Limited Partnership ....A 305 599-2337
Miami *(G-8869)*
Ccbcc Operations LLC ....D 850 785-6171
Panama City *(G-13238)*
Coca Cola Bottling Co ....F 813 569-3030
Brandon *(G-1087)*
Coca-Cola Beverages Fla LLC ....F 813 612-6631
Tampa *(G-16717)*
Coca-Cola Beverages Fla LLC ....C 813 623-5411
Tampa *(G-16718)*
Coca-Cola Beverages Fla LLC ....G....... 863 499-6300
Lakeland *(G-7294)*
Coca-Cola Beverages Fla LLC ....G....... 941 953-3151
Sarasota *(G-15636)*
Coca-Cola Beverages Fla LLC ....E 954 985-5000
Hollywood *(G-5553)*
Coca-Cola Beverages Fla LLC ....C 800 438-2653
Tampa *(G-16719)*
Coca-Cola Beverages Fla LLC ....B 904 786-2720
Jacksonville *(G-5991)*
Coca-Cola Beverages Fla LLC ....F 386 239-3100
Daytona Beach *(G-2532)*
Coca-Cola Beverages Fla LLC ....G....... 305 872-9715
Big Pine Key *(G-372)*
Coca-Cola Beverages Fla LLC ....C 305 378-1073
Miami *(G-8935)*
Coca-Cola Bottling Co ....F 305 378-1073
Miami *(G-8936)*
Coca-Cola Bottling Co Untd Inc ....D 850 785-0697
Panama City *(G-13248)*
Coca-Cola Bottling Co Untd Inc ....D 850 678-9370
Valparaiso *(G-17658)*
Coca-Cola Bottling Co Untd Inc ....C 850 478-4800
Pensacola *(G-13473)*
Coca-Cola Bottling Co Untd Inc ....C 850 575-6122
Tallahassee *(G-16426)*
Coca-Cola Btlg Centl Fla LLC ....F 832 260-0462
Brandon *(G-1088)*
Coca-Cola Company ....E 407 886-1568
Apopka *(G-111)*
Coca-Cola Company ....F 954 985-5000
Hollywood *(G-5554)*
Coca-Cola Company ....E 404 676-2121
Apopka *(G-112)*
Coca-Cola Company ....E 727 736-7101
Dunedin *(G-3446)*
Coca-Cola Company Distribution ....G....... 407 814-1327
Apopka *(G-115)*
Coca-Cola Refreshments USA Inc ....D 863 551-3700
Auburndale *(G-225)*
Cutrale Citrus Juices USA Inc ....A 352 728-7800
Leesburg *(G-7765)*
Florida Coca-Cola Bottling Co ....A 561 848-0055
Riviera Beach *(G-14623)*
Florida Coca-Cola Bottling Co ....B 813 569-2600
Brandon *(G-1093)*
Florida Coca-Cola Bottling Co ....A 772 461-3636
Fort Pierce *(G-4487)*
Kona Gold LLC ....F 844 714-2224
Melbourne *(G-8451)*
Milca Bottling Company ....F 305 365-0044
Key Biscayne *(G-6837)*
Opreme Beverage Corp ....G....... 954 699-0669
Jupiter *(G-6775)*
Panamco LLC ....F 305 856-7100
Miami *(G-9687)*
Pepsico Inc ....E 407 933-5542
Kissimmee *(G-6951)*
Primo Water Corporation ....A 844 237-7466
Tampa *(G-17181)*
Quaker Oats Company ....C 407 846-5926
Kissimmee *(G-6957)*
Sergeant Bretts Coffee LLC ....G....... 561 451-0048
Coconut Creek *(G-2004)*
Southeast Atlantic Bevera ....G....... 904 739-1000
Miami *(G-9926)*
Swire Pacific Holdings Inc ....D 305 371-3877
Miami *(G-9983)*
Titan Natural Focus Corp ....G....... 305 778-7005
West Palm Beach *(G-18182)*
Venga LLC ....G....... 561 665-8200
Delray Beach *(G-3033)*

Zephyrhills Corp ....D...... 813 778-0595
Zephyrhills *(G-18638)*

BEVERAGES, NONALCOHOLIC: Carbonated

APRU LLC..G....... 888 741-3777
Orlando *(G-11914)*

Buffalo Rock Company ....C...... 850 857-3774
Pensacola *(G-13465)*

Pepsi Beverages Company....................E...... 407 241-4110
Orlando *(G-12480)*

Pepsi Bottling Group ....G...... 863 452-9920
Avon Park *(G-284)*

Pepsi Bottling Group Inc ....G...... 863 687-7605
Lakeland *(G-7408)*

Pepsi St Pete ....F...... 727 527-8113
Saint Petersburg *(G-15149)*

Pepsi-Cola Bottling Co Tampa...............C...... 239 643-4642
Naples *(G-10852)*

Pepsi-Cola Bottling Co Tampa...............C...... 813 971-2550
Tampa *(G-17155)*

Pepsi-Cola Bottling Co Tampa...............B...... 941 378-1058
Sarasota *(G-15781)*

Pepsi-Cola Bottling Co Tampa...............F...... 407 857-3301
Orlando *(G-12481)*

Pepsi-Cola Bottling Co Tampa...............B...... 239 337-2011
Fort Myers *(G-4361)*

Pepsi-Cola Bottling Co Tampa...............C...... 727 942-3664
Holiday *(G-5503)*

Pepsi-Cola Bottling Co Tampa...............C...... 407 826-5929
Orlando *(G-12482)*

Pepsi-Cola Btlg Ft Ldrdl-Palm ....D...... 561 848-1000
Riviera Beach *(G-14659)*

Pepsi-Cola Metro Btlg Co Inc................C...... 904 733-1627
Jacksonville *(G-6367)*

Pepsi-Cola Metro Btlg Co Inc................D...... 407 354-5800
Orlando *(G-12483)*

Pepsi-Cola Metro Btlg Co Inc................F...... 352 376-8276
Gainesville *(G-4748)*

Pepsi-Cola Metro Btlg Co Inc................E...... 352 629-8911
Ocala *(G-11464)*

Pepsi-Cola Metro Btlg Co Inc................E...... 321 242-2984
Melbourne *(G-8493)*

Pepsi-Cola Metro Btlg Co Inc................C...... 772 464-6150
Fort Pierce *(G-4517)*

Pepsico Inc ....D...... 305 593-7500
Medley *(G-8297)*

Pepsico Beverage Distributors.............F...... 305 537-4477
Miami *(G-9704)*

Pepsico Latin America Beverage ....G....... 305 537-4477
Miami *(G-9705)*

BEVERAGES, NONALCOHOLIC: Carbonated, Canned & Bottled, Etc

Arkay Distributing Inc..........................G....... 954 536-8413
Fort Lauderdale *(G-3656)*

Asterion Beverages Inc ....G....... 866 335-2672
Doral *(G-3121)*

D D B Corporation ....G....... 305 721-9506
Miami *(G-8991)*

Everfresh Juice Co Inc ....E...... 954 581-0922
Plantation *(G-13849)*

Interbeverage LLC ....G....... 305 961-1110
Miami *(G-9323)*

Mipe Corp ....G....... 305 825-1195
Hialeah *(G-5261)*

Prodalim USA Inc ....G....... 407 656-1000
Winter Garden *(G-18401)*

Refresco Beverages US Inc ....C...... 813 241-0147
Tampa *(G-17211)*

Refresco US Holding Inc ....F...... 813 313-1863
Tampa *(G-17213)*

Shasta Beverages Intl Inc ....E...... 954 581-0922
Plantation *(G-13886)*

BEVERAGES, NONALCOHOLIC: Cider

Broski Ciderworks LLC ....G....... 954 657-8947
Pompano Beach *(G-13955)*

BEVERAGES, NONALCOHOLIC: Flavoring extracts & syrups, nec

Buddy Pauls Inc ....G....... 561 578-9813
West Palm Beach *(G-17953)*

Firmenich Incorporated........................E...... 863 646-0165
Lakeland *(G-7323)*

Florida Flvors Cncentrates Inc ....G....... 561 775-5714
Palm Beach Gardens *(G-12970)*

Florida Natural Flavors Inc ....E...... 407 834-5979
Casselberry *(G-1416)*

Givaudan Fragrances Corp...................E...... 863 667-0821
Lakeland *(G-7336)*

Interamericas Beverages Inc ....G....... 561 881-1340
Riviera Beach *(G-14630)*

Monin Inc ....E...... 727 461-3033
Clearwater *(G-1702)*

Royal Cup Inc ....G....... 813 664-8902
Tampa *(G-17235)*

Skinny Mixes LLC ....G....... 727 826-0306
Clearwater *(G-1785)*

Taste Advantage LLC ....G....... 863 619-8101
Lakeland *(G-7456)*

BEVERAGES, NONALCOHOLIC: Fruit Drnks, Under 100% Juice, Can

H & H Products Company ....E...... 407 299-5410
Orlando *(G-12205)*

Tropicana Products Inc ....A...... 941 747-4461
Bradenton *(G-1067)*

BEVERAGES, NONALCOHOLIC: Fruit Juices, Concentrtd, Fountain

Coca-Cola Company ....E...... 407 886-1568
Apopka *(G-111)*

Coca-Cola Company ....D...... 407 358-6758
Apopka *(G-114)*

BEVERAGES, NONALCOHOLIC: Lemonade, Bottled & Canned, Etc

Lorina Inc ....F...... 305 779-3085
Doral *(G-3286)*

BEVERAGES, NONALCOHOLIC: Soft Drinks, Canned & Bottled, Etc

7 Up Snapple Southeast........................G....... 407 839-1706
Orlando *(G-11855)*

American Bottling Company...................C...... 813 806-2931
Tampa *(G-16587)*

American Bottling Company...................C...... 561 732-7395
Boynton Beach *(G-839)*

American Bottling Company...................D...... 772 461-3383
Fort Pierce *(G-4463)*

American Bottling Company...................F...... 941 758-7010
Bradenton *(G-937)*

American Bottling Company...................D...... 863 665-6128
Lakeland *(G-7272)*

American Bottling Company...................D...... 239 489-0838
Fort Myers *(G-4171)*

American Bottling Company...................D...... 850 763-9069
Panama City *(G-13226)*

American Bottling Company...................C...... 904 739-1000
Jacksonville *(G-5882)*

American Bottling Company...................G....... 321 433-3622
Cocoa *(G-1902)*

Beverage Canners International............F...... 305 714-7000
Miami *(G-8822)*

Beverage Corp Intl Inc ....D...... 305 714-7000
Miami *(G-8823)*

Bighill Corporation ....G....... 786 497-1875
Miami Beach *(G-10170)*

Camel Enterprises Corp ....F...... 954 234-2559
Miami *(G-8881)*

Cawy Bottling Co Inc ....E...... 305 634-8669
Miami *(G-8903)*

Cloudkiss Beverages Inc ....E...... 407 324-8500
Sanford *(G-15285)*

Coca-Cola Beverages Fla LLC..............C...... 407 295-9290
Orlando *(G-12025)*

Coca-Cola Company ....G....... 407 295-9290
Orlando *(G-12026)*

Coca-Cola Company ....G....... 407 565-2465
Apopka *(G-113)*

Cola Group Riverside LLC ....G....... 305 940-0277
Sunny Isles Beach *(G-16269)*

Dr Pepper Bottling Co ....F...... 407 354-5800
Orlando *(G-12104)*

Dr Pepper/Seven Up Inc ....F...... 321 433-3622
Cocoa *(G-1921)*

Dr Pepper/Seven Up Inc ....E...... 352 732-9777
Ocala *(G-11372)*

Dr Pepper/Seven Up Inc ....F...... 561 995-6260
Boca Raton *(G-495)*

Ibs Partners Ltd ....E...... 954 581-0922
Plantation *(G-13857)*

National Beverage Corp ....D...... 954 581-0922
Plantation *(G-13872)*

Newbevco Inc ....E...... 954 581-0922
Plantation *(G-13874)*

Pepsi-Cola Metro Btlg Co Inc................F...... 863 551-4500
Winter Haven *(G-18456)*

R-Lines LLC ....G....... 954 457-7777
Hallandale Beach *(G-4968)*

Refresco Beverages US Inc ....F...... 352 567-2200
Dade City *(G-2322)*

Refresco Beverages US Inc ....C...... 813 313-1800
Tampa *(G-17212)*

Refreshment Services Inc ....D...... 850 574-0281
Tallahassee *(G-16493)*

Snapple Beverages...............................G....... 941 758-7010
Bradenton *(G-1047)*

Southeast Atlantic Bev Corp ....C...... 904 731-3644
Jacksonville *(G-6481)*

Sunshine Bottling Co ....E...... 305 592-4366
Doral *(G-3384)*

BEVERAGES, NONALCOHOLIC: Tea, Iced, Bottled & Canned, Etc

Florida Refresco Inc ....C...... 863 665-5515
Lakeland *(G-7332)*

BEVERAGES, WINE & DISTILLED ALCOHOLIC, WHOLESALE: Wine

Stripping Alpaca LLC ....F...... 207 208-9687
Miami Beach *(G-10236)*

Vicente Gandia Pla...............................C...... 310 699-8559
Miami *(G-10107)*

BEVERAGES, WINE/DISTILLED ALCOHOLIC, WHOL: Bttlg Wine/Liquor

Mango Bottling Inc................................E...... 321 631-1005
Cocoa *(G-1940)*

BICYCLE ASSEMBLY SVCS

Apollo Retail Specialists LLC ....D...... 813 712-2525
Tampa *(G-16600)*

BICYCLES, PARTS & ACCESS

Big Cat Humn Pwred Vhicles LLC.........F....... 407 999-0200
Orlando *(G-11949)*

Hawk Racing ....G....... 941 209-1790
Bradenton *(G-990)*

Profile Racing Inc.................................E...... 727 392-8307
Saint Petersburg *(G-15163)*

Trailmate Inc ....E...... 941 739-5743
Jacksonville *(G-6563)*

Ventum LLC ....G....... 786 838-1113
Miami Beach *(G-10245)*

Vet-Equip LLC ....G....... 239 537-3402
Naples *(G-10932)*

Worldglass Corporation ....G....... 813 609-2453
Tampa *(G-17439)*

BIDETS: Vitreous China

American Bidet Company ....F...... 954 981-1111
Sunrise *(G-16292)*

M F B International Inc ....G....... 305 436-6601
Miami *(G-9490)*

Rinseworks Inc ....F...... 954 946-0070
Pompano Beach *(G-14160)*

BILLFOLD INSERTS: Plastic

Sumiflex LLC ....G....... 954 578-6998
Sunrise *(G-16375)*

BILLIARD & POOL TABLES & SPLYS

Maitland Furniture Inc ....G....... 386 677-7711
Daytona Beach *(G-2572)*

Robertson Billiard Sups Inc...................G....... 813 229-2778
Tampa *(G-17228)*

BILLIARD EQPT & SPLYS WHOLESALERS

Robertson Billiard Sups Inc...................G....... 813 229-2778
Tampa *(G-17228)*

BILLING & BOOKKEEPING SVCS

Elements Accounting Inc ....G....... 305 662-4448
Miami *(G-9082)*

BINDING SVC: Books & Manuals

Abby Press Inc ....E 407 847-5565
Kissimmee *(G-6892)*

All-Star Sales Inc ....E 904 396-1653
Jacksonville *(G-5876)*

Allied General Engrv & Plas ....F 305 626-6585
Opa Locka *(G-11715)*

American Business Cards Inc ....E 314 739-0800
Naples *(G-10666)*

Apple Printing & Advg Spc Inc ....E 954 524-0493
Fort Lauderdale *(G-3653)*

Armstrongs Prtg & Graphics Inc ......G 850 243-6923
Fort Walton Beach *(G-4562)*

Assocated Prtg Productions Inc ....E 305 623-7600
Miami Lakes *(G-10282)*

B J and ME Inc ....G 561 368-5470
Boca Raton *(G-424)*

B R Q Grossmans Inc ....F 954 971-1077
Pompano Beach *(G-13943)*

Bava Inc ....F 850 893-4799
Tallahassee *(G-16417)*

Bayou Printing Inc ....F 850 678-5444
Valparaiso *(G-17656)*

Best Bindery Corp ....G 941 505-1779
Punta Gorda *(G-14498)*

Bill & Renee Enterprises Inc ....E 321 452-2800
Merritt Island *(G-8578)*

Bindery LLC ....G 407 647-7777
Winter Park *(G-18490)*

Bjm Enterprises Inc ....F 941 746-4171
Palmetto *(G-13157)*

Boca Color Graphics Inc ....F 561 391-2229
Boca Raton *(G-435)*

Bodree Printing Company Inc ....F 850 455-8511
Pensacola *(G-13459)*

Bros Williams Printing Inc ....G 305 769-9925
Hialeah *(G-5080)*

C & R Designs Inc ....E 321 383-2255
Titusville *(G-17577)*

C & R Designs Printing LLC ....E 321 383-2255
Titusville *(G-17578)*

Colonial Press Intl Inc ....C 305 633-1581
Miami *(G-8945)*

Color Concepts Prtg Design Co ....F 813 623-2921
Tampa *(G-16720)*

Color Express Inc ....G 305 558-2061
Hialeah *(G-5094)*

Coloramax Printing Inc ....F 305 541-0322
Miami *(G-8947)*

Commercial Printers Inc ....D 954 781-3737
Fort Lauderdale *(G-3738)*

Copy-Flow Inc ....F 305 592-0930
Davie *(G-2398)*

Creative Prtg Grphic Dsign Inc ....E 407 855-0202
Orlando *(G-12055)*

Csmc Inc ....E 407 246-1567
Orlando *(G-12060)*

Dahlquist Enterprises Inc ....G 407 896-2294
Orlando *(G-12071)*

Dannys Prtg Svc Sups & Eqp Inc .....G 305 757-2282
Miami *(G-9000)*

Donna Lynn Enterprises Inc ....G 772 286-2812
Palm Beach Gardens *(G-12966)*

Durra-Print Inc ....E 850 222-4768
Tallahassee *(G-16434)*

Ed Vance Printing Company Inc ....F 813 882-8888
Tampa *(G-16797)*

Fidelity Printing Corporation ....D 727 522-9557
Saint Petersburg *(G-15044)*

First Imprssons Prtg Cmmnctons ......E 407 831-6100
Longwood *(G-7896)*

Florida Graphic Printing Inc ....F 386 253-4532
Daytona Beach *(G-2553)*

G S Printers Inc ....G 305 931-2755
Fort Lauderdale *(G-3834)*

Gandy Printers Inc ....F 850 222-5847
Tallahassee *(G-16444)*

Gulf Coast Business World Inc ....F 850 864-1511
Fort Walton Beach *(G-4590)*

H & H Printing Inc ....G 407 422-2932
Orlando *(G-12204)*

H & M Printing Inc ....F 407 831-8030
Sanford *(G-15329)*

Hernandez Printing Service Inc ....F 305 642-0483
Miami *(G-9277)*

ICM Printing Co Inc ....F 352 377-7468
Gainesville *(G-4709)*

Instant Printing Services Inc ....F 727 546-8036
Floral City *(G-3611)*

Interprint Incorporated ....D 727 531-8957
Clearwater *(G-1646)*

J J M Services Inc ....G 954 437-1880
Miramar *(G-10507)*

J V G Inc ....G 727 584-7136
Largo *(G-7619)*

Jet Graphics Inc ....E 305 264-4333
Miami *(G-9365)*

Jet-Set Printing Inc ....G 407 339-1900
Casselberry *(G-1421)*

K R O Enterprises Ltd ....G 309 797-2213
Naples *(G-10795)*

Keithco Inc ....G 352 351-4741
Ocala *(G-11419)*

Kights Printing & Office Pdts ....G 904 731-7990
Jacksonville *(G-6242)*

L E M G Inc ....G 727 461-5300
Clearwater *(G-1668)*

Lake Worth Herald Press Inc ....F 561 585-9387
Lake Worth *(G-7214)*

Leda Printing Inc ....E 941 922-1563
Sarasota *(G-15724)*

Linden-Beals Corp ....G 772 562-0624
Vero Beach *(G-17773)*

Mailing & Bindery Systems Inc ....G 813 416-8965
Lutz *(G-8001)*

Midds Inc ....E 561 586-6220
Lake Worth Beach *(G-7258)*

Mikes Print Shop Inc ....G 407 718-4964
Winter Park *(G-18525)*

Multi-Color Printing Inc ....E 772 287-1676
Stuart *(G-16187)*

My Print Shop Inc ....F 954 973-9369
Deerfield Beach *(G-2773)*

Ngp Corporate Square Inc ....E 239 643-3430
Naples *(G-10836)*

Npc of Tampa Inc ....F 813 839-0035
Tampa *(G-17112)*

Ocala Print Quick Inc ....G 352 629-0736
Ocala *(G-11458)*

Oompha Inc ....G 850 222-7210
Tallahassee *(G-16486)*

Output Printing Corp ....F 813 228-8800
Tampa *(G-17134)*

Parkinson Enterprises Inc ....G 863 688-7900
Lakeland *(G-7406)*

PIP Printing ....G 352 622-3224
Ocala *(G-11467)*

Professional Bindery Inc ....F 305 633-3761
Miami *(G-9750)*

Quad/Graphics Inc ....D 813 837-3436
Tampa *(G-17198)*

Reimink Printing Inc ....E 813 289-4663
Tampa *(G-17214)*

Roberts Quality Printing Inc ....E 727 442-4011
Clearwater *(G-1769)*

Russells Bindery Inc ....G 904 829-3100
Saint Augustine *(G-14883)*

Saugus Valley Corp ....E 954 772-4077
Coral Springs *(G-2209)*

Schooner Prints Inc ....E 727 397-8572
Largo *(G-7676)*

South Broward Printing Inc ....G 954 962-1309
Hollywood *(G-5660)*

Southeast Finishing Group Inc ....E 407 299-4620
Orlando *(G-12613)*

Southeastern Printing Co Inc ....C 772 287-2141
Hialeah *(G-5357)*

Southeastern Printing Co Inc ....G 772 287-2141
Palm City *(G-13059)*

Spinnaker Holding Company ....E 561 392-8626
Boca Raton *(G-692)*

Steven K Bakum Inc ....G 561 804-9110
West Palm Beach *(G-18164)*

Sunshine Printing Inc ....F 561 478-2602
West Palm Beach *(G-18170)*

Taie Inc ....G 954 966-0233
Hollywood *(G-5668)*

Target Copy Gainesville Inc ....F 352 372-1171
Gainesville *(G-4774)*

Thalers Printing Center Inc ....G 954 741-6522
Lauderhill *(G-7744)*

Town Street Print Shop Inc ....G 850 432-8300
Gulf Breeze *(G-4895)*

United Seal & Tag Label Corp ....G 941 625-6799
Port Charlotte *(G-14321)*

Universal Graphics & Prtg Inc ....G 561 845-6404
North Palm Beach *(G-11184)*

V I P Printing ....G 386 258-3326
Daytona Beach *(G-2616)*

V P Press Inc ....F 954 581-7531
Fort Lauderdale *(G-4114)*

Vmak Corp ....F 407 260-1199
Longwood *(G-7958)*

Vowells Downtown Inc ....G 850 432-5175
Pensacola *(G-13622)*

W D H Enterprises Inc ....G 941 758-6500
Bradenton *(G-1073)*

BINDING SVC: Magazines

Rapid Rater Company ....E 850 893-7346
Tallahassee *(G-16492)*

BINDING SVC: Trade

Florida Print Finishers Inc ....G 850 877-8503
Tallahassee *(G-16441)*

BINOCULARS

Discipline Marketing Inc ....F 305 793-7358
Homestead *(G-5708)*

BINS: Prefabricated, Metal Plate

Myrlen Inc ....G 800 662-4762
Coral Springs *(G-2194)*

BIOLOGICAL PRDTS: Antitoxins

Vital Solutions LLC ....G 561 848-1717
West Palm Beach *(G-18198)*

BIOLOGICAL PRDTS: Bacteriological Media

Becker Microbial Products Inc ....G 954 345-9321
Parkland *(G-13344)*

BIOLOGICAL PRDTS: Blood Derivatives

Clearant Inc ....E 407 876-3134
Orlando *(G-12019)*

Immunotek Bio Centers LLC ....E 337 500-1175
Bradenton *(G-994)*

Immunotek Bio Centers LLC ....E 561 270-6712
Greenacres *(G-4849)*

Immunotek Bio Centers LLC ....E 772 577-7194
Fort Pierce *(G-4496)*

Immunotek Bio Centers LLC ....E 404 345-3570
Cocoa *(G-1936)*

BIOLOGICAL PRDTS: Exc Diagnostic

Adma Biomanufacturing LLC ....B 201 478-5552
Boca Raton *(G-389)*

Apexeon Biomedical LLC ....G 850 878-2150
Tallahassee *(G-16412)*

Applied Genetic Tech Corp ....D 386 462-2204
Alachua *(G-5)*

Bioresource Technology LLC ....E 954 792-5222
Weston *(G-18230)*

Biostem Technologies Inc ....E 954 380-8342
Pompano Beach *(G-13950)*

Custom Biologicals Inc ....G 561 998-1699
Deerfield Beach *(G-2697)*

Demerx Inc ....F 954 607-3670
Miami *(G-9016)*

Dyadic International Inc ....G 561 743-8333
Jupiter *(G-6713)*

Ecological Laboratories Inc ....E 239 573-6650
Cape Coral *(G-1336)*

Empowered Diagnostics LLC ....G 206 228-5990
Pompano Beach *(G-14010)*

HCW Biologics Inc ....E 954 842-2024
Miramar *(G-10500)*

Lactalogics Inc ....G 772 202-0407
Port Saint Lucie *(G-14421)*

Lillian Bay Medical Inc ....F 941 815-7373
Saint Petersburg *(G-15112)*

M-Biolabs Inc ....G 239 571-0435
Naples *(G-10809)*

Organabio LLC ....F 305 676-2586
South Miami *(G-16041)*

Radiation Shield Tech Inc ....F 866 733-6766
Coral Gables *(G-2102)*

Stat Biomedical LLC ....G 210 365-1495
Mims *(G-10450)*

Synergy Biologics LLC ....G 850 656-4277
Tallahassee *(G-16509)*

BIOLOGICAL PRDTS: Extracts

Citrus Extracts LLC ....F 772 464-9800
Fort Pierce **(G-4477)**
Real Extract Ventures Inc ....G 561 371-3532
Wellington **(G-17858)**

BIOLOGICAL PRDTS: Vaccines

Iliad Biotechnologies LLC ....G 954 336-0777
Weston **(G-18254)**
Pet Doc FL LLC ....G 407 437-6614
Oviedo **(G-12843)**

BIOLOGICAL PRDTS: Vaccines & Immunizing

Exosis Inc ....G 240 417-4477
Palm Beach **(G-12933)**
Healthy Schools LLC ....C 904 887-4540
Jacksonville **(G-6170)**

BIOLOGICAL PRDTS: Venoms

Biotoxins Inc ....G 407 892-6905
Saint Cloud **(G-14923)**
Venom Allstars LLC ....G 407 575-3484
Winter Garden **(G-18406)**

BIOLOGICAL PRDTS: Veterinary

Amino Cell Inc ....F 352 291-0200
Ocala **(G-11323)**
Bioivt LLC ....G 516 876-7902
Plantation **(G-13833)**
Medrx Inc ....E 727 584-9600
Largo **(G-7641)**

BIRTH CONTROL DEVICES: Rubber

Grove Medical LLC ....G 305 903-6402
Miami **(G-9254)**
Veru Inc ....D 305 509-6897
Miami **(G-10102)**

BITUMINOUS & LIGNITE COAL LOADING & PREPARATION

Progress Fuels Corporation ....D 727 824-6600
Saint Petersburg **(G-15164)**

BLADES: Saw, Hand Or Power

Elliott Diamond Tool Inc ....F 727 585-3839
Clearwater **(G-1583)**
Round Table Tools Inc ....G 850 877-7650
Tallahassee **(G-16496)**

BLANKBOOKS & LOOSELEAF BINDERS

Deluxe Shades Inc ....G 786 355-0086
Doral **(G-3190)**
Deluxe Stone Inc ....F 561 236-2322
Boynton Beach **(G-855)**
Dobbs & Brodeur Bookbinders ....F 305 885-5215
Hialeah **(G-5121)**
Fastkit Corp ....E 305 599-0839
Doral **(G-3212)**
Fastkit Corp ....G 754 227-8234
Sweetwater **(G-16402)**
Garcia Deluxe Services Corp ....G 786 291-4329
Hialeah **(G-5166)**
I Wentworth Inc ....G 561 231-7544
Vero Beach **(G-17761)**
Russells Bindery Inc ....G 904 829-3100
Saint Augustine **(G-14883)**

BLANKBOOKS: Account

All-Pro Accnting Bkkeeping LLC ......G 561 212-8418
Lake Worth Beach **(G-7247)**

BLANKBOOKS: Albums

Leather Craftsmen Inc ....D 631 752-9000
Sarasota **(G-15723)**

BLANKBOOKS: Albums, Record

Highrolla Empire LLC ....F 954 743-5324
Saint Petersburg **(G-15075)**
Rolo Gang LLC ....F 561 538-8173
Miramar **(G-10537)**

Umg Recordings Inc ....B 305 532-4754
Miami Beach **(G-10240)**

BLANKETS: Horse

Quality Shavings South Florida ....E 561 433-9955
Lake Worth **(G-7230)**

BLAST SAND MINING

Don Schick LLC ....G 954 491-9042
Oakland Park **(G-11261)**
In Diversified Plant Services ....F 813 453-7025
Lutz **(G-7995)**

BLASTING SVC: Sand, Metal Parts

First Cast Strpping MBL Sndbls ......G 904 733-5915
Jacksonville **(G-6092)**
Industrial Marine Inc ....F 904 781-4707
Jacksonville **(G-6195)**
Standard Sand & Silica Company .....G 863 419-9673
Haines City **(G-4916)**

BLINDS & SHADES: Micro

Fundamental Micro LP ....G 239 434-7434
Naples **(G-10754)**

BLINDS & SHADES: Vertical

1st Vertical Blind Company ....G 352 343-3363
Tavares **(G-17501)**
American Blind Corporation ....E 305 262-2009
Miami **(G-8714)**
Bornt Enterprises Inc ....E 813 623-1492
Tampa **(G-16658)**
Ceco Inc ....F 561 265-1111
Boynton Beach **(G-850)**
GK Window Treatments Inc ....F 954 786-2927
Pompano Beach **(G-14040)**
Myriam Interiors Inc ....G 305 626-9898
Hialeah **(G-5271)**
Ortega Industries and Mfg ....D 305 688-0090
Opa Locka **(G-11778)**
Shades To You LLC ....G 407 889-0049
Apopka **(G-176)**
Stand Vertical Inc ....G 407 474-0456
Orlando **(G-12621)**
Superior Shade & Blind Co Inc ....E 954 975-8122
Coral Springs **(G-2215)**
Thompson Awning & Shutter Co ....F 904 355-1616
Jacksonville **(G-6547)**
Tropic Shield Inc ....F 954 731-5553
Lauderdale Lakes **(G-7721)**
United Vertical Blinds LLC ....G 786 348-8000
Miami **(G-10069)**
Vertical Assesment Assoc LLC ....E 850 210-0401
Blountstown **(G-379)**
Vertical Flight Technology Inc ....F 407 687-3126
Melbourne **(G-8557)**
Vertical Land Inc ....F 850 244-5263
Panama City **(G-13318)**
Vertical Systems Inspctons Inc ....G 954 775-6023
Plantation **(G-13899)**
Vista Products Inc ....D 904 725-2242
Jacksonville **(G-6592)**

BLINDS : Window

5 Star Blinds and Shades LLC ....G 850 463-4155
Milton **(G-10415)**
A1cm Shades and Blind Inc ....F 305 726-3139
Miami **(G-8628)**
Blind Depot ....G 954 588-4580
Sunrise **(G-16298)**
Blinds 321 Inc ....G 305 336-9221
Miami **(G-8838)**
Blinds By Randy LLC ....G 305 300-1147
Miami Gardens **(G-10252)**
Blinds Side ....G 888 610-8366
Cape Canaveral **(G-1278)**
Blindsource Inc ....G 954 455-1965
Fort Lauderdale **(G-3690)**
BMW & Associates Inc ....G 352 694-2300
Ocala **(G-11336)**
Cardenas Roberto Blinds of Fla ....G 315 807-6878
Miami **(G-8890)**
Diy Blinds Inc ....G 305 692-8877
North Miami Beach **(G-11134)**
Dizenzo Manufacturing Intl Inc ....G 954 978-4624
Deerfield Beach **(G-2707)**

Ed Allen Inc ....G 941 743-2646
Port Charlotte **(G-14296)**
Florida Plntn Shutters LLC ....G 386 788-7766
South Daytona **(G-16021)**
Floridian Blinds Llc ....G 786 250-4697
Miami **(G-9160)**
Grannys Cheesecake & More Inc .....G 210 343-9610
Riverview **(G-14564)**
Grannys Cheesecake & More Inc .....G 561 847-6599
Okeechobee **(G-11607)**
Gulf Coast Shades & Blinds LLC ......F 850 332-2100
Gulf Breeze **(G-4883)**
J A Blnds Decorations More LLC ......G 754 422-4778
Miami **(G-9350)**
Jacqulnes Lvely Drpes Blnds LL ......G 407 826-1566
Orlando **(G-12264)**
Kelsies Blinds ....G 407 977-0827
Oviedo **(G-12834)**
Keys Blinds Inc ....G
Key West **(G-6870)**
Kristine Window Treatments LLC ......F 305 623-8302
Hialeah **(G-5214)**
Lg Smart Blinds Corp ....G 305 704-0696
Miami **(G-9456)**
Maggard Fndtion For Blind Phys ....G 407 637-5302
Altamonte Springs **(G-57)**
Mastercraft Shtters Blinds LLC ....G 904 379-7544
Jacksonville **(G-6279)**
Medmar Win Trtmnts Blinds Inc ....G 772 344-5714
Port Saint Lucie **(G-14425)**
MGM Blinds and Shutters Inc ....G
New Smyrna Beach **(G-11006)**
North W Fla Cncil of Blind Cor ....G 850 982-7867
Gulf Breeze **(G-4888)**
Orlando Blinds Factory ....G 407 697-0521
Orlando **(G-12450)**
Poseidon Window Treatments LLC ....F 954 920-1112
Dania Beach **(G-2358)**
Skagfield Corporation ....D 850 878-1144
Tallahassee **(G-16500)**
Srm Blinds Inc ....G 321 269-5332
Titusville **(G-17617)**
Statewide Blnds Shtters More I ....E 813 480-8638
New Port Richey **(G-10985)**
Sun City Blinds LLC ....G 727 522-6695
Ellenton **(G-3513)**
Sun Shell Blinds & Shades Corp ....G 678 975-1082
Miramar **(G-10549)**
Sunrise ....G 386 627-5029
Palm Coast **(G-13088)**
Sutton Draperies Inc ....F 305 653-7738
Miami **(G-9977)**
Top Trtment Cstomes Accesories .....G 239 936-4600
Fort Myers **(G-4426)**
Total Window Inc ....G 954 921-0109
Dania **(G-2345)**
Totally Glass & Blinds Llc ....G 561 929-6125
West Palm Beach **(G-18185)**

BLINDS, WOOD

Ramirez Cbnets Blnds Gran Mr ....G 352 606-0049
Spring Hill **(G-16076)**
Shades To You LLC ....G 407 889-0049
Apopka **(G-176)**
Srq Storm Protection LLC ....G 941 341-0334
Sarasota **(G-15834)**
Timbercraft of Naples Inc ....G 239 566-2559
Naples **(G-10927)**

BLOCKS & BRICKS: Concrete

Argos-US LLC ....F 407 298-1900
Orlando **(G-11918)**
Artistic Paver Mfg Inc ....E 305 653-7283
Miami **(G-8755)**
Bell Concrete Products Inc ....E 352 463-6103
Bell **(G-335)**
Bluegrass Materials Co LLC ....E 919 781-4550
Jacksonville **(G-5941)**
Cement Products Inc ....E 727 868-9226
Port Richey **(G-14357)**
Cemex Materials LLC ....C 561 746-4556
Jupiter **(G-6703)**
Cemex Materials LLC ....E 407 322-8862
Sanford **(G-15278)**
Cemex Materials LLC ....G 941 722-4578
Palmetto **(G-13159)**
Central Florida Cnstr Walls ....F 407 448-2350
Orlando **(G-11995)**
Devcon International Corp ....F 954 926-5200
Boca Raton **(G-482)**

PRODUCT

GLC 3 & Rental Corp ....G...... 954 916-1551
Plantation (G-13855)
Gulf Coast Ready Mix LLC ....E 352 621-3900
Homosassa (G-5749)
Jcs Contracting Inc ....G...... 407 348-4555
Kissimmee (G-6930)
Kenton Industries LLC ....G...... 863 675-8233
Labelle (G-6981)
McMaster Concrete Products LLC ....F 305 863-8854
Medley (G-8275)
Miami Quality Pavers Corp ....G...... 305 408-3444
Miami (G-9557)
New Line Transport LLC ....E 305 223-9200
Dade City (G-2321)
Paver Systems LLC ....E 407 859-9117
Orlando (G-12474)
Roof Tile Inc ....D...... 863 467-0042
Okeechobee (G-11615)
Royal Concrete Concepts Inc ......E 561 689-5398
Jupiter (G-6789)
Shealy Revel B Inc ....G...... 352 629-1552
Ocala (G-11489)
Titan America LLC ....D...... 954 523-9790
Fort Lauderdale (G-4092)
Whites Holdings Inc Centl Fla ......E 727 863-6072
Port Richey (G-14386)

BLOCKS: Acoustical, Concrete

Banaszak Concrete Corp ....F 954 476-1004
Davie (G-2391)
Cemex Cement Inc ....C...... 850 942-4582
Tallahassee (G-16421)

BLOCKS: Drystack Interlocking, Concrete

Labelle Brick Pavers Tile LLC ......F 863 230-3100
Labelle (G-6982)
Tremron Inc ....F 305 825-9000
Medley (G-8338)
Tremron LLC ....D...... 863 491-0990
Arcadia (G-195)

BLOCKS: Landscape Or Retaining Wall, Concrete

Blue Native of Fla Keys Inc ....G...... 305 345-5305
Big Pine Key (G-371)

BLOCKS: Paving

Masters Block - North LLC ....G...... 407 212-7704
Saint Cloud (G-14932)
Paver Technologies LLC ....G...... 772 213-8905
Vero Beach (G-17784)

BLOCKS: Paving, Asphalt, Not From Refineries

Atlantic Coast Asphalt Co ....F 904 268-0274
Jacksonville (G-5906)

BLOCKS: Paving, Concrete

American Pavers Manufacturing ....G...... 954 418-0000
Pompano Beach (G-13926)
Masters Block - North LLC ....G...... 407 212-7704
Saint Cloud (G-14932)
Sunshine Driveways Inc ....G...... 954 394-7373
Hollywood (G-5667)

BLOCKS: Paving, Cut Stone

Paver Systems LLC ....E 407 859-9117
Orlando (G-12474)

BLOCKS: Standard, Concrete Or Cinder

A and A Concrete Block Inc ....G...... 305 986-5128
Miami (G-8617)
A-1 Block Corporation ....E 407 422-3768
Orlando (G-11858)
Bedrock Industries Inc ....F 407 859-1300
Orlando (G-11943)
Cemex Materials LLC ....C...... 561 833-5555
West Palm Beach (G-17962)
Cemex Materials LLC ....E 321 636-5121
Titusville (G-17580)
Cemex Materials LLC ....C...... 352 435-0783
Okahumpka (G-11595)
Cemex Materials LLC ....C...... 305 558-0315
Miami (G-8910)

Cemex Materials LLC ....C...... 561 793-1442
West Palm Beach (G-17963)
Cemex Materials LLC ....C...... 561 743-4039
Jupiter (G-6704)
Cemex Pacific Holdings LLC ....D...... 239 992-1400
Bonita Springs (G-790)
Jahna Concrete Inc ....F 863 453-4353
Avon Park (G-282)
Legacy Vulcan LLC ....F 407 299-7494
Orlando (G-12320)
PM Engraving Corp ....F 786 573-5292
Miami (G-9723)
Titan America LLC ....F 800 396-3434
Delray Beach (G-3027)
Titan America LLC ....C...... 305 364-2200
Medley (G-8334)

BLOOD RELATED HEALTH SVCS

Morton Plant Mease Health Care ....A 727 462-7052
Clearwater (G-1704)

BLOWERS & FANS

A Mil Air ....F 813 417-9114
Brandon (G-1081)
Breezemaker Fan Company Inc ......E 813 248-5552
Tampa (G-16661)
Central Florida Central Fla ....F 407 674-2626
Orlando (G-11994)
Cool Components Inc ....G...... 813 322-3814
Tampa (G-16727)
Custom Masters Inc ....E 407 331-4634
Longwood (G-7885)
Eco Custom Filters Inc ....G...... 786 536-6764
Medley (G-8233)
Flaire Corporation ....C...... 352 237-1220
Ocala (G-11390)
Flanders Corp ....F 727 822-4411
Saint Petersburg (G-15048)
Hood Depot International Inc ....E 954 570-9860
Deerfield Beach (G-2740)
Merritt Mfg LLC ....G...... 407 481-1074
Land O Lakes (G-7499)
Metal Industries Inc ....E 352 793-8610
Bushnell (G-1247)
Moffitt Corporation Inc ....F 904 241-9944
Jacksonville Beach (G-6639)
Pall Aeropower Corporation ....B...... 727 849-9999
Deland (G-2893)
Plastec Ventilation Inc ....G...... 941 751-7596
Bradenton (G-1029)
Q-Pac Systems Inc ....D...... 904 863-5300
Elkton (G-3509)
R & J Mfg of Gainesville ....E 352 375-3130
Gainesville (G-4754)
Raytheon Technologies Corp ....A 860 565-4321
Jupiter (G-6786)
RB Kanalflakt Inc ....E 941 359-3267
Sarasota (G-15793)
Sunshine Filters Pinellas Inc ....E 727 530-3884
Largo (G-7694)
Sy-Klone Company LLC ....E 904 448-6563
Jacksonville (G-6525)
WSa Engineered Systems Inc ....F 414 481-4120
Pensacola (G-13628)

BLOWERS & FANS

Fanam Inc ....G...... 941 955-9788
Sarasota (G-15672)
Moffitt Fan Corporation ....F 585 768-7010
Jacksonville Beach (G-6640)
Robinson Fans Inc ....D...... 724 452-6121
Lakeland (G-7422)

BLUEPRINTING SVCS

Target Copy Gainesville Inc ....F 352 372-1171
Gainesville (G-4774)

BLUING

Felix Reynoso ....G...... 954 497-2330
Oakland Park (G-11266)

BOAT & BARGE COMPONENTS: Metal, Prefabricated

Calloway Barge Lines Inc ....F 904 284-0503
Green Cove Springs (G-4819)
Custom Marine Components Inc ......E 904 221-6412
Jacksonville (G-6018)

BOAT BUILDING & REPAIR

Aicon Yachts Americas LLC ....G...... 910 583-5299
Miami Beach (G-10162)
All Tank Services LLC ....G...... 954 260-9443
Pompano Beach (G-13918)
Ameracat Inc ....G...... 772 882-9186
Fort Pierce (G-4462)
Americraft Enterprises Inc ....G...... 386 756-1100
Daytona Beach (G-2510)
Arthur Cox ....G...... 772 286-5339
Stuart (G-16118)
Autocraft Manufacturing Co ....G...... 321 453-1850
Merritt Island (G-8577)
Bausch American Towers LLC ....F 772 283-2771
Stuart (G-16119)
Bausch Enterprises Inc ....F 772 220-6652
Stuart (G-16120)
Beavertail Skiffs Inc ....G...... 941 705-2090
Bradenton (G-947)
Bell Composites Inc ....G...... 561 575-9175
Jupiter (G-6690)
Bell Composites Inc ....F 561 714-9045
Riviera Beach (G-14597)
Belzona Inc ....E 305 512-3200
Doral (G-3133)
Bertram Yachts LLC ....G...... 813 527-9899
Tampa (G-16638)
Birdsall Marine Design Inc ....E 561 832-7879
West Palm Beach (G-17947)
Bms International Inc ....E 813 247-7040
Tampa (G-16651)
Boat Works ....G...... 904 389-0090
Jacksonville (G-5942)
Bonadeo Boat Works LLC ....G...... 772 341-9820
Stuart (G-16124)
C&A Boatworks Inc ....G...... 754 366-5549
Pompano Beach (G-13960)
C-Worthy Corp ....F 954 784-7370
Pompano Beach (G-13961)
Carey-Dunn Inc ....F 561 840-1694
Riviera Beach (G-14606)
CF Boatworks Inc ....G...... 954 325-6007
Fort Lauderdale (G-3721)
Chardonnay Boat Works LLC ....G...... 703 981-6339
Green Cove Springs (G-4821)
Chittum Yachts LLC ....E 386 589-7224
Stuart (G-16129)
CK Dockside Services Inc ....G...... 954 254-0263
Parkland (G-13345)
Composite Holdings Inc ....E 321 268-9625
Titusville (G-17582)
Concept Boats Inc ....G...... 305 635-8712
Opa Locka (G-11733)
Contender Boats Inc ....C...... 305 230-1600
Homestead (G-5704)
Corinthian Catamarans LLC ....F 813 334-1029
Palm Harbor (G-13107)
Craig Catamaran Corporation ....G...... 407 290-8778
Orlando (G-12052)
Creative Marine ....G...... 239 437-1010
Fort Myers (G-4222)
Custom Marine Components Inc ......E 904 221-6412
Jacksonville (G-6018)
Custom Marine Concepts Inc ....F 954 782-1111
Pompano Beach (G-13986)
Dennis Boatworks Inc ....G...... 954 260-6855
Oakland Park (G-11257)
Diamondback Manufacturing LLC ....F 321 305-5995
Cocoa (G-1918)
Diamondback Manufacturing LLC ....F 321 633-5624
Cocoa (G-1919)
Dig In Anchors LLC ....G...... 386 308-7745
Lakeland (G-7309)
Discount Boat Tops Inc ....G...... 727 536-4412
Largo (G-7571)
Dorado Custom Boats LLC ....G...... 727 786-3800
Tarpon Springs (G-17467)
Dorado Marine Inc ....G...... 727 786-3800
Ozona (G-12856)
Dos Amigos Boat Works LLC ....G...... 904 764-6541
Jacksonville (G-6039)
Double Down Boat Works Inc ....G...... 305 984-3000
Miami (G-9047)
Duckworth Steel Boats Inc ....G...... 727 934-2550
Tarpon Springs (G-17468)
Earl Parker Yacht Refinishing ....F 954 791-1811
Fort Lauderdale (G-3778)
Edgewater Power Boats LLC ....D...... 386 426-5457
Edgewater (G-3489)

(G-0000) Company's Geographic Section entry number

Engineered Yacht Solutions Inc ....D....... 954 993-6989
Fort Lauderdale ***(G-3795)***
EZ Boatworks Inc ....G....... 772 475-8721
Palm City ***(G-13035)***
Flat Island Boatworks LLC ....G....... 850 434-8295
Pensacola ***(G-13504)***
Flatsmaster Marine LLC ....G....... 239 574-7800
Cape Coral ***(G-1343)***
Flexiteek Americas Inc ....G....... 954 973-4335
Pompano Beach ***(G-14030)***
Floral City Airboat Co Inc ....F....... 352 637-4390
Inverness ***(G-5827)***
Florida Mkb Holdings LLC ....E....... 407 281-7909
Clermont ***(G-1867)***
Frank Murray & Sons Inc ....F....... 561 845-1366
Fort Lauderdale ***(G-3831)***
Gable Enterprises ....F....... 727 455-5576
Seffner ***(G-15959)***
Gilbane Boatworks LLC ....G....... 561 744-2223
Tequesta ***(G-17550)***
Glasser Boat Works Inc ....G....... 321 626-0061
Rockledge ***(G-14711)***
Good Time Outdoors Inc ....E....... 352 401-9070
Ocala ***(G-11401)***
Gulfstream Unsnkable Boats LLC ....F....... 813 820-6100
Tampa ***(G-16900)***
Hamant Airboats LLc ....G....... 321 259-6998
Melbourne ***(G-8432)***
Hinckley ....G....... 239 919-8142
Naples ***(G-10773)***
Hohol Marine Products ....G....... 386 734-0630
Deland ***(G-2874)***
Honest Hands LLC ....G....... 413 262-3892
Tampa ***(G-16921)***
Hutchins Co Inc ....F....... 727 442-6651
Clearwater ***(G-1631)***
Indian Rver HM Prfssionals Inc ....G....... 561 906-3881
Lake Worth ***(G-7205)***
Intrepid Powerboats Inc ....B....... 954 922-7544
Largo ***(G-7616)***
Invincible Boat Company LLC ....E....... 305 685-2704
Opa Locka ***(G-11756)***
Islamorada Boatworks LLC ....G....... 786 393-4752
Edgewater ***(G-3492)***
Jabm Advisors Inc ....G....... 727 458-3755
Tarpon Springs ***(G-17479)***
Jim Smith Boats Inc ....F....... 772 286-9049
Stuart ***(G-16171)***
Jlb Enterprises Tampa Inc ....G....... 813 545-3830
Tampa ***(G-16967)***
Jupiter Mar Intl Holdings Inc ....E....... 941 729-5000
Palmetto ***(G-13178)***
L & S Design & Construction ....G....... 772 220-1745
Palm City ***(G-13049)***
Lake & Bay Boats LLC ....G....... 813 949-7300
Naples ***(G-10800)***
Larsen ....G....... 305 989-4043
Stuart ***(G-16177)***
Lighthouse Boatworks Inc ....G....... 561 667-7382
Jupiter ***(G-6756)***
Littoral Marine LLC ....E....... 352 400-4222
Wildwood ***(G-18315)***
Mack Sales Inc ....G....... 772 283-2306
Stuart ***(G-16180)***
Marpro Marine Ways LLC ....G....... 727 447-4930
Clearwater ***(G-1684)***
Master Marine ....G....... 904 329-1541
Jacksonville ***(G-6278)***
Maverick Boat Group Inc ....C....... 772 465-0631
Fort Pierce ***(G-4504)***
Merrill-Stevens Dry Dock Co ....D....... 305 640-5676
Miami ***(G-9538)***
Michael Rybvich Sons Boat Wrks ....F....... 561 627-9168
Palm Beach Gardens ***(G-12989)***
Miller Marine Yacht Svc Inc ....E....... 850 265-6768
Panama City ***(G-13286)***
National Assemblers Inc ....E....... 877 915-5505
Lake Worth ***(G-7221)***
Novurania of America Inc ....D....... 772 567-9200
Vero Beach ***(G-17781)***
Parker Boatworks Inc ....F....... 954 585-1059
Fort Lauderdale ***(G-3977)***
Performance Sales and Svc Inc ....G....... 863 465-2814
Lake Placid ***(G-7146)***
Perry Composites LLC ....G....... 850 584-8400
Perry ***(G-13648)***
Piranha Boatworks LLC ....F....... 619 417-3592
Longwood ***(G-7938)***
Pitman Allen Boat Repr & Maint ....G....... 727 772-9848
Palm Harbor ***(G-13123)***

Premier Prfmce Interiors Inc ....E....... 941 752-6271
Sarasota ***(G-15539)***
Premium Marine Inc ....F....... 786 903-0851
Miami ***(G-9735)***
Progressive Industrial Inc ....F....... 941 723-0201
Palmetto ***(G-13187)***
Rabud Inc ....G....... 954 925-4199
Dania ***(G-2342)***
Resilient Group Inc ....E....... 518 434-4414
Jacksonville ***(G-6417)***
Roscioli International Inc ....E....... 941 755-7411
Fort Lauderdale ***(G-4026)***
Roscioli International Inc ....E....... 941 755-7411
Bradenton ***(G-1037)***
Rupp Marine Inc ....F....... 772 286-5300
Stuart ***(G-16210)***
S & S Performance Inc ....G....... 305 951-9846
Islamorada ***(G-5838)***
Salty Boats Rjl Inc ....G....... 863 802-0543
Wildwood ***(G-18320)***
Schurr Sails Inc ....F....... 850 438-9354
Pensacola ***(G-13601)***
Sdkc Corp ....F....... 305 469-7578
Doral ***(G-3358)***
Sea Breeze Marine Co ....G....... 561 368-0463
Deerfield Beach ***(G-2804)***
Sea Force Center Console LLC ....G....... 941 417-7017
Palmetto ***(G-13191)***
Sea Hawk Industries Inc ....G....... 863 385-1995
Sebring ***(G-15939)***
Sea Hunter Inc ....D....... 305 257-3344
Princeton ***(G-14489)***
Seavee Boats ....G....... 305 705-3158
North Miami ***(G-11120)***
Sheaffer Boats Inc ....G....... 813 872-7644
Tampa ***(G-17256)***
Shearwater Marine Fl Inc ....E....... 772 781-5553
Stuart ***(G-16216)***
Shurhold Products Company ....G....... 772 287-1313
Palm City ***(G-13058)***
SLM Boats Inc ....G....... 386 738-4425
Deland ***(G-2903)***
Smittys Boat Tops and Mar Eqp ....G....... 305 245-0229
Homestead ***(G-5740)***
Snug Harbor Dinghies Inc ....F....... 727 578-0618
Saint Petersburg ***(G-15188)***
Sonic Boatworks LLC ....F....... 561 631-6071
Fort Pierce ***(G-4529)***
South Bay Home Services LLC ....G....... 813 260-4708
Wimauma ***(G-18346)***
South Florida Field Techs Inc ....G....... 954 325-6548
West Palm Beach ***(G-18160)***
Southern Fiberglass Inc ....F....... 904 387-2246
Jacksonville ***(G-6490)***
Spice Island Boat Works Inc ....G....... 954 632-9453
Fort Lauderdale ***(G-4063)***
Statement Marine LLC ....F....... 727 525-5235
Clearwater ***(G-1796)***
Streamline Performance Boats C ....F....... 305 393-8848
Hialeah ***(G-5364)***
Stuart Boatworks Inc ....F....... 772 600-7121
Stuart ***(G-16228)***
Stuart Composites LLC ....E....... 772 266-4285
Miami ***(G-9960)***
Talaria Company LLC ....D....... 772 403-5387
Stuart ***(G-16236)***
Taylor Made Systems Brdnton In ....C....... 941 747-1900
Oviedo ***(G-12851)***
Tecnografic Inc ....E....... 954 928-1714
Fort Lauderdale ***(G-4085)***
Toledo Sales Inc ....G....... 305 389-3441
Miami ***(G-10021)***
Trolley Boats ....G....... 727 588-1100
Largo ***(G-7697)***
Ultimate Marine Centl Fla LLC ....F....... 407 849-1100
Orlando ***(G-12684)***
Ultrapanel Marine Inc ....E....... 772 285-4258
Miami ***(G-10058)***
US Spars Inc ....G....... 386 462-3760
Gainesville ***(G-4782)***
Vilano Interiors Inc ....G....... 904 824-3439
Saint Augustine ***(G-14911)***
Warbird Marine Holdings LLC ....F....... 844 341-2504
Opa Locka ***(G-11799)***
Williams Tenders Usa Inc ....F....... 954 648-6560
Pompano Beach ***(G-14243)***
Willis Marine Inc ....G....... 772 283-7189
Stuart ***(G-16252)***

BOAT BUILDING & REPAIRING: Fiberglass

Atlas Boat Works Inc ....G....... 239 574-2628
Cape Coral ***(G-1308)***
Bahama Boat Works LLC ....F....... 561 882-4069
Mangonia Park ***(G-8089)***
Blazer Boats Inc ....E....... 321 307-4761
Orlando ***(G-11957)***
Bonita Boats Inc ....F....... 321 978-1376
Melbourne ***(G-8380)***
Boston Whaler Inc ....B....... 386 428-0057
Edgewater ***(G-3483)***
Canaveral Custom Boats Inc ....G....... 321 783-3536
Cape Canaveral ***(G-1280)***
Chris Craft Corporation ....C....... 941 351-4900
Sarasota ***(G-15455)***
Copalo Inc ....C....... 941 753-7828
Sarasota ***(G-15462)***
Fabbro Marine Group Inc ....E....... 321 701-8141
Orlando ***(G-12143)***
Gulfshore Manufacturing Inc ....F....... 352 447-1330
Inglis ***(G-5818)***
Harley Boat Corporation ....G....... 863 533-2800
Bartow ***(G-309)***
Hells Bay Boatworks LLC ....E....... 321 383-8223
Titusville ***(G-17590)***
Hells Bay Marine Inc ....E....... 321 383-8223
Titusville ***(G-17591)***
Hydrofoils Incorporated ....G....... 561 964-6399
Lake Worth ***(G-7204)***
Intrepid Powerboats Inc ....E....... 954 324-4196
Dania ***(G-2333)***
Johannsen Boat Works Inc ....G....... 772 567-4612
Vero Beach ***(G-17769)***
Knowles Plastics Inc ....G....... 954 232-8756
Coral Springs ***(G-2175)***
Kz Manufacturing LLC ....G....... 305 257-2628
Princeton ***(G-14488)***
Land Marine Service Inc ....G....... 561 626-2947
West Palm Beach ***(G-18052)***
Little River Marine ....G....... 352 378-5025
Gainesville ***(G-4722)***
Magnum Marine Corporation ....F....... 305 931-4292
Miami ***(G-9498)***
Mark McManus Inc ....F....... 239 454-1300
Fort Myers ***(G-4317)***
Midnight Express Pwr Boats Inc ....E....... 954 745-8284
Miami ***(G-9566)***
Mirage & Co Inc ....F....... 407 301-5850
Saint Cloud ***(G-14935)***
Mirage Manufacturing Inc ....D....... 352 377-4146
Gainesville ***(G-4732)***
Patrick Industries Inc ....E....... 941 556-6311
Sarasota ***(G-15534)***
Pipe Welders Inc ....D....... 954 587-8400
Fort Lauderdale ***(G-3987)***
R J Dougherty Associates LLC ....C....... 386 409-2202
Edgewater ***(G-3499)***
Regal Marine Industries Inc ....B....... 407 851-4360
Orlando ***(G-12543)***
Revenge Advnced Composites LLC ....F....... 727 572-1410
Clearwater ***(G-1765)***
Sea Ray Boats Inc ....C....... 386 439-3401
Flagler Beach ***(G-3605)***
Sea Ray Boats Inc ....C....... 321 459-9463
Merritt Island ***(G-8593)***
Sea Ray Boats Inc ....C....... 321 459-2930
Merritt Island ***(G-8594)***
Sea Ray Boats Inc ....C....... 321 452-9876
Merritt Island ***(G-8595)***
Southern Cross Boatworks Inc ....F....... 954 467-5801
Fort Lauderdale ***(G-4060)***
Stamas Yacht Inc ....D....... 727 937-4118
Tarpon Springs ***(G-17494)***
Stinger Fiberglass Designs Inc ....F....... 321 268-1118
Titusville ***(G-17619)***
Talon Marine ....G....... 941 753-7400
Sarasota ***(G-15566)***
Target Marine Inc ....F....... 863 293-3592
Winter Haven ***(G-18473)***
Tiger Composites Inc ....F....... 386 334-0941
New Smyrna Beach ***(G-11014)***
W E Connery Boat Builders ....G....... 239 549-8014
Cape Coral ***(G-1405)***
Whitewater Boat Corp ....G....... 305 756-9191
Miami ***(G-10130)***
World Boat Manufacturing Inc ....G....... 863 824-0015
Okeechobee ***(G-11620)***

BOAT BUILDING & REPAIRING: Hydrofoil

Alumi Tech Inc ....F 407 826-5373
Orlando **(G-11898)**

BOAT BUILDING & REPAIRING: Kits, Not Models

Harley Shipbuilding Corp ....G 863 533-2800
Bartow **(G-310)**
Revere Survival Inc ....F 904 503-9733
Jacksonville **(G-6419)**

BOAT BUILDING & REPAIRING: Lifeboats

Survitec Survivor Cft Mar Inc ....G 954 374-4276
Miramar **(G-10551)**

BOAT BUILDING & REPAIRING: Motorboats, Inboard Or Outboard

Andros Boatworks Inc ....F 941 351-9702
Sarasota **(G-15595)**
Initial Marine Corporation ....E 407 321-1340
Sanford **(G-15337)**
P B C H Incorporated ....E 239 567-5030
Fort Myers **(G-4353)**
US Recreational Alliance Inc ....F 954 782-7279
Pompano Beach **(G-14232)**

BOAT BUILDING & REPAIRING: Motorized

Acrylico Inc ....G 561 304-2921
Lake Worth **(G-7181)**
All Craft Marine LLC ....E 813 236-8879
Zephyrhills **(G-18601)**
Bd Xtreme Holdings LLC ....F 850 703-1793
Bonifay **(G-767)**
Brunswick Commercial & ....D 386 423-2900
Edgewater **(G-3484)**
Cigarette Racing Team LLC ....D 305 769-4350
Opa Locka **(G-11729)**
CK Prime Investments Inc ....G 239 574-7800
Cape Coral **(G-1324)**
Forza X1 Inc ....D 772 202-8039
Fort Pierce **(G-4488)**
Performance Boats Inc ....F 305 956-9549
North Miami Beach **(G-11155)**
Ram Investments South Fla Inc ....E 305 759-6419
Medley **(G-8307)**
Smith Boat Designs Inc ....F 954 782-1000
Pompano Beach **(G-14182)**
Twin Vee Catamarans Inc ....F 772 429-2525
Fort Pierce **(G-4546)**
Whiticar Boat Works Inc ....E 772 287-2883
Stuart **(G-16250)**

BOAT BUILDING & REPAIRING: Pontoons, Exc Aircraft & Inflat

Fiesta Marine Products Inc ....F 727 856-6900
Hudson **(G-5772)**
Florida Trident Trading LLC ....F 352 253-1400
Tavares **(G-17507)**

BOAT BUILDING & REPAIRING: Rigid, Plastic

Acryplex Inc ....G 305 633-7636
Miami **(G-8648)**
American Plastic Sup & Mfg Inc ....E 727 573-0636
Clearwater **(G-1491)**
Pompanette LLC ....E 813 885-2182
Tampa **(G-17169)**

BOAT BUILDING & REPAIRING: Tenders, Small Motor Craft

Marine Exhaust Systems Inc ....D 561 848-1238
Riviera Beach **(G-14645)**

BOAT BUILDING & REPAIRING: Yachts

Adler Anb Inc ....G 954 581-2572
Davie **(G-2377)**
Admiral ....G 305 493-4355
Miami **(G-8651)**
Arkup Llc ....G 786 448-8635
Miami Beach **(G-10167)**
Big Eagle LLC ....G 305 586-8766
Fort Lauderdale **(G-3685)**
Bradford Yacht Limited Inc ....C 954 791-3800
Fort Lauderdale **(G-3702)**

Broward Yard & Marine LLC ....D 954 927-4119
Dania **(G-2329)**
Campeones Marina Corp ....F 305 491-5738
Miami **(G-8884)**
Camper & Nicholsons Usa Inc ....E 561 655-2121
Palm Beach **(G-12930)**
Chittum Yachts LLC ....F 386 589-7224
Palm City **(G-13029)**
Classic Yacht Refinishing Inc ....F 954 760-9626
Fort Lauderdale **(G-3731)**
Dania Cut Holdings Inc ....F 954 923-9545
Dania Beach **(G-2350)**
Diversified Yacht Services Inc ....E 239 765-8700
Fort Myers Beach **(G-4453)**
Endeavour Catamaran Corp ....F 727 573-5377
Clearwater **(G-1584)**
Florida Derecktor Inc ....C 954 920-5756
Dania Beach **(G-2351)**
G & S Boats Inc ....F 850 835-7700
Freeport **(G-4624)**
Garlington Landeweer Mar Inc ....E 772 283-7124
Stuart **(G-16152)**
Glass Tech Corp ....E 305 633-6491
Miami **(G-9215)**
Huckins Yacht Corporation ....E 904 389-1125
Jacksonville **(G-6186)**
Island Pcket Saward Yachts LLC ....G 727 535-6431
Largo **(G-7618)**
Ivm Usa Inc ....E 786 693-2755
Miami **(G-9347)**
Kc Marine Services Inc ....G 954 766-8100
Fort Lauderdale **(G-3902)**
Luxury Boat Services Inc ....G 360 451-2888
Port Saint Lucie **(G-14424)**
Mariner International Trvl Inc ....G 954 925-4150
Dania **(G-2336)**
Marlin Yacht Manufacturing ....G 305 586-3586
Pompano Beach **(G-14088)**
McKenzie Marine LLC ....G 904 770-2488
Saint Augustine **(G-14857)**
Moores Mar of Palm Beaches Inc ....G 561 841-2235
Riviera Beach **(G-14647)**
Multihull Technologies Inc ....G 305 296-2773
Key West **(G-6877)**
OP Yacht Services Corp ....F 954 451-3677
Fort Lauderdale **(G-3968)**
Ray Eaton Yacht Service Inc ....G 954 583-8762
Fort Lauderdale **(G-4012)**
Rmk Merrill Stevens Prpts LLC ....G 305 324-5211
Miami **(G-9813)**
Sea Force Ix Inc ....G 941 721-9009
Wimauma **(G-18345)**
Sheaffer Marine Inc ....F 813 872-7311
Tampa **(G-17257)**
Stuart Yacht Builders ....F 561 747-1947
Stuart **(G-16234)**
Talaria Company LLC ....D 239 261-2870
Naples **(G-10920)**
Tampa Yacht Manufacturing LLC ....F 813 792-2114
Clearwater **(G-1815)**
Tom George Yacht Group ....G 727 734-8707
Clearwater **(G-1834)**
Top Quality Yacht Refinishing ....F 954 522-5232
Fort Lauderdale **(G-4095)**
Tropical Dvrsons Mrina MGT Inc ....G 954 922-0387
Hollywood **(G-5676)**
Truesouth Marine Corp ....G 813 286-0716
Tampa **(G-17374)**
Willis Custom Yachts LLC ....C 772 221-9100
Stuart **(G-16251)**
Yacht 10 Inc ....G 954 759-9929
Fort Lauderdale **(G-4139)**

BOAT BUILDING & RPRG: Fishing, Small, Lobster, Crab, Oyster

Game Fisherman Inc ....F 772 220-4850
Stuart **(G-16151)**
L & H Boats Inc ....G 772 288-2291
Stuart **(G-16176)**
Maritec Industries Inc ....D 352 429-8888
Groveland **(G-4866)**
Maverick Boat Group Inc ....C 772 465-0631
Fort Pierce **(G-4505)**
Ocean Master Marine Inc ....G 561 840-0448
Riviera Beach **(G-14655)**
Pb Holdco LLC ....B 772 465-6006
Fort Pierce **(G-4516)**
Ros Holding Corporation ....E 954 581-9200
Fort Lauderdale **(G-4025)**

BOAT DEALERS

Camper & Nicholsons Usa Inc ....E 561 655-2121
Palm Beach **(G-12930)**
Concept Boats Inc ....E 305 635-8712
Opa Locka **(G-11733)**
Custom Marine Components Inc ....G 904 221-6412
Jacksonville **(G-6018)**
Florida Mkb Holdings LLC ....F 407 281-7909
Clermont **(G-1867)**
G & S Boats Inc ....F 850 835-7700
Freeport **(G-4624)**
Good Time Outdoors Inc ....G 352 401-9070
Ocala **(G-11401)**
Hohol Marine Products ....G 386 734-0630
Deland **(G-2874)**
Kz Manufacturing LLC ....G 305 257-2628
Princeton **(G-14488)**
Little River Marine ....G 352 378-5025
Gainesville **(G-4722)**
Marine Spc Cstm Fabricator ....G 813 855-0554
Oldsmar **(G-11672)**
Midnight Express Pwr Boats Inc ....E 954 745-8284
Miami **(G-9566)**
Model Shipways Inc ....E 800 222-3876
Miami **(G-9582)**
Multihull Technologies Inc ....G 305 296-2773
Key West **(G-6877)**
Nautical Acquisitions Corp ....D 727 541-6664
Largo **(G-7650)**
Pipewelders Marine Inc ....D 954 587-8400
Fort Lauderdale **(G-3988)**
Ram Investments South Fla Inc ....E 305 759-6419
Medley **(G-8307)**
Ray Electric Outboards Inc ....G 239 574-1948
Cape Coral **(G-1377)**
Southeastern Marine Power LLC ....E 727 545-2700
Saint Petersburg **(G-15190)**
T A C Armatures & Pumps Corp ....G 305 835-8845
Miami **(G-9989)**
Turning Point Propellers Inc ....G 904 900-7739
Jacksonville **(G-6569)**

BOAT DEALERS: Canoe & Kayak

Bote LLC ....F 888 855-4450
Miramar Beach **(G-10568)**

BOAT DEALERS: Marine Splys & Eqpt

Beachcomber Fibrgls Tech Inc ....G 772 283-0200
Stuart **(G-16122)**
Ros Holding Corporation ....E 954 581-9200
Fort Lauderdale **(G-4025)**

BOAT DEALERS: Outboard

Performance Sales and Svc Inc ....E 863 465-2814
Lake Placid **(G-7146)**

BOAT LIFTS

Ace Boat Lifts LLC ....E 941 493-8100
Venice **(G-17673)**
Boat Lift Pros of SW Fla Inc ....F 239 339-7080
Fort Myers **(G-4189)**
Boat Lifts By Synergy LLC ....G 641 676-4785
Fort Myers **(G-4190)**
Deco Power Lift Inc ....F 727 736-4529
Safety Harbor **(G-14785)**
Florida Boat Lift ....G 813 873-1614
Tampa **(G-16840)**
Golden Manufacturing Inc ....E 239 337-4141
North Fort Myers **(G-11061)**
Imm Survivor Inc ....F 239 454-7020
Fort Myers **(G-4287)**
Nbl1 Inc ....E 954 524-3616
Fort Lauderdale **(G-3957)**
Qlty Alumn Boat Lifts Inc ....G 850 434-6446
Pensacola **(G-13589)**
Quality Alum Boat Lifts Inc ....G 850 434-6446
Pensacola **(G-13590)**
R Js Boat Lifts Inc ....G 352 394-5666
Clermont **(G-1879)**
Rocky Bayou Enterprises Inc ....G 850 244-4567
Fort Walton Beach **(G-4606)**
SE Custom Lift Systems Inc ....G 954 941-8090
Pompano Beach **(G-14171)**
Touchless Cover LLC ....E 407 679-2217
Orlando **(G-12665)**

BOAT REPAIR SVCS

All Points Boats Inc ....D..... 954 767-8255
Fort Lauderdale (G-3639)
Florida Marine Joiner Svc Inc ....F..... 813 514-1125
Tampa (G-16849)
Kc Marine Services Inc ....G..... 954 766-8100
Fort Lauderdale (G-3902)

BOAT YARD: Boat yards, storage & incidental repair

Diversified Yacht Services Inc ....E..... 239 765-8700
Fort Myers Beach (G-4453)
Ros Holding Corporation ....E..... 954 581-9200
Fort Lauderdale (G-4025)

BOATS & OTHER MARINE EQPT: Plastic

Composite Holdings Inc ....E..... 321 268-9625
Titusville (G-17582)
Hc Grupo Inc ....G..... 954 227-0150
Coral Springs (G-2160)
Maritime Custom Designs Inc ....G..... 941 716-0255
Venice (G-17706)
Sargeant Marine Inc ....F..... 561 999-9916
Boca Raton (G-663)
Seacure Inc ....F..... 904 353-5353
Jacksonville (G-6459)
Structural Composites Inc ....F..... 321 951-9464
Melbourne (G-8534)
Taco Metals LLC ....F..... 727 224-4282
Seminole (G-15994)
W E Connery Boat Builders ....G..... 239 549-8014
Cape Coral (G-1405)

BOATS: Plastic, Nonrigid

Pompanette LLC ....E..... 813 885-2182
Tampa (G-17169)

BODIES: Truck & Bus

Amer-Con Corp ....E..... 786 293-8004
Palmetto Bay (G-13207)
Mickey Truck Bodies Inc ....F..... 352 620-0015
Ocala (G-11445)
Pierce Manufacturing Inc ....D..... 727 573-0400
Clearwater (G-1739)
Tesco Equipment LLC ....E..... 954 752-7994
Coral Springs (G-2220)
Tuflex Manufacturing Co ....E..... 954 781-0605
Davie (G-2493)

BODY PARTS: Automobile, Stamped Metal

AG Parts Corporation ....G..... 305 670-6227
Doral (G-3098)
Cooper-Standard Automotive Inc ......D..... 407 330-3323
Sanford (G-15294)
Direct Sales and Design Inc ....F..... 954 522-5477
Fort Lauderdale (G-3767)
Excellent Performance Inc ....G..... 561 296-0776
Riviera Beach (G-14620)
Glennmar Supply LLC ....G..... 727 536-1955
Largo (G-7596)
Lincoln Tactical LLC ....F..... 813 419-3110
Valrico (G-17667)
Marquez Brothers Inc ....F..... 305 888-0090
Medley (G-8272)
Priko Corp ....F..... 305 556-3558
Miami Lakes (G-10342)
Pro Trim of Central Florida ....G..... 863 294-4646
Winter Haven (G-18461)
Rotab Inc ....F..... 954 447-7746
Fort Lauderdale (G-4028)
Spicer Industries Inc ....F..... 352 732-5300
Ocala (G-11497)
Wish Inc ....F..... 305 653-9474
North Miami Beach (G-11171)

BOILER REPAIR SHOP

St Cloud Wldg Fabrication Inc ....E..... 407 957-2344
Saint Cloud (G-14939)

BOILERS & BOILER SHOP WORK

Fuse Fabrication Llc ....E..... 863 225-5698
Mulberry (G-10626)

BOILERS: Low-Pressure Heating, Steam Or Hot Water

Shilpico Inc ....G..... 561 306-5625
Boca Raton (G-671)

BOLTS: Metal

Sunpack of Pensacola Inc ....F..... 850 476-9838
Pensacola (G-13612)

BONDS, RAIL: Electric, Propulsion & Signal Circuit Uses

Douglas Abbott ....G..... 407 422-3597
Orlando (G-12102)

BOOK STORES

Books-A-Million Inc ....F..... 813 571-2062
Brandon (G-1084)
Ediciones Atenea Inc ....F..... 305 984-5483
Hialeah (G-5135)

BOOKS, WHOLESALE

Pro-Publishing Inc ....G..... 954 888-7726
Southwest Ranches (G-16057)
Spanish House Inc ....E..... 305 503-1191
Medley (G-8324)

BOOTHS: Spray, Sheet Metal, Prefabricated

Gibson Wldg Shetmetal Vent Inc ....G..... 850 837-6141
Destin (G-3067)
Tk - Autek Inc ....G..... 727 572-7473
Palm Harbor (G-13136)

BOOTS: Men's

Ronmar Industries Inc ....G..... 561 630-8035
West Palm Beach (G-18145)

BOOTS: Women's

Devon-Aire Inc ....F..... 813 884-9544
Tampa (G-16773)
Ronmar Industries Inc ....G..... 561 630-8035
West Palm Beach (G-18145)

BOTTLE CAPS & RESEALERS: Plastic

Amk Plastics LLC ....G..... 305 470-9088
Miami (G-8726)
Berry Global Inc ....D..... 941 355-7166
Sarasota (G-15446)
Berry Global Inc ....G..... 305 887-2040
Medley (G-8209)

BOTTLED GAS DEALERS: Propane

Airgas Usa LLC ....G..... 407 293-6630
Orlando (G-11884)

BOTTLED WATER DELIVERY

Keystone Water Company LLC ....F..... 863 465-1932
Lake Placid (G-7144)
Ultra-Pure Bottled Water Inc ....F..... 813 835-7873
Tampa (G-17384)

BOTTLES: Plastic

AC Plastics LLC ....G..... 305 826-6333
Hialeah (G-5024)
Advance Plastics Unlimited ....E..... 305 885-6266
Hialeah (G-5029)
Altira Inc ....D..... 305 687-8074
Miami (G-8702)
Altium Packaging LLC ....D..... 813 248-4300
Tampa (G-16582)
Amalie Oil Company ....C..... 813 248-1988
Tampa (G-16584)
Asi Global ....G..... 786 703-7155
Key Biscayne (G-6834)
Captiva Containers LLC ....D..... 800 861-3868
Miami (G-8888)
Cirkul Inc ....D..... 941 518-8596
Tampa (G-16707)
Cirkul Inc ....C..... 513 889-6708
Tampa (G-16708)
CKS Packaging Inc ....C..... 407 423-0333
Orlando (G-12015)

BOXES: Corrugated

CKS Packaging Inc ....D..... 954 925-9049
Hollywood (G-5551)
Compliance Meds Tech LLC ....F..... 786 319-9826
Miami (G-8952)
Island Bottles ....G..... 305 304-7673
Key West (G-6867)
Liqui-Box Corporation ....E..... 863 676-7602
Lake Wales (G-7166)
Mango Bottling Inc ....E..... 321 631-1005
Cocoa (G-1940)
Mfx Corp ....F..... 407 429-4051
Orlando (G-12376)
New Sentry Marketing Inc ....G..... 561 982-9599
Boca Raton (G-613)
Precision Concepts (miami) LLC ....D..... 305 825-5244
Hialeah (G-5299)
Rock Bottom Bottles LLC ....G..... 901 237-9929
Sarasota (G-15547)
Stretch Blow Systems LLC ....G..... 239 275-2207
Fort Myers (G-4407)
US Pack Group LLC ....G..... 954 556-1840
Sunrise (G-16387)
WR Kershaw Inc ....G..... 386 673-0602
Ormond Beach (G-12800)

BOULDER: Crushed & Broken

White County Stone LLC ....E..... 415 516-0849
West Palm Beach (G-18204)

BOXES & CRATES: Rectangular, Wood

Millenium Wood Boxes Inc ....G..... 305 969-5510
Miami (G-9571)

BOXES & SHOOK: Nailed Wood

Air-Flite Containers Inc ....G..... 407 679-1200
Orlando (G-11882)
Animal Air Service Inc ....E..... 305 218-1759
Doral (G-3116)
Cross City Veneer Company Inc ....D..... 352 498-3226
Cross City (G-2259)
Haman Industries Inc ....F..... 813 626-5700
Tampa (G-16903)
L & M Pallet Services Inc ....F..... 863 519-3502
Bartow (G-315)

BOXES, GARBAGE: Concrete

Florida Container Services ....F..... 407 302-2197
Sanford (G-15317)

BOXES: Corrugated

Advanced Design & Packg Inc ....F..... 904 356-6063
Jacksonville (G-5862)
Aggressive Box Inc ....F..... 813 901-9600
Tampa (G-16565)
Air-Flite Containers Inc ....G..... 407 679-1200
Orlando (G-11882)
American Container Conc ....G..... 631 737-6300
Oxford (G-12853)
Avatar Packaging Inc ....E..... 813 888-9141
Tampa (G-16618)
Avon Corrugated/Florida Corp ....F..... 305 770-3439
Miami (G-8779)
Birdiebox LLC ....E..... 786 762-2975
Miami (G-8832)
Central Florida Box Corp ....E..... 407 936-1277
Lake Mary (G-7064)
Cypress Folding Cartons Inc ....E..... 813 884-5418
Tampa (G-16757)
Dusobox Corporation ....D..... 407 855-5120
Orlando (G-12111)
Flamm Industries Inc ....G..... 904 356-2876
Jacksonville (G-6101)
Florida Packg & Graphics Inc ....F..... 954 781-1440
Fort Lauderdale (G-3823)
Gar Business Group LLC ....G..... 321 632-5133
Rockledge (G-14710)
Ic Industries Inc ....D..... 305 696-8330
Hialeah (G-5191)
International Paper Company ....E..... 407 855-2121
Orlando (G-12252)
International Paper Company ....D..... 813 717-9100
Plant City (G-13776)
International Paper Company ....G..... 813 621-0584
Tampa (G-16949)
K & G Box Inc ....D..... 904 356-6063
Jacksonville (G-6233)
Macpac Inc ....F..... 904 315-6457
Ponte Vedra Beach (G-14272)

PRODUCT

Mas Entrprses of Ft Lauderdale ....E 904 356-9606
Fort Lauderdale (G-3933)

Max-Pak Inc 863 682-0123
Lakeland (G-7392)

Metal Industries Inc ....E 813 855-4651
Oldsmar (G-11675)

Micon Packaging Inc ....C 813 855-4651
Oldsmar (G-11677)

Packaging Corporation America ....G 386 792-0810
Jasper (G-6646)

Packaging Corporation America ....G 407 299-1300
Orlando (G-12463)

Packaging Corporation America ....C 863 967-0641
Winter Haven (G-18454)

Packaging Corporation America ....C 904 757-8140
Jacksonville (G-6349)

Packaging Corporation America ....D 305 770-3439
Miami (G-9678)

Packaging Corporation America ....C 305 685-8956
Miami (G-9679)

Plant Foods Inc ....E 772 567-5741
Vero Beach (G-17787)

Pratt Industries Inc ....G 863 439-4184
Dundee (G-3437)

Schwarz Partners Packaging LLC ....C 863 682-0123
Lakeland (G-7430)

Schwarz Prtners Pckg Miami LLC ....G 305 693-1399
Hialeah (G-5342)

Sfbc LLC ....F 978 342-8921
Boca Raton (G-670)

Smurfit Kappa Packaging LLC ....F 954 838-9738
Sunrise (G-16369)

St Pete Paper Company ....G 727 572-9868
Palmetto (G-13192)

Suncoast Cartons & Crating LLC ....G 813 242-8477
Tampa (G-17311)

Sunshine Packaging Inc ....E 305 887-8141
Hialeah (G-5369)

TNT Packaging Inc ....F 305 769-0616
Miami (G-10016)

Ultrabox Inc ....G 941 371-0000
Bradenton (G-1069)

UNI-Box Inc ....E 954 733-3550
Oakland Park (G-11306)

Westrock Cp LLC ....C 904 261-5551
Fernandina Beach (G-3599)

Westrock Cp LLC ....D 850 785-4311
Panama City (G-13321)

Westrock Rkt LLC ....C 904 714-1643
Jacksonville (G-6606)

BOXES: Mail Or Post Office, Collection/Storage, Sheet Metal

Dhl Express (usa) Inc ....E 305 526-1112
Miami (G-9026)

United Express Intl Corp ....G 305 591-3292
Miami (G-10066)

Worlds Columbian Exonumis ....G 561 734-4433
Boynton Beach (G-925)

BOXES: Packing & Shipping, Metal

Desapro Inc ....E 321 674-6804
Rockledge (G-14699)

Edak Inc ....G 321 674-6804
Melbourne (G-8415)

Lotus Containers Inc ....G 786 590-1056
Miami (G-9480)

BOXES: Paperboard, Folding

Caribbean Box Company ....E 305 667-4900
Miami (G-8891)

Cypress Folding Cartons Inc ....E 813 884-5418
Tampa (G-16757)

Latham Marine Inc ....E 954 462-3055
Fort Lauderdale (G-3913)

R G Management Inc ....E 407 889-3100
Orlando (G-12525)

Richard C Good ....G 321 639-6383
Titusville (G-17613)

Southeast Finishing Group Inc ....E 407 299-4620
Orlando (G-12613)

Sunshine Packaging Inc ....E 305 887-8141
Hialeah (G-5369)

BOXES: Paperboard, Set-Up

Goldys Box Co ....G 954 648-1623
The Villages (G-17555)

McMill LLC ....G 561 279-3232
Boca Raton (G-589)

Simkins Industries Inc ....E 305 899-8184
Miami (G-9894)

Tropical Paper Box ....G 305 592-5520
Doral (G-3403)

BOXES: Plastic

New Generation Packaging LLC ....G 786 259-6670
Miami Gardens (G-10268)

Nfk Corporation ....F 305 378-2116
Miami (G-9618)

Profast Corporation ....E 305 827-7801
Miami Lakes (G-10343)

BRAKES & BRAKE PARTS

Coastal RE-Manufacturing Inc ....G 727 869-4808
Port Richey (G-14358)

Express Brake International ....F 352 304-6263
Ocala (G-11381)

Extreme Brake Integration Inc ....G 352 342-9596
Ocala (G-11382)

Mann+hummel Filtration Technol ....C 305 499-5100
Medley (G-8271)

SCI Undercar Inc ....G 727 327-2278
Saint Petersburg (G-15177)

Vette Brakes & Products Inc ....E 727 345-5292
Saint Petersburg (G-15225)

BRASS GOODS, WHOLESALE

James A De Flippo Co ....G 407 851-2765
Orlando (G-12265)

BRAZING SVCS

Precision Brazing Inc ....G 954 942-8971
Pompano Beach (G-14140)

Thermal Braze Inc ....G 561 746-6640
Jupiter (G-6808)

BRICK, STONE & RELATED PRDTS WHOLESALERS

A-1 Block Corporation ....E 407 422-3768
Orlando (G-11858)

Cement Industries Inc ....D 239 332-1440
Fort Myers (G-4204)

HG Trading Cia Inc ....G 305 986-5702
Hialeah (G-5183)

Quality Vaults Inc ....F 407 656-8781
Ocoee (G-11525)

Triton Stone Holdings LLC ....G 219 669-4890
Fort Lauderdale (G-4098)

Tropix Marble Company ....F 239 334-2371
Cape Coral (G-1401)

BRICKS & BLOCKS: Structural

Masters Block - North LLC ....G 407 212-7704
Saint Cloud (G-14932)

BRICKS : Ceramic Glazed, Clay

Three D Products Corp ....G 954 971-6511
Fort Lauderdale (G-4090)

BRICKS : Paving, Clay

Florida Brick and Clay Co Inc ....F 813 754-1521
Plant City (G-13766)

LLC Best Block ....G 239 789-3531
Orlando (G-12336)

LLC Best Block ....E 239 789-3531
Tampa (G-17019)

BRICKS: Concrete

Atlas Concrete Products Inc ....G 407 277-0841
Orlando (G-11930)

BROADCASTING & COMMS EQPT: Antennas, Transmitting/Comms

Altelix LLC ....F 561 660-9434
Boca Raton (G-400)

CF Motion Inc ....G 727 458-7092
Clearwater (G-1538)

Commstructures Inc ....D 850 968-9293
Pensacola (G-13476)

Denke Laboratories Inc ....E 941 721-0568
Palmetto (G-13164)

Gateway Wreless Communications ......F 561 732-6444
Boynton Beach (G-870)

Helical Communication Tech Inc ....G 561 762-2823
Rockledge (G-14713)

Myers Engineering Intl Inc ....E 954 975-2712
Margate (G-8144)

Vb-S1 Issuer LLC ....G 561 948-6367
Boca Raton (G-743)

Venti Group LLC ....G 949 264-3185
Miami Beach (G-10244)

Viatech of Delaware Inc ....E 321 308-6600
Melbourne (G-8558)

BROADCASTING & COMMS EQPT: Rcvr-Transmitter Unt, Transceiver

ACR Electronics Inc ....D 954 981-3333
Fort Lauderdale (G-3621)

Vela Research LP ....D 727 507-5300
Clearwater (G-1841)

BROADCASTING & COMMS EQPT: Trnsmttng TV Antennas/Grndng Eqpt

Maxxfi LLC ....F 513 289-6521
Cape Coral (G-1364)

BROADCASTING & COMMUNICATION EQPT: Transmit-Receiver, Radio

Trs Wireless Inc ....E 407 447-7333
Orlando (G-12675)

BROADCASTING & COMMUNICATIONS EQPT: Cellular Radio Telephone

Sky Phone LLC ....F 305 531-5218
Miami Beach (G-10228)

BROADCASTING & COMMUNICATIONS EQPT: Studio Eqpt, Radio & TV

Self Made Dynasty LLC ....G 754 303-3134
Fort Lauderdale (G-4043)

BROADCASTING & COMMUNICATIONS EQPT: Transmitting, Radio/TV

Vertical Bridge Towers LLC ....C 561 948-6367
Boca Raton (G-746)

BROADCASTING STATIONS, RADIO: News

Flickdirect Inc ....F 561 330-2987
Delray Beach (G-2963)

BROKERS' SVCS

Firefly Aircraft Parts Inc ....G 954 870-7833
Plantation (G-13852)

Global Ordnance LLC ....E 941 549-8388
Sarasota (G-15484)

BROKERS: Automotive

Uma Holdings Inc ....E 786 587-1349
Hollywood (G-5679)

BROKERS: Contract Basis

Imported Yarns LLC ....G 239 405-2974
Estero (G-3546)

BROKERS: Food

Ait USA Corp ....G 786 953-5918
Miami (G-8677)

Everglades Foods Inc ....G 863 655-2214
Sebring (G-15921)

Future Foods LLC ....G 786 390-5226
Lake Worth (G-7201)

Hispanic Certified Foods Inc ....G 305 772-6815
Pompano Beach (G-14050)

K and G Food Services LLC ....G 954 857-9283
West Palm Beach (G-18044)

BROKERS: Mortgage, Arranging For Loans

A M Coplan Associates ....G 904 737-6996
Jacksonville (G-5847)

BROKERS: Printing

Galleon Industries Inc ....G...... 708 478-5444
Altamonte Springs **(G-50)**
Kwikie Dup Ctr Pinellas Pk Inc ....G...... 727 544-7788
Pinellas Park **(G-13702)**
Power Point Graphics Inc ....G...... 561 351-5599
Boca Raton **(G-638)**

BROKERS: Yacht

Merrill-Stevens Dry Dock Co ....D...... 305 640-5676
Miami **(G-9538)**
Ros Holding Corporation ....E...... 954 581-9200
Fort Lauderdale **(G-4025)**
Tom George Yacht Group ....G...... 727 734-8707
Clearwater **(G-1834)**

BRONZE FOUNDRY, NEC

American Bronze Foundry Inc ....F...... 407 328-8090
Sanford **(G-15263)**
Arte Bronce Monuments Inc ....F...... 305 477-0813
Medley **(G-8200)**
Campbell Cnon Crrage Works Inc ....G...... 305 304-8528
East Palatka **(G-3471)**
We Bronze Wholesale LLC ....G...... 954 922-8826
Fort Lauderdale **(G-4126)**

BROOMS

Costa Broom Works Inc ....F...... 813 248-3397
Tampa **(G-16733)**

BROOMS & BRUSHES

A J Giammanco & Associates ....F...... 386 328-1254
Palatka **(G-12862)**
Industrial Brush Corporation ....F...... 863 647-5643
Lakeland **(G-7348)**
Smith Equipment & Supply Co ....E...... 863 665-4904
Lakeland **(G-7438)**
Torrington Brush Works Inc ....G...... 941 355-1499
Sarasota **(G-15855)**

BROOMS & BRUSHES: Household Or Indl

Boden Co Inc ....E...... 727 571-1234
Clearwater **(G-1522)**
Shurhold Products Company ....G...... 772 287-1313
Palm City **(G-13058)**

BROOMS & BRUSHES: Paint & Varnish

Elder & Jenks LLC ....G...... 727 538-5545
Largo **(G-7578)**

BROOMS & BRUSHES: Paint Rollers

Rollercoat Industries Inc ....E...... 813 621-4668
Tampa **(G-17231)**

BROOMS & BRUSHES: Paintbrushes

Brawley Distributing Co Inc ....F...... 727 539-8500
Largo **(G-7555)**
Corona Brushes Inc ....D...... 813 885-2525
Tampa **(G-16731)**

BRUCITE MINING

Jlt Custom Works Inc ....E...... 863 245-3371
Wauchula **(G-17829)**

BRUSHES

Premier Brush Inc ....G...... 850 271-5736
Panama City **(G-13299)**

BRUSHES: Rubber

Atlantech Process Technology ....G...... 352 751-4286
Lady Lake **(G-6994)**

BUFFING FOR THE TRADE

Shineline Buffing & Detail ....G...... 941 268-1033
Punta Gorda **(G-14530)**

BUILDING & STRUCTURAL WOOD MBRS: Timbers, Struct, Lam Lumber

Kennedy Craft Cabinets Inc ....G...... 239 598-1566
Naples **(G-10797)**

BUILDING & STRUCTURAL WOOD MEMBERS

American Truss ....G...... 352 493-9700
Chiefland **(G-1443)**
Architctral Mlding Mllwrks Inc ....F...... 305 638-8900
Miami **(G-8741)**
Fine Archtctral Mllwk Shutters ....F...... 954 491-2055
Fort Lauderdale **(G-3816)**
Florida Truss Corporation ....G...... 407 438-2553
Orlando **(G-12169)**
Georgia-Pacific LLC ....E...... 404 652-4000
Silver Springs **(G-16006)**
Joseph J Taylor Truss ....G...... 321 482-4039
Melbourne **(G-8443)**
Pacific Arches Corporation ....F...... 352 236-7787
Ocala **(G-11461)**
Park Place Manufacturing Inc ....F...... 863 382-0126
Sebring **(G-15934)**
Scosta Corp ....F...... 863 385-8242
Sebring **(G-15938)**
Truss William ....G...... 954 438-4710
Pembroke Pines **(G-13420)**

BUILDING BOARD & WALLBOARD, EXC GYPSUM

Continental Palatka LLC ....D...... 703 480-3800
Palatka **(G-12864)**

BUILDING BOARD: Gypsum

Continental Palatka LLC ....D...... 703 480-3800
Palatka **(G-12864)**
Proform Finishing Products LLC ....E...... 813 672-8269
Gibsonton **(G-4799)**

BUILDING CLEANING & MAINTENANCE SVCS

Apollo Retail Specialists LLC ....D...... 813 712-2525
Tampa **(G-16600)**
Joe Hearn Innovative Tech LLC ....F...... 850 898-3744
Pensacola **(G-13528)**

BUILDING CLEANING SVCS

Extra Time Solutions ....G...... 407 625-2198
Clermont **(G-1865)**

BUILDING COMPONENTS: Structural Steel

Ameribuilt Stl Structures LLC ....G...... 407 340-9401
Oviedo **(G-12803)**
Apex Metal Fabrication Inc ....F...... 386 328-2564
Jacksonville Beach **(G-6629)**
Banker Steel South LLC ....F...... 407 293-0120
Orlando **(G-11940)**
Bell Steel Company ....D...... 850 432-1545
Pensacola **(G-13453)**
Bell Steel Company ....F...... 850 479-2980
Pensacola **(G-13454)**
Canam Steel Corporation ....E...... 904 781-0898
Jacksonville **(G-5969)**
Central Fla Stl Bldg & Sup LLC ....G...... 352 266-6795
Ocala **(G-11348)**
Dade Engineering Group LLC ....D...... 305 885-2766
Miami **(G-8994)**
Division 5 Florida Inc ....E...... 904 964-4513
Starke **(G-16101)**
Fabricated Products Tampa Inc ....E...... 813 247-4001
Tampa **(G-16826)**
Gainesville Wldg & Fabrication ....G...... 352 373-0384
Gainesville **(G-4702)**
Gem Industries Inc ....E...... 321 302-8985
Cocoa **(G-1933)**
Hall Metal Corp ....G...... 772 460-0706
Fort Pierce **(G-4494)**
Hammer Haag Steel Inc ....C...... 727 216-6903
Clearwater **(G-1621)**
Hmb Steel Corporation ....F...... 321 636-6511
Rockledge **(G-14714)**
Imperial Industries Inc ....G...... 954 917-4114
Pompano Beach **(G-14060)**
Interstate Wldg & Fabrication ....F...... 727 446-1449
Clearwater **(G-1647)**
Met-Con Inc ....D...... 321 632-4880
Cocoa **(G-1941)**
Metal Systems Inc ....G...... 813 752-7088
Plant City **(G-13785)**
RDS Industrial Inc ....F...... 321 631-0121
Cocoa **(G-1951)**

Sea Cast Curb Adptors Crbs LLC ....F...... 772 466-2400
Fort Pierce **(G-4527)**
Storage Building Company LLC ....F...... 863 738-1319
Palmetto **(G-13193)**
Sunbelt Metals & Mfg Inc ....E...... 407 889-8960
Apopka **(G-179)**
Tampa Amalgamated Steel Corp ....F...... 813 621-0550
Tampa **(G-17324)**
West Point Industries Inc ....G...... 561 848-8381
Lake Park **(G-7135)**

BUILDING ITEM REPAIR SVCS, MISCELLANEOUS

Otis Elevator Company ....B...... 561 618-4831
West Palm Beach **(G-18100)**
Otis Elevator Company ....C...... 305 816-5740
Fort Lauderdale **(G-3970)**

BUILDING PRDTS & MATERIALS DEALERS

Aluma TEC Aluminun ....G...... 352 732-7362
Ocala **(G-11319)**
Cast-Crete Usa LLC ....D...... 813 621-4641
Seffner **(G-15954)**
Central Florida Lbr & Sup Co ....D...... 407 298-5600
Orlando **(G-11999)**
Cornerstone Kitchens Inc ....C...... 239 332-3020
Fort Myers **(G-4218)**
Finyl Products Inc ....G...... 352 351-4033
Ocala **(G-11388)**
Island Shutter Co Inc ....F...... 386 738-9455
Deland **(G-2876)**
Largo Aluminum Inc ....F...... 305 852-2390
Islamorada **(G-5837)**
Southern Fuelwood Inc ....E...... 352 472-4324
Newberry **(G-11027)**

BUILDING PRDTS: Concrete

Brown (usa) Inc ....F...... 305 593-9228
Miami **(G-8857)**
Knightsbridge Steel LLC ....G...... 786 532-0290
Hialeah **(G-5212)**
Lane Construction Corporation ....D...... 863 665-0457
Lakeland **(G-7374)**

BUILDING PRDTS: Stone

Borders & Accents Inc ....F...... 305 947-6200
North Miami **(G-11094)**
Florida Amico ....G...... 863 688-9256
Lakeland **(G-7328)**
Quartzo LLC ....F...... 888 813-3442
Tampa **(G-17203)**
Rising Stoners Inc ....G...... 305 300-7851
Miami **(G-9808)**
Stone Design By Santos LLC ....G...... 954 366-1919
Pompano Beach **(G-14201)**

BUILDING STONE, ARTIFICIAL: Concrete

Stonehardscapes Intl Inc ....F...... 954 989-4050
Fort Lauderdale **(G-4069)**

BUILDINGS & COMPONENTS: Prefabricated Metal

Adf International Inc ....F...... 954 931-5150
Pompano Beach **(G-13909)**
Advanced Alum Polk Cnty Inc ....E...... 863 648-5787
Lakeland **(G-7266)**
Affordable Scree Enclosure LLC ....F...... 800 900-8586
Pompano Beach **(G-13912)**
All American Building Products ....G...... 786 718-7300
Dania **(G-2326)**
All Amrcan Bldg Strctres Cntr ....G...... 407 466-4959
Apopka **(G-100)**
All Steel Bldngs Cmponents Inc ....E...... 813 671-8044
Gibsonton **(G-4793)**
Allied Insulated Panels Inc ....G...... 800 599-3905
Fort Lauderdale **(G-3643)**
Allied Steel Buildings Inc ....E...... 800 508-2718
Fort Lauderdale **(G-3644)**
Amazon Sheds and Gazebos Inc ....G...... 239 498-5558
Fort Myers **(G-4169)**
Amtex-Nms Holdings Inc ....F...... 352 728-2930
Leesburg **(G-7758)**
Bestway Portable Building Inc ....F...... 850 747-1984
Panama City **(G-13233)**
Carport Solution LLC ....F...... 352 789-1149
Ocala **(G-11345)**

PRODUCT

Carports Anywhere Inc................F..... 352 468-1116
Starke (G-16097)
Curvco Steel Structures Corp.................F..... 800 956-6341
Delray Beach (G-2952)
Defenshield Inc................................G..... 904 679-3942
Saint Augustine (G-14825)
Eds Aluminum Buildings Inc................G..... 850 476-2169
Molino (G-10578)
Grays Portable Buildings Inc................G..... 386 755-6449
Lake City (G-7020)
Gulfstream Alum & Shutter Corp.........E..... 772 287-6476
Stuart (G-16158)
Jacobsen Manufacturing Inc................C..... 727 726-1138
Safety Harbor (G-14788)
Jax Enterprises LLC.........................G..... 904 786-6909
Jacksonville (G-6220)
Kingspan Insulated Panels Inc.............E..... 386 626-6789
Deland (G-2881)
Kingspan Insulated Panels Inc.............C..... 386 626-6789
Deland (G-2882)
Kingspan-Medusa Inc..........................E..... 386 626-6789
Deland (G-2883)
Majestic Metals Inc............................G..... 813 380-6885
Valrico (G-17668)
Marinetek North America Inc................F..... 727 498-8741
Saint Petersburg (G-15120)
Mobile Mini Inc...................................G..... 954 745-0026
Opa Locka (G-11770)
Modular Life Solutions LLC..................G..... 904 900-7965
Jacksonville (G-6311)
Neopod Systems LLC...........................F..... 954 603-3100
Sunrise (G-16346)
Ocala Metal Products Inc.....................G..... 352 861-4500
Ocala (G-11456)
Orlando Mtal Bldg Erectors LLC...........F..... 407 917-9762
Umatilla (G-17648)
R & K Buildings Inc............................E..... 850 995-9525
Milton (G-10436)
R & K Portable Buildings.......................G..... 850 857-7899
Pensacola (G-13591)
Screens Fast.......................................G..... 239 565-1211
Fort Myers (G-4395)
Shed4less LLC....................................G..... 863 660-7300
Lakeland (G-7433)
Sheds Galore and More LLC..................G..... 386 362-1786
Live Oak (G-7855)
Shoreline Foundation Inc.....................C..... 954 985-0981
West Park (G-18216)
Snapspace Solutions LLC.....................E..... 561 756-6610
Daytona Beach (G-2600)
US Building Systems Corp....................E..... 954 281-2100
Deerfield Beach (G-2830)

BUILDINGS: Farm & Utility

Teds Sheds of Tampa..........................E..... 239 344-2900
Bonita Springs (G-825)

BUILDINGS: Mobile, For Commercial Use

Step Zone LLC....................................G..... 850 983-3758
Milton (G-10437)

BUILDINGS: Portable

Blue Water Dynamics LLC.....................D..... 386 957-5464
Edgewater (G-3482)
Eds Aluminum Buildings Inc................G..... 850 476-2169
Pensacola (G-13493)
Florida Pre-Fab Inc.............................F..... 813 247-3934
Tampa (G-16852)
Forts Services LLC..............................F..... 786 942-4389
Coconut Creek (G-1987)
Keens Portable Buildings.....................F..... 850 223-1939
Perry (G-13645)
Keens Portable Buildings Inc................F..... 386 364-7995
Live Oak (G-7849)
Langstons Utility Buildings....................G..... 813 659-0141
Mulberry (G-10630)
Leslie Industries Inc...........................F..... 850 422-0099
Tallahassee (G-16470)
M S Amtex-N Inc.................................C..... 352 326-9729
Leesburg (G-7784)
Mobile Mini Inc...................................G..... 866 344-4092
Orange Park (G-11834)
Smithbilt Industries Inc.......................D..... 321 690-0902
Auburndale (G-245)
Suncrest Sheds of South Fla.................F..... 305 231-1990
Miami Lakes (G-10362)
Superior Sheds Inc.............................E..... 386 774-9861
Orange City (G-11810)

BUILDINGS: Prefabricated, Metal

Dean Steel Buildings Inc......................D..... 239 334-1051
Fort Myers (G-4232)
Elite Outdoor Buildings LLC..................G..... 386 364-1364
Live Oak (G-7847)
Metal Building Kings............................G..... 412 522-4797
Tamarac (G-16536)
Scif Solutions Inc...............................F..... 904 298-0631
Jacksonville (G-6455)
Trident Building Systems Inc.................C..... 941 755-7073
Sarasota (G-15571)
Worth Metals Inc.................................F..... 904 626-1434
Green Cove Springs (G-4843)

BUILDINGS: Prefabricated, Plastic

Blue Water Dynamics LLC.....................D..... 386 957-5464
Edgewater (G-3482)

BUILDINGS: Prefabricated, Wood

Advanced Mdular Structures Inc...........G..... 954 960-1550
Pompano Beach (G-13911)
Amazon Sheds and Gazebos Inc...........G..... 239 498-5558
Fort Myers (G-4169)
Chariot Eagle Inc...............................D..... 623 936-7545
Ocala (G-11350)
Jacobsen Manufacturing Inc................C..... 727 726-1138
Safety Harbor (G-14788)
Neopod Systems LLC...........................F..... 954 603-3100
Sunrise (G-16346)
Peavy Enterprises Inc.........................G..... 863 297-6513
Winter Haven (G-18455)
Quality Cmpnents Tampa Bay LLC........G..... 727 623-4909
Largo (G-7666)
South Country Sheds LLC....................F..... 863 491-8700
Arcadia (G-194)
Southeastern Seating Inc....................F..... 813 273-9858
Tampa (G-17287)
Truss Systems of Vlsia Flgler................F..... 386 255-3009
Bunnell (G-1236)

BUILDINGS: Prefabricated, Wood

Florida Shed Company Inc....................E..... 727 524-9191
Saint Petersburg (G-15052)
Riverhead Housing Inc.........................G..... 630 688-6791
Fort Lauderdale (G-4019)
Suncrest Sheds Inc.............................G..... 863 675-8600
Labelle (G-6987)
Surepods LLC.....................................D..... 407 859-7034
Orlando (G-12640)

BULLETPROOF VESTS

Dhb Armor Group Inc...........................G..... 800 413-5155
Pompano Beach (G-13994)
Noguera Holdings LLC..........................G..... 305 846-9144
Hialeah (G-5281)
Onyx Protective Group Inc....................F..... 305 282-4455
Miami (G-9657)
Point Blank Enterprises Inc..................A..... 954 630-0900
Pompano Beach (G-14134)
Point Blank Enterprises Inc..................D..... 305 820-4270
Miami Lakes (G-10340)
Ppi International Corp..........................D..... 954 838-1008
Sunrise (G-16353)
Protective Group Inc...........................E..... 305 820-4266
Miami Lakes (G-10345)
Protective Products Entps Inc...............E..... 954 630-0900
Pompano Beach (G-14151)

BUMPERS: Motor Vehicle

Hope Technical Sales & Svcs................G..... 941 412-1204
Venice (G-17698)

BURGLAR ALARM MAINTENANCE & MONITORING SVCS

Cintas Corporation.............................G..... 239 693-8722
Fort Myers (G-4209)
Quality Cable Contractors Inc..............E..... 407 246-0606
Orlando (G-12520)
Vanguard Products Group Inc...............D..... 813 855-9639
Oldsmar (G-11705)

BURIAL VAULTS: Concrete Or Precast Terrazzo

Atlas Concrete Products Inc.................G..... 407 277-0841
Orlando (G-11930)

Atm Vault Corp....................................F..... 561 441-9294
Boca Raton (G-420)
Florida Wilbert Inc..............................G..... 904 765-2641
Jacksonville (G-6112)
Florida Wilbert Inc..............................G..... 352 728-3531
Okahumpka (G-11597)
Gulf Coast Wilbert Inc.........................G..... 850 682-8004
Crestview (G-2246)
Gun Vault...G..... 850 391-7651
Tallahassee (G-16455)
Hicks Industries Inc............................G..... 954 226-5148
Davie (G-2422)
Jewish Burial Society America..............G..... 954 424-1899
Delray Beach (G-2978)
Latteri & Sons Inc...............................G..... 813 876-1800
Tampa (G-17000)
Lewis Vault & Precast Inc.....................G..... 352 351-2992
Ocala (G-11426)
Mack Industries Inc............................E..... 352 742-2333
Astatula (G-201)
Quality Vaults Inc...............................F..... 407 656-8781
Ocoee (G-11525)
Roberts Vault Co Inc...........................G..... 352 567-0110
Dade City (G-2323)

BURIAL VAULTS: Stone

Florida Funeral Shipping Cntrs.............G..... 954 957-9259
Fort Lauderdale (G-3821)

BURNERS: Gas, Indl

Micron Fiber - Tech Inc........................F..... 386 668-7895
Debary (G-2638)

BURNERS: Gas-Oil, Combination

Intertech Worldwide Corp.....................G..... 561 395-5441
Boca Raton (G-551)

BUSHINGS: Cast Steel, Exc Investment

Contemporary Carbide Tech.................F..... 386 734-0080
Deland (G-2858)

BUSHINGS: Rubber

Stepincorp Auto Solutions LLC.............G..... 786 864-3222
Miami (G-9950)

BUSINESS ACTIVITIES: Non-Commercial Site

9t Technology LLC..............................G..... 904 703-9214
Jacksonville (G-5843)
Ajc Tiling Solutions LLC.......................G..... 863 274-1962
Winter Haven (G-18412)
American Metal Gate Corp....................F..... 516 659-7952
Bay Harbor Islands (G-331)
Aquino Trucks Center Corp...................G..... 239 327-9708
Cape Coral (G-1305)
Artvint Corp.......................................G..... 727 856-3565
Hudson (G-5762)
Blinds By Randy LLC............................G..... 305 300-1147
Miami Gardens (G-10252)
Boostane LLC.....................................F..... 239 908-1615
Bonita Springs (G-784)
Cavallo Estate Winery LLC...................G..... 352 500-9463
Lecanto (G-7749)
Cellec Games Inc...............................G..... 407 476-3590
Apopka (G-109)
Cnd Express Scooters LLC...................G..... 407 633-1079
Kissimmee (G-6975)
Comm Dots LLC Connecting..................F..... 305 505-6009
Miami (G-8951)
Common Sense Publishing LLC.............C..... 561 510-1713
Delray Beach (G-2949)
Connect Slutions Worldwide LLC...........G..... 407 492-9370
Vero Beach (G-17749)
Coqui Rdo Pharmaceuticals Corp..........G..... 787 685-5046
Doral (G-3172)
Courtney Allen Enterprises LLC.............F..... 571 314-4290
Sarasota (G-15643)
CP Logging Inc...................................F..... 850 379-8698
Hosford (G-5754)
Custom Carpentry Plus LLC..................F..... 305 972-3735
Cutler Bay (G-2286)
Custom Install Solutions Inc.................F..... 916 601-1190
Boca Raton (G-476)
Data Buoy Instrumentation LLC.............G..... 239 849-7063
Cape Coral (G-1330)
Day Shopping LLC...............................F..... 321 616-4504
Tampa (G-16766)

Demelle Biopharma LLC ....G..... 908 240-8939
Tarpon Springs (G-17466)
Deming Designs Inc ....F..... 850 478-5765
Pensacola (G-13488)
Dirtbag Choppers Inc ....F..... 904 725-7600
Atlantic Beach (G-207)
East Coast Metalworks LLC ....G..... 321 698-0624
Cocoa (G-1924)
Endurance Lasers LLC ....F..... 239 302-0053
Naples (G-10737)
Equiservisa USA Corp ....F..... 773 530-6964
Miami (G-9108)
Espace Inc ....E..... 802 735-7546
Stuart (G-16145)
Everyday Feminism LLC ....G..... 202 643-1001
Tallahassee (G-16437)
Exploration Resources Intn Geo ....G..... 601 747-0726
Lake Mary (G-7073)
Forward Inertia LLC ....G..... 617 794-8877
Miami (G-9169)
G Haddock Rowland Inc ....G..... 904 845-2725
Hilliard (G-5463)
GF & Associate Group LLC ....G..... 954 593-4788
West Palm Beach (G-18017)
H&K Home Supplies Distrs LLC ....F..... 786 308-6024
Homestead (G-5712)
Hollywood Cllctibles Group LLC ....G..... 407 985-4613
Orlando (G-12222)
Home Robot LLC ....G..... 850 826-8720
Fort Walton Beach (G-4592)
Hydrogen Innovations Co ....G..... 727 386-8805
Tarpon Springs (G-17477)
Ischa Products LLC ....F..... 305 609-8244
Homestead (G-5719)
Jadus Justice Apperal LLC ....F..... 954 394-6259
North Lauderdale (G-11081)
Jax Enterprises LLC ....G..... 904 786-6909
Jacksonville (G-6220)
Jsi Scientific Inc ....G..... 732 845-1925
Naples (G-10793)
Jwdi Realty LLC ....G..... 561 331-2481
Palm Beach Gardens (G-12981)
Karnak Corporation ....G..... 352 481-4145
East Palatka (G-3473)
Keepmefresh ....G..... 502 407-7902
Clermont (G-1872)
Kings Four Crners Auto Dtling ....G..... 866 886-4383
Clermont (G-1873)
Lamb Tec Inc ....G..... 305 798-6266
Cutler Bay (G-2293)
Maria Fuentes LLC ....G..... 305 717-3404
Miami (G-9511)
Mdy Services Inc ....G..... 954 392-1542
Miramar (G-10513)
Meridian Cable LLC ....F..... 904 770-4687
Saint Augustine (G-14858)
Mink Milli LLC ....F..... 813 606-0416
Tampa (G-17074)
Mito Corp ....F..... 786 208-3114
Pembroke Pines (G-13405)
Mmi North America Inc ....F..... 616 649-1912
Ponte Vedra Beach (G-14275)
Mobile Auto Solutions LLC ....G..... 561 903-5328
West Palm Beach (G-18080)
Morgannas Alchemy LLC ....G..... 727 505-8376
New Port Richey (G-10975)
Mr Next Level Investment LLC ....F..... 786 718-8056
Homestead (G-5732)
Natures Power and Energy LLC ....F..... 813 907-6279
Wesley Chapel (G-17883)
New Style Kit Cabinets Corp ....G..... 305 989-9665
Hialeah (G-5277)
North America Bio Fuel Corp ....G..... 877 877-9279
Bradenton (G-1019)
OGrady Tool Company ....F..... 239 560-3395
Fort Myers (G-4347)
Okee-B Inc ....D..... 561 996-3040
Belle Glade (G-342)
Ottica Dante Americas LLC ....G..... 561 322-0186
Boca Raton (G-627)
Pallet Direct Inc ....G..... 888 433-1727
Naples (G-10845)
Paper Free Technology Inc ....G..... 515 270-1505
Lehigh Acres (G-7819)
Pick-A-Load Dispatch LLC ....G..... 954 907-8245
Margate (G-8147)
Precision Infinity Systems Inc ....G..... 407 490-2320
Orlando (G-12501)
Pure Wave Organics Inc ....G..... 321 368-7002
Melbourne (G-8504)

Rapid Composites LLC ....G..... 941 322-6647
Sarasota (G-15544)
Recycled Vinyl ....G..... 727 434-1857
Sarasota (G-15794)
Reins Inc ....F..... 904 868-3381
Jacksonville (G-6414)
Reliable Site Solutions LLC ....G..... 904 238-3113
Callahan (G-1257)
Route4me Inc ....E..... 888 552-9045
Tampa (G-17234)
Roxy Lady LLC ....G..... 954 706-6735
Fort Lauderdale (G-4030)
Saf Aerospace LLC ....G..... 813 376-0883
Tampa (G-17243)
Sandy Lender Inc ....G..... 239 272-8613
Cape Coral (G-1380)
Sbm Beauty LLC ....F..... 850 567-7338
Quincy (G-14548)
Service Modern Trade LLC ....F..... 708 942-9154
Lakeland (G-7431)
Sleepy Dragon Studios Inc ....G..... 561 714-6156
Cutler Bay (G-2302)
Spectra Powder Coating Inc ....F..... 786 351-7448
Miami (G-9940)
Sterling Mdr Inc ....F..... 954 725-2777
Deerfield Beach (G-2815)
Stick With US Delivery Svc LLC ....G..... 561 425-4910
West Palm Beach (G-18165)
Stuart Boatworks Inc ....F..... 772 600-7121
Stuart (G-16228)
Super Swim Corp ....G..... 239 275-7600
Fort Myers (G-4414)
Swoogo LLC ....G..... 212 655-9810
Sarasota (G-15847)
Terfa Litter USA Inc ....F..... 416 358-4495
Sunny Isles Beach (G-16283)
Tropical Paver Sealing ....G..... 727 786-4011
Wesley Chapel (G-17889)
Trs Industries Inc ....G..... 561 880-0031
Lake Worth (G-7239)
Trugreen Products LLC ....G..... 954 629-5794
Pompano Beach (G-14221)
Tyson Petroleum Contrs LLC ....F..... 850 727-0082
Tallahassee (G-16518)
Unibeast Sports LLC ....G..... 813 255-2827
Riverview (G-14581)
USA Printing LLC ....G..... 754 275-5048
Hallandale Beach (G-4983)
Vuaant Inc ....G..... 407 701-6975
Orlando (G-12709)
W&I Properties LLC ....G..... 786 985-1642
Davie (G-2495)
West Texas Protein Inc ....F..... 806 250-5959
Jacksonville (G-6602)
Wiztel USA Inc ....G..... 416 457-5513
Miromar Lakes (G-10576)
Wonderworld 100 LLC ....F..... 407 618-3207
Orlando (G-12718)
Yesil Inc ....F..... 516 858-0244
Boca Raton (G-761)

BUSINESS FORMS WHOLESALERS

Dannys Prtg Svc Sups & Eqp Inc ....G..... 305 757-2282
Miami (G-9000)
Printed Systems Inc ....G..... 904 281-0909
Jacksonville (G-6388)

BUSINESS FORMS: Printed, Continuous

John Stewart Enterprises Inc ....F..... 904 356-9392
Jacksonville (G-6228)

BUSINESS FORMS: Printed, Manifold

Blackstone Legal Supplies Inc ....F..... 305 945-3450
Lauderhill (G-7727)
Business Card Ex Tampa Bay Inc ....D..... 727 535-7768
Clearwater (G-1532)
Economy Printing Co ....F..... 904 786-4070
Jacksonville (G-6065)
Herald-Advocate Publishing Co ....G..... 863 773-3255
Wauchula (G-17828)
Independent Resources Inc ....E..... 813 237-0945
Tampa (G-16937)
K R O Enterprises Ltd ....G..... 309 797-2213
Naples (G-10795)
Taylor Communications Inc ....F..... 813 689-5099
Seffner (G-15965)
Taylor Communications Inc ....E..... 813 886-5511
Tampa (G-17343)

Taylor Communications Inc ....F..... 954 632-6501
Sunrise (G-16380)
Tiger Business Forms Inc ....E..... 305 888-3528
Hialeah (G-5380)

BUSINESS FORMS: Strip, Manifold

Arlington Prtg Stationers Inc ....C..... 904 358-2928
Jacksonville (G-5901)

BUSINESS FORMS: Unit Sets, Manifold

Southeastern Peg Bd Prtrs Inc ....G..... 904 731-0357
Jacksonville (G-6488)

BUSINESS SUPPORT SVCS

Advanced Electronics Labs Inc ....G..... 305 255-6401
Pinecrest (G-13661)
Big Star Systems LLC ....G..... 954 243-7209
Lauderhill (G-7726)
Construction Software Inc ....G..... 888 801-0675
Fort Lauderdale (G-3743)
One Srce Prperty Solutions Inc ....G..... 239 800-9771
Fort Myers (G-4351)
Penngear LLC ....G..... 215 968-2403
Gainesville (G-4747)
Polaris Trading Corp ....G..... 954 956-6999
Coconut Creek (G-2002)
Quintessential Home Svcs LLC ....G..... 850 259-5064
Destin (G-3076)
R S S Partners Inc ....F..... 904 241-6144
Jacksonville Beach (G-6642)
Rbj Timber Inc ....G..... 904 879-1597
Callahan (G-1256)
Seal Outdoors Inc ....F..... 877 323-7325
South Miami (G-16045)
Steevie Stash LLC ....F..... 954 860-3138
Miami (G-9949)
Studio M LLC ....F..... 954 918-8528
Margate (G-8155)

BUSINESS TRAINING SVCS

Paradigm Leaders LLC ....G..... 850 441-3289
Panama City Beach (G-13336)

BUTTONS

M D R International Inc ....F..... 305 944-5335
North Miami (G-11110)
Maxant Button & Supply Inc ....G..... 770 460-2227
Plantation (G-13867)

CABINETS & CASES: Show, Display & Storage, Exc Wood

Bob & Lees Cabinets ....F..... 352 748-3553
Wildwood (G-18309)
Dyco Ventures LLC ....G..... 863 491-7211
Arcadia (G-192)
New River Cabinet & Fix Inc ....E..... 954 938-9200
Fort Lauderdale (G-3959)

CABINETS: Bathroom Vanities, Wood

Avon Cabinet Corporation ....C..... 941 755-2866
Bradenton (G-943)
Bailey Industries Inc ....E..... 352 326-2898
Leesburg (G-7761)
Beverly Acquisitions Inc ....F..... 561 746-3827
Jupiter (G-6692)
Braden Kitchens Inc ....E..... 321 636-4700
Cocoa (G-1907)
Clover Interior Systems Inc ....F..... 941 484-1300
Nokomis (G-11044)
Counter Productions Inc ....G..... 386 673-6500
Daytona Beach (G-2535)
Custom Klosets & Cabinets Inc ....E..... 813 246-4806
Tampa (G-16753)
Dj Cabinet Factory Inc ....G..... 786 483-8868
Hialeah (G-5120)
Home-Art Corporation ....E..... 352 326-3337
Fruitland Park (G-4641)
Jim Baird Cabinets ....G..... 772 569-0936
Vero Beach (G-17768)
Princeton Industries Inc ....E..... 954 344-9155
Margate (G-8149)
Smith Products Co Inc ....F..... 386 325-4534
Palatka (G-12880)
Star Quality Inc ....F..... 813 875-9955
Tampa (G-17300)

PRODUCT

CABINETS: Entertainment

Amick Cstm Woodcraft & Design ....G 407 324-8525
Sanford (G-15265)

Bon Vivant Interiors Inc ....E 305 576-8066
Opa Locka (G-11725)

Dons Cabinets and Woodworking ....F 727 863-3404
Hudson (G-5771)

Elegant House Intl LLC ....G 954 457-8836
Hallandale (G-4925)

Florida Designer Cabinets Inc ....F 352 793-8555
Sumterville (G-16263)

Home Pride Cabinets Inc ....F 813 887-3782
Tampa (G-16920)

J & J Custom Mica Inc ....F 239 433-2828
Fort Myers (G-4293)

McCallum Cabinets Inc ....F 352 372-2344
Gainesville (G-4725)

Spruce Creek Cabinetry Inc ....E 386 756-0041
Port Orange (G-14349)

Williams Minerals Co Inc ....G 304 897-6003
Winter Springs (G-18582)

Y F Leung Inc ....G 305 651-6851
North Miami Beach (G-11172)

CABINETS: Entertainment Units, Household, Wood

Still Water Industries Inc ....G 561 845-6033
West Palm Beach (G-18166)

CABINETS: Factory

Borgzinner Inc ....E 561 848-2538
Riviera Beach (G-14600)

Byblos Group Inc ....G 305 662-6666
Miami (G-8867)

Distinct Dsgns Cstm Coml Case ....G 727 530-0119
Largo (G-7572)

Florida Designer Cabinets Inc ....F 352 793-8555
Sumterville (G-16263)

Gulf South Distributors Inc ....F 850 244-1522
Fort Walton Beach (G-4591)

Guyton Industries LLC ....E 772 208-3019
Indiantown (G-5814)

James Spear Design Inc ....G 727 592-9600
Largo (G-7621)

Morris Mica Cabinets Inc ....G 954 979-6838
Pompano Beach (G-14105)

Regency Custom Cabinets Inc ....F 239 332-7977
Fort Myers (G-4377)

Werever Products Inc ....F 813 241-9701
Riverview (G-14582)

Wj Bergin Cabinetry LLC ....E 407 271-8982
Orlando (G-12715)

Wood Stile Inc ....G 561 329-4671
North Palm Beach (G-11185)

CABINETS: Filing, Wood

Casa Cabinets LLC ....G 850 459-3403
Port St Lucie (G-14473)

Kabinets By Kinsey Inc ....E 813 222-0460
Tampa (G-16974)

CABINETS: Kitchen, Metal

FL Central Cnstr & Rmdlg ....G 863 701-3548
Lakeland (G-7326)

Kit Residential Designs Inc ....G 305 796-5940
Hialeah (G-5211)

Mag Works Inc ....E 305 823-4440
Hialeah (G-5234)

Saint Petersburg Cabinets Inc ....G 727 327-4800
Saint Petersburg (G-15175)

Studio Luxe Cstm Cabinetry LLC ....G 941 371-4010
Sarasota (G-15842)

CABINETS: Kitchen, Wood

3 Stars Kitchen Cabinets Corp ....G 786 285-7147
Hialeah (G-5013)

A & R Kitchen Cabinet Corp ....G 305 333-3326
Cutler Bay (G-2281)

A A A Cabinets ....G 850 433-8337
Pensacola (G-13428)

A Better Kitchen Cabinets Inc ....G 786 234-1897
Homestead (G-5695)

A W R Cabinets Inc ....F 407 323-1415
Sanford (G-15257)

A-1 Custom Mica Inc ....G 954 893-0063
Hollywood (G-5519)

Aadi Inc ....E 407 957-4557
Saint Cloud (G-14919)

Abbot Hill LLC ....G 239 260-5246
Naples (G-10648)

About Face Cabinetry & Refacin ....F 813 777-4088
Lutz (G-7980)

Absolute Wood Creations LLC ....G 954 251-2202
Hallandale Beach (G-4933)

Adams Bros Cabinetry Inc ....G 863 993-0501
Arcadia (G-187)

Advanced Cabinetry Inventions ....G 305 866-1160
North Bay Village (G-11057)

Aj Originals Inc ....G 954 563-9911
Fort Lauderdale (G-3635)

Akiknav Inc ....F 561 842-8091
Riviera Beach (G-14591)

Al-FA Cabinets Inc ....F 813 876-4205
Tampa (G-16569)

Albrecht Consulting Inc ....F 941 377-7755
Sarasota (G-15591)

All Wood Cabinetry LLC ....E 866 367-2516
Bartow (G-297)

Alpha Kitchen Design LLC ....G 941 351-1659
Sarasota (G-15593)

AM Cabinets LLC ....G 321 663-4319
Altamonte Springs (G-30)

Amercn Cabinets Granite Floors ....G 727 303-0678
Palm Harbor (G-13097)

American Cab Connection LLC ....G 561 676-5875
West Palm Beach (G-17923)

Amick Cstm Woodcraft & Design ....G 407 324-8525
Sanford (G-15265)

Amy Cabinetry ....E 561 842-8091
Riviera Beach (G-14594)

Andersen Custom Cabinetry LLC ....G 407 702-4891
Orlando (G-11910)

Andrews Cabinets Inc ....F 850 994-0836
Milton (G-10417)

Antique & Modern Cabinets Inc ....E 904 393-9055
Jacksonville (G-5892)

Architctral Wdwrks Cbnetry Inc ....F 561 848-8595
Palm Beach Gardens (G-12949)

Argenal Cabinets Inc ....G 863 670-7973
Lakeland (G-7276)

Armando Grcia Cstm Cbinets Inc ....G 305 775-5674
Miami (G-8749)

Art Wood Cabinets Corp ....F 754 367-0742
Deerfield Beach (G-2670)

Assocate Cbinetmakers Palm Bch ......G 561 743-9566
Jupiter (G-6685)

B & K Discount Cabinets LLC ....G 321 254-2322
Melbourne (G-8373)

B H C P Inc ....G 850 444-9300
Pensacola (G-13450)

Bauformat South-East LLC ....G 201 693-6635
Fort Lauderdale (G-3676)

Bay Cabinets and Millworks ....G 850 215-1485
Panama City Beach (G-13326)

Beaches Woodcraft Inc ....F 904 249-0785
Atlantic Beach (G-205)

Beautiful Cabinets Corp ....G 813 486-9034
Tampa (G-16636)

Bennetts Custom Cabinets Inc ....G 904 751-1455
Jacksonville (G-5930)

Bob & Lees Cabinets ....F 352 748-3553
Wildwood (G-18309)

Brandon Crookes ....G 954 563-8584
Oakland Park (G-11247)

Braswell Custom Cabinets ....G 850 436-2645
Pensacola (G-13461)

Bresee Woodwork Inc ....F 941 355-2591
Sarasota (G-15615)

Broward Custom Woodwork LLC ....G 352 376-4732
Deerfield Beach (G-2682)

Bruno Danger Custom Cabinets ....G 754 366-1302
Sebastian (G-15888)

Built Rght Ktchens of Palm Cas ....G 386 437-7077
Bunnell (G-1228)

Built-Rite Cabinets Inc ....G 352 447-2238
Inglis (G-5816)

Busy Bee Cabinets Inc ....D 941 628-2025
North Port (G-11189)

Byerly Custom Design Inc ....G 941 371-7498
Sarasota (G-15622)

Cabinet Cnnction of Trsure Cas ....F 772 621-4882
Port Saint Lucie (G-14402)

Cabinet Collection Inc ....G 239 478-0359
Bonita Springs (G-788)

Cabinet Design and Cnstr LLC ....G 850 393-9724
Pensacola (G-13468)

Cabinet Designs of Central Fla ....G 321 636-1101
Rockledge (G-14695)

Cabinet Designs Sarasota Inc ....F 941 739-1607
Bradenton (G-955)

Cabinet Dreams & Things Inc ....G 727 514-0847
Hudson (G-5765)

Cabinet Factory Outlet ....G 386 323-0778
Daytona Beach (G-2525)

Cabinet Genies ....G 239 458-8563
Cape Coral (G-1318)

Cabinet Guy 2012 Inc ....G 305 796-5242
Davie (G-2394)

Cabinet Guy of Englewood Inc ....G 941 475-9454
Englewood (G-3526)

Cabinet Kings LLC ....G 239 288-6740
Fort Myers (G-4198)

Cabinet Masters Inc ....G 727 535-0020
Largo (G-7560)

Cabinet Options Inc ....G 904 434-1564
Saint Johns (G-14945)

Cabinet Startup LLC ....G 352 795-2655
Crystal River (G-2268)

Cabinet Systems Centl Fla Inc ....G 407 678-0994
Winter Park (G-18496)

Cabinet Wholesale LLC ....F 954 751-7200
Pompano Beach (G-13962)

Cabinetree Collection Inc ....G 772 569-4761
Vero Beach (G-17748)

Cabinetry Masters LLC ....G 954 549-8646
Jacksonville (G-5966)

Cabinets -N- More Inc ....G 321 355-9548
Cocoa (G-1910)

Cabinets By Marylin Inc ....G 954 729-3995
Pompano Beach (G-13963)

Cabinets By Wfc Inc ....F 941 355-2703
Sarasota (G-15623)

Cabinets Direct USA ....G 862 704-6138
Delray Beach (G-2940)

Cabinets Extraordinaire Inc ....G 941 961-8453
Sarasota (G-15624)

Cabinets Extraordinaire Inc ....F 618 925-0515
Bradenton (G-956)

Cabinets Moreunlimited Inc ....G 813 789-4203
Tampa (G-16669)

Cabinets One LLC ....G 407 227-1147
Orlando (G-11975)

Cabinets Plus Inc ....E 239 574-7020
Cape Coral (G-1319)

Cabinets Plus of America Inc ....G 813 408-0433
Tampa (G-16670)

Calti Cabinets Inc ....G 727 744-7844
Largo (G-7561)

Camelot Cabinets Inc ....F 813 876-9150
Tampa (G-16674)

Capri Kitchens Inc ....G 813 623-1424
Tampa (G-16676)

Captain Cabinets LLC ....G 813 685-7179
Seffner (G-15953)

Caravaggio Cabinetry Inc ....F 561 609-3355
Lake Worth (G-7190)

Carlos Velez Cabinets & Instal ....G 407 929-3402
Orlando (G-11982)

Carman Cabinets ....G 561 202-9871
Lantana (G-7508)

Carters Cabinetry Inc ....F 386 677-4192
Ormond Beach (G-12749)

Castor Inc ....G 813 254-1171
Tampa (G-16686)

Cayo Hueso Enterprises Inc ....E 305 747-0020
Key West (G-6858)

Century Millworks ....F 850 256-2565
Century (G-1442)

Cepero Remodeling Inc ....G 305 265-1888
Miami (G-8912)

Chief Cabinets LLC ....G 850 545-5055
Tallahassee (G-16423)

Chrisalen Cabinets Inc ....G 954 682-9390
Pembroke Pines (G-13381)

Cianos Tile & Marble Inc ....E 239 267-8453
Fort Myers (G-4208)

Classic Kitchens Brevard Inc ....G 321 327-5972
Melbourne (G-8389)

Clever Cabinetry LLC ....G 813 992-0020
Riverview (G-14559)

Cljp Inc ....E 850 678-8819
Niceville (G-11028)

Closet Rodz LLC ....G 386 212-8188
Ormond Beach (G-12750)

Cnc Cabinet Components Inc ....F 321 956-3470
Melbourne (G-8390)

Coastal Cabinets & Countertops G 850 424-3940
Miramar Beach *(G-10569)*

Coastline Cbntry Cstm Mllwk LL F 239 208-2876
Fort Myers *(G-4215)*

Coffin Cabinetry & Trim Michae G 352 217-3729
Umatilla *(G-17645)*

Concept One Custom Cabine G 954 829-3505
Hollywood *(G-5555)*

Contemporary Cabinets Gulf CST G 941 758-3060
Sarasota *(G-15459)*

Contractors Cabinet Company G 786 492-7118
Margate *(G-8126)*

Coral Cabinet Inc G 305 484-8702
Miami *(G-8967)*

Corn-E-Lee Woodcrafts G 239 574-2414
Cape Coral *(G-1327)*

Country Cabinets G 850 547-5477
Bonifay *(G-770)*

Creations In Cabinetry Inc G 386 237-3082
Palm Coast *(G-13075)*

Creative Cabinet Concepts Inc E 239 939-1313
Fort Myers *(G-4220)*

Creative Concepts Orlando Inc E 407 260-1435
Longwood *(G-7883)*

Csi Home Decor Inc G 754 301-2147
Sunrise *(G-16311)*

Curry Cabinetry Inc E 813 321-3650
Tampa *(G-16748)*

Curtis K Foulks G 239 454-9663
Fort Myers *(G-4226)*

Custom Cab Doors & More Inc F 954 318-1881
Fort Lauderdale *(G-3747)*

Custom Cabinet Designs Inc G 561 781-3251
Jupiter *(G-6707)*

Custom Cabinets G 727 392-1676
Seminole *(G-15973)*

Custom Cabinets By Jensen LLC G 813 250-0286
Tampa *(G-16750)*

Custom Cabinets Design Inc G 561 210-3423
Deerfield Beach *(G-2698)*

Custom Cabinets Inc F 941 366-0428
Sarasota *(G-15647)*

Custom Cabinets SW Florida LLC G 239 415-3350
Fort Myers *(G-4227)*

Custom Carpentry Plus LLC F 305 972-3735
Cutler Bay *(G-2286)*

Custom Craft Laminates Inc E 813 877-7100
Tampa *(G-16751)*

Custom Crafters G 954 792-6119
Pompano Beach *(G-13985)*

Custom WD Designs of Pensacola F 850 476-9663
Pensacola *(G-13481)*

Custom Wood Products Inc G 904 737-6906
Jacksonville *(G-6019)*

D & G Custom Cabinetry Inc F 954 561-8822
Tamarac *(G-16528)*

D & G Millwork & Cabinetry LLC G 305 830-3000
Miami *(G-8989)*

D & N Cabinetry Inc F 863 471-1500
Sebring *(G-15917)*

D R Nickelson & Company Inc F 386 755-6565
Lake City *(G-7017)*

D T Woodcrafters Corp F 305 556-3771
Hialeah *(G-5105)*

Da Vinci Cabinetry LLC F 239 633-7957
Bonita Springs *(G-794)*

Dade Doors Inc F 305 556-8980
Hialeah *(G-5107)*

Dale Mabry Heating & Metal Co G 813 877-1574
Tampa *(G-16761)*

Darmar Cabinets Inc G 786 556-5784
Miami Lakes *(G-10294)*

Daystar International Inc G 813 281-0200
Tampa *(G-16767)*

Debruyne Enterprise Inc F 850 562-0491
Tallahassee *(G-16431)*

Deem Cabinets Inc F 352 795-1402
Crystal River *(G-2274)*

Deluxe Clsets Cabinets Stn LLC G 786 879-3371
Miami *(G-9014)*

Demoss Cabinetry LLC G 863 738-0080
Lakeland *(G-7308)*

Design By Yogi LLC G 954 428-9797
Deerfield Beach *(G-2704)*

Design Your Kit Clset More Inc G 786 227-6412
Miami *(G-9021)*

Designers Choice Cabinetry F 321 632-0772
Rockledge *(G-14700)*

Designers Choice Cabinetry Inc G 321 632-0772
Rockledge *(G-14701)*

Diamond Cabinets & Service G 321 689-8289
Orlando *(G-12091)*

Distinctive Cabinet Designs G 239 641-5165
Naples *(G-10730)*

District 95 Wood Working Inc G 888 400-3136
Pompano Beach *(G-13998)*

Dixie Workshop Inc F 352 629-4699
Ocala *(G-11369)*

Dl Cabinetry Orlando LLC G 504 669-7847
Orlando *(G-12101)*

Dma Cabinets Inc G 352 249-8147
Lecanto *(G-7751)*

Doctor Granite and Cabinets G 321 368-1779
West Melbourne *(G-17898)*

Doerrs Cstm Cabinets Trim LLC F 904 540-7024
Saint Augustine *(G-14828)*

Doerrs Custom Cabinets & Trim G 904 540-7024
Saint Augustine *(G-14829)*

Dons Cabinets and Woodworking F 727 863-3404
Hudson *(G-5771)*

Doormark Inc E 954 418-4700
Deerfield Beach *(G-2709)*

Dukemans Custom Wdwkg Inc G 904 355-5188
Jacksonville *(G-6044)*

Dynamic Cabinets Inc G 813 891-0667
Oldsmar *(G-11645)*

E & D Kitchen Cabinet Inc G 786 343-8558
Hialeah *(G-5128)*

East Coast Cabinet Co G 321 392-4686
Rockledge *(G-14705)*

East Coast Fix & Mllwk Co Inc G 904 733-9711
Jacksonville *(G-6059)*

Eastburn Woodworks Inc F 850 456-8090
Pensacola *(G-13492)*

EC Cabinets Inc G 305 887-2091
Hialeah *(G-5132)*

Eco Woodwork and Design Inc G 954 326-8806
Oakland Park *(G-11263)*

Edymar Design Carpentry LLC F 954 822-0687
Hialeah *(G-5137)*

Elite Cabinet Coatings G 352 795-2655
Crystal River *(G-2275)*

Elite Cabinetry Inc G 239 262-1144
Naples *(G-10736)*

Emerald Coast Cabinets Inc F 850 267-2290
Santa Rosa Beach *(G-15424)*

Empire Stone and Cabinets E 305 885-7092
Hialeah *(G-5144)*

Esquadro Inc G 754 367-3098
Deerfield Beach *(G-2718)*

Eternity Cabinets F 239 482-7172
Fort Myers *(G-4248)*

Eurocraft Cabinets Inc G 561 948-3034
Boca Raton *(G-508)*

European Cabinets & Design LLC G 561 684-1440
West Palm Beach *(G-17989)*

European Custom Casework Inc G 401 356-0400
Stuart *(G-16146)*

Evans Custom Cabinetry LLC G 904 829-1973
Saint Augustine *(G-14831)*

Everest Cabinets Inc G 407 790-7819
Orlando *(G-12139)*

Excell Cabinet Corp G 561 628-9059
West Palm Beach *(G-17992)*

F & S Mill Works G 407 349-9948
Geneva *(G-4788)*

Faba Cabinets & Such LLC G 813 871-1529
Tampa *(G-16825)*

Factory Direct Cab Refacing G 954 445-6635
Hollywood *(G-5574)*

Falfas Cabinet & Stone LLC F 941 960-2065
Sarasota *(G-15670)*

Fgt Cabinetry LLC G 321 800-2036
Orlando *(G-12149)*

Final Touch Molding Cabinetry G 239 948-7856
Bonita Springs *(G-797)*

Final Tuch Mlding Cbinetry Inc G 239 298-0980
Bonita Springs *(G-798)*

Fine Archtctral Mllwk Shutters F 954 491-2055
Fort Lauderdale *(G-3816)*

Fine Wood Design Inc G 727 531-8000
Largo *(G-7585)*

Finecraft Custom Cabinetry G 941 378-1901
Sarasota *(G-15673)*

Fisher Cabinet Company LLC E 850 944-4171
Pensacola *(G-13503)*

FL Central Cnstr & Rmdlg G 863 701-3548
Lakeland *(G-7326)*

Florida Custom Cabinets Inc G 850 769-4781
Panama City *(G-13263)*

Florida Designer Cabinets Inc F 352 793-8555
Sumterville *(G-16263)*

Florida Kit Cbnets Amercn Corp G 305 828-2830
Hialeah *(G-5158)*

Florida Plywoods Inc D 850 948-2211
Greenville *(G-4854)*

Florida West Poggenpohl G 239 948-9005
Estero *(G-3544)*

Furniture Concepts 2000 Inc G 954 946-0310
Pompano Beach *(G-14036)*

Furnival Cabinetry LLC G 321 638-1223
Cocoa *(G-1931)*

Furnival Construction LLC F 321 638-1223
Cocoa *(G-1932)*

G K Woodworks G 941 232-3910
Sarasota *(G-15687)*

Garcia Custom Cabinetry G 864 420-3882
Miami *(G-9188)*

Gb Cabinets Incorporated G 863 446-0676
Sebring *(G-15925)*

Gc Cabinet Express LLC F 561 662-0369
Lake Park *(G-7128)*

Gemstone Cabinetry LLC G 941 426-5656
North Port *(G-11194)*

General Cabinets Inc E 727 863-3404
Port Richey *(G-14361)*

George Gillespie LLC G 561 744-6191
West Palm Beach *(G-18015)*

Gilmans Custom Furn & Cabinets F 352 746-3532
Lecanto *(G-7752)*

Glenny Stone Works Inc G 786 502-3918
Doral *(G-3233)*

Global Cabinet Distributors G 305 625-9814
Miami Lakes *(G-10305)*

Gontech Custom Wood Corp G 305 323-0765
Miami *(G-9226)*

Great American Imports Llc G 786 524-4120
Miami *(G-9238)*

Gulf Coast Cabinetry Inc G 850 769-3799
Panama City Beach *(G-13332)*

Gulf Coast Cabinets Carpentry G 239 222-2994
Fort Myers *(G-4274)*

Gulf Contours Inc G 941 639-3933
Punta Gorda *(G-14506)*

Hammond Kitchens & Bath LLC F 321 768-9549
Melbourne *(G-8433)*

Hand Carved Creations G 561 893-0292
Boca Raton *(G-536)*

Hector & Hector Inc F 305 629-8864
Miami *(G-9270)*

Heirloom Design Group LLC G 407 735-2224
Apopka *(G-139)*

Heller Cabinetry Inc F 321 729-9690
Melbourne *(G-8435)*

Herman Cabinets Inc G 727 459-6730
Largo *(G-7604)*

Highland Cabinet Inc G 863 385-4396
Sebring *(G-15926)*

HIS Cabinetry Inc D 727 527-7262
Pinellas Park *(G-13693)*

Home Design Group Corp G 305 888-5836
Hialeah *(G-5189)*

Home Pride Cabinets Inc F 813 887-3782
Tampa *(G-16920)*

Home Works Bay County Inc G 850 215-7880
Panama City *(G-13273)*

House of Cabinets Ltd Inc G 352 795-5300
Crystal River *(G-2277)*

Hudson Cabinets & Millwork LLC F 239 218-0451
Fort Myers *(G-4284)*

Imperial Kitchens Inc G 239 208-9359
Fort Myers *(G-4289)*

Infinite Ret Design & Mfg Corp F 305 967-8339
Miami *(G-9312)*

Innovtive Cabinets Closets Inc F 904 475-2336
Jacksonville *(G-6200)*

Integral WD Cstm Cabinetry LLC F 561 361-5111
Boca Raton *(G-546)*

Interlachen Cabinets Inc G 352 481-6078
Hawthorne *(G-5008)*

Interni Cucine LLC G 954 486-7000
Fort Lauderdale *(G-3882)*

Italian Cabinetry Inc F 786 534-2742
Miami *(G-9343)*

J & A Custom Cabinetry Inc G 786 255-4181
Homestead *(G-5720)*

J & D Oldja LLC F 727 526-3240
Saint Petersburg *(G-15087)*

J & E Custom Cabinets Inc F 727 868-2820
Port Richey *(G-14365)*

J & J Custom Mica Inc	F	239 433-2828	
Fort Myers (G-4293)			
J & J Door Manufacturing Inc	E	850 769-2554	
Panama City (G-13277)			
J & S Cypress Inc	F	352 383-3864	
Sorrento (G-16010)			
J & V Cabinets & More Inc	G	352 390-6378	
Ocala (G-11413)			
J J Cabinets Appliances	G	786 573-0300	
Miami (G-9351)			
J M Interiors Inc	G	305 891-6121	
North Miami (G-11107)			
Jaiba Cabinets Inc	G	305 364-3646	
Hialeah (G-5201)			
Jam Cabinets & Investments LLC	F	305 823-9020	
Hialeah (G-5202)			
James Simmons Cabinets Inc	G	407 468-1802	
Orlando (G-12266)			
Jamestown Kitchens Inc	G	941 359-1166	
Sarasota (G-15712)			
Jay Robinson Cabinet Sales Inc	G	954 298-3009	
Oakland Park (G-11274)			
JC Best Finish Cabinet Inc	G	786 216-5571	
Miami (G-9358)			
Jcs Limited Corporation	G	954 822-2887	
Tamarac (G-16534)			
Jeffrey Bowden Cabinets Llc	G	727 992-9187	
New Port Richey (G-10970)			
Jesus Cabinets Corp	G	786 285-1088	
Hialeah (G-5205)			
Jfaure LLC	F	239 631-5324	
Naples (G-10790)			
Jim Rinaldos Cabinetry Inc	F	813 788-2715	
Dade City (G-2320)			
JM Cabinets Incorp	G	863 699-2888	
Lake Placid (G-7143)			
Juan Rodriguez Cabinetry Corp	G	305 467-3878	
Hialeah (G-5209)			
JV Installations Corp	G	407 849-0262	
Orlando (G-12281)			
K & M Custom Cabinetry Inc	G	727 791-3993	
Safety Harbor (G-14789)			
K-Kraft Cabinets Inc	G	321 632-8800	
Rockledge (G-14722)			
K-Kraft Industries Inc	F	321 632-8800	
Rockledge (G-14723)			
Kbf Design Gallery Inc	G	407 830-7703	
Maitland (G-8063)			
Kc & B Custom Inc	G	561 276-1887	
Delray Beach (G-2981)			
Kea Kitchen Cabinetry Inc	F	954 639-6233	
Boca Raton (G-566)			
Kings & Queens Cabinets	G	863 646-6972	
Lakeland (G-7369)			
Kitchen and Bath Universe Inc	F	813 887-5658	
Tampa (G-16990)			
Kitchen Classics LLC	G	941 629-6990	
Punta Gorda (G-14511)			
Kitchen USA Inc	G	904 714-1970	
Jacksonville (G-6244)			
Kitchens By US	G	407 745-4923	
Orlando (G-12289)			
Kitchens Crafters Inc	G	407 788-0560	
Longwood (G-7911)			
Kitchens Rta LLC	G	407 969-0902	
Orlando (G-12290)			
Knothole Creations Inc	G	727 561-9107	
Clearwater (G-1664)			
KR Ward Inc	G	863 325-9070	
Winter Haven (G-18448)			
Lakeshore Custom Wood Pdts Inc	G	813 623-2790	
Tampa (G-16998)			
Larry Woleys Trim Cabinets LLC	G	850 526-3974	
Marianna (G-8168)			
Larsen Cabinetmaker Co	G	305 252-1212	
Miami (G-9426)			
Leiton Decor & Design	G	786 286-4776	
Miami (G-9450)			
Londos Fine Cabinetry LLC	G	727 544-2929	
Seminole (G-15980)			
Luxurable Kitchen & Bath Llc	G	727 286-8927	
Largo (G-7636)			
Lyndan Inc	E	813 977-6683	
Tampa (G-17028)			
M & E Kitchen Cabinets Inc	G	786 346-9987	
Hialeah (G-5231)			
M Wegener Inc	G	561 848-2408	
Palm Springs (G-13145)			
M X Corporation	G	305 597-9881	
Pembroke Pines (G-13401)			
M&L Cabinets Inc	G	941 761-8100	
Bradenton (G-1009)			
MAc Entps Tampa Bay Inc	G	813 363-2601	
New Port Richey (G-10973)			
Madewell Kitchens Inc	E	727 856-1014	
Port Richey (G-14368)			
Maggac Corporation	G	561 439-2707	
Lake Worth (G-7215)			
Magnolia Custom Cabinetry LLC	F	941 906-8744	
Sarasota (G-15733)			
Mahan Cabinets	G	305 255-3325	
Cutler Bay (G-2295)			
Majestic Woodworks	G	352 429-2520	
Groveland (G-4865)			
Manatee Cabinets Inc	G	941 792-8656	
Bradenton (G-1010)			
Marcos Professional Cabinets C	G	305 962-4378	
Hialeah (G-5240)			
Master Cabinet Maker Inc	G	941 723-0278	
Palmetto (G-13180)			
Master Kitchen Cabinets	G	239 225-9668	
Fort Myers (G-4318)			
Master-Kraft Cabinetry	G	863 661-2083	
Auburndale (G-240)			
McCallum Cabinets Inc	F	352 372-2344	
Gainesville (G-4725)			
Metro Door Brickell LLC	G	786 326-4748	
Miami (G-9541)			
Mg Cabinet Installers LLC	G	561 530-7961	
Palm Springs (G-13147)			
Miacucina LLC	G	305 792-9494	
Miami (G-9543)			
Miacucina LLC	F	305 444-7383	
Coral Gables (G-2086)			
Mica Craft & Design Inc	F	561 863-5354	
West Palm Beach (G-18077)			
Mica Pdts & WD Boca Raton Inc	E	561 395-4686	
Boca Raton (G-596)			
Micaworks Cabinetry Inc	G	352 336-1707	
Gainesville (G-4730)			
Michigan Avenue Bridge Inc	F	352 236-4044	
Ocala (G-11444)			
Midnite Son II of Sarasota	G	941 377-6029	
Sarasota (G-15746)			
Mike Pulver LLC	G	386 747-8951	
Deland (G-2885)			
Mister Cabinet Deluxe Inc	F	305 205-3601	
Hialeah (G-5263)			
MJM Cabinet Inc	G	786 953-5000	
Hialeah (G-5264)			
Mobius Business Group Inc	F	239 274-8900	
Fort Myers (G-4327)			
Moose Tracts Inc	G	407 491-1412	
Orlando (G-12391)			
Moralmar Kitchen Cabinets	E	305 819-8402	
Hialeah (G-5266)			
Morning Star of Sarasota Inc	G	941 371-0392	
Sarasota (G-15751)			
Morris Mica Cabinets Inc	G	954 979-6838	
Pompano Beach (G-14105)			
Myers Cabinetry LLC	G	850 872-1794	
Panama City (G-13288)			
Myers Cstm Cabinets Furn Corp	G	561 602-0755	
Boynton Beach (G-892)			
Nace Aircraft Cabinetry Inc	G	754 366-5799	
Fort Lauderdale (G-3950)			
National Stoneworks LLC	E	954 349-1609	
Weston (G-18271)			
Nautilus Cabinetry Inc	G	239 598-1011	
Naples (G-10835)			
Navigtor Kitchens Cabinets Inc	G	941 776-9482	
Parrish (G-13360)			
Neocabinet Inc	G	310 927-1008	
Hollywood (G-5632)			
Nfjb Inc	E	954 771-1100	
Fort Lauderdale (G-3962)			
Nickols Cbinetry Woodworks Inc	G	941 485-7894	
Venice (G-17707)			
Nosta Inc	G	305 634-1435	
Miami (G-9630)			
Nuform Cabinetry	G	954 532-2746	
Pompano Beach (G-14109)			
Ocean Kitchen Cabinets	G	352 745-7110	
Gainesville (G-4741)			
Oldja Enterprises Inc	G	727 526-3240	
Saint Petersburg (G-15146)			
Oliveira Services Corp	G	772 834-4803	
Port Saint Lucie (G-14430)			
Oly Custom Cabinets Miami Inc	G	305 216-3947	
Miami (G-9645)			
Omax Home Inc	F	239 980-2755	
Fort Myers (G-4350)			
Omt Inc	G	772 287-3762	
Stuart (G-16192)			
Orka Cabinets Inc	G	954 907-2456	
Coral Springs (G-2200)			
Ortega Custom Cabinets Inc	G	813 403-7101	
Tampa (G-17129)			
Oxley Cabinet Warehouse Inc	G	786 377-4281	
Miami (G-9672)			
Packard & Company Inc	G	941 451-8201	
Venice (G-17710)			
Palm Beach Trim Inc	G	561 588-8746	
Davie (G-2452)			
Peace Millwork Co Inc	E	305 573-6222	
Miami (G-9699)			
Peartree Cabinets & Design LLC	G	941 377-7655	
Sarasota (G-15778)			
Pedano Custom Furniture Inc	G	904 704-9329	
Jacksonville (G-6361)			
PGT American Inc	G	813 962-4400	
Tampa (G-17160)			
Pinellas Custom Cabinets Inc	G	727 864-4263	
Largo (G-7659)			
Pinnacle Cabinets Closets LLC	G	850 477-5402	
Pensacola (G-13575)			
Pinnacle Cbinets By Design Inc	G	239 440-2950	
Fort Myers (G-4362)			
Plastic and Products Mktg LLC	F	352 867-8078	
Ocala (G-11468)			
PLC Cabinets Installed Ltd	G	239 641-7565	
Naples (G-10862)			
Pohl Custom Cabinetry Inc	G	239 643-5661	
Naples (G-10864)			
Porath Fine Cabinetry Inc	F	561 616-9400	
West Palm Beach (G-18124)			
Precision Cabinetry LLC	G	386 218-3340	
Deltona (G-3051)			
Premier Cabinets LLC	G	407 760-9060	
Oviedo (G-12844)			
Premier Cabinets & Trim LLC	F	321 345-4923	
Palm Bay (G-12912)			
Pro Kitchen Cabinets Corp	G	786 768-4291	
Cutler Bay (G-2300)			
Procraft Cabinetry Florida LLC	G	754 212-2277	
Deerfield Beach (G-2791)			
Professional Kitchen Cabinets	G	305 888-5660	
Hialeah (G-5311)			
Progressive Cabinetry	G	941 866-6975	
Bradenton (G-1033)			
Project Pros Woodworking Inc	G	239 454-6800	
Fort Myers (G-4369)			
Prolific Cabinetry & More Inc	G	904 448-6575	
Jacksonville (G-6395)			
PS Cabinet Works Inc	G	239 850-2162	
Lehigh Acres (G-7823)			
Quality Cabinets & Counters	F	239 948-5364	
Fort Myers (G-4373)			
Quality Creations Inc	G	727 571-4332	
Clearwater (G-1761)			
Quality Custom Cabinet Design	G	352 728-4292	
Leesburg (G-7790)			
Quality Custom Cabinets LLC	E	201 873-6607	
Melbourne (G-8507)			
R & J Custom Cabinets Inc	G	813 871-5779	
Tampa (G-17205)			
R & R Designer Cabinets Inc	G	954 735-6435	
Oakland Park (G-11290)			
R & R Doors Corp	G	305 982-8106	
Hialeah (G-5324)			
Rainbow Cabinets Inc	F	352 236-4044	
Ocala (G-11477)			
RB Cabinetry LLC	E	850 685-5316	
Destin (G-3077)			
RCS Wood Crafters LLC	G	305 836-0120	
Hialeah (G-5327)			
Regal Cabinets Inc	F	407 678-1003	
Winter Park (G-18532)			
Regency Custom Cabinets Inc	F	239 332-7977	
Fort Myers (G-4377)			
Regent Cabinetry and More Inc	G	239 693-2207	
Fort Myers (G-4378)			
Reliable Cabinet Designs	F	941 473-3403	
Englewood (G-3523)			
Reso Inc	G	561 328-8539	
Riviera Beach (G-14668)			
Reyes Cabinets Installation	G	305 216-1683	
Miami (G-9800)			
Rich Maid Cabinets Inc	F	727 572-4857	
Clearwater (G-1766)			

Richard Bryan Ingram LLC	G	407 677-7779	
Orlando (G-12553)			
Richardsons Cabinet Works	G	850 832-8298	
Panama City (G-13302)			
Rider Kitchen Cabinets Inc	E	786 502-6663	
Miami Gardens (G-10272)			
Ritter Kit Bath & Closet LLC	G	239 272-4551	
Naples (G-10877)			
Rivercity Custom Cabinetry Inc	F	904 247-0807	
Jacksonville (G-6427)			
Rolu Woodcraft Inc	F	305 685-0914	
Hialeah (G-5336)			
Rt22 Creations Inc	G	954 254-8258	
Fort Lauderdale (G-4032)			
Rta Cabinets & More LLC	G	321 288-3068	
Indian Harbour Beach (G-5807)			
Rubens Custom Cabinets Inc	G	813 510-8397	
Tampa (G-17237)			
S M I Cabinetry Inc	E	407 841-0292	
Orlando (G-12565)			
Sarasota Cabinetry Inc	F	941 351-5588	
Sarasota (G-15811)			
Sarasota Kitchens Closets Inc	G	941 722-7505	
Bradenton (G-1041)			
Sasquatch Cabinet Company	G	941 365-4950	
Lakewood Ranch (G-7486)			
Sbr Custom Cabinets Inc	G	407 765-8134	
Orlando (G-12576)			
SC Cabinet LLC	G	561 429-5369	
Riviera Beach (G-14673)			
Sevilla Cabinets Inc	F	305 888-2174	
Hialeah (G-5346)			
Showcase Marble Inc	E	386 253-6646	
Daytona Beach (G-2598)			
Simply Cabinets LLC	F	850 541-3712	
Panama City Beach (G-13339)			
Simply Closets & Cabinets	G	239 994-4264	
Alva (G-84)			
Smokey Mountain Cabinets Inc	F	386 325-1677	
Palatka (G-12881)			
Snows Custom Furniture Inc	G	772 794-4430	
Vero Beach (G-17800)			
Sobrino Custom Cabinets Inc	G	786 564-2699	
Hialeah (G-5352)			
Southeast Woodcrafters Inc	F	561 392-2929	
Boca Raton (G-687)			
Southernstone Cabinets Inc	F	727 538-0123	
Clearwater (G-1791)			
Spacemakers Closets SW Fla Inc	F	239 598-0222	
Naples (G-10901)			
Sparks Cabinetry	G	954 367-2750	
Hollywood (G-5663)			
Speed Custom Cabinet Corp	G	407 953-1479	
Orlando (G-12616)			
Spruce Creek Cabinetry Inc	E	386 756-0041	
Port Orange (G-14349)			
St Marys Cabinetry Inc	G	239 331-1030	
Naples (G-10905)			
STA Cabinet Depot	G	719 502-5454	
Saint Augustine (G-14902)			
Statewide Cstm Cbinets Fla Inc	G	813 788-3856	
Zephyrhills (G-18631)			
Steve Unser Cabinetry Inc	F	239 631-2951	
Naples (G-10906)			
Studio Becker Florida LLC	G	305 514-0400	
Coral Gables (G-2112)			
Studio Luxe Cstm Cabinetry LLC	G	941 371-4010	
Sarasota (G-15842)			
Stylecraft Cabinets Mfg Inc	G	941 474-4824	
Englewood (G-3525)			
Sungraf Inc	G	954 456-8500	
Hallandale Beach (G-4976)			
Sunshine Alance Cabinets Mllwk	F	954 621-7444	
Deerfield Beach (G-2817)			
Superior Kitchens Inc	F	772 286-6801	
Stuart (G-16235)			
T & Y Cabinets Inc	G	305 512-0802	
Hialeah (G-5377)			
Tampa Bay Cabinets Inc	G	813 781-9468	
Apollo Beach (G-96)			
Techno Cabinets Inc	G	305 910-9929	
Doral (G-3393)			
Thomas C Gibbs Custom Cabinets	G	239 872-6279	
Fort Myers (G-4420)			
Thomas Rley Artisans Guild Inc	E	239 591-3203	
Naples (G-10925)			
Those Cabinet Guys Inc	G	703 927-2460	
Palm Coast (G-13090)			
Tiger Custom Cabinets Inc	G	813 748-7286	
Tampa (G-17352)			

TJ Cabinetry Inc	F	407 886-8294	
Orlando (G-12661)			
Tk Cabinets	G	386 325-6906	
Palatka (G-12884)			
Tm Cabinetry LLC	G	954 639-1725	
Hallandale Beach (G-4980)			
TNT Custom Cabinetry Inc	G	561 662-0964	
West Palm Beach (G-18183)			
Top Choice Cabinets and Tops	G	786 389-4590	
Miami (G-10023)			
Top Kitchen Cabinets	G	305 392-9938	
Medley (G-8336)			
Tops Kitchen Cabinet LLC	F	954 933-9988	
Pompano Beach (G-14215)			
Tradewind Custom Cabinetry LLC	G	239 257-3295	
Cape Coral (G-1400)			
Trim-Pak Corporation	E	407 851-8900	
Orlando (G-12673)			
Tws Cabinets LLC	F	863 614-4693	
Lakeland (G-7467)			
U C Cabinet Inc	G	407 322-0968	
Sanford (G-15401)			
Um Kitchen Cabinets Inc	G	772 224-5445	
Port Saint Lucie (G-14460)			
Underwood Butcher Block Co Inc	F	904 338-2348	
Jacksonville (G-6574)			
Unique Custom Cabinet Inc	F	786 247-4196	
Miami (G-10062)			
United Cabinets Corp	G	305 887-5050	
Hialeah (G-5393)			
Universal Kit Cabinets Closets	G	305 406-9096	
Kissimmee (G-6969)			
Universal Wood Design	F	772 569-5389	
Vero Beach (G-17812)			
Uptown Cstm Cabinets of Naples	G	239 825-8432	
Naples (G-10931)			
Ur Cabinets	G	813 434-6454	
Tampa (G-17395)			
V G Carpentry LLC	G	786 531-7824	
Hialeah (G-5404)			
Vanbert Corporation	G	561 945-5856	
Delray Beach (G-3031)			
Velez Custom Cabinetry Corp	G	772 418-9565	
Port Saint Lucie (G-14462)			
Veneta Cucine Inc	G	305 949-5223	
North Miami Beach (G-11167)			
Venice Custom Cabinets Inc	G	941 488-5000	
Nokomis (G-11056)			
Victory Custom Cabinetry	G	727 937-2284	
Holiday (G-5506)			
Viking Woodworking	G	352 237-5050	
Ocala (G-11509)			
W E W Enterprises Inc	F	941 751-6610	
Bradenton (G-1074)			
Walker Wood Products Inc	G	904 448-5202	
Jacksonville (G-6597)			
We RE Organized	G	407 323-5133	
Sanford (G-15409)			
Welshman Investment Corp	G	407 933-4444	
Kissimmee (G-6972)			
Wilson Custom Cabinets	G	954 296-1095	
Fort Lauderdale (G-4134)			
Windward Associates Corp	F	954 336-8085	
Dania (G-2346)			
Wood Aspects	G	321 800-8875	
Deland (G-2921)			
Wood Scapes Interiors	G	386 454-1540	
High Springs (G-5457)			
Wood U Envision	F	561 601-1973	
West Palm Beach (G-18208)			
Wood Zone Inc	G	305 971-5550	
Miami (G-10140)			
Woods Distinctive Designs Inc	F	941 698-7535	
Port Charlotte (G-14325)			
Woodtech Global Inc	F	941 371-0392	
Bradenton (G-1079)			
Woodwards Cabinets Inc	G	850 835-0071	
Freeport (G-4632)			
Woodworkers Cabinet Naples Inc	G	239 593-1718	
Naples (G-10943)			
Woodworks Cabinetry Inc	G	904 924-5300	
Jacksonville (G-6618)			
Woodworks Kit & Bath Designs	F	813 926-0570	
Odessa (G-11592)			
Woodworkx Unlimited Inc	G	772 882-4197	
Fort Pierce (G-4556)			
Y F Leung Inc	G	305 651-6851	
North Miami Beach (G-11172)			
Your Cabinet Source Inc	G	352 728-3806	
Leesburg (G-7802)			

Your Dreams Cabinets Corp	G	305 305-3729	
Hialeah (G-5427)			
Yp General Work & Cabinets	G	786 317-0973	
Miami (G-10154)			
Zbc Cabinetry	G	239 332-2940	
Fort Myers (G-4452)			
Zk Cabinets Inc	G	407 421-7307	
Orlando (G-12735)			

CABINETS: Office, Wood

Braden Kitchens Inc	E	321 636-4700	
Cocoa (G-1907)			
Creative Wdwkg Concepts Inc	E	727 937-4165	
Tarpon Springs (G-17462)			
District 95 Wood Working Inc	G	888 400-3136	
Pompano Beach (G-13998)			
F & S Cabinets Inc	E	386 822-9525	
Deland (G-2869)			
Furniture Design of Centl Fla	F	407 330-4430	
Sanford (G-15322)			
McCabinet Inc	G	727 608-5929	
Largo (G-7640)			
Star Quality Inc	G	813 875-9955	
Tampa (G-17300)			

CABINETS: Show, Display, Etc, Wood, Exc Refrigerated

Corry Cabinet Company Inc	E	850 539-6455	
Havana (G-4999)			
Creative Cabinet Concepts Inc	E	239 939-1313	
Fort Myers (G-4220)			
Excalibur Cabinetry LLC	E	248 697-6158	
Eustis (G-3557)			
Fisher Cabinet Company LLC	E	850 944-4171	
Pensacola (G-13503)			
Kitchen Dsgns By Joan E Rbbins	G	321 727-0012	
Melbourne (G-8450)			
Lyndan Inc	E	813 977-6683	
Tampa (G-17028)			
Mobius Business Group Inc	F	239 274-8900	
Fort Myers (G-4327)			
Mr Mica Wood Inc	F	561 278-5821	
Delray Beach (G-2990)			
New River Cabinet & Fix Inc	E	954 938-9200	
Fort Lauderdale (G-3959)			
Pro Tech Custom Cabinet	F	727 863-5143	
Port Richey (G-14372)			
S M I Cabinetry Inc	E	407 841-0292	
Orlando (G-12565)			
Spruce Creek Cabinetry Inc	E	386 756-0041	
Port Orange (G-14349)			
Still Water Industries Inc	G	561 845-6033	
West Palm Beach (G-18166)			
Trasport John	G	321 452-6789	
Merritt Island (G-8600)			

CABLE TELEVISION PRDTS

Componexx Corp	G	954 236-6569	
Sunrise (G-16306)			
NC IV Inc	F	941 378-9133	
Sarasota (G-15759)			
Quality Cable Contractors Inc	E	407 246-0606	
Orlando (G-12520)			
Ravic Technologies LLC	G	954 237-3241	
Medley (G-8308)			

CABLE: Fiber

American Wire Group LLC	F	954 455-3050	
Aventura (G-252)			
Applied Fiber Holdings LLC	E	850 539-7720	
Havana (G-4990)			
Applied Fiber Mfg LLC	E	850 539-7720	
Havana (G-4991)			
Chiptech Inc	F	954 454-3554	
Hallandale (G-4921)			
Conexus Technologies Inc	F	513 779-5448	
Sarasota (G-15640)			
Gulf Cable LLC	C	201 720-2417	
Milton (G-10428)			
Meridian Cable LLC	F	904 770-4687	
Saint Augustine (G-14858)			
Miami Cordage LLC	E	305 636-3000	
Miami (G-9549)			
Newlink Cabling Systems Inc	F	305 477-8063	
Medley (G-8289)			

PRODUCT

CABLE: Fiber Optic

AGS Enterprises Inc ....G....... 305 716-7660
Doral (G-3100)

Amphenol Custom Cable Inc ....C....... 813 623-2232
Tampa (G-16594)

Amphenol Custom Cable Inc ....E....... 407 393-3886
Orlando (G-11909)

Commski LLC ....G....... 813 501-0111
Spring Hill (G-16068)

Gulf Photonics Inc ....G....... 813 855-6618
Oldsmar (G-11656)

Managed Data Assoc Inc ....G....... 386 449-8419
Palm Coast (G-13082)

Newlink Cabling Systems Inc ....F....... 305 477-8063
Medley (G-8289)

Oceaneering International Inc ....C....... 985 329-3282
Panama City (G-13291)

CABLE: Ropes & Fiber

Bubba Rope LLC ....F....... 877 499-8494
Altamonte Springs (G-35)

Consolidated Cordage Corp ....F....... 561 347-7247
Stuart (G-16133)

Rope Works Inc ....F....... 954 525-6575
Fort Lauderdale (G-4024)

CABLE: Steel, Insulated Or Armored

Orbital Corporation of Tampa ....G....... 813 782-7300
Zephyrhills (G-18622)

Suncoast Post-Tension Ltd ....E....... 305 592-5075
Miami (G-9966)

CAFETERIAS

Tulipan Bakery Inc ....G....... 561 832-6107
West Palm Beach (G-18188)

CAGES: Wire

Animal Air Service Inc ....E....... 305 218-1759
Doral (G-3116)

CALCULATING & ACCOUNTING EQPT

Albert J Angel.....................G....... 954 718-3000
Miami (G-8681)

Blue Eagle Alliance Inc ....G....... 904 322-8067
Jacksonville (G-5938)

General Business Services ....G....... 904 260-1099
Jacksonville (G-6137)

R S S Partners Inc ....F....... 904 241-6144
Jacksonville Beach (G-6642)

Singletons AV Solutions Inc ....G....... 407 404-1506
Orlando (G-12605)

Szabo Pos Displays Inc ....G....... 941 778-0192
Bradenton (G-1057)

CALIBRATING SVCS, NEC

Aircon Fleet Management Corp ....E....... 305 234-8174
Miami (G-8674)

CAMERA & PHOTOGRAPHIC SPLYS STORES

Sunnypics LLC.....................G....... 407 992-6210
Orlando (G-12633)

CAMERA & PHOTOGRAPHIC SPLYS STORES: Cameras

Lester A Dine Inc ....G....... 561 624-3009
Palm Beach Gardens (G-12984)

CAMERAS & RELATED EQPT: Photographic

Ar2 Products LLC ....G....... 800 667-1263
Saint Johns (G-14944)

Drs Laurel Technologies ....E....... 727 541-6681
Largo (G-7574)

Eyeson Dgtal Srvllnce MGT Syst.........G....... 305 808-3344
Miami (G-9125)

Imperx Inc ....E....... 561 989-0006
Boca Raton (G-542)

Incity Security Inc ....F....... 561 306-9228
West Palm Beach (G-18031)

Westech Development Group Inc..........G....... 954 505-5090
Pompano Beach (G-14241)

Zd Realty LLC ....F....... 866 672-1212
Saint Petersburg (G-15244)

CAN LIDS & ENDS

Florida Can Manufacturing LLC ....G....... 863 356-5260
Winter Haven (G-18437)

CANDLE SHOPS

Love Is In The Air Corp................G....... 305 828-8181
Hialeah (G-5227)

Scentstional Soaps Candles Inc..........F....... 941 485-1443
Venice (G-17714)

CANDLES

2 Guys Company ....G....... 786 970-9275
Miami (G-8608)

Black Bee Aromatherapy LLC ....G....... 866 399-4233
Orlando (G-11955)

Desirous Candles Inc ....G....... 347 622-6987
Pembroke Pines (G-13384)

Eyes Med Billing & Consulting ....G....... 618 308-7016
Orange Park (G-11826)

Imagination Enterprises LLC ....F....... 504 289-9691
Orlando (G-12236)

Kaluz LLC ....E....... 786 991-2260
Miami (G-9383)

Kookie Kllection Kosmetics LLC..........F....... 888 811-1657
Weston (G-18262)

Lemon Grass Industries Inc ....G....... 954 418-6110
Parkland (G-13349)

Reflective Moments LLC ....G....... 561 716-2106
Boca Raton (G-651)

Scents of Nature Enterprises............E....... 305 547-2334
Miami Lakes (G-10351)

Scentsability Candles ....G....... 954 234-4405
Coral Springs (G-2210)

Scentstional Soaps Candles Inc..........F....... 941 485-1443
Venice (G-17714)

Vision Candles Inc ....G....... 305 836-8650
Miami (G-10115)

Wicks Unlimited Inc ....G....... 631 472-2010
Pompano Beach (G-14242)

CANDLES: Wholesalers

Kaluz LLC ....E....... 786 991-2260
Miami (G-9383)

Scentstional Soaps Candles Inc..........F....... 941 485-1443
Venice (G-17714)

CANDY & CONFECTIONS: Cake Ornaments

Signature Brands LLC ....C....... 352 622-3134
Ocala (G-11491)

Signature Brands LLC ....F....... 352 622-3134
Ocala (G-11493)

CANDY & CONFECTIONS: Candy Bars, Including Chocolate Covered

Cozy Bar ....G....... 305 532-2699
Miami Beach (G-10181)

Louis Sherry Company LLC..............G....... 904 482-1900
Jacksonville (G-6264)

Retreat ....G....... 813 254-2014
Tampa (G-17218)

CANDY & CONFECTIONS: Chocolate Candy, Exc Solid Chocolate

Bbx Sweet Holdings LLC ....F....... 954 940-4000
Fort Lauderdale (G-3679)

Sweet Tooth Inc....................G....... 305 682-1400
North Miami Beach (G-11164)

CANDY & CONFECTIONS: Fruit & Fruit Peel

Kizable LLC ....G....... 727 600-3469
Fort Lauderdale (G-3907)

CANDY & CONFECTIONS: Nuts, Candy Covered

Barnard Nut Company Inc...............D....... 305 836-9999
Miami (G-8799)

CANDY & CONFECTIONS: Popcorn Balls/Other Trtd Popcorn Prdts

Brownbag Popcorn Company LLC ....G....... 561 212-5664
Boca Raton (G-451)

CANDY, NUT & CONFECTIONERY STORE: Popcorn, Incl Caramel Corn

Popcorn Junkie LLC ....G....... 407 634-0042
Orlando (G-12494)

CANDY, NUT & CONFECTIONERY STORES: Candy

Bbx Sweet Holdings LLC ....F....... 954 940-4000
Fort Lauderdale (G-3679)

Sweet Tooth Inc....................G....... 305 682-1400
North Miami Beach (G-11164)

CANDY, NUT & CONFECTIONERY STORES: Produced For Direct Sale

Hoffman Commercial Group Inc ....E....... 561 967-2213
Orlando (G-12221)

CANDY: Chocolate From Cacao Beans

Behrs Chocolates By Design ....G....... 407 648-2020
Orlando (G-11944)

Hoffman Commercial Group Inc ....E....... 561 967-2213
Orlando (G-12221)

P B C Central ....G....... 407 648-2020
Orlando (G-12460)

CANDY: Hard

Candies and Beyond Inc ....G....... 954 828-2255
Miami Lakes (G-10290)

Lollipop Children Center Inc ....G....... 386 755-3953
Lake City (G-7030)

Lollipops and Gumdrops Inc ....G....... 954 389-7032
Weston (G-18264)

CANES & TRIMMINGS, EXC PRECIOUS METAL

Fashionable Canes ....F....... 727 547-8866
Largo (G-7580)

CANNED SPECIALTIES

Farm Cut LLC ....C....... 813 754-3321
Plant City (G-13765)

Kraft Heinz Foods Company ....G....... 407 786-8157
Longwood (G-7912)

Olas Foods Specialty Mkt Inc ....F....... 813 447-5127
Kenneth City (G-6832)

RL Schreiber Inc ....D....... 954 972-7102
Fort Lauderdale (G-4021)

Wittman Pharma Inc ....E....... 352 799-9813
Brooksville (G-1222)

CANOPIES: Sheet Metal

Consolidated Metal Products ....G....... 850 576-2167
Tallahassee (G-16427)

Sfa Systems Inc ....E....... 561 585-5927
Lake Worth (G-7232)

CANS: Aluminum

Andersons Can Line Fbrction Eq ....F....... 407 889-4665
Apopka (G-102)

S&J Aluminum Works Inc ....G....... 850 492-5700
Pensacola (G-13599)

CANS: Beverage, Metal, Exc Beer

Fire Brands LLC....................F....... 877 800-4398
Miami Beach (G-10189)

CANS: Composite Foil-Fiber, Made From Purchased Materials

Rapid Composites LLC ....G....... 941 322-6647
Sarasota (G-15544)

CANS: Metal

Ball Metal Beverage Cont Corp ....B....... 813 980-6073
Tampa (G-16627)

Metal Container Corporation ....C....... 904 695-7600
Jacksonville (G-6297)

CANVAS PRDTS

American Marine Coverings Inc...........F....... 305 889-5355
Hialeah (G-5048)

Bayside Cnvas Ycht Intrors Inc ....G.... 954 792-8535
Fort Lauderdale **(G-3678)**
BP International Inc ....D.... 386 943-6222
Deland **(G-2856)**
Busch Canvas ....G.... 561 881-1605
Riviera Beach **(G-14603)**
C&D Canvas Inc ....G.... 954 924-3433
Davie **(G-2393)**
Canvas Designers Inc ....E.... 561 881-7663
Riviera Beach **(G-14605)**
Canvas Spc Cstm Mar Fbrction I ....G.... 850 664-6200
Fort Walton Beach **(G-4569)**
Canvas West Inc ....G.... 941 355-0780
Sarasota **(G-15629)**
Creative Energies Inc ....G.... 352 351-9448
Ocala **(G-11360)**
Gar Industries Corp ....F.... 954 456-8088
Hollywood **(G-5581)**
Germain Canvas & Awning Co ....G.... 305 751-4963
Miami **(G-9206)**
Gioia Sails South LLC ....D.... 386 597-2876
Palm Coast **(G-13079)**
Innovative Indus Solutions Inc ....G.... 561 733-1548
Boynton Beach **(G-879)**
Mpc Group LLC ....G.... 773 927-4120
Deland **(G-2889)**
Picanova Inc ....F.... 786 705-2120
Miami **(G-9716)**
Pipe Welders Inc ....D.... 954 587-8400
Fort Lauderdale **(G-3987)**
Schnupp Manufacturing Co Inc ....G.... 305 325-0520
Miami **(G-9856)**
Scotties Canvas & Mar Sup LLC ....G.... 239 995-7479
North Fort Myers **(G-11068)**
Smittys Boat Tops and Mar Eqp ....G.... 305 245-0229
Homestead **(G-5740)**
Taylor Made Systems Brdnton In ....C.... 941 747-1900
Oviedo **(G-12851)**
Tip Top Canvas and Uphl Inc ....F.... 954 524-6214
Plantation **(G-13896)**
Utilis Usa LLC ....G.... 850 226-7043
Fort Walton Beach **(G-4614)**
World of Awnings Inc ....F.... 305 884-6699
Hialeah **(G-5422)**
Yacht Furn By Eclipse LLC ....G.... 954 792-7339
Davie **(G-2501)**

CANVAS PRDTS, WHOLESALE

Iis Incorporated ....G.... 561 547-4297
Boynton Beach **(G-878)**

CANVAS PRDTS: Boat Seats

Artful Canvas Design Inc ....F.... 727 521-0212
Saint Petersburg **(G-14973)**
Marine Customs Unlimited ....F.... 772 223-8005
Stuart **(G-16182)**

CANVAS PRDTS: Convertible Tops, Car/Boat, Fm Purchased Mtrl

Boatswains Locker Inc ....E.... 904 388-0231
Jacksonville **(G-5943)**
Discount Boat Tops Inc ....G.... 727 536-4412
Largo **(G-7571)**
J W L Trading Company Inc ....G.... 813 854-1128
Tampa **(G-16960)**

CANVAS PRDTS: Shades, Made From Purchased Materials

Awnings of Hollywood Inc ....E.... 954 963-7717
Hollywood **(G-5535)**
Sea King Kanvas & Shade Inc ....G.... 239 481-3535
Fort Myers **(G-4396)**

CAPACITORS & CONDENSERS

General Capacitor LLC ....G.... 510 371-2700
Tallahassee **(G-16446)**

CAPACITORS: NEC

ABB Inc ....B.... 407 732-2000
Lake Mary **(G-7056)**
ABB Inc ....D.... 305 471-0844
Miami **(G-8634)**
Dynamic Engrg Innovations Inc ....C.... 386 445-6000
Palm Coast **(G-13076)**
Exxelia Usa Inc ....E.... 407 695-6562
Longwood **(G-7893)**

General Capacitor LLC ....G.... 510 371-2700
Tallahassee **(G-16446)**
Kemet Corporation ....C.... 954 766-2800
Fort Lauderdale **(G-3903)**
Kemet Ventures LLC ....G.... 407 403-2958
Orlando **(G-12284)**
Kyocera AVX Cmpnnts Jcksnvlle ....D.... 904 724-2000
Jacksonville **(G-6252)**
Mat-Vac Technology Inc ....F.... 386 238-7017
Daytona Beach **(G-2573)**
Nordquist Dielectrics Inc ....E.... 727 585-7990
Clearwater **(G-1718)**
Nwl Inc ....C.... 561 848-9009
Riviera Beach **(G-14651)**
Vladmir Ltd ....E.... 386 445-6000
Palm Coast **(G-13092)**

CAPACITORS: Series

S&S Consulting Partners LLC ....G.... 850 803-8379
Niceville **(G-11037)**

CAPS: Plastic

Sun Coast Industries LLC ....D.... 941 355-7166
Sarasota **(G-15561)**

CAR WASH EQPT

Andre T Jean ....G.... 305 647-8744
Opa Locka **(G-11717)**
Bounce Back MBL Detailing LLC ....G.... 561 336-4626
Boynton Beach **(G-847)**
Car Wash Solutions Florida Inc ....E.... 941 323-8817
Ocala **(G-11343)**
Famous MBL Car Wash Prssure CL ....F.... 786 720-1326
Miami **(G-9132)**
J-Ko Company ....G.... 561 795-7377
Royal Palm Beach **(G-14768)**
Kings Four Crners Auto Dtling ....G.... 866 886-4383
Clermont **(G-1873)**
National Carwash Solutions Inc ....E.... 813 973-3507
Tampa **(G-17098)**
Wws Contracting LLC ....E.... 813 868-3100
Tampa **(G-17444)**

CAR WASH EQPT & SPLYS WHOLESALERS

OHanrahan Consultants Inc ....E.... 727 531-3375
Largo **(G-7652)**

CARBIDES

Caribe Express Associates Inc ....F.... 305 222-9057
Miami **(G-8896)**
Creative Carbide Inc ....F.... 239 567-0041
Fort Myers **(G-4221)**

CARBON REMOVING SOLVENT

Akj Industries Inc ....G.... 239 939-1696
Fort Myers **(G-4160)**
Magnatrade International Corp ....G.... 305 696-5694
Miami **(G-9496)**

CARBURETORS

Daytona Parts Company ....G.... 386 427-7108
New Smyrna Beach **(G-11000)**
Total Performance Inc ....F.... 203 265-5667
Palm Coast **(G-13091)**

CARDIOVASCULAR SYSTEM DRUGS, EXC DIAGNOSTIC

Cardiovasular Innovation Inc ....G.... 512 517-7761
Hollywood **(G-5547)**
Ivax Corporation ....C.... 305 329-3795
Miami **(G-9344)**

CARDS, PLASTIC, UNPRINTED, WHOLESALE

Card Usa Inc ....F.... 954 862-1300
Hollywood **(G-5546)**

CARDS: Greeting

Sincere Sentiments Inc ....G.... 352 287-1232
Inverness **(G-5834)**
Specialty Productions Inc ....G.... 786 399-1393
Miami **(G-9938)**
Starmakers Rising Inc ....F.... 561 989-8999
Boca Raton **(G-695)**

CARDS: Identification

Card Quest Inc ....G.... 813 288-0004
Tampa **(G-16678)**
Card Usa Inc ....F.... 954 862-1300
Hollywood **(G-5546)**
Checkpoint Card Group Inc ....G.... 954 426-1331
Deerfield Beach **(G-2691)**
Idproductsource LLC ....G.... 772 336-4269
Port Saint Lucie **(G-14417)**
J & P Deerfield Inc ....F.... 954 571-6665
Deerfield Beach **(G-2744)**
Southeast Id LLC ....F.... 954 571-6665
Miami Lakes **(G-10356)**
Your ID Guard ....G.... 904 354-8989
Jacksonville **(G-6622)**

CARDS: Playing

Marketshare LLC ....G.... 631 273-0598
Boca Raton **(G-585)**

CARNIVAL SPLYS, WHOLESALE

Sharp Marketing LLC ....G.... 954 565-2711
Oakland Park **(G-11293)**

CARPETS & RUGS: Tufted

Mohawk Industries Inc ....G.... 918 272-0184
Hollywood **(G-5628)**

CARPETS, RUGS & FLOOR COVERING

Carpet Clinic LLC ....G.... 850 232-1170
Pensacola **(G-13470)**
Drab To Fab ....G.... 941 475-7700
Englewood **(G-3529)**
Dyn-O-Mat Inc ....G.... 561 747-2301
Jupiter **(G-6715)**
Dynomat Inc ....E.... 561 747-2301
Jupiter **(G-6716)**
Hanteri Enterprises Corp ....F.... 813 949-8729
Lutz **(G-7993)**
International Mdse Sources Inc ....E.... 239 430-9993
Naples **(G-10784)**
Murse Properties LLC ....G.... 941 966-3380
Sarasota **(G-15755)**
Niba Designs Inc ....F.... 305 456-6230
Hollywood **(G-5634)**
Picket Fence Childrens ....G.... 813 713-8589
Zephyrhills **(G-18625)**
Proximity Mills LLC ....F.... 813 251-3060
Tampa **(G-17191)**
Rampell Software ....G.... 561 628-5102
Palm Beach **(G-12940)**
Ser-Mat International LLC ....E.... 954 525-1417
Pompano Beach **(G-14175)**

CARPETS: Hand & Machine Made

Design-A-Rug Inc ....F.... 954 943-7487
Deerfield Beach **(G-2705)**

CARPORTS: Prefabricated Metal

Storage and Canopy Inc ....G.... 863 840-4005
Venus **(G-17729)**

CARRIER EQPT: Telephone Or Telegraph

Allied Telecommunications Ltd ....F.... 954 370-9900
Plantation **(G-13824)**

CARRYING CASES, WHOLESALE

Bee Electronics Inc ....D.... 772 468-7477
Fort Pierce **(G-4469)**
Identity Stronghold LLC ....E.... 941 475-8480
Englewood **(G-3533)**

CARS: Electric

Electra Automotive Corp ....G.... 941 623-5563
Hollywood **(G-5570)**
Ev Pilotcar Inc ....G.... 239 243-8023
Fort Myers **(G-4249)**
Valiant Transport Group LLC ....E.... 855 648-7423
Boca Raton **(G-741)**

CARTS: Grocery

Load King Manufacturing Co ....C.... 904 354-8882
Jacksonville **(G-6263)**

PRODUCT

CASES, WOOD

Palm Beach Trim Inc............................E........ 561 588-8746
   Davie *(G-2452)*

CASES: Carrying

Agora Sales Inc..................................D........ 727 490-0499
   Clearwater *(G-1479)*
Agora Sales Inc..................................C........ 727 321-0707
   Saint Petersburg *(G-14957)*
Bee Electronics Inc...........................D........ 772 468-7477
   Fort Pierce *(G-4469)*
Gar Industries Corp..........................F........ 954 456-8088
   Hollywood *(G-5581)*
Hut Global Inc...................................G........ 561 571-2523
   Boca Raton *(G-540)*
Koszegi Industries Inc.....................E........ 954 419-9544
   Deerfield Beach *(G-2749)*
Stemler Corporation..........................E........ 727 577-1216
   Saint Petersburg *(G-15200)*
US Communications Industries.........E........ 772 468-7477
   Fort Pierce *(G-4551)*

CASES: Carrying, Clothing & Apparel

Forward Inertia LLC...........................G........ 617 794-8877
   Miami *(G-9169)*
Intradeco Apparel Inc.......................E........ 305 264-8888
   Medley *(G-8259)*
Spires Empire LLC.............................G........ 305 797-0622
   Key West *(G-6881)*

CASES: Jewelry

Yvel Usa Inc......................................G........ 561 391-5119
   Boca Raton *(G-763)*

CASES: Packing, Nailed Or Lock Corner, Wood

Custom Crate & Logistics Co.............G........ 954 527-5742
   Fort Lauderdale *(G-3748)*

CASES: Plastic

Homyn Enterprises Corp....................D........ 305 870-9720
   Miami *(G-9290)*
Rehrig Pacific Company.....................F........ 407 857-3888
   Orlando *(G-12544)*

CASES: Shipping, Nailed Or Lock Corner, Wood

Allcases Reekstin & Assoc Inc...........F........ 813 891-1313
   Oldsmar *(G-11624)*

CASES: Shipping, Wood, Wirebound

Allcases Reekstin & Assoc Inc...........F........ 813 891-1313
   Oldsmar *(G-11624)*

CASH REGISTERS WHOLESALERS

Eastern Ribbon & Roll Corp...............E........ 813 676-8600
   Odessa *(G-11548)*

CASINGS: Storage, Missile & Missile Components

C4 Advnced Tctical Systems LLC.........D........ 407 206-3886
   Orlando *(G-11974)*

CASKETS & ACCESS

Service Corp International.................G........ 321 636-6041
   Cocoa *(G-1956)*

CAST STONE: Concrete

AAA Cast Stone Inc...........................E........ 941 721-8092
   Palmetto *(G-13152)*
Art-Crete Products Inc.....................F........ 386 252-5118
   Daytona Beach *(G-2514)*
Hamner Parking Lot Service..............G........ 954 328-3216
   Fort Lauderdale *(G-3858)*
Marbon Inc...F........ 561 822-9999
   West Palm Beach *(G-18064)*
Palm Beach Cast Stone Inc................E........ 561 835-4085
   West Palm Beach *(G-18107)*
Pedronis Cast Stone Inc...................E........ 904 783-1690
   Jacksonville *(G-6363)*
Premier Stoneworks LLC....................D........ 561 330-3737
   Delray Beach *(G-3003)*

Stone Central of Central Fla..............F........ 352 689-0075
   Wildwood *(G-18321)*
True Stone Masonry LLC.....................F........ 772 334-9797
   Fort Pierce *(G-4544)*
VP Cast Stone Corp...........................G........ 305 691-9306
   Hialeah *(G-5415)*

CASTERS

Shadow-Caster Led Lighting LLC.........E........ 727 474-2877
   Clearwater *(G-1782)*

CASTINGS GRINDING: For The Trade

1842 Daily Grind & Mercantile............G........ 352 543-5004
   Cedar Key *(G-1437)*
Big OS Stump Grinding.......................G........ 904 945-5900
   Jacksonville *(G-5932)*
Grind It LLC.......................................G........ 813 310-9710
   Lutz *(G-7992)*
Gulfport Grind Inc............................G........ 727 343-2785
   Gulfport *(G-4899)*
James Caldwell Stump Grinding...........G........ 813 843-1262
   Plant City *(G-13777)*
Kens Stump Grinding LLC....................F........ 407 948-5031
   Orlando *(G-12286)*
Mr Bones Stump Grinding....................F........ 941 927-0790
   Sarasota *(G-15753)*
Vine and Grind LLC............................G........ 727 420-3122
   Treasure Island *(G-17628)*

CASTINGS: Aerospace Investment, Ferrous

Alm Technologies Inc.........................E........ 904 849-7212
   Yulee *(G-18587)*
Carson Innovation Inc........................G........ 727 348-0000
   Pinellas Park *(G-13674)*
Extant Cmpnnts Group Hldngs In.........G........ 321 254-1500
   Melbourne *(G-8423)*
General Pneumatics Inflation.............G........ 941 216-3500
   Sarasota *(G-15482)*
Kellstrom Aerospace Group Inc...........G........ 954 538-2482
   Boca Raton *(G-567)*

CASTINGS: Aerospace, Aluminum

Aerosapien Technologies LLC.............E........ 386 361-3838
   Daytona Beach *(G-2508)*
Gables Engineering Inc......................B........ 305 774-4400
   Coral Gables *(G-2058)*

CASTINGS: Aerospace, Nonferrous, Exc Aluminum

Gables Engineering Inc......................B........ 305 774-4400
   Coral Gables *(G-2058)*
Inspectech Aeroservice Inc................F........ 954 359-6766
   Fort Lauderdale *(G-3877)*
Kellstrom Aerospace Group Inc...........E........ 954 538-2482
   Boca Raton *(G-567)*
Shell Aerospace LLC..........................E........ 786 400-2660
   Miami *(G-9879)*

CASTINGS: Aluminum

RC Investment Casting........................G........ 305 801-9088
   Hialeah *(G-5326)*
West Coast Castings Inc.....................F........ 941 753-2969
   Bradenton *(G-1076)*

CASTINGS: Bronze, NEC, Exc Die

Bronzart Foundry Inc.........................F........ 941 922-9106
   Sarasota *(G-15617)*

CASTINGS: Commercial Investment, Ferrous

M Austin Forman................................D........ 954 763-8111
   Fort Lauderdale *(G-3925)*

CASTINGS: Die, Aluminum

Big Sun Equine Products Inc..............G........ 352 629-9645
   Ocala *(G-11334)*
Southern Die Casting Corp..................D........ 305 635-6571
   Miami *(G-9927)*
Southern Mfg Upholstery Inc...............F........ 727 573-1006
   Clearwater *(G-1790)*
Strive Development Corporation...........F........ 850 689-2124
   Crestview *(G-2255)*

CASTINGS: Die, Magnesium & Magnesium-Base Alloy

Fullerton 799 Inc..............................D........ 727 572-7040
   Clearwater *(G-1608)*

CASTINGS: Die, Nonferrous

Camp Aircraft Inc..............................F........ 727 397-6076
   Saint Petersburg *(G-14994)*
Motor City Classics Inc......................G........ 954 473-2201
   Sunrise *(G-16344)*
Target Manufacturing Inc....................G........ 305 633-0361
   Miami *(G-9994)*

CASTINGS: Die, Zinc

Southern Die Casting Corp..................D........ 305 635-6571
   Miami *(G-9927)*

CASTINGS: Gray Iron

Tld LLC...G........ 813 927-7554
   Tampa *(G-17358)*
U S Holdings Inc................................G........ 305 885-0301
   Hialeah *(G-5389)*
US Manufacturing Company.................C........ 305 885-0301
   Medley *(G-8346)*
US Manufacturing Company.................F........ 305 556-1661
   Hialeah *(G-5398)*

CASTINGS: Lead

Gypsy Mining Inc................................G........ 772 589-5547
   Roseland *(G-14757)*

CASTINGS: Machinery, Aluminum

Florida Machine & Casting Co.............G........ 561 655-3771
   Riviera Beach *(G-14624)*
Heroal USA Inc...................................A........ 888 437-6257
   Orlando *(G-12214)*
Simplimatic Automation......................G........ 941 360-6500
   Sarasota *(G-15557)*

CASTINGS: Machinery, Brass

Loren/Wtp..G........ 954 846-9800
   Hollywood *(G-5613)*

CASTINGS: Machinery, Nonferrous, Exc Die or Aluminum Copper

Chromalloy Castings Tampa Corp.........C........ 561 935-3571
   Palm Beach Gardens *(G-12958)*

CASTINGS: Precision

Collins Mfg Inc..................................D........ 407 889-9669
   Apopka *(G-116)*
XI Carts Inc.......................................G........ 904 277-7111
   Fernandina Beach *(G-3600)*

CASTINGS: Zinc

Camp Company St Petersburg..............E........ 727 397-6076
   Saint Petersburg *(G-14995)*

CAT BOX FILLER

Terfa Litter USA Inc...........................F........ 416 358-4495
   Sunny Isles Beach *(G-16283)*

CATALOG & MAIL-ORDER HOUSES

Blue Ocean Press Inc.........................E........ 954 973-1819
   Fort Lauderdale *(G-3693)*
Gleim Publications Inc........................D........ 352 375-0772
   Gainesville *(G-4703)*
Rainbow Lght Ntrtnal Systems I...........G........ 954 233-3300
   Sunrise *(G-16361)*
Warehouse Goods LLC........................E........ 877 865-2260
   Boca Raton *(G-753)*

CATALYSTS: Chemical

Nano Liquitec LLC..............................F........ 813 447-1742
   Lutz *(G-8006)*
Vanavac Inc.......................................G........ 813 752-1391
   Plant City *(G-13813)*
W R Grace & Co - Conn........................F........ 561 982-7776
   Boca Raton *(G-751)*

CATAPULTS

Catapult 13 Crtive Studios LLC ....G....... 305 788-6948
Miami **(G-8901)**
Catapult Lakeland Inc ....G....... 863 687-3788
Lakeland **(G-7289)**
Catapult Learning LL ....G....... 561 573-6025
Delray Beach **(G-2942)**
Chasco Machine & Manufacturing ....G....... 727 815-3510
Brooksville **(G-1144)**

CATCH BASIN CLEANING SVC

All Liquid Envmtl Svcs LLC ....E....... 800 767-9594
Fort Lauderdale **(G-3638)**

CATCH BASIN COVERS: Concrete

Oldcastle Coastal Inc ....G....... 813 932-1007
Tampa **(G-17125)**
Oldcastle Coastal Inc ....C....... 813 367-9780
Tampa **(G-17126)**

CATERERS

Big Bend Ice Cream Co ....G....... 850 539-7778
Havana **(G-4993)**
Madan Corporation ....G....... 954 925-0077
Dania Beach **(G-2353)**
Sweet Tooth Inc ....G....... 305 682-1400
North Miami Beach **(G-11164)**

CELLULOID PRDTS

Coffee Cllloid Productions LLC ....G....... 305 424-8900
Miami **(G-8941)**

CELLULOSE DERIVATIVE MATERIALS

Rayonier Advanced Mtls Inc ....C....... 904 357-4600
Jacksonville **(G-6406)**
Rayonier AM Sales and Tech Inc ....E....... 904 357-4600
Jacksonville **(G-6407)**

CEMENT, EXC LINOLEUM & TILE

Greencore LLC ....G....... 727 251-9837
Saint Petersburg **(G-15067)**
Lehigh White Cement Co LLC ....G....... 561 812-7439
West Palm Beach **(G-18055)**

CEMENT: Hydraulic

Argos Cement LLC ....F....... 813 247-4831
Tampa **(G-16603)**
Basecrete Technologies LLC ....F....... 941 312-5142
Sarasota **(G-15610)**
Bonsal American Inc ....G....... 813 621-2427
Tampa **(G-16657)**
Cement Products Inc ....E....... 727 868-9226
Port Richey **(G-14357)**
Fcs Holdings Inc ....G....... 352 787-0608
Leesburg **(G-7772)**
Gallop Group Inc ....G....... 813 251-6242
Tampa **(G-16868)**
Hco Holding I Corporation ....F....... 863 533-0522
Bartow **(G-311)**
Phg Kendall LLC ....F....... 954 392-8788
Hollywood **(G-5642)**
Quikrete Companies LLC ....E....... 850 623-0559
Milton **(G-10435)**
Titan America LLC ....F....... 800 396-3434
West Palm Beach **(G-18181)**
Titan America LLC ....C....... 305 364-2200
Medley **(G-8334)**

CEMENT: Linoleum & Tile

Proform Finishing Products LLC ....E....... 904 284-0221
Green Cove Springs **(G-4833)**

CEMENT: Masonry

David Sayne Masonry Inc ....F....... 386 873-4696
Deland **(G-2860)**

CEMENT: Natural

Euro Gear (usa) Inc ....E....... 518 578-1775
Miami **(G-9114)**

CEMETERY MEMORIAL DEALERS

Bricklser Engrv Monuments Corp ....F....... 786 806-0672
Doral **(G-3148)**

Campbells Ornamental Concrete ....G....... 239 458-0800
Cape Coral **(G-1321)**

CERAMIC FIBER

Florida Nonwovens Inc ....E....... 407 241-2701
Orlando **(G-12162)**

CERAMIC FLOOR & WALL TILE WHOLESALERS

Mosch International Corp ....G....... 786 616-9108
Miami **(G-9590)**
Salvia Tile & Stone Inc ....F....... 239 643-7770
Naples **(G-10881)**

CHAIN: Tire, Made From Purchased Wire

Las Zirh Americas Inc ....G....... 305 942-7597
Miami **(G-9428)**

CHAINS: Power Transmission

Orion Power Systems Inc ....G....... 877 385-1654
Jacksonville **(G-6343)**

CHAMBERS: Space Simulation, Metal Plate

Tru Simulation + Training Inc ....D....... 813 792-9300
Odessa **(G-11587)**

CHANGE MAKING MACHINES

American Changer Corp ....D....... 954 917-3009
Fort Lauderdale **(G-3648)**

CHARCOAL: Activated

American Carbons Inc ....G....... 850 265-4214
Lynn Haven **(G-8024)**
Carbonxt Inc ....E....... 352 378-4950
Gainesville **(G-4666)**
Donau Carbon US Lcc ....E....... 352 465-5959
Dunnellon **(G-3465)**
Puragen LLC ....E....... 561 907-5400
West Palm Beach **(G-18131)**
Puragen LLC ....E....... 760 630-5724
North Palm Beach **(G-11182)**

CHASING SVC: Metal

Extreme Coatings ....G....... 727 528-7998
Saint Petersburg **(G-15041)**

CHASSIS: Automobile Trailer

Safecraft Rstraint Systems Inc ....F....... 813 758-3571
Lutz **(G-8013)**

CHASSIS: Motor Vehicle

Shyft Group Inc ....E....... 954 946-9955
Jupiter **(G-6797)**

CHEESE WHOLESALERS

American Foods Intl LLC ....E....... 877 894-7675
Aventura **(G-251)**
Goloso Food Llc ....G....... 321 277-2055
Orlando **(G-12198)**
Latin Amercn Meats & Foods USA ....G....... 305 477-2700
Miami **(G-9434)**

CHEMICAL ELEMENTS

5thelement Indian Cuisine LLC ....G....... 386 302-0202
Palm Coast **(G-13066)**
Drywall Elements ....F....... 407 454-7293
Orlando **(G-12110)**
Element 26 LLC ....G....... 413 519-1146
Fort Pierce **(G-4482)**
Element Mtls Tech Jupiter LLC ....F....... 321 327-8985
West Melbourne **(G-17899)**
Element Solutions LLC ....G....... 352 279-3310
Tampa **(G-16801)**
Washington Shores Element ....G....... 407 250-6260
Orlando **(G-12711)**

CHEMICAL PROCESSING MACHINERY & EQPT

Dilution Solutions Inc ....G....... 800 451-6628
Clearwater **(G-1565)**

CHEMICAL SPLYS FOR FOUNDRIES

Global Materials Company ....E....... 800 797-3736
Riviera Beach **(G-14625)**

CHEMICALS & ALLIED PRDTS WHOLESALERS, NEC

Allied USA Incorporated ....G....... 305 235-3950
Miami **(G-8695)**
Ascend Prfmce Mtls Oprtons LLC ....A....... 850 968-7000
Cantonment **(G-1265)**
Auto Gard Qmi Inc ....F....... 727 847-5441
New Port Richey **(G-10962)**
B & R Products Inc ....F....... 305 238-1592
Cutler Bay **(G-2284)**
Bon Brands Inc ....F....... 800 590-7911
Royal Palm Beach **(G-14760)**
Ecological Laboratories Inc ....E....... 239 573-6650
Cape Coral **(G-1336)**
Goho Enterprises Inc ....F....... 407 884-0770
Zellwood **(G-18598)**
Hi-TEC Laboratories Inc ....E....... 850 835-6822
Freeport **(G-4627)**
Illinois Tool Works Inc ....F....... 561 422-9241
Riviera Beach **(G-14629)**
Illinois Tool Works Inc ....D....... 863 665-3338
Lakeland **(G-7347)**
Latam Group Corp ....G....... 305 793-8961
Miami **(G-9431)**
Mapei Corporation ....G....... 954 246-8888
Deerfield Beach **(G-2763)**
Thatcher Chemical Florida Inc ....G....... 386 734-3966
Deland **(G-2910)**

CHEMICALS & ALLIED PRDTS, WHOL: Chemical, Organic, Synthetic

Pure Wave Organics Inc ....G....... 321 368-7002
Melbourne **(G-8504)**

CHEMICALS & ALLIED PRDTS, WHOLESALE: Chemicals, Indl

Belzona Inc ....E....... 305 594-4994
Doral **(G-3134)**
Dyadic International USA Inc ....G....... 561 743-8333
Jupiter **(G-6714)**
Kraton Chemical LLC ....E....... 850 785-8521
Panama City **(G-13282)**
Morning Star Industries Inc ....E....... 800 440-6050
Jensen Beach **(G-6657)**

CHEMICALS & ALLIED PRDTS, WHOLESALE: Chemicals, Indl & Heavy

American Coatings Corporation ....G....... 954 970-7820
Margate **(G-8120)**
Hac International Inc ....E....... 954 584-4530
Davie **(G-2421)**

CHEMICALS & ALLIED PRDTS, WHOLESALE: Compressed Gas

Axi International ....E....... 239 690-9589
Fort Myers **(G-4184)**

CHEMICALS & ALLIED PRDTS, WHOLESALE: Detergents

Campos Chemicals ....G....... 727 412-2774
Saint Petersburg **(G-14996)**

CHEMICALS & ALLIED PRDTS, WHOLESALE: Dry Ice

Atlantic Dry Ice Corportion ....F....... 305 592-7000
Miami **(G-8763)**

CHEMICALS & ALLIED PRDTS, WHOLESALE: Essential Oils

Love Is In The Air Corp ....G....... 305 828-8181
Hialeah **(G-5227)**
Suns Eye Inc ....G....... 407 519-4904
Geneva **(G-4790)**

PRODUCT

CHEMICALS & ALLIED PRDTS, WHOLESALE: Indl Gases

Deland Metal Craft Company ....G....... 386 734-0828
Deland (G-2861)

CHEMICALS & ALLIED PRDTS, WHOLESALE: Oil Additives

Fuel Solutions Distrs LLC ....G....... 305 528-3758
North Miami Beach (G-11141)

CHEMICALS & ALLIED PRDTS, WHOLESALE: Plastics Materials, NEC

Melt-Tech Polymers Inc ....G....... 305 887-6148
Medley (G-8278)
Omnisphere Corporation ....F....... 305 388-4075
Miami (G-9648)
S V Bags America Inc ....G....... 954 577-9091
Weston (G-18285)
Seelye Acquisitions Inc ....G....... 407 656-6677
Apopka (G-174)

CHEMICALS & ALLIED PRDTS, WHOLESALE: Plastics Prdts, NEC

Action Plastics Inc ....G....... 352 342-4122
Belleview (G-357)
Doran Manufacturing Corp Fla ....G....... 904 731-3313
Jacksonville (G-6038)

CHEMICALS & ALLIED PRDTS, WHOLESALE: Plastics Sheets & Rods

American Plastic Sup & Mfg Inc ....E....... 727 573-0636
Clearwater (G-1491)
Piedmont Plastics Inc ....D....... 386 274-4627
Daytona Beach (G-2582)
Plastic and Products Mktg LLC ....F....... 352 867-8078
Ocala (G-11468)
Plastics America Inc ....G....... 813 620-3711
Tampa (G-17168)

CHEMICALS & ALLIED PRDTS, WHOLESALE: Resins

Composite Essential Mtls LLC ....G....... 772 344-0034
Port St Lucie (G-14475)
Pacific Limited International ....G....... 305 358-1900
Miami (G-9676)

CHEMICALS & ALLIED PRDTS, WHOLESALE: Resins, Plastics

Ravago Americas LLC ....A....... 407 773-7777
Orlando (G-12531)

CHEMICALS & ALLIED PRDTS, WHOLESALE: Spec Clean/Sanitation

Ciega Inc ....G....... 727 526-9048
Saint Petersburg (G-15007)

CHEMICALS & OTHER PRDTS DERIVED FROM COKING

Matschel of Flagler Inc ....G....... 386 446-4595
Saint Augustine (G-14856)

CHEMICALS, AGRICULTURE: Wholesalers

Chemical Dynamics Inc ....E....... 813 752-4950
Plant City (G-13755)

CHEMICALS/ALLIED PRDTS, WHOL: Coal Tar Prdts, Prim/Intermdt

Star-Seal of Florida Inc ....F....... 954 484-8402
Fort Lauderdale (G-4068)

CHEMICALS: Agricultural

Ai Thomas LLC ....E....... 904 553-6202
Ponte Vedra Beach (G-14260)
Ben Hill Griffin Inc ....D....... 863 635-2281
Frostproof (G-4634)
Brewer International Inc ....F....... 772 562-0555
Vero Beach (G-17743)
Chae Dupont PA ....G....... 305 697-7771
Miami (G-8918)

Custom Agronomics Inc ....F....... 772 223-0775
Palm City (G-13032)
Diamond R Fertilizer Co Inc ....E....... 863 763-2158
Okeechobee (G-11603)
E I Du Pont De Nemours & Co ....G....... 352 205-8103
The Villages (G-17554)
Excelag Corp ....G....... 305 670-0145
Miami (G-9119)
Gmx Technologies LLC ....G....... 917 697-0211
Highland Beach (G-5460)
Monsanto Company ....F....... 863 673-2157
Felda (G-3572)
Morse Enterprises Limited Inc ....G....... 407 682-6500
Miami (G-9589)
Numerator Technologies Inc ....G....... 941 807-5333
Sarasota (G-15763)
Rx For Fleas Inc ....F....... 954 351-9244
Fort Lauderdale (G-4034)
Sawyer Products Inc ....E....... 727 725-1177
Safety Harbor (G-14795)
Volac Inc ....G....... 800 759-7569
Pace (G-12859)

CHEMICALS: Alcohols

American Industrial Group Inc ....F....... 703 757-7683
North Miami Beach (G-11130)

CHEMICALS: Aluminum Compounds

Ceco & Associates Inc ....G....... 727 528-0075
Riverview (G-14558)

CHEMICALS: Anhydrous Ammonia

CF Industries Inc ....E....... 813 782-1591
Bartow (G-305)

CHEMICALS: Brine

H20logy Inc ....G....... 904 829-6098
Saint Augustine (G-14838)

CHEMICALS: Fire Retardant

Geltech Solutions Inc ....E....... 561 427-6144
Jupiter (G-6735)

CHEMICALS: Fluorine, Elemental

Vestagen Tchnical Textiles Inc ....G....... 407 781-2570
Orlando (G-12695)

CHEMICALS: Fuel Tank Or Engine Cleaning

Penek Chemical Industries Inc ....G....... 954 978-6501
Pompano Beach (G-14121)

CHEMICALS: High Purity Grade, Organic

Nu Earth Labs LLC ....E....... 727 648-4787
Dunedin (G-3455)

CHEMICALS: High Purity, Refined From Technical Grade

Cheltec Inc ....G....... 941 355-1045
Sarasota (G-15631)

CHEMICALS: Inorganic, NEC

5th Element Inc ....G....... 321 331-7028
Kissimmee (G-6890)
Affinity Chemical Woodbine LLC ....G....... 973 873-4070
Tampa (G-16563)
All Elements Mechanical Corp ....G....... 866 306-0359
Longwood (G-7864)
Artistic Elements Inc ....G....... 561 750-1554
Boca Raton (G-415)
Auto Gard Qmi Inc ....F....... 727 847-5441
New Port Richey (G-10962)
Avym LLC ....G....... 407 970-7746
Altamonte Springs (G-32)
Bio-Lab Inc ....F....... 863 709-1411
Lakeland (G-7282)
Caliber Elements LLC ....F....... 352 697-1415
Homosassa (G-5743)
Element Aircraft Sales LLC ....G....... 954 494-2242
Boca Raton (G-502)
Element Inc Co ....G....... 786 208-5693
Miami (G-9081)
Element International Dist Inc ....G....... 305 239-9228
Hollywood (G-5571)

Element Studios ....G....... 407 968-2192
Windermere (G-18350)
Element-M LLC ....G....... 954 288-8683
Plantation (G-13847)
Elemental Mobile Services LLC ....G....... 904 768-9840
Jacksonville (G-6069)
Elements Accounting Inc ....G....... 305 662-4448
Miami (G-9082)
Elements of Stylez ....G....... 813 575-8416
Wesley Chapel (G-17874)
Elementus Minerals LLC ....F....... 561 815-2617
Fort Lauderdale (G-3791)
Epic Elements LLC ....G....... 305 388-1384
Medley (G-8236)
Eternal Elements LLC ....G....... 407 830-6968
Altamonte Springs (G-45)
Gns Technologies LLC ....F....... 561 367-3774
Boca Raton (G-528)
Harcros Chemicals Inc ....E....... 813 247-4531
Tampa (G-16905)
Hi-TEC Laboratories Inc ....E....... 850 835-6822
Freeport (G-4627)
Home Elements St Petersburg Inc ....G....... 727 510-5700
Saint Petersburg (G-15077)
Jci Jones Chemicals Inc ....F....... 904 355-0779
Jacksonville (G-6222)
K C Industries LLC ....G....... 863 425-1195
Mulberry (G-10629)
K-Technologies Inc ....G....... 863 940-4815
Lakeland (G-7363)
Kraton Chemical LLC ....E....... 850 785-8521
Panama City (G-13282)
Lambert Corporation Florida ....E....... 407 841-2940
Orlando (G-12307)
National Chemical Sply ....F....... 800 515-9938
Davie (G-2444)
National Chemical Supply Inc ....G....... 954 683-1645
Plantation (G-13873)
P S Research Corp ....G....... 954 558-8727
Lauderhill (G-7738)
Plasmine Technology Inc ....G....... 850 438-8550
Pensacola (G-13576)
Plating Technologies Inc ....G....... 772 220-4201
Stuart (G-16197)
Prince Minerals Inc ....G....... 832 241-2169
Mount Dora (G-10611)
Productiv Elements LLC ....G....... 305 283-4790
Miami (G-9749)
Quest Environmental Pdts Inc ....G....... 321 984-4423
Melbourne (G-8508)
Sesolinc Grp Inc ....G....... 772 287-9090
Stuart (G-16215)
Shear Elements LLC ....G....... 954 678-8528
Lauderhill (G-7741)
Sinmat Commercial LLC ....F....... 352 334-7270
Gainesville (G-4762)
Sivance LLC ....D....... 352 376-8246
Gainesville (G-4764)
Standard Carbon LLC ....E....... 352 465-5959
Dunnellon (G-3467)
Syndesis Inc ....G....... 954 483-9548
Pembroke Pines (G-13417)
Taylor Building Elements LLC ....G....... 863 287-2228
Auburndale (G-246)
Thatcher Chemical Florida Inc ....G....... 386 734-3966
Deland (G-2910)
Trac Ecological America Inc ....G....... 954 583-4922
Fort Lauderdale (G-4096)
Trans-Resources LLC ....A....... 305 933-8301
Sunny Isles Beach (G-16284)
Waste Petro Recover ....G....... 305 345-4199
Hialeah (G-5419)

CHEMICALS: Iodine, Elemental

Isoaid LLC ....E....... 727 815-3262
Port Richey (G-14364)

CHEMICALS: Medicinal

Germkleen LLC ....G....... 954 947-5602
Fort Lauderdale (G-3838)
Mydor Industries Inc ....G....... 954 927-1140
Dania (G-2338)
South Walton Pharmacy LLC ....G....... 850 622-3313
Santa Rosa Beach (G-15432)

CHEMICALS: Medicinal, Inorganic, Uncompounded, Bulk

Real Ketones LLC ....F....... 801 244-8610
Saint Petersburg (G-15170)

CHEMICALS: Medicinal, Organic, Uncompounded, Bulk

Dragons Miracle LLC ....G...... 561 670-5546
Boca Raton (G-496)

One Bio Corp.................................B..... 305 328-8662
Aventura (G-268)

CHEMICALS: Muriate Of Potash, Not From Mines

Mosaic Company ....B..... 800 918-8270
Tampa (G-17086)

CHEMICALS: NEC

21st Century Chemical Inc ....G....... 954 689-7111
Fort Lauderdale (G-3615)

Agarose Unlimited Inc ....G...... 800 850-0659
Gainesville (G-4646)

Amaya Solutions Inc ....E...... 813 246-5448
Plant City (G-13736)

Arrmaz Products Inc........................D...... 863 578-1206
Mulberry (G-10619)

Aurum Chemicals Corp....................G...... 305 412-4141
Miami (G-8772)

B & R Products Inc ....F...... 305 238-1592
Cutler Bay (G-2284)

Bbj Environmental LLC ....G...... 813 622-8550
Tampa (G-16634)

Beesfree Inc ....G...... 561 939-4860
West Palm Beach (G-17942)

Belzona Inc ....E...... 305 594-4994
Doral (G-3134)

Blue Planet Envmtl Systems Inc ....G...... 321 255-1931
Palm Bay (G-12893)

Bonsal American Inc ....G...... 813 621-2427
Tampa (G-16657)

C W Products International.................G...... 407 831-4966
Longwood (G-7879)

Camco Chemical ....G...... 239 992-4100
Bonita Springs (G-789)

Cargill Incorporated ....F...... 813 241-4847
Tampa (G-16681)

Chem Guard Inc ....F...... 407 402-2798
Casselberry (G-1412)

Chemical Systems Orlando Inc ....G...... 407 886-2329
Zellwood (G-18597)

Cjb Industries Inc ....F...... 941 552-8397
Sarasota (G-15633)

Cleanpak Products LLC ....G...... 813 740-8611
Tampa (G-16714)

Clinical Dagnstc Solutions Inc ....E...... 954 791-1773
Plantation (G-13836)

Color-Chrome Technologies Inc..........G...... 954 335-0127
Fort Lauderdale (G-3737)

Confederated Specialty Assoc I ....G...... 904 751-4754
Jacksonville (G-5997)

Dovo Inc..F...... 754 244-5120
Boca Raton (G-493)

Dyadic International USA Inc ....G...... 561 743-8333
Jupiter (G-6714)

E-Liquids Investment Group LLC.........E...... 954 507-6060
Plantation (G-13845)

Element Solutions Inc ....D...... 561 207-9600
Fort Lauderdale (G-3790)

Enviroseal Corporation ....G...... 772 335-8225
Port Saint Lucie (G-14410)

Euclid Chemical Company.................F....... 813 886-8811
Odessa (G-11550)

Far Research Inc ....E...... 321 723-6160
Palm Bay (G-12899)

Freezetone Products LLC ....F...... 305 961-1116
Doral (G-3220)

Global Seven Inc ....G...... 973 664-1900
Sarasota (G-15693)

Illinois Tool Works Inc ....D...... 863 665-3338
Lakeland (G-7347)

Increte Systems ....F...... 813 886-8811
Odessa (G-11557)

Isoprenoids LLC.............................E...... 813 785-6446
Tampa (G-16955)

Jamo Inc ....D...... 305 885-3444
Medley (G-8264)

Kemira Water Solutions Inc ....E...... 863 533-5990
Lakeland (G-7365)

Kraton Chemical LLC ....E...... 850 785-8521
Panama City (G-13282)

Mapei Corporation..........................D...... 954 485-8637
Fort Lauderdale (G-3932)

Mk Monomers LLC ....G...... 732 928-5800
Miami (G-9578)

Natural Organic Products Intl ....G...... 352 383-8252
Mount Dora (G-10607)

P S Research Corp..........................G...... 954 558-8727
Lauderhill (G-7738)

Pharmco Laboratories Inc ....G...... 321 268-1313
Titusville (G-17607)

Plating Resources Inc ....F...... 321 632-2435
Cocoa (G-1946)

Proline Chemical & Plastics LL ....G...... 850 835-6822
Freeport (G-4628)

Pyrotecnico of Florida LLC ....F...... 352 588-5086
San Antonio (G-15251)

S M D Research Inc ....G...... 561 451-9895
Boca Raton (G-656)

Shield Products Inc ....G...... 904 880-6060
Doral (G-3363)

Two Little Fishies Inc ....G...... 305 623-7695
Miami (G-10050)

Universal Transactions Inc ....F...... 305 887-4677
Medley (G-8344)

Vass Holdings Inc ....G...... 863 295-5664
Winter Haven (G-18477)

CHEMICALS: Organic, NEC

Arrmaz Products Inc........................D...... 863 578-1206
Mulberry (G-10619)

Artech Systems Inc ....G...... 954 304-0430
Deerfield Beach (G-2671)

Bartow Ethanol Florida LC ....F...... 863 533-2498
Bartow (G-300)

BASF Corporation...........................G...... 850 627-7688
Quincy (G-14541)

Bastech LLC ....E...... 904 737-1722
Jacksonville (G-5925)

Carpenter Co ....D...... 863 687-9494
Lakeland (G-7288)

Divitae Inc ....G...... 786 585-5556
Hialeah (G-5119)

Eastman Chemical Company.............F....... 305 671-2800
Miami (G-9062)

Envirnmental Mfg Solutions LLC ....G...... 321 837-0050
Melbourne (G-8421)

Ethnergy International Inc ....E...... 954 499-1582
Pembroke Pines (G-13387)

Givaudan Fragrances Corp ....E...... 863 667-0821
Lakeland (G-7336)

Green Biofuels Miami LLC ....F...... 305 639-3030
Miami (G-9242)

Harcros Chemicals Inc ....E...... 813 247-4531
Tampa (G-16905)

Iff Chemical Holdings Inc ....D...... 904 783-2180
Jacksonville (G-6192)

Interntnal Flvors Frgrnces Inc ....D...... 904 783-2180
Jacksonville (G-6203)

Kraton Chemical LLC ....E...... 850 785-8521
Panama City (G-13282)

Lemnature Aquafarms Usa Inc ....C...... 772 207-4794
Vero Beach (G-17772)

Natural Organic Products Intl ....G...... 352 383-8252
Mount Dora (G-10607)

Parabel Inc ....E...... 321 409-7415
Melbourne (G-8491)

Phlexapeel LLC ....G...... 407 990-1854
Melbourne (G-8494)

Rat-Trap Bait Company Inc ....G...... 863 967-2148
Auburndale (G-243)

Rp International LLC.........................G...... 941 894-1228
Sarasota (G-15803)

Sivance LLC ....E...... 352 376-8246
Gainesville (G-4765)

St Marks Powder Inc ....B...... 850 577-2824
Crawfordville (G-2232)

Symrise Inc ....C...... 904 768-5800
Jacksonville (G-6526)

Terry Laboratories LLC ....F...... 321 259-1630
Melbourne (G-8549)

CHEMICALS: Reagent Grade, Refined From Technical Grade

Arj Medical Inc...............................F...... 813 855-1557
Oldsmar (G-11627)

Hac International Inc........................E...... 954 584-4530
Davie (G-2421)

CHEMICALS: Water Treatment

American Water Chemicals Inc ....F...... 813 246-5448
Plant City (G-13738)

Bluworld Innovations LLC ....D...... 888 499-5433
Orlando (G-11962)

Chemline Inc ....G...... 407 847-4181
Kissimmee (G-6906)

Duncanson Dynasty Inc ....G...... 561 288-1349
West Palm Beach (G-17982)

Ecological Laboratories Inc ....E...... 239 573-6650
Cape Coral (G-1336)

Jacks Magic Products Inc ....F...... 727 536-4500
Largo (G-7620)

Mydor Industries Inc........................G...... 954 927-1140
Dania (G-2338)

Northeast Water Reclamation.............G...... 727 893-7779
Saint Petersburg (G-15140)

Premier Water & Enrgy Tech Inc ....E...... 904 268-1152
Jacksonville (G-6384)

Siemens Industry Inc.......................D...... 941 355-2971
Sarasota (G-15554)

Terlyn Industries Inc........................F...... 727 592-0772
Clearwater (G-1826)

CHESTS: Bank, Metal

Zerons Metal Designers Inc ....F...... 305 688-2240
Hialeah (G-5429)

CHILD DAY CARE SVCS

Lincoln-Marti Cmnty Agcy Inc ....D...... 305 643-4888
Miami (G-9462)

CHILDREN'S & INFANTS' CLOTHING STORES

Bossy Princess LLC ....G...... 786 285-4435
Aventura (G-257)

CHINA & GLASS: Decalcomania Work

Martin Leonard Corporation ....G...... 850 434-2203
Pensacola (G-13543)

CHLORINE

Jci Jones Chemicals Inc ....F...... 904 355-0779
Jacksonville (G-6222)

Odyssey Manufacturing Co ....F...... 813 635-0339
Tampa (G-17116)

CHLOROPRENE RUBBER: Neoprene

Unaflex LLC ....E...... 954 943-5002
Pompano Beach (G-14224)

CHOCOLATE, EXC CANDY FROM BEANS: Chips, Powder, Block, Syrup

David Delights LLC ....G...... 407 648-2020
Orlando (G-12077)

Mvs International Inc ....G...... 954 727-3383
Weston (G-18270)

Pinnacle Foods Inc ....G...... 321 952-7926
Melbourne Beach (G-8568)

Sweet Tooth Inc..............................G...... 305 682-1400
North Miami Beach (G-11164)

CHOCOLATE, EXC CANDY FROM PURCH CHOC: Chips, Powder, Block

Araya Inc ....G...... 305 229-6868
Miami (G-8739)

Art Edibles Inc ....G...... 407 603-4043
Oviedo (G-12805)

Atlantic Candy Company ....E...... 904 429-7250
Saint Augustine (G-14811)

Fantasy Chocolates Inc ....E...... 561 276-9007
Orlando (G-12144)

Kay Peak Group Inc ....G...... 754 307-5400
Margate (G-8138)

Peterbrooke Choclat Fctry LLC ....G...... 904 273-7878
Ponte Vedra Beach (G-14276)

Venchi US Inc ....G...... 646 448-8663
Miami (G-10100)

Whole Coffee Company LLC...............D...... 786 364-4444
Miami (G-10131)

CHURCHES

Grace Bible Church ....F...... 850 623-4671
Milton (G-10426)

CHUTES: Metal Plate

US Chutes Corp ....F 860 567-4000
Boca Raton (G-737)
Valiant Products Inc ....E 863 688-7998
Lakeland (G-7469)

CIGAR & CIGARETTE HOLDERS

Innevape LLC ....G 631 957-6500
Hudson (G-5778)

CIGARETTE & CIGAR PRDTS & ACCESS

Double DS Tobaccco ....G 561 901-9145
Boynton Beach (G-857)
Gilla Inc ....G 416 843-2881
Daytona Beach (G-2556)
Goodcat LLC ....E 239 254-8288
Naples (G-10764)
Hmd Investment Group LLC ....G 305 244-1290
Doral (G-3250)
International Vapor Group LLC...........F 305 824-4027
Miami Lakes (G-10309)
Xikar Inc ....E 816 474-7555
Weston (G-18299)

CIRCUIT BOARD REPAIR SVCS

Denver Elevator Systems Inc.............G 800 633-9788
Cape Canaveral (G-1282)

CIRCUIT BOARDS, PRINTED: Television & Radio

Aw-Tronics LLC.............................E 786 228-7835
Miami (G-8781)
Bare Board Group Inc ....F 727 549-2200
Largo (G-7544)
Circuitronix LLC ....D 786 364-4458
Fort Lauderdale (G-3728)
Elreha Printed Circuits ....G 727 244-0130
Bradenton (G-975)
Jabil Circuit LLC ....G 727 577-9749
Saint Petersburg (G-15091)
Profab Electronics Inc ....E 954 917-1998
Pompano Beach (G-14150)
Ra Co AMO Inc ....F 561 626-7232
Palm Beach Gardens (G-13004)

CIRCUIT BOARDS: Wiring

American Auto / Mar Wirg Inc............G 954 782-0193
Pompano Beach (G-13923)

CIRCUIT BREAKERS

Southwire Company LLC ....E 727 535-0572
Largo (G-7689)

CIRCUITS, INTEGRATED: Hybrid

Micro Engineering Inc ....E 407 886-4849
Apopka (G-151)

CIRCUITS: Electronic

ACR Family Components LLC............E 352 243-0307
Groveland (G-4858)
Advanced Manufacturing Inc ....E 727 573-3300
Saint Petersburg (G-14954)
Allied Circuits LLC ....G 239 970-2299
Naples (G-10659)
American Fibertek Inc ....E 732 302-0660
Saint Petersburg (G-14961)
Aspen Electronics Inc ....F 305 863-2151
Miami (G-8760)
Best Circuits Inc............................E 321 425-6725
Melbourne (G-8376)
Bocatech Inc ....G 954 397-7070
Fort Lauderdale (G-3699)
Built Story LLC ....F 305 671-3890
Miami (G-8859)
Capacitor and Components LLC ....E 954 798-8943
Sunrise (G-16303)
Concurrent Mfg Solutions LLC..........E 512 637-2540
Doral (G-3168)
Continuity Unlimited Inc..................F 561 358-8171
Oviedo (G-12815)
Custom Mfg & Engrg Inc ....D 727 548-0522
Pinellas Park (G-13680)
Dbi Services LLC ....E 239 218-5204
Fort Myers (G-4230)

Delta Group Electronics Inc ....D 321 631-0799
Rockledge (G-14698)
Flint LLC ....G 813 622-8899
Tampa (G-16837)
Florida Microelectronics LLC ....E 561 845-8455
West Palm Beach (G-18005)
Hiltronics Corporation ....G 954 341-9100
Coral Springs (G-2162)
I-Con Systems Inc ....D 407 365-6241
Oviedo (G-12827)
Intellitec Motor Vehicles LLC ....G 386 738-7307
Deland (G-2875)
Just-In-Time Mfg Corp ....F 321 752-7552
Melbourne (G-8446)
Kai Limited ....C 954 957-8586
Fort Lauderdale (G-3899)
KID Group Inc ....G 888 805-8851
Greenacres (G-4850)
Kimball Electronics Tampa Inc ....B 813 814-5229
Tampa (G-16987)
Lgl Group Inc ....G 407 298-2000
Orlando (G-12325)
Mdco Inc ....F 813 855-4068
Tampa (G-17061)
Micro Cmpt Systems Sthwest Fla ......G 239 643-6672
Naples (G-10820)
Micro Technology of Brevard ....G 321 733-1766
Melbourne (G-8476)
MN Trades Inc...............................G 954 455-9320
Hallandale Beach (G-4962)
Monroe Cable LLC ....D 941 429-8484
North Port (G-11201)
New ERA Technology Corp................F 352 746-3569
Beverly Hills (G-368)
Phantom Technologies Inc ....E 407 265-2567
Longwood (G-7937)
Protek Electronics Inc ....E 941 351-4399
Sarasota (G-15789)
Rami Technology USA LLC ....G 305 593-6033
Doral (G-3345)
Relcom Industries Inc.....................G 561 304-7717
Greenacres (G-4852)
Samteck Inc ....G 813 210-6784
Brandon (G-1105)
Sibex Inc ....C 727 726-4343
Crystal River (G-2280)
Soltec Electronics LLC ....G 321 288-5689
Rockledge (G-14746)
Sparton Deleon Springs LLC ....G 386 985-4631
De Leon Springs (G-2629)
Syncron Ems LLC ....D 321 409-0025
Palm Bay (G-12924)
Sypris Electronics LLC....................G 813 972-6000
Tampa (G-17319)
Technical Service Labs Inc ....E 850 243-3722
Fort Walton Beach (G-4612)
Techtronics LLC ....G 407 738-4680
Kissimmee (G-6964)
Teledyne Technologies Inc ....C 805 373-4545
Daytona Beach (G-2611)
Telematic Systems Inc....................G 239 217-0629
North Fort Myers (G-11071)
Tri-Tech Electronics Inc...................D 407 277-2131
Orlando (G-12669)

CLAMPS: Metal

Safety Clamps Inc..........................F 904 781-2809
Jacksonville (G-6449)

CLAY PRDTS: Architectural

Glassarium LLC ....E 786 631-7080
Miami (G-9216)

CLAYS, EXC KAOLIN & BALL

C C Calhoun Inc ....F 863 292-9511
Winter Haven (G-18428)

CLEANERS: Boiler Tube

CT Natural ....G 813 996-6443
Tampa (G-16746)
Water Technology Pensacola Inc ....E 850 477-4789
Pensacola (G-13623)

CLEANING EQPT: Blast, Dustless

B E Pressure Supply Inc ....F 561 688-9246
West Palm Beach (G-17932)

CLEANING EQPT: Commercial

A&M Cleaning Solutions LLC............F 786 559-7093
West Palm Beach (G-17909)
Consumer Engineering Inc ....F 321 984-8550
Palm Bay (G-12895)
Douglas Machines Corp ....E 727 461-3477
Clearwater (G-1568)
Extra Time Solutions ....E 407 625-2198
Clermont (G-1865)
Kationx Corp ....G 321 338-5050
Melbourne (G-8448)
White Mop Wringer Company ....C 813 971-2223
Tampa (G-17430)
WSa Engineered Systems Inc............F 414 481-4120
Pensacola (G-13628)

CLEANING EQPT: Dirt Sweeping Units, Indl

Smith Equipment & Supply Co ....E 863 665-4904
Lakeland (G-7438)

CLEANING EQPT: Floor Washing & Polishing, Commercial

Genfloor LLC ....G 305 477-1557
Doral (G-3230)

CLEANING EQPT: High Pressure

A Clean Finish Inc ....G 407 516-1311
Jacksonville (G-5846)
A-1 Cleaning Concepts Inc ....G 772 288-7214
Stuart (G-16108)
American Pressure Systems Inc ....G 321 914-0827
West Melbourne (G-17892)
Blast Off Equipment Inc ....F 561 964-6199
West Palm Beach (G-17948)
Charles Gable Inc ....E 239 300-0220
Naples (G-10712)
Getitcleaned ....F 239 331-2891
Naples (G-10761)
Greenlam America Inc ....F 305 640-0388
Doral (G-3239)
Nilfisk Pressure-Pro LLC ....D 772 672-3697
Fort Pierce (G-4511)
Richard Lyn ....G 954 326-1017
North Lauderdale (G-11085)
Transition of Slc Inc.......................E 772 461-4486
Fort Pierce (G-4540)

CLEANING OR POLISHING PREPARATIONS, NEC

Chemco Corp ....E 305 623-4445
Miami Lakes (G-10292)
Crown Products LLC ....G 954 917-1118
Pompano Beach (G-13984)
Marinize Products Corp ....G 954 989-7990
Hollywood (G-5620)
Power Kleen Corporation ....E 813 854-2648
Oldsmar (G-11687)
Quality Industrial Chem Inc ....F 727 573-5760
Saint Petersburg (G-15167)
Sheila Shine Inc ....E 305 557-1729
Miami (G-9878)
Vin-Dotco Inc................................F 727 217-9200
Pinellas Park (G-13733)

CLEANING PRDTS: Automobile Polish

Clean & Shine Auto Marine ....G 239 261-6563
Naples (G-10717)
Distingshed Gntlman MBL Dtling........G 321 200-4331
Orlando (G-12098)
Gold Shine LLC ....E 561 419-3253
Coral Springs (G-2158)
Meticulous Detail Inc ....G 813 310-6440
Lutz (G-8004)

CLEANING PRDTS: Bleaches, Household, Dry Or Liquid

Odyssey Manufacturing Co ....E 813 635-0339
Tampa (G-17115)
Sewell Products Florida LLC ....D 863 967-4463
Auburndale (G-244)
United Sierra Group Corp ....D 305 297-5835
Miami Lakes (G-10369)
United Sierra Group Corp ....E 305 297-5835
Miami Lakes (G-10370)

CLEANING PRDTS: Degreasing Solvent

Asi Chemical Inc ....F ... 863 678-1814
  Lake Wales **(G-7152)**
Petruj Chemical Corp ....F ... 305 556-1271
  Hialeah Gardens **(G-5447)**
Quantum Envmtl Slutions St Inc ....G 800 975-8721
  Fort Lauderdale **(G-4007)**
Skymo LLC ....G 305 676-6739
  Cooper City **(G-2022)**

CLEANING PRDTS: Deodorants, Nonpersonal

Falconpro Industries Inc ....G 305 556-4456
  Hialeah **(G-5150)**
Hinsilblon Ltd Inc ....G 239 418-1133
  Fort Myers **(G-4281)**
OHanrahan Consultants Inc ....E ... 727 531-3375
  Largo **(G-7652)**

CLEANING PRDTS: Disinfectants, Household Or Indl Plant

Eco Concepts Inc ....F ... 954 920-9700
  Hollywood **(G-5569)**
Permasafe Prtctive Catings LLC ....E ... 866 372-9622
  Coconut Creek **(G-2001)**
Reliox Corporation ....G 904 729-5097
  Jacksonville **(G-6415)**
Seal Shield LLC ....E ... 877 325-7443
  Orlando **(G-12582)**

CLEANING PRDTS: Drain Pipe Solvents Or Cleaners

See-Ray Plumbing Inc ....E ... 772 489-2474
  Vero Beach **(G-17798)**

CLEANING PRDTS: Drycleaning Preparations

Holiday Cleaners Inc ....G 727 842-6989
  New Port Richey **(G-10968)**

CLEANING PRDTS: Indl Plant Disinfectants Or Deodorants

Lee Chemical Corporation ....G 407 843-6950
  Longwood **(G-7917)**
Northland Manufacturing Inc ....G 850 878-5149
  Tallahassee **(G-16484)**

CLEANING PRDTS: Laundry Preparations

Chhaya Corporation ....G 407 348-9400
  Kissimmee **(G-6907)**
Mollys Suds LLC ....G 678 361-5456
  Saint Petersburg **(G-15129)**
Renew Life Holdings Corp ....E ... 925 368-9711
  Davie **(G-2467)**

CLEANING PRDTS: Polishing Preparations & Related Prdts

Ibiz Inc ....F ... 954 781-4714
  Pompano Beach **(G-14058)**
N A Comandulli LLC ....G 941 870-2878
  Sarasota **(G-15522)**
Ocean Bio-Chem LLC ....E ... 954 587-6280
  Davie **(G-2448)**

CLEANING PRDTS: Sanitation Preparations

Ciega Inc ....G 727 526-9048
  Saint Petersburg **(G-15007)**

CLEANING PRDTS: Sanitation Preps, Disinfectants/Deodorants

Cogswell Innovations Inc ....G 954 245-8877
  Fort Lauderdale **(G-3734)**
Futurescape Inc ....G 386 679-4120
  Port Orange **(G-14334)**
Infinity Manufacturing LLC ....G 954 531-6918
  Coconut Creek **(G-1989)**
Inspec Solutions LLC ....F ... 866 467-7320
  Daytona Beach **(G-2563)**
Nvip LLC ....G 469 955-4427
  Naples **(G-10838)**

Paradise Air Fresh LLC ....F ... 561 972-0375
  Palm City **(G-13053)**
Relu Co ....E ... 786 717-5665
  Fort Lauderdale **(G-4014)**
Samarian Products LLC ....E ... 212 781-2121
  Naples **(G-10882)**
Saphire Services LLC ....G 386 247-1048
  Lake Butler **(G-7005)**
Veridien Corporation ....G 727 576-1600
  Saint Petersburg **(G-15224)**
Victory Valet Services LLC ....F ... 904 521-6517
  Jacksonville **(G-6590)**
Whr Holdings LLC ....G 954 342-4342
  Fort Lauderdale **(G-4130)**

CLEANING PRDTS: Specialty

1st Enviro-Safety Inc ....G 239 283-1222
  Saint James City **(G-14943)**
Amazon Cleaning & More Inc ....G 239 594-1733
  Naples **(G-10663)**
American Coatings Corporation..............G 954 970-7820
  Margate **(G-8120)**
Beyondclean LLC ....F ... 561 799-5710
  Jupiter **(G-6693)**
Brewer International Inc ....F ... 772 562-0555
  Vero Beach **(G-17743)**
Green Bull Products Inc ....G 386 402-0409
  New Smyrna **(G-10992)**
Impressions Dry Cleaners Inc ....F ... 561 988-3030
  Boca Raton **(G-543)**
Kmss Products Inc ....G 800 646-3005
  Largo **(G-7628)**
Services NS 18 LLC ....G 786 546-3295
  Aventura **(G-275)**
Spa Concepts Inc ....F ... 850 575-0921
  Tallahassee **(G-16502)**
Suncoast Research Labs Inc ....F ... 727 344-7627
  Saint Petersburg **(G-15201)**

CLEANING SVCS: Industrial Or Commercial

Florida Elc Mtr Co Miami Inc.................E ... 305 759-3835
  Miami **(G-9154)**

CLIPS & FASTENERS, MADE FROM PURCHASED WIRE

Mor EZ Clips ....G 352 867-1879
  Ocala **(G-11446)**

CLOSURES: Plastic

Marconi Line Inc....................................F ... 321 639-1130
  Rockledge **(G-14730)**

CLOTHING & ACCESS, WOMEN, CHILD & INFANT, WHOLESALE: Under

New Concepts Distrs Intl LLC.................F ... 305 463-8735
  Doral **(G-3311)**

CLOTHING & ACCESS, WOMEN, CHILD & INFANT, WHSLE: Sportswear

Sportailor Inc..D 305 754-3255
  Miami **(G-9944)**

CLOTHING & ACCESS, WOMEN, CHILDREN & INFANT, WHOL: Handbags

Excel Handbags Co Inc ....F ... 305 836-8800
  Miami **(G-9118)**

CLOTHING & ACCESS, WOMEN, CHILDREN & INFANT, WHOL: Uniforms

JA Uniforms Inc ....F ... 305 234-1231
  Miami **(G-9353)**

CLOTHING & ACCESS, WOMEN, CHILDREN/INFANT, WHOL: Baby Goods

Nissi & Jireh Inc ....E ... 866 897-7657
  Miramar **(G-10519)**

CLOTHING & ACCESS, WOMEN, CHILDREN/INFANT, WHOL: Outerwear

Fashion Pool USA Inc ....G 970 367-4797
  Jupiter **(G-6726)**

CLOTHING & ACCESS, WOMEN, CHILDREN/INFANT, WHOL: Swimsuits

Swim By Chuck Handy Inc.....................G 305 519-4946
  North Miami Beach **(G-11165)**

CLOTHING & ACCESS, WOMENS, CHILDREN & INFANTS, WHOL: Hats

Royal Headwear & EMB Inc ....F ... 305 889-8480
  Medley **(G-8316)**

CLOTHING & ACCESS: Arm bands, Elastic

Price Chopper Inc ....E ... 407 679-1600
  Orlando **(G-12504)**
Wristband Supply LLC ....F ... 954 571-3993
  Deerfield Beach **(G-2836)**

CLOTHING & ACCESS: Costumes, Lodge

Greater Miami Elks Lodge Inc................F ... 305 754-5899
  Miami **(G-9240)**

CLOTHING & ACCESS: Costumes, Theatrical

Algy Trimmings Co Inc ....D 954 457-8100
  Miami **(G-8686)**

CLOTHING & ACCESS: Footlets

Keepmefresh ....G 502 407-7902
  Clermont **(G-1872)**

CLOTHING & ACCESS: Handicapped

David Dobbs Enterprises Inc ....D 904 824-6171
  Saint Augustine **(G-14823)**
Geekshive Inc.......................................F ... 888 797-4335
  Miami **(G-9197)**
Stuntwear LLC ....G 305 842-2115
  Miami Beach **(G-10237)**

CLOTHING & ACCESS: Hospital Gowns

Carter-Health Disposables LLC ....G 407 296-6689
  Orlando **(G-11984)**
Prescient Logistics LLC ....F ... 407 547-2680
  Sanford **(G-15377)**
Universal HM Hlth Indus Sups I ....G 813 493-7904
  Tampa **(G-17393)**

CLOTHING & ACCESS: Men's Miscellaneous Access

Can Can Concealment LLC....................G 727 841-6930
  Odessa **(G-11542)**
Christy Lewis Sheek LLC ....G 786 512-2999
  Coral Springs **(G-2140)**
Davis-Wick Talent MGT LLC ....E ... 407 369-1614
  Margate **(G-8127)**
Exclusive Apparel LLC ....F ... 800 859-6260
  Fort Lauderdale **(G-3805)**
Lipscomb Finch Co................................F ... 904 415-4265
  Jacksonville **(G-6260)**
Slate Solutions LLC ....E ... 754 200-6752
  Davie **(G-2478)**
Walter Green Inc ....G 850 227-7946
  Port Saint Joe **(G-14392)**
Wayloo Inc ....G 954 914-3192
  Fort Lauderdale **(G-4125)**
Wesol Distribution LLC ....G 407 921-9248
  Casselberry **(G-1436)**
Zeppelin Products Inc ....F ... 954 989-8808
  Fort Lauderdale **(G-4146)**

CLOTHING & ACCESS: Suspenders

Sparkles and Suspenders FL.................G 754 701-4528
  Lauderhill **(G-7742)**

CLOTHING & APPAREL STORES: Custom

Cotton Pickin Shirts Plus ....G 850 435-3133
  Pensacola **(G-13478)**
Marlin Graphics Inc...............................G 561 743-5220
  Jupiter **(G-6761)**
Outdoor Products LLC ....G 352 473-0886
  Steinhatchee **(G-16106)**

PRODUCT

CLOTHING & FURNISHINGS, MEN'S & BOYS', WHOLESALE: Hats

Royal Headwear & EMB Inc ....F 305 889-8480
Medley (G-8316)

CLOTHING & FURNISHINGS, MEN'S & BOYS', WHOLESALE: Outerwear

American Lw & Promo Prods LLC ....G 954 946-5252
Pompano Beach (G-13924)
Fashion Pool USA Inc ....G 970 367-4797
Jupiter (G-6726)

CLOTHING & FURNISHINGS, MEN'S & BOYS', WHOLESALE: Shirts

CBI Industries Inc ....G 305 796-9346
Miami (G-8904)

CLOTHING & FURNISHINGS, MEN'S & BOYS', WHOLESALE: Uniforms

Interntnal Export Uniforms Inc ....F 305 869-9900
Miami (G-9330)

CLOTHING & FURNISHINGS, MENS & BOYS, WHOL: Sportswear/Work

Sportailor Inc ....D 305 754-3255
Miami (G-9944)
Stitch Count Inc ....G 609 929-9019
North Miami Beach (G-11162)

CLOTHING & FURNISHINGS, MENS & BOYS, WHOLESALE: Apprl Belts

Christy Lewis Sheek LLC ....G 786 512-2999
Coral Springs (G-2140)
Continental Belt Corp ....G 305 573-8871
Miami (G-8962)

CLOTHING STORES: Formal Wear

Designs To Shine Inc ....E 727 525-4297
Saint Petersburg (G-15023)

CLOTHING STORES: Jeans

Blue Light USA Corp ....G 954 766-4308
Sunrise (G-16299)

CLOTHING STORES: Shirts, Custom Made

CBI Industries Inc ....G 305 796-9346
Miami (G-8904)

CLOTHING STORES: T-Shirts, Printed, Custom

Above LLC ....F 850 469-9028
Pensacola (G-13431)
Expert TS of Jacksonville ....F 904 387-2500
Jacksonville (G-6084)
Kikisteescom LLC ....E 888 620-4110
Sunrise (G-16333)
Maddys Print Shop LLC ....G 954 749-0440
Fort Lauderdale (G-3926)
STS Apparel Corp ....F 305 628-4000
Hialeah (G-5366)

CLOTHING STORES: Uniforms & Work

A2z Uniforms Inc ....G 941 254-3194
Sarasota (G-15583)
Official Gear Company Inc ....G 407 721-9110
Ormond Beach (G-12782)
Rakiline LLC ....G 904 800-2632
Jacksonville (G-6404)
ST Action Pro Inc ....G 321 632-4111
Cocoa (G-1959)

CLOTHING STORES: Unisex

Bang Energy LLC ....F 954 641-0570
Weston (G-18227)
Shirts & Caps Inc ....F 813 788-7026
Tampa (G-17262)

CLOTHING, WOMEN & CHILD, WHLSE: Dress, Suit, Skirt & Blouse

Stush AP USA/Stush Style LLC ....F 404 940-3445
Sunrise (G-16374)

CLOTHING/ACCESS, WOMEN, CHILDREN/INFANT, WHOL: Apparel Belt

Christy Lewis Sheek LLC ....G 786 512-2999
Coral Springs (G-2140)

CLOTHING: Academic Vestments

Regency Cap & Gown Company ....F 904 724-3500
Jacksonville (G-6412)

CLOTHING: Access

Alluring Group Inc ....F 800 731-2280
Miramar (G-10466)
Antonyo Denard Llc ....F 904 290-1579
Jacksonville (G-5893)
C&D Sign and Lighting Svcs LLC ....G 863 937-9323
Lakeland (G-7287)
JADA Transitions LLC ....G 561 377-8194
Riviera Beach (G-14633)
Jewels Handmade LLC ....F 407 283-9951
Orlando (G-12273)
Lululemon ....G 813 973-3879
Wesley Chapel (G-17882)
Poof Game LLC ....G 239 245-2957
Lehigh Acres (G-7821)
Til Valhalla Project LLC ....D 904 579-3414
Saint Augustine (G-14906)

CLOTHING: Access, Women's & Misses'

Can Can Concealment LLC ....G 727 841-6930
Odessa (G-11542)
Christy Lewis Sheek LLC ....G 786 512-2999
Coral Springs (G-2140)
Coastal Paddle Co LLC ....G 850 916-1600
Gulf Breeze (G-4878)
Finesta Inc ....G 786 439-1647
Miami (G-9143)
Ischa Products LLC ....G 305 609-8244
Homestead (G-5719)
Maria Fuentes LLC ....G 305 717-3404
Miami (G-9511)
Mink Milli LLC ....F 813 606-0416
Tampa (G-17074)

CLOTHING: Aprons, Harness

Hallmark Emblems Inc ....D 813 223-5427
Tampa (G-16902)

CLOTHING: Aprons, Work, Exc Rubberized & Plastic, Men's

Cameron Textiles Inc ....G 954 454-6482
Palm City (G-13026)

CLOTHING: Athletic & Sportswear, Men's & Boys'

Anmapec Corporation ....F 786 897-5389
Miami (G-8731)
Armen Co Inc ....D 305 206-1601
Plantation (G-13827)
Arno Belo Inc ....G 800 734-2356
Hallandale Beach (G-4936)
Athco Inc ....E 941 351-1600
Sarasota (G-15444)
B & B Industries Orlando Inc ....G 407 366-1800
Oviedo (G-12809)
Bdc Florida LLC ....F 561 249-0900
West Palm Beach (G-17939)
Exist Inc ....D 954 739-7030
Fort Lauderdale (G-3806)
Fabrox LLC ....E 904 342-4048
Ormond Beach (G-12764)
Fitletic Sports LLC ....G 305 907-6663
Hallandale Beach (G-4947)
Golf America Southwest Fla Inc ....G 904 688-0280
Saint Augustine (G-14836)
Good Chance Textile Inc ....F 754 263-2792
Pembroke Pines (G-13393)
Icon Embroidery Inc ....G 407 858-0886
Windermere (G-18353)

In Gear Fashions Inc ....D 305 830-2900
Miami Gardens (G-10264)
J W Group Inc ....G 386 423-8828
Edgewater (G-3493)
JMP Fashion Inc ....G 305 633-9920
Miami (G-9369)
John M Caldwell Distrg Co Inc ....F 305 685-9822
Opa Locka (G-11758)
Onca Gear LLC ....G 857 253-8207
Hialeah (G-5287)
Outdoor Products LLC ....G 352 473-0886
Steinhatchee (G-16106)
Recover Gear LLC ....G 904 280-9660
Ponte Vedra Beach (G-14280)
Speedline Team Sports Inc ....F 813 876-1375
Tampa (G-17294)
Spirit Sales Corporation ....G 850 878-0366
Tallahassee (G-16503)
Sportailor Inc ....D 305 754-3255
Miami (G-9944)
Sports Structure Intl LLC ....G 305 777-2225
Miami Beach (G-10234)
Suncoast Trends Inc ....G 727 321-4948
Saint Petersburg (G-15202)
Surf Outfitter ....G 813 489-4587
Tampa (G-17317)
T Shirt Center Inc ....G 305 655-1955
Miami (G-9990)
Tactical Products Group LLC ....E 561 265-4066
Boynton Beach (G-918)
Ultimate Overstock LLC ....E 407 851-1017
Orlando (G-12685)
Val DOr Apparel LLC ....G 954 363-7340
Coconut Creek (G-2009)

CLOTHING: Athletic & Sportswear, Women's & Girls'

B & B Industries Orlando Inc ....G 407 366-1800
Oviedo (G-12809)
Excess Liquidator LLC ....G 407 247-9105
Oviedo (G-12820)
Gsg Group Inc ....E 954 733-8219
Lauderdale Lakes (G-7715)
J W Group Inc ....G 386 423-8828
Edgewater (G-3493)
Kamaj Business Group Inc ....F 813 863-9967
Tampa (G-16976)
New Concepts Distrs Intl LLC ....F 305 463-8735
Doral (G-3311)
Recover Gear LLC ....G 904 280-9660
Ponte Vedra Beach (G-14280)
Shgar Kane Couture Inc ....G 407 205-8038
Orlando (G-12591)
Workwear Outfitters LLC ....C 336 424-6000
Tampa (G-17436)

CLOTHING: Baker, Barber, Lab/Svc Ind Apparel, Washable, Men

Ivory International Inc ....C 305 687-2244
Medley (G-8261)
Uzzi Amphibious Gear LLC ....G 954 777-9595
Hallandale Beach (G-4984)

CLOTHING: Bathing Suits & Swimwear, Girls, Children & Infant

Rme Studio Inc ....G 305 409-0856
Miami (G-9812)
Shore Trendz LLC ....G 954 608-7375
Plantation (G-13887)
Surf Outfitter ....G 813 489-4587
Tampa (G-17317)

CLOTHING: Bathing Suits & Swimwear, Knit

House of Llull Atelier LLC ....G 305 964-7921
Miami (G-9291)
Reflections BEAch&resortwear ....G 954 776-1230
Laud By Sea (G-7711)
Swim By Chuck Handy Inc ....G 305 519-4946
North Miami Beach (G-11165)

CLOTHING: Bathrobes, Mens & Womens, From Purchased Materials

Terry Boca Inc ....G 561 893-0333
Deerfield Beach (G-2823)

CLOTHING: Beachwear, Knit

Nrz Inc .... G 305 345-7303
Pinecrest (G-13667)
Swf Bonita Beach Inc .... D 239 466-6600
Bonita Springs (G-824)

CLOTHING: Belts

Tagua Leather Corporation .... F 305 637-3014
Miami (G-9993)
Zeppelin Products Inc .... F 954 989-8808
Fort Lauderdale (G-4146)

CLOTHING: Blouses & Shirts, Girls' & Children's

Bossy Princess LLC .... G 786 285-4435
Aventura (G-257)

CLOTHING: Blouses, Women's & Girls'

Apyelen Curves LLC .... F 904 328-3390
Jacksonville (G-5895)
Daisy Crazy Inc .... G 305 300-5144
Doral (G-3183)
Decoy Inc .... G 305 633-6384
Miami (G-9006)
Dujon Inc .... F 813 770-3179
Saint Petersburg (G-15031)
Entire Select Inc .... G 954 674-2368
Sunrise (G-16316)
H M J Corporation .... F 954 229-1873
Fort Lauderdale (G-3855)
Kamtex USA Incorporated .... G 954 733-1044
Lauderdale Lakes (G-7717)
Matteo Graphics Inc .... G 239 652-1002
Cape Coral (G-1363)
R&S Intrnational Inv Group LLC .... F 305 576-3000
Miami (G-9774)
Stanley Industries of S Fla .... G 954 929-8770
Hollywood (G-5664)
Supreme International LLC .... A 305 592-2830
Doral (G-3386)
Vargas Enterprises Inc .... G 561 989-0908
Boca Raton (G-742)
Wbt Apparel Inc .... G 305 891-1107
North Miami (G-11127)

CLOTHING: Blouses, Womens & Juniors, From Purchased Mtrls

Argus International Inc .... E 305 888-4881
Weston (G-18226)
Goen3 Corporation .... G 407 601-6000
Orlando (G-12197)
Johnny Devil Inc .... G 305 634-0700
Miami (G-9370)
PJ Designs Inc .... E 727 525-0599
Saint Petersburg (G-15151)
Stush AP USA/Stush Style LLC .... F 404 940-3445
Sunrise (G-16374)
Suncoast Trends Inc .... G 727 321-4948
Saint Petersburg (G-15202)

CLOTHING: Brassieres

Universal Brass Fabrication .... F 561 691-5445
Palm Beach Gardens (G-13015)

CLOTHING: Bridal Gowns

Designs To Shine Inc .... E 727 525-4297
Saint Petersburg (G-15023)

CLOTHING: Children's, Girls'

Armen Co Inc .... D 305 206-1601
Plantation (G-13827)
Athco Inc .... E 941 351-1600
Sarasota (G-15444)
Dilan Enterprises Inc .... E 305 887-3051
Hialeah (G-5118)
Ivory International Inc .... C 305 687-2244
Medley (G-8261)
Manatee Bay Enterprises Inc .... F 407 245-3600
Orlando (G-12362)
Mishy Sportswear .... E 305 819-7556
Hialeah (G-5262)
Puppet Workshop Inc .... C 305 666-2655
Hialeah (G-5316)
Sarah Louise Inc .... F 941 377-9656
Sarasota (G-15808)

Suncoast Trends Inc .... G 727 321-4948
Saint Petersburg (G-15202)

CLOTHING: Coats & Jackets, Leather & Sheep-Lined

Tagua Leather Corporation .... F 305 637-3014
Miami (G-9993)

CLOTHING: Coats & Suits, Men's & Boys'

Harlan J Newman .... G 727 216-6419
Seminole (G-15977)
Lipscomb Finch Co .... F 904 415-4265
Jacksonville (G-6260)
Mario Kenny .... G 786 274-0527
Miami (G-9512)
Tycoon Tutti Inc .... E 305 624-7811
Miami (G-10052)

CLOTHING: Costumes

Goruck LLC .... G 904 708-2081
Jacksonville Beach (G-6633)
Goruck Holdings LLC .... G 904 708-2081
Jacksonville Beach (G-6634)
Miss BS Inc .... G 305 981-9900
North Miami Beach (G-11151)
Robot-Costumes Technologies .... G 904 535-0074
Saint Augustine (G-14880)

CLOTHING: Disposable

Mhms Corp .... E 813 948-0504
Lutz (G-8005)
Shore Trendz LLC .... G 954 608-7375
Plantation (G-13887)

CLOTHING: Dresses

Amj DOT LLC .... G 646 249-0273
Boca Raton (G-410)
Arde Apparel Inc .... E 305 326-0861
Miami (G-8744)
Janine of London Inc .... G 954 772-3593
Fort Lauderdale (G-3892)
Laura Knit Collection Inc .... C 305 945-8222
North Miami Beach (G-11148)
Nomi Rubinstein Inc .... G 305 467-7888
Miami (G-9624)
Stanley Industries of S Fla .... G 954 929-8770
Hollywood (G-5664)
Stush AP USA/Stush Style LLC .... F 404 940-3445
Sunrise (G-16374)

CLOTHING: Formal Jackets, Mens & Youth, From Purchased Matls

Apparel Imports Inc .... E 800 428-6849
Miami (G-8735)

CLOTHING: Garments, Indl, Men's & Boys

Garment Corporation of America .... B 305 531-4040
Miami Beach (G-10194)

CLOTHING: Gowns & Dresses, Wedding

AA Oldco Inc .... D 215 659-5300
Delray Beach (G-2923)
CD Greeting LLC .... G 954 530-1301
Fort Lauderdale (G-3717)
Classic Stars Inc .... G 305 871-6767
Miami (G-8930)
Miller Creative Works Inc .... G 904 504-3212
Jacksonville (G-6307)
Mori Lee LLC .... E 954 418-6165
Deerfield Beach (G-2771)
Weddings By Tina .... G 904 235-3740
Jacksonville (G-6599)

CLOTHING: Hats & Caps, NEC

Bernard Cap LLC .... D 305 822-4800
Hialeah (G-5073)
Ronmar Industries Inc .... G 561 630-8035
West Palm Beach (G-18145)

CLOTHING: Hats & Caps, Uniform

American Lw & Promo Prods LLC .... G 954 946-5252
Pompano Beach (G-13924)
Feds Apparel .... E 954 932-0685
Davie (G-2411)

CLOTHING: Hats, Harvest, Straw

John Lacquey Enterprises Inc .... F 386 935-1705
Branford (G-1113)

CLOTHING: Helmets, Jungle Cloth, Wool Lined

Casablanca Polo Co .... G 832 668-6804
Wellington (G-17847)
Coolhead Helmet LLC .... G 786 292-4829
Miami (G-8966)

CLOTHING: Hosiery, Men's & Boys'

Triumph Hosiery Corp .... G 954 929-6021
Hollywood (G-5675)

CLOTHING: Hosiery, Pantyhose & Knee Length, Sheer

New Concepts Distrs Intl LLC .... F 305 463-8735
Doral (G-3311)
Triumph Hosiery Corp .... G 954 929-6021
Hollywood (G-5675)

CLOTHING: Hospital, Men's

Affordable Med Scrubs LLC .... F 419 222-1088
Miami (G-8665)
Fabrox LLC .... E 904 342-4048
Ormond Beach (G-12764)
Samarian Products LLC .... E 212 781-2121
Naples (G-10882)

CLOTHING: Jackets, Knit

Bnj Noble Inc .... F 954 987-1040
Davie (G-2392)

CLOTHING: Knit Underwear & Nightwear

Sweet and Vicious LLC .... F 772 907-3030
Lake Worth (G-7234)

CLOTHING: Leather

Oceanstyle LLC .... G 305 672-9400
Miami Beach (G-10217)

CLOTHING: Leather & sheep-lined clothing

Shaikh Rizwan .... G 202 740-9796
Lakeland (G-7432)

CLOTHING: Lounge, Bed & Leisurewear

A & S Entertainment LLC .... F 305 627-3456
Miami (G-8615)

CLOTHING: Maternity

Olian Inc .... E 305 233-9116
Miami (G-9643)

CLOTHING: Men's & boy's clothing, nec

Jamerica Inc .... G 561 488-6247
Boca Raton (G-556)
Winntel USA .... F 863 451-1789
Sebring (G-15950)

CLOTHING: Men's & boy's underwear & nightwear

Val DOr Apparel LLC .... G 954 363-7340
Coconut Creek (G-2009)

CLOTHING: Neckwear

Chervo USA Inc .... G 561 510-2458
North Palm Beach (G-11179)
Element Outdoors LLC .... G 888 589-9589
Pace (G-12857)
Exces International LLC .... G 561 880-8920
Wellington (G-17850)
Jblaze Inc .... G 954 680-3962
Southwest Ranches (G-16055)
Orchid Envy .... G 941 485-1122
Venice (G-17709)
Prive Porter LLC .... G 561 479-9200
Boca Raton (G-641)

P R O D U C T

CLOTHING: Outerwear, Knit

Jonel Knitting Mills Inc ....E 305 887-7333
Hialeah *(G-5206)*

Two Mermaids Villages LLC ....G 352 259-4722
The Villages *(G-17558)*

CLOTHING: Outerwear, Lthr, Wool/Down-Filled, Men, Youth/Boy

Fashion Pool USA Inc ....G 970 367-4797
Jupiter *(G-6726)*

CLOTHING: Outerwear, Women's & Misses' NEC

A Living Testimony LLC ....G 352 406-0249
Eustis *(G-3551)*

Algy Trimmings Co Inc ....D 954 457-8100
Miami *(G-8686)*

ANue Ligne Inc ....G 305 638-7979
Miami *(G-8733)*

Big Fish Co Custom Creations ....G 727 525-5010
Saint Petersburg *(G-14981)*

Dilan Enterprises Inc ....E 305 887-3051
Hialeah *(G-5118)*

Fashion Pool USA Inc ....G 970 367-4797
Jupiter *(G-6726)*

Happy Kids For Kids Inc ....F 954 730-7922
Fort Lauderdale *(G-3860)*

Ivory International Inc ....C 305 687-2244
Medley *(G-8261)*

Joro Fashions Florida Inc ....F 305 888-8110
Pinecrest *(G-13666)*

Kacoo Usa LLC ....G 727 233-8237
Clearwater *(G-1658)*

Lagaci Inc ....F 954 929-1395
Fort Lauderdale *(G-3910)*

Lisa Todd International LLC ....G 305 445-2632
Miami *(G-9464)*

Manatee Bay Enterprises Inc ....F 407 245-3600
Orlando *(G-12362)*

Nordic Group LLC ....G 561 789-8676
Boca Raton *(G-619)*

Ocean Waves Inc ....F 904 372-4743
Jacksonville Beach *(G-6641)*

Perry Ellis International Inc ....B 305 592-2830
Doral *(G-3325)*

Salt Life LLC ....G 904 595-5370
Jacksonville Beach *(G-6644)*

South Florida Textile Inc ....F 954 973-5677
Pompano Beach *(G-14190)*

Speedline Team Sports Inc ....F 813 876-1375
Tampa *(G-17294)*

Sport Products of Tampa Inc ....G 813 630-5552
Tampa *(G-17296)*

Val DOr Apparel LLC ....G 954 363-7340
Coconut Creek *(G-2009)*

CLOTHING: Robes & Dressing Gowns

Boca Terry LLC ....F 954 312-4400
Deerfield Beach *(G-2679)*

Lyric Choir Gown Company ....G 904 725-7977
Jacksonville *(G-6266)*

PJ Designs Inc ....E 727 525-0599
Saint Petersburg *(G-15151)*

CLOTHING: Service Apparel, Women's

Momentum Comfort Gear Inc ....F 305 653-5050
Miami *(G-9586)*

Saint George Industries LLC ....E 786 212-1176
Miami *(G-9838)*

Uzzi Amphibious Gear LLC ....G 954 777-9595
Hallandale Beach *(G-4984)*

CLOTHING: Shirts

Dujon Inc ....F 813 770-3179
Saint Petersburg *(G-15031)*

Entire Select Inc ....G 954 674-2368
Sunrise *(G-16316)*

Feldenkreis Holdings LLC ....D 305 592-2830
Doral *(G-3214)*

La Providencia Express Co ....G 305 409-9894
Miami *(G-9412)*

Leo Fashions Inc ....F 305 887-1032
Hialeah *(G-5222)*

Ronmar Industries Inc ....G 561 630-8035
West Palm Beach *(G-18145)*

Stanley Industries of S Fla ....G 954 929-8770
Hollywood *(G-5664)*

Tycoon Tutti Inc ....E 305 624-7811
Miami *(G-10052)*

CLOTHING: Shirts & T-Shirts, Knit

Eyedose Inc ....G 786 853-6194
Miami *(G-9124)*

Monkey Shack ....G 850 234-0082
Panama City *(G-13287)*

CLOTHING: Shirts, Dress, Men's & Boys'

Perry Ellis International Inc ....B 305 592-2830
Doral *(G-3325)*

Pvh Corp ....F 850 269-0482
Miramar Beach *(G-10571)*

Regina Behar Enterprises Inc ....E 305 557-5212
Miramar *(G-10535)*

CLOTHING: Shirts, Sports & Polo, Men's & Boys'

A G A Electronics Corp ....F 305 592-1860
Miami *(G-8621)*

Dynasty Apparel Corp ....D 305 685-3490
Opa Locka *(G-11740)*

CLOTHING: Shirts, Uniform, From Purchased Materials

Feds Apparel ....F 954 932-0685
Davie *(G-2411)*

CLOTHING: Shirts, Women's & Juniors', From Purchased Mtrls

Leo Fashions Inc ....F 305 887-1032
Hialeah *(G-5222)*

CLOTHING: Skirts, Knit

Veronica Knits Inc ....F 305 887-7333
Hialeah *(G-5408)*

CLOTHING: Socks

American Stock LLC ....G 904 641-2055
Jacksonville *(G-5887)*

King of Socks ....G 772 204-3286
Port St Lucie *(G-14477)*

Leopard Brands Inc ....G 954 794-0007
Boca Raton *(G-577)*

Shashi LLC ....G 561 447-8800
Delray Beach *(G-3016)*

Skater Socks ....G 850 424-6764
Destin *(G-3079)*

Tox Manufacturing Group LLC ....F 310 909-4937
Vero Beach *(G-17809)*

Zokos Group Inc ....G 888 756-9769
Boca Raton *(G-764)*

CLOTHING: Sportswear, Women's

American Athletic Uniforms Inc ....F 850 729-1205
Valparaiso *(G-17654)*

Anmapec Corporation ....F 786 897-5389
Miami *(G-8731)*

Armen Co Inc ....G 305 206-1601
Plantation *(G-13827)*

Diane Dal Lago Limited Company ....F 813 374-2473
Tampa *(G-16775)*

Fitletic Sports LLC ....G 305 907-6663
Hallandale Beach *(G-4947)*

Great Cir Vntures Holdings LLC ....E 305 638-2650
Doral *(G-3238)*

Icon Embroidery Inc ....G 407 858-0886
Windermere *(G-18353)*

In Gear Fashions Inc ....D 305 830-2900
Miami Gardens *(G-10264)*

JMP Fashion Inc ....G 305 633-9920
Miami *(G-9369)*

John M Caldwell Distrg Co Inc ....F 305 685-9822
Opa Locka *(G-11758)*

Lear Investors Inc ....G 305 681-8582
Opa Locka *(G-11763)*

Matteo Graphics Inc ....G 239 652-1002
Cape Coral *(G-1363)*

Mishy Sportswear ....E 305 819-7556
Hialeah *(G-5262)*

Sir Winston Garments Inc ....F 305 499-3144
Miami *(G-9900)*

Southpoint Sportswear LLC ....G 305 885-3045
Medley *(G-8323)*

Suncoast Trends Inc ....G 727 321-4948
Saint Petersburg *(G-15202)*

T Shirt Center Inc ....G 305 655-1955
Miami *(G-9990)*

CLOTHING: Swimwear, Men's & Boys'

Ultimate Swimwear Inc ....F 386 668-8900
Altamonte Springs *(G-75)*

CLOTHING: Swimwear, Women's & Misses'

Double J of Broward Inc ....E 954 659-8880
Weston *(G-18238)*

Earth & Sea Wear LLC ....E 786 332-2236
Doral *(G-3202)*

Regency Cap & Gown Company ....F 904 724-3500
Jacksonville *(G-6412)*

Ultimate Swimwear Inc ....F 386 668-8900
Altamonte Springs *(G-75)*

Venus Manufacturing Co Inc ....D 904 645-3187
Jacksonville *(G-6589)*

CLOTHING: T-Shirts & Tops, Knit

Balzarano John ....F 239 455-1231
Naples *(G-10689)*

Coral Club Tee Shirts Inc ....G 305 828-6939
Hialeah *(G-5097)*

Daisy Crazy Inc ....G 305 300-5144
Doral *(G-3183)*

MK Brothers Inc ....G 407 847-9547
Kissimmee *(G-6944)*

CLOTHING: T-Shirts & Tops, Women's & Girls'

Kleids Enterprises Inc ....G 727 796-7900
Clearwater *(G-1662)*

Val DOr Apparel LLC ....G 954 363-7340
Coconut Creek *(G-2009)*

CLOTHING: Trousers & Slacks, Men's & Boys'

Goen3 Corporation ....G 407 601-6000
Orlando *(G-12197)*

Lagaci Inc ....F 954 929-1395
Fort Lauderdale *(G-3910)*

Original Pnguin Drect Oprtions ....F 305 592-2830
Doral *(G-3319)*

Perry Ellis International Inc ....B 305 592-2830
Doral *(G-3325)*

Stanley Industries of S Fla ....G 954 929-8770
Hollywood *(G-5664)*

Stush AP USA/Stush Style LLC ....F 404 940-3445
Sunrise *(G-16374)*

Supreme International LLC ....A 305 592-2830
Doral *(G-3386)*

CLOTHING: Underwear, Knit

Intradeco Apparel Inc ....E 305 264-8888
Medley *(G-8259)*

CLOTHING: Underwear, Women's & Children's

Apparel Machinery Services Inc ....G 772 335-5350
Port Saint Lucie *(G-14396)*

Decoy Inc ....G 305 633-6384
Miami *(G-9006)*

Eberjey Intimates ....G 305 260-0030
Miami *(G-9066)*

Fenix Wester Corp ....G 305 324-9105
Miami *(G-9137)*

Kamtex USA Incorporated ....G 954 733-1044
Lauderdale Lakes *(G-7717)*

Sweet and Vicious LLC ....G 305 576-0012
Miami *(G-9981)*

CLOTHING: Uniforms & Vestments

Bold Look Inc ....E 305 687-8725
Miami *(G-8844)*

Fashion Connection Miami Inc ....G 305 882-0782
Hialeah *(G-5151)*

Point Blank Enterprises Inc ....A 954 846-8222
Pompano Beach (G-14133)
Superior Group Companies Inc ....C 727 397-9611
Seminole (G-15991)

CLOTHING: Uniforms, Ex Athletic, Women's, Misses' & Juniors'

Cintas Corporation ....G 239 693-8722
Fort Myers (G-4209)
International Clothiers Inc ....F 914 715-5600
Miami (G-9325)
Interntnal Export Uniforms Inc ....F 305 869-9900
Miami (G-9330)

CLOTHING: Uniforms, Men's & Boys'

A G A Electronics Corp ....F 305 592-1860
Miami (G-8621)
Burn Proof Gear LLC ....G 786 634-7406
Miami (G-8862)
Global Trading Inc ....F 305 471-4455
Miami (G-9220)
Stitch Count Inc ....G 609 929-9019
North Miami Beach (G-11162)

CLOTHING: Uniforms, Military, Men/Youth, Purchased Materials

Cadre Holdings Inc ....E 904 741-5400
Jacksonville (G-5967)
Eglin Air Force Base ....C 850 882-5422
Eglin Afb (G-3504)
Eglin Air Force Base ....G 850 882-3315
Eglin Afb (G-3505)
L C Industries Inc ....F 850 581-0117
Hurlburt Field (G-5792)
Point Blank Protective Apprl ....E 954 630-0900
Pompano Beach (G-14136)
Tennier Industries Inc ....G 561 999-9710
Boca Raton (G-711)

CLOTHING: Uniforms, Policemen's, From Purchased Materials

Maui Holdings LLC ....A 904 741-5400
Palm Beach (G-12938)
Onyx Protective Group Inc ....F 305 282-4455
Miami (G-9657)

CLOTHING: Uniforms, Team Athletic

Bakers Sports Inc ....E 904 388-8126
Jacksonville (G-5921)
Speedline Athletic Wear Inc ....E 813 876-1375
Tampa (G-17293)

CLOTHING: Uniforms, Work

Cintas Corporation ....F 813 874-1401
Tampa (G-16706)
Cintas Corporation ....G 239 693-8722
Fort Myers (G-4209)
Global Trading Inc ....F 305 471-4455
Miami (G-9220)
International Clothiers Inc ....F 914 715-5600
Miami (G-9325)
JA Uniforms Inc ....F 305 234-1231
Miami (G-9353)
M R M S Inc ....G 305 576-3000
Miami (G-9492)
R&S Intrnational Inv Group LLC ....F 305 576-3000
Miami (G-9774)
Wayloo Inc ....G 954 914-3192
Fort Lauderdale (G-4125)

CLOTHING: Vests

Cameron Textiles Inc ....G 954 454-6482
Palm City (G-13026)

CLOTHING: Warm Weather Knit Outerwear, Including Beachwear

H2c Brands LLC ....G 904 342-7485
Saint Augustine (G-14839)
H2c Brands LLC ....E 360 338-0449
Atlantic Beach (G-211)

CLOTHING: Waterproof Outerwear

Loksak Inc ....G 239 331-5550
Naples (G-10806)
Monarch Safety Products Inc ....F 407 442-0269
Orlando (G-12388)
Sara Glove Company Inc ....G 866 664-7272
Naples (G-10884)
Seal Outdoors Inc ....F 877 323-7325
South Miami (G-16045)

CLOTHING: Work Apparel, Exc Uniforms

Dmr Creative Marketing LLC ....G 954 725-3750
Deerfield Beach (G-2708)
Gallant Inc ....G 800 330-1343
Winter Garden (G-18387)
Saint George Industries LLC ....E 786 212-1176
Miami (G-9838)
Stitch Count Inc ....G 609 929-9019
North Miami Beach (G-11162)
Workwear Outfitters LLC ....F 813 969-6481
Tampa (G-17437)

CLOTHING: Work, Men's

Anmapec Corporation ....F 786 897-5389
Miami (G-8731)
CSC Racing Corporation ....F 248 548-5727
Jupiter (G-6706)
Dujon Inc ....F 813 770-3179
Saint Petersburg (G-15031)
Ep Clothing LLC ....G 786 827-9187
Miami (G-9103)
Jackie Z Style Co St Pete LLC ....G 727 258-4849
Saint Petersburg (G-15099)
Jadus Justice Apperal LLC ....F 954 394-6259
North Lauderdale (G-11081)
Mario Kenny ....G 786 274-0527
Miami (G-9512)
Tees By Bo Inc ....G 305 382-8551
Miami (G-9999)
Zayas Fashions Inc ....E 305 823-1438
Hialeah (G-5428)

CLOTHS: Polishing, Plain

Coastal Wipers Inc ....E 813 628-4464
Tampa (G-16716)
Troy Industries Inc ....E 305 324-1742
Doral (G-3404)

COAL MINING EXPLORATION & TEST BORING SVC

Keystone Industries LLC ....F 239 337-7474
Jacksonville (G-6241)
US China Mining Group Inc ....D 813 514-2873
Tampa (G-17397)

COAL MINING SERVICES

Carbon Resources Inc ....G 941 746-8089
Lakewood Ranch (G-7482)
Cline Resource and Dev Co ....G 561 626-4999
Palm Beach Gardens (G-12961)
Diversified Mining Inc ....G 407 923-3194
Winter Park (G-18507)
Florida Crushed Stone Co ....G 352 799-7460
Bushnell (G-1243)
Foresight Reserves LP ....G 561 626-4999
Palm Beach Gardens (G-12971)
Mosaic ....D 863 860-1328
Lakeland (G-7399)
North American Mining ....F 305 824-3181
Medley (G-8290)
Oxbow Carbon LLC ....A 561 907-5400
West Palm Beach (G-18103)
Oxbow Enterprises Intl LLC ....G 561 907-5400
West Palm Beach (G-18104)
Weber South Fl LLC ....G 239 543-7240
Punta Gorda (G-14540)

COAL MINING: Bituminous Coal & Lignite-Surface Mining

North American Coal Corp ....G 305 824-9018
Miami (G-9628)
Teco Diversified Inc ....G 813 228-4111
Tampa (G-17345)

COAL PREPARATION PLANT: Bituminous or Lignite

Evolving Coal Corp ....G 813 944-3100
Saint Petersburg (G-15039)

COAL, MINERALS & ORES, WHOLESALE: Coal

Keystone Industries LLC ....F 239 337-7474
Jacksonville (G-6241)
Oxbow Carbon LLC ....A 561 907-5400
West Palm Beach (G-18103)
Oxbow Enterprises Intl LLC ....G 561 907-5400
West Palm Beach (G-18104)
Puragen LLC ....E 561 907-5400
West Palm Beach (G-18131)

COATING COMPOUNDS: Tar

Marbelite International Corp ....G 941 378-0860
Sarasota (G-15740)

COATING SVC

5 Star Coatings LLc ....G 850 628-3743
Panama City Beach (G-13324)
88 South Atlantic LLC ....G 386 253-0105
Daytona Beach (G-2504)
A Tek Steel Industries Inc ....G 561 745-2858
Jupiter (G-6676)
Aerospc/Dfense Coatings GA Inc ....G 407 843-1140
Altamonte Springs (G-27)
Alternative Coatings of SW Fla ....G 239 537-6153
Naples (G-10660)
Bacc Coatings LLC ....G 239 424-8843
Cape Coral (G-1310)
Boca Coatings Inc ....G 561 400-8183
Boca Raton (G-434)
Caliber Coating Inc ....G 813 928-1461
Zephyrhills (G-18607)
Custom Powder Coating LLC ....G 386 758-3973
Lake City (G-7016)
D and I Trucking Express Inc ....G 786 443-3320
Miami (G-8990)
Defend Coatings LLC ....G 954 612-5593
Plantation (G-13844)
Dna Surface Concepts Inc ....F 561 328-7302
Riviera Beach (G-14616)
Ds Coatings Inc ....G 321 848-4719
Avon Park (G-280)
Ecosmart Surface & Coating TEC ....G 402 319-1607
West Palm Beach (G-17986)
Emerald Coast Coatings LLC ....F 850 424-5244
Fort Walton Beach (G-4580)
Fuzion Prfmce Coatings LLC ....G 561 364-2474
Ocean Ridge (G-11517)
Genteel Coatings LLC ....G 772 708-1781
Inglis (G-5817)
Grindhard Coatings Inc ....G 772 221-9986
Stuart (G-16157)
Gwb Coatings LLC ....G 407 271-7732
Orlando (G-12203)
Hydrodynamic Coatings Llc ....G 954 344-8830
Parkland (G-13347)
Industrial Coating Solutions ....G 813 333-8988
Tampa (G-16940)
JM Coatings Inc ....G 407 312-1115
Longwood (G-7909)
KCS Professional Coatings Inc ....G 813 850-6386
Tampa (G-16978)
Kingdom Coatings Inc ....G 904 600-1424
Middleburg (G-10404)
Leisure Furniture Powder CT ....G 239 597-4343
Naples (G-10802)
M and T Pro Coating Inc ....G 727 272-4620
Clearwater (G-1677)
Magnum Coatings Inc ....G 407 704-0786
Brandon (G-1098)
Marlin Coatings LLC ....F 850 224-1370
Tallahassee (G-16475)
Monteocha Coatings Inc ....G 352 367-3136
Gainesville (G-4734)
Mtc Seal Coating Services Inc ....G 313 759-9423
Orlando (G-12397)
Nano Safe Coatings Inc ....F 561 747-5758
Jupiter (G-6769)
North FL Custom Coatings Inc ....G 904 251-4462
Jacksonville (G-6338)
Nu Tech Coating Systems ....G 813 448-9381
Oldsmar (G-11680)

Employee Codes: A=Over 500 employees, B=251-500
C=101-250, D=51-100, E=20-50, F=10-19, G=4-9

2022 Harris Florida
Manufacturers Directory

PRODUCT

1165

Nvs Coating Systems Inc ....G...... 239 784-3972
Naples *(G-10839)*

Orellana Coatings Inc ....F...... 305 389-4610
Miami *(G-9662)*

Performance Coatings Inc ....F...... 850 733-0082
Gulf Breeze *(G-4889)*

Petes Seal Coating 857 251-1912
Pompano Beach *(G-14123)*

Power Tek LLC ....G...... 904 814-7007
Saint Augustine *(G-14874)*

Pro Color Coating LLC ....G...... 941 661-4769
Port Charlotte *(G-14312)*

Protect All Coating Inc ....G...... 727 278-7454
Saint Petersburg *(G-15166)*

Protek Custom Coatings LLC ....G...... 850 656-7923
Tallahassee *(G-16491)*

Rigid Coatings & Castings Inc ....G...... 352 396-8738
Apopka *(G-169)*

Rigid Machine Services Inc ....G...... 352 396-8738
Apopka *(G-170)*

Ryans Custom Coatings ....G...... 863 669-3310
Lakeland *(G-7425)*

Southastern Specialty Coatings ....G...... 904 616-9186
Jacksonville *(G-6480)*

Southern Coating Systems Inc ....G...... 863 712-9900
Clearwater *(G-1789)*

Southern Coatings of Ts LLC ....G...... 727 858-6586
Tarpon Springs *(G-17492)*

Southwest Custom Coatings Inc ....G...... 239 682-9462
Naples *(G-10899)*

Titans Protective Coatings LLC ....G...... 561 370-2085
Jupiter *(G-6810)*

Top of The Line Coating Inc ....G...... 407 485-8546
Orlando *(G-12662)*

Tropic Seal Industries Inc ....G...... 239 543-8069
Fort Myers *(G-4434)*

Tropical Custom Coatings ....G...... 941 475-3663
Port Charlotte *(G-14319)*

U S A Coatings Inc ....F...... 904 477-0916
Jacksonville *(G-6571)*

United State Foam & Coatings ....G...... 954 972-5005
Pompano Beach *(G-14229)*

Universal Prof Coatings Inc ....G...... 954 294-5236
Middleburg *(G-10410)*

Victory Coatings Inc ....G...... 954 708-4388
Coconut Creek *(G-2010)*

Xtreme Powder Coating Inc ....G...... 352 219-3807
Trenton *(G-17631)*

COATING SVC: Aluminum, Metal Prdts

Coverall Aluminum Inc ....F...... 321 377-7874
Sanford *(G-15295)*

Every Thing Aluminum ....G...... 561 202-9900
Lantana *(G-7513)*

Ideal Deals LLC ....C...... 386 736-1700
Saint Augustine *(G-14844)*

Spectra Powder Coating Inc ....F...... 786 351-7448
Miami *(G-9940)*

COATING SVC: Metals & Formed Prdts

Abakan Inc ....G...... 786 206-5368
Miami *(G-8633)*

Absolute Powder Coating Inc ....F...... 954 917-2715
Pompano Beach *(G-13907)*

Accurate Powder Coating Inc ....G...... 321 269-6972
Titusville *(G-17568)*

Alpha Coatings Inc ....G...... 850 324-9454
Cantonment *(G-1263)*

Aluminum Powder Coating ....G...... 305 628-4155
Hialeah *(G-5042)*

Aluminum Powder Coating Lc ....G...... 305 628-4155
Hialeah *(G-5043)*

American Prtective Coating Inc ....F...... 954 561-0999
Fort Lauderdale *(G-3650)*

Americoat Corporation ....G...... 863 667-1035
Lakeland *(G-7274)*

Ameritech Powder Coating Inc ....F...... 239 274-8000
Fort Myers *(G-4175)*

Aml Extreme Powdercoating ....G...... 904 794-4313
Saint Augustine *(G-14809)*

Arcoat Coatings Corporation ....E...... 561 422-9900
West Palm Beach *(G-17926)*

Automated Services Inc ....F...... 772 461-3388
Fort Pierce *(G-4468)*

Azz Powder Coating - Tampa LLC ....G...... 813 390-2802
Tampa *(G-16624)*

Balpro Powder Coating Inc ....F...... 954 797-0520
Fort Lauderdale *(G-3672)*

Best Engineered Surfc Tech LLC ....D...... 407 932-0008
Kissimmee *(G-6898)*

Best Finisher ....F...... 305 688-8174
Miami *(G-8816)*

Best Powder Coatings Inc ....E...... 305 836-9460
Hialeah *(G-5074)*

Bethel Products LLC ....F...... 954 636-2645
Cape Coral *(G-1312)*

Blast Ctings Powdercoating LLC ....G...... 561 301-9538
Greenacres *(G-4844)*

Brothers Powder Coating Inc ....G...... 727 846-0717
New Port Richey *(G-10963)*

Brycoat Inc ....E...... 727 490-1000
Oldsmar *(G-11636)*

C Y A Powder Coating LLC ....G...... 727 299-9832
Clearwater *(G-1534)*

C2 Powder Coating LLC ....G...... 941 404-2671
Bradenton *(G-954)*

Centrex Powdercoating Inc ....G...... 813 390-2802
Tampa *(G-16694)*

Ceramlock Coatings Inc ....G...... 772 781-2141
Palm City *(G-13027)*

Champion Coatings Inc ....G...... 561 512-5985
Okeechobee *(G-11599)*

Coastal Powder Coatings Inc ....G...... 772 283-5311
Palm City *(G-13030)*

Corrocoat Usa Inc ....F...... 904 268-4559
Jacksonville *(G-6008)*

Custom Clors Powdercoating Inc ....G...... 941 953-7997
Sarasota *(G-15648)*

D and S Superior Coatings Inc ....G...... 360 388-6099
Fort Myers *(G-4229)*

Dads Powder Coating ....G...... 813 715-6561
Zephyrhills *(G-18611)*

Decortive Electro Coatings Inc ....F...... 386 255-7878
Daytona Beach *(G-2546)*

Dps Powder Coating Inc ....G...... 727 573-2797
Clearwater *(G-1571)*

Ds Powder Coating Inc ....G...... 561 660-7835
Lake Worth Beach *(G-7254)*

E G Coatings LLC ....F...... 407 624-2615
Kissimmee *(G-6915)*

East Coast Custom Coatings Inc ....G...... 954 914-6711
Coral Springs *(G-2152)*

Elite Powder Coating ....G...... 786 616-8084
Miami *(G-9087)*

Excell Coatings Inc ....E...... 321 868-7968
Cape Canaveral *(G-1284)*

Finns Brass and Silver Polsg ....G...... 904 387-1165
Jacksonville *(G-6091)*

Florida Pwdr Cting Shtters Inc ....F...... 561 588-2410
Lantana *(G-7514)*

Florida Spcialty Coatings Corp ....G...... 727 224-6883
Melbourne *(G-8427)*

Foot-In-Your-mouth Inc ....F...... 850 438-0876
Pensacola *(G-13508)*

Glassflake International Inc ....G...... 904 268-4000
Jacksonville *(G-6143)*

Glory Sandblasting Inc ....F...... 407 422-0078
Orlando *(G-12196)*

Gml Coatings LLC ....F...... 941 755-2176
Bradenton *(G-986)*

High Performance Systems Inc ....E...... 863 294-5566
Winter Haven *(G-18446)*

Innovative Powder Coating Inc ....F...... 954 537-2558
Oakland Park *(G-11272)*

JAS Powder Coating LLC ....G...... 386 410-6675
Edgewater *(G-3494)*

Levario Coatings Intl USA ....G...... 954 871-6461
Aventura *(G-265)*

Matrix Coatings Corp ....F...... 561 848-1288
West Palm Beach *(G-18069)*

Matrix Coatings Inc ....F...... 561 848-1288
West Palm Beach *(G-18070)*

Mineral Life Intl Inc ....G...... 305 661-9854
Miami *(G-9574)*

Mpp Coatings Inc ....G...... 386 334-4484
Port Orange *(G-14341)*

Naples Powder Coating LLC ....G...... 239 352-3500
Naples *(G-10830)*

National Powdr Coating Fla Inc ....G...... 941 756-1322
Bradenton *(G-1016)*

Nejat Arslaner ....G...... 321 300-5464
Orlando *(G-12410)*

Northeast Florida Coatings ....G...... 904 383-0749
Middleburg *(G-10407)*

Performance Powder Coating ....F...... 407 339-4000
Longwood *(G-7935)*

Powder Coating Factory LLC ....G...... 407 286-4550
Orlando *(G-12495)*

Powdertech Plus Inc ....G...... 904 269-1719
Orange Park *(G-11838)*

Premium Coating LLC ....G...... 727 270-1173
Clearwater *(G-1750)*

Premium Powder Coating ....G...... 386 789-0216
Deltona *(G-3052)*

Prime Tech Coatings Inc ....G...... 561 844-2312
Mangonia Park *(G-8099)*

Pro Powder Coating Inc ....F...... 941 505-8010
Punta Gorda *(G-14519)*

Quality Aerospace Coatings LLC ....G...... 863 619-2628
Lakeland *(G-7416)*

RSR Industrial Coatings Inc ....F...... 863 537-1110
Bartow *(G-324)*

S&H Arcylic Coatings Inc ....G...... 352 232-1249
Spring Hill *(G-16078)*

Special Coatings Inc ....G...... 239 301-2714
Naples *(G-10902)*

Specialty Powder Coating LLC ....G...... 813 782-2720
Zephyrhills *(G-18630)*

Tampa Bay Powder Coating Inc ....G...... 813 964-5667
Tampa *(G-17327)*

Taylors Indus Coatings Inc ....F...... 800 932-3049
Lake Wales *(G-7177)*

Td Coating Inc ....G...... 786 325-4211
North Miami *(G-11124)*

Tolliver Aluminum Service Inc ....F...... 561 582-8939
West Palm Beach *(G-18184)*

Trinu Powder Coating LLC ....G...... 727 316-6700
Port Richey *(G-14380)*

Trojan Fla Powdr Coating Inc ....F...... 941 351-0500
Sarasota *(G-15573)*

Tua Systems Inc ....G...... 321 453-3200
Merritt Island *(G-8602)*

Tua Systems of Florida Inc ....F...... 321 341-4944
Merritt Island *(G-8603)*

Uct Coatings Inc ....F...... 772 872-7110
Palm City *(G-13063)*

V and N Advanced Auto Sys LLC ....G...... 321 504-6440
Rockledge *(G-14753)*

Wheelblast Inc ....E...... 813 715-7117
Zephyrhills *(G-18636)*

COATING SVC: Rust Preventative

L A Rust Inc ....F...... 954 749-5009
Sunrise *(G-16335)*

COATING SVC: Silicon

Industrial Nanotech Inc ....G...... 800 767-3998
Naples *(G-10781)*

COATINGS: Epoxy

Aquatic Technologies Inc ....F...... 772 225-4389
Jensen Beach *(G-6652)*

Epoxy2u of Florida Inc ....F...... 239 772-0899
Cape Coral *(G-1338)*

Jodan Technology Inc ....F...... 561 515-5556
Lake Worth *(G-7211)*

Pro-Tech Coatings Inc ....G...... 813 248-1477
Tampa *(G-17186)*

COATINGS: Polyurethane

Soythane Technologies Inc ....F...... 904 225-1047
Yulee *(G-18594)*

COFFEE MAKERS: Electric

Grimes Aerospace Company ....D...... 407 276-6083
Delray Beach *(G-2971)*

Melitta North America Inc ....D...... 727 535-2111
Clearwater *(G-1691)*

Melitta Usa Inc ....D...... 727 535-2111
Clearwater *(G-1692)*

COFFEE SVCS

Potters Coffee Company ....G...... 850 525-1793
Pensacola *(G-13580)*

COILS & TRANSFORMERS

Exxelia Usa Inc ....E...... 407 695-6562
Longwood *(G-7893)*

OHM Americas LLC ....F...... 800 467-7275
Fort Lauderdale *(G-3966)*

Paal Technologies Holdings Inc ....F...... 954 368-5000
Sunrise *(G-16350)*

Spin Magnetics ....E...... 863 676-9333
Lake Wales *(G-7173)*

Standard Technology Inc ....F...... 386 671-7406
Ormond Beach *(G-12795)*

Wattcore Inc ....G....... 571 482-6777
　Palm Coast **(G-13093)**

COILS: Electric Motors Or Generators

Bethel Products LLC ....F...... 954 636-2645
　Cape Coral **(G-1312)**

COILS: Pipe

Custom Fab Inc ....D...... 407 859-3954
　Orlando **(G-12067)**

COIN COUNTERS

Klopp International Inc ....F..... 813 855-6789
　Oldsmar **(G-11666)**
Klopp of Florida Inc ....G..... 813 855-6789
　Oldsmar **(G-11667)**

COINS & TOKENS: Non-Currency

B-Token USA Inc ....G...... 305 735-2065
　Miami Beach **(G-10169)**
Promo Daddy LLC ....F..... 877 557-2336
　Melbourne **(G-8501)**

COKE: Calcined Petroleum, Made From Purchased Materials

Oxbow Carbon LLC ....A...... 561 907-5400
　West Palm Beach **(G-18103)**
Oxbow Enterprises Intl LLC................G...... 561 907-5400
　West Palm Beach **(G-18104)**

COKE: Petroleum & Coal Derivative

Agrotek Services Incorporated............G...... 305 599-3818
　Miami **(G-8667)**
Bradley Indus Textiles Inc ....F...... 850 678-6111
　Valparaiso **(G-17657)**

COKE: Petroleum, Not From Refineries

Oxbow Calcining Usa Inc ....C...... 580 874-2201
　West Palm Beach **(G-18102)**

COLOR PIGMENTS

Dry Color USA LLC ....G...... 407 856-7788
　Orlando **(G-12109)**
Dynamic Color Inc ....F...... 954 462-0261
　Pompano Beach **(G-14001)**

COLOR SEPARATION: Photographic & Movie Film

Columbia Films Inc ....G...... 800 531-3238
　Pompano Beach **(G-13972)**

COLORING & FINISHING SVC: Aluminum Or Formed Prdts

Titan Specialty Cnstr Inc ....E...... 850 916-7660
　Milton **(G-10440)**

COLORS: Pigments, Inorganic

Keystone Color Works Inc ....G...... 813 250-1313
　Tampa **(G-16981)**
Paver Systems LLC ....E...... 407 859-9117
　Orlando **(G-12474)**

COLORS: Pigments, Organic

Keystone Color Works Inc ....G...... 813 250-1313
　Tampa **(G-16981)**

COLUMNS: Concrete

Artistic Columns Inc ....G...... 954 530-5537
　Oakland Park **(G-11240)**
Ornamental Columns Statues Inc ....F...... 239 482-3911
　Fort Myers **(G-4352)**
Renaissance Entp Group LLC ....G...... 941 284-7854
　Englewood **(G-3536)**

COLUMNS: Paper-Mache Or Plaster Of Paris

Spaulding Craft Inc ....F...... 727 726-2316
　Safety Harbor **(G-14798)**

COMMERCIAL & OFFICE BUILDINGS RENOVATION & REPAIR

Moody Construction Svcs Inc ....E...... 941 776-1542
　Duette **(G-3432)**
New & Improved Services LLC.............F...... 904 323-2348
　Jacksonville **(G-6325)**

COMMERCIAL ART & GRAPHIC DESIGN SVCS

C & R Designs Inc ....G...... 321 383-2255
　Titusville **(G-17577)**
C & R Designs Printing LLC................G...... 321 383-2255
　Titusville **(G-17578)**
Continental Printing Svcs Inc ....G...... 904 743-6718
　Jacksonville **(G-6002)**
Customer First Inc Naples ....E...... 239 949-8518
　Bonita Springs **(G-793)**
E3 Graphics Inc ....G...... 954 510-1302
　Coral Springs **(G-2151)**
Fassidigitalcom Inc ....G...... 954 385-6555
　Weston **(G-18241)**
First Edition Design Inc ....G...... 941 921-2607
　Sarasota **(G-15675)**
Graphic Masters Inc ....D...... 800 230-3873
　Miami **(G-9234)**
Graphics Type Color Entps Inc.............G...... 305 591-7600
　Miami **(G-9236)**
Linographics Inc ....F...... 407 422-8700
　Orlando **(G-12331)**
MGM Cargo LLC ....G...... 407 770-1500
　Orlando **(G-12377)**
Oakhurst Marketing Inc ....G...... 727 532-8255
　Saint Petersburg **(G-15144)**
Proprint of Naples Inc.......................F...... 239 775-3553
　Fort Myers **(G-4370)**
Reliance Media Inc ....F...... 505 243-1821
　Apopka **(G-168)**
Sign Producers Inc ....E...... 407 855-8864
　Orlando **(G-12602)**
Sleepy Dragon Studios Inc ....G...... 561 714-6156
　Cutler Bay **(G-2302)**
Sonshine Digital Graphics Inc ....F...... 904 858-1000
　Jacksonville **(G-6479)**
Trial Exhibits Inc ....G...... 813 258-6153
　Tampa **(G-17369)**
Trim-Line of Miami Inc ....G...... 305 556-6210
　Hialeah **(G-5381)**
Two B Printing Inc............................G...... 954 566-4886
　Oakland Park **(G-11304)**

COMMERCIAL CONTAINERS WHOLESALERS

CKS Packaging Inc ....C...... 407 423-0333
　Orlando **(G-12015)**

COMMERCIAL EQPT WHOLESALERS, NEC

C & D Industrial Maint LLC..................E...... 833 776-5833
　Bradenton **(G-951)**
Decowall ....G...... 813 886-5226
　Tampa **(G-16770)**
Fast Signs ....G...... 239 498-7200
　Bonita Springs **(G-796)**
Lift Aerospace Corp..........................E...... 305 851-5237
　Miami **(G-9457)**
Profire Inc ....F...... 305 665-5313
　Pinecrest **(G-13669)**

COMMERCIAL EQPT, WHOLESALE: Neon Signs

Accent Neon & Sign Company ....G...... 727 784-8414
　Palm Harbor **(G-13095)**
Outdoor Images Central Fla Inc............G...... 407 825-9944
　Orlando **(G-12459)**

COMMERCIAL EQPT, WHOLESALE: Restaurant, NEC

American Metal Products Inc................G...... 407 293-0090
　Orlando **(G-11903)**
Vista Serv Corp ....G...... 239 275-1973
　Fort Myers **(G-4443)**

COMMERCIAL LAUNDRY EQPT

Kemco Systems Co LLC ....D...... 727 573-2323
　Clearwater **(G-1659)**

Psp Industrial Laundry Eqp LLC ....F....... 305 517-1421
　Pompano Beach **(G-14152)**

COMMERCIAL PRINTING & NEWSPAPER PUBLISHING COMBINED

Advanced Cmmncations Holdg Inc.......D...... 954 753-0100
　Coral Springs **(G-2126)**
Coinweek LLC ....G...... 407 786-5555
　Longwood **(G-7881)**
Cooke Communications Fla LLC............D...... 305 292-7777
　Key West **(G-6860)**
Cottonimagescom Inc ....E...... 305 251-2560
　Doral **(G-3176)**
D-R Media and Investments LLC...........D...... 941 207-1602
　Venice **(G-17682)**
Daily News Inc ....G...... 386 312-5200
　Palatka **(G-12865)**
Fishers of Keys Inc ....G...... 305 296-8671
　Key West **(G-6863)**
Florida Homes Magazine LLC ....G...... 941 549-5960
　Sarasota **(G-15679)**
Gadsden County Times Inc..................F...... 850 627-7649
　Quincy **(G-14545)**
Gainesville Sun Publishing Co ....B...... 352 378-1411
　Gainesville **(G-4701)**
Greentree Marketing Svcs Inc ....G...... 800 557-9567
　Fort Lauderdale **(G-3849)**
Herald-Advocate Publishing Co ....G...... 863 773-3255
　Wauchula **(G-17828)**
Image Experts Inc ....G...... 727 488-7556
　Saint Petersburg **(G-15083)**
Jewish Press Group of Tmpa Bay...........G...... 727 535-4400
　Largo **(G-7622)**
Newspaper Printing Company ....G...... 727 572-7488
　Clearwater **(G-1717)**
Npc of Tampa Inc ....F...... 813 839-0035
　Tampa **(G-17112)**
Observer Media Group Inc ....E...... 941 366-3468
　Sarasota **(G-15766)**
Osceola Woman Newspaper LLC..........G...... 407 891-9771
　Kissimmee **(G-6949)**
Perry Newspapers Inc ....F...... 850 584-5513
　Perry **(G-13649)**
Polk County Democrat ....F...... 863 533-4183
　Winter Haven **(G-18458)**
Princess Preserve Inc.......................E...... 954 771-7204
　Fort Lauderdale **(G-3998)**
Printing Services Plus LLC ....F...... 813 279-1903
　Tampa **(G-17185)**
Ronecker Holdings LLC ....G...... 813 855-5559
　Oldsmar **(G-11697)**
Santiago of Key West Inc ....G...... 305 304-6063
　Key West **(G-6880)**
Sarasota Herald-Tribune ....C...... 941 745-7808
　Bradenton **(G-1040)**
Sentinel Cmmnctons News Vntres........A...... 407 420-5000
　Orlando **(G-12584)**
Sentinel Cmmnctons News Vntres........G...... 352 742-5900
　Tavares **(G-17522)**
Sep Communications LLC ....F...... 561 998-0870
　Boca Raton **(G-669)**
Southeast Offset Inc ....F...... 305 623-7788
　Miami Lakes **(G-10357)**
The Scranton Times L P ....D...... 407 377-0400
　Orlando **(G-12655)**
Times Publishing Company ....A...... 727 893-8111
　Saint Petersburg **(G-15214)**
Washington County News.....................F...... 850 638-4242
　Chipley **(G-1458)**
Whatever Lo Que Sea LLC ....G...... 786 429-3462
　Miami **(G-10128)**
Your Hometown Newspaper Inc ....E...... 305 669-7355
　South Miami **(G-16049)**

COMMODITY CONTRACT TRADING COMPANIES

Del Prado Holdings LLC......................G...... 305 680-7425
　Hollywood **(G-5563)**
Heralpin Usa Inc ....G...... 305 218-0174
　Doral **(G-3245)**

COMMON SAND MINING

Bergeron Sand & Rock Min Inc ....E...... 954 680-6100
　Fort Lauderdale **(G-3682)**
ER Jahna Industries Inc ....F...... 863 675-3942
　La Belle **(G-6979)**

PRODUCT

COMMUNICATION HEADGEAR: Telephone

C & C Multiservices Corp ....F 305 200-5851
Miami *(G-8868)*

Ingeant Florida LLC ....G....... 954 868-2879
Coconut Creek *(G-1990)*

Synergy Communication MGT LLC.......F 800 749-3160
Cape Canaveral *(G-1294)*

COMMUNICATIONS EQPT & SYSTEMS, NEC

Nitv Federal Services LLC ....G....... 561 798-6280
West Palm Beach *(G-18093)*

COMMUNICATIONS EQPT: Microwave

E2g Partners LLC ....E 813 855-2251
Saint Petersburg *(G-15032)*

Millimeter Wave Products Inc ....E 727 563-0034
Saint Petersburg *(G-15126)*

U B Corp ....G....... 813 884-1463
Tampa *(G-17381)*

COMMUNICATIONS SVCS: Data

L3 Technologies Inc.....................G....... 904 269-5026
Orange Park *(G-11832)*

Satcom Scientific Inc ....F 407 856-1050
Orlando *(G-12574)*

COMMUNICATIONS SVCS: Internet Connectivity Svcs

Connected Life Solutions LLC.............F 214 507-9331
Altamonte Springs *(G-40)*

Sipradius LLC ....G....... 954 290-2434
Parkland *(G-13354)*

Wialan Technologies LLC ....G....... 954 749-3481
Sunrise *(G-16392)*

COMMUNICATIONS SVCS: Internet Host Svcs

Cloud Veneer LLC ....G....... 305 230-7379
Miami *(G-8931)*

COMMUNICATIONS SVCS: Online Svc Providers

Digi-Net Technologies Inc ....E 352 505-7450
Gainesville *(G-4677)*

Hardware Online Store ....G....... 954 565-5678
Fort Lauderdale *(G-3861)*

Kenexa Learning Inc ....G....... 407 548-0434
Lake Mary *(G-7089)*

Netexpressusa Inc ....G....... 888 575-1245
Fort Myers *(G-4338)*

COMMUNICATIONS SVCS: Proprietary Online Svcs Networks

Working Mother Media Inc ....D....... 212 351-6400
Winter Park *(G-18553)*

COMMUNICATIONS SVCS: Satellite Earth Stations

Nic4 Inc ....F 877 455-2131
Tampa *(G-17110)*

COMMUNITY SVCS EMPLOYMENT TRAINING PROGRAM

PHI CHI Foundation Inc ....G....... 561 526-3401
Margate *(G-8146)*

COMPACT LASER DISCS: Prerecorded

Akman Inc.....................................G....... 407 948-0562
Cocoa Beach *(G-1964)*

Captain Zoom Products Inc ....G....... 561 989-9119
Wellington *(G-17846)*

Dubhouse Inc ....G....... 954 524-3658
Fort Lauderdale *(G-3774)*

COMPACTORS: Trash & Garbage, Residential

Lean Green Enterprises LLC ....G....... 954 525-2971
Fort Lauderdale *(G-3916)*

COMPOSITION STONE: Plastic

Commercial Stone Cab Fbrctors ....F 727 209-1141
Saint Petersburg *(G-15011)*

Commercial Stone Fbrcators Inc..........F 727 209-1141
Saint Petersburg *(G-15012)*

COMPOST

Atlas Orgnics Indian River LLC............F 772 563-9336
Vero Beach *(G-17737)*

Consoldted Rsurce Recovery Inc...........E 813 262-8404
Tampa *(G-16724)*

Genesis II Systems Inc ....F 954 489-1124
Fort Lauderdale *(G-3837)*

Jfe Compost ....G....... 863 532-9629
Okeechobee *(G-11610)*

COMPRESSORS: Air & Gas

Aircel LLC ....E 865 681-7066
Naples *(G-10656)*

American Mfg & Mch Inc ....D....... 352 728-2222
Okahumpka *(G-11594)*

Atlas Copco Compressors LLC.............G....... 813 247-7231
Tampa *(G-16617)*

Brownies Marine Group Inc ....G....... 954 462-5570
Pompano Beach *(G-13956)*

Danfoss LLC ....C....... 850 504-4800
Tallahassee *(G-16430)*

Greengood Energy Corp ....G....... 954 417-6117
Hollywood *(G-5585)*

Hankison ....G....... 352 273-1220
Ocala *(G-11408)*

L M Compressor LLC ....G....... 352 484-0850
Ocala *(G-11424)*

Makai Marine Industries Inc ....G....... 954 425-0203
Deerfield Beach *(G-2762)*

Mat Industries LLC ....D....... 847 821-9630
Dania Beach *(G-2356)*

Q Industries Inc............................G....... 954 689-2263
Fort Lauderdale *(G-4003)*

Roper Technologies Inc ....E 941 556-2601
Sarasota *(G-15801)*

Southern Air Comprsr Svc Inc.............G....... 863 425-9111
Mulberry *(G-10639)*

Trane Technologies Company LLC........G....... 305 592-0672
Doral *(G-3401)*

Ultimate Compressor LLC..................G....... 305 720-3079
Pembroke Pines *(G-13422)*

COMPRESSORS: Air & Gas, Including Vacuum Pumps

America Energy Inc ....G....... 954 762-7763
Pembroke Pines *(G-13374)*

Interbay Air Compressors Inc.............G....... 813 831-8213
Tampa *(G-16948)*

Vac Cubes Inc...............................G....... 727 944-3337
Tarpon Springs *(G-17498)*

COMPRESSORS: Refrigeration & Air Conditioning Eqpt

Advanced Hermetics Inc ....G....... 407 464-0539
Apopka *(G-99)*

Frascold USA Corporation ....G....... 855 547-5600
Jacksonville *(G-6118)*

R & Y Automotive AC Cmpsr ....E 305 919-9232
North Miami Beach *(G-11158)*

R & Y Automotive AC Cmpsr ....F 305 947-1173
North Miami Beach *(G-11159)*

COMPRESSORS: Repairing

Aap Industrial Inc..........................E 941 377-4373
Sarasota *(G-15584)*

COMPUTER & COMPUTER SOFTWARE STORES

Bdt Concepts Inc ....G....... 904 730-2590
Jacksonville *(G-5926)*

Brainchild Corp ....F 239 263-0100
Naples *(G-10698)*

Brickmed LLC ....G....... 305 774-0081
Miami *(G-8852)*

Computers At Work Inc ....E 239 571-1050
Fort Myers *(G-4216)*

Information Mgt Svcs Inc ....F 386 677-5073
Ormond Beach *(G-12773)*

Intellgent Haring Systems Corp ....F 305 668-6102
Miami *(G-9321)*

Vensoft Corp ....F 786 991-2080
Miami *(G-10101)*

COMPUTER & COMPUTER SOFTWARE STORES: Peripheral Eqpt

P S T Computers Inc ....G....... 954 566-1600
Deerfield Beach *(G-2778)*

Thinglobal LLC ....G....... 561 923-8559
Boca Raton *(G-716)*

COMPUTER & COMPUTER SOFTWARE STORES: Personal Computers

Cloudfactors LLC ....G....... 407 768-3160
Orlando *(G-12022)*

COMPUTER & COMPUTER SOFTWARE STORES: Printers & Plotters

Light Source Business Systems ....F 772 562-5046
Port Saint Lucie *(G-14423)*

COMPUTER & COMPUTER SOFTWARE STORES: Software & Access

Advanced Software Inc ....F 215 369-7800
Jacksonville Beach *(G-6627)*

Express Badging Services Inc ....F 321 784-5925
Cocoa Beach *(G-1969)*

COMPUTER & COMPUTER SOFTWARE STORES: Software, Computer Game

Origin Pc LLC................................E 305 971-1000
Miami *(G-9667)*

COMPUTER & COMPUTER SOFTWARE STORES: Word Process Eqpt/Splys

Toner Technologies Inc ....G....... 561 547-9710
Boynton Beach *(G-920)*

COMPUTER & DATA PROCESSING EQPT REPAIR & MAINTENANCE

Computer Technician Inc ....G....... 941 479-0242
Palmetto *(G-13162)*

COMPUTER & OFFICE MACHINE MAINTENANCE & REPAIR

Buscar Inc ....G....... 813 877-7272
Tampa *(G-16664)*

Fis Avantgard LLC ....E 484 582-2000
Jacksonville *(G-6097)*

Kyocera Dcment Sltons Sthast L ....F 772 562-0511
Fort Pierce *(G-4499)*

Lightning Phase II Inc.....................G....... 727 539-1800
Seminole *(G-15979)*

COMPUTER & SFTWR STORE: Modem, Monitor, Terminal/Disk Drive

Incity Security Inc ....F 561 306-9228
West Palm Beach *(G-18031)*

COMPUTER DISKETTES WHOLESALERS

Tdk Electronics Inc ....F 561 509-7771
Ocean Ridge *(G-11518)*

COMPUTER FACILITIES MANAGEMENT SVCS

Arma Holdings Inc ....F 813 402-0667
Tampa *(G-16607)*

COMPUTER FORMS

Zilla Inc..F 904 610-1436
Orange Park *(G-11847)*

COMPUTER GRAPHICS SVCS

A Sanborn Corporation ....E 727 397-3073
Madeira Beach *(G-8039)*

Maddys Print Shop LLC ....G....... 954 749-0440
Fort Lauderdale *(G-3926)*

Networked Solutions Inc ....G...... 321 259-3242
Rockledge **(G-14735)**

Sep Communications LLC ....F...... 561 998-0870
Boca Raton **(G-669)**

Signsations Inc ....G...... 561 989-1900
Boca Raton **(G-675)**

Soren Technologies Inc ....F...... 954 236-9998
Plantation **(G-13892)**

Webcom Group Inc ....C...... 904 680-6600
Jacksonville **(G-6598)**

COMPUTER INTERFACE EQPT: Indl Process

Contrologix LLC....................................D....... 407 878-2774
Sanford **(G-15292)**

Intellgent Instrumentation Inc............F...... 520 573-0887
Naples **(G-10783)**

Mmats Inc ....E...... 561 842-0600
Jupiter **(G-6765)**

Noxtak Corp...G...... 786 586-7927
Pembroke Pines **(G-13408)**

COMPUTER PAPER WHOLESALERS

Computer Forms & Supplies ....G...... 727 535-0422
Largo **(G-7567)**

COMPUTER PERIPHERAL EQPT, NEC

Amag Technology Inc............................G...... 407 549-3882
Lake Mary **(G-7059)**

Arco Computer Products LLC ....G...... 954 925-2688
Hollywood **(G-5529)**

Best Iproductscom LLC ....G...... 386 402-7800
Edgewater **(G-3480)**

Blum & Company Inc............................G...... 941 922-3239
Sarasota **(G-15612)**

Boca Systems Inc ....C...... 561 998-9600
Boca Raton **(G-441)**

Braden & Son Construction Inc............G...... 239 694-8600
Fort Myers **(G-4194)**

Centurion Holdings I LLC ....E...... 636 349-5425
Tampa **(G-16696)**

Component General Inc ....E...... 727 376-6655
Odessa **(G-11544)**

Compro Solution..................................G...... 407 733-4130
Sanford **(G-15290)**

Conduent Image Solutions Inc ....C...... 407 849-0279
Orlando **(G-12041)**

Donovan Home Services LLC...............F...... 813 644-9488
Saint Petersburg **(G-15027)**

Electro-Comp Services Inc ....E...... 727 532-4262
Clearwater **(G-1581)**

Graphic Data Inc ....G...... 954 493-8003
Margate **(G-8134)**

Integrated Dealer Systems Inc............F...... 800 962-7872
Oldsmar **(G-11661)**

L3 Technologies Inc.............................C...... 321 409-6122
Melbourne **(G-8454)**

Lift Spectrum Technologies LLC...........G...... 407 228-8343
Orlando **(G-12328)**

Micro Crane Inc ....G...... 954 755-2225
Coral Springs **(G-2188)**

Nemal Electronics Intl Inc ....E...... 305 899-0900
North Miami **(G-11114)**

Select Engineered Systems Inc............E...... 305 823-5410
Hialeah **(G-5343)**

Signature Computer Svcs Inc...............G...... 954 421-0950
Boca Raton **(G-673)**

Smdk Corp..E...... 239 444-1736
Naples **(G-10895)**

Suncoast Identification Tech ....G...... 239 277-9922
Fort Myers **(G-4411)**

Synthes3d USA Inc ....G...... 321 946-1303
Orlando **(G-12643)**

Technetics Group Daytona Inc ....C...... 386 253-0628
Daytona Beach **(G-2607)**

Technologies For Tomorrow Inc...........F...... 850 478-5222
Pensacola **(G-13613)**

Thermal Scanning Inc...........................G...... 407 617-2927
Orlando **(G-12656)**

Thinglobal LLC ....G...... 561 923-8559
Boca Raton **(G-716)**

Thinktech Corporation ....F...... 954 501-3034
Margate **(G-8156)**

Tropical Pcb Design Svcs Inc ....F...... 561 784-9536
Loxahatchee **(G-7976)**

Verifone Inc..C...... 727 535-9200
Clearwater **(G-1843)**

Verifone Inc..C...... 800 837-4366
Coral Springs **(G-2224)**

Vertiv It Systems Inc ....A...... 954 746-9000
Fort Lauderdale **(G-4118)**

Western Microsystems Inc....................E...... 800 547-7082
Jacksonville **(G-6603)**

Zebra Technologies Corporation..........G...... 305 716-2200
Miramar **(G-10566)**

COMPUTER PERIPHERAL EQPT, WHOLESALE

Two Way Radio Gear Inc ....F...... 800 984-1534
Fort Pierce **(G-4547)**

COMPUTER PERIPHERAL EQPT: Decoders

McEs LLC ....G...... 321 363-4977
Sanford **(G-15357)**

COMPUTER PERIPHERAL EQPT: Encoders

AMC Development Group LLC ....F...... 305 597-8641
Doral **(G-3111)**

COMPUTER PERIPHERAL EQPT: Graphic Displays, Exc Terminals

Eizo Rugged Solutions Inc....................E...... 407 262-7100
Altamonte Springs **(G-44)**

In Touch Electronics LLC ....E...... 813 818-9990
Tampa **(G-16936)**

McKenny Printing Entp Inc ....G...... 727 420-4944
Saint Petersburg **(G-15125)**

Speedpro Imaging St Petersburg.........G...... 727 266-0956
Saint Petersburg **(G-15195)**

Suncoast Led Displays LLC..................F...... 727 683-2777
Palm Harbor **(G-13134)**

COMPUTER PERIPHERAL EQPT: Input Or Output

American Fibertek Inc ....E...... 732 302-0660
Saint Petersburg **(G-14961)**

Datamax International Corp...................C...... 407 578-8007
Orlando **(G-12075)**

Datamax-Oneil Corporation ....C...... 800 816-9649
Orlando **(G-12076)**

COMPUTER PROGRAMMING SVCS

Actigraph LLC ....F...... 850 332-7900
Pensacola **(G-13434)**

Ademero Inc ....F...... 863 937-0272
Lakeland **(G-7265)**

Asrc Aerospace Corp ....B...... 321 867-1462
Kennedy Space Center **(G-6830)**

Atris Technology LLC ....F...... 352 331-3100
Gainesville **(G-4655)**

Automation Consulting Inc ....F...... 850 477-6477
Pensacola **(G-13449)**

Cellec Games Inc ....G...... 407 476-3590
Apopka **(G-109)**

Eizo Rugged Solutions Inc....................E...... 407 262-7100
Altamonte Springs **(G-44)**

Engineerica Systems Inc.......................F...... 407 542-4982
Oviedo **(G-12819)**

Fathym Inc ....F...... 303 905-4402
Palmetto **(G-13166)**

Hispacom Inc..F...... 954 255-2622
Coral Springs **(G-2163)**

Information Builders Inc........................E...... 407 804-8000
Lake Mary **(G-7085)**

ITI Engineering LLC ....E...... 866 245-9356
Winter Springs **(G-18570)**

Kamel Software Inc...............................G...... 407 672-0202
Oviedo **(G-12833)**

Landtech Data Corporation...................F...... 561 790-1265
Royal Palm Beach **(G-14769)**

Lockheed Martin Corporation................B...... 813 855-5711
Oldsmar **(G-11671)**

Maxit Corporation ....G...... 904 998-9520
Ponte Vedra Beach **(G-14273)**

Mercury Systems Inc ....E...... 352 371-2567
Gainesville **(G-4729)**

Montague Enterprises Inc......................G...... 239 631-5292
Naples **(G-10823)**

Ncg Medical Systems Inc ....E...... 407 788-1906
Orlando **(G-12409)**

Praxis Software Inc...............................F...... 407 226-5691
Orlando **(G-12499)**

Tier5 Technical Services ....G...... 904 435-3484
Jacksonville **(G-6551)**

Trivantis Corporation............................D....... 513 929-0188
Deerfield Beach **(G-2828)**

Truecare24 Inc......................................E...... 240 434-0963
Tampa **(G-17373)**

Unicomp Corp of America ....G...... 954 755-1710
Coral Springs **(G-2223)**

Universal Software Solutions ....G...... 727 298-8877
Clearwater **(G-1839)**

Western Microsystems Inc....................E...... 800 547-7082
Jacksonville **(G-6603)**

Willsonet Inc...E...... 813 336-8175
Tampa **(G-17432)**

COMPUTER RELATED MAINTENANCE SVCS

Hatalom Corporation.............................E...... 407 567-2556
Orlando **(G-12211)**

Pulau International Corp ....F...... 407 380-9191
Orlando **(G-12517)**

COMPUTER SOFTWARE DEVELOPMENT

Axiom Services Inc...............................E...... 727 442-7774
Clearwater **(G-1504)**

Hatalom Corporation.............................E...... 407 567-2556
Orlando **(G-12211)**

It Labs LLC ....F...... 310 490-6142
Palm Beach Gardens **(G-12979)**

MEI Micro Inc..E...... 407 514-2619
Orlando **(G-12370)**

Pantograms Mfg Co Inc.........................E...... 813 839-5697
Tampa **(G-17145)**

Quadramed Corporation ....F...... 904 355-2900
Jacksonville **(G-6398)**

Retail Cloud Technologies LLC..............E...... 727 210-1700
Clearwater **(G-1764)**

Servos and Simulation Inc ....G...... 407 807-0208
Longwood **(G-7947)**

Summation Research Inc ....F...... 321 254-2580
Melbourne **(G-8536)**

COMPUTER SOFTWARE DEVELOPMENT & APPLICATIONS

Aqualogix Inc ....F...... 858 442-4550
Palm Beach Gardens **(G-12948)**

Bca Technologies Inc ....F...... 407 659-0653
Maitland **(G-8052)**

Caduceus International Pubg ....F...... 866 280-2900
Gainesville **(G-4664)**

Carlees Creations Inc ....G...... 786 232-0050
Miami **(G-8897)**

Cloudfactors LLC..................................G...... 407 768-3160
Orlando **(G-12022)**

Common Sense Publishing LLC.............C...... 561 510-1713
Delray Beach **(G-2949)**

Eventtracker Security LLC ....D....... 410 953-6776
Fort Lauderdale **(G-3799)**

Hensoldt Avionics Usa LLC....................G...... 941 306-1328
Sarasota **(G-15700)**

Igovsolutions LLC.................................E...... 407 574-3056
Lake Mary **(G-7084)**

Konnected Inc ....G...... 407 286-3138
Orlando **(G-12294)**

Lott Qa Group Inc ....G...... 201 693-2224
Bonita Springs **(G-810)**

One Milo Inc..F...... 305 804-0266
Miami **(G-9651)**

Original Impressions LLC ....C...... 305 233-1322
Weston **(G-18276)**

PNC Solutions Inc.................................G...... 407 401-8275
Orlando **(G-12492)**

Qsrr Corporation...................................G...... 305 322-9867
Hallandale Beach **(G-4967)**

SC Parent Corporation ....D....... 703 351-0200
Miami **(G-9852)**

SC Purchaser Corporation.....................D....... 703 351-0200
Miami **(G-9853)**

Starboard Consulting LLC ....E...... 407 622-6414
Longwood **(G-7950)**

Streamline Technologies Inc..................G...... 407 679-1696
Winter Springs **(G-18578)**

VIP Software Corporation ....F...... 813 837-4347
Lakeland **(G-7470)**

COMPUTER SOFTWARE SYSTEMS ANALYSIS & DESIGN: Custom

Informulate LLC ....G...... 866 222-2307
Oviedo **(G-12828)**

Employee Codes: A=Over 500 employees, B=251-500
C=101-250, D=51-100, E=20-50, F=10-19, G=4-9

2022 Harris Florida
Manufacturers Directory

1169

PRODUCT

Roper Technologies Inc ....E 941 556-2601
Sarasota **(G-15801)**
Utilitech Inc..F 863 767-0600
Wauchula **(G-17830)**
Vazkor Technologies S Fla Inc............G 561 357-9029
Boynton Beach **(G-922)**

COMPUTER STORAGE DEVICES, NEC

Computer Technician Inc ....G 941 479-0242
Palmetto **(G-13162)**
Computers At Work Inc ....E 239 571-1050
Fort Myers **(G-4216)**
EMC Quality Group Corp.....................G 786 501-5891
Miami Lakes **(G-10299)**
EMC Representations Corp ....G 305 305-1776
Hialeah **(G-5140)**
EMC Respiratory Care Inc ....G 305 829-5744
Hialeah **(G-5141)**
EMC Roofing LLC ....F 786 597-6604
Tampa **(G-16807)**
EMC South Florida LLC ....G 786 352-9327
South Miami **(G-16033)**
Emc2 Improvement Corporation ....G 786 564-9683
Miami **(G-9094)**
Hatalom Corporation ....G 407 567-2556
Orlando **(G-12211)**
Hill Donnelly Corporation.....................E 800 525-1242
Tampa **(G-16917)**
Hitachi Vantara Corporation ....G 407 517-4532
Orlando **(G-12219)**
Quantem Fbo Group Kssimmee LLC ....G 407 846-8001
Kissimmee **(G-6958)**
Quantum Assets LLC ....G 786 484-1187
Miami **(G-9763)**
Quantum Care R&D LLC ....G 407 365-1179
Winter Springs **(G-18577)**
Quantum Creations LLC ....F 786 233-6769
Miami Gardens **(G-10269)**
Quantum Group LLC ....G 305 926-1036
Miami **(G-9764)**
Quantum Limit Partners LLC ....G 954 849-3720
Fort Lauderdale **(G-4008)**
Quantum Reflex Integration Inc............G 352 228-0766
Crystal River **(G-2278)**
Quantum Safety Services Inc ....G 786 420-0735
Miami **(G-9765)**
Quantum Servicing Corporation ....G 305 229-6675
Miami **(G-9766)**
Refly of Miami Inc ....F 786 762-2748
Miami **(G-9787)**
Rela USA LLC ....G 786 656-5069
Miami **(G-9790)**
Seagate Productions LLC ....G 561 506-7750
Boynton Beach **(G-910)**
Simply Group II LLC ....G 407 960-4690
Sanford **(G-15386)**
Totally Storage Inc ....F 407 472-6000
Lake Mary **(G-7112)**

COMPUTER STORAGE UNITS: Auxiliary

IMC Storage...G 305 418-0069
Doral **(G-3256)**

COMPUTER SYSTEMS ANALYSIS & DESIGN

Applied Systems Integrator Inc ....G 321 259-6106
Melbourne **(G-8368)**

COMPUTER TERMINALS

Bioscuptor Corporation ....G 305 823-8300
Hialeah **(G-5076)**
Verifone Inc ....C 800 837-4366
Coral Springs **(G-2224)**

COMPUTER-AIDED MANUFACTURING SYSTEMS SVCS

Edumatics Inc...F 407 656-0661
Orlando **(G-12116)**

COMPUTER-AIDED SYSTEM SVCS

Backtocad Technologies LLC.................G 727 303-0383
Clearwater **(G-1508)**

COMPUTERS, NEC

9t Technology LLC ....G 904 703-9214
Jacksonville **(G-5843)**

Adsevero LLC ....G 813 508-0616
Tampa **(G-16559)**
Advanced Electronics Labs Inc ....G 305 255-6401
Pinecrest **(G-13661)**
Alienware Corp ....G 786 260-9625
Miami **(G-8687)**
Arctic Rays Llc ....G 321 223-5780
Satellite Beach **(G-15883)**
Ayon Cybersecurity Inc ....E 321 953-3033
Cocoa **(G-1906)**
Bio-Logic Systems Corp ....D 847 949-0456
Orlando **(G-11951)**
Black Diamond Systems Corp ....G 917 539-7309
Vero Beach **(G-17740)**
Buscar Inc ....G 813 877-7272
Tampa **(G-16664)**
Bytio Inc ....D 445 888-9999
Tampa **(G-16666)**
C & R Designs Inc ....G 321 383-2255
Titusville **(G-17577)**
C & R Designs Printing LLC ....G 321 383-2255
Titusville **(G-17578)**
Computer Technician Inc ....G 941 479-0242
Palmetto **(G-13162)**
Contec Americas Inc ....D 321 728-0172
Melbourne **(G-8394)**
Digital Asset MGT Group LLC ....F 877 507-5777
West Palm Beach **(G-17979)**
Enterprise Tech Partners LLC ....F 918 851-3285
Orlando **(G-12131)**
EPC Inc ....F 636 443-1999
Tampa **(G-16819)**
Essentials ....G 386 677-7444
Ormond Beach **(G-12762)**
Geekshive Inc ....F 888 797-4335
Miami **(G-9197)**
General Dynmics Mssion Systems ....E 407 823-7000
Orlando **(G-12190)**
Ibi Systems Inc ....G 954 978-9225
Fort Lauderdale **(G-3872)**
Industrial Technology LLC ....F 877 224-5534
Fort Myers **(G-4290)**
Konnected Inc ....G 407 286-3138
Orlando **(G-12294)**
Lockheed Martin Corporation................B 813 855-5711
Oldsmar **(G-11671)**
M & S Computer Products Inc ....G 561 244-5400
Boynton Beach **(G-888)**
McEs LLC ....G 321 363-4977
Sanford **(G-15357)**
Morgan Technical Services ....G 772 466-5757
Fort Pierce **(G-4508)**
Oriental Red Apple LLC ....G 646 853-1468
Miami **(G-9666)**
Orion Technologies LLC ....E 407 476-2120
Orlando **(G-12449)**
P S T Computers Inc ....G 954 566-1600
Deerfield Beach **(G-2778)**
Palm Tree Computer Systems Inc ....G 407 359-3356
Oviedo **(G-12842)**
PC Masters Corp ....G 305 582-5595
Miami Lakes **(G-10335)**
Phintec LLC ....G 321 214-2500
Orlando **(G-12485)**
Phone Wave Inc ....F 352 683-8101
Spring Hill **(G-16074)**
Ra Co AMO Inc ....F 561 626-7232
Palm Beach Gardens **(G-13004)**
Refly of Miami Inc ....F 786 762-2748
Miami **(G-9787)**
Scott-Clark LP ....G 512 756-7300
Ponce Inlet **(G-14252)**
Smartmatic Corporation ....F 561 862-0747
Boca Raton **(G-684)**
Superchips Inc ....G 407 585-7000
Sanford **(G-15393)**
Syn-Tech Systems Inc ....C 850 878-2558
Tallahassee **(G-16507)**
Tactical Phaser Corp ....G 321 262-4140
Oviedo **(G-12850)**
Titanus Technologies LLC ....G 888 378-2673
Hallandale Beach **(G-4979)**
United Wireless Tech Inc ....F 561 302-9350
Boca Raton **(G-735)**
Versatus Hpc Inc ....G 561 544-8862
Boca Raton **(G-745)**
Vinland International Inc ....E 954 316-2007
Plantation **(G-13901)**

COMPUTERS, NEC, WHOLESALE

Advanced Software Inc ....F 215 369-7800
Jacksonville Beach **(G-6627)**
Genel/Landec Inc ....G 305 591-9990
Doral **(G-3226)**

COMPUTERS, PERIPHERALS & SOFTWARE, WHOLESALE: Printers

Bluestar Latin America Inc....................E 954 485-1931
Miramar **(G-10475)**
Hut Global Inc ....G 561 571-2523
Boca Raton **(G-540)**

COMPUTERS, PERIPHERALS & SOFTWARE, WHOLESALE: Software

Above Property LLC ....E 239 263-7406
Naples **(G-10650)**
Aci Worldwide Inc ....B 305 894-2200
Coral Gables **(G-2024)**
Beachchip Technologies LLC ....G 727 643-8106
Clearwater **(G-1515)**
Brickmed LLC ....G 305 774-0081
Miami **(G-8852)**
Incity Security Inc ....F 561 306-9228
West Palm Beach **(G-18031)**
Intellgent Haring Systems Corp ....F 305 668-6102
Miami **(G-9321)**
Voyomotive LLC ....F 888 321-4633
Sarasota **(G-15869)**
Wialan Technologies LLC ....G 954 749-3481
Sunrise **(G-16392)**

COMPUTERS: Mini

Acer Latin America Inc ....G 305 392-7000
Doral **(G-3092)**
Artex Computer Llc ....G 407 844-2253
Miami **(G-8754)**
Energybionics LLC ....E 561 229-4985
Stuart **(G-16144)**
Oracle America Inc ....G 888 595-6310
Port Charlotte **(G-14310)**
Oracle America Inc ....F 407 380-0058
Orlando **(G-12445)**
Oracle America Inc ....E 407 458-1200
Orlando **(G-12446)**
Oracle America Inc ....G 813 287-1700
Orlando **(G-12447)**

COMPUTERS: Personal

Appel 26 Corp ....G 305 672-8645
Miami Beach **(G-10166)**
Atlantic Multi Family I LLC ....E 301 233-1261
Parkland **(G-13343)**
Dell USA LP ....F 512 728-8391
Miami **(G-9012)**
Evanios LLC ....F 617 233-4986
Orlando **(G-12138)**
Fun Electronics Inc ....F 305 933-4646
Miami **(G-9179)**
Gold Network of Miami Inc ....G 305 343-7355
Hialeah **(G-5174)**
Industry Standard Technology ....G 941 355-2100
Sarasota **(G-15499)**
Integrated Dealer Systems Inc..............F 800 962-7872
Oldsmar **(G-11661)**
Nortech Engineering Inc ....G 508 823-8520
Port Charlotte **(G-14309)**
Qtronics Inc ....G 850 267-0102
Santa Rosa Beach **(G-15431)**

CONCENTRATES, DRINK

Atlantic Bev Group USA Inc ....G 239 334-3016
Fort Myers **(G-4182)**
Coca-Cola Company ....G 407 565-2465
Apopka **(G-113)**
Prima Foods International Inc ....G 352 732-9148
Ocala **(G-11471)**

CONCENTRATES, FLAVORING, EXC DRINK

World Foods & Flavors USA LLC ....F 561 619-3655
Jupiter **(G-6828)**

CONCRETE BUGGIES: Powered

Sicoma North America Inc ....G 800 921-7559
Clearwater **(G-1783)**

CONCRETE MIXERS

Ficap ....F 407 302-3316
  Lake Mary *(G-7076)*
Tarmac America Inc ....F 386 427-0438
  Edgewater *(G-3502)*

CONCRETE PLANTS

Tensik Inc ....G 954 937-9505
  Winter Haven *(G-18474)*

CONCRETE PRDTS

A & C Concrete Products Inc ....G 305 232-1631
  Miami *(G-8613)*
Allstone Casting ....F 305 528-1677
  Medley *(G-8193)*
Americast Precast Generator ....G 772 971-1958
  Fort Pierce *(G-4465)*
Architectural Masters LLC ....G 239 290-2250
  Leesburg *(G-7760)*
Argos USA LLC ....D 352 472-4722
  Newberry *(G-11017)*
Barreiro Concrete Mtls Inc ....E 305 805-0095
  Princeton *(G-14486)*
Bayshore Con Prdcts/Chspake In ....D 757 331-2300
  Maitland *(G-8050)*
Bayshore Precast Concrete Inc ....G 239 543-3001
  Fort Myers *(G-4187)*
Bonsal American Inc ....G 904 783-0605
  Jacksonville *(G-5947)*
Cast-Stone International Corp ....F 561 625-0333
  Palm Beach Gardens *(G-12957)*
Caste Crete ....G 407 295-1959
  Orlando *(G-11985)*
Cement Products Inc ....E 727 868-9226
  Port Richey *(G-14357)*
Cemex Cnstr Mtls ATL LLC ....E 561 833-5555
  West Palm Beach *(G-17958)*
Cemex Cnstr Mtls PCF LLC ....E 561 833-5555
  West Palm Beach *(G-17961)*
Cemex Materials LLC ....C 561 746-4556
  Jupiter *(G-6703)*
Cemex Materials LLC ....E 561 793-1442
  West Palm Beach *(G-17963)*
Consolidated Minerals Inc ....F 352 365-6522
  Leesburg *(G-7764)*
Coreslab Strctures Orlando Inc ....E 407 855-3191
  Okahumpka *(G-11596)*
Cornerstone Interlocking Inc ....G 863 944-1609
  Lakeland *(G-7297)*
Crom Corporation ....B 352 372-3436
  Gainesville *(G-4673)*
Durlach Holdings Inc ....F 941 751-1672
  Bradenton *(G-970)*
Elite Cast Stone Inc ....G 305 904-3032
  Sun City Center *(G-16265)*
Finfrock Design Inc ....E 407 293-4000
  Apopka *(G-130)*
First Coast Concrete Pumping ....G 904 262-6488
  Jacksonville *(G-6094)*
Florida Engineered Constru ....G 727 863-7451
  Hudson *(G-5773)*
Florida Lift Stations Corp ....G 305 887-8485
  Medley *(G-8242)*
Florida Precast Industries Inc ....G 239 390-2868
  Estero *(G-3543)*
Florida Vault Service Inc ....G 727 527-4992
  Saint Petersburg *(G-15054)*
Forterra Pipe & Precast LLC ....F 386 734-6228
  Deland *(G-2872)*
Forterra Pressure Pipe Inc ....C 386 328-8841
  Palatka *(G-12868)*
Fsp-Ges Inc ....E 352 799-7933
  Brooksville *(G-1158)*
Gate Petroleum Company ....G 904 396-0517
  Jacksonville *(G-6128)*
Gulf Coast Precast Inc ....F 239 337-0021
  Fort Myers *(G-4276)*
Hall Fountains Inc ....F 954 484-8530
  Fort Lauderdale *(G-3857)*
Imperial Industries Inc ....G 954 917-4114
  Pompano Beach *(G-14060)*
Insteel Wire Products Company ....D 904 275-2100
  Sanderson *(G-15254)*
J R C Concrete Products Inc ....G 850 456-9665
  Pensacola *(G-13526)*
Jahna Concrete Inc ....F 863 453-4353
  Avon Park *(G-282)*
Janusz Art Stone Inc ....G 305 754-7171
  Miami *(G-9355)*

Lambert Corporation Florida ....E 407 841-2940
  Orlando *(G-12307)*
Landmark Precast LLC ....F 305 242-8888
  Homestead *(G-5726)*
Leesburg Concrete Company Inc ....E 352 787-4177
  Leesburg *(G-7782)*
Lindsay Precast Inc ....E 800 669-2278
  Alachua *(G-14)*
Lotts Concrete Products Inc ....E 407 656-2112
  Winter Garden *(G-18397)*
Lrg Solutions Inc ....G 321 978-1050
  Rockledge *(G-14726)*
Metro Roof Tile Inc ....F 863 467-0042
  Medley *(G-8280)*
Monroe Concrete Products Inc ....D 305 296-5606
  Key West *(G-6876)*
North Florida Vault LLC ....F 386 303-2267
  Lake City *(G-7034)*
Oldcastle Apg South Inc ....A 813 367-9780
  Palm Beach Gardens *(G-12995)*
Oldcastle Apg South Inc ....F 863 421-7422
  Haines City *(G-4911)*
Oldcastle Architectural Inc ....E 813 886-7761
  Tampa *(G-17120)*
Oldcastle Building Produc ....G 352 377-1699
  Gainesville *(G-4742)*
Oldcastle Coastal ....E 813 621-2427
  Tampa *(G-17123)*
Oldcastle Coastal Inc ....G 813 886-7761
  Tampa *(G-17124)*
Oldcastle Infrastructure Inc ....E 305 887-3527
  Medley *(G-8292)*
Oldcastle Infrastructure Inc ....E 800 642-1540
  Wildwood *(G-18316)*
Oldcastle Infrastructure Inc ....E 407 855-7580
  Orlando *(G-12438)*
Oldcastle Infrastructure Inc ....E 239 574-8896
  Cape Coral *(G-1370)*
Olde World Craftsmen Inc ....G 239 229-3806
  Fort Myers *(G-4348)*
Paver Systems LLC ....E 561 844-5202
  Riviera Beach *(G-14657)*
Paver Systems LLC ....E 407 859-9117
  Orlando *(G-12474)*
Pfci LLC ....E 239 435-3575
  Naples *(G-10853)*
Pollak Industries ....G 850 438-4651
  Pensacola *(G-13579)*
Ponce De Leon Construction ....G 786 554-3685
  Miami *(G-9729)*
Proform Finishing Products LLC ....E 904 284-0221
  Green Cove Springs *(G-4833)*
Quikrete Companies LLC ....E 850 623-0559
  Milton *(G-10435)*
Quikrete Companies LLC ....D 863 665-5127
  Lakeland *(G-7417)*
Ras Concrete Construction Inc ....E 239 775-3709
  Naples *(G-10873)*
Rinker Materials ....F 305 345-4127
  Medley *(G-8313)*
Roof Tile Inc ....D 863 467-0042
  Okeechobee *(G-11615)*
Silk Safari Inc ....G 561 689-3882
  West Palm Beach *(G-18154)*
Stabil Concrete Products LLC ....D 727 321-6000
  Saint Petersburg *(G-15198)*
Structural Cnstr Orlando Inc ....E 407 383-9719
  Oviedo *(G-12848)*
Superior Cast Stone LLC ....F 863 634-4771
  Okeechobee *(G-11618)*
Suwannee American Cem Co LLC ....E 352 569-5393
  Sumterville *(G-16264)*
Terrafuse USA Inc ....G 904 207-9564
  Jacksonville *(G-6545)*
Tremron LLC ....D 863 491-0990
  Arcadia *(G-195)*
US Paverscape Inc ....D 772 223-7287
  Stuart *(G-16245)*
US Precast Corporation ....G 305 885-8471
  Medley *(G-8347)*
Wall Way Corporation ....F 305 484-7600
  Medley *(G-8350)*
Wesco Partners Inc ....E 941 484-8224
  Sarasota *(G-15579)*
Zoho Stone LLC ....G 727 230-6956
  Palm Harbor *(G-13140)*

CONCRETE PRDTS, PRECAST, NEC

A-1 City Wide Sewer Svc Inc ....F 352 236-4456
  Silver Springs *(G-16004)*

Aercon Florida LLC ....D 863 422-6360
  Haines City *(G-4901)*
Allied Precast Products Co Inc ....E 407 745-5605
  Orlando *(G-11895)*
American Concrete Inds Inc ....E 772 464-1187
  Fort Pierce *(G-4464)*
Anderson Columbia Co Inc ....G 352 463-6342
  Chiefland *(G-1445)*
Artistic Fence Corporation ....G 305 805-1976
  Hialeah *(G-5060)*
Atlantic Cast Prcast S Fla LLC ....E 954 564-6245
  Oakland Park *(G-11243)*
Atlantic Concrete Products Inc ....D 941 355-2988
  Sarasota *(G-15604)*
Atlantic Tng LLC ....E 941 355-2988
  Sarasota *(G-15605)*
Bailey-Sigler Inc ....G 386 428-5566
  New Smyrna Beach *(G-10995)*
Barrier-1 Inc ....F 877 224-5850
  Winter Garden *(G-18376)*
Building Blocks Gfrc LLC ....D 312 243-9960
  Kissimmee *(G-6902)*
Cast Systems LLC ....G 941 625-3474
  Port Charlotte *(G-14291)*
Castone Creations Inc ....E 305 599-3367
  Doral *(G-3156)*
Cement Industries Inc ....D 239 332-1440
  Fort Myers *(G-4204)*
Cement Precast Products Inc ....E 352 372-0953
  Gainesville *(G-4668)*
Cemex Cnstr Mtls Fla LLC ....E 800 992-3639
  Sarasota *(G-15630)*
Coastal Concrete Products LLC ....E 239 208-4079
  Fort Myers *(G-4213)*
Commercial Concrete Pdts Inc ....E 813 659-3707
  Plant City *(G-13756)*
Concraft Inc ....G 561 689-0149
  Greenacres *(G-4845)*
Concrete Pdts of Palm Bches In ....E 561 842-2743
  Riviera Beach *(G-14611)*
Coreslab Structures Miami Inc ....B 305 823-8950
  Medley *(G-8222)*
Coreslab Structures Tampa Inc ....C 602 237-3875
  Tampa *(G-16729)*
D Maxwell Company Inc ....G 727 868-9151
  Port Richey *(G-14360)*
DC Kerckhoff Company ....F 239 597-7218
  Naples *(G-10725)*
Delzotto Products Florida Inc ....D 352 351-3834
  Ocala *(G-11365)*
F T F Construction Company ....E 772 571-1850
  Fellsmere *(G-3576)*
Florida Engineered Constru ....C 813 621-4641
  Seffner *(G-15958)*
Florida Silica Sand Company ....G 954 923-8323
  Fort Lauderdale *(G-3825)*
Forterra Pipe & Precast LLC ....D 863 401-6800
  Winter Haven *(G-18440)*
Gate Precast Company ....C 407 847-5285
  Kissimmee *(G-6923)*
International Casting Corp ....E 305 558-3515
  Miami Lakes *(G-10308)*
J & N Stone Inc ....E 941 924-6200
  Sarasota *(G-15711)*
Johnson Bros Prcsion Prcast Pd ....F 239 947-6734
  Bonita Springs *(G-807)*
Keystone Precast & Columns Cor ....G 305 216-5375
  Homestead *(G-5722)*
Mack Concrete Industries Inc ....C 352 742-2333
  Astatula *(G-200)*
Mother Earth Stone LLC ....F 407 878-2854
  Sanford *(G-15361)*
Oldcastle Retail Inc ....B 954 971-1200
  Pompano Beach *(G-14110)*
Phoscrete Corporation ....G 561 420-0595
  Pompano Beach *(G-14126)*
Polly Concrete Products Co ....F 850 897-3314
  Niceville *(G-11034)*
Pre-Cast Specialties Inc ....C 954 781-4040
  Sanford *(G-15373)*
Pre-Cast Specialties LLC ....G 954 781-4040
  Sanford *(G-15374)*
Precast Depot Inc ....E 305 885-2530
  Medley *(G-8302)*
Precast Designs Inc ....F 407 856-5444
  Orlando *(G-12500)*
Precast Solution System Inc ....F 813 949-7929
  Odessa *(G-11573)*
Pro-Crete Material Corporation ....F 352 748-1505
  Orlando *(G-12511)*

Quality Precast & Company .... F 407 877-1000
Winter Garden *(G-18402)*

Rj Staab Stone Co .... G 352 377-3313
Williston *(G-18334)*

Royal Concrete Concepts Inc .... E 561 689-5398
Jupiter *(G-6789)*

S & S Precast Inc .... F 239 992-8685
Bonita Springs *(G-816)*

Seminole Precast LLC .... F 386 668-7745
Debary *(G-2641)*

Solar Manufacturing Inc .... F 954 973-8488
Pompano Beach *(G-14185)*

Solar Manufacturing Inc .... E 954 973-8488
Pompano Beach *(G-14186)*

Southeastern Pipe Precast Inc .... E 850 587-7473
Cantonment *(G-1274)*

Spancrete of Florida LLC .... E 863 655-1515
Sebring *(G-15942)*

Spancrete Southeast Inc .... E 863 655-1515
Sebring *(G-15943)*

Stonehenge Architectural Corp .... G 954 325-6729
Dania *(G-2343)*

Treasure CST Curb & Therm Plas ...... G 772 287-0391
Palm City *(G-13062)*

Trenwa Inc .... F 863 666-1680
Lakeland *(G-7465)*

Urban Stone Works .... F 305 754-7171
Miami *(G-10078)*

US Concrete Products Corp .... D 954 973-0368
Pompano Beach *(G-14230)*

CONCRETE REINFORCING MATERIAL

Wire Products Inc of Florida .... E 954 772-1477
Fort Lauderdale *(G-4135)*

CONCRETE: Asphaltic, Not From Refineries

Advanta Asphalt Inc .... G 386 362-5580
Live Oak *(G-7841)*

CONCRETE: Dry Mixture

Bonsal American Inc .... G 813 621-2427
Tampa *(G-16657)*

Bonsal American Inc .... G 850 476-4223
Pensacola *(G-13460)*

Quikrete Companies LLC .... E 813 719-6612
Plant City *(G-13798)*

CONCRETE: Ready-Mixed

A & J Ready Mix Inc .... G 863 228-7154
Clewiston *(G-1885)*

A Materials Group Inc .... D 352 463-1254
Fanning Springs *(G-3571)*

A Materials Group Inc .... E 386 758-3164
Lake City *(G-7008)*

A-Mari-Mix LLC .... G 305 603-9134
Miami *(G-8626)*

Adonel Con Pmpg Fnshg S Fla In .... D 305 392-5416
Miami *(G-8653)*

All Star Materials LLC .... G 352 598-7590
Ocala *(G-11318)*

Anderson Columbia Co Inc .... G 352 463-6342
Chiefland *(G-1445)*

Argos .... F 678 368-4300
Jacksonville *(G-5899)*

Argos .... F 352 376-6491
Gainesville *(G-4650)*

Argos Ready Mix .... G 941 629-7713
Port Charlotte *(G-14286)*

Argos USA .... G 863 687-1898
Lakeland *(G-7277)*

Argos USA LLC .... E 850 872-1209
Panama City *(G-13228)*

Argos USA LLC .... E 850 235-9600
Panama City Beach *(G-13325)*

Argos USA LLC .... G 850 576-4141
Tallahassee *(G-16414)*

Argos USA LLC .... E 407 299-9924
Orlando *(G-11917)*

Argos USA LLC .... G 866 322-4547
Sarasota *(G-15600)*

Argos USA LLC .... E 813 962-3213
Tampa *(G-16604)*

B M H Concrete Inc .... F 561 615-0011
West Palm Beach *(G-17934)*

Banaszak Concrete Corp .... F 954 476-1004
Davie *(G-2391)*

Bell Concrete Products Inc .... E 352 463-6103
Bell *(G-335)*

Berkshire Managment Associates .... F 305 883-3277
Miami *(G-8815)*

Bet Er Mix Inc .... G 352 799-5538
Brooksville *(G-1140)*

BET-Er Mix Holding Inc .... G 727 868-9226
Port Richey *(G-14355)*

Bet-Er-Mixing .... F 813 779-2774
Zephyrhils *(G-18605)*

Better Mix .... F 800 232-6833
Hudson *(G-5764)*

Brooks Welding & Concrete Shop .... F 850 984-5279
Panacea *(G-13224)*

C-Mix Corp .... F 954 670-0208
Fort Lauderdale *(G-3711)*

Cement Miami Terminal .... G 305 221-2502
Miami *(G-8908)*

Cement Products Inc .... E 727 868-9226
Port Richey *(G-14357)*

Cement-It Inc .... G 954 565-7875
Fort Lauderdale *(G-3718)*

Cemex .... G 813 995-0396
Land O Lakes *(G-7490)*

Cemex Inc .... E 813 663-9712
Tampa *(G-16691)*

Cemex Cement Inc .... C 904 296-2400
Orange Park *(G-11817)*

Cemex Cement Inc .... C 352 867-5794
Ocala *(G-11346)*

Cemex Cement Inc .... C 727 327-5730
Saint Petersburg *(G-15003)*

Cemex Cement Inc .... C 407 877-9623
Winter Garden *(G-18378)*

Cemex Cement Inc .... C 850 942-4582
Tallahassee *(G-16421)*

Cemex Cnstr Mtls Fla LLC .... F 305 247-3011
Homestead *(G-5702)*

Cemex Cnstr Mtls Fla LLC .... G 321 636-5121
Cape Canaveral *(G-1281)*

Cemex Cnstr Mtls Fla LLC .... F 904 880-4958
Jacksonville *(G-5973)*

Cemex Cnstr Mtls Fla LLC .... G 800 992-3639
Fort Pierce *(G-4474)*

Cemex Cnstr Mtls Fla LLC .... G 954 977-9222
Pompano Beach *(G-13966)*

Cemex Cnstr Mtls Fla LLC .... G 561 996-5249
Belle Glade *(G-340)*

Cemex Cnstr Mtls Fla LLC .... F 352 330-1115
Wildwood *(G-18310)*

Cemex Cnstr Mtls Fla LLC .... G 352 746-0136
Lecanto *(G-7750)*

Cemex Cnstr Mtls Fla LLC .... G 813 621-5575
Tampa *(G-16692)*

Cemex Cnstr Mtls Fla LLC .... F 561 745-5240
Jupiter *(G-6702)*

Cemex Cnstr Mtls Fla LLC .... F 800 992-3639
Orange Park *(G-11818)*

Cemex Cnstr Mtls Fla LLC .... F 904 213-8860
Orange Park *(G-11819)*

Cemex Cnstr Mtls Fla LLC .... F 904 827-0369
Saint Augustine *(G-14820)*

Cemex Cnstr Mtls Fla LLC .... F 561 833-5555
West Palm Beach *(G-17960)*

Cemex Cnstr Mtls Fla LLC .... F 772 461-7102
Fort Pierce *(G-4475)*

Cemex Cnstr Mtls Fla LLC .... G 863 419-2875
Davenport *(G-2362)*

Cemex Cnstr Mtls Fla LLC .... F 800 992-3639
Oldsmar *(G-11637)*

Cemex Cnstr Mtls Fla LLC .... F 561 832-6646
West Palm Beach *(G-17959)*

Cemex Concrete Company .... F 305 558-0255
Medley *(G-8214)*

Cemex Materials LLC .... C 386 775-0790
Deland *(G-2857)*

Cemex Materials LLC .... C 305 223-6934
Miami *(G-8909)*

Cemex Materials LLC .... C 321 636-5121
Cocoa *(G-1911)*

Cemex Materials LLC .... D 305 821-5661
Medley *(G-8215)*

Cemex Materials LLC .... C 772 287-0502
Stuart *(G-16127)*

Cemex Materials LLC .... C 305 818-4941
Medley *(G-8216)*

Cemex Materials LLC .... D 904 296-2400
Jacksonville *(G-5974)*

Cemex Materials LLC .... C 941 722-4578
Palmetto *(G-13159)*

Cemex Materials LLC .... D 954 523-9978
Fort Lauderdale *(G-3719)*

Cemex Materials LLC .... E 407 322-8862
Sanford *(G-15278)*

Cemex Materials LLC .... D 850 769-2243
Panama City *(G-13240)*

Cemex Materials LLC .... F 863 688-2306
Lakeland *(G-7290)*

Cemex Materials LLC .... C 954 431-7655
Pembroke Pines *(G-13380)*

Cemex Materials LLC .... D 813 620-3760
Tampa *(G-16693)*

Cemex Materials LLC .... D 239 332-0135
Fort Myers *(G-4205)*

Cemex Materials LLC .... C 561 881-4472
Riviera Beach *(G-14608)*

Cemex Materials LLC .... E 863 678-3945
Lake Wales *(G-7154)*

Cemex Materials LLC .... C 561 833-5555
West Palm Beach *(G-17962)*

Cemex Materials LLC .... C 561 746-4556
Jupiter *(G-6703)*

Cemex Materials LLC .... C 352 435-0783
Okahumpka *(G-11595)*

Cemex Materials LLC .... C 305 558-0315
Miami *(G-8910)*

Cemex Materials LLC .... C 561 793-1442
West Palm Beach *(G-17963)*

Cemex Materials LLC .... C 561 743-4039
Jupiter *(G-6704)*

Central Concrete Supermix Inc .... F 954 480-9333
Deerfield Beach *(G-2689)*

Colonial Ready Mix LLC .... G 941 698-4022
Placida *(G-13734)*

Columbia Ready Mix Concrete .... F 386 755-2458
Lake City *(G-7014)*

Coreyco LLC .... G 813 469-1203
Wesley Chapel *(G-17872)*

Couch Ready Mix Usa Inc .... E 850 236-9042
Cantonment *(G-1267)*

Crestview Ready Mix Inc .... F 850 682-6117
Crestview *(G-2241)*

Crh Americas Inc .... A 843 672-5553
Lakeland *(G-7299)*

Custom Building Products LLC .... C 305 885-3444
Medley *(G-8227)*

Davis Concrete Inc .... E 727 733-3141
Clearwater *(G-1562)*

Devcon International Corp .... F 954 926-5200
Boca Raton *(G-482)*

Drake Inc .... F 239 590-9199
Fort Myers *(G-4239)*

Drake Ready Mix Inc .... D 239 590-9199
Fort Myers *(G-4240)*

Dunco Rock & Gravel Inc .... G 813 752-5622
Plant City *(G-13762)*

Eagle Ready Mix .... G 239 732-9333
Naples *(G-10734)*

Eagle Ready Mix LLC .... F 239 693-1500
Fort Myers *(G-4242)*

Elirpa Corporation .... G 813 986-8790
Tampa *(G-16803)*

Florida Block & Ready Mix LLC .... D 813 623-3700
Tampa *(G-16839)*

Florida Concrete Recycling Inc .... F 352 495-2044
Archer *(G-197)*

Florida Mining Enterprises LLC .... F 904 270-2646
Atlantic Beach *(G-208)*

Florida Rock .... G 941 625-1244
Port Charlotte *(G-14299)*

Florida Rock .... F 352 472-4722
Newberry *(G-11021)*

Florida Rock Concrete .... G 407 877-6180
Clermont *(G-1868)*

Florida Rock Concrete Inc .... C 904 355-1781
Jacksonville *(G-6107)*

Florida Rock Industries .... F 904 355-1781
Jacksonville *(G-6109)*

Fort Walton Concrete Co .... F 850 243-8114
Fort Walton Beach *(G-4583)*

Frako Concrete Services Inc .... G 305 551-8196
Miami *(G-9171)*

Frontier Ready Mix Inc .... F 727 544-1000
Pinellas Park *(G-13689)*

Griswold Ready Mix Con Inc .... F 904 751-3796
Jacksonville *(G-6158)*

Gulf Coast Ready Mix LLC .... E 352 621-3900
Homosassa *(G-5749)*

Hanson Lehigh Cement .... G 800 665-6006
Cape Canaveral *(G-1285)*

Hare Lumber & Ready Mix Inc .... F 863 983-8725
Clewiston *(G-1891)*

Harrison Concrete Inc ....G..... 321 276-0562
Orlando *(G-12209)*

Hicks Industries Inc ....E..... 863 425-4155
Mulberry *(G-10627)*

Instacrete Mobile Concrete ....F..... 813 956-3741
Zephyrhills *(G-18617)*

Jahna Concrete Inc ....E..... 863 453-4353
Avon Park *(G-283)*

Jahna Concrete Inc ....F..... 863 453-4353
Avon Park *(G-282)*

Jamo Inc ....D..... 305 885-3444
Medley *(G-8264)*

Kmr Concrete Inc ....F..... 863 519-9077
Bartow *(G-314)*

Larrys Mobilcrete Inc ....G..... 352 336-2525
Gainesville *(G-4718)*

Legacy Vulcan LLC ....G..... 407 855-9902
Orlando *(G-12319)*

Legacy Vulcan LLC ....G..... 407 321-5323
Sanford *(G-15351)*

Legacy Vulcan LLC ....F..... 352 796-5690
Brooksville *(G-1172)*

Legacy Vulcan LLC ....G..... 727 321-4667
Saint Petersburg *(G-15109)*

Legacy Vulcan LLC ....G..... 352 376-2182
Gainesville *(G-4720)*

Legacy Vulcan LLC ....F..... 352 394-6196
Clermont *(G-1874)*

Legacy Vulcan LLC ....G..... 850 951-0562
Defuniak Springs *(G-2840)*

Legacy Vulcan LLC ....G..... 863 687-7625
Lakeland *(G-7377)*

Legacy Vulcan LLC ....F..... 386 659-2477
Grandin *(G-4810)*

Legacy Vulcan LLC ....G..... 850 997-1490
Lloyd *(G-7857)*

Legacy Vulcan LLC ....F..... 407 299-7494
Orlando *(G-12320)*

Lehigh Cement Company LLC ....G..... 813 248-4000
Tampa *(G-17006)*

Lehigh Cement Company LLC ....F..... 954 581-2812
Davie *(G-2433)*

Lehigh Cement Company LLC ....F..... 321 323-5039
Cape Canaveral *(G-1289)*

Litecrete Inc ....E..... 305 500-9373
Miami *(G-9466)*

Market Ready ....G..... 407 324-4273
Sanford *(G-15353)*

Maschmeyer Concrete Co Fla ....E..... 386 668-7801
Debary *(G-2637)*

Maschmeyer Concrete Co Fla ....E..... 407 339-5311
Longwood *(G-7921)*

Maschmeyer Concrete Co Fla ....E..... 561 848-9112
Lake Park *(G-7131)*

Maschmeyer Concrete Co Fla ....E..... 863 420-6800
Davenport *(G-2368)*

Metropolitan Mix ....G..... 904 242-0743
Ponte Vedra Beach *(G-14274)*

Miami Mix Corp ....G..... 954 704-9682
Miramar *(G-10514)*

Mix It Loop Inc ....G..... 407 902-9334
Orlando *(G-12383)*

Mix Masters Inc ....G..... 386 846-9239
Port Orange *(G-14340)*

Ocala Concrete Services LLC ....G..... 352 694-4300
Ocala *(G-11453)*

Okeechbee Asp Rady Mxed Con In ....G..... 863 763-7373
Okeechobee *(G-11612)*

Organizacion Marketing Mix LLC ....G..... 407 924-2709
Kissimmee *(G-6946)*

Ozinga South Florida Inc ....E..... 305 594-2828
Doral *(G-3320)*

Ozinga South Florida Inc ....F..... 786 422-4694
Davie *(G-2451)*

Panama City Concrete Inc ....G..... 850 851-3637
Panama City *(G-13292)*

Pearsons Ready-Mix Con Inc ....F..... 386 294-3637
Mayo *(G-8185)*

Phoscrete Corporation ....G..... 561 420-0595
Pompano Beach *(G-14126)*

Polimix Usa LLC ....F..... 305 888-4752
Medley *(G-8301)*

Preferred Materials Inc ....E..... 904 288-0244
Lutz *(G-8011)*

Prestige/Ab Ready Mix LLC ....E..... 561 478-9980
West Palm Beach *(G-18129)*

Prestige/Ab Ready Mix LLC ....E..... 407 654-3330
Clermont *(G-1878)*

Prestige/Ab Ready Mix LLC ....D..... 321 751-2566
Melbourne *(G-8499)*

Prestige/Ab Ready Mix LLC ....E..... 772 468-4666
Fort Pierce *(G-4521)*

Pro-Mix Inc ....G..... 305 556-6699
Medley *(G-8304)*

Quality Block & Supply Inc ....G..... 863 425-3070
Mulberry *(G-10635)*

Quality Ready Mix Inc ....G..... 561 833-5555
West Palm Beach *(G-18135)*

Ready Mix Usa LLC ....F..... 850 227-7677
Port Saint Joe *(G-14391)*

Rinker Materials ....G..... 352 330-1115
Wildwood *(G-18319)*

Rinker Materials Corp ....G..... 352 799-7881
Brooksville *(G-1194)*

Rinker Materials Corp ....F..... 305 386-0078
Miami *(G-9807)*

Rinker Materials Corp ....G..... 386 775-0790
Deland *(G-2899)*

Rios Con Pmpg & Rentl Inc ....E..... 305 888-7909
Medley *(G-8315)*

RMC Ewell Inc ....F..... 850 879-0959
Niceville *(G-11036)*

RMC Ewell Inc ....F..... 850 863-5040
Fort Walton Beach *(G-4605)*

RMC Ewell Inc ....F..... 407 282-0984
Orlando *(G-12558)*

Rudys Ready Mix ....G..... 305 382-9283
Miami *(G-9828)*

South Florida Con Block LLC ....G..... 305 408-3444
Miami *(G-9924)*

South Florida Concrete & Rdymx ....E..... 305 888-0420
Medley *(G-8321)*

Srm Concrete ....G..... 850 588-7677
Panama City *(G-13310)*

Superior Redi-Mix ....F..... 850 575-1532
Midway *(G-10413)*

Supermix Concrete ....E..... 954 858-0780
Miami *(G-9973)*

Supermix Concrete ....D..... 305 265-4465
Fort Pierce *(G-4536)*

Sweet Mix LLC ....E..... 561 227-8332
West Palm Beach *(G-18173)*

Symrna Ready Mix ....G..... 352 330-1001
Wildwood *(G-18322)*

T Bower Enterprises Inc ....G..... 863 984-3050
Polk City *(G-13903)*

Taco Mix Corp ....G..... 239 498-9448
Naples *(G-10919)*

Takeria Mix Inc ....F..... 904 338-9157
Jacksonville *(G-6529)*

Tarmac Florida Inc ....F..... 954 481-2800
Deerfield Beach *(G-2821)*

Titan America LLC ....F..... 800 520-2083
Jacksonville *(G-6554)*

Titan America LLC ....D..... 954 523-9790
Fort Lauderdale *(G-4092)*

Titan America LLC ....F..... 904 296-0609
Jacksonville *(G-6555)*

Titan America LLC ....F..... 321 259-0490
Melbourne *(G-8551)*

Titan America LLC ....F..... 305 667-2522
Miami *(G-10013)*

Titan America LLC ....F..... 561 842-5309
Mangonia Park *(G-8103)*

Titan America LLC ....E..... 305 761-1944
Medley *(G-8332)*

Titan America LLC ....F..... 800 396-3434
Delray Beach *(G-3027)*

Titan America LLC ....F..... 954 481-2800
Medley *(G-8333)*

Titan America LLC ....F..... 904 296-0609
Jacksonville *(G-6556)*

Titan America LLC ....F..... 954 426-8407
Deerfield Beach *(G-2826)*

Titan America LLC ....F..... 772 467-2101
Fort Pierce *(G-4539)*

Titan America LLC ....F..... 407 240-9824
Orlando *(G-12659)*

Titan America LLC ....F..... 941 486-2220
Nokomis *(G-11054)*

Titan America LLC ....C..... 305 364-2200
Medley *(G-8334)*

Titan America Tarmac ....G..... 941 484-2276
Nokomis *(G-11055)*

Titan Florida LLC ....A..... 800 588-3939
Medley *(G-8335)*

Universal Con & Rdymx Corp ....E..... 305 512-3400
Hialeah *(G-5395)*

Universal Concrete & Ready Mix ....F..... 305 888-4101
Medley *(G-8343)*

Vulcan Construction Mtls LLC ....E..... 386 252-8581
Daytona Beach *(G-2618)*

Vulcan Materials Company ....F..... 205 298-3000
Tampa *(G-17419)*

We Mix You Match Inc ....G..... 561 615-0253
West Palm Beach *(G-18203)*

Whites Holdings Inc Centl Fla ....E..... 727 863-6072
Port Richey *(G-14386)*

Wpr Inc ....E..... 850 626-7713
Milton *(G-10445)*

Xpress Materials LLC ....F..... 352 748-2200
Wildwood *(G-18326)*

CONDENSERS & CONDENSING UNITS: Air Conditioner

Heat-Pipe Technology Inc ....E..... 813 470-4250
Tampa *(G-16911)*

Icecold2 LLC ....G..... 855 326-2665
Tampa *(G-16928)*

Preble Enterprises Inc ....G..... 954 480-6919
Deerfield Beach *(G-2785)*

CONDENSERS: Heat Transfer Eqpt, Evaporative

Cook Manufacturing Group Inc ....F..... 863 546-6183
Frostproof *(G-4635)*

CONDENSERS: Motors Or Generators

Air Temp of America Inc ....G..... 850 340-3017
Panama City *(G-13225)*

CONDUITS & FITTINGS: Electric

Camp Aircraft Inc ....F..... 727 397-6076
Saint Petersburg *(G-14994)*

Cantex Inc ....D..... 863 967-4161
Auburndale *(G-221)*

Reditek Corporation ....F..... 954 781-1069
Pompano Beach *(G-14156)*

CONFECTIONS & CANDY

Amazon Origins Inc ....G..... 239 404-1818
Naples *(G-10664)*

Behrs Chocolates By Design ....G..... 407 648-2020
Orlando *(G-11944)*

Florida Candy Factory Inc ....E..... 727 446-0024
Clearwater *(G-1599)*

Hoffman Commercial Group Inc ....E..... 561 967-2213
Orlando *(G-12221)*

Nestle Usa Inc ....C..... 813 301-4638
Thonotosassa *(G-17564)*

P B C Central ....G..... 407 648-2020
Orlando *(G-12460)*

Ricos Tostaditos Inc ....F..... 305 885-7392
Hialeah *(G-5333)*

Send It Sweetly LLC ....G..... 239 850-5500
Cape Coral *(G-1383)*

Signature Brands LLC ....B..... 352 622-3134
Ocala *(G-11492)*

CONFETTI: Made From Purchased Materials

Parti Line International Inc ....F..... 504 522-0300
Largo *(G-7655)*

CONFINEMENT SURVEILLANCE SYS MAINTENANCE & MONITORING SVCS

Chuxco Inc ....F..... 305 470-9595
Coral Gables *(G-2039)*

CONNECTORS & TERMINALS: Electrical Device Uses

ABB Installation Products Inc ....D..... 386 677-9110
Ormond Beach *(G-12740)*

Lynn Electronics LLC ....D..... 215 355-8200
Fort Lauderdale *(G-3924)*

Molex LLC ....F..... 727 521-2700
Pinellas Park *(G-13711)*

National Std Parts Assoc Inc ....D..... 850 456-5771
Pensacola *(G-13555)*

Polaris Sales Co Inc ....C..... 727 372-1703
Odessa *(G-11571)*

Top Flite Manufacturing Inc ....F..... 800 219-2601
Miami *(G-10025)*

CONNECTORS: Electrical

Gulf Connectors Inc .... G 239 657-2986
  Immokalee **(G-5797)**

Teledyne Instruments Inc .... G 386 888-0880
  Daytona Beach **(G-2610)**

Tensolite LLC .... A 904 829-5600
  Saint Augustine **(G-14905)**

CONNECTORS: Electronic

Altelix LLC .... F 561 660-9434
  Boca Raton **(G-400)**

Arrowhead Global LLC .... F 727 497-7340
  Clearwater **(G-1499)**

Backbone Interconnect LLC .... E 954 800-4749
  Sunrise **(G-16294)**

Benchmark Connector Corp .... E 954 746-9929
  Sunrise **(G-16295)**

Bocatech Inc .... G 954 397-7070
  Fort Lauderdale **(G-3699)**

Diversfied Mtl Specialists Inc .... G 941 244-0935
  North Venice **(G-11211)**

Eagle I Tech Inc .... E 772 221-8188
  Palm City **(G-13033)**

Interconnect Cable Tech Corp .... C 352 796-1716
  Brooksville **(G-1164)**

Lextm3 Systems LLC .... F 954 888-1024
  Davie **(G-2434)**

Logus Manufacturing Corp .... E 561 842-3550
  West Palm Beach **(G-18060)**

Molex LLC .... F 727 521-2700
  Pinellas Park **(G-13711)**

Rde Connectors & Cables Inc .... F 954 746-6400
  Sunrise **(G-16362)**

Rpp Devices .... G 772 807-7098
  Port Saint Lucie **(G-14443)**

Stratos Light Wave Inc .... G 321 308-4100
  Melbourne **(G-8533)**

Sv Microwave Inc .... C 561 840-1800
  West Palm Beach **(G-18172)**

Teledyne Instruments Inc .... C 386 236-0780
  Daytona Beach **(G-2609)**

Winchster Interconnect Rf Corp .... E 800 881-9689
  Melbourne **(G-8562)**

CONNECTORS: Power, Electric

National Std Parts Assoc Inc .... D 850 456-5771
  Pensacola **(G-13555)**

CONSTRUCTION & MINING MACHINERY WHOLESALERS

American Silica Holdings LLC .... G 352 796-8855
  Brooksville **(G-1136)**

Emergency Standby Power LLC .... G 850 259-2304
  Fort Walton Beach **(G-4581)**

Liebherr Cranes Inc .... G 305 817-7500
  Hialeah **(G-5223)**

Mwi Corporation .... F 239 337-4747
  Fort Myers **(G-4335)**

Pantropic Power Inc .... D 954 797-7972
  Fort Lauderdale **(G-3973)**

Tradewinds Power Corp .... F 863 382-2166
  Sebring **(G-15948)**

CONSTRUCTION EQPT: Airport

Apogee Services Inc .... F 561 441-5354
  Boynton Beach **(G-842)**

CONSTRUCTION EQPT: Attachments

Advanced Infrstrcture Tech Inc .... F 239 992-1700
  Bonita Springs **(G-779)**

Masaka LLC .... F 786 800-8337
  Doral **(G-3292)**

Patriot Foundation Systems LLC .... G 352 668-4842
  San Antonio **(G-15250)**

Pemberton Inc .... E 407 831-6688
  Longwood **(G-7934)**

CONSTRUCTION EQPT: Attachments, Backhoe Mounted, Hyd Pwrd

Zennergy LLC .... G 813 382-3460
  Tampa **(G-17455)**

CONSTRUCTION EQPT: Backhoes, Tractors, Cranes & Similar Eqpt

Bravo Inc .... G 239 471-8127
  Cape Coral **(G-1315)**

Supertrak Inc .... F 941 505-7800
  Punta Gorda **(G-14536)**

CONSTRUCTION EQPT: Cranes

Coastal Crane and Rigging Inc .... G 850 460-1766
  Santa Rosa Beach **(G-15423)**

CONSTRUCTION EQPT: Graders, Road

Duncan and Sons Cnstr Eqp Inc .... F 305 216-3115
  Miami Gardens **(G-10256)**

CONSTRUCTION EQPT: Ladder Ditchers, Vertical Boom Or Wheel

General Clamp Industries Inc .... F 407 859-6000
  Orlando **(G-12188)**

CONSTRUCTION EQPT: Roofing Eqpt

Gardner Asphalt Corporation .... C 813 248-2101
  Tampa **(G-16870)**

CONSTRUCTION EQPT: Trucks, Off-Highway

Iler Group Inc .... G 877 467-0326
  Wesley Chapel **(G-17879)**

CONSTRUCTION EQPT: Wellpoint Systems

Environmental Mfg & Supply Inc .... F 850 547-5287
  Bonifay **(G-771)**

CONSTRUCTION EQPT: Wrecker Hoists, Automobile

U Got Recovery Inc .... G 407 343-9919
  Kissimmee **(G-6967)**

Wanted Dead or Alive Inc .... G 239 633-5080
  North Fort Myers **(G-11073)**

CONSTRUCTION MATERIALS, WHOL: Concrete/Cinder Bldg Prdts

Florida Amico .... G 863 688-9256
  Lakeland **(G-7328)**

CONSTRUCTION MATERIALS, WHOLESALE: Aggregate

LV Thompson Inc .... C 813 248-3456
  Tampa **(G-17026)**

CONSTRUCTION MATERIALS, WHOLESALE: Air Ducts, Sheet Metal

Engineered Air Systems Inc .... F 813 881-9555
  Tampa **(G-16814)**

CONSTRUCTION MATERIALS, WHOLESALE: Awnings

Business World Trading Inc .... F 305 238-0724
  Miami **(G-8864)**

Iis Incorporated .... G 561 547-4297
  Boynton Beach **(G-878)**

CONSTRUCTION MATERIALS, WHOLESALE: Block, Concrete & Cinder

Bluegrass Materials Co LLC .... E 919 781-4550
  Jacksonville **(G-5941)**

Supermix Concrete .... E 954 858-0780
  Miami **(G-9973)**

CONSTRUCTION MATERIALS, WHOLESALE: Blocks, Building, NEC

Masters Block - North LLC .... M 407 212-7704
  Saint Cloud **(G-14932)**

Sg Blocks Inc .... G 646 240-4235
  Jacksonville **(G-6461)**

CONSTRUCTION MATERIALS, WHOLESALE: Brick, Exc Refractory

Lhoist North America Tenn Inc .... F 352 629-7990
  Ocala **(G-11427)**

CONSTRUCTION MATERIALS, WHOLESALE: Building Stone, Granite

Creta Granite & Marble Inc .... G 954 956-9993
  Pompano Beach **(G-13981)**

LAS & JB Inc .... G 772 672-5315
  Fort Pierce **(G-4500)**

CONSTRUCTION MATERIALS, WHOLESALE: Building Stone, Marble

Architctural MBL Importers Inc .... E 941 365-3552
  Sarasota **(G-15599)**

Azul Stone LLC .... G 561 655-9385
  West Palm Beach **(G-17931)**

C L Industries Inc .... E 800 333-2660
  Orlando **(G-11973)**

Exotic Countertop Inc .... G 954 979-8188
  Pompano Beach **(G-14015)**

Fantasy Marble & Granite Inc .... G 954 788-0433
  Pompano Beach **(G-14017)**

Quality Custom Cabinet Design .... G 352 728-4292
  Leesburg **(G-7790)**

Stone and Equipment Inc .... G 305 665-0002
  Miami **(G-9954)**

Stone Trend International Inc .... E 941 927-9113
  Sarasota **(G-15839)**

CONSTRUCTION MATERIALS, WHOLESALE: Building, Exterior

Arso Enterprises Inc .... E 305 681-2020
  Opa Locka **(G-11719)**

Best Manufacturing Company .... F 954 922-1443
  Hollywood **(G-5540)**

Florida Engineered Constru .... C 813 621-4641
  Seffner **(G-15958)**

CONSTRUCTION MATERIALS, WHOLESALE: Building, Interior

E-Stone USA Corp .... D 863 655-1273
  Sebring **(G-15919)**

CONSTRUCTION MATERIALS, WHOLESALE: Cement

Devcon International Corp .... F 954 926-5200
  Boca Raton **(G-482)**

CONSTRUCTION MATERIALS, WHOLESALE: Ceramic, Exc Refractory

Cug LLC .... F 786 858-0499
  Plantation **(G-13841)**

CONSTRUCTION MATERIALS, WHOLESALE: Concrete Mixtures

Cemex Cnstr Mtls Fla LLC .... F 561 832-6646
  West Palm Beach **(G-17959)**

Cemex Materials LLC .... C 386 775-0790
  Deland **(G-2857)**

Cemex Materials LLC .... C 772 287-0502
  Stuart **(G-16127)**

Cemex Materials LLC .... C 941 722-4578
  Palmetto **(G-13159)**

Cemex Materials LLC .... D 954 523-9978
  Fort Lauderdale **(G-3719)**

Cemex Materials LLC .... C 954 431-7655
  Pembroke Pines **(G-13380)**

Jahna Concrete Inc .... F 863 453-4353
  Avon Park **(G-282)**

CONSTRUCTION MATERIALS, WHOLESALE: Drywall Materials

Doral Building Supply Corp .... F 305 471-9797
  Doral **(G-3196)**

Grabber Construction Pdts Inc .... G 813 249-2281
  Tampa **(G-16888)**

CONSTRUCTION MATERIALS, WHOLESALE: Glass

Faours Mirror Corp ....E 813 884-3297
  Tampa (G-16827)
Florida A&G Co Inc ....A 800 432-8132
  Tamarac (G-16531)

CONSTRUCTION MATERIALS, WHOLESALE: Gravel

Legacy Vulcan LLC ....F 352 394-6196
  Clermont (G-1874)

CONSTRUCTION MATERIALS, WHOLESALE: Joists

Accu-Span Truss Co ....E 407 321-1440
  Longwood (G-7863)

CONSTRUCTION MATERIALS, WHOLESALE: Limestone

Helms Hauling & Materials Llc ....F 850 218-6895
  Niceville (G-11032)
Legacy Vulcan LLC ....F 352 796-5690
  Brooksville (G-1172)

CONSTRUCTION MATERIALS, WHOLESALE: Millwork

Builders Door and Supply Inc ....F 941 955-2311
  Sarasota (G-15619)
Synergy Thermal Foils Inc ....F 954 420-9553
  Coral Springs (G-2217)
Trusses Unlimited Inc ....E 904 355-6611
  Ponte Vedra Beach (G-14281)

CONSTRUCTION MATERIALS, WHOLESALE: Mobile Offices/Comm Units

GOTG LLC ....G 800 381-4684
  Brooksville (G-1159)

CONSTRUCTION MATERIALS, WHOLESALE: Molding, All Materials

Excel Millwork & Moulding Inc ....E 850 576-7228
  Midway (G-10412)

CONSTRUCTION MATERIALS, WHOLESALE: Pallets, Wood

Pallet Ex Jacksonville Inc ....E 904 781-2500
  Jacksonville (G-6352)

CONSTRUCTION MATERIALS, WHOLESALE: Paving Materials

Group III Asphalt Inc ....F 850 983-0611
  Milton (G-10427)
Paver Systems LLC ....E 407 859-9117
  Orlando (G-12474)
Paver Technologies LLC ....G 772 213-8905
  Vero Beach (G-17784)

CONSTRUCTION MATERIALS, WHOLESALE: Prefabricated Structures

ABC Screen Masters Inc ....G 239 772-7336
  Cape Coral (G-1295)
Consolidated Metal Products ....G 850 576-2167
  Tallahassee (G-16427)
Langstons Utility Buildings ....G 813 659-0141
  Mulberry (G-10630)

CONSTRUCTION MATERIALS, WHOLESALE: Roof, Asphalt/Sheet Metal

Hco Holding I Corporation ....F 863 533-0522
  Bartow (G-311)
Royal Westlake Roofing LLC ....F 863 676-9405
  Lake Wales (G-7172)
Southeast Gen Contrs Group Inc ....G 877 407-3535
  Port St Lucie (G-14483)

CONSTRUCTION MATERIALS, WHOLESALE: Roofing & Siding Material

Dj Roof and Solar Supply LLC ....G 954 557-1992
  Fort Lauderdale (G-3768)
Drexel Metals Inc ....E 727 572-7900
  Tampa (G-16786)
Kingspan Insulation LLC ....D 305 921-0100
  Opa Locka (G-11760)

CONSTRUCTION MATERIALS, WHOLESALE: Sand

Conrad Yelvington Distrs Inc ....F 352 336-5049
  Gainesville (G-4669)
Quikrete Companies LLC ....E 850 623-0559
  Milton (G-10435)

CONSTRUCTION MATERIALS, WHOLESALE: Septic Tanks

All Liquid Envmtl Svcs LLC ....E 800 767-9594
  Fort Lauderdale (G-3638)
Gunter Septic Tank Mfg ....G 813 654-1214
  Seffner (G-15962)

CONSTRUCTION MATERIALS, WHOLESALE: Skylights, All Materials

Logsdon and Associates Inc ....G 407 292-0084
  Windermere (G-18359)

CONSTRUCTION MATERIALS, WHOLESALE: Stone, Crushed Or Broken

Dyadic International USA Inc ....G 561 743-8333
  Jupiter (G-6714)
Martin Marietta Materials Inc ....F 850 913-0083
  Panama City (G-13285)
Rock Ridge Materials Inc ....F 321 268-8455
  Titusville (G-17615)

CONSTRUCTION MATERIALS, WHOLESALE: Stucco

Andrew Pratt Stucco & Plst Inc ....F 407 501-2609
  Orlando (G-11911)

CONSTRUCTION MATERIALS, WHOLESALE: Tile & Clay Prdts

Coma Cast Corp ....F 305 667-6797
  Miami (G-8950)

CONSTRUCTION MATERIALS, WHOLESALE: Tile, Clay/Other Ceramic

Design Works By Tech Pdts Inc ....E 941 355-2703
  Sarasota (G-15658)

CONSTRUCTION MATERIALS, WHOLESALE: Windows

Design Works By Tech Pdts Inc ....E 941 355-2703
  Sarasota (G-15658)

CONSTRUCTION MATLS, WHOL: Doors, Combination, Screen-Storm

Sunmaster of Naples Inc ....E 239 261-3581
  Naples (G-10914)

CONSTRUCTION MATLS, WHOLESALE: Struct Assy, Prefab, NonWood

Aldora Aluminum & GL Pdts Inc ....E 954 441-5057
  Miami (G-8683)
Atlantic Steel Inc ....E 407 599-3822
  Longwood (G-7871)
Clock Spring Company Inc ....F 561 683-6992
  Riviera Beach (G-14610)
Quality Custom Cabinet Design ....G 352 728-4292
  Leesburg (G-7790)

CONSTRUCTION MTRLS, WHOL: Exterior Flat Glass, Plate/Window

Gopi Glass Sales & Svcs Corp ....E 305 592-2089
  Miami (G-9228)

Oldcastle Buildingenvelope Inc ....C 305 651-6630
  Miami (G-9642)

CONSTRUCTION SAND MINING

Central Sand Inc ....G 321 632-0308
  Titusville (G-17581)
Charlotte County Min & Mtl Inc ....E 239 567-1800
  Punta Gorda (G-14501)
McDirt Industries Inc ....F 850 944-0112
  Pensacola (G-13545)
Quikrete Companies LLC ....E 850 623-0559
  Milton (G-10435)

CONSTRUCTION SITE PREPARATION SVCS

Arons Towing & Recovery Inc ....G 772 220-1151
  Hobe Sound (G-5479)
Consoldted Rsurce Recovery Inc ....E 813 262-8404
  Tampa (G-16724)

CONSTRUCTION: Airport Runway

Neubert Aero Corp ....G 352 345-4828
  Brooksville (G-1185)

CONSTRUCTION: Bridge

Atlantic Coast Asphalt Co ....F 904 268-0274
  Jacksonville (G-5906)

CONSTRUCTION: Commercial & Institutional Building

A Plus Construction Svcs Inc ....E 904 612-0597
  Jacksonville (G-5848)
Elements Restoration LLC ....F 813 330-2035
  Tampa (G-16802)
Waterfall Industries Inc ....F 407 330-2003
  Sanford (G-15406)

CONSTRUCTION: Commercial & Office Building, New

Dean Steel Buildings Inc ....D 239 334-1051
  Fort Myers (G-4232)
Premier Luxury Group LLC ....E 954 358-9885
  Fort Lauderdale (G-3995)

CONSTRUCTION: Dams, Waterways, Docks & Other Marine

Dolphin Boat Lifts Inc ....G 239 936-1782
  Fort Myers (G-4238)
Hydroplus Inc ....F 941 479-7473
  Palmetto (G-13175)
Rz Service Group LLC ....G 904 402-2313
  Jacksonville (G-6439)

CONSTRUCTION: Dock

Gator Dock & Marine LLC ....F 407 323-0190
  Sanford (G-15324)

CONSTRUCTION: Food Prdts Manufacturing or Packing Plant

Desirous Candles Inc ....G 347 622-6987
  Pembroke Pines (G-13384)
Sapphire Exchange LLC ....G 407 926-8305
  Edgewater (G-3500)

CONSTRUCTION: Foundation & Retaining Wall

Artistic Fence Corporation ....G 305 805-1976
  Hialeah (G-5060)

CONSTRUCTION: Heavy Highway & Street

Coastal Concrete Products LLC ....E 239 208-4079
  Fort Myers (G-4213)
Eagle Engrg & Land Dev Inc ....F 913 948-4320
  Boynton Beach (G-860)
Hamner Parking Lot Service ....G 954 328-3216
  Fort Lauderdale (G-3858)

CONSTRUCTION: Indl Building & Warehouse

Environmental Contractors Inc ....F 305 556-6942
  Hialeah (G-5146)
Industrial Construction & Wldg ....G 863 644-6124
  Lakeland (G-7350)

Waterfall Industries Inc ....F 407 330-2003
 Sanford *(G-15406)*

CONSTRUCTION: Indl Buildings, New, NEC

A Plus Construction Svcs Inc ....E 904 612-0597
 Jacksonville *(G-5848)*
Masters Block - North LLC ....G...... 407 212-7704
 Saint Cloud *(G-14932)*
Met-Con Inc ....D 321 632-4880
 Cocoa *(G-1941)*

CONSTRUCTION: Marine

Digital Antenna Inc ....F 954 747-7022
 Sunrise *(G-16313)*
Florida Floats Inc ....E 904 358-3362
 Jacksonville *(G-6105)*
Hendry Corporation ....D 813 241-9206
 Tampa *(G-16912)*
Hyper-Sub Platform Tech Inc ....F 386 365-6021
 Lake Butler *(G-7001)*

CONSTRUCTION: Nonresidential Buildings, Custom

A To Z Concrete Products Inc ....F 727 321-6000
 Saint Petersburg *(G-14950)*

CONSTRUCTION: Oil & Gas Pipeline Construction

Aei International Corp ....G...... 904 724-9771
 Jacksonville *(G-5865)*
Atomic Machine & Edm Inc ....G...... 239 353-9100
 Naples *(G-10682)*

CONSTRUCTION: Parking Lot

Platinium Rosis Inc ....G...... 786 617-9973
 Miami Beach *(G-10220)*

CONSTRUCTION: Pumping Station

Central Electric Motor Svc Inc ....F 863 422-4721
 Haines City *(G-4902)*

CONSTRUCTION: Residential, Nec

Elements Restoration LLC ....F 813 330-2035
 Tampa *(G-16802)*
Premier Luxury Group LLC ....E 954 358-9885
 Fort Lauderdale *(G-3995)*
Thomas Rley Artisans Guild Inc ....E 239 591-3203
 Naples *(G-10925)*

CONSTRUCTION: Single-Family Housing

A Plus Construction Svcs Inc ....E 904 612-0597
 Jacksonville *(G-5848)*
Alternative Cnstr Tech Inc ....G...... 321 421-6601
 Melbourne *(G-8363)*
Chuculu LLC ....F 305 595-4577
 Miami *(G-8924)*
D & D Building Contractors Inc ....G...... 954 791-2075
 Davie *(G-2402)*
F T F Construction Company ....E 772 571-1850
 Fellsmere *(G-3576)*
Realti Hub LLC ....G...... 754 242-4759
 Miami Gardens *(G-10270)*

CONSTRUCTION: Steel Buildings

Advanced Mdular Structures Inc ....G...... 954 960-1550
 Pompano Beach *(G-13911)*
Carport Solution LLC ....F 352 789-1149
 Ocala *(G-11345)*
Gulf Coast Rebar Inc ....E 813 247-1200
 Tampa *(G-16897)*

CONSTRUCTION: Swimming Pools

Jacks Magic Products Inc ....F 727 536-4500
 Largo *(G-7620)*
South West Adventure Team LLC ......G...... 903 288-4739
 Labelle *(G-6986)*

CONSTRUCTION: Tennis Court

Hamner Parking Lot Service ....G...... 954 328-3216
 Fort Lauderdale *(G-3858)*

CONSTRUCTION: Utility Line

Clearwater Engineering Inc ....G...... 727 573-2210
 Clearwater *(G-1542)*
Interntnal Drectional Drlg Inc ....F 954 890-1331
 Coconut Creek *(G-1994)*
Keller Industrial Inc ....E 813 831-1871
 Riverview *(G-14568)*

CONSTRUCTION: Waste Water & Sewage Treatment Plant

American Engineering Svcs Inc ....G...... 813 621-3932
 Plant City *(G-13737)*

CONSTRUCTION: Water Main

Hoover Pumping Systems Corp ....E 954 971-7350
 Pompano Beach *(G-14054)*

CONSULTING SVC: Business, NEC

Analytical Research Systems ....F 352 466-0051
 Micanopy *(G-10395)*
Archer Ellison Inc ....G...... 800 449-4095
 Lake Mary *(G-7060)*
Armbrust Aviation Group Inc ....E 561 355-8488
 West Palm Beach *(G-17927)*
Calev Systems Inc ....G...... 305 672-2900
 Miami Springs *(G-10387)*
Castle Software Inc ....G...... 800 345-7606
 Sebastian *(G-15889)*
Fournies Associates ....F 561 445-5102
 Delray Beach *(G-2964)*
Game Fisherman Inc ....F 772 220-4850
 Stuart *(G-16151)*
Global Diversified Products ....G...... 727 209-0854
 Pinellas Park *(G-13690)*
Logical Data Solutions Inc ....F 561 694-9229
 Palm Beach Gardens *(G-12986)*
Oracle America Inc ....F 813 287-1700
 Orlando *(G-12447)*
Ravenswood Import Export Ltd L ....G...... 863 800-0210
 Lake Placid *(G-7147)*
Sdi Industries Inc ....E 321 733-1128
 Melbourne *(G-8517)*
Solara Industries Inc ....E 863 688-3330
 Lakeland *(G-7439)*

CONSULTING SVC: Chemical

Color-Chrome Technologies Inc ....G...... 954 335-0127
 Fort Lauderdale *(G-3737)*

CONSULTING SVC: Computer

Betrock Info Systems Inc ....E 954 981-2821
 Cooper City *(G-2019)*
Cloud Veneer LLC ....G...... 305 230-7379
 Miami *(G-8931)*
Cyipcom Inc ....G...... 954 727-2500
 Oakland Park *(G-11255)*
Fis Avantgard LLC ....E 484 582-2000
 Jacksonville *(G-6097)*
Kenexa Learning Inc ....G...... 407 562-1905
 Maitland *(G-8064)*
Kenexa Learning Inc ....G...... 407 548-0434
 Lake Mary *(G-7089)*
Levitech Services LLC ....F 904 576-0562
 Jacksonville Beach *(G-6638)*
Lott Qa Group Inc ....G...... 201 693-2224
 Bonita Springs *(G-810)*
Mercury Systems Inc ....F 352 371-2567
 Gainesville *(G-4729)*
Microvision Technology Corp ....F 407 333-2943
 Lake Mary *(G-7095)*
Naztec International Group LLC ....F 561 802-4110
 West Palm Beach *(G-18088)*
Rperf Technologies Corp ....F 954 629-2359
 Coral Springs *(G-2207)*
Willsonet Inc ....E 813 336-8175
 Tampa *(G-17432)*

CONSULTING SVC: Data Processing

Microcomputer Services ....G...... 561 988-7000
 Boca Raton *(G-597)*

CONSULTING SVC: Educational

Rtj Group Inc ....G...... 954 999-4060
 Fort Lauderdale *(G-4033)*

CONSULTING SVC: Engineering

Calvert Manufacturing Inc ....E 407 331-5522
 Casselberry *(G-1411)*
Florida Turbine Tech Inc ....E 561 427-6400
 Jupiter *(G-6732)*
Survival Products Inc ....E 954 966-7329
 Sunrise *(G-16377)*
Yatfl Inc ....E 786 643-8660
 Miami *(G-10150)*

CONSULTING SVC: Financial Management

Dion Money Management LLC ....F 413 458-4700
 Naples *(G-10729)*

CONSULTING SVC: Management

Advantagecare Inc ....G...... 407 345-8877
 Orlando *(G-11873)*
Alterna Power Inc ....F 407 287-9148
 Orlando *(G-11897)*
Applied Technologies Group Inc ....G...... 813 413-7025
 Tampa *(G-16601)*
Coastal Communications Corp ....F 561 989-0600
 Boca Raton *(G-467)*
Custom Masters Inc ....E 407 331-4634
 Longwood *(G-7885)*
Darmiven Inc ....G...... 305 871-1157
 Virginia Gardens *(G-17821)*
Didna Inc ....G...... 239 851-0966
 Orlando *(G-12093)*
Diversfied Mtl Specialists Inc ....G...... 941 244-0935
 North Venice *(G-11211)*
East Coast Cooling Tower Inc ....F 904 551-5527
 Jacksonville *(G-6058)*
First Marketing Company ....C 954 979-0700
 Pompano Beach *(G-14021)*
Ilay Ventures LLC ....F 786 503-5335
 Miami Beach *(G-10203)*
Integritrust Solutions LLC ....G...... 850 685-9801
 Navarre *(G-10949)*
JKS Industries Inc ....F 727 573-1305
 Tampa *(G-16966)*
Pallet Consultants LLC ....E 954 946-2212
 Pompano Beach *(G-14115)*
Redstone Corporation ....G...... 321 213-2135
 Merritt Island *(G-8591)*
Riley Risk Inc ....G...... 202 601-0500
 Saint Augustine *(G-14879)*
Shaws Sthern Blle Frz Fods In ....D 904 768-1591
 Jacksonville *(G-6463)*
Smart Guides ....G...... 813 534-0940
 Tampa *(G-17274)*
Taylor Made Systems Brdnton In ......C 941 747-1900
 Oviedo *(G-12851)*
Trx Integration Inc ....F 727 797-4707
 Belleair *(G-353)*

CONSULTING SVC: Marketing Management

Comm Dots LLC Connecting ....F 305 505-6009
 Miami *(G-8951)*
Connected Life Solutions LLC ....F 214 507-9331
 Altamonte Springs *(G-40)*
Grand Cypress Group Inc ....G...... 407 622-1993
 Maitland *(G-8061)*
Graphic Masters Inc ....D 800 230-3873
 Miami *(G-9234)*
Greentree Marketing Svcs Inc ....G...... 800 557-9567
 Fort Lauderdale *(G-3849)*
Mc Squared Group Inc ....G...... 850 435-4600
 Pensacola *(G-13544)*
Mediware Info Systems Inc ....F 904 281-0467
 Jacksonville *(G-6289)*
Metalhouse LLC ....G...... 407 270-3000
 Orlando *(G-12373)*
Mfx Corp ....F 407 429-4051
 Orlando *(G-12376)*
Monumental Enterprises Inc ....G...... 305 803-8493
 Pembroke Pines *(G-13406)*
Myarea Network Inc ....F 800 830-7994
 Tampa *(G-17092)*
Pk Group Inc ....F 239 643-2442
 Naples *(G-10860)*
Smilefy Inc ....F 302 465-6606
 Hallandale Beach *(G-4972)*
Tm Marketing Group LLC ....G...... 954 848-9955
 Fort Lauderdale *(G-4094)*
Venice Quarters Inc ....E 954 318-3483
 Wilton Manors *(G-18344)*

Wingard LLC ....F 904 387-2570
Jacksonville (G-6614)
World Event Promotions LLC ....E 800 214-3408
Miami (G-10143)

CONSULTING SVC: Online Technology

Beachchip Technologies LLC ....G.... 727 643-8106
Clearwater (G-1515)
Connected Life Solutions LLC ....F 214 507-9331
Altamonte Springs (G-40)
Ebs Quality Service Inc ....F 305 595-4048
Miami (G-9067)

CONSULTING SVC: Sales Management

Flyteone Inc ....G.... 813 421-1410
Clearwater (G-1603)
James Reese Enterprises Inc ....F 727 386-5311
Clearwater (G-1652)
Terfa Litter USA Inc ....F 416 358-4495
Sunny Isles Beach (G-16283)

CONSULTING SVC: Telecommunications

Itelecom USA Inc ....G.... 305 557-4660
Weston (G-18257)
Lugloc LLC ....F 305 961-1765
Miami (G-9482)
Maxxfi LLC ....F 513 289-6521
Cape Coral (G-1364)
Prepaid Solutions LLC ....F 305 834-7422
Miami (G-9737)

CONSULTING SVCS, BUSINESS: Communications

Connected Life Solutions LLC ....F 214 507-9331
Altamonte Springs (G-40)
Primal Innovation Tech LLC ....F 407 558-9366
Tampa (G-17180)

CONSULTING SVCS, BUSINESS: Environmental

Cv Technology Inc ....E 561 694-9588
Jupiter (G-6708)

CONSULTING SVCS, BUSINESS: Lighting

Lightnet Usa Inc ....F 305 260-6444
Miami (G-9458)

CONSULTING SVCS, BUSINESS: Sys Engnrg, Exc Computer/Prof

Enablesoft Inc ....F 407 233-2626
Orlando (G-12128)
Hatalom Corporation ....E 407 567-2556
Orlando (G-12211)
Mantis Security Corporation ....E 571 418-3665
Sarasota (G-15739)

CONSULTING SVCS, BUSINESS: Systems Analysis & Engineering

Alterna Power Inc ....F 407 287-9148
Orlando (G-11897)
Concept Software Inc ....G.... 321 250-6670
Winter Garden (G-18381)
Jarden Plastic Solutions ....G.... 864 879-8100
Boca Raton (G-557)

CONSULTING SVCS, BUSINESS: Systems Analysis Or Design

Servos and Simulation Inc ....G.... 407 807-0208
Longwood (G-7947)
Vinland Corporation ....E 954 475-9093
Plantation (G-13900)

CONSULTING SVCS, BUSINESS: Test Development & Evaluation

Moore Solutions Inc ....G.... 772 337-4005
Port St Lucie (G-14478)

CONSULTING SVCS: Oil

Advance Green Energy Inc ....G.... 352 765-3850
Inverness (G-5821)

Foster & Foster Worldwide LLC ....F 352 362-9102
Apopka (G-135)
Gapv ....G.... 786 257-1681
South Miami (G-16034)

CONSULTING SVCS: Scientific

West Texas Protein Inc ....F 806 250-5959
Jacksonville (G-6602)

CONTACT LENSES

Danker Laboratories Inc ....F..... 941 758-7711
Sarasota (G-15467)
Express Vision Care Inc ....G.... 786 587-7404
Hialeah (G-5148)
Johnson Jhnson Vision Care Inc ....A 904 443-1000
Jacksonville (G-6230)
Unilens Corp USA ....E 727 544-2531
Clearwater (G-1837)
Universal Cntact Lenses of Fla ....G.... 904 731-3410
Jacksonville (G-6580)

CONTACTS: Electrical

Micro Contacts Inc ....F 954 973-6166
Pompano Beach (G-14098)
Southern Switch & Contacts ....F 727 789-0951
Palm Harbor (G-13133)

CONTAINERS, GLASS: Milk Bottles

Kiinde LLC ....G.... 914 303-6308
Melbourne (G-8449)

CONTAINERS, GLASS: Water Bottles

Best Quality Water Sys of Fla ....E 407 971-2537
Oviedo (G-12810)
Brand You Waters LLC ....G.... 786 312-0840
Pompano Beach (G-13953)

CONTAINERS: Air Cargo, Metal

Alpine Systems Associates Inc ....G.... 305 262-3263
Medley (G-8194)
John Bean Technologies Corp ....E 407 851-3377
Orlando (G-12275)

CONTAINERS: Cargo, Wood

Florida Funeral Shipping Cntrs ....G.... 954 957-9259
Fort Lauderdale (G-3821)
Williams Jewelry and Mfg Co ....G.... 727 823-7676
Saint Petersburg (G-15234)

CONTAINERS: Cargo, Wood & Metal Combination

Compact Container Systems LLC ....F 561 392-6910
Boca Raton (G-469)
Global Galan Logistics Inc ....G.... 754 263-2708
Miramar (G-10498)
Rima Cargo LLC ....G.... 305 477-8002
Miami (G-9806)
Sg Blocks Inc ....G.... 646 240-4235
Jacksonville (G-6461)

CONTAINERS: Cargo, Wood & Wood With Metal

Cal Air Forwarding ....G.... 305 871-4552
Miami (G-8880)
Container Mfg Solutions ....E 888 805-8785
Cutler Bay (G-2285)

CONTAINERS: Corrugated

Americans Gbc Corp ....G.... 407 371-9584
Orlando (G-11906)
Barco Sales & Mfg Inc ....F 954 563-3922
Oakland Park (G-11245)
Biodegradable Packaging Corp ....F 305 824-1164
Hialeah Gardens (G-5434)
Corrugated Creations By Alan ....G.... 904 683-4347
Jacksonville (G-6009)
Gbc By Glen Bergquist LLC ....G.... 352 348-7957
Leesburg (G-7778)
Gbc Interiors LLC ....G.... 386 624-8294
Deltona (G-3045)
Gbc Solutions LLC ....G.... 904 705-2415
Jacksonville (G-6133)
Mpc Company Inc ....G.... 863 802-1722
Lakeland (G-7400)

Packaging Alternatives Corp ....F 352 867-5050
Ocala (G-11462)
Packaging Corporation America ....D 813 626-7006
Tampa (G-17140)
Republic Packaging Florida Inc ....E 305 685-5175
Opa Locka (G-11785)
Two Paper Chasers LLC ....G.... 813 251-5090
Tampa (G-17379)
Westrock Cp LLC ....C 904 356-5611
Jacksonville (G-6604)
Westrock CP LLC ....E 407 859-9701
Orlando (G-12713)

CONTAINERS: Food & Beverage

Egd Euro Gourmet Deli Inc ....G.... 305 937-1515
Aventura (G-258)
La Perrada Del Gordo Boca LLC ....G.... 561 968-6978
West Palm Beach (G-18049)
Nardis Enterprises LLC ....G.... 954 529-0691
Fort Lauderdale (G-3952)
Outstanding Events Inc ....F 772 463-5406
Palm City (G-13051)
Weplenish LLC ....G.... 954 909-4183
Plantation (G-13902)

CONTAINERS: Food, Folding, Made From Purchased Materials

Beverage Blocks Inc ....F 813 309-8711
Tampa (G-16641)

CONTAINERS: Frozen Food, Made From Purchased Materials

Hg Brokerage Services Inc ....G.... 407 294-3507
Orlando (G-12215)

CONTAINERS: Glass

Anchor Glass Container Corp ....C 813 884-0000
Tampa (G-16596)
Anchor Glass Container Corp ....B 904 786-1010
Jacksonville (G-5888)
Rock Bottom Bottles LLC ....G.... 901 237-9929
Sarasota (G-15547)
Spiker USA Corporation ....G.... 850 710-3043
Pensacola (G-13610)
Van Teal Inc ....E 305 751-6767
Miami (G-10093)

CONTAINERS: Ice Cream, Made From Purchased Materials

Gesco Ice Cream Vending Corp ....F 718 782-3232
Sunny Isles Beach (G-16276)

CONTAINERS: Liquid Tight Fiber, From Purchased Materials

Custom Manufacturing Inc ....G.... 607 569-2738
Inverness (G-5824)

CONTAINERS: Metal

Standard Kegs LLC ....G.... 305 454-9721
Medley (G-8325)
Stemler Corporation ....E 727 577-1216
Saint Petersburg (G-15200)

CONTAINERS: Plastic

Action Plastics Inc ....G.... 352 342-4122
Belleview (G-357)
Altium Packaging LLC ....E 813 782-2695
Zephyrhills (G-18602)
Altium Packaging LLC ....D 813 248-4300
Tampa (G-16582)
Altium Packaging LLC ....F 386 246-4000
Palm Coast (G-13069)
Amcor Rigid Packaging Usa LLC ....G.... 407 859-7560
Orlando (G-11899)
American Composites Engrg ....E 352 528-5007
Williston (G-18329)
Amerikan LLC ....E 863 314-9417
Sebring (G-15914)
Associated Materials LLC ....G.... 813 621-7058
Tampa (G-16613)
Berry Global Inc ....G.... 727 447-8845
Clearwater (G-1517)
CKS Packaging Inc ....C 407 423-0333
Orlando (G-12015)

PRODUCT

CKS Packaging Inc .... D 407 420-9529
Orlando (G-12016)

CKS Packaging Inc .... D 954 925-9049
Hollywood (G-5551)

Cw21 Inc .... E 813 754-1760
Plant City (G-13759)

Dart Container Company Fla LLC .... C 813 752-1990
Plant City (G-13760)

Dart Industries Inc .... B 407 826-5050
Orlando (G-12074)

Delconte Packaging Inc .... F 305 885-2800
Hialeah (G-5113)

Genpak LLC .... G 863 243-1068
Lake Placid (G-7140)

Industrial Plastic Systems Inc .... E 863 646-8551
Lakeland (G-7351)

Jan and Jean Inc .... G 813 645-0680
Ruskin (G-14779)

K & I Plastics Inc .... G 904 387-0438
Jacksonville (G-6235)

MTS Sales & Marketing Inc .... D 727 812-2830
Clearwater (G-1707)

Myton Industries Inc .... F 954 989-0113
Hallandale (G-4927)

OPif- Our Plstic Is Fntstic .... G 954 636-4228
Lauderhill (G-7737)

Perry Fiberglas Products Inc .... E 321 609-9036
Rockledge (G-14737)

Plastic Specialties Inc .... F 239 643-0933
Naples (G-10861)

Prototype Plastics LLC .... G 941 371-3380
Sarasota (G-15790)

Sunbeam Products Inc .... B 561 912-4100
Boca Raton (G-703)

Ultratech International Inc .... E 904 292-9019
Jacksonville (G-6573)

CONTAINERS: Sanitary, Food

Estal Usa Inc .... F 305 728-3272
Miami (G-9112)

Tellus Products LLC .... F 561 996-5556
Belle Glade (G-344)

CONTAINERS: Shipping & Mailing, Fiber

May & Well Inc .... G 813 333-5806
Tampa (G-17057)

CONTAINERS: Shipping, Wood

Qps Companies Inc .... E 813 246-5525
Tampa (G-17197)

Stemler Corporation .... E 727 577-1216
Saint Petersburg (G-15200)

CONTAINERS: Wood

Mpc Company Inc .... G 863 802-1722
Lakeland (G-7400)

Southern Closet Systems Inc .... G 813 926-9348
Odessa (G-11579)

CONTRACT FOOD SVCS

GA Fd Svcs Pinellas Cnty LLC .... B 727 573-2211
Saint Petersburg (G-15057)

GA Fd Svcs Pinellas Cnty LLC .... D 954 972-8884
Fort Lauderdale (G-3835)

GA Fd Svcs Pinellas Cnty LLC .... E 239 693-5090
Fort Myers (G-4268)

Lincoln-Marti Cmnty Agcy Inc .... D 305 643-4888
Miami (G-9462)

CONTRACTOR: Framing

Alternative Cnstr Tech Inc .... G 321 421-6601
Melbourne (G-8363)

CONTRACTOR: Rigging & Scaffolding

Whitewater Boat Corp .... G 305 756-9191
Miami (G-10130)

CONTRACTORS: Access Control System Eqpt

L A Ornamental & Rack Corp .... G 305 696-0419
Miami (G-9403)

CONTRACTORS: Access Flooring System Installation

A Clean Finish Inc .... G 407 516-1311
Jacksonville (G-5846)

CONTRACTORS: Acoustical & Insulation Work

Florida Marine Joiner Svc Inc .... F 813 514-1125
Tampa (G-16849)

CONTRACTORS: Artificial Turf Installation

Easyturf Inc .... F 941 753-3312
Ellenton (G-3510)

CONTRACTORS: Asphalt

Superior Asphalt Inc .... D 941 755-2850
Bradenton (G-1056)

CONTRACTORS: Awning Installation

A & A Central Florida .... F 407 648-5666
Altamonte Springs (G-26)

Eddy Storm Protection .... G 386 248-1631
Daytona Beach (G-2548)

Florida Shutters Inc .... E 772 569-2200
Vero Beach (G-17755)

Germain Canvas & Awning Co .... G 305 751-4963
Miami (G-9206)

Miami Beach Awning Co .... E 305 576-2029
Miami (G-9546)

Paradise Awnings Corporation .... E 305 597-5714
Miami (G-9692)

CONTRACTORS: Banking Machine Installation & Svc

Crandon Enterprises Inc .... G 352 873-8400
Ocala (G-11359)

CONTRACTORS: Building Eqpt & Machinery Installation

Built Right Installers Intl .... F 305 362-6010
Hialeah (G-5082)

Millwork and Design Inc .... G 352 544-0444
Brooksville (G-1182)

Otis Elevator Company .... B 561 618-4831
West Palm Beach (G-18100)

Otis Elevator Company .... C 305 816-5740
Fort Lauderdale (G-3970)

CONTRACTORS: Building Sign Installation & Mntnce

Accent Neon & Sign Company .... G 727 784-8414
Palm Harbor (G-13095)

All-American Signs Inc .... G 863 665-7161
Lakeland (G-7270)

American Led Technology Inc .... F 850 863-8777
Naples (G-10667)

Art-Kraft Sign Co Inc .... E 321 727-7324
Palm Bay (G-12887)

Budget Signs Inc .... F 954 941-5710
Pompano Beach (G-13957)

Dakim Inc .... F 561 790-0884
Royal Palm Beach (G-14762)

Dynamic Aspects Inc .... G 407 322-1923
Debary (G-2634)

General Signs and Service Inc .... G 904 372-4238
Atlantic Beach (G-209)

Gould Signs Inc .... G 772 221-1218
Stuart (G-16155)

Guardfish Enterprises LLC .... G 850 455-4114
Pensacola (G-13513)

Interstate Signcrafters LLC .... D 561 547-3760
Boynton Beach (G-881)

Jayco Signs Inc .... F 407 339-5252
Maitland (G-8062)

Kenco - 2000 Inc .... F 386 672-1590
Daytona Beach (G-2565)

Oakhurst Marketing Inc .... G 727 532-8255
Saint Petersburg (G-15144)

Rogers Sign Corp .... F 352 799-1923
Brooksville (G-1195)

Signs Unlimited Bay County Inc .... G 850 785-1061
Panama City (G-13307)

Superior Signs Inc .... F 407 601-7964
Orlando (G-12639)

CONTRACTORS: Cable Laying

Quality Cable Contractors Inc .... E 407 246-0606
Orlando (G-12520)

CONTRACTORS: Cable Splicing Svcs

Quality Cable Contractors Inc .... E 407 246-0606
Orlando (G-12520)

CONTRACTORS: Carpentry Work

BMC Services Inc .... F 954 587-6337
Fort Lauderdale (G-3696)

Braden Kitchens Inc .... E 321 636-4700
Cocoa (G-1907)

Bresee Woodwork Inc .... F 941 355-2591
Sarasota (G-15615)

Florida Marine Joiner Svc Inc .... E 813 514-1125
Tampa (G-16849)

Hughes Trim LLC .... D 863 206-6048
Orlando (G-12231)

Kevco Builders Inc .... F 352 308-8025
Eustis (G-3561)

Melbourne Architectural Mllwk .... F 321 308-3297
Melbourne (G-8474)

Mirandas Woodcraft LLC .... G 954 306-3568
Lauderhill (G-7736)

CONTRACTORS: Carpentry, Cabinet & Finish Work

Acryplex Inc .... G 305 633-7636
Miami (G-8648)

Amick Cstm Woodcraft & Design .... G 407 324-8525
Sanford (G-15265)

Custom Cabinets SW Florida LLC .... G 239 415-3350
Fort Myers (G-4227)

Infinite Ret Design & Mfg Corp .... F 305 967-8339
Miami (G-9312)

Juan Pampanas Designs Inc .... G 305 573-7550
Miami (G-9381)

Madison Millwork & Cabinet Co .... E 954 966-7551
Hollywood (G-5619)

Princeton Industries Inc .... E 954 344-9155
Margate (G-8149)

Ramirez Cbnets Blnds Gran Mr .... G 352 606-0049
Spring Hill (G-16076)

Rik Enterprises Inc .... G 239 772-9485
Cape Coral (G-1378)

Rivercity Custom Cabinetry Inc .... F 904 247-0807
Jacksonville (G-6427)

S M I Cabinetry Inc .... E 407 841-0292
Orlando (G-12565)

Southern Woodworks Fine Wdwkg .... F 850 456-0550
Pensacola (G-13607)

Spruce Creek Cabinetry Inc .... E 386 756-0041
Port Orange (G-14349)

Welshman Investment Corp .... G 407 933-4444
Kissimmee (G-6972)

CONTRACTORS: Carpentry, Cabinet Building & Installation

Commercial Stone Cab Fbrctors .... F 727 209-1141
Saint Petersburg (G-15011)

Commercial Stone Fbrcators Inc .... F 727 209-1141
Saint Petersburg (G-15012)

Guyton Industries LLC .... E 772 208-3019
Indiantown (G-5814)

Institutional Products Inc .... E 305 248-4955
Homestead (G-5717)

Kc & B Custom Inc .... G 561 276-1887
Delray Beach (G-2981)

Roomy Design Organizers LLC .... F 407 703-9550
Apopka (G-172)

Southwest Woodwork Inc .... F 239 213-0126
Naples (G-10900)

CONTRACTORS: Carpentry, Finish & Trim Work

Daystar International Inc .... G 813 281-0200
Tampa (G-16767)

K M I International Inc .... E 561 588-5514
Lake Worth (G-7212)

CONTRACTORS: Ceramic Floor Tile Installation

Designer Lifestyles LLC ....F 904 631-8954
  Jacksonville (G-6030)

CONTRACTORS: Commercial & Office Building

Suncrest Sheds of South Fla................F 305 231-1990
  Miami Lakes (G-10362)

CONTRACTORS: Communications Svcs

Intercultural Communications ....G 813 926-2617
  Odessa (G-11558)

CONTRACTORS: Computer Installation

Incity Security Inc ....F 561 306-9228
  West Palm Beach (G-18031)
P S T Computers Inc ....G 954 566-1600
  Deerfield Beach (G-2778)

CONTRACTORS: Computer Power Conditioning Svcs

Air & Power Solutions Inc ....G 954 427-0019
  Coconut Creek (G-1976)

CONTRACTORS: Concrete

Coastal Concrete Products LLC...........E 239 208-4079
  Fort Myers (G-4213)
Foam By Design Inc..............................E 727 561-7479
  Clearwater (G-1604)
Mack Industries Inc..............................E 352 742-2333
  Astatula (G-201)
McMaster Concrete Products LLC ....F 305 863-8854
  Medley (G-8275)
Mother Earth Stone LLC........................F 407 878-2854
  Sanford (G-15361)
RG Groundworks LLC ....G 352 474-7949
  Newberry (G-11026)
Woodwork Unlimited Inc ....G 352 267-4051
  Oxford (G-12855)

CONTRACTORS: Concrete Breaking, Street & Highway

American Diamond Blades Corp ....F 561 571-2166
  Boca Raton (G-406)

CONTRACTORS: Concrete Pumping

Adonel Con Pmpg Fnshg S Fla In ....D 305 392-5416
  Miami (G-8653)

CONTRACTORS: Concrete Reinforcement Placing

Florida Wilbert Inc................................G 904 765-2641
  Jacksonville (G-6112)

CONTRACTORS: Concrete Repair

Dynamis Epoxy LLC ....G 941 488-3999
  Venice (G-17686)

CONTRACTORS: Construction Site Cleanup

Renovation Team Services LLC ....F 352 696-0215
  Saint Cloud (G-14937)
Rz Service Group LLC...........................G 904 402-2313
  Jacksonville (G-6439)

CONTRACTORS: Countertop Installation

Fellowship Enterprises Inc ....G 727 726-5997
  Safety Harbor (G-14787)
Florida Design Mfg Assoc Inc...............F 561 533-0733
  West Palm Beach (G-18004)
Heller Cabinetry Inc ....F 321 729-9690
  Melbourne (G-8435)
International Gran & Stone LLC ....E 813 920-6500
  Odessa (G-11559)
Natural Stone Sltons Fnest SRS............E 941 954-1100
  Sarasota (G-15756)

CONTRACTORS: Directional Oil & Gas Well Drilling Svc

Betwell Oil & Gas Company ....G 305 821-8300
  Hialeah Gardens (G-5433)
Bore Tech Inc ....G 904 262-0752
  Jacksonville (G-5948)
Centerline Drctnal Drlg Svc In ....E 863 674-0913
  Labelle (G-6980)
Full Bore Directional Inc......................G 727 327-7784
  Gulfport (G-4897)
Full Circle Directional Inc....................G 352 568-0639
  Bushnell (G-1244)
Interntnal Directional Drlg Inc..............F 954 890-1331
  Coconut Creek (G-1994)
Jaffer Wll Drlng A Div of AC ....E 954 523-6669
  Hialeah (G-5200)
Precision Directional Drlg LLC ....E 941 320-8308
  Bradenton (G-1032)
Pretec Directional Drlg LLC ....G 786 220-7667
  Coral Gables (G-2099)
Sabcon Underground LLC.....................G 863 268-8225
  Winter Haven (G-18466)

CONTRACTORS: Dock Eqpt Installation, Indl

Specialty Products Inc ....G 850 438-4264
  Pensacola (G-13608)

CONTRACTORS: Electric Power Systems

Cavok Capital LLC ....F 727 789-0951
  Palm Harbor (G-13105)
Megawattage LLC ....F 954 328-0232
  Fort Lauderdale (G-3937)

CONTRACTORS: Electrical

AL Covell Electric Inc ....G 352 544-0680
  Brooksville (G-1132)
ARC Electric Inc ....E 954 583-9800
  Davie (G-2388)
Capacity Inc ....F 855 440-7825
  Sarasota (G-15450)
Central Electric Motor Svc Inc..............F 863 422-4721
  Haines City (G-4902)
Coastal Electric ....G 239 245-7396
  Fort Myers (G-4214)
Del Air Electric Co ....G 407 531-1173
  Sanford (G-15303)
Ingram Signalization Inc.......................E 850 433-8267
  Pensacola (G-13524)
Johnson Controls Inc............................E 407 291-1971
  Orlando (G-12276)
Keltour US Inc ....E 239 424-8901
  Cape Coral (G-1361)
Walker Electric Inc ....G 941 729-5015
  Dunnellon (G-3469)

CONTRACTORS: Electronic Controls Installation

Commercial Gates and Elc LLC............F 386 454-2329
  High Springs (G-5454)
Electrical Controls Inc.........................F 954 801-6846
  Tamarac (G-16530)

CONTRACTORS: Energy Management Control

Integrated Surroundings Inc.................F 850 932-0848
  Gulf Breeze (G-4885)

CONTRACTORS: Excavating

H2r Corp...F 727 541-3444
  Pinellas Park (G-13692)
Keller Industrial Inc.............................E 813 831-1871
  Riverview (G-14568)

CONTRACTORS: Exterior Concrete Stucco

Trinity Exterior Solutions LLC ....G 850 393-9682
  Holt (G-5694)

CONTRACTORS: Exterior Insulation & Finish Application

Trinity Exterior Solutions LLC ....G 850 393-9682
  Holt (G-5694)

CONTRACTORS: Fence Construction

Arts Work Unlimited Inc ....G 305 247-9257
  Miami (G-8756)
Coastal Craftsmen Aluminum Inc ....E 727 868-8802
  Hudson (G-5767)
Danielle Fence Mfg Co Inc ....D 863 425-3182
  Mulberry (G-10621)
Df Multi Services LLC ....G 407 683-2223
  Orlando (G-12090)
Nationwide Industries Inc ....F 813 988-2628
  Tampa (G-17103)
RB Custom Welding LLC ....G 813 280-9860
  Tampa (G-17208)
Silverman Fence Mfg Inc ....G 904 730-0882
  Jacksonville (G-6471)

CONTRACTORS: Fiber Optic Cable Installation

C2c Innovated Technology LLC ....G 251 382-2277
  Bonifay (G-768)
Interntnal Drectional Drlg Inc................F 954 890-1331
  Coconut Creek (G-1994)
Quality Cable Contractors Inc ....E 407 246-0606
  Orlando (G-12520)

CONTRACTORS: Fiberglass Work

Hydes Screening Inc.............................G 954 345-6743
  Coral Springs (G-2165)
Precision Auto Tint Dsign Corp.............G 727 385-8788
  Tarpon Springs (G-17488)
Tampa Fiberglass Inc ....F 813 248-6828
  Tampa (G-17332)

CONTRACTORS: Fire Detection & Burglar Alarm Systems

Cv Technology Inc ....E 561 694-9588
  Jupiter (G-6708)
Security and Fire Elec Inc ....E 904 844-0964
  Saint Augustine (G-14890)

CONTRACTORS: Floor Laying & Other Floor Work

Cianos Tile & Marble Inc ....E 239 267-8453
  Fort Myers (G-4208)
Marlyn Steel Products Inc ....E 813 621-1375
  Tampa (G-17043)
Prestige Flrg Instllations Inc................F 407 291-0609
  Orlando (G-12503)
Triton Stone Holdings LLC....................G 219 669-4890
  Fort Lauderdale (G-4098)

CONTRACTORS: Flooring

Dekscape ....G 239 278-3325
  Fort Myers (G-4233)
Floors Inc...E 813 879-5720
  Tampa (G-16838)
Jdl Surface Innovations Inc ....F 239 772-0077
  Cape Coral (G-1359)
Renovation Flooring LLC ....E 850 460-7295
  Miramar Beach (G-10572)

CONTRACTORS: Foundation & Footing

Continental Concrete Products ....G 904 388-1390
  Jacksonville (G-6000)

CONTRACTORS: Garage Doors

A-1 Door Systems Inc............................F 904 327-7206
  Jacksonville (G-5850)

CONTRACTORS: Gas Detection & Analysis Svcs

Delacom Detection Systems LLC..........G 941 544-6636
  Sarasota (G-15655)

CONTRACTORS: Gas Field Svcs, NEC

Gexa Energy California LLC ....G 561 691-7171
  Juno Beach (G-6664)
Hess Express ....G 772 335-9975
  Port Saint Lucie (G-14416)
I C T S America Inc ....G 786 307-2993
  Doral (G-3252)

PRODUCT

CONTRACTORS: Gas Field Svcs, NEC

MCR Compression Services LLC ....G...... 432 552-8720
North Port *(G-11199)*
MCR Compression Services LLC ....F 210 760-7650
North Port *(G-11200)*
Repgas Inc ....G...... 786 202-8434
Port Saint Lucie *(G-14440)*

CONTRACTORS: General Electric

BJ Burns Incorporated ....E 305 572-9500
Sunrise *(G-16296)*
Freeman Electric Co Inc ....F 850 785-7448
Panama City *(G-13265)*
General Sign Service Inc ....F 904 355-5630
Jacksonville *(G-6140)*

CONTRACTORS: Glass Tinting, Architectural & Automotive

Solar Tint Inc ....G...... 305 663-4663
South Miami *(G-16046)*
Solar X ....G...... 386 673-2111
Ormond Beach *(G-12793)*

CONTRACTORS: Glass, Glazing & Tinting

Ad Investment Group LLC ....C 954 784-6900
Miramar *(G-10458)*
Arso Enterprises Inc ....E 305 681-2020
Opa Locka *(G-11719)*
BT Glass & Mirror Inc ....G...... 561 841-7676
West Palm Beach *(G-17952)*
Flat Glass Distributors LLC ....F 904 354-5413
Jacksonville *(G-6102)*
Greg Valentine LLC ....E 239 332-0855
Fort Myers *(G-4273)*
MA Glass & Mirror LLC ....F 305 593-8555
Miami *(G-9493)*
Michael Valentines Inc ....F 239 332-0855
Fort Myers *(G-4324)*
Plazadoor Corp ....E 561 578-5450
Palm City *(G-13056)*
Southeast Energy Inc ....G...... 561 883-1051
Boca Raton *(G-686)*

CONTRACTORS: Gutters & Downspouts

Titan Specialty Cnstr Inc ....E 850 916-7660
Milton *(G-10440)*

CONTRACTORS: Heating & Air Conditioning

Chiller Medic Inc ....G...... 904 814-9446
Jacksonville *(G-5978)*
Crown Seamless Gutters Inc ....E 561 748-9919
West Palm Beach *(G-17975)*
Everest Air Corp ....F 407 319-6204
Kissimmee *(G-6918)*
Miles of Smiles Rides Inc ....F 727 528-1227
Seminole *(G-15983)*

CONTRACTORS: Highway & Street Construction, General

Woodwork Unlimited Inc ....G...... 352 267-4051
Oxford *(G-12855)*

CONTRACTORS: Highway & Street Paving

Blue Water Industries LLC ....F 904 512-7706
Jacksonville *(G-5940)*

CONTRACTORS: Highway Sign & Guardrail Construction & Install

Scott Safety LLC ....E 239 340-8695
Moore Haven *(G-10592)*

CONTRACTORS: Home & Office Intrs Finish, Furnish/Remodel

Premier Coatings LLC ....E 954 797-9275
Fort Lauderdale *(G-3994)*
Y F Leung Inc ....G...... 305 651-6851
North Miami Beach *(G-11172)*

CONTRACTORS: Hydraulic Eqpt Installation & Svcs

Alpha Hydraulics LLC ....G...... 561 355-0318
Riviera Beach *(G-14592)*

CONTRACTORS: Hydraulic Well Fracturing Svcs

American Silica Holdings LLC ....G...... 352 796-8855
Brooksville *(G-1136)*

CONTRACTORS: Indl Building Renovation, Remodeling & Repair

Moody Construction Svcs Inc ....E 941 776-1542
Duette *(G-3432)*
Relu Co ....E 786 717-5665
Fort Lauderdale *(G-4014)*

CONTRACTORS: Kitchen & Bathroom Remodeling

FL Central Cnstr & Rmdlg ....G...... 863 701-3548
Lakeland *(G-7326)*
Jcs Limited Corporation ....G...... 954 822-2887
Tamarac *(G-16534)*

CONTRACTORS: Kitchen Cabinet Installation

Commercial Stone Cab Fbrctors ....F 727 209-1141
Saint Petersburg *(G-15011)*
Commercial Stone Fbrcators Inc ....F 727 209-1141
Saint Petersburg *(G-15012)*
Professnal Kit Instller Group ....G...... 954 436-1513
Miramar *(G-10533)*
Ramirez Cbnets Blnds Gran Mr ....G...... 352 606-0049
Spring Hill *(G-16076)*

CONTRACTORS: Land Reclamation

One Srce Prperty Solutions Inc ....G...... 239 800-9771
Fort Myers *(G-4351)*

CONTRACTORS: Machinery Installation

Sdi Industries Inc ....E 321 733-1128
Melbourne *(G-8517)*

CONTRACTORS: Marble Installation, Interior

Architctural MBL Importers Inc ....E 941 365-3552
Sarasota *(G-15599)*
New England Granite & Marble ....F 772 283-8667
Stuart *(G-16189)*
Puma Marble Co Inc ....F 305 758-6461
Miami *(G-9757)*

CONTRACTORS: Masonry & Stonework

All Granite & Marble Corp ....G...... 508 248-9393
Sarasota *(G-15592)*
LAS & JB Inc ....G...... 772 672-5315
Fort Pierce *(G-4500)*
Premier Stoneworks LLC ....D 561 330-3737
Delray Beach *(G-3003)*
True Stone Masonry LLC ....F 772 334-9797
Fort Pierce *(G-4544)*

CONTRACTORS: Mechanical

Mechanical Svcs Centl Fla Inc ....C 407 857-3510
Orlando *(G-12368)*
Southern Welding & Mechanics ....F 305 772-0961
Hialeah *(G-5358)*

CONTRACTORS: Millwrights

Diverse Co ....E 863 425-4251
Mulberry *(G-10623)*

CONTRACTORS: Multi-Family Home Remodeling

Jab-B-Inc ....G...... 813 803-3995
Lutz *(G-7997)*
Laser Cnstr & Restoration ....G...... 786 536-2065
Hialeah *(G-5221)*
Los Primos Express Svcs LLC ....G...... 786 701-3297
Miami *(G-9479)*

CONTRACTORS: Nonresidential Building Design & Construction

Division 5 Florida Inc ....E 904 964-4513
Starke *(G-16101)*

CONTRACTORS: Office Furniture Installation

Joe Hearn Innovative Tech LLC ....F 850 898-3744
Pensacola *(G-13528)*

CONTRACTORS: Oil & Gas Aerial Geophysical Exploration Svcs

Atlantic Gas Services LLC ....G...... 386 957-3668
New Smyrna Beach *(G-10994)*

CONTRACTORS: Oil & Gas Building, Repairing & Dismantling Svc

Sunshine Oil and Gas Inc ....G...... 305 367-3100
Miami *(G-9969)*
Warensford Well Drilling Inc ....G...... 386 738-3257
Deland *(G-2918)*

CONTRACTORS: Oil & Gas Field Salt Water Impound/Storing Svc

Worrell Water Technologies LLC ....G...... 434 973-6365
Delray Beach *(G-3038)*

CONTRACTORS: Oil & Gas Well Casing Cement Svcs

Bukkehave Inc ....G...... 954 525-9788
Fort Lauderdale *(G-3709)*

CONTRACTORS: Oil & Gas Well Drilling Svc

AES Services Inc ....G...... 941 237-1446
Venice *(G-17674)*
Old City Building ....G...... 850 432-7723
Pensacola *(G-13560)*
Perfect Oil Inc ....G...... 954 984-8944
Pompano Beach *(G-14122)*
Raven Forest Operating LLC ....F 727 497-2727
Tampa *(G-17207)*
US Natural Gas Corp ....G...... 727 482-1505
Saint Petersburg *(G-15222)*
Warensford Well Drilling Inc ....G...... 386 738-3257
Deland *(G-2918)*

CONTRACTORS: Oil & Gas Well Flow Rate Measurement Svcs

Five Star Feld Svcs Applchia L ....G...... 347 446-6816
Boynton Beach *(G-865)*

CONTRACTORS: Oil & Gas Wells Svcs

Puraglobe Florida LLC ....D 813 247-1754
Tampa *(G-17192)*

CONTRACTORS: Oil Field Haulage Svcs

D & S Pallets Inc ....D 727 540-0061
Clearwater *(G-1560)*

CONTRACTORS: Oil Field Lease Tanks: Erectg, Clng/Rprg Svcs

Ed-Gar Leasing Company Inc ....F 904 284-1900
Green Cove Springs *(G-4823)*

CONTRACTORS: Oil Field Pipe Testing Svcs

Mechanical Design Corp ....G...... 772 388-8782
Sebastian *(G-15902)*
Tricen Technologies Fla LLC ....F 866 620-9407
Fort Pierce *(G-4541)*

CONTRACTORS: Oil/Gas Field Casing,Tube/Rod Running,Cut/Pull

Mecol Oil Tools Corp ....F 305 638-7686
Miami *(G-9526)*

CONTRACTORS: Oil/Gas Well Construction, Rpr/Dismantling Svcs

A Plus Construction Svcs Inc ....E 904 612-0597
Jacksonville *(G-5848)*
Absolute Home Svcs Group Inc ....F 727 275-0020
Saint Petersburg *(G-14952)*
All-Jer Construction Usa Inc ....G...... 305 257-0225
Miami *(G-8692)*
Apps 47 Inc ....F 413 200-7533
Key West *(G-6854)*

Avco Materials and Svcs Inc ....E 727 233-2043
Hudson *(G-5763)*

Big Boy Inc ....G...... 407 434-9251
Orlando *(G-11948)*

Blue Tarpon Construction LLC ....G...... 251 223-3630
Pensacola *(G-13457)*

Bombastic Group Inc ....G...... 754 232-2932
Hollywood *(G-5543)*

Brace Integrated Services Inc ....E 813 248-6248
Tampa *(G-16659)*

Broit Builders Inc ....E 239 300-6900
Naples *(G-10700)*

Buena Vista Construction Co ....E 407 828-2104
Lake Buena Vista *(G-6998)*

Certified Mold Free Corp ....G...... 954 614-7100
Davie *(G-2397)*

Cohen Capital LLC ....G...... 954 661-8270
Fort Lauderdale *(G-3735)*

Compact Contract Inc ....G...... 352 817-8058
Ocala *(G-11356)*

Conquest Engineering LLC ....E 407 731-0519
Orlando *(G-12043)*

Dbn Investment LLC ....F 407 917-2525
Orlando *(G-12079)*

DDy Martinez LLC ....F 786 263-2672
Doral *(G-3187)*

DMC Industries Inc ....G...... 352 620-9322
Sparr *(G-16059)*

Downes Trading Co ....G...... 813 855-7122
Palm Harbor *(G-13109)*

Ducksteins Services ....G...... 352 449-5678
Leesburg *(G-7768)*

E 3 Maintenance ....E 904 708-7208
Jacksonville *(G-6053)*

Eco Restore LLC ....E 904 226-9265
Jacksonville *(G-6062)*

Elements Restoration LLC ....F 813 330-2035
Tampa *(G-16802)*

Elyse Installations LLC ....E 904 322-4754
Jacksonville *(G-6071)*

Equiservisa USA Corp ....F 773 530-6964
Miami *(G-9108)*

Freeman S Magic LLC ....G...... 786 286-8197
Miami *(G-9173)*

Fuse Builds LLC ....E 617 602-4001
Tampa *(G-16864)*

Genos Construction Inc ....D...... 234 303-3427
Dade City *(G-2318)*

Home Imprv & Developers LLC ....F 305 902-3015
Miramar *(G-10501)*

House Doctair Inc ....F 239 349-7497
Ave Maria *(G-248)*

Ingenria Prcura Y Cnstrccion C ....G...... 407 639-4288
Orlando *(G-12244)*

Jab-B-Inc ....G...... 813 803-3995
Lutz *(G-7997)*

Jfr Hazardous Services Inc ....G...... 716 313-2844
Tampa *(G-16965)*

Jordan Florida Group ....F 813 219-0100
Tampa *(G-16971)*

Kabrit Repair Services LLC ....F 407 714-1470
Windermere *(G-18357)*

Kr Solutions Group US LLC ....G...... 305 307-8353
Doral *(G-3277)*

Ladiesfitcamp LLC ....E 954 226-7034
North Lauderdale *(G-11083)*

Laser Cnstr & Restoration ....G...... 786 536-2065
Hialeah *(G-5221)*

Legacy Cnstr Rmdlg Clg Svcs LL ....E 800 638-9646
Hallandale Beach *(G-4958)*

Los Primos Express Svcs LLC ....G...... 786 701-3297
Miami *(G-9479)*

Loyalty Mechanical LLC ....F 718 502-0632
Riverview *(G-14569)*

Lucas Construction Inc ....G...... 386 623-0088
Ormond Beach *(G-12777)*

MEI Companies Inc ....G...... 352 361-6895
Citra *(G-1467)*

Michael L Larviere Inc ....G...... 239 267-2738
Fort Myers *(G-4323)*

Muelby Construction Services ....E 561 376-7614
North Palm Beach *(G-11180)*

Nivcoe International Dev ....F 321 282-3666
Winter Park *(G-18526)*

One Srce Prperty Solutions Inc ....G...... 239 800-9771
Fort Myers *(G-4351)*

Pearson Group LLC ....G...... 786 498-3532
Opa Locka *(G-11782)*

Pulling Inc ....G...... 305 224-2469
Sunrise *(G-16359)*

Quintessential Home Svcs LLC ....G...... 850 259-5064
Destin *(G-3076)*

Rachel Ally ....F 727 804-9596
Hudson *(G-5786)*

Ramirez Cbnets Blnds Gran Mr ....G...... 352 606-0049
Spring Hill *(G-16076)*

Randolph Cnstr Group Inc ....G...... 954 276-2889
Delray Beach *(G-3011)*

Rapid Response ....G...... 407 774-9877
Altamonte Springs *(G-69)*

Realti Hub LLC ....G...... 754 242-4759
Miami Gardens *(G-10270)*

Rekord Services LLC ....F 706 401-1791
Wellington *(G-17859)*

Renovation Team Services LLC ....F 352 696-0215
Saint Cloud *(G-14937)*

RG Mechanical USA LLC ....G...... 954 835-5287
Davie *(G-2470)*

Rippee Construction Inc ....G...... 850 668-6805
Tallahassee *(G-16494)*

Ryan Tire & Petroleum Inc ....G...... 239 334-1351
Fort Myers *(G-4386)*

Sherry J Bertucelli Inc ....G...... 407 760-7585
Orlando *(G-12590)*

Slg Solutions Inc ....G...... 786 379-4676
Miami *(G-9904)*

Solution Asset Management LLC ....G...... 786 288-9408
Hollywood *(G-5659)*

Sunshine Spray Foam Insulation ....G...... 239 221-8704
Bonita Springs *(G-823)*

Suvillaga Construction MGT LLC ....F 305 323-8380
Miami *(G-9979)*

Ten4 Solutions LLC ....G...... 302 544-1120
Nokomis *(G-11053)*

Tyson Petroleum Contrs LLC ....F 850 727-0082
Tallahassee *(G-16518)*

Ultra Airconditioning Inc ....F 877 333-0189
West Palm Beach *(G-18191)*

W&I Properties LLC ....G...... 786 985-1642
Davie *(G-2495)*

Weldcorp Industries ....E 561 339-7713
Jupiter *(G-6827)*

Williams Industrial Svcs LLC ....C...... 904 696-9994
Jacksonville *(G-6613)*

Yatfl Inc ....G...... 786 643-8660
Miami *(G-10150)*

CONTRACTORS: On-Site Welding

Bogue Executive Enterprises ....F 561 842-5336
Mangonia Park *(G-8090)*

C & H Baseball Inc ....G...... 941 727-1533
Bradenton *(G-952)*

Custom Wldg & Fabrication Inc ....D...... 863 967-1000
Auburndale *(G-227)*

D C Inc Prtble Wldg Fbrication ....G...... 863 533-4483
Frostproof *(G-4637)*

Deans Cstm Shtmtl Fbrction In ....G...... 813 757-6270
Dover *(G-3429)*

Gunns Welding & Fabricating ....G...... 727 393-5238
Saint Petersburg *(G-15070)*

Lm Industrial Inc ....G...... 407 240-8911
Orlando *(G-12337)*

St Cloud Wldg Fabrication Inc ....E 407 957-2344
Saint Cloud *(G-14939)*

Titan Service Industry Llc ....G...... 678 313-4707
Deland *(G-2912)*

CONTRACTORS: Ornamental Metal Work

Barrett Custom Designs LLC ....G...... 321 242-2002
Melbourne *(G-8374)*

Custom Fbrcations Freeport Inc ....F 850 729-0500
Valparaiso *(G-17659)*

Florida Aluminum and Steel Inc ....F 863 967-4191
Auburndale *(G-231)*

Metal Creations Sarasota Llc ....F 941 922-7096
Sarasota *(G-15744)*

CONTRACTORS: Painting & Wall Covering

A Clean Finish Inc ....G...... 407 516-1311
Jacksonville *(G-5846)*

Ken R Avery Painting Inc ....E 813 855-5037
Oldsmar *(G-11664)*

CONTRACTORS: Painting, Commercial, Exterior

Glory Sandblasting Inc ....F 407 422-0078
Orlando *(G-12196)*

CONTRACTORS: Painting, Indl

Industrial Marine Inc ....F 904 781-4707
Jacksonville *(G-6195)*

CONTRACTORS: Painting, Residential

Clear View Coatings LLC ....F 850 210-0155
Tallahassee *(G-16424)*

Thomas Smith & Company Inc ....E 863 858-2199
Lakeland *(G-7461)*

CONTRACTORS: Parking Lot Maintenance

Traffic Control Pdts Fla Inc ....E 352 372-7088
Jacksonville *(G-6562)*

CONTRACTORS: Patio & Deck Construction & Repair

Danielle Fence Mfg Co Inc ....D...... 863 425-3182
Mulberry *(G-10621)*

Fresco Group Inc ....E 239 936-8055
Fort Myers *(G-4263)*

Hydes Screening Inc ....G...... 954 345-6743
Coral Springs *(G-2165)*

K C Screen ....G...... 407 977-9636
Oviedo *(G-12831)*

R & K Portable Buildings ....G...... 850 857-7899
Pensacola *(G-13591)*

CONTRACTORS: Pile Driving

Shoreline Foundation Inc ....C...... 954 985-0981
West Park *(G-18216)*

CONTRACTORS: Playground Construction & Eqpt Installation

Southern Recreation Inc ....F 904 387-4390
Jacksonville *(G-6492)*

CONTRACTORS: Plumbing

RG Mechanical USA LLC ....G...... 954 835-5287
Davie *(G-2470)*

CONTRACTORS: Pole Cutting

Florida Pole Settlers & Crane ....F 772 283-6820
Palm City *(G-13039)*

CONTRACTORS: Post Disaster Renovations

Elements Restoration LLC ....F 813 330-2035
Tampa *(G-16802)*

Kustom Us Inc ....F 407 965-1940
Longwood *(G-7914)*

CONTRACTORS: Precast Concrete Struct Framing & Panel Placing

Orange State Steel Cnstr Inc ....E 727 544-3398
Pinellas Park *(G-13716)*

CONTRACTORS: Prefabricated Window & Door Installation

Absolute Window and Door Inc ....G...... 941 485-7774
Venice *(G-17672)*

Arso Enterprises Inc ....E 305 681-2020
Opa Locka *(G-11719)*

Clear-Vue Inc ....E 727 726-5386
Safety Harbor *(G-14784)*

Global Performance Windows Inc ....F 954 942-3322
Pompano Beach *(G-14042)*

Master Alum & SEC Shutter Co ....G...... 727 725-1744
Safety Harbor *(G-14790)*

CONTRACTORS: Pulpwood, Engaged In Cutting

Barnes & Sons Wood Producers ....G...... 386 935-2229
Branford *(G-1111)*

Breeden Pulpwood Inc ....F 352 528-5243
Williston *(G-18331)*

Creamer Corp ....G...... 850 265-2700
Panama City *(G-13250)*

Huntley Stemwood Inc ....G...... 904 237-4005
Middleburg *(G-10402)*

J Q Bell & Sons ....G...... 904 879-1597
Callahan *(G-1252)*

P R O D U C T

CONTRACTORS: Pulpwood, Engaged In Cutting

Joiner Land Clearing LLC ....F..... 850 997-5729
Monticello **(G-10582)**

Padgetts Pulpwood Inc ....G..... 904 282-5112
Middleburg **(G-10408)**

Stratton Inc Dm ....G..... 904 268-6052
Jacksonville **(G-6512)**

Whitfield Timber Company Inc ....E..... 850 639-5556
Wewahitchka **(G-18303)**

CONTRACTORS: Refrigeration

Kommercial Refrigeration Inc ....G..... 863 299-3000
Winter Haven **(G-18447)**

CONTRACTORS: Roofing

Chuculu LLC ....F..... 305 595-4577
Miami **(G-8924)**

Coastal Acquisitions Fla LLC ....F..... 850 769-9423
Panama City **(G-13244)**

Eco Restore LLC ....E..... 904 226-9265
Jacksonville **(G-6062)**

Largo Aluminum Inc ....F..... 305 852-2390
Islamorada **(G-5837)**

Southeast Gen Contrs Group Inc ....G..... 877 407-3535
Port St Lucie **(G-14483)**

CONTRACTORS: Roofing & Gutter Work

Thomas Smith & Company Inc ....E..... 863 858-2199
Lakeland **(G-7461)**

CONTRACTORS: Roustabout Svcs

Blue Chip Servicing Inc ....F..... 844 607-2029
Fort Lauderdale **(G-3691)**

Grms Servicing LLC ....G..... 850 278-1000
Santa Rosa Beach **(G-15426)**

Jdt Servicing LLC ....G..... 813 909-8640
Lutz **(G-7998)**

Srb Servicing LLC ....G..... 850 278-1000
Santa Rosa Beach **(G-15433)**

CONTRACTORS: Safe Or Vault Installation

Alternative Cnstr Tech Inc ....G..... 321 421-6601
Melbourne **(G-8363)**

CONTRACTORS: Safety & Security Eqpt

Amtel Security Systems Inc ....E..... 305 591-8200
Doral **(G-3115)**

Security Oracle Inc ....F..... 352 988-5985
Clermont **(G-1883)**

Titan Service Industry Llc ....G..... 678 313-4707
Deland **(G-2912)**

CONTRACTORS: Sandblasting Svc, Building Exteriors

RSR Industrial Coatings Inc ....F..... 863 537-1110
Bartow **(G-324)**

CONTRACTORS: Screening, Window & Door

ABC Screen Masters Inc ....G..... 239 772-7336
Cape Coral **(G-1295)**

British Boys & Associates ....G..... 305 278-1790
Miami **(G-8853)**

Liberty Aluminum Co ....E..... 239 369-3000
Lehigh Acres **(G-7815)**

Screen Monkey Corp ....G..... 352 746-7091
Homosassa **(G-5750)**

CONTRACTORS: Septic System

Averett Septic Tank Co Inc ....E..... 863 665-1748
Lakeland **(G-7278)**

Bingham On-Site Sewers Inc ....D..... 813 659-0003
Dover **(G-3428)**

Dixie Sptic Tank Orange Cy LLC ....E..... 386 775-3051
Orange City **(G-11805)**

Miller Brothers Contractors ....F..... 941 371-4162
Sarasota **(G-15748)**

Pilot Corp of Palm Beaches ....F..... 561 848-2928
Riviera Beach **(G-14661)**

Stans Septic Svc Con Pdts Inc ....G..... 941 639-3976
Punta Gorda **(G-14533)**

Taylor Concrete Inc ....G..... 941 737-7225
Palmetto **(G-13196)**

CONTRACTORS: Sheet Metal Work, NEC

Freeman Electric Co Inc ....F..... 850 785-7448
Panama City **(G-13265)**

Kohtler Elevator Inds Inc ....G..... 305 687-7037
Opa Locka **(G-11761)**

Mechanical Svcs Centl Fla Inc ....C..... 407 857-3510
Orlando **(G-12368)**

Ra Co AMO Inc ....F..... 561 626-7232
Palm Beach Gardens **(G-13004)**

CONTRACTORS: Single-Family Home Fire Damage Repair

Relu Co ....E..... 786 717-5665
Fort Lauderdale **(G-4014)**

CONTRACTORS: Single-family Home General Remodeling

British Boys & Associates ....G..... 305 278-1790
Miami **(G-8853)**

Kevco Builders Inc ....F..... 352 308-8025
Eustis **(G-3561)**

CONTRACTORS: Solar Energy Eqpt

Alterna Power Inc ....F..... 407 287-9148
Orlando **(G-11897)**

Wes Industries Inc ....F..... 941 371-7617
Sarasota **(G-15872)**

CONTRACTORS: Special Trades, NEC

East Coast Door Inc ....G..... 954 868-4700
Pompano Beach **(G-14004)**

CONTRACTORS: Store Front Construction

Florida Glass of Tampa Bay ....E..... 813 925-1330
Tampa **(G-16844)**

CONTRACTORS: Structural Iron Work, Structural

Fuse Fabrication Llc ....E..... 863 225-5698
Mulberry **(G-10626)**

CONTRACTORS: Structural Steel Erection

Aog Detailing Services Inc ....G..... 727 742-7321
Saint Petersburg **(G-14964)**

Central Maintenance & Wldg Inc ....C..... 813 229-0012
Lithia **(G-7831)**

Custom Fbrcations Freeport Inc ....F..... 850 729-0500
Valparaiso **(G-17659)**

Fitzlord Inc ....D..... 904 731-2041
Jacksonville **(G-6099)**

Met-Con Inc ....D..... 321 632-4880
Cocoa **(G-1941)**

Quality Industries America Inc ....G..... 386 755-0220
Lake City **(G-7041)**

Steel City Inc ....F..... 850 785-9596
Panama City **(G-13311)**

Storage Building Company LLC ....F..... 863 738-1319
Palmetto **(G-13193)**

United Fabrication & Maint ....G..... 863 295-9000
Eloise **(G-3514)**

Viper Communication Systems ....E..... 352 694-7030
Ocala **(G-11510)**

CONTRACTORS: Stucco, Interior

Central Florida Cnstr Walls ....F..... 407 448-2350
Orlando **(G-11995)**

CONTRACTORS: Textile Warping

Dillon Yarn Corporation ....D..... 973 684-1600
Fort Lauderdale **(G-3765)**

CONTRACTORS: Tile Installation, Ceramic

Designer Lifestyles LLC ....F..... 904 631-8954
Jacksonville **(G-6030)**

Renovation Flooring LLC ....E..... 850 460-7295
Miramar Beach **(G-10572)**

CONTRACTORS: Underground Utilities

Coastal Concrete Products LLC ....E..... 239 208-4079
Fort Myers **(G-4213)**

CONTRACTORS: Unit Paver Installation

Df Multi Services LLC ....G..... 407 683-2223
Orlando **(G-12090)**

CONTRACTORS: Wall Covering

Sanzogo Corporation ....G..... 561 334-2138
Boca Raton **(G-662)**

CONTRACTORS: Warm Air Heating & Air Conditioning

Airite Air Conditioning Inc ....E..... 813 886-0235
Tampa **(G-16567)**

Precision Resources Inc ....F..... 321 635-2000
Cocoa **(G-1949)**

CONTRACTORS: Water Well Drilling

Eagle Engrg & Land Dev Inc ....E..... 913 948-4320
Boynton Beach **(G-860)**

H2r Corp ....F..... 727 541-3444
Pinellas Park **(G-13692)**

CONTRACTORS: Well Acidizing Svcs

Rfg Consulting Services Inc ....G..... 832 298-5696
Medley **(G-8311)**

CONTRACTORS: Window Treatment Installation

Bornt Enterprises Inc ....E..... 813 623-1492
Tampa **(G-16658)**

Florida Wood Creations Inc ....G..... 239 561-5411
Punta Gorda **(G-14504)**

Timbercraft of Naples Inc ....G..... 239 566-2559
Naples **(G-10927)**

TMMR Holdings LLC ....E..... 407 295-5200
Ocoee **(G-11528)**

Top Trtment Cstomes Accesories ....G..... 239 936-4600
Fort Myers **(G-4426)**

CONTRACTORS: Windows & Doors

Gulfstream Alum & Shutter Corp ....E..... 772 287-6476
Stuart **(G-16158)**

Pinos Window Corporation ....F..... 305 888-9903
Medley **(G-8299)**

Rollshield LLC ....F..... 727 441-2243
Clearwater **(G-1771)**

Specialty Products Inc ....G..... 850 438-4264
Pensacola **(G-13608)**

Techno Cabinets Inc ....G..... 305 910-9929
Doral **(G-3393)**

CONTRACTORS: Wood Floor Installation & Refinishing

Eagle Prof Flrg Removal ....G..... 813 520-3027
Riverview **(G-14562)**

Global Prime Wood LLC ....G..... 770 292-9200
Aventura **(G-261)**

Renovation Flooring LLC ....E..... 850 460-7295
Miramar Beach **(G-10572)**

CONTRACTORS: Wrecking & Demolition

Platinum Rosis Inc ....G..... 786 617-9973
Miami Beach **(G-10220)**

CONTROL CIRCUIT DEVICES

Technical Drive Ctrl Svcs Inc ....G..... 954 471-6521
Davie **(G-2487)**

CONTROL EQPT: Electric

Barcode Automation Inc ....F..... 407 327-2177
Winter Springs **(G-18560)**

ICI Custom Parts Inc ....F..... 813 888-7979
Tampa **(G-16929)**

Metal-Tech Controls Corp ....G..... 941 575-7677
Punta Gorda **(G-14516)**

Phasetronics Inc ....C..... 727 573-1819
Clearwater **(G-1738)**

Pro Co Inc ....G..... 321 422-0900
Winter Springs **(G-18575)**

STA-Con Incorporated ....E..... 407 298-5940
Apopka **(G-177)**

Sun State Systems Inc ....F..... 904 269-2544
Orange Park **(G-11843)**

Tel-Tron Technologies Corp....................E...... 386 523-1070
Daytona Beach *(G-2608)*
Tentech Corporation.............................F...... 305 938-0389
Miami *(G-10001)*

CONTROL EQPT: Electric Buses & Locomotives

American Traction Systems Inc.............E...... 239 768-0757
Fort Myers *(G-4172)*

CONTROL PANELS: Electrical

America Energy Inc ....G...... 954 762-7763
Pembroke Pines *(G-13374)*
Champion Controls Inc ....E...... 954 318-3090
Fort Lauderdale *(G-3723)*
Consumer Engineering Inc ....F...... 321 984-8550
Palm Bay *(G-12895)*
Custom Control Solutions Inc ....E...... 850 937-8902
Cantonment *(G-1268)*
Ff Systems Inc ....G...... 239 288-4255
Fort Myers *(G-4253)*
Paneltronics Incorporated ....D...... 305 823-9777
Hialeah *(G-5291)*
Quality Building Controls Inc ....E...... 813 885-5005
Tampa *(G-17199)*
Technology Research LLC....................D...... 727 535-0572
Clearwater *(G-1822)*

CONTROLS & ACCESS: Indl, Electric

Automted Lgic Corp Kennesaw GA ......F...... 877 866-1226
Orlando *(G-11935)*
CC Control Corp....................................E...... 561 293-3975
West Palm Beach *(G-17957)*
Hale Products Inc ....C...... 352 629-5020
Ocala *(G-11407)*
Hf Scientific Inc ....E...... 888 203-7248
Fort Myers *(G-4279)*
Southern Automated Systems Inc ....G...... 863 815-7444
Lakeland *(G-7442)*
Sun Electronic Systems Inc ....F...... 321 383-9400
Titusville *(G-17621)*

CONTROLS & ACCESS: Motor

Eaton & Wolk ....G...... 305 249-1640
Miami *(G-9065)*
Eaton Law ....G...... 813 264-4800
Tampa *(G-16796)*
Motor Protection Electronics.................F...... 407 299-3825
Apopka *(G-155)*
Nidec Motor Corporation......................C...... 954 346-4900
Coral Springs *(G-2197)*
Saminco Inc ....E...... 239 561-1561
Fort Myers *(G-4390)*
Taylor Electronics Inc ....F...... 941 925-3605
Sarasota *(G-15852)*

CONTROLS: Air Flow, Refrigeration

Airflowbalance LLC ....F...... 386 871-8136
Lake Mary *(G-7057)*
Molekule Inc ....C...... 352 871-3803
Tampa *(G-17082)*
R & J Mfg of Gainesville.......................G...... 352 375-3130
Gainesville *(G-4754)*

CONTROLS: Automatic Temperature

Moisttech Corp......................................F...... 941 351-7870
Sarasota *(G-15519)*

CONTROLS: Electric Motor

Faac International Inc ....G...... 904 448-8952
Rockledge *(G-14709)*
Universal Precision Inds Inc ....G...... 727 581-7097
Largo *(G-7701)*

CONTROLS: Environmental

AVw Inc ....E...... 954 972-3338
Margate *(G-8122)*
Controls On Demand Llc.......................F...... 321 362-5485
Titusville *(G-17583)*
F & J Specialty Products Inc ....F...... 352 680-1177
Ocala *(G-11385)*
Florida Enviromental Cons ....G...... 407 402-2828
Clermont *(G-1866)*
Galtronics Telemetry Inc ....F...... 386 202-2055
Palm Coast *(G-13078)*

Kpa Llc ....F...... 352 671-9249
Ocala *(G-11421)*
Leslie Controls Inc ....C...... 813 978-1000
Temple Terrace *(G-17539)*
Melbourne-Tillman Wtr Ctrl Dst ....E...... 321 723-7233
Palm Bay *(G-12908)*
Micro Control Systems Inc ....E...... 239 694-0089
Fort Myers *(G-4325)*
Niagara Industries Inc ....F...... 305 876-9010
Miami *(G-9619)*
Noxtak Corp...G...... 786 586-7927
Pembroke Pines *(G-13408)*
Portalp Usa Inc ....F...... 800 474-3667
Naples *(G-10865)*
Sacyr Environment USA LLC.................F...... 202 361-4568
Miami *(G-9834)*
Sampletech ....G...... 727 239-7055
Clearwater *(G-1776)*
Suntree Technologies Inc ....F...... 321 637-7552
Cocoa *(G-1960)*
Technico ....F...... 561 588-8300
Lake Worth *(G-7235)*
Triumvirate Environmental ....E...... 407 859-4441
Orlando *(G-12674)*
Two Tree Inc ....G...... 352 284-1763
Gainesville *(G-4781)*

CONTROLS: Hydronic

Oil Water Separator Tech LLC ....G...... 561 693-3250
West Palm Beach *(G-18095)*

CONTROLS: Marine & Navy, Auxiliary

Arctic Rays Llc ....G...... 321 223-5780
Satellite Beach *(G-15883)*
Artful Arnautic Assemblies LLC ....G...... 727 522-0055
Saint Petersburg *(G-14972)*
L-3 Cmmnctons Ntronix Holdings........D...... 212 697-1111
Melbourne *(G-8453)*
Marine Engine Controls Inc ....F...... 727 518-8080
Hudson *(G-5782)*
Seatorque Control Systems LLC ....F...... 772 220-3020
Stuart *(G-16213)*
Southeastern Marine Power LLC.........F...... 727 545-2700
Saint Petersburg *(G-15190)*

CONTROLS: Relay & Ind

ABB Enterprise Software Inc ....C...... 954 752-6700
Coral Springs *(G-2124)*
ABB Inc ....B...... 407 732-2000
Lake Mary *(G-7056)*
ABB Inc ....D...... 305 471-0844
Miami *(G-8634)*
Action Controls Inc ....G...... 253 243-7703
Aventura *(G-250)*
Advance Ctrl Mfg Jean Annette ....G...... 941 697-0846
Englewood *(G-3515)*
Alttec Corporation ....G...... 727 547-1622
Clearwater *(G-1489)*
Coast Controls Inc ....F...... 941 355-7555
Sarasota *(G-15456)*
Custom Controls Technology Inc..........E...... 305 805-3700
Hialeah *(G-5103)*
D & L Auto & Marine Supplies ....G...... 305 593-0560
Doral *(G-3181)*
Dynalco Controls Corporation ....E...... 323 589-6181
Fort Lauderdale *(G-3775)*
E G Pump Controls Inc ....E...... 904 292-0110
Jacksonville *(G-6054)*
Electrical Controls Inc ....F...... 954 801-6846
Tamarac *(G-16530)*
Entech Controls Corp ....G...... 954 613-2971
Miami *(G-9100)*
Ese & Assoc Inc ....G...... 718 767-2367
Miami *(G-9110)*
Everaxis Usa Inc ....D...... 239 263-3102
Naples *(G-10743)*
Facts Engineering LLC ....E...... 727 375-8888
Trinity *(G-17636)*
Intelligent Heater LLC..........................G...... 305 248-4971
Homestead *(G-5718)*
Jenzano Incorporated...........................F...... 386 761-4474
Port Orange *(G-14336)*
Kemco Industries LLC...........................D...... 407 322-1230
Sanford *(G-15348)*
Kinematics and Controls Corp ....G...... 352 796-0300
Brooksville *(G-1169)*
Lextm3 Systems LLC.............................F...... 954 888-1024
Davie *(G-2434)*

Micro Control Systems Inc ....E...... 239 694-0089
Fort Myers *(G-4325)*
Quest Controls Inc ....F...... 941 729-4799
Palmetto *(G-13189)*
Rockwell Automation Inc ....G...... 954 306-7900
Weston *(G-18283)*
Rockwell Automation Inc ....F...... 813 466-6400
Tampa *(G-17230)*
RTC Solutions Inc ....G...... 919 439-8680
Davie *(G-2472)*
Scientific Instruments Inc ....E...... 561 881-8500
Mangonia Park *(G-8100)*
Select Engineered Systems Inc ....G...... 305 823-5410
Hialeah *(G-5343)*
Sepac Corp..F...... 305 718-3379
Miami *(G-9868)*
Song-Chuan USA Inc ....F...... 954 788-5889
Pompano Beach *(G-14187)*
Ultrapanel Marine Inc.........................E...... 772 285-4258
Miami *(G-10058)*

CONTROLS: Remote, Boat

Alamo USA Inc ....G...... 954 774-3747
Hallandale Beach *(G-4934)*
Dukane Seacom Inc ....C...... 941 739-3200
Sarasota *(G-15472)*
Gem Remotes Inc..................................F...... 239 642-0873
Naples *(G-10759)*

CONTROLS: Thermostats

Simplexgrinnell Holdings LLC...............G...... 978 731-2500
Boca Raton *(G-677)*
Southern Environmental Inc ....E...... 850 944-4475
Pensacola *(G-13605)*

CONTROLS: Thermostats, Exc Built-in

Mold Control Systems Inc.....................G...... 561 316-5412
Palm Beach Gardens *(G-12990)*
Vtronix LLC..G...... 305 471-7600
Miami *(G-10122)*

CONTROLS: Truck, Indl Battery

Lithium Battery Co Intl ....F...... 813 504-0074
Tampa *(G-17015)*
Mia Consulting & Trading Inc ....G...... 305 640-3077
Miami *(G-9542)*

CONVERTERS: Data

Cisco Systems Inc ....F...... 305 718-2600
Doral *(G-3163)*
Crucial Cllsion Prductions LLC ....F...... 321 501-1722
Melbourne *(G-8395)*
Cyipcom Inc...G...... 954 727-2500
Oakland Park *(G-11255)*
Global Mind USA LLC ....D...... 305 402-2190
Miami *(G-9218)*
Multimedia Effects Inc ....F...... 800 367-3054
Plantation *(G-13871)*
Ten In Motion LLC ....F...... 407 226-0204
Orlando *(G-12651)*
Wau USA Corp.......................................F...... 305 361-6110
Key Biscayne *(G-6841)*

CONVERTERS: Power, AC to DC

Creating Tech Solutions LLC.................E...... 727 914-3001
Clearwater *(G-1555)*
OHM Americas LLC ....F...... 800 467-7275
Fort Lauderdale *(G-3966)*

CONVEYOR SYSTEMS

Built Right Installers Intl......................F...... 305 362-6010
Hialeah *(G-5082)*
UNI-Pak Corp...E...... 407 830-9300
Longwood *(G-7956)*

CONVEYOR SYSTEMS: Pneumatic Tube

Eagle Pneumatic Inc.............................E...... 863 644-4870
Lakeland *(G-7314)*
JDB Dense Flow Inc..............................F...... 727 785-8500
Palm Harbor *(G-13116)*

CONVEYOR SYSTEMS: Robotic

American Automtn Systems Inc ....G...... 305 620-0077
Miami Lakes *(G-10281)*

P
R
O
D
U
C
T

Emmeti USA LLC ....F 813 490-6252
Safety Harbor *(G-14786)*
Sunshine Tool LLC ....G 941 351-6330
Sarasota *(G-15564)*

CONVEYORS & CONVEYING EQPT

Agri Machinery & Parts Inc ....F 407 299-1592
Orlando *(G-11878)*
Anchor Machine & Fabricating ....F 813 247-3099
Tampa *(G-16597)*
Andersons Can Line Fbrction Eq ....F 407 889-4665
Apopka *(G-102)*
Atlas Metal Industries Inc.................C 305 625-2451
Miami *(G-8767)*
Automated Parking Corporation ....G 754 200-8441
Fort Lauderdale *(G-3667)*
Capitol Conveyors Inc ....G 727 314-7474
Trinity *(G-17633)*
Chris Industries Corp ....G 941 729-7600
Palmetto *(G-13160)*
Container Handling Solutions ....G 941 359-2095
Sarasota *(G-15458)*
Conveyor Concepts Corporation ....G 941 751-1200
Sarasota *(G-15460)*
Conveyor Consulting & Rbr Corp ....F 813 385-1254
Odessa *(G-11545)*
Custom Metal Designs Inc ....D 407 656-7771
Oakland *(G-11228)*
Epperson & Company ....D 813 626-6125
Tampa *(G-16820)*
Erie Manufacturing Inc ....F 863 534-3743
Bartow *(G-308)*
Flite Technology Inc ....G 321 631-2050
Cocoa *(G-1928)*
Gaemmerler (us) Corporation.................G 941 465-4400
Palmetto *(G-13168)*
ISA Group Corp ....G 305 748-1578
Miami *(G-9341)*
Jepsen Tool Company Inc ....F 904 262-2793
Jacksonville *(G-6223)*
Keller-Nglillis Design Mfg Inc ....F 727 733-4111
Dunedin *(G-3452)*
Lynx Products Corp Inc ....G 941 727-9676
Bradenton *(G-1008)*
M A K Manufacturing Inc ....G 352 343-5881
Tavares *(G-17517)*
Material Conveying Maint Inc ....E 813 677-3740
Apollo Beach *(G-95)*
Material Conveying Maint Inc ....G 813 740-1111
Tampa *(G-17056)*
Multi-Flex LLC ....G 941 360-6500
Sarasota *(G-15520)*
Novak Machining Inc ....G 727 527-5473
Pinellas Park *(G-13714)*
Padgett Manufacturing Inc.................D 941 756-8566
Bradenton *(G-1025)*
Quality Fbrction Mch Works Inc ....F 386 755-0220
Lake City *(G-7040)*
Sdi Industries Inc ....E 321 733-1128
Melbourne *(G-8517)*
Titan Service Industry Llc 678 313-4707
Deland *(G-2912)*
US Conveyor Solutions Inc ....G 352 343-0085
Tavares *(G-17526)*
Ver-Val Enterprises Inc ....F 850 244-7931
Fort Walton Beach *(G-4616)*
William Laroque Installers Inc ....E 305 769-1717
Hollywood *(G-5684)*

COOKING & FOOD WARMING EQPT: Commercial

Argosy Group International LLC ....G 888 350-7643
Orlando *(G-11919)*
Atlas Metal Industries Inc.................C 305 625-2451
Miami *(G-8767)*
Brake-Funderburk Entps Inc.................E 904 730-6788
Jacksonville *(G-5951)*
Crystal Pool Service Inc ....G 954 444-8282
Sunrise *(G-16310)*
Enodis Holdings Inc ....E 727 375-7010
Trinity *(G-17635)*
Louis Di Rmndo Wrldwide Invstm ....F 786 536-7578
Miami Beach *(G-10209)*
Mvp Group LLC ....D 786 600-4687
Fort Lauderdale *(G-3948)*
Welbilt Inc ....C 727 375-7010
Trinity *(G-17641)*

COOKING & FOODWARMING EQPT: Coffee Brewing

Jiva Cubes Inc ....F 305 788-1200
Surfside *(G-16396)*

COOKING & FOODWARMING EQPT: Commercial

Euroasia Products Inc ....G 321 221-9398
Orlando *(G-12136)*

COOKING & FOODWARMING EQPT: Microwave Ovens, Commercial

Accommodating Services Inc.................G 863 528-3231
Lake Wales *(G-7151)*
Apollo Worldwide Inc ....G 561 585-3865
Hypoluxo *(G-5794)*

COOKING EQPT, HOUSEHOLD: Convection Ovens, Incldg Portable

Strategic Products Inc.................F 321 752-0441
Melbourne *(G-8532)*

COOKING EQPT, HOUSEHOLD: Ranges, Electric

Tannous Innovations LLC ....G 754 220-6645
Pompano Beach *(G-14210)*

COOKWARE: Fine Earthenware

Comerint Inc ....G 813 443-2466
Tampa *(G-16721)*

COOLERS & ICE CHESTS: Polystyrene Foam

Icemule Company Inc ....F 904 325-9012
Saint Augustine *(G-14843)*

COOLING TOWERS: Wood

East Coast Cooling Tower Inc ....F 904 551-5527
Jacksonville *(G-6058)*

COPPER ORES

Chemours Company Fc LLC.................D 904 964-1200
Starke *(G-16099)*
Goldfield Cnsld Mines Co ....D 321 724-1700
Melbourne *(G-8430)*
US Precious Metals Inc ....G 786 814-5804
Coral Gables *(G-2118)*

COPPER: Rolling & Drawing

Technetics Group LLC.................B 386 736-7373
Deland *(G-2908)*
Technetics Group LLC.................G 386 736-7373
De Land *(G-2620)*

CORD & TWINE

Rat-Trap Bait Company Inc ....G 863 967-2148
Auburndale *(G-243)*
Shurhold Products Company ....G 772 287-1313
Palm City *(G-13058)*

CORK & CORK PRDTS

Amorim Cork Composites Inc ....E 800 558-3206
Tampa *(G-16593)*
Art & Frame Drct/Timeless Inds ....F 407 857-6000
Orlando *(G-11924)*

CORK & CORK PRDTS: Tiles

Delta Mg ....G 561 840-0577
West Palm Beach *(G-17977)*
Designer Lifestyles LLC ....F 904 631-8954
Jacksonville *(G-6030)*

CORRUGATED PRDTS: Boxes, Partition, Display Items, Sheet/Pad

Givr Packaging LLC ....G 321 345-6875
Melbourne *(G-8429)*
Omni Displays LLC ....E 352 799-9997
Brooksville *(G-1186)*

COSMETIC PREPARATIONS

Agustin Reyes Inc.................F 305 558-8870
Hialeah *(G-5034)*
Alfa Manufacturing Group LLC ....G 305 979-7344
Miami Gardens *(G-10250)*
American Hygenic Laboratories...........F 305 891-9518
Miami *(G-8717)*
Audrey Morris Cosmt Intl LLC ....E 954 332-2000
Deerfield Beach *(G-2674)*
Biddiscombe International LLC.................F 727 299-9287
Saint Petersburg *(G-14980)*
Bobbie Weiner Enterprises LLC ....G 817 615-8610
North Miami *(G-11093)*
Bpj International LLC.................G 305 507-8971
Doral *(G-3147)*
Brand Labs USA ....E 954 532-5390
Pompano Beach *(G-13952)*
Carfore Ltd ....G 239 415-2275
Fort Myers *(G-4201)*
Caribbean Breeze Inc ....G 904 261-7831
Fernandina Beach *(G-3582)*
Cemi International Inc ....C 407 859-7701
Orlando *(G-11992)*
Coco Cosmetics Inc ....F 305 622-3488
Miami *(G-8937)*
Cofran International Corp ....E 305 592-2644
Doral *(G-3166)*
Contours Rx LLC ....G 727 827-7321
Saint Petersburg *(G-15015)*
Cosmetic Corp of America Inc ....E 305 883-8434
Medley *(G-8223)*
Cosmetic Solutions LLC ....E 561 226-8600
Boca Raton *(G-472)*
Cosmetics & Cleaners Intl LLC ....E 305 592-5504
Doral *(G-3175)*
Custom Manufacturing Corp ....F 305 863-1001
Medley *(G-8228)*
Daby Products Carisen ....G 305 559-3018
West Miami *(G-17904)*
Danibella Inc 561 307-9274
Loxahatchee *(G-7968)*
Dermazone Solutions Inc ....E 727 446-6882
Saint Petersburg *(G-15022)*
Eagle Labs Incorporated ....E 727 548-1816
Saint Petersburg *(G-15033)*
F&J USA LLC.................F 800 406-6190
Fort Lauderdale *(G-3808)*
Formulated Solutions LLC.................D 727 373-3970
Largo *(G-7589)*
Formulated Solutions LLC.................G 727 456-0302
Saint Petersburg *(G-15055)*
Glamer Medspa LLC ....F 305 744-6908
Pembroke Pines *(G-13391)*
Image International Inc.................E 561 793-9560
West Palm Beach *(G-18030)*
Instanatural LLC.................E 800 290-6932
Orlando *(G-12248)*
K-Plex LLC 239 963-2280
Bonita Springs *(G-808)*
Kira Labs Inc ....F 954 978-4549
Pompano Beach *(G-14071)*
Kookie Kllection Kosmetics LLC.................F 888 811-1657
Weston *(G-18262)*
Lf of America Corp.................G 561 988-0303
Boca Raton *(G-579)*
M D Nutra-Luxe LLC ....F 239 561-9699
Fort Myers *(G-4313)*
Matherson Organics LLC.................G 647 801-6977
Tallahassee *(G-16477)*
Mazi Group Inc ....E 786 800-2425
Miami *(G-9522)*
Mcilpack Inc ....F 561 988-8545
Pompano Beach *(G-14091)*
Michael Giordano Intl Inc.................F 305 948-6673
North Miami *(G-11112)*
Nohbo Labs LLC ....G 321 345-5319
Palm Bay *(G-12910)*
Nutraceutical Corporation.................E 813 877-4186
Tampa *(G-17113)*
Ollie Pippa International Inc ....G 888 851-6533
Boca Raton *(G-623)*
Prime Enterprises LLC ....D 305 625-4929
Hialeah *(G-5304)*
Prime Packaging Inc ....E 305 625-6737
Hialeah *(G-5305)*
Prive International Inc ....E 888 750-5850
North Miami Beach *(G-11156)*
Products By O2 Inc.................E 561 392-1892
Boynton Beach *(G-902)*

Promoitalia LLC ....F 305 347-5178
Miami (G-9752)
Pulsaderm LLC ....G.. 877 474-4038
Fort Myers (G-4371)
Pure Source LLC ....E .. 305 477-8111
Doral (G-3340)
Rev Personal Care LLC ....G.. 832 217-8585
Wellington (G-17860)
Revlon Inc ....E .. 904 693-1254
Jacksonville (G-6420)
Revlon Consumer Products Corp ...E .. 904 378-4167
Jacksonville (G-6421)
Romano Group LLC ....G.. 305 255-4242
Miami (G-9822)
Rxgenesys LLC ....G.. 786 220-8366
Miami (G-9830)
Shiseido Americas Corporation ....F .. 305 416-6021
Miami (G-9882)
Sincerus Pharmaceuticals Inc .....F .. 800 604-5032
Pompano Beach (G-14180)
Skinmetics Inc ....F .. 305 663-5750
Miami (G-9902)
Sloan Health Products LLC ...G.. 727 504-3915
Tampa (G-17273)
South Beach Skin Care Inc ...F .. 954 606-5057
Hallandale Beach (G-4973)
Stream2sea LLC ....F .. 866 960-9513
Bowling Green (G-833)
Swisscosmet Corp ....G.. 727 842-9419
New Port Richey (G-10987)
Tanning Research Labs LLC ...E .. 386 677-9559
Ormond Beach (G-12797)
Tend Skin International Inc ....F .. 954 382-0800
Davie (G-2488)

COSMETICS & TOILETRIES

4elementum LLC ....G.. 305 989-1106
Miami (G-8611)
Aleavia Brands LLC ....G.. 407 289-2632
Orlando (G-11889)
Aquarian Bath Inc ....G.. 310 919-0220
Holly Hill (G-5511)
Aromavalue Inc ....G.. 866 223-7561
Oldsmar (G-11629)
Ayurdevas Natural Products LLC ....G.. 786 322-0909
Miami (G-8784)
Berkant Corp ....F .. 305 771-5578
Miami (G-8814)
Brand Builders Rx LLC ....G.. 727 576-4013
Saint Petersburg (G-14988)
Cbd Brands Inc ....G.. 561 325-0482
Jupiter (G-6701)
Chelly Cosmetics Manufacturing ...F .. 305 471-9608
Miami (G-8922)
Christian L International Inc ..G.. 305 947-1722
Miami (G-8923)
Cosmo International Corp .....E .. 954 798-4500
Deerfield Beach (G-2695)
Coughlan Products Corp ......F .. 973 904-1500
Punta Gorda (G-14502)
Crunchi LLC ....G.. 772 600-8082
Stuart (G-16135)
Delab Care USA LLC ....G.. 754 317-5678
North Miami (G-11102)
Ecomkbiz LLC ....F .. 786 477-1865
Sunny Isles Beach (G-16271)
Esteemed Brands Inc ....G.. 954 442-3923
Miramar (G-10489)
Ewhite LLC ....G.. 954 530-3382
Fort Lauderdale (G-3803)
Extreme Care Inc ....G.. 239 898-3709
Cape Coral (G-1341)
Facelove Cosmetics Inc ....G.. 786 346-7357
Miami (G-9128)
Fhs Enterprises LLC ....G.. 754 214-9379
Delray Beach (G-2962)
Filorga Americas Inc ....E .. 786 266-7429
Miami Beach (G-10188)
Four X Four Organics ....G.. 561 687-1514
West Palm Beach (G-18009)
Fragrance Expresscom LLC ...G.. 800 372-4726
Miami (G-9170)
Fresh Brandz LLC ....G.. 813 880-7110
Tampa (G-16862)
Fruitful LLC ....G.. 954 534-9828
Hialeah Gardens (G-5437)
Hydron Technologies Inc ......G.. 727 342-5050
Saint Petersburg (G-15079)
Inspec Solutions SLLC ....F .. 866 467-7320
Holly Hill (G-5514)

Kayva Distribution LLC ....G.. 305 428-2816
Doral (G-3271)
Keratronix Inc ....F .. 954 753-5741
Coral Springs (G-2173)
Kreyol Essence LLC ....F .. 786 453-8287
Miami (G-9399)
Luxe Brands Inc ....E .. 954 791-6050
Plantation (G-13864)
Luxury World LLC ....F .. 954 746-8776
Sunrise (G-16339)
Natural4naturalz LLC ....G.. 561 621-1546
Clewiston (G-1894)
Odara Kanvas Cosmetics ......F .. 239 785-8013
Lehigh Acres (G-7818)
OL Products Inc ....D .. 813 854-3575
Oldsmar (G-11681)
Old 97 Company ....G.. 813 246-4180
Tampa (G-17117)
Oxygen Development LLC ......D .. 954 480-2675
Palm Springs (G-13148)
Oz Naturals LLC ....G.. 561 602-2932
West Palm Beach (G-18105)
Palladio Beauty Group LLC ...E .. 954 922-4311
Hollywood (G-5637)
Pb Group LLC ....E .. 954 922-4311
Hollywood (G-5638)
Personal Brands LLC ....E .. 855 426-7765
Deerfield Beach (G-2782)
Pretty Vulgar LLC ....G.. 561 465-8831
Boca Raton (G-640)
Prevail Solutions LLC ....G.. 727 210-6600
Clearwater (G-1752)
Prime Topco LLC ....G.. 305 625-4929
Hialeah (G-5306)
Private Label Skin Na LLC .....C .. 877 516-2200
Saint Petersburg (G-15162)
Promex LLC ....G.. 305 884-2400
Hialeah (G-5314)
Pure Labs LLC ....G.. 561 659-2229
West Palm Beach (G-18132)
Skin Combat LLC ....G.. 727 517-3376
Saint Petersburg (G-15186)
Skin Pro International Inc ......G.. 305 528-9095
Southwest Ranches (G-16058)
Sky Organics LLC ....G.. 561 295-1890
Boca Raton (G-682)
Terry Laboratories LLC ....F .. 321 259-1630
Melbourne (G-8549)
Three Cay G LLC ....G.. 904 930-4554
Jacksonville (G-6549)
Tupperware Brands Corporation ...B .. 407 826-5050
Orlando (G-12677)
Tupperware Intl Holdings Corp ...F .. 407 826-5050
Orlando (G-12678)
Unilever ....E .. 904 378-0298
Jacksonville (G-6575)
V P R A R T LLC ....E .. 786 205-4526
Hialeah (G-5405)
Vianny Corporation ....F .. 239 888-4536
Fort Myers (G-4440)
Wps Skincare LLC ....D .. 877 516-2200
Saint Petersburg (G-15239)

COSMETICS WHOLESALERS

Bobbie Weiner Enterprises LLC ...G.. 817 615-8610
North Miami (G-11093)
Brand Builders Rx LLC ....G.. 727 576-4013
Saint Petersburg (G-14988)
Chelly Cosmetics Manufacturing ...F .. 305 471-9608
Miami (G-8922)
Dermazone Solutions Inc ......E .. 727 446-6882
Saint Petersburg (G-15022)
Instanatural LLC ....E .. 800 290-6932
Orlando (G-12248)
K-Plex LLC ....E .. 239 963-2280
Bonita Springs (G-808)
Mazi Group Inc ....E .. 786 800-2425
Miami (G-9522)
Newbeauty Media Group LLC ...E .. 561 961-7600
Boca Raton (G-615)
Palladio Beauty Group LLC ...E .. 954 922-4311
Hollywood (G-5637)
Shiseido Americas Corporation ...F .. 305 416-6021
Miami (G-9882)
Sincerus Pharmaceuticals Inc ...F .. 800 604-5032
Pompano Beach (G-14180)
Swisscosmet Corp ....G.. 727 842-9419
New Port Richey (G-10987)

COSTUME JEWELRY & NOVELTIES: Apparel, Exc Precious Metals

Pret-EE LLC ....G.. 561 839-4338
Palm Beach Gardens (G-13001)

COSTUME JEWELRY & NOVELTIES: Bracelets, Exc Precious Metals

Inspire ME Bracelets ....F .. 404 644-7771
Fort Lauderdale (G-3878)

COSTUME JEWELRY & NOVELTIES: Exc Semi & Precious

Accent Jewelry Inc ....F .. 941 391-6687
Punta Gorda (G-14490)
Firstline Products Inc ....G.. 401 219-0378
Lakewood Ranch (G-7478)
James A De Flippo Co ....G.. 407 851-2765
Orlando (G-12265)
Sonnys Strings Inc ....G.. 407 862-4905
Winter Park (G-18538)

COSTUME JEWELRY & NOVELTIES: Pins, Exc Precious Metals

Delray Pin Factory Intl Inc .....G.. 561 994-1680
Casselberry (G-1415)

COUGH MEDICINES

Ingenus Pharmaceuticals LLC ...F .. 407 354-5365
Orlando (G-12245)

COUNTER & SINK TOPS

AGR Fabricators Inc ....F .. 904 733-9393
Jacksonville (G-5869)
AGR of Florida Inc ....E .. 904 733-9393
Jacksonville (G-5870)
Amercn Cabinets Granite Floors ...G.. 727 303-0678
Palm Harbor (G-13097)
Blues Design Group LLC ....G.. 305 586-3630
Miami (G-8840)
Byblos Group Inc ....G.. 305 662-6666
Miami (G-8867)
Cianos Tile & Marble Inc ......G.. 239 267-8453
Fort Myers (G-4208)
Commercial Stone Cab Fbrctors ...F .. 727 209-1141
Saint Petersburg (G-15011)
Commercial Stone Fbrcators Inc ...F .. 727 209-1141
Saint Petersburg (G-15012)
Counter Active Inc ....F .. 813 626-0022
Ponte Vedra (G-14255)
Countertop Solutions Inc ......G.. 239 961-0663
Naples (G-10721)
Countrkraft Solid Surfaces Inc ...F .. 321 456-5928
Merritt Island (G-8582)
Designers Tops Inc ....E .. 305 599-9973
Miami (G-9023)
Furniture Concepts Inc ....G.. 727 535-0093
Largo (G-7590)
Just Counters Other Stuff Inc ...F .. 941 235-1300
Port Charlotte (G-14304)
Lx Hausys America Inc ....D .. 813 249-7658
Tampa (G-17027)
Orange County Countertops ...F .. 407 294-8677
Apopka (G-159)
Salvia Tile & Stone Inc ....G.. 239 643-7770
Naples (G-10881)
Ssvm Partners Inc ....D .. 239 825-6282
Sarasota (G-15835)
Superior Solid Surface Inc .....F .. 727 842-9947
Port Richey (G-14377)
Venice Granit & Marble Inc ....G.. 941 483-4363
Venice (G-17728)

COUNTERS & COUNTING DEVICES

Building Management Group ...G.. 305 440-9101
Doral (G-3151)
Hedrick Walker & Assoc Inc ...G.. 352 735-2600
Mount Dora (G-10603)
Maxogen Group LLC ....E .. 305 814-0734
Hollywood (G-5622)
Power Plus Inc ....G.. 386 672-7579
Ormond Beach (G-12787)
Trumeter Company Inc ....G.. 954 725-6699
Coconut Creek (G-2008)

PRODUCT

COUNTERS OR COUNTER DISPLAY CASES, EXC WOOD

East Coast Fix & Mllwk Co Inc .... G 904 733-9711
  Jacksonville *(G-6059)*

Emjac Industries Inc .... D 305 883-2194
  Hialeah *(G-5142)*

Florida Design Mfg Assoc Inc .... F 561 533-0733
  West Palm Beach *(G-18004)*

Kitchen Counter Connections .... F 386 677-9471
  Ormond Beach *(G-12775)*

Load King Manufacturing Co .... C 904 354-8882
  Jacksonville *(G-6263)*

COUNTERS OR COUNTER DISPLAY CASES, WOOD

Akiknav Inc .... F 561 842-8091
  Riviera Beach *(G-14591)*

COUNTING DEVICES: Gauges, Press Temp Corrections Computing

Suncoast Tool & Gage Inds Inc .... F 727 572-8000
  Clearwater *(G-1801)*

COUNTING DEVICES: Production

Del Monte Fresh Production Inc .... F 863 844-5836
  Mulberry *(G-10622)*

COUNTING DEVICES: Tally

Countwise Llc .... F 954 846-7011
  Sunrise *(G-16308)*

R S S Partners Inc .... F 904 241-6144
  Jacksonville Beach *(G-6642)*

COUPLINGS: Hose & Tube, Hydraulic Or Pneumatic

Florida Hose & Hydraulics Inc .... G 305 887-9577
  Miami *(G-9157)*

STS Distribution Solutions LLC .... F 844 359-4673
  Miramar *(G-10548)*

COURIER SVCS, AIR: Package Delivery, Private

Leeward Tech .... G 305 215-4526
  Homestead *(G-5727)*

COVERS: Automobile Seat

Sargent Seat Cover Co Inc .... E 904 355-2529
  Jacksonville *(G-6452)*

Seat Savers Plus Inc .... G 305 256-7863
  Miami *(G-9862)*

Universal Seat Cvers Auto ACC .... G 305 262-3955
  Miami *(G-10073)*

COVERS: Automotive, Exc Seat & Tire

Rolin Industries Inc .... G 850 654-1704
  Fort Walton Beach *(G-4608)*

COVERS: Canvas

C-Worthy Corp .... F 954 784-7370
  Pompano Beach *(G-13961)*

Evora Enterprises Inc .... F 305 261-4522
  Ocala *(G-11380)*

Industrial Shadeports Inc .... G 954 755-0661
  Fort Lauderdale *(G-3876)*

COVERS: Hot Tub & Spa

Bdjl Enterprises LLC .... F 407 678-9960
  Apopka *(G-105)*

Prestige Spas Inc .... D 727 576-8600
  Pinellas Park *(G-13722)*

Spa Cover Inc .... F 954 923-8801
  Hollywood *(G-5662)*

CRADLES: Boat

Gyro-Gale Inc .... G 772 283-1711
  Stuart *(G-16160)*

CRANE & AERIAL LIFT SVCS

Jayco Signs Inc .... F 407 339-5252
  Maitland *(G-8062)*

Perl Inc .... F 352 726-2483
  Inverness *(G-5833)*

CRANES & MONORAIL SYSTEMS

J Herbert Corporation .... F 407 846-0588
  Kissimmee *(G-6928)*

PM Enterprises Holdings LLC .... G 407 846-0588
  Kissimmee *(G-6952)*

CRANES: Indl Plant

Coastal Crane and Rigging Inc .... G 850 460-1766
  Santa Rosa Beach *(G-15423)*

CRANES: Overhead

Equipment Fabricators Inc .... E 321 632-0990
  Cocoa *(G-1926)*

Nautical Acquisitions Corp .... D 727 541-6664
  Largo *(G-7650)*

CRANKSHAFTS & CAMSHAFTS: Machining

Crankshaft Rebuilders Inc .... D 407 323-4870
  Sanford *(G-15296)*

Delta Machine LLC .... F 386 738-2204
  Deland *(G-2862)*

Diamondback Cnc LLC .... E 321 305-5995
  Cocoa *(G-1916)*

CRANKSHAFTS: Motor Vehicle

La Experiencia Crankshaft .... G 305 823-6161
  Hialeah Gardens *(G-5440)*

CRATES: Fruit, Wood Wirebound

Walling Crate Company .... F 352 787-5211
  Leesburg *(G-7801)*

CROWNS & CLOSURES

Amcor Flexibles LLC .... E 954 499-4800
  Miramar *(G-10468)*

CRUDE PETROLEUM & NATURAL GAS PRODUCTION

Breitburn Operating LP .... C 850 675-1704
  Jay *(G-6649)*

C & C Diversified Services LLC .... G 772 597-1022
  Stuart *(G-16125)*

CRUDE PETROLEUM & NATURAL GAS PRODUCTION

Carpenter Co .... D 863 687-9494
  Lakeland *(G-7288)*

Fromkin Energy LLC .... G 954 683-2509
  Coral Springs *(G-2157)*

Jones Field Services Pamela .... G 904 368-9777
  Starke *(G-16103)*

K20 Oil LLC .... G 954 421-1735
  Deerfield Beach *(G-2747)*

Neptune Petroleum LLC .... G 561 684-2844
  West Palm Beach *(G-18089)*

Noumenon Corporation .... G 302 296-5460
  Cape Coral *(G-1368)*

South Florida Petro Svcs LLC .... G 561 793-2102
  Fort Lauderdale *(G-4058)*

Speed Mobile Oil Change Inc .... G 305 763-4352
  Miami *(G-9941)*

SPS Drilling Exploration Prod .... F 305 777-3553
  Coral Gables *(G-2111)*

US Natural Gas Corp .... G 727 482-1505
  Saint Petersburg *(G-15222)*

CRUDE PETROLEUM PRODUCTION

Delta Oil .... G 813 323-3113
  Brandon *(G-1089)*

Dorward Energy Corporation .... G 727 490-1778
  Saint Petersburg *(G-15030)*

Tg Oil Services .... G 407 576-9571
  Davie *(G-2489)*

Venkata SAI Corporation .... F 352 746-7076
  Beverly Hills *(G-370)*

CRYSTALS

Tdk Electronics Inc .... F 561 509-7771
  Ocean Ridge *(G-11518)*

V-Blox Corporation .... G 904 425-4908
  Jacksonville *(G-6584)*

CRYSTALS & CRYSTAL ASSEMBLIES: Radio

Crystek Crystals Corporation .... E 239 561-3311
  Fort Myers *(G-4224)*

CUBICLES: Electric Switchboard Eqpt

B & J Atlantic Inc .... E 904 338-0088
  Jacksonville *(G-5916)*

CULTURE MEDIA

Acuderm Inc .... D 954 733-6935
  Fort Lauderdale *(G-3623)*

Assoction Hspnic Hritg Fstival .... G 305 885-5613
  Hialeah *(G-5063)*

Caregivercom Inc .... G 954 893-0550
  Oakland Park *(G-11250)*

Larrick Group Inc .... E 941 351-2700
  Sarasota *(G-15509)*

One Biotechnology Company .... F 941 355-8451
  Sarasota *(G-15528)*

P B C Cultural Counsel .... F 561 471-2903
  West Palm Beach *(G-18106)*

Players Media Group Inc .... F 509 254-4949
  Brooksville *(G-1190)*

CULVERTS: Sheet Metal

Metal Culverts Inc .... F 727 531-1431
  Clearwater *(G-1694)*

CUPS & PLATES: Foamed Plastics

Dart Container Company Fla LLC .... C 813 752-1990
  Plant City *(G-13760)*

Key Packaging Company Inc .... E 941 355-2728
  Sarasota *(G-15507)*

CUPS: Plastic Exc Polystyrene Foam

Compak Companies LLC .... F 321 249-9590
  Sanford *(G-15288)*

Grupo Phoenix Corp Svcs LLC .... E 954 241-0023
  Miami *(G-9257)*

Tervis Tumbler Company .... C 941 966-2114
  North Venice *(G-11220)*

CURBING: Granite Or Stone

Airam Stone Designs Inc .... G 305 477-8009
  Miami *(G-8672)*

Fusion Industries Intl LLC .... G 239 415-7554
  Fort Myers *(G-4265)*

Kadassa Inc .... F 954 684-8361
  Riviera Beach *(G-14636)*

New England Granite & Marble .... F 772 283-8667
  Stuart *(G-16189)*

Terrastone Inc .... G 305 234-8384
  Miami *(G-10003)*

CURLING FEATHERS

Fi-Foil Company Inc .... E 863 965-1846
  Auburndale *(G-230)*

CURTAIN & DRAPERY FIXTURES: Poles, Rods & Rollers

A Albrtini Cstm Win Treatments .... G 941 925-2556
  Sarasota *(G-15581)*

Awnit Corporation .... G ....
  Okeechobee *(G-11598)*

B & D Precision Tools Inc .... E 305 885-1583
  Hialeah *(G-5065)*

Biscayne Awning & Shade Co .... E 305 638-7933
  Miami *(G-8833)*

Coverall Interiors .... G 813 961-8261
  Tampa *(G-16734)*

Deco Abrusci International LLC .... F 305 406-3401
  Doral *(G-3188)*

Deco Shades Solutions Inc .... G 305 558-9800
  Hialeah *(G-5112)*

Designers Whl Workroom Inc .... F 239 434-7633
  Naples *(G-10728)*

Etchart LLC .... G 321 504-4060
  Cocoa *(G-1927)*

Island Shutter Co Inc .... F 386 738-9455
  Deland *(G-2876)*

Orlando Shutters LLC .... G 407 495-5250
  Lake Mary *(G-7098)*

Premier Blinds & Verticals ....G....... 305 244-0598
Hialeah (G-5301)
Ramirez Cbnets Blnds Gran Mr ....G.......... 352 606-0049
Spring Hill (G-16076)
Reah Group LLC ....G....... 727 423-0668
Tampa (G-17210)
Resort Window Treatments Inc ....G....... 813 355-4877
Zephyrhills (G-18629)
Sanzogo Corporation ....G....... 561 334-2138
Boca Raton (G-662)
Southeast Window Coverings ....G....... 904 372-0326
Jacksonville (G-6485)
TMMR Holdings LLC ....E....... 407 295-5200
Ocoee (G-11528)
USA Recmar Corp ....G....... 786 554-3505
Miami (G-10083)
Vertical Village Inc ....G....... 772 340-0400
Port Saint Lucie (G-14464)

CURTAIN WALLS: Building, Steel

Fenwall LLC ....G....... 813 343-5979
Tampa (G-16831)
Freedom Steel Building Corp ....E....... 561 330-0447
Fort Lauderdale (G-3832)

CURTAINS & BEDDING: Knit

Andirali Corporation ....G....... 305 542-5374
Miami (G-8730)

CUSHIONS & PILLOWS

Andirali Corporation ....G....... 305 542-5374
Miami (G-8730)
Bedding Acquisition LLC ....G....... 561 997-6900
Boca Raton (G-428)
Cushion Solutions Incorporated ....G....... 813 253-2131
Tampa (G-16749)
Elaine Smith Inc ....F....... 561 863-3333
Riviera Beach (G-14619)
Florida Pillow Company ....G....... 407 648-9121
Orlando (G-12163)
General Pillows & Fiber Inc ....G....... 305 884-8300
Hialeah (G-5169)
Pacific Coast Feather LLC ....C....... 206 624-1057
Boca Raton (G-628)
Superior Sleep Technology Inc ....F....... 305 888-0953
Hialeah (G-5374)
V M Visual Mdsg Dctr Group Inc ....F....... 305 759-9910
Miami (G-10088)

CUSHIONS & PILLOWS: Bed, From Purchased Materials

Design Works By Tech Pdts Inc ....E....... 941 355-2703
Sarasota (G-15658)
Hygenator Pillow Service Inc ....G....... 305 325-0250
Miami (G-9294)
United Pillow Mfg Inc ....F....... 305 636-9747
Miami (G-10068)

CUSHIONS & PILLOWS: Boat

Affordable Boat Cushions Inc ....G....... 877 350-2628
Riverview (G-14556)
Canvas Spc Cstm Mar Fbrction I.........G....... 850 664-6200
Fort Walton Beach (G-4569)
Miami Prestige Interiors Inc ....E....... 305 685-3343
Miami (G-9555)

CUSHIONS: Carpet & Rug, Foamed Plastics

Pmh Homes Inc ....G....... 941 234-5121
Bradenton (G-1030)

CUSHIONS: Textile, Exc Spring & Carpet

Advanced Sewing ....G....... 954 484-2100
Fort Lauderdale (G-3626)
Shelleys Cushions Mfg Inc ....E....... 305 633-1790
Miami (G-9880)

CUT STONE & STONE PRODUCTS

Affordable Granite Concepts ....F....... 407 332-0057
Altamonte Springs (G-28)
American MBL Restoration Inc ....G....... 561 502-0764
Palm Springs (G-13143)
Artistic Columns Inc ....G....... 954 530-5537
Oakland Park (G-11240)
Baro Granite Inc ....G....... 786 663-2514
Hialeah (G-5067)

Bathroom World Manufacturing ....G....... 954 566-0451
Oakland Park (G-11246)
Cemex Materials LLC ....C....... 561 746-4556
Jupiter (G-6703)
Designers Tops Inc ....E....... 305 599-9973
Miami (G-9023)
Dyadic International USA Inc ....G....... 561 743-8333
Jupiter (G-6714)
Englert Arts Inc ....G....... 561 241-9924
Boca Raton (G-504)
F T F Construction Company ....G....... 772 571-1850
Fellsmere (G-3576)
First Coast Granite & MBL Inc ....F....... 904 388-1217
Jacksonville (G-6095)
Five Star Marble and Stone ....G....... 904 887-4736
Ponte Vedra (G-14257)
Global Stone Corp ....F....... 786 601-2459
Cutler Bay (G-2289)
Granite World Inc ....E....... 813 243-6556
Tampa (G-16890)
Highlander Stone Corp ....F....... 786 333-1151
Opa Locka (G-11753)
House of Marble & Granite Inc ....G....... 239 261-0099
Naples (G-10777)
International Gran & Stone LLC ....G....... 813 920-6500
Odessa (G-11559)
J & N Stone Inc ....G....... 863 422-7369
Davenport (G-2367)
Mannys Stone Depot Corp ....G....... 954 744-2506
Hialeah (G-5237)
Moderno Porcelain Works LLC ....F....... 954 607-3535
Sunrise (G-16341)
Mother Earth Stone LLC ....F....... 407 878-2854
Sanford (G-15361)
PSC Building Group Inc ....E....... 561 756-6811
Delray Beach (G-3008)
Stone Craft Masters LLC ....F....... 786 401-7060
Doral (G-3377)
Stone Palace ....F....... 407 896-0872
Orlando (G-12627)
Stone Trend International Inc ....E....... 941 927-9113
Sarasota (G-15839)
Stonecrfters Archtctral Prcast ....F....... 727 544-1210
Seminole (G-15990)
Suncoast Stone Inc ....E....... 561 364-2061
Delray Beach (G-3024)
T H Stone ....F....... 561 361-3966
Boca Raton (G-706)
Titan America LLC ....F....... 954 523-9790
Fort Lauderdale (G-4092)
Unique Marble Inc ....F....... 772 766-4432
Vero Beach (G-17810)

CUTLERY

Andritz Iggesund Tools Inc ....E....... 813 855-6902
Oldsmar (G-11626)
Edgewell Per Care Brands LLC ....F....... 386 677-9559
Ormond Beach (G-12760)
Mondolfo LLC ....F....... 954 523-1115
Fort Lauderdale (G-3943)
Novelty Crystal Corp ....D....... 352 429-9036
Orlando (G-12426)

CUTLERY, STAINLESS STEEL

Bastinelli Creations LLC ....F....... 407 572-8073
Kissimmee (G-6897)

CUTTING EQPT: Milling

Hayley Carson Odom Cordrays............G....... 850 830-8270
Destin (G-3069)

CYCLIC CRUDES & INTERMEDIATES

Eastman Chemical Company...............F....... 305 671-2800
Miami (G-9062)

CYLINDER & ACTUATORS: Fluid Power

Dynalco Controls Corporation.............E....... 323 589-6181
Fort Lauderdale (G-3775)
Easylift N Bansbach Amer Inc ....E....... 321 253-1999
Melbourne (G-8414)
Leslie Controls Inc........................C....... 813 978-1000
Temple Terrace (G-17539)

DAIRY PRDTS STORE: Ice Cream, Packaged

Big Bend Ice Cream Co ....G....... 850 539-7778
Havana (G-4993)

Lefab Commercial LLC ....F....... 305 456-1306
Coral Gables (G-2082)
McConnell Corp ....G....... 305 296-6124
Key West (G-6875)
Worlds Greatest Ice Cream Inc...........F....... 305 538-0207
Miami Beach (G-10247)

DAIRY PRDTS WHOLESALERS: Fresh

Borden Dairy Company Fla LLC ....E....... 863 298-9742
Winter Haven (G-18423)
Dean Dairy Holdings LLC ....D....... 239 334-1114
Fort Myers (G-4231)
Rubix Foods LLC ....E....... 904 268-8999
Jacksonville (G-6437)

DAIRY PRDTS: Butter

Carrollwood Creamery ....G....... 813 926-2023
Tampa (G-16682)
Gw Creamery LLC ....G....... 904 509-6202
Macclenny (G-8037)
Magical Creamery LLC ....G....... 407 719-6866
Lake Mary (G-7090)
Trinity Creamery Inc ....G....... 813 926-2023
Odessa (G-11586)

DAIRY PRDTS: Cheese

Goloso Food Llc ....G....... 321 277-2055
Orlando (G-12198)

DAIRY PRDTS: Cream Substitutes

Saputo Dairy Foods Usa LLC ....G....... 904 354-0406
Jacksonville (G-6451)

DAIRY PRDTS: Custard, Frozen

Lilas Desserts Inc ....F....... 305 252-1441
Miami (G-9460)

DAIRY PRDTS: Dairy Based Desserts, Frozen

Latin Dairy Foods LLC.....................F....... 305 888-1788
Miami (G-9436)
Todays Frozen Desserts Inc ....F....... 305 994-9940
Miami (G-10018)
Verdu-Us LLC ....F....... 407 776-3017
Davenport (G-2373)

DAIRY PRDTS: Dietary Supplements, Dairy & Non-Dairy Based

123 Diet LLC ....G....... 954 643-2522
Deerfield Beach (G-2647)
Allegro Nutrition Inc ....E....... 732 364-3777
Palmetto (G-13153)
AMC Pharma Usa LLC ....G....... 813 508-0160
Tampa (G-16585)
Amino Cell Inc ....F....... 352 291-0200
Ocala (G-11323)
Betancourt Sports Ntrtn LLC ....G....... 305 593-9296
Miami Lakes (G-10285)
Bkn International Inc ....G....... 301 518-7153
Miami Beach (G-10171)
BI Bio Lab LLC ....F....... 727 900-2707
Clearwater (G-1521)
Blue Sky Labs LLC ....G....... 901 268-6988
Jacksonville (G-5939)
Cerno Pharmaceuticals LLC................G....... 786 763-2766
Miami (G-8915)
Cyber Group USA LLC ....F....... 888 574-9555
Pompano Beach (G-13987)
Dmso Store Inc.............................G....... 954 616-5699
Fort Lauderdale (G-3770)
Fleda Pharmaceuticals Corp...............G....... 813 920-9882
Odessa (G-11551)
Fresh Start Beverage Company ....G....... 561 757-6541
Boca Raton (G-524)
Full Lf Natural Hlth Pdts LLC ....G....... 954 889-4019
Hollywood (G-5577)
Function Please LLC ....G....... 305 792-7900
Hollywood (G-5579)
Green Essentials LLC ....E....... 786 584-4377
Miami (G-9243)
Health & Muscles ....G....... 305 225-2929
Miami (G-9266)
Ianorod JB LLC ....F....... 954 217-3014
Weston (G-18253)
Iq Formulations Llc ....D....... 954 533-9256
Tamarac (G-16533)

Maxam Group LLC ....F 305 952-3227
Miami *(G-9521)*

My Adventure To Fit Inc ....F 727 200-3081
Clearwater *(G-1708)*

Naturecity LLC ....G 800 593-2563
Boca Raton *(G-609)*

Nutraceuticals Factory LLC ....E 727 692-7294
Saint Petersburg *(G-15141)*

Nutrition Laboratories Inc ....E 915 496-7531
Clearwater *(G-1723)*

Nutritorch ....G 561 777-9079
Lake Worth *(G-7223)*

Ohana Liquids LLC ....G 888 642-6244
New Smyrna Beach *(G-11007)*

Omnimark Enterprises LLC ....G 516 351-9075
Orlando *(G-12439)*

Pangenex Corporation ....G 352 346-4045
Tampa *(G-17143)*

Peak Nutritional Products LLC ....E 813 884-4989
Tampa *(G-17153)*

Prime Life Ntrtn Companyllc ....G 754 307-7137
Deerfield Beach *(G-2786)*

Sawgrass Nutra Labs LLC ....G 844 688-7244
Jacksonville *(G-6453)*

Sea 21-21 LLC ....G 954 366-4677
Pompano Beach *(G-14172)*

Sun-Pac Manufacturing Inc ....E 813 925-8787
Tampa *(G-17310)*

Sunshine Supplements Inc ....G 407 751-4299
Orlando *(G-12635)*

Twinlab Cnsld Holdings Inc ....G 561 443-4301
Boca Raton *(G-726)*

Vital Health Corporation ....G 407 522-1125
Orlando *(G-12702)*

Vitapak LLC ....G 954 661-0390
Fort Lauderdale *(G-4119)*

DAIRY PRDTS: Dried & Powdered Milk & Milk Prdts

S A Gloria Corp ....C 305 575-2900
South Miami *(G-16044)*

DAIRY PRDTS: Fermented & Cultured Milk Prdts

Borden Dairy Company Fla LLC ....E 863 298-9742
Winter Haven *(G-18423)*

Rubix Foods LLC ....E 904 268-8999
Jacksonville *(G-6437)*

DAIRY PRDTS: Frozen Desserts & Novelties

Big Bend Ice Cream Co ....G 850 539-7778
Havana *(G-4993)*

C&A Lozaro Inc ....G 407 671-8809
Winter Park *(G-18495)*

Carpe Diem Ice Cream LLC ....G 305 504-4469
Key West *(G-6857)*

Chikitas LLC ....G 561 401-5033
West Palm Beach *(G-17966)*

Cold Stone Creamery-Parkland ....G 954 341-8033
Coral Springs *(G-2142)*

Cross Atlantic Commodities Inc ....G 954 678-0698
Weston *(G-18235)*

Dean Dairy Holdings LLC ....D 239 334-1114
Fort Myers *(G-4231)*

Deliciosa Food Group Inc ....F 954 492-6131
Miami *(G-9011)*

Dolci Peccati LLC ....G 954 632-8551
Miami *(G-9039)*

Eden Fast Frozen Dessert LLC ....F 787 375-0826
Kissimmee *(G-6917)*

Eds Delight LLC ....G 305 632-3051
North Miami Beach *(G-11135)*

Florida Candy Buffets LLC ....G 407 529-5880
Lake Mary *(G-7078)*

Gourmet Parisien Inc ....G 305 778-0756
Hollywood *(G-5582)*

GS Gelato and Desserts Inc ....E 850 243-5455
Fort Walton Beach *(G-4589)*

Hj German Corner LLC ....G 239 672-8462
Fort Myers *(G-4282)*

HM Factory LLC ....F 305 897-0004
Miami *(G-9286)*

Ice Cream Club Inc ....E 561 731-3331
Boynton Beach *(G-877)*

Island Dream Itln Ice Dssrts L ....F 904 778-6839
Jacksonville *(G-6207)*

Ispy Equities LLC ....G 813 731-0676
Spring Hill *(G-16085)*

Jimmy & Toons Icecream Sp LLC ....G 850 752-2291
Quincy *(G-14547)*

Just Now Jennings LLC ....G 239 331-0315
Naples *(G-10794)*

Lavish Ice Cream LLC ....F 561 408-1616
West Palm Beach *(G-18054)*

Lefab Commercial LLC ....F 305 456-1306
Coral Gables *(G-2082)*

Los Coquitos ....G 407 289-9315
Kissimmee *(G-6940)*

Maria E Acosta ....G 305 231-5543
Hialeah *(G-5241)*

Mercy D LLC ....G 321 212-7712
Rockledge *(G-14732)*

Mia Products Company ....E 786 479-4021
Hialeah *(G-5247)*

Old Meeting House Home Made Ic ....F 813 254-0977
Tampa *(G-17119)*

Rd Abukaf 1 Inc ....G 239 390-8788
Estero *(G-3549)*

Renacer Bros LLC ....G 305 935-6777
Miami *(G-9792)*

Rhonda Clanton ....G 305 502-7050
Hialeah *(G-5331)*

Romeo Ohana LLC ....F 808 500-3420
Spring Hill *(G-16077)*

Ronnie & Moes Italian Ice LLC ....G 786 970-1805
Miami *(G-9824)*

Royaltea ....G 407 401-9969
Orlando *(G-12561)*

Rubix Foods LLC ....E 904 268-8999
Jacksonville *(G-6437)*

Simply Sweet Company Inc ....G 386 873-6516
Deland *(G-2902)*

Smart Stream Inc ....F 904 223-1511
Jacksonville *(G-6477)*

Sunnibunni ....G 941 554-8744
Sarasota *(G-15844)*

Sweet Treats ....G 239 598-3311
Naples *(G-10916)*

Sweetreats of Naples Inc ....G 239 598-3311
Naples *(G-10917)*

Tiempo LLC ....G 941 780-9900
Sarasota *(G-15854)*

Tropical Skoops Llc ....F 954 440-8736
Miramar *(G-10555)*

Vegan Suckers LLC ....F 904 265-5263
Jacksonville *(G-6588)*

Working Cow Homemade Inc ....F 727 572-7251
Saint Petersburg *(G-15238)*

Y3k LLC ....G 561 835-0404
Palm Beach *(G-12943)*

Yogurt Breeze LLC ....G 407 412-5939
Orlando *(G-12729)*

DAIRY PRDTS: Ice Cream & Ice Milk

Coco Gelato Corp ....E 786 621-2444
Miami *(G-8938)*

Happy Mix LLC ....G 954 880-0160
Cooper City *(G-2021)*

Peekaboo Organics LLC ....G 305 527-7162
Surfside *(G-16398)*

DAIRY PRDTS: Ice Cream, Bulk

A Means To A Vend Inc ....F 954 533-8330
Oakland Park *(G-11232)*

Cesibon ....G 239 682-5028
Naples *(G-10711)*

Cholados Y Mas ....G 813 935-9262
Tampa *(G-16702)*

Coneheads Frozen Custards ....G 772 600-7730
Stuart *(G-16131)*

Cool Treat ....G 407 248-0743
Orlando *(G-12047)*

Eighteen Degrees Eighteen ....G 904 686-1892
Ponte Vedra Beach *(G-14267)*

Food Marketing Consultants Inc ....F 954 322-2668
Miramar *(G-10492)*

Gelateria Milani LLC ....F 305 532-8562
Miami Beach *(G-10196)*

Gelato Petrini LLC ....F 561 600-4088
Delray Beach *(G-2968)*

Kevin M Lukasiewicz ....F 561 588-5853
Riviera Beach *(G-14638)*

Mattheessons ....G 305 296-1616
Key West *(G-6874)*

McConnell Corp ....G 305 296-6124
Key West *(G-6875)*

Mix It At Loop ....F 407 201-8948
Kissimmee *(G-6943)*

Muse Gelato Inc ....F 407 363-1443
Orlando *(G-12402)*

Rich Ice Cream Co ....C 561 833-7585
West Palm Beach *(G-18141)*

Uncle Carlos Gelatos ....G 810 523-8506
Fort Pierce *(G-4548)*

Valentini Italian Spc Co ....G 305 638-0822
Miami *(G-10091)*

Worlds Greatest Ice Cream Inc ....F 305 538-0207
Miami Beach *(G-10247)*

Yogurtology ....G 727 895-1393
Saint Petersburg *(G-15240)*

DAIRY PRDTS: Ice Cream, Packaged, Molded, On Sticks, Etc.

Alcas USA Corp ....G 305 591-3325
Fort Lauderdale *(G-3636)*

Clondalkin LLC ....F 866 545-8703
Largo *(G-7566)*

DAIRY PRDTS: Milk, Chocolate

Chocolate Compass LLC ....G 407 600-0145
Sanford *(G-15283)*

Louis Sherry Company LLC ....G 904 482-1900
Jacksonville *(G-6264)*

Whetstone Industries Inc ....F 904 824-0888
Saint Augustine *(G-14913)*

DAIRY PRDTS: Milk, Condensed & Evaporated

Climb Your Mountain Inc ....E 571 571-8623
Medley *(G-8219)*

Flayco Products Inc ....E 813 879-1356
Tampa *(G-16835)*

Nestle Usa Inc ....B 813 273-5355
Thonotosassa *(G-17563)*

New Dairy Opco LLC ....E 305 652-3720
North Miami Beach *(G-11153)*

DAIRY PRDTS: Milk, Fluid

Dfa Dairy Brands Fluid LLC ....F 386 775-6700
Jacksonville *(G-6032)*

Dfa Dairy Brands Fluid LLC ....G 386 775-6700
Melbourne *(G-8400)*

Dfa Dairy Brands Fluid LLC ....F 352 622-4666
Ocala *(G-11366)*

Dfa Dairy Brands Fluid LLC ....E 813 621-7805
Tampa *(G-16774)*

Fluid Handling Support Corp ....F 786 623-2105
Doral *(G-3219)*

DAIRY PRDTS: Milk, Processed, Pasteurized, Homogenized/Btld

Dfa Dairy Brands Fluid LLC ....G 352 754-1750
Brooksville *(G-1153)*

Southeast Dairy Processors Inc ....E 813 620-1516
Tampa *(G-17284)*

Wwf Operating Company LLC ....D 904 354-0406
Jacksonville *(G-6620)*

DAIRY PRDTS: Natural Cheese

Bufalinda USA LLC ....G 305 979-9258
Miami Beach *(G-10173)*

Lanzas Distributor Inc ....G 305 885-5966
Miami *(G-9423)*

Mambi Cheese Company Inc ....E 305 324-5282
Miami *(G-9504)*

DAIRY PRDTS: Processed Cheese

Mondelez Global LLC ....D 305 774-6273
Coral Gables *(G-2089)*

DAIRY PRDTS: Spreads, Cheese

Massachusetts Bay Clam Co Inc ....F 813 855-4599
Tampa *(G-17053)*

DAIRY PRDTS: Whey, Powdered

Naked Whey Inc ....G 352 246-7294
Miami *(G-9605)*

DAIRY PRDTS: Yogurt, Exc Frozen

Colormet Foods LLC ....F 888 775-3966
Miami *(G-8948)*

Dairy Fairy LLC ....G..... 305 865-1506
Surfside (G-16395)

Powerful Foods LLC ....G..... 305 637-7300
Pinecrest (G-13668)

Pura Vida Dairy Inc ....F..... 305 817-1762
Hialeah (G-5317)

Spoons Chilly ....G..... 321 610-8966
Melbourne (G-8529)

Tias Milkshakes and More ....G..... 954 391-8753
Hollywood (G-5671)

Yogurt Breeze LLC ....G..... 407 412-5939
Orlando (G-12729)

Yogurtology ....G..... 813 839-4200
Tampa (G-17448)

Yogurtology ....G..... 813 969-2500
Tampa (G-17449)

Yogurtology ....G..... 813 926-9090
Tampa (G-17450)

DAIRY PRDTS: Yogurt, Frozen

Faithful Heart Froyo LLC ....G..... 407 325-3052
Winter Park (G-18512)

Florida Froyo Inc ....G..... 407 977-4911
Lake Mary (G-7079)

HM Froyos LLC ....G..... 561 339-0603
Orlando (G-12220)

Miami Foods Distrs USA Inc ....F..... 305 512-3246
Hialeah (G-5250)

Millenia Froyo LLC ....G..... 407 694-9938
Windermere (G-18362)

Supersweet Frog LLC ....G..... 863 386-4917
Sebring (G-15945)

Top Hat Food Services LLC ....G..... 630 825-2800
Venice (G-17724)

DATA PROCESSING & PREPARATION SVCS

Image One Corporation ....D..... 813 888-8288
Tampa (G-16933)

ITI Engineering LLC ....E..... 866 245-9356
Winter Springs (G-18570)

Metavante Holdings LLC ....G..... 904 438-6000
Jacksonville (G-6301)

Neptune Tech Services Inc ....E..... 904 646-2700
Jacksonville (G-6323)

Northrop Grumman Systems Corp ....D..... 850 863-8000
Fort Walton Beach (G-4598)

Oracle America Inc ....F..... 813 287-1700
Orlando (G-12447)

DATA PROCESSING SVCS

Advanced Xrgrphics Imging Syst..........E..... 407 351-0232
Orlando (G-11872)

Locus Solutions LLC ....D..... 561 575-7600
Palm Beach Gardens (G-12985)

DAVITS

Davit Master Corp ....F..... 727 573-4414
Clearwater (G-1563)

Quick Lift Inc ....G..... 305 471-0147
Doral (G-3342)

V-Bro Products LLC ....F..... 352 267-6235
Tavares (G-17528)

DECORATIVE WOOD & WOODWORK

Amick Cstm Woodcraft & Design ....G..... 407 324-8525
Sanford (G-15265)

Coral Gables Custom Design Inc ....F..... 305 591-7575
Miami (G-8968)

Cubos LLC ....G..... 786 299-2671
Miami (G-8983)

Dixie Workshop Inc ....F..... 352 629-4699
Ocala (G-11369)

Excel Millwork & Moulding Inc ....E..... 850 576-7228
Midway (G-10412)

G and W Craftsman LLC ....G..... 440 453-2770
Naples (G-10757)

Home Works Bay County Inc ....G..... 850 215-7880
Panama City (G-13273)

JTS Woodworking Inc ....G..... 561 272-7996
Delray Beach (G-2980)

K K Woodworking ....G..... 321 724-1298
Malabar (G-8084)

Madden Millworks ....G..... 310 514-2640
Jacksonville (G-6271)

Noveltex Miami Inc ....E..... 305 887-8191
Hialeah (G-5282)

Pleasure Interiors LLC ....E..... 941 756-9969
Sarasota (G-15783)

Round Table Tools Inc ....G..... 850 877-7650
Tallahassee (G-16496)

Sira ....G..... 352 377-4947
Gainesville (G-4763)

Strasser Enterprises............................G..... 386 677-5163
Daytona Beach (G-2605)

Summit ATL Productions LLC ....G..... 407 930-5488
Orlando (G-12630)

Welshman Investment Corp ....G..... 407 933-4444
Kissimmee (G-6972)

Woodcrafts By Angel Inc ....G..... 352 754-9335
Brooksville (G-1223)

DEFENSE SYSTEMS & EQPT

55 Group LLC ....G..... 954 427-8405
Deerfield Beach (G-2648)

Acet Joint Venture (ajv) LLC ....G..... 240 509-1360
Loxahatchee (G-7965)

Aerojet Rcktdyne Clman Arspc I ....D..... 407 354-0047
Orlando (G-11877)

Alonso Defense Group LLC ....G..... 305 989-0927
Miami (G-8699)

American Payment Systems ....G..... 954 968-6920
North Lauderdale (G-11075)

Cubic Advnced Lrng Sltions Inc ....E..... 407 859-7410
Orlando (G-12061)

Cubic Corporation ....C..... 407 859-7410
Orlando (G-12062)

Defenstech International Inc ....F..... 202 688-1988
Boca Raton (G-480)

Enki Group Inc ....G..... 305 773-3502
Coral Gables (G-2054)

Fab Defense Inc ....G..... 386 263-3054
Ormond Beach (G-12763)

Full Circle Integration LLC ....F..... 504 615-5501
Valparaiso (G-17660)

Global Supply Solutions LLC ....F..... 757 227-6757
Fort Walton Beach (G-4586)

Hyper-Sub Platform Tech Inc ....F..... 386 365-6021
Lake Butler (G-7001)

Linx Defense LLC................................F..... 805 233-2472
Destin (G-3073)

Lockheed Martin Corporation ....B..... 813 855-5711
Oldsmar (G-11671)

Metro Defense Services Inc ....E..... 407 285-2304
Winter Park (G-18522)

Microgerm Defense LLC.......................E..... 561 309-0842
West Palm Beach (G-18078)

Neuro20 Technologies Corp ....G..... 813 990-7138
Tampa (G-17107)

Nxgen Brands Inc ....E..... 954 329-2205
Cape Coral (G-1369)

Orbital Sciences LLC ....C..... 703 406-5474
Merritt Island (G-8589)

Patriot Person Defense ....G..... 813 470-8025
Brandon (G-1102)

Phoenix Defense Group LLC ....G..... 941 776-8714
Parrish (G-13361)

Polyhistor International Inc ....G..... 904 646-5666
Jacksonville (G-6377)

Raytheon Company ....F..... 321 235-1700
Orlando (G-12534)

Sas R & D Services Inc ....F..... 954 432-2345
Miramar (G-10540)

Seven Defenses Corporation ....F..... 786 448-5701
Doral (G-3361)

Space Cast Intllgent Sltons In ....F..... 321 622-6858
Melbourne (G-8525)

Steele Industries Inc ....F..... 800 674-7302
Bradenton (G-1052)

Stout Defense PA ....G..... 352 665-9266
Gainesville (G-4767)

Telesis Technology Corporation ....F..... 941 795-7441
Palmetto (G-13197)

Tf Defense LLC....................................G..... 321 961-7596
Kissimmee (G-6966)

Ticket Drop Traffic Defense ....G..... 305 332-3186
Miami (G-10009)

Truenorth Iq Inc ....G..... 678 849-5000
Port Saint Lucie (G-14459)

DEGREASING MACHINES

Akj Industries Inc ....G..... 239 939-1696
Fort Myers (G-4160)

Global Manufacturing Tech Inc.............G..... 239 657-3720
Immokalee (G-5796)

Instazorb International Inc ....G..... 561 416-7302
Boca Raton (G-545)

Systemone Technologies Inc................G..... 305 593-8015
Doral (G-3389)

DEHYDRATION EQPT

Cummins-Wagner-Florida LLC ....F..... 813 630-2220
Tampa (G-16747)

DENTAL EQPT

Blitz Micro Turning Inc ....G..... 727 725-5005
Safety Harbor (G-14783)

Med Dental Equipment (import)............G..... 786 417-8486
Miami (G-9527)

Parkway Dental Services LLC...............E..... 800 257-0400
Hudson (G-5784)

SDS Dental Inc ....E..... 954 730-3636
Pompano Beach (G-14170)

Vet Sonic Inc ....G..... 305 681-4486
Hialeah (G-5409)

DENTAL EQPT & SPLYS

Boca Dental Supply LLC ....G..... 800 768-5691
Boca Raton (G-436)

Dentsply Sirona Inc ....E..... 262 752-4040
Sarasota (G-15468)

Dentsply Sirona Inc ....D..... 941 527-4450
Sarasota (G-15469)

Dotamed LLC ....G..... 786 594-0144
Doral (G-3199)

Economy Dntres Jcksonville LLC ....E..... 904 696-6767
Jacksonville (G-6064)

Glenroe Technologies Inc ....F..... 941 554-5262
Sarasota (G-15483)

Impress3d LLC ....G..... 312 339-0215
Highland Beach (G-5461)

Intralock International Inc ....G..... 561 447-8282
Boca Raton (G-552)

Omnia Incorporated.............................E..... 863 619-8100
Lakeland (G-7404)

Oralbiolife Inc ....F..... 305 401-2622
Miami Beach (G-10218)

Regent Labs Inc ....G..... 954 426-4889
Deerfield Beach (G-2798)

Regent Labs Inc ....G..... 954 426-4889
Deerfield Beach (G-2799)

Showerfloss Inc ....G..... 239 947-2855
Estero (G-3550)

Sunoptic Technologies LLC..................D..... 877 677-2832
Jacksonville (G-6516)

Superior Dental & Surgical Mfg ....E..... 772 335-5200
Port Saint Lucie (G-14452)

Valley Surgical Inc ....G..... 954 768-9886
Pompano Beach (G-14234)

White Square Chemical Inc..................G..... 302 212-4555
Tavernier (G-17533)

DENTAL EQPT & SPLYS WHOLESALERS

Florida Probe Corporation ....G..... 352 372-1142
Gainesville (G-4694)

DENTAL EQPT & SPLYS: Autoclaves

Orion Dntl Sls Trning Repr LLC.............G..... 888 674-6657
Kissimmee (G-6947)

DENTAL EQPT & SPLYS: Dental Materials

Biomet 3i LLC ....A..... 561 775-9928
Palm Beach Gardens (G-12951)

Custom Atmated Prosthetics LLC.........G..... 781 279-2771
Clearwater (G-1557)

Denterprise International Inc ....F..... 386 672-0450
Ormond Beach (G-12756)

Sunshine Health Products Inc ....F..... 954 493-5469
Fort Lauderdale (G-4075)

DENTAL EQPT & SPLYS: Enamels

Dentate Porcelain Inc ....G..... 917 359-7696
Pompano Beach (G-13992)

Katherine Scures ....G..... 772 589-7409
Sebastian (G-15896)

DENTAL EQPT & SPLYS: Laboratory

Dsg Clearwater Laboratory ....F..... 727 530-9444
Clearwater (G-1572)

DENTAL EQPT & SPLYS: Metal

L A R Manufacturing LLC ....G..... 727 846-7860
Port Richey (G-14367)

Employee Codes: A=Over 500 employees, B=251-500
C=101-250, D=51-100, E=20-50, F=10-19, G=4-9

2022 Harris Florida
Manufacturers Directory

PRODUCT

1189

DENTAL EQPT & SPLYS: Orthodontic Appliances

Inman Orthodontic Labs Inc ....F 954 340-8477
Coral Springs (G-2166)

DENTAL EQPT & SPLYS: Sterilizers

3b Global LLC...G....... 813 350-7872
Tampa (G-16546)
Wayne Metal Products Inc ....G....... 407 321-7168
Sanford (G-15408)

DENTAL EQPT & SPLYS: Tools, NEC

Florida Probe Corporation ....G....... 352 372-1142
Gainesville (G-4694)

DEPARTMENT STORES: Army-Navy Goods

Heralpin Usa Inc ....G....... 305 218-0174
Doral (G-3245)

DERMATOLOGICALS

Clearly Derm LLC...................................F 561 353-3376
Boca Raton (G-465)
Diva Stuff ....G....... 386 256-2521
Ormond Beach (G-12757)
ERA Organics Inc ....G....... 800 579-9817
Clearwater (G-1589)
Genesis Health Institute Inc ....G....... 954 561-3175
Wilton Manors (G-18340)
Heritage Skin Care Inc..........................F 305 757-9264
Miami Shores (G-10383)
North Fort Myers Prescr Sp ....G....... 239 599-4120
North Fort Myers (G-11063)
Pure Wave Organics Inc ....G....... 321 368-7002
Melbourne (G-8504)
Sincerus Pharmaceuticals Inc ....F 800 604-5032
Pompano Beach (G-14180)

DERRICKS

Altec Inc ....E 813 372-0058
Tampa (G-16580)

DESIGN SVCS, NEC

L and C Science and Tech Inc ....G....... 305 200-3531
Hialeah (G-5215)
Metal Creations Sarasota Llc ....F 941 922-7096
Sarasota (G-15744)
Ollo Usa LLC ....G....... 941 366-0600
Sarasota (G-15769)
Virginia Electronic & Ltg Corp..............G....... 904 230-2840
Green Cove Springs (G-4842)

DESIGN SVCS: Commercial & Indl

Idea Design Studio Inc ....F 305 823-6008
Doral (G-3254)
Integrted Dsign Dev Cntl Fla I ....G....... 407 268-4300
Sanford (G-15339)
Nypro Inc ....F 727 577-9749
Saint Petersburg (G-15143)
Precision Analog Systems Co ....G....... 954 587-0668
Plantation (G-13878)
Robotic Parking Systems Inc ....F 727 539-7275
Clearwater (G-1770)
Royal Foam US LLC ....E 904 345-5400
Jacksonville (G-6434)

DESIGN SVCS: Computer Integrated Systems

Aeb Technologies Inc ....G....... 352 417-0009
Homosassa (G-5742)
Applied Technologies Group Inc ....G....... 813 413-7025
Tampa (G-16601)
Arma Holdings Inc ....F 813 402-0667
Tampa (G-16607)
Arrowhead Global LLC ....F 727 497-7340
Clearwater (G-1499)
Asrc Aerospace Corp ....B 321 867-1462
Kennedy Space Center (G-6830)
Black Knight Inc ....B 904 854-5100
Jacksonville (G-5933)
C2c Innovated Technology LLC ....G....... 251 382-2277
Bonifay (G-768)
Cae USA Inc ....A 813 885-7481
Tampa (G-16672)

Contec Americas Inc ....D 321 728-0172
Melbourne (G-8394)
Donnelley Financial LLC ....F 305 371-3900
Miami (G-9042)
Eci Telecom Inc.....................................E 954 772-3070
Fort Lauderdale (G-3783)
Inceptra LLC ....E 954 442-5400
Weston (G-18255)
ITI Engineering LLC ....E 866 245-9356
Winter Springs (G-18570)
Kreateck International Corp ....G....... 772 925-1216
Vero Beach (G-17771)
Lightning Phase II Inc ....G....... 727 539-1800
Seminole (G-15979)
Mantis Security Corporation ....E 571 418-3665
Sarasota (G-15739)
Myers Engineering Intl Inc ....E 954 975-2712
Margate (G-8144)
Oracle America Inc ....F 813 287-1700
Orlando (G-12447)
Simpleshow USA Corp ....E 844 468-5447
Miami (G-9896)
Uts Systems LLC ....G....... 850 226-4301
Fort Walton Beach (G-4615)
Willsonet Inc ....E 813 336-8175
Tampa (G-17432)

DETECTION APPARATUS: Electronic/Magnetic Field, Light/Heat

Senelco Iberia Inc ....A 561 912-6000
Deerfield Beach (G-2807)
Sentech Eas Corporation ....G....... 954 426-2965
Coconut Creek (G-2003)
Teledyne Flir LLC ....D 407 816-0091
Orlando (G-12649)

DETECTION EQPT: Aeronautical Electronic Field

We Love Tec LLC ....G....... 305 433-4453
North Miami Beach (G-11169)

DETECTIVE & ARMORED CAR SERVICES

Jade Tactical Disaster Relief.................C 850 270-4077
Tampa (G-16961)
Metal 2 Metal Inc ....G....... 954 253-9450
Palmetto Bay (G-13214)

DETECTORS: Water Leak

Sleuth Inc ....F 941 745-9903
Bradenton (G-1046)

DIAGNOSTIC SUBSTANCES

Alere Inc ....G....... 813 898-5709
Tampa (G-16571)
Cojali Usa Inc ....G....... 305 960-7651
Doral (G-3167)
Continental Services Group Inc ....E 305 633-7700
Miami (G-8963)
Continental Services Group Inc ....G....... 954 327-0809
Fort Lauderdale (G-3745)
Doctorxs Allergy Formula ....G....... 904 758-2088
Jacksonville (G-6037)
Nilsson Nils ....G....... 561 790-2400
Royal Palm Beach (G-14771)
Opko Health Inc ....C 305 575-4100
Miami (G-9660)
Physicians Imaging LLC ....G....... 352 383-3716
Mount Dora (G-10610)
Sanzay Corporation ....F 305 826-9886
Miami (G-9846)
Suntree Diagnostic Center ....G....... 321 259-8800
Melbourne (G-8540)
US Diagnostics Inc ....E 866 216-5308
Plantation (G-13898)
US Pet Imaging LLC ....G....... 941 921-0383
Sarasota (G-15865)

DIAGNOSTIC SUBSTANCES OR AGENTS: Enzyme & Isoenzyme

Genzyme Corporation ....D 800 245-4363
Miami (G-9203)
Inter Cell Technologies Inc ....G....... 561 575-6868
Jupiter (G-6747)

DIAGNOSTIC SUBSTANCES OR AGENTS: Hematology

Clinical Dagnstc Solutions Inc ....E 954 791-1773
Plantation (G-13836)

DIAGNOSTIC SUBSTANCES OR AGENTS: In Vitro

AP Lifesciences LLC ....F 954 300-7469
Alachua (G-3)
Cambridge Diagnostic Pdts Inc ....F 954 971-4040
Fort Lauderdale (G-3712)
Lumos Diagnostics Inc..........................E 941 556-1850
Lakewood Ranch (G-7485)

DIAGNOSTIC SUBSTANCES OR AGENTS: In Vivo

Positiveid Corporation ....G....... 561 805-8000
Delray Beach (G-3001)

DIAGNOSTIC SUBSTANCES OR AGENTS: Microbiology & Virology

Advanced Bioprocess LLC ....G....... 305 927-3661
Miami (G-8657)
Infinity Genome Sciences Inc ....G....... 321 327-7365
Melbourne Beach (G-8566)
La Genomics LLC ....G....... 407 909-1120
Windermere (G-18358)
Meridian Life Science Inc ....F 561 241-0223
Boca Raton (G-594)
Sun & Earth Microbiology Llc................G....... 786 354-8894
Cutler Bay (G-2305)

DIAGNOSTIC SUBSTANCES OR AGENTS: Radioactive

Cardinal Health 414 LLC.......................G....... 813 972-1351
Tampa (G-16679)
Evolvegene LLC ....G....... 727 623-4052
Saint Petersburg (G-15038)
Petnet Solutions Inc ....G....... 813 627-0022
Tampa (G-17157)

DIAMONDS: Cutting & Polishing

Bach Diamonds......................................G....... 954 921-4069
Hollywood (G-5537)
Bashert Diamonds Inc ....G....... 305 466-1881
Aventura (G-255)
Giraldo & Donalisio Corp ....F 239 567-2206
Cape Coral (G-1348)
Suncoast Accrdted Gmlgical Lab...........G....... 941 756-8787
Bradenton (G-1054)

DIAPERS: Disposable

Impex of Doral Inc ....E 305 470-0041
Medley (G-8257)

DIATOMACEOUS EARTH: Ground Or Treated

Atlas Peat & Soil Inc ....E 561 734-7300
Boynton Beach (G-845)

DICE & DICE CUPS

Master Mold Corp..................................G....... 941 486-0000
North Venice (G-11214)

DIE CUTTING SVC: Paper

Top Notch Diecutting Foil STA ....G....... 904 346-3511
Jacksonville (G-6560)

DIE SETS: Presses, Metal Stamping

Ebway LLC..E 954 971-4911
Fort Lauderdale (G-3780)
Ebway LLC..D 954 971-4911
Fort Lauderdale (G-3781)
Miami Quality Graphics Inc ....E 305 634-9506
Miami (G-9556)
Sohacki Industries Inc ....E 904 826-0130
Saint Augustine (G-14894)
Versatile Manufacturing Inc ....E 954 561-8083
Oakland Park (G-11310)
Versatile Manufacturing Inc ....F 954 561-8083
Oakland Park (G-11311)

DIES & TOOLS: Special

Accu Metal ....G...... 850 912-4855
  Pensacola (G-13432)
Cob Industries Inc ....G...... 321 723-3200
  West Melbourne (G-17897)
Crenshaw Die & Manufacturing ....G...... 949 475-5505
  Daytona Beach (G-2536)
FDM of Clearwater Inc ....F...... 727 544-8801
  Largo (G-7582)
Gregg Tool & Die Co Inc ....G...... 305 685-6309
  Hialeah (G-5177)
Gulf Tool Corporation ....F...... 850 456-0840
  Pensacola (G-13517)
Innovative Carbide Inc ....F...... 863 696-7999
  Lake Wales (G-7165)
Kirtech Enterprises Inc ....F...... 352 742-7222
  Tavares (G-17515)
Moloney Die Company ....G...... 904 388-3654
  Jacksonville (G-6313)
Pace Machine & Tool Inc ....F...... 561 747-5444
  Stuart (G-16194)
Pacific Die Cast Inc ....F...... 813 316-2221
  Tampa (G-17137)
Rafferty Holdings LLC ....E...... 352 248-0906
  Gainesville (G-4756)
Roller Die + Forming ....F...... 502 804-5571
  Green Cove Springs (G-4834)
Savage Ventures Inc ....E...... 772 335-5655
  Port Saint Lucie (G-14444)
Schwarz Bros Manufacturing Co ....G...... 309 342-5814
  Pensacola (G-13602)
Southpointe Precision ....G...... 239 225-1350
  Fort Myers (G-4402)
Tennessee Tool and Fixture LLC ....F...... 931 954-5316
  Winter Park (G-18544)
Tibor Inc ....E...... 561 272-0770
  Delray Beach (G-3026)
Triad Edm Inc ....G...... 352 489-5336
  Dunnellon (G-3468)
Unique Tool & Die LLC ....F...... 772 464-5006
  Fort Pierce (G-4549)
Universal Die Services Inc ....G...... 863 665-6092
  Lakeland (G-7468)
Versacomp Inc ....G...... 954 561-8778
  Oakland Park (G-11309)

DIES: Cutting, Exc Metal

Nessmith Dye Cutting & Finshg ....G...... 904 353-6317
  Jacksonville (G-6324)

DIES: Steel Rule

Victors Die Cutting Inc ....G...... 305 599-0255
  Hialeah (G-5411)

DIETICIANS' OFFICES

Kulfi LLC ....E...... 855 488-4273
  Boca Raton (G-573)

DIMENSION STONE: Buildings

Breton USA Customers Svc Corp ....F...... 941 360-2700
  Sarasota (G-15616)

DIODES: Light Emitting

Absen Inc ....F...... 407 203-8870
  Orlando (G-11862)
American Led Display Solutions ....G...... 561 227-8048
  Miami (G-8718)
Apollo Metro Solutions Inc ....F...... 239 444-6934
  Naples (G-10671)
Apure Distribution LLC ....F...... 305 351-1025
  Miami (G-8737)
Aqualuma LLC ....G...... 954 234-2512
  Deerfield Beach (G-2669)
Itelecom USA Inc ....G...... 305 557-4660
  Weston (G-18257)
Keytroller LLC ....F...... 813 877-4500
  Tampa (G-16984)
Led Are US LLC ....G...... 305 823-2803
  Hialeah Gardens (G-5441)
Luminoso LLC ....G...... 305 364-8099
  Hialeah Gardens (G-5442)
Lumiron Inc ....G...... 305 652-2599
  Miami (G-9485)
Nebula Led Lighting Systems of ....G...... 813 907-0001
  Wesley Chapel (G-17884)
Suncoast Led Displays LLC ....F...... 727 683-2777
  Palm Harbor (G-13134)

Tesco of Swfl Inc ....G...... 239 234-6490
  Naples (G-10923)
Tm USA Inc ....G...... 954 801-4649
  Doral (G-3397)
Viva Led LLC ....F...... 786 491-9290
  Miami (G-10118)
Wbn LLC ....G...... 786 870-4172
  Doral (G-3418)

DIODES: Solid State, Germanium, Silicon, Etc

US Applied Physics Group LLC ....G...... 321 607-9023
  Titusville (G-17626)

DIRECT SELLING ESTABLISHMENTS, NEC

Shaws Sthern Blle Frz Fods In ....D...... 904 768-1591
  Jacksonville (G-6463)

DIRECT SELLING ESTABLISHMENTS: Bakery Goods, House-To-House

904 Sweet Treatz Street LLC ....G...... 800 889-3298
  Jacksonville (G-5842)
I Be Cakin LLC ....G...... 954 707-3865
  Pompano Beach (G-14057)

DIRECT SELLING ESTABLISHMENTS: Clothing, House-To-House

Harlan J Newman ....G...... 727 216-6419
  Seminole (G-15977)

DIRECT SELLING ESTABLISHMENTS: Cosmetic, House-To-House

Mazi Group Inc ....E...... 786 800-2425
  Miami (G-9522)

DIRECT SELLING ESTABLISHMENTS: Encyclopedias & Publications

Great Hse Mdia Group of Pbls I ....F...... 407 779-3846
  Orlando (G-12200)

DIRECT SELLING ESTABLISHMENTS: Food Svcs

All Naturals Direct ....G...... 813 792-3777
  Tampa (G-16573)

DIRECT SELLING ESTABLISHMENTS: Snacks

Mvs International Inc ....G...... 954 727-3383
  Weston (G-18270)

DISCS & TAPE: Optical, Blank

Twinstar Optics & Coatings Inc ....F...... 727 847-2300
  Port Richey (G-14381)

DISHWASHING EQPT: Commercial

Bar Maid Corporation ....F...... 954 960-1468
  Pompano Beach (G-13948)
ICI Custom Parts Inc ....F...... 813 888-7979
  Tampa (G-16929)

DISPENSERS, TISSUE: Plastic

Hernon Manufacturing Inc ....D...... 407 322-4000
  Sanford (G-15331)

DISPENSERS: Soap

Ecolab Inc ....F...... 800 931-8911
  Jupiter (G-6717)
Ultraclenz LLC ....F...... 800 931-8911
  Jupiter (G-6817)

DISPENSING EQPT & PARTS, BEVERAGE: Coolers, Milk/Water, Elec

International H20 Inc ....G...... 954 854-1638
  North Miami Beach (G-11144)

DISPENSING EQPT & PARTS, BEVERAGE: Fountain/Other Beverage

Dcg Enterprises LLC ....G...... 813 931-4303
  Tampa (G-16768)
Gate Cfv Solutions Inc ....G...... 772 388-3387
  Sebastian (G-15893)
Juice Culture LLC ....G...... 407 312-8079
  Winter Park (G-18517)
Micro Matic Usa Inc ....E...... 352 544-1081
  Brooksville (G-1181)

DISPLAY FIXTURES: Wood

Capital Contracting & Design ....F...... 908 561-8411
  Fort Lauderdale (G-3713)
Nauset Enterprises Inc ....G...... 727 443-3469
  Clearwater (G-1713)

DISPLAY ITEMS: Corrugated, Made From Purchased Materials

Hitex Marketing Group Inc ....G...... 305 406-1150
  Miami (G-9285)

DISPLAY LETTERING SVCS

Firedrake Inc ....G...... 813 713-8902
  Zephyrhills (G-18614)

DISPLAY STANDS: Merchandise, Exc Wood

La Fabrika Retail Services LLC ....G...... 786 525-4491
  Miami (G-9406)

DISTANCE MEASURING EQPT OR DME: Aeronautical

Trumeter Company Inc ....G...... 954 725-6699
  Coconut Creek (G-2008)

DISTILLATION PRDTS: Wood

Kraton Chemical LLC ....C...... 904 928-8700
  Jacksonville (G-6250)

DISTILLERS DRIED GRAIN & SOLUBLES

Drum Circle Distilling LLC ....F...... 941 358-1900
  Sarasota (G-15662)
Florida Distillers Co ....F...... 863 967-4481
  Auburndale (G-233)

DISTRIBUTORS: Motor Vehicle Engine

Carbel LLC ....C...... 305 599-0832
  Doral (G-3153)
Central Turbos Corp ....G...... 305 406-3933
  Doral (G-3159)
Daikin Comfort Tech Mfg LP ....G...... 904 355-4520
  Jacksonville (G-6023)
South Florida Core Distrs ....G...... 954 452-9091
  Davie (G-2480)

DIVING EQPT STORES

Gigli Enterprises Inc ....G...... 850 871-4777
  Panama City (G-13267)

DOCK EQPT & SPLYS, INDL

Gator Dock & Marine LLC ....F...... 407 323-0190
  Sanford (G-15324)
International Dock Pdts Inc ....F...... 954 964-5315
  Hallandale Beach (G-4952)
Keys Deck & Dock Supplies Inc ....G...... 305 451-8001
  Key Largo (G-6848)

DOCKS: Floating, Wood

Crowell Marine Inc ....G...... 813 236-3625
  Tampa (G-16742)
Hohol Marine Products ....G...... 386 734-0630
  Deland (G-2874)
W R Williams Enterprises Inc ....G...... 813 677-2000
  Gibsonton (G-4803)

DOCKS: Prefabricated Metal

Bluewater Marine Systems Inc ....G...... 619 499-7507
  Saint Petersburg (G-14985)
Florida Floats Inc ....E...... 904 358-3362
  Jacksonville (G-6105)

Employee Codes: A=Over 500 employees, B=251-500
C=101-250, D=51-100, E=20-50, F=10-19, G=4-9

2022 Harris Florida
Manufacturers Directory

1191

PRODUCT

DOCUMENT DESTRUCTION SVC

Bay Area Security Shred ....F 877 974-7337
Palm Harbor *(G-13102)*

DOLOMITE: Crushed & Broken

Crystal River Quarries Inc ....E 352 795-2828
Crystal River *(G-2273)*
Dolomite Inc ....F 850 482-4962
Marianna *(G-8163)*

DOLOMITE: Dimension

Hatch Enterprises Inc ....G 386 935-1419
Branford *(G-1112)*

DOOR & WINDOW REPAIR SVCS

Shutterman Storm & Security ....E 239 455-9166
Naples *(G-10891)*

DOOR FRAMES: Wood

Al & Sons Millwork Inc ....E 352 245-9191
Belleview *(G-358)*
Dayoris Doors ....G 954 374-8538
Hollywood *(G-5562)*
Door Styles Inc ....E 305 653-4447
Miami *(G-9043)*
Doors 4 U Inc ....F 786 400-2298
Medley *(G-8231)*
East Coast Door Inc ....G 954 868-4700
Pompano Beach *(G-14004)*
Mills & Nebraska Door & Trim ....F 407 472-2742
Orlando *(G-12381)*
Southern Door Technologies ....G 386 496-3844
Lake Butler *(G-7006)*
Taylor-Cotton-Ridley Inc ....D 904 733-8373
Jacksonville *(G-6535)*

DOOR MATS: Rubber

Gallant Inc..................................G 800 330-1343
Winter Garden *(G-18387)*

DOOR OPERATING SYSTEMS: Electric

First Mate Inc...............................G 954 475-2750
Plantation *(G-13853)*
Somfy Systems Inc ....F 561 292-3483
Boynton Beach *(G-914)*

DOOR PARTS: Sashes, Wood

Hill Enterprises LLC.........................G 850 478-4455
Pensacola *(G-13519)*

DOORS & WINDOWS WHOLESALERS: All Materials

Custom Cft Windows & Doors Inc..............F 407 834-5400
Winter Springs *(G-18563)*
Gulfport Industries Inc ....F 813 885-1000
Tampa *(G-16899)*
Hartman Windows and Doors LLC.............D 561 296-9600
Riviera Beach *(G-14628)*
Jeld-Wen Inc ....D 407 343-8596
Kissimmee *(G-6931)*
Quality Engineered Products Co ....E 813 885-1693
Tampa *(G-17200)*
R & R Door and Trim Inc.....................G 561 844-5496
West Palm Beach *(G-18136)*
Superior Quality Contractors.................G 786 371-7991
Hialeah *(G-5373)*

DOORS & WINDOWS: Screen & Storm

Ashton Manufacturing LLC...................F 941 351-5529
Sarasota *(G-15601)*
Defender Screens Intl LLC ....E 866 802-0400
Sarasota *(G-15654)*
Dependable Shutter Service Inc ....E 954 583-1411
Davie *(G-2404)*
Fortress Impact Wndows Dors LL.............G 954 621-2395
Fort Lauderdale *(G-3828)*
G F E Inc ....E 954 583-7005
Davie *(G-2416)*
Levinson Built LLC..........................G 561 712-9882
West Palm Beach *(G-18057)*
Pioneer Screen Inc..........................G 772 260-3068
Palm City *(G-13055)*
Russell Home Imprvmnt Ctr Inc ....S 954 436-9186
Davie *(G-2473)*

Window Craftsmen Inc ....E 941 922-1844
Sarasota *(G-15876)*

DOORS & WINDOWS: Storm, Metal

American Marine Mfg Inc ....G 305 497-7723
Hialeah *(G-5049)*
Coastal Awngs Hrrcane Prtction ....G 407 923-9482
Orlando *(G-12023)*
Poma Corporation ....D 561 790-5799
West Palm Beach *(G-18123)*
Rolladen Inc.................................F 954 454-4114
Longwood *(G-7943)*
Rolsafe LLC ....F 239 225-2487
Fort Myers *(G-4385)*
Style-View Products Inc ....E 305 634-9688
Miami *(G-9962)*
Superior Quality Contractors.................G 786 371-7991
Hialeah *(G-5373)*

DOORS: Fiberglass

My Shower Door Tampa LLC ....G 239 337-3667
Fort Myers *(G-4336)*
Plazadoor Corp ....F 561 578-5450
Palm City *(G-13056)*
Quality Molds USA Inc........................F 321 632-6066
Cocoa *(G-1950)*
Sunflex Wall Systems LP ....G 239 220-1570
Naples *(G-10912)*

DOORS: Fire, Metal

Omega Garage Doors Inc ....F 352 620-8830
Melbourne *(G-8488)*

DOORS: Folding, Plastic Or Plastic Coated Fabric

Overhead Door Corporation ....D 850 474-9890
Pensacola *(G-13563)*

DOORS: Garage, Overhead, Metal

A Superior Garage Door Company ....E 305 556-6624
Hialeah *(G-5017)*
Best Rolling Manufacturer Inc ....D 305 821-4276
Hialeah Gardens *(G-5432)*
C & D Industrial Maint LLC...................G 833 776-5833
Bradenton *(G-951)*
Hrh Door Corp ....F 850 474-9890
Pensacola *(G-13521)*
Overhead Door Corporation ....D 850 474-9890
Pensacola *(G-13563)*
Specialty Products Inc ....G 850 438-4264
Pensacola *(G-13608)*

DOORS: Garage, Overhead, Wood

A-1 Door Systems Inc ....F 904 327-7206
Jacksonville *(G-5850)*
All Pro Chelo Corp ....G 786 317-3914
Hialeah *(G-5039)*
Hire Authority ....F 561 477-6663
Miami *(G-9283)*
Hrh Door Corp ....F 850 474-9890
Pensacola *(G-13521)*
Marko Garage Doors & Gates Inc ....G 561 547-4001
Palm Springs *(G-13146)*
Old City Gates ....G 904 669-7938
Saint Augustine *(G-14867)*
Specialty Products Inc ....G 850 438-4264
Pensacola *(G-13608)*

DOORS: Glass

Acryplex Inc.................................G 305 633-7636
Miami *(G-8648)*
Coastal Industries Inc ....C 904 642-3970
Jacksonville *(G-5990)*
Crawford Glass Door Co ....F 954 480-6820
Deerfield Beach *(G-2696)*
Enviralum Industries Inc ....F 305 752-4411
Miami *(G-9101)*
Florida Glass of Tampa Bay ....E 813 925-1330
Tampa *(G-16844)*
Lawson Industries Inc ....B 305 696-8660
Medley *(G-8267)*
Martell Glass ....G 786 336-0142
Miami *(G-9514)*
Sarasota Shower Door Company ....G 941 378-0051
Sarasota *(G-15815)*

Sea Products Inc ....D 904 781-8200
Jacksonville *(G-6458)*
Southeastern Aluminum Pdts LLC.......G 800 243-8200
Jacksonville *(G-6486)*
Sunshine Windows Mfg Inc ....D 305 364-9952
Hialeah *(G-5370)*
Windoor Incorporated ....C 407 481-8400
North Venice *(G-11222)*

DOORS: Hangar, Metal

Hangar Door Spclsts Design Inc ....F 772 266-9070
Stuart *(G-16162)*
M Bilt Enterprises Inc ....F 352 528-5566
Ocala *(G-11434)*
Well Bilt Industries Usa LLC ....F 352 528-5566
Ocala *(G-11512)*

DOORS: Rolling, Indl Building Or Warehouse, Metal

Rolling Door Parts Inc ....G 305 888-5020
Miami *(G-9820)*

DOORS: Safe & Vault, Metal

Fbs Fortified & Ballistic SEC ....G 561 409-6300
Boca Raton *(G-513)*

DOORS: Screen, Metal

Simplex Inc ....E 352 357-2828
Mount Dora *(G-10613)*
Simpson Screens Inc ....F 904 757-1498
Jacksonville *(G-6474)*
Southeastern Door Company LLC ....F 561 746-5493
Jupiter *(G-6803)*
Yale Ogron Mfg Co Inc........................G 305 687-0424
Opa Locka *(G-11802)*

DOORS: Wooden

Absolute Window and Door Inc............G 941 485-7774
Venice *(G-17672)*
Algoma Hardwoods Inc ....E 865 471-6300
Orlando *(G-11890)*
Builders Door and Supply Inc................F 941 955-2311
Sarasota *(G-15619)*
Century Millworks ....F 850 256-2565
Century *(G-1442)*
D R Nickelson & Company Inc................F 386 755-6565
Lake City *(G-7017)*
DTF Woodworks LLC..........................F 954 317-6443
Southwest Ranches *(G-16053)*
Florida Made Door Co ....C 352 742-1000
Tampa *(G-16848)*
Gulfport Industries Inc ....F 813 885-1000
Tampa *(G-16899)*
Hartman Windows and Doors LLC.......D 561 296-9600
Riviera Beach *(G-14628)*
Islandoor Company ....G 954 524-3667
Fort Lauderdale *(G-3885)*
Jambco Millwork Inc ....F 954 977-4998
Margate *(G-8136)*
Jeld-Wen Inc ....D 407 343-8596
Kissimmee *(G-6931)*
K M I International Inc ....E 561 588-5514
Lake Worth *(G-7212)*
Lake Door and Trim Inc ....F 352 589-5566
Eustis *(G-3562)*
Masonite Corporation ....D 813 877-2726
Tampa *(G-17046)*
Masonite Corporation ....D 715 354-3441
Tampa *(G-17047)*
Masonite Holdings Inc ....E 813 877-2726
Tampa *(G-17048)*
Masonite International Corp ....E 813 889-3861
Tampa *(G-17049)*
Masonite International Corp ....D 813 877-2726
Tampa *(G-17050)*
Masonite International Corp ....D 904 225-3889
Yulee *(G-18591)*
Masonite International Corp ....D 813 877-2726
Tampa *(G-17051)*
Masonite US Corporation ....D 813 877-2726
Tampa *(G-17052)*
Mill-Rite Woodworking Co Inc ....D 727 527-7808
Pinellas Park *(G-13708)*
Overhead Door Corporation ....D 850 474-9890
Pensacola *(G-13563)*
Premdor Finance LLC.........................D 813 877-2726
Tampa *(G-17177)*

Quality Engineered Products Co ....E 813 885-1693
Tampa (G-17200)

R & R Door and Trim Inc ....G...... 561 844-5496
West Palm Beach (G-18136)

Reso Inc ....G...... 561 328-8539
Riviera Beach (G-14668)

Shaver Properties Inc ....E 772 569-3466
Vero Beach (G-17799)

Siw Solutions LLC ....C 561 274-9392
Delray Beach (G-3017)

Superior Trim & Door Inc ....E 407 408-7624
Apopka (G-180)

Ultimate Door Palm Beach Inc............F 561 642-2828
Lake Worth (G-7240)

Wow Business ....F 813 301-2620
Tampa (G-17442)

DRAINAGE PRDTS: Concrete

Cemex Materials LLC ....C 561 743-4039
Jupiter (G-6704)

DRAPERIES & CURTAINS

Andirali Corporation ....G...... 305 542-5374
Miami (G-8730)

Associated Intr Desgr Svc Inc ....F 561 655-4926
West Palm Beach (G-17930)

Bkbl Holdings Ltd ....G...... 954 920-6772
Sunrise (G-16297)

Dwa Inc ....F 941 444-1134
Sarasota (G-15663)

Fabric Innovations Inc ....E 305 860-5757
Miami (G-9127)

GK Window Treatments Inc ....F 954 786-2927
Pompano Beach (G-14040)

Kenco Hospitality Inc ....D 954 921-5434
Fort Lauderdale (G-3904)

Mws Drapery Inc ....E 305 794-3811
Hialeah (G-5269)

Quest Drape ....G...... 407 888-8164
Orlando (G-12521)

Remas Draperies Etc Inc ....G...... 904 845-9300
Hilliard (G-5474)

Residential Acoustics LLC ....F 813 922-2390
Tampa (G-17216)

Solar Shades Draperies & More ....G...... 954 600-3419
Plantation (G-13891)

Top Trtment Cstomes Accesories ....G...... 239 936-4600
Fort Myers (G-4426)

Vertical Land Inc ....F 850 244-5263
Panama City (G-13318)

Westpoint Home Inc ....A 850 415-4100
Chipley (G-1461)

DRAPERIES & DRAPERY FABRICS, COTTON

Ards Awning & Upholstery Inc ....F 863 293-2442
Winter Haven (G-18418)

Associated Intr Desgr Svc Inc ....F 561 655-4926
West Palm Beach (G-17930)

Designers Whl Workroom Inc...............F 239 434-7633
Naples (G-10728)

Dhf Marketing Inc ....F 305 884-8077
Hialeah (G-5116)

Distinctive Creat Intr Wkshp I.............F 954 921-1861
Hollywood (G-5567)

Dwa Inc ....F 941 444-1134
Sarasota (G-15663)

Interior Views Inc ....G...... 727 527-8899
Pinellas Park (G-13694)

Sanzogo Corporation ....G...... 561 334-2138
Boca Raton (G-662)

DRAPERIES: Plastic & Textile, From Purchased Materials

Lasalle Bristol Corporation.................F 352 687-2151
Ocala (G-11425)

Paul Himber Inc ....F 561 586-3741
West Palm Beach (G-18115)

Powless Drapery Service Inc ....F 954 566-7863
Oakland Park (G-11287)

Shades By Ana Inc ....G...... 305 238-4858
Miami (G-9876)

Suncoast Fabrics Inc ....G...... 239 566-3313
Naples (G-10911)

Sutton Draperies Inc ....F 305 653-7738
Miami (G-9977)

Tiffany Quilting & Drapery ....F 407 834-6386
Longwood (G-7952)

DRAPERY & UPHOLSTERY STORES: Curtains

Sanzogo Corporation ....G...... 561 334-2138
Boca Raton (G-662)

DRAPERY & UPHOLSTERY STORES: Draperies

Dwa Inc ....F 941 444-1134
Sarasota (G-15663)

Myriam Interiors Inc ....G...... 305 626-9898
Hialeah (G-5271)

Remas Draperies Etc Inc ....G...... 904 845-9300
Hilliard (G-5474)

Vertical Land Inc ....F 850 819-2535
Panama City (G-13317)

Vertical Village Inc ....G...... 772 340-0400
Port Saint Lucie (G-14464)

DRAPES & DRAPERY FABRICS, FROM MANMADE FIBER

Dti Design Trend Inc ....F 954 680-8370
Hialeah (G-5124)

Remas Draperies Etc Inc ....G...... 904 845-9300
Hilliard (G-5474)

Vertical Village Inc ....G...... 772 340-0400
Port Saint Lucie (G-14464)

DRILL BITS

Approved Performance Tooling ....E 305 592-7775
Miami (G-8736)

B & A Manufacturing Co ....E 561 848-8648
Riviera Beach (G-14596)

DRILLING MACHINERY & EQPT: Oil & Gas

Logistic Systems Inc ....G...... 305 477-4999
Miami (G-9472)

DRILLING MACHINERY & EQPT: Water Well

Jayco Screens Inc...............................G...... 850 456-0673
Pensacola (G-13527)

Krausz Usa Inc ....F 352 509-3600
Ocala (G-11422)

Phoenix Dewatering Inc ....F 407 330-7015
Sanford (G-15371)

DRILLS & DRILLING EQPT: Mining

Ronnies Welding & Machine Inc...........G...... 305 238-0972
Cutler Bay (G-2301)

Wolf Americas LLC ....G...... 407 704-2051
Orlando (G-12716)

DRILLS: Core

Sandvik Mining & Cnstr USA LLC ....C 386 462-4100
Alachua (G-21)

DRINK MIXES, NONALCOHOLIC: Cocktail

Lemon-X Corporation ....G...... 863 635-8400
Frostproof (G-4638)

DRINKING PLACES: Bars & Lounges

Burn By Rocky Patel.............................G...... 239 653-9013
Naples (G-10701)

DRIVE SHAFTS

Broward Power Train Co Inc ....E 954 772-0881
Fort Lauderdale (G-3705)

Central Florida Driveshaft....................G...... 407 299-1100
Orlando (G-11997)

DRIVES: High Speed Indl, Exc Hydrostatic

ABB Enterprise Software Inc ....C 954 752-6700
Coral Springs (G-2124)

DRUG STORES

Kashiben Say LLC ....G...... 352 489-4960
Dunnellon (G-3466)

St Mary Pharmacy LLC ....F 727 585-1333
Largo (G-7690)

DRUG TESTING KITS: Blood & Urine

Advantagecare Inc...............................G...... 407 345-8877
Orlando (G-11873)

Arcpoint of Tallahassee Inc ....G...... 850 201-2500
Tallahassee (G-16413)

Five Star Screening LLC ....G...... 800 788-8315
Ruskin (G-14778)

Intrinsic Interventions Inc ....F 614 205-8465
Bonita Springs (G-806)

DRUGS & DRUG PROPRIETARIES, WHOLESALE

Sancilio & Company Inc ....E 561 847-2302
Riviera Beach (G-14672)

DRUGS & DRUG PROPRIETARIES, WHOLESALE: Medicinals/Botanicals

Diamond Wellness Holdings Inc ....G...... 800 433-0127
Fort Lauderdale (G-3764)

Lftd Partners Inc ....F 847 915-2446
Jacksonville (G-6256)

Upexi Inc ....G...... 701 353-5425
Clearwater (G-1840)

DRUGS & DRUG PROPRIETARIES, WHOLESALE: Pharmaceuticals

Andrx Corporation ....C 954 585-1400
Davie (G-2387)

Camphor Technologies Inc ....F 941 360-0025
Sarasota (G-15627)

Ceautamed Worldwide LLC ....G...... 866 409-6262
Boca Raton (G-456)

Lupin Research Inc ....E 800 466-1450
Coral Springs (G-2180)

Max Avw Professional LLC ....F 954 972-3338
Margate (G-8143)

Rowell Laboratories Inc ....F 407 929-9445
Apopka (G-173)

Shriji Swami LLC ....G...... 904 727-3434
Jacksonville (G-6467)

Specialty Pharmacy Svcs Inc ....G...... 321 953-2004
Melbourne (G-8528)

Uspharma Ltd ....D 954 817-4418
Miami Lakes (G-10374)

DRUGS & DRUG PROPRIETARIES, WHOLESALE: Vitamins & Minerals

Be Whole Nutrition LLC.........................G...... 813 420-3057
Plant City (G-13746)

Boston Ntrceutical Science LLC ....F 617 848-4560
Miami (G-8849)

Mr Gummy Vitamins LLC ....G...... 855 674-8669
Opa Locka (G-11771)

Taylor L Max L C ....G...... 833 346-9963
Fort Myers (G-4419)

DRUGS: Parasitic & Infective Disease Affecting

Sinofresh Healthcare Inc ....G...... 941 270-2627
Venice (G-17715)

DRUMS: Brake

Multi Parts Supply Usa Inc....................E 561 748-1515
Jupiter (G-6767)

DRUMS: Fiber

Design Containers Inc ....E 904 764-6541
Jacksonville (G-6029)

DRYCLEANING & LAUNDRY SVCS: Commercial & Family

One Price Drycleaners Tampa ....F 727 734-3353
Dunedin (G-3456)

DRYCLEANING EQPT & SPLYS WHOLESALERS

Power Kleen Corporation.......................E 813 854-2648
Oldsmar (G-11687)

Employee Codes: A=Over 500 employees, B=251-500
C=101-250, D=51-100, E=20-50, F=10-19, G=4-9

2022 Harris Florida
Manufacturers Directory

PRODUCT

1193

DRYCLEANING EQPT & SPLYS: Commercial

Steiner-Atlantic LLC .... E 305 754-4551
Miami Gardens (G-10275)

DUCTS: Sheet Metal

Advanced Metals LLC .... G 352 494-2476
Hawthorne (G-5005)

Badger Corporation .... G 954 942-5277
Pompano Beach (G-13945)

Duct Design Corporation .... E 305 827-0110
Hialeah (G-5125)

Impulse Air Inc .... E 904 475-1822
Jacksonville (G-6194)

Jer-Air Manufacturing Inc .... E 352 591-2674
Micanopy (G-10398)

Lapin Sheet Metal Company .... D 407 423-9897
Orlando (G-12310)

Metal Mart Systems Inc .... E 863 533-4040
Bartow (G-317)

South Florida Sheet Metal .... G 954 647-6457
Pembroke Pines (G-13415)

US Sheet Metal Inc .... F 305 884-7705
Miami (G-10081)

DUMPSTERS: Garbage

Dumpstermaxx .... G 805 552-6299
University Park (G-17653)

Dumpsterme LLC .... G 904 647-1945
Jacksonville (G-6045)

Elevated Dumpsters LLC .... G 813 732-6338
Zephyrhills (G-18613)

Interstate Recycling Waste Inc .... F 407 812-5555
Orlando (G-12254)

Need A Dumpster LLC .... G 888 407-3867
Apopka (G-156)

Platinium Rosis Inc .... G 786 617-9973
Miami Beach (G-10220)

Pro Dumpsters Inc .... F 407 910-6341
Kissimmee (G-6956)

Service D N D Dumpster .... G 813 989-3867
Tampa (G-17252)

Trash Express SW Inc .... G 239 340-5291
Fort Myers (G-4433)

U-Load Dumpsters LLC .... G 352 318-3045
Ponce De Leon (G-14250)

Wastequip Manufacturing Co LLC ... D 704 900-4654
Lakeland (G-7471)

Xtreme Dumpster Services Corp ..... G 407 272-8899
Orlando (G-12722)

DYES & TINTS: Household

Southeast Energy Inc .... G 561 883-1051
Boca Raton (G-686)

DYES OR COLORS: Food, Synthetic

Allied USA Incorporated .... G 305 235-3950
Miami (G-8695)

EATING PLACES

Choctaw Trading Co Inc .... F 407 905-9917
Winter Garden (G-18380)

Culinary Concepts Inc .... E 407 228-0069
Orlando (G-12064)

Grand Buffet .... G 941 752-3388
Bradenton (G-988)

Magnolias Gurmet Bky Itln Deli ..... G 352 207-2667
Ocala (G-11435)

Ronnie & Moes Italian Ice LLC ...... G 786 970-1805
Miami (G-9824)

Suzanne Chalet Foods Inc .... G 863 676-6011
Lake Wales (G-7176)

White Publishing Co Inc .... F 904 389-3622
Jacksonville (G-6610)

EDUCATIONAL SVCS

Drazcanna Inc .... E 786 618-1472
Miami (G-9048)

EDUCATIONAL SVCS, NONDEGREE GRANTING: Continuing Education

Rtj Group Inc .... G 954 999-4060
Fort Lauderdale (G-4033)

ELASTOMERS

Linvatec Corporation .... B 727 392-6464
Largo (G-7633)

ELECTRIC MOTOR REPAIR SVCS

A & A Electric Mtrs & Pump Svc ..... G 407 843-5005
Orlando (G-11856)

Aap Industrial Inc .... E 941 377-4373
Sarasota (G-15584)

AC Industrial Service Inc .... F 305 887-5541
Miami (G-8639)

AL Covell Electric Inc .... G 352 544-0680
Brooksville (G-1132)

Allapattah Electric Motor Repr .... G 305 325-0330
Miami (G-8693)

American International Mtr Svc .... G 727 573-9501
Clearwater (G-1490)

Belle Glade Electric Motor Svc .... G 561 996-3333
Belle Glade (G-339)

Biscayne Electric Motor & Pump ..... G 305 681-8171
Miami (G-8834)

Blueocean Marine Services LLC ...... F 954 583-9888
Fort Lauderdale (G-3694)

Central Electric Motor Svc Inc .... F 863 422-4721
Haines City (G-4902)

Condo Electric Motor Repr Corp ..... E 305 691-5400
Hialeah (G-5095)

Dade Pump & Supply Co .... G 305 235-5000
Miami (G-8996)

Done Rite Pumps .... G 305 953-3380
Opa Locka (G-11738)

Electrcal Systems Cmmnications ..... G 813 248-4275
Tampa (G-16799)

Electro Mechanical South Inc .... E 941 342-9111
Bradenton (G-974)

Florida Elc Mtr Co Miami Inc .... E 305 759-3835
Miami (G-9154)

Genesis Electric Motors Inc .... G 727 572-1414
Largo (G-7592)

Indian River Armature Inc .... G 772 461-2067
Fort Pierce (G-4497)

John Mader Enterprises Inc .... E 239 731-5455
Fort Myers (G-4300)

K C W Electric Company Inc .... G 850 878-2051
Tallahassee (G-16465)

Kolich Electric Motor Co Inc .... G 954 969-8605
Pompano Beach (G-14072)

M & W Electric Motors Inc .... G 850 433-0400
Pensacola (G-13541)

Miami Industrial Motor Inc .... G 305 593-2370
Doral (G-3299)

Michigan Pmps Elc Mtrs Repr Co .... G 407 841-6800
Orlando (G-12378)

Morgans Elc Mtr & Pump Svc .... F 321 960-2209
Cocoa Beach (G-1974)

Pinellas Electric Mtr Repr Inc .... G 727 572-0777
Clearwater (G-1741)

Robert E Weissenborn Sr .... E 239 262-1771
Naples (G-10879)

Southern Winding Service Inc .... E 813 621-6555
Tampa (G-17291)

St Agustine Elc Mtr Works Inc .... F 904 829-8211
Saint Augustine (G-14897)

Stewarts Elc Mtr Works Inc .... E 407 859-1837
Orlando (G-12626)

Suncoast Electric Mtr Svc Inc .... E 813 247-4104
Tampa (G-17312)

T A C Armatures & Pumps Corp ...... F 305 835-8845
Miami (G-9989)

Tampa Armature Works Inc .... D 904 757-7790
Jacksonville (G-6531)

Tampa Armature Works Inc .... C 813 612-2600
Tampa (G-17325)

Taw Payroll Inc .... E 813 621-5661
Tampa (G-17342)

TEam Service Corp New York .... E 410 365-1574
Marco Island (G-8113)

Tripp Electric Motors Inc .... G 561 996-3333
Belle Glade (G-345)

United Electric Motor Inc .... G 813 238-7872
Tampa (G-17391)

V A Electrical Motors Ctr Inc .... G 305 825-3327
Hialeah (G-5403)

ELECTRIC POWER DISTRIBUTION TO CONSUMERS

Tuscola Wind II LLC .... G 561 691-7171
Juno Beach (G-6668)

ELECTRIC SERVICES

Fcs Holdings Inc .... G 352 787-0608
Leesburg (G-7772)

Florida Crystals Corporation .... D 561 655-6303
West Palm Beach (G-18000)

Florida Crystals Corporation .... C 561 515-8080
West Palm Beach (G-18002)

Vasco Winds LLC .... G 561 691-7171
Juno Beach (G-6669)

White Oak Energy Backleverage ..... G 561 691-7171
Juno Beach (G-6670)

Wilton Wind II LLC .... G 561 691-7171
Juno Beach (G-6672)

ELECTRIC WATER HEATERS WHOLESALERS

Niagara Industries Inc .... F 305 876-9010
Miami (G-9619)

ELECTRICAL APPARATUS & EQPT WHOLESALERS

Anuva Manufacturing Svcs Inc .... E 321 821-4900
Melbourne (G-8366)

Apollo Sunguard Systems Inc .... F 941 925-3000
Sarasota (G-15596)

Arco Marine Inc .... E 850 455-5476
Pensacola (G-13444)

Edashop Inc .... F 786 565-9197
Winter Garden (G-18384)

Englander Enterprises Inc .... E 727 461-4755
Clearwater (G-1586)

Gfx Inc .... E 305 499-9789
Miami (G-9209)

Morning Star Industries Inc .... E 800 440-6050
Jensen Beach (G-6657)

Robertson Transformer Co .... G 917 603-8530
Sarasota (G-15797)

US Generator Inc .... G 772 778-0131
Sebastian (G-15907)

ELECTRICAL APPLIANCES, TELEVISIONS & RADIOS WHOLESALERS

AVI-Spl Holdings Inc .... A 866 708-5034
Tampa (G-16619)

AVI-Spl LLC .... B 813 884-7168
Tampa (G-16620)

Flash Sales Inc .... G 954 914-2689
Miami Gardens (G-10258)

La Cuisine Intl Distrs Inc .... E 305 418-0010
Miami (G-9405)

ELECTRICAL CURRENT CARRYING WIRING DEVICES

B G Service Company Inc .... E 561 659-1471
West Palm Beach (G-17933)

Compulink Corporation .... B 727 579-1500
Saint Petersburg (G-15014)

Data Phone Wire & Cable Corp .... F 954 761-7171
Fort Lauderdale (G-3756)

Dayton-Granger Inc .... C 954 463-3451
Fort Lauderdale (G-3758)

Evolution Intrcnnect Systems I .... F 954 217-6223
Davie (G-2409)

Five Oceans Florida Inc .... E 772 221-8188
Palm City (G-13037)

Hytronics Corp .... D 727 535-0413
Clearwater (G-1635)

I C Probotics Inc .... D 407 339-8298
Longwood (G-7902)

Interconnect Cable Tech Corp .... C 352 796-1716
Brooksville (G-1164)

J B Nottingham & Co Inc .... E 386 873-2990
Deland (G-2877)

Kbn Corporation .... G 321 327-9792
Palm Bay (G-12905)

Kleen Wheels Corporation .... G 954 791-9112
Davie (G-2430)

Lextm3 Systems LLC .... F 954 888-1024
Davie (G-2434)

Lightning Specialists Inc .... G 727 938-3560
Odessa (G-11564)

Logus Manufacturing Corp .... E 561 842-3550
West Palm Beach (G-18060)

Panamtech Inc .... G 954 587-3769
Plantation (G-13876)

Paramount Industries Inc ....E 954 781-3755
  Pompano Beach *(G-14118)*
Scan Technology Inc ....G 931 723-0304
  Gainesville *(G-4758)*
Select Engineered Systems Inc ....E 305 823-5410
  Hialeah *(G-5343)*
Superior Electronics Inc ....E 727 733-0700
  Clearwater *(G-1804)*
Technipower LLC ....F 954 346-2442
  Coral Springs *(G-2219)*
United Electronics Corporation ....D 954 888-1024
  Miami *(G-10065)*
Vee Industries Inc ....G 561 732-1083
  Boynton Beach *(G-923)*
Verifone Inc ....C 800 837-4366
  Coral Springs *(G-2224)*

ELECTRICAL DISCHARGE MACHINING, EDM

Phoenix Trinity Mfg Inc ....G 937 619-0172
  Hudson *(G-5785)*
Savvy Associate Inc ....F 954 941-6986
  Pompano Beach *(G-14167)*
Triad Edm Inc ....G 352 489-5336
  Dunnellon *(G-3468)*

ELECTRICAL EQPT & SPLYS

Advance Solder Technology Inc ....F 321 633-4777
  Rockledge *(G-14690)*
Aero-Tel Wire Harness Corp ....E 407 445-1722
  Orlando *(G-11876)*
Aeronautical Systems Engrg Inc ....G 727 375-2520
  Odessa *(G-11534)*
Airo Industries Inc ....G 239 229-5273
  Fort Myers *(G-4159)*
Alectron Inc ....G 786 397-6827
  Doral *(G-3105)*
ARC Electric Inc ....E 954 583-9800
  Davie *(G-2388)*
Asco Power Technologies LP ....G 727 450-2730
  Clearwater *(G-1502)*
Astronics Test Systems Inc ....C 407 381-6062
  Orlando *(G-11929)*
Be Power Tech Inc ....F 954 543-5370
  Deerfield Beach *(G-2676)*
BJ Burns Incorporated ....E 305 572-9500
  Sunrise *(G-16296)*
Canam Electric ....G 305 534-7903
  Miami Beach *(G-10174)*
Carling Technologies Inc ....E 561 745-0405
  Jupiter *(G-6700)*
Clare Instruments (us) Inc ....G 813 886-2775
  Tampa *(G-16711)*
Coastal Electric ....G 239 245-7396
  Fort Myers *(G-4214)*
Commercial Gates and Elc LLC ....F 386 454-2329
  High Springs *(G-5454)*
Custom Mfg & Engrg Inc ....D 727 548-0522
  Pinellas Park *(G-13680)*
Del Air Electric Co ....G 407 531-1173
  Sanford *(G-15303)*
DMC Components Intl LLC ....G 407 478-4064
  Winter Park *(G-18508)*
Eaton Corporation ....G 813 281-8069
  Tampa *(G-16795)*
Exploration Resources Intn Geo ....G 601 747-0726
  Lake Mary *(G-7073)*
Explotrain LLC ....G 850 862-5344
  Fort Walton Beach *(G-4582)*
Famatel USA LLC ....G 754 217-4841
  Medley *(G-8240)*
Geddis Inc ....F 800 844-6792
  Dunedin *(G-3450)*
General Electric Company ....C 203 796-1000
  Jacksonville *(G-6138)*
Guerilla Technologies Inc ....F 772 283-0500
  Palm City *(G-13043)*
Hale Products Inc ....C 352 629-5020
  Ocala *(G-11407)*
Holly Sargent ....G 954 560-6973
  Fort Lauderdale *(G-3867)*
Hooper Corp ....F 954 382-5711
  Davie *(G-2424)*
Hose-Mccann Telephone Co Inc ....E 954 429-1110
  Deerfield Beach *(G-2741)*
Interrail Power Inc ....F 904 268-6411
  Jacksonville *(G-6206)*
Inviro Tek Inc ....G 215 499-1209
  Orlando *(G-12256)*
Invision Industries Inc ....G 407 451-8353
  Orlando *(G-12259)*

J B Nottingham & Co Inc ....E 386 873-2990
  Deland *(G-2877)*
L3harris Technologies Inc ....A 321 309-7848
  Melbourne *(G-8456)*
Laser Interceptor Usa LLC ....G 352 688-0708
  Brooksville *(G-1170)*
Laserstar Technologies Corp ....G 407 248-1142
  Orlando *(G-12314)*
Lightworks Inc ....G 305 456-3520
  Miami *(G-9459)*
Load Banks Direct LLC ....F 859 554-2522
  Venice *(G-17705)*
Lockheed Martin Corporation ....A 407 306-1000
  Orlando *(G-12340)*
Lui Technical Services Inc ....G 954 803-7610
  Sunrise *(G-16338)*
M Micro Technologies Inc ....B 954 973-6166
  Pompano Beach *(G-14083)*
Marine Digital Integrators LLC ....E 772 210-2403
  Stuart *(G-16183)*
Microsemi Corp ....F 407 965-5687
  Lake Mary *(G-7094)*
Nuenergy Technologies Corp ....G 866 895-6838
  Clearwater *(G-1721)*
Pfi Inc ....G 407 822-4499
  Longwood *(G-7936)*
Probotix ....G 844 472-9262
  Fort Walton Beach *(G-4603)*
Salco Electric Supply LLC ....F 305 777-0200
  Coral Gables *(G-2106)*
Semilab USA LLC ....E 813 977-2244
  Temple Terrace *(G-17545)*
Sibex Inc ....C 727 726-4343
  Crystal River *(G-2280)*
Superior Metal Fabricators Inc ....E 407 295-5772
  Orlando *(G-12638)*
Surf Lighting Inc ....F 305 888-7851
  Hialeah *(G-5375)*
Symetrics Industries LLC ....C 321 254-1500
  Melbourne *(G-8543)*
T V Trac Ltd 516 371-1111
  Boynton Beach *(G-917)*
Technipower LLC ....F 954 346-2442
  Coral Springs *(G-2219)*
Top Sales Co ....G 561 852-4311
  Boca Raton *(G-719)*
United Space Coast Cables Inc ....E 321 952-1040
  West Melbourne *(G-17902)*
Vinland Corporation ....E 954 475-9093
  Plantation *(G-13900)*
Vos Systems LLC ....G 352 317-2954
  Gainesville *(G-4784)*
Walker Electric Inc ....G 941 729-5015
  Dunnellon *(G-3469)*

ELECTRICAL EQPT FOR ENGINES

American Auto / Mar Wirg Inc ....G 954 782-0193
  Pompano Beach *(G-13923)*
Arco Marine Inc ....E 850 455-5476
  Pensacola *(G-13444)*
B G Service Company Inc ....E 561 659-1471
  West Palm Beach *(G-17933)*
Battery Power Solutions Inc ....G 727 446-8400
  Clearwater *(G-1511)*
Bobcat of Wiregrass Inc ....F 334 792-5121
  Panama City Beach *(G-13327)*
Competition Specialties Inc ....F 386 776-1476
  Mc Alpin *(G-8188)*
Dynalco Controls Corporation ....E 323 589-6181
  Fort Lauderdale *(G-3775)*
Ibtm Engineering Inc ....G 239 246-1876
  Sanibel *(G-15415)*
L & L Automotive Electric Inc ....G 631 471-5230
  Melbourne *(G-8452)*
Reynoso & Associates Inc ....G 954 360-0601
  Deerfield Beach *(G-2800)*
Tradewinds Power Corp ....F 863 382-2166
  Sebring *(G-15948)*

ELECTRICAL EQPT REPAIR & MAINTENANCE

Delta Regis Tools Inc ....E 772 465-4302
  Fort Pierce *(G-4480)*
Electro Mechanical South Inc ....E 941 342-9111
  Bradenton *(G-974)*
GE Medcal Systems Info Tech In ....D 561 575-5000
  Jupiter *(G-6734)*
Megin Us LLC ....G 954 341-2965
  Coral Springs *(G-2182)*

Money Tree Atm Mfg LLC ....G 850 244-5543
  Fort Walton Beach *(G-4597)*
Virginia Electronic & Ltg Corp ....G 904 230-2840
  Green Cove Springs *(G-4842)*

ELECTRICAL EQPT REPAIR SVCS

3d Perception Inc ....F 321 235-7999
  Orlando *(G-11850)*
Automted Lgic Corp Kennesaw GA ....F 877 866-1226
  Orlando *(G-11935)*
Megawattage LLC ....F 954 328-0232
  Fort Lauderdale *(G-3937)*
Sanbur Inc ....F 941 371-7446
  Sarasota *(G-15807)*

ELECTRICAL EQPT: Automotive, NEC

Advanced Automotive Designs ....G 561 499-8812
  Delray Beach *(G-2925)*
D & L Auto & Marine Supplies ....G 305 593-0560
  Doral *(G-3181)*
Euromotion Inc ....G 954 612-0354
  Delray Beach *(G-2960)*

ELECTRICAL EQPT: Household

David Chittum ....G 386 754-6127
  Saint Petersburg *(G-15020)*
Portalp Usa Inc ....F 800 474-3667
  Naples *(G-10865)*

ELECTRICAL GOODS, WHOLESALE: Answering Machines, Telephone

Tier5 Technical Services ....G 904 435-3484
  Jacksonville *(G-6551)*

ELECTRICAL GOODS, WHOLESALE: Boxes & Fittings

BJ Burns Incorporated ....E 305 572-9500
  Sunrise *(G-16296)*
Tic Light Electrical Corp ....G 305 712-3499
  Miami *(G-10008)*

ELECTRICAL GOODS, WHOLESALE: Cable Conduit

Electriduct Inc ....E 954 867-9100
  Pompano Beach *(G-14007)*
Quality Cable Contractors Inc ....E 407 246-0606
  Orlando *(G-12520)*

ELECTRICAL GOODS, WHOLESALE: Capacitors

Aero Uno Llc ....G 561 767-5597
  Coconut Creek *(G-1975)*

ELECTRICAL GOODS, WHOLESALE: Connectors

Kai Limited ....C 954 957-8586
  Fort Lauderdale *(G-3899)*

ELECTRICAL GOODS, WHOLESALE: Electrical Appliances, Major

Quality Custom Cabinet Design ....G 352 728-4292
  Leesburg *(G-7790)*
US Generator Inc ....G 772 778-0131
  Sebastian *(G-15907)*

ELECTRICAL GOODS, WHOLESALE: Electronic Parts

Compulink Corporation ....B 727 579-1500
  Saint Petersburg *(G-15014)*
Next Generation Home Pdts Inc ....G 727 834-9400
  Tampa *(G-17109)*

ELECTRICAL GOODS, WHOLESALE: Fire Alarm Systems

AB Fire Sprinklers LLC ....G 954 973-8054
  Pompano Beach *(G-13905)*

Employee Codes: A=Over 500 employees, B=251-500
C=101-250, D=51-100, E=20-50, F=10-19, G=4-9

2022 Harris Florida
Manufacturers Directory

1195

PRODUCT

ELECTRICAL GOODS, WHOLESALE: Fittings & Construction Mat

Citel America Inc ....F 954 430-6310
Miramar *(G-10480)*

ELECTRICAL GOODS, WHOLESALE: Flashlights

Emergency Vehicle Sup Co LLC ....E 954 428-5201
Pompano Beach *(G-14009)*

ELECTRICAL GOODS, WHOLESALE: Generators

Armstrong Power Systems LLC ....G 305 470-0058
Miami *(G-8750)*

ELECTRICAL GOODS, WHOLESALE: Light Bulbs & Related Splys

Roth Southeast Lighting LLC ....G 954 423-6640
Fort Lauderdale *(G-4029)*

ELECTRICAL GOODS, WHOLESALE: Lighting Fixtures, Comm & Indl

Lumilum LLC ....F 305 233-2844
Miami *(G-9484)*
Solar Electric Power Company ....F 772 220-6615
Stuart *(G-16224)*

ELECTRICAL GOODS, WHOLESALE: Lugs & Connectors

Arrowhead Global LLC ....F 727 497-7340
Clearwater *(G-1499)*

ELECTRICAL GOODS, WHOLESALE: Mobile telephone Eqpt

Sky Phone LLC ....F 305 531-5218
Miami Beach *(G-10228)*

ELECTRICAL GOODS, WHOLESALE: Motor Ctrls, Starters & Relays

T R S ....D 407 298-5490
Orlando *(G-12644)*

ELECTRICAL GOODS, WHOLESALE: Motors

Biscayne Electric Motor & Pump ....G 305 681-8171
Miami *(G-8834)*
Dade Pump & Supply Co ....G 305 235-5000
Miami *(G-8996)*
Electrcal Systems Cmmnications ....G 813 248-4275
Tampa *(G-16799)*
Florida Elc Mtr Co Miami Inc ....E 305 759-3835
Miami *(G-9154)*
Indian River Armature Inc ....G 772 461-2067
Fort Pierce *(G-4497)*
M & W Electric Motors Inc ....G 850 433-0400
Pensacola *(G-13541)*
Robert E Weissenborn Sr ....G 239 262-1771
Naples *(G-10879)*
Tampa Armature Works Inc ....D 904 757-7790
Jacksonville *(G-6531)*
Tampa Armature Works Inc ....C 813 612-2600
Tampa *(G-17325)*
TEam Service Corp New York ....E 410 365-1574
Marco Island *(G-8113)*
United Electric Motor Inc ....G 813 238-7872
Tampa *(G-17391)*

ELECTRICAL GOODS, WHOLESALE: Panelboards

Champion Controls Inc ....E 954 318-3090
Fort Lauderdale *(G-3723)*

ELECTRICAL GOODS, WHOLESALE: Radio & TV Or TV Eqpt & Parts

Da Vinci Systems Inc ....E 954 688-5600
Coral Springs *(G-2146)*
Dayton Industrial Corporation ....G 941 351-4454
Sarasota *(G-15651)*

ELECTRICAL GOODS, WHOLESALE: Security Control Eqpt & Systems

Edgewater Technologies Inc ....F 954 565-9898
Fort Lauderdale *(G-3785)*
Salco Industries Inc ....F 941 377-7717
Sarasota *(G-15806)*
Senelco Iberia Inc ....A 561 912-6000
Deerfield Beach *(G-2807)*

ELECTRICAL GOODS, WHOLESALE: Semiconductor Devices

Boca Semiconductor Corporation ....E 561 226-8500
Boca Raton *(G-438)*
V and N Advanced Auto Sys LLC ....G 321 504-6440
Rockledge *(G-14753)*

ELECTRICAL GOODS, WHOLESALE: Switchboards

Axon Circuit Inc ....F 407 265-7980
Longwood *(G-7873)*

ELECTRICAL GOODS, WHOLESALE: Switchgear

Resa Pwr Slutions Plant Cy LLC ....F 813 752-6550
Plant City *(G-13799)*

ELECTRICAL GOODS, WHOLESALE: Telephone & Telegraphic Eqpt

Prime Meridian Trading Corp ....G 954 727-2152
Sunrise *(G-16355)*

ELECTRICAL GOODS, WHOLESALE: Telephone Eqpt

Allied Telecommunications Ltd ....F 954 370-9900
Plantation *(G-13824)*
Cyipcom Inc ....G 954 727-2500
Oakland Park *(G-11255)*

ELECTRICAL GOODS, WHOLESALE: Transformer & Transmission Eqpt

Man-Trans LLC ....F 850 222-6993
Tallahassee *(G-16474)*

ELECTRICAL GOODS, WHOLESALE: Transformers

Exxelia Usa Inc ....E 407 695-6562
Longwood *(G-7893)*

ELECTRICAL GOODS, WHOLESALE: Tubes, Rcvg & Txmtg Or Indl

Renco Usa Inc ....F 321 637-1000
Miami *(G-9793)*

ELECTRICAL GOODS, WHOLESALE: Video Eqpt

Interntnal Srvillance Tech Inc ....E 954 574-1100
Deerfield Beach *(G-2742)*

ELECTRICAL GOODS, WHOLESALE: Wire & Cable

American Wire Group LLC ....F 954 455-3050
Aventura *(G-252)*
Commski LLC ....G 813 501-0111
Spring Hill *(G-16068)*
Stampco Inc ....F 904 737-6144
Jacksonville *(G-6503)*

ELECTRICAL GOODS, WHOLESALE: Wire/Cable, Telephone/Telegraph

Managed Data Assoc Inc ....G 386 449-8419
Palm Coast *(G-13082)*

ELECTRICAL INDL APPARATUS, NEC

Burlakoff Manufacturing Co ....G 972 889-2502
Ocala *(G-11340)*
First Look Inc ....G 954 240-0530
Fort Lauderdale *(G-3818)*

Kbn Corporation ....G 321 327-9792
Palm Bay *(G-12905)*

ELECTRICAL MEASURING INSTRUMENT REPAIR & CALIBRATION SVCS

International Ozone Svcs LLC ....G 352 978-9785
Mount Dora *(G-10604)*

ELECTRICAL SPLYS

Advance Controls Inc ....F 941 746-3221
Bradenton *(G-933)*
Eaton Corporation ....G 813 281-8069
Tampa *(G-16795)*
Pressure Systems Innvtions LLC ....F 561 249-2708
West Palm Beach *(G-18128)*
Ryan Scientific LLC ....F 904 284-6025
Green Cove Springs *(G-4835)*

ELECTRICAL SUPPLIES: Porcelain

Rock Intl Distributors Inc ....E 305 513-3314
Miami *(G-9815)*

ELECTROMEDICAL EQPT

Actigraph LLC ....G 850 332-7900
Pensacola *(G-13433)*
Bio-Logic Systems Corp ....D 847 949-0456
Orlando *(G-11951)*
Biofuse Medical Tech Inc ....F 877 466-2434
Melbourne *(G-8378)*
Critical Disposables Inc ....E 407 330-1154
Sanford *(G-15297)*
Diapulse Corporation America ....G 516 466-3030
Hollywood *(G-5566)*
Evren Technologies Inc ....G 352 494-0950
Newberry *(G-11020)*
GAp Imaging Intl LLC ....G 407 268-9746
Lake Mary *(G-7081)*
Geddis Inc ....F 800 844-6792
Dunedin *(G-3450)*
Invivo Corporation ....E 352 336-0010
Gainesville *(G-4714)*
Iris International Inc ....D 818 709-1244
Miami *(G-9338)*
Lasersight Incorporated ....G 407 678-9900
Orlando *(G-12311)*
Lasersight Technologies Inc ....F 407 678-9900
Orlando *(G-12312)*
Natus Medical Incorporated ....E 321 235-8213
Orlando *(G-12407)*
Natus Medical Incorporated ....F 847 949-5200
Orlando *(G-12408)*
Somatics LLC ....G 847 234-6761
Venice *(G-17716)*
Stimwave LLC ....F 800 965-5134
Pompano Beach *(G-14199)*
Twinstar Optics & Coatings Inc ....F 727 847-2300
Port Richey *(G-14381)*

ELECTROMETALLURGICAL PRDTS

Bayside Small Cap Senior Loan ....G 305 381-4100
Miami *(G-8805)*
Chance Aluminum Corp ....F 407 789-1606
Orlando *(G-12002)*

ELECTRON BEAM: Cutting, Forming, Welding

Advanced Metal Works Inc ....F 727 449-9353
Clearwater *(G-1476)*

ELECTRON TUBES

Advanced Manufacturing Inc ....E 727 573-3300
Saint Petersburg *(G-14954)*
Cathodic Prtection Tech of Fla ....G 321 799-0046
Cocoa Beach *(G-1966)*
Citel America Inc ....F 954 430-6310
Miramar *(G-10480)*
L3harris Technologies Inc ....C 321 727-9100
Melbourne *(G-8459)*
Lextm3 Systems LLC ....F 954 888-1024
Davie *(G-2434)*
Video Display Corporation ....D 321 784-4427
Cocoa *(G-1963)*

2022 Harris Florida
Manufacturers Directory

(G-0000) Company's Geographic Section entry number

ELECTRON TUBES: Cathode Ray

Ecoatm LLC ....D 858 766-7250
Clearwater *(G-1576)*

Passur Aerospace Inc ....G 631 589-6800
Orlando *(G-12470)*

Video Display Corporation ....E 800 241-5005
Cocoa *(G-1962)*

ELECTRONIC COMPONENTS

2204 Avenue X LLC ....G 407 619-1410
Vero Beach *(G-17730)*

Arcco Inc ....G 954 564-0827
Oakland Park *(G-11239)*

J and A Maintenance ....G 754 234-0708
Sunrise *(G-16327)*

Leeward Tech ....G 305 215-4526
Homestead *(G-5727)*

Phil Lau ....F 813 631-8643
Tampa *(G-17162)*

Pro Fuse ....G 305 982-8457
Miami *(G-9747)*

Trademark Components Inc ....G 813 948-2233
Lutz *(G-8018)*

Unno Tekno LLC ....G 786 536-5992
Doral *(G-3408)*

Workforce Audio Inc ....E 866 360-6416
Tampa *(G-17435)*

ELECTRONIC DETECTION SYSTEMS: Aeronautical

Moog Inc ....F 321 435-8722
Orlando *(G-12389)*

ELECTRONIC DEVICES: Solid State, NEC

Aero Uno Llc ....G 561 767-5597
Coconut Creek *(G-1975)*

Gen-Prodics Inc ....G 772 221-8464
Palm City *(G-13041)*

JAs Business Solutions Inc ......E 954 975-0025
Pompano Beach *(G-14065)*

ELECTRONIC EQPT REPAIR SVCS

Industry Standard Technology ...G 941 355-2100
Sarasota *(G-15499)*

Ra Co AMO Inc ....F 561 626-7232
Palm Beach Gardens *(G-13004)*

ELECTRONIC LOADS & POWER SPLYS

Atlas Marine Systems Inc ....F 954 735-6767
Fort Lauderdale *(G-3664)*

Edge Power Solutions Inc ....F 321 499-1919
Melbourne *(G-8416)*

OHM Americas LLC ....F 800 467-7275
Fort Lauderdale *(G-3966)*

Powerficient LLC ....E 800 320-2535
Fort Lauderdale *(G-3990)*

ELECTRONIC PARTS & EQPT WHOLESALERS

Argos Global Partner Svcs LLC ...G 305 365-1096
Key Biscayne *(G-6833)*

AVw Inc ....E 954 972-3338
Margate *(G-8122)*

Cisco Systems Inc ....F 305 718-2600
Doral *(G-3163)*

Component General Inc ....E 727 376-6655
Odessa *(G-11544)*

Englander Enterprises Inc ....E 727 461-4755
Clearwater *(G-1586)*

Entech Controls Corp ....G 954 613-2971
Miami *(G-9100)*

Hensoldt Avionics Usa LLC ....G 941 306-1328
Sarasota *(G-15700)*

Interconnect Cable Tech Corp ....C 352 796-1716
Brooksville *(G-1164)*

Lexmark International Inc ....F 305 467-2200
Miami *(G-9454)*

Lift Aerospace Corp ....E 305 851-5237
Miami *(G-9457)*

Logus Manufacturing Corp ....F 561 842-3550
West Palm Beach *(G-18060)*

Marware Inc ....E 954 927-6031
Dania Beach *(G-2354)*

Mat-Vac Technology Inc ....F 386 238-7017
Daytona Beach *(G-2573)*

Minuteman Industries Inc ....G 813 248-1776
Tampa *(G-17075)*

Nemal Electronics Intl Inc ....E 305 899-0900
North Miami *(G-11114)*

Phototelesis LP ....F 321 254-1500
Melbourne *(G-8495)*

Sagrad Inc ....F 321 726-9400
Melbourne *(G-8513)*

Superior Electronics ....G 941 355-9500
Sarasota *(G-15565)*

Sv Microwave Inc ....C 561 840-1800
West Palm Beach *(G-18172)*

Vc Displays Inc ....G 352 796-0060
Brooksville *(G-1218)*

Voxx International Corporation ....B 800 645-7750
Orlando *(G-12706)*

ELECTRONIC SECRETARIES

Omnisys LLC ....E 800 325-2017
Sarasota *(G-15770)*

ELECTRONIC SHOPPING

Flavcity Corp ....G 413 221-0041
Boynton Beach *(G-867)*

Ischa Products LLC ....F 305 609-8244
Homestead *(G-5719)*

Youmop LLC ....G 248 343-2013
Boynton Beach *(G-929)*

ELECTRONIC TRAINING DEVICES

Cae USA Inc ....A 813 885-7481
Tampa *(G-16672)*

Cubic Simulation Systems Inc ....C 407 641-2037
Orlando *(G-12063)*

Environmental Tectonics Corp ...F 407 282-3378
Orlando *(G-12132)*

Nida Corporation ....G 321 727-2265
Melbourne *(G-8480)*

Nkc Electronics Inc ....G 954 471-8368
Weston *(G-18273)*

Pulau International Corp ....F 407 380-9191
Orlando *(G-12517)*

ELECTROPLATING & PLATING SVC

Biomedtech Laboratories Inc .....G 813 558-2000
Tampa *(G-16644)*

Freedom Metal Finishing Inc ......E 727 573-2464
Clearwater *(G-1607)*

ELEMENTARY & SECONDARY MILITARY ACADEMIES

United Ntons Space Crps Mltary ...G 702 373-2351
Ponce De Leon *(G-14251)*

ELEMENTARY & SECONDARY SCHOOLS, PUBLIC

Brevard Achievement Center Inc ...B 321 632-8610
Rockledge *(G-14693)*

ELEMENTARY & SECONDARY SCHOOLS, SPECIAL EDUCATION

Lincoln-Marti Cmnty Agcy Inc ....D 305 643-4888
Miami *(G-9462)*

ELEVATORS & EQPT

Concept Elevator Group LLC ......E 786 845-8955
Miami *(G-8954)*

Emac Inc ....E 850 526-4111
Marianna *(G-8164)*

Gunderlin Ltd Inc ....D 305 696-6071
Hialeah *(G-5180)*

International Mch Works Inc ....F 305 635-3585
Miami *(G-9328)*

Kohtler Elevator Inds Inc ....G 305 687-7037
Opa Locka *(G-11761)*

Otis Elevator Company ....B 561 618-4831
West Palm Beach *(G-18100)*

Otis Elevator Company ....A 561 623-4594
Palm Beach Gardens *(G-12996)*

Otis Elevator Company ....C 305 816-5740
Fort Lauderdale *(G-3970)*

Precision Lift Industries LLC ......G 877 770-5862
Pensacola *(G-13582)*

ELEVATORS: Automobile

Madiera Service Group Inc ....G 727 323-3800
Largo *(G-7637)*

ELEVATORS: Stair, Motor Powered

A1 Elevators LLC ....G 954 773-4443
North Lauderdale *(G-11074)*

Beautiful Homes Inc ....G 800 403-1480
Spring Hill *(G-16065)*

EMBALMING FLUID

Hepburn Industries Inc ....G 305 757-6688
Miami *(G-9275)*

EMBLEMS: Embroidered

Atticus Screen Printing T ....G 407 365-9911
Oviedo *(G-12807)*

Bakers Sports Inc ....E 904 388-8126
Jacksonville *(G-5921)*

Blackwell Family Corporation .....G 941 639-0200
Punta Gorda *(G-14499)*

Clothesline Inc ....E 850 877-9171
Tallahassee *(G-16425)*

Florida Embroidered Patch & .....F 561 748-9356
Jupiter *(G-6731)*

Ssh Holding Inc ....D 678 942-1800
Seminole *(G-15988)*

STS Apparel Corp ....F 305 628-4000
Hialeah *(G-5366)*

Wings Things Monogramming Inc ...F 850 455-3081
Pensacola *(G-13626)*

World Emblem International Inc ...C 305 899-9006
Hollywood *(G-5685)*

EMBOSSING SVC: Paper

Elton Foil Embossing Inc ....G 904 399-1510
Jacksonville *(G-6070)*

H A Friend & Company Inc ....E 847 746-1248
Boynton Beach *(G-876)*

Miami Quality Graphics Inc ....E 305 634-9506
Miami *(G-9556)*

Tektrol Inc ....F 305 305-0937
Doral *(G-3395)*

EMBROIDERING & ART NEEDLEWORK FOR THE TRADE

A2z Uniforms Inc ....G 941 254-3194
Sarasota *(G-15583)*

Active Line Corp ....F 786 766-1944
Hialeah *(G-5026)*

American S-Shore Plting Sttchi ...G 305 978-9934
Hialeah *(G-5050)*

Brooklyn Stitch Inc ....G 786 280-1730
Miami *(G-8856)*

Capsmith Inc ....E 407 328-7660
Sanford *(G-15277)*

CC Sportswear Inc ....G 941 351-4205
Sarasota *(G-15452)*

Creative Shirts Intl Inc ....F 954 351-0909
Oakland Park *(G-11253)*

Designers Top Shop Inc ....G 863 453-3855
Avon Park *(G-279)*

DP EMB & Screen Prints Inc ......F 954 245-5902
Sunrise *(G-16314)*

Embroidery Chimp LLC ....F 561 775-9195
Palm Beach Gardens *(G-12967)*

Embroidery USA Inc ....G 305 477-9973
Miami *(G-9092)*

Embroidmecom Inc ....E 813 878-2400
Tampa *(G-16806)*

Fully Promoted ....G 561 615-8655
West Palm Beach *(G-18014)*

Gravity Ink & Stitch Inc ....G 954 558-0119
Sunrise *(G-16322)*

Hitmaster Graphics LLC ....F 267 269-8220
Thonotosassa *(G-17562)*

Jr Embroidery Inc ....G 305 253-6968
Miami *(G-9376)*

Lifes A Stitch ....G 386 385-3079
Palatka *(G-12873)*

Mid-Florida Sportswear LLC ....E 386 258-5632
Daytona Beach *(G-2575)*

Overstitch Inc ....G 954 505-8567
Hollywood *(G-5636)*

Paradise Cstm Screening & EMB ...E 954 566-9096
Davie *(G-2453)*

PRODUCT

Pei Shores Inc ....G..... 407 523-2899
Orlando (G-12477)

Preferred Stitching Inc ....G..... 813 737-3996
Lithia (G-7837)

Print Art Screen Printing Inc ....F 386 258-5186
Daytona Beach (G-2585)

Prodigy Customs ....G..... 407 832-1752
Altamonte Springs (G-66)

Reliable Custom Imprints Corp ....G..... 407 834-0571
Longwood (G-7942)

Rhinestntransfersdirectcom Inc ......G..... 484 254-6410
Orlando (G-12550)

Say What Screen Prtg & EMB Inc ....F 941 745-5822
Bradenton (G-1042)

Stitch By Stitch ....G..... 305 979-2275
Hialeah (G-5363)

Stitch Ink Inc ....G..... 954 203-0868
Lauderdale Lakes (G-7720)

Stitched National Harbor LLC ....G..... 786 483-8740
Miami (G-9952)

Stitchez LLC ....G..... 904 221-9148
Jacksonville (G-6509)

Stitching Heart LLC ....G..... 904 379-7990
Jacksonville (G-6510)

T-Wiz Prtg & EMB Designs LLC ....E 954 280-8949
Fort Lauderdale (G-4083)

Turin Em Inc ....F 305 825-2004
Hialeah (G-5385)

Tys Variety Co ....G..... 813 643-1515
Tampa (G-17380)

Wearable Nalia LLC ....G..... 561 629-5804
Haverhill (G-5004)

Workwear Outfitters LLC ....E 813 671-2986
Riverview (G-14583)

EMBROIDERING SVC

Above LLC ....F 850 469-9028
Pensacola (G-13431)

Acme Cap & Clothing Inc ....G..... 407 321-5100
Sanford (G-15258)

Apparel Expressions LLC ....G..... 850 314-0100
Fort Walton Beach (G-4561)

Apparel Printers ....G..... 352 463-8850
Alachua (G-4)

Atlas Embroidery LLC ....D 954 625-2411
Fort Lauderdale (G-3663)

Bartman Enterprises Inc ....G..... 321 259-4898
Melbourne (G-8375)

Bc Sales ....F 941 708-2727
Bradenton (G-944)

Ben Kaufman Sales Co Inc ....E 305 688-2144
Medley (G-8208)

Blue Ocean Press Inc ....G..... 954 973-1819
Fort Lauderdale (G-3693)

Briesa Inc ....G..... 407 830-5307
Longwood (G-7877)

Caribbean Emblems ....G..... 305 593-8183
Doral (G-3154)

Cotton Pickin Shirts Plus ....G..... 850 435-3133
Pensacola (G-13478)

Creative Images Embroidery ....G..... 904 730-5660
Jacksonville (G-6013)

Dapp Embroidery Inc ....G..... 407 260-1600
Longwood (G-7887)

Eagle Athletic Wear Inc ....F 727 937-6147
Tarpon Springs (G-17469)

Embroidery Plus ....G..... 561 439-8943
Lantana (G-7512)

Embroservice LLC ....F 305 267-2323
Miami (G-9093)

G J Embroidery Inc ....G..... 407 284-8036
Orlando (G-12180)

G6 Embroidery LLC ....G..... 904 729-1191
Jacksonville (G-6126)

Gle Holdings Inc ....G..... 305 295-7585
Key West (G-6865)

Gns Embroidery ....G..... 850 775-1147
Panama City Beach (G-13331)

Good Catch Inc ....G..... 305 757-7700
Miami (G-9227)

Hamburg House Inc ....F 305 557-9913
Hialeah (G-5182)

Island Designs Outlet Inc ....E 813 855-0020
Tampa (G-16954)

Logoxpress Inc ....G..... 954 973-4994
Pompano Beach (G-14081)

Palm Beach Embroidery USA Inc ....G..... 561 506-6307
West Palm Beach (G-4078)

Paradise EMB & Silkscreen Inc ....G..... 305 595-6441
Miami (G-9693)

Promowear ....G..... 561 372-0505
Parkland (G-13350)

R Y D Enterprises Inc ....E 305 655-1045
Miami (G-9773)

Ray Graphics Inc ....G..... 863 325-0911
Winter Haven (G-18464)

Royal Headwear & EMB Inc ....G..... 305 889-8480
Medley (G-8316)

S S Designs Inc ....D 863 965-2576
Winter Haven (G-18465)

Sharp Marketing LLC ....G..... 954 565-2711
Oakland Park (G-11293)

Southern International Svcs ....F 954 349-7321
Miami (G-9929)

Stitch Logo Inc ....G..... 727 446-0228
Clearwater (G-1797)

Stitching Around Inc ....G..... 305 665-1600
Miami (G-9953)

Thread Graphics Embroidery ....G..... 407 688-7026
Deland (G-2911)

Uniform Nametape Company Inc .....G..... 813 839-6737
Tampa (G-17388)

VSF Corp ....E 305 769-2202
Hialeah (G-5416)

Vyp Services LLC ....G..... 305 593-8183
Doral (G-3417)

Were In Stitches ....G..... 813 264-4804
Tampa (G-17426)

Worldwide Embroidery Inc ....F 386 761-2688
Port Orange (G-14353)

Young Guns Embroidery Inc ....G..... 813 814-9172
Oldsmar (G-11708)

EMBROIDERING SVC: Schiffli Machine

Bnj Noble Inc ....F 954 987-1040
Davie (G-2392)

Gattas Corp ....G..... 727 733-5886
Dunedin (G-3449)

Pantograms Mfg Co Inc ....E 813 839-5697
Tampa (G-17145)

Royal Headwear & EMB Inc ....G..... 305 889-8480
Medley (G-8316)

Screenprint Plus Inc ....D 239 549-7284
Cape Coral (G-1382)

EMBROIDERY ADVERTISING SVCS

Acm Screen Printing Inc ....G..... 305 547-1552
Miami (G-8646)

Briesa Inc ....G..... 407 830-5307
Longwood (G-7877)

Dowling Graphics Inc ....E 727 573-5997
Clearwater (G-1570)

Hes Products Inc ....G..... 407 834-0741
Ormond Beach (G-12769)

Kikisteescom LLC ....E 888 620-4110
Sunrise (G-16333)

Koala Tee Inc (usa) ....E 941 954-7700
Sarasota (G-15720)

Lucky Dog Screen Printing Mg ....G..... 407 629-8838
Winter Park (G-18520)

Shipping + Business Svcs LLC ....G..... 904 240-1737
Jacksonville (G-6465)

Signs Unlimited - Sea Inc ....G..... 352 732-7341
Ocala (G-11494)

EMERGENCY ALARMS

Advantor Systems Corporation ....C..... 407 859-3350
Orlando (G-11874)

Asp Alarm & Elec Sups Inc ....G..... 305 556-9047
Hialeah (G-5062)

Heritage Medcall LLC ....F 813 221-1000
Tampa (G-16915)

Med Alert Response Inc ....G..... 407 730-3571
Orlando (G-12369)

Medattend LLC ....F 561 465-2735
Boca Raton (G-590)

Morganelli & Associates Inc ....G..... 386 738-3669
Deland (G-2887)

Old Heritage Medcall Inc ....F 813 221-1000
Tampa (G-17118)

Potter Roemer LLC ....F 786 845-0842
Doral (G-3331)

Prime Meridian Trading Corp ....G..... 954 727-2152
Sunrise (G-16355)

Rossam Industries Inc ....E 305 493-5111
Fort Lauderdale (G-4027)

Simplex Time Recorder Co ....G..... 561 988-7200
Boca Raton (G-676)

Spec-TEC Manufacturing Inc ....G..... 954 749-4204
Sunrise (G-16370)

Zom Monterra LP ....F 407 644-6300
Orlando (G-12737)

Zumro Manufacturing Inc ....E 954 782-7779
Pompano Beach (G-14247)

EMERGENCY SHELTERS

Air Shelters USA LLC ....E 215 957-6128
Pompano Beach (G-13913)

EMPLOYMENT AGENCY SVCS

Windermere Nannies LLC ....F 407 782-2057
Windermere (G-18371)

ENAMELS

Caribbean Paint Company Inc ....G..... 305 594-4500
Doral (G-3155)

ENCLOSURES: Electronic

Edwin B Stimpson Company Inc ....C..... 954 946-3500
Pompano Beach (G-14006)

ENCLOSURES: Screen

ABC Screen Masters Inc ....G..... 239 772-7336
Cape Coral (G-1295)

Affordble Screen Enclosure LLC ......G..... 561 900-8868
Delray Beach (G-2927)

Allstar Screen Enclosures & St ....G..... 954 266-9757
Davie (G-2382)

Aluma TEC Aluminun ....G..... 352 732-7362
Ocala (G-11319)

Alumicenter Inc ....G..... 954 674-2631
Miramar (G-10467)

Aluminum Creations ....F 386 451-0113
De Leon Springs (G-2622)

Brian Schatzman ....G..... 239 398-1798
Bonita Springs (G-786)

British Boys & Associates ....G..... 305 278-1790
Miami (G-8853)

Cage Works ....G..... 239 707-0847
Naples (G-10702)

Charles Screening & Alum LLC ....G..... 239 369-0551
Lehigh Acres (G-7807)

Clupper LLC ....F 386 956-6396
Deltona (G-3042)

Coastal Craftsmen Aluminum Inc .....E 727 868-8802
Hudson (G-5767)

Coastal Screen & Rail LLC ....G..... 321 917-4605
Delray Beach (G-2948)

Custom Built Screen Enclosures ......F 239 242-0224
Cape Coral (G-1329)

Design Pro Screens Inc ....G..... 407 831-6541
Longwood (G-7888)

Df Multi Services LLC ....G..... 407 683-2223
Orlando (G-12090)

Gardners Screen Enclosures ....F 813 843-8527
Seffner (G-15960)

General Metals & Plastics Inc ....G..... 904 354-8224
Jacksonville (G-6139)

Harper Screen Enclosures LLC ....G..... 813 417-5937
Riverview (G-14565)

Housmans Alum & Screening Inc .....F 321 255-2778
Melbourne (G-8438)

Hydes Screening Inc ....G..... 954 345-6743
Coral Springs (G-2165)

J D Aluminum ....G..... 239 543-3558
Fort Myers (G-4295)

Jbr Exteriors Inc ....G..... 772 873-0600
Port Saint Lucie (G-14418)

Jennifer Yoder Sung ....G..... 352 748-6655
Wildwood (G-18314)

K C Screen ....G..... 407 977-9636
Oviedo (G-12831)

Knox Aluminum Inc ....F 813 645-3529
Ruskin (G-14780)

Mark Housman Screen RPS Inc ....E 321 255-2778
Melbourne (G-8469)

New World Enclosures Inc ....F 904 334-4752
Green Cove Springs (G-4831)

Pace Enclosures Inc ....E 239 275-3818
Fort Myers (G-4354)

Pioneer Development Entps Inc ....F 239 592-0001
Naples (G-10859)

Quality Rescreening ....G..... 941 625-9765
Fort Myers (G-4374)

Quality Screen Enclosure LLC ....G..... 954 226-1980
Hollywood (G-5649)

R Townsend Rescreens Inc ....G...... 239 244-4759
Punta Gorda (G-14524)
Royal Screen Enclosures Inc............F...... 407 970-0864
Groveland (G-4869)
Screen Enclosure Services Inc............G...... 239 334-6528
Fort Myers (G-4394)
Screenco North Inc ....E...... 561 840-3300
Palm Beach Gardens (G-13007)
Tdse Inc ....E...... 352 399-6413
Wildwood (G-18324)

ENERGY MEASUREMENT EQPT

MP&tr Corp ....G...... 305 456-9292
Miami (G-9594)

ENGINE PARTS & ACCESS: Internal Combustion

Advanced Engine Tech LLC ....G...... 727 744-2935
Clearwater (G-1475)
Diesel Pro Power Inc ....F...... 305 545-5588
Miami (G-9031)

ENGINE REBUILDING: Diesel

Diesel Machinery Intl USA............G...... 305 551-4424
Miami (G-9030)
Gfs Corp ....E...... 954 693-9657
Weston (G-18247)
National Diesel Engine Inc ....F...... 810 516-6855
Tampa (G-17101)

ENGINE REBUILDING: Gas

360 Energy Solutions LLC ....E...... 786 348-2156
Miami (G-8609)
Engine Lab of Tampa Inc ....G...... 813 630-2422
Tampa (G-16813)

ENGINEERING SVCS

3d Perception Inc ....F...... 321 235-7999
Orlando (G-11850)
Aerosapien Technologies LLC ....E...... 386 361-3838
Daytona Beach (G-2508)
Agteck Inc ....E...... 321 305-5930
Cocoa (G-1900)
Aker Data LLC ....F...... 385 394-2537
Ormond Beach (G-12741)
Analytical Research Systems ....F...... 352 466-0051
Micanopy (G-10395)
Aog Detailing Services Inc ....G...... 727 742-7321
Saint Petersburg (G-14964)
ARC Acquisition Corp ....E...... 386 626-0005
Deland (G-2852)
Atsg Logistic Support Service............E...... 904 479-3808
Jacksonville (G-5911)
Bca Technologies Inc ....F...... 407 659-0653
Maitland (G-8052)
Big Bend Truss Components Inc ....F...... 850 539-5351
Havana (G-4994)
Cae USA Inc ....A...... 813 885-7481
Tampa (G-16672)
Circuitronics LLC ....F...... 407 322-8300
Sanford (G-15284)
Corporate One Hundred Inc ....E...... 352 335-0901
Gainesville (G-4672)
Custom Mfg & Engrg Inc ....D...... 727 548-0522
Pinellas Park (G-13680)
Deep Planet Research LLC ....G...... 517 740-1526
Melbourne (G-8398)
Defenshield Inc ....G...... 904 679-3942
Saint Augustine (G-14825)
Diversfied Mtl Specialists Inc ....G...... 941 244-0935
North Venice (G-11211)
Dutchy Enterprises LLC ....G...... 321 877-0700
Cocoa (G-1922)
Entech Onsite Services LLC ....G...... 407 956-8980
Rockledge (G-14707)
Exploration Resources Intn Geo ....G...... 601 747-0726
Lake Mary (G-7073)
Fathym Inc ....F...... 303 905-4402
Palmetto (G-13166)
Full Circle Integration LLC ....F...... 504 615-5501
Valparaiso (G-17660)
Goodrich Corporation ....C...... 904 757-3660
Jacksonville (G-6146)
Granite Services Intl Inc ....F...... 813 242-7400
Tampa (G-16889)
H2r Corp ....F...... 727 541-3444
Pinellas Park (G-13692)

Holtec International ....D...... 561 745-7772
Jupiter (G-6742)
Interface Technology Group Inc ....G...... 321 433-1165
Rockledge (G-14718)
ITI Engineering LLC ....E...... 866 245-9356
Winter Springs (G-18570)
J A Custom Fabricators Inc ....F...... 561 615-4680
Lake Worth (G-7208)
Lrm Industries Intl Inc ....G...... 321 635-9797
Rockledge (G-14727)
Mgl Engineering Inc ....E...... 863 648-0320
Lakeland (G-7394)
Neptune Tech Services Inc ....E...... 904 646-2700
Jacksonville (G-6323)
Nypro Inc ....F...... 727 577-9749
Saint Petersburg (G-15143)
Osgood Industries LLC ....C...... 813 448-9041
Oldsmar (G-11683)
Patrick Industries Inc ....E...... 941 556-6311
Sarasota (G-15534)
Polyhistor International Inc ....G...... 904 646-5666
Jacksonville (G-6377)
Power Systems Mfg LLC ....B...... 561 354-1100
Jupiter (G-6779)
Pyramid Imaging Inc ....G...... 813 984-0125
Tampa (G-17196)
Redstone Corporation ....G...... 321 213-2135
Merritt Island (G-8591)
Sdi Industries Inc ....E...... 321 733-1128
Melbourne (G-8517)
Serf Inc ....E...... 850 476-8203
Cantonment (G-1273)
Sg Blocks Inc ....G...... 646 240-4235
Jacksonville (G-6461)
Spectrum Engineering & Mfg Inc ....G...... 727 376-5510
Odessa (G-11580)
Tactical Air Support Inc ....C...... 229 563-7502
Jacksonville (G-6528)
Tropical Pcb Design Svcs Inc ....F...... 561 784-9536
Loxahatchee (G-7976)
UDC Usa Inc ....E...... 813 281-0200
Tampa (G-17382)
United Rail Inc ....F...... 904 503-9757
Jacksonville (G-6577)
Verifone ....G...... 800 837-4366
Coral Springs (G-2224)

ENGINEERING SVCS: Acoustical

Acoustic Communications LLC............G...... 305 463-9485
Doral (G-3095)
Belquette Inc ....G...... 727 329-9483
Clearwater (G-1516)
Spectrum Engineering Inc ....G...... 239 277-1182
Fort Myers (G-4405)

ENGINEERING SVCS: Aviation Or Aeronautical

Aercap Inc ....D...... 954 760-7777
Fort Lauderdale (G-3627)
Aercap Leasing USA I LLC............F...... 425 237-4000
Miami (G-8661)
Avalon Aviation Inc ....G...... 954 655-0256
Fort Lauderdale (G-3668)
R4 Integration Inc ....E...... 850 226-6913
Fort Walton Beach (G-4604)

ENGINEERING SVCS: Chemical

E3 Fluid Recovery Eng ....G...... 727 754-9792
Largo (G-7577)

ENGINEERING SVCS: Construction & Civil

Ingenria Prcura Y Cnstrccion C............G...... 407 639-4288
Orlando (G-12244)

ENGINEERING SVCS: Electrical Or Electronic

Digital Lighting Systems Inc............G...... 305 264-8391
Miami (G-9032)
Gadgetcat LLC ....G...... 802 238-3671
Cocoa Beach (G-1971)
OHM Americas LLC ....F...... 800 467-7275
Fort Lauderdale (G-3966)
Prime Technological Svcs LLC............D...... 850 539-2500
Havana (G-5002)
Smartsat Inc ....F...... 727 535-6880
Largo (G-7684)

ENGINEERING SVCS: Energy conservation

DOT Green Energy Inc............G...... 717 505-8686
Clearwater (G-1567)

ENGINEERING SVCS: Industrial

Phantom Sales Group Inc ....G...... 888 614-1232
Bartow (G-322)

ENGINEERING SVCS: Marine

L-3 Cmmnctons Ntronix Holdings........D...... 212 697-1111
Melbourne (G-8453)
Structural Composites Inc ....F...... 321 951-9464
Melbourne (G-8534)

ENGINEERING SVCS: Mechanical

Electro Mech Solutions Inc ....E...... 813 792-0400
Odessa (G-11549)
Lumitec LLC ....E...... 561 272-9840
Delray Beach (G-2983)
Praesto Enterprises LLC ....E...... 407 298-9171
Orlando (G-12498)
Rapid Composites LLC ....G...... 941 322-6647
Sarasota (G-15544)

ENGINEERING SVCS: Petroleum

Gas Turbine Efficiency LLC ....E...... 407 304-5200
Orlando (G-12183)

ENGINEERING SVCS: Professional

Consumer Engineering Inc ....F...... 321 984-8550
Palm Bay (G-12895)
I-Con Systems Inc ....D...... 407 365-6241
Oviedo (G-12827)

ENGINEERING SVCS: Sanitary

Tri-Tech Electronics Inc............D...... 407 277-2131
Orlando (G-12669)

ENGINES & ENGINE PARTS: Guided Missile

Topline Hy-Lift Johnson Inc............F...... 352 799-4668
Brooksville (G-1212)

ENGINES & ENGINE PARTS: Guided Missile, Research & Develpt

Terran Orbital Operating Corp ....E...... 561 988-1704
Boca Raton (G-713)
Troxel Aerospace Inds Inc ....F...... 720 626-0454
Gainesville (G-4780)

ENGINES: Diesel & Semi-Diesel Or Duel Fuel

American Diesel and Gas Inc............F...... 561 447-8500
Deerfield Beach (G-2667)

ENGINES: Gasoline, NEC

Fka Racing Inc............G...... 386 938-4211
Jennings (G-6650)
Granite Services Intl Inc ....F...... 813 242-7400
Tampa (G-16889)

ENGINES: Internal Combustion, NEC

2g Cenrgy Pwr Systems Tech Inc........E...... 904 342-5988
Saint Augustine (G-14804)
Cummins-Wagner-Florida LLC............F...... 813 630-2220
Tampa (G-16747)
Cyclone Power Technologies Inc ....F...... 954 943-8721
Pompano Beach (G-13988)
Enginesaver............G...... 813 493-3861
Ruskin (G-14776)
Environmental Recovery Systems........G...... 727 344-3301
Saint Petersburg (G-15037)
Hybrid Engines Corp ....G...... 954 591-5303
Pompano Beach (G-14056)
Innovation Marine Corporation............E...... 941 355-7852
Sarasota (G-15500)
Just Engines............G...... 561 575-2681
Jupiter (G-6753)
Mars Precision Products Inc............G...... 727 846-0505
Port Richey (G-14369)
Progress Rail Services Corp............D...... 239 643-3013
Naples (G-10868)
Spectrumit Inc............F...... 850 202-5263
Pensacola (G-13609)

P
R
O
D
U
C
T

Topline Hy-Lift Johnson Inc..................F...... 352 799-4668
Brooksville (G-1212)

ENGINES: Jet Propulsion

Gem Aerospace............................G....... 786 464-5900
Doral (G-3224)

ENGINES: Marine

ABB Inc...E...... 954 450-9544
Miramar (G-10457)
Aylynn Maritime LLC ....G...... 954 564-6134
Jupiter (G-6687)
Boat Energy LLC..............................G...... 954 501-2628
Fort Lauderdale (G-3697)
Brunswick Corporation ....E...... 954 744-3500
Miramar (G-10476)
Cobra Power Corporation ....G...... 305 893-5018
North Miami (G-11099)
Emerald Coast Mfg LLC ....G...... 850 469-1133
Pensacola (G-13497)
Gull Tool & Machine Inc ....G...... 727 527-0808
Saint Petersburg (G-15069)
Keith Eickert Power Pdts LLC ....F...... 386 446-0660
Palm Coast (G-13081)
Marine Electronics Engine ....G...... 727 459-5593
Saint Petersburg (G-15118)
Offshore Performance Spc Inc ....F...... 239 481-2768
Fort Myers (G-4346)
PMC North America Inc ....F...... 727 530-0714
Largo (G-7661)
Raider Outboards Inc ....E...... 321 383-9585
Titusville (G-17610)
Sen-Dure Products Inc ....D...... 954 973-1260
Fort Lauderdale (G-4044)
USA Marine Engines ....F...... 954 614-4810
Fort Lauderdale (G-4112)
Xcessive Inc ....G...... 866 919-9527
Miami Lakes (G-10380)

ENGRAVING SVC, NEC

Allied General Engrv & Plas ....F...... 305 626-6585
Opa Locka (G-11715)
Friends Professional Sty....................G...... 561 734-4660
Boynton Beach (G-869)

ENGRAVING SVC: Jewelry & Personal Goods

Finlayson Enterprises Inc ....G...... 850 785-7953
Panama City (G-13262)

ENGRAVING SVCS

Carlaron Inc ....G...... 386 258-1183
Daytona Beach (G-2526)
Kemco Industries LLC......................D...... 407 322-1230
Sanford (G-15348)
PM Engraving Corp...........................F 786 573-5292
Miami (G-9723)
Shirts & Caps Inc ....F...... 813 788-7026
Tampa (G-17262)

ENGRAVING: Currency

Seattle Engraving Center LLC ....G...... 813 330-7620
Brandon (G-1106)

ENGRAVINGS: Plastic

Holmes Stamp Company....................E...... 904 396-2291
Jacksonville (G-6183)
Lean Design & Mfg Inc ....F 727 415-3504
Lutz (G-7999)

ENTERTAINERS

Legacy Delights LLC ....G...... 321 222-9330
Orlando (G-12318)

ENTERTAINERS & ENTERTAINMENT GROUPS

Premier Parties Entertainment ....E....... 352 375-6122
Gainesville (G-4750)

ENTERTAINMENT GROUP

Davis-Wick Talent MGT LLC ....E....... 407 369-1614
Margate (G-8127)
Great Hse Mdia Group of Pbls I ....F....... 407 779-3846
Orlando (G-12200)

ENTERTAINMENT PROMOTION SVCS

A2f LLC ....G....... 305 984-9205
Miami (G-8629)
D-R Media and Investments LLC..........D....... 941 207-1602
Venice (G-17682)
Davis-Wick Talent MGT LLC ....E...... 407 369-1614
Margate (G-8127)

ENVELOPES

Double Envelope Corporation ....B...... 352 375-0738
Gainesville (G-4679)
Everglades Envelope Co Inc ....F...... 954 783-7920
Fort Lauderdale (G-3800)
Mac Paper Converters LLC ....G...... 800 334-7026
Jacksonville (G-6269)
Services On Demand Print Inc...........F...... 305 681-5345
Hallandale Beach (G-4970)
Starlock Inc.....................................G...... 305 477-2303
Doral (G-3375)
Winsted Thermographers Inc ....F...... 305 944-7862
Hallandale Beach (G-4985)

ENZYMES

AB Enzymes Inc ....G...... 954 278-3975
Plantation (G-13818)

EPOXY RESINS

American Epoxy Coatings LLC ....F...... 954 850-1169
Dania Beach (G-2348)

EQUIPMENT: Pedestrian Traffic Control

Dynasystems LLC.............................G...... 410 343-7759
Melbourne (G-8412)
N & H Construction Inc......................F...... 904 282-2224
Middleburg (G-10405)

EQUIPMENT: Rental & Leasing, NEC

Agrifleet Leasing Corporation ....E...... 239 293-3976
Auburndale (G-218)
Ashberry Acquisition Company...........F...... 813 248-0055
Tampa (G-16612)
Holiday Ice Inc................................E...... 407 831-2077
Longwood (G-7901)
Holland Pump Company ....G...... 561 697-3333
West Palm Beach (G-18025)
Holland Pump Company ....G...... 904 880-0010
Jacksonville (G-6181)
Mwi Corporation ....E...... 954 426-1500
Deerfield Beach (G-2772)
Mwi Corporation ....G...... 239 337-4747
Fort Myers (G-4335)
Southeastern Seating Inc..................F...... 813 273-9858
Tampa (G-17287)

ETCHING & ENGRAVING SVC

Blast Ctings Powdercoating LLC ....F...... 561 635-7605
Lake Worth Beach (G-7252)
Bricklser Engrv Monuments Corp........F...... 786 806-0672
Doral (G-3148)
Clear View Coatings LLC ....F...... 850 210-0155
Tallahassee (G-16424)
Gws Tool LLC...................................E...... 352 343-8778
Tavares (G-17510)
Hialeah Powder Coating Corp ....F...... 786 275-4107
Hialeah (G-5186)
JAS Powder Coating LLC....................G...... 954 916-7711
Fort Lauderdale (G-3893)
Sea Site Inc....................................G...... 305 403-3002
Miami (G-9859)

ETCHING SVC: Metal

Cm2 Industries Inc...........................G...... 305 685-4812
Opa Locka (G-11731)

ETCHING SVC: Photochemical

Pcm Products Inc.............................E...... 321 267-7500
Titusville (G-17606)
Southern Micro Etch Inc....................F...... 954 781-5999
Pompano Beach (G-14194)

ETHYLENE-PROPYLENE RUBBERS: EPDM Polymers

Fatovich Technologies LLC ....G...... 772 597-1326
Palm City (G-13036)

International Polymer Svcs LLC...........G...... 401 529-6855
Pensacola (G-13525)
Rayonier AM Sales and Tech Inc ....E...... 904 357-4600
Jacksonville (G-6407)
Vinavil Americas Corporation ....F...... 954 246-8888
Deerfield Beach (G-2831)

EXCAVATING EQPT

Florida Dragline Operation.................F...... 305 824-9755
Hialeah (G-5156)

EXHAUST SYSTEMS: Eqpt & Parts

Remetall USA Inc ....F...... 888 212-3812
Aventura (G-273)
Shaw Development LLC ....C...... 239 405-6100
Bonita Springs (G-817)

EXPLOSIVES

Austin Powder Company ....G...... 352 690-7060
Anthony (G-86)
Austin Powder Company ....G...... 863 674-0504
Fort Denaud (G-3613)
General Dynmics Ord Tctcal Sys........C...... 727 578-8100
Saint Petersburg (G-15060)
Ireco Inc ....F...... 239 593-3749
Naples (G-10787)
J & G Explosives LLC........................G...... 407 883-0734
Fort Lauderdale (G-3889)

EXPLOSIVES: Secondary High

Boland Production Supply Inc............G...... 863 324-7784
Winter Haven (G-18422)

EXTENSION CORDS

Evolution Intrcnnect Systems I ....F...... 954 217-6223
Davie (G-2409)

EXTRACTS, FLAVORING

Aromatech Flavorings Inc..................G...... 407 277-5727
Orlando (G-11921)
Cvista LLC......................................E...... 813 405-3000
Riverview (G-14560)
Flayco Products Inc..........................E...... 813 879-1356
Tampa (G-16835)

EYEGLASSES

Bajio Inc...G...... 630 461-0915
New Smyrna Beach (G-10996)
For Eyes Optcal Ccnut Grove In.........C...... 305 557-9004
Miramar (G-10493)
Miraflex Corporation ....G...... 786 380-4494
Doral (G-3304)
Pasco Vision Center ....G...... 813 788-7656
Zephyrhills (G-18623)

EYEGLASSES: Sunglasses

Costa Inc ....G...... 386 274-4000
Daytona Beach (G-2534)
Ocean Waves Inc ....F...... 904 372-4743
Jacksonville Beach (G-6641)

EYELASHES, ARTIFICIAL

Bare Arii LLC ....G...... 352 701-6625
Tampa (G-16628)
Lash Makers LLC ....G...... 800 989-6912
Miami (G-9430)
Mink Bar LLC...................................G...... 954 758-2085
Pembroke Pines (G-13404)

FABRIC SOFTENERS

Dyadic International USA Inc..............G...... 561 743-8333
Jupiter (G-6714)

FABRICATED METAL PRODUCTS, NEC

Adec Metal Fabrication Inc ....G...... 305 401-5073
Hialeah (G-5028)
All Metal Fabrication.........................G...... 305 666-3312
Pinecrest (G-13662)
All Metals Custom Inc ....G...... 727 709-4297
Pinellas Park (G-13671)
American Metal Fabrication LLC ....G...... 954 736-9819
Tamarac (G-16524)
Anna Florer ....G...... 352 424-2210
Dade City (G-2313)

Atlantic Coast Roofing & Metal ....G.... 321 449-9494
Merritt Island *(G-8576)*

BHd Precision Products Inc ....G.... 941 753-0003
Sarasota *(G-15448)*

Customer 1st LLC ....G.... 941 585-5123
North Port *(G-11192)*

David Gill Enterprises ....G.... 863 422-5711
Davenport *(G-2363)*

Doll Marine Metal Fabrica ....G.... 954 941-5093
Fort Lauderdale *(G-3771)*

East Coast Metalworks LLC ....G.... 321 698-0624
Cocoa *(G-1924)*

Ernies Metal Fabricating ....G.... 813 679-0816
Brandon *(G-1090)*

International Vault Inc ....E.... 941 390-4505
Lakewood Ranch *(G-7479)*

J&J Sheet Mtal Fabercation LLC ....G.... 941 752-0569
Sarasota *(G-15503)*

Jetstream Fabrication LLC ....G.... 772 287-3338
Stuart *(G-16169)*

JHK LLC ....G.... 786 871-0150
Miami *(G-9367)*

Jose Rodriguez Met Fabrication ....G.... 305 305-6110
Miami *(G-9374)*

Lakes Metal Fabrication Inc ....G.... 954 731-2010
Oakland Park *(G-11275)*

Marble Bridge Inc ....F.... 239 213-1411
Naples *(G-10811)*

Merritt Hollow Metal Inc ....G.... 727 656-4380
Largo *(G-7643)*

Metal Express LLC ....G.... 786 391-0093
Miami *(G-9539)*

Pitts Fabrication LLC ....G.... 850 259-4548
Fort Walton Beach *(G-4602)*

R H Quality Metal LLC ....G.... 407 279-2454
Davenport *(G-2369)*

Robert James Cstm Met Fabg LLC ......F.... 772 214-0996
Jacksonville *(G-6432)*

Soto Metal Fabrication Inc ....G.... 786 486-7125
Miami *(G-9921)*

Spot-On Wldg Met Fbrcation LLC ....G.... 239 825-7452
Naples *(G-10904)*

Srq Fabrications Inc ....G.... 941 780-5496
Sarasota *(G-15833)*

Sunset Metal Fabrication Inc ....G.... 386 215-4520
Sarasota *(G-15846)*

Tpi Aluminum ....G.... 239 332-3900
Fort Myers *(G-4430)*

United Metal Fabrications Inc ....G.... 305 962-1608
North Miami *(G-11126)*

Worth Metals Inc ....F.... 904 626-1434
Green Cove Springs *(G-4843)*

Yeager Manufacturing Tech LLC ....F.... 407 573-7033
Winter Park *(G-18555)*

FABRICS: Apparel & Outerwear, Cotton

Ata Group of Companies Inc ....G.... 352 735-1588
Mount Dora *(G-10597)*

Chrome Connection Corp ....F.... 305 947-9191
North Miami Beach *(G-11132)*

Emilio Craig Footwear LLC ....G.... 954 999-8302
Montverde *(G-10588)*

Fbo Key Largo LLC ....G.... 305 451-3018
Key Largo *(G-6845)*

Fury Surf Shack ....G.... 305 747-0799
Key West *(G-6864)*

Indigo Mountain Inc ....G.... 239 947-0023
Naples *(G-10780)*

Jesus In Trenches Inc ....F.... 800 865-8274
Fort Lauderdale *(G-3896)*

Jode Corporation ....G.... 321 684-1769
Sebastian *(G-15887)*

Kikisteescom LLC ....E.... 888 620-4110
Sunrise *(G-16333)*

New Breed Clothing llc ....G.... 941 773-7406
Sarasota *(G-15526)*

Newflo LLC ....G.... 718 795-5691
Coral Springs *(G-2196)*

Official Gear Company Inc ....G.... 407 721-9110
Ormond Beach *(G-12782)*

Phoenix Custom Gear LLC ....G.... 561 808-7181
Delray Beach *(G-2996)*

Poof Game LLC ....E.... 239 245-2957
Lehigh Acres *(G-7821)*

RAD Wear Inc ....G.... 352 727-4498
Gainesville *(G-4755)*

FABRICS: Apparel & Outerwear, From Manmade Fiber Or Silk

R S Apparel Inc ....F.... 305 599-4939
Doral *(G-3343)*

FABRICS: Awning Stripes, Cotton

Business World Trading Inc ....F.... 305 238-0724
Miami *(G-8864)*

FABRICS: Bags & Bagging, Cotton

Zellermayer Supply Corp ....F.... 561 848-0057
Mangonia Park *(G-8104)*

FABRICS: Balloon Cloth, Cotton

Southern Balloon Works Inc ....G.... 727 388-8360
Jacksonville *(G-6489)*

FABRICS: Broadwoven, Cotton

Energy Services Providers Inc ....G.... 305 947-7880
Miramar *(G-10488)*

Superior Fabrics Inc ....E.... 954 975-8122
Parkland *(G-13355)*

Tex Z-E Corp ....G.... 305 769-0202
Opa Locka *(G-11793)*

Unique Originals Inc ....E.... 305 634-2274
Fort Lauderdale *(G-4106)*

West Point Stevens ....G.... 850 638-9421
Chipley *(G-1459)*

Westpoint Home Inc ....A.... 850 415-4100
Chipley *(G-1461)*

FABRICS: Broadwoven, Synthetic Manmade Fiber & Silk

Anglo Silver Liner Co ....F.... 508 943-1440
Parrish *(G-13356)*

Bradley Indus Textiles Inc ....F.... 850 678-6111
Valparaiso *(G-17657)*

Legend Moto LLC ....G.... 863 946-2002
Moore Haven *(G-10590)*

Point Blank Enterprises Inc ....A.... 954 846-8222
Pompano Beach *(G-14133)*

Reliatex Inc ....E.... 813 621-6021
Tampa *(G-17215)*

Rfl & Figlio LLC ....F.... 904 765-2222
Jacksonville *(G-6422)*

Stylors Inc ....F.... 904 765-4453
Jacksonville *(G-6514)*

Sunshine Nylon Products Inc ....G.... 352 754-9932
Brooksville *(G-1208)*

Superior Fabrics Inc ....E.... 954 975-8122
Parkland *(G-13355)*

Valley Forge Textiles LLC ....G.... 954 971-1776
Pompano Beach *(G-14233)*

FABRICS: Broadwoven, Wool

Valley Forge Textiles LLC ....G.... 954 971-1776
Pompano Beach *(G-14233)*

FABRICS: Canvas

Bahamas Uphl & Mar Canvas Inc ....F.... 305 992-4346
Miami *(G-8794)*

Bay Networks Inc ....F.... 813 249-8103
Tampa *(G-16632)*

Bestcanvas Inc ....F.... 305 759-7800
Miami *(G-8818)*

Busch Canvas & Interiors Inc ....G.... 561 881-1605
Riviera Beach *(G-14604)*

Camera2canvas LLC ....G.... 850 276-6990
Lynn Haven *(G-8027)*

Canvas ....G.... 727 317-5572
Saint Petersburg *(G-14997)*

Canvas Clinical Research ....F.... 561 229-0002
Palm Beach Gardens *(G-12954)*

Canvas Clinical Research ....G.... 561 229-0002
Lake Worth *(G-7189)*

Canvas Foods Corp ....G.... 786 529-8041
Weston *(G-18232)*

Canvas Freaks LLC ....F.... 407 978-6224
Orlando *(G-11979)*

Canvas Land Surveying LLC ....G.... 321 689-5330
Longwood *(G-7880)*

Cape Canvas Inc ....G.... 239 772-0300
Cape Coral *(G-1322)*

Caribbean Canvas and Mari ....G.... 786 972-6377
Miami *(G-8892)*

Christopher R Shuman ....G.... 561 800-8541
Riviera Beach *(G-14609)*

Classic Canvas & Upholstery ....G.... 954 850-4994
Hollywood *(G-5552)*

Consultcanvas LLC ....G.... 863 214-3115
Miami *(G-8958)*

Creative Canvas Centl Fla Inc ....G.... 407 661-1211
Altamonte Springs *(G-41)*

Discovery Canvas East Coast Co........G.... 786 487-8897
Miami *(G-9035)*

Fit Canvas Inc ....G.... 954 258-9352
Margate *(G-8130)*

JM Ocean Mar Canvas & Uphl Inc ......G.... 786 473-7143
Hallandale *(G-4926)*

Mollys Marine Service LLC ....G.... 239 262-2628
Naples *(G-10822)*

Sea and Shore Custom Canvas Up ......G.... 954 983-3060
Hollywood *(G-5655)*

Sunshine Canvas Inc ....F.... 352 787-4436
Leesburg *(G-7796)*

Tk Custom Canvas & Upholstery ....G.... 954 609-3477
Pompano Beach *(G-14213)*

Tony William Sitko ....G.... 772 321-6361
Vero Beach *(G-17808)*

Traveling Canvas Corporation ....G.... 305 259-2001
Palmetto Bay *(G-13221)*

Wine and Canvas Dev LLC ....G.... 239 980-9138
Fort Myers *(G-4449)*

FABRICS: Canvas & Heavy Coarse, Cotton

BP International Inc ....D.... 386 943-6222
Deland *(G-2856)*

FABRICS: Chemically Coated & Treated

Clock Spring Company Inc ....F.... 561 683-6992
Riviera Beach *(G-14610)*

Enviroworks Inc ....E.... 407 889-5533
Apopka *(G-127)*

Fiskars Brands Inc ....D.... 407 889-5533
Apopka *(G-132)*

FABRICS: Coated Or Treated

Carolina Company USA LLC ....G.... 401 487-2749
Lady Lake *(G-6989)*

Drezo Manufacturing Inc ....G.... 305 864-9814
Miami Beach *(G-10185)*

Mundi Intl Trading Corp ....G.... 305 205-0062
Weston *(G-18269)*

FABRICS: Cotton, Narrow

Mansfield International Inc...............G.... 954 632-3280
Fort Lauderdale *(G-3931)*

FABRICS: Decorative Trim & Specialty, Including Twist Weave

Lead 2 Design ....G.... 954 757-6116
Coral Springs *(G-2177)*

FABRICS: Denims

Denim Lily LLC ....G.... 754 264-9331
Pompano Beach *(G-13991)*

Genuine Denim ....G.... 305 491-1326
North Miami Beach *(G-11142)*

Intertex Miami LLC ....G.... 305 627-3536
Miami *(G-9332)*

FABRICS: Dress, Cotton

Tropical Textiles Intl Inc ....G.... 305 364-4595
Hialeah *(G-5383)*

FABRICS: Felts, Blanketing & Upholstery, Wool

Vertical Land Inc ....F.... 850 819-2535
Panama City *(G-13317)*

FABRICS: Fiberglass, Broadwoven

AA Fiberglass Inc ....G.... 904 355-5511
Jacksonville *(G-5852)*

Accurate Reproductions Inc ....G.... 407 814-1622
Apopka *(G-98)*

Alta Technologies Inc ....G.... 609 538-9500
Ponte Vedra Beach *(G-14262)*

Fastglas ....G.... 904 765-2222
Jacksonville *(G-6089)*

PRODUCT

Glasrite Inc ....F...... 863 967-8151
Auburndale *(G-234)*
Merritt Precision Tech Inc ....G..... 321 453-2334
Merritt Island *(G-8587)*
Nida-Core Corporation ....E..... 772 343-7300
Port Saint Lucie *(G-14428)*

FABRICS: Furniture Denim

Guyton Industries LLC ....E..... 772 208-3019
Indiantown *(G-5814)*

FABRICS: Gauze

Ijkb LLC ....G..... 941 953-9046
Sarasota *(G-15704)*

FABRICS: Glass & Fiberglass, Broadwoven

Smittys Boat Tops and Mar Eqp .....G...... 305 245-0229
Homestead *(G-5740)*

FABRICS: Hand Woven

South Florida Cutting ....F..... 305 693-6711
Hialeah *(G-5354)*

FABRICS: Jean

Blue Light USA Corp ....,.....G...... 954 766-4308
Sunrise *(G-16299)*

FABRICS: Lace & Lace Prdts

Wyla Inc ....F...... 904 886-4338
Jacksonville *(G-6621)*

FABRICS: Lace, Knit, NEC

Metritek Corporation ....E..... 561 995-2414
Coral Springs *(G-2186)*

FABRICS: Laminated

Madico Inc ....D..... 727 327-2544
Pinellas Park *(G-13707)*
Trann Technologies Inc ....G...... 888 668-6700
Mossy Head *(G-10595)*

FABRICS: Lawns, Cotton

N3xt L3vel 2 Point 0 LLC ....F..... 863 777-3778
Tampa *(G-17096)*

FABRICS: Metallized

Metalex LLC ....D..... 941 918-4431
Nokomis *(G-11051)*

FABRICS: Nonwoven

Cerex Advanced Fabrics Inc ....D...... 850 968-0100
Cantonment *(G-1266)*
Mutual Industries North Inc ....D...... 239 332-2400
Fort Myers *(G-4334)*
Superior Fabrics Inc ....E..... 954 975-8122
Parkland *(G-13355)*

FABRICS: Nylon, Broadwoven

Sport Products of Tampa Inc ....G...... 813 630-5552
Tampa *(G-17296)*

FABRICS: Polyethylene, Broadwoven

K Pro Supply Co Inc ....G...... 941 758-1226
Sarasota *(G-15506)*

FABRICS: Print, Cotton

Team Hammer Screen Printing ....G...... 863 666-1108
Lakeland *(G-7458)*
Team Ip Sports LLC ....F...... 772 398-4664
Stuart *(G-16237)*

FABRICS: Resin Or Plastic Coated

C M I Enterprises Inc ....E..... 305 622-6410
Opa Locka *(G-11726)*
Sabic Innovative Plastics ....F..... 386 409-5540
New Smyrna Beach *(G-11008)*

FABRICS: Rubber & Elastic Yarns & Fabrics

Garware Fulflex USA Inc ....G...... 305 436-8915
Miami *(G-9190)*

FABRICS: Sail Cloth

Palafox Marine Inc ....F..... 850 438-9354
Pensacola *(G-13565)*

FABRICS: Satin

Cathy Minh Lee ....G..... 626 827-3214
Dunedin *(G-3443)*
Saten Leaf Nursery Inc ....F..... 305 216-5340
Homestead *(G-5738)*
Satin Sensation Co ....G..... 786 290-4114
Miami *(G-9850)*

FABRICS: Scrub Cloths

Firebird Scrubs and More LLC ....G...... 904 258-7514
Orange Park *(G-11828)*
Taylor Made Scrub Hats LLC ....G...... 615 348-7802
Riverview *(G-14579)*

FABRICS: Shirting, From Manmade Fiber Or Silk

CBI Industries Inc ....E..... 305 796-9346
Miami *(G-8904)*

FABRICS: Specialty Including Twisted Weaves, Broadwoven

Mutual Industries North Inc ....D..... 239 332-2400
Fort Myers *(G-4334)*

FABRICS: Tapestry, Cotton

Holyland Tapestries Inc ....G..... 305 255-7955
Palmetto Bay *(G-13211)*

FABRICS: Trimmings

Adva-Lite Inc ....C..... 727 369-5319
Seminole *(G-15967)*
Ampersand Graphics Inc ....F..... 772 283-1359
Stuart *(G-16115)*
Automated Services Inc ....F..... 772 461-3388
Fort Pierce *(G-4468)*
Buchanan Signs Screen Process ....F..... 904 725-5500
Jacksonville *(G-5962)*
Classic Trim Wtp Inc ....G..... 305 258-3090
Princeton *(G-14487)*
Custom Grafix Industries Inc ....G..... 727 530-7300
Pinellas Park *(G-13678)*
Eastern Shores Printing ....E..... 305 685-8976
Opa Locka *(G-11741)*
Florida Screen Services Inc ....F..... 407 316-0466
Orlando *(G-12166)*
Florida Tape & Labels Inc ....F..... 941 921-5788
Sarasota *(G-15681)*
Full Press Apparel Inc ....F..... 850 222-1003
Tallahassee *(G-16443)*
H Sixto Distributors Inc ....E..... 305 688-5242
Opa Locka *(G-11752)*
Hes Products Inc ....G..... 407 834-0741
Ormond Beach *(G-12769)*
Icon Embroidery Inc ....G..... 407 858-0886
Windermere *(G-18353)*
Image Depot ....G..... 813 685-7116
Tampa *(G-16932)*
Island Designs Outlet Inc ....E..... 813 855-0020
Tampa *(G-16954)*
Joni Industries Inc ....F..... 352 799-5456
Brooksville *(G-1166)*
Lorente International LLC ....E..... 877 281-6469
Seminole *(G-15981)*
Moser Automotive ....E..... 561 881-5665
Riviera Beach *(G-14648)*
National Traffic Signs Inc ....G..... 727 446-7983
Clearwater *(G-1712)*
Philias Supreme LLC ....G..... 786 865-1335
Miami *(G-9710)*
Playa Perfection Inc ....E..... 440 670-8154
Fort Myers *(G-4363)*
Premier Manufacturing Pdts LLC ......F..... 239 542-0260
Cape Coral *(G-1374)*
Print Shack ....G..... 352 799-2972
Brooksville *(G-1192)*
Ray Graphics Inc ....G..... 863 325-0911
Winter Haven *(G-18464)*
Royal Tees Inc ....F..... 941 366-0056
Sarasota *(G-15802)*
Southern Business Card Inc ....G..... 305 944-2931
Delray Beach *(G-3020)*

Southern International Svcs ....F..... 954 349-7321
Miami *(G-9929)*
Steven Chancas ....G..... 352 629-5016
Ocala *(G-11499)*
Universal Screen Graphics Inc ......E..... 813 623-5335
Tampa *(G-17394)*
Vivid Images USA Inc ....F..... 904 620-0303
Jacksonville *(G-6594)*

FABRICS: Trimmings, Textile

M & H Enterprises Inc ....G..... 305 885-5945
Hialeah *(G-5232)*

FABRICS: Umbrella Cloth, Cotton

Fiberbuilt Umbrellas Inc ....E..... 954 484-9139
Pompano Beach *(G-14020)*
Windbrella Products Corp ....E..... 561 734-5222
Boynton Beach *(G-924)*

FABRICS: Upholstery, Cotton

Anderson Mfg & Upholstery Inc ....G..... 321 267-7028
Titusville *(G-17571)*

FABRICS: Varnished Glass & Coated Fiberglass

Blutec Glass Fabrication LLC ....G..... 941 232-1600
Sarasota *(G-15613)*

FABRICS: Woven, Narrow Cotton, Wool, Silk

American Elastic & Tape Inc ....G..... 305 888-0303
Hialeah *(G-5045)*
Eastern Shores Printing ....E..... 305 685-8976
Opa Locka *(G-11741)*
Valley Forge Textiles LLC ....G..... 954 971-1776
Pompano Beach *(G-14233)*

FACIAL SALONS

Florida Keys Keylime Products ....G..... 305 853-0378
Key Largo *(G-6846)*
Tend Skin International Inc ....F..... 954 382-0800
Davie *(G-2488)*

FACILITIES SUPPORT SVCS

Atsg Logistic Support Service ....E..... 904 479-3808
Jacksonville *(G-5911)*
GE Medcal Systems Info Tech In ......D..... 561 575-5000
Jupiter *(G-6734)*
Kratos Def & SEC Solutions Inc ......E..... 866 606-5867
Orlando *(G-12296)*

FAMILY CLOTHING STORES

Clothesline Inc ....E..... 850 877-9171
Tallahassee *(G-16425)*
Simons Hallandale Inc ....E..... 561 468-1174
Miami *(G-9895)*
T-Shirt Express ....G..... 904 448-3761
Jacksonville *(G-6527)*

FANS, BLOWING: Indl Or Commercial

Certainteed Corporation ....F..... 863 294-3206
Winter Haven *(G-18431)*
Fan America Inc ....G..... 941 955-9788
Sarasota *(G-15671)*
Kanalflakt Inc ....F..... 941 359-3267
Sarasota *(G-15717)*
S&P USA Vntilation Systems LLC ......D..... 904 731-4711
Jacksonville *(G-6442)*

FANS, VENTILATING: Indl Or Commercial

Air Flow Specialists ....G..... 954 727-9507
Davie *(G-2379)*
TNT Transfer Inc ....G..... 561 594-0123
Stuart *(G-16238)*
Upton House Cooler Corporation ......G..... 305 633-2531
Miami *(G-10076)*
Ventilex Inc ....G..... 954 433-1321
Pembroke Pines *(G-13423)*
Warren Technology Inc ....C..... 305 556-6933
Hialeah *(G-5418)*

FANS: Ceiling

Suns Up of Swf LLC ....G..... 301 470-2678
Venice *(G-17721)*

FARM MACHINERY REPAIR SVCS

Channel Industries Inc ....F 561 214-0637
   West Palm Beach (G-17965)

FARM SPLY STORES

Branch Properties Inc............................D 352 732-4143
   Ocala (G-11338)
Seminole Stores Inc ....F 352 732-4143
   Ocala (G-11485)

FARM SPLYS WHOLESALERS

Branch Properties Inc............................D 352 732-4143
   Ocala (G-11338)
Brinsea Products Inc ....G 321 267-7009
   Titusville (G-17576)
Farmers Cooperative Inc........................E 386 362-1459
   Live Oak (G-7848)
Morse Enterprises Limited Inc..............G 407 682-6500
   Miami (G-9589)

FARM SPLYS, WHOLESALE: Feed

Barber Fertilizer Company ....E 850 263-6324
   Campbellton (G-1259)

FARM SPLYS, WHOLESALE: Fertilizers & Agricultural Chemicals

Calcium Silicate Corp Inc.......................F 863 902-0217
   Lake Harbor (G-7054)
Harrells LLC...E 863 687-2774
   Lakeland (G-7341)
Pioneer Ag-Chem Inc.............................E 772 464-9300
   Fort Pierce (G-4519)

FARM SPLYS, WHOLESALE: Garden Splys

Pottre Gardening Products LLC.............G 941 224-8856
   Bradenton (G-1031)

FASTENERS WHOLESALERS

Scott Slide Fasteners Inc ....G 305 576-3328
   Miami (G-9858)

FASTENERS: Metal

Fk Irons Inc...E 855 354-7667
   Doral (G-3217)
Shashy Enterprises Inc ....G 352 732-3904
   Ocala (G-11488)

FASTENERS: Notions, NEC

Arrowhead Global LLC ....F 727 497-7340
   Clearwater (G-1499)
Bisi Fasteners LLC ....G 850 913-0101
   Panama City (G-13235)
Captains Fasteners Corp ....G 954 533-9259
   Fort Lauderdale (G-3714)
Ceco & Associates Inc ....G 727 528-0075
   Riverview (G-14558)
Coll Builders Supply Inc ....F 407 745-4641
   Orlando (G-12029)
E-Z Fastening Solutions Inc...................G 813 854-3937
   Oldsmar (G-11646)
Fastener Specialty Corp ....G 631 903-4453
   Port Charlotte (G-14298)
Innovative Fasteners LLc.......................F 561 542-2152
   Coconut Creek (G-1992)
Tekk Supply Inc.....................................G 954 444-5782
   Pompano Beach (G-14211)
Zoag LLC...G 862 591-2969
   Palm Beach Gardens (G-13020)

FASTENERS: Notions, Zippers

Ideal Fastener Corporation ....D 201 207-6722
   Miami (G-9301)

FASTENERS: Wire, Made From Purchased Wire

Southwire Company LLC ....C 850 423-4680
   Crestview (G-2254)

FATTY ACID ESTERS & AMINOS

Originates Inc..F 954 233-2500
   Aventura (G-269)

FAUCETS & SPIGOTS: Metal & Plastic

Ecolab Inc...F 800 931-8911
   Jupiter (G-6717)
OMalley Manufacturing Inc ....G 727 327-6817
   Saint Petersburg (G-15147)
Ultraclenz LLC.......................................F 800 931-8911
   Jupiter (G-6817)

FEATHERS & FEATHER PRODUCTS

S A Feather Co Inc ....F 239 693-6363
   Fort Myers (G-4388)

FELT: Acoustic

Valley Forge Textiles LLC.......................G 954 971-1776
   Pompano Beach (G-14233)

FENCE POSTS: Iron & Steel

Father & Son Fence Supply LLC ....F 352 848-3180
   Brooksville (G-1156)
Friedman & Greenberg PA.....................G 954 370-4774
   Plantation (G-13854)
Just Steel Inc...F 941 755-7811
   Sarasota (G-15504)

FENCES & FENCING MATERIALS

Merchants Metals LLC............................F 813 980-0938
   Tampa (G-17065)
Merchants Metals LLC............................F 561 478-0059
   West Palm Beach (G-18075)

FENCES OR POSTS: Ornamental Iron Or Steel

Iron-Art & Fence Inc..............................F 407 699-1734
   Longwood (G-7906)
L A Ornamental & Rack Corp ....G 305 696-0419
   Miami (G-9403)

FENCING DEALERS

Baby Guard Inc ....F 954 741-6351
   Coral Springs (G-2133)
Father & Son Fence Supply LLC ....F 352 848-3180
   Brooksville (G-1156)
Florida Fence Post Co Inc ....G 863 735-1361
   Ona (G-11709)
Luv Enterprises Inc................................F 352 867-8440
   Ocala (G-11433)

FENCING MADE IN WIREDRAWING PLANTS

Baby Guard Inc ....F 954 741-6351
   Coral Springs (G-2133)

FENCING MATERIALS: Docks & Other Outdoor Prdts, Wood

Core Outdoors Inc ....F 904 215-6866
   Saint Augustine (G-14822)
John Hurst Outdoor Svcs LLC ....G 850 556-7459
   Tallahassee (G-16463)

FENCING MATERIALS: Plastic

Brill Hygienic Products Inc ....F 561 278-5600
   Delray Beach (G-2938)
Father & Son Fence Supply LLC ....F 352 848-3180
   Brooksville (G-1156)
V & C Supply Ornamental Corp ....G 305 634-9040
   Miami (G-10086)

FENCING MATERIALS: Wood

ABC Fence Systems Inc ....F 850 638-8876
   Chipley (G-1452)
Consolidated Forest Pdts Inc ....G 407 830-7723
   Perry (G-13635)
Consolidated Forest Pdts Inc ....F 407 830-7723
   Longwood (G-7882)
Danielle Fence Mfg Co Inc ....D 863 425-3182
   Mulberry (G-10621)
Florida Cypress & Fence Co ....G 561 392-3011
   Palm City (G-13038)
Mc Connie Enterprises Inc.....................G 813 247-3827
   Tampa (G-17059)
Silverman Fence Mfg Inc........................G 904 730-0882
   Jacksonville (G-6471)
Spray-Tech Staining Inc ....F 407 443-4239
   Longwood (G-7949)

FENCING: Chain Link

Father & Son Fence Supply LLC ....F 352 848-3180
   Brooksville (G-1156)

FERROSILICON, EXC MADE IN BLAST FURNACES

Globe Specialty Metals Inc.....................F 786 509-6900
   Miami (G-9222)

FERTILIZER MINERAL MINING

Ostara Usa LLC ....G 813 666-8123
   Riverview (G-14572)

FERTILIZERS: NEC

Barber Fertilizer Company ....E 850 263-6324
   Campbellton (G-1259)
Ben Hill Griffin Inc.................................E 863 635-2281
   Frostproof (G-4633)
Ben Hill Griffin Inc.................................D 863 635-2281
   Frostproof (G-4634)
Carrabelle Beach An Rvc ....G 850 697-8813
   Carrabelle (G-1409)
CF Industries Inc...................................D 813 782-1591
   Plant City (G-13753)
Chemical Dynamics Inc..........................E 813 752-4950
   Plant City (G-13755)
Diamond R Fertilizer Co Inc ....E 863 763-2158
   Okeechobee (G-11603)
Farmers Cooperative Inc........................E 386 362-1459
   Live Oak (G-7848)
Harrells LLC...E 863 687-2774
   Lakeland (G-7341)
Lesco Inc...E 863 655-2424
   Sebring (G-15929)
Plant Foods Inc ....E 772 567-5741
   Vero Beach (G-17787)
S A Florikan-E LLC ....D 800 322-8666
   Bowling Green (G-832)
Scotts Company LLC..............................D 352 429-0066
   Groveland (G-4870)
Sun Gro Horticulture Dist Inc ....E 407 291-1676
   Orlando (G-12631)
Sunshine Organics Compost LLC...........G 904 900-3072
   Jacksonville (G-6519)
Wedgworth Farms Inc ....G 561 996-2076
   Plant City (G-13815)
Wedgworths Inc ....G 561 996-2076
   Belle Glade (G-347)

FERTILIZERS: Nitrogen Solutions

Pioneer Ag-Chem Inc.............................E 772 464-9300
   Fort Pierce (G-4519)
Trans-Resources LLC ....A 305 933-8301
   Sunny Isles Beach (G-16284)

FERTILIZERS: Nitrogenous

Agrium Advanced Tech US Inc...............F 407 302-2024
   Sanford (G-15260)
Anuvia Plant Nutrients Corp ....G 689 407-3430
   Winter Garden (G-18373)
Ben Hill Griffin Inc.................................D 863 635-2281
   Frostproof (G-4634)
Bionitrogen Holdings Corp ....G 561 600-9550
   West Palm Beach (G-17945)
Growers Fertilizer Corporation ....E 863 956-1101
   Lake Alfred (G-6995)
Natural Organic Products Intl ....G 352 383-8252
   Mount Dora (G-10607)
Nurserymens Sure-Gro Corp ....G 772 770-0462
   Vero Beach (G-17782)
Stoller Chemical Co of Florida................F 352 357-3173
   Eustis (G-3566)
T-Brand Fertilizer Inc ....G 386 437-2970
   Bunnell (G-1235)
Turf Care Supply LLC ....D 863 655-0700
   Sebring (G-15949)

FERTILIZERS: Phosphatic

CF Industries Inc...................................D 813 782-1591
   Plant City (G-13753)
Growers Fertilizer Corporation ....E 863 956-1101
   Lake Alfred (G-6995)
Mos Holdings Inc ....D 763 577-2700
   Mulberry (G-10634)
Mosaic Company ....F 813 775-2827
   Riverview (G-14570)

PRODUCT

Mosaic Company ....B 800 918-8270
Tampa *(G-17086)*
Mosaic Crop Nutrition LLC ....D 813 500-6800
Lithia *(G-7835)*
Mosaic Fertilizer LLC ....A 813 500-6300
Lithia *(G-7836)*
Mosaic Global Sales LLC ....E 763 577-2700
Tampa *(G-17087)*
Nurserymens Sure-Gro Corp ....G 772 770-0462
Vero Beach *(G-17782)*

FIBER & FIBER PRDTS: Acrylic

Mirart Inc ....E 954 974-5230
Pompano Beach *(G-14101)*
Sterling Fibers Inc ....D 850 994-5311
Milton *(G-10438)*

FIBER & FIBER PRDTS: Organic, Noncellulose

Ascend Prfmce Mtls Oprtons LLC ....A 850 968-7000
Cantonment *(G-1265)*
Two Brothers Cultivation LLC ....E 954 478-2402
Fort Lauderdale *(G-4102)*

FIBER & FIBER PRDTS: Synthetic Cellulosic

Composite Holdings Inc ....E 321 268-9625
Titusville *(G-17582)*
Eastman Chemical Company ....F 305 671-2800
Miami *(G-9062)*
Rayonier Advanced Mtls Inc ....C 904 357-4600
Jacksonville *(G-6406)*
Rayonier Inc ....E 904 277-1343
Yulee *(G-18592)*

FIBER & FIBER PRDTS: Vinyl

American Trffic Sfety Mtls Inc ....E 904 284-0284
Green Cove Springs *(G-4814)*
Bay City Window Company ....F 727 323-5443
Saint Petersburg *(G-14978)*
Uniroyal Engineered Pdts LLC ....F 941 906-8580
Sarasota *(G-15862)*
Uniroyal Globl Engnred Pdts In ....F 941 906-8580
Sarasota *(G-15863)*

FIBER OPTICS

Gulf Fiberoptics Inc ....E 813 891-1993
Oldsmar *(G-11654)*
Southern Lights ....G 727 849-4442
New Port Richey *(G-10984)*

FIBER PRDTS: Pressed, Wood Pulp, From Purchased Materials

A M Rayonier Products Inc ....B 904 261-3611
Yulee *(G-18585)*

FIBERS: Carbon & Graphite

Rapid Composites LLC ....G 941 322-6647
Sarasota *(G-15544)*

FILLERS & SEALERS: Putty

Rezolin LLC ....G 386 677-8238
Ormond Beach *(G-12791)*

FILM & SHEET: Unsuppported Plastic

Berry Global Inc ....D 941 355-7166
Sarasota *(G-15446)*
Dairy-Mix Inc ....F 813 621-8098
Tampa *(G-16759)*
Inpro Corp Ike ....G 407 342-9912
Orlando *(G-12247)*
Madico Inc ....D 727 327-2544
Pinellas Park *(G-13707)*
Miami Cellophane Inc ....E 786 293-2212
Hialeah *(G-5248)*
Nina Plastic Bags Inc ....D 407 802-6828
Orlando *(G-12417)*
Ped-Stuart Corporation ....E 352 754-6001
Brooksville *(G-1188)*
Protex Inc ....F 727 573-4665
Clearwater *(G-1757)*
Seal-Tite Plastic Packg Co Inc ....D 305 264-9015
Miami *(G-9860)*
Solar X ....G 386 673-2111
Ormond Beach *(G-12793)*

Tape Technologies Inc ....E 904 284-0284
Green Cove Springs *(G-4838)*

FILM: Motion Picture

Columbia Films Inc ....G 800 531-3238
Pompano Beach *(G-13972)*
Planet Inhouse Inc ....G 321 216-2189
Melbourne *(G-8496)*
Sonia Land Inc ....G 305 798-4912
Coral Gables *(G-2110)*
Trap World LLC ....D 305 517-5676
Miami *(G-10038)*
VIP 2000 Tv Inc ....F 305 373-2400
Miami *(G-10113)*

FILTERS

Federal Eastern Intl Inc ....F 954 533-4506
Fort Lauderdale *(G-3813)*
Filter Specialists Inc ....G 516 801-9944
Deland *(G-2871)*
Ingelub Corp ....G 407 656-8800
Winter Garden *(G-18392)*
Noflood Inc ....G 239 776-1671
Fort Myers *(G-4341)*
Pall Aeropower Corporation ....B 727 849-9999
Deland *(G-2893)*
Safetek International Inc ....G 702 558-8202
Boca Raton *(G-658)*
Siemens Industry Inc ....G 407 650-3570
Orlando *(G-12598)*
Suinpla LLC ....F 786 747-4829
Medley *(G-8328)*
United States Filter Corp ....G 772 466-5955
Fort Pierce *(G-4550)*

FILTERS & SOFTENERS: Water, Household

Ashberry Acquisition Company ....F 813 248-0055
Tampa *(G-16612)*
Atlantic Drinking Water Systms ....G 252 255-1110
Fort Myers *(G-4183)*
Enviro Water Solutions LLC ....D 877 842-1635
Deland *(G-2868)*
Johnson Well Equipment Inc ....G 850 453-3131
Pensacola *(G-13530)*
Michael P Wahlquist ....G 850 643-5139
Bristol *(G-1124)*
Paragon Water Systems Inc ....E 727 538-4704
Tampa *(G-17149)*
Sawyer Products Inc ....E 727 725-1177
Safety Harbor *(G-14795)*
Voda Technologies LLC ....G 727 645-6030
Palm Harbor *(G-13137)*
Waterfilterusa ....G 386 469-0138
Deland *(G-2919)*

FILTERS: Air

Air Sponge Filter Company Inc ....G 954 752-1836
Coral Springs *(G-2129)*
Andrews Filter and Supply Corp ....E 407 423-3310
Orlando *(G-11912)*
Boair Inc ....G 954 426-9226
Deerfield Beach *(G-2678)*
DOT Blue Trading Inc ....G 954 646-0448
Miami *(G-9045)*
Duststop Filters Inc ....G 904 725-1001
Jacksonville *(G-6049)*
Energenics Corporation ....E 239 643-1711
Naples *(G-10738)*
Filter King LLC ....F 877 570-9755
Miami *(G-9141)*
Filters Plus Inc ....G 813 232-2000
Tampa *(G-16832)*
Glasfloss Industries Inc ....E 904 741-9922
Jacksonville *(G-6142)*
Pall Filtration and Sep ....C 386 822-8000
Deland *(G-2894)*
Polk Air Filter Sales Inc ....G 863 688-4436
Lakeland *(G-7411)*
Rv Air Inc ....G 309 657-4300
Clearwater *(G-1773)*

FILTERS: Air Intake, Internal Combustion Engine, Exc Auto

Lawrence Factor Inc ....E 305 430-9152
Miami Lakes *(G-10353)*
Sunshine Filters Pinellas Inc ....E 727 530-3884
Largo *(G-7694)*

FILTERS: Gasoline, Internal Combustion Engine, Exc Auto

Suinpla LLC ....F 786 747-4829
Medley *(G-8328)*

FILTERS: General Line, Indl

Custom Masters Inc ....E 407 331-4634
Longwood *(G-7885)*
Darly Filtration Inc ....E 727 318-7064
Saint Petersburg *(G-15019)*
Industrial Filter Pump Mfg Co ....G 708 656-7800
Mims *(G-10448)*
Miami Filter LLC ....E 772 466-1440
Fort Pierce *(G-4507)*
Pall Aeropower Corporation ....B 727 849-9999
New Port Richey *(G-10980)*
Vuflow Filters Co Inc ....G 352 597-2607
Brooksville *(G-1220)*

FILTERS: Motor Vehicle

Puradyn Filter Tech Inc ....E 561 547-9499
Boynton Beach *(G-903)*

FILTRATION DEVICES: Electronic

E3 Fluid Recovery Eng ....G 727 754-9792
Largo *(G-7577)*
Filta Group Inc ....F 407 996-5550
Orlando *(G-12150)*
Nordquist Dielectrics Inc ....G 727 585-7990
Clearwater *(G-1718)*
Pall Filtration and Sep ....C 386 822-8000
Deland *(G-2894)*
Piezo Technology Inc ....D 407 298-2000
Orlando *(G-12486)*
Rusco Inc ....F 352 597-2522
Brooksville *(G-1196)*
Two Little Fishies Inc ....G 305 623-7695
Miami *(G-10050)*

FINANCIAL INVESTMENT ADVICE

Weiss Research Inc ....C 561 627-3300
Jupiter *(G-6826)*

FINDINGS & TRIMMINGS: Apparel

Hofmann & Leavy Inc ....D 954 698-0000
Deerfield Beach *(G-2738)*

FINDINGS & TRIMMINGS: Fabric

Uniroyal Globl Engnred Pdts In ....F 941 906-8580
Sarasota *(G-15863)*

FINGERNAILS, ARTIFICIAL

Chelly Cosmetics Manufacturing ....F 305 471-9608
Miami *(G-8922)*
Vicx LLC ....F 407 674-2073
Winter Garden *(G-18407)*

FINGERPRINT EQPT

Armor Holdings Forensics LLC ....E 904 485-1836
Jacksonville *(G-5903)*
Cross Match Technologies Inc ....C 561 622-1650
Palm Beach Gardens *(G-12963)*

FINISHING AGENTS

International Finishes Inc ....F 561 948-1066
Boca Raton *(G-550)*

FINISHING AGENTS: Textile

Vestagen Tchnical Textiles Inc ....G 407 781-2570
Orlando *(G-12695)*

FIRE ARMS, SMALL: Guns Or Gun Parts, 30 mm & Below

Adams Arms Holdings LLC ....E 727 853-0550
Brooksville *(G-1130)*
Artisan Arms Inc ....G 321 299-4053
Apopka *(G-103)*
C Products Defense Inc ....E 941 727-0009
Bradenton *(G-953)*
Diamondback Firearms LLC ....F 321 305-5995
Cocoa *(G-1917)*

Hitman Industries LLC..............F 321 735-8562
Cocoa (G-1935)
Kel-TEC Cnc Industries Inc.............F 321 631-0068
Cocoa (G-1939)
Khaled W Akkawi ....G 321 396-3108
Apopka (G-145)
Knights Manufacturing Company .....D 321 607-9900
Titusville (G-17599)
Mwg Company Inc ....G 305 232-7344
Cutler Bay (G-2298)
Naroh Manufacturing LLC ....F 321 806-4875
Rockledge (G-14734)
Precision Machine Tech LLC ....F 305 594-1789
Doral (G-3334)
R M Equipment Inc ....F 305 477-9312
Miami (G-9772)
Rwc Group LLC.............................E 754 222-1407
Pompano Beach (G-14164)
Sccy Industries LLC ....C 386 322-6336
Daytona Beach (G-2593)
US Security Defense Corp ....E 407 979-1478
Tavares (G-17527)

FIRE ARMS, SMALL: Machine Guns & Grenade Launchers

Arsenal Democracy LLC ....F 850 296-2122
Freeport (G-4621)

FIRE ARMS, SMALL: Machine Guns/Machine Gun Parts, 30mm/below

Premiere Manufacturing Co LLC ....G 407 747-3955
Sanford (G-15376)

FIRE ARMS, SMALL: Shotguns Or Shotgun Parts, 30 mm & Below

Ttc Performance Products Inc ....F 407 630-9359
Longwood (G-7955)

FIRE CONTROL EQPT REPAIR SVCS, MILITARY

Done Right Fire Gear Repr Inc..............G 727 848-9019
Hudson (G-5770)

FIRE CONTROL OR BOMBING EQPT: Electronic

Lehigh Acrs Fre Cnrl & Rscue ....E 239 303-5300
Lehigh Acres (G-7814)

FIRE DETECTION SYSTEMS

Simplexgrinnell Holdings LLC..............G 978 731-2500
Boca Raton (G-677)

FIRE EXTINGUISHER CHARGES

Patriot Fire Defense Inc ....G 321 313-2265
Melbourne (G-8492)

FIRE OR BURGLARY RESISTIVE PRDTS

Argonide Corporation.........................F 407 322-2500
Sanford (G-15266)
Centerline Steel LLC ....E 904 217-4186
Saint Augustine (G-14821)
Champion Shtmtl Fabrication ....G 407 509-7439
Winter Park (G-18498)
Custom Mfg & Engrg Inc ....D 727 548-0522
Pinellas Park (G-13680)
East Coast Machine Inc ....F 321 632-4817
Cocoa (G-1923)
Fire Technologies Corp ....G 305 592-1914
Coconut Creek (G-1986)
J A Custom Fabricators Inc ....F 561 615-4680
Lake Worth (G-7208)
Metal Creations Sarasota Llc..............F 941 922-7096
Sarasota (G-15744)
Preston Works Inc ....G 850 932-0888
Holt (G-5693)
Telese Properties Inc ....D 813 752-6015
Plant City (G-13809)
Theissen Training Systems Inc ....D 352 490-8020
Gainesville (G-4775)

FIRE PROTECTION EQPT

911 Equipment Inc ....G 954 217-1745
Weston (G-18217)

Done Right Fire Gear Repr Inc..............G 727 848-9019
Hudson (G-5770)
Elite Fire Protection Inc ....F 352 639-4119
Tavares (G-17505)
Magenav Inc ....G 718 551-1815
Fort Lauderdale (G-3927)
Target Manufacturing Inc ....G 305 633-0361
Miami (G-9994)

FIREARMS & AMMUNITION, EXC SPORTING, WHOLESALE

Boland Production Supply Inc..............G 863 324-7784
Winter Haven (G-18422)

FIREARMS: Large, Greater Than 30mm

Ballista Tactical Systems ....G 954 260-0765
Fort Lauderdale (G-3671)
Nst Global LLC ....E 941 748-2270
Bradenton (G-1020)
Syrac Ordnance Inc ....G 727 612-6090
New Port Richey (G-10988)

FIREARMS: Small, 30mm or Less

Ao Precision Manufacturing LLC ....C 386 274-5882
Daytona Beach (G-2511)
Arma Holdings Inc ....F 813 402-0667
Tampa (G-16607)
Atomic Machine & Edm Inc ....G 239 353-9100
Naples (G-10682)
Ballista Tactical Systems ....G 954 260-0765
Fort Lauderdale (G-3671)
Bauer Small Arms Trning Ctr In ....G 850 862-1811
Pensacola (G-13452)
Crosstac Corporation ....G 406 522-9300
Medley (G-8225)
Dark Storm Manufacturing LLC ....G 516 983-3473
Merritt Island (G-8583)
Eric Lemoine ....G 407 919-9783
Longwood (G-7890)
Global Ordnance LLC ....E 941 549-8388
Sarasota (G-15484)
Gtgjfe LLC...G 904 800-6333
Jacksonville (G-6160)
Mossberg Group Inc ....F 386 274-5882
Ormond Beach (G-12781)
O I Inc ....E 321 212-7801
Melbourne (G-8486)
Oath Corporation ....G 407 221-7288
Rockledge (G-14736)
Right To Bear Arms LLC.......................G 772 794-1188
Vero Beach (G-17793)
Wide Open Armory LLC ....G 727 202-5980
Seminole (G-15998)

FIREPLACE & CHIMNEY MATERIAL: Concrete

Earthcore Industries LLC ....G 904 363-3417
Jacksonville (G-6057)

FIREPLACE EQPT & ACCESS

Grate Ideas of America LLC................G 844 292-6044
Fort Lauderdale (G-3845)

FIREPLACES: Concrete

Grate Fireplace & Stone Shoppe ....E 239 939-7187
Fort Myers (G-4272)

FIREWORKS

Ralph Santore & Sons Inc ....E 386 437-2242
Bunnell (G-1233)

FIREWORKS DISPLAY SVCS

Ralph Santore & Sons Inc ....E 386 437-2242
Bunnell (G-1233)

FISH & SEAFOOD MARKETS

Captain Rustys....................................G 813 244-2799
Lorida (G-7963)

FISH & SEAFOOD PROCESSORS: Canned Or Cured

M & R Seafood Inc ....F 352 498-5150
Cross City (G-2261)

FISH & SEAFOOD PROCESSORS: Fresh Or Frozen

Cypress Pensacola LLC.......................G 850 724-1124
Pensacola (G-13482)
Del Rosario Enterprises Inc ....F 786 547-6812
Medley (G-8230)
M & R Seafood Inc ....F 352 498-5150
Cross City (G-2261)
Mestizo Peruvian Cuisine Llc ....G 561 469-1164
West Palm Beach (G-18076)
Miracle Seafood Manufacturers...........G 850 653-2114
Apalachicola (G-89)
Modern Garden Miami LLC ....G 305 440-4200
Miami (G-9583)
Pier 220 Inc ....G 321 264-2011
Titusville (G-17608)

FISH & SEAFOOD WHOLESALERS

M & R Seafood Inc ....F 352 498-5150
Cross City (G-2261)
Select Europe Inc...............................F 866 204-0899
Deerfield Beach (G-2806)

FISHING EQPT: Lures

Boone Bait Co Inc ....F 407 975-8775
Winter Park (G-18492)
Cind-Al Inc ....G 863 401-8700
Clermont (G-1863)
Classic Fishing Products Inc ....E 407 656-6133
Clermont (G-1864)
Highroller Fishing Lure Co LLC ....G 352 215-2925
Gainesville (G-4706)
L & S Bait Co Inc ....E 727 584-7691
Largo (G-7631)
Mayo Plastics Mfg Inc ....F 386 294-1049
Mayo (G-8183)
Ryman Hospitality Prpts Inc ....A 904 284-2770
Green Cove Springs (G-4836)
Stuart Industries Inc ....F 305 651-3474
Miami (G-9961)

FISHING EQPT: Nets & Seines

Frank Murray & Sons Inc......................F 561 845-1366
Fort Lauderdale (G-3831)
Lee Fisher International Inc ....E 813 875-6296
Tampa (G-17004)
Mc Connie Enterprises Inc ....G 813 247-3827
Tampa (G-17059)

FITTINGS & ASSEMBLIES: Hose & Tube, Hydraulic Or Pneumatic

Awab LLC ....G 954 763-3003
Fort Lauderdale (G-3669)
Ibd Industrial LLC ....G 786 655-7577
Coral Gables (G-2069)
Mako Hose & Rubber Co ....G 561 795-6200
West Palm Beach (G-18063)
Space Coast Hydraulics Inc.................F 321 504-6006
Rockledge (G-14748)

FITTINGS: Pipe

Azex Flow Technologies Inc ....G 305 393-8037
Miami (G-8785)
Napac Inc...G 904 766-4470
Jacksonville (G-6318)
Nuflo Inc..E 904 265-4001
Jacksonville (G-6340)
Southeast Power Group Inc ....G 305 592-9745
Doral (G-3370)
Teckno Corp ....G 305 677-3487
Doral (G-3394)
Tradewinds Power Corp ....D 305 592-9745
Doral (G-3400)

FIXTURES & EQPT: Kitchen, Metal, Exc Cast Aluminum

Accurate Metal Fabricators ....F 407 933-2666
Kissimmee (G-6893)
LAtelier Pris Hute Design LLC..............F 800 792-3550
Miami (G-9433)
Officine Gullo USA LLC ....G 800 781-7125
Miami (G-9639)
Professnl Kit Instller Group ....F 954 436-1513
Miramar (G-10533)

Employee Codes: A=Over 500 employees, B=251-500
C=101-250, D=51-100, E=20-50, F=10-19, G=4-9

2022 Harris Florida
Manufacturers Directory

1205

PRODUCT

FIXTURES: Cut Stone

Tropix Marble Company ....F 239 334-2371
Cape Coral **(G-1401)**

FLAGS: Fabric

Buchanan Signs Screen Process ....F 904 725-5500
Jacksonville **(G-5962)**

FLAGSTONES

Flagstone Pavers South ....G 239 225-5646
Pompano Beach **(G-14028)**

FLARES

Edible Flair Inc ....G 954 321-3608
Fort Lauderdale **(G-3786)**
Flare Clothing Inc ....G 863 859-1800
Lakeland **(G-7327)**

FLAT GLASS: Antique

Antique Crystal Glass & Prcln ....G 352 220-2666
Crystal River **(G-2266)**

FLAT GLASS: Construction

Dynamic Visions Inc ....E 941 497-1984
Venice **(G-17685)**
King Construction & Glass LLC ....G 407 508-6286
Kissimmee **(G-6933)**

FLAT GLASS: Laminated

Advanced Impact Tech Inc ....F 727 287-4620
Largo **(G-7522)**
National Glass Pdts & Distrs ....G 303 762-9768
Coral Gables **(G-2090)**
PGT Innovations Inc ....C 941 480-1600
North Venice **(G-11218)**

FLAT GLASS: Picture

Giz Studio Inc ....F 305 416-5001
Miami **(G-9214)**

FLAT GLASS: Skylight

Kenny Skylights LLC ....G 407 330-5150
Sanford **(G-15349)**
Sun-Tek Manufacturing Inc ....E 407 859-2117
Orlando **(G-12632)**

FLAT GLASS: Window, Clear & Colored

Assura Windows and Doors LLC ....G 954 781-4430
Pompano Beach **(G-13940)**
Coastal Hurricane Film LLC ....G 941 268-9693
Port Charlotte **(G-14293)**
Cws Holding Company LLC ....G 352 368-6922
Ocala **(G-11362)**
Erickson International LLC ....G 702 853-4800
Boynton Beach **(G-864)**
Global Performance Windows Inc ....F 954 942-3322
Pompano Beach **(G-14042)**
Panama City Tint Center ....G 850 640-0167
Panama City **(G-13295)**
US Global Glass LLC ....F 305 651-6630
Miami **(G-10080)**
Vistamatic LLC ....E 866 466-9525
Coral Springs **(G-2226)**
Windoor Incorporated ....C 407 481-8400
North Venice **(G-11222)**

FLEA MARKET

United Trophy Manufacturing ....E 407 841-2525
Orlando **(G-12690)**

FLIGHT TRAINING SCHOOLS

Cae USA Inc ....A 813 885-7481
Tampa **(G-16672)**

FLOATING DRY DOCKS

Jmh Marine Inc ....F 954 785-7557
Pompano Beach **(G-14067)**

FLOOR CLEANING & MAINTENANCE EQPT: Household

Flexshopper LLC ....E 561 922-6609
Boca Raton **(G-516)**

FLOOR COVERING STORES: Carpets

Design-A-Rug Inc ....F 954 943-7487
Deerfield Beach **(G-2705)**
Tropic Shield Inc ....F 954 731-5553
Lauderdale Lakes **(G-7721)**

FLOOR COVERING STORES: Rugs

Murse Properties LLC ....G 941 966-3380
Sarasota **(G-15755)**

FLOOR COVERINGS WHOLESALERS

Eagle Prof Flrg Removal ....G 813 520-3027
Riverview **(G-14562)**

FLOOR COVERINGS: Rubber

Abco Products Inc ....E 888 694-2226
Miami **(G-8636)**
Impact Molding Clearwater LLC ....E 847 718-9300
Clearwater **(G-1641)**

FLOOR COVERINGS: Textile Fiber

Englert Arts Inc ....G 561 241-9924
Boca Raton **(G-504)**
Floors Inc ....E 813 879-5720
Tampa **(G-16838)**
Glassflake International Inc ....G 904 268-4000
Jacksonville **(G-6143)**
Milliken & Company ....G 352 244-2267
Gainesville **(G-4731)**

FLOORING & GRATINGS: Open, Construction Applications

Alabama Metal Industries Corp ....D 863 688-9256
Lakeland **(G-7269)**

FLOORING: Baseboards, Wood

Eagle Prof Flrg Removal ....G 813 520-3027
Riverview **(G-14562)**

FLOORING: Hard Surface

Amercn Cabinets Granite Floors ....G 727 303-0678
Palm Harbor **(G-13097)**

FLOORING: Hardwood

Bona Enterprises Inc ....G 954 927-4889
Dania **(G-2327)**
Designer Lifestyles LLC ....F 904 631-8954
Jacksonville **(G-6030)**
Goodwin Lumber Company Inc ....F 352 466-0339
Micanopy **(G-10397)**
It Is Finished Inc ....G 813 598-9585
Land O Lakes **(G-7494)**
New T Management Inc ....G 954 927-4889
Dania **(G-2339)**
Renovation Flooring LLC ....E 850 460-7295
Miramar Beach **(G-10572)**
Reso Inc ....G 561 328-8539
Riviera Beach **(G-14668)**
Upstream Installation Inc ....G 904 829-3507
Saint Augustine **(G-14908)**

FLOORING: Parquet, Hardwood

Cryntel Enterprises Ltd Inc ....G 954 577-7844
Davie **(G-2400)**

FLOORING: Rubber

A Clean Finish Inc ....G 407 516-1311
Jacksonville **(G-5846)**
Ajc Tiling Solutions LLC ....G 863 274-1962
Winter Haven **(G-18412)**
Bolidt Cruise Control Corp ....F 305 607-4172
Opa Locka **(G-11724)**
Ffo Leesburg LLC ....G 352 315-0783
Leesburg **(G-7773)**

FLOORING: Tile

Arcana Tileworks ....G 407 492-0668
Winter Garden **(G-18374)**
Asd Surfaces LLC ....G 561 845-5009
North Palm Beach **(G-11174)**

FLORISTS

Always Flowers Inc ....F 305 572-1122
Miami **(G-8706)**
Ebs Quality Service Inc ....F 305 595-4048
Miami **(G-9067)**

FLOWER ARRANGEMENTS: Artificial

1800flowerscom ....G 954 683-1246
Fort Lauderdale **(G-3614)**
Dianthus Miami Inc ....F 786 800-8365
Miami **(G-9028)**
Nearly Natural LLC ....F 800 711-0544
Hialeah **(G-5274)**

FLOWER POTS Plastic

Enviroworks Inc ....E 407 889-5533
Apopka **(G-127)**
Fiskars Brands Inc ....D 407 889-5533
Apopka **(G-132)**
Nursery Supplies Inc ....B 407 846-9750
Kissimmee **(G-6945)**

FLOWERS & FLORISTS' SPLYS WHOLESALERS

Ebs Quality Service Inc ....F 305 595-4048
Miami **(G-9067)**

FLOWERS, ARTIFICIAL, WHOLESALE

Nearly Natural LLC ....F 800 711-0544
Hialeah **(G-5274)**

FLOWERS: Artificial & Preserved

Always Flowers Inc ....F 305 572-1122
Miami **(G-8706)**

FLUES & PIPES: Stove Or Furnace

Crown Products Company Inc ....C 904 737-7144
Jacksonville **(G-6015)**

FLUID METERS & COUNTING DEVICES

Trak Engineering Incorporated ....E 850 878-4585
Tallahassee **(G-16514)**

FLUID POWER PUMPS & MOTORS

Flaire Corporation ....C 352 237-1220
Ocala **(G-11390)**
Motors Pumps and Accessories ....G 305 883-3181
Medley **(G-8284)**
Scott Industrial Systems Inc ....F 904 693-3318
Jacksonville **(G-6456)**

FLUID POWER VALVES & HOSE FITTINGS

Helios Technologies Inc ....E 941 351-6648
Sarasota **(G-15490)**
Helios Technologies Inc ....F 941 362-1200
Sarasota **(G-15493)**
Hose Power USA ....G 863 669-9333
Lakeland **(G-7345)**
Kinetics Usa Inc ....E 561 988-8826
Boca Raton **(G-569)**
Leslie Controls Inc ....C 813 978-1000
Temple Terrace **(G-17539)**
Sun Hydraulics Corporation ....E 941 362-1300
Sarasota **(G-15563)**
Teknocraft Inc ....E 321 729-9634
Melbourne **(G-8548)**

FLY TRAPS: Electrical

Pestwest Usa LLC ....G 941 358-1983
Sarasota **(G-15536)**

FOAM CHARGE MIXTURES

Blue Earth Solutions Inc ....E 352 729-0150
Clermont **(G-1861)**

FOAM RUBBER

Inspiration Foam Inc ....F 407 498-0040
Kissimmee *(G-6927)*

Lapolla Industries LLC ....F 954 379-0241
Deerfield Beach *(G-2751)*

Reliatex Inc ....E 813 621-6021
Tampa *(G-17215)*

Treadway Industries LLC ....E 352 326-3313
Minneola *(G-10453)*

FOIL & LEAF: Metal

Vega...G 239 574-1798
Cape Coral *(G-1403)*

FOOD CONTAMINATION TESTING OR SCREENING KITS

Elisa Technologies Inc ....F 352 337-3929
Gainesville *(G-4685)*

FOOD PRDTS & SEAFOOD: Shellfish, Fresh, Shucked

Juniors Bait and Seafood Inc ....E 321 480-5492
Melbourne *(G-8445)*

FOOD PRDTS, BREAKFAST: Cereal, Wheat Flakes

General Mills Inc ....E 305 591-1771
Doral *(G-3227)*

FOOD PRDTS, CANNED OR FRESH PACK: Fruit Juices

Apple Rush Company Inc ....G 888 741-3777
Titusville *(G-17572)*

Coco Lopez Inc ....G 954 450-3100
Miramar *(G-10481)*

Cutrale Citrus Juices USA Inc ....A 352 728-7800
Leesburg *(G-7765)*

Florida Refresco Inc ....C 863 665-5515
Lakeland *(G-7332)*

Gem Freshco LLC ....D 772 595-0070
Fort Pierce *(G-4489)*

M & B Products Inc ....C 813 988-2211
Temple Terrace *(G-17540)*

Ouhlala Gourmet Corp ....F 305 774-7332
Coral Gables *(G-2093)*

Pepsico Inc ....E 407 933-5542
Kissimmee *(G-6951)*

Raw Foods International Llc ....F 305 856-1991
Coral Gables *(G-2103)*

Tropicana Products Inc ....F 772 465-2030
Fort Pierce *(G-4542)*

United Jice Companies Amer Inc ....D 772 562-5442
Vero Beach *(G-17811)*

FOOD PRDTS, CANNED OR FRESH PACK: Vegetable Juices

Benfresh LLC ....G 786 403-5046
Miami *(G-8813)*

FOOD PRDTS, CANNED OR FRESH PACK: Vegetable Juices

Florida Food Products LLC...............D 352 357-4141
Eustis *(G-3558)*

FOOD PRDTS, CANNED: Barbecue Sauce

Barbecue Superstore.....................G 305 635-4427
Miami *(G-8796)*

Choctaw Trading Co Inc ....F 407 905-9917
Winter Garden *(G-18380)*

Cordoba Foods LLC ....E 305 733-4768
Hialeah *(G-5098)*

Flayco Products Inc ....E 813 879-1356
Tampa *(G-16835)*

Hot Sauce Harrys Inc...................G 941 423-7092
North Port *(G-11195)*

FOOD PRDTS, CANNED: Beans, With Meat

Conchita Foods Inc ....D 305 888-9703
Medley *(G-8220)*

FOOD PRDTS, CANNED: Chili Sauce, Tomato

Wharton Pepper Co ....G 850 997-4359
Monticello *(G-10587)*

FOOD PRDTS, CANNED: Ethnic

All Naturals Direct.......................G 813 792-3777
Tampa *(G-16573)*

Alpha Omega Commercial Limited ....G 407 925-7913
Windermere *(G-18347)*

FOOD PRDTS, CANNED: Fruit Juices, Concentrated

Tropicana Manufacturing Co Inc ....A 800 237-7799
Bradenton *(G-1066)*

FOOD PRDTS, CANNED: Fruit Juices, Fresh

Brown International Corp LLC...........G 863 299-2111
Winter Haven *(G-18424)*

Coca-Cola Company ....G 407 565-2465
Apopka *(G-113)*

Cutrale Farms Inc ....D 863 965-5000
Auburndale *(G-228)*

Lakewood Organics LLC ....D 305 324-5900
Miami *(G-9418)*

Sun Orchard LLC ....E 786 646-9200
Doral *(G-3382)*

Tropicana Products Inc ....A 941 747-4461
Bradenton *(G-1067)*

Watts Juicery ....F 904 372-0693
Atlantic Beach *(G-217)*

Wm G Roe & Sons Inc ....B 863 294-3577
Winter Haven *(G-18478)*

FOOD PRDTS, CANNED: Fruits

Ben Hill Griffin Inc......................E 863 635-2281
Frostproof *(G-4633)*

Conchita Foods Inc ....D 305 888-9703
Medley *(G-8220)*

Fruselva Usa LLC ....F 949 798-0061
Miami *(G-9178)*

FOOD PRDTS, CANNED: Fruits

Allapattah Industries Inc ....E 305 324-5900
Miami *(G-8694)*

Ardmore Farms LLC ....D 386 734-4634
Deland *(G-2854)*

Coca-Cola Company ....E 727 736-7101
Dunedin *(G-3446)*

Gma-Food LLC ....G 646 469-8599
Lutz *(G-7991)*

Kraft Heinz Foods Company.............G 727 459-4527
Saint Petersburg *(G-15106)*

Kraft Heinz Foods Company ....G 239 694-3663
Fort Myers *(G-4307)*

Mancini Packing Company ....D 863 735-2000
Zolfo Springs *(G-18640)*

Sun Orchard LLC ....D 863 422-5062
Haines City *(G-4918)*

FOOD PRDTS, CANNED: Fruits & Fruit Prdts

Del Monte Fresh Produce NA Inc ....E 305 520-8400
Coral Gables *(G-2047)*

Freshco Ltd ....E 772 287-2111
Stuart *(G-16149)*

R & Z Ventures Inc ....D 954 532-7938
Pompano Beach *(G-14154)*

FOOD PRDTS, CANNED: Italian

Ait USA Corp ....G 786 953-5918
Miami *(G-8677)*

Delarosa Real Foods LLC ....D 718 333-0333
Lauderdale Lakes *(G-7712)*

Magnificat Holdings LLC................G 727 798-0512
Clearwater *(G-1681)*

Nanas Original Stromboli Inc............G 954 771-6262
Fort Lauderdale *(G-3951)*

Richard Meer Investments Inc...........G 941 484-6551
Venice *(G-17713)*

FOOD PRDTS, CANNED: Jams, Jellies & Preserves

Good Jams LLC ....F 702 379-5551
Boca Raton *(G-530)*

Kraft Heinz Foods Company.................D 904 695-1300
Jacksonville *(G-6249)*

FOOD PRDTS, CANNED: Jellies, Edible, Including Imitation

Palmetto Canning Company ....F 941 722-1100
Palmetto *(G-13183)*

Seven Keys Co of Florida................G 954 946-5010
Pompano Beach *(G-14176)*

FOOD PRDTS, CANNED: Mexican, NEC

Rancheritos ....G 561 479-0046
Boca Raton *(G-647)*

Whole Enchilada Fresh Mxcan Gri........F 954 561-4040
Fort Lauderdale *(G-4129)*

FOOD PRDTS, CANNED: Mushrooms

Ida Solutions ....G 305 603-9835
Medley *(G-8256)*

FOOD PRDTS, CANNED: Pizza Sauce

Chiantis..................................G 407 484-6510
Sanford *(G-15282)*

FOOD PRDTS, CANNED: Soups, Exc Seafood

Suzanne Chalet Foods Inc ....G 863 676-6011
Lake Wales *(G-7176)*

FOOD PRDTS, CANNED: Tamales

Catalina Finer Food Corp ....E 813 872-6359
Tampa *(G-16687)*

FOOD PRDTS, CANNED: Tomato Purees

Gulf Coast Growers Florida LLC ....D 941 981-3888
Palmetto *(G-13170)*

FOOD PRDTS, CANNED: Vegetables

Sam S Accrsio Sons Pkg Prod In ....F 305 246-3455
Homestead *(G-5737)*

Vazko LLC ....G 786 521-0808
Medley *(G-8348)*

FOOD PRDTS, CANNED: Vegetables

Fruit Dynamics LLC ....C 239 643-7373
Naples *(G-10752)*

FOOD PRDTS, CONFECTIONERY, WHOLESALE: Candy

Hoffman Commercial Group Inc..........E 561 967-2213
Orlando *(G-12221)*

Peterbrooke Choclat Fctry LLC...........G 904 273-7878
Ponte Vedra Beach *(G-14276)*

FOOD PRDTS, DAIRY, WHOLESALE: Frozen Dairy Desserts

Latin Dairy Foods LLC...................F 305 888-1788
Miami *(G-9436)*

Miami Foods Distrs USA Inc ....F 305 512-3246
Hialeah *(G-5250)*

FOOD PRDTS, FISH & SEAFOOD, WHOLESALE: Seafood

Florida Fresh Seafood Corp..............F 305 694-1733
Miami *(G-9156)*

FOOD PRDTS, FISH & SEAFOOD: Canned & Jarred, Etc

Select Europe Inc.......................F 866 204-0899
Deerfield Beach *(G-2806)*

FOOD PRDTS, FISH & SEAFOOD: Crab cakes, Frozen

Santos Frozen Foods Inc ....F 813 875-4901
Tampa *(G-17247)*

FOOD PRDTS, FISH & SEAFOOD: Crabmeat, Fresh, Pkgd Nonsealed

Chiefland Crab Company Inc ....E 352 493-4887
Chiefland (G-1447)

FOOD PRDTS, FISH & SEAFOOD: Fish, Frozen, Prepared

Masa Trading LLC ....F 561 729-3293
Pompano Beach (G-14089)

FOOD PRDTS, FISH & SEAFOOD: Fish, Smoked

Captain Rustys ....G 813 244-2799
Lorida (G-7963)

FOOD PRDTS, FISH & SEAFOOD: Fresh, Prepared

Buddy Ward & Sons Seafood ....G 850 653-8522
Apalachicola (G-88)
Florida Fresh Seafood Corp ....F 305 694-1733
Miami (G-9156)
Massachusetts Bay Clam Co Inc ....F 813 855-4599
Tampa (G-17053)
Sahlman Holding Company Inc ....G 813 248-5726
Tampa (G-17244)
Shaws Sthern Blle Frz Fods In ....D 904 768-1591
Jacksonville (G-6463)

FOOD PRDTS, FISH & SEAFOOD: Fresh/Frozen Chowder, Soup/Stew

Skip One Seafood Inc ....G 239 463-8788
Fort Myers Beach (G-4456)

FOOD PRDTS, FISH & SEAFOOD: Oysters, Canned, Jarred, Etc

Miracle Seafood Manufacturers ....G 850 653-2114
Apalachicola (G-89)

FOOD PRDTS, FISH & SEAFOOD: Seafood, Frozen, Prepared

Framors Trading Inc ....G 305 382-8782
Miami (G-9172)
Global Aliment Inc ....G 786 536-5261
Doral (G-3234)

FOOD PRDTS, FISH & SEAFOOD: Shrimp, Frozen, Prepared

Thetradebaycom LLC ....G 954 607-2405
Weston (G-18291)

FOOD PRDTS, FROZEN, WHOLESALE: Dinners

Jo MO Enterprises Inc ....G 708 599-8098
Boca Raton (G-563)

FOOD PRDTS, FROZEN: Breakfasts, Packaged

Uren North America LLC ....G 410 924-3478
Coral Gables (G-2117)

FOOD PRDTS, FROZEN: Ethnic Foods, NEC

Asian Food Solutions Inc ....E 888 499-6888
Oviedo (G-12806)
Comida Vida Inc ....G 855 720-7663
Oviedo (G-12814)
International Fd Solutions Inc ....E 888 499-6888
Oviedo (G-12829)
Patty King Inc ....E 305 817-1888
Hialeah (G-5292)
Very Tasty LLC ....F 305 636-4140
Miami (G-10103)

FOOD PRDTS, FROZEN: Fruit Juice, Concentrates

Citrus World Inc ....A 863 676-1411
Lake Wales (G-7155)
Coca-Cola Company ....G 407 565-2465
Apopka (G-113)

Country Pure Foods Inc ....B 904 734-4634
Deland (G-2859)
Tropicana Products Inc ....A 941 747-4461
Bradenton (G-1067)
Tropicana Products Inc ....F 772 465-2030
Fort Pierce (G-4542)

FOOD PRDTS, FROZEN: Fruit Juices

Ardmore Farms LLC ....D 386 734-4634
Deland (G-2854)
Florida Food Products LLC ....D 352 357-4141
Eustis (G-3558)
Food Partners Inc ....F 863 298-8771
Winter Haven (G-18439)
Silver Springs Citrus Inc ....C 352 324-2101
Howey In The Hills (G-5759)
Sun Orchard LLC ....E 786 646-9200
Doral (G-3382)

FOOD PRDTS, FROZEN: Fruits

Totally Bananas LLC ....F 954 674-9421
Davie (G-2492)

FOOD PRDTS, FROZEN: Fruits & Vegetables

World Wide Frozen Foods LLC ....G 954 266-8500
Fort Lauderdale (G-4137)

FOOD PRDTS, FROZEN: Fruits, Juices & Vegetables

Ata Group of Companies Inc ....G 352 735-1588
Mount Dora (G-10597)
Borden Dairy Company Fla LLC ....E 863 298-9742
Winter Haven (G-18423)
Brazilian Smoothie Inc ....G 305 233-5543
Pinecrest (G-13663)
Chunky Plates LLC ....G 321 746-3346
Orlando (G-12012)
Clonts Groves Inc ....F 407 359-4103
Oviedo (G-12813)
Crop LLC ....F 941 923-8640
Sarasota (G-15645)
Floridas Natural Food Svc Inc ....E 888 657-6600
Lake Wales (G-7161)
Fresh Blends North America Inc ....F 531 665-8200
Delray Beach (G-2966)
Green Plant LLC ....E 305 397-9394
Miami (G-9246)
Kerry Inc ....D 813 359-5181
Plant City (G-13782)
Key Biscayne Smoothie Company ....G 305 441-7882
Coral Gables (G-2076)
Manatee Smoothies LLC ....G 985 640-3088
Lakewood Ranch (G-7480)
Natural Fruit Corp ....E 305 887-7525
Hialeah (G-5272)
Palm Beach Smoothies Com Inc ....G 561 379-8647
Tequesta (G-17551)
PI Smoothie LLC ....G 954 554-0450
Davie (G-2459)
Refreshing Smoothie ....G 904 549-5366
Jacksonville (G-6411)
Shri Guru Krupa Smoothies Inc ....F 904 461-9090
Saint Augustine (G-14891)
Smoothie Corp ....D 305 588-0867
Miami (G-9908)
Smoothies Recharge ....G 954 999-0332
Sunrise (G-16368)
Sunluver Smoothies Inc ....G 239 331-5431
Naples (G-10913)
Sunnyland Usa Inc ....F 772 293-0293
Fort Pierce (G-4535)

FOOD PRDTS, FROZEN: NEC

Charles Bryant Enterprises ....G 850 785-3604
Panama City (G-13241)
Chefs Commissary LLC ....D 321 303-2947
Orlando (G-12007)
Discos Y Empanadas Argentina ....F 305 326-9300
Miami (G-9033)
GA Fd Svcs Pinellas Cnty LLC ....B 727 573-2211
Saint Petersburg (G-15057)
GA Fd Svcs Pinellas Cnty LLC ....D 954 972-8884
Fort Lauderdale (G-3835)
GA Fd Svcs Pinellas Cnty LLC ....E 239 693-5090
Fort Myers (G-4268)
Greenie Tots Inc ....G 888 316-6126
Plantation (G-13856)

Kibby Foods LLC ....G 305 456-3635
Hialeah (G-5210)
Lillys Gstrnmia Itlana Fla Inc ....G 305 655-2111
Hallandale Beach (G-4959)
Madan Corporation ....G 954 925-0077
Dania Beach (G-2353)
Sukalde Inc ....G 786 399-0087
Coral Gables (G-2113)

FOOD PRDTS, FROZEN: Pizza

Classic Pizza Crusts Inc ....G 954 570-8383
Plantation (G-13835)
Pizza Spice Packet LLC ....G 718 831-7036
Boca Raton (G-635)

FOOD PRDTS, FROZEN: Potato Prdts

Interfries Inc ....G 786 427-1427
Miami (G-9324)

FOOD PRDTS, FROZEN: Snack Items

Krunchy Krisps LLC ....G 561 309-7049
Palm City (G-13048)
Zesty Brands LLC ....F 954 348-2827
Orlando (G-12732)

FOOD PRDTS, FROZEN: Spaghetti & Meatballs

Jo MO Enterprises Inc ....G 708 599-8098
Boca Raton (G-563)

FOOD PRDTS, FRUITS & VEGETABLES, FRESH, WHOLESALE

Del Monte Fresh Produce NA Inc ....E 305 520-8400
Coral Gables (G-2047)

FOOD PRDTS, FRUITS & VEGETABLES, FRESH, WHOLESALE: Vegetable

Farm Cut LLC ....C 813 754-3321
Plant City (G-13765)

FOOD PRDTS, MEAT & MEAT PRDTS, WHOLESALE: Cured Or Smoked

La Villarena Meat & Pork Inc ....F 305 759-0555
Miami (G-9415)

FOOD PRDTS, MEAT & MEAT PRDTS, WHOLESALE: Fresh

Bush Brothers Provision Co ....E 561 832-6666
West Palm Beach (G-17954)
Latin Amercn Meats & Foods USA ....G 305 477-2700
Miami (G-9434)
Pinellas Provision Corporation ....E 727 822-2701
Saint Petersburg (G-15150)

FOOD PRDTS, WHOLESALE: Beverage Concentrates

Egd Euro Gourmet Deli Inc ....G 305 937-1515
Aventura (G-258)
Nutrition Laboratories Inc ....E 727 442-2747
Clearwater (G-1724)

FOOD PRDTS, WHOLESALE: Beverages, Exc Coffee & Tea

Candies and Beyond Inc ....G 954 828-2255
Miami Lakes (G-10290)
Shasta Beverages Intl Inc ....E 954 581-0922
Plantation (G-13886)

FOOD PRDTS, WHOLESALE: Coffee & Tea

Babys Coffee LLC ....G 305 744-9866
Key West (G-6855)
De Luna Coffee Intl Inc ....G 850 478-6371
Pensacola (G-13486)
Grand Havana Inc ....G 305 297-2207
Miami Beach (G-10197)
Latitude 235 Coffee and Tea ....G 941 556-2600
Sarasota (G-15511)
Royal Cup Inc ....G 813 664-8902
Tampa (G-17235)

FOOD PRDTS, WHOLESALE: Coffee, Green Or Roasted

Aroma Coffee Service Inc ....G...... 239 481-7262
Fort Myers (G-4181)
Potters Coffee Company ....G...... 850 525-1793
Pensacola (G-13580)
Rae Launo Corporation ....G...... 813 242-4281
Valrico (G-17669)

FOOD PRDTS, WHOLESALE: Flavorings & Fragrances

Two Scents LLC DBA Vinevida ....E 888 527-6805
Opa Locka (G-11796)

FOOD PRDTS, WHOLESALE: Grains

Southland Milling Co ....G...... 850 674-8448
Blountstown (G-378)

FOOD PRDTS, WHOLESALE: Health

Powerful Foods LLC ....G...... 305 637-7300
Pinecrest (G-13668)

FOOD PRDTS, WHOLESALE: Macaroni

Termine Ravioli Manufacturing ....F 954 983-3711
Hollywood (G-5669)

FOOD PRDTS, WHOLESALE: Natural & Organic

Shining Tree Inc ....F 855 688-7987
Wellington (G-17863)

FOOD PRDTS, WHOLESALE: Sandwiches

Los Atntcos Sndwich Cuban Cafe ....G...... 407 282-2322
Orlando (G-12352)

FOOD PRDTS, WHOLESALE: Sauces

Joys International Foods Inc ....G...... 321 242-6520
Melbourne (G-8444)

FOOD PRDTS, WHOLESALE: Spaghetti

Cheney Ofs Inc ....A 407 292-3223
Orlando (G-12008)

FOOD PRDTS, WHOLESALE: Specialty

All Naturals Direct...................G...... 813 792-3777
Tampa (G-16573)
Vigo Importing Company ....C 813 884-3491
Tampa (G-17417)

FOOD PRDTS, WHOLESALE: Spices & Seasonings

El Sabor Spices Inc...................F 305 691-2300
Miami (G-9076)

FOOD PRDTS, WHOLESALE: Sugar, Refined

Evergreen Sweeteners Inc ....F 954 381-7776
Hollywood (G-5573)

FOOD PRDTS, WHOLESALE: Water, Distilled

Ultra-Pure Bottled Water Inc ....F 813 835-7873
Tampa (G-17384)

FOOD PRDTS, WHOLESALE: Water, Mineral Or Spring, Bottled

Aqua Pure LLC...................G...... 407 521-3055
Orlando (G-11915)

FOOD PRDTS: Animal & marine fats & oils

Conchita Foods Inc...................D 305 888-9703
Medley (G-8220)
Darling Ingredients Inc ....G...... 904 964-8083
Starke (G-16100)
Darling Ingredients Inc ....F 863 425-0065
Tampa (G-16762)
Griffin Industries LLC ....E 407 857-5474
Orlando (G-12201)
Valley Proteins (de) Inc ....E 704 718-6568
Jacksonville (G-6585)

Valley Proteins (de) Inc ....E 910 282-7900
Mulberry (G-10643)

FOOD PRDTS: Bread Crumbs, Exc Made In Bakeries

Quality Bakery Products LLC ....G...... 954 779-3663
Fort Lauderdale (G-4005)

FOOD PRDTS: Butter, Renovated & Processed

Belgium Co Inc ....F 407 957-1886
Saint Cloud (G-14921)

FOOD PRDTS: Cheese Curls & Puffs

Super-Pufft Snacks Usa Inc ....E 905 564-1180
Perry (G-13654)

FOOD PRDTS: Chili Pepper Or Powder

Shiloh Import/Export LLC ....G...... 404 514-4109
Tamarac (G-16542)

FOOD PRDTS: Citrus Pulp, Dried

Citrus World Services Inc ....F 863 676-1411
Lake Wales (G-7156)
Cvista LLC ....E 813 405-3000
Riverview (G-14560)

FOOD PRDTS: Coffee

Adrenaline Productions LLC ....G...... 305 697-6445
Miami (G-8655)
Allcoffee LLC ....G...... 305 685-6856
Opa Locka (G-11714)
Aroma Coffee Service Inc ....G...... 239 481-7262
Fort Myers (G-4181)
Babys Coffee LLC...................G...... 305 744-9866
Key West (G-6855)
C&D Purveyors Inc ....F 305 562-8541
Miami (G-8871)
Carefree Group Inc ....G...... 866 800-1007
Miami Beach (G-10175)
Clr Roasters LLC...................E 305 591-0040
Miami (G-8932)
De Luna Coffee Intl Inc ....G...... 850 478-6371
Pensacola (G-13486)
Distribuidora Giorgio Usa LLC ....F 305 685-6366
Opa Locka (G-11737)
Grand Havana Inc ....G...... 305 297-2207
Miami Beach (G-10197)
Javalution Coffee Company...................F 954 568-1747
Fort Lauderdale (G-3894)
Kafe PA Nou LLC...................G...... 305 953-3344
Sunny Isles Beach (G-16278)
List + Beisler Corp ....E 646 866-6960
Miami (G-9465)
Melitta North America Inc...................D 727 535-2111
Clearwater (G-1691)
Mercers Fresh Roasted Coffees ....G...... 941 286-7054
Punta Gorda (G-14515)
Potters Coffee Company ....G...... 850 525-1793
Pensacola (G-13580)
Rae Launo Corporation ....G...... 813 242-4281
Valrico (G-17669)
Royal Cup Inc ....G...... 813 664-8902
Tampa (G-17235)
Sergeant Bretts Coffee LLC...................G...... 561 451-0048
Coconut Creek (G-2004)
Whole Coffee Company LLC...................D 786 364-4444
Miami (G-10131)

FOOD PRDTS: Coffee Extracts

Dupuy Silo Facility LLC...................G...... 904 899-7200
Jacksonville (G-6048)
Larson Industries Incorporated...........G...... 352 262-0566
Gainesville (G-4719)

FOOD PRDTS: Coffee Roasting, Exc Wholesale Grocers

Burke Brands LLC ....E 305 249-5628
Miami (G-8861)
Coffee Unlimited LLC ....F 305 685-6366
Opa Locka (G-11732)
Conali Express Corp...................G...... 954 531-9573
Fort Lauderdale (G-3741)

Day Shopping LLC...................F 321 616-4504
Tampa (G-16766)
Espresso Disposition Corp 1...................D 305 594-9062
Miami (G-9111)
Gold Coffee Roasters Inc ....F 561 746-8110
Jupiter (G-6737)
Kraft Heinz Foods Company ....C 904 632-3400
Jacksonville (G-6248)
Latitude 235 Coffee and Tea ....G...... 941 556-2600
Sarasota (G-15511)
Melitta Usa Inc ....D 727 535-2111
Clearwater (G-1692)
Naviera Coffee Mills Inc ....E 813 248-2521
Tampa (G-17104)
New Dawn Coffee Company Inc ....G...... 727 321-5155
Saint Petersburg (G-15138)
Rcr Coffee Company Inc ....E 813 248-6264
Tampa (G-17209)

FOOD PRDTS: Coffee Substitutes

Ilex Organics LLC ....F 386 566-3826
Edgewater (G-3491)

FOOD PRDTS: Cooking Oils, Refined Vegetable, Exc Corn

Grease TEC Holding LLC ....G...... 352 742-2440
Tavares (G-17509)

FOOD PRDTS: Corn Chips & Other Corn-Based Snacks

Specialty Food Group LLC ....G...... 305 392-5000
Doral (G-3372)

FOOD PRDTS: Dessert Mixes & Fillings

Body LLC...................F 850 888-2639
Saint Petersburg (G-14986)
General Mills Inc ....E 305 591-1771
Doral (G-3227)

FOOD PRDTS: Dips, Exc Cheese & Sour Cream Based

Salsa Cuba Inc ....G...... 305 993-9757
Hialeah (G-5341)
Salsa Pembroke Pines Inc ....E 954 461-0532
Pembroke Pines (G-13412)
Salsa Three Inc...................G...... 954 990-2223
Plantation (G-13885)
Salsa Tropical LLC...................G...... 786 362-9034
Miami (G-9840)
Sheas Salsa LLC...................G...... 954 371-7781
Wellington (G-17862)

FOOD PRDTS: Dough, Pizza, Prepared

Classic Pizza Crusts Inc...................G...... 954 570-8383
Plantation (G-13835)

FOOD PRDTS: Doughs, Frozen Or Refrig From Purchased Flour

Burris Investment Group Inc ....E 850 623-3845
Pensacola (G-13467)

FOOD PRDTS: Dressings, Salad, Raw & Cooked Exc Dry Mixes

Mizkan America Inc...................F 863 956-0391
Lake Alfred (G-6996)

FOOD PRDTS: Dried & Dehydrated Fruits, Vegetables & Soup Mix

Conchita Foods Inc...................D 305 888-9703
Medley (G-8220)
Culinary Concepts Inc ....E 407 228-0069
Orlando (G-12064)
Green Leaf Foods LLC ....G...... 305 308-9167
Miramar (G-10499)
Isofrut Company Inc ....G...... 305 961-1681
Miami (G-9342)
Kerry Inc ....D 813 359-5181
Plant City (G-13782)
Presage Analytics Inc ....G...... 800 309-1704
Bonita Springs (G-814)
Story Citrus Inc ....E 863 638-1619
Lake Wales (G-7175)

PRODUCT

FOOD PRDTS: Edible fats & oils

Ventura Foods LLC ....D...... 772 878-1400
Port Saint Lucie (G-14463)

FOOD PRDTS: Flavored Ices, Frozen

Phillys Famous Water Ice Inc ....C...... 813 248-8644
Tampa (G-17163)

FOOD PRDTS: Flour

General Mills Inc ....E...... 305 591-1771
Doral (G-3227)

FOOD PRDTS: Flour & Other Grain Mill Products

Bay State Milling Company ....F...... 630 427-3400
Fort Lauderdale (G-3677)
Change This World ....G...... 407 900-8840
Orlando (G-12003)
Shining Tree Inc ....F...... 855 688-7987
Wellington (G-17863)

FOOD PRDTS: Flour Mixes & Doughs

Big L Brands Inc ....G...... 888 552-9768
Boca Raton (G-431)
General Mills Inc ....E...... 305 591-1771
Doral (G-3227)

FOOD PRDTS: Freeze-Dried Coffee

Coca-Cola Company ....D...... 407 358-6758
Apopka (G-114)

FOOD PRDTS: Fresh Vegetables, Peeled Or Processed

Stripping Alpaca LLC ....F...... 207 208-9687
Miami Beach (G-10236)

FOOD PRDTS: Fruit Juices

Allapattah Industries Inc ....E...... 305 324-5900
Miami (G-8694)
Bru Bottling Inc ....F...... 561 324-5053
Juno Beach (G-6661)
Cebev LLC ....G...... 918 830-4417
Boca Raton (G-457)
Country Frits Juices Nurs Corp...........G...... 786 302-8487
Miami (G-8976)
Cutrale Citrus Juices USA Inc ....A...... 352 728-7800
Leesburg (G-7765)
Healtheintentions Inc ....G...... 954 394-8867
Miami (G-9268)
King Brands LLC ....E...... 239 313-2057
Fort Myers (G-4305)
Orchid Island Juice Co Inc ....D...... 772 465-1122
Fort Pierce (G-4514)
Raw Foods International Llc ....F...... 305 856-1991
Coral Gables (G-2103)
Southern Grdns Ctrus Hldg Corp.........G...... 863 983-8121
Clewiston (G-1895)

FOOD PRDTS: Fruits & Vegetables, Pickled

Pickled Art Inc ....G...... 954 635-7370
Fort Lauderdale (G-3986)
Pickles Plus ....G...... 941 661-6139
North Port (G-11203)

FOOD PRDTS: Fruits, Dehydrated Or Dried

Ritco Foods LLC ....G...... 954 727-3554
Sunrise (G-16364)

FOOD PRDTS: Ham, Poultry

American Foods Intl LLC ....E...... 877 894-7675
Aventura (G-251)

FOOD PRDTS: Honey

Bees Brothers LLC ....G...... 305 529-5789
Coral Gables (G-2033)

FOOD PRDTS: Ice, Blocks

Nucycle Energy of Tampa LLC ....E...... 813 848-0509
Plant City (G-13787)
Reddy Ice Corporation ....F...... 850 433-2191
Pensacola (G-13595)

FOOD PRDTS: Instant Coffee

Kraken Koffee LLC ....G...... 833 546-3725
Coral Gables (G-2079)

FOOD PRDTS: Juice Pops, Frozen

Frio Distributors Inc ....F...... 813 567-1493
Plant City (G-13769)
Guanabana & Co LLC ....F...... 904 891-5256
Jacksonville (G-6161)

FOOD PRDTS: Macaroni Prdts, Dry, Alphabet, Rings Or Shells

Termine Ravioli Manufacturing.............F........ 954 983-3711
Hollywood (G-5669)

FOOD PRDTS: Macaroni, Noodles, Spaghetti, Pasta, Etc

First Grade Food Corporation ....E...... 813 886-6118
Tampa (G-16833)
Jo MO Enterprises Inc ....G...... 708 599-8098
Boca Raton (G-563)
Lillys Gstrnmia Itlana Fla Inc ....G...... 305 655-2111
Hallandale Beach (G-4959)

FOOD PRDTS: Malt

Florida Brewery Inc ....E...... 863 965-1825
Auburndale (G-232)
Great Western Malting Co ....D...... 360 991-0888
Plant City (G-13774)

FOOD PRDTS: Mixes, Bread & Bread-Type Roll

Majesty Foods LLC ....E...... 305 817-1888
Hialeah (G-5235)

FOOD PRDTS: Mixes, Salad Dressings, Dry

Cranco Industries Inc ....G...... 321 690-2695
Rockledge (G-14697)

FOOD PRDTS: Mixes, Sauces, Dry

Sunshine Packing & Noodle Co ....G...... 904 355-7561
Jacksonville (G-6520)

FOOD PRDTS: Mixes, Seasonings, Dry

Everglades Foods Inc ....G...... 863 655-2214
Sebring (G-15921)
My Familys Seasonings LLC ....F...... 863 698-7968
Clearwater (G-1709)

FOOD PRDTS: Noodles, Uncooked, Packaged W/Other Ingredients

Massimo & Umberto Inc ....G...... 954 993-0842
Dania Beach (G-2355)
Strumba Media LLC ....G...... 800 948-4205
Miami (G-9959)

FOOD PRDTS: Nuts & Seeds

Papa Johns Peanuts Inc ....F...... 904 389-2511
Jacksonville (G-6354)
Veronicas Health Crunch LLC ....G...... 352 409-1124
Freeport (G-4631)

FOOD PRDTS: Oils & Fats, Marine

Openwater Seafood LLC ....G...... 407 440-0656
Orlando (G-12442)

FOOD PRDTS: Olive Oil

Bella Blsmic Pressed Olive Inc............F...... 941 249-3571
Punta Gorda (G-14496)
Estero FL ....G...... 239 289-9511
Estero (G-3542)
Miami Oliveoil & Beyond Llc ....G...... 954 632-2762
Doral (G-3301)
Mount Dora Olive Oil Company ....G...... 352 735-8481
Mount Dora (G-10606)
Olive Florida Oil Company ....G...... 941 483-1865
Venice (G-17708)
Olive Naples Oil Company ....F...... 239 275-5100
Fort Myers (G-4349)
Olive Naples Oil Company ....G...... 239 596-3000
Naples (G-10842)

Olive Tree II ....G...... 813 991-8781
Wesley Chapel (G-17885)
Olive Zarzis Oil LLC ....F...... 941 284-0291
Ellenton (G-3511)
Tomatoes & Olive Oil LLC ....G...... 941 822-9709
Venice (G-17723)
United Oil Packers Inc ....E...... 305 687-6457
Miami (G-10067)
Vigo Importing Company ....C...... 813 884-3491
Tampa (G-17417)

FOOD PRDTS: Olives, Brine, Bulk

Filthy Food LLC ....D...... 786 916-5556
Miami (G-9142)

FOOD PRDTS: Pasta, Rice/Potatoes, Uncooked, Pkgd

Jo MO Enterprises Inc ....G...... 708 599-8098
Boca Raton (G-563)
Lillys Gstrnmia Itlana Fla Inc ....G...... 305 655-2111
Hallandale Beach (G-4959)
Nex-Xos Worldwide LLC ....G...... 305 433-8376
Hollywood (G-5633)

FOOD PRDTS: Pasta, Uncooked, Packaged With Other Ingredients

Brefaros Nobile Food LLC ....E...... 305 621-0074
Miami Lakes (G-10287)

FOOD PRDTS: Peanut Oil, Cake & Meal

Hawks Nuts Inc ....F...... 813 872-0900
Tampa (G-16909)

FOOD PRDTS: Popcorn, Unpopped

Barnard Nut Company Inc.................D...... 305 836-9999
Miami (G-8799)
Popcorn Junkie LLC ....G...... 407 634-0042
Orlando (G-12494)

FOOD PRDTS: Potato & Corn Chips & Similar Prdts

Frito-Lay North America Inc ....C...... 407 295-1810
Orlando (G-12177)
Ggs Snacks & Things Inc.................G...... 954 297-9375
Pembroke Pines (G-13390)
Kerry Consulting Corp ....F...... 561 364-9969
Boynton Beach (G-883)
Mio Gourmet Products LLC ....F...... 305 219-0253
Hialeah (G-5260)
Polaris Trading Corp ....G...... 954 956-6999
Coconut Creek (G-2002)
R & S Snacks LLC ....G...... 954 839-5482
Port Saint Lucie (G-14437)
Rap Snacks Inc ....G...... 305 926-9594
Miami (G-9780)

FOOD PRDTS: Potatoes, Fresh Cut & Peeled

Santos Frozen Foods Inc ....F...... 813 875-4901
Tampa (G-17247)

FOOD PRDTS: Poultry Sausage, Lunch Meats/Other Poultry Prdts

E&M Innovative Forager LLC ....E...... 954 923-0056
Deerfield Beach (G-2713)
Premium Quality Meats Inc ....F...... 239 309-4418
Miramar (G-10528)

FOOD PRDTS: Poultry, Processed, Fresh

Chick N Portions Inc ....D...... 305 687-0000
Opa Locka (G-11728)

FOOD PRDTS: Poultry, Processed, Frozen

Asian Food Solutions Inc ....E...... 888 499-6888
Oviedo (G-12806)
International Fd Solutions Inc ....E...... 888 499-6888
Oviedo (G-12829)

FOOD PRDTS: Preparations

10x Vegan LLC ....F...... 954 256-4094
Pompano Beach (G-13904)
20-100 Delicious Seasoning LLC..........G...... 954 687-5124
Miramar (G-10454)

Abraaham Rosa Seasonings Inc	G	386 453-4827
Deland (G-2847)		
Adelheidis Commercial Inc	G	239 384-8642
Naples (G-10652)		
Al-Rite Fruits and Syrups Inc	G	305 652-2540
Miami (G-8679)		
Alnoor Import Inc	G	954 683-9897
Plantation (G-13825)		
Amaranth Lf Sciences Phrm Inc	F	561 756-8291
Boca Raton (G-403)		
ARA Food Corporation	D	305 592-5558
Miami (G-8738)		
Argen Foods	G	305 884-0037
Medley (G-8198)		
Aztlan Foods Corp	F	786 202-8301
Medley (G-8204)		
Baby Food Chef LLC	G	305 335-5990
Hollywood (G-5536)		
Best Brand Bottlers Inc	F	941 755-1941
Sarasota (G-15447)		
Bio-Revival LLC	F	561 667-3990
Jupiter (G-6694)		
Blue Stone Usa LLC	G	305 494-1141
Coral Gables (G-2035)		
C & E Innovative MGT LLC	G	727 408-5146
Clearwater (G-1533)		
Cacao Fruit Company	G	954 449-8704
Weston (G-18231)		
Captain Foods Inc	G	386 428-5833
New Smyrna Beach (G-10998)		
Carvalho Naturals LLC	G	813 833-8229
Tampa (G-16683)		
Catalina Finer Food Corp	E	813 872-6359
Tampa (G-16687)		
CFM&d LLC	G	772 220-8938
Stuart (G-16128)		
Champion Nutrition Inc	G	954 233-3300
Sunrise (G-16304)		
Charles Bryant Enterprises	G	850 785-3604
Panama City (G-13241)		
Coco Lopez Inc	G	954 450-3100
Miramar (G-10481)		
Culinary Concepts Inc	E	407 228-0069
Orlando (G-12064)		
Delicae Gourmet LLC	G	727 942-2502
Tarpon Springs (G-17465)		
Dole	G	305 925-7900
Doral (G-3195)		
Dolmar Foods Inc	F	262 303-6026
Belleview (G-360)		
Easy Foods Inc	C	321 300-1104
Kissimmee (G-6916)		
Egg Roll Skins Inc	F	305 836-0571
Hialeah (G-5138)		
Evergreen Sweeteners Inc	F	305 835-6907
Miami (G-9115)		
Farm Cut LLC	C	813 754-3321
Plant City (G-13765)		
Fathers Table LLC	C	407 324-1200
Sanford (G-15315)		
Flavorworks Inc	E	561 588-8246
West Palm Beach (G-17998)		
Floribbean Inc	G	844 282-8459
Miami (G-9153)		
Frito-Lay North America Inc	C	407 295-1810
Orlando (G-12177)		
G & G Latin Business Inc	G	954 385-8085
Weston (G-18245)		
GA Fd Svcs Pinellas Cnty LLC	E	239 693-5090
Fort Myers (G-4268)		
Geneva Foods LLC	F	407 302-4751
Sanford (G-15325)		
Greenes Reserve Inc	F	954 304-0791
Ocala (G-11405)		
Handal Foods LLC	G	954 753-0649
Coral Springs (G-2159)		
Hispanic Certified Foods Inc	G	305 772-6815
Pompano Beach (G-14050)		
Jenard Fresh Incorporated	D	407 240-4545
Orlando (G-12272)		
K and G Food Services LLC	G	954 857-9283
West Palm Beach (G-18044)		
Kerry I&F Contracting Company	F	813 359-5182
Plant City (G-13781)		
Kulfi LLC	E	855 488-4273
Boca Raton (G-573)		
L & A Quality Products Inc	G	305 326-9300
Miami (G-9402)		
Lifeco Foods North America	G	321 348-5896
Winter Garden (G-18396)		

Mabels Place Corp	G	786 355-0435
Hallandale Beach (G-4960)		
McM Food Corp	G	305 885-9254
Medley (G-8274)		
Mestizo Foods LLC	C	352 414-4900
Ocala (G-11442)		
Mobile Meals	G	813 907-6325
Tampa (G-17080)		
Mr Bills Fine Foods	G	727 581-9850
Clearwater (G-1705)		
Nana Foods Inc	G	407 363-7183
Orlando (G-12403)		
Native Vanilla LLC	F	407 724-1995
Sanford (G-15362)		
Natures Heathy Gourmet	E	772 873-0180
Port St Lucie (G-14479)		
New Hope Sugar Company	F	561 366-5120
West Palm Beach (G-18090)		
Nutrifusion LLC	G	404 240-0030
Naples (G-10837)		
Nutritious You LLC	G	941 203-5203
Sarasota (G-15764)		
Oakbrook Sales Inc	F	800 773-0979
Boca Raton (G-622)		
OH Catering Inc	G	305 903-9271
Miami (G-9640)		
Organic Amazon Corp	G	305 365-7811
Key Biscayne (G-6838)		
Paca Foods LLC	E	813 628-8228
Tampa (G-17136)		
Pikantitos LLC	F	305 937-4827
Aventura (G-271)		
Plantain Products Company	E	800 477-2447
Miami (G-9720)		
Port Saint Wich LLC	G	772 237-2000
Port Saint Lucie (G-14433)		
Prege	G	954 908-1535
Fort Lauderdale (G-3993)		
Prima Food Corp	E	954 788-0411
Pompano Beach (G-14145)		
Qsrr Corporation	G	305 322-9867
Hallandale Beach (G-4967)		
Respect Foods	G	561 557-2832
Palm Beach Gardens (G-13006)		
Rj Foods	G	863 425-3282
Mulberry (G-10636)		
Roxy Lady LLC	F	954 706-6735
Fort Lauderdale (G-4030)		
Royal Cup Inc	G	813 664-8902
Tampa (G-17235)		
Sage Imports Corp	F	305 962-0631
Coral Gables (G-2105)		
Savory Life LLC	G	813 981-2022
Riverview (G-14576)		
Sentry Food Solutions LLC	F	904 482-1900
Jacksonville (G-6460)		
SOS Food Lab LLC	E	305 594-9933
Hialeah Gardens (G-5451)		
Southeast Corn Traders LLC	E	843 372-4315
Hollywood (G-5661)		
Spice World LLC	C	407 851-9432
Orlando (G-12617)		
Sunrise Foods LLC	G	904 613-4756
Jacksonville (G-6517)		
Sunshine Peanut Company	G	813 988-6987
Temple Terrace (G-17547)		
Survivor Industries Inc	E	805 385-5560
Doral (G-3388)		
Suviche International LLC	F	305 777-3530
Miami (G-9978)		
Sweet Additions LLC	F	561 472-0178
Palm Beach Gardens (G-13012)		
T&S Kitchen and Bbq LLC	G	863 608-6223
Lakeland (G-7455)		
Tasteful Delight LLC	F	305 879-6487
Lakeland (G-7457)		
Tastyz LLC	G	772 480-5741
Sunrise (G-16379)		
Teaposh Naturals LLC	F	904 683-2099
Jacksonville (G-6536)		
Thunder Bay Foods Corporation	F	727 943-0606
Clearwater (G-1830)		
Torro Foods LLC	G	305 558-3212
Miami Lakes (G-10368)		
Total Nutrition Technology LLC	E	352 435-0050
Leesburg (G-7799)		
Triton Seafood Co	F	305 888-8999
Medley (G-8339)		
Ultra-Max LLC	F	850 728-8442
Tallahassee (G-16519)		

Yaadie Fiesta Group Inc	G	562 766-8033
Coral Springs (G-2227)		
Yfan LLC	G	786 453-3724
Miami Lakes (G-10381)		

FOOD PRDTS: Prepared Meat Sauces Exc Tomato & Dry

Hoerndler Inc	G	239 643-2008
Naples (G-10775)		
La Lechonera Products Inc	F	305 635-2303
Miami (G-9407)		

FOOD PRDTS: Prepared Sauces, Exc Tomato Based

Farm Cut LLC	C	813 754-3321
Plant City (G-13765)		

FOOD PRDTS: Prepared Seafood Sauces Exc Tomato & Dry

Destination Bvi II Inc	G	850 699-9551
Destin (G-3064)		

FOOD PRDTS: Raw cane sugar

Florida Crystals Food Corp	A	561 366-5100
West Palm Beach (G-18003)		
Okeelanta Corporation	C	561 996-9072
South Bay (G-16016)		
Organic Cane Company Inc	G	561 385-4081
Stuart (G-16193)		
Tru Cane Sugar Corp	G	561 833-1731
West Palm Beach (G-18187)		

FOOD PRDTS: Rice, Milled

Conchita Foods Inc	D	305 888-9703
Medley (G-8220)		
Deeja Foods Inc	G	321 402-8300
Kissimmee (G-6911)		
Florida Crystals Corporation	D	561 655-6303
West Palm Beach (G-18000)		
Florida Crystals Corporation	C	561 515-8080
West Palm Beach (G-18002)		
Florida Gold Foods LLC	F	347 595-1983
Kissimmee (G-6920)		
Poinciana Milling Complex Inc	G	407 587-5525
Kissimmee (G-6954)		

FOOD PRDTS: Rice, Packaged & Seasoned

Vigo Importing Company	C	813 884-3491
Tampa (G-17417)		

FOOD PRDTS: Salads

Brianas Salad LLC	G	954 608-0953
Boca Raton (G-448)		

FOOD PRDTS: Sandwiches

Axrdham Corp	G	813 653-9588
Valrico (G-17662)		
Deli Fresh Foods Inc	F	305 652-2848
Miami (G-9009)		
ME Thompson Inc	G	904 356-6258
Jacksonville (G-6287)		
ME Thompson Inc	D	863 667-3732
Lakeland (G-7393)		

FOOD PRDTS: Seasonings & Spices

Bavaria Corporation	F	407 880-0322
Apopka (G-104)		
Broth Bomb LLC	F	813 278-1912
Clearwater (G-1527)		
Burma Spice Inc	G	863 254-0960
Fort Myers (G-4196)		
El Jaliciense Inc	F	850 481-1232
Panama City (G-13259)		
Flayco Products Inc	E	813 879-1356
Tampa (G-16835)		
Greek Island Spice Inc	G	954 761-7161
Fort Lauderdale (G-3847)		
Italian Rose Garlic Pdts LLC	C	561 863-5556
Riviera Beach (G-14632)		
Jayshree Holdings Inc	F	352 429-1000
Groveland (G-4864)		
Kenart Holdings Llc	C	561 863-5556
Riviera Beach (G-14637)		

PRODUCT

FOOD PRDTS: Sorbets, Non-dairy Based

Buzz Pop Cocktails Corporation ....F 727 275-9848
Holiday *(G-5491)*

FOOD PRDTS: Soup Mixes

Major Products Company ....E 386 673-8381
Ormond Beach *(G-12778)*

RL Schreiber Inc ....D 954 972-7102
Fort Lauderdale *(G-4021)*

FOOD PRDTS: Soup Mixes, Dried

Flayco Products Inc ....E 813 879-1356
Tampa *(G-16835)*

FOOD PRDTS: Spices, Including Ground

Bijol and Spices Inc ....G 305 634-9030
Miami *(G-8826)*

Chili Produkt Kft ....E 954 655-4111
Wellington *(G-17848)*

El Sabor Spices Inc ....F 305 691-2300
Miami *(G-9076)*

Life Spice and Ingredients LLC ....G 708 301-0447
Palm Beach *(G-12937)*

McCormick Restaurant Services ....E 561 706-5554
Boca Raton *(G-588)*

Oriental Packing Company Inc ....F 305 235-1829
Miami *(G-9665)*

RL Schreiber Inc ....D 954 972-7102
Fort Lauderdale *(G-4021)*

Sazon Inc ....E 305 591-9785
Doral *(G-3357)*

Service Modern Trade LLC ....F 708 942-9154
Lakeland *(G-7431)*

FOOD PRDTS: Spreads, Garlic

Joys International Foods Inc ....G 321 242-6520
Melbourne *(G-8444)*

Stripping Alpaca LLC ....F 207 208-9687
Miami Beach *(G-10236)*

FOOD PRDTS: Spreads, Sandwich, Salad Dressing Base

Los Atntcos Sndwich Cuban Cafe ....G 407 282-2322
Orlando *(G-12352)*

FOOD PRDTS: Starch, Liquid

Element Eliquid LLC ....G 754 260-5500
Miramar *(G-10487)*

FOOD PRDTS: Sugar

Evergreen Sweeteners Inc ....F 954 381-7776
Hollywood *(G-5573)*

Evergreen Sweeteners Inc ....F 407 323-4250
Sanford *(G-15313)*

Pantaleon Commodities Corp ....F 786 542-6333
Miami *(G-9689)*

FOOD PRDTS: Sugar, Cane

Atlantic Sugar Association ....F 561 996-6541
Belle Glade *(G-338)*

B and M Sugar Products LLC ....G 305 897-8427
Miami *(G-8788)*

Florida Crystal Refinery Inc ....G 561 366-5200
West Palm Beach *(G-17999)*

Florida Crystals Corporation ....D 561 655-6303
West Palm Beach *(G-18000)*

Florida Crystals Corporation ....B 561 366-5000
West Palm Beach *(G-18001)*

Florida Crystals Corporation ....B 561 992-5635
South Bay *(G-16015)*

Florida Crystals Corporation ....C 561 515-8080
West Palm Beach *(G-18002)*

Florida Sugar Distributors ....E 561 655-6303
West Palm Beach *(G-18006)*

Florida Sugar Farmers ....F 863 983-7276
Clewiston *(G-1889)*

Merkavah International Inc ....G 305 909-6798
Miami *(G-9536)*

Okeelanta Corporation ....E 561 366-5100
West Palm Beach *(G-18097)*

Osceola Farms Co ....A 561 924-7156
Pahokee *(G-12860)*

FOOD PRDTS: Sugar, Dry Cane Prdts, Exc Refined

Add-V LLC ....G 305 496-2445
Lauderhill *(G-7724)*

FOOD PRDTS: Sugar, Ground

Flo Sun Land Corporation ....D 561 655-6303
Palm Beach *(G-12934)*

Osceola Farms Co ....E 561 655-6303
Palm Beach *(G-12939)*

Osceola Farms Co ....A 561 924-7156
Pahokee *(G-12860)*

FOOD PRDTS: Sugar, Raw Cane

Alvean Americas Inc ....G 305 606-0770
Coral Gables *(G-2027)*

Atlantic Sugar Association ....F 561 996-6541
Belle Glade *(G-338)*

Florida Crystals Corporation ....D 561 655-6303
West Palm Beach *(G-18000)*

Florida Crystals Corporation ....B 561 366-5000
West Palm Beach *(G-18001)*

Florida Crystals Corporation ....B 561 992-5635
South Bay *(G-16015)*

Florida Crystals Corporation ....F 561 515-8080
West Palm Beach *(G-18002)*

Okeelanta Corporation ....E 561 366-5100
West Palm Beach *(G-18097)*

Sugar Cane Growers Coop Fla ....B 561 996-5556
Belle Glade *(G-343)*

FOOD PRDTS: Tapioca

Tapioca Fit ....G 954 842-3924
Pembroke Pines *(G-13418)*

FOOD PRDTS: Tea

Grand Havana Inc ....G 305 297-2207
Miami Beach *(G-10197)*

Mad At SAD LLC ....F 941 203-8854
Sarasota *(G-15732)*

Mother Kombucha LLC ....F 727 767-0408
Saint Petersburg *(G-15131)*

New Dawn Coffee Company Inc ....G 727 321-5155
Saint Petersburg *(G-15138)*

Tata Tea Extractions Inc ....G 813 754-2602
Plant City *(G-13807)*

Twinlab Corporation ....G 800 645-5626
Boca Raton *(G-728)*

FOOD PRDTS: Tortilla Chips

El Mira Sol Inc ....D 813 754-5857
Plant City *(G-13764)*

FOOD PRDTS: Tortillas

Carne Asada Tortilleria Nica ....G 305 221-7001
Miami *(G-8898)*

De Todos Tortillas Inc ....G 305 248-4402
Homestead *(G-5706)*

Easy Foods Inc ....E 305 599-0357
Miami *(G-9064)*

Fritanga Y Tortilla Modra ....G 305 649-9377
Miami *(G-9174)*

Ipac Inc ....G 407 699-7507
Winter Springs *(G-18568)*

La Autentica Foods Inc ....F 305 888-6727
Hialeah *(G-5219)*

La Chiquita Tortilla Mfr ....F 407 251-8290
Orlando *(G-12303)*

La Real Foods Inc ....E 305 232-6449
Miami *(G-9414)*

Latino Entps La Chqita Trtilla ....F 407 251-8290
Orlando *(G-12315)*

Tortilla Bay ....G 941 778-3663
Holmes Beach *(G-5692)*

Tortilleria America Inc ....G 239 462-2175
Fort Myers *(G-4427)*

Tortilleria Dona Chela ....G 941 953-4045
Sarasota *(G-15856)*

Tortilleria Gallo De Oro LLC ....F 561 818-7829
Stuart *(G-16239)*

Tortilleria La Rancherita ....G 941 747-7949
Bradenton *(G-1061)*

Tortilleria Lamexicana 7 Inc ....F 407 324-3100
Sanford *(G-15399)*

Tortilleria Santa Rosa ....G 239 839-0832
Fort Myers *(G-4428)*

FOOD PRDTS: Vegetable Oil Mills, NEC

C P Vegetable Oil Inc ....F 954 584-0420
Fort Lauderdale *(G-3710)*

Trujillo Oil Plant Inc ....F 305 696-8701
Miami *(G-10043)*

FOOD PRDTS: Vegetables, Dehydrated Or Dried

Wedgworths Inc ....G 561 996-2076
Lake Placid *(G-7149)*

FOOD PRDTS: Vinegar

Delarosa Real Foods LLC ....D 718 333-0333
Lauderdale Lakes *(G-7712)*

Miami Oliveoil & Beyond Llc ....G 954 632-2762
Doral *(G-3301)*

Mizkan America Inc ....F 863 956-0391
Lake Alfred *(G-6996)*

FOOD PRODUCTS MACHINERY

Alexander Industries Inc ....G 305 888-9840
Hialeah *(G-5036)*

Emerge Interactive Inc ....E 772 563-0570
Vero Beach *(G-17753)*

Gruenewald Mfg Co Inc ....F 978 777-0200
Ocklawaha *(G-11519)*

Hoppin Pop Kettle Stop LLC ....G 502 220-2372
Jacksonville *(G-6184)*

Jbt Foodtech Citrus Systems ....D 863 683-5411
Lakeland *(G-7359)*

Jbt LLC ....G 407 463-2045
Orlando *(G-12269)*

Jbt LLC ....D 513 238-4218
Naples *(G-10789)*

John Bean Technologies Corp ....C 863 683-5411
Lakeland *(G-7361)*

John Bean Technologies Corp ....E 407 851-3377
Orlando *(G-12275)*

Remco Industries International ....F 954 462-0000
Fort Lauderdale *(G-4015)*

Rice Machinery Supply Co Inc ....F 305 620-2274
Miami *(G-9805)*

Sen-Pack Inc ....E 386 763-3312
New Smyrna Beach *(G-11010)*

Thinking Foods Inc ....G 305 433-8287
Miami *(G-10006)*

FOOD STORES: Frozen Food &Freezer Plans, Exc Meat

Pizza Spice Packet LLC ....G 718 831-7036
Boca Raton *(G-635)*

FOOD STORES: Grocery, Independent

El Mira Sol Inc ....D 813 754-5857
Plant City *(G-13764)*

FOOD WARMING EQPT: Commercial

International Food Eqp Inc ....G 305 785-5100
Miami Springs *(G-10389)*

FOOTWEAR, WHOLESALE: Boots

Interntnal Tech Sltons Sup LLC ....G 305 364-5229
Doral *(G-3259)*

FOOTWEAR: Cut Stock

Latin Quarters LLC ....G 954 470-8034
Margate *(G-8141)*

Upper Keys Snacks Llc ....G 305 298-6109
Miramar *(G-10559)*

FORGINGS

American Professional Ir Work ....G 305 556-9522
Hialeah Gardens *(G-5430)*

Enstar Holdings (us) LLC ....E 727 217-2900
Saint Petersburg *(G-15036)*

Grizzly Manufacturing Inc ....E 386 755-0220
Lake City *(G-7024)*

Lubov Manufacturing Inc ....G 813 873-2640
Tampa *(G-17023)*

Nav-X LLC ....E 954 978-9988
Fort Lauderdale *(G-3956)*

Profile Racing Inc ....E 727 392-8307
Saint Petersburg *(G-15163)*

FORGINGS: Aluminum

Lawrence Commercial Systems ....G..... 850 574-8723
Tallahassee (G-16468)

Nav-X LLC ....E...... 954 978-9988
Fort Lauderdale (G-3956)

Sapa Prcsion Tubing Adrian Inc ....D..... 321 636-8147
Rockledge (G-14745)

FORGINGS: Anchors

Anchor & Docking Inc ....G..... 239 770-2030
Cape Coral (G-1302)

Profast Usa Inc ....F...... 305 827-7801
Miami Lakes (G-10344)

FORGINGS: Armor Plate, Iron Or Steel

Point Blank Enterprises Inc ....A..... 954 630-0900
Pompano Beach (G-14134)

Survival Armor Inc ....E...... 239 210-0891
Fort Myers (G-4415)

FORGINGS: Automotive & Internal Combustion Engine

Scorpion Equity LLC ....E...... 352 512-0800
Ocala (G-11484)

Xcessive Inc ....G..... 866 919-9527
Miami Lakes (G-10380)

FORGINGS: Construction Or Mining Eqpt, Ferrous

Masaka LLC ....F...... 786 800-8337
Doral (G-3292)

FORGINGS: Engine Or Turbine, Nonferrous

Advanced Engine Tech LLC ....G..... 727 744-2935
Clearwater (G-1475)

FORGINGS: Gear & Chain

Rosuca International LLC ....G..... 305 332-5572
Doral (G-3351)

FORGINGS: Iron & Steel

Project and Cnstr Wldg Inc ....F...... 239 772-9299
Cape Coral (G-1376)

FORGINGS: Mechanical Power Transmission, Ferrous

North Amrcn Prtection Ctrl LLC ....G..... 407 788-3717
Altamonte Springs (G-59)

FORMS HANDLING EQPT

New Market Enterprises Ltd.................F...... 484 341-8004
Palm Harbor (G-13121)

FORMS: Concrete, Sheet Metal

Dayton Superior Corporation ....G..... 407 859-4541
Orlando (G-12078)

FOUNDRIES: Aluminum

Broward Casting Foundry Inc...............E...... 954 584-6400
Fort Lauderdale (G-3704)

Cost Cast Aluminum Corp ....E...... 863 422-5617
Haines City (G-4904)

G & K Aluminum Inc ....F...... 772 283-1297
Stuart (G-16150)

Harberson Rv Pinellas LLC...................E...... 727 937-6176
Holiday (G-5497)

HP Preferred Ltd Partners ....F...... 407 298-4470
Orlando (G-12229)

Luv Enterprises Inc...........................F...... 352 867-8440
Ocala (G-11433)

Rebah Fabrication Inc ....F...... 407 857-3232
Orlando (G-12537)

Sapa Extrsons St Augustine LLC ....C...... 904 794-1500
Saint Augustine (G-14886)

Southern Die Casting Corp ....D...... 305 635-6571
Miami (G-9927)

Tarvin Mobile Home Service ....G..... 727 734-3400
Palm Harbor (G-13135)

Town Country Industries.....................G..... 727 862-5483
Hudson (G-5790)

FOUNDRIES: Brass, Bronze & Copper

Florida Airboat Propeller ....G..... 863 324-1653
Winter Haven (G-18436)

Florida Machine & Casting Co ....G..... 561 655-3771
Riviera Beach (G-14624)

Foundry ....G..... 904 257-5020
Daytona Beach (G-2554)

Hawver Aluminum Foundry Inc ....G..... 813 961-1497
Tampa (G-16910)

Henefelt Precision Pdts Inc..................F...... 727 531-0406
Largo (G-7603)

PM Craftsman ....E...... 863 665-0815
Lakeland (G-7410)

Robert St Croix Sculpture Stu ....G..... 561 835-1753
West Palm Beach (G-18143)

FOUNDRIES: Gray & Ductile Iron

Maddox Foundry & Mch Works LLC .....E...... 352 495-2121
Archer (G-198)

Nusfc LLC ....C...... 920 725-7000
Medley (G-8291)

FOUNDRIES: Iron

US Manufacturing Company..................C...... 305 885-0301
Medley (G-8346)

FOUNDRIES: Nonferrous

Altis Aju Kingwood LLC ....G..... 305 338-5232
Miami (G-8703)

Cost Cast Aluminum Corp ....E...... 863 422-5617
Haines City (G-4904)

Flotech LLC ....D...... 904 358-1849
Jacksonville (G-6113)

J&N Keystone of Florida ....G..... 305 528-1677
Medley (G-8263)

Nav-X LLC ....E...... 954 978-9988
Fort Lauderdale (G-3956)

Southern Die Casting Corp ....D...... 305 635-6571
Miami (G-9927)

Tampa Brass and Aluminum Corp ....C...... 813 885-6064
Tampa (G-17330)

FOUNDRIES: Steel

Hardware Parts Corporation ....G..... 561 994-2121
Boca Raton (G-538)

Maddox Foundry & Mch Works LLC .....E...... 352 495-2121
Archer (G-198)

FOUNDRIES: Steel Investment

R B Casting Inc ....G..... 407 648-2005
Orlando (G-12524)

FOUNDRY MACHINERY & EQPT

Safetarp Corp ....D...... 904 824-7277
Saint Augustine (G-14884)

FOUNTAINS, METAL, EXC DRINKING

Aquatectonica LLC ....F...... 941 592-3071
Bradenton (G-940)

Architectural Fountains Inc ....G..... 727 323-6068
Saint Petersburg (G-14969)

Johnston Archtctral Systems In ....E...... 904 886-9030
Jacksonville (G-6231)

Waltzing Waters Inc ....G..... 239 574-5181
Cape Coral (G-1406)

Wesco Partners Inc...........................E...... 941 484-8224
Sarasota (G-15579)

FOUNTAINS: Concrete

Aquatectonica LLC ....F...... 941 592-3071
Bradenton (G-940)

Architectural Fountains Inc ....G..... 727 323-6068
Saint Petersburg (G-14969)

Artistic Statuary Inc ....E...... 954 975-9533
Pompano Beach (G-13937)

Com Pac Filtration Inc........................E...... 904 356-4003
Jacksonville (G-5993)

Freeport Fountains LLC ....E...... 407 330-1150
Sanford (G-15320)

FOUNTAINS: Plaster Of Paris

Architectural Fountains Inc ....G..... 727 323-6068
Saint Petersburg (G-14969)

FRACTIONATION PRDTS OF CRUDE PETROLEUM, HYDROCARBONS, NEC

Kraton Chemical LLC ....C...... 904 928-8700
Jacksonville (G-6250)

FRAMES & FRAMING WHOLESALE

Artworks International ....G..... 561 833-9165
West Palm Beach (G-17929)

Chez Industries LLC ....F...... 386 698-4414
Crescent City (G-2235)

FRANCHISES, SELLING OR LICENSING

BCT International Inc ....E...... 305 563-1224
Fort Lauderdale (G-3680)

Ciao Group Inc ....E...... 347 560-5040
Boca Raton (G-460)

Matrix Packaging of Florida...................G..... 305 358-9696
Miami (G-9520)

FREIGHT FORWARDING ARRANGEMENTS

Custom Crate & Logistics Co ....G..... 954 527-5742
Fort Lauderdale (G-3748)

Wetherill Associates Inc......................C...... 800 877-3340
Miramar (G-10564)

FREIGHT FORWARDING ARRANGEMENTS: Foreign

Rosuca International LLC ....G..... 305 332-5572
Doral (G-3351)

FREIGHT TRANSPORTATION ARRANGEMENTS

Lift Aerospace Corp............................E...... 305 851-5237
Miami (G-9457)

FREON

Brian Reck Valenzuela ....G..... 386 801-5096
Deltona (G-3041)

FRICTION MATERIAL, MADE FROM POWDERED METAL

ARC Group Worldwide Inc ....E...... 303 467-5236
Deland (G-2853)

Atlantic Central Entps Inc ....F...... 386 255-6227
Daytona Beach (G-2515)

FRITS

Stylepoint Us LLC ....G..... 954 990-6778
Fort Lauderdale (G-4071)

FRUITS & VEGETABLES WHOLESALERS: Fresh

Florida Flvors Cncentrates Inc ....G..... 561 775-5714
Palm Beach Gardens (G-12970)

Ritco Foods LLC ....G..... 954 727-3554
Sunrise (G-16364)

FUEL ADDITIVES

Boostane LLC....................................F...... 239 908-1615
Bonita Springs (G-784)

Fuel Solutions Distrs LLC ....G..... 305 528-3758
North Miami Beach (G-11141)

Mega Power ....F...... 813 855-6664
Largo (G-7642)

Purify Fuels Inc ....G..... 949 842-6159
Davie (G-2462)

FUEL OIL DEALERS

Taronis Fuels Inc ....C...... 727 934-3448
Clearwater (G-1816)

FUEL TREATING

Bell Performance Inc ....F...... 407 831-5021
Longwood (G-7875)

FUEL: Rocket Engine, Organic

Aerojet Rocketdyne De Inc ....C...... 561 882-5150
Jupiter (G-6680)

FUELS: Diesel

Clean Energy ESb Inc ....E 202 905-6726
Coral Gables *(G-2040)*

Export Diesel LLC ....G 305 396-1943
Miami *(G-9122)*

Indian River Biodiesel LLC ....G 321 586-7670
West Palm Beach *(G-18032)*

New Energy Fuels LLC ....G 281 205-0153
Labelle *(G-6984)*

FUELS: Ethanol

ACC Fuels Operation LLC ....G 305 246-8214
Homestead *(G-5696)*

Aero Fuel LLC ....G 352 728-2018
Leesburg *(G-7756)*

Agri-Source Fuels LLC ....E 352 521-3460
Pensacola *(G-13439)*

Ameri Food & Fuel Inc ....F 727 584-0120
Largo *(G-7530)*

America Marine & Fuel Inc ....G 239 261-3715
Naples *(G-10665)*

American Carbons Inc ....G 850 265-4214
Lynn Haven *(G-8024)*

Baa LLC ....F 954 292-9449
Miramar *(G-10473)*

Big Bend Fuel Inc ....F 727 946-8727
Gibsonton *(G-4796)*

Bio Fuel Professionals ....F 239 591-3835
Naples *(G-10695)*

Blue Biofuels Inc ....G 561 693-1943
Palm Beach Gardens *(G-12952)*

Brooklink Green Fuels Inc ....G 561 514-1725
Royal Palm Beach *(G-14761)*

Caribbean Fuels Inc ....F 305 233-3016
Miami *(G-8894)*

Coastal Fuels Mktg Inc ....G 941 722-7753
Palmetto *(G-13161)*

Consolidated Forest Pdts Inc ....F 407 830-7723
Longwood *(G-7882)*

Consolidated Forest Pdts Inc ....G 407 830-7723
Perry *(G-13635)*

Douglas Fuel II Inc ....G 305 620-0707
Miami Gardens *(G-10255)*

Excel Fuel Inc ....G 727 547-5511
Saint Petersburg *(G-15040)*

Fast Fuel Corp ....G 786 251-0373
Hialeah *(G-5152)*

Fire Fly Fuels Inc ....G 941 404-6820
Sarasota *(G-15674)*

Fuel Connection ....G 305 354-8115
North Miami *(G-11105)*

Fuel N Go LLC ....G 239 656-1072
Estero *(G-3545)*

Fuel Productions LLC ....G 904 342-7826
Saint Augustine *(G-14834)*

Fuel Solutions LLC ....G 813 969-2506
Tampa *(G-16863)*

Fuel U Fast Inc ....G 561 654-0212
Boca Raton *(G-525)*

Fuelmyschool ....G 407 952-1030
Windermere *(G-18351)*

Gaseous Fuel Systems Corp ....G 954 693-9475
Weston *(G-18246)*

Green Biofuels LLC ....F 305 639-3030
Miami *(G-9241)*

Green Fuel Systems LLC ....G 352 483-5005
Eustis *(G-3559)*

Green Marine Fuels Inc ....G 305 775-3546
Miami *(G-9245)*

Greenwave Biodiesel LLC ....G 239 682-7700
Fort Lauderdale *(G-3850)*

Kendall Fuel Inc ....G 305 270-7735
Miami *(G-9388)*

Largent Fuels USA LLC ....G 786 431-5981
Miami *(G-9425)*

Lee County Fuels Inc ....G 239 349-5322
Fort Myers *(G-4310)*

Liles Oil Company ....F 407 739-2083
Casselberry *(G-1422)*

Living Fuel Inc ....G 813 254-0777
Tampa *(G-17017)*

Lutz Fuel Inc ....G 727 376-3013
Trinity *(G-17639)*

Mendez Fuel ....G 305 227-0470
Coral Gables *(G-2084)*

Montebana Fuels LLC ....G 954 385-5374
Weston *(G-18268)*

Montedana Fuels ....G 305 887-6754
Hialeah *(G-5265)*

Natures Fuel Inc ....G 407 808-4272
Orlando *(G-12406)*

Nb Fuel LLC ....G 954 382-3893
Davie *(G-2445)*

On The Go Food & Fuel Inc ....G 727 815-0823
New Port Richey *(G-10979)*

Originclear Inc ....G 323 939-6645
Clearwater *(G-1731)*

Pentacles Energy GP LLC ....G 786 552-9931
Coral Gables *(G-2096)*

Phillips Energy Inc ....G 850 682-5127
Crestview *(G-2250)*

Pine Fuel LLC ....G 407 345-7960
Orlando *(G-12488)*

R & A Performance Fuel Inc ....G 954 237-9824
Pembroke Pines *(G-13410)*

Renewable Fuels Group LLC ....G 305 388-3028
Miami *(G-9794)*

Rhodes Brothers Miami Inc ....G 305 456-9682
Miami Springs *(G-10393)*

Romco Fuels Inc ....G 954 474-5392
Davie *(G-2471)*

Sab Fuels Inc ....G 786 213-3399
Sarasota *(G-15805)*

Safe Industries Inc ....F 321 639-8646
Rockledge *(G-14743)*

Sincere Fuel Inc ....G 954 433-3577
Miramar *(G-10544)*

South East Fuel LLC ....G 407 392-4668
Orlando *(G-12612)*

Southern Fuel Inc ....G 904 545-5163
Glen Saint Mary *(G-4805)*

Taronis Fuels Inc ....C 727 934-3448
Clearwater *(G-1816)*

US Fuels Inc ....F 254 559-1212
Rotonda West *(G-14758)*

Viesel Fuel LLC ....E 772 781-4300
Stuart *(G-16247)*

Wesley Chapel Fuel Inc ....G 813 907-9994
Wesley Chapel *(G-17891)*

Wf Fuel ....G 941 706-4953
Sarasota *(G-15873)*

Wise Gas Fuel Card LLC ....G 954 636-4291
Weston *(G-18298)*

World Fuel Cx LLC ....F 305 428-8000
Doral *(G-3422)*

Yudkin Fuel Co ....G 561 487-0418
Boca Raton *(G-762)*

FUELS: Jet

Atlantic Jet Center Inc ....G 321 255-7111
Melbourne *(G-8369)*

Jet Fuel Catering LLC ....G 954 804-1146
Pembroke Pines *(G-13398)*

Sellink Aviation Fuel Div LLC ....G 305 336-6627
Miami *(G-9864)*

Sheltair Daytona Beach LLC ....E 386 255-0471
Daytona Beach *(G-2597)*

FUELS: Oil

Otus Corp Intl LLC ....G 305 833-6078
Miami *(G-9670)*

Repgas Inc ....G 786 202-8434
Port Saint Lucie *(G-14440)*

Taronis Fuels Inc ....C 727 934-3448
Clearwater *(G-1816)*

FUNGICIDES OR HERBICIDES

Trans-Resources LLC ....A 305 933-8301
Sunny Isles Beach *(G-16284)*

FUR CLOTHING WHOLESALERS

Blum & Fink Inc ....F 212 695-2606
Boca Raton *(G-433)*

FUR: Coats & Other Apparel

Blum & Fink Inc ....F 212 695-2606
Boca Raton *(G-433)*

FURNACES & OVENS: Indl

Air Burners Inc ....F 772 220-7303
Palm City *(G-13022)*

Clarios LLC ....B 727 541-3531
Largo *(G-7564)*

Matthews International Corp ....C 407 886-5533
Apopka *(G-149)*

Pillar Inc ....G 904 545-4993
Jacksonville *(G-6370)*

FURNITURE & CABINET STORES: Cabinets, Custom Work

A A A Cabinets ....G 850 438-8337
Pensacola *(G-13428)*

Castor Inc ....G 813 254-1171
Tampa *(G-16686)*

Custom Cabinets SW Florida LLC ....G 239 415-3350
Fort Myers *(G-4227)*

Guyton Industries LLC ....E 772 208-3019
Indiantown *(G-5814)*

Italkraft LLC ....F 305 406-1301
Doral *(G-3262)*

McCabinet Inc ....G 727 608-5929
Largo *(G-7640)*

Schrappers Fine Cabinetry Inc ....F 561 746-3827
Jupiter *(G-6792)*

FURNITURE & CABINET STORES: Custom

Carsons Cabinetry & Design Inc ....G 352 373-8292
Archer *(G-196)*

Kennedy Craft Cabinets Inc ....G 239 598-1566
Naples *(G-10797)*

Lioher Enterprise Corp ....G 305 685-0005
Miami Lakes *(G-10314)*

FURNITURE & FIXTURES Factory

American Technical Furn LLC ....G 866 239-4204
Holly Hill *(G-5509)*

England Trading Company LLC ....E 888 969-4190
Jacksonville *(G-6076)*

Great American Woodworks Inc ....E 727 375-1212
Odessa *(G-11555)*

Ultima Design South Fla Inc ....F 305 477-9300
Medley *(G-8341)*

FURNITURE COMPONENTS: Porcelain Enameled

Famatel USA LLC ....G 754 217-4841
Medley *(G-8240)*

FURNITURE PARTS: Metal

MA Metal Fabricators Inc ....G 786 343-0268
Miami *(G-9494)*

S & S Metal and Plastics Inc ....E 904 731-4655
Jacksonville *(G-6440)*

Spicer Industries Inc ....F 352 732-5300
Ocala *(G-11497)*

FURNITURE STOCK & PARTS: Carvings, Wood

Cut Services LLC ....G 305 560-0905
Doral *(G-3180)*

Giovanni Art In Cstm Furn Inc ....G 954 698-1008
Deerfield Beach *(G-2726)*

Juan Pampanas Designs Inc ....G 305 573-7550
Miami *(G-9381)*

FURNITURE STOCK & PARTS: Chair Seats, Hardwood

Smittys Boat Tops and Mar Eqp ....G 305 245-0229
Homestead *(G-5740)*

FURNITURE STOCK & PARTS: Dimension Stock, Hardwood

Maggac Corporation ....G 561 439-2707
Lake Worth *(G-7215)*

FURNITURE STOCK & PARTS: Frames, Upholstered Furniture, Wood

Iverica Industrial Inc ....F 305 691-1659
Hialeah *(G-5198)*

Roorda Buiders Inc ....G 727 410-7776
Odessa *(G-11575)*

FURNITURE STOCK & PARTS: Hardwood

David R Nassivera Inc ....E 352 351-1176
Ocala *(G-11364)*

Stuart Stair & Furniture Mfg ....G 772 287-4097
Stuart *(G-16232)*

FURNITURE STORES

Alumatech Manufacturing Inc..............E...... 941 748-8880
Bradenton *(G-936)*

Closetmaid LLC..............C...... 352 401-6000
Orlando *(G-12021)*

Contemporary Interiors Inc..............F...... 352 620-8686
Ocala *(G-11357)*

Cordaroys Wholesale Inc..............G...... 352 332-1837
Gainesville *(G-4671)*

Custom Cabinets Inc..............F...... 941 366-0428
Sarasota *(G-15647)*

Florida Finisher Inc..............G...... 941 722-5643
Palmetto *(G-13167)*

Garcia Iron Works..............G...... 305 888-0080
Hialeah *(G-5167)*

Lakewood Manufacturing Co Inc..............C...... 443 398-5015
West Palm Beach *(G-18051)*

Rex Fox Enterprises Inc..............F...... 386 677-3752
Daytona Beach *(G-2590)*

Thayer Industries Inc..............G...... 813 719-6597
Dundee *(G-3438)*

The Natural Light Inc..............E...... 850 265-0800
Lynn Haven *(G-8034)*

Wall Bed Systems Inc..............G...... 419 738-5207
Clearwater *(G-1848)*

Werever Products Inc..............F...... 813 241-9701
Riverview *(G-14582)*

FURNITURE STORES: Cabinets, Kitchen, Exc Custom Made

R & R Designer Cabinets Inc..............G...... 954 735-6435
Oakland Park *(G-11290)*

FURNITURE STORES: Custom Made, Exc Cabinets

Leandro Mora Studio LLC..............G...... 786 376-9166
Miami *(G-9447)*

Southwest Woodwork Inc..............F...... 239 213-0126
Naples *(G-10900)*

FURNITURE STORES: Office

Altamonte Office Supply Inc..............G...... 407 339-6911
Longwood *(G-7866)*

New Vision Furniture Inc..............G...... 305 562-9428
Opa Locka *(G-11776)*

FURNITURE UPHOLSTERY REPAIR SVCS

Ards Awning & Upholstery Inc..............F...... 863 293-2442
Winter Haven *(G-18418)*

Jose Leal Enterprises Inc..............D...... 305 887-9611
Hialeah *(G-5207)*

FURNITURE WHOLESALERS

Contemporary Interiors Inc..............F...... 352 620-8686
Ocala *(G-11357)*

Nordic Line Inc..............F...... 561 338-5545
Boca Raton *(G-620)*

S&S Global Supply LLC..............G...... 786 529-4799
Hialeah *(G-5339)*

Shores Global LLC..............G...... 305 716-0848
Miami *(G-9883)*

FURNITURE, BARBER & BEAUTY SHOP

Classic Hardwood Design..............G...... 850 232-6473
Molino *(G-10577)*

FURNITURE, CHURCH: Concrete

Helping Adlscnts Live Optmstcl..............G...... 407 257-8221
Orlando *(G-12213)*

FURNITURE, HOUSEHOLD: Wholesalers

Glodea Store Corp..............G...... 888 400-4937
Jacksonville *(G-6145)*

FURNITURE, OFFICE: Wholesalers

H A Friend & Company Inc..............E...... 847 746-1248
Boynton Beach *(G-876)*

FURNITURE, OUTDOOR & LAWN: Wholesalers

Advanced Sewing..............G...... 954 484-2100
Fort Lauderdale *(G-3626)*

FURNITURE, WHOLESALE: Chairs

United Chair Industries LLC..............G...... 386 333-0800
Odessa *(G-11588)*

FURNITURE, WHOLESALE: Lockers

Broward Custom Woodwork LLC..............G...... 352 376-4732
Deerfield Beach *(G-2682)*

List Industries Inc..............C...... 954 429-9155
Deerfield Beach *(G-2753)*

List Plymouth LLC..............D...... 954 429-9155
Deerfield Beach *(G-2755)*

FURNITURE, WHOLESALE: Restaurant, NEC

Raytash Inc..............G...... 561 347-8863
Boca Raton *(G-648)*

FURNITURE, WHOLESALE: Waterbeds

Waterfall Industries Inc..............F...... 407 330-2003
Sanford *(G-15406)*

FURNITURE: Assembly Hall

Apollo Retail Specialists LLC..............D...... 813 712-2525
Tampa *(G-16600)*

I-Pop Inc..............E...... 561 567-9000
West Palm Beach *(G-18028)*

FURNITURE: Backs & Seats, Metal Household

Tuuci LLC..............B...... 305 634-5116
Hialeah *(G-5386)*

FURNITURE: Bar furniture

Design Furnishings Inc..............E...... 407 294-0507
Orlando *(G-12086)*

FURNITURE: Bean Bag Chairs

Cordaroys Wholesale Inc..............G...... 352 332-1837
Gainesville *(G-4671)*

E-Sea Rider LLC..............G...... 727 863-3333
Holiday *(G-5493)*

FURNITURE: Bed Frames & Headboards, Wood

Saint Petersburg Cabinets Inc..............G...... 727 327-4800
Saint Petersburg *(G-15175)*

FURNITURE: Bedroom, Wood

Capitol Furniture Mfg LLC..............G...... 954 485-5000
Boca Raton *(G-453)*

FURNITURE: Beds, Household, Incl Folding & Cabinet, Metal

Cadence Keen Innovations Inc..............G...... 561 249-2219
West Palm Beach *(G-17955)*

Mobilite Corporation..............E...... 407 321-5630
Sanford *(G-15360)*

Murphy Bed USA Inc..............E...... 954 493-9001
Fort Lauderdale *(G-3947)*

Wall Bed Systems Inc..............G...... 419 738-5207
Clearwater *(G-1848)*

FURNITURE: Box Springs, Assembled

Leggett & Platt Incorporated..............E...... 863 666-8999
Lakeland *(G-7378)*

Star Bedding Mfg Corp..............E...... 305 887-5209
Hialeah *(G-5361)*

FURNITURE: Buffets

Grand Buffet..............G...... 941 752-3388
Bradenton *(G-988)*

FURNITURE: Cabinets & Filing Drawers, Office, Exc Wood

Cayman Nat Mfg Instllation Inc..............D...... 954 421-1170
Deerfield Beach *(G-2688)*

FURNITURE: Cabinets & Vanities, Medicine, Metal

Gk Inc..............E...... 215 223-7207
Fort Lauderdale *(G-3840)*

FURNITURE: Chairs & Couches, Wood, Upholstered

Andrews Warehouse Partnership..............G...... 954 524-3330
Fort Lauderdale *(G-3652)*

Capris Furniture Inds Inc..............C...... 352 629-8889
Ocala *(G-11342)*

Devon Chase & Company..............G...... 407 438-6466
Orlando *(G-12089)*

FURNITURE: Chairs, Dental

Boyd Industries Inc..............D...... 727 561-9292
Clearwater *(G-1524)*

FURNITURE: Chairs, Household Upholstered

Design Furnishings Inc..............E...... 407 294-0507
Orlando *(G-12086)*

Jordan Brown Inc..............G...... 904 495-0717
Saint Augustine *(G-14851)*

Pendulum One Inc..............G...... 561 844-8169
Riviera Beach *(G-14658)*

FURNITURE: Chairs, Household Wood

Bluewater Chairs Inc..............F...... 954 318-0840
Fort Lauderdale *(G-3695)*

FURNITURE: Chairs, Office Exc Wood

Systematix Inc..............E...... 850 983-2213
Milton *(G-10439)*

FURNITURE: Chairs, Office Wood

Camilo Office Furniture Inc..............D...... 305 261-5366
Miami *(G-8882)*

Pradere Manufacturing Corp..............F...... 305 823-0190
Hialeah *(G-5298)*

Tockwogh LLC..............G...... 813 920-3413
Odessa *(G-11584)*

FURNITURE: Chests, Cedar

Cedar Fresh Home Products LLC..............G...... 305 975-8524
Miami *(G-8906)*

FURNITURE: China Closets

Accent Closets Inc..............F...... 954 561-8800
Deerfield Beach *(G-2653)*

FURNITURE: Desks, Wood

S M I Cabinetry Inc..............E...... 407 841-0292
Orlando *(G-12565)*

FURNITURE: Fiberglass & Plastic

Arcadia Thrift LLC..............G...... 863 993-2004
Arcadia *(G-188)*

FURNITURE: Frames, Box Springs Or Bedsprings, Metal

Mantua Manufacturing Co..............G...... 813 621-3714
Tampa *(G-17037)*

FURNITURE: Garden, Exc Wood, Metal, Stone Or Concrete

Sole Inc..............G...... 305 513-2603
Doral *(G-3368)*

FURNITURE: Hospital

Custom Comfort Medtek LLC..............E...... 407 332-0062
Winter Park *(G-18502)*

Winco Mfg LLC..............D...... 352 854-2929
Ocala *(G-11513)*

FURNITURE: Hotel

Blue Leaf Hospitality Inc..............F...... 305 668-3000
Coral Gables *(G-2034)*

Bryan Ashley Inc..............E...... 954 351-1199
Deerfield Beach *(G-2684)*

PRODUCT

Deepstream Designs Inc ....G 305 857-0466
Miami **(G-9007)**

Italian Cabinetry Inc ....F 786 534-2742
Miami **(G-9343)**

Kron Designs LLC ....G 954 941-0800
Fort Lauderdale **(G-3908)**

One World Resource LLC ....E 305 445-9199
Miami **(G-9653)**

FURNITURE: Household, Metal

Cramco Inc ....G 305 634-7500
Miami **(G-8977)**

J M Interiors Inc ....G 305 891-6121
North Miami **(G-11107)**

Jordan Brown Inc ....G 904 495-0717
Saint Augustine **(G-14851)**

Suncoast Aluminum Furn Inc ....E 239 267-8300
Fort Myers **(G-4410)**

Sungraf Inc ....G 954 456-8500
Hallandale Beach **(G-4976)**

Tuuci Worldwide ....G 305 634-5116
Hialeah **(G-5387)**

Tuuci Worldwide LLC ....B 305 823-3480
Hialeah **(G-5388)**

Tuuci Worldwide LLC ....G 305 634-5116
Miami **(G-10047)**

FURNITURE: Household, NEC

Blue Hippo LLC ....F 407 325-4090
Orlando **(G-11960)**

Cnd Express Scooters LLC ....G 407 633-1079
Kissimmee **(G-6975)**

Growth Logistics Inc ....F 800 846-2363
Miami Gardens **(G-10262)**

Lx Limited LLC ....G 888 610-0642
Melbourne **(G-8465)**

FURNITURE: Household, Upholstered On Metal Frames

Built LLC ....G 813 512-6250
Tampa **(G-16663)**

FURNITURE: Household, Upholstered, Exc Wood Or Metal

Flexshopper LLC ....E 561 922-6609
Boca Raton **(G-516)**

Outpost 30a LLC ....F 850 909-0138
Inlet Beach **(G-5819)**

FURNITURE: Household, Wood

A A A Cabinets ....G 850 438-8337
Pensacola **(G-13428)**

Ahus Inc ....E 305 572-9052
Miami Gardens **(G-10249)**

Aj Originals Inc ....G 954 563-9911
Fort Lauderdale **(G-3635)**

American Frame Furniture Inc ....G 305 548-3018
Miami **(G-8716)**

Annette M Wellington-Hall Inc ....F 954 437-9880
Hollywood **(G-5528)**

Avrora Inc ....G 386 246-9112
Palm Coast **(G-13071)**

B C Cabinetry ....G 561 393-8937
Boca Raton **(G-422)**

Beaches Woodcraft Inc ....F 904 249-0785
Atlantic Beach **(G-205)**

Belle Isle Furniture LLC ....G 407 408-1266
Belle Isle **(G-348)**

Bon Vivant Interiors Inc ....E 305 576-8066
Opa Locka **(G-11725)**

Carsons Cabinetry & Design Inc ....G 352 373-8292
Archer **(G-196)**

Contemporary Design Concepts ....F 305 253-2044
Miami **(G-8961)**

Contemporary Interiors Inc ....F 352 620-8686
Ocala **(G-11357)**

Cramco Inc ....G 305 634-7500
Miami **(G-8977)**

Creative Woodwork Miami Inc ....F 305 634-3100
Miami **(G-8978)**

Custom Beach Huts LLC ....F 305 439-3991
Coral Gables **(G-2044)**

Custom Cabinets Inc ....F 941 366-0428
Sarasota **(G-15647)**

Custom Mica Furniture Inc ....G 305 888-8480
Hialeah **(G-5104)**

Davila Woodworking Inc ....G 954 458-0460
Hallandale Beach **(G-4943)**

Dixie Workshop Inc ....F 352 629-4699
Ocala **(G-11369)**

Ecco Doors LLC ....G 561 392-3533
Boynton Beach **(G-861)**

Ecco Doors Manufacturing LLC ....G 561 721-6660
Boynton Beach **(G-862)**

Elegant House Intl LLC ....G 954 457-8836
Hallandale **(G-4925)**

Fine Archtctral Mllwk Shutters ....F 954 491-2055
Fort Lauderdale **(G-3816)**

Furniture Concepts 2000 Inc ....G 954 946-0310
Pompano Beach **(G-14036)**

Furniture Design of Centl Fla ....F 407 330-4430
Sanford **(G-15322)**

Genie Shelf ....G 305 213-4382
Miami **(G-9202)**

Gilmans Custom Furn & Cabinets ....F 352 746-3532
Lecanto **(G-7752)**

Glodea Store Corp ....G 888 400-4937
Jacksonville **(G-6145)**

Gulf South Distributors Inc ....E 850 244-1522
Fort Walton Beach **(G-4591)**

I B Furniture Inc ....G 941 371-5764
Sarasota **(G-15703)**

Infinite Ret Design & Mfg Corp ....F 305 967-8339
Miami **(G-9312)**

J & S Cypress Inc ....F 352 383-3864
Sorrento **(G-16010)**

J M Interiors Inc ....G 305 891-6121
North Miami **(G-11107)**

JTS Woodworking Inc ....G 561 272-7996
Delray Beach **(G-2980)**

Ken Clearys Two LLC ....F 727 573-0700
Clearwater **(G-1660)**

Lakewood Manufacturing Co Inc ....C 443 398-5015
West Palm Beach **(G-18051)**

Madison Millwork & Cabinet Co ....G 954 966-7551
Hollywood **(G-5619)**

Maggac Corporation ....G 561 439-2707
Lake Worth **(G-7215)**

Mantua Manufacturing Co ....G 813 621-3714
Tampa **(G-17037)**

Manufacturing By Skema Inc ....G 954 797-7325
Davie **(G-2435)**

McCallum Cabinets Inc ....F 352 372-2344
Gainesville **(G-4725)**

Mica Visions Inc ....G 727 712-3213
Clearwater **(G-1697)**

Mobius Business Group Inc ....F 239 274-8900
Fort Myers **(G-4327)**

Mr Mica Wood Inc ....F 561 278-5821
Delray Beach **(G-2990)**

N & N Investment Corporation ....G 954 590-3800
Pompano Beach **(G-14106)**

Nfjb Inc ....E 954 771-1100
Fort Lauderdale **(G-3962)**

Noell Design Group Inc ....G 561 391-9942
Boca Raton **(G-618)**

Nosta Inc ....G 305 634-1435
Miami **(G-9630)**

Perri Brothers and Associates ....G 305 887-8686
Medley **(G-8298)**

Pinellas Custom Cabinets Inc ....G 727 864-4263
Largo **(G-7659)**

PKolino LLC ....G 888 403-8992
Miami **(G-9719)**

Princeton Industries Inc ....E 954 344-9155
Margate **(G-8149)**

Raytash Inc ....G 561 347-8863
Boca Raton **(G-648)**

Riverstone Snctary - Cbd - Inc ....G 954 473-1254
Fort Lauderdale **(G-4020)**

Rm Custom Woodcraft Inc ....G 786 355-7387
Miami **(G-9811)**

Rolu Woodcraft Inc ....F 305 685-0914
Hialeah **(G-5336)**

Shelfgenie ....G 877 814-3643
Naples **(G-10890)**

Shelfgenie-Orlando ....G 407 808-5925
Orlando **(G-12589)**

Silverline Furniture Corp ....G 305 663-9560
Miami **(G-9893)**

Smith Products Co Inc ....G 386 325-4534
Palatka **(G-12880)**

Spacios Design Group Inc ....F 305 696-1766
Miami **(G-9932)**

Thomas Rley Artisans Guild Inc ....E 239 591-3203
Naples **(G-10925)**

TPL Manufacturing Inc ....G 954 783-3400
Lake Worth **(G-7237)**

Unlimited Cabinet Designs Inc ....F 954 923-3269
Hallandale **(G-4931)**

Via Cabinets Corp ....G 407 633-1915
Orlando **(G-12696)**

Viking Kabinets Inc ....E 305 238-9025
Cutler Bay **(G-2311)**

Waterfall Industries Inc ....F 407 330-2003
Sanford **(G-15406)**

Willson & Son Industry Inc ....G 954 972-5073
Margate **(G-8160)**

Winston & Sons Inc ....F 954 562-1984
Tamarac **(G-16544)**

Woodcraft LLC ....G 850 217-7757
Navarre **(G-10957)**

Woodcrafts By Angel Inc ....G 352 754-9335
Brooksville **(G-1223)**

Y F Leung Inc ....G 305 651-6851
North Miami Beach **(G-11172)**

Yonder Woodworks Inc ....G 561 547-5777
West Palm Beach **(G-18209)**

FURNITURE: Hydraulic Barber & Beauty Shop Chairs

Advanced Vacuum Systems LLC ....G 941 378-4565
Sarasota **(G-15588)**

Sustainable Casework Inds LLC ....G 954 980-6506
Deerfield Beach **(G-2818)**

FURNITURE: Institutional, Exc Wood

A & J Commercial Seating Inc ....G 352 288-2022
Summerfield **(G-16255)**

Allied Plastics Co Inc ....E 904 359-0386
Jacksonville **(G-5877)**

Antique & Modern Cabinets Inc ....E 904 393-9055
Jacksonville **(G-5892)**

Ashley Bryan International Inc ....E 954 351-1199
Deerfield Beach **(G-2672)**

Benchmark Design Group Inc ....F 904 246-5060
Jacksonville Beach **(G-6630)**

Contemporary Interiors Inc ....F 352 620-8686
Ocala **(G-11357)**

Divatti & Co LLC ....G 786 354-1888
Miramar **(G-10485)**

Gt Grandstands Inc ....E 813 305-1415
Plant City **(G-13775)**

Kron Designs LLC ....G 954 941-0800
Fort Lauderdale **(G-3908)**

FURNITURE: Kitchen & Dining Room

Pastrana Prime LLC ....F 407 470-9339
Orlando **(G-12471)**

Utopia Grilling LLC ....G 727 488-1355
New Port Richey **(G-10991)**

FURNITURE: Kitchen & Dining Room, Metal

Florida Custom Fabricators Inc ....F 407 892-8538
Saint Cloud **(G-14925)**

FURNITURE: Lawn & Garden, Except Wood & Metal

Alumatech Manufacturing Inc ....E 941 748-8880
Bradenton **(G-936)**

Armored Frog Inc ....G 850 418-2048
Pensacola **(G-13445)**

Keter North America LLC ....G 765 298-6800
Boca Raton **(G-568)**

Morning Star of Sarasota Inc ....G 941 371-0392
Sarasota **(G-15751)**

FURNITURE: Lawn & Garden, Metal

American Household Inc ....D 561 912-4100
Boca Raton **(G-407)**

Brown Jordan Company LLC ....D 904 495-0717
Saint Augustine **(G-14818)**

Casual Tone Inc ....F 941 722-5643
Palmetto **(G-13158)**

Florida Finisher Inc ....G 941 722-5643
Palmetto **(G-13167)**

Got It Inc ....G 954 899-0001
Boca Raton **(G-531)**

Sunbeam Americas Holdings LLC ....E 561 912-4100
Boca Raton **(G-702)**

Trainor Metal Products Inc ....G 561 395-5520
Boca Raton **(G-721)**

FURNITURE: Lawn, Metal

Medallion Leisure Furniture ....F 305 626-0000
Miami (G-9528)
Metal Craft of Pensacola Inc ....F 850 478-8333
Pensacola (G-13550)

FURNITURE: Lawn, Wood

Lifetime Environmental Designs ....G 352 237-7177
Ocala (G-11428)

FURNITURE: Living Room, Upholstered On Wood Frames

Associated Intr Desgr Svc Inc ....F 561 655-4926
West Palm Beach (G-17930)
Carlton Mfg Inc ....G 352 465-2153
Dunnellon (G-3463)
Koki Interiors Furn Mfg Inc ....F 305 558-6573
Hialeah (G-5213)
Ruby Vanrum ....G 850 643-5155
Bristol (G-1127)
Spring Oaks LLC ....G 352 592-1150
Brooksville (G-1207)

FURNITURE: Mattresses & Foundations

Devon Chase & Company ....G 407 438-6466
Orlando (G-12089)
Florida Mattress Wholesale ....G 941 244-2139
Venice (G-17692)
Rex Fox Enterprises Inc ....F 386 677-3752
Daytona Beach (G-2590)

FURNITURE: Mattresses, Box & Bedsprings

Blu Sleep Products LLC ....G 866 973-7614
Deerfield Beach (G-2677)
Diaz Brothers Corp ....F 305 364-4911
Hialeah (G-5117)
Leggett & Platt Incorporated ....E 727 856-3154
Spring Hill (G-16086)
Leggett & Platt Incorporated ....D 954 846-0300
Sunrise (G-16336)
Leggett & Platt Incorporated ....D 904 786-0750
Jacksonville (G-6255)
Mattress Makers USA Inc ....E 904 906-2793
Jacksonville (G-6280)
Murphy Bed USA Inc ....E 954 493-9001
Fort Lauderdale (G-3947)
Plushbeds Inc ....G 888 449-5738
Boca Raton (G-636)
Sealy Mattress Mfg Co LLC ....D 407 855-8523
Orlando (G-12583)
Sleep International LLC ....E 813 247-5337
Tampa (G-17272)

FURNITURE: Mattresses, Innerspring Or Box Spring

Biscayne Bedding Intl LLC ....E 305 633-4634
Hialeah (G-5077)
Corsicana Bedding LLC ....D 863 534-3450
Bartow (G-306)
Zeno Furniture & Mat Mfg Co ....G 954 764-1212
Fort Lauderdale (G-4145)

FURNITURE: NEC

Aloqua Gms Inc ....D 786 673-6838
Miami (G-8700)
Asemblu Inc ....F 800 827-4419
Hialeah (G-5061)
Octametro LLC ....G 305 715-9713
Doral (G-3316)
SC Gastronomic Crew Inc ....E 786 864-1212
Coral Gables (G-2107)
Smarte Carte Inc ....G 407 857-5841
Orlando (G-12610)

FURNITURE: Novelty, Wood

Yield Design ....G 402 321-2196
Saint Augustine (G-14917)

FURNITURE: Office Panel Systems, Exc Wood

Avl Systems Inc ....E 352 854-1170
Ocala (G-11330)

FURNITURE: Office Panel Systems, Wood

Engineered Equipment Corp ....F 561 839-4008
West Palm Beach (G-17987)

FURNITURE: Office, Exc Wood

Advanced Furniture Svcs Inc ....F 850 390-3442
Pensacola (G-13438)
Allied Plastics Co Inc ....E 904 359-0386
Jacksonville (G-5877)
Buckeye Used Office Furn Inc ....G 727 457-5287
Largo (G-7558)
Cayman Manufacturing Inc ....E 954 421-1170
Deerfield Beach (G-2687)
Dons Cabinets and Woodworking ....F 727 863-3404
Hudson (G-5771)
Gk Inc ....E 215 223-7207
Fort Lauderdale (G-3840)
Manning Company ....G 954 523-9355
Fort Lauderdale (G-3930)
New Vision Furniture Inc ....G 305 562-9428
Opa Locka (G-11776)
Office Express Corp ....F 786 503-6800
Miami (G-9638)
Sullenberger Inc ....F 813 988-4525
Tampa (G-17306)
Sungraf Inc ....G 954 456-8500
Hallandale Beach (G-4976)
Winston & Sons Inc ....G 954 562-1984
Tamarac (G-16544)

FURNITURE: Office, Wood

Allied Plastics Co Inc ....E 904 359-0386
Jacksonville (G-5877)
Antique & Modern Cabinets Inc ....E 904 393-9055
Jacksonville (G-5892)
Cabinet Masters Inc ....G 727 535-0020
Largo (G-7560)
Camilo Office Furniture Inc ....G 305 261-5366
Miami (G-8883)
Contemporary Interiors Inc ....F 352 620-8686
Ocala (G-11357)
Corpdesign ....G 866 323-6055
Miami (G-8972)
Creative Concepts Orlando Inc ....E 407 260-1435
Longwood (G-7883)
Custom Craft Laminates Inc ....E 813 877-7100
Tampa (G-16751)
Dons Cabinets and Woodworking ....F 727 863-3404
Hudson (G-5771)
Edgeline Industries LLC ....G 954 727-5272
Deerfield Beach (G-2716)
Gilmans Custom Furn & Cabinets ....G 352 746-3532
Lecanto (G-7752)
Home Pride Cabinets Inc ....F 813 887-3782
Tampa (G-16920)
J F V Designs Inc ....F 321 228-7469
Tavares (G-17513)
JTS Woodworking Inc ....G 561 272-7996
Delray Beach (G-2980)
Ken Clearys Two LLC ....F 727 573-0700
Clearwater (G-1660)
Kings & Queens Cabinets ....G 863 646-6972
Lakeland (G-7369)
McCallum Cabinets Inc ....F 352 372-2344
Gainesville (G-4725)
Millerknoll Inc ....E 904 858-9918
Jacksonville (G-6308)
Millerknoll Inc ....E 305 572-2909
Miami (G-9573)
N & N Investment Corporation ....F 954 590-3800
Pompano Beach (G-14106)
Office Furniture By Tempo Inc ....F 305 685-3077
Hialeah (G-5286)
Pinellas Custom Cabinets Inc ....G 727 864-4263
Largo (G-7659)
Rolu Woodcraft Inc ....F 305 685-0914
Hialeah (G-5336)
Roque Brothers Corp ....E 305 885-6995
Miami (G-9825)
Sullenberger Inc ....F 813 988-4525
Tampa (G-17306)
TOS Manufacturing Inc ....F 407 330-3880
Sanford (G-15400)
Viccarbe Inc ....E 305 670-0979
Miami (G-10106)
Wonder Emporium Millwork Fab ....F 407 850-3131
Orlando (G-12717)

FURNITURE: Outdoor, Wood

Brown Jordan Company LLC ....D 904 495-0717
Saint Augustine (G-14818)

FURNITURE: Rattan

Capris Furniture Inds Inc ....C 352 629-8889
Ocala (G-11342)

FURNITURE: Restaurant

A & J Commercial Seating Inc ....G 352 288-2022
Summerfield (G-16255)
Eldorado Miranda Mfg Co Inc ....G 727 586-0707
Largo (G-7579)
Vista Serv Corp ....G 239 275-1973
Fort Myers (G-4443)

FURNITURE: School

Cayman Manufacturing Inc ....E 954 421-1170
Deerfield Beach (G-2687)
Griffin & Holman Inc ....G 904 781-4531
Jacksonville (G-6157)
Series Usa LLC ....G 305 932-4626
Miami (G-9870)

FURNITURE: Ship

Aj Originals Inc ....G 954 563-9911
Fort Lauderdale (G-3635)
BMC Services Inc ....F 954 587-6337
Fort Lauderdale (G-3696)

FURNITURE: Sleep

Symbol Mattress Florida Inc ....G 407 343-4626
Kissimmee (G-6963)

FURNITURE: Stadium

Southeastern Seating Inc ....F 813 273-9858
Tampa (G-17287)

FURNITURE: Stools, Household, Wood

Simply45 LLC ....G 954 982-2017
Fort Lauderdale (G-4049)

FURNITURE: Storage Chests, Household, Wood

Closetmaid LLC ....C 352 401-6000
Orlando (G-12021)

FURNITURE: Table Tops, Marble

Ametrine LLC ....F 786 300-7946
Brandon (G-1083)
Ancient Mosaic Studios LLC ....E 772 460-3145
Fort Pierce (G-4466)
Galaxy Custom Granite Inc ....G 352 220-2822
Inverness (G-5828)
J & J Stone Tops Inc ....G 305 305-8993
Opa Locka (G-11757)
National Stoneworks LLC ....E 954 349-1609
Weston (G-18271)
Stone and Equipment Inc ....E 305 665-0002
Miami (G-9954)
Venice Granit & Marble Inc ....G 941 483-4363
Venice (G-17728)

FURNITURE: Tables & Table Tops, Wood

Allied Plastics Co Inc ....E 904 359-0386
Jacksonville (G-5877)
R & R Mica Works Inc ....G 305 231-1887
Miami Lakes (G-10346)

FURNITURE: Theater

Cinema Crafters Inc ....G 305 891-6121
North Miami (G-11098)

FURNITURE: Unfinished, Wood

Lawko Inc ....G 904 389-2850
Jacksonville (G-6253)

FURNITURE: Upholstered

American Marine Coverings Inc ....F 305 889-5355
Hialeah (G-5048)

PRODUCT

Architctral Wdwkg Concepts Inc ....G...... 239 434-0549
Naples (G-10672)
Bon Vivant Interiors Inc ....E...... 305 576-8066
Opa Locka (G-11725)
Capitol Furniture Mfg LLC ....G...... 954 485-5000
Boca Raton (G-453)
Contemporary Interiors Inc ....F...... 352 620-8686
Ocala (G-11357)
Elegant House Intl LLC ....G...... 954 457-8836
Hallandale (G-4925)
Expressions In Wood ....G...... 954 956-0005
Pompano Beach (G-14016)
Grafton Furniture Company ....E...... 305 696-3811
Miami (G-9231)
H317 Logistics LLC ....G...... 404 307-1621
Vero Beach (G-17758)
Home-Art Corporation ....E...... 352 326-3337
Fruitland Park (G-4641)
Martinson Mica Wood Pdts Inc ....G...... 305 688-4445
Opa Locka (G-11765)
Modern Happy Home Llc ....G...... 954 436-0055
Fort Lauderdale (G-3942)
Nordic Line Inc ....F...... 561 338-5545
Boca Raton (G-620)
Palm Furniture Systems Inc ....G...... 305 888-7009
Medley (G-8294)
S&S Global Supply LLC ....G...... 786 529-4799
Hialeah (G-5339)
Shores Global LLC ....G...... 305 716-0848
Miami (G-9883)
Stanley Chair Company Inc ....E...... 813 884-1436
Tampa (G-17299)
Twin Upholstery & Furn Mfg ....F...... 954 791-0744
Fort Lauderdale (G-4101)
Unimat Industries LLC ....G...... 305 716-0358
Miami (G-10061)
Unique Originals Inc ....E...... 305 634-2274
Fort Lauderdale (G-4106)

FURNITURE: Vanity Dressers, Wood

Italkraft LLC ....F...... 305 406-1301
Doral (G-3262)

FURNITURE: Wicker & Rattan

Ashley Bryan International Inc ....E...... 954 351-1199
Deerfield Beach (G-2672)
Conquest Financial Management ....D...... 305 630-8950
Miami (G-8957)
Source Contract LLC ....F...... 305 630-8950
Miami (G-9922)

FUSES: Electric

Power Grid Pros Inc ....G...... 716 378-1419
Weston (G-18279)

Furs

Made Fur You Inc ....F...... 813 444-7707
Hudson (G-5781)
Vanity Furs of Avondale LLC ....G...... 904 387-9900
Jacksonville (G-6587)

GAMES & TOYS: Automobiles, Children's, Pedal Driven

Prime Pedal Karts LLC ....F...... 850 475-0450
Pensacola (G-13584)

GAMES & TOYS: Banks

Kidstance LLC ....G...... 954 245-9916
Pompano Beach (G-14070)

GAMES & TOYS: Board Games, Children's & Adults'

Hasbro Latin America Inc ....G...... 305 931-3180
Miami (G-9263)
Victory Tailgate LLC ....C...... 407 704-8775
Orlando (G-12698)

GAMES & TOYS: Child Restraint Seats, Automotive

Smart Kid USA Inc ....G...... 754 366-6666
Pompano Beach (G-14181)

GAMES & TOYS: Craft & Hobby Kits & Sets

Bob Violett Models Inc ....E...... 407 327-6333
Winter Springs (G-18561)
Brandine Woodcraft Inc ....G...... 561 266-9360
Delray Beach (G-2937)
Safari Programs Inc ....D...... 305 621-1000
Jacksonville (G-6443)

GAMES & TOYS: Dolls & Doll Clothing

American Girl Brands LLC ....E...... 407 852-9771
Orlando (G-11901)

GAMES & TOYS: Dolls, Exc Stuffed Toy Animals

Doll Maker LLC ....G...... 800 851-5183
Naples (G-10732)

GAMES & TOYS: Electronic

Benchmark Entertainment LC ....E...... 561 588-5200
Lake Worth Beach (G-7250)
Benchmark Games Intl LLC ....D...... 561 588-5200
Lake Worth Beach (G-7251)
Etronics4u Inc ....F...... 786 303-8429
Sunny Isles Beach (G-16274)

GAMES & TOYS: Game Machines, Exc Coin-Operated

Misfit Gaming ....D...... 954 347-0906
Boca Raton (G-600)

GAMES & TOYS: Hobby Horses

Galaxy America Inc ....F...... 941 697-0324
Port Charlotte (G-14302)

GAMES & TOYS: Kits, Science, Incl Microscopes/Chemistry Sets

Triops Inc ....G...... 850 479-4415
Pensacola (G-13615)

GAMES & TOYS: Miniature Dolls, Collectors'

Timeless Treasures Doll Club ....E...... 813 854-6208
Tampa (G-17353)

GAMES & TOYS: Models, Airplane, Toy & Hobby

Atlantic Models Inc ....E...... 305 883-2012
Medley (G-8203)

GAMES & TOYS: Models, Boat & Ship, Toy & Hobby

Maritime Replicas Usa LLC ....E...... 305 921-9690
Boca Raton (G-583)

GAMES & TOYS: Musical Instruments

Schoenhut LLC ....G...... 904 810-1945
Saint Augustine (G-14887)

GAMES & TOYS: Scooters, Children's

Ev Rider LLC ....G...... 239 278-5054
Fort Myers (G-4250)

GAMES & TOYS: Strollers, Baby, Vehicle

Nikiani Inc ....G...... 305 606-1104
West Palm Beach (G-18092)

GARAGES: Portable, Prefabricated Metal

Wheel Systems Intl Inc ....F...... 920 235-9888
Bradenton (G-1078)

GARBAGE CONTAINERS: Plastic

Hippo Tampa LLC ....G...... 813 391-9152
Tampa (G-16918)
Quick Cans Inc ....G...... 407 415-1361
Winter Park (G-18529)
Ultimate Containers Pro LLC ....F...... 786 241-4306
Miami Gardens (G-10277)
Volusia Waste Inc ....F...... 386 878-3322
Deltona (G-3056)

Z Cans LLC ....G...... 941 748-6688
Bradenton (G-1080)

GARBAGE DISPOSERS & COMPACTORS: Commercial

C & D Industrial Maint LLC ....E...... 833 776-5833
Bradenton (G-951)
Ebco Envmtl Bins & Cntrs Inc ....F...... 954 967-9999
West Park (G-18211)

GAS & HYDROCARBON LIQUEFACTION FROM COAL

Cleancor Eqp Solutions LLC ....G...... 954 523-2200
Fort Lauderdale (G-3732)

GAS & OIL FIELD EXPLORATION SVCS

Albasol LLC ....G...... 830 334-3280
Miami (G-8680)
CP Royalties LLC ....G...... 888 694-9265
Tampa (G-16735)
Dauntless Usa Inc ....E...... 904 996-8800
Jacksonville (G-6026)
DM Oil Corp ....G...... 954 835-5468
Wilton Manors (G-18338)
Exploration Services LLC ....G...... 352 505-3578
Gainesville (G-4688)
Fuels Unlimited Inc ....G...... 407 302-3193
Sanford (G-15321)
Gulfstream Natural Gas Sys LLC ....G...... 941 723-7000
Palmetto (G-13171)
Hess Logistics Inc ....G...... 954 668-7101
Parkland (G-13346)
Hess Station 09307 ....F...... 407 891-7156
Saint Cloud (G-14928)
HRF Exploration & Prod LLC ....G...... 561 847-4743
Palm Beach (G-12936)
Hunt Ventures Inc ....F...... 941 375-3699
Venice (G-17699)
Interntnal Tech Sltons Sup LLC ....G...... 305 364-5229
Doral (G-3259)
Kelton Company LLC ....G...... 850 434-6830
Pensacola (G-13533)
Kens Gas Piping Inc ....G...... 850 897-4149
Valparaiso (G-17661)
Maverick Natural Resources LLC ....F...... 239 657-2171
Immokalee (G-5799)
Oil For Amer Exploration LLC ....G...... 701 690-2407
Tallahassee (G-16485)
ONeill Industries Intl Inc ....G...... 850 754-0312
Cantonment (G-1272)
Platinum Group Usa Inc ....F...... 561 274-7553
Delray Beach (G-2999)
Reliance Petro Holdings LLC ....F...... 352 390-8039
Ocala (G-11480)
Seacor Marine LLC ....D...... 954 523-2200
Fort Lauderdale (G-4042)
Shaka Energy Exploration Inc ....G...... 561 279-1379
Delray Beach (G-3015)
Superior Oil 2016 Inc ....G...... 305 851-5140
Miami (G-9971)
Sylios Corp ....F...... 727 821-6200
Saint Petersburg (G-15206)
Tri C Petroleum Inc ....G...... 941 756-3370
Bradenton (G-1063)
Western Intl Gas Cylinders Inc ....G...... 813 635-9321
Tampa (G-17428)
Whittington Energy Co ....G...... 321 984-2128
Melbourne (G-8561)

GAS & OIL FIELD SVCS, NEC

Alfresco Air ....F...... 786 275-5111
Miami (G-8685)
Bodman Oil & Gas LLC ....G...... 239 430-8545
Naples (G-10697)
Charuvil Oil Inc DBA Valero ....G...... 772 871-9050
Port Saint Lucie (G-14404)
Euramerica Gas and Oil Corp ....G...... 954 858-5714
Plantation (G-13848)
Expressway Oil Corp ....G...... 786 302-9534
Medley (G-8239)
Proserv Technologies Inc ....F...... 727 265-3190
Palm Harbor (G-13125)
Thompsons Arprt Hnger Svcs LLC ....G...... 239 825-7466
Naples (G-10926)
W2e International Corp ....G...... 561 362-9595
Boca Raton (G-752)

GAS FIELD MACHINERY & EQPT

Carib Energy (usa) LLC ....A 904 727-2559
Jacksonville **(G-5971)**

GAS STATIONS

Reliance Petro Holdings LLC ....F 352 390-8039
Ocala **(G-11480)**

GAS STATIONS WITH CONVENIENCE STORES

Kendall Fuel Inc ....G 305 270-7735
Miami **(G-9388)**

GAS: Refinery

DOT Green Energy Inc ....G 717 505-8686
Clearwater **(G-1567)**
Port Hmlton Rfinery Trnsp Lllp ....A ... 305 299-0251
Coral Gables **(G-2097)**

GASES & LIQUIFIED PETROLEUM GASES

Donald Ross Gas Inc ....F 561 776-1324
Jupiter **(G-6712)**
NPC&ug Inc ....G 239 694-7255
Alva **(G-82)**
Omega Gas Inc ....G 786 277-2176
Miami **(G-9647)**

GASES: Flourinated Hydrocarbon

North America Bio Fuel Corp ....G 877 877-9279
Bradenton **(G-1019)**

GASES: Helium

Add Helium ....G 239 300-0913
Fort Lauderdale **(G-3624)**

GASES: Hydrogen

Genh2 Inc...G 321 223-5950
Titusville **(G-17587)**
Genh2 Corp ....E 530 654-3642
Titusville **(G-17588)**
Hydrogen Innovations Co ....G 727 386-8805
Tarpon Springs **(G-17477)**
Hydrogen One Inc ....G 352 361-6974
Belleview **(G-363)**

GASES: Indl

Air Liquide America LP ....E 407 855-8286
Orlando **(G-11880)**
Air Liquide Large Inds US LP ....G 321 452-2214
Merritt Island **(G-8572)**
Air Products and Chemicals Inc............F 407 859-5141
Orlando **(G-11881)**
Bridge Chemicals Inc ....G 954 545-9459
Pompano Beach **(G-13954)**
Equipment Sales & Service Inc ....G 727 572-9197
Clearwater **(G-1588)**
Linde Inc ....F 813 626-3636
Tampa **(G-17011)**
Liquid Technolgy Corp ....G 832 804-8650
Oldsmar **(G-11670)**
Matheson Tri-Gas Inc..........................E 561 615-3000
Jupiter **(G-6763)**
Matheson Tri-Gas Inc..........................G 727 572-8737
Clearwater **(G-1686)**
Prodair Corporation ....G 850 994-5511
Milton **(G-10433)**
Vs Carbonics Inc ....F 305 903-6501
Miami **(G-10120)**

GASES: Neon

EZ Neon Inc ....G 561 262-7813
Jupiter **(G-6724)**
Neon Cowboys LLC ....G 949 514-5557
Apopka **(G-157)**
Neon Workforce Technologies ....G 305 458-8244
Hialeah **(G-5275)**

GASES: Nitrogen

Frostbite Nitrogen Ice Cream.................G 305 933-5482
Miami **(G-9176)**
Linde Inc ....E 321 267-2311
Mims **(G-10449)**

Nitrogen Jupiter LLC ....G 561 662-2150
Jupiter **(G-6772)**
Rz Service Group LLC ....G 904 402-2313
Jacksonville **(G-6439)**

GASES: Oxygen

Airgas Usa LLC ....G 407 293-6630
Orlando **(G-11884)**
Messer LLC ....F 925 606-2000
Delray Beach **(G-2987)**

GASKETS & SEALING DEVICES

Construction and Elec Pdts Inc............F 954 972-9787
Pompano Beach **(G-13976)**
Fabrico Inc ....C 386 736-7373
Deland **(G-2870)**
Guy Gasket Inc ....E 561 703-1774
Lake Worth **(G-7203)**
Technetics Group LLC ....B 386 736-7373
Deland **(G-2908)**
Technetics Group LLC ....E 386 736-7373
De Land **(G-2620)**

GASOLINE BLENDING PLANT

Ares Distributors Inc ....G 305 858-0163
Miami **(G-8745)**
Dion Fuels LLC ....F 305 296-2000
Key West **(G-6862)**

GATES: Dam, Metal Plate

Ppa Miami Corp ....G 305 436-0460
Miami **(G-9733)**

GATES: Ornamental Metal

American Metal Gate Corp ....F 516 659-7952
Bay Harbor Islands **(G-331)**
Greg Valentine LLC ....E 239 332-0855
Fort Myers **(G-4273)**
Precision Gate & Security Inc ....G 813 404-6278
Sarasota **(G-15785)**

GAUGES

Sohacki Industries Inc ....E 904 826-0130
Saint Augustine **(G-14894)**
Tom Sweet ....G 727 515-9015
Pinellas Park **(G-13731)**

GAUGES: Pressure

Uniweld Products Inc ....G 954 584-2000
Fort Lauderdale **(G-4111)**

GEARS

Riley Gear Corporation ....D 904 829-5652
Saint Augustine **(G-14878)**

GEARS & GEAR UNITS: Reduction, Exc Auto

Hydraulicnet LLC ....F 630 543-7630
Saint Augustine **(G-14840)**

GEARS: Power Transmission, Exc Auto

Lubov Manufacturing Inc ....G 813 873-2640
Tampa **(G-17023)**
Martin Sprocket & Gear Inc ....E 813 623-1705
Tampa **(G-17045)**
S I P Corporation ....F 813 884-8300
Tampa **(G-17239)**
Snow-Nabstedt Power Transmissi ....G 603 661-5551
Bradenton **(G-1048)**

GELATIN CAPSULES

Catalent Pharma Solutions Inc ....A 727 572-4000
Saint Petersburg **(G-14999)**
Enzymedica Inc ....E 941 505-5565
Venice **(G-17690)**

GEM STONES MINING, NEC: Natural

4 Power International Stones.................G 407 286-4677
Orlando **(G-11852)**

GEMSTONE & INDL DIAMOND MINING SVCS

ER Jahna Industries Inc ....E 863 424-0730
Davenport **(G-2364)**

Waste Management Inc Florida ....E 954 984-2000
Winter Garden **(G-18408)**

GENERAL MERCHANDISE STORES, NEC

Artvint Corp...G 727 856-3565
Hudson **(G-5762)**

GENERAL MERCHANDISE, NONDURABLE, WHOLESALE

Argos Global Partner Svcs LLC ....G 305 365-1096
Key Biscayne **(G-6833)**
Artvint Corp...G 727 856-3565
Hudson **(G-5762)**
Lakay Vita LLC ....G 786 985-7552
Hallandale Beach **(G-4957)**
Pb Group LLC ....E 954 922-4311
Hollywood **(G-5638)**
Premier Luxury Group LLC ....E 954 358-9885
Fort Lauderdale **(G-3995)**
Rokey Corporation ....G 561 470-0164
Boca Raton **(G-654)**

GENERATING APPARATUS & PARTS: Electrical

Adtec Productions Incorporated ....F 904 720-2003
Jacksonville **(G-5859)**
Illinois Tool Works Inc ....E 941 721-1000
Palmetto **(G-13176)**

GENERATION EQPT: Electronic

American Payment Systems ....F 407 856-8524
Orlando **(G-11904)**
Apollo Energy Systems Inc...................G 954 969-7755
Pompano Beach **(G-13930)**
Axis Group ....F 954 580-6000
Pompano Beach **(G-13942)**
Chenega Manufacturing Svcs LLC........E 850 763-6013
Panama City **(G-13242)**
Coastland Specialties LLC ....G 239 910-5401
Bonita Springs **(G-791)**
Electrnic Systems Sutheast LLC ....F 561 955-9006
Fort Myers **(G-4245)**
Industry Standard Technology ....G 941 355-2100
Sarasota **(G-15499)**
Keytroller LLC ....F 813 877-4500
Tampa **(G-16984)**
Keytroller LLC ....F 813 877-4500
Tampa **(G-16985)**
Lightning Master Corporation ....E 800 749-6800
Clearwater **(G-1673)**
M Micro Technologies Inc ....B 954 973-6166
Pompano Beach **(G-14083)**
Mathews Associates Inc.......................C 407 323-3390
Sanford **(G-15354)**
Omniaelectronics LLC ....G 631 742-5719
North Bay Village **(G-11059)**
Sagrad Inc..F 321 726-9400
Melbourne **(G-8513)**
Sepac Corp ....F 305 718-3379
Miami **(G-9868)**
Ultrasonic Technologies Inc ....G 813 973-1702
Wesley Chapel **(G-17890)**
Universal Networking Svcs Co ....G 281 825-9790
Saint Petersburg **(G-15220)**
Veethree Electronics & Mar LLC...........D 941 538-7775
Bradenton **(G-1072)**
Watts Technologies LLC ....F 407 512-5750
Sanford **(G-15407)**

GENERATOR REPAIR SVCS

Pinnacle Central Company Inc ....F 904 354-5746
Jacksonville **(G-6371)**
Santanas Pwrsprts Small Eng Rp ....G 813 658-3530
Tampa **(G-17246)**

GENERATORS SETS: Steam

Southern Innovative Energy Inc ....G 321 747-9205
Titusville **(G-17616)**

GENERATORS: Automotive & Aircraft

Create and Company Inc......................F 813 393-8778
Tampa **(G-16737)**
Pcm and S L Plota Co LLC ....F 727 547-6277
Largo **(G-7656)**

PRODUCT

GENERATORS: Electric

Armstrong Power Systems LLC ....G....... 305 470-0058
Miami (G-8750)

Bgt Holdings LLC ....G....... 239 643-9949
Naples (G-10694)

Cummins Power Generation Inc...........E....... 239 337-1211
Fort Myers (G-4225)

Emergency Standby Power LLC ....G....... 850 259-2304
Fort Walton Beach (G-4581)

Jat Power LLC ....F....... 305 592-0103
Doral (G-3266)

Mtservicer LLC ....G....... 305 200-1254
Miami Lakes (G-10328)

Southeast Power Group Inc ....D....... 305 592-9745
Doral (G-3370)

Tradewinds Power Corp ....D....... 305 592-9745
Doral (G-3400)

GENERATORS: Electrochemical, Fuel Cell

Dioxide Materials Inc ....F....... 217 239-1400
Boca Raton (G-485)

Kollsman Inc ....G....... 407 312-1384
Orlando (G-12293)

GENERATORS: Gas

Sams Gas...........G....... 386 698-1033
Crescent City (G-2237)

GENERATORS: Storage Battery Chargers

Amper Usa LLC ....G....... 305 717-3101
Doral (G-3114)

Enersys...........G....... 863 577-3900
Lakeland (G-7316)

Lithium Battery Co Intl ....F....... 813 504-0074
Tampa (G-17015)

Solar Stik Inc ....E....... 800 793-4364
Saint Augustine (G-14895)

GENERATORS: Thermo-Electric

Mitsubishi Power Americas Inc ....D....... 407 688-6100
Lake Mary (G-7096)

GIFT SHOP

Baker County Press Inc ....G....... 904 259-2400
Macclenny (G-8036)

Thayer Industries Inc...........G....... 813 719-6597
Dundee (G-3438)

Treasure Cove II Inc ....F....... 941 966-2004
Sarasota (G-15858)

GIFT WRAP: Paper, Made From Purchased Materials

Wrap-Art Inc ....G....... 954 428-1819
Deerfield Beach (G-2835)

GIFT, NOVELTY & SOUVENIR STORES: Gifts & Novelties

Big Bend Ice Cream Co ....G....... 850 539-7778
Havana (G-4993)

GIFTS & NOVELTIES: Wholesalers

Birdiebox LLC ....E....... 786 762-2975
Miami (G-8832)

Fanatics Mounted Memories Inc ....E....... 866 578-9115
Jacksonville (G-6087)

Mounted Memories Inc ....F....... 866 236-2541
Miramar (G-10516)

PM Craftsman ....E....... 863 665-0815
Lakeland (G-7410)

Suncoast Identification Tech ....G....... 239 277-9922
Fort Myers (G-4411)

GLASS & GLASS CERAMIC PRDTS, PRESSED OR BLOWN: Tableware

Anchor Glass Container Corp ....B....... 904 786-1010
Jacksonville (G-5888)

Ecosoulife USA Dist LLC ....F....... 754 212-5456
Boca Raton (G-499)

GLASS FABRICATORS

Adams Glass Co ....G....... 816 842-8686
Indialantic (G-5801)

American Woodwork Specialty Co...........F....... 937 263-1053
Santa Rosa Beach (G-15421)

Ameriglass Engineering Inc...........F....... 305 558-6227
Hialeah (G-5053)

Arso Enterprises Inc ....E....... 305 681-2020
Opa Locka (G-11719)

B & K Installations Inc ....G....... 305 245-6968
Homestead (G-5701)

Buchelli Glass Inc ....G....... 954 695-8067
Coconut Creek (G-1980)

Cardinal Lg Company ....D....... 352 237-4410
Ocala (G-11344)

Clear View Glass & Glazing ....G....... 561 441-7675
Delray Beach (G-2946)

Commercial Insulating Glass Co...........E....... 941 378-9100
Sarasota (G-15638)

Commercial Rfrg Door Co Inc ....G....... 941 371-8110
Sarasota (G-15639)

Custom Cft Windows & Doors Inc...........F....... 407 834-5400
Winter Springs (G-18563)

Darren Thomas Glass Co Inc...........G....... 863 655-9500
Sebring (G-15918)

Defenshield Inc ....G....... 904 679-3942
Saint Augustine (G-14825)

Downey Group LLC ....E....... 954 972-0026
Pompano Beach (G-14000)

G F E Inc ....G....... 954 583-7005
Davie (G-2416)

GE Glass Inc ....F....... 305 599-7725
Miami (G-9195)

Geltech Inc ....C....... 407 382-4003
Orlando (G-12185)

Jambco Millwork Inc ....F....... 954 977-4998
Margate (G-8136)

Jensen Scientific Products Inc...........E....... 954 344-2006
Coral Springs (G-2169)

Jsl Enterprises of Orlando ....F....... 386 767-9653
Chuluota (G-1465)

Justi Group Inc ....E....... 813 855-5779
Oldsmar (G-11663)

Living Color Aquarium Corp ....E....... 844 522-8265
Deerfield Beach (G-2756)

Luv Enterprises Inc...........F....... 352 867-8440
Ocala (G-11433)

MA Glass & Mirror LLC...........F....... 305 593-8555
Miami (G-9493)

Ocean Dynamics USA Inc ....G....... 305 770-1800
Miami (G-9637)

PGT Industries Inc ....A....... 941 480-1600
North Venice (G-11216)

Pompanette LLC ....E....... 813 885-2182
Tampa (G-17169)

Security Impact GL Hldings LLC ....G....... 561 844-3100
Riviera Beach (G-14674)

Shower Doors Unlimited Inc ....G....... 561 547-0702
Boynton Beach (G-912)

Smart Glass Systems Inc ....G....... 954 801-5349
Plantation (G-13889)

Square One Armoring Svcs Co ....D....... 305 477-1109
Miami (G-9945)

Stony Coral Investments LLC...........F....... 941 704-5391
Myakka City (G-10647)

Sunoptic Technologies LLC...........D....... 877 677-2832
Jacksonville (G-6516)

Universal Alum Windows & Doors ....F....... 305 825-7900
Hialeah (G-5394)

Worldglass Corporation ....G....... 813 609-2453
Tampa (G-17439)

Yale Ogron Mfg Co Inc ....E....... 305 687-0424
Opa Locka (G-11803)

GLASS PRDTS, FROM PURCHASED GLASS: Art

Prestige Glass Art LLC...........G....... 941 921-6758
Sarasota (G-15786)

GLASS PRDTS, FROM PURCHASED GLASS: Enameled

LP Auto & Home Glass...........F....... 772 335-3697
Fort Pierce (G-4502)

GLASS PRDTS, FROM PURCHASED GLASS: Glass Beads, Reflecting

Flexstake Inc ....E....... 239 481-3539
Fort Myers (G-4254)

Oldcastle Buildingenvelope Inc...........C....... 305 651-6630
Miami (G-9642)

GLASS PRDTS, FROM PURCHASED GLASS: Glassware

Terraferma USA Corporation ....F....... 305 994-7892
Doral (G-3396)

GLASS PRDTS, FROM PURCHASED GLASS: Insulating

Omega Garage Doors Inc ....F....... 352 620-8830
Melbourne (G-8488)

GLASS PRDTS, FROM PURCHASED GLASS: Mirrored

AGM Industries Inc ....F....... 954 486-1112
Fort Lauderdale (G-3631)

All Glass & Mirror LLC ....F....... 561 914-5277
Pompano Beach (G-13916)

Art & Frame Direct Inc ....C....... 407 857-6000
Orlando (G-11923)

BT Glass & Mirror Inc ....G....... 561 841-7676
West Palm Beach (G-17952)

Friedman Bros Dcrtive Arts Inc ....D....... 800 327-1065
Medley (G-8243)

Mirrors & More Inc ....G....... 954 782-7272
Pompano Beach (G-14102)

GLASS PRDTS, FROM PURCHASED GLASS: Mirrors, Framed

Venture Circle Intl LLC ....F....... 407 677-6004
Sanford (G-15403)

GLASS PRDTS, PRESSED OR BLOWN: Barware

Foh Inc ....C....... 305 757-7940
Miami (G-9165)

GLASS PRDTS, PRESSED OR BLOWN: Bowls

Eco Cups International Corp ....F....... 407 308-1764
Orlando (G-12115)

Water Works Tech Group LLC ....F....... 954 979-2480
Pompano Beach (G-14240)

GLASS PRDTS, PRESSED OR BLOWN: Bulbs, Electric Lights

DK International Group Corp ....G....... 954 391-8969
Hollywood (G-5568)

Jga Lighting LLC...........G....... 772 408-8224
Grant (G-4812)

Ledradiant LLC...........G....... 305 901-1313
Hollywood (G-5609)

GLASS PRDTS, PRESSED OR BLOWN: Glass Fibers, Textile

Owens Corning Sales LLC ....E....... 863 291-3046
Winter Haven (G-18453)

GLASS PRDTS, PRESSED OR BLOWN: Glassware, Art Or Decorative

Miracles For Fun Usa Inc ....F....... 561 702-8217
Hallandale Beach (G-4961)

GLASS PRDTS, PRESSED OR BLOWN: Ophthalmic, Exc Flat

Transitions Optical Inc ....B....... 727 545-0400
Pinellas Park (G-13732)

GLASS PRDTS, PRESSED OR BLOWN: Optical

Safilo Usa Inc ....D....... 305 262-5727
Miami (G-9837)

GLASS PRDTS, PRESSED OR BLOWN: Ornaments, Christmas Tree

Edmund C Miga...........G....... 941 628-5951
Port Charlotte (G-14297)

2022 Harris Florida
Manufacturers Directory

(G-0000) Company's Geographic Section entry number

GLASS PRDTS, PRESSED OR BLOWN: Tubing

Charles Composites LLC ....F 863 357-2500
Okeechobee *(G-11600)*

GLASS PRDTS, PRESSED/BLOWN: Glassware, Art, Decor/Novelty

A Sanborn Corporation ....E 727 397-3073
Madeira Beach *(G-8039)*
Madart ....G 321 961-9264
Titusville *(G-17600)*
Milano Worldwide Corp ....G 561 266-0201
Boca Raton *(G-599)*
Nebula Glass International Inc ....E 954 975-3233
Pompano Beach *(G-14107)*

GLASS PRDTS, PURCHASED GLASS: Glassware, Scientific/Tech

Florida Style Aluminum Inc ....F 239 689-8662
Fort Myers *(G-4257)*

GLASS PRDTS, PURCHASED GLASS: Insulating, Multiple-Glazed

Global Performance Windows Inc........F 954 942-3322
Pompano Beach *(G-14042)*

GLASS PRDTS, PURCHD GLASS: Furniture Top, Cut, Beveld/Polshd

Circle Redmont Inc ....F 321 259-7374
Satellite Beach *(G-15884)*
Kron Designs LLC ....G 954 941-0800
Fort Lauderdale *(G-3908)*

GLASS PRDTS, PURCHSD GLASS: Ornamental, Cut, Engraved/Décor

Ace Mirror & Glass Works Inc ....G....... 561 792-7478
Loxahatchee *(G-7964)*
Global Porte...G..... 305 416-5001
Miami *(G-9219)*

GLASS STORE: Leaded Or Stained

Jsl Enterprises of Orlando ....F 386 767-9653
Chuluota *(G-1465)*

GLASS STORES

American Archtctral Mtls GL LL ....G....... 305 688-8778
Hialeah *(G-5044)*
Blutec Glass Fabrication LLC ....G....... 941 232-1600
Sarasota *(G-15613)*
Creative Glassworks.............................G..... 904 860-0865
Jacksonville *(G-6012)*
Faours Mirror Corp ....E 813 884-3297
Tampa *(G-16827)*
Oldcastle Buildingenvelope Inc..........D 813 247-3184
Tampa *(G-17121)*
Oldcastle Buildingenvelope Inc..........E 813 663-0949
Tampa *(G-17122)*
Simplex Inc ....E 352 357-2828
Mount Dora *(G-10613)*

GLASS: Broadwoven Fabrics

Security Impact GL Hldings LLC ....G....... 561 844-3100
Riviera Beach *(G-14674)*

GLASS: Fiber

Allied Molded Products LLC ....E 941 723-3072
Palmetto *(G-13154)*
Merritt Precision Tech Inc ....G....... 321 453-2334
Merritt Island *(G-8587)*
Perry Composites LLC ....G....... 850 584-8400
Perry *(G-13648)*
Spectra Composites East Fla ....G....... 772 461-7747
Fort Pierce *(G-4532)*

GLASS: Flat

Faours Mirror Corp ....E 813 884-3297
Tampa *(G-16827)*
FMC/Rhyno LLC....................................E 813 838-2264
Tampa *(G-16856)*
Guardian Industries Cor......................G..... 954 525-3481
Fort Lauderdale *(G-3853)*

Jsl Enterprises of Orlando ....F 386 767-9653
Chuluota *(G-1465)*
Pilkington North America Inc ....G..... 305 470-1813
Doral *(G-3329)*
Pilkington North America Inc ....G..... 800 759-0940
Tallahassee *(G-16487)*
Pilkington North America Inc ....F 407 295-8560
Orlando *(G-12487)*
Precision Auto Tint Dsign Corp............G..... 727 385-8788
Tarpon Springs *(G-17488)*
Schott Solutions Inc.............................G..... 786 340-5116
Pembroke Pines *(G-13413)*

GLASS: Indl Prdts

Flat Glass Distributors LLC ....F 904 354-5413
Jacksonville *(G-6102)*

GLASS: Insulating

Commercial Insulating Glass Co.........E 941 378-9100
Sarasota *(G-15638)*
Impact Safe Glass Corporation ....G....... 813 247-5528
Tampa *(G-16934)*

GLASS: Pressed & Blown, NEC

Hoya Largo ....E 727 531-8964
Largo *(G-7609)*
Mjr Enterprises Inc...............................G..... 352 483-0735
Eustis *(G-3564)*
Perfect Reflections Inc ....G..... 813 991-4361
Zephyrhills *(G-18624)*

GLASS: Safety

Dependable Shutter Service Inc ....E 954 583-1411
Davie *(G-2404)*
Vision Blocks Inc ....F 321 254-7478
Melbourne *(G-8559)*

GLASS: Stained

Advent Glass Works Inc ....G..... 386 497-2050
Fort White *(G-4618)*
Conrad Pickel Studio Inc......................G..... 772 567-1710
Vero Beach *(G-17750)*
Creative Glassworks.............................G..... 904 860-0865
Jacksonville *(G-6012)*
Mtg Designs Inc ....G..... 904 923-1620
Jacksonville *(G-6626)*

GLASS: Structural

Aldora Aluminum & GL Pdts Inc...........E 954 441-5057
Miami *(G-8683)*
Structure Glass Solutions LLC............F 954 499-9450
Hialeah *(G-5365)*

GLASS: Tempered

Oldcastle Buildingenvelope Inc............D 813 247-3184
Tampa *(G-17121)*
Oldcastle Buildingenvelope Inc............E 813 663-0949
Tampa *(G-17122)*
Tempered Glass Industries Inc.............E 727 499-0284
Clearwater *(G-1825)*

GLASSWARE WHOLESALERS

Mjr Enterprises Inc...............................G..... 352 483-0735
Eustis *(G-3564)*
Premier Lab Supply Inc ....G..... 772 873-1700
Port Saint Lucie *(G-14434)*

GLASSWARE: Cut & Engraved

Hartmans Canine Center LLC ....G....... 352 978-6592
Clermont *(G-1871)*

GLOBAL POSITIONING SYSTEMS & EQPT

Anywhere Gps LLC...............................G..... 949 468-6842
Saint Augustine *(G-14810)*
Fleetboss Globl Pstning Sltons...........E 407 265-9559
Fern Park *(G-3578)*
Joe Hearn Innovative Tech LLC............F 850 898-3744
Pensacola *(G-13528)*
Locus Solutions LLC ....D 561 575-7600
Palm Beach Gardens *(G-12985)*
Nxgen Brands LLC................................E 888 315-6339
Plantation *(G-13875)*
Rgrauto Inc ....E 305 952-5522
Aventura *(G-274)*

GLOVES: Fabric

Dion Atelier Inc....................................G..... 305 389-9711
Miami Beach *(G-10183)*
I ABC Corp ....G..... 904 645-6000
Jacksonville *(G-6191)*
Parker Protective Products LLC...........F 800 879-0329
North Miami *(G-11115)*
Warren Heim Corp ....F 772 466-8265
Fort Pierce *(G-4553)*

GLOVES: Leather, Work

Sara Glove Company Inc.......................G..... 866 664-7272
Naples *(G-10884)*

GLOVES: Work

Niefeld Group LLC ....G..... 786 587-7423
Hialeah *(G-5279)*

GLUE

Craig Armstrong ....F 786 319-6514
Miami Beach *(G-10182)*

GLYCERIN

World Hlth Enrgy Holdings Inc ....F 561 870-0440
Boca Raton *(G-755)*

GLYCOL ETHERS

Mmt Technologies Inc ....G..... 863 619-2926
Lakeland *(G-7397)*

GOLD ORE MINING

Bromide Mining LLC ....F 786 477-6229
Doral *(G-3149)*
Iamgold Purchasing Svcs Inc...............G..... 713 671-5973
Doral *(G-3253)*

GOLD ORES

Astor Explorations Corp ....G..... 561 241-3621
Boca Raton *(G-417)*
Chemours Company Fc LLC...................D 904 964-1200
Starke *(G-16099)*
Goldfield Cnsld Mines Co ....D 321 724-1700
Melbourne *(G-8430)*
US Precious Metals Inc ....G..... 786 814-5804
Coral Gables *(G-2118)*

GOLD ORES PROCESSING

New World Gold Corporation................F 561 962-4139
Boca Raton *(G-614)*

GOLF CARTS: Powered

Columbia Parcar Corp ....F 352 753-0244
Leesburg *(G-7763)*
Cricket Mini Golf Carts Inc....................F 386 220-3536
Daytona Beach *(G-2537)*
Elite Enclosures ....G..... 352 323-6005
Leesburg *(G-7771)*
Ljs Tops & Bottoms ....E 561 736-7868
Boynton Beach *(G-887)*
Maria Dill Inc ....G..... 352 394-0418
Clermont *(G-1876)*
Nivel Holdings LLC ....G..... 904 741-6161
Jacksonville *(G-6335)*
Nivel Parts & Mfg Co LLC......................E 904 741-6161
Jacksonville *(G-6336)*
Streetrod Productions Inc.....................G..... 352 751-3953
The Villages *(G-17557)*

GOLF CARTS: Wholesalers

Nivel Holdings LLC ....G..... 904 741-6161
Jacksonville *(G-6335)*
Nivel Parts & Mfg Co LLC......................G..... 904 741-6161
Jacksonville *(G-6336)*

GOLF EQPT

Biomech Golf Equipment LLC..............F 401 932-0479
Naples *(G-10696)*
Custom Design Golf LLC ....G..... 770 926-4653
Ormond Beach *(G-12754)*
Kent Manufacturing Venice Inc.............F 941 485-8871
Nokomis *(G-11049)*
Laird International Corp ....G..... 954 532-3794
Pompano Beach *(G-14075)*

PRODUCT

Liquid Ed Inc ....G....... 727 943-8616
Tarpon Springs **(G-17480)**

Qwikpik Golf LLC ....G....... 407 505-5546
Orlando **(G-12522)**

US Golf Liquidators Inc ....E....... 407 677-1118
Orlando **(G-12693)**

Whole 9 Golf & Cigars ....G....... 407 814-9994
Apopka **(G-185)**

GOLF GOODS & EQPT

Custom Design Golf LLC ....G....... 770 926-4653
Ormond Beach **(G-12754)**

GOURMET FOOD STORES

Classica & Telecard Corp ....G....... 239 354-3727
Naples **(G-10716)**

Termine Ravioli Manufacturing ....F....... 954 983-3711
Hollywood **(G-5669)**

GOVERNMENT, EXECUTIVE OFFICES:
Mayors'

City of Ocala ....E....... 352 622-6803
Ocala **(G-11352)**

GRANITE: Crushed & Broken

Blue Water Industries LLC ....F....... 904 512-7706
Jacksonville **(G-5940)**

Granite World Inc ....E....... 813 243-6556
Tampa **(G-16890)**

Rock Ridge Materials Inc ....F....... 321 268-8455
Titusville **(G-17615)**

GRANITE: Cut & Shaped

All Granite & Marble Corp ....G....... 508 248-9393
Sarasota **(G-15592)**

Cantor Design On Granite ....G....... 407 230-1568
Orlando **(G-11978)**

Creta Granite & Marble Inc ....G....... 954 956-9993
Pompano Beach **(G-13981)**

Cug LLC ....F....... 786 858-0499
Plantation **(G-13841)**

D G Morrison Inc ....F....... 813 865-0208
Odessa **(G-11546)**

Exotic Countertop Inc ....G....... 954 979-8188
Pompano Beach **(G-14015)**

Fantasy Marble & Granite Inc ....G....... 954 788-0433
Pompano Beach **(G-14017)**

Fasulo Granite & Marble Inc ....G....... 561 371-5410
Jupiter **(G-6727)**

Fine Surfaces and More Inc ....F....... 305 691-5752
Doral **(G-3215)**

Grevan Artistic Ventures Inc ....F....... 850 243-8111
Fort Walton Beach **(G-4588)**

HI Tech Granite and Marble ....G....... 407 230-4363
Orlando **(G-12217)**

JV Installations Corp ....E....... 407 849-0262
Orlando **(G-12281)**

Kusser Graniteworks Usa Inc ....G....... 813 248-3428
Tampa **(G-16993)**

LAS & JB Inc ....G....... 772 672-5315
Fort Pierce **(G-4500)**

Naples Stone Consulting LLC ....F....... 239 325-8653
Naples **(G-10832)**

Natural Stone Sltons Fnest SRS ....E....... 941 954-1100
Sarasota **(G-15756)**

Prestige Flrg Instllations Inc ....F....... 407 291-0609
Orlando **(G-12503)**

Ramirez Cbnets Blnds Gran Mr ....G....... 352 606-0049
Spring Hill **(G-16076)**

Reyes Granite & Marble Corp ....F....... 305 599-7330
Miami **(G-9801)**

Ribeiro Stones LLC ....G....... 407 723-8802
Orlando **(G-12552)**

Rik Enterprises Inc ....G....... 239 772-9485
Cape Coral **(G-1378)**

Sarasotas Finest MBL Gran Inc ....G....... 941 365-9697
Sarasota **(G-15818)**

Signature Granite Inc ....F....... 813 443-5597
Tampa **(G-17266)**

Taken For Granite ....G....... 727 235-1559
Saint Petersburg **(G-15207)**

Triton Stone Holdings LLC ....G....... 219 669-4890
Fort Lauderdale **(G-4098)**

GRANITE: Dimension

Commercial Stone Cab Fbrctors ....F....... 727 209-1141
Saint Petersburg **(G-15011)**

Commercial Stone Fbrcators Inc...........F....... 727 209-1141
Saint Petersburg **(G-15012)**

Granite Imports Inc ....G....... 732 500-2549
Boynton Beach **(G-875)**

OCC My Stone LLC ....G....... 786 352-1567
Hialeah Gardens **(G-5445)**

Paramount Depot LLC ....F....... 786 275-0107
Doral **(G-3321)**

Quality Stones R US LLC ....G....... 904 551-5619
Jacksonville **(G-6400)**

GRAPHIC ARTS & RELATED DESIGN SVCS

A-Plus Prtg & Graphic Ctr Inc ....E....... 954 327-7315
Plantation **(G-13817)**

Amelia Island Graphics ....G....... 904 261-0740
Fernandina Beach **(G-3581)**

Baru Agency Incorporated ....G....... 305 259-8800
Doral **(G-3129)**

Bg Expo Group LLC ....G....... 305 428-3576
Doral **(G-3136)**

Blue Ocean Press Inc ....E....... 954 973-1819
Fort Lauderdale **(G-3693)**

Design & Print ....G....... 561 361-8299
Boca Raton **(G-481)**

Fresh Ink Print LLC ....G....... 407 412-5905
Orlando **(G-12175)**

Graphic Center Group Corp ....G....... 305 961-1649
Coral Gables **(G-2065)**

Mc Squared Group Inc ....G....... 850 435-4600
Pensacola **(G-13544)**

McKenny Printing Entp Inc ....G....... 727 420-4944
Saint Petersburg **(G-15125)**

Outdoor America Images Inc ....E....... 813 888-8796
Tampa **(G-17133)**

Speedpro Imaging St Petersburg ....G....... 727 266-0956
Saint Petersburg **(G-15195)**

Zeeeees Corporation ....G....... 407 624-3796
Saint Cloud **(G-14942)**

GRAPHITE MINING SVCS

Western Graphite Inc ....G....... 850 270-2808
Monticello **(G-10586)**

GRASSES: Artificial & Preserved

Easyturf Inc ....F....... 941 753-3312
Ellenton **(G-3510)**

Sike Usa Inc ....G....... 786 331-4020
Doral **(G-3366)**

GRAVEL & PEBBLE MINING

Atlantic Earth Materials ....F....... 321 631-0600
Cocoa **(G-1904)**

GRAVEL MINING

Bdc Shell & Aggregate LLC ....G....... 941 875-6615
Punta Gorda **(G-14495)**

Geotechnical & Materials Inc ....G....... 813 814-0671
Oldsmar **(G-11651)**

GRAVEL: Painted

Ipg Network Corp ....F....... 305 681-4001
Miami **(G-9335)**

GREASES & INEDIBLE FATS, RENDERED

Griffin Industries LLC ....D....... 904 964-8083
Starke **(G-16102)**

GREASES: Lubricating

Aoclsc Inc ....D....... 813 248-1988
Tampa **(G-16599)**

GREENHOUSES: Prefabricated Metal

B & K Installations Inc ....E....... 305 245-6968
Homestead **(G-5701)**

C P Enterprises of Apopka Inc...........G....... 407 886-3321
Mount Dora **(G-10598)**

GRILLS & GRILLWORK: Woven Wire, Made
From Purchased Wire

Grille Tech Inc ....E....... 305 537-0053
Miami **(G-9249)**

Grille Tech Inc ....F....... 305 537-0053
Miami **(G-9250)**

GRIT: Steel

Navatech Usa LLC ....G....... 305 600-4458
Miami **(G-9608)**

GRITS: Crushed & Broken

South Carolina Minerals Inc ....G....... 352 365-6522
Leesburg **(G-7795)**

GROCERIES WHOLESALERS, NEC

Big L Brands Inc ....G....... 888 552-9768
Boca Raton **(G-431)**

Cirkul Inc ....D....... 941 518-8596
Tampa **(G-16707)**

Cirkul Inc ....C....... 513 889-6708
Tampa **(G-16708)**

Coca-Cola Bottling Co Untd Inc ....C....... 850 478-4800
Pensacola **(G-13473)**

Conchita Foods Inc ....D....... 305 888-9703
Medley **(G-8220)**

Fresh Start Beverage Company ....G....... 561 757-6541
Boca Raton **(G-524)**

Hot Sauce Harrys Inc ....G....... 941 423-7092
North Port **(G-11195)**

La Province Inc ....F....... 305 538-2406
Miami **(G-9413)**

ME Thompson Inc ....D....... 863 667-3732
Lakeland **(G-7393)**

Pepsi-Cola Metro Btlg Co Inc ....C....... 904 733-1627
Jacksonville **(G-6367)**

Pepsi-Cola Metro Btlg Co Inc ....F....... 352 376-8276
Gainesville **(G-4748)**

Rcr Coffee Company Inc ....E....... 813 248-6264
Tampa **(G-17209)**

Refresco Beverages US Inc ....C....... 813 241-0147
Tampa **(G-17211)**

Twinlab Holdings Inc ....E....... 800 645-5626
Boca Raton **(G-729)**

GROCERIES, GENERAL LINE
WHOLESALERS

El Mira Sol Inc ....D....... 813 754-5857
Plant City **(G-13764)**

Johnson Brothers Whl Meats Inc ....E....... 850 763-2828
Panama City **(G-13280)**

La Autentica Foods Inc ....F....... 305 888-6727
Hialeah **(G-5219)**

My Familys Seasonings LLC ....F....... 863 698-7968
Clearwater **(G-1709)**

Vigo Importing Company ....C....... 813 884-3491
Tampa **(G-17417)**

GUARD PROTECTIVE SVCS

Tactical Products Group LLC ....E....... 561 265-4066
Boynton Beach **(G-918)**

GUARDRAILS

Scott Safety LLC ....E....... 239 340-8695
Moore Haven **(G-10592)**

GUIDANCE SYSTEMS & EQPT: Space Vehicle

Lockheed Martin Corporation ....F....... 321 853-5194
Cape Canaveral **(G-1290)**

GUIDED MISSILES & SPACE VEHICLES

Blue Origin Florida LLC ....G....... 253 437-9300
Merritt Island **(G-8579)**

Boeing Company ....B....... 321 853-6647
Cape Canaveral **(G-1279)**

Chad ....G....... 727 433-0404
Tampa **(G-16699)**

Kratos Def & SEC Solutions Inc ....E....... 866 606-5867
Orlando **(G-12296)**

Lockheed Martin Corporation ....F....... 321 853-5194
Cape Canaveral **(G-1290)**

Lockheed Martin Corporation ....E....... 407 356-2000
Orlando **(G-12345)**

Micro Systems Inc ....C....... 850 244-2332
Fort Walton Beach **(G-4596)**

Mishaal Aerospace Corporation ....G....... 786 353-2685
Miami **(G-9576)**

Moon Express Inc ....E....... 650 241-8577
Cape Canaveral **(G-1291)**

Northrop Grmman Feld Spport Sv ....D....... 904 810-4665
Saint Augustine **(G-14861)**

2022 Harris Florida
Manufacturers Directory

(G-0000) Company's Geographic Section entry number

Redwire Corporation ....F 650 701-7722
Jacksonville (G-6410)

Space Machine & Engrg Corp............E 727 323-2221
Saint Petersburg (G-15194)

United Space Alliance ....G 321 853-3417
Orlando (G-12689)

GUIDED MISSILES & SPACE VEHICLES: Research & Development

Trailblazerai Inc ....G 727 859-2732
Saint Petersburg (G-15215)

Troxel Aerospace Inds Inc ....F 720 626-0454
Gainesville (G-4780)

GUIDED MISSILES/SPACE VEHICLE PARTS/AUX EQPT: Research/Devel

H H Terry Co Inc ....F 239 593-0132
Naples (G-10769)

L3 Aviation Products Inc ....C 941 371-0811
Saint Petersburg (G-15107)

Moog Inc ....F 321 435-8722
Orlando (G-12389)

GUM & WOOD CHEMICALS

AZ Chem Holdings LP ....C 800 526-5294
Jacksonville (G-5914)

Lignotech Florida LLC ....E 904 577-9077
Fernandina Beach (G-3592)

Taber Incorporated ....G 401 245-2800
Port St Lucie (G-14484)

GUN SIGHTS: Optical

Knight Vision Lllp ....F 321 607-9900
Titusville (G-17598)

GUTTERS

Estradas Fiberglass Mfg Corp ....G 954 924-8778
Sunny Isles Beach (G-16273)

GUTTERS: Sheet Metal

Benchmark Quality Gutters Inc ....G 904 759-9800
Jacksonville (G-5928)

Crown Seamless Gutters Inc ....E 561 748-9919
West Palm Beach (G-17975)

Mr Gutter Cutter Inc ....F 772 286-7780
Stuart (G-16186)

S&L Cnstrction Specialists Inc ....G 407 300-5080
Orlando (G-12566)

GYPSUM & CALCITE MINING SVCS

Copaco Inc............F 407 333-3041
Orange City (G-11804)

GYPSUM BOARD

Gypsum Bd Specialists USA Corp ....G 954 348-8869
Pembroke Pines (G-13394)

United States Gypsum Company ....F 305 688-8744
Miami Shores (G-10384)

GYPSUM MINING

Harrison Gypsum LLC ....E 850 762-4315
Marianna (G-8165)

GYPSUM PRDTS

Certanteed Gyps Ciling Mfg Inc............E 813 286-3900
Tampa (G-16698)

E2 Walls Inc ....E 813 374-2010
Tampa (G-16791)

H & H Gypsum LLC............G 321 972-5571
Casselberry (G-1417)

Lambert Corporation Florida ....E 407 841-2940
Orlando (G-12307)

Premix-Marbletite Mfg Co............F 407 327-0830
Winter Springs (G-18574)

Proform Finishing Products LLC ....E 407 438-3450
Orlando (G-12514)

Proform Finishing Products LLC ....E 904 284-0221
Green Cove Springs (G-4833)

United States Gypsum Company ....D 904 768-2501
Jacksonville (G-6579)

HAIR & HAIR BASED PRDTS

Beauty Cosmetica............F 305 406-1022
Opa Locka (G-11722)

Condition Culture LLC............G 786 433-8279
Boynton Beach (G-852)

Flex Beauty Labs LLC............F 646 302-8542
Orlando (G-12155)

Fusion Industries LLC............F 239 415-7554
Fort Myers (G-4264)

Italian Hair Extension Inc ....G 954 839-5366
Sunrise (G-16325)

Its A 10 Inc ....G 954 227-7813
Coral Springs (G-2168)

Katcheri Davis Services LLC ....G 754 222-4464
Jacksonville (G-6239)

Lion Locs LLC ....F 704 802-2752
Orlando (G-12333)

Sbm Beauty LLC ....F 850 567-7338
Quincy (G-14548)

Serenity Hair Extensions LLC............F 407 917-1788
Deltona (G-3053)

HAIR CARE PRDTS

365 Sun LLC ....G 208 357-8062
Nokomis (G-11041)

Abdiversified LLC ....D 954 791-6050
Plantation (G-13820)

AIG Technologies Inc ....F 954 433-0618
Deerfield Beach (G-2660)

B & R Products Inc ....F 305 238-1592
Cutler Bay (G-2284)

Beauty Lab Inc ....E 305 687-0071
Opa Locka (G-11723)

Blaq Luxury Collection LLC............G 407 496-7517
Apopka (G-107)

Celeb Luxury LLC ....F 954 763-0333
Davie (G-2396)

Ds Healthcare Group Inc ....E 888 829-4212
Doral (G-3200)

Ds Healthcare Group Inc ....C 888 404-7770
Miami (G-9052)

Fekkai Retail LLC ....F 866 514-8048
Plantation (G-13851)

Katcheri Davis Services LLC ....G 754 222-4464
Jacksonville (G-6239)

Ladove Industries Inc ....G 305 624-2456
Miami Lakes (G-10312)

Luxebrands LLC ....D 866 514-8048
Plantation (G-13865)

Sabrosol Laboratories LLC............G 305 290-4038
North Miami (G-11119)

Scientific Research Products ....E 954 971-0600
Fort Lauderdale (G-4038)

Terra Beauty Products Inc ....G 561 674-2136
Deerfield Beach (G-2822)

HAIR CARE PRDTS: Hair Coloring Preparations

Beautyge Brands Usa Inc............C 904 693-1200
Jacksonville (G-5927)

Dyebar Express Ltd ....F 954 298-5171
Deerfield Beach (G-2711)

Epitomi Inc ....E 305 971-5370
Miami (G-9105)

Pure-Chlor Systems Florida Inc ....F 305 437-9937
Tampa (G-17194)

Xtreme Tools International Inc............E 305 622-7474
Opa Locka (G-11801)

HAIR CARE PRDTS: Home Permanent Kits

Stylors Inc............F 904 765-4453
Jacksonville (G-6514)

HAIR CARE PRDTS: Tonics

M & S Computer Products Inc ....G 561 244-5400
Boynton Beach (G-888)

Van Tibolli Beauty Corp............E 305 390-0044
Fort Lauderdale (G-4116)

HAIR CURLERS: Beauty Shop

Stylors Inc............F 904 765-4453
Jacksonville (G-6514)

HAIR DRESSING, FOR THE TRADE

Destiny & Light Inc ....F 813 476-8386
Tampa (G-16772)

Jaydad LLC............G 407 508-6267
Kissimmee (G-6929)

Queen B Hair Collection LLC............F 954 393-2791
Miami (G-9768)

HAIRPINS: Rubber

Hnc Enterprises Inc ....G 904 448-9387
Jacksonville (G-6178)

HAND TOOLS, NEC: Wholesalers

Db Tucker LLC............G 561 301-4974
Jupiter (G-6709)

Marbelite International Corp ....G 941 378-0860
Sarasota (G-15740)

HANDBAGS

Italian Idea Srq LLC ....G 941 330-0525
Sarasota (G-15710)

HANDBAGS: Men's

Gar Industries Corp ....F 954 456-8088
Hollywood (G-5581)

HANDBAGS: Women's

Becarro International Corp ....G 561 737-5585
West Palm Beach (G-17940)

Excel Handbags Co Inc ....F 305 836-8800
Miami (G-9118)

Gar Industries Corp ....G 954 456-8088
Hollywood (G-5581)

Stark Enterprises Inc ....G 941 341-0319
Sarasota (G-15837)

HANDYMAN SVCS

Los Primos Express Svcs LLC............G 786 701-3297
Miami (G-9479)

New & Improved Services LLC............F 904 323-2348
Jacksonville (G-6325)

HANG GLIDERS

Miami Hang Gliding Corp ....G 863 805-0440
Clewiston (G-1893)

HARDWARE

Alpine Engineered Products............F 954 781-3333
Pompano Beach (G-13922)

American Marine Coverings Inc............F 305 889-5355
Hialeah (G-5048)

Atkinson Marine Inc ....G 954 763-1652
Fort Lauderdale (G-3662)

Automation Consulting Inc ....F 850 477-6477
Pensacola (G-13449)

Beachcomber Fibrgls Tech Inc ....G 772 283-0200
Stuart (G-16122)

Biosculptor Corporation ....G 305 823-8300
Hialeah (G-5076)

Bms International Inc ....E 813 247-7040
Tampa (G-16651)

Brown (usa) Inc ....F 305 593-9228
Miami (G-8857)

Consolidated Ace Hdwr Sup Inc............F 850 939-9800
Navarre (G-10947)

Countryside Locks LLC............G 631 561-5006
Estero (G-3541)

CT Hydraulics Inc............F 724 342-3089
Sanibel (G-15414)

Custom Marble Works Inc ....E 813 620-0475
Tampa (G-16754)

E-Z Fastening Solutions Inc............G 813 854-3937
Oldsmar (G-11646)

Florida Pool Products Inc ....E 727 531-8913
Clearwater (G-1602)

General Clamp Industries Inc ....F 407 859-6000
Orlando (G-12188)

Goodrich Corporation ....C 904 757-3660
Jacksonville (G-6146)

Greenway Bridge LLC ....G 631 901-4561
Saint Augustine (G-14837)

Halliday Products Inc ....D 407 298-4470
Orlando (G-12208)

Hardware Concepts Inc ....G 305 685-1337
Miami (G-9262)

Hardware Online Store ....G 954 565-5678
Fort Lauderdale (G-3861)

Inter Gard R&D LLC ....F 954 476-5574
Sunrise (G-16323)

PRODUCT

International Dock Pdts Inc..................F.......954 964-5315
Hallandale Beach *(G-4952)*

Ipline LLC.......................................F.......305 675-4235
Miami *(G-9336)*

James D Nall Co Inc.......................E.......305 884-8363
Fort Lauderdale *(G-3891)*

Jefco Manufacturing Inc...................E.......954 527-4220
Fort Lauderdale *(G-3895)*

Loos & Co Inc................................D.......239 643-5667
Naples *(G-10807)*

Mermaid Mfg Southwest Fla Inc........F.......239 418-0535
Fort Myers *(G-4321)*

Mitek Inc.......................................D.......813 675-1224
Tampa *(G-17077)*

Mobile Rugged Tech Corp.................G.......781 771-6743
Orlando *(G-12384)*

Pompanette LLC.............................E.......813 885-2182
Tampa *(G-17169)*

Practical Design Products Co.............F.......561 995-4023
Boca Raton *(G-639)*

Precise Technologies Inc..................G.......727 535-5594
Largo *(G-7662)*

Press-Rite Inc................................G.......954 963-7373
Miramar *(G-10529)*

Rampmaster Inc..............................G.......305 691-9090
Miami *(G-9779)*

Savvy Associate Inc.......................F.......954 941-6986
Pompano Beach *(G-14167)*

SBs Precision Shtmtl Inc..................G.......321 951-7411
Melbourne *(G-8516)*

Southern Die Casting Corp................D.......305 635-6571
Miami *(G-9927)*

Stainless Fabricators Inc..................E.......813 926-7113
Odessa *(G-11581)*

Taylor Made Systems Brdnton In ....C.......941 747-1900
Oviedo *(G-12851)*

Window Craftsmen Inc......................F.......941 922-1844
Sarasota *(G-15876)*

HARDWARE & BUILDING PRDTS: Plastic

Bruce R Ely Enterprise Inc................F.......727 573-1643
Clearwater *(G-1528)*

Dillco Inc......................................F.......386 734-7510
Deland *(G-2865)*

Florida Amico..................................G.......863 688-9256
Lakeland *(G-7328)*

Mercer Products Company Inc............G.......352 357-0057
Umatilla *(G-17647)*

Paragon Plastics Inc.......................E.......321 631-6212
Titusville *(G-17604)*

Plastic Components Inc....................E.......305 885-0561
Medley *(G-8300)*

Protective Enclosures Co LLC............G.......321 441-9689
Altamonte Springs *(G-67)*

Shwinco Industries Inc.....................E.......850 271-8900
Lynn Haven *(G-8032)*

Vinyl Corp.....................................F.......305 477-6464
Miami *(G-10112)*

Walt Dittmer and Sons Inc................E.......407 699-1755
Winter Springs *(G-18581)*

HARDWARE STORES

Panhandle Paint & Dctg LLC..............G.......850 596-9248
Panama City Beach *(G-13335)*

HARDWARE STORES: Builders'

Hare Lumber & Ready Mix Inc............F.......863 983-8725
Clewiston *(G-1891)*

Trim-Pak Corporation.......................G.......407 851-8900
Orlando *(G-12673)*

W R Williams Enterprises Inc.............G.......813 677-2000
Gibsonton *(G-4803)*

HARDWARE STORES: Door Locks & Lock Sets

Architctral Mllwk Slutions Inc.............G.......727 441-1409
Largo *(G-7538)*

Visions Millwork Inc........................F.......239 390-0811
Fort Myers *(G-4442)*

HARDWARE STORES: Pumps & Pumping Eqpt

Oase North America Inc....................G.......800 365-3880
Riviera Beach *(G-14652)*

HARDWARE STORES: Tools

Tekk Supply Inc..............................G.......954 444-5782
Pompano Beach *(G-14211)*

HARDWARE WHOLESALERS

Deco Truss Company Inc..................E.......305 257-1910
Homestead *(G-5707)*

E-Z Fastening Solutions Inc..............G.......813 854-3937
Oldsmar *(G-11646)*

Lockheed Martin Corporation.............E.......407 517-6627
Orlando *(G-12341)*

Round Table Tools Inc.....................G.......850 877-7650
Tallahassee *(G-16496)*

Shashy Enterprises Inc....................G.......352 732-3904
Ocala *(G-11488)*

HARDWARE, WHOLESALE: Builders', NEC

A-Fabco Inc...................................E.......813 677-8790
Gibsonton *(G-4792)*

Certified Whl Exterior Pdts................G.......407 654-7170
Winter Garden *(G-18379)*

Hare Lumber & Ready Mix Inc............F.......863 983-8725
Clewiston *(G-1891)*

Suncoast Post-Tension Ltd................E.......305 592-5075
Miami *(G-9966)*

Trim-Pak Corporation.......................E.......407 851-8900
Orlando *(G-12673)*

W R Williams Enterprises Inc.............G.......813 677-2000
Gibsonton *(G-4803)*

HARDWARE, WHOLESALE: Saw Blades

American Diamond Blades Corp...........E.......561 571-2166
Boca Raton *(G-406)*

HARDWARE: Aircraft

Altum Aerospace.............................F.......954 618-6573
Sunrise *(G-16291)*

Atomic Machine & Edm Inc................E.......239 353-9100
Naples *(G-10682)*

Avian Inventory Management LLC........G.......407 787-9100
Orlando *(G-11936)*

Aviation Parts & Trade Corp..............G.......954 944-2828
Plantation *(G-13830)*

D I R Inc.......................................G.......863 661-5360
Lakeland *(G-7303)*

Precision Shapes Inc.......................E.......321 269-2555
Titusville *(G-17609)*

Tactical Air Support Inc....................C.......229 563-7502
Jacksonville *(G-6528)*

Ver-Val Enterprises Inc....................F.......850 244-7931
Fort Walton Beach *(G-4616)*

HARDWARE: Aircraft & Marine, Incl Pulleys & Similar Items

Longbow Marine Inc.........................G.......954 616-5737
Fort Lauderdale *(G-3921)*

Warfighter Fcsed Logistics Inc...........F.......740 513-4692
Fort Lauderdale *(G-4122)*

HARDWARE: Builders'

Dayton Superior Corporation..............G.......407 859-4541
Orlando *(G-12078)*

Doorknob Discount Center LLC...........G.......813 963-3104
Lutz *(G-7989)*

Phg Kendall LLC.............................F.......954 392-8788
Hollywood *(G-5642)*

Td Tra -Dix Supply Inc.....................G.......727 869-8662
Hudson *(G-5788)*

Venture Circle Enterprises LLC...........F.......407 678-7489
Sanford *(G-15402)*

HARDWARE: Cabinet

Barr Systems LLC............................E.......352 491-3100
Gainesville *(G-4657)*

Divine Dovetail...............................G.......561 245-7601
Boca Raton *(G-488)*

Strategic Brands Inc........................F.......516 745-6100
Pompano Beach *(G-14203)*

Woodies Inc...................................G.......305 266-9209
Miami *(G-10142)*

HARDWARE: Door Opening & Closing Devices, Exc Electrical

Marko Garage Doors & Gates Inc........G.......561 547-4001
Palm Springs *(G-13146)*

HARDWARE: Furniture

C & S Plastics................................E.......863 294-5628
Winter Haven *(G-18427)*

HARDWARE: Furniture, Builders' & Other Household

Mica Craft & Design Inc...................F.......561 863-5354
West Palm Beach *(G-18077)*

Ocean Dynamics USA Inc..................G.......305 770-1800
Miami *(G-9637)*

Salt International Corp......................G.......305 698-8889
Pembroke Park *(G-13366)*

Shorr Enterprises Inc.......................F.......954 733-9840
Lauderdale Lakes *(G-7719)*

HARDWARE: Parachute

Jco Metals Inc................................F.......386 734-5867
Deland *(G-2878)*

Mirage Systems Inc.........................F.......386 740-9222
Deland *(G-2886)*

Uninsred Untd Prchute Tech LLC........D.......386 736-7589
Deland *(G-2915)*

HARDWARE: Rubber

Shaw Development LLC.....................C.......239 405-6100
Bonita Springs *(G-817)*

Warfighter Fcsed Logistics Inc...........F.......740 513-4692
Fort Lauderdale *(G-4122)*

HARNESS ASSEMBLIES: Cable & Wire

Aero Electronics Systems Inc............G.......321 269-0478
Titusville *(G-17569)*

Automatic Coax and Cable Inc...........E.......407 322-7622
Sanford *(G-15269)*

Backbone Interconnect LLC...............E.......954 800-4749
Sunrise *(G-16294)*

Dse Inc...E.......863 425-1745
Mulberry *(G-10624)*

Electro Technik Industries Inc............D.......727 530-9555
Clearwater *(G-1580)*

G2 Harness LLC..............................915 892-2494
Saint Petersburg *(G-15056)*

Interconnect Cable Tech Corp............C.......352 796-1716
Brooksville *(G-1164)*

Ksm Electronics Inc.........................D.......954 642-7050
Fort Lauderdale *(G-3909)*

Lynn Electronics LLC.......................D.......215 355-8200
Fort Lauderdale *(G-3924)*

Pacer Electronics Florida Inc.............E.......941 378-5774
Sarasota *(G-15772)*

Paradise Cable Industries.................F.......941 488-6092
Venice *(G-17711)*

Paramount Electronic Mfg Co.............E.......954 781-3755
Boca Raton *(G-631)*

Paramount Industries Inc...................E.......954 781-3755
Pompano Beach *(G-14118)*

Sound Connections Intl.....................G.......813 948-2707
Lutz *(G-8016)*

Spectraflex Inc...............................G.......850 892-3900
Defuniak Springs *(G-2843)*

Stern Brands Inc.............................F.......321 622-8584
Melbourne *(G-8531)*

Superior Electronics........................G.......941 355-9500
Sarasota *(G-15565)*

Tensolite LLC.................................A.......904 829-5600
Saint Augustine *(G-14905)*

Trinity Manufacturing Corp................E.......941 727-9595
Bradenton *(G-1065)*

Unique Electronics Inc.....................C.......407 422-3051
Orlando *(G-12687)*

HARNESSES, HALTERS, SADDLERY & STRAPS

Leatherworks Inc............................G.......305 471-4430
Doral *(G-3281)*

Longchamp Usa Inc.........................D.......305 372-1628
Miami *(G-9474)*

2022 Harris Florida
Manufacturers Directory

(G-0000) Company's Geographic Section entry number

HEADPHONES: Radio

Joyce Telectronics Corp .... F 727 461-3525
Zephyrhills (G-18618)

HEALTH AIDS: Exercise Eqpt

American Quality Mfg Inc .... F 321 636-3434
Cocoa (G-1903)
Bodylastics International Inc .... G 561 254-0475
Boca Raton (G-442)
Bodylastics International Inc .... F 561 562-4745
Boca Raton (G-443)
Lifetime Wellness Centers Inc .... F 321 693-8698
Melbourne (G-8460)
Medx Corporation .... E 352 351-2005
Ocala (G-11441)
Super Swim Corp .... G 239 275-7600
Fort Myers (G-4414)
Vertimax LLC .... G 800 699-5867
Tampa (G-17411)

HEALTH AIDS: Vaporizers

Warehouse Goods LLC .... E 877 865-2260
Boca Raton (G-753)

HEALTH FOOD & SUPPLEMENT STORES

Natural Immunogenics Corp .... D 888 328-8840
Sarasota (G-15525)
Organic Amazon Corp .... G 305 365-7811
Key Biscayne (G-6838)

HEARING AIDS

Affordable At Home Has Inc .... G 786 200-0484
Miami (G-8664)
Audina Hearing Instruments Inc .... D 407 331-0077
Longwood (G-7872)
Bell Hearing Instruments Inc .... F 813 814-2355
Oldsmar (G-11635)
Captel Inc .... B 407 730-3397
Orlando (G-11981)
Ear-Tronics Inc .... G 239 275-7655
Fort Myers (G-4243)
Eartech Inc .... G 941 747-8193
Bradenton (G-972)
Florida Best Hearing .... E 863 402-0094
Boynton Beach (G-868)
Florida North Hearing Solution .... G 386 466-0902
Gainesville (G-4693)
Miami .... E 954 874-7707
Miami (G-9544)
Morton Plant Mease Health Care ...... A 727 462-7052
Clearwater (G-1704)
N-Ear Pro Inc .... E 877 290-4599
Tampa (G-17095)
Physician Hearing Care .... F 239 261-7722
Naples (G-10857)
Precision Laboratories Inc .... E 407 774-4261
Longwood (G-7940)
Truear Inc .... F 352 314-8805
Mount Dora (G-10617)

HEARING TESTING SVCS

Florida Best Hearing .... E 863 402-0094
Boynton Beach (G-868)

HEAT EXCHANGERS

Monitor Products Inc .... D 352 544-2620
Brooksville (G-1183)

HEAT TREATING: Metal

Braddck Mtllgl Arsp Ser Inc .... F 561 622-2200
Boynton Beach (G-848)
Braddock Metallurgical Inc .... F 386 267-0955
Jacksonville (G-5950)
Braddock Metallurgical GA Inc .... E 386 267-0955
Daytona Beach (G-2520)
Braddock Metallurgical MGT LLC ...... F 386 267-0955
Daytona Beach (G-2521)
Braddock Mtllrgcal - Dytona In .... G 386 267-0955
Daytona Beach (G-2522)
Braddck Mtllurgical Holdg Inc .... G 386 323-1500
Daytona Beach (G-2523)
Dynamic Alloy .... F 352 728-7600
Leesburg (G-7770)
Heat Treating Incorporated .... D 352 245-8811
Belleview (G-362)

Nelco Products Inc .... G 727 533-8282
Clearwater (G-1715)
Suncoast Heat Treat Inc .... F 386 267-0955
Daytona Beach (G-2606)
Suncoast Heat Treat Inc .... F 561 776-7763
Boynton Beach (G-916)
Superheat Fgh Services Inc .... G 519 396-1324
Bartow (G-327)
Tech To Site .... G 813 253-9381
Homosassa (G-5752)
Thermal Braze Inc .... G 561 746-6640
Jupiter (G-6808)
Whertec Inc .... E 904 278-6503
Jacksonville (G-6608)

HEATERS: Swimming Pool, Electric

Aquacal Autopilot Inc .... C 727 823-5642
Saint Petersburg (G-14966)

HEATERS: Swimming Pool, Oil Or Gas

Gulf Associates Control Inc .... E 954 426-0536
Deerfield Beach (G-2728)

HEATING & AIR CONDITIONING UNITS, COMBINATION

Addison Hvac LLC .... C 407 292-4400
Orlando (G-11867)
Air & Power Solutions Inc .... G 954 427-0019
Coconut Creek (G-1976)
Air Infinity Inc .... G 941 423-1355
North Port (G-11187)
Data Cooling Tech Canada LLC .... E 813 865-4701
Tampa (G-16763)
Filter King LLC .... F 877 570-9755
Miami (G-9141)
Lorenze & Associates Inc .... G 407 682-7570
Altamonte Springs (G-55)
Miles of Smiles Rides Inc .... F 727 528-1227
Seminole (G-15983)
Ross Slade Inc .... G 813 250-0488
Tampa (G-17233)
Woodys Heating & AC LLC .... G 651 829-4570
Fort Myers (G-4450)

HEATING APPARATUS: Steam

Leslie Controls Inc .... C 813 978-1000
Temple Terrace (G-17539)

HEATING EQPT & SPLYS

Alfa Laval Inc .... F 941 727-1900
Sarasota (G-15439)
Duststop Filters Inc .... G 904 725-1001
Jacksonville (G-6049)
Innovative Heat Concepts LLC .... G 305 248-4971
Homestead (G-5716)
Jer-Air Manufacturing Inc .... E 352 591-2674
Micanopy (G-10398)
Metal Industries Inc .... D 352 793-8610
Bushnell (G-1247)
R & J Mfg of Gainesville .... G 352 375-3130
Gainesville (G-4754)
Southland Power & Enrgy Co LLC ..... F 800 217-6040
Fort Lauderdale (G-4061)

HEATING EQPT: Complete

Trane Inc .... E 772 621-3200
Port Saint Lucie (G-14457)

HEATING UNITS & DEVICES: Indl, Electric

Aruki Services LLC .... F 850 364-5206
Havana (G-4992)

HELICOPTERS

Blue Hole Helicopters Inc .... F 561 723-0378
Jupiter (G-6697)
Florida Sncast Helicopters LLC .... F 941 355-1525
Sarasota (G-15477)
Heli Aviation Florida LLC .... G 941 355-1525
Sarasota (G-15489)
Heli-Tech Inc .... F 850 763-9000
Panama City (G-13272)
Rockymountain Lifenet .... G 863 533-5168
Bartow (G-323)
Sikorsky Aircraft Corporation .... F 561 775-5142
Jupiter (G-6799)

Traumaone Helicopter Base .... G 386 755-9294
Lake City (G-7049)
Van Nevel Aerospace LLC .... G 337 936-2504
Cottondale (G-2230)
Vertical Aviation Tech Inc .... F 407 322-9488
Sanford (G-15404)

HELMETS: Athletic

Jay Squared LLC .... F 386 677-7700
Daytona Beach (G-2564)
Tavarez Sporting Goods Inc .... G 347 441-9690
Miami (G-9995)

HELMETS: Steel

Helicopter Helmet LLC .... G 843 556-0405
Melbourne (G-8434)

HELP SUPPLY SERVICES

Granite Services Intl Inc .... F 813 242-7400
Tampa (G-16889)

HIGH ENERGY PARTICLE PHYSICS EQPT

Natures Power and Energy LLC .... F 813 907-6279
Wesley Chapel (G-17883)
Novena TEC LLC .... G 407 392-1868
Orlando (G-12427)

HITCHES: Trailer

Rvcc of Florida .... F 352 569-5870
Bushnell (G-1248)

HOBBY, TOY & GAME STORES: Hobbies, NEC

Daytona Magic Inc .... G 386 252-6767
Daytona Beach (G-2543)

HOISTS

Beta Max Inc .... E 321 727-3737
Palm Bay (G-12890)
High Tech Hoist Corp .... F 321 733-3387
Melbourne (G-8436)
Hook International Inc .... G 727 209-0855
Largo (G-7607)

HOLDING COMPANIES, NEC

New World Holdings Inc .... E 561 888-4939
Delray Beach (G-2992)

HOLDING COMPANIES: Investment, Exc Banks

Blue Summit Wind LLC .... G 561 691-7171
Juno Beach (G-6660)
Laporte Inv Holdings Inc .... G 863 294-4498
Winter Haven (G-18449)
Ronecker Holdings LLC .... G 813 855-5559
Oldsmar (G-11697)

HOME ENTERTAINMENT EQPT: Electronic, NEC

A-N-L Home Solutions LLC .... F 954 648-2623
Miami (G-8627)
Freshetech LLC .... F 516 519-3453
Orlando (G-12176)
Mdy Services Inc .... G 954 392-1542
Miramar (G-10513)
Visual Acoustics LLC .... G 786 390-6128
Miami (G-10116)

HOME ENTERTAINMENT REPAIR SVCS

Visual Acoustics LLC .... G 786 390-6128
Miami (G-10116)

HOME FURNISHINGS WHOLESALERS

Art & Frame Source Inc .... E 727 329-6502
Saint Petersburg (G-14971)
Ben Kaufman Sales Co Inc .... E 305 688-2144
Medley (G-8208)
Euroasia Products Inc .... G 321 221-9398
Orlando (G-12136)
Gfx Inc .... E 305 499-9789
Miami (G-9209)

PRODUCT

Kasulik II LLC ....F 786 629-8978
  Hallandale Beach (G-4956)
Venture Circle Enterprises LLC ....F 407 678-7489
  Sanford (G-15402)

HOME IMPROVEMENT & RENOVATION CONTRACTOR AGENCY

Tropic Shield Inc ....F 954 731-5553
  Lauderdale Lakes (G-7721)

HOME MOVIES DEVELOPING & PROCESSING

Columbia Films Inc ....G 800 531-3238
  Pompano Beach (G-13972)

HOMEFURNISHING STORES: Barbeque Grills

Werever Products Inc ....F 813 241-9701
  Riverview (G-14582)

HOMEFURNISHING STORES: Beddings & Linens

Fabric Innovations Inc ....E 305 860-5757
  Miami (G-9127)

HOMEFURNISHING STORES: Brushes

Torrington Brush Works Inc ....F 941 355-1499
  Sarasota (G-15855)

HOMEFURNISHING STORES: Lighting Fixtures

Lumilum LLC ....F 305 233-2844
  Miami (G-9484)

HOMEFURNISHING STORES: Vertical Blinds

Tropic Shield Inc ....F 954 731-5553
  Lauderdale Lakes (G-7721)
Vertical Village Inc ....G 772 340-0400
  Port Saint Lucie (G-14464)

HOMEFURNISHING STORES: Window Shades, NEC

Kelsies Blinds ....G 407 977-0827
  Oviedo (G-12834)
Vertical Land Inc ....F 850 819-2535
  Panama City (G-13317)

HOMEFURNISHINGS & SPLYS, WHOLESALE: Decorative

Pastrana Prime LLC ....F 407 470-9339
  Orlando (G-12471)
Royal Foam US LLC ....E 904 345-5400
  Jacksonville (G-6434)

HOMEFURNISHINGS, WHOLESALE: Blinds, Venetian

Total Window Inc ....G 954 921-0109
  Dania (G-2345)

HOMEFURNISHINGS, WHOLESALE: Blinds, Vertical

Bornt Enterprises Inc ....E 813 623-1492
  Tampa (G-16658)
Florida Pwdr Cting Shtters Inc ....F 561 588-2410
  Lantana (G-7514)
Sutton Draperies Inc ....F 305 653-7738
  Miami (G-9977)

HOMEFURNISHINGS, WHOLESALE: Decorating Splys

Fleurissima Inc ....F 305 572-0203
  Miami (G-9149)

HOMEFURNISHINGS, WHOLESALE: Draperies

Paul Himber Inc ....F 561 586-3741
  West Palm Beach (G-18115)

HOMEFURNISHINGS, WHOLESALE: Kitchenware

Distrivalto USA Inc ....E 305 715-0366
  Coral Gables (G-2049)
La Cuisine Intl Distrs Inc ....E 305 418-0010
  Miami (G-9405)

HOMEFURNISHINGS, WHOLESALE: Linens, Table

Sobel Westex ....D 954 942-5777
  Pompano Beach (G-14184)

HOMEFURNISHINGS, WHOLESALE: Mirrors/Pictures, Framed/Unframd

Art Connection Usa LLC ....E 954 781-0125
  Pompano Beach (G-13935)

HOMEFURNISHINGS, WHOLESALE: Pillowcases

Elaine Smith Inc ....F 561 863-3333
  Riviera Beach (G-14619)
Fabric Innovations Inc ....E 305 860-5757
  Miami (G-9127)

HOMEFURNISHINGS, WHOLESALE: Sheets, Textile

Vestagen Tchnical Textiles Inc ....G 407 781-2570
  Orlando (G-12695)

HOMEFURNISHINGS, WHOLESALE: Window Covering Parts & Access

Ortega Industries and Mfg ....D 305 688-0090
  Opa Locka (G-11778)
West Coast Shutters Sunburst ....F 727 894-0044
  Saint Petersburg (G-15230)

HOMEFURNISHINGS, WHOLESALE: Wood Flooring

Asd Surfaces LLC ....G 561 845-5009
  North Palm Beach (G-11174)
Designer Lifestyles LLC ....F 904 631-8954
  Jacksonville (G-6030)

HOMES, MODULAR: Wooden

All Modular Service Inc ....E 352 429-0868
  Mascotte (G-8181)
HI Tech Construction Svc Inc ....E 863 968-0731
  Winter Haven (G-18445)
Island Style Homes Inc ....G 772 464-6259
  Fort Pierce (G-4498)
Jennings Mobile HM Set Up LLC ....F 863 965-0883
  Auburndale (G-238)

HONEYCOMB CORE & BOARD: Made From Purchased Materials

Nida-Core Corporation ....E 772 343-7300
  Port Saint Lucie (G-14428)

HORMONES OR DERIVATIVES

Bodylogicmd Franchise Corp ....D 561 972-9580
  Boca Raton (G-444)

HORSE & PET ACCESSORIES: Textile

Ronmar Industries Inc ....G 561 630-8035
  West Palm Beach (G-18145)

HORSESHOES

Blue Horseshoe RES Group LLC ....G 561 429-2030
  Wellington (G-17845)
Dockside At Horseshoe Beach L ....G 352 377-4616
  Gainesville (G-4678)
Horseshoe ....G 863 438-6632
  Davenport (G-2366)
Horseshoe Picking Inc ....G 305 345-5778
  Homestead (G-5715)
Horseshoe Shrimp Boat LLC ....G 352 356-1982
  Horseshoe Beach (G-5753)
Jmg Strategies LLC ....G 305 606-2117
  Miami Beach (G-10207)

HOSE: Automobile, Rubber

Hitachi Cable America Inc ....C 850 476-0907
  Pensacola (G-13520)

HOSE: Flexible Metal

Microflex Inc ....E 386 672-1945
  Ormond Beach (G-12780)
Space Coast Hydraulics Inc ....F 321 504-6006
  Rockledge (G-14748)
Unaflex LLC ....F 954 943-5002
  Pompano Beach (G-14224)

HOSE: Plastic

Uip International Inc ....G 954 785-3539
  Pompano Beach (G-14222)

HOSE: Pneumatic, Rubber Or Rubberized Fabric, NEC

Space Coast Hydraulics Inc ....F 321 504-6006
  Rockledge (G-14748)
Unaflex LLC ....F 954 943-5002
  Pompano Beach (G-14224)

HOSE: Rubber

Fluid Routing Solutions LLC ....B 352 732-0222
  Ocala (G-11393)
Space Coast Distributors ....G 386 239-0305
  Daytona Beach (G-2603)

HOSES & BELTING: Rubber & Plastic

Ghx Industrial LLC ....F 305 620-4313
  Miami (G-9212)
Ghx Industrial LLC ....G 813 223-7554
  Tampa (G-16879)
Ghx Industrial LLC ....G 407 843-8190
  Orlando (G-12195)
Hecht Rubber Corporation ....D 904 731-3401
  Jacksonville (G-6171)
Varibelt Incorporated ....G 305 775-1568
  Miami (G-10097)

HOSPITAL EQPT REPAIR SVCS

Mobility Freedom Inc ....F 407 495-1333
  Orlando (G-12385)

HOT TUBS

Aquacal ....G 727 898-2412
  Saint Petersburg (G-14965)

HOT TUBS: Plastic & Fiberglass

Gatsby Spas Inc ....C 813 754-4122
  Plant City (G-13770)
Hot Tub Parts LLC ....G 727 573-9611
  Saint Petersburg (G-15078)

HOUSEHOLD APPLIANCE STORES

AAA Able Appliance Service Inc ....G 954 791-5222
  Fort Lauderdale (G-3617)

HOUSEHOLD ARTICLES, EXC FURNITURE: Cut Stone

Architctural MBL Importers Inc ....E 941 365-3552
  Sarasota (G-15599)
Italian Cast Stones Inc ....E 813 902-8900
  Tampa (G-16956)

HOUSEHOLD ARTICLES: Metal

6 Ports LLC ....F 561 743-8696
  Jupiter (G-6673)
Edwards Co ....G 215 343-2133
  Nokomis (G-11045)

HOUSEHOLD FURNISHINGS, NEC

Brenda Naused ....G 352 344-4729
  Daytona Beach (G-2524)
C-Worthy Corp ....F 954 784-7370
  Pompano Beach (G-13961)
Dwa Inc ....F 941 444-1134
  Sarasota (G-15663)
Elegant House Intl LLC ....G 954 457-8836
  Hallandale (G-4925)

Home Source Manufacturing Inc..........E 404 663-0647
 Marianna *(G-8166)*
Keter North America LLC.....................G...... 765 298-6800
 Boca Raton *(G-568)*
Lasalle Bristol Corporation.................F 352 687-2151
 Ocala *(G-11425)*
Q Squared Design LLC........................F 212 686-8860
 Fort Myers *(G-4372)*
Remas Draperies Etc Inc.....................G...... 904 845-9300
 Hilliard *(G-5474)*
Top Trtment Cstomes Accesories ....G...... 239 936-4600
 Fort Myers *(G-4426)*
Victors Cstm Qlting Bdspread I...........G...... 305 362-1990
 Hialeah *(G-5410)*
Westpoint Home Inc...........................A 850 415-4100
 Chipley *(G-1461)*

HOUSEWARES, ELECTRIC, EXC COOKING APPLIANCES & UTENSILS

Db Tucker LLC.....................................G...... 561 301-4974
 Jupiter *(G-6709)*

HOUSEWARES, ELECTRIC: Air Purifiers, Portable

Airfree USA LLC ....G...... 305 772-6577
 Miami *(G-8676)*
Healthquest Technologies LLC ....G...... 850 997-6300
 Monticello *(G-10581)*
Pyure Company Inc ....E 561 735-3701
 Boynton Beach *(G-904)*

HOUSEWARES, ELECTRIC: Appliances, Personal

Alton Manufacturing Inc......................G...... 305 821-0701
 Miami *(G-8704)*
Distrivalto USA Inc ....E 305 715-0366
 Coral Gables *(G-2049)*

HOUSEWARES, ELECTRIC: Broilers

Charcoal Chef Usa LLC.......................G...... 786 273-6511
 Miami *(G-8921)*

HOUSEWARES, ELECTRIC: Cooking Appliances

Russell Hobbs Inc...............................D...... 954 883-1000
 Miramar *(G-10538)*

HOUSEWARES, ELECTRIC: Curlers, Hair

Charles & Co LLC ....F 404 592-1190
 Fort Lauderdale *(G-3724)*
Van Tibolli Beauty Corp.......................E 305 390-0044
 Fort Lauderdale *(G-4116)*

HOUSEWARES, ELECTRIC: Dryers, Hand & Face

Saniflow Corporation...........................G...... 305 424-2433
 Miami *(G-9844)*

HOUSEWARES, ELECTRIC: Fans, Exhaust & Ventilating

Air-Tech of Pensacola Inc ....F 850 433-6443
 Pensacola *(G-13441)*
Fan America Inc ....G...... 941 955-9788
 Sarasota *(G-15671)*

HOUSEWARES, ELECTRIC: Heaters, Immersion

Intelligent Heater LLC.........................G...... 305 248-4971
 Homestead *(G-5718)*

HOUSEWARES, ELECTRIC: Heating, Bsbrd/Wall, Radiant Heat

and-Dell Corporation ....E 954 523-6478
 Fort Lauderdale *(G-3651)*

HOUSEWARES, ELECTRIC: Lighters, Cigarette

Lightfire Holdings LLC.........................G...... 866 375-0541
 Tamarac *(G-16535)*

Vapor Group Inc..................................G...... 954 792-8450
 Miami *(G-10096)*

HOUSEWARES, ELECTRIC: Massage Machines, Exc Beauty/Barber

Simulated Envmt Concepts Inc ....E 754 263-3184
 Hollywood *(G-5657)*

HOUSEWARES: Dishes, Plastic

Corkcicle LLC.....................................E 866 780-0007
 Orlando *(G-12048)*
D&W Fine Pack LLC............................E 305 592-4329
 Doral *(G-3182)*
Hans-Mill Corp....................................C 904 395-2288
 Jacksonville *(G-6165)*
Kasulik II LLC.....................................F 786 629-8978
 Hallandale Beach *(G-4956)*
Newell Brands Inc...............................D...... 858 729-4138
 Boca Raton *(G-616)*
Novelty Crystal Corp ....D...... 352 429-9036
 Orlando *(G-12426)*
Tupperware Intl Holdings Corp............F 407 826-5050
 Orlando *(G-12678)*
Tupperware Turkey Inc ....F 407 826-5050
 Orlando *(G-12680)*
Vista Serv Corp ....G...... 239 275-1973
 Fort Myers *(G-4443)*

HOUSEWARES: Toothpicks, Wood

Pixotine Products Inc ....G...... 305 479-1335
 Jupiter *(G-6777)*

HOUSINGS: Pressure

Djfs LLC ....G...... 727 551-1391
 Saint Petersburg *(G-15026)*

HUB CAPS: Automobile, Stamped Metal

Clever Covers Inc................................G...... 407 423-5959
 Orlando *(G-12020)*

HYDRAULIC EQPT REPAIR SVC

Alpha Hydraulics LLC..........................G...... 561 355-0318
 Riviera Beach *(G-14592)*
Chuxco Inc..F 305 470-9595
 Coral Gables *(G-2039)*

HYDRAULIC FLUIDS: Synthetic Based

Element Solutions Inc ....D...... 561 207-9600
 Fort Lauderdale *(G-3790)*
HB Sealing Products Inc ....C 727 796-1300
 Clearwater *(G-1623)*

HYDROELECTRIC POWER GENERATION

Sepac Corp...F 305 718-3379
 Miami *(G-9868)*

Hard Rubber & Molded Rubber Prdts

Hernol Usa Inc....................................E 786 263-3341
 Coral Gables *(G-2068)*
Lakeland Lures Inc..............................F 863 644-3127
 Lakeland *(G-7373)*
Revere Manufactured Pdts Inc ....G...... 904 503-9733
 Jacksonville *(G-6418)*
Tomsons Inc..G...... 248 646-0677
 Englewood *(G-3539)*

ICE

Atlantic Dry Ice Corportion ....F 305 592-7000
 Miami *(G-8763)*
Btu Reps LLC......................................G...... 727 235-3591
 Saint Petersburg *(G-14990)*
Central Florida Ice Services.................F 407 779-0161
 Orlando *(G-11998)*
Florida Ice Corporation ....F 305 685-9377
 Opa Locka *(G-11747)*
Gainesville Ice Company.....................F 352 378-2604
 Gainesville *(G-4698)*
Hialeah Distribution Corp....................E 786 200-2498
 Hialeah *(G-5184)*
Ice Magic-Orlando Inc.........................G...... 407 816-1905
 Orlando *(G-12234)*
Orlando Ice Servive Corp....................G...... 407 999-4940
 Orlando *(G-12452)*

Reddy Ice Corporation ....G...... 772 461-5046
 Fort Pierce *(G-4524)*
Reddy Ice Corporation ....F 904 388-2653
 Jacksonville *(G-6409)*
Reddy Ice Corporation ....G...... 850 233-0128
 Panama City *(G-13301)*
Reddy Ice Corporation ....F 561 881-9501
 West Palm Beach *(G-18138)*
Reddy Ice Inc......................................G...... 407 296-8300
 Orlando *(G-12540)*

ICE CREAM & ICES WHOLESALERS

Cross Atlantic Commodities Inc...........G...... 954 678-0698
 Weston *(G-18235)*
Lefab Commercial LLC........................F 305 456-1306
 Coral Gables *(G-2082)*
Muse Gelato Inc ....F 407 363-1443
 Orlando *(G-12402)*

ICE: Dry

Atlantic Dry Ice Corportion ....F 305 592-7000
 Miami *(G-8763)*

IDENTIFICATION PLATES

Commercial Metal Photography ....G...... 407 295-8182
 Orlando *(G-12033)*

IGNITION APPARATUS & DISTRIBUTORS

Alcolock FL Inc ....G...... 407 207-3337
 Orlando *(G-11888)*
Smartcart Ev LLC ....F 727 906-7001
 Safety Harbor *(G-14797)*

IGNITION COILS: Automotive

T C B Products Inc..............................E 941 723-9820
 Palmetto *(G-13195)*

INCENSE

Kenneth S Jarrell Inc ....F 334 215-7774
 Pensacola *(G-13534)*
Love Is In The Air Corp.......................G...... 305 828-8181
 Hialeah *(G-5227)*
Scents Nature Enterprises Corp...........F 305 547-2334
 Miami Lakes *(G-10350)*

INCUBATORS & BROODERS: Farm

Brinsea Products Inc ....G...... 321 267-7009
 Titusville *(G-17576)*
Hawkhead International Inc ....G...... 904 264-4295
 Orange Park *(G-11831)*
Pas Reform North America LLC ....E 904 358-0355
 Jacksonville *(G-6356)*

INDICATORS: Cabin Environment

Drs Advanced Isr LLC ....F 321 622-1202
 Melbourne *(G-8403)*

INDICATORS: Horizon Flight

Utility Services Authority LLC ....E 772 344-9339
 Fort Pierce *(G-4552)*

INDL & PERSONAL SVC PAPER WHOLESALERS

Atlas Paper Mills LLC ....C 305 835-8046
 Hialeah *(G-5064)*
Latam Group Corp...............................G...... 305 793-8961
 Miami *(G-9431)*
World Indus Resources Corp ....E 727 572-9991
 Clearwater *(G-1856)*

INDL & PERSONAL SVC PAPER, WHOL: Bags, Paper/Disp Plastic

Dairy-Mix Inc.......................................F 813 621-8098
 Tampa *(G-16759)*

INDL & PERSONAL SVC PAPER, WHOL: Boxes, Corrugtd/Solid Fiber

Avatar Packaging Inc...........................E 813 888-9141
 Tampa *(G-16618)*

Employee Codes: A=Over 500 employees, B=251-500
C=101-250, D=51-100, E=20-50, F=10-19, G=4-9 2022 Harris Florida
Manufacturers Directory 1227

P
R
O
D
U
C
T

INDL EQPT SVCS

Chemko Technical Services Inc ....E 954 783-7673
Pompano Beach *(G-13969)*

Done Rite Pumps ....G 305 953-3380
Opa Locka *(G-11738)*

G S Servicore Corp ....E 305 888-0189
Hialeah *(G-5163)*

James O Corbett Inc ....G 352 483-1222
Eustis *(G-3560)*

Mat-Vac Technology Inc ....F 386 238-7017
Daytona Beach *(G-2573)*

Star-Seal of Florida Inc ....F 954 484-8402
Fort Lauderdale *(G-4068)*

INDL GASES WHOLESALERS

Air Products and Chemicals Inc ....F 407 859-5141
Orlando *(G-11881)*

Airgas Usa LLC ....G 407 293-6630
Orlando *(G-11884)*

INDL HELP SVCS

Azex Flow Technologies Inc ....G 305 393-8037
Miami *(G-8785)*

INDL MACHINERY & EQPT WHOLESALERS

Black Damnd Drill Grinders Inc ....F 978 465-3799
Windermere *(G-18348)*

Breezemaker Fan Company Inc ....E 813 248-5552
Tampa *(G-16661)*

Contemprary McHnrey Engrg Svcs ....E 386 439-0937
Flagler Beach *(G-3603)*

Costex Corporation ....C 305 592-9769
Miami *(G-8975)*

Crown Equipment Corporation ....D 954 786-8889
Pompano Beach *(G-13983)*

Duramaster Cylinders ....G 813 882-0040
Tampa *(G-16788)*

Eidschun Engineering Inc ....E 727 647-2300
Clearwater *(G-1578)*

Gas Turbine Efficiency LLC ....E 407 304-5200
Orlando *(G-12183)*

Gem Remotes Inc ....F 239 642-0873
Naples *(G-10759)*

International Baler Corp ....E 904 358-3812
Jacksonville *(G-6202)*

JDB Dense Flow Inc ....F 727 785-8500
Palm Harbor *(G-13116)*

Keytroller LLC ....E 813 877-4500
Tampa *(G-16984)*

Knight Industrial Eqp Inc ....G 863 646-2997
Lakeland *(G-7370)*

Lee Chemical Corporation ....G 407 843-6950
Longwood *(G-7917)*

Lexington Cutter Inc ....E 941 739-2726
Bradenton *(G-1004)*

Lynx Products Corp Inc ....G 941 727-9676
Bradenton *(G-1008)*

Madan Corporation ....G 954 925-0077
Dania Beach *(G-2353)*

Marden Industries Inc ....F 863 682-7882
Punta Gorda *(G-14513)*

Marine Exhaust Systems Inc ....D 561 848-1238
Riviera Beach *(G-14645)*

Parker-Hannifin Corporation ....E 305 470-8800
Miami *(G-9694)*

Performance Pumps Inc ....E 407 339-6700
Casselberry *(G-1427)*

Pinellas Electric Mtr Repr Inc ....G 727 572-0777
Clearwater *(G-1741)*

Pixe International Corp ....F 850 574-6469
Tallahassee *(G-16488)*

Rios Con Pmpg & Rentl Inc ....E 305 888-7909
Medley *(G-8315)*

Sensidyne LP ....D 727 530-3602
Saint Petersburg *(G-15180)*

Southeast Power Group Inc ....D 305 592-9745
Doral *(G-3370)*

Southern Packaging McHy Corp ....E 305 245-3045
Florida City *(G-3612)*

SPS Drilling Exploration Prod ....F 305 777-3553
Coral Gables *(G-2111)*

Teknocraft Inc ....E 321 729-9634
Melbourne *(G-8548)*

Tradewinds Power Corp ....E 305 592-9745
Doral *(G-3400)*

William Laroque Installers Inc ....E 305 769-1717
Hollywood *(G-5684)*

INDL MACHINERY REPAIR & MAINTENANCE

Diverse Co ....E 863 425-4251
Mulberry *(G-10623)*

Matthews International Corp ....C 407 886-5533
Apopka *(G-149)*

Megawattage LLC ....F 954 328-0232
Fort Lauderdale *(G-3937)*

Power Kleen Corporation ....E 813 854-2648
Oldsmar *(G-11687)*

INDL PATTERNS: Foundry Patternmaking

U S Holdings Inc ....G 305 885-0301
Hialeah *(G-5389)*

INDL PROCESS INSTR: Transmit, Process Variables

For-A Latin America Inc ....G 305 261-2345
Miami *(G-9166)*

INDL PROCESS INSTRUMENTS: Chromatographs

Jsi Scientific Inc ....G 732 845-1925
Naples *(G-10793)*

INDL PROCESS INSTRUMENTS: Control

Blue Siren Inc ....E 321 242-0300
Melbourne *(G-8379)*

Facts Engineering LLC ....E 727 375-8888
Trinity *(G-17636)*

James O Corbett Inc ....G 352 483-1222
Eustis *(G-3560)*

Sepac Corp ....F 305 718-3379
Miami *(G-9868)*

INDL PROCESS INSTRUMENTS: Controllers, Process Variables

ABB Enterprise Software Inc ....C 954 752-6700
Coral Springs *(G-2124)*

Precision Analog Systems Co ....G 954 587-0668
Plantation *(G-13878)*

Riegl Usa Inc ....E 407 248-9927
Winter Garden *(G-18403)*

INDL PROCESS INSTRUMENTS: Digital Display, Process Variables

Digital Living ....G 407 332-9998
Altamonte Springs *(G-42)*

Electric Pcture Dsplay Systems ....G 321 757-8484
Melbourne *(G-8417)*

Infiniti Digital Equipment Inc ....G 305 477-6333
Doral *(G-3258)*

Outform Inc ....G 800 204-0524
Miami *(G-9671)*

INDL PROCESS INSTRUMENTS: Elements, Primary

AP Buck Inc ....F 407 851-8602
Orlando *(G-11913)*

INDL PROCESS INSTRUMENTS: Fluidic Devices, Circuit & Systems

Bar Beverage Ctrl Systems Fla ....G 239 213-3301
Naples *(G-10690)*

Chicago Electronic Distrs Inc ....F 312 985-6175
Port Charlotte *(G-14292)*

Kinetics Usa Inc ....E 561 988-8826
Boca Raton *(G-569)*

Real-Time Laboratories LLC ....D 561 988-8826
Boca Raton *(G-649)*

INDL PROCESS INSTRUMENTS: Temperature

Atkins Technical Inc ....E 860 349-3473
Gainesville *(G-4654)*

Roper Technologies Inc ....E 941 556-2601
Sarasota *(G-15801)*

INDL PROCESS INSTRUMENTS: Water Quality Monitoring/Cntrl Sys

Aqualogix Inc ....F 858 442-4550
Palm Beach Gardens *(G-12948)*

Coffman Systems Inc ....F 813 891-1300
Oldsmar *(G-11640)*

Engineer Service Corporation ....G 904 268-0482
Jacksonville *(G-6075)*

Wes Holdings Corp ....F 941 371-4995
Sarasota *(G-15871)*

INDL SPLYS WHOLESALERS

American Coatings Corporation ....G 954 970-7820
Margate *(G-8120)*

Bryan Nelco Inc ....G 727 533-8282
Clearwater *(G-1529)*

Del Prado Holdings LLC ....G 305 680-7425
Hollywood *(G-5563)*

Henefelt Precision Pdts Inc ....F 727 531-0406
Largo *(G-7603)*

J C S Engineering & Dev ....F 305 888-7911
Hialeah *(G-5199)*

Lap of Amer Lser Applctons LLC ....G 561 416-9250
Boynton Beach *(G-884)*

Lodex Enterprises Corp ....G 954 442-3843
Miramar *(G-10509)*

Matthews International Corp ....C 407 886-5533
Apopka *(G-149)*

Nasco Industries Inc ....E 954 733-8665
Fort Lauderdale *(G-3953)*

NSK Latin America Inc ....G 305 477-0605
Miami *(G-9633)*

Plastics America Inc ....E 813 620-3711
Tampa *(G-17168)*

Rock River Tool Inc ....F 941 753-6343
Bradenton *(G-1036)*

SPS Drilling Exploration Prod ....F 305 777-3553
Coral Gables *(G-2111)*

Tekk Supply Inc ....G 954 444-5782
Pompano Beach *(G-14211)*

INDL SPLYS, WHOL: Fasteners, Incl Nuts, Bolts, Screws, Etc

Grabber Construction Pdts Inc ....G 813 249-2281
Tampa *(G-16888)*

Merit Fastener Corporation ....E 407 331-4815
Longwood *(G-7922)*

INDL SPLYS, WHOLESALE: Abrasives

True Grit Abrasives Inc ....F 813 247-5219
Tampa *(G-17372)*

INDL SPLYS, WHOLESALE: Bearings

Shark Skinz ....G 772 388-9621
Sebastian *(G-15904)*

INDL SPLYS, WHOLESALE: Bins & Containers, Storage

Container of America LLC ....F 954 772-5519
Fort Lauderdale *(G-3744)*

INDL SPLYS, WHOLESALE: Brushes, Indl

Torrington Brush Works Inc ....F 941 355-1499
Sarasota *(G-15855)*

INDL SPLYS, WHOLESALE: Fasteners & Fastening Eqpt

National Std Parts Assoc Inc ....D 850 456-5771
Pensacola *(G-13555)*

INDL SPLYS, WHOLESALE: Gaskets

Construction and Elec Pdts Inc ....F 954 972-9787
Pompano Beach *(G-13976)*

Hisco Pump South LLC ....F 904 786-4488
Jacksonville *(G-6177)*

Siligom USA LLC ....G 786 406-6262
Doral *(G-3367)*

Sunpack of Pensacola Inc ....F 850 476-9838
Pensacola *(G-13612)*

INDL SPLYS, WHOLESALE: Glass Bottles

Liquid Bottles LLC ....E... 888 222-5232
Bradenton *(G-1006)*

INDL SPLYS, WHOLESALE: Hydraulic & Pneumatic Pistons/Valves

Alpha Hydraulics LLC ....G... 561 355-0318
Riviera Beach *(G-14592)*
Bridgestone Hosepower LLC...........D... 904 264-1267
Orange Park *(G-11816)*
Space Coast Hydraulics Inc ....F... 321 504-6006
Rockledge *(G-14748)*

INDL SPLYS, WHOLESALE: Mill Splys

Quality Industries America Inc ....G... 386 755-0220
Lake City *(G-7041)*

INDL SPLYS, WHOLESALE: Power Transmission, Eqpt & Apparatus

Man-Trans LLC ....F... 850 222-6993
Tallahassee *(G-16474)*
Robert E Weissenborn Sr.................G... 239 262-1771
Naples *(G-10879)*

INDL SPLYS, WHOLESALE: Seals

HB Sealing Products Inc ....C... 727 796-1300
Clearwater *(G-1623)*

INDL SPLYS, WHOLESALE: Signmaker Eqpt & Splys

National Traffic Signs Inc ....G... 727 446-7983
Clearwater *(G-1712)*
Poli Group Intl Inc ....F... 305 468-8986
Miami *(G-9726)*
Rogers Sign Corp ....F... 352 799-1923
Brooksville *(G-1195)*

INDL SPLYS, WHOLESALE: Tools

Delta Regis Tools Inc...................E... 772 465-4302
Fort Pierce *(G-4480)*

INDL SPLYS, WHOLESALE: Valves & Fittings

Azex Flow Technologies Inc ....G... 305 393-8037
Miami *(G-8785)*

INDL TRUCK REPAIR SVCS

Nichols Truck Bodies LLC ....F... 904 781-5080
Jacksonville *(G-6333)*

INDUCTORS

Manutech Assembly Inc ....G... 305 888-2800
Miami *(G-9506)*

INDUSTRIAL & COMMERCIAL EQPT INSPECTION SVCS

C & D Industrial Maint LLC...................E... 833 776-5833
Bradenton *(G-951)*
Megawattage LLC ....F... 954 328-0232
Fort Lauderdale *(G-3937)*
Pdma Corporation........................E... 813 621-6463
Tampa *(G-17152)*

INFORMATION SVCS: Consumer

Brigiz Inc..................................F... 404 400-5399
Riviera Beach *(G-14601)*

INFRARED OBJECT DETECTION EQPT

Eltec Instruments Inc........................E... 386 252-0411
Daytona Beach *(G-2549)*

INK OR WRITING FLUIDS

International Imaging Mtls Inc ....F... 727 834-8200
Odessa *(G-11560)*

INK: Letterpress Or Offset

Folders Tabs Et Cetera ....F... 813 884-3651
Tampa *(G-16858)*

INK: Printing

Amrob Inc ....G... 813 238-6041
Tampa *(G-16595)*
Florida Ink Mfg Co Inc ....G... 813 247-2911
Tampa *(G-16846)*
Hailey Cian LLC.........................G... 954 895-7143
Fort Lauderdale *(G-3856)*
J&S Inks LLC ....G... 305 999-0304
North Miami Beach *(G-11146)*
One Step Papers LLC ....G... 305 238-2296
Miami *(G-9652)*
Rainbow Ink Products Inc ....G... 954 252-6030
Davie *(G-2464)*
T C Deliveries ....G... 813 881-1830
Tampa *(G-17320)*
Yes Solutions Gallery LLC ....G... 352 622-7937
Ocala *(G-11516)*

INK: Screen process

Instorescreen LLC ....G... 646 301-4690
Naples *(G-10782)*

INSECTICIDES

Agrosource Inc.........................F... 908 251-3500
Jupiter *(G-6682)*
Fresh Mark Corporation ....F... 352 394-7746
Clermont *(G-1869)*
Growers Fertilizer Corporation ......E... 863 956-1101
Lake Alfred *(G-6995)*

INSECTICIDES & PESTICIDES

Lenoc Chemical Solutions Inc.............G... 229 499-0665
Bowling Green *(G-830)*
Matrix24 Laboratories LLC..............F... 941 879-3048
Sarasota *(G-15514)*
Natures Own Pest Control Inc ....G... 941 378-3334
Sarasota *(G-15758)*
Ticks-N-All LLC ....G... 321 445-9497
Orlando *(G-12658)*
Velmaxxx Enterprises Inc................G... 239 689-4343
Fort Myers *(G-4439)*

INSPECTION & TESTING SVCS

Bogue Executive Enterprises ....F... 561 842-5336
Mangonia Park *(G-8090)*
Tricen Technologies Fla LLC ....F... 866 620-9407
Fort Pierce *(G-4541)*

INSTALLATION OF CITIZENS BAND ANTENNAS

C2c Innovated Technology LLC ....G... 251 382-2277
Bonifay *(G-768)*

INSTRUMENTS & ACCESSORIES: Surveying

Datagrid Inc ....G... 352 371-7608
Gainesville *(G-4676)*
Leadair Inc ....E... 407 343-7571
Kissimmee *(G-6937)*

INSTRUMENTS & METERS: Measuring, Electric

Emcee Electronics Inc..................F... 941 485-1515
Venice *(G-17689)*
Hughes Corporation ....E... 954 755-7111
Coral Springs *(G-2164)*

INSTRUMENTS, LAB: Spectroscopic/Optical Properties Measuring

Chemplex Industries Inc ....F... 772 283-2700
Palm City *(G-13028)*

INSTRUMENTS, LABORATORY: Gas Chromatographic

Separation Systems Inc ....F... 850 932-1433
Gulf Breeze *(G-4891)*

INSTRUMENTS, LABORATORY: Photometers

Mip-Technology Corp ....G... 239 221-3604
Bonita Springs *(G-811)*

INSTRUMENTS, LABORATORY: Spectrometers

Stellarnet Inc...........................F... 813 855-8687
Tampa *(G-17301)*
Thermo Arl US Inc......................E... 800 532-4752
West Palm Beach *(G-18177)*

INSTRUMENTS, MEASURING & CNTRL: Geophysical/Meteorological

Drew Scientific Inc.......................E... 305 418-2320
Miami Lakes *(G-10297)*

INSTRUMENTS, MEASURING & CNTRL: Radiation & Testing, Nuclear

Sun Nuclear Corp......................E... 321 259-6862
Melbourne *(G-8537)*
Sun Nuclear Corp......................C... 321 259-6862
Melbourne *(G-8538)*

INSTRUMENTS, MEASURING & CNTRL: Testing, Abrasion, Etc

AVK Industries Inc ....F... 904 998-8400
Jacksonville *(G-5913)*
Veroch LLC.........................G... 954 990-7544
Sunrise *(G-16388)*

INSTRUMENTS, MEASURING & CNTRLG: Aircraft & Motor Vehicle

Suncoast Tool & Gage Inds Inc ......F... 727 572-8000
Clearwater *(G-1801)*

INSTRUMENTS, MEASURING & CNTRLG: Fatigue Test, Indl, Mech

Qualitest USA Lc........................F... 877 884-8378
Fort Lauderdale *(G-4004)*

INSTRUMENTS, MEASURING & CNTRLG: Thermometers/Temp Sensors

American Household Inc.....................D... 561 912-4100
Boca Raton *(G-407)*
Co2meter Inc.........................F... 386 310-4933
Ormond Beach *(G-12751)*
Electro-Optix Inc ....F... 954 973-2800
Pompano Beach *(G-14008)*
Marathon Technology Corp ....F... 305 592-1340
Doral *(G-3291)*
Sunbeam Americas Holdings LLC ......E... 561 912-4100
Boca Raton *(G-702)*

INSTRUMENTS, MEASURING & CNTRLNG: Press & Vac Ind, Acft Eng

Hydroplus...........................G... 386 341-2768
Edgewater *(G-3490)*

INSTRUMENTS, MEASURING & CONTROLLING: Breathalyzers

Alcohol Cntrmasure Systems Inc..........C... 407 207-3337
Orlando *(G-11887)*

INSTRUMENTS, MEASURING & CONTROLLING: Fuel System, Aircraft

AMD Aero Inc ....F... 239 561-8622
Fort Myers *(G-4170)*

INSTRUMENTS, MEASURING & CONTROLLING: Gas Detectors

Core Enterprises Incorporated...........G... 954 227-0781
Coral Springs *(G-2144)*
LDS Vacuum Products Inc ....E... 407 862-4643
Longwood *(G-7916)*

INSTRUMENTS, MEASURING & CONTROLLING: Gauges, Rain

K-Rain Manufacturing Corp.................E... 561 844-1002
Riviera Beach *(G-14635)*

INSTRUMENTS, MEASURING & CONTROLLING: Leak Detection, Liquid

Oriflow ....F 727 400-4881
Clearwater *(G-1730)*

Precision Leak Detection Inc ....G 904 996-9290
Jacksonville *(G-6380)*

INSTRUMENTS, MEASURING & CONTROLLING: Photogrammetrical

Geodetic Services Inc ....F 321 724-6831
Melbourne *(G-8428)*

INSTRUMENTS, MEASURING & CONTROLLING: Polygraph

Asset Guardian Inc ....G 727 942-2246
Palm Harbor *(G-13099)*

INSTRUMENTS, MEASURING & CONTROLLING: Ultrasonic Testing

Applus Laboratories USA Inc ....G 941 205-5700
Punta Gorda *(G-14491)*

Mri Depot Inc ....G 407 696-9822
Longwood *(G-7925)*

INSTRUMENTS, MEASURING/CNTRLG: Fare Registers, St Cars/Buses

Umbrella Buses Inc ....G 754 457-4004
Davenport *(G-2372)*

INSTRUMENTS, MEASURING/CNTRLNG: Med Diagnostic Sys, Nuclear

Brrh Corporation ....D 954 427-9665
Deerfield Beach *(G-2683)*

Faro Technologies Inc ....B 407 333-9911
Lake Mary *(G-7075)*

Homestead Diagnostic Ctr Inc ....F 305 246-5600
Homestead *(G-5713)*

New World Holdings Inc ....E 561 888-4939
Delray Beach *(G-2992)*

Pet Services of Florida LLC ....G 352 746-6888
Beverly Hills *(G-369)*

Vital Imging Diagnstc Ctrs LLC .....F 305 569-9992
Miami *(G-10117)*

Whk Biosystems LLC ....G 727 209-8402
Clearwater *(G-1851)*

INSTRUMENTS, OPTICAL: Aiming Circles, Fire Control

Konus USA Corporation ....G 305 884-7618
Medley *(G-8266)*

Oasis Alignment Services Inc ....F 850 484-2994
Pensacola *(G-13558)*

INSTRUMENTS, OPTICAL: Elements & Assemblies, Exc Ophthalmic

Ii-VI Aerospace & Defense Inc ....C 727 375-8562
Port Richey *(G-14363)*

Optigrate Corporation ....E 407 542-7704
Oviedo *(G-12840)*

Vloc Incorporated ....C 727 375-8562
Port Richey *(G-14385)*

INSTRUMENTS, OPTICAL: Lenses, All Types Exc Ophthalmic

Benz Research and Dev LLC ....E 941 758-8256
Sarasota *(G-15445)*

Graflex Inc ....G 561 691-5959
Jupiter *(G-6738)*

Meopta USA Inc ....C 631 436-5900
Trinity *(G-17640)*

Twinstar Optics & Coatings Inc ......F 727 847-2300
Port Richey *(G-14381)*

INSTRUMENTS, OPTICAL: Magnifying, NEC

Electro-Optix Inc ....F 954 973-2800
Pompano Beach *(G-14008)*

INSTRUMENTS, OPTICAL: Test & Inspection

Direct Optical Research Co ....G 727 319-9000
Largo *(G-7570)*

Fiberoptic Engineering Corp ....F 850 763-2289
Panama City *(G-13261)*

INSTRUMENTS, SURGICAL & MED: Fixation Appliances, Internal

Treace Medical Concepts Inc ....C 904 373-5940
Ponte Vedra *(G-14259)*

INSTRUMENTS, SURGICAL & MED: Gastroscopes, Exc Electromedcal

Endo-Gear LLC ....F 305 710-6662
Miami *(G-9098)*

INSTRUMENTS, SURGICAL & MEDICAL: Biopsy

Mobilehelp LLC ....D 561 347-6255
Boca Raton *(G-602)*

INSTRUMENTS, SURGICAL & MEDICAL: Blood & Bone Work

Alpha Industries Inc ....G 727 443-2673
Clearwater *(G-1488)*

Anew Inc ....G 386 668-7785
Debary *(G-2630)*

Betawave LLC ....F 954 223-8298
Fort Lauderdale *(G-3683)*

Biosafe Supplies LLC ....F 407 281-6658
Orlando *(G-11952)*

Byomed LLC ....F 305 634-6763
North Miami *(G-11095)*

Chuxco Inc ....F 305 470-9595
Coral Gables *(G-2039)*

David Perkins Enterprises Inc ....G 850 234-0002
Panama City Beach *(G-13329)*

Drew Scientific Inc ....E 305 418-2320
Miami Lakes *(G-10297)*

Endo-Therapeutics Inc ....D 727 538-9570
Clearwater *(G-1585)*

Gulf Coast Hyperberic Inc ....G 850 271-1441
Panama City *(G-13269)*

Hdl Therapeutics Inc ....F 772 453-2770
Vero Beach *(G-17759)*

Medtronic ....E 305 458-7260
Miami Lakes *(G-10319)*

New World Holdings Inc ....E 561 888-4939
Delray Beach *(G-2992)*

North American Diagnostics LLC .....C 855 752-6879
Holly Hill *(G-5517)*

Steripack (usa) Limited LLC ....E 863 648-2333
Lakeland *(G-7449)*

Surgentec LLC ....G 561 990-7882
Boca Raton *(G-705)*

INSTRUMENTS, SURGICAL & MEDICAL: Blood Pressure

American Household Inc ....D 561 912-4100
Boca Raton *(G-407)*

Sunbeam Americas Holdings LLC ...E 561 912-4100
Boca Raton *(G-702)*

Technicuff Corp ....F 352 326-2833
Leesburg *(G-7797)*

INSTRUMENTS, SURGICAL & MEDICAL: Catheters

Inneuroco Inc ....E 954 742-5988
Southwest Ranches *(G-16054)*

INSTRUMENTS, SURGICAL & MEDICAL: Clamps

Bravo Inc ....G 239 471-8127
Cape Coral *(G-1315)*

INSTRUMENTS, SURGICAL & MEDICAL: Inhalation Therapy

Mobilite Corporation ....E 407 321-5630
Sanford *(G-15360)*

INSTRUMENTS, SURGICAL & MEDICAL: Inhalators

Lor-Ed Enterprises LLC ....G 352 750-1999
Lady Lake *(G-6992)*

INSTRUMENTS, SURGICAL & MEDICAL: Lasers, Surgical

Aesthetic MBL Laser Svcs Inc ....G 954 480-2600
Deerfield Beach *(G-2659)*

Family of Smith Inc ....G 941 726-0873
Sarasota *(G-15476)*

Ideal Image Brandon ....G 813 982-3420
Brandon *(G-1095)*

Marysol Technologies Inc ....G 727 712-1523
Clearwater *(G-1685)*

INSTRUMENTS, SURGICAL & MEDICAL: Needles, Suture

Rochester Electro-Medical Inc ....E 813 994-7519
Coral Springs *(G-2206)*

INSTRUMENTS, SURGICAL & MEDICAL: Ophthalmic

Adamas Instrument Corporation ......F 727 540-0033
Clearwater *(G-1474)*

Brain Power Incorporated ....E 305 264-4465
Miami *(G-8851)*

Clinicon Corporation ....F 239 939-1345
Fort Myers *(G-4211)*

Hansa Ophthalmics LLC ....E 305 594-1789
Doral *(G-3244)*

Innovative Designs of Sarasota ......G 941 752-7779
Bradenton *(G-995)*

Morcent Import Export Inc ....E 727 442-9735
Belleair *(G-352)*

INSTRUMENTS, SURGICAL & MEDICAL: Plates & Screws, Bone

Orthopedic Designs N Amer Inc ......G 813 443-4905
Tampa *(G-17130)*

INSTRUMENTS, SURGICAL & MEDICAL: Skin Grafting

Sensus Healthcare Inc ....E 561 922-5808
Boca Raton *(G-668)*

INSTRUMENTS, SURGICAL/MED: Microsurgical, Exc Electromedical

Medtronic Xomed Inc ....A 904 296-9600
Jacksonville *(G-6293)*

Medtronic Xomed Inc ....B 904 296-9600
Jacksonville *(G-6294)*

Mmi North America Inc ....F 616 649-1912
Ponte Vedra Beach *(G-14275)*

INSTRUMENTS: Analytical

Analytical Research Systems ....F 352 466-0051
Micanopy *(G-10395)*

Anton Paar Quantatec Inc ....G 561 731-4999
Boynton Beach *(G-841)*

Awareness Technology Inc ....D 772 283-6540
Palm City *(G-13023)*

Awareness Technology Inc ....E 772 283-6540
Palm City *(G-13024)*

Beckman Coulter Inc ....F 305 380-2175
Miami *(G-8810)*

Beckman Coulter Inc ....C 305 380-3800
Miami *(G-8811)*

Beckman Coulter Inc ....F 954 432-4336
Pembroke Pines *(G-13377)*

Block Engineering Incorporated ......G 508 251-3100
Vero Beach *(G-17742)*

Bowman Analytics Inc ....G 847 781-3523
Sarasota *(G-15614)*

Cellmic LLC ....G 310 443-2070
Palm Harbor *(G-13106)*

Cole-Parmer Instrument Co LLC .....D 352 854-8080
Ocala *(G-11355)*

DOE & Ingalls Florida Oper LLC .....G 813 347-4741
Tampa *(G-16784)*

Edgeone LLC ....E 561 995-7767
Boca Raton *(G-500)*

Field Forensics Inc ....F 727 490-3609
Saint Petersburg *(G-15045)*

Gilson Inc ....G 904 725-7612
Jacksonville *(G-6141)*

Hf Scientific Inc ....E 888 203-7248
Fort Myers *(G-4279)*

L and C Science and Tech Inc ....G....... 305 200-3531
Hialeah (G-5215)
Lablogic Systems Inc ....F...... 813 626-6848
Tampa (G-16997)
Multicore Photonics Inc ....G...... 407 325-7800
Orlando (G-12398)
Npact America Inc ....G...... 904 755-6259
Jacksonville (G-6339)
Ocean Optics Inc ....E...... 407 673-0041
Orlando (G-12431)
Ocean Optics Inc ....E...... 407 673-0041
Orlando (G-12432)
Ocean Optics Inc ....E...... 727 545-0741
Orlando (G-12433)
P S Analytical Inc ....G...... 954 429-1577
Deerfield Beach (G-2777)
Pipette Solutions LLC ....G...... 877 974-7388
Casselberry (G-1428)
Rave LLC ....E...... 561 330-0411
Delray Beach (G-3012)
Teledyne Flir LLC ....G...... 850 678-4503
Niceville (G-11038)
Thermo Electron North Amer LLC ....E...... 561 688-8700
West Palm Beach (G-18178)
Thermo Fisher Scientific Inc................B...... 561 688-8700
West Palm Beach (G-18179)
Ultrafast Systems LLC ....F...... 941 360-2161
Sarasota (G-15859)
USA Scientific Inc ....E...... 352 237-6288
Ocala (G-11508)
Vision Analytical Inc ....G...... 305 801-7140
Miami (G-10114)
World Precision Instrs LLC ....E...... 941 371-1003
Sarasota (G-15879)
Ysi Inc ....F...... 727 565-2201
Saint Petersburg (G-15242)

INSTRUMENTS: Analyzers, Internal Combustion Eng, Electronic

Baytronics Manufacturing Inc ....F...... 813 434-0401
Tampa (G-16633)
Performance Technology 2000 ....G....... 772 463-1056
Stuart (G-16196)
Rjh Technical Services Inc ....G...... 813 655-7947
Brandon (G-1104)

INSTRUMENTS: Analyzers, Spectrum

Spectrum Bridge Inc............................F 407 792-1570
Lake Mary (G-7107)

INSTRUMENTS: Colonoscopes, Electromedical

Eurospa...G...... 904 242-8200
Neptune Beach (G-10958)

INSTRUMENTS: Combustion Control, Indl

Axi International..................................E 239 690-9589
Fort Myers (G-4184)
Ecombustible Products LLC ....F...... 786 565-8610
Sunny Isles Beach (G-16270)
Gencor Industries Inc ....C..... 407 290-6000
Orlando (G-12187)

INSTRUMENTS: Endoscopic Eqpt, Electromedical

Endo-Gear LLC....................................F...... 305 710-6662
Miami (G-9098)

INSTRUMENTS: Eye Examination

Sinocare Meditech Inc ....F 800 342-7226
Fort Lauderdale (G-4051)
Vmax Vision Inc ....G...... 321 972-1823
Maitland (G-8078)

INSTRUMENTS: Frequency Meters, Electrical, Mech & Electronic

King Han Inc ....G...... 860 933-8574
Englewood (G-3519)
Next Generation Home Pdts Inc ....G....... 727 834-9400
Tampa (G-17109)

INSTRUMENTS: Indl Process Control

Advanced Manufacturing Inc................E 727 573-3300
Saint Petersburg (G-14954)

Amci Technologies Inc ....F 561 596-6288
Boynton Beach (G-838)
Ametek Inc ....D....... 800 527-9999
Largo (G-7534)
Ametek Power Instrument Inc ....D...... 954 344-9822
Coral Springs (G-2131)
Applied Technologies Group Inc..........G...... 813 413-7025
Tampa (G-16601)
Automated Sonix Corporation..............G...... 941 964-1361
Boca Grande (G-380)
Bestest International Inc ....F 714 974-8837
Saint Augustine (G-14815)
Calibrated Controls LLC.......................G...... 904 718-0541
Middleburg (G-10401)
Centroid Products Inc ....G...... 386 423-3574
Edgewater (G-3486)
Chem-TEC Equipment Co ....G...... 954 428-8259
Deerfield Beach (G-2692)
Clearwater Engineering Inc..................G...... 727 573-2210
Clearwater (G-1542)
Coast Controls Inc ....F 941 355-7555
Sarasota (G-15456)
Complete Instrmnttion Cntrls I ....G...... 813 340-8545
Lithia (G-7832)
Computational Systems Inc ....C...... 954 846-5030
Sunrise (G-16307)
Computational Systems Inc ....C...... 863 648-9044
Lakeland (G-7295)
Control Solutions Inc ....F...... 813 247-2136
Tampa (G-16725)
CPS Products Inc ....D....... 305 687-4121
Miramar (G-10482)
Crystal Photonics Inc ....E...... 407 328-9111
Sanford (G-15298)
Dynalco Controls Corporation..............E...... 323 589-6181
Fort Lauderdale (G-3775)
Emcee Electronics Inc.........................E...... 941 485-1515
Venice (G-17688)
Emerson Electric Co ....E...... 904 741-6800
Jacksonville (G-6073)
Energy Control Tech Inc ....G...... 954 739-8400
Davie (G-2406)
Fct-Combustion Inc ....E...... 610 725-8840
Fort Lauderdale (G-3812)
Gkwf Inc ....G...... 863 644-6925
Lakeland (G-7337)
H Q Inc ....F...... 941 721-7588
Palmetto (G-13172)
Hf Scientific Inc ....E...... 888 203-7248
Fort Myers (G-4279)
Hughes Corporation ....E...... 954 755-7111
Coral Springs (G-2164)
I C Probotics Inc.................................D....... 407 339-8298
Longwood (G-7902)
Ian-Conrad Bergan LLC ....E...... 850 434-1286
Pensacola (G-13522)
Instrument & Valve Services Co ....G...... 904 741-6800
Jacksonville (G-6201)
Jhn North LLC ....E...... 561 294-5613
Boynton Beach (G-882)
L3harris Technologies Inc ....C....... 260 451-6814
Tampa (G-16995)
Malema Engineering Corporation ....F...... 561 995-0595
Boca Raton (G-582)
Onicon Incorporated............................E 727 447-6140
Largo (G-7654)
Optoelectronics Inc ....F...... 954 642-8997
Boca Raton (G-625)
Precision Fabg & Clg Co Inc.................D....... 321 635-2000
Cocoa (G-1948)
Precision Resources Inc ....F...... 321 635-2000
Cocoa (G-1949)
Presys Instruments Inc ....G...... 305 495-3335
Miami (G-9739)
Pyramid Imaging Inc............................F...... 813 984-0125
Tampa (G-17196)
Red Meters LLC ....F...... 407 337-0110
Orlando (G-12538)
Roper Industrial Pdts Inv Co.................F...... 941 556-2601
Sarasota (G-15800)
Saikou Optics Incorporated ....E...... 407 986-4200
Orlando (G-12569)
Scientific Instruments Inc ....E...... 561 881-8500
Mangonia Park (G-8100)
Sensidyne LP ....G...... 727 530-3602
Saint Petersburg (G-15180)
Sunoptic Technologies LLC...................D....... 877 677-2832
Jacksonville (G-6516)
Teledyne Flir LLC ....D....... 407 816-0091
Orlando (G-12649)

Tutela Monitoring Systems LLC ....G...... 941 462-1067
Spring Hill (G-16083)
Utilytech Company ....F...... 813 778-6952
Kissimmee (G-6970)
Wilkerson Instrument Co Inc ....F...... 863 647-2000
Lakeland (G-7473)
Xothermic Inc ....G...... 407 951-8008
Longwood (G-7961)

INSTRUMENTS: Infrared, Indl Process

Cv Technology Inc ....E...... 561 694-9588
Jupiter (G-6708)
Eltec Instruments Inc..........................E...... 386 252-0411
Daytona Beach (G-2549)
Infrared Associates Inc ....F...... 772 223-6670
Stuart (G-16166)

INSTRUMENTS: Instrument Relays, All Types

Creating Tech Solutions LLC.................G...... 727 914-3001
Clearwater (G-1555)
Creating Tech Solutions LLC.................E...... 727 914-3001
Clearwater (G-1554)

INSTRUMENTS: Laser, Scientific & Engineering

Belquette Inc ....G...... 727 329-9483
Clearwater (G-1516)
Data Buoy Instrumentation LLC ....G...... 239 849-7063
Cape Coral (G-1330)
Gam Laser Inc ....F...... 407 851-8999
Orlando (G-12181)
Haas Laser Technologies Inc.................G...... 954 529-7273
Weston (G-18252)
Infrared Systems Dev Corp ....F...... 407 679-5101
Winter Park (G-18515)
Marysol Technologies Inc ....G...... 727 712-1523
Clearwater (G-1685)
South Florida Institut ....G...... 305 668-2853
South Miami (G-16048)
St Johns Optical Systems LLC...............G...... 407 280-3787
Sanford (G-15390)
Twinstar Optics & Coatings Inc ....F...... 727 847-2300
Port Richey (G-14381)

INSTRUMENTS: Liquid Level, Indl Process

Kus Usa Inc ....E...... 954 463-1075
Davie (G-2431)

INSTRUMENTS: Measurement, Indl Process

Core Enterprises Incorporated ....G...... 954 227-0781
Coral Springs (G-2144)
Gas Turbine Efficiency LLC ....E...... 407 304-5200
Orlando (G-12183)
Pulsar Process Measurement Inc...........G...... 850 279-4882
Largo (G-7664)
Vertec Inc ....F...... 850 478-6480
Pensacola (G-13620)

INSTRUMENTS: Measuring & Controlling

Advanced Manufacturing Inc ....E...... 727 573-3300
Saint Petersburg (G-14954)
Airpro Diagnostics LLC.........................F...... 904 717-1711
Jacksonville (G-5871)
Alertgy Inc ....G...... 321 914-3199
Melbourne (G-8359)
Anton Paar Quantatec Inc ....G...... 561 731-4999
Boynton Beach (G-841)
Awe Diagnostics LLC ....E...... 786 285-0755
Miami (G-8782)
B & G Instruments Inc ....F...... 305 871-4445
Miami (G-8787)
Collins Research Inc............................F...... 321 401-6060
Orlando (G-12031)
Colloidal Dynamics LLC ....G...... 904 686-1536
Ponte Vedra Beach (G-14265)
Comten Industries Inc ....G...... 727 520-1200
Pinellas Park (G-13677)
Crumbliss Manufacturing Co.................F...... 239 693-8588
Fort Myers (G-4223)
Dynalco Controls Corporation...............E...... 323 589-6181
Fort Lauderdale (G-3775)
Emcee Electronics Inc.........................E...... 941 485-1515
Venice (G-17688)
Exploration Resources Intn Geo ....G...... 601 747-0726
Lake Mary (G-7073)
F & J Specialty Products Inc ....F...... 352 680-1177
Ocala (G-11385)

PRODUCT

Florida Level & Transit Co Inc ....G.... 813 623-3307
Tampa *(G-16847)*

Forceleader Inc ....G.... 727 521-1808
Pinellas Park *(G-13687)*

General Oceanics Inc ....F.... 305 621-2882
Miami *(G-9200)*

Gray Seismic Monitoring LLC ....F.... 904 728-3299
Jacksonville *(G-6625)*

Guardian Ign Interlock Mfg Inc ....D.... 321 205-1730
Cocoa *(G-1934)*

Hytronics Corp ....D.... 727 535-0413
Clearwater *(G-1635)*

Innovative Tech By Design Inc ....F.... 321 676-3194
Palm Bay *(G-12904)*

Intelligent Operating Tech Inc ....E.... 303 400-9640
Palm City *(G-13045)*

Invivo Corporation ....B.... 301 525-9683
Gainesville *(G-4713)*

IPC Global ....G.... 727 470-2134
Clearwater *(G-1648)*

James O Corbett Inc ....G.... 352 483-1222
Eustis *(G-3560)*

Life Proteomics Inc ....F.... 813 864-7646
Tampa *(G-17009)*

Lockheed Martin Corporation ....E.... 407 356-2000
Orlando *(G-12345)*

Magnetic Automation Corp ....E.... 321 635-8585
Rockledge *(G-14728)*

MC Miller Co Inc ....E.... 772 794-9448
Sebastian *(G-15900)*

Micro Typing Systems Inc ....E.... 954 970-9500
Pompano Beach *(G-14100)*

Molekule Inc ....C.... 352 871-3803
Tampa *(G-17082)*

Neubert Aero Corp ....G.... 352 345-4828
Brooksville *(G-1185)*

Parker Research Corporation ....F.... 727 796-4066
Clearwater *(G-1735)*

Pixe International Corp ....G.... 850 574-6469
Tallahassee *(G-16488)*

Quest Controls Inc ....F.... 941 729-4799
Palmetto *(G-13189)*

Redington Counters Inc ....G.... 954 725-6699
Deerfield Beach *(G-2797)*

Riegl Usa Inc ....E.... 407 248-9927
Winter Garden *(G-18403)*

Rieker LLC ....G.... 407 496-1555
Orlando *(G-12554)*

Scientific Instruments Inc ....E.... 561 881-8500
Mangonia Park *(G-8100)*

Select Engineered Systems Inc ....E.... 305 823-5410
Hialeah *(G-5343)*

Sensor Systems LLC ....C.... 727 347-2181
Saint Petersburg *(G-15181)*

Sepac Corp ....F.... 305 718-3379
Miami *(G-9868)*

Sigma Netics LLC ....G.... 954 473-2106
Davie *(G-2476)*

Smart Material Corp ....G.... 941 870-3337
Sarasota *(G-15831)*

Stellarnet Inc ....F.... 813 855-8687
Tampa *(G-17301)*

Superflow Inc ....G.... 786 238-8253
Miami Beach *(G-10238)*

Survey Supplies Inc ....G.... 305 477-1555
Doral *(G-3387)*

Tectron Engineering Company ....F.... 904 394-0683
Jacksonville *(G-6541)*

Thermo Arl US Inc ....E.... 800 532-4752
West Palm Beach *(G-18177)*

Tucker-Davis Technologies Inc ....E.... 386 462-9622
Alachua *(G-23)*

Veracity Tech Solutions LLC ....F.... 402 658-4113
Pensacola *(G-13618)*

World Precision Instrs LLC ....E.... 941 371-1003
Sarasota *(G-15879)*

INSTRUMENTS: Measuring Electricity

Amascott LLC ....G.... 352 683-4895
Spring Hill *(G-16062)*

CPS Products Inc ....D.... 305 687-4121
Miramar *(G-10482)*

Crumbliss Manufacturing Co ....F.... 239 693-8588
Fort Myers *(G-4223)*

Crystek Crystals Corporation ....E.... 239 561-3311
Fort Myers *(G-4224)*

Dynalco Controls Corporation ....E.... 323 589-6181
Fort Lauderdale *(G-3775)*

Hid Global Corp ....F.... 561 622-9013
Palm Beach Gardens *(G-12973)*

Klaaventura LLC ....G.... 305 931-2322
Miami *(G-9392)*

L3harris Interstate Elec Corp ....E.... 321 730-0119
Cocoa Beach *(G-1973)*

Logus Manufacturing Corp ....E.... 561 842-3550
West Palm Beach *(G-18060)*

MC Miller Co Inc ....E.... 772 794-9448
Sebastian *(G-15900)*

Measurements International Inc ....E.... 315 393-1323
Lake Mary *(G-7093)*

Nci ....G.... 813 749-1799
Tampa *(G-17105)*

Optronic Laboratories LLC ....F.... 407 422-3171
Orlando *(G-12444)*

Piezo Technology Inc ....D.... 407 298-2000
Orlando *(G-12486)*

Salco Industries Inc ....F.... 941 377-7717
Sarasota *(G-15806)*

Semilab USA LLC ....E.... 813 977-2244
Temple Terrace *(G-17545)*

Smartsat Inc ....F.... 727 535-6880
Largo *(G-7684)*

T & M Atlantic Inc ....G.... 786 332-4773
Miami *(G-9987)*

Techtron Corporation ....F.... 239 513-0800
Naples *(G-10922)*

Tektronix Inc ....F.... 407 660-2727
Maitland *(G-8075)*

Universal Microwave Corp ....E.... 352 754-2200
Brooksville *(G-1216)*

W & W Manufacturing Co ....G.... 516 942-0011
Tampa *(G-17420)*

Wdc Miami Inc ....G.... 305 884-2800
Medley *(G-8351)*

INSTRUMENTS: Measuring, Electrical Energy

Data Flow Systems Inc ....D.... 321 259-5009
Melbourne *(G-8397)*

Energy Control Tech Inc ....G.... 954 739-8400
Davie *(G-2406)*

Omega Power Systems Inc ....G.... 772 219-0045
Stuart *(G-16191)*

Sota Manufacturing Inc ....G.... 561 368-8007
Boca Raton *(G-685)*

Technical International Corp ....G.... 305 374-1054
Miami *(G-9996)*

Vertiv Corporation ....D.... 954 377-7101
Sunrise *(G-16389)*

INSTRUMENTS: Measuring, Electrical Power

AB Ampere Industrial Panels ....G.... 904 379-4168
Yulee *(G-18586)*

Belle Glade Electric Motor Svc ....G.... 561 996-3333
Belle Glade *(G-339)*

TCS Electrical Co ....F.... 844 827-1040
Fort Walton Beach *(G-4611)*

INSTRUMENTS: Medical & Surgical

3d Medical Manufacturing Inc ....C.... 561 842-7175
Riviera Beach *(G-14584)*

Aaron Medical Industries Inc ....F.... 727 384-2323
Saint Petersburg *(G-14951)*

Abbott Labs US Sbsdries Alere ....D.... 877 441-7440
Orlando *(G-11859)*

ABC Enterprises ....G.... 407 656-6503
Oakland *(G-11226)*

Adatif Medical Incorporated ....F.... 561 840-0395
Riviera Beach *(G-14586)*

Advanced Prosthetics Amer Inc ....F.... 904 269-4993
Orange Park *(G-11811)*

Advantage Medical Elec LLC ....G.... 954 345-9800
Coral Springs *(G-2127)*

Ahc Ventures Corp ....F.... 954 978-9290
Margate *(G-8118)*

Aiolos Group Inc ....G.... 305 496-7674
Miami *(G-8668)*

Airon Corporation ....G.... 321 821-9433
Melbourne *(G-8358)*

Alicia Diagnostic Inc ....F.... 407 365-8498
Chuluota *(G-1463)*

Amend Surgical Inc ....F.... 844 281-3169
Alachua *(G-2)*

Anew International Corporation ....F.... 386 668-7785
Debary *(G-2631)*

Apollo Renal Therapeutics LLC ....E.... 202 413-0963
Ocala *(G-11326)*

Apyx Medical Corporation ....C.... 727 384-2323
Clearwater *(G-1496)*

Arthrex Inc ....C.... 239 643-5553
Naples *(G-10674)*

Arthrex California Inc ....F.... 239 643-5553
Naples *(G-10675)*

Arthrex Trauma Inc ....F.... 239 643-5553
Naples *(G-10677)*

Avra Medical Robotics Inc ....F.... 407 956-2250
Orlando *(G-11937)*

B & M Precision Inc ....B.... 813 645-1188
Ruskin *(G-14774)*

B Braun Medical Inc ....E.... 386 274-1837
Daytona Beach *(G-2516)*

B Braun Medical Inc ....E.... 386 888-2000
Daytona Beach *(G-2517)*

B Braun Medical Inc ....E.... 866 388-5120
Daytona Beach *(G-2518)*

B F Industries Inc ....E.... 561 368-6662
Boca Raton *(G-423)*

Back Lory Lee ....G.... 850 638-5430
Chipley *(G-1453)*

Bestest International Inc ....F.... 714 974-8837
Saint Augustine *(G-14815)*

Bio Ceps Inc ....G.... 727 669-7544
Clearwater *(G-1520)*

Bio-Logic Systems Corp ....D.... 847 949-0456
Orlando *(G-11951)*

Bioderm Inc ....G.... 727 507-7655
Largo *(G-7550)*

Bionebicine Corp ....G.... 401 648-0695
Saint Petersburg *(G-14983)*

Biosculpture Technology Inc ....E.... 561 651-7816
West Palm Beach *(G-17946)*

Bolton Medical Inc ....B.... 954 838-9699
Sunrise *(G-16300)*

Bowen Medical Services Inc ....G.... 386 362-1345
Live Oak *(G-7842)*

Breathing Systems Inc ....G.... 850 477-2324
Pensacola *(G-13462)*

Central Fla Attrnsfsonists Inc ....G.... 321 299-6019
Oviedo *(G-12812)*

Cerenovas Inc ....E.... 800 255-2500
Miami *(G-8914)*

CMF Medicon Surgical Inc ....G.... 904 642-7500
Jacksonville *(G-5987)*

Command Medical Products Inc ....C.... 386 677-7775
Ormond Beach *(G-12752)*

Contract Mfg Solutions Inc ....F.... 954 424-9813
Weston *(G-18234)*

Cordis Corporation ....C.... 786 313-2000
Miami Lakes *(G-10293)*

Corin USA Limited Inc ....F.... 813 977-4469
Tampa *(G-16730)*

Critical Disposables Inc ....E.... 407 330-1154
Sanford *(G-15297)*

Custom Medical Products Inc ....G.... 407 865-7211
Apopka *(G-119)*

Depuy Synthes Products Inc ....F.... 305 265-6842
Miami *(G-9018)*

Derm-Buro Inc ....E.... 305 953-4025
Hialeah *(G-5114)*

Dhss LLC ....E.... 305 405-4001
North Miami Beach *(G-11133)*

Diabetex Care ....G.... 954 427-9510
Deerfield Beach *(G-2706)*

Digicare Biomedical Tech Inc ....G.... 561 689-0408
Boynton Beach *(G-856)*

Doctor Easy Medical Pdts LLC ....G.... 904 276-7200
Orange Park *(G-11823)*

Dwyer Precision Products Inc ....F.... 904 249-3545
Jacksonville *(G-6051)*

EM Adams Inc ....D.... 772 468-6550
Fort Pierce *(G-4483)*

Emcyte Corp ....E.... 239 481-7725
Fort Myers *(G-4246)*

Eusa Global LLC ....G.... 786 483-7490
Medley *(G-8238)*

Evren Technologies Inc ....G.... 352 494-0950
Newberry *(G-11020)*

Flospine LLC ....G.... 561 705-3080
Boca Raton *(G-520)*

Gaumard Scientific Company Inc ....E.... 305 971-3790
Miami *(G-9192)*

Geddis Inc ....F.... 800 844-6792
Dunedin *(G-3450)*

Genicon Inc ....E.... 407 657-4851
Orlando *(G-12193)*

Globalink Mfg Solutions ....F.... 239 455-5166
Naples *(G-10763)*

Gremed Group Corp ....F.... 305 392-5331
Doral *(G-3240)*

Gyrx LLC ....F 904 641-2599
Jacksonville *(G-6162)*

Halma Holdings Inc ....E 973 832-2658
Seminole *(G-15976)*

Harts Mobility LLC ....G 404 769-4234
Port St Lucie *(G-14476)*

Health Star Inc ....G 321 914-6012
Merritt Island *(G-8586)*

Hnm Medical LLC ....E 866 291-8498
Miami *(G-9288)*

Howmedica Osteonics Corp ....C 954 714-7933
Fort Lauderdale *(G-3869)*

Hti ....G 941 723-4570
Palmetto *(G-13174)*

Hurricane Medical Inc ....E 941 753-1517
Bradenton *(G-993)*

Hydrogel Vision Corporation ....D 941 739-1382
Sarasota *(G-15496)*

Hygreen Inc ....F 352 327-9747
Gainesville *(G-4708)*

Imaging Diagnostic Systems Inc ...F 954 581-9800
Orlando *(G-12237)*

Innfocus Inc ....F 305 378-2651
Miami *(G-9315)*

Innomed Technologies Inc ....G 800 200-9842
Coconut Creek *(G-1991)*

Innovative Mfg Solutions LLC ......G 904 647-5300
Jacksonville *(G-6199)*

Inspired Therapeutics LLC ....G 339 222-0847
Melbourne Beach *(G-8567)*

Integrity Implants Inc ....E 561 529-3861
Palm Beach Gardens *(G-12978)*

Intermed Group Inc ....E 561 586-3667
Alachua *(G-12)*

International Medical Inds Inc ....E 954 917-9570
Pompano Beach *(G-14063)*

Invo Bioscience Inc ....G 978 878-9505
Lakewood Ranch *(G-7484)*

Iris International Inc ....D 818 709-1244
Miami *(G-9338)*

Ispg Inc ....F 941 896-3999
Bradenton *(G-998)*

Ivan & Ivan LLC ....G 305 507-8793
Doral *(G-3263)*

Jepsen Tool Company Inc ....F 904 262-2793
Jacksonville *(G-6223)*

Jimenez Enterprises Group ....E 561 391-6800
Parkland *(G-13348)*

JTL Enterprises (delaware) ....E 727 536-5566
Clearwater *(G-1656)*

Kalitec Direct LLC ....G 407 545-2063
Oviedo *(G-12832)*

Kawasumi Laboratories Amer Inc ...F 813 630-5554
Tampa *(G-16977)*

Klyo Medical Systems Inc ....F 305 330-5025
Doral *(G-3275)*

Kms Medical LLC ....F 305 266-3388
Miami *(G-9394)*

Kollsut International Inc ....G 305 438-6877
North Miami Beach *(G-11147)*

Lane Care LLC ....F 727 316-3708
Palm Harbor *(G-13118)*

Laser Surgical Florida Inc ....G 954 609-7633
Miami *(G-9429)*

Led Technologies Incorporated .....F 800 337-9565
Largo *(G-7632)*

Lenkbar LLC ....D 239 732-5915
Naples *(G-10803)*

Lensar Inc ....E 888 536-7271
Orlando *(G-12322)*

Liviliti Health Products Corp ....G 888 987-0744
Lake City *(G-7029)*

Lumenis Ltd ....F 305 508-5052
Miami *(G-9483)*

Marina Medical Instruments Inc ....E 954 924-4418
Davie *(G-2436)*

Martin-Weston Co ....F 727 545-8877
Largo *(G-7638)*

Maven Medical Mfg Inc ....E 727 518-0555
Largo *(G-7639)*

MC Johnson Co ....F 239 293-0901
Naples *(G-10815)*

Medic Healthcare LLC ....G 954 336-1776
Fort Lauderdale *(G-3935)*

Medica360 LLC ....G 941 500-2890
Osprey *(G-12802)*

Medical Energy Inc ....G 850 313-6277
Pensacola *(G-13547)*

Medical Magnetics Inc ....F 954 565-8500
Fort Lauderdale *(G-3936)*

Medine Industries LP ....F 863 337-4797
Auburndale *(G-241)*

Medone Surgical Inc ....F 941 359-3129
Sarasota *(G-15516)*

Medrx Inc ....E 727 584-9600
Largo *(G-7641)*

Medtrnic Sofamor Danek USA Inc ...G 904 645-6925
Jacksonville *(G-6290)*

Medtronic ....D 305 818-4100
Miami Lakes *(G-10320)*

Medtronic Inc ....F 904 296-9600
Jacksonville *(G-6291)*

Medtronic Usa Inc ....A 702 308-1302
Jacksonville *(G-6292)*

Medtronic Usa Inc ....A 786 709-4200
Doral *(G-3296)*

Mergenet Medical Inc ....E 561 208-3770
Deerfield Beach *(G-2765)*

Merlola Industries LLC ....G 888 418-0408
Miami *(G-9537)*

Micro Tool & Engineering Inc ....F 561 842-7381
Riviera Beach *(G-14646)*

Microtek Medical Inc ....B 904 741-2964
Jacksonville *(G-6304)*

Motus Gi LLC ....G 954 541-8000
Fort Lauderdale *(G-3945)*

Motus GI Holdings Inc ....G 954 541-8000
Fort Lauderdale *(G-3946)*

N E D LLC ....G 610 442-1017
Boca Raton *(G-607)*

Nb Products Inc ....E 904 807-0140
Jacksonville *(G-6321)*

Neocis Inc ....D 855 963-6247
Miami *(G-9611)*

Neurotronics Inc ....G 352 372-9955
Alachua *(G-15)*

New Wave Surgical Corp ....F 866 346-8883
Coral Springs *(G-2195)*

Nkem Inc ....G 800 582-0707
Sarasota *(G-15762)*

Nouveau Cosmetique Usa Inc ......G 321 332-6976
Orlando *(G-12424)*

Oculus Surgical Inc ....E 772 236-2622
Port St Lucie *(G-14480)*

One Milo Inc ....G 305 804-0266
Miami *(G-9651)*

Opko Curna LLC ....G 305 575-4100
Miami *(G-9659)*

Orbusneich Medical Inc ....E 954 730-0711
Fort Lauderdale *(G-3969)*

Oscor Inc ....C 727 937-2511
Palm Harbor *(G-13122)*

Parcus Medical LLC ....F 941 755-7965
Sarasota *(G-15531)*

Ped-Stuart Corporation ....E 352 754-6001
Brooksville *(G-1188)*

Pedicraft Inc ....F 904 348-3170
Jacksonville *(G-6362)*

Perry Baromedical Corporation .....E 561 840-0395
Riviera Beach *(G-14660)*

Pioneer Surgical Technology ....F 906 225-5629
Alachua *(G-17)*

Polyhistor International Inc ....G 904 646-5666
Jacksonville *(G-6377)*

Precision Machine Tech LLC ....F 305 594-1789
Doral *(G-3334)*

Professional Pet Products Inc ....E 305 592-1992
Doral *(G-3339)*

Promedica Inc ....B 813 854-1905
Oldsmar *(G-11694)*

Qhslab Inc ....G 929 379-6503
West Palm Beach *(G-18134)*

Quick-Med Technologies Inc ....G 352 379-0611
Gainesville *(G-4753)*

Radiaction Inc ....F 561 351-3697
Dania Beach *(G-2359)*

Regeneration Technologies Inc .....E 386 418-8888
Alachua *(G-18)*

Rhythm Healthcare LLC ....F 877 843-6464
Saint Petersburg *(G-15174)*

Rolls Axle Lc ....G 813 764-0242
Plant City *(G-13801)*

Rti Donor Services Inc ....C 321 431-2464
Melbourne *(G-8512)*

Rti Surgical Inc ....C 386 418-8888
Alachua *(G-19)*

Rxenergy LLC ....F 727 726-4204
Clearwater *(G-1774)*

S4j Manufacturing Services Inc .....F 239 574-9400
Cape Coral *(G-1379)*

Savvy Associate Inc ....F 954 941-6986
Pompano Beach *(G-14167)*

Shl Pharma LLC ....E 954 725-2008
Deerfield Beach *(G-2808)*

Simplified Systems Inc ....F 305 672-7676
Miami Beach *(G-10227)*

Sky Medical Inc ....F 954 747-3188
Sunrise *(G-16366)*

Sleepmed Incorporated ....E 941 361-3035
Sarasota *(G-15830)*

Spacelabs Healthcare Inc ....E 904 786-5113
Jacksonville *(G-6497)*

Speranza Therapeutics Corp ....F 844 477-3726
Boca Raton *(G-690)*

Strena Medical LLC ....G 305 406-3931
Doral *(G-3379)*

Stryker Orthopedics ....G 904 296-6000
Jacksonville *(G-6513)*

Summit Orthopedic Tech Inc ....E 239 919-8081
Naples *(G-10909)*

Sun Coast Surgical & Med Sup .....G 813 881-0065
Tampa *(G-17307)*

Sunoptic Technologies LLC ....D 877 677-2832
Jacksonville *(G-6516)*

Surgimed Corporation ....F 912 674-7660
Coral Springs *(G-2216)*

Synold LLC ....G 305 266-3388
Miami *(G-9986)*

Techtrade LLC ....G 201 706-8130
Orlando *(G-12647)*

Tequesta Community Health Ctr ....E 561 713-0798
Jupiter *(G-6807)*

Tutogen Medical Inc ....E 386 418-8888
Alachua *(G-24)*

Ultra Clean Systems Inc ....F 813 925-1003
Oldsmar *(G-11700)*

Ultroid Technologies Inc ....G 877 858-0555
Tampa *(G-17386)*

Universal HM Hlth Indus Sups I .....G 813 493-7904
Tampa *(G-17393)*

Universal Surgical Appliance ....G 305 652-0810
Miami *(G-10074)*

Uroshape LLC ....F 321 960-2484
Melbourne *(G-8555)*

Vgi Medical LLC ....F 727 565-1235
Largo *(G-7702)*

Vital Usa Inc ....F 561 282-6074
West Palm Beach *(G-18199)*

Vivonex LLC ....D 210 695-9244
Key Largo *(G-6852)*

Viztek Inc ....F 904 448-9936
Jacksonville *(G-6595)*

Vuessence Inc ....G 813 792-7123
Odessa *(G-11591)*

Wayne Metal Products Inc ....G 407 321-7168
Sanford *(G-15408)*

Xhale Inc ....G 352 371-8488
Gainesville *(G-4785)*

Xymogen Manufacturing LLC ....G 800 647-6100
Orlando *(G-12726)*

Ziptek LLC ....F 941 953-5509
Sarasota *(G-15881)*

INSTRUMENTS: Meters, Integrating Electricity

Frank Theodore Johanson ....F 800 607-0690
West Palm Beach *(G-18012)*

INSTRUMENTS: Nautical

Kus Usa Inc ....E 954 463-1075
Davie *(G-2431)*

Ocean Test Equipment Inc ....G 954 474-6603
Davie *(G-2449)*

Waterproof Charters Inc ....G 941 639-7626
Punta Gorda *(G-14539)*

INSTRUMENTS: Power Measuring, Electrical

Relm Communications Inc ....C 321 953-7800
Melbourne *(G-8510)*

INSTRUMENTS: Radio Frequency Measuring

Hid Global Corporation ....E 954 990-2782
Fort Lauderdale *(G-3865)*

Locus Diagnostics LLC ....F 321 727-3077
Melbourne *(G-8463)*

Pinnacle Cmmncations Group LLC ...F 904 910-0444
Jacksonville *(G-6372)*

P
R
O
D
U
C
T

INSTRUMENTS: Standards & Calibration, Electrical Measuring

Rail Scale Inc ....E 904 302-5154
  Saint Augustine *(G-14876)*

INSTRUMENTS: Temperature Measurement, Indl

Chilly Willys Heating & A Inc ....G 904 772-1164
  Jacksonville *(G-5979)*
Cobex Recorders Inc ....F 954 425-0003
  Coconut Creek *(G-1981)*
Ipeg Corporation ....F 239 963-1470
  Naples *(G-10786)*

INSTRUMENTS: Test, Digital, Electronic & Electrical Circuits

Florida Veex Inc ....F 727 442-6677
  Largo *(G-7588)*
Sjostrom Industries Inc ....F 561 368-2000
  Boca Raton *(G-681)*
Tucker-Davis Technologies Inc ....E 386 462-9622
  Alachua *(G-23)*
Victus Capital Enterprises Inc ....F 727 442-6677
  Saint Petersburg *(G-15227)*

INSTRUMENTS: Test, Electrical, Engine

Corporate One Hundred Inc ....E 352 335-0901
  Gainesville *(G-4672)*

INSTRUMENTS: Test, Electronic & Electric Measurement

Core Enterprises Incorporated ....G 954 227-0781
  Coral Springs *(G-2144)*
EMC Test Design LLC ....G 508 292-1833
  Sarasota *(G-15664)*
Indra Systems Inc ....E 407 567-1977
  Orlando *(G-12241)*
L3harris Interstate Elec Corp ....D 321 730-0119
  Cape Canaveral *(G-1288)*
Pdma Corporation ....E 813 621-6463
  Tampa *(G-17152)*
Peak Electronics Inc ....G 305 888-1588
  Miami *(G-9700)*
Testmaxx Services Corporation ....F 954 946-7100
  Fort Lauderdale *(G-4088)*

INSTRUMENTS: Test, Electronic & Electrical Circuits

I C Probotics Inc ....D 407 339-8298
  Longwood *(G-7902)*
Kobetron LLC ....F 850 939-5222
  Navarre *(G-10951)*
Mc Assembly International LLC ....F 321 253-0541
  Melbourne *(G-8471)*
Optoelectronics Inc ....F 954 642-8997
  Boca Raton *(G-625)*
Ra Co AMO Inc ....F 561 626-7232
  Palm Beach Gardens *(G-13004)*
Servos and Simulation Inc ....G 407 807-0208
  Longwood *(G-7947)*

INSTRUMENTS: Vibration

Roper Technologies Inc ....E 941 556-2601
  Sarasota *(G-15801)*

INSULATING BOARD, CELLULAR FIBER

Chicago Electronic Distrs Inc ....F 312 985-6175
  Port Charlotte *(G-14292)*

INSULATING COMPOUNDS

Southeast Intl Chem Co Inc ....G 904 992-4007
  Jacksonville *(G-6483)*

INSULATION & CUSHIONING FOAM: Polystyrene

Atlantic Insulation Inc ....D 904 354-2217
  Jacksonville *(G-5908)*
Carpenter Co ....D 863 687-9494
  Lakeland *(G-7288)*
Coastal Foam Systems LLC ....G 850 470-9827
  Pensacola *(G-13472)*

Compsys Inc ....D 321 255-0399
  Melbourne *(G-8393)*
Foam Masters Inc ....E 239 403-0755
  Naples *(G-10749)*
Future Foam Inc ....D 407 857-2510
  Orlando *(G-12178)*
Hickory Springs Mfg Co ....D 352 622-7583
  Ocala *(G-11409)*
Imperial Foam & Insul Mfg Co ....D 386 673-4177
  Ormond Beach *(G-12772)*
Kingspan Insulation LLC ....D 305 921-0100
  Opa Locka *(G-11760)*

INSULATION & ROOFING MATERIALS: Wood, Reconstituted

Marsig Group Inc ....G 813 840-3714
  Lutz *(G-8002)*
Polyglass USA Inc ....D 954 246-8888
  Deerfield Beach *(G-2784)*
Standard Industries Inc ....G 813 248-7000
  Tampa *(G-17298)*

INSULATION MATERIALS WHOLESALERS

Carpenter Co ....G 863 687-9494
  Lakeland *(G-7288)*

INSULATION: Fiberglass

Owens Corning Sales LLC ....E 863 291-3046
  Winter Haven *(G-18453)*
Ryan Scientific LLC ....F 904 284-6025
  Green Cove Springs *(G-4835)*

INSULATORS & INSULATION MATERIALS: Electrical

Gamma Insulators Corp ....G 585 302-0878
  Coral Gables *(G-2059)*
Insulator Seal Incorporated ....E 941 751-2880
  Sarasota *(G-15502)*

INSULATORS, PORCELAIN: Electrical

Famatel USA LLC ....G 754 217-4841
  Medley *(G-8240)*
Insulator Seal Incorporated ....E 941 751-2880
  Sarasota *(G-15502)*

INSURANCE: Agents, Brokers & Service

Stripping Alpaca LLC ....F 207 208-9687
  Miami Beach *(G-10236)*

INTEGRATED CIRCUITS, SEMICONDUCTOR NETWORKS, ETC

Advanced Micro Devices Inc ....F 407 541-6800
  Orlando *(G-11870)*
Akuwa Solutions Group Inc ....F 941 343-9947
  Sarasota *(G-15589)*
Hybrid Sources Inc ....F 772 563-9100
  Vero Beach *(G-17760)*
L3harris Technologies Inc ....B 321 727-9100
  Melbourne *(G-8455)*
Solitron Devices Inc ....D 561 848-4311
  West Palm Beach *(G-18158)*
Source 1 Solutions Inc ....D 727 538-4114
  Clearwater *(G-1787)*
Visiontech Components LLC ....F 727 547-5466
  Clearwater *(G-1845)*
Wafer World Inc ....F 561 842-4441
  West Palm Beach *(G-18201)*

INTERCOMMUNICATIONS SYSTEMS: Electric

Access Wrless Data Sltions LLC ....G 813 751-2039
  Lutz *(G-7981)*
Acoustic Communications LLC ....G 305 463-9485
  Doral *(G-3095)*
Attenti Us Inc ....D 813 749-5454
  Odessa *(G-11538)*
Automation Consulting Inc ....F 850 477-6477
  Pensacola *(G-13449)*
AVI-Spl Holdings Inc ....A 866 708-5034
  Tampa *(G-16619)*
AVI-Spl LLC ....B 813 884-7168
  Tampa *(G-16620)*
Gresso LLC ....G 305 515-8677
  Miami *(G-9248)*

Lugloc LLC ....F 305 961-1765
  Miami *(G-9482)*
Padgett Communications Inc ....E 727 323-5800
  Tampa *(G-17141)*
Smiths Interconnect Inc ....C 813 901-7200
  Tampa *(G-17276)*
Two Way Radio Gear Inc ....F 800 984-1534
  Fort Pierce *(G-4547)*
Vecom Usa LLC ....G 813 901-5300
  Tampa *(G-17404)*
Walkup Enterprises Inc ....F 727 571-1244
  Clearwater *(G-1847)*

INTERIOR DECORATING SVCS

Fleurissima Inc ....F 305 572-0203
  Miami *(G-9149)*

INTERIOR DESIGN SVCS, NEC

Hygenator Pillow Service Inc ....G 305 325-0250
  Miami *(G-9294)*
Lastrada Furniture Inc ....F 954 485-6000
  Fort Lauderdale *(G-3912)*

INTERIOR DESIGNING SVCS

Thayer Industries Inc ....G 813 719-6597
  Dundee *(G-3438)*

INVERTERS: Nonrotating Electrical

GOTG LLC ....G 800 381-4684
  Brooksville *(G-1159)*

INVERTERS: Rotating Electrical

Multi-Commercial Services Corp ....G 305 235-1373
  Miami *(G-9600)*

INVESTMENT ADVISORY SVCS

Italian Rose Garlic Pdts LLC ....C 561 863-5556
  Riviera Beach *(G-14632)*

IRON & STEEL PRDTS: Hot-Rolled

Garcia Iron Works ....G 305 888-0080
  Hialeah *(G-5167)*
Gerdau Ameristeel US Inc ....B 813 286-8383
  Tampa *(G-16877)*
Gerdau USA Inc ....B 813 286-8383
  Tampa *(G-16878)*
Techno Trading Manufacturing ....G 689 777-0755
  Deland *(G-2909)*

IRON ORE MINING

Tyrex Ore & Minerals Company ....G 305 333-5288
  Miami *(G-10053)*
US Iron LLC ....F 765 210-4111
  Miramar Beach *(G-10574)*

IRON ORE PELLETIZING

Meelko Co ....G 845 600-3379
  Opa Locka *(G-11767)*

IRON ORES

Chemours Company Fc LLC ....D 904 964-1200
  Starke *(G-16099)*

IRRIGATION EQPT WHOLESALERS

Robert E Weissenborn Sr ....G 239 262-1771
  Naples *(G-10879)*

IRRIGATION SYSTEMS, NEC Water Distribution Or Sply Systems

Eagle Engrg & Land Dev Inc ....F 913 948-4320
  Boynton Beach *(G-860)*
Sergeant Bretts Coffee LLC ....G 561 451-0048
  Coconut Creek *(G-2004)*

JACKS: Hydraulic

Sealift LLC ....F 321 638-0301
  Merritt Island *(G-8596)*

JANITORIAL & CUSTODIAL SVCS

Slg Solutions Inc ....G 786 379-4676
  Miami *(G-9904)*

JANITORIAL EQPT & SPLYS WHOLESALERS

Skymo LLC ....G....... 305 676-6739
Cooper City *(G-2022)*

JARS: Plastic

Tupperware US Inc ....D...... 407 826-5050
Orlando *(G-12681)*

JEWELERS' FINDINGS & MATERIALS

Modern Settings LLC ....G...... 800 645-5585
Sarasota *(G-15750)*
Our Warehouse Inc ....G...... 954 786-1234
Pompano Beach *(G-14113)*

JEWELERS' FINDINGS & MATERIALS: Castings

Roma Casting Inc......................................G...... 305 577-0289
Miami *(G-9821)*

JEWELERS' FINDINGS & MTLS: Jewel Prep, Instr, Tools, Watches

Adamas Instrument Corporation...........F...... 727 540-0033
Clearwater *(G-1474)*

JEWELRY & PRECIOUS STONES WHOLESALERS

Accar Ltd Inc ....G...... 305 375-0620
Miami *(G-8641)*
Buvin Jewelry Florida Inc ....F...... 305 358-0170
Miami *(G-8866)*

JEWELRY APPAREL

Arty-Sun LLC...G...... 561 705-2222
Boca Raton *(G-416)*
Corporcion Intrncnal De Jyas V ....G...... 772 343-1721
Port Saint Lucie *(G-14406)*
Finger Mate Inc...E...... 954 458-2700
Hallandale Beach *(G-4945)*
Gnj Manufacturing Inc ....E...... 305 651-8644
West Park *(G-18212)*
Too Many Ideas Inc ....G...... 904 396-9245
Jacksonville *(G-6559)*
Zulkifal Kiani LLC ....F...... 765 291-4529
Saint Petersburg *(G-15245)*

JEWELRY FINDINGS & LAPIDARY WORK

Finger Mate Inc...E...... 954 458-2700
Hallandale Beach *(G-4945)*
Jewelnet Corp ....G...... 561 989-8383
Delray Beach *(G-2977)*
Marios Casting Jewelry Inc......................G...... 305 374-2894
Miami *(G-9513)*
National Custom Insignia Inc...................F...... 813 313-2561
Tampa *(G-17099)*

JEWELRY REPAIR SVCS

Amber Jewelers Corp ....G...... 305 373-8089
Miami *(G-8711)*

JEWELRY STORES

Finger Mate Inc...E...... 954 458-2700
Hallandale Beach *(G-4945)*
Patrice Inc...F...... 941 359-2577
Sarasota *(G-15775)*

JEWELRY STORES: Precious Stones & Precious Metals

Cabus USA Inc ....G...... 305 681-0872
North Miami *(G-11096)*
Jon Paul Inc..G...... 954 564-4221
Fort Lauderdale *(G-3897)*
Marios Casting Jewelry Inc......................G...... 305 374-2894
Miami *(G-9513)*
Neptune Designs Inc ....G...... 305 294-8131
Key West *(G-6878)*

JEWELRY STORES: Watches

Original Pnguin Drect Oprtions ....F...... 305 592-2830
Doral *(G-3319)*

JEWELRY, PRECIOUS METAL: Bracelets

Montesino International Corp ....G....... 954 767-6185
Fort Lauderdale *(G-3944)*
Zedora Inc ....E...... 954 332-3322
Fort Lauderdale *(G-4143)*

JEWELRY, PRECIOUS METAL: Cigar & Cigarette Access

Burn By Rocky Patel..............................G....... 239 653-9013
Naples *(G-10701)*
Lightfire Holdings LLC ....G...... 866 375-0541
Tamarac *(G-16535)*
Orlando Novelty LLC ....G...... 407 858-9499
Orlando *(G-12454)*
Smokersvaporcom Incorporated..........G...... 727 258-4942
Largo *(G-7685)*

JEWELRY, PRECIOUS METAL: Cigarette Lighters

Sunshine Lighters.....................................G...... 386 322-1300
Port Orange *(G-14351)*

JEWELRY, PRECIOUS METAL: Medals, Precious Or Semiprecious

Larter & Sons ....D...... 732 290-1515
Jupiter *(G-6755)*
Williams Jewelry and Mfg Co...................G...... 727 823-7676
Saint Petersburg *(G-15234)*

JEWELRY, PRECIOUS METAL: Necklaces

Liza Gold Corp ....G...... 305 885-0731
Hialeah *(G-5225)*
Richline Group Inc ....B...... 954 718-3200
Tamarac *(G-16540)*

JEWELRY, PRECIOUS METAL: Settings & Mountings

Amber Jewelers Corp ....G...... 305 373-8089
Miami *(G-8711)*

JEWELRY, WHOLESALE

Hidalgo Corp ....G...... 305 379-0110
Miami *(G-9279)*
International Jwly Designs Inc ....G...... 954 577-9099
Oakland Park *(G-11273)*
James A De Flippo Co ....G...... 407 851-2765
Orlando *(G-12265)*
OCon Enterprise Inc ....D...... 954 920-6700
Hollywood *(G-5635)*
Our Warehouse Inc ....G...... 954 786-1234
Pompano Beach *(G-14113)*
Phoenix Jewelry Mfg Inc ....F...... 305 477-2515
Doral *(G-3327)*

JEWELRY: Decorative, Fashion & Costume

D Turin & Company Inc ....E...... 305 825-2004
Hialeah *(G-5106)*
Galaxy Medals Inc ....G...... 321 269-0840
Titusville *(G-17586)*
International Jwly Designs Inc ....G...... 954 577-9099
Oakland Park *(G-11273)*
Liza Gold Corp ....G...... 305 885-0731
Hialeah *(G-5225)*
Magnetic Jewellry Inc ....G...... 954 975-5868
Pompano Beach *(G-14084)*
Patrice Inc...F...... 941 359-2577
Sarasota *(G-15775)*
Swatch Group Caribbean ....F...... 877 839-5224
Miami *(G-9980)*

JEWELRY: Precious Metal

Accar Ltd Inc ....G...... 305 375-0620
Miami *(G-8641)*
American Diamond Distributors ....G...... 954 485-7808
Fort Lauderdale *(G-3649)*
Arriaga Originals ....F...... 850 231-0084
Panama City *(G-13323)*
Bashert Diamonds Inc ....G...... 305 466-1881
Aventura *(G-255)*
Bullion International Inc ....C...... 321 773-2727
Indian Harbour Beach *(G-5804)*
Buvin Jewelry Florida Inc ....F...... 305 358-0170
Miami *(G-8866)*

Classique Style Inc ....G...... 561 995-7557
Boca Raton *(G-464)*
D Turin & Company Inc ....E...... 305 825-2004
Hialeah *(G-5106)*
Delevoes Lobby LLC ....F...... 305 906-0475
Havana *(G-5000)*
Deluxe Gems LLC ....G...... 407 513-2004
Windermere *(G-18349)*
Dolphine Jewelry Contracting ....G...... 561 488-0355
Boca Raton *(G-490)*
Evan Lloyd Designs..................................G...... 772 286-7723
Stuart *(G-16147)*
Golden Century Inc ....G...... 954 933-2911
Margate *(G-8133)*
Green Bullion Fincl Svcs LLC ....G...... 954 960-7000
Hollywood *(G-5584)*
Hidalgo Corp ....G...... 305 379-0110
Miami *(G-9279)*
Jld Manufacturing Corp............................G...... 877 358-5462
Sunrise *(G-16331)*
Jon Paul Inc..G...... 954 564-4221
Fort Lauderdale *(G-3897)*
Lau International Inc ....G...... 305 381-9855
Miami *(G-9438)*
Marios Casting Jewelry Inc ....G...... 305 374-2894
Miami *(G-9513)*
Mayers Jwly Co Hollywood Inc................E...... 954 921-1422
Hollywood *(G-5623)*
Merit Diamond Corporation ....E...... 954 883-3660
Hollywood *(G-5625)*
Metal Rock Inc ....F...... 407 886-6440
Apopka *(G-150)*
Moba Corp ....F...... 305 868-3700
Bal Harbour *(G-295)*
Neptune Designs Inc ....G...... 305 294-8131
Key West *(G-6878)*
OCon Enterprise Inc ....D...... 954 920-6700
Hollywood *(G-5635)*
Phoenix Jewelry Mfg Inc ....F...... 305 477-2515
Doral *(G-3327)*
Reese Corporation ....G...... 305 653-1000
Parkland *(G-13352)*
Reyes Jewelers Corp.................................G...... 305 431-8303
Miami *(G-9802)*
Roma Casting Inc......................................G...... 305 577-0289
Miami *(G-9821)*
Sal Praschnik Inc ....F...... 305 866-4323
Bay Harbor Islands *(G-333)*
Suncoast Accrdted Gmlgical Lab...........G...... 941 756-8787
Bradenton *(G-1054)*
Westchster Gold Fbricators Inc.............G...... 941 625-0666
Port Charlotte *(G-14324)*

JOB PRINTING & NEWSPAPER PUBLISHING COMBINED

American Classifieds.................................F...... 850 747-1155
Panama City *(G-13227)*
Lake Worth Herald Press Inc ....F...... 561 585-9387
Lake Worth *(G-7214)*
Observer Group and Gulf Coast...........G...... 239 263-0122
Naples *(G-10840)*

JOB TRAINING & VOCATIONAL REHABILITATION SVCS

Miami Hang Gliding Corp ....G...... 863 805-0440
Clewiston *(G-1893)*
Paradigm Leaders LLC ....G...... 850 441-3289
Panama City Beach *(G-13336)*

JOB TRAINING SVCS

Bluedrop USA Inc ....G...... 800 563-3638
Orlando *(G-11961)*
Veracity Tech Solutions LLC.................F...... 402 658-4113
Pensacola *(G-13618)*

JOINTS: Expansion

Fox Equipment LLC ....E...... 904 531-3150
Green Cove Springs *(G-4824)*

JOINTS: Expansion, Pipe

Microflex Inc..E...... 386 672-1945
Ormond Beach *(G-12780)*

JOINTS: Concrete

Structral Prestressed Inds Inc ....D...... 305 556-6699
Doral *(G-3380)*

PRODUCT

JOISTS: Long-Span Series, Open Web Steel

New Mllennium Bldg Systems LLC ....C 386 466-1300
Lake City (G-7031)

JUICE, FROZEN: Wholesalers

Gem Freshco LLC ....D 772 595-0070
Fort Pierce (G-4489)

Raw Foods International Llc ....F 305 856-1991
Coral Gables (G-2103)

KEYBOARDS: Computer Or Office Machine

Seal Shield LLC ....E 877 325-7443
Orlando (G-12582)

KEYS, KEY BLANKS

Rokey Corporation ....G 561 470-0164
Boca Raton (G-654)

KITCHEN CABINET STORES, EXC CUSTOM

Contractors Cabinet Company ....G 786 492-7118
Margate (G-8126)

Grevan Artistic Ventures Inc ....F 850 243-8111
Fort Walton Beach (G-4588)

Guyton Industries LLC ....E 772 208-3019
Indiantown (G-5814)

Kc & B Custom Inc ....G 561 276-1887
Delray Beach (G-2981)

Oliveri Woodworking Inc ....E 561 478-7233
West Palm Beach (G-18098)

Princeton Industries Inc ....E 954 344-9155
Margate (G-8149)

Rta Cabinets & More LLC ....G 321 288-3068
Indian Harbour Beach (G-5807)

KITCHEN CABINETS WHOLESALERS

Design Your Kit Clset More Inc ....G 786 227-6412
Miami (G-9021)

Kit Residential Designs Inc ....G 305 796-5940
Hialeah (G-5211)

Regency Custom Cabinets Inc ....F 239 332-7977
Fort Myers (G-4377)

Richard Bryan Ingram LLC ....G 407 677-7779
Orlando (G-12553)

Spruce Creek Cabinetry Inc ....E 386 756-0041
Port Orange (G-14349)

KITCHEN TOOLS & UTENSILS WHOLESALERS

Classica & Telecard Corp ....G 239 354-3727
Naples (G-10716)

KITCHEN UTENSILS: Food Handling & Processing Prdts, Wood

Genesis Caribbean Cuisine LLC ....G 718 503-4308
Lakeland (G-7334)

Vista Serv Corp ....G 239 275-1973
Fort Myers (G-4443)

KITCHEN UTENSILS: Wooden

Big Kitchen ....F 813 254-6112
Tampa (G-16643)

Delet Doors Inc ....F 786 250-4506
Miami (G-9008)

Mr Next Level Investment LLC ....F 786 718-8056
Homestead (G-5732)

KITCHENWARE: Plastic

Classica & Telecard Corp ....G 239 354-3727
Naples (G-10716)

Tupperware Brands Corporation ....B 407 826-5050
Orlando (G-12677)

KITS: Plastic

Tearepair Inc ....E 813 948-6898
Land O Lakes (G-7506)

KNIT OUTERWEAR DYEING & FINISHING, EXC HOSIERY & GLOVE

Color Touch Inc ....F 954 444-1999
Lauderhill (G-7728)

KNIVES: Agricultural Or indl

Andritz Iggesund Tools Inc ....E 813 855-6902
Oldsmar (G-11626)

LABELS: Cotton, Printed

Finotex USA Corp ....E 305 593-1102
Miami (G-9144)

Florida Marking Products LLC ....E 407 834-3000
Longwood (G-7897)

LABELS: Paper, Made From Purchased Materials

Consolidated Label Co ....C 407 339-2626
Sanford (G-15291)

En-Vision America Inc ....E 309 452-3088
Palmetto (G-13165)

Express Label Co Inc ....E 407 332-4774
Longwood (G-7892)

Palmas Printing Inc ....E 321 984-4451
Melbourne (G-8490)

Paradise Label Inc ....F 863 860-8779
Plant City (G-13793)

LABELS: Woven

Express Label Co Inc ....E 407 332-4774
Longwood (G-7892)

LABORATORIES, TESTING: Food

Elisa Technologies Inc ....F 352 337-3929
Gainesville (G-4685)

LABORATORIES: Biological Research

Applied Genetic Tech Corp ....D 386 462-2204
Alachua (G-5)

Bpc Plasma Inc ....F 561 989-5800
Boca Raton (G-445)

Bpc Plasma Inc ....E 561 569-3100
Boca Raton (G-446)

Sea Gear Corporation ....G 321 728-9116
Melbourne (G-8518)

LABORATORIES: Biotechnology

Gmx Technologies LLC ....G 917 697-0211
Highland Beach (G-5460)

Longeveron Inc ....F 305 909-0840
Miami (G-9475)

Opko Health Inc ....C 305 575-4100
Miami (G-9660)

LABORATORIES: Commercial Nonphysical Research

Cole Enterprises Inc ....G 727 441-4101
Clearwater (G-1546)

LABORATORIES: Dental

Inman Orthodontic Labs Inc ....F 954 340-8477
Coral Springs (G-2166)

LABORATORIES: Dental, Artificial Teeth Production

Dsg Clearwater Laboratory ....F 727 530-9444
Clearwater (G-1572)

LABORATORIES: Environmental Research

Greentechnologies LLC ....G 352 379-7780
Gainesville (G-4704)

LABORATORIES: Medical

Adams Bros Cabinetry Inc ....D 941 639-7188
North Port (G-11186)

Clinicon Corporation ....F 239 939-1345
Fort Myers (G-4211)

Logan Laboratories LLC ....G 813 316-4824
Tampa (G-17021)

Mri Specialists ....G 561 369-2144
Boynton Beach (G-891)

RM Imaging Incorporated ....E 561 361-8090
Boca Raton (G-652)

Sanzay Corporation ....F 305 826-9886
Miami (G-9846)

LABORATORIES: Noncommercial Research

Uts Systems LLC ....G 850 226-4301
Fort Walton Beach (G-4615)

LABORATORIES: Physical Research, Commercial

Beacon Phrm Jupiter LLC ....E 212 991-8988
Jupiter (G-6689)

Environmental Recovery Systems ....G 727 344-3301
Saint Petersburg (G-15037)

Intellgent Haring Systems Corp ....F 305 668-6102
Miami (G-9321)

Knights Manufacturing Company ....D 321 607-9900
Titusville (G-17599)

Larrick Group Inc ....E 941 351-2700
Sarasota (G-15509)

Mercury Systems Inc ....E 352 371-2567
Gainesville (G-4729)

Northrop Grumman Systems Corp ....D 850 863-8000
Fort Walton Beach (G-4598)

Sancilio & Company Inc ....E 561 847-2302
Riviera Beach (G-14672)

Sensatek Propulsion Tech Inc ....F 850 321-5993
Daytona Beach (G-2596)

Teledyne Flir LLC ....D 407 816-0091
Orlando (G-12649)

Uts Systems LLC ....G 850 226-4301
Fort Walton Beach (G-4615)

Vestagen Tchnical Textiles Inc ....G 407 781-2570
Orlando (G-12695)

LABORATORIES: Testing

Homestead Diagnostic Ctr Inc ....F 305 246-5600
Homestead (G-5713)

LABORATORIES: Testing

Genesis Reference Laboratories ....D 407 232-7130
Orlando (G-12191)

H2r Corp ....F 727 541-3444
Pinellas Park (G-13692)

Intelligent Operating Tech Inc ....E 303 400-9640
Palm City (G-13045)

Knights Manufacturing Company ....D 321 607-9900
Titusville (G-17599)

Lockheed Martin Corporation ....F 321 853-5194
Cape Canaveral (G-1290)

Mc Assembly Holdings Inc ....G 321 253-0541
Melbourne (G-8470)

Pharmatech LLC ....G 954 581-7881
Davie (G-2457)

Sun Nuclear Corp ....G 321 259-6862
Melbourne (G-8538)

Veracity Tech Solutions LLC ....F 402 658-4113
Pensacola (G-13618)

LABORATORY APPARATUS & FURNITURE

Comprhnsive Sleep Disorder Ctr ....F 407 834-1023
Altamonte Springs (G-39)

Corp Comfort Finisher Mr ....G 786 332-3655
Hialeah (G-5100)

Ga-MA & Associates Inc ....G 352 687-8840
Ocala (G-11398)

Hemco Corporation ....G 904 993-0380
Altamonte Springs (G-52)

Hf Scientific Inc ....E 888 203-7248
Fort Myers (G-4279)

Jensen Scientific Products Inc ....E 954 344-2006
Coral Springs (G-2169)

Phy-Med ....G 305 925-0141
Miami (G-9715)

LABORATORY APPARATUS & FURNITURE: Worktables

AGR of Florida Inc ....E 904 733-9393
Jacksonville (G-5870)

LABORATORY APPARATUS, EXC HEATING & MEASURING

Arj Medical Inc ....F 813 855-1557
Oldsmar (G-11627)

Cbg Biotech Ltd Co ....G 239 514-1148
Naples (G-10707)

Precision Coating Rods Inc ....F 813 855-5054
Oldsmar (G-11688)

Tintometer Inc ....F 941 756-6410
Sarasota **(G-15568)**

LABORATORY APPARATUS: Particle Size Reduction

Colloidal Dynamics LLC ....G..... 904 686-1536
Ponte Vedra Beach **(G-14265)**

LABORATORY APPARATUS: Sample Preparation Apparatus

Premier Lab Supply Inc ....G..... 772 873-1700
Port Saint Lucie **(G-14434)**

LABORATORY CHEMICALS: Organic

Awareness Technology Inc ....D...... 772 283-6540
Palm City **(G-13023)**
Awareness Technology Inc ....E...... 772 283-6540
Palm City **(G-13024)**
Firstpath Laboratory Svcs LLC ....G...... 954 977-6977
Pompano Beach **(G-14023)**
Synergy Ancillary Services LLC ....F 561 249-7238
Port Saint Lucie **(G-14453)**
W & B Scientific Inc ....F 954 607-1500
Pompano Beach **(G-14239)**

LABORATORY EQPT: Chemical

South Bay Hospital ....B 813 634-3301
Sun City Center **(G-16267)**
W & B Scientific Inc ....F 954 607-1500
Pompano Beach **(G-14239)**

LABORATORY EQPT: Clinical Instruments Exc Medical

Axiom Diagnostics Inc ....G...... 813 902-9888
Tampa **(G-16622)**
Etectrx Inc ....F 352 262-8054
Gainesville **(G-4686)**
Genesis Reference Laboratories ....D...... 407 232-7130
Orlando **(G-12191)**
Logan Laboratories LLC ....G...... 813 316-4824
Tampa **(G-17021)**
Mrn Biologics LLC ....F 508 989-6090
Coral Springs **(G-2193)**
Ormond Beach Clinical RES LLC ....F 386 310-7462
Ormond Beach **(G-12783)**
South Florida Laboratory Llc ....F 954 889-0335
Palm Springs **(G-13150)**
Southeast Clinical RES LLC ....F 904 296-3260
Jacksonville **(G-6482)**
Versea Diagnostics LLC ....E 800 397-0670
Tampa **(G-17409)**

LABORATORY EQPT: Incubators

Nfi Masks LLC ....E 239 990-6546
Fort Myers **(G-4339)**
Oculus Surgical Inc ....E 772 236-2622
Port St Lucie **(G-14480)**

LADDERS: Metal

Garelick Mfg Co ....D...... 727 545-4571
Largo **(G-7591)**
Leesburg Concrete Company Inc..........E 352 787-4177
Leesburg **(G-7782)**

LADDERS: Permanent Installation, Metal

Rampmaster Inc ....F 305 691-9090
Miami **(G-9779)**

LADDERS: Wood

Abbott Citrus Ladders Inc....................G...... 863 773-6322
Bowling Green **(G-828)**

LAMINATED PLASTICS: Plate, Sheet, Rod & Tubes

AA Fiberglass Inc...............................G...... 904 355-5511
Jacksonville **(G-5851)**
American Thrmplastic Extrusion...........C...... 305 769-9566
Opa Locka **(G-11716)**
Chemclad LLC ....F 863 967-1156
Auburndale **(G-224)**
Echo Plastic Systems ....F 305 655-1300
Deerfield Beach **(G-2715)**

Fun Marine Inc ....G...... 321 576-1100
Cocoa **(G-1930)**
Innovatier Inc ....G...... 863 688-4548
Lakeland **(G-7352)**
J Schor R Inc ....F 954 621-5279
Plantation **(G-13861)**
Seal-Tite Plastic Packg Co Inc.............D...... 305 264-9015
Miami **(G-9860)**
Southern Fiberglass Inc ....F 904 387-2246
Jacksonville **(G-6490)**
Sungraf Inc ....G...... 954 456-8500
Hallandale Beach **(G-4976)**

LAMINATING SVCS

Plastic Sealing Company Inc ....G...... 954 956-9797
Pompano Beach **(G-14130)**
Serigraphic Arts Inc ....F 813 626-1070
Tampa **(G-17251)**
Suncoast Identification Tech ....G...... 239 277-9922
Fort Myers **(G-4411)**
Target Copy Gainesville Inc ....F 352 372-1171
Gainesville **(G-4774)**

LAMP & LIGHT BULBS & TUBES

Bella Luna Inc ....E 305 696-0310
Hialeah **(G-5071)**
Digecon Plastics International ....F 850 477-5483
Pensacola **(G-13489)**
Energy Management Products LLC ......G...... 410 320-0200
Bradenton **(G-977)**
Johnston Archtctral Systems In ....E 904 886-9030
Jacksonville **(G-6231)**
Kyp Go Inc ....F 386 736-3770
Deland **(G-2884)**
Light Solutions Inc ....G...... 305 884-3468
Medley **(G-8268)**
Pearl Academy LLC ....F 904 619-6419
Jacksonville **(G-6360)**
Sun Catalina Holdings LLC ....E 305 558-4777
Miami Lakes **(G-10361)**
Surf Lighting Inc ....F 305 888-7851
Hialeah **(G-5375)**
Vision Engineering Labs ....E 727 812-2000
Largo **(G-7704)**

LAMP BULBS & TUBES, ELECTRIC: For Specialized Applications

Eag-Led LLC ....E 813 463-2420
Tampa **(G-16792)**
Oceanic Electrical Mfg Co Inc..............F 908 355-1900
Clearwater **(G-1725)**

LAMP BULBS & TUBES, ELECTRIC: Light, Complete

AMS Global Suppliers Group LLC........G...... 305 714-9441
Miami **(G-8728)**
City Electric Supply Company ....G...... 772 879-7440
Port Saint Lucie **(G-14405)**

LAMP SHADES: Plastic

Advanced Components Solutions ....G...... 813 884-1600
Lutz **(G-7982)**

LAMPS: Arc Units, Electrotherapeutic

Nuline Sensors LLC ....G...... 407 473-0765
Sanford **(G-15363)**

LAMPS: Desk, Commercial

Evolution Lighting LLC ....E 305 558-4777
Pembroke Pines **(G-13388)**
Systematix Inc....................................E 850 983-2213
Milton **(G-10439)**

LAMPS: Floor, Residential

Studio 21 Lighting Inc ....E 941 355-2677
Sarasota **(G-15841)**

LAMPS: Table, Residential

Marios Metalcraft ....G...... 239 649-0085
Naples **(G-10813)**
Papila Design Inc ....G...... 407 240-2992
Orlando **(G-12468)**
The Natural Light Inc ....E 850 265-0800
Lynn Haven **(G-8034)**

LAMPS: Ultraviolet

Robertson Transformer Co ....G...... 917 603-8530
Sarasota **(G-15797)**
Seal Shield LLC ....E 877 325-7443
Orlando **(G-12582)**

LAMPS: Wall, Residential

Gq Investments LLC ....C...... 305 821-3850
Hialeah **(G-5176)**

LAND SUBDIVISION & DEVELOPMENT

Diatomite Corp of America...................G...... 305 466-0075
Miami **(G-9029)**
Flo Sun Land Corporation ....D...... 561 655-6303
Palm Beach **(G-12934)**
Richland Towers Inc ....E 813 286-4140
Tampa **(G-17219)**
Vector Group Ltd ....D...... 305 579-8000
Miami **(G-10099)**
Vgr Holding LLC.................................F 305 579-8000
Miami **(G-10104)**

LAPIDARY WORK: Contract Or Other

Vee Enterprises Inc ....G...... 954 960-0300
Pompano Beach **(G-14235)**

LASER SYSTEMS & EQPT

905 East Hillsboro LLC ....F 954 480-2600
Deerfield Beach **(G-2651)**
Armalaser Inc ....G...... 954 937-6054
Pompano Beach **(G-13934)**
Boss Laser LLC ....D...... 407 878-0880
Sanford **(G-15275)**
Control Laser Corporation ....E 407 926-3500
Orlando **(G-12045)**
Control Micro Systems Inc...................E 407 679-9716
Winter Park **(G-18500)**
Edmund Optics Inc ....E 813 855-1900
Oldsmar **(G-11647)**
Faro Technologies Inc ....E 800 736-0234
Lake Mary **(G-7074)**
Integrated Laser Systems Inc ....G...... 954 489-8282
Coral Springs **(G-2167)**
L-3 Cmmnctons Advnced Lser Sys.......D...... 407 295-5878
Orlando **(G-12299)**
L3 Technologies Inc ....D...... 407 295-5878
Orlando **(G-12300)**
Lap of Amer Lser Applctons LLC ....G...... 561 416-9250
Boynton Beach **(G-884)**
Laser Assault ....G...... 801 374-3400
Navarre **(G-10952)**
Laserpath Technologies LLC ....G...... 407 247-3930
Oviedo **(G-12835)**
Lasersight Incorporated......................G...... 407 678-9900
Orlando **(G-12311)**
New Laser Tech Inc............................G...... 305 450-0456
Miami Lakes **(G-10331)**
Schwartz Electro-Optics Inc ....E 407 297-8988
Orlando **(G-12578)**
T J Sales Associates Inc ....G...... 407 328-0777
Sanford **(G-15394)**

LASERS: Welding, Drilling & Cutting Eqpt

A and J Sheet Metal Inc ....G...... 561 746-4048
Jupiter **(G-6674)**
Fonon Technologies Inc......................E 407 477-5618
Orlando **(G-12172)**

LATH: Woven Wire, Made From Purchased Wire

Best Manufacturing Company ....F 954 922-1443
Hollywood **(G-5540)**

LATHES

Chase Metals Inc................................E 352 669-1254
Umatilla **(G-17644)**
D & D Plastering & Lath Inc ....G...... 561 312-7256
Lake Worth **(G-7194)**
E T Plastering Inc..............................F 305 874-7082
Virginia Gardens **(G-17823)**
El Jefe Stucco Lath Inc.......................G...... 352 399-4837
Plant City **(G-13763)**
LJ&j Lathing Inc ....G...... 386 325-5040
Palatka **(G-12874)**

P R O D U C T

LATHES

LPs Lath Plst & Stucco Inc ....F 954 444-3727
Fort Lauderdale (G-3923)

Patriot Building & Cnstr Inc ....G....... 863 634-8489
Fort Pierce (G-4515)

LAUNDRIES, EXC POWER & COIN-OPERATED

Southern International Svcs ....F 954 349-7321
Miami (G-9929)

LAUNDRY & DRYCLEANER AGENTS

Holiday Cleaners Inc.............G....... 727 842-6989
New Port Richey (G-10968)

LAUNDRY EQPT: Commercial

PWS International ....G....... 850 432-4222
Pensacola (G-13588)

LAWN & GARDEN EQPT

Brandfx LLC ....E 321 632-2063
Cocoa (G-1908)

Electrolux Professional LLC............F 954 327-6778
Fort Lauderdale (G-3789)

Iceblox Inc ....G....... 717 697-1900
New Port Richey (G-10969)

Morning Glory Lawn Maint Inc............G....... 407 376-5833
Orlando (G-12392)

Mulch & Stone Emporium Inc ....G....... 352 237-7870
Ocala (G-11448)

Oase North America Inc ....G....... 800 365-3880
Riviera Beach (G-14652)

Pickhardt Professional Sr ....G....... 941 737-7262
Palmetto (G-13185)

Pottre Gardening Products LLC...........G....... 941 224-8856
Bradenton (G-1031)

Precision Small Engine Company.......E 954 974-1960
Pompano Beach (G-14142)

Toro Company............F 407 321-2901
Sanford (G-15398)

LAWN & GARDEN EQPT STORES

Peterson Enterprises LLC............G....... 386 456-3400
Mc Alpin (G-8189)

Santanas Pwrsprts Small Eng Rp ....G....... 813 658-3530
Tampa (G-17246)

LAWN & GARDEN EQPT: Blowers & Vacuums

Greg Franklin Enterprises Inc...........F 904 675-9129
Hilliard (G-5465)

LAWN & GARDEN EQPT: Grass Catchers, Lawn Mower

Robomow USA Inc ....G....... 844 762-6669
Vero Beach (G-17794)

LAWN & GARDEN EQPT: Lawnmowers, Residential, Hand Or Power

Santanas Pwrsprts Small Eng Rp ....G....... 813 658-3530
Tampa (G-17246)

Trailmate Inc ....E 941 739-5743
Jacksonville (G-6563)

LAWN & GARDEN EQPT: Tractors & Eqpt

All-Pro Equipment & Rental Inc...........F 850 656-0208
Tallahassee (G-16410)

Bravo Inc............G....... 239 471-8127
Cape Coral (G-1315)

Peterson Enterprises LLC............G....... 386 456-3400
Mc Alpin (G-8189)

LAWN & GARDEN EQPT: Trimmers

Woodys Hedging LLC............G....... 863 557-4525
Lake Hamilton (G-7053)

LAWN MOWER REPAIR SHOP

Peterson Enterprises LLC............G....... 386 456-3400
Mc Alpin (G-8189)

LEAD & ZINC

Envirofocus Technologies LLC...........D 813 620-3260
Tampa (G-16818)

LEAD & ZINC ORES

Chemours Company Fc LLC............D 904 964-1200
Starke (G-16099)

LEAD PENCILS & ART GOODS

Bic Corporation............A 727 536-7895
Clearwater (G-1519)

LEASING & RENTAL SVCS: Cranes & Aerial Lift Eqpt

Big Iron Intl Inc ....G....... 407 222-2573
Orlando (G-11950)

Key West Wldg Fabrication Inc ....G....... 305 296-5555
Key West (G-6869)

Steel City Inc ....F 850 785-9596
Panama City (G-13311)

LEASING & RENTAL: Construction & Mining Eqpt

Bobs Barricades Inc ....E 813 886-0518
Tampa (G-16652)

Repco Equipment Leasing Inc...........F 727 584-3329
Largo (G-7671)

LEASING & RENTAL: Medical Machinery & Eqpt

Compliance Meds Tech LLC ....F 786 319-9826
Miami (G-8952)

Vet-Equip LLC ....G....... 239 537-3402
Naples (G-10932)

LEASING & RENTAL: Trucks, Indl

Southern States Toyota Lift ....D 904 764-7662
Tampa (G-17290)

LEASING & RENTAL: Utility Trailers & RV's

Agrifleet Leasing Corporation ....E 239 293-3976
Auburndale (G-218)

LEATHER GOODS, EXC FOOTWEAR, GLOVES, LUGGAGE/BELTING, WHOL

Land Leather Inc ....G....... 305 594-2260
Miami (G-9422)

LEATHER GOODS: Aprons, Welders', Blacksmiths', Etc

Southern-Bartlett Intl LLC ....F 407 374-1613
Lakeland (G-7445)

LEATHER GOODS: Boxes

Allcases Reekstin & Assoc Inc...........F 813 891-1313
Oldsmar (G-11624)

American Commodity Exch Corp...........G....... 904 687-0588
Jacksonville (G-5883)

Sarasota Leather Gallery Inc ....G....... 800 741-4336
Hudson (G-5787)

Wellington Leather LLC ....G....... 561 790-0034
Royal Palm Beach (G-14773)

LEATHER GOODS: Card Cases

Identity Stronghold LLC ....E 941 475-8480
Englewood (G-3533)

LEATHER GOODS: Desk Sets

Creative Colors International............F 239 573-8883
Cape Coral (G-1328)

LEATHER GOODS: Harnesses Or Harness Parts

Milcom Services Inc............G....... 561 907-6816
Lake Worth Beach (G-7259)

LEATHER GOODS: Holsters

Cadre Holdings Inc ....E 904 741-5400
Jacksonville (G-5967)

High Noon Unlimited Inc ....G....... 727 939-2701
Holiday (G-5499)

Safariland LLC ....D 904 741-5400
Jacksonville (G-6446)

Summit Holsters LLC ....G....... 386 383-4090
Deltona (G-3054)

Zen Distributors Group II LLC ....F 305 637-3014
Miami (G-10156)

LEATHER GOODS: NEC

Eileen Kramer Inc............G....... 315 395-3831
Aventura (G-259)

Land Leather Inc ....G....... 305 594-2260
Miami (G-9422)

Leather or Not ....G....... 813 972-9667
Tampa (G-17003)

Roof-A-Cide West LLC ....G....... 877 258-8998
Sarasota (G-15799)

LEATHER GOODS: Personal

Abco Industries LLC ....G....... 813 605-5900
Tampa (G-16554)

Bespoke Stitchery LLC ....G....... 407 412-9937
Orlando (G-11945)

Christian Workshop LLC ....G....... 321 676-2396
Melbourne (G-8387)

Continental Belt Corp............G....... 305 573-8871
Miami (G-8962)

Everglades Creations Inc ....E 305 822-3344
Opa Locka (G-11744)

Group III International Inc ....D 954 984-1607
Pompano Beach (G-14046)

Koszegi Industries Inc............E 954 419-9544
Deerfield Beach (G-2749)

Leon Leather Company Inc............G....... 386 304-1902
Edgewater (G-3496)

Ostrich Market Inc............G....... 954 873-1957
Melbourne (G-8489)

Soul Kass Boutique LLC ....F 682 429-4323
Molino (G-10579)

Winston Manufacturing Corp............F 305 822-3344
Hialeah (G-5421)

Zpacks Corp ....F 321 215-5658
West Melbourne (G-17903)

LEATHER GOODS: Sewing Cases

Sea Link International Irb Inc............F 727 523-8660
Largo (G-7679)

LEATHER GOODS: Stirrups, Wood Or Metal

Ontyte LLC............G....... 561 880-8920
Wellington (G-17857)

LEATHER GOODS: Wallets

J Lea LLC............G....... 954 921-1422
Hollywood (G-5602)

LEATHER TANNING & FINISHING

Ti-Pagos Usa Inc ....G....... 786 310-7423
Miami (G-10007)

LEATHER: Artificial

Uniroyal Engineered Pdts LLC ....F 941 906-8580
Sarasota (G-15862)

Windsor & York Inc ....G....... 561 687-8424
West Palm Beach (G-18207)

LEGAL OFFICES & SVCS

Lawex Corporation ....F 305 259-9755
Coral Gables (G-2081)

Pageantry Tlent Entrmt Svcs In...........G....... 407 260-2262
Longwood (G-7930)

Rtj Group Inc ....G....... 954 999-4060
Fort Lauderdale (G-4033)

Time Adjusters Conference Inc ....G....... 386 274-4210
Port Orange (G-14352)

Watermakers Inc ....F 954 467-8920
Fort Lauderdale (G-4123)

LEGAL PROCESS SERVERS

Builders Notice Corporation ....G...... 954 764-1322
Fort Lauderdale (G-3708)

LENSES: Plastic, Exc Optical

Latam Optical LLC ....G...... 786 275-3284
Miami (G-9432)

Optical Hong Kong ....F 305 200-5522
Hialeah (G-5289)

LICENSE TAGS: Automobile, Stamped Metal

Eurosign Metalwerke Inc ....G...... 954 717-4426
Fort Lauderdale (G-3797)

Highway Sfety Mtr Vhcles Fla D ....F 561 640-6826
West Palm Beach (G-18024)

LIFE RAFTS: Rubber

Eastern Aero Marine Inc ....C...... 305 871-4050
Miami (G-9061)

Patten Co Inc ....E 707 826-2887
Lake Worth Beach (G-7260)

Winslow Marine Products Corp ....D...... 941 613-6666
Lake Suzy (G-7150)

LIFE SAVING & SURVIVAL EQPT REPAIR SVCS, NON-MEDICAL

Eastern Aero Marine Inc ....C...... 305 871-4050
Miami (G-9061)

LIFESAVING & SURVIVAL EQPT, EXC MEDICAL, WHOLESALE

Throw Raft LLC ....G...... 954 366-8004
Fort Lauderdale (G-4091)

LIGHT DISTILLATES

Cyber Fuels Inc ....G...... 866 771-3580
Palm Beach Gardens (G-12964)

LIGHT SENSITIVE DEVICES

B & R Profiles LLC ....E 305 479-8308
Bartow (G-299)

LIGHTING EQPT: Area & Sports Luminaries

Lightnet Usa Inc ....F 305 260-6444
Miami (G-9458)

LIGHTING EQPT: Flashlights

Adva-Lite Inc ....C...... 727 369-5319
Seminole (G-15967)

Siglo Holdings LLC ....C...... 727 369-5220
Largo (G-7682)

LIGHTING EQPT: Floodlights

Eag-Led LLC ....E 813 463-2420
Tampa (G-16792)

LIGHTING EQPT: Motor Vehicle

Rontan North America Inc ....E 305 599-2974
Doral (G-3350)

LIGHTING EQPT: Motor Vehicle, Dome Lights

Emergency Vehicle Sup Co LLC ....E 954 428-5201
Pompano Beach (G-14009)

LIGHTING EQPT: Motor Vehicle, NEC

Sea Link International Irb Inc ....F 727 523-8660
Largo (G-7679)

LIGHTING EQPT: Outdoor

Airstar America Inc ....F 407 851-7830
Orlando (G-11885)

Lighting Technologies ....F 850 462-1790
Pensacola (G-13536)

Logic Illumination LLC ....F 407 906-0126
Kissimmee (G-6939)

Nightscenes Inc ....F 813 855-9416
Tampa (G-17111)

Saltage Inc ....G...... 305 462-8960
Medley (G-8318)

LIGHTING EQPT: Searchlights

Rand Search Light Advertising ....G...... 954 476-7620
Davie (G-2465)

LIGHTING EQPT: Spotlights

Art In Spotlight ....G...... 904 853-6661
Atlantic Beach (G-204)

LIGHTING FIXTURES WHOLESALERS

Digecon Plastics International ....F 850 477-5483
Pensacola (G-13489)

Green Applications LLC ....E 954 900-2290
Fort Lauderdale (G-3848)

Green Global Energy Systems ....F 305 253-3413
Cutler Bay (G-2290)

Led Are US LLC ....G...... 305 823-2803
Hialeah Gardens (G-5441)

Louis Poulsen USA Inc ....D...... 954 349-2525
Weston (G-18265)

Nebula Led Lighting Systems of ....G...... 813 907-0001
Wesley Chapel (G-17884)

Versailles Lighting Inc ....F 561 945-5744
Delray Beach (G-3035)

LIGHTING FIXTURES, NEC

0energy Lighting Inc ....F 855 955-1055
Orlando (G-11848)

ACR Electronics Inc ....D...... 954 981-3333
Fort Lauderdale (G-3621)

Ameritech Energy Corporation ....G...... 610 730-1733
Holly Hill (G-5510)

Apollo Metro Solutions Inc ....F 239 444-6934
Naples (G-10671)

Brite Shot Inc ....F 954 418-7125
Deerfield Beach (G-2681)

Candela Controls Inc ....E 407 654-2420
Winter Garden (G-18377)

CC Lighting Inc ....F 805 302-5321
Boynton Beach (G-849)

Christie Lites Entps USA LLC ....C...... 407 856-0016
Orlando (G-12010)

Christie Lites Orlando LLC ....G...... 206 223-7200
Orlando (G-12011)

Creative Lighting & Power LLC ....F 407 967-0957
Lakeland (G-7298)

Cyalume Tech Holdings Inc ....G...... 954 315-4939
Fort Lauderdale (G-3749)

Digital Lighting Systems Inc ....G...... 305 264-8391
Miami (G-9032)

Energyware LLC ....F 540 809-5902
Davie (G-2407)

Evolution Lighting LLC ....E 305 558-4777
Pembroke Pines (G-13388)

Fanto Group LLC ....G...... 407 857-5101
Orlando (G-12145)

First Block LLC ....D...... 727 462-2526
Clearwater (G-1595)

Fusion Energy Solutions LLC ....G...... 941 366-9936
Punta Gorda (G-14505)

Hoosier Lightening Inc ....G...... 407 290-3323
Orlando (G-12223)

Illuminated Lightpanels Inc ....G...... 954 484-6633
Oakland Park (G-11271)

IMC Lighting Inc ....G...... 305 373-4422
Miami (G-9305)

Jay Strong Lighting Inc ....G...... 813 253-0490
Tampa (G-16964)

Jng Lighting ....G...... 561 707-2028
West Palm Beach (G-18041)

Krohn Lighting LLC ....G...... 407 949-7231
Altamonte Springs (G-54)

Lanai Lights LLC ....G...... 239 415-2561
Fort Myers (G-4308)

Led Surf Lighting Inc ....G...... 239 687-4458
Naples (G-10801)

Light and Sound Equipment Inc ....G...... 305 233-3737
Cutler Bay (G-2294)

Lps Production LLC ....F 786 208-6217
Miami Lakes (G-10315)

Lux Unlimited Inc ....G...... 305 871-8774
Miami (G-9488)

Next Step Products LLC ....G...... 407 857-9900
Orlando (G-12415)

Professional Holiday Lighting ....G...... 208 709-2968
Ormond Beach (G-12789)

Pure Bright Lighting LLC ....G...... 954 780-8700
Fort Lauderdale (G-4001)

Reward Lighting Net LLC ....G...... 561 832-1819
West Palm Beach (G-18140)

Roth Southeast Lighting LLC ....G...... 954 423-6640
Fort Lauderdale (G-4029)

Russell Hobbs Inc ....D...... 954 883-1000
Miramar (G-10538)

S B Lighting LLC ....G...... 850 687-1166
Ponce De Leon (G-14249)

Sgm Lighting Inc ....G...... 407 440-3601
Orlando (G-12587)

State Lighting Co Inc ....G...... 561 371-9529
West Palm Beach (G-18161)

Stonelight Inc ....G...... 239 514-3272
Naples (G-10907)

Sun Catalina Holdings LLC ....E 305 558-4777
Miami Lakes (G-10361)

Sundown Lighting ....G...... 561 254-3738
Lantana (G-7515)

Tamlite Lighting - New Whse ....G...... 772 879-7440
Port Saint Lucie (G-14455)

Titans USA Ltd ....G...... 727 290-9897
Clearwater (G-1833)

Triarch International Inc ....F 305 622-3400
Hollywood (G-5674)

Van Teal Inc ....E 305 751-6767
Miami (G-10093)

Volt Lighting ....F 813 978-3700
Lutz (G-8020)

Zaniboni Lighting LLC ....D...... 727 213-0410
Clearwater (G-1859)

LIGHTING FIXTURES: Airport

Neubert Aero Corp ....G...... 352 345-4828
Brooksville (G-1185)

Virginia Electronic & Ltg Corp ....G...... 904 230-2840
Green Cove Springs (G-4842)

LIGHTING FIXTURES: Decorative Area

Bluegate Inc ....F 305 628-8391
Miami Gardens (G-10253)

Jsm Creations Inc ....G...... 239 229-8746
Cape Coral (G-1360)

LIGHTING FIXTURES: Fluorescent, Commercial

Paramount Depot LLC ....F 786 275-0107
Doral (G-3321)

Surf Lighting Inc ....F 305 888-7851
Hialeah (G-5375)

LIGHTING FIXTURES: Fluorescent, Residential

Blu Sense ....G...... 786 616-8628
Doral (G-3143)

LIGHTING FIXTURES: Fountain

Bluworld of Water LLC ....D...... 407 426-7674
Orlando (G-11963)

LIGHTING FIXTURES: Gas

Gas Light Services Inc ....G...... 941 232-8668
Sarasota (G-15689)

LIGHTING FIXTURES: Indl & Commercial

Affineon Lighting ....G...... 407 448-3434
Weston (G-18221)

Anarchy Offroad LLC ....G...... 239 919-6681
Naples (G-10668)

Apollo Metro Solutions Inc ....F 239 444-6934
Naples (G-10671)

Brownlee Lighting Inc ....E 407 297-3677
Orlando (G-11970)

Candela Controls Inc ....E 407 654-2420
Winter Garden (G-18377)

City Electric Supply Company ....C...... 772 878-4944
Port St Lucie (G-14474)

Commercial Energy Services ....F 904 589-1059
Green Cove Springs (G-4822)

Coresential Energy & Lighting ....E 919 602-0849
Tampa (G-16728)

Dauer Manufacturing Corp ....G...... 800 883-2590
Medley (G-8229)

Digecon Plastics International ....F 850 477-5483
Pensacola (G-13489)

Employee Codes: A=Over 500 employees, B=251-500
C=101-250, D=51-100, E=20-50, F=10-19, G=4-9

2022 Harris Florida
Manufacturers Directory

PRODUCT

1239

LIGHTING FIXTURES: Indl & Commercial (continued)

Edsun Lighting Fixtures Mfg ....F 305 888-8849
Hialeah (G-5136)

Electraled Inc ....F 727 561-7610
Clearwater (G-1579)

Energy Harness Corporation ....G 239 790-3300
Cape Coral (G-1337)

Energy Management Products LLC ....G 410 320-0200
Bradenton (G-977)

Energy Sving Solutions USA LLC ....F 305 735-2878
Miami (G-9099)

Eran Group Inc ....F 561 289-5021
Boca Raton (G-506)

Global Tech Led LLC ....E 877 748-5533
Fort Lauderdale (G-3842)

Green Applications LLC ....E 954 900-2290
Fort Lauderdale (G-3848)

Green Creative LLC ....E 866 774-5433
Sanford (G-15327)

Green Global Energy Systems ....F 305 253-3413
Cutler Bay (G-2290)

H I T Lighting Corp ....G 772 221-1155
Palm City (G-13044)

Harris Manufacturing Inc ....D 877 204-7540
Jacksonville (G-6166)

Icpf Development Group LLC ....G 727 474-9927
Clearwater (G-1637)

Impexpar LLC ....G 786 238-5700
Doral (G-3257)

J B Nottingham & Co Inc ....E 386 873-2990
Deland (G-2877)

Janoro Fixture Mfg Corp ....G 305 887-2524
Hialeah (G-5203)

Keylon Lighting Services Inc ....G 352 279-3249
Brooksville (G-1167)

Koncept Systems LLC ....G 786 610-0122
Homestead (G-5724)

Led Lghting Slutions Globl LLC ....G 855 309-1702
Bradenton (G-1003)

Ledradiant LLC ....G 305 901-1313
Hollywood (G-5609)

Lighting Science Group Corp ....G 321 779-5520
Melbourne (G-8461)

Lightn Up Inc ....F 954 797-7778
Sunrise (G-16337)

Louis Poulsen USA Inc ....D 954 349-2525
Weston (G-18265)

Lumastream Inc ....E 727 827-2805
Saint Petersburg (G-15115)

Lumilum LLC ....F 305 233-2844
Miami (G-9484)

Metrotech Media & Lighting Inc ....G 844 463-8761
Pensacola (G-13552)

Morning Star Industries Inc ....E 800 440-6050
Jensen Beach (G-6657)

Municipal Lighting Systems Inc ....G 305 666-4210
Miami (G-9601)

Orion Energy Systems Inc ....E 920 892-5825
Jacksonville (G-6342)

Pioneer Led Lighting Corp ....G 305 620-5300
Miami Lakes (G-10339)

Remcraft Lighting Products Inc ....E 305 687-9031
Opa Locka (G-11784)

Restoration Arts ....G 305 953-9755
Miami Gardens (G-10271)

Safetogether Ltd Liability Co ....G 954 227-2236
Parkland (G-13353)

Sun Catalina Holdings LLC ....E 305 558-4777
Miami Lakes (G-10361)

Tek-Lite Inc ....G 410 775-7123
Melbourne (G-8546)

Underwater Lights Usa LLC ....F 954 760-4447
Fort Lauderdale (G-4103)

Versailles Lighting Inc ....F 561 945-5744
Delray Beach (G-3035)

Violet Defense LLC ....E 407 433-1104
Orlando (G-12699)

Vision Engineering Labs ....D 727 812-2035
Largo (G-7705)

Vonn LLC ....F 888 604-8666
North Miami Beach (G-11168)

Xeleum Lighting LLC ....F 954 617-8170
Boca Raton (G-759)

LIGHTING FIXTURES: Marine

Lumishore Usa LLC ....F 941 405-3302
Sarasota (G-15512)

Lumitec LLC ....E 561 272-9840
Delray Beach (G-2983)

LIGHTING FIXTURES: Motor Vehicle

Autocraft Manufacturing Co ....E 321 453-1850
Merritt Island (G-8577)

Basewest Inc ....E 727 573-2700
Clearwater (G-1509)

Energy Management Products LLC ....G 410 320-0200
Bradenton (G-977)

Hg2 Emergency Lighting LLC ....G 407 426-7700
Orlando (G-12216)

Light Integration Inc ....G 407 681-0072
Longwood (G-7918)

Luminar LLC ....B 407 900-5259
Orlando (G-12355)

Phantom Products Inc ....F 321 690-6729
Rockledge (G-14738)

LIGHTING FIXTURES: Residential

Brian Slater & Associates LLC ....G 561 886-7705
Boca Raton (G-447)

Brownlee Lighting Inc ....E 407 297-3677
Orlando (G-11970)

City Electric Supply Company ....C 772 878-4944
Port St Lucie (G-14474)

Dauer Manufacturing Corp ....G 800 883-2590
Medley (G-8229)

Edsun Lighting Fixtures Mfg ....F 305 888-8849
Hialeah (G-5136)

Evolution Lighting LLC ....G 305 558-4777
Pembroke Pines (G-13388)

Janoro Fixture Mfg Corp ....G 305 887-2524
Hialeah (G-5203)

Logic Illumination LLC ....F 407 906-0126
Kissimmee (G-6939)

Louis Poulsen USA Inc ....D 954 349-2525
Weston (G-18265)

Remcraft Lighting Products Inc ....E 305 687-9031
Opa Locka (G-11784)

Smarthome-Products Inc ....F 727 490-7260
Clearwater (G-1786)

Sun Catalina Holdings LLC ....E 305 558-4777
Miami Lakes (G-10361)

Tamlite ....G 772 878-4944
Port St Lucie (G-14485)

Van Teal Inc ....E 305 751-6767
Miami (G-10093)

Versailles Lighting Inc ....F 561 945-5744
Delray Beach (G-3035)

Vonn LLC ....F 888 604-8666
North Miami Beach (G-11168)

LIGHTING FIXTURES: Residential, Electric

Bella Luna Inc ....E 305 696-0310
Hialeah (G-5071)

Jibe Ltg N Amer Ltd Lblty Co ....F 954 899-4040
Boca Raton (G-561)

Triple Seven Home LLC ....G 321 652-5151
Grant (G-4813)

LIGHTING FIXTURES: Street

Lighting Science Group Corp ....G 321 779-5520
Melbourne (G-8461)

Southwest Signal Inc ....E 813 621-4949
Englewood (G-3524)

Street Lighting Equipment Corp ....F 954 961-9140
Davie (G-2483)

LIGHTING FIXTURES: Swimming Pool

A J Giammanco & Associates ....F 386 328-1254
Palatka (G-12862)

Aquacomfort Solutions LLC ....E 407 831-1941
Delray Beach (G-2932)

LIGHTING FIXTURES: Underwater

Lumitec LLC ....E 561 272-9840
Delray Beach (G-2983)

Underwter Fish Light Ltd Lblty ....G 941 391-5846
Port Charlotte (G-14320)

LIGHTING MAINTENANCE SVC

Apure Distribution LLC ....F 305 351-1025
Miami (G-8737)

Itelecom USA Inc ....G 305 557-4660
Weston (G-18257)

Signs Unlimited Inc ....G 727 845-0330
Saint Augustine (G-14893)

LIGHTS: Trouble lights

Safety Zone Specialists Inc ....G 863 984-1385
Lakeland (G-7427)

LIME

Crystal River Quarries Inc ....E 352 795-2828
Crystal River (G-2273)

Lhoist North America Ala LLC ....G 352 585-3488
Brooksville (G-1174)

Lhoist North America Ala LLC ....E 817 732-8164
Pompano Beach (G-14077)

Lime Group ....G 941 485-0272
Nokomis (G-11050)

Marianna Lime Products Inc ....E 850 526-3580
Marianna (G-8170)

Mineral Life Intl Inc ....G 305 661-9854
Miami (G-9574)

Silver Star On Lime LLC ....G 941 312-4566
Sarasota (G-15828)

LIME ROCK: Ground

Anderson Mining Corporation ....G 352 542-7942
Old Town (G-11621)

Blue Rock Inc ....G 850 584-4324
Perry (G-13633)

Florida Rock Industries ....C 904 355-1781
Jacksonville (G-6108)

Florida Rock Industries ....E 407 847-6457
Kissimmee (G-6921)

LIME: Agricultural

Marianna Limestone LLC ....F 954 581-1220
Marianna (G-8171)

LIMESTONE & MARBLE: Dimension

ARC Stone III LLC ....F 561 478-8805
Lake Worth Beach (G-7248)

Asd Surfaces LLC ....G 561 845-5009
North Palm Beach (G-11174)

Azul Stone LLC ....G 561 655-9385
West Palm Beach (G-17931)

Southern Contracting N FL Inc ....G 850 674-3570
Blountstown (G-377)

Stone Metals LLC ....G 813 605-7363
Plant City (G-13806)

LIMESTONE: Crushed & Broken

A Mining Group LLC ....E 386 752-7585
Lake City (G-7009)

Argos ....G 305 592-3501
Miami (G-8746)

Blue Water Industries LLC ....F 904 512-7706
Jacksonville (G-5940)

Cemex Cnstr Mtls Fla LLC ....F 855 292-8453
Naples (G-10708)

Cemex Materials LLC ....C 561 833-5555
West Palm Beach (G-17962)

Cemex Materials LLC ....C 352 435-0783
Okahumpka (G-11595)

Cemex Materials LLC ....C 305 558-0315
Miami (G-8910)

Cemex Materials LLC ....C 561 793-1442
West Palm Beach (G-17963)

Cemex Materials LLC ....C 561 743-4039
Jupiter (G-6704)

Dixie Lime Andstone Co ....G 352 512-0180
Ocala (G-11367)

Eagle Engrg & Land Dev Inc ....F 913 948-4320
Boynton Beach (G-860)

Evolving Coal Corp ....G 813 944-3100
Saint Petersburg (G-15039)

Fcs Holdings Inc ....G 352 787-0608
Leesburg (G-7772)

Helms Hauling & Materials Llc ....F 850 218-6895
Niceville (G-11032)

Lake Point Restoration LLC ....E 561 924-9100
Wellington (G-17854)

Lakeview Dirt Co Inc ....E 904 824-2586
Welaka (G-17840)

Lhoist North America Tenn Inc ....F 352 629-7990
Ocala (G-11427)

Martin Marietta Materials Inc ....G 904 596-0230
Jacksonville (G-6277)

Martin Marietta Materials Inc ....F 850 981-9020
Milton (G-10430)

Martin Marietta Materials Inc ....F 850 913-0083
Panama City (G-13285)

Rinker Materials Corp Con .... G 305 818-4952
Medley *(G-8314)*

Rock Ridge Materials Inc .... F 321 268-8455
Titusville *(G-17615)*

Waste Management Inc Florida .... E 954 984-2000
Winter Garden *(G-18408)*

LIMESTONE: Dimension

Denali Investments Inc .... G 386 364-2979
Live Oak *(G-7845)*

Five Stones Mine LLC .... F 813 967-2123
Canal Point *(G-1260)*

LIMESTONE: Ground

Bedrock Resources LLC .... E 352 369-8600
Ocala *(G-11333)*

Colitz Mining Co Inc .... F 352 795-2409
Crystal River *(G-2272)*

SCI Materials LLC .... E 352 878-4979
Reddick *(G-14553)*

Vecellio & Grogan Inc .... D 305 822-5322
Hialeah *(G-5406)*

LINENS & TOWELS WHOLESALERS

Harbor Linen LLC .... D 305 805-8085
Medley *(G-8251)*

LINENS: Tablecloths, From Purchased Materials

Jewm Inc .... F 973 942-1555
Lake Worth *(G-7210)*

Sperry Marketing Group Inc .... F 941 483-4667
Venice *(G-17718)*

LINER BRICK OR PLATES: Sewer Or Tank Lining, Vitrified Clay

Infrastructure Repair Systems .... G 727 327-4216
Saint Petersburg *(G-15084)*

LININGS: Apparel, Made From Purchased Materials

Saint George Industries LLC .... E 786 212-1176
Miami *(G-9838)*

LININGS: Fabric, Apparel & Other, Exc Millinery

Catalyst Fabric Solutions LLC .... E 850 396-4325
Marianna *(G-8162)*

S 3 Marketing Group LLC .... E 317 491-3398
Sanibel *(G-15417)*

World Event Promotions LLC .... E 800 214-3408
Miami *(G-10143)*

LINTELS

Cast-Crete Usa LLC .... D 813 621-4641
Seffner *(G-15954)*

LINTELS: Steel, Light Gauge

Nichols Truck Bodies LLC .... F 904 781-5080
Jacksonville *(G-6333)*

LIP BALMS

Floridas Best Inc .... G 407 682-9570
Altamonte Springs *(G-48)*

LIPSTICK

Suits Stlttos Lpstick Fndtion .... G 954 903-9426
Fort Lauderdale *(G-4072)*

LIQUEFIED PETROLEUM GAS DEALERS

Farmers Cooperative Inc .... E 386 362-1459
Live Oak *(G-7848)*

LIQUEFIED PETROLEUM GAS WHOLESALERS

Sams Gas .... G 386 698-1033
Crescent City *(G-2237)*

LIQUID CRYSTAL DISPLAYS

Digital Pixel Displays LLC .... G 321 948-3751
Orlando *(G-12096)*

DMC Components Intl LLC .... G 407 478-4064
Winter Park *(G-18508)*

New Vision Display Inc .... G 407 480-5800
Orlando *(G-12413)*

Vc Displays Inc .... E 352 796-0060
Brooksville *(G-1218)*

Via Optronics LLC .... E 407 745-5031
Orlando *(G-12697)*

Video Display Corporation .... E 813 854-2259
Tampa *(G-17416)*

LITHIUM MINERAL MINING

USA Rare Earth LLC .... F 813 867-6155
Tampa *(G-17399)*

LITHOGRAPHIC PLATES

Elicar Printing .... G 305 324-5252
Miami *(G-9084)*

LOADS: Electronic

Concept 2 Market Inc .... F 954 974-0022
Pompano Beach *(G-13974)*

LOCK & KEY SVCS

Safe Banks and Lock .... G 954 762-3565
Fort Lauderdale *(G-4035)*

LOCKERS

List Industries Inc .... C 954 429-9155
Deerfield Beach *(G-2753)*

List Plymouth LLC .... D 954 429-9155
Deerfield Beach *(G-2755)*

Valiant Products Inc .... E 863 688-7998
Lakeland *(G-7469)*

LOCKERS: Wood, Exc Refrigerated

List Industries Inc .... C 954 429-9155
Deerfield Beach *(G-2753)*

LOCKS

Assa Abloy Hospitality Inc .... G 954 920-0772
Fort Lauderdale *(G-3661)*

Brandon Lock & Safe Inc .... G 813 655-4200
Tampa *(G-16660)*

Gator Door East Inc .... E 904 824-2827
Saint Augustine *(G-14835)*

LOCKS & LOCK SETS, WHOLESALE

Visions Millwork Inc .... F 239 390-0811
Fort Myers *(G-4442)*

LOCKS: Safe & Vault, Metal

Safe Banks and Lock .... G 954 762-3565
Fort Lauderdale *(G-4035)*

LOGGING

Agner Timber Services Inc .... G 850 251-6615
Perry *(G-13629)*

Bernice I Finch .... G 850 638-0082
Wausau *(G-17831)*

Black Creek Logging .... G 904 591-9681
Middleburg *(G-10400)*

Bushnell Sawmill Inc .... G 352 793-2740
Bushnell *(G-1240)*

Coastal Logging Inc .... F 850 832-0133
Panama City *(G-13245)*

Donald Smith Logging Inc .... G 850 697-3975
Carrabelle *(G-1410)*

Feagle Logging LLC .... G 386 365-2689
Lake City *(G-7018)*

Florida Cental Logging Inc .... F 863 272-5364
Lakeland *(G-7329)*

G Black Logging LLC .... G 850 379-8747
Hosford *(G-5755)*

G Haddock Rowland Inc .... G 904 845-2725
Hilliard *(G-5463)*

Gulf Coast Timber Company .... G 850 271-8818
Panama City *(G-13270)*

H Jones Timber LLC .... G 386 312-0603
Palatka *(G-12871)*

LOGGING CAMPS & CONTRACTORS

Hardy Logging Company Inc .... G 850 994-1955
Pace *(G-12858)*

Hbt Forestry Services Inc .... F 850 584-9324
Perry *(G-13643)*

Hobbs Trucking LLC .... G 904 463-5681
Hilliard *(G-5467)*

John Harvey Green .... G 850 643-2544
Bristol *(G-1120)*

John L Shadd Enterprises .... E 386 496-3989
Lake Butler *(G-7002)*

Joiners Enterprises Inc .... F 850 623-5593
Milton *(G-10429)*

Joyner Inc .... G 850 832-6326
Panama City Beach *(G-13333)*

Justin Bell Logging Inc .... G 904 759-9006
Callahan *(G-1254)*

Pearce Logging LLC .... G 386 365-1880
Lake Butler *(G-7004)*

Randall Birge .... G 850 373-6131
Bonifay *(G-777)*

Tucker Trckg Log Jhnny E Tcker .... G 850 258-1982
Wewahitchka *(G-18302)*

Usher Land & Timber Inc .... E 352 493-4221
Chiefland *(G-1451)*

Van Zant Timber Incorporated .... G 904 845-4661
Hilliard *(G-5478)*

West Fraser Inc .... C 904 786-4155
Jacksonville *(G-6601)*

LOGGING CAMPS & CONTRACTORS

4 C Timber Inc .... G 386 937-0806
Palatka *(G-12861)*

A and H Logging Inc .... G 352 528-3868
Williston *(G-18328)*

A L Baxley & Sons Inc .... F 352 629-5137
Citra *(G-1466)*

A&H Logging Inc .... G 352 528-3868
Morriston *(G-10593)*

B&M Logging Inc .... G 386 397-1145
White Springs *(G-18304)*

Bbts Logging LLC .... G 850 997-2436
Monticello *(G-10580)*

Boland Timber Company Inc .... E 850 997-5270
Perry *(G-13634)*

BTR Logging Inc .... G 386 397-0730
White Springs *(G-18305)*

C & G Timber Harvesters Inc .... G 850 643-1340
Bristol *(G-1117)*

C F Webb and Sons Logging LLC .... F 850 971-5565
Lee *(G-7755)*

Cedar Creek Logging Inc .... F 850 832-0133
Panama City *(G-13239)*

Circle C Timber Inc .... G 863 735-0383
Zolfo Springs *(G-18639)*

Cooper Timber Harvesting Inc .... F 863 494-0240
Arcadia *(G-190)*

CP Logging Inc .... F 850 379-8698
Hosford *(G-5754)*

D & S Logging Inc .... G 850 638-5500
Chipley *(G-1455)*

Flatwoods Forest Products Inc .... F 352 787-1161
Leesburg *(G-7774)*

Flowers Logging Co Inc .... G 850 639-2856
Kinard *(G-6889)*

Geiger Logging Inc .... E 904 845-7534
Hilliard *(G-5464)*

Gray Logging LLC .... G 850 973-3863
Madison *(G-8042)*

Gray Logging LLC .... G 850 973-3863
Madison *(G-8043)*

H B Tutun Jr Logging Inc .... G 850 584-9324
Perry *(G-13641)*

Harrison Logging .... E 352 591-2779
Williston *(G-18332)*

Harry Pickett .... G 904 845-4643
Hilliard *(G-5466)*

HB Tuten Jr Logging Inc .... E 850 584-9324
Perry *(G-13642)*

Henry W Long .... G 352 542-7068
Old Town *(G-11622)*

Howell Logging & Land Clearing .... G 352 528-2698
Williston *(G-18333)*

John A Cruce Jr Inc .... E 850 584-9755
Perry *(G-13644)*

Johnny Sellers Logging Inc .... G 850 643-5214
Bristol *(G-1121)*

Johns & Conner Inc .... G 904 845-4430
Hilliard *(G-5468)*

Johns & Conner Logging Inc .... G 904 845-4430
Hilliard *(G-5469)*

Johns & Connor Inc ....F 904 845-4541
Hilliard *(G-5470)*
Key Logging ....G 386 328-6984
Hollister *(G-5508)*
L and D Logging ....G 850 859-1013
Westville *(G-18301)*
M & L Timber Inc ....F 386 437-0895
Bunnell *(G-1230)*
McClellan Logging Inc ....G 352 468-1856
Hampton *(G-4986)*
McMillan Logging Inc ....F 850 643-4819
Bristol *(G-1123)*
P & S Logging Inc ....G 904 845-4256
Hilliard *(G-5472)*
Pine Top Logging LLC ....G 386 365-0857
Branford *(G-1114)*
R & M Logging Inc ....G 904 813-4877
Hilliard *(G-5473)*
Randy Morris Logging Inc ....F 850 773-9010
Chipley *(G-1457)*
Reagan H Fox III Inc ....F 850 584-9229
Perry *(G-13651)*
Ridgeway Timber Inc ....G 352 463-6013
Bell *(G-336)*
Riverland Logging Inc ....G 904 845-4326
Hilliard *(G-5475)*
Tumbling Pines Inc ....G 386 437-2668
Bunnell *(G-1237)*
TW Byrds Sons Inc ....E 386 935-1544
Branford *(G-1115)*
Van Aernam Logging & Trucking ....G 352 498-5809
Cross City *(G-2265)*
Walden Timber Harvesting Inc ....F 850 674-4884
Altha *(G-79)*
Warwick Logging ....G 386 328-9358
East Palatka *(G-3478)*
Williams Timber Inc ....E 850 584-2760
Perry *(G-13658)*

LOGGING: Timber, Cut At Logging Camp

Ata Group of Companies Inc ....G 352 735-1588
Mount Dora *(G-10597)*
B & B Timber Company ....G 904 284-5541
Green Cove Springs *(G-4818)*
Bailey Timber Co Inc ....F 850 674-2080
Blountstown *(G-375)*
Griffis Timber Inc ....G 904 275-2372
Sanderson *(G-15253)*
L W Timber Co Inc ....G 850 592-2597
Greenwood *(G-4855)*
M&E Timber Inc ....G 850 584-6650
Perry *(G-13647)*
Paul White Logging Inc ....G 850 379-8651
Hosford *(G-5757)*
Rbj Timber Inc ....G 904 879-1597
Callahan *(G-1256)*
Southern Wood Services LLC ....G 352 279-3208
Brooksville *(G-1203)*

LOGGING: Wooden Logs

South Amercn Lbr & Timber LLC ....G 786 280-8326
Miami *(G-9923)*
Underwood Butcher Block Co Inc ....F 904 338-2348
Jacksonville *(G-6574)*

LOOSELEAF BINDERS

Allied Decals-Fla Inc ....F 800 940-2233
Fort Lauderdale *(G-3642)*

LOOSELEAF BINDERS: Library

County of Hernando ....F 352 754-4042
Brooksville *(G-1149)*

LOTIONS OR CREAMS: Face

Cosmesis Skincare Inc ....G 954 963-5090
Hollywood *(G-5556)*
Doerfler Manufacturing Inc ....G 763 772-3728
Umatilla *(G-17646)*
Florida Keys Keylime Products ....G 305 853-0378
Key Largo *(G-6846)*
Health and Beauty Mfg LLC ....G 727 565-0797
Saint Petersburg *(G-15073)*
JP Cosmetics Inc ....F 305 231-4963
Hialeah *(G-5208)*
Miramar Cosmetic Inc ....F 305 455-5016
Doral *(G-3305)*
Nac USA Corporation ....G 800 396-0149
Miami *(G-9603)*

Product Max Group Inc ....G 813 949-5061
Land O Lakes *(G-7500)*
Tropical Enterprises Intl Inc ....E 813 837-9800
Tampa *(G-17371)*
Vienna Beauty Products Co ....F 937 228-7109
Naples *(G-10934)*
Younger You Inc ....G 954 924-4462
Fort Lauderdale *(G-4142)*

LOUDSPEAKERS

Advanced Cmmnications Tech Inc ....F 954 444-4119
Boca Raton *(G-390)*
Eminent Technology Inc ....G 850 575-5655
Tallahassee *(G-16436)*

LUBRICATING EQPT: Indl

Airgroup Inc ....F 561 279-0680
Boca Raton *(G-395)*
Phantom Sales Group Inc ....G 888 614-1232
Bartow *(G-322)*
Travis Lh LLC ....F 863 967-0628
Winter Haven *(G-18475)*

LUBRICATING SYSTEMS: Centralized

Cirven Usa LLC ....G 305 815-2545
Doral *(G-3162)*

LUGGAGE & BRIEFCASES

Fussion International Inc ....G 305 662-4848
Coral Gables *(G-2057)*
Lug Usa LLC ....F 855 584-5433
Orlando *(G-12354)*
Maleta Import ....G 305 592-2410
Miami *(G-9502)*
Qps Companies Inc ....E 813 246-5525
Tampa *(G-17197)*

LUGGAGE & LEATHER GOODS STORES: Leather, Exc Luggage & Shoes

Land Leather Inc ....G 305 594-2260
Miami *(G-9422)*

LUGGAGE WHOLESALERS

Group III International Inc ....D 954 984-1607
Pompano Beach *(G-14046)*

LUGGAGE: Traveling Bags

My Focus Inc ....G 305 826-4480
Hialeah *(G-5270)*

LUGGAGE: Wardrobe Bags

Goyard Miami LLC ....D 305 894-9235
Bal Harbour *(G-294)*
Hontus Ltd ....G 786 322-3022
Medley *(G-8255)*

LUMBER & BLDG MATLS DEALER, RET: Garage Doors, Sell/Install

All Pro Chelo Corp ....G 786 317-3914
Hialeah *(G-5039)*
Specialty Products Inc ....G 850 438-4264
Pensacola *(G-13608)*

LUMBER & BLDG MATLS DEALERS, RET: Energy Conservation Prdts

A & A Central Florida ....F 407 648-5666
Altamonte Springs *(G-26)*

LUMBER & BLDG MATRLS DEALERS, RET: Bath Fixtures, Eqpt/Sply

Kitchen & Bath Center Inc ....E 850 244-3996
Fort Walton Beach *(G-4594)*
Location 3 Holdings LLC ....F 941 342-3443
Sarasota *(G-15726)*
Unique Marble Inc ....F 772 766-4432
Vero Beach *(G-17810)*

LUMBER & BLDG MTRLS DEALERS, RET: Closets, Interiors/Access

Cast Art International Corp ....G 727 807-3395
Dunedin *(G-3442)*

Southern Closet Systems Inc ....G 813 926-9348
Odessa *(G-11579)*

LUMBER & BLDG MTRLS DEALERS, RET: Doors, Storm, Wood/Metal

Trim-Pak Corporation ....E 407 851-8900
Orlando *(G-12673)*

LUMBER & BLDG MTRLS DEALERS, RET: Windows, Storm, Wood/Metal

Absolute Window and Door Inc ....G 941 485-7774
Venice *(G-17672)*
Leon Screening & Repair Inc ....F 850 575-2840
Tallahassee *(G-16469)*
Tropic Shield Inc ....F 954 731-5553
Lauderdale Lakes *(G-7721)*
Winsulator Corporation ....G 941 365-7901
Sarasota *(G-15877)*

LUMBER & BUILDING MATERIAL DEALERS, RETAIL: Roofing Material

Yandles Quality Roof Trusses ....G 352 732-3000
Ocala *(G-11515)*

LUMBER & BUILDING MATERIALS DEALER, RET: Door & Window Prdts

Architctral Mllwk Slutions Inc ....G 727 441-1409
Largo *(G-7538)*
Custom Cft Windows & Doors Inc ....F 407 834-5400
Winter Springs *(G-18563)*
Rolladen Inc ....F 954 454-4114
Longwood *(G-7943)*
Solar X ....G 386 673-2111
Ormond Beach *(G-12793)*
Sun Barrier Products Inc ....F 407 830-9085
Longwood *(G-7951)*
USA Shutter Company LLC ....G 239 596-8883
Fort Myers *(G-4436)*
West Coast Shutters Sunburst ....F 727 894-0044
Saint Petersburg *(G-15230)*

LUMBER & BUILDING MATERIALS DEALER, RET: Masonry Matls/Splys

Art-Crete Products Inc ....F 386 252-5118
Daytona Beach *(G-2514)*
Concrete Edge Company ....G 407 658-2788
Orlando *(G-12040)*
Marble Designs of FL Inc ....G 321 269-6920
Titusville *(G-17601)*
Paver Systems LLC ....E 407 859-9117
Orlando *(G-12474)*
Quikrete Companies LLC ....E 850 623-0559
Milton *(G-10435)*
Trenwa Inc ....F 863 666-1680
Lakeland *(G-7465)*

LUMBER & BUILDING MATERIALS DEALERS, RETAIL: Cement

Anderson Columbia Co Inc ....G 352 463-6342
Chiefland *(G-1445)*

LUMBER & BUILDING MATERIALS DEALERS, RETAIL: Flooring, Wood

Designer Lifestyles LLC ....F 904 631-8954
Jacksonville *(G-6030)*
Renovation Flooring LLC ....E 850 460-7295
Miramar Beach *(G-10572)*

LUMBER & BUILDING MATERIALS DEALERS, RETAIL: Sand & Gravel

Bdc Shell & Aggregate LLC ....G 941 875-6615
Punta Gorda *(G-14495)*
Helms Hauling & Materials Llc ....F 850 218-6895
Niceville *(G-11032)*
Rock Ridge Materials Inc ....F 321 268-8455
Titusville *(G-17615)*

LUMBER & BUILDING MATERIALS DEALERS, RETAIL: Tile, Ceramic

Asd Surfaces LLC ....G 561 845-5009
North Palm Beach *(G-11174)*

Techno Cabinets Inc ....G 305 910-9929
  Doral **(G-3393)**

LUMBER & BUILDING MATERIALS RET DEALERS: Millwork & Lumber

Architctural WD Pdts of Naples ....G 239 260-7156
  Naples **(G-10673)**
Bay Meadow Architectural Mllwk ....E 407 332-7992
  Longwood **(G-7874)**
Cross City Lumber LLC ....F 352 578-8078
  Cross City **(G-2258)**
Magnolia Millwork Intl Inc ....G 407 585-3470
  Casselberry **(G-1424)**
Millwork and Design Inc ....G 352 544-0444
  Brooksville **(G-1182)**

LUMBER & BUILDING MATLS DEALERS, RET: Concrete/Cinder Block

Cemex Cnstr Mtls Fla LLC ....F 561 832-6646
  West Palm Beach **(G-17959)**
Cemex Materials LLC ....C 386 775-0790
  Deland **(G-2857)**
Cemex Materials LLC ....C 772 287-0502
  Stuart **(G-16127)**
Cemex Materials LLC ....C 941 722-4578
  Palmetto **(G-13159)**
Cemex Materials LLC ....D 954 523-9978
  Fort Lauderdale **(G-3719)**
Cemex Materials LLC ....C 954 431-7655
  Pembroke Pines **(G-13380)**
Commercial Concrete Pdts Inc ....E 813 659-3707
  Plant City **(G-13756)**

LUMBER & BUILDING MATLS DEALERS, RET: Screens, Door/Window

ABC Screen Masters Inc ....G 239 772-7336
  Cape Coral **(G-1295)**
Greg Valley ....F 941 739-6628
  Sarasota **(G-15487)**
Tag Media Group LLC ....F 239 288-0499
  Fort Myers **(G-4417)**

LUMBER & BUILDING MTRLS DEALERS, RET: Insulation Mtrl, Bldg

Carpenter Co ....D 863 687-9494
  Lakeland **(G-7288)**

LUMBER: Dimension, Hardwood

Resolute Cross City LLC ....G 352 498-3363
  Cross City **(G-2263)**

LUMBER: Furniture Dimension Stock, Softwood

Inox LLC ....G 305 409-2764
  Sunny Isles Beach **(G-16277)**

LUMBER: Hardboard

Custom Cornhole Boards Inc ....E 407 203-6886
  Orlando **(G-12066)**

LUMBER: Hardwood Dimension

Boyett Timber Inc ....G 352 583-2138
  Webster **(G-17832)**

LUMBER: Hardwood Dimension & Flooring Mills

A L Baxley & Sons Inc ....F 352 629-5137
  Citra **(G-1466)**
Aj Originals Inc ....G 954 563-9911
  Fort Lauderdale **(G-3635)**
Bushnell Sawmill Inc ....G 352 793-2740
  Bushnell **(G-1240)**
Resolute Cross Cy RE Hldngs LL ....F 352 498-3363
  Cross City **(G-2264)**
Roberts Lumber Company Inc ....F 850 584-4573
  Perry **(G-13652)**
West Fraser Inc ....C 850 587-1000
  Mc David **(G-8190)**
West Fraser Inc ....C 904 786-4155
  Jacksonville **(G-6601)**

LUMBER: Kiln Dried

Roberts Lumber Company Inc ....F 850 584-4573
  Perry **(G-13652)**

LUMBER: Plywood, Hardwood

Boise Cascade Company ....G 800 359-6432
  Havana **(G-4995)**
Coastal Plywood LLC ....B 800 359-6432
  Havana **(G-4997)**
Dackor Inc ....F 407 654-5013
  Winter Garden **(G-18382)**
Goodwin Lumber Company Inc ....F 352 466-0339
  Micanopy **(G-10397)**
Plywood Express Inc ....E 954 956-7576
  Pompano Beach **(G-14132)**
Thomas Rley Artisans Guild Inc ....E 239 591-3203
  Naples **(G-10925)**

LUMBER: Plywood, Hardwood or Hardwood Faced

Esco Industries Inc ....F 863 666-3696
  Lakeland **(G-7317)**

LUMBER: Plywood, Softwood

Coastal Forest Resources Co ....B 850 539-6432
  Havana **(G-4996)**
Cross City Veneer Company Inc ....D 352 498-3226
  Cross City **(G-2259)**

LUMBER: Plywood, Softwood

Corelite Inc ....F 305 921-4292
  Hialeah **(G-5099)**
Thomas Rley Artisans Guild Inc ....E 239 591-3203
  Naples **(G-10925)**

LUMBER: Poles & Pole Crossarms, Treated

Apalachee Pole Company Inc ....E 850 643-2121
  Bristol **(G-1116)**

LUMBER: Poles, Wood, Untreated

Apalachee Pole Company Inc ....E 850 643-2121
  Bristol **(G-1116)**

LUMBER: Rails, Fence, Round Or Split

Equity Group Usa Inc ....G 407 421-6464
  Winter Springs **(G-18565)**
L A Ornamental & Rack Corp ....G 305 696-0419
  Miami **(G-9403)**

LUMBER: Treated

Arnold Lumber Company Inc ....F 850 547-5733
  Bonifay **(G-766)**
Great Southern Wood Prsv Inc ....E 352 793-9410
  Lake Panasoffkee **(G-7119)**
Johnny Under Pressure LLC ....G 850 530-8763
  Pensacola **(G-13529)**
Pensacola Wood Treating Co ....E 850 433-1300
  Pensacola **(G-13573)**
Robbins Manufacturing Company ....C 813 971-3030
  Tampa **(G-17226)**
Southern Lbr & Treating Co Inc ....F 904 695-0784
  Jacksonville **(G-6491)**

MACHINE PARTS: Stamped Or Pressed Metal

Aero Technology Mfg Inc ....F 305 345-7747
  Miami **(G-8662)**
Aircraft Tbular Components Inc ....E 321 757-9020
  Melbourne **(G-8357)**
Benton Machine Works Inc ....G 904 768-9161
  Jacksonville **(G-5931)**
Bonato & Pires LLC ....G 727 581-1220
  Largo **(G-7553)**
Chasco Machine & Mfg Inc ....E 352 678-4188
  Brooksville **(G-1145)**
Cnc Works Service Inc ....F 813 777-8642
  Clearwater **(G-1544)**
Fuse Fabrication Llc ....E 863 225-5698
  Mulberry **(G-10626)**
Icosi Manufacturing LLC ....F 813 854-1333
  Odessa **(G-11530)**
Iva Parts Broker LLC ....G 239 222-2604
  Miramar **(G-10506)**
SBs Precision Shtmtl Inc ....E 321 951-7411
  Melbourne **(G-8516)**

Sohacki Industries Inc ....E 904 826-0130
  Saint Augustine **(G-14894)**

MACHINE SHOPS

10858 Opco LLC ....E 949 697-6737
  Starke **(G-16094)**
Aba Engineering & Mfg Inc ....F 386 672-9665
  Ormond Beach **(G-12739)**
Addtad Partners Inc ....G 727 863-0847
  Hudson **(G-5761)**
Aero Technology Mfg Inc ....F 305 345-7747
  Miami **(G-8662)**
AL Garey & Associates Inc ....C 954 975-7992
  Coral Springs **(G-2130)**
Arnold Industries South Inc ....C 352 867-0190
  Ocala **(G-11327)**
Automated Production Eqp Ape ....G 305 451-4722
  Key Largo **(G-6843)**
C4 Group LLC ....F 850 230-4541
  Panama City **(G-13237)**
Dj/Pj Inc ....E 813 907-6359
  Clearwater **(G-1566)**
Euro Gear (usa) Inc ....E 518 578-1775
  Miami **(G-9114)**
Grinder Wear Parts Inc ....E 503 982-0881
  Largo **(G-7600)**
Hammer Haag Steel Inc ....C 727 216-6903
  Clearwater **(G-1621)**
Integritrust Solutions LLC ....E 850 685-9801
  Navarre **(G-10949)**
Koral Precision LLC ....F 727 548-5040
  Pinellas Park **(G-13701)**
Machine Tool Masters Inc ....F 850 432-2829
  Pensacola **(G-13542)**
Madson Inc ....G 305 863-7390
  Medley **(G-8270)**
Marden Industries Inc ....G 863 682-7882
  Punta Gorda **(G-14513)**
Merit Fastener Corporation ....E 407 331-4815
  Longwood **(G-7922)**
Merit Fastener Corporation ....G 813 626-3748
  Tampa **(G-17066)**
Mid-State Machine & Fabg Corp ....C 863 665-6233
  Lakeland **(G-7395)**
Novak Machining Inc ....G 727 527-5473
  Pinellas Park **(G-13714)**
Production Metal Stampings Inc ....F 850 981-8240
  Milton **(G-10434)**
Responsive Machining Inc ....F 321 225-4011
  Titusville **(G-17612)**
Rfg Consulting Services Inc ....G 786 498-2177
  Miami **(G-9803)**
Rodriguez Welding ....G 305 856-3749
  Miami **(G-9803)**
Santa Rosa Auto Parts Inc ....E 850 477-7747
  Pensacola **(G-13600)**
Stemworks LLC ....E 407 595-8451
  Orlando **(G-12625)**
Sulzer Ems Inc ....E 407 858-9447
  Orlando **(G-12629)**
Sunshine Tool LLC ....G 941 351-6330
  Sarasota **(G-15564)**
Sy-Klone Company LLC ....E 904 448-6563
  Jacksonville **(G-6525)**
Tep Manufacturing Co ....G 321 632-1417
  Rockledge **(G-14751)**
Ttc-The Trading Company Inc ....E 503 982-0880
  Largo **(G-7699)**
Van Linda Iron Works Inc ....E 561 586-8400
  Lake Worth Beach **(G-7263)**
Weber Mfg & Supplies Inc ....F 941 488-5185
  North Venice **(G-11221)**

MACHINE TOOL ACCESS: Broaches

Turbine Broach Company ....F 352 795-1163
  Hernando **(G-5010)**

MACHINE TOOL ACCESS: Cutting

Agi-Vr/Wesson Inc ....E 239 573-5132
  Cape Coral **(G-1299)**
Rock River Tool Inc ....F 941 753-6343
  Bradenton **(G-1036)**

MACHINE TOOL ACCESS: Diamond Cutting, For Turning, Etc

Gws Tool LLC ....E 352 343-8778
  Tavares **(G-17510)**

Microtool and Instrument Inc.................E...... 786 242-8780
Palmetto Bay (G-13215)

Thermocarbon Inc.................................E...... 407 834-7800
Casselberry (G-1435)

MACHINE TOOL ACCESS: Drills

Elliott Diamond Tool Inc......................F...... 727 585-3839
Clearwater (G-1583)

MACHINE TOOL ACCESS: Files

Mastercut Tool Corp............................E...... 727 726-5336
Safety Harbor (G-14791)

MACHINE TOOL ACCESS: Knives, Metalworking

Florida Knife Co.................................F...... 941 371-2104
Sarasota (G-15680)

MACHINE TOOL ACCESS: Machine Attachments & Access, Drilling

Tom Burke Services..............................G...... 863 940-4504
Lakeland (G-7463)

MACHINE TOOL ACCESS: Tool Holders

Aaw Products Inc................................G...... 305 330-6863
Miami (G-8630)

MACHINE TOOL ATTACHMENTS & ACCESS

Dan Lipman and Associates ....G...... 561 245-8672
Delray Beach (G-2953)

Nasco Industries Inc............................E...... 954 733-8665
Fort Lauderdale (G-3953)

Polygon Solutions Inc..........................G...... 239 628-4800
Fort Myers (G-4365)

MACHINE TOOLS & ACCESS

A B & B Manufacturing Inc....................F...... 904 378-3350
Jacksonville (G-5845)

Andritz Iggesund Tools Inc...................E...... 813 855-6902
Oldsmar (G-11626)

B & P Motors Inc.................................G...... 305 687-7337
Opa Locka (G-11721)

Construction and Elec Pdts Inc.............F...... 954 972-9787
Pompano Beach (G-13976)

Creative Carbide Inc............................F...... 239 567-0041
Fort Myers (G-4221)

Delta International Inc.........................F...... 305 665-6573
Miami (G-9013)

Dse Inc...F...... 813 443-4809
Riverview (G-14561)

Gulf Tool Corporation..........................F...... 850 456-0840
Pensacola (G-13517)

Henefelt Precision Pdts Inc...................F...... 727 531-0406
Largo (G-7603)

Jacksnvlle Advnced McHning LLC ....G...... 904 292-2999
Jacksonville (G-6212)

Lexington Cutter Inc............................E...... 941 739-2726
Bradenton (G-1004)

Micro Quality Corp..............................G...... 954 354-5572
Deerfield Beach (G-2767)

Mitts and Merrill LP.............................G...... 352 343-7001
Tavares (G-17519)

Rhino Tools Inc..................................F...... 305 332-7750
Hialeah (G-5330)

Shaw Development LLC.........................C...... 239 405-6100
Bonita Springs (G-817)

Suncoast Tool & Gage Inds Inc.............F...... 727 572-8000
Clearwater (G-1801)

Swisstech Machinery LLC......................G...... 407 416-2383
Orlando (G-12641)

MACHINE TOOLS, METAL CUTTING: Drilling

Aerowest Mfg Corp..............................G...... 786 367-6948
Hialeah (G-5032)

Levil Technology Corp.........................G...... 407 542-3971
Oviedo (G-12836)

M Vb Industries Inc..............................E...... 954 480-6448
Deerfield Beach (G-2758)

Technical Ord Solutions LLC..................G...... 850 223-2393
Perry (G-13656)

MACHINE TOOLS, METAL CUTTING: Exotic, Including Explosive

Metal Supply and Machining Inc............F...... 561 276-4941
Delray Beach (G-2988)

Mitts and Merrill LP.............................G...... 352 343-7001
Tavares (G-17519)

MACHINE TOOLS, METAL CUTTING: Jig, Boring & Grinding

Reinecker Grinders Corp.......................G...... 954 974-6190
Pompano Beach (G-14157)

MACHINE TOOLS, METAL CUTTING: Numerically Controlled

Gulf Machining Inc..............................F...... 727 571-1244
Clearwater (G-1618)

MACHINE TOOLS, METAL CUTTING: Plasma Process

Machitech Automation LLC ....F...... 314 756-2288
Deerfield Beach (G-2759)

MACHINE TOOLS, METAL CUTTING: Sawing & Cutoff

Americut of Florida Inc........................F...... 800 692-2187
Fort Myers (G-4174)

MACHINE TOOLS, METAL CUTTING: Tool Replacement & Rpr Parts

Bonato & Pires LLC.............................G...... 727 581-1220
Largo (G-7553)

Icosi Manufacturing LLC.......................F...... 813 854-1333
Odessa (G-11530)

International Tool Mchs of Fla ....E...... 386 446-0500
Palm Coast (G-13080)

Lundy Enterprises Inc..........................F...... 727 549-1292
Largo (G-7635)

MACHINE TOOLS, METAL FORMING: Bending

Phoenix Enterprises Fla LLC ....F...... 813 986-9000
Temple Terrace (G-17542)

MACHINE TOOLS, METAL FORMING: Container, Metal Incl Cans

Sequa Corporation...............................A...... 561 935-3571
Palm Beach Gardens (G-13008)

Sunrise Manufacturing Intl Inc ....F...... 813 780-7369
Zephyrhills (G-18632)

MACHINE TOOLS, METAL FORMING: Crimping, Metal

Bridgestone Hosepower LLC...................D...... 904 264-1267
Orange Park (G-11816)

MACHINE TOOLS, METAL FORMING: Forging Machinery & Hammers

G & R Machine Inc...............................G...... 407 324-1600
Sanford (G-15323)

MACHINE TOOLS, METAL FORMING: Gear Rolling

B&M RC Racing....................................G...... 313 518-3999
Winter Haven (G-18419)

MACHINE TOOLS, METAL FORMING: Headers

Double Header Fish Charter ....G...... 772 388-5741
Sebastian (G-15890)

MACHINE TOOLS, METAL FORMING: High Energy Rate

Bedeschi America Inc..........................D...... 954 602-2175
Pembroke Pines (G-13378)

MACHINE TOOLS, METAL FORMING: Mechanical, Pneumatic Or Hyd

Aflg Invstmnts-Industrials LLC..............G...... 813 443-8203
Tampa (G-16564)

Aflg Invstmnts-Industrials LLC..............F...... 813 443-8203
Hernando Beach (G-5011)

Lenco Holdings LLC.............................G...... 305 360-0895
Deerfield Beach (G-2752)

MACHINE TOOLS, METAL FORMING: Shearing, Power

Hydrapower International Inc ....A...... 239 642-5379
Marco Island (G-8112)

MACHINE TOOLS: Metal Cutting

Acu-Grind Tool Works Inc.....................F...... 941 758-6963
Bradenton (G-931)

Agi-Vr/Wesson Inc...............................E...... 239 573-5132
Cape Coral (G-1299)

Andritz Iggesund Tools Inc...................E...... 813 855-6902
Oldsmar (G-11626)

Armada Systems Inc............................G...... 850 664-5197
Destin (G-3058)

Azt Technology LLC..............................C...... 239 352-0600
Naples (G-10687)

Coastal Machine LLC............................G...... 850 769-6117
Panama City (G-13246)

Elliott Diamond Tool Inc.......................F...... 727 585-3839
Clearwater (G-1583)

Ems Technologies NA LLC......................F...... 321 259-5979
Orlando (G-12127)

Florida Hytorc.....................................F...... 813 990-9470
Clearwater (G-1601)

Florida Knife Co.................................F...... 941 371-2104
Sarasota (G-15680)

Giraldo & Donalisio Corp......................F...... 239 567-2206
Cape Coral (G-1348)

Grizzly Manufacturing Inc.....................E...... 386 755-0220
Lake City (G-7024)

Heath Corporation...............................G...... 863 638-1819
Lake Wales (G-7164)

High Performance Holdings Ltd ....F...... 815 874-9421
Lakeland (G-7344)

Highvac Co LLC...................................F...... 407 969-0399
Orlando (G-12218)

Huff Carbide Tool Inc...........................F...... 727 848-4001
Port Richey (G-14362)

Lexington Cutter Inc............................E...... 941 739-2726
Bradenton (G-1004)

Precision Metal Parts Inc ....F...... 727 526-9165
Saint Petersburg (G-15160)

Rankine-Hinman Mfg Co ....F...... 904 808-0404
Saint Augustine (G-14877)

Reiley Tool Company LLC.......................G...... 360 929-0350
Middleburg (G-10409)

Republic Drill/Apt Corp........................D...... 305 592-7777
Miami (G-9797)

Skill-Metric Machine & TI Inc ....E...... 561 454-8900
Delray Beach (G-3018)

Snk America Inc..................................F...... 407 831-7766
Sanford (G-15387)

Super Tool Inc...................................F...... 941 751-9677
Bradenton (G-1055)

Unbridled Technologies LLC ....G...... 888 334-8402
Brooksville (G-1215)

Walin Tools LLC..................................G...... 850 226-8632
Fort Walton Beach (G-4617)

Zel Tech Trining Solutions LLC...............E...... 757 722-5565
Winter Park (G-18556)

MACHINE TOOLS: Metal Forming

Coastal Machine LLC............................G...... 850 769-6117
Panama City (G-13246)

Daigle Tool & Die Inc...........................G...... 954 785-9989
Deerfield Beach (G-2703)

Delta Machine & Tool Inc......................E...... 386 738-2204
Deland (G-2863)

Fuji International LLC...........................F...... 941 961-5472
Sarasota (G-15685)

Jenzano Incorporated...........................F...... 386 761-4474
Port Orange (G-14336)

Mitek Inc..D...... 813 675-1224
Tampa (G-17077)

Production Metal Stampings Inc ....F...... 850 981-8240
Milton (G-10434)

U S Hardware Supply Inc ....E...... 407 657-1551
Winter Park (G-18547)

MACHINERY & EQPT, AGRICULTURAL, WHOLESALE: Agricultural, NEC

Florida Sprayers Inc ....G....... 813 989-0500
Temple Terrace *(G-17538)*

MACHINERY & EQPT, AGRICULTURAL, WHOLESALE: Dairy

Sanchelima International Inc ....F....... 305 591-4343
Doral *(G-3356)*

MACHINERY & EQPT, AGRICULTURAL, WHOLESALE: Landscaping Eqpt

Concrete Edge Company ....G....... 407 658-2788
Orlando *(G-12040)*

MACHINERY & EQPT, AGRICULTURAL, WHOLESALE: Poultry Eqpt

Hawkhead International Inc ....G..... 904 264-4295
Orange Park *(G-11831)*

MACHINERY & EQPT, INDL, WHOL: Brewery Prdts Mfrg, Commercial

Brewfab LLC ....F....... 727 823-8333
Saint Petersburg *(G-14989)*
Canarchy Craft ....C....... 813 348-6363
Tampa *(G-16675)*
Cigar City Brewpub LLC ....G....... 813 348-6363
Tampa *(G-16703)*

MACHINERY & EQPT, INDL, WHOLESALE: Cranes

Coastal Crane and Rigging Inc..............G....... 850 460-1766
Santa Rosa Beach *(G-15423)*

MACHINERY & EQPT, INDL, WHOLESALE: Drilling, Exc Bits

Ronnies Welding & Machine Inc............G....... 305 238-0972
Cutler Bay *(G-2301)*

MACHINERY & EQPT, INDL, WHOLESALE: Engines & Parts, Diesel

All Power Pro Inc ....G....... 904 310-3069
Fernandina Beach *(G-3580)*
Diesel Pro Power Inc ....F....... 305 545-5588
Miami *(G-9031)*

MACHINERY & EQPT, INDL, WHOLESALE: Engs & Parts, Air-Cooled

AC Industrial Service Inc......................F....... 305 887-5541
Miami *(G-8639)*

MACHINERY & EQPT, INDL, WHOLESALE: Fans

Kanalflakt Inc.......................................F....... 941 359-3267
Sarasota *(G-15717)*

MACHINERY & EQPT, INDL, WHOLESALE: Fuel Injection Systems

Progress Rail Services Corp.................D....... 239 643-3013
Naples *(G-10868)*

MACHINERY & EQPT, INDL, WHOLESALE: Instruments & Cntrl Eqpt

Automted Lgic Corp Kennesaw GA ......F....... 877 866-1226
Orlando *(G-11935)*

MACHINERY & EQPT, INDL, WHOLESALE: Machine Tools & Access

Chasco Machine & Mfg Inc ....E....... 352 678-4188
Brooksville *(G-1145)*

MACHINERY & EQPT, INDL, WHOLESALE: Packaging

Profile Packaging Inc............................E....... 941 359-6678
Sarasota *(G-15788)*

MACHINERY & EQPT, INDL, WHOLESALE: Paper Manufacturing

Sandar Industries Inc ....E....... 904 246-4309
Atlantic Beach *(G-215)*

MACHINERY & EQPT, INDL, WHOLESALE: Processing & Packaging

Aircel LLC ....E....... 865 681-7066
Naples *(G-10656)*
Wilkinson Hi-Rise LLC...........................C....... 954 342-4400
Fort Lauderdale *(G-4132)*

MACHINERY & EQPT, INDL, WHOLESALE: Propane Conversion

Aei International Corp ....G....... 904 724-9771
Jacksonville *(G-5865)*

MACHINERY & EQPT, INDL, WHOLESALE: Safety Eqpt

Cintas Corporation ....G....... 239 693-8722
Fort Myers *(G-4209)*
Primetime Industries LLC ....G....... 813 781-0196
Wesley Chapel *(G-17886)*

MACHINERY & EQPT, INDL, WHOLESALE: Waste Compactors

C & D Industrial Maint LLC....................E....... 833 776-5833
Bradenton *(G-951)*

MACHINERY & EQPT, TEXTILE: Fabric Forming

Hills Inc ....D....... 321 723-5560
Melbourne *(G-8437)*

MACHINERY & EQPT, WHOLESALE: Construction & Mining, Ladders

Atlantic Insulation Inc...........................D....... 904 354-2217
Jacksonville *(G-5908)*

MACHINERY & EQPT, WHOLESALE: Construction, Cranes

Coastal Crane and Rigging Inc..............G....... 850 460-1766
Santa Rosa Beach *(G-15423)*

MACHINERY & EQPT, WHOLESALE: Construction, General

Dhs Unlimited Inc.................................G....... 954 532-2142
Pompano Beach *(G-13995)*

MACHINERY & EQPT, WHOLESALE: Drilling, Wellpoints

Jayco Screens Inc.................................G....... 850 456-0673
Pensacola *(G-13527)*

MACHINERY & EQPT: Electroplating

Eidschun Engineering Inc......................E....... 727 647-2300
Clearwater *(G-1578)*
Surface Finishing Tech Inc ....E....... 727 577-7777
Clearwater *(G-1807)*

MACHINERY & EQPT: Farm

Agri Machinery & Parts Inc ....F....... 407 299-1592
Orlando *(G-11878)*
Agro & Cnstr Solutions Inc ....F....... 305 593-7011
Doral *(G-3099)*
Alpha Technology USA Corp ....F....... 407 571-2060
Sanford *(G-15261)*
Animal Air Service Inc ....E....... 305 218-1759
Doral *(G-3116)*
Black Widow Custom Cases ....G....... 321 327-8058
Palm Bay *(G-12892)*
Bushhog N Blade Work ....G....... 904 669-2764
Saint Augustine *(G-14819)*
Chargers and Cases LLC ....F....... 352 587-2539
Orlando *(G-12004)*
Cnh Industrial America LLC ....F....... 954 389-9779
Weston *(G-18233)*
David R Case ....G....... 727 808-9330
Spring Hill *(G-16084)*

Erb Roberts Tillage LLC.........................G....... 352 376-4888
Fort Lauderdale *(G-3796)*
Farmco Manufacturers Inc ....F....... 813 645-0611
Ruskin *(G-14777)*
First Case Cash LLC ....G....... 954 200-5374
Hallandale Beach *(G-4946)*
Foley Air LLC ....F....... 904 379-2243
Jacksonville *(G-6117)*
Franz A Ullrich Jr ....G....... 863 773-4653
Wauchula *(G-17827)*
Hera Cases LLC ....G....... 305 322-8960
Coral Gables *(G-2067)*
Home & Garden Industries Inc ....F....... 305 634-0681
Miami *(G-9289)*
International Packaging Mchs ....G....... 239 643-2020
Naples *(G-10785)*
John W Hock Company ....G....... 352 378-3209
Gainesville *(G-4716)*
Marden Industries Inc...........................F....... 863 682-7882
Punta Gorda *(G-14513)*
Marine Metal Products Co ....G....... 727 461-5575
Clearwater *(G-1683)*
Niteo Products LLC ....G....... 561 745-1812
Jupiter *(G-6771)*
OSteen Plastic Inc................................G....... 954 434-4921
Southwest Ranches *(G-16056)*
Ovipost Inc ....F....... 707 776-6108
Labelle *(G-6985)*
Petersen Industries Inc ....C....... 863 676-1493
Lake Wales *(G-7169)*
Powercases Inc ....G....... 239 415-3846
Miromar Lakes *(G-10575)*
R & C Sales & Mfg Inc...........................F....... 904 824-2223
Palm Coast *(G-13085)*
R & S Metalworks & Co LLC ....F....... 772 466-3303
Port Saint Lucie *(G-14436)*
Ryan Manufacturing Inc ....F....... 386 325-3644
East Palatka *(G-3475)*
Sebring Septic Tank Precast Co ....E....... 863 655-2030
Sebring *(G-15941)*
Southern Fiberglass Inc ....F....... 904 387-2246
Jacksonville *(G-6490)*
St Johns Turf Care LLC ....F....... 352 258-3314
East Palatka *(G-3476)*
Ted Cases Inc ....G....... 561 809-1030
Boca Raton *(G-709)*
Tracto Parts Corp.................................G....... 305 972-1357
Miami *(G-10032)*
Tru-Flo Corp ....F....... 561 996-5850
Belle Glade *(G-346)*
Turner Machine & Supply Co ....G....... 772 464-4550
Fort Pierce *(G-4545)*

MACHINERY & EQPT: Gas Producers, Generators/Other Rltd Eqpt

Casper Engineering Corp.......................G....... 305 666-4046
Pinecrest *(G-13664)*

MACHINERY & EQPT: Liquid Automation

Aflg Invstmnts-Industrials LLC...............G....... 813 443-8203
Tampa *(G-16564)*
Aflg Invstmnts-Industrials LLC...............F....... 813 443-8203
Hernando Beach *(G-5011)*
Keltour US Inc ....F....... 239 424-8901
Cape Coral *(G-1361)*
Syn-Tech Systems Inc ....C....... 850 878-2558
Tallahassee *(G-16507)*

MACHINERY & EQPT: Metal Finishing, Plating Etc

Prestige Service Group ....G....... 954 532-9014
Pompano Beach *(G-14144)*
Recycling Center..................................G....... 386 364-5865
Live Oak *(G-7854)*

MACHINERY & EQPT: Petroleum Refinery

Logistic Systems Inc ....G....... 305 477-4999
Miami *(G-9472)*

MACHINERY BASES

Brady Built Technologies Inc..................G....... 270 692-6866
Melbourne *(G-8381)*
Dj/Pj Inc ....E....... 813 907-6359
Clearwater *(G-1566)*
JP Donvan Prcsion McHining LLC ....G....... 321 383-1171
Rockledge *(G-14720)*

PRODUCT

Tru Mension Mfg Solutions ....G..... 321 255-4665
 Melbourne *(G-8554)*
Vested Metals Intl LLC ....G..... 904 495-7278
 Saint Augustine *(G-14909)*

MACHINERY, COMMERCIAL LAUNDRY & Drycleaning: Ironers

Klinco Inc ....G..... 734 949-4999
 Miami *(G-9393)*

MACHINERY, COMMERCIAL LAUNDRY & Drycleaning: Pressing

Unipress Corporation ....D..... 813 623-3731
 Tampa *(G-17389)*

MACHINERY, COMMERCIAL LAUNDRY: Washing, Incl Coin-Operated

Coin-O-Matic Inc ....E..... 305 635-4141
 Miami *(G-8942)*
R&K Mehall Inc ....G..... 727 781-8780
 Palm Harbor *(G-13126)*

MACHINERY, EQPT & SUPPLIES: Parking Facility

Lcn Incorporated ....E..... 305 461-2770
 Miami *(G-9440)*
Park Plus Florida Inc ....F..... 954 929-7511
 Dania *(G-2341)*
Robotic Parking Systems Inc ....F..... 727 539-7275
 Clearwater *(G-1770)*

MACHINERY, FOOD PRDTS: Dairy & Milk

Authentic Trading Inc ....G..... 347 866-7241
 Davie *(G-2390)*
Carter Day Holding Inc ....D..... 239 280-0361
 Naples *(G-10704)*
Sanchelima International Inc ....F..... 305 591-4343
 Doral *(G-3356)*

MACHINERY, FOOD PRDTS: Distillery

Aquaback Technologies Inc ....F..... 978 863-1000
 Port Saint Lucie *(G-14397)*
Muscle LLC ....G..... 772 678-6176
 Stuart *(G-16188)*
Point Distillery LLC ....F..... 727 269-5588
 New Port Richey *(G-10981)*

MACHINERY, FOOD PRDTS: Juice Extractors, Fruit & Veg, Comm

Zumex Usa Inc ....G..... 305 591-0061
 Doral *(G-3424)*

MACHINERY, FOOD PRDTS: Mixers, Commercial

Cei Liquidation Inc ....G..... 281 541-2444
 Fort Pierce *(G-4473)*

MACHINERY, FOOD PRDTS: Ovens, Bakery

Californo Corp ....G..... 855 553-6766
 Hallandale Beach *(G-4940)*

MACHINERY, FOOD PRDTS: Packing House

Whigham Citrus Packing House ....G..... 772 569-7190
 Vero Beach *(G-17818)*

MACHINERY, FOOD PRDTS: Pasta

Defrancisci Machine Co LLC ....F..... 321 952-6600
 Melbourne *(G-8399)*

MACHINERY, FOOD PRDTS: Sugar Plant

Alvean Americas Inc ....G..... 305 606-0770
 Coral Gables *(G-2027)*
Czarnikow Group Ltd ....G..... 786 476-0000
 Miami *(G-8988)*

MACHINERY, MAILING: Mailing

Sure-Feed Engineering Inc ....D..... 727 571-3330
 Clearwater *(G-1806)*

MACHINERY, MAILING: Postage Meters

Pitney Bowes Inc ....D..... 813 639-1110
 Tampa *(G-17167)*

MACHINERY, METALWORKING: Assembly, Including Robotic

Alh Systems Inc ....G..... 727 787-6306
 Palm Harbor *(G-13096)*
Centurion Armoring Intl Inc ....G..... 813 426-3385
 Tampa *(G-16695)*
Robotics Fabrication Inc ....E..... 850 896-4987
 Panama City *(G-13304)*
Waterjet Robotics USA LLC ....G..... 772 403-2192
 Palm Beach Gardens *(G-13016)*
Westlund Engineering Inc ....G..... 727 572-4343
 Palm Harbor *(G-13139)*

MACHINERY, METALWORKING: Coilers, Metalworking

Best Closures Inc ....G..... 305 821-6607
 Miami Lakes *(G-10284)*

MACHINERY, METALWORKING: Coiling

Prime Global Group Inc ....E..... 386 676-2200
 Ormond Beach *(G-12788)*

MACHINERY, OFFICE: Dictating

Dictaphone Corporation ....C..... 321 255-8668
 Melbourne *(G-8402)*
Hth Engineering Inc ....E..... 727 939-8853
 Tarpon Springs *(G-17476)*

MACHINERY, OFFICE: Duplicating

R & K Marketing Inc ....G..... 904 745-0022
 Jacksonville *(G-6401)*

MACHINERY, OFFICE: Embossing, Store Or Office

Cim USA Inc ....G..... 305 369-1040
 Doral *(G-3161)*
Diversified Performance System ....G..... 904 765-7181
 Jacksonville *(G-6034)*

MACHINERY, OFFICE: Ticket Counting

MC Mieth Manufacturing Inc ....F..... 386 767-3494
 Port Orange *(G-14339)*

MACHINERY, OFFICE: Time Clocks &Time Recording Devices

Simplexgrinnell Holdings LLC ....G..... 978 731-2500
 Boca Raton *(G-677)*

MACHINERY, PACKAGING: Carton Packing

Endflex LLC ....E..... 305 622-4070
 Opa Locka *(G-11742)*

MACHINERY, PACKAGING: Vacuum

MDC Engineering Inc ....G..... 941 358-0610
 Sarasota *(G-15742)*

MACHINERY, PACKAGING: Wrapping

International Packaging Mchs ....G..... 239 643-2020
 Naples *(G-10785)*
Polypack Inc ....D..... 727 578-5000
 Pinellas Park *(G-13720)*

MACHINERY, PAPER INDUSTRY: Paper Mill, Plating, Etc

Industrial Cnstr Svcs Dsign In ....D..... 904 827-9795
 Saint Augustine *(G-14846)*

MACHINERY, PRINTING TRADES: Bookbinding Machinery

Instabook Corp ....G..... 352 332-1311
 Gainesville *(G-4712)*

MACHINERY, PRINTING TRADES: Copy Holders

Kyocera Dcment Sltons Sthast L ....F..... 772 562-0511
 Fort Pierce *(G-4499)*

MACHINERY, PRINTING TRADES: Plates

Trinity Graphic Usa Inc ....F..... 941 355-2636
 Sarasota *(G-15572)*

MACHINERY, PRINTING TRADES: Printing Trade Parts & Attchts

Equigraph Trading Corp ....G..... 786 237-5665
 Miami *(G-9107)*
William B Rudow Inc ....G..... 941 957-4200
 Sarasota *(G-15875)*

MACHINERY, SERVICING: Coin-Operated, Exc Dry Clean & Laundry

Sergeant Bretts Coffee LLC ....G..... 561 451-0048
 Coconut Creek *(G-2004)*

MACHINERY, SEWING: Sewing & Hat & Zipper Making

Toucan Industries Inc ....E..... 954 590-2222
 Pompano Beach *(G-14216)*

MACHINERY, TEXTILE: Card Clothing

Baylee & Company LLC ....G..... 305 333-6464
 Hialeah *(G-5069)*

MACHINERY, TEXTILE: Cloth Spreading

Unicraft Corp ....F..... 305 633-4945
 Miami *(G-10059)*

MACHINERY, TEXTILE: Embroidery

Lac Inc ....F..... 407 671-6610
 Winter Park *(G-18518)*
Pantograms Inc ....G..... 813 839-5697
 Tampa *(G-17144)*
Pantograms Mfg Co Inc ....E..... 813 839-5697
 Tampa *(G-17145)*

MACHINERY, TEXTILE: Silk Screens

B Line Apparel Inc ....F..... 305 953-8300
 Hialeah *(G-5066)*
Imprints International Inc ....G..... 561 202-0105
 Royal Palm Beach *(G-14767)*
Joni Industries Inc ....F..... 352 799-5456
 Brooksville *(G-1166)*

MACHINERY, TEXTILE: Winders

Prime Global Group Inc ....E..... 386 676-2200
 Ormond Beach *(G-12788)*
Progressive Machine Co Inc ....F..... 386 333-6850
 Ormond Beach *(G-12790)*

MACHINERY, WOODWORKING: Bandsaws

A H Woodcrafter ....G..... 305 885-2136
 Miami *(G-8622)*

MACHINERY, WOODWORKING: Cabinet Makers'

Artemisa Escobar Brothers Inc ....G..... 786 286-1493
 Medley *(G-8201)*
Commercial Cabinetry LLC ....G..... 407 440-4601
 Orlando *(G-12032)*
Generations Metier Inc ....E..... 239 458-8127
 Cape Coral *(G-1347)*
Thomas Mix Kitchens Baths Inc ....G..... 239 229-4323
 Fort Myers *(G-4421)*
Up - N - Atom ....G..... 904 716-5431
 Jacksonville *(G-6582)*

MACHINERY, WOODWORKING: Furniture Makers

Designers Mfg Ctr Inc ....G..... 954 530-7622
 Oakland Park *(G-11259)*
Lastrada Furniture Inc ....F..... 954 485-6000
 Fort Lauderdale *(G-3912)*

Pleasure Interiors LLC..................E......941 756-9969
Sarasota **(G-15783)**

MACHINERY, WOODWORKING: Planing Mill

County of Sumter.....................G......352 689-4460
Bushnell **(G-1242)**

MACHINERY, WOODWORKING: Veneer Mill

Calvert Manufacturing Inc...................E......407 331-5522
Casselberry **(G-1411)**

MACHINERY/EQPT, INDL, WHOL: Cleaning, High Press, Sand/Steam

Cress Chemical & Eqp Co Inc..............G......407 425-2846
Orlando **(G-12056)**

MACHINERY: Ammunition & Explosives Loading

Amtec Less Lethal Systems Inc ....D......850 223-4066
Perry **(G-13631)**
M Seven Holdings LLC......................F......888 462-7577
Fort Myers **(G-4314)**

MACHINERY: Assembly, Exc Metalworking

Automatic Mfg Systems Inc..................E......954 791-1500
Plantation **(G-13829)**
Buffalo Machine Manufacturing ....G......727 321-1905
Saint Petersburg **(G-14991)**
Carter Day Holding Inc......................D......239 280-0361
Naples **(G-10704)**
Innovated Industrial Svcs Inc..............F......863 701-2711
Bartow **(G-313)**
Jenzano Incorporated......................F......386 761-4474
Port Orange **(G-14336)**
Serf Inc................................E......850 476-8203
Cantonment **(G-1273)**

MACHINERY: Automobile Garage, Frame Straighteners

Popstops Marketing Inc ....G......800 209-4571
Saint Petersburg **(G-15155)**

MACHINERY: Automotive Maintenance

Florida Oil Service Inc ....F......813 655-4753
Lithia **(G-7834)**
Solid Start Inc.............................E......863 937-9297
Lakeland **(G-7440)**
Star Envirotech Inc........................F......714 427-1244
Hialeah **(G-5362)**
Sun Nation Corp.........................F......954 822-5460
Pompano Beach **(G-14205)**

MACHINERY: Automotive Related

Archimaze Logistics Inc...................G......954 615-7485
Fort Lauderdale **(G-3654)**
Pcm and S L Plota Co LLC...............F......727 547-6277
Largo **(G-7656)**
Shirley L Jordan Company Inc............F......352 754-1117
Brooksville **(G-1199)**

MACHINERY: Banking

Greenwise Bankcard ....G......954 673-0406
Coconut Creek **(G-1988)**
Metavante Holdings LLC.................G......904 438-6000
Jacksonville **(G-6301)**

MACHINERY: Billing

American Respiratory Solutions ....G......386 698-4446
Crescent City **(G-2234)**

MACHINERY: Bottle Washing & Sterilzing

Kiinde LLC..............................G......914 303-6308
Melbourne **(G-8449)**

MACHINERY: Bottling & Canning

Emhart Glass Manufacturing Inc..........E......727 535-5502
Saint Petersburg **(G-15035)**

MACHINERY: Brewery & Malting

Union Engineering N Amer LLC ....F......386 445-4200
Daytona Beach **(G-2615)**

MACHINERY: Coin Wrapping

Klopp International Inc ....F......813 855-6789
Oldsmar **(G-11666)**

MACHINERY: Concrete Prdts

Concrete Edge Company ....G......407 658-2788
Orlando **(G-12040)**
Somero Enterprises Inc..................D......906 482-7252
Fort Myers **(G-4401)**

MACHINERY: Construction

AA Casey Company ....F......813 234-8831
Tampa **(G-16549)**
All Points Boats Inc......................D......954 767-8255
Fort Lauderdale **(G-3639)**
Altec Industries Inc......................G......904 647-5219
Jacksonville **(G-5879)**
Altec Industries Inc......................F......561 686-8550
Riviera Beach **(G-14593)**
Amer-Con Corp ....E......786 293-8004
Palmetto Bay **(G-13207)**
American Mfg & Mch Inc ....D......352 728-2222
Okahumpka **(G-11594)**
Ammann America Inc ....F......954 907-5776
Davie **(G-2386)**
Blasters Ready Jet Inc ....E......813 985-4500
Tampa **(G-16647)**
Bromma Conquip.......................G......786 501-7130
Miami **(G-8855)**
Charles Machine Works Inc ....F......813 704-4865
Plant City **(G-13754)**
Cme Arma Inc ....E......305 633-1524
Miami **(G-8933)**
Costex Corporation ....C......305 592-9769
Miami **(G-8975)**
Cross Construction Svcs Inc.............D......813 907-1013
Lutz **(G-7987)**
Dade Equipment.........................G......305 717-9901
Miami **(G-8995)**
Dave Siler Transport ....G......239 348-3283
Naples **(G-10724)**
Dhs Unlimited Inc.......................G......954 532-2142
Pompano Beach **(G-13995)**
Equipment Fabricators Inc...............E......321 632-0990
Cocoa **(G-1926)**
Faver Inc ....G......305 448-6060
Miami **(G-9135)**
Florida General Trading Inc ....G......813 391-2149
Ocala **(G-11392)**
Form-Co Inc.............................G......800 745-3700
Orlando **(G-12173)**
Fw Shoring Company ....F......813 248-2495
Tampa **(G-16867)**
Fw Shoring Company ....G......517 676-8800
Orlando **(G-12179)**
Gar International ....G......954 704-9590
Miramar **(G-10495)**
Industrial Cnveyor Systems Inc ....F......305 255-0200
Cutler Bay **(G-2292)**
Jlg Industries Inc ....F......786 558-8909
Doral **(G-3269)**
Jones Communications Inc ....G......407 448-6615
Sanford **(G-15345)**
Michigan Group Inc ....G......954 328-6341
Coconut Creek **(G-1998)**
Nippon Maciwumei Co..................F......954 533-7747
Sunrise **(G-16347)**
P3 Fleet LLC............................F......904 549-5500
Jacksonville **(G-6348)**
Pantropic Power Inc ....D......954 797-7972
Fort Lauderdale **(G-3973)**
Puzzled Caterpillars Inc.................G......904 379-9219
Jacksonville **(G-6397)**
Roadsafe Traffic Systems Inc ....E......386 755-0140
Lake City **(G-7043)**
Ronnies Welding & Machine Inc..........G......305 238-0972
Cutler Bay **(G-2301)**
Shantui America Corp ....F......786 491-9114
Miami **(G-9877)**
Sipp Technologies LLC ....E......904 374-5606
Jacksonville **(G-6475)**
Smith Challenger Mfg Svcs Inc ....F......863 248-2624
Lakeland **(G-7437)**
Southland Services LLC.................G......850 393-2444
Freeport **(G-4630)**
Space Coast Hydraulics Inc..............F......321 504-6006
Rockledge **(G-14748)**
Spin Free LLC...........................F......561 775-2534
Palm Beach Gardens **(G-13010)**

Townley Engrg & Mfg Co Inc ....C......352 687-3001
Candler **(G-1261)**
Tyco Machine Inc ....G......352 544-0210
Brooksville **(G-1214)**
Waterblasting Technologies Inc ....D......772 223-7393
Stuart **(G-16248)**

MACHINERY: Cryogenic, Industrial

Mec Cryo LLC...........................E......813 644-3764
Tampa **(G-17062)**

MACHINERY: Custom

Blair Machine & Tool Inc ....F......904 731-4377
Jacksonville **(G-5935)**
Builders Automtn McHy Co LLC ....E......727 538-2180
Largo **(G-7559)**
Cole Machine LLC.......................G......239 571-4364
Naples **(G-10718)**
Flc Machines Inc ....E......352 728-2303
Leesburg **(G-7775)**
Gunns Welding & Fabricating............G......727 393-5238
Saint Petersburg **(G-15070)**
La Zero Inc..............................G......727 545-1175
Pinellas Park **(G-13703)**
Larson-Burton Incorporated ....F......815 637-9500
Daytona Beach **(G-2569)**
P D I S Inc..............................F......561 243-8442
Jacksonville **(G-6347)**
Parker-Hannifin Corporation ....E......305 470-8800
Miami **(G-9694)**
Precision Qulty Machining Inc............G......407 831-7240
Sanford **(G-15375)**
Real Fleet Solutions LLC.................E......321 631-2414
Cocoa **(G-1952)**
Riegl Usa Inc ....E......407 248-9927
Winter Garden **(G-18403)**
Schur & Company LLC ....D......904 353-8075
Jacksonville **(G-6454)**
Special Tool Solutions Inc ....E......904 356-5671
Jacksonville **(G-6498)**

MACHINERY: Dredging

Cavo Development Inc ....F......305 255-7465
Miami **(G-8902)**

MACHINERY: Electrical Discharge Erosion

Mew Automation LLC ....G......305 319-9199
Medley **(G-8281)**

MACHINERY: Electronic Component Making

Andrew Martin Swift ....G......321 409-0509
Melbourne **(G-8365)**
Automated Production Eqp Ape..........F......631 654-1197
Key Largo **(G-6842)**
Beachchip Technologies LLC.............G......727 643-8106
Clearwater **(G-1515)**
Cannon T4 Inc ....G......347 583-0477
Naples **(G-10703)**
Connectronics US Inc....................G......954 534-3335
Palm Beach **(G-12931)**
Hilton International Inds..................E......941 371-2600
Sarasota **(G-15701)**
Interactive Cards Inc.....................F......863 688-4548
Lakeland **(G-7354)**
Lgl Group Inc...........................G......407 298-2000
Orlando **(G-12325)**
Rubyquartz Technology LLC ....F......305 406-0211
Doral **(G-3354)**
Skylink Technology Inc ....G......609 689-9200
Windermere **(G-18366)**

MACHINERY: Electronic Teaching Aids

Gadgetcat LLC ....G......802 238-3671
Cocoa Beach **(G-1971)**

MACHINERY: Engraving

Elements of Space LLC..................G......407 718-9690
Orlando **(G-12120)**

MACHINERY: Extruding

Bedeschi America Inc....................G......954 602-2175
Boca Raton **(G-429)**

MACHINERY: Fiber Optics Strand Coating

Force Enterprises Coatings LLC ....F 561 480-7298
West Palm Beach **(G-18007)**

MACHINERY: Folding

Profold Inc ....E 772 589-0063
Sebastian **(G-15903)**

MACHINERY: Gas Producers

Union Engineering N Amer LLC ....F 386 445-4200
Daytona Beach **(G-2615)**

MACHINERY: General, Industrial, NEC

Pneumatic Products Corporation ....G 352 873-5793
Ocala **(G-11469)**

MACHINERY: Ice Cream

Kenfar Corporation ....G 813 443-5222
Tampa **(G-16980)**

MACHINERY: Ice Making

A & V Refrigeration Corp ....G 305 883-0733
Hialeah **(G-5015)**
Asbury Manufacturing Co LLC ....E 954 202-7419
Fort Lauderdale **(G-3660)**
Holiday Ice Inc ....E 407 831-2077
Longwood **(G-7901)**
Ice Link 2018 LLC ....G 305 988-4023
Lake Worth Beach **(G-7256)**
Welbilt Inc ....C 727 375-7010
Trinity **(G-17641)**

MACHINERY: Industrial, NEC

Ace Tools ....G 386 302-5152
Palm Coast **(G-13067)**
Bryan Nelco Inc ....G 727 533-8282
Clearwater **(G-1529)**
Custom Watersports Eqp Inc ....G 941 753-9949
Bradenton **(G-965)**
Donaldson Enterprises ....G 850 934-5030
Gulf Breeze **(G-4880)**
Express Tools Inc ....G 954 663-4333
Davie **(G-2410)**
Fast Lane Autoshop LLC ....G 954 835-5728
Fort Lauderdale **(G-3810)**
RPM Crushers and Screens ....F 941 769-0420
Punta Gorda **(G-14529)**
Select Machinery Inc ....G 941 960-1970
Sarasota **(G-15823)**
Southridge Outdoor Storage ....G 352 516-5598
Tavares **(G-17523)**
System 48 Plus Inc ....G 561 844-5305
West Palm Beach **(G-18174)**
Turbo Parts LLC ....F 352 351-4510
Ocala **(G-11504)**
Tws Fabricators ....G 954 983-9749
Pembroke Pines **(G-13421)**

MACHINERY: Jewelers

Laserstar Technologies Corp ....G 407 248-1142
Orlando **(G-12314)**

MACHINERY: Labeling

Booth Manufacturing Company ....E 772 465-4441
Fort Pierce **(G-4471)**
Flexo Concepts Manufacturing ....G 305 233-7075
Miami **(G-9150)**
Industrial Marking Eqp Co Inc ....G 561 626-8520
Palm Beach Gardens **(G-12975)**
Universal Labeling Systems Inc ....E 727 327-2123
Saint Petersburg **(G-15219)**

MACHINERY: Marking, Metalworking

Tophet-Blyth LLC ....F 239 594-5477
Naples **(G-10928)**

MACHINERY: Metalworking

Ace Metalworks & Mfg Inc ....E 239 666-1103
Fort Myers **(G-4155)**
American Cmmerce Solutions Inc ....G 863 533-0326
Bartow **(G-298)**
Automatic Mfg Systems Inc ....E 954 791-1500
Plantation **(G-13829)**

Custom Instruments LLC ....G 561 735-9971
Boynton Beach **(G-853)**
Decoral System USA Corporation ....E 954 755-6021
Coral Springs **(G-2149)**
Ebway LLC ....E 954 971-4911
Fort Lauderdale **(G-3780)**
Hilton International Inds ....E 941 371-2600
Sarasota **(G-15701)**
Inen USA Corp ....G 305 343-6666
Opa Locka **(G-11754)**
Jrmetal Ornamental ....G 954 989-2607
Hollywood **(G-5607)**
KCm Mch Sp Broward Cnty Inc ....F 954 475-8732
Davie **(G-2429)**
Marchant Machine Corporation ....G 301 937-4481
Sarasota **(G-15741)**
Mid-State Machine Company LLC ....F 704 636-7029
Fort Myers **(G-4326)**
Precision TI Engrg Gnsvlle Inc ....E 352 376-2533
Gainesville **(G-4749)**
Servo Tech Inc ....G 727 573-7998
Clearwater **(G-1781)**
Smith Machine Services Inc ....G 904 845-2002
Hilliard **(G-5476)**
Symme3d LLC ....F 321 220-1584
Orlando **(G-12642)**
TL Fahringer Co Inc ....G 813 681-2373
Tampa **(G-17356)**
United Machining Service Inc ....G 407 422-7710
Orlando **(G-12688)**

MACHINERY: Mining

B & A Manufacturing Co ....E 561 848-8648
Riviera Beach **(G-14596)**
Chemours Company Fc LLC ....D 904 964-1230
Starke **(G-16098)**
Knight Industrial Eqp Inc ....G 863 646-2997
Lakeland **(G-7370)**
Komatsu Mining Corp ....E 407 491-0758
Winter Garden **(G-18393)**
Komatsu Mining Corp ....E 863 804-0131
Fort Meade **(G-4150)**
Microtool and Instrument Inc ....E 786 242-8780
Palmetto Bay **(G-13215)**
Quality Fbrction Mch Works Inc ....F 386 755-0220
Lake City **(G-7040)**
Technical International Corp ....G 305 374-1054
Miami **(G-9996)**
Townley Engrg & Mfg Co Inc ....C 352 687-3001
Candler **(G-1261)**
Townley Foundry & Mch Co Inc ....D 352 687-3001
Candler **(G-1262)**
Vertex Precision Inc ....F 561 582-6171
Lake Worth **(G-7242)**

MACHINERY: Optical Lens

Automated Vacuum Systems Inc ....G 941 378-4565
Sarasota **(G-15607)**
Intuitos LLC ....F 727 522-2301
Largo **(G-7617)**

MACHINERY: Ozone

International Ozone Svcs LLC ....G 352 978-9785
Mount Dora **(G-10604)**
Worldwide Technology Inc ....E 813 855-2443
Oldsmar **(G-11707)**

MACHINERY: Packaging

A & B of Tarpon Corporation ....G 727 940-5333
Tarpon Springs **(G-17456)**
Acasi Machinery Inc ....F 305 805-8533
Miami **(G-8640)**
B & M Industries Inc ....G 813 754-9960
Plant City **(G-13742)**
B H Bunn Company ....F 863 647-1555
Lakeland **(G-7279)**
Balpack Incorporated ....G 941 371-7323
Sarasota **(G-15608)**
Bbull Usa Inc ....G 813 855-1400
Oldsmar **(G-11632)**
Central Florida Sales & Svc ....E 863 967-6678
Auburndale **(G-223)**
Diamond Moba Americas Inc ....D 954 384-5828
Weston **(G-18237)**
Fill Tech Solutions Inc 200 ....E 727 572-8550
Largo **(G-7584)**
Gevas Pckg Converting Tech Ltd ....G 561 202-0800
Boynton Beach **(G-871)**

Hdh Agri Products LLC ....G 352 343-3484
Tavares **(G-17512)**
Hussmann Corporation ....E 813 623-1199
Tampa **(G-16927)**
Ics Inex Inspection Systems ....F 727 535-5502
Clearwater **(G-1638)**
Intellitech Inc ....E 727 914-7000
Saint Petersburg **(G-15086)**
ISA Group Corp ....G 305 748-1578
Miami **(G-9341)**
JV&h Corporation ....G 954 305-9043
Weston **(G-18261)**
K H S Inc ....D 941 359-4000
Sarasota **(G-15505)**
Kinematics and Controls Corp ....G 352 796-0300
Brooksville **(G-1169)**
Lanfranchi North America Inc ....F 813 901-5333
Tampa **(G-16999)**
MTS Medication Tech Inc ....C 727 576-6311
Saint Petersburg **(G-15133)**
Orkan18 ....G 855 675-2618
Lake Worth **(G-7224)**
Osgood Industries LLC ....C 813 448-9041
Oldsmar **(G-11683)**
Pelliconi Florida LLC ....E 407 855-6984
Orlando **(G-12478)**
Pepsico Inc ....D 305 593-7500
Medley **(G-8297)**
Pharmaworks LLC ....C 727 232-8200
Odessa **(G-11569)**
Plan Automation LLC ....G 786 502-1812
Miami Beach **(G-10219)**
Pneumatic Scale Angelus ....D 727 535-4100
Clearwater **(G-1743)**
Polypack Limited Partnership ....E 727 578-5000
Pinellas Park **(G-13721)**
Production System Engineering ....F 863 299-7330
Winter Haven **(G-18462)**
R & L Manufacturing Inc ....F 772 770-9300
Vero Beach **(G-17792)**
Southern Packaging McHy Corp ....E 305 245-3045
Florida City **(G-3612)**
Sweepy Group Products LLC ....G 305 556-3450
Miami Lakes **(G-10363)**
Trepko Inc ....F 813 443-0794
Tampa **(G-17367)**
VMS Usa Inc ....F 727 434-1577
Seminole **(G-15997)**
Westlund Engineering Inc ....G 727 572-4343
Palm Harbor **(G-13139)**

MACHINERY: Paper Industry Miscellaneous

J and L Artistry ....G 904 701-3070
Jacksonville **(G-6210)**
Kazdin Industries Inc ....G 772 223-5511
Palm City **(G-13047)**
Ronco Machine Inc ....G 904 827-9795
Jacksonville **(G-6433)**
Southeastern Paper Group Inc ....C 864 574-0440
Lakeland **(G-7441)**
Sure-Feed Engineering Inc ....D 727 571-3330
Clearwater **(G-1806)**

MACHINERY: Pharmaciutical

Pharmacy Automtn Systems LLC ....G 727 544-6522
Pinellas Park **(G-13718)**

MACHINERY: Photoengraving

Guided Particle Systems Inc ....G 727 424-8790
Pensacola **(G-13514)**

MACHINERY: Photographic Reproduction

Mac Gregor Smith Blueprinters ....F 407 423-5944
Orlando **(G-12360)**

MACHINERY: Plastic Working

Flite Technology Inc ....F 321 631-2050
Cocoa **(G-1928)**
Midgard Inc ....D 863 696-1224
Lake Wales **(G-7168)**
Mold Control Systems Inc ....G 561 316-5412
Palm Beach Gardens **(G-12990)**
Polyumac Inc ....E 305 691-9093
Hialeah **(G-5297)**
Reduction International LLC ....G 954 905-5999
Weston **(G-18282)**

MACHINERY: Polishing & Buffing

Gaynor Group Inc ....G...... 954 749-1228
Sunrise (G-16320)

MACHINERY: Printing Presses

Altamonte Office Supply Inc ....G...... 407 339-6911
Longwood (G-7866)
Palm Prnting/Printers Ink Corp...........E...... 239 332-8600
Fort Myers (G-4355)
Southwest Eqp For Hrnando Cnty .....G...... 352 596-5142
Brooksville (G-1204)

MACHINERY: Recycling

Alto Recycling LLC ....G...... 813 962-0140
Tampa (G-16583)
Progress Rail Services Corp ....F...... 352 748-8008
Wildwood (G-18318)
Tin Man Co..G...... 305 365-1926
Coral Gables (G-2114)
Wilkinson Hi-Rise LLC.......................C...... 954 342-4400
Fort Lauderdale (G-4132)

MACHINERY: Riveting

Fabco-Air Inc ....D...... 352 373-3578
Gainesville (G-4689)
Standard Rivet Company Inc ....F...... 386 872-6477
South Daytona (G-16029)

MACHINERY: Robots, Molding & Forming Plastics

Nypro Inc ....F...... 727 577-9749
Saint Petersburg (G-15143)
Sunshine Tool LLC ....G...... 941 351-6330
Sarasota (G-15564)

MACHINERY: Rubber Working

BBH General Partnership.....................F...... 863 425-5626
Mulberry (G-10620)
Omega Lift Corporation ....F...... 561 840-0088
Riviera Beach (G-14656)

MACHINERY: Screening Eqpt, Electric

Pe Manufacturing Company Fla ....E...... 727 823-8172
Clearwater (G-1736)

MACHINERY: Semiconductor Manufacturing

Adamas Instrument Corporation..........F...... 727 540-0033
Clearwater (G-1474)
Baytronics Manufacturing Inc ....F...... 813 434-0401
Tampa (G-16633)
Guided Particle Systems Inc................G...... 727 424-8790
Pensacola (G-13514)
Novena TEC LLC ....G...... 407 392-1868
Orlando (G-12427)

MACHINERY: Service Industry, NEC

Defense Flight Aerospace LLC ....F...... 321 442-7255
Orlando (G-12081)
Jamuna1 LLC ....G...... 407 313-5927
Windermere (G-18355)

MACHINERY: Sheet Metal Working

Electro Mech Solutions Inc ....E...... 813 792-0400
Odessa (G-11549)

MACHINERY: Specialty

Aaxon Laundry Systems LLC ....F...... 954 772-7100
Fort Lauderdale (G-3618)
Cisam LLC ....G...... 813 404-4180
Zephyrhills (G-18609)
Demaco LLC ....G...... 321 952-6600
Miami (G-9015)
Fueltec Systems LLC...........................G...... 828 212-1141
Royal Palm Beach (G-14764)
Overture Life Inc ....G...... 323 420-6343
Coral Gables (G-2095)
Southern Fabricating Machinery ....G...... 813 966-3983
Lithia (G-7838)

MACHINERY: Stone Working

Poseidon Industries Inc ....G...... 305 812-2582
Punta Gorda (G-14518)

MACHINERY: Tapping

Rockford Ettco Procunier Inc ....F...... 863 688-0071
Lakeland (G-7423)

MACHINERY: Textile

Alpine Industries Corporation ....F...... 941 749-1900
Bradenton (G-935)
ISA Group Corp..................................G...... 305 748-1578
Miami (G-9341)
ISA Group Corp..................................G...... 786 201-8360
Coral Gables (G-2074)
Legacy Wdm LLC ....G...... 352 799-5434
Brooksville (G-1173)
Ricoma International Corp ....G...... 305 418-4421
Medley (G-8312)
Tekmatic Corp ....G...... 305 972-1300
Miami (G-10000)
United Associates Group Inc................E...... 561 840-0050
Palm Beach Gardens (G-13014)

MACHINERY: Tire Retreading

Vampa Tires Supplies Inc....................G...... 305 888-1001
Miami (G-10092)

MACHINERY: Tire Shredding

Quik Shred ....G...... 561 841-1822
Jupiter (G-6784)

MACHINERY: Voting

Naztec International Group LLC ....F...... 561 802-4110
West Palm Beach (G-18087)
Naztec International Group LLC ....F...... 561 802-4110
West Palm Beach (G-18088)
Smartmatic Corporation ....F...... 561 862-0747
Boca Raton (G-684)

MACHINERY: Woodworking

Braid Sales and Marketing Inc.............E...... 321 752-8180
Melbourne (G-8382)
Dimar Usa Inc ....G...... 954 590-8573
Fort Lauderdale (G-3766)
Lioher Enterprise Corp ....G...... 305 685-0005
Miami Lakes (G-10314)
Quality Fbrction Mch Works Inc ....F...... 386 755-0220
Lake City (G-7040)
Quickwood LLC ....G...... 866 888-5858
Windermere (G-18364)
Teknatool Usa Inc ....G...... 727 954-3433
Clearwater (G-1824)

MACHINES: Forming, Sheet Metal

AL Garey & Associates Inc ....C...... 954 975-7992
Coral Springs (G-2130)

MACHINISTS' TOOLS: Measuring, Precision

Gws Tool Holdings LLC.......................D...... 352 343-8778
Tavares (G-17511)
Time Industries Inc ....G...... 321 676-2080
Melbourne (G-8550)
Trumeter Company Inc ....G...... 954 725-6699
Coconut Creek (G-2008)

MACHINISTS' TOOLS: Precision

Armorit Precision LLC ....F...... 941 751-1292
Sarasota (G-15442)
E-Z Fastening Solutions Inc.................G...... 813 854-3937
Oldsmar (G-11646)
Elite Aero LLC ....F...... 727 244-3382
Saint Petersburg (G-15034)
Goss Inc ....E...... 386 423-0311
New Smyrna Beach (G-11001)
OGrady Tool Company ....F...... 239 560-3395
Fort Myers (G-4347)
Omega One Research Inc ....G...... 561 995-9611
Boca Raton (G-624)
Sandar Industries Inc ....E...... 904 246-4309
Atlantic Beach (G-215)
Selectwo Machine Company Inc ....G...... 407 788-3102
Longwood (G-7945)

MACHINISTS' TOOLS: Scales, Measuring, Precision

Outline Technologies Inc ....G...... 904 858-9933
Jacksonville (G-6345)

MAGAZINES, WHOLESALE

Spanish Peri & Bk Sls Inc ....D...... 305 592-3919
Doral (G-3371)

MAGNETIC INK & OPTICAL SCANNING EQPT

Uniscan LLC ....G...... 305 322-7669
Doral (G-3406)

MAGNETIC INK RECOGNITION DEVICES

Scan Technology Inc ....G...... 931 723-0304
Gainesville (G-4758)

MAGNETIC RESONANCE IMAGING DEVICES: Nonmedical

Invivo Corporation ....E...... 352 336-0010
Gainesville (G-4714)
Medical Outfitters Inc ....G...... 305 885-4045
Miami (G-9529)
Medical Outfitters Inc ....E...... 305 332-9103
North Bay Village (G-11058)
Open Magnetic Scanning Ltd ....G...... 954 202-5097
Oakland Park (G-11282)
Radiance Radiology Inc ....G...... 727 934-5500
Palm Harbor (G-13127)
Tonbo Imaging Inc ....G...... 814 441-0475
Sunrise (G-16383)

MAGNETIC SHIELDS, METAL

Manufacturers Inv Group LLC ....F...... 630 285-0800
Keystone Heights (G-6887)

MAGNETIC TAPE, AUDIO: Prerecorded

Bible Alliance Inc ....E...... 941 748-3031
Bradenton (G-949)
Miami Tape Inc ....F...... 305 558-9211
Hialeah (G-5253)

MAGNETS: Ceramic

Smart Material Corp............................G...... 941 870-3337
Sarasota (G-15831)

MAGNETS: Permanent

USA Rare Earth LLC ....F...... 813 867-6155
Tampa (G-17399)

MAGNIFIERS

Vision Source Inc...............................G...... 407 435-9958
Apopka (G-184)

MAIL-ORDER BOOK CLUBS

Pro-Publishing Inc ....G...... 954 888-7726
Southwest Ranches (G-16057)

MAIL-ORDER HOUSE, NEC

Gulf Glo Banners and Signs LLC ....G...... 850 234-0952
Panama City (G-13271)
J W Group Inc.....................................G...... 386 423-8828
Edgewater (G-3493)

MAIL-ORDER HOUSES: Collectibles & Antiques

Hollywood Cllctibles Group LLC ....G...... 407 985-4613
Orlando (G-12222)

MAIL-ORDER HOUSES: Computer Eqpt & Electronics

Gadgetcat LLC ....G...... 802 238-3671
Cocoa Beach (G-1971)

MAIL-ORDER HOUSES: Cosmetics & Perfumes

Xtreme Tools International Inc..............E...... 305 622-7474
Opa Locka (G-11801)

Employee Codes: A=Over 500 employees, B=251-500
C=101-250, D=51-100, E=20-50, F=10-19, G=4-9

2022 Harris Florida
Manufacturers Directory

PRODUCT

1249

MAIL-ORDER HOUSES: Fitness & Sporting Goods

Onetown Boards ....G...... 786 704-5921
Miami **(G-9654)**

Ventum LLC ....G...... 786 838-1113
Miami Beach **(G-10245)**

MAIL-ORDER HOUSES: General Merchandise

Imagination Enterprises LLC ....F...... 504 289-9691
Orlando **(G-12236)**

New ERA Music Group LLC ....F...... 800 454-9751
Miami **(G-9613)**

Rokey Corporation ....G...... 561 470-0164
Boca Raton **(G-654)**

MAIL-ORDER HOUSES: Magazines

Mojowax Media Inc ....G...... 805 550-6013
Bradenton **(G-1013)**

MAIL-ORDER HOUSES: Order Taking Office Only

Birdsall Marine Design Inc ....E...... 561 832-7879
West Palm Beach **(G-17947)**

MAIL-ORDER HOUSES: Tools & Hardware

Brown (usa) Inc ....F...... 305 593-9228
Miami **(G-8857)**

Doorknob Discount Center LLC ....G...... 813 963-3104
Lutz **(G-7989)**

Electriduct Inc ....E...... 954 867-9100
Pompano Beach **(G-14007)**

MAILING SVCS, NEC

Advanced Xrgrphics Imging Syst ....E...... 407 351-0232
Orlando **(G-11872)**

Princess Preserve Inc ....E...... 954 771-7204
Fort Lauderdale **(G-3998)**

Reimink Printing Inc ....G...... 813 289-4663
Tampa **(G-17214)**

Southeast Print Programs Inc ....E...... 813 885-3203
Tampa **(G-17286)**

Town Street Print Shop Inc ....G...... 850 432-8300
Gulf Breeze **(G-4895)**

MALLETS: Rubber

General Rubber Corporation ....F...... 941 412-0001
Venice **(G-17693)**

MANAGEMENT CONSULTING SVCS: Automation & Robotics

Fuelmatics Corp ....G...... 305 807-4923
Palmetto Bay **(G-13209)**

V and N Advanced Auto Sys LLC ....G...... 321 504-6440
Rockledge **(G-14753)**

MANAGEMENT CONSULTING SVCS: Business

Hogan Assessment Systems Inc ....G...... 904 992-0302
Jacksonville **(G-6179)**

MANAGEMENT CONSULTING SVCS: Business Planning & Organizing

Informa Usa Inc ....A...... 561 361-6017
Sarasota **(G-15705)**

MANAGEMENT CONSULTING SVCS: Corporate Objectives & Policies

Interntnal Synrgy For Tchncal ....G...... 321 305-0863
Orlando **(G-12253)**

MANAGEMENT CONSULTING SVCS: Incentive Or Award Program

Gallant Inc ....G...... 800 330-1343
Winter Garden **(G-18387)**

MANAGEMENT CONSULTING SVCS: Industrial

Phelps Dodge Intl Corp ....E...... 305 648-7888
Doral **(G-3326)**

MANAGEMENT CONSULTING SVCS: Industry Specialist

Skide Llc ....F...... 305 537-4275
Miami **(G-9901)**

MANAGEMENT CONSULTING SVCS: Information Systems

Donovan Home Services LLC ....F...... 813 644-9488
Saint Petersburg **(G-15027)**

MANAGEMENT CONSULTING SVCS: Manufacturing

ALLEZ LLC ....F...... 205 216-6330
Plantation **(G-13823)**

Smartscience Laboratories Inc ....F...... 813 925-8454
Tampa **(G-17275)**

MANAGEMENT CONSULTING SVCS: Retail Trade Consultant

Black Bee Aromatherapy LLC ....G...... 866 399-4233
Orlando **(G-11955)**

Firefly Aircraft Parts Inc ....G...... 954 870-7833
Plantation **(G-13852)**

Tin Man Co ....G...... 305 365-1926
Coral Gables **(G-2114)**

MANAGEMENT CONSULTING SVCS: Transportation

E&P Solutions and Services Inc ....G...... 305 715-9545
Miami **(G-9058)**

MANAGEMENT SERVICES

Aircon Fleet Management Corp ....E...... 305 234-8174
Miami **(G-8674)**

All Power Pro Inc ....G...... 904 310-3069
Fernandina Beach **(G-3580)**

Archer Ellison Inc ....G...... 800 449-4095
Lake Mary **(G-7060)**

Brickmed LLC ....G...... 305 774-0081
Miami **(G-8852)**

C & E Innovative MGT LLC ....G...... 727 408-5146
Clearwater **(G-1533)**

Legacy Vulcan LLC ....F...... 407 299-7494
Orlando **(G-12320)**

Merchspin Inc ....E...... 877 306-3651
Orlando **(G-12372)**

Nexogy Inc ....D...... 305 358-8952
Coral Gables **(G-2091)**

Pearsons Ready-Mix Con Inc ....F...... 386 294-3637
Mayo **(G-8185)**

Vulcan Construction Mtls LLC ....E...... 386 252-8581
Daytona Beach **(G-2618)**

MANAGEMENT SVCS, FACILITIES SUPPORT: Environ Remediation

Robotics Fabrication Inc ....E...... 850 896-4987
Panama City **(G-13304)**

MANAGEMENT SVCS: Administrative

Precision Resources Inc ....F...... 321 635-2000
Cocoa **(G-1949)**

MANAGEMENT SVCS: Business

Consultant MGT Group LLC ....G...... 352 344-4001
Inverness **(G-5823)**

Davis-Wick Talent MGT LLC ....E...... 407 369-1614
Margate **(G-8127)**

MANAGEMENT SVCS: Construction

Sg Blocks Inc ....G...... 646 240-4235
Jacksonville **(G-6461)**

MANAGEMENT SVCS: Personnel

Atsg Logistic Support Service ....E...... 904 479-3808
Jacksonville **(G-5911)**

MANGANESE ORES MINING

Georgian American Alloys Inc ....E...... 305 375-7560
Miami **(G-9204)**

MANHOLES & COVERS: Metal

Halliday Products Inc ....D...... 407 298-4470
Orlando **(G-12208)**

MANHOLES COVERS: Concrete

Standard Precast Inc ....D...... 904 268-0466
Jacksonville **(G-6504)**

MANICURE PREPARATIONS

Alt Thuyan ....G...... 407 302-3655
Sanford **(G-15262)**

Merchant Central Plaza ....G...... 239 574-7166
Cape Coral **(G-1365)**

MANNEQUINS

Simetri Inc ....E...... 321 972-9980
Winter Park **(G-18537)**

MANUFACTURED & MOBILE HOME DEALERS

Nobility Homes Inc ....E...... 352 732-5157
Ocala **(G-11451)**

MANUFACTURING INDUSTRIES, NEC

3fdm Inc ....F...... 727 877-3336
Largo **(G-7518)**

A Morris Industries LLC ....F...... 239 308-2199
Lehigh Acres **(G-7803)**

Aara Industries ....G...... 954 342-9526
Miramar **(G-10456)**

AB Used Pallets Inc ....E...... 305 594-2776
Miami **(G-8631)**

Acroturn Industries Usa LLC ....F...... 754 205-7178
Tavares **(G-17502)**

Adma ....G...... 561 989-5800
Boca Raton **(G-387)**

Adonel Block Mfg Corp ....F...... 561 615-9500
Miami **(G-8652)**

Air Technical LLC ....F...... 305 837-3274
Saint Petersburg **(G-14958)**

AK Industries LLC ....G...... 954 662-7038
West Park **(G-18210)**

Allan Industries ....G...... 407 875-0897
Orlando **(G-11892)**

Almar Industries Inc ....G...... 305 385-8284
Miami **(G-8698)**

Alvis Industries Inc ....G...... 941 377-7800
Sarasota **(G-15594)**

Argos Nautic Manufacturing LLC ....G...... 305 856-7586
Miami **(G-8747)**

ARI Specialties LLC ....G...... 321 269-2244
Mims **(G-10446)**

Arm Almnum Rling Mnfctures LLC ......G...... 813 626-2264
Tampa **(G-16606)**

Arsenal Industries LLC ....F...... 407 506-2698
Winter Park **(G-18488)**

Arsenal Venture Partners Fla ....F...... 407 838-1400
Winter Park **(G-18489)**

Artec Manufacturing LLC ....F...... 305 888-4375
Hialeah **(G-5058)**

ASG Corp ....G...... 718 641-4500
Miami Beach **(G-10168)**

Associated Carbonic Inds LLC ....G...... 786 464-1260
Miami **(G-8761)**

Astroted Inc ....G...... 786 220-5898
Doral **(G-3122)**

Atria Industry ....G...... 786 334-6621
Doral **(G-3125)**

Aurel Partners LLC ....E...... 203 300-7470
Lake Mary **(G-7061)**

Axiom Manufacturing Inc ....G...... 321 223-3394
West Melbourne **(G-17893)**

Axop Industries Inc ....G...... 239 273-0911
Naples **(G-10686)**

Axtonne Inc ....F...... 510 755-7480
Delray Beach **(G-2934)**

Bahri Industries Inc ....G...... 904 744-4472
Jacksonville **(G-5920)**

Balistic 2400 LLC ....F...... 407 955-0065
Naples **(G-10688)**

Barth Industries ....F...... 727 787-6392
Dunedin **(G-3440)**

Bass Auto Industries LLC G 727 446-4051
Clearwater *(G-1510)*
Biochem Manufacturing Inc G 786 210-1290
Miami *(G-8830)*
Biochemical Manufacturing Inc G 561 799-1590
Jupiter *(G-6696)*
Black Oak Industries Inc G 863 307-1566
Winter Haven *(G-18421)*
Blackfin Manufacturing LLC G 314 482-2766
Rockledge *(G-14692)*
Bruns Mfg Homes G 863 294-4949
Winter Haven *(G-18425)*
Bubblemac Industries Inc G 352 396-8043
Mc Alpin *(G-8187)*
Cannon Industries Inc G 727 320-5040
New Port Richey *(G-10964)*
Caribbean Basin Industries Inc G 941 726-7272
Nokomis *(G-11043)*
Cas Industries LLC G 813 986-2694
Plant City *(G-13751)*
Castle Distributing Inds Inc G 305 336-0855
Miramar *(G-10479)*
Category 5 Manufacturing Inc F 561 777-2491
Lantana *(G-7509)*
Cavok Capital LLC F 727 789-0951
Palm Harbor *(G-13105)*
CCA Industries Inc G 813 601-6238
Dade City *(G-2314)*
Celios Corporation G 833 235-4671
Tampa *(G-16690)*
Centurion Residential Inds F 561 574-1483
West Palm Beach *(G-17964)*
Cgc Industries Inc G 954 923-2428
Hollywood *(G-5549)*
Classic Industries Inc G 561 855-4609
Wellington *(G-17849)*
Cloud Industries G 816 213-2730
Sarasota *(G-15634)*
Codsworth Industries Inc G 203 622-5151
North Miami *(G-11100)*
Colonial Industries Centl Fla G 407 484-5239
Lake Mary *(G-7066)*
Conquest Manufacturing Fla LLC F 954 655-0139
Pompano Beach *(G-13975)*
Costech Lab LLC G 407 476-3488
Orlando *(G-12050)*
Covalent Industries Inc G 727 381-2739
Clearwater *(G-1553)*
Crowe Manufacturing G 813 334-1921
Tampa *(G-16741)*
Crown Industries of Florida G 321 432-0014
Orlando *(G-12058)*
Crown Leao Industries Inc G 561 866-1218
Boca Raton *(G-475)*
Crows Nest Industries Inc G 740 466-2926
Orange Park *(G-11821)*
Ctr Industries G 321 264-1458
Mims *(G-10447)*
Desco G 941 284-1160
Sarasota *(G-15656)*
Disruptor Manufacturing G 407 900-2868
Sanford *(G-15306)*
Dkm Machine Manufacturing F 904 733-0103
Jacksonville *(G-6036)*
Dontech Industries Inc G 847 682-1776
Saint Petersburg *(G-15028)*
Double R Manufacturing G 352 878-4009
Reddick *(G-14552)*
E & A Industries Inc F 954 278-2428
Fort Lauderdale *(G-3777)*
E Benton Grimsley Inc G 850 863-4064
Fort Walton Beach *(G-4579)*
E M Chadbourne Inds LLC G 850 429-1797
Pensacola *(G-13491)*
E-Z Anchor Puller Mfg Co LLC G 800 800-1640
Parrish *(G-13358)*
Echodog Industries Inc G 407 909-1636
Orlando *(G-12114)*
El Teide North Industries G 786 830-7506
Miami *(G-9077)*
Emerging Mfg Tech Inc G 407 341-3476
Lake Mary *(G-7071)*
Empire Enterprises G 786 373-8003
Hialeah *(G-5143)*
Endeavor Manufacturing Inc F 954 752-6828
Deerfield Beach *(G-2717)*
Engitork Industries Llc G 239 877-8499
Naples *(G-10739)*
Europe Coating Industries LLC G 786 535-4143
Medley *(G-8237)*
Everest Industries LLC G 786 210-0662
Doral *(G-3210)*
Evergreen Rush Industries Inc F 954 825-9291
Davie *(G-2408)*
Everlast Industries Corp G 239 689-3837
Fort Myers *(G-4251)*
Eye Wall Industries Inc G 850 607-2288
Pensacola *(G-13499)*
Fagerberg Industries LLC G 352 318-2254
Gainesville *(G-4690)*
Falco Industries Inc G 407 956-0045
Longwood *(G-7895)*
FBI Industries Inc G 239 462-1176
Fort Myers *(G-4252)*
Fcs Industries Corp G 407 947-3127
Ocoee *(G-11521)*
Fcs Industries Corp F 407 412-5642
Orlando *(G-12147)*
Finger Lakes Custom Mfg LLC G 315 283-4849
Ocala *(G-11387)*
Five Star Quality Mfg Corp G 954 972-4772
Fort Lauderdale *(G-3819)*
FL Industries Inc G 954 422-3766
Pompano Beach *(G-14027)*
Flex Innovations LLC F 866 310-3539
Venice *(G-17691)*
Florida Freshner Corp G 954 349-0348
Weston *(G-18242)*
Florida Nbty Manufacturing F 561 922-4800
Boca Raton *(G-518)*
Floridas Finest Industries F 239 333-1777
Fort Myers *(G-4259)*
Fox Industries of Swfl Inc F 239 732-6199
Naples *(G-10750)*
Fox Manufacturing LLC G 904 531-3150
Green Cove Springs *(G-4825)*
Fraziers Fbrication Prfmce LLC G 813 928-1449
Dover *(G-3430)*
Fusion Industries G 239 592-7070
Naples *(G-10755)*
Fuzion Digital Signs G 844 529-0505
Tampa *(G-16866)*
Gator Fabrications LLC G 352 245-7227
Belleview *(G-361)*
Global Composite USA Inc E 813 898-7987
Tampa *(G-16881)*
Global Seashell Industries LLC G 813 677-6674
Tampa *(G-16885)*
Gloves USA Corp F 786 536-2905
Miami *(G-9223)*
Green Touch Industries Inc G 561 659-5525
West Palm Beach *(G-18020)*
GT Industries Inc G 954 962-9700
Fort Lauderdale *(G-3851)*
GTM Manufacturing Inc G 407 654-6598
Groveland *(G-4861)*
H & F Industries Corp G 727 271-4974
Holiday *(G-5496)*
H V Payne Mfg LLC G 941 773-1112
Sarasota *(G-15697)*
Halliday Industries LLC G 321 288-3979
Melbourne *(G-8431)*
Hardrives Industries Inc F 561 278-0456
Delray Beach *(G-2974)*
Hawthorne & Son Industries LLC G 954 980-8427
Fort Lauderdale *(G-3862)*
High Five Industries Inc G 954 673-1811
Hollywood *(G-5595)*
High Temp Industries G 215 794-0864
Cape Coral *(G-1353)*
Holcomb Industries Flp G 480 363-9988
Clearwater *(G-1626)*
Hopkins Manufacturing Co G 620 591-8229
Tarpon Springs *(G-17475)*
Hough Industries Inc G 863 634-1664
O Brien *(G-11224)*
Hughes Fabrication G 239 481-1376
Fort Myers *(G-4285)*
Hurricane Marine Mfg Inc F 772 260-3950
Stuart *(G-16163)*
Hurricane Marine Mfg S Inc G 305 735-4461
Tavernier *(G-17531)*
Hyend Mfg Inc G 727 828-0826
Clearwater *(G-1633)*
Ice Bunker A&M Corp F 786 368-0924
Hialeah *(G-5192)*
Icon Industries G 352 988-3895
Groveland *(G-4862)*
Insight Optical Mfg Co Fla Inc G 787 758-9096
Miramar *(G-10505)*
Instatech Industries Inc G 954 415-4392
Lake Worth *(G-7206)*
Intouch Inc F 702 572-4786
Orlando *(G-12255)*
Iver Services F 786 329-3018
North Miami Beach *(G-11145)*
J C Industries Inc G 863 773-9199
Bradenton *(G-999)*
Jamali Industries LLC G 954 908-5075
Sunrise *(G-16328)*
Jane and George Industries G 727 698-4903
Saint Petersburg *(G-15100)*
Jay More Corporation F 786 384-1299
Miami *(G-9356)*
Jet Factory LLC G 786 387-6865
Pompano Beach *(G-14066)*
Jfliszo Industries Inc G 239 215-6965
Fort Myers *(G-4298)*
Jsp Manufacturing Holdings LLC G 727 488-5353
Pinellas Park *(G-13698)*
Jta Industries LLC G 407 352-4255
Orlando *(G-12279)*
Jwo Industries Inc F 352 551-6943
Tavares *(G-17514)*
K & N Industries Inc G 850 939-7722
Navarre *(G-10950)*
K Bausch Mfg Corp G 772 485-2426
Stuart *(G-16173)*
Kamco Industries LLC G 772 299-1401
Vero Beach *(G-17770)*
Keller Manufacturing Inc F 863 937-8928
Lakeland *(G-7364)*
Kent Mfg Fla Keys Inc G 941 488-0355
Venice *(G-17703)*
KLA Industries G 727 315-4719
Largo *(G-7626)*
Km Coatings Mfg Jr F 602 253-1168
Deerfield Beach *(G-2748)*
Knb Manufacturers G 407 733-0364
Orlando *(G-12292)*
Knight Industries G 772 344-2053
Port Saint Lucie *(G-14420)*
Laal Manufacturing Inc G 786 859-3613
Miami *(G-9416)*
LDM Industries Inc G 305 216-1545
Miami *(G-9441)*
Load King Manufacturing G 904 633-7352
Jacksonville *(G-6262)*
Lobo Industries LLC G 407 310-3219
Orlando *(G-12338)*
Ls Industries LLC G 850 278-6215
Santa Rosa Beach *(G-15428)*
Luther Industries LLC F 813 833-5652
Tampa *(G-17025)*
M J Boturla Industries Inc G 386 574-0811
Deltona *(G-3048)*
Maddox Industries Inc G 561 529-2165
Jupiter *(G-6759)*
Maher Industries Inc G 407 928-5288
Orlando *(G-12361)*
Manns Diversified Inds Inc G 407 310-5938
Altamonte Springs *(G-58)*
Manufacturing Inc Sp F 305 362-0456
Hialeah *(G-5238)*
Marker Industries LLC G 954 907-2647
Pompano Beach *(G-14087)*
Maskco Technologies Inc F 877 261-6405
Miami Beach *(G-10210)*
Maxeff Industries Inc G 941 893-5804
Sarasota *(G-15515)*
McM Industries Inc F 727 259-9894
Clearwater *(G-1689)*
Medical Waste Industries Inc G 407 325-4832
New Smyrna Beach *(G-11005)*
Memon Industries LLC G 772 204-3131
Stuart *(G-16184)*
Metropolis Corp E 954 951-1011
Fort Lauderdale *(G-3939)*
Mf Industries LLC G 407 457-7531
Casselberry *(G-1425)*
Mfr Empire Corp G 786 558-7122
Miami Lakes *(G-10323)*
Mft Stamps G 352 360-5797
Eustis *(G-3563)*
Miami Asphalt Striping G 305 386-3253
Cutler Bay *(G-2296)*
Milbank Manufacturing Co G 813 623-2681
Tampa *(G-17072)*
Mitten Manufacturing G 941 722-1818
Palmetto *(G-13182)*

MJK Industries Inc ....G 954 788-7494
Pompano Beach *(G-14103)*

Mmo Industries Inc ....G 727 452-8665
Tampa *(G-17079)*

Mmx Manufacturing LLC ....F 786 456-5072
Miami *(G-9579)*

Multiple Tech Industries Inc ....G 561 795-0759
Tamarac *(G-16537)*

Mumford Micro Mch Works LLC ......G 814 720-7291
Sarasota *(G-15754)*

Mytek Industries ....F 727 536-7891
Largo *(G-7648)*

N Y I Industries Inc ....G 561 248-6760
Lake Worth *(G-7220)*

Namro Industries Inc ....G 561 704-8063
Boynton Beach *(G-893)*

Nature Coast Precision Mfg LLC .....G 727 424-3848
Spring Hill *(G-16087)*

Nbs Prformance Fabrication Inc ......G 727 541-1833
Pinellas Park *(G-13713)*

Newvida Products LLC ....G 863 781-9232
Zolfo Springs *(G-18641)*

Niagratech Industries Inc ....G 305 876-9010
Miami *(G-9620)*

Norton Manufacturing & Svc Inc ....G 352 225-1225
Morriston *(G-10594)*

Nova Solid Surfaces Inc ....G 239 888-0975
Fort Myers *(G-4343)*

NTS Industries Inc ....F 317 847-6675
Orlando *(G-12429)*

Oberon Industries Inc ....G 321 245-7338
Orlando *(G-12430)*

Ocala Manufacturing ....G 352 433-6643
Ocala *(G-11455)*

Odyssey Manufacturing Co ....G 407 582-9051
Orlando *(G-12436)*

Panel Armor Products LLC ....G 407 960-5946
Longwood *(G-7932)*

Paradise Building Mtls LLC ....G 407 267-3378
Altamonte Springs *(G-61)*

Patio Products Mfg Inc ....G 813 681-3806
Brandon *(G-1100)*

Patrick German Industries Inc ....G 727 251-3015
Brandon *(G-1101)*

Paveway Systems Inc ....F 386 659-1316
Florahome *(G-3610)*

Pembroke Office Industries LLC ......G 954 589-1329
Hollywood *(G-5640)*

Penguin Door Holding Co LLC ....G 904 540-4450
Jacksonville *(G-6364)*

Pg5 Industries LLC ....G 786 256-0896
Palmetto Bay *(G-13217)*

Pgh Industries Ltd ....G 847 849-0800
Highland Beach *(G-5462)*

Phoenix Mountain Inds LLC ....G 239 348-9895
Naples *(G-10855)*

Platinum Mfg Intl Inc ....F 727 544-4555
Pinellas Park *(G-13719)*

PNC Manufacturing Leather ....G 407 201-2069
Kissimmee *(G-6953)*

Pond Industries Inc ....G 727 526-5483
Saint Petersburg *(G-15154)*

Poseidon Boat Manufacturing ....G 239 362-3736
Fort Myers *(G-4366)*

Printing Services Plus LLC ....F 813 279-1903
Tampa *(G-17185)*

Product Dev Experts Inc ....F 714 366-9000
Stuart *(G-16201)*

Professnal Mtal Innovation Inc ....G 786 354-3091
Hialeah *(G-5312)*

Prowin Industries Inc ....G 954 584-5686
Sunrise *(G-16358)*

R & A Industries Inc ....G 352 307-6655
Oviedo *(G-12845)*

R C R Manufacturing Inc ....G 786 499-9245
Miami *(G-9771)*

R T Industries Inc ....G 352 427-2632
Crystal River *(G-2279)*

R&D Manufacturing Inds Inc ....G 352 351-8800
Ocala *(G-11476)*

Rail Tech ....G 407 834-6966
Altamonte Springs *(G-68)*

Rapid Industries Inc ....F 772 287-0651
Stuart *(G-16205)*

Rdc Manufacturing Inc ....G 772 286-6921
Stuart *(G-16206)*

Resell Mfg LLC ....G 407 478-8181
Maitland *(G-8071)*

Resharp Industries ....G 352 362-1730
Ocala *(G-11481)*

Richard K Pratt LLC ....G 321 482-9494
Titusville *(G-17614)*

Rizo Industries Inc ....F 561 420-2548
West Palm Beach *(G-18142)*

Rogue Industries LLC ....G 850 797-9228
Fort Walton Beach *(G-4607)*

Romax Industries Inc ....G 305 773-6657
Hialeah *(G-5337)*

Royal Canes ....G 727 474-0792
Largo *(G-7673)*

Royal Industries Inc ....G 954 871-6807
Weston *(G-18284)*

S & B Industries Inc ....G 305 367-1068
Miami *(G-9831)*

S3 Industries Inc ....G 305 498-8364
Miami *(G-9833)*

Salty Industries LLC ....G 321 626-6331
Melbourne *(G-8514)*

Schneider Industries LLC ....F 850 207-0929
Daytona Beach *(G-2594)*

Schoen Industries Inc ....G 305 491-5993
Saint Cloud *(G-14938)*

Scky Industries Inc ....G 352 595-7782
Citra *(G-1468)*

Scully Industries ....G 941 349-5561
Sarasota *(G-15821)*

Sdm Industries Inc ....G 904 814-2814
Palm Coast *(G-13086)*

Sebastian Sea Products In ....G 772 321-3997
Vero Beach *(G-17797)*

Seyer - Tech Industries Inc ....G 305 233-2672
Miami *(G-9872)*

Shade Experts USA LLC ....G 561 422-3200
Wellington *(G-17861)*

Shifted Industries ....G 561 302-8915
Groveland *(G-4871)*

Sinclair Industries LLC ....G 305 215-0990
Key Largo *(G-6849)*

Soto Industries LLC ....G 941 830-6000
Punta Gorda *(G-14532)*

South Florida Fabricators LLC ....G 954 802-6782
Cooper City *(G-2023)*

Southeast Manufacturing Inc ....G 866 550-2511
Tampa *(G-17285)*

Spector Manufacturing Inc ....G 860 559-6068
Palm City *(G-13060)*

Squire Industries Inc ....G 813 523-1505
Plant City *(G-13805)*

Ss & S Industries Inc ....F 321 327-2500
Melbourne *(G-8530)*

State of Florida ....F 850 488-1234
Tallahassee *(G-16505)*

Steeda Engineering and Mfg LLC ....G 954 960-0774
Pompano Beach *(G-14198)*

Stover Manufacturing Inc ....G 386 238-3775
Daytona Beach *(G-2604)*

Stover Manufacturing LLC ....F 386 235-7060
Port Orange *(G-14350)*

Stump Industries LLC ....D 239 940-5754
Fort Myers *(G-4409)*

Sunciti Industries Inc ....G 407 877-8081
Winter Garden *(G-11593)*

Suncoast Assemblers LLC ....G 407 947-8835
Belle Isle *(G-351)*

Sundown Manufacturing Inc ....F 727 828-0826
Clearwater *(G-1802)*

Sunnman Inc ....G 305 505-6615
Hialeah *(G-5367)*

T & M Industries Inc ....G 954 778-2238
Deerfield Beach *(G-2819)*

Talon Industries Inc ....G 727 517-0052
Belleair Beach *(G-354)*

Tdt Manufacturing LLC ....G 239 573-7498
Cape Coral *(G-1398)*

Team Solutions Dental LLC ....D 407 542-1552
Sanford *(G-15395)*

Tehgol Industries LLC ....G 904 439-5623
Jacksonville *(G-6542)*

Thompson Manufacturing Inc ....G 239 332-0446
Fort Myers *(G-4423)*

Thriv Industries LLC ....F 404 436-3230
Delray Beach *(G-3025)*

Tikore Industries LLC ....G 954 616-5902
Miami *(G-10010)*

Titan Trailers LLC ....G 813 298-8597
Valrico *(G-17670)*

Toogle Industries LLC ....G 863 688-8975
Lakeland *(G-7464)*

Treetop Industries LLC ....G 904 471-4412
Saint Augustine *(G-14907)*

Tri-Edge Industries LLC ....G 561 703-5961
Lake Worth *(G-7238)*

Trine Industries Inc ....G 561 995-1995
Boca Raton *(G-724)*

Trividia Meditech LLC ....F 954 677-9201
Fort Lauderdale *(G-4100)*

Tropic Guard Industries LLC ....G 813 447-3938
Apollo Beach *(G-97)*

Tropic Manufacturing Inc ....G 863 673-3179
Labelle *(G-6988)*

Tropical Mfg Inc ....G 305 394-6280
Hialeah *(G-5382)*

True Line Industries Inc ....G 561 745-4828
Jupiter *(G-6816)*

Tsn Manufacturing ....G 813 740-1876
Tampa *(G-17377)*

Tsn Manufacturing Inc ....G 727 709-9802
Seffner *(G-15966)*

TST Industries LLC ....G 386 868-2011
Lake Helen *(G-7055)*

Turn Key Industries ....G 813 671-3446
Gibsonton *(G-4802)*

Union Pvc Industries Inc ....G 305 883-1640
Hialeah *(G-5391)*

United Manufacturing Svcs LLC ....G 941 224-1692
Bradenton *(G-1070)*

US Patriot Industries Inc ....G 954 802-7402
Hallandale Beach *(G-4981)*

V & G Industries Inc ....G 786 853-1265
Hialeah *(G-5402)*

Vandalay Inds Manatee Cnty LLC .....G 941 756-6028
Bradenton *(G-1071)*

Volcano Industries Inc ....F 770 300-0041
Sarasota *(G-15578)*

Vplenish Nutritionals Inc ....F 954 304-4000
Boca Raton *(G-749)*

Wallace Industries Inc ....G 561 833-8554
West Palm Beach *(G-18202)*

Wallace Industries Inc ....G 561 301-0811
Lake Worth *(G-7244)*

Westrock Lake Mary ....G 407 936-1277
Lake Mary *(G-7117)*

Whitman Industries LLC ....G 239 216-6171
Marco Island *(G-8114)*

Willis Industries Inc ....G 954 830-6163
Davie *(G-2498)*

Wiltcher Industries Inc ....G 704 907-9838
Ormond Beach *(G-12799)*

Worldwide Building Intl Inc ....C 786 744-7076
Miami *(G-10146)*

Worthington Industries LLC ....G 813 979-1000
Tampa *(G-17441)*

Wrobel Industries Inc ....G 727 560-6850
Holiday *(G-5507)*

WW Timber LLC ....G 352 584-4550
Perry *(G-13660)*

Yeager Manufacturing Tech LLC ......F 407 573-7033
Winter Park *(G-18555)*

Z & N Manufacturing Corp ....G 407 518-1114
Kissimmee *(G-6974)*

Zel Custom Manufacturing LLC ....G 303 880-8701
Odessa *(G-11593)*

Zenithtech Industries Inc ....G 386 454-7630
High Springs *(G-5458)*

Zepsa Industries ....G 754 307-2173
Pompano Beach *(G-14246)*

MAPS

Quantum Spatial Inc ....D 920 457-3631
Saint Petersburg *(G-15168)*

MARBLE BOARD

Jabs Investors Corp ....F 561 540-2693
Lake Worth Beach *(G-7257)*

R & S Marble Designs Inc ....F 941 475-3111
Englewood *(G-3535)*

Sarasotas Finest MBL Gran Inc ....G 941 365-9697
Sarasota *(G-15818)*

MARBLE, BUILDING: Cut & Shaped

Atlantic Marble Company Inc ....F 904 262-6262
Jacksonville *(G-5909)*

Custom Marble Works Inc ....E 813 620-0475
Tampa *(G-16754)*

Debanie Inc ....E 239 254-1222
Naples *(G-10726)*

Gold Granite & Marble ....F 863 439-9794
Lake Hamilton *(G-7050)*

Marble Designs of FL Inc .... G 321 269-6920
Titusville (G-17601)

Marble Lite Products Corp .... E 305 557-8766
Hialeah Gardens (G-5443)

Mont Everest Inc .... G 727 209-0864
Largo (G-7646)

Old World Marble and Gran Inc .... G 239 596-4777
Naples (G-10841)

Puma Marble Co Inc .... F 305 758-6461
Miami (G-9757)

Showcase Marble Inc .... E 386 253-6646
Daytona Beach (G-2598)

Stoneworks Inc .... F 305 666-6676
Miami (G-9955)

Unisource Stone Inc .... G 561 493-0660
Stuart (G-16244)

Yarey Inc .... F 954 520-6015
Boca Raton (G-760)

Zachey Design Marble Inc .... G 754 367-6261
Hollywood (G-5688)

MARBLE: Dimension

Baltic Marble Inc .... G 561 436-3774
West Palm Beach (G-17937)

MARINAS

Gulfstream Land Company LLC .... F 772 286-3456
Stuart (G-16159)

Performance Sales and Svc Inc .... G 863 465-2814
Lake Placid (G-7146)

MARINE ENGINE REPAIR SVCS

Cobra Power Corporation .... G 305 893-5018
North Miami (G-11099)

Offshore Performance Spc Inc .... F 239 481-2768
Fort Myers (G-4346)

MARINE HARDWARE

Accon Marine Inc .... F 727 572-9202
Clearwater (G-1471)

Acryplex Inc .... G 305 633-7636
Miami (G-8648)

Arctic Rays Llc .... G 321 223-5780
Satellite Beach (G-15883)

Batech Inc .... E 321 784-4838
Cape Canaveral (G-1277)

Birdsall Marine Design Inc .... E 561 832-7879
West Palm Beach (G-17947)

Boatrax Corp .... G 855 727-5647
Miami (G-8842)

Byrd Technologies Inc .... E 954 957-8333
Pompano Beach (G-13959)

Dolphin Boat Lifts Inc .... G 239 936-1782
Fort Myers (G-4238)

G G Schmitt & Sons Inc .... C 717 394-3701
Sarasota (G-15479)

Galley Maid Marine Pdts Inc .... F 863 467-6070
Okeechobee (G-11605)

Garelick Mfg Co .... D 727 545-4571
Largo (G-7591)

General Hydrulic Solutions Inc .... G 727 561-0719
Clearwater (G-1613)

Hc Grupo Inc .... G 954 227-0150
Coral Springs (G-2160)

Headhunter Inc .... E 954 462-5953
Fort Lauderdale (G-3863)

Latham Marine Inc .... E 954 462-3055
Fort Lauderdale (G-3913)

Lenco Marine Solutions LLC .... E 772 288-2662
Stuart (G-16179)

Marine Hdwr Specialists Inc .... G 561 766-1987
West Palm Beach (G-18065)

Marine Manufacturing Inc .... G 305 885-3493
Hialeah (G-5242)

Orbe Inc .... G 954 534-2264
Oakland Park (G-11283)

Patrick Industries Inc .... C 941 556-6311
Sarasota (G-15533)

Patrick Industries Inc .... D 239 283-0800
Cape Coral (G-1372)

Pipewelders Marine Inc .... D 954 587-8400
Fort Lauderdale (G-3988)

R J Marine Group Inc .... G 772 232-6590
Stuart (G-16203)

Rupp Marine Inc .... F 772 286-5300
Stuart (G-16210)

Southcoast Marine Products Inc .... C 727 573-4821
Clearwater (G-1788)

Stainless Marine Inc .... E 305 681-7893
Opa Locka (G-11790)

Stuart Industries Inc .... F 305 651-3474
Miami (G-9961)

T & R Marine Corp .... G 850 584-4261
Perry (G-13655)

Tides Marine Inc .... G 954 420-0949
Deerfield Beach (G-2824)

Vitsur Industries Inc .... E 561 744-1290
Jupiter (G-6821)

W D Wilson Inc .... G 813 626-6989
Tampa (G-17421)

MARINE RELATED EQPT

American Boom and Barrier Inc .... E 321 784-2110
Cape Canaveral (G-1276)

Bogantec Corp .... G 954 217-0023
Dania Beach (G-2349)

Csa International Inc .... E 561 746-7946
Jupiter (G-6705)

Enviro-USA American Mfr LLC .... E 321 222-9551
Cape Canaveral (G-1283)

Flagship Marine Inc .... G 772 781-4242
Stuart (G-16148)

Frz Marine .... G 941 322-2631
Sarasota (G-15683)

Jetboatpilot LLC .... F 850 960-3236
Panama City (G-13279)

Marine Spc Cstm Fabricator .... G 813 855-0554
Oldsmar (G-11672)

South Florida Marine .... G 305 232-8788
Cutler Bay (G-2304)

Taco Metals LLC .... G 305 652-8566
Miramar (G-10552)

Tecnografic Inc .... E 954 928-1714
Fort Lauderdale (G-4085)

Uflex Usa Inc .... G 941 351-2628
Sarasota (G-15575)

Zinc Guy Inc .... G 954 907-2752
Davie (G-2503)

MARINE RELATED EQPT: Cranes, Ship

Liebherr Cranes Inc .... G 305 817-7500
Hialeah (G-5223)

MARINE SPLY DEALERS

Davit Master Corp .... F 727 573-4414
Clearwater (G-1563)

Headhunter Inc .... E 954 462-5953
Fort Lauderdale (G-3863)

Rocky Bayou Enterprises Inc .... G 850 244-4567
Fort Walton Beach (G-4606)

Whiticar Boat Works Inc .... E 772 287-2883
Stuart (G-16250)

MARINE SPLYS WHOLESALERS

Jetboatpilot LLC .... F 850 960-3236
Panama City (G-13279)

Veethree Electronics & Mar LLC .... D 941 538-7775
Bradenton (G-1072)

Zinc Guy Inc .... G 954 907-2752
Davie (G-2503)

MARINE SVC STATIONS

S & S Performance Inc .... G 305 951-9846
Islamorada (G-5838)

MARKERS

Trs Industries Inc .... G 561 880-0031
Lake Worth (G-7239)

MARKING DEVICES

Ace Printing Inc .... F 305 358-2572
Miami (G-8643)

Burr Printing Co Inc .... G 863 294-3166
Winter Haven (G-18426)

Four G Enterprises Inc .... E 407 834-4143
Longwood (G-7898)

GBIG Corporation .... G 866 998-8466
Miami (G-9194)

Identity Holding Company LLC .... D 941 355-5171
Sarasota (G-15498)

Mark Master Inc .... D 813 988-6000
Tampa (G-17040)

One Price Drycleaners Tampa .... F 727 734-3353
Dunedin (G-3456)

Sun Graphic Technologies Inc .... E 941 753-7541
Sarasota (G-15562)

MARKING DEVICES: Canceling Stamps, Hand, Rubber Or Metal

Holmes Stamp Company .... E 904 396-2291
Jacksonville (G-6183)

MARKING DEVICES: Embossing Seals & Hand Stamps

Ace Marking Devices Corp .... G 561 833-4073
West Palm Beach (G-17911)

Finlayson Enterprises Inc .... G 850 785-7953
Panama City (G-13262)

MARKING DEVICES: Irons, Marking Or Branding

Sequoia Brands Inc .... E 813 969-2000
Odessa (G-11576)

MARKING DEVICES: Screens, Textile Printing

Say What Screen Prtg & EMB Inc .... F 941 745-5822
Bradenton (G-1042)

Southeast Marketing Concepts .... G 561 747-7010
Jupiter (G-6802)

Vanlex Clothing Inc .... G 305 431-4669
Miami Lakes (G-10375)

Wholesale Screen Prtg Nples In .... G 239 263-7061
Naples (G-10938)

MARKING DEVICES: Stencil Machines

Universal Stncling Mkg Systems .... E 727 894-3027
Saint Petersburg (G-15221)

MASSAGE MACHINES, ELECTRIC: Barber & Beauty Shops

Elastec Inc .... E 618 382-2525
Cocoa (G-1925)

MASSAGE PARLORS

Tom Watson Enterprises Inc .... G 352 683-5097
Hudson (G-5789)

MASTS: Cast Aluminum

Sinobec Resources LLC .... G 561 409-2205
Deerfield Beach (G-2810)

St Judas Tadeus Foundry Inc .... G 305 512-3612
Hialeah (G-5360)

MATERIAL GRINDING & PULVERIZING SVCS NEC

Apex Grinding Inc .... G 386 624-7350
Daytona Beach (G-2512)

MATERIALS HANDLING EQPT WHOLESALERS

Ring Power Corporation .... G 863 606-0512
Lakeland (G-7421)

MATS & MATTING, MADE FROM PURCHASED WIRE

D & D Manufacturing LLC .... F 321 652-4509
Titusville (G-17584)

MATS, MATTING & PADS: Auto, Floor, Exc Rubber Or Plastic

Mobile Auto Solutions LLC .... G 561 903-5328
West Palm Beach (G-18080)

MATS, MATTING & PADS: Door, Paper, Grass, Reed, Coir, Etc

Woovfu Inc .... F 719 301-1661
Saint Petersburg (G-15237)

PRODUCT

MATS: Blasting, Rope

Nets Depot Inc ....F 305 215-5579
Medley *(G-8286)*

MATTRESS PROTECTORS: Rubber

Levita LLC ....G 954 227-7468
Coral Springs *(G-2178)*

MATTRESS STORES

Plushbeds Inc ....G 888 449-5738
Boca Raton *(G-636)*
Zeno Furniture & Mat Mfg Co ....G 954 764-1212
Fort Lauderdale *(G-4145)*

MEAT & MEAT PRDTS WHOLESALERS

Catalina Finer Meat Corp ....E 813 876-3910
Tampa *(G-16688)*
Del Rosario Enterprises Inc ....F 786 547-6812
Medley *(G-8230)*

MEAT CUTTING & PACKING

Apakus Inc ....G 305 403-2603
Coral Gables *(G-2029)*
Azar Industries Inc ....E 904 358-2354
Jacksonville *(G-5915)*
Bubba Foods LLC ....E 904 482-1900
Jacksonville *(G-5961)*
Cargill Meat Solutions Corp ....D 305 826-3699
Hialeah *(G-5086)*
Dutch Packing Co Inc ....G 305 871-3640
Miami *(G-9054)*
Egea Food LLC ....F 833 353-6637
Miami *(G-9074)*
El Toro Meat Packing Corp ....E 305 836-4461
Miami *(G-9078)*
FM Meat Products Ltd Partnr ....E 352 546-3000
Fort Mc Coy *(G-4149)*
Johnson Brothers Whl Meats Inc ....E 850 763-2828
Panama City *(G-13280)*
Justice Government Supply Inc ....G 954 559-3038
West Palm Beach *(G-18043)*
Kelly Foods ....G 904 354-7600
Jacksonville *(G-6240)*
La Montina Inc ....E 305 324-0083
Miami *(G-9410)*
Madson Inc ....F 305 863-7390
Medley *(G-8270)*
Martinez Distributors Corp ....F 305 882-8282
Miami *(G-9515)*
Prg Packing Corp ....E 201 242-5500
Madison *(G-8046)*
South Marion Meats ....G 352 245-2096
Summerfield *(G-16259)*
Special Americas Bbq Inc ....E 305 637-7377
Miami *(G-9936)*

MEAT MARKETS

South Marion Meats ....G 352 245-2096
Summerfield *(G-16259)*

MEAT PRDTS: Bacon, Slab & Sliced, From Slaughtered Meat

Gourmet 3005 Inc ....G 786 334-6250
Hialeah *(G-5175)*

MEAT PRDTS: Calf's Foot Jelly, From Purchased Meat

Immokalee Ranch ....G 239 657-2000
Immokalee *(G-5798)*

MEAT PRDTS: Canned

Pamplona Foods Inc ....G 305 970-4120
Miami *(G-9686)*

MEAT PRDTS: Dried Beef, From Purchased Meat

Moroccan Khlii Inc ....G 813 699-0096
Tampa *(G-17085)*

MEAT PRDTS: Frozen

Kuando Trading Corp ....F 786 603-3772
Miami *(G-9401)*

La Villarena Meat & Pork Inc ....F 305 759-0555
Miami *(G-9415)*
Southast Protein Purveyors LLC ....G 912 354-2770
Winter Haven *(G-18469)*

MEAT PRDTS: Ham, Boiled, From Purchased Meat

Amba Ham Company Inc ....G 305 754-0001
Miami *(G-8710)*
Golden Boar Product Corp ....G 305 500-9392
Miami *(G-9225)*

MEAT PRDTS: Ham, Boneless, From Purchased Meat

High Top Products Corp ....D 305 633-3287
Miami *(G-9281)*

MEAT PRDTS: Ham, Canned, From Purchased Meat

La Montina Inc ....E 305 324-0083
Miami *(G-9410)*

MEAT PRDTS: Pork, From Slaughtered Meat

American Foods Intl LLC ....E 877 894-7675
Aventura *(G-251)*
Henrys Hickory House Inc ....D 904 493-4420
Jacksonville *(G-6174)*

MEAT PRDTS: Prepared Beef Prdts From Purchased Beef

Vienna Beef Ltd ....B 941 723-7234
Palmetto *(G-13203)*

MEAT PRDTS: Prepared Pork Prdts, From Purchased Meat

Get Hams Inc ....G 850 386-7123
Tallahassee *(G-16449)*
La Coronella Meat Processing ....F 305 691-2630
Miami *(G-9404)*
La Esquina Del Le Billto ....E 305 477-4225
Doral *(G-3280)*

MEAT PRDTS: Sausages, From Purchased Meat

Cabreras Spanish Sausages LLC ....G 305 882-1040
Hialeah *(G-5085)*
Elore Enterprises LLC ....E 305 477-1650
Miami *(G-9090)*
Elore Holdings Inc ....G 305 477-1650
Miami *(G-9091)*
Hot Dog Shoppe LLC ....G 850 682-3649
Crestview *(G-2247)*
New Best Packers Inc ....E 386 328-5127
Palatka *(G-12875)*
Red Smith Foods Inc ....E 954 581-1996
Davie *(G-2466)*

MEAT PRDTS: Smoked

Blue Planet Holdings LLC ....F 863 559-1236
Lakeland *(G-7283)*
Uncle Johns Pride LLC ....D 813 685-7745
Tampa *(G-17387)*

MEAT PRDTS: Snack Sticks, Incl Jerky, From Purchased Meat

Country Prime Meats USA Inc ....G 250 396-4111
Plantation *(G-13839)*
Grub Company ....F 347 464-9770
Ormond Beach *(G-12767)*
Silver Horn Jerky Inc ....F 850 208-1433
Pensacola *(G-13603)*

MEAT PRDTS: Variety, Fresh Edible Organs

High Top Products Corp ....D 305 633-3287
Miami *(G-9281)*

MEAT PROCESSED FROM PURCHASED CARCASSES

Bush Brothers Provision Co ....E 561 832-6666
West Palm Beach *(G-17954)*

Catalina Finer Meat Corp ....E 813 876-3910
Tampa *(G-16688)*
Cheney Ofs Inc ....A 407 292-3223
Orlando *(G-12008)*
Discos Y Empanadas Argentina ....F 305 326-9300
Miami *(G-9033)*
Dutch Packing Co Inc ....G 305 871-3640
Miami *(G-9054)*
E&M Innovative Forager LLC ....E 954 923-0056
Deerfield Beach *(G-2713)*
Future Foods LLC ....G 786 390-5226
Lake Worth *(G-7201)*
Henrys Hickory House Inc ....D 904 493-4420
Jacksonville *(G-6174)*
Johnson Brothers Whl Meats Inc ....E 850 763-2828
Panama City *(G-13280)*
Latin Amercn Meats & Foods USA ......G 305 477-2700
Miami *(G-9434)*
Pinellas Provision Corporation ....E 727 822-2701
Saint Petersburg *(G-15150)*
Port Palm Cold Storage Inc ....E 386 328-5127
Palatka *(G-12877)*
Richards Brazilian Sausage LLC ....G 786 609-3554
Pembroke Pines *(G-13411)*
South Marion Meats ....G 352 245-2096
Summerfield *(G-16259)*
Special Americas Bbq Inc ....E 305 637-7377
Miami *(G-9936)*

MEATS, PACKAGED FROZEN: Wholesalers

Latin Amercn Meats & Foods USA ......G 305 477-2700
Miami *(G-9434)*

MECHANICAL INSTRUMENT REPAIR SVCS

Weimer Mechanical Services Inc ....G 813 645-2258
Ruskin *(G-14781)*

MEDIA: Magnetic & Optical Recording

New ERA Music Group LLC ....F 800 454-9751
Miami *(G-9613)*

MEDICAL & HOSPITAL EQPT WHOLESALERS

Allied Pharmacy Products Inc ....G 516 374-8862
Delray Beach *(G-2928)*
Bellatrix Trade LLC ....F 786 536-2905
Miami *(G-8812)*
Dhss LLC ....E 305 405-4001
North Miami Beach *(G-11133)*
Great Northern Rehab PC ....G 352 732-8868
Ocala *(G-11403)*
Great Northern Rehab PC ....F 352 732-8868
Ocala *(G-11404)*
Hygreen Inc ....F 352 327-9747
Gainesville *(G-4708)*
Mahnkes Orthtics Prsthtics of ....G 954 772-1299
Miami *(G-9499)*
Medical Outfitters Inc ....G 305 885-4045
Miami *(G-9529)*
Merits Health Products Inc ....E 239 772-0579
Fort Myers *(G-4320)*
Neuro20 Technologies Corp ....G 813 990-7138
Tampa *(G-17107)*
Oculus Surgical Inc ....E 772 236-2622
Port St Lucie *(G-14480)*
Pride Florida ....F 813 621-9262
Tampa *(G-17179)*
Sunoptic Technologies LLC ....D 877 677-2832
Jacksonville *(G-6516)*

MEDICAL & HOSPITAL SPLYS: Radiation Shielding Garments

Burkhart Roentgen Intl Inc ....F 727 327-6950
Saint Petersburg *(G-14992)*

MEDICAL & SURGICAL SPLYS: Abdominal Support, Braces/Trusses

A & A Orthopedics Mfg ....G 305 256-8119
Miami *(G-8612)*
North Shore Hldngs Lghthuse Pt ....E 954 785-1055
Lighthouse Point *(G-7828)*

2022 Harris Florida
Manufacturers Directory

(G-0000) Company's Geographic Section entry number

MEDICAL & SURGICAL SPLYS: Belts, Linemen's Safety

Ace Sales Corp.................................F 305 835-0310
Miami (G-8645)

MEDICAL & SURGICAL SPLYS: Braces, Orthopedic

Anjon Inc....................................E 904 730-9373
Jacksonville (G-5891)
Bolt Systems Inc............................G 407 425-0012
Orlando (G-11966)
Bremer Group Company Inc..................F 904 645-0004
Jacksonville (G-5956)
Restorative Care America Inc ....D 727 573-1595
Saint Petersburg (G-15171)
Restorative Products Inc...................F 813 342-4432
Tampa (G-17217)
Tendonease LLC.............................G 888 224-0319
Palm City (G-13061)

MEDICAL & SURGICAL SPLYS: Clothing, Fire Resistant & Protect

Simpson Construction and Roofg........F 863 443-0710
Avon Park (G-288)
Straw Giant Company.......................G 561 430-0729
Delray Beach (G-3022)

MEDICAL & SURGICAL SPLYS: Cosmetic Restorations

Ace Restoration Services LLC.............F 786 487-1870
Miami (G-8644)
Debut Development LLC....................E 863 448-9081
Wauchula (G-17825)

MEDICAL & SURGICAL SPLYS: Cotton & Cotton Applicators

Juvent Medical Inc..........................G 732 748-8866
Fort Myers Beach (G-4455)

MEDICAL & SURGICAL SPLYS: Dressings, Surgical

Depuy Inc.....................................E 305 412-8010
Miami (G-9017)

MEDICAL & SURGICAL SPLYS: Foot Appliances, Orthopedic

Dr Jills Foot Pads Inc ....F 954 573-6557
Deerfield Beach (G-2710)
Orcom Labs Inc...............................G 321 773-0741
Indian Harbour Beach (G-5805)
Rlcjc Inc.......................................G 407 370-3338
Orlando (G-12557)
Southern Surgical Consultants ....G...... 904 296-7828
Jacksonville (G-6493)

MEDICAL & SURGICAL SPLYS: Ligatures

Southwest Florida Regional..................C 615 344-9551
Largo (G-7688)

MEDICAL & SURGICAL SPLYS: Limbs, Artificial

Advanced Prosthetics Amer Inc............F 352 383-0396
Eustis (G-3552)
Around and About Inc ....F 954 584-1954
Plantation (G-13828)
Grace Prsthtic Fabrication Inc...............G 727 842-2265
New Port Richey (G-10967)
Hanger Prsthetcs & Ortho Inc...............G...... 850 216-2392
Tallahassee (G-16457)
Institute For Prosthetic Advan................G...... 850 784-0320
Panama City (G-13276)
Jrs Limb Tree & Farm LLC ....G...... 407 383-4843
Sanford (G-15346)
Limbitless Solutions Inc....................G...... 407 494-3661
Orlando (G-12330)
Orthotic Prsthtic Rhblttion As ....G...... 352 331-3399
Gainesville (G-4744)
Ryder Orthopedics Inc ....G...... 239 939-0009
Fort Myers (G-4387)
Westcoast Brace & Limb Inc...............F 813 985-5000
Temple Terrace (G-17549)

MEDICAL & SURGICAL SPLYS: Models, Anatomical

Digital Antomy Smltons For HLT..........G 937 623-7377
Orlando (G-12094)

MEDICAL & SURGICAL SPLYS: Orthopedic Appliances

Biomet Inc....................................F 561 385-8405
Palm Beach Gardens (G-12950)
Euroinsoles Incorporated ....G 786 206-6117
Coral Gables (G-2055)
Evolution Orthotics Inc ....F 407 688-2860
Lake Mary (G-7072)
Freedom Fabrication Inc ....F 850 539-4194
Havana (G-5001)
Great Northern Rehab PC ....G 352 732-8868
Ocala (G-11403)
Great Northern Rehab PC ....F 352 732-8868
Ocala (G-11404)
Hanger Prsthtics Orthotics Inc ....F 239 772-4510
Cape Coral (G-1352)
Integrity Prsthetics Orthotics ....G...... 813 416-5905
Tampa (G-16947)
Ko Orthotics Inc ....G 954 570-8096
Coconut Creek (G-1996)
Leeder Group Inc ....G 305 436-5030
Miami (G-9449)
Mako Surgical Corp ....B 866 647-6256
Weston (G-18266)
McCluneys Orthpd Prsthetis Svc ....G 352 373-5754
Gainesville (G-4726)
Ongoing Care Solutions Inc................E 727 526-0707
Clearwater (G-1727)
Orthomerica Products Inc...................C 407 290-6592
Orlando (G-12458)
Pensacola Orthtc & Prostetic ....G 850 478-7676
Pensacola (G-13570)
Potenza Services Inc ....G 305 400-4938
Miami (G-9732)
Professional Products Inc...................C 850 892-5731
Defuniak Springs (G-2842)
Quirantes Orthopedics Inc..................G 305 261-1382
Miami (G-9769)
R&M Orthotics Inc...........................G 954 547-6722
Parkland (G-13351)
South Bch Orthtics Prsthtics I ....F 352 512-0262
Stuart (G-16225)
Structure Medical LLC......................D 239 262-5551
Naples (G-10908)
Tidwells Orthotics and Prosthe..............G 954 346-5402
Coral Springs (G-2222)
US Orthotics Inc.............................F 813 621-7797
Tampa (G-17398)
Visionare LLC................................G 305 989-7271
Fort Myers (G-4441)
Williams Orthtc-Prosthetic Inc..............G 850 385-6655
Tallahassee (G-16522)
Zimmer Dental Inc...........................D 561 776-6700
Palm Beach Gardens (G-13019)

MEDICAL & SURGICAL SPLYS: Personal Safety Eqpt

Cadre Holdings Inc ....E 904 741-5400
Jacksonville (G-5967)
Cameron Textiles Inc ....G 954 454-6482
Palm City (G-13026)
Decimal LLC ....E 407 330-3300
Sanford (G-15301)
Hawk Protection Incorporated.............G 954 980-9631
Pembroke Pines (G-13395)
Lifesaving Systems Corporation..........E 813 645-2748
Apollo Beach (G-94)
Primetime Industries LLC ....G 813 781-0196
Wesley Chapel (G-17886)
Universal HM Hlth Indus Sups I............G 813 493-7904
Tampa (G-17393)

MEDICAL & SURGICAL SPLYS: Prosthetic Appliances

A and A Orthopedics Inc ....G 305 256-8119
Miami (G-8618)
All American Amputee ....G 352 383-0396
Eustis (G-3554)
Alps South LLC...............................D 727 528-8566
Saint Petersburg (G-14959)

Bader Prosthetics & Orthotics.............F 813 962-6100
Tampa (G-16626)
Evolution Liners Inc ....G 407 839-6213
Orlando (G-12140)
Florida Prsthtics Orthtics Inc...............G 305 553-1217
Miami (G-9159)
Innovative Spine Care Inc ....G 813 920-3022
Tampa (G-16945)
Kinetic Research Inc ....F 813 962-6300
Tampa (G-16988)
Mahnkes Orthtics Prsthtics of ....G...... 954 772-1299
Miami (G-9499)
Maramed Precision Corporation ....E 305 823-8300
Hialeah (G-5239)
Prosthetic Laboratories.....................G 305 250-9900
Coral Gables (G-2100)
Son Life Prsthtics Orthtics In ....F 352 596-2257
Hernando Beach (G-5012)
South Broward Brace Inc ....F 954 458-0656
Hallandale Beach (G-4974)
TLC Recovery Center S Fla LLC............G 954 533-0783
Fort Lauderdale (G-4093)

MEDICAL & SURGICAL SPLYS: Sponges

Sponge Merchant International ....G 727 919-3523
Tarpon Springs (G-17493)

MEDICAL & SURGICAL SPLYS: Sutures, Non & Absorbable

Demetech Corporation ....E 305 824-1048
Miami Lakes (G-10296)

MEDICAL & SURGICAL SPLYS: Traction Apparatus

C Dyer Development Group LLC ....G 727 423-6169
Tarpon Springs (G-17460)

MEDICAL & SURGICAL SPLYS: Walkers

Donna M Walker PA ....G 561 289-0437
Boca Raton (G-491)

MEDICAL & SURGICAL SPLYS: Welders' Hoods

Alloy Cladding.................................E 561 625-4550
Jupiter (G-6683)

MEDICAL EQPT: Cardiographs

Medicomp Inc ....D 321 676-0010
Melbourne (G-8473)

MEDICAL EQPT: Defibrillators

US Defib Medical Tech LLC.................G 305 887-7552
Medley (G-8345)

MEDICAL EQPT: Diagnostic

Abbott Rapid Diagnostics ....G 877 441-7440
Orlando (G-11860)
Abbott Rapid Dx North Amer LLC ....F 877 441-7440
Orlando (G-11861)
Advanced Dagnstc Solutions Inc ....F 352 293-2810
Trinity (G-17632)
Clinical Chmstry Spclists Corp ....F 919 554-1424
West Palm Beach (G-17967)
Dhss LLC ....E 305 830-0327
Hollywood (G-5565)
Diagnostic Test Group LLC..................F 561 347-5760
Boca Raton (G-483)
Doral Imaging Institute LLC ....G 305 594-2881
Miami (G-9044)
Erba Diagnostics Inc ....E 305 324-2300
Miami Lakes (G-10300)
First Check Diagnostics LLC ....E 858 805-2425
Orlando (G-12153)
Galix Bmedical Instrumentation............F 305 534-5905
Doral (G-3223)
Home Aide Diagnostics Inc.................F 954 794-0212
Deerfield Beach (G-2739)
Intellgent Haring Systems Corp ....F 305 668-6102
Miami (G-9321)
Invivo Corporation ....B 301 525-9683
Gainesville (G-4713)
Iradimed Corporation ....C 407 677-8022
Winter Springs (G-18569)

PRODUCT

MEI Development Corporation ....F 954 341-3302
Coral Springs (G-2183)
Nuline Sensors LLC ....G 407 473-0765
Sanford (G-15363)
Pace Tech Inc ....E 727 442-8118
Clearwater (G-1733)
RM Imaging Incorporated ....E 561 361-8090
Boca Raton (G-652)
Sota Manufacturing Inc ....G 561 368-8007
Boca Raton (G-685)
Twins & Martin Equipment Corp..........G 954 802-0345
Miami (G-10049)
Welch Allyn Inc ....E 305 669-9003
Doral (G-3419)

MEDICAL EQPT: Electromedical Apparatus

Conmed Corporation ....B 727 392-6464
Largo (G-7568)
H Q Inc ....F 941 721-7588
Palmetto (G-13172)
Healthlight LLC ....F 224 231-0342
Jupiter (G-6740)
Motus GI Holdings Inc ....F 954 541-8000
Fort Lauderdale (G-3946)
Sequa Corporation ....A 561 935-3571
Palm Beach Gardens (G-13008)
Tri-Tech Electronics Inc ....D 407 277-2131
Orlando (G-12669)
Vertec Inc ....F 850 478-6480
Pensacola (G-13620)
Zassi Holdings Inc ....G 904 432-8315
Ponte Vedra Beach (G-14283)

MEDICAL EQPT: Electrotherapeutic Apparatus

Axogen Inc ....D 386 462-6800
Alachua (G-6)
Curallux LLC ....E 786 888-1875
Doral (G-3179)
Orthosensor Inc ....D 954 577-7770
Dania Beach (G-2357)

MEDICAL EQPT: Laser Systems

Anti-Ging Asthtic Lser Ctr Inc ....G 786 539-4901
Miami Beach (G-10165)
Channel Investments LLC ....G 727 599-1360
Tampa (G-16700)
Erchonia Corporation LLC ....E 321 473-1251
Melbourne (G-8422)
Estetika Skin & Laser Spe ....G 262 646-9222
Sarasota (G-15667)
Home Healthcare 2000 Inc ....G 954 977-4450
Pompano Beach (G-14053)
K-O Concepts Inc ....G 407 296-7788
Titusville (G-17596)
Lexington International LLC ....E 800 973-4769
Boca Raton (G-578)
Meditek-Icot Inc ....F 813 909-7476
Lutz (G-8003)
Nova Laserlight LLC ....F 407 226-0609
Orlando (G-12425)
Pristine Laser Center ....G 407 389-1200
Altamonte Springs (G-65)
Silver Bay LLC ....F 941 306-5812
Sarasota (G-15556)
Stimwave Technologies Inc ....G 800 965-5134
Pompano Beach (G-14200)
Touchpoint Medical Inc ....E 813 854-1905
Odessa (G-11585)

MEDICAL EQPT: MRI/Magnetic Resonance Imaging Devs, Nuclear

L&R Imaging ....G 678 691-3204
Pompano Beach (G-14074)
Mri Specialists ....G 561 369-2144
Boynton Beach (G-891)

MEDICAL EQPT: Patient Monitoring

3M Resident Monitoring Inc ....E 813 749-5453
Odessa (G-11531)
Actigraph LLC ....E 850 332-7900
Pensacola (G-13434)
Compliance Meds Tech LLC ....F 786 319-9826
Miami (G-8952)
GE Medcal Systems Info Tech In ....D 561 575-5000
Jupiter (G-6734)

Infopia USA LLC..........F 321 225-3620
Cocoa (G-1937)

MEDICAL EQPT: Sterilizers

Internl Sterilization Lab LLC ....G 352 429-3200
Groveland (G-4863)
Primus Sterilizer Company LLC ....F 402 344-4200
Orlando (G-12506)

MEDICAL EQPT: Ultrasonic Scanning Devices

Harbor Imaging ....E 941 883-8383
Port Charlotte (G-14303)
Mri Depot Inc ....G 407 696-9822
Longwood (G-7925)
Shenk Enterprises LLC ....F 386 753-1959
Orange City (G-11809)
Supersonic Imagine Inc ....G 954 660-3528
Weston (G-18287)

MEDICAL EQPT: X-Ray Apparatus & Tubes, Therapeutic

Power Wthin Cnsling Cnsltn LLC..........G 863 242-3023
Haines City (G-4912)

MEDICAL HELP SVCS

Medtek Medical Solutions LLC ....F 786 458-8080
Miami (G-9530)

MEDICAL SUNDRIES: Rubber

Medical Defense Company Inc ....F 954 614-3266
Doral (G-3295)

MEDICAL SVCS ORGANIZATION

Advantagecare Inc ....G 407 345-8877
Orlando (G-11873)
Modernzing Mdcine Gstrntrlogy..........C 561 880-2998
Boca Raton (G-604)

MEDICAL, DENTAL & HOSPITAL EQPT, WHOL: Hospital Eqpt & Splys

Steripack (usa) Limited LLC ....E 863 648-2333
Lakeland (G-7449)

MEDICAL, DENTAL & HOSPITAL EQPT, WHOL: Hosptl Eqpt/Furniture

Decimal LLC ....E 407 330-3300
Sanford (G-15301)
Galix Bmedical Instrumentation ....F 305 534-5905
Doral (G-3223)
Omega Medical Imaging LLC ....E 407 323-9400
Sanford (G-15364)

MEDICAL, DENTAL & HOSPITAL EQPT, WHOL: Surgical Eqpt & Splys

Kollsut International Inc ....G 305 438-6877
North Miami Beach (G-11147)
Zimmer Biomet CMF Thoracic LLC..........C 574 267-6639
Jacksonville (G-6623)

MEDICAL, DENTAL & HOSPITAL EQPT, WHOLESALE: Hearing Aids

Audina Hearing Instruments Inc..........D 407 331-0077
Longwood (G-7872)
Miami ....E 954 874-7707
Miami (G-9544)

MEDICAL, DENTAL & HOSPITAL EQPT, WHOLESALE: Med Eqpt & Splys

CMF Medicon Surgical Inc ....G 904 642-7500
Jacksonville (G-5987)
Erchonia Corporation LLC ....E 321 473-1251
Melbourne (G-8422)
Healthline Medical Pdts Inc..........F 407 656-0704
Winter Garden (G-18389)
Intermed Group Inc ....E 561 586-3667
Alachua (G-12)
Lane Care LLC ....E 727 316-3708
Palm Harbor (G-13118)
Liviliti Health Products Corp..........G 888 987-0744
Lake City (G-7029)

Medone Surgical Inc ....F 941 359-3129
Sarasota (G-15516)
Mmx Manufacturing LLC ....F 786 456-5072
Miami (G-9579)
New World Holdings Inc ....E 561 888-4939
Delray Beach (G-2992)
Oscor Inc ....C 727 937-2511
Palm Harbor (G-13122)
Professional Products Inc..........C 850 892-5731
Defuniak Springs (G-2842)
Technicuff Corp..........F 352 326-2833
Leesburg (G-7797)
Universal HM Hlth Indus Sups I..........G 813 493-7904
Tampa (G-17393)
Warehouse Goods LLC ....E 877 865-2260
Boca Raton (G-753)

MEDICAL, DENTAL & HOSPITAL EQPT, WHOLESALE: Orthopedic

EM Adams Inc ....D 772 468-6550
Fort Pierce (G-4483)
Imc-Heartway LLC..........G 239 275-6767
Fort Myers (G-4286)

MEDICAL, DENTAL & HOSPITAL EQPT, WHOLESALE: Oxygen Therapy

Lor-Ed Enterprises LLC..........G 352 750-1999
Lady Lake (G-6992)

MEDICAL, DENTAL & HOSPITAL EQPT, WHOLESALE: Safety

Cameron Textiles Inc ....G 954 454-6482
Palm City (G-13026)

MEDITATION THERAPY

Stripping Alpaca LLC ....F 207 208-9687
Miami Beach (G-10236)

MEMBERSHIP ORGANIZATIONS, NEC: Charitable

Jade Tactical Disaster Relief..........C 850 270-4077
Tampa (G-16961)

MEMBERSHIP ORGANIZATIONS, PROFESSIONAL: Accounting Assoc

Automated Accounting Assoc Inc..........G 512 669-1000
Pensacola (G-13448)

MEMBERSHIP ORGANIZATIONS, RELIGIOUS: Pentecostal Church

Great Hse Mdia Group of Pbls I..........F 407 779-3846
Orlando (G-12200)

MEN'S & BOYS' CLOTHING STORES

Perry Ellis International Inc..........B 305 592-2830
Doral (G-3325)

MEN'S & BOYS' CLOTHING WHOLESALERS, NEC

Apparel Imports Inc ....E 800 428-6849
Miami (G-8735)
Carpe Diem Sales & Mktg Inc ....E 407 682-1400
Orlando (G-11983)
Fresh Thread Llc..........F 904 677-9505
Jacksonville (G-6122)
Indigo Mountain Inc..........G 239 947-0023
Naples (G-10780)
Official Gear Company Inc ....G 407 721-9110
Ormond Beach (G-12782)
Pattern Grading & Marker Svcs ....G 305 495-9963
Miramar (G-10525)
Sarah Louise Inc ....F 941 377-9656
Sarasota (G-15808)
Stush AP USA/Stush Style LLC ....F 404 940-3445
Sunrise (G-16374)
Workwear Outfitters LLC..........E 813 671-2986
Riverview (G-14583)

MEN'S & BOYS' SPORTSWEAR CLOTHING STORES

Kikisteescom LLC ....E 888 620-4110
  Sunrise (G-16333)
Resort Poolside Shops Inc ....G 407 256-5853
  Belle Isle (G-350)

MEN'S & BOYS' SPORTSWEAR WHOLESALERS

Rock N Roll Custom Screened S ....G 727 528-2111
  Pinellas Park (G-13727)
Spirit Sales Corporation ....G 850 878-0366
  Tallahassee (G-16503)
T Shirt Center Inc ....G 305 655-1955
  Miami (G-9990)

MESSAGE CONCENTRATORS

American Impact Media Corp ....F 954 457-9003
  Hallandale Beach (G-4935)

METAL & STEEL PRDTS: Abrasive

Liquid Metal Products Inc ....G 402 895-4436
  Ocala (G-11430)
Lorefice Steel Corp ....G 786 609-1593
  Miami (G-9478)
Monstertech Corporation ....E 813 898-0405
  Tampa (G-17084)
Tyrex Ore & Minerals Company ....G 305 333-5288
  Miami (G-10053)

METAL COMPONENTS: Prefabricated

American Projects Brokers Inc ....G 904 343-5424
  Jacksonville (G-5884)
Ferrera Tooling Inc ....F 863 646-8500
  Lakeland (G-7321)
Fertec Inc ....F 850 478-6480
  Pensacola (G-13502)
Sesolinc Grp Inc ....G 772 287-9090
  Stuart (G-16215)
U C Fab of Florida LLC ....G 407 614-4210
  Ocoee (G-11529)

METAL CUTTING SVCS

All Points Boats Inc ....D 954 767-8255
  Fort Lauderdale (G-3639)
P3d Creations LLC ....F 407 801-9126
  Maitland (G-8068)

METAL DETECTORS

Tectron Engineering Company ....F 904 394-0683
  Jacksonville (G-6541)

METAL FABRICATORS: Architechtural

Aerotec Aluminium Inc ....G 407 324-5400
  Sanford (G-15259)
Agri Metal Supply Inc ....G 386 294-1720
  Mayo (G-8182)
Airguide Manufacturing LLC ....C 305 888-1631
  Hialeah (G-5035)
Alenac Metals Corp ....E 561 877-4109
  Palm Springs (G-13141)
Alse Industries LLC ....F 305 688-8778
  Miami Gardens (G-10251)
Alumacart Inc ....F 772 675-2158
  Indiantown (G-5811)
Amazon Metal Fabricators Inc ....F 321 631-7574
  Cocoa (G-1901)
Ambiance Interiors Mfg Corp ....G 305 668-4995
  Miami (G-8712)
Architectural Metal Systems ....F 407 277-1364
  Orlando (G-11916)
Bachiller Iron Works Inc ....E 305 751-7773
  Miami (G-8792)
Bausch American Towers LLC ....F 772 283-2771
  Stuart (G-16119)
Brownsville Orna Ir Works Inc ....E 850 433-0521
  Pensacola (G-13463)
Buchanan Signs Screen Process ....F 904 725-5500
  Jacksonville (G-5962)
Caballero Metals Corp ....G 305 266-9085
  Miami (G-8876)
Caballero Metals Corp ....F 305 266-9085
  Miami (G-8877)
Casco Services Inc ....F 727 942-1888
  Tarpon Springs (G-17461)

Cement Precast Products Inc ....E 352 372-0953
  Gainesville (G-4668)
Chancey Metal Products Inc ....E 904 260-6880
  Jacksonville (G-5976)
Citory Solutions LLC ....F 407 766-6533
  Orlando (G-12013)
Classic Iron Decor Inc ....F 904 241-5022
  Jacksonville Beach (G-6631)
Creative Metal Studio Inc ....G 321 206-6112
  Apopka (G-117)
D & D MBL Wldg Fabrication Inc ....D 772 489-7900
  Fort Pierce (G-4479)
D G Morrison Inc ....F 813 865-0208
  Odessa (G-11546)
David Viera LLC ....G 305 218-3401
  Hialeah (G-5109)
Deland Metal Craft Company ....G 386 734-0828
  Deland (G-2861)
English Ironworks Inc ....G 941 364-9120
  Sarasota (G-15665)
Fluid Metalworks Inc -105 ....G 850 332-0103
  Pensacola (G-13506)
Glassarium LLC ....E 786 631-7080
  Miami (G-9216)
Halliday Products Inc ....D 407 298-4470
  Orlando (G-12208)
Icon Welding & Fabrication LLC ....F 941 822-8822
  Sarasota (G-15497)
Ironworks Inc of Orange Park ....F 904 291-9330
  Middleburg (G-10403)
ITW Blding Cmponents Group Inc ....G 863 422-8685
  Haines City (G-4908)
ITW Bldng Cmponents Group Inc ....E 954 781-3333
  Fort Lauderdale (G-3888)
Jace Fabrication Inc ....G 727 547-6873
  Pinellas Park (G-13697)
Kawneer Company Inc ....C 407 648-4511
  Orlando (G-12283)
L & L Orna Alum Ironworks Inc ....F 561 547-5605
  West Palm Beach (G-18048)
Largo Aluminum Inc ....G 305 852-2390
  Islamorada (G-5837)
Laza Iron Works Inc ....E 305 754-8200
  Miami (G-9439)
Liberty Aluminum Co ....E 239 369-3000
  Lehigh Acres (G-7815)
Litecrete Inc ....E 305 500-9373
  Miami (G-9466)
Mantua Manufacturing Co ....G 813 621-3714
  Tampa (G-17037)
Mary Lame Wrought Iron & Alum ....G 727 934-2879
  Holiday (G-5502)
Metal Creations Sarasota Llc ....F 941 922-7096
  Sarasota (G-15744)
Metal Industries Inc ....D 352 793-8610
  Bushnell (G-1247)
Metal Supply and Machining Inc ....F 561 276-4941
  Delray Beach (G-2988)
Miami Railing Design Corp ....G 305 926-0062
  Miami (G-9558)
Monummtal Fabrication Amer Inc ....G 850 227-9500
  Port Saint Joe (G-14389)
Naples Iron Works Inc ....E 239 649-7265
  Naples (G-10829)
New England Crftsmen Bston Irn ....G 727 789-1618
  Palm Harbor (G-13120)
Ornamntal Design Ironworks Inc ....E 813 626-8449
  Tampa (G-17128)
Ornamntal Metal Specialist Inc ....G 786 360-5727
  Hialeah (G-5290)
RDS Industrial Inc ....F 321 631-0121
  Cocoa (G-1951)
Regional Cnstr Resources Inc ....E 713 789-5131
  Sarasota (G-15795)
Reich Metal Fabricators Inc ....E 561 585-3173
  West Palm Beach (G-18139)
Rustwerks ....F 407 399-2262
  Orlando (G-12562)
S & S Welding Inc ....F 863 533-2888
  Bartow (G-325)
Saftron Manufacturing LLC ....F 305 233-5511
  Bradenton (G-1039)
Screenco North Inc ....E 561 840-3300
  Palm Beach Gardens (G-13007)
Sfa Systems Inc ....E 561 585-5927
  Lake Worth (G-7232)
Statements 2000 LLC ....G 561 249-1587
  West Palm Beach (G-18162)
Sunbelt Metals & Mfg Inc ....E 407 889-8960
  Apopka (G-179)

Tampa Tank & Welding Inc ....F 813 241-0123
  Gibsonton (G-4801)
Toledo Doors Inc ....F 305 633-4352
  Miami (G-10020)
US Ironworks Company ....F 850 588-5995
  Panama City (G-13316)
Vintage Ironworks LLC ....F 407 339-2555
  Altamonte Springs (G-77)
W D Wilson Inc ....G 813 626-6989
  Tampa (G-17421)
Wesco Partners Inc ....E 941 484-8224
  Sarasota (G-15579)
Wilcox Steel Company LLC ....G 727 443-0461
  Clearwater (G-1852)
Ymg Iron Work & Metal Design ....G 305 343-2537
  Pembroke Pines (G-13425)

METAL FABRICATORS: Plate

Aluminum Tank Industries Inc ....G 863 401-9474
  Winter Haven (G-18415)
American Aluminum ACC Inc ....E 850 277-0869
  Perry (G-13630)
Central Metal Fabricators Inc ....E 305 261-6262
  Miami (G-8911)
Coastal Machine LLC ....G 850 769-6117
  Panama City (G-13246)
Contech Engnered Solutions LLC ....F 561 582-2558
  Miami (G-8960)
Duramaster Cylinders ....G 813 882-0040
  Tampa (G-16788)
Formweld Fitting Inc ....E 850 626-4888
  Milton (G-10424)
Greenco Manufacturing Corp ....F 813 882-4400
  Tampa (G-16892)
Halliday Products Inc ....D 407 298-4470
  Orlando (G-12208)
Hutchins Co Inc ....F 727 442-6651
  Clearwater (G-1631)
Jacksonville Steel Pdts Inc ....G 904 268-3364
  Jacksonville (G-6216)
Jim Appleys Tru-Arc Inc ....F 727 571-3007
  Clearwater (G-1653)
Mantua Manufacturing Co ....G 813 621-3714
  Tampa (G-17037)
Mid-State Machine & Fabg Corp ....C 863 665-6233
  Lakeland (G-7395)
Mpc Containment Systems LLC ....D 773 927-4121
  Deland (G-2888)
Ofab Inc ....D 352 629-0040
  Ocala (G-11460)
Permasteelisa North Amer Corp ....E 305 265-4405
  Miami (G-9707)
Quality Fbrction Mch Works Inc ....F 386 755-0220
  Lake City (G-7040)
Riw of Jacksonville Inc ....F 904 356-5635
  Jacksonville (G-6429)
Ryan Manufacturing Inc ....F 386 325-3644
  East Palatka (G-3475)
Serf Inc ....E 850 476-8203
  Cantonment (G-1273)
Spencer Fabrications Inc ....E 352 343-0014
  Tavares (G-17524)
SPX Flow Technology Usa Inc ....C 352 237-1220
  Ocala (G-11498)
Style-View Products Inc ....E 305 634-9688
  Miami (G-9962)
Sunbelt Metals & Mfg Inc ....E 407 889-8960
  Apopka (G-179)
Swiss Components Inc ....F 321 723-6729
  Melbourne (G-8542)
Tampa Tank & Welding Inc ....F 813 241-0123
  Gibsonton (G-4801)
Universal Metal Works Inc ....G 904 765-2600
  Jacksonville (G-6581)
W D Wilson Inc ....G 813 626-6989
  Tampa (G-17421)
Walker Stainless Eqp Co LLC ....G 352 343-2606
  Tavares (G-17530)
World Stone and Design LLC ....G 850 235-0399
  Panama City (G-13322)
Zahn Builders Inc ....G 718 885-2202
  Lighthouse Point (G-7829)

METAL FABRICATORS: Sheet

A & A Sheetmetal Contr Corp ....D 305 592-2217
  Doral (G-3087)
A A Sheet Metal Corp ....G 305 592-2217
  Doral (G-3089)
Aba Engineering & Mfg Inc ....F 386 672-9665
  Ormond Beach (G-12739)

PRODUCT

Abele Sheetmetal Works Inc ....F 561 471-1134
Riviera Beach *(G-14585)*

Accord Industries LLC ....D 407 671-6989
Winter Park *(G-18480)*

Adeptus Industries Inc ....F 941 756-7636
Bradenton *(G-932)*

Advanced Alum Polk Cnty Inc ....E 863 648-5787
Lakeland *(G-7266)*

Advanced Sheet Metal & Welding ....G 239 430-1155
Naples *(G-10653)*

Air Balance Corp ....G 305 401-8780
Palm Bay *(G-12886)*

Air Distributors Inc ....E 352 522-0006
Dunnellon *(G-3461)*

Airite Air Conditioning Inc ....E 813 886-0235
Tampa *(G-16567)*

AJF Sheet Metals Inc ....F 305 970-6359
North Miami *(G-11088)*

Alacriant Holdings LLC ....E 330 233-0523
Lake Mary *(G-7058)*

All Metal Fab Inc ....F 904 570-9772
Jacksonville *(G-5873)*

All Phase Construction USA LLC ....F 754 227-5605
Deerfield Beach *(G-2663)*

All Southern Fabricators Inc ....E 727 573-4846
Clearwater *(G-1486)*

American Metal Fabricators Inc ....E 561 790-5799
Mangonia Park *(G-8087)*

AMS Fabrications Inc ....G 813 420-0784
Oakland Park *(G-11236)*

Anvil Iron Works Inc ....E 727 375-2884
Odessa *(G-11536)*

Apache Sheet Metal ....G 954 214-4468
Weston *(G-18224)*

Architctral Shtmtl Fbrctors In ....G 407 672-9086
Winter Park *(G-18487)*

Architectural Metal Systems ....F 407 277-1364
Orlando *(G-11916)*

Architectural Metals S W FL ....E 239 334-7433
Fort Myers *(G-4179)*

B & C Sheet Metal Duct Corp ....G 305 316-9212
Miami *(G-8786)*

B & K Installations Inc ....E 305 245-6968
Homestead *(G-5701)*

B&B Custom Sheet Metal Inc ....E 727 938-8083
Tarpon Springs *(G-17458)*

Bamco Inc ....G 303 886-5992
Seminole *(G-15970)*

Barrett Custom Designs LLC ....G 321 242-2002
Melbourne *(G-8374)*

Bausch American Towers LLC ....F 772 283-2771
Stuart *(G-16119)*

Bausch Enterprises Inc ....F 772 220-6652
Stuart *(G-16120)*

Bay Harbor Sheet Metal Inc ....F 813 740-8662
Tampa *(G-16631)*

Beautiful Mailbox Co ....E 305 403-4820
Hialeah *(G-5070)*

Birdsall Marine Design Inc ....E 561 832-7879
West Palm Beach *(G-17947)*

Blackwater Folk Art Inc ....G 850 623-3470
Milton *(G-10419)*

Breiner Machine Co Inc ....F 352 544-0463
Brooksville *(G-1142)*

C C Lead Inc ....F 863 465-6458
Lake Placid *(G-7139)*

Camcorp Industries Inc ....G 941 488-5000
Venice *(G-17679)*

Captive-Aire Systems Inc ....E 813 448-7884
Tampa *(G-16677)*

Carpenters Roofg & Shtmtl Inc ....E 561 833-0341
Riviera Beach *(G-14607)*

Cato Steel Co ....F 407 671-3333
Winter Park *(G-18497)*

Cemex Cnstr Mtls Fla LLC ....F 561 832-6646
West Palm Beach *(G-17959)*

Cemex Materials LLC ....C 561 746-4556
Jupiter *(G-6703)*

Central Metal Fabricators Inc ....E 305 261-6262
Miami *(G-8911)*

Century Metal Products Inc ....E 407 293-8871
Orlando *(G-12000)*

Cladding Systems Inc ....E 813 250-0786
Tampa *(G-16710)*

Clarkwstern Dtrich Bldg System ....E 800 543-7140
Dade City *(G-2316)*

Clear-Vue Inc ....E 727 726-5386
Safety Harbor *(G-14784)*

Conklin Metal Industries Inc ....F 407 688-0900
Orlando *(G-12042)*

Contech Engnered Solutions LLC ....F 561 582-2558
Miami *(G-8960)*

Corrugated Industries Fla Inc ....F 813 623-6606
Tampa *(G-16732)*

Custom Cft Windows & Doors Inc ....F 407 834-5400
Winter Springs *(G-18563)*

Custom Metal Specialties Inc ....E 727 522-3986
Pinellas Park *(G-13679)*

D C Inc Prtble Wldg Fbrication ....G 863 533-4483
Frostproof *(G-4637)*

Day Metal Products LLC ....G 352 799-9258
Brooksville *(G-1151)*

Deans Cstm Shtmtl Fbrction In ....G 813 757-6270
Dover *(G-3429)*

Decon USA ....G 440 610-5009
Tarpon Springs *(G-17464)*

Delta International Inc ....G 305 665-6573
Miami *(G-9013)*

Dills Enterprises LLC ....G 941 493-1993
Venice *(G-17683)*

Dixie Metalcraft Incorporated ....F 239 337-4299
Fort Myers *(G-4235)*

Dynamic Precision Group Inc ....F 772 287-7770
Stuart *(G-16141)*

Earnest Products Inc ....D 407 831-1588
Sanford *(G-15308)*

Electro Mech Solutions Inc ....E 813 792-0400
Odessa *(G-11549)*

Europa Manufacturing Inc ....F 954 426-2965
Coconut Creek *(G-1985)*

Flash Roofing and Shtmtl LLC ....G 786 237-9440
Miami *(G-9148)*

Flite Technology Inc ....F 321 631-2050
Cocoa *(G-1928)*

Float-On Corporation ....F 772 569-4440
Vero Beach *(G-17754)*

Florida Aluminum and Steel Inc ....F 863 967-4191
Auburndale *(G-231)*

Florida Metal-Craft Inc ....F 407 656-1100
Winter Garden *(G-18386)*

Florida Roofing & Shtmtl LLC ....F 561 517-9675
Loxahatchee *(G-7969)*

Flotech LLC ....D 904 358-1849
Jacksonville *(G-6113)*

Fowlers Sheet Metal Inc ....F 561 659-3309
West Palm Beach *(G-18011)*

Frc Electrical Industries Inc ....G 321 676-3300
Palm Bay *(G-12902)*

G & K Aluminum Inc ....F 772 283-1297
Stuart *(G-16150)*

G F E Inc ....F 954 583-7005
Davie *(G-2416)*

G J Sheet Metal Corp ....G 954 709-9011
Deerfield Beach *(G-2723)*

Gautier Fabrication Inc ....F 941 485-2464
North Venice *(G-11212)*

Gizmos Lion Sheet Metal Inc ....F 561 684-8480
West Palm Beach *(G-18018)*

Gms Sheet Metal & AC Inc ....F 772 221-0585
Palm City *(G-13042)*

H Lamm Industries Inc ....C 954 491-8929
Oakland Park *(G-11270)*

Halliday Products Inc ....D 407 298-4470
Orlando *(G-12208)*

Hollywood Design & Concepts ....F 954 458-4634
Yalaha *(G-18583)*

Hood Depot International Inc ....E 954 570-9860
Deerfield Beach *(G-2740)*

Hurricane Roofing & Shtmtl Inc ....G 954 968-8155
Margate *(G-8135)*

Hydro Extrusion Usa LLC ....B 904 794-1500
Saint Augustine *(G-14841)*

Ice Sheet Metal LLC ....E 850 872-2129
Panama City *(G-13274)*

Infinity Manufactured Inds ....F 727 532-4453
Largo *(G-7613)*

Integrated Metal Products Inc ....D 863 687-4110
Lakeland *(G-7353)*

International Dock Pdts Inc ....F 954 964-5315
Hallandale Beach *(G-4952)*

Interstate Wldg & Fabrication ....F 727 446-1449
Clearwater *(G-1647)*

ITW Blding Cmponents Group Inc ....E 954 781-3333
Fort Lauderdale *(G-3888)*

J & J Steel Services Corp ....G 305 878-8929
Medley *(G-8262)*

Jax Metals LLC ....G 904 731-4655
Jacksonville *(G-6221)*

JC Industrial Mfg Corp ....E 305 634-5280
Miami *(G-9359)*

Jim Appleys Tru-Arc Inc ....F 727 571-3007
Clearwater *(G-1653)*

JP Custom Metals Inc ....F 786 318-2855
Miami *(G-9375)*

Keene Metal Fabricators Inc ....E 813 621-2455
Tampa *(G-16979)*

Kemco Industries LLC ....D 407 322-1230
Sanford *(G-15348)*

Kling Fabrication Inc ....F 727 321-7233
Pinellas Park *(G-13699)*

Kustom Industrial Fabricators ....F 407 965-1940
Longwood *(G-7913)*

Kustom Us Inc ....F 407 965-1940
Longwood *(G-7914)*

L D F Services ....F 386 947-9256
Daytona Beach *(G-2567)*

Largo Aluminum Inc ....F 305 852-2390
Islamorada *(G-5837)*

Liberty Aluminum Co ....G 239 369-3000
Lehigh Acres *(G-7815)*

Lion Sheet Metal Inc ....F 561 840-0540
West Palm Beach *(G-18059)*

Lloyd Industries Inc ....F 904 541-1655
Orange Park *(G-11833)*

Manning Company ....G 954 523-9355
Fort Lauderdale *(G-3930)*

Marion Metal Works Inc ....E 352 351-4221
Ocala *(G-11437)*

Marlyn Steel Decks Inc ....F 813 621-1375
Tampa *(G-17042)*

Marlyn Steel Products Inc ....F 813 621-1375
Tampa *(G-17043)*

Memphis Metal Manufacturing Co ....F 901 276-6363
Tampa *(G-17063)*

Metal Creations Sarasota Llc ....F 941 922-7096
Sarasota *(G-15744)*

Metal Essence Inc ....G 407 478-8480
Longwood *(G-7923)*

Metal Industries Inc ....D 727 441-2651
Clearwater *(G-1696)*

Metal Products Company LC ....G 850 526-5593
Marianna *(G-8173)*

Metal Sales Manufacturing Corp ....E 904 783-3660
Jacksonville *(G-6298)*

Metal Supply and Machining Inc ....F 561 276-4941
Delray Beach *(G-2988)*

Metal Works By Gal ....G 407 486-7198
Sanford *(G-15358)*

Metalco Mfg Inc ....F 305 592-0704
Hialeah *(G-5245)*

Metalcraft Industries Inc ....F 352 680-3555
Ocala *(G-11443)*

Metalcrafters LLC ....F 904 257-9036
Jacksonville *(G-6299)*

Metalfab Inc ....G 352 588-9901
San Antonio *(G-15249)*

Metalworks Engineering Corp ....F 305 223-0011
Hialeah *(G-5246)*

Miami Tech Inc ....F 786 354-1115
Hialeah *(G-5254)*

Mid-State Machine & Fabg Corp ....C 863 665-6233
Lakeland *(G-7395)*

N C A Manufacturing Inc ....D 727 441-2651
Clearwater *(G-1710)*

Naples Iron Works Inc ....E 239 649-7265
Naples *(G-10829)*

Nautical Structures Inds Inc ....E 727 541-6664
Largo *(G-7651)*

Normandin LLC ....F 941 739-8046
Sarasota *(G-15527)*

Northside Sheet Metal Inc ....G 850 769-1461
Panama City *(G-13290)*

Ornamntal Design Ironworks Inc ....E 813 626-8449
Tampa *(G-17128)*

Osborne Metals ....G 727 441-1703
Clearwater *(G-1732)*

Oscar E Perez ....G 786 442-6889
Miami *(G-9669)*

Osgood Industries LLC ....C 813 448-9041
Oldsmar *(G-11683)*

P & M Sheet Metal Corp ....G 954 618-8513
Ave Maria *(G-249)*

Peak Sheet Metal Solutions Inc ....G 954 775-6393
Palm City *(G-13054)*

Perez Industries Inc ....F 239 992-2444
Bonita Springs *(G-812)*

Pioneer Development Entps Inc ....F 239 592-0001
Naples *(G-10859)*

Pipewelders Marine Inc ....D 954 587-8400
Fort Lauderdale *(G-3988)*

Plan B Manufacturing Inc.................G...... 904 633-7888
Jacksonville (G-6374)
Plotkowski Inc.................................G..... 561 740-2226
Boynton Beach (G-896)
Preferred Metal Products Inc..........F..... 407 296-4449
Orlando (G-12502)
Premier Archtctural Shtmtl Inc.......F..... 727 373-8937
Odessa (G-11574)
Premier Fabricating Llc...................F..... 813 855-4633
Oldsmar (G-11689)
Production Metal Stampings Inc.......F...... 850 981-8240
Milton (G-10434)
Rafab Spcialty Fabrication Inc.........F..... 407 422-3750
Orlando (G-12530)
Rankine-Hinman Mfg Co..................F..... 904 808-0404
Saint Augustine (G-14877)
Rapid Metal Products Inc................E..... 863 701-0058
Lakeland (G-7418)
Reading Truck Body LLC..................E..... 727 943-8911
Tarpon Springs (G-17490)
Responsive Machining Inc................F..... 321 225-4011
Titusville (G-17612)
Road Block Fabrication Inc..............G..... 708 417-6091
Fort Myers (G-4381)
S & B Metal Products S Fla Inc........C..... 941 727-3669
Bradenton (G-1038)
S & B Metal Products S Fla Inc........F..... 941 727-3669
Lakeland (G-7426)
S & S Welding Inc...........................F..... 863 533-2888
Bartow (G-325)
Seacoast Air Conditioning & Sh......F..... 772 466-2400
Fort Pierce (G-4528)
Sfi Inc..E..... 407 834-2258
Orlando (G-12586)
Sheet Metal Unlimited.....................F..... 772 872-7440
Stuart (G-16217)
Silver Sheet-Florida Inc..................F..... 850 230-9711
Panama City (G-13308)
Spectrum Engineering & Mfg Inc......G..... 727 376-5510
Odessa (G-11580)
Spencer Fabrications Inc.................E..... 352 343-0014
Tavares (G-17524)
Stainless Fabricators Inc................E..... 813 926-7113
Odessa (G-11581)
Stampco Inc....................................F..... 904 737-6144
Jacksonville (G-6503)
Stanron Corporation.......................E..... 954 974-8050
Fort Lauderdale (G-4066)
Steel City Inc.................................F..... 850 785-9596
Panama City (G-13311)
Sterling Industry LLC.....................E..... 561 845-2440
Riviera Beach (G-14677)
Sunbelt Metals & Mfg Inc................E..... 407 889-8960
Apopka (G-179)
Sunshine Metal Products Inc..........G..... 407 331-1300
Altamonte Springs (G-72)
Superior Metal................................F..... 407 522-8100
Orlando (G-12637)
Superior Metal Fabricators Inc.........E..... 407 295-5772
Orlando (G-12638)
Supply Network Inc.........................G..... 954 791-2287
Fort Lauderdale (G-4078)
Tampa Metal Works Inc...................F..... 813 628-9223
Tampa (G-17336)
Tampa Sheet Metal Company...........E...... 813 251-1845
Tampa (G-17338)
Taurus Chutes Inc..........................G..... 954 445-0146
Oakland Park (G-11300)
Tejeda Sheet Metal & Aluminum.......G..... 305 609-5477
Hialeah (G-5378)
Tibor Inc..E..... 561 272-0770
Delray Beach (G-3026)
Townsend Signs Inc........................G..... 386 255-1955
Holly Hill (G-5518)
Tri County Metals...........................G..... 850 574-4001
Tallahassee (G-16516)
Tri-H Metal Products Inc.................G..... 941 753-7311
Bradenton (G-1064)
Tri-Tech of Florida Inc....................F..... 727 544-8836
Saint Petersburg (G-15217)
Turbocombustor Technology Inc......B..... 772 287-7770
Stuart (G-16243)
Upton House Cooler Corporation......G..... 305 633-2531
Miami (G-10076)
USA Sheet Metal Inc......................... 786 517-3482
Hialeah (G-5400)
Ventilation Air Inc..........................G..... 954 975-9501
Pompano Beach (G-14236)
Versatile Manufacturing Inc............E..... 954 561-8083
Oakland Park (G-11310)

Versatile Manufacturing Inc............F..... 954 561-8083
Oakland Park (G-11311)
W D Wilson Inc................................G..... 813 626-6989
Tampa (G-17421)
Wheeler Lumber LLC.......................F...... 772 464-4400
Fort Pierce (G-4554)
White Rose Installation....................F...... 772 562-6698
Vero Beach (G-17819)
Window Craftsmen Inc.....................E..... 941 922-1844
Sarasota (G-15876)

METAL FABRICATORS: Structural, Ship

All Points Boats Inc.......................D..... 954 767-8255
Fort Lauderdale (G-3639)
Artful Canvas Design Inc.................F..... 727 521-0212
Saint Petersburg (G-14973)
Bausch American Towers LLC..........F..... 772 283-2771
Stuart (G-16119)
Blue Marlin Towers Inc....................G..... 954 530-9140
Fort Lauderdale (G-3692)
Eastern Shipbuilding Group Inc.......A..... 850 522-7400
Panama City (G-13257)
Pipe Welders Inc............................D..... 954 587-8400
Fort Lauderdale (G-3987)

METAL FINISHING SVCS

Best Engineered Surfc Tech LLC.......D..... 407 932-0008
Kissimmee (G-6898)
C Y A Powder Coating LLC...............G..... 727 299-9832
Clearwater (G-1534)
Chem-Tek Metal Finishing Corp.......F..... 321 722-2227
Melbourne (G-8386)
D R C Industries Inc.......................G..... 954 971-0699
Pompano Beach (G-13989)
Eps Metal Finishing.........................G..... 954 782-3073
Pompano Beach (G-14013)
Metal Spray Painting Powder...........G..... 954 227-2744
Coral Springs (G-2184)
Orlando Plating Co.........................G..... 407 843-1140
Orlando (G-12455)
Poly Coatings of South Inc.............F..... 941 371-8555
Sarasota (G-15784)
Pozin Enterprises Inc.....................E..... 800 741-1456
Clearwater (G-1745)
Quality Finishers Inc.......................G..... 954 782-3073
Pompano Beach (G-14153)
Quality Powder Coating Inc.............F..... 941 378-0051
Sarasota (G-15792)
Sintavia LLC..................................G..... 954 474-7800
Fort Lauderdale (G-4052)
Stuart-Dean Co Inc.........................E..... 305 652-9595
Doral (G-3381)

METAL MINING SVCS

American Aggregates LLC................F..... 813 352-2124
Boca Raton (G-404)
Evolution Metals Corp.....................E..... 561 531-2314
West Palm Beach (G-17990)
Golden Global Corp.........................G..... 954 695-7025
Boca Raton (G-529)
Nyrstar Us Inc...............................D..... 954 400-6464
Fort Lauderdale (G-3965)
Ssemiami Corporation.....................E..... 305 322-1890
Doral (G-3374)
USA Rare Earth LLC........................F..... 813 867-6155
Tampa (G-17399)

METAL SERVICE CENTERS & OFFICES

Lloyd Industries Inc.......................D..... 904 541-1655
Orange Park (G-11833)
LV Thompson Inc............................C..... 813 248-3456
Tampa (G-17026)
Metal Supply and Machining Inc.......F..... 561 276-4941
Delray Beach (G-2988)
Primary Metals Intl LLC...................... 800 243-1923
Cape Coral (G-1375)
Spectra Metal Sales Inc..................F..... 727 530-5435
Clearwater (G-1795)
Urban Metals LLC...........................E..... 813 241-2801
Tampa (G-17396)
Vested Metals Intl LLC....................G..... 904 495-7278
Saint Augustine (G-14909)

METAL SPINNING FOR THE TRADE

Accurate Metals Spinning Inc..........G..... 305 885-9988
Medley (G-8192)

METAL STAMPING, FOR THE TRADE

Aero Precision Products Inc............D..... 305 688-2565
Opa Locka (G-11712)
Atlantic Tool & Mfg Corp S..............F..... 727 546-2250
Largo (G-7539)
D & A Machine Inc..........................G..... 407 275-5770
Orlando (G-12069)
ES Investments LLC........................C..... 727 536-8822
Clearwater (G-1590)
Florida Metal Services Inc...............D..... 727 541-6441
Largo (G-7586)
Gator Stampings Intl Inc..................D..... 941 753-9598
Sarasota (G-15481)
Griffiths Corporation......................D..... 407 851-8342
Orlando (G-12202)
Hudson Tool & Die Company Inc.......C..... 386 672-2000
Ormond Beach (G-12771)
Interlake Industries Inc..................F..... 863 688-5665
Lakeland (G-7356)
Interlake Stamping Florida Inc.........D..... 863 688-5665
Lakeland (G-7357)
Kwikprint Manufacturing Co Inc.......G..... 904 737-3755
Jacksonville (G-6251)
Masonite Corporation.....................D..... 813 877-2726
Tampa (G-17046)
Masonite International Corp.............D..... 904 225-3889
Yulee (G-18591)
Mitek Inc.......................................E..... 727 536-7891
Largo (G-7645)
Mohawk Manufacturing Company......F..... 407 849-0333
Longwood (G-7924)
P&A Machine..................................G..... 407 275-5770
Orlando (G-12461)
Peterson Manufacturing LLC............E..... 941 371-4989
Sarasota (G-15782)
Stanron Corporation.......................E..... 954 974-8050
Fort Lauderdale (G-4066)

METAL STAMPINGS: Ornamental

Blue Water Dynamics LLC................D..... 386 957-5464
Edgewater (G-3482)

METAL STAMPINGS: Patterned

Creative Concepts Ncj LLC..............G..... 352 302-8100
Homosassa (G-5745)
Creative Concepts Ncj LLC..............G..... 352 302-8100
Homosassa (G-5746)

METAL: Heavy, Perforated

Supply Expediters Intl Inc................F..... 305 805-4255
Pembroke Pines (G-13416)

METALS SVC CENTERS & WHOL: Structural Shapes, Iron Or Steel

J & J Wldg Stl Fbrction Fla In..........F..... 813 754-0771
Auburndale (G-237)

METALS SVC CENTERS & WHOLESALERS: Cable, Wire

Meridian Cable LLC.........................F..... 904 770-4687
Saint Augustine (G-14858)

METALS SVC CENTERS & WHOLESALERS: Iron & Steel Prdt, Ferrous

Pioneer Welding & Fabrication..........G..... 407 880-4997
Apopka (G-161)

METALS SVC CENTERS & WHOLESALERS: Pipe & Tubing, Steel

Advanced Drainage Systems Inc.......C..... 407 654-3989
Winter Garden (G-18372)

METALS SVC CENTERS & WHOLESALERS: Rails & Access

United Rail Inc...............................F..... 904 503-9757
Jacksonville (G-6577)

METALS SVC CENTERS & WHOLESALERS: Reinforcement Mesh, Wire

Metalhouse LLC..............................G..... 407 270-3000
Orlando (G-12373)

PRODUCT

METALS SVC CENTERS & WHOLESALERS: Steel

Bell Steel Company .... D 850 432-1545
Pensacola (G-13453)

Central Fla Stl Bldg & Sup LLC .... G 352 266-6795
Ocala (G-11348)

Modern Welding Company Fla Inc .... D 407 843-1270
Orlando (G-12386)

Quality Industries America Inc .... G 386 755-0220
Lake City (G-7041)

Steel City Inc .... F 850 785-9596
Panama City (G-13311)

METALS SVC CTRS & WHOLESALERS: Aluminum Bars, Rods, Etc

Ceco & Associates Inc .... G 727 528-0075
Riverview (G-14558)

Eastern Metal Supply Inc .... F 863 682-6660
Lakeland (G-7315)

METALS: Honeycombed

Composite Essential Mtls LLC .... G 772 344-0034
Port St Lucie (G-14475)

METALS: Precious NEC

Allliance Precious Mtls Group .... G 954 480-8676
Coconut Creek (G-1977)

C B Precious Metals LLC .... F 407 790-1585
Longwood (G-7878)

Crains Precious Metals LLC .... G 954 536-8334
Hollywood (G-5557)

Crypto Cpitl Precious Mtls Inc .... G 727 200-2108
Saint Petersburg (G-15017)

Enviro Gold Ref Systems LLC .... G 813 390-7043
Tampa (G-16817)

I J Precious Metals Inc .... G 305 371-3009
Miami (G-9295)

ICM Precious Metals Inc .... G 917 327-8171
Miami (G-9299)

Miami Metals II Inc .... C 305 685-8505
Opa Locka (G-11769)

Palm Beach Precious Metals .... G 561 662-6025
Palm Springs (G-13149)

Pmr Gestion Inc .... F 561 501-5190
Delray Beach (G-3000)

Precious Metal Exchange .... G 321 727-2278
Melbourne (G-8497)

Precious Metal Group LLC .... G 904 219-8358
Jacksonville (G-6379)

Precious Metals Buyers LLC .... G 813 880-9544
Tampa (G-17173)

Precious Metals Buyers LLC .... F 813 417-7857
Tampa (G-17174)

SPI LLC .... C 786 907-4022
Miami (G-9943)

METALS: Primary Nonferrous, NEC

C C Lead Inc .... F 863 465-6458
Lake Placid (G-7139)

Flotech LLC .... D 904 358-1849
Jacksonville (G-6113)

METALWORK: Miscellaneous

Ace Construction Management .... G 407 704-7803
Orlando (G-11866)

Alumacart Inc .... F 772 675-2158
Indiantown (G-5811)

Anvil Iron Works Inc .... E 727 375-2884
Odessa (G-11536)

Fuse Fabrication Llc .... E 863 225-5698
Mulberry (G-10626)

Gerdau Ameristeel US Inc .... D 813 752-7550
Plant City (G-13771)

GMF Industries Inc .... D 863 646-5081
Lakeland (G-7338)

Hanaya LLC .... F 904 285-7575
Ponte Vedra Beach (G-14268)

ITW Blding Cmponents Group Inc ...... E 863 422-8685
Haines City (G-4908)

Mid Florida Steel Corp .... E 321 632-8228
Cocoa (G-1942)

Midwest Mtal Fbrction Cstm Rll .... F 317 769-6489
North Fort Myers (G-11062)

Q2 Aerospace LLC .... G 305 591-9469
Miami (G-9760)

Specialty Fabrication LLC .... E 863 683-0708
Lakeland (G-7446)

Structall Building Systems Inc .... E 813 855-2627
Oldsmar (G-11698)

Tri Tech Metal Inc .... G 727 946-1229
New Port Richey (G-10989)

METALWORK: Ornamental

AMD Ornamental Inc .... G 239 458-7437
Cape Coral (G-1300)

Artistic Welding Inc .... G 954 563-3098
Oakland Park (G-11242)

Arts Work Unlimited Inc .... G 305 247-9257
Miami (G-8756)

Barrette Outdoor Living Inc .... D 352 754-8555
Brooksville (G-1139)

Custom Metal Creations LLC .... G 772 807-0000
Fort Pierce (G-4478)

Edwards Ornamental Iron Inc .... F 904 354-4282
Jacksonville (G-6066)

Gurtan Designs .... G 954 972-6100
Pompano Beach (G-14047)

Hernandez Ornamental Inc .... G 305 592-7296
Doral (G-3247)

Iacono Iron LLC .... G 561 640-1696
West Palm Beach (G-18029)

J A Custom .... G 561 615-4680
West Palm Beach (G-18038)

M&B Steel Fabricators Inc .... F 407 486-1774
Orlando (G-12359)

Shanker Industries Realty Inc .... G 631 940-9889
West Palm Beach (G-18150)

Southern Aluminum Inc .... F 239 275-3367
Cape Coral (G-1388)

Wonderland Products Inc .... G 904 786-0144
Jacksonville (G-6617)

METALWORKING MACHINERY WHOLESALERS

Lloyd Industries Inc .... D 904 541-1655
Orange Park (G-11833)

METEOROLOGIC TRACKING SYSTEMS

Embrace Telecom Inc .... F 866 933-8986
Fort Lauderdale (G-3792)

METERING DEVICES: Gas Meters, Domestic & Large Cap, Indl

Ronaele Mustang Inc .... G 954 319-7433
Tamarac (G-16541)

METERING DEVICES: Gasoline Dispensing

Repgas Inc .... G 786 202-8434
Port Saint Lucie (G-14440)

METERING DEVICES: Measuring, Mechanical

Edc Corporation .... G 386 951-4075
Deland (G-2867)

Qualitest USA Lc .... F 877 884-8378
Fort Lauderdale (G-4004)

METERING DEVICES: Water Quality Monitoring & Control Systems

Elster Amco Water LLC .... F 352 369-6500
Ocala (G-11377)

Fewtek Inc .... F 727 736-0533
Dunedin (G-3448)

METERS: Altimeters

Alti-2 Inc .... F 386 943-9333
Deland (G-2851)

METERS: Liquid

Kus Usa Inc .... E 954 463-1075
Davie (G-2431)

METERS: Power Factor & Phase Angle

Powerficient LLC .... E 800 320-2535
Fort Lauderdale (G-3990)

MGMT CONSULTING SVCS: Matls, Incl Purch, Handle & Invntry

Hatalom Corporation .... E 407 567-2556
Orlando (G-12211)

Management Hlth Solutions Inc .... B 888 647-4621
Tampa (G-17034)

Rz Service Group LLC .... G 904 402-2313
Jacksonville (G-6439)

MICA PRDTS

Braden Kitchens Inc .... E 321 636-4700
Cocoa (G-1907)

MICROCIRCUITS, INTEGRATED: Semiconductor

Chip Supply Inc .... E 407 298-7100
Apopka (G-110)

Florida Micro Devices Inc .... G 954 973-7200
Coral Springs (G-2153)

MEI Micro Inc .... E 407 514-2619
Orlando (G-12370)

Micross Minco LLC .... D 512 339-3422
Apopka (G-153)

Xilinx Inc .... F 407 365-8644
Oviedo (G-12852)

MICROMETERS

Microtex Electronics Inc .... G 386 426-1922
Weeki Wachee (G-17838)

MICROPROCESSORS

Intelbase Security Corporation .... F 703 371-9181
Saint Augustine (G-14848)

Micro Control Systems Inc .... E 239 694-0089
Fort Myers (G-4325)

Spartronics Brooksville LLC .... D 352 799-6520
Brooksville (G-1205)

MICROSCOPES

A&C Microscopes LLC .... F 786 514-3967
Doral (G-3090)

MICROSCOPES: Electron & Proton

JI Optical Inc .... G 386 428-6928
New Smyrna Beach (G-11003)

MICROWAVE COMPONENTS

Electrosource Inc .... F 954 723-0840
Plantation (G-13846)

Logus Manufacturing Corp .... G 561 842-3550
West Palm Beach (G-18060)

Microwave Electronics .... G 561 432-8511
Lake Worth (G-7216)

RES-Net Microwave Inc .... E 727 530-9555
Clearwater (G-1763)

Smiths Interconnect Inc .... C 813 901-7200
Tampa (G-17277)

Smiths Interconnect Group Ltd .... G 805 370-5580
Stuart (G-16222)

Smiths Intrcnnect Americas Inc .... B 772 286-9300
Stuart (G-16223)

Sv Microwave Inc .... C 561 840-1800
West Palm Beach (G-18172)

MICROWAVE OVENS: Household

Apollo Worldwide Inc .... G 561 585-3865
Hypoluxo (G-5794)

MILITARY GOODS & REGALIA STORES

M/V Marine Inc .... F 904 633-7992
Jacksonville (G-6268)

MILK, FLUID: Wholesalers

Dfa Dairy Brands Fluid LLC .... G 352 754-1750
Brooksville (G-1153)

MILLING: Cereal Flour, Exc Rice

Bay State Milling Company .... E 772 597-2056
Indiantown (G-5812)

MILLING: Chemical

Powder Systems Inc ....G..... 352 680-3558
Ocala **(G-11470)**

MILLING: Grains, Exc Rice

Southland Milling Co ....G....... 850 674-8448
Blountstown **(G-378)**

MILLWORK

1565 Woodworks LLC ....G..... 904 347-7664
Saint Augustine **(G-14803)**

A Gs Mica and Custom Wdwrk LLC ......G....... 561 351-5429
West Palm Beach **(G-17907)**

A L Custom Wood Corp ....G....... 305 557-2434
Hialeah **(G-5016)**

A Wsco ....G....... 937 263-1053
Santa Rosa Beach **(G-15420)**

A&D Woodwork Florida LLC ....E..... 561 465-2863
Boca Raton **(G-385)**

AB Wood Work Inc ....G..... 786 701-3611
Miami **(G-8632)**

Accent Woodworking Inc ....G..... 727 522-2700
Largo **(G-7520)**

Actual Woodworking Inc ....G..... 305 606-7849
Naples **(G-10651)**

Adams Bros Cabinetry Inc ....D..... 941 639-7188
North Port **(G-11186)**

Advanced Millwork Inc ....E..... 407 294-1927
Orlando **(G-11871)**

AJ AZ Woodwork Inc ....G..... 561 859-4963
Margate **(G-8119)**

Akira Wood Inc ....E..... 352 375-0691
Gainesville **(G-4647)**

Al-FA Cabinets Inc ....F..... 813 876-4205
Tampa **(G-16569)**

All Phase Custom Mill Shop Inc ....E..... 941 474-0903
Port Charlotte **(G-14284)**

Alliance Cabinets & Millwork ....G..... 407 802-9921
Deerfield Beach **(G-2665)**

Allstair ....G..... 239 313-5574
Fort Myers **(G-4167)**

Alpha Woodwork Inc ....G..... 954 347-6251
Pompano Beach **(G-13921)**

American Archtctural Mllwk LLC ....F..... 844 307-9571
Venice **(G-17677)**

American Fine Woodwork LLC ....G..... 954 261-9793
Davie **(G-2384)**

Amets Woodworks Corp ....G..... 786 537-5982
Miami **(G-8723)**

Antifaz Woodwork Inc ....G..... 786 306-7740
Miami **(G-8732)**

Apperals Custom Finish Wdwrk ....G..... 754 264-2296
Boca Raton **(G-413)**

Architctral WD Wkg Mlding Div ....F..... 727 527-7400
Saint Petersburg **(G-14968)**

Architctural WD Pdts of Naples ....G..... 239 260-7156
Naples **(G-10673)**

Architectural Detail & Wdwkg ....G..... 561 835-4005
West Palm Beach **(G-17925)**

Architectural Moulding Corp ....G..... 305 638-8900
Miami **(G-8742)**

Architectural Spc Trdg Co ....D..... 850 435-2507
Pensacola **(G-13443)**

Art Staircase & Woodwork Llc ....F..... 239 440-6591
Cape Coral **(G-1307)**

Artisan Wood Works Inc ....E..... 239 321-9122
Naples **(G-10678)**

Artisanis Guild ....G..... 239 591-3203
Naples **(G-10679)**

Artistic Doors Inc ....G..... 561 582-0348
Lake Worth Beach **(G-7249)**

Atelier Woodworking ....F..... 561 386-0811
Royal Palm Beach **(G-14759)**

Atlantic Custom Woodcraft Corp ......E..... 727 645-6905
Odessa **(G-11537)**

Atlantic West Molding & Mllwk ....F..... 239 261-2874
Naples **(G-10681)**

Aventura Custom Woodwork ....G..... 305 891-9093
North Miami **(G-11091)**

Badger Woodworks LLC ....F..... 386 860-9600
Sanford **(G-15270)**

Bari Millwork & Supply LLC ....E..... 954 969-9440
Pompano Beach **(G-13949)**

Bay Meadow Architectural Mllwk ......E..... 407 332-7992
Longwood **(G-7874)**

Blumer & Stanton Entps Inc ....F..... 561 585-2525
West Palm Beach **(G-17949)**

Blumer & Stanton Inc ....F..... 561 585-2525
West Palm Beach **(G-17950)**

Blums Woodworking LLC ....F..... 850 449-7729
Pensacola **(G-13458)**

Bodhi Tree Woodwork Inc ....G..... 904 540-2655
Saint Augustine **(G-14816)**

C & M Millwork Inc ....F..... 352 588-5050
San Antonio **(G-15246)**

Cabinet Design and Cnstr LLC ....G..... 850 393-9724
Pensacola **(G-13468)**

Carolina Woodworks Inc ....G..... 954 692-4662
Deerfield Beach **(G-2686)**

Casons Quality Care Svcs LLC ....G..... 386 365-1016
Lulu **(G-7977)**

CG Quality Woodworks Inc ....G..... 305 231-3480
Hialeah **(G-5089)**

Coastal Awngs Hrrcane Prtction ....G..... 407 923-9482
Orlando **(G-12023)**

Coastal Door & Mllwk Svcs LLC ....G..... 561 266-3716
Delray Beach **(G-2947)**

Coastal Millworks Inc ....E..... 561 881-7755
West Palm Beach **(G-17968)**

Coastal Millworx LLC ....G..... 850 250-6672
Panama City **(G-13247)**

Coastal Woodwork Inc ....G..... 561 218-3353
Pompano Beach **(G-13971)**

Commercial Instllation Systems ....G..... 727 525-2372
Saint Petersburg **(G-15010)**

Commercial Millworks Inc ....F..... 407 648-2787
Orlanco **(G-12034)**

Conrad Markle Bldr & Cbnt ....G..... 904 744-4569
Jacksonville **(G-5998)**

Conway Bldg Cstm Woodworks LLC ....G..... 407 738-9266
Kissimmee **(G-6908)**

Crawfords Custom Woodwork ....G..... 904 782-1375
Lawtey **(G-7745)**

Creative Concepts Orlando Inc ....E..... 407 260-1435
Longwood **(G-7883)**

Creative Custom Stairs ....G..... 941 505-0336
Punta Gorda **(G-14503)**

Creative Millwork Inc ....G..... 305 885-5474
Hialeah **(G-5101)**

Creative Wdwkg Concepts Inc ....G..... 727 937-4165
Tarpon Springs **(G-17462)**

Custom Cft Windows & Doors Inc ....F..... 407 834-5400
Winter Springs **(G-18563)**

Custom Install Solutions Inc ....F..... 916 601-1190
Boca Raton **(G-476)**

Custom Marine Joinery Inc ....G..... 954 822-6057
Oakland Park **(G-11254)**

Custom Teak Marine Woodwork ....G..... 727 768-6065
Saint Petersburg **(G-15018)**

Custom WD Architectural Mllwk ....G..... 786 290-5412
Miami **(G-8985)**

Custom WD Designs of Pensacola ......F..... 850 476-9663
Pensacola **(G-13481)**

D & D Building Contractors Inc ....G..... 954 791-2075
Davie **(G-2402)**

D&D Wood Working Inc ....G..... 407 427-0106
Orlando **(G-12070)**

Dac Wood Work Inc ....G..... 954 729-9232
Deerfield Beach **(G-2702)**

Dade Truss Company Inc ....C..... 305 592-8245
Miami **(G-8997)**

Dana Andrews Woodworking ....G..... 561 882-0444
Riviera Beach **(G-14614)**

Db Doors Inc ....F..... 561 798-6684
West Palm Beach **(G-17976)**

Decowall ....G..... 813 886-5226
Tampa **(G-16770)**

Deep Ocean Woodworks Inc ....G..... 407 687-2773
Sanford **(G-15302)**

Design Custom Millwork Inc ....E..... 407 878-1267
Sanford **(G-15304)**

Designers Specialty Cab Co Inc ....E..... 954 776-4500
Miami **(G-9022)**

E & E Woodcraft Corp ....F..... 305 556-1443
Hialeah **(G-5129)**

E B Custom Cabinets LLC ....G..... 407 927-2346
Kissimmee **(G-6914)**

Effearredi Usa Inc ....G..... 786 725-4948
Miami **(G-9073)**

El Custom Wood Creations Inc ....G..... 786 337-0014
Dania **(G-2331)**

Evm Woodwork Corp ....G..... 954 970-4352
North Lauderdale **(G-11079)**

Evm Woodworks Corp ....G..... 954 655-6414
North Lauderdale **(G-11080)**

Evolution Woodworking ....G..... 407 221-5031
Geneva **(G-4787)**

Excell Woodwork Corp ....G..... 954 461-0465
Margate **(G-8128)**

Exquisite Wood Works By Al ....G..... 321 634-5398
Rockledge **(G-14708)**

F W I Inc ....F..... 407 509-9739
Longwood **(G-7894)**

Fine Archtctral Mllwk Shutters ....F..... 954 491-2055
Fort Lauderdale **(G-3816)**

Fine Woodworks ....G..... 954 448-9206
Weirsdale **(G-17839)**

First Imprssion Doors More Inc ....G..... 561 798-6684
West Palm Beach **(G-17997)**

Five Star Millwork Inc ....F..... 954 956-7665
Pompano Beach **(G-14026)**

Florida Frames Inc ....F..... 727 572-4064
Clearwater **(G-1600)**

Florida Heritage Wdwkg LLC ....G..... 941 705-9980
Sarasota **(G-15677)**

Florida Marine Joiner Svc Llc ....F..... 813 514-1125
Tampa **(G-16849)**

Foote Woodworking Inc ....F..... 941 923-6553
Sarasota **(G-15682)**

Fort Lauderdale Wdwkg Inc ....E..... 954 935-0366
Pompano Beach **(G-14035)**

Fraser Millworks Inc ....G..... 904 768-7710
Jacksonville **(G-6119)**

Fraser West Inc ....C..... 904 289-7261
Jacksonville **(G-6120)**

Fraser West Inc ....C..... 904 290-6460
Lake Butler **(G-7000)**

Fuentes Custom Woodwork LLC ....G..... 941 232-0635
Sarasota **(G-15684)**

G G Millwork Contractor Inc ....E..... 305 522-6333
Howey In The Hills **(G-5758)**

G G Millwork Contractor Inc ....G..... 305 852-1718
Key Largo **(G-6847)**

Garcia Woodwork Entps Inc ....G..... 954 226-3906
Oakland Park **(G-11268)**

GF Woodworks ....G..... 407 716-3712
Altamonte Springs **(G-51)**

Gleman Sons Cstm Woodworks LLC ....F..... 407 314-9638
Sanford **(G-15326)**

Gloval Displays Inc ....E..... 800 972-0353
Miami Gardens **(G-10259)**

Golden Wood Works LLC ....G..... 239 677-8540
Cape Coral **(G-1349)**

Goodwin Lumber Company Inc ....F..... 352 466-0339
Micanopy **(G-10397)**

Grand Woodworking Llc ....F..... 239 594-9663
Naples **(G-10765)**

Green Forest Industries Inc ....E..... 941 721-0504
Palmetto **(G-13169)**

Gulfshore Custom Woodworks LLC .....G..... 239 205-0777
Cape Coral **(G-1351)**

Handcraft Woodworking Inc ....G..... 561 241-9911
Boca Raton **(G-537)**

Handcraft Woodworking Inc ....E..... 954 418-6356
Deerfield Beach **(G-2730)**

Harlen S Woodworking ....G..... 850 774-2224
Lynn Haven **(G-8028)**

Harris Woodworks LLC ....G..... 561 543-3265
Palm Beach Gardens **(G-12972)**

Hollywood Woodwork Inc ....D..... 954 920-5009
Hollywood **(G-5598)**

Ilan Custom Woodwork LLC ....E..... 727 272-5070
Clearwater **(G-1639)**

Infinite Ret Design & Mfg Corp ....F..... 305 967-8339
Miami **(G-9312)**

Island Millwork Inc ....F..... 352 694-5565
Ocala **(G-11412)**

J-Coast Woodworks LLC ....G..... 561 262-6144
Jupiter **(G-6748)**

Jayco Woodworks Inc ....G..... 850 814-3041
Panama City **(G-13278)**

JB Wood Werks LLC ....G..... 239 314-4462
Cape Coral **(G-1358)**

Jireh Woodwork Inc ....G..... 954 515-8041
Deerfield Beach **(G-2746)**

Jk2 Scenic LLC ....E..... 407 703-2977
Apopka **(G-141)**

JM Custom Millworks Inc ....F..... 561 582-5600
Mangonia Park **(G-8094)**

JM Custom Woodworking ....F..... 561 582-5600
Mangonia Park **(G-8095)**

John S Wilson Inc ....F..... 410 442-2400
Naples **(G-10791)**

Johnson Woodworking ....G..... 772 473-1404
Malabar **(G-8083)**

JR Wood Works Inc ....G..... 305 401-6056
Miami **(G-9377)**

Kdavid Woodwork + Design Inc ....F..... 754 205-2433
North Lauderdale **(G-11082)**

Employee Codes: A=Over 500 employees, B=251-500
C=101-250, D=51-100, E=20-50, F=10-19, G=4-9

2022 Harris Florida
Manufacturers Directory

1261

PRODUCT

Kevins Custom Woodworking ....G..... 727 804-8422
Palm Harbor *(G-13117)*

L and T W Oodwork LLC ....G..... 305 742-4362
Homestead *(G-5725)*

LE Wood Work Inc ....G..... 786 269-4275
Miami *(G-9444)*

Leandro Mora Studio LLC ....G..... 786 376-9166
Miami *(G-9447)*

Liberty Woodworking Inc ....G..... 727 642-9652
Pinellas Park *(G-13705)*

Local Woodwork LLC ....G..... 954 551-1515
Margate *(G-8142)*

Lombardis Woodworking ....G..... 305 439-7208
Miami Springs *(G-10391)*

Losobe LLC ....G..... 850 748-3162
Pensacola *(G-13540)*

Lra Architectural WD Work Inc ....G..... 305 801-5573
Hialeah *(G-5228)*

Luxury Woodworking Soluti ....G..... 786 398-1785
Hialeah *(G-5230)*

Lyndan Inc ....E..... 813 977-6683
Tampa *(G-17028)*

Magnolia Millwork Intl Inc ....G..... 407 585-3470
Casselberry *(G-1424)*

Mayworth Showcase Works Inc ....G..... 813 251-1558
Tampa *(G-17058)*

McMullen Road LLC ....E..... 813 854-3100
Tampa *(G-17060)*

Melbourne Architectural Mllwk ....F..... 321 308-3297
Melbourne *(G-8474)*

Mg Woodwork Inc ....F..... 561 459-7552
Pompano Beach *(G-14097)*

Mike C Lohmeyer ....G..... 727 669-0808
Safety Harbor *(G-14792)*

Miles of Wood Inc ....G..... 305 300-6370
Miami *(G-9569)*

Millennium Glass Inc ....G..... 305 638-1785
Miami *(G-9572)*

Millwork and Design Inc ....G..... 352 544-0444
Brooksville *(G-1182)*

Millwork Masters LLC ....F..... 727 807-6221
New Port Richey *(G-10974)*

Millwork Plus Inc ....G..... 352 343-2121
Tavares *(G-17518)*

Mjr Woodworks LLC ....F..... 407 403-5430
Apopka *(G-154)*

Mm Wood Designs Inc ....G..... 561 602-2775
Delray Beach *(G-2989)*

N & N Investment Corporation ....E..... 954 590-3800
Pompano Beach *(G-14106)*

Naples Woodworks Inc ....G..... 239 287-1632
Naples *(G-10833)*

National Woodworks Inc ....G..... 407 489-3572
Orlando *(G-12405)*

Natural Wood Works LLC ....G..... 954 445-1493
Hialeah *(G-5273)*

New Style Kit Cabinets Corp ....G..... 305 989-9665
Hialeah *(G-5277)*

Noble Wood Works ....G..... 561 702-2889
Pompano Beach *(G-14108)*

Ocean Woodworks Inc ....G..... 904 246-7178
Atlantic Beach *(G-213)*

Ouro Custom Woodwork Inc ....E..... 954 428-0735
Deerfield Beach *(G-2776)*

Palm Beach Cstm Woodworks LLC .....F..... 561 575-5335
Mangonia Park *(G-8097)*

Paradise Oaks Woodworking Inc ....G..... 863 206-0858
Tampa *(G-17147)*

Pat Clark Custom Woodworking L ....G..... 941 376-1387
Sarasota *(G-15774)*

Pelican Woodworks Inc ....G..... 904 687-5759
Saint Augustine *(G-14871)*

Pineapple Grove Woodworks Inc ....G..... 561 676-1287
West Palm Beach *(G-18121)*

Powell Woodworking LLC ....F..... 407 883-9181
Sanford *(G-15372)*

Pradere Manufacturing Corp ....F..... 305 823-0190
Hialeah *(G-5298)*

Pro Millwork Installations ....G..... 561 302-5869
Boynton Beach *(G-901)*

Pro-Trim Millwork Inc ....G..... 239 592-5454
Naples *(G-10867)*

Quality 1 Appraisal Inc ....G..... 786 859-4085
Hialeah *(G-5319)*

R Dorian Millworks LLC ....F..... 561 863-9125
West Palm Beach *(G-18137)*

R K Constructors of Centl Fla ....G..... 407 222-5376
Orlando *(G-12527)*

Ramos Woodwork LLC ....F..... 954 861-7679
Deerfield Beach *(G-2795)*

Rbs Woodwork Corp ....F..... 754 214-7682
Margate *(G-8152)*

Rich Woodturning Inc ....G..... 305 573-9142
Miami Lakes *(G-10349)*

Rick Ernissee Woodworks LLC ....G..... 727 421-7711
Clearwater *(G-1767)*

River Craft LLC ....F..... 407 867-0584
Orlando *(G-12556)*

Riverview Millworks Inc ....G..... 904 764-9571
Jacksonville *(G-6428)*

Rolu Woodcraft Inc ....F..... 305 685-0914
Hialeah *(G-5336)*

Rubinelli Woodwork Inc ....G..... 954 445-0537
Boca Raton *(G-655)*

S M I Cabinetry Inc ....E..... 407 841-0292
Orlando *(G-12565)*

Sailor Made Cstm Woodworks LLC .....G..... 805 587-1197
Palm Bay *(G-12916)*

Sailor Made Custom Woodworks L .....G..... 805 587-1197
Rockledge *(G-14744)*

Sarasota Archtctural Wdwkg LLC ....G..... 941 684-1614
Sarasota *(G-15809)*

SCi Architectural Wdwrk Inc ....F..... 954 247-9601
Fort Lauderdale *(G-4037)*

Security World Electronics ....G..... 786 285-5303
Miami Gardens *(G-10273)*

Simpson ....F..... 954 804-0829
Coconut Creek *(G-2005)*

Smiths Woodworks Inc ....G..... 863 381-6564
Lake Placid *(G-7148)*

South Florida Woodworkers Inc ....G..... 954 868-5043
Fort Lauderdale *(G-4059)*

Southwest Woodwork Inc ....G..... 239 213-0126
Naples *(G-10900)*

Splinter Woodworking Inc ....G..... 305 731-9334
Delray Beach *(G-3021)*

Steadfast Woodworking Inc ....G..... 386 748-1744
Deland *(G-2904)*

Stephs Woodworking LLC ....G..... 772 571-2661
Vero Beach *(G-17803)*

Straight Line Mllwk & Sup Inc ....G..... 561 422-0444
West Palm Beach *(G-18168)*

Sullivan Penny Woodworking ....G..... 561 860-1163
Delray Beach *(G-3023)*

T and M Woodworking Inc ....G..... 352 748-6655
Wildwood *(G-18323)*

Tampa Contractors Supply Inc ....E..... 813 418-7284
Tampa *(G-17331)*

Teak Isle Inc ....C..... 407 656-8885
Ocoee *(G-11527)*

Terrades Custom Woodworks Inc ....G..... 305 316-2908
Hialeah *(G-5379)*

Thomas Rley Artisans Guild Inc ....E..... 239 591-3203
Naples *(G-10925)*

Top Notch Wood Works Inc ....G..... 954 445-7861
Miami *(G-10026)*

Tri-County Cabinetry Wdwrk LLC ....G..... 850 238-6226
Altha *(G-78)*

Tri-County Woodworking LLC ....F..... 954 850-2222
Pompano Beach *(G-14218)*

Tru Craft Woodworks LLC ....G..... 561 441-2742
Delray Beach *(G-3029)*

Trucraft Specialties Inc ....G..... 561 441-2742
Delray Beach *(G-3030)*

Universal Wood Design ....F..... 772 569-5389
Vero Beach *(G-17812)*

Vc Atlantic Woodwork ....G..... 305 219-9411
Miami *(G-10098)*

Vera Custom Woodworking I ....G..... 941 726-8831
Palmetto *(G-13200)*

Vera Custom Woodworking Inc ....G..... 321 355-0161
Palmetto *(G-13201)*

Vesten Woodworks LLC ....G..... 407 780-9295
Saint Augustine *(G-14910)*

Viking Kabinets Inc ....E..... 305 238-9025
Cutler Bay *(G-2311)*

Vreeland Woodworking LLC ....G..... 727 365-0241
Palm Harbor *(G-13138)*

Waterhuse Archtctral Wdwrk LLC ....F..... 786 534-4943
Miami *(G-10125)*

West Harbour Woodworking LLC ....G..... 954 822-7543
Lauderdale Lakes *(G-7722)*

Wicked Woodworks Inc ....G..... 305 714-2209
Fort Lauderdale *(G-4131)*

William Leupold Sr ....G..... 727 527-7400
Saint Petersburg *(G-15233)*

Wishbone Woodworking Inc ....G..... 239 262-7230
Naples *(G-10941)*

Wonder Emporium Millwork Fab ....F..... 407 850-3131
Orlando *(G-12717)*

Wood One LLC ....G..... 727 639-5620
Saint Petersburg *(G-15236)*

Woodwork Unlimited Inc ....G..... 352 267-4051
Oxford *(G-12855)*

Woodworkers Cabinet Inc ....F..... 239 593-1718
Naples *(G-10942)*

Woodworks of Tampa Bay LLC ....G..... 813 330-5836
Tampa *(G-17434)*

Worthington Millwork LLC ....G..... 800 872-1608
Panama City Beach *(G-13341)*

Wylde Woodworking Co ....G..... 954 942-7630
Pompano Beach *(G-14245)*

Y F Leung Inc ....G..... 305 651-6851
North Miami Beach *(G-11172)*

Zaho Global Enterprises LLC ....G..... 321 239-0653
Orlando *(G-12731)*

MIMEOGRAPHING SVCS

L E M G Inc ....G..... 727 461-5300
Clearwater *(G-1668)*

MINE & QUARRY SVCS: Nonmetallic Minerals

Kiskeya Minerals Usa LLC ....G..... 305 328-5082
Miami *(G-9391)*

Standard Sand & Silica Company ....G..... 352 625-2385
Silver Springs *(G-16008)*

MINE DEVELOPMENT SVCS: Nonmetallic Minerals

Diatomite Corp of America ....G..... 305 466-0075
Miami *(G-9029)*

MINE EXPLORATION SVCS: Nonmetallic Minerals

H2r Corp ....F..... 727 541-3444
Pinellas Park *(G-13692)*

MINERAL ABRASIVES MINING SVCS

Marion Rock Inc ....E..... 352 687-2023
Ocala *(G-11439)*

MINERAL MINING: Nonmetallic

Acg Materials ....G..... 405 366-9500
Marianna *(G-8161)*

Resources In Rare Mining ....G..... 954 800-5251
Fort Lauderdale *(G-4018)*

MINERAL WOOL

Johns Manville Corporation ....D..... 904 786-0298
Jacksonville *(G-6229)*

Magnum Venus Plastech ....F..... 727 573-2955
Clearwater *(G-1682)*

Quiet Flex ....F..... 352 429-3286
Groveland *(G-4868)*

Tubos Inc ....G..... 727 504-0633
Largo *(G-7700)*

MINERAL WOOL INSULATION PRDTS

Bigham Insulation & Sup Co Inc ....E..... 954 522-2887
Fort Lauderdale *(G-3686)*

MINERALS: Ground or Treated

Chemours Company Fc LLC ....D..... 904 964-1200
Starke *(G-16099)*

Diatomite Corp of America ....G..... 305 466-0075
Miami *(G-9029)*

Imerys Perlite Usa Inc ....E..... 850 875-1282
Quincy *(G-14546)*

MINING EXPLORATION & DEVELOPMENT SVCS

Benchmark Metals Inc ....G..... 239 699-0802
Cape Coral *(G-1311)*

James Fletcher Cnstr Inc ....F..... 619 405-9316
Bonifay *(G-773)*

Tri-State Demolition LLC ....G..... 850 597-8722
Tallahassee *(G-16517)*

US Precious Metals Inc ....G..... 786 814-5804
Coral Gables *(G-2118)*

MINING MACHINES & EQPT: Concentration, Metallurgical/Mining

Tmg Manufacturing Corp ....F 813 464-2299
Tampa *(G-17359)*

MINING MACHINES & EQPT: Washers, Aggregate & Sand

Bluegrass Materials Co LLC ....E 919 781-4550
Jacksonville *(G-5941)*

MINING SVCS, NEC: Lignite

Vecellio Management Svcs Inc ....F 561 793-2102
Palm Beach *(G-12942)*

MISSILES: Ballistic, Complete

Lockheed Martin Corporation ....A 407 306-1000
Orlando *(G-12340)*
Rocket Crafters Launch LLC ....F 321 222-0858
Cocoa *(G-1955)*

MISSILES: Guided

Northrop Grumman Systems Corp ....C 904 825-3300
Saint Augustine *(G-14865)*

MIXING EQPT

Premix-Marbletite Mfg Co ....F 954 970-6540
Pompano Beach *(G-14143)*

MIXTURES & BLOCKS: Asphalt Paving

A & F Paving LLC ....G 352 359-2282
Ocala *(G-11313)*
A&W Brick Pavers of North Fla ....G 904 672-7112
Jacksonville *(G-5849)*
Aldanas Pavers Inc ....G 305 970-5339
Miami *(G-8682)*
All In One Cmplete Hndyman Svc ....F 954 708-3463
Deerfield Beach *(G-2662)*
All Pro Pavers Hardscapes Inc ....G 954 300-6281
Pompano Beach *(G-13917)*
Andrade Professional Pavers ....G 904 504-3257
Jacksonville *(G-5889)*
Artistic Paver Mfg Inc ....E 305 653-7283
Miami *(G-8755)*
ASAP Brick Pavers and More ....G 850 522-7123
Panama City *(G-13230)*
Authentic Pavers LLC ....G 850 687-1678
Destin *(G-3059)*
Beauty Pavers LLC ....G 941 720-3655
Bradenton *(G-946)*
Best Pavers LLC ....G 407 259-9020
Orlando *(G-11946)*
Blacklidge Emulsions Inc ....G 850 432-3496
Pensacola *(G-13456)*
Bolivian Pavers LLC ....G 813 952-0608
Tampa *(G-16653)*
Brick Pavers By Mendoza Inc ....G 772 925-1666
Vero Beach *(G-17744)*
Brick Pavers By Mendoza Inc ....D 772 408-2005
Vero Beach *(G-17745)*
Brick Pvers Drveway Big Pavers ....G 407 928-1217
· Orlando *(G-11968)*
Btb Refining LLC ....F 561 999-9916
Boca Raton *(G-452)*
Butler Pavers Inc ....G 941 423-3977
North Port *(G-11190)*
CJL Bricks & Pavers Inc ....G 305 527-4240
Miami *(G-8929)*
Clever Pavers Inc ....G 239 633-7048
Fort Myers *(G-4210)*
Colossus Pavers LLC ....G 239 601-5230
Cape Coral *(G-1326)*
Costa Brick Pavers Inc ....G 904 535-5009
Jacksonville *(G-6010)*
Crystal River Quarries Inc ....E 352 795-2828
Crystal River *(G-2273)*
Devcon International Corp ....F 954 926-5200
Boca Raton *(G-482)*
Eagle Pavers Inc ....G 954 822-1137
Deerfield Beach *(G-2714)*
Easy Pavers Corp ....G 407 967-0511
Winter Garden *(G-18383)*
Flamingo Pavers Inc ....F 850 974-0094
Freeport *(G-4622)*
Florida North Emulsions Inc ....G 386 328-1733
Palatka *(G-12867)*

Freedom Brick Pavers LLC ....G 863 224-6008
Lake Wales *(G-7162)*
Gardner Asphalt Corporation ....D 813 248-2101
Tampa *(G-16869)*
Gardner-Gibson Mfg Inc ....E 813 248-2101
Tampa *(G-16871)*
Gb Brick Pavers Inc ....G 407 453-5505
Orlando *(G-12184)*
Gem Asset Acquisition LLC ....E 904 268-6063
Jacksonville *(G-6136)*
Gem Asset Acquisition LLC ....E 407 888-2080
Orlando *(G-12186)*
Gem Asset Acquisition LLC ....E 813 630-1695
Tampa *(G-16872)*
Gemseal Pavement Products ....G 305 328-9159
Tampa *(G-16873)*
General Asphalt Co Inc ....C 305 592-6005
Miami *(G-9199)*
H & J Asphalt Inc ....G 305 635-8110
Miami *(G-9260)*
Impressive Pavers Inc ....G 321 508-9991
West Melbourne *(G-17901)*
Innovation Pavers Llc ....G 850 687-2864
Destin *(G-3072)*
J & A Big Pavers LLC ....G 321 948-0019
Orlando *(G-12263)*
J & V Paverscorp ....G 786 510-4389
Miami *(G-9349)*
JD Pavers Inc ....G 904 245-9183
Jacksonville Beach *(G-6636)*
Jml Pavers LLC ....G 239 240-0082
Fort Myers *(G-4299)*
Karnak South Inc ....F 954 761-7606
Fort Lauderdale *(G-3900)*
La Pavers Inc ....G 407 209-9163
Orlando *(G-12305)*
Lcf Pavers Inc ....G 239 826-8177
Fort Myers *(G-4309)*
Limas Pavers and Services Inc ....G 904 314-7719
Jacksonville *(G-6259)*
Magnum Pavers Corp ....G 754 367-1832
Deerfield Beach *(G-2760)*
Melanie R Bush Pavers ....G 772 501-7295
Vero Beach *(G-17777)*
Mfjr Pavers LLC ....G 239 440-2580
Fort Myers *(G-4322)*
Most Valuable Pavers ....G 239 590-5217
Cape Coral *(G-1366)*
Msh Brick Pavers Inc ....F 941 822-6472
Bradenton *(G-1015)*
OB Inc ....G 321 223-0332
Cocoa *(G-1945)*
Old & New Brick Pavers LLC ....G 908 249-6130
Orlando *(G-12437)*
Omega Prof Brick Pavers Inc ....G 727 243-4659
Largo *(G-7653)*
Owens Corning Sales LLC ....D 904 353-7361
Jacksonville *(G-6346)*
P&G Pavers Inc ....G 561 716-5113
Jupiter *(G-6776)*
Pan American Cnstr Plant ....F 305 477-5058
Medley *(G-8295)*
Pavemax ....G 386 206-3113
Daytona Beach *(G-2581)*
Paver Action Inc ....G 954 868-1468
Pompano Beach *(G-14120)*
Pavers & Bricks Services Corp ....G 305 986-2544
Miami *(G-9697)*
Pavers By Leandro Peralta Corp ....G 941 323-7338
Sarasota *(G-15777)*
Pavers Professional Inc ....G 239 878-6989
Jacksonville *(G-6357)*
Pavers Solutions Inc ....G 754 551-1924
Deerfield Beach *(G-2780)*
Paverscape Solutions LLC ....G 850 497-5557
Miramar Beach *(G-10570)*
Paversealingcom Corp ....G 407 951-6437
Longwood *(G-7933)*
Pbc Pavers Borba Co ....G 407 296-7727
Orlando *(G-12476)*
PDM LLC ....E 317 605-6656
Tarpon Springs *(G-17486)*
Perfect Brick Pavers Inc ....G 727 534-2506
Port Richey *(G-14370)*
Prime Pavers Inc ....E 941 320-7878
Sarasota *(G-15787)*
Quality Pavers South Fla LLC ....G 954 881-1919
Plantation *(G-13879)*
RG Groundworks LLC ....G 352 474-7949
Newberry *(G-11026)*

Riani Pavers Inc ....G 239 321-1875
Fort Myers *(G-4380)*
Rock Brick Pavers Inc ....G 407 692-6816
Orlando *(G-12559)*
SGS Pavers Inc ....F 561 436-7276
Boynton Beach *(G-911)*
Spiegel Pavers Inc ....G 954 687-5797
Pompano Beach *(G-14196)*
Spiegel Pavers Inc ....G 954 687-5797
Coral Springs *(G-2213)*
Standard Industries Inc ....D 813 248-7000
Tampa *(G-17298)*
Sunset Pavers Inc ....G 239 208-7293
Fort Myers *(G-4413)*
Superior Asphalt Inc ....D 941 755-2850
Bradenton *(G-1056)*
Symmetry Pavers Inc ....G 813 340-0724
Lutz *(G-8017)*
Terra Nova Pvers Hrdscape Slto ....G 904 662-2999
Jacksonville *(G-6544)*
Tikal Pavers Inc ....G 850 892-2207
Defuniak Springs *(G-2845)*
Total Pavers Corp ....F 561 902-7665
Port Saint Lucie *(G-14456)*
Tremron LLC ....D 863 491-0990
Arcadia *(G-195)*
Tsb Emulsions LLC ....G 904 249-5115
Neptune Beach *(G-10959)*
V L Pavers Corp ....G 954 605-0061
Margate *(G-8158)*
Yolo Consulting LLC ....G 954 993-4517
Pembroke Pines *(G-13426)*

MOBILE COMMUNICATIONS EQPT

Artex Computer Llc ....G 407 844-2253
Miami *(G-8754)*
Brightsky LLC ....F 239 919-8551
Naples *(G-10699)*
C E S Wireless Tech Corp ....E 407 681-0869
Winter Park *(G-18494)*
Limitless Mobile Wholesale Inc ....F 321 710-6936
Ocoee *(G-11523)*
Niobium Technology Group LLC ....G 786 292-2613
Miami *(G-9622)*
Relm Communications Inc ....C 321 953-7800
Melbourne *(G-8510)*
Tridor Group Inc ....G 786 707-2241
Miami *(G-10040)*
TX Trading Inc ....G 786 303-9950
Miami *(G-10051)*
Wpp Group Usa Inc ....F 305 341-8132
Miami *(G-10147)*

MOBILE HOMES

Alternative Cnstr Tech Inc ....G 321 421-6601
Melbourne *(G-8363)*
America Trading Inc ....F 305 256-0101
Miami *(G-8713)*
Blevins Inc ....F 904 562-7428
Jacksonville *(G-5937)*
Celltronix ....F 407 610-7852
Orlando *(G-11991)*
Center Seal Inc ....G 863 965-7124
Auburndale *(G-222)*
Chariot Eagle Inc ....D 623 936-7545
Ocala *(G-11350)*
Dills Enterprises LLC ....G 941 493-1993
Venice *(G-17683)*
Eiq Mobility Inc ....G 561 691-7171
Juno Beach *(G-6663)*
Good Rep Inc ....G 407 869-6531
Longwood *(G-7899)*
Marlin Darlin Air LLC ....G 727 726-1136
Belleair Bluffs *(G-355)*
Mobile Home Rebuilders LLC ....G 863 838-9547
Lakeland *(G-7398)*
Mobile4lessusa Corp ....G 954 706-0582
Deerfield Beach *(G-2770)*
Nobility Homes Inc ....E 352 732-5157
Ocala *(G-11451)*
Southern Pines Inc ....G 239 947-1515
Bonita Springs *(G-820)*
Tropic Isles Co-Op Inc ....F 941 721-8888
Palmetto *(G-13199)*
Wayne Dixon LLC ....G 352 279-6886
Brooksville *(G-1221)*

Employee Codes: A=Over 500 employees, B=251-500
C=101-250, D=51-100, E=20-50, F=10-19, G=4-9

2022 Harris Florida
Manufacturers Directory

1263

PRODUCT

MOBILE HOMES, EXC RECREATIONAL

Jacobsen Manufacturing Inc ....C 727 726-1138
Safety Harbor *(G-14788)*
Linman Inc ....B 904 755-6800
Lake City *(G-7028)*
Nobility Homes Inc ....E 352 245-5126
Belleview *(G-364)*
Realty Systems Inc ....F 386 439-0460
Flagler Beach *(G-3604)*
Rolling Greens Mobile Home Pk ....G 352 624-0022
Ocala *(G-11482)*

MOBILE HOMES: Indl Or Commercial Use

Tridor Group Inc ....G 786 707-2241
Miami *(G-10040)*

MOBILE HOMES: Personal Or Private Use

Florida Harbor Homes Inc ....F 941 284-8363
Englewood *(G-3531)*
Harbor Homes ....G 941 320-2670
Sarasota *(G-15699)*
Stone Harbor Homes LLC ....G 239 672-7687
Cape Coral *(G-1393)*

MODELS: Airplane, Exc Toy

Aeroessentials LLC ....G 239 263-9915
Naples *(G-10654)*
Coastal Aircraft Parts LLC ....G 954 980-6929
Sunrise *(G-16305)*

MODELS: Boat, Exc Toy

C M I Enterprises Inc ....E 305 622-6410
Opa Locka *(G-11726)*
Maritime Replicas America Inc ....G 305 386-1958
Hialeah *(G-5243)*

MODELS: General, Exc Toy

Designer Svcs of Trsure Cast I ....G 772 286-0855
Stuart *(G-16138)*
Hollywood Clictibles Group LLC ....G 407 985-4613
Orlando *(G-12222)*
Scale Models Arts & Tech ....F 305 949-1706
North Miami Beach *(G-11161)*

MODULES: Computer Logic

David S Stoyka ....G 561 848-2599
Riviera Beach *(G-14615)*

MODULES: Solid State

Analog Modules Inc ....D 407 339-4355
Longwood *(G-7868)*
Smiths Interconnect Inc ....C 813 901-7200
Tampa *(G-17276)*

MOLDED RUBBER PRDTS

Medfab Corporation ....G 813 854-2646
Oldsmar *(G-11673)*

MOLDING COMPOUNDS

American Sperior Compounds Inc ....G 716 873-1209
Lithia *(G-7830)*
Southern Plastics & Rubber Co ....E 386 672-1167
Ormond Beach *(G-12794)*
Tupperware Products Inc ....F 407 826-5050
Orlando *(G-12679)*

MOLDING SAND MINING

Marine Concepts ....F 239 283-0800
Cape Coral *(G-1362)*

MOLDINGS & TRIM: Metal, Exc Automobile

Oliveri Woodworking Inc ....E 561 478-7233
West Palm Beach *(G-18098)*
Windsor Window Company ....F 321 385-3880
Titusville *(G-17627)*

MOLDINGS OR TRIM: Automobile, Stamped Metal

Florida Production Engrg Inc ....C 386 677-2566
Ormond Beach *(G-12765)*
Sterling Eqp Mfg Centl Fla Inc ....G 352 669-3255
Umatilla *(G-17652)*

MOLDINGS, ARCHITECTURAL: Plaster Of Paris

Cutting Edge Archtctral Mldngs ....G 941 727-1111
Bradenton *(G-966)*
Cutting Edge Moldings LLC ....G 734 649-1500
Sarasota *(G-15465)*
Sun-Rock Inc ....F 727 938-0013
Tarpon Springs *(G-17495)*
Tri Inc ....F 813 267-1201
Tampa *(G-17368)*

MOLDINGS: Picture Frame

Artworks International ....G 561 833-9165
West Palm Beach *(G-17929)*
Cinega Cstm Frmng & Design Inc ....E 904 686-5654
Orange Park *(G-11820)*
Jem Art Inc ....E 954 966-7078
Sunrise *(G-16330)*

MOLDS: Indl

American Mfg & Mch Inc ....D 352 728-2222
Okahumpka *(G-11594)*
American Mold Detectives Inc ....G 954 729-0640
Tamarac *(G-16525)*
American Mold Removal Inc ....G 561 575-7757
Loxahatchee *(G-7967)*
Ameritech Die & Mold South Inc ....E 386 677-1770
Ormond Beach *(G-12742)*
Apex Flood Fire Mold Clnup Inc ....G 305 975-1710
Boca Raton *(G-412)*
Armoury Property & Mold Inspec ....F 813 503-9765
Port Charlotte *(G-14287)*
C & C Tool & Mold ....G 863 699-5337
Lake Placid *(G-7138)*
Cavaform International LLC ....D 727 384-3676
Saint Petersburg *(G-15001)*
Certified Mold Treatment LLC ....G 305 879-1839
Summerland Key *(G-16261)*
Complete Mold Remediators Inc ....F 305 903-8885
Homestead *(G-5703)*
D M T Inc ....F 321 267-3931
Cocoa *(G-1914)*
Danly Corporation ....G 305 285-0111
Miami *(G-8999)*
Diemold Machine Company Inc ....E 239 482-1400
Fort Myers *(G-4234)*
Expert Mold Removal Inc ....G 407 925-6443
Tavares *(G-17506)*
Florida Mold Stoppers Inc ....G 954 445-5560
Davie *(G-2413)*
Fullerton 799 Inc ....D 727 572-7040
Clearwater *(G-1608)*
Gama TEC Corporation ....G 305 362-0456
Hialeah *(G-5165)*
M D Mold LLC ....G 941 214-0854
Port Charlotte *(G-14307)*
Mold Be Gone Plus ....G 239 672-5321
Fort Myers *(G-4328)*
Mold Busters LLC ....G 786 360-6464
Miami *(G-9585)*
Mold Expert ....G 954 829-3102
Coral Springs *(G-2189)*
Mold Pros Franchising Inc ....F 239 262-6653
Naples *(G-10821)*
Mold R US Inc ....G 954 850-6653
Hollywood *(G-5629)*
Moldsbiz ....G 352 327-2720
Gainesville *(G-4733)*
Mommy & ME Molds LLC ....G 727 460-0335
Saint Petersburg *(G-15130)*
National Mold Testing ....G 561 626-7418
West Palm Beach *(G-18085)*
Oxygenix Mold and Odor LLC ....G 850 926-5421
Crawfordville *(G-2231)*
Papenfuss Holdings Inc ....G 239 775-9090
Naples *(G-10848)*
PMC Enterprises Mgmt Division ....F 239 949-6566
Naples *(G-10863)*
Project Mold ....G 561 213-6167
Boca Raton *(G-642)*
Robert Petrucci Inc ....F 954 772-2333
Fort Lauderdale *(G-4023)*
Spaulding Craft Inc ....G 727 726-2316
Safety Harbor *(G-14798)*
Technamold Inc ....G 727 561-0030
Clearwater *(G-1820)*
US Mold Inc ....G 561 748-2223
Jupiter *(G-6818)*

MOLDS: Plastic Working & Foundry

American Plastic Sup & Mfg Inc ....E 727 573-0636
Clearwater *(G-1491)*

MONUMENTS & GRAVE MARKERS, EXC TERRAZZO

Mc Monumental Group Inc ....G 305 651-9113
North Miami Beach *(G-11149)*
Monumental Air Inc ....F 954 383-9507
Coral Springs *(G-2192)*
Monumental Enterprises Inc ....G 305 803-8493
Pembroke Pines *(G-13406)*

MOPS: Floor & Dust

Costa Broom Works Inc ....F 813 248-3397
Tampa *(G-16733)*
Youmop LLC ....G 248 343-2013
Boynton Beach *(G-929)*

MOTION PICTURE & VIDEO PRODUCTION SVCS

Sleepy Dragon Studios Inc ....G 561 714-6156
Cutler Bay *(G-2302)*

MOTION PICTURE & VIDEO PRODUCTION SVCS: Educational, TV

Edumatics Inc ....F 407 656-0661
Orlando *(G-12116)*
Protege Media LLC ....G 310 738-9567
Port Saint Lucie *(G-14435)*

MOTION PICTURE PRODUCTION ALLIED SVCS

On-Board Media Inc ....D 305 673-0400
Doral *(G-3318)*

MOTOR & GENERATOR PARTS: Electric

AB Electric Motors & Pumps ....E 954 322-6900
Hollywood *(G-5520)*
Advanced Mfg & Pwr Systems Inc ....E 386 822-5565
Deland *(G-2848)*
Technet Corp ....G 305 582-5369
Doral *(G-3392)*

MOTOR REBUILDING SVCS, EXC AUTOMOTIVE

Electric Motors Lift Stn Svcs ....G 727 538-4778
Pinellas Park *(G-13683)*
Miami Compressor Rbldrs Inc ....F 305 303-2251
Miami *(G-9548)*

MOTOR REPAIR SVCS

Quality Driven ....G 941 923-3322
Sarasota *(G-15791)*

MOTOR SCOOTERS & PARTS

Adir Scooters Inc ....G 305 532-0019
Miami Beach *(G-10161)*

MOTOR VEHICLE ASSEMBLY, COMPLETE: Ambulances

Rev Amblance Group Orlando Inc ....B 407 677-7777
Winter Park *(G-18533)*
Worldwide Auto Systems Corp ....F 954 439-6332
Hollywood *(G-5686)*

MOTOR VEHICLE ASSEMBLY, COMPLETE: Autos, Incl Specialty

Alevo Automotive Inc ....G 954 593-4215
Boca Raton *(G-397)*
Barron Boyz Auto ....F 229 403-2656
Fleming Island *(G-3608)*
Delaware Chassis Works ....G 302 378-3013
Stuart *(G-16137)*
Emergency Vehicles Inc ....F 561 848-6652
Lake Park *(G-7124)*
Giliberti Inc ....F 772 597-1870
Indiantown *(G-5813)*
Mike Cope Race Cars LLC ....G 352 585-2810
Clearwater *(G-1700)*

2022 Harris Florida
Manufacturers Directory

(G-0000) Company's Geographic Section entry number

Phelps Motorsports LLC ....G...... 239 417-2042
Naples (G-10854)

Revology Cars LLC.............................F 800 974-4463
Orlando (G-12549)

Rp High Performance Inc ....F 561 863-2800
Riviera Beach (G-14671)

Uma Holdings Inc ....E 786 587-1349
Hollywood (G-5679)

MOTOR VEHICLE ASSEMBLY, COMPLETE: Bus/Large Spclty Vehicles

Amer-Con Corp ....E 786 293-8004
Palmetto Bay (G-13207)

MOTOR VEHICLE ASSEMBLY, COMPLETE: Buses, All Types

Florida Bus Unlimited Inc....................E 407 656-1175
Orlando (G-12158)

MOTOR VEHICLE ASSEMBLY, COMPLETE: Cars, Armored

Armour Group Inc ....E 954 767-2030
Fort Lauderdale (G-3657)

F I B US Corp.......................................G 239 262-6070
Naples (G-10744)

Metal 2 Metal Inc ....G 954 253-9450
Palmetto Bay (G-13214)

Noguera Holdings LLC ....G 305 846-9144
Hialeah (G-5281)

Nu Trek Inc ....F 813 920-4348
Odessa (G-11568)

Square One Armoring Svcs Co ....D 305 477-1109
Miami (G-9945)

MOTOR VEHICLE ASSEMBLY, COMPLETE: Fire Department Vehicles

E-One Inc ....B 352 237-1122
Ocala (G-11375)

E-One Inc ....D 352 237-1122
Ocala (G-11376)

Pierce Manufacturing Inc ....D 941 748-3900
Bradenton (G-1028)

MOTOR VEHICLE ASSEMBLY, COMPLETE: Military Motor Vehicle

Fea Inc ....F 407 330-3535
Sanford (G-15316)

MOTOR VEHICLE ASSEMBLY, COMPLETE: Patrol Wagons

Emergency Vehicle Sup Co LLC............E 954 428-5201
Pompano Beach (G-14009)

MOTOR VEHICLE ASSEMBLY, COMPLETE: Personnel Carriers

Elite Enclosures ....G 352 323-6005
Leesburg (G-7771)

MOTOR VEHICLE ASSEMBLY, COMPLETE: Truck & Tractor Trucks

Navistar Inc..F 305 513-2255
Doral (G-3310)

MOTOR VEHICLE ASSEMBLY, COMPLETE: Truck Tractors, Highway

Shirley Simon & Associates LLC ....G 813 247-2100
Tampa (G-17261)

MOTOR VEHICLE ASSEMBLY, COMPLETE: Wreckers, Tow Truck

Alert Towing Inc ....F 561 586-5504
West Palm Beach (G-17918)

Arons Towing & Recovery Inc ....G 772 220-1151
Hobe Sound (G-5479)

Flints Wrecker Service Inc ....G 863 676-1318
Lake Wales (G-7160)

MOTOR VEHICLE DEALERS: Automobiles, New & Used

Southern States Toyota Lift ....D 904 764-7662
Tampa (G-17290)

MOTOR VEHICLE DEALERS: Cars, Used Only

Diamond Wellness Holdings Inc ....G 800 433-0127
Fort Lauderdale (G-3764)

MOTOR VEHICLE DEALERS: Trucks, Tractors/Trailers, New & Used

All Amrcan Trlr Connection Inc ....G 561 582-1800
Palm Springs (G-13142)

East 46th Auto Sales Inc ....F 407 322-3100
Sanford (G-15309)

MOTOR VEHICLE PARTS & ACCESS: Acceleration Eqpt

Creative Auto Boutique Llc...................G 407 654-7300
Oakland (G-11227)

Onaris ....F 305 579-0056
Miami (G-9650)

MOTOR VEHICLE PARTS & ACCESS: Air Conditioner Parts

Commercial Duct Systems LLC............D 877 237-3828
Thonotosassa (G-17561)

MOTOR VEHICLE PARTS & ACCESS: Body Components & Frames

Argos Global Partner Svcs LLC ....G 305 365-1096
Key Biscayne (G-6833)

Clarios LLC..E 407 850-0147
Orlando (G-12017)

Thule Inc ....D 850 584-3448
Perry (G-13657)

MOTOR VEHICLE PARTS & ACCESS: Booster Cables, Jump-Start

Epower 360 LLC ....G 305 330-6684
Miami (G-9106)

MOTOR VEHICLE PARTS & ACCESS: Clutches

Warden Enterprises Inc ....G 954 463-4404
Fort Lauderdale (G-4121)

MOTOR VEHICLE PARTS & ACCESS: Cylinder Heads

Dover Cylinder Head of Jackson...........F .....
Orange Park (G-11824)

National Cylinder Services LLC............E 407 299-8454
Orlando (G-12404)

MOTOR VEHICLE PARTS & ACCESS: Electrical Eqpt

Advanced Automotive Designs ....G 561 499-8812
Delray Beach (G-2925)

Apollo Sunguard Systems Inc ....F 941 925-3000
Sarasota (G-15596)

Daytona Parts Company ....G 386 427-7108
New Smyrna Beach (G-11000)

MOTOR VEHICLE PARTS & ACCESS: Engines & Parts

Delray Tropic Holdings Inc....................G 561 342-1501
Delray Beach (G-2955)

Gt Technologies Inc ....C 850 575-8181
Tallahassee (G-16451)

Gt Technologies I Inc ....C 850 575-8181
Tallahassee (G-16452)

Hoerbger Auto Cmfort Systems L ....E 334 321-2292
Deerfield Beach (G-2734)

Kleen Wheels Corporation ....G 954 791-9112
Davie (G-2430)

Kysor Industrial Corporation ....F 727 376-8600
Trinity (G-17638)

Pops Turn LLC ....F 843 725-8890
Fernandina Beach (G-3596)

Premier Services of Fl Inc ....G 678 815-6078
Tallahassee (G-16489)

MOTOR VEHICLE PARTS & ACCESS: Engs & Trans,Factory, Rebuilt

Avalanche Corporation ....D 800 708-0087
Brooksville (G-1138)

Sun Coast Converters Inc ....G 850 864-2361
Fort Walton Beach (G-4610)

MOTOR VEHICLE PARTS & ACCESS: Frames

Marden Industries Inc..........................F 863 682-7882
Punta Gorda (G-14513)

MOTOR VEHICLE PARTS & ACCESS: Fuel Pumps

Progress Rail Services Corp..................D 239 643-3013
Naples (G-10868)

MOTOR VEHICLE PARTS & ACCESS: Fuel Systems & Parts

National Carburetors Inc ....E 904 636-9400
Jacksonville (G-6319)

MOTOR VEHICLE PARTS & ACCESS: Gears

Coast Wcp ....E 727 572-4249
Odessa (G-11543)

Gear Dynamics Inc...............................G 305 691-0151
Miami (G-9196)

Profile Racing Inc.................................E 727 392-8307
Saint Petersburg (G-15163)

MOTOR VEHICLE PARTS & ACCESS: Horns

Hornblasters Inc...................................E 813 783-8058
Tampa (G-16922)

MOTOR VEHICLE PARTS & ACCESS: Lubrication Systems & Parts

Improved Racing Products LLC ....G 407 705-3054
Orlando (G-12240)

MOTOR VEHICLE PARTS & ACCESS: Manifolds

Professional Products...........................G 323 754-1287
Tampa (G-17189)

Wilson Manifolds Inc ....E 954 771-6216
Oakland Park (G-11312)

MOTOR VEHICLE PARTS & ACCESS: PCV Valves

Shipping Depot Inc ....E 813 347-2494
Tampa (G-17260)

MOTOR VEHICLE PARTS & ACCESS: Pumps, Hydraulic Fluid Power

Alpha Hydraulics LLC...........................G 561 355-0318
Riviera Beach (G-14592)

MOTOR VEHICLE PARTS & ACCESS: Trailer Hitches

B & B Trailers and Accessories ....F 904 829-6855
Saint Augustine (G-14813)

Bulletproof Hitches LLC.......................G 941 251-8110
Bradenton (G-950)

MOTOR VEHICLE PARTS & ACCESS: Transmission Housings Or Parts

Gfx Inc ....E 305 499-9789
Miami (G-9209)

Style Crest Products.............................G 863 709-8735
Lakeland (G-7451)

MOTOR VEHICLE PARTS & ACCESS: Transmissions

JW Performance Transm Inc.................E 321 632-6205
Rockledge (G-14721)

PRODUCT

Suncoast Rebuild Center Inc ....F 813 238-3433
Tampa (G-17313)

MOTOR VEHICLE PARTS & ACCESS: Universal Joints

Cairo JM Car Parts Inc ....G 305 688-4044
Opa Locka (G-11727)

MOTOR VEHICLE PARTS & ACCESS: Water Pumps

Lusa Supplier LLC ....G 305 885-7634
Miami (G-9487)

MOTOR VEHICLE PARTS & ACCESS: Wipers, Windshield

Pylon Manufacturing Corp ....E 800 626-4902
Deerfield Beach (G-2794)

MOTOR VEHICLE PARTS & ACCESS: Wiring Harness Sets

Iron Strength Corp ....F 305 226-6866
Miami (G-9340)

MOTOR VEHICLE RADIOS WHOLESALERS

Drivers World Corp ....G 561 852-5545
Boca Raton (G-497)

MOTOR VEHICLE SPLYS & PARTS WHOLESALERS: New

B & B Trailers and Accessories ....F 904 829-6855
Saint Augustine (G-14813)
Florida Dacco/Detroit Inc ....E 813 879-4131
Tampa (G-16841)
National Carburetors Inc ....E 904 636-9400
Jacksonville (G-6319)
Southeast Power Group Inc ....D 305 592-9745
Doral (G-3370)
Tradewinds Power Corp ....D 305 592-9745
Doral (G-3400)
Viatek Consumer Pdts Group Inc ....E 423 402-9010
Stuart (G-16246)

MOTOR VEHICLE SPLYS & PARTS WHOLESALERS: Used

Battery Usa Inc ....E 863 665-6317
Lakeland (G-7280)

MOTOR VEHICLE: Hardware

AME Triton LLC ....E 352 799-1111
Brooksville (G-1134)
Dse Inc ....F 813 443-4809
Riverview (G-14561)
Vehicle Maint Program Inc ....F 561 362-6080
Boca Raton (G-744)

MOTOR VEHICLE: Steering Mechanisms

Ezy-Glide Inc ....G 850 638-4403
Chipley (G-1456)
G-Car Inc ....D 305 883-8223
Hialeah (G-5164)

MOTOR VEHICLE: Wheels

Jpm Import LLC ....E 800 753-3009
Margate (G-8137)
Rhino Tire Usa Llc ....G 407 777-5598
Orlando (G-12551)
Southern Wheel & Rim Inc ....F 904 786-7542
Jacksonville (G-6495)

MOTOR VEHICLES & CAR BODIES

Citrus Motorsports ....F 352 564-2453
Crystal River (G-2270)
Composite Holdings Inc ....E 321 268-9625
Titusville (G-17582)
FCA North America Holdings LLC ....E 407 826-7021
Orlando (G-12146)
Gar-P Industries Inc ....E 305 888-7252
Medley (G-8245)
Jade Tactical Disaster Relief ....C 850 270-4077
Tampa (G-16961)

Kovatch Mobile Equipment Corp ....G 800 235-3928
Ocala (G-11420)
Lions Intl MGT Group Inc ....F 813 367-2517
Tampa (G-17013)
Lippert Components Inc ....F 267 825-0665
Bradenton (G-1005)
Moser Automotive ....E 561 881-5665
Riviera Beach (G-14648)
Naples Hotrods & Prfmce LLC ....G 239 653-9076
Naples (G-10827)
Nev International Inc ....F 407 671-0045
Casselberry (G-1426)
Pegasus Clean Air Mtr Cars Inc ....F 954 682-2000
Fort Lauderdale (G-3980)
Pierce Manufacturing Inc ....D 727 573-0400
Clearwater (G-1739)
Total Performance Inc ....F 203 265-5667
Palm Coast (G-13091)
Trikaroo ....G 800 679-3415
Orlando (G-12672)
Vac-Con Inc ....G 904 284-4200
Green Cove Springs (G-4841)
Voxx Automotive Corporation ....G 407 842-7000
Orlando (G-12705)
Voxx International Corporation ....B 800 645-7750
Orlando (G-12706)

MOTOR VEHICLES, WHOLESALE: Motor scooters

Best Price Mobility Inc ....F 321 402-5955
Kissimmee (G-6899)

MOTOR VEHICLES, WHOLESALE: Truck bodies

A&L Hall Investments Inc ....E 904 781-5080
Bryceville (G-1225)

MOTOR VEHICLES, WHOLESALE: Truck tractors

Heralpin Usa Inc ....G 305 218-0174
Doral (G-3245)

MOTOR VEHICLES, WHOLESALE: Trucks, commercial

Iler Group Inc ....G 877 467-0326
Wesley Chapel (G-17879)

MOTORCYCLE & BICYCLE PARTS: Saddles & Seat Posts

Hartco International ....G 386 698-4668
Crescent City (G-2236)

MOTORCYCLE ACCESS

A1a Sportbike LLC ....F 321 806-3995
Titusville (G-17566)
Dirtrbags Chopper ....G 904 725-7600
Jacksonville (G-6033)
Scott Fischer Enterprises LLC ....E 844 749-2363
Fort Myers (G-4393)

MOTORCYCLE DEALERS

Tampa Bay Powersports LLC ....E 813 968-7888
Tampa (G-17328)
Versacomp Inc ....G 954 561-8778
Oakland Park (G-11309)

MOTORCYCLE DEALERS: All-Terrain Vehicle Parts & Access

Partsvu LLC ....C 239 643-2292
Naples (G-10851)

MOTORCYCLE DEALERS: Motor Scooters

Vapor Group Inc ....G 954 792-8450
Miami (G-10095)

MOTORCYCLE PARTS & ACCESS DEALERS

Jay Squared LLC ....F 386 677-7700
Daytona Beach (G-2564)
Shark Skinz ....G 772 388-9621
Sebastian (G-15904)

MOTORCYCLES & RELATED PARTS

Dirtbag Choppers Inc ....F 904 725-7600
Atlantic Beach (G-207)
Grass Choppers ....G 305 253-1217
Miami (G-9237)
Powersports 911 Inc ....E 813 769-2468
Tampa (G-17170)
Pro Street Choppers Inc ....E 407 389-2047
Apopka (G-163)
Southwest Choppers Inc ....G 239 242-1101
Cape Coral (G-1389)
Wmr Cycle Performance Inc ....E 772 426-3000
Stuart (G-16253)
Worldwide Intl Trade LLC ....E 305 414-9774
Hollywood (G-5687)

MOTORCYCLES: Wholesalers

Worldwide Intl Trade LLC ....E 305 414-9774
Hollywood (G-5687)

MOTORS: Electric

Discovery Technology Intl Inc ....G 941 907-4444
Lakewood Ranch (G-7483)
Motor Magnetics Inc ....E 727 873-3180
Saint Petersburg (G-15132)
Nidec Motor Corporation ....C 954 346-4900
Coral Springs (G-2197)
Ray Electric Outboards Inc ....G 239 574-1948
Cape Coral (G-1377)

MOTORS: Generators

360 Energy Solutions LLC ....E 786 348-2156
Miami (G-8609)
Acme Service Corp ....F 305 836-4800
Miami (G-8647)
Advanced Manufacturing Inc ....E 727 573-3300
Saint Petersburg (G-14954)
All Power Pro Inc ....G 904 310-3069
Fernandina Beach (G-3580)
American Generator Svcs LLC ....F 954 965-1210
Davie (G-2385)
Anko Products Inc ....E 941 748-2307
Bradenton (G-939)
Fischer Panda Generators Inc ....F 954 462-2800
Pompano Beach (G-14024)
Fischer Panda Generators LLC ....E 954 462-2800
Pompano Beach (G-14025)
Fisher Electric Technology Inc ....F 727 345-9122
Saint Petersburg (G-15046)
G S Servicore Corp ....E 305 888-0189
Hialeah (G-5163)
GE Aviation Systems LLC ....B 727 531-7781
Clearwater (G-1610)
Grove Power Inc ....G 305 599-2045
Doral (G-3241)
Hts Controls Inc ....F 813 287-5512
Tampa (G-16926)
Hydrogen Diesel Prfmce Inc ....G 407 847-6064
Kissimmee (G-6925)
Hytronics Corp ....D 727 535-0413
Clearwater (G-1635)
Innovative Power Solutions LLC ....E 732 544-1075
Sarasota (G-15501)
JDM of Miami LLC ....G 305 253-4650
Miami (G-9362)
K&M Power Systems LLC ....G 866 945-9100
Riviera Beach (G-14634)
Kbn Corporation ....G 321 327-9792
Palm Bay (G-12905)
Marine Exhaust Systems Inc ....D 561 848-1238
Riviera Beach (G-14645)
Maymaan Research LLC ....G 954 374-9376
Hollywood (G-5624)
One Stop Generator Shop Inc ....G 561 840-0009
West Palm Beach (G-18099)
Peerless Wind Systems ....G 516 249-6900
Boynton Beach (G-895)
Perkins Power Corp ....F 904 278-9919
Doral (G-3324)
Robertson Transformer Co ....G 917 603-8530
Sarasota (G-15797)
Tampa Armature Works Inc ....C 813 612-2600
Tampa (G-17325)
US Generator Inc ....G 772 778-0131
Sebastian (G-15907)
Winans Electric Motors LLC ....G 863 875-5710
Auburndale (G-247)

MOTORS: Pneumatic

Evo Motors LLC ....G...... 813 621-7799
Seffner (G-15957)

MOUNTING SVC: Display

Gloval Displays Inc ....E...... 800 972-0353
Miami Gardens (G-10259)
Ollo Usa LLC ....G...... 941 366-0600
Sarasota (G-15769)

MOUTHWASHES

H2ocean LLC ....F...... 866 420-2326
Stuart (G-16161)

MOVING SVC: Local

Los Primos Express Svcs LLC ....G....... 786 701-3297
Miami (G-9479)

MUSIC BOXES

World Indus Resources Corp ....E...... 727 572-9991
Clearwater (G-1856)

MUSIC DISTRIBUTION APPARATUS

Fgmg International ....F...... 305 988-7436
Deltona (G-3044)
Time Is Money Campaign LLC ....F....... 352 255-5273
Clermont (G-1884)

MUSIC VIDEO PRODUCTION SVCS

Spanish House Inc ....E...... 305 503-1191
Medley (G-8324)

MUSICAL INSTRUMENTS & ACCESS: NEC

Englert Arts Inc ....G...... 561 241-9924
Boca Raton (G-504)
Flexshopper LLC ....E...... 561 922-6609
Boca Raton (G-516)
Isla Instruments LLC ....G...... 561 603-4685
West Palm Beach (G-18036)
Lan Music Corp ....G...... 305 722-5842
Miami (G-9421)
Mars Talent Agency ....G...... 561 748-6566
Jupiter (G-6762)

MUSICAL INSTRUMENTS & PARTS: String

Sabine Inc ....D...... 386 418-2000
Alachua (G-20)

MUSICAL INSTRUMENTS WHOLESALERS

Lewis-Riggs Custom Guitars Inc...........G...... 407 538-3710
Orlando (G-12323)

MUSICAL INSTRUMENTS: Bells

Belsnickel Enterprises Inc ....F...... 386 256-5367
South Daytona (G-16018)

MUSICAL INSTRUMENTS: Electric & Electronic

Dok Solution Inc ....G...... 727 209-1313
Largo (G-7573)

MUSICAL INSTRUMENTS: Guitars & Parts, Electric & Acoustic

Lewis-Riggs Custom Guitars Inc...........G...... 407 538-3710
Orlando (G-12323)

MUSICAL INSTRUMENTS: Marimbas

Marimba Cocina Mexicana II Inc ....F...... 321 268-6960
Titusville (G-17602)
Mode Marimba Inc ....G...... 561 512-5001
Jupiter (G-6766)

MUSICAL INSTRUMENTS: Reeds

Bari Associates Inc ....F...... 941 342-9385
Sarasota (G-15609)

MUSICAL INSTRUMENTS: Violins & Parts

Gatchell Violins Company Inc ....F...... 321 733-1499
West Melbourne (G-17900)

NAME PLATES: Engraved Or Etched

Labelpro Inc....................................F...... 727 538-2149
Clearwater (G-1670)

NAMEPLATES

Hallmark Nameplate Inc ....D...... 352 383-8142
Mount Dora (G-10602)

NATIONAL SECURITY FORCES

Dla Document Services ....F...... 813 828-4646
Tampa (G-16782)

NATIONAL SECURITY, GOVERNMENT: Air Force

United Ntons Space Crps Mltary ....G...... 702 373-2351
Ponce De Leon (G-14251)

NATURAL GAS COMPRESSING SVC, On-Site

Hoerbiger America Holding Inc ....B...... 954 422-9850
Deerfield Beach (G-2735)
Hoerbiger America Holding Inc ....A...... 954 422-9850
Deerfield Beach (G-2736)

NATURAL GAS LIQUIDS PRODUCTION

Mar-Co Gas Services Inc....................G...... 561 745-0085
Jupiter (G-6760)
Nopetro LLC ....G...... 305 441-9059
Tallahassee (G-16483)

NATURAL PROPANE PRODUCTION

Ideal Gas LLC..................................G...... 904 417-6470
Saint Augustine (G-14845)

NAUTICAL REPAIR SVCS

Centrifugal Rebabbitting Inc ....F...... 954 522-3003
Fort Lauderdale (G-3720)
SDr Specialties Services LLC ....G...... 386 878-6771
De Leon Springs (G-2627)

NAVIGATIONAL SYSTEMS & INSTRUMENTS

Weibel Equipment Inc.......................G...... 571 278-1989
Sarasota (G-15870)

NET & NETTING PRDTS

Burbank Trawl Makers Inc ....E...... 904 321-0976
Jacksonville (G-5963)
Intermas Nets USA Inc ....F...... 305 442-1416
Coral Gables (G-2073)

NETS: Laundry

Superior Group Companies Inc............G...... 727 397-9611
Seminole (G-15992)

NETTING: Plastic

Intermas Nets USA Inc ....F...... 305 442-1416
Coral Gables (G-2073)

NETTING: Rope

Csl of America Inc.............................G...... 407 849-7070
Orlando (G-12059)

NETTING: Woven Wire, Made From Purchased Wire

Octal Ventures Inc............................F...... 727 526-9288
Pinellas Park (G-13715)

NEW & USED CAR DEALERS

Evo Motors LLC ....G...... 813 621-7799
Seffner (G-15957)
Obd Genie LLC ....G...... 321 250-3650
Oviedo (G-12839)
Revology Cars LLC ....F...... 800 974-4463
Orlando (G-12549)
Sfada Tag Agency Inc ....F...... 305 981-1077
North Miami (G-11121)

NEWS SYNDICATES

Tribune Media Services Inc ....D...... 407 420-6200
Orlando (G-12671)

NEWSPAPERS & PERIODICALS NEWS REPORTING SVCS

Overseas Radio LLC..........................G...... 305 296-1630
Key West (G-6879)

NEWSSTAND

Weekly Newspaper ....F...... 305 743-0844
Marathon (G-8109)

NONCURRENT CARRYING WIRING DEVICES

Afc Cable Systems Inc ....G...... 813 539-0588
Largo (G-7524)
Alta Technologies Inc ....G...... 609 538-9500
Ponte Vedra Beach (G-14262)
Backbone Interconnect LLC ....E...... 954 800-4749
Sunrise (G-16294)
Microlumen Inc ....D...... 813 886-1200
Oldsmar (G-11678)

NONDURABLE GOODS WHOLESALERS, NEC

Downes Trading Co ....G...... 813 855-7122
Palm Harbor (G-13109)
T-Shirt Express.................................G...... 904 448-3761
Jacksonville (G-6527)

NONFERROUS: Rolling & Drawing, NEC

Heartland Metals Inc ....E...... 863 465-7501
Lake Placid (G-7141)
Lata LLC ....G...... 772 324-8170
Stuart (G-16178)
Leadex ....F...... 305 266-2028
Miami (G-9446)
Nexus Mint LLC ....G...... 561 306-9898
Palm Beach Gardens (G-12991)
Shar Family Enterprises Llc................G...... 352 365-6988
Leesburg (G-7792)

NONMETALLIC MINERALS: Support Activities, Exc Fuels

Fcs Holdings Inc ....E...... 352 793-5151
Center Hill (G-1441)
Qci Britannic Inc ....G...... 305 860-0102
Coral Gables (G-2101)

NOTARIES PUBLIC

Carlees Creations Inc ....G...... 786 232-0050
Miami (G-8897)
New & Improved Services LLC............F...... 904 323-2348
Jacksonville (G-6325)

NOVELTIES

Collectibles of SW Florida ....G...... 239 332-2344
Cape Coral (G-1325)
Joni Industries Inc ....F...... 352 799-5456
Brooksville (G-1166)
Marcela Creations Inc ....G...... 813 253-0556
Tampa (G-17038)
Significant Solutions Corp ....G...... 561 703-7703
Boca Raton (G-674)

NOVELTIES, DURABLE, WHOLESALE

Williams Minerals Co Inc....................G...... 304 897-6003
Winter Springs (G-18582)

NOVELTIES: Plastic

Ei Global Group Llc ....G...... 561 999-8989
Boca Raton (G-501)
Pompadour Products Inc ....E...... 954 345-2700
Coral Springs (G-2203)

NOZZLES & SPRINKLERS Lawn Hose

AB Fire Sprinklers LLC.......................G...... 954 973-8054
Pompano Beach (G-13905)
C Mike Roach Inc ....F...... 864 882-1101
Hobe Sound (G-5480)
K-Rain Manufacturing Corp ....E...... 561 844-1002
Riviera Beach (G-14635)
Star Sight Innovations ....G...... 307 786-2911
Crescent City (G-2239)

PRODUCT

NOZZLES: Spray, Aerosol, Paint Or Insecticide

Spraying Systems Co ....G....... 813 259-9400
Bradenton *(G-1051)*

NUCLEAR FUELS SCRAP REPROCESSING

Holtec International ....D.... 561 745-7772
Jupiter *(G-6742)*

NUCLEAR REACTORS: Military Or Indl

United Ntons Space Crps Mltary ....G..... 702 373-2351
Ponce De Leon *(G-14251)*

NUCLEAR SHIELDING: Metal Plate

A-Fabco Inc ....E..... 813 677-8790
Gibsonton *(G-4792)*

NURSERIES & LAWN & GARDEN SPLY STORES, RETAIL

Ronald M Hart Inc ....G....... 772 600-8497
Stuart *(G-16209)*

NURSERIES & LAWN & GARDEN SPLY STORES, RETAIL: Fertilizer

Clean Energy ESb Inc ....E...... 202 905-6726
Coral Gables *(G-2040)*

NURSERIES & LAWN & GARDEN SPLY STORES, RETAIL: Sod

Conrad Yelvington Distrs Inc ....F 352 336-5049
Gainesville *(G-4669)*

NURSERIES/LAWN/GARDEN SPLY STORES, RET: Hydroponic Eqpt/Sply

Morgans Elc Mtr & Pump Svc ....F...... 321 960-2209
Cocoa Beach *(G-1974)*

NURSERIES/LAWN/GRDN SPLY STORE, RET: Nursery Stck, Seed/Bulb

Vertpac LLC ....E...... 407 886-9010
Apopka *(G-183)*

NURSERY STOCK, WHOLESALE

J T Walker Industries Inc ....E...... 727 461-0501
Clearwater *(G-1650)*

NUTS: Metal

Henefelt Precision Pdts Inc ....F...... 727 531-0406
Largo *(G-7603)*

NYLON FIBERS

Redsled DBA Bulldog Equipment ....F 954 448-5221
Stuart *(G-16207)*

Tagalong Inc ....G...... 561 585-7400
Lantana *(G-7516)*

OFFICE EQPT WHOLESALERS

H A Friend & Company Inc ....E...... 847 746-1248
Boynton Beach *(G-876)*

Kyocera Dcment Sltons Sthast L ....F.... 772 562-0511
Fort Pierce *(G-4499)*

New Market Enterprises Ltd ....F...... 484 341-8004
Palm Harbor *(G-13121)*

Totalprint USA ....G...... 855 915-1300
Tampa *(G-17363)*

OFFICE EQPT, WHOLESALE: Blueprinting

Reprographic Solutions Inc ....G....... 772 340-3430
Port Saint Lucie *(G-14441)*

OFFICE EQPT, WHOLESALE: Dictating Machines

Hth Engineering Inc ....E...... 727 939-8853
Tarpon Springs *(G-17476)*

OFFICE EQPT, WHOLESALE: Photocopy Machines

R & K Marketing Inc ....G...... 904 745-0022
Jacksonville *(G-6401)*

OFFICE FIXTURES: Wood

Antique & Modern Cabinets Inc ....E.... 904 393-9055
Jacksonville *(G-5892)*

Duval Fixtures Inc ....E.... 904 757-3964
Jacksonville *(G-6050)*

OFFICE MACHINES, NEC

Solunet ....G..... 321 369-9719
Palm Bay *(G-12919)*

OFFICE SPLY & STATIONERY STORES

Light Source Business Systems ....F.... 772 562-5046
Port Saint Lucie *(G-14423)*

Mark Master Inc ....D.... 813 988-6000
Tampa *(G-17040)*

OFFICE SPLY & STATIONERY STORES: Office Forms & Splys

Ace Marking Devices Corp ....G..... 561 833-4073
West Palm Beach *(G-17911)*

Ayers Publishing Inc ....G..... 352 463-7135
Trenton *(G-17629)*

Baker County Press Inc ....G..... 904 259-2400
Macclenny *(G-8036)*

Bradford County Telegraph Inc ....F..... 904 964-6305
Starke *(G-16096)*

Eclipse Development LLC ....F..... 520 370-7358
Weston *(G-18239)*

Express Printing & Office Sups ....G..... 904 765-9696
Jacksonville *(G-6085)*

Formsystems Inc ....G..... 850 479-0800
Pensacola *(G-13509)*

Gulf Coast Business World Inc ....F..... 850 864-1511
Fort Walton Beach *(G-4590)*

H D Quickprint & Disc Off Sups ....G..... 407 678-1355
Orlando *(G-12206)*

Independent Resources Inc ....E..... 813 237-0945
Tampa *(G-16937)*

Marlin Graphics Inc ....G..... 561 743-5220
Jupiter *(G-6761)*

Nassau Printing & Off Sup Inc ....G..... 904 879-2305
Callahan *(G-1255)*

Scott Brevard Inc ....G..... 386 698-1121
Crescent City *(G-2238)*

Steven M Roessler LLC ....G..... 321 773-2300
Indian Harbour Beach *(G-5808)*

Thalers Printing Center Inc ....G..... 954 741-6522
Lauderhill *(G-7744)*

Wakulla News ....F..... 850 926-7102
Crawfordville *(G-2233)*

Weidenhamer Corporation ....G..... 850 837-3190
Destin *(G-3082)*

Wells Legal Supply Inc ....G..... 904 399-1510
Jacksonville *(G-6600)*

OFFICE SPLYS, NEC, WHOLESALE

Baker County Press Inc ....G..... 904 259-2400
Macclenny *(G-8036)*

H A Friend & Company Inc ....E..... 847 746-1248
Boynton Beach *(G-876)*

Replenish Ink Inc ....G..... 818 206-2424
Miami *(G-9795)*

OFFICES & CLINICS OF DRS OF MED: Em Med Ctr, Freestanding

Worldwide Auto Systems Corp ....F.... 954 439-6332
Hollywood *(G-5686)*

OFFICES & CLINICS OF DRS, MED: Specialized Practitioners

Advanced Prosthetics Amer Inc ....F.... 904 269-4993
Orange Park *(G-11811)*

OFFICES & CLINICS OF HEALTH PRACTITIONERS: Physical Therapy

Great Northern Rehab PC ....G....... 352 732-8868
Ocala *(G-11403)*

Great Northern Rehab PC ....F 352 732-8868
Ocala *(G-11404)*

OFFICES & CLINICS OF OPTOMETRISTS: Specialist, Optometrists

Institutional Eye Care LLC ....F..... 866 604-2931
Bonita Springs *(G-804)*

OIL & GAS FIELD MACHINERY

Bioenersource Inc ....G...... 786 797-0496
Miami *(G-8831)*

Chromalloy Gas Turbine LLC ....A..... 561 935-3571
Palm Beach Gardens *(G-12959)*

Enviro Petroleum Inc ....G...... 713 896-6996
Jensen Beach *(G-6654)*

Fred International LLC ....F 786 539-1600
Miramar *(G-10494)*

Skide Llc ....G...... 305 537-4275
Miami *(G-9901)*

Tecvalco USA Inc ....E..... 866 427-3444
Rockledge *(G-14750)*

OIL FIELD MACHINERY & EQPT

Sandvik Mining & Cnstr USA LLC ....C..... 386 462-4100
Alachua *(G-21)*

OIL FIELD SVCS, NEC

CA Pipeline Inc ....G..... 305 969-4655
Miami *(G-8875)*

J&D Oil Field Intl Inc ....G..... 305 436-0024
Doral *(G-3265)*

Mc Oil and Gas LLC ....G..... 239 649-7013
Naples *(G-10816)*

Mll Oil Holding Inc ....C..... 321 200-0039
Tallahassee *(G-16480)*

North America Wireline LLC ....G..... 870 365-5401
Gulf Breeze *(G-4887)*

Offshore Inland Mar Olfld Svcs ....C..... 251 443-5550
Pensacola *(G-13559)*

Oils R US 1 800 ....G..... 305 681-0909
Miami *(G-9641)*

Southern Underground Inds ....G..... 954 226-3865
Miami Lakes *(G-10359)*

Titan Oil Tools LLC ....G..... 941 356-3010
Sarasota *(G-15569)*

Walters Tools LLC ....G..... 321 537-4788
Palm Bay *(G-12927)*

OILS & ESSENTIAL OILS

Florida Kolmiami Corporation ....G..... 305 582-0114
Miami Lakes *(G-10304)*

Intercit Inc ....B..... 863 646-0165
Lakeland *(G-7355)*

Suns Eye Inc ....G..... 407 519-4904
Geneva *(G-4790)*

Two Scents LLC DBA Vinevida ....E..... 888 527-6805
Opa Locka *(G-11796)*

Vaprzone LLC ....G..... 941 882-4841
Venice *(G-17727)*

OILS & GREASES: Blended & Compounded

Bell Performance Inc ....F 407 831-5021
Longwood *(G-7875)*

Remcoda LLC ....C..... 908 239-4137
Sunny Isles Beach *(G-16281)*

OILS & GREASES: Lubricating

Advanced Engine Tech LLC ....G..... 727 744-2935
Clearwater *(G-1475)*

Am2f Energy Inc ....G..... 407 505-1127
Winter Park *(G-18484)*

Armor Oil Products LLC ....G..... 813 248-1988
Tampa *(G-16608)*

Break-Free Inc ....F 800 347-1200
Jacksonville *(G-5955)*

Carolina Company USA LLC ....G..... 401 487-2749
Lady Lake *(G-6989)*

Eng Group LLC ....G..... 954 323-2024
Fort Lauderdale *(G-3794)*

Gb Energy Management LLC ....G..... 305 792-4650
Miami *(G-9193)*

Global Diversified Products ....E..... 727 209-0854
Pinellas Park *(G-13690)*

Illinois Tool Works Inc ....D..... 863 665-3338
Lakeland *(G-7347)*

Lubrication Global LLC ....F 954 239-9522
Doral *(G-3288)*
Magellan Intl Lbrction Chem Te ....G 386 257-3456
Daytona Beach *(G-2571)*
Ocean Bio-Chem LLC ....E 954 587-6280
Davie *(G-2448)*
Otus Corp Intl LLC ....G 305 833-6078
Miami *(G-9670)*
Pro-Tech Coatings Inc ....G 813 248-1477
Tampa *(G-17186)*

OILS, ANIMAL OR VEGETABLE, WHOLESALE

Griffin Industries LLC ....D 813 626-1135
Tampa *(G-16893)*

OILS: Essential

Firmenich Incorporated ....F 863 292-7456
Lakeland *(G-7322)*
Firmenich Incorporated ....C 863 646-0165
Lakeland *(G-7324)*

OILS: Lubricating

All American Lube ....G 561 432-0476
Lake Worth *(G-7183)*
Citilube Inc ....F 305 681-6064
Miami *(G-8926)*
Global GI Lc ....G 863 551-1079
Winter Haven *(G-18443)*
Mobile 1 Inc ....G 954 283-8100
Lauderdale Lakes *(G-7718)*

OILS: Lubricating

Amalie Oil Company ....C 813 248-1988
Tampa *(G-16584)*
D N L Performance Inc ....G 786 295-8831
Opa Locka *(G-11735)*
Lubrexx Specialty Products LLC ....G 561 988-7500
Pompano Beach *(G-14082)*
United Armour Products LLC ....G 813 767-9624
Tampa *(G-17390)*
Wd-40 Company ....F 305 463-9158
Miami *(G-10127)*

OILS: Mineral, Natural

Island Natural Originals LLC ....G 561 287-0095
Boca Raton *(G-553)*

OINTMENTS

Amerx Health Care Corp ....F 727 443-0530
Oldsmar *(G-11625)*
Transdermal Technologies Inc ....G 561 848-2345
North Palm Beach *(G-11183)*

OLEFINS

Texene LLC ....F 305 200-5001
Miami Lakes *(G-10364)*

OPEN PIT GOLD MINING

Construmining Inc ....G 786 217-3146
Doral *(G-3169)*

OPERATOR TRAINING, COMPUTER

Inceptra LLC ....E 954 442-5400
Weston *(G-18255)*

OPHTHALMIC GOODS

Achievia Direct Inc ....F 386 615-8708
Daytona Beach *(G-2505)*
Bausch & Lomb Incorporated ....C 813 975-7700
Tampa *(G-16629)*
Bausch Lomb Surgical Inc ....F 727 724-6600
Clearwater *(G-1513)*
Best Price Digital Lenses Inc ....G 850 361-4401
Pensacola *(G-13455)*
Bicentrics Inc ....F 813 649-0225
Ruskin *(G-14775)*
CL Gardens LLC ....G 561 567-0504
Palm Beach Gardens *(G-12960)*
CL Waterside Naples LLC ....F 239 734-8534
Naples *(G-10714)*
Ditas Corp ....G 305 558-5766
Miami *(G-9036)*

Electro-Optix Inc ....F 954 973-2800
Pompano Beach *(G-14008)*
Gerber Coburn Optical Inc ....E 305 592-4705
Miami *(G-9205)*
Icare Industries Inc ....C 727 512-3000
Saint Petersburg *(G-15081)*
M12 Lenses Inc ....G 407 973-4403
Altamonte Springs *(G-56)*
Medical Developmental Research ....G 727 793-0170
Clearwater *(G-1690)*
Premium Dynamic Lens ....G 813 891-9912
Oldsmar *(G-11690)*
Solidar Express Coatings LLC ....G 727 585-2192
Largo *(G-7687)*
Techtran Lenses Inc ....F 561 623-5490
Jupiter *(G-6806)*
Top Optical Lab ....F 305 662-2893
Miami *(G-10027)*
Veriteq Acquisition Corp ....G 561 805-8007
Delray Beach *(G-3034)*

OPHTHALMIC GOODS WHOLESALERS

Lip Trading Co ....G 954 987-0306
Hollywood *(G-5612)*

OPHTHALMIC GOODS, NEC, WHOLESALE: Contact Lenses

Danker Laboratories Inc ....F 941 758-7711
Sarasota *(G-15467)*

OPHTHALMIC GOODS: Eyewear, Protective

Group Tws LLC ....F 337 499-2928
Tampa *(G-16895)*
Inspecs USA LC ....F 727 771-7710
Palm Harbor *(G-13114)*

OPHTHALMIC GOODS: Frames & Parts, Eyeglass & Spectacle

Ottica Dante Americas LLC ....G 561 322-0186
Boca Raton *(G-627)*

OPHTHALMIC GOODS: Frames, Lenses & Parts, Eyeglasses

Institutional Eye Care LLC ....F 866 604-2931
Bonita Springs *(G-804)*
Miami Eyeworks Inc ....G 954 316-6757
Pembroke Pines *(G-13403)*
Pixeloptics Inc ....G 954 376-1542
Fort Lauderdale *(G-3989)*

OPHTHALMIC GOODS: Lenses, Intraocular

Bausch & Lomb Incorporated ....C 727 724-6600
Clearwater *(G-1512)*

OPHTHALMIC GOODS: Lenses, Ophthalmic

Hoya Largo ....E 727 531-8964
Largo *(G-7609)*
Transitions Optical Inc ....B 727 545-0400
Pinellas Park *(G-13732)*

OPTICAL GOODS STORES

Premium Dynamic Lens ....G 813 891-9912
Oldsmar *(G-11690)*

OPTICAL GOODS STORES: Contact Lenses, Prescription

Icare Industries Inc ....C 727 512-3000
Saint Petersburg *(G-15081)*

OPTICAL GOODS STORES: Opticians

For Eyes Optcal Ccnut Grove In ....C 305 557-9004
Miramar *(G-10493)*

OPTICAL INSTRUMENTS & APPARATUS

ER Precision Optical Corp ....F 407 292-5395
Apopka *(G-128)*
Isp Optics Corporation ....F 914 591-3070
Orlando *(G-12261)*
Lenstec Inc ....F 727 571-2272
Saint Petersburg *(G-15111)*
Light-Tech Inc ....G 863 385-6000
Sebring *(G-15930)*

Low Vision Aids Inc ....G 954 722-1580
Ocala *(G-11432)*
Manasota Optics Inc ....G 941 359-1748
Sarasota *(G-15737)*
Multicore Photonics Inc ....G 407 325-7800
Orlando *(G-12398)*
Tower Optical Corporation ....F 561 740-2525
Boynton Beach *(G-921)*

OPTICAL INSTRUMENTS & LENSES

Aldana Laser Miami Inc ....G 786 681-7752
Doral *(G-3104)*
Align Optics Inc ....G 954 748-1715
Sunrise *(G-16289)*
American Tech Netwrk Corp ....E 800 910-2862
Doral *(G-3112)*
Amphenol Custom Cable Inc ....C 813 623-2232
Tampa *(G-16594)*
Amphenol Custom Cable Inc ....E 407 393-3886
Orlando *(G-11909)*
Asphericon Inc ....F 941 564-0890
Sarasota *(G-15603)*
Brain Power Incorporated ....E 305 264-4465
Miami *(G-8851)*
Carl Zeiss Vision Inc ....G 727 528-8873
Clearwater *(G-1536)*
D R S Optronics Inc ....F 321 309-1500
Melbourne *(G-8396)*
Eye Specialists Mid Florida PA ....F 863 937-4515
Lakeland *(G-7320)*
Family Vision Center ....G 321 454-3002
Merritt Island *(G-8585)*
Grampus Enterprises Inc ....G 305 491-9827
Weston *(G-18249)*
Innovative Optics LLC ....G 239 994-0695
North Port *(G-11196)*
Jenoptik North America Inc ....C 561 881-7400
Jupiter *(G-6749)*
Jenoptik Optical Systems LLC ....C 561 881-7400
Jupiter *(G-6750)*
Laser Lens Tek Inc ....F 941 752-5811
Sarasota *(G-15510)*
Levenhuk Inc ....G 800 342-1706
Tampa *(G-17008)*
Lightpath Technologies Inc ....D 407 382-4003
Orlando *(G-12329)*
Mercoframes Optical Corp ....G 305 882-0120
Miami *(G-9534)*
Ocean Optics Inc ....E 407 673-0041
Orlando *(G-12432)*
Ocean Optics Inc ....E 727 545-0741
Orlando *(G-12433)*
Oculus Surgical Inc ....E 772 236-2622
Port St Lucie *(G-14480)*
Pixelteq Inc ....G 727 545-0741
Orlando *(G-12489)*
Plastics For Mankind Inc ....G 305 687-5917
Opa Locka *(G-11783)*
Pyramid Imaging Inc ....G 813 984-0125
Tampa *(G-17196)*
Saikou Optics Incorporated ....G 407 986-4200
Orlando *(G-12569)*
Sunoptic Technologies LLC ....D 877 677-2832
Jacksonville *(G-6516)*
Tecport Optics Inc ....F 407 855-1212
Orlando *(G-12648)*
Thermal Matrix Intl LLC ....F 813 222-3274
Tampa *(G-17351)*
Thermo Arl US Inc ....E 800 532-4752
West Palm Beach *(G-18177)*
Vision Solution Technology LL ....G 305 477-4480
Doral *(G-3414)*
Zyloware Corporation ....F 561 479-4640
Boca Raton *(G-765)*

OPTOMETRIC EQPT & SPLYS WHOLESALERS

Bausch & Lomb Incorporated ....C 727 724-6600
Clearwater *(G-1512)*
Vision Solution Technology LL ....G 305 477-4480
Doral *(G-3414)*

ORAL PREPARATIONS

Probiora Health LLC ....F 214 850-2519
Tampa *(G-17187)*

Employee Codes: A=Over 500 employees, B=251-500
C=101-250, D=51-100, E=20-50, F=10-19, G=4-9

2022 Harris Florida
Manufacturers Directory

1269

PRODUCT

ORDNANCE

Ao Precision Manufacturing LLC ....C 386 274-5882
Daytona Beach *(G-2511)*

Avasar Corp ....E 321 723-3456
Melbourne *(G-8371)*

Break-Free Inc ....F 800 347-1200
Jacksonville *(G-5955)*

C4 Advnced Tctical Systems LLC ....D 407 206-3886
Orlando *(G-11974)*

Fairbanks and Fairbanks Inc ....G 850 293-1184
Pensacola *(G-13500)*

General Defense Corporation ....G 954 444-0155
Davie *(G-2419)*

General Dynmics Ord Tctcal Sys ....C 727 578-8100
Saint Petersburg *(G-15060)*

Global Ordnance LLC ....E 941 549-8388
Sarasota *(G-15484)*

Gr Dynamics LLC ....F 850 897-9700
Niceville *(G-11031)*

Integrted Dsign Dev Cntl Fla I ....C 407 268-4300
Sanford *(G-15339)*

Kaman Precision Products Inc ....C 407 282-1000
Orlando *(G-12282)*

L2d Outdoors Inc ....G 954 757-6116
Coral Springs *(G-2176)*

Mabel Lake Loop LLC ....G 863 326-7144
Winter Haven *(G-18450)*

Slr Rifleworks LLC ....G 855 757-7435
Winter Garden *(G-18404)*

ORDNANCE: Smoke Generators

Elite Distributors LLC ....F 407 601-6665
Orlando *(G-12121)*

ORGANIZATIONS: Bacteriological Research

Becker Microbial Products Inc ....G 954 345-9321
Parkland *(G-13344)*

ORGANIZATIONS: Civic & Social

Brevard Softball Magazine Inc ....F 321 453-3711
Merritt Island *(G-8580)*

ORGANIZATIONS: Medical Research

Bio Therapeutics Inc ....G 954 321-5553
Plantation *(G-13832)*

Biorep Technologies Inc ....F 305 330-4449
Miami Lakes *(G-10286)*

ORGANIZATIONS: Professional

Netexpressusa Inc ....G 888 575-1245
Fort Myers *(G-4338)*

ORGANIZATIONS: Religious

Action Weekly Corp ....G 561 586-8699
West Palm Beach *(G-17914)*

Florida Catholic Media Inc ....G 407 373-0075
Orlando *(G-12159)*

Orlando Times Inc ....G 407 841-3052
Orlando *(G-12456)*

Shalom Adventure ....G 727 375-7502
New Port Richey *(G-10983)*

ORNAMENTS: Christmas Tree, Exc Electrical & Glass

Stocking Factory ....G 305 745-2681
Big Pine Key *(G-373)*

OSCILLATORS

APA Wireless Technologies Inc ....F 954 563-8833
Oakland Park *(G-11237)*

Piezo Technology Inc ....D 407 298-2000
Orlando *(G-12486)*

OSCILLATORS

All-Tag Corporation ....E 561 998-9983
Boca Raton *(G-398)*

OUTBOARD MOTORS & PARTS

Brunswick Corporation ....G 850 769-1011
Panama City *(G-13236)*

OUTLETS: Electric, Convenience

123 Dollar Plus Inc ....G 305 456-4561
Miami *(G-8605)*

Tienda Maya ....G 561 965-0900
Lake Worth *(G-7236)*

OUTREACH PROGRAM

Quality Life Publishing Co ....G 239 513-9907
Naples *(G-10871)*

OVENS: Cremating

B & L Cremation Systems Inc ....D 727 541-4666
Largo *(G-7543)*

Matthews International Corp ....C 407 886-5533
Apopka *(G-149)*

OVERBURDEN REMOVAL SVCS: Nonmetallic Minerals

Environmental Contractors Inc ....F 305 556-6942
Hialeah *(G-5146)*

PACKAGE DESIGN SVCS

Private Label Skin Na LLC ....C 877 516-2200
Saint Petersburg *(G-15162)*

PACKAGED FROZEN FOODS WHOLESALERS, NEC

Allapattah Industries Inc ....E 305 324-5900
Miami *(G-8694)*

Borden Dairy Company Fla LLC ....E 863 298-9742
Winter Haven *(G-18423)*

Coca-Cola Company ....E 727 736-7101
Dunedin *(G-3446)*

GA Fd Svcs Pinellas Cnty LLC ....D 954 972-8884
Fort Lauderdale *(G-3835)*

Pizza Spice Packet LLC ....G 718 831-7036
Boca Raton *(G-635)*

PACKAGING & LABELING SVCS

Birdiebox LLC ....E 786 762-2975
Miami *(G-8832)*

Cofran International Corp ....E 305 592-2644
Doral *(G-3166)*

Compliance Meds Tech LLC ....F 786 319-9826
Miami *(G-8952)*

Florida Candy Factory Inc ....E 727 446-0024
Clearwater *(G-1599)*

Scan Technology Inc ....G 931 723-0304
Gainesville *(G-4758)*

Sunsof Inc ....E 305 691-1875
Hialeah *(G-5371)*

PACKAGING MATERIALS, INDL: Wholesalers

Waterbrick International Inc ....G 877 420-9283
Windermere *(G-18370)*

PACKAGING MATERIALS, WHOLESALE

JV&h Corporation ....G 954 305-9043
Weston *(G-18261)*

Peter T Amann ....G 561 848-2770
West Palm Beach *(G-18118)*

Storopack Inc ....G 305 805-9696
Medley *(G-8327)*

PACKAGING MATERIALS: Paper

Apakus Inc ....G 305 403-2603
Coral Gables *(G-2029)*

Dairy-Mix Inc ....F 813 621-8098
Tampa *(G-16759)*

Estal Usa Inc ....F 305 728-3272
Miami *(G-9112)*

Four G Enterprises Inc ....E 407 834-4143
Longwood *(G-7898)*

Full Cut Tabs LLC ....F 941 316-1510
Sarasota *(G-15686)*

Graphics Designer Inc ....F 561 687-7993
West Palm Beach *(G-18019)*

Great Northern Corporation ....G 920 739-3671
Jacksonville *(G-6150)*

Gulf Packaging Co ....F 727 441-1117
Clearwater *(G-1619)*

Holmes Stamp Company ....E 904 396-2291
Jacksonville *(G-6183)*

J & J International Corp ....E 407 349-7114
Sanford *(G-15341)*

Label Graphics Inc ....G 561 798-8180
Lake Worth *(G-7213)*

Labelpro Inc ....F 727 538-2149
Clearwater *(G-1670)*

Stephen Gould Corporation ....F 813 886-8460
Tampa *(G-17302)*

Storopack Inc ....E 305 805-9696
Medley *(G-8327)*

Trend At LLC ....E 786 300-2550
Miami *(G-10039)*

Tutti Hogar International LLC ....G 305 705-4735
Miami *(G-10046)*

United Seal & Tag Label Corp ....G 941 625-6799
Port Charlotte *(G-14321)*

Zellwin Farms Company ....E 407 886-9241
Zellwood *(G-18600)*

PACKAGING MATERIALS: Paper, Coated Or Laminated

A Plus Lamination & Finshg Inc ....F 305 636-9888
Miami *(G-8623)*

Legar Inc ....F 561 635-5882
Boynton Beach *(G-885)*

Plastic Coated Papers Inc ....D 850 968-6100
Pensacola *(G-13578)*

Southeast Packg Sanitation LLC ....G 904 634-7911
Jacksonville *(G-6484)*

PACKAGING MATERIALS: Paperboard Backs For Blister/Skin Pkgs

Gulf Packaging Co ....F 727 441-1117
Clearwater *(G-1619)*

Uvisors ....G 813 716-1113
Tampa *(G-17401)*

PACKAGING MATERIALS: Plastic Film, Coated Or Laminated

Almi Intl Plastic Inds Inc ....G 954 920-6836
Hollywood *(G-5527)*

Amcor Flexibles LLC ....E 954 499-4800
Miramar *(G-10468)*

Attesa Holdings Group LLC ....G 305 777-3567
Miami *(G-8771)*

Jr Plastics Corporation ....D 352 401-0880
Ocala *(G-11414)*

Mr Cool Waters Inc ....F 305 234-6311
Miami *(G-9596)*

PACKAGING MATERIALS: Polystyrene Foam

3a Products LLC ....G 754 263-2968
Miramar *(G-10455)*

Allied Foam Fabricators LLC ....E 813 626-0090
Tampa *(G-16575)*

Architectural Foam Supply Inc ....F 954 943-6949
Pompano Beach *(G-13933)*

Autopax Inc ....G 772 563-0131
Vero Beach *(G-17738)*

Drb Packaging LLC ....G 321 877-2802
Rockledge *(G-14703)*

Drb Packaging LLC ....G 321 877-2802
Rockledge *(G-14704)*

Foam By Design Inc ....E 727 561-7479
Clearwater *(G-1604)*

Foam Factory Inc ....E 954 485-6700
Boca Raton *(G-521)*

JC & A of South Florida Inc ....G 305 445-6665
Miami *(G-9357)*

Kitko Corp ....G 786 287-8900
Doral *(G-3273)*

Magna Manufacturing Inc ....E 850 243-1112
Fort Walton Beach *(G-4595)*

Merry Mailman Inc ....G 954 786-1146
Pompano Beach *(G-14095)*

Plastix Usa LLC ....D 305 891-0091
Hollywood *(G-5643)*

Republic Packaging Florida Inc ....E 305 685-5175
Opa Locka *(G-11785)*

Root International Inc ....G 813 482-1732
Redington Shores *(G-14554)*

Root International Inc ....F 813 265-1808
Clearwater *(G-1772)*

Seven Group USA Inc ....G 305 392-9193
Doral *(G-3362)*

Source Sup In Plyurethanes Inc ....G 239 573-3637
Cape Coral *(G-1387)*

Storopack Inc ....G 305 805-9696
Medley (G-8327)

Ufp Technologies Inc ....E 407 933-4880
Kissimmee (G-6968)

Unity Marine Inc ....F 954 321-1727
Fort Lauderdale (G-4109)

W R Grace & Co - Conn ....F 561 982-7776
Boca Raton (G-751)

PACKAGING MATERIALS: Resinous Impregnated Paper

Signode Industrial Group LLC ....F 866 347-1820
Tampa (G-17267)

PACKAGING: Blister Or Bubble Formed, Plastic

Holpack Corp ....F 786 565-3969
Hialeah (G-5188)

MTS Medication Tech Inc ....C 727 576-6311
Saint Petersburg (G-15133)

MTS Packaging Systems Inc ....C 727 576-6311
Saint Petersburg (G-15134)

Southeast Packg Sanitation LLC ....G 904 634-7911
Jacksonville (G-6484)

PACKING & CRATING SVC

Homyn Enterprises Corp ....D 305 870-9720
Miami (G-9290)

PADS: Mattress

Pillow Plus Manufacturing Inc ....G 305 652-2218
Miami (G-9717)

PAGERS: One-way

R F Laboratories Inc ....F 920 564-2700
Sorrento (G-16013)

PAINT & PAINTING SPLYS STORE: Brushes, Rollers, Sprayers

Greg Franklin Enterprises Inc ....F 904 675-9129
Hilliard (G-5465)

PAINT STORE

Acrylux Paint Mfg Co Inc ....F 954 772-0300
Fort Lauderdale (G-3622)

Anvil Paints & Coatings Inc ....F 727 535-1411
Largo (G-7535)

Hy-Tech Thermal Solutions LLC ....G 321 984-9777
Melbourne (G-8439)

Povia Paints Inc ....G 239 791-0011
Fort Myers (G-4367)

Richards Paint Mfg Co Inc ....D 321 636-6200
Rockledge (G-14741)

PAINTING SVC: Metal Prdts

Allstar Lighting & Sound Inc ....F 407 767-0111
Longwood (G-7865)

Bumper Doctor ....G 850 341-1771
Pensacola (G-13466)

Electrostatic Industrial Pntg ....G 305 696-4556
Miami (G-9080)

Industrial Marine Inc ....F 904 781-4707
Jacksonville (G-6195)

Leto LLC ....G 813 486-8049
Clearwater (G-1671)

Pozin Enterprises Inc ....E 800 741-1456
Clearwater (G-1745)

Precision Metal Services Inc ....F 407 843-3682
Sorrento (G-16012)

Reliable Finishes ....G 321 723-3334
Melbourne (G-8509)

PAINTS & ADDITIVES

Anchor Coatings Leesburg Inc ....G 352 728-0777
Leesburg (G-7759)

Anvil Paints & Coatings Inc ....F 727 535-1411
Largo (G-7535)

Associated Paint Inc ....F 305 885-1964
Medley (G-8202)

Hy-Tech Thermal Solutions LLC ....G 321 984-9777
Melbourne (G-8439)

Lapolla Industries LLC ....F 954 379-0241
Deerfield Beach (G-2751)

Marine Industrial Paint Co Inc ....F 727 527-3382
Saint Petersburg (G-15119)

Povia Paints Inc ....G 239 791-0011
Fort Myers (G-4367)

Richards Paint Mfg Co Inc ....D 321 636-6200
Rockledge (G-14741)

Semg Incorporated ....G 407 777-6860
Davenport (G-2370)

Sun Coatings LLC ....E 727 531-4100
Tampa (G-17308)

Tex-Cote LLC ....E 800 454-0340
Panama City (G-13313)

Union Chemical Industries Corp ....F 954 581-6060
Fort Lauderdale (G-4105)

PAINTS & ALLIED PRODUCTS

Adsil Inc ....G 386 274-1382
Daytona Beach (G-2506)

All Florida Marketing ....G 813 281-4641
Rocky Point (G-14756)

Assis Master Paint Corp ....E 786 797-6106
Margate (G-8121)

Autek Spray Booths ....G 727 709-4373
Largo (G-7540)

Black Diamond Coatings Inc ....E 800 270-4050
Brooksville (G-1141)

Coating Application Tech Inc ....F 781 850-5080
Sarasota (G-15457)

Complementary Coatings Corp ....C 386 428-6461
Orlando (G-12036)

Cork Industries Inc ....E 904 695-2400
Jacksonville (G-6007)

Coronado Paint Co Inc ....G 386 428-6461
Orlando (G-12049)

Deako Coatings Chemical ....F 305 323-9914
Cutler Bay (G-2288)

Ecosmart ....E 561 328-6488
Lake Park (G-7123)

Epoxy Experts LLC ....G 941 565-3785
Sarasota (G-15475)

Faux Effects International Inc ....E 800 270-8871
Fort Pierce (G-4486)

Florida Prtctive Ctngs Cons In ....G 407 322-1243
Lake Mary (G-7080)

Gulf Coast Paint & Supplies ....F 813 932-3093
Tampa (G-16896)

Hco Holding I Corporation ....F 863 533-0522
Bartow (G-311)

Inseco Inc ....F 239 939-1072
Fort Myers (G-4291)

International Paint LLC ....G 321 636-9722
Cocoa (G-1938)

International Paint LLC ....G 305 620-9220
Opa Locka (G-11755)

J & J Inc ....G 954 746-7300
Sunrise (G-16326)

Ken R Avery Painting Inc ....E 813 855-5037
Oldsmar (G-11664)

Lambert Corporation Florida ....E 407 841-2940
Orlando (G-12307)

Lanco & Harris Corp ....D 407 240-4000
Orlando (G-12308)

Nationwide Prtctive Cting Mfrs ....E 941 753-7500
Sarasota (G-15524)

P S Research Corp ....G 954 558-8727
Lauderhill (G-7738)

Panhandle Paint & Dctg LLC ....G 850 596-9248
Panama City Beach (G-13335)

Parasol Films Inc ....G 954 478-8661
Tamarac (G-16539)

Poly Coatings of South Inc ....F 941 371-8555
Sarasota (G-15784)

PPG Industries Inc ....E 305 477-0541
Doral (G-3333)

Prestige Construction Jax LLC ....G 904 334-4772
Jacksonville (G-6385)

Reliance Supply Co USA LLC ....G 954 971-9111
Pompano Beach (G-14158)

Rexpro Services ....G 561 328-6488
Jupiter (G-6787)

Roberlo Usa Inc ....E 786 334-6191
Doral (G-3349)

Somay Manufacturing Inc ....G 305 637-4757
Miami (G-9916)

Suncoast Coatings ....G 954 306-2149
Sunrise (G-16376)

Textured Coatings ....G 850 360-1451
Panama City Beach (G-13340)

Tuf Top Coatings ....F 727 527-3382
Saint Petersburg (G-15218)

Ultra Tuff Manufacturing Inc ....G 970 252-9457
Hobe Sound (G-5486)

Vinavil Americas Corporation ....F 954 246-8888
Deerfield Beach (G-2831)

Zurigo Trading Inc ....G 305 244-4681
Miami (G-10158)

PAINTS, VARNISHES & SPLYS, WHOLESALE: Paints

Hy-Tech Thermal Solutions LLC ....G 321 984-9777
Melbourne (G-8439)

Povia Paints Inc ....G 239 791-0011
Fort Myers (G-4367)

PAINTS: Asphalt Or Bituminous

Good 4 Tklc Inc ....G 321 632-4340
Rockledge (G-14712)

PAINTS: Marine

All Tank Services LLC ....G 954 260-9443
Pompano Beach (G-13918)

Dynamis Epoxy LLC ....G 941 488-3999
Venice (G-17686)

New Nautical Coatings Inc ....E 727 523-8053
Clearwater (G-1716)

PAINTS: Oil Or Alkyd Vehicle Or Water Thinned

Deako Coating & Chemical Inc ....G 305 634-5162
Miami (G-9005)

Kel Glo Corp ....G 305 751-5641
Miami (G-9387)

PAINTS: Waterproof

Acrylux Paint Mfg Co Inc ....F 954 772-0300
Fort Lauderdale (G-3622)

PALLET REPAIR SVCS

Pallet Consultants LLC ....E 954 946-2212
Pompano Beach (G-14115)

Pallet Ex Jacksonville Inc ....E 904 781-2500
Jacksonville (G-6352)

PALLETS

Aaa-Affordable Pallets & Reels ....G 813 740-8009
Tampa (G-16550)

Amigo Pallets Inc ....F 305 302-9751
Miami (G-8725)

Chicos Pallets Corp ....G 904 236-3607
Jacksonville (G-5977)

Diversified Pallets Inc ....G 904 491-6800
Fernandina Beach (G-3585)

Gt Pallets LLC ....G 786 541-6532
Miami (G-9258)

Pallet Exchange Inc ....F 386 734-0133
Orange City (G-11808)

Preferred Pallets Llc ....G 863 401-9517
Winter Haven (G-18460)

Raymond Newkirk ....G 772 359-0237
Fort Pierce (G-4522)

Xtreme Pallets Inc ....G 954 302-8915
Coconut Creek (G-2013)

PALLETS & SKIDS: Wood

Buckley Pallets LLC ....F 727 415-4497
Clearwater (G-1531)

Camara Industries LLC ....F 407 879-2549
Orlando (G-11977)

Global Bamboo Technologies Inc ....E 707 730-0288
Ocala (G-11399)

Marianna Truss Inc ....F 850 594-5420
Marianna (G-8172)

Pallet Holdings LLC ....D 561 367-0009
Boca Raton (G-629)

Tg Expess Services LLC ....G 862 218-7752
Miami Gardens (G-10276)

PALLETS: Plastic

Craemer US Corporation ....G 727 312-8859
Palm Harbor (G-13108)

Mason Ways Indstrctble Plas LL ....E 561 478-8838
West Palm Beach (G-18068)

PALLETS: Wooden

A Pallet Co Inc .... G 561 798-1564
  West Palm Beach (G-17908)
A Plus Lumber Corp .... G 786 899-0535
  Miami Springs (G-10385)
A Quallity Pallet Company .... G 239 245-0900
  Fort Myers (G-4153)
A1 Pallets LLC .... G 813 598-9165
  Thonotosassa (G-17560)
Aarons Pallets .... G 813 627-3225
  Tampa (G-16551)
AB Used Pallets Inc .... F 305 594-2776
  Miami (G-8631)
Advanced Pallets Inc .... E 954 785-1215
  Margate (G-8117)
All State Pallets Company LLC .... F 407 855-8087
  Orlando (G-11891)
Amigo Pallets Inc .... G 305 631-2452
  Medley (G-8195)
Amware Logistics Services Inc .... F 970 337-7000
  Pompano Beach (G-13929)
Best Pallets of Fl LLC .... G 386 624-5575
  Deland (G-2855)
Brothers Pallets .... G 863 944-5278
  Lakeland (G-7286)
Buckley Pallets .... G 727 415-4497
  Clearwater (G-1530)
Cienfuegos Pallets Corp .... G 786 703-3686
  Medley (G-8217)
D & S Pallet Recycle Center .... G 352 351-0070
  Ocala (G-11363)
D & S Pallets Inc .... D 727 540-0061
  Clearwater (G-1560)
Floor Tech LLC .... F 407 855-8087
  Orlando (G-12157)
Florida AA Pallets Inc .... G 305 805-1522
  Medley (G-8241)
Freeman Pallets Inc .... G 352 328-9326
  Gainesville (G-4696)
G D Pallets LLC .... G 772 713-8251
  Vero Beach (G-17757)
Haman Industries Inc .... F 813 626-5700
  Tampa (G-16903)
Jacksonville Box & Woodwork Co .... F 904 354-1441
  Jacksonville (G-6214)
L & M Pallet Services Inc .... F 863 519-3502
  Bartow (G-315)
Manasota Pallets Inc .... G 941 360-0562
  Sarasota (G-15738)
Monison Pallets Inc .... F 904 359-0235
  Jacksonville (G-6314)
Monison Pallets Inc .... F 305 637-1600
  Miami (G-9587)
National Pallets .... E 305 324-1021
  Miami (G-9607)
Opa-Locka Pallets Inc .... F 305 681-8212
  Opa Locka (G-11777)
Pal-King Inc .... E 904 334-8797
  Jacksonville (G-6350)
Pallet Consultants LLC .... E 954 946-2212
  Pompano Beach (G-14115)
Pallet Creations Inc .... G 239 601-0606
  Naples (G-10844)
Pallet Depot LLC .... E 863 686-6245
  Lakeland (G-7405)
Pallet Direct Inc .... G 888 433-1727
  Naples (G-10845)
Pallet Doctor Inc .... G 904 444-2514
  Jacksonville (G-6351)
Pallet Dude LLC .... F 941 720-1667
  Sarasota (G-15773)
Pallet Enterprises of Florida .... G 305 836-3204
  Miami (G-9682)
Pallet Ex Jacksonville Inc .... E 904 781-2500
  Jacksonville (G-6352)
Pallet Express Inc .... F 813 752-1600
  Plant City (G-13789)
Pallet Express of Jkvl Inc .... F 904 781-2500
  Jacksonville (G-6353)
Pallet Industries Inc .... G 954 935-5804
  Deerfield Beach (G-2779)
Pallet Logix Corp .... G 407 834-2336
  Longwood (G-7931)
Pallet One of Mobile LLC .... F 251 960-1107
  Bartow (G-319)
Pallet Recall Inc .... G 941 727-1944
  Sarasota (G-15530)
Pallet Services Inc .... G 813 754-7719
  Plant City (G-13790)

Pallet Services Plant City LLC .... F 813 752-1600
  Plant City (G-13791)
Pallet Solutions Inc .... G 305 801-8314
  Miami (G-9683)
Palletone Inc .... E 800 771-1147
  Bartow (G-320)
Palletone of Texas LP .... D 903 628-5695
  Bartow (G-321)
Pallets Plus Inc .... G 813 759-6355
  Plant City (G-13792)
Pallets To Go Inc .... F 305 654-0303
  Miami (G-9684)
Panama City Pallet Inc .... E 850 769-1040
  Panama City (G-13294)
Panama Pallets Co Inc .... G 850 769-1040
  Panama City (G-13296)
Phoenix Wood Products Inc .... F 888 304-1131
  Ocala (G-11466)
Placetas Pallet Corp .... G 305 633-4262
  Hialeah (G-5295)
Premier Pallet Recycler LLC .... G 561 722-0457
  West Palm Beach (G-18127)
Premier Pallets Inc .... G 813 986-4889
  Tampa (G-17178)
Ralph & Llerena Pallets Inc .... G 305 446-2651
  Hialeah (G-5325)
Rass Fast Pallet Inc .... G 786 877-2854
  Miami (G-9782)
Regional Trailer Repair Inc .... F 912 484-7729
  Jacksonville (G-6413)
Ricks Pallet Co Inc .... G 305 884-4896
  Hialeah (G-5332)
Sanchez Brothers Corp .... F 561 992-0062
  South Bay (G-16017)
South Florida Pallet Inc .... G 305 330-7663
  Miami (G-9925)
South Florida Pallets Dist .... G 305 330-7663
  Doral (G-3369)
Southeastern Pallets Inc .... G 904 783-8363
  Jacksonville (G-6487)
Sunbelt Forest Ventures LLC .... G 863 496-3054
  Bartow (G-326)
Suncoast Pallets Inc .... G 813 988-1623
  Temple Terrace (G-17546)
Superior Pallets Llc .... G 863 875-4041
  Winter Haven (G-18471)
USA Express Pallets Corp .... G 786 251-9543
  Miami (G-10082)
Usmi Pallets Inc .... G 813 765-4309
  Plant City (G-13812)
V-Lumber LLC .... F 305 510-4458
  Opa Locka (G-11798)
Walling Crate Company .... F 352 787-5211
  Leesburg (G-7801)
Worldwide Pallet LLC .... G 205 671-5210
  Naples (G-10944)

PANEL & DISTRIBUTION BOARDS & OTHER RELATED APPARATUS

Hallmark Nameplate Inc .... D 352 383-8142
  Mount Dora (G-10602)
Techno-Solis Inc .... F 727 823-6766
  Saint Petersburg (G-15211)

PANEL & DISTRIBUTION BOARDS: Electric

Electrical Controls Inc .... F 954 801-6846
  Tamarac (G-16530)
Ultrapanel Marine Inc .... E 772 285-4258
  Miami (G-10058)

PANELS, CORRUGATED: Plastic

Multi-Panels Corporation .... G 800 723-8620
  Saint Petersburg (G-15135)

PANELS, FLAT: Plastic

Innovative Base Tech LLC .... G 727 391-9009
  Saint Petersburg (G-15085)
Nida-Core Corporation .... E 772 343-7300
  Port Saint Lucie (G-14428)

PANELS: Building, Metal

Alternative Cnstr Tech Inc .... G 321 421-6601
  Melbourne (G-8363)
Dade Engineering Corp .... F 305 885-2766
  Coral Gables (G-2045)
Metal Building Supplies LLC .... F 407 935-9714
  Kissimmee (G-6942)

Ring Power Corporation .... C 904 354-1858
  Jacksonville (G-6423)

PANELS: Building, Plastic, NEC

Elite Aluminum Corporation .... D 954 949-3200
  Coconut Creek (G-1984)

PANELS: Building, Wood

Innova Eco Bldg Systems LLC .... E 305 455-7707
  Miami (G-9317)

PAPER & BOARD: Die-cut

Advanced Printing Finshg Inc .... F 305 836-8581
  Hialeah (G-5031)
Bros Williams Printing Inc .... G 305 769-9925
  Hialeah (G-5080)
C & R Designs Inc .... G 321 383-2255
  Titusville (G-17577)
Florida Print Finishers Inc .... G 850 877-8503
  Tallahassee (G-16441)
Folders Tabs Et Cetera .... F 813 884-3651
  Tampa (G-16858)
Intertape Polymer US Inc .... G 941 727-5788
  Bradenton (G-997)
Knopf & Sons Bindery Inc .... F 904 355-4411
  Jacksonville (G-6247)
Maq Investments Group Inc .... E 305 691-1468
  Miami Lakes (G-10316)
Packaging Alternatives Corp .... F 352 867-5050
  Ocala (G-11462)
Service Bindery Entps Inc .... F 727 823-9866
  Saint Petersburg (G-15182)
Southeast Finishing Group Inc .... E 407 299-4620
  Orlando (G-12613)
Specialty Fin Consulting Corp .... B 717 246-1661
  Longboat Key (G-7860)

PAPER CONVERTING

Amerifax Acquisition Corp .... G 305 828-1701
  Hialeah (G-5052)
Automated Paper Converters .... G 954 925-0721
  Hollywood (G-5534)
Dietzgen Corporation .... E 813 286-4767
  Tampa (G-16776)
Express Paper Company Inc .... F 305 685-4929
  Miami Lakes (G-10301)
Gainesville Sun .... F 352 374-5000
  Gainesville (G-4700)
Omnisphere Corporation .... F 305 388-4075
  Miami (G-9648)
Palmland Paper Co Inc .... G 954 764-6910
  Fort Lauderdale (G-3971)
Putnam Paper & Packaging Inc .... F 904 328-5101
  Palatka (G-12879)
R & D Sleeves Llc .... E 407 886-9010
  Apopka (G-167)
Specialty Fin Consulting Corp .... B 717 246-1661
  Longboat Key (G-7860)
Vinland Marketing Inc .... G 954 602-2177
  Pembroke Pines (G-13424)

PAPER MANUFACTURERS: Exc Newsprint

Amcor Flexibles LLC .... E 954 499-4800
  Miramar (G-10468)
Bristol Venture Service LLC .... G 407 844-8629
  Orlando (G-11969)
Commonwealth Brands Inc .... C 800 481-5814
  Fort Lauderdale (G-3739)
Excel Converting Inc .... F 786 318-2222
  Miami (G-9117)
Georgia-Pacific LLC .... D 386 328-8826
  Palatka (G-12869)
Georgia-Pacific LLC .... D 850 379-4000
  Hosford (G-5756)
Georgia-Pacific LLC .... E 386 328-8826
  Palatka (G-12870)
Gold Bond Building Pdts LLC .... F 813 672-8269
  Gibsonton (G-4797)
J Bristol LLC .... G 407 488-6744
  Winter Park (G-18516)
N V Texpack Group .... E 305 358-9696
  Miami (G-9602)
Paper Chase .... G 561 641-5319
  Lake Worth (G-7226)
Paper Machine Services Inc .... G 608 365-8095
  Fort Myers (G-4359)
Peninsula Tissue Corporation .... G 305 863-0704
  Miami (G-9703)

(G-0000) Company's Geographic Section entry number

PAPER PRDTS

Randal R Young ....G...... 800 584-9937
Oviedo (G-12846)
Resolute Tissue LLC ....F...... 305 636-5741
Miami (G-9799)
Suzano Pulp & Paper ....G...... 954 772-7716
Fort Lauderdale (G-4080)
Vinland Marketing Inc ....G...... 954 602-2177
Pembroke Pines (G-13424)
West Fraser Inc ....C...... 850 587-1000
Mc David (G-8190)

PAPER PRDTS

Andrews Sales Agency Manufactu ......G...... 813 254-4959
Tampa (G-16598)
Contact Enterprises Inc ....G...... 561 900-5134
Pompano Beach (G-13978)

PAPER PRDTS: Book Covers

David Dobbs Enterprises Inc ....D...... 904 824-6171
Saint Augustine (G-14823)

PAPER PRDTS: Cleansing Tissues, Made From Purchased Material

Anthem South LLC ....E...... 973 779-1982
Medley (G-8196)

PAPER PRDTS: Feminine Hygiene Prdts

All About Her ....F...... 954 559-5175
Davie (G-2380)
Esteemed Brands Inc ....F...... 954 442-3923
Miramar (G-10489)
Johnson & Johnson ....D...... 954 534-1141
Dania Beach (G-2352)
Steevie Stash LLC....................F...... 954 860-3138
Miami (G-9949)

PAPER PRDTS: Infant & Baby Prdts

Wonderworld 100 LLC ....E...... 407 618-3207
Orlando (G-12718)

PAPER PRDTS: Napkin Stock

Sun Paper Company ....E...... 305 887-0040
Doral (G-3383)

PAPER PRDTS: Pin Tickets, Made From Purchased Paper

Amtec Sales Inc ....F...... 800 994-3318
Miami (G-8729)

PAPER PRDTS: Sanitary

Diversitypro Corp........................D...... 305 691-2348
South Miami (G-16032)
Georgia-Pacific LLC...............................G...... 850 584-1121
Perry (G-13639)
Playtex Manufacturing Inc ....E...... 386 677-9559
Ormond Beach (G-12785)

PAPER PRDTS: Toilet Tissue, Stock

Atlas Paper Mills LLC ....F...... 800 562-2860
Miami (G-8768)
Atlas Paper Mills LLC ....C...... 305 835-8046
Hialeah (G-5064)
Resolute FP Florida Inc ....C...... 800 562-2860
Miami (G-9798)

PAPER PRDTS: Toweling Tissue

Clean Skin LLC..........................G...... 203 997-2491
Delray Beach (G-2945)

PAPER PRDTS: Towels, Napkins/Tissue Paper, From Purchd Mtrls

Green Leaf Foods LLC ....G...... 305 308-9167
Miramar (G-10499)
Lifelink Foundation Inc......................E...... 407 218-8783
Orlando (G-12327)
Papers Unlimited Plus Inc...............G...... 215 947-1155
Palm Beach Gardens (G-12997)
Softex Paper Inc...........................D...... 386 328-8488
Palatka (G-12882)
SW Premier Products LLC ....G...... 941 275-6677
Punta Gorda (G-14537)

Threez Company LLC..................G...... 904 422-9224
Jacksonville (G-6550)

PAPER PRDTS: Wrappers, Blank, Made From Purchased Materials

Versatile Packagers LLC ....F...... 813 664-1171
Tampa (G-17408)

PAPER, WHOLESALE: Printing

PHI CHI Foundation Inc ....G...... 561 526-3401
Margate (G-8146)
Trend At LLC ....E...... 786 300-2550
Miami (G-10039)

PAPER: Adhesive

Automatic Business Products Co ....F...... 888 742-7639
Port Orange (G-14326)
Avery Dennison Corporation ....G...... 727 787-1651
Palm Harbor (G-13100)
Online Labels LLC ....E...... 407 936-3900
Sanford (G-15366)
Southeast Packg Sanitation LLC.......G...... 904 634-7911
Jacksonville (G-6484)
Southern States Gluing Svcs................G...... 850 469-9667
Pensacola (G-13606)
Tapesouth Inc ....G...... 904 642-1800
Gainesville (G-4773)

PAPER: Art

Pro Edge Cutlery LLC ....G...... 239 304-8000
Naples (G-10866)

PAPER: Bag

Probag Inc ....F...... 305 883-3266
Medley (G-8305)

PAPER: Book

John Franklin Mowery ....G...... 202 468-8644
Venice (G-17701)

PAPER: Cardboard

Cardboard Only Inc........................G...... 352 345-5060
Weeki Wachee (G-17835)
County Cardboard LLC ....G...... 772 546-1983
Hobe Sound (G-5481)
Tommy & Giordy Buy/Sell ....G...... 786 797-6973
Opa Locka (G-11794)
White Cardboard Corp......................G...... 786 260-4692
Miami (G-10129)

PAPER: Cloth, Lined, Made From Purchased Materials

Terry Boca Inc ....G...... 561 893-0333
Deerfield Beach (G-2823)

PAPER: Coated & Laminated, NEC

Avery Dennison Corporation ....G...... 305 228-8740
Miami (G-8776)
Florida Tape & Labels Inc....................F...... 941 921-5788
Sarasota (G-15681)
Folders Tabs Et Cetera ....F...... 813 884-3651
Tampa (G-16858)
J & P Deerfield Inc ....F...... 954 571-6665
Deerfield Beach (G-2744)
Keithco Inc ....G...... 352 351-4741
Ocala (G-11419)
Labelpro Inc.....................................F...... 727 538-2149
Clearwater (G-1670)
Midds Inc ....E...... 561 586-6220
Lake Worth Beach (G-7258)
Mikes Print Shop Inc.......................G...... 407 718-4964
Winter Park (G-18525)
Southeast Id LLC ....F...... 954 571-6665
Miami Lakes (G-10356)
Suncoast Identification Tech ....G...... 239 277-9922
Fort Myers (G-4411)
Tampa Bay Coatings Inc ....F...... 727 823-9866
Saint Petersburg (G-15208)
Taylor Communications Inc ....E...... 813 886-5511
Tampa (G-17343)

PAPER: Gift Wrap

Gwmf Holdings LLC.........................F...... 305 788-1473
Weston (G-18250)

PAPER: Kraft

Vertpac LLC..........................E...... 407 886-9010
Apopka (G-183)

PAPER: Packaging

Papers Unlimited Plus Inc..................G...... 215 947-1155
Palm Beach Gardens (G-12997)

PAPER: Specialty

Superior Leaf Inc...................................G...... 561 480-2464
West Palm Beach (G-18171)

PAPER: Tissue

3tissue LLC.................................G...... 904 540-4335
Jacksonville (G-5840)
Atlas Southeast Papers Inc................D...... 407 330-9118
Sanford (G-15268)
Gtg-Jax LLC..................................E...... 904 861-3290
Jacksonville (G-6159)
Resolute Tissue Sales ....C...... 800 562-2860
Hialeah (G-5329)

PAPER: Transfer, Gold Or Silver, From Purchased Materials

One Step Papers LLC ....G...... 305 238-2296
Miami (G-9652)

PAPER: Waxed, Made From Purchased Materials

World Indus Resources Corp ....E...... 727 572-9991
Clearwater (G-1856)

PAPER: Wrapping & Packaging

Hammer Head Group Inc......................E...... 305 436-5691
Doral (G-3243)
Main Packaging Supply ....E...... 305 863-7176
Miami (G-9500)
Stephen Gould Corporation ....F...... 813 886-8460
Tampa (G-17302)

PAPERBOARD

Biodegradable Packaging Corp............F...... 305 824-1164
Hialeah Gardens (G-5434)
Design Containers Inc........................E...... 904 764-6541
Jacksonville (G-6029)
Matrix Packaging of Florida ....G...... 305 358-9696
Miami (G-9520)
Sonoco Products Company ....E...... 386 424-0970
New Smyrna Beach (G-11012)
Westrock Cp LLC ....E...... 407 843-1300
Orlando (G-12712)

PAPERBOARD PRDTS: Container Board

Packaging Corporation America ....D...... 813 626-7006
Tampa (G-17140)
Westrock Cp LLC ....C...... 904 714-7151
Jacksonville (G-6605)

PAPERBOARD PRDTS: Tagboard

Sfada Tag Agency Inc ....F...... 305 981-1077
North Miami (G-11121)

PAPERBOARD: Corrugated

Porter Pizza Box Florida Inc ....E...... 800 626-0828
Lakeland (G-7412)

PARACHUTES

Aerodyne Research LLC ....F...... 813 891-6300
Deland (G-2849)
Performance Designs Inc ....C...... 386 738-2224
Deland (G-2896)
S E Inc ....E...... 407 859-9317
Orlando (G-12564)
Tactical Prchute Dlvry Systems..........F...... 813 782-7482
Zephyrhills (G-18634)
USA Vigil ....G...... 386 736-8404
Deland (G-2917)

PARKING STRUCTURE

Magnetic Automation Corp ....E...... 321 635-8585
Rockledge (G-14728)

PRODUCT

PARTICLEBOARD

Florida Plywoods Inc ....D 850 948-2211
Greenville (G-4854)

PARTICLEBOARD: Laminated, Plastic

Allied Plastics Co Inc ....E 904 359-0386
Jacksonville (G-5877)

PARTITIONS & FIXTURES: Except Wood

Akiknav Inc ....F 561 842-8091
Riviera Beach (G-14591)
Bass Industries Inc ....E 305 751-2716
Hialeah (G-5068)
Bruce R Ely Enterprise Inc ....F 727 573-1643
Clearwater (G-1528)
Ccp of Miami Inc ....F 305 233-6534
Miami (G-8905)
Dons Cabinets and Woodworking ....F 727 863-3404
Hudson (G-5771)
Gulf South Distributors Inc ....F 850 244-1522
Fort Walton Beach (G-4591)
Iverica Industrial Inc ....F 305 691-1659
Hialeah (G-5198)
James Spear Design Inc ....G 727 592-9600
Largo (G-7621)
N & N Investment Corporation ....E 954 590-3800
Pompano Beach (G-14106)
Sam Weiss Woodworking Inc ....G 954 975-8158
Margate (G-8153)
T & R Store Fixtures Inc ....E 305 751-0377
Miami (G-9988)
Tcm Imagineering Inc ....F 407 323-6494
Deland (G-2906)
Teak Isle Inc ....C 407 656-8885
Ocoee (G-11527)
Telese Inc ....E 813 752-6015
Plant City (G-13808)

PARTITIONS: Nonwood, Floor Attached

American Sani Partition Corp ....E 407 656-0611
Ocoee (G-11520)

PARTITIONS: Wood & Fixtures

Amick Cstm Woodcraft & Design ....G 407 324-8525
Sanford (G-15265)
Braden Kitchens Inc ....E 321 636-4700
Cocoa (G-1907)
Central Fla Kit Bath Srfces In ....F 352 307-2333
Ocala (G-11347)
Corn-E-Lee Woodcrafts ....G 239 574-2414
Cape Coral (G-1327)
Creative Countertops Inc ....F 904 387-2800
Jacksonville (G-6011)
Custom Cabinets Inc ....F 941 366-0428
Sarasota (G-15647)
Custom Marble Works Inc ....E 813 620-0475
Tampa (G-16754)
Daystar International Inc ....G 813 281-0200
Tampa (G-16767)
EMI Industries LLC ....C 813 626-3166
Tampa (G-16808)
Extreme Wood Works S Fla Inc ....F 305 463-8614
Doral (G-3211)
Featherlite Exhibits ....G 800 229-5533
Tampa (G-16830)
Florida Designer Cabinets Inc ....F 352 793-8555
Sumterville (G-16263)
Home Pride Cabinets Inc..........................F 813 887-3782
Tampa (G-16920)
Inspired Closets Central FL ....G 352 748-0770
Wildwood (G-18313)
J & J Custom Mica Inc ....F 239 433-2828
Fort Myers (G-4293)
J M Interiors Inc ....G 305 891-6121
North Miami (G-11107)
Kitchen Counter Connections ....F 386 677-9471
Ormond Beach (G-12775)
Larsen Cabinetmaker Co ....F 305 252-1212
Miami (G-9426)
Mahan Cabinets ....G 305 255-3325
Cutler Bay (G-2295)
Mayworth Showcase Works Inc ....G 813 251-1558
Tampa (G-17058)
McCallum Cabinets Inc. ....F 352 372-2344
Gainesville (G-4725)
Morning Star of Sarasota Inc ....G 941 371-0392
Sarasota (G-15751)

N & N Investment Corporation ....E 954 590-3800
Pompano Beach (G-14106)
Princeton Industries Inc ....E 954 344-9155
Margate (G-8149)
Sand Dollar Charters LLC ....G 903 734-5376
New Smyrna Beach (G-11009)
Southern Woodworks Fine Wdwkg ....F 850 456-0550
Pensacola (G-13607)
Tizzoni Cucine Inc ....G 305 698-8889
Hollywood (G-5672)
Wilwoodman Inc ....G 386 334-7929
Palm Coast (G-13094)
Wonder Emporium Millwork Fab ....F 407 850-3131
Orlando (G-12717)
Y F Leung Inc ....G 305 651-6851
North Miami Beach (G-11172)

PARTITIONS: Wood, Floor Attached

East Coast Fix & Mllwk Co Inc ....G 904 733-9711
Jacksonville (G-6059)
Hugh Robinson Inc ....G 954 484-0660
Lauderdale Lakes (G-7716)

PARTS: Metal

Ameri Produ Produ Compa of Pin ....G 813 925-0144
Tampa (G-16586)
American Products Inc ....G 813 925-0144
Tampa (G-16590)
G Metal Industries Inc ....F 305 633-0300
Miami (G-9182)
Heritage Manufacturing Svcs ....G 727 906-5599
Saint Petersburg (G-15074)
Nautical Structures Inds Inc ....E 727 541-6664
Largo (G-7651)
Phoenix Trinity Mfg Inc ....G 937 619-0172
Hudson (G-5785)

PARTY & SPECIAL EVENT PLANNING SVCS

Premier Parties Entertainment ....E 352 375-6122
Gainesville (G-4750)

PATENT OWNERS & LESSORS

Lasersight Incorporated ....G 407 678-9900
Orlando (G-12311)

PATIENT MONITORING EQPT WHOLESALERS

Chuxco Inc ....F 305 470-9595
Coral Gables (G-2039)
Nuline Sensors LLC ....G 407 473-0765
Sanford (G-15363)

PATROL SVCS: Electric Transmission Or Gas Lines

Mitsubishi Power Americas Inc ....D 407 688-6100
Lake Mary (G-7096)

PATTERNS: Indl

Cost Cast Aluminum Corp ....E 863 422-5617
Haines City (G-4904)
Pattern Grading & Marker Svcs ....G 305 495-9963
Miramar (G-10525)

PAVERS

Adriano Gb Brick Pavers LLC ....G 407 497-1517
Orlando (G-11869)
AM Pavers Inc ....P 954 275-1590
Boca Raton (G-402)
Artistic Pavers LLC ....F 727 573-0918
Clearwater (G-1500)
Atm Pavers Inc ....G 239 322-7010
Cape Coral (G-1309)
Baju Professional Brick Pavers ....G 727 234-5300
Pinellas Park (G-13672)
Baron Pavers Corp ....G 786 389-2894
Miami (G-8800)
Brazilian Brickpavers Inc ....G 850 699-7833
Fort Walton Beach (G-4568)
Brito Brick & Pavers Corp ....G 727 214-8760
Clearwater (G-1526)
C&C Brick Pavers Inc ....G 813 716-8291
Tampa (G-16668)
Destination Pavers LLC ....G 850 319-6551
Panama City (G-13252)

EMK Brick Pavers LLC ....G 813 500-9663
Tampa (G-16809)
Fine Line Pavers Inc ....G 561 389-9819
West Palm Beach (G-17996)
First Coast Pavers Corp ....F 904 410-0278
Orange Park (G-11830)
Herbert Pavers Inc ....G 941 447-4909
Bradenton (G-991)
Homewood Holdings LLC ....F 941 740-3655
Cape Coral (G-1356)
Jessica Pavers Inc ....G 305 970-4879
Miami (G-9364)
Jf Flakes and Powers Inc ....G 407 414-6467
Orlando (G-12274)
Labelle Brick Pavers Tile LLC ....F 863 230-3100
Labelle (G-6982)
Lentus Products LLC ....G 203 913-7600
Kissimmee (G-6938)
Martins Pavers & Pools Corp ....G 754 368-4413
Deerfield Beach (G-2764)
Mr Alex Pavers Corp ....G 941 726-7273
Sarasota (G-15752)
Naia Brick Pavers Inc ....G 727 638-4734
Pinellas Park (G-13712)
North Florida Brick Pavers LLC ....G 850 255-0336
Santa Rosa Beach (G-15429)
North Port Pavers Inc ....G 941 391-7557
North Port (G-11202)
Pacific Pavers Inc ....G 941 238-7854
Bradenton (G-1022)
Paver Paradise LLC ....G 561 843-3031
Port St Lucie (G-14481)
Paver Way LLC ....F 321 303-0968
Altamonte Springs (G-63)
Pavers Inc ....G 352 754-3875
Brooksville (G-1187)
Paverscape Inc ....F 407 381-1022
Orlando (G-12475)
Payless Brick Pavers LLC ....G 904 629-7436
Jacksonville (G-6359)
Perfect Pavers South Fla LLC ....F 954 779-1855
Fort Lauderdale (G-3981)
Precise Pavers Inc ....G 863 528-8000
Auburndale (G-242)
Professional Paver Restorations ....G 352 797-8411
Spring Hill (G-16075)
Reef Pavers Inc ....G 904 471-0859
Jacksonville Beach (G-6643)
Reyes Interlocking Pavers Inc ....G 863 698-9179
Plant City (G-13800)
Rio Pavers Inc ....G 321 388-6757
Orlando (G-12555)
South Florida Pavers Corp ....G 786 517-9100
Hialeah (G-5355)
Stabil Concrete Pavers LLC ....E 941 739-7823
Sarasota (G-15559)
Stamp Concrete & Pavers Inc ....G 561 880-1527
Merritt Island (G-8597)
Stone Brick Pavers Inc ....G 407 844-1455
Ocoee (G-11526)
Superior Pavers and Stone LLC ....G 904 887-7831
Jacksonville (G-6522)
Sws Services Inc ....F 904 802-2120
Fernandina Beach (G-3598)
T & E Pavers Inc ....G 239 243-6229
Cape Coral (G-1397)
Tremron LLC ....G 904 359-5900
Jacksonville (G-6565)
Tropical Paver Sealing ....G 727 786-4011
Wesley Chapel (G-17889)
US Paver Co ....G 954 292-4373
Boca Raton (G-738)
Villar Stone & Paver Works LLC ....G 860 209-2907
Sarasota (G-15867)
Wagner Pavers Contractor ....G 321 633-5131
Rockledge (G-14754)
Wf Brick Pavers Inc ....G 813 506-1941
Tampa (G-17429)

PAVING MATERIALS: Coal Tar, Not From Refineries

Star-Seal of Florida Inc ....F 954 484-8402
Fort Lauderdale (G-4068)

PAVING MATERIALS: Prefabricated, Concrete

Encore Stone Products LLC ....E 352 428-1542
Holly Hill (G-5513)

PAWN SHOPS

Westchster Gold Fbricators Inc............G....... 941 625-0666
Port Charlotte (G-14324)

PEAT GRINDING SVCS

Sun Gro Horticulture Dist Inc ....E....... 407 291-1676
Orlando (G-12631)

PEDESTALS: Marble

C L Industries Inc........................E....... 800 333-2660
Orlando (G-11973)

PENCILS & PARTS: Mechanical

Dixon Ticonderoga Company ....D....... 407 829-9000
Lake Mary (G-7070)

PENS & PENCILS: Mechanical, NEC

Bic Corporation.........................A....... 727 536-7895
Clearwater (G-1519)
Ross Industries Inc......................D....... 954 752-2800
Pompano Beach (G-14162)
Scribe Manufacturing Inc ....F....... 727 524-7482
Clearwater (G-1777)
Scribe Manufacturing Inc ....C....... 727 536-7895
Saint Petersburg (G-15178)
Scribe Opco Inc..........................E....... 727 536-7895
Clearwater (G-1778)
Sharp Marketing LLC......................G....... 954 565-2711
Oakland Park (G-11293)

PERFUME: Concentrated

Mar Company Distributors LLC...........E....... 786 477-4174
Miami (G-9507)

PERFUME: Perfumes, Natural Or Synthetic

Crusellas & Co Inc ....F....... 305 261-9580
Miami (G-8980)
Grafton Products Corp....................E....... 561 738-2886
Boynton Beach (G-874)
It Smells Good ....G....... 904 899-2818
Jacksonville (G-6208)

PERFUMES

B224 USA Co ....G....... 786 598-8805
Holiday (G-5490)
Beloved Inc ....F....... 404 643-5177
North Miami Beach (G-11131)
Desire Fragrances Inc ....G....... 646 832-3051
Miami (G-9024)
Firmenich Lakeland ....F....... 863 646-0165
Lakeland (G-7325)
Le Labo ....G....... 786 636-6928
Miami (G-9442)
Megamaxmoney LLC ....F....... 561 523-4458
West Palm Beach (G-18072)
Megamaxmoney LLC ....G....... 561 523-4458
West Palm Beach (G-18073)
Perfumeland ....F....... 407 354-3342
Orlando (G-12484)
Wake Up Beautiful ....G....... 941 792-6500
Bradenton (G-1075)

PERLITE: Processed

Conrad Yelvington Distrs Inc.............F....... 352 336-5049
Gainesville (G-4669)

PERMANENT WAVE EQPT & MACHINES

Sox LLC ....G....... 561 501-0057
Boca Raton (G-689)

PEST CONTROL IN STRUCTURES SVCS

50 50 Parmley Envmtl Svcs LLC...........G....... 407 593-1165
Saint Cloud (G-14918)
Zap Mosquito Solutions Inc ....G....... 786 732-0772
Miami (G-10155)

PEST CONTROL SVCS

Natures Own Pest Control Inc ....G....... 941 378-3334
Sarasota (G-15758)

PESTICIDES

Brandfx LLC ....E....... 321 632-2063
Cocoa (G-1908)
Glades Formulating Corporation..........F....... 561 996-4200
Belle Glade (G-341)
Levita LLC...............................F....... 954 227-7468
Coral Springs (G-2178)
North Florida AG Services Inc ....G....... 352 494-3978
Lake City (G-7033)
Pbi/Gordon Corp.........................G....... 850 478-2770
Pensacola (G-13568)
Permasafe Prtctive Catings LLC ....E....... 866 372-9622
Coconut Creek (G-2001)

PESTICIDES WHOLESALERS

Glades Formulating Corporation..........F....... 561 996-4200
Belle Glade (G-341)

PET COLLARS, LEASHES, MUZZLES & HARNESSES: Leather

Dp Pet Products Inc.....................F....... 407 888-4627
Orlando (G-12103)
N3xt Up Exotic LLC.......................G....... 863 777-3778
Tampa (G-17097)
Old Kentucky Leather Works Inc..........G....... 904 269-1369
Orange Park (G-11835)

PET SPLYS

Be The Solution Inc ....G....... 850 545-2043
Tallahassee (G-16418)
Cafco LLC...............................G....... 240 848-5574
Miami (G-8879)
Crown Products LLC......................G....... 954 917-1118
Pompano Beach (G-13984)
Higgins Group Corp......................E....... 305 681-4444
Miami (G-9280)
King Kanine LLC ....G....... 833 546-4738
Plantation (G-13863)
M Pet Group Corp........................G....... 954 455-5003
Aventura (G-266)
Matry Group LLC.........................F....... 407 461-9797
Kissimmee (G-6977)
Miami Tbr LLC...........................G....... 786 275-4773
Doral (G-3302)
Munro International Inc ....E....... 352 337-1535
Gainesville (G-4736)
Nava Pets Inc...........................F....... 407 982-7256
Longwood (G-7926)
Professional Pet Products Inc ....E....... 305 592-1992
Doral (G-3339)
RDt Business Enterprises Inc............F....... 954 525-1133
Fort Lauderdale (G-4013)
Reef Cleaners Inc.......................G....... 772 905-7166
Port St Lucie (G-14482)
Sunshine Nylon Products Inc ....G....... 352 754-9932
Brooksville (G-1208)
Synergylabs LLC.........................G....... 954 525-1133
Fort Lauderdale (G-4082)
Timberwolf Organics Ltd Lblty ....F....... 407 877-8779
Windermere (G-18367)
Tropichem Research Labs LLC ....E....... 314 686-4614
Jupiter (G-6815)
Tropichem Research Labs LLC ....D....... 561 804-7603
Jupiter (G-6814)
West Texas Protein Inc ....F....... 806 250-5959
Jacksonville (G-6602)

PET SPLYS WHOLESALERS

Miami Tbr LLC...........................G....... 786 275-4773
Doral (G-3302)

PETROLEUM PRDTS WHOLESALERS

Armor Oil Products LLC..................G....... 813 248-1988
Tampa (G-16608)
Enviro Petroleum Inc....................G....... 713 896-6996
Jensen Beach (G-6654)

PETS & PET SPLYS, WHOLESALE

Reef Cleaners Inc.......................G....... 772 905-7166
Port St Lucie (G-14482)

PEWTER WARE

Accent Jewelry Inc......................F....... 941 391-6687
Punta Gorda (G-14490)

Metal Rock Inc..........................F....... 407 886-6440
Apopka (G-150)

PHARMACEUTICAL PREPARATIONS: Adrenal

Caq International LLC....................G....... 305 744-1472
Miami (G-8889)
Tg United Inc ....G....... 888 627-9139
Brooksville (G-1210)

PHARMACEUTICAL PREPARATIONS: Druggists' Preparations

Ajenat Pharmaceuticals LLC ....C....... 727 471-0850
Tampa (G-16568)
Ambo Health LLC..........................G....... 866 414-0188
Venice (G-17676)
Beutlich Pharmaceuticals LLC ....F....... 386 263-8860
Bunnell (G-1226)
Exactus Pharmacy Solutions Inc ....B....... 888 314-3874
Tampa (G-16823)
Navinta III Inc ....G....... 561 997-6959
Boca Raton (G-611)
Pack4u LLC ....F....... 407 857-2871
Orlando (G-12462)

PHARMACEUTICAL PREPARATIONS: Emulsions

Nanocann Research Labs LLC ....G....... 850 630-4676
Miami (G-9606)

PHARMACEUTICAL PREPARATIONS: Medicines, Capsule Or Ampule

Assistrx Inc ....D....... 855 421-4607
Orlando (G-11927)
Assistrx Inc ....D....... 855 382-2533
Orlando (G-11928)
Nutrakey LLC ....G....... 321 234-6282
Longwood (G-7929)
Nutricorp LLC ....F....... 305 680-4896
Hialeah (G-5285)

PHARMACEUTICAL PREPARATIONS: Pills

American Bhvioral RES Inst LLC ....D....... 888 353-1205
Boca Raton (G-405)
Kesin Pharma Corporation ....G....... 833 537-4679
Oldsmar (G-11665)
Liquidcapsule Mfg LLC ....F....... 813 431-0532
Tampa (G-17014)
Neuro Pharmalogics Inc ....G....... 240 476-4491
Boca Raton (G-612)
Qol Medical LLC.........................G....... 772 584-3640
Vero Beach (G-17790)

PHARMACEUTICAL PREPARATIONS: Powders

Biolife LLC.............................E....... 941 360-1300
Sarasota (G-15449)
Rx For Fleas Inc........................F....... 954 351-9244
Fort Lauderdale (G-4034)
Xcelience LLC ....E....... 813 286-0404
Tampa (G-17445)

PHARMACEUTICAL PREPARATIONS: Proprietary Drug PRDTS

Lf of America Corp......................G....... 561 988-0303
Boca Raton (G-579)
Peak Nutritional Products LLC...........E....... 813 884-4989
Tampa (G-17153)
Quantum Pharmaceuticals Llc ....G....... 321 724-0625
Melbourne Beach (G-8569)
Rockledge Phrm Mfg LLC ....F....... 321 636-0717
Rockledge (G-14742)
Speer Laboratories LLC ....F....... 954 586-8700
Fort Lauderdale (G-4062)
Vistapharm Inc ....E....... 727 530-1633
Largo (G-7707)

PHARMACEUTICAL PREPARATIONS: Solutions

Abhai LLC...............................G....... 215 579-1842
Saint Augustine (G-14805)
Gand Inc................................G....... 240 575-0622
Miami Beach (G-10193)

PRODUCT

PHARMACEUTICAL PREPARATIONS: Tablets

Capzerpharma Manufacturing LLC ......G...... 561 493-4000
Lake Worth Beach **(G-7253)**

Corerx Pharmaceuticals Inc ......E...... 727 259-6950
Clearwater **(G-1552)**

PHARMACEUTICALS

1source Biotechnology LLC ....G...... 305 668-5888
Miami **(G-8607)**

5d Bio Gold LLC ....G...... 561 756-8291
Boca Raton **(G-382)**

AC Pharma Corp ....G...... 954 773-9735
Margate **(G-8115)**

Accentia Biopharmaceuticals ....F...... 813 864-2554
Tampa **(G-16556)**

Acic Pharmaceuticals Inc ....G...... 954 341-0795
Coral Springs **(G-2125)**

Actavis Laboratories FI Inc ....G...... 954 585-1400
Davie **(G-2375)**

Actavis Laboratories FL Inc ....F...... 954 358-6100
Weston **(G-18220)**

Actavis Laboratories FL Inc ....F...... 954 585-1400
Davie **(G-2376)**

Adma Biologics Inc ....D...... 561 989-5800
Boca Raton **(G-388)**

Advanced Pharma Research Inc ....F...... 786 234-3709
Cutler Bay **(G-2282)**

Advanced Pharmaceutical Inc ....G...... 866 259-7122
North Miami **(G-11087)**

Aenova Doral Manufacturing Inc ....G...... 305 463-2270
Doral **(G-3096)**

Aenova Doral Manufacturing Inc ....C...... 305 463-2263
Doral **(G-3097)**

Aenova North America Inc ....E...... 786 345-5505
Miami **(G-8660)**

Aim Immunotech Inc ....F...... 352 448-7797
Ocala **(G-11317)**

Allay Pharmaceutical LLC ....G...... 954 336-1136
Hialeah **(G-5040)**

Allergan Sales LLC ....F...... 787 406-1203
Sunrise **(G-16290)**

Allied Pharmacy Products Inc ....G...... 516 374-8862
Delray Beach **(G-2928)**

Alta Pharma LLC ....G...... 727 942-7645
Tarpon Springs **(G-17457)**

Alternative Medical Entps LLC ....F...... 941 702-9955
Apollo Beach **(G-90)**

Alvita Pharma Usa Inc ....G...... 305 961-1623
Doral **(G-3110)**

American Injectables Inc ....F...... 813 435-6014
Brooksville **(G-1135)**

American Pharmaceutical Svcs ....F...... 407 704-5937
Orlando **(G-11905)**

Andrx Corporation ....C...... 954 217-4500
Weston **(G-18223)**

Andrx Corporation ....C...... 954 585-1770
Sunrise **(G-16293)**

Andrx Corporation ....C...... 954 585-1400
Davie **(G-2387)**

Annona Biosciences Inc ....G...... 888 204-4980
Palm Beach Gardens **(G-12947)**

Apical Pharmaceutical Corp ....G...... 786 331-7200
Doral **(G-3117)**

Apotex Corp ....E...... 954 384-8007
Weston **(G-18225)**

Archer Pharmaceuticals Inc ....F...... 941 752-2949
Sarasota **(G-15441)**

Arnet Pharmaceutical Corp ....B...... 954 236-9053
Davie **(G-2389)**

Arxada LLC ....E...... 813 286-0404
Tampa **(G-16610)**

Aveva Drug Dlvry Systems Inc ....D...... 954 430-3340
Miramar **(G-10470)**

Aveva Drug Dlvry Systems Inc ....E...... 954 430-3340
Miramar **(G-10471)**

Axis Phrm Partners LLC ....F...... 407 936-2949
Lake Mary **(G-7062)**

Azopharma Inc ....G...... 954 536-4738
Miramar **(G-10472)**

Baker Norton US Inc ....D...... 305 575-6000
Miami **(G-8795)**

Beach Products Inc ....G...... 813 839-6565
Tampa **(G-16635)**

Beacon Phrm Jupiter LLC ....E...... 212 991-8988
Jupiter **(G-6689)**

Belcher Holdings Inc ....E...... 727 530-1585
Largo **(G-7547)**

Belcher Holdings Inc ....C...... 727 471-0850
Largo **(G-7548)**

Belcher Pharmaceuticals LLC ....C...... 727 471-0850
Largo **(G-7549)**

Berman Products LLC ....F...... 561 743-5197
Jupiter **(G-6691)**

Bio Therapeutics Inc ....G...... 954 321-5553
Plantation **(G-13832)**

Bio-Nucleonics Pharma Inc ....F...... 305 576-0996
Miami **(G-8829)**

Bio-Pharm LLC ....G...... 973 223-7163
Hallandale Beach **(G-4938)**

Bpc Plasma Inc ....F...... 407 207-1932
Orlando **(G-11967)**

Bpc Plasma Inc ....F...... 561 989-5800
Boca Raton **(G-445)**

Bpc Plasma Inc ....E...... 561 569-3100
Boca Raton **(G-446)**

Bpi Labs LLC ....C...... 727 471-0850
Largo **(G-7554)**

Brammer Bio LLC ....B...... 386 418-8199
Alachua **(G-10)**

Briemad Inc ....G...... 561 626-4377
Palm Beach Gardens **(G-12953)**

Bristol-Myers Squibb Company ....E...... 212 546-4000
Temple Terrace **(G-17535)**

Bristol-Myers Squibb Company ....G...... 813 881-7000
Tampa **(G-16662)**

Britvic North America LLC ....E...... 786 641-5041
Miami **(G-8854)**

California Greens Corporation ....G...... 630 423-5760
Pompano Beach **(G-13964)**

Camphor Technologies Inc ....F...... 941 360-0025
Sarasota **(G-15627)**

Cardinal Health 414 LLC ....G...... 813 972-1351
Tampa **(G-16679)**

Casa De Rprsntcones Jmw CA LLC ....F...... 754 707-1689
Miramar **(G-10478)**

Catalent Inc ....F...... 727 803-2832
Saint Petersburg **(G-14998)**

Catalent Pharma Solutions Inc ....A...... 727 572-4000
Saint Petersburg **(G-14999)**

Catalyst Pharmaceuticals Inc ....E...... 305 420-3200
Coral Gables **(G-2038)**

Centro De Diagnostico ....G...... 407 865-7020
Sanford **(G-15280)**

Cerno Pharmaceuticals LLC ....G...... 786 763-2766
Miami **(G-8915)**

Cleveland Diabetes Care Inc ....F...... 904 394-2620
Jacksonville **(G-5983)**

Clinical Dagnstc Solutions Inc ....E...... 954 791-1773
Plantation **(G-13836)**

Cobalt Laboratories Inc ....F...... 239 390-0245
Bonita Springs **(G-792)**

Cocrystal Discovery Inc ....A...... 425 750-7208
Miami **(G-8939)**

Cocrystal Pharma Inc ....G...... 877 262-7123
Miami **(G-8940)**

Collfix Inc ....G...... 754 264-0959
Boca Raton **(G-468)**

Community Pharmacy Svcs LLC ....G...... 727 431-8261
Clearwater **(G-1548)**

Concordia Pharmaceuticals Inc ....G...... 786 304-2083
Miami **(G-8955)**

Coqui Rdo Pharmaceuticals Corp ....G...... 787 685-5046
Doral **(G-3172)**

Cor International (not Inc) ....G...... 850 766-2866
Tallahassee **(G-16429)**

Corerx Inc ....F...... 727 259-6950
Clearwater **(G-1550)**

Corerx Inc ....C...... 727 259-6950
Clearwater **(G-1551)**

Cryothrapy Pain Rlief Pdts Inc ....G...... 954 364-8192
Hollywood **(G-5558)**

Cyto Dyncorp Inc ....G...... 813 527-6969
Lutz **(G-7988)**

Dain M Bayer ....G...... 407 647-0679
Winter Park **(G-18504)**

Darmerica LLC ....G...... 321 219-9111
Casselberry **(G-1414)**

Dazmed Inc ....G...... 561 571-2020
Boca Raton **(G-478)**

Demelle Biopharma LLC ....G...... 908 240-8939
Tarpon Springs **(G-17466)**

Dermatonus ....G...... 305 229-3923
Miramar **(G-10483)**

Devatis Inc ....G...... 954 316-4844
Fort Lauderdale **(G-3763)**

Diabetic Care Rx LLC ....E...... 866 348-0441
Pompano Beach **(G-13996)**

Doctors Scentific Organica LLC ....F...... 888 455-9031
Riviera Beach **(G-14617)**

Dr Lips LLC ....G...... 352 203-3182
Boca Raton **(G-494)**

Duy Drugs Inc ....F...... 305 594-3667
Doral **(G-3201)**

Eci Pharmaceuticals LLC ....E...... 954 486-8181
Fort Lauderdale **(G-3782)**

Eli Lilly and Company ....F...... 305 987-7000
Miami **(G-9083)**

Elite Fitforever LLC ....G...... 305 902-2358
Miami Beach **(G-10186)**

EMD Serono Research & Dev Inst ....G...... 978 715-1804
Miami **(G-9095)**

Emerge Nutraceuticals Inc ....F...... 888 352-1683
Mount Dora **(G-10601)**

EMJ Pharma Inc ....G...... 973 600-9087
Palm Beach Gardens **(G-12968)**

Engage Surgical Knee LLC ....G...... 614 915-2960
Maitland **(G-8057)**

Envoy Therapeutics Inc ....F...... 561 210-7705
Jupiter **(G-6722)**

Epigenetix Inc ....G...... 561 543-7569
Delray Beach **(G-2959)**

Erba Diagnostics Inc ....E...... 305 324-2300
Miami Lakes **(G-10300)**

Exelan Pharmaceuticals Inc ....G...... 561 287-6631
Boca Raton **(G-509)**

Farma International Inc ....F...... 305 670-4416
Miami **(G-9134)**

First Wave Biopharma Inc ....F...... 561 589-7020
Boca Raton **(G-515)**

Fitteam Global LLC ....G...... 586 260-1487
Palm Beach Gardens **(G-12969)**

Forest Research Institute Inc ....F...... 631 436-4600
Weston **(G-18243)**

Forest Research Institute Inc ....E...... 954 622-5600
Sunrise **(G-16319)**

Fresenius Kabi Usa LLC ....E...... 847 550-2300
Doral **(G-3221)**

Gadal Laboratories Inc ....G...... 786 732-2571
Miami **(G-9184)**

Gild Corporation ....G...... 305 378-6982
Miami **(G-9213)**

Global Life Technologies Corp ....G...... 301 337-2059
Coral Gables **(G-2061)**

Global Pharma Analytics LLC ....G...... 701 491-7770
Jupiter **(G-6736)**

Global Reach Rx Pbf LLC ....F...... 786 703-1988
Doral **(G-3235)**

Green Roads of Florida ....G...... 954 626-0574
Davie **(G-2420)**

Growhealthy Holdings LLC ....F...... 863 223-8882
West Palm Beach **(G-18021)**

Hill Dermaceuticals Inc ....E...... 407 323-1887
Sanford **(G-15332)**

Hill Labs Inc ....E...... 407 323-1887
Sanford **(G-15333)**

Horizon Pharmaceuticals Inc ....D...... 561 844-7227
Palm Beach Gardens **(G-12974)**

Infupharma LLC ....G...... 305 301-3389
Hollywood **(G-5601)**

Innova Softgel LLC ....C...... 855 536-8872
Miami **(G-9318)**

Inter Cell Technologies Inc ....G...... 561 575-6868
Jupiter **(G-6747)**

Ivax Pharmaceuticals LLC ....C...... 305 575-6000
Miami **(G-9345)**

Ivax Research Inc ....D...... 305 668-7688
Miami **(G-9346)**

Ivax Teva ....G...... 954 384-5316
Weston **(G-18258)**

Jmi-Dniels Pharmaceuticals Inc ....C...... 727 323-5151
Saint Petersburg **(G-15101)**

JNJ & Company Inc ....F...... 239 489-0053
Alva **(G-81)**

Kashiben Say LLC ....G...... 352 489-4960
Dunnellon **(G-3466)**

Kavi Skin Solutions Inc ....E...... 415 839-5156
Titusville **(G-17597)**

Kd-Pharma Usa Inc ....G...... 786 345-5500
Miami **(G-9386)**

Kempharm Inc ....G...... 321 939-3416
Celebration **(G-1438)**

King Pharmaceuticals LLC ....G...... 954 575-7085
Coral Springs **(G-2174)**

King Pharmaceuticals LLC ....D...... 423 989-8000
Saint Petersburg **(G-15104)**

Kova Laboratories Inc ....G...... 954 978-8730
Margate **(G-8139)**

Kramer Pharmacal Inc ....F...... 305 226-0641
Miami **(G-9397)**

(G-0000) Company's Geographic Section entry number

Krs Global Biotechnology Inc ....E 888 502-2050
Boca Raton *(G-572)*

Krs MSA LLC ....G 727 264-7605
New Port Richey *(G-10971)*

Labelclick Inc ....G 727 548-8345
Oldsmar *(G-11669)*

Linpharma Inc ....G 888 989-3237
Orlando *(G-12332)*

Linpharma Inc ....G 888 989-3237
Tampa *(G-17012)*

Llorens Phrm Intl Div Inc ....F 305 716-0595
Miami *(G-9469)*

Longeveron Inc ....F 305 909-0840
Miami *(G-9475)*

Lonza ....F 727 608-6802
Tampa *(G-17022)*

Lupin Oncology Inc ....F 239 316-1900
Naples *(G-10808)*

Lupin Research Inc ....E 800 466-1450
Coral Springs *(G-2180)*

M3 Biopharma Inc ....G 858 603-8296
Sarasota *(G-15731)*

Magellan Pharmaceuticals Inc ....G 813 623-6800
Tampa *(G-17031)*

Max Avw Professional LLC ....F 954 972-3338
Margate *(G-8143)*

Maximilian Zenho & Co Inc ....G 352 875-1190
Ocala *(G-11440)*

Mayo Clinic ....G 904 953-2000
Jacksonville *(G-6282)*

Mayo Clinic ....G 904 953-2000
Jacksonville *(G-6283)*

MCR Amrcan Pharmaceuticals Inc ....E 352 754-8587
Brooksville *(G-1178)*

Medstone Pharma LLC ....G 305 777-7872
Weston *(G-18267)*

Merck Sharp & Dohme Corp ....D 305 512-6062
Miami Lakes *(G-10321)*

Merck Sharp & Dohme LLC ....C 305 698-4600
Miami Lakes *(G-10322)*

Methapharm Inc ....G 954 341-0795
Coral Springs *(G-2185)*

Millennium Pharmaceuticals Inc ....D 866 466-7779
Orlando *(G-12380)*

Mohnark Pharmaceuticals Inc ....G 954 607-4559
Davie *(G-2442)*

Mpact Sales Solutions ....G 630 669-5937
Oakland *(G-11229)*

Mymd Pharmaceuticals Fla Inc ....F 813 864-2566
Tampa *(G-17094)*

Nabi ....F 561 989-5800
Boca Raton *(G-608)*

Natural Immunogenics Corp ....D 888 328-8840
Sarasota *(G-15525)*

Natures Bioscience LLC ....G 800 570-7450
Sarasota *(G-15757)*

Neglex Inc ....F 305 551-4177
Miami *(G-9609)*

Nephron Pharmaceuticals ....F 407 913-3142
Orlando *(G-12411)*

Nephron Pharmaceuticals Corp ....F 407 999-2225
Orlando *(G-12412)*

New Vision Pharmaceuticals LLC ....C 954 721-5000
Tamarac *(G-16538)*

New World Holdings Inc ....E 561 888-4939
Delray Beach *(G-2992)*

Nextsource Biotechnology LLC ....G 305 753-6360
Miami *(G-9617)*

Nexus Alliance Corp ....G 321 945-4283
Longwood *(G-7928)*

Northside Pharmacy LLC ....G 256 398-7500
Destin *(G-3074)*

Noven Pharmaceuticals Inc ....C 305 964-3393
Miami *(G-9631)*

Noven Therapeutics LLC ....B 212 682-4420
Miami *(G-9632)*

Nutra Pharma Corp ....G 954 509-0911
Coral Springs *(G-2198)*

Nutra Sciences World Inc ....G 305 302-8870
Hialeah *(G-5284)*

Nxgen Brands LLC ....E 888 315-6339
Plantation *(G-13875)*

Ocala Pharmacy LLC ....G 352 509-7890
Ocala *(G-11457)*

Ocean Pharmaceuticals Inc ....F 954 473-4717
Sunrise *(G-16348)*

One Nursing Care LLC ....C 954 441-6644
Miramar *(G-10523)*

Opko Health Inc ....C 305 575-4100
Miami *(G-9660)*

Oryza Pharmaceuticals Inc ....E 954 881-5481
Coral Springs *(G-2202)*

Pacira Biosciences Inc ....C 813 553-6680
Tampa *(G-17138)*

Pacira Pharmaceuticals Inc ....A 813 553-6680
Tampa *(G-17139)*

PDC ....F 386 322-2808
Port Orange *(G-14343)*

Pfmc Bayer Limited Partnership ....F 850 244-1310
Mary Esther *(G-8179)*

Pharma Resources Inc ....F 973 780-5241
Altamonte Springs *(G-64)*

Pharmacy Hn Llc ....F 786 307-0509
Miami *(G-9709)*

Pharmalink Inc ....C 800 257-3527
Largo *(G-7657)*

Pharmamed USA Inc ....G 954 533-4462
Fort Lauderdale *(G-3982)*

Pharmatech LLC ....G 954 581-7881
Davie *(G-2457)*

Pharmatech LLC ....F 954 629-2444
Davie *(G-2458)*

Pharmatech Pharmatech LLC ....G 954 583-8778
Fort Lauderdale *(G-3983)*

Phoenix Medical Research LLC ....G 786 762-2040
Miami *(G-9712)*

Platinum Group Usa Inc ....F 561 274-7553
Delray Beach *(G-2999)*

PLD Acquisitions LLC ....D 305 463-2270
Miami *(G-9722)*

PQ Pharmacy LLC ....G 352 477-8977
Brooksville *(G-1191)*

Prestige Brands International ....E 914 524-6800
Bonita Springs *(G-815)*

Procyon Corporation ....G 727 447-2998
Clearwater *(G-1756)*

Product Dev Partners LLC ....F 813 908-6775
Tampa *(G-17188)*

Profounda Health & Beauty ....F 407 270-7792
Orlando *(G-12515)*

Prosolus Inc ....G 305 514-0270
Miami *(G-9754)*

R-Da Trading LLC ....G 954 278-6983
Weston *(G-18281)*

Rainbow Lght Ntrtnal Systems I ....G 954 233-3300
Sunrise *(G-16361)*

Regenerative Proc Plant LLC ....E 727 781-0818
Palm Harbor *(G-13130)*

Relmada Therapeutics Inc ....E 646 876-3459
Coral Gables *(G-2104)*

Rls (usa) Inc ....A 561 596-0556
Tampa *(G-17224)*

Romark Laboratories LC ....E 813 282-8544
Tampa *(G-17232)*

Rowell Laboratories Inc ....F 407 929-9445
Apopka *(G-173)*

Sancilio & Company Inc ....E 561 847-2302
Riviera Beach *(G-14672)*

Sanofi US Services Inc ....E 407 736-0226
Orlando *(G-12573)*

Script Central LLC ....G 954 805-8581
Miami Beach *(G-10225)*

Shriji Swami LLC ....G 904 727-3434
Jacksonville *(G-6467)*

Smartscience Laboratories Inc ....F 813 925-8454
Tampa *(G-17275)*

Sofie Co ....E 407 321-9076
Sanford *(G-15388)*

Southeast Compounding Phrm LLC ....G 813 644-7700
Tampa *(G-17283)*

Specialty Pharmacy Svcs Inc ....G 321 953-2004
Melbourne *(G-8528)*

St Mary Pharmacy LLC ....F 727 585-1333
Largo *(G-7690)*

Star Pharmaceuticals LLC ....G 800 845-7827
Fort Lauderdale *(G-4067)*

Stemtech Healthsciences Corp ....E 954 715-6000
Miramar *(G-10547)*

Steriline North America I ....G 941 405-2039
Bradenton *(G-1053)*

Stratco Pharmaceuticals LLC ....F 813 403-5060
Odessa *(G-11582)*

Stratus Pharmaceuticals Inc ....E 305 254-6793
Miami *(G-9958)*

Teva Pharmaceuticals ....F 954 382-7729
Sunrise *(G-16381)*

Teva Pharmaceuticals Usa Inc ....E 305 575-6000
Miami *(G-10004)*

Therapeuticsmd Inc ....D 561 961-1900
Boca Raton *(G-715)*

Theretbicom Inc ....G 917 796-1443
Weston *(G-18289)*

Tri-Fecta Solutions LLC ....G 954 908-1669
Fort Lauderdale *(G-4097)*

Triad Isotopes Inc ....E 407 455-6700
Orlando *(G-12670)*

Trifecta Phrmceuticals USA LLC ....G 888 296-9067
Pompano Beach *(G-14219)*

Trivecta Pharmaceuticals Inc ....F 561 856-0842
Fort Lauderdale *(G-4099)*

Tropichem Research Labs LLC ....D 561 804-7603
Jupiter *(G-6814)*

Tropichem Research Labs LLC ....E 314 686-4614
Jupiter *(G-6815)*

Trxade Inc ....G 727 230-1915
Land O Lakes *(G-7507)*

Twinlab Holdings Inc ....E 800 645-5626
Boca Raton *(G-729)*

Ultimaxx Health LLC ....G 877 300-3424
Boca Raton *(G-732)*

Ultra Pharma LLC ....G 954 532-7539
Pompano Beach *(G-14223)*

United Biosource LLC (ubc) ....G 877 599-7748
Lake Mary *(G-7114)*

USA and International RES Inc ....G 786 558-5115
Doral *(G-3409)*

Uspharma Ltd ....D 954 817-4418
Miami Lakes *(G-10374)*

Usvi Pharmaceuticals LLC ....F 305 643-8841
Doral *(G-3410)*

Uvlrx Therapeutics Inc ....F 813 309-1976
Oldsmar *(G-11704)*

Versea Holdings Inc ....E 800 397-0670
Tampa *(G-17410)*

Veru Inc ....D 305 509-6897
Miami *(G-10102)*

Vistakon Pharmaceuticals LLC ....G 904 443-1000
Jacksonville *(G-6593)*

Vistapharm Inc ....E 727 530-1633
Largo *(G-7706)*

Vital Pharma Research Inc ....G 786 666-0592
Hialeah *(G-5413)*

Vividus LLC ....G 954 326-1954
Pompano Beach *(G-14237)*

Watson Therapeutics Inc ....E 954 266-1000
Miramar *(G-10563)*

West Pharmaceutical Svcs Inc ....G 727 546-2402
Clearwater *(G-1850)*

West Phrm Svcs Fla Inc ....B 727 546-2402
Saint Petersburg *(G-15231)*

Woodfield Pharmaceutical LLC ....D 281 530-3077
Miami *(G-10141)*

PHARMACEUTICALS: Medicinal & Botanical Prdts

Atlantic Medical Products LLC ....F 727 535-0022
Saint Petersburg *(G-14974)*

Biobotanical LLC ....G 239 458-4534
Cape Coral *(G-1314)*

Botanica Odomiwale Corp ....G 305 381-5834
Hialeah *(G-5078)*

Cansortium Charities Inc ....E 305 902-2720
Miami *(G-8885)*

Cls Holdings Usa Inc ....E 888 438-9132
Pinecrest *(G-13665)*

Concentrated Aloe Corp ....G 386 673-7566
Ormond Beach *(G-12753)*

Coterie Care Inc ....F 850 325-0422
Fort Walton Beach *(G-4571)*

Diamond Wellness Holdings Inc ....G 800 433-0127
Fort Lauderdale *(G-3764)*

Generex Laboratories LLC ....G 239 592-7255
Naples *(G-10760)*

Immudyne Nutritional LLC ....G 914 714-8901
Pensacola *(G-13523)*

Lotus Stress Relief LLC ....F 941 706-2778
Sarasota *(G-15727)*

Macrocap Labs Inc ....E 321 234-6282
Longwood *(G-7919)*

Midway Labs Usa LLC ....F 561 571-6252
Boca Raton *(G-598)*

Morgannas Alchemy LLC ....G 727 505-8376
New Port Richey *(G-10975)*

Natural Immunogenics Corp ....D 888 328-8840
Sarasota *(G-15525)*

Natures Bounty Co ....D 800 327-0908
Boca Raton *(G-610)*

Natures Clear LLC ....G 561 503-1751
Lake Worth *(G-7222)*

One Innovation Labs Llc ....E 305 985-3950
  Miami Lakes (G-10333)
Pain Away LLC ....F 800 215-8739
  Deland (G-2892)
Palmate LLC ....E 352 508-7800
  Tavares (G-17520)
Pharmco Laboratories Inc ....G 321 268-1313
  Titusville (G-17607)
Purovite Inc ....F 305 364-5727
  Miami (G-9759)
Socati Corp ....F 503 634-2378
  Plantation (G-13890)
Socratic Solutions Inc ....G 813 324-7018
  Brandon (G-1109)
Stem Holdings Inc ....E 561 948-5410
  Boca Raton (G-696)
Stem Holdings Florida Inc ....G 561 948-5410
  Boca Raton (G-697)
Terry Laboratories LLC ....F 321 259-1630
  Melbourne (G-8549)
Thunder Energies Corporation ....G 786 855-6190
  Hollywood (G-5670)
Twinlab Corporation ....G 800 645-5626
  Boca Raton (G-728)
Twinlab Holdings Inc ....D 800 645-5626
  Boca Raton (G-730)
Ultimaxx Inc ....F 877 300-3424
  Boca Raton (G-731)
Upexi Inc ....G 701 353-5425
  Clearwater (G-1840)
Veritas Farms Inc ....F 561 288-6603
  Fort Lauderdale (G-4117)
World Perfumes Inc ....F 305 822-0004
  Opa Locka (G-11800)

PHOSPHATE ROCK MINING

Mineral Development LLC ....F 863 354-3113
  Mulberry (G-10633)
White Springs AG Chem Inc ......A 386 397-8101
  White Springs (G-18307)

PHOSPHATES

Bastech Inc ....F 904 737-1722
  Jacksonville (G-5924)
Novaphos Inc ....E 863 285-8607
  Fort Meade (G-4151)
White Springs AG Chem Inc ......A 386 397-8101
  White Springs (G-18307)

PHOTO RECONNAISSANCE SYSTEMS

Moog Inc ....F 321 435-8722
  Orlando (G-12389)

PHOTOCOPY MACHINE REPAIR SVCS

Sun Print Management LLC ....E 727 945-0255
  Holiday (G-5504)
Toner Technologies Inc ....G 561 547-9710
  Boynton Beach (G-920)

PHOTOCOPY MACHINES

Florida Copier Connections ......G 407 844-9690
  Orlando (G-12160)

PHOTOCOPY SPLYS WHOLESALERS

Discount Distributors Inc ....G 772 336-0092
  Port Saint Lucie (G-14407)

PHOTOCOPYING & DUPLICATING SVCS

352ink Corp ....G 352 373-7547
  Gainesville (G-4643)
B J and ME Inc ....G 561 368-5470
  Boca Raton (G-424)
Customer First Inc Naples ....E 239 949-8518
  Bonita Springs (G-793)
G S Printers Inc ....G 305 931-2755
  Fort Lauderdale (G-3834)
Garvin Management Company Inc ......G 850 893-4719
  Tallahassee (G-16445)
Goforit Inc ....G 727 785-7616
  Palm Harbor (G-13111)
Hobby Press Inc ....E 305 887-4333
  Medley (G-8253)
Instant Printing Services Inc ......F 727 546-8036
  Floral City (G-3611)
J V G Inc ....G 727 584-7136
  Largo (G-7619)

Linden-Beals Corp ....G 772 562-0624
  Vero Beach (G-17773)
Ocala Print Quick Inc ....G 352 629-0736
  Ocala (G-11458)
Palm Prnting/Printers Ink Corp ....E 239 332-8600
  Fort Myers (G-4355)
Palmetto Printing Inc ....F 305 253-2444
  Miami (G-9685)
Print One Inc ....G 813 273-0240
  Oldsmar (G-11691)
Printers of Pensacola LLC ....G 850 434-2588
  Pensacola (G-13585)
Reimink Printing Inc ....G 813 289-4663
  Tampa (G-17214)
Tru Dimensions Printing Inc ......G 407 339-3410
  Longwood (G-7954)

PHOTOGRAPHIC EQPT & SPLYS

Aigean Networks ....G 754 223-2240
  Oakland Park (G-11234)
AVI-Spl Holdings Inc ....A 866 708-5034
  Tampa (G-16619)
AVI-Spl LLC ....B 813 884-7168
  Tampa (G-16620)
Cinidyne Sales Inc ....G 941 473-3914
  Englewood (G-3527)
Dale Photo and Digital Inc ....F 954 925-0103
  Hollywood (G-5560)
Discount Distributors Inc ....G 772 336-0092
  Port Saint Lucie (G-14407)
Faf Distribution LLC ....G 561 717-3353
  Boca Raton (G-511)
Innovate Audio Visual Inc ....G 561 249-1117
  Wellington (G-17853)
Lester A Dine Inc ....G 561 624-3009
  Palm Beach Gardens (G-12984)
Light Source Business Systems ....F 772 562-5046
  Port Saint Lucie (G-14423)
Lip Trading Co ....G 954 987-0306
  Hollywood (G-5612)
Teledyne Flir LLC ....D 407 816-0091
  Orlando (G-12649)
Xerox Business Services LLC ......G 407 926-4228
  Orlando (G-12721)

PHOTOGRAPHIC EQPT & SPLYS WHOLESALERS

Lip Trading Co ....G 954 987-0306
  Hollywood (G-5612)

PHOTOGRAPHIC EQPT & SPLYS, WHOLESALE: Project, Motion/Slide

AVI-Spl LLC ....B 813 884-7168
  Tampa (G-16620)

PHOTOGRAPHIC EQPT & SPLYS: Cameras, Aerial

Harris Aerial LLC ....F 407 725-7886
  Casselberry (G-1418)

PHOTOGRAPHIC EQPT & SPLYS: Film, Sensitized

Eastman Kodak Company ....D 813 908-7910
  Tampa (G-16794)

PHOTOGRAPHIC EQPT & SPLYS: Plates, Sensitized

Photoengraving Inc ....E 813 253-3427
  Tampa (G-17165)

PHOTOGRAPHIC EQPT & SPLYS: Printing Eqpt

ID Print Inc ....G 954 923-8374
  Plantation (G-13858)
Tonertype Inc ....E 813 915-1300
  Tampa (G-17360)

PHOTOGRAPHIC EQPT & SPLYS: Printing Frames

Chez Industries LLC ....F 386 698-4414
  Crescent City (G-2235)

PHOTOGRAPHIC EQPT & SPLYS: Reels, Film

Premier Plastics LLC ....G 305 805-3333
  Boynton Beach (G-899)

PHOTOGRAPHIC EQPT & SPLYS: Toners, Prprd, Not Chem Plnts

Bdt Concepts Inc ....G 904 730-2590
  Jacksonville (G-5926)
Globaltek Office Supply Inc ....G 305 477-2988
  Sweetwater (G-16403)
Ink & Toner Plus ....G 813 783-1650
  Dade City (G-2319)
Toner City Corp ....G 954 945-5392
  Davie (G-2491)

PHOTOVOLTAIC Solid State

Solar Electric Power Company ....F 772 220-6615
  Stuart (G-16224)
Sollunar Energy Inc ....G 352 293-2347
  Spring Hill (G-16080)

PICTURE FRAMES: Metal

Dillco Inc ....F 386 734-7510
  Deland (G-2865)
Russell Hobbs Inc ....D 954 883-1000
  Miramar (G-10538)

PICTURE FRAMES: Wood

Art & Frame Direct Inc ....C 407 857-6000
  Orlando (G-11923)
Art Connection Usa LLC ....E 954 781-0125
  Pompano Beach (G-13935)
Florida Frames Inc ....F 727 572-4064
  Clearwater (G-1600)
Frametastic Inc ....E 954 567-2800
  Fort Lauderdale (G-3830)
Miami Decor Inc ....G 800 235-2197
  Miami (G-9550)
Russell Hobbs Inc ....D 954 883-1000
  Miramar (G-10538)
Total Vision Design Group ....F 407 438-6933
  Orlando (G-12663)

PICTURE PROJECTION EQPT

3d Perception Inc ....F 321 235-7999
  Orlando (G-11850)

PIECE GOODS & NOTIONS WHOLESALERS

Bespoke Stitchery LLC ....G 407 412-9937
  Orlando (G-11945)
Valley Forge Textiles LLC ....G 954 971-1776
  Pompano Beach (G-14233)

PIECE GOODS, NOTIONS & DRY GOODS, WHOL: Textiles, Woven

Stanley Industries of S Fla ....G 954 929-8770
  Hollywood (G-5664)

PIECE GOODS, NOTIONS & DRY GOODS, WHOLESALE: Fabrics

Andirali Corporation ....G 305 542-5374
  Miami (G-8730)
J & H Supply Co Inc ....G 561 582-3346
  Lake Worth (G-7207)

PIECE GOODS, NOTIONS & DRY GOODS, WHOLESALE: Fabrics, Knit

Superior Shade & Blind Co Inc ....E 954 975-8122
  Coral Springs (G-2215)

PIECE GOODS, NOTIONS & OTHER DRY GOODS, WHOLESALE: Buttons

Promo Daddy LLC ....F 877 557-2336
  Melbourne (G-8501)

PIECE GOODS, NOTIONS & OTHER DRY GOODS, WHOLESALE: Notions

Florida Thread & Trimming ....F 954 240-2474
  Hialeah (G-5159)

PIECE GOODS, NOTIONS & OTHER DRY GOODS, WHOLESALE: Ribbons

Design Services Inc ....G...... 813 949-4748
   Land O Lakes (G-7491)

PIECE GOODS, NOTIONS/DRY GOODS, WHOL: Drapery Mtrl, Woven

Kenco Quilting & Textiles Inc ....F 954 921-5434
   Fort Lauderdale (G-3905)

PIECE GOODS, NOTIONS/DRY GOODS, WHOL: Fabrics, Synthetic

Ascend Prfmce Mtls Oprtons LLC........A 850 968-7000
   Cantonment (G-1265)
Texene LLC ....F 305 200-5001
   Miami Lakes (G-10364)

PIGMENTS, INORGANIC: Black

Pigments Black Diamond ....G 904 241-2533
   Saint Augustine (G-14872)

PILING: Prefabricated, Concrete

Henderson Prestress Con Inc................F 727 938-2828
   Tarpon Springs (G-17474)
Wills Prestress Inc ....F 239 417-9117
   Naples (G-10939)

PILOT SVCS: Aviation

ELite Intl Group LLC ....F 305 901-5005
   Miami (G-9086)
Florida Sncast Helicopters LLC............F 941 355-1525
   Sarasota (G-15477)
Flyteone Inc ....G 813 421-1410
   Clearwater (G-1603)
Heli Aviation Florida LLC ....G 941 355-1525
   Sarasota (G-15489)
Helicopter Helmet LLC ....G 843 556-0405
   Melbourne (G-8434)

PINS

Naples Hma LLC ....F 239 390-2174
   Estero (G-3547)
Pin King LLC ....G 561 622-6367
   Palm Beach Gardens (G-12999)
Pin-N-Win Wrestling Club Inc ....G 904 276-8038
   Orange Park (G-11837)
Sin Pin Inc ....G 877 805-5665
   Stuart (G-16221)
Xue Wu Inc ....G 727 532-4571
   Clearwater (G-1858)

PINS: Dowel

Dowels Pins & Shafts Inc ....F 727 461-1255
   Clearwater (G-1569)

PIPE & FITTING: Fabrication

Alumacart Inc ....F 772 675-2158
   Indiantown (G-5811)
ARC-Rite Inc ....E 386 325-3523
   Jacksonville (G-5897)
Cantex Inc ....D 863 967-4161
   Auburndale (G-221)
Custom Tube Products Inc ....F 386 426-0670
   Edgewater (G-3488)
Customfab Inc ....G 786 339-9158
   Homestead (G-5705)
Energy Task Force LLC ....F 407 523-3770
   Apopka (G-126)
Etf West LLC ....F 407 523-3770
   Apopka (G-129)
Formweld Fitting Inc ....E 850 626-4888
   Milton (G-10424)
GPM Fab & Supply LLC ....G 813 689-7107
   Seffner (G-15961)
Gulf Atlantic Culvert Company ....F 850 562-2384
   Tallahassee (G-16454)
Hines Bending Systems Inc ....F 239 433-2132
   Fort Myers (G-4280)
Insulation Design & Dist LLC ....G 850 332-7312
   Cantonment (G-1269)
Jensen Scientific Products Inc.............E 954 344-2006
   Coral Springs (G-2169)
Marine Exhaust Systems Inc ....D 561 848-1238
   Riviera Beach (G-14645)

MPH Industries Inc ....F 352 372-9533
   Gainesville (G-4735)
Peterson Manufacturing LLC ....E 941 371-4989
   Sarasota (G-15782)
Petrotech Services Inc ....D 813 248-0743
   Tampa (G-17158)
Petrotech Services Inc ....G 813 248-0743
   Tampa (G-17159)
Pipeline Fabricators Inc ....F 863 678-0977
   Lake Wales (G-7170)
Price Brothers Company ....G 386 328-8841
   Palatka (G-12878)
Shafers Clssic Rprductions Inc ....G 813 622-7091
   Tampa (G-17255)
Specialty Maintenance & Constr ....G 863 644-8432
   Lakeland (G-7447)
Star Products ....G 407 929-6969
   Orlando (G-12622)
Strongbridge International LLC ....E 904 278-7499
   Orange Park (G-11842)
Sunshine Piping Inc ....E 850 763-4834
   Panama City (G-13312)
Townley Engrg & Mfg Co Inc ....C 352 687-3001
   Candler (G-1261)
US Pipe Fabrication LLC ....D 860 769-6097
   Orlando (G-12694)

PIPE & FITTINGS: Cast Iron

Custom Flange Pipe LLC ....E 863 353-6602
   Winter Haven (G-18433)
Urecon Systems Inc.............................E 904 695-3332
   Winter Park (G-18549)

PIPE & FITTINGS: Pressure, Cast Iron

Forterra Pressure Pipe Inc ....C 386 328-8841
   Palatka (G-12868)

PIPE & TUBES: Copper & Copper Alloy

Kme Amrica Mar Tube Ftting LLC ....D 904 265-4001
   Jacksonville (G-6245)
Mueller Industries Inc ....C 901 753-3200
   West Palm Beach (G-18082)

PIPE JOINT COMPOUNDS

Continental Palatka LLC.......................D 703 480-3800
   Palatka (G-12864)

PIPE, CULVERT: Concrete

Wheeler Lumber LLC ....F 772 464-4400
   Fort Pierce (G-4554)

PIPE, CYLINDER: Concrete, Prestressed Or Pretensioned

Nuflo Inc ....E 904 265-4001
   Jacksonville (G-6340)

PIPE: Concrete

Cemex Cnstr Mtls Fla LLC ....G 800 992-3639
   Oldsmar (G-11637)
Cemex Materials LLC............................C 561 833-5555
   West Palm Beach (G-17962)
Cemex Materials LLC............................C 352 435-0783
   Okahumpka (G-11595)
Cemex Materials LLC............................C 305 558-0315
   Miami (G-8910)
Florida Concrete Pipe Corp ....E 352 742-2232
   Astatula (G-199)
Mancini Inc ....E 954 583-7220
   Pompano Beach (G-14086)
RMC Ewell Inc ....E 850 879-0959
   Niceville (G-11036)
RMC Ewell Inc ....G 850 863-5040
   Fort Walton Beach (G-4605)
RMC Ewell Inc ....F 407 282-0984
   Orlando (G-12558)
Valmont Newmark Inc ....E 863 533-6465
   Bartow (G-328)

PIPE: Irrigation, Sheet Metal

Home & Garden Industries Inc ....F 305 634-0681
   Miami (G-9289)

PIPE: Plastic

Accord Industries LLC ....D 407 671-6989
   Winter Park (G-18480)

Advanced Drainage Systems Inc ....C 407 654-3989
   Winter Garden (G-18372)
Advantage Earth Products Inc..............F 904 329-1430
   Saint Augustine (G-14806)
Aei International Corp ....G 904 724-9771
   Jacksonville (G-5865)
Atkore Plastic Pipe Corp ....F 813 884-2525
   Tampa (G-16616)
C & S Plastics ....E 863 294-5628
   Winter Haven (G-18427)
Cantex Inc ....D 863 967-4161
   Auburndale (G-221)
Ciro Manufacturing Corporation ....E 561 988-2139
   Deerfield Beach (G-2693)
Dixie Sptic Tank Orange Cy LLC ....E 386 775-3051
   Orange City (G-11805)
Hancor Inc ....E 863 655-5499
   Winter Garden (G-18388)
Maruti Technology Inc ....G 407 704-4775
   Orlando (G-12364)
Sanderson Pipe Corporation ....E 904 275-3289
   Sanderson (G-15255)
Taylor Made Plastics Inc ....G 941 926-0200
   Sarasota (G-15853)
Wellstream International Ltd..................C 850 636-4800
   Panama City (G-13320)

PIPE: Seamless Steel

Berg Pipe Panama City Corp ....C 850 769-2273
   Panama City (G-13232)

PIPE: Sheet Metal

Dcr Fabrication Inc ....E 863 709-1121
   Lakeland (G-7306)
Gulf Atlantic Culvert Company ....F 850 562-2384
   Tallahassee (G-16454)
Mechanical Svcs Centl Fla Inc ....C 407 857-3510
   Orlando (G-12368)
Metal 2 Metal Inc ....G 954 253-9450
   Palmetto Bay (G-13214)

PIPES & FITTINGS: Fiber, Made From Purchased Materials

Rotary Manufacturing LLC....................G 941 564-8038
   North Port (G-11204)

PIPES & TUBES

American Vinyl Company.......................F 813 663-0157
   Tampa (G-16592)

PIPES & TUBES: Steel

Accord Industries LLC ....D 407 671-6989
   Winter Park (G-18480)
Allied Tube & Conduit...........................G 813 623-2681
   Tampa (G-16577)
Allsteel Processing LC ....F 954 587-1900
   Fort Lauderdale (G-3646)
Alpha Advantage America LLC ....G 305 671-3990
   Sunny Isles Beach (G-16268)
Atkore International Inc.........................F 800 882-5543
   Boca Raton (G-419)
Cmn Steel Fabricators Inc....................D 305 592-5466
   Miami (G-8934)
Custom Fab Inc ....D 407 859-3954
   Orlando (G-12067)
GPM Fab & Supply LLC ....G 813 689-7107
   Seffner (G-15961)
Metal Culverts Inc ....F 727 531-1431
   Clearwater (G-1694)
Neptune Research Inc ....E 561 683-6992
   Riviera Beach (G-14650)
Primary Metals Intl LLC ....G 800 243-1923
   Cape Coral (G-1375)
Sanitube LLC ....G 863 606-5960
   Lakeland (G-7429)
Southstern Indus Fbrcators LLC...........E 941 776-1211
   Duette (G-3433)
Specialty Steel Holdco Inc ....G 305 375-7560
   Miami (G-9939)
Theclipcom Inc ....G 305 599-3871
   Tavernier (G-17532)
Value Providers LLC ....G 321 567-0919
   Daytona Beach (G-2617)
Wellstream International Ltd..................C 850 636-4800
   Panama City (G-13320)

PIPES & TUBES: Welded

Florida Steam Services Inc ....G....... 407 247-8250
Geneva **(G-4789)**

PIPES: Steel & Iron

Berg Europipe Holding Corp ....C....... 850 769-2273
Panama City **(G-13231)**

Chemko Technical Services Inc ....E....... 954 783-7673
Pompano Beach **(G-13969)**

H & M Steel ....G....... 904 765-3465
Jacksonville **(G-6163)**

US Pipe Fabrication LLC ....D....... 860 769-6097
Orlando **(G-12694)**

PIPES: Tobacco

Spliffpuff LLC ....F....... 786 493-4529
Doral **(G-3373)**

PLANING MILL, NEC

Idaho Timber LLC ....D....... 386 758-8111
Lake City **(G-7025)**

PLANING MILLS: Millwork

Synergy Thermal Foils Inc ....F....... 954 420-9553
Coral Springs **(G-2217)**

PLANTERS: Plastic

Bloem LLC ....F....... 407 889-5533
Apopka **(G-108)**

PLAQUES: Picture, Laminated

American Trophy Co ....G....... 954 782-2250
Pompano Beach **(G-13928)**

Art & Frame Direct Inc ....C....... 407 857-6000
Orlando **(G-11923)**

Clifton Studio Inc ....G....... 813 240-0286
Tampa **(G-16715)**

In The News Inc ....D....... 813 882-8886
Tampa **(G-16935)**

Parrillo Inc ....G....... 386 767-8011
South Daytona **(G-16026)**

Williams Jewelry and Mfg Co ....G....... 727 823-7676
Saint Petersburg **(G-15234)**

PLASMAS

Advanced Bioservices LLC................C....... 850 476-7999
Pensacola **(G-13436)**

Hemarus Llc-Jcksnvle Plsma Ctr ....G....... 904 642-1005
Jupiter **(G-6741)**

Inter Cell Technologies Inc ....G....... 561 575-6868
Jupiter **(G-6747)**

Plasma Biolife Services L P ....G....... 407 388-1052
Casselberry **(G-1429)**

Plasma Creations LLC......................G....... 561 324-8214
West Palm Beach **(G-18122)**

Plasma Cutting LLC ....G....... 954 558-1371
Hallandale **(G-4928)**

Plasma Energy Group LLC ....F....... 813 760-6385
Odessa **(G-11570)**

PLASTER WORK: Ornamental & Architectural

Green Forest Industries Inc ....E....... 941 721-0504
Palmetto **(G-13169)**

PLASTIC PRDTS

Acacia Inc ....F....... 813 253-2789
Tampa **(G-16555)**

Aqua Technologies ....G....... 305 246-2125
Homestead **(G-5699)**

Envirosafe Technologies Inc ....G....... 904 646-3456
Jacksonville **(G-6077)**

Jar-Den Llc ....G....... 860 334-7539
Port Richey **(G-14366)**

Latham Plastics Inc ....G....... 813 783-7212
Zephyrhills **(G-18619)**

Parras Plastic Inc ....G....... 305 972-9537
Miami **(G-9695)**

Profbox of America Inc ....G....... 786 454-8148
North Miami Beach **(G-11157)**

Rosier Manufacturing Company........G....... 386 409-7223
Daytona Beach **(G-2591)**

Semplastics ....F....... 407 353-6885
Oviedo **(G-12847)**

Specialties Unlimited ....G....... 239 482-8433
Fort Myers **(G-4404)**

Wb Medical Transport LLC ....G....... 561 827-8877
Port Saint Lucie **(G-14465)**

Zeus Industries ....G....... 727 530-4373
Largo **(G-7710)**

PLASTICS FILM & SHEET

Designer Films Inc ....F....... 305 828-0605
Hialeah **(G-5115)**

Falken Design Corporation ....G....... 765 688-0809
Miami **(G-9131)**

Flexsol Holding Corp........................E....... 954 941-6333
Pompano Beach **(G-14031)**

King Plastic Corporation ....C....... 941 423-8666
North Port **(G-11197)**

Piedmont Plastics Inc ....D....... 386 274-4627
Daytona Beach **(G-2582)**

Sungraf Inc ....G....... 954 456-8500
Hallandale Beach **(G-4976)**

PLASTICS FILM & SHEET: Polyethylene

Essex Plastics Midwest LLC Lc ....A....... 954 956-1100
Pompano Beach **(G-14014)**

PLASTICS FILM & SHEET: Vinyl

Dynamic Visions Inc ....E....... 941 497-1984
Venice **(G-17685)**

Real Gold Inc ....G....... 386 873-4849
Deland **(G-2897)**

Recycled Vinyl ....G....... 727 434-1857
Sarasota **(G-15794)**

PLASTICS FINISHED PRDTS: Laminated

Acryplex Inc ....G....... 305 633-7636
Miami **(G-8648)**

Enduris Extrusions Inc ....E....... 904 421-3304
Jacksonville **(G-6074)**

Fisher Cabinet Company LLC ....E....... 850 944-4171
Pensacola **(G-13503)**

Institutional Products Inc ....E....... 305 248-4955
Homestead **(G-5717)**

Neptune Tech Services Inc ....E....... 904 646-2700
Jacksonville **(G-6323)**

Redbud Enterprises Inc ....E....... 386 752-5696
Lake City **(G-7042)**

Streamline Extrusion Inc ....F....... 727 796-4277
Safety Harbor **(G-14799)**

Suncoast Identification Tech ....G....... 239 277-9922
Fort Myers **(G-4411)**

PLASTICS MATERIAL & RESINS

3 Miracles Corporation ....G....... 407 796-9292
Orlando **(G-11849)**

Advanced Composite Systems ....F....... 904 765-6502
Jacksonville **(G-5861)**

ALLEZ LLC ....F....... 205 216-6330
Plantation **(G-13823)**

Amcor Flexibles LLC ....E....... 954 499-4800
Miramar **(G-10468)**

American Polymer Company ....F....... 786 877-4690
Pompano Beach **(G-13927)**

Anchor Coatings Leesburg Inc..........E....... 352 728-0777
Leesburg **(G-7759)**

Ascend Performance Mtls Inc............B....... 850 968-7000
Cantonment **(G-1264)**

Ascend Prfmce Mtls Oprtons LLC........C....... 734 819-0656
Gulf Breeze **(G-4876)**

Ascend Prfmce Mtls Oprtons LLC........A....... 850 968-7000
Cantonment **(G-1265)**

Atlantic Marble Company Inc............F....... 904 262-6262
Jacksonville **(G-5909)**

Atlas Polymers Corp........................F....... 786 312-2131
Miami **(G-8769)**

Autisan International Inc ....G....... 941 349-7029
Sarasota **(G-15606)**

Automated Services Inc ....F....... 772 461-3388
Fort Pierce **(G-4468)**

Avon Assoc ....G....... 561 391-7188
Boca Raton **(G-421)**

Blue Water Dynamics LLC ....D....... 386 957-5464
Edgewater **(G-3482)**

Braden Kitchens Inc ....E....... 321 636-4700
Cocoa **(G-1907)**

Carpenter Co ....D....... 863 687-9494
Lakeland **(G-7288)**

Cellofoam North America Inc ....D....... 407 888-4667
Orlando **(G-11990)**

Charles K Sewell ....G....... 407 423-1870
Orlando **(G-12005)**

Coosa LLC ....G....... 904 268-1187
Jacksonville **(G-6004)**

Creative Countertops Inc ....F....... 904 387-2800
Jacksonville **(G-6011)**

Cup Plus USA ....G....... 321 972-1968
Winter Park **(G-18501)**

Designers Tops Inc ....G....... 305 599-9973
Miami **(G-9023)**

Dynamic Material Systems LLC ....G....... 407 353-6885
Oviedo **(G-12818)**

Eastman Chemical Company ....G....... 305 671-2800
Miami **(G-9062)**

F O F Plastics Inc ....G....... 727 937-2144
Tarpon Springs **(G-17471)**

Fairing Xchange LLC ....G....... 904 589-5253
Orange Park **(G-11827)**

Fiberflon Usa Inc ....G....... 786 953-7329
Miami **(G-9140)**

G Phillips and Sons LLC ....F....... 248 705-5873
Sarasota **(G-15688)**

Global Holdings and Dev LLC ....G....... 949 500-4997
Pompano Beach **(G-14041)**

Huntsman Properties LLC ....E....... 305 653-2288
Miami **(G-9292)**

Industrial Plastic Pdts Inc ....E....... 305 822-3223
Miami Lakes **(G-10307)**

Ineos New Planet Bioenergy LLC........E....... 772 794-7900
Vero Beach **(G-17764)**

International Composite ....E....... 206 349-7468
Sarasota **(G-15706)**

Jrf Technology LLC ....F....... 813 443-5273
Tampa **(G-16972)**

Linkpoint LLC ....F....... 305 903-9191
Key Biscayne **(G-6836)**

Matrix Composites Inc......................C....... 321 633-4480
Rockledge **(G-14731)**

Nida-Core Corporation ....E....... 772 343-7300
Port Saint Lucie **(G-14428)**

Olevin Compounds LLC ....E....... 954 993-5148
Miramar **(G-10522)**

Orca Composites LLC ....E....... 206 349-5300
Sarasota **(G-15771)**

Pacific Limited International ....G....... 305 358-1900
Miami **(G-9676)**

Pacific Ltd Corp ....G....... 305 358-1900
Miami **(G-9677)**

Paradigm Plastics Inc ....G....... 727 797-3555
Safety Harbor **(G-14794)**

Plastic Masters International ....F....... 386 312-9775
East Palatka **(G-3474)**

Plastic Trading Intl Inc ....E....... 863 688-1983
Lakeland **(G-7409)**

Plastics America Inc ....G....... 813 620-3711
Tampa **(G-17168)**

Poly-Chem Corp ....G....... 305 593-1928
Miami **(G-9728)**

Polymersan LLC ....G....... 305 887-3824
Hialeah **(G-5296)**

Pro Poly of America Inc ....E....... 352 629-1414
Ocala **(G-11473)**

Profab Corporation ....G....... 352 369-5010
Ocala **(G-11474)**

Profab Corporation ....F....... 352 369-5515
Ocala **(G-11475)**

Ravago Americas LLC ....A....... 407 773-7777
Orlando **(G-12531)**

Ravago Holdings America Inc ....D....... 407 875-9595
Orlando **(G-12532)**

Rayonier A M Products Inc ....D....... 904 357-9100
Jacksonville **(G-6405)**

Rayonier Advanced Mtls Inc ....G....... 904 261-3611
Fernandina Beach **(G-3597)**

Saint-Gobain Prfmce Plas Corp........C....... 727 531-4191
Clearwater **(G-1775)**

Stm Industries LLC ....F....... 813 854-3544
Tampa **(G-17304)**

Stoltz Industries Inc ....F....... 954 792-3270
Davie **(G-2482)**

Teak Isle Inc ....C....... 407 656-8885
Ocoee **(G-11527)**

TEC Composites Inc ....G....... 904 765-6502
Jacksonville **(G-6537)**

The Hc Companies Inc ....D....... 863 314-9417
Sebring **(G-15947)**

Thermo Compaction Systems Inc........G....... 863 370-3799
Lakeland **(G-7460)**

Tradepak Inc ....G....... 305 871-2247
Miami **(G-10033)**

2022 Harris Florida
Manufacturers Directory

(G-0000) Company's Geographic Section entry number

U S Composites Inc ....G.....561 588-1001
West Palm Beach (G-18189)
US Blanks LLC ....E.....321 253-3626
Melbourne (G-8556)
US Composites ....G.....561 588-1001
Riviera Beach (G-14685)
Wheeler Lumber LLC ....F.....772 464-4400
Fort Pierce (G-4554)

PLASTICS MATERIALS, BASIC FORMS & SHAPES WHOLESALERS

Finyl Products Inc.....................G.....352 351-4033
Ocala (G-11388)
Peter T Amann..........................G.....561 848-2770
West Palm Beach (G-18118)

PLASTICS PROCESSING

Bio Bubble Pets LLC ....F.....561 998-5350
West Palm Beach (G-17944)
Conrad Plastics LLC ....G.....954 391-9515
Hallandale Beach (G-4942)
JW Austin Industries Inc ....G.....321 723-2422
Melbourne (G-8447)
Laser Creations Incorporated ....E.....800 771-7151
Apopka (G-146)
Marlon Inc ....F.....813 901-8488
Tampa (G-17041)
Maxi-Blast of Florida Inc ....G.....727 572-0909
Saint Petersburg (G-15122)
Midgard Inc ....D.....863 696-1224
Lake Wales (G-7168)
Mpc Group LLC ....G.....773 927-4120
Deland (G-2889)
Noveltex Miami Inc ....E.....305 887-8191
Hialeah (G-5282)
Plastic Composites Inc ....F.....352 669-5822
Umatilla (G-17650)
Precision Concepts (miami) LLC...........D.....305 825-5244
Hialeah (G-5299)
Rainbow Pool Supply Inc ....F.....407 324-9616
Sanford (G-15380)
Sippers By Design ....G.....305 371-5087
Miami (G-9899)

PLASTICS SHEET: Packing Materials

Barco Sales & Mfg Inc ....F.....954 563-3922
Oakland Park (G-11245)
Ifco Systems Us LLC ....E.....813 463-4103
Tampa (G-16931)
J & D Manufacturing Inc ....F.....813 854-1700
Oldsmar (G-11662)
Serv-Pak Corp ....F.....954 962-4262
Hollywood (G-5656)

PLASTICS: Blow Molded

Chrom Industries LLC ....E.....954 400-5135
Fort Lauderdale (G-3725)
Liqui-Box Corporation ....E.....863 676-7602
Lake Wales (G-7166)
Safariland LLC ....E.....904 646-0141
Jacksonville (G-6445)

PLASTICS: Carbohydrate

Plastirex LLC ....F.....305 471-1111
Avon Park (G-285)

PLASTICS: Extruded

American Products Inc..............G.....813 925-0144
Tampa (G-16590)
American Thrmplastic Extrusion...........C.....305 769-9566
Opa Locka (G-11716)
C & S Plastics..........................E.....863 294-5628
Winter Haven (G-18427)
Emmanuel Holdings Inc ....E.....305 558-3088
Miami (G-9096)
Jmh Marine Inc.........................F.....954 785-7557
Pompano Beach (G-14067)
Melt-Tech Polymers Inc ....G.....305 887-6148
Medley (G-8278)
Shoreline Plastics LLC ....E.....904 696-2981
Jacksonville (G-6466)

PLASTICS: Finished Injection Molded

Apollo Renal Therapeutics LLC.........E.....202 413-0963
Ocala (G-11326)

ARC Acquisition Corp ....E.....386 626-0005
Deland (G-2852)
Delta Machine & Tool Inc ....E.....386 738-2204
Deland (G-2863)
Diamond Precision Machine Inc...........F.....321 729-8453
Palm Bay (G-12896)
Ehud Industries Inc ....G.....904 803-0873
Jacksonville (G-6068)
Eurogan-Usa Inc ....F.....321 356-5248
Orlando (G-12137)
Florida Production Engrg Inc ....C.....386 677-2566
Ormond Beach (G-12765)
Hardware Concepts Inc ....G.....305 685-1337
Miami (G-9262)
Integrated Components Corp ....F.....305 824-0484
Hialeah (G-5194)
M O Precision Molders Inc ....F.....727 573-4466
Clearwater (G-1678)
Mid-Florida Plastics Inc ....E.....407 856-1805
Orlando (G-12379)
Nanotechnovation Corporation...........E.....352 732-3244
Ocala (G-11449)
National Molding LLC ....F.....727 546-7470
Largo (G-7649)
Plastic Concepts & Designs Inc...........G.....904 396-7500
Jacksonville (G-6375)
Rainbow Precision Mfg Corp ....G.....561 691-1658
Palm Beach Gardens (G-13005)
Tuthill Corporation ....D.....727 446-8593
Clearwater (G-1836)
William B Rudow Inc ....G.....941 957-4200
Sarasota (G-15875)

PLASTICS: Injection Molded

7 Plastics Inc ....F.....407 321-5441
Longwood (G-7862)
A 1 Fabrications Inc ....G.....352 410-0752
Weeki Wachee (G-17834)
Absolute Plastic Solutions Inc ....E.....239 313-7779
Fort Myers (G-4154)
Acai Investments Llc ....G.....305 821-8872
Hialeah (G-5025)
Accu Metal ....G.....850 912-4855
Pensacola (G-13432)
Accu Tech LLC ....G.....407 446-6676
Groveland (G-4857)
Acrylic Images Inc ....F.....954 484-6633
Oakland Park (G-11233)
Advanced Air International Inc ....E.....561 845-8212
Riviera Beach (G-14588)
AIN Plastics of Florida Inc ....F.....813 242-6400
Riverview (G-14557)
Allied General Engrv & Plas...........F.....305 626-6585
Opa Locka (G-11715)
American Molding & Plas LLC...........G.....561 734-4194
Delray Beach (G-2931)
American Molding and Plas LLC...........F.....561 676-1987
Boynton Beach (G-840)
American Plastic Sup & Mfg Inc...........E.....727 573-0636
Clearwater (G-1491)
American Technical Molding Inc...........D.....727 447-7377
Clearwater (G-1492)
American Tool & Mold Inc ....C.....727 447-7377
Clearwater (G-1493)
Atlantic Molding Inc..................F.....954 781-9340
Pompano Beach (G-13941)
Automated Mfg Systems Inc...........G.....561 833-9898
Mangonia Park (G-8088)
Ayanna Plastics & Engrg Inc ....E.....727 561-4329
Clearwater (G-1505)
B & D Precision Tools Inc ....E.....305 885-1583
Hialeah (G-5065)
B & R Sales Corporation ....G.....727 571-2231
Clearwater (G-1507)
Better Plastics Inc....................G.....407 480-2909
Orlando (G-11947)
Big Sun Plastics Inc ....G.....352 671-1844
Ocala (G-11335)
C & J Industries Inc ....F.....386 589-4907
Ormond Beach (G-12748)
Cavaform Inc ....G.....727 384-3676
Saint Petersburg (G-15000)
Choice Tool & Mold LLC ....F.....941 371-6767
Sarasota (G-15632)
Covington Plastics Inc ....F.....321 632-6775
Cocoa (G-1912)
Covocup LLC............................G.....855 204-5106
Sarasota (G-15463)
Custom Plastic Card Company...........D.....954 426-1331
Deerfield Beach (G-2700)

Custom Plastic Developments...........D.....407 847-3054
Kissimmee (G-6910)
D M T Inc ....F.....321 267-3931
Cocoa (G-1914)
D-Rep Plastics Inc....................G.....407 240-4154
Clearwater (G-1561)
Diemold Machine Company Inc...........E.....239 482-1400
Fort Myers (G-4234)
Donarra Extrusions LLC ....G.....352 369-5552
Ocala (G-11370)
Doran Manufacturing Corp Fla...........G.....904 731-3313
Jacksonville (G-6038)
Dura-Cast Products Inc ....D.....863 638-3200
Lake Wales (G-7158)
Dynotec Plastic Inc ....G.....813 248-5335
Tampa (G-16790)
Ellis Family Holdings Inc ....F.....503 785-7400
Hialeah (G-5139)
Epic Extrusion Inc ....G.....941 378-0835
Sarasota (G-15666)
Euro Trim Inc ....F.....239 574-6646
Cape Coral (G-1339)
Excalibur Manufacturing Corp...........F.....352 544-0055
Brooksville (G-1155)
Extreme Coatings ....G.....727 528-7998
Saint Petersburg (G-15041)
Faulkner Inc of Miami ....F.....305 885-4731
Hialeah (G-5153)
Fimco Manufacturing Inc ....G.....561 624-3308
Jupiter (G-6728)
First Shot Mold and Tool ....G.....321 269-0031
Titusville (G-17585)
Florida Central Extrusion Inc...........G.....863 324-2541
Winter Haven (G-18438)
Florida Custom Mold Inc ....D.....813 343-5080
Odessa (G-11552)
Gator Polymers LLC ....G.....866 292-7306
Cape Coral (G-1346)
Gemini Group USA Inc ....F.....305 338-1066
Miami (G-9198)
Genca Corp..............................E.....727 524-3622
Clearwater (G-1612)
Gerogari Dsplay Mnfacture Corp...........G.....305 888-0993
Miami (G-9207)
Graduate Plastics Inc ....C.....305 687-0405
Miami (G-9230)
Gulf View Plastics Inc ....G.....727 379-3072
Hudson (G-5777)
Harbortech Plastics LLC ....F.....727 944-2425
Holiday (G-5498)
House Plastics Unlimited Inc...........E.....407 843-3290
Orlando (G-12227)
Industrial Plastic Pdts Inc ....E.....305 822-3223
Miami Lakes (G-10307)
Jarden Plastic Solutions ....G.....864 879-8100
Boca Raton (G-557)
Jdr and Associates Inc ....G.....941 926-1800
Sarasota (G-15713)
Jtf Ventures LLC ....G.....305 556-5156
Hialeah Gardens (G-5439)
K & I Creative Plas & WD LLC...........G.....904 923-0409
Jacksonville (G-6234)
Kinetic Industries LLC ....G.....727 572-7604
Clearwater (G-1661)
Kramski North America Inc...........F.....727 828-1500
Largo (G-7629)
L C Southwind Manufacturing...........F.....352 687-1999
Ocala (G-11423)
M & M Plastics Inc ....E.....305 688-4335
Miami (G-9489)
M & N Plastics ....G.....863 646-0208
Lakeland (G-7385)
M D R International Inc ....F.....305 944-5335
North Miami (G-11110)
Master Mold Corp ....G.....941 486-0000
North Venice (G-11214)
Master Tool Co Inc ....E.....305 557-1020
Miami Lakes (G-10318)
Mdi Products LLC ....F.....772 228-7371
Sebastian (G-15901)
Meltpoint Plastics Intl Inc ....E.....305 887-8020
Medley (G-8279)
Mikes Precision Inc..................G.....305 558-6421
Hialeah (G-5257)
Modern Tchncal Molding Dev LLC...........F.....727 343-2942
Saint Petersburg (G-15128)
Modular Molding Intl Inc ....E.....727 541-1333
Seminole (G-15984)
Molds and Plastic McHy Inc...........G.....305 828-3456
North Miami (G-11113)

National Molding LLC ....C 305 823-5440
Miami Lakes *(G-10329)*

Nelson Plastics Inc ....E 407 339-3570
Longwood *(G-7927)*

Novelty Crystal Corp ....G 352 429-9036
Groveland *(G-4867)*

Nylacarb Corp ....E 772 569-5999
Vero Beach *(G-17783)*

Nypro Inc ....F 727 577-9749
Saint Petersburg *(G-15143)*

Octex Holdings LLC ....E 941 371-6767
Sarasota *(G-15768)*

Paradigm Leaders LLC ....G 850 441-3289
Panama City Beach *(G-13336)*

Paragon Globl Sup Slutions LLC ....F 813 745-9902
Tampa *(G-17148)*

Paramount Mold LLC ....E 954 772-2333
Fort Lauderdale *(G-3975)*

Paramount Molded Products Inc ....E 954 772-2333
Fort Lauderdale *(G-3976)*

Plastic Concepts Ltd Inc ....F 727 942-6684
Tarpon Springs *(G-17487)*

Plastic Kingdom Inc ....G 561 586-9300
Lake Worth *(G-7227)*

Plastic Parts Inc ....E 954 974-3051
Pompano Beach *(G-14129)*

Plastic Solutions Inc ....G 727 202-6815
Largo *(G-7660)*

Plastic Solutions of Pompano ....G 800 331-7081
Pompano Beach *(G-14131)*

Plastimold Products Inc ....G 561 869-0183
Delray Beach *(G-2998)*

Precision Mold & Tool Inc ....E 407 847-5687
Kissimmee *(G-6955)*

Precision Plastics Group Inc ....E 863 299-6639
Winter Haven *(G-18459)*

Precision Tool & Mold Inc ....E 727 573-4441
Clearwater *(G-1749)*

Premier Lab Supply Inc ....G 772 873-1700
Port Saint Lucie *(G-14434)*

Prime Molding Technologies Inc ....E 561 721-2799
Riviera Beach *(G-14663)*

Prospect Plastics Inc ....G 954 564-7282
Oakland Park *(G-11289)*

Proto Corp ....D 727 573-4665
Clearwater *(G-1758)*

Prototype Plstic Extrusion Inc ....E 727 572-0803
Clearwater *(G-1759)*

R S Design Inc ....F 727 525-8292
Pinellas Park *(G-13726)*

Ranger Plastic Extrusions Inc ....E 817 640-6067
Fort Myers *(G-4375)*

RSC Molding Inc ....F 516 351-9871
West Palm Beach *(G-18147)*

S Gager Industries Inc ....E 904 268-6727
Jacksonville *(G-6441)*

Salva Enterprises Inc ....F 863 291-4407
Winter Haven *(G-18467)*

Scf Processing LLC ....G 352 377-0858
Gainesville *(G-4759)*

Scott Sign Systems Inc ....E 941 355-5171
Sarasota *(G-15553)*

Seaway Plastics Engrg LLC ....E 352 799-3167
Brooksville *(G-1198)*

Seaway Plastics Engrg LLC ....E 727 777-6032
Port Richey *(G-14374)*

Seaway Plastics Engrg LLC ....D 727 845-3235
Port Richey *(G-14375)*

Silcar Corp ....G 305 557-8391
Hialeah *(G-5349)*

Simco Machine and Tool Inc ....F 863 452-1151
Avon Park *(G-287)*

Simtec Silicone Parts LLC ....E 954 656-4212
Miramar *(G-10543)*

Southern Reinforced Plas Inc ....G 941 746-8793
Bradenton *(G-1050)*

Standard Injection Molding Inc ....F 863 452-9090
Avon Park *(G-289)*

Steven R Durante ....G 954 564-9913
Oakland Park *(G-11299)*

Sun Works Plastics Inc ....G 727 573-2343
Clearwater *(G-1800)*

Sunco Plastics Inc ....F 305 238-2864
Miami *(G-9965)*

Suncoast Molders Inc ....F 727 546-0041
Largo *(G-7693)*

Sunrise Fiberglass Inc ....G 305 636-4111
Palmetto Bay *(G-13219)*

Team Plastics Inc ....E 386 740-9555
Deland *(G-2907)*

TEC Air Inc ....G 772 335-8220
Fort Pierce *(G-4537)*

Technicraft Plastics Inc ....F 954 927-2575
Dania *(G-2344)*

Tmf Plastic Solutions LLC ....E 941 748-2946
Bradenton *(G-1060)*

Tomsons Inc ....G 248 646-0677
Englewood *(G-3539)*

United Plastic Fabricating Inc ....D 352 291-2477
Ocala *(G-11506)*

USB Plastics ....G 727 375-8840
Odessa *(G-11589)*

Usbev Products Inc ....F 727 375-8840
Odessa *(G-11590)*

Valintech ....G 941 366-8885
Sarasota *(G-15577)*

Vanguard Systems Corp ....G 727 528-0121
Saint Petersburg *(G-15223)*

Victors Trim Molding Crown Bas ....G 727 403-6057
Saint Petersburg *(G-15226)*

Wattera LLC ....E 954 400-5135
Fort Lauderdale *(G-4124)*

Winslow Microplastics Corp ....G 305 493-3501
Miami *(G-10135)*

WR Kershaw Inc ....G 386 673-0602
Ormond Beach *(G-12800)*

PLASTICS: Molded

A Crown Molding Specialist ....G 954 665-5640
Pembroke Pines *(G-13367)*

American Moulding Corporation ....F 321 676-8929
Melbourne *(G-8364)*

Bas Plastics Inc ....G 954 202-9080
Fort Lauderdale *(G-3675)*

Beachcomber Fibrgls Tech Inc ....G 772 283-0200
Stuart *(G-16122)*

Boyce Engineering Inc ....F 727 572-6318
Saint Petersburg *(G-14987)*

C Q Molding Inc ....G 786 314-1312
Miramar *(G-10477)*

Concealment Express LLC ....D 888 904-2722
Jacksonville *(G-5996)*

Creative Molding Corp ....F 786 251-4241
Doral *(G-3178)*

Custom Molding & Casework Inc ....G 407 709-7377
Deltona *(G-3043)*

Custom Plastic Fabricators ....G 813 884-5200
Tampa *(G-16755)*

Daigle Tool & Die Inc ....G 954 785-9989
Deerfield Beach *(G-2703)*

Darnel Inc ....G 954 929-0085
Hollywood *(G-5561)*

Doors Molding and More ....F 727 498-8552
Saint Petersburg *(G-15029)*

Firstcut ....G 786 740-3683
Miami *(G-9147)*

Foam Molding LLC ....G 813 434-7044
Tampa *(G-16857)*

Glass Works of Largo Inc ....G 727 535-9808
Largo *(G-7595)*

Kincaid Plastics Inc ....D 352 754-9979
Brooksville *(G-1168)*

Molded Moments Art ....G 954 913-0793
Royal Palm Beach *(G-14770)*

Molding Depot Inc ....E 813 348-4837
Tampa *(G-17081)*

Mtng Usa Corp ....G 305 670-0979
Miami *(G-9597)*

Paradise Inc ....D 813 752-1155
Tampa *(G-17146)*

Plastics Dynamics Inc ....G 954 565-7122
Oakland Park *(G-11284)*

Plastics For Mankind Inc ....G 305 687-5917
Opa Locka *(G-11783)*

Sands Molding Inc ....G 813 345-8646
Land O Lakes *(G-7504)*

T S E Industries Inc ....D 727 573-7676
Clearwater *(G-1809)*

T S E Industries Inc ....D 727 540-1368
Clearwater *(G-1810)*

Usbev Plastics LLC ....F 813 855-0700
Oldsmar *(G-11703)*

PLASTICS: Polystyrene Foam

AAA Architectural Elements ....F 941 722-1910
Palmetto *(G-13151)*

Allied Aerofoam Products LLC ....F 731 660-2705
Fort Lauderdale *(G-3640)*

Allied Aerofoam Products LLC ....D 813 626-0090
Fort Lauderdale *(G-3641)*

Barco Sales & Mfg Inc ....F 954 563-3922
Oakland Park *(G-11245)*

Caribbean Foam Products Inc ....F 786 431-5024
Hialeah *(G-5087)*

Dart Container Corp Florida ....E 941 358-1202
Sarasota *(G-15650)*

Design Works By Tech Pdts Inc ....G 941 355-2703
Sarasota *(G-15658)*

Dwm-2021 Inc ....F 813 443-0791
Tampa *(G-16789)*

East Coast Foam Supply Inc ....G 321 433-8231
Rockledge *(G-14706)*

Foam & Psp Inc ....G 954 816-5648
Fort Lauderdale *(G-3826)*

Foam Decoration Inc ....G 786 293-8813
Miami *(G-9164)*

Icorp-Ifoam Specialty Products ....G 407 328-8500
Sanford *(G-15334)*

Innocor Foam Tech - Acp Inc ....D 305 685-6341
Miami *(G-9316)*

Italian Cast Stones Inc ....E 813 902-8900
Tampa *(G-16956)*

Medfab Corporation ....G 813 854-2646
Oldsmar *(G-11673)*

Nida-Core Corporation ....E 772 343-7300
Port Saint Lucie *(G-14428)*

Novicon Industries ....G 813 854-3235
Oldsmar *(G-11679)*

Reilly Foam Corp ....F 561 842-8090
Riviera Beach *(G-14665)*

Scott Sign Systems Inc ....E 941 355-5171
Sarasota *(G-15553)*

Stephen Gould Corporation ....F 813 886-8460
Tampa *(G-17302)*

Wind Blue Technology LLC ....F 850 218-9398
Pensacola *(G-13625)*

PLASTICS: Thermoformed

Bk Plastics Industry Inc ....F 813 920-3628
Odessa *(G-11541)*

Dj Plastics Inc ....G 407 656-6677
Apopka *(G-122)*

Saint-Gobain Prfmce Plas Corp ....D 727 373-1299
Largo *(G-7675)*

Sibe Automation LLC ....F 352 690-1741
Ocala *(G-11490)*

Stockdale Technologies Inc ....D 407 323-5121
Lake Mary *(G-7108)*

PLATEMAKING SVC: Color Separations, For The Printing Trade

Diversified Graphics Inc ....F 407 425-9443
Orlando *(G-12099)*

Miami Trucolor Offset Svc Co ....G 954 962-5230
West Park *(G-18215)*

Rex Three Inc ....C 954 452-8301
Davie *(G-2469)*

Venue Advertising Inc ....E 561 844-1778
Jupiter *(G-6820)*

PLATES

Ace Printing Inc ....F 305 358-2572
Miami *(G-8643)*

All-Star Sales Inc ....E 904 396-1653
Jacksonville *(G-5876)*

American Business Cards Inc ....E 314 739-0800
Naples *(G-10666)*

Assocated Prtg Productions Inc ....E 305 623-7600
Miami Lakes *(G-10282)*

Bellak Color Corporation ....E 305 854-8525
Doral *(G-3132)*

Bjm Enterprises Inc ....F 941 746-4171
Palmetto *(G-13157)*

Boca Color Graphics Inc ....F 561 391-2229
Boca Raton *(G-435)*

Boca Raton Printing Co ....G 561 395-8404
Boca Raton *(G-437)*

Coastal Printing Inc Sarasota ....E 941 351-1515
Sarasota *(G-15635)*

Creative Prtg Grphic Dsign Inc ....E 407 855-0202
Orlando *(G-12055)*

Dobbs & Brodeur Bookbinders ....F 305 885-5215
Hialeah *(G-5121)*

Durra-Print Inc ....E 850 222-4768
Tallahassee *(G-16434)*

H & M Printing Inc ....F 407 831-8030
Sanford *(G-15329)*

Impact Design Group Inc ....E 904 636-8989
Jacksonville *(G-6193)*

Interprint Incorporated ....D...... 727 531-8957
Clearwater (G-1646)
Keithco Inc ....G...... 352 351-4741
Ocala (G-11419)
Linographics Inc ....F...... 407 422-8700
Orlando (G-12331)
Pfaffco Inc ....F...... 305 635-0986
Miami Lakes (G-10337)
Photoengraving Inc ....E...... 813 253-3427
Tampa (G-17165)
Press Printing Enterprises Inc ....E...... 239 598-1500
Fort Myers (G-4368)
Roberts Quality Printing Inc ....E...... 727 442-4011
Clearwater (G-1769)
Southeast Finishing Group Inc ....E...... 407 299-4620
Orlando (G-12613)
Trinity Graphic Usa Inc ....F...... 941 355-2636
Sarasota (G-15572)
Vowells Downtown Inc ....G...... 850 432-5175
Pensacola (G-13622)
Walker Graphics Inc ....G...... 954 964-1688
Hollywood (G-5683)

PLATES: Steel

Renaissance Steel LLC ....E...... 941 773-7290
Temple Terrace (G-17544)

PLATES: Truss, Metal

Blackwater Truss Systems LLC ....G...... 850 623-1414
Milton (G-10420)
ITW Blding Cmponents Group Inc ....E...... 863 422-8685
Haines City (G-4908)
ITW Blding Cmponents Group Inc ....E...... 954 781-3333
Fort Lauderdale (G-3888)
Mitek Inc ....D...... 813 675-1224
Tampa (G-17077)
Mitek USA Inc ....G...... 813 906-3122
Tampa (G-17078)

PLATING & FINISHING SVC: Decorative, Formed Prdts

Kerno LLC ....G...... 954 261-5854
Fort Lauderdale (G-3906)
Mil-Spec Metal Finishing Inc ....G...... 386 426-7188
Edgewater (G-3498)

PLATING & POLISHING SVC

Accurate Metal Finshg Fla Inc ....F...... 321 636-4900
Rockledge (G-14688)
Exact Inc ....C...... 904 783-6640
Jacksonville (G-6082)
Finishing Group Florida Inc ....G...... 954 981-2171
Hollywood (G-5576)
Finns Brass and Silver Polsg ....G...... 904 387-1165
Jacksonville (G-6091)
Marios Metalcraft ....G...... 239 649-0085
Naples (G-10813)
World Plate ....G...... 386 597-7832
Bunnell (G-1239)

PLATING SVC: Chromium, Metals Or Formed Prdts

Ni-Chro Plating Corp ....G...... 727 327-5118
Saint Petersburg (G-15139)

PLATING SVC: Electro

Accurate Metal Finshg Fla Inc ....F...... 321 636-4900
Rockledge (G-14689)
Airco Plating Company Inc ....E...... 305 633-2476
Miami (G-8673)
All Brght Electropolishing Inc ....G...... 727 449-9353
Clearwater (G-1485)
B4c Technologies Inc ....G...... 772 463-1557
Palm City (G-13025)
Central Florida Plating Inc ....G...... 321 452-7234
Merritt Island (G-8581)
Coating Technology Inc ....E...... 813 854-3674
Oldsmar (G-11639)
Crown Plating Inc ....E...... 904 783-6640
Jacksonville (G-6014)
Delta Metal Finishing Inc ....E...... 954 953-9898
Fort Lauderdale (G-3760)
Electro Lab Inc ....F...... 813 818-7605
Oldsmar (G-11648)
Gold Effects Inc ....G...... 727 573-1990
Clearwater (G-1615)

Hard Chrome Enterprises Inc ....G...... 561 844-2529
Lake Park (G-7129)
Hialeah Plating ....G...... 305 953-4143
Hialeah (G-5185)
Jssa Inc ....E...... 321 383-7798
Titusville (G-17594)
Melmar Cstm Met Finshg Svc Inc ....G...... 954 327-5788
Davie (G-2438)
Millenium Engine Plating Inc ....G...... 305 688-0098
Hialeah (G-5258)
Purecoat International LLC ....E...... 561 844-0100
West Palm Beach (G-18133)
Quality Anodizing Inc ....G...... 954 791-8711
Davie (G-2463)
Spectra Chrome LLC ....G...... 727 573-1990
Clearwater (G-1794)
Yosniel Finishing Inc ....G...... 305 890-3287
Hialeah (G-5426)

PLATING SVC: NEC

Action Plating Corp ....F...... 305 685-6313
Opa Locka (G-11711)
Alex Robert Silversmith Inc ....G...... 727 442-7333
Clearwater (G-1484)
Cfu Plating ....G...... 386 795-5198
Ocala (G-11349)
Gold Plating Specialties ....G...... 239 851-9323
Fort Myers (G-4270)
KPc Southern Industries Inc ....G...... 954 943-0254
Pompano Beach (G-14073)
Mark Plating Co ....G...... 561 655-4370
West Palm Beach (G-18066)
PC of Titusville Inc ....E...... 321 267-1161
Titusville (G-17605)
Space Coast Map LLC ....G...... 321 242-4538
Melbourne (G-8526)
Spacecast Pltg Met Rfnshing In ....G...... 321 254-2880
Melbourne (G-8527)
Superior Chrome Plating Inc ....F...... 832 659-0873
Naples (G-10915)
Techno-Coatings Inc ....G...... 305 945-2220
North Miami (G-11125)

PLAYGROUND EQPT

Florida Playground & Steel Co ....G...... 813 247-2812
Tampa (G-16851)
Southern Recreation Inc ....F...... 904 387-4390
Jacksonville (G-6492)
Urban Extreme LLC ....F...... 954 248-9007
Hollywood (G-5680)

PLEATING & STITCHING SVC

Cubco Inc ....F...... 386 254-2706
Daytona Beach (G-2538)
Full Press Apparel Inc ....F...... 850 222-1003
Tallahassee (G-16443)
Hes Products Inc ....G...... 407 834-0741
Ormond Beach (G-12769)
HOB Corporation ....G...... 813 988-2272
Tampa (G-16919)
Icon Embroidery Inc ....G...... 407 858-0886
Windermere (G-18353)
Image Depot ....G...... 813 685-7116
Tampa (G-16932)
Joni Industries Inc ....F...... 352 799-5456
Brooksville (G-1166)
Mid West Lettering Company ....E...... 850 477-6522
Pensacola (G-13553)
Shirts & Caps Inc ....E...... 813 788-7026
Tampa (G-17262)
Tiffany Quilting & Drapery ....F...... 407 834-6386
Longwood (G-7952)
Vivid Images USA Inc ....F...... 904 620-0303
Jacksonville (G-6594)

PLUGS: Electric

Broadband International Inc ....G...... 305 882-0505
Medley (G-8212)

PLUMBING & HEATING EQPT & SPLY, WHOL: Htg Eqpt/Panels, Solar

Ameritech Energy Corporation ....G...... 610 730-1733
Holly Hill (G-5510)

PLUMBING & HEATING EQPT & SPLY, WHOLESALE: Hydronic Htg Eqpt

Aruki Services LLC ....F...... 850 364-5206
Havana (G-4992)
St Cloud Wldg Fabrication Inc ....E...... 407 957-2344
Saint Cloud (G-14939)
Vickery and Company ....F...... 813 987-2100
Tampa (G-17415)

PLUMBING & HEATING EQPT & SPLYS WHOLESALERS

Sunset Power Inc ....F...... 866 485-2757
Jacksonville (G-6518)
Wool Wholesale Plumbing Supply ....D...... 954 763-3632
Fort Lauderdale (G-4136)

PLUMBING & HEATING EQPT & SPLYS, WHOL: Pipe/Fitting, Plastic

Sun Pipe and Valves LLC ....F...... 772 408-5530
Port Saint Lucie (G-14451)

PLUMBING & HEATING EQPT & SPLYS, WHOL: Plumbing Fitting/Sply

Design Works By Tech Pdts Inc ....E...... 941 355-2703
Sarasota (G-15658)

PLUMBING & HEATING EQPT & SPLYS, WHOL: Water Purif Eqpt

Aqua Engineering & Eqp Inc ....F...... 407 599-2123
Winter Park (G-18486)
Fshs Inc ....G...... 941 625-5929
Port Charlotte (G-14301)
H20logy Inc ....G...... 904 829-6098
Saint Augustine (G-14838)
H2o International Inc ....F...... 954 570-3464
Deerfield Beach (G-2729)
Siemens Industry Inc ....G...... 407 650-3570
Orlando (G-12598)

PLUMBING FIXTURES

Apollo Retail Specialists LLC ....D...... 813 712-2525
Tampa (G-16600)
Averett Septic Tank Co Inc ....E...... 863 665-1748
Lakeland (G-7278)
Bobs Backflow & Plumbing Co ....G...... 904 268-8009
Jacksonville (G-5944)
BSK USA LLC ....G...... 786 328-5395
Coral Gables (G-2036)
Coolcraft Inc ....G...... 954 946-0070
Pompano Beach (G-13979)
Dakota Plumbing Products LLC ....F...... 954 987-3430
Fort Lauderdale (G-3753)
Ddp Holdings LLC ....D...... 813 712-2515
Tampa (G-16769)
Designers Plumbing Studio Inc ....G...... 954 920-5997
Hollywood (G-5564)
Enolgas Usa Inc ....G...... 754 205-7902
Pompano Beach (G-14012)
Home & Garden Industries Inc ....F...... 305 634-0681
Miami (G-9289)
Johnston Archtctral Systems In ....E...... 904 886-9030
Jacksonville (G-6231)
M F B International Inc ....G...... 305 436-6601
Miami (G-9490)
Plumb Rite of Central Florida ....G...... 407 292-0750
Apopka (G-162)
Target Manufacturing Inc ....G...... 305 633-0361
Miami (G-9994)
True Plumbing Svc Inc ....G...... 941 296-5123
Bradenton (G-1068)
Wool Wholesale Plumbing Supply ....D...... 954 763-3632
Fort Lauderdale (G-4136)

PLUMBING FIXTURES: Plastic

Bathroom World Manufacturing ....G...... 954 566-0451
Oakland Park (G-11246)
Coast Products LLC ....F...... 850 235-2090
Panama City Beach (G-13328)
East Coast Fix & Mllwk Co Inc ....G...... 904 733-9711
Jacksonville (G-6059)
Elstons Inc ....G...... 727 527-7929
Apollo Beach (G-91)
Hale Products Inc ....C...... 352 629-5020
Ocala (G-11407)

PRODUCT

Home & Garden Industries Inc ....F 305 634-0681
Miami (G-9289)
Lions Intl MGT Group Inc ....F 813 367-2517
Tampa (G-17013)
Lpi Inc ....F 702 403-8555
Saint Petersburg (G-15113)
Paramount Depot LLC ....F 786 275-0107
Doral (G-3321)
Sh Shower & Tub Enclosures LLC ....G 786 229-2529
Miami (G-9875)
Trane Inc ....E 772 621-3200
Port Saint Lucie (G-14457)
Tuflex Manufacturing Co ....E 954 781-0605
Davie (G-2493)
Two Guys Plumbing Supply LLc ....G 321 263-0021
Altamonte Springs (G-74)

PLUMBING FIXTURES: Vitreous

Custom Marble Works Inc ....E 813 620-0475
Tampa (G-16754)
Ecotech Water LLC ....G 877 341-9500
St Pete Beach (G-16089)

PLUMBING FIXTURES: Vitreous China

Wool Wholesale Plumbing Supply ....D 954 763-3632
Fort Lauderdale (G-4136)

POINT OF SALE DEVICES

Bluestar Latin America Inc ....E 954 485-1931
Miramar (G-10475)
Verifone Inc ....C 800 837-4366
Coral Springs (G-2224)
Verifone Inc ....B 727 953-4000
Clearwater (G-1842)
Verifone Inc ....C 727 535-9200
Clearwater (G-1843)
Verifone Systems Inc ....C 408 232-7800
Coral Springs (G-2225)
Zhyno Inc ....G 844 313-1900
Hollywood (G-5689)

POLES & POSTS: Concrete

D & S Logging Inc ....G 850 638-5500
Chipley (G-1455)
Utilities Structures Inc ....F 239 334-7757
Fort Myers (G-4437)

POLICE PROTECTION: Bureau Of Criminal Investigation, Govt

United Ntons Space Crps Mltary ....G 702 373-2351
Ponce De Leon (G-14251)

POLISHING SVC: Metals Or Formed Prdts

A Sotolongo Polishing Marble C ....G 305 271-7957
Miami (G-8625)
Amado Wheel Finishing ....G 786 732-6249
Miami (G-8708)
Big Dogs Mobile Polishing LLC ....G 813 312-6892
Zephyrhills (G-18606)
Exotic Marble Polishing Inc ....G 786 318-6568
North Miami (G-11104)
Florida Polsg & Restoration ....G 305 688-2988
Opa Locka (G-11748)
Unique Marble Polishing Inc ....G 305 969-1554
Miami (G-10064)
Universal Polishing Systems ....G 407 227-9516
Orlando (G-12692)
Wicked Polishing Inc ....G 561 255-7554
West Palm Beach (G-18205)
Xe Global Polsg Systems LLC ....G 941 685-9788
Sarasota (G-15880)

POLYCARBONATE RESINS

Midgard Inc ....D 863 696-1224
Lake Wales (G-7168)

POLYESTERS

Code 1 Inc ....G 786 347-7755
Jacksonville (G-5992)
Lrm Industries Intl Inc ....E 321 635-9797
Rockledge (G-14727)

POLYETHYLENE RESINS

Flying W Plastics Fl Inc ....F 904 800-2451
Jacksonville (G-6116)

POLYPROPYLENE RESINS

Composite Essential Mtls LLC ....G 772 344-0034
Port St Lucie (G-14475)
Purecycle Technologies Inc ....F 877 648-3565
Orlando (G-12518)

POLYSTYRENE RESINS

Dioxide Materials Inc ....F 217 239-1400
Boca Raton (G-485)

POLYURETHANE RESINS

Hancor Inc ....E 863 655-5499
Winter Garden (G-18388)

POLYVINYL CHLORIDE RESINS

Ultraflex Systems Florida Inc ....F 973 664-6739
Riverview (G-14580)

POPCORN & SUPPLIES WHOLESALERS

Barnard Nut Company Inc ....D 305 836-9999
Miami (G-8799)
Brownbag Popcorn Company LLC ....G 561 212-5664
Boca Raton (G-451)

PORCELAIN ENAMELED PRDTS & UTENSILS

Hycomb Usa Inc ....F 954 251-1691
Hallandale Beach (G-4950)

POSTAL EQPT: Locker Boxes, Exc Wood

Davis Mail Services Inc ....C 904 477-7970
Jacksonville (G-6027)

POSTERS

Paris Ink Inc ....G 561 990-1194
Boca Raton (G-632)
Starmakers Rising Inc ....F 561 989-8999
Boca Raton (G-695)
Tropicolor Photo Service Inc ....G 305 672-3720
Miami Beach (G-10239)

POTTERY

Florida Cool Ring Company ....F 863 858-2211
Lakeland (G-7330)
Hart S Ceramic & Stone Inc ....G 850 217-6145
Destin (G-3068)
Kreative Ceramics Inc ....G 321 278-9889
Ocoee (G-11522)
Precision Ceramic & Stone Llc ....G .....
Vero Beach (G-17788)
Slipaway Ceramics Inc ....G 727 577-1936
Saint Petersburg (G-15187)

POTTING SOILS

Forestry Resources LLC ....E 239 332-3966
Fort Myers (G-4261)
Margo Outdoor Living Inc ....F 912 496-2999
Jacksonville (G-6276)
United AG Svcs Amer Inc ....E 352 793-1682
Lake Panasoffkee (G-7120)

POULTRY & POULTRY PRDTS WHOLESALERS

La Villarena Meat & Pork Inc ....F 305 759-0555
Miami (G-9415)

POULTRY & SMALL GAME SLAUGHTERING & PROCESSING

Cedars Food Inc ....F 321 724-2624
West Melbourne (G-17896)
Johnson Brothers Whl Meats Inc ....E 850 763-2828
Panama City (G-13280)
Pilgrims Pride Corporation ....D 386 362-4171
Live Oak (G-7851)

POWDER: Metal

Azz Powder Coating - Tampa LLC ....G 813 390-2802
Tampa (G-16624)
Drakon Coatings Industries Inc ....G 810 875-3874
Venice (G-17684)

POWDER: Silver

B-N-J Powder Coatings LLC ....G 407 999-8448
Orlando (G-11938)

POWER GENERATORS

GE Renewables North Amer LLC ....D 850 474-4011
Pensacola (G-13512)
General Power Limited Inc ....F 800 763-0359
Doral (G-3228)
Green Rhino Enrgy Slutions LLC ....E 407 925-5868
Apopka (G-137)
Megawattage LLC ....F 954 328-0232
Fort Lauderdale (G-3937)
Silent Standby Power Sup LLC ....G 954 253-9557
West Palm Beach (G-18153)

POWER OUTLETS & SOCKETS

Terracassa LLC ....G 786 581-7741
Miami (G-10002)

POWER SUPPLIES: All Types, Static

Electriduct Inc ....E 954 867-9100
Pompano Beach (G-14007)
Jfh Technologies LLC ....E 407 938-9336
Lake Buena Vista (G-6999)
North Erie Electronics Inc ....F 561 839-8127
Jupiter (G-6773)
Technipower LLC ....F 954 346-2442
Coral Springs (G-2219)
Vision Engineering Labs ....D 727 812-2035
Largo (G-7705)

POWER TOOLS, HAND: Drills & Drilling Tools

Delta International Inc ....F 305 665-6573
Miami (G-9013)

POWER TOOLS, HAND: Grinders, Portable, Electric Or Pneumatic

S I P Corporation ....F 813 884-8300
Tampa (G-17239)

POWER TRANSMISSION EQPT: Aircraft

Dukane Seacom Inc ....C 941 739-3200
Sarasota (G-15472)

POWER TRANSMISSION EQPT: Mechanical

Consultant MGT Group LLC ....G 352 344-4001
Inverness (G-5823)
Creative Carbide Inc ....F 239 567-0041
Fort Myers (G-4221)
Dowels Pins & Shafts Inc ....F 727 461-1255
Clearwater (G-1569)
Enstar Holdings (us) LLC ....E 727 217-2900
Saint Petersburg (G-15036)
Gfx Inc ....E 305 499-9789
Miami (G-9209)
Ggb1 LLC ....G 305 387-5334
Miami (G-9211)
Ipts Inc ....F 561 844-8216
Riviera Beach (G-14631)
JW Performance Transm Inc ....E 321 632-6205
Rockledge (G-14721)
Man-Trans LLC ....F 850 222-6993
Tallahassee (G-16474)
Martin Sprocket & Gear Inc ....E 813 623-1705
Tampa (G-17045)
North Amrcn Prtection Ctrl LLC ....G 407 788-3717
Altamonte Springs (G-59)
NSK Latin America Inc ....G 305 477-0605
Miami (G-9633)
Suncoast Rebuild Center Inc ....F 813 238-3433
Tampa (G-17313)
Torque Technologies Products ....G 630 462-1188
Sarasota (G-15570)

POWER TRANSMISSION EQPT: Vehicle

Progressive Power Products Inc ....G 904 354-1819
Jacksonville (G-6393)

PRECAST TERRAZZO OR CONCRETE PRDTS

Cds Manufacturing Inc ....D...... 850 875-4651
  Gretna (G-4856)
Central Florida Precast Inc ....G...... 941 730-2158
  Bradenton (G-960)
Concrete Structures Inc ....F...... 305 597-9393
  Miami (G-8956)
Decorative Precast LLC ....F...... 239 566-9503
  Naples (G-10727)
Florida Engineered Constru.................G...... 321 953-5161
  Palm Bay (G-12901)
Gate Precast Company........................C...... 904 520-5795
  Jacksonville (G-6129)
Hbp Pipe & Precast LLC ....E...... 904 529-8228
  Green Cove Springs (G-4828)
Km Precast Inc ....F...... 239 438-2146
  Naples (G-10799)
Master Construction Pdts Inc ....E...... 407 857-1221
  Orlando (G-12365)
Perry Precast Inc ....G...... 386 294-2710
  Mayo (G-8186)
Precast and Foam Works LLC ....G...... 727 657-9195
  Clearwater (G-1746)
Precast Technical Assistance...............G...... 850 432-8446
  Pensacola (G-13581)
Rmmj Inc ....E...... 239 597-2486
  Naples (G-10878)
Southern Pre Cast Structures L ....G...... 352 569-1128
  Bushnell (G-1249)
United Concrete Products LLC............G...... 786 402-3536
  Medley (G-8342)
US Precast Corp...............................E...... 305 364-8253
  Hialeah (G-5399)

PRECIOUS METALS

Gold Buyers of America LLC ....C...... 877 721-8033
  Greenacres (G-4848)

PREFABRICATED BUILDING DEALERS

Eds Aluminum Buildings Inc ....G....... 850 476-2169
  Pensacola (G-13493)
Eds Aluminum Buildings Inc ....G....... 850 476-2169
  Molino (G-10578)

PRERECORDED TAPE, CD & RECORD STORE: Record, Disc/Tape

Singing Machine Company Inc............F...... 954 596-1000
  Fort Lauderdale (G-4050)

PRERECORDED TAPE, CD/RECORD STORES: Audio Tapes, Prerecorded

Muscle Mixes Inc...............................F...... 407 872-7576
  Orlando (G-12401)

PRERECORDED TAPE, COMPACT DISC & RECORD STORES: Compact Disc

Horizon Duplication Inc.......................G....... 407 767-5000
  Winter Park (G-18514)

PRESS CLIPPING SVC

Cole Enterprises Inc ....G....... 727 441-4101
  Clearwater (G-1546)

PRESSED & MOLDED PULP PRDTS, NEC: From Purchased Materials

Inovart Inc ....G....... 941 751-2324
  Bradenton (G-996)

PRESTRESSED CONCRETE PRDTS

Accord Industries LLC ....D...... 407 671-6989
  Winter Park (G-18480)
Bayshore Concrete Pdts Corp...............C...... 757 331-2300
  Maitland (G-8051)
Dura-Stress Inc ....C...... 352 787-1422
  Leesburg (G-7769)
Finfrock Industries Inc ....C...... 407 293-4000
  Apopka (G-131)
Prestressed Systems Inc ....F...... 305 556-6699
  Doral (G-3336)
South Estrn Prstressed Con Inc...........F...... 561 793-1177
  West Palm Beach (G-18159)

Spancrete Inc ....E...... 305 599-8885
  Miami (G-9933)

PRIMARY METAL PRODUCTS

Accurate Metal Finshg Fla Inc ....F...... 321 636-4900
  Rockledge (G-14688)
AP Richter Holding Co LLC ....F...... 239 732-9440
  Naples (G-10670)
Klocke of America Inc ....D...... 239 561-5800
  Fort Myers (G-4306)
Ogre Custom Fabrications LLC.............G...... 321 544-2142
  Melbourne (G-8487)
Tom Haggetts Pressure Cleaning.........G...... 407 932-0140
  Merritt Island (G-8599)

PRINT CARTRIDGES: Laser & Other Computer Printers

Computer Forms & Supplies ....G...... 727 535-0422
  Largo (G-7567)
Micromicr Corporation ....E...... 954 922-8044
  Dania (G-2337)
Replenish Ink Inc ....G...... 818 206-2424
  Miami (G-9795)
Sun Print Management LLC ....E...... 727 945-0255
  Holiday (G-5504)
Suncoast Toner Cartridge Inc...............F...... 727 945-0255
  Holiday (G-5505)
Team Inkjet ....G...... 954 554-3250
  Coral Springs (G-2218)
Toner Cartridge Recharge Inc..............G...... 305 968-1045
  Miami Lakes (G-10365)
Toner Technologies Inc ....G...... 561 547-9710
  Boynton Beach (G-920)
Universal Ribbon Corporation ....F...... 305 471-0828
  Miami (G-10072)
Well Made Bus Solutions LLC ....G...... 754 227-7268
  Coconut Creek (G-2011)

PRINTED CIRCUIT BOARDS

4front Solutions LLC ....D...... 814 464-2000
  Deland (G-2846)
ACt USA International LLC ....G...... 321 725-4200
  Melbourne (G-8354)
Advanced Manufacturing Inc................E...... 727 573-3300
  Saint Petersburg (G-14954)
Alegro Industries Inc ....D...... 702 943-0978
  Tamarac (G-16523)
AOC Technologies Inc........................G...... 727 577-9749
  Saint Petersburg (G-14963)
Ateei International Corp ....G...... 305 597-6408
  Doral (G-3123)
Axon Circuit Inc ....F...... 407 265-7980
  Longwood (G-7873)
Axon Circuit Inc ....E...... 407 265-7980
  Tampa (G-16623)
Bare Board Group Intl LLC ....F...... 727 549-2200
  Largo (G-7545)
Board Shark Pcb Inc...........................G...... 352 759-2100
  Astor (G-202)
Cem Ltd ....E...... 321 253-1160
  Melbourne (G-8384)
Circuit Works Co................................G...... 727 544-5336
  Pinellas Park (G-13675)
Circuitronics LLC ....F...... 407 322-8300
  Sanford (G-15284)
Ckc Industries Inc ....G...... 813 888-9468
  Tampa (G-16709)
Concept 2 Market Inc ....F...... 954 974-0022
  Pompano Beach (G-13974)
Continuity Unlimited Inc......................F...... 561 358-8171
  Oviedo (G-12815)
Delta Group Electronics Inc.................D...... 321 631-0799
  Rockledge (G-14698)
Denver Elevator Systems Inc................G...... 800 633-9788
  Cape Canaveral (G-1282)
Diamond Mt Inc ....F...... 321 339-3377
  Melbourne (G-8401)
Electrotek Inc ....G...... 321 231-6846
  Sanford (G-15311)
Englander Enterprises Inc ....E...... 727 461-4755
  Clearwater (G-1586)
Florida Elreha Corporation ....E...... 727 327-6236
  Saint Petersburg (G-15049)
Global Intrcnnect Slutions LLC.............G...... 239 254-0326
  Naples (G-10762)
H & T Global Circuit Fctry LLC ....D...... 727 327-6236
  Saint Petersburg (G-15071)
I3 Microsystems Inc ....E...... 727 235-6532
  Saint Petersburg (G-15080)

Icmfg & Associates Inc.......................G...... 727 258-4995
  Clearwater (G-1636)
Jabil Advnced Mech Sltions Inc ....E...... 727 577-9749
  Saint Petersburg (G-15089)
Jabil Circuit ....G...... 727 577-9749
  Saint Petersburg (G-15090)
Jabil Circuit LLC ....D...... 727 577-9749
  Saint Petersburg (G-15092)
Jabil Def & Arospc Svcs LLC ....E...... 727 577-9749
  Saint Petersburg (G-15093)
Jabil Def & Arospc Svcs LLC ....F...... 727 577-9749
  Saint Petersburg (G-15094)
Jabil Inc...A...... 727 577-9749
  Saint Petersburg (G-15095)
Jabil Inc...E...... 727 577-9749
  Saint Petersburg (G-15096)
Jabil Inc...C...... 727 803-3110
  Saint Petersburg (G-15097)
Jabil Inc...D...... 727 577-9749
  Saint Petersburg (G-15098)
Jrt Manufacturing LLC........................F...... 321 363-4133
  Sanford (G-15347)
Kimball Electronics Group LLC............D...... 813 854-2000
  Tampa (G-16986)
Kimball Electronics Tampa Inc.............B...... 813 814-5229
  Tampa (G-16987)
Laser Photo-Tooling Svcs Inc...............F...... 561 393-4710
  Boca Raton (G-574)
M C Test Service Inc ....C...... 321 253-0541
  Melbourne (G-8466)
Mack Technologies Florida Inc..............C...... 321 725-6993
  Melbourne (G-8467)
Marlo Electronics Inc ....E...... 561 477-0856
  Boca Raton (G-586)
Mathews Associates Inc......................C...... 407 323-3390
  Sanford (G-15354)
Mc Assembly Holdings Inc ....G...... 321 253-0541
  Melbourne (G-8470)
Mc Assembly LLC ....B...... 321 253-0541
  Melbourne (G-8472)
Memo Labs Inc ....F...... 561 842-0586
  West Palm Beach (G-18074)
Micro Engineering Inc ....E...... 407 886-4849
  Apopka (G-151)
Nano Dimension USA Inc ....E...... 650 209-2866
  Sunrise (G-16345)
Neotech Company ....G...... 954 570-5833
  Deerfield Beach (G-2774)
Nypro Healthcare LLC ....E...... 727 577-9749
  Saint Petersburg (G-15142)
Oum LLC...F...... 407 886-1511
  Apopka (G-160)
Paramount Industries Inc.....................E...... 954 781-3755
  Pompano Beach (G-14118)
Pica Sales and Engineering..................G...... 239 992-9079
  Estero (G-3548)
Precision Circuits Inc ....E...... 321 632-8629
  Rockledge (G-14739)
Prime Technological Svcs LLC..............D...... 850 539-2500
  Havana (G-5002)
Protek Electronics Inc ....E...... 941 351-4399
  Sarasota (G-15789)
Qualitel Inc.......................................F...... 954 464-3991
  Hollywood (G-5648)
Quality Manufacturing Svcs Inc ....D...... 407 531-6000
  Lake Mary (G-7104)
Rtp Corp..G...... 954 597-5333
  Pompano Beach (G-14163)
Sibex Inc ....C...... 727 726-4343
  Crystal River (G-2280)
Smiths Interconnect Inc ....C...... 813 901-7200
  Tampa (G-17276)
Solutions Manufacturing Inc.................D...... 321 848-0848
  Rockledge (G-14747)
Sparton Corporation...........................C...... 847 762-5800
  De Leon Springs (G-2628)
Sparton Deleon Springs LLC ....C...... 386 985-4631
  De Leon Springs (G-2629)
Specialty Fin Consulting Corp...............B...... 717 246-1661
  Longboat Key (G-7860)
Superior Electronics Inc......................E...... 727 733-0700
  Clearwater (G-1804)
Sypris Electronics LLC........................C...... 813 972-6000
  Tampa (G-17319)
Tms Enterprises LLC ....B...... 850 539-2500
  Havana (G-5003)
Tropical Assemblies Inc ....D...... 954 396-9999
  Oakland Park (G-11302)
Tropical Stencil Pcb Inc......................F...... 561 972-5133
  Jupiter (G-6813)

Employee Codes: A=Over 500 employees, B=251-500
C=101-250, D=51-100, E=20-50, F=10-19, G=4-9

2022 Harris Florida
Manufacturers Directory

1285

PRODUCT

United Circuits Inc ....F 954 971-6860
Pompano Beach *(G-14226)*
Xtreme Electronic Designs Inc ....G 561 557-3667
Lake Worth *(G-7245)*

PRINTERS & PLOTTERS

Barrett & Company ....G 305 293-4501
Key West *(G-6856)*
I T Management Express Inc ....G 954 237-6999
Miramar *(G-10502)*
Knight Bacon Associates ....G 772 388-5115
Sebastian *(G-15897)*
Roberto Valverde ....G 305 324-5252
Miami *(G-9814)*
Zsno Ft Lauderdale ....G 954 792-2223
Miramar *(G-10567)*

PRINTERS' SVCS: Folding, Collating, Etc

Midds Inc ....E 561 586-6220
Lake Worth Beach *(G-7258)*

PRINTERS: Computer

AAA Index Tabs LLC ....G 954 457-7777
Hallandale Beach *(G-4932)*
Evolis Inc ....F 954 777-9262
Fort Lauderdale *(G-3801)*
Lexmark International Inc ....C 954 345-2442
Coral Springs *(G-2179)*
Lexmark International Inc ....F 305 467-2200
Miami *(G-9454)*
Nscrypt Inc ....E 407 275-4720
Orlando *(G-12428)*
Peripheral Services Inc ....E 813 854-1181
Oldsmar *(G-11685)*
Totalprint USA ....G 855 915-1300
Tampa *(G-17363)*

PRINTERS: Magnetic Ink, Bar Code

Logiscenter LLC ....G 800 729-0236
Miami *(G-9471)*
US Barcodes Inc ....G 727 849-1196
Port Richey *(G-14382)*

PRINTING & BINDING: Books

Sosumi Holdings Inc ....E 239 634-3430
Naples *(G-10896)*

PRINTING & BINDING: Pamphlets

Tone Printing LLC ....G 855 505-8663
Miami *(G-10022)*

PRINTING & EMBOSSING: Plastic Fabric Articles

PHI CHI Foundation Inc ....G 561 526-3401
Margate *(G-8146)*
Williams Specialties Inc ....G 305 769-9925
Hialeah *(G-5420)*

PRINTING & ENGRAVING: Card, Exc Greeting

Alpha Card Compact Media LLC ....G 407 698-3592
Winter Park *(G-18483)*

PRINTING & ENGRAVING: Invitation & Stationery

Hey Day ....G 305 763-8660
Miami Beach *(G-10199)*
Miami Engrv Co-Oxford Prtg Co ....G 305 371-9595
Miami *(G-9551)*

PRINTING & STAMPING: Fabric Articles

McGee Enterprises Inc ....G 904 328-3226
Jacksonville *(G-6284)*
Open Market Enterprises LLC ....G 407 322-5434
Orlando *(G-12440)*
Parthenon Prints Inc ....E 850 769-8321
Panama City *(G-13297)*
Preferred Custom Printing LLC ....F 727 443-1900
Seminole *(G-15987)*
Walter Haas Graphics Inc ....E 305 883-2257
Hialeah *(G-5417)*

PRINTING MACHINERY

Amrav Inc ....G 407 831-1550
Altamonte Springs *(G-31)*
Apex Machine Company ....D 954 563-0209
Oakland Park *(G-11238)*
CST USA Inc ....F 404 695-2249
Miami *(G-8981)*
EL Harley Inc ....F 561 841-9887
Delray Beach *(G-2957)*
Gammerlertech Corporation ....F 941 803-0150
Bradenton *(G-981)*
Gto USA Inc ....G 727 216-6907
Clearwater *(G-1617)*
Howard Imprinting Machine Co ....G 813 884-2398
Tampa *(G-16923)*
Mark/Trece Inc ....F 863 647-4372
Lakeland *(G-7390)*
MGI Usa Inc ....F 321 751-6755
Melbourne *(G-8475)*
Southern Graphic Machine LLC ....G 615 812-0778
Edgewater *(G-3501)*
Universal Stncling Mkg Systems ....E 727 894-3027
Saint Petersburg *(G-15221)*
Zenith Rollers Llc ....G 954 493-6484
Fort Lauderdale *(G-4144)*

PRINTING MACHINERY, EQPT & SPLYS: Wholesalers

Amrav Inc ....G 407 831-1550
Altamonte Springs *(G-31)*
Howard Imprinting Machine Co ....G 813 884-2398
Tampa *(G-16923)*

PRINTING TRADES MACHINERY & EQPT REPAIR SVCS

Light Source Business Systems ....F 772 562-5046
Port Saint Lucie *(G-14423)*
Peripheral Services Inc ....E 813 854-1181
Oldsmar *(G-11685)*

PRINTING, COMMERCIAL: Announcements, NEC

Rapid Rater Company ....E 850 893-7346
Tallahassee *(G-16492)*

PRINTING, COMMERCIAL: Bags, Plastic, NEC

Vicbag LLC ....G 305 423-7042
Miami *(G-10105)*

PRINTING, COMMERCIAL: Business Forms, NEC

Easy Rent Inc ....G 904 443-7446
Jacksonville *(G-6061)*
Ef Enterprises of North Fla ....G 904 739-5995
Jacksonville *(G-6067)*
Express Printing Center Inc ....F 813 909-1085
Land O Lakes *(G-7492)*
M & M Studios Inc ....G 561 744-2754
Jupiter *(G-6758)*
Standard Register Inc ....F 954 492-9986
Fort Lauderdale *(G-4065)*

PRINTING, COMMERCIAL: Cards, Playing, NEC

Buddy Bridge Inc ....G 941 488-0799
Nokomis *(G-11042)*
Buddy Bridge Inc ....E 941 586-8281
Venice *(G-17678)*
Sun Business Systems Inc ....G 727 547-6540
Clearwater *(G-1799)*

PRINTING, COMMERCIAL: Cards, Visiting, Incl Business, NEC

Jrg Systems Inc ....F 954 962-1020
Fort Lauderdale *(G-3898)*
Print Shop of Chiefland Inc ....G 352 493-0322
Chiefland *(G-1449)*

PRINTING, COMMERCIAL: Certificates, Security, NEC

Pasa Services Inc ....E 305 594-8662
Opa Locka *(G-11780)*

PRINTING, COMMERCIAL: Decals, NEC

Martin Leonard Corporation ....G 850 434-2203
Pensacola *(G-13543)*

PRINTING, COMMERCIAL: Directories, Telephone, NEC

Safari Sun LLC ....E 407 339-7291
Altamonte Springs *(G-70)*

PRINTING, COMMERCIAL: Envelopes, NEC

Services On Demand Print Inc ....F 305 681-5345
Hallandale Beach *(G-4970)*

PRINTING, COMMERCIAL: Fashion Plates, NEC

PHI CHI Foundation Inc ....G 561 526-3401
Margate *(G-8146)*

PRINTING, COMMERCIAL: Imprinting

Imprint Promotions LLC ....G 321 622-8946
Melbourne *(G-8441)*
Put Your Name On It LLC ....G 813 972-1460
Tampa *(G-17195)*
Sunybell LLC ....F 727 301-2832
New Port Richey *(G-10986)*

PRINTING, COMMERCIAL: Labels & Seals, NEC

A Bar Code Business Inc ....G 352 750-0077
The Villages *(G-17552)*
Brightfish Label LLC ....G 727 521-7900
Largo *(G-7557)*
Dongili Investment Group Inc ....F 941 927-3003
Sarasota *(G-15660)*
Executive Label Inc ....F 954 978-6983
Margate *(G-8129)*
Fast Labels ....G 904 626-0508
Jacksonville *(G-6088)*
Florida Tape & Labels Inc ....F 941 921-5788
Sarasota *(G-15681)*
L & N Label Company Inc ....E 727 442-5400
Clearwater *(G-1667)*
Label Graphics Inc ....G 561 798-8180
Lake Worth *(G-7213)*
Prolabel Inc ....F 305 620-2202
Hialeah *(G-5313)*
Southern Tape & Label Inc ....F 321 632-5275
Cocoa *(G-1957)*
Tradingflex Inc ....F 877 522-3535
Miami *(G-10034)*
United Seal & Tag Label Corp ....G 941 625-6799
Port Charlotte *(G-14321)*

PRINTING, COMMERCIAL: Letterpress & Screen

Elite Printing & Marketing Inc ....G 850 474-0894
Pensacola *(G-13494)*
Endangered Species Designs LLC ....F 954 613-2111
Boynton Beach *(G-863)*
Sealmaster of Wisconsin ....E 954 979-5458
Pompano Beach *(G-14173)*

PRINTING, COMMERCIAL: Literature, Advertising, NEC

Aacecorp Inc ....G 904 353-7878
Jacksonville *(G-5853)*
Corporate Printing & Advg Inc ....F 305 273-6000
Miami *(G-8973)*
Dxm Marketing Group LLC ....F 904 332-6490
Jacksonville *(G-6052)*
Image Depot ....G 813 685-7116
Tampa *(G-16932)*
Mark Wsser Grphic Prdctons Inc ....G 305 888-7445
Boynton Beach *(G-889)*
Tone Printing LLC ....G 855 505-8663
Miami *(G-10022)*

PRINTING, COMMERCIAL: Magazines, NEC

Vision Web Offset LLC.........................F....... 305 433-6188
Miami Lakes *(G-10376)*

PRINTING, COMMERCIAL: Maps, NEC

Reprographic Solutions Inc..................G....... 772 340-3430
Port Saint Lucie *(G-14441)*

PRINTING, COMMERCIAL: Menus, NEC

David Dobbs Enterprises Inc...............D....... 904 824-6171
Saint Augustine *(G-14823)*

PRINTING, COMMERCIAL: Promotional

Clear Choice Inc.................................G....... 407 830-6968
Altamonte Springs *(G-38)*
Creative Promotional Products............G....... 407 383-7114
Orlando *(G-12054)*
Drip Communication LLC......................F....... 407 730-5519
Orlando *(G-12107)*
Gdp Consulting Inc..............................G....... 561 401-9195
Jupiter *(G-6733)*
Hit Promotional Products Inc..............B....... 727 541-5561
Largo *(G-7605)*
Inflatable Design Works Corp...............F....... 786 242-1049
Miami *(G-9313)*
New Image Printing Promotion............G....... 904 240-1516
Jacksonville *(G-6327)*
Promotional Mktg Online LLC..............G....... 941 347-8564
Punta Gorda *(G-14520)*
Tattoo Factory Inc................................E....... 941 923-4110
Sarasota *(G-15850)*
Vurb LLC...G....... 561 441-8870
Pompano Beach *(G-14238)*
Whitecap Promotions LLC...................G....... 813 960-4918
Tampa *(G-17431)*
World Event Promotions LLC...............E....... 800 214-3408
Miami *(G-10143)*

PRINTING, COMMERCIAL: Publications

ABC Imaging of Washington................F....... 954 759-2037
Fort Lauderdale *(G-3619)*
Academic Publication Svcs Inc............G....... 941 925-4474
Sarasota *(G-15585)*
Baptist Mid-Missions Inc.......................F....... 863 382-6350
Sebring *(G-15915)*
Greentex America LLC..........................F....... 305 908-8580
Hallandale Beach *(G-4949)*
Mango Publications..............................G....... 863 583-4773
Lakeland *(G-7388)*
Marco Polo Publications Inc.................G....... 866 610-9441
Saint Petersburg *(G-15117)*
Mojowax Media Inc................................G....... 805 550-6013
Bradenton *(G-1013)*
Morris Visitor Publications...................F....... 407 423-0618
Orlando *(G-12393)*
Newbeauty Media Group LLC..............E....... 561 961-7600
Boca Raton *(G-615)*

PRINTING, COMMERCIAL: Schedules, Transportation, NEC

Aw Publishing.......................................F....... 305 856-7000
Miami *(G-8780)*

PRINTING, COMMERCIAL: Screen

850 Screen Printing LLC......................G....... 850 549-7861
Pensacola *(G-13427)*
A D Coaches Corner Inc........................G....... 786 242-2229
Miami *(G-8619)*
Above LLC..F....... 850 469-9028
Pensacola *(G-13431)*
Accuprint My Print Shop.......................F....... 954 973-9369
Deerfield Beach *(G-2655)*
Acm Screen Printing Inc......................G....... 305 547-1552
Miami *(G-8646)*
Active Sole...G....... 941 923-4840
Sarasota *(G-15586)*
Admiral Printing Inc...............................G....... 727 938-9589
Holiday *(G-5487)*
Adver-T Screen Printing Inc.................F....... 727 443-5525
Clearwater *(G-1477)*
All Florida Engraving............................G....... 352 213-4572
Hawthorne *(G-5006)*
All Pro Ink LLC......................................G....... 305 252-7644
Cutler Bay *(G-2283)*
All Purpose Prtg Graphics Inc...............F....... 904 346-0999
Jacksonville *(G-5875)*
All Star Graphix Inc...............................G....... 954 772-1972
Oakland Park *(G-11235)*
Allgeo & Yerkes Entps Inc.....................F....... 321 255-9030
Melbourne *(G-8361)*
Allied Decals-Fla Inc.............................F....... 800 940-2233
Fort Lauderdale *(G-3642)*
Aloha Screen Printing Inc.....................G....... 850 934-4716
Gulf Breeze *(G-4875)*
American Mentality Inc..........................G....... 407 599-7255
Longwood *(G-7867)*
American Screen Print Inc....................G....... 904 443-0071
Jacksonville *(G-5885)*
Ampersand Graphics Inc......................F....... 772 283-1359
Stuart *(G-16115)*
Ampersand Shirt Shack........................F....... 772 600-8743
Stuart *(G-16116)*
Anchor Screen Printing LLC.................G....... 850 243-4200
Fort Walton Beach *(G-4559)*
Apparel Printers....................................G....... 352 463-8850
Alachua *(G-4)*
APS Promotional Solutions Inc.............F....... 904 721-4977
Jacksonville *(G-5894)*
Arj Art Inc..G....... 727 535-8633
Saint Petersburg *(G-14970)*
Artworks Printing Entps Inc..................G....... 954 893-7984
Hollywood *(G-5530)*
ASAP Screen Printing Inc.....................G....... 352 505-7574
Gainesville *(G-4652)*
Atticus Screen Printing T......................G....... 407 365-9911
Oviedo *(G-12807)*
Bam Enterprises Inc..............................F....... 850 469-8872
Pensacola *(G-13451)*
Beach Embroidery & Screen Ptg..........G....... 386 478-3931
New Smyrna Beach *(G-10997)*
Benner China and Glwr of Fla..............E....... 904 733-4620
Jacksonville *(G-5929)*
Bl Brandhouse LLC...............................G....... 305 600-7181
Doral *(G-3141)*
CAM Broc Sports Inc.............................G....... 407 933-6524
Kissimmee *(G-6904)*
Capsmith Inc..E....... 407 328-7660
Sanford *(G-15277)*
Carpe Diem Sales & Mktg Inc...............E....... 407 682-1400
Orlando *(G-11983)*
CC Sportswear Inc................................G....... 941 351-4205
Sarasota *(G-15452)*
Classic Screen Prtg Design Inc............G....... 407 850-0112
Orlando *(G-12018)*
Classic Shirts Inc..................................F....... 850 875-2200
Quincy *(G-14543)*
Coral Club Tee Shirts Inc......................G....... 305 828-6939
Hialeah *(G-5097)*
Cotton Pickin Shirts Plus......................G....... 850 435-3133
Pensacola *(G-13478)*
Cubco Inc..F....... 386 254-2706
Daytona Beach *(G-2538)*
Currin Graphics.....................................G....... 850 505-0955
Pensacola *(G-13480)*
Custom Graphics Inc..............................G....... 954 563-6756
Deerfield Beach *(G-2699)*
DAccord Shirts & Guayaberas...............G....... 305 576-0926
Miami *(G-8993)*
Davie Embroidme..................................G....... 954 452-0600
Davie *(G-2403)*
DC Apparel Inc......................................G....... 863 325-9273
Winter Haven *(G-18434)*
Designated Sports Inc...........................F....... 904 797-9469
Saint Augustine *(G-14827)*
Designers Top Shop Inc........................G....... 863 453-3855
Avon Park *(G-279)*
Dillco Inc...F....... 386 734-7510
Deland *(G-2865)*
DNE Pot Sbob Inc..................................F....... 239 936-8880
Fort Myers *(G-4237)*
Double H Enterprises Inc......................G....... 972 562-8588
Ormond Beach *(G-12758)*
Douglass Screen Printers Inc................E....... 863 687-8545
Lakeland *(G-7312)*
Dragonfly Graphics...............................G....... 772 879-9800
Port Saint Lucie *(G-14408)*
Dragonfly Graphics Inc..........................G....... 352 375-2144
Gainesville *(G-4681)*
Embroidery Solutions Inc......................G....... 407 438-8188
Orlando *(G-12124)*
Engead Gb Design & Prtg Inc................G....... 954 783-5161
Pompano Beach *(G-14011)*
Epic Promos LLC...................................G....... 561 479-8055
Boca Raton *(G-505)*
Evolutionary Screen Printing L.............G....... 863 248-2692
Lakeland *(G-7318)*
Fassi Equipment Inc..............................G....... 954 385-6555
Weston *(G-18240)*
Fassidigitalcom Inc................................G....... 954 385-6555
Weston *(G-18241)*
Ferrera Embroidery & Prtg Ser..............G....... 786 667-2680
Christmas *(G-1462)*
First Coast Tee Shirt Co Inc..................G....... 904 737-1985
Jacksonville *(G-6096)*
Fla Property Holdings Inc......................E....... 813 888-8796
Miami Lakes *(G-10303)*
Florida Flexible.....................................G....... 305 512-2222
Hialeah *(G-5157)*
Florida Screen Services Inc..................F....... 407 316-0466
Orlando *(G-12166)*
Full Press Apparel Inc...........................F....... 850 222-1003
Tallahassee *(G-16443)*
Galaxy Screenprinting Inc......................G....... 407 862-2224
Altamonte Springs *(G-49)*
Galleon Industries Inc...........................G....... 708 478-5444
Altamonte Springs *(G-50)*
Garment Gear Inc..................................F....... 850 215-2121
Panama City *(G-13266)*
Good Catch Inc......................................G....... 305 757-7700
Miami *(G-9227)*
Grand Cypress Group Inc......................G....... 407 622-1993
Maitland *(G-8061)*
Graphix By Fran Inc...............................G....... 239 939-3125
Fort Myers *(G-4271)*
Great Atlantic Outfitters.........................G....... 904 722-0196
Jacksonville *(G-6149)*
Gulf Breeze Apparel LLC........................G....... 941 488-8337
Venice *(G-17695)*
Halifax Plastic Inc..................................F....... 386 252-2442
Daytona Beach *(G-2560)*
Happy Endings of Miami Inc..................G....... 305 759-4467
Miami *(G-9261)*
Hes Products Inc...................................G....... 407 834-0741
Ormond Beach *(G-12769)*
Hitmaster Graphics LLC.........................F....... 267 269-8220
Thonotosassa *(G-17562)*
Hot Action Sportswear Inc.....................E....... 386 677-5680
Ormond Beach *(G-12770)*
I P Team Inc...E....... 772 398-4664
Stuart *(G-16164)*
Imperial Imprinting LLC..........................G....... 772 633-8256
Vero Beach *(G-17762)*
Impress Ink LLC.....................................G....... 407 982-5646
Orlando *(G-12238)*
Impress Ink LLC.....................................G....... 561 635-6442
Orlando *(G-12239)*
Industrial Marking Svcs Inc....................G....... 727 541-7622
Largo *(G-7612)*
Ink-Trax Inc..F....... 850 235-4849
Panama City *(G-13275)*
International Prtg Ad Spc Inc..................E....... 772 398-4664
Stuart *(G-16167)*
Izabellas Creations Inc...........................G....... 786 429-3441
Miami *(G-9348)*
James Hines Printing.............................G....... 904 398-5110
Jacksonville *(G-6219)*
Jet-Set Printing Inc.................................G....... 407 339-1900
Casselberry *(G-1421)*
Joni Industries Inc..................................F....... 352 799-5456
Brooksville *(G-1166)*
Jose Polanco..G....... 305 631-1784
Miami *(G-9373)*
Kenny-Ts Inc...F....... 850 575-6644
Tallahassee *(G-16467)*
Kikisteescom LLC...................................E....... 888 620-4110
Sunrise *(G-16333)*
Koala Tee Inc (usa)................................E....... 941 954-7700
Sarasota *(G-15720)*
Local Enterprises Inc..............................G....... 305 295-0026
Key West *(G-6873)*
Logos Promote Inc.................................G....... 407 447-5646
Orlando *(G-12351)*
Looper Sports Connection Inc...............G....... 352 796-7974
Brooksville *(G-1175)*
Lowe Gear Printing................................G....... 866 714-9965
Lutz *(G-8000)*
Lr Printing LLC.......................................G....... 407 558-0543
Orange City *(G-11806)*
Lucky Dog Screen Printing Mg...............G....... 407 629-8838
Winter Park *(G-18520)*
Merchspin Inc...E....... 877 306-3651
Orlando *(G-12372)*
Metropolis Graphics Inc..........................G....... 407 740-5455
Winter Park *(G-18523)*
Miami Epic Tees Corp.............................G....... 305 224-3465
Hialeah *(G-5249)*

PRODUCT

Employee Codes: A=Over 500 employees, B=251-500
C=101-250, D=51-100, E=20-50, F=10-19, G=4-9

2022 Harris Florida
Manufacturers Directory

1287

Miami Screenprint Supply Inc..............G...... 305 622-7532
Miami Lakes *(G-10324)*

Miami Tees Inc..............................D...... 305 623-3908
Miami Lakes *(G-10325)*

Mid State Screen Graphics LLC.........E...... 727 573-2299
Clearwater *(G-1699)*

Mlxl Productions Inx.......................G...... 904 350-0048
Jacksonville *(G-6310)*

Morning Star Personalized AP...........G...... 772 569-8412
Vero Beach *(G-17778)*

Ocean Blue Graphics Inc.................G...... 561 881-2022
Riviera Beach *(G-14653)*

Ocean Blue Graphics Design Inc......G...... 561 881-2022
Riviera Beach *(G-14654)*

Outdoor America Images Inc...........E...... 813 888-8796
Miami Lakes *(G-10334)*

Palmas Printing Inc........................E...... 321 984-4451
Melbourne *(G-8490)*

Pathfinder Shirts............................G...... 407 865-6530
Altamonte Springs *(G-62)*

Paul Wales Inc...............................E...... 352 371-2120
Gainesville *(G-4746)*

Picasso Embroidery Systems...........F...... 305 827-9666
Miramar *(G-10527)*

Point Blank Scrnprnting Design.........G...... 850 234-9745
Panama City *(G-13298)*

Premier Tees.................................G...... 941 681-2688
Englewood *(G-3521)*

Print Art Screen Printing Inc............F...... 386 258-5186
Daytona Beach *(G-2585)*

Print Shack..................................G...... 352 799-2972
Brooksville *(G-1192)*

Printec Inc...................................G...... 813 854-1075
Oldsmar *(G-11692)*

Printex Worldwide Inc.....................G...... 954 518-0722
Hallandale *(G-4929)*

Productive Products Inc..................G...... 904 570-5553
Saint Augustine *(G-14875)*

Prographix Inc..............................G...... 863 298-8081
Winter Haven *(G-18463)*

Proud Tshirts Corp.........................F...... 888 233-3426
North Miami *(G-11116)*

Racerink LLC................................G...... 239 470-0872
Jupiter *(G-6785)*

Ranger Associates Inc...................G...... 407 869-0024
Longwood *(G-7941)*

Ray Graphics Inc...........................G...... 863 325-0911
Winter Haven *(G-18464)*

Real Thread Inc.............................E...... 407 679-3895
Orlando *(G-12536)*

Red 7 Tees LLC.............................G...... 850 612-7007
Crestview *(G-2251)*

Red Hot Trends Inc........................G...... 305 888-6951
Medley *(G-8309)*

Rex Three Inc...............................C...... 954 452-8301
Davie *(G-2469)*

Rinehart Corp...............................G...... 850 271-5600
Lynn Haven *(G-8031)*

RMR Distributors Inc......................E...... 813 908-1141
Tampa *(G-17225)*

Schimmbros Inc............................G...... 407 796-8361
Kissimmee *(G-6960)*

Schooner Prints Inc.......................D...... 727 397-8572
Largo *(G-7676)*

Screen Graphics Florida Inc.............E...... 800 346-4420
Pompano Beach *(G-14169)*

Screen Process Printers Inc............G...... 904 354-8708
Jacksonville *(G-6457)*

Screen Tech.................................G...... 321 536-6091
Merritt Island *(G-8592)*

Seaside Graphics Inc.....................G...... 954 782-7151
Pompano Beach *(G-14174)*

Seemore Shirts & Tees LLC.............G...... 954 708-1100
Coral Springs *(G-2211)*

Serigraphic Arts Inc.......................F...... 813 626-1070
Tampa *(G-17251)*

SGS Designs Inc...........................G...... 813 258-2691
Tampa *(G-17254)*

Shirts n Things Inc........................G...... 954 434-7480
Davie *(G-2475)*

Shocksocks LLC...........................F...... 352 258-0496
Stuart *(G-16218)*

Sign Depot Co..............................F...... 407 894-0090
Orlando *(G-12601)*

Silkmasters Inc.............................G...... 904 372-8958
Gainesville *(G-4761)*

Slick Designs & AP Miami Inc...........F...... 305 836-7950
Hialeah *(G-5351)*

Societees Inc...............................G...... 786 208-9880
Miami Beach *(G-10230)*

Solseen LLC.................................G...... 727 322-3131
Saint Petersburg *(G-15189)*

Southeast Marketing Concepts.........G...... 561 747-7010
Jupiter *(G-6802)*

Splash of Color LLC.......................E...... 732 735-3090
Jacksonville *(G-6501)*

Sports N Stuff Screen Printing.........G...... 407 859-0437
Orlando *(G-12618)*

Sublimation Station Inc...................G...... 407 605-5300
Orlando *(G-12628)*

Sun Graphic Technologies Inc.........E...... 941 753-7541
Sarasota *(G-15562)*

T Sals Shirt Co.............................G...... 850 916-9229
Gulf Breeze *(G-4893)*

T-Shirt Express.............................G...... 904 448-3761
Jacksonville *(G-6527)*

T-Shirts Plus Color Inc...................G...... 305 267-7664
Miami *(G-9991)*

Tampa Bay Print Shop LLC..............G...... 813 321-8790
Riverview *(G-14578)*

Tee Line Corp...............................F...... 786 350-9526
West Palm Beach *(G-18176)*

Tee-Hee Corp...............................G...... 754 200-4962
Wilton Manors *(G-18343)*

Teeko Graphics Inc........................G...... 386 754-5600
Lake City *(G-7048)*

Tees Please Inc.............................G...... 857 472-3391
Hobe Sound *(G-5484)*

Ten Star Supply Co Inc...................G...... 813 254-6921
Tampa *(G-17348)*

Think Outloud Printing....................G...... 239 800-3219
Cape Coral *(G-1399)*

Thread Pit Inc...............................G...... 352 505-0065
Gainesville *(G-4776)*

Threadbird LLC.............................G...... 407 545-6506
Orlando *(G-12657)*

Tidewater Incentives Group Ltd.........F...... 410 734-0691
Venice *(G-17722)*

Til Valhalla Project LLC...................D...... 904 579-3414
Saint Augustine *(G-14906)*

Tip Tops of America Inc...................F...... 352 357-9559
Eustis *(G-3567)*

Trim-Line of Miami Inc....................G...... 305 556-6210
Hialeah *(G-5381)*

Universal Screen Graphics Inc..........E...... 813 623-5335
Tampa *(G-17394)*

Vanlex Clothing Inc........................E...... 305 431-4669
Miami Lakes *(G-10375)*

Vivid Images USA Inc......................F...... 904 620-0303
Jacksonville *(G-6594)*

Walter Haas Graphics Inc................E...... 305 883-2257
Hialeah *(G-5417)*

Waterboyz-Wbz Inc........................G...... 850 433-2929
Pensacola *(G-13624)*

Wear Fund LLC.............................F...... 239 313-3907
Fort Myers *(G-4446)*

Westview Corp Inc.........................G...... 239 643-5699
Naples *(G-10937)*

Whitehouse Custom Scrn PR.............G...... 727 321-7398
Saint Petersburg *(G-15232)*

Wholesale Screen Prtg Nples In........G...... 239 263-7061
Naples *(G-10938)*

Worldwide Sportswear Inc................E...... 386 761-2688
Port Orange *(G-14354)*

PRINTING, COMMERCIAL: Stationery, NEC

Pfaffco Inc...................................F...... 305 635-0986
Miami Lakes *(G-10337)*

PRINTING, COMMERCIAL: Tags, NEC

Blue Ribbon Tag & Label of PR.........F...... 787 858-5300
Hollywood *(G-5542)*

PRINTING, LITHOGRAPHIC: Advertising Posters

Firehouse Promotions Inc................G...... 407 990-1600
Maitland *(G-8058)*

Mc Squared Group Inc....................G...... 850 435-4600
Pensacola *(G-13544)*

Outdoor Media Inc.........................G...... 305 529-1400
Coral Gables *(G-2094)*

PRINTING, LITHOGRAPHIC: Calendars & Cards

Write Stuff Enterprises LLC..............E...... 954 462-6657
Fort Lauderdale *(G-4138)*

PRINTING, LITHOGRAPHIC: Color

Colorprint Design...........................G...... 305 229-8880
Miami *(G-8949)*

Printing Corp of Americas Inc...........E...... 954 943-6087
Pompano Beach *(G-14147)*

Sun Belt Graphics Inc.....................F...... 954 424-3139
Davie *(G-2484)*

PRINTING, LITHOGRAPHIC: Decals

National Traffic Signs Inc.................G...... 727 446-7983
Clearwater *(G-1712)*

SMc Diversified Services Inc.............G...... 863 698-9696
Lakeland *(G-7436)*

PRINTING, LITHOGRAPHIC: Forms & Cards, Business

Amtec Sales Inc............................F...... 800 994-3318
Miami *(G-8729)*

Delicate Designs Event Plg Inc..........G...... 305 833-8725
Miami *(G-9010)*

Graphink Incorporated....................G...... 305 468-9463
Doral *(G-3236)*

Ncp Solutions LLC.........................D...... 205 849-5200
Jacksonville *(G-6322)*

PRINTING, LITHOGRAPHIC: Letters, Circular Or Form

Print Rite Co................................G...... 305 757-0611
Miami *(G-9743)*

Scott Brevard Inc..........................G...... 386 698-1121
Crescent City *(G-2238)*

PRINTING, LITHOGRAPHIC: Menus

Plastic Sealing Company Inc............G...... 954 956-9797
Pompano Beach *(G-14130)*

PRINTING, LITHOGRAPHIC: Newspapers

Heritage Cntl Fla Jwish News I..........F...... 407 834-8277
Fern Park *(G-3579)*

PRINTING, LITHOGRAPHIC: Offset & photolithographic printing

Playlist Live Inc............................E...... 877 306-3651
Orlando *(G-12491)*

Screen Machine.............................G...... 941 962-0395
Bradenton *(G-1043)*

Screen Machines LLC......................G...... 386 527-1368
Port Orange *(G-14346)*

Tone Printing LLC...........................G...... 855 505-8663
Miami *(G-10022)*

PRINTING, LITHOGRAPHIC: On Metal

Burr Printing Co Inc.......................G...... 863 294-3166
Winter Haven *(G-18426)*

C & S Press Inc.............................D...... 407 841-3000
Orlando *(G-11972)*

Coastal Printing Inc Sarasota...........E...... 941 351-1515
Sarasota *(G-15635)*

Eastern Shores Printing...................E...... 305 685-8976
Opa Locka *(G-11741)*

John Stewart Enterprises Inc............F...... 904 356-9392
Jacksonville *(G-6228)*

Lake Worth Herald Press Inc............F...... 561 585-9387
Lake Worth *(G-7214)*

Tiffany and Associates Inc...............E...... 386 252-7351
Daytona Beach *(G-2613)*

PRINTING, LITHOGRAPHIC: Post Cards, Picture

Hill Printing Inc.............................G...... 407 654-4282
Winter Garden *(G-18390)*

PRINTING, LITHOGRAPHIC: Promotional

Area Litho Inc...............................G...... 863 687-4656
Lakeland *(G-7275)*

Blue Ocean Press Inc.....................E...... 954 973-1819
Fort Lauderdale *(G-3693)*

Pure Postcards Inc.........................F...... 877 446-2434
Clearwater *(G-1760)*

PRINTING, LITHOGRAPHIC: Publications

Green Papers Inc ....G....... 305 956-3535
  North Miami Beach (G-11143)
Guest Service Publications Inc ....F 516 333-3474
  Bonita Springs (G-801)

PRINTING, LITHOGRAPHIC: Tags

Blue Ribbon Tag & Label Corp ....E 954 922-9292
  Hollywood (G-5541)

PRINTING, LITHOGRAPHIC: Trading Stamps

Miami Quality Graphics Inc ....E 305 634-9506
  Miami (G-9556)

PRINTING, LITHOGRAPHIC: Transfers, Decalcomania Or Dry

Dowling Graphics Inc ....E 727 573-5997
  Clearwater (G-1570)
Global Impressions Inc ....F 727 531-1290
  Largo (G-7597)

PRINTING: Books

Jrg Systems Inc ....F 954 962-1020
  Fort Lauderdale (G-3898)
Marquis Media Group ....G....... 941 255-0087
  Punta Gorda (G-14514)

PRINTING: Books

Creative Tech Sarasota Inc ....F 941 371-2743
  Sarasota (G-15644)
Digital Direct Corporation ....G....... 813 448-9071
  Oldsmar (G-11642)
Florida Graphic Printing Inc..............F 386 253-4532
  Daytona Beach (G-2553)
Lincoln-Marti Cmnty Agcy Inc ....D 305 643-4888
  Miami (G-9462)
Lincoln-Marti Cmnty Agcy Inc ....C 646 463-6120
  Miami (G-9463)
On Demand Spclty Envelope Corp...........F 305 681-5345
  Hallandale Beach (G-4965)
Power Printing of Florida ....G .....
  Saint Petersburg (G-15156)
Prisna Latino ....G....... 305 525-9292
  Miami (G-9746)
Reliance Media Inc ....F 505 243-1821
  Apopka (G-168)
Royal Palm Press Inc ....G....... 941 575-4299
  Punta Gorda (G-14528)
Seminole County Public Schools...........E 407 320-0393
  Sanford (G-15385)
Southeastern Printing Co Inc ....G....... 772 287-2141
  Palm City (G-13059)
Southeastern Printing Co Inc ....C 772 287-2141
  Hialeah (G-5357)

PRINTING: Broadwoven Fabrics. Cotton

JADA Transitions LLC ....G....... 561 377-8194
  Riviera Beach (G-14633)

PRINTING: Checkbooks

Deluxe Cars LLC ....G....... 407 982-7978
  Orlando (G-12084)

PRINTING: Commercial, NEC

A Z Printing Delray ....G....... 561 330-4154
  Delray Beach (G-2922)
Abby Press Inc ....E 407 847-5565
  Kissimmee (G-6892)
Abeka Print Shop Inc ....E 850 478-8496
  Pensacola (G-13430)
Absolute Graphics Inc ....F 954 792-3488
  Davie (G-2374)
Academy Publishing Inc ....E 407 736-0100
  Orlando (G-11864)
Advanced Cmmncations Holdg Inc.......D 954 753-0100
  Coral Springs (G-2126)
Advantage Prtg Lmnting Fla Inc...........G....... 904 737-1613
  Jacksonville (G-5864)
Agility Press Inc ....F 904 731-8989
  Jacksonville (G-5868)
All-Star Sales Inc ....E 904 396-1653
  Jacksonville (G-5876)
Alm Global LLC ....D 305 347-6650
  Miami (G-8696)

Altira Inc ....D 305 687-8074
  Miami (G-8702)
Amelia Island Graphics ....G....... 904 261-0740
  Fernandina Beach (G-3581)
Apis Cor Inc ....E 347 404-1481
  Melbourne (G-8367)
Arrow Embroidery ....F 850 626-1796
  Milton (G-10418)
Art of Printing Inc ....F 561 640-7344
  West Palm Beach (G-17928)
Artvint Corp ....G....... 727 856-3565
  Hudson (G-5762)
Automated Services Inc ....F 772 461-3388
  Fort Pierce (G-4468)
B R Q Grossmans Inc ....F 954 971-1077
  Pompano Beach (G-13943)
Barjo Printing and Sign ....F 786 332-2661
  Medley (G-8207)
Bros Williams Printing ....G....... 305 769-9925
  Hialeah (G-5079)
Bros Williams Printing Inc ....G....... 305 769-9925
  Hialeah (G-5080)
Business Card Ex Tampa Bay Inc ....D 727 535-7768
  Clearwater (G-1532)
Century Graphics & Metals Inc ....E 407 262-8290
  Altamonte Springs (G-37)
China Public Security Tech Inc ....E 866 821-9004
  Saint Petersburg (G-15005)
Commercial Printers Inc ....D 954 781-3737
  Fort Lauderdale (G-3738)
Concept Design and Printing ....G....... 813 516-9798
  Tampa (G-16723)
Cor Label LLC ....G....... 407 402-6633
  Debary (G-2632)
Core Label LLC ....F 772 287-2141
  Palm City (G-13031)
Couchman Printing Company ....G....... 386 756-3052
  South Daytona (G-16020)
Creative Prtg Grphic Dsign Inc ....E 407 855-0202
  Orlando (G-12055)
Csmc Inc ....E 407 246-1567
  Orlando (G-12060)
D G Morrison Inc ....F 813 865-0208
  Odessa (G-11546)
Dahlquist Enterprises Inc ....G....... 407 896-2294
  Orlando (G-12071)
Dandy Media Corporation ....F 954 616-6800
  Hallandale (G-4923)
Dannys Prtg Svc Sups & Eqp Inc ....G....... 305 757-2282
  Miami (G-9000)
Davis Franklin Printing Co ....G....... 813 259-2500
  Tampa (G-16765)
Designers Press Inc ....D 407 843-3141
  Orlando (G-12087)
Dobbs & Brodeur Bookbinders ....F 305 885-5215
  Hialeah (G-5121)
Doral Dgtal Reprographics Corp ....G....... 305 704-3194
  Doral (G-3197)
Durra Quick Print Inc ....G....... 850 681-2900
  Tallahassee (G-16433)
Durra-Print Inc ....E 850 222-4768
  Tallahassee (G-16434)
E&P Solutions and Services Inc ....G....... 305 715-9545
  Miami (G-9058)
Easy Digital Corp ....G....... 305 940-1001
  Miami (G-9063)
Envision Graphics Inc ....E 305 470-0083
  Miami (G-9102)
Fdc Print LLC ....D 305 885-8707
  Hialeah (G-5154)
FGA Printing ....G....... 954 763-1122
  Pompano Beach (G-14019)
Fidelity Printing Corporation ....D 727 522-9557
  Saint Petersburg (G-15044)
Five Star Sports Tickets ....F 440 899-2000
  Hallandale Beach (G-4948)
Florida Graphic Printing Inc..............F 386 253-4532
  Daytona Beach (G-2554)
Florida Sncast Trism Prmtons I ....F 727 544-1212
  Largo (G-7587)
Formsystems Inc ....G....... 850 479-0800
  Pensacola (G-13509)
Four G Enterprises Inc ....E 407 834-4143
  Longwood (G-7898)
Fritz Commercial Printing Inc ....G....... 561 585-6869
  West Palm Beach (G-18013)
G S Printers Inc ....G....... 305 931-2755
  Fort Lauderdale (G-3834)
Gabrielas Memoirs Inc ....G....... 305 666-9991
  Miami (G-9183)

Gadsden County Times Inc..............F 850 627-7649
  Quincy (G-14545)
Gandy Printers Inc ....F 850 222-5847
  Tallahassee (G-16444)
Genuine Ad Inc.......................G....... 786 399-6484
  Sunny Isles Beach (G-16275)
Go 2 Print Now Inc ....E 800 500-4276
  Saint Petersburg (G-15063)
Grace Bible Church ....G....... 850 623-4671
  Milton (G-10426)
Granada Prtg & Graphics Corp...........F 305 593-5266
  Miami (G-9233)
Graphic and Printing Svcs Corp...........G....... 954 486-8868
  Tamarac (G-16532)
Graphics Type Color Entps Inc ....E 305 591-7600
  Miami (G-9236)
Graphix Solutions of America ....F 727 898-6744
  Parrish (G-13359)
Greater 7th Digital Press Inc ....G....... 305 681-2412
  Miami (G-9239)
Greg Allens Inc ....E 904 262-8912
  Jacksonville (G-6155)
Gulf Coast Printing ....E 239 482-5555
  Fort Myers (G-4277)
H & H Printing Inc ....G....... 407 422-2932
  Orlando (G-12204)
Harvey Branker and Assoc PA ....E 954 966-4445
  Hollywood (G-5588)
Herald-Advocate Publishing Co ....G....... 863 773-3255
  Wauchula (G-17828)
Hernandez Printing Service Inc ....F 305 642-0483
  Miami (G-9277)
Hilcraft Engraving Inc ....G....... 305 871-6100
  Miami (G-9282)
Holland Creative Services Inc ....G....... 904 732-4932
  Jacksonville (G-6180)
Holmes Stamp Company ....E 904 396-2291
  Jacksonville (G-6183)
Howies Instant Printing Inc ....F 561 686-8699
  West Palm Beach (G-18027)
ICM Printing Co Inc ....F 352 377-7468
  Gainesville (G-4709)
Image Graphics 2000 Inc ....F 954 332-3380
  Pompano Beach (G-14059)
Impact Design Group Inc ....E 904 636-8989
  Jacksonville (G-6193)
Impressions of Miami Inc ....G....... 305 666-0277
  Miami (G-9307)
Instant Printing Services Inc..............F 727 546-8036
  Floral City (G-3611)
J J M Services Inc ....G....... 954 437-1880
  Miramar (G-10507)
Jdjsis Inc ....G....... 561 732-2388
  West Palm Beach (G-18039)
JMS Designs of Florida Inc ....G....... 954 572-6100
  Sunrise (G-16332)
Keithco Inc ....G....... 352 351-4741
  Ocala (G-11419)
Kights Printing & Office Pdts ....G....... 904 731-7990
  Jacksonville (G-6242)
King Printing & Graphics Inc ....G....... 813 681-5060
  Brandon (G-1097)
Kj Reynolds Inc ....G....... 904 829-6488
  Saint Augustine (G-14853)
Knopf & Sons Bindery Inc...............F 904 355-4411
  Jacksonville (G-6247)
Kover Corp ....G....... 305 888-0146
  Doral (G-3276)
Lauderdale Graphics Corp...............E 954 450-0800
  Davie (G-2432)
Leda Printing Inc ....E 941 922-1563
  Sarasota (G-15724)
Ledger ....B 863 802-7000
  Lakeland (G-7376)
Limited Designs LLC ....G....... 305 547-9909
  Miami (G-9461)
Lrp Conferences LLC ....E 215 784-0860
  Palm Beach Gardens (G-12987)
Lujotex LLC ....G....... 954 322-1001
  Miramar (G-10510)
Marlin Graphics Inc ....G....... 561 743-5220
  Jupiter (G-6761)
Maxigraphics Inc ....F 954 978-0740
  Pompano Beach (G-14090)
Media Works Inc ....F 904 398-5518
  Jacksonville (G-6288)
Mendez Brothers LLC..................F 305 685-3490
  Opa Locka (G-11768)
Microcomputer Services ....G....... 561 988-7000
  Boca Raton (G-597)

PRODUCT

Miller Creative Graphics	G	904 771-5855
Jacksonville (G-6306)		
Minuteman Press	G	386 255-2767
Daytona Beach (G-2577)		
Newspaper Printing Company	G	727 572-7488
Clearwater (G-1717)		
Nis Print Inc	E	407 423-7575
Orlando (G-12418)		
Platecrafters Corporation	F	215 997-1990
Longwood (G-7939)		
Pod All Solutions Corp	G	805 291-2675
Miami (G-9724)		
Poms Enterprises Inc	G	954 358-1359
Margate (G-8148)		
Power Point Graphics Inc	G	561 351-5599
Boca Raton (G-638)		
Premier Parties Entertainment	E	352 375-6122
Gainesville (G-4750)		
Print Mart Inc	G	727 796-0064
Dunedin (G-3457)		
Printers Printer Inc	F	954 917-2773
Pompano Beach (G-14146)		
Printhouseusacom Inc	G	305 231-0202
Hialeah (G-5309)		
Printing Mart Inc South Fla	F	954 753-0323
Pompano Beach (G-14149)		
Printing Services Plus LLC	F	813 279-1903
Tampa (G-17185)		
Procorp LLC	G	904 477-6762
Jacksonville (G-6390)		
Quad/Graphics Inc	D	813 837-3436
Tampa (G-17198)		
R R Donnelley & Sons Company	E	407 859-2030
Orlando (G-12528)		
Rakiline LLC	G	904 800-2632
Jacksonville (G-6404)		
Reporgraphics Unlimited Inc	G	386 253-7990
Daytona Beach (G-2589)		
Roberts Quality Printing Inc	E	727 442-4011
Clearwater (G-1769)		
Scp Commercial Printing	F	561 998-0870
Boca Raton (G-664)		
Screen Monkey Corp	G	352 746-7091
Homosassa (G-5750)		
Seabreeze Publication Centl FL	E	561 741-7770
Jupiter (G-6793)		
Serv-Pak Corp	F	954 962-4262
Hollywood (G-5656)		
Signarama	G	239 997-1644
North Fort Myers (G-11070)		
Skies Limit Printing	G	772 340-1090
Port Saint Lucie (G-14446)		
Slasher Printing Center Inc	G	305 835-7366
Sunrise (G-16367)		
South Florida Finger Printing	G	305 661-1636
South Miami (G-16047)		
Southeast Finishing Group Inc	E	407 299-4620
Orlando (G-12613)		
Southeastern Printing Co Inc	G	772 287-2141
Palm City (G-13059)		
St Ives Burrups	G	305 685-7381
Opa Locka (G-11789)		
Storterchilds Printing Co Inc	E	352 376-2658
Gainesville (G-4766)		
Suncoast Specialty Prtg Inc	G	813 951-0899
Tampa (G-17315)		
Super Color Digital LLC	F	407 240-1660
Orlando (G-12636)		
T-Wiz Prtg & EMB Designs LLC	E	954 280-8949
Fort Lauderdale (G-4083)		
Taie Inc	G	954 966-0233
Hollywood (G-5668)		
Tampa Printing Company	E	813 612-7746
Tampa (G-17337)		
Target Copy Gainesville Inc	F	352 372-1171
Gainesville (G-4774)		
Tonertype Inc	E	813 915-1300
Tampa (G-17360)		
Treasured Photo Gifts LLC	F	407 324-4816
Lake Mary (G-7113)		
Trend At LLC	E	786 300-2550
Miami (G-10039)		
Triple Crown Printing	E	561 939-6440
Boca Raton (G-725)		
Tru Dimensions Printing Inc	E	407 339-3410
Longwood (G-7954)		
Venue Advertising Inc	E	561 844-1778
Jupiter (G-6820)		
W D H Enterprises Inc	G	941 758-6500
Bradenton (G-1073)		

Walruss Enterprises Inc	G	954 525-0342
Fort Lauderdale (G-4120)		
Wingard LLC	F	904 387-2570
Jacksonville (G-6614)		

PRINTING: Engraving & Plate

Hilcraft Engraving Inc	G	305 871-6100
Miami (G-9282)		

PRINTING: Fabric, Narrow

PHI CHI Foundation Inc	G	561 526-3401
Margate (G-8146)		

PRINTING: Flexographic

Fort Dearborn Company	D	772 600-2756
Palm City (G-13040)		
Graphic Printing Corp	E	561 994-3586
Boca Raton (G-532)		
Passion Labels & Packaging	G	941 312-5003
Sarasota (G-15532)		
Safeprints LLC	G	305 960-7391
Miami (G-9836)		
Southeastern Printing Co Inc	C	772 287-2141
Hialeah (G-5357)		
Southeastern Printing Co Inc	F	305 885-8707
Boca Raton (G-688)		
Worldwide Tickets & Labels Inc	D	877 426-5754
Boynton Beach (G-926)		

PRINTING: Gravure, Business Form & Card

Amtec Sales Inc	F	800 994-3318
Miami (G-8729)		
Collier Business Systems	G	239 649-5554
Naples (G-10719)		

PRINTING: Gravure, Envelopes

Sun Coast Paper & Envelope Inc	F	727 545-9566
Largo (G-7692)		

PRINTING: Gravure, Forms, Business

Ef Enterprises of North Fla	G	904 739-5995
Jacksonville (G-6067)		

PRINTING: Gravure, Job

Brut Printing Co Inc	E	904 354-5055
Jacksonville (G-5960)		
Reprographic Services Inc	F	305 859-8282
Miami (G-9796)		

PRINTING: Gravure, Labels

Datamax International Corp	C	407 578-8007
Orlando (G-12075)		
Datamax-Oneil Corporation	C	800 816-9649
Orlando (G-12076)		
Dongili Investment Group Inc	F	941 927-3003
Sarasota (G-15660)		

PRINTING: Gravure, Rotogravure

A-Plus Prtg & Graphic Ctr Inc	E	954 327-7315
Plantation (G-13817)		
Collins Media & Advg LLC	F	954 688-9758
Margate (G-8124)		
Eti-Label Inc	G	305 716-0094
Miami (G-9113)		
Miami Engrv Co-Oxford Prtg Co	G	305 371-9595
Miami (G-9551)		
Restifo Investments LLC	F	305 468-0013
Doral (G-3348)		
Screen Graphics Florida Inc	E	800 346-4420
Pompano Beach (G-14169)		
Tone Printing LLC	G	855 505-8663
Miami (G-10022)		

PRINTING: Gravure, Seals

Starlock Inc	G	305 477-2303
Doral (G-3375)		
Wells Legal Supply Inc	E	904 399-1510
Jacksonville (G-6600)		

PRINTING: Gravure, Stationery & Invitation

Kreative Drive Inc	G	786 845-8605
Doral (G-3278)		

PRINTING: Gravure, Visiting Cards

Business Card Ex Tampa Bay Inc	D	727 535-7768
Clearwater (G-1532)		

PRINTING: Laser

Advanced Xrgrphics Imging Syst	E	407 351-0232
Orlando (G-11872)		
Endurance Lasers LLC	F	239 302-0053
Naples (G-10737)		
Light Source Business Systems	F	772 562-5046
Port Saint Lucie (G-14423)		
Pad Printing Technology Corp	G	941 739-8667
Bradenton (G-1023)		
Target Graphics Inc	F	941 365-8809
Sarasota (G-15849)		

PRINTING: Letterpress

Crain Ventures Inc	G	407 933-1820
Kissimmee (G-6909)		
Futch Printing & Mailing Inc	F	904 388-3995
Jacksonville (G-6124)		
Rinaldi Printing Company	E	813 569-0033
Tampa (G-17221)		
Spett Printing Co Inc	G	561 241-9758
Boca Raton (G-691)		
Steven Chancas	G	352 629-5016
Ocala (G-11499)		
Woods Printing Ocala Inc	G	352 629-1665
Ocala (G-11514)		

PRINTING: Lithographic

3d Printing Solutions	G	850 443-4200
Ponte Vedra (G-14254)		
3g Enterprises Inc	F	754 366-7643
Boynton Beach (G-834)		
5301 Realty LLC	C	305 633-9779
Hialeah (G-5014)		
5hp Investments LLC	G	561 655-5355
West Palm Beach (G-17905)		
Accuprint My Print Shop	F	954 973-9369
Deerfield Beach (G-2655)		
Adorgraf Corp	G	786 752-1680
Miami (G-8654)		
Advanced Cmmncations Holdg Inc	D	954 753-0100
Coral Springs (G-2126)		
Aether Media USA Inc	G	863 647-5500
Lakeland (G-7268)		
Agpb LLC	F	561 935-4147
Jupiter (G-6681)		
Aleph Graphics Inc	G	305 994-9933
Doral (G-3106)		
All-Star Sales Inc	E	904 396-1653
Jacksonville (G-5876)		
AlphaGraphics Us658	G	813 689-7788
Tampa (G-16579)		
American Business Cards Inc	E	314 739-0800
Naples (G-10666)		
Anderson Printing Services Inc	E	727 545-9000
Seminole (G-15969)		
Ard Printing Solutions LL	G	305 785-7200
Miami (G-8743)		
Arfona Printing LLC	G	312 339-0215
Highland Beach (G-5459)		
Artistic Label Company Inc	G	401 737-0666
Estero (G-3540)		
Baker County Press Inc	G	904 259-2400
Macclenny (G-8036)		
Banks Sign Systems Inc	G	954 979-0055
Pompano Beach (G-13947)		
Barnett & Pugliano Inc	G	727 826-6075
Saint Petersburg (G-14977)		
Bayfront Printing Company	G	727 823-1965
Saint Petersburg (G-14979)		
Bayshore Professional LLC	G	941 787-3023
Punta Gorda (G-14494)		
BCT International Inc	E	305 563-1224
Fort Lauderdale (G-3680)		
Bdd International Corp	G	305 573-2416
Miami (G-8808)		
Bema Inc	G	954 761-1919
Fort Lauderdale (G-3681)		
Bestprintingonlinecom LLC	E	239 263-2106
Naples (G-10693)		
Bi-Ads Inc	F	954 525-1489
Fort Lauderdale (G-3684)		
Big Biz Direct	G	813 978-0584
Tampa (G-16642)		

(G-0000) Company's Geographic Section entry number

Company	Code	Phone
Bill & Renee Enterprises Inc	G	321 452-2800
Merritt Island (G-8578)		
Blix Corporate Image LLC	F	305 572-9001
Doral (G-3142)		
Boostan Inc	G	305 223-5981
Miami (G-8846)		
Business Clinic Inc	G	786 473-4573
Hialeah (G-5084)		
C & R Designs Inc	G	321 383-2255
Titusville (G-17577)		
C&D Sign and Lighting Svcs LLC	G	863 937-9323
Lakeland (G-7287)		
Caxton Newspapers Inc	E	305 538-9700
Miami Beach (G-10176)		
Cbm Printing Worldwide Inc	G	786 531-1834
Hialeah (G-5088)		
Cigar City Printing	G	813 843-2751
Tampa (G-16704)		
City Prints LLC	G	407 409-0509
Orlando (G-12014)		
Classic Screen	G	407 699-2473
Winter Springs (G-18562)		
Cobalt Laser	G	407 855-2833
Orlando (G-12024)		
Compass Banners & Printing LLC	G	727 522-7414
Saint Petersburg (G-15013)		
Convicted Printing LLC	G	813 431-6286
Tampa (G-16726)		
Corona Printing Company Inc	G	754 263-2914
Hallandale (G-4922)		
Couchman Printing Company	G	386 756-3052
South Daytona (G-16020)		
Creative Biz Center Inc	G	954 918-7322
Lauderhill (G-7729)		
Cronus Litho LLC	G	239 325-4846
Naples (G-10722)		
D Turin & Company Inc	E	305 825-2004
Hialeah (G-5106)		
Danifer Printing Inc	G	727 849-5883
New Port Richey (G-10966)		
Dark Horse Signs and Prtg LLC	G	850 684-3833
Gulf Breeze (G-4879)		
Dentz Design Screen Prtg LLC	G	609 303-0827
Saint Augustine (G-14826)		
Design & Print	G	561 361-8299
Boca Raton (G-481)		
Design & Print Solutions Inc	G	407 703-7861
Apopka (G-120)		
Designers Press Inc	D	407 843-3141
Orlando (G-12087)		
Dg Design and Print Co LLC	G	321 446-6435
Rockledge (G-14702)		
Di Jam Holdings Inc	F	863 967-6949
Auburndale (G-229)		
Direct Mail Velocity LLC	G	561 393-4722
Boca Raton (G-486)		
Disbrow Corporation	G	813 621-9444
Tampa (G-16779)		
Diversified Graphics Inc	F	407 425-9443
Orlando (G-12099)		
Dla Document Services	F	813 828-4646
Tampa (G-16782)		
Docuvision Incorporated	E	954 791-0091
Davie (G-2405)		
Donald Art Company Inc	G	407 831-2525
Longwood (G-7889)		
Donna Lynn Enterprises Inc	G	772 286-2812
Palm Beach Gardens (G-12966)		
Doral Dgtal Reprographics Corp	G	305 704-3194
Doral (G-3197)		
Dvh Macleod Corp	F	850 224-6760
Tallahassee (G-16435)		
E3 Graphics Inc	G	954 510-1302
Coral Springs (G-2151)		
Eco Print Inc	G	305 248-1478
Homestead (G-5710)		
Economy Printing Co	F	904 786-4070
Jacksonville (G-6065)		
Editcar Printing Corp	G	305 324-5252
Miami (G-9072)		
Elite Power Prtg Solutions Inc	G	786 387-7164
Miami (G-9088)		
Emerald Prints LLC	G	850 460-5532
Niceville (G-11029)		
Envision Graphics Inc	E	305 470-0083
Miami (G-9102)		
Evolution Signs and Print Inc	G	904 634-5666
Jacksonville (G-6081)		
Express Prtg Winter Haven Inc	G	863 294-3286
Winter Haven (G-18435)		
Express Signs & Graphics Inc	F	407 889-4433
Winter Garden (G-18385)		
F2f Inc	G	561 833-9661
Delray Beach (G-2961)		
Fast Frontier Printing	G	407 538-5621
Largo (G-7581)		
Feria De Artesania Para TI	G	407 545-0909
Kissimmee (G-6919)		
Five Star Sports Tickets	F	440 899-2000
Hallandale Beach (G-4948)		
Flash Prints LLC	G	786 422-3195
Miami Gardens (G-10257)		
Flexible Prtg Solutions LLC	G	727 446-3014
Clearwater (G-1597)		
Florida Hospital Assn MGT Corp	G	407 841-6230
Orlando (G-12161)		
Florida Sentinel Publishing Co	E	813 248-1921
Tampa (G-16855)		
Florida State Graphics Inc	G	727 328-0733
Saint Petersburg (G-15053)		
Florida Tape & Labels Inc	F	941 921-5788
Sarasota (G-15681)		
Foot Print To Sccess Clbhuse I	F	954 657-8010
Lauderhill (G-7732)		
Form Script - Form Print LLC	G	954 345-3727
Coral Springs (G-2155)		
Formica Print Solutions LLC	E	800 669-5601
Clearwater (G-1606)		
Four G Enterprises Inc	E	407 834-4143
Longwood (G-7898)		
Fresh Thread Llc	G	904 677-9505
Jacksonville (G-6122)		
Fretto Prints Inc	G	904 687-1985
Crystal River (G-2276)		
G Print Inc	G	305 316-2266
Hialeah (G-5162)		
Gabol Screen Printing Co	G	305 681-3882
Opa Locka (G-2883)		
Gadsden County Times Inc	F	850 627-7649
Quincy (G-14545)		
General & Duplicating Services	G	305 541-2116
Coral Gables (G-2060)		
GLo Consumer Svcs & Prtg Co	G	954 977-5450
Margate (G-8131)		
Global Printing Services Inc	G	305 446-7628
Coral Gables (G-2062)		
Goforit Inc	G	727 785-7616
Palm Harbor (G-13111)		
Gold Coast Printing Inc	G	813 853-2219
Tampa (G-16886)		
Graphics Designer Inc	F	561 687-7993
West Palm Beach (G-18019)		
Graphics Type Color Entps Inc	G	305 591-7600
Miami (G-9236)		
Grizzly Printing Parlour LLC	G	786 416-2494
Miami (G-9251)		
Guerrilla Prtg Solutions LLC	G	352 394-7770
Minneola (G-10451)		
Guimar Inc	F	305 888-1547
Hialeah (G-5179)		
Gulfstream Graphics Inc	G	561 276-0006
Delray Beach (G-2973)		
Hartco Inc	G	904 353-5259
Jacksonville (G-6167)		
Herff Jones Inc	G	407 647-4373
Winter Park (G-18513)		
Herff Jones LLC	G	904 641-4060
Jacksonville (G-6175)		
HOB Corporation	G	813 988-2272
Tampa (G-16919)		
Hoipong Customs Inc	G	954 684-9232
Pembroke Pines (G-13396)		
Hybrid Impressions Inc	F	305 392-5029
Hialeah (G-5190)		
In Stock Printers Inc	G	727 447-2515
Oldsmar (G-11659)		
Ink Bros Printing LLC	G	407 494-9585
Longwood (G-7904)		
Instant Garden Inc	G	305 815-1090
Hialeah (G-5193)		
Instant Locate Inc	G	800 431-0812
Casselberry (G-1419)		
It Busness Solutions Group Inc	F	407 260-0116
Longwood (G-7907)		
J & J International Corp	E	407 349-7114
Sanford (G-15341)		
J J M Services Inc	G	954 437-1880
Miramar (G-10507)		
J V G Inc	G	727 584-7136
Largo (G-7619)		
J-Kup Corp	F	352 683-5629
Spring Hill (G-16073)		
Jet-Set Printing Inc	G	407 339-1900
Casselberry (G-1421)		
Jj Screenprint LLC	G	941 587-1801
Sarasota (G-15714)		
Jjaz Enterprises Inc	G	407 330-0245
Lake Mary (G-7087)		
Jmf Dgital Print Solutions Inc	G	954 362-4929
Pembroke Pines (G-13399)		
JPS Digital LLC	F	813 501-6040
Inverness (G-5831)		
Just Say Print Inc	G	954 254-7793
Coral Springs (G-2172)		
Kee Kreative LLC	G	954 931-2579
Lauderhill (G-7734)		
Kindorf Enterprises Inc	G	407 858-0331
Orlando (G-12287)		
King Tech Print LLC	G	786 362-6249
Miami (G-9390)		
L E M G Inc	G	727 461-5300
Clearwater (G-1668)		
La Mar Orlando LLC	E	407 423-2051
Orlando (G-12304)		
Label Printing Service	G	727 820-1226
Clearwater (G-1669)		
Labelpro Inc	F	727 538-2149
Clearwater (G-1670)		
Landmark Fingerprinting	G	754 205-6505
Margate (G-8140)		
Leda Printing Inc	E	941 922-1563
Sarasota (G-15724)		
Leila K Moavero	G	954 978-0018
Pompano Beach (G-14076)		
Lincoln Smith Ventures LLC	G	863 337-6670
Lakeland (G-7379)		
Linographics Inc	F	407 422-8700
Orlando (G-12331)		
Lion Ink Print Inc	G	561 358-8925
West Palm Beach (G-18058)		
Lionheart Printers LLC	G	561 781-8300
Jupiter (G-6757)		
Ljk & TS Partners Inc	G	941 661-5675
Tampa (G-17018)		
Luxe Prints LLC	G	941 484-4500
Sarasota (G-15730)		
M L Solutions Inc	G	305 506-5113
Miami (G-9491)		
Maki Printing LLC	F	941 809-7574
Sarasota (G-15735)		
Maki Printing LLC	G	941 925-4802
Sarasota (G-15736)		
Masc Aspen Partners LLC	G	212 545-1076
Boca Raton (G-587)		
Matrix Marketing Solutions Inc	F	407 654-5736
Windermere (G-18360)		
Maxigraphics Inc	F	954 978-0740
Pompano Beach (G-14090)		
McGee Enterprises Inc	G	904 328-3226
Jacksonville (G-6284)		
Mid West Lettering Company	E	850 477-6522
Pensacola (G-13553)		
Milton Newspapers Inc	A	850 623-2120
Milton (G-10431)		
Minute Man Press	G	727 791-1115
Dunedin (G-3454)		
Minuteman Press	F	727 535-3800
Largo (G-7644)		
Minuteman Press	F	813 884-2476
Tampa (G-17076)		
Minuteman Press	G	904 733-5578
Jacksonville (G-6309)		
Minuteman Press	G	305 242-6800
Cutler Bay (G-2297)		
Minuteman Press	G	863 337-6670
Lakeland (G-7396)		
Minuteman Press	G	386 255-2767
Daytona Beach (G-2577)		
Minuteman Press	G	352 728-6333
Leesburg (G-7786)		
Minuteman Press	G	772 301-0222
Port Saint Lucie (G-14426)		
Minuteman Press	G	727 214-2275
Pinellas Park (G-13709)		
Minuteman Press	G	954 804-8304
Lake Worth (G-7219)		
Mp 93 Screen Print and EMB LLC	F	407 592-3657
Orlando (G-12394)		
MRM Creative LLC	G	386 218-5940
Orange City (G-11807)		

PRODUCT

Mxn Inc ....G.......813 654-3173
Tampa (G-17089)
Navarre 3d Printing LLC ....G.......850 281-6780
Mary Esther (G-8178)
Navarre 3d Printing LLC ....F.......850 281-6780
Navarre (G-10953)
Neat Print Inc ....G.......941 545-1517
Sarasota (G-15760)
New Gnrtion Abndant Mssion Ch ...E.......772 497-5871
Port Saint Lucie (G-14427)
Onesource of Florida Inc ....G.......904 620-0003
Jacksonville (G-6341)
Open Market Enterprises LLC .....G.......407 322-5434
Orlando (G-12440)
Orellana Investments Inc ....G.......305 477-2817
Miami (G-9663)
Palm Print Inc ....F.......561 833-9661
West Palm Beach (G-18112)
Pamatian Group Inc ....G.......407 291-8387
Orlando (G-12464)
Panda Printing LLC ....F.......239 970-9727
Naples (G-10847)
Paper Palm LLC ....G.......407 647-3328
Orlando (G-12467)
Paper Pushers of America Inc ....G.......386 872-7025
Daytona Beach (G-2580)
Pasa Services Inc ....E.......305 594-8662
Opa Locka (G-11780)
Paulas Dves Sign TS Other Prtg ..G.......239 673-8923
Cape Coral (G-1373)
Pfaffco Inc ....F.......305 635-0986
Miami Lakes (G-10337)
Phantom Usa LLC ....F.......863 353-5972
Dundee (G-3436)
Phil & Brenda Johnson Inc ....F.......813 623-5478
Tampa (G-17161)
Phoenix Group Florida Inc ....G.......954 563-1224
Fort Lauderdale (G-3985)
Photoengraving Inc ....E.......813 253-3427
Tampa (G-17165)
PNC Solutions Inc ....G.......407 401-8275
Orlando (G-12492)
Power Printing of Florida ....F.......727 823-1162
Saint Petersburg (G-15157)
Precise Print Florida ....G.......813 960-4958
Lutz (G-8010)
Precision Printing of Columbus ..G.......561 509-7269
Boynton Beach (G-898)
Premier Global Enterprises .....G.......561 747-7303
Palm Beach Gardens (G-13000)
Print Administrate ....G.......407 877-5923
Winter Garden (G-18400)
Print All Promotions LLC ....G.......800 971-3209
Wildwood (G-18317)
Print Pro Shop Inc ....F.......305 859-8282
Miami (G-9742)
Print Production Services Inc ...G.......321 557-4414
Melbourne (G-8500)
Print This and That LLC ....E.......386 344-4420
Lake City (G-7038)
Printing and Labels Inc ....G.......954 578-4411
Sunrise (G-16356)
Printing Department LLC ....G.......386 253-7990
Daytona Beach (G-2586)
Printing For A Cause LLC ....E.......786 496-0637
Saint Petersburg (G-15161)
Printing Services Plus LLC ......F.......813 279-1903
Tampa (G-17185)
Printmor ....F.......954 247-9405
Coral Springs (G-2204)
Printrust Inc ....F.......954 572-0790
Sunrise (G-16357)
Prints 2 Go Inc ....G.......727 725-1700
Clearwater (G-1753)
Printshaqcom Inc ....G.......954 678-7286
Hollywood (G-5646)
Priority Printing Inc ....G.......727 446-6605
Clearwater (G-1754)
PS & QS Custom Prints LLC ....F.......352 231-3961
Gainesville (G-4751)
Push Designs Printing Inc ....G.......321 591-1645
Melbourne (G-8505)
Quality Arts Lcp LLC ....G.......305 735-2310
Hialeah (G-5320)
R A Printing Inc ....G.......904 733-5578
Jacksonville (G-6402)
Ramseys Prtg & Off Pdts Inc .....G.......850 227-7468
Port Saint Joe (G-14390)
Ranger Associates Inc ....G.......407 869-0024
Longwood (G-7941)

Real Print & Ship Inc ....F.......727 787-1949
Palm Harbor (G-13129)
Reimink Printing Inc ....G.......813 289-4663
Tampa (G-17214)
Relion Enterprises LLC ....G.......321 287-4225
Orlando (G-12546)
Rennak Inc ....G.......305 558-0144
Miami Lakes (G-10348)
San Marco Place Condo Assn .....G.......504 812-0352
Jacksonville (G-6450)
Sand Dollar Printing Inc ....G.......813 740-1953
Tampa (G-17245)
Sandy-Alexander Inc ....D.......727 579-1527
Saint Petersburg (G-15176)
Saugus Valley Corp ....G.......954 772-4077
Coral Springs (G-2209)
Securus Brot LLC ....G.......954 532-8065
Miramar (G-10542)
Semprun & Morales Corporation ..G.......305 698-2554
Hialeah (G-5345)
Sergios Printing Inc ....F.......305 971-4112
Miami (G-9869)
Services On Demand Print Inc ....F.......305 681-5345
Hallandale Beach (G-4970)
Shiny Prints ....F.......561 200-2872
Jupiter (G-6795)
Sir Speedy Printing Center .....F.......352 683-8758
Spring Hill (G-16079)
Sirs Publishing Inc ....D.......800 521-0600
Boca Raton (G-680)
Sonshine Digital Graphics Inc ...F.......904 858-1000
Jacksonville (G-6479)
SOs Services On Prtg Corp ......G.......305 225-6000
Hialeah (G-5353)
South Broward Printing Inc .....G.......954 962-1309
Hollywood (G-5660)
Southeastern Printing Co Inc ....G.......772 287-2141
Palm City (G-13059)
Southern Litho II LLC ....E.......724 394-3693
Naples (G-10898)
Spanglish Advertising Cor ......G.......305 244-0918
Miami (G-9934)
Spinnaker Holding Company ......E.......561 392-8626
Boca Raton (G-692)
Spinnaker Vero Inc ....F.......772 567-4645
Vero Beach (G-17802)
Steven Chancas ....G.......352 629-5016
Ocala (G-11499)
Steven K Bakum Inc ....G.......561 804-9110
West Palm Beach (G-18164)
Sun Coast Media Group Inc ......D.......941 206-1300
Port Charlotte (G-14317)
Sun Graphic Technologies Inc ....E.......941 753-7541
Sarasota (G-15562)
Sun Print Management LLC ....E.......727 945-0255
Holiday (G-5504)
Sunrise Printing & Signs ....G.......321 284-3803
Kissimmee (G-6962)
Superior Signs and Prints ......G.......954 780-6351
Pompano Beach (G-14207)
Taie Inc ....G.......954 966-0233
Hollywood (G-5668)
Three60printing LLC ....F.......954 271-2701
Miramar (G-10553)
Tiba Enterprises Inc ....G.......561 575-3037
Jupiter (G-6809)
Tks Printing & Promo Products ...D.......904 469-0968
Jacksonville (G-6557)
Totalprint USA ....G.......855 915-1300
Tampa (G-17363)
Tri County Printing Co In ......G.......561 477-8487
Boca Raton (G-722)
Tropical Prints Inc A Corp .....G.......305 261-9926
Miami (G-10041)
Tucker Lithographic Co ....G.......904 276-0568
Orange Park (G-11844)
United Printing LLC ....G.......954 554-7969
Pompano Beach (G-14227)
United Printing Sales Inc ......G.......954 942-4300
Pompano Beach (G-14228)
Urbaprint LLC ....G.......786 502-3223
Weston (G-18296)
USA Printing LLC ....G.......754 275-5048
Hallandale Beach (G-4983)
Van Charles Inc ....G.......954 394-3242
Oakland Park (G-11308)
Vinylot of Florida Inc ....G.......954 978-8424
Margate (G-8159)
Vision Concepts Ink Inc ....F.......305 463-8003
Doral (G-3413)

Vmak Corp ....F.......407 260-1199
Longwood (G-7958)
W H L Business Communications ...G.......561 361-9202
Boca Raton (G-750)
Walter Haas Graphics Inc ....E.......305 883-2257
Hialeah (G-5417)
Wayloo Inc ....G.......954 914-3192
Fort Lauderdale (G-4125)
Wild Prints LLC ....G.......561 800-6536
West Palm Beach (G-18206)
Wildas Jean-Joseph ....G.......561 929-1907
Lantana (G-7517)
Will-Rite Industries Inc ....G.......305 253-1985
Cutler Bay (G-2312)
Winwood Print ....G.......786 615-3188
Miami (G-10136)
Xymoprint LLC ....C.......407 504-2170
Orlando (G-12727)

PRINTING: Offset

24hour Printing Inc ....G.......954 247-9575
Lauderhill (G-7723)
3-Dimension Graphics Inc ....E.......305 599-3277
Doral (G-3084)
352ink Corp ....G.......352 373-7547
Gainesville (G-4643)
A Fine Print of Miami LLC ......G.......305 441-5263
Miami (G-8620)
A-Plus Prtg & Graphic Ctr Inc ...E.......954 327-7315
Plantation (G-13817)
Abbott Printing Co ....D.......407 831-2999
Maitland (G-8049)
Abby Press Inc ....E.......407 847-5565
Kissimmee (G-6892)
Absolute Graphics Inc ....F.......954 792-3488
Davie (G-2374)
AC Graphics Inc ....E.......305 691-3778
Hialeah (G-5023)
Accuprint Corporation ....F.......954 973-9369
Deerfield Beach (G-2654)
Ace Blueprinting Inc ....F.......954 771-0104
Fort Lauderdale (G-3620)
Ace High Printing LLC ....G.......727 542-3897
Saint Petersburg (G-14953)
Ace Press Inc ....G.......239 334-1118
Fort Myers (G-4156)
Ace Printing Inc ....E.......305 358-2572
Miami (G-8643)
Action Printers Inc ....G.......772 567-4377
Vero Beach (G-17732)
Action Printing Inc ....G.......305 592-4646
Miami (G-8649)
Admask Inc ....G.......954 962-2040
Plantation (G-13821)
Advermarket Corp ....G.......239 541-1144
Cape Coral (G-1297)
Advermarket Corp ....G.......239 542-1020
Cape Coral (G-1298)
Aesthetic Print & Design Inc ...G.......352 278-3714
Gainesville (G-4645)
Agape Graphics & Printing Inc ...G.......305 252-9147
Miami (G-8666)
All Because LLC ....G.......407 884-6700
Apopka (G-101)
All In One Mail Shop Inc ....F.......305 233-6100
Miami (G-8689)
All Service Graphics Inc ....F.......321 259-8957
Melbourne (G-8360)
All Star Printing Intl ....G.......954 974-0333
Deerfield Beach (G-2664)
Allegra Direct - South Inc .....G.......586 226-1400
Orlando (G-11893)
Allegra Fort Myers ....G.......239 275-5797
Fort Myers (G-4163)
Allegra Marketing ....G.......813 664-1129
Tampa (G-16574)
Allegra Print Signs Mail ....G.......954 963-3886
Hollywood (G-5526)
Allied Printing Inc ....D.......800 749-7683
Jacksonville (G-5878)
Alpha Commercial Printing ......G.......561 841-1415
North Palm Beach (G-11173)
Alpha Press Inc ....F.......407 299-2121
Orlando (G-11896)
Alta Systems Inc ....E.......352 372-2534
Gainesville (G-4648)
Amazon Services Inc ....F.......305 663-0585
Miami (G-8709)
Ambassador Printing Company ....G.......561 330-3668
Delray Beach (G-2930)

American Specialty Sales Corp............G......305 947-9700 North Miami (G-11089)	Central Fla Prtg Graphics LLC............G......321 752-8753 Melbourne (G-8385)	Daniels Offset Printing Inc............G......305 261-3263 Cutler Bay (G-2287)
AMG Printing Solutions Corp............G......954 235-8007 Miami (G-8724)	Central Ink International............G......786 747-8411 Doral (G-3158)	Dannys Prtg Svc Sups & Eqp Inc............G......305 757-2282 Miami (G-9000)
Apple Printing & Advg Spc Inc............E......954 524-0493 Fort Lauderdale (G-3653)	Central Printers Inc............G......727 527-5879 Saint Petersburg (G-15004)	Dax Copying and Printing Inc............G......954 236-3000 Plantation (G-13843)
Aquaflex Printing LLC............G......727 914-4922 Saint Petersburg (G-14967)	Chromatech Digital Inc............E......727 528-4711 Saint Petersburg (G-15006)	DEb Printing & Graphics Inc............G......954 968-0060 Fort Lauderdale (G-3759)
Aquarius Press Inc............F......305 688-0066 Opa Locka (G-11718)	Cincinnati Printing Service............G......239 455-0960 Naples (G-10713)	Design Litho Inc............G......813 238-7494 Tampa (G-16771)
Aquinas Inc............G......727 842-2254 New Port Richey (G-10961)	City Clors Dgital Prtg Ctr Inc............F......305 471-0816 Doral (G-3164)	Detailed Services Inc............F......239 542-2452 Cape Coral (G-1332)
Arjay Printing Company Inc............G......904 764-6070 Oldsmar (G-11628)	Class A Printing LLC............G......386 447-0520 Palm Coast (G-13073)	Digital Printing Solutions Inc............E......407 671-8715 Winter Park (G-18506)
Armstrongs Prtg & Graphics Inc............G......850 243-6923 Fort Walton Beach (G-4562)	Clear Copy Inc............E......561 369-3900 Boynton Beach (G-851)	Dimension Photo Engrv Co Inc............E......813 251-0244 Tampa (G-16777)
Art In Print Inc............F......561 877-0995 Delray Beach (G-2933)	Colonial Press Intl Inc............C......305 633-1581 Miami (G-8945)	Dimensnal Imprssion Hldngs Inc............E......813 251-0244 Tampa (G-16778)
Artcraft Engraving & Prtg Inc............F......305 557-9449 Hialeah (G-5057)	Color Concepts Prtg Design Co............F......813 623-2921 Tampa (G-16720)	Direct Impressions Inc............E......239 549-4484 Cape Coral (G-1335)
Artworks Printing Entps Inc............G......954 893-7984 Hollywood (G-5530)	Color Express Inc............G......305 558-2061 Hialeah (G-5094)	Docuprint Corporation............F......305 639-8618 Miami (G-9038)
Automated Printing Services............G......904 731-3244 Jacksonville (G-5912)	Color Press Print Inc............G......850 763-9884 Panama City (G-13249)	Dominion Printers Inc............G......757 340-1300 Port Charlotte (G-14295)
B J and ME Inc............G......561 368-5470 Boca Raton (G-424)	Coloramax Printing Inc............F......305 541-0322 Miami (G-8947)	Donnelley Financial LLC............F......305 371-3900 Miami (G-9042)
B R Q Grossmans Inc............F......954 971-1077 Pompano Beach (G-13943)	Colorfast Printing & Graphics............G......727 531-9506 Clearwater (G-1547)	Donoso Printing Corp............G......786 508-9426 Hialeah Gardens (G-5435)
Ballard Printing Inc............G......904 783-4430 Jacksonville (G-5922)	Colorgraphx Inc............E......727 572-6364 Saint Petersburg (G-15009)	Dpdm Inc............G......561 327-4150 Lake Worth (G-7196)
Bama Printing LLC............E......561 855-7641 West Palm Beach (G-17938)	Commercial Printers Inc............D......954 781-3737 Fort Lauderdale (G-3738)	Drewlu Enterprises Inc............E......407 478-7872 Winter Park (G-18509)
Bandart Enterprises Inc............F......954 564-1224 Fort Lauderdale (G-3673)	Compass Printing and Marketing............G......954 856-8331 Margate (G-8125)	Drummond Press Inc............E......904 354-2818 Jacksonville (G-6042)
Bava Inc............F......850 893-4799 Tallahassee (G-16417)	Consolidated Label Co............C......407 339-2626 Sanford (G-15291)	Durra Quick Print Inc............G......850 681-2900 Tallahassee (G-16433)
Bay Area Graphics............G......813 247-2400 Tampa (G-16630)	Continental Printing............G......904 731-8989 Jacksonville (G-6001)	Durra-Print Inc............E......850 222-4768 Tallahassee (G-16434)
Bayou Printing Inc............F......850 678-5444 Valparaiso (G-17656)	Continental Printing Svcs Inc............G......904 743-6718 Jacksonville (G-6002)	Dynacolor Graphics Inc............E......305 625-5388 Hialeah (G-5127)
Beck Graphics Inc............F......727 443-3803 Palm Harbor (G-13104)	Copy Cat Printing LLC............G......850 438-5566 Pensacola (G-13477)	Dynamic Printing of Brandon............G......813 664-6880 Lithia (G-7833)
Bellak Color Corporation............E......305 854-8525 Doral (G-3132)	Copy Right Bgmd Inc............F......904 680-0343 Jacksonville (G-6006)	Dynastic Investments Inc............E......513 570-7153 Miami (G-9055)
Bizcard Xpress Sanford LLC............G......407 688-8902 Sanford (G-15273)	Copy Van of Florida Inc............G......407 366-7126 Oviedo (G-12816)	E & P Printing Corp............G......305 715-9545 Miami (G-9056)
Bjm Enterprises Inc............F......941 746-4171 Palmetto (G-13157)	Copy Well Inc............G......850 222-9777 Tallahassee (G-16428)	Eagle Artistic Printing Inc............G......973 476-6301 Boca Raton (G-498)
Blackstone Legal Supplies Inc............F......305 945-3450 Lauderhill (G-7727)	Copy-Flow Inc............F......305 592-0930 Davie (G-2398)	Ed Vance Printing Company Inc............F......813 882-8888 Tampa (G-16797)
Blackwell Family Corporation............G......941 639-0200 Punta Gorda (G-14499)	Corporate Printing Svcs Inc............G......305 273-6000 Miami (G-8974)	Edigitalprintingcom Inc............G......305 378-2325 Miami (G-9071)
Bladorn Investments Inc............G......941 627-0014 Port Charlotte (G-14288)	Crain Ventures Inc............G......407 933-1820 Kissimmee (G-6909)	Edward Thomas Company............G......561 746-1441 Jupiter (G-6718)
Bobs Quick Prtg & Copy Ctr............G......561 278-0203 Boynton Beach (G-846)	Creative Color Printing Inc............G......954 701-6763 Davie (G-2399)	Ejco Inc............G......352 375-0797 Gainesville (G-4684)
Boca Color Graphics Inc............F......561 391-2229 Boca Raton (G-435)	Creative Printing Bay Cnty Inc............F......850 784-1645 Panama City (G-13251)	Elite Printing & Marketing Inc............G......850 474-0894 Pensacola (G-13494)
Boca Raton Printing Co............G......561 395-8404 Boca Raton (G-437)	Creative Prtg & Graphics Inc............G......954 242-2562 Coconut Creek (G-1982)	Ellison Graphics Corp............F......561 746-9256 Jupiter (G-6720)
Bodree Printing Company Inc............F......850 455-8511 Pensacola (G-13459)	Creative Prtg Grphic Dsign Inc............E......407 855-0202 Orlando (G-12055)	Empire Corp Kit of............G......800 432-3028 Doral (G-3208)
Bonita Printshop Inc............G......239 992-8522 Bonita Springs (G-783)	Creative Svcs Centl Fla Inc............G......863 385-8383 Sebring (G-15916)	EO Painter Printing Company............F......386 985-4877 De Leon Springs (G-2624)
Bradford County Telegraph Inc............F......904 964-6305 Starke (G-16096)	Cromer Printing Inc............E......863 422-8651 Haines City (G-4905)	Everything Printing Inc............G......239 541-2679 Cape Coral (G-1340)
Brooksville Printing Inc............G......352 848-0016 Brooksville (G-1143)	Crompco Inc............G......954 584-8488 Plantation (G-13840)	Express Press Inc............F......813 884-3310 Tampa (G-16824)
Bros Williams Printing Inc............G......305 769-9925 Hialeah (G-5080)	Crown Printing Inc............G......863 682-4881 Lakeland (G-7301)	Express Printing & Office Sups............G......904 765-9696 Jacksonville (G-6085)
Brut Printing Co Inc............E......904 354-5055 Jacksonville (G-5960)	Csba Digital Printing............G......813 482-1608 Tampa (G-16744)	Express Printing Center Inc............F......813 909-1085 Land O Lakes (G-7492)
Budget Printing Center LLC............G......561 848-5700 Riviera Beach (G-14602)	Csmc Inc............G......407 246-1567 Orlando (G-12060)	Factorymart Inc............F......561 202-9820 West Palm Beach (G-17994)
Business Center & Printshop............G......786 547-6681 Miami (G-8863)	Curry & Sons Inc............G......305 296-8781 Key West (G-6861)	Fermatex Enterprises Inc............G......407 332-8320 Orlando (G-12148)
Butler Graphics Inc............G......305 477-1344 Miami (G-8865)	Custom Graphics and Plates Inc............F......407 696-5448 Longwood (G-7884)	FGA Printing............G......954 763-1122 Pompano Beach (G-14019)
C & D Printing Company............D......727 572-9999 Saint Petersburg (G-14993)	Customer First Inc Naples............E......239 949-8518 Bonita Springs (G-793)	Fidelity Printing Corporation............D......727 522-9557 Saint Petersburg (G-15044)
C & H Printing Inc............G......904 620-8444 Jacksonville (G-5965)	D&R Printing LLC............G......941 378-3311 Sarasota (G-15649)	First Impressions Printing............F......352 237-6141 Ocala (G-11389)
C F Print Ltd Inc............F......631 567-2110 The Villages (G-17553)	D-Lux Printing Inc............F......850 457-8494 Pensacola (G-13485)	First Imprseesion South Flo............G......954 525-0342 Fort Lauderdale (G-3817)
Calev Systems Inc............E......305 672-2900 Miami Springs (G-10387)	Dagher & Sons Inc............F......904 998-0911 Jacksonville (G-6022)	First Imprssons Prtg Cmmnctons............G......407 831-6100 Longwood (G-7896)
Capra Graphics Inc............G......305 418-4582 Doral (G-3152)	Dahlquist Enterprises Inc............G......407 896-2294 Orlando (G-12071)	Flamingo Printing Brevard Inc............G......321 723-2771 Melbourne (G-8426)
Catapult Print and Packg LLC............F......407 717-4323 Orlando (G-11986)	Dakim Inc............F......561 790-0884 Royal Palm Beach (G-14762)	Florida Graphic Printing Inc............F......386 253-4532 Daytona Beach (G-2553)

Florida Print Solutions Inc ....G 727 327-5500	Howies Instant Printing Inc ....F 561 686-8699	Kwikie Dup Ctr Pinellas Pk Inc ...G 727 544-7788
Saint Petersburg (G-15051)	West Palm Beach (G-18027)	Pinellas Park (G-13702)
Florida Printing Group Inc ....G 954 956-8570	Hughes Consolidated Services ....G 904 438-5710	L & N Label Company Inc ....E 727 442-5400
Pompano Beach (G-14032)	Jacksonville (G-6187)	Clearwater (G-1667)
Flyer Studios Inc ....G 786 402-9596	Hunt Enterprises Inc ....G 863 682-6187	Label Company ....E 850 438-7334
Davie (G-2414)	Lakeland (G-7346)	Pensacola (G-13535)
Ford Press Inc ....F 352 787-4650	Hurricane Graphics Inc ....E 305 760-9154	Laser Light Litho Corp ....F 305 899-0713
Leesburg (G-7777)	Miami Gardens (G-10263)	North Miami (G-11108)
Fort Dearborn Company ....D 772 600-2756	ICM Printing Co Inc ....F 352 377-7468	Lauderdale Graphics Corp ....G 954 450-0800
Palm City (G-13040)	Gainesville (G-4709)	Davie (G-2432)
Fort Myers Digital LLC ....G 239 482-3086	Ideal Publishing Co Inc ....G 727 321-0785	Lawton Printers Inc ....E 407 260-0400
Fort Myers (G-4262)	Saint Petersburg (G-15082)	Orlando (G-12316)
Free Press Publishing Company ...E 813 254-5888	Iguana Graphics Inc ....G 813 657-7800	Lee Printing Inc ....F 904 396-5715
Tampa (G-16860)	Brandon (G-1096)	Jacksonville Beach (G-6637)
G S Printers Inc ....G 305 931-2755	Image Printing & Graphics LLC ...G 321 783-5555	Leesburg Printing Company ....F 352 787-3348
Fort Lauderdale (G-3834)	Cape Canaveral (G-1286)	Leesburg (G-7783)
Gandy Printers Inc ....G 850 222-5847	Image Prtg & Digital Svcs Inc ...G 850 244-3380	Lexprint LLC ....G 305 661-2424
Tallahassee (G-16444)	Mary Esther (G-8177)	Miami (G-9455)
Garvin Management Company Inc ...G 850 893-4719	Imprint ....G 941 484-5151	Linden-Beals Corp ....G 772 562-0624
Tallahassee (G-16445)	Nokomis (G-11046)	Vero Beach (G-17773)
Gb Printing ....F 954 941-3778	Independent Resources Inc ....E 813 237-0945	Lindsey Macke Bindery Printing ...G 727 514-3570
Pompano Beach (G-14037)	Tampa (G-16937)	Odessa (G-11565)
Gentry Printing Company LLC .....G 727 441-1914	Infinite Print LLC ....G 727 942-2121	Lion Press Inc ....G 954 971-6193
Clearwater (G-1614)	Holiday (G-5500)	Pompano Beach (G-14078)
Glider Printing LLC ....G 813 601-8907	Inkpressions Inc ....F 305 261-0872	Litho Art Inc ....G 305 232-7098
Tampa (G-16880)	Palmetto Bay (G-13213)	Miami (G-9467)
Global Printing Solutions Inc .....G 727 458-3483	Inky Fingers Printing Inc ....G 904 384-1900	Litho Haus Printers Inc ....G 850 671-6600
Saint Petersburg (G-15062)	Jacksonville (G-6197)	Tallahassee (G-16471)
Gobczynskis Printery Inc ....G 941 758-5734	Instant Printing & Copy Center ...G 727 849-1199	Lithocraft Inc ....G 386 761-3584
Sarasota (G-15485)	Holiday (G-5501)	Port Orange (G-14338)
Golden Print Inc ....G 561 833-9661	Instant Printing Services Inc .....G 727 546-8036	Lithotec Commercial Printing .....F 727 541-4614
Boynton Beach (G-873)	Floral City (G-3611)	Clearwater (G-1675)
Goodtime Printing Inc ....G 352 629-8838	Intec Printing Solutions Corp .....G 813 949-7799	Lmb Consultants Inc ....G 954 537-9590
Ocala (G-11402)	Lutz (G-7996)	Pompano Beach (G-14080)
Gpt Media Group Corporation .....E 954 315-0990	Integrity Business Svcs Inc ....G 321 267-9294	Lmn Printing Co Inc ....F 386 428-9928
Pompano Beach (G-14043)	Titusville (G-17592)	Edgewater (G-3497)
Graphic and Printing Svcs Corp ...G 954 486-8868	International Printing & Copyi .....G 954 295-5239	Lori Roberts Print Shop I ....G 813 882-8456
Tamarac (G-16532)	Coconut Creek (G-1993)	Brooksville (G-1176)
Graphic Dynamics Inc ....G 954 728-8452	Interprint Incorporated ....D 727 531-8957	Lucky Dog Printing Inc ....G 407 346-1663
Fort Lauderdale (G-3844)	Clearwater (G-1646)	Saint Cloud (G-14931)
Graphic Masters Inc ....D 800 230-3873	Ironhorse Pressworks Inc ....G 727 462-9988	Lufemor Inc ....G 305 557-2162
Miami (G-9234)	Clearwater (G-1649)	Hialeah (G-5229)
Graphic Press Corporation ....G 850 562-2262	Ironside Press ....G 772 569-8484	Lumo Print Inc ....G 305 246-0003
Tallahassee (G-16450)	Vero Beach (G-17767)	Homestead (G-5728)
Graphic Reproductions Inc ....G 321 267-1111	Island Print Shop ....G 239 642-0077	M Victoria Enterprises Inc ....F 727 576-8090
Titusville (G-17589)	Naples (G-10788)	Saint Petersburg (G-15116)
Graphica Services Inc ....G 305 232-5333	J K & M Ink Corporation ....G 813 875-3106	Mad Inc ....G 813 251-9334
Miami (G-9235)	Tampa (G-16959)	Tampa (G-17030)
Graphix Solutions of America .....F 727 898-6744	J M Econo-Print Inc ....G 305 591-3620	Maddys Print Shop LLC ....G 954 749-0440
Parrish (G-13359)	Coral Gables (G-2075)	Fort Lauderdale (G-3926)
Green Light Printing Inc ....G 305 576-5858	Jak Corporate Holdings Inc ....F 813 289-1660	Magic Print Copy Center ....G 239 332-4456
Miami (G-9244)	Tampa (G-16962)	Fort Myers (G-4315)
Gulf Coast Business World Inc .....F 850 864-1511	Jet Graphics Inc ....E 305 264-4333	Magnaprint Corp ....G 954 376-8416
Fort Walton Beach (G-4590)	Miami (G-9365)	Oakland Park (G-11276)
Gunn Prtg & Lithography Inc .....F 813 870-6010	Jimbob Printing Inc ....F 850 973-2633	Manatee Printers Inc ....E 941 746-9100
Tampa (G-16901)	Madison (G-8045)	Bradenton (G-1011)
H & H Printing Inc ....G 407 422-2932	Jkg Group ....G 561 866-2850	Manci Graphics Corp ....G 813 664-1129
Orlando (G-12204)	Boca Raton (G-562)	Tampa (G-17035)
H & M Printing Inc ....F 407 831-8030	Jordan Norris Inc ....G 407 846-1400	Mark V Printing LLC ....G 954 563-2505
Sanford (G-15329)	Orlando (G-12278)	Oakland Park (G-11278)
H D Quickprint & Disc Off Sups ...G 407 678-1355	Jrg Systems Inc ....F 954 962-1020	Market Ink Usa Inc ....G 561 502-3438
Orlando (G-12206)	Fort Lauderdale (G-3898)	West Palm Beach (G-18067)
H&M Phillips Inc ....G 727 797-4600	K Color Corp ....F 305 579-2290	Marrakech Inc ....G 727 942-2218
Odessa (G-11556)	Miami (G-9382)	Tarpon Springs (G-17482)
Hamilton Printing Inc ....G 772 334-0151	K R O Enterprises Ltd ....G 309 797-2213	Martin Lithograph Inc ....E 813 254-1553
Jensen Beach (G-6655)	Naples (G-10795)	Tampa (G-17044)
Hartley Press Inc ....D 904 398-5141	K12 Print Inc ....G 800 764-7600	Master Screen Printing ....G 407 625-8902
Jacksonville (G-6168)	West Palm Beach (G-18046)	Orlando (G-12366)
Hartmans Print Center Inc ....G 941 475-2220	Keithco Inc ....G 352 351-4741	Mc Graphics LLC ....G 727 579-1527
Englewood (G-3518)	Ocala (G-11419)	Saint Petersburg (G-15124)
Harvest Print & Bus Svcs Inc .....F 850 681-2488	Key West Printing LLC ....G 305 517-6711	Mdh Graphic Services Inc ....F 561 533-9000
Tallahassee (G-16459)	Key West (G-6868)	West Palm Beach (G-18071)
Harvest Print Mktg Sltions LLC ...G 850 681-2488	Kights Printing & Office Pdts .....G 904 731-7990	Medfare LLC ....F 561 998-9444
Tallahassee (G-16460)	Jacksonville (G-6242)	Boca Raton (G-591)
Harvest Prtg & Copy Ctr Inc .....F 850 681-2488	Kinane Corp ....F 772 288-6580	Media Systems Inc ....G 954 427-4411
Tallahassee (G-16461)	Stuart (G-16174)	Coral Springs (G-2181)
Herald-Advocate Publishing Co ...G 863 773-3255	King & Grube Advg & Prtg LLC ...G 727 327-6033	Megacolor Print LLC ....G 305 499-9395
Wauchula (G-17828)	Largo (G-7624)	Miami Beach (G-10212)
Hernandez Printing Service Inc ...F 305 642-0483	King & Grube Inc ....F 727 327-6033	Megamalls Inc ....F 407 891-2111
Miami (G-9277)	Largo (G-7625)	Saint Cloud (G-14933)
Hernando Lithoprinting Inc ....G 352 796-4136	King Printing & Graphics Inc .....G 813 681-5060	Menu Men Inc ....F 305 633-7925
Brooksville (G-1160)	Brandon (G-1097)	Miami (G-9532)
HI Tech Printing Systems Inc .....E 954 933-9155	Kissimmee Printing ....G 407 518-2514	Miami Trucolor Offset Svc Co .....G 954 962-5230
Pompano Beach (G-14049)	Kissimmee (G-6935)	West Park (G-18215)
Hilcraft Engraving Inc ....G 305 871-6100	Kmg Marketing LLC ....G 727 376-7200	Micro Printing Inc ....F 954 676-5757
Miami (G-9282)	Odessa (G-11563)	Fort Lauderdale (G-3940)
Hobby Press Inc ....E 305 887-4333	Kopy Kats Club Ormond Bch Inc ...G 386 437-3281	Midds Inc ....F 561 586-6220
Medley (G-8253)	Ormond Beach (G-12776)	Lake Worth (G-7217)
Hoffman Brothers Inc ....E 407 563-5004	Kreate Printing Inc ....G 305 542-1336	Midds Inc ....E 561 586-6220
Debary (G-2636)	Miami (G-9398)	Lake Worth Beach (G-7258)

(G-0000) Company's Geographic Section entry number

Mikes Print Shop Inc	G	407 718-4964	
Winter Park *(G-18525)*			
Mmp-Boca Raton LLC	F	561 392-8626	
Boca Raton *(G-601)*			
Modern Digital Imaging Inc	F	850 222-7514	
Tallahassee *(G-16481)*			
Modern Mail Print Slutions Inc	E	727 572-6245	
Clearwater *(G-1701)*			
MOR Printing Inc	F	954 377-1197	
Plantation *(G-13869)*			
Morten Enterprises Inc	F	727 531-8957	
Clearwater *(G-1703)*			
Multi-Color Printing Inc	G	772 287-1676	
Stuart *(G-16187)*			
My Print Shop Inc	F	954 973-9369	
Deerfield Beach *(G-2773)*			
Myers Printing Inc	G	813 237-0288	
Tampa *(G-17093)*			
Nai Print Solutions LLC	G	850 637-1260	
Pensacola *(G-13554)*			
Naples Printing Inc	G	239 643-2442	
Naples *(G-10831)*			
Nassau Printing & Off Sup Inc	G	904 879-2305	
Callahan *(G-1255)*			
National Multiple Listing Inc	E	954 772-8880	
Fort Lauderdale *(G-3954)*			
Nebraska Printing Inc	E	813 870-6871	
Tampa *(G-17106)*			
Newspaper Printing Company	C	813 839-0035	
Tampa *(G-17108)*			
Nexpub Inc	F	954 392-5889	
Miramar *(G-10518)*			
Ngp Corporate Square Inc	E	239 643-3430	
Naples *(G-10836)*			
North Florida Printing Inc	G	386 362-1080	
Live Oak *(G-7850)*			
North Palm Printing Center	G	561 622-2839	
Palm Beach Gardens *(G-12993)*			
Nupress of Miami Inc	E	305 594-2100	
Doral *(G-3314)*			
Ocala Print Quick Inc	G	352 629-0736	
Ocala *(G-11458)*			
Olmedo Printing Corp	G	305 262-4666	
Miami *(G-9644)*			
One Hour Printing	G	386 763-3111	
South Daytona *(G-16025)*			
Oompha Inc	G	850 222-7210	
Tallahassee *(G-16486)*			
Original Impressions LLC	C	305 233-1322	
Weston *(G-18276)*			
Output Printing Corp	F	813 228-8800	
Tampa *(G-17134)*			
P & G Printing Group Inc	F	954 971-2511	
Margate *(G-8145)*			
P & J Graphics Inc	F	813 626-3243	
Temple Terrace *(G-17541)*			
Pad Printing Technology Corp	G	941 739-8667	
Bradenton *(G-1023)*			
Pad Printing Technology Group	F	941 739-8667	
Bradenton *(G-1024)*			
Palm Beach Junior Clg Prnt Shp	F	561 969-0122	
Lake Worth *(G-7225)*			
Palm Prnting/Printers Ink Corp	E	239 332-8600	
Fort Myers *(G-4355)*			
Palm Prtg Strgc Solutions LLC	G	239 332-8600	
Fort Myers *(G-4356)*			
Palmetto Printing Inc	F	305 253-2444	
Miami *(G-9685)*			
Pan American Graphic Inc	E	305 885-1962	
Hialeah Gardens *(G-5446)*			
Panther Printing Inc	E	239 936-5050	
Fort Myers *(G-4357)*			
Panther Printing LLC	G	239 936-5050	
Pompano Beach *(G-14116)*			
Panther Printing LLC	F	954 651-7766	
Pompano Beach *(G-14117)*			
Paper Fish Printing Inc	G	239 481-3555	
Fort Myers *(G-4358)*			
Paragon Products Inc	E	407 302-9147	
Sanford *(G-15369)*			
Parkinson Enterprises Inc	E	863 688-7900	
Lakeland *(G-7406)*			
Parkway Printing Inc	G	239 936-6970	
Fort Myers *(G-4360)*			
Patriot Press Inc	F	407 625-7516	
Orlando *(G-12472)*			
Paw Print Co	G	561 753-5588	
West Palm Beach *(G-18116)*			
PCI Communications Inc	G	941 729-5202	
Ellenton *(G-3512)*			

Penstripe Graphics	G	904 726-0200	
Jacksonville *(G-6365)*			
Perfect Copy & Print Inc	G	727 743-0913	
Pinellas Park *(G-13717)*			
Peter Printer Inc	G	305 558-0147	
Hialeah *(G-5293)*			
Phillips Graphics Inc	G	352 622-1776	
Ocala *(G-11465)*			
Phillips Printing Services LLC	G	941 526-6570	
Bradenton *(G-1027)*			
Photo Offset Inc	F	305 666-1067	
Miami *(G-9713)*			
PIP Marketing Signs Print	F	904 825-2372	
Saint Augustine *(G-14873)*			
PIP Printing	G	352 622-3224	
Ocala *(G-11467)*			
PIP Printing	G	386 258-3326	
Daytona Beach *(G-2583)*			
PIP Printing 622 Inc	G	813 935-8113	
Tampa *(G-17166)*			
Pk Graphicz	G	305 534-2184	
Pompano Beach *(G-14128)*			
Pk Group Inc	F	239 643-2442	
Naples *(G-10860)*			
Plasti-Card Corporation	E	305 944-2726	
Delray Beach *(G-2997)*			
Podgo Printing LLC	G	954 874-9100	
Hollywood *(G-5644)*			
Port Printing Co	G	561 848-1402	
Riviera Beach *(G-14662)*			
PPG Inc	F	813 831-9902	
Tampa *(G-17172)*			
Precision Litho Service Inc	D	727 573-1763	
Clearwater *(G-1747)*			
Premier Corporate Printing	G	305 378-8480	
Jacksonville *(G-6382)*			
Premier Corporate Printing LLC	F	305 378-8480	
Jacksonville *(G-6383)*			
Premier Printing Signs	G	727 849-2493	
Port Richey *(G-14371)*			
Premier Printing Solutions Inc	G	305 490-0244	
Fort Lauderdale *(G-3996)*			
Press Ex Inc	F	727 532-4177	
Largo *(G-7663)*			
Press Print Graphics LLC	F	850 249-3700	
Panama City Beach *(G-13337)*			
Press Printing Enterprises Inc	E	239 598-1500	
Fort Myers *(G-4368)*			
Press Room Inc	G	954 792-6729	
Pembroke Pines *(G-13409)*			
Pressex Inc	F	727 299-8500	
Clearwater *(G-1751)*			
Print & Post Inc	G	786 603-9279	
Aventura *(G-272)*			
Print Basics Inc	G	954 354-0700	
Deerfield Beach *(G-2787)*			
Print Big Inc	G	305 398-8898	
Hialeah *(G-5307)*			
Print Bold Corp	E	305 517-1281	
Miami *(G-9740)*			
Print Dynamics	F	954 524-9294	
Fort Lauderdale *(G-3999)*			
Print E-Solution Inc	G	954 588-5454	
Deerfield Beach *(G-2788)*			
Print Etc Inc	G	813 972-2800	
Tampa *(G-17183)*			
Print Express	G	904 737-6641	
Jacksonville *(G-6386)*			
Print Factory LLC	G	954 392-5889	
Miramar *(G-10530)*			
Print Farm Inc	E	305 592-2895	
Miami *(G-9741)*			
Print Headquarters	F	772 286-2812	
Palm Beach Gardens *(G-13002)*			
Print Motion Inc	G	786 212-1817	
Doral *(G-3337)*			
Print One Inc	G	813 273-0240	
Oldsmar *(G-11691)*			
Print Resources	G	904 316-0373	
Jacksonville *(G-6387)*			
Print Shop of Chiefland Inc	G	352 493-0322	
Chiefland *(G-1449)*			
Print Solution Digital LLC	G	305 819-7420	
Hialeah *(G-5308)*			
Print Store LLC	G	727 656-1376	
Palm Harbor *(G-13124)*			
Print-It Usacom Inc	G	954 370-2200	
Davie *(G-2460)*			
Printed Systems Inc	G	904 281-0909	
Jacksonville *(G-6388)*			

Printer Pix	G	863 273-3447	
Sanford *(G-15378)*			
Printers Edge LLC	F	407 294-8542	
Orlando *(G-12507)*			
Printers of Pensacola LLC	G	850 434-2588	
Pensacola *(G-13585)*			
Printers Pride Inc	G	813 932-8683	
Tampa *(G-17184)*			
Printing Connection Too Inc	G	954 584-4197	
Davie *(G-2461)*			
Printing Depot Inc	G	813 855-6758	
Oldsmar *(G-11693)*			
Printing Edge Inc	G	904 399-3343	
Jacksonville *(G-6389)*			
Printing Express	G	305 512-0900	
Hialeah *(G-5310)*			
Printing Grphics Cnnection Inc	G	305 222-6144	
Miami *(G-9745)*			
Printing Mart Inc	G	954 753-0323	
Pompano Beach *(G-14148)*			
Printing Usa Inc	F	407 857-7468	
Orlando *(G-12508)*			
Printmaster Inc	G	954 771-6104	
Oakland Park *(G-11288)*			
Printnow Inc	G	850 435-1149	
Pensacola *(G-13586)*			
Printworks	G	850 681-6909	
Tallahassee *(G-16490)*			
Pro-Copy Inc	E	813 988-5900	
Temple Terrace *(G-17543)*			
Professnal Reproduction of Jax	G	904 389-4141	
Jacksonville *(G-6391)*			
Progressive Printing Co Inc	F	904 388-0746	
Jacksonville *(G-6394)*			
Progressive Printing Solutions	G	800 370-5591	
Delray Beach *(G-3005)*			
Prolific Resource Inc	G	727 868-9341	
Port Richey *(G-14373)*			
Promo Printing Group Inc	G	813 541-3509	
Tampa *(G-17190)*			
Proprint of Naples Inc	F	239 775-3553	
Fort Myers *(G-4370)*			
Psb Miami Corp	G	786 870-4880	
Miami *(G-9755)*			
Public Image Printing Inc	G	727 363-1800	
St Pete Beach *(G-16092)*			
QP Consulting Inc	G	321 727-2442	
Melbourne *(G-8506)*			
Quad/Graphics Inc	D	813 837-3436	
Tampa *(G-17198)*			
Quality Printing Inc	G	386 255-1565	
Daytona Beach *(G-2588)*			
Quick Prints LLC	G	954 526-9013	
Fort Lauderdale *(G-4010)*			
Quick Prints LLC	G	954 594-9415	
Plantation *(G-13880)*			
Quickprint Line	G	561 740-9930	
Boynton Beach *(G-905)*			
Quicksilver Prtg & Copying Inc	G	813 888-6811	
Tampa *(G-17204)*			
R K L Enterprises of Pensacola	F	850 432-2335	
Pensacola *(G-13592)*			
R R H Inc	F	954 966-1209	
Hollywood *(G-5651)*			
R Smith Printing Inc	G	518 827-7700	
Hastings *(G-4989)*			
Rainbow Printing Inc	G	561 364-9000	
Boynton Beach *(G-907)*			
Rapid Graphix Inc	G	941 639-2043	
Punta Gorda *(G-14525)*			
Rapid Print Southwest Fla Inc	G	239 590-9797	
Fort Myers *(G-4376)*			
Rapid Rater Company	E	850 893-7346	
Tallahassee *(G-16492)*			
Rapid Reproductions LLC	G	607 843-2221	
Melbourne Beach *(G-8570)*			
Redberd Printing	G	407 622-2292	
Winter Park *(G-18530)*			
Redbird Printing	G	904 654-8371	
Winter Park *(G-18531)*			
Repro Plus Inc	F	407 843-1492	
Orlando *(G-12547)*			
Rgu Color Inc	G	386 252-9979	
South Daytona *(G-16027)*			
Rinaldi Printing Company	E	813 569-0033	
Tampa *(G-17221)*			
Roberts Quality Printing Inc	E	727 442-4011	
Clearwater *(G-1769)*			
Rodes Printing Corp	G	305 559-5263	
Miami *(G-9817)*			

PRODUCT

Rose Printing Co Inc .... F 850 339-8093
Tallahassee (G-16495)
Rush Flyers .... G 954 332-0509
Plantation (G-13883)
Rush To Excellence Prtg Inc .... G 904 367-0100
Jacksonville (G-6438)
Rxprinting and Graphics LLC .... G 407 965-3039
Orlando (G-12563)
S Printing Inc .... G 305 633-3343
Miami (G-9832)
Salt 1 To 1 .... G 407 538-2134
Orlando (G-12571)
Sameday Printing Inc .... G 800 411-3106
Miami (G-9842)
Sanibel Print & Graphics .... G 239 454-1001
Fort Myers (G-4391)
SBT River PIP Project .... F 919 469-5095
Orlando (G-12577)
Seapress Inc .... G 941 366-8494
Sarasota (G-15822)
Seminole Paper & Printing Co .... G 305 379-8481
Miami (G-9865)
Seminole Printing Inc .... G 305 823-7204
Hialeah (G-5344)
Serbin Printing Inc .... E 941 366-0755
Sarasota (G-15825)
Shelbie Press Inc .... G 407 896-4600
Orlando (G-12588)
Shima Group Corp .... G 305 463-0288
Doral (G-3364)
Shoreline Printing Company .... G 954 491-0311
Oakland Park (G-11294)
Short Stop Print Inc .... G 941 474-4313
Englewood (G-3537)
Signature Printing Inc .... F 305 828-9992
Miami Lakes (G-10352)
Sobe Express .... G 305 674-4454
Miami Beach (G-10229)
Sol Davis Printing Inc .... F 813 353-3609
Tampa (G-17279)
Solid Print Solutions Inc .... G 561 670-4391
Lake Worth Beach (G-7261)
Solo Printing LLC .... C 305 594-8699
Miami (G-9914)
Sosumi Holdings Inc .... E 239 634-3430
Naples (G-10896)
South Florida Graphics Corp .... G 954 917-0606
Fort Lauderdale (G-4057)
Southeast Print Programs Inc .... E 813 885-3203
Tampa (G-17286)
Southeastern Printing Co Inc .... C 772 287-2141
Hialeah (G-5357)
Southeastern Printing Co Inc .... F 305 885-8707
Boca Raton (G-688)
Southern Business Card Inc .... G 305 944-2931
Delray Beach (G-3020)
Southern Company Entp Inc .... E 904 879-2101
Callahan (G-1258)
Southprint Corp .... G 813 237-8000
Tampa (G-17292)
Space Flyers Inc .... G 305 219-6990
Hialeah Gardens (G-5452)
Speed Print One Inc .... G 305 374-5936
Miami (G-9942)
Spett Printing Co Inc .... G 561 241-9758
Boca Raton (G-691)
Spiritwear Today .... G 239 676-7384
Bonita Springs (G-821)
Spotlight Graphics Inc .... E 941 929-1500
Sarasota (G-15832)
Sprint Printing Company LLC .... G 239 947-2221
Bonita Springs (G-822)
Spyder Graphics Inc .... G 954 561-9725
Oakland Park (G-11297)
Stacy Lee Montgomery .... G 863 662-3163
Winter Haven (G-18470)
Steve Printer Inc .... G 941 375-8657
Venice (G-17719)
Steven M Roessler LLC .... G 321 773-2300
Indian Harbour Beach (G-5808)
Stewart-Hedrick Inc .... E 941 907-0090
Lakewood Ranch (G-7487)
Stuart Web Inc .... E 772 287-8022
Stuart (G-16233)
Sun 3d Corporation .... G 954 210-6010
Pompano Beach (G-14204)
Sun Screen Print Inc .... G 904 674-0520
Jacksonville (G-6515)
Sunbelt Usa Inc .... F 239 353-5519
Naples (G-10910)

Suniland Press Inc .... E 305 235-8811
Miami (G-9967)
Sunshine Printing Inc .... F 561 478-2602
West Palm Beach (G-18170)
Super Color Inc .... E 954 964-4656
Davie (G-2485)
Superior Printers Inc .... D 407 644-3344
Winter Park (G-18541)
Swift Print Service Inc .... G 239 458-2212
Cape Coral (G-1396)
T Beattie Enterprises .... F 407 679-2000
Winter Park (G-18542)
Tag & Label of Florida Inc .... G 305 255-1050
Miami (G-9992)
Tags & Labels Printing Inc .... E 954 455-2867
Hallandale Beach (G-4977)
Tampa Bay Press Inc .... G 813 886-1415
Tampa (G-17329)
Tampa Printing Company .... E 813 612-7746
Tampa (G-17337)
Tan Printing Inc .... G 954 986-9869
Hallandale Beach (G-4978)
Target Graphics Inc .... F 941 365-8809
Sarasota (G-15849)
Target Print & Mail .... F 850 671-6600
Tallahassee (G-16512)
Thalers Printing Center Inc .... G 954 741-6522
Lauderhill (G-7744)
The Sobe Group Inc .... G 305 884-4008
Medley (G-8330)
Thunderbird Press Inc .... F 321 269-7616
Titusville (G-17622)
Tiger Business Forms Inc .... E 305 888-3528
Hialeah (G-5380)
Time Printing Co Inc .... G 904 396-9967
Jacksonville (G-6552)
Tip Top Prtg of Volusia Cnty .... G 386 760-7701
Daytona Beach (G-2614)
Tko Print Solutions Inc .... E 954 315-0990
Pompano Beach (G-14214)
Toms Instant Printing Inc .... G 904 396-0686
Jacksonville (G-6558)
Top Drawer Inc .... F 305 620-1102
Miami Lakes (G-10366)
Top Drawer Printers Inc .... E 305 620-1102
Miami Lakes (G-10367)
Topline Prtg & Graphics Inc .... E 561 881-2267
Riviera Beach (G-14683)
Total Print Inc .... G 772 589-9658
Sebastian (G-15905)
Town Street Print Shop Inc .... G 850 432-8300
Gulf Breeze (G-4895)
Trend Offset Printing Svcs Inc .... D 562 598-2446
Jacksonville (G-6567)
Trese Inc .... F 321 632-7272
Rockledge (G-14752)
Two B Printing Inc .... G 954 566-4886
Oakland Park (G-11304)
Ultra Graphics Corp .... G 305 593-0202
Miami (G-10057)
Universal Graphics & Prtg Inc .... G 561 845-6404
North Palm Beach (G-11184)
Universal Printing Company .... E 305 592-5387
Miami (G-10071)
Up2speed Printing Inc .... F 850 508-2620
Hialeah (G-5397)
V I P Printing .... G 386 258-3326
Daytona Beach (G-2616)
V P Press Inc .... F 954 581-7531
Fort Lauderdale (G-4114)
Verified Label & Print Inc .... F 813 290-7721
Tampa (G-17407)
Vero Beach Printing Inc .... G 772 562-4267
Vero Beach (G-17814)
Village Scribe Printing Co .... F 727 585-7388
Largo (G-7703)
Villagran Printing Corp .... G 786 230-6638
Miami (G-10111)
Vlp Prtg Night CLB Sups LLC .... G 561 603-2846
Boca Raton (G-748)
Vista Color Corporation .... D 305 635-2000
Doral (G-3415)
Vital Graphics and Signs Inc .... G 305 557-8181
Hialeah (G-5412)
Vital Printing Corporation .... F 561 659-2367
Lake Worth Beach (G-7264)
Vowells Downtown Inc .... G 850 432-5175
Pensacola (G-13622)
W D H Enterprises Inc .... G 941 758-6500
Bradenton (G-1073)

Web Offset Printing Co Inc .... D 727 572-7488
Clearwater (G-1849)
Webb-Mason Inc .... G 727 531-1112
Largo (G-7708)
Wecando Print LLC .... G 754 222-9144
Deerfield Beach (G-2833)
Weidenhamer Corporation .... G 850 837-3190
Destin (G-3082)
Wells Legal Supply Inc .... E 904 399-1510
Jacksonville (G-6600)
William Burns .... G 877 462-5872
Lakeland (G-7474)
Willy Walt Inc .... G 727 209-2872
Saint Petersburg (G-15235)
Wilson Printing USA LLC .... G 727 536-4173
Clearwater (G-1854)
WJS Printing Partners Inc .... G 904 731-0357
Jacksonville (G-6616)
Woods Printing Ocala Inc .... G 352 629-1665
Ocala (G-11514)
Wright Printery Inc .... G 386 252-6571
Daytona Beach (G-2619)
Xperient LLC .... G 407 265-8000
Longwood (G-7962)
Your Name Printing .... G 813 621-2400
Tampa (G-17452)

PRINTING: Pamphlets

Dasops Inc .... G 386 258-6230
Daytona Beach (G-2540)
McGee Enterprises Inc .... G 904 328-3226
Jacksonville (G-6284)
Peter T Amann .... E 561 848-2770
West Palm Beach (G-18118)

PRINTING: Photolithographic

Lutimi Nr Corp .... G 954 245-7986
Miramar (G-10511)

PRINTING: Roller, Broadwoven Fabrics, Cotton

Ripa & Associates Inc .... C 813 623-6777
Tampa (G-17222)

PRINTING: Screen, Broadwoven Fabrics, Cotton

American Mentality Inc .... G 407 599-7255
Longwood (G-7867)
Aquarius Silk Screen Inc .... G 941 377-3059
Sarasota (G-15598)
Blackwell Family Corporation .... G 941 639-0200
Punta Gorda (G-14499)
Capsmith Inc .... E 407 328-7660
Sanford (G-15277)
Cubco Inc .... F 386 254-2706
Daytona Beach (G-2538)
Daytona Trophy Inc .... F 386 253-2806
Daytona Beach (G-2544)
Happy Endings of Miami Inc .... G 305 759-4467
Miami (G-9261)
Michelle Lynn Solutions Inc .... G 786 413-0455
Miami (G-9564)
Mid-Florida Sportswear LLC .... E 386 258-5632
Daytona Beach (G-2575)
Rock N Roll Custom Screened S .... G 727 528-2111
Pinellas Park (G-13727)
Royal Tees Inc .... F 941 366-0056
Sarasota (G-15802)
Screenprint Plus Inc .... D 239 549-7284
Cape Coral (G-1382)
Screenworks Usa Inc .... C 407 426-9999
Orlando (G-12580)
Sherry Manufacturing Co Inc .... C 305 693-7000
Miami (G-9881)
South Florida Strip-Tees Inc .... F 954 972-4899
Pompano Beach (G-14189)

PRINTING: Screen, Fabric

Aloha Screen Printing Inc .... G 850 934-4716
Gulf Breeze (G-4875)
Ataly Inc .... E 813 880-9142
Tampa (G-16614)
Bakers Sports Inc .... E 904 388-8126
Jacksonville (G-5921)
Baru Agency Incorporated .... G 305 259-8800
Doral (G-3129)

Clothesline Inc ....E 850 877-9171
   Tallahassee (G-16425)

Dixon Screen Printing LLC ....G 850 476-3924
   Pensacola (G-13490)

Eagle Athletic Wear Inc ....F 727 937-6147
   Tarpon Springs (G-17469)

Expert TS of Jacksonville ....F 904 387-2500
   Jacksonville (G-6084)

HOB Corporation ....G 813 988-2272
   Tampa (G-16919)

Kid-U-Not Inc ....E 407 324-2112
   Sanford (G-15350)

Manatee Bay Enterprises Inc ....F 407 245-3600
   Orlando (G-12362)

Paradise Cstm Screening & EMB ....E 954 566-9096
   Davie (G-2453)

Promo Daddy LLC ....F 877 557-2336
   Melbourne (G-8501)

Reliable Custom Imprints Corp ....G 407 834-0571
   Longwood (G-7942)

S S Designs Inc ....D 863 965-2576
   Winter Haven (G-18465)

Serigraphia Inc ....F 850 243-9743
   Fort Walton Beach (G-4609)

Shirts & Caps Inc ....F 813 788-7026
   Tampa (G-17262)

Synergy Sports LLC ....G 239 593-9374
   Naples (G-10918)

Team Edition Apparel Inc ....C 941 744-2041
   Bradenton (G-1058)

Tiptops Inc ....G 352 357-9559
   Eustis (G-3568)

Vanlex Clothing Inc ....E 305 431-4669
   Miami Lakes (G-10375)

PRINTING: Screen, Manmade Fiber & Silk, Broadwoven Fabric

Apparel Printers ....G 352 463-8850
   Alachua (G-4)

Bagindd Prints ....F 954 971-9000
   Coral Springs (G-2134)

Blue Ocean Press Inc ....E 954 973-1819
   Fort Lauderdale (G-3693)

Cottonimagescom Inc ....E 305 251-2560
   Doral (G-3176)

Creative Shirts Intl Inc ....F 954 351-0909
   Oakland Park (G-11253)

Dowling Graphics Inc ....E 727 573-5997
   Clearwater (G-1570)

Metal Spray Painting Powder ....G 954 227-2744
   Coral Springs (G-2184)

Orange Sunshine Graphics Inc ....G 954 797-7425
   Davie (G-2450)

PRINTING: Thermography

American Business Cards Inc ....E 314 739-0800
   Naples (G-10666)

Boostan Inc ....G 305 223-5981
   Miami (G-8846)

J & J Litho Enterprises Inc ....F 239 433-2311
   Fort Myers (G-4294)

Winsted Thermographers Inc ....F 305 944-7862
   Hallandale Beach (G-4985)

PRODUCT STERILIZATION SVCS

Clearant Inc ....G 407 876-3134
   Orlando (G-12019)

PROFESSIONAL EQPT & SPLYS, WHOLESALE: Bank

Diebold Nixdorf Incorporated ....F 407 549-2000
   Lake Mary (G-7069)

Metavante Holdings LLC ....G 904 438-6000
   Jacksonville (G-6301)

PROFESSIONAL EQPT & SPLYS, WHOLESALE: Engineers', NEC

Naztec International Group LLC ....F 561 802-4110
   West Palm Beach (G-18088)

PROFESSIONAL EQPT & SPLYS, WHOLESALE: Optical Goods

Lasersight Technologies Inc ....F 407 678-9900
   Orlando (G-12312)

Low Vision Aids Inc ....G 954 722-1580
   Ocala (G-11432)

Premium Dynamic Lens ....G 813 891-9912
   Oldsmar (G-11690)

PROFESSIONAL EQPT & SPLYS, WHOLESALE: Scientific & Engineerg

A B Survey Supply Entps Inc ....G 772 464-9500
   Fort Pierce (G-4457)

Jensen Scientific Products Inc ....E 954 344-2006
   Coral Springs (G-2169)

PROFESSIONAL EQPT & SPLYS, WHOLESALE: Theatrical

Cinema Crafters Inc ....G 305 891-6121
   North Miami (G-11098)

PROFESSIONAL INSTRUMENT REPAIR SVCS

Marine Exhaust Systems Inc ....D 561 848-1238
   Riviera Beach (G-14645)

Santanas Pwrsprts Small Eng Rp ....G 813 658-3530
   Tampa (G-17246)

Sun Nuclear Corp ....C 321 259-6862
   Melbourne (G-8538)

Superior Unlimited Entps Inc ....G 863 294-1683
   Winter Haven (G-18472)

PROFILE SHAPES: Unsupported Plastics

Daniel Bustamante ....G 305 779-7777
   Coral Gables (G-2046)

Firedrake Inc ....G 813 713-8902
   Zephyrhills (G-18614)

PROMOTION SVCS

Grand Cypress Group Inc ....D 407 622-1993
   Maitland (G-8061)

Toms Instant Printing Inc ....G 904 396-0686
   Jacksonville (G-6558)

PROPELLERS: Boat & Ship, Cast

Blair Propeller MA ....G 772 283-1453
   Stuart (G-16123)

Turning Point Propellers Inc ....G 904 900-7739
   Jacksonville (G-6569)

PROPELLERS: Boat & Ship, Machined

E M P Inc ....G 772 286-7343
   Stuart (G-16142)

PROPELLERS: Ship, Nec

S & S Propeller Co Inc ....G 718 359-3393
   Pompano Beach (G-14165)

PROPULSION UNITS: Guided Missiles & Space Vehicles

American Maglev Tech Fla Inc ....F 404 386-4036
   Amelia Island (G-85)

Atk Sales Corp ....G 954 701-0465
   Hollywood (G-5532)

PROTECTION EQPT: Lightning

Alico Lighting Group Inc ....G 305 542-2648
   Hollywood (G-5524)

Allstate Lghtning Prtction LLC ....G 813 240-2736
   Tampa (G-16578)

Bren Tuck Inc ....F 727 561-7697
   Clearwater (G-1525)

Lightning Prtction Systems Inc ....F 239 643-4323
   Naples (G-10804)

Omega Power Systems Inc ....G 772 219-0045
   Stuart (G-16191)

Thor Guard Inc ....F 954 835-0900
   Sunrise (G-16382)

PROTECTIVE FOOTWEAR: Rubber Or Plastic

Global Trading Inc ....F 305 471-4455
   Miami (G-9220)

PUBLIC RELATIONS SVCS

Conric Holdings LLC ....F 239 690-9840
   Fort Myers (G-4217)

Quality Life Publishing Co ....G 239 513-9907
   Naples (G-10871)

PUBLISHERS: Art Copy & Poster

Sinergie Printing Inc ....G 786 493-6167
   Miami (G-9898)

PUBLISHERS: Book

2leaf Press Inc ....G 646 801-4227
   Plantation (G-13816)

Armbrust Aviation Group Inc ....E 561 355-8488
   West Palm Beach (G-17927)

Athletic Guide Publishing ....G 386 439-2250
   Flagler Beach (G-3601)

Belvoir Publications Inc ....D 941 929-1720
   Sarasota (G-15611)

Bisk Education Inc ....C 813 621-6200
   Tampa (G-16645)

Builders Publishing Group LLC ....G 407 539-2938
   Altamonte Springs (G-36)

Casebriefs LLC ....G 646 240-4401
   Boca Raton (G-454)

Coeur De Lion Inc ....E 727 442-4808
   Clearwater (G-1545)

Darmiven Inc ....G 305 871-1157
   Virginia Gardens (G-17821)

Ediciones Atenea Inc ....F 305 984-5483
   Hialeah (G-5135)

Elibro Corporation ....F 305 466-0155
   Sunny Isles Beach (G-16272)

First Edition Design Inc ....G 941 921-2607
   Sarasota (G-15675)

Fournies Associates ....G 561 445-5102
   Delray Beach (G-2964)

Getabstract Inc ....E 305 936-2626
   Miami (G-9208)

Great Hse Mdia Group of Pbls I ....F 407 779-3846
   Orlando (G-12200)

Houghton Mifflin Harcourt ....E 407 345-2000
   Orlando (G-12225)

Houghton Mifflin Harcourt Pubg ....C 407 345-2000
   Orlando (G-12226)

Jabberwocky LLC ....G 310 717-3343
   Miami (G-9354)

Legacy Publishing Services ....G 407 647-3787
   Winter Park (G-18519)

Lmn Printing Co Inc ....F 386 428-9928
   Edgewater (G-3497)

Meadowbrook Inc ....E 800 338-2232
   Naples (G-10817)

Mega Book Inc ....G 352 378-4567
   Gainesville (G-4728)

MPS North America LLC ....G 407 472-1280
   Orlando (G-12395)

Municipal Code Corporation ....F 850 576-3171
   Tallahassee (G-16482)

New Underground RR Pubg Co ....F 305 825-1444
   Miami Lakes (G-10332)

On-Board Media Inc ....D 305 673-0400
   Doral (G-3318)

Phidal Inc ....G 786 288-0339
   Aventura (G-270)

Plus Communications Inc ....E 407 333-0600
   Lake Mary (G-7101)

Printers Printer Inc ....F 954 917-2773
   Pompano Beach (G-14146)

Samjay Media Group Orlando LLC ....G 407 865-7526
   Longwood (G-7944)

Scribe Inc ....F 215 336-5094
   Fort Lauderdale (G-4040)

Signcraft Publishing Co Inc ....F 239 939-4644
   Fort Myers (G-4399)

Starline Education Inc ....G 808 631-1818
   Titusville (G-17618)

Stephens Group ....G 941 623-9689
   Port Charlotte (G-14316)

Vr Preserve Development LLC ....E 561 370-3617
   West Palm Beach (G-18200)

PUBLISHERS: Book Clubs, No Printing

Rourke Ray Publishing Co Inc ....G 772 234-6001
   Vero Beach (G-17796)

Employee Codes: A=Over 500 employees, B=251-500
C=101-250, D=51-100, E=20-50, F=10-19, G=4-9

2022 Harris Florida
Manufacturers Directory

PRODUCT

1297

PUBLISHERS: Books, No Printing

90-Minute Books LLC ..... G 863 318-0464
Winter Haven *(G-18410)*

American Accounting Assn ..... E 941 921-7747
Lakewood Ranch *(G-7475)*

Archer Ellison Inc ..... G 800 449-4095
Lake Mary *(G-7060)*

Artex Publishing Inc ..... G 727 944-4117
Holiday *(G-5489)*

Buck Pile Inc ..... G 772 492-1056
Vero Beach *(G-17747)*

Center For Business Ownership ..... G 239 455-9393
Naples *(G-10709)*

Comex Systems Inc ..... G 908 881-6301
Port Charlotte *(G-14294)*

CRC Press LLC ..... E 561 994-0555
Boca Raton *(G-473)*

CRC Press LLC ..... D 561 361-6000
Boca Raton *(G-474)*

Direct Response Publication ..... F 561 620-3010
Boca Raton *(G-487)*

Esperanto Inc ..... F 305 513-8980
Doral *(G-3209)*

Frederic Thomas USA Inc ..... F 239 593-8000
Naples *(G-10751)*

Gleim Publications Inc ..... D 352 375-0772
Gainesville *(G-4703)*

Great Locations Inc ..... G 954 943-1188
Pompano Beach *(G-14045)*

Management International Inc ..... F 954 763-8811
Fort Lauderdale *(G-3929)*

Maupin House Publishing Inc ..... G 800 524-0634
Gainesville *(G-4724)*

Netexpressusa Inc ..... G 888 575-1245
Fort Myers *(G-4338)*

New World Publications Inc ..... G 904 737-6558
Jacksonville *(G-6330)*

Penguin Random House LLC ..... F 305 206-8715
Miami *(G-9702)*

Printing For A Cause LLC ..... E 786 496-0637
Saint Petersburg *(G-15161)*

Pro-Publishing Inc ..... G 954 888-7726
Southwest Ranches *(G-16057)*

Reliance Media Inc ..... F 505 243-1821
Apopka *(G-168)*

Rourke Educational Media LLC ..... F 772 234-6001
Vero Beach *(G-17795)*

Santillana USA Pubg Co Inc ..... E 305 591-9522
Miami *(G-9845)*

Senda De Vida Publishers ..... E 305 262-2627
Miami *(G-9866)*

Spanish House Inc ..... E 305 503-1191
Medley *(G-8324)*

Taylor & Francis Group LLC ..... C 561 994-0555
Boca Raton *(G-707)*

Twinlab Corporation ..... G 800 645-5626
Boca Raton *(G-728)*

Two Little Fishies Inc ..... G 305 623-7695
Miami *(G-10050)*

Write Stuff Enterprises LLC ..... E 954 462-6657
Fort Lauderdale *(G-4138)*

PUBLISHERS: Directories, NEC

ED Publications Inc ..... F 727 726-3592
Clearwater *(G-1577)*

Gulf Publishing Company Inc ..... F 727 596-2863
Largo *(G-7602)*

Homes Magazine Inc ..... F 239 334-7168
Fort Myers *(G-4283)*

Yp Advrtising Pubg LLC Not LLC ..... B 321 956-5400
Melbourne *(G-8565)*

PUBLISHERS: Directories, Telephone

Supermedia LLC ..... F 972 453-7000
Saint Petersburg *(G-15204)*

PUBLISHERS: Guides

Sun Publications Florida Inc ..... D 321 402-0257
Kissimmee *(G-6961)*

Waterford Press Inc ..... E 727 812-0140
Safety Harbor *(G-14801)*

Waterford Publishing Group LLC ..... F 727 812-0140
Safety Harbor *(G-14802)*

PUBLISHERS: Magazines, No Printing

A & A Publishing Corp ..... F 561 982-8960
Boca Raton *(G-383)*

Action Weekly Corp ..... G 561 586-8699
West Palm Beach *(G-17914)*

Agnet Media Inc ..... F 352 671-1909
Newberry *(G-11016)*

American Accounting Assn ..... E 941 921-7747
Lakewood Ranch *(G-7475)*

American Welding Society Inc ..... D 305 443-9353
Doral *(G-3113)*

Around House Publishing Inc ..... F 561 969-7412
Lake Worth *(G-7185)*

Back To Godhead Inc ..... F 386 462-0481
Alachua *(G-8)*

Betrock Info Systems Inc ..... E 954 981-2821
Cooper City *(G-2019)*

Blackfist Magazine LLC ..... G 904 864-8695
Miami *(G-8836)*

Boat International Media Inc ..... G 954 522-2628
Fort Lauderdale *(G-3698)*

Bocadelray Life Magazine ..... G 954 421-9797
Coconut Creek *(G-1979)*

Bonnier Corporation ..... F 954 830-4460
Fort Lauderdale *(G-3701)*

Bonnier Corporation ..... C 407 628-4802
Winter Park *(G-18491)*

Brooklands New Media LLC ..... E 305 370-3867
Miami Beach *(G-10172)*

CJ Publishers Inc ..... F 727 521-6277
Pinellas Park *(G-13676)*

Coastal Communications Corp ..... F 561 989-0600
Boca Raton *(G-467)*

Conric Holdings LLC ..... F 239 690-9840
Fort Myers *(G-4217)*

Constructconnect Inc ..... C 772 770-6003
Vero Beach *(G-17751)*

Country Club Concierge Mag Inc ..... G 904 223-0204
Ponte Vedra Beach *(G-14266)*

Desh-Videsh Media Group Inc ..... F 954 784-8100
Tamarac *(G-16529)*

Direct Response Publication ..... F 561 620-3010
Boca Raton *(G-487)*

Distribuidora Continental SA ..... F 305 374-4474
Virginia Gardens *(G-17822)*

Diversityinc Media LLC ..... F 973 494-0539
Palm Beach *(G-12932)*

Dolphin/Curtis Publishing Co ..... G 305 594-0508
Miami Springs *(G-10388)*

Dupont Publishing Inc ..... D 727 573-9339
Clearwater *(G-1574)*

Ebella Magazine ..... G 239 431-7231
Naples *(G-10735)*

Entree Magazine Florida LLC ..... G 239 354-1245
Naples *(G-10740)*

Et Publishing International ..... D 305 871-6400
Virginia Gardens *(G-17824)*

Florida Bid Reporting Service ..... F 850 539-7522
Tallahassee *(G-16440)*

Florida Design Inc ..... E 561 997-1660
Boca Raton *(G-517)*

Florida Eqine Publications Inc ..... F 352 732-8686
Ocala *(G-11391)*

Florida Family Magazine Inc ..... G 941 922-5437
Sarasota *(G-15676)*

Florida Homes Magazine ..... G 941 227-7331
Sarasota *(G-15678)*

Florida Media Inc ..... F 407 816-9596
Altamonte Springs *(G-47)*

Floridas Hotspots Publishing ..... F 954 928-1862
Oakland Park *(G-11267)*

Grandstand Publishing LLC ..... G 847 491-6440
Orlando *(G-12199)*

Gulfstream Media Group Inc ..... E 954 462-4488
Fort Lauderdale *(G-3854)*

Haute Living Inc ..... E 305 798-1373
Miami *(G-9264)*

Home and Design Magazine ..... G 239 598-4826
Naples *(G-10776)*

Home Improver Inc ..... F 239 549-6901
Cape Coral *(G-1354)*

Homemag Inc ..... E 239 549-6960
Cape Coral *(G-1355)*

Homes Media Solutions LLC ..... F 850 350-7800
Tallahassee *(G-16462)*

Howard Publications Inc ..... G 904 355-2601
Jacksonville *(G-6185)*

IMS Publishing Inc ..... G 954 761-8777
Fort Lauderdale *(G-3874)*

Interior Design ..... F 646 805-0200
Boca Raton *(G-548)*

Interior Dsign Media Group LLC ..... D 561 750-0151
Boca Raton *(G-549)*

International Guidelines Ctr ..... G 407 878-7606
Lake Mary *(G-7086)*

Jazziz Magazine Inc ..... E 561 893-6868
Boca Raton *(G-558)*

Jes Publishing Corp ..... E 561 997-8683
Boca Raton *(G-560)*

Judicial & ADM RES Assoc ..... F 850 222-3171
Tallahassee *(G-16464)*

Kenney Communications Inc ..... F 407 859-3113
Orlando *(G-12285)*

L C Clark Publishing Inc ..... F 561 627-3393
Palm Beach Gardens *(G-12982)*

Lakeside Publishing Co LLC ..... G 847 491-6440
Palm Beach Gardens *(G-12983)*

Latin Amrcn Fncl Pblctions Inc ..... F 305 416-5261
Miami *(G-9435)*

Latin Press Inc ..... F 305 285-3133
Miami *(G-9437)*

Los Latinos Magazine Inc ..... F 305 882-9074
Hialeah *(G-5226)*

Lrp Publications Inc ..... C 215 784-0860
Palm Beach Gardens *(G-12988)*

Mailbox Publishing Inc ..... F 772 334-2121
Stuart *(G-16181)*

Maritime Executive LLC ..... G 954 848-9955
Plantation *(G-13866)*

Mary Lake Life Mag Inc ..... G 407 324-2644
Lake Mary *(G-7091)*

Mary Lake Life Magazine Inc ..... F 407 324-2644
Lake Mary *(G-7092)*

Mercantile Two ..... G 941 388-0059
Sarasota *(G-15743)*

Miles Partnership II LLC ..... C 941 342-2300
Sarasota *(G-15747)*

Mio Publication Inc ..... G 941 351-2411
Sarasota *(G-15517)*

Motorsport Marketing Inc ..... E 386 239-0523
Holly Hill *(G-5516)*

Moulton Publications Inc ..... G 772 234-8871
Vero Beach *(G-17779)*

Netexpressusa Inc ..... G 888 575-1245
Fort Myers *(G-4338)*

Nostalgic America Inc ..... F 561 585-1724
Boca Raton *(G-621)*

Ocala Magazine ..... E 352 622-2995
Ocala *(G-11454)*

Ocala Publication Incorporated ..... E 352 732-0073
Ocala *(G-11459)*

On-Board Media Inc ..... D 305 673-0400
Doral *(G-3318)*

Open House Magazine Inc ..... G 305 576-6011
Miami *(G-9658)*

Oxendine Publishing Inc ..... E 352 373-6907
Gainesville *(G-4745)*

Oxpecker Enterprise Inc ..... G 305 253-5301
Miami *(G-9673)*

PA C Publishing Inc ..... G 813 814-1505
Oldsmar *(G-11684)*

Pageantry Tlent Entrmt Svcs In ..... G 407 260-2262
Longwood *(G-7930)*

Palm Beach Liquidation Company ..... E 561 659-0210
West Palm Beach *(G-18110)*

Palm Beach Media Group Inc ..... G 239 434-6966
Naples *(G-10846)*

Passport Pblcations Media Corp ..... E 561 615-3900
West Palm Beach *(G-18113)*

PCI Communications Inc ..... G 941 729-5202
Ellenton *(G-3512)*

Phoenix Media Network Inc ..... E 561 994-1118
Boca Raton *(G-633)*

Polo Players Edition ..... G 561 968-5208
Lake Worth *(G-7228)*

Quanturo Publishing Inc ..... E 305 373-3700
Miami *(G-9767)*

R T Publishing Inc ..... G 904 886-4919
Jacksonville *(G-6403)*

Recommend Travel Publications ..... F 305 826-4763
Miami Lakes *(G-10347)*

Rowland Publishing Inc ..... E 850 878-0554
Tallahassee *(G-16497)*

Rwla Enterprises LLC ..... F 772 334-1248
Stuart *(G-16211)*

Sandow Media LLC ..... F 646 805-0200
Boca Raton *(G-659)*

Sandow Media LLC ..... D 561 961-7749
Boca Raton *(G-660)*

Sandy Lender Inc ..... G 239 272-8613
Cape Coral *(G-1380)*

Sarasota Cottages LLC ..... G 941 724-2245
Sarasota *(G-15812)*

Seabreze Cmmncations Group Inc	F	239 278-4222	Fort Myers (G-4397)
South Florida Parenting	D	954 747-3050	Tamarac (G-16543)
Southern Boating & Yachting	E	954 522-5515	Pompano Beach (G-14192)
Spanish Peri & Bk Sls Inc	D	305 592-3919	Doral (G-3371)
Special Editionspublishing	G	407 862-7737	Altamonte Springs (G-71)
Sport America Magazine	G	727 391-3099	Madeira Beach (G-8041)
Stern Bloom Media Inc	G	954 454-8522	Miami (G-9951)
Stream Line Publishing Inc	F	561 655-8778	Boca Raton (G-698)
Street Elements Magazine Inc	F	813 935-5894	Tampa (G-17305)
Stuart Magazine	F	954 332-3214	Fort Lauderdale (G-4070)
Swapper	G	850 973-6653	Madison (G-8047)
T T Publications Inc	E	407 327-4817	Winter Springs (G-18579)
Tampa Bay Publications Inc	F	727 791-4800	Clearwater (G-1812)
Teeze International Inc	F	727 726-3592	Clearwater (G-1823)
Time Adjusters Conference Inc	G	386 274-4210	Port Orange (G-14352)
Tm Marketing Group LLC	G	954 848-9955	Fort Lauderdale (G-4094)
Toti Media Inc	G	239 472-0205	Sanibel (G-15419)
Trafalger Communications Inc	E	941 365-7702	Sarasota (G-15857)
Treasure Cast Prenting Mag Inc	F	772 672-8588	Port Saint Lucie (G-14458)
Trend Magazines Inc	E	727 821-5800	Saint Petersburg (G-15216)
Turnstile Publishing Company	D	407 563-7000	Orlando (G-12682)
Valleymedia Inc	E	510 565-7559	Fort Lauderdale (G-4115)
Venice Quarters Inc	E	954 318-3483	Wilton Manors (G-18344)
Weiss Group LLC	C	561 627-3300	Jupiter (G-6825)
Weiss Research Inc	C	561 627-3300	Jupiter (G-6826)
White Publishing Co Inc	F	904 389-3622	Jacksonville (G-6610)
Woods n Water Magazine Inc	G	850 584-3824	Perry (G-13659)
Working Mother Media Inc	D	212 351-6400	Winter Park (G-18553)
World Publications Inc	G	407 628-4802	Winter Park (G-18554)
Worldwide Challenge Magazine	E	407 826-2390	Orlando (G-12720)
Worth Intl Media Group	E	305 826-4763	Miami Lakes (G-10379)
Write Stuff Enterprises LLC	E	954 462-6657	Fort Lauderdale (G-4138)

PUBLISHERS: Maps

Map & Globe LLC	G	407 898-0757	Maitland (G-8067)
Streetwise Maps Inc	G	941 358-1956	Sarasota (G-15840)

PUBLISHERS: Miscellaneous

A Beka Book Inc	F	850 478-8933	Pensacola (G-13429)
A Cappela Publishing Inc	G	941 351-2050	Sarasota (G-15582)
A2f LLC	G	305 984-9205	Miami (G-8629)
ABC Book Publishers Inc	G	904 230-0737	Jacksonville (G-6624)
Academic Publication Svcs Inc	G	941 925-4474	Sarasota (G-15585)
Advertisers Press	G	305 879-3227	Miami (G-8658)
AGM Publishing Inc	G	727 934-9993	Holiday (G-5488)
Alexander Publications LLC	G	727 596-4544	Largo (G-7528)
Ali Tamposi Publishing Inc	G	561 306-6597	West Palm Beach (G-17919)

Aluminum Express Inc	G	954 868-2628	Hialeah (G-5041)
American Classifieds	F	850 747-1155	Panama City (G-13227)
AMI Celebrity Publications LLC	C	561 997-7733	Boca Raton (G-408)
AMI Digital Inc	B	561 997-7733	Boca Raton (G-409)
Antwon Publishing Company Inc	G	863 508-0825	Winter Haven (G-18417)
Armstrong Press Inc	G	561 247-1071	Port Saint Lucie (G-14398)
Ascendants Publishing LLC	G	813 391-2745	Gainesville (G-4653)
Atlantic Publishing Group Inc	E	352 622-6220	Ocala (G-11329)
B&C Publishing Inc	G	305 385-8216	Miami (G-8789)
Banyan Hill	G	561 455-9045	Delray Beach (G-2935)
Barbes Publishing Inc	F	904 992-9945	Jacksonville (G-5923)
Beano Publishing LLC	F	954 689-8339	Weston (G-18228)
Best Publishing Company	F	561 776-6066	North Palm Beach (G-11177)
Bevel Express & Tops Lac	G	813 887-3174	Tampa (G-16639)
BHF Publishing Inc	G	727 536-2245	Clearwater (G-1518)
Bioenergetics Press	F	386 462-5155	Alachua (G-9)
Birdie Publishing LLC	G	561 332-1826	Delray Beach (G-2936)
Black-Tie Publishing Inc	G	954 472-6003	Plantation (G-13834)
Bluetoad Inc	E	407 992-8744	Gotha (G-4806)
Bonita Daily News	E	239 213-6060	Fort Myers (G-4193)
Books-A-Million Inc	F	813 571-2062	Brandon (G-1084)
Boyle Publications Inc	G	941 255-0187	Port Charlotte (G-14289)
Breath Life Music Publishing	G	407 350-4669	Kissimmee (G-6900)
Builders Publishing Group LLC	G	407 539-2938	Altamonte Springs (G-36)
Caduceus International Pubg	F	866 280-2900	Gainesville (G-4664)
Campus Publications Inc	G	941 780-1326	Sarasota (G-15628)
Capital Publishing Inc	G	813 286-8444	Spring Hill (G-16067)
Carbon Press LLC	F	239 689-4406	Fort Myers (G-4200)
Casey Research LLC	F	561 455-9043	Delray Beach (G-2941)
Catskill Express LLC	G	954 784-5151	Pompano Beach (G-13965)
Cda Ventures Inc	F	305 428-2857	Miami Beach (G-10177)
Central Florida Publishing Inc	F	407 323-5204	Sanford (G-15279)
Circle Press	G	561 213-5831	Boca Raton (G-461)
City Debate Publishing Company	G	305 868-1161	Miami Beach (G-10179)
City News Publishing LLC	G	305 332-9101	Boca Raton (G-462)
City Publications South FL	G	305 495-3311	Virginia Gardens (G-17820)
CJ Publishers Inc	F	727 521-6277	Pinellas Park (G-13676)
Classic Mail Corp	G	386 290-0309	Daytona Beach (G-2529)
Classics Reborn Publishing LLC	G	727 232-6739	New Port Richey (G-10965)
Color Press Corp	G	786 621-8491	Miami (G-8946)
Common Sense Publishing LLC	C	561 510-1713	Delray Beach (G-2949)
Compass Publishing LLC	G	407 328-0970	Sanford (G-15289)
Competitor Group Inc	F	858 450-6510	Tampa (G-16722)
Connectpress Ltd	G	505 629-0695	Sarasota (G-15641)
Consumer Source Inc	G	407 888-0745	Orlando (G-12044)

Convivium Press Inc	G	305 889-0489	Miami (G-8964)
Countryside Publishing Co Inc	E	813 925-0195	Oldsmar (G-11641)
County of Orange	D	407 649-0076	Orlando (G-12051)
Croft Publishing Inc	G	352 473-3159	Keystone Heights (G-6884)
Cycling Quarterly LLC	E	786 367-2497	Fort Lauderdale (G-3750)
David Jacobs Pubg Group LLC	F	813 321-4119	Tampa (G-16764)
Delure Publishing LLC	G	407 866-5448	Orlando (G-12083)
Digital Publishing LLC	G	813 749-8640	Oldsmar (G-11643)
Dion Money Management LLC	G	413 458-4700	Naples (G-10729)
Diversified Pubg & Design	G	239 598-4826	Naples (G-10731)
Dolph Map Company Inc	F	954 763-4732	Oakland Park (G-11260)
Double R Publishing	G	305 525-3573	Boynton Beach (G-858)
Dreamspinner Press LLC	F	800 970-3759	Tallahassee (G-16432)
Elsevier Inc	F	813 579-3866	Pinellas Park (G-13684)
Empyre Music Publishing LLC	G	813 873-7700	Tampa (G-16811)
Essential Publishing Group LLC	G	410 440-5777	Boca Raton (G-507)
Essential Publishing Group LLC	G	561 570-7165	Greenacres (G-4846)
Everyday Feminism LLC	G	202 643-1001	Tallahassee (G-16437)
Ew Publishing LLC	G	305 358-1100	Fort Lauderdale (G-3802)
Express Ironing Inc	G	305 261-1072	Miami (G-9123)
F L F Corp	G	561 747-7077	Jupiter (G-6725)
Faulkner Media LLC	E	855 393-3393	Gainesville (G-4691)
Ferrari Express Inc	E	305 374-5003	Miami (G-9138)
Florida Living LLC	G	352 556-9691	Brooksville (G-1157)
Floyd Publications Inc	G	813 707-8783	Plant City (G-13767)
FM Publications Enterprise Inc	G	561 670-7205	Greenacres (G-4847)
Fng Express Inc	G	863 471-9669	Sebring (G-15923)
Focal Point Publishing LLC	G	877 469-9530	Gainesville (G-4695)
Focus Community Publications	G	407 892-0019	Saint Cloud (G-14926)
Forever Current Studios LLC	G	561 544-7303	Boca Raton (G-522)
Forum Publishing Group Inc	D	954 596-5650	Deerfield Beach (G-2722)
Four WD Consulting & Pubg LLC	G	561 969-7412	West Palm Beach (G-18008)
Fresh Press	G	305 942-8571	North Miami Beach (G-11140)
Frog Publications Inc	G	352 588-2082	San Antonio (G-15247)
G S Printers Inc	G	305 931-2755	Fort Lauderdale (G-3834)
Galan Express Inc	F	305 438-8738	Miami (G-9185)
Gatehouse Media LLC	D	863 401-6900	Winter Haven (G-18442)
Genie Publishing	G	863 937-7769	Lakeland (G-7335)
GLM Publishing LLC	G	561 409-7696	Boca Raton (G-527)
Global Media Press Corp	G	813 857-5898	Tampa (G-16883)
Global Publishing Inc	E	904 262-0491	Jacksonville (G-6144)
Grapevine Usa Inc	G	786 510-9122	Fort Lauderdale (G-3843)
Great Escape Publishing	G	561 860-8266	Delray Beach (G-2970)
Great Hse Mdia Group of Pbls I	F	407 779-3846	Orlando (G-12200)
Great Virtualworks LLC	F	800 606-6518	Fort Lauderdale (G-3846)

Employee Codes: A=Over 500 employees, B=251-500
C=101-250, D=51-100, E=20-50, F=10-19, G=4-9

2022 Harris Florida
Manufacturers Directory

1299

PRODUCT

Guerrilla Press ....G....... 352 281-7420	Mariner Publications LLC ....G....... 941 426-9645	Red Brick Publishing LLC ....G....... 718 208-3600
Gainesville (G-4705)	North Port (G-11198)	Boynton Beach (G-908)
Halldale Media Inc ....E....... 407 322-5605	Mark Walters LLC ....G....... 727 742-3091	Robert Gomes Publishing Inc ......G....... 941 637-6080
Lake Mary (G-7082)	Saint Petersburg (G-15121)	Punta Gorda (G-14527)
Health Communications Inc ....D....... 954 360-0909	Mark Wayne Adams Inc ....G....... 407 756-5862	Russanos Express LLC ....G....... 772 220-3329
Deerfield Beach (G-2731)	Longwood (G-7920)	Palm City (G-13057)
Hogan Assessment Systems Inc ....G....... 904 992-0302	Media Creations Inc ....G....... 954 726-0902	Safety Compliance Publ Inc ....G....... 844 556-3149
Jacksonville (G-6179)	Fort Lauderdale (G-3934)	Miramar (G-10539)
Hoot/Wisdom Music Pubg LLC ......G....... 561 297-3205	Media Edge Communications LLC ....G....... 352 313-6700	Sandpaper Publishing Inc ....G....... 850 939-8040
Boca Raton (G-539)	Gainesville (G-4727)	Gulf Breeze (G-4890)
Hot Off Press ....G....... 386 238-8700	Messner Publications Inc ....F....... 863 318-1595	Scheduall Scheduall Scheduall ....G....... 954 334-5400
South Daytona (G-16022)	Winter Haven (G-18452)	Hollywood (G-5654)
Howard Scripts Inc ....F....... 561 746-5111	Milenium Publishing LLC ....G....... 786 573-9974	Seahill Press Inc ....G....... 805 845-8636
Jupiter (G-6743)	Miami (G-9568)	Leesburg (G-7791)
I M I Publishing Inc ....G....... 615 957-9288	Miramar Publishing Inc ....G....... 305 695-0639	Sentinel Cmmnctons News Vntres ....G....... 407 420-5291
Naples (G-10778)	Miami Beach (G-10213)	Orlando (G-12585)
Icat Resource LLC ....F....... 410 908-9369	Mobile Rving ....G....... 954 870-7095	Sentinel Cmmnctons News Vntres ....G....... 352 742-5900
Clearwater Beach (G-1860)	Deerfield Beach (G-2769)	Tavares (G-17522)
IMI Publishing Inc ....G....... 239 529-5081	New Life Publishing Inc ....G....... 239 549-9152	Sigma Press Inc ....F....... 904 264-6006
Naples (G-10779)	Cape Coral (G-1367)	Orange Park (G-11840)
Impact Promotional Pubg LLC ......F....... 727 736-6228	New You Media LLC ....F....... 800 606-6518	Silent Giant Publishing Co ....G....... 305 725-7911
Dunedin (G-3451)	Fort Lauderdale (G-3960)	Miami (G-9892)
Ink Publishing Corporation ....F....... 786 206-9867	Newsmax Media Inc ....F....... 561 686-1165	Sirs Publishing Inc ....D....... 800 521-0600
Coral Gables (G-2070)	West Palm Beach (G-18091)	Boca Raton (G-680)
Ink Publishing Corporation ....F....... 786 482-2065	Nikki Beach Publishing LLC ....G....... 305 538-1111	Snookton Inc ....G....... 352 429-1133
Coral Gables (G-2071)	Miami Beach (G-10216)	Groveland (G-4872)
Insanejournalcom ....G....... 561 315-9311	Nwh Publishing Llc ....G....... 904 217-3911	Sony Discos ....G....... 305 420-4540
West Palm Beach (G-18034)	Saint Augustine (G-14866)	Miami (G-9919)
Internet Marketing Press ....G....... 850 271-4333	Omega Publishing ....G....... 727 815-0402	Sophist Research LLC ....G....... 305 763-8184
Lynn Haven (G-8029)	New Port Richey (G-10977)	Miami Beach (G-10232)
Irving Publications LLC ....F....... 352 219-4688	Online German Publisher LLC ......G....... 239 344-8953	Southeast Publications USA Inc ....E....... 954 368-4686
Gainesville (G-4715)	Cape Coral (G-1371)	Deerfield Beach (G-2813)
Island Media Publishing LLC ......G....... 904 556-3002	Open Palm Press Inc ....G....... 813 870-3839	SP Publications LLC ....G....... 239 595-9040
Fernandina Beach (G-3590)	Tampa (G-17127)	Miramar Beach (G-10573)
J & Z Production and Pblcy Inc ....G....... 786 718-8204	Orlando Branding Agency LLC ......F....... 407 692-8868	Spanish Publishers LLC ....G....... 305 233-3365
Homestead (G-5721)	Oviedo (G-12841)	Miami (G-9935)
J Ross Publishing Inc ....G....... 954 727-9333	Palm Beach Newspapers Inc ....C....... 561 820-3800	Spikes Press & Printhouse LLC ....G....... 850 438-2293
Plantation (G-13859)	West Palm Beach (G-18111)	Pensacola (G-13611)
Jazzy Dogs Publishing LLC ....G....... 941 726-0343	Palm Pheon Music Pubg LLC ....F....... 305 705-2405	SSE Publications LLC ....F....... 954 835-7616
Nokomis (G-11048)	North Miami Beach (G-11154)	Sunrise (G-16372)
JC 323 Media Pubg Group Inc ......G....... 772 940-3510	Pandia Press Inc ....G....... 352 789-8156	Strong Publications LLC ....E....... 813 362-8224
Lake Worth (G-7209)	Mount Dora (G-10609)	Land O Lakes (G-7505)
Jeanius Publishing LLC ....G....... 239 560-5229	Panoff Publishing Inc ....D....... 954 377-7777	Sun Publications Florida Inc ....E....... 863 583-1202
Lehigh Acres (G-7811)	Fort Lauderdale (G-3972)	Lakeland (G-7452)
Kameleon Press Inc ....G....... 850 566-2522	Paramount Digital Pubg LLC ....G....... 813 489-5029	Sun-Sentinel Company LLC ....D....... 954 356-4000
Tallahassee (G-16466)	Brandon (G-1099)	Deerfield Beach (G-2816)
Kenney Communications Inc ....F....... 407 859-3113	Paramount Marketing Inc ....G....... 352 608-8801	Sunset Publications Inc ....G....... 321 727-8500
Orlando (G-12285)	Ocala (G-11463)	Melbourne (G-8539)
Km Press Dental Ceramics LLC ....G....... 828 299-8500	Parkside Publishing LLC ....G....... 888 386-1115	Swi Publishing Inc ....G....... 352 538-1438
Sarasota (G-15719)	Delray Beach (G-2993)	Gainesville (G-4771)
Korangy Publishing Inc ....D....... 786 334-5052	Parkstone International Inc ....G....... 954 205-0075	Taylor & Francis Group LLC ....D....... 800 516-0186
Miami (G-9396)	Fort Lauderdale (G-3979)	Sarasota (G-15851)
Krieger Publishing Co Inc ....F....... 321 724-9542	Patterson Publishing LLC ....F....... 863 701-2707	Taylor Media LLC ....C....... 727 317-5800
Malabar (G-8085)	Lakeland (G-7407)	Saint Petersburg (G-15210)
Ksr Publishing Inc ....F....... 941 388-7050	Paxen Publishing LLC ....G....... 321 425-3030	Telexpress La Musica Inc ....G....... 813 879-1914
Sarasota (G-15721)	Indian Harbour Beach (G-5806)	Tampa (G-17347)
Kulaga William John ....G....... 727 536-3180	Peniel Inc ....F....... 305 594-2739	Tightline Publications Inc ....G....... 954 570-7174
Clearwater (G-1666)	Miramar (G-10526)	Deerfield Beach (G-2825)
Latin Goddess Press Inc ....G....... 917 703-1356	Peppertree Press LLC ....G....... 941 922-2662	Total Spcalty Publications LLC ....G....... 813 405-2610
Winter Springs (G-18571)	Sarasota (G-15780)	Tampa (G-17362)
Latitude 29 Publishing ....G....... 904 429-7889	Pfa Publishing ....G....... 727 512-5814	Tower Publications Inc ....F....... 352 372-5468
Saint Augustine (G-14854)	Gulfport (G-4900)	Gainesville (G-4777)
Le Publications Inc ....G....... 954 766-8433	Phoenix Publications ....G....... 954 609-7586	Toys For Boys Miami LLC ....G....... 786 464-0160
Fort Lauderdale (G-3915)	Pompano Beach (G-14125)	Miami (G-10030)
Learning For Life Press LLC ......G....... 352 234-0472	Preferred Pcks Pblications Inc ......F....... 954 377-8000	Trifecta Publishing ....G....... 863 676-6311
Venice (G-17704)	Sunrise (G-16354)	Lake Wales (G-7178)
Lifegate Publishing LLC ....G....... 561 602-0089	Premium Latin Music Inc ....F....... 212 873-1472	Turtle Publishing Co ....G....... 904 568-1484
Greenacres (G-4851)	Miami (G-9734)	Jacksonville (G-6570)
Lifestyle Publications LLC ....G....... 954 217-1165	Press Gourmet Sandwiches ....F....... 954 440-0422	United Advg Publications ....G....... 954 730-9700
Weston (G-18263)	Fort Lauderdale (G-3997)	Fort Lauderdale (G-4107)
Light Age Press Inc ....G....... 352 242-4530	Prs In Vivo Holdings Inc ....G....... 305 420-5935	Urano Publishing Inc ....F....... 305 233-3365
Clermont (G-1875)	Miami Beach (G-10223)	Miami (G-10077)
Lighthouse Express World Inc ......G....... 754 210-6196	Psychlgcal Asssment Rsrces In ....D....... 813 968-3003	Usdirectorycom LLC ....G....... 561 989-7400
Hollywood (G-5611)	Lutz (G-8012)	Boca Raton (G-740)
Lions Gate Publishing Prod LLC ....G....... 954 733-9576	Publify Press Inc ....F....... 774 248-4056	Vj Publications Inc ....G....... 407 461-0707
Fort Lauderdale (G-3919)	Melbourne (G-8503)	Longwood (G-7957)
Living Well Spending Less Inc ......G....... 941 209-1811	Publishers Crcltion Flfllment ......D....... 877 723-6668	Vlex 1450 LLC ....G....... 954 218-5443
Punta Gorda (G-14512)	Pensacola (G-13587)	Weston (G-18297)
LTSC LLC ....G....... 863 678-0011	Publishers Direct Choice LLC ......G....... 305 264-5998	Want ADS of Hot Springs Inc ......G....... 501 623-4404
Lake Wales (G-7167)	Miami (G-9756)	Panama City (G-13319)
M30 Freedom Inc ....G....... 813 433-1776	Publishing Research Inc ....G....... 954 921-4026	War Chest River LLC ....G....... 954 736-7704
Land O Lakes (G-7497)	North Miami (G-11117)	Miami (G-10123)
Madow Group ....G....... 410 526-4780	Purplefly Press LLC ....G....... 954 682-2726	Waterhouse Press LLC ....G....... 781 975-6191
Port Charlotte (G-14308)	Sunrise (G-16360)	Destin (G-3081)
Mama Bear Lawn Care Press ....G....... 863 517-5322	Quad Intl Incorporated ....E....... 305 662-5959	Weider Publications LLC ....G....... 561 998-7424
Clewiston (G-1892)	Doral (G-3341)	Boca Raton (G-754)
Management International Inc ......F....... 954 763-8811	Quality Life Publishing Co ....G....... 239 513-9907	Wemerge Inc ....G....... 561 305-2070
Fort Lauderdale (G-3929)	Naples (G-10871)	Coconut Creek (G-2012)
Manatee Media Inc ....F....... 813 909-2800	Quickseries Publishing Inc ....D....... 954 584-1606	Whats Wrong Publishing Co ....G....... 904 388-3494
Land O Lakes (G-7498)	Fort Lauderdale (G-4011)	Jacksonville (G-6607)

Whiz Bang LLC ....F 305 296-0160
Key West (G-6882)

Windward Communications Inc ....G 727 584-7191
Largo (G-7709)

Winter Park Publishing Co LLC ....G 941 320-6627
Winter Park (G-18552)

Wohlers Publishing Inc ....G 305 289-1644
Marathon (G-8110)

Worldwide Media Svcs Group Inc ....F 212 545-4800
Boca Raton (G-757)

Wrongs Without Wremedies LLC ....G 850 423-0828
Crestview (G-2257)

Xpress Finance Inc ....G 407 629-0095
Deltona (G-3057)

Xx Press One Inc ....G 407 287-2673
Orlando (G-12724)

PUBLISHERS: Music Book & Sheet Music

Bigg D Entertainment LLC ....G 917 204-0292
Weston (G-18229)

Fjh Music Company Inc ....E 954 382-6061
Davie (G-2412)

Kobalt Music Pubg Amer Inc ....D 305 200-5682
Coral Gables (G-2078)

Laras ....G 305 576-0036
Miami (G-9424)

Luna Negra Productions Inc ....G 786 247-1215
Miami (G-9486)

South Florida Jazz Inc ....E 954 474-8889
Plantation (G-13893)

Yung Payper Chasers Entrmt LLC ....F 727 239-2880
Saint Petersburg (G-15243)

PUBLISHERS: Newsletter

Bayou Printing Inc ....F 850 678-5444
Valparaiso (G-17656)

Builders Notice Corporation ....G 954 764-1322
Fort Lauderdale (G-3708)

Eastgate Publishing Inc ....G 772 286-0101
Hobe Sound (G-5482)

Netexpressusa Inc ....G 888 575-1245
Fort Myers (G-4338)

PUBLISHERS: Newspaper

Alm Global LLC ....F 954 468-2600
Fort Lauderdale (G-3647)

Alm Global LLC ....D 305 347-6650
Miami (G-8696)

Almanac LLC ....E 305 570-4311
Miami (G-8697)

Alternative Daily ....G 561 628-4711
West Palm Beach (G-17920)

ASAP Magazine & Newspaper ....G 813 238-0184
Tampa (G-16611)

Aw Publishing ....F 305 856-7000
Miami (G-8780)

Better Built Group Inc ....G 850 803-4044
Destin (G-3083)

Charisma Media ....D 407 333-0600
Lake Mary (G-7065)

Community News Publications ....F 813 909-2800
Lutz (G-7986)

Dailys 1113 Shell ....G 904 608-0219
Ponte Vedra (G-14256)

Distribuidora Continental SA ....F 305 374-4474
Virginia Gardens (G-17822)

Eco Informativo ....G 786 362-6789
Miami (G-9069)

Europrint Inc ....F 407 869-9955
Altamonte Springs (G-46)

Fernandina Observer Inc ....G 904 261-4372
Fernandina Beach (G-3587)

First Class Media Inc ....G 561 719-3433
Jupiter (G-6730)

Five Star Sports Tickets ....F 440 899-2000
Hallandale Beach (G-4948)

Future House ....G 904 683-9177
Jacksonville (G-6125)

Galactic News Service ....G 239 431-7470
Naples (G-10758)

Gatehouse Media LLC ....D 863 401-6900
Winter Haven (G-18442)

Hammond Enterprises ....G 386 575-2402
Leesburg (G-7779)

Horizon Publications Inc ....G 386 427-1000
New Smyrna Beach (G-11002)

Intercultural Communications ....G 813 926-2617
Odessa (G-11558)

Nexstar Broadcasting Inc ....F 863 683-6531
Lakeland (G-7402)

Next Step Advertising Inc ....G 305 371-4428
Miami (G-9616)

North Central Advertiser Inc ....G 386 755-2917
Lake City (G-7032)

Republic Newspapers Inc ....F 352 394-2183
Clermont (G-1881)

Seabreze Cmmncations Group Inc ....G 239 278-4222
Fort Myers (G-4397)

Southeast Publishing Co Inc ....G 239 213-1277
Naples (G-10897)

Sweetwater Today Inc ....G 305 456-4724
Miami (G-9982)

Triumphant Magazine LLC ....G 407 549-5443
Deltona (G-3055)

Unidad Editorial ....F 305 371-4428
Miami (G-10060)

Various Inc ....E 561 900-3691
Delray Beach (G-3032)

Voice Publishing Co Inc ....G 305 687-5555
Hialeah (G-5414)

Weekly Schulte Valdes ....G 813 221-1154
Tampa (G-17425)

Worldbox Corporation ....G 305 253-8800
Miami (G-10145)

Worldcity Inc ....G 305 441-2244
Coral Gables (G-2120)

Www Tcpalm Company ....E 772 287-1550
Stuart (G-16254)

PUBLISHERS: Newspapers, No Printing

A M Coplan Associates ....G 904 737-6996
Jacksonville (G-5847)

Ali Kamakhi ....F 850 405-8591
Tallahassee (G-16409)

American City Bus Journals Inc ....G 813 873-8225
Tampa (G-16588)

Ayers Publishing Inc ....G 352 463-7135
Trenton (G-17629)

Baker County Press Inc ....G 904 259-2400
Macclenny (G-8036)

Breeze Corporation ....G 239 574-1110
Cape Coral (G-1316)

Breeze Newspapers ....F 239 574-1116
Fort Myers (G-4195)

Breeze Newspapers ....G 239 574-1110
Cape Coral (G-1317)

Buck Pile Inc ....G 772 492-1056
Vero Beach (G-17747)

Business Jrnl Publications Inc ....E 813 342-2472
Tampa (G-16665)

Captiva Current Inc ....F 239 574-1110
Sanibel (G-15413)

Caxton Newspapers Inc ....E 305 538-9700
Miami Beach (G-10176)

Citrus Publishing LLC ....C 352 563-6363
Crystal River (G-2271)

Creative Loafing Inc ....G 813 739-4800
Tampa (G-16739)

Dixie County Advocate ....G 352 498-3312
Cross City (G-2260)

Downtown Projects I LLC ....G 352 226-8288
Gainesville (G-4680)

Florida Catholic Media Inc ....G 407 373-0075
Orlando (G-12159)

Florida Sentinel Publishing Co ....G 813 248-1921
Tampa (G-16855)

Forum Publishing Group Inc ....D 954 596-5650
Deerfield Beach (G-2722)

Greenwood Lake News Inc ....F 845 477-2575
Hudson (G-5776)

Griffon Graphics Inc ....F 954 922-1800
Hollywood (G-5587)

Grupo De Diarios America LLC ....G 305 577-0094
Miami (G-9256)

Hopkins & Daughter Inc ....G 941 964-2995
Boca Grande (G-381)

Howard Scripts Inc ....F 561 746-5111
Jupiter (G-6743)

Job News ....F 904 296-3006
Jacksonville (G-6227)

La Gaceta Publishing Inc ....F 813 248-3921
Tampa (G-16996)

Las Amrcas Mltimedia Group LLC ....F 305 633-3341
Miami (G-9427)

Lorken Publications Inc ....G 239 395-1213
Sanibel (G-15416)

Macbonner Inc ....F 941 778-7978
Holmes Beach (G-5690)

Miami News 24 Inc ....G 786 331-8141
Doral (G-3300)

Newspaper Publishers Inc ....E 561 793-7606
Wellington (G-17855)

Observer Media Group Inc ....E 941 349-4949
Sarasota (G-15767)

Orange Peel Gazette Inc ....G 407 892-5556
Saint Cloud (G-14936)

Orlando Times Inc ....G 407 841-3052
Orlando (G-12456)

Osceola Star ....G 407 933-0174
Kissimmee (G-6948)

Pensacola Voice Inc ....G 850 434-6963
Pensacola (G-13572)

Photo Finishing News Inc ....G 239 992-4421
Naples (G-10856)

Reed Brennan Media Associates ....E 407 894-7300
Orlando (G-12541)

Samara Publishing ....G 305 361-3333
Key Biscayne (G-6839)

Senior Lf Cmmnctions Group Inc ....F 561 392-4550
Boca Raton (G-665)

Southwest Fla Newspapers Inc ....G 239 574-9733
Cape Coral (G-1390)

Swapper ....G 850 973-6653
Madison (G-8047)

Tom Watson Enterprises Inc ....G 352 683-5097
Hudson (G-5789)

Voice of South Marion ....G 352 245-3161
Belleview (G-367)

Wakulla News ....F 850 926-7102
Crawfordville (G-2233)

Want ADS of Hot Springs Inc ....G 501 623-4404
Panama City (G-13319)

Washington CL Inc ....E 813 739-4800
Tampa (G-17422)

West Bolusia Beacon ....F 386 734-4622
Deland (G-2920)

Worldwide Media Svcs Group Inc ....F 212 545-4800
Boca Raton (G-757)

PUBLISHERS: Pamphlets, No Printing

Informa Usa Inc ....A 561 361-6017
Sarasota (G-15705)

PUBLISHERS: Periodical Statistical Reports, No Printing

Twinlab Corporation ....G 800 645-5626
Boca Raton (G-728)

PUBLISHERS: Periodical, With Printing

Cole Enterprises Inc ....G 727 441-4101
Clearwater (G-1546)

N Media Group LLC ....E 239 594-1322
Naples (G-10826)

Sep Communications LLC ....F 561 998-0870
Boca Raton (G-669)

PUBLISHERS: Periodicals, Magazines

954 Savings Magazine ....G 954 900-4649
Weston (G-18218)

Aacecorp Inc ....G 904 353-7878
Jacksonville (G-5853)

Academy Publishing Inc ....E 407 736-0100
Orlando (G-11864)

Always Fun Inc ....G 954 258-4377
Cooper City (G-2016)

Armbrust Aviation Group Inc ....E 561 355-8488
West Palm Beach (G-17927)

Best Community Magazine ....G 407 571-2980
Altamonte Springs (G-33)

Born To Ride ....F 813 661-9402
Brandon (G-1085)

Boswell JM & Associates Inc ....G 239 949-2311
Bonita Springs (G-785)

Central Florida Publishing Inc ....F 407 323-5204
Sanford (G-15279)

Community News Publications ....F 813 909-2800
Lutz (G-7986)

Construction Bulletin Inc ....F 904 388-0336
Jacksonville (G-5999)

Data Publishers Inc ....F 954 752-2332
Coral Springs (G-2147)

Fathym Inc ....F 303 905-4402
Palmetto (G-13166)

Gatehouse Media LLC ....D 863 401-6900
Winter Haven (G-18442)

PRODUCT

Gulf Publishing Company Inc..............F 727 596-2863
Largo (G-7602)
Hispanic Amercn Pubg Group Inc........G 305 961-1132
Miami (G-9284)
In Focus Interactive Magazine ....G 954 966-1233
Miramar (G-10503)
Lifestyle Magazine ....G 386 423-2772
New Smyrna Beach (G-11004)
Mercaworld and CIA LLC ....G 786 212-5905
Pembroke Pines (G-13402)
Municipal Code Corporation ....F 850 576-3171
Tallahassee (G-16482)
Newsmax Media Inc ....F 561 686-1165
West Palm Beach (G-18091)
Quad Intl Incorporated ....E 305 662-5959
Doral (G-3341)
Senior Lf Cmmnctions Group Inc.........F 561 392-4550
Boca Raton (G-665)
Showcase Publications Inc ....G 863 687-4377
Lakeland (G-7434)
Solution Publishing LLC ....F 813 291-0840
Tampa (G-17281)
Southeast Review Inc ....G 850 644-4230
Tallahassee (G-16501)
Spanish House Inc ....E 305 503-1191
Medley (G-8324)
Streamline Publishing Inc ....G 561 655-8778
Boca Raton (G-699)
Tampa Media Group LLC ....G 813 259-7100
Tampa (G-17335)
Twinlab Holdings Inc ....E 800 645-5626
Boca Raton (G-729)
Wheelhouse Direct LLC ....G 239 246-8788
Fort Myers (G-4448)
World Politics Review LLC ....F 202 903-8398
Tampa (G-17438)

PUBLISHERS: Periodicals, No Printing

Coral Gables Living ....G 786 552-6464
Coral Gables (G-2043)
In The Bite ....F 561 529-3940
Jupiter (G-6745)
Naples Illustrated ....G 239 434-6966
Naples (G-10828)
Our Seniors Guidecom Inc ....G 904 655-2130
Jacksonville (G-6344)
Taylor & Francis Group LLC ....C 561 994-0555
Boca Raton (G-707)
Waste Advantage Corporation ....G 800 358-2873
Jupiter (G-6823)

PUBLISHERS: Posters

Publishers Guild Inc ....G 904 273-5394
Ponte Vedra Beach (G-14278)

PUBLISHERS: Technical Manuals

Tomsons Inc ....G 248 646-0677
Englewood (G-3539)

PUBLISHERS: Technical Manuals & Papers

Bot International Inc ....G 407 366-6547
Oviedo (G-12811)
Digital Direct Corporation ....G 813 448-9071
Oldsmar (G-11642)

PUBLISHERS: Telephone & Other Directory

Coastal Directory Company ....F 321 777-7076
Melbourne (G-8391)
Global Directories Inc ....F 954 571-8283
Deerfield Beach (G-2727)
Guest Service Publications Inc ....F 516 333-3474
Bonita Springs (G-801)
Heritage Publishing Inc ....F 904 296-1304
Jacksonville (G-6176)
Hill Donnelly Corporation ....G 800 525-1242
Tampa (G-16917)
Nationwide Publishing Company ....E 352 253-0017
Deltona (G-3049)
North Metro Media ....G 850 650-1014
Niceville (G-11033)
Page Golfs Yellow Directory ....F 305 378-8038
Palmetto Bay (G-13216)
Supermedia LLC ....G 813 402-3753
Tampa (G-17316)
Supermedia LLC ....D 727 576-1300
Saint Petersburg (G-15203)
Time Adjusters Conference Inc ....G 386 274-4210
Port Orange (G-14352)

PUBLISHERS: Textbooks, No Printing

Houghton Mifflin Harcourt Pubg ....F 561 951-5518
Royal Palm Beach (G-14766)
Houghton Mifflin Harcourt Pubg ....F 954 975-0508
Pompano Beach (G-14055)
Logoi Inc ....G 305 232-5880
Miami (G-9473)
Phillip Roy Inc ....F 727 593-2700
Largo (G-7658)

PUBLISHERS: Trade journals, No Printing

First Marketing Company ....C 954 979-0700
Pompano Beach (G-14021)
Industrial Projects Services ....G 813 265-2957
Tampa (G-16942)
Uproxx Media Inc ....F 917 603-2374
Miami Beach (G-10241)

PUBLISHING & BROADCASTING: Internet Only

Aero-News Network Inc ....G 863 299-8680
Orange Park (G-11813)
Akua Rage Entertainment Inc ....G 904 627-5312
Jacksonville (G-5872)
Altered Media Inc ....E 813 397-3892
Tampa (G-16581)
Bg Expo Group LLC ....G 305 428-3576
Doral (G-3136)
Brazilian Clssfied ADS-Chei In ....G 954 570-7568
Deerfield Beach (G-2680)
Broadcast Tech Inc ....G 786 351-4227
Medley (G-8213)
Collidecom LLC ....F 407 903-5626
Orlando (G-12030)
Comm Dots LLC Connecting ....F 305 505-6009
Miami (G-8951)
D1 Locker LLC ....G 305 446-9041
Miami (G-8992)
Digicrib LLC ....G 833 932-8800
Destin (G-3065)
Do You Remember Inc ....G 305 987-9111
Miami Beach (G-10184)
E1w Games LLC ....G 561 255-7370
Delray Beach (G-2956)
El American LLC ....E 305 902-8051
Coral Gables (G-2053)
Fbr 1804 Inc ....F 305 340-3114
North Miami Beach (G-11139)
Flowhance Inc ....F 305 690-0784
Miami (G-9163)
Gcn Publishing Inc ....G 203 665-6211
Pompano Beach (G-14039)
Icome2fix LLC ....F 954 789-4102
Miami (G-9300)
Igbo Network LLC ....F 352 727-4113
Gainesville (G-4710)
Isocialmedia Digital Marketing ....G 561 510-1124
Boca Raton (G-554)
Jjj & H Inc ....G 904 389-1130
Jacksonville (G-6224)
Levatas ....D 561 622-4511
West Palm Beach (G-18056)
Media Digittal LLC ....G 305 506-0470
Doral (G-3294)
Myarea Network Inc ....F 800 830-7994
Tampa (G-17092)
Page One LLC ....F 833 467-2431
Dania (G-2340)
Printing For A Cause LLC ....E 786 496-0637
Saint Petersburg (G-15161)
Romeo Roseau Ecommerce ....F 561 633-1352
Boynton Beach (G-909)
Sarasota Byfront Plg Orgnztion ....G 941 203-5316
Sarasota (G-15810)
Saving For College LLC ....F 954 770-5136
Miami (G-9851)
Simpleshow USA Corp ....E 844 468-5447
Miami (G-9896)
Sipradius LLC ....G 954 290-2434
Parkland (G-13354)
Slate Group LLC ....G 786 484-9408
Miami (G-9903)
Smilefy Inc ....F 302 465-6606
Hallandale Beach (G-4972)
Videolinq Streaming Svcs LLC ....G 904 330-1026
Jacksonville (G-6591)
Vlex LLC ....G 800 335-6202
Miami (G-10119)

PUBLISHING & PRINTING: Art Copy

Afrikin LLC ....G 646 296-3613
West Palm Beach (G-17916)
Dakim Inc ....F 561 790-0884
Royal Palm Beach (G-14762)
Palm Prnting/Printers Ink Corp ....E 239 332-8600
Fort Myers (G-4355)
Preferred Custom Printing LLC ....F 727 443-1900
Seminole (G-15987)

PUBLISHING & PRINTING: Book Music

4ever Music LLC ....E 407 490-0977
Orlando (G-11853)

PUBLISHING & PRINTING: Books

Beacon Publishing Inc ....G 888 618-5253
North Palm Beach (G-11176)
Creative Tech Sarasota Inc ....F 941 371-2743
Sarasota (G-15644)
Plus Communications Inc ....E 407 333-0600
Lake Mary (G-7100)
Red Giant Entertainment Inc ....G 877 904-7334
Clermont (G-1880)
Speech Bin ....F 772 770-0006
Vero Beach (G-17801)
Starlite Inc ....F 727 392-2929
Seminole (G-15989)
Tra Publishing LLP ....F 305 424-6468
Miami (G-10031)

PUBLISHING & PRINTING: Catalogs

Sony Music Publishing (us) LLC ....G 305 532-9064
Miami Beach (G-10231)

PUBLISHING & PRINTING: Directories, NEC

American Computer & Tech Corp ....G 786 738-3220
Miami Beach (G-10164)
Municipal Code Corporation ....F 850 576-3171
Tallahassee (G-16482)

PUBLISHING & PRINTING: Guides

Enterra Inc ....F 813 514-0531
Tampa (G-16815)

PUBLISHING & PRINTING: Magazines: publishing & printing

Akers Media Group Inc ....E 352 787-4112
Leesburg (G-7757)
American Chiropractor ....F 305 434-8865
Miami (G-8715)
Artnexus Online Inc ....E 305 891-7270
North Miami (G-11090)
Automundo Productions Inc ....G 305 541-4198
Coral Gables (G-2031)
Black College Monthly Inc ....G 352 335-5771
Gainesville (G-4661)
Black College Today Inc ....G 954 344-4469
Coral Springs (G-2137)
Brevard Softball Magazine Inc ....F 321 453-3711
Merritt Island (G-8580)
Conde Nast Americas ....G 305 371-9393
Coral Gables (G-2042)
Diamond Advertising & Mktg ....F 561 833-5129
West Palm Beach (G-17978)
Endeavor Publications Inc ....G 352 369-1104
Ocala (G-11378)
Five Sports Inc ....G 727 209-1750
Saint Petersburg (G-15047)
Franja Corp ....G 954 659-1950
Weston (G-18244)
Goodpress Publishing LLC ....G 561 865-8101
Delray Beach (G-2969)
Grupo Editorial Expansion ....G 305 374-9003
Coral Gables (G-2066)
Insurance Plus ....G 904 567-1553
Ponte Vedra Beach (G-14269)
International Cnstr Pubg ....G 305 668-4999
Miami (G-9326)
Lifestyle Media Group LLC ....F 954 377-9470
Fort Lauderdale (G-3918)
Mas Editorial Corp ....G 305 748-0124
Hollywood (G-5621)
Metro Life Media Inc ....G 813 745-3658
Tampa (G-17070)
Npc of Tampa Inc ....F 813 839-0035
Tampa (G-17112)

Old Port Group LLC ....F 904 819-5812
Saint Augustine (G-14869)
Our City Media of Florida LLC ....F 954 306-1007
Sunrise (G-16349)
Palm Beach Newspapers Inc ....C 561 820-3800
West Palm Beach (G-18111)
Playbill Southern Publishing ....F 305 595-1984
Miami (G-9721)
Plus Communications Inc ....E 407 333-0600
Lake Mary (G-7100)
Shalom Adventure ....G 727 375-7502
New Port Richey (G-10983)
Shelton Group LLC ....G 321 676-8981
Melbourne (G-8520)
Special Publications Inc ....F 352 622-2995
Ocala (G-11496)
T V HI Lites Penny Saver Inc ....F 941 378-5353
Sarasota (G-15848)
Times Holding Co ....D 727 893-8111
Saint Petersburg (G-15212)
Times Publishing Company ....A 727 893-8111
Saint Petersburg (G-15214)
Vista Publishing Corporation ....F 305 416-4644
Miami Beach (G-10246)

PUBLISHING & PRINTING: Music, Book

Globe Boyz International LLC ....F 305 308-8160
Miami (G-9221)

PUBLISHING & PRINTING: Newsletters, Business Svc

Avprinting Solutions LLC ....G 866 207-6295
Pembroke Pines (G-13376)
Construction Bulletin Inc ....F 904 388-0336
Jacksonville (G-5999)
Leila K Moavero ....G 954 978-0018
Pompano Beach (G-14076)

PUBLISHING & PRINTING: Newspapers

925 Nuevos Cubanos Inc ....G 954 806-8375
Fort Lauderdale (G-3616)
Alachua Today Inc ....G 386 462-3355
Alachua (G-1)
Anna Andres ....F 239 335-0233
Fort Myers (G-4177)
B Squared of Chiefland LLC ....G 352 507-2195
Chiefland (G-1446)
Bcc-Bgle Cmmnctons Crp-Clrin L ....F 305 270-3333
Miami (G-8806)
Beach Beacon ....F 727 397-5563
Seminole (G-15971)
Bi-Ads Inc ....F 954 525-1489
Fort Lauderdale (G-3684)
Bonita Daily News ....E 239 213-6060
Fort Myers (G-4193)
Bradford County Telegraph Inc ....F 904 964-6305
Starke (G-16096)
Brazilian Clssfied ADS-Chei In ....G 954 570-7568
Deerfield Beach (G-2680)
Brevard Business News ....F 321 951-7777
Melbourne (G-8383)
Bulletin Net Inc ....F 941 468-2569
Sarasota (G-15620)
Business Report of N Cntrl FL ....G 352 275-9469
Gainesville (G-4663)
Campus Communications Inc ....C 352 376-4482
Gainesville (G-4665)
Caribbean Today News Magazine ....F 305 238-2868
Palmetto Bay (G-13208)
Carol City Opa Locka News ....E 305 669-7355
South Miami (G-16031)
Central Florida Publishing Inc ....F 407 323-5204
Sanford (G-15279)
Chipley Newspapers Inc ....G 850 638-0212
Bonifay (G-769)
Community News Papers Inc ....E 386 752-1293
Lake City (G-7015)
Cooppa News Reporter ....F 954 437-8864
Pembroke Pines (G-13383)
Current ....F 954 262-8455
Davie (G-2401)
Cve Reporter Inc ....F 954 421-5566
Deerfield Beach (G-2701)
Daily Buzz ....G 407 673-5400
Winter Park (G-18503)
Daily Green ....G 352 226-8288
Gainesville (G-4675)
Daily Melt ....G 305 519-2585
Miami (G-8998)

Daily Racing Enterprises Inc ....G 772 287-9106
Stuart (G-16136)
Daily Room ....G 754 200-5153
Plantation (G-13842)
Daily Therapy Services Inc ....G 954 649-3620
Lauderhill (G-7730)
Dailys ....F 904 448-0562
Jacksonville (G-6024)
Dailys ....G 904 880-4784
Jacksonville (G-6025)
Doral Family Journal LLC ....G 305 300-4594
Doral (G-3198)
El Colusa News ....G 786 845-6868
Miami (G-9075)
El Hispano ....G 772 878-6488
Port Saint Lucie (G-14409)
Emerald Coast Media & Mktg ....E 850 267-4555
Santa Rosa Beach (G-15425)
EW Scripps Company ....C 772 408-5300
Port Saint Lucie (G-14411)
F S View Fla Flambeau Newsppr ....E 850 561-6653
Tallahassee (G-16438)
Florida Health Care News Inc ....E 813 989-1330
Temple Terrace (G-17537)
Florida Star Inc ....F 904 766-8834
Jacksonville (G-6110)
Florida Weekly ....D 239 333-2135
Fort Myers (G-4258)
Foliage Enterprises Inc ....E 407 886-2777
Apopka (G-134)
Forum Publishing Group Inc ....F 954 698-6397
Deerfield Beach (G-2721)
Free Press Publishing Company ....E 813 254-5888
Tampa (G-16860)
Gainesville ....G 352 339-0294
Gainesville (G-4697)
Go Latinos Magazine LLC ....G 786 601-7693
Homestead (G-5711)
Greene Publishing Inc ....E 850 973-6397
Madison (G-8044)
Gulf Breeze News Inc ....G 850 932-8986
Gulf Breeze (G-4882)
Gulf Coast Business Review ....G 941 906-9386
Sarasota (G-15695)
Gulfcoast Gabber Inc ....G 727 321-6965
Gulfport (G-4898)
Halifax Media Group LLC ....B 386 265-6700
Daytona Beach (G-2558)
Halifax Media Group LLC ....E 941 361-4800
Sarasota (G-15698)
Halifax Media Holdings LLC ....E 386 681-2404
Daytona Beach (G-2559)
Harborpoint Media LLC ....C 352 365-8200
Leesburg (G-7780)
Harold Brley For Ormond Bch Cy ....G 386 853-9000
Ormond Beach (G-12768)
Heritage Cntl Fla Jwish News I ....F 407 834-8277
Fern Park (G-3579)
Homestead Newspapers Inc ....A 305 245-2311
Homestead (G-5714)
Hometown News LC ....E 772 465-5656
Fort Pierce (G-4495)
Impremedia LLC ....F 407 767-0070
Longwood (G-7903)
Independent Newsmedia Inc USA ....G 863 983-9148
Okeechobee (G-11609)
Inquirer Newspapers Inc ....E 772 257-6230
Vero Beach (G-17765)
Jacksonville Free Press ....F 904 634-1993
Jacksonville (G-6215)
Jls of St Augustine Inc ....G 904 797-6098
Saint Augustine (G-14849)
Kenneth A Jeffus Fine Art LLC ....G 954 849-0553
Plantation (G-13862)
Key West Printing LLC ....G 305 517-6711
Key West (G-6868)
Keynoter Publishing Co Inc ....F 305 743-5551
Marathon (G-8108)
Knight-Rddr/Miami Herald Cr Un ....G 305 376-2181
Miami (G-9395)
Lake News LLC ....G 407 251-1314
Orlando (G-12306)
Ledger ....B 863 802-7000
Lakeland (G-7376)
Liberty Calhoun Journal Inc ....G 850 643-3333
Bristol (G-1122)
Linville Enterprises LLC ....G 813 782-1558
Zephyrhills (G-18620)
Localtoolbox Inc ....G 415 250-3232
Pensacola (G-13538)

Longboat Key News Inc ....F 941 387-2200
Longboat Key (G-7858)
M C H Journal Services Inc ....G 352 336-4215
Gainesville (G-4723)
McClatchy Shared Services Ctr ....E 305 740-8800
Doral (G-3293)
Medleycom Incorporated ....E 408 745-5418
Delray Beach (G-2986)
Merle Harris Enterprises Inc ....G 386 677-7060
South Daytona (G-16024)
Miami Herald ....E 305 269-7768
Miami (G-9552)
Miami Herald ....G 800 843-4372
Doral (G-3298)
Miami Times ....E 305 694-6210
Miami (G-9561)
Mid-Florida Publications Inc ....G 352 589-8811
Mount Dora (G-10605)
Miller Publishing Co Inc ....F 305 669-7355
South Miami (G-16039)
Milton Newspapers Inc ....A 850 623-2120
Milton (G-10431)
Monticello News ....F 850 997-3568
Monticello (G-10584)
National Newspaper Placem ....G 866 404-5913
Lake Mary (G-7097)
Ne Media Group Inc ....G 954 733-8393
Oakland Park (G-11280)
Neighbor To Neighbor Newspaper ....G 904 278-7256
Middleburg (G-10406)
Neighborhood News & Lifestyles ....F 727 943-0551
Tarpon Springs (G-17483)
News Features USA Inc ....G 305 298-5313
Miami Beach (G-10215)
News Herald ....G 850 785-6550
Panama City (G-13289)
News Leader Inc ....F 352 242-9818
Clermont (G-1877)
News-Journal Corporation ....A 386 252-1511
Daytona Beach (G-2578)
News-Journal Corporation ....F 386 283-5664
Palm Coast (G-13083)
North Orange Avenue Properties ....G 407 420-5000
Orlando (G-12421)
Northwest Florida Daily News ....E 850 863-1111
Fort Walton Beach (G-4599)
Observer Group ....G 407 654-5500
Winter Garden (G-18399)
Observer Group Inc ....F 941 383-5509
Sarasota (G-15765)
Ocala Star Banner Corporation ....C 352 867-4010
Gainesville (G-4740)
Office of Medical Examiner ....G 772 464-7378
Fort Pierce (G-4512)
Ord of Ahepa Ch 356 Daily & T ....G 727 791-1040
Clearwater (G-1729)
Ormond Beach Observer ....G 386 492-2784
Ormond Beach (G-12784)
Our Village Okeechobee Inc ....F 863 467-0158
Okeechobee (G-11613)
Outpost North Lake ....G 352 669-2430
Umatilla (G-17649)
Overseas Radio LLC ....G 305 296-1630
Key West (G-6879)
P A Vivid Pathology ....G 850 416-7780
Pensacola (G-13564)
Palm Beach Newspapers Inc ....C 561 820-3800
West Palm Beach (G-18111)
Palm Coast Observer LLC ....E 386 447-9723
Palm Coast (G-13084)
Panama City News Herald ....D 850 747-5000
Panama City (G-13293)
Panama City News Herald ....B 850 863-1111
Fort Walton Beach (G-4601)
Pathfnders Palm Bch-Mrtin Cnty ....E 561 820-4262
West Palm Beach (G-18114)
Pearcey Enterprise ....G 904 235-3096
Tampa (G-17154)
Pinecrest Tribune ....F 305 662-2277
South Miami (G-16042)
Plant City Observer LLC ....G 813 704-6850
Plant City (G-13796)
Plantation Journal Corporation ....G 954 226-6170
Plantation (G-13877)
Ponte Vedra Wns Civic Aliance ....G 904 834-3543
Ponte Vedra Beach (G-14277)
Port St Lucie News ....E 772 287-1550
Stuart (G-16199)
Pressnet Corp ....G 786 728-1369
Miami (G-9738)

Employee Codes: A=Over 500 employees, B=251-500
C=101-250, D=51-100, E=20-50, F=10-19, G=4-9

2022 Harris Florida
Manufacturers Directory

PRODUCT

1303

Prestige Publication Group .... E 305 538-9700
Miami Beach *(G-10222)*

Prison Legal News .... F 561 360-2523
Lake Worth *(G-7229)*

Republic Newspapers Inc .... G 813 782-1558
Zephyrhills *(G-18628)*

Resident Cmnty News Group Inc .... F 904 962-6876
Jacksonville *(G-6416)*

Ring of Fire Radio LLC .... G 866 666-6114
Pensacola *(G-13597)*

Santiva Chronicle LLC .... G 239 472-0559
Sanibel *(G-15418)*

Sarasota Herald-Tribune .... C 941 358-4000
Sarasota *(G-15551)*

Sarasota Herald-Tribune .... B 941 953-7755
Sarasota *(G-15813)*

Sarasota Herald-Tribune .... G 941 953-7755
Sarasota *(G-15814)*

Sathyam Publications Inc .... F 562 667-6622
Miami *(G-9849)*

Science Daily LLC .... G 239 596-2624
Sarasota *(G-15820)*

Senior Life of Florida .... F 321 242-1235
Melbourne *(G-8519)*

Senior Voice America Inc .... G 813 444-1011
Tampa *(G-17250)*

Sentinel Cmmnctons News Vntres .... E 407 420-6229
Longwood *(G-7946)*

Sentinel Cmmnctons News Vntres .... G 407 420-5291
Orlando *(G-12585)*

Sentinel Sq Off Bldg MGT & Lsg .... G 727 461-7700
Clearwater *(G-1780)*

South Florida Digest Inc .... F 954 458-0635
Hallandale Beach *(G-4975)*

Southfloridagaynewscom .... E 954 530-4970
Wilton Manors *(G-18342)*

St Augustine Record .... E 904 829-6562
Saint Augustine *(G-14900)*

Stuart News .... C 772 287-1550
Stuart *(G-16229)*

Stuart News .... C 772 287-1550
Stuart *(G-16230)*

Sun Coast Media Group Inc .... D 941 206-1300
Port Charlotte *(G-14317)*

Sun Coast Media Group Inc .... D 941 207-1000
Venice *(G-17720)*

Sun Coast Media Group Inc .... G 863 494-7600
Punta Gorda *(G-14534)*

Sun Coast Media Group Inc .... E 941 681-3000
Englewood *(G-3538)*

Sun Coast Media Group Inc .... F 941 206-1900
Port Charlotte *(G-14318)*

Sun-Sentinel Company LLC .... B 954 356-4000
Fort Lauderdale *(G-4073)*

Sun-Sentinel Company LLC .... D 954 356-4000
Deerfield Beach *(G-2816)*

Sun-Sentinel Company Inc .... F 954 735-6414
Fort Lauderdale *(G-4074)*

Suncoast News .... F 727 815-1023
Port Richey *(G-14376)*

Syndicated Programming Inc .... G 850 877-0105
Tallahassee *(G-16508)*

Tallahassee Democrat .... E 850 599-2100
Tallahassee *(G-16510)*

Tampa Bay Newspapers Inc .... D 727 397-5563
Seminole *(G-15995)*

Tampa Bay Sports Entrmt LLC .... D 727 893-8111
Saint Petersburg *(G-15209)*

Tampa Bay Times .... G 352 754-6100
Brooksville *(G-1209)*

Tampa Media Group Inc .... C 813 259-7711
Tampa *(G-17333)*

Tampa Media Group Inc .... B 813 259-7711
Tampa *(G-17334)*

Tampa Media Group LLC .... G 813 259-7100
Tampa *(G-17335)*

Times Holding Co .... B 727 445-4249
Clearwater *(G-1831)*

Times Holding Co .... B 813 226-3300
Tampa *(G-17354)*

Times Holding Co .... D 727 893-8111
Saint Petersburg *(G-15212)*

Times Media Services Inc .... E 727 893-8111
Saint Petersburg *(G-15213)*

Times Publishing Company .... E 727 849-6397
Port Richey *(G-14379)*

Times Publishing Company .... F 352 567-6660
Inverness *(G-5835)*

Todays Restaurant News Inc .... G 561 620-8888
Boca Raton *(G-718)*

Treasure Chest of Sweetwater .... G 407 788-0020
Longwood *(G-7953)*

Triangle Shopping Guide Inc .... G 352 589-8811
Mount Dora *(G-10616)*

Venice Herald Tribune .... G 941 486-3000
Sarasota *(G-15866)*

Vero News .... G 772 234-5727
Vero Beach *(G-17815)*

Weekly Challenger Newspaper .... F 727 896-2922
Saint Petersburg *(G-15229)*

Weekly Newspaper .... F 305 743-0844
Marathon *(G-8109)*

Weekly Planet of Sarasota Inc .... E 813 739-4800
Tampa *(G-17424)*

Will & Mia Corp .... G 617 943-6914
Miami *(G-10132)*

Winter Garden Times Inc .... G 407 656-2121
Winter Garden *(G-18409)*

Woody Hatcher .... G 850 526-1501
Marianna *(G-8176)*

Worldwide Media Svcs Group Inc .... C 561 989-1342
Boca Raton *(G-758)*

PUBLISHING & PRINTING: Pamphlets

Baptist Communications Mission .... F 954 981-2271
Hollywood *(G-5538)*

Digital Propaganda Inc .... F 407 644-8444
Orlando *(G-12097)*

Florida Sncast Trism Prmtons I .... F 727 544-1212
Largo *(G-7587)*

PUBLISHING & PRINTING: Posters

Cutting Edge Sgns Grphics of P .... G 727 546-3700
Clearwater *(G-1559)*

Reimink Printing Inc .... G 813 289-4663
Tampa *(G-17214)*

PUBLISHING & PRINTING: Shopping News

Fpc Printing Inc .... C 813 626-9430
Tampa *(G-16859)*

Observer Media Group Inc .... E 941 349-4949
Sarasota *(G-15767)*

Trading Post of Central Fla .... G 954 675-2149
Margate *(G-8157)*

PUBLISHING & PRINTING: Technical Manuals

Rapid Rater Company .... E 850 893-7346
Tallahassee *(G-16492)*

PUBLISHING & PRINTING: Textbooks

H & H Publishing Co Inc .... G 727 442-7760
Clearwater *(G-1620)*

Sirs Publishing Inc .... D 800 521-0600
Boca Raton *(G-680)*

PUBLISHING & PRINTING: Trade Journals

Signcraft Publishing Co Inc .... F 239 939-4644
Fort Myers *(G-4399)*

Ural & Associates Inc .... G 305 446-9462
Coral Gables *(G-2116)*

PULP MILLS

Foley Cellulose LLC .... A 850 584-1121
Perry *(G-13637)*

Rayonier Inc .... E 904 277-1343
Yulee *(G-18592)*

Suzano Pulp & Paper .... G 954 772-7716
Fort Lauderdale *(G-4080)*

PULP MILLS: Mechanical & Recycling Processing

Ies Sales and Service LLC .... G 305 525-6079
Miami *(G-9303)*

Platinium Rosis Inc .... G 786 617-9973
Miami Beach *(G-10220)*

Southern Wood Services LLC .... G 352 279-3208
Brooksville *(G-1203)*

Stellar On-Site Llc .... F 904 945-1908
Hilliard *(G-5477)*

Universal PC Organization Inc .... G 321 285-9206
Orlando *(G-12691)*

PULSE FORMING NETWORKS

Akuwa Solutions Group Inc .... F 941 343-9947
Sarasota *(G-15589)*

PUMP JACKS & OTHER PUMPING EQPT: Indl

Stenner Pump Company Inc .... D 904 641-1666
Jacksonville *(G-6506)*

PUMPS

Acme Service Corp .... F 305 836-4800
Miami *(G-8647)*

Air Supply of Future Inc .... F 954 977-0877
Pompano Beach *(G-13914)*

American Incinerators Corp .... E 321 282-7357
Orlando *(G-11902)*

American-Marsh Pumps LLC .... G 863 646-5689
Lakeland *(G-7273)*

Anko Products Inc .... E 941 748-2307
Bradenton *(G-939)*

Channel Industries Inc .... F 561 214-0637
West Palm Beach *(G-17965)*

Custom Masters Inc .... E 407 331-4634
Longwood *(G-7885)*

D & D Machine & Hydraulics Inc .... E 239 275-7177
Fort Myers *(G-4228)*

Del Prado Holdings LLC .... G 305 680-7425
Hollywood *(G-5563)*

Delta P Systems Inc .... F 386 236-0950
Ormond Beach *(G-12755)*

Gulf ATL Pump & Dredge LLC .... G 386 362-2761
Newberry *(G-11022)*

Hamworthy Inc .... G 305 597-7520
Fort Lauderdale *(G-3859)*

Hisco Pump South LLC .... F 904 786-4488
Jacksonville *(G-6177)*

Hizer Machine Mfg Inc .... G 386 755-3155
White Springs *(G-18306)*

Holland Pump Company .... G 561 697-3333
West Palm Beach *(G-18025)*

Holland Pump Company .... G 904 880-0010
Jacksonville *(G-6181)*

Hydrolec Inc .... G 904 730-3766
Jacksonville *(G-6189)*

Innovation Marine Corporation .... E 941 355-7852
Sarasota *(G-15500)*

ITT Water & Wastewater USA Inc .... G 407 880-2900
Apopka *(G-140)*

John Mader Enterprises Inc .... E 239 731-5455
Fort Myers *(G-4300)*

Johnston Archtctral Systems In .... E 904 886-9030
Jacksonville *(G-6231)*

Keller Industrial Inc .... E 813 831-1871
Riverview *(G-14568)*

Lodex Enterprises Corp .... G 954 442-3843
Miramar *(G-10509)*

Marine Metal Products Co .... G 727 461-5575
Clearwater *(G-1683)*

Multitrode Inc .... E 561 737-1210
Boca Raton *(G-606)*

Mwi Corporation .... E 954 426-1500
Deerfield Beach *(G-2772)*

Osgood Industries LLC .... C 813 448-9041
Oldsmar *(G-11683)*

Parker-Hannifin Corporation .... E 305 470-8800
Miami *(G-9694)*

Performance Pumps Inc .... E 407 339-6700
Casselberry *(G-1427)*

Phoenix Dewatering Inc .... F 407 330-7015
Sanford *(G-15371)*

Portable Pumping Systems Inc .... G 727 518-9191
Clearwater *(G-1744)*

Pulsafeeder Inc .... D 941 575-2900
Punta Gorda *(G-14521)*

Pulsafeeder Spo Inc .... G 941 575-3800
Punta Gorda *(G-14522)*

Rev Old Inc .... F 954 523-9396
Davie *(G-2468)*

RG Groundworks LLC .... G 352 474-7949
Newberry *(G-11026)*

Schwing Bioset .... F 239 237-2174
Fort Myers *(G-4392)*

Serf Inc .... E 850 476-8203
Cantonment *(G-1273)*

Southern Innovative Energy Inc .... G 321 747-9205
Titusville *(G-17616)*

Thermo King of Ocala Inc .... G 352 867-7700
Ocala *(G-11500)*

Townley Engrg & Mfg Co Inc .... C 352 687-3001
Candler *(G-1261)*

Tradewinds Power Corp ....F 863 382-2166
Sebring *(G-15948)*
Turner Machine & Supply Co ....G 772 464-4550
Fort Pierce *(G-4545)*
Wilo USA LLC ....D 954 524-6776
Fort Lauderdale *(G-4133)*
Xylem Water Solutions Fla LLC ....E 561 848-1200
Apopka *(G-186)*
Xylem Water Solutions USA Inc ....D 407 880-2900
Sanford *(G-15411)*

PUMPS & PARTS: Indl

Air Dimensions Inc ....E 954 428-7333
Deerfield Beach *(G-2661)*
Azcue Pumps USA Inc ....G 954 597-7602
Tamarac *(G-16527)*
G & F Manufacturing Inc ....F 239 939-7446
Fort Myers *(G-4267)*
Greylor Dynesco Co Inc ....G 239 574-2011
Cape Coral *(G-1350)*
Hoover Pumping Systems Corp ....E 954 971-7350
Pompano Beach *(G-14054)*
Jka Pump Specialists ....G 561 686-4455
West Palm Beach *(G-18040)*
Pioneer Dredge Inc ....G 904 732-2151
Jacksonville *(G-6373)*
Quantumfly Enterprises Inc ....E 407 807-7050
Sanford *(G-15379)*
Smith Surface Prep Systems Inc ....E 954 941-9744
Pompano Beach *(G-14183)*
Tru-Flo Corp ....F 561 996-5850
Belle Glade *(G-346)*

PUMPS & PUMPING EQPT REPAIR SVCS

Central Electric Motor Svc Inc ....F 863 422-4721
Haines City *(G-4902)*
Dade Pump & Supply Co ....G 305 235-5000
Miami *(G-8996)*
Gulf Coast Elc Mtr Svc Inc ....E 850 433-5134
Pensacola *(G-13515)*
John Mader Enterprises Inc ....E 239 731-5455
Fort Myers *(G-4300)*
K C W Electric Company Inc ....G 850 878-2051
Tallahassee *(G-16465)*
Morgans Elc Mtr & Pump Svc ....F 321 960-2209
Cocoa Beach *(G-1974)*
Robert E Weissenborn Sr ....G 239 262-1771
Naples *(G-10879)*

PUMPS & PUMPING EQPT WHOLESALERS

Dade Pump & Supply Co ....G 305 235-5000
Miami *(G-8996)*
Greylor Dynesco Co Inc ....G 239 574-2011
Cape Coral *(G-1350)*
Keller Industrial Inc ....E 813 831-1871
Riverview *(G-14568)*

PUMPS, HEAT: Electric

Built Right Pool Heaters LLC ....G 941 505-1600
Punta Gorda *(G-14500)*
Calorex USA LLC ....G 239 482-0606
Fort Myers *(G-4199)*

PUMPS: Aircraft, Hydraulic

Leading Edge Aerospace Llc ....G 305 608-6826
Miami Gardens *(G-10267)*

PUMPS: Domestic, Water Or Sump

Awl Manufacturing Inc ....G 239 643-5780
Naples *(G-10685)*
Vickery and Company ....F 813 987-2100
Tampa *(G-17415)*

PUMPS: Fluid Power

Eem Technologies Corp ....G 786 606-5993
Doral *(G-3205)*
Oase North America Inc ....G 800 365-3880
Riviera Beach *(G-14652)*

PUMPS: Hydraulic Power Transfer

Mwi Corporation ....F 239 337-4747
Fort Myers *(G-4335)*

PUMPS: Measuring & Dispensing

Stenner Pump Company Inc ....D 904 641-1666
Jacksonville *(G-6506)*

PUMPS: Oil Well & Field

Acme Dynamics Inc ....F 813 752-3137
Winter Haven *(G-18411)*

PUMPS: Vacuum, Exc Laboratory

Graham & Company LLC ....G 904 281-0003
Jacksonville *(G-6148)*
Hisco Pump South LLC ....G 904 786-4488
Jacksonville *(G-6177)*
Mat-Vac Technology Inc ....F 386 238-7017
Daytona Beach *(G-2573)*

PUPPETS & MARIONETTES

Duck In Truck Puppets Inc ....G 772 334-3022
Jensen Beach *(G-6653)*
Puppet Workshop Inc ....E 305 666-2655
Miami *(G-9758)*

PURIFICATION & DUST COLLECTION EQPT

Rgf Environmental Group Inc ....C 800 842-7771
Riviera Beach *(G-14669)*

PURSES: Women's

Christy Lewis Sheek LLC ....G 786 512-2999
Coral Springs *(G-2140)*

QUARTZ CRYSTALS: Electronic

Daytona Glass Works LLC ....F 386 274-2550
Daytona Beach *(G-2542)*
Mtn Government Services Inc ....F 954 538-4000
Miramar *(G-10517)*
Quartz Unlimited Inc ....E 561 720-7460
Boca Raton *(G-644)*

QUARTZITE: Dimension

Hs Stone Gallery LLC ....G 305 200-5810
Doral *(G-3251)*

QUILTING SVC & SPLYS, FOR THE TRADE

Rainbows End ....F 727 733-8572
Palm Harbor *(G-13128)*

RACEWAYS

Apw ....G 850 332-7023
Pensacola *(G-13442)*
Gaukaupa Raceway ....G 904 483-3473
Jacksonville *(G-6132)*
Golden Glades Raceway LLC ....G 305 321-9627
Miami Gardens *(G-10260)*
Holeshot Raceway Inc ....G 407 864-1095
Oviedo *(G-12825)*
Mary Symon ....G 813 986-4676
Dover *(G-3431)*
Montalvos Raceway LLC ....G 239 289-6931
Naples *(G-10824)*
Nelson Raceway LLC ....G 904 206-1625
Fernandina Beach *(G-3594)*
Nine Mile Raceway Inc ....G 850 937-1845
Cantonment *(G-1271)*
Raceway 6852 ....G 850 944-8212
Pensacola *(G-13593)*
Raceway Electric LLC ....G 772 260-6530
Port Saint Lucie *(G-14439)*
Raceway Towing LLC ....G 754 244-9597
Oakland Park *(G-11291)*
Shalimar Raceway DBA Gulfcoast ....G 850 651-7848
Shalimar *(G-16002)*

RACKS: Bicycle, Automotive

Bikekeeper LLC ....G 561 209-6863
Lake Worth *(G-7187)*
Weehoo Inc ....G 720 477-3700
Tarpon Springs *(G-17499)*

RACKS: Display

Szabo Pos Displays Inc ....G 941 778-0192
Bradenton *(G-1057)*

RACKS: Pallet, Exc Wood

Km Industrial Racking Inc ....G 813 900-7457
Largo *(G-7627)*
SC Capital Ventures Inc ....D 954 657-8563
Pompano Beach *(G-14168)*

RACKS: Railroad Car, Vehicle Transportation, Steel

First Class Liaisons LLC ....G 954 882-8634
Wellington *(G-17851)*
Inversnes Wlldel Asociados Inc ....D 305 591-0931
Doral *(G-3260)*
Inversnes Wlldel Asociados Inc ....G 305 591-0118
Miami *(G-9333)*
Stick With US Delivery Svc LLC ....G 561 425-4910
West Palm Beach *(G-18165)*

RADAR SYSTEMS & EQPT

C Speed LLC ....G 321 336-7939
Titusville *(G-17579)*
Detect Inc ....F 850 763-7200
Panama City *(G-13253)*
Drs Training Ctrl Systems LLC ....E 850 302-3000
Fort Walton Beach *(G-4578)*
Northrop Grumman Systems Corp ....A 321 951-5000
Melbourne *(G-8484)*
Raytheon Company ....E 727 768-8468
Largo *(G-7669)*
Raytheon Company ....E 310 647-9438
Saint Petersburg *(G-15169)*
Stormquant Inc ....F 408 840-2003
Titusville *(G-17620)*

RADIATORS: Stationary Engine

Luminar LLC ....B 407 900-5259
Orlando *(G-12355)*

RADIO & TELEVISION COMMUNICATIONS EQUIPMENT

Aero-Mach TCO Manufacturing ....G 239 936-7570
Fort Myers *(G-4158)*
Airspan Networks Inc ....E 561 893-8670
Boca Raton *(G-396)*
Aska Communication Corp ....G 954 708-2387
Miami *(G-8759)*
AVI-Spl Holdings Inc ....A 866 708-5034
Tampa *(G-16619)*
AVI-Spl LLC ....B 813 884-7168
Tampa *(G-16620)*
Azimuth Communications Corp ....G 727 573-5735
Clearwater *(G-1506)*
Barco LLC ....G 305 677-9600
Miami *(G-8797)*
Bluazu LLC ....F 386 697-3743
Gainesville *(G-4662)*
Commscope Technologies LLC ....F 407 944-9116
Orlando *(G-12035)*
Component General Inc ....E 727 376-6655
Odessa *(G-11544)*
Da Vinci Systems Inc ....E 954 688-5600
Coral Springs *(G-2146)*
Electro Technik Industries Inc ....D 727 530-9555
Clearwater *(G-1580)*
Ericsson Inc ....F 856 230-6268
Orlando *(G-12133)*
Fiplex Communications Inc ....E 305 884-8991
Doral *(G-3216)*
Fortune Media Group Inc ....F 954 379-4321
Coral Springs *(G-2156)*
Gap Antenna Products Inc ....G 772 571-9922
Fellsmere *(G-3577)*
Global Wrless Sltions Tech Inc ....G 941 744-2511
Bradenton *(G-984)*
Gogps USA Inc ....F 941 751-2363
Sarasota *(G-15486)*
Gps Education LLC ....F 386 756-7575
Port Orange *(G-14335)*
Hilomast LLC ....G 386 668-6784
Debary *(G-2635)*
Hoverfly Technologies Inc ....D 407 985-4500
Orlando *(G-12228)*
Imagik International Corp ....F 786 631-5003
Doral *(G-3255)*
Interface Technology Group Inc ....G 321 433-1165
Rockledge *(G-14718)*
L3harris Interstate Elec Corp ....D 321 730-0119
Cape Canaveral *(G-1288)*

Employee Codes: A=Over 500 employees, B=251-500
C=101-250, D=51-100, E=20-50, F=10-19, G=4-9

2022 Harris Florida
Manufacturers Directory

1305

PRODUCT

L3harris Technologies Inc............A..... 321 309-7848
Melbourne *(G-8456)*
L3harris Technologies Inc............B..... 321 727-9100
Melbourne *(G-8455)*
L3harris Technologies Inc............D..... 321 768-4660
Malabar *(G-8086)*
M C Test Service Inc............C..... 321 253-0541
Melbourne *(G-8466)*
Mambo LLC............E..... 305 860-2544
Doral *(G-3289)*
Micro Systems Inc............C..... 850 244-2332
Fort Walton Beach *(G-4596)*
Motorola Solutions............F..... 239 939-7717
Fort Myers *(G-4331)*
Phototelesis LP............F..... 321 254-1500
Melbourne *(G-8495)*
Radiotronics Inc............F..... 772 600-7574
Stuart *(G-16204)*
Raytheon Company............E..... 727 768-8468
Largo *(G-7669)*
Rockwell Collins Inc............D..... 321 768-7303
Melbourne *(G-8511)*
RVR USA LLC............G..... 305 471-9091
Doral *(G-3355)*
Satcom Scientific Inc............F..... 407 856-1050
Orlando *(G-12574)*
Sierra Nevada Corporation............F..... 850 659-3600
Shalimar *(G-16003)*
Tampa Microwave LLC............F..... 813 855-2251
Clearwater *(G-1813)*
Thunderforce Inc............F..... 315 403-8026
Port Richey *(G-14378)*
Transamerica Intl Brdcstg Inc............G..... 305 477-0973
Miami *(G-10037)*
TV Film International Inc............G..... 305 671-3265
Miami *(G-10048)*
United Wireless Tech Inc............F..... 561 302-9350
Boca Raton *(G-735)*
Viasat Inc............E..... 813 880-5000
Tampa *(G-17414)*
Video Display Corporation............D..... 321 784-4427
Cocoa *(G-1963)*
Visual Comm Specialists Inc............G..... 407 936-7300
Lake Mary *(G-7116)*
Vmoviles Inc............G..... 954 609-2510
Aventura *(G-276)*
Voxx International Corporation............B..... 800 645-7750
Orlando *(G-12706)*
W & W Manufacturing Co............F..... 516 942-0011
Tampa *(G-17420)*
Williams Communications Inc............G..... 850 689-6651
Crestview *(G-2256)*

RADIO & TELEVISION REPAIR

Gulf Electronics............F..... 727 595-3840
Largo *(G-7601)*

RADIO BROADCASTING & COMMUNICATIONS EQPT

Bk Technologies Inc............F..... 321 984-1414
West Melbourne *(G-17894)*
Bk Technologies Corporation............F..... 321 984-1414
West Melbourne *(G-17895)*
Cooper Notification Inc............D..... 941 487-2300
Sarasota *(G-15461)*
First Communications Inc............D..... 850 668-7990
Tallahassee *(G-16439)*
Intercultural Communications............G..... 813 926-2617
Odessa *(G-11558)*
Motorola Solutions Inc............A..... 954 723-5000
Plantation *(G-13870)*
Pax Ctholic Communications Inc............E..... 305 638-9729
Miami *(G-9698)*
Pinnacle Cmmncations Group LLC............F..... 904 910-0444
Jacksonville *(G-6372)*
Sports Radar Ltd............G..... 352 503-6825
Homosassa *(G-5751)*
Tech Comm Inc............F..... 954 712-7777
Fort Lauderdale *(G-4084)*
Tecore Government Services LLC............G..... 410 872-6000
Melbourne *(G-8545)*

RADIO COMMUNICATIONS: Airborne Eqpt

Becker Avionics Inc............F..... 954 450-3137
Miramar *(G-10474)*
Dayton-Granger Inc............C..... 954 463-3451
Fort Lauderdale *(G-3758)*
Smiths Interconnect Inc............C..... 813 901-7200
Tampa *(G-17276)*

Wialan Technologies LLC............G..... 954 749-3481
Sunrise *(G-16392)*

RADIO EQPT: Citizens Band

Wiztel USA Inc............G..... 416 457-5513
Miromar Lakes *(G-10576)*

RADIO MAGNETIC INSTRUMENTATION

General Dynmics Land Systems I............B..... 850 574-4700
Tallahassee *(G-16447)*

RADIO PRODUCERS

American Impact Media Corp............F..... 954 457-9003
Hallandale Beach *(G-4935)*

RADIO RECEIVER NETWORKS

Antique Automobile Radio Inc............G..... 727 785-8733
Palm Harbor *(G-13098)*

RADIO, TELEVISION & CONSUMER ELECTRONICS STORES: Eqpt, NEC

Fun Electronics Inc............F..... 305 933-4646
Miami *(G-9179)*

RADIOS WHOLESALERS

Marathon Technology Corp............F..... 305 592-1340
Doral *(G-3291)*

RAIL & STRUCTURAL SHAPES: Aluminum rail & structural shapes

Custom Fbrcations Freeport Inc............F..... 850 729-0500
Valparaiso *(G-17659)*
Fabworx LLC............F..... 239 573-9353
Cape Coral *(G-1342)*
Prestige Aluminum Railing Inc............G..... 904 966-2163
Starke *(G-16104)*
White Aluminum Fabrication Inc............E..... 772 219-3245
Stuart *(G-16249)*

RAILINGS: Prefabricated, Metal

Delamere Industries Inc............E..... 813 929-0841
Brooksville *(G-1152)*
Fab Rite Inc............G..... 561 848-8181
Riviera Beach *(G-14621)*
Gelander Industries Inc............F..... 352 343-3100
Tavares *(G-17508)*
Greco Alum Railings USA Inc............D..... 727 372-4545
Hudson *(G-5775)*
Quality Railings Miami Corp............G..... 786 400-0462
Hialeah *(G-5322)*

RAILROAD EQPT

CAF USA Inc............G..... 305 753-5371
Miami *(G-8878)*
Contemprary McHnrey Engrg Svcs............E..... 386 439-0937
Flagler Beach *(G-3603)*
G G Schmitt & Sons Inc............C..... 717 394-3701
Sarasota *(G-15479)*
Progress Rail Services Corp............F..... 904 783-1143
Jacksonville *(G-6392)*
Railings Plus Inc............G..... 386 437-4501
Bunnell *(G-1232)*
Rov Railway Industry LLC............F..... 305 299-8264
Plantation *(G-13882)*
Silver Enterprises Assoc Inc............G..... 239 542-0068
Cape Coral *(G-1386)*

RAILROAD EQPT: Cars & Eqpt, Dining

Doglips Logistics LLC............G..... 407 704-0097
Groveland *(G-4859)*
New & Improved Services LLC............F..... 904 323-2348
Jacksonville *(G-6325)*
No Boundaries Transportation............G..... 850 263-1903
Bonifay *(G-774)*

RAILROAD EQPT: Cars & Eqpt, Train, Freight Or Passenger

Hitachi Rail STS Usa Inc............D..... 415 397-7010
Medley *(G-8252)*

RAILROAD EQPT: Cars, Rebuilt

Southstern Rail Svcs Mlbrry FL............F..... 863 425-4986
Mulberry *(G-10640)*

RAILROAD RELATED EQPT: Railway Track

Florida E Coast Holdings Corp............E..... 904 279-3152
Jacksonville *(G-6104)*
Mafeks International LLC............F..... 561 997-2080
Boca Raton *(G-580)*

RAILROAD TIES: Concrete

Rocla Concrete Tie Inc............C..... 772 800-1855
Fort Pierce *(G-4525)*

RAILROADS: Long Haul

New Underground RR Pubg Co............F..... 305 825-1444
Miami Lakes *(G-10332)*

RAILS: Rails, rolled & drawn, aluminum

Barrows Aluminum Inc............F..... 386 767-3445
Port Orange *(G-14329)*
Largo Aluminum Inc............F..... 305 852-2390
Islamorada *(G-5837)*
Poma Corporation............D..... 561 790-5799
West Palm Beach *(G-18123)*

RAILS: Steel Or Iron

Rq Welding Inc............G..... 786 609-3384
Miami *(G-9826)*
Sfa Systems Inc............E..... 561 585-5927
Lake Worth *(G-7232)*

RAMPS: Prefabricated Metal

Rampmaster Inc............F..... 305 691-9090
Miami *(G-9779)*
Unifi Aviation LLC............A..... 954 377-2724
Fort Lauderdale *(G-4104)*

RARE EARTH METAL ORE MINING

USA Rare Earth LLC............F..... 813 867-6155
Tampa *(G-17399)*

REAL ESTATE AGENCIES & BROKERS

Jwdi Realty LLC............G..... 561 331-2481
Palm Beach Gardens *(G-12981)*

REAL ESTATE AGENCIES: Residential

Volvox Inc Hollywood............G..... 954 961-4942
Hollywood *(G-5682)*

REAL ESTATE AGENTS & MANAGERS

Feick Corporation............D..... 305 271-8550
Miami *(G-9136)*
Sal Praschnik Inc............F..... 305 866-4323
Bay Harbor Islands *(G-333)*
Seabreze Cmmncations Group Inc............F..... 239 278-4222
Fort Myers *(G-4397)*
Sun Publications Florida Inc............D..... 321 402-0257
Kissimmee *(G-6961)*

REAL ESTATE APPRAISERS

Suncoast Accrdted Gmlgical Lab............G..... 941 756-8787
Bradenton *(G-1054)*

REAL ESTATE INVESTMENT TRUSTS

Bricklser Engrv Monuments Corp............F..... 786 806-0672
Doral *(G-3148)*

REAL ESTATE OPERATORS, EXC DEVELOPERS: Commercial/Indl Bldg

A M Coplan Associates............G..... 904 737-6996
Jacksonville *(G-5847)*
Atlantic Jet Center Inc............G..... 321 255-7111
Melbourne *(G-8369)*
Pulau International Corp............F..... 407 380-9191
Orlando *(G-12517)*

REAL ESTATE OPERATORS, EXC DEVELOPERS: Property, Retail

Ddp Holdings LLC ....D 813 712-2515
Tampa (G-16769)

RECEIVERS: Radio Communications

Dayton Industrial Corporation ....G 941 351-4454
Sarasota (G-15651)
Summation Research Inc ....F 321 254-2580
Melbourne (G-8536)

RECORDING TAPE: Video, Blank

Triple J Marketing LLC ....E 813 247-6999
Tampa (G-17370)

RECORDS & TAPES: Prerecorded

Axzes LLC ....G 786 626-1611
Doral (G-3126)
Capital Technology Solutions ....G 850 562-3321
Tallahassee (G-16420)
Devscape Software LLC ....G 904 625-6510
Jacksonville (G-6031)
Jazziz Magazine Inc ....E 561 893-6868
Boca Raton (G-558)
Latamready LLC ....G 786 600-2641
North Miami (G-11109)
Mahigaming LLC ....G 561 504-1534
Deerfield Beach (G-2761)
Muscle Mixes Inc ....F 407 872-7576
Orlando (G-12401)
Ocoa LLC ....E 407 898-1961
Orlando (G-12435)
Panoptex Technologies Inc ....E 407 412-0222
Orlando (G-12466)
Piergate LLC ....G 813 938-9170
Zephyrhills (G-18626)
Runaware Inc ....G 954 907-9052
Coral Springs (G-2208)
Singing Machine Company Inc ....F 954 596-1000
Fort Lauderdale (G-4050)
Workep Inc ....G 787 634-1115
North Miami (G-11129)

RECOVERY SVC: Iron Ore, From Open Hearth Slag

Quest Manufacturing Corp ....F 305 513-8583
Medley (G-8306)

RECREATIONAL VEHICLE DEALERS

Florida Bus Unlimited Inc ....E 407 656-1175
Orlando (G-12158)
Harberson Rv Pinellas LLC ....E 727 937-6176
Holiday (G-5497)

RECREATIONAL VEHICLE PARTS & ACCESS STORES

Offshore Performance Spc Inc ....F 239 481-2768
Fort Myers (G-4346)

RECYCLING: Paper

ABC Recyclers Collier Cnty Inc ....G 239 643-2302
Naples (G-10649)
All Green Recycling Inc ....G 754 204-3707
Hollywood (G-5525)
Hogenkamp Research Inc ....F 850 677-1072
Gulf Breeze (G-4884)
Reuse Salvage Inc ....G 772 485-3248
Port Salerno (G-14468)

REELS: Wood

Temple Terrace Industries Inc ....E 813 752-7546
Plant City (G-13810)

REFINERS & SMELTERS: Aluminum

Alliance Metals LLC ....G 305 343-9536
Bay Harbor Islands (G-330)
Wise Recycling 1 LLC ....F 850 477-5273
Pensacola (G-13627)

REFINERS & SMELTERS: Copper

EJM Copper Inc ....F 407 447-0074
Orlando (G-12118)

REFINERS & SMELTERS: Nonferrous Metal

All Metals Fabrication LLC ....G 904 862-6885
Jacksonville (G-5874)
Enviro Focus Technology ....G 813 744-5000
Tampa (G-16816)
Flotech LLC ....D 904 358-1849
Jacksonville (G-6113)
Troika Group Inc ....G 561 313-1119
Wellington (G-17867)

REFINERS & SMELTERS: Silicon, Primary, Over 99% Pure

Globe Specialty Metals Inc ....F 786 509-6900
Miami (G-9222)

REFINING: Petroleum

AZ Chem Holdings LP ....C 800 526-5294
Jacksonville (G-5914)
Comoderm Corp ....G 561 756-2929
Pompano Beach (G-13973)
Ipro Force LLC ....G 603 766-8716
Windermere (G-18354)
Jupiter Petroleum Inc ....G 561 622-1276
Jupiter (G-6751)
Kimberlyn Investments Co ....G 305 448-6328
Coral Gables (G-2077)
Okeechobee Petroleum LLC ....F 561 478-1083
West Palm Beach (G-18096)
Oxbow Calcining LLC ....D 580 874-2201
West Palm Beach (G-18101)
Petroleum Group LLC ....F 352 304-5500
Belleview (G-365)
Petroleum Marine LLC ....G 561 422-9018
West Palm Beach (G-18119)
Petrosol Processing & Refining ....F 305 442-7400
Miami (G-9708)
Quality Petroleum Corp ....G 863 635-6708
Frostproof (G-4640)
Searaven Glauben LLC ....F 727 230-8840
Saint Augustine (G-14888)

REFRACTORIES: Brick

Gem Paver Systems Inc ....E 305 805-0000
Medley (G-8246)

REFRACTORIES: Cement, nonclay

Natures Earth Products Inc ....E 561 688-8101
West Palm Beach (G-18086)

REFRACTORIES: Clay

Jamo Inc ....D 305 885-3444
Medley (G-8264)

REFRACTORIES: Nonclay

Matthews International Corp ....C 407 886-5533
Apopka (G-149)
Osmi Inc ....F 561 330-9300
Boca Raton (G-626)

REFRACTORIES: Tile & Brick, Exc Plastic

Oldcastle Retail Inc ....B 954 971-1200
Pompano Beach (G-14110)

REFRIGERATION & HEATING EQUIPMENT

1600 Lenox LLC ....G 786 360-2553
Miami (G-8606)
2951 SE Dominica Holding LLC ....F 772 220-0038
Stuart (G-16107)
AAA Able Appliance Service Inc ....G 954 791-5222
Fort Lauderdale (G-3617)
Adrick Marine Group Inc ....F 321 631-0776
Cocoa (G-1898)
All Power Pro Inc ....G 904 310-3069
Fernandina Beach (G-3580)
Allied Manufacturing Inc ....F 813 502-0300
Tampa (G-16576)
American Standards Inc ....G 904 683-2189
Jacksonville (G-5886)
Andrews Filter and Supply Corp ......E 407 423-3310
Orlando (G-11912)
Beam Associates LLC ....G 813 855-5695
Oldsmar (G-11633)
Beverage Equipment Repair Co ....F 239 573-0683
Cape Coral (G-1313)

Bmp Usa Inc ....D 813 443-0757
Tampa (G-16650)
Carrier Global Corporation ....C 561 365-2000
Palm Beach Gardens (G-12956)
Climax Inc ....G 786 264-6082
Doral (G-3165)
Con-Air Industries Inc ....D 407 298-5733
Orlando (G-12039)
CPS Products Inc ....G 305 687-4121
Miramar (G-10482)
Crown Products Company Inc ....D 904 924-8340
Jacksonville (G-6016)
Dade Engineering Group LLC ....F 305 885-2766
Miami (G-8994)
Danfoss LLC ....C 850 504-4800
Tallahassee (G-16430)
Drinkable Air Inc ....F 954 533-6415
Lauderdale Lakes (G-7713)
Duststop Filters Inc ....G 904 725-1001
Jacksonville (G-6049)
Engineered Air Systems Inc ....F 813 881-9555
Tampa (G-16814)
Fireside Holdings Inc ....G 941 371-0300
Bradenton (G-979)
Green Air Group LLC ....D 850 608-3065
Freeport (G-4625)
Hoseline Inc ....F 541 258-8984
Ocala (G-11410)
Jer-Air Manufacturing Inc ....E 352 591-2674
Micanopy (G-10398)
John Bean Technologies Corp ....E 407 851-3377
Orlando (G-12275)
Lajoie Investment Corp ....F 954 463-3271
Fort Lauderdale (G-3911)
Lasalle Bristol Corporation ....F 863 680-1729
Lakeland (G-7375)
Lennox Global Ltd ....E 305 718-2921
Doral (G-3283)
Lennox International Inc ....G 352 379-9630
Gainesville (G-4721)
Lennox Letts ....G 954 630-5989
Fort Lauderdale (G-3917)
Lennox Miami Corp ....E 305 763-8655
Miami Beach (G-10208)
Lennox National Account S ....G 954 745-3482
Miami (G-9451)
Metal Industries Inc ....D 352 793-8610
Bushnell (G-1247)
MI Metals Inc ....G 813 855-5695
Oldsmar (G-11676)
Micro Matic Usa Inc ....G 352 799-6331
Brooksville (G-1180)
Munters Corporation ....G 239 936-1555
Fort Myers (G-4333)
Nortek Global Hvac LLC ....D 305 592-6154
Miami (G-9627)
R & J Mfg of Gainesville ....G 352 375-3130
Gainesville (G-4754)
Reftec International Inc ....E 800 214-4883
Bradenton (G-1035)
Reftec Intl Systems LLC ....F 727 290-9830
Largo (G-7670)
Sharing Three Inc ....F 305 884-8384
Hialeah (G-5347)
Soda Service of Florida LLC ....G 727 595-7632
Largo (G-7686)
Stan Weaver and Company ....E 407 581-6940
Orlando (G-12620)
Store It Cold LLC ....G 720 456-1178
Medley (G-8326)
Trane Inc ....F 352 237-0136
Ocala (G-11502)
Trane Inc ....E 954 421-7133
Pompano Beach (G-14217)
Trane US Inc ....D 813 877-8251
Tampa (G-17364)
Trane US Inc ....G 239 277-0344
Fort Myers (G-4432)
Trane US Inc ....D 904 538-8600
Jacksonville (G-6564)
Trane US Inc ....D 954 499-6900
Miramar (G-10554)
Trane US Inc ....E 561 683-1521
West Palm Beach (G-18186)
Trane US Inc ....F 850 574-1726
Tallahassee (G-16515)
Trane US Inc ....F 813 877-8253
Tampa (G-17365)
Trane US Inc ....G 305 592-8646
Miami (G-10036)

PRODUCT

Tsm Champ LLC ....D 615 806-7900
  Sarasota (G-15574)
Verde GSE Inc ....E 888 837-5221
  Palmetto (G-13202)
Westran Corporation ....E 727 375-7010
  Trinity (G-17642)
York International Corporation ....F 407 850-0147
  Orlando (G-12730)
York International Corporation ....F 813 663-9332
  Tampa (G-17451)
York International Corporation ....F 305 805-5600
  Medley (G-8352)

REFRIGERATION EQPT: Complete

Acme Service Corp ....F 305 836-4800
  Miami (G-8647)
American Panel Corporation ....C 352 245-7055
  Ocala (G-11320)
Arctic Industries LLC ....D 305 883-5581
  Medley (G-8197)
Banks Airconditioning & Rfrgn ....G 813 917-8685
  Plant City (G-13744)
Cold Storage Engineering Co ....G 305 448-0099
  Miami (G-8943)
Kysor Industrial Corporation ....F 727 376-8600
  Trinity (G-17638)
Mainstream Engineering Corp ....E 321 631-3550
  Rockledge (G-14729)
Mr Winter Inc ....E 800 327-3371
  Medley (G-8285)
Refrigeration Panels Inc ....F 305 836-6900
  Miami (G-9788)
Refrigrtion Engnred Systems In ....E 305 836-6900
  Miami (G-9789)

REFRIGERATION REPAIR SVCS

A & V Refrigeration Corp ....G 305 883-0733
  Hialeah (G-5015)
Mechanical Svcs Centl Fla Inc ....C 407 857-3510
  Orlando (G-12368)

REFRIGERATION SVC & REPAIR

AAA Able Appliance Service Inc ....G 954 791-5222
  Fort Lauderdale (G-3617)
AAA Monterey Discount Vacuum ....G 772 288-5233
  Stuart (G-16109)

REFRIGERATORS & FREEZERS WHOLESALERS

Apollo Worldwide Inc ....G 561 585-3865
  Hypoluxo (G-5794)

REFUSE SYSTEMS

Dixie Sptic Tank Orange Cy LLC ....E 386 775-3051
  Orange City (G-11805)
Wise Recycling 1 LLC ....F 850 477-5273
  Pensacola (G-13627)

REGULATORS: Power

Ring Power Corporation ....C 904 354-1858
  Jacksonville (G-6423)

REGULATORS: Transmission & Distribution Voltage

Universal Microwave Corp ....E 352 754-2200
  Brooksville (G-1216)

RELAYS & SWITCHES: Indl, Electric

Hts Controls Inc ....F 813 287-5512
  Tampa (G-16926)
Southern Switch & Contacts ....F 727 789-0951
  Palm Harbor (G-13133)
Tic Light Electrical Corp ....G 305 712-3499
  Miami (G-10008)

REMOVERS & CLEANERS

Cress Chemical & Eqp Co Inc ....G 407 425-2846
  Orlando (G-12056)

RENTAL CENTERS: General

Lotus Containers Inc ....G 786 590-1056
  Miami (G-9480)

RENTAL SVCS: Aircraft

Aercap Inc ....D 954 760-7777
  Fort Lauderdale (G-3627)
Aercap Group Services Inc ....F 954 760-7777
  Fort Lauderdale (G-3628)
Aercap Leasing USA I LLC ....F 425 237-4000
  Miami (G-8661)

RENTAL SVCS: Books

Ediciones Atenea Inc ....F 305 984-5483
  Hialeah (G-5135)

RENTAL SVCS: Business Machine & Electronic Eqpt

International Keg Rental LLC ....F 407 900-9992
  Orlando (G-12251)
Sun Print Management LLC ....E 727 945-0255
  Holiday (G-5504)

RENTAL SVCS: Eqpt & Prop, Motion Picture Production

Boland Production Supply Inc ....G 863 324-7784
  Winter Haven (G-18422)

RENTAL SVCS: Floor Maintenance Eqpt

Jdl Surface Innovations Inc ....F 239 772-0077
  Cape Coral (G-1359)

RENTAL SVCS: Sound & Lighting Eqpt

Airstar America Inc ....F 407 851-7830
  Orlando (G-11885)

RENTAL SVCS: Work Zone Traffic Eqpt, Flags, Cones, Etc

Traffic Control Pdts Fla Inc ....E 813 621-8484
  Fort Myers (G-4431)

RENTAL: Passenger Car

Premier Luxury Group LLC ....E 954 358-9885
  Fort Lauderdale (G-3995)

RENTAL: Portable Toilet

AAA Event Services LLC ....F 386 454-0929
  Newberry (G-11015)
Monty Sanitation Inc ....G 239 597-2486
  Naples (G-10825)
P & L Creech Inc ....G 386 547-4182
  Daytona Beach (G-2579)

RESEARCH, DEVELOPMENT & TEST SVCS, COMM: Cmptr Hardware Dev

Diversfied Mtl Specialists Inc ....G 941 244-0935
  North Venice (G-11211)
Kreateck International Corp ....G 772 925-1216
  Vero Beach (G-17771)

RESEARCH, DEVELOPMENT & TEST SVCS, COMM: Research, Exc Lab

David Perkins Enterprises Inc ....G 850 234-0002
  Panama City Beach (G-13329)
Dermazone Solutions Inc ....E 727 446-6882
  Saint Petersburg (G-15022)

RESEARCH, DEVELOPMENT & TESTING SVCS, COMM: Research Lab

Dermazone Solutions Inc ....E 727 446-6882
  Saint Petersburg (G-15022)
Dioxide Materials Inc ....F 217 239-1400
  Boca Raton (G-485)
General Oceanics Inc ....F 305 621-2882
  Miami (G-9200)

RESEARCH, DEVELOPMENT & TESTING SVCS, COMMERCIAL: Business

Analytical Research Systems ....F 352 466-0051
  Micanopy (G-10395)
Smx-US Inc ....E 914 840-5631
  Miami (G-9909)

RESEARCH, DEVELOPMENT & TESTING SVCS, COMMERCIAL: Energy

Authentic Trading Inc ....G 347 866-7241
  Davie (G-2390)

RESEARCH, DEVELOPMENT & TESTING SVCS, COMMERCIAL: Medical

Kms Medical LLC ....F 305 266-3388
  Miami (G-9394)
Life Proteomics Inc ....F 813 864-7646
  Tampa (G-17009)
Quick-Med Technologies Inc ....G 352 379-0611
  Gainesville (G-4753)
Sinocare Meditech Inc ....G 800 342-7226
  Fort Lauderdale (G-4051)

RESEARCH, DVLPT & TEST SVCS, COMM: Mkt Analysis or Research

Original Impressions LLC ....C 305 233-1322
  Weston (G-18276)

RESIDENTIAL REMODELERS

New & Improved Services LLC ....F 904 323-2348
  Jacksonville (G-6325)

RESIDUES

JKS Residual Assets LLC ....G 904 346-3200
  Jacksonville (G-6225)
R Residual Corp ....G 810 874-6727
  Ponte Vedra Beach (G-14279)
Referral & Residual Exchange L ....G 813 655-5000
  Riverview (G-14574)
Residual Innovations LLC ....G 407 459-5497
  Orlando (G-12548)

RESINS: Custom Compound Purchased

Bath Junkie of Gainesville ....G 352 331-3012
  Gainesville (G-4658)
City of Lakeland ....F 863 834-6780
  Lakeland (G-7292)
Seelye Acquisitions Inc ....G 407 656-6677
  Apopka (G-174)

RESISTORS

Casa Del Marinero Corp ....G 305 374-5386
  Miami (G-8899)
Component General Inc ....E 727 376-6655
  Odessa (G-11544)
Electro Technik Industries Inc ....D 727 530-9555
  Clearwater (G-1580)
Nasco Aerospace and Elec LLC ....F 727 344-7554
  Saint Petersburg (G-15136)
Precision Resistor Co Inc ....E 727 541-5771
  Seminole (G-15986)
Solitron Devices Inc ....D 561 848-4311
  West Palm Beach (G-18158)
Vishay Americas Inc ....A 407 804-2567
  Lake Mary (G-7115)

RESISTORS & RESISTOR UNITS

Hymeg Corporation ....G 800 322-1953
  Clearwater (G-1634)

RESOLVERS

Resolver Group Inc ....E 941 387-7410
  Longboat Key (G-7859)

RESORT HOTELS

Arkup Llc ....G 786 448-8635
  Miami Beach (G-10167)

RESPIRATORY SYSTEM DRUGS

Wonder Holdings Acquisition ....F 305 379-2322
  Miami (G-10138)

RESTAURANT EQPT: Carts

American Metal Products Inc ....G 407 293-0090
  Orlando (G-11903)
Klugman Enterprises LLC ....G 352 318-9623
  Sarasota (G-15508)
Load King Manufacturing Co ....C 904 354-8882
  Jacksonville (G-6263)

RESTAURANT EQPT: Food Wagons

Aquino Trucks Center Corp ....F   239 327-9708
Cape Coral (G-1305)
Carley Nigel Holdings LLC.................F   407 212-9341
Rockledge (G-14696)
Cg Burgers ....G   954 618-6450
Fort Lauderdale (G-3722)
Chin & Chin Enterprises Inc ....F   407 478-8726
Winter Park (G-18499)
Drinks On ME 305 LLC.......................F   786 488-2356
Miami (G-9050)
Gcato 1959 Enterprises LLC...............G   954 937-6282
Pompano Beach (G-14038)
Honduras Food Services Inc ....E   310 940-2071
Gainesville (G-4707)
Legacy Delights LLC..........................G   321 222-9330
Orlando (G-12318)
Luong Moc III Inc ....E   407 478-8726
Winter Park (G-18521)
Mrreal Deal Barbque LLC ....G   561 271-8749
Delray Beach (G-2991)
My Passion On A Plate LLC ....F   954 857-6382
North Lauderdale (G-11084)
TLC Food Truck LLC...........................F   305 879-2488
Miami (G-10014)
Wynot International LLC......................F   305 218-8794
Miami (G-10148)

RESTAURANT EQPT: Sheet Metal

Tarpon Stnless Fabricators Inc ....E   727 942-1821
Tarpon Springs (G-17496)

RESTAURANTS:Full Svc, Cajun

Titanic Brewing Company Inc..............F   305 668-1742
Coral Gables (G-2115)

RESTAURANTS:Full Svc, Chinese

Egg Roll Skins Inc..............................F   305 836-0571
Hialeah (G-5138)

RESTAURANTS:Full Svc, Ethnic Food

Patty King Inc...................................E   305 817-1888
Hialeah (G-5292)

RESTAURANTS:Full Svc, Italian

Richard Meer Investments Inc.............G   941 484-6551
Venice (G-17713)

RESTAURANTS:Full Svc, Mexican

La Esquina Del Le Billto ....E   305 477-4225
Doral (G-3280)

RESTAURANTS:Limited Svc, Coffee Shop

Buttercream Cpcakes Cof Sp Inc ....F   305 669-8181
Coral Gables (G-2037)
Outpost 30a LLC ....F   850 909-0138
Inlet Beach (G-5819)

RESTAURANTS:Limited Svc, Frozen Yogurt Stand

Top Hat Food Services LLC ....G   630 825-2800
Venice (G-17724)

RESTAURANTS:Limited Svc, Ice Cream Stands Or Dairy Bars

Coco Gelato Corp ....E   786 621-2444
Miami (G-8938)
Cold Stone Creamery-Parkland............G   954 341-8033
Coral Springs (G-2142)

RESTAURANTS:Limited Svc, Pizza

Classic Pizza Crusts Inc.....................G   954 570-8383
Plantation (G-13835)
Pizza Spice Packet LLC.....................G   718 831-7036
Boca Raton (G-635)

RESTRAINTS

Safety Intl Bags & Straps Inc ....F   407 830-0888
Casselberry (G-1432)

RESTROOM CLEANING SVCS

Lions Intl MGT Group Inc....................F   813 367-2517
Tampa (G-17013)

RETAIL BAKERY: Cakes

Carlees Creations Inc ....G   786 232-0050
Miami (G-8897)

RETAIL BAKERY: Cookies

Selmas Cookies Inc ....E   407 884-9433
Apopka (G-175)

RETAIL BAKERY: Doughnuts

Dip-A-Dee Donuts ....E   352 460-4266
Leesburg (G-7766)

RETAIL FIREPLACE STORES

Grate Fireplace & Stone Shoppe ....E   239 939-7187
Fort Myers (G-4272)

RETAIL LUMBER YARDS

Bushnell Truss Enterprises LLC ....F   352 793-6090
Bushnell (G-1241)

RETAIL STORES, NEC

A Living Testimony LLC ....G   352 406-0249
Eustis (G-3551)
Apyelen Curves LLC ....F   904 328-3390
Jacksonville (G-5895)
Big Boy Inc ....G   407 434-9251
Orlando (G-11948)
Splinter Woodworking Inc...................G   305 731-9334
Delray Beach (G-3021)

RETAIL STORES: Alcoholic Beverage Making Eqpt & Splys

Martin Leonard Corporation ....G   850 434-2203
Pensacola (G-13543)

RETAIL STORES: Aquarium Splys

Endless Oceans LLC...........................G   561 274-1990
Delray Beach (G-2958)
Waterbox Usa LLC ....G   800 674-2608
Longwood (G-7959)

RETAIL STORES: Architectural Splys

Taco Metals LLC................................F   305 652-8566
Miramar (G-10552)

RETAIL STORES: Artificial Limbs

Son Life Prsthtics Orthtics In ....F   352 596-2257
Hernando Beach (G-5012)

RETAIL STORES: Audio-Visual Eqpt & Splys

Dj Live Productions LLC ....G   407 383-1740
Altamonte Springs (G-43)

RETAIL STORES: Autograph Splys

Eartech Inc...G   941 747-8193
Bradenton (G-972)

RETAIL STORES: Awnings

A & A Central Florida ....F   407 648-5666
Altamonte Springs (G-26)
Business World Trading Inc.................F   305 238-0724
Miami (G-8864)
John R Caito ....G   850 612-0179
Fort Walton Beach (G-4593)
Milliken & Milliken Inc.........................E   941 474-0223
Englewood (G-3534)
Rolling Shield Parts Inc......................F   305 436-6661
Hialeah Gardens (G-5450)
Southern Awning Inc ....E   561 586-0464
Lake Worth (G-7233)
Sunmaster of Naples Inc ....E   239 261-3581
Naples (G-10914)

RETAIL STORES: Baby Carriages & Strollers

Best Price Mobility Inc.......................F   321 402-5955
Kissimmee (G-6899)

RETAIL STORES: Banners

C&D Sign and Lighting Svcs LLC ....G   863 937-9323
Lakeland (G-7287)
Carlaron Inc ....G   386 258-1183
Daytona Beach (G-2526)
Fastsigns ....G   850 477-9744
Pensacola (G-13501)
International Quiksigns Inc..................F   954 462-7446
Fort Lauderdale (G-3880)
Maddys Print Shop LLC ....G   954 749-0440
Fort Lauderdale (G-3926)
Thomas United Inc............................G   239 561-7446
Fort Myers (G-4422)

RETAIL STORES: Binoculars & Telescopes

JI Optical Inc.....................................G   386 428-6928
New Smyrna Beach (G-11003)

RETAIL STORES: Business Machines & Eqpt

M & S Computer Products Inc ....G   561 244-5400
Boynton Beach (G-888)

RETAIL STORES: Cake Decorating Splys

Carlees Creations Inc ....G   786 232-0050
Miami (G-8897)

RETAIL STORES: Canvas Prdts

Canvas West Inc ....G   941 355-0780
Sarasota (G-15629)
Sea King Kanvas & Shade Inc ....G   239 481-3535
Fort Myers (G-4396)

RETAIL STORES: Cleaning Eqpt & Splys

Campos Chemicals..............................G   727 412-2774
Saint Petersburg (G-14996)

RETAIL STORES: Concrete Prdts, Precast

Concraft Inc ....G   561 689-0149
Greenacres (G-4845)

RETAIL STORES: Cosmetics

Inspec Solutions LLC ....F   866 467-7320
Holly Hill (G-5514)
Matrix Packaging of Florida.................G   305 358-9696
Miami (G-9520)

RETAIL STORES: Educational Aids & Electronic Training Mat

Gadgetcat LLC ....G   802 238-3671
Cocoa Beach (G-1971)
Paradigm Leaders LLC.......................G   850 441-3289
Panama City Beach (G-13336)

RETAIL STORES: Electronic Parts & Eqpt

Interntnal Synrgy For Tchncal ....G   321 305-0863
Orlando (G-12253)
Spin Magnetics...................................E   863 676-9333
Lake Wales (G-7173)

RETAIL STORES: Farm Eqpt & Splys

Marden Industries Inc........................F   863 682-7882
Punta Gorda (G-14513)

RETAIL STORES: Fiberglass Materials, Exc Insulation

Ryan Scientific LLC ....F   904 284-6025
Green Cove Springs (G-4835)
Stm Industries LLC ....F   813 854-3544
Tampa (G-17304)
Tiki Water Sports Inc ....G   305 852-9298
Key Largo (G-6851)

RETAIL STORES: Flags

Keystone 75 Inc..................................G   954 430-1880
Hollywood (G-5608)

RETAIL STORES: Hair Care Prdts

Brand Labs USA..................................E   954 532-5390
Pompano Beach (G-13952)
Katcheri Davis Services LLC ....G   754 222-4464
Jacksonville (G-6239)

RETAIL STORES: Hearing Aids

Audina Hearing Instruments Inc ....D 407 331-0077
Longwood (G-7872)
Bell Hearing Instruments Inc ....F 813 814-2355
Oldsmar (G-11635)
Ear-Tronics Inc ....G 239 275-7655
Fort Myers (G-4243)
Miami ....E 954 874-7707
Miami (G-9544)

RETAIL STORES: Hospital Eqpt & Splys

Med Alert Response Inc ....G 407 730-3571
Orlando (G-12369)

RETAIL STORES: Ice

Reddy Ice Corporation ....F 850 433-2191
Pensacola (G-13595)

RETAIL STORES: Infant Furnishings & Eqpt

Nissi & Jireh Inc ....E 866 897-7657
Miramar (G-10519)

RETAIL STORES: Maps & Charts

Map & Globe LLC ....G 407 898-0757
Maitland (G-8067)

RETAIL STORES: Medical Apparatus & Splys

Cables and Sensors LLC ....G 866 373-6767
Orlando (G-11976)
En-Vision America Inc ....E 309 452-3088
Palmetto (G-13165)

RETAIL STORES: Mobile Telephones & Eqpt

Gnj Manufacturing Inc ....E 305 651-8644
West Park (G-18212)
Sky Phone LLC ....F 305 531-5218
Miami Beach (G-10228)

RETAIL STORES: Monuments, Finished To Custom Order

Latteri & Sons Inc ....G 813 876-1800
Tampa (G-17000)

RETAIL STORES: Motors, Electric

AL Covell Electric Inc ....G 352 544-0680
Brooksville (G-1132)
Biscayne Electric Motor & Pump ....G 305 681-8171
Miami (G-8834)
Electrcal Systems Cmmnications ....G 813 248-4275
Tampa (G-16799)
M & W Electric Motors Inc ....G 850 433-0400
Pensacola (G-13541)
Stewarts Elc Mtr Works Inc ....E 407 859-1837
Orlando (G-12626)
Suncoast Electric Mtr Svc Inc ....F 813 247-4104
Tampa (G-17312)
United Electric Motor Inc ....G 813 238-7872
Tampa (G-17391)

RETAIL STORES: Orthopedic & Prosthesis Applications

Bolt Systems Inc ....G 407 425-0012
Orlando (G-11966)
Institute For Prosthetic Advan ....G 850 784-0320
Panama City (G-13276)
Orthotic Prsthtic Rhbltttion As ....G 352 331-3399
Gainesville (G-4744)
Prosthetic Laboratories ....G 305 250-9900
Coral Gables (G-2100)
Quirantes Orthopedics Inc ....G 305 261-1382
Miami (G-9769)

RETAIL STORES: Pet Food

Advanced Household MGT Inc ....G 941 322-9638
Sarasota (G-15438)

RETAIL STORES: Pet Splys

King Kanine LLC ....G 833 546-4738
Plantation (G-13863)
Miami Tbr LLC ....G 786 275-4773
Doral (G-3302)

RETAIL STORES: Photocopy Machines

Toner Technologies Inc ....G 561 547-9710
Boynton Beach (G-920)

RETAIL STORES: Rubber Stamps

Print Shop of Chiefland Inc ....G 352 493-0322
Chiefland (G-1449)

RETAIL STORES: Safety Splys & Eqpt

Lifesaving Systems Corporation ....E 813 645-2748
Apollo Beach (G-94)

RETAIL STORES: Sunglasses

Waterboyz-Wbz Inc ....F 850 433-2929
Pensacola (G-13624)

RETAIL STORES: Telephone & Communication Eqpt

Cyipcom Inc ....G 954 727-2500
Oakland Park (G-11255)
Trs Wireless Inc ....E 407 447-7333
Orlando (G-12675)

RETAIL STORES: Water Purification Eqpt

Ashberry Acquisition Company ....F 813 248-0055
Tampa (G-16612)
Siemens Industry Inc ....G 407 650-3570
Orlando (G-12598)

RETREADING MATERIALS: Tire

Fedan Corp ....G 305 885-5415
Hialeah (G-5155)

REUPHOLSTERY & FURNITURE REPAIR

Antique & Modern Cabinets Inc ....E 904 393-9055
Jacksonville (G-5892)

REUPHOLSTERY SVCS

Designers Mfg Ctr Inc ....G 954 530-7622
Oakland Park (G-11259)
Grafton Furniture Company ....E 305 696-3811
Miami (G-9231)
Shorr Enterprises Inc ....F 954 733-9840
Lauderdale Lakes (G-7719)

REWINDING SVCS

Aircraft Electric Motors Inc ....D 305 885-9476
Miami Lakes (G-10280)
Tri-County Aerospace Inc ....F 305 639-3356
Doral (G-3402)
TSA Rewinds Florida Inc ....G 305 681-2030
Opa Locka (G-11795)

RIBBONS: Machine, Inked Or Carbon

Eastern Ribbon & Roll Corp ....E 813 676-8600
Odessa (G-11548)
Golden Ribbon Corporation ....E 727 545-4499
Largo (G-7598)
Ribbon Wholesale Corp ....G 786 457-0555
Miami (G-9804)

RIPRAP QUARRYING

Rock Ridge Materials Inc ....F 321 268-8455
Titusville (G-17615)

RIVETS: Metal

Standard Rivet Company Inc ....F 386 872-6477
South Daytona (G-16029)

ROAD MATERIALS: Bituminous

Ellison Rbm Inc ....G 863 679-5283
Lake Wales (G-7159)

ROAD MATERIALS: Bituminous, Not From Refineries

Blacklidge Emulsions Inc ....F 813 247-5699
Tampa (G-16646)

ROBOTS: Assembly Line

Bcdirect Corp ....F 305 623-3838
Miami (G-8807)
Health Robotics Canada LLC ....F 786 388-5339
Miami (G-9267)
Sims Machine & Controls Inc ....E 352 799-2405
Brooksville (G-1201)

ROCKETS: Space & Military

Space Exploration Tech Corp ....A 310 363-6000
Cape Canaveral (G-1293)
United Drones LLC ....G 305 978-1480
Naples (G-10930)

ROD & BAR: Aluminum

Winrise Enterprises LLC ....G 786 621-6705
Miramar (G-10565)

RODS: Plastic

American Plastic Sup & Mfg Inc ....E 727 573-0636
Clearwater (G-1491)
King Plastic Corporation ....C 941 423-8666
North Port (G-11197)
Piedmont Plastics Inc ....D 386 274-4627
Daytona Beach (G-2582)

RODS: Steel & Iron, Made In Steel Mills

Durbal Inc ....G 727 531-3040
Clearwater (G-1575)
Kissimmee Iron Works Inc ....G 407 870-8872
Kissimmee (G-6934)

RODS: Welding

Dons Custom Service Inc ....G 954 491-4043
Fort Lauderdale (G-3772)

ROLLERS & FITTINGS: Window Shade

Solar Venetian Blinds Inc ....G 305 634-4553
Miami (G-9913)

ROLLING MILL EQPT: Galvanizing Lines

Industrial Galvanizers Miami ....E 305 681-8844
Miami (G-9309)
Metalplate Galvanizing LP ....D 904 768-6330
Jacksonville (G-6300)

ROLLING MILL MACHINERY

Metalhouse LLC ....G 407 270-3000
Orlando (G-12373)

ROOF DECKS

Dynamic Metals LLC ....F 561 629-7304
West Palm Beach (G-17984)
Epic Metals Corporation ....G 863 533-7404
Bartow (G-307)

ROOFING MATERIALS: Asphalt

American Roofing Services LLC ....G 305 250-7115
Coral Gables (G-2028)
Chuculu LLC ....F 305 595-4577
Miami (G-8924)
Coastal Acquisitions Fla LLC ....F 850 769-9423
Panama City (G-13244)
Dj Roof and Solar Supply LLC ....G 954 557-1992
Fort Lauderdale (G-3768)
Drexel Metals Inc ....E 727 572-7900
Tampa (G-16786)
Karnak South Inc ....F 954 761-7606
Fort Lauderdale (G-3900)
Miami Metal Roofing LLC ....F 305 749-6356
Hialeah (G-5252)
P&S Industries LLC ....F 954 975-3384
Pompano Beach (G-14114)
Thomas White LLC ....G 813 704-4406
Plant City (G-13811)

ROOFING MATERIALS: Sheet Metal

Baker Metal Works & Supply LLC ....G 850 537-2010
Baker (G-291)
Dans Custom Sheet Metal Inc ....E 239 594-0530
Naples (G-10723)
LV Thompson Inc ....C 813 248-3456
Tampa (G-17026)

Metal Roof Factory Inc ....G..... 321 632-8300
Rockledge *(G-14733)*

Thomas Smith & Company Inc ....E..... 863 858-2199
Lakeland *(G-7461)*

ROOFING MEMBRANE: Rubber

Shredded Tire Inc ....F..... 954 970-8565
Fort Lauderdale *(G-4045)*

Southeast Gen Contrs Group Inc ....G..... 877 407-3535
Port St Lucie *(G-14483)*

ROOM COOLERS: Portable

Amerikooler LLC ....C..... 305 884-8384
Hialeah *(G-5054)*

ROPE

Sunshine Cordage Corporation ....G..... 305 592-3750
Miami *(G-9968)*

RUBBER

Daytona Rubber Company Inc ....F..... 305 513-4105
Doral *(G-3186)*

Goodrich Corporation ....C..... 904 757-3660
Jacksonville *(G-6146)*

Latam Group Corp ....G..... 305 793-8961
Miami *(G-9431)*

Maclan Corporation Inc ....E..... 863 665-4814
Lakeland *(G-7387)*

Modern Silicone Tech Inc ....C..... 727 873-1805
Pinellas Park *(G-13710)*

T S E Industries Inc ....D..... 727 573-7676
Clearwater *(G-1809)*

RUBBER BANDS

Premium Rubber Bands Inc ....G..... 305 321-0333
Miami *(G-9736)*

RUBBER PRDTS

Arca Pro Retractables LLC ....G..... 407 844-5013
Oviedo *(G-12804)*

Bellatrix Trade LLC ....F..... 786 536-2905
Miami *(G-8812)*

Global Force Enterprises LLC ....G..... 786 317-8197
Miramar *(G-10497)*

Liberty Balloons LLC ....G..... 239 947-3338
Bonita Springs *(G-809)*

Professional Ctr At Gardens ....F..... 561 394-5200
Delray Beach *(G-3004)*

Racing Shell Covers LLC ....G..... 732 236-0435
Naples *(G-10872)*

Submersible Systems LLC ....G..... 714 842-6566
Tallahassee *(G-16506)*

RUBBER PRDTS: Automotive, Mechanical

Archimaze Logistics Inc ....G..... 954 615-7485
Fort Lauderdale *(G-3654)*

RUBBER PRDTS: Mechanical

Etco Incorporated ....C..... 941 756-8426
Bradenton *(G-978)*

J B Nottingham & Co Inc ....E..... 386 873-2990
Deland *(G-2877)*

Modern Silicone Tech Inc ....C..... 727 873-1805
Pinellas Park *(G-13710)*

Otoc LLC ....G..... 813 265-8352
Tampa *(G-17132)*

Pompadour Products Inc ....E..... 954 345-2700
Coral Springs *(G-2203)*

Southern Plastics & Rubber Co ....E..... 386 672-1167
Ormond Beach *(G-12794)*

T S E Industries Inc ....D..... 727 573-7676
Clearwater *(G-1809)*

RUBBER PRDTS: Oil & Gas Field Machinery, Mechanical

Cables and Sensors LLC ....G..... 866 373-6767
Orlando *(G-11976)*

RUBBER PRDTS: Reclaimed

Global Tire Rcycl of Smter CNT ....E..... 352 330-2213
Wildwood *(G-18311)*

Global Tire Recycling Inc ....F..... 352 330-2213
Wildwood *(G-18312)*

RUBBER PRDTS: Sheeting

Mako Hose & Rubber Co ....G..... 561 795-6200
West Palm Beach *(G-18063)*

RUBBER PRDTS: Silicone

Rowe Industries Inc ....F..... 302 855-0585
Pembroke Park *(G-13365)*

Venair Inc ....G..... 305 362-8920
Miami Gardens *(G-10278)*

RUBBER PRDTS: Sponge

Re-Think It Inc ....F..... 407 671-6000
Orlando *(G-12535)*

RUBBER PRDTS: Wet Suits

Aquatic Fabricators of S Fla ....G..... 954 458-0400
Hallandale *(G-4919)*

J & I Ventures Inc ....E..... 561 845-0030
West Palm Beach *(G-18037)*

Sport Products of Tampa Inc ....G..... 813 630-5552
Tampa *(G-17296)*

RUG BINDING

Area Rugs Mfg Inc ....G..... 904 398-5481
Jacksonville *(G-5898)*

RUGS : Hand & Machine Made

Area Rugs Mfg Inc ....G..... 904 398-5481
Jacksonville *(G-5898)*

SAFES & VAULTS: Metal

Blue Chip Group LLC ....G..... 305 863-9094
Doral *(G-3144)*

Brandon Lock & Safe Inc ....G..... 813 655-4200
Tampa *(G-16660)*

CE Safes and SEC Pdts Inc ....F..... 239 561-1260
Fort Myers *(G-4203)*

Hayman Safe Co Inc ....E..... 407 365-5434
Oviedo *(G-12824)*

Valuesafes Inc ....G..... 877 629-6214
Port Charlotte *(G-14322)*

Vault Structures Inc ....E..... 239 332-3270
Fort Myers *(G-4438)*

SAFETY EQPT & SPLYS WHOLESALERS

Lifesaving Systems Corporation ....E..... 813 645-2748
Apollo Beach *(G-94)*

Safariland LLC ....D..... 904 741-5400
Jacksonville *(G-6446)*

Sara Glove Company Inc ....G..... 866 664-7272
Naples *(G-10884)*

Threez Company LLC ....G..... 904 422-9224
Jacksonville *(G-6550)*

Troy Industries Inc ....E..... 305 324-1742
Doral *(G-3404)*

SAFETY INSPECTION SVCS

Titan Service Industry Llc ....G..... 678 313-4707
Deland *(G-2912)*

SAILBOAT BUILDING & REPAIR

Catalina Yachts Inc ....C..... 727 544-6681
Largo *(G-7562)*

Gause Built Marine Inc ....F..... 727 937-9113
Tarpon Springs *(G-17473)*

Sino Eagle Usa Inc ....F..... 727 259-3570
Dunedin *(G-3458)*

Uk Sailmakers Inc ....G..... 941 365-7245
Sarasota *(G-15576)*

SAILS

Atlantic Sails Makers ....G..... 305 567-1773
Miami *(G-8764)*

Douglas A Fisher Inc ....G..... 941 951-0189
Sarasota *(G-15661)*

Doyle Sailmakers Inc ....F..... 772 219-4024
Stuart *(G-16139)*

Gulfcoast Sailing Inc ....G..... 727 823-1968
Saint Petersburg *(G-15068)*

Schurr Sails Inc ....F..... 850 438-9354
Pensacola *(G-13601)*

Southern Interest Co Inc ....F..... 727 471-2040
Saint Petersburg *(G-15191)*

US Spars Inc ....G..... 386 462-3760
Gainesville *(G-4782)*

SALES PROMOTION SVCS

Deco Abrusci International LLC ....F..... 305 406-3401
Doral *(G-3188)*

SALT

A 2 Z of Lake City Inc ....G..... 386 755-0235
Lake City *(G-7007)*

Lake City Mediplex LLC ....G..... 386 752-2209
Lake City *(G-7026)*

Microsalt Inc ....F..... 877 825-0655
West Palm Beach *(G-18079)*

Morton Salt Inc ....C..... 321 868-7136
Cape Canaveral *(G-1292)*

OMI of Lake City LLC ....G..... 386 288-5632
Lake City *(G-7035)*

Panda Moni Yum Lake City LL ....G..... 352 494-5193
Lake City *(G-7037)*

Salt 1to1 Inc ....F..... 407 721-8107
Orlando *(G-12572)*

Startech Lake City Inc ....F..... 386 466-1969
Lake City *(G-7047)*

SAMPLE BOOKS

Hofmann & Leavy Inc ....D..... 954 698-0000
Deerfield Beach *(G-2738)*

US Sample Corp ....E..... 954 495-4525
Boca Raton *(G-739)*

SAND & GRAVEL

Aurora Stone & Gravel LLC ....G..... 321 253-4808
Melbourne *(G-8370)*

Bermont Excavating LLC ....F..... 866 367-9557
Punta Gorda *(G-14497)*

Blue Water Industries LLC ....F..... 904 512-7706
Jacksonville *(G-5940)*

Cemex Cnstr Mtls Fla LLC ....F..... 800 992-3639
Moore Haven *(G-10589)*

Clrs Solutions LLC ....G..... 612 481-9244
Trinity *(G-17634)*

Corbin Sand and Clay Inc ....G..... 850 638-8462
Chipley *(G-1454)*

Dan Frame & Trim Inc ....G..... 352 726-4567
Inverness *(G-5825)*

ER Jahna Industries Inc ....G..... 863 422-7617
Haines City *(G-4906)*

G2c Enterprises Inc ....G..... 850 398-5368
Crestview *(G-2244)*

G2c Enterprises Inc ....F..... 850 585-4166
Crestview *(G-2245)*

Hector Corporation ....G..... 786 308-5853
Miami *(G-9271)*

Helms Hauling & Materials Llc ....F..... 850 218-6895
Niceville *(G-11032)*

James G Dowling Inc ....G..... 407 509-9484
Sanford *(G-15344)*

Professional Site & Trnspt Inc ....F..... 386 239-6800
Daytona Beach *(G-2587)*

Reliable Site Solutions LLC ....G..... 904 238-3113
Callahan *(G-1257)*

Rockpack Inc ....E..... 407 757-0798
Apopka *(G-171)*

Sesame Flyers of South Florida ....G..... 954 274-7233
Lauderhill *(G-7740)*

Sod Depot & Gravel Inc ....G..... 321 728-2766
Palm Bay *(G-12918)*

Stewart Materials Inc ....G..... 561 972-4517
Jupiter *(G-6805)*

Stony Creek Sand & Gravel LLC ....G..... 804 229-0015
Pompano Beach *(G-14202)*

Titan America LLC ....D..... 954 523-9790
Fort Lauderdale *(G-4092)*

Tropical Sands ....G..... 786 573-3094
Miami *(G-10042)*

Vecellio & Grogan Inc ....D..... 305 822-5322
Hialeah *(G-5406)*

SAND MINING

Bonita Grande Mining LLC ....E..... 239 947-6402
Bonita Springs *(G-782)*

C C Calhoun Inc ....F..... 863 292-9511
Winter Haven *(G-18428)*

Garcia Mining Company LLC ....G..... 863 902-9777
Clewiston *(G-1890)*

Legacy Vulcan Corp ....G..... 352 742-2122
Tavares *(G-17516)*

PRODUCT

SAND: Hygrade

Chemours Company Fc LLC ....D 904 964-1200
Starke (G-16099)
Standard Sand & Silica Company ....E 863 422-7100
Davenport (G-2371)

SAND: Silica

Sand Hill Rock LLC ....G 772 216-4852
Okeechobee (G-11616)

SANDBLASTING EQPT

Industrial Marine Inc ....F 904 781-4707
Jacksonville (G-6195)
N-Viro Inc ....F 904 781-4707
Jacksonville (G-6317)

SANDBLASTING SVC: Building Exterior

C Y A Powder Coating LLC ....G 727 299-9832
Clearwater (G-1534)

SANITARY SVC, NEC

Bingham On-Site Sewers Inc ....D 813 659-0003
Dover (G-3428)
Joe Hearn Innovative Tech LLC ....F 850 898-3744
Pensacola (G-13528)

SANITARY SVCS: Liquid Waste Collection & Disposal

All Liquid Envmtl Svcs LLC ....E 800 767-9594
Fort Lauderdale (G-3638)

SANITARY SVCS: Sanitary Landfill, Operation Of

Waste Management Inc Florida ....E 954 984-2000
Winter Garden (G-18408)

SANITARY SVCS: Waste Materials, Recycling

D & S Pallets Inc ....D 727 540-0061
Clearwater (G-1560)
Global Holdings and Dev LLC ....G 949 500-4997
Pompano Beach (G-14041)
Purecycle Technologies Inc ....F 877 648-3565
Orlando (G-12518)
Yahl Mulching & Recycling Inc ....F 239 352-7888
Naples (G-10945)

SANITARY WARE: Metal

Arya Group LLC ....G 561 792-9992
Wellington (G-17843)
Bathroom World Manufacturing ....G 954 566-0451
Oakland Park (G-11246)
East Coast Fix & Mllwk Co Inc ....G 904 733-9711
Jacksonville (G-6059)
Jambco Millwork Inc ....F 954 977-4998
Margate (G-8136)
Wool Wholesale Plumbing Supply ....D 954 763-3632
Fort Lauderdale (G-4136)

SANITATION CHEMICALS & CLEANING AGENTS

Allen Shuffleboard LLC ....G 727 399-8877
Seminole (G-15968)
and Services ....G 850 805-6455
Fort Walton Beach (G-4560)
Campos Chemicals ....G 727 412-2774
Saint Petersburg (G-14996)
Caribbean Global Group Corp ....G 786 449-2767
Port St Lucie (G-14471)
Chemical Systems Orlando Inc ....G 407 886-2329
Zellwood (G-18597)
Clorox Healthcare Holdings LLC ....E 904 996-7758
Jacksonville (G-5985)
Enozo Technologies Inc ....G 512 944-7772
Lakewood Ranch (G-7477)
Freezetone Products LLC ....F 305 961-1116
Doral (G-3220)
Goho Enterprises Inc ....F 407 884-0770
Zellwood (G-18598)
Illinois Tool Works Inc ....D 863 665-3338
Lakeland (G-7347)
NCH (fl) Funding LLC ....G 321 777-7777
Melbourne (G-8478)

NCH Marine LLC ....G 754 422-4237
Davie (G-2446)
Pro Chem Products Inc ....G 407 425-5533
Orlando (G-12509)
Puritair LLC ....F 954 281-5105
Fort Lauderdale (G-4002)
Roebic Laboratories Inc ....F 561 799-3380
Jupiter (G-6788)
Rolite Co ....G 920 251-1006
Sarasota (G-15798)
Sicamu Inc ....G 850 270-6283
Quincy (G-14549)
Sltons Envirnmntal Group Assoc ....F 305 665-5594
Miami (G-9905)
Star-Brite Distributing Inc ....E 954 587-6280
Davie (G-2481)
Stratford Corporation ....G 727 443-1573
Clearwater (G-1798)
Super Cleaning Woman Services ....G 954 670-7527
Fort Lauderdale (G-4076)
Troy Industries Inc ....E 305 324-1742
Doral (G-3404)
Venco Marine Inc ....G 954 923-0036
Hollywood (G-5681)

SASHES: Door Or Window, Metal

Building Envelope Systems Inc ....G 305 693-0683
Hialeah (G-5081)
Curv-A-Tech Corp ....F 305 888-9631
Hialeah (G-5102)
Hill Enterprises LLC ....G 850 478-4455
Pensacola (G-13519)
Hollow Metal Inc ....F 813 246-4112
Valrico (G-17665)
Panelfold Inc ....C 305 688-3501
Miami (G-9688)
Sea Products Inc ....D 904 781-8200
Jacksonville (G-6458)
T M Building Products Ltd ....G 954 781-4430
Pompano Beach (G-14209)
Universal Alum Windows & Doors ....F 305 825-7900
Hialeah (G-5394)
YKK AP America Inc ....G 561 736-7808
Boynton Beach (G-928)
YKK AP America Inc ....F 407 856-0660
Orlando (G-12728)

SATCHELS

Jasmine Purkiss ....F 386 244-7726
Edgewater (G-3495)

SATELLITE COMMUNICATIONS EQPT

Airbus Onweb Stlltes N Amer LL ....E 321 522-6645
Merritt Island (G-8574)
Airbus Onweb Stlltes N Amer LL ....D 321 522-6645
Merritt Island (G-8575)
Julio Garcia Satellite ....G 407 414-3223
Kissimmee (G-6932)
Nic4 Inc ....F 877 455-2131
Tampa (G-17110)
Satellite Now Inc ....G 239 945-0520
Cape Coral (G-1381)
Terran Orbital Corporation ....F 561 988-1704
Boca Raton (G-712)

SATELLITES: Communications

Airbus Oneweb Satellites LLC ....E 321 522-6645
Merritt Island (G-8573)
Alphatec Communications ....G 518 580-0520
Doral (G-3109)
Antennas For Cmmnctons Ocala F ......E 352 687-4121
Ocala (G-11325)
Applied Systems Integrator Inc ....G 321 259-6106
Melbourne (G-8368)
Astrumsat Communications LLC ....G 954 368-9980
Sanford (G-15267)
Comtech Antenna Systems Inc ....C 407 854-1950
Orlando (G-12037)
Comtech Systems Inc ....D 407 854-1950
Orlando (G-12038)
Crystal Communications Inc ....G 954 474-3072
Sunrise (G-16309)
Espace Inc ....E 802 735-7546
Stuart (G-16145)
Global Satellite Prpts LLC ....G 954 459-3000
Fort Lauderdale (G-3841)
Itelecom USA Inc ....G 305 557-4660
Weston (G-18257)

J&B Cmmnication Solutions Corp ....G 786 346-7449
Davie (G-2427)
Mil-Sat LLC ....G 954 862-3613
Davie (G-2441)
Nextplat Corp ....G 305 560-5355
Aventura (G-267)
Qualitysat Corp ....G 305 232-4211
Miami (G-9762)
Satcom Direct Government Inc ....F 321 777-3000
Melbourne (G-8515)
Southeastern Engineering Inc ....E 321 984-2521
Palm Bay (G-12921)
Srt Wireless LLC ....G 954 797-7850
Sunrise (G-16371)

SAUNA ROOMS: Prefabricated

East Coast Floats LLC ....G 407 203-5628
Orlando (G-12113)

SAVINGS INSTITUTIONS: Federally Chartered

Southwest Florida Regional ....C 615 344-9551
Largo (G-7688)

SAW BLADES

American Diamond Blades Corp ....F 561 571-2166
Boca Raton (G-406)
Blades Direct LLC ....G 855 225-2337
Coral Springs (G-2138)
Global Diversified Products ....E 727 209-0854
Pinellas Park (G-13690)
Microtool and Instrument Inc ....E 786 242-8780
Palmetto Bay (G-13215)
RSC Industries Inc ....E 813 886-4711
Tampa (G-17236)

SAWDUST & SHAVINGS

J W Dawson Co Inc ....E 305 634-8618
Miami (G-9352)
Tatum Brothers Lumber Co Inc ....E 904 782-3690
Lawtey (G-7747)

SAWING & PLANING MILLS

A L Baxley & Sons Inc ....F 352 629-5137
Citra (G-1466)
Apalachee Pole Company Inc ....G 850 263-4457
Graceville (G-4807)
Bailey Timber Co Inc ....F 850 674-2080
Blountstown (G-375)
Creamer Corp ....G 850 265-2700
Panama City (G-13250)
Cross City Lumber LLC ....F 352 578-8078
Cross City (G-2258)
David E Ashe Sawmill ....F 904 377-4800
Saint Augustine (G-14824)
Florida North Lumber Inc ....G 850 263-4457
Bristol (G-1119)
Fraser West ....G 850 601-2560
Perry (G-13638)
Gilman Building Products LLC ....G 904 548-1000
Yulee (G-18590)
Great South Timber & Lbr Inc ....F 386 755-3046
Lake City (G-7022)
International Closet Center ....G 305 883-6551
Medley (G-8258)
J & S Cypress Inc ....F 352 383-3864
Sorrento (G-16010)
John A Cruce Jr Inc ....E 850 584-9755
Perry (G-13644)
Kempfer Sawmill Inc ....F 407 892-2955
Saint Cloud (G-14930)
McCain Mills Inc ....G 813 752-6478
Plant City (G-13784)
North Florida Woodlands Inc ....F 850 643-2238
Bristol (G-1125)
Rex Lumber Graceville LLC ....C 850 263-2056
Graceville (G-4808)
Rex Lumber LLC ....F 850 643-2172
Bristol (G-1126)
Rex Lumber LLC ....F 850 263-2056
Graceville (G-4809)
Robbins Manufactuing Co ....D 352 793-2443
Webster (G-17833)
Rulon Company of Georgia ....C 904 584-1400
Saint Augustine (G-14882)
West Fraser Inc ....C 904 786-4155
Jacksonville (G-6601)

West Fraser Inc ....C 850 587-1000
  Mc David *(G-8190)*
Whitfield Timber Company Inc ....E 850 639-5556
  Wewahitchka *(G-18303)*
Williston Timber Co Inc ....E 352 528-2699
  Williston *(G-18336)*

SAWING & PLANING MILLS: Custom

Fuqua Sawmill Inc.............................G 352 236-3456
  Ocala *(G-11397)*

SAWS & SAWING EQPT

Bayou Outdoor Equipment ....F 850 729-2711
  Valparaiso *(G-17655)*
Tct Manufacturing ....F 352 735-5070
  Mount Dora *(G-10615)*

SCALES & BALANCES, EXC LABORATORY

Intercomp...G 407 637-9766
  Delray Beach *(G-2975)*

SCALES: Indl

Atlas Industrial Scales Inc ....G 352 610-9989
  Spring Hill *(G-16063)*
Mettler-Toledo Inc ....F 407 423-3856
  Orlando *(G-12375)*

SCALES: Truck

Pinto Palma Sound LLC ....E 877 959-1815
  Cutler Bay *(G-2299)*
US 1 Truck Sales LLC........................G 904 545-1233
  Jacksonville *(G-6583)*

SCANNING DEVICES: Optical

Dtsystems Inc...................................G 813 994-0030
  Tampa *(G-16787)*
Industrial Scan Inc ....F 407 322-3664
  Sanford *(G-15336)*

SCHOOL BUS SVC

Amer-Con Corp ....E 786 293-8004
  Palmetto Bay *(G-13207)*

SCHOOLS & EDUCATIONAL SVCS, NEC

Titan Tools LLC ....E 818 984-1001
  Clearwater *(G-1832)*

SCIENTIFIC INSTRUMENTS WHOLESALERS

Analytical Research Systems ....F 352 466-0051
  Micanopy *(G-10395)*
Ocean Test Equipment Inc ....G 954 474-6603
  Davie *(G-2449)*
Thermo Fisher Scientific Inc ....B 561 688-8700
  West Palm Beach *(G-18179)*

SCRAP & WASTE MATERIALS, WHOLESALE: Paper

Omnisphere Corporation ....F 305 388-4075
  Miami *(G-9648)*

SCREENS: Door, Metal Covered Wood

Omega Garage Doors Inc....................F 352 620-8830
  Melbourne *(G-8488)*
Tag Media Group LLC ....F 239 288-0499
  Fort Myers *(G-4417)*

SCREENS: Door, Wood Frame

Unique Technology Inds LLC ....F 941 358-5410
  Sarasota *(G-15861)*

SCREENS: Projection

General Screen Service Co ....G 305 226-0741
  Miami *(G-9201)*
Vutec Corporation ....C 954 545-9000
  Vero Beach *(G-17816)*

SCREENS: Window, Metal

Brevard Aluminum Cnstr Co.................G 321 383-9255
  Titusville *(G-17575)*
J T Walker Industries Inc ....E 727 461-0501
  Clearwater *(G-1650)*

Leon Screening & Repair Inc ....F 850 575-2840
  Tallahassee *(G-16469)*
Plotkowski Inc ....G 561 740-2226
  Boynton Beach *(G-896)*
Reliable Pool Enclsres Screns ....G 407 731-3408
  Orlando *(G-12545)*
Tag Media Group LLC ....F 239 288-0499
  Fort Myers *(G-4417)*

SCREENS: Window, Wood Framed

Eagle View Windows Inc ....F 904 647-8221
  Jacksonville *(G-6055)*

SCREENS: Woven Wire

Harpers Manufacturing Spc ....G 941 629-3490
  Punta Gorda *(G-14508)*
Yale Ogron Mfg Co Inc........................G 305 687-0424
  Opa Locka *(G-11803)*

SCREW MACHINE PRDTS

Ashley F Ward Inc ....F 904 284-2848
  Green Cove Springs *(G-4817)*
Atomic Machine & Edm Inc ....G 239 353-9100
  Naples *(G-10682)*
Blitz Micro Turning Inc ....G 727 725-5005
  Safety Harbor *(G-14783)*
Coastal Machine LLC..........................G 850 769-6117
  Panama City *(G-13246)*
Consoldted Mch Tl Holdings LLC ....F 888 317-9990
  Flagler Beach *(G-3602)*
Construction and Elec Pdts Inc............F 954 972-9787
  Pompano Beach *(G-13976)*
D J Camco Corporation ....G 904 355-5995
  Jacksonville *(G-6020)*
Danco Machine Inc ....G 727 501-0460
  Largo *(G-7569)*
Forcon Precision Products LLC ....F 239 574-4543
  Cape Coral *(G-1345)*
Gti Systems Inc.................................E 863 965-2002
  Auburndale *(G-236)*
Hunter Aerospace Supply LLC ....G 954 321-8848
  Fort Lauderdale *(G-3871)*
Integrted Dsign Dev Cntl Fla I ....G 407 268-4300
  Sanford *(G-15339)*
Klopfer Holdings Inc ....D 727 472-2002
  Clearwater *(G-1663)*
Merit Screw.......................................G 352 344-3744
  Hernando *(G-5009)*
Mkm Sarasota LLC.............................E 941 358-0383
  Sarasota *(G-15749)*
MSP Industries LLC ....C 727 443-5764
  Clearwater *(G-1706)*
Mtec Trailer Supply ....F 813 659-1647
  Plant City *(G-13786)*
OMalley Manufacturing Inc ....G 727 327-6817
  Saint Petersburg *(G-15147)*
Praesto Enterprises LLC ....G 407 298-9171
  Orlando *(G-12498)*
Precision Metal Parts Inc ....F 727 526-9165
  Saint Petersburg *(G-15160)*
Precision Shapes Inc..........................E 321 269-2555
  Titusville *(G-17609)*
Precision Turning Corporation ....F 386 364-5788
  Live Oak *(G-7852)*
Quality Precision Pdts Co Inc...............F 305 885-4596
  Hialeah *(G-5321)*
Royal Precision Products Inc ....E 305 685-5490
  Opa Locka *(G-11786)*
Walkup Enterprises Inc ....F 727 571-1244
  Clearwater *(G-1847)*
Weber Mfg & Supplies Inc....................F 941 488-5185
  North Venice *(G-11221)*

SCREW MACHINES

Precision Turning Corporation ....F 386 364-5788
  Live Oak *(G-7852)*

SCREWS: Metal

Grabber Construction Pdts Inc.............G 813 249-2281
  Tampa *(G-16888)*
Migrandy Corp ....G 321 459-0044
  Merritt Island *(G-8588)*
Quality Socket Screw Mfg Corp...........F 941 475-9585
  Englewood *(G-3522)*
Sockets & Specials Inc........................F 561 582-7022
  West Palm Beach *(G-18156)*

SEALANTS

386 Nanotech Inc ....F 727 252-9580
  South Pasadena *(G-16050)*
Master Painting & Sealants LLC ....G 305 910-5104
  Miami *(G-9518)*
Mg Coating and Sealants LLC ....G 305 409-0915
  North Miami *(G-11111)*
Southast Clking Slant Svcs LLC ....G 813 731-8778
  Plant City *(G-13804)*
Srm Waterproofing Sealants Inc ....G 407 963-3619
  Orlando *(G-12619)*
Ussi LLC ....F 941 244-2408
  Venice *(G-17726)*

SEALS: Hermetic

Frc Electrical Industries Inc ....G 321 676-3300
  Palm Bay *(G-12902)*
Winchster Intrcnnect Hrmtics L............D 321 254-4067
  Melbourne *(G-8563)*

SEALS: Oil, Rubber

Bxd Enterprises Inc ....G 727 937-4100
  Holiday *(G-5492)*

SEARCH & DETECTION SYSTEMS, EXC RADAR

Northrop Grumman Corporation ....A 321 951-5000
  Melbourne *(G-8482)*

SEARCH & NAVIGATION SYSTEMS

Aero-Trim Control Systems Inc ....G 954 321-1936
  Davie *(G-2378)*
Alakai Defense Systems Inc ....F 727 541-1600
  Largo *(G-7527)*
Alliant Tchsystems Oprtons LLC ....E 561 776-9876
  Palm Beach Gardens *(G-12946)*
Asrc Aerospace Corp ....B 321 867-1462
  Kennedy Space Center *(G-6830)*
Astronics Test Systems Inc ....C 407 381-6062
  Orlando *(G-11929)*
Bae Systems Tech Sltons Svcs I ....E 850 664-6070
  Fort Walton Beach *(G-4563)*
Bae Systems Tech Sltons Svcs I ....D 850 244-6433
  Fort Walton Beach *(G-4564)*
Bae Systems Tech Sltons Svcs I ....G 850 344-0832
  Fort Walton Beach *(G-4565)*
Carbonara Labs Inc ....F 321 952-1303
  Grant *(G-4811)*
Cobham Mission System Corp ....G 850 226-6717
  Fort Walton Beach *(G-4570)*
Cobham Satcom ....E 407 650-9054
  Sanford *(G-15286)*
Coda Octopus Group Inc ....F 407 735-2402
  Orlando *(G-12027)*
CPS Products Inc ....D 305 687-4121
  Miramar *(G-10482)*
Drs Advanced Isr LLC ....F 850 226-4888
  Fort Walton Beach *(G-4573)*
Drs C3 Systems Inc ....E 850 302-3909
  Fort Walton Beach *(G-4574)*
Drs Cengen Llc ....B 321 622-1500
  Melbourne *(G-8404)*
Drs Consolidated Controls ....F 850 302-3000
  Fort Walton Beach *(G-4575)*
Drs Land Electronics ....G 321 622-1435
  Melbourne *(G-8405)*
Drs Leonardo Inc ....C 850 302-3000
  Fort Walton Beach *(G-4576)*
Drs Leonardo Inc ....D 850 302-3514
  Fort Walton Beach *(G-4577)*
Drs Ntwork Imaging Systems LLC ....B 321 309-1500
  Melbourne *(G-8406)*
Drs S and T Optronics Div ....F 321 309-1500
  Melbourne *(G-8407)*
Drs Sensors Targeting Systems............E 321 309-1500
  Melbourne *(G-8408)*
Drs Soneticom Inc ....E 321 733-0400
  Melbourne *(G-8409)*
Drs Systems Inc ....G 973 451-3525
  Melbourne *(G-8410)*
Drs Tactical Systems Inc ....D 321 727-3672
  Melbourne *(G-8411)*
Edgeone LLC ....E 561 995-7767
  Boca Raton *(G-500)*
Eve Uam LLC ....G 954 359-3700
  Fort Lauderdale *(G-3798)*

PRODUCT

Gannet Technologies LLC	F	941 870-3444
Sarasota *(G-15480)*		
Garmin International Inc	B	305 674-7701
Miami Beach *(G-10195)*		
GE Aviation Systems LLC	B	727 531-7781
Clearwater *(G-1610)*		
General Dynamics-Ots Inc	D	727 578-8100
Saint Petersburg *(G-15058)*		
Heico Aerospace Corporation	E	954 987-6101
Hollywood *(G-5590)*		
Hensoldt Avionics Usa LLC	G	941 306-1328
Sarasota *(G-15700)*		
Honeywell International Inc	D	505 358-0676
Largo *(G-7606)*		
Ilsc Holdings Lc	G	480 935-4230
Orlando *(G-12235)*		
Jade Tactical Disaster Relief	C	850 270-4077
Tampa *(G-16961)*		
Joe Hearn Innovative Tech LLC	F	850 898-3744
Pensacola *(G-13528)*		
Kollsman Inc	G	407 312-1384
Orlando *(G-12293)*		
L3 Crestview Aerospace	F	850 682-2746
Crestview *(G-2249)*		
L3 Technologies Inc	C	321 409-6122
Melbourne *(G-8454)*		
L3 Technologies Inc	F	941 371-0811
Saint Petersburg *(G-15108)*		
L3harris Interstate Elec Corp	D	321 730-0119
Cape Canaveral *(G-1288)*		
L3harris Technologies Inc	B	321 727-9100
Melbourne *(G-8455)*		
L3harris Technologies Inc	E	407 581-3782
Orlando *(G-12302)*		
L3harris Technologies Inc	D	321 768-4660
Malabar *(G-8086)*		
L3harris Technologies Inc	D	321 727-4000
Melbourne *(G-8458)*		
L3harris Technologies Inc	C	260 451-6814
Tampa *(G-16995)*		
Lockheed Martin Corporation	A	407 306-6405
Orlando *(G-12339)*		
Lockheed Martin Corporation	E	407 517-6627
Orlando *(G-12341)*		
Lockheed Martin Corporation	D	863 647-0100
Lakeland *(G-7380)*		
Lockheed Martin Corporation	C	407 306-4803
Orlando *(G-12342)*		
Lockheed Martin Corporation	C	727 578-6940
Pinellas Park *(G-13706)*		
Lockheed Martin Corporation	B	321 635-7621
Rockledge *(G-14725)*		
Lockheed Martin Corporation	F	407 356-2000
Orlando *(G-12343)*		
Lockheed Martin Corporation	D	352 687-2163
Ocala *(G-11431)*		
Lockheed Martin Corporation	E	407 356-1034
Orlando *(G-12344)*		
Lockheed Martin Corporation	F	863 647-0100
Lakeland *(G-7381)*		
Lockheed Martin Corporation	B	863 647-0558
Lakeland *(G-7382)*		
Lockheed Martin Corporation	E	863 647-0100
Lakeland *(G-7383)*		
Lockheed Martin Corporation	F	863 647-0303
Lakeland *(G-7384)*		
Lockheed Martin Corporation	D	301 897-6000
Riviera Beach *(G-14643)*		
Lockheed Martin Corporation	E	407 356-2000
Orlando *(G-12345)*		
Lockheed Mrtin Gyrcam Systems	C	407 356-6500
Orlando *(G-12346)*		
Lockheed Mrtin Intgrted System	C	407 356-2000
Orlando *(G-12347)*		
Lockheed Mrtin Trning Sltons I	D	856 722-3317
Orlando *(G-12349)*		
Loos & Co Inc	D	239 643-5667
Naples *(G-10807)*		
Luminar LLC	B	407 900-5259
Orlando *(G-12355)*		
Mathews Associates Inc	C	407 323-3390
Sanford *(G-15354)*		
Meads International Inc	D	407 356-8400
Orlando *(G-12367)*		
Micro Systems Inc	C	850 244-2332
Fort Walton Beach *(G-4596)*		
Moog	F	305 471-0444
Doral *(G-3307)*		
Moog Inc	G	407 451-9534
Orlando *(G-12390)*		

Northrop Grmman Tchncal Svcs I	G	321 837-7000
Melbourne *(G-8481)*		
Northrop Grmman Tchncal Svcs I	E	904 825-3300
Saint Augustine *(G-14862)*		
Northrop Grumman ISS Intl Inc	F	321 951-5695
Melbourne *(G-8483)*		
Northrop Grumman Systems Corp	G	904 810-5957
Saint Augustine *(G-14864)*		
Northrop Grumman Systems Corp	G	850 452-7970
Pensacola *(G-13557)*		
Northrop Grumman Systems Corp	D	850 863-8000
Fort Walton Beach *(G-4598)*		
Northrop Grumman Systems Corp	E	321 235-3800
Orlando *(G-12422)*		
Northrop Grumman Systems Corp	E	561 515-3651
Palm Beach Gardens *(G-12994)*		
Northrop Grumman Systems Corp	C	407 737-4900
Orlando *(G-12423)*		
Northrop Grumman Systems Corp	B	407 295-4010
Apopka *(G-158)*		
Passur Aerospace Inc	F	203 622-4086
Orlando *(G-12469)*		
Phoenix Navtech LLC	G	407 285-4536
Harmony *(G-4987)*		
Pixels On Target LLC	E	305 614-0890
Sunrise *(G-16352)*		
Radiant Power Corp	D	941 739-3200
Sarasota *(G-15541)*		
Raytheon Company	D	407 207-9223
Orlando *(G-12533)*		
Raytheon Technologies Corp	A	860 565-4321
Jupiter *(G-6786)*		
Riegl Usa Inc	E	407 248-9927
Winter Garden *(G-18403)*		
Ritchie	G	904 783-0416
Jacksonville *(G-6424)*		
Rockwell Collins Inc	D	321 768-7303
Melbourne *(G-8511)*		
Saikou Optics Incorporated	G	407 986-4200
Orlando *(G-12569)*		
Searobotics Corporation	E	772 742-3700
Stuart *(G-16212)*		
Segers Aerospace Corporation	D	850 689-2198
Crestview *(G-2252)*		
Sensormatic	F	561 912-6429
Boca Raton *(G-666)*		
Sensormatic Electronics Corp	G	561 989-7000
Boca Raton *(G-667)*		
Sequa Corporation	A	561 935-3571
Palm Beach Gardens *(G-13008)*		
Sierra Nevada Corporation	F	850 659-3600
Shalimar *(G-16003)*		
Sikorsky Aircraft Corp	G	772 210-0849
Stuart *(G-16220)*		
Smiths Interconnect Inc	C	813 901-7200
Tampa *(G-17276)*		
Sports Radar Ltd	G	352 503-6825
Homosassa *(G-5751)*		
Streamline Numerics Inc	G	352 271-8841
Gainesville *(G-4768)*		
Technologies Drs Unmanned Inc	D	850 302-3909
Fort Walton Beach *(G-4613)*		
Trakka USA LLC	G	505 345-0270
Bradenton *(G-1062)*		
Viewpoint Systems LLC	F	850 450-0681
Pensacola *(G-13621)*		

SEARCH & RESCUE SVCS

Exploration Services LLC	G	352 505-3578
Gainesville *(G-4688)*		

SEASHELLS, WHOLESALE

Sun Krafts of Volusia County	G	386 441-1961
Ormond Beach *(G-12796)*		

SEAT BELTS: Automobile & Aircraft

CSC Racing Corporation	F	248 548-5727
Jupiter *(G-6706)*		
Key Safety Systems Inc	C	863 668-6000
Lakeland *(G-7367)*		
Seatbelt Solutions Llc	E	855 642-3964
Jupiter *(G-6794)*		

SEATING: Bleacher, Portable

Miami Grandstand Entrmt Corp	G	305 636-9665
Hialeah *(G-5251)*		

SEATING: Chairs, Table & Arm

F & R General Interiors Corp	F	305 635-4747
Hialeah *(G-5149)*		

SEATING: Stadium

Seating Constructors Usa Inc	F	813 505-7560
Brooksville *(G-1197)*		
Seating Installation Group LLC	F	727 289-7652
Saint Petersburg *(G-15179)*		

SECRETARIAL & COURT REPORTING

Pensacola Voice Inc	G	850 434-6963
Pensacola *(G-13572)*		

SECRETARIAL SVCS

Mdintouch Us Inc	G	786 268-1161
Miami *(G-9525)*		
Paper Free Technology Inc	G	515 270-1505
Lehigh Acres *(G-7819)*		

SECURITY CONTROL EQPT & SYSTEMS

AAA Security Depot Corp	E	305 652-8567
Opa Locka *(G-11710)*		
Absolute Automation & Security	G	321 505-9989
Cocoa *(G-1897)*		
Abz Marketing Solutions Corp	E	305 340-1887
Doral *(G-3091)*		
Advanced Dsign Tech Systems In	E	850 462-2868
Pensacola *(G-13437)*		
Advanced Intelligence Group	G	904 565-1004
Jacksonville *(G-5863)*		
Alco Advanced Technologies	G	305 333-0831
Doral *(G-3103)*		
Amtel Security Systems Inc	E	305 591-8200
Doral *(G-3115)*		
Aressco Technologies Inc	G	305 245-5854
Homestead *(G-5700)*		
Audio Intelligence Devices	E	954 418-1400
Deerfield Beach *(G-2673)*		
Centrys LLC	E	407 476-4786
Sanford *(G-15281)*		
Communcations Surveillance Inc	F	305 377-1211
Coral Gables *(G-2041)*		
Control and Automtn Cons Inc	G	305 823-8670
Hialeah *(G-5096)*		
Control Investments Inc	F	954 491-6660
Fort Lauderdale *(G-3746)*		
Edgewater Technologies Inc	F	954 565-9898
Fort Lauderdale *(G-3785)*		
Elipter Corp	G	305 593-8355
Doral *(G-3207)*		
Etc Palm Beach LLC	D	561 881-8118
West Palm Beach *(G-17988)*		
ICO USA Corp	G	305 253-0871
Palmetto Bay *(G-13212)*		
Industrial Smoke & Mirrors Inc	E	407 299-9400
Orlando *(G-12242)*		
Integrated Surroundings Inc	F	850 932-0848
Gulf Breeze *(G-4885)*		
L3harris Technologies Inc	B	321 727-9100
Melbourne *(G-8455)*		
Salco Industries Inc	F	941 377-7717
Sarasota *(G-15806)*		
Saltex Group Corp	G	305 477-3187
Miami *(G-9841)*		
Select Engineered Systems Inc	E	305 823-5410
Hialeah *(G-5343)*		
Sepronet Inc	F	305 463-8551
Doral *(G-3360)*		
Simplexgrinnell Holdings LLC	G	978 731-2500
Boca Raton *(G-677)*		
Smart Access Inc	G	407 331-4724
Lake Mary *(G-7106)*		
Source 1 Solutions Inc	D	727 538-4114
Clearwater *(G-1787)*		
Southeast Security Products	G	954 786-5900
Pompano Beach *(G-14191)*		
Sunrise Financial Assoc Inc	G	321 439-9797
Orlando *(G-12634)*		
Telsec Corporation	G	561 998-9983
Boca Raton *(G-710)*		
Validsoft	G	813 334-9745
Lutz *(G-8019)*		
Venco Marine Inc	G	954 923-0036
Hollywood *(G-5681)*		
World Electronics Inc	G	954 318-1044
Sunrise *(G-16393)*		

Xpondr Corporation ....E 727 541-4149
Seminole **(G-15999)**

SECURITY DEVICES

Appointment Team Inc ....F 561 314-5471
Boynton Beach **(G-843)**
Armor Accessories Inc ....E 904 741-1717
Jacksonville **(G-5902)**
Asecure America Inc ....G...... 352 347-7951
Belleview **(G-359)**
Brijot Imaging Systems Inc ....E 407 641-4370
Boca Raton **(G-449)**
C-Note Solutions Inc ....G...... 321 952-2490
Indialantic **(G-5802)**
Came Americas Automation LLC ....F 305 433-3307
Miami Lakes **(G-10289)**
Danielle Fence Mfg Co Inc ....D 863 425-3182
Mulberry **(G-10621)**
Deggy Corp ....G...... 305 377-2233
Miami Lakes **(G-10295)**
Devcon International Corp ....F 954 926-5200
Boca Raton **(G-482)**
Devcon Security Services Corp ....E 813 386-3849
Pompano Beach **(G-13993)**
Gatecrafterscom ....F 800 537-4283
Odessa **(G-11553)**
Gess Technologies LLC ....F 305 231-6322
Hialeah **(G-5171)**
Gto Access Systems LLC ....D 850 575-0176
Tallahassee **(G-16453)**
Hemco Industries Inc ....F 305 769-0606
North Miami **(G-11106)**
Hummingbirds Ai Inc ....E 305 432-2787
Miami Beach **(G-10201)**
Knight Fire & Security Inc ....E 561 471-8221
Riviera Beach **(G-14639)**
Point Blank Enterprises Inc ....D 305 820-4270
Miami Lakes **(G-10340)**
Protective Group Inc ....E 305 820-4266
Miami Lakes **(G-10345)**
Rm Brands Inc ....G...... 904 356-0092
Jacksonville **(G-6431)**
Safeguard America Inc ....G...... 305 859-9000
Miami **(G-9835)**
Secure Biometric Corporation ....G...... 813 832-1164
Tampa **(G-17249)**
Security and Fire Elec Inc ....G...... 904 844-0964
Saint Augustine **(G-14890)**
Segutronic International Inc ....G...... 305 463-8551
Doral **(G-3359)**
Servision Inc ....G...... 305 900-4999
Hallandale Beach **(G-4971)**
Signalvault LLC ....G...... 407 878-6365
Debary **(G-2642)**
Symetrics Technology Group LLC ....F 321 254-1500
Melbourne **(G-8544)**
Theft Protection Com Corp ....F 772 231-6677
Vero Beach **(G-17806)**
Vanguard Products Group Inc ....D 813 855-9639
Oldsmar **(G-11705)**
Xts Corp ....F 305 863-7779
Doral **(G-3423)**

SECURITY EQPT STORES

Florida Fence Post Co Inc ....G...... 863 735-1361
Ona **(G-11709)**
Throw Raft LLC ....G...... 954 366-8004
Fort Lauderdale **(G-4091)**

SECURITY PROTECTIVE DEVICES
MAINTENANCE & MONITORING SVCS

Express Badging Services Inc ....F 321 784-5925
Cocoa Beach **(G-1969)**
Lions Intl MGT Group Inc ....F 813 367-2517
Tampa **(G-17013)**
Security Oracle Inc ....F 352 988-5985
Clermont **(G-1883)**

SECURITY SYSTEMS SERVICES

Ad America ....G...... 904 781-5900
Jacksonville **(G-5858)**
Amtel Security Systems Inc ....E 305 591-8200
Doral **(G-3115)**
Defenshield Inc ....G...... 904 679-3942
Saint Augustine **(G-14825)**
Del Prado Holdings LLC ....G...... 305 680-7425
Hollywood **(G-5563)**

Eyeson Dgtal Srvllnce MGT Syst ....G...... 305 808-3344
Miami **(G-9125)**
Jade Tactical Disaster Relief ....C 850 270-4077
Tampa **(G-16961)**
Kratos Def & SEC Solutions Inc ....E 866 606-5867
Orlando **(G-12296)**
Protext Mobility Inc ....G...... 435 881-3611
Delray Beach **(G-3007)**
Safe Banks and Lock ....G...... 954 762-3565
Fort Lauderdale **(G-4035)**
Source 1 Solutions Inc ....D 727 538-4114
Clearwater **(G-1787)**
Top Line Installation Inc ....G...... 352 636-4192
Leesburg **(G-7798)**

SELF-PROPELLED AIRCRAFT DEALER

Atlantic Jet Center Inc ....G...... 321 255-7111
Melbourne **(G-8369)**

SEMICONDUCTOR CIRCUIT NETWORKS

Aurora Semiconductor LLC ....E 727 235-6500
Saint Petersburg **(G-14976)**

SEMICONDUCTOR DEVICES: Wafers

Hine Automation LLC ....G...... 813 749-7519
Saint Petersburg **(G-15076)**

SEMICONDUCTORS & RELATED DEVICES

AGS Electronics Inc ....G...... 850 471-1551
Pensacola **(G-13440)**
American All ....G...... 561 401-0885
Loxahatchee **(G-7966)**
American Technology Pdts Inc ....F 407 960-1722
Sanford **(G-15264)**
API Tech North America Inc ....F 929 255-1231
Winter Park **(G-18485)**
Baytronics Manufacturing Inc ....F 813 434-0401
Tampa **(G-16633)**
Convergent Engineering Inc ....F 352 378-4899
Gainesville **(G-4670)**
Convergent Marketing LLC ....F 561 270-7081
Delray Beach **(G-2950)**
Convergent Technologies ....F 407 482-4381
Orlando **(G-12046)**
Cybortrack Solutions Inc ....G...... 805 904-5677
Longwood **(G-7886)**
Drt Services ....G...... 321 549-1431
Palm Bay **(G-12898)**
Everaxis Usa Inc ....F 239 263-3102
Naples **(G-10742)**
Exalos Inc ....E 215 669-4488
Fort Lauderdale **(G-3804)**
Intertech Supply Inc ....G...... 786 200-0561
Miami **(G-9331)**
Led Nation Corp ....G...... 888 590-1720
Doral **(G-3282)**
Legacy Components LLC ....F 813 964-6805
Tampa **(G-17005)**
Mercury Systems Inc ....E 352 371-2567
Gainesville **(G-4729)**
Micross Inc ....D 407 298-7100
Apopka **(G-152)**
Micross Prmier Smcdtr Svcs LLC ....E 727 532-1777
Clearwater **(G-1698)**
Multicore Photonics Inc ....G...... 407 325-7800
Orlando **(G-12398)**
Multicore Technologies LLC ....G...... 407 325-7800
Orlando **(G-12400)**
Nasco Aerospace and Elec LLC ....F 727 344-7554
Saint Petersburg **(G-15136)**
Neos Technologies Inc ....G...... 321 242-7818
Melbourne **(G-8479)**
Notice Four LLC ....G...... 954 652-1168
Fort Lauderdale **(G-3963)**
Oerlikon USA Inc ....F 727 577-4999
Saint Petersburg **(G-15145)**
One Resonance Sensors LLC ....F 407 637-0771
Sanford **(G-15365)**
Planar Energy Devices Inc ....F 407 459-1440
Orlando **(G-12490)**
Plasma-Therm Inc ....E 856 753-8111
Saint Petersburg **(G-15152)**
Plasma-Therm LLC ....C 727 577-4999
Saint Petersburg **(G-15153)**
Qorvo Inc ....B 407 886-8860
Apopka **(G-164)**
Qorvo Us Inc ....B 407 886-8860
Apopka **(G-165)**

Qualcomm Atheros Inc ....F 407 284-7314
Orlando **(G-12519)**
Quantum Technology Inc ....G...... 407 333-9348
Lake Mary **(G-7105)**
Quartz Unlimited LLC ....G...... 561 306-1243
Boca Raton **(G-645)**
Raytheon Company ....C 310 647-9438
Largo **(G-7668)**
Reflectivity Inc ....F 386 738-1008
Deland **(G-2898)**
Renesas Electronics Amer Inc ....A 321 724-7000
Palm Bay **(G-12914)**
Sawstreet LLC ....E 407 601-4907
Orlando **(G-12575)**
Scientific Instruments Inc ....E 561 881-8500
Mangonia Park **(G-8100)**
Semiconductor Technology Inc ....G...... 772 341-0800
Stuart **(G-16214)**
Semilab USA LLC ....G...... 813 977-2244
Temple Terrace **(G-17545)**
Sepac Corp ....F 305 718-3379
Miami **(G-9868)**
Spartronics Brooksville LLC ....B 352 799-6520
Brooksville **(G-1206)**
Supliaereos USA LLC ....G...... 727 754-4915
Clearwater **(G-1805)**
Technology Products Design Inc ....F 321 432-3537
Palm Bay **(G-12925)**
Triple Play Cmmunications Corp ....G...... 321 327-8997
Melbourne **(G-8553)**
US Applied Phys Ics Group ....G...... 321 567-7270
Titusville **(G-17625)**

SENSORS: Infrared, Solid State

Drs Ntwork Imaging Systems LLC ....C 321 309-1500
Palm Bay **(G-12897)**
Northrop Grumman Systems Corp ....B 407 295-4010
Apopka **(G-158)**

SENSORS: Radiation

Integrated Sensors LLC ....G...... 419 536-3212
Palm Beach Gardens **(G-12977)**
Tesseract Sensors LLC ....F 407 385-2498
Sanford **(G-15396)**

SENSORS: Temperature, Exc Indl Process

Ckc Industries Inc ....G...... 813 888-9468
Tampa **(G-16709)**

SEPTIC TANK CLEANING SVCS

A & L Septic Tank Products Inc ....G...... 407 273-2149
Orlando **(G-11857)**
Averett Septic Tank Co Inc ....E 863 665-1748
Lakeland **(G-7278)**
Bingham On-Site Sewers Inc ....D 813 659-0003
Dover **(G-3428)**
Miller Brothers Contractors ....F 941 371-4162
Sarasota **(G-15748)**
Monty Sanitation Inc ....G...... 239 597-2486
Naples **(G-10825)**
P & L Creech Inc ....G...... 386 547-4182
Daytona Beach **(G-2579)**

SEPTIC TANKS: Concrete

A & L Septic Tank Products Inc ....G...... 407 273-2149
Orlando **(G-11857)**
Averett Septic Tank Co Inc ....E 863 665-1748
Lakeland **(G-7278)**
Bingham On-Site Sewers Inc ....D 813 659-0003
Dover **(G-3428)**
Dixie Sptic Tank Orange Cy LLC ....E 386 775-3051
Orange City **(G-11805)**
Florida Septic Inc ....E 352 481-2455
Hawthorne **(G-5007)**
Gunter Septic Tank Mfg ....G...... 813 654-1214
Seffner **(G-15962)**
Kt Properties & Dev Inc ....F 386 253-0610
Daytona Beach **(G-2566)**
Miller Brothers Contractors ....F 941 371-4162
Sarasota **(G-15748)**
Monty Sanitation Inc ....G...... 239 597-2486
Naples **(G-10825)**
Pilot Corp of Palm Beaches ....F 561 848-2928
Riviera Beach **(G-14661)**
Rogers Septic Tanks Inc ....G...... 203 259-9947
Port Saint Lucie **(G-14442)**
Sebring Septic Tank Precast Co ....E 863 655-2030
Sebring **(G-15941)**

Stans Septic Svc Con Pdts Inc ....G....... 941 639-3976
Punta Gorda *(G-14533)*

Taylor Concrete Inc ....G....... 941 737-7225
Palmetto *(G-13196)*

Wpr Inc ....E........ 850 626-7713
Milton *(G-10445)*

SEPTIC TANKS: Plastic

All Liquid Envmtl Svcs LLC ....E....... 800 767-9594
Fort Lauderdale *(G-3638)*

Alpha General Services Inc ....E....... 863 382-1544
Sebring *(G-15913)*

P & L Creech Inc ....G....... 386 547-4182
Daytona Beach *(G-2579)*

SEWAGE & WATER TREATMENT EQPT

American Boom and Barrier Inc ....E....... 321 784-2110
Cape Canaveral *(G-1276)*

Bogue Executive Enterprises ....F....... 561 842-5336
Mangonia Park *(G-8090)*

City of Cocoa Beach ....E....... 321 868-3342
Cocoa Beach *(G-1967)*

Dais Corp ....F....... 727 375-8484
Odessa *(G-11547)*

Eco World Water Corp ....G....... 954 599-3672
Fort Lauderdale *(G-3784)*

Enviro-USA American Mfr LLC ....E....... 321 222-9551
Cape Canaveral *(G-1283)*

Pulsafeeder Inc ....D....... 941 575-2900
Punta Gorda *(G-14521)*

Pulsafeeder Spo Inc ....G....... 941 575-3800
Punta Gorda *(G-14522)*

Science of Water LLC ....G....... 904 654-0778
Orange Park *(G-11839)*

Tetra Process Technology ....G....... 813 886-9331
Tampa *(G-17349)*

SEWAGE FACILITIES

Alpha General Services Inc ....E....... 863 382-1544
Sebring *(G-15913)*

SEWAGE TREATMENT SYSTEMS & EQPT

American Engineering Svcs Inc ....G....... 813 621-3932
Plant City *(G-13737)*

Environmental Services ....E....... 727 518-3080
Clearwater *(G-1587)*

Resource Management Associates ......G....... 239 656-0818
Fort Myers *(G-4379)*

SEWER CLEANING EQPT: Power

Gator Drain Cleaning Equipment ....G....... 954 584-4441
Davie *(G-2418)*

Vac-Con Inc ....B....... 904 284-4200
Green Cove Springs *(G-4841)*

SEWING CONTRACTORS

Advanced Sewing ....G....... 954 484-2100
Fort Lauderdale *(G-3626)*

SEWING KITS: Novelty

Dyno LLC ....E....... 954 971-2910
Pompano Beach *(G-14002)*

SEWING MACHINES & PARTS: Indl

Mid West Lettering Company ....E....... 850 477-6522
Pensacola *(G-13553)*

SEWING, NEEDLEWORK & PIECE GOODS STORES: Sewing & Needlework

Looper Sports Connection Inc ....G....... 352 796-7974
Brooksville *(G-1175)*

T-Shirt Express ....G....... 904 448-3761
Jacksonville *(G-6527)*

SEXTANTS

Sextant Marketing LLC ....F....... 800 691-9980
Tampa *(G-17253)*

SHADES: Lamp & Light, Residential

Allure Shades Inc ....F....... 954 543-6259
Lauderhill *(G-7725)*

General Metal Intl Inc ....G....... 305 628-2052
Miramar *(G-10496)*

Morlee Lampshade Co Inc ....E....... 305 500-9310
Miami *(G-9588)*

Stateside Indus Solutions LLC ....E....... 305 301-4052
Miramar *(G-10546)*

SHADES: Lamp Or Candle

Lampshades of Florida Inc ....F....... 954 491-3377
Deerfield Beach *(G-2750)*

SHADES: Window

Aero Shade Technologies Inc ....G....... 772 562-2243
Fort Pierce *(G-4460)*

Aerospace Tech Group Inc ....D....... 561 244-7400
Boca Raton *(G-392)*

Eddy Storm Protection ....G....... 386 248-1631
Daytona Beach *(G-2548)*

SHAFTS: Flexible

American Vulkan Corporation ....E....... 863 324-2424
Winter Haven *(G-18416)*

Schur & Company LLC ....D....... 904 353-8075
Jacksonville *(G-6454)*

SS White Technologies Inc ....C....... 727 626-2800
Saint Petersburg *(G-15196)*

SHAPES & PILINGS, STRUCTURAL: Steel

ABS Structural Corp ....F....... 321 768-2067
Melbourne *(G-8353)*

Dixie Structures & Maintenance ....F....... 205 274-4525
Fort Myers *(G-4236)*

Florida Aluminum and Steel Inc ....F....... 863 967-4191
Auburndale *(G-231)*

Harbor Entps Ltd Lblty Co ....F....... 229 403-0756
Tallahassee *(G-16458)*

Hollywood Iron Works Inc ....F....... 954 962-0556
West Park *(G-18213)*

International Iron Works LLC ....G....... 305 835-0190
Hialeah *(G-5195)*

Mgl Engineering Inc ....E....... 863 648-0320
Lakeland *(G-7394)*

Renovaship Inc ....G....... 954 342-9062
Hallandale Beach *(G-4969)*

SHAPES: Extruded, Aluminum, NEC

Anchor Aluminum Products South ....G....... 305 293-7965
Key West *(G-6853)*

Golden Aluminum Extrusion LLC ....E....... 330 372-2300
Plant City *(G-13773)*

Hydro Precision Tubing USA LLC ....C....... 321 636-8147
Rockledge *(G-14716)*

Plastic and Products Mktg LLC ....F....... 352 867-8078
Ocala *(G-11468)*

Walt Dittmer and Sons Inc ....E....... 407 699-1755
Winter Springs *(G-18581)*

SHEARS

Southern Supply and Mfg Co ....E....... 727 323-7099
Saint Petersburg *(G-15193)*

SHEET METAL SPECIALTIES, EXC STAMPED

Actron Entities Inc ....D....... 727 531-5871
Clearwater *(G-1473)*

Affordable Metal Inc ....F....... 305 691-8082
Hialeah *(G-5033)*

All County Sheet Metal Inc ....G....... 561 588-0099
Lake Worth Beach *(G-7246)*

Arrow Sheet Metal Works Inc ....E....... 813 247-2179
Tampa *(G-16609)*

B & T Metalworks Inc ....E....... 352 236-6000
Ocala *(G-11332)*

Bob Kline Quality Metal Inc ....G....... 561 659-4245
West Palm Beach *(G-17951)*

Bohnert Sheet Metal & Roofg Co ....F....... 305 696-6851
Miami *(G-8843)*

Cornerstone Fabrication LLC ....E....... 386 310-1110
Debary *(G-2633)*

Crown Products Company Inc ....D....... 904 924-8340
Jacksonville *(G-6016)*

Custom Metal Fabricators Inc ....G....... 407 841-8551
Orlando *(G-12068)*

Cwp Sheet Metal Inc ....E....... 407 349-0926
Geneva *(G-4786)*

Electrnic Shtmtl Crftsmen Fla ....E....... 321 727-0633
Melbourne *(G-8418)*

Exact Inc ....C....... 904 783-6640
Jacksonville *(G-6082)*

Florida Storm Panels Inc ....F....... 305 685-9000
Opa Locka *(G-11749)*

Lajoie Investment Corp ....F....... 954 463-3271
Fort Lauderdale *(G-3911)*

Magnus Hitech Industries Inc ....E....... 321 724-9731
Melbourne *(G-8468)*

Masseys Metals ....E....... 813 626-8275
Tampa *(G-17054)*

Miami Tech Inc ....E....... 305 693-7054
Miami *(G-9560)*

MJM Manufacturing Inc ....D....... 305 620-2020
Miami Lakes *(G-10327)*

Pomper Sheet Metal Inc ....F....... 954 492-9717
Oakland Park *(G-11285)*

Precision Fabrication Corp ....F....... 941 488-2474
Nokomis *(G-11052)*

Precision Metal Industries Inc ....D....... 954 942-6303
Pompano Beach *(G-14141)*

Precision Metal Services Inc ....F....... 407 843-3682
Sorrento *(G-16012)*

S P Sheet Metal Co Inc ....F....... 609 698-8800
Jupiter *(G-6790)*

SBs Precision Shtmtl Inc ....F....... 321 951-7411
Melbourne *(G-8516)*

Simar Industries Inc ....F....... 352 622-2287
Ocala *(G-11495)*

Singer Holdings Inc ....F....... 321 724-0900
Melbourne *(G-8523)*

Telese Inc ....E....... 813 752-6015
Plant City *(G-13808)*

Ver-Val Enterprises Inc ....F....... 850 244-7931
Fort Walton Beach *(G-4616)*

Vertec Inc ....F....... 850 478-6480
Pensacola *(G-13620)*

SHEETING: Window, Plastic

Clear-Vue Inc ....E....... 727 726-5386
Safety Harbor *(G-14784)*

SHELL MINING

Blackhawk Construction Co Inc ....F....... 321 258-4957
Vero Beach *(G-17741)*

Charlotte County Min & Mtl Inc ....E....... 239 567-1800
Punta Gorda *(G-14501)*

SHELLAC

Cathodic Prtection Tech of Fla ....G....... 321 799-0046
Cocoa Beach *(G-1966)*

Kiss Polymers LLC ....F....... 813 962-2703
Tampa *(G-16989)*

SHELVING, MADE FROM PURCHASED WIRE

Closetmaid LLC ....D....... 352 351-6100
Ocala *(G-11354)*

SHELVING: Office & Store, Exc Wood

Adapto Storage Products ....E....... 305 887-9563
Hialeah *(G-5027)*

SHIP BUILDING & REPAIRING: Cargo Vessels

Bae Systems Sthast Shpyrds Amh ....B....... 904 251-3111
Jacksonville *(G-5918)*

World Container Services LLC ....E....... 305 400-4850
Doral *(G-3421)*

SHIP BUILDING & REPAIRING: Cargo, Commercial

All Points Boats Inc ....D....... 954 767-8255
Fort Lauderdale *(G-3639)*

Premier Luxury Group LLC ....E....... 954 358-9885
Fort Lauderdale *(G-3995)*

SHIP BUILDING & REPAIRING: Dredges

Florida Dredge and Dock LLC ....E....... 727 942-7888
Tarpon Springs *(G-17472)*

SHIP BUILDING & REPAIRING: Ferryboats

Trident Pontoons Inc ....G....... 352 253-1400
Tavares *(G-17525)*

SHIP BUILDING & REPAIRING: Landing

Merced Industrial Corp ....G....... 908 309-0170
Miami *(G-9533)*

USA Maritime Enterprises Inc ....G 954 764-8360
Fort Lauderdale (G-4113)

SHIP BUILDING & REPAIRING: Lighters, Marine

American Marine Mfg Inc ....G 305 497-7723
Hialeah (G-5049)

SHIP BUILDING & REPAIRING: Patrol Boats

Old City Marine LLC ....G 904 252-6887
Saint Augustine (G-14868)

SHIP BUILDING & REPAIRING: Rigging, Marine

TNT Custom Marine Inc ....G 305 931-3157
Miami (G-10015)
Unlimited Marine Mfg Inc ....G 305 420-6034
Hialeah (G-5396)

SHIP BUILDING & REPAIRING: Tugboats

Progressive Industrial Inc ....F 941 723-0201
Palmetto (G-13187)

SHIP COMPONENTS: Metal, Prefabricated

D W Allen Marine Svcs Inc ....E 904 358-1933
Jacksonville (G-6021)

SHIPBUILDING & REPAIR

A Better Choice Marine LLC ....G 941 264-5019
Sarasota (G-15435)
A Mobile Tech Llc ....G 561 631-4563
Jupiter (G-6675)
Advanced Mechanical Entps Inc ....E 954 764-2678
Fort Lauderdale (G-3625)
Almaco Group Inc ....F 561 558-1600
Boca Raton (G-399)
Amee Bay LLC ....E 904 553-9873
Atlantic Beach (G-203)
Atlantic Dry Dock ....E 904 251-1545
Jacksonville (G-5907)
Atlantic Marine Inc ....G 904 251-1580
Jacksonville (G-5910)
Barnacle King LLC ....G 954 952-9140
Fort Lauderdale (G-3674)
Capt Latham LLC ....G 904 483-6118
Green Cove Springs (G-4820)
Colonna Shipyard ....G 904 246-1183
Atlantic Beach (G-206)
D W Allen Marine Svcs Inc ....E 904 358-1933
Jacksonville (G-6021)
Derecktor Ship Yard ....G 772 595-9326
Fort Pierce (G-4481)
Eastern Shipbuilding Group Inc ....B 850 763-1900
Panama City (G-13256)
Eastern Shipyards Inc ....D 850 763-1900
Panama City (G-13258)
Edison Chouest Offshore ....G 813 241-2165
Tampa (G-16798)
Ellisons Premier Mar Svcs LLC ....G 561 570-9807
Jupiter (G-6721)
Fassmer Service America LLC ....E 305 557-8875
Lauderhill (G-7731)
Fincantieri Marine Repair LLC ....E 904 990-5869
Jacksonville (G-6090)
Gable Enterprises ....F 727 455-5576
Seffner (G-15959)
General Dynamics Corporation ....E 407 380-9384
Orlando (G-12189)
Gulf County Ship Building Inc ....G 850 229-9300
Port Saint Joe (G-14388)
Gulf Marine Repair Corporation ....C 813 247-3153
Tampa (G-16898)
Gulfstream Land Company LLC ....F 772 286-3456
Stuart (G-16159)
Gulfstream Shipbuilding LLC ....G 850 835-5125
Freeport (G-4626)
Hendry Corporation ....D 813 241-9206
Tampa (G-16912)
Hendry Marine Industries Inc ....E 813 241-9206
Tampa (G-16913)
Hydrex LLC ....G 727 443-3900
Clearwater (G-1632)
Integrity Engineering Corp ....G 954 458-0500
Hallandale Beach (G-4951)
International Ship Repair & MA ....F 813 247-1118
Tampa (G-16950)

International Shipyards Ancona ....F 305 371-7722
Fort Lauderdale (G-3881)
M/V Marine Inc ....F 904 633-7992
Jacksonville (G-6268)
Maritime SEC Strtegies Fla LLC ....G 912 704-0300
Tampa (G-17039)
Metalcraft of Pensacola Inc ....G 850 478-8333
Pensacola (G-13551)
Metro Machine Corp ....D 904 249-7772
Jacksonville (G-6302)
Miller Marine Yacht Svc Inc ....E 850 265-6768
Panama City (G-13286)
Model Shipways Inc ....E 800 222-3876
Miami (G-9582)
Naiad Dynamics Us Inc ....E 954 797-7566
Davie (G-2443)
Newcastle Shipyards LLC ....C 386 312-0000
Saint Augustine (G-14860)
Nordic Made Inc ....F 954 651-6208
Davie (G-2447)
Norseman Shipbuilding Corp ....E 305 545-6815
Miami (G-9626)
OSG America LLC ....E 813 209-0600
Tampa (G-17131)
Patti Marine Enterprises Inc ....F 850 453-1282
Pensacola (G-13567)
Port Manatee Ship Repair ....F 941 417-2613
Palmetto (G-13186)
Professional Coating Systems ....G 904 477-7138
Lawtey (G-7746)
Propel Builders Inc ....F 407 960-5116
Maitland (G-8070)
Puma Aero Marine Inc ....G 904 638-5888
Fort Lauderdale (G-4000)
Riverhawk Fast Sea Frames LLC ....G 912 484-3112
Tampa (G-17223)
Rmk Merrill Stevens Prpts LLC ....G 305 324-5211
Miami (G-9813)
Salmi and Company Inc ....G 443 243-8537
Navarre (G-10955)
Seaquest Marine LLC ....E 781 888-8850
Miami (G-9861)
SGS US East Coast LLC ....E 305 571-9700
Miami (G-9874)
Shearwater Marine Fl Inc ....E 772 781-5553
Stuart (G-16216)
Shell Producers Corp ....F 813 247-3153
Tampa (G-17259)
Sisco Marine LLC ....F 850 265-1383
Panama City (G-13309)
Southern Drydock Inc ....F 904 355-9945
Saint Augustine (G-14896)
St Augustine Marina Inc ....E 904 824-4394
Saint Augustine (G-14899)
St Augustine Trawlers Inc ....F 904 824-4394
Saint Augustine (G-14901)
St Johns Ship Building Inc ....C 386 328-6054
Palatka (G-12883)
Superformance Mfg Inc ....G 305 420-6034
Hialeah (G-5372)
Tampa Ship LLC ....B 813 248-9310
Tampa (G-17339)
Tecnico Corporation ....F 904 853-6118
Atlantic Beach (G-216)
United Ship Service Corp ....G 954 583-4588
Fort Lauderdale (G-4108)
Vandalize Boat Works ....G 305 450-2014
Miami (G-10094)

SHIPPING AGENTS

USA Maritime Enterprises Inc ....G 954 764-8360
Fort Lauderdale (G-4113)

SHOCK ABSORBERS: Indl

Mustang Vacuum Systems Inc ....E 941 377-1440
Sarasota (G-15521)

SHOE MATERIALS: Counters

AGM Kitchen & Bath LLC ....G 239 300-4739
Naples (G-10655)
Choice Cabinets & Counters ....G 407 670-8944
Orlando (G-12009)
Counter ....F 239 566-0644
Naples (G-10720)
Counter Impressions LLC ....F 352 589-4966
Eustis (G-3556)
Creative Countertops Inc ....F 904 387-2800
Jacksonville (G-6011)

Jmg Counters LLC ....F 904 551-7006
Jacksonville (G-6226)

SHOE MATERIALS: Heel Parts

Tap Express Inc ....G 305 468-0038
Doral (G-3391)

SHOE MATERIALS: Plastic

Kino Sandals Inc ....F 305 294-5044
Key West (G-6871)

SHOE MATERIALS: Quarters

Advanced Living Quarters Inc ....G 954 684-9392
Pembroke Pines (G-13369)

SHOE MATERIALS: Rands

Ingersoll Rand ....F 954 391-4500
Miramar (G-10504)

SHOE STORES: Orthopedic

Son Life Prsthtics Orthtics In ....F 352 596-2257
Hernando Beach (G-5012)

SHOE STORES: Women's

Lerness Shoe Corp ....G 305 643-6525
Miami (G-9452)

SHOES: Canvas, Rubber Soled

Gold Banner USA Inc ....F 305 576-2215
Miami (G-9224)

SHOES: Men's

Kino Sandals Inc ....F 305 294-5044
Key West (G-6871)
Lerness Shoe Corp ....G 305 643-6525
Miami (G-9452)

SHOES: Men's, Sandals

Zeppelin Products Inc ....F 954 989-8808
Fort Lauderdale (G-4146)

SHOES: Plastic Or Rubber

Protege Media LLC ....G 310 738-9567
Port Saint Lucie (G-14435)

SHOES: Sandals, Rubber

Rebuild Globally Inc ....E 407 801-9936
Lake Worth (G-7231)

SHOES: Women's

Grezzo Usa Llc ....G 954 885-0331
Hollywood (G-5586)
Kino Sandals Inc ....F 305 294-5044
Key West (G-6871)
Kloth Inc ....G 954 578-5687
Sunrise (G-16334)
Lerness Shoe Corp ....G 305 643-6525
Miami (G-9452)
Stush AP USA/Stush Style LLC ....F 404 940-3445
Sunrise (G-16374)

SHOES: Women's, Dress

Cedrick McDonald ....G 813 279-1442
Tampa (G-16689)

SHOES: Women's, Sandals

Zeppelin Products Inc ....F 954 989-8808
Fort Lauderdale (G-4146)

SHOT PEENING SVC

Metal Improvement Company LLC ....G 305 592-5960
Miami (G-9540)

SHOWCASES & DISPLAY FIXTURES: Office & Store

Acryplex Inc ....G 305 633-7636
Miami (G-8648)
Asottu Inc ....F 626 627-6021
Orlando (G-11926)

Caddie Company Inc ....F 267 332-0976
Tampa **(G-16671)**
Gulf Coast Installers LLC ....F 239 273-4663
Bonita Springs **(G-802)**
Synergy Custom Fixtures Corp .....C 305 693-0055
Hialeah **(G-5376)**

SHOWER STALLS: Metal

Martell Glass ....G 786 336-0142
Miami **(G-9514)**
Shower Doors Unlimited Inc ....G 561 547-0702
Boynton Beach **(G-912)**

SHOWER STALLS: Plastic & Fiberglass

AGM Orlando Inc ....G 407 865-9522
Altamonte Springs **(G-29)**
Brian Belitz ....G 407 924-5543
Kissimmee **(G-6901)**
Central Fla Kit Bath Srfces In .....F 352 307-2333
Ocala **(G-11347)**
KDD Inc ....F 239 689-8402
Fort Myers **(G-4304)**
Martell Glass ....G 786 336-0142
Miami **(G-9514)**
Sea Products Inc ....D 904 781-8200
Jacksonville **(G-6458)**
Woodys Enterprises LLC ....F 407 892-1900
Saint Cloud **(G-14941)**

SHREDDERS: Indl & Commercial

Bay Area Security Shred ....F 877 974-7337
Palm Harbor **(G-13102)**
R & R Stone Industries Inc ....G 888 999-4921
Miami **(G-9770)**

SHUTTERS, DOOR & WINDOW: Metal

Aabc Inc ....F 727 434-4444
Largo **(G-7519)**
ABC Shutters Protection Corp .....G 785 547-9527
Miami **(G-8635)**
Adams Hurricane Protection Inc ...F 850 434-2336
Pensacola **(G-13435)**
Addison Metal Additions Inc ....G 305 245-9860
Homestead **(G-5698)**
Advanced Hurricane Protection .....G 772 220-1200
Stuart **(G-16112)**
ANC Shutters LLC ....F 561 966-8336
Lake Worth **(G-7184)**
Anchor Aluminum Products South ...G 305 293-7965
Key West **(G-6853)**
Before Wind Blows LLC ....G 407 977-4833
Chuluota **(G-1464)**
California Shutters Inc ....G 305 827-9333
Miami Lakes **(G-10288)**
Camco Corp ....G 561 427-0433
Jupiter **(G-6699)**
Cat 5 Hurricane Products LLC ......F 941 752-4692
Bradenton **(G-958)**
Eclipse Screen and Shutters ......G 305 216-4716
Miami **(G-9068)**
Eddy Storm Protection ....G 386 248-1631
Daytona Beach **(G-2548)**
Florida Shutters Inc ....E 772 569-2200
Vero Beach **(G-17755)**
Future Modes Inc ....G 305 654-9995
Miami **(G-9180)**
General Impact GL Windows Corp ...F 305 558-8103
Hialeah **(G-5168)**
Guardian Hurricane Protection .....F 305 805-7050
Miami Lakes **(G-10306)**
Hurricane Shutter & Plus Inc ......F 786 287-0007
Miami **(G-9293)**
Jansen Shutters & Spc Ltd ....G 941 484-4700
North Venice **(G-11213)**
Jose Morales Hurricane Shutter ....G 786 315-1835
Miami **(G-9372)**
Lifetime Shutters Inc ....G 407 402-3365
Oviedo **(G-12837)**
Loxahatchee Shutter & Alum Inc ...G 561 513-9581
Loxahatchee **(G-7973)**
Master Alum & SEC Shutter Co .....G 727 725-1744
Safety Harbor **(G-14790)**
Orlando Shutters LLC ....G 407 495-5250
Lake Mary **(G-7098)**
Pinellas Blind and Shutter Inc .....G 727 481-4461
Clearwater **(G-1740)**
Plantation Shutters Inc ....F 772 208-8245
Port Saint Lucie **(G-14432)**

Rollertech Corp ....G 239 645-6698
Fort Myers **(G-4384)**
Rolling Shield Incorporated ....E 305 436-6661
Hialeah Gardens **(G-5449)**
Rolling Shield Parts Inc ....F 305 436-6661
Hialeah Gardens **(G-5450)**
Rollshield LLC ....F 727 441-2243
Clearwater **(G-1771)**
Sano Associates Inc ....G 239 403-2650
Naples **(G-10883)**
Sentinel Inc ....F 239 263-9888
Naples **(G-10889)**
Shoreline Shutter Systems Inc .....G 386 299-2219
Port Orange **(G-14347)**
Shutter Down Storm Protection ....F 813 957-8936
Plant City **(G-13803)**
Shutter Lubrication & Service ......F 561 745-8956
Jupiter **(G-6796)**
Shutter2think Inc ....G 850 291-8301
Palm Beach Gardens **(G-13009)**
Shutterreflections ....G 813 351-9979
Odessa **(G-11577)**
Shutters On Sale Inc ....G 386 756-0009
Port Orange **(G-14348)**
Shuttertek Inc ....G 772 828-6149
Port Saint Lucie **(G-14445)**
Smart Guard Shutters LLC ....G 386 227-6295
Palm Coast **(G-13087)**
Smart Shutters Inc ....G 786 391-1100
Miami **(G-9907)**
Southern Cross Shutter Systems ...G 941 585-2152
Port Charlotte **(G-14315)**
Sun Barrier Products Inc ....F 407 830-9085
Longwood **(G-7951)**
Swfl Hurricane Shutters Inc ....G 239 454-4944
Cape Coral **(G-1395)**
Tropic Shield Inc ....F 954 731-5553
Lauderdale Lakes **(G-7721)**
USA Aluminum ....G 305 303-9121
Hallandale Beach **(G-4982)**
Valco Group Inc ....C 813 870-0482
Tampa **(G-17402)**
Valiant Products Inc ....E 863 688-7998
Lakeland **(G-7469)**
West Coast Shutters Sunburst .....F 727 894-0044
Saint Petersburg **(G-15230)**
West Palm Installers Inc ....F 305 406-3575
Doral **(G-3420)**
Will Shutter U Inc ....F 772 285-3600
Jensen Beach **(G-6659)**

SHUTTERS, DOOR & WINDOW: Plastic

Future Modes Inc ....G 305 654-9995
Miami **(G-9180)**
USA Shutter Company LLC ....G 239 596-8883
Fort Myers **(G-4436)**
Viterra Affordable Shutters ....G 239 738-6364
Cape Coral **(G-1404)**

SHUTTERS: Door, Wood

1st Chice Hrrcane Prtction LLC ....F 239 325-3400
Bonita Springs **(G-778)**
American Louvered Products Co ....F 813 884-1441
Tampa **(G-16589)**
Dependable Shutter Service Inc ....E 954 583-1411
Davie **(G-2404)**
Future Modes Inc ....G 305 654-9995
Miami **(G-9180)**
Guardian Hurricane Protection .....F 305 805-7050
Miami Lakes **(G-10306)**
Hurricane Shtters Cntl Fla Inc .....G 321 639-2622
Rockledge **(G-14715)**
Roy Smith S Screen ....F 561 792-3381
Loxahatchee **(G-7975)**
Shutterman Storm & Security ......E 239 455-9166
Naples **(G-10891)**

SHUTTERS: Window, Wood

Florida Wood Creations Inc ....G 239 561-5411
Punta Gorda **(G-14504)**
Greg Valley ....F 941 739-6628
Sarasota **(G-15487)**
Island Shutter Co Inc ....F 386 738-9455
Deland **(G-2876)**
Ita Inc ....F 386 301-5172
Ormond Beach **(G-12774)**
Orlando Shutters LLC ....G 407 495-5250
Lake Mary **(G-7098)**

W C H Enterprises Inc ....G 239 267-7549
Fort Myers **(G-4444)**

SIDING & STRUCTURAL MATERIALS: Wood

AW Gates Inc ....G 954 341-2180
Coral Springs **(G-2132)**
Innovative Cnstr Group LLC ....E 904 398-5690
Jacksonville **(G-6198)**
Maxville LLC ....C 904 289-7261
Jacksonville **(G-6281)**
Meridian Centre ....G 253 620-4542
Boca Raton **(G-593)**

SIDING MATERIALS

Aluminum Products ....G 904 829-9995
Saint Augustine **(G-14807)**
S&L Cnstrction Specialists Inc .....G 407 300-5080
Orlando **(G-12566)**

SIDING: Precast Stone

Headwaters Incorporated ....E 407 273-9221
Orlando **(G-12212)**
Stonecrfters Archtctral Prcast .....F 727 544-1210
Seminole **(G-15990)**

SIDING: Sheet Metal

Millennium Metals Inc ....E 904 358-8366
Jacksonville **(G-6305)**

SIGN LETTERING & PAINTING SVCS

Productive Products Inc ....G 904 570-5553
Saint Augustine **(G-14875)**

SIGN PAINTING & LETTERING SHOP

Apparel Printers ....G 352 463-8850
Alachua **(G-4)**
Guardfish Enterprises LLC ....G 850 455-4114
Pensacola **(G-13513)**
Kevin Jeffers Inc ....G 352 377-2322
Gainesville **(G-4717)**
Sign Design of Florida Inc ....E 352 787-3882
Leesburg **(G-7793)**

SIGNALS: Railroad, Electric

Alstom Signaling Operation LLC ...C 781 740-8111
Melbourne **(G-8362)**
Interrail Engineering Inc ....E 904 268-6411
Jacksonville **(G-6205)**
United Rail Inc ....F 904 503-9757
Jacksonville **(G-6577)**

SIGNALS: Traffic Control, Electric

City of Ocala ....E 352 622-6803
Ocala **(G-11352)**
North American Signal LLC ....G 850 462-1790
Pensacola **(G-13556)**
North Amrcn Signal Systems LLC ...G 352 376-8341
Gainesville **(G-4739)**
Southwest Signal Inc ....E 813 621-4949
Englewood **(G-3524)**
Traffipax LLC ....B 561 881-7400
Jupiter **(G-6811)**
Transprtation Ctrl Systems Inc .....E 813 630-2800
Tampa **(G-17366)**

SIGNALS: Transportation

Ingram Signalization Inc ....E 850 433-8267
Pensacola **(G-13524)**
International C & C Corp ....E 727 249-0675
Largo **(G-7614)**
Peek Traffic Corporation ....C 941 366-8770
Sarasota **(G-15535)**
Traffic Control Pdts Fla Inc ....E 352 372-7088
Jacksonville **(G-6562)**

SIGNS & ADVERTISING SPECIALTIES

3dfx Inc ....F 407 237-6249
Orlando **(G-11851)**
A Complete Sign Service Inc ....G 407 328-7714
Sanford **(G-15256)**
A J Trophies & Awards Inc ....E 850 878-7187
Tallahassee **(G-16404)**
A Sign ....G 321 264-0077
Titusville **(G-17565)**

A&C Signs Solutions Corp ....F 786 953-5600
  Hialeah *(G-5018)*

Aardvark Sgns Prperty Svcs LLC ....G 407 348-7446
  Kissimmee *(G-6891)*

Abalux Inc ....F 305 698-9192
  Hialeah *(G-5022)*

Abby Press Inc ....E 407 847-5565
  Kissimmee *(G-6892)*

Accuform Global Inc ....F 800 237-1001
  Brooksville *(G-1128)*

Accuform Signs ....F 800 237-1001
  Spring Hill *(G-16060)*

Ace Custom Signs of Winter Pk ....G 407 257-6475
  Winter Park *(G-18481)*

Action Signs & Graphics Inc ....G 386 752-0121
  Lake City *(G-7010)*

ADM II Exhibits & Displays Inc ......F 813 887-1960
  Tampa *(G-16558)*

Aerial Banners Inc ....F 954 893-0099
  Pembroke Pines *(G-13370)*

AG Signs Plus Inc ....G 954 709-8422
  Boca Raton *(G-393)*

All Miami Signs Inc ....F 305 406-2420
  Miami *(G-8690)*

All Venue Graphics and Signs ....G 954 399-7446
  Pompano Beach *(G-13919)*

Allegra Print Signs Mail ....G 954 963-3886
  Hollywood *(G-5526)*

Alli Cats Inc ....G 239 274-0744
  Fort Myers *(G-4165)*

Alternative Sign Group Inc ....G 561 722-9272
  West Palm Beach *(G-17921)*

American Led Technology Inc ....F 850 863-8777
  Naples *(G-10667)*

American Lw & Promo Prods LLC ....G 954 946-5252
  Pompano Beach *(G-13924)*

American Sign Letters ....G 772 643-4012
  Sebastian *(G-15886)*

Anything Display ....G 239 433-9738
  Fort Myers *(G-4178)*

Aonea ....G 561 989-0067
  Boca Raton *(G-411)*

ARC Creative Inc ....G 904 996-7773
  Jacksonville *(G-5896)*

Architctral Sgnage Systems Inc ......G 813 996-6777
  Land O Lakes *(G-7488)*

Architectural Signcrafters ....G 772 600-5032
  Stuart *(G-16117)*

Arrive Alive Traffic Ctrl LLC ....F 407 578-5431
  Orlando *(G-11922)*

Artech ....G 813 929-0754
  Land O Lakes *(G-7489)*

Ash Signs Inc ....G 904 724-7446
  Jacksonville *(G-5904)*

Atlas Sign Industries Fla LLC ....C 561 863-6659
  Riviera Beach *(G-14595)*

Automotive Advertising Assoc ....G 954 389-6500
  Cooper City *(G-2018)*

Axion Signs Inc ....G 954 274-1146
  Oakland Park *(G-11244)*

B & B Signs & Awnings Inc ....G 727 507-0600
  Largo *(G-7542)*

B R Signs Inc ....G 954 973-7700
  Pompano Beach *(G-13944)*

B2b Sign Resource ....G 813 855-7446
  Tampa *(G-16625)*

B4 Enterprises Inc ....G 352 529-1114
  Williston *(G-18330)*

Backyard Canvas & Signs Inc ....G 813 672-2660
  Gibsonton *(G-4794)*

Baron International LLC ....F 800 531-9558
  Jupiter *(G-6688)*

Barrau & Coirin Inc ....G 305 571-5051
  Miami *(G-8801)*

Bayfront Printing Company ....G 727 823-1965
  Saint Petersburg *(G-14979)*

Bdnz Associates Inc ....G 305 379-7993
  Miami *(G-8809)*

Beautiful Mailbox Co ....E 305 403-4820
  Hialeah *(G-5070)*

Big Digital Graphics LLC ....G 561 844-4708
  Lake Park *(G-7122)*

Binca LLC ....F 305 698-8883
  Doral *(G-3138)*

Binick Digital Imaging LLC ....F 786 420-2067
  Miami *(G-8828)*

Binney Family of Florida Inc ....F 727 376-5596
  Odessa *(G-11540)*

Bolt Signs & Marketing LLC ....F 407 865-7446
  Longwood *(G-7876)*

BR Signs International In ....G 954 464-7999
  Coral Springs *(G-2139)*

Brite Lite Tribe ....G 561 250-6824
  Jupiter *(G-6698)*

Bruce R Ely Enterprise Inc ....F 727 573-1643
  Clearwater *(G-1528)*

Buchanan Signs Screen Process .....F 904 725-5500
  Jacksonville *(G-5962)*

Bucks Corporation Inc ....F 850 894-2400
  Tallahassee *(G-16419)*

Bundy Signs LLC ....G 954 296-0784
  Sunrise *(G-16301)*

Business Forward Inc ....G 954 967-6730
  Hollywood *(G-5544)*

C & E Cabinets Design LLC ....G 386 410-4281
  Edgewater *(G-3485)*

C & H Sign Enterprises Inc ....G 407 826-0155
  Orlando *(G-11971)*

C&D Sign and Lighting Svcs LLC .....G 863 937-9323
  Lakeland *(G-7287)*

Calmac Corporation ....G 813 493-8700
  Tampa *(G-16673)*

Cardinal Signs Inc ....G 352 376-8494
  Gainesville *(G-4667)*

Carlaron Inc ....G 386 258-1183
  Daytona Beach *(G-2526)*

Carter Signs Inc ....G 239 543-4004
  Fort Myers *(G-4202)*

Catch One Comm ....G 772 221-0225
  Port Saint Lucie *(G-14403)*

Central Signs Volusia Cnty Inc ....G 386 341-4842
  South Daytona *(G-16019)*

Century Graphics & Metals Inc ....E 407 262-8290
  Altamonte Springs *(G-37)*

Channel Letter USA Corp ....G 561 243-9699
  Delray Beach *(G-2943)*

Charles Thaggard Inc ....G 239 936-8059
  Fort Myers *(G-4206)*

Chiliprint LLC ....G 863 547-6930
  Dundee *(G-3434)*

Chilton Signs & Designs LLC ....G 863 438-0880
  Winter Haven *(G-18432)*

Clari Solutions LLC ....G 813 679-4848
  Brandon *(G-1086)*

Clark Craig Enterprises ....G 813 287-0110
  Tampa *(G-16712)*

Clarks Electrical Signs & Svcs ....G 561 248-5932
  Lake Worth *(G-7191)*

Classic Shirts Inc ....F 850 875-2200
  Quincy *(G-14543)*

Cns Signs Inc ....G 904 733-4806
  Jacksonville *(G-5988)*

Collins Media & Advg LLC ....F 954 688-9758
  Margate *(G-8124)*

Corporate Signs Inc ....G 305 500-9313
  Doral *(G-3174)*

Crazy 4 Signs LLC ....G 813 239-3085
  Zephyrhills *(G-18610)*

Creative Printing Bay Cnty Inc ....F 850 784-1645
  Panama City *(G-13251)*

Creative Sign Designs LLC ....D 800 804-4809
  Tampa *(G-16740)*

Creative Signs Inc ....E 407 293-9393
  Apopka *(G-118)*

Crf Group Inc ....F 954 428-7446
  Pompano Beach *(G-13982)*

Cso Systems Inc ....F 941 355-5653
  Sarasota *(G-15646)*

Custom Sign & Awning ....F 727 210-0941
  Clearwater *(G-1558)*

D & R Signs Inc ....G 386 252-2777
  Daytona Beach *(G-2539)*

D E E Custom Fabricators Inc ....E 863 667-1850
  Lakeland *(G-7302)*

D G Morrison Inc ....F 813 865-0208
  Odessa *(G-11546)*

Dakim Inc ....F 561 790-0884
  Royal Palm Beach *(G-14762)*

Daniels Whl Sign & Plas Inc ....G 386 736-4918
  Sanford *(G-15299)*

Darkhorse Inc ....G 954 849-4440
  Fort Lauderdale *(G-3754)*

Data Graphics Inc ....D 352 589-1312
  Mount Dora *(G-10600)*

David Dobbs Enterprises Inc ....D 904 824-6171
  Saint Augustine *(G-14823)*

Daytona Trophy Inc ....F 386 253-2806
  Daytona Beach *(G-2544)*

Dcp Holdings ....E 863 644-0030
  Lakeland *(G-7305)*

Delconte Packaging Inc ....F 305 885-2800
  Hialeah *(G-5113)*

Design Communications Ltd ....F 407 856-9661
  Orlando *(G-12085)*

Design It Wraps & Graphics LLC .....E 904 310-6032
  Fernandina Beach *(G-3584)*

Designer Sign Systems Inc ....G 954 972-0707
  Fort Lauderdale *(G-3761)*

Designstogo Inc ....G 561 432-1313
  Palm Springs *(G-13144)*

Dgs Retail LLC ....F 727 388-4975
  Saint Petersburg *(G-15025)*

Digiprint & Design Corp ....G 786 464-1770
  Sweetwater *(G-16401)*

Digital Tech of Lakeland Inc ....F 863 668-8770
  Lakeland *(G-7310)*

Dimensional Americas Inc ....G 786 417-9370
  Doral *(G-3194)*

Divinitas Displays LLC ....G 407 660-6625
  Orlando *(G-12100)*

Don Signs Inc ....G 407 344-9444
  Kissimmee *(G-6976)*

Doug Bloodworth Enterprises ....G 407 247-9728
  Lady Lake *(G-6990)*

Dynamic Aspects Inc ....G 407 322-1923
  Debary *(G-2634)*

Eastern Signs LLC ....G 305 542-8274
  Hialeah *(G-5131)*

Easy Rent Inc ....G 904 443-7446
  Jacksonville *(G-6061)*

Easy Signs Inc ....G 954 673-0118
  Oakland Park *(G-11262)*

Econochannel Inc ....E 305 255-2113
  Hialeah *(G-5133)*

Eidolon Analytics Inc ....G 239 288-6951
  Fort Myers *(G-4244)*

Electronic Sign Supply Corp ....G 305 477-0555
  Medley *(G-8235)*

Elite Printing & Marketing Inc ....G 850 474-0894
  Pensacola *(G-13494)*

Emerald Coast Signs ....G 850 398-1712
  Crestview *(G-2243)*

Ernies Signs ....G 239 992-0800
  Bonita Springs *(G-795)*

Everything Communicates Inc ....G 407 578-6616
  Winter Park *(G-18510)*

Exotics Car Wraps ....G 786 768-6798
  Miami *(G-9121)*

F D Signworks LLC ....G 561 248-6323
  West Palm Beach *(G-17993)*

Fast Signs ....F 813 999-4981
  Tampa *(G-16829)*

Fast Signs ....G 239 498-7200
  Bonita Springs *(G-796)*

Fast Signs of Brandon ....G 813 655-9036
  Brandon *(G-1092)*

Fastsigns ....F 305 628-3278
  Miami Lakes *(G-10302)*

Fastsigns ....G 727 341-0084
  Saint Petersburg *(G-15043)*

Fastsigns ....G 305 747-7115
  Coral Gables *(G-2056)*

Fastsigns ....F 305 945-4700
  North Miami Beach *(G-11138)*

Fastsigns ....G 954 404-8341
  Fort Lauderdale *(G-3811)*

Fastsigns ....G 954 416-3434
  Hollywood *(G-5575)*

Fastsigns ....G 407 542-1234
  Oviedo *(G-12821)*

Fastsigns ....G 850 477-9744
  Pensacola *(G-13501)*

Fastsigns 176101 ....F 321 307-2400
  Melbourne *(G-8424)*

Fastsigns2043 ....F 305 988-5264
  Boca Raton *(G-512)*

FDA Signs LLC ....F 904 800-1776
  Saint Augustine *(G-14832)*

Federal Heath Sign Company LLC ...E 817 685-9075
  Daytona Beach *(G-2552)*

Firedrake Inc ....G 813 713-8902
  Zephyrhills *(G-18614)*

Flexofferscom Inc ....G 305 999-9940
  Miami *(G-9151)*

Florida Rdway Grdrail Sgns Inc ....G 561 719-7478
  Lake Park *(G-7126)*

Florida Roadway Signs Inc ....G 561 722-4067
  Lake Park *(G-7127)*

Florida Sign Source ....G 407 316-0466
  Orlando *(G-12167)*

Forge Unlimited Co .... G 727 900-7600	**Jte Inc** .... G 941 925-2605	**Onsight Industries LLC** .... D 407 830-8861
Clearwater *(G-1605)*	Sarasota *(G-15715)*	Sanford *(G-15367)*
Foundry-Mill Ltd .... G 954 467-0287	**Jwn Family Partners LP Ltd** .... G 352 628-4910	**Outdoor Images Central Fla Inc** ... G 407 825-9944
Fort Lauderdale *(G-3829)*	Lecanto *(G-7753)*	Orlando *(G-12459)*
Galea Corporation .... G 305 663-0244	**K & I Plastics Inc** .... G 904 387-0438	**Pacheco Creative Group Inc** .... G 305 541-1400
Miami *(G-9186)*	Jacksonville *(G-6235)*	Miami *(G-9674)*
Georgia Mktg & Sign Co LLC ..... G 800 286-8671	**K R O Enterprises Ltd** .... G 309 797-2213	**Paints N Cocktails Inc** .... F 954 514-7383
West Palm Beach *(G-18016)*	Naples *(G-10795)*	Miami *(G-9680)*
Gillette Sign & Lighting Inc .... G 352 256-2225	**Kay Enterprises** .... G 352 732-5770	**Pattison Sign Lease (us) LLC** ..... G 407 345-8010
Zephyrhills *(G-18616)*	Ocala *(G-11418)*	Orlando *(G-12473)*
Gjcb Signs Graphics Inc .... F 352 429-0803	**Kendall Sign and Design Inc** ...... G 305 595-2000	**Pavement Marking & Signs Inc** ..... G 786 431-6788
Groveland *(G-4860)*	Miami *(G-9389)*	Opa Locka *(G-11781)*
Glow Bench Systems Intl .... G 954 315-4615	**Kids Wood** .... F 407 332-9663	**Phil Rowe Signs Inc** .... G 561 832-8688
Sunrise *(G-16321)*	Longwood *(G-7910)*	West Palm Beach *(G-18120)*
Graph-Plex Corp .... G 772 766-3866	**L R Gator Corporation** .... G 407 578-6616	**Pivotal Sign & Graphics Inc** ...... G 727 462-2266
Sebastian *(G-15894)*	Orlando *(G-12298)*	Clearwater *(G-1742)*
Graphic Banner LLP .... G 954 491-9441	**L4 Design LLC** .... G 224 612-5045	**Pk Group Inc** .... F 239 643-2442
Oakland Park *(G-11269)*	Maitland *(G-8066)*	Naples *(G-10860)*
Graphic Designs Intl Inc .... F 772 287-0000	**Labelpro Inc** .... F 727 538-2149	**Plastic Art Sign Company Inc** ..... F 850 455-4114
Stuart *(G-16156)*	Clearwater *(G-1670)*	Pensacola *(G-13577)*
Graphic Difference Inc A .... G 954 748-6990	**Lambs Signs Inc** .... F 941 792-4453	**Platinum Signs and Design LLC** .... G 407 971-3640
Lauderhill *(G-7733)*	Bradenton *(G-1002)*	Casselberry *(G-1430)*
Graphic Images Inc .... F 954 984-0015	**Laporte Inv Holdings Inc** .... G 863 294-4498	**Poblocki Sign Co Southeast LLC** ... G 407 660-3174
Pompano Beach *(G-14044)*	Winter Haven *(G-18449)*	Orlando *(G-12493)*
Graphic Installers Inc .... G 863 646-5543	**Lcr Signs & Services** .... G 772 882-5276	**Poli Group Intl Inc** .... F 305 468-8986
Lakeland *(G-7339)*	Port Saint Lucie *(G-14422)*	Miami *(G-9726)*
Graphic Sign Dsgin Cntl Fla LL .. G 386 547-4569	**Liquid Soul Dgtal Graphics LLC** ... G 407 948-6973	**Precision Auto Tint Dsign Corp** ... G 727 385-8788
Daytona Beach *(G-2557)*	Orlando *(G-12334)*	Tarpon Springs *(G-17488)*
Graphics Designer Inc .... F 561 687-7993	**Local Biz Spot Inc** .... G 866 446-1790	**Premier Printing Signs** .... G 727 849-2493
West Palm Beach *(G-18019)*	Wesley Chapel *(G-17881)*	Port Richey *(G-14371)*
Graphics Pdts Excellence Inc .... F 813 884-1578	**Lsj Corp** .... G 954 920-0905	**Premier Sign & Service Inc** .... G 239 258-6979
Wesley Chapel *(G-17878)*	Hollywood *(G-5616)*	Lehigh Acres *(G-7822)*
Great Bay Signs Inc .... G 727 437-1091	**Lucke Enterprises Inc** .... G 727 797-1177	**Print Signs & Banners** .... G 305 600-1349
Indian Shores *(G-5810)*	Clearwater *(G-1676)*	Miami *(G-9744)*
Greathouse Signs LLC .... G 407 247-2668	**Lucke Group Inc** .... G 727 525-4949	**Priority 1 Signs** .... G 954 971-8689
Apopka *(G-136)*	Saint Petersburg *(G-15114)*	Deerfield Beach *(G-2789)*
Greyfield Holdings Inc .... G 407 927-4476	**M & M Signs** .... G 904 381-7353	**Professional Signs** .... G 305 662-5957
Winter Springs *(G-18566)*	Jacksonville *(G-6267)*	Miami *(G-9751)*
Greyson Corp .... F 407 830-7443	**M&D Signs** .... G 561 296-3636	**Quick Advertising Inc** .... F 407 774-0003
Longwood *(G-7900)*	West Palm Beach *(G-18061)*	Apopka *(G-166)*
Guardfish Enterprises LLC .... G 850 455-4114	**Major League Signs Inc** .... G 954 600-5505	**R & A Power Graphics Inc** .... F 407 898-5770
Pensacola *(G-13513)*	Hialeah *(G-5236)*	Orlando *(G-12523)*
Gulf Coast Business World Inc ... F 850 864-1511	**Max Graphix LLC** .... G 904 408-1543	**Raimonda Investment Group Inc** .... G 352 347-8899
Fort Walton Beach *(G-4590)*	Macclenny *(G-8038)*	Belleview *(G-366)*
Guthman Signs LLC .... G 941 218-0014	**McColl Display Solutions** .... G 813 333-6613	**Rapid Signs and T Shirts** .... G 786 486-2804
Bradenton *(G-989)*	Windermere *(G-18361)*	Homestead *(G-5736)*
Heritage Signs .... G 904 529-7446	**McGrail Signs & Graphics LLC** ..... G 850 435-1017	**Ricks Quality Prtg & Signs** ...... G 321 504-7446
Green Cove Springs *(G-4829)*	Pensacola *(G-13954)*	Cocoa *(G-1954)*
Hermes 7 Communications LLC ..... F 954 426-1998	**McKenny Printing Entp Inc** .... G 727 420-4944	**River City Advg Objectional** ...... G 904 731-3452
Deerfield Beach *(G-2733)*	Saint Petersburg *(G-15125)*	Jacksonville *(G-6425)*
Hit Promotional Products Inc .... B 727 541-5561	**MGM Cargo Inc** .... G 407 770-1500	**Rocket Sign Supplies LLC** .... G 239 995-4684
Largo *(G-7605)*	Orlando *(G-12377)*	Fort Myers *(G-4383)*
HOB Corporation .... G 813 988-2272	**Miami Banners & Signs Inc** .... G 305 262-4460	**Royal Atlantic Ventures LLC** ...... G 561 243-9699
Tampa *(G-16919)*	Miami *(G-9545)*	Delray Beach *(G-3013)*
Holmes Stamp Company .... E 904 396-2291	**Miami Sign Shop Inc** .... G 305 431-2455	**RPM Graphics Inc** .... G 239 275-3278
Jacksonville *(G-6183)*	North Miami Beach *(G-11150)*	Lehigh Acres *(G-7824)*
Honchin Inc .... G 305 235-3800	**Miller Signs LLC** .... G 786 395-9420	**Sam Weiss Woodworking Inc** .... G 954 975-8158
Cutler Bay *(G-2291)*	Hollywood *(G-5627)*	Margate *(G-8153)*
Human Sign .... G 239 573-4292	**Milliken & Milliken Inc** .... E 941 474-0223	**Sapphire LLC** .... G 561 346-7449
Cape Coral *(G-1357)*	Englewood *(G-3534)*	Greenacres *(G-4853)*
Hunt RDS Inc .... F 813 249-7551	**Mobile Sign Service Inc** .... G 954 579-8628	**Sarasota Signs and Visuals** .... G 941 355-5746
Oldsmar *(G-11657)*	Coconut Creek *(G-1999)*	Sarasota *(G-15816)*
I2k Digital Solutions LLC .... F 305 507-0707	**Monsta Performance Inc** .... G 321 848-7256	**Saul Signs Inc** .... F 305 266-8484
Miami *(G-9296)*	Melbourne *(G-8477)*	Medley *(G-8319)*
Image 360 .... G 561 395-0745	**Mr Graphic Prtg & Signs LLC** ...... G 561 424-1724	**Sb Signs Inc** .... G 561 688-9100
Boca Raton *(G-541)*	West Palm Beach *(G-18081)*	West Palm Beach *(G-18148)*
Imprint Promotions LLC .... G 321 622-8946	**Mwr Sign Enterprises Inc** .... G 954 914-2709	**Screen Process Printers Inc** ...... G 904 354-8708
Melbourne *(G-8441)*	Pembroke Pines *(G-13407)*	Jacksonville *(G-6457)*
Infinity Signs & Graphix LLC .... F 407 270-6733	**N & N Investment Corporation** ..... E 954 590-3800	**Sebco Industries Inc** .... G 954 566-8500
Orlando *(G-12243)*	Pompano Beach *(G-14106)*	Oakland Park *(G-11292)*
Inklab Signs Inc .... G 786 430-8100	**National Direct Signs LLC** .... E 561 320-2102	**Seminole Sign Company LLC** .... G 863 623-6600
Miami *(G-9314)*	West Palm Beach *(G-18084)*	Okeechobee *(G-11617)*
International Sign Design Corp ... E 727 541-5573	**National Sign Inc** .... F 727 572-1503	**Seminole State Signs & Ltg** .... G 954 316-6030
Largo *(G-7615)*	Clearwater *(G-1711)*	Davie *(G-2474)*
Island Life Graphics Inc .... G 904 206-6997	**Nauset Enterprises Inc** .... G 727 443-3469	**Sep Communications LLC** .... F 561 998-0870
Fernandina Beach *(G-3588)*	Clearwater *(G-1713)*	Boca Raton *(G-669)*
Island Life Graphics Inc .... E 904 261-0340	**New Vision Signs Corp** .... G 786 514-6822	**Shipping + Business Svcs LLC** ..... G 904 240-1737
Fernandina Beach *(G-3589)*	Miami *(G-9614)*	Jacksonville *(G-6465)*
J R Wheeler Corporation .... G 954 585-8950	**Nine Enterprises Inc** .... G 904 998-8880	**Shirts & Caps Inc** .... F 813 788-7026
Fort Lauderdale *(G-3890)*	Jacksonville *(G-6334)*	Tampa *(G-17262)*
Jay Berry Signs .... G 352 805-4050	**Nitesol Inc** .... G 407 557-4042	**Sign & Vehicle Wraps Inc** .... G 407 859-8631
Leesburg *(G-7781)*	Orlando *(G-12419)*	Orlando *(G-12600)*
Jbjb Holdings LLC .... G 239 267-1975	**Novus Clip Signs & Video Prod** .... G 239 471-5639	**Sign A Rama** .... G 954 796-1644
Fort Myers *(G-4296)*	Fort Myers *(G-4344)*	Coral Springs *(G-2212)*
JCP Signs Inc .... G 305 790-5336	**Nu-Art Signs Inc** .... G 305 531-9850	**Sign A Rama** .... G 813 264-0022
Miami *(G-9361)*	Miami *(G-9634)*	Tampa *(G-17263)*
Joni Industries Inc .... F 352 799-5456	**Omega Sign Service Corporation** ... F 727 505-7833	**Sign A Rama Inc** .... E 561 640-5570
Brooksville *(G-1166)*	New Port Richey *(G-10978)*	West Palm Beach *(G-18152)*
Jpl Associates Inc .... F 954 929-6024	**On-Site Lighting & Sign Svcs** ..... G 256 693-1018	**Sign A Rama Inc** .... G 904 998-8880
Hallandale Beach *(G-4955)*	Pensacola *(G-13561)*	Jacksonville *(G-6468)*

2022 Harris Florida
Manufacturers Directory

(G-0000) Company's Geographic Section entry number

Sign and Design Depot LLC ....G...... 239 995-7446
North Fort Myers (G-11069)

Sign Design and Creations ....G...... 954 724-2884
Margate (G-8154)

Sign Design of Florida Inc ....E...... 352 787-3882
Leesburg (G-7793)

Sign Development Corporation ....G...... 305 227-6250
Miami (G-9884)

Sign Graphix Inc ....G...... 954 571-7131
Deerfield Beach (G-2809)

Sign Man Inc ....G...... 321 259-1703
Melbourne (G-8521)

Sign On LLC ....F...... 239 800-9454
Cape Coral (G-1385)

Sign Pro America ....F...... 412 908-9832
Jacksonville (G-6469)

Sign Rockers LLC ....E...... 866 212-9697
Miami (G-9885)

Sign Savers Corp ....G...... 305 909-9967
Miami (G-9886)

Sign Space ....G...... 786 360-2670
Miami (G-9887)

Sign Stapler ....G...... 800 775-3971
Orlando (G-12603)

Sign Tech Inc ....G...... 941 575-1349
Punta Gorda (G-14531)

Sign Up Now Sign Company LLC ....G...... 754 224-9091
Pompano Beach (G-14177)

Sign Wizard ....G...... 352 365-6922
Fruitland Park (G-4642)

Signage Pro LLC ....G...... 813 671-4272
Riverview (G-14577)

Signarama ....G...... 239 997-1644
North Fort Myers (G-11070)

Signarama Dwntwn Fort Lderdale ....F...... 954 990-4749
Fort Lauderdale (G-4047)

Signarama Naples ....G...... 239 330-3737
Naples (G-10893)

Signarama-Sarasota ....G...... 941 554-8798
Sarasota (G-15826)

Signcraft LLC ....G...... 561 543-0034
Wellington (G-17864)

Signcraft & More Inc ....G...... 386 755-4754
Lake City (G-7044)

Signcraft Publishing Co Inc ....F...... 239 939-4644
Fort Myers (G-4399)

Signpost LLC ....G...... 813 334-7678
Maitland (G-8073)

Signs 2 Sell LLC ....G...... 850 277-0518
Panama City (G-13306)

Signs 2 U Inc ....G...... 305 227-6250
Miami (G-9888)

Signs By Akos LLC ....G...... 941 625-6845
Port Charlotte (G-14314)

Signs Connection Inc ....G...... 305 978-5777
Miami (G-9889)

Signs International Distr Corp ....G...... 305 715-0017
Miami (G-9891)

Signs Now ....G...... 386 238-5507
Daytona Beach (G-2599)

Signs Now ....F...... 727 524-8500
Largo (G-7683)

Signs Now ....G...... 850 383-6500
Tallahassee (G-16499)

Signs Now Inc ....G...... 407 628-2410
Winter Park (G-18535)

Signs Now of Brandon Inc ....G...... 813 684-0047
Brandon (G-1108)

Signs Now St Augustine Inc ....G...... 904 810-5838
Saint Augustine (G-14892)

Signs of America Tampa Corp ....G...... 813 243-9243
Tampa (G-17268)

Signs of Reilly ....G...... 954 263-7829
Pompano Beach (G-14178)

Signs of Tampa Bay LLC ....E...... 813 526-0484
Lutz (G-8015)

Signs of Time Inc ....G...... 772 240-9590
Stuart (G-16219)

Signs Plus New IDS-New Tech In ....F...... 941 378-4262
Sarasota (G-15827)

Signs Supreme Inc ....G...... 561 795-0111
Wellington (G-17865)

Signs Unlimited - Sea Inc ....F...... 352 732-7341
Ocala (G-11494)

Signs Unlimited Inc ....G...... 727 845-0330
Saint Augustine (G-14893)

Signs Usa Inc ....F...... 813 901-9333
Tampa (G-17269)

Signsations Inc ....G...... 561 989-1900
Boca Raton (G-675)

Signsitecom Inc ....G...... 386 487-0265
Lake City (G-7045)

Signsourse USA Incorporated ....G...... 954 561-1234
Fort Lauderdale (G-4048)

Sitecrafters of Florida Inc ....E...... 813 258-4696
Tampa (G-17270)

Skylite Signs & Services Inc ....G...... 305 362-5015
Hialeah (G-5350)

Slaton & Sons Enterprises Inc ....G...... 561 308-7187
Port Saint Lucie (G-14447)

Smart Signs Inc ....G...... 754 701-8910
Davie (G-2479)

Sneids Inc ....G...... 561 278-7446
Delray Beach (G-3019)

Solar Enterprises Inc ....E...... 904 724-2262
Jacksonville (G-6478)

Southeastern Ltg Solutions ....G...... 386 238-1711
Daytona Beach (G-2601)

Southern Exhibits Graphics Inc ....G...... 407 423-2860
Orlando (G-12614)

Sp Sign LLC ....F...... 772 562-0955
Stuart (G-16226)

Spectrum Signworks LLC ....G...... 239 908-0505
Naples (G-10903)

Speed Pro Miami ....G...... 954 534-9503
Miramar (G-10545)

Speedpro Imaging St Petersburg ....G...... 727 266-0956
Saint Petersburg (G-15195)

Speedysigns Com Inc ....E...... 386 755-2006
Lake City (G-7046)

Sposen Signature Homes LLC ....F...... 239 244-8886
Cape Coral (G-1392)

Srq Sign Partners LLC ....G...... 941 357-0319
Sarasota (G-15558)

St Lucie Signs LLC ....G...... 772 971-6363
Fort Pierce (G-4533)

Stellar Signs Grap ....G...... 561 721-6060
West Palm Beach (G-18163)

Steven Chancas ....G...... 352 629-5016
Ocala (G-11499)

Street Signs USA Inc ....G...... 561 848-1411
Lake Park (G-7134)

Sun Graphic Technologies Inc ....E...... 941 753-7541
Sarasota (G-15562)

Suncoast Investmens of PA ....G...... 941 722-5391
Palmetto (G-13194)

Suncoast Sign Shop Inc ....G...... 941 448-5835
Sarasota (G-15843)

Sunray Reflections Inc ....G...... 305 305-6350
Hollywood (G-5666)

Superior Signs Inc ....F...... 407 601-7964
Orlando (G-12639)

Szabo Pos Displays Inc ....G...... 941 778-0192
Bradenton (G-1057)

T & C Godby Enterprises Inc ....F...... 407 831-6334
Casselberry (G-1434)

Tattoo Factory Inc ....E...... 941 923-4110
Sarasota (G-15850)

Thomas United Inc ....G...... 239 561-7446
Fort Myers (G-4422)

Tigo Inc ....E...... 954 935-5990
Weston (G-18292)

Tone Printing LLC ....G...... 855 505-8663
Miami (G-10022)

Total Sign Solutions ....G...... 561 264-2551
Riviera Beach (G-14684)

Trademark Signs LLC ....G...... 954 859-6220
Deerfield Beach (G-2827)

Traffic Control Pdts Fla Inc ....E...... 352 372-7088
Jacksonville (G-6562)

Tropical Signs & Graphics ....G...... 321 458-7742
Merritt Island (G-8601)

Ufg Group Inc ....G...... 561 425-6829
West Palm Beach (G-18190)

Unique Led Products LLC ....G...... 440 520-4959
North Port (G-11205)

Unisigns Usa Inc ....G...... 305 509-5232
Doral (G-3407)

United Visual Branding LLC ....D...... 813 855-3300
Oldsmar (G-11702)

Universal Signs ....G...... 954 366-1535
Fort Lauderdale (G-4110)

US Sign and Mill Inc ....E...... 239 936-9154
Fort Myers (G-4435)

Van Gogh Signs & Displays ....G...... 813 849-7446
Tampa (G-17403)

Vintage Art and Sign LLC ....G...... 770 815-7887
Niceville (G-11039)

Vinyl Bros ....G...... 850 396-5977
Gulf Breeze (G-4896)

Vinyl Etchings Inc ....G...... 727 845-5300
Port Richey (G-14384)

Vinyl Lettering and Signs ....G...... 239 537-7355
Naples (G-10935)

Vinylize Creation LLC ....G...... 954 478-3172
Miramar (G-10561)

Vista System LLC ....E...... 941 365-4646
Sarasota (G-15868)

Visual Signs LLC ....G...... 407 693-0200
Orlando (G-12701)

Vivid Images USA Inc ....F...... 904 620-0303
Jacksonville (G-6594)

Vizcom Enterprises Llc ....G...... 407 324-8338
Sanford (G-15405)

Volunteer Capital LLC ....G...... 954 366-6659
Deerfield Beach (G-2832)

Waterboyz-Wbz Inc ....F...... 850 433-2929
Pensacola (G-13624)

Way Bright Sign Systems ....G...... 615 480-4602
Santa Rosa Beach (G-15434)

We Sign It Inc ....G...... 561 310-2542
Port Saint Lucie (G-14466)

We Sign It Inc ....F...... 772 800-7373
Port Saint Lucie (G-14467)

West Coast Signs Inc ....G...... 941 755-5686
Bradenton (G-1077)

White Sands Dmg Inc ....G...... 305 947-7731
North Miami Beach (G-11170)

White Sign Company LLC ....G...... 407 342-7887
Debary (G-2645)

Wholesale Sign Superstore Inc ....G...... 321 212-8458
Rockledge (G-14755)

Wildner Sign & Paint Co ....G...... 239 997-5155
Cape Coral (G-1408)

Windstone Development Intl Lc ....F...... 954 370-7201
Davie (G-2499)

Wrap Installers Inc ....G...... 407 404-2914
Debary (G-2646)

Xtreme Signs & Printing Inc ....G...... 321 438-3954
Orlando (G-12723)

Yesco Orlando South ....G...... 407 922-5856
Kissimmee (G-6973)

Yesco Sign and Lighting ....G...... 407 321-3577
Sanford (G-15412)

Ysl Graphics LLC ....G...... 954 916-7255
Sunrise (G-16394)

Z & L Partners Inc ....G...... 813 639-0066
Tampa (G-17454)

Zebra Stripes Inc ....G...... 561 685-0654
Dania (G-2347)

Zoo Holdings LLC ....G...... 941 355-5653
Sarasota (G-15882)

SIGNS & ADVERTISING SPECIALTIES: Artwork, Advertising

DSign Solutions Inc ....G...... 786 447-4165
Miami (G-9053)

Royal Foam US LLC ....E...... 904 345-5400
Jacksonville (G-6434)

Tribune Media Services Inc ....D...... 407 420-6200
Orlando (G-12671)

SIGNS & ADVERTISING SPECIALTIES: Novelties

Ataly Inc ....E...... 813 880-9142
Tampa (G-16614)

Bullet Line LLC ....C...... 305 623-9223
Hialeah (G-5083)

Delray Pin Factory Intl Inc ....G...... 561 994-1680
Casselberry (G-1415)

Ellis Family Holdings Inc ....F...... 503 785-7400
Hialeah (G-5139)

Inflatable Design Works Corp ....F...... 786 242-1049
Miami (G-9313)

Laser Creations Incorporated ....E...... 800 771-7151
Apopka (G-146)

Lorente International LLC ....E...... 877 281-6469
Seminole (G-15981)

Process Automation Corporation ....G...... 727 541-6280
Pinellas Park (G-13724)

Promo Daddy LLC ....F...... 877 557-2336
Melbourne (G-8501)

Promo Daddy LLC ....E...... 352 390-3081
Melbourne (G-8502)

Put Your Name On It LLC ....G...... 813 972-1460
Tampa (G-17195)

Ross Industries Inc ....D...... 954 752-2800
Pompano Beach (G-14162)

PRODUCT

SIGNS & ADVERTISING SPECIALTIES: Signs

AC Signs LLC ....E 407 857-5565
Orlando (G-11863)

Accuform Manufacturing Inc ....B 352 799-5434
Brooksville (G-1129)

Ad America ....G 904 781-5900
Jacksonville (G-5858)

Allen Industries Inc ....D 727 573-3076
Clearwater (G-1487)

Annat Inc ....F 239 262-4639
Naples (G-10669)

Architectural Graphics Inc ....F 757 427-1900
Clearwater (G-1497)

ASAP Signs & Graphics of Fla ......G 727 443-4878
Clearwater (G-1501)

Banks Sign Systems Inc ....G 954 979-0055
Pompano Beach (G-13947)

Banners-N-Signs Etc Inc ....G 904 272-3395
Orange Park (G-11815)

Boardwalk Designs Inc ....G 850 265-0988
Lynn Haven (G-8026)

Boca Signworks ....G 561 393-6010
Boca Raton (G-439)

C & S Graphics Inc ....G 813 251-4411
Tampa (G-16667)

Classic Design and Mfg ....G 850 433-4981
Pensacola (G-13471)

Compliancesigns LLC ....G 800 578-1245
Brooksville (G-1148)

Custom Illusionz ....G 386 330-5245
Live Oak (G-7844)

Cutting Edge Sgns Grphics of P .....G 727 546-3700
Clearwater (G-1559)

Delivery Signs LLC ....G 407 362-7896
Orlando (G-12082)

Dgs Retail LLC ....C 727 388-4975
Saint Petersburg (G-15024)

Dragonfire Industries Inc ....G 407 999-2215
Orlando (G-12105)

Finlayson Enterprises Inc ....G 850 785-7953
Panama City (G-13262)

First Sign Corp ....F 954 972-7222
Pompano Beach (G-14022)

Glomaster Signs Inc ....G 772 464-0718
Fort Pierce (G-4492)

Go Mobile Signs ....G 239 245-7803
Fort Myers (G-4269)

H & H Signs Inc ....G 941 485-0556
Venice (G-17696)

Innovative Signs Inc ....G 407 830-5155
Sanford (G-15338)

International Quiksigns Inc ....F 954 462-7446
Fort Lauderdale (G-3880)

James Testa ....F 954 962-5840
Hollywood (G-5604)

Kemp Signs Inc ....F 561 840-6382
Mangonia Park (G-8096)

L4 Design LLC ....E 407 262-8200
Maitland (G-8065)

Mag-Tags Inc ....G 850 294-1809
Tallahassee (G-16473)

McCain Sales of Florida Inc ....E 772 461-0665
Fort Pierce (G-4506)

National Traffic Signs Inc ....G 727 446-7983
Clearwater (G-1712)

Nite-Bright Sign Company Inc ....E 239 466-2616
Fort Myers (G-4340)

Oakhurst Marketing Inc ....G 727 532-8255
Saint Petersburg (G-15144)

Pensacola Sign & Graphics Inc ....G 850 433-7878
Pensacola (G-13571)

Pope Enterprises Inc ....F 850 729-7446
Niceville (G-11035)

Productive Products Inc ....G 904 570-5553
Saint Augustine (G-14875)

Reddi Sign Corporation ....G 904 757-0680
Jacksonville (G-6408)

S & S Metal and Plastics Inc ....E 904 731-4655
Jacksonville (G-6440)

Sanbur Inc ....F 941 371-7446
Sarasota (G-15807)

Sign Partners Inc ....G 561 270-6919
Boca Raton (G-672)

Sign Producers Inc ....E 407 855-8864
Orlando (G-12602)

Sign Solutions of Tampa Bay ....G 813 269-5990
Tampa (G-17264)

Sign Systems Grphic Dsigns Inc .....G,.... 813 281-2400
Tampa (G-17265)

Sign-O-Saurus Daytona Inc ....G 386 322-5222
South Daytona (G-16028)

Sign-O-Saurus Inc ....G 407 677-8965
Casselberry (G-1433)

Signature Signs Inc ....F 727 725-1044
Safety Harbor (G-14796)

Signway Inc ....G 407 696-7446
Winter Park (G-18536)

Suncoast Signs Inc ....G 813 664-0699
Tampa (G-17314)

Superior Unlimited Entps Inc ....G 863 294-1683
Winter Haven (G-18472)

Universal 3d Innovation Inc ....F 516 837-9423
Miramar (G-10558)

Vital Signs of Orlando Inc ....G 407 297-0680
Orlando (G-12703)

Zeeeees Corporation ....G 407 624-3796
Saint Cloud (G-14942)

SIGNS & ADVERTSG SPECIALTIES: Displays/Cutouts Window/Lobby

Artistic Adventures Inc ....G 407 297-0557
Orlando (G-11925)

Bass Industries Inc ....E 305 751-2716
Hialeah (G-5068)

Bay Area Signs Inc ....F 813 677-0237
Plant City (G-13745)

D I H Corporation ....G 561 881-8705
Riviera Beach (G-14613)

Fiero Enterprises Inc ....F 954 454-5004
Hallandale Beach (G-4944)

Graph-Plex Inc ....G 954 920-0905
Hollywood (G-5583)

Pro-Ad Media Inc ....G 863 802-5043
Lakeland (G-7413)

Sdm Acquisition Corporation ....G 954 462-1919
Fort Lauderdale (G-4041)

SIGNS, EXC ELECTRIC, WHOLESALE

River City Advg Objectional ....G 904 731-3452
Jacksonville (G-6425)

Sign Depot Co ....F 407 894-0090
Orlando (G-12601)

Signsource USA Incorporated ....G 954 561-1234
Fort Lauderdale (G-4048)

Suncoast Signs Inc ....G 813 664-0699
Tampa (G-17314)

Superior Signs Inc ....F 407 601-7964
Orlando (G-12639)

SIGNS: Electrical

A 1 A Signs & Service Inc ....G 305 757-6950
Miami (G-8616)

A A A Signs Inc ....G 813 949-8397
Lutz (G-7978)

Acolite Claude Untd Sign Inc ....E 305 362-3333
Doral (G-3093)

Acolite Sign Company Inc ....G 305 362-3333
Doral (G-3094)

Amerisigns ....F 407 492-5644
Orlando (G-11907)

Apple Sign & Awning LLC ....F 813 948-2220
Lutz (G-7983)

Art Sign Co Inc ....D 954 763-4410
Fort Lauderdale (G-3659)

Art-Kraft Sign Co Inc ....E 321 727-7324
Palm Bay (G-12887)

B&C Signs ....G 386 426-2373
Edgewater (G-3479)

Bengis Signs Inc ....G 305 592-3860
Hialeah Gardens (G-5431)

Berry Signs Inc ....G 321 631-6150
Rockledge (G-14691)

Brite Lite Service Company ....F 904 398-5305
Jacksonville (G-5957)

Broward Signs ....G 954 320-9903
Fort Lauderdale (G-3706)

Bryson of Brevard Inc ....E 321 636-5116
Rockledge (G-14694)

Budget Signs Inc ....F 954 941-5710
Pompano Beach (G-13957)

C & S Signs Inc ....G 850 983-9540
Milton (G-10421)

C L F Enterprises ....G 305 643-3222
Miami (G-8870)

Cadillac Graphics Inc ....G 954 772-2440
Oakland Park (G-11249)

Central Signs LLC ....F 386 322-7446
Daytona Beach (G-2528)

Channel Letter Network Corp ....F 305 594-3360
Miami (G-8919)

Coastline Whl Sgns Led Disp LL ....F 386 238-6200
Daytona Beach (G-2530)

Coastline Whl Signs Svcs Ltd ....F 386 238-6200
Daytona Beach (G-2531)

Corporate Signs Inc ....G 305 500-9313
Doral (G-3173)

Custom Graphics & Sign Design ....G 904 264-7667
Orange Park (G-11822)

Digital Outdoor LLC ....E 305 944-7945
Doral (G-3192)

Dixie Signs Inc ....E 863 644-3521
Lakeland (G-7311)

Don Bell Signs LLC ....D 800 824-0080
Port Orange (G-14332)

Dvc Signs LLC ....G 727 524-8543
Largo (G-7575)

Erimark Electric Sign Co Inc ....G 954 423-1364
Opa Locka (G-11743)

Express Signs & Graphics Inc ....F 407 889-4433
Winter Garden (G-18385)

Ferrin Signs Inc ....E 561 802-4242
West Palm Beach (G-17995)

Forever Signs Inc ....F 305 885-3411
Hialeah (G-5160)

Freeman Electric Co Inc ....F 850 785-7448
Panama City (G-13265)

Fresh Ink Print LLC ....G 407 412-5905
Orlando (G-12175)

General Sign Service Inc ....F 904 355-5630
Jacksonville (G-6140)

General Signs and Service Inc ....G 904 372-4238
Atlantic Beach (G-209)

Gould Signs Inc ....G 772 221-1218
Stuart (G-16155)

Greyfield Holdings Inc ....F 407 830-8861
Sanford (G-15328)

Gulf Coast Signs Sarasota Inc ....G 941 355-8841
Sarasota (G-15696)

Guy Wingo Signs ....F 407 578-1132
Apopka (G-138)

Hanes-Harris Design Cons ....G 813 237-0202
Tampa (G-16904)

Himes Signs Inc ....F 850 837-1159
Destin (G-3070)

International Signs & Ltg Inc ....F 407 332-9663
Longwood (G-7905)

Interstate Signcrafters LLC ....D 561 547-3760
Boynton Beach (G-881)

J D M Corp ....G 305 947-5876
Doral (G-3264)

Jayco Signs Inc ....F 407 339-5252
Maitland (G-8062)

Kenco - 2000 Inc ....G 386 672-1590
Daytona Beach (G-2565)

Kenco Signs Awning LLC ....F 386 672-1590
Holly Hill (G-5515)

Kendal Signs Inc ....E 321 636-5116
Rockledge (G-14724)

Kevin Jeffers Inc ....G 352 377-2322
Gainesville (G-4717)

Lee Designs Llc ....F 239 278-4245
Fort Myers (G-4311)

Machin Signs Inc ....G 305 694-0464
Miami (G-9495)

Metro Signs Inc ....E 954 410-4343
Hollywood (G-5626)

Micole Electric Sign Company ....G 954 796-4293
Coral Springs (G-2187)

Modulex Miami LLC ....F 786 424-0857
Miami (G-9584)

Olympian Led Inc ....E 321 747-3220
Titusville (G-17603)

Pete Peterson Signs Inc ....G 352 625-2307
Silver Springs (G-16007)

Preferred Signs Inc ....F 954 922-0126
Hollywood (G-5645)

Publi Signs ....G 954 927-4411
Hollywood (G-5647)

Quality Neon Sign Company ....E 904 268-4681
Jacksonville (G-6399)

Road Signs Inc ....G 941 321-0695
Sarasota (G-15545)

Rogers Sign Corp ....F 352 799-1923
Brooksville (G-1195)

Sar Wholesale Sign Factory ....F 813 949-8397
Lutz (G-8014)

Shark Signs of Ne Fl Inc ....G 904 766-6222
Jacksonville (G-6462)

2022 Harris Florida
Manufacturers Directory

(G-0000) Company's Geographic Section entry number

SIGNS (continued)

Sign One Inc ....G...... 305 888-6565
Hialeah (G-5348)
Signcrafters of Central Fla ....F...... 352 323-1862
· Leesburg (G-7794)
Signs For You Inc ....E...... 305 635-6662
Miami (G-9890)
Signs Galore Inc ....G...... 850 683-8010
Crestview (G-2253)
Signs Unlimited Bay County Inc ....G...... 850 785-1061
Panama City (G-13307)
Signsharks Sign Service ....G...... 904 766-6222
Jacksonville (G-6470)
Sky-High Sign & Lighting Inc ....G...... 813 994-3954
Palm Harbor (G-13132)
Stellar Sign and Design LLC ....F...... 407 660-3174
Orlando (G-12624)
Stephens Advertising Inc ....G...... 904 354-7004
Jacksonville (G-6507)
Sungraf Inc ....G...... 954 456-8500
Hallandale Beach (G-4976)
Taylor Sign & Design Inc ....F...... 904 396-4652
Jacksonville (G-6534)
Thomas Sign and Awning Co Inc ....C...... 727 573-7757
Clearwater (G-1828)
Townsend Signs Inc ....G...... 386 255-1955
Holly Hill (G-5518)
United Advantage Signs Inc ....D...... 813 855-3300
Oldsmar (G-11701)
US Signs Inc ....E...... 727 862-7933
Port Richey (G-14383)
USA Signs Inc ....G...... 305 470-2333
Miami (G-10084)
West Coast Signs ....E...... 941 755-5686
Sarasota (G-15580)

SIGNS: Neon

A1a Electric Signs & Neon Inc ....F...... 305 757-6950
Hialeah (G-5020)
Accent Neon & Sign Company ....G...... 727 784-8414
Palm Harbor (G-13095)
All-American Signs Inc ....G...... 863 665-7161
Lakeland (G-7270)
Bulldog Neon Sign Company Inc ....G...... 786 277-6366
Miami (G-8860)
Expert Promotions LLC.....................F...... 772 643-4012
Sebastian (G-15891)
McNeill Signs Inc ....F...... 561 737-6304
Pompano Beach (G-14092)
McNeill Signs Inc ....G...... 386 586-7100
Bunnell (G-1231)
Parrillo Inc ....G...... 386 767-8011
South Daytona (G-16026)
Robson Corporation ....E...... 941 753-6935
Sarasota (G-15546)
Signing Off Now Inc ....F...... 941 747-1000
Bradenton (G-1045)
Tropic Signs Inc ....G...... 727 942-4129
Tarpon Springs (G-17497)
West Central Signs Inc ....E...... 813 980-6763
Tampa (G-17427)

SILICONE RESINS

Syi Inc ....G...... 954 323-2483
Sunrise (G-16378)

SILICONES

Aerialife Inc....................................G...... 561 990-9299
Lake Worth (G-7182)
Clock Spring Company Inc ....F...... 561 683-6992
· Riviera Beach (G-14610)
E T I Incorporated ....E...... 727 546-6472
Largo (G-7576)
Syi Inc ....G...... 954 323-2483
Sunrise (G-16378)

SILK SCREEN DESIGN SVCS

Commercial Metal Photography ....G...... 407 295-8182
Orlando (G-12033)
Koala Tee Inc (usa) ....E...... 941 954-7700
Sarasota (G-15720)
Signs Unlimited - Sea Inc ....F...... 352 732-7341
Ocala (G-11494)
Sun-Art Designs Inc ....E...... 954 929-6622
Hollywood (G-5665)

SILLS, WINDOW: Cast Stone

FL Precast LLC................................G...... 321 356-9673
Orlando (G-12154)

SILO STAVES: Concrete Or Cast Stone

Cast Art International Corp ....G...... 727 807-3395
Dunedin (G-3442)

SILVER ORES

Goldfield Cnsld Mines Co ....D...... 321 724-1700
Melbourne (G-8430)
US Precious Metals Inc ....G...... 786 814-5804
Coral Gables (G-2118)

SIMULATORS: Electronic Countermeasure

Sierra Nevada Corporation ....F...... 850 659-3600
Shalimar (G-16003)

SIMULATORS: Flight

5dt Inc ....E...... 407 734-5377
Orlando (G-11854)
Aero Simulation Inc ....C...... 813 628-4447
Tampa (G-16562)
Aviation Instrument Tech Inc ....G...... 813 783-3361
Zephyrhills (G-18604)
Aviation Trning Foundation LLC ....G...... 844 746-4968
Port Orange (G-14327)
Bluedrop USA Inc ....G...... 800 563-3638
Orlando (G-11961)
Cae Healthcare USA Inc ....E...... 941 377-5562
Sarasota (G-15626)
Cubic Advnced Lrng Sltions Inc ....E...... 407 859-7410
Orlando (G-12061)
Indra Systems Inc ....E...... 407 567-1977
Orlando (G-12241)
James Taylor ....F...... 850 882-5148
Eglin Afb (G-3506)
Microsimulators Inc ....G...... 407 696-8722
Winter Springs (G-18573)
Opinicus Textron Inc ....D...... 813 792-9300
Lutz (G-8008)
Sequa Corporation...........................A...... 561 935-3571
Palm Beach Gardens (G-13008)
Servos and Simulation Inc ....G...... 407 807-0208
Longwood (G-7947)
Tru Simulation + Training Inc..............D...... 813 792-9300
Odessa (G-11587)

SIRENS: Vehicle, Marine, Indl & Warning

Bay Design Marine Group Inc..............G...... 239 825-8094
Naples (G-10691)
Danas Safty Supply Inc ....F...... 305 639-6024
Doral (G-3185)

SKILL TRAINING CENTER

Vertimax LLC ....G...... 800 699-5867
Tampa (G-17411)

SKIN CARE PRDTS: Suntan Lotions & Oils

Breeze Products Inc ....E...... 727 521-4482
Largo (G-7556)
Edgewell Personal Care Company ....B...... 386 673-2024
Ormond Beach (G-12761)
Florida Glsd Holdings Inc ....C...... 321 633-4644
Cocoa (G-1929)
Panama Jack Inc ....F...... 407 843-8110
Orlando (G-12465)
Salon Technologies Intl......................G...... 407 301-3726
Orlando (G-12570)

SKYLIGHTS

Circle Redmont Inc ....F...... 321 259-7374
Satellite Beach (G-15884)

SLAB & TILE, ROOFING: Concrete

Coma Cast Corp...............................F...... 305 667-6797
Miami (G-8950)
La Moti Roof & Tile Inc ....G...... 305 635-2641
Miami (G-9411)
Rival Roof Tile Delivery Corp................G...... 786 251-2631
Miami (G-9809)
Roof Tile Administration Inc ....F...... 863 467-0042
Okeechobee (G-11614)
Royal Westlake Roofing LLC ....F...... 863 676-9405
Lake Wales (G-7172)
Superior Roof Tile Mfg ....F...... 850 892-2299
Defuniak Springs (G-2844)

SLAB & TILE: Precast Concrete, Floor

Atlas Walls LLC...............................G...... 800 951-9201
Orlando (G-11931)
Cug LLC ....F...... 786 858-0499
Plantation (G-13841)
E T C R Inc ....E...... 305 637-0999
Miami (G-9057)
E-Stone USA Corporation ....C...... 954 266-6793
Sebring (G-15920)
E-Stone USA Corporation ....G...... 863 214-8281
Miami (G-9059)
Heavy Hwy Infrastructure LLC ....D...... 407 323-8853
Sanford (G-15330)
Itiles LLC ....G...... 954 609-0984
Boca Raton (G-555)
Kingman Cstm Stairs & Trim LLC ....G...... 561 547-9888
West Palm Beach (G-18047)
US Bullnosing ....F...... 954 567-0404
Oakland Park (G-11307)

SLAG: Crushed Or Ground

Calcium Silicate Corp Inc...................F...... 863 902-0217
Lake Harbor (G-7054)
Harsco Corporation ....F...... 717 506-2071
Tampa (G-16907)

SLAUGHTERING & MEAT PACKING

Bruss Company ....C...... 904 693-0688
Jacksonville (G-5959)
Central Beef Ind LLC ....C...... 352 793-3671
Center Hill (G-1440)

SLIDES & EXHIBITS: Prepared

Gloval Displays Inc ....E...... 800 972-0353
Miami Gardens (G-10259)
Trial Exhibits Inc ....G...... 813 258-6153
Tampa (G-17369)

SLINGS: Rope

Atlantic Wire and Rigging Inc ....G...... 321 633-1552
Cocoa (G-1905)

SLIP RINGS

Everaxis Usa Inc ....D...... 239 263-3102
Naples (G-10743)

SLIPPERS: House

Margarita Internl Trading Inc................F...... 305 688-1300
Miami (G-9510)

SLOT MACHINES

Banyan Gaming LLC.........................G...... 954 951-7094
Deerfield Beach (G-2675)

SLUGS: Slugs, aluminum

Aludisc LLC ....E...... 910 299-0911
Boca Raton (G-401)

SMOKING ACCESS: Rubber

Pipes R US.....................................G...... 813 661-4420
Seffner (G-15964)

SNACK & NONALCOHOLIC BEVERAGE BARS

Mishas Cupcakes Inc........................F...... 786 200-6153
Miami (G-9577)

SOAPS & DETERGENTS

Asi Chemical Inc ....F...... 863 678-1814
Lake Wales (G-7152)
Bar Maid Corporation ....F...... 954 960-1468
Pompano Beach (G-13948)
Bon Brands Inc ....F...... 800 590-7911
Royal Palm Beach (G-14760)
Cambridge Diagnostic Pdts Inc...........F...... 954 971-4040
Fort Lauderdale (G-3712)
Care-Metix Products Inc ....F...... 813 628-8801
Tampa (G-16680)
Chemline Products Inc ....G...... 727 573-2436
Clearwater (G-1541)
Eco Concepts Inc ....F...... 954 920-9700
Hollywood (G-5569)

Employee Codes: A=Over 500 employees, B=251-500
C=101-250, D=51-100, E=20-50, F=10-19, G=4-9

2022 Harris Florida
Manufacturers Directory

1323

PRODUCT

Loris 1 Inc G 727 847-4499
New Port Richey *(G-10972)*

Mollys Suds LLC G 678 361-5456
Saint Petersburg *(G-15129)*

Pro Chem Products Inc G 407 425-5533
Orlando *(G-12509)*

Purox Brands Corp F 305 392-0738
Hialeah *(G-5318)*

Sanit Technologies LLC E 941 351-9114
Sarasota *(G-15550)*

Scentstional Soaps Candles Inc F 941 485-1443
Venice *(G-17714)*

Sicamu Inc G 850 270-6283
Quincy *(G-14549)*

Skampas Performance Group G 305 974-0047
Sunny Isles Beach *(G-16282)*

Skymo LLC G 305 676-6739
Cooper City *(G-2022)*

Trugreen Products LLC G 954 629-5794
Pompano Beach *(G-14221)*

Whip-It Inventions Inc E 850 626-6300
Milton *(G-10444)*

SOFT DRINKS WHOLESALERS

Coca-Cola Beverages Fla LLC F 813 612-6631
Tampa *(G-16717)*

Coca-Cola Beverages Fla LLC G 941 953-3151
Sarasota *(G-15636)*

Coca-Cola Beverages Fla LLC E 954 985-5000
Hollywood *(G-5553)*

Coca-Cola Beverages Fla LLC C 407 295-9290
Orlando *(G-12025)*

Coca-Cola Beverages Fla LLC B 904 786-2720
Jacksonville *(G-5991)*

Coca-Cola Beverages Fla LLC G 305 378-1073
Miami *(G-8935)*

Hialeah Distribution Corp E 786 200-2498
Hialeah *(G-5184)*

Pepsico Inc D 305 593-7500
Medley *(G-8297)*

SOFTWARE PUBLISHERS: Application

Abawi Fit LLC G 813 215-1833
Tampa *(G-16552)*

Acucall LLC F 855 799-7905
Jupiter *(G-6677)*

Advtravl Inc G 978 549-5013
Ocala *(G-11315)*

Applied Software Inc G 215 297-9441
West Palm Beach *(G-17924)*

Atris Technology LLC F 352 331-3100
Gainesville *(G-4655)*

Blackcloak Inc F 833 882-5625
Lake Mary *(G-7063)*

Bond-Pro Inc C 888 789-4985
Tampa *(G-16655)*

Bond-Pro LLC F 813 413-7576
Tampa *(G-16656)*

Chen Technology Inc F 305 621-0023
Miami Gardens *(G-10254)*

Cloudfactors LLC G 407 768-3160
Orlando *(G-12022)*

Colorproof Software Inc G 813 963-0241
Lutz *(G-7985)*

Community MGT Systems LLC G 561 214-4780
West Palm Beach *(G-17971)*

Cubic Advnced Lrng Sltions Inc E 407 859-7410
Orlando *(G-12061)*

Dark Lake Software Inc F 407 602-8046
Winter Park *(G-18505)*

Duenas Mobile Applications LLC F 305 851-3397
Homestead *(G-5709)*

Dynamic Glucose Hlth Ctrs LLC G 800 610-6422
Fort Lauderdale *(G-3776)*

Elliot Technologies Inc E 203 548-0069
Miami *(G-9089)*

Encore Analytics LLC G 866 890-4331
Destin *(G-3066)*

Fizgig LLC F 754 423-0349
Pembroke Pines *(G-13389)*

Flexiinternational Sftwr Inc G 239 298-5700
Naples *(G-10748)*

Flickdirect Inc F 561 330-2987
Delray Beach *(G-2963)*

Foris Inc E 904 394-2618
Miami *(G-9167)*

Gbi Intralogistics Solutions F 954 596-5000
Deerfield Beach *(G-2724)*

Genius Central Systems Inc E 800 360-2231
Bradenton *(G-982)*

Georgesoft Inc G 850 329-5517
Tallahassee *(G-16448)*

Hcr Software Solutions Inc E 904 638-6177
Jacksonville *(G-6169)*

Healthme Technology Inc G 888 994-3627
Naples *(G-10772)*

Himgc Limited D 213 443-8729
Daytona Beach *(G-2562)*

Hipaat International Inc F 905 405-6299
Naples *(G-10774)*

Hydrogen Technology Corp E 800 315-9554
Miami Beach *(G-10202)*

Icarecom LLC F 954 768-7100
Fort Lauderdale *(G-3873)*

Ilay Ventures LLC F 786 503-5335
Miami Beach *(G-10203)*

Industry Weapon Inc E 877 344-8450
Oldsmar *(G-11660)*

Informulate LLC G 866 222-2307
Oviedo *(G-12828)*

Innovative Software Tech Inc F 813 920-9435
Tampa *(G-16944)*

Interactyx Americas Inc E 888 575-2266
Bonita Springs *(G-805)*

Iq Formulations Llc D 954 533-9256
Tamarac *(G-16533)*

It Labs LLC F 310 490-6142
Palm Beach Gardens *(G-12979)*

Keith Dennis Markham G 239 353-4122
Naples *(G-10796)*

Kirchman Corporation E 877 384-0936
Orlando *(G-12288)*

Kony Inc E 407 730-5669
Orlando *(G-12295)*

Ld Telecommunications Inc D 954 628-3029
Fort Lauderdale *(G-3914)*

Lightning Phase II Inc G 727 539-1800
Seminole *(G-15979)*

Mantis Security Corporation E 571 418-3665
Sarasota *(G-15739)*

Maxord LLC F 405 256-2381
Boynton Beach *(G-890)*

Merkari Group Inc F 305 748-3260
Coral Gables *(G-2085)*

Microsoft Corporation F 813 281-3900
Tampa *(G-17071)*

Microsoft Corporation C 425 882-8080
Fort Lauderdale *(G-3941)*

Modernizing Medicine Inc C 561 880-2998
Boca Raton *(G-603)*

Modernzing Mdcine Gstrntrlogy C 561 880-2998
Boca Raton *(G-604)*

Multi Soft II Inc F 305 579-8000
Miami *(G-9599)*

Niftys Inc F 786 878-4725
Miami *(G-9621)*

Note Bin Inc F 727 642-8530
Clearwater *(G-1720)*

Nvaulted Enterprises Inc G 305 632-0525
Hallandale Beach *(G-4964)*

On-Q Software Inc G 305 553-6566
Miami *(G-9649)*

Open International LLC G 305 265-0310
Coral Gables *(G-2092)*

Opie Choice LLC G 352 331-3741
Gainesville *(G-4743)*

Opie Choice LLC F 727 726-5157
Clearwater *(G-1728)*

Painassist Inc G 248 875-4222
Saint Petersburg *(G-15148)*

Peeks Mobile App Corp F 407 931-3878
Kissimmee *(G-6950)*

Perch Security Inc E 844 500-1810
Tampa *(G-17156)*

Phase Integration LLC G 877 778-8885
Jacksonville *(G-6369)*

Powerline Group Inc C 631 828-1183
Delray Beach *(G-3002)*

Precision Infinity Systems Inc G 407 490-2320
Orlando *(G-12501)*

Provictus Inc E 561 437-0232
Palm Beach Gardens *(G-13003)*

Ranorex Inc E 727 835-5570
Clearwater *(G-1762)*

Reins Inc F 904 868-3381
Jacksonville *(G-6414)*

Reliable Business Technologies G 386 561-9944
Ocala *(G-11479)*

Riley Risk Inc G 202 601-0500
Saint Augustine *(G-14879)*

Saas Transportation Inc F 850 650-7709
Destin *(G-3078)*

Sage Implementations LLC G 407 290-6952
Orlando *(G-12567)*

SAI Super Software Solutions G 407 445-2520
Orlando *(G-12568)*

Sas Usa Inc G 305 428-0200
Miami *(G-9848)*

SC Parent Corporation D 703 351-0200
Miami *(G-9852)*

SC Purchaser Corporation D 703 351-0200
Miami *(G-9853)*

Seronix Corporation G 352 406-1698
Mount Dora *(G-10612)*

Sighthound Inc E 407 974-5694
Winter Park *(G-18534)*

Simplepin LLC F 800 727-4136
Hobe Sound *(G-5483)*

Simplicity Esports LLC F 855 345-9467
Boca Raton *(G-678)*

Simplicity Esports & Gaming Co G 855 345-9467
Boca Raton *(G-679)*

Smx-US Inc E 914 840-5631
Miami *(G-9909)*

Starboard Consulting LLC E 407 622-6414
Longwood *(G-7950)*

Stay Smart Care LLC G 321 682-7113
Winter Park *(G-18540)*

Stayfilm Inc G 786 961-1007
Miami *(G-9947)*

Streamline Technologies Inc G 407 679-1696
Winter Springs *(G-18578)*

Sun Valley Tech Solutions Inc G 480 463-4101
Wesley Chapel *(G-17887)*

Synergistic Office Solutions F 352 242-9100
Minneola *(G-10452)*

Thalo Assist LLC G 786 340-6892
Weston *(G-18288)*

Theater Ears Inc G 561 305-0519
Boca Raton *(G-714)*

Thermaband Inc G 248 497-1665
Weston *(G-18290)*

Titan Tools LLC E 818 984-1001
Clearwater *(G-1832)*

Tropical MBC LLC G 727 498-6511
St Pete Beach *(G-16093)*

Truecare24 Inc E 240 434-0963
Tampa *(G-17373)*

U2 Cloud LLC F 888 370-5433
Green Cove Springs *(G-4840)*

Unicomp Corp of America G 954 755-1710
Coral Springs *(G-2223)*

Universal Training Sftwr Inc F 561 981-6421
Boca Raton *(G-736)*

Utilitech Inc F 863 767-0600
Wauchula *(G-17830)*

Vuaant Inc G 407 701-6975
Orlando *(G-12709)*

Webvoip Inc G 305 793-2061
Fort Lauderdale *(G-4127)*

Westrom Software G 866 480-1879
Vero Beach *(G-17817)*

Wind River Systems Inc G 321 726-9463
Melbourne *(G-8564)*

Windermere Nannies LLC F 407 782-2057
Windermere *(G-18371)*

Yieldx Inc F 646 328-9803
Aventura *(G-277)*

Yourmembershipcom Inc E 727 827-0046
Saint Petersburg *(G-15241)*

Zeroc Inc G 561 283-1480
Jupiter *(G-6829)*

SOFTWARE PUBLISHERS: Business & Professional

Aci Worldwide Inc B 305 894-2200
Coral Gables *(G-2024)*

Adaptive Insights Inc E 800 303-6346
Winter Springs *(G-18558)*

Advanced Public Safety LLC G 954 354-3000
Deerfield Beach *(G-2658)*

Advanced Software Inc F 215 369-7800
Jacksonville Beach *(G-6627)*

Advantage Software Inc E 772 288-3266
Stuart *(G-16113)*

Agile Risk Management LLC G 800 317-5497
Tampa *(G-16566)*

Alliance Rsrvations Netwrk LLC F 602 889-5505
Orlando *(G-11894)*

Aptum Technologies (usa) Inc	D	877 504-0091	Doral (G-3118)
Bca Technologies Inc	F	407 659-0653	Maitland (G-8052)
Bio-Tech Medical Software Inc	D	800 797-4711	Fort Lauderdale (G-3688)
Bla Software Inc	G	407 355-0800	Orlando (G-11954)
Broadsword Solutions Corp	F	248 341-3367	Marathon (G-8106)
Ca Inc	C	305 559-4640	Miami (G-8873)
Capstorm LLC		314 403-2143	Santa Rosa Beach (G-15422)
Carpediem LLC	F	229 230-1453	Destin (G-3061)
Central Fla Bus Solutions Inc	E	863 297-9293	Winter Haven (G-18430)
CFS Inc	F	850 386-2902	Tallahassee (G-16422)
Channel Logistics LLC	F	856 614-5441	Miami (G-8920)
Cloud Veneer LLC	G	305 230-7379	Miami (G-8931)
Collegefrog Inc	G	850 696-1500	Pensacola (G-13474)
Connectyx Technologies Corp	G	772 221-8240	Stuart (G-16132)
Consumer Information Bur Inc	G	954 971-5079	Pompano Beach (G-13977)
Contact Center Solutions Inc	E	305 499-0163	Miami (G-8959)
Coresystems Software USA Inc	G	786 497-4477	Miami (G-8971)
Crichlow Data Sciences Inc	G	863 616-1222	Lakeland (G-7300)
Datamentors LLC	E	813 960-7800	Wesley Chapel (G-17873)
Dealer It Group LLC	F	904 518-3379	Jacksonville (G-6028)
Digiportal Software Inc	G	407 333-2488	Sanford (G-15305)
Drsingh Technologies Inc	F	352 334-7270	Gainesville (G-4682)
Duos Technologies Group Inc	F	904 652-1601	Jacksonville (G-6047)
Eclipse Ehr Solutions LLC	F	352 488-0081	Weeki Wachee (G-17836)
Ei Interactive LLC	G	407 579-0993	Orlando (G-12117)
Enablesoft Inc	F	407 233-2626	Orlando (G-12128)
Enterprise System Assoc Inc	F	407 275-0220	Orlando (G-12130)
Eventtracker Security LLC	D	410 953-6776	Fort Lauderdale (G-3799)
Evolution Voice Inc	F	407 204-1614	Orlando (G-12141)
Excelor LLC	F	321 300-3315	Orlando (G-12142)
Fis Avantgard LLC	E	484 582-2000	Jacksonville (G-6097)
Fis Kiodex LLC	F	904 438-6000	Jacksonville (G-6098)
Flagshipmd LLC	G	904 302-6160	Jacksonville (G-6100)
Genensys LLC	G	407 701-4158	Oviedo (G-12823)
Genesys Band	G	347 701-5670	Orlando (G-12192)
Geocommand Inc	G	561 347-9215	Boca Raton (G-526)
Global Recash LLC	D	818 297-4437	Coral Gables (G-2063)
Gooee LLC	F	727 510-0663	Clearwater (G-1616)
Gotobilling LLC	F	800 305-1534	Tampa (G-16887)
Govpay Network LLC	G	866 893-9678	Miami (G-9229)
Green Shades Software Inc	F	904 807-0160	Jacksonville (G-6154)
Guardia LLC	G	954 670-2900	Fort Lauderdale (G-3852)
H Park Services LLC	G	844 607-2142	Orlando (G-12207)
Hr Ease Inc	G	813 414-0040	Tampa (G-16925)
Igovsolutions LLC		407 574-3056	Lake Mary (G-7084)

Ils Management LLC	E	321 252-0100	Melbourne (G-8440)
Information Mgt Svcs Inc	F	386 677-5073	Ormond Beach (G-12773)
Inperium Corp	E	305 901-5650	Miami Beach (G-10205)
Integra Connect LLC		800 742-3069	West Palm Beach (G-18035)
Intermedix Corporation	D	954 308-8700	Fort Lauderdale (G-3879)
Iomartcloud Inc	G	954 880-1680	Vero Beach (G-17766)
Iris Inc	G	561 921-0847	Delray Beach (G-2976)
Ironwifi LLC	F	800 963-6221	Orlando (G-12260)
Juritis USA LLC	G	954 529-2168	Weston (G-18260)
Kenexa Learning Inc	G	407 562-1905	Maitland (G-8064)
Kenexa Learning Inc	G	407 548-0434	Lake Mary (G-7089)
Kronos Incorporated	G	813 207-1987	Tampa (G-16992)
Lamb Tec Inc	G	305 798-6266	Cutler Bay (G-2293)
Lawex Corporation	G	305 259-9755	Coral Gables (G-2081)
Levitech Services LLC	F	904 576-0562	Jacksonville Beach (G-6638)
Linqs Inc	F	321 244-2626	Winter Springs (G-18572)
Lobby Docs LLC	G	850 294-0013	Tallahassee (G-16472)
Lott Qa Group Inc	G	201 693-2224	Bonita Springs (G-810)
Lps Group LLC	G	305 668-8780	South Miami (G-16038)
Management Hlth Solutions Inc	B	888 647-4621	Tampa (G-17034)
Mdintouch Us Inc	G	786 268-1161	Miami (G-9525)
Method Merchant Inc	F	954 745-7998	Plantation (G-13868)
Microvision Technology Corp	F	407 333-2943	Lake Mary (G-7095)
Momenry Inc	F	318 668-0888	Tampa (G-17083)
Ncg Medical Systems Inc	E	407 788-1906	Orlando (G-12409)
New Generation Computing Inc	D	800 690-0642	Miami Lakes (G-10330)
Nexogy Inc	D	305 358-8952	Coral Gables (G-2091)
Nphase Inc	D	805 750-8580	Atlantic Beach (G-212)
Omnivore Technologies Inc	D	800 293-4058	Clearwater (G-1726)
Oracle Systems Corporation	E	650 506-7000	Naples (G-10843)
Ordercounter Inc	F	850 332-5540	Pensacola (G-13562)
Orion Travel Technologies Inc	F	407 574-6649	Celebration (G-1439)
Outreach Corporation	C	888 938-7356	Tampa (G-17135)
Pacemate LLC	G	305 322-5074	Bradenton (G-1021)
Phocas Software	E	863 738-9107	Maitland (G-8069)
Powerchord Inc	E	727 823-1530	Saint Petersburg (G-15158)
Premieretrade Forex LLC	G	407 287-4149	Lake Mary (G-7102)
Profitsword LLC	E	407 909-8822	Orlando (G-12513)
Projstream LLC	F	407 476-1084	Lake Mary (G-7103)
Qgiv Inc	E	888 855-9595	Lakeland (G-7415)
Quadramed Corporation	F	904 355-2900	Jacksonville (G-6398)
Radial Inc	F	561 737-5151	Boynton Beach (G-906)
Raynetcrm LLC	G	813 489-9565	Venice (G-17712)
Razient LLC	G	855 747-5911	Miami (G-9784)
Recordsone LLC	F	301 440-8119	Naples (G-10874)

Retail Cloud Technologies LLC	E	727 210-1700	Clearwater (G-1764)
Route4me Inc	E	888 552-9045	Tampa (G-17234)
Ruvos LLC	G	850 254-7270	Tallahassee (G-16498)
Siemens Industry Software Inc	E	407 517-5919	Orlando (G-12599)
Signingordercom LLC		904 300-0104	Orange Park (G-11841)
Silvershore Partners LLC	F	904 562-0812	Jacksonville (G-6472)
Simply Reliable Inc		800 209-9332	Saint Petersburg (G-15184)
Singular Grape Inc	G	305 508-4000	Orlando (G-12606)
Smart Guides	G	813 534-0940	Tampa (G-17274)
Smartadvocate LLC	E	239 390-1000	Bonita Springs (G-819)
Soe Software Corporation	E	813 490-7150	Tampa (G-17278)
Softech International Inc	F	305 233-4813	Miami (G-9911)
Sophio Software Inc	F	323 446-2172	Fort Lauderdale (G-4056)
Sophix Solutions Inc	G	813 837-9555	Tampa (G-17282)
Sphere Access Inc	F	336 501-6159	Tampa (G-17295)
Stature Software LLC	G	888 782-8881	Saint Augustine (G-14903)
Strands Inc	G	415 398-4333	Miami (G-9956)
Strata Analytics Holdg US LLC	D	954 349-4630	Sunrise (G-16373)
Sundog Software LLC	G	425 635-8683	Merritt Island (G-8598)
Supply Chain Technologies LLC	F	732 282-1000	Vero Beach (G-17804)
Swoogo LLC	G	212 655-9810	Sarasota (G-15847)
Tapinfluence Inc	E	720 726-4071	Winter Park (G-18543)
Technolgy Training Associates	E	813 249-0303	Tampa (G-17344)
Telephony Partners LLC	E	813 769-4690	Tampa (G-17346)
Threattrack Security Inc	C	855 885-5566	Clearwater (G-1829)
Timus Inc	G	904 614-4342	Jacksonville (G-6553)
Trx Integration Inc	F	727 797-4707	Belleair (G-353)
Two Roads Consulting LLC	G	305 395-8821	Dunedin (G-3460)
Ukg Inc	D	954 331-7000	Weston (G-18293)
Ukg Inc	C	954 331-7000	Weston (G-18294)
Unite Parent Corp	F	800 432-1729	Weston (G-18295)
VIP Software Corporation	F	813 837-4347	Lakeland (G-7470)
Vuram Inc		813 421-8000	Temple Terrace (G-17548)
World Hlth Enrgy Holdings Inc	F	561 870-0440	Boca Raton (G-755)
Yippy Inc	G	877 947-7901	Miami (G-10151)
Zerion Group LLC	F	877 872-1726	Maitland (G-8080)

SOFTWARE PUBLISHERS: Computer Utilities

Green Power Systems LLC	G	904 545-1311	Jacksonville (G-6153)
Lidarit Inc	E	407 632-2622	Orlando (G-12326)
N2w Software Inc	F	561 225-2483	West Palm Beach (G-18083)

SOFTWARE PUBLISHERS: Education

Ai2 Inc	G	407 645-3234	Winter Park (G-18482)
Brainchild Corp	F	239 263-0100	Naples (G-10698)
Cellec Games Inc	G	407 476-3590	Apopka (G-109)

PRODUCT

Cookie App LLC ....G...... 305 330-5099
Miami (G-8965)
Devclan Inc ....G...... 407 933-8212
Kissimmee (G-6913)
Drazcanna Inc ....E...... 786 618-1472
Miami (G-9048)
Educational Networks Inc ....G...... 866 526-0200
Coral Gables (G-2052)
Elogic Learning LLC ....E...... 813 901-8600
Tampa (G-16805)
Fluenz Inc ....G...... 305 209-1695
Miami Beach (G-10190)
Genel/Landec Inc ....G...... 305 591-9990
Doral (G-3226)
Hopscotch Technology Group Inc ....F 305 846-0942
Oviedo (G-12826)
Impact Education Inc ....G...... 239 482-0202
Fort Myers (G-4288)
IT Pacs Pro Software Inc ....G...... 954 678-1270
West Park (G-18214)
Maxit Corporation ....G...... 904 998-9520
Ponte Vedra Beach (G-14273)
Moore Solutions Inc ....G...... 772 337-4005
Port St Lucie (G-14478)
My Reviewers LLC ....G...... 813 404-9734
Tampa (G-17091)
Ngweb Solutions LLC ....G...... 904 332-9001
Jacksonville (G-6332)
Pogi Beauty LLC ....G...... 305 600-1305
Miami (G-9725)
Prekcom LLC ....G...... 877 773-5669
Miami Beach (G-10221)
Rperf Technologies Corp ....F 954 629-2359
Coral Springs (G-2207)
Rtj Group Inc ....G...... 954 999-4060
Fort Lauderdale (G-4033)
Stallion King LLC ....G...... 321 503-7368
Saint Petersburg (G-15199)
Unfoldingword Corporation ....F 407 900-3005
Orlando (G-12686)
Vector-Solutionscom Inc ....E...... 813 207-0012
Tampa (G-17406)

SOFTWARE PUBLISHERS: Home Entertainment

Electronic Arts Inc ....F 407 838-8000
Orlando (G-12119)
Nuevo Mundo Company ....F 305 207-8155
Miami (G-9635)
Sleepy Dragon Studios Inc ....G...... 561 714-6156
Cutler Bay (G-2302)
Studio M LLC ....F 954 918-8528
Margate (G-8155)

SOFTWARE PUBLISHERS: NEC

1425 N Washington Street LLC..........G...... 904 680-6600
Jacksonville (G-5839)
180bytwo ....G...... 202 403-7097
Clearwater (G-1469)
24/7 Software Inc......................F 954 514-8988
Coral Springs (G-2122)
5nine Software Inc ....E...... 561 898-1100
West Palm Beach (G-17906)
Above Property LLC ....E...... 239 263-7406
Naples (G-10650)
Accounting & Computer Systems ....G...... 407 353-1570
Orlando (G-11865)
Accuware Inc ....G...... 305 894-6874
Miami Beach (G-10160)
Actionable Quality Assurance ....G...... 352 562-0005
Gainesville (G-4644)
Ademero Inc ....G...... 863 937-0272
Lakeland (G-7265)
Aderant North America Inc ....F 850 224-2200
Tallahassee (G-16406)
Advanced Services Intl Inc ....G...... 954 889-1366
Miramar (G-10459)
Adventurous Entertainment LLC..........F 407 483-4057
Orlando (G-11875)
Afina Systems Inc ....G...... 305 261-1433
Miramar (G-10461)
Alchiba Inc ....G...... 561 832-9292
West Palm Beach (G-17917)
American Optimal Decisions Inc ......G...... 352 278-2034
Gainesville (G-4649)
Appgate Inc ....G...... 866 524-4782
Coral Gables (G-2030)
Appo Group Inc ....G...... 410 992-5500
Aventura (G-253)

ASG Federal Inc ....E...... 239 435-2200
Naples (G-10680)
Asysco Inc ....F 850 383-2522
Tallahassee (G-16415)
Authority Software LLC ....G...... 877 603-9653
Tamarac (G-16526)
Automated Accounting Assoc Inc.......G...... 512 669-1000
Pensacola (G-13448)
Avt Technology Solutions LLC ....C...... 727 539-7429
Clearwater (G-1503)
Axiom Services Inc ....E...... 727 442-7774
Clearwater (G-1504)
B-Scada Inc ....G...... 352 564-9610
Crystal River (G-2267)
Backtocad Technologies LLC ....G...... 727 303-0383
Clearwater (G-1508)
Bankingly Inc ....G...... 734 201-0007
North Miami (G-11092)
Belatrix Software Inc ....E...... 801 673-8331
Naples (G-10692)
Bellini Systems Inc ....G...... 813 264-9252
Tampa (G-16637)
Best Choice Software Inc ....F 941 747-5858
Bradenton (G-948)
Betablocks Company ....G...... 424 353-1978
Miami (G-8819)
Big Star Systems LLC ....G...... 954 243-7209
Lauderhill (G-7726)
Bigbyte Software Systems Inc..........G...... 917 370-1733
Pembroke Pines (G-13379)
Biosculptor Corporation ....G...... 305 823-8300
Hialeah (G-5076)
Black Ice Software LLC ....G...... 561 757-4107
Boca Raton (G-432)
Black Knight Inc ....B...... 904 854-5100
Jacksonville (G-5933)
Black Knight Fincl Svcs Inc ....C...... 904 854-5100
Jacksonville (G-5934)
BMC Software Inc ....F 813 227-4500
Tampa (G-16649)
Bohemia Intrctive Smltions Inc ....F 407 608-7000
Orlando (G-11965)
Bond Medical Group Inc ....F 813 264-5951
Tampa (G-16654)
Brigiz Inc ....F 404 400-5399
Riviera Beach (G-14601)
Brokerage MGT Solutions Inc ....F 561 766-0409
Boca Raton (G-450)
C-Horse Software Inc ....G...... 321 952-0692
Palm Bay (G-12894)
Ca Inc ....E...... 305 347-5140
Miami (G-8874)
Cadcam Software Co ....G...... 727 450-6440
Clearwater (G-1535)
Cafm ....F 407 658-6531
Cocoa Beach (G-1965)
Castle Software Inc ....G...... 800 345-7606
Sebastian (G-15889)
CB Parent Holdco GP LLC ....A...... 727 827-0046
Saint Petersburg (G-15002)
CCT Software LLC ....G...... 305 747-5682
North Miami (G-11097)
Certek Software Designs Inc ....G...... 727 738-8188
Dunedin (G-3444)
Checksum Software LLC ....G...... 786 375-8091
Doral (G-3160)
Chicago Soft Ltd ....F 863 940-2066
Lakeland (G-7291)
Cielo Enterprise Solutions LLC ....F 786 292-4111
Miami (G-8925)
Citadinos Corp ....G...... 954 435-7529
Pembroke Pines (G-13382)
Citrix Systems Inc ....A...... 954 267-3000
Fort Lauderdale (G-3729)
CMA Interactive Corporation ....F 954 336-6403
Fort Lauderdale (G-3733)
Collaborative Sftwr Solutions ....G...... 954 753-2025
Coral Springs (G-2143)
Comcept Solutions LLC ....E...... 727 535-1900
Seminole (G-15972)
Comp U Netcom Inc ....G...... 407 539-1800
Maitland (G-8054)
Concept Software Inc ....G...... 321 250-6670
Winter Garden (G-18381)
Connect Slutions Worldwide LLC ....G...... 407 492-9370
Vero Beach (G-17749)
Connected Life Solutions LLC ....F 214 507-9331
Altamonte Springs (G-40)
Construction Software Inc ....G...... 888 801-0675
Fort Lauderdale (G-3743)

Cooltech Holding Corp ....G...... 786 675-5236
Doral (G-3171)
Corellium Inc ....E...... 561 502-2420
Delray Beach (G-2951)
Creative Data Solutions Inc ....F 407 333-4770
Lake Mary (G-7067)
Creative Vtran Productions LLC ....F 407 656-2743
Maitland (G-8055)
Customer Success LLC ....G...... 386 265-4882
Port Orange (G-14331)
Cyber Manufacturing Inc ....G...... 786 457-1973
Miami (G-8987)
Daniel Lampert Communications ....F 407 327-7000
Winter Springs (G-18564)
Dashclicks LLC ....G...... 866 600-3369
Fort Lauderdale (G-3755)
Dat Software Inc ....G...... 305 266-5150
Miami (G-9003)
Data Access International Inc ....D...... 305 238-0012
Miami (G-9004)
Datacore Software Corporation ....D...... 954 377-6000
Fort Lauderdale (G-3757)
Ddi System LLC ....E...... 203 364-1200
Sarasota (G-15653)
Dealerups Inc ....F 407 557-5368
Lake Mary (G-7068)
Digi-Net Technologies Inc ....G...... 352 505-7450
Gainesville (G-4677)
Dignitas Software Development ....G...... 727 392-2004
Seminole (G-15974)
Dnt Software Corp ....G...... 407 323-0987
Sanford (G-15307)
Duos Technologies Inc ....E...... 904 652-1601
Jacksonville (G-6046)
Edashop Inc ....F 786 565-9197
Winter Garden (G-18384)
Electus Global Educatn Co Inc ....G...... 813 885-4122
Tampa (G-16800)
Ellis & Associates of Sanford ....G...... 407 322-1128
Sanford (G-15312)
Emerald Technologies Corp ....F 773 244-0092
St Pete Beach (G-16090)
Emphasys Cmpt Solutions Inc ....F 305 599-2531
Pembroke Pines (G-13386)
Empower Software Solutions Inc ....B...... 407 233-2000
Orlando (G-12126)
Engineerica Systems Inc ....F 407 542-4982
Oviedo (G-12819)
Enhancell Inc ....G...... 469 363-2038
Miami Beach (G-10187)
Erwin Inc ....F 813 933-3323
Tampa (G-16821)
Esterel Technologies Inc ....F 724 746-3304
Orlando (G-12134)
Everything Blockchain Inc ....E...... 904 454-2111
Jacksonville (G-6080)
Evolve Technologies Inc ....G...... 239 963-8037
Marco Island (G-8111)
Exec Technology Corp ....G...... 305 394-8132
Miami (G-9120)
Ezverify & Validate LLC ....G...... 855 398-3981
Sunrise (G-16318)
Factorfox Software LLC ....G...... 305 671-9526
Miami (G-9129)
Fcbn LLC ....G...... 408 505-1324
Pompano Beach (G-14018)
Feick Corporation ....D...... 305 271-8550
Miami (G-9136)
Finastra USA Corporation ....C...... 800 989-9009
Lake Mary (G-7077)
Finastra USA Corporation ....D...... 800 394-8778
Orlando (G-12151)
Fleetmatics ....G...... 727 483-9016
Tampa (G-16836)
Forewarn LLC ....G...... 561 757-4550
Boca Raton (G-523)
Fyi Software Inc ....E...... 239 272-6016
Naples (G-10756)
Geonova Gaming LLC ....G...... 908 414-5874
Kissimmee (G-6924)
Gleim Publications Inc ....D...... 352 375-0772
Gainesville (G-4703)
Goengineer Inc ....G...... 800 688-3234
Windermere (G-18352)
Gold-Rep Corporation ....G...... 954 892-5868
Weston (G-18248)
Goodrich Corporation ....G...... 305 622-4500
Miami Gardens (G-10261)
Goverlan LLC ....E...... 888 330-4188
Coral Gables (G-2064)

Graphic Center Group Corp	G	305 961-1649	
Coral Gables *(G-2065)*			
Grom Social Enterprises Inc	E	561 287-5776	
Boca Raton *(G-534)*			
Gulf Coast Program	G	727 945-1402	
Palm Harbor *(G-13112)*			
Hazmat Software LLC	F	407 416-5434	
Lake Mary *(G-7083)*			
Hilton Software LLC	F	954 323-2244	
Coral Springs *(G-2161)*			
Hispacom Inc	F	954 255-2622	
Coral Springs *(G-2163)*			
Ichosen1 Inc	F	844 403-4055	
Miami *(G-9298)*			
Image One Corporation	D	813 888-8288	
Tampa *(G-16933)*			
IMD Software Inc	G	813 685-2138	
Valrico *(G-17666)*			
Inceptra LLC	E	954 442-5400	
Weston *(G-18255)*			
Infor (us) LLC	E	407 916-9100	
Boca Raton *(G-544)*			
Infor Public Sector Inc	E	813 207-6911	
Tampa *(G-16943)*			
Information Builders Inc	E	407 804-8000	
Lake Mary *(G-7085)*			
Innergy	G	941 815-8655	
Punta Gorda *(G-14509)*			
Innquest Corporation	F	813 288-4900	
Clearwater *(G-1643)*			
Insight Software LLC	D	305 495-0022	
Weston *(G-18256)*			
Intouch Gps LLC	E	877 593-2981	
Lakeland *(G-7358)*			
Ipvision Software LLC	F	813 728-3175	
Tampa *(G-16953)*			
Itqlick Inc	G	855 487-5425	
Hallandale Beach *(G-4953)*			
Ityx Solutions Inc	F	407 474-4383	
Orlando *(G-12262)*			
Jade Software Corporation USA	F	904 677-5133	
Jacksonville *(G-6218)*			
Jonas Software USA Inc	G	800 476-0094	
Pensacola *(G-13531)*			
Jupiter Compass LLC	G	561 444-6740	
Palm Beach Gardens *(G-12980)*			
Kamel Software Inc	G	407 672-0202	
Oviedo *(G-12833)*			
Kaseya US LLC	E	415 694-5700	
Miami *(G-9385)*			
Kodiak Software Inc	F	727 599-8839	
Clearwater *(G-1665)*			
Koho Software Inc	G	813 390-1309	
Tampa *(G-16991)*			
Kommander Software LLC	G	407 906-2121	
Inverness *(G-5832)*			
Kreateck International Corp	G	772 925-1216	
Vero Beach *(G-17771)*			
Landtech Data Corporation	F	561 790-1265	
Royal Palm Beach *(G-14769)*			
Lenz Group LLC	G	305 467-5351	
Miramar *(G-10508)*			
Levelblox Inc	G	941 907-8822	
Sarasota *(G-15725)*			
Lifeline Software Inc	F	866 592-1343	
Boynton Beach *(G-886)*			
Linenmaster LLC	E	772 212-2710	
Vero Beach *(G-17774)*			
Linga Pos LLC	G	800 619-5931	
Naples *(G-10805)*			
Logical Data Solutions Inc	F	561 694-9229	
Palm Beach Gardens *(G-12986)*			
Low Code Ip Holding LLC	G	833 260-2151	
Fort Lauderdale *(G-3922)*			
Luminar LLC	B	407 900-5259	
Orlando *(G-12355)*			
Marquis Software Dev Inc	D	850 877-8864	
Tallahassee *(G-16476)*			
Marware Inc	E	954 927-6031	
Dania Beach *(G-2354)*			
Matchware Inc	G	800 880-2810	
Tampa *(G-17055)*			
Mau Mau Corporation	E	305 440-5203	
Miami Beach *(G-10211)*			
Med X Change LLC	E	941 746-0538	
Bradenton *(G-1012)*			
Medaffinity Corporation	G	850 254-9690	
Tallahassee *(G-16478)*			
Mediaops Inc	E	516 857-7409	
Boca Raton *(G-592)*			
Medical Sftwr Integrators Inc	F	561 570-4680	
Pensacola *(G-13548)*			
Mediware Info Systems Inc	F	904 281-0467	
Jacksonville *(G-6289)*			
Melodon Software Inc	G	407 654-1234	
Orlando *(G-12371)*			
Mercury Systems Inc	E	352 371-2567	
Gainesville *(G-4729)*			
Mills & Murphy Sftwr Systems	F	727 577-1236	
Saint Petersburg *(G-15127)*			
Mobilebits Holdings Corp	G	941 225-6115	
Sarasota *(G-15518)*			
Mobvious Corp	F	786 497-6620	
Miami *(G-9581)*			
Moduslink Corporation	E	305 888-8091	
Medley *(G-8283)*			
Montague Enterprises Inc	G	239 631-5292	
Naples *(G-10823)*			
Morrissy & Co	G	850 934-4243	
Gulf Breeze *(G-4886)*			
Motionvibe Innovations LLC	F	202 285-0235	
Bradenton *(G-1014)*			
Motorsport Games Inc	F	305 507-8799	
Miami *(G-9593)*			
My Clone Solution	F	813 442-9925	
Tampa *(G-17090)*			
Networked Solutions Inc	G	321 259-3242	
Rockledge *(G-14735)*			
Newmile Partners LLC	G	800 674-3474	
Riverview *(G-14571)*			
Nex Software LLC	G	786 200-3396	
Homestead *(G-5734)*			
Nicraf Software & Creat Inc	G	813 842-9648	
Odessa *(G-11567)*			
Northpointe Bank	G	239 308-4532	
Fort Myers *(G-4342)*			
Oaktree Software Inc	F	407 339-5855	
Altamonte Springs *(G-60)*			
Obd Genie LLC	G	321 250-3650	
Oviedo *(G-12839)*			
Oceana Software LLC	G	813 335-6966	
Tampa *(G-17114)*			
Onezeno LLC	G	407 539-1665	
Winter Park *(G-18527)*			
Openkm Usa LLC	G	407 257-2640	
Orlando *(G-12441)*			
Oracle America Inc	G	305 260-7200	
Miami *(G-9661)*			
Oracle Corporation	C	772 337-4141	
Port Saint Lucie *(G-14431)*			
Oracle Corporation	B	772 466-0704	
Fort Pierce *(G-4513)*			
Oracle Essence Inc	G	786 258-8153	
Weston *(G-18275)*			
Oracle Systems Corporation	E	407 458-1200	
Orlando *(G-12448)*			
Panther Software Inc	F	800 856-8729	
Miami *(G-9690)*			
Paper Free Technology Inc	G	515 270-1505	
Lehigh Acres *(G-7819)*			
Patient Portal Tech Inc	F	877 779-6627	
North Palm Beach *(G-11181)*			
Paylocity Holding Corporation	A	407 878-6585	
Lake Mary *(G-7099)*			
Perii Inc	G	321 253-2269	
Merritt Island *(G-8590)*			
Platesmart Technologies	F	813 749-0892	
Oldsmar *(G-11686)*			
Playoff Technologies LLC	G	407 497-2202	
Winter Park *(G-18528)*			
Powerdms Inc	D	407 992-6000	
Orlando *(G-12497)*			
Praxis Software Inc	F	407 226-5691	
Orlando *(G-12499)*			
Primal Innovation Tech LLC	F	407 558-9366	
Tampa *(G-17180)*			
Prism Venture Partners LLC	G	561 427-6565	
Jupiter *(G-6782)*			
Professor Software Company	G	561 691-5455	
Jupiter *(G-6783)*			
Program Works Inc	F	407 489-4140	
Winter Springs *(G-18576)*			
Prolink Software Corporation	G	860 659-5928	
Naples *(G-10869)*			
Protext Mobility Inc	G	435 881-3611	
Delray Beach *(G-3007)*			
Qhslab Inc	G	929 379-6503	
West Palm Beach *(G-18134)*			
Quality Software LLC	E	561 714-2314	
Delray Beach *(G-3009)*			
Queuelogix LLC	G	404 721-3928	
Fort Lauderdale *(G-4009)*			
Radixx Solutions Intl Inc	G	407 856-9009	
Orlando *(G-12529)*			
Rational Ediscovery LLC	G	518 489-3000	
Miami *(G-9783)*			
Recon Group LLP	F	855 874-8741	
Miami *(G-9786)*			
Red Oak Software Inc	G	973 316-6064	
Holmes Beach *(G-5691)*			
Restoration Games LLC	G	954 937-1970	
Sunrise *(G-16363)*			
Sachi Tech Inc	G	813 649-8028	
Tampa *(G-17242)*			
Safco Software	F	561 750-7879	
Boca Raton *(G-657)*			
Safe Passage Home Inc	G	904 241-4211	
Jacksonville *(G-6448)*			
Safeboot Corp	D	239 298-7000	
Naples *(G-10880)*			
SC Elearning LLC	D	561 293-2543	
Deerfield Beach *(G-2803)*			
Scalable Software Inc	G	239 603-7090	
Naples *(G-10887)*			
Scanid Inc	G	305 607-3523	
Miami *(G-9854)*			
Scope Worker LLC	E	917 855-5379	
Miami *(G-9857)*			
Scs Software Inc	F	727 871-8366	
Belleair Bluffs *(G-356)*			
Security Oracle Inc	F	352 988-5985	
Clermont *(G-1883)*			
Seniors Vent Mgmt Inc	G	305 266-0988	
Miami *(G-9867)*			
Servdata Inc	G	305 269-7374	
Palmetto Bay *(G-13218)*			
Shopworks LLC	G	561 491-6000	
West Palm Beach *(G-18151)*			
Silco Software Technology Inc	F	813 475-4591	
Odessa *(G-11578)*			
SIS Holdings LP	F	855 699-8372	
Coral Gables *(G-2108)*			
Slappey Communications LLC	G	863 619-5600	
Lakeland *(G-7435)*			
Smartbear Software	F	954 312-0188	
Coconut Creek *(G-2006)*			
Smartcop Inc	E	850 429-0082	
Pensacola *(G-13604)*			
Smartmatic Corporation	F	561 862-0747	
Boca Raton *(G-684)*			
Smdk Corp	E	239 444-1736	
Naples *(G-10895)*			
Soft Tech America Inc	F	954 563-3198	
Fort Lauderdale *(G-4053)*			
Software Product Solutions LLC	G	561 798-6727	
West Palm Beach *(G-18157)*			
Software To Systems Inc	G	513 893-4367	
Port Saint Lucie *(G-14449)*			
Softwareteacher Inc	G	954 593-3333	
Jupiter *(G-6801)*			
Solidexperts Inc	F	954 772-1903	
Fort Lauderdale *(G-4055)*			
Soren Technologies Inc	F	954 236-9998	
Plantation *(G-13892)*			
SOS Software Corp	G	786 237-4903	
Miami *(G-9920)*			
Southeastern Mktg Assoc Inc	G	954 421-7388	
Deerfield Beach *(G-2814)*			
Springbig Holdings Inc	C	800 772-9172	
Boca Raton *(G-693)*			
SRS Software LLC	G	201 802-1300	
Tampa *(G-17297)*			
Stadium 1 Software LLC	E	561 498-8356	
Miami Beach *(G-10235)*			
Stadson Technology Corporation	E	561 372-2648	
Boca Raton *(G-694)*			
Stratonet Inc	G	863 382-8503	
Sebring *(G-15944)*			
Sungard Asset MGT Systems Inc	F	561 656-2007	
Palm Beach Gardens *(G-13011)*			
Superion LLC	A	407 304-3235	
Lake Mary *(G-7109)*			
Synkt Games Inc	F	305 779-5611	
Miami *(G-9085)*			
System Data Resource	G	954 213-8008	
Port Saint Lucie *(G-14454)*			
Team Cymru Inc	C	847 378-3300	
Lake Mary *(G-7111)*			
Tech Data Education Inc	F	727 539-7429	
Clearwater *(G-1817)*			

P
R
O
D
U
C
T

Tech Data Resources LLC ....E   727 539-7429
Clearwater (G-1818)

Tech Data Tennessee Inc ....E   727 539-7429
Clearwater (G-1819)

Technisys LLC ....B   305 728-5372
Miami (G-9997)

Teledyne Flir LLC ....D   407 816-0091
Orlando (G-12649)

Thales Dis Cpl Usa Inc ....F   954 888-6200
Plantation (G-13894)

Thales Esecurity Inc C   954 888-6200
Plantation (G-13895)

That Software Guy Inc ....G   727 533-8109
Largo (G-7695)

Think Education Solutions LLC ....G   954 345-7839
Coral Springs (G-2221)

Tops Software ....G   813 960-8300
Clearwater (G-1835)

Touche Software LLC ....G   786 241-9907
Miami (G-10029)

Tracking Solutions Corp ....E   877 477-2922
Doral (G-3398)

Tradestation Technologies Inc ....E   954 652-7000
Plantation (G-13897)

Trendy Entertainment Inc ....E   814 384-7123
Gainesville (G-4778)

Unique Recording Software Inc ....E   917 854-5403
Boca Raton (G-734)

Universal Software Solutions ....G   727 298-8877
Clearwater (G-1839)

Utopic Software LLC ....E   813 444-2231
Tampa (G-17400)

Vanguardistas LLC ....G   386 868-2919
Ormond Beach (G-12798)

Vazkor Technologies S Fla Inc ....G   561 357-9029
Boynton Beach (G-922)

Veeam Software Corporation ....D   614 339-8200
Davie (G-2494)

Vensoft Corp ....F   786 991-2080
Miami (G-10101)

Vertaeon LLC ....G   404 823-6232
Gainesville (G-4783)

Vfinity Inc ....F   239 244-2555
Naples (G-10933)

Visible Results USA Inc ....F   913 706-8248
Reunion (G-14555)

Visions Sky Corp ....G   888 788-8609
Orlando (G-12700)

Vx Technologies ....F   608 774-5221
Delray Beach (G-3036)

Webcom Group Inc C   904 680-6600
Jacksonville (G-6598)

Webidcard Inc ....G   443 280-1577
Saint Augustine (G-14912)

Western Microsystems Inc ....E   800 547-7082
Jacksonville (G-6603)

Whole Tomato Software Inc ....G   408 323-1590
Sarasota (G-15874)

Willsonet Inc ....E   813 336-8175
Tampa (G-17432)

Windowware Pro ....G   904 584-9191
Saint Augustine (G-14915)

Xcape Solutions Inc ....F   813 369-5261
Lutz (G-8021)

SOFTWARE PUBLISHERS: Operating Systems

Audio Storage Technologies ....G   954 229-5050
Fort Lauderdale (G-3666)

Dpi Information Inc ....F   813 258-8004
Tampa (G-16785)

Ecoprintq Inc ....F   305 681-7445
Miami Lakes (G-10298)

Optimus Fleet LLC ....F   407 590-5060
Orlando (G-12443)

Sipradius LLC ....G   954 290-2434
Parkland (G-13354)

Verifone Inc C   800 837-4366
Coral Springs (G-2224)

Verifone Systems Inc C   408 232-7800
Coral Springs (G-2225)

SOFTWARE PUBLISHERS: Publisher's

Azure Computing Inc ....G   407 359-8787
Oviedo (G-12808)

Didna Inc ....G   239 851-0966
Orlando (G-12093)

Mas Editorial Corp ....G   305 748-0124
Hollywood (G-5621)

Pepper Tree ....G   941 922-2662
Sarasota (G-15779)

Sna Software LLC ....G   866 389-6750
Orlando (G-12611)

Synnova Health Inc ....G   305 253-5433
Palmetto Bay (G-13220)

Trivantis Corporation ....D   513 929-0188
Deerfield Beach (G-2828)

SOFTWARE PUBLISHERS: Word Processing

Emerson Prcess MGT Pwr Wtr Slt ....E   941 748-8100
Bradenton (G-976)

SOFTWARE TRAINING, COMPUTER

C2c Innovated Technology LLC ....G   251 382-2277
Bonifay (G-768)

Utilitech Inc ....F   863 767-0600
Wauchula (G-17830)

SOIL CONDITIONERS

Humic Growth Solutions Inc ....F   904 392-7201
Jacksonville (G-6188)

Humic Growth Solutions Inc ....G   904 329-1012
Green Cove Springs (G-4830)

Humic Growth Solutions Inc ....G   904 329-1012
Saint Johns (G-14946)

SOLAR CELLS

Alterna Power Inc ....F   407 287-9143
Orlando (G-11897)

Atlas Renewable Energy USA LLC .....F   786 358-5614
Miami (G-8770)

Brightwatts Inc ....F   954 513-3352
Oakland Park (G-11248)

Gb Energy Tech ....F   561 450-6047
Delray Beach (G-2967)

Guardian Solar LLC ....F   727 504-2790
Holiday (G-5495)

Solarbeam International Inc ....G   305 248-8400
Homestead (G-5741)

Solartech Universal LLC ....E   561 440-8000
Riviera Beach (G-14676)

SOLAR HEATING EQPT

Coast To Coast Solar Inc ....F   813 406-6501
Lutz (G-7984)

Eco Solar Technology ....G   904 219-0807
Jacksonville (G-6063)

Gain Solar LLC ....G   305 933-1060
Aventura (G-260)

Solar Energy Specialist Corp ....G   863 514-9532
Winter Haven (G-18468)

Sunset Power Inc ....F   866 485-2757
Jacksonville (G-6518)

Thermal Conversion Tech Inc ....E   904 358-3720
Jacksonville (G-6546)

United States Green Enrgy Corp ....E   540 295-4843
Pensacola (G-13617)

SOLVENTS

Skymo LLC ....G   305 676-6739
Cooper City (G-2022)

SOLVENTS: Organic

Skymo LLC ....G   305 676-6739
Cooper City (G-2022)

SONAR SYSTEMS & EQPT

Erapsco ....G   386 740-5335
De Leon Springs (G-2625)

Goodrich Corporation C   904 757-3660
Jacksonville (G-6146)

Raytheon Company C   310 647-9433
Largo (G-7668)

SOUND EQPT: Electric

35 Technologies Group Inc ....E   407 402-2119
Longwood (G-7861)

Bongiovi Aviation LLC ....F   772 879-0578
Port Saint Lucie (G-14401)

Sabine Inc ....D   386 418-2000
Alachua (G-20)

SOUND EQPT: Underwater

Argotec Inc ....F   954 491-6550
Fort Lauderdale (G-3655)

Argotec Inc ....G   407 331-9372
Longwood (G-7870)

L-3 Cmmnctons Ntronix Holdings .....D   212 697-1111
Melbourne (G-8453)

SOUVENIRS, WHOLESALE

Image Depot ....G   813 685-7116
Tampa (G-16932)

SOYBEAN PRDTS

Amerifood Corp ....G   305 305-5951
Miami (G-8722)

SPACE PROPULSION UNITS & PARTS

Aerojet Rocketdyne Inc ....B   561 796-2000
Jupiter (G-6679)

Boeing Company ....B   321 853-6647
Cape Canaveral (G-1279)

Chromalloy Gas Turbine LLC ....A   561 935-3571
Palm Beach Gardens (G-12959)

Sensatek Propulsion Tech Inc ....F   850 321-5993
Daytona Beach (G-2596)

Sequa Corporation ....A   561 935-3571
Palm Beach Gardens (G-13008)

SPACE VEHICLE EQPT

Chromalloy Gas Turbine LLC ....A   561 935-3571
Palm Beach Gardens (G-12959)

Kaman Aerospace Corporation ....B   904 485-1410
Jacksonville (G-6236)

Livetv ....F   321 722-0783
Melbourne (G-8462)

Lockheed Martin Corporation ....D   352 687-2163
Ocala (G-11431)

Micro Systems Inc C   850 244-2332
Fort Walton Beach (G-4596)

Micro Tool & Engineering Inc ....F   561 842-7381
Riviera Beach (G-14646)

Precise Technologies Inc ....F   727 535-5594
Largo (G-7662)

Precision Fabg & Clg Co Inc ....D   321 635-2000
Cocoa (G-1948)

Savvy Associate Inc ....F   954 941-6986
Pompano Beach (G-14167)

Stuart Industries Inc ....F   305 651-3474
Miami (G-9961)

SPACE VEHICLES

Terran Orbital Corporation ....F   561 988-1704
Boca Raton (G-712)

Terran Orbital Operating Corp ....F   561 988-1704
Boca Raton (G-713)

SPARK PLUGS: Internal Combustion Engines

Wiretec Ignition Inc ....F   407 578-4569
Palmetto (G-13206)

SPEAKER SYSTEMS

Light and Sound Equipment Inc ....G   305 233-3737
Cutler Bay (G-2294)

Peter Fogel ....G   561 245-5252
Delray Beach (G-2995)

SPECIALTY FOOD STORES: Coffee

Aroma Coffee Service Inc ....G   239 481-7262
Fort Myers (G-4181)

Melitta North America Inc ....D   727 535-2111
Clearwater (G-1691)

SPECIALTY FOOD STORES: Dietetic Foods

Real Ketones LLC ....F   801 244-8610
Saint Petersburg (G-15170)

SPECIALTY FOOD STORES: Health & Dietetic Food

Great Amercn Natural Pdts Inc ....F   727 521-4372
Saint Petersburg (G-15066)

Pure Solutions Inc ....E   813 925-1098
Tampa (G-17193)

SPECIALTY FOOD STORES: Juices, Fruit Or Vegetable

Healtheintentions Inc......................G......954 394-8867
  Miami (G-9268)
Watts Juicery.................................F......904 372-0693
  Atlantic Beach (G-217)

SPECIALTY FOOD STORES: Tea

Socratic Solutions Inc....................G......813 324-7018
  Brandon (G-1109)

SPECIALTY FOOD STORES: Vitamin

Function Please LLC.......................G......305 792-7900
  Hollywood (G-5579)

SPECIALTY SAWMILL PRDTS

Griffin Sawmill & Woodworking..........G......863 241-5180
  Lake Wales (G-7163)

SPECULATIVE BUILDERS: Single-Family Housing

Lucas Construction Inc....................G......386 623-0088
  Ormond Beach (G-12777)

SPICE & HERB STORES

Bijol and Spices Inc.......................G......305 634-9030
  Miami (G-8826)
El Sabor Spices Inc........................F......305 691-2300
  Miami (G-9076)
Everglades Foods Inc.....................G......863 655-2214
  Sebring (G-15921)

SPIKES: Steel, Wire Or Cut

Gerdau Ameristeel US Inc................B......813 286-8383
  Tampa (G-16877)
Gerdau USA Inc.............................B......813 286-8383
  Tampa (G-16878)

SPINDLES: Textile

Levil Technology Corp.....................G......407 542-3971
  Oviedo (G-12836)

SPORTING & ATHLETIC GOODS: Arrows, Archery

United Strings Intl LLC....................G......561 790-4191
  West Palm Beach (G-18192)

SPORTING & ATHLETIC GOODS: Balls, Baseball, Football, Etc

Nitro Leisure Products Inc................E......414 272-5084
  Stuart (G-16190)

SPORTING & ATHLETIC GOODS: Boomerangs

Aussie Boomerang Bar On Ave In........G......561 436-9741
  Lake Worth (G-7186)

SPORTING & ATHLETIC GOODS: Bowling Alleys & Access

50 Hwy 17 S Inc............................G......904 225-1077
  Yulee (G-18584)

SPORTING & ATHLETIC GOODS: Bows, Archery

S G F Inc.....................................G......813 996-2528
  Land O Lakes (G-7503)

SPORTING & ATHLETIC GOODS: Buckets, Fish & Bait

Marine Metal Products Co................G......727 461-5575
  Clearwater (G-1683)

SPORTING & ATHLETIC GOODS: Driving Ranges, Golf, Electronic

Custom Carts of Sarasota LLC..........E......941 953-4445
  Bradenton (G-964)

Easy Picker Golf Products Inc............E......239 368-6600
  Lehigh Acres (G-7808)
Evies Golf Center..........................G......941 377-2399
  Sarasota (G-15668)
Topgolf International Inc..................G......813 298-1811
  Tampa (G-17361)

SPORTING & ATHLETIC GOODS: Dumbbells & Other Weight Eqpt

Everslim LLC................................G......813 265-2100
  Brandon (G-1091)

SPORTING & ATHLETIC GOODS: Fishing Bait, Artificial

Fishgum.....................................G......256 394-2761
  Navarre (G-10948)
Fishgum.....................................G......256 394-2760
  Gulf Breeze (G-4881)

SPORTING & ATHLETIC GOODS: Fishing Eqpt

Black Bart International LLC..............G......561 842-4045
  Riviera Beach (G-14598)
Crowder Custom Rods Inc................G......772 220-8108
  Stuart (G-16134)
Renzetti.....................................F......321 267-7705
  Titusville (G-17611)
Volvox Inc Hollywood.....................G......954 961-4942
  Hollywood (G-5682)

SPORTING & ATHLETIC GOODS: Fishing Tackle, General

Fishermans Center Inc....................G......561 844-5150
  Riviera Beach (G-14622)
Gypsy Mining Inc..........................G......772 589-5547
  Roseland (G-14757)
Larrys Rigs.................................B......561 967-7791
  West Palm Beach (G-18053)
Lead Enterprises Inc......................F......305 635-8644
  Miami (G-9445)
New World Trade Inc......................E......941 205-5873
  Punta Gorda (G-14517)
No Live Bait Needed LLC..................G......305 479-8719
  Miramar (G-10520)
Rat-Trap Bait Company Inc...............G......863 967-2148
  Auburndale (G-243)

SPORTING & ATHLETIC GOODS: Football Eqpt & Splys, NEC

Unibeast Sports LLC.......................F......813 255-2827
  Riverview (G-14581)

SPORTING & ATHLETIC GOODS: Hooks, Fishing

O Mustad & Son USA Inc..................E......206 284-7871
  Doral (G-3315)

SPORTING & ATHLETIC GOODS: Hunting Eqpt

Jrh Sport Industries Inc...................G......904 940-3381
  Saint Augustine (G-14852)

SPORTING & ATHLETIC GOODS: Pools, Swimming, Exc Plastic

Tri-County Chemical Co...................G......407 682-3550
  Apopka (G-181)

SPORTING & ATHLETIC GOODS: Pools, Swimming, Plastic

Blue Hawaiian Products Inc..............E......727 535-5677
  Largo (G-7551)
Florida North Inc...........................G......352 606-2408
  Weeki Wachee (G-17837)

SPORTING & ATHLETIC GOODS: Protective Sporting Eqpt

Macho Products Inc.......................E......800 327-6812
  Sebastian (G-15899)

SPORTING & ATHLETIC GOODS: Racket Sports Eqpt

Diadem Sports LLC........................G......844 434-2336
  Pompano Beach (G-13997)

SPORTING & ATHLETIC GOODS: Rackets/Frames, Tennis, Etc

Bard Sports Corp...........................G......305 233-2200
  Miami (G-8798)
Pickle Pro LLC..............................G......844 332-7069
  Naples (G-10858)

SPORTING & ATHLETIC GOODS: Reels, Fishing

Tibor Inc.....................................E......561 272-0770
  Delray Beach (G-3026)

SPORTING & ATHLETIC GOODS: Rods & Rod Parts, Fishing

Halo Fishing LLC...........................G......321 373-2055
  Malabar (G-8082)
Rod Biscayne Manufacturing............G......305 884-0808
  Hialeah (G-5335)

SPORTING & ATHLETIC GOODS: Shafts, Golf Club

Buy Golf Grips 4 Less.....................G......352 256-7577
  Spring Hill (G-16066)
Cheval Country Club.......................G......813 279-5122
  Dunedin (G-3445)
First Tee Miami Daga.......................F......305 633-4583
  Miami (G-9146)
Golf Shaft Deals Inc.......................G......321 591-7824
  Indialantic (G-5803)
Pro Duffers Orlando.......................G......407 641-7626
  Orlando (G-12510)
Quail Height Golf Club.....................F......386 752-3339
  Lake City (G-7039)

SPORTING & ATHLETIC GOODS: Shooting Eqpt & Splys, General

Atg Specialty Products Corp.............G......888 455-5499
  Doral (G-3124)
Bag-A-Nut LLC.............................G......904 641-3934
  Jacksonville (G-5919)

SPORTING & ATHLETIC GOODS: Shuffleboards & Shuffleboard Eqpt

Allen Shuffleboard LLC....................G......727 399-8877
  Seminole (G-15968)

SPORTING & ATHLETIC GOODS: Skateboards

Boris Skateboards Mfg Inc................G......305 519-3544
  Miami (G-8848)
Fiik Skateboards LLC......................F......561 405-9541
  Fort Lauderdale (G-3815)
Fiik Skateboards LLC......................G......561 316-8234
  Boca Raton (G-514)
Magneto Sports LLC.......................G......760 593-4589
  Miami (G-9497)
Onetown Boards............................G......786 704-5921
  Miami (G-9654)
Skateboard Supercross LLC..............F......786 529-8187
  Surfside (G-16400)
Tri-Deck LLC................................G......386 748-3239
  Deland (G-2914)

SPORTING & ATHLETIC GOODS: Team Sports Eqpt

Sterling Facility Services LLC............F......772 871-2161
  Port Saint Lucie (G-14450)
Tendonease LLC............................G......888 224-0319
  Palm City (G-13061)

SPORTING & ATHLETIC GOODS: Tennis Eqpt & Splys

All Tennis LLC..............................G......561 842-0070
  Lake Park (G-7121)

Employee Codes: A=Over 500 employees, B=251-500
C=101-250, D=51-100, E=20-50, F=10-19, G=4-9
      2022 Harris Florida
     Manufacturers Directory
                       1329

PRODUCT

Biscayne Tennis LLC ....G...... 786 231-8372
Miami *(G-8835)*

Mp Tennis Inc 813 961-8844
Tampa *(G-17088)*

SPORTING & ATHLETIC GOODS: Trampolines & Eqpt

Indoor Trampoline Arena Inc ....F 321 222-1300
Sanford *(G-15335)*

Sunrise Trampolines and Nets ....G...... 727 526-9288
Pinellas Park *(G-13730)*

SPORTING & ATHLETIC GOODS: Treadmills

Treadmill Parts Zone.............................G...... 305 336-5600
Medley *(G-8337)*

SPORTING & ATHLETIC GOODS: Water Skis

Diamondback Towers LLC ....E 800 424-5624
Cocoa *(G-1920)*

Ski Rixen - Quiet Waters Inc ....G...... 954 429-0215
Deerfield Beach *(G-2811)*

SPORTING & ATHLETIC GOODS: Water Sports Eqpt

Cayago Americas Inc ....F 754 216-4600
Fort Lauderdale *(G-3715)*

Foil Inc ....G........ 442 233-3645
Pensacola *(G-13507)*

Island Fever LLC ....G...... 941 639-6400
Punta Gorda *(G-14510)*

Lake Area Watersports LLC ....G...... 352 475-3434
Melrose *(G-8571)*

SPORTING & REC GOODS, WHOLESALE: Ammunition, Sporting

O I Inc ....E 321 212-7801
Melbourne *(G-8486)*

SPORTING & REC GOODS, WHOLESALE: Boats, Canoes, Etc/Eqpt

Lake Area Watersports LLC ....G...... 352 475-3434
Melrose *(G-8571)*

Nautical Acquisitions Corp ....D...... 727 541-6664
Largo *(G-7650)*

Survitec Survivor Cft Mar Inc ....G...... 954 374-4276
Miramar *(G-10551)*

Waterbrick International Inc ....G...... 877 420-9283
Windermere *(G-18370)*

SPORTING & RECREATIONAL GOODS & SPLYS WHOLESALERS

Bote LLC ....F 888 855-4450
Miramar Beach *(G-10568)*

Jmh Marine Inc ....F 954 785-7557
Pompano Beach *(G-14067)*

Salt Life LLC ....G...... 904 595-5370
Jacksonville Beach *(G-6644)*

Sergeant Bretts Coffee LLC ....G...... 561 451-0048
Coconut Creek *(G-2004)*

Stuart Yacht Builders ....G...... 561 747-1947
Stuart *(G-16234)*

SPORTING & RECREATIONAL GOODS, WHOLESALE: Boat Access & Part

Beach House Engineering ....G....... 941 727-4488
Bradenton *(G-945)*

Uflex Usa Inc ....E 941 351-2628
Sarasota *(G-15575)*

SPORTING & RECREATIONAL GOODS, WHOLESALE: Diving

A Plus Marine Supply Inc ....G....... 850 934-3890
Gulf Breeze *(G-4874)*

Lamartek Inc ....E 386 752-1087
Lake City *(G-7027)*

Undersea Breathing Systems ....G...... 561 588-7698
Lake Worth *(G-7241)*

SPORTING & RECREATIONAL GOODS, WHOLESALE: Fitness

Neuro20 Technologies Corp ....G...... 813 990-7138
Tampa *(G-17107)*

SPORTING & RECREATIONAL GOODS, WHOLESALE: Golf

Flexstake Inc ....E 239 481-3539
Fort Myers *(G-4254)*

Liquid Ed Inc ....G...... 727 943-8616
Tarpon Springs *(G-17480)*

Whole 9 Golf & Cigars ....G...... 407 814-9994
Apopka *(G-185)*

SPORTING & RECREATIONAL GOODS, WHOLESALE: Watersports

Crystal Pool Service Inc ....G...... 954 444-8282
Sunrise *(G-16310)*

SPORTING GOODS

3n2 LLC ....G...... 407 862-3622
Maitland *(G-8048)*

All Golf ....G...... 954 441-1333
Pembroke Pines *(G-13373)*

Anzio Ironworks Corp ....G...... 727 895-2019
Clearwater *(G-1495)*

Armalaser Inc ....F 800 680-5020
Gainesville *(G-4651)*

Arno Belo Inc ....G...... 800 734-2355
Hallandale Beach *(G-4936)*

Asb Sports Group LLC ....G...... 305 775-4689
Miami *(G-8757)*

B & D Precision Tools Inc ....E 305 885-1583
Hialeah *(G-5065)*

Baby Guard Inc ....F 954 741-6351
Coral Springs *(G-2133)*

Blue Gardenia LLC ....G...... 727 560-0040
Saint Petersburg *(G-14984)*

BP International Inc ....D...... 386 943-6222
Deland *(G-2856)*

BRC Sports Llc ....G...... 904 388-8126
Jacksonville *(G-5954)*

Brownies Marine Group Inc ....G...... 954 462-5570
Pompano Beach *(G-13956)*

Burn Proof Gear LLC ....G...... 786 634-7406
Miami *(G-8862)*

Carolina Company USA LLC ....G...... 401 487-2749
Lady Lake *(G-6989)*

Clawson Custom Cues Inc ....F 904 448-8748
Jacksonville *(G-5981)*

Covert Armor LLC ....G...... 561 459-8077
West Palm Beach *(G-17974)*

D G Morrison Inc ....F 813 865-0208
Odessa *(G-11546)*

Deers Holdings Inc ....E 805 323-6899
Bay Harbor Islands *(G-332)*

Durabody Usa LLC ....G...... 954 357-2333
Miramar *(G-10486)*

Eagle Athletica LLC ....G...... 305 209-7002
Miami *(G-9060)*

Exclusive Bats LLC ....G...... 305 450-3858
Hialeah *(G-5147)*

Florida Fishing Products ....G...... 239 938-4612
Tampa *(G-16843)*

Florida Pool Products Inc ....E 727 531-8913
Clearwater *(G-1602)*

Florida Stucco Corp ....E 561 487-1301
Boca Raton *(G-519)*

G & K Aluminum Inc ....F 772 283-1297
Stuart *(G-16150)*

Gar Industries Corp ....F 954 456-8088
Hollywood *(G-5581)*

Garbo Sport International Inc ....G...... 305 599-8797
Miami *(G-9187)*

Gorilla Bats LLC ....G...... 813 285-9409
Riverview *(G-14563)*

Headhunter Spearfishing Co ....G...... 954 745-0747
Fort Lauderdale *(G-3864)*

Homerun Derby Bats Only LLC ....G...... 813 545-3887
Riverview *(G-14566)*

Just For Nets ....G...... 813 871-1133
Tampa *(G-16973)*

Ljs Tops & Bottoms ....E 561 736-7868
Boynton Beach *(G-887)*

Lucas 5135 Inc ....G...... 800 835-7665
Jacksonville *(G-6265)*

Lynn Jackson Kimberly ....G...... 904 285-7745
Ponte Vedra Beach *(G-14271)*

Marconi Line Inc ....F 321 639-1130
Rockledge *(G-14730)*

Mirage Systems Inc ....F 386 740-9222
Deland *(G-2886)*

Moreno & Sons Inc ....G...... 786 402-8919
Hollywood *(G-5630)*

Nighthawk Running LLC ....G...... 407 443-8404
Orlando *(G-12416)*

Pocketec Inc ....G...... 772 692-8020
Stuart *(G-16198)*

Pompanette LLC ....G...... 813 885-2182
Tampa *(G-17169)*

Precision Paddleboards ....G...... 954 616-8046
Fort Lauderdale *(G-3992)*

Racing Spirit Llc ....G...... 305 373-6671
Miami *(G-9775)*

Salt Life LLC ....G...... 904 595-5370
Jacksonville Beach *(G-6644)*

Seasucker LLC ....F 941 586-2664
Bradenton *(G-1044)*

Seattle Engraving Center LLC ....G...... 813 330-7620
Brandon *(G-1106)*

Showcase Marble Inc ....G...... 386 253-6646
Daytona Beach *(G-2598)*

Simons Hallandale Inc ....E 561 468-1174
Miami *(G-9895)*

Sogofishing LLC ....G...... 800 308-0259
Fort Lauderdale *(G-4054)*

Sport Products of Tampa Inc ....G...... 813 630-5552
Tampa *(G-17296)*

Sports Radar Ltd ....G...... 352 503-6825
Homosassa *(G-5751)*

SSE and Associates Inc ....E 954 973-7144
Pompano Beach *(G-14197)*

Stuart Yacht Builders ....F 561 747-1947
Stuart *(G-16234)*

Swim Buoy ....G...... 305 953-4101
Opa Locka *(G-11792)*

Tess Enterprises Inc ....G...... 727 573-9701
Clearwater *(G-1827)*

Top Spec US Inc ....G...... 904 345-0814
Jacksonville *(G-6561)*

Uninsured Relative Workshop ....F 386 736-7589
Deland *(G-2916)*

Vertical Reality Inc ....G...... 305 238-4522
Palmetto Bay *(G-13222)*

Wayloomoto LLC ....G...... 954 636-1510
Davie *(G-2496)*

Wemi Sports ....G...... 305 446-5178
Coral Gables *(G-2119)*

Your Performance Solutions ....G...... 305 278-2762
Miami *(G-10153)*

SPORTING GOODS STORES, NEC

Bakers Sports Inc ....E 904 388-8126
Jacksonville *(G-5921)*

Boone Bait Co Inc ....F 407 975-8775
Winter Park *(G-18492)*

Classic Fishing Products Inc ....E 407 656-6133
Clermont *(G-1864)*

Crowder Custom Rods Inc ....G...... 772 220-8108
Stuart *(G-16134)*

L & S Bait Co Inc ....E 727 584-7691
Largo *(G-7631)*

Looper Sports Connection Inc ....G...... 352 796-7974
Brooksville *(G-1175)*

Synergy Sports LLC ....G...... 239 593-9374
Naples *(G-10918)*

SPORTING GOODS STORES: Firearms

Nst Global LLC ....E 941 748-2270
Bradenton *(G-1020)*

SPORTING GOODS STORES: Fishing Eqpt

Fishermans Center Inc ....G...... 561 844-5150
Riviera Beach *(G-14622)*

Toledo Sales Inc ....G...... 305 389-3441
Miami *(G-10021)*

SPORTING GOODS STORES: Pool & Billiard Tables

Robertson Billiard Sups Inc ....G...... 813 229-2778
Tampa *(G-17228)*

SPORTING GOODS STORES: Surfing Eqpt & Splys

Bote LLC .... F 888 855-4450
Miramar Beach (G-10568)

Waterboyz-Wbz Inc .... F 850 433-2929
Pensacola (G-13624)

SPORTING GOODS STORES: Team sports Eqpt

Dixon Screen Printing LLC .... G 850 476-3924
Pensacola (G-13490)

SPORTING GOODS: Archery

Bear Archery Inc .... C 352 376-2327
Gainesville (G-4659)

SPORTING GOODS: Fishing Nets

Brunken Manufacturing Co Inc .... G 850 438-2478
Pensacola (G-13464)

Burbank Trawl Makers Inc .... E 904 321-0976
Jacksonville (G-5963)

Lee Fisher International Inc .... E 813 875-6296
Tampa (G-17004)

SPORTING GOODS: Skin Diving Eqpt

A Plus Marine Supply Inc .... G 850 934-3890
Gulf Breeze (G-4874)

Halcyon Manufacturing Inc .... E 386 454-0811
High Springs (G-5455)

Lamartek Inc .... E 386 752-1087
Lake City (G-7027)

Mine Survival Inc .... G 850 774-0025
Panama City Beach (G-13334)

Undersea Breathing Systems .... G 561 588-7698
Lake Worth (G-7241)

SPORTING GOODS: Surfboards

Bote LLC .... F 888 855-4450
Miramar Beach (G-10568)

Bote Boards .... G 850 855-4046
Fort Walton Beach (G-4567)

Bote Paddle Boards .... F 850 460-2250
Destin (G-3060)

Glaspro .... E 941 488-4586
Venice (G-17694)

Hyperform Inc .... E 321 632-6503
Rockledge (G-14717)

Inspired Surf Boards .... G 904 347-8879
Saint Augustine (G-14847)

R & D Surf .... F 321 636-4456
Rockledge (G-14740)

SPORTS APPAREL STORES

Concealment Express LLC .... D 888 904-2722
Jacksonville (G-5996)

Rock N Roll Custom Screened S .... G 727 528-2111
Pinellas Park (G-13727)

Spirit Sales Corporation .... G 850 878-0366
Tallahassee (G-16503)

SPOUTING: Plastic & Fiberglass Reinforced

Building Blocks Management Inc .... F 214 289-9737
Kissimmee (G-6903)

Saint-Gobain Vetrotex Amer Inc .... C 407 834-8968
Maitland (G-8072)

SPRAYING & DUSTING EQPT

Desco Manufacturing Inc .... F 941 925-7029
Sarasota (G-15657)

Irms Inc .... F 321 631-1161
Rockledge (G-14719)

SPRAYING EQPT: Agricultural

Castillos Farms Inc .... G 305 232-0771
Miami (G-8900)

Florida Sprayers Inc .... G 813 989-0500
Temple Terrace (G-17538)

Spray Box LLC .... G 850 567-2724
Tallahassee (G-16504)

SPRINGS: Automobile

S N S Auto Sports LLC .... G 727 546-2700
Pinellas Park (G-13728)

SPRINGS: Clock, Precision

Forceleader Inc .... G 727 521-1808
Pinellas Park (G-13687)

SPRINGS: Mechanical, Precision

Harper Limbach LLC .... F 813 207-0057
Tampa (G-16906)

SPRINGS: Precision

SOUTHERN SPRING & STAMPING INC E 941 488-2276
Venice (G-17717)

SPRINGS: Steel

Goodrich Corporation .... C 904 757-3660
Jacksonville (G-6146)

Industrial Spring Corp .... F 954 524-2558
Davie (G-2425)

J C S Engineering & Dev .... F 305 888-7911
Hialeah (G-5199)

SOUTHERN SPRING & STAMPING INC E 941 488-2276
Venice (G-17717)

Vette Brakes & Products Inc .... E 727 345-5292
Saint Petersburg (G-15225)

SPRINGS: Wire

Carlo Morelli .... G 954 241-1426
Hollywood (G-5548)

Cook Spring Co .... D 941 377-5766
Sarasota (G-15642)

Crawford Manufacturing Company ..... F 513 548-6890
Tampa (G-16736)

Gilco Spring of Florida Inc .... E 813 855-4631
Oldsmar (G-11652)

Goodrich Corporation .... C 904 757-3660
Jacksonville (G-6146)

J C S Engineering & Dev .... F 305 888-7911
Hialeah (G-5199)

Optimum Spring Mfg Inc .... G 904 567-5999
Ponte Vedra (G-14258)

SPRINKLER SYSTEMS: Field

K-Rain Manufacturing Corp .... E 561 844-1002
Riviera Beach (G-14635)

SPRINKLING SYSTEMS: Fire Control

Grinnell LLC .... B 561 988-3658
Boca Raton (G-533)

Muller Fire Protection Inc .... E 305 636-9780
Miami (G-9598)

SPROCKETS: Power Transmission

Grizzly Manufacturing Inc .... E 386 755-0220
Lake City (G-7024)

Quality Industries America Inc .... G 386 755-0220
Lake City (G-7041)

Southern Gear & Machine Inc .... D 305 691-6300
Miami (G-9928)

STAGE LIGHTING SYSTEMS

Armadillo Sounds Inc .... G 305 801-7906
Miami (G-8748)

Dj Live Productions LLC .... G 407 383-1740
Altamonte Springs (G-43)

Koncept Systems LLC .... E 786 610-0122
Homestead (G-5724)

Liteworks Lighting Productions .... F 407 888-8677
Orlando (G-12335)

Platinum Ltg Productions LLC .... G 941 320-1906
Sarasota (G-15538)

Sweetlight Systems .... G 239 245-8159
Fort Myers (G-4416)

STAINLESS STEEL

American Stainless Mfrs .... G 786 275-4458
Miami (G-8720)

ATI Accurate Technology .... G 239 206-1240
Palmetto (G-13155)

ATI Agency Inc .... F 954 895-7909
Boca Raton (G-418)

ATI By Sea Co .... G 954 483-0526
Hollywood (G-5531)

Ati2 Inc .... G 904 396-3766
Jacksonville (G-5905)

Brewfab LLC .... F 727 823-8333
Saint Petersburg (G-14989)

Custom Stainless Stl Eqp Inc .... E 305 627-6049
Miami (G-8984)

Fabmaster Inc .... G 727 216-6750
Clearwater (G-1593)

Florida Stainless Steel ACC .... G 727 207-2575
Spring Hill (G-16071)

Quality Stinless Stl Works Inc .... G 305 519-0142
Hialeah (G-5323)

Shaws Fiberglass Inc .... G 863 425-9176
Mulberry (G-10638)

Stainless Steel Kitchens Corp .... G 305 999-1543
North Bay Village (G-11060)

Zerons Metal Designers Inc .... F 305 688-2240
Hialeah (G-5429)

STAINLESS STEEL WARE

Roden International Inc .... F 954 929-1900
Hollywood (G-5653)

STAINS: Biological

Inter Cell Technologies Inc .... G 561 575-6868
Jupiter (G-6747)

STAIRCASES & STAIRS, WOOD

Cedrus Inc .... E 772 286-2082
Stuart (G-16126)

General Stair Corporation .... E 305 769-9900
Hialeah (G-5170)

Remior Industries Inc .... E 305 883-8722
Miami (G-9791)

Scott-Douglas Design Inc .... G 727 535-7900
Largo (G-7677)

Symmetrical Stair Inc .... F 561 228-4800
Pompano Beach (G-14208)

STAMPED ART GOODS FOR EMBROIDERING

Ocean Blue Graphics Inc .... G 561 881-2022
Riviera Beach (G-14653)

STAMPINGS: Metal

Blackwater Folk Art Inc .... G 850 623-3470
Milton (G-10419)

Chasco Machine & Manufacturing ..... G 727 815-3510
Brooksville (G-1144)

Defense Stampings & Engrg Inc .... E 850 438-6105
Pensacola (G-13487)

Ebway LLC .... E 954 971-4911
Fort Lauderdale (G-3780)

Exact Inc .... C 904 783-6640
Jacksonville (G-6082)

Global Friction Products Inc .... F 813 241-2700
Tampa (G-16882)

Gregg Tool & Die Co Inc .... G 305 685-6309
Hialeah (G-5177)

Hoffstetter Tool & Die Inc .... F 727 573-7775
Clearwater (G-1625)

Industrial Spring Corp .... F 954 524-2558
Davie (G-2425)

Iron Container LLC .... E 305 726-2150
Miami (G-9339)

Koszegi Industries Inc .... E 954 419-9544
Deerfield Beach (G-2749)

Leader Tech Inc .... D 813 855-6921
Tampa (G-17002)

Metal Products Company LC .... E 850 526-5593
Marianna (G-8173)

Mikes Aluminum Products LLC .... G 407 855-1989
Saint Cloud (G-14934)

Plastic and Products Mktg LLC .... F 352 867-8078
Ocala (G-11468)

Premier Fabricating Llc .... F 813 855-4633
Oldsmar (G-11689)

Press-Rite Inc .... G 954 963-7373
Miramar (G-10529)

Production Metal Stampings Inc .... F 850 981-8240
Milton (G-10434)

RDS Manufacturing Inc .... C 850 584-6898
Perry (G-13650)

SOUTHERN SPRING & STAMPING INC E 941 488-2276
Venice (G-17717)

Spicer Industries Inc .... F 352 732-5300
Ocala (G-11497)

Strictly Toolboxes .... G 352 672-6566
Gainesville (G-4770)

PRODUCT

Top Notch Diecutting Foil STA ....G...... 904 346-3511
Jacksonville (G-6560)
U S Hardware Supply Inc ....E...... 407 657-1551
Winter Park (G-18547)

STAPLES

CMC Steel Us LLC ....E...... 904 266-4261
Jacksonville (G-5986)

STAPLES: Steel, Wire Or Cut

Tecnometales Onis Cnc LLC ....G...... 786 637-8316
Pembroke Pines (G-13419)

STARTERS: Electric Motor

T R S ....D...... 407 298-5490
Orlando (G-12644)

STARTERS: Motor

Central Fla Remanufacturing ....G...... 407 299-9011
Orlando (G-11993)

STATIC ELIMINATORS: Ind

Desco Industries Inc ....E...... 305 255-7744
Miami (G-9020)
Kinetronics Corporation ....F...... 941 951-2432
Bradenton (G-1001)
Ksm Electronics Inc ....D...... 954 642-7050
Fort Lauderdale (G-3909)
Patlon Industries Inc ....G...... 305 255-7744
Miami (G-9696)

STATIONARY & OFFICE SPLYS, WHOL: Computer/Photocopying Splys

I T Management Express Inc ....G...... 954 237-6999
Miramar (G-10502)

STATIONARY & OFFICE SPLYS, WHOLESALE: Laser Printer Splys

Sun Print Management LLC ....E...... 727 945-0255
Holiday (G-5504)
Totalprint USA ....G...... 855 915-1300
Tampa (G-17363)

STATIONERY & OFFICE SPLYS WHOLESALERS

Eclipse Development LLC ....F...... 520 370-7358
Weston (G-18239)
Greg Allens Inc ....E...... 904 262-8912
Jacksonville (G-6155)
Ramseys Prtg & Off Pdts Inc ....G...... 850 227-7468
Port Saint Joe (G-14390)
Toner Technologies Inc ....G...... 561 547-9710
Boynton Beach (G-920)
Well Made Bus Solutions LLC ....G...... 754 227-7268
Coconut Creek (G-2011)

STATIONERY PRDTS

Universal Tech Inc ....G...... 786 220-8032
Miami (G-10075)

STATORS REWINDING SVCS

Gulf Coast Elc Mtr Svc Inc ....E...... 850 433-5134
Pensacola (G-13515)

STATUARY & OTHER DECORATIVE PRDTS: Nonmetallic

Fleurissima Inc ....F...... 305 572-0203
Miami (G-9149)
Treasure Cove II Inc ....F...... 941 966-2004
Sarasota (G-15858)

STATUARY GOODS, EXC RELIGIOUS: Wholesalers

3dfx Inc ....F...... 407 237-6249
Orlando (G-11851)

STATUES: Nonmetal

Campbells Ornamental Concrete ....G...... 239 458-0800
Cape Coral (G-1321)

STEEL & ALLOYS: Tool & Die

Alpine Tool Inc ....G...... 727 587-0407
Largo (G-7529)
Sarasota Precision Engrg Inc ....F...... 941 727-3444
Sarasota (G-15552)

STEEL FABRICATORS

3dfx Inc ....F...... 407 237-6249
Orlando (G-11851)
3Imetals Inc ....F...... 305 497-4038
Miami (G-8610)
A & K Machine & Fab Shop Inc ....F...... 904 388-7772
Jacksonville (G-5844)
A&L Hall Investments Inc ....E...... 904 781-5080
Bryceville (G-1225)
A/C Cages ....G...... 407 446-9259
Deltona (G-3039)
AAA Steel Fabricators Inc ....G...... 954 570-7211
Deerfield Beach (G-2652)
Aat Omega LLC ....E...... 352 473-6673
Keystone Heights (G-6883)
Ace Fabricators Inc ....F...... 904 355-3724
Jacksonville (G-5856)
Adelman Steel Corp ....F...... 305 691-7740
Miami (G-8650)
Advanced Manufacturing & Engrg ....G...... 352 629-1494
Ocala (G-11314)
AGIsupreme Llc ....G...... 818 232-6699
Hollywood (G-5521)
Air Duct Systems Inc ....F...... 407 839-3313
Orlando (G-11879)
Al-Mar Metals Inc ....G...... 386 734-3377
De Leon Springs (G-2621)
Alchemist Holdings LLC ....E...... 772 340-7774
Port Saint Lucie (G-14394)
Alchemist Holdings LLC ....F...... 772 343-1111
Port Saint Lucie (G-14395)
Alico Metal Fabricators LLC ....G...... 239 454-4766
Fort Myers (G-4161)
Allensteel Inc ....E...... 239 454-1331
Fort Myers (G-4164)
Allied-360 LLC ....G...... 954 590-4940
Fort Lauderdale (G-3645)
Allpro Fbricators Erectors Inc ....G...... 954 797-7300
Davie (G-2381)
Alse Industries LLC ....G...... 305 688-8778
Miami Gardens (G-10251)
Aluminum Designs LLC ....G...... 239 289-3388
Naples (G-10662)
American Archtctral Mtls GL LL ....G...... 305 688-8778
Hialeah (G-5044)
American Metal Fab of Ctrl Fl ....G...... 813 653-2788
Brandon (G-1082)
Aminsa Corp ....G...... 954 865-1289
Weston (G-18222)
Anthony Spagna Svc & Maint Inc ....G...... 352 796-2109
Brooksville (G-1137)
Aog Detailing Services Inc ....G...... 727 742-7321
Saint Petersburg (G-14964)
Apex Fabrication Inc ....F...... 904 259-4666
Macclenny (G-8035)
ARC Transition LLC ....G...... 386 626-0001
Daytona Beach (G-2513)
ARC-Rite Inc ....E...... 386 325-3523
Jacksonville (G-5897)
Arcosa Trffic Ltg Strctres LLC ....E...... 352 748-4258
Sumterville (G-16262)
Artec Metal Fabrication Inc ....G...... 305 888-4375
Hialeah (G-5059)
Artemis Holdings Llc ....G...... 904 284-5611
Green Cove Springs (G-4816)
Artistic Gate Railing ....F...... 954 348-9752
Oakland Park (G-11241)
Atlantic Central Entps Inc ....F...... 386 255-6227
Daytona Beach (G-2515)
Atlantic Steel Inc ....E...... 407 599-3822
Longwood (G-7871)
Automated Metal Products Inc ....G...... 863 638-4404
Lake Wales (G-7153)
B & K Installations Inc ....G...... 305 245-6968
Homestead (G-5701)
Baker Metalworks and Sup Inc ....F...... 850 537-2010
Baker (G-292)
Barrett Custom Designs LLC ....G...... 321 242-2002
Melbourne (G-8374)
Best Fabrications Inc ....F...... 863 519-6611
Bartow (G-303)
Best Industries Inc ....F...... 772 460-8310
Fort Pierce (G-4470)

Big Bend Rebar Inc ....F...... 850 875-8000
Quincy (G-14542)
Big Iron Intl Inc ....G...... 407 222-2573
Orlando (G-11950)
Bostic Steel Inc ....D...... 305 592-7276
Doral (G-3146)
Brantley Machine & Fabrication ....F...... 904 359-0554
Jacksonville (G-5953)
Breton USA Customers Svc Corp ....F...... 941 360-2700
Sarasota (G-15616)
Burch Welding & Fabrication ....G...... 904 353-6513
Jacksonville (G-5964)
C M C Steel Fabricators Inc ....E...... 239 337-3480
Fort Myers (G-4197)
Capital Steel Inc ....F...... 352 628-1700
Homosassa (G-5744)
Capitol Rental Bldg Eqp Inc ....G...... 305 633-5008
Miami (G-8887)
Cato Steel Co ....F...... 407 671-3333
Winter Park (G-18497)
CC Welding & Construction LLC ....G...... 407 884-7474
Zellwood (G-18596)
Cemex Materials LLC ....C...... 941 722-4578
Palmetto (G-13159)
Central Metal Fabricators Inc ....E...... 305 261-6262
Miami (G-8911)
Central Steel Fabricators LLC ....G...... 904 503-1660
Jacksonville (G-5975)
Clarkwestern Dietrich Building ....D...... 800 693-3018
Ocala (G-11353)
Clarkwstern Dtrich Bldg System ....E...... 954 772-6300
Fort Lauderdale (G-3730)
Classic Metal Fabrication Inc ....F...... 561 305-9532
Boca Raton (G-463)
Coastal Acquisitions Fla LLC ....G...... 850 769-9423
Panama City (G-13243)
Coastal Mfg & Fabrication Inc ....G...... 352 799-8706
Brooksville (G-1147)
Coastal Sheet Mtalof S Fla LLC ....E...... 561 718-6044
Lake Worth (G-7192)
Commercial Metals Company ....G...... 904 262-9770
Jacksonville (G-5994)
Complete Metal Solutions Intl ....G...... 954 560-0583
Fort Lauderdale (G-3740)
Cornerstone Fabrication LLC ....E...... 386 310-1110
Debary (G-2633)
Custom Fabrication Inc ....E...... 813 754-7571
Plant City (G-13758)
Custom Metal Specialties Inc ....E...... 727 522-3986
Pinellas Park (G-13679)
Custom Wldg & Fabrication Inc ....D...... 863 967-1000
Auburndale (G-227)
D & D MBL Wldg Fabrication Inc ....F...... 954 791-3385
Fort Lauderdale (G-3751)
D & D MBL Wldg Fabrication Inc ....D...... 772 489-7900
Fort Pierce (G-4479)
D & D Wldg & Fabrication LLC ....G...... 954 791-3385
Fort Lauderdale (G-3752)
D & I Carbide Tool Co Inc ....F...... 727 848-3356
Hudson (G-5768)
Daytona Welding & Fabrication ....F...... 386 562-0093
Daytona Beach (G-2545)
DEC Sheet Metal Inc ....F...... 863 669-0707
Lakeland (G-7307)
Deltana Enterprises Inc ....E...... 305 592-8188
Doral (G-3189)
Dixie Metal Products Inc ....D...... 352 873-2554
Ocala (G-11368)
Dixie-Southern Arkansas LLC ....G...... 479 751-9183
Bradenton (G-969)
DK International Assoc Inc ....E...... 954 828-1256
Fort Lauderdale (G-3769)
Domestic Custom Metals Company ....G...... 239 643-2422
Naples (G-10733)
Dutchy Enterprises LLC ....G...... 321 877-0700
Cocoa (G-1922)
Dynabilt Technologies Corp ....F...... 305 919-9800
Hialeah (G-5126)
E-Z Metals Inc ....E...... 239 936-7887
Fort Myers (G-4241)
Eagle Metal Products Inc ....F...... 561 964-4192
Lake Worth (G-7200)
East Coast Medal ....G...... 561 619-6753
Lantana (G-7510)
East Coast Metal Decks Inc ....E...... 561 433-8259
Lantana (G-7511)
East Coast Steel Inc ....G...... 386 233-1385
Ormond Beach (G-12759)
Eastern Metal Supply NC Inc ....F...... 800 432-2204
West Palm Beach (G-17985)

Ed Steel Fabricator Inc .... G 305 926-4904
Hialeah *(G-5134)*
Elite Metal Manufacturing LLC .... G 386 364-0777
Live Oak *(G-7846)*
Elro Manufacturing LLC .... F 407 410-6006
Apopka *(G-125)*
Emerald Coast Fabricators .... G 850 554-6172
Pensacola *(G-13496)*
Emf Inc .... C 321 453-3670
Merritt Island *(G-8584)*
Emjac Industries Inc .... D 305 883-2194
Hialeah *(G-5142)*
Entertainment Metals Inc .... E 800 817-2683
Fort Myers *(G-4247)*
Fab Rite Inc .... G 561 848-8181
Riviera Beach *(G-14621)*
Fabco Metal Products LLC .... D 386 252-3730
Daytona Beach *(G-2551)*
Fabricating Technologies LLC .... G 352 473-6673
Keystone Heights *(G-6885)*
Fabsouth LLC .... F 954 938-5800
Oakland Park *(G-11265)*
Fis Group Inc .... G 786 622-3308
Opa Locka *(G-11746)*
Fitzlord Inc .... D 904 731-2041
Jacksonville *(G-6099)*
FK Instrument Co LLC .... D 727 472-2003
Clearwater *(G-1596)*
Florida Aluminum and Steel Inc .... F 863 967-4191
Auburndale *(G-231)*
Florida CMC Rebar .... G 407 518-5101
Jacksonville *(G-6103)*
Florida Custom Fabricators Inc .... F 407 892-8538
Saint Cloud *(G-14925)*
Florida Fabrication Inc .... F 407 212-0105
Apopka *(G-133)*
Florida Glass of Tampa Bay .... E 813 925-1330
Tampa *(G-16844)*
Fluid Metalworks Inc .... F 850 332-0103
Pensacola *(G-13505)*
Fsf Manufacturing Inc .... C 407 971-8280
Oviedo *(G-12822)*
Fuse Fabrication Llc .... E 863 225-5698
Mulberry *(G-10626)*
G & A Manufacturing Inc .... F 352 473-6882
Keystone Heights *(G-6886)*
Gardner-Watson Decking Inc .... E 813 891-9849
Oldsmar *(G-11650)*
General Saw Company .... F 813 231-3167
Tampa *(G-16874)*
Georges Welding Services Inc .... D 305 822-2445
Medley *(G-8248)*
Gerdau Ameristeel US Inc .... D 813 752-7550
Plant City *(G-13771)*
Gill Manufacturing Inc .... F 863 422-5711
Davenport *(G-2365)*
Grizzly Products Corp .... F 813 545-3828
Tampa *(G-16894)*
Group Steel Inc .... G 786 319-1222
Hialeah *(G-5178)*
Group Steel Inc .... G 305 965-0614
Miami *(G-9253)*
Gulf Coast Fabricators Inc .... G 850 584-5979
Perry *(G-13640)*
Gunns Welding & Fabricating .... G 727 393-5238
Saint Petersburg *(G-15070)*
Harrison Metals Inc .... G 352 588-2436
San Antonio *(G-15248)*
Henley Metal LLC .... F 904 353-4770
Jacksonville *(G-6173)*
Hernandez Metal Fabricators .... G 305 970-4145
Miami *(G-9276)*
Highway Systems Incorporated .... G 813 907-7512
Lutz *(G-7994)*
Holbrook Metal Fabrication LLC .... F 386 937-5441
Palatka *(G-12872)*
Hollywood Iron Works Inc .... F 954 962-0556
West Park *(G-18213)*
Imagine That Inc .... F 813 728-8324
Tarpon Springs *(G-17478)*
Industrial Welding & Maint .... G 352 799-3432
Brooksville *(G-1163)*
Innovative Fabricators Fla Inc .... G 941 375-8668
Nokomis *(G-11047)*
Inox Stainless Specialist LLC .... G 407 764-2456
Pompano Beach *(G-14062)*
Inprodelca Inc .... G 865 687-7921
Pembroke Pines *(G-13397)*
Iron Metal USA Corp .... G 786 757-3263
Medley *(G-8260)*

ITW Blding Cmponents Group Inc .... E 863 422-8685
Haines City *(G-4908)*
ITW Blding Cmponents Group Inc .... E 954 781-3333
Fort Lauderdale *(G-3888)*
J & J Steel Services Corp .... G 305 878-8929
Medley *(G-8262)*
J & J Wldg Stl Fbrction Fla In .... F 813 754-0771
Auburndale *(G-237)*
J A Custom .... G 561 615-4680
West Palm Beach *(G-18038)*
J2b Industrial LLC .... F 904 574-8919
Jacksonville *(G-6211)*
Jacksonville Steel Pdts Inc .... G 904 268-3364
Jacksonville *(G-6216)*
Jamar Cnstr Fabrication Inc .... G 321 400-0333
Sanford *(G-15342)*
Jax Truss Inc .... G 904 710-8198
Callahan *(G-1253)*
Jglc Enterprises LLC .... E 772 223-7393
Stuart *(G-16170)*
Jnc Welding & Fabricating Inc .... F 954 227-9424
Coral Springs *(G-2171)*
Jomar Metal Fabrication Inc .... G 407 857-1259
Orlando *(G-12277)*
Juno Ironcraft .... G 561 352-0471
Lake Park *(G-7130)*
Just Steel Inc .... F 941 755-7811
Sarasota *(G-15504)*
Just-In-Time Mfg Corp .... F 321 752-7552
Melbourne *(G-8446)*
K & T Manufacturing Inc .... G 407 814-7700
Apopka *(G-143)*
Keene Metal Fabricators Inc .... E 813 621-2455
Tampa *(G-16979)*
Kemco Industries LLC .... D 407 322-1230
Sanford *(G-15348)*
L & D Steel USA Inc .... F 727 538-9917
Largo *(G-7630)*
Latham Marine Inc .... E 954 462-3055
Fort Lauderdale *(G-3913)*
Lexington Dsign + Fbrction E L .... F 407 578-4720
Orlando *(G-12324)*
Lm Industrial Inc .... G 407 240-8911
Orlando *(G-12337)*
Lost Fabrication LLC .... G 772 971-3467
Fort Pierce *(G-4501)*
Magic Fabricators Inc .... F 407 332-0722
Casselberry *(G-1423)*
Manning Company .... G 954 523-9355
Fort Lauderdale *(G-3930)*
Manor Steel Fabricators .... G 941 722-8077
Palmetto *(G-13179)*
Mares Services Corp .... F 305 752-0093
Miami *(G-9508)*
Marlyn Steel Products Inc .... E 813 621-1375
Tampa *(G-17043)*
Martin & Vleminckx Rides LLC .... G 407 566-0036
Haines City *(G-4910)*
Master Fabricators Inc .... F 786 537-7440
Miami *(G-9517)*
McCarthy Fabrication LLC .... F 407 943-4909
Sanford *(G-15356)*
McDs Pro LLC .... G 954 302-3054
Davie *(G-2437)*
Meachem Steel Inc .... G 352 735-7333
Sorrento *(G-16011)*
Mechanical Dynamics Inc .... F 863 292-0709
Winter Haven *(G-18451)*
Merit Investments Inc .... F 877 997-8335
Fort Lauderdale *(G-3938)*
Merlin Industries Inc .... F 954 472-6891
Davie *(G-2439)*
Metal Magix Inc .... G 754 235-9996
Pompano Beach *(G-14096)*
Metal Supply and Machining Inc .... F 561 276-4941
Delray Beach *(G-2988)*
Metalcraft Services Tampa Inc .... F 813 558-8700
Tampa *(G-17068)*
Metpro Supply Inc .... E 863 425-7155
Mulberry *(G-10632)*
Michael Valentines Inc .... F 239 332-0855
Fort Myers *(G-4324)*
Mid Florida Steel Corp .... E 321 632-8228
Cocoa *(G-1942)*
Miller-Leaman Inc .... E 386 248-0500
Daytona Beach *(G-2576)*
Misc Metal Fabrication LLC .... F 754 264-1026
Deerfield Beach *(G-2768)*
MO Steel Fbricator Erector Inc .... G 305 945-4855
Miami *(G-9580)*

Moody Construction Svcs Inc .... E 941 776-1542
Duette *(G-3432)*
MPH Industries Inc .... F 352 372-9533
Gainesville *(G-4735)*
Naples Iron Works Inc .... E 239 649-7265
Naples *(G-10829)*
Nautical Structures Inds Inc .... E 727 541-6664
Largo *(G-7651)*
Orange State Steel Cnstr Inc .... E 727 544-3398
Pinellas Park *(G-13716)*
Orlando Metal Fabrication Inc .... F 407 850-4313
Orlando *(G-12453)*
Palatka Welding Shop Inc .... E 386 328-1507
Palatka *(G-12876)*
Palm Beach Iron Works Inc .... E 561 683-1816
West Palm Beach *(G-18109)*
Peters Structural Products .... G 863 229-5275
Winter Haven *(G-18457)*
Petrotech Services Inc .... G 813 248-0743
Tampa *(G-17159)*
Phoenix Metal Products Inc .... E 772 595-6386
Fort Pierce *(G-4518)*
Piecemakers LLC .... F 786 517-1829
Doral *(G-3328)*
Piecemakers Llc .... F 786 517-1829
Brandon *(G-1103)*
Pilot Steel Inc .... E 954 978-3615
Pompano Beach *(G-14127)*
Pipewelders Marine Inc .... D 954 587-8400
Fort Lauderdale *(G-3988)*
Powell Steel LLC .... G 386 406-1017
Ormond Beach *(G-12786)*
Precision Mtal Fbrications Inc .... G 305 691-0616
Hialeah *(G-5300)*
Premier Fabricators LLC .... G 772 323-2042
Fort Pierce *(G-4520)*
Protek Systems Inc .... G 561 395-8155
Delray Beach *(G-3006)*
Quality Fbrction Mch Works Inc .... F 386 755-0220
Lake City *(G-7040)*
Quality Industries America Inc .... G 386 755-0220
Lake City *(G-7041)*
Quality Metal Fabricators Inc .... E 813 831-7320
Tampa *(G-17201)*
Quality Metal Worx LLC .... F 863 353-6638
Haines City *(G-4914)*
Quality Steel Fabricators Inc .... F 813 247-7110
Tampa *(G-17202)*
Raber Industries Inc .... G 239 728-5527
Alva *(G-83)*
Rafab Spcialty Fabrication Inc .... F 407 422-3750
Orlando *(G-12530)*
Rebah Fabrication Inc .... F 407 857-3232
Orlando *(G-12537)*
Reeds Metal Manufacturing Inc .... E 352 498-0100
Cross City *(G-2262)*
Renaissance Man Incorporated .... G 850 432-1177
Pensacola *(G-13596)*
Renova Land and Sea LLC .... G 786 916-2695
Miramar *(G-10536)*
Rev-Tech Mfg Solutions LLC .... E 727 577-4999
Saint Petersburg *(G-15172)*
Rm Brands Inc .... G 904 356-0092
Jacksonville *(G-6431)*
Robert Ojeda Metalsmith Inc .... G 561 507-5511
Royal Palm Beach *(G-14772)*
Robotic Security Systems Inc .... E 850 871-9300
Panama City *(G-13303)*
Rubin Iron Works LLC .... F 904 356-5635
Jacksonville *(G-6436)*
Ryder Welding Service Inc .... F 305 685-6630
Opa Locka *(G-11787)*
S & B Metal Products E Fla Inc .... E 386 274-0092
Daytona Beach *(G-2592)*
SBs Precision Shtmtl Inc .... E 321 951-7411
Melbourne *(G-8516)*
Seaside Aluminum llc .... F 386 252-4940
Daytona Beach *(G-2595)*
Seatech Fabrication Inc .... G 954 410-0524
Deerfield Beach *(G-2805)*
Seiter Enterprises Inc .... F 813 728-8324
Tarpon Springs *(G-17491)*
Sembco Stl Erection Met Bldg .... F 561 863-0606
Riviera Beach *(G-14675)*
Shapes Group Ltd Co .... D 321 837-0500
Palm Bay *(G-12917)*
Shaws Fiberglass Inc .... G 863 425-9176
Mulberry *(G-10638)*
Sheet Metal Systems Inc .... F 727 548-1711
Pinellas Park *(G-13729)*

Snappy Structures Inc ....F...... 954 926-6611
Hollywood *(G-5658)*

Southern Aluminum and Stl Inc ....G...... 850 484-4700
Cantonment *(G-1275)*

Southern Custom Iron & Art LLC ....E...... 561 586-8400
Lake Worth Beach *(G-7262)*

Southern Strl Stl Fla Inc ....F...... 727 327-7123
Saint Petersburg *(G-15192)*

Southstern Stnless Fbrctors In ....F...... 904 354-4381
Jacksonville *(G-6496)*

Southwest Steel Group Inc ....G...... 239 283-8980
Cape Coral *(G-1391)*

Specialty Structures Inc ....F...... 386 668-0474
Debary *(G-2643)*

Spencer Fabrications Inc ....E...... 352 343-0014
Tavares *(G-17524)*

Spring Loaded Inc ....F...... 561 747-8785
Jupiter *(G-6804)*

Star Fabricators ....G...... 904 899-6569
Jacksonville *(G-6505)*

Steel City Inc ....F...... 850 785-9596
Panama City *(G-13311)*

Steel Components Inc ....F...... 954 427-6820
Coconut Creek *(G-2007)*

Steel Fabricators LLC ....C...... 954 772-0440
Oakland Park *(G-11298)*

Steel Products Inc ....G...... 941 351-8128
Sarasota *(G-15838)*

Sterling Steel Fabrications ....E...... 561 366-8600
Mangonia Park *(G-8101)*

Sterling Stl Cstm Alum Fbrcton ....E...... 561 386-7166
Riviera Beach *(G-14678)*

Structural Steel of Brevard ....F...... 321 726-0271
Melbourne *(G-8535)*

Stuart Yacht Builders ....F...... 561 747-1947
Stuart *(G-16234)*

Suncoast Projects LLC ....E...... 407 581-0665
Groveland *(G-4873)*

Tampa Steel Erecting Company ....D...... 813 677-7184
Tampa *(G-17340)*

Tampa Tank & Welding Inc ....F...... 813 241-0123
Gibsonton *(G-4801)*

Teknifab Industries Inc ....G...... 321 722-1922
Melbourne *(G-8547)*

Tidal Wave Tanks Fabrications ....G...... 863 425-7795
Mulberry *(G-10642)*

Titan Dealer Services LLC ....E...... 813 839-7406
Tampa *(G-17355)*

TL Sheet Metal Inc ....G...... 813 871-3780
Tampa *(G-17357)*

Trinity Fabricators Inc ....E...... 904 284-9657
Green Cove Springs *(G-4839)*

Tryana LLC ....G...... 813 467-9916
Tampa *(G-17376)*

TTI Holdings Inc ....G...... 813 623-2675
Tampa *(G-17378)*

Tuckers Machine & Stl Svc Inc ....D...... 352 787-3157
Leesburg *(G-7800)*

United Fabrication & Maint ....G...... 863 295-9000
Eloise *(G-3514)*

United Granite Inc ....F...... 813 391-4323
Tampa *(G-17392)*

Universal Erectors Inc ....G...... 813 621-8111
Lithia *(G-7840)*

Universal Welding Service Co ....G...... 305 898-9130
Hialeah Gardens *(G-5453)*

Unlimited Welding Inc ....E...... 407 327-3333
Winter Springs *(G-18580)*

US Custom Fabrication Inc ....G...... 954 917-6161
Pompano Beach *(G-14231)*

US Manufacturing Company ....C...... 305 885-0301
Medley *(G-8346)*

US Manufacturing Company ....F...... 305 556-1661
Hialeah *(G-5398)*

US Metal Fabricators Inc ....F...... 954 921-0800
Dania Beach *(G-2360)*

USF Fabrication Inc ....C...... 305 556-1661
Hialeah *(G-5401)*

Van Linda Iron Works Inc ....E...... 561 586-8400
Lake Worth Beach *(G-7263)*

Veatic ....G...... 888 474-2999
Kissimmee *(G-6971)*

Viper Communication Systems ....E...... 352 694-7030
Ocala *(G-11510)*

Vision Conveyor Inc ....F...... 352 343-3300
Tavares *(G-17529)*

Vulcan Steel ....G...... 561 945-1259
Jupiter *(G-6822)*

W D Wilson Inc ....G...... 813 626-6989
Tampa *(G-17421)*

Western Fabricating LLC ....G...... 239 676-5382
Fort Myers *(G-4447)*

Wheeler Lumber LLC ....F...... 772 464-4400
Fort Pierce *(G-4554)*

Wilcox Steel Company LLC ....G...... 727 443-0461
Clearwater *(G-1852)*

Wilkinson Steel Supply LLC ....G...... 904 757-1522
Jacksonville *(G-6611)*

STEEL MILLS

Associated Steel & Alum Co Inc ....F...... 954 974-7890
Pompano Beach *(G-13938)*

Associated Steel & Alum Ltd ....G...... 954 974-7890
Pompano Beach *(G-13939)*

Belt Corp ....F...... 954 505-7400
Hollywood *(G-5539)*

Berg LLC ....F...... 786 201-2625
Aventura *(G-256)*

Commercial Metals Company ....F...... 904 781-4780
Jacksonville *(G-5995)*

Conc-Steel Inc ....G...... 516 882-5551
Palm Coast *(G-13074)*

Diverse Co ....E...... 863 425-4251
Mulberry *(G-10623)*

Gerdau Ameristeel Corp ....A...... 813 286-8383
Tampa *(G-16876)*

Gerdau Ameristeel US Inc ....E...... 813 752-7550
Plant City *(G-13772)*

Gulf Atlantic Culvert Company ....F...... 850 562-2384
Tallahassee *(G-16454)*

Home & Garden Industries Inc ....F...... 305 634-0681
Miami *(G-9289)*

Inductoweld Tube Corp ....G...... 646 734-7094
Fort Lauderdale *(G-3875)*

Industrial Galvanizers Miami ....E...... 305 681-8844
Miami *(G-9309)*

Innovative Steel Tech Inc ....F...... 813 767-1746
Gibsonton *(G-4798)*

ITW Blding Cmponents Group Inc ....E...... 863 422-8685
Haines City *(G-4908)*

Latham Marine Inc ....E...... 954 462-3055
Fort Lauderdale *(G-3913)*

Maclan Corporation Inc ....E...... 863 665-4814
Lakeland *(G-7387)*

Metal Culverts Inc ....F...... 727 531-1431
Clearwater *(G-1694)*

Metal Processors Inc ....E...... 813 654-0050
Tampa *(G-17067)*

Nucor LLC ....G...... 786 290-9328
Surfside *(G-16397)*

Nucor Steel Florida Inc ....G...... 863 546-5800
Frostproof *(G-4639)*

Phlebotomists On Wheels Inc ....F...... 954 873-7591
Fort Lauderdale *(G-3984)*

Sea Side Specialties ....G...... 561 276-6518
Delray Beach *(G-3014)*

Sel West Coast Inc ....E...... 352 373-6354
Gainesville *(G-4760)*

Spectrum Engineering Inc ....G...... 239 277-1182
Fort Myers *(G-4405)*

Stainless Fabricators Inc ....E...... 813 926-7113
Odessa *(G-11581)*

T&T Sons Inc ....G...... 859 576-3316
Oviedo *(G-12849)*

Wheel Wright ....G...... 850 626-2662
Milton *(G-10443)*

Wheels For You Inc ....F...... 772 485-0162
Fort Pierce *(G-4555)*

Yale Ogron Mfg Co Inc ....E...... 305 687-0424
Opa Locka *(G-11803)*

STEEL: Cold-Rolled

Hydro Extrusion Usa LLC ....B...... 904 794-1500
Saint Augustine *(G-14841)*

Hydro Precision Tubing USA LLC ....C...... 321 636-8147
Rockledge *(G-14716)*

Suncoast Post-Tension Ltd ....E...... 305 592-5075
Miami *(G-9966)*

STEEL: Laminated

Poly Coatings of South Inc ....F...... 941 371-8555
Sarasota *(G-15784)*

STENCILS

Design Services Inc ....G...... 813 949-4748
Land O Lakes *(G-7491)*

Ipg (us) Holdings Inc ....D...... 941 727-5788
Sarasota *(G-15708)*

Ipg (us) Inc ....G...... 941 727-5788
Sarasota *(G-15709)*

STENCILS & LETTERING MATERIALS: Die-Cut

Super Grafix Inc ....F...... 561 585-1519
Boca Raton *(G-704)*

STOCK CAR RACING

Tom Watson Enterprises Inc ....G...... 352 683-5097
Hudson *(G-5789)*

STONE: Cast Concrete

Coral Reef Cast Stone Inc ....F...... 561 586-1900
West Palm Beach *(G-17973)*

K&T Stoneworks Inc ....G...... 561 798-8486
West Palm Beach *(G-18045)*

Saint Augustine Cast Stone ....G...... 904 794-2626
Saint Augustine *(G-14885)*

True Stone Corp ....E...... 772 334-9797
Fort Pierce *(G-4543)*

STONE: Dimension, NEC

Cavastone LLC ....G...... 561 994-9100
Boca Raton *(G-455)*

Central State Aggregates LLC ....F...... 813 788-0454
Zephyrhills *(G-18608)*

Custom Marble Works Inc ....E...... 813 620-0475
Tampa *(G-16754)*

Keystone Products Inc ....F...... 305 245-4716
Homestead *(G-5723)*

LW Rozzo Inc ....E...... 954 435-8501
Pembroke Pines *(G-13400)*

Old World Marble and Gran Inc ....G...... 239 596-4777
Naples *(G-10841)*

Plaza Materials Corp ....D...... 813 788-0454
Zephyrhills *(G-18627)*

Reyes Granite & Marble Corp ....F...... 305 599-7330
Miami *(G-9801)*

Rockers Stone Inc ....G...... 305 447-1231
Miami *(G-9816)*

Stone Center Inc ....F...... 863 669-0292
Lakeland *(G-7450)*

Stone Mosaics ....G...... 321 773-3635
Palm Bay *(G-12923)*

Stone Systems South Fla LLC ....F...... 954 584-4058
Lauderhill *(G-7743)*

Stone Trend International Inc ....E...... 941 927-9113
Sarasota *(G-15839)*

Vgcm LLC ....F...... 813 247-7625
Tampa *(G-17412)*

Vgcm LLC ....E...... 813 620-4889
Tampa *(G-17413)*

STONE: Quarrying & Processing, Own Stone Prdts

Center Sand Mine ....G...... 800 366-7263
Clermont *(G-1862)*

Devcon International Corp ....F...... 954 926-5200
Boca Raton *(G-482)*

Florida Crushed Stone Co ....G...... 352 799-7460
Bushnell *(G-1243)*

Keystone Products Inc ....F...... 305 245-4716
Homestead *(G-5723)*

Palm Beach Aggregates LLC ....E...... 561 795-6550
Loxahatchee *(G-7974)*

STONES: Abrasive

Martin Marietta Materials Inc ....G...... 904 596-0230
Jacksonville *(G-6277)*

STOOLS: Factory

E&T Horizons Ltd Liability Co ....F...... 321 704-1244
Melbourne *(G-8413)*

STORE FIXTURES: Wood

Artco Group Inc ....D...... 305 638-1785
Miami *(G-8753)*

Load King Manufacturing Co ....C...... 904 354-8882
Jacksonville *(G-6263)*

Synergy Custom Fixtures Corp ....C...... 305 693-0055
Hialeah *(G-5376)*

T & R Store Fixtures Inc ....E...... 305 751-0377
Miami *(G-9988)*

STORE FRONTS: Prefabricated, Metal

Architectural Metal Systems...............F..... 407 277-1364
Orlando *(G-11916)*

Gopi Glass Sales & Svcs Corp............E..... 305 592-2089
Miami *(G-9228)*

Metal Fronts Inc............G..... 727 547-6700
Seminole *(G-15982)*

STORES: Auto & Home Supply

Shafers Clssic Rprductions Inc............G..... 813 622-7091
Tampa *(G-17255)*

STORES: Drapery & Upholstery

Southeast Energy Inc............G..... 561 883-1051
Boca Raton *(G-686)*

STRAPPING

JKS Industries Inc............E..... 863 425-1745
Mulberry *(G-10628)*

JKS Industries Inc............F..... 727 573-1305
Tampa *(G-16966)*

STRAW GOODS

Straw Life Inc............G..... 386 935-2850
O Brien *(G-11225)*

STRAWS: Drinking, Made From Purchased Materials

CU Holdings LLC............D..... 904 483-5700
Jacksonville *(G-6017)*

STRUCTURAL SUPPORT & BUILDING MATERIAL: Concrete

A To Z Concrete Products Inc............F..... 727 321-6000
Saint Petersburg *(G-14950)*

Gate Precast Company............G..... 904 732-7668
Jacksonville *(G-6130)*

Gate Precast Erection Co............D..... 904 737-7220
Jacksonville *(G-6131)*

Solar Erectors US Inc............F..... 305 823-8950
Medley *(G-8320)*

Thompson Sales Group Inc............E..... 239 332-0446
Fort Myers *(G-4424)*

STUCCO

Andrew Pratt Stucco & Plst Inc............F..... 407 501-2609
Orlando *(G-11911)*

Best of Orlando Pntg & Stucco............G..... 407 947-4174
Apopka *(G-106)*

Best Products Mix Inc............G..... 305 512-9920
Hialeah *(G-5075)*

Bluewater Finishing LLC............G..... 772 460-9457
Port Saint Lucie *(G-14400)*

Classic Stucco & Stone LLC............F..... 850 892-1045
Defuniak Springs *(G-2838)*

Custom Stucco Inc............G..... 941 650-5649
Englewood *(G-3517)*

Custom Wall Systems Inc............G..... 772 408-3006
Vero Beach *(G-17752)*

E T Plastering Inc............F..... 305 874-7082
Virginia Gardens *(G-17823)*

Fekel Stucco Plastering Inc............G..... 239 571-5464
Naples *(G-10746)*

Florida Stucco Corp............E..... 561 487-1301
Boca Raton *(G-519)*

Florida Sunshine Stucco LLC............G..... 407 947-2088
Orlando *(G-12168)*

Gold Coast Plst & Stucco Inc............F..... 954 275-9132
Margate *(G-8132)*

Gsw Stucco LLC............G..... 904 246-0783
Jacksonville Beach *(G-6635)*

Harry Cashatt Stucco LLC............G..... 941 468-2166
Englewood *(G-3532)*

J&Jh Stucco Inc............G..... 813 482-5282
Riverview *(G-14567)*

Jag Stucco Inc............G..... 813 210-6577
Land O Lakes *(G-7495)*

MDK Enterpises Inc............F..... 904 288-6855
Jacksonville *(G-6286)*

Pre-Mix Marble Tite Inc............E..... 954 917-7665
Pompano Beach *(G-14139)*

Premix-Marbletite Mfg Co............F..... 954 970-6540
Pompano Beach *(G-14143)*

Premix-Marbletite Mfg Co............F..... 407 327-0830
Winter Springs *(G-18574)*

Q Plastering and Stucco Inc............G..... 239 530-1712
Naples *(G-10870)*

Reyes Stucco Inc............G..... 321 557-1319
Cocoa *(G-1953)*

River City Stucco Inc............G..... 904 234-9526
Jacksonville *(G-6426)*

S&L Cnstrction Specialists Inc............G..... 407 300-5080
Orlando *(G-12566)*

Trinity Exterior Solutions LLC............G..... 850 393-9682
Holt *(G-5694)*

STUDIOS: Artist

Seaboard Manufacturing LLC............G..... 727 497-3572
Clearwater *(G-1779)*

STUDS & JOISTS: Sheet Metal

Doral Building Supply Corp............F..... 305 471-9797
Doral *(G-3196)*

Steel Cnstr Systems Holdg Co............E..... 407 438-1664
Orlando *(G-12623)*

SUBMARINE BUILDING & REPAIR

Triton Submarines LLC............E..... 772 770-1995
Sebastian *(G-15906)*

US Submarines Inc............E..... 208 687-9057
Vero Beach *(G-17813)*

SUNDRIES & RELATED PRDTS: Medical & Laboratory, Rubber

Acuderm Inc............D..... 954 733-6935
Fort Lauderdale *(G-3623)*

Ga-MA & Associates Inc............G..... 352 687-8840
Ocala *(G-11398)*

Integrity Technologies LLC............G..... 561 768-9023
Jupiter *(G-6746)*

Liquiguard Technologies Inc............E..... 954 566-0996
Fort Lauderdale *(G-3920)*

Omt LLC............F..... 954 327-1447
Fort Lauderdale *(G-3967)*

Rubber 2 Go Llc............E..... 305 688-8566
Miami *(G-9827)*

Victus LLC............E..... 305 663-2129
Miami *(G-10109)*

SUNGLASSES, WHOLESALE

Miami Eyeworks Inc............G..... 954 316-6757
Pembroke Pines *(G-13403)*

SUNROOMS: Prefabricated Metal

Titan Specialty Cnstr Inc............E..... 850 916-7660
Milton *(G-10440)*

SUPERMARKETS & OTHER GROCERY STORES

ABC Fence Systems Inc............F..... 850 638-8876
Chipley *(G-1452)*

Delarosa Real Foods LLC............D..... 718 333-0333
Lauderdale Lakes *(G-7712)*

Healthier Choices MGT Corp............E..... 305 600-5004
Hollywood *(G-5589)*

SURFACE ACTIVE AGENTS

Paraflow Energy Solutions LLC............E..... 713 239-0336
Boca Raton *(G-630)*

SURFACE ACTIVE AGENTS: Oils & Greases

Global GI Lc............G..... 863 551-1079
Winter Haven *(G-18443)*

SURFACERS: Concrete Grinding

A Clean Finish Inc............G..... 407 516-1311
Jacksonville *(G-5846)*

Jdl Surface Innovations Inc............F..... 239 772-0077
Cape Coral *(G-1359)*

SURGICAL & MEDICAL INSTRUMENTS WHOLESALERS

Camel Enterprises Corp............F..... 954 234-2559
Miami *(G-8881)*

Gremed Group Corp............F..... 305 392-5331
Doral *(G-3240)*

Uroshape LLC............F..... 321 960-2484
Melbourne *(G-8555)*

SURGICAL APPLIANCES & SPLYS

Consolidated Polymer Tech............E..... 727 531-4191
Clearwater *(G-1549)*

Halkey-Roberts Corporation............C..... 727 471-4200
Saint Petersburg *(G-15072)*

Johnson & Johnson............E..... 305 261-3500
Miami *(G-9371)*

Singletary Systems Inc............E..... 508 865-4445
Saint Petersburg *(G-15185)*

Universal Surgical Appliance............G..... 305 652-0810
Miami *(G-10074)*

SURGICAL APPLIANCES & SPLYS

360 O and P Inc............G..... 813 985-5000
Temple Terrace *(G-17534)*

Advanced Prosthetics Amer Inc............F..... 813 631-9400
Tampa *(G-16560)*

Aso Corporation............E..... 941 378-6600
Sarasota *(G-15602)*

Baycare Home Care Inc............F..... 727 461-5878
Clearwater *(G-1514)*

Biosculptor Corporation............G..... 305 823-8300
Hialeah *(G-5076)*

Blue Diamond Orthopedic LLC............G..... 407 613-2001
Orlando *(G-11959)*

C C Lead Inc............F..... 863 465-6458
Lake Placid *(G-7139)*

Cesar E Rodriguez............G..... 561 305-1312
Deerfield Beach *(G-2690)*

Comfort Brace LLC............G..... 954 899-1563
Lighthouse Point *(G-7826)*

Cordis Corporation............C..... 786 313-2000
Miami Lakes *(G-10293)*

Core Oncology Inc............G..... 206 236-2100
Miami *(G-8970)*

Elmridge Protection Pdts LLC............G..... 561 244-8337
Boca Raton *(G-503)*

Encore Inc............F..... 941 359-3599
Sarasota *(G-15474)*

Exactech Inc............D..... 352 377-1140
Gainesville *(G-4687)*

Foot Function Lab Inc............G..... 954 753-2500
Coral Springs *(G-2154)*

Harts Mobility LLC............G..... 404 769-4234
Port St Lucie *(G-14476)*

Healthline Medical Pdts Inc............F..... 407 656-0704
Winter Garden *(G-18389)*

Howmedica Osteonics Corp............G..... 941 378-4600
Sarasota *(G-15702)*

Howmedica Osteonics Corp............G..... 813 886-3450
Tampa *(G-16924)*

Intermed Group Inc............E..... 561 586-3667
Alachua *(G-12)*

Invacare Corporation............G..... 800 532-8677
Pinellas Park *(G-13695)*

Invacare Florida Corporation............B..... 407 321-5630
Sanford *(G-15340)*

Johnson & Johnson............G..... 813 972-0204
Tampa *(G-16969)*

Johnson & Johnson Services Inc............C..... 239 598-4444
Naples *(G-10792)*

Kericure Inc............F..... 855 888-5374
Wesley Chapel *(G-17880)*

Linvatec Corporation............B..... 727 392-6464
Largo *(G-7633)*

Main Tape Co Inc............G..... 561 248-8867
West Palm Beach *(G-18062)*

Maven Medical Mfg Inc............E..... 727 518-0555
Largo *(G-7639)*

Medtronic Usa Inc............A..... 702 308-1302
Jacksonville *(G-6292)*

Neutral Guard LLC............G..... 954 249-6600
Fort Lauderdale *(G-3958)*

Quick Protective Systems Inc............G..... 772 220-3315
Stuart *(G-16202)*

Restoration Medical LLC............G..... 863 272-0250
Lakeland *(G-7420)*

Safariland LLC............F..... 904 741-5400
Jacksonville *(G-6444)*

Safariland LLC............E..... 904 741-5400
Jacksonville *(G-6447)*

Shukla Medical Inc............E..... 732 474-1769
Saint Petersburg *(G-15183)*

Sientra Inc............G..... 813 751-7576
Brandon *(G-1107)*

Sky Medical Inc............F..... 954 747-3188
Sunrise *(G-16366)*

Employee Codes: A=Over 500 employees, B=251-500
C=101-250, D=51-100, E=20-50, F=10-19, G=4-9

2022 Harris Florida
Manufacturers Directory

1335

PRODUCT

Specialty Def Systems KY Inc ....G..... 904 741-5400
Jacksonville *(G-6499)*
Steris Corporation ....C..... 813 852-8002
Tampa *(G-17303)*
Superior Surgical Mfg Co ....F..... 800 727-8643
Seminole *(G-15993)*
Surefire Strgc Solutions LLC ....G..... 305 720-7118
Miami *(G-9976)*
Syndaver Labs Inc ....E..... 813 600-5530
Tampa *(G-17318)*
Vy Spine LLC ....G..... 866 489-7746
Tallahassee *(G-16521)*
Westcoast Brace & Limb Inc ....D..... 407 502-0024
Maitland *(G-8079)*
Zassi Holdings Inc ....G..... 904 432-8315
Ponte Vedra Beach *(G-14283)*

SURGICAL EQPT: See Also Instruments

American Surgical Mask LLC ....E..... 813 606-4510
Tampa *(G-16591)*
Arthrex Manufacturing Inc ....C..... 239 643-5553
Naples *(G-10676)*
Baxter Healthcare Corporation ....B..... 727 544-5050
Largo *(G-7546)*
Cae Healthcare Inc ....E..... 941 377-5562
Sarasota *(G-15625)*
Conmed Corporation ....B..... 727 392-6464
Largo *(G-7568)*
Gulf Medical Fiberoptics Inc ....G..... 813 855-6618
Oldsmar *(G-11655)*
Howmedica Osteonics Corp ....C..... 954 791-6078
Fort Lauderdale *(G-3870)*
Linvatec Corporation ....B..... 727 392-6464
Largo *(G-7633)*
Maxxim Medical Group Inc ....F..... 727 571-3717
Clearwater *(G-1688)*
Ndh Medical Inc ....G..... 727 570-2293
Saint Petersburg *(G-15137)*
Rotburg Instruments Amer Inc ....F..... 954 331-8046
Sunrise *(G-16365)*
Unimed Surgical Products Inc ....E..... 727 546-1900
Seminole *(G-15996)*
Zimmer Biomet CMF Thoracic LLC ......C..... 574 267-6639
Jacksonville *(G-6623)*

SURGICAL IMPLANTS

Axogen Corporation ....E..... 386 462-6800
Alachua *(G-7)*
Catalyst Orthoscience Inc ....G..... 239 325-9976
Naples *(G-10705)*
Catalyst Orthoscience Inc ....G..... 317 625-7548
Naples *(G-10706)*
Ctm Biomedical LLC ....F..... 561 650-4027
Miami *(G-8982)*
Engage UNI LLC ....F..... 833 364-2432
Orlando *(G-12129)*
Ht Medical LLC ....G..... 888 594-8633
Orlando *(G-12230)*
Innovative Mfg Solutions LLC ....G..... 904 647-5300
Jacksonville *(G-6199)*
Medtronic Xomed Inc ....A..... 904 296-9600
Jacksonville *(G-6293)*
Medtronic Xomed Inc ....B..... 904 296-9600
Jacksonville *(G-6294)*
Physiorx LLC ....G..... 407 718-5549
Ocoee *(G-11524)*
Spinenet LLC ....G..... 321 439-1806
Winter Park *(G-18539)*
US Implant Solutions LLC ....G..... 407 971-8054
Maitland *(G-8077)*

SURVEYING & MAPPING: Land Parcels

A B Survey Supply Entps Inc ....G..... 772 464-9500
Fort Pierce *(G-4457)*
Quantum Spatial Inc ....D..... 920 457-3631
Saint Petersburg *(G-15168)*

SURVEYING SVCS: Aerial Digital Imaging

Drs Training Ctrl Systems LLC ....E..... 850 302-3000
Fort Walton Beach *(G-4578)*

SVC ESTABLISHMENT EQPT & SPLYS WHOLESALERS

Quality Industrial Chem Inc ....F..... 727 573-5760
Saint Petersburg *(G-15167)*

SVC ESTABLISHMENT EQPT, WHOL: Cleaning & Maint Eqpt & Splys

Threez Company LLC ....G..... 904 422-9224
Jacksonville *(G-6550)*

SVC ESTABLISHMENT EQPT, WHOL: Liquor Dispensing Eqpt/Sys

Micro Matic Usa Inc ....E..... 352 544-1081
Brooksville *(G-1181)*

SVC ESTABLISHMENT EQPT, WHOLESALE: Beauty Parlor Eqpt & Sply

Matrix Packaging of Florida ....G..... 305 358-9696
Miami *(G-9520)*
No 1 Beauty Salon Furniture ....G..... 954 981-0403
Oakland Park *(G-11281)*

SVC ESTABLISHMENT EQPT, WHOLESALE: Vending Machines & Splys

Sunnypics LLC ....G..... 407 992-6210
Orlando *(G-12633)*

SWIMMING POOL & HOT TUB CLEANING & MAINTENANCE SVCS

Fibre Tech Inc ....E..... 727 539-0844
Largo *(G-7583)*
National Chemical Sply ....F..... 800 515-9938
Davie *(G-2444)*
South West Adventure Team LLC ......G..... 903 288-4739
Labelle *(G-6986)*

SWIMMING POOL ACCESS: Leaf Skimmers Or Pool Rakes

Skim-A-Round Inc ....G..... 631 223-5072
Bonita Springs *(G-818)*

SWIMMING POOL EQPT: Filters & Water Conditioning Systems

Aladdin Equipment Company ....D..... 941 371-3732
Sarasota *(G-15590)*
Com Pac Filtration Inc ....E..... 904 356-4003
Jacksonville *(G-5993)*
Esse Sales Inc ....G..... 954 368-3900
Oakland Park *(G-11264)*
Fluidra Usa LLC ....F..... 904 378-4486
Jacksonville *(G-6115)*
Harmsco Inc ....D..... 561 848-9628
Riviera Beach *(G-14626)*
Paradise Pool Care & Co LLC ....G..... 239 338-7715
Lehigh Acres *(G-7820)*
South West Adventure Team LLC ......G..... 903 288-4739
Labelle *(G-6986)*
Yauchler Properties LLC ....F..... 863 662-5570
Winter Haven *(G-18479)*

SWIMMING POOL SPLY STORES

Jacks Magic Products Inc ....F..... 727 536-4500
Largo *(G-7620)*
South West Adventure Team LLC ......G..... 903 288-4739
Labelle *(G-6986)*
Tri-County Chemical Co ....G..... 407 682-3550
Apopka *(G-181)*

SWIMMING POOLS, EQPT & SPLYS: Wholesalers

South West Adventure Team LLC ......G..... 903 288-4739
Labelle *(G-6986)*

SWITCHBOARD APPARATUS, EXC INSTRUMENTS

Siemens Industry Inc ....D..... 954 436-8848
Pembroke Pines *(G-13414)*

SWITCHES

Everaxis Usa Inc ....D..... 239 263-3102
Naples *(G-10743)*
S A Microtechnologies LLC ....F..... 954 973-6166
Pompano Beach *(G-14166)*

SWITCHES: Electric Power

Resa Pwr Slutions Plant Cy LLC ......F..... 813 752-6550
Plant City *(G-13799)*

SWITCHES: Electric Power, Exc Snap, Push Button, Etc

Entech Controls Corp ....G..... 954 613-2971
Miami *(G-9100)*
Powerficient LLC ....E..... 800 320-2535
Fort Lauderdale *(G-3990)*

SWITCHES: Electronic

Mini Circuits Lab Inc ....E..... 305 558-6381
Hialeah *(G-5259)*
Molex LLC ....F..... 727 521-2700
Pinellas Park *(G-13711)*

SWITCHES: Flow Actuated, Electrical

Malema Engineering Corporation .....F..... 561 995-0595
Boca Raton *(G-582)*

SWITCHES: Solenoid

Standard Technology Inc ....F..... 386 671-7406
Ormond Beach *(G-12795)*

SWITCHES: Time, Electrical Switchgear Apparatus

Miami Switchgear Company ....G..... 786 336-5783
Miami *(G-9559)*

SWITCHGEAR & SWITCHBOARD APPARATUS

ABB Enterprise Software Inc ....C..... 954 752-6700
Coral Springs *(G-2124)*
ABB Inc ....B..... 407 732-2000
Lake Mary *(G-7056)*
ABB Inc ....D..... 305 471-0844
Miami *(G-8634)*
Control Solutions Inc ....F..... 813 247-2136
Tampa *(G-16725)*
Evolution Intrcnnect Systems I ......F..... 954 217-6223
Davie *(G-2409)*
Gas Turbine Efficiency LLC ....E..... 407 304-5200
Orlando *(G-12183)*
Hughes Corporation ....E..... 954 755-7111
Coral Springs *(G-2164)*
J B Nottingham & Co Inc ....E..... 386 873-2990
Deland *(G-2877)*
Kbn Corporation ....G..... 321 327-9792
Palm Bay *(G-12905)*
Kemco Industries LLC ....D..... 407 322-1230
Sanford *(G-15348)*
Lextm3 Systems LLC ....F..... 954 888-1024
Davie *(G-2434)*
Motor Protection Electronics ....F..... 407 299-3825
Apopka *(G-155)*
New IEM Power Systems LLC ......C..... 904 365-4444
Jacksonville *(G-6326)*
Rapid Switch Systems LLC ....G..... 941 720-7380
Bradenton *(G-1034)*
TESS LLC ....F..... 954 583-6262
Fort Lauderdale *(G-4087)*

SYNCHROS

Miramar Mrmids Synchro Team LL ....G..... 786 520-6678
Miramar *(G-10515)*

SYNTHETIC RESIN FINISHED PRDTS, NEC

County Plastics Corp ....F..... 954 971-9205
Pompano Beach *(G-13980)*
Creative Archtctral Resin Pdts ....G..... 239 939-0034
Fort Myers *(G-4219)*
Fellowship Enterprises Inc ....G..... 727 726-5997
Safety Harbor *(G-14787)*
Octal Ventures Inc ....F..... 727 526-9288
Pinellas Park *(G-13715)*
Petroleum Containment Inc ....E..... 904 358-1700
Jacksonville *(G-6368)*

SYRUPS, FLAVORING, EXC DRINK

H & H Products Company ....E..... 407 299-5410
Orlando *(G-12205)*

Pinzon Caramel Syrup..................G...... 305 591-2472
Miami (G-9718)

SYSTEMS ENGINEERING: Computer Related

R4 Integration Inc.................E...... 850 226-6913
Fort Walton Beach (G-4604)
Rapid Composites LLC ....G...... 941 322-6647
Sarasota (G-15544)

SYSTEMS INTEGRATION SVCS

Diversfied Mtl Specialists Inc ....G...... 941 244-0935
North Venice (G-11211)
Trx Integration Inc.................F...... 727 797-4707
Belleair (G-353)
UDC Usa Inc ....E...... 813 281-0200
Tampa (G-17382)

SYSTEMS INTEGRATION SVCS: Local Area Network

Akuwa Solutions Group Inc ....F...... 941 343-9947
Sarasota (G-15589)

SYSTEMS SOFTWARE DEVELOPMENT SVCS

5dt Inc ....E...... 407 734-5377
Orlando (G-11854)
Bca Technologies Inc ....F...... 407 659-0653
Maitland (G-8052)
It Labs LLC ....F...... 310 490-6142
Palm Beach Gardens (G-12979)
Itelecom USA Inc................G...... 305 557-4660
Weston (G-18257)

TABLE OR COUNTERTOPS, PLASTIC LAMINATED

Bevel Top Shop Express LLC ....G...... 813 299-1250
Tampa (G-16640)
Cabinet Cnnction of Trsure Cas ....F...... 772 621-4882
Port Saint Lucie (G-14402)
Front of House Inc ....E...... 305 757-7940
Miami (G-9175)
Global Stone Collection LLC ....E...... 772 467-1924
Fort Pierce (G-4490)
Global Stone Collection LLC ....G...... 772 467-1924
Fort Pierce (G-4491)

TABLE TOPS: Porcelain Enameled

Roden International Inc ....F...... 954 929-1900
Hollywood (G-5653)

TABLECLOTHS & SETTINGS

Bust Out Promotions LLC ....G...... 561 305-8313
Pompano Beach (G-13958)
Centered Memories LLC................G...... 915 308-3224
Pompano Beach (G-13967)

TABLETS & PADS

3nstar Inc ....F...... 786 233-7011
Doral (G-3085)

TABLETS & PADS: Book & Writing, Made From Purchased Material

Peter T Amann................G...... 561 848-2770
West Palm Beach (G-18118)

TABLEWARE: Plastic

Q Squared Design LLC................F...... 212 686-8860
Fort Myers (G-4372)

TAGS & LABELS: Paper

American Label Group Inc ....F...... 386 274-5234
Daytona Beach (G-2509)
Force Imaging Group LLC................G...... 888 406-2120
Wesley Chapel (G-17877)
Nadco Tapes & Labels Inc ....E...... 941 751-6693
Sarasota (G-15523)
Passion Labels & Packaging ....G...... 941 312-5003
Sarasota (G-15532)
Prosegur Eas Usa LLC ....E...... 561 900-2744
Deerfield Beach (G-2793)
Southeast Packg Sanitation LLC..........G...... 904 634-7911
Jacksonville (G-6484)

TAGS: Paper, Blank, Made From Purchased Paper

Auto Tag of America Inc ....G...... 941 739-8841
Bradenton (G-942)

TALLOW: Animal

Griffin Industries LLC ....D...... 813 626-1135
Tampa (G-16893)
Kane-Miller Corp ....G...... 941 346-2003
Sarasota (G-15718)

TANK COMPONENTS: Military, Specialized

C4 Advnced Tctical Systems LLC ....F...... 407 206-3886
Orlando (G-11974)
Florida Ordnance Corporation................F...... 954 493-8691
Fort Lauderdale (G-3822)

TANK TOWERS: Metal Plate

Vertarib Inc ....E...... 877 815-8610
West Palm Beach (G-18195)

TANKS & OTHER TRACKED VEHICLE CMPNTS

Aba-Con Inc ....F...... 321 567-4967
Titusville (G-17567)
Fidelity Manufacturing LLC................E...... 352 414-4700
Ocala (G-11386)
Memco Inc ....G...... 352 241-2302
Bushnell (G-1246)

TANKS: Concrete

Heralpin Usa Inc................G...... 305 218-0174
Doral (G-3245)
Precon Corporation................C...... 352 332-1200
Newberry (G-11025)

TANKS: Fuel, Including Oil & Gas, Metal Plate

DI Myers Corp................F...... 609 698-8800
Jupiter (G-6710)
Envirovault LLC ....F...... 904 354-1858
Jacksonville (G-6078)
Fuel Tanks To Go LLC ....G...... 865 604-4726
Ocala (G-11395)
Midwest Mtal Fbrction Cstm RII..........F...... 317 769-6489
North Fort Myers (G-11062)
RDS Manufacturing Inc ....C...... 850 584-6898
Perry (G-13650)

TANKS: Lined, Metal

Keller-Nglillis Design Mfg Inc ....F...... 727 733-4111
Dunedin (G-3452)

TANKS: Plastic & Fiberglass

Big Slide Enterprises Inc................G...... 727 329-8845
Saint Petersburg (G-14982)
Dura-Weld Inc ....G...... 561 586-0180
Lake Worth Beach (G-7255)
Industrial Cmpsite Systems LLC..........F...... 863 646-8551
Lakeland (G-7349)
Tiki Water Sports Inc ....G...... 305 852-9298
Key Largo (G-6851)
Tuflex Manufacturing Co ....E...... 954 781-0605
Davie (G-2493)
Waterbrick International Inc................G...... 877 420-9283
Windermere (G-18370)

TANKS: Standard Or Custom Fabricated, Metal Plate

Aly Fabrication Inc................G...... 724 898-2990
Saint Augustine (G-14808)
American Stainless & Alum Pdts ....G...... 423 472-4832
Kissimmee (G-6894)
ARC-Rite Inc ....E...... 386 325-3523
Jacksonville (G-5897)
Modern Welding Company Fla Inc..........D...... 407 843-1270
Orlando (G-12386)
Ring Power Corporation................C...... 904 354-1858
Jacksonville (G-6423)
Southern Mfg & Fabrication LLC..........F...... 407 894-8851
Sanford (G-15389)

Specialty Tank and Eqp Co ....G...... 904 353-8761
Jacksonville (G-6500)
Sunshine Marine Tanks Inc ....G...... 305 805-9898
Medley (G-8329)
TTI Holdings Inc ....G...... 813 623-2675
Tampa (G-17378)

TANKS: Storage, Farm, Metal Plate

Nelson and Affiliates Inc ....E...... 352 316-5641
Gainesville (G-4737)

TANKS: Water, Metal Plate

Dixie Tank Company ....E...... 904 781-9500
Jacksonville (G-6035)
Durapoly Industries Inc ....G...... 352 622-3455
Silver Springs (G-16005)
Krausz Usa Inc ....F...... 352 509-3600
Ocala (G-11422)
Premier Water Tanks LLC................F...... 352 910-0188
Leesburg (G-7788)
Wes Industries Inc ....F...... 941 371-7617
Sarasota (G-15872)

TANNERIES: Leather

Sebring Custom Tanning Inc ....G...... 863 655-1600
Sebring (G-15940)

TAPE DRIVES

Quality Contract Mfg Svcs LLC ....F...... 941 355-7787
Sarasota (G-15540)

TAPES: Coated Fiberglass, Pipe Sealing Or Insulating

Access-Able Technologies Inc ....G...... 407 834-2999
Winter Springs (G-18557)
RSR Industrial Coatings Inc................F...... 863 537-1110
Bartow (G-324)
Urecon Systems Inc................C...... 321 638-2364
Winter Park (G-18548)

TAPES: Fabric

Nadco Tapes & Labels Inc................E...... 941 751-6693
Sarasota (G-15523)

TAPES: Pressure Sensitive

Intertape Polymer Corp ....C...... 888 898-7834
Sarasota (G-15707)
Intertape Polymer Corp ....D...... 813 621-8410
Tampa (G-16951)
Ipg (us) Holdings Inc ....D...... 941 727-5788
Sarasota (G-15708)
Ipg (us) Inc ....G...... 941 727-5788
Sarasota (G-15709)
Sunshine Ltd Tape & Label Spc ....F...... 561 832-9656
West Palm Beach (G-18169)

TAPES: Pressure Sensitive, Rubber

Florida Tape & Labels Inc................F...... 941 921-5788
Sarasota (G-15681)

TAPES: Tie, Woven Or Braided

Tie Collection LLC ....G...... 305 323-1420
Vero Beach (G-17807)

TAPES: Zipper

Lg-TEC Corporation................G...... 305 770-4005
Hollywood (G-5610)

TAPS

Widell Industries Inc ....D...... 800 237-5963
Port Richey (G-14387)

TAR

Ad-Tar................G...... 561 732-2055
Boynton Beach (G-836)
Tar Building LLC ....G...... 407 896-7252
Orlando (G-12645)

TARGET DRONES

Censys Technologies Corp................F...... 386 314-3599
Daytona Beach (G-2527)

PRODUCT

Drones Shop LLC............................G...... 772 224-8118
Stuart *(G-16140)*

Sunstate Uav LLC.............................F...... 904 580-4828
Saint Augustine *(G-14904)*

Working Drones Inc...........................G...... 904 647-4511
Jacksonville *(G-6619)*

TARPAULINS

Aer-Flo Canvas Products Inc.............D...... 941 747-4151
Bradenton *(G-934)*

Cosner Manufacturing LLC................F...... 863 676-2579
Lake Wales *(G-7157)*

Texene LLC.......................................F...... 305 200-5001
Miami Lakes *(G-10364)*

TEETHING RINGS: Rubber

Babbala LLC.....................................G...... 844 869-5747
Boca Raton *(G-426)*

TELECOMMUNICATION EQPT REPAIR SVCS, EXC TELEPHONES

Tridor Group Inc...............................G...... 786 707-2241
Miami *(G-10040)*

Wintel...F...... 407 834-1188
Longwood *(G-7960)*

TELECOMMUNICATION SYSTEMS & EQPT

Antennas For Cmmnctons Ocala F......E...... 352 687-4121
Ocala *(G-11325)*

Avaya Inc..F...... 239 498-2737
Bonita Springs *(G-781)*

Avaya Inc..C...... 305 264-7021
Miami *(G-8773)*

Cellphone Parts Express LLC..............G...... 954 635-5525
Hallandale Beach *(G-4941)*

Ciao Group Inc.................................E...... 347 560-5040
Boca Raton *(G-460)*

Communication Eqp & Engrg Co.........F...... 863 357-0798
Okeechobee *(G-11601)*

Communications Labs Inc..................F...... 321 701-9000
Melbourne *(G-8392)*

Converlogic Inter LLC.......................G...... 786 623-4747
Doral *(G-3170)*

Coppercom Inc.................................D...... 561 322-4000
Boca Raton *(G-471)*

Dasan Zhone Solutions Inc................F...... 305 789-6680
Miami *(G-9002)*

Eci Telecom Inc................................E...... 954 772-3070
Fort Lauderdale *(G-3783)*

Hemco Industries Inc.........................F...... 305 769-0606
North Miami *(G-11106)*

J I S Associates...............................G...... 321 777-6829
Satellite Beach *(G-15885)*

L3harris Technologies Inc..................E...... 321 727-4255
Palm Bay *(G-12906)*

L3harris Technologies Inc..................E...... 321 984-0782
Melbourne *(G-8457)*

L3harris Technologies Inc..................C...... 321 727-9100
Melbourne *(G-8459)*

Monroe Cable LLC............................D...... 941 429-8484
North Port *(G-11201)*

Primal Innovation Tech LLC...............F...... 407 558-9366
Tampa *(G-17180)*

Raytheon Company...........................C...... 310 647-9438
Largo *(G-7668)*

Recall Technologies Inc......................G...... 321 952-4422
Palm Bay *(G-12913)*

Select Engineered Systems Inc............E...... 305 823-5410
Hialeah *(G-5343)*

Tellabs International Inc.....................E...... 954 492-0120
Fort Lauderdale *(G-4086)*

Wave Tech Plus Corp.........................F...... 813 855-7007
Tampa *(G-17423)*

Wintel...F...... 407 834-1188
Longwood *(G-7960)*

TELECOMMUNICATIONS CARRIERS & SVCS: Wired

Ciao Group Inc.................................E...... 347 560-5040
Boca Raton *(G-460)*

TELECOMMUNICATIONS CARRIERS & SVCS: Wireless

Eng Group LLC.................................G...... 954 323-2024
Fort Lauderdale *(G-3794)*

First Communications Inc...................D...... 850 668-7990
Tallahassee *(G-16439)*

TELEGRAPH EQPT WHOLESALERS

Engineered Air Systems Inc................F...... 813 881-9555
Tampa *(G-16814)*

TELEMARKETING BUREAUS

Superior Group Companies Inc............C...... 727 397-9611
Seminole *(G-15991)*

TELEMETERING EQPT

L3 Technologies Inc..........................G...... 904 269-5026
Orange Park *(G-11832)*

L3 Technologies Inc..........................G...... 407 354-0047
Orlando *(G-12301)*

Leidos SEC Dtction Automtn Inc..........F...... 407 926-1900
Orlando *(G-12321)*

TELEPHONE ANSWERING SVCS

US Communications Industries............E...... 772 468-7477
Fort Pierce *(G-4551)*

TELEPHONE EQPT INSTALLATION

Tier5 Technical Services.....................G...... 904 435-3484
Jacksonville *(G-6551)*

TELEPHONE EQPT: Modems

Baila Con Micho Inc.........................G...... 786 953-8566
Medley *(G-8206)*

TELEPHONE EQPT: NEC

CCM Clllar Cnnection Miami Inc...........E...... 305 406-1656
Doral *(G-3157)*

Comdial Real Estate Co Inc...............G...... 941 564-9208
Sarasota *(G-15637)*

Cyipcom Inc.....................................G...... 954 727-2500
Oakland Park *(G-11255)*

L3harris Technologies Inc..................B...... 321 727-9100
Melbourne *(G-8455)*

Medtel Services LLC..........................E...... 941 753-5000
Palmetto *(G-13181)*

Networks Assets LLC.........................F...... 954 334-1390
Weston *(G-18272)*

Pss Communications Inc.....................F...... 408 496-3330
Sun City Center *(G-16266)*

Siemens AG......................................G...... 386 822-8000
Deland *(G-2900)*

Siemens Corporation.........................E...... 407 736-5629
Orlando *(G-12592)*

Sk Worldwide LLC............................G...... 786 360-4842
Surfside *(G-16399)*

Steve Baie Enterprises Inc..................G...... 407 822-3997
Apopka *(G-178)*

Tier5 Technical Services.....................G...... 904 435-3484
Jacksonville *(G-6551)*

TELEPHONE STATION EQPT & PARTS: Wire

Altanet Corporation...........................G...... 786 228-5758
Miami *(G-8701)*

Smiths Interconnect Inc.....................C...... 813 901-7200
Tampa *(G-17276)*

TELEPHONE SVCS

Cyipcom Inc.....................................G...... 954 727-2500
Oakland Park *(G-11255)*

Interactive Media Tech Inc..................F...... 561 999-9116
Boca Raton *(G-547)*

Telephony Partners LLC......................E...... 813 769-4690
Tampa *(G-17346)*

TELEPHONE: Fiber Optic Systems

Adcon Telemetry Inc.........................G...... 561 989-5309
Boca Raton *(G-386)*

Arden Photonics LLC.........................F...... 727 478-2651
Clearwater *(G-1498)*

Florida Veex Inc................................F...... 727 442-6677
Largo *(G-7588)*

Multicore Photonics Inc......................G...... 407 325-7800
Orlando *(G-12399)*

Nextera Fibernet LLC.........................A...... 866 787-2637
Juno Beach *(G-6665)*

Photon Towers Inc.............................G...... 305 235-7337
Miami *(G-9714)*

Prime Meridian Trading Corp...............G...... 954 727-2152
Sunrise *(G-16355)*

Victus Capital Enterprises Inc.............F...... 727 442-6677
Saint Petersburg *(G-15227)*

Zhone Technologies Inc......................F...... 510 777-7151
Seminole *(G-16000)*

TELEPHONE: Headsets

Truvoice Telecom Inc.........................E...... 888 448-5556
Tampa *(G-17375)*

TELEPHONE: Sets, Exc Cellular Radio

Anuva Manufacturing Svcs Inc.............E...... 321 821-4900
Melbourne *(G-8366)*

Milsav LLC.......................................G...... 407 556-5055
Orlando *(G-12382)*

Prepaid Solutions LLC........................F...... 305 834-7422
Miami *(G-9737)*

TELEPHONES: Sound Powered, Without Battery

Hose-Mccann Telephone Co Inc...........E...... 954 429-1110
Deerfield Beach *(G-2741)*

TELEVISION BROADCASTING & COMMUNICATIONS EQPT

Balsys Technology Group Inc...............G...... 407 656-3719
Winter Garden *(G-18375)*

Flickdirect Inc...................................F...... 561 330-2987
Delray Beach *(G-2963)*

Florical Systems Inc...........................E...... 352 372-8326
Gainesville *(G-4692)*

International Sound Corp.....................C...... 305 556-1000
Hialeah *(G-5196)*

Lit TV Network Llc.............................G...... 904 274-0732
Jacksonville *(G-6261)*

Nahuel Trading Corp..........................F...... 305 999-9944
Miami *(G-9604)*

RES-Net Microwave Inc......................E...... 727 530-9555
Clearwater *(G-1763)*

TELEVISION: Closed Circuit Eqpt

Flagship Marine Inc...........................G...... 772 781-4242
Stuart *(G-16148)*

Keytroller LLC...................................F...... 813 877-4500
Tampa *(G-16984)*

TELEVISION: Monitors

Monroe Cable LLC............................D...... 941 429-8484
North Port *(G-11201)*

TEMPERING: Metal

American Metal Processors Inc............F...... 386 754-9367
Lake City *(G-7011)*

TEMPORARY RELIEF SVCS

Waterbrick International Inc.................G...... 877 420-9283
Windermere *(G-18370)*

TENTS: All Materials

Ae Tent LLC.....................................E...... 305 691-0191
Miami *(G-8659)*

Economy Tent International Inc............E...... 305 691-0191
Miami *(G-9070)*

M & N Capital Enterprises LLC............E...... 800 865-5064
Tampa *(G-17029)*

Uts Systems LLC..............................G...... 850 226-4301
Fort Walton Beach *(G-4615)*

TERMINAL BOARDS

Etco Incorporated.............................C...... 941 756-8426
Bradenton *(G-978)*

TESTERS: Battery

Alber Corp..D...... 954 377-7101
Sunrise *(G-16288)*

TESTERS: Environmental

Clearwater Engineering Inc..................G...... 727 573-2210
Clearwater *(G-1542)*

F & J Specialty Products Inc...............F...... 352 680-1177
Ocala *(G-11385)*

Lindorm Inc ....F 305 888-0762
Miami Springs *(G-10390)*
Professional Laboratories Inc ....E 954 384-4446
Weston *(G-18280)*
Sun Electronic Systems Inc................F 321 383-9400
Titusville *(G-17621)*

TESTERS: Physical Property

Giebner Enterprises Inc ....F 727 520-1200
Saint Petersburg *(G-15061)*
St Acquisitions LLC ....G 941 753-1095
Sarasota *(G-15836)*

TESTERS: Spark Plug

Awl Manufacturing Inc.......................G 239 643-5780
Naples *(G-10685)*

TESTERS: Water, Exc Indl Process

Mydor Industries Inc ....G 954 927-1140
Dania *(G-2338)*
Sea Gear Corporation ....G 321 728-9116
Melbourne *(G-8518)*

TESTING SVCS

Testmaxx Services Corporation ....F 954 946-7100
Fort Lauderdale *(G-4088)*

TEXTILE & APPAREL SVCS

Lipscomb Finch Co............................F 904 415-4265
Jacksonville *(G-6260)*
Royal Tees Inc ....F 941 366-0056
Sarasota *(G-15802)*

TEXTILE FABRICATORS

Paradigm Parachute and Defense........F 928 580-9013
Pensacola *(G-13566)*
South Florida Cutting ....F 305 693-6711
Hialeah *(G-5354)*

TEXTILE FINISHING: Chemical Coating Or Treating, Narrow

Colortone Inc ....E 954 455-0200
Plantation *(G-13837)*

TEXTILE FINISHING: Dyeing, Broadwoven, Cotton

Arca Knitting Inc ....D 305 836-0155
Hialeah *(G-5056)*
Bam Enterprises Inc ....F 850 469-8872
Pensacola *(G-13451)*

TEXTILE: Finishing, Cotton Broadwoven

Armen Co Inc ....D 305 206-1601
Plantation *(G-13827)*
Colortone Inc ....E 954 455-0200
Plantation *(G-13837)*

TEXTILE: Finishing, Raw Stock NEC

Armen Co Inc ....D 305 206-1601
Plantation *(G-13827)*
Technifinish Inc ....F 727 576-5955
Clearwater *(G-1821)*

TEXTILE: Goods, NEC

Good Chance Inc ....G 754 263-2792
Pembroke Pines *(G-13392)*
Lahia America Corp ....F 305 254-6212
Miami *(G-9417)*
White Horse Fashion Cuisine ....G 561 847-4549
Wellington *(G-17869)*

TEXTILES: Jute & Flax Prdts

Divas Fashion...................................G 786 717-7039
Miami *(G-9037)*

TEXTILES: Linen Fabrics

Hamburg House Inc ....F 305 557-9913
Hialeah *(G-5182)*
Harbor Linen LLC..............................D 305 805-8085
Medley *(G-8251)*
Niba Designs Inc ....F 305 456-6230
Hollywood *(G-5634)*

TEXTILES: Recovering Textile Fibers From Clippings & Rags

Yesil Inc..F 516 858-0244
Boca Raton *(G-761)*

THEATRICAL SCENERY

Themeworks Incorporated ....C 386 454-7500
High Springs *(G-5456)*

THERMOMETERS: Medical, Digital

7 Holdings Group LLC ....E 754 200-1365
Doral *(G-3086)*
Oculus Surgical Inc ....E 772 236-2622
Port St Lucie *(G-14480)*
Potenza Services Inc ....G 305 400-4938
Miami *(G-9732)*
Sanomedics Inc ....G 305 433-7814
Boca Raton *(G-661)*

THERMOPLASTIC MATERIALS

Dj Plastics Inc ....G 407 656-6677
Apopka *(G-122)*
Plastic and Products Mktg LLC............F 352 867-8078
Ocala *(G-11468)*
T S E Industries Inc ....D 727 540-1368
Clearwater *(G-1810)*

THERMOSETTING MATERIALS

Hexion Inc ....E 863 669-2565
Lakeland *(G-7343)*
Preform LLC ....F 888 826-5161
Elkton *(G-3508)*
Pro Poly of America Inc ....G 352 629-1414
Ocala *(G-11472)*

THERMOSTAT REPAIR SVCS

Johnson Controls Inc ....E 407 291-1971
Orlando *(G-12276)*

THREAD: All Fibers

American Quality Embroidery ....D 239 772-8687
Cape Coral *(G-1301)*

THREAD: Embroidery

John & Betsy Hovland.........................G 727 449-2032
Clearwater *(G-1654)*

THREAD: Thread, From Manmade Fiber

Florida Thread & Trimming ....F 954 240-2474
Hialeah *(G-5159)*

TIE SHOPS

Tie Collection LLC ....G 305 323-1420
Vero Beach *(G-17807)*

TILE: Brick & Structural, Clay

Acme Brick Company ....F 850 531-0725
Tallahassee *(G-16405)*
American Pavers Consultants ....E 954 418-0000
Pompano Beach *(G-13925)*
Artistic Paver Mfg Inc ....E 305 653-7283
Miami *(G-8755)*
Brick Markers USA Inc ....F 561 842-1338
Mangonia Park *(G-8091)*
Cemex Materials LLC ....C 941 722-4578
Palmetto *(G-13159)*
Dyadic International USA Inc ....G 561 743-8333
Jupiter *(G-6714)*
HG Trading Cia Inc ....G 305 986-5702
Hialeah *(G-5183)*
International Whl Tile LLC....................D 772 223-5151
Palm City *(G-13046)*
Quikrete Companies LLC ....E 813 719-6612
Plant City *(G-13798)*

TILE: Clay, Drain & Structural

Crown Building Pdts Fla LLC ....D 863 993-4004
Arcadia *(G-191)*
James Hardie Building Pdts Inc ....D 813 478-1758
Plant City *(G-13778)*

TILE: Clay, Roof

Ceramica Verea USA Corp ....F 305 665-3923
Miami *(G-8913)*
Metro Roof Tile Inc............................F 863 467-0042
Medley *(G-8280)*
Southeast Gen Contrs Group Inc ....G 877 407-3535
Port St Lucie *(G-14483)*

TILE: Mosaic, Ceramic

Custom Mosaics Inc ....G 954 610-9436
Sunrise *(G-16312)*
Manotiles LLC ....G 954 803-3303
Delray Beach *(G-2985)*
Vidrepur of America LLC ....F 305 468-9008
Miami *(G-10110)*

TILE: Quarry, Clay

Florida Brick and Clay Co Inc ....F 813 754-1521
Plant City *(G-13766)*

TILE: Stamped Metal, Floor Or Wall

Floor and Bath Solutions ....G 954 368-6698
Wilton Manors *(G-18339)*
Floridian Title Group Inc ....G 305 792-4911
Miami *(G-9161)*

TILE: Terrazzo Or Concrete, Precast

E-Stone USA Corp ....D 863 655-1273
Sebring *(G-15919)*
Herpel Inc..G 561 585-5573
West Palm Beach *(G-18023)*

TILE: Wall, Ceramic

Colaianni Italian Flr Tile Mfg ....G 954 321-8244
Fort Lauderdale *(G-3736)*
Precision Ceramics Usa Inc.................F 727 388-5060
Saint Petersburg *(G-15159)*

TIMERS, APPLIANCE

Watchfacts Inc..................................E 786 797-5705
Miami *(G-10124)*

TIN

A Perfect View Window Tint.................G 954 937-0400
Boca Raton *(G-384)*
Ashtin Inc..G 352 867-1900
Ocala *(G-11328)*
Garrett Tin & Brother Inc ....G 727 236-5434
Trinity *(G-17637)*
Larrys Extreme Audio Tint LLC ....G 941 766-8468
Port Charlotte *(G-14305)*
Something In A Tin Inc ....G 305 785-6891
Miami *(G-9917)*
Tin-Rez Corp Inc ....F 561 654-3133
Boynton Beach *(G-919)*

TIRE & INNER TUBE MATERIALS & RELATED PRDTS

Elite Wheel Distributors Inc ....G 813 673-8393
Tampa *(G-16804)*
Eminel Corporation Inc ....F 407 900-0190
Orlando *(G-12125)*
Noahs MBL Tire Auto Solutions ....F 904 250-1502
Jacksonville *(G-6337)*
Tire Experts LLC ....G 305 663-3508
Medley *(G-8331)*

TIRE DEALERS

Fedan Corp ....G 305 885-5415
Hialeah *(G-5155)*

TIRE RECAPPING & RETREADING

Fedan Corp ....G 305 885-5415
Hialeah *(G-5155)*

TIRES & INNER TUBES

BF American Business LLC ....G 561 856-7094
Boca Raton *(G-430)*
BF One LLC ....F 239 939-5251
Fort Myers *(G-4188)*
BF Weston LLC ....G 561 844-5528
North Palm Beach *(G-11178)*

TIRES & INNER TUBES

Bridgestone Americas Inc..............E....... 941 235-0445
  Port Charlotte *(G-14290)*
Db Motoring Group Inc..............G....... 305 685-0707
  Hialeah *(G-5110)*
Jacksonville Tire Rescue Inc..............F....... 904 783-1296
  Jacksonville *(G-6217)*
S N S Auto Sports LLC..............G....... 727 546-2700
  Pinellas Park *(G-13728)*
Tbc Retail Group Inc..............G....... 702 395-2100
  Juno Beach *(G-6667)*

TIRES & TUBES WHOLESALERS

Db Motoring Group Inc..............G....... 305 685-0707
  Hialeah *(G-5110)*
Fedan Corp..............G....... 305 885-5415
  Hialeah *(G-5155)*
Rhino Tire Usa Llc..............G....... 407 777-5598
  Orlando *(G-12551)*

TIRES: Auto

McLaren Industries Inc..............E....... 310 212-1333
  Jacksonville *(G-6285)*
Vossen Wheels Inc..............G....... 305 463-7778
  Doral *(G-3416)*

TIRES: Motorcycle, Pneumatic

Rhino Tire Usa Llc..............G....... 407 777-5598
  Orlando *(G-12551)*

TIRES: Plastic

Chacho Customs..............G....... 239 369-4664
  Lehigh Acres *(G-7806)*
Jerae Inc..............F....... 954 989-6665
  Hollywood *(G-5605)*

TITANIUM MILL PRDTS

Sunrui Ttnium Prcsion Pdts Inc..............G....... 727 953-7101
  Clearwater *(G-1803)*
Titanium Development LLC..............G....... 407 844-8664
  Orlando *(G-12660)*
Titanium Gymnastics & Cheer..............G....... 813 689-2200
  Lithia *(G-7839)*
Titanium Integration LLC..............G....... 561 775-1898
  Palm Beach Gardens *(G-13013)*
Titanium Performance LLC..............G....... 407 712-5770
  Winter Park *(G-18546)*
Titanium Prof Hyraulics..............G....... 917 929-5044
  Riviera Beach *(G-14682)*
Titanium Real Estate LLC..............G....... 863 808-0445
  Lakeland *(G-7462)*

TOBACCO & PRDTS, WHOLESALE: Cigarettes

International Vapor Group LLC..............F....... 305 824-4027
  Miami Lakes *(G-10309)*

TOBACCO & PRDTS, WHOLESALE: Cigars

J C Newman Cigar Co..............D....... 813 248-2124
  Tampa *(G-16958)*

TOBACCO: Chewing & Snuff

Drew Estate LLC..............E....... 786 581-1800
  Miami *(G-9049)*
Jti Duty-Free USA Inc..............G....... 305 377-3922
  Miami *(G-9379)*

TOBACCO: Cigarettes

Commonwealth Brands Inc..............C....... 800 481-5814
  Fort Lauderdale *(G-3739)*
Dosal Tobacco Corporation..............E....... 305 685-2949
  Opa Locka *(G-11739)*
Flavana LLC..............G....... 561 285-7034
  Pompano Beach *(G-14029)*
Healthier Choices MGT Corp..............E....... 305 600-5004
  Hollywood *(G-5589)*
R J Reynolds Tobacco Company..............D....... 772 873-6955
  Port Saint Lucie *(G-14438)*
V2 Cigs..............G....... 305 517-1149
  Miami Beach *(G-10243)*
V2 Cigs..............E....... 305 240-6387
  Miami *(G-10089)*
Vapor Group Inc..............G....... 954 792-8450
  Miami *(G-10095)*
Vaporbrands International Inc..............F....... 352 573-6130
  West Palm Beach *(G-18194)*

Vaprzone LLC..............G....... 941 882-4841
  Venice *(G-17727)*
Vector Group Ltd..............D....... 305 579-8000
  Miami *(G-10099)*
Vgr Holding LLC..............F....... 305 579-8000
  Miami *(G-10104)*
Vpr Brands LP..............G....... 954 715-7001
  Sunrise *(G-16391)*

TOBACCO: Cigars

Consolidated Cigr Holdings Inc..............A....... 954 772-9000
  Fort Lauderdale *(G-3742)*
Domrey Cigar Ltd Company..............G....... 941 360-8200
  Pinellas Park *(G-13682)*
Dosal Tobacco Corporation..............E....... 305 685-2949
  Opa Locka *(G-11739)*
Havana Dreams LLC..............G....... 305 322-7599
  Miami *(G-9265)*
Itg Cigars Inc..............D....... 813 623-2262
  Tampa *(G-16957)*
Itg Cigars Inc..............G....... 954 772-9000
  Fort Lauderdale *(G-3887)*
J C Newman Cigar Co..............D....... 813 248-2124
  Tampa *(G-16958)*
La Luna Ltd..............G....... 305 644-0444
  Miami *(G-9408)*
Luis Martinez Cigar Co..............G....... 800 822-4427
  Tampa *(G-17024)*
Moore & Bode Group LLC..............G....... 786 615-9389
  Homestead *(G-5731)*
New Century..............G....... 305 670-3510
  Miami *(G-9612)*
South Beach Cigar Factory LLC..............G....... 786 216-7475
  Miami Beach *(G-10233)*
Swisher International Inc..............G....... 904 353-4311
  Jacksonville *(G-6523)*

TOBACCO: Smoking

Accendo Tobacco LLC..............G....... 305 407-2222
  Miami *(G-8642)*
Commonwealth Brands Inc..............C....... 800 481-5814
  Fort Lauderdale *(G-3739)*
Eternal Smoke Inc..............G....... 407 984-5090
  Orlando *(G-12135)*
Lakay Vita LLC..............G....... 786 985-7552
  Hallandale Beach *(G-4957)*
Swisher Intl Group Inc..............F....... 904 353-4311
  Jacksonville *(G-6524)*

TOILET PREPARATIONS

Cosmetic Creations Inc..............G....... 904 261-7831
  Fernandina Beach *(G-3583)*
Solar Packaging Corp..............G....... 305 621-5551
  Miami Lakes *(G-10354)*
World Perfumes Inc..............F....... 305 822-0004
  Opa Locka *(G-11800)*

TOILETRIES, COSMETICS & PERFUME STORES

Dermazone Solutions Inc..............E....... 727 446-6882
  Saint Petersburg *(G-15022)*
Mazi Group Inc..............E....... 786 800-2425
  Miami *(G-9522)*
Nu Earth Labs LLC..............E....... 727 648-4787
  Dunedin *(G-3455)*
Tend Skin International Inc..............F....... 954 382-0800
  Davie *(G-2488)*

TOILETRIES, WHOLESALE: Toilet Preparations

Vianny Corporation..............F....... 239 888-4536
  Fort Myers *(G-4440)*

TOILETRIES, WHOLESALE: Toiletries

Fresh Brandz LLC..............G....... 813 880-7110
  Tampa *(G-16862)*
T H Stone..............G....... 561 361-3966
  Boca Raton *(G-706)*
Tend Skin International Inc..............F....... 954 382-0800
  Davie *(G-2488)*

TOILETS: Metal

AAA Event Services LLC..............F....... 386 454-0929
  Newberry *(G-11015)*

TOILETS: Portable Chemical, Plastics

Bingham On Site Portables LLC..............G....... 813 659-0003
  Dover *(G-3427)*

TOMBSTONES: Terrazzo Or Concrete, Precast

Perl Inc..............F....... 352 726-2483
  Inverness *(G-5833)*

TOOL & DIE STEEL

Defense Stampings & Engrg Inc..............E....... 850 438-6105
  Pensacola *(G-13487)*

TOOLS & EQPT: Used With Sporting Arms

Applied Fiber Concepts Inc..............G....... 754 581-2744
  Hialeah *(G-5055)*

TOOLS: Carpenters', Including Levels & Chisels, Exc Saws

Dovetails A Precision..............G....... 561 818-6323
  West Palm Beach *(G-17981)*
Just Door Toolz LLC..............G....... 954 448-6872
  Port Saint Lucie *(G-14419)*
Thomas A Glassman LLC..............G....... 239 822-2219
  Naples *(G-10924)*

TOOLS: Hand

ABC Hammers..............G....... 708 343-9900
  Sarasota *(G-15436)*
Automated Production Eqp Ape..............F....... 631 654-1197
  Key Largo *(G-6842)*
B & A Manufacturing Co..............E....... 561 848-8648
  Riviera Beach *(G-14596)*
Daniels Manufacturing Corp..............C....... 407 855-6161
  Orlando *(G-12072)*
Es Manufacturing Inc..............F....... 727 323-4040
  Pinellas Park *(G-13686)*
Florida Knife Co..............F....... 941 371-2104
  Sarasota *(G-15680)*
Grip Tooling Technologies LLC..............F....... 813 654-6832
  Brandon *(G-1094)*
Halex Corporation..............G....... 239 216-4444
  Naples *(G-10770)*
Iron Bridge Tools Inc..............G....... 954 596-1090
  Fort Lauderdale *(G-3883)*
Merit International Entps Inc..............E....... 305 635-1011
  Miami *(G-9535)*
Microjig Inc..............G....... 855 747-7233
  Winter Park *(G-18524)*
Nasco Industries Inc..............E....... 954 733-8665
  Fort Lauderdale *(G-3953)*
Pettit Tools & Supplies Inc..............F....... 954 781-2640
  Pompano Beach *(G-14124)*
QEP Co Inc..............G....... 561 994-5550
  Boca Raton *(G-643)*
Skyo Industries Inc..............E....... 631 586-4702
  Ormond Beach *(G-12792)*
Steritool Inc..............F....... 904 388-3672
  Jacksonville *(G-6508)*
Vs Coatings LLC..............G....... 305 677-6224
  Miami *(G-10121)*

TOOLS: Hand, Engravers'

Imperial Photoengraving..............G....... 772 924-1731
  Stuart *(G-16165)*
Infinite Lasers LLC..............G....... 850 424-3759
  Destin *(G-3071)*

TOOLS: Hand, Jewelers'

Arca LLC..............F....... 305 470-1430
  Miami *(G-8740)*
Benchmark of Palm Beach..............G....... 706 258-3553
  Palm Beach *(G-12929)*
Filthy Rich of Jacksonville..............G....... 904 342-5092
  Saint Augustine *(G-14833)*
George Birney Jr..............G....... 407 851-5604
  Orlando *(G-12194)*
La Perlelle LLC..............G....... 941 388-2458
  Sarasota *(G-15722)*
Prisma Direct..............G....... 954 638-4753
  Miramar *(G-10531)*
Thida Thai Jewelry..............G....... 561 455-4249
  Miami *(G-10005)*
Volpino Corp..............F....... 904 264-8808
  Orange Park *(G-11846)*

TOOLS: Hand, Masons'

Exit Ten Inc ....G... 407 574-2433
  Longwood (G-7891)

TOOLS: Hand, Mechanics

Cob Industries Inc ....G... 321 723-3200
  West Melbourne (G-17897)
Mayhew/Bestway LLC ....E... 631 586-4702
  Ormond Beach (G-12779)

TOOLS: Hand, Power

Air Turbine Technology Inc ....F... 561 994-0500
  Boca Raton (G-394)
Daniels Manufacturing Corp ....C... 407 855-6161
  Orlando (G-12072)
Delta Regis Tools Inc ....E... 772 465-4302
  Fort Pierce (G-4480)
Es Manufacturing Inc ....F... 727 323-4040
  Pinellas Park (G-13686)
Fabco-Air Inc ....D... 352 373-3578
  Gainesville (G-4689)
Laycock Systems Inc ....F... 813 248-3555
  Tampa (G-17001)
Nasco Industries Inc ....E... 954 733-8665
  Fort Lauderdale (G-3953)
Ronnies Welding & Machine Inc ....G... 305 238-0972
  Cutler Bay (G-2301)
Tdk Electronics Inc ....F... 561 509-7771
  Ocean Ridge (G-11518)

TOOTHBRUSHES: Exc Electric

Marketshare LLC ....G... 631 273-0598
  Boca Raton (G-585)

TOOTHPASTES, GELS & TOOTHPOWDERS

Lively Company LLC ....F... 617 737-1199
  Tampa (G-17016)

TOPS, DISPENSER OR SHAKER, ETC: Plastic

Proandre Hygiene Systems Inc ....F... 305 433-3493
  Miami (G-9748)

TOWELETTES: Premoistened

Med-Nap LLC ....F... 352 796-6020
  Brooksville (G-1179)
Unico International Trdg Corp ....G... 561 338-3338
  Boca Raton (G-733)

TOWELS: Fabric & Nonwoven, Made From Purchased Materials

Beyond White Spa LLC ....E... 866 399-8867
  Miami (G-8824)

TOWELS: Indl

Alcee Industries Inc ....F... 407 468-4573
  Orlando (G-11886)

TOWERS, SECTIONS: Transmission, Radio & Television

Aluma Tower Company Inc ....E... 772 567-3423
  Vero Beach (G-17734)
Aluma Tower Company Inc ....F... 772 567-3423
  Vero Beach (G-17735)
Chism Manufacturing Svcs LLC ....F... 941 896-9671
  Sarasota (G-15454)
Heights Tower Systems Inc ....G... 850 455-1210
  Pensacola (G-13518)
Locus Location Systems LLC ....E... 321 727-3077
  Melbourne (G-8464)
Nextower LLC ....G... 407 907-7984
  Gainesville (G-4738)
Richland Towers Inc ....E... 813 286-4140
  Tampa (G-17219)
Ridan Industries LLC ....G... 813 258-8334
  Tampa (G-17220)

TOWING BARS & SYSTEMS

Pauls Twing Dsptch Cntl Fla I ....F... 407 323-4446
  Sanford (G-15370)

TOYS

Basic Fun Inc ....E... 561 997-8901
  Boca Raton (G-427)
Daytona Magic Inc ....G... 386 252-6767
  Daytona Beach (G-2543)
Dennys Electronics Inc ....E... 941 485-5400
  North Venice (G-11210)
Florida Pool Products Inc ....E... 727 531-8913
  Clearwater (G-1602)
Furrytails LLC ....F... 407 654-1465
  Maitland (G-8059)
George & Company LLC ....E... 239 949-3650
  Bonita Springs (G-800)
Getfpv LLC ....E... 941 444-0021
  Sarasota (G-15692)
Groovy Toys LLC ....G... 772 878-0790
  Port Saint Lucie (G-14415)
Herbko Inc ....G... 305 932-3572
  Aventura (G-263)
Jazwares LLC ....D... 954 845-0800
  Sunrise (G-16329)
JC Toys Group Inc ....F... 305 592-3541
  Doral (G-3267)
KNex Ltd Partnership Group ....D... 215 997-7722
  Boca Raton (G-570)
Leisure Activities Usa LLC ....G... 727 417-7128
  Saint Petersburg (G-15110)
Lumenier Holdco LLC ....G... 941 444-0021
  Sarasota (G-15728)
Majic Wheels Corp ....G... 239 313-5672
  Fort Myers (G-4316)
Never Wrong Toys & Games LLC .....G... 941 371-0909
  Sarasota (G-15761)
Scale Models Arts & Tech ....F... 305 949-1706
  North Miami Beach (G-11161)
Schick LLC ....G... 718 810-3804
  Miami (G-9855)
Simplicity Esports ....G... 386 479-9091
  Deland (G-2901)
System Enterprises LLC ....G... 888 898-3600
  Clearwater (G-1808)
Tangle Corporation ....G... 904 712-0042
  Jacksonville (G-6533)

TOYS & HOBBY GOODS & SPLYS, WHOLESALE: Amusement Goods

Daytona Magic Inc ....G... 386 252-6767
  Daytona Beach (G-2543)

TOYS & HOBBY GOODS & SPLYS, WHOLESALE: Toys & Games

Jazwares LLC ....D... 954 845-0800
  Sunrise (G-16329)
Safari Programs Inc ....D... 305 621-1000
  Jacksonville (G-6443)

TOYS, HOBBY GOODS & SPLYS WHOLESALERS

Hasbro Latin America Inc ....G... 305 931-3180
  Miami (G-9263)

TOYS: Dolls, Stuffed Animals & Parts

Baby Abuelita Productions LLC ....G... 305 662-7320
  Miami (G-8791)
Basic Fun Inc ....E... 561 997-8901
  Boca Raton (G-427)
JC Toys Group Inc ....F... 305 592-3541
  Doral (G-3267)
Teddy Mountain LLC ....G... 877 480-2327
  Kissimmee (G-6965)

TOYS: Kites

Core Kites USA ....G... 321 302-0693
  Cocoa Beach (G-1968)
Kite Technology Group LLC ....F... 407 557-0512
  Kissimmee (G-6936)
Red Kite Group Inc ....G... 305 665-7620
  South Miami (G-16043)

TOYS: Video Game Machines

Blingka Inc ....G... 800 485-6793
  Tampa (G-16648)

TRADERS: Commodity, Contracts

Bellatrix Trade LLC ....F... 786 536-2905
  Miami (G-8812)

TRAFFIC CONTROL FLAGGING SVCS

Acme Barricades LC ....E... 904 781-1950
  Jacksonville (G-5857)
L C Acme Barricades ....G... 863 816-5874
  Lakeland (G-7372)
L C Acme Barricades ....G... 561 657-8222
  Riviera Beach (G-14640)

TRAILER COACHES: Automobile

Excalibur Coach Svc & Sls LLC ....G... 407 302-9139
  Sanford (G-15314)

TRAILERS & PARTS: Boat

Amera Trail Inc ....E... 407 892-1100
  Saint Cloud (G-14920)
Boat Master Aluminum Trailers ....G... 239 768-2224
  Fort Myers (G-4191)
Caribbean Trailers Corp ....G... 305 256-1505
  Miami (G-8895)
EZ Loder Adjstble Boat Trlrs S ....G... 800 323-8190
  Port Saint Lucie (G-14413)
Float-On Corporation ....E... 772 569-4440
  Vero Beach (G-17754)
Harbor View Boat Trailers ....G... 941 916-3777
  Punta Gorda (G-14507)
J & J Marine Service Inc ....G... 813 741-2190
  Saint Petersburg (G-15088)
Jdci Enterprises Inc ....E... 239 768-2292
  Fort Myers (G-4297)
Magic Tilt Trailer Mfg Co Inc ....E... 727 535-5561
  Clearwater (G-1679)
Rocket Marine Inc ....F... 239 275-0880
  Fort Myers (G-4382)
Rolls Axle Lc ....G... 813 764-0242
  Plant City (G-13801)
Thule Inc ....D... 850 584-3448
  Perry (G-13657)

TRAILERS & PARTS: Horse

East 46th Auto Sales Inc ....F... 407 322-3100
  Sanford (G-15309)
Florida Trailer Ranch LLC ....F... 904 289-7710
  Jacksonville (G-6111)

TRAILERS & PARTS: Truck & Semi's

All Amrcan Trlr Connection Inc ....G... 561 582-1800
  Palm Springs (G-13142)
Alumne Manufacturing Inc ....G... 352 748-3229
  Wildwood (G-18308)
Axxium Engineering LLC ....G... 786 573-9808
  Miami (G-8783)
Dills Enterprises LLC ....G... 941 493-1993
  Venice (G-17683)
Draggin Trailers Inc ....G... 352 351-8790
  Ocala (G-11374)
EZ Truck Services Inc ....F... 239 728-3022
  Alva (G-80)
Freight Train Trucking Corp ....G... 407 509-0611
  Saint Cloud (G-14927)
Interglobal Capital Inc ....G... 727 585-1500
  Clearwater (G-1645)
Nelsons Truck and Trlr Sls LLC ....G... 352 732-8908
  Ocala (G-11450)
Pierce Manufacturing Inc ....D... 941 748-3900
  Bradenton (G-1028)
Rolls Rite Trailers Inc ....F... 850 526-2290
  Marianna (G-8174)
Terminal Service Company ....C... 850 739-5702
  Tallahassee (G-16513)
Thunder Bay Enterprises Inc ....E... 352 796-9551
  Brooksville (G-1211)
U-Dump Trailers LLC ....D... 352 351-8510
  Ocala (G-11505)
Unique Custom Truck & Trlr LLC ....F... 305 403-7042
  Miami (G-10063)
Warren Equipment Inc ....E... 813 752-5126
  Plant City (G-13814)

TRAILERS & TRAILER EQPT

Central Florida Cstm Trlrs Inc ....E... 407 851-1144
  Orlando (G-11996)

PRODUCT

Chambers Body Works Inc ....G...... 352 588-3072
Dade City (G-2315)
Liles Custom Trailers.......................G...... 352 368-2652
Ocala (G-11429)
Mbf Industries Inc ....E....... 407 323-9414
Sanford (G-15355)
Precision Equipment Co Inc ....G...... 561 689-4400
West Palm Beach (G-18125)
Space Coast Industries Inc ....G...... 321 633-9336
Cocoa (G-1958)
Ver-Val Enterprises Inc ....F....... 850 244-7931
Fort Walton Beach (G-4616)

TRAILERS OR VANS: Horse Transportation, Fifth-Wheel Type

RPM Co ....G...... 352 542-3110
Old Town (G-11623)
Shadow Trailers Inc ....E....... 352 529-2190
Williston (G-18335)

TRAILERS: Bodies

Loadmaster Alum Boat Trlrs Inc...........E....... 813 689-3096
Tampa (G-17020)

TRAILERS: Demountable Cargo Containers

Cepods LLC ....G...... 786 520-1412
Miami Beach (G-10178)

TRAILERS: House, Exc Permanent Dwellings

Chariot Eagle Inc..............................D....... 623 936-7545
Ocala (G-11350)

TRAILERS: Semitrailers, Missile Transportation

Ultimate Cargo Services LLC...............F....... 954 251-1680
Jacksonville (G-6572)

TRAILERS: Semitrailers, Truck Tractors

Arnold Manufacturing Inc ....G...... 850 470-9200
Pensacola (G-13447)
Globe Trailers Florida Inc...................E....... 941 753-6425
Bradenton (G-985)

TRAILERS: Truck, Chassis

Chassis King LLC..............................G...... 727 585-1500
Clearwater (G-1540)

TRANSFORMERS: Control

Wired Rite Systems Inc ....F....... 707 838-1122
Sarasota (G-15878)

TRANSFORMERS: Distribution

ABB Inc ....B....... 407 732-2000
Lake Mary (G-7056)
ABB Inc ....D....... 305 471-0844
Miami (G-8634)
Digitrax Inc ....E....... 850 872-9890
Panama City (G-13254)
Evolution Intrcnnect Systems I ....F....... 954 217-6223
Davie (G-2409)
OHM Americas LLC ....F....... 800 467-7275
Fort Lauderdale (G-3966)
Power Quality Intl LLC.......................G...... 727 478-7284
Odessa (G-11572)
Sunbelt Transformer Ltd ....G...... 305 517-3657
Pompano Beach (G-14206)

TRANSFORMERS: Distribution, Electric

Everybodywinco ....G...... 954 214-4172
Miami (G-9116)

TRANSFORMERS: Electric

Bright Manufacturing LLC..................G...... 954 603-4950
Fort Lauderdale (G-3703)
Manutech Assembly Inc ....G...... 305 888-2800
Miami (G-9506)
Nwl Inc ....D....... 800 742-5695
Lake Hamilton (G-7051)
Nwl Inc ....C....... 561 848-9009
Riviera Beach (G-14651)
Payton America Inc ....F....... 954 428-3326
Deerfield Beach (G-2781)

TRANSFORMERS: Electronic

Bocatech Inc ....G...... 954 397-7070
Fort Lauderdale (G-3699)
Cooper Bussmann LLC ....C....... 561 998-4100
Boca Raton (G-470)
Filter Research Corporation ....E....... 321 802-3444
Palm Bay (G-12900)
Renco Usa Inc ....F....... 321 637-1000
Miami (G-9793)
Vision Engineering Labs ....D....... 727 812-2035
Largo (G-7705)

TRANSFORMERS: Florescent Lighting

Robertson Transformer Co ....G...... 917 603-8530
Sarasota (G-15797)

TRANSFORMERS: Fluorescent Lighting

Hatch Transformers Inc ....E....... 813 288-8006
Tampa (G-16908)

TRANSFORMERS: Furnace, Electric

Solucnes Elctrcas Intgrles LLC............F....... 305 804-4201
Miami (G-9915)

TRANSFORMERS: Instrument

Arteche USA Inc ....F....... 954 438-9499
Miramar (G-10469)
Instrument Transformers LLC ....A....... 727 229-0616
Clearwater (G-1644)

TRANSFORMERS: Lighting, Street & Airport

Neubert Aero Corp ....G...... 352 345-4828
Brooksville (G-1185)

TRANSFORMERS: Power Related

ABB Partners LLC..............................F....... 917 843-4430
Palm Beach (G-12928)
Central Turbos Corp ....G...... 305 406-3933
Doral (G-3159)
Control Solutions Inc ....F....... 813 247-2136
Tampa (G-16725)
Edisonecoenergycom Corporation ....G...... 954 417-5326
Fort Lauderdale (G-3787)
Exxelia Usa Inc ....E....... 407 695-6562
Longwood (G-7893)
Florida Transformer Inc ....G...... 850 892-2711
Defuniak Springs (G-2839)
Gfsf Inc...G...... 727 478-7284
Odessa (G-11554)
Hytronics Corp ....D....... 727 535-0413
Clearwater (G-1635)
Inductive Technologies Inc ....F....... 727 536-7861
Clearwater (G-1642)
Kbn Corporation ....G...... 321 327-9792
Palm Bay (G-12905)
Lextm3 Systems LLC ....F....... 954 888-1024
Davie (G-2434)
Miami Transformers Corp ....F....... 305 257-1491
Homestead (G-5730)
Spin Magnetics ....B....... 863 676-9333
Lake Wales (G-7173)
Technipower LLC ....F....... 954 346-2442
Coral Springs (G-2219)

TRANSFORMERS: Specialty

Magnatronix Corporation Inc ....F....... 727 536-7861
Clearwater (G-1680)
Ventex Technology Inc ....F....... 561 354-6300
Jupiter (G-6819)

TRANSFORMERS: Voltage Regulating

Powerficient LLC...............................E....... 800 320-2535
Fort Lauderdale (G-3990)

TRANSISTORS

Boca Semiconductor Corporation ....E....... 561 226-8500
Boca Raton (G-438)

TRANSPORTATION ARRANGEMNT SVCS, PASS: Travel Tour Pkgs, Whol

Mario Kenny ....G...... 786 274-0527
Miami (G-9512)

TRANSPORTATION BROKERS: Truck

Amware Logistics Services Inc ....F....... 970 337-7000
Pompano Beach (G-13929)

TRANSPORTATION EPQT & SPLYS, WHOL: Aeronautical Eqpt & Splys

Aero-Marine Technologies Inc.............G...... 941 205-5420
Englewood (G-3516)
Sky Technics Aviation Sls Inc ....G...... 305 885-7499
Miami Lakes (G-10353)

TRANSPORTATION EPQT & SPLYS, WHOLESALE: Helicopter Parts

Florida Sncast Helicopters LLC...........F....... 941 355-1525
Sarasota (G-15477)

TRANSPORTATION EPQT & SPLYS, WHOLESALE: Marine Crafts/Splys

Keith Eickert Power Pdts LLC ....F....... 386 446-0660
Palm Coast (G-13081)
Miami Cordage LLC ....E....... 305 636-3000
Miami (G-9549)
Turning Point Propellers Inc ....G...... 904 900-7739
Jacksonville (G-6569)

TRANSPORTATION EPQT & SPLYS, WHOLESALE: Nav Eqpt & Splys

L3harris Technologies Inc..................D....... 321 727-4000
Melbourne (G-8458)

TRANSPORTATION EPQT/SPLYS, WHOL: Marine Propulsn Mach/Eqpt

E M P Inc ....G...... 772 286-7343
Stuart (G-16142)

TRANSPORTATION EPQT/SPLYS, WHOL: Space Propulsion Unit/Part

Troxel Aerospace Inds Inc ....F....... 720 626-0454
Gainesville (G-4780)

TRANSPORTATION EQPT & SPLYS WHOLESALERS, NEC

Advanced Air West Palm Bch Inc.........E....... 561 845-8289
Riviera Beach (G-14589)
Asrc Aerospace Corp ....B....... 321 867-1462
Kennedy Space Center (G-6830)
Cme Arma Inc....................................E....... 305 633-1524
Miami (G-8933)
Lift Aerospace Corp ....E....... 305 851-5237
Miami (G-9457)
Marine Exhaust Systems Inc ....D....... 561 848-1238
Riviera Beach (G-14645)
Radiant Power Corp ....D....... 941 739-3200
Sarasota (G-15541)
Ultimate Cargo Services LLC...............F....... 954 251-1680
Jacksonville (G-6572)
XI Carts Inc ....G...... 904 277-7111
Fernandina Beach (G-3600)

TRANSPORTATION EQUIPMENT, NEC

A Cheaper Shot LLC ....F....... 727 221-3237
Saint Petersburg (G-14949)
Agile Cargo Transportation LLC............F....... 407 747-0812
Jacksonville (G-5867)
Andrews 1st Choice Trckg LLC ....G...... 205 703-5717
Jacksonville (G-5890)
Bollou Transportation LLC..................F....... 800 548-1768
Miami (G-8845)
D & R Delivery Services of Pb ....F....... 561 602-6427
Riviera Beach (G-14612)
Lnl Logistics LLC...............................G...... 386 977-9276
Deltona (G-3047)
Lotus Containers Inc ....G...... 786 590-1056
Miami (G-9480)
Sodikart USA ....G...... 561 493-0290
Boynton Beach (G-913)
Triumph Transport Inc ....G...... 863 226-7276
Lakeland (G-7466)

TRANSPORTATION PROGRAM REGULATION & ADMIN, GOVT: State

Highway Sfety Mtr Vhcles Fla D ....F 561 640-6826
  West Palm Beach **(G-18024)**

TRANSPORTATION SVCS, AIR, SCHEDULED: Helicopter Carriers

Heli Aviation Florida LLC ....G....... 941 355-1525
  Sarasota **(G-15489)**

TRANSPORTATION SVCS, DEEP SEA: Intercoastal, Freight

Ultimate Cargo Services LLC ....F 954 251-1680
  Jacksonville **(G-6572)**

TRANSPORTATION SVCS, WATER: Boathouses, Commercial

Arkup Llc ....G....... 786 448-8635
  Miami Beach **(G-10167)**

TRANSPORTATION SVCS, WATER: Canal & Intracoastal, Freight

Copaco Inc ....F 407 333-3041
  Orange City **(G-11804)**

TRANSPORTATION: Bus Transit Systems

Amer-Con Corp ....E 786 293-8004
  Palmetto Bay **(G-13207)**

TRAP ROCK: Dimension

Youngquist Brothers Rock Inc ....D 239 267-6000
  Fort Myers **(G-4451)**

TRAPS: Animal & Fish, Wire

Aquateko International LLC ....G....... 904 273-7200
  Ponte Vedra Beach **(G-14264)**
Ellis Trap and Cage Mfg Inc ....G....... 850 969-1302
  Pensacola **(G-13495)**

TRAPS: Animal, Iron Or Steel

Ellis Trap and Cage Mfg Inc ....G....... 850 969-1302
  Pensacola **(G-13495)**
H B Sherman Traps Inc ....G....... 850 575-8727
  Tallahassee **(G-16456)**

TRAVEL AGENCIES

Mariner International Trvl Inc ....G....... 954 925-4150
  Dania **(G-2336)**
On-Board Media Inc ....D....... 305 673-0400
  Doral **(G-3318)**
Thalo Assist LLC ....G....... 786 340-6892
  Weston **(G-18288)**

TRAVEL TRAILERS & CAMPERS

East 46th Auto Sales Inc ....F 407 322-3100
  Sanford **(G-15309)**
Pierce Manufacturing Inc ....D....... 941 748-3900
  Bradenton **(G-1028)**
Rolls Axle Lc ....G....... 813 764-0242
  Plant City **(G-13801)**
Southeastern Truck Tops Inc ....F 386 761-0002
  Daytona Beach **(G-2602)**
Stephen Shives ....G....... 352 454-6522
  Summerfield **(G-16260)**

TRAVELER ACCOMMODATIONS, NEC

Allen Shuffleboard LLC ....G....... 727 399-8877
  Seminole **(G-15968)**

TRAVELERS' AID

Built Story LLC ....F 305 671-3890
  Miami **(G-8859)**

TROPHIES, NEC

A J Trophies & Awards Inc ....E 850 878-7187
  Tallahassee **(G-16404)**
American Trophy Co ....G....... 954 782-2250
  Pompano Beach **(G-13928)**

M D R International Inc ....F 305 944-5335
  North Miami **(G-11110)**
Michelsons Trophies Inc ....G....... 305 687-9898
  Miami **(G-9565)**
Parrillo Inc ....G....... 386 767-8011
  South Daytona **(G-16026)**

TROPHIES, PLATED, ALL METALS

United Trophy Manufacturing ....E 407 841-2525
  Orlando **(G-12690)**

TROPHIES: Metal, Exc Silver

Cabus USA Inc ....G....... 305 681-0872
  North Miami **(G-11096)**

TROPHY & PLAQUE STORES

Daytona Trophy Inc ....F 386 253-2806
  Daytona Beach **(G-2544)**
In The News Inc ....D....... 813 882-8886
  Tampa **(G-16935)**
Looper Sports Connection Inc ....G....... 352 796-7974
  Brooksville **(G-1175)**

TRUCK & BUS BODIES: Bus Bodies

Temsa North America Inc ....E 407 807-6950
  Orlando **(G-12650)**

TRUCK & BUS BODIES: Cement Mixer

McNeilus Truck and Mfg Inc ....E 954 366-4769
  Pompano Beach **(G-14093)**

TRUCK & BUS BODIES: Dump Truck

Armor Supply Metals LLC ....G....... 305 640-9901
  Medley **(G-8199)**
Nichols Truck Bodies LLC ....F 904 781-5080
  Jacksonville **(G-6333)**
T Disney Trucking & Grading ....E 813 443-6258
  Tampa **(G-17321)**
Warren Equipment Inc ....E 813 752-5126
  Plant City **(G-13814)**

TRUCK & BUS BODIES: Tank Truck

Bulk Manufacturing Florida Inc ....F 813 757-2313
  Plant City **(G-13747)**
Terminal Service Company ....C....... 850 739-5702
  Tallahassee **(G-16513)**

TRUCK & BUS BODIES: Truck Beds

Miami-Dade Truck & Eqp Svc Inc ....F 305 691-2932
  Miami **(G-9562)**
Reading Truck Body LLC ....E 727 943-8911
  Tarpon Springs **(G-17490)**

TRUCK & BUS BODIES: Truck Tops

Southeastern Truck Tops Inc ....F 386 761-0002
  Daytona Beach **(G-2602)**

TRUCK & BUS BODIES: Truck, Motor Vehicle

A&L Hall Investments Inc ....E 904 781-5080
  Bryceville **(G-1225)**
Advanced Truck Equipment Inc ....E 561 424-0442
  Boynton Beach **(G-837)**
Gar-P Industries Inc ....E 305 888-7252
  Medley **(G-8245)**
Reading Truck Body LLC ....E 727 943-8911
  Tarpon Springs **(G-17489)**
Transtat Equipment Inc ....F 407 857-2040
  Orlando **(G-12668)**

TRUCK BODIES: Body Parts

Florida Truck Parts ....G....... 786 251-8614
  Hialeah Gardens **(G-5436)**
Simplified Fabricators Inc ....E 561 335-3488
  West Palm Beach **(G-18155)**
World Industrial Equipment Inc ....E 772 461-6056
  Fort Pierce **(G-4557)**

TRUCK BODY SHOP

Gar-P Industries Inc ....E 305 888-7252
  Medley **(G-8245)**
Reading Truck Body LLC ....E 727 943-8911
  Tarpon Springs **(G-17489)**

Transtat Equipment Inc ....F 407 857-2040
  Orlando **(G-12668)**

TRUCK PAINTING & LETTERING SVCS

Suncoast Signs Inc ....G....... 813 664-0699
  Tampa **(G-17314)**

TRUCK PARTS & ACCESSORIES: Wholesalers

Gar-P Industries Inc ....E 305 888-7252
  Medley **(G-8245)**
Warren Equipment Inc ....E 813 752-5126
  Plant City **(G-13814)**

TRUCKING & HAULING SVCS: Hazardous Waste

ALLEZ LLC ....F 205 216-6330
  Plantation **(G-13823)**
Environmental Contractors Inc ....F 305 556-6942
  Hialeah **(G-5146)**

TRUCKING & HAULING SVCS: Lumber & Timber

Southern Wood Services LLC ....G....... 352 279-3208
  Brooksville **(G-1203)**

TRUCKING & HAULING SVCS: Timber, Local

Paul White Logging Inc ....G....... 850 379-8651
  Hosford **(G-5757)**

TRUCKING, AUTOMOBILE CARRIER

Trio Envmtl Solutions LLC ....F 850 543-9125
  Mary Esther **(G-8180)**

TRUCKING, DUMP

Rock Ridge Materials Inc ....F 321 268-8455
  Titusville **(G-17615)**

TRUCKING: Except Local

Harrison Gypsum LLC ....E 850 762-4315
  Marianna **(G-8165)**
Titan America LLC ....C....... 305 364-2200
  Medley **(G-8334)**

TRUCKING: Local, With Storage

Ofab Inc ....D....... 352 629-0040
  Ocala **(G-11460)**

TRUCKING: Local, Without Storage

Buddy Ward & Sons Seafood ....G....... 850 653-8522
  Apalachicola **(G-88)**
Donald Smith Logging Inc ....G....... 850 697-3975
  Carrabelle **(G-1410)**
Tumbling Pines Inc ....F 386 437-2668
  Bunnell **(G-1237)**
Usher Land & Timber Inc ....E 352 493-4221
  Chiefland **(G-1451)**
Yahl Mulching & Recycling Inc ....F 239 352-7888
  Naples **(G-10945)**

TRUCKS & TRACTORS: Industrial

Alliance Commercial Eqp Inc ....F 772 232-8149
  Pompano Beach **(G-13920)**
Amer-Con Corp ....E 786 293-8004
  Palmetto Bay **(G-13207)**
Amera Trail Inc ....E 407 892-1100
  Saint Cloud **(G-14920)**
Bms International Inc ....E 813 247-7040
  Tampa **(G-16651)**
Dhs Power Corp ....G....... 305 599-1022
  Miami **(G-9027)**
Earthmover Cnstr Eqp LLC ....F 407 401-8956
  Apopka **(G-124)**
Grass Pro Shops Inc ....F 813 381-3890
  Tampa **(G-16891)**
Illinois Tool Works Inc ....E 941 721-1000
  Palmetto **(G-13176)**
Lite Cart Corp ....G....... 954 659-7671
  Largo **(G-7634)**
Loxahatchee Mobile Equipment R ....G....... 561 723-6378
  Loxahatchee **(G-7972)**

Employee Codes: A=Over 500 employees, B=251-500
C=101-250, D=51-100, E=20-50, F=10-19, G=4-9
                    2022 Harris Florida
                   Manufacturers Directory   1343

PRODUCT

Rampmaster Inc ....F 305 691-9090
Miami *(G-9779)*

Rolls Rite Trailers Inc ....F 850 526-2290
Marianna *(G-8174)*

Sdi Industries Inc ....E 321 733-1128
Melbourne *(G-8517)*

Terex Corporation ....G 352 330-4044
Wildwood *(G-18325)*

Tesco Equipment LLC ....E 954 752-7994
Coral Springs *(G-2220)*

Tfl of Orlando ....G 407 936-1553
Orlando *(G-12654)*

The Forklift Company Inc ....F 863 595-8156
Lake Alfred *(G-6997)*

Windstar Express Inc ....G 786 252-1569
Miami *(G-10133)*

World Industrial Equipment Inc ..E 772 461-6056
Fort Pierce *(G-4557)*

TRUCKS: Forklift

A & S Equipment Co ....F 305 436-8207
Doral *(G-3088)*

Benitez Forklift Corp ....G 786 307-3872
Hialeah *(G-5072)*

Florida Jacksonville Forklift ....G 904 674-6898
Jacksonville *(G-6106)*

Jamco Industrial Inc ....F 866 848-5400
Sanford *(G-15343)*

Onsite Rlble Forklift Svcs Inc .....G 305 305-8638
Hialeah *(G-5288)*

Orlandos Forklift Service LLC .....G 407 761-9104
Orlando *(G-12457)*

Petlift S & B Mfg Inc ....G 941 346-2211
Bradenton *(G-1026)*

Ring Power Corporation ....G 863 606-0512
Lakeland *(G-7421)*

RJ Forklift Services Inc ....G 786 539-6613
Miami *(G-9810)*

Southern States Toyota Lift ....D 904 764-7662
Tampa *(G-17290)*

Tampa Fork Lift Inc ....F 904 674-6899
Jacksonville *(G-6532)*

TRUCKS: Indl

Belamour Logistics LLC ....G 813 540-2199
Gibsonton *(G-4795)*

Big Man Friendly Trnsp LLC ....G 941 229-3454
Lakewood Ranch *(G-7476)*

Carriers Direct Inc ....F 941 776-2979
Parrish *(G-13357)*

Courtney Allen Enterprises LLC ...F 571 314-4290
Sarasota *(G-15643)*

Dmoney365 Logistic LLC ....F 954 529-8202
North Lauderdale *(G-11078)*

First Coast Cargo Inc ....F 844 774-7711
Jacksonville *(G-6093)*

GF & Associate Group LLC ....G 954 593-4788
West Palm Beach *(G-18017)*

Iscar GSE Corp ....E 305 364-8886
Miami Gardens *(G-10265)*

Iscar GSE Corp ....E 305 364-8886
Miami Gardens *(G-10266)*

Jordan Logistics Co LLC ....F 813 787-7791
Apollo Beach *(G-93)*

Lofton Enterprises Trckg LLC ....F 786 220-6053
Miami *(G-9470)*

LUnion Logistics LLC ....F 866 586-4660
Hollywood *(G-5618)*

MC Intl Transportation ....F 305 805-8228
Miami *(G-9523)*

Modest Logistics LLC ....F 321 314-2825
Orlando *(G-12387)*

Nuwas Deva LLC ....G 786 859-2819
Miramar *(G-10521)*

Runn-It LLC ....G 800 932-8052
Miami *(G-9829)*

Sep National Logistics LLC ....G 239 439-2239
Fort Myers *(G-4398)*

Toteum All Trckg Trnsprting L ....E 888 506-5890
Orlando *(G-12664)*

TRUSSES & FRAMING: Prefabricated Metal

A-1 Industries Florida Inc ....F 270 316-9409
Coral Springs *(G-2123)*

Cmn Steel Fabricators Inc ....D 305 592-5466
Miami *(G-8934)*

Park Place Manufacturing Inc ....F 863 382-0126
Sebring *(G-15934)*

Scosta Corp ....F 863 385-8242
Sebring *(G-15938)*

Steel Technology & Design ....F 863 665-2525
Lakeland *(G-7448)*

TRUSSES: Wood, Floor

True House Inc ....F 904 757-7500
Jacksonville *(G-6568)*

TRUSSES: Wood, Roof

A-1 Industries Florida Inc ....F 270 316-9409
Coral Springs *(G-2123)*

A-1 Roof Trusses Ltd Company .....C 772 409-1010
Fort Pierce *(G-4458)*

ABT Trusses Inc ....F 352 221-4867
Bell *(G-334)*

Accu-Span Truss Co ....E 407 321-1440
Longwood *(G-7863)*

American Truss Chiefland LL ....G 352 493-9700
Chiefland *(G-1444)*

Anderson Truss LLC ....E 386 752-3103
Lake City *(G-7012)*

Angle Truss Co Inc ....F 352 343-7477
Tavares *(G-17503)*

Arban & Associates Inc ....E 850 836-4362
Ponce De Leon *(G-14248)*

B and B Roof and Floor Trusses ...G 850 265-4119
Lynn Haven *(G-8025)*

Banks Lumber Co Inc ....G 863 687-6068
Auburndale *(G-219)*

Best Truss Company ....E 305 667-6797
Miami *(G-8817)*

Big Bend Truss Components Inc .....F 850 539-5351
Havana *(G-4994)*

Bruce Component Systems Inc ....F 352 628-0522
Lecanto *(G-7748)*

Bushnell Truss Enterprises LLC .....F 352 793-6090
Bushnell *(G-1241)*

Casmin Inc ....G 352 253-5000
Mount Dora *(G-10599)*

Central Florida Truss Inc ....E 863 533-0821
Bartow *(G-304)*

Chambers Truss Inc ....D 772 465-2012
Fort Pierce *(G-4476)*

Charity Homes LLC ....G 352 274-0306
Ocala *(G-11351)*

CMF Truss Inc ....E 352 796-5805
Brooksville *(G-1146)*

Custom Truss LLC ....F 561 266-3451
Boynton Beach *(G-854)*

D & M Truss Co ....F 850 944-4864
Pensacola *(G-13484)*

D J Trusses Unlimited Inc ....F 863 687-4796
Lakeland *(G-7304)*

Dade Truss Company Inc ....C 305 592-8245
Miami *(G-8997)*

Dan Boudreau Inc ....G 407 491-7611
Oviedo *(G-12817)*

Deco Truss Company Inc ....E 305 257-1910
Homestead *(G-5707)*

Duley Truss Inc ....E 352 465-0964
Dunnellon *(G-3462)*

Emerald Coast Truss LLC ....E 850 623-1967
Milton *(G-10423)*

Florida Engineered Constru ....C 813 621-4641
Seffner *(G-15958)*

Florida Forest Products LLC ....E 727 585-2067
Saint Petersburg *(G-15050)*

Florida Quality Truss Inc ....G 954 975-3384
Pompano Beach *(G-14033)*

Florida Quality Truss Inds Inc .....F 954 971-3167
Pompano Beach *(G-14034)*

Freeport Truss Company Inc ....G 850 835-4541
Freeport *(G-4623)*

Hitech Truss Inc ....F 352 797-0877
Brooksville *(G-1161)*

Hitek Property LLC ....F 352 797-0877
Brooksville *(G-1162)*

K & M Truss Inc ....G 407 880-4551
Zellwood *(G-18599)*

Lemon Bay Truss & Supply Co ....G 941 698-0800
Placida *(G-13735)*

Marianna Truss Inc ....F 850 594-5420
Marianna *(G-8172)*

Martinez Builders Supply LLC ....D 772 466-2480
Fort Pierce *(G-4503)*

Martinez Truss Company Inc ....F 305 883-6261
Medley *(G-8273)*

Mayo Truss Co Inc ....F 386 294-3988
Mayo *(G-8184)*

Mid-Flrida Lbr Acqisitions Inc ......E 863 533-0155
Bartow *(G-318)*

Nexgen Framing System LLC ....F 321 508-6763
Palm Bay *(G-12909)*

Old Oak Truss Company ....G 813 689-6597
Seffner *(G-15963)*

Park Place Truss Inc ....F 863 382-0126
Sebring *(G-15935)*

Park Place Truss & Design Inc ......F 863 382-0126
Sebring *(G-15936)*

Pelliccione Builders Sup Inc ....F 941 334-3014
North Fort Myers *(G-11066)*

Ridgway Roof Truss Company ....D 352 376-4436
Gainesville *(G-4757)*

Royal Truss Corp ....F 786 222-1100
Medley *(G-8317)*

Santa Fe Truss Company Inc ....E 386 454-7711
Bell *(G-337)*

Scosta Corp ....E 863 385-8242
Sebring *(G-15937)*

Southern Truss Companies Inc ....D 772 464-4160
Fort Pierce *(G-4531)*

Southwest Strl Systems Inc ....E 239 693-6000
Fort Myers *(G-4403)*

Standard Truss & Roof Sup Inc ......E 863 422-8293
Haines City *(G-4917)*

Superior Truss Systems Inc ....D 305 591-9918
Doral *(G-3385)*

True House Inc ....C 386 325-9085
East Palatka *(G-3477)*

Truss Systems of Vlsia Flgler ....F 386 255-3009
Bunnell *(G-1236)*

Trusscorp International Inc ....E 305 882-8826
Medley *(G-8340)*

Trusses Unlimited Inc ....E 904 355-6611
Ponte Vedra Beach *(G-14281)*

Trussway Manufacturing Inc ....E 407 857-2777
Orlando *(G-12676)*

Trusswood Inc ....D 321 383-0366
Titusville *(G-17624)*

US Truss Inc ....E 561 686-4000
West Palm Beach *(G-18193)*

W Kost Inc ....E 772 286-3700
Palm City *(G-13064)*

Wood Product Services Inc ....E 813 248-2221
Tampa *(G-17433)*

Yandles Quality Roof Trusses ....G 352 732-3000
Ocala *(G-11515)*

TUBE & TUBING FABRICATORS

Blue Water Dynamics LLC ....D 386 957-5464
Edgewater *(G-3482)*

Gunns Welding & Fabricating ....G 727 393-5238
Saint Petersburg *(G-15070)*

SCR Precision Tube Bending Inc .....F 813 622-7091
Tampa *(G-17248)*

Trubendz Technology Inc ....E 305 378-9337
Cutler Bay *(G-2308)*

Trubendz Technology Inc ....G 305 378-9337
Cutler Bay *(G-2309)*

TUBES: Extruded Or Drawn, Aluminum

Hydro Extrusion Usa LLC ....B 904 794-1500
Saint Augustine *(G-14841)*

Sapa Extrsons St Augustine LLC ...C 904 794-1500
Saint Augustine *(G-14886)*

TUBES: Finned, For Heat Transfer

Applied Cooling Technology LLC .....G 239 217-5080
Cape Coral *(G-1304)*

TUBES: Paper Or Fiber, Chemical Or Electrical Uses

Caraustar Indus Cnsmr Pdts Gro ...D 386 328-8335
Palatka *(G-12863)*

TUBES: Steel & Iron

Calnat International Inc ....G 239 839-2581
Cape Coral *(G-1320)*

TUBING, COLD-DRAWN: Mech Or Hypodermic Sizes, Stainless

Ace Mechanical Inc ....G 727 304-6277
Clearwater *(G-1472)*

TUBING: Flexible, Metallic

Custom Tube Products Inc ....F 386 426-0670
Edgewater (G-3488)

TUBING: Plastic

Consolidated Polymer Tech ....E 727 531-4191
Clearwater (G-1549)

Flexsol Holding Corp..........................E 954 941-6333
Pompano Beach (G-14031)

Microlumen Inc..................................D 813 886-1200
Oldsmar (G-11678)

TUBING: Rubber

Florida Pool Products Inc ....E 727 531-8913
Clearwater (G-1602)

TUBING: Seamless

Driveshaft Power Inc ....G....... 561 433-0022
Lake Worth (G-7198)

TUCKING FOR THE TRADE

Wheeler Trading Inc............................F 305 430-7100
Miami Lakes (G-10378)

TURBINE GENERATOR SET UNITS: Hydraulic, Complete

Hoerbger Auto Cmfort Systems L ......E 334 321-2292
Deerfield Beach (G-2734)

Hydroplus Inc....................................F 941 479-7473
Palmetto (G-13175)

TURBINES & TURBINE GENERATOR SET UNITS, COMPLETE

Jupiter Bach North America Inc ....C 850 476-6304
Pensacola (G-13532)

Marajo Diesel Power Corp....................G 786 212-1485
Doral (G-3290)

TURBINES & TURBINE GENERATOR SET UNITS: Gas, Complete

2jcp LLC..G....... 904 834-3818
Ponte Vedra (G-14253)

Power Systems Inc.............................D 561 354-1100
Jupiter (G-6778)

Powerphase LLC.................................F 561 299-3970
Jupiter (G-6780)

Solar Turbines Incorporated ....F 305 476-6855
Miami (G-9912)

Turbine Resources Intl LLC ....G....... 850 377-0449
Pensacola (G-13616)

TURBINES & TURBINE GENERATOR SETS

Alterntive Repr McHning Svcs L ....E 904 861-3040
Jacksonville (G-5880)

Belac LLC ....D 813 749-3200
Oldsmar (G-11634)

Chromalloy Castings Tampa Corp ....C 561 935-3571
Palm Beach Gardens (G-12958)

Diemech Turbine Solution Inc ....G....... 386 804-0179
Deland (G-2864)

Escue Energy LLC ....G....... 561 762-1486
Royal Palm Beach (G-14763)

Florida Hydro Power & Light Co...........G....... 386 328-2470
Palatka (G-12866)

GE...G....... 904 570-3151
Jacksonville (G-6134)

GSE Jetall Inc...................................G....... 305 688-2111
Opa Locka (G-11751)

Locust Usa Inc ....F 305 889-5410
Medley (G-8269)

Peerless Wind Systems.......................G....... 516 249-6900
Boynton Beach (G-895)

Siemens Energy Inc ....A 407 736-1400
Orlando (G-12593)

Siemens Energy Inc ....G....... 407 206-5008
Orlando (G-12594)

Siemens Gmesa Rnwble Enrgy Inc ....E 407 736-2000
Orlando (G-12596)

Siemens Gmesa Rnwble Enrgy Inc ....A 407 721-3273
Orlando (G-12597)

Southwest Turbine Inc........................G....... 305 769-1765
Hialeah (G-5359)

Turbine Generator Maint Inc ....E 239 573-1233
Cape Coral (G-1402)

Vesta T Hetherington ....G 561 588-9933
West Palm Beach (G-18196)

TURBINES & TURBINE GENERATOR SETS & PARTS

Chromalloy Mtl Solutions LLC...............E 954 378-1999
Fort Lauderdale (G-3727)

Sandpiper Turbine LLC ....F 407 377-7220
Kissimmee (G-6959)

TURBINES: Gas, Mechanical Drive

Mitsubishi Power Americas Inc ....D 407 688-6100
Lake Mary (G-7096)

Power Systems Mfg LLC ....B 561 354-1100
Jupiter (G-6779)

Raytheon Technologies Corp ....A 860 565-4321
Jupiter (G-6786)

TURBINES: Hydraulic, Complete

Southstern Indus Fbrcators LLC...........E 941 776-1211
Duette (G-3433)

TURBINES: Steam

Babcock & Wilcox Company ....G 561 478-3800
West Palm Beach (G-17936)

Gas Turbine Efficiency Inc ....E 407 304-5200
Orlando (G-12182)

Gas Turbine Efficiency LLC ....G 407 304-5200
Orlando (G-12183)

Siemens Energy Inc............................D 407 736-7957
Orlando (G-12595)

TURBO-SUPERCHARGERS: Aircraft

Approved Turbo Components Inc ....F 559 627-3600
Vero Beach (G-17736)

TURKISH BATH

Rfg Consulting Services Inc ....G 832 298-5696
Medley (G-8311)

TYPESETTING SVC

Abby Press Inc ....E 407 847-5565
Kissimmee (G-6892)

Aether Media USA Inc ....G 863 647-5500
Lakeland (G-7268)

Alta Systems Inc ....E 352 372-2534
Gainesville (G-4648)

American Business Cards Inc ....E 314 739-0800
Naples (G-10666)

Apple Printing & Advg Spc Inc ....G 954 524-0493
Fort Lauderdale (G-3653)

Armstrongs Prtg & Graphics Inc ....G 850 243-6923
Fort Walton Beach (G-4562)

Assocated Prtg Productions Inc ....E 305 623-7600
Miami Lakes (G-10282)

B J and ME Inc ....G 561 368-5470
Boca Raton (G-424)

B R Q Grossmans Inc ....F 954 971-1077
Pompano Beach (G-13943)

Bava Inc ....F 850 893-4799
Tallahassee (G-16417)

Bayou Printing Inc ....F 850 678-5444
Valparaiso (G-17656)

Bjm Enterprises Inc ....F 941 746-4171
Palmetto (G-13157)

Boca Color Graphics Inc ....F 561 391-2229
Boca Raton (G-435)

Boca Raton Printing Co ....G 561 395-8404
Boca Raton (G-437)

Bros Williams Printing Inc ....G 305 769-9925
Hialeah (G-5080)

Burr Printing Co Inc ....G 863 294-3166
Winter Haven (G-18426)

Caxton Newspapers Inc ....E 305 538-9700
Miami Beach (G-10176)

Central Florida Publishing Inc ....F 407 323-5204
Sanford (G-15279)

Coastal Printing Inc Sarasota ....E 941 351-1515
Sarasota (G-15635)

Color Concepts Prtg Design Co ....F 813 623-2921
Tampa (G-16720)

Color Express Inc ....G 305 558-2061
Hialeah (G-5094)

Coloramax Printing Inc........................F 305 541-0322
Miami (G-8947)

Commercial Printers Inc......................D 954 781-3737
Fort Lauderdale (G-3738)

Creative Prtg Grphic Dsign Inc ....E 407 855-0202
Orlando (G-12055)

Csmc Inc ....E 407 246-1567
Orlando (G-12060)

Dahlquist Enterprises Inc ....G 407 896-2294
Orlando (G-12071)

Dannys Prtg Svc Sups & Eqp Inc ....G 305 757-2282
Miami (G-9000)

Durra-Print Inc ....E 850 222-4768
Tallahassee (G-16434)

Dvh Macleod Corp ....F 850 224-6760
Tallahassee (G-16435)

Ed Vance Printing Company Inc............F 813 882-8888
Tampa (G-16797)

Edward Thomas Company ....G 561 746-1441
Jupiter (G-6718)

Express Printing & Office Sups ....G 904 765-9696
Jacksonville (G-6085)

FGA Printing ....G 954 763-1122
Pompano Beach (G-14019)

Fidelity Printing Corporation ....D 727 522-9557
Saint Petersburg (G-15044)

First Imprssons Prtg Cmmnctons ....G 407 831-6100
Longwood (G-7896)

Florida Graphic Printing Inc ....F 386 253-4532
Daytona Beach (G-2553)

Ford Press Inc ....F 352 787-4650
Leesburg (G-7777)

Four G Enterprises Inc ....E 407 834-4143
Longwood (G-7898)

G S Printers Inc ....G 305 931-2755
Fort Lauderdale (G-3834)

Graphics Type Color Entps Inc..............E 305 591-7600
Miami (G-9236)

Gulf Coast Business World Inc ....F 850 864-1511
Fort Walton Beach (G-4590)

Halifax Media Holdings LLC...................E 386 681-2404
Daytona Beach (G-2559)

Hartco Inc ....G 904 353-5259
Jacksonville (G-6167)

Hilcraft Engraving Inc.........................G 305 871-6100
Miami (G-9282)

ICM Printing Co Inc ....F 352 377-7468
Gainesville (G-4709)

Image Prtg & Digital Svcs Inc ....G 850 244-3380
Mary Esther (G-8177)

Impact Design Group Inc ....E 904 636-8989
Jacksonville (G-6193)

Instant Printing Services Inc ....F 727 546-8036
Floral City (G-3611)

J J M Services Inc ....G 954 437-1880
Miramar (G-10507)

J V G Inc ....G 727 584-7136
Largo (G-7619)

Jeffrey B Gould ....G 410 463-0796
Orlando (G-12271)

Jet Graphics Inc ....E 305 264-4333
Miami (G-9365)

Jet-Set Printing Inc ....E 407 339-1900
Casselberry (G-1421)

K R O Enterprises Ltd ....G 309 797-2213
Naples (G-10795)

Keithco Inc ....G 352 351-4741
Ocala (G-11419)

Kights Printing & Office Pdts ....G 904 731-7990
Jacksonville (G-6242)

Lake Worth Herald Press Inc ....F 561 585-9387
Lake Worth (G-7214)

Lauderdale Graphics Corp ....E 954 450-0800
Davie (G-2432)

Leda Printing Inc ....E 941 922-1563
Sarasota (G-15724)

Leila K Moavero ....G 954 978-0018
Pompano Beach (G-14076)

Liberty Calhoun Journal Inc ....G 850 643-3333
Bristol (G-1122)

Linden-Beals Corp ....G 772 562-0624
Vero Beach (G-17773)

Linographics Inc ....F 407 422-8700
Orlando (G-12331)

Menu Men Inc ....F 305 633-7925
Miami (G-9532)

Mikes Print Shop Inc...........................G 407 718-4964
Winter Park (G-18525)

Multi-Color Printing Inc ....G 772 287-1676
Stuart (G-16187)

My Print Shop Inc...............................F 954 973-9369
Deerfield Beach (G-2773)

Employee Codes: A=Over 500 employees, B=251-500
C=101-250, D=51-100, E=20-50, F=10-19, G=4-9

2022 Harris Florida
Manufacturers Directory

1345

PRODUCT

Ngp Corporate Square Inc ....E 239 643-3430
Naples (G-10836)
Ocala Print Quick Inc ....G 352 629-0736
Ocala (G-11458)
Oompha Inc ....G 850 222-7210
Tallahassee (G-16486)
Output Printing Corp ....F 813 228-8800
Tampa (G-17134)
Paper Fish Printing Inc ....G 239 481-3555
Fort Myers (G-4358)
Parkinson Enterprises Inc ....E 863 688-7900
Lakeland (G-7406)
PIP Printing ....G 352 622-3224
Ocala (G-11467)
Precision Printing of Columbus ....G 561 509-7269
Boynton Beach (G-898)
Premier Global Enterprises ....G 561 747-7303
Palm Beach Gardens (G-13000)
Print One Inc ....G 813 273-0240
Oldsmar (G-11691)
Printers of Pensacola LLC ....G 850 434-2588
Pensacola (G-13585)
Reimink Printing Inc ....G 813 289-4663
Tampa (G-17214)
Roberts Quality Printing Inc ....E 727 442-4011
Clearwater (G-1769)
S Printing Inc ....G 305 633-3343
Miami (G-9832)
Saugus Valley Corp ....G 954 772-4077
Coral Springs (G-2209)
Sergios Printing Inc ....F 305 971-4112
Miami (G-9869)
Set Up Inc ....G 239 542-4142
Cape Coral (G-1384)
South Broward Printing Inc ....G 954 962-1309
Hollywood (G-5660)
Spinnaker Holding Company ....E 561 392-8626
Boca Raton (G-692)
Steven K Bakum Inc ....G 561 804-9110
West Palm Beach (G-18164)
Sunshine Printing Inc ....F 561 478-2602
West Palm Beach (G-18170)
Tampa Printing Company ....E 813 612-7746
Tampa (G-17337)
Thalers Printing Center Inc ....G 954 741-6522
Lauderhill (G-7744)
Toms Instant Printing Inc ....G 904 396-0686
Jacksonville (G-6558)
Town Street Print Shop Inc ....G 850 432-8300
Gulf Breeze (G-4895)
Universal Graphics & Prtg Inc ....G 561 845-6404
North Palm Beach (G-11184)
Universal Screen Graphics Inc ....E 813 623-5335
Tampa (G-17394)
V I P Printing ....G 386 258-3326
Daytona Beach (G-2616)
V P Press Inc ....F 954 581-7531
Fort Lauderdale (G-4114)
Vmak Corp ....F 407 260-1199
Longwood (G-7958)
Vowells Downtown Inc ....G 850 432-5175
Pensacola (G-13622)
W D H Enterprises Inc ....G 941 758-6500
Bradenton (G-1073)
Walker Graphics Inc ....G 954 964-1688
Hollywood (G-5683)

ULTRASONIC EQPT: Cleaning, Exc Med & Dental

Geneva Systems Inc ....G 352 235-2990
Green Cove Springs (G-4826)
Kenneth Jake Linton ....G 850 526-0121
Marianna (G-8167)
Neat Clean Group Inc ....F 727 459-6079
Clearwater (G-1714)
Power Vac Corporation ....G 954 491-0188
Oakland Park (G-11286)
Pressure Systems Innvtions LLC ....F 561 249-2708
West Palm Beach (G-18128)

ULTRASONIC EQPT: Dental

Simplified Systems Inc ....F 305 672-7676
Miami Beach (G-10227)

UMBRELLAS & CANES

Ultimate Umbrella Company Inc ....E 305 634-5116
Hialeah (G-5390)

UMBRELLAS: Garden Or Wagon

Advanced Sewing ....G 954 484-2100
Fort Lauderdale (G-3626)
Schnupp Manufacturing Co Inc ....G 305 325-0520
Miami (G-9856)
Shelleys Cushions Mfg Inc ....E 305 633-1790
Miami (G-9880)
Suntyx LLC ....E 786 558-2233
Miramar (G-10550)

UNDERCOATINGS: Paint

Paints & Coatings Inc ....E 239 997-6645
North Fort Myers (G-11065)
Sfa Systems Inc ....E 561 585-5927
Lake Worth (G-7232)
Techncal Pntg Jacksonville Inc ....D 904 652-1129
Jacksonville (G-6538)

UNIFORM SPLY SVCS: Indl

Cintas Corporation ....G 239 693-8722
Fort Myers (G-4209)

UNIFORM STORES

Bnj Noble Inc ....F 954 987-1040
Davie (G-2392)
Sharp Marketing LLC ....G 954 565-2711
Oakland Park (G-11293)

UNISEX HAIR SALONS

Fekkai Retail LLC ....F 866 514-8048
Plantation (G-13851)

UNIVERSITY

Current ....F 954 262-8455
Davie (G-2401)

UPHOLSTERERS' EQPT & SPLYS WHOLESALERS

Design Works By Tech Pdts Inc ....E 941 355-2703
Sarasota (G-15658)

UPHOLSTERY MATERIALS, BROADWOVEN

J & H Supply Co Inc ....G 561 582-3346
Lake Worth (G-7207)
Miami Prestige Interiors Inc ....E 305 685-3343
Miami (G-9555)

UPHOLSTERY WORK SVCS

Top Trtment Cstomes Accesories ....G 239 936-4600
Fort Myers (G-4426)

URNS: Cut Stone

Eterna Urn Co Inc ....G 386 258-6491
Daytona Beach (G-2550)

USED CAR DEALERS

Addco Manufacturing Company ....E 828 733-1560
Riviera Beach (G-14587)
Evo Motors LLC ....G 813 621-7799
Seffner (G-15957)

USED MERCHANDISE STORES

Nfjb Inc ....E 954 771-1100
Fort Lauderdale (G-3962)

UTENSILS: Cast Aluminum, Household

Kitchen Sink Express LLC ....G 800 888-6604
Dunedin (G-3453)

UTENSILS: Household, Cooking & Kitchen, Metal

All Southern Fabricators Inc ....E 727 573-4846
Clearwater (G-1486)
Epare LLC ....G 347 682-5121
Miami (G-9104)
Global Marketing Corp ....D 973 426-1088
Bradenton (G-983)
Royal Prestige ....E 813 464-9872
Fort Lauderdale (G-4031)

UTENSILS: Household, Metal, Exc Cast

Zeroll Co ....E 772 461-3811
Weston (G-18300)

UTILITY TRAILER DEALERS

All Amrcan Trlr Connection Inc ....G 561 582-1800
Palm Springs (G-13142)
Amera Trail Inc ....E 407 892-1100
Saint Cloud (G-14920)
Eds Aluminum Buildings Inc ....G 850 476-2169
Pensacola (G-13493)
Loadmaster Alum Boat Trlrs Inc ....E 813 689-3096
Tampa (G-17020)

VACUUM CLEANER REPAIR SVCS

AAA Monterey Discount Vacuum ....G 772 288-5233
Stuart (G-16109)

VACUUM CLEANERS: Household

AAA Monterey Discount Vacuum ....G 772 288-5233
Stuart (G-16109)
Intelliclean Solutions LLC ....G 615 293-2299
Miami (G-9322)

VACUUM CLEANERS: Indl Type

LDS Vacuum Products Inc ....E 407 862-4643
Longwood (G-7916)

VACUUM CLEANERS: Wholesalers

Pro Chem Products Inc ....E 407 425-5533
Orlando (G-12509)

VACUUM PUMPS & EQPT: Laboratory

Walden Consulting LLC ....G 407 563-3620
Orlando (G-12710)

VALUE-ADDED RESELLERS: Computer Systems

Cloudfactors LLC ....G 407 768-3160
Orlando (G-12022)
Commski LLC ....G 813 501-0111
Spring Hill (G-16068)
Phintec LLC ....G 321 214-2500
Orlando (G-12485)

VALVE REPAIR SVCS, INDL

Flotech LLC ....D 904 358-1849
Jacksonville (G-6113)
Hoerbger Cmprssion Tech Amer H ......B 954 974-5700
Pompano Beach (G-14051)

VALVES

Control Southern Inc ....E 904 353-0004
Jacksonville (G-6003)
Florida Marine Products Inc ....F 813 248-2283
Tampa (G-16850)

VALVES & PARTS: Gas, Indl

Petroleum Equipment and Mfg Co ....F 305 558-9573
Hialeah (G-5294)

VALVES & PIPE FITTINGS

A & N Corporation ....D 352 528-4100
Williston (G-18327)
Andersons Can Line Fbrction Eq ....F 407 889-4665
Apopka (G-102)
Depend-O-Drain Inc ....E 941 756-1710
Bradenton (G-968)
Eagle Pneumatic Inc ....E 863 644-4870
Lakeland (G-7314)
Enolgas Usa Inc ....G 754 205-7902
Pompano Beach (G-14012)
Flotech LLC ....D 904 358-1849
Jacksonville (G-6113)
Formweld Fitting Inc ....E 850 626-4888
Milton (G-10424)
Gate Cfv Solutions Inc ....G 772 388-3387
Sebastian (G-15893)
Helios Technologies Inc ....F 941 362-1200
Sarasota (G-15493)
Hoerbger Cmprssion Tech Amer H ......B 954 974-5700
Pompano Beach (G-14051)

Leslie Controls Inc............................C...... 813 978-1000
Temple Terrace *(G-17539)*
Mat-Vac Technology Inc.......................F...... 386 238-7017
Daytona Beach *(G-2573)*
Parker-Hannifin Corporation.............E...... 305 470-8800
Miami *(G-9694)*
Precision Fabg & Clg Co Inc............D...... 321 635-2000
Cocoa *(G-1948)*
Serf Inc...E...... 850 476-8203
Cantonment *(G-1273)*
Southern Innovative Energy Inc.........G...... 321 747-9205
Titusville *(G-17616)*
Sun Pipe and Valves LLC....................F...... 772 408-5530
Port Saint Lucie *(G-14451)*
Target Manufacturing Inc...................G...... 305 633-0361
Miami *(G-9994)*
Teknocraft Inc......................................E...... 321 729-9634
Melbourne *(G-8548)*
WSa Engineered Systems Inc..............F...... 414 481-4120
Pensacola *(G-13628)*

VALVES Solenoid

Jefferson Slnoid Vlves USA Inc...........D...... 305 249-8120
Miami *(G-9363)*
Thermoval Solenoid Valves Usa...........G...... 954 835-5523
Davie *(G-2490)*

VALVES: Aerosol, Metal

Ees Design LLC.....................................F...... 954 541-2660
Fort Lauderdale *(G-3788)*
Medway Hall Dev Group Inc..................F...... 904 786-0622
Jacksonville *(G-6295)*
Sfi Inc...E...... 407 834-2258
Orlando *(G-12586)*

VALVES: Aircraft

Flyteone Inc...G...... 813 421-1410
Clearwater *(G-1603)*

VALVES: Aircraft, Control, Hydraulic & Pneumatic

Micro Pneumatic Logic Inc.................C...... 954 935-6821
Pompano Beach *(G-14099)*

VALVES: Aircraft, Hydraulic

Chuxco Inc..F...... 305 470-9595
Coral Gables *(G-2039)*
Jet Research Development Inc............D...... 954 427-0404
Deerfield Beach *(G-2745)*

VALVES: Control, Automatic

Doch LLC...G...... 571 491-7578
Tampa *(G-16783)*
Roper Technologies Inc.......................E...... 941 556-2601
Sarasota *(G-15801)*

VALVES: Fluid Power, Control, Hydraulic & pneumatic

Eem Technologies Corp.......................G...... 786 606-5993
Doral *(G-3205)*
Helios Technologies Inc.......................C...... 941 362-1200
Sarasota *(G-15491)*
Helios Technologies Inc.......................C...... 941 328-1769
Sarasota *(G-15492)*
Industrial Mobile Hydraulics..............G...... 904 866-7592
Jacksonville *(G-6196)*
Zennergy LLC..G...... 813 382-3460
Tampa *(G-17455)*

VALVES: Gas Cylinder, Compressed

S A Microtechnologies LLC...................F...... 954 973-6166
Pompano Beach *(G-14166)*

VALVES: Indl

Alfa Laval Inc......................................F...... 941 727-1900
Sarasota *(G-15439)*
Chem-TEC Equipment Co......................F...... 954 428-8259
Deerfield Beach *(G-2692)*
Chemseal Inc..G...... 305 433-8362
Hialeah *(G-5091)*
Circor International Inc......................G...... 813 978-1000
Temple Terrace *(G-17536)*
Dresser Inc...E...... 318 640-2250
Jacksonville *(G-6040)*

Dresser LLC..B...... 904 781-7071
Jacksonville *(G-6041)*
Hoerbiger Corp America Inc.................B...... 954 974-5700
Pompano Beach *(G-14052)*
Hoerbiger Service Inc...........................E...... 954 422-9850
Deerfield Beach *(G-2737)*
Hose Power USA...................................G...... 863 669-9333
Lakeland *(G-7345)*
Inovinox Usa LLC..................................G...... 800 780-1017
Miami *(G-9319)*
Iq Valves Co...E...... 321 729-9634
Melbourne *(G-8442)*
Merit Fastener Corporation.................G...... 813 626-3748
Tampa *(G-17066)*
Micro Matic Usa Inc............................E...... 352 544-1081
Brooksville *(G-1181)*
Morris Valves Inc.................................G...... 305 477-6525
Doral *(G-3308)*
Pentair Flow Technologies...................G...... 904 538-0894
Jacksonville *(G-6366)*
Pentair LLC...G...... 386 469-0566
Deland *(G-2895)*
Target Manufacturing Inc...................G...... 305 633-0361
Miami *(G-9994)*
Tsm Champ LLC....................................D...... 615 806-7900
Sarasota *(G-15574)*
Watts One LLC......................................F...... 305 606-1816
Wellington *(G-17868)*

VALVES: Regulating & Control, Automatic

Azex Flow Technologies Inc.................G...... 305 393-8037
Miami *(G-8785)*
Chicago Electronic Distrs Inc...............F...... 312 985-6175
Port Charlotte *(G-14292)*
Del Prado Holdings LLC........................G...... 305 680-7425
Hollywood *(G-5563)*
Fabco-Air Inc..D...... 352 373-3578
Gainesville *(G-4689)*
Grinnell LLC..B...... 561 988-3658
Boca Raton *(G-533)*
Guard Dog Valves Inc..........................G...... 239 793-6886
Naples *(G-10767)*
Leslie Controls Inc..............................C...... 813 978-1000
Temple Terrace *(G-17539)*

VALVES: Regulating, Process Control

Abbey Rogers..G...... 813 645-1400
Tampa *(G-16553)*

VALVES: Water Works

Gate Cfv Solutions Inc.........................G...... 772 388-3387
Sebastian *(G-15893)*
Harrington Corporation........................F...... 863 326-6130
Winter Haven *(G-18444)*

VAN CONVERSIONS

Interntnal Srvillance Tech Inc..............E...... 954 574-1100
Deerfield Beach *(G-2742)*

VAN CONVERSIONS

Interntnal Srvillance Tech Inc..............E...... 954 574-1100
Deerfield Beach *(G-2742)*
Master Overland LLC............................G...... 727 255-3764
Brooksville *(G-1177)*

VASES: Pottery

Americraft Cookware LLC.....................E...... 352 483-7600
Mount Dora *(G-10596)*

VAULTS & SAFES WHOLESALERS

Safe Banks and Lock...........................G...... 954 762-3565
Fort Lauderdale *(G-4035)*

VEGETABLE OILS: Medicinal Grade, Refined Or Concentrated

Ravenswood Import Export Ltd L.........G...... 863 800-0210
Lake Placid *(G-7147)*

VEHICLES FINANCE LEASING, EXC AUTOMOBILES & TRUCKS

Bulk Resources Inc..............................G...... 813 764-8420
Plant City *(G-13748)*

VEHICLES: All Terrain

Power Sports Treasure Coast..............G...... 772 463-6428
Stuart *(G-16200)*
River City Powersports LLC..................G...... 386 259-5724
Debary *(G-2640)*
Southern Brothers Racing LLC.............G...... 850 509-2223
Quincy *(G-14550)*
Viper 4x4...F...... 305 468-9818
Windermere *(G-18369)*
Xscream Inc..G...... 727 449-9353
Clearwater *(G-1857)*

VEHICLES: Recreational

B & E Rv Service & Repair LLC............G...... 352 401-7930
Ocala *(G-11331)*
Lakeside Recreational Inc.....................G...... 863 467-1530
Okeechobee *(G-11611)*

VENDING MACHINES & PARTS

Dgw Technologies LLC.........................F...... 407 930-4437
Apopka *(G-121)*
Hylton & Assoc.....................................G...... 321 303-2862
Orlando *(G-12232)*
Optima Associates Inc..........................F...... 877 371-1555
Lake City *(G-7036)*
Optimal Vending Systems LLC.............G...... 301 633-2353
Alachua *(G-16)*
Rocket Vending Inc...............................F...... 561 672-1373
Boca Raton *(G-653)*
SAP Enterprises Inc.............................F...... 954 871-8688
North Lauderdale *(G-11086)*
Sunnypics LLC.......................................G...... 407 992-6210
Orlando *(G-12633)*
Vendapin LLC..F...... 352 796-2693
Brooksville *(G-1219)*

VENETIAN BLINDS & SHADES

Blinds R Us Corp..................................G...... 305 303-2072
Miami *(G-8839)*
Dwa Inc...F...... 941 444-1134
Sarasota *(G-15663)*
Privacy Window Design Inc...................G...... 386 761-7306
Port Orange *(G-14345)*

VENTURE CAPITAL COMPANIES

Sphere Access Inc................................F...... 336 501-6159
Tampa *(G-17295)*

VESSELS: Process, Indl, Metal Plate

Brewfab LLC..F...... 727 823-8333
Saint Petersburg *(G-14989)*

VETERINARY PHARMACEUTICAL PREPARATIONS

American Vet Sciences LLC..................G...... 727 471-0850
Largo *(G-7533)*
Amino Cell Inc......................................F...... 352 291-0200
Ocala *(G-11323)*
D V M Pharmaceuticals Inc..................D...... 305 575-6950
Weston *(G-18236)*
Dr Xies Jing-Tang Herbal Inc...............F...... 352 591-2141
Ocala *(G-11373)*
Pegasus Laboratories Inc.....................E...... 850 478-2770
Pensacola *(G-13569)*
Synergylabs LLC...................................E...... 954 525-1133
Fort Lauderdale *(G-4082)*
Vetbiotek Inc..F...... 727 308-2030
Oldsmar *(G-11706)*

VETERINARY PRDTS: Instruments & Apparatus

Earth Vets Inc......................................G...... 352 332-9991
Fernandina Beach *(G-3586)*

VIALS: Glass

Jensen Scientific Products Inc..............E...... 954 344-2006
Coral Springs *(G-2169)*

VIDEO & AUDIO EQPT, WHOLESALE

Armadillo Sounds Inc...........................G...... 305 801-7906
Miami *(G-8748)*
Hitex Marketing Group Inc....................G...... 305 406-1150
Miami *(G-9285)*

Employee Codes: A=Over 500 employees, B=251-500
C=101-250, D=51-100, E=20-50, F=10-19, G=4-9

2022 Harris Florida
Manufacturers Directory

PRODUCT

1347

Interntnal Srvillance Tech Inc ....E 954 574-1100
Deerfield Beach **(G-2742)**

Perpetual Marketing Assoc Inc ....G 813 949-9385
Lutz **(G-8009)**

VIDEO PRODUCTION SVCS

Collins Media & Advg LLC ....F 954 688-9758
Margate **(G-8124)**

VIDEO TRIGGERS EXC REMOTE CONTROL TV DEVICES

Adtec Productions Incorporated ....F 904 720-2003
Jacksonville **(G-5859)**

VINYL RESINS, NEC

American Vinyl Company ....E 305 687-1863
Hialeah **(G-5051)**

Certified Whl Exterior Pdts ....G 407 654-7170
Winter Garden **(G-18379)**

Leather or Not ....G 813 972-9667
Tampa **(G-17003)**

VISUAL COMMUNICATIONS SYSTEMS

First Communications Inc ....D 850 668-7990
Tallahassee **(G-16439)**

Kaltec Electronics Inc ....F 813 888-9555
Tampa **(G-16975)**

Viper Communication Systems ....E 352 694-7030
Ocala **(G-11510)**

VISUAL EFFECTS PRODUCTION SVCS

3d Perception Inc ....F 321 235-7999
Orlando **(G-11850)**

VITAMINS: Natural Or Synthetic, Uncompounded, Bulk

Alfa Manufacturing LLC ....F 305 436-8150
Miami **(G-8684)**

Alive By Nature Inc ....F 800 810-1935
Ponte Vedra Beach **(G-14261)**

American Natural Pdts Lab Inc ....G 305 261-5152
Miami **(G-8719)**

Boston Ntrceutical Science LLC ....F 617 848-4560
Miami **(G-8849)**

CJ Labs Inc ....F 305 234-9644
Miami **(G-8928)**

De Lima Consultants Group Inc ....G 954 933-7030
Coral Springs **(G-2148)**

Great Amercn Natural Pdts Inc ....F 727 521-4372
Saint Petersburg **(G-15066)**

Guardian Essentials LLC ....G 817 401-0200
Delray Beach **(G-2972)**

Interactive Media Tech Inc ....F 561 999-9116
Boca Raton **(G-547)**

Lab Kingz LLC ....G 561 808-4216
Delray Beach **(G-2982)**

Lan Industries LLC ....F 305 889-2087
Miami **(G-9420)**

Live Wise Naturals LLC ....G 866 866-0075
Bradenton **(G-1007)**

Modular Thermal Tech LLC ....E 954 785-1055
Pompano Beach **(G-14104)**

National Health Alliance LLC ....G 727 504-3915
Tampa **(G-17102)**

Nulab Inc ....D 727 446-1126
Clearwater **(G-1722)**

Nutop International LLC ....G 954 909-0010
Fort Lauderdale **(G-3964)**

Rainbow Lght Ntrtnal Systems I ....G 954 233-3300
Sunrise **(G-16361)**

Totally Products LLC ....G 786 942-9218
Boca Raton **(G-720)**

Twinlab Cnsld Holdings Inc ....G 561 443-4301
Boca Raton **(G-726)**

Twinlab Consolidation Corp ....G 800 645-5626
Boca Raton **(G-727)**

Twinlab Holdings Inc ....E 800 645-5626
Boca Raton **(G-729)**

Vedic Origins Inc ....G 407 712-5614
Altamonte Springs **(G-76)**

Vitalleo LLC ....G 904 474-5330
Neptune Beach **(G-10960)**

Vitamin Shoppe Florida LLC ....E 305 468-1600
Miami Lakes **(G-10377)**

Vitaminmed LLC ....G 727 443-7008
Clearwater **(G-1846)**

Viva 5 LLC ....E 561 239-2239
Saint Petersburg **(G-15228)**

We Make Vitamins LLC ....G 863 607-6708
Lakeland **(G-7472)**

VITAMINS: Pharmaceutical Preparations

Avanti Nutritional Labs LLC ....E 305 822-3880
Miami Lakes **(G-10283)**

Be Whole Nutrition LLC ....G 813 420-3057
Plant City **(G-13746)**

Ceautamed Worldwide LLC ....G 866 409-6262
Boca Raton **(G-456)**

Dextrum Laboratories Inc ....G 305 594-4020
Miami **(G-9025)**

Florida Nutri Labs LLC ....F 863 607-6708
Lakeland **(G-7331)**

Full Life Direct LLC ....F 800 305-3043
Hollywood **(G-5578)**

Glucorell Inc ....G 407 384-3388
Maitland **(G-8060)**

Interntnal Ntrctcals Group Inc ....G 786 518-2903
Sunrise **(G-16324)**

Master Nutrition Labs Inc ....G 786 847-2000
Opa Locka **(G-11766)**

Mdr LLC ....C 954 845-9500
Sunrise **(G-16340)**

Natural Vitamins Lab Corp ....C 305 265-1660
Opa Locka **(G-11773)**

Natural Vitamins Lab Corp ....C 305 265-1660
Opa Locka **(G-11774)**

Nutrition Laboratories Inc ....E 727 442-2747
Clearwater **(G-1724)**

Pharmalab Enterprises Inc ....F 305 821-4002
Miami Lakes **(G-10338)**

Roja Med Inc ....E 305 381-5803
Miami **(G-9819)**

Taylor L Max L C ....G 833 346-9963
Fort Myers **(G-4419)**

Twinlab Corporation ....G 800 645-5626
Boca Raton **(G-728)**

VOCATIONAL REHABILITATION AGENCY

Brevard Achievement Center Inc ....B 321 632-8610
Rockledge **(G-14693)**

WALKWAYS: Moving

Mobile Specialties Inc ....G 407 878-5469
Sanford **(G-15359)**

WALL & CEILING SQUARES: Concrete

Armstrong World Industries Inc ....D 850 433-8321
Pensacola **(G-13446)**

Jenasis Structures Inc ....F 813 238-7620
Odessa **(G-11562)**

USG International Ltd ....F 305 688-8744
Miami **(G-10085)**

WALLBOARD: Decorated, Made From Purchased Materials

Panelfold Inc ....C 305 688-3501
Miami **(G-9688)**

WALLPAPER & WALL COVERINGS

Nicolette Mayer Collection Inc ....G 561 241-6906
Boca Raton **(G-617)**

Parthenon Prints Inc ....E 850 769-8321
Panama City **(G-13297)**

Richard Wagner LLC ....G 239 450-1721
Naples **(G-10875)**

WALLPAPER STORE

Sanzogo Corporation ....G 561 334-2138
Boca Raton **(G-662)**

WALLS: Curtain, Metal

Johnson & Jackson GL Pdts Inc ....F 813 630-9774
Tampa **(G-16968)**

WAREHOUSING & STORAGE FACILITIES, NEC

Refreshment Services Inc ....D 850 574-0281
Tallahassee **(G-16493)**

WAREHOUSING & STORAGE, REFRIGERATED: Cold Storage Or Refrig

West Texas Protein Inc ....F 806 250-5959
Jacksonville **(G-6602)**

WAREHOUSING & STORAGE: General

Boeing Company ....B 321 853-6647
Cape Canaveral **(G-1279)**

CF Industries Inc ....E 813 782-1591
Bartow **(G-305)**

Dip-A-Dee Donuts ....E 352 460-4266
Leesburg **(G-7766)**

Regent Labs Inc ....G 954 426-4889
Deerfield Beach **(G-2799)**

WAREHOUSING & STORAGE: Liquid

Kus Usa Inc ....E 954 463-1075
Davie **(G-2431)**

WAREHOUSING & STORAGE: Lumber Terminal Or Storage For Hire

Mid-Flrida Lbr Acqisitions Inc ....E 863 533-0155
Bartow **(G-318)**

WAREHOUSING & STORAGE: Self Storage

GOTG LLC ....G 800 381-4684
Brooksville **(G-1159)**

WARFARE COUNTER-MEASURE EQPT

Sparton Deleon Springs LLC ....C 386 985-4631
De Leon Springs **(G-2629)**

Spartronics Brooksville LLC ....B 352 799-6520
Brooksville **(G-1206)**

WARM AIR HEATING & AC EQPT & SPLYS, WHOLESALE Air Filters

Air Sponge Filter Company Inc ....G 954 752-1836
Coral Springs **(G-2129)**

Andrews Filter and Supply Corp ....E 407 423-3310
Orlando **(G-11912)**

Con-Air Industries Inc ....D 407 298-5733
Orlando **(G-12039)**

Rv Air Inc ....G 309 657-4300
Clearwater **(G-1773)**

WARM AIR HEATING/AC EQPT/SPLYS, WHOL Warm Air Htg Eqpt/Splys

Innovative Support Systems Inc ....G 407 682-7570
Altamonte Springs **(G-53)**

Lasalle Bristol Corporation ....F 863 680-1729
Lakeland **(G-7375)**

WASHERS

Color Mstr Pressure Washer Inc ....G 561 366-7747
Lake Worth **(G-7193)**

G & G Pressure Washers Inc ....G 786 376-1800
Hollywood **(G-5580)**

Pressure Washers USA ....G 561 848-7970
Lake Park **(G-7133)**

Scott Washer Inc ....G 407 432-2648
Orlando **(G-12579)**

Siligom USA LLC ....G 786 406-6262
Doral **(G-3367)**

Washers-R-Us Inc ....G 850 573-0221
Alford **(G-25)**

WASHERS: Metal

Edwin B Stimpson Company Inc ....C 954 946-3500
Pompano Beach **(G-14006)**

WASHROOM SANITATION SVCS

AAA Event Services LLC ....F 386 454-0929
Newberry **(G-11015)**

WATCH STRAPS, EXC METAL

Rubber B LLC ....G 305 771-2369
Miami Beach **(G-10224)**

WATCHES

Lucien Piccard/Arnex Watch Co ....D 954 241-2745
Hollywood **(G-5617)**

WATCHES & PARTS, WHOLESALE

LP Watch Group Inc ....E..... 954 985-3827
Hollywood **(G-5614)**

WATER HEATERS

Marey International LLC ....G..... 787 727-0277
Miami **(G-9509)**

Peralta Group Inc ....G..... 954 502-8100
Sunrise **(G-16351)**

Stiebel Eltron Inc ....F..... 800 826-5537
Sarasota **(G-15560)**

WATER HEATERS WHOLESALERS EXCEPT ELECTRIC

Marey International LLC ....G..... 787 727-0277
Miami **(G-9509)**

WATER PURIFICATION EQPT: Household

Action Manufacturing & Sup Inc ....F..... 239 574-3443
Cape Coral **(G-1296)**

Aquathin Corp ....E..... 800 462-7634
Pompano Beach **(G-13931)**

Astro Pure Incorporated ....F..... 954 422-8966
Lighthouse Point **(G-7825)**

Atmospheric Wtr Solutions Inc ....F..... 954 306-6763
Cooper City **(G-2017)**

Biozone Scientific Intl Inc ....G..... 407 876-2000
Orlando **(G-11953)**

Clearwater Enviro Tech Inc ....E..... 727 209-6400
Largo **(G-7565)**

Focus On Water Inc ....G..... 239 275-1880
Fort Myers **(G-4260)**

Great Lakes Wtr Trtmnt Systems ....G..... 269 381-0210
Naples **(G-10766)**

H2o International Inc ....F..... 954 570-3464
Deerfield Beach **(G-2729)**

Hydro-Dyne Engineering Inc ....E..... 727 532-0777
Oldsmar **(G-11658)**

K V Water Equipment & Krane Co ....G..... 941 723-0707
Venice **(G-17702)**

Lapure Water Products Inc ....G..... 727 521-3993
Pinellas Park **(G-13704)**

Lifegard Prfcation Systems LLC ....G..... 813 875-7777
Tampa **(G-17010)**

Main USA Corp ....G..... 305 499-4994
Miami **(G-9501)**

Pristine Environment LLC ....F..... 727 541-5748
Pinellas Park **(G-13723)**

Rgf Environmental Group Inc ....C..... 800 842-7771
Riviera Beach **(G-14669)**

Watermakers Inc ....F..... 954 467-8920
Fort Lauderdale **(G-4123)**

Watts Water Technologies Inc ....E..... 352 465-2000
Dunnellon **(G-3470)**

Worldwide Technology Inc ....E..... 813 855-2443
Oldsmar **(G-11707)**

WATER PURIFICATION PRDTS: Chlorination Tablets & Kits

Biomar Products LLC ....G..... 800 216-2080
Doral **(G-3139)**

Xcelience LLC ....F..... 813 286-0404
Tampa **(G-17446)**

Xcelience Holdings LLC ....B..... 813 286-0404
Tampa **(G-17447)**

WATER SOFTENER SVCS

Aqualogix Inc ....F..... 858 442-4550
Palm Beach Gardens **(G-12948)**

WATER SOFTENING WHOLESALERS

Enviro Water Solutions LLC ....D..... 877 842-1635
Deland **(G-2868)**

WATER SUPPLY

City of Hollywood ....E..... 954 967-4230
Hollywood **(G-5550)**

Lapure Water Products Inc ....G..... 727 521-3993
Pinellas Park **(G-13704)**

Sergeant Bretts Coffee LLC ....G..... 561 451-0048
Coconut Creek **(G-2004)**

WATER TREATMENT EQPT: Indl

A1 Balers and Compators LLC ....F..... 561 792-3399
West Palm Beach **(G-17910)**

Action Mfg & Sup WPB LLC ....G..... 239 574-3443
West Palm Beach **(G-17913)**

Advatech Corporation ....G..... 732 803-8000
West Palm Beach **(G-17915)**

Aesinc Advanced Eqp & Svcs ....G..... 954 857-1895
Coral Springs **(G-2128)**

AFL Industries Inc ....G..... 561 848-1826
Riviera Beach **(G-14590)**

Aqua Engineering & Eqp Inc ....F..... 407 599-2123
Winter Park **(G-18486)**

Aqua Wholesale Inc ....G..... 941 341-0847
Sarasota **(G-15597)**

Aquatec Solutions LLC ....F..... 561 717-6933
Boca Raton **(G-414)**

Aquatech Inc ....F..... 727 559-8084
Largo **(G-7536)**

Aquatech Manufacturing LLC ....F..... 813 664-0300
Tampa **(G-16602)**

Ce Hooton Sales LLC ....F..... 305 255-9722
Sarasota **(G-15453)**

Central Processing Corp ....G..... 352 787-3004
Leesburg **(G-7762)**

Chlorinators Inc ....E..... 772 288-4854
Stuart **(G-16130)**

City of Bradenton ....D..... 941 727-6360
Bradenton **(G-961)**

City of Hollywood ....E..... 954 967-4230
Hollywood **(G-5550)**

Crane Co ....F..... 941 480-9101
Venice **(G-17680)**

Crane Environmental Inc ....C..... 941 480-9101
Venice **(G-17681)**

Ecosphere Technologies Inc ....F..... 772 287-4846
Stuart **(G-16143)**

Electrolytic Tech Svcs LLC ....G..... 305 655-2755
North Miami Beach **(G-11136)**

Electrolytic Technologies Corp ....F..... 305 655-2755
Miami **(G-9079)**

Esd Waste2water Inc ....D..... 800 277-3279
Ocala **(G-11379)**

Evoqua Water Technologies LLC ....F..... 813 620-0900
Tampa **(G-16822)**

Fovico Inc ....F..... 561 624-5400
West Palm Beach **(G-18010)**

Fshs Inc ....G..... 941 625-5929
Port Charlotte **(G-14301)**

Genesis Systems LLC ....G..... 417 499-3301
Tampa **(G-16875)**

Harn Ro Systems Inc ....E..... 941 488-9671
Venice **(G-17697)**

Kemco Systems Co LLC ....D..... 727 573-2323
Clearwater **(G-1659)**

Latitude Clean Tech Group Inc ....F..... 561 417-0687
Boca Raton **(G-575)**

Lenntech USA LLC ....F..... 877 453-8095
South Miami **(G-16037)**

Lodex Enterprises Corp ....G..... 954 442-3843
Miramar **(G-10509)**

Mar Cor Purification Inc ....E..... 484 991-0220
Lakeland **(G-7389)**

Originclear Inc ....G..... 323 939-6645
Clearwater **(G-1731)**

Parkson Corporation ....G..... 954 974-6610
Fort Lauderdale **(G-3978)**

Phoenix Catastrophe Svcs LLC ....F..... 918 321-2100
Santa Rosa Beach **(G-15430)**

Poseidon Services Inc ....G..... 786 294-8529
Miami **(G-9730)**

Premier Water & Enrgy Tech Inc ....E..... 904 268-1152
Jacksonville **(G-6384)**

Pro Water Treatment Inc ....G..... 954 650-1955
Margate **(G-8150)**

Pure Water Changes Inc ....F..... 407 699-2837
Windermere **(G-18363)**

Randazza Enterprises Inc ....F..... 813 677-0041
Riverview **(G-14573)**

Rgf Marine Envmtl Tech Inc ....E..... 561 848-1826
Riviera Beach **(G-14670)**

Rz Service Group LLC ....G..... 904 402-2313
Jacksonville **(G-6439)**

Starke Waste Wtr Trtmnt Plant ....G..... 904 964-7999
Starke **(G-16105)**

Superior Waterway Services Inc ....F..... 561 799-5852
Riviera Beach **(G-14680)**

Tampa Fiberglass Inc ....F..... 813 248-6828
Tampa **(G-17332)**

Technical International Corp ....G..... 305 374-1054
Miami **(G-9996)**

Twinoxide-Usa Inc ....G..... 321 207-8524
Merritt Island **(G-8604)**

Vapex Environmental Tech Inc ....G..... 407 277-0900
Cocoa **(G-1961)**

Water Bagel Boca East Lllp ....G..... 347 661-7171
Jupiter **(G-6824)**

Yacht-Mate Products Inc ....G..... 954 527-0112
Fort Lauderdale **(G-4140)**

WATER: Mineral, Carbonated, Canned & Bottled, Etc

Aqua Pure LLC ....G..... 407 521-3055
Orlando **(G-11915)**

Chem-Free System Inc ....G..... 954 258-5415
Delray Beach **(G-2944)**

Clewiston Water Btlg Co LLC ....G..... 863 902-1317
Clewiston **(G-1886)**

South Pacific Trading Company ....E..... 352 567-2200
Dade City **(G-2324)**

WATER: Pasteurized & Mineral, Bottled & Canned

AMA Waters LLC ....G..... 786 400-1630
Miami **(G-8707)**

Silver Springs Citrus Inc ....C..... 352 324-2101
Howey In The Hills **(G-5759)**

Silver Springs Citrus LLC ....F..... 352 324-2101
Howey In The Hills **(G-5760)**

WATER: Pasteurized, Canned & Bottled, Etc

Beverage Blocks Inc ....F..... 813 309-8711
Tampa **(G-16641)**

Cg Roxane LLC ....E..... 407 241-1640
Orlando **(G-12001)**

Isobev Inc ....G..... 561 701-5385
Stuart **(G-16168)**

Keystone Water Company LLC ....F..... 863 465-1932
Lake Placid **(G-7144)**

Lee McCullough Inc ....G..... 352 796-7100
Brooksville **(G-1171)**

Mvs International Inc ....G..... 954 727-3383
Weston **(G-18270)**

Nubo Bottle Company LLC ....G..... 954 283-9057
Port Saint Lucie **(G-14429)**

SOS Food Lab LLC ....E..... 305 594-9933
Hialeah Gardens **(G-5451)**

Ultra-Pure Bottled Water Inc ....F..... 813 835-7873
Tampa **(G-17384)**

Water Boy Inc ....F..... 239 461-0860
Fort Myers **(G-4445)**

WATERING POTS Plastic

Peaktop Technologies Inc ....F..... 561 598-6005
West Palm Beach **(G-18117)**

WAX REMOVERS

Ft Lauderdale Wax ....G..... 954 256-9291
Fort Lauderdale **(G-3833)**

WAXES: Petroleum, Not Produced In Petroleum Refineries

Gaynor Group Inc ....G..... 954 749-1228
Sunrise **(G-16320)**

Trigeant Ep Ltd ....F..... 561 999-9916
Boca Raton **(G-723)**

WEATHER FORECASTING SVCS

Stormquant Inc ....F..... 408 840-2003
Titusville **(G-17620)**

WEAVING MILL, BROADWOVEN FABRICS: Wool Or Similar Fabric

Cool Ocean LLC ....G..... 954 848-4060
Plantation **(G-13838)**

WEDDING CHAPEL: Privately Operated

Carlees Creations Inc ....G..... 786 232-0050
Miami **(G-8897)**

PRODUCT

WEIGHING MACHINERY & APPARATUS

Keytroller LLC ....F 813 877-4500
Tampa *(G-16984)*

Merrick Industries Inc ....C 850 265-3611
Lynn Haven *(G-8030)*

Radwag USA LLC ....G 305 651-3522
North Miami Beach *(G-11160)*

Tannehill Intl Inds Inc ....C 850 265-3611
Lynn Haven *(G-8033)*

Weightech USA LLC ....G 954 666-0877
Davie *(G-2497)*

WELDING & CUTTING APPARATUS & ACCESS, NEC

Applied Design & Fabrication ....G 954 524-6619
Lake Placid *(G-7137)*

Jdci Enterprises Inc ....E 239 768-2292
Fort Myers *(G-4297)*

Seelye Acquisitions Inc ....G 407 656-6677
Apopka *(G-174)*

Smittys Boat Tops and Mar Eqp ....G 305 245-0229
Homestead *(G-5740)*

WELDING EQPT

Alloy Cladding Company LLC ....F 561 625-4550
Fort Myers *(G-4166)*

American Torch Tip Company ....C 941 753-7557
Bradenton *(G-938)*

Automated Production Eqp Ape ....F 631 654-1197
Key Largo *(G-6842)*

Goss Inc ....E 386 423-0311
New Smyrna Beach *(G-11001)*

TL Fahringer Co Inc ....G 813 681-2373
Tampa *(G-17356)*

V & C Supply Ornamental Corp ....G 305 634-9040
Miami *(G-10086)*

WELDING EQPT & SPLYS WHOLESALERS

Matheson Tri-Gas Inc ....E 561 615-3000
Jupiter *(G-6763)*

Matheson Tri-Gas Inc ....G 727 572-8737
Clearwater *(G-1686)*

R & S Metalworks & Co LLC ....F 772 466-3303
Port Saint Lucie *(G-14436)*

Seelye Acquisitions Inc ....G 407 656-6677
Apopka *(G-174)*

WELDING EQPT & SPLYS: Arc Welders, Transformer-Rectifier

R & S Metalworks & Co LLC ....F 772 466-3303
Port Saint Lucie *(G-14436)*

WELDING EQPT & SPLYS: Gas

Uniweld Products Inc ....C 954 584-2000
Fort Lauderdale *(G-4111)*

WELDING EQPT & SPLYS: Resistance, Electric

Alphatron Industries Inc ....G 954 581-1418
Davie *(G-2383)*

WELDING EQPT: Electric

J B Nottingham & Co Inc ....E 386 873-2990
Deland *(G-2877)*

Parodi General Group Corp ....G 954 306-1098
Coconut Creek *(G-2000)*

WELDING EQPT: Electrical

Crandon Enterprises Inc ....G 352 873-8400
Ocala *(G-11359)*

WELDING MACHINES & EQPT: Ultrasonic

Complete Access Ctrl Centl Fla ....G 407 498-0067
Saint Cloud *(G-14924)*

Surface Engrg & Alloy Co Inc ....D 727 528-3734
Saint Petersburg *(G-15205)*

WELDING REPAIR SVC

4f Mobile Welding LLC ....G 850 537-2290
Baker *(G-290)*

5571 Halifax Inc ....E 239 454-4999
Fort Myers *(G-4152)*

A & E Machine Inc ....E 321 636-3110
Cocoa *(G-1896)*

Aarons Equipment Repair Inc ....G 904 879-3249
Callahan *(G-1251)*

Able Railing & Welding LLC ....G 850 243-5444
Fort Walton Beach *(G-4558)*

Accurate Wldg Fabrication LLC ....G 727 483-3125
Tampa *(G-16557)*

Ace-Pipe Welding LLC ....G 561 727-6345
Palm Beach Gardens *(G-12944)*

Advanced Machine and Tool Inc ....D 772 465-6546
Fort Pierce *(G-4459)*

Advanced Wldg Fbrction Dsign L ....G 352 237-9800
Summerfield *(G-16256)*

Ajs Fabrication Llc ....G 863 514-9630
Winter Haven *(G-18413)*

Alexis Welding Express Corp ....G 786 626-4090
Opa Locka *(G-11713)*

Alfredo Welding Service LLC ....G 954 770-8744
Winter Haven *(G-18414)*

All Phase Welding LLC ....G 772 834-2980
Vero Beach *(G-17733)*

All Weld Inc ....G 239 348-9550
Naples *(G-10658)*

Alpha Omega MBL Wldg Svcs Inc ....G 813 629-5777
Dover *(G-3426)*

Amax Welding & Fabrication ....G 352 544-8484
Brooksville *(G-1133)*

American Fence Shop LLC ....F 305 681-3511
Hialeah *(G-5046)*

American Wldg & Installation ....G 786 391-4800
Miami *(G-8721)*

Andys Welding Services Inc ....G 239 478-4907
Immokalee *(G-5795)*

Anthony Wright Welding ....G 850 544-1831
Tallahassee *(G-16411)*

ARC Dimensions Inc ....G 727 524-6139
Largo *(G-7537)*

ARC-Rite Inc ....E 386 325-3523
Jacksonville *(G-5897)*

Armor Supply Metals LLC ....G 305 640-9901
Medley *(G-8199)*

Arnold Industries South Inc ....G 352 867-0190
Ocala *(G-11327)*

Art of Iron Inc ....G 850 819-1500
Panama City *(G-13229)*

Atlas Innovative Services Inc ....G 617 259-4529
Punta Gorda *(G-14493)*

B & B of Saint Augustine Inc ....G 904 829-6855
Saint Augustine *(G-14812)*

B & N Wldg & Fabrication Inc ....E 813 719-3956
Plant City *(G-13743)*

Badger Welding Orlando LLC ....G 407 648-1100
Orlando *(G-11939)*

Barrs Equipment Service Inc ....F 407 999-5214
Orlando *(G-11941)*

Bartow Machine Works Inc ....G 863 533-6361
Bartow *(G-301)*

Baxley Services Inc ....G 850 675-4459
Jay *(G-6648)*

Bee Welding Inc ....F 561 616-9003
West Palm Beach *(G-17941)*

Beyers Welding Inc ....G 407 892-2834
Saint Cloud *(G-14922)*

Blane E Taylor Welding Inc ....G 386 931-1242
Bunnell *(G-1227)*

Blane E Taylor Welding Inc ....G 386 931-1240
Ormond Beach *(G-12746)*

Blue Point Fabrication Inc ....F 321 269-0073
Titusville *(G-17573)*

Bob Kline Quality Metal Inc ....G 561 659-4245
West Palm Beach *(G-17951)*

Bobs Wldg Fbrcation Maint Inc ....F 863 665-0135
Lakeland *(G-7284)*

Boyd Welding LLC ....G 352 447-2405
Ocala *(G-11337)*

Brandon Alan Chapman ....G 863 651-9189
Auburndale *(G-220)*

Bray Welding Inc ....G 352 622-7780
Ocala *(G-11339)*

Burton JC Companies Inc ....G 239 992-2377
Bonita Springs *(G-787)*

Cannons of Jack LLC ....G 904 733-3524
Jacksonville *(G-5970)*

Central Maintenance & Wldg Inc ....D 352 795-2817
Crystal River *(G-2269)*

Central Maintenance & Wldg Inc ....C 813 229-0012
Lithia *(G-7831)*

Champion Welding Services LLC ....G 786 262-5727
Miami Lakes *(G-10291)*

Channel Industries Inc ....F 561 214-0637
West Palm Beach *(G-17965)*

Ciron Custom Welding Inc ....G 786 259-7589
Hialeah *(G-5092)*

Coastal Wldg Fabrications Inc ....F 954 938-7933
Oakland Park *(G-11252)*

Copeland Welding & Muffler Sp ....G 904 355-6383
Jacksonville *(G-6005)*

Cornelius Welding Inc ....E 863 635-3668
Frostproof *(G-4636)*

Crown Welding & Fabg Inc ....G 941 737-6844
Myakka City *(G-10645)*

Crumpton Welding Sup & Eqp Inc ....G 863 965-8423
Auburndale *(G-226)*

D & D MBL Wldg Fabrication Inc ....F 954 791-3385
Fort Lauderdale *(G-3751)*

D & D Welding Inc ....G 850 438-9011
Pensacola *(G-13483)*

D & S Steel ....G 352 489-8791
Dunnellon *(G-3464)*

D D Welding ....G 732 998-1100
Spring Hill *(G-16070)*

Dade Made ....G 305 846-9482
Hialeah *(G-5108)*

Dannys Welding Services Inc ....G 786 436-8087
Miami *(G-9001)*

Dcwfab LLC ....G 941 320-6095
Sarasota *(G-15652)*

Dennys Welding Service Corp ....G 321 494-2608
Kissimmee *(G-6912)*

Diligent Wldg Fabrication LLC ....G 561 620-4900
Boca Raton *(G-484)*

Discount Welds LLC ....G 305 637-3939
Miami *(G-9034)*

Diversified Welding Inc ....G 561 996-9398
Perry *(G-13636)*

Doll Marine Metal Fabrication ....G 954 941-5093
Pompano Beach *(G-13999)*

Double R Mfg Ocala Inc ....F 352 873-1441
Ocala *(G-11371)*

Duke Custom Fabrication LLC ....G 954 707-1722
Cooper City *(G-2020)*

E M P Inc ....G 772 286-7343
Stuart *(G-16142)*

East Coast Metalworks LLC ....G 321 698-0624
Cocoa *(G-1924)*

East Coast Ornamental Wldg Inc ....F 386 672-4340
Daytona Beach *(G-2547)*

Electron Beam Development ....E 772 219-4600
Palm City *(G-13034)*

Emf Inc ....G 321 453-3670
Merritt Island *(G-8584)*

ENG Manufacturing Inc ....G 727 942-3868
Tarpon Springs *(G-17470)*

Escambia Welding and Fab Inc ....G 850 477-3901
Pensacola *(G-13498)*

Evolution Wldngs Fbrcation LLC ....G 786 702-4703
Opa Locka *(G-11745)*

Exact Inc ....C 904 783-6640
Jacksonville *(G-6082)*

First Coast Fabrication Inc ....G 904 849-7426
Yulee *(G-18588)*

Floyd Fabrication LLC ....G 330 289-7351
Haines City *(G-4907)*

Franz A Ullrich Jr ....G 863 773-4653
Wauchula *(G-17827)*

Friendly Welding Inc ....F 786 953-8413
Hialeah *(G-5161)*

Fusion Welding ....F 239 288-6530
Fort Myers *(G-4266)*

G B Welding & Fabrication LLC ....F 954 967-2573
Davie *(G-2415)*

Gator Welding Inc ....F 561 746-0049
Stuart *(G-16153)*

General Welding Svc Entps Inc ....G 305 592-9483
Doral *(G-3229)*

Golden Hands Welding Inc ....F 786 728-6838
Palmetto Bay *(G-13210)*

Grahams Welding Fabrication ....G 850 865-0899
Fort Walton Beach *(G-4587)*

Greg Clark Welding Inc ....G 904 226-2952
Jacksonville *(G-6156)*

Griffiths Corporation ....D 407 851-8342
Orlando *(G-12202)*

Gunns Welding & Fabricating ....G 727 393-5238
Saint Petersburg *(G-15070)*

HA Morton Corp ....E 352 220-9790
Ocala *(G-11406)*

Hay Tech ....G 850 592-2424
Bascom *(G-329)*

Hernandez Mobile Welding Inc ....G....... 954 347-4071
Okeechobee *(G-11608)*
HI Tech Aviation Welding LLC ....G....... 305 591-3393
Miami *(G-9278)*
Holland Welding LLC...........................G....... 904 675-6106
Jacksonville *(G-6182)*
Holmes Tool & Engineering Inc ....E....... 850 547-4417
Bonifay *(G-772)*
Hot Shot Welding Inc ....F....... 727 585-1900
Largo *(G-7608)*
House of Metal LLC ....G....... 727 540-0637
Clearwater *(G-1630)*
Hudsons Wldg & Fabrication Inc...........G....... 941 355-4858
Bradenton *(G-992)*
Industrial & Marine Maint Inc ....G....... 813 622-8338
Tampa *(G-16939)*
Industrial Construction & Wldg ....G....... 863 644-6124
Lakeland *(G-7350)*
Industrial Repair Inc ....F....... 239 368-7435
Lehigh Acres *(G-7810)*
Interstate Wldg & Fabrication ....F....... 727 446-1449
Clearwater *(G-1647)*
Ironclad Welding Inc............................G....... 954 925-7987
Dania *(G-2334)*
J L M Machine Co Inc ....F....... 941 748-4288
Bradenton *(G-1000)*
Jackson Equipment Inc ....G....... 904 845-3696
Jacksonville *(G-6213)*
JAM Welding Service Inc ....F....... 305 662-3787
South Miami *(G-16035)*
JC Industrial Mfg Corp ....E....... 305 634-5280
Miami *(G-9359)*
Jim Appleys Tru-Arc Inc ....F....... 727 571-3007
Clearwater *(G-1653)*
JL Welding Inc......................................F....... 786 442-4319
South Miami *(G-16036)*
Jordan Weld Fabrication ....G....... 386 789-3606
Deltona *(G-3046)*
Jupiter Welding LLC ....G....... 561 801-3585
Jupiter *(G-6752)*
Just Steel Inc ....F....... 941 755-7811
Sarasota *(G-15504)*
Kentucky Welding LLC ....G....... 305 852-7433
Islamorada *(G-5836)*
Key West Wldg Fabrication Inc ....G....... 305 296-5555
Key West *(G-6869)*
King Mobile Welding Andrew.................G....... 386 437-1007
Bunnell *(G-1229)*
Knight Welding Supply LLC..................G....... 561 889-5342
Stuart *(G-16175)*
L & C Metals LLC ....G....... 407 859-2600
Orlando *(G-12297)*
Lynn Industrial Welding Inc ....G....... 850 584-4494
Perry *(G-13646)*
Madson Inc ....F....... 305 863-7390
Medley *(G-8270)*
Maguires Welding Services Inc ....G....... 813 382-3558
Zephyrhills *(G-18621)*
MB Welding Inc ....F....... 727 548-0923
Saint Petersburg *(G-15123)*
Metal Craft of Pensacola Inc ....F....... 850 478-8333
Pensacola *(G-13550)*
Metal Fabrication and ....G....... 850 205-2300
Tallahassee *(G-16479)*
Miami Ship Repair & Wldg Svcs ....G....... 305 491-4161
Oakland Park *(G-11279)*
Mid-State Machine & Fabg Corp ....C....... 863 665-6233
Lakeland *(G-7395)*
Mike Blackburn Welding LLC ....G....... 850 643-8464
Blountstown *(G-376)*
Milans Machine Shop & Wldg Svc ....E....... 305 592-2447
Doral *(G-3303)*
MPH Industries Inc ....F....... 352 372-9533
Gainesville *(G-4735)*
Ms Mobile Wldg & Fabrication ....G....... 904 591-1488
Jacksonville *(G-6316)*
National Pipe Welding Inc ....F....... 904 588-2589
Glen Saint Mary *(G-4804)*
New World Welding Inc ....G....... 786 423-1575
Miami *(G-9615)*
Omni Marine Enterprises LLC ....G....... 941 474-4614
Englewood *(G-3520)*
On Site Svcs of Mid FL.........................G....... 407 444-2951
Deland *(G-2891)*
Palatka Welding Shop Inc ....E....... 386 328-1507
Palatka *(G-12876)*
Paradise Wldg Cstm Fabrication ....G....... 239 961-8864
Naples *(G-10849)*
Parts Central Inc ....F....... 850 547-1660
Bonifay *(G-776)*

Patriot Welding Inc ....G....... 954 798-8819
Pompano Beach *(G-14119)*
Pena General Welding Inc ....G....... 786 255-2153
Miami *(G-9701)*
Precision Svcs Jcksonville Inc ....F....... 904 781-3770
Jacksonville *(G-6381)*
Pro Weld of South Florida Inc ....G....... 954 984-0104
Margate *(G-8151)*
Pro-Weld Inc ....G....... 863 453-9353
Avon Park *(G-286)*
Production Metal Stampings Inc ....F....... 850 981-8240
Milton *(G-10434)*
Quality Metal Worx LLC ....F....... 863 353-6638
Haines City *(G-4914)*
R & K Welding and Fabrication ....G....... 863 422-8728
Lake Hamilton *(G-7052)*
Ramsay Marine Services LLC ....F....... 561 881-1234
Riviera Beach *(G-14664)*
Rankine-Hinman Mfg Co ....F....... 904 808-0404
Saint Augustine *(G-14877)*
RB Custom Welding LLC ....G....... 813 280-9860
Tampa *(G-17208)*
Real Pro Welding Inc ....G....... 850 939-3469
Navarre *(G-10954)*
Responsive Machining Inc ....F....... 321 225-4011
Titusville *(G-17612)*
Richards Mobile Welding ....G....... 954 913-0487
Coral Springs *(G-2205)*
Rodriguez Welding ....G....... 305 856-3749
Miami *(G-9818)*
Rudd & Son Welding Inc ....F....... 850 476-2110
Pensacola *(G-13598)*
Ryder Welding Service Inc ....F....... 305 685-6630
Opa Locka *(G-11787)*
S & S Welding Inc ....G....... 863 533-2888
Bartow *(G-325)*
SDr Specialties Services LLC ....G....... 386 878-6771
De Leon Springs *(G-2627)*
Serf Inc ....E....... 850 476-8203
Cantonment *(G-1273)*
Shaws Welding Inc ....F....... 850 584-7197
Perry *(G-13653)*
Sheps Welding Inc ....G....... 352 493-1730
Chiefland *(G-1450)*
Shermans Welding & Maintence ....F....... 904 731-3460
Jacksonville *(G-6464)*
Smittys Boat Tops and Mar Eqp ....G....... 305 245-0229
Homestead *(G-5740)*
Smittys Welding Shop ....G....... 321 723-4533
Melbourne *(G-8524)*
Southern Awning Inc ....G....... 561 586-0464
Lake Worth *(G-7233)*
Southern Welding & Mechanics ....F....... 305 772-0961
Hialeah *(G-5358)*
Specialty Fabrication Wldg Inc ....F....... 352 669-9353
Umatilla *(G-17651)*
Srq Welding Inc ....G....... 941 484-5947
North Venice *(G-11219)*
St Cloud Wldg Fabrication Inc ....E....... 407 957-2344
Saint Cloud *(G-14939)*
Steel Plus Service Center Inc ....G....... 407 328-7169
Sanford *(G-15391)*
Steel Products Inc ....G....... 941 351-8128
Sarasota *(G-15838)*
Straight Polarity Welding Inc ....G....... 727 530-7224
Largo *(G-7691)*
Superior Fabrication Inc........................G....... 941 639-2966
Punta Gorda *(G-14535)*
Sureweld Welding Inc ....E....... 813 918-1857
Lakeland *(G-7454)*
Tallahassee Welding & Mch Sp ....E....... 850 576-9596
Tallahassee *(G-16511)*
Tampa Amalgamated Steel Corp ....F....... 813 621-0550
Tampa *(G-17324)*
Tera Industries Inc ....E....... 561 848-7272
Riviera Beach *(G-14681)*
Tig Technologies Inc ....G....... 561 691-3633
Fort Pierce *(G-4538)*
Tigart Welding LLC ....G....... 407 371-1820
Winter Park *(G-18545)*
Titan Mfg Inc ....F....... 239 939-5152
Fort Myers *(G-4425)*
Titan Service Industry Llc ....G....... 678 313-4707
Deland *(G-2912)*
Unlimited Welding Inc ....E....... 407 327-3333
Winter Springs *(G-18580)*
Voyager Offroad LLC ....F....... 941 235-7225
Port Charlotte *(G-14323)*
Watts Welding Inc ....G....... 863 978-3371
Lake Wales *(G-7179)*

Weimer Mechanical Services Inc..........G....... 813 645-2258
Ruskin *(G-14781)*
Welding Anything Anywhere LLC ....G....... 561 762-1404
Palm Beach Gardens *(G-13017)*
Welding Around ....G....... 772 342-3233
Palm City *(G-13065)*
West Palm Machining & Welding ....G....... 561 841-2725
Riviera Beach *(G-14686)*
West Point Industries Inc ....G....... 561 848-8381
Lake Park *(G-7135)*
Westcoast Metalworks Inc ....G....... 941 920-3201
Palmetto *(G-13205)*
Whitley Welding Company L ....G....... 904 576-3410
Middleburg *(G-10411)*
Wilson Mch & Wldg Works Inc ....G....... 904 829-3737
Saint Augustine *(G-14914)*
World Class Machining Inc ....F....... 386 437-7036
Bunnell *(G-1238)*
Xpress Precision Products Inc ....G....... 305 685-2127
Hialeah *(G-5424)*

WELDMENTS

Metal 2 Metal Inc ....G....... 954 253-9450
Palmetto Bay *(G-13214)*

WESTERN APPAREL STORES

Farmers Cooperative Inc ....E....... 386 362-1459
Live Oak *(G-7848)*

WHEELCHAIRS

Best Price Mobility Inc ....F....... 321 402-5955
Kissimmee *(G-6899)*
Buffalo Wheelchair Inc ....G....... 941 921-6331
Sarasota *(G-15618)*
Custom Medical Systems Inc ....G....... 941 722-3434
Palmetto *(G-13163)*
Deming Designs Inc ....F....... 850 478-5765
Pensacola *(G-13488)*
Gulf Coast Non Emergency Trans ....G....... 239 825-1350
Fort Myers *(G-4275)*
Hoveround Corporation ....B....... 941 739-6200
Sarasota *(G-15495)*
Imc-Heartway LLC................................G....... 239 275-6767
Fort Myers *(G-4286)*
Invacare Corporation ....F....... 727 522-8677
Pinellas Park *(G-13696)*
Merits Health Products Inc ....E....... 239 772-0579
Fort Myers *(G-4320)*
Mobility Freedom Inc ....F....... 407 495-1333
Orlando *(G-12385)*
Noa International Inc ....G....... 954 835-5258
Wellington *(G-17856)*
Pride Florida..F....... 813 621-9262
Tampa *(G-17179)*
Synergy Rehab Technologies Inc..........G....... 407 943-7500
Saint Cloud *(G-14940)*
Trinity Mobility Inc ....G....... 727 389-1438
New Port Richey *(G-10990)*
Verhi Inc ....E....... 850 477-4880
Pensacola *(G-13619)*

WHEELS

Advance One Wheels Inc ....F....... 305 238-5833
Miami *(G-8656)*
American Force Wheels Inc ....F....... 786 345-6301
Hialeah *(G-5047)*
Bigg Wills Wheels LLC ....G....... 352 222-6170
Gainesville *(G-4660)*
Drt Express Inc....................................G....... 305 827-5005
Hialeah *(G-5123)*
Elite Wheel Distributors Inc ....G....... 813 673-8393
Tampa *(G-16804)*
Family System Solution Whl Inc ....G....... 954 431-5254
Miramar *(G-10490)*
Frozen Wheels LLC..............................F....... 305 799-2258
Miami *(G-9177)*
Leals Tires & Wheels ....G....... 239 491-2214
Lehigh Acres *(G-7813)*
Miami Power Wheels ....G....... 305 553-1888
Miami *(G-9554)*
School-On-Wheels.................................F....... 239 530-8522
Naples *(G-10888)*
Sg Global LLC ....G....... 305 726-3439
Miami *(G-9873)*
Specialty Forged Wheels Inc ....G....... 786 332-5925
Miami *(G-9937)*
Starr Wheel Group Inc ....F....... 954 935-5536
Coral Springs *(G-2214)*

WHEELS

TK Tires & Wheels Inc ....G...... 321 473-8945
Melbourne *(G-8552)*

WHEELS & GRINDSTONES, EXC ARTIFICIAL: Abrasive

American Diamond Blades Corp ....F 561 571-2166
Boca Raton *(G-406)*

WHEELS, GRINDING: Artificial

Global Diversified Products ....E 727 209-0854
Pinellas Park *(G-13690)*

WHEELS: Iron & Steel, Locomotive & Car

Skipper Wright Inc ....E 904 354-4381
Jacksonville *(G-6476)*

WHIRLPOOL BATHS: Hydrotherapy

Bathroom World Manufacturing ....G...... 954 566-0451
Oakland Park *(G-11246)*
Royal Baths Manufacturing Co ....D...... 407 854-1740
Orlando *(G-12560)*

WIGS & HAIRPIECES

Advanced Hair Products Inc ....G...... 561 347-2799
Deerfield Beach *(G-2656)*

WINDINGS: Coil, Electronic

Electro Technik Industries Inc ....D...... 727 530-9555
Clearwater *(G-1580)*
Hytronics Corp ....D...... 727 535-0413
Clearwater *(G-1635)*
Jst Power Equipment Inc ....D...... 844 631-9046
Lake Mary *(G-7088)*
Precision Econowind LLC ....F 239 997-3860
North Fort Myers *(G-11067)*
Winatic Corporation ....C...... 727 538-8917
Clearwater *(G-1855)*

WINDMILLS: Electric Power Generation

Blue Summit Wind LLC ....G...... 561 691-7171
Juno Beach *(G-6660)*
Pheasant Run Wind LLC ....G...... 561 691-7171
Juno Beach *(G-6666)*
Tuscola Wind II LLC ....G...... 561 691-7171
Juno Beach *(G-6668)*
Vasco Winds LLC ....G...... 561 691-7171
Juno Beach *(G-6669)*
White Oak Energy Backleverage ....G...... 561 691-7171
Juno Beach *(G-6670)*
White Oak Energy Holdings LLC ....G...... 561 691-7171
Juno Beach *(G-6671)*
Wilton Wind II LLC ....G...... 561 691-7171
Juno Beach *(G-6672)*

WINDMILLS: Farm Type

Jmp Marine LLC ....E 305 599-0009
Doral *(G-3270)*

WINDOW & DOOR FRAMES

Alutech Corporation ....G...... 305 593-2080
Miami *(G-8705)*
Arso Enterprises Inc ....E 305 681-2020
Opa Locka *(G-11719)*
Coyote Acquisition Co ....E 941 480-1600
North Venice *(G-11209)*
Custom Cft Windows & Doors Inc ....F 407 834-5400
Winter Springs *(G-18563)*
Custom Window Systems Inc ....A...... 352 368-6922
Ocala *(G-11361)*
Eastman Performance Films LLC ....G...... 954 920-2001
Fort Lauderdale *(G-3779)*
First Windows Incorporated ....G...... 813 508-9388
Wesley Chapel *(G-17875)*
Garcia Door & Window Inc ....G...... 305 635-0644
Miami *(G-9189)*
Innovtive Win Cncpts Doors Inc ....F 561 493-2303
Boynton Beach *(G-880)*
Larry Johnson Inc ....F 305 888-2300
Hialeah *(G-5220)*
Majestic Ultimate Design Inc ....F 954 533-8677
Oakland Park *(G-11277)*
Masonite International Corp ....E 813 889-3861
Tampa *(G-17049)*
Miami Wall Systems Inc ....C...... 305 888-2300
Hialeah *(G-5255)*

PGT Industries Inc ....A...... 941 480-1600
North Venice *(G-11216)*
PGT Innovations Inc ....D...... 941 480-1600
North Venice *(G-11217)*
PGT Innovations Inc ....C...... 941 480-1600
North Venice *(G-11218)*
Pinos Window Corporation ....F 305 888-9903
Medley *(G-8299)*
Quality Engineered Products Co ....E 813 885-1693
Tampa *(G-17200)*
Ram Sales LLC ....D...... 844 726-6382
Miami *(G-9778)*

WINDOW CLEANING SVCS

Island Shutter Co Inc ....F 386 738-9455
Deland *(G-2876)*

WINDOW FRAMES & SASHES: Plastic

Bay City Window Company ....F 727 323-5443
Saint Petersburg *(G-14978)*
J T Walker Industries Inc ....E 727 461-0501
Clearwater *(G-1650)*
Pvc Windoors Inc ....F 305 940-3608
North Miami *(G-11118)*
Southern Die Casting Corp ....D...... 305 635-6571
Miami *(G-9927)*

WINDOW FRAMES, MOLDING & TRIM: Vinyl

Sun-Tek Manufacturing Inc ....E 407 859-2117
Orlando *(G-12632)*

WINDOW FURNISHINGS WHOLESALERS

BMW & Associates Inc ....G...... 352 694-2300
Ocala *(G-11336)*
Greg Valley ....F 941 739-6628
Sarasota *(G-15487)*
Swfl Hurricane Shutters Inc ....G...... 239 454-4944
Cape Coral *(G-1395)*

WINDOWS: Frames, Wood

American Woodwork Specialty Co ....F 937 263-1053
Santa Rosa Beach *(G-15421)*
Cws Holding Company LLC ....E 352 368-6922
Ocala *(G-11362)*

WINDOWS: Storm, Wood

Eco Window Systems LLC ....A...... 305 885-5299
Medley *(G-8234)*
Gravitystorm Inc ....F 772 519-3009
Fort Pierce *(G-4493)*
Innovtive Win Cncpts Doors Inc ....F 561 493-2303
Boynton Beach *(G-880)*

WINDOWS: Wood

Delet Doors Inc ....F 786 250-4506
Miami *(G-9008)*

WINE & DISTILLED ALCOHOLIC BEVERAGES WHOLESALERS

D G Yuengling and Son Inc ....D...... 813 972-8500
Tampa *(G-16758)*

WINE CELLARS, BONDED: Wine, Blended

Luxe Vintages LLC ....G...... 561 558-7399
Delray Beach *(G-2984)*

WIRE

Broadband Fibers & Supplies ....G...... 786 258-5746
Bal Harbour *(G-293)*
Merchants Metals Inc ....D...... 813 333-5515
Tampa *(G-17064)*
Repwire LLC ....G...... 786 486-1823
Doral *(G-3347)*
Wire Products Inc of Florida ....E 954 772-1477
Fort Lauderdale *(G-4135)*

WIRE & CABLE: Aluminum

American Wire Group LLC ....F 954 455-3050
Aventura *(G-252)*

WIRE & CABLE: Nonferrous, Aircraft

Aerosapien Technologies LLC ....E 386 361-3838
Daytona Beach *(G-2508)*

Sunmaster of Naples Inc ....E 239 261-3581
Naples *(G-10914)*

WIRE & CABLE: Nonferrous, Automotive, Exc Ignition Sets

Wiretec Ignition Inc ....F 407 578-4569
Palmetto *(G-13206)*

WIRE & CABLE: Nonferrous, Building

Conduit Space Rcvery Systems L ....F 330 416-0887
Bradenton *(G-963)*
Ford Wire and Cable Corp ....E 772 388-3660
Sebastian *(G-15892)*
Technlogy Integration Svcs LLC ....G...... 904 565-4050
Jacksonville *(G-6539)*

WIRE & WIRE PRDTS

Alp Industries Inc ....E 786 845-8617
Doral *(G-3108)*
Artistic Fence Corporation ....G...... 305 805-1976
Hialeah *(G-5060)*
Baby Guard Inc ....F 954 741-6351
Coral Springs *(G-2133)*
Blue Water Dynamics LLC ....D...... 386 957-5464
Edgewater *(G-3482)*
Brandano Displays Inc ....E 954 956-7266
Margate *(G-8123)*
Central Wire Industries LLC ....E 850 983-9926
Milton *(G-10422)*
Clear-Vue Inc ....E 727 726-5386
Safety Harbor *(G-14784)*
Commercial Metals Company ....E 954 921-2500
Dania *(G-2330)*
Cross City Veneer Company Inc ....D...... 352 498-3226
Cross City *(G-2259)*
Eastern Wire Products Inc ....E 904 781-6775
Jacksonville *(G-6060)*
Fabricated Wire Products Inc ....G...... 813 802-8463
Valrico *(G-17663)*
Florida Wire & Rigging Sup Inc ....G...... 407 422-6218
Orlando *(G-12170)*
Insteel Wire Products Company ....D...... 904 275-2100
Sanderson *(G-15254)*
Jayco Screens Inc ....G...... 850 456-0673
Pensacola *(G-13527)*
Johnson Well Equipment Inc ....E 850 453-3131
Pensacola *(G-13530)*
Ludlow Fibc Corp ....G...... 305 702-5000
Opa Locka *(G-11764)*
Marmon Aerospace & Defense LLC ......D...... 239 643-6400
Naples *(G-10814)*
Merchants Metals LLC ....D...... 904 781-3920
Jacksonville *(G-6296)*
Miami Cordage LLC ....E 305 636-3000
Miami *(G-9549)*
Mutual Industries North Inc ....D...... 239 332-2400
Fort Myers *(G-4334)*
Proform Finishing Products LLC ....E 904 284-0221
Green Cove Springs *(G-4833)*
Rat-Trap Bait Company Inc ....G...... 863 967-2148
Auburndale *(G-243)*
Rowe Industries Inc ....F 302 855-0585
Pembroke Park *(G-13365)*
SOUTHERN SPRING & STAMPING INC E 941 488-2276
Venice *(G-17717)*
St Judas Tadeus Foundry Inc ....G...... 305 512-3612
Hialeah *(G-5360)*
TL Fahringer Co Inc ....G...... 813 681-2373
Tampa *(G-17356)*
Vutec Corporation ....C...... 954 545-9000
Vero Beach *(G-17816)*
Wire Experts Group Inc ....D...... 239 597-8555
Naples *(G-10940)*

WIRE CLOTH & WOVEN WIRE PRDTS, MADE FROM PURCHASED WIRE

John W Hock Company ....G...... 352 378-3209
Gainesville *(G-4716)*

WIRE FENCING & ACCESS WHOLESALERS

American All Scure Gtes Fnce L ....F 407 423-4962
Orlando *(G-11900)*
Father & Son Fence Supply LLC ....F 352 848-3180
Brooksville *(G-1156)*

2022 Harris Florida
Manufacturers Directory

(G-0000) Company's Geographic Section entry number

WIRE MATERIALS: Copper

American Wire Group LLC ....F 954 455-3050
Aventura *(G-252)*

WIRE MATERIALS: Steel

Green Mountain Specialties ....G 386 469-0057
Deland *(G-2873)*
Keystone Steel Products Co ....G 813 248-9828
Tampa *(G-16983)*
List Manufacturing Inc ....D 954 429-9155
Deerfield Beach *(G-2754)*
Macias Gabions Inc ....G 850 910-8000
Lauderhill *(G-7735)*
Metalhouse LLC ....G 407 270-3000
Orlando *(G-12373)*
Peninsula Steel Inc ....E 813 473-8133
Plant City *(G-13794)*
Peninsula Steel Inc ....E 956 795-1966
Plant City *(G-13795)*
Phelps Dodge Intl Corp ....E 305 648-7888
Doral *(G-3326)*
Pte Systems International LLC ....G 305 863-3409
Hialeah *(G-5315)*

WIRE PRDTS: Steel & Iron

Atlantic Wire and Rigging Inc ....G 321 633-1552
Cocoa *(G-1905)*
Industrial Spring Corp ....F 954 524-2558
Davie *(G-2425)*
Maschmeyer Concrete Co Fla ....E 561 848-9112
Lake Park *(G-7131)*

WIRE ROPE CENTERS

Hofmann & Leavy Inc ....D 954 698-0000
Deerfield Beach *(G-2738)*

WIRE WHOLESALERS

Southwire Company LLC ....C 850 423-4680
Crestview *(G-2254)*

WIRE WINDING OF PURCHASED WIRE

Wire Mesh Corp ....F 706 922-5179
Jacksonville *(G-6615)*

WIRE: Communication

Diversfied Mtl Specialists Inc ....G 941 244-0935
North Venice *(G-11211)*
Fibertronics Inc ....E 321 473-8933
Melbourne *(G-8425)*
Molex LLC ....F 727 521-2700
Pinellas Park *(G-13711)*
Novagroup LLC ....G 305 471-4824
Doral *(G-3313)*
Wireless Latin Entrmt Inc ....G 305 858-7740
Miami *(G-10137)*

WIRE: Magnet

Advanced Magnet Lab Inc ....F 321 728-7543
Melbourne *(G-8355)*

WIRE: Mesh

Equity Group Usa Inc ....G 407 421-6464
Winter Springs *(G-18565)*
R & R Livestock Solutions Inc ....G 863 223-8443
Lake Wales *(G-7171)*

WIRE: Nonferrous

Dekoron Unitherm LLC ....E 800 633-5015
Cape Coral *(G-1331)*
Electro Technik Industries Inc ....D 727 530-9555
Clearwater *(G-1580)*
Equity Group Usa Inc ....G 407 421-6464
Winter Springs *(G-18565)*
Integrated Cable Solutions ....E 813 769-5740
Tampa *(G-16946)*
Kai Limited ....C 954 957-8586
Fort Lauderdale *(G-3899)*
Logus Manufacturing Corp ....E 561 842-3550
West Palm Beach *(G-18060)*
Monroe Cable LLC ....D 941 429-8484
North Port *(G-11201)*
Phelps Dodge Intl Corp ....E 305 648-7888
Doral *(G-3326)*

Tensolite LLC ....A 904 829-5600
Saint Augustine *(G-14905)*
Times Microwave Systems Inc ....F 203 949-8400
West Palm Beach *(G-18180)*

WIRING DEVICES WHOLESALERS

Pacer Electronics Florida Inc ....E 941 378-5774
Sarasota *(G-15772)*

WOMEN'S & CHILDREN'S CLOTHING WHOLESALERS, NEC

Apparel Imports Inc ....E 800 428-6849
Miami *(G-8735)*
Carpe Diem Sales & Mktg Inc ....E 407 682-1400
Orlando *(G-11983)*
Chrome Connection Corp ....F 305 947-9191
North Miami Beach *(G-11132)*
Decoy Inc ....G 305 633-6384
Miami *(G-9006)*
Kamtex USA Incorporated ....G 954 733-1044
Lauderdale Lakes *(G-7717)*
La Providencia Express Co ....G 305 409-9894
Miami *(G-9412)*
Pattern Grading & Marker Svcs ....G 305 495-9963
Miramar *(G-10525)*
Sarah Louise Inc ....F 941 377-9656
Sarasota *(G-15808)*
Sharp Marketing LLC ....G 954 565-2711
Oakland Park *(G-11293)*
Workwear Outfitters LLC ....E 813 671-2986
Riverview *(G-14583)*

WOMEN'S & GIRLS' SPORTSWEAR WHOLESALERS

Lear Investors Inc ....G 305 681-8582
Opa Locka *(G-11763)*
T Shirt Center Inc ....G 305 655-1955
Miami *(G-9990)*

WOMEN'S CLOTHING STORES

Amj DOT LLC ....G 646 249-0273
Boca Raton *(G-410)*
Excess Liquidator LLC ....G 407 247-9105
Oviedo *(G-12820)*
Exist Inc ....D 954 739-7030
Fort Lauderdale *(G-3806)*
Jackie Z Style Co St Pete LLC ....G 727 258-4849
Saint Petersburg *(G-15099)*
Original Pnguin Drect Oprtions ....F 305 592-2830
Doral *(G-3319)*
Perry Ellis International Inc ....B 305 592-2830
Doral *(G-3325)*

WOMEN'S CLOTHING STORES: Ready-To-Wear

Yoly Munoz Corp ....G 305 860-3839
Miami *(G-10152)*

WOMEN'S SPORTSWEAR STORES

JMP Fashion Inc ....G 305 633-9920
Miami *(G-9369)*
Lan Designs Inc ....G 305 661-7878
Miami *(G-9419)*

WOOD FENCING WHOLESALERS

Florida Cypress & Fence Co ....G 561 392-3011
Palm City *(G-13038)*

WOOD PRDTS

4303 Silverwood LLC ....G 904 900-1702
Jacksonville *(G-5841)*
Axley Brothers Saw Mill Inc ....G 727 531-8724
Largo *(G-7541)*
Backwoods Crossing Llc ....F 850 765-3753
Tallahassee *(G-16416)*
Burnham Woods Untd Civic Group ....G 954 532-2675
North Lauderdale *(G-11076)*
Hollywood Houndz LLC ....G 407 614-2108
Winter Garden *(G-18391)*
Hollywood Lodging Inc ....F 305 803-7455
Hollywood *(G-5596)*
Linenwood Home LLC ....G 850 607-7445
Pensacola *(G-13537)*

Mamalu Wood LLC ....G 305 261-6332
Miami *(G-9503)*
Wlc Wood Works Inc ....G 305 896-6460
Deerfield Beach *(G-2834)*
Wood Splinter Corp ....G 305 721-7215
Miami *(G-10139)*

WOOD PRDTS: Applicators

Carpentree Creation ....G 904 300-4008
Jacksonville *(G-5972)*
Konadocks LLC ....G 407 909-0606
Winter Garden *(G-18394)*
Teakdecking Systems Inc ....D 941 756-0600
Sarasota *(G-15567)*

WOOD PRDTS: Barrels & Barrel Parts

Diamondback Barrels LLC ....F 321 305-5995
Cocoa *(G-1915)*

WOOD PRDTS: Beekeeping Splys

Agp Holding Corp ....G 850 668-0006
Tallahassee *(G-16407)*
Agri-Products Inc ....G 850 668-0006
Tallahassee *(G-16408)*

WOOD PRDTS: Door Trim

Joshua Throckmorton ....G 561 236-3349
Loxahatchee *(G-7971)*

WOOD PRDTS: Extension Planks

Wurth Wood Group Inc ....F 800 432-1149
Tampa *(G-17443)*

WOOD PRDTS: Hampers, Laundry

Laundromart ....G 561 487-4343
Boca Raton *(G-576)*

WOOD PRDTS: Laundry

Fine Line Custom Millwork LLC ....E 941 628-9611
Arcadia *(G-193)*
Petit Custom Wood Works ....G 954 200-3111
Davie *(G-2456)*
Sandy Finished Wood Inc ....E 954 615-7271
Fort Lauderdale *(G-4036)*

WOOD PRDTS: Mauls

Boyett Timber Inc ....G 352 583-2138
Webster *(G-17832)*

WOOD PRDTS: Moldings, Unfinished & Prefinished

Architctral Mlding Mllwrks Inc ....F 305 638-8900
Miami *(G-8741)*
Excel Millwork & Moulding Inc ....E 850 576-7228
Midway *(G-10412)*
Hughes Trim LLC ....D 863 206-6048
Orlando *(G-12231)*
M & M Enterprises Daytona LLC ....G 386 672-1554
Daytona Beach *(G-2570)*
S&S Craftsmen Inc ....F 813 247-4429
Tampa *(G-17241)*
Spacewerks Inc ....F 727 540-9714
Clearwater *(G-1793)*
Terry D Triplett Inc ....G 561 251-3641
Mangonia Park *(G-8102)*
Windsor Window Company ....F 321 385-3880
Titusville *(G-17627)*

WOOD PRDTS: Mulch Or Sawdust

Agri - Source Inc ....E 352 351-2700
Ocala *(G-11316)*
E & M Recycling Inc ....G 561 718-1092
Lake Worth *(G-7199)*

WOOD PRDTS: Mulch, Wood & Bark

Forestry Resources LLC ....E 239 332-3966
Fort Myers *(G-4261)*
K & B Landscape Supplies Inc ....G 800 330-8816
Deland *(G-2880)*
Margo Outdoor Living Inc ....F 912 496-2999
Jacksonville *(G-6276)*
Randy Wheeler ....G 850 997-1248
Monticello *(G-10585)*

PRODUCT

Southern Softwoods Inc ....E 863 666-1404
Lakeland (G-7444)
Yahl Mulching & Recycling Inc ....F 239 352-7888
Naples (G-10945)

WOOD PRDTS: Novelties, Fiber

Fanatics Mounted Memories Inc ....E 866 578-9115
Jacksonville (G-6087)
Mounted Memories Inc ....F 866 236-2541
Miramar (G-10516)

WOOD PRDTS: Oars & Paddles

Coastal Paddle Co LLC ....G 850 916-1600
Gulf Breeze (G-4878)
Dolphin Paddlesports Inc ....F 941 924-2785
Sarasota (G-15659)
Three Brothers Boards ....G 386 310-4927
Daytona Beach (G-2612)

WOOD PRDTS: Outdoor, Structural

Ecosan LLC ....G 954 446-5929
Coral Gables (G-2050)
Global Prime Wood LLC ....G 770 292-9200
Aventura (G-261)
Shade Systems Inc ....E 352 237-0135
Ocala (G-11487)
Ufp Palm Bch LLC DBA Ufp Mami ....E 786 837-0552
Miami (G-10055)

WOOD PRDTS: Panel Work

Unique Originals Inc ....E 305 634-2274
Fort Lauderdale (G-4106)

WOOD PRDTS: Poles

Banaghan Wood Products Inc ....E 386 788-6114
Port Orange (G-14328)

WOOD PRDTS: Shavings & Packaging, Excelsior

Southeast Packg Sanitation LLC...........G 904 634-7911
Jacksonville (G-6484)

WOOD PRDTS: Survey Stakes

A B Survey Supply Entps Inc ....G 772 464-9500
Fort Pierce (G-4457)

WOOD PRODUCTS: Reconstituted

Enviva Pellets Cottondale LLC ....E 850 557-7357
Cottondale (G-2228)

WOOD TREATING: Bridges & Trestles

York Bridge Concepts Inc ....E 813 482-0613
Lutz (G-8022)

WOOD TREATING: Flooring, Block

Coastal Treated Products LLC...............G 850 539-6432
Havana (G-4998)

WOOD TREATING: Millwork

Commercial Wood Designs Inc ....F 407 302-9063
Sanford (G-15287)

F & R General Interiors Corp ....F 305 635-4747
Hialeah (G-5149)
Infinite Ret Design & Mfg Corp ....F 305 967-8339
Miami (G-9312)
Ufp Orlando LLC ....F 407 982-3312
Orlando (G-12683)
Ufp Tampa LLC ....E 813 971-3030
Tampa (G-17383)

WOOD TREATING: Structural Lumber & Timber

All Moldings Inc ....G 305 556-6171
Hialeah (G-5038)
Coastal Forest Resources Co ....B 850 539-6432
Havana (G-4996)
John Andersen ....G 407 702-4891
Apopka (G-142)
Larry C Cribb ....G 904 845-2804
Hilliard (G-5471)

WOOD TREATING: Wood Prdts, Creosoted

Mirandas Woodcraft LLC ....G 954 306-3568
Lauderhill (G-7736)

WOODWORK & TRIM: Exterior & Ornamental

Mr Foamy Southwest Fl LLC..................F 239 461-3110
Fort Myers (G-4332)

WOODWORK & TRIM: Interior & Ornamental

Designers Specialty Cab Co Inc ....E 954 868-3440
Fort Lauderdale (G-3762)
Hollywood Woodwork LLC ....F 954 920-5009
Hollywood (G-5599)
Peace Millwork Co Inc ....E 305 573-6222
Miami (G-9699)
Pleasure Interiors LLC...........................E 941 756-9969
Sarasota (G-15783)
Visions Millwork Inc ....F 239 390-0811
Fort Myers (G-4442)

WOODWORK: Carved & Turned

Rich Woodturning Inc ....F 305 573-9142
Miami Lakes (G-10349)

WOODWORK: Interior & Ornamental, NEC

Architctral Wdwrks Cbnetry Inc ....F 561 848-8595
Palm Beach Gardens (G-12949)
Cubos LLC ....G 786 299-2671
Miami (G-8983)
Johnsons Woodwork Incorporated........G 904 826-4100
Saint Augustine (G-14850)
Newmil Inc ....F 954 444-4471
Fort Lauderdale (G-3961)
Oliveri Woodworking Inc ....E 561 478-7233
West Palm Beach (G-18098)
Superior Millwork Company Inc ....F 904 355-5676
Jacksonville (G-6521)
Wicked Woodworks Inc ....E 352 455-8402
Eustis (G-3570)
Woodshed Woodworks LLC ....F 904 540-0354
Saint Augustine (G-14916)

WOODWORK: Ornamental, Cornices, Mantels, Etc.

Federal Millwork Corp ....E 954 522-0653
Fort Lauderdale (G-3814)
Palm Beach Woodwork Co Inc ....G 561 844-8818
Mangonia Park (G-8098)

WRENCHES

James Reese Enterprises Inc ....F 727 386-5311
Clearwater (G-1652)

X-RAY EQPT & TUBES

Atlantic MBL Imaging Svcs Inc ....F 386 239-8271
Ormond Beach (G-12744)
L and C Science and Tech Inc ....G 305 200-3531
Hialeah (G-5215)
Lead Enterprises Inc ....F 305 635-8644
Miami (G-9445)
Omega Medical Imaging LLC ....E 407 323-9400
Sanford (G-15364)
Orlando Flores ....G 305 898-2111
Miami (G-9668)
Osko Inc ....F 305 599-7161
Medley (G-8293)
Ziehm Imaging Inc ....E 407 615-8560
Orlando (G-12734)

YACHT BASIN OPERATIONS

Broward Yard & Marine LLC ....D 954 927-4119
Dania (G-2329)

YARN : Crochet, Spun

Four Purls ....G 863 293-6261
Winter Haven (G-18441)

YARN MILLS: Texturizing

Dillon Yarn Corporation.........................D 973 684-1600
Fort Lauderdale (G-3765)

YARN, ELASTIC: Fabric Covered

Nissi Elastic Corp ....G 305 968-3812
Hialeah (G-5280)

YARN: Manmade & Synthetic Fiber, Spun

Southern Fiber Inc ....G 786 916-3052
Miami Lakes (G-10358)

YARN: Manmade & Synthetic Fiber, Twisting Or Winding

Eastman Chemical Company ....F 305 671-2800
Miami (G-9062)

YOGURT WHOLESALERS

Colormet Foods LLC ....F 888 775-3966
Miami (G-8948)

ZINC OINTMENT

Gensco Laboratories LLC ....F 754 263-2898
Doral (G-3231)